WHO'S WHO 2002

WHO'S WHO 2002

AN ANNUAL
BIOGRAPHICAL DICTIONARY

ONE HUNDRED AND FIFTY-FOURTH
YEAR OF ISSUE

A & C BLACK
LONDON

PUBLISHED BY A&C BLACK (PUBLISHERS) LIMITED, 37 SOHO SQUARE, LONDON W1D 3QZ

ISBN 0 7136 6055 4

The United States
PALGRAVE PRESS, NEW YORK

Australia and New Zealand
ALLEN & UNWIN, SYDNEY

Canada
FITZHENRY & WHITESIDE, MARKHAM, ONTARIO

Southern Africa
BOOK PROMOTIONS (PTY) LTD, PLUMSTEAD, CAPE TOWN

Middle East
PENGUIN INTERNATIONAL

India
MAYA PUBLISHERS PVT LTD, NEW DELHI

Hong Kong
ROGER WARD, ENGLAND

Singapore
STP DISTRIBUTORS (PTE) LTD

Malaysia
STP DISTRIBUTORS (M) SDN BHD, SHAH ALAM, SELANGOR

PRINTED AND BOUND IN GREAT BRITAIN BY
WILLIAM CLOWES LIMITED, BECCLES AND LONDON

TEROPAQUE CREAM 40 g/m² SUPPLIED BY PRECISION PUBLISHING PAPERS LIMITED, YEOVIL

CONTENTS

PREFACE

Who's Who is the recognised source book of information on people of influence and interest in all fields.

This, the 2002 edition, contains more than 30,000 biographies, approximately one thousand of these making their first appearance in *Who's Who*. They are of all kinds of people from all parts of the world and from all walks of life: the arts, business and finance, the church, the civil service, education, entertainment and sport, government, the law, local government, the media, medicine, professional institutions, science and the trade unions.

Each entry is in a standard form, full name and present post being followed by date of birth and family details, education, career in date order, publications, recreations and address.

The entries are carefully updated both from information supplied by biographees on their annual proofs and from many independent sources of reference. As a result, tens of thousands of amendments are made, more than half the entries requiring change. The book includes an obituary and a comprehensive list of abbreviations used in the entries.

HISTORICAL NOTE

The first edition of *Who's Who* was published in 1849. It consisted of an almanac followed by thirty-nine lists of ranks and appointments and the names of those holding them. As might be expected, there were lists of peers, members of the House of Commons, judges, archbishops and bishops. Additionally, however, there were the names of the Governor and board of directors of the Bank of England, of British envoys abroad, of the directors of the East India Company and of the officers (including the actuaries) of the life and fire assurance companies in London.

The range of lists was expanded over the next half century to more than two hundred and fifty, to include, amongst others, the Police Commissioners, the officers of the principal railways, the members of the London School Board and the Crown Agents – together with the editors of significant newspapers and magazines whose names, the editor noted, were ''given here, not for contributors, but that the public may know who lead public opinion''.

In 1897 substantial changes were made to the nature and content of the book. The major change was the addition of a section of biographies in which details were given of the lives of some five and a half thousand leading figures of the day.

Now as then the book aims to list people who, through their careers, affect the political, economic, scientific and artistic life of the country. *Who's Who* places its emphasis on careers whilst giving opportunity for the inclusion of family and other individual details, such as the recreations which have become a distinctive feature of the book.

An invitation to appear in *Who's Who* has, on occasion, been thought of as conferring distinction; that is the last thing it can do. It recognises distinction and influence. The attitude of the present editorial board remains that of the editor of the 1897 edition, who stated in his preface that the book seeks to recognise people whose ''prominence is inherited, or depending upon office, or the result of ability which singles them out from their fellows in occupations open to every educated man or woman''.

INDEX TO ADVERTISERS

OBITUARY

Deaths notified from October 2000 to October 2001.

Aagaard, Robert, OBE, 1 April 2001.
Abraham, Maj.-Gen. (Sutton) Martin (O'Heguerty), CB, MC, 15 May 2001.
Adam, Madge Gertrude, 25 Aug. 2001.
Adams, Bernard Charles, 10 Sept. 2001.
Adams, Douglas Noël, 11 May 2001.
Adams, Frederick Baldwin, Jr, 7 Jan. 2001.
Adams, Sir Philip George Doyne, KCMG, 14 Oct. 2001.
Adler, Larry, (Lawrence Cecil Adler), 7 Aug. 2001.
Airey, Sir Lawrence, KCB, 21 June 2001.
Aldington, 1st Baron; Toby Austin Richard William Low, KCMG, CBE, DSO, TD, PC, 7 Dec. 2000.
Alexander, Sir Kenneth John Wilson, 27 March 2001.
Allan, (Charles) Lewis (Cuthbert), 9 Aug. 2000.
Allen, Prof. John Frank, FRS, 22 April 2001.
Anderson, Prof. John Allan Dalrymple, TD, 21 Oct. 2000.
Anderson, Prof. Sir (William) Ferguson, OBE, 28 June 2001.
Andrew, Prof. Edward Raymond, FRS, 27 May 2001.
Andrews, Brig. George Lewis Williams, CBE, DSO, 27 Aug. 2001.
Anscombe, Prof. Gertrude Elizabeth Margaret, FBA, 5 Jan. 2001.
Ansell, Dr Barbara May, CBE, 14 Sept. 2001.
ap Robert, His Honour Hywel Wyn Jones, 30 July 2001.
Aquilecchia, Prof. Giovanni, 3 Aug. 2001.
Argyll, 12th Duke of; Ian Campbell, 21 April 2001.
Ashcroft, James Geoffrey, CB, 21 July 2000.
Ashley, Prof. Francis Paul, 3 Sept. 2000.
Ashton, Rt Rev. Leonard James, CB, 19 Jan. 2001.
Ashworth, Sir Herbert, 29 Dec. 2000.
Aske, Rev. Sir Conan, 2nd Bt, 7 May 2001.
Atwill, Sir (Milton) John (Napier), 27 Aug. 2001.
Aylmer, Gerald Edward, FBA, 17 Dec. 2000.

Bagot, 9th Baron; Heneage Charles Bagot, 19 Jan. 2001.
Bailey, John Everett Creighton, CBE, 21 Dec. 2000.
Baird, Sir David Charles, 5th Bt, 15 Nov. 2000.
Baker, Alex Anthony, CBE, 8 Oct 2001.
Baker, Willfred Harold Kerton, TD, 9 Nov. 2000.
Balfour, David Mathers, CBE, 21 Jan. 2001.
Bamford, Joseph Cyril, CBE, 1 March 2001.
Bandaranaike, Sirimavo Ratwatte Dias, 10 Oct. 2000.
Barker, Sir Alwyn Bowman, CMG, 25 Sept. 1998.
Barker, Arthur Vincent, CBE, 4 March 2001.
Barnard, Prof. Christiaan Neethling, 2 Sept. 2001.
Barraclough, Sir Kenneth James Priestley, CBE, TD, 3 April 2001.
Barrett, William Spencer, FBA, 23 Sept. 2001.
Barton, Maj.-Gen. Francis Christopher, CB, CBE, 26 April 2001.
Barwick, David Robert, CBE, QC, 25 April 2001.
Basov, Prof. Nikolai Gennadievich, 1 July 2001.
Basset, Lady Elizabeth, DCVO, 30 Nov. 2000.
Bate, Sir (Walter) Edwin, OBE, 12 Sept. 1999.
Bates, Ralph, 26 Nov. 2000.
Bath, Alan Alfred, 8 July 2001.
Beagley, Thomas Lorne, CB, 5 Jan. 2001.
Bean, Dame Marjorie Louise, DBE, 16 March 2001.
Beattie, Hon. Sir David Stuart, GCMG, GCVO, QSO, 4 Feb. 2001.
Beattie-Moriarty, Brigid Mary, CBE, 7 March 2001.
Beckett, Sir Martyn Gervase, 2nd Bt, MC, 5 Aug. 2001.
Beddington, Rosa Susan Penelope, (Mrs R. A. Denniston), FRS, 18 May 2001.
Beeley, Sir Harold, KCMG, CBE, 27 July 2001.
Begg, Robert William, CBE, 1 March 2001.
Behr, Norman Isaac, 30 May 2001.
Beishon, (Ronald) John, 28 April 2001.
Bell, Archibald Angus, QC (Scot.), 2 Oct. 2001.
Bell, Sir (William) Ewart, KCB, 2 Jan. 2001.
Bellamy, Alexander William, 3 Dec. 1999.
Bellwin, Baron (Life Peer); Irwin Norman Bellow, 11 Feb. 2001.
Bennett, Sir Hubert, 13 Dec. 2000.
Bennett, Sir Reginald Frederick Brittain, VRD, 19 Dec. 2000.
Bernstein, Prof. Basil Bernard, 24 Sept. 2000.
Bessey, Gordon Scott, CBE, 2 April 2001.
Bevins, Anthony John, 23 March 2001.
Bevins, Kenneth Milton, CBE, TD, 30 June 2001.
Bierich, Marcus, 25 Nov. 2000.
Bignall, John Reginald, 15 Nov. 2000.
Bird-Wilson, Air Vice-Marshal Harold Arthur Cooper, CBE, DSO, DFC, AFC, 27 Dec. 2000.
Birkmyre, Sir Archibald, 3rd Bt, 7 May 2001.
Birks, Jack, CBE, 27 June 2001.
Black, Prof. Archibald Niel, 14 Jan. 2001.
Bloch, Prof. Konrad Emil, 15 Oct. 2000.
Block, Brig. David Arthur Kennedy William, CBE, DSO, MC, 26 June 2001.
Bolland, Group Captain Guy Alfred, CBE, 20 Jan. 2001.
Bolton, 7th Baron; Richard William Algar Orde-Powlett, 29 July 2001.
Bonner, Frederick Ernest, CBE, 20 Oct. 2000.
Booth, His Honour James, 31 Aug. 2000.
Borrett, Ven. Charles Walter, 30 Nov. 2000.
Botha, Matthys Izak, 1 June 1999.
Bowen, (Evan) Roderic, QC, 18 July 2001.
Bowring, Edgar Rennie Harvey, MC, 29 June 2001.
Boydell, Peter Thomas Sherrington, QC, 23 Feb. 2001.
Boyles, Edgar William, 7 May 2001.
Bradbury, Sir Malcolm Stanley, CBE, 27 Nov. 2000.
Bradman, Sir Donald George, AC, 25 Feb. 2001.
Branigan, Sir Patrick Francis, QC (Gold Coast), 2 Nov. 2000.
Bray, Sir Theodor Charles, CBE, 10 Aug. 2000.
Braybrook, Edward John, CB, 14 Sept. 2001.
Braybrooke, Neville Patrick Bellairs, 14 July 2001.
Bridge, Ronald George Blacker, CBE, 14 April 2001.
Broughton, Leonard, 29 May 2000.
Brown, Alexander Cosens Lindsay, CB, 23 July 1999.
Brown, Sir John, 27 Dec. 2000
Brown, Sir John Douglas Keith, 13 Oct. 2000.
Brown, Ven. Robert Saville, 20 April 2001.
Buchan, Ven. Eric Ancrum, 27 April 2001.
Buckle, (Christopher) Richard (Sandford), CBE, 12 Oct. 2001.
Buckley, Sir John William, 19 Nov. 2000.
Bull, George Anthony, OBE, 6 April 2001.
Bullus, Wing Comdr Sir Eric Edward, 31 Aug. 2001.
Bunting, John Reginald, CBE, 21 Sept. 2001.
Burgner, Thomas Ulric, 14 July 2001.
Burke-Gaffney, Michael Anthony Bowes, QC, 3 June 2001.
Burns, Anne, (Mrs D. O. Burns), 22 Jan. 2001.
Burns, Dr B(enedict) Delisle, FRS, 6 Sept. 2001.
Burns, Prof. Tom, FBA, 20 June 2001.
Bury, John, OBE, 12 Nov. 2000.
Butler, Ian Geoffrey, CBE, 4 March 2001.
Byers, Sir Maurice Hearne, CBE, QC (Aust.), 16 Jan. 1999.

Cable, Sir James Eric, KCVO, CMG, 27 Sept. 2001.
Cameron, Prof. Kenneth, CBE, FBA, 10 March 2001.
Campos, Roberto de Oliveira, Hon. GCVO, 9 Oct. 2001.
Cann, James Charles, MP, 15 Oct. 2001.
Caplan, Leonard, QC, 18 Jan. 2001.
Carless, Prof. John Edward, 12 Sept. 2001.
Carman, George Alfred, QC, 2 Jan. 2001.
Carmichael of Kelvingrove, Baron (Life Peer); Neil George Carmichael, 19 July 2001.
Carnarvon, 7th Earl of; Henry George Reginald Molyneux Herbert, KCVO, KBE, 11 Sept. 2001.
Carrick, Maj.- Gen. Thomas Welsh, OBE, 4 Oct. 2000.
Carter, Peers Lee, CMG, 8 Feb. 2001.
Carter, Robert William Bernard, CMG, 11 July 2001.
Carter, William Nicholas, OBE, 17 March 2001.
Carter, Sir William Oscar, 11 Dec. 2000.
Casey, Dame Stella Katherine, DBE, 7 July 2000.
Cassel, His Honour Sir Harold Felix, 3rd Bt, TD, QC, 17 Sept. 2001.
Catto, 2nd Baron; Stephen Gordon Catto, 3 Sept. 2001.
Cave, Prof. Alexander James Edward, 17 May 2001.
Cawley, 3rd Baron; Frederick Lee Cawley, 13 April 2001.
Cawley, Sir Charles Mills, CBE, 8 Nov. 2000.
Chaban-Delmas, Jacques Pierre Michel, 10 Nov. 2000.
Chadwick, Gerald William St John, (John), CMG, 5 May 2001.
Charles, Leslie Stanley Francis, 12 Dec. 2000.
Charlesworth, Arthur Leonard, 16 Jan. 2001.
Christian, Prof. John Wyrill, FRS, 27 Feb. 2001.
Christopherson, Sir Derman Guy, OBE, FRS, 7 Nov. 2000.
Chubb, Andrew Vyvyan; His Honour Judge Chubb, 27 July 2001.
Chumas, Henry John, CMG, TD, 27 June 2001.
Clarke, Prof. Sir Cyril Astley, KBE, FRS, 21 Nov. 2000.
Cledwyn of Penrhos, Baron (Life Peer); Cledwyn Hughes, CH, PC, 22 Feb. 2001.
Clive, Nigel David, CMG, OBE, MC, TD, 6 May 2001.
Close, Richard Charles, 6 April 2000.
Cocks of Hartcliffe, Baron (Life Peer); Michael Francis Lovell Cocks, PC, 26 March 2001.

Cohen, Lt-Col Nathan Leslie, OBE, CPM, TD, 27 Sept. 2000.
Colchester, Trevor Charles, CMG, 26 Jan. 2001.
Coldwells, Rev. Canon Alan Alfred, 8 Feb. 2001.
Cole, Sir (Alexander) Colin, KCB, KCVO, TD, 18 Feb. 2001.
Colegate, Raymond, CBE, 10 July 2001.
Coleman, Arthur Percy, 31 July 2000.
Coleman, Prof. Robert George Gilbert, 18 Jan. 2001.
Collins, Sir Arthur James Robert, KCVO, ERD, 28 Dec. 2000.
Combermere, 5th Viscount; Michael Wellington Stapleton-Cotton, 3 Nov. 2000.
Condon, Denis David, OBE, 6 June 2000.
Connell, John Morris, OBE, 8 Sept. 1999.
Cook, Maj.-Gen. Arthur Thompson, 10 Dec. 2000.
Cook, Brig. Richard Arthur, CBE, 23 Sept. 2001.
Cooke, His Honour (Richard) Kenneth, OBE, 25 Oct. 2000.
Cooper, John Newton, CBE, 24 Dec. 2000.
Cooper, Joseph, OBE, 4 Aug. 2001.
Cope, Prof. F(rederick) Wolverson, 4 May 2000.
Cosgrave, Patrick John, 15 Sept. 2001.
Cottenham, 8th Earl of; Kenelm Charles Everard Digby Pepys, 20 Oct. 2000.
Cotter, Lt-Col Sir Delaval James Alfred, 6th Bt, DSO, 2 April 2001.
Coven, Frank, 7 Sept. 2001.
Cowdrey of Tonbridge, Baron (Life Peer); Michael Colin Cowdrey, CBE, 4 Dec. 2000.
Cox, Peter Richmond, CB, 1 Sept. 2001.
Craib, Douglas Duncan Simpson, CBE, 9 June 2001.
Cram, Prof. Donald James, 17 June 2001.
Crane, Prof. (Francis) Roger, 12 Jan. 2001.
Crook, 2nd Baron; Douglas Edwin Crook, 18 June 2001.
Croom-Johnson, Rt Hon. Sir David Powell, DSC, VRD, PC, 21 Nov. 2000.
Crowley, Niall, Hon. CBE, 9 June 1998.
Cruddas, Rear-Adm. Thomas Rennison, CB, 22 Nov. 2000.
Cullen of Ashbourne, 2nd Baron; Charles Borlase Marsham Cokayne, MBE, 17 Dec. 2000.
Curtis, Sir (Edward) Leo, 20 Feb. 2001.

Davies, Sir Alun Talfan, QC, 11 Nov. 2000.
Davies, Robert Henry, MBE, DFC, 17 Feb. 2001.
Davis, Brian Michael, 23 Jan. 2001.
Dearnley, Christopher Hugh, LVO, 15 Dec. 2000.
Debenham, Sir Gilbert Ridley, 3rd Bt, 3 June 2001.
Denby, Patrick Morris Coventry, CMG, 3 July 2001.
Denton of Wakefield, Baroness (Life Peer); Jean Denton, CBE, 5 Feb. 2001.
Denton, Anthony Albert, CBE, 3 March 2001.
de Pury, David, 26 Dec. 2000.
Derry, Thomas Kingston, OBE, 11 July 2001.
de Valois, Dame Ninette, OM, CH, DBE, 8 March 2001.
Dewar, Rt Hon. Donald Campbell, PC, MP, 11 Oct. 2000.
de Winton, Michael Geoffrey, CBE, MC, 23 April 2001.
De Wolf, Vice-Adm. Harry George, CBE, DSO, DSC, 2000.
Dickens, Prof. Arthur Geoffrey, CMG, FBA, 31 July 2001.
Dickinson, John Lawrence, (Bob), CBE, 1 Sept. 2001.
Disbrey, Air Vice-Marshal William Daniel, CB, CBE, AFC, 26 June 2001.
Dixon, Sir Ian Leonard, CBE, 20 July 2001.
Dixon, Peter Vibart, 11 June 2001.
Dixon, Stanley, 8 Sept. 2000.
Doniach, Prof. Israel, 11 Feb. 2001.
Donkin, Alexander Sim, 11 Sept. 2001.
Douglas, Prof. Ronald Walter, 14 Nov. 2000.
Dumbutshena, Hon. Enoch, 14 Dec. 2000.
Dummett, George Anthony, 13 June 2001.
Dunham, Sir Kingsley Charles, FRS, 5 April 2001.
Durie, Sir Alexander Charles, CBE, 5 Jan. 2001.
Dymond, Michael John, 21 Feb. 2001.

Eadie, Douglas George Arnott, 5 Dec. 2000.
Eadie, Ellice Aylmer, CBE, 31 March 2001.
Eklund, (Arne) Sigvard, 30 Jan. 2000.
Ellis, Humphry Francis, MBE, 8 Dec. 2000.
Else, John, MBE, TD, 8 Sept. 1996.
Elyan, Prof. Sir (Isadore) Victor, 16 Feb. 2000.
Everson, Sir Frederick Charles, KCMG, 27 May 2001.

Farmer, Frank Reginald, OBE, FRS, 10 June 2001.
Farnham, 12th Baron; Barry Owen Somerset Maxwell, 22 March 2001.
Feld, Valerie, 17 July 2001.
Ferrall, Sir Raymond Alfred, CBE, 1 June 2000.
Ffitch, George Norman, 5 July 2001.
Fisher, Harold Wallace, 8 Dec. 2000.
Fisher, Rev. James Atherton, 12 Feb. 2001.
FitzGerald, Sir George Peter Maurice, 5th Bt, MC, 6 April 2001.
Fleming, John, 29 May 2001.
Fletcher, Major John Antony, MBE, 20 Aug. 2001.
Fletcher-Cooke, Sir Charles Fletcher, QC, 24 Feb. 2001.
Fogarty, Michael Patrick, 20 Jan. 2001.
Forbes, Hon. Sir Alastair Granville, 19 July 2001.
Forbes-Leith of Fyvie, Sir Andrew George, 3rd Bt, 4 Nov. 2000.
Forder, Kenneth John, 13 July 2001.
Forsberg, (Charles) Gerald, OBE, 24 Oct. 2000.
Forshaw, Brig. Peter, CBE, 6 Aug. 2001.
Forster, Sir Archibald William, 14 Feb. 2001.
Forster, His Honour Donald Murray, 12 Oct. 2000.
Forwood, Sir Dudley Richard, 3rd Bt, 25 Jan. 2001.
Foster, Sir Richard Anthony, 8 March 2001.
Foxon, David Fairweather, FBA, 5 June 2001.
Foxon, Harold Peter, OBE, 19 Jan. 2001.
Frank, Air Vice-Marshal Alan Donald, CB, CBE, DSO, DFC, 6 Oct. 2001.
Fraser, Sir Angus McKay, KCB, TD, 27 May 2001.
Fraser, Air Marshal Rev. Sir (Henry) Paterson, KBE, CB, AFC, 4 Aug. 2001.
Frederick, Sir Charles Boscawen, 10th Bt, 21 March 2001.
French, Henry William, CBE, 3 July 2001.
Fry, Sir William Gordon, 29 Sept. 2000.
Fugard, Maj.-Gen. Michael Teape, CB, 25 March 2001.
Fulthorpe, Henry Joseph, 31 Jan. 1999.

Gammie, Gordon Edward, CB, QC, 19 July 2001.
Gardner, Sir Edward Lucas, QC, 22 Aug. 2001.
Gardner, William Maving, 28 Dec. 2000.
Garland, (Frederick) Peter (Collison), CVO, QPM, 2 Nov. 2000.
Gaskell, (John) Philip (Wellesley), 31 July 2001.
Gell, Prof. Philip George Houthem, FRS, 3 May 2001.
Gershevitch, Ilya, FBA, 11 April 2001.
Gibson, Vice-Adm. Sir Donald Cameron Ernest Forbes, KCB, DSC, 22 Nov. 2000.
Gibson, Wilford Henry, CBE, QPM, 30 July 2001.
Gidden, Barry Owen Barton, CMG, 29 Dec. 1997.
Gilbert, Sir Arthur, 2 Sept. 2001.
Gillespie, Dr William Hewitt, 30 June 2001.
Gilmour, Alan Breck, CVO, CBE, 18 July 2001.
Glasgow, Archbishop of, (RC); His Eminence Cardinal Thomas J. Winning, 17 June 2001.
Glasspole, Most Hon. Sir Florizel Augustus, ON, GCMG, GCVO, CD, 25 Nov. 2000.
Glover, Robert Finlay, TD, 2 May 2001.
Godwin, Peter Raymond, CBE, 26 April 2001.
Goodall, His Honour Anthony Charles, MC, 3 Feb. 2001.
Gooding, Air Vice-Marshal Keith Horace, CB, OBE, 4 March 2001.
Goodman, Maj.-Gen. (John) David (Whitlock), CB, 29 Sept. 2000.
Goodrich, Rt Rev. Philip Harold Ernest, 22 Jan. 2001.
Goodwin, Prof. John Forrest, 7 June 2001.
Gordon, Aubrey Abraham, 11 Sept. 2000.
Gordon, Prof. Cyrus H., 30 March 2001.
Gordon-Finlayson, Maj.-Gen. Robert, OBE, 19 June 2001.
Goschen, Sir Edward Christian, 3rd Bt, DSO, 8 March 2001.
Graham, Prof. Alastair, FRS, 12 Dec. 2000.
Grant, Sir (Matthew) Alistair, 22 Jan. 2001.
Grebenik, Eugene, CB, 14 Oct. 2001.
Greenhill of Harrow, Baron (Life Peer); Denis Arthur Greenhill, GCMG, OBE, 8 Nov. 2000.
Greetham, John Francis, CBE, 16 April 2001.
Greswell, Air Cdre Jeaffreson Herbert, CB, CBE, DSO, DFC, 19 Nov. 2000.
Griffith, Owen Glyn, CBE, MVO, 16 June 2001.
Griffiths, Islwyn Owen, QC, 5 May 2001.
Grint, Edmund Thomas Charles, CBE, 8 Feb. 2001.
Grunfeld, Prof. Cyril, 20 Sept. 2001.
Grylls, Sir (William) Michael (John), 7 Feb. 2001.
Gunn, (Alan) Richard, CBE, 6 April 1998.
Gurney, Prof. Oliver Robert, FBA, 11 Jan. 2001.

Haigh, Clement Percy, 25 Feb. 2001.
Hailsham of Saint Marylebone, Baron (Life Peer); Quintin McGarel Hogg, KG, CH, PC, FRS, 12 Oct. 2001.
Hall, Prof. Edward Thomas, CBE, 11 Aug. 2001.
Hall, Prof. Geoffrey Ronald, CBE, 3 Feb. 2001.
Hamburger, Sir Sidney Cyril, CBE, 6 June 2001.
Hamilton, Sir (Robert Charles) Richard (Caradoc), 9th Bt, 27 Sept. 2001.
Hamilton, Hon. William, (Liam), 29 Nov. 2000.
Hamlyn, Baron (Life Peer); Paul Bertrand Hamlyn, CBE, 31 Aug. 2001.
Hammond, Prof. Nicholas Geoffrey Lemprière, CBE, DSO, FBA, 24 March 2001.
Hands, David Richard Granville, QC, 10 Dec. 2000.
Hanley, Howard Granville, CBE, 18 Feb. 2001.
Hanley, Sir Michael Bowen, KCB, 1 Jan. 2001.
Harden, Major James Richard Edwards, DSO, OBE, MC, 22 Oct. 2000.
Hardman, Sir Henry, KCB, 17 Jan. 2001.

Harris of Greenwich, Baron (Life Peer); John Henry Harris, PC, 11 April 2001.
Harris, Prof. Sir Alan James, CBE, 26 Dec. 2000.
Harris, Brig. Lewis John, CBE, 24 Jan. 2001.
Harris, Martin Richard, 20 Sept. 2001.
Hart, Thomas Mure, CMG, 16 Jan. 2001.
Hart, Maj.-Gen. Trevor Stuart, CB, 7 Oct. 2000.
Hartwell, Baron (Life Peer); William Michael Berry, MBE, TD, 3 April 2001.
Hartwell, Eric, CBE, 11 Feb. 2001.
Harvey, Major Thomas Cockayne, CVO, DSO, ERD, 11 June 2001.
Hastings, Rev. Prof. Adrian Christopher, 30 May 2001.
Hatty, Hon. Sir Cyril James, 19 Aug. 2001.
Hayes, John Philip, CB, 25 Feb. 2001.
Hayes, Walter Leopold Arthur, CBE, 26 Dec. 2000.
Hayr, Air Marshal Sir Kenneth William, KCB, KBE, AFC, 2 June 2001.
Heaney, Leonard Martin, CMG, 16 July 2001.
Hector, Gordon Matthews, CMG, CBE, 4 Oct. 2001.
Heenan, Maurice, CMG, QC (Hong Kong), 26 Sept. 2000.
Hellaby, Sir (Frederick Reed) Alan, 19 May 2001.
Hemlow, Prof. Joyce, 3 Sept. 2001.
Henderson, Sir William MacGregor, FRS, 29 Nov. 2000.
Henri, Adrian Maurice, 20 Dec. 2000.
Heptinstall, Leslie George *[Deceased.*
Hewett, Sir Peter John Smithson, 6th Bt, MM, 1 June 2001.
Hickman, John Kyrle, CMG, 23 Feb. 2001.
Higson, Gordon Robert, 9 Aug. 2001.
Hindley-Smith, David Dury, CBE, 23 April 2001.
Hippisley-Cox, Peter Denzil John, 21 June 2001.
Hobbs, Rev. Canon Keith, 11 June 2001.
Hoddinott, Sir John Charles, CBE, QPM, 13 Aug. 2001.
Hodgson, Stanley Ernest, CBE, 28 April 2001.
Hogg, Sir Michael David, 8th Bt, 12 July 2001.
Hohler, Henry Arthur Frederick, CMG, 19 May 2001.
Holder, Air Marshal Sir Paul Davie, KBE, CB, DSO, DFC, 22 April 2001.
Holland, Arthur David, CB, TD, 4 Sept. 2001.
Holland-Martin, Rosamund Mary, (Lady Holland-Martin), DBE, 18 June 2001.
Holt, Richard Anthony Appleby, 18 May 2001.
Howard, Sir (Hamilton) Edward (de Coucey), 2nd Bt, GBE, 16 March 2001.
Howarth, Prof. Leslie, OBE, FRS, 22 Sept. 2001.
Howd, Isobel, 11 Dec. 2000.
Howe, Rt Rev. John William Alexander, 26 April 2001.
Hoyle, Prof. Sir Fred, FRS, 20 Aug. 2001.
Hoyos, Hon. Sir (Fabriciano) Alexander, 23 Aug. 2001.
Hudson, Frank Michael Stanislaus, 13 April 2001.
Hughes, Rt Rev. John Taylor, CBE, 21 July 2001.
Humphrey, Arthur Hugh Peters, CMG, OBE, 10 Sept. 2001.
Hunter, Dame Pamela, DBE, 30 May 2001.
Hunter, Rita, CBE, 29 April 2001.
Hutchison, (Joseph) Douglas, CBE, MC, TD, 6 Oct. 2001.
Hutton-Williams, Derek Alfred, MBE, 22 Feb. 2001.
Hyatali, Sir Isaac Emanuel, TC, 2 Dec. 2000.
Hyde, W(illiam) Leonard, 11 Nov. 2000.

Inglis, James Craufuird Roger, WS, 26 May 2001.
Ingram, Prof. David John Edward, CBE, 15 Jan. 2001.
Innes, Maughan William, 1 April 2001.

Jackson, Gerald Breck, 1 Dec. 2000.
Jackson, Sir Robert, 7th Bt, 17 April 2000.
Jacob, Sir Isaac Hai, (Sir Jack), QC, 26 Dec. 2000.
Jahoda, Prof. Marie, (Mrs A. H. Albu), CBE, 28 April 2001.
James, Prof. John Ivor Pulsford, 11 July 2001.
James, Prof. Philip Seaforth, 5 May 2001.
Jamieson, Major David Auldjo, VC, CVO, 5 May 2001.
Jehangir, Sir Hirji, 3rd Bt, 24 Feb. 2000.
Jocelyn, Prof. Henry David, FBA, 22 Oct. 2000.
Johnson, David John, CMG, CVO, 23 Dec. 2000.
Johnson, Air Vice-Marshal James Edgar, (Johnnie), CB, CBE, DSO, DFC, 30 Jan. 2001.
Johnson, (Reginald) Stuart, CBE, 22 June 2001.
Johnston, Ian Henderson, CB, 13 Sept. 2001.
Johnston, John Douglas Hartley, 10 March 2000.
Johnstone, Air Vice-Marshal Alexander Vallance Riddell, CB, DFC, AE, 13 Dec. 2000.
Johnstone, Michael Anthony, 10 Oct. 2001.
Jones, Rachel Marianne, 19 March 2001.
Jones, R(obin) Huws, CBE, 16 June 2001.

Keeling, Robert William Maynard, 16 March 2001.
Kelbie, Sheriff David, 30 May 2001.
Kennaway, Prof. Alexander, 1 May 2000.
Kennedy, Eamon, 12 Dec. 2000.
Kent, John Philip Cozens, FBA, 22 Oct. 2000.
Kilburn, Prof. Tom, CBE, FRS, 17 Jan. 2001.
King, Prof. (John) Oliver (Letts), 11 Dec. 2000.
Kiralfy, Prof. Albert Kenneth Roland, 27 April 2001.
Kitchen, Stanley, 22 July 2001.
Knapp, James, 13 Aug. 2001.
Knowles, Sir Leonard Joseph, CBE, 23 Sept. 1999.
Kolane, John Teboho, ODSM, OL, 1999.
Kraft, Rt Rev. Richard Austin, 17 Jan. 2001.
Kuenssberg, Ekkehard von, CBE, 27 Dec. 2000.

Ladas, Diana Margaret, 8 Oct. 2001.
Laister, Peter, 14 April 2001.
Lang, Lt-Gen. Sir Derek Boileau, KCB, DSO, MC, 7 April 2001.
Lasdun, Sir Denys Louis, CH, CBE, RA, 11 Jan. 2001.
Law, James, QC (Scot.), 6 March 2001.
Lawrence, Sir Guy Kempton, DSO, OBE, DFC, 30 Nov. 2000.
Lawton, Rt Hon. Sir Frederick Horace, PC, 3 Feb. 2001.
Leadbeater, Howell, 3 March 2001.
Lechmere, Sir Berwick Hungerford, 6th Bt, 24 June 2001.
Lees-Spalding, Rear-Adm. Ian Jaffery, (Tim), CB, 20 July 2001.
Lemieux, Prof. Raymond Urgel, CC, FRS, 22 July 2000.
Leonard, Michael William, CVO, 30 May 2001.
Leslie, (Percy) Theodore, 28 July 2001.
Lewis-Jones, Captain (Robert) Gwilym, CBE, RN, 18 Sept. 2001.
Lincoln, 18th Earl of; Edward Horace Fiennes-Clinton, 7 July 2001.
Lindbergh, Anne Spencer Morrow, 7 Feb. 2001.
Lindsay, John Vliet, 19 Dec. 2000.
Livingston Booth, John Dick, OBE, 16 July 2001.
Llewellyn, Rt Rev. William Somers, 22 July 2001.
Lloyd, Very Rev. Henry Morgan, DSO, OBE, 16 April 2001.
Lloyd Owen, Maj.-Gen. David Lanyon, CB, DSO, OBE, MC, 5 April 2001.
Longford, 7th Earl of; Francis Aungier Pakenham, KG, PC, 3 Aug. 2001.
Love, Prof. Andrew Henry Garmany, CBE, 3 Jan. 2001.
Lovell-Davis, Baron (Life Peer); Peter Lovell Lovell-Davis, 6 Jan. 2001.
Low, Sir Alan Roberts, 18 April 1999.
Lowrey, Air Comdt Dame Alice, DBE, RRC, 19 May 2001.
Lowry, Sir John Patrick, (Sir Pat), CBE, 30 May 2001.
Lowry, His Honour Richard John, QC, 17 Sept. 2001.
Loxam, John Gordon, 13 Dec. 2000.
Loyn, Prof. Henry Royston, FBA, 9 Oct. 2000.
Lunt, Maj.-Gen. James Doiran, CBE, 1 Oct. 2001.
Lyle, Lt-Col (Archibald) Michael, OBE, 3 Jan. 2001.
Lynch, Rev. Preb. Donald MacLeod, CBE, 27 Nov. 2000.
Lythall, Basil Wilfrid, CB, 22 Sept. 2001.

Maby, (Alfred) Cedric, CBE, 28 Nov. 2000.
Macaulay, Janet Stewart Alison, 10 Dec. 2000.
McConnell, Baron (Life Peer); Robert William Brian McConnell, PC (NI), 25 Oct. 2000.
Macdonald, Vice-Adm. Sir Roderick Douglas, KBE, 19 Jan. 2001.
MacGill, (George) Roy (Buchanan), CBE, 14 Nov. 2000.
MacIntyre, Rt Hon. Duncan, CMG, DSO, OBE, ED, PC (NZ), 7 June 2001.
Mack, Keith Robert, 11 March 2001.
Mackay of Ardbrecknish, Baron (Life Peer); John Jackson Mackay, PC, 21 Feb. 2001.
McKean, Douglas CB, 28 May 2001.
MacKenzie, Prof. David Neil, FBA, 13 Oct. 2001.
MacKenzie, James Sargent Porteous, OBE, 6 Dec. 2000.
Mackeown, Thomas Frederick William, 29 Aug. 2001.
Macklin, Sir Bruce Roy, OBE, 29 Aug. 2000.
Mackworth-Young, Sir Robert Christopher, (Sir Robin), GCVO, 5 Dec. 2000.
McLeod, Sir Ian George, 18 Jan. 2001.
MacMahon, Gerald John, CB, CMG, 23 July 2001.
McMillan, Rt Rev. Mgr Donald Neil, 16 March 2001.
Macpherson, Fiona Mary, (Mrs Adrian Bailey), 28 Nov. 2000.
Madden, Adm. Sir Charles Edward, 2nd Bt, GCB, 23 April 2001.
Maddocks, Sir Kenneth Phipson, KCMG, KCVO, 28 Aug. 2001.
Maguire, Air Marshal Sir Harold John, KCB, DSO, OBE, 1 Feb. 2001.
Maguire, Rt Rev. Robert Kenneth, 14 Oct. 2000.
Major, Kathleen, FBA, 19 Dec. 2000.
Malcolm, Prof. John Laurence, 9 Oct. 2001.
Mallet, Roger, 21 June 2001.
Malmesbury, 6th Earl of; William James Harris, TD, 11 Nov. 2000.
Mann, (Francis) George, CBE, DSO, MC, 8 Aug. 2001.
Mann, Dr William Neville, 25 June 2001.
Mant, Prof. (Arthur) Keith, 12 Oct. 2000.
Manthorp, Brian Robert, 21 April 2001.
Maples, Ven. Jeffrey Stanley, 14 Sept. 2001.
Mark, James, MBE, 7 Jan. 2001.
Marriott, Sir John Brook, KCVO, 3 July 2001.
Marshall, Sir Robert Braithwaite, KCB, MBE, 25 Dec. 2000.
Martin, Patrick William, TD, 17 Nov. 2000.

Martin, Samuel Frederick Radcliffe, CB, 20 Nov. 2000.
Martin, Victor Cecil, OBE, 6 April 2001.
Matthews, Prof. Walter Bryan, 12 July 2001.
Maynard, Brian Alfred, CBE, 15 Aug. 2001.
Melville, Sir Ronald Henry, KCB, 4 June 2001.
Mendoza, Maurice, CVO, MSM, 11 Oct. 2000.
Miller, Alastair Cheape, MBE, TD, 16 July 2001.
Miller, Edward, FBA, 21 Dec. 2000.
Miller, Rev. Canon Paul William, 18 Oct. 2000.
Mills, Air Cdre Stanley Edwin Druce, CB, CBE, 19 Jan. 2001.
Molloy, Baron (Life Peer); William John Molloy, TD, 26 May 2001.
Monod, Prof. Théodore, 22 Nov. 2000.
Montgomery, (Charles) John, CBE, 29 May 2001.
Moore, Antony Ross, CMG, 3 Nov. 2000.
Moore, Brian Baden, 1 Sept. 2001.
Moore, Sir Henry Roderick (Sir Harry), CBE, 7 May 2001.
Morley, Eric Douglas, 9 Nov. 2000.
Morley, John Harwood, 3 May 2001.
Morris of Castle Morris, Baron (Life Peer); Brian Robert Morris, 30 April 2001.
Morrison, Prof. John Lamb Murray, CBE, 6 Feb. 2001.
Morrison, John Sinclair, CBE, 25 Oct. 2000.
Morrison, Margaret, OBE, BEM, 5 March 2001.
Morton-Saner, Robert, CVO, CBE, 26 Sept. 2001.
Mulligan, Andrew Armstrong, 24 Feb. 2001.
Munster, 7th Earl of; Anthony Charles FitzClarence, 30 Dec. 2000 (*ext*).
Murdoch, William Ridley Morton, CBE, DSC, VRD, 31 July 2000.
Musgrave, Sir Richard James, 7th Bt, 2 Dec. 2000.

Nall, Sir Michael Joseph, 2nd Bt, 8 Sept. 2001.
Napper, John Pelham, 17 March 2001.
Narayan, Rasipuram Krishnaswamy, (R. K. Narayan), 13 May 2001.
Nath, (Dhurma) Gian, 19 Oct. 1997.
Néel, Prof. Louis Eugène Félix, 17 Nov. 2000.
Neill, Very Rev. Ivan Delacherois, CB, OBE, 18 June 2001.
Nelson, St Elmo Dudley, CMG, 18 July 2001.
Nevin, His Honour (Thomas) Richard, TD, 24 Dec. 2000.
Newhouse, Ven. (Robert) John (Darrell), 27 Nov. 2000.
Newman, Karl Max, CB, 12 Jan. 2001.
Nicholson, (Edward) Rupert, 15 Dec. 2000.
Niklaus, Prof. Robert, 16 Jan. 2001.
Norwood, Sir Walter Neville, 1 April 2000.
Nunburnholme, 5th Baron; Charles Thomas Wilson, 20 Nov. 2000.

O'Connell, John Eugene Anthony, 27 April 2001.
O'Connor, Air Vice-Marshal Patrick Joseph, CB, OBE, 5 March 2001.
O'Connor, Rt Hon. Sir Patrick McCarthy, PC, 3 May 2001.
Olivier, Henry, CMG, 6 Oct. 1994.
Ongley, Hon. Sir Joseph Augustine, 22 Oct. 2000.
Onslow of Woking, Baron (Life Peer); Cranley Gordon Douglas Onslow, KCMG, PC, 13 March 2001.
Oram, Rt Rev. Kenneth Cyril, 7 Jan. 2001.
O'Sullivan, Rt Rev. Mgr James, CBE, 7 March 2001.
Ousby, Ian Vaughan Kenneth, 6 Aug. 2001.
Owen, Philip Loscombe Wintringham, TD, QC, 3 April 2001.
Oxlee, Colin Hamilton, 27 July 2001.

Page, Maj.-Gen. Charles Edward, CB, MBE, 31 Jan. 2001.
Palmer, Charles Stuart William, OBE, 17 Aug. 2001.
Palmer, Sidney John, CB, OBE, 14 April 2001.
Park, Hon. Sir Hugh Eames, 24 Jan. 2001.
Pasterfield, Rt Rev. Philip John, 29 Jan. 2001.
Peat, (William Wood) Watson, CBE, 1 May 2001.
Peirson, Margaret Ellen, CB, 5 May 2001.
Penlington, Ross Grange, CBE, AE, 12 May 2001.
Pennant, His Honour David Edward Thornton, 7 Oct. 2001.
Perrin, John Henry, 18 Jan. 2001.
Petrie, Prof. James Colquhoun, CBE, 31 Aug. 2001.
Peyrefitte, (Pierre-) Roger, 5 Nov. 2000.
Philipson, John Trevor Graham, QC, 17 April 2001.
Phillimore, John Gore, CMG, 22 Sept. 2001.
Phillips, Prof. Neville Crompton, CMG, 29 June 2001.
Phipps, Rt Rev. Simon Wilton, MC, 29 Jan. 2001.
Plowden, Baron (Life Peer); Edwin Noel Plowden, GBE, KCB, 15 Feb. 2001.
Pocock, Kenneth Walter, (Peter), MBE, 12 Nov. 2000.
Pollard, Maj.-Gen. (Charles) Barry, 18 Oct. 2000.
Popham, Mervyn Reddaway, FBA, 24 Oct. 2000.
Popplewell, (Catherine) Margaret, (Lady Popplewell), 20 April 2001.
Porteous, Col Patrick Anthony, VC, 9 Oct. 2000.
Power, Michael George, 27 March 2001.
Prebble, John Edward Curtis, OBE, 30 Jan. 2001.
Prentice, Baron (Life Peer); Reginald Ernest Prentice, PC, 18 Jan. 2001.
Price, Rear-Adm. Cecil Ernest, CB, AFC, 22 June 2001.
Prichard, Air Cdre Richard Julian Paget, CB, CBE, DFC, AFC, 26 April 2001.
Proctor, Ven. Jesse Heighton, 21 May 2001.
Proom, Major William Arthur, TD, 3 Oct. 2000.
Pullinger, John Elphick; His Honour Judge Pullinger, 31 Dec. 2000.
Puttick, Richard George, 20 Feb. 2001.
Pyke, David Alan, CBE, 12 Jan. 2001.

Quine, Prof. Willard Van Orman, 25 Dec. 2000.
Quinlan, Maj.-Gen. Henry, CB, 29 Oct. 2000.

Railton, Dame Ruth, DBE, 23 Feb. 2001.
Rankin, Lady Jean Margaret, DCVO, 3 Oct. 2001.
Rankin, Prof. Robert Alexander, 27 Jan. 2001.
Raven, Simon Arthur Noël, 12 May 2001.
Rea, James Taylor, CMG, 23 Sept. 2001.
Read, Rev. David Haxton Carswell, 6 Jan. 2001.
Reece, Sir (James) Gordon, 22 Sept. 2001.
Rees, Sir (Charles William) Stanley, TD, 2 Dec. 2000.
Rhea, Alexander Dodson, III, 1 Sept. 2000.
Rhodes, Reginald Paul, 2 July 2001.
Richardson, Hugh Edward, CIE, OBE, 3 Dec. 2000.
Richler, Mordecai, OC, 3 July 2001.
Ridler, Anne Barbara, OBE, 15 Oct. 2001.
Ridley, Sir (Nicholas) Harold (Lloyd), FRS, 25 May 2001.
Ripley, (Sidney) Dillon, II, Hon. KBE, 12 March 2001.
Rob, Prof. Charles Granville, MC, 26 July 2001.
Roberts, Albert, 11 May 2000.
Roberts, Rt Rev. Edward James Keymer, 29 June 2001.
Roberts, (Herbert) John, CMG, 29 Dec. 1999.
Robertson, Comdt Dame Nancy Margaret, DBE, 26 Dec. 2000.
Robertson, Prof. Sir Rutherford Ness, AC, CMG, FRS, 5 March 2001.
Robey, Douglas John Brett, CMG, 30 May 2001.
Rodgers, Prof. Harold William, OBE, 24 June 2001.
Roffey, Harry Norman, CMG, 27 Feb. 2001.
Rogers, Rev. Percival Hallewell, MBE, 24 April 2001.
Rogers, William Pierce, 2 Jan. 2001.
Rolf, Percy Henry, 5 July 2001.
Romer, Mark Lemon Robert, 22 July 2001.
Roscoe, Sir Robert Bell, KBE, 24 July 2000.
Rosehill, Lord; Alexander Robert MacRae Carnegie, 31 Aug. 2001.
Ross, Alan, CBE, 14 Feb. 2001.
Rosser, Sir Melvyn Wynne, 4 Feb. 2001.
Rotherham, Leonard, CBE, FRS, 23 March 2001.
Rowell, Sir John Joseph, CBE, 5 May 1996.
Roy, Ian, 17 Feb. 2001.
Rubinstein, Michael Bernard, 12 Jan. 2001.
Rudden, James, 16 Nov. 2000.
Ruggles-Brise, Captain Guy Edward, TD, 14 Nov. 2000.
Runciman, Hon. Sir James Cochran Stevenson, (Hon. Sir Steven), CH, CLit, FBA, 1 Nov. 2000.
Russell, Prof. Roger Wolcott, 25 July 1998.
Ryder of Warsaw, Baroness (Life Peer); Margaret Susan, (Sue), Ryder, CMG, OBE, 2 Nov. 2000.

Sage, Prof. Lorna, 11 Jan. 2001.
Salmon, Brian Lawson, CBE, 28 May 2001.
Salmon, Col William Alexander, (Alec), OBE, 2 Nov. 2000.
Sanger, Ruth Ann, (Mrs R. R. Race), FRS, 4 June 2001.
Sarell, Sir Roderick Francis Gisbert, KCMG, KCVO, 15 Aug. 2001.
Savory, Hubert Newman, 21 Feb. 2001.
Scatchard, Vice-Adm. John Percival, CB, DSC, 22 June 2001.
Scoble, (Arthur William) John, 10 Jan. 2001.
Scrivener, Ronald Stratford, CMG, 14 Jan. 2001.
Seccombe, Hugh Digorie, CBE, 11 June 2001.
Secombe, Sir Harry Donald, CBE, 11 April 2001.
Sefton of Garston, Baron (Life Peer); William Henry Sefton, 9 Sept. 2001.
Selby, 5th Viscount; Edward Thomas William Gully, 23 Jan. 2001.
Seymour, Francis, 16 March 2001.
Shackleton, Prof. Robert Millner, FRS, 3 May 2001.
Shand, Sir James, MBE, 23 Dec. 2000.
Sharp, Derek Joseph, 14 March 2001.
Sharpe, Peter Samuel, QPM, 1 Dec. 2000.
Shaw, Robert Macdonald, CB, 9 Nov. 2000.
Shearer, Very Rev. John, (Jack), OBE, 12 Jan. 2001.
Sheehy, Terence Joseph, 30 Aug. 2001.
Shelford, Cornelius William, 16 Jan. 2001.
Shepherd, 2nd Baron; Malcolm Newton Shepherd, PC, 5 April 2001.
Shergold, Harold Taplin, CMG, OBE, 25 Dec. 2000.
Sherlock, Sir Philip Manderson, KBE, 4 Dec. 2000.
Shillington, Sir (Robert Edward) Graham, CBE, 14 Aug. 2001.
Shore of Stepney, Baron (Life Peer); Peter David Shore, PC, 24 Sept. 2001.
Short, Sir Noel Edward Vivian, MBE, MC, 12 June 2001.
Sidebottom, Edward John, 9 April 2001.

Sieff of Brimpton, Baron (Life Peer); Marcus Joseph Sieff, OBE, 23 Feb. 2001.
Simeon, John Power Barrington, OBE, 16 Nov. 2000.
Simon, Prof. Herbert Alexander, 9 Feb. 2001.
Simpson, Ffreebairn Liddon, CMG, 25 Jan. 2001.
Sinopoli, Giuseppe, 20 April 2001.
Skempton, Sir Alec Westley, FRS, 9 Aug. 2001.
Slater, John Fell, CMG, 14 Oct. 2001.
Slater, Richard Mercer Keene, CMG, 8 Oct. 2001.
Slaughter, Frank Gill, MC, 17 May 2001.
Smart, Prof. (Roderick) Ninian, 29 Jan. 2001.
Smith, Ven. Arthur Cyril, VRD, 3 April 2001.
Smith, Brian Percival, 29 Nov. 2000.
Smith, Colin, 26 Sept. 2001.
Smith, Rev. Francis Taylor, 25 Dec. 2000.
Smith, Kenneth Graeme Stewart, CMG, 14 April 2001.
Smith, Prof. Michael, CC, OBC, FRS, 4 Oct. 2000.
Smith, William McGregor, OBE, 16 Feb. 2001.
Sneddon, Prof. Ian Naismith, OBE, FRS, 4 Nov. 2000.
Solomon, His Honour (Alan) Peter, 17 Sept. 2001.
Southam, Gordon Ronald, 13 Aug. 2000.
Southern, Michael William, 21 Sept. 2001.
Southern, Sir Richard William, FBA, 6 Feb. 2001.
Sowry, Dr (George Stephen) Clive, 4 Sept. 2001.
Spedding, Sir David Rolland, KCMG, CVO, OBE, 13 June 2001.
Spens, 3rd Baron; Patrick Michael Rex Spens, 5 Jan. 2001.
Stafford, John, OBE, 16 Feb. 2001.
Stainforth, Maj.-Gen. Charles Herbert, CB, OBE, 22 March 2001.
Stakis, Sir Reo Argyros, 28 Aug. 2001.
Stassen, Harold Edward, 4 March 2001.
Stead, Robert, CBE, 3 April 2001.
Stearn, William Thomas, CBE, 8 May 2001.
Stephen, Harbourne Mackay, CBE, DSO, DFC, AE, 20 Aug. 2001.
Stephen, John Low, 17 May 2001.
Stephens, William Henry, CB, 12 Aug. 2001.
Stern, Isaac, 22 Sept. 2001.
Sterne, Laurence Henry Gordon, 30 May 2001.
Stevens, Prof. Thomas Stevens, FRS, 12 Nov. 2000.
Stevenson, Derek Paul, CBE, 4 March 2001.
Stewart, Ewen, 9 Oct. 2000.
Stewart, Dame Muriel Acadia, DBE, 7 Oct. 2001.
Stewart-Smith, Rev. Canon David Cree, 1 May 2001.
Stock, His Honour Raymond, QC, 17 May 2001.
Storr, (Charles) Anthony, 17 March 2001.
Stout, Samuel Coredon, 21 Jan. 2001.
Strachan, Michael Francis, CBE, 30 Nov. 2000.
Subramaniam, Chidambaram, 7 Nov. 2000.
Sutherland, James, CBE, 21 Sept. 2001.
Sutherland, Sir Maurice, 11 March 2001.
Swales, Prof. John Douglas, 17 Oct. 2000.
Swynnerton, Sir Roger John Massy, CMG, OBE, MC, 30 Dec. 2000.
Sykes, Sir John Charles Anthony le Gallais, 3rd Bt, 12 May 2001.
Sylvester, (Anthony) David (Bernard), CBE, 19 June 2001.
Symmers, Prof. William St Clair, 25 Oct. 2000.
Synge, Henry Millington, 24 April 2001.
Synnot, Adm. Sir Anthony Monckton, KBE, AO, 4 July 2001.

Tange, Sir Arthur Harold, AC, CBE, 10 May 2001.
Taylor of Gryfe, Baron (Life Peer); Thomas Johnston Taylor, 13 July 2001.
Taylor, Andrew James, CBE, 17 March 2001.
Taylor, Hermon, 10 Jan. 2001.
Taylor, Rt Rev. John Vernon, 30 Jan. 2001.
Taylor, Ronald Oliver, 13 Oct. 2000.
Taylor, William Bernard, 5 March 1999.
Temple, Rt Rev. Frederick Stephen, 26 Nov. 2000.
Tench, William Henry, CBE, 20 Oct. 2000.
Terrington, 5th Baron; Christopher Montague Woodhouse, DSO, OBE, 13 Feb. 2001.
Tett, Sir Hugh Charles, 2 Jan. 2001.
Thirkettle, (William) Ellis, CBE, 25 Oct. 2000.
Thirlwall, Air Vice-Marshal George Edwin, CB, 19 Oct. 2000.
Thomas, (John) Frank (Phillips), 14 Oct. 2000.
Thomas, Ralph Philip, MC, 17 March 2001.
Thompson, John Alan, CMG, 5 Feb. 2001.
Thompson, Prof. William Bell, 17 Oct. 1995.
Thomson, Rt Hon. David Spence, CMG, MC, ED, PC, 25 Oct. 1999.
Thomson, Ian Mackenzie, WS, 4 Nov. 2000.
Tillotson, Prof. Kathleen Mary, CBE, FBA, 3 June 2001.
Tonkin, Hon. David Oliver, AO, 2 Oct. 2000.
Trewby, Vice-Adm. Sir (George Francis) Allan, KCB, 23 July 2001.
Troup, His Honour Alistair Mewburn, 10 May 2001.
Trowbridge, George William Job, CBE, 8 March 2001.
Trubshaw, (Ernest) Brian, CBE, MVO, 24 March 2001.
Tryon-Wilson, Brig. Charles Edward, CBE, DSO, 18 April 2001.
Tuke, Sir Anthony Favill, 6 March 2001.
Turnbull, Ven. David Charles, 5 May 2001.
Turner, Hon. Joanna Elizabeth, (Hon. Mrs Turner), 10 Feb. 2001.
Turner, Patricia, OBE, 22 July 2000.
Tutin, Dame Dorothy, DBE, 6 Aug. 2001.
Twigg, Patrick Alan, QC, 14 May 2001.
Tyson, Alan Walker, CBE, FBA, 10 Nov. 2000.

Unwin, Rayner Stephens, CBE, 23 Nov. 2000.
Upjohn, Maj.-Gen. Gordon Farleigh, CB, CBE, 19 March 2001.
Urie, Wing Comdr (John) Dunlop, AE, 20 July 2001.
Uvarov, Dame Olga Nikolaevna, DBE, 29 Aug. 2001.

Verco, Sir Walter John George, KCVO, 10 March 2001.
Vereker, Peter William Medlicott, 12 Sept. 2001.
Verey, Michael John, TD, 13 Oct. 2000.
Verey, Rosemary Isabel Baird, OBE, 31 May 2001.
Vermeule, Prof. Emily Dickinson Townsend, 6 Feb. 2001.
Verney, Sir Ralph Bruce, 5th Bt, KBE, 17 Aug. 2001.
Vernon, Sir James, AC, CBE, 10 July 2000.
Vial, Sir Kenneth Harold, CBE, 29 Jan. 2001.
Vincent, Prof. John Joseph, 24 April 2001.

Wain, Prof. (Ralph) Louis, CBE, FRS, 14 Dec. 2000.
Walker, Prof. Arthur Geoffrey, FRS, 31 March 2001.
Walker, Sir Gervas George, 19 Aug. 2001.
Walker, John Malcolm, 26 March 2001.
Walker, Gen. Sir Walter Colyear, KCB, CBE, DSO, 12 Aug. 2001.
Wall, Prof. Patrick David, FRS, 8 Aug. 2001.
Wallington, Jeremy Francis, 14 Aug. 2001.
Walls, Prof. John, 1 March 2001.
Walton, Anthony Michael, QC, 18 Nov. 2000.
Ward, Donald Albert, 12 Oct. 2001.
Waterhouse, Douglas Frew, AO, CMG, FRS, Dec. 2000.
Watson, Arthur Christopher, CMG, 7 May 2001.
Waugh, Auberon Alexander, 16 Jan. 2001.
Waymouth, Charity, 31 Oct. 2000.
Weatherley, Prof. Paul Egerton, FRS, 8 Aug. 2001.
Weaver, Sir Tobias Rushton, (Sir Toby), CB, 10 June 2001.
Webster, Alen Gregg, CMG, 22 July 2001.
Weighill, Air Cdre Robert Harold George, CBE, DFC, 27 Oct. 2000.
Wellings, Victor Gordon, QC, 19 June 2001.
Wells, Thomas Leonard, OOnt, 11 Oct. 2000.
Welty, Eudora, 23 July 2001.
Westbury, 5th Baron; David Alan Bethell, CBE, MC, 12 Oct. 2001.
Westerman, Sir (Wilfred) Alan, CBE, 20 May 2001.
Whippman, Michael Lewis, CB, 1 Oct. 2001.
Whistler, Sir (Alan Charles) Laurence, CBE, 19 Dec. 2000.
Whitfield, Rev. George Joshua Newbold, 28 Oct. 2000.
Whittome, Sir (Leslie) Alan, 21 Jan. 2001.
Wigram, Rev. Canon Sir Clifford Woolmore, 7th Bt, 11 Dec. 2000.
Wilberforce, William John Antony, CMG, 2 Sept. 2001.
Wilkinson, Prof. Elizabeth Mary, FBA, 2 Jan. 2001.
Williams, Michael Leonard, 11 Jan. 2001.
Williams, Prof. Thomas Eifion Hopkins, CBE, 17 June 2001.
Williamson, Sir Nicholas Frederick Hedworth, 11th Bt, 31 Dec. 2000 (*ext*).
Willis, Joseph Robert McKenzie, CB, CMG, 14 Feb. 2001.
Willman, George, 13 April 2001.
Willmer, Prof. (Edward) Nevill, FRS, 8 April 2001.
Wilson, Henry Braithwaite, 29 April 2001.
Wilson, Sir (Robert) Donald, KBE, 29 July 2001.
Wilson, Prof. Thomas, OBE, FBA, 27 July 2001.
Wood, Leonard George, CBE, 16 Feb. 2001.
Woodruff, Harry Wells, CMG, 19 June 2000.
Woodruff, Prof. Sir Michael Francis Addison, FRS, 10 March 2001.
Woods, Sir Colin Philip Joseph, KCVO, CBE, QPM, 27 Jan. 2001.
Worswick, (George) David (Norman), CBE, FBA, 18 May 2001.
Wraxall, 2nd Baron; George Richard Lawley Gibbs, 19 July 2001.
Wyatt, Gavin Edward, CMG, 17 July 2001.
Wynn, Arthur Henry Ashford, 23 Sept. 2001.

Xenakis, Prof. Iannis, 4 Feb. 2001.

Young, Bertram Alfred, OBE, 17 Sept. 2001.
Young, Gavin David, 18 Jan. 2001.

ABBREVIATIONS USED IN THIS BOOK

Some of the designatory letters in this list are used merely for economy of space and do not necessarily imply any professional or other qualification.

A

AA Anti-aircraft; Automobile Association; Architectural Association; Augustinians of the Assumption; Associate in Arts

AAA Amateur Athletic Association; American Accounting Association

AAAL American Academy of Arts and Letters

AA&QMG Assistant Adjutant and Quartermaster-General

AAArb Member, Association of Arbitrators (South Africa)

AAAS American Association for the Advancement of Science

AAC Army Air Corps

AACCA Associate, Association of Certified and Corporate Accountants (*now see* ACCA)

AACE Association for Adult and Continuing Education

AAF Auxiliary Air Force (*now see* RAux AF)

AAFCE Allied Air Forces in Central Europe

AAG Assistant Adjutant-General

AAI Associate, Chartered Auctioneers' and Estate Agents' Institute (*now* (after amalgamation) *see* ARICS)

AAIL American Academy and Institute of Arts and Letters (*now see* AAAL)

AAM Association of Assistant Mistresses in Secondary Schools

AAMC Australian Army Medical Corps (*now see* RAAMC)

A&AEE Aeroplane and Armament Experimental Establishment

A&E Accident and Emergency

A and SH Argyll and Sutherland Highlanders

AAPS Aquatic and Atmospheric Physical Sciences

AAS American Astronomical Society

AASA Associate, Australian Society of Accountants (*now see* FCPA)

AASC Australian Army Service Corps

AATSE Australian Academy of Technological Sciences and Engineering

AAUQ Associate in Accountancy, University of Queensland

AB Bachelor of Arts (US); able-bodied seaman; airborne; Alberta (postal)

ABA Amateur Boxing Association; Antiquarian Booksellers' Association; American Bar Association

ABBSI Associate Member, British Boot and Shoe Institute

ABC Australian Broadcasting Commission; American Broadcasting Companies; Amateur Boxing Club; Associate, Birmingham Conservatoire

ABCC Association of British Chambers of Commerce

ABI Association of British Insurers

ABIA Associate, Bankers' Institute of Australasia

ABINZ Associate, Bankers' Institute of New Zealand

ABIS Association of Burglary Insurance Surveyors

ABM Advisory Board of Ministry

ABNM American Board of Nuclear Medicine

ABP Associated British Ports

Abp Archbishop

ABPI Association of British Pharmaceutical Industry

ABPsS Associate, British Psychological Society (*now see* AFBPsS)

ABRC Advisory Board for the Research Councils

ABS Associate, Building Societies' Institute (*now see* ACBSI)

ABSA Association for Business Sponsorship of the Arts

ABSM Associate, Birmingham and Midland Institute School of Music

ABTA Association of British Travel Agents

ABTAPL Association of British Theological and Philosophical Libraries

AC Companion, Order of Australia; *Ante Christum* (before Christ)

ACA Associate, Institute of Chartered Accountants

Acad. Academy

ACARD Advisory Council for Applied Research and Development

ACAS Advisory, Conciliation and Arbitration Service; Assistant Chief of the Air Staff

ACBSI Associate, Chartered Building Societies Institute

ACC Association of County Councils; Anglican Consultative Council

ACCA Associate, Association of Chartered Certified Accountants (*formerly* Chartered Association of Certified Accountants)

ACCE Association of County Chief Executives

ACCEL American College of Cardiology Extended Learning

ACCM Advisory Council for the Church's Ministry (*now see* ABM)

ACCS Associate, Corporation of Secretaries (*formerly* of Certified Secretaries)

ACDP Australian Committee of Directors and Principals

ACDS Assistant Chief of Defence Staff

ACE Association of Consulting Engineers; Member, Association of Conference Executives; Allied Command Europe

ACENVO Association of Chief Executives of National Voluntary Organisations

ACEO Association of Chief Education Officers

ACertCM Archbishops' Certificate in Church Music

ACF Army Cadet Force

ACFA Army Cadet Force Association

ACFAS Association Canadienne-Française pour l'avancement des sciences

ACFHE Association of Colleges for Further and Higher Education

ACG Assistant Chaplain-General

ACGI Associate, City and Guilds of London Institute

ACGS Assistant Chief of the General Staff

ACI Airports Council International (Europe)

ACIArb Associate, Chartered Institute of Arbitrators

ACIB Associate, Chartered Institute of Bankers

ACII Associate, Chartered Insurance Institute

ACIS Associate, Institute of Chartered Secretaries and Administrators (*formerly* Chartered Institute of Secretaries)

ACIT Associate, Chartered Institute of Transport

ACLS American Council of Learned Societies

ACM Association of Computing Machinery

ACMA Associate, Chartered Institute of Management Accountants (*formerly* Institute of Cost and Management Accountants)

ACNS Assistant Chief of Naval Staff

ACommA Associate, Society of Commercial Accountants (*now see* ASCA)

ACORD Advisory Committee on Research and Development

ACOS Assistant Chief of Staff

ACOST Advisory Council on Science and Technology

ACP Association of Clinical Pathologists; Associate, College of Preceptors; African/Caribbean/Pacific

ACPO Association of Chief Police Officers

ACR Accredited Conservator-Restorer

ACRE Action with Rural Communities in England

ACS American Chemical Society; Additional Curates Society

ACSEA Allied Command South East Asia

ACSM Associate, Camborne School of Mines

AcSS Member, Academy of Learned Societies for the Social Sciences

ACT Australian Capital Territory; Australian College of Theology; Associate, College of Technology; Association of Corporate Treasurers

ACTSS Association of Clerical, Technical and Supervisory Staff

ACTT Association of Cinematograph, Television and Allied Technicians

ACTU Australian Council of Trade Unions

ACU Association of Commonwealth Universities

ACWA Associate, Institute of Cost and Works Accountants (*now see* ACMA)

AD Dame of the Order of Australia; *Anno Domini* (in the year of the Lord); Air Defence

aD ausser Dienst

ADAS Agricultural Development and Advisory Service

ADB Asian Development Bank; Associate of the Drama Board (Education)

ADB/F African Development Bank/Fund

ADC Aide-de-camp; Association of District Councils

ADCM Archbishop of Canterbury's Diploma in Church Music

AD Corps Army Dental Corps (*now* RADC)

ADC(P) Personal Aide-de-camp to HM The Queen

ADEME Assistant Director Electrical and Mechanical Engineering

Ad eund *Ad eundem gradum*; and *see under* aeg

ADFManc Art and Design Fellow, Manchester

ADGMS Assistant Director-General of Medical Services

Adjt Adjutant

ADJAG Assistant Deputy Judge Advocate General

ADK Order of Ahli Darjah Kinabalu

ADM Advanced Diploma in Midwifery

Adm. Admiral

ADMS Assistant Director of Medical Services

ADOS Assistant Director of Ordnance Services

ADP Automatic Data Processing

ADPA Associate Diploma of Public Administration

ADS&T Assistant Director of Supplies and Transport
Adv. Advisory; Advocate
AdvDip Advanced Diploma
ADVS Assistant Director of Veterinary Services
ADWE&M Assistant Director of Works, Electrical and Mechanical
AE Air Efficiency Award
AEA Atomic Energy Authority; Air Efficiency Award (*now see* AE)
AEAF Allied Expeditionary Air Force
AEC Agriculture Executive Council; Army Educational Corps (*now see* RAEC); Atomic Energy Commission
AECMA Association Européenne des Constructeurs de Matériel Aérospatial
AEE Atomic Energy Establishment
AEEU Amalgamated Engineering and Electrical Union
AEF Amalgamated Union of Engineering and Foundry Workers (later AEU, *now see* AEEU); American Expeditionary Forces
aeg *ad eundem gradum* (to the same degree—of the admission of a graduate of one university to the same degree at another without examination)
AEI Associated Electrical Industries
AEM Air Efficiency Medal
AER Army Emergency Reserve
AERE Atomic Energy Research Establishment (Harwell)
Æt., Ætat. *Ætatis* (aged)
AEU Amalgamated Engineering Union (*now see* AEEU)
AF Admiral of the Fleet
AFA Amateur Football Alliance; Associate, Institute of Financial Accountants
AFAIAA Associate Fellow, American Institute of Aeronautics and Astronautics
AFASIC Association for All Speech Impaired Children
AFB Air Force Base
AFBPsS Associate Fellow, British Psychological Society
AFC Air Force Cross; Association Football Club
AFCAI Associate Fellow, Canadian Aeronautical Institute
AFCEA Armed Forces Communications and Electronics Association
AFCENT Allied Forces in Central Europe
AFD Doctor of Fine Arts (US)
AFDS Air Fighting Development Squadron
AFGE Associate Fellow, Guild of Glass Engravers
AFHQ Allied Force Headquarters
AFI American Film Institute
AFIA Associate, Federal Institute of Accountants (Australia)
AFIAP Artiste, Fédération Internationale de l'Art Photographique
AFIAS Associate Fellow, Institute of Aeronautical Sciences (US) (*now see* AFAIAA)
AFIMA Associate Fellow, Institute of Mathematics and its Applications
AFM Air Force Medal
AFNORTH Allied Forces in Northern Europe
AFOM Associate, Faculty of Occupational Medicine
AFRAeS Associate Fellow, Royal Aeronautical Society (*now see* MRAeS)
AFRC Agricultural and Food Research Council (*now see* BBSRC)
AFV Armoured Fighting Vehicles
AG Attorney-General
AGAC American Guild of Authors and Composers
AGARD Advisory Group for Aerospace Research and Development
AGC Adjutant General's Corps
AGH Australian General Hospital
AGI Alliance Graphique Internationale; Associate, Institute of Certificated Grocers
AGR Advanced Gas-cooled Reactor
AGRA Army Group Royal Artillery; Association of Genealogists and Record Agents
AGSM Associate, Guildhall School of Music and Drama; Australian Graduate School of Management
AHA Area Health Authority; American Hospitals Association; Associate, Institute of Health Service Administrators (*now see* AHSM)
AHA(T) Area Health Authority (Teaching)
AHQ Army Headquarters
AHRB Arts and Humanities Research Board
AHSM Associate, Institute of Health Services Management
AH-WC Associate, Heriot-Watt College, Edinburgh
ai *ad interim*
AIA Associate, Institute of Actuaries; American Institute of Architects; Association of International Artists
AIAA American Institute of Aeronautics and Astronautics
AIAgrE Associate, Institution of Agricultural Engineers
AIAL Associate Member, International Institute of Arts and Letters
AIArb Associate, Institute of Arbitrators (*now see* ACIArb)
AIAS Associate Surveyor Member, Incorporated Association of Architects and Surveyors
AIB Associate, Institute of Bankers (*now see* ACIB)
AIBD Associate, Institute of British Decorators
AIBP Associate, Institute of British Photographers
AIBScot Associate, Institute of Bankers in Scotland
AIC Agricultural Improvement Council; Associate of the Institute of Chemistry (later ARIC, MRIC; *now see* MRSC)
aic armour infantry course
AICA Associate Member, Commonwealth Institute of Accountants; Association Internationale des Critiques d'Art
AICE Associate, Institution of Civil Engineers
AIChE American Institute of Chemical Engineers
AICPA American Institute of Certified Public Accountants
AICS Associate, Institute of Chartered Shipbrokers
AICTA Associate, Imperial College of Tropical Agriculture
AIDS Acquired Immunity Deficiency Syndrome
AIE Associate, Institute of Education
AIEE Associate, Institution of Electrical Engineers
AIF Australian Imperial Forces
AIFireE Associate, Institution of Fire Engineers
AIG Adjutant-Inspector-General
AIH Associate, Institute of Housing
AIHort Associate, Institute of Horticulture
AIIA Associate, Insurance Institute of America; Associate, Indian Institute of Architects
AIIMR Associate, Institute of Investment Management and Research
AIInfSc Associate, Institute of Information Scientists
AIIRA Associate, International Industrial Relations Association
AIL Associate, Institute of Linguists
AILA Associate, Institute of Landscape Architects (*now see* ALI)
AIM Associate, Institution of Metallurgists (*now see* MIM); Australian Institute of Management; Alternative Investment Market
AIMarE Associate, Institute of Marine Engineers
AIMC Associate, Institute of Management Consultants
AIME American Institute of Mechanical Engineers
AIMgt Associate, Institute of Management
AIMSW Associate, Institute of Medical Social Work
AInstM Associate Member, Institute of Marketing
AInstP Associate, Institute of Physics
AInstPI Associate, Institute of Patentees and Inventors
AIP Association of Independent Producers
AIPR Associate, Institute of Public Relations
AIProdE Associate, Institution of Production Engineers
AIQS Associate Member, Institute of Quantity Surveyors
AIRCENT Allied Air Forces Central Europe
AIRTE Associate, Institute of Road Transport Engineers
AIRTO Association of Independent Research and Technology Organizations
AIS Associate, Institute of Statisticians (*later* MIS)
AISA Associate, Incorporated Secretaries' Association
AIStructE Associate, Institution of Structural Engineers
AITI Associate, Institute of Translators and Interpreters
AITP Associate, Institute of Town Planners, India
AJAG Assistant Judge Advocate General
AJEX Association of Jewish Ex-Service Men and Women
AK Knight, Order of Australia; Alaska (postal)
AKC Associate, King's College London
AL Alabama (postal)
ALA Associate, Library Association; Association of London Authorities
Ala Alabama
ALAA Associate, Library Association of Australia
ALAI Associate, Library Association of Ireland
ALAM Associate, London Academy of Music and Dramatic Art
ALCD Associate, London College of Divinity
ALCM Associate, London College of Music
ALCM (TD) Associate, London College of Music (Teaching Diploma)
ALCS Authors Lending and Copyright Society
ALFSEA Allied Land Forces South-East Asia
ALI Argyll Light Infantry; Associate, Landscape Institute (*now see* MLI)
ALICE Autistic and Language Impaired Children's Education
ALLC Association for Literary and Linguistic Computing
ALP Australian Labor Party
ALPSP Association of Learned and Professional Society Publishers
ALS Associate, Linnean Society; Amyotrophic Lateral Sclerosis
Alta Alberta
ALVA Association of Leading Visitor Attractions
AM Albert Medal; Member, Order of Australia; Master of Arts (US); Alpes Maritimes
AMA Association of Metropolitan Authorities; Assistant Masters Association (later AMMA, *now see* ATL); Associate, Museums Association; Australian Medical Association
AMARC Associated Marine and Related Charities
Amb. Ambulance; Ambassador
AMBDA Associate Member, British Dyslexia Association
AMBIM Associate Member, British Institute of Management (*now see* AIMgt)

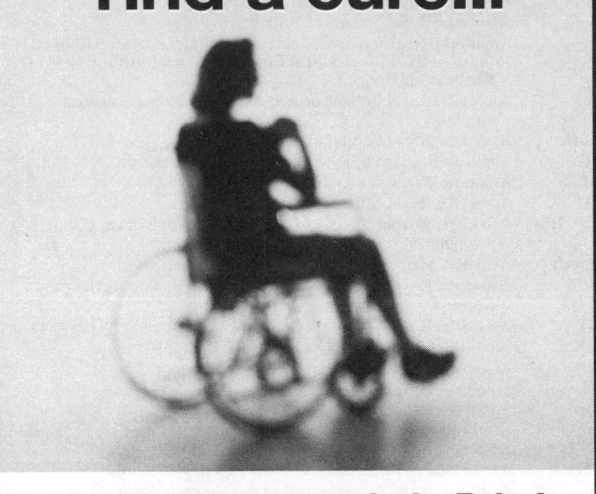

AMBritIRE Associate Member, British Institution of Radio Engineers (*now see* AMIERE)
AMC Association of Municipal Corporations
AMCST Associate, Manchester College of Science and Technology
AMCT Associate, Manchester College of Technology
AME Association of Municipal Engineers
AMEME Association of Mining Electrical and Mechanical Engineers
AMet Associate of Metallurgy
AMF Australian Military Forces
AMIAE Associate Member, Institution of Automobile Engineers
AMIAgrE Associate Member, Institution of Agricultural Engineers
AMICE Associate Member, Institution of Civil Engineers (*now see* MICE)
AMIChemE Associate Member, Institution of Chemical Engineers
AMIE(Aust) Associate Member, Institution of Engineers, Australia
AMIED Associate Member, Institution of Engineering Designers
AMIEE Associate Member, Institution of Electrical Engineers (*now see* MIEE)
AMIE(Ind) Associate Member, Institution of Engineers, India
AMIERE Associate Member, Institution of Electronic and Radio Engineers
AMIH Associate Member, Institute of Housing
AMIMechE Associate Member, Institution of Mechanical Engineers (*now see* MIMechE)
AMIMinE Associate Member, Institution of Mining Engineers (*now see* AMIMM)
AMIMM Associate Member, Institution of Mining and Metallurgy
AMInstBE Associate Member, Institution of British Engineers
AMInstCE Associate Member, Institution of Civil Engineers (*now see* MICE)
AmInstEE American Institute of Electrical Engineers
AMInstR Associate Member, Institute of Refrigeration
AMInstT Associate Member, Institute of Transport (*now see* ACIT)
AMInstTA Associate Member, Institute of Traffic Administration
AMINucE Associate Member, Institution of Nuclear Engineers
AMIRSE Associate Member, Institute of Railway Signalling Engineers
AMIStructE Associate Member, Institution of Structural Engineers
AMMA Assistant Masters & Mistresses Association (*now see* ATL)
AMN Ahli Mangku Negara (Malaysia)
AMP Advanced Management Program; Air Member for Personnel
AMRC Association of Medical Research Charities
AMRINA Associate Member, Royal Institution of Naval Architects
AMRSH Associate Member, Royal Society of Health
AMS Assistant Military Secretary; Army Medical Services
AMSO Air Member for Supply and Organisation
AMTE Admiralty Marine Technology Establishment
AMTRI Advanced Manufacturing Technology Research Institute
ANA Associate National Academician (US)
ANAF Arab Non-Arab Friendship
Anat. Anatomy; Anatomical
ANC African National Congress
ANECInst Associate, NE Coast Institution of Engineers and Shipbuilders
Anon. Anonymously
ANU Australian National University
ANZAAS Australian and New Zealand Association for the Advancement of Science
Anzac Australian and New Zealand Army Corps
AO Officer, Order of Australia; Air Officer
AOA Air Officer in charge of Administration
AOC Air Officer Commanding
AOC-in-C Air Officer Commanding-in-Chief
AOD Army Ordnance Department
AOER Army Officers Emergency Reserve
APA American Psychiatric Association
APACS Association of Payment and Clearing Systems
APD Army Pay Department
APEX Association of Professional, Executive, Clerical and Computer Staff
APHA American Public Health Association
APIS Army Photographic Intelligence Service
APM Assistant Provost Marshal
APMI Associate, Pensions Management Institute
APR Accredited Public Relations Practitioner
APS Aborigines Protection Society; American Physical Society
APsSI Associate, Psychological Society of Ireland
APSW Association of Psychiatric Social Workers
APT&C Administrative, Professional, Technical and Clerical
APTC Army Physical Training Corps
AQ Administration and Quartering
AQMG Assistant Quartermaster-General
AR Associated Rediffusion (Television); Arkansas (postal)
ARA Associate, Royal Academy
ARACI Associate, Royal Australian Chemical Institute
ARAD Associate, Royal Academy of Dancing
ARAeS Associate, Royal Aeronautical Society
ARAgS Associate, Royal Agricultural Societies (*ie* of England, Scotland and Wales)
ARAIA Associate, Royal Australian Institute of Architects
ARAM Associate, Royal Academy of Music
ARAS Associate, Royal Astronomical Society
ARBA Associate, Royal Society of British Artists
ARBS Associate, Royal Society of British Sculptors
ARC Architects' Registration Council; Agricultural Research Council (later AFRC); Aeronautical Research Council; Arthritis and Rheumatism Council
ARCA Associate, Royal College of Art; Associate, Royal Canadian Academy
ARCamA Associate, Royal Cambrian Academy of Art
ARCIC Anglican-Roman Catholic International Commission
ARCM Associate, Royal College of Music
ARCO Associate, Royal College of Organists
ARCO(CHM) Associate, Royal College of Organists with Diploma in Choir Training
ARCPsych Associate Member, Royal College of Psychiatrists
ARCS Associate, Royal College of Science; Accreditation Review and Consulting Service (*now see* ISI)
ARCST Associate, Royal College of Science and Technology (Glasgow)
ARCUK Architects' Registration Council of the United Kingdom
ARCVS Associate, Royal College of Veterinary Surgeons
ARE Associate, Royal Society of Painter-Printmakers (*formerly* of Painter-Etchers and Engravers); Arab Republic of Egypt; Admiralty Research Establishment
AREINZ Associate, Real Estate Institute, New Zealand
ARELS Association of Recognised English Language Schools
ARIAS Associate, Royal Incorporation of Architects in Scotland
ARIBA Associate, Royal Institute of British Architects (*now see* RIBA)
ARIC Associate, Royal Institute of Chemistry (later MRIC; *now see* MRSC)
ARICS Professional Associate, Royal Institution of Chartered Surveyors (*now see* MRICS)
ARINA Associate, Royal Institution of Naval Architects
ARLT Association for the Reform of Latin Teaching
ARMS Associate, Royal Society of Miniature Painters
ARP Air Raid Precautions
ARPS Associate, Royal Photographic Society
ARR Association of Radiation Research
ARRC Associate, Royal Red Cross; Allied Command Europe Rapid Reaction Corps
ARSA Associate, Royal Scottish Academy
ARSC Association of Recorded Sound Collections
ARSCM Associate, Royal School of Church Music
ARSM Associate, Royal School of Mines
ARTC Associate, Royal Technical College (Glasgow) (*now see* ARCST)
ARWA Associate, Royal West of England Academy
ARWS Associate, Royal Society of Painters in Water-Colours
AS Anglo-Saxon
ASA Associate Member, Society of Actuaries; Associate of Society of Actuaries (US); Australian Society of Accountants; Army Sailing Association; Advertising Standards Authority; Alment Aksjeselskap
ASAA Associate, Society of Incorporated Accountants and Auditors
ASAI Associate, Society of Architectural Illustrators
AS&TS of SA Associated Scientific and Technical Societies of South Africa
ASAQS Association of South African Quantity Surveyors
ASBAH Association for Spina Bifida and Hydrocephalus
ASC Administrative Staff College, Henley
ASCA Associate, Society of Company and Commercial Accountants
ASCAB Armed Services Consultant Approval Board
ASCAP American Society of Composers, Authors and Publishers
ASCE American Society of Civil Engineers
ASCHB Association for Study of Conservation of Historic Buildings
AScW Association of Scientific Workers (*now see* ASTMS)
ASD Armament Supply Department
ASE Amalgamated Society of Engineers (later AUEW, then AEU; *now see* AEEU); Association for Science Education
ASEAN Association of South East Asian Nations
ASH Action on Smoking and Health
ASIAD Associate, Society of Industrial Artists and Designers
ASLE American Society of Lubrication Engineers
ASLEF Associated Society of Locomotive Engineers and Firemen
ASLIB or Aslib Association for Information Management (*formerly* Association of Special Libraries and Information Bureaux)
ASM Association of Senior Members; Australian Service Medal
ASME American Society of Mechanical Engineers; Association for the Study of Medical Education
ASO Air Staff Officer
ASSC Accounting Standards Steering Committee
ASSET Association of Supervisory Staffs, Executives and Technicians (*now see* ASTMS)
AssocEng Associate of Engineering
AssocISI Associate, Iron and Steel Institute

AssocMCT Associateship of Manchester College of Technology
AssocMIAeE Associate Member, Institution of Aeronautical Engineers
AssocRINA Associate, Royal Institution of Naval Architects
AssocSc Associate in Science
Asst Assistant
ASTA Association of Short Circuit Testing Authorities
ASTC Administrative Service Training Course
ASTMS Association of Scientific, Technical and Managerial Staffs (now part of MSF)
ASVU Army Security Vetting Unit
ASWE Admiralty Surface Weapons Establishment
ATA Air Transport Auxiliary
ATAE Association of Tutors in Adult Education
ATAF Allied Tactical Air Force
ATC Air Training Corps; Art Teacher's Certificate
ATCDE Association of Teachers in Colleges and Departments of Education (*now see* NATFHE)
ATCL Associate, Trinity College of Music, London
ATD Art Teacher's Diploma
ATI Associate, Textile Institute
ATII Associate Member, Chartered Institute (*formerly* Incorporated Institute, then Institute) of Taxation
ATL Association of Teachers and Lecturers
ato Ammunition Technical Officer
ATP Association of Tennis Players
ATPL (A) or (H) Airline Transport Pilot's Licence (Aeroplanes), or (Helicopters)
ATR Art Therapist Registered
ATS Auxiliary Territorial Service (*now see* WRAC)
ATTI Association of Teachers in Technical Institutions (*now see* NATFHE)
ATV Associated Television (*formerly* Association TeleVision)
AUA American Urological Association
AUCAS Association of University Clinical Academic Staff
AUEW Amalgamated Union of Engineering Workers (later AEU, *now see* AEEU)
AUS Army of the United States
AUT Association of University Teachers
AVCC Australian Vice-Chancellors' Committee
AVCM Associate, Victoria College of Music
AVD Army Veterinary Department
AVLA Audio Visual Language Association
AVR Army Volunteer Reserve
AWA Anglian Water Authority
AWHCT Associate, West Ham College of Technology
AWO Association of Water Officers (*now see* IWO)
AWRE Atomic Weapons Research Establishment
aws Graduate of Air Warfare Course
AZ Arizona (postal)

B

b born; brother
BA Bachelor of Arts
BAA British Airports Authority
BAAB British Amateur Athletic Board
BAAL British Association for Applied Linguistics
BAAS British Association for the Advancement of Science
BAB British Airways Board
BAC British Aircraft Corporation
BAcc Bachelor of Accountancy
BaccPhil Baccalaureate in Philosophy
BACM British Association of Colliery Management
BACUP British Association of Cancer United Patients
BAe British Aerospace
BAED Bachelor of Arts in Environmental Design
B&FBS British and Foreign Bible Society
BAFO British Air Forces of Occupation
BAFPA British Association of Fitness Promotion Agencies
BAFTA British Academy of Film and Television Arts
BAG Business Art Galleries
BAgrSc Bachelor of Agricultural Science
BAI *Baccalarius in Arte Ingeniaria* (Bachelor of Engineering)
BAIE British Association of Industrial Editors
BALPA British Air Line Pilots' Association
BAO Bachelor of Art of Obstetrics
BAOMS British Association of Oral and Maxillo-Facial Surgeons
BAOR British Army of the Rhine (*formerly* on the Rhine)
BAOS British Association of Oral Surgeons (*now see* BAOMS)
BAppSc(MT) Bachelor of Applied Science (Medical Technology)
BAPS British Association of Plastic Surgeons
BARB Broadcasters' Audience Research Board
BARC British Automobile Racing Club
BArch Bachelor of Architecture
Bart Baronet
BAS Bachelor in Agricultural Science
BASc Bachelor of Applied Science
BASCA British Academy of Songwriters, Composers and Authors
BASEEFA British Approvals Service for Electrical Equipment in Flammable Atmospheres
BASW British Association of Social Workers
Batt. Battery
BBA British Bankers' Association; Bachelor of Business Administration
BBB of C British Boxing Board of Control
BBC British Broadcasting Corporation
BBFC British Board of Film Classification
BBS Bachelor of Business Studies
BBSRC Biotechnology and Biological Sciences Research Council
BC Before Christ; British Columbia; Borough Council
BCAR British Civil Airworthiness Requirements
BCC British Council of Churches (*now see* CCBI)
BCE Bachelor of Civil Engineering; Before the Christian Era
BCh or **BChir** Bachelor of Surgery
BChD Bachelor of Dental Surgery
BCIA British Clothing Industries Association
BCL Bachelor of Civil Law
BCMF British Ceramic Manufacturers' Federation
BCMS Bible Churchmen's Missionary Society
BCOF British Commonwealth Occupation Force
BCom or **BComm** Bachelor of Commerce
BComSc Bachelor of Commercial Science
BCPC British Crop Protection Council
BCS Bengal Civil Service; British Computer Society
BCSA British Constructional Steelwork Association
BCTS Bristol Certificate in Theological Studies
BCURA British Coal Utilization Research Association
BCYC British Corinthian Yacht Club
BD Bachelor of Divinity
Bd Board
BDA British Dental Association; British Deaf Association; British Dyslexia Association
Bde Brigade
BDQ Bachelor of Divinity Qualifying
BDS Bachelor of Dental Surgery
BDSc Bachelor of Dental Science
BE Bachelor of Engineering; British Element
BEA British East Africa; British European Airways; British Epilepsy Association
BEAMA Federation of British Electrotechnical and Allied Manufacturers' Associations (*formerly* British Electrical and Allied Manufacturers' Association)
BE&A Bachelor of Engineering and Architecture (Malta)
BEARR British Emergency Aid for Russia and the Republics
BEC Business Education Council (*now see* BTEC)
BEc Bachelor of Economics
BECTU Broadcasting, Entertainment, Cinematograph and Theatre Union
BEd Bachelor of Education
Beds Bedfordshire
BEE Bachelor of Electrical Engineering
BEF British Expeditionary Force; British Equestrian Federation
BEM British Empire Medal
BEMAS British Educational Management and Administration Society
BEME Brigade Electrical and Mechanical Engineer
BEng Bachelor of Engineering
BEO Base Engineer Officer
Berks Berkshire
BES Bachelor of Environmental Studies
BESO British Executive Service Overseas
BEVA British Equine Veterinary Association
BFI British Film Institute
BFMIRA British Food Manufacturing Industries Research Association
BFPO British Forces Post Office
BFSS British Field Sports Society
BFUW British Federation of University Women (*now see* BFWG)
BFWG British Federation of Women Graduates
BGS Brigadier General Staff
BHA British Hospitality Association
Bhd Berhad
BHF British Heart Foundation
BHL Bachelor of Hebrew Letters
BHRA British Hydromechanics Research Association
BHRCA British Hotels, Restaurants and Caterers' Association (*now see* BHA)
BHS British Horse Society
BI British Invisibles
BIBA British Insurance Brokers' Association (*now see* BIIBA)

BIBRA British Industrial Biological Research Association
BICC British Insulated Callender's Cables
BICERA British Internal Combustion Engine Research Association (*now see* BICERI)
BICERI British Internal Combustion Engine Research Institute
BICSc British Institute of Cleaning Science
BIEC British Invisible Exports Council (*now see* BI)
BIEE British Institute of Energy Economics
BIF British Industries Fair
BIFU Banking Insurance and Finance Union
BIIBA British Insurance & Investment Brokers' Association
BIM British Institute of Management
BIR British Institute of Radiology
BIS Bank for International Settlements
BISF British Iron and Steel Federation
BISFA British Industrial and Scientific Film Association
BISPA British Independent Steel Producers Association
BISRA British Iron and Steel Research Association
BITC Business in the Community
BJ Bachelor of Journalism
BJP Bharatiya Janata Party
BJSM British Joint Services Mission
BJur Bachelor of Law
BKSTS British Kinematograph, Sound and Television Society
BL Bachelor of Law; British Library
BLA British Liberation Army
BLDSA British Long Distance Swimming Association
BLE Bachelor of Land Economy
BLegS Bachelor of Legal Studies
BLESMA British Limbless Ex-Servicemen's Association
BLitt Bachelor of Letters
BM British Museum; Bachelor of Medicine; Brigade Major; British Monomark
BMA British Medical Association
BMedSci Bachelor of Medical Science
BMEO British Middle East Office
BMet Bachelor of Metallurgy
BMEWS Ballistic Missile Early Warning System
BMG British Military Government
BMH British Military Hospital
BMilSc Bachelor of Military Science
BMJ British Medical Journal
BMM British Military Mission
BMR Bureau of Mineral Resources
BMRA Brigade Major Royal Artillery
Bn Battalion
BNA British Nursing Association
BNAF British North Africa Force
BNC Brasenose College
BNEC British National Export Council
BNF British National Formulary
BNFL British Nuclear Fuels Ltd
BNOC British National Oil Corporation; British National Opera Company
BNP Banque Nationale de Paris
BNSC British National Space Centre
BNSc Bachelor of Nursing Science
BOAC British Overseas Airways Corporation
BoT Board of Trade
Bot. Botany; Botanical
BOTB British Overseas Trade Board
BOU British Ornithologists' Union
Bp Bishop
BPA British Paediatric Association (later CPCH; *now see* RCPCH)
BPG Broadcasting Press Guild
BPharm Bachelor of Pharmacy
BPIF British Printing Industries Federation
BPMF British Postgraduate Medical Federation
BProc Bachelor of Procurationis
BPsS British Psychological Society
BR British Rail
Br. Branch
BRA Brigadier Royal Artillery; British Rheumatism & Arthritis Association
BRB British Railways Board
BRCS British Red Cross Society
BRE Building Research Establishment
Brig. Brigadier
BRIT British Recording Industry Trust
BritIRE British Institution of Radio Engineers (*now see* IERE)
BRNC Britannia Royal Naval College
BRS British Road Services
BRurSc Bachelor of Rural Science
BS Bachelor of Surgery; Bachelor of Science; British Standard
BSA Bachelor of Scientific Agriculture; Birmingham Small Arms; Building Societies' Association
BSAA British South American Airways
BSAP British South Africa Police
BSAS British Society of Animal Science
BSBI Botanical Society of the British Isles
BSC British Steel Corporation; Bengal Staff Corps
BSc Bachelor of Science
BScA, BScAgr Bachelor of Science in Agriculture
BSc(Dent) Bachelor of Science in Dentistry
BScEng Bachelor of Science in Engineering
BSc (Est. Man.) Bachelor of Science in Estate Management
BScN Bachelor of Science in Nursing
BScSoc Bachelor of Social Sciences
BSE Bachelor of Science in Engineering (US); Bovine Spongiform Encephalopathy
BSES British Schools Exploring Society
BSF British Salonica Force
BSFA British Science Fiction Association
BSI British Standards Institution
BSIA British Security Industry Association
BSJA British Show Jumping Association
BSME Bachelor of Science in Mechanical Engineering; British Society of Magazine Editors
BSN Bachelor of Science in Nursing
BSNS Bachelor of Naval Science
BSocSc Bachelor of Social Science
BSRA British Ship Research Association
BSRIA Building Services Research and Information Association
BSS Bachelor of Science (Social Science)
BST Bachelor of Sacred Theology
BSurv Bachelor of Surveying
BSW Bachelor of Social Work
BT Bachelor of Teaching; British Telecommunications
Bt Baronet; Brevet
BTA British Tourist Authority (*formerly* British Travel Association)
BTC British Transport Commission
BTCV British Trust for Conservation Volunteers
BTDB British Transport Docks Board (*now see* ABP)
BTEC Business and Technology (*formerly* Technician) Education Council
BTh Bachelor of Theology
BTP Bachelor of Town Planning
Btss Baronetess
BUAS British Universities Association of Slavists
Bucks Buckinghamshire
BUGB Baptist Union of Great Britain
BUPA British United Provident Association
BURA British Urban Regeneration Association
BV Besloten Vennootschap
BVA British Veterinary Association
BVetMed Bachelor of Veterinary Medicine
BVI British Virgin Islands
BVM Blessed Virgin Mary
BVMS Bachelor of Veterinary Medicine and Surgery
BVSc Bachelor of Veterinary Science
BWI British West Indies
BWM British War Medal

C

C Conservative: 100
c child; cousin; *circa* (about)
CA Central America; County Alderman; Chartered Accountant (Scotland and Canada); California (postal)
CAA Civil Aviation Authority
CAABU Council for the Advancement of Arab and British Understanding
CAAV (Member of) Central Association of Agricultural Valuers
CAB Citizens' Advice Bureau; Centre for Agricultural and Biosciences (*formerly* Commonwealth Agricultural Bureau)
CACTM Central Advisory Council of Training for the Ministry (later ACCM; *now see* ABM)
CAER Conservative Action for Electoral Reform
CAF Charities Aid Foundation
CAFOD Catholic Fund for Overseas Development
CAJ Committee on the Administration of Justice
CALE Canadian Army Liaison Executive
Calif California
CAM Communications, Advertising and Marketing
Cambs Cambridgeshire
CAMC Canadian Army Medical Corps
CAMRA Campaign for Real Ale

CAMS Certificate of Advanced Musical Study
CAMW Central Association for Mental Welfare
C&G City and Guilds of London Institute
Cantab *Cantabrigiensis* (of Cambridge)
Cantuar *Cantuariensis* (of Canterbury)
CARD Campaign against Racial Discrimination
CARE Cottage and Rural Enterprises
CARICOM Caribbean Community
CARIFTA Caribbean Free Trade Area (*now see* CARICOM)
Carms Carmarthenshire
CAS Chief of the Air Staff
CASI Canadian Aeronautics and Space Institute
CAT College of Advanced Technology; Countryside Around Towns
CATE Council for the Accreditation of Teacher Education
Cav. Cavalry
CAWU Clerical and Administrative Workers' Union (later APEX)
CB Companion, Order of the Bath; County Borough
CBC County Borough Council
CBCO Central Board for Conscientious Objectors
CBE Commander, Order of the British Empire
CBI Confederation of British Industry
CBIM Companion, British Institute of Management (*now see* CIMgt)
CBiol Chartered Biologist
CBNS Commander British Navy Staff
CBS Columbia Broadcasting System; Confraternity of the Blessed Sacrament
CBSI Chartered Building Societies Institute (*now see* CIB)
CBSO City of Birmingham Symphony Orchestra
CC Companion, Order of Canada; City Council; County Council; Cricket Club; Cycling Club; County Court
CCAB Consultative Committee of Accountancy Bodies
CCAHC Central Council for Agricultural and Horticultural Co-operation
CCBE Commission Consultative des Barreaux de la Communauté Européenne
CCBI Council of Churches for Britain and Ireland (*now see* CTBI)
CCC Corpus Christi College; Central Criminal Court; County Cricket Club
CCE Chartered Civil Engineer
CCETSW Central Council for Education and Training in Social Work
CCF Combined Cadet Force
CCFM Combined Cadet Forces Medal
CCG Control Commission Germany
CCH Cacique's Crown of Honour, Order of Service of Guyana
CChem Chartered Chemist
CCHMS Central Committee for Hospital Medical Services
CCIA Commission of Churches on International Affairs
CCIPD Companion, Chartered Institute of Personnel and Development
CCIS Command Control Information System
CCJ Council of Christians and Jews
CCLRC Council for the Central Laboratory of the Research Councils
CCPR Central Council of Physical Recreation
CCRA Commander Corps of Royal Artillery
CCRE Commander Corps of Royal Engineers
CCREME Commander Corps of Royal Electrical and Mechanical Engineers
CCRSigs Commander Corps of Royal Signals
CCS Casualty Clearing Station; Ceylon Civil Service; Countryside Commission for Scotland
CCSU Council of Civil Service Unions
CCTA Commission de Coopération Technique pour l'Afrique; Central Computer and Telecommunications Authority
CCTS Combat Crew Training Squadron
CD Canadian Forces Decoration; Commander, Order of Distinction (Jamaica); Civil Defence; Compact Disc
CDA Co-operative Development Agency
CDC Centers for Disease Control and Prevention
CDEE Chemical Defence Experimental Establishment
CDipAF Certified Diploma in Accounting and Finance
CDir Chartered Director
Cdo Commando
CDRA Committee of Directors of Research Associations
Cdre Commodore
CDS Chief of the Defence Staff
CDU Christlich-Demokratische Union
CE Civil Engineer
CEA Central Electricity Authority
CEC Commission of the European Communities
CECD Confédération Européenne du Commerce de Détail
CECG Consumers in European Community Group
CEDEP Centre Européen d'Education Permanente
CEDR Centre for Effective Dispute Resolution
CEE Communauté Economique Européenne
CEED Centre for Economic and Environmental Development
CEF Canadian Expeditionary Force
CEFIC Conseil Européen des Fédérations de l'Industrie Chimique
CEGB Central Electricity Generating Board
CEH Centre for Ecology & Hydrology
CEI Council of Engineering Institutions
CEIR Corporation for Economic and Industrial Research
CEM Council of European Municipalities (*now see* CEMR)
CEMA Council for the Encouragement of Music and Arts
CEMR Council of European Municipalities and Regions
CEMS Church of England Men's Society
CEN Comité Européen de Normalisation
CENELEC European Committee for Electrotechnical Standardization
CEng Chartered Engineer
Cento Central Treaty Organisation
CEO Chief Executive Officer
CEPES Comité européen pour le progrès économique et social
CEPS Center for Economic Policy Studies
CEPT Conférence Européenne des Postes et des Télécommunications
CERL Central Electricity Research Laboratories
CERN Organisation (*formerly* Centre) Européenne pour la Recherche Nucléaire
CERT Charities Effectiveness Review Trust
CertCPE Certificate in Clinical Pastoral Education
Cert Ed Certificate of Education
CertITP Certificate of International Teachers' Program (Harvard)
CertTP Certificate in Town Planning
CEST Centre for Exploitation of Science and Technology
CET Council for Educational Technology
CETSW Council for Education and Training in Social Work
CF Chaplain to the Forces; Companion, Order of Fiji
CFA Canadian Field Artillery
CFE Central Fighter Establishment
CFM Cadet Forces Medal
CFPS Certificate of Further Professional Studies
CFR Commander, Order of the Federal Republic of Nigeria
CFS Central Flying School
CGA Community of the Glorious Ascension; Country Gentlemen's Association
CGeol Chartered Geologist
CGIA Insignia Award of City and Guilds of London Institute (*now see* FCGI)
CGLI City and Guilds of London Institute (*now see* C&G)
CGM Conspicuous Gallantry Medal
CGRM Commandant-General Royal Marines
CGS Chief of the General Staff
CH Companion of Honour
Chanc. Chancellor; Chancery
Chap. Chaplain
ChapStJ Chaplain, Order of St John of Jerusalem (*now see* ChStJ)
CHAR Campaign for the Homeless and Rootless
CHB Companion of Honour of Barbados
ChB Bachelor of Surgery
CHC Community Health Council
Ch.Ch. Christ Church
CHE Campaign for Homosexual Equality
ChLJ Chaplain, Order of St Lazarus of Jerusalem
(CHM) *See under* ARCO(CHM), FRCO(CHM)
ChM Master of Surgery
Chm. Chairman or Chairwoman
CHN Community of the Holy Name
CHSC Central Health Services Council
ChStJ Chaplain, Most Venerable Order of the Hospital of St John of Jerusalem
CI Imperial Order of the Crown of India; Channel Islands
CIA Chemical Industries Association; Central Intelligence Agency
CIAD Central Institute of Art and Design
CIAgrE Companion, Institution of Agricultural Engineers
CIAL Corresponding Member of the International Institute of Arts and Letters
CIArb Chartered Institute of Arbitrators
CIB Chartered Institute of Bankers
CIBS Chartered Institution of Building Services (*now see* CIBSE)
CIBSE Chartered Institution of Building Services Engineers
CIC Chemical Institute of Canada
CICB Criminal Injuries Compensation Board
CICHE Committee for International Co-operation in Higher Education
CICI Confederation of Information Communication Industries
CID Criminal Investigation Department
CIE Companion, Order of the Indian Empire; Confédération Internationale des Etudiants
CIEx Companion, Institute of Export
CIFE Conference for Independent Further Education
CIGasE Companion, Institution of Gas Engineers
CIGRE Conférence Internationale des Grands Réseaux Electriques
CIGS Chief of the Imperial General Staff (*now see* CGS)
CIIA Canadian Institute of International Affairs
CIL *Corpus inscriptionum latinarum*

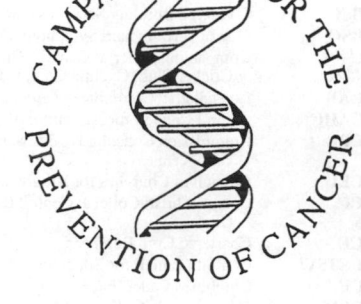

CIM China Inland Mission; Chartered Institute of Marketing
CIMA Chartered Institute of Management Accountants
CIMarE Companion, Institute of Marine Engineers
CIMEMME Companion, Institution of Mining Electrical and Mining Mechanical Engineers
CIMgt Companion, Institute of Management
CIMGTechE Companion, Institution of Mechanical and General Technician Engineers
CIMR Cambridge Institute for Medical Research
C-in-C Commander-in-Chief
CINCHAN Allied Commander-in-Chief Channel
CIOB Chartered Institute of Building
CIPD Companion, Institute of Personnel and Development (*now see* CCIPD)
CIPFA Chartered Institute of Public Finance and Accountancy
CIPL Comité International Permanent des Linguistes
CIPM Companion, Institute of Personnel Management (*now see* CIPD)
CIR Commission on Industrial Relations
CIRES Co-operative Institute for Research in Environmental Sciences
CIRIA Construction Industry Research and Information Association
CIRP Collège Internationale pour Recherche et Production
CIS Institute of Chartered Secretaries and Administrators (*formerly* Chartered Institute of Secretaries); Command Control Communications and Information Systems; Commonwealth of Independent States
CISAC Confédération Internationale des Sociétés d'Auteurs et Compositeurs; Centre for International Security and Arms Control
CIT Chartered Institute of Transport; California Institute of Technology
CITB Construction Industry Training Board
CITD Certificate of Institute of Training and Development
CIU Club and Institute Union
CIV City Imperial Volunteers
CIWEM Chartered Institution of Water and Environmental Management
CJ Chief Justice
CJC Companions of Jesus Christ
CJM Congregation of Jesus and Mary (Eudist Fathers)
CL Commander, Order of Leopold
cl *cum laude*
Cl. Class
CLA Country Landowners' Association
CLIC Cancer and Leukemia in Childhood
CLIP Common Law Institute of Intellectual Property
CLit Companion of Literature (Royal Society of Literature Award)
CLJ Commander, Order of St Lazarus of Jerusalem
CLP Constituency Labour Party
CLRAE Congress (*formerly* Conference) of Local and Regional Authorities of Europe
CLY City of London Yeomanry
CM Member, Order of Canada; Congregation of the Mission (Vincentians); Master in Surgery; Certificated Master; Canadian Militia
CMA Canadian Medical Association; Cost and Management Accountant (NZ)
CMAC Catholic Marriage Advisory Council
CMath Chartered Mathematician
CMB Central Midwives' Board
CMC Certified Management Consultant
CME Continuing Ministerial Education
CMet Chartered Meteorologist
CMF Commonwealth Military Forces; Central Mediterranean Force
CMG Companion, Order of St Michael and St George
CMIWSc Certified Member, Institute of Wood Science
CMJ Commander, Supreme Military Order of the Temple of Jerusalem
CMLJ Commander of Merit, Order of St Lazarus of Jerusalem
CMM Commander, Order of Military Merit (Canada)
CMO Chief Medical Officer
CMP Corps of Military Police (*now see* CRMP)
CMS Church Mission (*formerly* Church Missionary) Society; Certificate in Management Studies
CMT Chaconia Medal of Trinidad
CNAA Council for National Academic Awards
CND Campaign for Nuclear Disarmament
CNI Companion, Nautical Institute
CNO Chief of Naval Operations
CNR Canadian National Railways
CNRS Centre National de la Recherche Scientifique
CNZM Companion, New Zealand Order of Merit
CO Commanding Officer; Commonwealth Office (after Aug. 1966) (*now see* FCO); Colonial Office (before Aug. 1966); Conscientious Objector; Colorado (postal)
Co. County; Company
Coal.L or **Co.L** Coalition Liberal
Coal.U or **Co.U** Coalition Unionist
CODEST Committee for the Development of European Science and Technology
C of E Church of England
C of I Church of Ireland
C of S Chief of Staff; Church of Scotland
COHSE Confederation of Health Service Employees
COI Central Office of Information
CoID Council of Industrial Design (*now* Design Council)
Col Colonel
Coll. College; Collegiate
Colo Colorado
Col.-Sergt Colour-Sergeant
Com Communist
Comd Command
Comdg Commanding
Comdr Commander
Comdt Commandant
COMEC Council of the Military Education Committees of the Universities of the UK
COMET Committee for Middle East Trade
Commn Commission
Commnd Commissioned
CompAMEME Companion, Association of Mining Electrical and Mechanical Engineers
CompICE Companion, Institution of Civil Engineers
CompIEE Companion, Institution of Electrical Engineers
CompIERE Companion, Institution of Electronic and Radio Engineers
CompIGasE Companion, Institution of Gas Engineers
CompIMechE Companion, Institution of Mechanical Engineers
CompInstMC Companion, Institute of Measurement and Control
CompIWES Companion, Institution of Water Engineers and Scientists
CompOR Companion, Operational Research Society
CompTI Companion of the Textile Institute
Comr Commissioner
Comy-Gen. Commissary-General
CON Commander, Order of the Niger
Conn Connecticut
Const. Constitutional
CONUL Council of National and University Librarians
Co-op. Co-operative
COPA Comité des Organisations Professionels Agricoles de la CEE
COPEC Conference of Politics, Economics and Christianity
COPUS Committee on the Public Understanding of Science
Corp. Corporation; Corporal
Corresp. Mem. Corresponding Member
COS Chief of Staff; Charity Organization Society
COSA Colliery Officials and Staffs Association
CoSIRA Council for Small Industries in Rural Areas
COSLA Convention of Scottish Local Authorities
COSPAR Committee on Space Research
COSSAC Chief of Staff to Supreme Allied Commander
COTC Canadian Officers' Training Corps
CP Central Provinces; Cape Province; Congregation of the Passion
CPA Commonwealth Parliamentary Association; Chartered Patent Agent; Certified Public Accountant (USA)
CPAG Child Poverty Action Group
CPAS Church Pastoral Aid Society
CPC Conservative Political Centre
CPCH College of Paediatrics and Child Health (*now see* RCPCH)
CPE Common Professional Examination
CPEng Chartered Professional Engineer (of Institution of Engineers of Australia)
CPFA Member or Associate, Chartered Institute of Public Finance and Accountancy
CPHVA Community Practitioners & Health Visitors' Association
CPhys Chartered Physicist
CPL Chief Personnel and Logistics
CPLS Certificate of Professional Legal Studies
CPM Colonial Police Medal
CPR Canadian Pacific Railway
CPRE Council for the Protection of Rural England
CPRW Campaign for the Protection of Rural Wales
CPS Crown Prosecution Service
CPSA Civil and Public Services Association; Church of the Province of South Africa
CPSM Council for Professions Supplementary to Medicine
CPSU Communist Party of the Soviet Union
CPsychol Chartered Psychologist
CPU Commonwealth Press Union
CQSW Certificate of Qualification in Social Work
CR Community of the Resurrection
cr created or creation
CRA Commander, Royal Artillery
CRAC Careers Research and Advisory Centre
CRAeS Companion, Royal Aeronautical Society

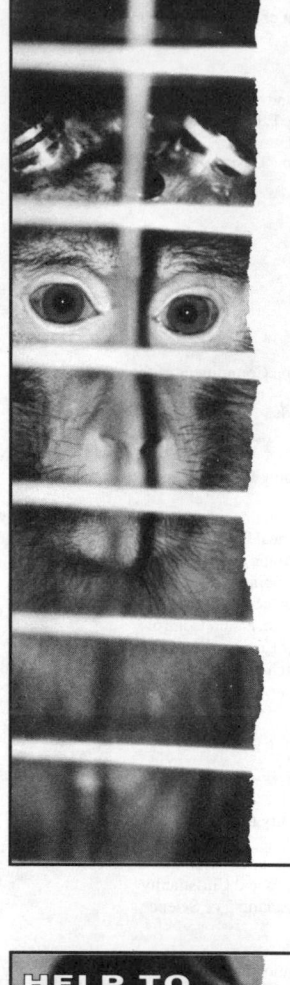

CRAG Clinical Resources and Audit Group
CRASC Commander, Royal Army Service Corps
CRC Cancer Research Campaign; Community Relations Council
CRCP(C) Certificant, Royal College of Physicians of Canada
CRE Commander, Royal Engineers; Commission for Racial Equality; Commercial Relations and Exports; Conference of Rectors of European Universities (*formerly* Association of European Universities)
Cres. Crescent
CRMP Corps of Royal Military Police
CRNCM Companion, Royal Northern College of Music
CRO Commonwealth Relations Office (*now see* FCO)
CS Civil Service; Clerk to the Signet
CSA Confederate States of America; Child Support Agency
CSAB Civil Service Appeal Board
CSB Bachelor of Christian Science
CSC Conspicuous Service Cross; Congregation of the Holy Cross
CSCA Civil Service Clerical Association (*now see* CPSA)
CSCE Conference on Security and Co-operation in Europe
CSD Civil Service Department; Co-operative Secretaries Diploma; Chartered Society of Designers
CSDE Central Servicing Development Establishment
CSEU Confederation of Shipbuilding and Engineering Unions
CSG Companion, Order of the Star of Ghana; Company of the Servants of God
CSI Companion, Order of the Star of India
CSIR Commonwealth Council for Scientific and Industrial Research (*now see* CSIRO)
CSIRO Commonwealth Scientific and Industrial Research Organization (Australia)
CSO Chief Scientific Officer; Chief Signal Officer; Chief Staff Officer; Central Statistical Office (*now see* ONS)
CSP Chartered Society of Physiotherapists; Civil Service of Pakistan
CSS Companion, Star of Sarawak; Council for Science and Society
CSSB Civil Service Selection Board
CSSp Holy Ghost Father
CSSR Congregation of the Most Holy Redeemer (Redemptorist Order)
CStat Chartered Statistician
CSTI Council of Science and Technology Institutes
CStJ Commander, Most Venerable Order of the Hospital of St John of Jerusalem
CSU Christlich-Soziale Union in Bayern
CSV Community Service Volunteers
CSW Certificate in Social Work
CT Connecticut (postal)
CTA Chaplain Territorial Army
CTB College of Teachers of the Blind
CTBI Churches Together in Britain and Ireland
CTC Cyclists' Touring Club; Commando Training Centre; City Training College
CText Chartered Textile Technologist
CTR(Harwell) Controlled Thermonuclear Research
CU Cambridge University
CUAC Cambridge University Athletic Club; Colleges and Universities of the Anglican Communion
CUAFC Cambridge University Association Football Club
CUBC Cambridge University Boat Club
CUCC Cambridge University Cricket Club
CUF Common University Fund
CUHC Cambridge University Hockey Club
CUMS Cambridge University Musical Society
CUNY City University of New York
CUP Cambridge University Press
CURUFC Cambridge University Rugby Union Football Club
CV Cross of Valour (Canada)
CVCP Committee of Vice-Chancellors and Principals of the Universities of the United Kingdom (*now see* UUK)
CVO Commander, Royal Victorian Order
CVS Council for Voluntary Service
CVSNA Council of Voluntary Service National Association
CWA Crime Writers Association
CWGC Commonwealth War Graves Commission
CWS Co-operative Wholesale Society
CWU Communication Workers Union

D

D Duke
d died; daughter
DA Dame of St Andrew, Order of Barbados; Diploma in Anaesthesia; Diploma in Art; Doctor of Arts
DAA&QMG Deputy Assistant Adjutant and Quartermaster-General
DAAD Designers and Art Directors Association
DAAG Deputy Assistant Adjutant-General
DA&QMG Deputy Adjutant and Quartermaster-General
DAC Development Assistance Committee; Diocesan Advisory Committee
DACG Deputy Assistant Chaplain-General
DAD Deputy Assistant Director
DAdmin Doctor of Administration
DADMS Deputy Assistant Director of Medical Services
DADOS Deputy Assistant Director of Ordnance Services
DADQ Deputy Assistant Director of Quartering
DADST Deputy Assistant Director of Supplies and Transport
DAEd Diploma in Art Education
DAG Deputy Adjutant-General
DAgr Doctor of Agriculture
DAgrFor Doctor of Agriculture and Forestry
DAMS Deputy Assistant Military Secretary
D&AD Designers and Art Directors Association
DAppSc Doctor of Applied Science
DAQMG Deputy Assistant Quartermaster-General
DArch Doctor of Architecture
DArt Doctor of Art
DArts Doctor of Arts
DASc Doctor in Agricultural Sciences
DASS Diploma in Applied Social Studies
DATA Draughtsmen's and Allied Technicians' Association (later AUEW(TASS))
DATEC Art and Design Committee, Technician Education Council
DAvMed Diploma in Aviation Medicine, Royal College of Physicians
DBA Doctor of Business Administration
DBE Dame Commander, Order of the British Empire
DC District Council; District of Columbia
DCAe Diploma of College of Aeronautics
DCAS Deputy Chief of the Air Staff
DCB Dame Commander, Order of the Bath
DCC Diploma of Chelsea College
DCCH Diploma in Community Child Health
DCDS Deputy Chief of Defence Staff
DCE Diploma of a College of Education
DCG Deputy Chaplain-General
DCGRM Department of the Commandant General Royal Marines
DCGS Deputy Chief of the General Staff
DCh Doctor of Surgery
DCH Diploma in Child Health
DCHS Dame Commander, Order of the Holy Sepulchre
DCIGS Deputy Chief of the Imperial General Staff (*now see* DCGS)
DCL Doctor of Civil Law; Dr of Canon Law
DCLI Duke of Cornwall's Light Infantry
DCLJ Dame Commander, Order of St Lazarus of Jerusalem
DCM Distinguished Conduct Medal
DCMG Dame Commander, Order of St Michael and St George
DCMHE Diploma of Contents and Methods in Health Education
DCMS Department for Culture, Media and Sport
DCnL Doctor of Canon Law
DCNZM Distinguished Companion, New Zealand Order of Merit
DCO Duke of Cambridge's Own
DCom or **DComm** Doctor of Commerce
DCP Diploma in Clinical Pathology; Diploma in Conservation of Paintings
DCS Deputy Chief of Staff; Doctor of Commercial Sciences
DCSG Dame Commander, Order of St Gregory the Great
DCSO Deputy Chief Scientific Officer
DCT Doctor of Christian Theology
DCVO Dame Commander, Royal Victorian Order
DD Doctor of Divinity
DDes Doctor of Design
DDGAMS Deputy Director General, Army Medical Services
DDH Diploma in Dental Health
DDL Deputy Director of Labour
DDME Deputy Director of Mechanical Engineering
DDMI Deputy Director of Military Intelligence
DDMO Deputy Director of Military Operations
DDMS Deputy Director of Medical Services
DDMT Deputy Director of Military Training
DDNI Deputy Director of Naval Intelligence
DDO Diploma in Dental Orthopaedics
DDPH Diploma in Dental Public Health
DDPR Deputy Director of Public Relations
DDPS Deputy Director of Personal Services
DDR Deutsche Demokratische Republik
DDRA Deputy Director Royal Artillery
DDra Doctor of Drama
DDS Doctor of Dental Surgery; Director of Dental Services
DDSc Doctor of Dental Science
DDSD Deputy Director Staff Duties
DDSM Defense Distinguished Service Medal
DDST Deputy Director of Supplies and Transport

DDWE&M Deputy Director of Works, Electrical and Mechanical
DE Doctor of Engineering; Delaware (postal)
DEA Department of Economic Affairs
DEc Doctor of Economics
decd deceased
DEconSc Doctor of Economic Science
DEd Doctor of Education
DEFRA Department for Environment, Food and Rural Affairs
Deleg. Delegate
DEME Directorate of Electrical and Mechanical Engineering
DEMS Defensively Equipped Merchant Ships
(DemU) Democratic Unionist
DenD Docteur en Droit
DEng Doctor of Engineering
DenM Docteur en Médicine
DEOVR Duke of Edinburgh's Own Volunteer Rifles
DEP Department of Employment and Productivity; European Progressive Democrats
Dep. Deputy
DERA Defence Evaluation and Research Agency
DES Department of Education and Science (later DFE; *now see* DFEE); Dr in Environmental Studies
DèsL Docteur ès lettres
DèS or **DèsSc** Docteur ès sciences
DesRCA Designer of the Royal College of Art
DESU Diplôme d'Etudes Supérieures d'Université
DETR Department of the Environment, Transport and the Regions
DFA Doctor of Fine Arts
DFAS Decorative and Fine Art Society
DFC Distinguished Flying Cross
DFE Department for Education (*now see* DFEE)
DFEE or **DfEE** Department for Education and Employment
DfES Department for Education and Skills
DFFP Diploma in Fertility and Family Planning
DFH Diploma of Faraday House
DFID Department for International Development
DFLS Day Fighter Leaders' School
DFM Distinguished Flying Medal
DFPHM Diplomate Member, Faculty of Public Health Medicine
DG Director General; Dragoon Guards
DGAA Distressed Gentlefolks Aid Association
DGAMS Director-General Army Medical Services
DGCHS Dame Grand Cross, Order of the Holy Sepulchre
DGDP Diploma in General Dental Practice, Royal College of Physicians
DGEME Director General Electrical and Mechanical Engineering
DGLP(A) Director General Logistic Policy (Army)
DGMS Director-General of Medical Services
DGMT Director-General of Military Training
DGMW Director-General of Military Works
DGNPS Director-General of Naval Personal Services
DGP Director-General of Personnel
DGPS Director-General of Personal Services
DGS Diploma in Graduate Studies
DGStJ Dame of Grace, Order of St John of Jerusalem (*now see* DStJ)
DGU Doctor of Griffith University
DH Doctor of Humanities
DHA District Health Authority
Dhc Doctor *honoris causa*
DHEW Department of Health Education and Welfare (US)
DHL Doctor of Humane Letters; Doctor of Hebrew Literature
DHM Dean Hole Medal
DHMSA Diploma in the History of Medicine (Society of Apothecaries)
DHQ District Headquarters
DHS Dame, Order of the Holy Sepulchre
DHSS Department of Health and Social Security (*now see* DoH *and* DSS)
DHum Doctor of Humanities
DHumLit Doctor of Humane Letters
DIA Diploma in Industrial Administration
DIAS Dublin Institute of Advanced Sciences
DIC Diploma of the Imperial College
DICTA Diploma of Imperial College of Tropical Agriculture
DIG Deputy Inspector-General
DIH Diploma in Industrial Health
DIMP Darjah Indera Mahkota Pahang
DIntLaw Diploma in International Law
Dio. Diocese
DipA Diploma of Arts in Theology
DipAA Diploma in Applied Art
DipAD Diploma in Art and Design
DipAE Diploma in Adult Education
DipAe Diploma in Aeronautics
DipAgr Diploma in Agriculture
DipArch Diploma in Architecture
DipASE Diploma in Advanced Study of Education, College of Preceptors
DipAvMed Diploma in Aviation Medicine, Royal College of Physicians
DipBA Diploma in Business Administration
DipBS Diploma in Fine Art, Byam Shaw School
DipCAM Diploma in Communications, Advertising and Marketing of CAM Foundation
DipCC Diploma of the Central College
DipCD Diploma in Civic Design
DipCE Diploma in Civil Engineering; Diploma of a College of Education (Scotland)
DipEcon Diploma in Economics
DipEd Diploma in Education
DipEE Diploma in Electrical Engineering
DipEl Diploma in Electronics
DipESL Diploma in English as a Second Language
DipEth Diploma in Ethnology
DipEurHum Diploma in European Humanities
DipFBOM Diploma in Farm Business Organisation and Management
DipFD Diploma in Funeral Directing
DipFE Diploma in Further Education
DipFM Diploma in Forensic Medicine
DipGSM Diploma in Music, Guildhall School of Music and Drama
DipHA Diploma in Hospital Administration
DipHE Diploma in Higher Education
DipHSM Diploma in Health Services Management
DipHIC Diploma in Hospital Infection Control
DipHum Diploma in Humanities
DipHV Diploma in Health Visiting
DipICArb Diploma in International Commercial Arbitration
DipLA Diploma in Landscape Architecture
DipLib Diploma of Librarianship
DipLP Diploma in Legal Practice
DipM Diploma in Marketing
DipN Diploma in Nursing
DipNEC Diploma of Northampton Engineering College (*now* City University)
DipPA Diploma of Practitioners in Advertising (*now see* DipCAM)
DipPE Diploma in Physical Education
DipPSA Diploma in Public Service Administration
DipPSW Diploma in Psychiatric Social Work
DipRE Diploma in Religious Education
DipREM Diploma in Rural Estate Management
DipSMS Diploma in School Management Studies
DipSoc Diploma in Sociology
DipSocSc Diploma in Social Science
DipTA Diploma in Tropical Agriculture
DipT&CP Diploma in Town and Country Planning
DipTh Diploma in Theology
DipTMHA Diploma in Training and Further Education of Mentally Handicapped Adults
DipTP Diploma in Town Planning
DipTPT Diploma in Theory and Practice of Teaching
DipTRP Diploma in Town and Regional Planning
DIS Diploma in Industrial Studies
DistTP Distinction in Town Planning
DIur Doctor of Law
Div. Division; Divorced
Div.Test Divinity Testimonium (of Trinity College, Dublin)
DJAG Deputy Judge Advocate General
DJPD Dato Jasa Purba Di-Raja Negeri Sembilan (Malaysia)
DJStJ Dame of Justice, Order of St John of Jerusalem (*now see* DStJ)
DJur *Doctor Juris* (Doctor of Law)
DK Most Esteemed Family Order (Brunei)
DL Deputy Lieutenant
DLC Diploma of Loughborough College
DLES Doctor of Letters in Economic Studies
DLI Durham Light Infantry
DLit or **DLitt** Doctor of Literature; Doctor of Letters
DLittS Doctor of Sacred Letters
DLJ Dame of Grace, Order of St Lazarus of Jerusalem
DLO Diploma in Laryngology and Otology
DLP Diploma in Legal Practice
DLR Docklands Light Railway
DM Doctor of Medicine
DMA Diploma in Municipal Administration
DMCC Diploma in the Medical Care of Catastrophe, Society of Apothecaries
DMD Doctor of Medical Dentistry (Australia)
DME Director of Mechanical Engineering
DMet Doctor of Metallurgy
DMI Director of Military Intelligence
DMin Doctor of Ministry

DMiss Doctor of Missiology
DMJ Diploma in Medical Jurisprudence
DMJ(Path) Diploma in Medical Jurisprudence (Pathology)
DMLJ Dame of Merit, Order of St Lazarus of Jerusalem
DMO Director of Military Operations
DMR Diploma in Medical Radiology
DMRD Diploma in Medical Radiological Diagnosis
DMRE Diploma in Medical Radiology and Electrology
DMRT Diploma in Medical Radio-Therapy
DMS Director of Medical Services; Decoration for Meritorious Service (South Africa); Diploma in Management Studies
DMSc Doctor of Medical Science
DMSSB Direct Mail Services Standards Board
DMT Director of Military Training
DMus Doctor of Music
DN Diploma in Nursing
DNB Dictionary of National Biography
DNE Director of Naval Equipment
DNH Department of National Heritage
DNI Director of Naval Intelligence
DNZM Dame Companion, New Zealand Order of Merit
DO Diploma in Ophthalmology
DOAE Defence Operational Analysis Establishment
DObstRCOG Diploma of Royal College of Obstetricians and Gynaecologists (*now see* DRCOG)
DOC District Officer Commanding
DocArts Doctor of Arts
DocEng Doctor of Engineering
DoE Department of the Environment
DoH Department of Health
DoI Department of Industry
DOL Doctor of Oriental Learning
Dom. *Dominus* (Lord)
DOMS Diploma in Ophthalmic Medicine and Surgery
DOR Director of Operational Requirements
DOrthRCS Diploma in Orthodontics, Royal College of Surgeons
DOS Director of Ordnance Services; Doctor of Ocular Science
Dow. Dowager
DP Data Processing
DPA Diploma in Public Administration; Discharged Prisoners' Aid; Doctor of Public Administration
DPD Diploma in Public Dentistry
DPEc Doctor of Political Economy
DPed Doctor of Pedagogy
DPH Diploma in Public Health
DPh or **DPhil** Doctor of Philosophy
DPharm Doctor of Pharmacy
DPhilMed Diploma in Philosophy of Medicine
DPhysMed Diploma in Physical Medicine
DPLG Diplômé par le Gouvernement
DPM Diploma in Psychological Medicine; Diploma in Personnel Management
DPMS Dato Paduka Mahkota Selangor (Malaysia)
DPMSA Diploma in Philosophy and Ethics of Medicine, Society of Apothecaries
DPP Director of Public Prosecutions
DPR Director of Public Relations
DPS Director of Postal Services; Director of Personal Services; Doctor of Public Service; Diploma in Pastoral Studies
DPSA Diploma in Public and Social Administration
DPSE Diploma in Professional Studies in Education
DPSM Diploma in Public Sector Management
DPsych Doctor of Psychology
DQMG Deputy Quartermaster-General
Dr Doctor
DRA Defence Research Agency (*now see* DERA)
DRAC Director Royal Armoured Corps
DRC Diploma of Royal College of Science and Technology, Glasgow
DRCOG Diploma of Royal College of Obstetricians and Gynaecologists
DRD Diploma in Restorative Dentistry
Dr ing Doctor of Engineering
Dr jur Doctor of Laws
DrŒcPol *Doctor Œconomiæ Politicæ* (Doctor of Political Economy)
Dr rer. nat. Doctor of Natural Science
Dr rer. pol. Doctor of Political Science
DRS Diploma in Religious Studies
Drs Doctorandus
DRSAMD Diploma of the Royal Scottish Academy of Music and Drama
DS Directing Staff; Doctor of Science
DSA Diploma in Social Administration
DSAC Defence Scientific Advisory Council
DSAO Diplomatic Service Administration Office
DSC Distinguished Service Cross
DSc Doctor of Science
DScA Docteur en sciences agricoles
DSc(Eng) Doctor of Engineering Science
DSCHE Diploma of the Scottish Council for Health Education
DScMil Doctor of Military Science
DSc (SocSci) Doctor of Science in Social Science
DSD Director Staff Duties
DSF Director Special Forces
DSG Dame, Order of St Gregory the Great
DSIR Department of Scientific and Industrial Research (later SRC; then SERC)
DSL Doctor of Sacred Letters
DSLJ Dato Seri Laila Jasa (Brunei)
DSM Distinguished Service Medal
DSNB Dato Setia Negara Brunei
DSNS Dato Setia Negeri Sembilan (Malaysia)
DSO Companion of the Distinguished Service Order
DSocSc Doctor of Social Science
DSP Director of Selection of Personnel; Docteur en sciences politiques (Montreal)
dsp *decessit sine prole* (died without issue)
DSS Department of Social Security; Doctor of Sacred Scripture
Dss Deaconess
DSSc Doctor of Social Science
DST Director of Supplies and Transport
DStJ Dame of Grace, Most Venerable Order of the Hospital of St John of Jerusalem; Dame of Justice, Most Venerable Order of the Hospital of St John of Jerusalem
DTA Diploma in Tropical Agriculture
DTD Dekoratie voor Trouwe Dienst (Decoration for Devoted Service)
DTech Doctor of Technology
DTH Diploma in Tropical Hygiene
DTh or **DTheol** Doctor of Theology
DThPT Diploma in Theory and Practice of Teaching
DTI Department of Trade and Industry
DTLR Department for Transport, Local Government and the Regions
DTM&H Diploma in Tropical Medicine and Hygiene
DU or **DUniv** Honorary Doctor of the University
Dunelm *Dunelmensis* (of Durham)
DUP Democratic Unionist Party; Docteur de l'Université de Paris
DVA Diploma of Veterinary Anaesthesia
DVH Diploma in Veterinary Hygiene
DVLA Driver and Vehicle Licensing Authority
DVLC Driver and Vehicle Licensing Centre
DVM Doctor of Veterinary Medicine
DVMS or **DVM&S** Doctor of Veterinary Medicine and Surgery
DVR Diploma in Veterinary Radiology
DVSc Doctor of Veterinary Science
DVSM Diploma in Veterinary State Medicine
DWP Department for Work and Pensions

E

E East; Earl; England
e eldest
EA Environment Agency
EAA Edinburgh Architectural Association
EACR European Association for Cancer Research
EADS European Aeronautics Defence and Space Company
EAF East African Forces
EAGA Energy Action Grants Agency
EAHY European Architectural Heritage Year
EAP East Africa Protectorate
EASD European Association of Securities Dealers
EAW Electrical Association for Women
EBC English Benedictine Congregation
Ebor *Eboracensis* (of York)
EBRD European Bank for Reconstruction and Development
EBU European Broadcasting Union
EC Etoile du Courage (Canada); European Community; European Commission; Emergency Commission
ECA Economic Co-operation Administration; Economic Commission for Africa
ECAFE Economic Commission for Asia and the Far East (*now see* ESCAP)
ECB England and Wales Cricket Board
ECCTIS Education Courses and Credit Transfer Information Systems
ECE Economic Commission for Europe
ECGD Export Credits Guarantee Department
ECHR European Court of Human Rights
ECLA Economic Commission for Latin America
ECLAC United Nations Economic Commission for Latin America and the Caribbean
ECOSOC Economic and Social Committee of the United Nations

ECSC European Coal and Steel Community
ED Efficiency Decoration; Doctor of Engineering (US); European Democrat
ed edited
EdB Bachelor of Education
EDC Economic Development Committee
EdD Doctor of Education
EDF European Development Fund
EDG European Democratic Group; Employment Department Group
Edin. Edinburgh
Edn Edition
EDP Executive Development Programme
EdS Specialist in Education
Educ Educated
Educn Education
EEA European Environment Agency
EEC European Economic Community (*now see* EC); Commission of the European Communities
EEF Engineering Employers' Federation; Egyptian Expeditionary Force
EEIBA Electrical and Electronic Industries Benevolent Association
EETPU Electrical Electronic Telecommunication & Plumbing Union (*now see* AEEU)
EETS Early English Text Society
EFCE European Federation of Chemical Engineering
EFTA European Free Trade Association
eh ehrenhalber (honorary)
EI East Indian; East Indies
EIA Engineering Industries Association
EIB European Investment Bank
E-in-C Engineer-in-Chief
EIS Educational Institute of Scotland
EISCAT European Incoherent Scatter Association
EIU Economist Intelligence Unit
ELBS English Language Book Society
ELSE European Life Science Editors
ELT English Language Teaching
EM Edward Medal; Earl Marshal
EMBL European Molecular Biology Laboratory
EMBO European Molecular Biology Organisation
EMEA European Agency for the Evaluation of Medical Products
EMP Electro Magnetic Pulse; Executive Management Program Diploma
EMS Emergency Medical Service
Enc.Brit. Encylopaedia Britannica
Eng. England
Engr Engineer
ENO English National Opera
ENSA Entertainments National Service Association
ENT Ear Nose and Throat
EO Executive Officer
EOC Equal Opportunities Commission
EOPH Examined Officer of Public Health
EORTC European Organisation for Research on Treatment of Cancer
EP European Parliament
EPICC European Process Industries Competitiveness Centre
EPP European People's Party
EPSRC Engineering and Physical Sciences Research Council
EPsS Experimental Psychology Society
er elder
ER Eastern Region (BR); East Riding
ERA Electrical Research Association
ERC Electronics Research Council
ERD Emergency Reserve Decoration (Army)
ESA European Space Agency
ESART Environmental Services Association Research Trust
ESCAP Economic and Social Commission for Asia and the Pacific
ESF European Science Foundation
ESL English as a Second Language
ESNS Educational Sub-Normal Serious
ESOL English for Speakers of Other Languages
ESRC Economic and Social Research Council; Electricity Supply Research Council
ESRO European Space Research Organization (*now see* ESA)
ESTA European Science and Technology Assembly
ESU English-Speaking Union
ETA Engineering Training Authority
ETH Eidgenössische Technische Hochschule
ETUC European Trade Union Confederation
ETUCE European Trade Union Committee for Education
EU European Union
EUDISED European Documentation and Information Service for Education
Euratom European Atomic Energy Community
EurBiol European Biologist (*now see* EurProBiol)
EurChem European Chemist
Eur Ing European Engineer
EUROM European Federation for Optics and Precision Mechanics
EurProBiol European Professional Biologist
EUW European Union of Women
eV eingetragener Verein
Ext Extinct

F

FA Football Association
FAA Fellow, Australian Academy of Science; Fleet Air Arm
FAAAI Fellow, American Association for Artificial Intelligence
FAAAS Fellow, American Association for the Advancement of Science
FAAO Fellow, American Academy of Optometry
FAAP Fellow, American Academy of Pediatrics
FAARM Fellow, American Academy of Reproductive Medicine
FAAV Fellow, Central Association of Agricultural Valuers
FAAVCT Fellow, American Academy of Veterinary and Comparative Toxicology
FABE Fellow, Association of Building Engineers
FACC Fellow, American College of Cardiology
FACCA Fellow, Association of Certified and Corporate Accountants (*now see* FCCA)
FACCP Fellow, American College of Chest Physicians
FACD Fellow, American College of Dentistry
FACDS Fellow, Australian College of Dental Surgeons (*now see* FRACDS)
FACE Fellow, Australian College of Education
FACerS Fellow, American Ceramic Society
FACHSE Fellow, Australian College of Health Service Executives
FACI Fellow, Australian Chemical Institute (*now see* FRACI)
FACMA Fellow, Australian College of Medical Administrators (*now see* FRACMA)
FACMG Fellow, American College of Medicinal Genetics
FACOG Fellow, American College of Obstetricians and Gynæcologists
FACOM Fellow, Australian College of Occupational Medicine
FACP Fellow, American College of Physicians
FACPM Fellow, American College of Preventive Medicine
FACR Fellow, American College of Radiology
FACRM Fellow, Australian College of Rehabilitation Medicine
FACS Fellow, American College of Surgeons
FACVT Fellow, American College of Veterinary Toxicology (*now see* FAAVCT)
FADM Fellow, Academy of Dental Materials
FADO Fellow, Association of Dispensing Opticians
FAeSI Fellow, Aeronautical Society of India
FAFPHM Fellow, Australian Faculty of Public Health Medicine
FAGO Fellowship in Australia in Obstetrics and Gynaecology
FAGS Fellow, American Geographical Society
FAHA Fellow, Australian Academy of the Humanities
FAI Fellow, Chartered Auctioneers' and Estate Agents' Institute (*now* (after amalgamation) *see* FRICS); Fédération Aéronautique Internationale
FAIA Fellow, American Institute of Architects
FAIAA Fellow, American Institute of Aeronautics and Astronautics
FAIAS Fellow, Australian Institute of Agricultural Science (*now see* FAIAST)
FAIAST Fellow, Australian Institute of Agricultural Science and Technology
FAIB Fellow, Australian Institute of Bankers
FAIBiol Fellow, Australian Institute of Biology
FAICD Fellow, Australian Institute of Company Directors
FAIE Fellow, Australian Institute of Energy
FAIEx Fellow, Australian Institute of Export
FAIFST Fellow, Australian Institute of Food Science and Technology
FAII Fellow, Australian Insurance Institute
FAIM Fellow, Australian Institute of Management
FAIP Fellow, Australian Institute of Physics
FAISB Fellow, Society for the Study of Artificial Intelligence and the Simulation of Behaviour
FAMA Fellow, Australian Medical Association
FAMI Fellow, Australian Marketing Institute
FAMINZ(Arb) Fellow, Arbitrators and Mediators Institute of New Zealand
FAmNucSoc Fellow, American Nuclear Society
FAMS Fellow, Ancient Monuments Society
F and GP Finance and General Purposes
FANY First Aid Nursing Yeomanry
FANZCA Fellow, Australian and New Zealand College of Anaesthetists
FANZCP Fellow, Australian and New Zealand College of Psychiatrists (*now see* FRANZCP)
FAO Food and Agriculture Organization of the United Nations
FAOrthA Fellow, Australian Orthopaedic Association
FAPA Fellow, American Psychiatric Association

FAPHA Fellow, American Public Health Association
FAPI Fellow, Australian Planning Institute (*now see* FRAPI)
FAPM Fellow, Association of Project Managers
FAPS Fellow, American Phytopathological Society
FArborA Fellow, Aboricultural Association
FARE Federation of Alcoholic Rehabilitation Establishments
FARELF Far East Land Forces
FAS Fellow, Antiquarian Society; Fellow, Nigerian Academy of Science; Funding Agency for Schools
FASA Fellow, Australian Society of Accountants (*now see* FCPA)
FASc Fellow, Indian Academy of Sciences
fasc. fascicule
FASCE Fellow, American Society of Civil Engineers
FASI Fellow, Architects' and Surveyors' Institute
FASME Fellow, American Society of Mechanical Engineers
FASPOG Fellow, Australian Society for Psychosomatic Obstetrics and Gynaecology
FASSA Fellow, Academy of the Social Sciences in Australia
FAusIMM Fellow, Australasian Institute of Mining and Metallurgy
FAustCOG Fellow, Australian College of Obstetricians and Gynæcologists (later FRACOG; *now see* FRANZCOG)
FBA Fellow, British Academy; Federation of British Artists
FBAHA Fellow, British Association of Hotel Accountants
FBCartS Fellow, British Cartographic Society
FBCO Fellow, British College of Optometrists (*formerly* of Ophthalmic Opticians (Optometrists)) (*now see* FCOptom)
FBCS Fellow, British Computer Society
FBEC(S) Fellow, Business Education Council (Scotland)
FBEng Fellow, Association of Building Engineers
FBES Fellow, Biological Engineering Society (*now see* FIPEMB)
FBHA Fellow, British Hospitality Association
FBHI Fellow, British Horological Institute
FBHS Fellow, British Horse Society
FBI Federation of British Industries (*now see* CBI); Federal Bureau of Investigation
FBIA Fellow, Bankers' Institute of Australasia (*now see* FAIB)
FBIAT Fellow, British Institute of Architectural Technicians
FBIBA Fellow, British Insurance Brokers' Association (*now see* FBIIBA)
FBID Fellow, British Institute of Interior Design
FBII Fellow, British Institute of Innkeeping
FBIIBA Fellow, British Insurance and Investment Brokers' Association
FBIM Fellow, British Institute of Management (*now see* FIMgt)
FBINZ Fellow, Bankers' Institute of New Zealand
FBIPM Fellow, British Institute of Payroll Management
FBIPP Fellow, British Institute of Professional Photography
FBIRA Fellow, British Institute of Regulatory Affairs
FBIS Fellow, British Interplanetary Society
FBKS Fellow, British Kinematograph Society (*now see* FBKSTS)
FBKSTS Fellow, British Kinematograph, Sound and Television Society
FBOA Fellow, British Optical Association
FBOU Fellow, British Ornithologists' Union
FBPICS Fellow, British Production and Inventory Control Society
FBPsS Fellow, British Psychological Society
FBritIRE Fellow, British Institution of Radio Engineers (later FIERE)
FBS Fellow, Building Societies Institute (later FCBSI; *now see* FCIB)
FBSI Fellow, Boot and Shoe Institution (*now see* FCFI)
FBSM Fellow, Birmingham School of Music
FC Football Club
FCA Fellow, Institute of Chartered Accountants; Fellow, Institute of Chartered Accountants in Australia; Fellow, New Zealand Society of Accountants; Federation of Canadian Artists
FCAI Fellow, New Zealand Institute of Cost Accountants; Fellow, Canadian Aeronautical Institute (*now see* FCASI)
FCAM Fellow, CAM Foundation
FCAnaes Fellow, College of Anaesthetists (*now see* FRCA)
FCA(SA) Fellow, College of Anaesthetists (South Africa)
FCASI Fellow, Canadian Aeronautics and Space Institute
FCBSI Fellow, Chartered Building Societies Institute (merged with Chartered Institute of Bankers; *now see* FCIB)
FCCA Fellow, Chartered Association of Certified Accountants
FCCEA Fellow, Commonwealth Council for Educational Administration
FCCS Fellow, Corporation of Secretaries (*formerly* of Certified Secretaries)
FCCT Fellow, Canadian College of Teachers
FCEC Federation of Civil Engineering Contractors
FCFI Fellow, Clothing and Footwear Institute
FCGA Fellow, Certified General Accountants of Canada
FCGI Fellow, City and Guilds of London Institute
FCGP Fellow, College of General Practitioners (*now see* FRCGP)
FChS Fellow, Society of Chiropodists
FCI Fellow, Institute of Commerce
FCIA Fellow, Corporation of Insurance Agents
FCIArb Fellow, Chartered Institute of Arbitrators
FCIB Fellow, Corporation of Insurance Brokers; Fellow, Chartered Institute of Bankers
FCIBS Fellow, Chartered Institution of Building Services (*now see* FCIBSE); Fellow, Chartered Institute of Bankers in Scotland
FCIBSE Fellow, Chartered Institution of Building Services Engineers
FCIC Fellow, Chemical Institute of Canada (*formerly* Canadian Institute of Chemistry)
FCIEH Fellow, Chartered Institute of Environmental Health
FCIH Fellow, Chartered Institute of Housing
FCII Fellow, Chartered Insurance Institute
FCIJ Fellow, Chartered Institute of Journalists
FCILA Fellow, Chartered Institute of Loss Adjusters
FCIM Fellow, Chartered Institute of Marketing; Fellow, Institute of Corporate Managers (Australia)
FCIOB Fellow, Chartered Institute of Building
FCIPA Fellow, Chartered Institute of Patent Agents (*now see* CPA)
FCIPD Fellow, Chartered Institute of Personnel and Development
FCIPS Fellow, Chartered Institute of Purchasing and Supply
FCIS Fellow, Institute of Chartered Secretaries and Administrators (*formerly* Chartered Institute of Secretaries)
FCISA Fellow, Chartered Institute of Secretaries and Administrators (Australia)
FCIT Fellow, Chartered Institute of Transport
FCIWEM Fellow, Chartered Institution of Water and Environmental Management
FCM Faculty of Community Medicine
FCMA Fellow, Chartered Institute of Management Accountants (*formerly* Institute of Cost and Management Accountants); Fellow, Communications Management Association
FCMC Fellow grade, Certified Management Consultant
FCMSA Fellow, College of Medicine of South Africa
FCNA Fellow, College of Nursing, Australia
FCO Foreign and Commonwealth Office
FCOG(SA) Fellow, South African College of Obstetrics and Gynæcology
FCollH Fellow, College of Handicraft
FCollP Fellow, College of Preceptors
FCommA Fellow, Society of Commercial Accountants (*now see* FSCA)
FCOphth Fellow, College of Ophthalmologists (*now see* FRCOphth)
FCOptom Fellow, College of Optometrists
FCP Fellow, College of Preceptors
FCPA Fellow, Australian Society of Certified Practising Accountants
FCPath Fellow, College of Pathologists (*now see* FRCPath)
FCPCH Fellow, College of Paediatrics and Child Health (*now see* FRCPCH)
FCPS Fellow, College of Physicians and Surgeons
FCP(SoAf) Fellow, College of Physicians, South Africa
FCPSO(SoAf) Fellow, College of Physicians and Surgeons and Obstetricians, South Africa
FCPS (Pak) Fellow, College of Physicians and Surgeons of Pakistan
FCRA Fellow, College of Radiologists of Australia (*now see* FRACR)
FCS Federation of Conservative Students
FCS or **FChemSoc** Fellow, Chemical Society (now absorbed into Royal Society of Chemistry)
FCSD Fellow, Chartered Society of Designers
FCSHK Fellow, College of Surgeons of Hong Kong
FCSLT Fellow, College of Speech and Language Therapists (*now see* FRCSLT)
FCSM Fellow, Cambridge School of Music
FCSP Fellow, Chartered Society of Physiotherapy
FCSSA or **FCS(SoAf)** Fellow, College of Surgeons, South Africa
FCSSL Fellow, College of Surgeons of Sri Lanka
FCST Fellow, College of Speech Therapists (later FCSLT; *now see* FRCSLT)
FCT Federal Capital Territory (*now see* ACT); Fellow, Association of Corporate Treasurers; Fellow, College of Teachers
FCTB Fellow, College of Teachers of the Blind
FCU Fighter Control Unit
FCWA Fellow, Institute of Costs and Works Accountants (*now see* FCMA)
FDA Association of First Division Civil Servants
FDF Food and Drink Federation
FDI Fédération Dentaire Internationale
FDP Freie Demokratische Partei
FDS Fellow in Dental Surgery
FDSRCPSGlas Fellow in Dental Surgery, Royal College of Physicians and Surgeons of Glasgow
FDSRCS or **FDS RCS** Fellow in Dental Surgery, Royal College of Surgeons of England
FDSRCSE Fellow in Dental Surgery, Royal College of Surgeons of Edinburgh
FE Far East
FEA Fellow, English Association
FEAF Far East Air Force
FEANI Fédération Européenne d'Associations Nationales d'Ingénieurs
FEBS Federation of European Biochemical Societies
FECI Fellow, Institute of Employment Consultants

FECTS Fellow, European Association for Cardiothoracic Surgery

FEE Fédération des Expertes Comptables Européens

FEF Far East Fleet

FEFC or **FEFCE** Further Education Funding Council for England

FEI Fédération Equestre Internationale

FEIDCT Fellow, Educational Institute of Design Craft and Technology

FEIS Fellow, Educational Institute of Scotland

FELCO Federation of English Language Course Opportunities

FEng Fellow, Royal Academy (*formerly* Fellowship) of Engineering

FEPS Federation of European Physiological Societies

FES Fellow, Entomological Society; Fellow, Ethnological Society

FESC Fellow, European Society of Cardiology

FF Fianna Fáil; Field Force

FFA Fellow, Faculty of Actuaries (in Scotland); Fellow, Institute of Financial Accountants

FFAEM Fellow, Faculty of Accident and Emergency Medicine

FFARACS Fellow, Faculty of Anaesthetists, Royal Australasian College of Surgeons (*now see* FANZCA)

FFARCS Fellow, Faculty of Anaesthetists, Royal College of Surgeons of England (*now see* FRCA)

FFARCSI Fellow, Faculty of Anaesthetists, Royal College of Surgeons in Ireland

FFAS Fellow, Faculty of Architects and Surveyors, London (*now see* FASI)

FFA(SA) Fellow, Faculty of Anaesthetists (South Africa) (*now see* FCA(SA))

FFB Fellow, Faculty of Building

FFCM Fellow, Faculty of Community Medicine (*now see* FFPHM); Fellow, Faculty of Church Music

FFCMI Fellow, Faculty of Community Medicine of Ireland

FFDRCSI Fellow, Faculty of Dentistry, Royal College of Surgeons in Ireland

FFFP Fellow, Faculty of Family Planning of the Royal College of Obstetricians and Gynaecologists

FFHC Freedom from Hunger Campaign

FFHom Fellow, Faculty of Homœopathy

FFI Finance for Industry; Fauna & Flora International

FFOM Fellow, Faculty of Occupational Medicine

FFOMI Fellow, Faculty of Occupational Medicine of Ireland

FFOP (RCPA) Fellow, Faculty of Oral Pathology, Royal College of Pathologists of Australasia

FFPath, RCPI Fellow, Faculty of Pathologists of the Royal College of Physicians of Ireland

FFPHM Fellow, Faculty of Public Health Medicine

FFPHMI Fellow, Faculty of Public Health Medicine of Ireland

FFPM Fellow, Faculty of Pharmaceutical Medicine

FFPS Fauna and Flora Preservation Society (*now see* FFI)

FFR Fellow, Faculty of Radiologists (*now see* FRCR)

FG Fine Gael

FGA Fellow, Gemmological Association

FGCL Fellow, Goldsmiths' College, London

FGCM Fellow, Guild of Church Musicians

FGDS Fédération de la Gauche Démocratique et Socialiste

FGGE Fellow, Guild of Glass Engineers

FGI Fellow, Institute of Certificated Grocers

FGMS Fellow, Guild of Musicians and Singers

FGS Fellow, Geological Society

FGSM Fellow, Guildhall School of Music and Drama

FGSM(MT) Fellow, Guildhall School of Music and Drama (Music Therapy)

FHA Fellow, Institute of Health Service Administrators (*formerly* Hospital Administrators) (*now see* FHSM)

FHAS Fellow, Highland and Agricultural Society of Scotland

FHCIMA Fellow, Hotel Catering and Institutional Management Association

FHKAES Fellow, Hong Kong Academy of Engineering Sciences

FHKIE Fellow, Hong Kong Institution of Engineers

FHMAAAS Foreign Honorary Member, American Academy of Arts and Sciences

FHS Fellow, Heraldry Society; Forces Help Society and Lord Roberts Workshops (*now see* SSAFA)

FHSA Family Health Services Authority

FHSM Fellow, Institute of Health Services Management (*now see* FIHM)

FH-WC Fellow, Heriot-Watt College (*now* University), Edinburgh

FIA Fellow, Institute of Actuaries

FIAA Fellow, Institute of Actuaries of Australia

FIAAS Fellow, Institute of Australian Agricultural Science

FIAA&S Fellow, Incorporated Association of Architects and Surveyors

FIACM Fellow, International Association of Computational Mechanics

FIAE Fellow, Irish Academy of Engineering

FIAgrE Fellow, Institution of Agricultural Engineers

FIAgrM Fellow, Institute of Agricultural Management

FIAI Fellow, Institute of Industrial and Commercial Accountants

FIAL Fellow, International Institute of Arts and Letters

FIAM Fellow, International Academy of Management

FIAP Fellow, Institution of Analysts and Programmers

FIArb Fellow, Institute of Arbitrators (*now see* FCIArb)

FIArbA Fellow, Institute of Arbitrators of Australia

FIAS Fellow, Institute of Aeronautical Sciences (US) (*now see* FAIAA)

FIASc Fellow, Indian Academy of Sciences

FIAWS Fellow, International Academy of Wood Sciences

FIB Fellow, Institute of Bankers (*now see* FCIB)

FIBA Fellow, Institute of Business Administration, Australia (*now see* FCIM)

FIBD Fellow, Institute of British Decorators

FIBI Fellow, Institute of Bankers of Ireland

FIBiol Fellow, Institute of Biology

FIBiotech Fellow, Institute for Biotechnical Studies

FIBMS Fellow, Institute of Biomedical Sciences

FIBP Fellow, Institute of British Photographers

FIBScot Fellow, Institute of Bankers in Scotland (*now see* FCIBS)

FIC Fellow, Institute of Chemistry (*now see* FRIC, FRSC); Fellow, Imperial College, London

FICA Fellow, Commonwealth Institute of Accountants; Fellow, Institute of Chartered Accountants in England and Wales (*now see* FCA)

FICAI Fellow, Institute of Chartered Accountants in Ireland

FICB Fellow, Institute of Canadian Bankers

FICD Fellow, Institute of Civil Defence (*now see* FICDDS); Fellow, Indian College of Dentists; Fellow, International College of Dentists

FICDDS Fellow, Institute of Civil Defence and Disaster Studies

FICE Fellow, Institution of Civil Engineers

FICeram Fellow, Institute of Ceramics (*now see* FIM)

FICFM Fellow, Institute of Charity Fundraising Managers

FICFor Fellow, Institute of Chartered Foresters

FIChemE Fellow, Institution of Chemical Engineers

FICI Fellow, Institute of Chemistry of Ireland; Fellow, International Colonial Institute

FICM Fellow, Institute of Credit Management

FICMA Fellow, Institute of Cost and Management Accountants

FICOG Fellow, Indian College of Obstetricians and Gynaecologists

FICorr Fellow, Institute of Corrosion

FICorrST Fellow, Institution of Corrosion Science and Technology (*now see* FICorr)

FICPD Fellow, Institute of Continuing Professional Development

FICS Fellow, Institute of Chartered Shipbrokers; Fellow, International College of Surgeons

FICT Fellow, Institute of Concrete Technologists

FICW Fellow, Institute of Clerks of Works of Great Britain

FIDA Fellow, Institute of Directors, Australia (*now see* FAICD)

FIDCA Fellow, Industrial Design Council of Australia

FIDDA Fellow, Interior Decorators and Designers Association

FIDE Fédération Internationale des Echecs; Fellow, Institute of Design Engineers; Fédération Internationale pour le Droit Européen

FIDEM Fédération Internationale de la Médaille

FIDPM Fellow, Institute of Data Processing Management

FIEAust Fellow, Institution of Engineers, Australia

FIEC Fellow, Institute of Employment Consultants

FIED Fellow, Institution of Engineering Designers

FIEE Fellow, Institution of Electrical Engineers

FIEEE Fellow, Institute of Electrical and Electronics Engineers (NY)

FIEEIE Fellow, Institution of Electronics and Electrical Incorporated Engineers (*now see* FIIE)

FIEHK Fellow, Institution of Engineering, Hong Kong

FIEI Fellow, Institution of Engineering Inspection (*now see* FIQA); Fellow, Institution of Engineers of Ireland

FIEIE Fellow, Institution of Electronic Incorporated Engineers (later FIEEIE; *now see* FIIE)

FIEJ Fédération Internationale des Editeurs de Journaux et Publications

FIERE Fellow, Institution of Electronic and Radio Engineers (*now see* FIEE)

FIES Fellow, Illuminating Engineering Society (later FIllumES; *now see* FCIBSE); Fellow, Institution of Engineers and Shipbuilders, Scotland

FIET Fédération Internationale des Employés, Techniciens et Cadres

FIEx Fellow, Institute of Export

FIExpE Fellow, Institute of Explosives Engineers

FIFA Fédération Internationale de Football Association

FIFF Fellow, Institute of Freight Forwarders (*now see* FIFP)

FIFireE Fellow, Institution of Fire Engineers

FIFM Fellow, Institute of Fisheries Management

FIFor Fellow, Institute of Foresters (*now see* FICFor)

FIFP Fellow, Institute of Freight Professionals

FIFST Fellow, Institute of Food Science and Technology

FIGasE Fellow, Institution of Gas Engineers

FIGCM Fellow, Incorporated Guild of Church Musicians

FIGD Fellow, Institute of Grocery Distribution

FIGO International Federation of Gynaecology and Obstetrics

FIH Fellow, Institute of Housing (*now see* FCIH); Fellow, Institute of the Horse
FIHE Fellow, Institute of Health Education
FIHEEM Fellow, Institute of Healthcare Engineering and Estate Management
FIHM Fellow, Institute of Housing Managers (later FIH; *now see* FCIH); Fellow, Institute of Healthcare Management
FIHort Fellow, Institute of Horticulture
FIHospE Fellow, Institute of Hospital Engineering
FIHT Fellow, Institution of Highways and Transportation
FIHVE Fellow, Institution of Heating & Ventilating Engineers (later FCIBS and MCIBS; *now see* FCIBSE)
FIIA Fellow, Institute of Industrial Administration (later CBIM and FBIM); Fellow, Institute of Internal Auditors
FIIB Fellow, International Institute of Biotechnology
FIIC Fellow, International Institute for Conservation of Historic and Artistic Works
FIIDA Fellow, International Interior Design Association
FIIE Fellow, Institution of Incorporated Engineers in Electronic, Electrical and Mechanical Engineering
FIIM Fellow, Institution of Industrial Managers
FIInfSc Fellow, Institute of Information Scientists
FIIP Fellow, Institute of Incorporated Photographers (*now see* FBIPP)
FIIPC Fellow, India International Photographic Council
FIIPE Fellow, Indian Institution of Production Engineers
FIL Fellow, Institute of Linguists
FILA Fellow, Institute of Landscape Architects (*now see* FLI)
FILDM Fellow, Institute of Logistics and Distribution Management (*now see* FILog)
FilDr Doctor of Philosophy
Fil.Hed. Filosofie Hedersdoktor
FILLM Fédération Internationale des Langues et Littératures Modernes
FIllumES Fellow, Illuminating Engineering Society (*now see* FCIBSE)
FILog Fellow, Institute of Logistics (*now see* FILT)
FILT Fellow, Institute of Logistics and Transport
FIM Fellow, Institute of Materials (*formerly* Institution of Metallurgists, then Institute of Metals)
FIMA Fellow, Institute of Mathematics and its Applications
FIMarE Fellow, Institute of Marine Engineers
FIMatM Fellow, Institute of Materials Management (later FILog)
FIMBRA Financial Intermediaries, Managers and Brokers Regulatory Association
FIMC Fellow, Institute of Management Consultants (*now see* FCMC)
FIMCB Fellow, International Management Centre from Buckingham
FIMechE Fellow, Institution of Mechanical Engineers
FIMfgE Fellow, Institution of Manufacturing Engineers (*now see* FIEE)
FIMFT Fellow, Institute of Maxillo-facial Technology
FIMgt Fellow, Institute of Management
FIMGTechE Fellow, Institution of Mechanical and General Technician Engineers
FIMH Fellow, Institute of Materials Handling (later FIMatM); Fellow, Institute of Military History
FIMI Fellow, Institute of the Motor Industry
FIMinE Fellow, Institution of Mining Engineers (*now see* FIMM)
FIMIT Fellow, Institute of Musical Instrument Technology
FIMLS Fellow, Institute of Medical Laboratory Sciences (*now see* FIBMS)
FIMLT Fellow, Institute of Medical Laboratory Technology (later FIMLS)
FIMM Fellow, Institution of Mining and Metallurgy
FIMMA Fellow, Institute of Metals and Materials Australasia
FIMS Fellow, Institute of Mathematical Statistics
FIMT Fellow, Institute of the Motor Trade (*now see* FIMI)
FIMTA Fellow, Institute of Municipal Treasurers and Accountants (*now see* IPFA)
FIMunE Fellow, Institution of Municipal Engineers (now amalgamated with Institution of Civil Engineers)
FIN Fellow, Institute of Navigation (*now see* FRIN)
FINA Fédération Internationale de Natation Amateur
FInstAM Fellow, Institute of Administrative Management
FInstArb(NZ) Fellow, Institute of Arbitrators of New Zealand
FInstB Fellow, Institution of Buyers
FInstBiol Fellow, Institute of Biology (*now see* FIBiol)
FInstCES Fellow, Institution of Civil Engineering Surveyors
FInstD Fellow, Institute of Directors
FInstE Fellow, Institute of Energy
FInstEnvSci Fellow, Institute of Environmental Sciences
FInstF Fellow, Institute of Fuel (*now see* FInstE)
FInstFF Fellow, Institute of Freight Forwarders Ltd (*now see* FIFF)
FInstHE Fellow, Institution of Highways Engineers (*now see* FIHT)
FInstLEx Fellow, Institute of Legal Executives
FInstM Fellow, Institute of Meat; Fellow, Institute of Marketing (*now see* FCIM)
FInstMC Fellow, Institute of Measurement and Control
FInstMSM Fellow, Institute of Marketing and Sales Management (later FInstM; *now see* FCIM)
FInstMet Fellow, Institute of Metals (later part of Metals Society; *now see* FIM)
FInstNDT Fellow, Institute of Non-Destructive Testing
FInstP Fellow, Institute of Physics
FInstPet Fellow, Institute of Petroleum
FInstPI Fellow, Institute of Patentees and Inventors
FInstPkg Fellow, Institute of Packaging
FInstPS Fellow, Institute of Purchasing and Supply (*now see* FCIPS)
FInstSM Fellow, Institute of Sales Management (*now see* FInstSMM)
FInstSMM Fellow, Institute of Sales and Marketing Management
FInstW Fellow, Institute of Welding (*now see* FWeldI)
FINucE Fellow, Institution of Nuclear Engineers
FIOA Fellow, Institute of Acoustics
FIOB Fellow, Institute of Building (*now see* FCIOB)
FIOH Fellow, Institute of Occupational Hygiene
FIOM Fellow, Institute of Office Management (*now see* FIAM)
FIOP Fellow, Institute of Printing
FIOSH Fellow, Institute of Occupational Safety and Health
FIP Fellow, Australian Institute of Petroleum
FIPA Fellow, Institute of Practitioners in Advertising
FIPD Fellow, Institute of Personnel and Development (*now see* FCIPD)
FIPDM Fellow, Institute of Physical Distribution Management (later FILDM)
FIPEM Fellow, Institute of Physics and Engineering in Medicine
FIPENZ Fellow, Institution of Professional Engineers, New Zealand
FIPG Fellow, Institute of Professional Goldsmiths
FIPHE Fellow, Institution of Public Health Engineers (*now see* FIWEM)
FIPlantE Fellow, Institute of Plant Engineers (*now see* FIIM)
FIPM Fellow, Institute of Personnel Management (*now see* FIPD)
FIPR Fellow, Institute of Public Relations
FIProdE Fellow, Institution of Production Engineers (later FIMfgE; *now see* FIEE)
FIPSM Fellow, Institute of Physical Sciences in Medicine (*now see* FIPEM)
FIQ Fellow, Institute of Quarrying
FIQA Fellow, Institute of Quality Assurance
FIQS Fellow, Institute of Quantity Surveyors
FIRA Furniture Industry Research Association
FIRI Fellow, Institution of the Rubber Industry (later FPRI)
FIRM Fellow, Institute of Risk Management
FIRSE Fellow, Institute of Railway Signalling Engineers
FIRTE Fellow, Institute of Road Transport Engineers
FIS Fellow, Institute of Statisticians
FISA Fellow, Incorporated Secretaries' Association; Fédération Internationale des Sociétés d'Aviron
FISE Fellow, Institution of Sales Engineers; Fellow, Institution of Sanitary Engineers
FISITA Fédération Internationale des Sociétés d'Ingénieurs des Techniques de l'Automobile
FISM Fellow, Institute of Supervisory Managers; Fellow, Institute of Sports Medicine
FISOB Fellow, Incorporated Society of Organ Builders
FIST Fellow, Institute of Science Technology
FISTC Fellow, Institute of Scientific and Technical Communicators
FISTD Fellow, Imperial Society of Teachers of Dancing
FIStructE Fellow, Institution of Structural Engineers
FISW Fellow, Institute of Social Work
FITD Fellow, Institute of Training and Development (*now see* FIPD)
FITE Fellow, Institution of Electrical and Electronics Technician Engineers
FITSA Fellow, Institute of Trading Standards Administration
FIW Fellow, Welding Institute (*now see* FWeldI)
FIWE Fellow, Institution of Water Engineers (later FIWES; then FIWEM; *now see* FCIWEM)
FIWEM Fellow, Institution of Water and Environmental Management (*now see* FCIWEM)
FIWES Fellow, Institution of Water Engineers and Scientists (later FIWEM; *now see* FCIWEM)
FIWM Fellow, Institution of Works Managers (*now see* FIIM); Fellow, Institute of Wastes Management
FIWO Fellow, Institute of Water Officers
FIWPC Fellow, Institute of Water Pollution Control (later FIWEM; *now see* FCIWEM)
FIWSc Fellow, Institute of Wood Science
FIWSP Fellow, Institute of Work Study Practitioners (*now see* FMS)
FJI Fellow, Institute of Journalists (*now see* FCIJ)
FJIE Fellow, Junior Institution of Engineers (*now see* CIMGTechE)
FKC Fellow, King's College London
FKCHMS Fellow, King's College Hospital Medical School
FL Florida (postal)
FLA Fellow, Library Association
Fla Florida
FLAI Fellow, Library Association of Ireland

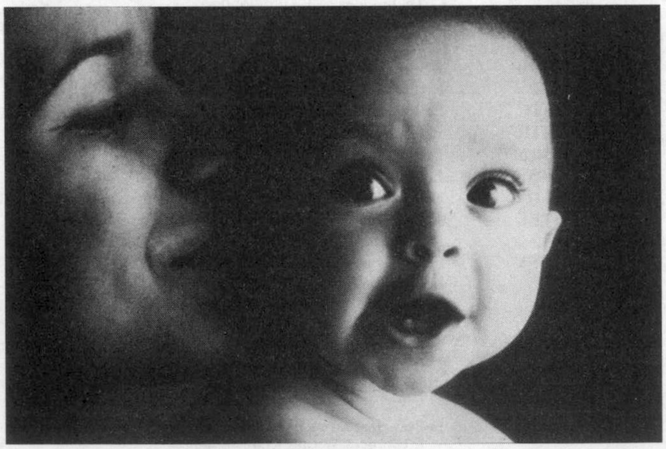

FLAS Fellow, Chartered Land Agents' Society (*now* (after amalgamation) *see* FRICS)
FLCM Fellow, London College of Music
FLHS Fellow, London Historical Society
FLI Fellow, Landscape Institute
FLIA Fellow, Life Insurance Association
FLS Fellow, Linnean Society
Flt Flight
FM Field-Marshal
FMA Fellow, Museums Association
FMAAT Fellow Member, Association of Accounting Technicians
FMedSci Fellow, Academy of Medical Sciences
FMES Fellow, Minerals Engineering Society
FMI Foundation for Manufacturing and Industry
FMinSoc Fellow, Mineralogical Society of Great Britain and Ireland
FMS Federated Malay States; Fellow, Medical Society; Fellow, Institute of Management Services
FMSA Fellow, Mineralogical Society of America
FNA Fellow, Indian National Science Academy
FNAEA Fellow, National Association of Estate Agents
FNCO Fleet Naval Constructor Officer
FNECInst Fellow, North East Coast Institution of Engineers and Shipbuilders
FNI Fellow, Nautical Institute; Fellow, National Institute of Sciences in India (*now see* FNA)
FNIA Fellow, Nigerian Institute of Architects
FNM Free National Movement
FNZEI Fellow, New Zealand Educational Institute
FNZIA Fellow, New Zealand Institute of Architects
FNZIAS Fellow, New Zealand Institute of Agricultural Science
FNZIC Fellow, New Zealand Institute of Chemistry
FNZIE Fellow, New Zealand Institution of Engineers (*now see* FIPENZ)
FNZIM Fellow, New Zealand Institute of Management
FNZPsS Fellow, New Zealand Psychological Society
FO Foreign Office (*now see* FCO); Field Officer; Flag Officer; Flying Officer
FODA Fellow, Overseas Doctors' Association
FODC Franciscan Order of the Divine Compassion
FOIC Flag Officer in charge
FOMA Flag Officer, Maritime Aviation
FOMI Faculty of Occupational Medicine of Ireland
FONA Flag Officer, Naval Aviation
FONAC Flag Officer, Naval Air Command
FOR Fellowship of Operational Research
For. Foreign
FOREST Freedom Organisation for the Right to Enjoy Smoking Tobacco
FOX Futures and Options Exchange
FPA Family Planning Association
FPC Family Practitioner Committee (later FHSA); Financial Planning Certificate
FPEA Fellow, Physical Education Association
FPHM Faculty of Public Health Medicine
FPhS Fellow, Philosophical Society of England
FPI Fellow, Plastics Institute (later FPRI)
FPIA Fellow, Plastics Institute of Australia
FPMI Fellow, Pensions Management Institute
FPRI Fellow, Plastics and Rubber Institute (*now see* FIM)
FPS Fellow, Pharmaceutical Society (*now also* FRPharmS); Fauna Preservation Society (*now see* FFPS)
FPhysS Fellow, Physical Society
f r fuori ruole
FRA Fellow, Royal Academy
FRAC Fellow, Royal Agricultural College
FRACDS Fellow, Royal Australian College of Dental Surgeons
FRACGP Fellow, Royal Australian College of General Practitioners
FRACI Fellow, Royal Australian Chemical Institute
FRACMA Fellow, Royal Australian College of Medical Administrators
FRACO Fellow, Royal Australian College of Ophthalmologists
FRACOG Fellow, Royal Australian College of Obstetricians and Gynaecologists (*now see* FRANZCOG)
FRACP Fellow, Royal Australasian College of Physicians
FRACR Fellow, Royal Australasian College of Radiologists
FRACS Fellow, Royal Australasian College of Surgeons
FRAD Fellow, Royal Academy of Dancing
FRAeS Fellow, Royal Aeronautical Society
FRAgS Fellow, Royal Agricultural Societies (*ie* of England, Scotland and Wales)
FRAHS Fellow, Royal Australian Historical Society
FRAI Fellow, Royal Anthropological Institute of Great Britain & Ireland
FRAIA Fellow, Royal Australian Institute of Architects
FRAIB Fellow, Royal Australian Institute of Building
FRAIC Fellow, Royal Architectural Institute of Canada
FRAIPA Fellow, Royal Australian Institute of Public Administration
FRAM Fellow, Royal Academy of Music
FRAME Fund for the Replacement of Animals in Medical Experiments
FRANZCOG Fellow, Royal Australian and New Zealand College of Obstetricians and Gynaecologists
FRANZCP Fellow, Royal Australian and New Zealand College of Psychiatrists
FRAPI Fellow, Royal Australian Planning Institute
FRAS Fellow, Royal Astronomical Society; Fellow, Royal Asiatic Society
FRASE Fellow, Royal Agricultural Society of England
FRBS Fellow, Royal Society of British Sculptors; Fellow, Royal Botanic Society
FRCA Fellow, Royal College of Art; Fellow, Royal College of Anaesthetists
FRCCO Fellow, Royal Canadian College of Organists
FRCD(Can.) Fellow, Royal College of Dentists of Canada
FRCGP Fellow, Royal College of General Practitioners
FRCM Fellow, Royal College of Music
FRCN Fellow, Royal College of Nursing
FRCO Fellow, Royal College of Organists
FRCO(CHM) Fellow, Royal College of Organists with Diploma in Choir Training
FRCOG Fellow, Royal College of Obstetricians and Gynaecologists
FRCOphth Fellow, Royal College of Ophthalmologists
FRCP Fellow, Royal College of Physicians, London
FRCPA Fellow, Royal College of Pathologists of Australasia
FRCP&S (Canada) Fellow, Royal College of Physicians and Surgeons of Canada
FRCPath Fellow, Royal College of Pathologists
FRCPC Fellow, Royal College of Physicians of Canada
FRCPCH Fellow, Royal College of Paediatrics and Child Health
FRCPE or **FRCPEd** Fellow, Royal College of Physicians, Edinburgh
FRCPGlas Fellow, Royal College of Physicians and Surgeons of Glasgow
FRCPI Fellow, Royal College of Physicians of Ireland
FRCPSGlas Hon. Fellow, Royal College of Physicians and Surgeons of Glasgow
FRCPsych Fellow, Royal College of Psychiatrists
FRCR Fellow, Royal College of Radiologists
FRCS Fellow, Royal College of Surgeons of England
FRCSCan Fellow, Royal College of Surgeons of Canada
FRCSE or **FRCSEd** Fellow, Royal College of Surgeons of Edinburgh
FRCSGlas Fellow, Royal College of Physicians and Surgeons of Glasgow
FRCSI Fellow, Royal College of Surgeons in Ireland
FRCSLT Fellow, Royal College of Speech and Language Therapists
FRCSoc Fellow, Royal Commonwealth Society
FRCUS Fellow, Royal College of University Surgeons (Denmark)
FRCVS Fellow, Royal College of Veterinary Surgeons
FREconS Fellow, Royal Economic Society
FREng Fellow, Royal Academy of Engineering
FRES Fellow, Royal Entomological Society of London
FRFPSG Fellow, Royal Faculty of Physicians and Surgeons, Glasgow (*now see* FRCPGlas)
FRG Federal Republic of Germany
FRGS Fellow, Royal Geographical Society
FRGSA Fellow, Royal Geographical Society of Australasia
FRHistS Fellow, Royal Historical Society
FRHS Fellow, Royal Horticultural Society (*now see* MRHS)
FRIAS Fellow, Royal Incorporation of Architects of Scotland; Royal Institute for the Advancement of Science
FRIBA Fellow, Royal Institute of British Architects (*and see* RIBA)
FRIC Fellow, Royal Institute of Chemistry (*now see* FRSC)
FRICS Fellow, Royal Institution of Chartered Surveyors
FRIH Fellow, Royal Institute of Horticulture (NZ)
FRIN Fellow, Royal Institute of Navigation
FRINA Fellow, Royal Institution of Naval Architects
FRIPA Fellow, Royal Institute of Public Administration (the Institute no longer has Fellows)
FRIPHH Fellow, Royal Institute of Public Health and Hygiene
FRMCM Fellow, Royal Manchester College of Music
FRMedSoc Fellow, Royal Medical Society
FRMetS Fellow, Royal Meteorological Society
FRMIA Fellow, Retail Management Institute of Australia
FRMS Fellow, Royal Microscopical Society
FRNCM Fellow, Royal Northern College of Music
FRNS Fellow, Royal Numismatic Society
FRPharmS Fellow, Royal Pharmaceutical Society
FRPS Fellow, Royal Photographic Society
FRPSL Fellow, Royal Philatelic Society, London
FRS Fellow, Royal Society
FRSA Fellow, Royal Society of Arts
FRSAI Fellow, Royal Society of Antiquaries of Ireland
FRSAMD Fellow, Royal Scottish Academy of Music and Drama
FRSanI Fellow, Royal Sanitary Institute (*now see* FRSH)
FRSC Fellow, Royal Society of Canada; Fellow, Royal Society of Chemistry

FRS(Can) Fellow, Royal Society of Canada (used when a person is also a Fellow of the Royal Society of Chemistry)
FRSCM Hon. Fellow, Royal School of Church Music
FRSC (UK) Fellow, Royal Society of Chemistry (used when a person is also a Fellow of the Royal Society of Canada)
FRSE Fellow, Royal Society of Edinburgh
FRSGS Fellow, Royal Scottish Geographical Society
FRSH Fellow, Royal Society for the Promotion of Health
FRSL Fellow, Royal Society of Literature
FRSocMed Fellow, Royal Society of Medicine
FRSNZ Fellow, Royal Society of New Zealand
FRSSAf Fellow, Royal Society of South Africa
FRSTM&H Fellow, Royal Society of Tropical Medicine and Hygiene
FRTPI Fellow, Royal Town Planning Institute
FRTS Fellow, Royal Television Society
FRUSI Fellow, Royal United Services Institute
FRVA Fellow, Rating and Valuation Association (*now see* IRRV)
FRVC Fellow, Royal Veterinary College
FRZSScot Fellow, Royal Zoological Society of Scotland
FS Field Security
fs Graduate, Royal Air Force Staff College
FSA Fellow, Society of Antiquaries; Financial Services Authority
FSAA Fellow, Society of Incorporated Accountants and Auditors
FSACOG Fellow, South African College of Obstetricians and Gynaecologists
FSAE Fellow, Society of Automotive Engineers; Fellow, Society of Art Education
FSAI Fellow, Society of Architectural Illustrators
FSAIEE Fellow, South African Institute of Electrical Engineers
FSArc Fellow, Society of Architects (merged with the RIBA 1952)
FSaRS Fellow, Safety and Reliability Society
FSAScot Fellow, Society of Antiquaries of Scotland
FSASM Fellow, South Australian School of Mines
fsc Foreign Staff College
FSCA Fellow, Society of Company and Commercial Accountants
FScotvec Fellow, Scottish Vocational Education Council
FSCRE Fellow, Scottish Council for Research in Education
FSDC Fellow, Society of Dyers and Colourists
FSE Fellow, Society of Engineers
FSG Fellow, Society of Genealogists
FSGD Fellow, Society of Garden Designers
FSGT Fellow, Society of Glass Technology
FSI Fellow, Chartered Surveyors' Institution (*now see* FRICS); Fellow, Securities Institute
FSIA Fellow, Securities Institute of Australia
FSIAD Fellow, Society of Industrial Artists and Designers (*now see* FCSD)
FSLAET Fellow, Society of Licensed Aircraft Engineers and Technologists
FSLCOG Fellow, Sri Lankan College of Obstetrics and Gynaecology
FSLTC Fellow, Society of Leather Technologists and Chemists
FSMA Fellow, Incorporated Sales Managers' Association (later FInstMSM, then FInstM)
FSMC Freeman of the Spectacle-Makers' Company
FSME Fellow, Society of Manufacturing Engineers
FSMPTE Fellow, Society of Motion Picture and Television Engineers (US)
FSNAD Fellow, Society of Numismatic Artists and Designers
FSNAME Fellow, American Society of Naval Architects and Marine Engineers
FSOGC Fellow, Society of Obstetricians and Gynaecologists of Canada
FSPI Fellow, Society of Practitioners of Insolvency
FSQA Fellow, Scottish Qualifications Authority
FSRHE Fellow, Society for Research into Higher Education
FSRP Fellow, Society for Radiological Protection
FSS Fellow, Royal Statistical Society
FSSI Fellow, Society of Scribes and Illuminators
FSTD Fellow, Society of Typographic Designers
FSVA Fellow, Incorporated Society of Valuers and Auctioneers (*now see* RICS)
FT Financial Times
FTAT Furniture, Timber and Allied Trades Union
FTC Flying Training Command; Full Technological Certificate, City and Guilds of London Institute
FTCD Fellow, Trinity College, Dublin
FTCL Fellow, Trinity College of Music, London
FTI Fellow, Textile Institute
FTII Fellow, Chartered Institute (*formerly* Incorporated Institute, then Institute) of Taxation
FTMA Fellow, Telecommunications Managers Association (*now see* FCMA)
FTP Fellow, Thames Polytechnic
FTS Fellow, Australian Academy of Technological Sciences and Engineering (*now see* FTSE); Flying Training School; Fellow, Tourism Society
FTSC Fellow, Tonic Sol-fa College
FTSE Fellow, Australian Academy of Technological Sciences and Engineering
FUCEB Fellow, University of Central England in Birmingham
FUCUA Federation of University Conservative and Unionist Associations (*now see* FCS)
FUMDS Fellow, United Medical and Dental Schools
FUMIST Fellow, University of Manchester Institute of Science and Technology
FVRDE Fighting Vehicles Research and Development Establishment
FWAAS Fellow, World Academy of Arts and Sciences
FWACP Fellow, West African College of Physicians
FWCMD Fellow, Welsh College of Music and Drama
FWeldI Fellow, Welding Institute
FWSOM Fellow, Institute of Practitioners in Work Study, Organisation and Method (*now see* FMS)
FZS Fellow, Zoological Society
FZSScot Fellow, Zoological Society of Scotland (*now see* FRZSScot)

G

GA Geologists' Association; Gaelic Athletic (Club); Georgia (postal)
Ga Georgia
GAI Guild of Architectural Ironmongers
GAP Gap Activity Projects
GAPAN Guild of Air Pilots and Air Navigators
GATT General Agreement on Tariffs and Trade (*now* World Trade Organisation)
GB Great Britain
GBA Governing Bodies Association
GBE Knight or Dame Grand Cross, Order of the British Empire
GBGSA Governing Bodies of Girls' Schools Association (*formerly* Association of Governing Bodies of Girls' Public Schools)
GBM Grand Bauhinia Medal (Hong Kong)
GBS Gold Bauhinia Star (Hong Kong)
GBSM Graduate of Birmingham and Midland Institute School of Music
GC George Cross
GCB Knight or Dame Grand Cross, Order of the Bath
GCBS General Council of British Shipping
GCC General Chiropractic Council
GCCC Gonville and Caius College, Cambridge
GCCS Government Code and Cipher School
GCFR Grand Commander, Order of the Federal Republic of Nigeria
GCH Knight Grand Cross, Hanoverian Order
GCHQ Government Communications Headquarters
GCIE Knight Grand Commander, Order of the Indian Empire
GCLJ Grand Cross, Order of St Lazarus of Jerusalem
GCLM Grand Commander, Order of the Legion of Merit of Rhodesia
GCM Gold Crown of Merit (Barbados)
GCMG Knight or Dame Grand Cross, Order of St Michael and St George
GCON Grand Cross, Order of the Niger
GCSE General Certificate of Secondary Education
GCSG Knight Grand Cross, Order of St Gregory the Great
GCSI Knight Grand Commander, Order of the Star of India
GCSJ Knight Grand Cross of Justice, Sovereign Order of St John of Jerusalem (Knights Hospitaller)
GCSL Grand Cross, Order of St Lucia
GCStJ Bailiff or Dame Grand Cross, Most Venerable Order of the Hospital of St John of Jerusalem
GCVO Knight or Dame Grand Cross, Royal Victorian Order
gd grand-daughter
GDBA Guide Dogs for the Blind Association
GDC General Dental Council
Gdns Gardens
GDR German Democratic Republic
GDST Girls' Day School Trust
Gen. General
Ges. Gesellschaft
GFD Geophysical Fluid Dynamics
GFS Girls' Friendly Society
ggd great-grand-daughter
ggs great-grandson
GGSM Graduate in Music, Guildhall School of Music and Drama
GHQ General Headquarters
Gib. Gibraltar
GIMechE Graduate, Institution of Mechanical Engineers
GKT Guy's, King's and St Thomas' (Medical and Dental School of King's College London)
GL Grand Lodge
GLA Greater London Authority
GLAA Greater London Arts Association (*now see* GLAB)
GLAB Greater London Arts Board
GLC Greater London Council

Glos Gloucestershire
GM George Medal; Grand Medal (Ghana)
GMB (Union for) General, Municipal, Boilermakers
GMBATU General, Municipal, Boilermakers and Allied Trades Union (*now see* GMB)
GmbH Gesellschaft mit beschränkter Haftung
GMC General Medical Council; Guild of Memorial Craftsmen; General Management Course (Henley)
GMWU General and Municipal Workers' Union (later GMBATU; *now see* GMB)
GNC General Nursing Council
GNVQ General National Vocational Qualification
GNZM Knight or Dame Grand Companion, New Zealand Order of Merit
GOC General Officer Commanding
GOC-in-C General Officer Commanding-in-Chief
GOE General Ordination Examination
GOMLJ Grand Officer of Merit, Order of St Lazarus of Jerusalem
GOQ Grand Officer, National Order of Quebec
GOSK Grand Officer, Order of the Star and Key (Mauritius)
Gov. Governor
Govt Government
GP General Practitioner; Grand Prix
GPDST Girls' Public Day School Trust (*now see* GDST)
GPMU Graphical, Paper and Media Union
GPO General Post Office
GR General Reconaissance
Gr. Greek
GRSM Graduate of the Royal Schools of Music
GS General Staff; Grammar School
g s grandson
GSA Girls' Schools Association
GSD Gibraltar Social Democrats
GSM General Service Medal; (Member of) Guildhall School of Music and Drama
GSMD Guildhall School of Music and Drama
GSO General Staff Officer
GTCL Graduate, Trinity College of Music
GTS General Theological Seminary (New York)
GUI Golfing Union of Ireland
GWR Great Western Railway

H

HA Historical Association; Health Authority
HAA Heavy Anti-Aircraft
HAC Honourable Artillery Company
HACAS Housing Association Consultancy and Advisory Service
Hants Hampshire
HARCVS Honorary Associate, Royal College of Veterinary Surgeons
Harv. Harvard
HAT Housing Action Trust
HBM His (or Her) Britannic Majesty (Majesty's); Humming Bird Gold Medal (Trinidad)
hc *honoris causa* (honorary)
HCEG Honourable Company of Edinburgh Golfers
HCF Honorary Chaplain to the Forces
HCIMA Hotel, Catering and Institutional Management Association
HCO Higher Clerical Officer
HCSC Higher Command and Staff Course
HDA Hawkesbury Diploma in Agriculture (Australia); Health Development Agency
HDD Higher Dental Diploma
HDFA Higher Diploma in Fine Art
HDipEd Higher Diploma in Education
HE His (or Her) Excellency; His Eminence
HEA Health Education Authority (*now see* HDA)
HEC Ecole des Hautes Etudes Commerciales; Higher Education Corporation
HEFCE Higher Education Funding Council for England
HEFCW Higher Education Funding Council for Wales
HEH His (or Her) Exalted Highness
Heir-pres. Heir-presumptive
HEO Higher Executive Officer
HEQC Higher Education Quality Council (*now see* QAA)
HERO Higher Education Research Opportunities
Herts Hertfordshire
HFEA Human Fertilisation and Embryology Authority
HG Home Guard
HGTAC Home Grown Timber Advisory Committee
HH His (or Her) Highness; His Holiness; Member, Hesketh Hubbard Art Society
HHA Historic Houses Association
HHD Doctor of Humanities (US)
HI Hawaii (postal)
HIH His (or Her) Imperial Highness
HIM His (or Her) Imperial Majesty
HIV Human Immunodeficiency Virus
HJ Hilal-e-Jurat (Pakistan)
HKIA Hong Kong Institute of Architects
HKIPM Hong Kong Institute of Personnel Management
HKSAR Hong Kong Special Administrative Region
HLD Doctor of Humane Letters
HLI Highland Light Infantry
HM His (or Her) Majesty, or Majesty's
HMA Head Masters' Association
HMAS His (or Her) Majesty's Australian Ship
HMC Headmasters' and Headmistresses' (*formerly* Headmasters') Conference; Hospital Management Committee
HMCIC His (or Her) Majesty's Chief Inspector of Constabulary
HMCS His (or Her) Majesty's Canadian Ship
HMHS His (or Her) Majesty's Hospital Ship
HMI His (or Her) Majesty's Inspector
HMIED Honorary Member, Institute of Engineering Designers
HMMTB His (or Her) Majesty's Motor Torpedo Boat
HMNZS His (or Her) Majesty's New Zealand Ship
HMOCS His (or Her) Majesty's Overseas Civil Service
HMS His (or Her) Majesty's Ship
HMSO His (or Her) Majesty's Stationery Office
HNC Higher National Certificate
HND Higher National Diploma
H of C House of Commons
H of L House of Lords
Hon. Honourable; Honorary
HPk Hilal-e-Pakistan
HQ Headquarters
HQA Hilali-Quaid-i-Azam (Pakistan)
HRGI Honorary Member, The Royal Glasgow Institute of the Fine Arts
HRH His (or Her) Royal Highness
HRHA Honorary Member, Royal Hibernian Academy
HRI Honorary Member, Royal Institute of Painters in Water Colours
HROI Honorary Member, Royal Institute of Oil Painters
HRSA Honorary Member, Royal Scottish Academy
HRSW Honorary Member, Royal Scottish Water Colour Society
HRUA Hon. Member, Royal Ulster Academy
HSC Health and Safety Commission
HSE Health and Safety Executive
HSH His (or Her) Serene Highness
HSS Health and Social Services
Hum. Humanity, Humanities (Classics)
Hunts Huntingdonshire
HVCert Health Visitor's Certificate

I

I Island; Ireland
IA Indian Army; Iowa (postal)
IAA International Academy of Architecture
IAAF International Amateur Athletic Federation
IAC Indian Armoured Corps; Institute of Amateur Cinematographers
IACP International Association of Chiefs of Police
IACR Institute of Arable Crops Research
IADB Inter American Development Bank
IADR International Association for Dental Research
IAEA International Atomic Energy Agency
IAF Indian Air Force; Indian Auxiliary Force
IAHM Incorporated Association of Headmasters
IAM Institute of Advanced Motorists; Institute of Aviation Medicine
IAMAS International Association of Meteorology and Atmospheric Sciences
IAMC Indian Army Medical Corps
IAML International Association of Music Libraries
IAMTACT Institute of Advanced Machine Tool and Control Technology
IAO Incorporated Association of Organists
IAOC Indian Army Ordnance Corps
IAPS Incorporated Association of Preparatory Schools
IAPSO International Association for the Physical Sciences of the Oceans
IARO Indian Army Reserve of Officers
IAS Indian Administrative Service; Institute for Advanced Studies; International Academy of Science
IASC International Arctic Science Committee
IASS International Association for Scandinavian Studies
IATA International Air Transport Association
IATUL International Association of Technological University Libraries
IAU International Astronomical Union

IAWPRC International Association on Water Pollution Research and Control
ib. or ibid. *ibidem* (in the same place)
IBA Independent Broadcasting Authority; International Bar Association
IBBY International Board for Books for Young People
IBCA International Braille Chess Association
IBG Institute of British Geographers (now part of RGS)
IBRD International Bank for Reconstruction and Development (World Bank)
IBRO International Bank Research Organisation; International Brain Research Organisation
IBTE Institution of British Telecommunications Engineers
IBVM Institute of the Blessed Virgin Mary
i/c in charge; in command
ICA Institute of Contemporary Arts; Institute of Chartered Accountants in England and Wales (*now see* ICAEW)
ICAA Invalid Children's Aid Association
ICAC Independent Commission Against Corruption, Hong Kong
ICAEW Institute of Chartered Accountants in England and Wales
ICAI Institute of Chartered Accountants in Ireland
ICAO International Civil Aviation Organization
ICAS Institute of Chartered Accountants of Scotland
ICBP International Council for Bird Preservation
ICBS Irish Christian Brothers' School
ICC International Chamber of Commerce; International Cricket Council (*formerly* International Cricket Conference)
ICCA International Council for Commercial Arbitration
ICCROM International Centre for Conservation at Rome
ICD *Iuris Canonici Doctor* (Doctor of Canon Law); Independence Commemorative Decoration (Rhodesia)
ICE Institution of Civil Engineers
ICED International Council for Educational Development
ICEF International Federation of Chemical, Energy and General Workers' Unions
Icel. Icelandic
ICES International Council for the Exploration of the Sea
ICF International Federation of Chemical and General Workers' Unions (*now see* ICEF)
ICFC Industrial and Commercial Finance Corporation (later part of Investors in Industry)
ICFTU International Confederation of Free Trade Unions
ICHCA International Cargo Handling Co-ordination Association
IChemE Institution of Chemical Engineers
ICI Imperial Chemical Industries
ICJ International Commission of Jurists
ICL International Computers Ltd
ICM International Confederation of Midwives
ICMA Institute of Cost and Management Accountants (*now see* CIMA)
ICME International Commission for Mathematical Education
ICNL International Center for Not for Profit Law
ICOM International Council of Museums
ICOMOS International Council on Monuments and Sites
ICorr Institute of Corrosion
ICorrST Institution of Corrosion Science and Technology (*now see* ICorr)
ICPO International Criminal Police Organization (Interpol)
ICRC International Committee of the Red Cross
ICRF Imperial Cancer Research Fund
ICS Indian Civil Service
ICSA Institute of Chartered Secretaries and Administrators
ICSD International Council for Scientific Development
ICSID International Council of Societies of Industrial Design; International Centre for Settlement of Investment Disputes
ICSM Imperial College School of Medicine
ICSS International Committee for the Sociology of Sport
ICSTIS Independent Committee for Supervision of Telephone Information Services
ICSTM Imperial College of Science, Technology and Medicine, London
ICSU International Council of Scientific Unions
ICT International Computers and Tabulators Ltd (*now see* ICL)
ID Independence Decoration (Rhodesia); Idaho (postal)
IDA International Development Association
IDB Internal Drainage Board; Industrial Development Board
IDC Imperial Defence College (*now see* RCDS); Inter-Diocesan Certificate
idc completed a course at, or served for a year on the Staff of, the Imperial Defence College (*now see* rcds)
IDDA Interior Decorators and Designers Association
IDRC International Development Research Centre
IDS Institute of Development Studies; Industry Department for Scotland
IEA Institute of Economic Affairs
IEC International Electrotechnical Commission
IEE Institution of Electrical Engineers
IEEE Institute of Electrical and Electronics Engineers (NY)
IEEIE Institution of Electrical and Electronics Incorporated Engineers (*now see* IIE)
IEETE Institution of Electrical and Electronics Technician Engineers (*now see* IIE)
IEI Institution of Engineers of Ireland
IEIE Institution of Electronics and Electrical Incorporated Engineers (*now see* IIE)
IEME Inspectorate of Electrical and Mechanical Engineering
IEng Incorporated Engineer
IERE Institution of Electronic and Radio Engineers
IES Indian Educational Service; Institution of Engineers and Shipbuilders in Scotland; International Electron Paramagnetic Resonance Society
IExpE Institute of Explosives Engineers
IFAC International Federation of Automatic Control
IFAD International Fund for Agricultural Development (UNO)
IFAW International Fund for Animal Welfare
IFBWW International Federation of Building Woodworkers
IFC International Finance Corporation
IFIAS International Federation of Institutes of Advanced Study
IFIP International Federation for Information Processing
IFLA International Federation of Library Associations
IFOR Implementation Force
IFORS International Federation of Operational Research Societies
IFPI International Federation of the Phonographic Industry
IFRA World Press Research Association
IFS Irish Free State; Indian Forest Service
IG Instructor in Gunnery
IGasE Institution of Gas Engineers
IGPP Institute of Geophysics and Planetary Physics
IGS Independent Grammar School
IGU International Geographical Union; International Gas Union
IHA Institute of Health Service Administrators (*now see* IHSM)
IHBC (Member of) Institute of Historic Building Conservation
IHospE Institute of Hospital Engineering
IHSM Institute of Health Services Management
IHVE Institution of Heating and Ventilating Engineers (later CIBS)
IIE Institution of Incorporated Engineers
IIExE Institution of Incorporated Executive Engineers
IILS International Institute for Labour Studies
IIM Institution of Industrial Managers
IIMR Institute of Investment Management and Research
IIMT International Institute for the Management of Technology
IInfSc Institute of Information Scientists
IIS International Institute of Sociology
IISI International Iron and Steel Institute
IISS International Institute of Strategic Studies
IIT Indian Institute of Technology
IL Illinois (postal)
ILA International Law Association
ILAC International Laboratory Accreditation Co-operation
ILEA Inner London Education Authority
ILEC Inner London Education Committee
Ill Illinois
ILO International Labour Office; International Labour Organisation
ILP Independent Labour Party
ILR Independent Local Radio; International Labour Review
IM Individual Merit
IMA International Music Association; Institute of Mathematics and its Applications
IMCB International Management Centre from Buckingham
IMCO Inter-Governmental Maritime Consultative Organization (*now see* IMO)
IME Institute of Medical Ethics
IMEA Incorporated Municipal Electrical Association
IMechE Institution of Mechanical Engineers
IMechIE Institution of Mechanical Incorporated Engineers (*now see* IIE)
IMEDE Institut pour l'Etude des Méthodes de Direction de l'Entreprise
IMF International Monetary Fund
IMGTechE Institution of Mechanical and General Technician Engineers
IMinE Institution of Mining Engineers
IMM Institution of Mining and Metallurgy
IMMLEP Immunology of Leprosy
IMO International Maritime Organization
Imp. Imperial
IMRO Investment Management Regulatory Organisation
IMS Indian Medical Service; Institute of Management Services; International Military Staff
IMTA Institute of Municipal Treasurers and Accountants (*now see* CIPFA)
IMU International Mathematical Union
IMunE Institution of Municipal Engineers (now amalgamated with Institution of Civil Engineers)
IN Indian Navy; Indiana (postal)
INASFMH International Sports Association for People with Mental Handicap

Inc. Incorporated
INCA International Newspaper Colour Association
Incog. Incognito
Ind. Independent
Inf. Infantry
INFORM Information Network Focus on New Religious Movements
INSA Indian National Science Academy
INSEA International Society for Education through Art
INSEAD or **Insead** Institut Européen d'Administration des Affaires
Insp. Inspector
INSS Institute of Nuclear Systems Safety
Inst. Institute
InstBE Institution of British Engineers
Instn Institution
InstSMM Institute of Sales and Marketing Management
InstT Institute of Transport (*now see* CIT)
INTELSAT International Telecommunications Satellite Organisation
IOB Institute of Banking (*now see* CIOB)
IOC International Olympic Committee; Intergovernmental Oceanographic Commission
IOCD International Organisation for Chemical Science in Development
IoD Institute of Directors
IODE Imperial Order of the Daughters of the Empire
I of M Isle of Man
IOM Isle of Man; Indian Order of Merit
IOP Institute of Painters in Oil Colours
IOTA (Fellow of) Institute of Transport Administration
IoW Isle of Wight
IPA International Publishers' Association
IPCIS International Institute for Practitioners in Credit Insurance and Surety
IPCS Institution of Professional Civil Servants
IPFA Member or Associate, Chartered Institute of Public Finance and Accountancy (*now see* CPFA)
IPHE Institution of Public Health Engineers (*now see* IWEM)
IPI International Press Institute; Institute of Patentees and Inventors
IPlantE Institution of Plant Engineers (*now see* IIM)
IPM Institute of Personnel Management
IPPA Independent Programme Producers' Association
IPPF International Planned Parenthood Federation
IPPR Institute for Public Policy Research
IPPS Institute of Physics and The Physical Society
IPR Institute of Public Relations
IProdE Institution of Production Engineers (later Institution of Manufacturing Engineering; *now see* IEE)
IPS Indian Police Service; Indian Political Service; Institute of Purchasing and Supply
IPSM Institute of Public Sector Managers
IPU Inter-Parliamentary Union
IRA Irish Republican Army
IRAD Institute for Research on Animal Diseases
IRC Industrial Reorganization Corporation; Interdisciplinary Research Centre
IRCAM Institute for Research and Co-ordination in Acoustics and Music
IRCert Industrial Relations Certificate
IREE(Aust) Institution of Radio and Electronics Engineers (Australia)
IRI Institution of the Rubber Industry (*now see* PRI)
IRO International Refugee Organization
IRPA International Radiation Protection Association
IRRV (Fellow/Member of) Institute of Revenues, Rating and Valuation
IRTE Institute of Road Transport Engineers
IS International Society of Sculptors, Painters and Gravers
Is Island(s)
ISAF International Sailing Federation
ISBA Incorporated Society of British Advertisers
ISC Imperial Service College, Haileybury; Indian Staff Corps; Independent Schools Council
ISCM International Society for Contemporary Music
ISCO Independent Schools Careers Organisation
ISE Indian Service of Engineers
ISI International Statistical Institute; Independent Schools Inspectorate
ISIS Independent Schools Information Service
ISJC Independent Schools Joint Council (*now see* ISC)
ISM Incorporated Society of Musicians
ISMAR International Society of Magnetic Resonance
ISME International Society for Musical Education
ISMRC Inter-Services Metallurgical Research Council
ISO Imperial Service Order; International Organization for Standardization
ISSA International Social Security Association
ISSTIP International Society for Study of Tension in Performance
ISTC Iron and Steel Trades Confederation; Institute of Scientific and Technical Communicators
ISTD Imperial Society of Teachers of Dancing; Institute for the Study and Treatment of Delinquency
IStructE Institution of Structural Engineers
ISVA Incorporated Society of Valuers and Auctioneers
IT Information Technology; Indian Territory (US)
It. or Ital. Italian
ITA Independent Television Authority (later IBA)
ITAB Information Technology Advisory Board
ITB Industry Training Board
ITC International Trade Centre; Independent Television Commission
ITCA Independent Television Association (*formerly* Independent Television Companies Association Ltd)
ITDG Intermediate Technology Development Group
ITEME Institution of Technician Engineers in Mechanical Engineering
ITF International Transport Workers' Federation
ITN Independent Television News
ITO International Trade Organization
ITSA Information Technology Services Agency
ITU International Telecommunication Union
ITV Independent Television
ITVA International Television Association
IUA International Union of Architects
IUB International Union of Biochemistry (*now see* IUBMB)
IUBMB International Union of Biochemistry and Molecular Biology
IUC Inter-University Council for Higher Education Overseas (*now see* IUPC)
IUCN World Conservation Union (*formerly* International Union for the Conservation of Nature and Natural Resources)
IUCW International Union for Child Welfare
IUGG International Union of Geodesy & Geophysics
IUGS International Union of Geological Sciences
IUHPS International Union of the History and Philosophy of Science
IULA International Union of Local Authorities
IUPAB International Union of Pure and Applied Biophysics
IUPAC International Union of Pure and Applied Chemistry
IUPAP International Union of Pure and Applied Physics
IUPC Inter-University and Polytechnic Council for Higher Education Overseas
IUPS International Union of Physiological Sciences
IUSSP International Union for the Scientific Study of Population
IUTAM International Union of Theoretical and Applied Mechanics
IVF In-vitro Fertilisation
IVS International Voluntary Service
IWA Inland Waterways Association
IWEM Institution of Water and Environmental Management (*now see* CIWEM)
IWES Institution of Water Engineers and Scientists (later IWEM)
IWGC Imperial War Graves Commission (*now see* CWGC)
IWM Institution of Works Managers (*now see* IIM)
IWO Institution of Water Officers
IWPC Institute of Water Pollution Control (later IWEM)
IWS International Wool Secretariat
IWSA International Water Supply Association
IWSOM Institute of Practitioners in Work Study Organisation and Methods (*now see* IMS)
IWSP Institute of Work Study Practitioners (*now see* IMS)
IYRU International Yacht Racing Union (*now see* ISAF)
IZ I Zingari

J

JA Judge Advocate
JACT Joint Association of Classical Teachers
JAG Judge Advocate General
Jas James
JCB *Juris Canonici* (or *Civilis*) *Baccalaureus* (Bachelor of Canon (or Civil) Law)
JCR Junior Common Room
JCS Journal of the Chemical Society
JCD *Juris Canonici* (or *Civilis*) *Doctor* (Doctor of Canon (or Civil) Law)
JCI Junior Chamber International
JCL *Juris Canonici* (or *Civilis*) *Licentiatus* (Licentiate in Canon (or Civil) Law)
JCO Joint Consultative Organisation (of AFRC, MAFF, and Department of Agriculture and Fisheries for Scotland)
JD Doctor of Jurisprudence
jd *jure dignitatis* (by virtue of status)
JDipMA Joint Diploma in Management Accounting Services
JG Junior Grade
JInstE Junior Institution of Engineers (*now see* IMGTechE)
jl(s) journal(s)

JMB Joint Matriculation Board
JMN Johan Mangku Negara (Malaysia)
JMOTS Joint Maritime Operational Training Staff
JNCC Joint Nature Conservation Committee
Jno. or **Joh.** John
JP Justice of the Peace
Jr Junior
jsc qualified at a Junior Staff Course, or the equivalent, 1942–46
JSD Doctor of Juristic Science
JSDC Joint Service Defence College
jsdc completed a course at Joint Service Defence College
JSLS Joint Services Liaison Staff
JSM Johan Setia Mahkota (Malaysia); Master of the Science of Jurisprudence
JSPS Japan Society for the Promotion of Science
JSSC Joint Services Staff College
jssc completed a course at Joint Services Staff College
JSU Joint Support Unit
jt, jtly joint, jointly
JUD *Juris Utriusque Doctor* (Doctor of Both Laws (Canon and Civil))
Jun. Junior
Jun.Opt. Junior Optime
JWS or **jws** Joint Warfare Staff

K

KA Knight of St Andrew, Order of Barbados
Kans Kansas
KAR King's African Rifles
KBE Knight Commander, Order of the British Empire
KC King's Counsel
KCB Knight Commander, Order of the Bath
KCC Commander, Order of the Crown, Belgium and Congo Free State
KCGSJ Knight Commander of Magisterial Grace, Order of St John of Jerusalem (Knights Hospitaller)
KCH King's College Hospital; Knight Commander, Hanoverian Order
KCHS Knight Commander, Order of the Holy Sepulchre
KCIE Knight Commander, Order of the Indian Empire
KCL King's College London
KCLJ Knight Commander, Order of St Lazarus of Jerusalem
KCMG Knight Commander, Order of St Michael and St George
KCN Knight Commander, Most Distinguished Order of the Nation (Antigua and Barbuda)
KCSA Knight Commander, Military Order of the Collar of St Agatha of Paternò
KCSG Knight Commander, Order of St Gregory the Great
KCSHS Knight Commander with Star, Order of the Holy Sepulchre
KCSI Knight Commander, Order of the Star of India
KCSJ Knight Commander, Sovereign Order of St John of Jerusalem (Knights Hospitaller)
KCSS Knight Commander, Order of St Silvester
KCVO Knight Commander, Royal Victorian Order
KDG King's Dragoon Guards
KEO King Edward's Own
KG Knight, Order of the Garter
KGB Komitet Gosudarstvennoi Bezopanosti (Committee of State Security, USSR)
KGCSS Knight Grand Cross, Order of St Silvester
KGN Knight Grand Collar, Most Distinguished Order of the Nation (Antigua and Barbuda)
KGSJ Knight of Grace, Sovereign Order of St John of Jerusalem (Knights Hospitaller)
KGStJ Knight of Grace, Order of St John of Jerusalem (*now see* KStJ)
KH Knight, Hanoverian Order
KHC Hon. Chaplain to the King
KHDS Hon. Dental Surgeon to the King
KHNS Hon. Nursing Sister to the King
KHP Hon. Physician to the King
KHS Hon. Surgeon to the King; Knight, Order of the Holy Sepulchre
K-i-H Kaisar-i-Hind
KJStJ Knight of Justice, Order of St John of Jerusalem (*now see* KStJ)
KLJ Knight, Order of St Lazarus of Jerusalem
KM Knight of Malta
KMLJ Knight of Merit, Order of St Lazarus of Jerusalem
KNH Knight Companion, Most Exalted Order of National Hero (Antigua and Barbuda)
KNZM Knight Companion, New Zealand Order of Merit
KOM Companion, National Order of Merit (Malta)
KORR King's Own Royal Regiment
KOSB King's Own Scottish Borderers
KOYLI King's Own Yorkshire Light Infantry
KP Knight, Order of St Patrick
KPM King's Police Medal
KrF Kristelig Folkeparti
KRRC King's Royal Rifle Corps
KS King's Scholar; Kansas (postal)
KSC Knight of St Columba
KSG Knight, Order of St Gregory the Great
KSJ Knight, Sovereign Order of St John of Jerusalem (Knights Hospitaller)
KSLI King's Shropshire Light Infantry
KSS Knight, Order of St Silvester
KStJ Knight, Most Venerable Order of the Hospital of St John of Jerusalem
KStJ(A) Associate Knight of Justice, Most Venerable Order of the Hospital of St John of Jerusalem
KT Knight, Order of the Thistle
Kt Knight
KUOM Companion of Honour, National Order of Merit (Malta)
KY Kentucky (postal)
Ky Kentucky

L

L Liberal
LA Los Angeles; Library Association; Liverpool Academy; Louisiana (postal)
La Louisiana
LAA Light Anti-Aircraft
Lab Labour
LAC London Athletic Club
LACSAB Local Authorities Conditions of Service Advisory Board
LAE London Association of Engineers
LAMDA London Academy of Music and Dramatic Art
LAMSAC Local Authorities' Management Services and Computer Committee
LAMTPI Legal Associate Member, Town Planning Institute (*now see* LMRTPI)
Lance-Corp. Lance-Corporal
Lancs Lancashire
LAPADA London & Provincial Antique Dealers' Association
LARSP Language Assessment, Remediation and Screening Procedure
Lautro Life Assurance and Unit Trust Regulatory Organisation
LBC London Broadcasting Company; London Borough Council
LBHI Licentiate, British Horological Institute
LC Cross of Leo
LCAD London Certificate in Art and Design (University of London)
LCC London County Council (later GLC)
LCD Lord Chancellor's Department
LCh Licentiate in Surgery
LCJ Lord Chief Justice
LCL Licentiate of Canon Law
LCP Licentiate, College of Preceptors
LCSP London and Counties Society of Physiologists
LCST Licentiate, College of Speech Therapists
LD Liberal and Democratic; Licentiate in Divinity
LDC Limited Duration Company (US)
LDDC London Docklands Development Corporation
LDiv Licentiate in Divinity
LDP Liberal Democratic Party (Japan)
LDS Licentiate in Dental Surgery
LDV Local Defence Volunteers
LEA Local Education Authority
LEADR Lawyers Engaged in Alternative Dispute Resolution
LEDU Local Enterprise Development Unit
LEP Local Ecumenical Project
LEPRA British Leprosy Relief Association
LèsL Licencié ès lettres
LèsSc Licencié ès Sciences
LG Lady Companion, Order of the Garter
LGA Local Government Association
LGSM Licentiate, Guildhall School of Music and Drama
LGTB Local Government Training Board
LH Light Horse
LHD *Literarum Humaniorum Doctor* (Doctor of Literature)
LHSM Licentiate, Institute of Health Services Management
LI Light Infantry; Long Island
LIBA Lloyd's Insurance Brokers' Association
Lib Dem Liberal Democrat
LIBER Ligue des Bibliothèques Européennes de Recherche
LicMed Licentiate in Medicine
Lieut Lieutenant
LIFFE London International Financial Futures and Options Exchange
LIMA Licentiate, Institute of Mathematics and its Applications
Lincs Lincolnshire

LIOB Licentiate, Institute of Building
Lit. Literature; Literary
LitD Doctor of Literature; Doctor of Letters
Lit.Hum. *Literae Humaniores* (Classics)
LittD Doctor of Literature; Doctor of Letters
LJ Lord Justice
LLB Bachelor of Laws
LLC Limited Liability Company
LLCM Licentiate, London College of Music
LLD Doctor of Laws
LLL Licentiate in Laws
LLM Master of Laws
LLP Limited Liability Partnership
LM Licentiate in Midwifery
LMBC Lady Margaret Boat Club
LMC Local Medical Committee
LMCC Licentiate, Medical Council of Canada
LMed Licentiate in Medicine
LMH Lady Margaret Hall, Oxford
LMR London Midland Region (BR)
LMS London, Midland and Scottish Railway; London Missionary Society; London Mathematical Society
LMSSA Licentiate in Medicine and Surgery, Society of Apothecaries
LMRTPI Legal Member, Royal Town Planning Institute
LNat Liberal National
LNER London and North Eastern Railway
LOB Location of Offices Bureau
L of C Library of Congress; Lines of Communication
LP Limited Partnership
LPh Licentiate in Philosophy
LPO London Philharmonic Orchestra
LPTB London Passenger Transport Board (later LTE; *now see* LRT)
LRAD Licentiate, Royal Academy of Dancing
LRAM Licentiate, Royal Academy of Music
LRCP Licentiate, Royal College of Physicians, London
LRCPE Licentiate, Royal College of Physicians, Edinburgh
LRCPI Licentiate, Royal College of Physicians of Ireland
LRCPSGlas Licentiate, Royal College of Physicians and Surgeons of Glasgow
LRCS Licentiate, Royal College of Surgeons of England
LRCSE Licentiate, Royal College of Surgeons, Edinburgh
LRCSI Licentiate, Royal College of Surgeons in Ireland
LRelSc Licentiate in Religious Sciences
LRFPS(G) Licentiate, Royal Faculty of Physicians and Surgeons, Glasgow (*now see* LRCPSGlas)
LRIBA Licentiate, Royal Institute of British Architects (*now see* RIBA)
LRPS Licentiate, Royal Photographic Society
LRSM Licentiate, Royal Schools of Music
LRT London Regional Transport
LSA Licentiate, Society of Apothecaries; Licence in Agricultural Sciences
LSE London School of Economics and Political Science
LSHTM London School of Hygiene and Tropical Medicine
LSO London Symphony Orchestra
Lt Lieutenant; Light
LT Lady, Order of the Thistle; London Transport (*now see* LRT); Licentiate in Teaching
LTA Lawn Tennis Association
LTB London Transport Board (later LTE; *now see* LRT)
LTCL Licentiate of Trinity College of Music, London
Lt Col Lieutenant Colonel
LTE London Transport Executive (*now see* LRT)
Lt Gen. Lieutenant General
LTh Licentiate in Theology
LTS London Topographical Society
LU Liberal Unionist
LUOTC London University Officers' Training Corps
LVO Lieutenant, Royal Victorian Order (*formerly* MVO (Fourth Class))
LWT London Weekend Television
LXX Septuagint

M

M Marquess; Member; Monsieur
m married
MA Master of Arts; Military Assistant; Massachusetts (postal)
MAA Manufacturers' Agents Association of Great Britain
MAAF Mediterranean Allied Air Forces
MAAT Member, Association of Accounting Technicians
MACE Member, Australian College of Education; Member, Association of Conference Executives
MACI Member, American Concrete Institute
MACM Member, Association of Computing Machines
MACS Member, American Chemical Society
MADO Member, Association of Dispensing Opticians
MAE Member, Academia Europaea
MAEE Marine Aircraft Experimental Establishment
MAF Ministry of Agriculture and Fisheries
MAFF Ministry of Agriculture, Fisheries and Food
MAHL Master of Arts in Hebrew Letters
MAI *Magister in Arte Ingeniaria* (Master of Engineering)
MAIAA Member, American Institute of Aeronautics and Astronautics
MAICE Member, American Institute of Consulting Engineers
MAIChE Member, American Institute of Chemical Engineers
Maj. Gen. Major General
MALD Master of Arts in Law and Diplomacy
Man Manitoba
M&A Mergers and Acquisitions
MAO Master of Obstetric Art
MAOT Member, Association of Occupational Therapists
MAOU Member, American Ornithologists' Union
MAP Ministry of Aircraft Production
MAPsS Member, Australian Psychological Society
MARAC Member, Australasian Register of Agricultural Consultants
MArch Master of Architecture
Marq. Marquess
MAS Minimal Access Surgery
MASAE Member, American Society of Agricultural Engineers
MASC Member, Australian Society of Calligraphers
MASc Master of Applied Science
MASCE Member, American Society of Civil Engineers
MASME Member, American Society of Mechanical Engineers
Mass Massachusetts
MAT Master of Arts and Teaching (US)
MATh Master of Arts in Theology
Math. Mathematics; Mathematical
MATSA Managerial Administrative Technical Staff Association
MAusIMM Member, Australasian Institute of Mining and Metallurgy
MB Medal of Bravery (Canada); Bachelor of Medicine; Manitoba (postal)
MBA Master of Business Administration
MBASW Member, British Association of Social Workers
MBC Metropolitan/Municipal Borough Council
MBCS Member, British Computer Society
MBE Member, Order of the British Empire
MBES Member, Biological Engineering Society
MBFR Mutual and Balanced Force Reductions (negotiations)
MBHI Member, British Horological Institute
MBIFD Member, British Institute of Funeral Directors
MBIM Member, British Institute of Management (*now see* MIMgt)
MBKS Member, British Kinematograph Society (*now see* MBKSTS)
MBKSTS Member, British Kinematograph, Sound and Television Society
MBOU Member, British Ornithologists' Union
MBPICS Member, British Production and Inventory Control Society
MBritIRE Member, British Institution of Radio Engineers (later MIERE; *now see* MIEE)
MBS Member, Building Societies Institute (*now see* MCBSI)
MBSc Master of Business Science
MC Military Cross; Missionaries of Charity
MCAM Member, CAM Foundation
MCB Master in Clinical Biochemistry
MCBSI Member, Chartered Building Societies Institute
MCC Marylebone Cricket Club; Metropolitan County Council
MCCDRCS Member in Clinical Community Dentistry, Royal College of Surgeons
MCD Master of Civic Design
MCE Master of Civil Engineering
MCFP Member, College of Family Physicians (Canada)
MCGI Member, City and Guilds of London Institute
MCh or MChir Master in Surgery
MChD Master of Dental Surgery
MChE Master of Chemical Engineering
MChemA Master in Chemical Analysis
MChOrth Master of Orthopaedic Surgery
MCIArb Member, Chartered Institute of Arbitrators
MCIBS Member, Chartered Institution of Building Services (*now see* MCIBSE)
MCIBSE Member, Chartered Institution of Building Services Engineers
MCIH Member, Chartered Institute of Housing
MCIJ Member, Chartered Institute of Journalists
MCIM Member, Chartered Institute of Marketing
MCIMarE Member, Canadian Institute of Marine Engineers
MCIOB Member, Chartered Institute of Building
MCIPD Member, Charted Institute of Personnel and Development
MCIPS Member, Chartered Institute of Purchasing and Supply
M.CIRP Member, International Institution for Production Engineering Research
MCIS Member, Institute of Chartered Secretaries and Administrators

MCIT Member, Chartered Institute of Transport
MCIWEM Member, Chartered Institution of Water and Environmental Management
MCL Master in Civil Law
MCom Master of Commerce
MConsE Member, Association of Consulting Engineers
MConsEI Member, Association of Consulting Engineers of Ireland
MCOphth Member, College of Ophthalmologists (*now see* MRCOphth)
MCP Member of Colonial Parliament; Master of City Planning (US)
MCPA Member, College of Pathologists of Australia (*now see* MRCPA)
MCPath Member, College of Pathologists (*now see* MRCPath)
MCPP Member, College of Pharmacy Practice
MCPS Member, College of Physicians and Surgeons
MCS Malayan Civil Service
MCSD Member, Chartered Society of Designers
MCSEE Member, Canadian Society of Electrical Engineers
MCSP Member, Chartered Society of Physiotherapy
MCST Member, College of Speech Therapists
MCT Member, Association of Corporate Treasurers
MD Doctor of Medicine; Military District; Maryland (postal)
Md Maryland
MDC Metropolitan District Council
MDes Master of Design
MDiv Master of Divinity
MDS Master of Dental Surgery
MDSc Master of Dental Science
ME Mining Engineer; Middle East; Master of Engineering; Maine (postal)
MEAF Middle East Air Force
MEC Member of Executive Council; Middle East Command
MEc Master of Economics
MECAS Middle East Centre for Arab Studies
Mech. Mechanics; Mechanical
MECI Member, Institute of Employment Consultants
Med. Medical
MEd Master of Education
MEdSt Master of Educational Studies
MEF Middle East Force
MEIC Member, Engineering Institute of Canada
MELF Middle East Land Forces
Mencap Royal Society for Mentally Handicapped Children and Adults
MEng Master of Engineering
MEO Marine Engineering Officer
MEP Member of the European Parliament
MESc Master of Engineering Science
MetR Metropolitan Railway
MetSoc Metals Society (formed by amalgamation of Institute of Metals and Iron and Steel Institute; now merged with Institution of Metallurgists to form Institute of Metals)
MEXE Military Engineering Experimental Establishment
MF Master of Forestry
MFA Master of Fine Arts
MFC Mastership in Food Control
MFCM Member, Faculty of Community Medicine (*now see* MFPHM)
MFFP Member, Faculty of Family Planning, Royal College of Obstetricians and Gynaecologists
MFGB Miners' Federation of Great Britain (*now see* NUM)
MFH Master of Foxhounds
MFHom Member, Faculty of Homœopathy
MFOM Member, Faculty of Occupational Medicine
MFPaed Member, Faculty of Paediatrics, Royal College of Physicians of Ireland
MFPHM Member, Faculty of Public Health Medicine
MFPHMI Member, Faculty of Public Health Medicine of Ireland
MGA Major General in charge of Administration
MGC Machine Gun Corps
MGDSRCS Member in General Dental Surgery, Royal College of Surgeons
MGGS Major General, General Staff
MGI Member, Institute of Certificated Grocers
MGO Master General of the Ordnance; Master of Gynaecology and Obstetrics
Mgr Monsignor
MHA Member of House of Assembly
MHCIMA Member, Hotel Catering and Institutional Management Association
MHK Member of the House of Keys
MHort (RHS) Master of Horticulture, Royal Horticultural Society
MHR Member of the House of Representatives
MHRA Modern Humanities Research Association
MHRF Mental Health Research Fund
MHSM Member, Institute of Health Services Management
MI Military Intelligence; Michigan (postal)
MIAeE Member, Institute of Aeronautical Engineers
MIAgrE Member, Institution of Agricultural Engineers
MIAM Member, Institute of Administrative Management
MIAS Member, Institute of Aeronautical Science (US) (*now see* MAIAA)
MIBC Member, Institute of Business Counsellors
MIBF Member, Institute of British Foundrymen
MIBiol Member, Institute of Biology
MIBritE Member, Institution of British Engineers
MIB(Scot) Member, Institute of Bankers in Scotland
MICE Member, Institution of Civil Engineers
MICEI Member, Institution of Civil Engineers of Ireland
MICFor Member, Institute of Chartered Foresters
Mich Michigan
MIChemE Member, Institution of Chemical Engineers
MICM Member, Institute of Credit Management
MICorr Member, Institute of Corrosion
MICorrST Member, Institution of Corrosion Science and Technology (*now see* MICorr)
MICS Member, Institute of Chartered Shipbrokers
MIDPM Member, Institute of Data Processing Management
MIE(Aust) Member, Institution of Engineers, Australia
MIED Member, Institution of Engineering Designers
MIEE Member, Institution of Electrical Engineers
MIEEE Member, Institute of Electrical and Electronics Engineers (NY)
MIEEM Member, Institute of Ecology and Environmental Management
MIEI Member, Institution of Engineering Inspection
MIEMA Member, Institute of Environmental Management and Assessment
MIEMgt Member, Institute of Environmental Management (*now see* MIEMA)
MIEnvSc Member, Institute of Environmental Science
MIERE Member, Institution of Electronic and Radio Engineers (*now see* MIEE)
MIES Member, Institution of Engineers and Shipbuilders, Scotland
MIET Member, Institute of Engineers and Technicians
MIEx Member, Institute of Export
MIExpE Member, Institute of Explosives Engineers
MIFA Member, Institute of Field Archaeologists
MIFF Member, Institute of Freight Forwarders (*now see* MIFP)
MIFireE Member, Institution of Fire Engineers
MIFM Member, Institute of Fisheries Management
MIFor Member, Institute of Foresters (*now see* MICFor)
MIFP Member, Institute of Freight Professionals
MIGasE Member, Institution of Gas Engineers
MIGeol Member, Institution of Geologists
MIH Member, Institute of Housing (*now see* MCIH)
MIHM Member, Institute of Housing Managers (later MIH); Member, Institute of Healthcare Management
MIHort Member, Institute of Horticulture
MIHT Member, Institution of Highways and Transportation
MIHVE Member, Institution of Heating and Ventilating Engineers (later MCIBS)
MIIA Member, Institute of Industrial Administration (later FBIM)
MIIM Member, Institution of Industrial Managers
MIInfSc Member, Institute of Information Sciences
MIL Member, Institute of Linguists
Mil. Military
MILGA Member, Institute of Local Government Administrators
MILocoE Member, Institution of Locomotive Engineers
MILog Member, Institute of Logistics (*now see* MILT)
MILT Member, Institute of Logistics and Transport
MIM Member, Institute of Materials (*formerly* Institution of Metallurgists, then Institute of Metals)
MIMarE Member, Institute of Marine Engineers
MIMC Member, Institute of Management Consultants
MIMechE Member, Institution of Mechanical Engineers
MIMEMME Member, Institution of Mining Electrical & Mining Mechanical Engineers (*now see* MIMinE)
MIMgt Member, Institute of Management
MIMGTechE Member, Institution of Mechanical and General Technician Engineers
MIMI Member, Institute of the Motor Industry
MIMinE Member, Institution of Mining Engineers (*now see* MIMM)
MIMM Member, Institution of Mining and Metallurgy
MIMunE Member, Institution of Municipal Engineers (now amalgamated with Institution of Civil Engineers)
MIN Member, Institute of Navigation (*now see* MRIN)
Min. Ministry
Minn Minnesota
MInstAM Member, Institute of Administrative Management
MInstBE Member, Institution of British Engineers
MInstCE Member, Institution of Civil Engineers (*now see* FICE)
MInstD Member, Institute of Directors
MInstE Member, Institute of Energy
MInstEnvSci Member, Institute of Environmental Sciences
MInstF Member, Institute of Fuel (*now see* MInstE)
MInstHE Member, Institution of Highway Engineers (*now see* MIHT)
MInstM Member, Institute of Marketing (*now see* MCIM)

MInstMC Member, Institute of Measurement and Control
MInstME Member, Institution of Mining Engineers
MInstMet Member, Institute of Metals (later part of Metals Society; *now see* MIM)
MInstP Member, Institute of Physics
MInstPet Member, Institute of Petroleum
MInstPI Member, Institute of Patentees and Inventors
MInstPkg Member, Institute of Packaging
MInstPS Member, Institute of Purchasing and Supply
MInstR Member, Institute of Refrigeration
MInstRA Member, Institute of Registered Architects
MInstT Member, Institute of Transport (*now see* MCIT)
MInstTA Member, Institute of Transport Administration
MInstTM Member, Institute of Travel Managers in Industry and Commerce
MInstW Member, Institute of Welding (*now see* MWeldI)
MInstWM Member, Institute of Wastes Management
MINucE Member, Institution of Nuclear Engineers
MIOA Member, Institute of Acoustics
MIOB Member, Institute of Building (*now see* MCIOB)
MIOM Member, Institute of Office Management (*now see* MIAM)
MIOSH Member, Institution of Occupational Safety and Health
MIPA Member, Institute of Practitioners in Advertising
MIPD Member, Institute of Personnel and Development (*now see* MCIPD)
MIPlantE Member, Institution of Plant Engineers (*now see* MIIM)
MIPM Member, Institute of Personnel Management (*now see* MIPD)
MIPR Member, Institute of Public Relations
MIProdE Member, Institution of Production Engineers (*now see* MIEE)
MIQ Member, Institute of Quarrying
MIQA Member, Institute of Quality Assurance
MIRE Member, Institution of Radio Engineers (later MIERE)
MIREE(Aust) Member, Institution of Radio and Electronics Engineers (Australia)
MIRM Member, Institute of Risk Management
MIRO Mineral Industry Research Organisation
MIRT Member, Institute of Reprographic Technicians
MIRTE Member, Institute of Road Transport Engineers
MIS Member, Institute of Statisticians
MISI Member, Iron and Steel Institute (later part of Metals Society)
MIStructE Member, Institution of Structural Engineers
MIT Massachusetts Institute of Technology
MITA Member, Industrial Transport Association
MITD Member, Institute of Training and Development (*now see* MIPD)
MITE Member, Institution of Electrical and Electronics Technician Engineers
MITI Member, Institute of Translation & Interpreting
MITSA Member, Institute of Trading Standards Administration
MITT Member, Institute of Travel and Tourism
MIWE Member, Institution of Water Engineers (later MIWES; then MIWEM; *now see* MCIWEM)
MIWEM Member, Institution of Water and Environmental Management (*now see* MCIWEM)
MIWES Member, Institution of Water Engineers and Scientists (later MIWEM; *now see* MCIWEM)
MIWM Member, Institution of Works Managers (*now see* MIIM)
MIWPC Member, Institute of Water Pollution Control (later MIWEM; *now see* MCIWEM)
MIWSP Member, Institute of Work Study Practitioners (*now see* MMS)
MJA Medical Journalists Association
MJI Member, Institute of Journalists (*now see* MCIJ)
MJIE Member, Junior Institution of Engineers (*now see* MIGTechE)
MJS Member, Japan Society
MJur *Magister Juris* (Master of Law)
ML Licentiate in Medicine; Master of Laws
MLA Member of Legislative Assembly; Modern Language Association; Master in Landscape Architecture
MLC Member of Legislative Council; Meat and Livestock Commission
MLCOM Member, London College of Osteopathic Medicine
MLI Member, Landscape Institute
MLitt Master of Letters
Mlle Mademoiselle
MLO Military Liaison Officer
MLR Modern Language Review
MM Military Medal; Merchant Marine
MMA Metropolitan Museum of Art
MMB Milk Marketing Board
MMD Movement for Multi-Party Democracy
MME Master of Mining Engineering
Mme Madame
MMechE Master of Mechanical Engineering
MMet Master of Metallurgy
MMGI Member, Mining, Geological and Metallurgical Institute of India
MMin Master of Ministry
MMM Member, Order of Military Merit (Canada)
MMRS Member, Market Research Society
MMS Member, Institute of Management Services
MMSA Master of Midwifery, Society of Apothecaries
MMus Master of Music
MN Merchant Navy; Minnesota (postal)
MNAS Member, National Academy of Sciences (US)
MND Motor Neurone Disease
MNECInst Member, North East Coast Institution of Engineers and Shipbuilders
MNI Member, Nautical Institute
MNIMH Member, National Institute of Medical Herbalists
MNSE Member, Nigerian Society of Engineers
MNZIS Member, New Zealand Institute of Surveyors
MNZPI Member, New Zealand Planning Institute
MO Medical Officer; Military Operations; Missouri (postal)
Mo Missouri
MoD Ministry of Defence
Mods Moderations (Oxford)
MOF Ministry of Food
MOH Medical Officer(s) of Health
MOI Ministry of Information
MOM Member, Order of Merit (Malta)
MOMA Museum of Modern Art
MOMI Museum of the Moving Image
Mon Monmouthshire
Mont Montgomeryshire
MOP Ministry of Power
MOrthRCS Member in Orthodontics, Royal College of Surgeons
MoS Ministry of Supply
Most Rev. Most Reverend
MoT Ministry of Transport
MOV Member, Order of Volta (Ghana)
MP Member of Parliament
MPA Master of Public Administration; Member, Parliamentary Assembly, Northern Ireland
MPBW Ministry of Public Building and Works
MPH Master of Public Health
MPhil Master of Philosophy
MPIA Master of Public and International Affairs
MPMI Member, Property Management Institute
MPO Management and Personnel Office
MPP Member, Provincial Parliament; Master in Public Policy (Harvard)
MPRISA Member, Public Relations Institute of South Africa
MPS Member, Pharmaceutical Society (*now see* MRPharmS)
MR Master of the Rolls; Municipal Reform
MRAC Member, Royal Agricultural College
MRACP Member, Royal Australasian College of Physicians
MRACS Member, Royal Australasian College of Surgeons
MRad Master of Radiology
MRAeS Member, Royal Aeronautical Society
MRAIC Member, Royal Architectural Institute of Canada
MRAS Member, Royal Asiatic Society
MRC Medical Research Council
MRCA Multi-Role Combat Aircraft
MRCGP Member, Royal College of General Practitioners
MRC-LMB Medical Research Council Laboratory of Molecular Biology
MRCOG Member, Royal College of Obstetricians and Gynaecologists
MRCOphth Member, Royal College of Ophthalmologists
MRCP Member, Royal College of Physicians, London
MRCPA Member, Royal College of Pathologists of Australia
MRCPath Member, Royal College of Pathologists
MRCPCH Member, Royal College of Paediatrics and Child Health
MRCPE Member, Royal College of Physicians, Edinburgh
MRCPGlas Member, Royal College of Physicians and Surgeons of Glasgow
MRCPI Member, Royal College of Physicians of Ireland
MRCPsych Member, Royal College of Psychiatrists
MRCS Member, Royal College of Surgeons of England
MRCSE Member, Royal College of Surgeons of Edinburgh
MRCSI Member, Royal College of Surgeons in Ireland
MRCVS Member, Royal College of Veterinary Surgeons
MRE Master of Religious Education
MRHS Member, Royal Horticultural Society
MRI Member, Royal Institution
MRIA Member, Royal Irish Academy
MRIAI Member, Royal Institute of the Architects of Ireland
MRIC Member, Royal Institute of Chemistry (*now see* MRSC)
MRICS Member, Royal Institution of Chartered Surveyors
MRIN Member, Royal Institute of Navigation
MRINA Member, Royal Institution of Naval Architects
MRNZCGP Member, Royal New Zealand College of General Practitioners
MRPharmS Member, Royal Pharmaceutical Society
MRSanI Member, Royal Sanitary Institute (*now see* MRSH)

MRSC Member, Royal Society of Chemistry
MRSH Member, Royal Society for the Promotion of Health
MRSL Member, Order of the Republic of Sierra Leone
MRSocMed Member, Royal Society of Medicine
MRST Member, Royal Society of Teachers
MRTPI Member, Royal Town Planning Institute
MRurSc Master of Rural Science
MRUSI Member, Royal United Service Institution
MRVA Member, Rating and Valuation Association
MS Master of Surgery; Master of Science (US); Mississippi (postal); Multiple Sclerosis
MS, MSS Manuscript, Manuscripts
MSA Master of Science, Agriculture (US); Mineralogical Society of America
MSAAIE Member, Southern African Association of Industrial Editors
MSAE Member, Society of Automotive Engineeers (US)
MSAICE Member, South African Institution of Civil Engineers
MSAInstMM Member, South African Institute of Mining and Metallurgy
MS&R Merchant Shipbuilding and Repairs
MSC Manpower Services Commission; Missionaries of the Sacred Heart
MSc Master of Science
MScD Master of Dental Science
MScSoc Master of Social Sciences
MScSocMed Master of Science in Social Medicine
MSD Meritorious Service Decoration (Fiji)
MSE Master of Science in Engineering (US)
MSF (Union for) Manufacturing, Science, Finance
MSFA Member, Society of Financial Advisers
MSI Member, Securities Institute
MSIA Member, Society of Industrial Artists
MSIAD Member, Society of Industrial Artists and Designers (*now see* MCSD)
MSIT Member, Society of Instrument Technology (*now see* MInstMC)
MSM Meritorious Service Medal; Madras Sappers and Miners; Master in Science Management
MSN Master of Science in Nursing
MSocAdmin Master of Social Administration
MSocIS Member, Société des Ingénieurs et Scientifiques de France
MSocSc Master of Social Sciences
MSocWork Master of Social Work
MSoFHT Member, Society of Food Hygiene Technology
MSR Member, Society of Radiographers
MSSc Master of Social Sciences
MSt Master of Studies
MSTD Member, Society of Typographic Designers
MSzP Magyar Szocialista Párt
MT Mechanical Transport; Montana (postal)
Mt Mount, Mountain
MTA Music Trades Association
MTAI Member, Institute of Travel Agents
MTB Motor Torpedo Boat
MTCA Ministry of Transport and Civil Aviation
MTD Midwife Teachers' Diploma
MTech Master of Technology
MTEFL Master in the Teaching of English as a Foreign or Second Language
MTh Master of Theology
MTIA Metal Trades Industry Association
MTIRA Machine Tool Industry Research Association (*now see* AMTRI)
MTPI Member, Town Planning Institute (*now see* MRTPI)
MTS Master of Theological Studies; Ministerial Training Scheme
MUniv Honorary Master of the University
MusB Bachelor of Music
MusD Doctor of Music
MusM Master of Music
MV Merchant Vessel, Motor Vessel (naval)
MVEE Military Vehicles and Engineering Establishment
MVO Member, Royal Victorian Order
MVSc Master of Veterinary Science
MW Master of Wine
MWA Mystery Writers of America
MWeldI Member, Welding Institute
MWSOM Member, Institute of Practitioners in Work Study Organisation and Methods (*now see* MMS)

N

N Nationalist; Navigating Duties; North
n nephew
NA National Academician (America)
NAACP National Association for the Advancement of Colored People
NAAFI Navy, Army and Air Force Institutes
NAAS National Agricultural Advisory Service
NAB National Advisory Body for Public Sector Higher Education
NABC National Association of Boys' Clubs (*now see* NABC-CYP)
NABC-CYP National Association of Boys' Clubs - Clubs for Young People
NAC National Agriculture Centre
NACAB National Association of Citizens' Advice Bureaux
NACCB National Accreditation Council for Certification Bodies
NACETT National Advisory Council for Education and Training Targets
NACF National Art-Collections Fund
NACRO National Association for the Care and Resettlement of Offenders
NADFAS National Association of Decorative and Fine Arts Societies
NAE National Academy of Engineering
NAEW Nato Airborn Early Warning
NAHA National Association of Health Authorities (*now see* NAHAT)
NAHAT National Association of Health Authorities and Trusts
NAHT National Association of Head Teachers
NALGO or **Nalgo** National and Local Government Officers' Association
NAMAS National Measurement and Accreditation Service
NAMCW National Association for Maternal and Child Welfare
NAMH MIND (National Association for Mental Health)
NAMMA NATO MRCA Management Agency
NAPAG National Academies Policy Advisory Group
NARM National Association of Recording Merchandisers (US)
NAS National Academy of Sciences
NASA National Aeronautics and Space Administration (US)
NASDAQ National Association of Securities Dealers Automated Quotation System
NASDIM National Association of Security Dealers and Investment Managers (later FIMBRA)
NAS/UWT National Association of Schoolmasters/Union of Women Teachers
NATCS National Air Traffic Control Services (*now see* NATS)
NATFHE National Association of Teachers in Further and Higher Education (combining ATCDE and ATTI)
NATLAS National Testing Laboratory Accreditation Scheme
NATO North Atlantic Treaty Organisation
NATS National Air Traffic Services
Nat. Sci. Natural Sciences
NATSOPA National Society of Operative Printers, Graphical and Media Personnel (*formerly* of Operative Printers and Assistants)
NAYC Youth Clubs UK (*formerly* National Association of Youth Clubs)
NB New Brunswick; Nebraska (postal)
NBA North British Academy
NBC National Book Council (later NBL); National Broadcasting Company (US)
NBL National Book League
NBPI National Board for Prices and Incomes
NC National Certificate; North Carolina
NCA National Certificate of Agriculture
NCARB National Council of Architectural Registration Boards
NCB National Coal Board
NCC National Computing Centre; Nature Conservancy Council (*now see* NCCE); National Consumer Council
NCCE Nature Conservancy Council for England (English Nature)
NCCI National Committee for Commonwealth Immigrants
NCCL National Council for Civil Liberties
NCD National Capital District, Papua New Guinea
NCDAD National Council for Diplomas in Art and Design
NCEA National Council for Educational Awards
NCET National Council for Educational Technology
NCH National Children's Homes
NCLC National Council of Labour Colleges
NCOP National Council of Provinces (South Africa)
NCOPF National Council for One Parent Families
NCSE National Council for Special Education
NCSS National Council of Social Service
NCTA National Community Television Association (US)
NCTJ National Council for the Training of Journalists
NCU National Cyclists' Union
NCVCCO National Council of Voluntary Child Care Organisations
NCVO National Council for Voluntary Organisations
NCVQ National Council for Vocational Qualifications
ND North Dakota
NDA National Diploma in Agriculture
NDC National Defence College; NATO Defence College
NDD National Diploma in Dairying; National Diploma in Design
NDEA National Defense Education Act
NDH National Diploma in Horticulture
NDIC National Defence Industries Council
NDP New Democratic Party
NDTA National Defense Transportation Association (US)
NE North-east
NEAB Northern Examinations and Assessment Board

NEAC New English Art Club
NEAF Near East Air Force
NEARELF Near East Land Forces
NEB National Enterprise Board
NEBSS National Examinations Board for Supervisory Studies
NEC National Executive Committee
NECCTA National Education Closed Circuit Television Association
NECInst North East Coast Institution of Engineers and Shipbuilders
NEDC National Economic Development Council; North East Development Council
NEDO National Economic Development Office
NEH National Endowment for the Humanities
NEL National Engineering Laboratory
NERC Natural Environment Research Council
NESTA National Endowment for Science, Technology and the Arts
NF Newfoundland and Labrador (postal)
NFC National Freight Consortium (*formerly* Corporation, then Company)
NFCG National Federation of Consumer Groups
NFER National Foundation for Educational Research
NFHA National Federation of Housing Associations
NFMS National Federation of Music Societies
NFS National Fire Service
NFSH National Federation of Spiritual Healers
NFT National Film Theatre
NFU National Farmers' Union
NFWI National Federation of Women's Institutes
NGO Non-Governmental Organisation(s)
NGTE National Gas Turbine Establishment
NH New Hampshire
NH&MRC National Health and Medical Research Council (Australia)
NHBC National House-Building Council
NHS National Health Service
NI Northern Ireland; Native Infantry
NIAB National Institute of Agricultural Botany
NIACRO Northern Ireland Association for the Care and Resettlement of Offenders
NIAE National Institute of Agricultural Engineering
NIAID National Institute of Allergy and Infectious Diseases
NICE National Institute of Clinical Excellence
NICEC National Institute for Careers Education and Counselling
NICG Nationalised Industries Chairmen's Group
NICS Northern Ireland Civil Service
NID Naval Intelligence Division; National Institute for the Deaf; Northern Ireland District; National Institute of Design (India)
NIESR National Institute of Economic and Social Research
NIH National Institutes of Health (US)
NIHCA Northern Ireland Hotels and Caterers Association
NIHEC Northern Ireland Higher Education Council
NII Nuclear Installations Inspectorate
NILP Northern Ireland Labour Party
NIMR National Institute for Medical Research
NISA National Ice Skating Association of UK
NISTRO Northern Ireland Science and Technology Regional Organisation
NISW National Institute of Social Work
NIU Northern Ireland Unionist
NJ New Jersey
NL National Liberal; No Liability
NLCS North London Collegiate School
NLF National Liberal Federation
NLYL National League of Young Liberals
NM New Mexico (postal)
NMR Nuclear Magnetic Resonance
NNMA Nigerian National Merit Award
NNOM Nigerian National Order of Merit
NODA National Operatic and Dramatic Association
Northants Northamptonshire
NOTB National Ophthalmic Treatment Board
Notts Nottinghamshire
NP Notary Public
NPA Newspaper Publishers' Association
NPFA National Playing Fields Association
NPG National Portrait Gallery
NPk Nishan-e-Pakistan
NPL National Physical Laboratory
NPQH National Professional Qualification for Headship
NRA National Rifle Association; National Recovery Administration (US); National Rivers Authority
NRAO National Radio Astronomy Observatory
NRCC National Research Council of Canada
NRD National Registered Designer
NRDC National Research Development Corporation
NRPB National Radiological Protection Board
NRR Northern Rhodesia Regiment
NS Nova Scotia; New Style in the Calendar (in Great Britain since 1752); National Society; National Service
ns Graduate of Royal Naval Staff College, Greenwich
NSA National Skating Association (*now see* NISA)
NSAIV Distinguished Order of Shaheed Ali (Maldives)
NSERC Natural Sciences and Engineering Research Council, Canada
NSF National Science Foundation (US)
NSM Non-Stipendiary Minister
NSMHC National Society for Mentally Handicapped Children (*now see* Mencap)
NSPCC National Society for Prevention of Cruelty to Children
NSQT National Society for Quality through Teamwork
NSRA National Small-bore Rifle Association
N/SSF Novice, Society of St Francis
NSTC Nova Scotia Technical College
NSW New South Wales
NT New Testament; Northern Territory (Australia); Northwest Territories (Canada); National Theatre (*now see* RNT); National Trust
NT&SA National Trust & Savings Association
NTDA National Trade Development Association
NTO National Training Organisation
NTUC National Trades Union Congress
NUAAW National Union of Agricultural and Allied Workers
NUBE National Union of Bank Employees (*now see* BIFU)
NUFLAT National Union of Footwear Leather and Allied Trades (*now see* NUKFAT)
NUGMW National Union of General and Municipal Workers (later GMBATU)
NUHKW National Union of Hosiery and Knitwear Workers (*now see* NUKFAT)
NUI National University of Ireland
NUJ National Union of Journalists
NUJMB Northern Universities Joint Matriculation Board
NUKFAT National Union of Knitwear, Footwear and Apparel Trades
NUM National Union of Mineworkers
NUMAST National Union of Marine, Aviation and Shipping Transport Officers
NUPE National Union of Public Employees
NUR National Union of Railwaymen (*now see* RMT)
NUS National Union of Students
NUT National Union of Teachers
NUTG National Union of Townswomen's Guilds
NUTGW National Union of Tailors and Garment Workers
NUTN National Union of Trained Nurses
NUU New University of Ulster
NV Nevada (postal)
NVQ National Vocational Qualification
NW North-west
NWC National Water Council
NWFP North-West Frontier Province
NWP North-Western Province
NWT North-Western Territories
NY New York
NYC New York City
NYO National Youth Orchestra
NYT National Youth Theatre
NZ New Zealand
NZEF New Zealand Expeditionary Force
NZIA New Zealand Institute of Architects
NZRSA New Zealand Retired Services Association

O

o only
OA Officier d'Académie
OAM Medal of the Order of Australia
O & E Operations and Engineers (US)
O & M organisation and method
O & O Oriental and Occidental Steamship Co.
OAS Organisation of American States; On Active Service
OASC Officer Aircrew Selection Centre
OAU Organisation for African Unity
OB Order of Barbados
ob *obiit* (died)
OBC Order of British Columbia
OBE Officer, Order of the British Empire
OBI Order of British India
OC Officer, Order of Canada (equivalent to former award SM)
OC or **o/c** Officer Commanding
o c only child
OCC Order of the Caribbean Community
OCDS or **ocds Can** Overseas College of Defence Studies (Canada)

OCF Officiating Chaplain to the Forces
OCS Officer Candidates School
OCSS Oxford and Cambridge Shakespeare Society
OCTU Officer Cadet Training Unit
OCU Operational Conversion Unit
OD Officer, Order of Distinction (Jamaica); Order of Distinction (Antigua)
ODA Overseas Development Administration
ODI Overseas Development Institute
ODM Ministry of Overseas Development
ODSM Order of Diplomatic Service Merit (Lesotho)
OE Order of Excellence (Guyana)
OEA Overseas Education Association
OECD Organization for Economic Co-operation and Development
OED Oxford English Dictionary
OEEC Organization for European Economic Co-operation (*now see* OECD)
OF Order of the Founder, Salvation Army
OFEMA Office Française d'Exportation de Matériel Aéronautique
OFFER Office of Electricity Regulation
Ofgem Office of Gas and Electricity Markets
OFM Order of Friars Minor (Franciscans)
OFMCap Order of Friars Minor Capuchin (Franciscans)
OFMConv Order of Friars Minor Conventual (Franciscans)
OFR Order of the Federal Republic of Nigeria
OFS Orange Free State
OFSTED Office for Standards in Education
OFT Office of Fair Trading
Oftel Office of Telecommunications
Ofwat Office of Water Services
OGS Oratory of the Good Shepherd
OH Ohio (postal)
OHMS On His (or Her) Majesty's Service
O i/c Officer in charge
OJ Order of Jamaica
OK Oklahoma (postal)
OL Officer, Order of Leopold; Order of the Leopard (Lesotho)
OLJ Officer, Order of St Lazarus of Jerusalem
OLM Officer, Legion of Merit (Rhodesia)
OM Order of Merit
OMCS Office of the Minister for the Civil Service
OMI Oblate of Mary Immaculate
OMM Officer, Order of Military Merit (Canada)
ON Order of the Nation (Jamaica); Ontario (postal)
OND Ordinary National Diploma
ONDA Ordinary National Diploma in Agriculture
ONS Office for National Statistics
Ont Ontario
ONZ Order of New Zealand
ONZM Officer, New Zealand Order of Merit
OON Officer, Order of the Niger
OOnt Order of Ontario
OP *Ordinis Praedicatorum* (of the Order of Preachers (Dominican)); Observation Post
OPCON Operational Control
OPCS Office of Population Censuses and Surveys (*now see* ONS)
OPRA Occupational Pensions Regulatory Authority
OPS Office of Public Service
OPSS Office of Public Service and Science (*now see* OPS)
OQ Officer, National Order of Quebec
OR Order of Rorima (Guyana); Operational Research; Oregon (postal)
ORC Orange River Colony
ORGALIME Organisme de Liaison des Industries Métalliques Européennes
ORL Otorhinolaryngology
ORS Operational Research Society
ORSA Operations Research Society of America
ORSL Order of the Republic of Sierra Leone
ORT Organization for Rehabilitation through Training
ORTF Office de la Radiodiffusion et Télévision Française
o s only son
OSA Order of St Augustine (Augustinian); Ontario Society of Artists
OSB Order of St Benedict (Benedictine)
osc Graduate of Overseas Staff College
OSCE Organisation for Security and Co-operation in Europe
OSFC Franciscan (Capuchin) Order
O/Sig Ordinary Signalman
OSMTH Ordo Supremus Militaris Templi Hierosolymitani (Supreme Military Order of the Temple of Jerusalem)
OSNC Orient Steam Navigation Co.
o s p *obiit sine prole* (died without issue)
OSRD Office of Scientific Research and Development
OSS Office of Strategic Services
OST Office of Science and Technology
OStJ Officer, Most Venerable Order of the Hospital of St John of Jerusalem
OSUK Ophthalmological Society of the United Kingdom
OT Old Testament
OTC Officers' Training Corps
OTL Officer, Order of Toussaint L'Ouverture (Haiti)
OTU Operational Training Unit
OTWSA Ou-Testamentiese Werkgemeenskap in Suider-Afrika
OU Oxford University; Open University
OUAC Oxford University Athletic Club
OUAFC Oxford University Association Football Club
OUBC Oxford University Boat Club
OUCC Oxford University Cricket Club
OUDS Oxford University Dramatic Society
OUP Oxford University Press; Official Unionist Party
OURC Oxford University Rifle Club
OURFC Oxford University Rugby Football Club
OURT Order of the United Republic of Tanzania
Oxon Oxfordshire; *Oxoniensis* (of Oxford)

P

PA Pakistan Army; Personal Assistant; Pennsylvania (postal)
PAA President, Australian Academy of Science
pac passed the final examination of the Advanced Class, The Military College of Science
PACE Protestant and Catholic Encounter; Property Advisers to the Civil Estate
PACTA Professional Associate, Clinical Theology Association
PAg Professional Agronomist
P&O Peninsular and Oriental Steamship Co.
P&OSNCo. Peninsular and Oriental Steam Navigation Co.
PAO Prince Albert's Own
PASI Professional Associate, Chartered Surveyors' Institution (*now see* ARICS)
PASOK Panhellenic Socialist Movement
PBS Public Broadcasting Service
PC Privy Counsellor; Police Constable; Perpetual Curate; Peace Commissioner (Ireland); Progressive Conservative (Canada)
pc *per centum* (in the hundred)
PCC Parochial Church Council; Protected Cell Company (Guernsey)
PCE Postgraduate Certificate of Education
PCEF Polytechnic and Colleges Employers' Forum
PCFC Polytechnics and Colleges Funding Council
PCL Polytechnic of Central London
PCMO Principal Colonial Medical Officer
PCNZM Principal Companion, New Zealand Order of Merit
PCS Parti Chrétien-Social; Public and Commercial Services Union
PdD Doctor of Pedagogy (US)
PDG Président Directeur Général
PDipHEd Postgraduate Diploma in Health Education
PDR People's Democratic Republic
PDRA post doctoral research assistant
PDSA People's Dispensary for Sick Animals
PDTC Professional Dancer's Training Course Diploma
PE Procurement Executive; Prince Edward Island (postal)
PEI Prince Edward Island
PEN Poets, Playwrights, Editors, Essayists, Novelists (Club)
PEng Registered Professional Engineer (Canada); Member, Society of Professional Engineers
Penn Pennsylvania
PEP Political and Economic Planning (*now see* PSI)
PER Professional and Executive Recruitment
PEST Pressure for Economic and Social Toryism
PETRAS Polytechnic Educational Technology Resources Advisory Service
PF Procurator-Fiscal
PFA Professional Footballers' Association
pfc Graduate of RAF Flying College
PFE Program for Executives
PFI Private Finance Initiative
PGA Professional Golfers' Association
PGCE Post Graduate Certificate of Education
PGTC Postgraduate Teaching Certificate
PH Presidential Order of Honour (Botswana)
PHAB Physically Handicapped & Able-bodied
PhB Bachelor of Philosophy
PhC Pharmaceutical Chemist
PhD Doctor of Philosophy
Phil. Philology, Philological; Philosophy, Philosophical
PhL Licentiate in Philosophy
PHLS Public Health Laboratory Service
PhM Master of Philosophy (USA)
PhmB Bachelor of Pharmacy

Phys. Physical
PIA Personal Investment Authority
PIARC Permanent International Association of Road Congresses
PIB Prices and Incomes Board (later NBPI)
PICAO Provisional International Civil Aviation Organization (*now* ICAO)
pinx. *pinxit* (he painted it)
PIRA Paper Industries Research Association
PITCOM Parliamentary Information Technology Committee
PJG Pingat Jasa Gemilang (Singapore)
PJK Pingkat Jasa Kebaktian (Malaysia)
Pl. Place; Plural
PLA Port of London Authority
PLC or plc public limited company
Plen. Plenipotentiary
PLI President, Landscape Institute
PLP Parliamentary Labour Party; Progressive Liberal Party (Bahamas)
PLR Public Lending Right
PMA Personal Military Assistant
PMC Personnel Management Centre
PMD Program for Management Development
PMedSci President, Academy of Medical Sciences
PMG Postmaster-General
PMN Panglima Mangku Negara (Malaysia)
PMO Principal Medical Officer
PMRAFNS Princess Mary's Royal Air Force Nursing Service
PMS Presidential Order of Meritorious Service (Botswana); President, Miniature Society
PNBS Panglima Negara Bintang Sarawak
PNEU Parents' National Educational Union
PNG Papua New Guinea
PNP People's National Party
PO Post Office
POB Presidential Order of Botswana
POMEF Political Office Middle East Force
Pop. Population
POST Parliamentary Office of Science and Technology
POUNC Post Office Users' National Council
POW Prisoner of War; Prince of Wales's
PP Parish Priest; Past President
pp pages
PPA Periodical Publishers Association
PPARC Particle Physics and Astronomy Research Council
PPCLI Princess Patricia's Canadian Light Infantry
PPDF Parti Populaire pour la Démocratie Française
PPE Philosophy, Politics and Economics
PPInstHE Past President, Institution of Highway Engineers
PPIStructE Past President, Institution of Structural Engineers
PPITB Printing and Publishing Industry Training Board
PPP Private Patients Plan
PPRA Past President, Royal Academy
PPRBA Past President, Royal Society of British Artists
PPRBS Past President, Royal Society of British Sculptors
PPRE Past President, Royal Society of Painter-Printmakers (*formerly* of Painter-Etchers and Engravers)
PPRIBA Past President, Royal Institute of British Architects
PPROI Past President, Royal Institute of Oil Painters
PPRP Past President, Royal Society of Portrait Painters
PPRTPI Past President, Royal Town Planning Institute
PPRWA Past President, Royal Watercolour Association
PPS Parliamentary Private Secretary
PPSIAD Past President, Society of Industrial Artists and Designers
PQ Province of Quebec
PQE Professional Qualifying Examination
PR Public Relations; Parti républicain
PRA President, Royal Academy
PRBS President, Royal Society of British Sculptors
PRCS President, Royal College of Surgeons
PrD Doctor of Professional Practice
PRE President, Royal Society of Painter-Printmakers (*formerly* of Painter-Etchers and Engravers)
Preb. Prebendary
PrEng. Professional Engineer
Prep. Preparatory
Pres. President
PRHA President, Royal Hibernian Academy
PRI President, Royal Institute of Painters in Water Colours; Plastics and Rubber Institute
PRIA President, Royal Irish Academy
PRIAS President, Royal Incorporation of Architects in Scotland
Prin. Principal
PRISA Public Relations Institute of South Africa
PRL Liberal Reform Party (Belgium)
PRO Public Relations Officer; Public Records Office
Proc. Proctor; Proceedings
Prof. Professor; Professional
PROI President, Royal Institute of Oil Painters
PRO NED Promotion of Non-Executive Directors
PRORM Pay and Records Office, Royal Marines
Pro tem. *Pro tempore* (for the time being)
Prov. Provost; Provincial
Prox. *Proximo* (next)
Prox.acc. *Proxime accessit* (next in order of merit to the winner)
PRS President, Royal Society; Performing Right Society Ltd
PRSA President, Royal Scottish Academy
PRSE President, Royal Society of Edinburgh
PRSH President, Royal Society for the Promotion of Health
PRSW President, Royal Scottish Water Colour Society
PRUAA President, Royal Ulster Academy of Arts
PRWA President, Royal West of England Academy
PRWS President, Royal Society of Painters in Water Colours
PS Pastel Society; Paddle Steamer
ps passed School of Instruction (of Officers)
PSA Property Services Agency; Petty Sessions Area
psa Graduate of RAF Staff College
psc Graduate of Staff College († indicates Graduate of Senior Wing Staff College)
PSD Petty Sessional Division; Social Democratic Party (Portugal)
PSE Party of European Socialists
PSGB Pharmaceutical Society of Great Britain (*now see* RPSGB)
PSI Policy Studies Institute
PSIAD President, Society of Industrial Artists and Designers
PSM Panglima Setia Mahkota (Malaysia)
psm Certificate of Royal Military School of Music
PSMA President, Society of Marine Artists
PSNC Pacific Steam Navigation Co.
PSO Principal Scientific Officer; Personal Staff Officer
PSOE Partido Socialista Obrero Español
PSSC Personal Social Services Council
PTA Passenger Transport Authority; Parent-Teacher Association
PTC Personnel and Training Command
PTE Passenger Transport Executive
Pte Private
ptsc passed Technical Staff College
Pty Proprietary
PUP People's United Party; Progressive Unionist Party
PVSM Param Vishisht Seva Medal (India)
PWD Public Works Department
PWE Political Welfare Executive
PWO Prince of Wales's Own
PWR Pressurized Water Reactor
PYBT Prince's Youth Business Trust

Q

Q Queen
QAA Quality Assurance Agency for Higher Education
QAIMNS Queen Alexandra's Imperial Military Nursing Service
QALAS Qualified Associate, Chartered Land Agents' Society (*now* (after amalgamation) *see* ARICS)
QARANC Queen Alexandra's Royal Army Nursing Corps
QARNNS Queen Alexandra's Royal Naval Nursing Service
QBD Queen's Bench Division
QC Queen's Counsel; Quebec (postal)
QCA Qualifications and Curriculum Authority
QCVS Queen's Commendation for Valuable Service
QCVSA Queen's Commendation for Valuable Service in the Air
QEH Queen Elizabeth Hall
QEO Queen Elizabeth's Own
QFSM Queen's Fire Service Medal for Distinguished Service
QGM Queen's Gallantry Medal
QHC Honorary Chaplain to the Queen
QHDS Honorary Dental Surgeon to the Queen
QHNS Honorary Nursing Sister to the Queen
QHP Honorary Physician to the Queen
QHS Honorary Surgeon to the Queen
Qld Queensland
Qly Quarterly
QMAAC Queen Mary's Army Auxiliary Corps
QMC Queen Mary College, London (*now see* QMW)
QMG Quartermaster-General
QMO Queen Mary's Own
QMW Queen Mary and Westfield College, London
QO Qualified Officer
QOOH Queen's Own Oxfordshire Hussars
Q(ops) Quartering (operations)
QOY Queen's Own Yeomanry

QPM Queen's Police Medal
QPSM Queen's Public Service Medal (New Zealand)
Qr Quarter
QRIH Queen's Royal Irish Hussars
QS Quarter Sessions; Quantity Surveying
qs RAF graduates of the Military or Naval Staff College
QSM Queen's Service Medal (NZ)
QSO Queen's Service Order (NZ)
QTS Qualified Teacher Status
QUB Queen's University, Belfast
qv *quod vide* (which see)
QVRM Queen's Volunteer Reserve Medal
qwi Qualified Weapons Instructor

R

(R) Reserve
RA Royal Academician; Royal Academy; Royal (Regiment of) Artillery
RAA Regional Arts Association; Royal Australian Artillery
RAAF Royal Australian Air Force
RAAMC Royal Australian Army Medical Corps
RABI Royal Agricultural Benevolent Institution
RAC Royal Automobile Club; Royal Agricultural College; Royal Armoured Corps
RACDS Royal Australian College of Dental Surgeons
RACGP Royal Australian College of General Practitioners
RAChD Royal Army Chaplains' Department
RACI Royal Australian Chemical Institute
RACO Royal Australian College of Ophthalmologists
RACOG Royal Australian College of Obstetricians and Gynaecologists
RACP Royal Australasian College of Physicians
RACS Royal Australasian College of Surgeons; Royal Arsenal Co-operative Society
RADA Royal Academy of Dramatic Art
RADAR Royal Association for Disability and Rehabilitation
RADC Royal Army Dental Corps
RADIUS Religious Drama Society of Great Britain
RAE Royal Australian Engineers; Royal Aerospace Establishment (*formerly* Royal Aircraft Establishment); Research Assessment Exercise
RAEC Royal Army Educational Corps
RAeS Royal Aeronautical Society
RAF Royal Air Force
RAFA Royal Air Force Association
RAFO Reserve of Air Force Officers (*now see* RAFRO)
RAFR Royal Air Force Reserve
RAFRO Royal Air Force Reserve of Officers
RAFVR Royal Air Force Volunteer Reserve
RAI Royal Anthropological Institute of Great Britain & Ireland; Radio Audizioni Italiane
RAIA Royal Australian Institute of Architects
RAIC Royal Architectural Institute of Canada
RAM (Member of) Royal Academy of Music
RAMC Royal Army Medical Corps
RAN Royal Australian Navy
R&D Research and Development
RANR Royal Australian Naval Reserve
RANVR Royal Australian Naval Volunteer Reserve
RAOC Royal Army Ordnance Corps
RAPC Royal Army Pay Corps
RARDE Royal Armament Research and Development Establishment
RARO Regular Army Reserve of Officers
RAS Royal Astronomical Society; Royal Asiatic Society; Recruitment and Assessment Services
RASC Royal Army Service Corps (*now see* RCT)
RASE Royal Agricultural Society of England
RAuxAF Royal Auxiliary Air Force
RAVC Royal Army Veterinary Corps
RB Rifle Brigade
RBA Member, Royal Society of British Artists
RBK&C Royal Borough of Kensington and Chelsea
RBL Royal British Legion
RBS Royal Society of British Sculptors
RBSA (Member of) Royal Birmingham Society of Artists
RBY Royal Bucks Yeomanry
RC Roman Catholic
RCA Member, Royal Canadian Academy of Arts; Royal College of Art; (Member of) Royal Cambrian Academy
RCAC Royal Canadian Armoured Corps
RCAF Royal Canadian Air Force
RCamA Member, Royal Cambrian Academy
RCAnaes Royal College of Anaesthetists
RCAS Royal Central Asian Society (*now see* RSAA)
RCCM Research Council for Complementary Medicine
RCDS Royal College of Defence Studies
rcds completed a course at, or served for a year on the Staff of, the Royal College of Defence Studies
RCGP Royal College of General Practitioners
RCHA Royal Canadian Horse Artillery
RCHME Royal Commission on Historical Monuments of England
RCM (Member of) Royal College of Music
RCN Royal Canadian Navy; Royal College of Nursing
RCNC Royal Corps of Naval Constructors
RCNR Royal Canadian Naval Reserve
RCNVR Royal Canadian Naval Volunteer Reserve
RCO Royal College of Organists
RCOG Royal College of Obstetricians and Gynaecologists
RCP Royal College of Physicians, London
RCPA Royal College of Pathologists of Australia
RCPath Royal College of Pathologists
RCPCH Royal College of Paediatrics and Child Health
RCPE or RCPEd Royal College of Physicians, Edinburgh
RCPI Royal College of Physicians of Ireland
RCPSG Royal College of Physicians and Surgeons of Glasgow
RCPsych Royal College of Psychiatrists
RCR Royal College of Radiologists
RCS Royal College of Surgeons of England; Royal Corps of Signals; Royal College of Science
RCSE or RCSEd Royal College of Surgeons of Edinburgh
RCSI Royal College of Surgeons in Ireland
RCT Royal Corps of Transport
RCVS Royal College of Veterinary Surgeons
RD Rural Dean; Royal Naval and Royal Marine Forces Reserve Decoration
Rd Road
RDA Diploma of Roseworthy Agricultural College, South Australia; Regional Development Agency
RDC Rural District Council
RDF Royal Dublin Fusiliers
RDI Royal Designer for Industry (Royal Society of Arts)
RDS Royal Dublin Society
RE Royal Engineers; Fellow, Royal Society of Painter-Printmakers (*formerly* of Painter-Etchers and Engravers); Religious Education
REACH Retired Executives Action Clearing House
react Research Education and Aid for Children with potentially Terminal illness
Rear Adm. Rear Admiral
REconS Royal Economic Society
Regt Regiment
REME Royal Electrical and Mechanical Engineers
REngDes Registered Engineering Designer
REOWS Royal Engineers Officers' Widows' Society
REPC Regional Economic Planning Council
RERO Royal Engineers Reserve of Officers
Res. Resigned; Reserve; Resident; Research
RETI Association of Traditional Industrial Regions
Rev. Reverend; Review
RFA Royal Field Artillery
RFC Royal Flying Corps (*now* RAF); Rugby Football Club
RFCA Reserve Forces and Cadets Association
RFD Reserve Force Decoration
RFH Royal Festival Hall
RFN Registered Fever Nurse
RFPS(G) Royal Faculty of Physicians and Surgeons, Glasgow (*now see* RCPSG)
RFR Rassemblement des Français pour la République
RFU Rugby Football Union
RGA Royal Garrison Artillery
RGI Royal Glasgow Institute of the Fine Arts
RGJ Royal Green Jackets
RGN Registered General Nurse
RGS Royal Geographical Society
RGSA Royal Geographical Society of Australasia
RHA Royal Hibernian Academy; Royal Horse Artillery; Regional Health Authority
RHASS Royal Highland and Agricultural Society of Scotland
RHB Regional Hospital Board
RHBNC Royal Holloway and Bedford New College, London
RHC Royal Holloway College, London (*now see* RHBNC)
RHF Royal Highland Fusiliers
RHG Royal Horse Guards
RHistS Royal Historical Society
RHQ Regional Headquarters
RHR Royal Highland Regiment
RHS Royal Horticultural Society; Royal Humane Society
RHV Royal Health Visitor

RI (Member of) Royal Institute of Painters in Water Colours; Rhode Island
RIA Royal Irish Academy
RIAI Royal Institute of the Architects of Ireland
RIAM Royal Irish Academy of Music
RIAS Royal Incorporation of Architects in Scotland
RIASC Royal Indian Army Service Corps
RIBA (Member of) Royal Institute of British Architects
RIBI Rotary International in Great Britain and Ireland
RIC Royal Irish Constabulary; Royal Institute of Chemistry (*now see* RSC)
RICS (Member of) Royal Institution of Chartered Surveyors
RIE Royal Indian Engineering (College)
RIF Royal Inniskilling Fusiliers
RIIA Royal Institute of International Affairs
RILEM Réunion internationale des laboratoires d'essais et de recherches sur les matériaux et les constructions
RIM Royal Indian Marines
RIN Royal Indian Navy
RINA Royal Institution of Naval Architects
RINVR Royal Indian Naval Volunteer Reserve
RIPA Royal Institute of Public Administration
RIPH&H Royal Institute of Public Health and Hygiene
RIrF Royal Irish Fusiliers
RLC Royal Logistic Corps
RLSS Royal Life Saving Society
RM Royal Marines; Resident Magistrate; Registered Midwife
RMA Royal Marine Artillery; Royal Military Academy Sandhurst (*now* incorporating Royal Military Academy, Woolwich)
RMB Rural Mail Base
RMC Royal Military College Sandhurst (*now see* RMA)
RMCM (Member of) Royal Manchester College of Music
RMCS Royal Military College of Science
RMedSoc Royal Medical Society, Edinburgh
RMetS Royal Meteorological Society
RMFVR Royal Marine Forces Volunteer Reserve
RMIT Royal Melbourne Institute of Technology
RMLI Royal Marine Light Infantry
RMN Registered Mental Nurse
RMO Resident Medical Officer(s)
RMP Royal Military Police
RMPA Royal Medico-Psychological Association
RMS Royal Microscopical Society; Royal Mail Steamer; Royal Society of Miniature Painters
RMT Rail, Maritime and Transport Union
RN Royal Navy; Royal Naval; Registered Nurse
RNAS Royal Naval Air Service
RNAY Royal Naval Aircraft Yard
RNC Royal Naval College
RNCM (Member of) Royal Northern College of Music
RNEC Royal Naval Engineering College
RNIB Royal National Institute for the Blind
RNID Royal National Institute for Deaf People (*formerly* Royal National Institute for the Deaf)
RNLI Royal National Life-boat Institution
RNLO Royal Naval Liaison Officer
RNR Royal Naval Reserve
RNRU Royal Navy Rugby Union
RNS Royal Numismatic Society
RNSA Royal Naval Sailing Association
RNSC Royal Naval Staff College
RNT Registered Nurse Tutor; Royal National Theatre
RNTNEH Royal National Throat, Nose and Ear Hospital
RNUR Régie Nationale des Usines Renault
RNVR Royal Naval Volunteer Reserve
RNVSR Royal Naval Volunteer Supplementary Reserve
RNXS Royal Naval Auxiliary Service
RNZA Royal New Zealand Artillery
RNZAC Royal New Zealand Armoured Corps
RNZAF Royal New Zealand Air Force
RNZIR Royal New Zealand Infantry Regiment
RNZN Royal New Zealand Navy
RNZNVR Royal New Zealand Naval Volunteer Reserve
ROC Royal Observer Corps
ROF Royal Ordnance Factories
R of O Reserve of Officers
ROI Member, Royal Institute of Oil Painters
RoSPA Royal Society for the Prevention of Accidents
(Rot.) Rotunda Hospital, Dublin (after degree)
RP (Member of) Royal Society of Portrait Painters
RPC Royal Pioneer Corps
RPE Rocket Propulsion Establishment
RPF Rassemblement pour la France
RPMS Royal Postgraduate Medical School
RPO Royal Philharmonic Orchestra
RPR Rassemblement pour la République
RPS Royal Photographic Society
RPSGB Royal Pharmaceutical Society of Great Britain
RRC Royal Red Cross; Rapid Reaction Corps
RRE Royal Radar Establishment (*now see* RSRE)
RRF Royal Regiment of Fusiliers
RRS Royal Research Ship
RSA Royal Scottish Academician; Royal Society of Arts; Republic of South Africa
RSAA Royal Society for Asian Affairs
RSAF Royal Small Arms Factory
RSAI Royal Society of Antiquaries of Ireland
RSAMD Royal Scottish Academy of Music and Drama
RSanI Royal Sanitary Institute (*now see* RSH)
RSAS Royal Surgical Aid Society
RSC Royal Society of Canada; Royal Society of Chemistry; Royal Shakespeare Company
RSCM Royal School of Church Music
RSCN Registered Sick Children's Nurse
RSE Royal Society of Edinburgh
RSF Royal Scots Fusiliers
RSFSR Russian Soviet Federated Socialist Republic
RSGS Royal Scottish Geographical Society
RSH Royal Society for the Promotion of Health
RSL Royal Society of Literature; Returned Services League of Australia
RSM Royal School of Mines
RSM or **RSocMed** Royal Society of Medicine
RSMA Royal Society of Marine Artists
RSME Royal School of Military Engineering
RSMHCA Royal Society for Mentally Handicapped Children and Adults (*see* Mencap)
RSNC Royal Society for Nature Conservation
RSO Rural Sub-Office; Railway Sub-Office; Resident Surgical Officer
RSPB Royal Society for Protection of Birds
RSPCA Royal Society for Prevention of Cruelty to Animals
RSRE Royal Signals and Radar Establishment
RSSAf Royal Society of South Africa
RSSAILA Returned Sailors, Soldiers and Airmen's Imperial League of Australia (*now see* RSL)
RSSPCC Royal Scottish Society for Prevention of Cruelty to Children
RSTM&H Royal Society of Tropical Medicine and Hygiene
RSUA Royal Society of Ulster Architects
RSV Revised Standard Version
RSW Member, Royal Scottish Society of Painters in Water Colours
RTE Radio Telefis Eireann
Rt Hon. Right Honourable
RTL Radio-Télévision Luxembourg
RTO Railway Transport Officer
RTPI Royal Town Planning Institute
RTR Royal Tank Regiment
Rt Rev. Right Reverend
RTS Religious Tract Society; Royal Toxophilite Society; Royal Television Society
RTYC Royal Thames Yacht Club
RU Rugby Union
RUA Royal Ulster Academy
RUC Royal Ulster Constabulary
RUI Royal University of Ireland
RUKBA Royal United Kingdom Beneficent Association
RUR Royal Ulster Regiment
RURAL Society for the Responsible Use of Resources in Agriculture & on the Land
RUSI Royal United Services Institute for Defence Studies (*formerly* Royal United Service Institution)
RVC Royal Veterinary College
RWA (Member of) Royal West of England Academy
RWAFF Royal West African Frontier Force
RWF Royal Welch Fusiliers
RWS (Member of) Royal Society of Painters in Water Colours
RYA Royal Yachting Association
RYS Royal Yacht Squadron
RZSScot Royal Zoological Society of Scotland

S

(S) (in Navy) Paymaster; Scotland
S Succeeded; South; Saint
s son
SA South Australia; South Africa; Société Anonyme; Society of the Atonement
SAAF South African Air Force

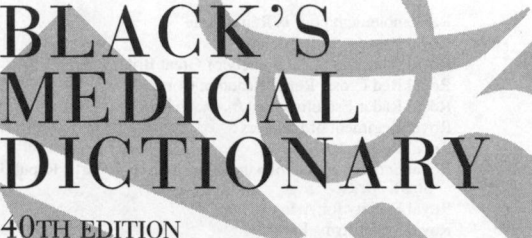

SABC South African Broadcasting Corporation
SAC Scientific Advisory Committee
sac qualified at small arms technical long course
SACC South African Council of Churches
SACEUR Supreme Allied Commander Europe
SACIF sociedad anónima commercial industrial financiera
SACLANT Supreme Allied Commander Atlantic
SACRO Scottish Association for the Care and Resettlement of Offenders
SACSEA Supreme Allied Command, SE Asia
SA de CV sociedad anónima de capital variable
SADF Sudanese Auxiliary Defence Force
SADG Société des Architectes Diplômés par le Gouvernement
SAE Society of Automobile Engineers (US)
SAHFOS Sir Alister Hardy Foundation for Ocean Science
SAMC South African Medical Corps
SAN Senior Advocate of Nigeria
SARL Société à Responsabilité Limitée
Sarum Salisbury
SAS Special Air Service
Sask Saskatchewan
SASO Senior Air Staff Officer
SAT Senior Member, Association of Accounting Technicians
SATB Soprano, Alto, Tenor, Bass
SATRO Science and Technology Regional Organisation
SB Bachelor of Science (US)
SBAA Sovereign Base Areas Administration
SBAC Society of British Aerospace Companies (*formerly* Society of British Aircraft Constructors)
SBS Special Boat Service
SBStJ Serving Brother, Most Venerable Order of the Hospital of St John of Jerusalem
SC Star of Courage (Canada); Senior Counsel; South Carolina
sc student at the Staff College
SCA Society of Catholic Apostolate (Pallottine Fathers); Société en Commandité par Actions
SCAA School Curriculum and Assessment Authority
SCAO Senior Civil Affairs Officer
SCAPA Society for Checking the Abuses of Public Advertising
SCAR Scientific Committee for Antarctic Research
ScD Doctor of Science
SCDC Schools Curriculum Development Committee
SCF Senior Chaplain to the Forces; Save the Children Fund
Sch. School
SCI Society of Chemical Industry
SCIS Scottish Council of Independent Schools
SCL Student in Civil Law
SCLC Short Service Limited Commission
SCM State Certified Midwife; Student Christian Movement
SCONUL Standing Conference of National and University Libraries
SCOP Standing Conference of Principals
Scot. Scotland
ScotBIC Scottish Business in the Community
SCOTMEG Scottish Management Efficiency Group
SCOTVEC Scottish Vocational Education Council
SD Staff Duties; South Dakota (postal)
SDA Social Democratic Alliance; Scottish Diploma in Agriculture; Scottish Development Agency
SDF Sudan Defence Force; Social Democratic Federation
SDI Strategic Defence Initiative
SDLP Social Democratic and Labour Party
SDP Social Democratic Party
SE South-east
SEAC South-East Asia Command
SEALF South-East Asia Land Forces
SEATO South-East Asia Treaty Organization
SEC Security Exchange Commission
Sec. Secretary
SED Scottish Education Department
SEE Society of Environmental Engineers
SEEDA South East England Development Agency
SEFI European Society for Engineering Education
SEN State Enrolled Nurse
SEPA Scottish Environmental Protection Agency
SEPM Society of Economic Palaeontologists and Mineralogists
SERC Science and Engineering Research Council (*now see* EPSRC and PPARC)
SERT Society of Electronic and Radio Technicians (*now see* IEIE)
SESO Senior Equipment Staff Officer
SF Sinn Féin
SFA Securities and Futures Authority
SFInstE Senior Fellow, Institute of Energy
SFInstF Senior Fellow, Institute of Fuel (*now see* SFInstE)
SFOR Stabilisation Force
SFTA Society of Film and Television Arts (*now see* BAFTA)
SFTCD Senior Fellow, Trinity College Dublin
SG Solicitor-General
SGA Member, Society of Graphic Art
Sgt Sergeant
SHA Secondary Heads Association; Special Health Authority
SHAC London Housing Aid Centre
SHAEF Supreme Headquarters, Allied Expeditionary Force
SHAPE Supreme Headquarters, Allied Powers, Europe
SHEFC Scottish Higher Education Funding Council
SHHD Scottish Home and Health Department
SHO Senior House Officer
SIAD Society of Industrial Artists and Designers (*now see* CSD)
SIAM Society of Industrial and Applied Mathematics (US)
SIB Shipbuilding Industry Board; Securities and Investments Board (*now see* FSA)
SICAV Société d'Investissement à Capital Variable
SICOT Société Internationale de Chirurgie Orthopédique et de Traumatologie
SID Society for International Development
SIESO Society of Industrial and Emergency Services Officers
SIMA Scientific Instrument Manufacturers' Association of Great Britain
SIME Security Intelligence Middle East
SIMG *Societas Internationalis Medicinae Generalis*
SinDrs Doctor of Chinese
SIROT Société Internationale pour Recherche en Orthopédie et Traumatologie
SIS Secret Intelligence Service
SITA Société Internationale de Télécommunications Aéronautiques
SITPRO Simpler Trade Procedures Board (*formerly* Simplification of International Trade Procedures)
SJ Society of Jesus (Jesuits)
SJAB St John Ambulance Brigade
SJD Doctor of Juristic Science
SJJ Setia Jubli Perak Tuanku Ja'afar
SK Saskatchewan (postal)
SL Serjeant-at-Law; Sociedad Limitada
SLA Special Libraries Association
SLAC Stanford Linear Accelerator Centre
SLAET Society of Licensed Aircraft Engineers and Technologists
SLAS Society for Latin-American Studies
SLD Social and Liberal Democrats
SLP Scottish Labour Party
SM Medal of Service (Canada) (*now see* OC); Master of Science; Officer qualified for Submarine Duties
SMA Society of Marine Artists (*now see* RSMA)
SMB Setia Mahkota Brunei
SMCC Submarine Commanding Officers' Command Course
SME School of Military Engineering (*now see* RSME)
SMEO Squadron Marine Engineer Officer
SMHO Sovereign Military Hospitaller Order (Malta)
SMIEE Senior Member, Institute of Electrical and Electronics Engineers (New York)
SMIRE Senior Member, Institute of Radio Engineers (New York)
SMMT Society of Motor Manufacturers and Traders Ltd
SMN Seri Maharaja Mangku Negara (Malaysia)
SMO Senior Medical Officer; Sovereign Military Order
SMP Senior Managers' Program
SMPTE Society of Motion Picture and Television Engineers (US)
SMRTB Ship and Marine Requirements Technology Board
SNAME Society of Naval Architects and Marine Engineers (US)
SNCF Société Nationale des Chemins de Fer Français
SND Sisters of Notre Dame
SNH Scottish Natural Heritage
SNP Scottish National Party
SNTS Society for New Testament Studies
SO Staff Officer; Scientific Officer; Symphony Orchestra
SOAF Sultan of Oman's Air Force
SOAS School of Oriental and African Studies
Soc. Society; Socialist (France)
Soc & Lib Dem Social and Liberal Democrats (*now see* Lib Dem)
SocCE(France) Société des Ingénieurs Civils de France
SODEPAX Committee on Society, Development and Peace
SOE Special Operations Executive
SOGAT Society of Graphical and Allied Trades (*now see* GPMU)
SOLACE or Solace Society of Local Authority Chief Executives
SOLT Society of London Theatre
SOM Society of Occupational Medicine
SOSc Society of Ordained Scientists
SOTS Society for Old Testament Study
sowc Senior Officers' War Course
SP Self-Propelled (Anti-Tank Regiment)
sp *sine prole* (without issue)
SpA Società per Azioni
SPAB Society for the Protection of Ancient Buildings

SPARKS Sport Aiding Medical Research for Children
SPCA Society for the Prevention of Cruelty to Animals
SPCK Society for Promoting Christian Knowledge
SPCM Darjah Seri Paduka Cura Si Manja Kini (Malaysia)
SPD Salisbury Plain District; Sozialdemokratische Partei Deutschlands
SPDK Seri Panglima Darjal Kinabalu
SPG Society for the Propagation of the Gospel (*now see* USPG)
SPk Sitara-e-Pakistan
SPMB Seri Paduka Makhota Brunei
SPMK Darjah Kebasaran Seri Paduka Mahkota Kelantan (Malaysia)
SPMO Senior Principal Medical Officer
SPNC Society for the Promotion of Nature Conservation (*now see* RSNC)
SPNM Society for the Promotion of New Music
SPR Society for Psychical Research
SPRC Society for Prevention and Relief of Cancer
sprl société de personnes à responsabilité limitée
SPSO Senior Principal Scientific Officer
SPTL Society of Public Teachers of Law
SPUC Society for the Protection of the Unborn Child
Sq. Square
sq staff qualified
SQA Sitara-i-Quaid-i-Azam (Pakistan)
Sqdn or **Sqn** Squadron
SR Special Reserve; Southern Railway; Southern Region (BR)
SRC Science Research Council (later SERC); Students' Representative Council
SRCh State Registered Chiropodist
SRHE Society for Research into Higher Education
SRIS Science Reference Information Service
SRN State Registered Nurse
SRNA Shipbuilders and Repairers National Association
SRO Supplementary Reserve of Officers; Self-Regulatory Organisation
SRP State Registered Physiotherapist
SRY Sherwood Rangers Yeomanry
SS Saints; Straits Settlements; Steamship
SSA Society of Scottish Artists; Side Saddle Association
SSAC Social Security Advisory Committee
SSAFA Soldiers, Sailors, Airmens and Families Association—Forces Help (formerly Soldiers', Sailors', and Airmen's Families Association)
SSBN Nuclear Submarine, Ballistic
SSC Solicitor before Supreme Court (Scotland); Sculptors Society of Canada; *Societas Sanctae Crucis* (Society of the Holy Cross); Short Service Commission
SSEB South of Scotland Electricity Board
SSEES School of Slavonic and East European Studies
SSF Society of St Francis
SSJE Society of St John the Evangelist
SSM Society of the Sacred Mission; Seri Setia Mahkota (Malaysia)
SSO Senior Supply Officer; Senior Scientific Officer
SSR Soviet Socialist Republic
SSRC Social Science Research Council (*now see* ESRC)
SSSI Sites of Special Scientific Interest
SSSR Society for the Scientific Study of Religion
SSStJ Serving Sister, Most Venerable Order of the Hospital of St John of Jerusalem
St Street; Saint
STA Sail Training Association
STB *Sacrae Theologiae Baccalaureus* (Bachelor of Sacred Theology)
STC Senior Training Corps
STD *Sacrae Theologiae Doctor* (Doctor of Sacred Theology)
STETS Southern Theological Education and Training Scheme
STh Scholar in Theology
Stip. Stipend; Stipendiary
STL *Sacrae Theologiae Lector* (Reader or a Professor of Sacred Theology)
STM *Sacrae Theologiae Magister* (Master of Sacred Theology)
STP *Sacrae Theologiae Professor* (Professor of Divinity, old form of DD)
STSO Senior Technical Staff Officer
STV Scottish Television
SUNY State University of New York
Supp. Res. Supplementary Reserve (of Officers)
Supt Superintendent
Surg. Surgeon
Surv. Surviving
SW South-west
SWET Society of West End Theatre (*now see* SOLT)
SWIA Society of Wildlife Artists
SWPA South West Pacific Area
SWRB Sadler's Wells Royal Ballet
Syd. Sydney

T

T Telephone; Territorial
TA Telegraphic Address; Territorial Army
TAA Territorial Army Association
TAF Tactical Air Force
T&AFA Territorial and Auxiliary Forces Association
T&AVR Territorial and Army Volunteer Reserve
TANS Territorial Army Nursing Service
TANU Tanganyika African National Union
TARO Territorial Army Reserve of Officers
TAS Torpedo and Anti Submarine Course
TASS Technical, Administrative and Supervisory Section of AUEW (now part of MSF)
TAVRA or **TA&VRA** Territorial Auxiliary and Volunteer Reserve Association (*now see* RFCA)
TC Order of the Trinity Cross (Trinidad and Tobago)
TCCB Test and County Cricket Board (*now see* ECB)
TCD Trinity College, Dublin (University of Dublin, Trinity College)
TCF Temporary Chaplain to the Forces
TCPA Town and Country Planning Association
TD Territorial Efficiency Decoration; Efficiency Decoration (T&AVR) (since April 1967); Teachta Dala (Member of the Dáil, Eire)
TDD Tubercular Diseases Diploma
TE Technical Engineer
TEAC Technical Educational Advisory Council
TEC Technician Education Council (*now see* BTEC); Training and Enterprise Council
Tech(CEI) Technician
TechRICS Technical Member, Royal Institution of Chartered Surveyors
TEFL Teaching English as a Foreign Language
TEFLA Teaching English as a Foreign Language to Adults
TEM Territorial Efficiency Medal
TEMA Telecommunication Engineering and Manufacturing Association
Temp. Temperature; Temporary
TEng(CEI) Technician Engineer (*now see* IEng)
Tenn Tennessee
TeolD Doctor of Theology
TES Times Educational Supplement
TESL Teaching English as a Second Language
TESOL Teaching English to Speakers of other Languages
TET Teacher of Electrotherapy
Tex Texas
TF Territorial Force
TFR Territorial Force Reserve
TFTS Tactical Fighter Training Squadron
TGEW Timber Growers England and Wales Ltd
TGO Timber Growers' Organisation (*now see* TGEW)
TGWU Transport and General Workers' Union
ThD Doctor of Theology
THED Transvaal Higher Education Diploma
THELEP Therapy of Leprosy
THES Times Higher Education Supplement
ThL Theological Licentiate
ThSchol Scholar in Theology
TIMS The Institute of Management Sciences
TLS Times Literary Supplement
TMA Theatrical Management Association
TMMG Teacher of Massage and Medical Gymnastics
TN Tennessee (postal)
TNC Theatres National Committee
TOSD Tertiary Order of St Dominic
TPI Town Planning Institute (*now see* RTPI)
Trans. Translation; Translated
Transf. Transferred
TRC Thames Rowing Club
TRE Telecommunications Research Establishment (later RRE)
TRH Their Royal Highnesses
TRIC Television and Radio Industries Club
Trin. Trinity
TRL Transport Research Laboratory
TRRL Transport and Road Research Laboratory (*now see* TRL)
TS Training Ship
TSB Trustee Savings Bank
tsc passed a Territorial Army Course in Staff Duties
TSD Tertiary of St Dominic
TSSA Transport Salaried Staffs' Association
TSSF Tertiary, Society of St Francis
TTA Teacher Training Agency
TUC Trades Union Congress
TULV Trade Unions for a Labour Victory
TUS Trade Union Side
TV Television

TVEI Technical and Vocational Education Initiative
TWA Thames Water Authority
TX Texas (postal)
TYC Thames Yacht Club (*now see* RTYC)

U

U Unionist
u uncle
UA Unitary Authority
UACE Universities Association for Continuing Education
UAE United Arab Emirates
UAR United Arab Republic
UAU Universities Athletic Union
UBC University of British Columbia
UBI Understanding British Industry
UC University College
UCAS Universities and Colleges Admissions Service
UCCA Universities Central Council on Admissions
UCCF Universities and Colleges Christian Fellowship of Evangelical Unions
UCE University of Central England
UCET Universities Council for Education of Teachers
UCH University College Hospital (London)
UCL University College London
UCLA University of California at Los Angeles
UCLES University of Cambridge Local Examinations Syndicate
UCMSM University College and Middlesex School of Medicine
UCNS Universities' Council for Non-academic Staff
UCNW University College of North Wales
UCRN University College of Rhodesia and Nyasaland
UCS University College School
UCSB University of California at Santa Barbara
UCSD University of California at San Diego
UCW University College of Wales; Union of Communication Workers (*now see* CWU)
UDC Urban District Council; Urban Development Corporation
UDF Union Defence Force; Union pour la démocratie française
UDM United Democratic Movement (South Africa)
UDR Ulster Defence Regiment; Union des Démocrates pour la Vème République (*now see* RPR)
UDSR Union Démocratique et Socialiste de la Résistance
UE United Empire Loyalist (Canada)
UEA University of East Anglia
UED University Education Diploma
UEFA Union of European Football Associations
UF United Free Church
UFAW Universities Federation for Animal Welfare
UFC Universities' Funding Council
UGC University Grants Committee (later UFC)
UIAA Union Internationale des Associations d'Alpinisme
UICC Union Internationale contre le Cancer
UIE Union Internationale des Etudiants
UISPP Union Internationale des Sciences Préhistoriques et Protohistoriques
UITP International Union of Public Transport
UJD *Utriusque Juris Doctor* (Doctor of both Laws, Doctor of Canon and Civil Law)
UK United Kingdom
UKAC United Kingdom Automation Council
UKAEA United Kingdom Atomic Energy Authority
UKCC United Kingdom Central Council for Nursing, Midwifery and Health Visiting
UKCCCR United Kingdom Co-ordinating Committee on Cancer Research
UKCIS United Kingdom Chemical Information Service
UKCP United Kingdom Council for Psychotherapy
UKERNA United Kingdom Education and Research Networking Association
UKIAS United Kingdom Immigrants' Advisory Service
UKIC United Kingdom Institute for Convservation
UKISC United Kingdom Industrial Space Committee
UKLF United Kingdom Land Forces
UKMF(L) United Kingdom Military Forces (Land)
UKMIS United Kingdom Mission
UKOOA United Kingdom Offshore Operators Association
UKPIA United Kingdom Petroleum Industry Association Ltd
UKSC United Kingdom Support Command
UKSLS United Kingdom Services Liaison Staff
UKU United Kingdom Unionist
ULPS Union of Liberal and Progressive Synagogues
UMDS United Medical and Dental Schools
UMIST University of Manchester Institute of Science and Technology
UN United Nations
UNA United Nations Association
UNCAST United Nations Conference on the Applications of Science and Technology
UNCIO United Nations Conference on International Organisation
UNCITRAL United Nations Commission on International Trade Law
UNCSTD United Nations Conference on Science and Technology for Development
UNCTAD or **Unctad** United Nations Commission for Trade and Development
UNDP United Nations Development Programme
UNDRO United Nations Disaster Relief Organisation
UNECA United Nations Economic Commission for Asia
UNECE United Nations Economic Commission for Europe
UNEP United Nations Environment Programme
UNESCO or **Unesco** United Nations Educational, Scientific and Cultural Organisation
UNFAO United Nations Food and Agriculture Organisation
UNFICYP United Nations Force in Cyprus
UNHCR United Nations High Commissioner for Refugees
UNICE Union des Industries de la Communauté Européenne
UNICEF or **Unicef** United Nations Children's Fund (*formerly* United Nations International Children's Emergency Fund)
UNIDO United Nations Industrial Development Organisation
UNIDROIT Institut International pour l'Unification du Droit Privé
UNIFEM United Nations Development Fund for Women
UNIFIL United Nations Interim Force in Lebanon
UNIPEDE Union Internationale des Producteurs et Distributeurs d'Energie Electrique
UNISIST Universal System for Information in Science and Technology
UNITAR United Nations Institute of Training and Research
Univ. University
UNO United Nations Organization
UNRRA United Nations Relief and Rehabilitation Administration
UNRWA United Nations Relief and Works Agency
UNSCOB United Nations Special Commission on the Balkans
UP United Provinces; Uttar Pradesh; United Presbyterian
UPGC University and Polytechnic Grants Committee
UPNI Unionist Party of Northern Ireland
UPU Universal Postal Union
UPUP Ulster Popular Unionist Party
URC United Reformed Church
URSI Union Radio-Scientifique Internationale
US United States
USA United States of America
USAAF United States Army Air Force
USAF United States Air Force
USAID United States Agency for International Development
USAR United States Army Reserve
USC University of Southern California
USDAW Union of Shop Distributive and Allied Workers
USM Unlisted Securities Market
USMA United States Military Academy
USMC United States Marine Corps
USN United States Navy
USNR United States Naval Reserve
USPG United Society for the Propagation of the Gospel
USPHS United States Public Health Service
USPS United States Postal Service
USS United States Ship
USSR Union of Soviet Socialist Republics
USVI United States Virgin Islands
UT Utah (postal)
UTC University Training Corps
UTS University of Technology, Sydney
UU Ulster Unionist
UUK Universities UK
UUUC United Ulster Unionist Coalition
UUUP United Ulster Unionist Party
UWCC University of Wales College of Cardiff
UWE University of the West of England
UWIC University of Wales Institute, Cardiff
UWIST University of Wales Institute of Science and Technology
UWP United Workers' Party (Dominica)
UWT Union of Women Teachers

V

V Five (Roman numerals); Version; Vicar; Viscount; Vice
v *versus* (against)
v or vid. *vide* (see)
VA Virginia (postal)
Va Virginia
VAD Voluntary Aid Detachment

V&A Victoria and Albert
VAT Value Added Tax
VC Victoria Cross; Voluntary Controlled
VCAS Vice Chief of the Air Staff
VCDS Vice Chief of the Defence Staff
VCGS Vice Chief of the General Staff
VCNS Vice Chief of the Naval Staff
VD Royal Naval Volunteer Reserve Officers' Decoration (*now* VRD); Volunteer Officers' Decoration; Victorian Decoration
VDC Volunteer Defence Corps
Ven. Venerable
Vet. Veterinary
VetMB Bachelor of Veterinary Medicine
VG Vicar-General
Vice Adm. Vice Admiral
Visc. Viscount
VM Victory Medal
VMH Victoria Medal of Honour (Royal Horticultural Society)
VMSM Voluntary Medical Services Medal
Vol. Volume; Voluntary; Volunteers
VP Vice-President
VPP Volunteer Political Party
VPRP Vice-President, Royal Society of Portrait Painters
VQMG Vice-Quartermaster-General
VR *Victoria Regina* (Queen Victoria); Volunteer Reserve
VRD Royal Naval Volunteer Reserve Officers' Decoration
VSO Voluntary Service Overseas
VT Vermont (postal)
Vt Vermont
VUP Vanguard Unionist Party
VVD Volkspartij voor Vrijheiden Democratie

W

W West
WA Western Australia; Washington (postal)
WAAF Women's Auxiliary Air Force (later WRAF)
WAOS Welsh Agricultural Organisations Society
Wash Washington State
WCC World Council of Churches
W/Cdr Wing Commander
WCMD Welsh College of Music and Drama
WDA Welsh Development Agency
WEA Workers' Educational Association; Royal West of England Academy
WEU Western European Union
WFEO World Federation of Engineering Organisations
WFSW World Federation of Scientific Workers
WFTU World Federation of Trade Unions
WhF Whitworth Fellow
WHO World Health Organization
WhSch Whitworth Scholar
WI West Indies; Women's Institute; Wisconsin (postal)
Wilts Wiltshire
WIPO World Intellectual Property Organization
Wis Wisconsin
Wits Witwatersrand
WJEC Welsh Joint Education Committee
WLA Women's Land Army
WLD Women Liberal Democrats
WLF Women's Liberal Federation
Wm William
WMO World Meteorological Organization
WNO Welsh National Opera
WO War Office; Warrant Officer
Worcs Worcestershire
WOSB War Office Selection Board
WR West Riding; Western Region (BR)
WRAC Women's Royal Army Corps
WRAF Women's Royal Air Force
WRNS Women's Royal Naval Service
WRVS Women's Royal Voluntary Service
WS Writer to the Signet
WSAVA World Small Animal Veterinary Association
WSPA World Society for the Protection of Animals
WSPU Women's Social and Political Union
WTO World Trade Organisation
WUS World University Service
WV West Virginia (postal)
WVS Women's Voluntary Services (*now see* WRVS)
WWF World Wide Fund for Nature (*formerly* World Wildlife Fund)
WY Wyoming (postal)

X

X Ten (Roman numerals)
XO Executive Officer

Y

y youngest
YC Young Conservative
YCNAC Young Conservatives National Advisory Committee
Yeo. Yeomanry
YES Youth Enterprise Scheme
YHA Youth Hostels Association
YMCA Young Men's Christian Association
YOI Young Offenders Institute
Yorks Yorkshire
YPTES Young People's Trust for Endangered Species
yr younger
yrs years
YT Yukon Territory (postal)
YTS Youth Training Scheme
YVFF Young Volunteer Force Foundation
YWCA Young Women's Christian Association

Z

ZANU Zimbabwe African National Union
ZAPU Zimbabwe African People's Union

THE ROYAL FAMILY

THE SOVEREIGN

Born

Her Majesty Queen Elizabeth II, (Elizabeth Alexandra Mary). . . . . 21 April 1926

Succeeded her father, King George VI, 6 February 1952

Married 20 Nov. 1947, HRH The Duke of Edinburgh, *now* HRH The Prince Philip, Duke of Edinburgh, KG, KT, OM, GBE (*b* 10 June 1921, *s* of HRH Prince Andrew of Greece (*d* 1944) and of HRH Princess Andrew of Greece (*d* 1969), *gg-d* of Queen Victoria; *cr* 1947, Baron Greenwich, Earl of Merioneth and Duke of Edinburgh)

Residences: Buckingham Palace, SW1A 1AA; Windsor Castle, Berkshire SL4 1NJ; Sandringham House, Norfolk PE35 6EN; Balmoral Castle, Aberdeenshire AB35 5TB.

SONS AND DAUGHTER OF HER MAJESTY

HRH The Prince of Wales, (Prince Charles Philip Arthur George), KG, KT, GCB; . . . . 14 Nov. 1948

cr 1958, Prince of Wales and Earl of Chester; Duke of Cornwall; Duke of Rothesay, Earl of Carrick and Baron of Renfrew; Lord of the Isles and Great Steward of Scotland

Married 29 July 1981, Lady Diana Frances Spencer (*b* 1 July 1961, *y d* of 8th Earl Spencer, LVO, she *d* 31 Aug. 1997), (marriage dissolved, 1996), and has issue –

HRH PRINCE WILLIAM OF WALES, (PRINCE WILLIAM ARTHUR PHILIP LOUIS) . . . . 21 June 1982

HRH PRINCE HENRY OF WALES, (PRINCE HENRY CHARLES ALBERT DAVID) . . . . 15 Sept. 1984

Office: St James's Palace, SW1A 1BS; *residence:* Highgrove, Doughton, Tetbury, Gloucestershire GL8 8TN.

HRH The Duke of York, (Prince Andrew Albert Christian Edward), CVO; . . . . . 19 Feb. 1960

cr 1986, Baron Killyleagh, Earl of Inverness and Duke of York

Married 23 July 1986, Sarah Margaret Ferguson, *now* Sarah, Duchess of York (*b* 15 Oct. 1959, 2nd *d* of Major Ronald Ivor Ferguson, Life Guards (retired)), (marriage dissolved, 1996) and has issue –

HRH PRINCESS BEATRICE OF YORK, (PRINCESS BEATRICE ELIZABETH MARY). . . . . 8 Aug. 1988

HRH PRINCESS EUGENIE OF YORK, (PRINCESS EUGENIE VICTORIA HELENA) . . . . . 23 March 1990

Office: Buckingham Palace, SW1A 1AA; *residence:* Sunninghill Park, Ascot, Berkshire SL5 7TH.

HRH The Earl of Wessex, (Prince Edward Antony Richard Louis), CVO; . . . . . . 10 March 1964

cr 1999, Viscount Severn and Earl of Wessex

Married 19 June 1999, Sophie Helen Rhys-Jones (*b* 20 Jan. 1965, *d* of Christopher and Mary Rhys-Jones)

Residence: Bagshot Park, Bagshot, Surrey GU19 5PL.

HRH The Princess Royal, (Princess Anne Elizabeth Alice Louise), ... 15 Aug. 1950

Lady of the Order of the Garter, Royal Lady of the Order of the Thistle, GCVO

Married 1st, 14 Nov. 1973, Captain Mark Anthony Peter Phillips, *qv* (marriage dissolved, 1992), and has issue –

PETER MARK ANDREW PHILLIPS . . . . 15 Nov. 1977

ZARA ANNE ELIZABETH PHILLIPS . . . . 15 May 1981

Married 2nd, 12 Dec. 1992, Commodore Timothy James Hamilton Laurence, *qv*

Office: Buckingham Palace, SW1A 1AA; *residence:* Gatcombe Park, Minchinhampton, Stroud, Gloucestershire GL6 9AT.

SISTER OF HER MAJESTY

HRH The Princess Margaret (Rose), Countess of Snowdon, CI, GCVO . . . . . . 21 Aug. 1930

Married 6 May 1960, Antony Charles Robert Armstrong-Jones, *now* 1st Earl of Snowdon, *qv* (marriage dissolved, 1978), and has issue –

DAVID ALBERT CHARLES ARMSTRONG-JONES, (VISCOUNT LINLEY, *qv*) . . . . . . 3 Nov. 1961

SARAH FRANCES ELIZABETH ARMSTRONG-JONES, (LADY SARAH CHATTO) . . . . . 1 May 1964

Married 14 July 1994, Daniel Chatto, *s* of late Thomas Chatto and of Rosalind Chatto, and has issue –

SAMUEL DAVID BENEDICT CHATTO . . . . 28 July 1996

ARTHUR ROBERT NATHANIEL CHATTO . . . . 5 Feb. 1999

Residence: Kensington Palace, W8 4PU.

MOTHER OF HER MAJESTY

Her Majesty Queen Elizabeth The Queen Mother, (Elizabeth Angela Marguerite), . . . 4 Aug. 1900
Lady of the Order of the Garter, Lady of the Order of the Thistle, CI, GCVO, GBE

Married 26 April 1923 (as Lady Elizabeth Bowes-Lyon, *d* of 14th Earl of Strathmore and Kinghorne), HRH The Duke of York (Prince Albert), who succeeded as King George VI, 11 Dec. 1936 and *d* 6 Feb. 1952

Residences: Clarence House, St James's, SW1A 1BA; Royal Lodge, The Great Park, Windsor, Berkshire; Birkhall, Ballater, Aberdeenshire; Castle of Mey, Caithness-shire.

WIDOW OF UNCLE OF HER MAJESTY

HRH Princess Alice (Christabel), Duchess of Gloucester, GCB, CI, GCVO, GBE, ... 25 Dec. 1901
3rd *d* of 7th Duke of Buccleuch

Married 6 Nov. 1935, HRH The Duke of Gloucester (Prince Henry William Frederick Albert, *b* 31 March 1900, *d* 10 June 1974), and has issue –

HRH PRINCE WILLIAM OF GLOUCESTER, (PRINCE WILLIAM HENRY ANDREW FREDERICK), *b* 18 Dec. 1941, *d* 28 Aug. 1972

HRH THE DUKE OF GLOUCESTER, (PRINCE RICHARD ALEXANDER WALTER GEORGE) (*see below*)

Residence: Kensington Palace, W8 4PU.

COUSINS OF HER MAJESTY

Child of HRH The Duke of Gloucester and of HRH Princess Alice, Duchess of Gloucester (*see above*)

HRH The Duke of Gloucester, (Prince Richard Alexander Walter George), KG, GCVO . . 26 Aug. 1944

Married 8 July 1972, Birgitte Eva van Deurs, GCVO (*b* 20 June 1946, *d* of Asger Preben Wissing Henriksen), and has issue –

ALEXANDER PATRICK GREGERS RICHARD, (EARL OF ULSTER, *qv*) . . . . 24 Oct. 1974

DAVINA ELIZABETH ALICE BENEDIKTE, (LADY DAVINA WINDSOR) . . . . . . 19 Nov. 1977

ROSE VICTORIA BIRGITTE LOUISE, (LADY ROSE WINDSOR) . . . . 1 March 1980

Residence: Kensington Palace, W8 4PU.

Children of HRH The Duke of Kent (Prince George Edward Alexander Edmund, *b* 20 Dec. 1902, *d* 25 Aug. 1942) and HRH Princess Marina, Duchess of Kent (*b* 13 Dec. 1906, *d* 27 Aug. 1968), *y d* of late Prince Nicholas of Greece

HRH The Duke of Kent, (Prince Edward George Nicholas Paul Patrick), KG, GCMG, GCVO 9 Oct. 1935

Married 8 June 1961, Katharine Lucy Mary Worsley, GCVO (*b* 22 Feb. 1933, *o d* of Sir William Worsley, 4th Bt) and has issue –

GEORGE PHILIP NICHOLAS, (EARL OF ST ANDREWS, *qv*) . . . . 26 June 1962

NICHOLAS CHARLES EDWARD JONATHAN, (LORD NICHOLAS WINDSOR) . . . . . 25 July 1970

HELEN MARINA LUCY, (LADY HELEN TAYLOR) . . . . 28 April 1964

Married 18 July 1992, Timothy Verner Taylor, *e s* of Commander Michael Taylor, RN and Mrs Colin Walkinshaw, and has issue –

COLUMBUS GEORGE DONALD TAYLOR . . . . 6 Aug. 1994

CASSIUS EDWARD TAYLOR . . . . 26 Dec. 1996

Residence: Wren House, Palace Green, W8 4PY.

HRH Prince Michael of Kent, (Prince Michael George Charles Franklin), KCVO. . . . . 4 July 1942

Married 30 June 1978, Baroness Marie-Christine Agnes Hedwig Ida von Reibnitz (*b* 15 Jan. 1945, *d* of Baron Günther Hubertus von Reibnitz), and has issue –

FREDERICK MICHAEL GEORGE DAVID LOUIS, (LORD FREDERICK WINDSOR) . . . 6 April 1979

GABRIELLA MARINA ALEXANDRA OPHELIA, (LADY GABRIELLA WINDSOR) . . . . 23 April 1981

Residences: Kensington Palace, W8 4PU; Nether Lypiatt Manor, Stroud, Gloucestershire GL6 7LS.

HRH Princess Alexandra (Helen Elizabeth Olga Christabel), The Hon. Lady Ogilvy, GCVO 25 Dec. 1936

Married 24 April 1963, Rt Hon. Sir Angus (James Bruce) Ogilvy, *qv*, and has issue –

JAMES ROBERT BRUCE OGILVY . . . . 29 Feb. 1964

Married 30 July 1988, Julia, *d* of Charles Frederick Melville Rawlinson, *qv*, and has issue –

ALEXANDER CHARLES OGILVY . . . . 12 Nov. 1996

FLORA ALEXANDRA OGILVY . . . . 15 Dec. 1994

MARINA VICTORIA ALEXANDRA . . . . 31 July 1966

Married 2 Feb. 1990, Paul Julian Mowatt (marriage dissolved, 1997), and has issue –

CHRISTIAN ALEXANDER MOWATT . . . . 4 June 1993

ZENOUSKA MAY MOWATT . . . . 26 May 1990

Office: Buckingham Palace, SW1A 1AA; *residence:* Thatched House Lodge, Richmond, Surrey TW10 5HP.

EDITORS' NOTE

A proof of each entry is posted to its subject every year for personal revision. Addresses printed in *Who's Who* are those which the subjects of the entries have submitted for publication. Addresses in London, and the names of London clubs, are unaccompanied by the word 'London'.

Entries are listed alphabetically by surname; forenames follow, those which are not customarily used by the subject being placed within brackets. Where a diminutive or alternative name is preferred, this is shown in brackets after all the given names.

Inclusion in *Who's Who* has never, at any time, been a matter for payment or of obligation to purchase.

A

AARONSON, Graham Raphael; QC 1982; *b* 31 Dec. 1944; *s* of late John Aaronson and of Dora Aaronson (*née* Franks); *m*; two *s* one *d*; *m* 1993, Pearl Isobel Buchler; two step *s* one step *d*. *Educ:* City of London Sch.; Trinity Hall, Cambridge (Thomas Waraker Law Schol.; MA). Called to the Bar, Middle Temple, 1966 (Bencher 1991); practised Revenue law, 1968–73 and 1978–. Chairman: Tax Law Review Cttee, 1994–97; Revenue Bar Assoc., 1995–98. Advr on tax reform to Treasury, Israel, 1986–90. Chm., Dietary Res. Foundn, 1989–. Founder, Standford Grange residential rehabilitation centre for ex-offenders, 1974; Man. Dir, Worldwide Plastics Development, 1973–77; Dir, Bridgend Group PLC, 1973–92. *Address:* Pump Court Tax Chambers, 16 Bedford Row, WC1R 4EB.

AARONSON, Michael John, CBE 2000; Director-General, Save the Children Fund, since 1995; *b* 8 Sept. 1947; *s* of Edward John Aaronson and Marian Aaronson (*née* Davies); *m* 1988, Andrene Margaret Sutherland; two *s* one *d*. *Educ:* Merchant Taylors' Sch.; St John's Coll., Oxford (Sir Thomas White Scholar, Trevelyan Scholar; MA). Field Co-ordinator, SCF, Nigeria, 1969–71; HM Diplomatic Service, 1972–88, served Paris, Lagos, Rangoon; Overseas Dir, SCF, 1988–95. Freeman: City of London, 1989; Merchant Taylors' Co., 1989. *Recreations:* sports, the performing arts. *Address:* Dingley Dell, Glaziers Lane, Normandy, Surrey GU3 2EB. *T:* (01483) 811655; Save the Children, 17 Grove Lane, SE5 8RD. *T:* (020) 7703 5400, *Fax:* (020) 7793 7466. *Club:* MCC.

ABBADO, Claudio; Artistic Director, Berlin Philharmonic Orchestra, 1989–Sept. 2002; Generalmusikdirektor of Vienna, since 1987; *b* Milan, 26 June 1933. Music Dir, La Scala, Milan, 1968–86; Principal Conductor, LSO, 1979–88; Music Director, Vienna State Opera, 1986–91. Founder, European Community Youth Orch., 1978; Artistic Advr, Chamber Orchestra of Europe, 1981–; Founder and Artistic Director: Gustav Mahler Jugend Orchester, 1988; Festival, Wien Modern, 1988; Artistic Dir, Salzburg Easter Fest., 1994. Dr *hc*: Aberdeen, 1986; Ferrara, 1990; Cambridge, 1994. Mozart-Medaille, Mozart-Gemeinde, Vienna, 1973; Goldmedaille der Internat. Gustav Mahler Gesellschaft, Vienna, 1985; winner of major international prizes for recordings. Ehrenring, City of Vienna, 1994. Gran Croce d'Italia, 1984; Cross, Légion d'Honneur; Bundesverdienstkreuz (Germany), 1992. *Address:* Berliner Philharmonisches Orchester, Herbert von Karajan Strasse 1, 10785 Berlin, Germany.

ABBOTT, Sir Albert Francis, Kt 1981; CBE 1974; Mayor, City of Mackay, Queensland, 1970–88; *b* Marvel Loch, WA, 10 Dec. 1913; *s* of late Albert Victor and Diana Abbott; *m* 1941, Gwendoline Joyce Maclean; two *s* four *d*. *Educ:* Mount Martin and Mackay State Schs, Qld. Served RAAF, 1941–45. Sugar cane farmer, 1950–; has given twenty years service to sugar industry organisations. Member: Picture, Theatre and Films Commn, 1975–90; Qld Local Govt Grants Commn, 1977–85. Returned Services League of Australia: Mem., 1946–; Pres., Mackay Sub-Br., 1960–65; Dist Pres., Mackay, 1965–74; Pres., Qld State, 1974–90; Hon. Life Pres., Qld State, 1991–; Hon. Life Vice Pres., Nat. Br., 1995–. President: N Qld Local Govt Assoc., 1975–84; Qld Local Govt Assoc., 1983–88; Aust. Local Govt Assoc., 1986–87; Lifeline Mackay, 1990–. Mem., Mackay Rotary Club. Governor, Utah Foundn, 1975–88. Hon. Dr Central Qld Univ., 1996. *Recreations:* golf, tennis, racing. *Address:* 2 Tudor Court, Mackay, Qld 4740, Australia. *Clubs:* United Services (Brisbane); RSL Ex-Services, Bowls, Golf, Trotting, Turf, Amateur Race, Diggers Race, Legacy (all in Mackay).

ABBOTT, Anthony John, CMG 2001; OBE 1997 (MBE 1986); HM Diplomatic Service, retired; Head, Pitcairn Logistics Team, New Zealand, since 2001; *b* Ashton-under-Lyne, 9 Sept. 1941; *s* of Walter Abbott and Mary Abbott (*née* Delaney); *m* 1962, Margaret Stuart Green; three *s* one *d*. *Educ:* All Souls' Sch., Salford; De La Salle Coll., Pendleton. Joined HM Diplomatic Service, 1959: Vice-Consul, Khorramshahr, 1963–65; Helsinki, 1965–68; Press Officer, FCO, 1969–72; Passport Officer, Lusaka, 1972–75; Consul, Santiago, 1976–80; UK Presidency Secretariat to EC, 1981; on secondment to BOTB, 1981–82; Consul, Lisbon, 1983–87; First Sec., Calcutta, 1987–91; EC Monitor, Croatia and Bosnia Herzogovina, 1991; Dep. Head, Trng Dept, FCO, 1992–93; Consul-Gen., Perth, 1993–97; Governor, Montserrat, 1997–2001. EC Monitoring Medal, 1994. Officer, Order of Enfante Dom Henrique (Portugal), 1985. *Recreations:* travel, driving, golf, spectator (all sports). *Address:* c/o Foreign and Commonwealth Office, King Charles Street, SW1A 2AH; 5 Rye View Maisonettes, The Gardens, East Dulwich, SE22 9QB. *Club:* Royal Over-Seas League.

ABBOTT, Diane Julie; MP (Lab) Hackney North and Stoke Newington, since 1987; *b* 27 Sept. 1953; *d* of late Reginald and Julia Abbott; *m* 1991, David Thompson (marr. diss.); one *s*. *Educ:* Harrow County Girls' Grammar Sch.; Newnham Coll., Cambridge. Formerly: Admin. Trainee, Home Office; Race Relations Officer, NCCL; Researcher, Thames Television; Reporter, TV-am; Equality Officer, ACTT; Press and PR Officer, GLC; Principal Press Officer, Lambeth Borough Council. Joined Labour Party, 1971; Mem., NEC, 1994–. Mem., Westminster City Council, 1982–86. Mem. resp. for equality and women's issues, Mayor of London's Cabinet, 2000–. *Address:* House of Commons, SW1A 0AA.

ABBOTT, James Alan, PhD; Manager and Director of Research, Koninklijk/Shell Laboratorium, Amsterdam, Shell Research BV, 1981–88, retired; *b* 2 Dec. 1928; *s* of George Oswald and Eva Abbott; *m* 1954, Rita Marjorie Galloway; one *s* one *d*. *Educ:* Ilkeston Grammar School; University of Nottingham (BSc, PhD). Post-doctoral research, Univ. of Durham, 1952–53; served Royal Air Force, 1953–56 (Flt Lt RAF Technical Coll., Henlow). Shell companies, UK and Holland, 1956–88: Dir, Shell Research Ltd, Sittingbourne Research Centre, 1980–81. Officer, Order of Oranje-Nassau (The Netherlands), 1988. *Publications:* papers in Trans Faraday Soc., Proc. Royal Society. *Recreation:* golf.

ABBOTT, John Martin, CBE 2000; QPM 1996; Director General, National Criminal Intelligence Service, since 1997; Vice President, Interpol, since 1999; *b* 22 March 1949; *s* of late Geoffrey Lowick Abbott and of Gladys Lilian Abbott; *m* 1972, Christine Sowter; two *d*. *Educ:* Univ. of Sussex (BA Hons History 1982). Joined Sussex Police, 1968: served in various ranks throughout Sussex, 1968–86; Supt, seconded to Royal Hong Kong Police, 1986–88; Chief Supt, seconded to Police Staff Coll., Bramshill, 1989–91; Asst Chief Constable, 1991–94; Asst Insp. of Constabulary, 1994–96. *Recreations:* reading, history, cricket, keeping fit. *Club:* St Michaels (Lewes).

ABBOTT, Adm. Sir Peter (Charles), GBE 1999; KCB 1994; Vice Chief of the Defence Staff, 1997–2001; Commissioner, Commonwealth War Graves Commission, since 2001; *b* 12 Feb. 1942; *s* of late Lieut-Col Dennis Abbott, Royal Garwhal Rifles and Delphine McConaghey; *m* 1965, Susan Phillippa Grey; three *d*. *Educ:* St Edward's Sch., Oxford; Queens' College, Cambridge (MA 1966). Articled Clerk, Blackburn, Robson Coates, 1963; 2nd Lieut, RMFVR 1963; Sub Lieut, RN 1964; Commanding Officer, HM Ships Chawton, 1972, Ambuscade, 1976, Ajax, 1983 (and First Frigate Sqdn); RCDS 1985; Flag Officer, Flotilla Two, 1989; ACNS, 1991–93; Dep. SACLANT, 1993–95; C-in-C Fleet, C-in-C Eastern Atlantic Area and Comdr Naval Forces N Western Europe, 1995–97. Officer, US Legion of Merit, 1995.

ABBOTT, Roderick Evelyn; Deputy Director-General, Trade, European Commission, since 2000; *b* 16 April 1938; *e s* of late Stuart Abbott, OBE; *m* 1963, Elizabeth Isobel McLean; three *d*. *Educ:* Rugby Sch.; Merton Coll., Oxford. Board of Trade, 1962–68 (Private Sec. to Pres. of BoT, 1965–66; seconded to DEA, 1966–68); UK Mission to UN, Geneva, 1968–71; Foreign Office, London, 1971–73; EEC, Brussels, 1973–75; EEC Delegation, Geneva, 1975–79; EEC, Brussels, 1979–82; Dir, D-G of External Relns, then External Econ. Relns, EC, Brussels, 1982–96; Ambassador and Perm. Rep. of EC to UN and other internat. orgns, Geneva, 1996–2000. *Recreation:* travel. *Address:* c/o European Commission, Rue de la Loi 200, 1049 Brussels, Belgium. *Club:* Royal Commonwealth Society.

ABBOTT, Ronald William, CVO 1989; CBE 1979; FIA, ASA, FPMI; Consultant Partner, Bacon & Woodrow, Consulting Actuaries, 1982–94 (Senior Partner, 1972–81); *b* 18 Jan. 1917; *s* of late Edgar Abbott and Susan Mary Ann Abbott; *m* 1st, 1948, Hilda Mary Hampson (*d* 1972), *d* of late William George Clarke and Emily Jane Clarke; two *d*; 2nd, 1973, Barbara Constance, *d* of late Gilbert Hugh Clough and Harriet Clough. *Educ:* St Olave's Grammar Sch. FIA 1946; FPMI 1976. Actuarial Assistant: Atlas Assce Co., 1934–38; Friends Provident & Century Life Office, 1938–46; Sen. Actuary, Bacon & Woodrow, 1946, Partner 1948. Mem., Deptl Cttee on Property Bonds and Equity Linked Life Assce, 1971–73. Dep. Chm., 1973–82, Chm., 1982–87, Occupational Pensions Bd. Mem. Council: Inst. of Actuaries, 1966–74 (Hon. Treasurer, 1971–73); Indust. Soc., 1964–84 (Life Mem., 1984); Pensions Management Inst., 1977–81 (Vice-Pres., 1978–80). Master, Worshipful Co. of Ironmongers, 1986–87. FRSA. Finlaison Medal, Inst. of Actuaries, 1988. *Publications:* A Short History of the Association of Consulting Actuaries, 1991; contrib. to Jl of Inst. of Actuaries. *Recreation:* music. *Club:* Royal Automobile.

ABDELA, Lesley Julia, MBE 1990; journalist and broadcaster, since 1986; Chief Executive, Project Parity, since 1996; Senior Partner: Eyecatcher Associates, since 1986; Shevolution, since 1998; *b* London, 17 Nov. 1945; *d* of late Frederick Abdela and Henrietta (*née* Hardy); *m* 1972 (marr. diss.); one *s*; partner, Tim Symonds. *Educ:* Queen Anne's Sch., Caversham; Châtelard Sch., Les Avants, Switzerland; Queen's Coll., Harley Street; Hammersmith Coll of Art and Building; London Coll. of Printing. Advertising Exec., Royds of London, 1968–72; Derek Forsyth Design Partnership, 1972–73; researcher for Liberal Party, H of C, 1977–79; Founder, 1980, Chair, 1980–85, Trustee, 1980–95, 300 Group (for women in politics). UK Consultant, Project Liberty, Kennedy Sch. of Govt, Harvard Univ., 1992–98. OSCE Dep. Dir for Democracy, UN Interim Admin in Kosovo, 1999. Political Editor: Cosmopolitan, 1993–96 (first Pol Ed. of a women's mag.); Radio Viva!, 1995; regular contributor to Exec. Woman mag., Woman's Jl, Mail on Sunday, Sunday Times, Guardian, Times, Independent, Glasgow Herald, etc; writer, researcher and presenter of radio and TV documentaries, incl. Women with X Appeal, 1993, Breaking Glass, 1994. Board Member: Internat. Inst. for Envmt and Develt, 1992–96; British Council, 1995–2000; Mem. Exec. Bd, Women in Mgt, 1985–88. Vice Pres., Electoral Reform Soc., 1995–. Contested (L) E Herts, 1979. Gov., Nottingham Trent Univ., 1997–2000. FRGS; FRSA; MCIJ. Hon. DLitt Nottingham Trent, 1996. *Publications:* Women with X Appeal, 1989; Breaking Through the Glass Ceilings, 1991; What Women Want, 1994; Do It!-Walk the Talk, 1995. *Recreations:* painting, ski-ing, scuba, reading, looking forward to true equality between women and men in politics and society. *Address:* Lower Windmill Oast, Lamberhurst, Kent TN3 8AL; Harper's Marsh, King's Saltern Road, Lymington, Hants SO41 9QG; *e-mail:* lesley.abdela@shevolution.com.

ABDIN, Dr Hasan; Ambassador of Sudan to the Court of St James's, since 2000; *b* 1 Jan. 1939; *m* 1966, Manahil A. Abu Kashwa; two *s* three *d*. *Educ:* Univ. of Khartoum (BA 1965); Univ. of Wisconsin (MA 1967; PhD 1970). Lectr in African Hist., Univ. of Khartoum, 1970–77; State Minister, Sudan, 1977–78; Mem., Nat. Assembly, 1978–80; Asst Prof. of Hist., Univ. of King Saud, Riyyadh, Saudi Arabia, 1983–88; Prof. of Hist., Inst. of Asian and African Studies, Univ. of Khartoum, 1988–90; Ambassador to: Algeria, 1990–92; Iraq, 1993–97; Under Sec., Min. of Foreign Affairs, Khartoum, 1998–2000. *Publications:* Introduction to African History (in Arabic), 1974; Early Sudanese Nationalism, 1986. *Recreations:* reading, walking. *Address:* Embassy of the Republic of the Sudan, 3 Cleveland Row, St James's, SW1A 1DD. *T:* (020) 7839 8080, *Fax:* (020) 7839 7560.

ABDULAH, Frank Owen; Deputy Secretary-General, Caribbean Community Secretariat, Guyana, 1989–93; *b* 8 Nov. 1928; *m*; four *d*. *Educ:* Queen's Royal Coll., Trinidad; Oxford (MA, DipEd Oxon). Held several govt posts, 1953–62, before entering Diplomatic Service at Trinidad and Tobago's Independence, 1962; Dep. Perm. Rep. (Minister Counsellor), 1970–73, Perm. Rep. (Ambassador), 1975–83, Trinidad and Tobago Perm. Mission to UN, NY; Perm. Sec. (Acting), Ministry of External Affairs, Port of Spain, 1973–75; High Comr for Trinidad and Tobago in London with concurrent accreditations as Ambassador to Denmark, Finland, France, FRG, Norway and Sweden, 1983–85; Permanent Sec., Min. of External Affairs and Internat. Trade, Trinidad and Tobago, 1985–88. Pres., UNA Trinidad and Tobago, 1987–88. *Recreations:* music, sports. *Address:* 8 Nock Road, Maraval, Trinidad.

ABDY, Sir Valentine (Robert Duff), 6th Bt *cr* 1850; European Representative, Smithsonian Institution, Washington, 1983–95 and since 1998 (Member, National Board, 1995–98; Member, National Board, Alumni); *b* 11 Sept. 1937; *s* of Sir Robert Henry Edward Abdy, 5th Bt, and Lady Diana Bridgeman (*d* 1967), *e d* of 5th Earl of Bradford; *S* father, 1976; *m* 1971, Mathilde Coche de la Ferté (marr. diss. 1982); one *s*. *Educ:* Eton. Administrator, Musée des Arts Décoratifs, Paris; Mem., Scientific Committee, Conservatoire Nationale des Arts et Métiers, 1992–; Special Advr, Internat. Fund for Promotion of Culture, UNESCO, 1991–. FRSA 1998. Chevalier des Arts et des Lettres (France), 1995. *Heir: s* Robert Etienne Eric Abdy, *b* 22 Feb. 1978. *Address:* 11 avenue de Brétigny, Garches 92380, France; Hadsley House, Lefebvre Street, St Peter Port, Guernsey. *Clubs:* Travellers, Jockey (Paris).

ABEL, Prof. Edward William, CBE 1997; PhD, DSc; FRSC; Professor of Inorganic Chemistry, University of Exeter, 1972–97, now Emeritus (Head of Department of Chemistry, 1977–88; Deputy Vice-Chancellor, 1991–94); *b* 3 Dec. 1931; *s* of Sydney and Donna Abel; *m* 1960, Margaret R. Edwards; one *s* one *d*. *Educ:* Bridgend Grammar Sch.; University Coll., Cardiff (BSc 1952); Northern Polytechnic, London (PhD 1957); *e-mail:* Served Army, 1953–55. Research Fellow, Imperial Coll., 1957–59; Lectr, later Reader, Univ. of Bristol, 1957–71. Vis. Professor: Univ. of British Columbia, 1970; Japanese Soc. for Promotion of Science, 1971; Tech. Univ. of Braunschweig, 1973; ANU, Canberra, 1990; Robert E.Welch Lectures, Texas, 1994. Royal Society of Chemistry: Mem. Council, 1977–82, 1983–87 and 1989–99; Pres., 1996–98; Chm., Local Affairs Bd, 1983–87; Chm., Divl Affairs Bd, 1989–2002; Chm., Scientific Affairs Bd, 1992–95. Main Group Chem. Medal, 1976; Tilden Medal and Lectr, 1981; Mem., Dalton Div. Council, 1977–83, 1987–91 (Sec./Treasurer, 1977–82; Vice-Pres., 1983, 1989–91; Pres., 1987–89). Perm. Sec., Internat. Confs on Organometallic Chem., 1972–89; Mem., UGC, 1986–89 (Chm., Phys. Scis Sub-Cttee, 1986–89); Nat. Advr for Chem., UFC, 1989–92; CNAA: Mem., 1991–93; Chm., Phys. Scis Cttee, 1987–91; Mem., Cttee for Academic Affairs, 1989–91. DUniv North London, 1998; Hon. DSc Exeter, 2000. *Publications:* (ed jtly) Organometallic Chemistry, vols 1–25, 1970–95; (exec. editor) Comprehensive Organometallic Chemistry, 9 vols, 1984; (exec. editor) Comprehensive Organometallic Chemistry II, 14 vols, 1995; papers to learned jls. *Address:* 1A Rosebarn Avenue, Exeter EX4 6DY. *T:* (01392) 270272; Department of Chemistry, University of Exeter, Exeter EX4 4QD. *T:* (01392) 263489, *Fax:* (01392) 263434; *e-mail:* EWAbel@ex.ac.uk.

ABEL, Kenneth Arthur, CBE 1984; DL; Clerk and Chief Executive, Dorset County Council, 1967–91 (Clerk of the Peace, 1967–73); *b* 4 April 1926; *s* of late Arthur Abel, CBE and Frances Ethel Abel; *m* 1955, Sarah Matilda, *d* of late Capt. M. P. Poynor, TD and Norah Elizabeth Poynor; three *s*. *Educ:* Durham Sch.; Glasgow Univ.; Durham Univ. (LLB). Served RA, 1944–48. Admitted Solicitor, 1953; Assistant Solicitor: Warwicks CC, 1953–54; Leics CC, 1954–59; Sen. Asst Solicitor, Northants CC, 1959–63. Chm., Assoc. of County Chief Execs, 1982–83. Past Pres., Dorset County Golf Union. DL Dorset, 1977. *Recreations:* golf, gardening. *Address:* Herne's Oak, Bradford Road, Sherborne, Dorset DT9 6BP. *T:* (01935) 813200. *Club:* Sherborne Golf (Sherborne).

ABEL, Roger Lee; Executive Vice President, Occidental Petroleum Corporation, 1999–2000, now Consultant; *b* Nebraska, 12 Aug. 1943. *Educ:* Colorado Sch. of Mines (BSc Petroleum Engrg 1965); MIT (MSc 1979). FInstPet. Served US Army, 1966–68 (Capt.). Joined Conoco Inc., 1968: prodn engr, 1968–72; Supervising Reservoir Engr, Lake Charles, Louisiana, 1972–73; Staff Engr, N America, 1973–74; Co-ordinator for W Hemisphere Planning Dept, 1974–75; Manager, Planning and Budgets, 1975–77; Exec. Asst to Conoco's Dep. Chm., 1977–78; Sloan Fellow, MIT, 1978–79; Asst Div. Manager, Offshore Div., 1979–80; Vice Pres. and Gen. Manager of Ops for Dubai Petroleum Co., 1980–82; Manager: of Ops, UK and Europe, 1982–84; of Planning, Admin and Engrg, N American Prodn, 1984–86; General Manager: Offshore and Frontier, N American Prodn, 1986–88; Prodn Engrg and Res. Dept, 1988–90; Vice-Pres. and Gen. Manager, Prodn Engrg and Res., 1990–91; Vice Pres., Exploration Prodn–Russia, 1991–93; Chm., Conoco Exploration Prodn Europe Ltd, 1993–97; Pres. and Chief Operating Officer, Occidental Oil & Gas Corp., 1997–99. Distinguished Mem., Soc. of Petroleum Engrs (Pres., 1992). *Address:* 2300 Barton Creek Boulevard #2, Austin, TX 78735, USA. *T:* (512) 3309052; *e-mail:* RLAbel@aol.com.

ABEL SMITH, Henriette Alice, (Lady Abel Smith), DCVO 1977 (CVO 1964); JP; an Extra Lady-in-Waiting to the Queen (formerly as HRH Princess Elizabeth), since 1987 (a Lady-in-Waiting, 1949–87); *b* 6 June 1914; *d* of late Comdr Francis Charles Cadogan, RN, and late Ruth Evelyn (*née* Howard, *widow* of Captain Gardner Sebastian Bazley); *m* 1st, 1939, Sir Anthony Frederick Mark Palmer, 4th Bt (killed in action, 1941); one *s* one *d*; 2nd, 1953, Sir Alexander Abel Smith, KCVO, TD (*d* 1980); one *s* one *d*. JP Tunbridge Wells 1955, Gloucestershire 1971. *Address:* The Garden House, Quenington, Cirencester, Glos GL7 5BN. *T:* (01285) 750231.

See also Sir C. M. Palmer, Bt.

ABEL SMITH, Col Richard Francis; Vice Lord-Lieutenant of Nottinghamshire, 1991–99; *b* 11 Oct. 1933; *s* of Col Sir Henry Abel Smith, KCMG, KCVO, DSO and late Lady May Cambridge, *o d* of Earl of Athlone, KG, GCB, GCMG, GCVO, DSO, PC, FRS and Princess Alice, Countess of Athlone, VA, GCVO, GBE; *m* 1960, Marcia Kendrew, JP, DL (High Sherrif, Notts, 1990–91); one *d*. *Educ:* Eton; RMA Sandhurst; Royal Agric. Coll., Cirencester. Commissioned, 1954, Royal Horse Guards (The Blues); Escort Comdr and ADC to Govs of Cyprus, 1957–60; Adjutant, 1960–63; Instr, Sandhurst, 1961–63. Comdr, Sherwood Rangers Sqn, Royal Yeomanry Regt, 1967–69, Hon. Col, 1979–89. Chm., Sports Aid Foundn (E Midlands), 1979–90. County Comr, Scouts (Notts), 1966–75. DL 1970, High Sheriff, 1978, Notts. *Recreations:* fishing, shooting, riding. *Address:* Blidworth Dale, Ravenshead, Notts NG15 9AL. *Clubs:* White's, Army and Navy.

ABELL, (John) David; Chairman, Jourdan (formerly Thomas Jourdan) plc, since 1997; Director, Leicester Football Club plc; *b* 15 Dec. 1942; *s* of Leonard Abell and Irene (*née* Anderson); *m* 1st, 1967, Anne Janette Priestley (marr. diss. 1977); three *s*; 2nd, 1981, Sandra Dawn Atkinson (marr. diss. 1986); one *s* one *d*; 3rd, 1988, Juliana, *d* of late Prof. J. L. I. Fennell, PhD, FRSL and of Marina Lopukhin. *Educ:* Univ. of Leeds (BAEcon); London School of Economics (Dip. Business Admin). Assistant to Cash and Investment Manager, Ford Motor Co., 1962–65; Asst, Treasurer's Office, AEI, 1965–67; British Leyland: Central Staffs, 1968–69; Manager, Investments and Banking, 1969–70; Chm. and Chief Exec., Prestcold Div., 1970–72; Corporate Treasurer, 1972; First Nat. Finance Corp., Nov. 1972–Aug. 1973; re-joined British Leyland as Man. Dir, Leyland Australia, 1974–75; Group Man. Dir, Leyland Special Products, 1975; Man. Dir, BL Commercial Vehicles, Chm. and Chief Exec., Leyland Vehicles Ltd, 1978–81; Chm. and Chief Exec., Suter Electrical, subseq. Suter plc, 1981–96. *Recreations:* horse racing and breeding, wine, tennis, music, Rugby, soccer. *Address:* Jourdan plc, Elm House, Elmer Street North, Grantham, Lincs NG31 6RE.

ABELL, John Norman; Chairman, Europe, CIBC Wood Gundy Inc., 1990–91; Vice-Chairman, Wood Gundy Inc., London, 1988–91; *b* 18 Sept. 1931; *s* of Sir George Edmond Brackenbury Abell; *m* 1957, Mora Delia (*née* Clifton-Brown); two *s* one *d*. *Educ:* Marlborough Coll.; Worcester Coll., Oxford (MA). Wood Gundy Ltd: joined in Vancouver, Canada, 1955; Internat. Man. Dir, Toronto, 1962; Director and Vice-Pres., 1966; Pres., Wood Gundy Inc., New York, 1966; Vice-Chm., Wood Gundy Ltd, Toronto, 1977; Dep. Chm. and Chief Exec., Orion Royal Bank Ltd, 1982, Chm. and Chief Exec. Officer, 1983–85; Vice-Chm., Wood Gundy Inc., Toronto, 1986–88; Director: Echo Bay Mines, Edmonton, Canada, 1980–; First Australia Prime Income Investment Co. Ltd, 1986–92; Minerals & Resources Corp. Ltd, 1985–89; Scotia Synfuels Ltd, Toronto, 1987–97; Euro-clear Clearance System, 1989–92; Stelco Inc., Hamilton, Ont, 1993–; A. T. Plastics Inc., Brampton, Ont, 1993–; Longwall Internat., 1993–95; Investec Bank (UK), 1993–. Mem., Securities and Investments Bd, 1985–86; Gov., Toronto Stock Exchange, 1987–88. Chairman: Arthritis Soc. of Canada, 1981–82; Canada Meml Foundn, 1992–. Mem. Council, GAP Activity Projects, 1983–98. Dir, London House for Overseas Graduates, 1984; Mem. Council, Reading Univ., 1984. *Address:* Whittonditch House, Ramsbury, Marlborough, Wilts SN8 2PZ. *T:* (01672) 520449. *Clubs:* Boodle's, MCC; Toronto, York (Toronto).

ABELSON, Michael Andrew; a District Judge (Magistrates' Courts), Merseyside, since 2001; a Recorder, since 2000; *b* 22 March 1952; *s* of Harvey Abelson and Eva Abelson (*née* Newman); *m* 1994, Angela Bernadette Therese Walsh, BEd, DipEFL, *d* of Joseph Walsh and Frances Walsh (*née* Begley); one *s*. *Educ:* Leyton County High Sch.; University Coll., London (LLB Hons 1975). Called to the Bar, Middle Temple, 1976; in practice at the Bar, Northern, and Wales and Chester Circuits, 1977–98; Asst Recorder, 1997–2000; acting Stipendiary Magistrate: S Yorks, 1993–98; Gtr Manchester, 1995–98; Stipendiary Magistrate, later a Dist Judge (Magistrates' Courts), Gtr Manchester, 1998–2001. *Recreations:* travel, ski-ing, tennis. *Address:* Liverpool City Magistrates' Court, Dale Street, Liverpool L2 2JQ. *T:* (0151) 243 5596.

ABER, Prof. Geoffrey Michael, FRCP; Professor of Renal Medicine, University of Keele, 1982–93; *b* 19 Feb. 1928; *s* of David and Hilda Aber; *m* 1964, Eleanor Maureen; one *s* one *d*. *Educ:* Leeds Grammar School; University of Leeds (MB, ChB, MD with distinction); PhD Birmingham. Leeds Gen. Infirmary, 1952–54; RAMC, 1954–56; Queen Elizabeth Hosp., Birmingham (Univ. of Birmingham), 1956–57, 1958–65; Brompton Hosp., London, 1957–58; Research Fellow: Univ. of Birmingham (Depts of Exptl Path. and Medicine), 1958–59 and 1960–64; McGill Univ., 1959–60; Wellcome Sen. Res. Fellow in Clinical Sci., 1964–65; Keele University: Prof. and Adviser in Clinical Res., 1979–82; Head of Dept. of Postgrad. Medicine, 1982–89; Dean of Postgrad. Medicine, 1989–91. *Publications:* contribs to: Recent Advances in Renal Medicine, 1983; Postgraduate Nephrology, 1985; Textbook of Genitourinary Surgery, 1985; scientific papers in learned jls. *Recreations:* music, sport, motor cars. *Address:* Mill Green House, Stone Rings Grange, Harrogate HG2 9HU. *T:* (01423) 871737; *e-mail:* g.m.aber@btinternet.com.

ABERCONWAY, 3rd Baron, *cr* 1911, of Bodnant; **Charles Melville McLaren,** Bt 1902; JP; President: John Brown & Co. Ltd, 1978–85 (Director, 1939–85; Chairman, 1953–78); English China Clays Ltd, since 1984 (Director, 1935–87; Chairman, 1963–84); President, Royal Horticultural Society, 1961–84, now President Emeritus; *b* 16 April 1913; *e s* of 2nd Baron Aberconway, CBE, LLD and Christabel (*d* 1974), *y d* of Sir Melville Macnaghten, CB; *S* father, 1953; *m* 1st, 1941, Deirdre Knewstub (marr. diss. 1949); one *s* two *d*; 2nd, 1949, Ann Lindsay Bullard, *o d* of Mrs A. L. Aymer, New York City; one *s*. *Educ:* Eton; New Coll., Oxford. Barrister, Middle Temple, 1937. Served War of 1939–45, 2nd Lieut RA. Deputy Chairman: Sun Alliance & London Insurance, 1976–85 (Dir, London Assurance, 1953); Westland Aircraft, 1979–84 (Dir, 1947–85); Dir, National Westminster Bank (formerly National Provincial Bank), 1953–83. Comr-Gen., Internat. Garden Fest., Liverpool, 1984; Director: Nat. Garden Fest. (Stoke on Trent) 1986 Ltd; Glasgow Garden Fest. Ltd, 1988; Gateshead Garden Fest. Ltd, 1990; Ebbw Vale Garden Fest. Ltd, 1992. JP Denbighshire 1946; High Sheriff of Denbighshire 1950. *Recreations:* gardening, travel. *Heir: s* Hon. Henry Charles McLaren [*b* 26 May 1948; *m* 1981, Sally, *yr d* of Captain C. N. Lentaigne; one *s* two *d*]. *Address:* 25 Egerton Terrace, SW3 2DP; Bodnant, Tal-y-cafn, Colwyn Bay, Clwyd.

ABERCORN, 5th Duke of, *cr* 1868; **James Hamilton,** KG 1999; Lord of Paisley, 1587; Lord of Abercorn, 1603; Earl of Abercorn and Lord of Hamilton, Mountcastle and Kilpatrick, 1606; Baron of Strabane, 1617; Viscount of Strabane, 1701; Viscount Hamilton, 1786; Marquess of Abercorn, 1790; Marquess of Hamilton, 1868; Bt 1660; Lord Lieutenant of Co. Tyrone, since 1987; Lord Steward of HM Household, since 2001; company director; *b* 4 July 1934; *er s* of 4th Duke of Abercorn, and Lady Mary Kathleen Crichton (Dowager Duchess of Abercorn, GCVO) (*d* 1990); *S* father, 1979; *m* 1966, Anastasia Alexandra, *e d* of late Lt-Col Harold Phillips, Checkendon Court, Reading; two *s* one *d*. *Educ:* Eton Coll.; Royal Agricultural Coll., Cirencester, Glos. Joined HM Army, Oct. 1952; Lieut, Grenadier Guards. MP (UU) Fermanagh and South Tyrone, 1964–70. Dir, Northern Bank Ltd, 1970–97. Chm., Laganside Develt Corp., 1989–96 (Laganside Ltd, 1986–89); Dir, NI Industrial Develt Bd, 1982–87. Member: Council of Europe, 1968–70; European Economic and Social Cttee, 1973–78. President: Royal UK Beneficent Assoc., 1979–; Building Socs Assoc., 1986–92; Patron, Royal Ulster Agricl Soc., 1990–96. Trustee, Winston Churchill Meml Trust, 1991–. Col, Irish Guards, 2000. High Sheriff of Co. Tyrone, 1970. Hon. Mem., RICS, 1995. Hon. LLB QUB, 1997. *Recreations:* shooting, ski-ing. *Heir: s* Marquess of Hamilton, *qv*. *Address:* Barons Court, Omagh, Northern Ireland BT78 4EZ. *T:* (028) 8166 1470, *Fax:* (028) 8166 2231; 10 Little Chester Street, SW1X 7AL. *T:* (020) 7235 5518. *Club:* Brooks's.

ABERCROMBIE, Ian Ralph; QC (Scot.) 1994; *b* 7 July 1955; *s* of Ralph Abercrombie and of late Jean Abercrombie (*née* Lithgow). *Educ:* Edinburgh Univ. (LLB Hons 1978). Called to the Bar: Scotland, 1981; Lincoln's Inn, 1992. *Address:* Advocates' Library, Parliament House, Edinburgh EH1 1RF. *T:* (0131) 226 5071; 7 Lauder Road, Edinburgh EH9 2EW. *T:* (0131) 668 2489.

ABERCROMBY, Sir Ian George, 10th Bt *cr* 1636, of Birkenbog; *b* 30 June 1925; *s* of Robert Ogilvie Abercromby (*g s* of 5th Bt); *S* kinsman, 1972; *m* 1st, 1950, Joyce Beryl, *d* of Leonard Griffiths; 2nd, 1959, Fanny Mary, *d* of late Dr Graham Udale-Smith; one *d*; 3rd, 1976, Diana Marjorie, *d* of H. G. Cockell, and *widow* of Captain Ian Charles Palliser

Galloway. *Educ:* Lancing Coll.; Bloxham Sch. *Heir:* none. *Clubs:* Ski Club of Great Britain; Kandahar; Kildare Street (Dublin).

ABERDARE, 4th Baron, *cr* 1873, of Duffryn; **Morys George Lyndhurst Bruce,** KBE 1984; PC 1974; DL; a Deputy Speaker, House of Lords; *b* 16 June 1919; *s* of 3rd Baron Aberdare, GBE, and Margaret Bethune (*née* Black); *S* father 1957; *m* 1946, Maud Helen Sarah, *o d* of Sir John Dashwood, 10th Bt, CVO; four *s*. *Educ:* Winchester; New College, Oxford (MA). Welsh Guards, 1939–46. Minister of State, DHSS, 1970–74; Minister Without Portfolio, 1974; Chm. of Cttees, H of L, 1976–92; elected Mem., H of L, 1999. Chairman: Albany Life Assurance Co. Ltd, 1975–92; Metlife (UK) Ltd, 1986–92. Chm., The Football Trust, 1979–98; President: Welsh Nat. Council of YMCAs; Kidney Res. Unit for Wales Foundn; Tennis and Rackets Assoc. Hon. LLD Wales, 1985. DL Dyfed, 1985. Bailiff Grand Cross, 1974, Prior for Wales, 1958–88, OStJ. *Publications:* The Story of Tennis, 1959; Willis Faber Book of Tennis and Rackets, 1980. *Recreations:* Real tennis and rackets. *Heir: s* Hon. Alastair John Lyndhurst Bruce [*b* 2 May 1947; *m* 1971, Elizabeth Mary Culbert, *d* of John Foulkes; one *s* one *d*]. *Address:* 26 Crown Lodge, 12 Elystan Street, SW3 3PP. *Clubs:* Boodle's, Lansdowne, MCC, Queen's (Pres., 1993–96).

ABERDEEN, Bishop of, (RC), since 1977; **Rt Rev. Mario Joseph Conti;** *b* Elgin, Moray, 20 March 1934; *s* of Louis Joseph Conti and Josephine Quintilia Panicali. *Educ:* St Marie's Convent School and Springfield, Elgin; Blairs Coll., Aberdeen; Pontifical Gregorian Univ. (Scots College), Rome. PhL 1955, STL 1959. FRSE 1995. Ordained, Rome, 1958; Curate, St Mary's Cathedral, Aberdeen, 1959–62; Parish Priest, St Joachim's, Wick and St Anne's, Thurso (joint charge), 1962–77. Chairman: Scottish Catholic Heritage Commn, 1980–; Commn for the Pastoral Care of Migrant Workers and Tourists (incl. Apostleship of the Sea, Scotland), 1978–85; Pres.-Treasurer, Scottish Catholic Internat. Aid Fund, 1978–85; Pres., National Liturgy Commn, 1981–85; Scottish Mem., Episcopal Bd, Internat. Commn for English in the Liturgy, 1978–87; Mem., Bishops' Jt Bio-ethics Cttee (formerly Cttee for Bio-ethical Issues), 1982–; Pres., Nat. Christian Doctrine and Unity Commn, 1985–; Consultor-Mem., Secretariat, later Council, for Promotion of Christian Unity (Rome), 1984–; Convener, Action of Churches Together in Scotland, 1990–93; Co-moderator, Jt Working Gp, WCC and RC Church, 1996–; Member: Pontifical Commn for Cultural Heritage of the Church, Rome, 1994–; Historic Bldgs Council of Scotland, 2000–. Conventual Chaplain *ad honorem*, British Assoc., SMO Malta, 1991– (Principal Chaplain, 1995–2000). Hon. DD Aberdeen, 1989. KCHS 1989. Commendatore, Order of Merit of the Italian Republic, 1981. *Recreations:* music, art, book browsing, TV, travel, swimming. *Address:* Bishop's House, 3 Queen's Cross, Aberdeen AB15 4XU. *T:* (01224) 319154.

ABERDEEN, (St Andrew's Cathedral), Provost of; *see* Wightman, Very Rev. W. D.

ABERDEEN AND ORKNEY, Bishop of, since 1992; **Most Rev. Andrew Bruce Cameron;** Primus of the Episcopal Church in Scotland, since 2000; *b* 2 May 1941; *s* of Andrew and Helen Cameron; *m* 1974, Elaine Gingles; two *s*. *Educ:* Eastwood Secondary Sch., Glasgow; Edinburgh Theol Coll.; Edinburgh Univ. (Cert. in Past. Studies); Urban Theology Unit, Sheffield (Dip. in Theology and Mission). Ordained deacon 1964, priest 1965; Assistant Curate: St Michael and All Angels, Helensburgh, 1964–67; Holy Cross, Edinburgh, 1967–70; Diocesan and Provincial Youth Chaplain and Chaplain, St Mary's Cathedral, Edinburgh, 1970–75; Rector, St Mary's, Dalmahoy and Anglican Chaplain Heriot-Watt Univ., 1975–82; Churches Develt Officer in Livingston Ecumenical Parish, 1982–88; Rector, St John's, Perth and Convenor of Provincial Mission Bd, 1988–92. *Recreations:* golf, swimming, walking, singing, listening to music, theatre, reading 'whodunnits'. *Address:* Ashley House, 16 Ashley Gardens, Aberdeen AB10 6RQ. *T:* (01224) 208142, *Fax:* (01224) 312141; (office) *T:* (01224) 636653, *Fax:* (01224) 636186; *e-mail:* bishop@aberdeen.anglican.org.
See also Bishop of Argyll and the Isles.

ABERDEEN AND ORKNEY, Dean of; *see* Stranraer-Mull, Very Rev. G.

ABERDEEN AND TEMAIR, 6th Marquess of, *cr* 1916; **Alastair Ninian John Gordon;** Bt (NS) 1642; Earl of Aberdeen, Viscount Formartine, Lord Haddo, Methlic, Tarves and Kellie, 1682 (Scot.); Viscount Gordon 1814, Earl of Haddo 1916 (UK); painter; exhibitions of botanical painting in London, New York, Chicago, Sydney; *b* 20 July 1920; *s* of 3rd Marquess of Aberdeen and Temair, DSO, and Cécile Elizabeth (*d* 1948), *d* of George Drummond, Swaylands, Penshurst, Kent; *S* brother, 1984; *m* 1950, Anne (ceramic sculptor), *d* of late Lt-Col Gerald Barry, MC; one *s* two *d*. *Educ:* Harrow; Camberwell Sch. of Art. Served War of 1939–45, Captain Scots Guards. Member: Internat. Assoc. of Art Critics; Bach Choir, 1939–82. *Recreations:* wine, women and song. *Heir: s* Earl of Haddo, *qv*. *Address:* Quick's Green, near Pangbourne, Berks RG8 8SN. *Clubs:* Arts (Chm., 1966–76), MCC; Puffins (Edinburgh).

ABERDEEN AND TEMAIR, June Marchioness of; (Beatrice Mary) June Gordon, CBE 1989 (MBE 1971); DL; Musical Director and Conductor, Haddo House Choral and Operatic Society (formerly Haddo House Choral Society), since 1945; *d* of Arthur Paul Boissier, MA, and Dorothy Christina Leslie Smith; *m* 1939, David George Ian Alexander Gordon (later 4th Marquess of Aberdeen and Temair, CBE, TD) (*d* 1974); two adopted *s* two adopted *d*. *Educ:* Southlands School, Harrow; Royal Coll. of Music. GRSM, ARCM. Teacher of Music, Bromley High School for Girls, 1936–39. Director of Haddo House Choral and Operatic Soc. and Arts Centre, 1945–. Chairman: Scottish Children's League, 1969–94; NE Scotland Music School, 1975–; Adv. Council, Scottish Opera, 1979–92; Chm. (local), Adv. Cttee, Aberdeen Internat. Festival of Music and the Performing Arts, 1980–96. Governor: Gordonstoun Sch., 1971–86; Royal Scottish Acad. of Music and Drama, 1979–82. FRCM 1967; FRSE 1983; FRSAMD 1985. DStJ 1977; GCStJ 1995. DL Aberdeenshire, 1971. Hon. LLD Aberdeen, 1968; Hon. DMus CNAA, 1991. *Publications:* contribs to Aberdeen Univ. Jl, RCM magazine. *Address:* Haddo House, Aberdeen AB41 7EQ. *T:* (01651) 851216. *Club:* New (Edinburgh).

ABERDOUR, Lord; John Stewart Sholto Douglas; *b* 17 Jan. 1952; *s* and *heir* of 22nd Earl of Morton, *qv*; *m* 1985, Amanda, *yr d* of David Mitchell, Kirkcudbright; one *s* two *d*. *Educ:* Dunrobin Castle School. Studied Agriculture, Aberdeen Univ. *Heir: s* Master of Aberdour, *qv*. *Address:* Haggs Farm, Kirknewton, Midlothian EH27 8EE.

ABERDOUR, Master of; Hon. John David Sholto Douglas; *b* 28 May 1986; *s* and *heir* of Lord Aberdour, *qv*.

ABERGAVENNY, 6th Marquess of, *cr* 1876; **Christopher George Charles Nevill;** Baron Abergavenny 1450; Earl of Abergavenny and Viscount Nevill 1784; Earl of Lewes 1876; *b* 23 April 1955; *yr s* of Lord Rupert Charles Montacute Nevill, CVO, *yr s* of 4th Marquess of Abergavenny and of Lady Anne Camilla Eveline Wallop, *d* of 9th Earl of Portsmouth; *S* uncle, 2000; *m* 1985, Venetia Jane, *er d* of late Frederick Gerard Maynard; one *d* (one *s* decd). *Educ:* Harrow. Dir, Nevill Estate Co. Ltd, 1985–. Mem., Wealden DC, 1999–. *Heir:* (to Earldom and Barony of Abergavenny and Viscountcy of Nevill only) *kinsman* David Michael Ralph Nevill [*b* 20 June 1941; *m* 1972, Katherine Mary, *d* of Rossmore Derrick Westenra; one *s* two *d*]. *Address:* Eridge Park, Eridge, Tunbridge Wells, Kent TN3 9JT. *T:* (01892) 750766. *Club:* White's.

ABERGAVENNY, Marchioness of; Mary Patricia Nevill, DCVO 1981 (CVO 1970); an Extra Lady of the Bedchamber to the Queen, 1960–66 and since 1987 (a Lady of the Bedchamber, 1966–87); *b* 20 Oct. 1915; *d* of late Lt-Col John Fenwick Harrison, Royal Horse Guards, and Hon. Margery Olive Edith, *d* of 3rd Baron Burnham, DSO; *m* 1938, 5th Marquess of Abergavenny, KG, OBE; three *d* (and one *s* one *d* decd). *Address:* c/o Freemantle Farmhouse, North Oakley, Tadley, Hants.

ABERNETHY, Hon. Lord; John Alastair Cameron; a Senator of the College of Justice in Scotland, since 1992; *b* 1 Feb. 1938; *s* of William Philip Legerwood Cameron and Kathleen Milthorpe (*née* Parker); *m* 1968, Elspeth Mary Dunlop Miller; three *s*. *Educ:* St Mary's, Melrose; Trinity Coll., Glenalmond; Pembroke Coll., Oxford (MA 1961; Hon. Fellow, 1993). Nat. Service, 1956–58 (2nd Lieut, RASC). Called to the Bar, Inner Temple, 1963; admitted Mem., Faculty of Advocates, 1966, Vice-Dean, 1983–92; QC (Scotland) 1979. Advocate-Depute, 1972–75; Standing Jun. Counsel; to Dept of Energy, 1976–79; to Scottish Develt Dept, 1978–79. Legal Chm., Pensions Appeal Tribunals for Scotland, 1979–92 (Pres., 1985–92). International Bar Association: Chm., Judges' Forum, 1994–98 (Vice-Chm., 1993–94); Mem. Council, Section on Legal Practice, 1998–; Mem. Council, Human Rights Inst., 1998–2000. Pres., Scottish Medico-Legal Soc., 1996–2000. Mem. Exec. Cttee, Soc. for Welfare and Teaching of the Blind (Edinburgh and SE Scotland), 1979–92. Trustee, Arthur Smith Meml Trust, 1975– (Chm., 1990–). *Publications:* Medical Negligence: an introduction, 1983; (contrib.) Reproductive Medicine and the Law, 1990. *Recreations:* travel, sport, nature conservation, Africana. *Address:* Court of Session, Parliament House, Edinburgh EH1 1RQ. *T:* (0131) 225 2595, *Fax:* (0131) 240 6711.

ABERNETHY, William Leslie, CBE 1972; FCA, CPFA; Managing Trustee, Municipal Mutual Insurance Ltd, and Director of associated companies, 1973–87; Comptroller of Financial Services, Greater London Council, 1972–73 (Treasurer, 1964–72) and Chief Financial Officer, Inner London Education Authority, 1967–73; *b* 10 June 1910; *s* of Robert and Margaret Abernethy; *m* 1937, Irene Holden (*d* 1998); one *s*. *Educ:* Darwen Grammar Sch., Lancs. Hindle & Jepson, Chartered Accts, Darwen, 1925–31; Borough Treasurer's Dept, Darwen, 1931–37; Derbyshire CC, Treasurer's Dept, 1937–48 (Dep. Co. Treas., 1944–48); 1st Treas., Newcastle upon Tyne Regional Hosp. Bd, 1948–50. LCC: Asst Comptroller, 1950–56; Dep. Comptroller, 1956–64; Comptroller, Sept. 1964–Mar. 1965. Chm. Exec. Council, RIPA, 1959–60. Mem. Council, IMTA, 1966–73. *Publications:* Housing Finance and Accounts (with A. R. Holmes), 1953; Internal Audit in Local Authorities and Hospitals, 1957; Internal Audit in the Public Boards, 1957; contribs professional jls. *Address:* 6 Thornhill Close, Port Erin, Isle of Man IM9 6NF. *T:* (01624) 835316.

ABINGDON, Earl of; *see* Lindsey and Abingdon, Earl of.

ABINGER, 8th Baron *cr* 1835; **James Richard Scarlett;** DL; Lieutenant-Colonel, late Royal Artillery; farmer and company director, retired; *b* 28 Sept. 1914; *e s* of 7th Baron and Marjorie (*d* 1965), 2nd *d* of John McPhillamy, Blair Athol, Bathurst, NSW; *S* father, 1943; *m* 1957, Isla Carolyn, *o d* of late Vice-Adm. J. W. Rivett-Carnac, CB, CBE, DSC; two *s*. *Educ:* Eton; Magdalene College, Cambridge (MA 1952). India, France, Airborne Corps, and attached RAF; RNXS, 1968. DL Essex, 1968. KStJ. *Heir: s* Hon. James Harry Scarlett [*b* 28 May 1959; *m* 1995, Tracy, *d* of N. Cloutier]. *Address:* Sheepcote House, Queen Street, Castle Hedingham, Halstead, Essex CO9 3HA. *T:* (01787) 460388; 7 Cumberland Street, SW1V 4LS. *T:* (020) 7828 4708. *Clubs:* Carlton, Royal Automobile.

ABLE, Graham George; Master, Dulwich College, since 1997; *b* 28 July 1947; *s* of George Jasper Able and Irene Helen Able (*née* Gaff); *m* 1969, Mary Susan Munro; one *s* one *d*. *Educ:* Worksop Coll.; Trinity Coll., Cambridge (MA Nat. Scis 1968, PGCE 1969); MA Social Scis Dunelm 1983. Teacher, Sutton Valence Sch., 1969–83 (Boarding Housemaster, 1976–83); Second Master, Barnard Castle Sch., 1983–88; Headmaster, Hampton Sch., 1988–96. Co-Chm., HMC and GSA Educn and Academic Policy Cttee, 1998–; Mem. Council, Edexcel, 1998–. Member: Council and Court, ICSTM, 1999–; Council, Roedean Sch., 2000–. FRSA 1994. MInstD 1995. *Publications:* (jtly) Head to Head, 1992; (jtly) Head to HoD, 1998. *Recreations:* cricket, golf, sailing, contract bridge. *Address:* Elm Lawn, Dulwich Common, Dulwich, SE21 7EW. *T:* (020) 8693 3601. *Clubs:* MCC, East India (Hon. Mem.).

ABNEY-HASTINGS, family name of **Countess of Loudoun.**

ABOYNE, Earl of; Alistair Granville Gordon; *b* 26 July 1973; *s* and *heir* of Marquess of Huntly, *qv*. *Educ:* Harrow. *Address:* c/o Aboyne Castle, Aberdeenshire.

ABRAHAM, Ann; Legal Services Ombudsman for England and Wales, since 1997; *b* 25 Aug. 1952; *d* of John Kenneth and Kathleen Mary Marsden. *Educ:* Bedford Coll., Univ. of London (BA Hons German); Postgrad. DMS. MCIH. Housing Manager, Local Govt, 1975–80; Ops Manager, Regional Dir and Ops Dir, Housing Corp., 1980–90; Chief Exec., NACAB, 1991–97. Non-exec. Dir, Benefits Agency, 1997–2001. Mem., Cttee on Standards in Public Life, 2000–. *Recreations:* walking, family, friends, football. *Address:* Office of the Legal Services Ombudsman, 22 Oxford Court, Oxford Street, Manchester M2 3WQ.

ABRAHAM, Neville Victor, CBE 2001; Chairman, Groupe Chez Gérard plc, since 1994 (Joint Founder, 1986; Chief Executive, 1994–99); *b* 22 Jan. 1937; *s* of late Solomon Abraham and of Sarah (*née* Raphael). *Educ:* Brighton Coll.; London Sch. of Econs (BSc Hons). Marketing Asst, Young & Rubicam, 1961–63; Sen. Principal, DTI, 1963–71; Corporate Policy Advr, Harold Whitehead & Partners, 1971–74; Founder, Les Amis du Vin, 1974 (Man. Dir, 1974–86); Chm., Amis du Vin Gp, 1980–84; Dir, Kennedy Brookes plc, 1984–86. Vis. Lectr, several business schools, 1972–81. Chairman: Exec. Cttee, Covent Garden Fest., 1993–; London Internat. String Quartet Comp., 2000–. *Publication:* Big Business and Government: the new disorder, 1974. *Recreations:* music, opera, walking, good food and wine, cricket. *Address:* (office) 8 Shelton Street, WC2H 9UW. *Clubs:* Royal Automobile, Home House, MCC.

ABRAHAM-WILLIAMS, Rev. Gethin; General Secretary, CYTÛN: Churches Together in Wales, since 1998; *s* of late Lt Col Emlyn Abraham-Williams, DL, and of Anne Elizabeth Abraham-Williams; *m* 1977, Denise Frances Harding; one *s* one *d*. *Educ:* Ysgol yr Urdd, Aberystwyth; Ardwyn Grammar Sch., Aberystwyth; UC of Wales, Aberystwyth; Regent's Park Coll., Oxford (BA Hons Theol. 1964; MA 1967; Chm., Oxford Theol Colls' Union, 1963). Ordained 1965; Asst Minister, Queen's Road Baptist Ch (with Lenton's Lane, Hawkesbury), Coventry, 1964–68; Minister: Chester Rd Baptist Ch, Sutton Coldfield, 1968–73; Sutton Baptist Ch, Surrey, 1973–80; Ecumenical Officer and Exec. Sec., Milton Keynes Christian Council, 1981–90; Bp of Oxford's Ecumenical Officer, Milton Keynes, 1981–90; Gen. Sec., ENFYS: Covenanted Churches in Wales, with Provincial Officer for Ecumenism, Ch in Wales, 1990–98. Ed., Baptist Ministers'

Fellowship Jl, 1998–. Baptist Union of GB: Member: Council, 1971–73 and 1993–95; Wkg Gp on LEPs, 1982–90; Worship and Doctrine Cttee, 1993–95. Mem., 1981–90, Moderator, 1988–90, Consultative Cttee for LEPs in England; British Council of Churches: Mem., Bd for Ecumenical Affairs, 1987–90; Observer: Nat. (RC) Conf. of Priests, 1983 and 1984; English ARC, 1988–90; Mem., Steering Cttee, CCBI, 1992–96, 1998–; Mem., Free Church Fed. Council, 1991–96; Mem. Council, CYTÛN, 1995–; Mem., Ecumenical Adv. Gp, ACC, 1997. Member: Warwicks Probationery and After Care Service, 1970–73; Marjory Fry and St Leonard's Trust Housing Cttee, 1970–73; Westlake Pastoral Lectr, Regent's Pk Coll., Oxford, 1973. Mem., Order of St Luke, 1961–. Radio presenter, BBC World Service, Radio 4, Radio Wales, etc. *Publications:* (ed) Christian Baptism and Church Membership, Vol. II, 1994; (ed jtly) Letters to Friends, 1996; (ed) Towards the Making of an Ecumenical Bishop in Wales, 1997; contrib. to Birmingham Post, Expository Times, Epworth Rev., Baptist Times, Cristion, etc. *Recreations:* radio, travel, theatre, books, eating out. *Address:* CYTÛN, 11 St Helen's Road, Swansea SA1 4AL. *T:* (01792) 460876, *Fax:* (01792) 469391. *Club:* Rotary (Sutton Coldfield).

ABRAHAMS, Anthony Claud Walter; advocate and solicitor, Brunei Darussalam, since 1987; *b* 16 June 1923; *s* of late Rt Hon. Sir Sidney Abrahams, QC, and of Ruth Bowman; *m* 1st, 1950, Laila Myking; two *s* one *d*; 2nd, 1982, Elizabeth, *d* of late Comdr A. E. Bryant, RN. *Educ:* Bedford Sch.; Emmanuel Coll., Cambridge (MA). Barrister-at-law. Served War: Wavell Cadet, Bangalore, 1942–43; commnd 3/12 Royal Bn, Frontier Force Regt, 1943–45; India, N Africa, Italy, Greece (despatches). Called to the Bar, Middle Temple, 1951; practised Midland Circuit, 1951–64. Gov., 1966–88, Chm., 1978–88, Harpur Trust (the Bedford Charity). Centre for British Teachers: Founder, 1964; Dir, 1973–82; Life Pres., 1982. Mem., Educn Cttee, British-Malaysian Soc., 1986–. Liveryman, Worshipful Co. of Glaziers, 1976. Kt, Order of Uggla (Norway), 1962. *Recreations:* golf, watching cricket and Rugby, wine, travel. *Address:* Goldsmith Building, Temple, EC4Y 7BL. *T:* (020) 7353 7913. *Clubs:* Garrick, MCC, Jesters.

ABRAHAMS, Ivor, RA 1991 (ARA 1989); FRBS 1996; sculptor; *b* 10 Jan. 1935; *s* of Harry Abrahams and Rachel Kalisky; *m* 1st, 1966, Victoria Taylor; (one *s* decd); 2nd, 1974, Evelyne Horvais; one *s*. *Educ:* Wigan Grammar Sch.; St Martin's and Camberwell Schools of Art. NDD(ScSp). Visiting Lecturer: Birmingham College of Art, 1960–63; Coventry College of Art, 1963–66; RCA, Slade Sch., 1980–82. *Major Exhibitions:* Kölnischer Kunstverein, Cologne, 1973; Ikon Gall., Birmingham, 1976; Yorkshire Sculpture Park, Wakefield, 1984. *Public Collections:* Arts Council of GB; Bibliotheque Nat., Paris; Brit. Council; Denver Mus., Colorado; Metropolitan Mus., NY; Nat. Gall. of Australia, Canberra; Tate Gall.; Mus. of Modern Art, NY; V&A Mus.; Wilhelm Lembruck Mus., Duisburg, W Germany; Boymans Mus., Rotterdam, etc. Winston Churchill Fellow, 1990. *Publications:* E. A. Poe: poems and tales (foreword Norbert Lynton), 1976; Oxford Garden Sketchbook (foreword Robert Melville), 1977. *Recreations:* golf, photography. *Address:* c/o Royal Academy, Burlington House, W1V 0DS. *Clubs:* Chelsea Arts, Colony Rooms.

ABRAHAMS, Michael David, CBE 1994 (MBE 1988); DL; Chairman: The London Clinic, since 1996; Kingston Communications plc, since 1999; *b* 23 Nov. 1937; *s* of Alexander Abrahams and Anne Abrahams (*née* Sokoloff); *m* 1968, Amanda Atha; one *s* two *d*. *Educ:* Shrewsbury; Worcester Coll., Oxford. Nat. Service, RM (commnd). Man. Dir, AW (Securities) Ltd, 1968–73; Chairman: Champion Associated Weavers Ltd, 1974–80; Associated Weavers Europe NV, 1974–83; Weavercraft Carpets Ltd, 1980–85; Dep. Chm., John Crowther PLC, 1985–88; Director: Prudential Corp. plc, 1984–2000 (Dep. Chm., 1991–2000); John Waddington plc, 1984–2000; Cavaghan & Gray plc, 1987–98 (Chm., 1992–98); Drummond Gp plc, 1989–2001; Minorplanet Systems plc, 1997– (Chm., 1997–). Pres., British Carpet Mfrs Assoc., 1979–80. Dep. Chm. Council, Prince of Wales's Inst. of Architecture, 1991–96; Dir, Rank Foundn, 1992–; Regl Chm., NT for Yorks, 1996–. Jt Chm., Yorks Children's Hosp. Fund (Co-founder), 1989–; Trustee, Hackfall Trust, 1987–. Master, Woolmen's Co., 1996–97. High Sheriff, 1993–94, DL, 1994, N Yorks. *Recreations:* hunting, shooting, sailing, art, architecture. *Address:* Newfield, Mickley, Ripon, N Yorks HG4 3JH. *T:* (01765) 635348. *Clubs:* Garrick, Pratt's.

ABRAHAMSEN, Egil; Comdr, Order of St Olav, 1987 (Kt Comdr 1979); Chairman, Norwegian Telecommunications, 1980–95; *b* 7 Feb. 1923; *s* of Anker Christian Abrahamsen and Aagot (*née* Kjølberg); *m* 1950, Randi Wiborg; one *s* two *d*. *Educ:* Technical Univ. of Norway (Naval Architect, 1949); Durham Univ., King's Coll., Newcastle upon Tyne (post-grad. studies and res.); Univ. of Calif, Berkeley (post-grad. studies). Sales Engr, Maschienen-Fabrik Augsburg-Nürnberg, and Karlstads Mekaniska Verkstad AB, Sweden, 1949–50; projects and planning, A/S Rosenberg Mekanisk Verksted, Stavanger, 1951–52; Det Norske Veritas, 1952–85: Surveyor, 1952; Sen. Surveyor, 1954 (resp. for building up Res. Dept); Principal Surveyor, 1957; Dep. Pres., 1966; Vice Pres., 1966; Pres., 1967. Chairman: Norsk Hydro, 1985–92; OPAK, 1985–; Royal Caribbean Cruise-Line, 1987–88; Kosmos, 1988–99; IKO Group, 1988–; Eikland, 1990–99; IM Skaugen A.S, 1990–99. Editor, European Shipbuilding, 1952–60. Fellow, Nat. Acad. of Engrg, USA, 1978; Member: Norwegian Acad. of Technical Scis, 1968; Royal Swedish Acad. of Engrg Scis, 1979; Hon. Mem., Soc. of Naval Architects and Marine Engrs, USA, 1987. DTech *hc* Royal Inst. of Technol., Sweden, 1977. Owes Hon. Prize, for contribn to res. and educn, 1971. Grand Officer, Order of Infante Dom Henrique (Portugal), 1977; Comdr, Order of the Lion (Finland), 1982; Kt, Nat. Order of Merit (France), 1982. *Address:* Maaltrostveien 35, 0786 Oslo, Norway.

ABRAM, Henry Charles, VRD 1958 (bar 1968); Chairman: Henry Abram Ltd, since 1955; Henry Abram & Sons, since 1989; Vice Lord-Lieutenant of Renfrewshire, since 1995; *b* 3 March 1924; *s* of Henry Kerr Abram and Madge Ballantyne, Glasgow; *m* 1950, Marie Kathleen Janet Paterson, *d* of Andrew Paterson, Glasgow; four *s*. *Educ:* Kelvinside Acad. Joined family shipping firm, Henry Abram Ltd, 1941; Dir, 1948–; Man. Dir, 1953. Joined RNVR, 1942; served in HMSs Ganges, Porcupine (torpedoed) and Meadowsweet; Lieut, 1946; Lieut-Comdr, 1954; Comdr, 1963; assumed comd and commnd HMS Dalriada, RNR Trg Estabt, Greenock, 1965; retd 1972. Dir, Glasgow Aged Seamen Relief Fund, 1974–; Pres., Glasgow Shipowners' and Shipbrokers' Benevolent Assoc., 1976–77; Hon. Vice-Pres., Clyde Maritime Trust, 1990; Mem., Scottish Council, King George's Fund for Sailors, 1988–. Deacon Convenor, Trades House of Glasgow, 1978–79; Chm., Trades Hall of Glasgow Trust, 1987–. Dir, Glasgow Sch. of Art, 1977– (Vice-Chm., 1985; Chm., 1989–92). MRIN 1957; FRSA 1987. DL Strathclyde, 1987. OStJ 1978. *Recreations:* sailing, shooting, stalking, golf, gardening. *Address:* Enterkin, Kilmacolm, Renfrewshire PA13 4NR. *T:* (01505) 872018. *Clubs:* Caledonian, Royal Thames Yacht; Western (Glasgow); Kilmacolm Golf, Prestwick Golf.

ABRAM, Rev. Paul Robert Carrington; a Chaplain to the Queen, since 1996; Chaplain of the Chapel Royal of St Peter ad Vincula, Tower of London, since 1996; *b* 21 July 1936; *s* of Norman and Madge Alice Abram; *m* 1961, Joanna Rose (*née* Headley); four *d*. *Educ:* The English Sch., Cairo; King Alfred Sch., Plon; Hymers Coll., Hull; Keble Coll., Oxford (BA 1962; MA 1965); Chichester Theol Coll. Ordained deacon, 1962, priest, 1963; Asst Curate, Redcar, 1962–65; Chaplain to the Forces, 1965–89; Vicar of Salcombe and Chaplain, Missions to Seamen, 1989–96; Chaplain for the Pool of London, Missions to Seamen, 1996–. *Recreations:* sailing, pre-nineteenth century maps, travel, people. *Address:* 1 The Green, HM Tower of London, EC3N 4AB. *T:* (020) 7488 5689. *Club:* Special Forces.

ABRAMS, Dr Michael Ellis, CB 1992; FRCP, FFPHM; public health consultant, since 1992; Chairman, Whittington Hospital NHS Trust, since 1998; Deputy Chief Medical Officer, Department of Health (formerly of Health and Social Security), 1985–92; *b* 17 Sept. 1932; *s* of late Sam Philip and Ruhamah Emmie Abrams; *m* 1962, Rosalind J. Beckman; four *c*. *Educ:* King Edward's Sch., Birmingham; Univ. of Birmingham (BSc 1st Cl. Anat. and Physiol. 1953; MB ChB Distinction in Medicine 1956). FRCP 1972; MFCM (Founder Mem.) 1972, FFCM 1983. Ho. Officer posts in United Birmingham Hosps, 1957–58; Univ. Research Fellow, Dept of Exp. Pathology, Univ. of Birmingham, and Medical Registrar, Queen Elizabeth Hosp., Birmingham, 1959; Medical Registrar and MRC Clinical Res. Fellow, Queen Elizabeth Hosp., Birmingham, 1959–62; MRC Clin. Res. Fellow, Dept of Medicine, Guy's Hosp., London, 1962–63; Rockefeller Travelling Fellow, Cardiovascular Res. Inst., Univ. of California Med. Centre, San Francisco, 1963–64; Lectr/Sen. Lectr and Hon. Cons. Phys., Guy's Hosp., 1964–75; Chief Med. Adviser, Guy's Hosp./Essex Gen. Practice Computing Unit, 1968–73; Dir, Inter-Deptl Laboratory, Guy's Hosp., 1971–75; DHSS: SMO, 1975–78; PMO, 1978–79; SPMO, 1979–85. Vice-Chm., Haringey Healthcare NHS Trust, 1993–98; Chm., N Thames Reg., Metropolitan Housing Trust, 1999– (Vice-Chm., 1998–99). Mem. Bd, Dalco Homes Ltd, 1997–. UK Deleg., Council of Europe Steering Cttee on Bioethics, 1990–97; Mem., WHO Council on Earth Summit Action Prog. for Health and Envmt, 1993–. Hon. Cons. Phys. Emeritus, Guy's Hosp. and Hon. Lectr in Medicine, Guy's Hosp. Med. Sch.; Examr in Human Communication, London Univ., 1972–84. President, Section of Measurement in Medicine, RSM, 1981–83; Chm., Computer Cttee, RCP, 1981–89. Gov., Moselle Sch., 2000–. Chm. Editl Bd, Health Trends, 1988–99. *Publications:* (ed) Medical Computing Progress and Problems, 1970; (ed) Spectrum 71, 1971; (ed) The Computer in the Doctor's Office, 1980; articles on medical manpower planning, biomedical computing, pulmonary surfactant and glucose tolerance in diabetes. *Recreations:* reading, gardening, beachcombing. *Address:* 97 Wood Vale, N10 3DL. *Club:* Athenæum.

ABRAMSKY, Jennifer, (Mrs Alasdair Liddell), CBE 2001; Director, BBC Radio and Music, since 2000; *b* 7 Oct. 1946; *d* of Chimen Abramsky and late Miriam (*née* Nirenstein); *m* 1976, Alasdair D. MacDuff Liddell, *qv*; one *s* one *d*. *Educ:* Holland Park Sch.; Univ. of East Anglia (BA Hons English) (Dep. Chm., New Univs Fest., 1968). BBC: joined as Prog. Operations Asst, 1969; Producer, World at One, 1973; Jt Producer and Compiler of Special Prog. on 'Nixon', 1974; Editor: PM Prog., 1978–81; Radio Four Budget Prog., 1979–86; World at One, 1981–86; Today, 1986–87; News and Current Affairs, BBC Radio, 1987–93; set up Radio 4 News FM for duration of Gulf War, 1991; Controller, BBC Radio Five Live, 1993–96; Dir, Continuous News Services, BBC, incl. Radio 5 Live, BBC World, 24 Hour UK TV News, Ceefax and Multimedia News, 1996–98; Dir, BBC Radio, 1999–2000. Member: ESRC, 1992–96; Editl Bd, British Journalism Rev., 1993–. A Governor, BFI, 2000–. Hon. Prof., Univ. of Thames Valley, 1994. Fellow, Radio Acad., 1998. Hon. MA Salford, 1997. Woman of Distinction, Jewish Care, 1990; Sony Radio Acad. Award, 1995. *Recreations:* theatre, music. *Address:* BBC, Broadcasting House, W1A 1AA.

ABRAMSKY, Prof. Samson, PhD; FRSE; Christopher Strachey Professor of Computing, University of Oxford, since 2000; Fellow, Wolfson College, Oxford, since 2000; *b* 12 March 1953; *s* of Moshe and Chaya-Sarah Abramsky; *m* 1976, Rosalind Susan Herman; two *s*. *Educ:* King's Coll., Cambridge (BA 1975; MA Philosophy 1979; Dip. Computer Sci.); Queen Mary Coll., London (PhD Computer Sci. 1988). FRSE 2000. Programmer, GEC Computers Ltd, 1976–78; Lectr, Dept of Computer Sci. and Stats, QMC, 1980–83; Lectr, 1983–88, Reader, 1988–90, Prof., 1990–95, Dept of Computing, Imperial Coll., London; Prof. of Theoretical Computer Sci., Univ. of Edinburgh, 1996–2000. MAE 1993. *Publications:* (ed jtly) Handbook of Logic in Computer Science, 5 vols, 1992–2000; contrib. numerous articles to computer sci. jls and confs. *Recreations:* reading, music, walking. *Address:* Computing Laboratory, Wolfson Building, Parks Road, Oxford OX1 3QD. *T:* (01865) 283558; Wolfson College, Linton Road, Oxford OX2 6UD.

ABSE, Dr Dannie, FRSL; Specialist in charge of chest clinic, Central Medical Establishment, London, 1954–89; writer; *b* 22 Sept. 1923; *s* of Rudolph Abse and Kate (*née* Shepherd); *m* 1951, Joan (*née* Mercer); one *s* two *d*. *Educ:* St Illtyd's Coll., Cardiff; University Coll., Cardiff; King's Coll., London; Westminster Hosp., London. MRCS, LRCP. First book of poems accepted for publication, 1946. Qualified at Westminster Hosp., 1950; RAF, 1951–54, Sqdn Ldr; Sen. Fellow of the Humanities, Princeton Univ., 1973–74. Pres., Poetry Soc., 1978–92. FRSL 1983; Fellow, Welsh Acad. of Letters, 1992 (Pres., 1995). Hon. Fellow, Univ. of Wales Coll. of Med., 1999. Hon. DLitt: Wales, 1989; Glamorgan, 1997. *Publications: poetry:* After Every Green Thing, 1948; Walking Under Water, 1952; Tenants of the House, 1957; Poems, Golders Green, 1962; A Small Desperation, 1968; Funland and other Poems, 1973; Collected Poems, 1977; Way Out in the Centre, 1981; Ask the Bloody Horse, 1986; White Coat, Purple Coat, 1989; Remembrance of Crimes Past, 1990; Selected Poems, 1994; On the Evening Road, 1994; Welsh Retrospective, 1997; Arcadia, One Mile, 1998; *prose:* A Strong Dose of Myself, 1983; Journals from the Ant Heap, 1986; Intermittent Journals, 1994; *novels:* Ash on a Young Man's Sleeve, 1954; Some Corner of an English Field, 1957; O. Jones, O. Jones, 1970; There Was a Young Man from Cardiff, 1991; *autobiography:* A Poet in the Family, 1974; *plays:* House of Cowards, (first prod.) Questors Theatre, Ealing, 1960; The Dogs of Pavlov, (first prod.) Questors, 1969; Pythagoras, (first prod.) Birmingham Rep. Th., 1976; Gone in January, (first prod.) Young Vic, 1978; *anthologies edited:* (with Howard Sergeant) Mavericks, 1957; Modern European Verse, 1964; (with Joan Abse) Voices in the Gallery, 1986; (with Joan Abse) The Music Lover's Literary Companion, 1988; The Hutchinson Book of Post-War British Poets, 1989; Twentieth Century Anglo-Welsh Poetry, 1997. *Recreations:* chess, watching Cardiff City FC. *Address:* 85 Hodford Road, NW11 8NH; Green Hollows, Craig-yr-Eos Road, Ogmore-by-Sea, Glamorgan, South Wales.

See also L. Abse.

ABSE, Leo; *b* 22 April 1917; *s* of Rudolph and Kate Abse; *m* 1st, 1955, Marjorie Davies (*d* 1996); one *s* one *d*; 2nd, 2000, Ania Czeputkowska. *Educ:* Howard Gardens High Sch.; LSE. Served RAF, 1941–46 (arrest for political activities in ME, 1944, precipitated parly debate). Solicitor; sen. partner, subseq. consultant in Cardiff law firm; first solicitor to be granted audience in High Court, 1986. Chm., Cardiff City Lab Party, 1951–53; Mem., Cardiff CC, 1953–58. Contested (Lab) Cardiff N, 1955. Fought a record 17 UK parly and local elections. MP (Lab): Pontypool, Nov. 1958–1983; Torfaen, 1983–87. Chm., Welsh Parly Party, 1976–87. Mem., Home Office Adv. Cttees on the Penal System, 1968, on adoption, 1972; first Chm., Select Cttee on Welsh Affairs, 1980; Mem., Select Cttee on Abortion, 1975–76; Sec., British-Taiwan Parly Gp, 1983–87. Led agitation for Suicide Act (ending criminality of attempted suicide), 1961; led final parly campaign for abolition of

capital punishment, 1969; sponsor or co-sponsor of Private Mem.'s Acts relating to divorce, homosexuality, family planning, legitimacy, widows' damages, industrial injuries, congenital disabilities and relief from forfeiture; sponsored Children's Bill, 1973, later taken over by Govt to become Children's Act, 1975; sponsored Divorce Bill, 1983, later taken over by Govt to become Matrimonial and Family Proceedings Act, 1985; initiated first Commons debates on genetic engineering, Windscale, *in vitro* pregnancies. Led Labour anti-devolution campaign in Wales, 1979. Mem. Council, Inst. for Study and Treatment of Delinquency, 1964–94, Vice-Pres., 1995–; Chm., Winnicott Clinic of Psychotherapy, 1988–91 (Trustee, 1980–); Pres., National Council for the Divorced and Separated, 1974–92; Vice-Pres., British Assoc. for Counselling, 1985–90; Chm., Parly Friends of WNO, 1985–87. Gov., Nat. Mus. of Wales, 1981–87; Member of Court: Univ. of Wales, 1981–87; UWIST. Regents' Lectr, Univ. of Calif, 1984. Received best dressed man award of Clothing Fedn, 1962. Order of Brilliant Star (China), 1988. *Publications:* Private Member: a psychoanalytically orientated study of contemporary politics, 1973; (contrib.) In Vitro Fertilisation: past, present and future, 1986; Margaret, daughter of Beatrice: a psychobiography of Margaret Thatcher, 1989; Wotan, my enemy: can Britain live with the Germans?, 1994 (Wingate prize, Jewish Qly, 1994); The Man Behind the Smile: Tony Blair and the politics of perversion, 1996, rev. edn 2001; Fellatio, Masochism, Politics and Love, 2000. *Recreations:* Italian wines, psycho-biography. *Address:* 54 Strand-on-the-Green, W4 3PD. *T:* (020) 8994 1166; Via Poggio di Mezzo, Nugola Vecchia, Livorno, Italy. *T:* (586) 977022. *Club:* Savile.
See also D. Abse.

ABUBAKAR, Prof. Iya; Galadima of Mubi; Senator, Federal Republic of Nigeria; Pro-Chancellor and Chairman of Council, University of Ibadan, since 1993; *b* 14 Dec. 1934; *s* of Buba Abubakar, Wali of Mubi, and Fatima Abubakar; *m* 1963, Ummu; one *s* three *d*. *Educ:* Univ. of Ibadan (BSc London (External)); Cambridge Univ. (PhD). FRAS, FIMA. Ahmadu Bello Univ., Zaria, Nigeria: Prof. of Maths, 1967–75, 1978; Dean, Faculty of Science, 1968–69, 1973–75; Vice-Chancellor, 1975–78. Former Dir, Nat. Mathematical Centre, Abuja. Minister of Defence, Nigeria, 1979–82. Chm., Senate Cttee on Finance and Appropriation. Visiting Professor: Univ. of Michigan, 1965–66; City Univ. of New York, 1971–72. Chairman: Natural Sciences Reg. Council of Nigeria, 1972–75; Nat. Manpower Commn of Nigeria, 1992–. Mem., Nigerian Univs Commn, 1968–73. Dir, Central Bank of Nigeria, 1972–75. Hon. DSc Ife, 1977; Ahmadu Bello, 1980. *Publications:* Entebbe Modern Mathematics, 1970; several research papers on mathematics in internat. jls. *Recreations:* chess, golf, horse riding. *Address:* The Senate, National Assembly, PMB 141, Abuja, Nigeria.

ABULAFIA, Prof. David Samuel Harvard, PhD, LittD; FRHistS; Professor of Mediterranean History, University of Cambridge, since 2000; Fellow, Gonville and Caius College, Cambridge, since 1974; *b* Twickenham, 12 Dec. 1949; *s* of Leon Abulafia and Rachel (*née* Zafransky); *m* 1979, Anna Sapir; two *d*. *Educ:* St Paul's Sch.; King's Coll., Cambridge (BA 1971; MA); PhD 1975, LittD 1994, Cantab. FRHistS 1981. Rome Schol., British Sch. at Rome, 1972–74; Asst Lectr, 1978–83, Lectr, 1983–91, Reader, 1991–2000, History Faculty, Cambridge Univ.; Tutor for Grad. Students, Gonville and Caius Coll., Cambridge, 1984–91. Dorfler Meml Lectr, Leo Baeck Coll., 1992; Guest Lectr, project on Objective Cultural Resources, Tokyo Univ., 2000. Project co-ordinator, EU Culture 2000, 2000–. Mem., Rev. Cttee, Ben Gurion Univ. of the Negev, 1999–2000. Mem. Council, Mediterranean Studies Assoc., 1999–; Gen. Ed., Jl of Medieval Hist., 1989–95. *Publications:* The Two Italies, 1977 (trans. Italian 1991); Italy, Sicily and the Mediterranean, 1987; Frederick II, 1988, 3rd edn 2002 (trans. Italian 1990, German 1991); Spain and 1492, 1992; (ed jtly) Church and City, 1992; Commerce and Conquest in the Mediterranean, 1993; A Mediterranean Emporium, 1994 (trans. Spanish 1996); (ed) The French Descent into Renaissance Italy, 1995; The Western Mediterranean Kingdoms, 1997 (trans. Italian 1999); (ed jtly) En las costas del Mediterráneo occidental, 1997; (ed) New Cambridge Medieval History, vol. 5, 1999; Mediterranean Encounters, 2000; (ed jtly) The Medieval Frontier, 2002. *Recreation:* travel. *Address:* Gonville and Caius College, Cambridge CB2 1TA. *T:* (01223) 332473.

ACHEBE, Prof. Chinua, FRSL 1983; author; Professor Emeritus, University of Nigeria, since 1984; Pro-Chancellor and Chairman of Council, Anambra State University of Technology, Enugu, 1986–88; *b* 16 Nov. 1930; *s* of Isaiah and Janet Achebe; *m* 1961, Christiana Okoli; two *s* two *d*. *Educ:* Univ. of Ibadan. Nigerian Broadcasting Corp.: Talks Producer, 1954; Controller, 1959; Dir, 1961–66. Rockefeller Fellowship, 1960; Unesco Fellowship, 1963; Professor of English: Univ. of Massachusetts, 1972–75; Univ. of Connecticut, Storrs, 1975–76; Univ. of Nigeria, Nsukka, 1973–81. Fulbright Prof., Univ. of Massachusetts, 1987–88; Vis. Distinguished Prof. of English, City Coll., City Univ. of NY, 1989; Vis. Fellow and Ashby Lectr, Clare Hall, Cambridge, 1993. Chairman: Soc. of Nigerian Authors, 1966; Assoc. of Nigerian Authors, 1982–86. Hon. Vice-Pres., Royal Africa Soc., 1999. Member: Council, Univ. of Lagos, 1966; Exec. Cttee, Commonwealth Arts Orgn, London, 1981. Neil Gunn Internat. Fellowship, Scottish Arts Council, 1975; Hon. Fellow: Modern Language Assoc. of America, 1975; Amer. Acad. of Arts and Letters, 1982. Editor, Okike, 1971–84. Patron, Writers and Scholars Educnl Trust, London, and Writers and Scholars Internat., 1972–; Governor, Newsconcern Internat. Foundn, London, 1983–90. Goodwill Ambassador, UN Population Fund, 1999–. Hon. DLitt: Dartmouth Coll., 1972; Southampton, 1975; Ife, 1978; Nigeria, 1981; Kent, 1982; Guelph and Mount Allison, 1984; Franklin Pierce Coll., 1985; Ibadan, 1989; Skidmore Coll., 1990; Harvard, 1996; Syracuse, 1998; Brown, 1998; Witwatersrand, 2000; DUniv: Open, 1989; Stirling, 1975; Hon. LLD Prince Edward Island, 1976; Hon. DHL: Massachusetts, 1977; Westfield Coll., 1989; Georgetown Univ., 1990. Jock Campbell New Statesman Award, 1965; Commonwealth Poetry Prize, 1972; Commonwealth Foundn Sen. Vis. Practitioner Award, 1983. Nat. Order of Merit (Nigeria), 1979; Order of the Fed. Repub. (Nigeria), 1979. *Publications: fiction:* Things Fall Apart, 1958; No Longer at Ease, 1960; Arrow of God, 1964; A Man of the People, 1966; Girls at War (short stories), 1972; Anthills of the Savannah, 1987; Home and Exile, 2000; *essays:* Morning Yet on Creation Days, 1975; The Trouble with Nigeria, 1983; Hopes and Impediments, 1987; Beware Soul-brother (poems), 1971; (with Robert Lyons) Another Africa (poetry, prose and photographs), 1998; *for children:* Chike and the River, 1966; (jt) How the Leopard Got its Claws, 1971; The Flute, 1978; The Drum, 1978. *Recreation:* music. *Address:* Bard College, PO Box 41, Annandale–on–Hudson, NY 12504, USA.

ACHER, Gerald, CBE 1999; Member, UK Board, since 1987, Senior Partner, London Office, since 1998, KPMG; *b* 30 April 1945; *s* of David Acher and Andrée Diana Acher (*née* Laredo); *m* 1970, Joyce Kathleen White; two *s*. *Educ:* King's Coll. Sch., Wimbledon. Articled clerk, Bird Potter & Co., 1961-66; Peat, Marwick, Mitchell & Co., subseq. KPMG: Asst Manager, 1967-73; Manager, 1973-75; Sen. Manager, 1975-80; Partner, 1980-; Hd, Corporate Finance, 1990-93; UK Hd of Audit and Accounting, 1993-98; Chairman: Worldwide Audit and Accounting Cttee, 1995-98; UK Client Service Bd, 1998-2001. Member: Adv. Cttee on Business and the Envmt, 1999–; DTI Foresight Panel on Crime and Business, 2001–. Dep. Chm., London First, 2000–; Dir, London First Centre, 1998–. Institute of Chartered Accountants in England and Wales: Mem., 1967–; Mem. Council, 1995-; Chm., Audit and Assce Faculty, 1995-. MSI 1992 . Gov., 1990–, and Vice Chm., 1995–, Motability; Trustee, Motability Tenth Anniversary Trust, 1991–. Royal Society of Arts: Fellow, 1998; Treas., 1999–; Trustee, 2000–; Mem. Council, 2000–. Liveryman, Chartered Accountants' Co. (Mem., Ct of Assistants). Chm. Govs, Milbourne Lodge Jun. Sch., 1986–. *Recreations:* classic and vintage car rallying, mountain walking, opera, classical music, travel, watching sport (especially Rugby), gardening. *Address:* KPMG, 8 Salisbury Square, EC4Y 8BB. *T:* (020) 7311 8640. *Club:* Travellers.

ACHESON, family name of **Earl of Gosford**.

ACHESON, Sir (Ernest) Donald, KBE 1986; Chief Medical Officer, Departments of Health and of Social Security (formerly Department of Health and Social Security), Department of Education and Science and Home Office, 1983–91; *b* 17 Sept. 1926; *s* of Malcolm King Acheson, MC, MD, and Dorothy Josephine Rennoldson; *m* Barbara Mary Castle; one *s* four *d* (and one *d* decd). *Educ:* Merchiston Castle Sch., Edinburgh; Brasenose Coll., Oxford (Theodore Williams Schol. in pathology, 1946; MA, DM; Hon. Fellow, 1989); Middlesex Hospital (Sen. Broderip Schol. in Med., Surg. and Pathol., 1950). FRCP; FRCS; FFPHM; FFOM; FRCOG 1992. Acting Sqdn Leader, RAF Med. Br., 1953–55. Medical Practitioner, 1951; various clinical posts at Middlesex Hosp.; Radcliffe Trav. Fellow of University Coll., Oxford, 1957–59; Medical Tutor, Nuffield Dept of Medicine, Radcliffe Infirmary, Oxford, 1960; Dir, Oxford Record Linkage Study and Unit of Clin. Epidemiology, 1962; May Reader in Medicine, 1965; Fellow, Brasenose Coll., Oxford, 1968; Prof. of Clinical Epidemiology, Univ. of Southampton, and Hon. Consultant Physician, Royal South Hants Hosp., 1968–83; Foundation Dean, Faculty of Med., Southampton Univ., 1968–78; Dir, MRC Unit in Environmental Epidemiology, 1979–83. Member: Wessex Regional Hosp. Bd, 1968–74; Hampshire AHA (Teaching) 1974–78; Chm., SW Hants and Southampton DHA, 1981–83; Member: Adv. Cttee on Asbestos, Health and Safety Exec., 1978; Royal Commn on Environmental Pollution, 1979–83; UGC, 1982–83; GMC, 1984–91; MRC, 1984–91; Chairman: Slow Virus Group, DHSS, 1979–80; Primary Health Care Inner London Gp, DHSS, 1980–81; Enquiry into Public Health in England, 1988; Home Office Adv. Cttee on Health of Prisoners, 1992–; Internat. Centre for Health and Society, UCL, 1996–; Ind. Inquiry into Inequalities in Health, DoH, 1997–98. UK Rep., Exec. Bd, WHO, 1988–90; Special Rep. of WHO in former Yugoslavia, 1992–93. Trustee, SCF, 1991–93. R. Samuel McLaughlin Vis. Prof., McMaster Univ., 1977; King's Fund Travelling Fellow, NZ Postgrad. Med. Fedn, 1979; Vis. Prof. of Internat. Health, Dept of Public Health and Policy, LSHTM, 1991–98. Lectures include: inaugural Adolf Streicher Meml, Stoke-on-Trent, 1978; Walter Hubert, British Assoc. for Cancer Res., 1981; Christie Gordon, Univ. of Birmingham, 1982; Edwin Chadwick Centennial, LSHTM, 1990; Harveian Orator, RCP, 1998. Examiner in Community Medicine: Univ. of Aberdeen, 1971–74; Univ. of Leicester, 1981–82; Examiner in Medicine, Univ. of Newcastle upon Tyne, 1975. Mem., Assoc. of Physicians of GB and Ire, 1965– (Pres. 1979); Pres., RIPH&H, 1999–. Founder FMedSci 1998. Hon. Fellow: LSHTM 1985; UCL, 1994. Hon. FRSocMed 1994. Hon. DM Southampton, 1984; Hon. DSc: Newcastle, 1984; Salford, 1991; Ulster, 1998; Hon. MD: QUB, 1987; Nottingham, 1989; Birmingham, 1991; Hon. LLD Aberdeen, 1988. Leon Bernard Foundn Prize, WHO, 1994. *Publications:* Medical Record Linkage, 1967; Multiple Sclerosis, a reappraisal, 1966; Medicine, an outline for the intending student, 1970; scientific papers on epidemiology of cancer and chronic disease, medical education and organisation of medical care. *Recreations:* family, gardening, music. *Address:* Department of Epidemiology and Public Health, University College London, Torrington Place, WC1E 6BT. *Club:* Athenæum.
See also R. M. Acheson.

ACHESON, Prof. Roy Malcolm, ScD, DM; FRCP, FFCM, FFOM; Professor of Community Medicine, University of Cambridge, 1976–88, now Emeritus; Fellow, Churchill College, Cambridge, since 1976; *b* 18 Aug. 1921; *s* of Malcolm King Acheson, MC, MD and Dorothy Rennoldson; *m* 1950, Fiona Marigo O'Brien (marr. diss. 1990); two *s* one *d*. *Educ:* Merchiston Castle Sch., Edinburgh; TCD (MA, ScD); Brasenose Coll., Oxford (MA, DM); Radcliffe Infirmary, Oxford. FRCP 1973; FFCM 1972; FFOM (by distinction) 1984. Clin. and res. posts, Radcliffe Infirmary, Oxford; Rockefeller Trav. Fellow, Western Reserve and Harvard Univs, 1955–56; Radcliffe Trav. Fellow, Univ. of Oxford, 1955–57; Lectr in Social Med., Univ. of Dublin, 1955–59; FTCD, 1957–59; Sen. Lectr, then Reader in Social and Preventive Med., Guy's Hosp. Med. Sch. and London Sch. of Hygiene and Trop. Med., 1959–62; Yale University: Associate Prof. of Epidemiology, 1962; Prof. of Epidemiology, 1964–72; Fellow, Jonathan Edwards Coll., 1966–75; London Sch. of Hygiene and Tropical Medicine: Commonwealth Fund Sen. Trav. Fellow in Med., 1968–69; Dir, Centre for Extension Trng in Community Med., 1972–76. Hon. Cons. in Community Med., NE Thames RHA (formerly NE Metrop. RHB), 1972–76, E Anglian RHA, 1976–88; Prof. of Health Service Studies, Univ. of London, 1974–76. Samuel R. McLaughlin Vis. Prof. in Med., McMaster Univ., Hamilton, Ont, 1976. Member: Exec. Cttee and Council, Internat. Epidemiol Soc., 1964–75; Expert Cttee, Methods in Chronic Disease Epidemiol., WHO, 1966; GMC, 1979–88 (Mem. Exec. Cttee, 1979–88; Mem. Educn Cttee, 1979–86); GDC, 1985–88 (Mem. Educn Cttee, 1985–88); Cambridge HA, 1986–88. Cons., Argentina, Colombia, Guatemala, India, Venezuela, WHO, 1965–76; Rapporteur, Adv. Cttee on Med. Res., WHO, 1976–79. Faculty of Community Medicine: Mem. Bd, 1974–84; Sec. to Examrs, 1974–77; Vice Pres., 1986–88; and Mem., numerous cttees. Gov., Action in Internat. Medicine, 1989–92; Councillor, Oral and Dental Res. Trust, 1989–91. Hon. Fellow: Buenos Aires Acad. of Medicine, 1980; Singapore Acad. of Medicine, 1988. Hon. MA Yale, 1964. *Publications:* (ed) Comparability in International Epidemiology, 1965; Seminars in Community Medicine: (ed with L. Aird) I: Sociology, 1976; (ed with L. Aird and D. J. Hall) II: Health Information, Planning and Monitoring, 1971; (with S. Hagard) Health, Society and Medicine: an introduction to community medicine, 1985; (jtly) Costs and Benefits of the Heart Transplantation Programmes at Harefield and Papworth Hospitals, 1985; (jtly) History of Education in Public Health, 1991. *Recreations:* golf, choral singing, country matters, meditating in the bath. *Address:* 21 The Cliff, Brighton BN2 5RF. *T:* (01273) 698518. *Clubs:* Oxford and Cambridge; Seaford Golf.
See also Sir E. D. Acheson.

ACHONRY, Bishop of, (RC), since 1977; **Most Rev. Thomas Flynn,** DD; *b* 8 July 1931; *s* of Robert and Margaret Flynn. *Educ:* St Nathy's, Ballaghaderreen; Maynooth College. BD, LPh, MA. Diocesan Religious Inspector of Schools, 1957–64; teaching in St Nathy's College, Ballaghaderreen, 1964–73; President and Headmaster of St Nathy's Coll., 1973–77. DD 1977. *Recreations:* gardening, fishing, golf. *Address:* St Nathy's, Ballaghaderreen, Co. Roscommon, Eire. *T:* (907) 60021.

ACKERMANN, Georg K.; *see* Kahn-Ackermann.

ACKERS, Sir James George, Kt 1987; Chairman, West Midlands Regional Health Authority, 1982–93; *b* 20 Oct. 1935; *s* of James Ackers and Vera Harriet Ackers (*née* Edwards). *Educ:* Oundle Sch., Northants; LSE. BSc(Econ). Man. Dir, 1963, Chm., 1974–91, Ackers Jarrett Ltd; Chm., Ackers Jarrett Leasing Ltd, 1982–91; Vice Pres., Michael Doud Gill & Associates, Washington, DC, 1968–71. Pres., Walsall Chamber of

Industry and Commerce, 1978; Association of British Chambers of Commerce, 1982–: Dep. Chm., 1982–84; Chm., 1984–86; Pres., 1986–90. Member: Cttee of Inquiry into Civil Service Pay, 1981–; Monopolies and Mergers Commn, 1981–90; Nat. Trng Task Force, 1989–91; NEDC, 1989–92. Chm., Fedn of Univ. Conservative Assocs, 1958; Vice-Chm., Bow Group, 1962–63. Pres., Jerome K. Jerome Soc., 1985–93. *Address:* 7 Gainsborough Drive, Mile Oak, Tamworth, Staffordshire B78 3PJ.

ACKLAND, Joss, (Sidney Edmond Jocelyn), CBE 2001; actor; *b* 29 Feb. 1928; *s* of Norman Ackland and Ruth Izod; *m* 1951, Rosemary Jean Kirkcaldy; one *s* five *d* (and one *s* decd). *Educ:* Dame Alice Owens Sch.; Central Sch. of Speech Training and Dramatic Art. Has worked in theatre, 1945–; repertory includes Stratford-upon-Avon, Arts Th., Buxton, Croydon, Embassy, Coventry, Oxford, Chesterfield, Windsor, Pitlochry; tea planter, Central Africa, 1954–55; disc jockey, Cape Town, 1955–57; Mem., Old Vic Theatre Co., 1958–61: parts include Toby Belch, in Twelfth Night, Caliban, in The Tempest, Pistol, in Henry IV, Lord Froth, in The Double Dealer, Aegisthus, in The Oresteia, Falstaff, in Henry IV Pt I and the Merry Wives of Windsor; Associate Dir, Mermaid Theatre, 1961–63: dir, The Plough and the Stars; parts include title rôle, Galileo, Bluntschli, in Arms and the Man, Scrofulovsky, in The Bedbug, Kirilov, in The Possessed. *West End theatre* rôles include: title rôle,The Professor, 1966; Gus, in Hotel in Amsterdam, 1968–69; Come As You Are, 1969–70; Brassbound, in Captain Brassbound's Conversion, 1971; Sam, in The Collaborators, 1973; Mitch, in A Streetcar Named Desire, 1974; Stewart, in A Pack of Lies, 1984; Clarence Darrow, in Never the Sinner, 1990; Weller Martin, in The Gin Game, 1999; *West End musicals:* Justice Squeezum, in Lock up your Daughters, 1962; title rôle, Jorrocks, 1967; Frederik, in a Little Night Music, 1975–76; Juan Perón, in Evita, 1978; Captain Hook and Mr Darling, in Peter Pan—the musical, 1985–86; *National Theatre:* Eustace Perry State, in The Madras House, 1977; Romain Gary, in Jean Seburg (musical), 1983; *Barbican Theatre:* Falstaff, in Henry IV pts I and II (opening prodn), 1982; Captain Hook and Mr Darling, in Peter Pan, 1982; *Chichester Theatre:* Gaev, in The Cherry Orchard, 1981; Ill, in The Visit, 1995; John Tarleton in Misalliance, 1997; Captain Shotover, in Heartbreak House, 2000; *tours:* Petruchio, in The Taming of the Shrew, 1977; Sir, in The Dresser, 1981. *Films* include: Seven Days to Noon, 1949; Crescendo, 1969; The House that Dripped Blood, Villain, 1970; The Happiness Cage, England Made Me, 1971; The Little Prince, The Black Windmill, S-P-Y-S, The Three Musketeers, 1973; Great Expectations, One of our Dinosaurs is Missing, 1974; Operation Daybreak, Royal Flash, 1975; The Silver Bears, 1976; The End of Civilisation as we know it, The Greek Tycoon, Who is killing the Great Chefs of Europe, 1977; Saint Jack, The Apple, Rough Cut, 1978; Lady Jane, 1984; A Zed and Two Noughts, 1985; Don Masino, in The Sicilian, 1987; Sir Jock Broughton, in White Mischief, The Colonel, in To Kill a Priest, 1988; Lethal Weapon II, The Hunt for Red October, The Palermo Connection, 1989; The Object of Beauty, The Sheltering Desert, 1991; The Bridge, Nowhere to Run, Pin for the Butterfly, The Mighty Ducks, 1992; Occhio Pinocchio (Italy), 1993; Miracle on 34th Street, Mad Dogs and Englishmen, A Kid in King Arthur's Court, Citizen X, 1994; Daisies in December, 'Til the End of Time, Mighty Ducks 3, Surviving Picasso, Deadly Voyage, Giorgino (France), 1995; Firelight, Swept from the Sea, 1996; Son of Sandokan, Game of Mirrors, Milk, 1999; Mumbo Jumbo, 2000. Numerous TV plays and serials, incl. Kipling, Alan Holly in First and Last, C. S. Lewis in Shadowlands, Barrett in The Barretts of Wimpole Street, Voices in the Garden, A Murder of Quality, Isaac in The Bible, Onassis in A Woman Named Jackie, Goering in The Man who stayed at the Ritz, Heat of the Sun, The Sport of Kings, K-19 The Widowmaker. Member: Drug Helpline; Amnesty Internat. *Publication:* I Must Be in There Somewhere (autobiog), 1989. *Recreations:* writing, painting, twenty-nine grandchildren, one great-grandchild.

ACKNER, family name of **Baron Ackner**.

ACKNER, Baron *cr* 1986 (Life Peer), of Sutton in the county of West Sussex; **Desmond James Conrad Ackner;** Kt 1971; PC 1980; a Lord of Appeal in Ordinary, 1986–92; *b* 18 Sept. 1920; *s* of Dr Conrad and Rhoda Ackner; *m* 1946, Joan, *d* of late John Evans, JP, and widow of K. B. Spence; one *s* two *d*. *Educ:* Highgate Sch.; Clare Coll., Cambridge (MA; Hon. Fellow, 1983). Served in RA, 1941–42; Admty Naval Law Br., 1942–45. Called to Bar, Middle Temple, 1945; QC 1961; Recorder of Swindon, 1962–71; Judge of Courts of Appeal of Jersey and Guernsey, 1967–71; a Judge of the High Court of Justice, Queen's Bench Div., 1971–80; Judge of the Commercial Court, 1973–80; Presiding Judge, Western Circuit, 1976–79; a Lord Justice of Appeal, 1980–86. Mem. Gen. Council of Bar, 1957–61, 1963–70 (Hon. Treas., 1964–66; Vice-Chm., 1966–68; Chm., 1968–70); Bencher Middle Temple, 1965, Dep. Treasurer, 1983, Treasurer, 1984; Mem. Senate of the Four Inns of Court, 1966–70 (Vice-Pres., 1968–70); Pres., Senate of the Inns of Court and the Bar, 1980–82. Chm., Law Adv. Cttee, British Council, 1980–90 (Mem., 1991–); Mem., Lloyd's Arbitration Panel, 1992–. Pres., Arb. Appeal Tribunal, SFA, 1994–. Appeal Comr, PIA, 1994–; Dir, City Disputes Panel, 1994–98. Hon. Mem., Canadian Bar Assoc., 1973–. Pres., Soc. of Sussex Downsmen, 1993–96. Hon. Fellow, Soc. of Advanced Legal Studies, 1997. *Recreations:* swimming, theatre. *Address:* House of Lords, SW1A 0PW. *T:* (020) 7219 3295; 4 Pump Court, Temple, EC4Y 7AN. *T:* (020) 7353 2656; The Flat, Lobs House, South Road, Liphook, Hants GU30 7HS.

See also I. H. D. Hughes.

ACKRILL, Prof. John Lloyd, FBA 1981; Professor of the History of Philosophy, Oxford University, 1966–89, now Emeritus; Fellow of Brasenose College, Oxford, 1953–89, now Emeritus; *b* 30 Dec. 1921; *s* of late Frederick William Ackrill and Jessie Anne Ackrill; *m* 1953, Margaret Walker Kerr; one *s* three *d*. *Educ:* Reading School; St John's Coll., Oxford (Scholar) (1940–41 and 1945–48; Hon. Fellow, 1996). War service (Royal Berks Regt and GS, Capt.), 1941–45. Assistant Lecturer in Logic, Glasgow Univ., 1948–49; Univ. Lectr in Ancient Philosophy, Oxford, 1951–52; Tutorial Fellow, Brasenose Coll., 1953–66. Mem., Inst. for Adv. Study, Princeton, 1950–51, 1961–62; Fellow Coun. of Humanities, and Vis. Prof., Princeton Univ., 1955, 1964. *Publications:* Aristotle's *Categories* and *De Interpretatione* (trans. with notes), 1963; Aristotle's Ethics, 1973; Aristotle the Philosopher, 1981; New Aristotle Reader, 1987; Essays on Plato and Aristotle, 1997; articles in philos. and class. jls. *Address:* 22 Charlbury Road, Oxford OX2 6UU. *T:* (01865) 556098.

ACKROYD, Keith, CBE 1994; FRPharmS; Chairman, Silentnight Holdings plc, since 1995 (Director, since 1993); *b* 6 July 1934; *s* of Edward Ackroyd and Ethel (*née* Bate); *m* 1958, Ellen Gwenda Thomas; two *s* one *d*. *Educ:* Heath Grammar Sch.; Bradford Sch. of Pharmacy; London Business Sch. FRPharmS 1981. Boots The Chemists Ltd: Apprentice Pharmacist, 1952; Dir, 1975–94; Midlands Area Dir, 1976–77; Man. Dir, 1983–89; Pres., Boots Drug Stores (Canada) Ltd, 1977–79; Boots Company plc: Dir, 1979–94; Man. Dir, Retail Div., 1984–94; Chairman: Halfords Ltd, 1989–94; A. G. Stanley, 1989–94; Do It All Ltd, 1992–94; Director: Carefirst (formerly Takare) plc, 1994–98 (Dep. Chm., 1996–98); Navara (formerly Nottingham Gp) plc, 1994–; Cowie plc, 1994–96; Victoria plc, 1998–. Chairman: Company Chemists Assoc., 1983–89; British Retailers Assoc., 1988–92; British Retail Consortium, 1992–94; Regl Chm., Trent RHA, later NHS Exec., Trent, 1994–97; Mem., NHS Policy Bd, 1994–97. Member: Passport Agency Bd, 1991–2000; Nat. Bd for Crime Prevention, 1993–95. CIMgt 1981; FInstD 1979. Liveryman, Soc. of Apothecaries, 1990–. *Recreations:* drinking wine, country sport. *Address:* Millfield, Bradmore, Nottingham NG11 6PF. *T:* (0115) 921 6052. *Club:* Royal Automobile.

ACKROYD, Norman, RA 1991 (ARA 1988); RE 1985; artist (painter and etcher); *b* 26 March 1938; *s* of late Albert Ackroyd, master butcher, and Clara Briggs, weaver; *m* 1st, 1963, Sylvia Buckland (marr. diss. 1975); two *d*; 2nd, 1978, Penelope Hughes-Stanton; one *s* one *d*. *Educ:* Cockburn High Sch., Leeds; Leeds Coll. of Art; Royal Coll. of Art (ARCA 1964; Sen. FRCA 2000). Teaches occasionally at RA, Slade, RCA and in N America; Tutor in Etching, Central Sch. of Arts, London, 1965–93; Prof. of Etching, London Inst., 1992. Over 50 one-man exhibns, 1970–, mainly in UK and USA; work in public collections includes: Tate Gall.; BM; V&A; Arts Council; British Council; Mus. of Modern Art, NY; Nat. Galls of Scotland, Norway, Canada, S Africa; Albertina, Vienna; Rijksmus. and Stedelyk, Amsterdam; Musée d'Art Histoire, Geneva; Nat. Gall. of Art, Washington. Mural commissions include: Albany, Glasgow, 1975; Haringey Cultural Centre, 1985; Lloyds Bank Technol. Centre, London, 1990; British Airways, 1991; Freshfields, London, 1992; Tetrapak, London, 1993; British Embassy, Moscow, 2000. TV work includes: Artists in Print (etching), 1981; A Prospect of Rivers, 1988; Painting with Acid, 2000. Awards: Bradford Internat. Biennale, 1972, 1982; Royal Soc. of Etchers and Engravers, 1984, 1985; Bronze Medal, Frechen, Germany, 1986. *Publications:* A Cumberland Journey, 1981; Travels with Copper and Zinc, 1983; (with Douglas Dunn) The Pictish Coast, 1988; St Kilda: the furthest land, 1989; Windrush, 1990; A Song for Ireland, 1999; numerous collections of etchings from travels in the British Isles, occasionally with poets. *Recreations:* cricket, archæology. *Address:* Royal Academy of Arts, Piccadilly, W1V 0DS. *T:* (020) 7378 6001. *Clubs:* Chelsea Arts, Arts.

ACKROYD, Peter; writer; Chief Book Reviewer, The Times, since 1986; *b* 5 Oct. 1949; *s* of Graham Ackroyd and Audrey Whiteside. *Educ:* St Benedict's Sch., Ealing; Clare Coll., Cambridge (MA); Yale Univ. (Mellon Fellow). Literary Editor, 1973–77, Jt Managing Editor, 1978–82, The Spectator. FRSL 1984. Hon. DLitt: Exeter, 1992; London Guildhall. *Publications: poetry:* London Lickpenny, 1973; Country Life, 1978; The Diversions of Purley, 1987; *novels:* The Great Fire of London, 1982; The Last Testament of Oscar Wilde, 1983 (Somerset Maugham Prize, 1984); Hawksmoor, 1985 (Whitbread Award; Guardian Fiction Prize); Chatterton, 1987; First Light, 1989; English Music, 1992; The House of Doctor Dee, 1993; Dan Leno and the Limehouse Golem, 1994; The Plato Papers, 1999; *non-fiction:* Notes for a New Culture, 1976; Dressing Up, 1979; Ezra Pound and his World, 1980; T. S. Eliot, 1984 (Whitbread Award; Heinemann Award); Dickens, 1990; Introduction to Dickens, 1991; Blake, 1995; Milton in America, 1996; The Life of Thomas More, 1998; London: the biography, 2000. *Address:* c/o Anthony Sheil Associates Ltd, 43 Doughty Street, WC1N 2LF. *T:* (020) 7405 9351.

ACKROYD, Rev. Prof. Peter Runham, MA, PhD Cantab, BD, MTh, DD London; Samuel Davidson Professor of Old Testament Studies, University of London, 1961–82, now Emeritus Professor; *b* 15 Sept. 1917; *s* of Jabez Robert Ackroyd and Winifred (*née* Brown); *m* 1st, 1940, Evelyn Alice Nutt (*d* 1990), BSc (Manch.), *d* of William Young Nutt; two *s* three *d*; 2nd, 1991, Ann, MA (Oxon), *d* of James Golden. *Educ:* Harrow County School for Boys; Downing and Trinity Colleges, Cambridge. Open Exhibition in Modern Languages, Downing Coll., Cambridge, 1935; Mod. and Med. Langs Tripos, Pt I, 1936, Pt II, 1938; BDHons London, 1940; Stanton Student, Trin. Coll., Cambridge, 1941–43; Dr Williams's Trust Exhibnr, 1941; MTh London, 1942; PhD Cambridge, 1945; DD London, 1970. Minister of: Roydon Congregational Church, Essex, 1943–47; Balham Congregational Church, London, 1947–48; Lectr in Old Testament and Biblical Hebrew, Leeds Univ., 1948–52; Cambridge University: Univ. Lectr in Divinity, 1952–61; Select Preacher, 1955; Mem. Council of Senate, 1957–61; Hulsean Lectr, 1960–62; Select Preacher, Oxford, 1962, 1981 (McBride Sermon); Dean of Faculty of Theology, King's Coll., London, 1968–69; FKC 1969; Mem. Senate, London Univ., 1971–79; Dean, Univ. Faculty of Theology, 1976–80. Vis. Professor: Lutheran Sch. of Theology, Chicago, 1967 and 1976; Univ. of Toronto, 1972; Univ. of Notre Dame, Indiana, 1982; Emory Univ., Atlanta, 1984. Lectures: Selwyn, NZ, 1970; Ethel M. Wood, Univ. of London, 1982; (first) Walter S. Williams, Denver, 1982; Tübingen, 1983; Haskell, Oberlin, Ohio, 1984; series of lectures, Japan, 1983. External Examiner, Belfast, Bristol, Durham, Cambridge, Edinburgh, Leeds, Nottingham, Exeter, West Indies. Ordained Deacon, 1957; Priest, 1958; Hon. Curate, Holy Trinity, Cambridge, 1957–61. Proctor in Convocation, Cambridge Univ., 1960–64. Pres., Soc. for Old Testament Study, 1972 (Foreign Sec., 1986–89); Hon. Mem., Soc. of Biblical Literature, 1982–; Chairman: Council, British Sch. of Archaeology in Jerusalem, 1979–83; Palestine Exploration Fund, 1986–90 (Hon. Sec., 1962–70). Hon. DD St Andrews, 1970. *Publications:* Freedom in Action, 1951; The People of the Old Testament, 1959, new edn 1981; Continuity, 1962; The Old Testament Tradition, 1963; Exile and Restoration, 1968; Israel under Babylon and Persia, 1970; 1 & 2 Chronicles, Ezra, Nehemiah, Ruth, Jonah, Maccabees, 1970; 1 Samuel (Cambridge Bible Commentary), 1971; I & II Chronicles, Ezra, Nehemiah (Torch Bible Commentary), 1973; 2 Samuel, 1977; Doors of Perception, 1978, new edn 1983; Studies in the Religious Tradition of the Old Testament, 1987; The Chronicler in His Age, 1991; articles and reviews in various learned jls, dictionaries, etc; *translations:* E. Würthein's The Text of the Old Testament, 1957; L. Köhler's Hebrew Man, 1957, repr. 1973; O. Eissfeldt's The Old Testament: An Introduction, 1965; *editor:* Bible Key Words, 1961–64; Society for Old Testament Study Book List, 1967–73; Palestine Exploration Quarterly, 1971–86; *joint editor:* SCM Press OT Library, 1960–80; Cambridge Bible Commentary, 1961–79; SCM Studies in Biblical Theol., 1962–77; Words and Meanings: Essays presented to D. W. Thomas, 1968; Cambridge History of the Bible, vol. I, 1970; Oxford Bible Series, 1979–92; Cambridge Commentaries: Jewish and Christian Writings of the period 200 BC to AD 200, 1979–. *Recreations:* reading, music. *Address:* 155 Northumberland Road, North Harrow, Middlesex HA2 7RB. *T:* (020) 8429 0396.

ACKROYD, Sir Timothy Robert Whyte, 3rd Bt *cr* 1956, of Dewsbury, West Riding of Yorkshire; actor; *b* 7 Oct. 1958; *er s* of Sir John Robert Whyte Ackroyd, 2nd Bt and Jennifer Eileen McLeod (*d* 1997), *d* of H. G. S. Bishop; *S* father, 1995. *Educ:* Bradfield; LAMDA. *Theatre* includes: Agamemnon, 1976; On Approval, 1979; Much Ado About Nothing, 1980; Macbeth, Old Vic. Co., 1980; Man and Superman, 1982; A Sleep of Prisoners, 1983; Pygmalian, 1984; Another Country, 1986; No Sex Please – We're British, 1987; Black Coffee, 1988; Jeffrey Bernard is Unwell, 1989, 1999 (televised); Journey's End, 1993; Bad Soldier Smith, 1995; Saki, 1997; The Rivals, Iphigenia at Aulis, A Step Out of Time, 2000; *television:* Jack Be Nimble, 1979; Luther, 1983; Man and Superman, 1985; Pied Piper, 1989; A Royal Scandal, 1996; The New Professionals, 1998; *films:* Creator, 1984; Bullseye, 1990; Tembo Kali, 1992; *radio* includes Fugitive Pieces, 1999. Director: Martingale Productions, 1985–86; Archview Films, 1991–95; Ackroyd Pullan, 1995–98; Zuma Productions, 2000; Messiah Pictures, 2001. Hon. Mem., Theatre of Comedy, 1984. Chm., Ackroyd Trust; Trustee and Patron, Tusk Trust; Trustee, Marjorie and Dorothy Whyte Meml Fund; Patron, London & Internat. Sch. of Acting. Freeman and Liveryman, Carpenters' Co., 1982. *Recreations:* Rugby, cricket, literature, Sumo wrestling. *Heir: b* Andrew John Armitage Ackroyd, *b* 17 Sept. 1961. *Clubs:* Garrick, MCC; Lazarusians.

ACLAND, Sir Antony (Arthur), KG 2001; GCMG 1986 (KCMG 1982; CMG 1976); GCVO 1991 (KCVO 1976); HM Diplomatic Service, retired; Provost of Eton, 1991–2000; *b* 12 March 1930; *s* of late Brig. P. B. E. Acland, OBE, MC, TD and Bridget Susan Acland; *m* 1956, Clare Anne Verdon (*d* 1984); two *s* one *d*; *m* 1987, Jennifer McGougan (*née* Dyke). *Educ:* Eton; Christ Church, Oxford (MA 1956). Joined Diplomatic Service, 1953; ME Centre for Arab Studies, 1954; Dubai, 1955; Kuwait, 1956; FO, 1958–62; Asst Private Sec. to Sec. of State, 1959–62; UK Mission to UN, 1962–66; Head of Chancery, UK Mission, Geneva, 1966–68; FCO, 1968, Hd of Arabian Dept, 1970–72; Principal Private Sec. to Foreign and Commonwealth Sec., 1972–75; Ambassador to Luxembourg, 1975–77, to Spain, 1977–79; Deputy Under-Sec. of State, FCO, 1980–82, Perm. Under-Sec. of State, FCO, and Head of Diplomatic Service, 1982–86; Ambassador to Washington, 1986–91. Director: Shell Transport and Trading, 1991–2000; Booker plc, 1992–99. Chairman: Council, Ditchley Foundn, 1991–96; Tidy Britain Gp, 1992–96 (Pres., 1996–). Trustee, Nat. Portrait Gall., 1991–98. Chancellor, Order of St Michael and St George, 1994–. Hon. DCL: Exeter, 1988; William and Mary Coll., USA, 1990; Reading, 1992. *Address:* Staddon Farm, near Winsford, Minehead, Som TA24 7HY. *T:* (01643) 831489. *Club:* Brooks's.
See also Maj.-Gen. Sir J. H. B. Acland.

ACLAND, Lt-Col Sir (Christopher) Guy (Dyke), 6th Bt *cr* 1890; LVO 1999 (MVO 1990); an Extra Equerry to the Queen, since 1999; Administrator, HSA Charitable Trust, since 2000; *b* 24 March 1946; *s* of Major Sir Antony Guy Acland, 5th Bt, and of Margaret Joan, *e d* of late Major Nelson Rooke; *S* father, 1983; *m* 1971, Christine Mary Carden, *y d* of late Dr John Waring, Totland Bay, Isle of Wight; two *s*. *Educ:* Allhallows School; RMA Sandhurst. Commissioned RA, 1966; served BAOR (26 Field Regt), 1967–70; UK and Hong Kong (3 RHA), 1970–73; BAOR and UK (22 AD Regt), 1974–77; Staff Coll., Camberley, 1978 (psc); served on Staff of HQ Eastern District, 1979–80; commanded Q (Sanna's Post) Bty in BAOR (5 Regt), 1981–83; SO2, Army Staff Duties Directorate, MoD, 1983–85; 2 i/c 1 RHA BAOR, 1986–88; Equerry to HRH The Duke of Edinburgh, 1988–90; SO1, Management Services Orgn 3, MoD, 1990–92; CO, Southampton Univ. OTC, 1992–94; retired 1994. Dep. Master of the Household and Equerry to the Queen, 1994–99. *Recreations:* sailing, shooting, gardening. *Heir: s* Alexander John Dyke Acland, *b* 29 May 1973. *Clubs:* Royal Yacht Squadron, Royal Solent Yacht, Royal Artillery Yacht.

ACLAND, Sir John (Dyke), 16th Bt *cr* 1644, of Columb John, Devon; *b* 13 May 1939; *s* of Sir Richard Thomas Dyke Acland, 15th Bt and Anne Stella (*née* Alford) (*d* 1992); *S* father, 1990; *m* 1961, Virginia, *yr d* of Roland Forge; two *s* one *d*. *Educ:* Clifton; Magdalene Coll., Cambridge; Univ. of West Indies (MSc). *Heir: s* Dominic Dyke Acland [*b* 19 Nov. 1962; *m* 1990, Sarah Anne, 3rd *d* of Ven. Kenneth Unwin, *qv*; two *s* two *d* (of whom one *s* one *d* are twins)]. *Address:* Sprydon, Broadclyst, Exeter, Devon EX5 3JN.

ACLAND, Maj.-Gen. Sir John (Hugh Bevil), KCB 1980; CBE 1978; Vice Lord-Lieutenant of Devon, 1994–99; farmer; *b* 26 Nov. 1928; *s* of late Brig. Peter Acland, OBE, MC, TD and Bridget Susan Acland; *m* 1953, Myrtle Christian Euing, *d* of Brig. and Mrs Alastair Crawford, Auchentroig, Stirlingshire; one *s* one *d*. *Educ:* Eton. Enlisted Scots Guards, 1946; commnd, 1948; served with 1st or 2nd Bn in Malaya, Cyprus, Egypt, Germany, Kenya, Zanzibar and NI, 1949–70; Equerry to HRH the Duke of Gloucester, 1957–59; Staff Coll., 1959; Bde Major, 4th Guards Armoured Bde, 1964–66; CO 2nd Bn Scots Guards, 1968–71; Col GS ASD, MoD, 1971–74; BGS, MoD, 1975; Comd Land Forces and Dep. Comd British Forces Cyprus, 1976–78; GOC South West Dist, 1978–81; Comd Monitoring Force, Southern Rhodesia, and Military Advr to the Governor, 1979–80; retired 1981. Dir of Liaison Res., Allied Vintners, 1982–93. Hon. Colonel: Exeter Univ. OTC, 1980–90; Royal Devon Yeomanry, 1983–92; Royal Wessex Yeomanry, 1989–92. Pres., Royal British Legion, Devon, 1982–90; Mem., Dartmoor National Park Authority, 1986. Chm., SW Regl Working Party on Alcohol, 1987–93. Mem. Steering Gp, Schools Health Educn Unit, Exeter Univ., 1986–92. Trustee, Exeter Cathedral Preservation Trust, 1994– (Chm., 1997–). Governor: Allhallows Sch., 1982–94; King's Sch., Ottery St Mary, 1994–99. Pres., Honiton and Dist Agricl Assoc., 1995–. DL Devon, 1984. *Publications:* articles in Country and other jls. *Recreations:* fishing, arboriculture, destroying vermin. *Address:* Feniton Court, Honiton, Devon EX14 0BE. *Clubs:* Army and Navy, MCC, Blue Seal.
See also Sir A. A. Acland.

ACRES, Dr Douglas Ian, CBE 1987 (OBE 1981); JP; DL; Vice President, Magistrates' Association, since 1988 (Chairman of Council, 1984–87); *b* Brockley, 21 Nov. 1924; *y s* of Sydney Herbert and Hilda Emily Acres; *m* Joan Marjorie, *o d* of William Charles and Alice Emily Bloxham, Benfleet. *Educ:* Westcliff High Sch.; Borland's, Victoria; London Hosp. Med. Coll. MRCS, LRCP 1949; DMJ (Clin.); MRCGP 1968. House Surgeon and Casualty Registrar, King George Hosp., Ilford, 1949–51; RAF Med. Branch, 1951–53 (Dep. Pres., Air Crew Med. Bd, Hornchurch; AOC's Commendation and Vote of Thanks, OStJ, East Coast Flood Disaster, 1953); gen. med. practice, Benfleet, 1953–84; MO, Remploy Ltd, 1965–99. Med. Adviser, Congregational Fedn, 1985–; Member: Cttee on Mentally Abnormal Offenders, 1972–75; Barclay Cttee on Role and Task of Social Worker, 1979; Parole Bd, 1984–87; Sec., Fedn of Alcohol Rehab. Estabts, 1980–82; Mem., Exec. Cttee, Alcohol Concern, 1983–87; Chairman: Essex Council on Alcoholism, 1981–86; Out of Court (Alt. for Drunkenness Offenders), 1982–89; Churches' Council on Alcohol and Drugs, 1986–89; Mem., Interdeptl Cttee on Alcoholism, 1975–78; Chm., Educn Cttee, Inst. for Study and Treatment and Delinquency, 1985–89. Cropwood Fellow, Inst. of Criminology, 1973; Mem., BMA (Chm., SE Essex Div., 1979). Magistrates' Association: Dep. Chm., 1983; Chm., Sentencing of Offenders Cttee, 1978–83; Chm., Essex and NE London Br., 1975–78; Chm., Trng Sub-Cttee, 1978–91. JP Essex, 1958; Chm., Rochford Bench, 1974–84; Member: Lord Chancellor's Essex Adv. Cttee, 1973–87; Essex Magistrates' Courts Cttee, 1973–92 (Chm., Trng Sub-Cttee, 1978–92); Essex Probation Cttee, 1972–92 (Chm., R&D Sub-Cttee, 1980–90); Pres., Essex Br., Nat. Assoc. of Probation Officers, 1983–89. Indep. Mem., Benfleet UDC, 1960–65 (Chm., Public Health Cttee). Mem., Board of Visitors, HM Borstal, Bullwood Hall, 1970–83 (Vice-Chm., 1976–82); Member, Governing Body: King John Sch., Thundersley, 1967–89 (Chm., 1971–89); SE Essex Sixth Form Coll., 1982–88. Lay Pastor: Battlesbridge Free Church, 1984–99, now Pastor Emeritus; Woodham Ferrers Congregational Church, 1984–92; Chaplain to Chm., Rochford DC, 1996–97. DL Essex 1978. CStJ. Med. corresp., SE Essex Evening Echo, 1968–95. *Publications:* articles and chapters on medico-legal matters. *Address:* Thundersley Lodge, Runnymede Chase, Thundersley, Benfleet, Essex SS7 3DB. *T:* (01268) 793241.

ACRES, Paul, QPM 1997; Chief Constable of Hertfordshire, since 2000; *b* 15 April 1948; *s* of Albert George Acres and Kathleen Acres (*née* Jones); *m* 1971, Jean Parsons; three *s*. *Educ:* City of Bath Boys' Sch. Liverpool and Bootle Constabulary, 1968–74; joined Merseyside Police, 1974: Asst Chief Constable, 1992–94; rcds, 1994; Dep. Chief Constable, 1995–2000. Police Long Service and Good Conduct Medal, 1991. *Recreations:* walking, motor cycling, golf, cycling. *Address:* Hertfordshire Police HQ, Stanborough Road, Welwyn Garden City, Herts AL8 6XF. *Club:* West Lancashire Golf.

ACTON, 4th Baron *cr* 1869, of Aldenham, Salop; **Richard Gerald Lyon-Dalberg-Acton;** Baron Acton of Bridgnorth (Life Peer) 2000; Bt 1644; Patrician of Naples, 1802; writer; *b* 30 July 1941; *s* of 3rd Baron Acton, CMG, MBE, TD and of Daphne, *o d* of 4th Baron Rayleigh, FRS and late Mary Hilda, 2nd *d* of 4th Earl of Leitrim; *S* father, 1989; *m* 1st, 1965, Hilary Juliet Sarah (*d* 1973), *d* of Dr Osmond Laurence Charles Cookson, Perth, WA; one *s*; 2nd, 1974, Judith (writer) (marr. diss. 1987), *d* of Hon. Sir Garfield Todd, *qv*; 3rd, 1988, Patricia (Law Professor and writer), *o d* of late M. Morey Nassif and of Mrs Nassif, Iowa, USA. *Educ:* St George's Coll., Salisbury, Rhodesia; Trinity Coll., Oxford (BA History 1963, MA 1988). Mgt trainee, Amalgamated Packaging Industries Ltd, Britain, Rhodesia, USA and S Africa, 1963–66; Trainee Dir, 1967–70, Dir, 1970–74, Coutts & Co.; law student, Council of Legal Educn Inns of Court Sch. of Law, 1974–76; called to the Bar, Inner Temple, 1976; practising barrister, 1977–81; a Senior Law Officer, Min. of Justice, Legal and Parly Affairs, Zimbabwe, 1981–85. A cross-bencher, H of L, 1989–97; joined Lab. Party, 1997; Mem., H of L Constitution Cttee, 2001–. Sponsor, British Defence & Aid Fund for Southern Africa, 1980–94; Patron: Jubilee Appeal, MIND, 1996–; The Mulberry Bush Sch., 1998–; Vice-Patron: APEX Trust, 1995–; 2000 Appeal, British Sch. of Osteopathy, 1999–. Mem. Court, Oxford Brookes Univ., 1999–. Throne/Aldrich Award, State Historical Soc. of Iowa, 1995. *Publications:* (with Prof. P. Acton) To Go Free: a treasury of Iowa's legal heritage, 1995 (Benjamin F. Shambaugh award, 1996); A Brit Among the Hawkeyes, 1998; (contrib.) Outside In: African-American history in Iowa 1838–2000, 2001; contribs anthologies and periodicals. *Heir: s* Hon. John Charles Ferdinand Harold Lyon-Dalberg-Acton [*b* 19 Aug. 1966; *m* 1998, Lucinda, *d* of Brig. James Percival]. *Address:* 152 Whitehall Court, SW1A 2EL. *T:* (020) 7839 3077; 100 Red Oak Lane SE, Cedar Rapids, IA 52403, USA. *T:* (319) 3626181.

ACTON DAVIS, Jonathan James; QC 1996; a Recorder, since 2000; *b* 15 Jan. 1953; *s* of Michael James and Elizabeth Acton Davis; *m* 1987, Lindsay Alice Boswell, *qv*; one *s*. *Educ:* Harrow Sch.; Poly. of Central London (LLB London). Called to the Bar, Inner Temple, 1977 (Bencher, 1995, Master of the House, 1999–); an Asst Recorder, 1997–2000. General Council of the Bar: Mem., 1993–98; Chm., Professional Conduct and Complaints Cttee, 2001 (Vice-Chm., 1999–2000). *Recreations:* cricket, walking, South West France. *Address:* 1 Atkin Building, Gray's Inn, WC1R 5AT. *T:* (020) 7404 0102. *Clubs:* Garrick, MCC.

ACTON DAVIS, Lindsay Alice; *see* Boswell, L. A.

ACWORTH, Ven. Richard Foote; Archdeacon of Wells, since 1993; *b* 19 Oct. 1936, *s* of late Rev. Oswald Roney Acworth and Jean Margaret Acworth; *m* 1966, Margaret Caroline Marie Jennings; two *s* one *d*. *Educ:* St John's Sch., Leatherhead; Sidney Sussex Coll., Cambridge (BA Hist. and Theol. 1962; MA 1965); Cuddesdon Theol Coll. Nat. service, RNVR, 1956–58. Ordained deacon, 1963, priest, 1964; Assistant Curate: St Etheldreda's, Fulham, 1963; All Saints and Martyrs, Langley, Mancs, 1964–66; St Mary's, Bridgwater, 1966–69; Vicar, Yatton, 1969–81; Priest-in-charge, St John's and St Mary's, Taunton, 1981–85; Vicar of St Mary Magdalene, Taunton, 1985–93. *Recreations:* walking, gardening, DIY, ornithology. *Address:* The Old Rectory, Croscombe, Wells, Som BA5 3QN. *T:* (01749) 342242, *Fax:* (01749) 330060.
See also Brig. R. W. Acworth.

ACWORTH, Brig. Robert William, CBE 1986; Registrar of St Paul's Cathedral, 1991–2001; *b* 11 Dec. 1938; *s* of late Rev. Oswald Roney Acworth and of Jean Margaret (*née* Coupland); *m* 1967, Elizabeth Mary, *e d* of late J. N. S. Ridgers; two *s* one *d*. *Educ:* St John's Sch., Leatherhead; RMA, Sandhurst. Commnd, Queen's Royal Regt, 1958; served in Germany, Holland, Norway, Gibraltar, Aden, Oman, Hong Kong, UK and NI; sc 1970; staff and regtl duty, 1971–81; Comdr, 10 UDR, 1981–83; Asst COS, HQ NI, 1983–85; Coll. Comdr, RMA, Sandhurst, 1985–87; Asst COS (Intelligence), HQ AFCENT, 1987–90; Dep. Comdr and COS, SE Dist, 1990–91, retd. Deputy Colonel: Queen's Regt, 1986–92; Princess of Wales's Royal Regt, 1992–94. Pres., Queen's Royal Surrey Regt Assoc., 1995–. *Recreations:* gardening, shooting, fishing, tennis. *Address:* The Old Rectory, Great Wishford, Salisbury, Wilts SP2 0NN. *T:* (01722) 790583. *Club:* Army and Navy.
See also Ven. R. F. Acworth.

ADAIR, Brian Campbell, TD 1979; NP 1975; Senior Partner, Adairs, Solicitors, Dumbarton, since 1973; President, Law Society of Scotland, 1992–93; *b* 28 Aug. 1945; *s* of Alan William Adair and Helen Mary Scott or Adair; *m* 1969, Elaine Jean Morrison; one *s* two *d*. *Educ:* Milngavie Primary Sch.; High Sch., Glasgow; Glasgow Univ. (LLB). Apprentice Solicitor, McGrigor Donald, Glasgow, 1967–70; Solicitor, Dumbarton CC, 1970–73; constituted own firm, 1973. Temp. Sheriff, 1995–99; part-time Sheriff, 2000–. Mem., Scottish Legal Aid Bd, 1998–. Mem. Council, Law Soc. of Scotland, 1980–94 (Vice Pres., 1991–92). Elder, St Paul's Church, Milngavie. Gov., High Sch. of Glasgow, 1992–. *Recreations:* holidaying in Arran, entertaining, golf. *Address:* (office) 3/13 Castle Street, Dumbarton G82 1QS. *T:* (01389) 767625; 21 James Watt Road, Milngavie, Glasgow G62 7JX. *T:* (0141) 956 3070. *Club:* Milngavie Golf (Captain, Centenary Year, 1995).

ADAM, Brian James; Member (SNP) NE Scotland, Scottish Parliament, since 1999; *b* 10 June 1948; *s* of James Pirie Adam and Isabella Adam (now Geddes); *m* 1975, Dorothy McKillip Mann; four *s* one *d*. *Educ:* Keith Grammar Sch.; Aberdeen Univ. (BSc, MSc). Principal Biochemist: City Hosp., Aberdeen, 1973–88; Aberdeen Royal Infirmary, 1988–99. Mem. (SNP) Aberdeen CC, 1988–99. Joined SNP, 1974. Contested (SNP): Gordon, 1992; Aberdeen N, 1997. *Address:* 8 Newburgh Drive, Aberdeen AB22 8SR. *T:* (01224) 704917.

ADAM, Sir Christopher Eric Forbes, 3rd Bt *cr* 1917; *b* 12 Feb. 1920; *s* of Eric Graham Forbes Adam, CMG (*d* 1925) (2nd *s* of 1st Bt) and of Agatha Perrin, *d* of Reginald Walter Macan; *S* uncle, 1982; *m* 1957, Patricia Ann Wreford, *y d* of late John Neville Wreford Brown; one adopted *d*. *Heir: cousin* Rev. (Stephen) Timothy Beilby Forbes Adam [*b* 19 Nov. 1923; *m* 1954, Penelope, *d* of George Campbell Munday, MC; four *d*]. *Address:* 46 Rawlings Street, SW3 2LS.

ADAM, Gordon Johnston, PhD; Member (Lab) North East Region, England, European Parliament, since Feb. 2000; *b* 28 March 1934; *s* of John Craig Adam and Deborah Armstrong Johnston; *m* 1973, Sarah Jane Seely; one *s*. *Educ:* Leeds Univ. (BSc Hons, PhD). CEng, MIMM. NCB, 1959–79. Mem., Whitley Bay Bor. Council, 1971–74; Mem. 1973–80, and Dep. Leader 1975–80, North Tyneside Metrop. Bor. Council (Chm., 1973–74; Mayor, 1974–75). Mem., Whitley Bay Playhouse Theatre Trust, 1975– (Chm., 1975–80). MEP (Lab) Northumbria, 1979–99; contested (Lab) NE Region, 1999; Vice-Chm., Energy, Res. and Technol. Cttee, EP, 1984–99. Chm., Northern Energy Initiative, 1996–; Member: Northern Econ. Planning Council, 1974–79; Northern Arts Gen.

Council, 1975–78; Northern Sinfonia Management Cttee, 1978–80; Bd, Northern Stage Co., 1989–. Contested (Lab): Tynemouth, 1966; Berwick-upon-Tweed, Nov. 1973 (by-election), Feb. 1974 and 1992. *Recreation:* gardening. *Address:* The Old Farm House, East House Farm, Killingworth Village, Newcastle upon Tyne NE12 6BQ. *T:* (0191) 216 0154.

ADAM, Robert, RIBA; Director, Robert Adam Architects, since 1995; *b* 10 April 1948; *s* of Dr Robert Wilson Adam and Jessie Margaret Adam; *m* 1970, Sarah Jane Chalcraft; one *s* one *d.* *Educ:* Canford Sch., Dorset; Regent Street Poly. (DipArch 1973). RIBA 1977. Partner, 1977–, Dir, 1987–, Roberts & Partners, subseq. Winchester Design (Architects) Ltd. Trustee, 1989–98, Chm., Faculty of Fine Arts, 1993–97, British Sch. at Rome; Chm., Popular Housing Forum, 1997–; Mem. Council, RIBA, 1999–. *Publications:* Classical Architecture: a complete handbook, 1990; (contrib.) Building Classical, 1993; (contrib.) Companion to Contemporary Architectural Thought, 1993; Buildings by Design, 1994; papers in Architectl Review, Architects Jl, RIBA Jl, Architectl Design, City Jl (USA), Archis (Holland). *Recreations:* medieval history, ceramics. *Address:* 9 Upper High Street, Winchester, Hants SO23 8UT. *T:* (01962) 843843. *Clubs:* Athenæum, Home House.

ADAM, Sheila Anne, QHP; MD; FRCP, FFPHM; Deputy Chief Medical Officer, since 1999, and Director of Policy, since 2001, NHS Executive, Department of Health; *b* 24 Nov. 1949. *Educ:* Nottingham High Sch. for Girls; Edinburgh Univ. (MB ChB 1972; MD 1983); DCH 1974. MRCP 1976, FRCP 1993; MFPHM 1981, FFPHM 1986. Public Health Registrar, 1975–77, Sen. Registrar and MRC Trng Fellow in Public Health, 1977–81, Oxford RHA; Public Health Consultant, Brent HA, 1981–83; Public Health Consultant, 1983–89, Dir of Public Health, 1989–95, NW Thames RHA; NHS Executive, Department of Health: Hd of Mental Health and NHS Community Care, 1995–97; Dep. Dir of Health Services, 1997–99; Dir of Health Services, 1999–2001. QHP 1996–. *Address:* Department of Health, Richmond House, 79 Whitehall, SW1A 7NS.

ADAMI, Edward F.; *see* Fenech-Adami.

ADAMISHIN, Anatoly; Vice President, International Affairs, Sistema Joint-Stock Financial Corporation, Russia, since 1998; *b* 11 Oct. 1934; *s* of Leonid Adamishin and Vera Gusovskaya; *m* 1979, Olga Vtorova; one *d*; *m* 2000, Svetlana Kharlamova. *Educ:* Lomonosov Moscow State Univ. Joined USSR Diplomatic Service, 1957; First European Dept, Min. of Foreign Affairs, 1957–59; served embassy in Italy, 1959–65; First European Dept, 1965–71; Foreign Policy Planning Dept, 1971–73; Head, Gen. Internat. Issues Dept, 1973–78; Head, First European Dept and Mem., Min. of Foreign Affairs Collegium, 1978–86; Dep. Minister for Foreign Affairs, 1986–90; also Head, USSR Commn for UNESCO Affairs, 1987–90; Ambassador to Italy, 1990–92; First Dep. Minister for Foreign Affairs of Russia, 1992–94; Ambassador to UK, 1994–97; Minister for relations with CIS, Min. of Foreign Affairs, 1997–98. *Publications:* Tramonto e rinascita di una grande potenza, 1995; The White Sun of Angola, 2001. *Recreation:* lawn tennis. *Address:* (office) Leontyevski per. 10, 103009 Moscow, Russia.

ADAMKUS, Valdas; President, Republic of Lithuania, since 1998; *b* Kaunas, 3 Nov. 1926; *s* of Ignas Adamkavičius and Genovaite Bacevičiūte; *m* 1951, Alma Adamkiene. *Educ:* Munich Univ.; Illinois Inst. of Technology, Chicago. Qualified civil engr, 1960; Chicago Car Plant, 1949–50; Draftsman, Meissner Consulting Engrs, 1950–59; owner and operator, summer resort, Sodus, Michigan, 1960–69; Dir, Envmt Res. Centre, US Envmt Protection Agency, 1969–71; Dep. Adminr, 1971–81, Adminr, 1981–97, Reg. 5 (Great Lakes), US Envmt Protection Agency. Mem., US Delegn in Co-operation with USSR under bilateral envmtl agreement, 1972–91; Chm., US Delegn, Internat. Jt Commn for Great Lakes (US-Canada), 1980–97. Vice Chm., 1958–65, Chm., 1967–97, Santara-Sviesa Cultural-political Fedn; Vice-Chm., Exec. Cttee, American-Lithuanian Community; Mem., American-Lithuanian Council. Hon. Dr: Vilnius, 1989; Indiana St Joseph Coll., 1991; Northwestern, 1994; Kaunas Technology Univ., 1998. *Publication:* Lithuania: the name of my destiny, 1997. *Recreations:* sport activities (golf, swimming), classical music. *Address:* 3 S Daukanto Square, 2600 Vilnius, Lithuania. *T:* (2) 628986.

ADAMS, Dr Aileen Kirkpatrick, CBE 1988; FRCS; FRCA; Emeritus Consultant Anaesthetist, Addenbrooke's Hospital, Cambridge, since 1983; *b* 5 Sept. 1923; *d* of F. Joseph Adams and M. Agnes Adams (*née* Munro). *Educ:* Farringtons School, Chislehurst; Sheffield Univ. MB ChB Sheffield, 1945; MA Cantab 1977; FFARCS 1954; FFA(SA) 1987; FRCS 1988; FDSRCS 1989. Fellow in anaesthesia, Harvard Univ. and Mass. Gen. Hosp., Boston, 1955–57; Consultant Anaesthetist, Addenbrooke's Hosp., Cambridge, 1960–83; Associate Lectr, Univ. of Cambridge, 1977–85; Dean, Faculty of Anaesthetists, RCS, 1985–88. Sen. Lectr, Lagos Univ. Med. Sch., Nigeria, 1963–64. Mem., Cambridge Health Authy, 1978–82. Royal College of Surgeons of England: Mem. Council, 1982–88; Hunterian Prof., 1993; Trustee, Hunterian Collection, 1996–; Royal Society of Medicine: Hon. Treas., 1995–99; formerly Pres., Anaesthetic Section; Pres., History of Medicine Section, 1994–95; Pres., History of Anaesthesia Soc., 1990–92. Hon. Archivist, Royal Coll. of Anaesthetists, 1989–98. Former Examr, Cambridge Univ. and FFARCS. Hon. Mem., Assoc. of Anaesthetists, GB and Ire. Mem., Editl Bd, Anaesthesia, 1972–85. Silver Jubilee Medal, 1977. *Publications:* book chapters and papers in med. jls on anaesthetic and related topics, and on history of medicine. *Recreations:* choral singing, outdoor activities, including walking, ski-ing, history. *Address:* 12 Redwood Lodge, Grange Road, Cambridge CB3 9AR. *T:* and *Fax:* (01223) 356460.

ADAMS, Alec Cecil Stanley, CMG 1960; CBE 1952; HM Diplomatic Service, retired; *b* 25 July 1909; *e s* of late Stanley A. Adams. *Educ:* King's School, Canterbury; Corpus Christi Coll., Cambridge. One of HM Vice-Consuls in Siam, 1933; served in Portuguese East Africa (acting Consul at Beira, June 1936–Feb. 1937); local rank 2nd Secretary, Bangkok Legation, 1937; Acting Consul, Sourabaya, 1938; Bangkok Legation, 1939–40; Foreign Office, Ministry of Information, 1940; Consul, in Foreign Office, 1945; Bangkok, 1946, Acting Consul-General and Chargé d'Affaires, 1948; Consul, Cincinnati, 1949; HM Chargé d'Affaires in Korea, 1950; HM Consul-General at Houston, Texas, 1953–55; Counsellor and Consul-General at HM Embassy, Bangkok, 1956–62; Deputy Commissioner-General for South East Asia, 1962–63; Political Advisor to C-in-C (Far East) at Singapore, 1963–67; retired 1967. *Address:* Flat 513, 97 Southampton Row, WC1B 4HH. *Club:* Travellers.

ADAMS, Prof. Alfred Rodney, FRS 1996; Professor of Physics, University of Surrey, since 1987; *b* 11 Nov. 1939; *s* of Alfred Walter Adams and Lucie Elisabeth Adams; *m* 1966, Helga Fehringer; two *d.* *Educ:* Rayleigh Technical Sch.; Westcliff High Sch.; Univ. of Leicester (BSc, PhD, DSc). FInstP, FIEE, FIEEE. Research Fellow: Univ. of Leicester, 1964; Univ. of Karlsruhe, 1965; Lectr, 1967, Reader, 1984, Univ. of Surrey. Royal Soc./Japanese Soc. for Promotion of Science Fellow, 1980, Hitachi Prof., 1992, Tokyo Inst. Tech; CNRS Vis. Researcher, Univ. of Montpellier, 1993. Duddell Medal and Prize, Inst. of Physics, 1995. *Publications:* (ed with Y. Suematsu) Semiconductor Lasers and Photonic Integrated Circuits, 1994; numerous papers in jls on physics and on quantum electronics. *Recreations:* walking, travel. *Address:* Department of Physics, University of Surrey, Guildford, Surrey GU2 5XH. *T:* (01483) 259310.

ADAMS, Prof. Anthony Peter, FRCA, FANZCA; Professor of Anaesthetics in the University of London, 1979–2001, and Joint Vice-Chairman, Division of Surgery and Anaesthesia, 1998–2001, at Guy's, King's and St Thomas' Medical and Dental School of King's College, London; *b* 17 Oct. 1936; *s* of late H. W. J. Adams and W. L. Adams; *m* 1973, Veronica Rosemary John; three *s* one *d.* *Educ:* Epsom College; London Univ. MB BS 1960, PhD 1970; DA 1962; MRCS 1960, LRCP 1960, FRCA (FFARCS 1964); FANZCA (FFARACS 1987). Wellcome Res. Fellow, RPMS, 1964–66; Consultant Anaesthetist and Clinical Lectr, Nuffield Dept of Anaesthetics, Univ. of Oxford, 1968–79; Guy's Hosp. Med. Sch., subseq. UMDS of Guy's and St Thomas' Hospitals, 1979–98: Chm., Div. of Anaesthetics, 1984–89, 1996–97; Vice-Chm., Div. of Surgery and Anaesthesia, 1997–98; Mem., Council of Govs, 1997–98. Member: Standing Cttee, Bd of Studies in Surgery, London Univ., 1979–92; Academic Bd of Medicine, London Univ., 1980–83; Jt Cttee for Higher Trng of Anaesthetists, 1985–90; Specialist Adv. Cttee on Accident and Emergency Medicine, Jt Cttee for Higher Trng in Medicine, 1986–90; Exec. Cttee, Fedn of Assocs of Clin. Profs, 1979–87; Exec. Cttee, Anaesthetic Res. Soc., 1983–94 (Chm., 1991–94); Council, Assoc. of Anaesthetists of GB and Ireland, 1984–89 (Chm., Safety Cttee, 1987–89); Council, Royal Coll. of Anaesthetists, 1989–97; Chm., Assoc. of Profs of Anaesthesia, 1984–88; Senator, Eur. Acad. of Anaesthesiology, 1985–95, 2000– (Mem. Exec. Cttee, 1997–). Regional Educnl Adviser (SE Thames RHA) to Faculty of Anaesthetists of RCS, 1980–87; Examiner: FFARCS, 1974–86; DVA, 1986–93; DA and DM, Univ. of WI, 1986–88, 1995, 1997, 1998; MSc, Univ. of Wales Coll. of Medicine, 1988–93; PhD: Univ. of London, 1989, 1997, 1999, 2001; Univ. of Manchester, 1993; Univ. of Liverpool, 1995; NUI, Galway, 2000; MB ChB Chinese Univ. of Hong Kong, 1990. Asst Editor, Anaesthesia, 1976–82; Associate Editor: Survey of Anesthesiology, 1984–2001; European Jl of Anaesthesiology, 1987–94; Jl of Anesthesia (Japan), 1995–; Mem. Editl Bd, British Jl of Anaesthesia, 1984–97; Chm. Editl Bd, 1997–2000, Editor-in-Chief, 2000–, European Jl of Anaesthesiology. Mem. Bd of Govs, Sutton High Sch. for Girls, 1988–95 (Chm., 1991–95). *Publications:* Principles and Practice of Blood Gas Analysis, 1979, 2nd edn 1982; Intensive Care, 1984; (ed jtly) Recent Advances in Anaesthesia and Analgesia, vol. 15, 1985, vol. 16, 1989, vol. 17, 1992, vol. 18, 1994, vol. 19, 1995, vol. 20, 1998, vol. 21, 2000; Emergency Anaesthesia, 1986 and 1988; (ed jtly) Anaesthesia, Analgesia and Intensive Care, 1991; contribs to medical jls. *Recreations:* badger watching, English castles, history, tennis, croquet, cinema, theatre, ballet. *Clubs:* Royal Society of Medicine; Halifax House (Oxford).

ADAMS, Rev. David; *see* Adams, Rev. J. D. A.

ADAMS, David H.; *see* Hempleman-Adams.

ADAMS, Ernest Victor, CB 1978; Deputy Secretary and Commissioner, Inland Revenue, 1975–81; *b* 17 Jan. 1920; *s* of Ernest and Amelia Adams; *m* 1st, 1943, Joan Bastin, Halesworth, Suffolk (*d* 1985); one *s* one *d*; 2nd, 1987, Mavisse Evelyn Surtees, Henley-on-Thames. *Educ:* Manchester Grammar Sch.; Keble Coll., Oxford (MA). HM Forces, RA, 1940–45. Inland Revenue Dept, 1947; Sen. Inspector of Taxes, 1956; Principal Inspector of Taxes, 1961; Sen. Principal Inspector of Taxes, 1966; Dep. Chief Inspector of Taxes, 1969. *Address:* 5 Northfield Court, Henley-on-Thames RG9 2LH. *T:* (01491) 572586. *Club:* Phyllis Court (Henley).

ADAMS, Gerard, (Gerry); MP (SF) Belfast West, since 1997; Member (SF) Belfast West, Northern Ireland Assembly, since 1998; President, Sinn Féin, since 1983 (Vice-President, 1978–83); *b* 6 Oct. 1948; *s* of Gerard Adams and Annie (*née* Hannaway); *m* 1971, Colette McArdle; one *s.* *Educ:* St Mary's Christian Brothers' Sch., Belfast. Interned for suspected terrorist activity, 1971, 1973; subseq. imprisoned; released, 1976. Mem., NI Assembly, 1982; MP (Provisional Sinn Féin) Belfast W, 1983–92. Thorr Award, Switzerland, 1995. *Publications:* Falls Memories (autobiog.), 1982; Politics of Irish Freedom; Pathway to Peace, 1988; Cage Eleven (autobiog.), 1990; The Street and Other Stories, 1992; Selected Writings, 1994; Before the Dawn (autobiog.), 1996; An Irish Voice: the quest for peace, 1997. *Address:* Sinn Féin, 55 Falls Road, Belfast, N Ireland BT12 4PD.

ADAMS, Irene; *see* Adams, Katherine.

ADAMS, Sir James; *see* Adams, Sir W. J.

ADAMS, James Noel, DPhil; FBA 1992; Senior Research Fellow, All Souls College, Oxford, since 1998; *b* 24 Sept. 1943; *m* 1971, Geneviève Lucienne Baudon; one *s.* *Educ:* North Sydney Boys' High Sch.; Univ. of Sydney (BA); Brasenose Coll., Oxford (DPhil). MA Cantab. Teaching Fellow, Dept of Latin, Univ. of Sydney, 1965–66; Commonwealth Schol., Brasenose Coll., Oxford, 1967–70; Rouse Res. Fellow in Classics, Christ's Coll., Cambridge, 1970–72; University of Manchester: Lectr and Sen. Lectr in Greek and Latin, 1972–82; Reader in Latin, 1982–93; Prof. of Latin, 1993–95; Prof. of Latin, Univ. of Reading, 1995–97. Vis. Sen. Res. Fellow, St John's Coll., Oxford, 1994–95. *Publications:* The Text and Language of a Vulgar Latin Chronicle (Anonymus Valesianus), 1976; The Vulgar Latin of the Letters of Claudius Terentianus, 1977; The Latin Sexual Vocabulary, 1982; Wackernagel's Law and the Placement of the Copula *Esse* in Classical Latin, 1994; Pelagonius and Latin Veterinary Terminology in the Roman Empire, 1995; articles in learned jls. *Recreation:* cricket. *Address:* All Souls College, Oxford OX1 4AL.

ADAMS, Jennifer, LVO 1993; Director of Open Spaces, Corporation of London, since 2001; *b* 1 Feb. 1948; *d* of Arthur Roy Thomas Crisp and Joyce Muriel Crisp (*née* Davey); *m* 1968, Terence William Adams. *Educ:* City of London School for Girls. Final Diploma, Inst. of Leisure and Amenity (FILAM DipPRA); FIHort. Various positions in Parks Dept, London Borough of Wandsworth, 1971–83; Superintendent, Central Royal Parks, later Manager, Inner Royal Parks, 1983–97; Hd of Inner Parks and Commerce, Royal Parks, 1997 –2001. Pres., Inst. of Horticulture, 1996–98. Liveryman, Gardeners' Co., 1985. Associate of Honour, RHS, 1999. *Recreations:* walking, gardening, nature conservation.

ADAMS, John; composer; *b* 15 Feb. 1947. *Educ:* Harvard Univ. (scholar). Teacher, San Francisco Conservatory of Music, 1972–82; Music Advr, 1978–82, Composer-in-Residence, 1982–85, San Francisco Symphony. *Compositions include: opera:* Nixon in China, 1987; The Death of Klinghoffer, 1990; I Was Looking at the Ceiling and Then I Saw the Sky, 1995; El niño, 2000; *orchestral works:* Shaker Loops, 1978; Common Tones in Simple Time, 1979; Harmonium, 1980–81; Grand Pianola Music, 1981–82; Harmonielehre, 1984–85; The Chairman Dances, 1985; Short Ride in a Fast Machine, 1986; Tromba Lontana, 1986; Fearful Symmetries, 1988; The Wound-Dresser, 1988–89; Eros Piano, 1989; El Dorado, 1991; Violin Concerto, 1993 (Grawemeyer Award for Music Composition, 1995); Gnarly Buttons, 1996; Century Rolls, piano concerto, 1998; *chamber and ensemble works:* Christian Zeal and Activity, 1973; China Gates, 1977; Phrygian Gates, 1977; Chamber Symphony, 1992; John's Book of Alleged Dances, 1994; Road Movies, 1995; numerous recordings. *Address:* c/o Boosey & Hawkes Music Publishers Ltd, 295 Regent Street, W1R 8JH.

ADAMS, John Crawford, OBE 1977; MD, MS, FRCS; in consulting orthopaedic practice; Hon. Consulting Orthopaedic Surgeon, St Mary's Hospital, London, since 1979;

Hon. Civil Consultant in Orthopædic Surgery, Royal Air Force, since 1984 (Civil Consultant, 1964–84); *b* 25 Sept. 1913; *s* of Archibald Crawford Adams, W Hallam, Derbys; *m* 1940, Joan Bower Elphinstone (*d* 1981); *m* 1990, Marguerite Kyle. MB, BS 1937; MRCS 1937; LRCP 1937; FRCS 1941; MD (London) 1943; MS (London) 1965. Formerly: Chief Asst, Orthopædic and Accident Dept, London Hosp.; Orthopædic Specialist, RAFVR; Resident Surgical Officer, Wingfield-Morris Orthopædic Hosp., Oxford; Consultant Orthopaedic Surgeon: St Mary's Hosp., London and Paddington Green Children's Hosp., 1948–79; Brighton Gen. Hosp., 1948–58; St Vincent's Orthopaedic Hosp., Pinner, 1952–65. FRSocMed 1948 (Hon. Mem., Sect. of Orthopædics, 1986); Hon. Fellow: British Orthopædic Assoc., 1994 (Hon. Sec., 1959–62; Vice-Pres., 1974–75; Robert Jones Gold Medal and Prize, 1961); Amer. Acad. of Orthopædic Surgeons, 1975. Mem, Council, Jl of Bone and Joint Surgery, 1974–84 (formerly Production Editor). *Publications:* Outline of Orthopædics, 1956, 13th edn 2001; Outline of Fractures, 1957, 11th edn 1999; Ischio-femoral Arthrodesis, 1966; Arthritis and Back Pain, 1972; Standard Orthopaedic Operations, 1976, 4th edn 1992; Recurrent Dislocation of Shoulder (chapter in Techniques in British Surgery, ed Maingot), 1950; Francis, Forgiven Fraud, 1991; Shakespeare's Physic, 2000; Associate Editor and contributor, Operative Surgery (ed Rob and Smith); contributions to the Journal of Bone and Joint Surgery, etc. *Recreations:* history, writing, silversmithing. *Address:* 126 Harley Street, W1N 1AH; The Old H H Inn, Cheriton, Alresford, Hampshire SO24 0PY.

ADAMS, Rev. (John) David (Andrew); Headmaster, Weydon School, 1982–98; Chaplain to the Queen, since 1994; Secondary School consultant, since 1998; *b* 27 Nov. 1937; *s* of John McCullough McConnell Adams and Sylvia Pansy (*née* Pinner); *m* 1970, Maria Carmen de Azpiazu-Cruz; one *s* one *d*. *Educ:* Trinity Coll., Dublin (BA 1960; Div. Test. 1961; MA 1964; BD 1965); Univ. of Reading (MEd 1974). Curate, St Stephen's, Belfast, 1962–65; part-time teaching and vol. chaplaincy in Europe, 1965–67; Hd, Religious Educn, Tower Ramparts, Ipswich, 1967–70; Counsellor, later Sen. Teacher, Robert Haining Sch., Surrey, 1970–74; Headmaster, St Paul's, Addlestone, 1974–82. Non-stipendiary Curate, St Thomas-on-the-Bourne, Farnham, 1976–. *Recreations:* gardening, household chores, birding; the life of George Morley, Bishop of Winchester, 1597–1684. *Address:* Brookside Farm, Oast House Crescent, Farnham, Surrey GU9 0NP. *T:* (01252) 652737.

ADAMS, John Douglas Richard; His Honour Judge John Adams; a Circuit Judge, since 1998; *b* 19 March 1940; *o s* of late Gordon Arthur Richard Adams and Marjorie Ethel Adams (*née* Ongley); *m* 1966, Anne Easton Todd, *o d* of late Robert Easton Todd and Mary Ann Margaret Todd (*née* Isaac); two *d*. *Educ:* Watford Grammar School; Durham Univ. (LLB 1963). Called to Bar, Lincoln's Inn, 1967; Bencher, Inner Temple, 1997. Lecturer: Newcastle Univ., 1963–71; University College London, 1971–78; also practised at Revenue Bar until 1978; Special Comr of Income Tax, 1978–82; Registrar of Civil Appeals, 1982–98; a Recorder, 1992–98. Hon. Lecturer, St Edmund Hall, Oxford, 1978–; Vis. Lectr, Oxford Univ., 1995–. *Publications:* (with J. Whalley) The International Taxation of Multinational Enterprises, 1977; (contrib.) Atkin's Court Forms, 1984, 1992; (ed jtly) Supreme Court Practice, 1985, 1991, 1993, 1995, 1997, 1999; (ed jtly) Chitty and Jacob's Queen's Bench Forms, 21st edn, 1986; (ed jtly) Sweet & Maxwell's County Court Litigation, 1993; (ed jtly) Emergency Remedies in the Family Courts, 3rd edn, 1997. *Recreations:* music, walking, dining. *Address:* Barnet County Court, St Mary's Court, Regent's Park Road, Finchley Central, N3 1BQ.

ADAMS, Rear-Adm. John Harold, CB 1967; LVO 1957; Senior Partner, John Adams Interviews, 1993–99; *b* Newcastle-on-Tyne, 19 Dec. 1918; *m* 1st, 1943, Mary Parker (marr. diss. 1961); one *s* decd; 2nd, 1961, Ione Eadie, MVO, JP (*d* 1998); two *s* two *d*. *Educ:* Glenalmond. Joined Navy, 1936; Home Fleet, 1937–39; Western Approaches, Channel and N Africa, 1939–42 (despatches); Staff Capt. (D), Liverpool, 1943–45; Staff Course, Greenwich, 1945; HMS Solebay, 1945–47; HMS Vernon, 1947–49; jssc 1949; comd HMS Creole, 1950; Staff Flag Officer Submarines, 1951–52; TAS, Warfare Div., Admty, 1953; Comdr, HM Yacht Britannia, 1954–57; Asst Dir, Underwater Weapons Matériel Dept, 1957–58; Capt. (SM) 3rd Submarine Sqdn, HMS Adamant, 1958–60; Captain Supt, Underwater Detection Estab., Portland, subseq. Admty Underwater Weapons Estab., 1960–62; idc 1963; comd HMS Albion, 1964–66; Asst Chief of Naval Staff (Policy), 1966–68; retd 1968. Lieut 1941; Lieut-Comdr 1949; Comdr 1951; Capt. 1957; Rear-Adm. 1966. Dir, Paper and Paper Products Industry Training Bd, 1968–71; Dir, Employers' Federation of Papermakers and Boardmakers, 1972–73; Dir Gen., British Paper and Board Industry Fedn, 1974–83. Dir, DUO (UK) Ltd, 1983–93. Chm. Governors, Cheam Sch, 1975–87. Paper Industry Gold Medal, 1984. *Recreations:* fishing, photography. *Address:* The Coach House, Greywell Hill, Hook, Hants RG29 1DG. *Club:* Army and Navy.

ADAMS, John Kenneth; Editor of Country Life, 1958–73; Editorial Director, Country Life Ltd, 1959–73; *b* 3 June 1915; *o c* of late Thomas John Adams and late Mabel Adams (*née* Jarvis), Oxford; *m* 1944, Margaret (*d* 2000), *o c* of late Edward Claude Fortescue, Banbury, Oxon. *Educ:* City of Oxford Sch.; Balliol Coll., Oxford. Asst Master, Stonyhurst Coll., 1939–40; served with RAFVR, 1940–41 (invalided); Asst Master, Wellington Coll., 1941–44; attached to Manchester Guardian as Leader-writer, 1942–44; Leader-writer, The Scotsman, 1944–46; joined editorial staff of Country Life, 1946; Asst Editor, 1952; Deputy Editor, 1956; Editor, 1958; Editorial Director, 1959. *Recreations:* gardening, ornithology, travel. *Address:* 95 Alleyn Park, West Dulwich, SE21 8AA. *T:* (020) 8693 1736. *Club:* Athenæum.

ADAMS, Prof. John Norman; Professor of Intellectual Property, University of Sheffield, since 1994; barrister; *b* 24 Dec. 1939; *s* of Vincent Smith Adams and Elsie Adams (*née* Davison), Gateshead. *Educ:* Newcastle upon Tyne Royal GS; Univ. of Durham. Called to the Bar, Inner Temple, 1984. Solicitor in private practice, 1965–71; Lectr in Law, Univ. of Sheffield, 1971–79; Sen. Lectr, 1979–87, Prof. of Commercial Law, 1987–94, Univ. of Kent. Dir, Intellectual Property Inst., 1991–99. *Publications include:* (with K. V. Prichard-Jones) Franchising, 1981, 4th edn 1997; (with G. Averley) A Bibliography of Eighteenth Century Legal Literature, 1982; Character Merchandising, 1987, 2nd edn 1996; (with R. Brownsword) Understanding Contract Law, 1987, 3rd edn 2000; Commercial Hiring and Leasing, 1989; (with R. Brownsword) Understanding Law, 1992, 2nd edn 1999; (with R. Brownsword) Key Issues in Contract, 1995; Atiyah's Sale of Goods, 10th edn 2000. *Recreations:* music, walking. *Address:* 26 Priory Terrace, NW6 4DM. *T:* (020) 7328 8676; 49 Endcliffe Hall Avenue, Sheffield S10 3EL. *T:* (0114) 268 7311; One Raymond Buildings, Gray's Inn, WC1R 5BN; Faculty of Law, University of Sheffield, Sheffield S10 1FL. *Clubs:* Savage, Lansdowne.

ADAMS, John Roderick Seton; His Honour Judge Adams; a Circuit Judge, since 1990; *b* 29 Feb. 1936; *s* of George Adams and Winifred (*née* Wilson); *m* 1965, Pamela Bridget, *e d* of Rev. D. E. Rice, MC; three *s*. *Educ:* Whitgift Sch.; Trinity Coll., Cambridge. BA, 1959, MA 1963. Commnd, Seaforth Highlanders, 1955–56; Parachute Regt, TA, 1959–66. Legal Adviser in industry, 1960–66. Called to the Bar, Inner Temple, 1962; began practice at the Bar, 1967; Dep. Circuit Judge, 1978–80; a Recorder, 1980–90. *Recreations:* music, fishing, growing old roses. *Address:* 6 Pump Court, Temple, EC4Y 7AR. *T:* (020) 7583 6013; Melness House, Sutherland IV27 4YR. *T:* (01847) 601255. *Club:* Bradford.

ADAMS, Katherine, (Irene); JP; MP (Lab) Paisley North, since Nov. 1990; *b* 27 Dec. 1947; *m* 1968, Allen S. Adams (*d* 1990), MP Paisley North; one *s* two *d*. *Educ:* Stanley Green High Sch., Paisley. Councillor, Paisley Town, 1970; Member: Renfrew DC, 1974–78; Strathclyde Regl Council, 1979–84. *Address:* c/o House of Commons, SW1A 0AA.

ADAMS, Major Kenneth Galt, CVO 1979; CBE 1989; Hon. Industry Fellow, Comino Foundation, since 1997; *b* 6 Jan. 1920; *s* of late William Adams, OBE, and Christina Elisabeth (*née* Hall); *m* 1988, Sally, *d* of late Col John Middleton and *widow* of Douglas Long. *Educ:* Doncaster Grammar Sch.; Staff Coll., Camberley (psc 1953). Served RASC, 1940–59: War Service, ME and N Africa; DADST WO, 1946–48; DAA&QMG, Aldershot, 1952; DAQMG HQ Northern Comd, 1954–56; Sen. Instr, RASC Officers Sch., 1956–59. Sec., S London Indust. Mission, 1959–61; Proprietors of Hay's Wharf Ltd, 1960–70, Exec. Dir, 1966–70; non-exec. dir and consultant, other cos, until 1985. St George's House, Windsor Castle: Dir of Studies, 1969–76; Fellow, 1976–82; Hon. Fellow, 1990. Comino Fellow, RSA, 1979–89; Industry Fellow, Comino Foundn, 1989–96. Chairman: S London Indust. Mission, 1971–74; Indust. Christian Fellowship, 1977–86; Vice Chairman: Archbishops' Council on Evangelism, 1965–77; Southwark Cathedral Council, 1967–70; Member: Indust. Cttee, Bd for Social Responsibility of C of E, 1973–81; Bldg EDC, NEDC, 1977–81; Prof. Standards Cttee, BIM, 1976–81; Dept of Employment's Services Resettlement Cttee for SE England, 1967–77; Adv. Cttee, Christian Assoc. of Business Execs, 1975–96; Adv. Cttee, Inst. of Business Ethics, 1986–96; Hon. Mem., Foundn for Manufg and Industry (Chm., 1993); Trustee, Industrial Trng Foundn, 1980–91. Lay Steward, St George's Chapel, Windsor, 1969–. Freeman, City of London, 1967; Liveryman, Pattenmakers' Co., 1976–96. CIMgt (CBIM 1972); FRSA 1979; FCIT 1981. MA Lambeth, 1979; Hon. DPhil Internat. Management Centres, 1991. Templeton Award, 1996. *Publications:* lectures and papers on developing an affirmative cultural attitude to industry in Britain, and on Christianity and wealth creation. *Recreations:* 19th century novels, pilgrimages. *Address:* 8 Datchet Road, Windsor, Berks SL4 1QE. *T:* (01753) 869708. *Club:* Army and Navy.

ADAMS, Lewis Drummond, OBE 1999; Board Member, Strategic Rail Authority, since 1999; General Secretary, Associated Society of Locomotive Engineers and Firemen, 1994–99; *b* London, 16 Aug. 1939; *s* of Lewis John Adams and Margaret (*née* Drummond); *m* 1958, Jean Marion Bass; one *s* one *d*. *Educ:* Impington Coll., Cambridge; NCLC; Tavistock Inst., London. British Railways: engine cleaner, 1954–55; engine fireman and driver asst, 1955–67; engine driver, 1967–80. Associated Society of Locomotive Engineers and Firemen: Sec., London Dist Council No 1, 1970–80; Executive Committee: Mem., 1981–90; Vice-Pres., 1985–90; Asst Gen. Sec., 1990–93. British Railways: Mem., later Chm., Pension Fund, 1982–93; Member: Wages Grade Pension Fund, 1982–93; Superannuation Fund, 1982–93. Dir, Millennium Drivers Ltd, 1998–. Member: TUC Pension Cttee, 1987–90; Railway Industries Adv. Cttee, 1985–90. *Recreations:* travel, gardening.

ADAMS, Air Vice-Marshal Michael Keith, CB 1986; AFC 1970; FRAeS; *b* 23 Jan. 1934; *s* of late William Frederick Adams and Jean Mary Adams; *m* 1966, Susan (*née* Trudgian); two *s* one *d*. *Educ:* Bedford Sch.; City of London Sch. FRAeS 1978. Joined RAF, 1952; qualified Pilot, 1954; Flying Instr, 1960; Test Pilot, 1963 (QCVSA 1967); Staff Coll., Toronto, 1969; CO Empire Test Pilots' Sch., 1975; Dir of Operational Requirements, 1978–81; RCDS, 1982; AOC Training Units, 1983; ACAS (Op. Requirements), MoD, 1984; ACDS (Op. Requirements) Air, MoD, 1985–86; Sen. Directing Staff (Air), RCDS, 1987–88; retd. Dir, Thomson-CSF (UK) Ltd, 1988–94; Dir, International Aerospace, 1989–96 (Chm., 1996). Vice-Pres., RAeS, 1992–95. Chm. Govs, Duke of Kent Sch., Cranleigh, Surrey, 1997–. *Recreations:* walking, silversmithing. *Club:* Royal Air Force.

ADAMS, Norman (Edward Albert), RA 1972 (ARA 1967); ARCA 1951; artist (painter); Professor of Painting in Royal Academy schools, since 1995; *b* 9 Feb. 1927; *s* of Albert Henry Adams and Winifred Elizabeth Rose Adams; *m* 1947, Anna Theresa; two *s*. *Educ:* Royal Coll. of Art. Head of Sch. of Painting, Manchester Coll. of Art and Design, 1962–70; Lectr, Leeds Univ., 1975–78; Prof. of Fine Art, and Dir of King Edward VII Coll. (formerly Sch.), Univ. of Newcastle upon Tyne, 1981–86; Keeper, Royal Acad., 1986–95. Exhibitions in America (New York, Pittsburgh); Retrospective exhibns, Royal College of Art, 1969, Whitechapel Gall., RA, 1988. Paintings in collections of: most British Provincial Art Galleries; Tate Gall., London; Nat. Galls, New Zealand; Gulbenkian Mus., Lisbon; work purchased by: Arts Coun. of Gt Brit.; Contemp. Art Soc.; Chantrey Bequest; various Educn Authorities. Murals at: Broad Lane Comprehensive Sch., Coventry; St Anselm's Church, S London; Our Lady of Lourdes, Milton Keynes; Stations of the Cross, St Mary's RC Church, Mulberry Street, Manchester, 1994–95. Decor for ballets, Covent Garden and Sadler's Wells. Kornferry Prize, RA Summer exhibn. *Publications:* Alibis and Convictions, 1978; A Decade of Painting, 1971–81, 1981; (with A. Adams): Angels of Soho, 1988; Island Chapters, 1991; Life on Limestone, 1994. *Address:* Butts, Horton-in-Ribblesdale, Settle, North Yorks BD24 0HD. *T:* (01729) 860284; 6 Gainsborough Road, Chiswick, W4 1NJ.

ADAMS, Sir Philip (George Doyne), KCMG 1969 (CMG 1959); HM Diplomatic Service, retired; *b* 17 Dec. 1915; *s* of late George Basil Doyne Adams, MD, and Arline Maud Adams (*née* Dodgson); *m* 1954, Hon. (Mary) Elizabeth Lawrence, *e d* of Baron Trevethin and Oaksey (3rd and 1st Baron respectively); two *s* two *d*. *Educ:* Lancing Coll.; Christ Church, Oxford. Entered Consular Service, 1939; served at: Beirut, 1939; Cairo, 1941; Jedda, 1945; FO, 1947; First Sec., 1948; Vienna, 1951; Counsellor, Khartoum, 1954; Beirut, 1956; FO, 1959; Chicago, 1963; Ambassador to Jordan, 1966–70; Asst Under-Sec., FCO, 1970; Dep. Sec., Cabinet Office, 1971–72; Ambassador to Egypt, 1973–75. Dir, Ditchley Foundn, 1977–82. Member: Board, British Council, 1977–82; Marshall Aid Commem. Commn, 1979–88. *Address:* 54 Sussex Square, W2 2SR. *Club:* Brooks's.

ADAMS, Richard Borlase, CBE 1983; Managing Director, Peninsular & Oriental Steam Navigation Co., 1979–84 (Director, 1970, Deputy Managing Director, 1974); *b* 9 Sept. 1921; *s* of James Elwin Cokayne Adams and Susan Mercer Porter; *m* 1951, Susan Elizabeth Lambert; two *s* one *d*. *Educ:* Winchester Coll.; Trinity Coll., Oxford, 1940. War service, Rifle Bde, 1940–46 (Major). Mackinnon Mackenzie Gp of Cos, Calcutta, New Delhi and Hongkong, 1947–63; Chm., Islay Kerr & Co. Ltd, Singapore, 1963–66; British India Steam Navigation Co. Ltd: Dir, 1966; Man. Dir, 1969; Chm., 1970. Dir, Clerical, Medical & General Life Assurance Soc., 1975–88. *Recreation:* gardening. *Address:* 6 Leicester Close, Henley-on-Thames, Oxon RG9 2LD. *T:* (01491) 574184.

ADAMS, Richard Clive; consultant; Secretary to the Post Office, 1997–99; *b* 22 June 1945; *s* of William Henry Adams and Alberta Sarah Adams (*née* Steed); *m* 1971, Elizabeth

Anne Coleman; two *s. Educ:* Cotham Grammar Sch., Bristol; Exeter Univ. (BA). Post Office: Asst Postal Controller, 1966–78; Dir of Studies, PO Mgt Coll., 1978–82; Head Postmaster, Northampton, 1982–85; Asst Dir, Corporate Planning, 1985–92; Gp Planning Dir, 1992–97. Mem. Council, CBI, 1998–. *Recreations:* antique silver and plate, railways, wine. *Address:* 48 Overton Drive, Wanstead, E11 2NJ. *T:* (020) 8989 0021.

ADAMS, Richard George; author; *b* 9 May 1920; *s* of Evelyn George Beadon Adams, FRCS, and Lilian Rosa Adams (*née* Button); *m* 1949, Barbara Elizabeth Acland; two *d. Educ:* Bradfield Coll., Berks; Worcester Coll., Oxford (MA, Mod. Hist.). Entered Home Civil Service, 1948; retd as Asst Sec., DoE, 1974. Writer-in-residence: Univ. of Florida, 1975; Hollins Univ., Virginia, 1976. Pres., RSPCA, 1980–82. Carnegie Medal, 1972; Guardian Award for Children's Literature, 1972. FRSL 1975; FRSA. *Publications:* Watership Down, 1972 (numerous subseq. edns in various languages; filmed 1978); Shardik, 1974; (with Max Hooper) Nature through the Seasons, 1975; The Tyger Voyage, 1976; The Ship's Cat, 1977; The Plague Dogs, 1977 (filmed 1982); (with Max Hooper) Nature Day and Night, 1978; The Girl in a Swing, 1980 (filmed 1988); The Iron Wolf, 1980; (with Ronald Lockley) Voyage through the Antarctic, 1982; Maia, 1984; The Bureaucats, 1985; A Nature Diary, 1985; (ed and contrib.) Occasional Poets (anthology), 1986; The Legend of Te Tuna, 1986; Traveller, 1988; The Day Gone By (autobiog.), 1990; Tales from Watership Down, 1996; The Outlandish Knight, 2000. *Recreations:* folk-song, chess, country pursuits, fly-fishing, travel. *Address:* 26 Church Street, Whitchurch, Hants RG28 7AR.

ADAMS, Suzanne; *see* Cory, S.

ADAMS, Terence David, CMG 1997; FGS; Managing Director, Monument Oil and Gas, since 1998; *b* 22 Feb. 1938; *s* of F. E. Adams and E. S. Adams; *m* 1990, Caroline Mary (*née* Hartley); two *s* four *d* by previous marriage. *Educ:* UCW, Aberystwyth (BSc Hons; PhD 1963; Fellow). FGS 1963. International service in petroleum industry with Shell and BP, 1959–98; served in N America, Europe, ME and SE Asia. Pres., Azerbaijan Internat. Operating Co., Baku, 1994–98. Sen. Associate, Cambridge Energy Associates, Cambridge, Mass. Dir, Caspian Studies, CEPMLP, Univ. Dundee. Fellow, East-West Inst., NY. Medal of Honour, Republic of Azerbaijan, 1998; Hon. Citizen, Republic of Georgia, 1999. *Publications:* numerous scientific articles on micropalaeontology, geomorphology and world energy predictions. *Recreations:* archaeology, palaeontology, music, literature. *Address:* Old Manor House, High Street, Cley next the Sea, Norfolk NR25 7RN. *T:* (01263) 740066. *Clubs:* Travellers, Royal Commonwealth Society; Tanglin (Singapore).

ADAMS, Sir (William) James, KCMG 1991 (CMG 1976); HM Diplomatic Service, retired; Consultant, Control Risks Group, 1992–2001; *b* 30 April 1932; *s* of late William Adams and late Norah (*née* Walker); *m* 1961, Donatella, *d* of late Andrea Pais-Tarsilia; two *s* one *d. Educ:* Wolverhampton Grammar Sch.; Shrewsbury Sch.; Queen's Coll., Oxford. 2nd Lieut RA, MELF, 1950–51. Foreign Office, 1954; MECAS, 1955; 3rd Sec., Bahrain, 1956; Asst Political Agent, Trucial States, 1957; FO, 1958; 2nd Sec., 1959; Manila, 1960; 1st Sec. and Private Sec. to Minister of State, FO, 1963; 1st Sec. (Information), Paris, 1965–69; FCO, 1969; Counsellor, 1971; Head of European Integration Dept (2), FCO, 1971–72; seconded to Economic Commn for Africa, Addis Ababa, 1972–73; Counsellor (Developing Countries), UK Permanent Representation to EEC, 1973–77; Head of Chancery and Counsellor (Economic), Rome, 1977–80; Asst Under-Sec. of State (Public Depts, then Energy), FCO, 1980–84; Ambassador to Tunisia, 1984–87, to Egypt, 1987–92. Chm., Egyptian-British Chamber of Commerce, 1992–99. Mem., RC Cttee for Other Faiths, 1995–. Chm., Egyptian Growth Investment Co. Ltd, 1997–. Order of the Star of Honour (Hon.), Ethiopia, 1965; Order of the Two Niles (Hon.), Sudan, 1965. *Address:* 13 Kensington Court Place, W8 5BJ. *Club:* Reform.

ADAMS-CAIRNS, (Andrew) Ruaraidh; Head of Litigation Support, since 1995, Director, and Head of Residential Valuations, since 1998, FPD Savills (formerly Savills); *b* 12 Oct. 1953; *s* of late Alastair Adams-Cairns and Fiona Lauder (*née* Paton of Grandhome); *m* 1983, Susan Ann Foll; two *s. Educ:* Gordonstoun Sch.; Reading Univ. (BSc Est. Man.); RMA Sandhurst. FRICS; ACIArb. Commissioned Queen's Own Highlanders, 1971; Platoon Comdr, Germany, UK, Belize, Gibraltar; Royal Guard, Balmoral (Capt.); Intell. Officer, NI, 1978–79. Joined Savills, 1980; Partner in charge, Salisbury office, 1985–87; Dir, Mixed Develt, 1987–91; Man. Dir, Savills Propriedades, Portugal, 1989–96; Dir, Land and Property, 1987–97. *Publications:* occasional contribs to Estates Gazette, Family Law and Liability Today. *Recreations:* field sports, carpentry. *Address:* FPD Savills, 20 Grosvenor Hill, Berkeley Square, W1X 0HQ. *T:* (020) 7535 2972. *Club:* Army and Navy.

ADAMSON, Hamish Christopher, OBE 1996; Director (International), The Law Society, 1987–95; *b* 17 Sept. 1935; *s* of John Adamson, Perth, Scotland, and Denise Adamson (*née* Colman-Sadd). *Educ:* Stonyhurst Coll.; Lincoln Coll., Oxford (Schol.; MA Hons Jurisprudence). Solicitor (Hons). Law Society: Asst Sec., then Sen. Asst Sec. (Law Reform), 1966–81; Sec., Law Reform and Internat. Relations, 1981–87. Sec., UK Delegn, Council of the Bars and Law Socs of EC, 1981–95; Exec. Sec., Commonwealth Lawyers' Assoc., 1983–95. Chm., Trustee Cttee, Commonwealth Human Rights Initiative, 1993–95; Mem. Bd Trustees, Acad. of European Law, 1995–. Dir, Franco-British Lawyers' Soc., 1991–. *Publications:* The Solicitors Act 1974, 1975; Free Movement of Lawyers, 1992, 2nd edn 1998. *Recreations:* plants, books, travel. *Address:* 133 Hartington Road, SW8 2EY.

ADAMSON, Ian; *see* Adamson, S. I. G.

ADAMSON, Nicolas Clark, OBE 1982; Private Secretary to the Duke and Duchess of Kent, since 1993; *b* 5 Sept. 1938; *s* of Joseph Clark Adamson and Prudence Mary (*née* Gleeson); *m* 1971, Hilary Jane Edwards; two *d. Educ:* St Edward's Sch., Oxford; RAF Coll., Cranwell. Commnd RAF, 1959; served various fighter Sqdns, UK and ME, 1960–65; Flt Lieut 1962; Flying Instructor, 1965–67; ADC to Chief of Defence Staff, MoD, 1967–69; transferred to FCO, 1969 as First Sec.; served: Brussels (EC), 1972–75; Islamabad, 1979–82; Paris, 1985–90; Counsellor, FCO, 1990–92; attached CBI, 1992–93; retd from FCO, 1993. *Address:* York House, St James's Palace, SW1A 1BQ. *T:* (020) 7930 4872. *Clubs:* Athenæum, Royal Air Force.

ADAMSON, Norman Joseph, CB 1981; QC (Scot.) 1979; Legal Secretary to the Lord Advocate and First Parliamentary Draftsman for Scotland, 1979–89, retired; Assistant Counsel to the Lord Chairman of Committees, House of Lords, 1989–95, retired; *b* 29 Sept. 1930; *o s* of Joseph Adamson, wine and spirit merchant, and Lily Thorrat, Glasgow; *m* 1961, Patricia Mary, *er d* of Walter Scott Murray Guthrie and Christine Gillies Greenfield, Edinburgh; four *d. Educ:* Hillhead High Sch., Glasgow; Glasgow Univ. MA (Hons Philosophy and Economics) 1952; LLB 1955; Faculty of Advocates, Scotland, 1957; called to English Bar, Gray's Inn, 1959. Army Legal Aid (Civil) (UK), 1956–57; practice at Scottish Bar, 1957–65; Partner, Joseph Adamson & Co., 1965–82; Standing Jun. Counsel, Bible Board, 1962; Standing Jun. Counsel, MoD (Army), 1963–65; Hon. Sheriff Substitute, 1963–65; Parly Draftsman and Legal Sec., Lord Advocate's Dept, London, 1965–89. Underwriting Mem. of Lloyd's, 1976–91. Jt Convener, Scottish YCs, 1953–55. Founder Chm., Laleham Soc. (Civic Trust), 1970–72. Pres., Woking and Dist Scottish Soc., 1980–81. Governor, Ashford (Middx) Secondary Schs, 1968–72. Contested (C) Glasgow (Maryhill), 1959 and 1964. TA, 1948–55. Elder of the Church of Scotland. *Publications:* (contrib.) Stair Memorial Encyclopedia of the Laws of Scotland, 1995; contribs to legal jls. *Recreations:* music, theatre. *Address:* Prospect House, 53 Lodge Hill Road, Lower Bourne, Farnham, Surrey GU10 3RD. *T:* (01252) 721988. *Club:* Civil Service.

ADAMSON, (Samuel) Ian (Gamble), OBE 1998; medical practitioner; Member (UU) Belfast East, Northern Ireland Assembly, since 1998; Member (UU), Belfast City Council, since 1989 (Lord Mayor of Belfast, 1996–97); *b* 28 June 1944; *s* of John Gamble Sloan Adamson and Jane (*née* Kerr); *m* 1998, Kerry Christian Carson. *Educ:* Bangor GS; Queen's Univ., Belfast (MB, BCh; BAO 1969). DCH RCSI 1974; DCH RCPSG 1974; MFCH 1988; FRIPHH 1998. Registrar in Paediatrics: Royal Belfast Hosp. for Sick Children, 1975–76; Ulster Hosp., Dundonald, 1976–77; specialist in community child health and travel medicine, N and W Belfast HSS Trust (formerly Community Unit of Mgt), 1981–. Chm., Farset Youth and Community Develt, 1988–90. Founder Rector, Ulster-Scots Acad., 1994–. Founder Chairman: Somme Assoc., 1989–; Ulster-Scots Lang. Soc., 1992–; Founder Member: Cultural Traditions Gp, NI CRC, 1988; Ultach Trust, 1990; Pres., Belfast Civic Trust, 2001. SBStJ 1998. Fluent in ten langs, incl. Lakota; holds Wisdom-Keeper status among Lakota (Sioux) nation. *Publications:* The Cruthin, 1974, 5th edn 1995; Bangor: light of the world, 1979, 2nd edn 1987; The Battle of Moira, 1980; The Identity of Ulster, 1982, 4th edn 1995; The Ulster People, 1991; 1690, William and the Boyne, 1995; Dalaradia: kingdom of the Cruthin, 1998. *Recreations:* oil painting, theatre, travel. *Address:* 4 Cherryvalley Gardens, Belfast, N Ireland BT5 6PQ. *T:* (028) 9079 3017. *Clubs:* Ulster Reform (Belfast); Clandeboye Golf.

ADAMSON-MACEDO, Prof. Emeritus Colin, DSc; FIEE; engineering and higher education consultant; *b* 23 Nov. 1922; British; *m* 1983, Dr Elvidina Nabuco Macedo; one *s* (one *d*, and one *s* decd, of former marriage). *Educ:* Pocklington Sch., Yorks. BSc 1947, MSc(Eng.) 1952, London; DSc Manchester, 1961. REME (Capt.), 1942–46. Asst Lectr, then with A. Reyrolle & Co. (power systems analysis), 1946–52; Sen. Lectr, then Reader, in Electrical Power Systems Engrg, UMIST, 1952–61; Chm., Dept of Electrical Engineering and Electronics, Univ. of Manchester Institute of Science and Technology, 1961–70; Rector, The Polytechnic of Central London, 1970–83; Overseas Adviser to Univ. of Salford, 1983–86. Mem., Conference Internationale des Grands Réseaux Electriques; Chm. of Consultants, Educational Overseas Services, 1975–90; Chm. of Panel 1 (and Mem. Council), British Calibration Service, 1969–83. Mem., Exec. Cttee, Inter-Univ. Council for Service Overseas, 1972–82. Mem., Bd of Trustees, Ecole Supérieure Interafricaine d'Electricité, Abidjan, 1979–90; UN Team leader for Yarmouk Univ. of Technology, Jordan, 1978–80. Vis. Professor: Univ. of Roorkee, India, 1954–55; Univs of Washington and Wisconsin, 1959; Middle East Techn. Univ., Ankara, 1967–68; Univ. of Technology, Baghdad, 1975–83; Fed. Univ. of Rio de Janeiro, 1983–93 (UNESCO Energy Conslt to Coordenação dos Programas de Pós-graduação de Engenharia, 1986); Advisor to Rector, Mahidol Univ., Thailand, 1984–92; NATO Fellow, Electrical/Electronics Res. Inst., ME Technical Univ., Ankara, 1987; Vis. Prof. and Energy Conslt, Inst. de Pesquisas Tecnológicas, Univ. of São Paulo, 1987–88; Consultant, Trng Policy Div., ILO, 1991–92. Mem. Governing Council, Polytechnic of Huddersfield HEC, 1989–92. Blumlein Meml Lectr, IEE, 1998. Bailie Meml Prize, IEE, 1948–49. *Publications:* (jtly) High Voltage Direct Current Power Transmission, 1960; High Voltage DC Power Convertors and Systems, 1963; University Perspectives, 1970; UNESCO reports: Higher Technical Education (Egypt), 1972; Alternative University Structures (UK), 1973, 3rd edn 1977; Technical Higher Education (Iraq), 1974; Post-secondary Education for Persons Gainfully-employed, 1976 and 1977; contribs to Proc. IEE and other learned jls. *Recreations:* yachting, oriental science and technology. *Address:* Yetts o' Huaxu, Glendevon by Dollar, Clackmannanshire FK14 7JY. *T:* (01259) 781641; Rua Tonelero 27/201, Edificio Yapa, Copacabana, 22030-000 Rio de Janeiro-RJ, Brazil. *Club:* Athenæum.

ADCOCK, Robert Wadsworth, CBE 1992; DL; Chief Executive and Clerk, Essex County Council, 1976–95; *b* 29 Dec. 1932; *s* of Sir Robert Adcock, CBE; *m* 1957, Valerie Colston Robins; one *d* (one *s* decd). *Educ:* Rugby Sch. Solicitor. Asst Solicitor, Lancs CC, 1955–56; Asst Solicitor, Manchester City Council, 1956–59; Sen. Solicitor, Berks CC, 1959–63; Asst Clerk, later Dep. Clerk, Northumberland CC, 1963–70; Dep. Chief Exec., Essex CC, 1970–76; Clerk of Essex Lieutenancy, 1976–95. Assoc. of County Councils: Advisor, Police Cttee, 1976–83; Advisor, Policy Cttee, 1983–95; Chm., Officers Adv. Gp, 1987–95. Hon. Sec., Assoc. of County Chief Executives, 1983–90 (Chm., 1991–92); Chm., Officers Adv. Panel, SE Regional Planning Conference, 1984–88. DL Essex, 1978. *Recreations:* gardening, ornithology. *Address:* The Christmas Cottage, Great Sampford, Saffron Walden, Essex CB10 2RQ. *T:* (01799) 586363. *Club:* Law Society.

ADDERLEY, family name of **Baron Norton**.

ADDINGTON, family name of **Viscount Sidmouth**.

ADDINGTON, 6th Baron *cr* 1887; **Dominic Bryce Hubbard;** *b* 24 Aug. 1963; *s* of 5th Baron Addington and of Alexandra Patricia, *yr d* of late Norman Ford Millar; *S* father, 1982; *m* 1999, (Elizabeth) Ann Morris. *Educ:* Aberdeen Univ. (MA Hons). Lib Dem spokesman on disability and on sport, H of L; elected Mem., H of L, 1999. Vice President: British Dyslexia Assoc.; Adult Dyslexia Orgn; UK Sport Assoc. for People with Learning Disability; Lonsdale Sporting Club; Lakenham Hewett RFC. *Recreation:* Rugby football. *Heir: b* Hon. Michael Walter Leslie Hubbard, *b* 6 July 1965. *Address:* 11 Chalk Hill Road, Norwich NR1 1SL.

ADDIS, Richard James; Editor, The Globe and Mail, Toronto, since 1999; *b* 23 Aug. 1956; *s* of Richard Thomas Addis and Jane Addis; *m* 1983, Eunice Minogue; one *s* two *d. Educ:* West Downs Prep. Sch.; Rugby; Downing Coll., Cambridge (MA). Evening Standard, 1985–89; Dep. Editor, Sunday Telegraph, 1989–91; Exec. Editor, Daily Mail, 1991–95; Editor, The Express, 1995–98; Consultant Editor, Mail on Sunday, 1998–99. *Recreations:* dancing, tennis, ski-ing, flute. *Address:* (office) 444 Front Street West, Toronto, Ont M5V 2S9, Canada. *T:* (416) 5853329. *Clubs:* Boodle's, Beefsteak; Royal Canadian Yacht.

ADDISON, family name of **Viscount Addison**.

ADDISON, 4th Viscount *cr* 1945, of Stallingborough; **William Matthew Wand Addison;** Baron Addison 1937; Chairman, DCL Telecommunications, since 1997; *b* 13 June 1945; *s* of 3rd Viscount and of Kathleen Amy, *d* of Rt Rev. and Rt Hon. J. W. C. Wand, PC, KCVO; *S* father, 1992; *m* 1st, 1970, Joanna Mary (marr. diss. 1990), *e d* of late J. I. C. Dickinson; one *s* two *d*; 2nd, 1991, Lesley Ann, *d* of George Colin Mawer. *Educ:* King's Sch., Bruton; Essex Inst. of Agriculture. Mem., Cttee on Jt Statutory Instruments, 1993–. Vice President: Council for Nat. Parks, 1994–; British Trust for Conservation

Volunteers, 1996–. Pres., Motor Activities Trng Council, 1996–. *Heir:* *s* Hon. Paul Wand Addison, *b* 18 March 1973.

ADDISON, Kenneth George, OBE 1978; company director; Director, 1971–89, and Deputy Chief General Manager, 1976–84, Sun Alliance & London Insurance Group; *b* 1 Jan. 1923; *s* of Herbert George Addison and Ruby (*née* Leathers); *m* 1945, Maureen Newman; one *s* one *d*. *Educ:* Felixstowe Grammar Sch. LLB Hons London. Served RAF, 1942–46. Joined Alliance Assurance Co. Ltd, 1939; various subsequent appts; Asst Sec., Law Fire Insurance Office, 1960–64; Gen. Manager, Sun Alliance & London Insurance Group, 1971. Chm., Bourne Home Develts Ltd, 1989–93; Dir, Sabre Insurance Co. Ltd, 1990–96. Chairman: Fire Insurers' Res. & Testing Orgn, 1977–84; Management Cttee, Associated Insurers (British Electricity), 1977–84; Internat. Oil Insurers, 1979–82; Dir, Insurance Technical Bureau, 1977–84; Advr, Med. Defence Union, 1986–94 (Dir, 1991–94). Chm., Hearing Aid Council, 1971–78. Dir, Croydon Community Trust, 1990–94. FCIS; FCII (Pres., 1980); FCIArb (Pres., 1968–69). *Publications:* papers on insurance and allied subjects. *Recreations:* swimming, carpentry, gardening. *Address:* Ockley, 13 Hillcroft Avenue, Purley, Surrey CR8 3DJ. *T:* (020) 8660 2793.

ADDISON, Mark Eric; Director General for Operations and Service Delivery, Department for Environment, Food and Rural Affairs, since 2001; *b* 22 Jan. 1951; *s* of Sydney Robert James Addison and Prudence Margaret Addison (*née* Russell); *m* 1987, Lucinda Clare Booth. *Educ:* Marlborough Coll.; St John's Coll., Cambridge (BA, MA); City Univ. (MSc); Imperial Coll. (DIC, PhD). Department of Employment, 1978–95: Private Sec. to Parly Under-Sec. of State, 1982; Private Sec. to Prime Minister (Home Affairs, then Parly Affairs), 1985–88; Regl Dir for London, Training Agency, 1988–91; Dir, Finance and Resource Management, 1991–94; DoE, 1995–97; Dir, Safety Policy, HSE, 1994–97; Dir, Better Regulation Unit, OPS, 1997–98; Chief Exec., Crown Prosecution Service, 1998–2001. *Recreations:* British motorbikes, windsurfing, photography. *Address:* Department for Environment, Food and Rural Affairs, 1A Page Street, SW1P 4PQ.

ADDISON, Michael Francis; His Honour Judge Addison; a Circuit Judge, since 1987; *b* 14 Sept. 1942; *s* of late Joseph Addison and Wendy Blyth Addison; *m* 1979, Rosemary Hardy (*d* 1994); one *s*. *Educ:* Eton; Trinity College, Cambridge (BA). Called to the Bar, Inner Temple, 1965. *Recreation:* gardening. *Address:* 2 Harcourt Buildings, Temple, EC4Y 9DB. *T:* (020) 7353 2112.

ADDISON, Mira; *see* Bar-Hillel, M.

ADDYMAN, Peter Vincent, CBE 2000; FSA; Director, York Archaeological Trust, since 1972; *b* 12 July 1939; *y s* of Erik Thomas Waterhouse Addyman and Evelyn Mary (*née* Fisher); *m* 1965, Shelton (*née* Oliver), Atlanta, Ga; one *s* one *d*. *Educ:* Sedbergh Sch.; Peterhouse, Cambridge (MA). MIFA 1982; FSA 1967. Asst Lectr in Archaeology, 1962–64, Lectr, 1964–67, QUB; Lectr in Archaeol., Univ. of Southampton, 1967–72. Hon. Fellow, Univ. of York, 1972–; Hon. Reader, Univ. of Bradford, 1974–81. Directed excavations: Maxey, 1960; Lydford, 1964–67; Ludgershall Castle, 1964–72; Chalton, 1970–72. Vice-President: Council for British Archaeol., 1981–85 (Pres., 1992–95); Royal Archaeol. Inst., 1979–83; Chairman: Standing Conf. of Archaeol Unit Managers, 1975–78; Inst. of Field Archaeologists, 1983–85; Standing Conf. on Portable Antiquities, 1995–; Member: RCHM of England, 1997–99; Ancient Monuments Adv. Cttee, English Heritage, 1998–. Chm., Cultural Resource Management Ltd, 1989–95 (Dir, 1979–95); Academic Dir, Heritage Projects Ltd, 1984–; Jt Instigator, Jorvik Viking Centre, York. Honorary Professor: Univ. of Bradford, 1998; Univ. of York, 1998. Hon. DSc Bradford, 1984; DUniv York, 1985. *Publications:* (gen. editor) The Archaeology of York, vols 1–20, 1976–2000; (ed with V. E. Black) Archaeological Papers from York, 1984; papers in archaeol jls. *Recreations:* gardening, watercolours, travel. *Address:* 50 Bootham, York YO30 7BZ. *T:* (01904) 624311; York Archaeological Trust, Cromwell House, 13 Ogleforth, York YO1 7FG. *T:* (01904) 663001. *Club:* Athenæum.

ADEANE, Hon. (George) Edward, CVO 1985; an Extra Equerry to HRH the Prince of Wales, since 1985; Director: English and Scottish Investors plc, since 1986; BNP Paribas UK Holdings Ltd, since 1998; *b* 4 Oct. 1939; *s* of Baron Adeane, GCB, GCVO, PC and Lady Adeane. *Educ:* Eton; Magdalene College, Cambridge (MA). Called to Bar, Middle Temple, July 1962. Page of Honour to HM the Queen, 1954–55; Private Sec. and Treas. to HRH the Prince of Wales, 1979–85; Treas. to TRH the Prince and Princess of Wales, 1981–85; Private Sec. to HRH the Princess of Wales, 1984–85. Director: Guardian Royal Exchange plc, 1985–99; Hambros plc, 1992–98; Hambros Bank Ltd, 1986–98 (Exec. Dir, 1991–98). Mem., British Library Bd, 1993–99. Trustee: Leeds Castle Foundn, 1991–; Lambeth Palace Liby, 1991–. *Address:* B4 Albany, Piccadilly, W1J 0AN. *T:* (020) 7734 9410.

ADEBOWALE, Baron *cr* 2001 (Life Peer), of Thornes in the County of West Yorkshire; **Victor Olufemi Adebowale,** CBE 2000; Chief Executive, Centrepoint, since 1995; *b* 21 July 1962; *s* of Ezekiel Adebowale and Grace Adebowale. *Educ:* Thornes House Sch., Wakefield; Poly of E London. London Borough of Newham: Private Sector Repairs Administrator and Estate Officer, 1983–84; Sen. Estate Manager, 1984–86; Perm. Property Manager, Patchwork Community Housing Assoc., 1986–88; Regl Dir, Ujima Housing Assoc., 1988–90; Dir, Alcohol Recovery Project, 1990–95. Member: Nat. Council, NFHA, 1991–; Adv. Gp, New Deal Task Force, 1997–. Trustee, Public Mgt Foundn, 1998–. DUniv UCE, 2001. *Recreations:* poetry writing, kite flying, music, playing the saxophone. *Address:* Centrepoint, Neil House, 7 Whitechapel Road, E1 1DU. *T:* (020) 7426 5300.

ADELAIDE, Archbishop of, and Metropolitan of South Australia, since 1991; **Most Rev. Ian Gordon Combe George,** AO 2001 (AM 1989); *b* 12 Aug. 1934; *s* of late Gordon Frank George and Kathleen Mary George (*née* Combe); *m* 1964, Barbara Dorothy (*née* Peterson); one *d* (one *s* decd). *Educ:* St Peter's Coll., Adelaide; Univ. of Adelaide (LLB 1957); Gen. Theol Seminary, NY (MDiv 1964). Judges' Associate, Supreme Court of S Australia, 1955–57; barrister and solicitor, Australia, 1957–61. Ordained deacon and priest, New York, 1964; Assistant Curate: St Thomas', Mamaroneck, NY, USA, 1964–65; St David's, Burnside, SA, 1966–67; Priest-in-charge, St Barbara's, Woomera, SA and Chaplain and Welfare Officer, Australian Regular Army, 1967–69; Sub-Warden and Chaplain, St George's Coll., 1969–73, Lectr in History, 1969–73, Univ. of W Australia; Dean of Brisbane, Qld, 1973–81; Senior Chaplain (Army), Qld, 1975–81; Archdeacon of Canberra, 1981–89; Rector, St John's Church, Canberra, 1981–89; Asst Bp, Dio. of Canberra and Goulburn, 1989–91. Art Critic, The News, Adelaide, 1965–67. Trustee, Qld Art Gall., 1974–81. Founding Pres., Alcohol and Drug Problems Assoc. of Qld, 1975–81. Hon. DD Gen. Theol Seminary, NY, 1990. ChStJ 1992; ChLJ 1995. *Publications:* Meditations on the Life of Jesus, 1991; Making Worship Work, 1992; many articles in theol, church and aesthetics jls on art and religion. *Recreations:* gardening, reading, the Arts, wine, ski-ing. *Address:* Bishop's Court, 45 Palmer Place, North Adelaide, SA 5006, Australia. *T:* (8) 82672364; Church Office, 26 King William Road, North Adelaide, SA 5006, Australia. *T:* (8) 83059353, *Fax:* (8) 83059399.

ADELAIDE, Archbishop of, (RC), since 1985; **Most Rev. Leonard Anthony Faulkner;** *b* Booleroo Centre, South Australia, 5 Dec. 1926. *Educ:* Sacred Heart Coll., Glenelg; Corpus Christi Coll., Werribee; Pontifical Urban University, Rome. Ordained Propaganda Fide Coll., Rome, 1 Jan. 1950. Asst Priest, Woodville, SA, 1950–57; Administrator, St Francis Xavier Cathedral, Adelaide, 1957–67; Diocesan Chaplain, Young Christian Workers, 1955–67; Mem., Nat. Fitness Council of SA, 1958–67; Bishop of Townsville, 1967–83; Coadjutor Archbishop of Adelaide, 1983–85. Chm., Aust. Catholic Bishops' Conf. Cttee for the Family and for Life, 1993–. *Address:* Catholic Diocesan Centre, Box 1364 GPO, Adelaide, SA 5001, Australia.

ADELAIDE, Assistant Bishop of; *see* Aspinall, Rt Rev. P. J.

ADELAIDE, Dean of; *see* Renfrey, Rt Rev. L. E. W.

ADER, Peter Charles; His Honour Judge Ader; a Circuit Judge, since 1999; *b* 14 May 1950; *s* of late Max Ader and of Inge Ader (*née* Nord); *m* 1979, Margaret Taylor; one *s* two *d*. *Educ:* Highgate Sch.; Southampton Univ. (LLB). Called to the Bar, Middle Temple, 1973; a Recorder, 1995–99. Freeman, Clockmakers' Co., 1998. *Recreations:* squash, tennis, golf, ski-ing, travel. *Address:* 3 Temple Gardens, Temple, EC4Y 9AU. *T:* (020) 7353 3102. *Clubs:* Cumberland Tennis, Hampstead Cricket.

ADÈS, Prof. (Josephine) Dawn, FBA 1996; Professor of Art History and Theory, University of Essex, since 1989; *b* 6 May 1943; *d* of A. E. Tylden-Pattenson, CSI; *m* 1966, Timothy Raymond Adès; three *s*. *Educ:* St Hilda's Coll., Oxford (BA 1965); MA London 1968. Essex University: Lectr, 1971–85; Sen. Lectr, 1985–88; Reader, 1988–89; Head of Dept of Art History and Theory, 1989–92. Trustee: Tate Gall., 1995–; Nat. Gall., 1998–. *Publications:* Dada and Surrealism Reviewed, 1978; Salvador Dali, 1982, 2nd edn 1995; (jtly) The Twentieth Century Poster: design of the avant garde, 1984; (jtly) Francis Bacon, 1985; Photomontage, 1986; Art in Latin America: the modern era 1820–1980, 1989; Andre Masson, 1994; Figures and Likenesses: the paintings of Siron Franco, 1995; Surrealist Art: the Bergman Collection in the Art Institute of Chicago, 1997; (jtly) Marcel Duchamp, 1999; Salvador Dali's Optical Illusions, 2000. *Address:* Department of Art History and Theory, Essex University, Wivenhoe Park, Colchester, Essex CO4 3SQ.
See also T. J. E. Adès.

ADÈS, Thomas Joseph Edmund; composer and pianist; Artistic Director, Aldeburgh Festival, since 1999; *b* 1 March 1971; *s* of Timothy Adès and Prof. Dawn Adès, *qv*. *Educ:* University Coll. Sch.; Guildhall Sch. of Music and Drama; King's Coll., Cambridge (MA); St John's Coll., Cambridge (MPhil). Composer in Association, Hallé Orch., 1993–95; Lectr, Univ. of Manchester, 1993–94; Fellow Commoner in Creative Arts, Trinity Coll., Cambridge, 1995–97; Benjamin Britten Prof. of Music, RAM, 1997-2000; Musical Dir, Birmingham Contemporary Music Gp, 1998–2000. *Principal compositions:* Five Eliot Landscapes, 1990; Chamber Symphony, 1990; Catch, 1991; Darknesse Visible, 1992; Still Sorrowing, 1993; Life Story, 1993; Living Toys, 1993; … but all shall be well, 1993; Sonata da Caccia, 1993; Arcadiana (for string quartet), 1994; Powder Her Face (Chamber opera), 1995; Traced Overhead, 1996; These Premises are Alarmed, 1996; Asyla, 1997; Concerto Conciso, 1997–98; America (A Prophecy), 1999; Piano Quintet, 2000. *Address:* c/o Faber Music, 3 Queen Square, WC1N 3AU. *T:* (020) 7833 7911, *Fax:* (020) 7833 7939. *Club:* Black's.

ADETILOYE, Most Rev. Joseph Abiodun; *see* Nigeria, Metropolitan Archbishop and Primate of.

ADEY, John Fuller; company director; Chief Executive, National Blood Authority, 1993–98; *b* 12 May 1941; *s* of Frank Douglas Adey and Doreen Adey (*née* Fuller); *m* 1965, Marianne Alyce Banning; two *s* two *d*. *Educ:* Glyn GS, Epsom; St Edmund Hall, Oxford (MA); Harvard Univ. (MBA). CEng 1970; MIMechE 1970; MIEE 1976. Graduate Trainee, AEI Ltd, 1963–65; Design Engineer: Montreal Engrg, 1965–67; Nat. Steel & Shipbuilding, San Diego, 1967–70; various positions, Raychem Ltd, 1972–83; Chief Exec., Chemicals and Plastics, Courtaulds, 1983–86; Man. Dir, Baxter Healthcare, 1986–93. Director: API, 1987–97; Seton Healthcare Gp, 1996–98; non-exec. Chm., Adams Healthcare, 1999-2000. A Gen. Comr of Income Tax, 1985–. Trustee, Royal Merchant Navy Sch. Foundn, 1999–; Gov., John o'Gaunt Sch., Hungerford, 2000–. *Recreations:* tennis, tinkering with old cars, village life. *Address:* The Old Malt House, Aldbourne, Marlborough, Wilts SN8 2DW.

ADIE, Kathryn, (Kate), OBE 1993; Chief News Correspondent, BBC TV, since 1989; *b* 19 Sept. 1945; *d* of Babe Dunnet (*née* Issitt), and adopted *d* of late John Wilfrid Adie and Maud Adie (*née* Fambely). *Educ:* Sunderland Church High Sch.; Newcastle Univ. (BA Hons Scandinavian Studies). FJI 1990. Technician and Producer, BBC Radio, 1969–76; Reporter, BBC TV South, 1977–78; Reporter, TV News, 1979–81, Correspondent, 1982. Hon. Prof., Broadcasting and Journalism, Univ. of Sunderland, 1995. Hon. Fellow, Royal Holloway, London Univ., 1996. Hon. MA: Bath, 1987; Newcastle upon Tyne, 1990; Hon. DLitt: City, 1989; Loughborough, 1991; Sunderland, 1993; Robert Gordon, 1996; Nottingham, 1998; Nottingham Trent, 1998; MUniv Open, 1996. RTS News Award, 1981 and 1987, Judges' Award, 1989; Monte Carlo Internat. TV News Award, 1981 and 1990; BAFTA Richard Dimbleby Award, 1989. Hon. Freeman, Borough of Sunderland, 1989. *Address:* c/o BBC TV, Wood Lane, W12 7RJ. *T:* (020) 8576 8830.

ADIE, Rt Rev. Michael Edgar, CBE 1994; Bishop of Guildford, 1983–94; *b* 22 Nov. 1929; *s* of Walter Granville Adie and Kate Emily Adie (*née* Parish); *m* 1957, Anne Devonald Roynon; one *s* three *d*. *Educ:* Westminster School; St John's Coll., Oxford (MA). Assistant Curate, St Luke, Pallion, Sunderland, 1954–57; Resident Chaplain to the Archbishop of Canterbury, 1957–60; Vicar of St Mark, Sheffield, 1960–69; Rural Dean of Hallam, 1966–69; Rector of Louth, 1969–76; Vicar of Morton with Hacconby, 1976–83; Archdeacon of Lincoln, 1977–83. Chm., Gen. Synod Bd of Education and of National Soc., 1989–94. DUniv Surrey, 1995. *Publication:* Held Together: an exploration of coherence, 1997. *Recreations:* gardening, walking, sneezing. *Address:* Greenslade, Froxfield, Petersfield, Hants GU32 1EB.

ADKINS, Richard David; QC 1995; *b* 21 Oct. 1954; *s* of Walter David Adkins and Patricia (*née* Chimes); *m* 1977, Jane Margaret, *d* of Derek and Ella Sparrow; two *s* one *d*. *Educ:* Leamington Coll. for Boys; Hertford Coll., Oxford (MA). Admitted as solicitor, 1978; called to the Bar, Middle Temple, 1982. Cttee Mem., Chancery Bar Assoc., 1991–93. *Publications:* Encyclopaedia of Forms and Precedents, Vol. 3: Arrangements with Creditors, 1985; Company Receivers: a new status?, 1988; contrib. Gore Browne on Companies, 44th edn, 1992–. *Recreations:* opera, tennis. *Address:* 3–4 South Square, Gray's Inn, WC1R 5HP. *T:* (020) 7696 9900. *Club:* Bromley Cricket.

ADLER, George Fritz Werner, OBE 1982; FREng; FIMechE; FICE; Director of Research, British Hydromechanics Research Association, 1971–86; *b* 12 Jan. 1926; *s* of Fritz Jacob Sigismund Adler and Hildegard Julie Adler (*née* Lippmann); *m* 1949, June Moonaheim Margaret Nash; three *d*. *Educ:* Penarth County School; Cardiff Technical Coll.; University Coll., Cardiff (Fellow 1984); Imperial Coll., London. BSc (Eng), DIC.

FICE 1980; FREng (FEng 1981). Design Engineer, 1948, Chief, Mechanical Develt, 1953, English Electric, Rugby; Chief Mechanical Engineer, 1958, Gen. Manager Mech. Products, Marconi, 1962; Manager, Mech. Products Div., English Electric, 1966. Dir, Fluid Engineering Products Ltd, 1982–84. Vice-Pres., 1979, Pres., 1983, IMechE; Chm., CDRA (Fedn of Technology Centres), 1981–83; Vice-Pres., FEANI, 1987–89; Mem., Engineering Council, 1986–89; Treasurer, Fellowship of Engrg, 1988–91. FIMgt (FBIM 1979); FInstD 1985. Eur Ing, FEANI, 1987. Freeman, City of London, 1984; Liveryman, Co. of Engrs, 1984–. *Publications:* chapter, Water Turbines (jtly), in Kempe's Engineers' Year Book, 1956; articles in technical jls. *Recreations:* gardening, swimming, music. *Address:* The Haining, Orchard Close, Longburton, Sherborne, Dorset DT9 5PP. *T:* (01963) 210641. *Club:* Carlton.

ADLER, Prof. Jeremy David, PhD; Professor of German, King's College London, since 1994; *b* 1 Oct. 1947; *s* of H. G. and Bettina Adler; *m* 1983, Eva Mikulašová. *Educ:* St Marylebone GS; Queen Mary Coll., Univ. of London (BA 1st cl. Hons 1969); Westfield Coll., Univ. of London (PhD 1977). Lectr in German, Westfield Coll., 1970–89; Queen Mary and Westfield College, London: Reader, 1989–91; Prof. of German, 1991–94; Founding Chm., Centre for Modern European Studies, 1990–94. Mem. Council, Poetry Soc., 1973–77; Jt Hon. Sec., English Goethe Soc., 1987–; Member: Bielefeld Colloquium für Neue Poesie, 1979–; Council, Goethe Gesellschaft, Weimar, 1995–; Council, 1997–99, Senate, 2000–01, London Univ. Chm., M. L.v. Motesiczky Trust, 1997–. Schol., Herzog August Bibliothek, Wolfenbüttel, 1979; Fellow, Inst. of Advanced Study, Berlin, 1985–86. Goethe Prize, English Goethe Soc., 1977. *Publications:* (ed with J. J. White) August Stramm: Kritische Essays und unveröffentliches Quellenmaterial aus dem Nachlass des Dichters, 1979; (ed) Allegorie und Eros: Texte von und über Albert Paris Gütersloh, 1986; Eine fast magische Anziehungskraft: Goethes Wahlverwandtschaften und die Chemie seiner Zeit, 1987; (with Ulrich Ernst) Text als Figur: Visuelle Poesie von der Antike bis zur Moderne, 1987, 3rd edn 1990; (ed) August Stramm: Die Dichtungen, Sämtliche Gedichte, Dramen, Prosa, 1990; (ed) August Stramm: Alles ist Gedicht: Briefe, Gedichte, Bilder, Dokumente, 1990; (ed) Friedrich Hölderlin: Poems and Fragments, 1998; (ed) H. G. Adler: Der Wahrheit verpflichtet, 1998; (ed) E. T. A. Hoffmann: The Life and Opinions of the Tomcat Murr, 1999; (ed) H. G. Adler: Eine Reise, 1999; (ed jtly) F. B. Steiner: Selected Writings, 2 vols, 1999; (ed jtly) Goethe at 250, 2000; (ed) F. B. Steiner: Am Stürzenden Pfad, gesammelte Gedichte, 2000; Kafka: a biography, 2001; *poetry:* Alphabox, 1973; Alphabet Music, 1974; Fragments Towards the City, 1977; Even in April, Ferrara and Liberty, 1978; A Short History of London, 1979; The Wedding and Other Marriages, 1980; Triplets, 1980; Homage to Theocritus, 1985; Notes from the Correspondence, 1983; The Electric Alphabet, 1986, 3rd edn 2001; To Cythera!, 1993; At the Edge of the World, 1994; Big Skies and Little Stones, 1997; pamphlets; articles in learned jls, daily press, New York Times and TLS. *Recreations:* mountaineering, painting and drawing, listening to music. *Address:* Department of German, King's College London, WC2R 2LS. *T:* (020) 7873 2090.

ADLER, Prof. Michael William, CBE 1999; MD; FRCP, FFPHM; Professor of Genito Urinary Medicine, and Consultant Physician, University College London (formerly Middlesex Hospital) Medical School, since 1979; *b* 12 June 1939; *s* of late Gerhard and of Hella Adler; *m* 1st, 1966, Susan Jean (marr. diss. 1978); 2nd, 1979, Karen Hope Dunnell (marr. diss. 1994); two *d*; 3rd, 1994, Margaret Jay (*see* Baroness Jay of Paddington). *Educ:* Bryanston Sch.; Middlesex Hosp. Med. Sch. MB BS 1965, MD 1977; MRCP 1970, FRCP 1984; FFPHM (MFCM 1977, FFCM 1983). House Officer and Registrar in Medicine, Middlesex, Central Middlesex and Whittington Hosps, 1965–69; Lectr, St Thomas' Hosp. Med. Sch., 1970–75; Sen. Lectr, Middlesex Hosp. Med. Sch., 1975–79. Consultant Physician: Middlesex Hosp., 1979–; Camden and Islington Community Health Services NHS Trust, 1992– (non-exec. Dir, 1992–94); non-exec. Dir, Health Develt Agency, 1999–. Advr in Venereology, WHO, 1983–; Department of Health (formerly DHSS): Mem., Expert Adv. Gp on AIDS, 1984–92; Mem., Sub-Gps on Monitoring and Surveillance, 1987–88 and Health Care Workers, 1987–92; Mem., AIDS Action Gp, 1991–92; Mem., Stocktake Gp, 1997–99; Chief Scientist's Advr, Res. Liaison Gp (Child Health), 1985–90. Medical Research Council: Member: Res. Adv. Gp on Epidemiol Studies of Sexually Transmitted Diseases, 1975–80; Working Party to co-ordinate Lab. Studies on the Gonococcus, 1979–83; Working Party on AIDS, 1981–87; Sub-Cttee on Therapeutic Studies, 1985–87; Cttee on Epidemiol Studies on AIDS, 1985–94; Cttee on Clinical Studies of Prototype Vaccines against AIDS, 1987–89; RCS Cttee on HIV infection/AIDS, 1991–96. Member: Med. Adv. Cttee, Brook Adv. Centres, 1984–94; Working Gp on AIDS, European Commn, 1985–; AIDS Working Party, BMA, 1986–92; Exec. Cttee, Internat. Union Against Sexually Transmitted Infections (formerly Against the Venereal Diseases and Treponematoses), 1986–; DFID (formerly ODA) Health and Population Adv. Cttee on R&D, 1995–99; Steering Cttee, Assoc. of NHS Pioneers of AIDS Care and Treatment, 1996–; Exec. Cttee, Assoc. of Genito Urinary Medicine, 1997–99. Mem., Specialist Adv. Cttee on Genito Urinary Medicine, Jt Cttee of Higher Med. Trng, 1981–86 (Sec., 1981–82; Chm., 1983–86). Royal College of Physicians: Member: Cttee on Genito Urinary Medicine, 1984– (Sec., 1984–87; Chm., 1987–91); Working Gp on AIDS, FCM (now FPHM), 1985–; Lumleian Lectr, 1996; Member Council: Med. Soc. for the Study of Venereal Diseases (Pres., 1997–99); RIPH&H, 1993–94; RCP, 1999–. Dir, Terrence Higgins Trust, 1982–88; Mem. Governing Council, Internat. AIDS Soc., 1993–98; Trustee, 1987–2000, Chm., 1991–2000, Nat. AIDS Trust (Chm., Grants and Gen. Purposes Cttee, 1988–91); Adviser: AIDS Crisis Trust, 1986–98; Parly All Party Cttee on AIDS, 1987–. Patron, Albany Soc., 1987–91. Evian Health Award, 1990. Member, Editorial Panel: Genito Urinary Medicine; Current Opinion on Infections Diseases; Enfermedades de Transmission Sexual; Venereology; also Ed., AIDS, 1986–94; Consultant Editor, AIDS Letter, RSM, 1987–89. *Publications:* ABC of Sexually Transmitted Diseases, 1984, 4th edn 1998; (ed) ABC of AIDS, 1987, 5th edn 2001; (ed) Diseases in the Homosexual Male, 1988; (jtly) Sexual Health and Care Guidelines for Prevention and Treatment, 1998; articles on sexually transmitted diseases and AIDS in med. jls. *Recreations:* yoga, jogging. *Address:* Department of Sexually Transmitted Diseases, Mortimer Market Centre, Capper Street, WC1E 6AU. *T:* (020) 7380 9892.

ADMANI, Dr (Abdul) Karim, OBE 1987; JP; consultant physician, with special interest in strokes and the elderly; *b* 19 Sept. 1937; *s* of late Haji Razzak Admani, Palitana, India, and of Hajiani Rahima Admani; *m* Seema, *d* of late Charles Robson, South Shields; one *s* one *d*. *Educ:* Gujarat Univ., India (BSc 1st cl. Hons); Karachi Univ., Pakistan (MB, BS); Univ. of London. DTM&H 1963; FRCP; FRCPE 1979; FRCPGlas 1988; FRSocMed 1988; FRIPHH. Teacher, Trent RHA (formerly Sheffield AHA), 1970–; Clin. Lectr, Sheffield Med. Sch., 1972–; Clin. Dir of Medicine, Northern Gen. Hosp. Trust, 1990–92. Vis. Prof. of Medicine and Neurol., Quaide-Azam Med. Coll., Bahawalpur, Pakistan, 1990–. WHO External Examr, Coll. of Physicians and Surgeons of Bangladesh, 1990–93. Director: Ranmoor Grange Nursing Home Ltd, 1975–80; Sunningdale Yorks Ltd, 1983–. Overseas Doctors' Association in UK: Dir, 1976–; Chm., 1981–87; Pres., 1987–94; Chm., ODTS, 1979– (Chm., Educn and Post-grad. Trng Cttee, 1982–). General Medical Council: Mem., 1979–; Chm., L Cttee, 1990–92; Member: Prof. Conduct Cttee, 1979–91; Preliminary Proc. Council, 1991–; Educn Cttee, 1990–92 and 1994; Racial Equality Cttee, 1994–. Member: Exec. Cttee, BMA, Sheffield, 1974–; Central Cttee of Consultants and Specialists, 1979–93; Sheffield HA, 1977–82; Council, British Geriatric Soc., 1989–93 (Chm., Trent Region, 1989–93); Council, BRCS, 1991–94 (Chm., Region III, 1991–94; Pres., S Yorks 1982–); Exec. Cttee for Racial Equality in Sheffield, 1972–90 (Chm., 1978–); Exec. Cttee, Age Concern, Sheffield, 1982–90; Management Bd, Pakistan Muslim Centre, 1987–; NHS Nursing Home Tribunal, 1989–; Medico-Chirurgical Soc. of Sheffield. Chm., Inst. of Transcultural Health Care, 1991–. President: Muslim Council of Sheffield, Rotherham and Dists, 1978–; Union of Pakistani Orgns in UK and Europe, 1979–94. Chm., Pakistan Enterprise Center, 1993–. JP City of Sheffield, 1974. Member, Editorial Board: Pakistan Medical Bull., 1974–; Medi-Scene, 1981–; ODA News Rev., 1985–. *Publication:* (ed) Guidance for Overseas Doctors in National Health Service in UK, 1982, 1991. *Recreations:* tennis, table tennis, snooker, chess. *Address:* 1 Derriman Glen, Silverdale Road, Sheffield S11 9LQ. *T:* (0114) 236 0465; Northern General Hospital, Barnsley Road, Sheffield. *Clubs:* Abbeydale Rotary (Pres., 1995), Conservative (Sheffield).

ADONIS, Andrew; Prime Minister's Head of Policy, since 2001; *b* 22 Feb. 1963; *m* 1994, Kathryn Davies; one *s* one *d*. *Educ:* Kingham Hill Sch., Oxon; Keble Coll., Oxford (BA 1st Cl. Hons Modern Hist.); Christ Church, Oxford (DPhil 1988). Mem., HQ Secretariat, British Gas Corp., 1984–85; Nuffield College, University of Oxford: Res. student, 1985–86; Fellow in Politics, 1988–91; Financial Times: Public Policy corresp., 1991–93; Industry corresp., 1993–94; Public Policy Editor, 1994–96; political columnist and contributing editor, The Observer, 1996–98; Mem., Prime Minister's Policy Unit, 1998–2001. Vice-Pres., Oxford Graduate Union, 1987–88. Mem., Oxford City Council, 1987–91. *Publications:* Parliament Today, 1990; Making Aristocracy Work: the peerage and the political system in Britain 1884–1914, 1993; (with T. Hames) A Conservative Revolution?: the Thatcher-Reagan decade in perspective, 1994; (with D. Butler and T. Travers) Failure in British Government: the politics of the poll tax, 1994; (with S. Pollard) A Class Act: the myth of Britain's classless society, 1997. *Address:* c/o 10 Downing Street, SW1A 2AA.

ADRIANO, Dino, FCCA; Director, 1990–2000, Group Chief Executive, 1998–2000, J. Sainsbury plc (Joint Group Chief Executive, 1997–98); Chairman and Chief Executive, Sainsbury's Supermarkets Ltd, 1997–2000; *b* 24 April 1943; *s* of Dante Adriano and Yole Adriano; *m* 1966, Susan Rivett; two *d*. *Educ:* Highgate Coll.; Strand Grammar Sch. ACCA 1965, FCCA 1980. Articled clerk, George W. Spencer & Co., Chartered Accountants, 1959–64; joined J. Sainsbury plc, 1964: trainee, Accounting Dept, 1964–65; Financial Accounts Dept, 1965–73; Br. Financial Control Manager, 1973–80; Gen. Manager, Homebase, 1981–86; Area Dir, Sainsbury's Central and Western Area, 1986–89; Homebase: Man. Dir, 1989–95; Chm., 1991–96; Shaw's Supermarkets Inc.: Dep. Chm., 1994; Chm., 1994–96; Dir, Giant Food Inc., 1994–96; J. Sainsbury plc: Asst Man. Dir, 1995–96; Dep. Chief Exec., 1996–97. Dir, Laura Ashley plc, 1996–98. Oxfam: Trustee, 1990–96, 1998–; Advr on Retail Matters, 1996–98. *Recreations:* opera, music, soccer, culinary arts.

ADRIEN, Hon. Sir Maurice L.; *see* Latour-Adrien.

ADSETTS, Sir (William) Norman, Kt 1999; OBE 1988; Chairman, Sheffield Theatres Trust, since 1996; *b* 6 April 1931; *s* of Ernest Norman Adsetts and Hilda Rachel Adsetts (*née* Wheeler); *m* 1956, Eve Stefanuti; one *s* one *d*. *Educ:* King Edward VII Sch., Sheffield; Queen's Coll., Oxford (BA 1955; MA). Commissioned RAF, 1950–52; Marketing Manager, Fibreglass Ltd, 1955–66; Sheffield Insulating Co.: Dir, 1966–89; Man. Dir, 1970–85; Chm., 1985–89; Chm., Sheffield Insulations Gp, 1989–96. Dir, 1988–91, Dep. Chm., 1991–97, Sheffield Develt Corp.; Chairman: Kelham Riverside Develt Agency, 1998–; Sheffield Supertram Trust, 1993–98; Sheffield Partnerships, 1988–93; Sheffield First for Investment, 1999–. Chairman: Assoc. for Conservation of Energy, 1985–90, 1993–95; Yorkshire Humberside CBI, 1989–91; Pres., Sheffield Chamber of Commerce, 1988–89. Chairman of Governors: Sheffield Hallam Univ., 1993–99; Mount St Mary's Coll., 1999–. Patron of local charities. *Recreations:* reading, family and local history, grandchildren. *Address:* Churchfield House, Rotherham Road, Eckington, Sheffield S21 4FH. *T:* (01246) 431008, *Fax:* (01246) 431006. *Club:* Oxford and Cambridge.

ADYE, Sir John (Anthony), KCMG 1993; Chairman, Country Houses Association, since 1999; *b* 24 Oct. 1939; *s* of Arthur Francis Capel Adye and Hilda Marjorie Adye (*née* Elkes); *m* 1961, Anne Barbara, *d* of Dr John Aeschlimann, Montclair, NJ; two *s* one *d*. *Educ:* Leighton Park Sch.; Lincoln Coll., Oxford (MA). Joined GCHQ, 1962; Principal, 1968; British Embassy, Washington, 1973–75; Nat. Defence Coll., Latimer, 1975–76; Asst Sec., 1977–83; Under Sec., 1983–89; Dir, GCHQ, 1989–96; Dep. Sec., 1989–92; 2nd Perm. Sec., 1992–96. Gov., Dean Close Sch., Cheltenham. *Address:* c/o Country Houses Association, Aynhoe Park, Aynhoe, Banbury OX17 3BQ. *Club:* Naval and Military.

AGA KHAN (IV), His Highness Prince Karim, granted title His Highness by the Queen, 1957, granted title His Royal Highness by the Shah of Iran, 1959; *b* Genthod, Geneva, 13 Dec. 1936; *s* of late Prince Aly Salomon Khan and Princess Joan Aly Khan, later Viscountess Camrose (*née* Joan Barbara Yarde-Buller, *e d* of 3rd Baron Churston, MVO, OBE); became Aga Khan, spiritual leader and hereditary Imam of Ismaili Muslims all over the world on the death of his grandfather, Sir Sultan Mahomed Shah, Aga Khan III, GCSI, GCIE, GCVO, 11 July 1957; *m* 1969, Sarah Frances Croker-Poole (marr. diss. 1995); two *s* one *d*; *m* 1998, Princess Gabriele zu Leiningen (Begum Inaara Aga Khan); one *s*, and one step *d*. *Educ:* Le Rosey, Switzerland; Harvard University (BA Hons 1959). Founder and Chairman: Aga Khan Foundn, Geneva, 1967 (also branches/affiliates in Bangladesh, Canada, India, Kenya, Tanzania, Pakistan, Portugal, Tajikistan, Uganda, UK and US); Aga Khan Award for Architecture, 1977–; Inst. of Ismaili Studies, 1977–; Aga Khan Fund for Econ. Develt, Geneva, 1984–; Aga Khan Trust for Culture, Geneva, 1988. Founder and Chancellor, Aga Khan Univ., Pakistan, 1983. Leading owner and breeder of race horses in France, Ireland and UK; won: Derby, 1981 (Shergar), 1986 (Shahrastani), 1988 (Kahyasi), 2000 (Sinndar); Irish Derby, 1981 (Shergar), 1986 (Shahrastani), 1988 (Kahyasi), 2000 (Sinndar); Prix de L'Arc de Triomphe, 1982 (Akiyda), 2000 (Sinndar); Prix du Jockey Club, 1960 (Charlottesville), 1979 (Top Ville), 1984 (Darshaan), 1985 (Mouktar), 1987 (Natroun); Prix de Diane, 1993 (Shemaka), 1997 (Vereva), 1998 (Zainta), 1999 (Daryaba). Hon. FRIBA 1991; Hon. Mem., AIA, 1992. Doctor of Laws (*hc*): Peshawar Univ., Pakistan, 1967; Sind Univ., Pakistan, 1970; McGill, 1983; McMaster, 1987; Wales, 1993; Brown, 1996; Hon. DLitt London, 1989. Thomas Jefferson Meml Foundn Medal in Architecture, 1984; Amer. Inst. of Architects' Inst. Honor, 1984; Medalla de Oro, Consejo Superior de Colegios de Arquitectos, Spain, 1987; Médaille d'argent, Académie d'Architecture, Paris 1991; Huésped de Honor de Granada, Spain, 1991; Hadrian Award, World Monuments Fund, 1996; Gold Medal, City of Granada, 1998. Commandeur, Ordre du Mérite Mauritanien, 1960; Grand Croix: Order of Prince Henry the Navigator, Portugal, 1960; Ordre National de la Côte d'Ivoire, 1965; Ordre National de la Haute-Volta, 1965; Ordre Malgache, 1966; Ordre du Croissant Vert des Comores, 1966; Order of Merit, Portugal, 1998; Grand Cordon, Order of the Taj,

Iran, 1967; Nishan-i-Imtiaz, Pakistan, 1970; Cavaliere, Gran Croce, Ordine al Merito della Republica Italiana, 1977; Grand Officier, Ordre National du Lion, Sénégal, 1982; Nishan-e-Pakistan, Pakistan, 1983; Grand Cordon, Ouissam-al Arch, Morocco, 1986; Cavaliere del Lavoro, Italy, 1988; Commandeur, Légion d'Honneur, France, 1990; Gran Cruz, Orden del Mérito Civil, Spain, 1991; Order of Friendship, Tajikistan, 1998. *Address:* Aiglemont, 60270 Gouvieux, France. *Clubs:* Royal Yacht Squadron; Yacht Club Costa Smeralda (Founder Pres.) (Sardinia).

AGA KHAN, Prince Sadruddin; Consultant and Chargé de Mission to the Secretary-General of the UN, since 1978; Founding Member and President, Groupe de Bellerive; Founding Member and Chairman, Independent Commission on Internal Humanitarian Issues, 1983; *b* 17 Jan. 1933; *s* of His late Highness Sir Sultan Mohamed Shah, Aga Khan III, GCSI, GCIE, GCVO and of Andrée Joséphine Caron; *m* 1957, Nina Sheila Dyer (marr. diss., 1962); *m* 1972, Catherine Aleya Sursock. *Educ:* Harvard Univ. (BA); Harvard Grad. Sch. Arts and Sciences; Centre of Middle Eastern Studies. Unesco Consultant for Afro-Asian Projects, 1958; Head of Mission and Adviser to UN High Comr for Refugees, 1959–60; Unesco Special Consultant to Dir-Gen., 1961; Exec. Sec., Internat. Action Cttee for Preservation of Nubian Monuments, 1961; UN Dep. High Comr for Refugees, 1962–65; UN High Comr for Refugees, 1965–77; Co-ordinator, UN Humanitarian and Econ. Assistance Progs relating to Afghanistan, 1988–90; Personal Rep. of UN Sec.-Gen. for Humanitarian Assistance relating to Iraq-Kuwait crisis, 1990–91. Vice Pres., WWF, 1986–. Hon. Fellow, Amer. Acad. of Arts and Scis. Dr *hc* Fletcher Sch. of Law and Diplomacy, 1986; Univ. of Nice, 1988; Hon. LLD Leeds, 1992. Hon. Citizen Geneva, 1978. UN Human Rights Award, 1978; Hammarsköld Medal, German UN Assoc., 1979; Olympia Prize, Alexander S. Onassis Foundn, 1982; Man of Peace Award, Together for Peace Foundn, 1989; Freedom Award, Internat. Rescue Cttee, USA. Grand Cross: Order of St Silvestro (Papal), 1963; Order of Homayoun (Iran), 1967; Order of the Royal Star of Great Comoro (Comoro Is), 1970; Order of the Two Niles (First Class) Sudan, 1973; Commander's Cross with Star, Order of Merit of Polish People's Republic, 1977; Commandeur de la Légion d'Honneur (France), 1979; Hilal-e-Pakistan, 1991; Commander of Golden Ark (Netherlands). *Publications:* Lectures on refugee problems delivered to RSA and Acad. Internat. Law, The Hague; Violations of Human Rights and Mass Exodus, study for UN Commn on Human Rights, 1981. *Recreations:* Islamic art, sailing, ski-ing, hiking, kite-flying. *Address:* Château de Bellerive, 1245 Collonge-Bellerive, Canton of Geneva, Switzerland. *Clubs:* Travellers (Paris); Knickerbocker (New York).

AGAR, family name of **Earl of Normanton**.

AGASSI, André; tennis player; *b* Las Vegas, 29 April 1970; *s* of Emmanuel (Mike) and Betty Agassi; *m* 1997, Brooke Shields (marr. diss.). Trained at Nick Bollettieri Tennis Acad., Fla. Professional tennis player, 1986–; winner: (inaugural) ATP World Championship, Frankfurt, 1991; Wimbledon, 1992; US Open, 1994, 1999; Australian Open, 1995, 2000, 2001; French Open, 1999 (one of only five players ever to win all four men's grand-slam titles); Gold Medallist, Olympic Games, 1996. *Address:* c/o IMG, Suite 1300, 1 Brieview Plaza, Cleveland, OH 44114, USA.

AGIUS, Marcus Ambrose Paul; Chairman, Lazard Brothers & Co. Ltd, since 2001; *b* 22 July 1946; *s* of late Lt-Col Alfred Victor Louis Benedict Agius, MC, TD and Ena Eleanora Alberta Agius (*née* Hueffer); *m* 1971, Kate Juliette de Rothschild; two *d*. *Educ:* Trinity Hall, Cambridge (MA); Harvard Business Sch. (MBA). With Vickers plc, 1968–70; Lazard Brothers & Co. Ltd, 1972–: Dir, 1981–83; Man. Dir, 1984–89; Vice-Chm., 1990–2001; Lazard Frères & Co., New York, 1987–: Limited Partner, 1987–88; Gen. Partner, 1989–95; Man. Dir, 1995–. Non-exec. Director: Exbury Gardens Ltd, 1977–; BAA plc, 1995– (Dep. Chm., 1998–April 2002; Chm., April 2002–). Trustee: Southampton Univ. Develt Trust, 1995–; Restoration of Appearance and Function Trust, 1998–. *Recreations:* gardening, shooting, ski-ing, tennis, sailing. *Address:* 7 South Terrace, SW7 2TB. *T:* (020) 7589 9440; Marise Cottage, Exbury, Hants SO45 1AH. *T:* (023) 8089 1195. *Clubs:* White's; Swinley Forest Golf; Beaulieu River Sailing.

AGLIONBY, His Honour Francis John; a Circuit Judge, 1980–97, a Deputy Circuit Judge, since 1997; *b* 17 May 1932; *s* of Francis Basil and Marjorie Wycliffe Aglionby; *m* 1967, Susan Victoria Mary Vaughan; one *s* one *d*. *Educ:* Charterhouse; Corpus Christi Coll., Oxford (MA). Nat. Service, 1950–52, commnd Nigeria Regt. Barrister, Inner Temple, 1956, Bencher, 1976; a Recorder of the Crown Court, 1975–80. Chancellor of Diocese: of Birmingham, 1971–; of Portsmouth, 1978–; of Carlisle, 1991–. Mem., Adv. Bd for Redundant Churches, 1999–. Held Home Office enquiry into Horserace Totalisator Bd's bets transmissions procedures, 1979. *Recreations:* variable. *Address:* The Croft, Houghton, Carlisle, Cumbria CA3 0LD. *T:* (01228) 523747. *Club:* Brooks's.

AGNELLI, Dr Giovanni; industrialist; Chairman: Fiat, 1966–96 (Hon. Chairman, since 1996); Istituto Finanziario Industriale, since 1959; EXOR, SA, Luxembourg, since 1974; Giovanni Agnelli Foundation, since 1968; Chairman, Editrice La Stampa, since 1982; *b* Turin, Italy, 12 March 1921; *s* of Edoardo Agnelli, and *g s* of Giovanni Agnelli, founder of Fabbrica Italiana Automobili Torino (FIAT); *m* 1953, Princess Marella Caracciolo di Castagneto. *Educ:* Turin Univ. (DrJur, 1943). Member Board: Eurafrance, Paris; Italian Stock Cos Assoc.; Turin Industrial Assoc.; Member: Exec. Bd, Confedn of Italian Industry; Internat. Adv. Council, Chase Manhattan Corp., NY; Adv. Bd, Bilderberg Meetings. Hon. Vice-Pres., Assoc. for Monetary Union of Europe. Hon. Chm., Council for US and Italy. Romanes Lectr, Univ. of Oxford, 1991. Hon. Fellow, Magdalen Coll., Oxford, 1991. Corresp. Mem., Moral and Political Scis Acad., Institut de France. *Address:* c/o Fiat SpA, 250 via Nizza, Turin 10126, Italy. *T:* (11) 6861111.

AGNEW OF LOCHNAW, Sir Crispin Hamlyn, 11th Bt *cr* 1629; QC (Scot.) 1995; Rothesay Herald of Arms, since 1986; Chief of the Name and Arms of Agnew; *b* 13 May 1944; *s* of (Sir) Fulque Melville Gerald Noel Agnew of Lochnaw, 10th Bt and Swanzie, *d* of late Major Esmé Nourse Erskine, CMG, MC; *S* father, 1975; *m* 1980, Susan (formerly journalist, broadcaster, Advertising Exec.), *yr d* of late J. W. Strang Steel, Logie, Kirriemuir, Angus; one *s* three *d*. *Educ:* Uppingham; RMA, Sandhurst. Major (retd 1981), late RHF. Admitted to Faculty of Advocates, 1982. Dep. Social Security and Child Support Comr, 2000–. Slains Pursuivant of Arms to Lord High Constable of Scotland, 1978–81; Unicorn Pursuivant of Arms, 1981–86. Trustee, John Muir Trust, 1989–. Leader: Army Expedn to E Greenland, 1968; Jt Services Expedn to Chilean Patagonia, 1972–73; Army Expedn to Api, NW Nepal, 1980; Member: RN Expedn to E Greenland, 1966; Jt Services to Elephant Island (Antarctica), 1970–71; Army Nuptse Expedn, 1975; Jt British and Royal Nepalese Army Everest Expedn, 1976 (reached the South Col). *Publications:* (jtly) Allan and Chapman, Licensing (Scotland) Act 1976, 2nd edn 1989, 4th edn 1996; (jtly) Connell on the Agricultural Holdings Acts, 7th edn 1996; Agricultural Law in Scotland, 1996; Land Obligations, 1999; Crofting Law, 2000; articles in newspapers and magazines, and in legal and heraldic jls. *Recreations:* mountaineering, sailing (Yacht Pippa's Song), heraldry. *Heir: s* Mark Douglas Noel Agnew of Lochnaw, yr, *b* 24 April 1991. *Address:* 6 Palmerston Road, Edinburgh EH9 1TN. *Club:* Army and Navy.

AGNEW, Sir John (Keith), 6th Bt *cr* 1895, of Great Stanhope Street, London; *b* 19 Dec. 1950; *er s* of Major Sir (George) Keith Agnew, 5th Bt, TD, and of Anne Merete Louise, *yr d* of Baron Johann Schaffalitzky de Muckadell, Fyn, Denmark; *S* father, 1994. *Educ:* Gresham's Sch., Holt. *Heir: b* George Anthony Agnew, *b* 18 Aug. 1953. *Address:* Rougham Estate Office, Rougham, Bury St Edmunds, Suffolk IP30 9LZ.

AGNEW, Jonathan Geoffrey William; Chairman, Henderson Geared Income and Growth Trust (formerly HTR Income and Growth Split Trust) plc, since 1995; Deputy Chairman, Nationwide Building Society, since 1999 (non-executive Director, since 1997); *b* 30 July 1941; *er s* of Sir Geoffrey Agnew and Hon. Doreen Maud, *y d* of 1st Baron Jessel, CB, CMG; *m* 1st, 1966, Hon. Joanna Campbell (marr. diss. 1985); one *s* two *d*; 2nd, 1990, Marie-Claire Dreesmann; one *s* one *d*. *Educ:* Eton College; Trinity College, Cambridge (MA). The Economist, 1964–65; World Bank, 1965–67; Hill Samuel & Co., 1967–73, Dir, 1971–73; Morgan Stanley & Co., 1973–82, a Managing Dir, 1977–83; financial consultant, 1983–86; Chief Exec., ISRO, 1986; Kleinwort Benson Gp, 1987–93 (Gp Chief Exec., 1989–93); Chairman: London Insce Market Investment Trust, subseq. Limit, 1993–2000; Gerrard Gp, 1998–2000. Non-exec. Dir, Thos Agnew & Sons Ltd, 1969–. Mem. Council, Lloyd's, 1995–99. *Address:* Flat E, 51 Eaton Square, SW1W 9BE. *Clubs:* White's; Automobile (Paris); Brook (New York).

AGNEW, Jonathan Philip; cricket correspondent, BBC, since 1991; *b* 4 April 1960; *s* of Philip Agnew and Margaret Agnew; *m* 1996, Emma Norris; two *d* by former marriage. *Educ:* Uppingham Sch. Professional cricketer: début, Leics CCC, 1978; played for England, 1984–85; retd from first class cricket, 1990; cricket corresp., Today, 1990–91. Sports Reporter of Year, Sony, 1992. *Publications:* 8 Days a Week, 1988; Over to You, Aggers, 1997. *Address:* BBC Radio, Broadcasting House, W1A 1AA.

AGNEW, Peter Graeme, MBE 1946; BA; retired; Deputy Chairman, Bradbury Agnew & Co. Ltd (Proprietors of Punch), 1969–84; *b* 7 April 1914; *s* of late Alan Graeme Agnew; *m* 1937, Mary Diana (*née* Hervey) (*d* 2000); two *s* two *d*. *Educ:* Kingsmead, Seaford; Stowe School; Trinity College, Cambridge. Student Printer, 1935–37. Joined Bradbury Agnew & Co. Ltd, 1937. RAFVR 1937. Served War of 1939–45; demobilised, 1945, as Wing Commander. *Recreations:* sailing, gardening.

See also Col N.T. Davies.

AGNEW, Rudolph Ion Joseph; Chairman: Stena International BV, since 1990; LASMO PLC, 1994–2000; *b* 12 March 1934; *s* of Rudolph John Agnew and Pamela Geraldine (*née* Campbell); *m* 1980, Whitney Warren. *Educ:* Downside School. Commissioned officer, 8th King's Royal Irish Hussars, 1953–57. Joined Consolidated Gold Fields, 1957; Dep. Chm., 1978–82; Gp Chief Exec., 1978–89; Chm., 1983–89; Mem., Cttee of Man. Dirs, 1986–89. Chairman: TVS Entertainment, 1990–93; Federated Aggregates PLC, 1991–95; Bona Shipholding Ltd, Bermuda, 1993–98; Redland plc, 1995–97; Star Mining Corp., 1995–98; Jt Chm., Global Stone Corp. (Canada), 1993–94; Non-executive Director: Internat. Tool and Supply (formerly New London) PLC, 1985–96; Standard Chartered PLC, 1988–97; Newmont Mining Corp., USA, 1989–98; Newmont Gold Co., USA, 1989–98; Stena (UK) Ltd, 1990–99; Director: Gold Fields of South Africa Ltd, 1978–89; Renison Goldfields Consolidated, 1978–90; Anglo American Corp. of South Africa, 1980–88; Hanson PLC, 1989–91. Vice President: Nat. Assoc. of Boys' Clubs; Game Conservancy (Fellow); Hawk Trust; Chm., World Conservation Monitoring Centre, 1989–; Mem. Council, WWF (UK), 1989– (Trustee, 1983–89). CIMgt (FBIM 1980). FRSA. *Recreation:* shooting. *Address:* 7 Eccleston Street, SW1W 9LX. *Clubs:* Cavalry and Guards, White's.

AGNEW, Stanley Clarke, CB 1985; FREng; FICE; Chief Engineer, Scottish Development Department, 1976–87, retired; *b* 18 May 1926; *s* of Christopher Gerald Agnew and Margaret Eleanor Agnew (*née* Clarke); *m* 1950, Isbell Evelyn Parker (*née* Davidson); two *d*. *Educ:* Royal Belfast Academical Instn; Queen's Univ., Belfast (BSc Civil Eng., 1947). FIWEM. Service with contractors, consulting engineers and local authorities, 1947–62; Eng. Inspector, Scottish Develt Dept, 1962–68, Dep. Chief Engr, 1968–75. FREng (FEng 1985). *Recreations:* golf, photography, motoring, gardening. *Address:* Duncraig, 52 Blinkbonny Road, Edinburgh EH4 3HX. *T:* (0131) 332 4072. *Club:* Murrayfield Golf (Edinburgh).

AGNEW, William Alexander Fraser; Member (UU) Belfast North, Northern Ireland Assembly, since 1998; Cultural Co-ordinator, Newtownabbey Borough Council, since 1981; *b* 16 Aug. 1942; *s* of late James Agnew and Maureen Barbara Agnew (*née* Fraser); *m* 1972, Lila McCausland; one *s*. *Educ:* Ballyclare High Sch.; Univ. of Ulster at Jordanstown; Belfast Tech. Coll.; Coll. of Business Studies. MCIOB (MIOB 1968). Architectural draughtsman and company dir, until 1990; part-time sports journalist; presenter, history programmes on community radio; lecturer. Mem., NI Assembly, 1982–86. Mem. (UU) Newtownabbey BC, 1980– (Chairman: Corporate Services Cttee, 1993–94, 1995–96; Culture and Tourism Cttee, 1995–); Mayor, Newtownabbey, 1990–91. Chm., Ulster Tourist Develt Assoc. Chm., Ulster Young Unionist Council, 1970. Associate Mem., Inst. of Engrg Technol., 1969. *Publications:* numerous pamphlets on aspects of Ireland's history. *Recreations:* soccer coaching for children (qualified coach), 5-a-side football, golf. *Address:* 1 Knockview Crescent, Newtownabbey BT36 6UD. *T:* (028) 9084 1097; (office) 1 The Square, Ballyclare, Co. Antrim BT39 9BA.

AGNEW-SOMERVILLE, Sir Quentin (Charles Somerville), 2nd Bt *cr* 1957, of Clendry, Co. Wigtown; insurance consultant; *b* 8 March 1929; *s* of Comdr Sir Peter Agnew, 1st Bt and Enid Frances (*d* 1982), *d* of late Henry Boan; assumed additional name of Somerville by Royal licence, 1950; *S* father, 1990; *m* 1963, Hon. April, *y d* and a *co-heiress* of 15th Baron Strange; one *s* two *d*. *Educ:* RNC Dartmouth. *Heir: s* James Lockett Charles Agnew-Somerville, *b* 26 May 1970. *Address:* Mount Auldyn House, Ramsey, Isle of Man IM8 3PF. *T:* (01624) 813724, *Fax:* (01624) 816498; *e-mail:* agsom@enterprise.net.

AGRAN, Linda Valerie; Joint Chief Executive, Agran Barton Television Ltd, since 1993; *b* 9 May 1947; *d* of Albert and Gertrude Agran; *m* 1991, Alexander Gordon Scott. *Educ:* Queen Elizabeth's Girls' Grammar Sch., Barnet. William Morris Agency, Columbia Pictures, Paramount Pictures, Warner Bros, 1973–76; Head of Development, 1976, Director, 1982, Euston Films; Writer in Residence, Aust. Film & TV Sch.; Dep. Controller of Drama and Arts, LWT, 1986; Chief Exec., Paravision (UK) Ltd, 1989; completed management buyout to form Agran Barton TV, 1993. FRSA. *Television* (as producer or executive producer): series include: Minder; Widows; Paradise Postponed; London's Burning; Hercule Poirot; Moving Story. *Recreations:* cooking good food, drinking fine wines, horse racing, reading, all in the company of close friends. *Address:* Saddlewood Manor, Saddlewood, Leighterton, Glos GL8 8UQ.

AGUIRRE, Marcelino O.; *see* Oreja Aguirre.

ÁGÚSTSSON, Helgi, Hon. GCVO 1990; Icelandic Grand Order of the Falcon, 1990 (Order of the Falcon, 1979); Ambassador of Iceland to Denmark, since 1998, also accredited to Lithuania, Turkey, Israel and Romania; *b* 16 Oct. 1941; *s* of Ágúst Pétursson and Helga Jóhannesdóttir; *m* 1963, Hervör Jónasdóttir; three *s* one *d.* *Educ:* Univ. of Iceland (Law degree 1970). Joined Foreign Ministry, 1970; served London, 1973–77; Counsellor, 1977; Dir, Defence Div., Foreign Min., 1979 and Chm., US-Icelandic Defence Council; Minister-Counsellor, 1980; served Washington, 1983–87; Dep. Perm. Under-Sec., Foreign Min., 1987, in rank of Ambassador; Ambassador to UK, 1989–94, and to Ireland, Holland and Nigeria, 1990–94; Perm. Under-Sec., Min. for Foreign Affairs, Iceland, 1995–98. Former Pres., Icelandic Basketball Fedn. Mem., Rotary Club of Copenhagen. Decorations from Finland, Denmark, Sweden, Norway, Italy, Spain, Netherlands. *Recreations:* theatre, music, reading. *Address:* Embassy of Iceland, Dantes Plads 3, 1556 Copenhagen V, Denmark.

AGUTTER, Jennifer Ann; actress; *b* 20 Dec. 1952; *d* of Derek and Catherine Agutter; *m* 1990, Johan Tham; one *s.* *Educ:* Elmhurst Ballet School, Camberley. *Films:* East of Sudan, 1964; Ballerina, 1964; Gates of Paradise, 1967; Star, 1968; Walkabout, I Start Counting, The Railway Children, 1969 (Royal Variety Club Most Promising Artist, 1971); Logan's Run, 1975; The Eagle Has Landed, Equus (BAFTA Best Supporting Actress, 1977), The Man In The Iron Mask, 1976; Dominique, Clayton and Catherine, 1977; The Riddle of the Sands, Sweet William, 1978; The Survivor, 1980; An American Werewolf in London, 1981; Secret Places, 1983; Dark Tower, 1987; King of the Wind, 1989; Child's Play 2, 1991; Freddie as Fro7, 1992; Blue Juice, 1995; *stage:* School for Scandal, 1972; Rooted, Arms and the Man, The Ride Across Lake Constance, 1973; National Theatre: The Tempest, Spring Awakening, 1974; Hedda, Betrayal, 1980; Peter Pan, 1997; Royal Shakespeare Co.: Arden of Faversham, Lear, King Lear, The Body, 1982–83; Breaking the Silence, 1985; Shrew, The Unified Field, LA, 1987; Breaking the Code, NY, 1987; Love's Labour's Lost, Barbican, 1995; Mothers and Daughters, Chichester, 1996; *television includes:* Long After Summer, 1967; The Wild Duck, The Cherry Orchard, The Snow Goose (Emmy Best Supporting Actress), 1971; A War of Children, 1972; School Play, 1979; Amy, 1980; Love's Labour's Lost, This Office Life, 1984; Silas Marner, 1985; Murder She Wrote, 1986; The Equaliser, Magnum, 1988; Dear John, 1989; Not a Penny More, Not a Penny Less, Tecx, 1990; The Good Guys, Puss in Boots, 1991; The Buccaneers, 1995; And the Beat Goes On, 1996; Bramwell, A Respectable Trade, 1998; The Railway Children, 2000. *Publication:* Snap, 1983. *Address:* c/o JY Publicity, 54A Ebury Street, SW1W 0LU. *T:* (020) 7730 2112.

AGUTTER, Richard Devenish; Senior Adviser, KPMG, since 1998; *b* 17 Sept. 1941; *s* of late Anthony Tom Devenish Agutter and of Joan Hildegare Sabina (*née* Machen, now Fleming); *m* 1968, Lesley Anne Ballard; three *s*; Educ: Marlborough Coll. CA 1964. With W. T. Walton, 1960–64; joined Peat Marwick Mitchell, subsequently KPMG, 1964: Partner, 1977–98; Chm., KPMG Internat. Corporate Finance, 1990–96. City of London: Alderman, Ward of Castle Baynard, 1995–; Sheriff, 2000–01. Liveryman: Co. of Chartered Accountants, 1977–; Goldsmiths' Co., 1979–; Mem., Ct of Assts, Co. of Marketors, 1999–; Jun. Warden, Guild of Freemen, 2001. *Recreations:* wine, gardening, sailing. *Address:* Great Frenches Park, Snow Hill, Crawley Down, Sussex RH10 3EE. *T:* (01342) 716816.

AHEARNE, Stephen James, FCA; Chief Financial Officer, 1990–96, and Managing Director, 1992–96, British Petroleum Company PLC; *b* 7 Sept. 1939; *s* of James Joseph Ahearne and Phyllis Eva (*née* Grigsby); *m* 1965, Janet Elizabeth Edwards; two *s.* Qualified as Chartered Accountant, 1962; joined British Petroleum, 1964: Man. Dir, BP Denmark, 1978–81; Exec. Dir, BP Chems, 1981–86; Gp Controller, 1986–88; Gp Planner, 1988–90. Mem., Restrictive Practices Court, 1993–. Gov., Felsted Sch., 1996–. *Recreations:* tennis, gardening, sailing, walking, reading.

AHERN, Bertie; Member of the Dáil (TD) (FF), since 1977; Taoiseach (Prime Minister of Ireland), since 1997; President, Fianna Fáil, since 1994; *b* 12 Sept. 1951; *s* of Cornelius and Julia Ahern; *m* 1975 (separated); two *d.* *Educ:* Rathmines Coll. of Commerce; University Coll., Dublin. Accountant. Asst Chief Whip, 1980–81; spokesman on youth affairs, 1981; Govt Chief Whip and Minister of State at Depts of Taoiseach and Defence, 1982; Minister for Labour, 1987–91; Minister for Finance, 1991–94; Leader of the Opposition, 1994–97. Lord Mayor of Dublin, 1986–87. Member, Board of Governors, 1991–94: IMF; World Bank; EIB (Chm., 1991–92). Grand Cross, Order of Merit with Star and Sash (Germany), 1991. *Recreations:* sports, reading. *Address:* St Luke's, 161 Lower Drumcondra Road, Dublin 9, Ireland.

AHMAD, Khurshid; Chairman: Institute of Policy Studies, Islamabad, Pakistan, since 1979; Board of Trustees, Islamic Foundation, Leicester, since 1985; Member, Senate of Pakistan, 1985–97; *b* 23 March 1934; three *s* three *d.* *Educ:* Karachi Univ. (LLB; MA Economics; MA Islamic Studies). Dir-Gen., Islamic Foundn, Leicester, 1973–78; Federal Minister for Planning and Develt and Dep. Chm., Planning Commn, Govt of Pakistan, 1978–79. Chm., Internat. Inst. of Islamic Econs, Islamic Univ., Islamabad, 1983–87. Hon. PhD Educn, Nat. Univ. of Malaya. Islamic Develt Bank Laureate for dist. contribn to Islamic econs, 1988; King Faisal, Internat. Prize for service to Islam, 1990. *Publications:* Essays on Pakistan Economy (Karachi), 1958; An Analysis of Munir Report (Lahore), 1958; (ed) Studies in the Family Law of Islam (Karachi), 1960; (ed) The Quran: an Introduction (Karachi), 1966; The Prophet of Islam (Karachi), 1967; Principles of Islamic Education (Lahore), 1970; Fanaticism, Intolerance and Islam (Lahore), 1970; Islam and the West (Lahore), 1972; The Religion of Islam (Lahore), 1973; (ed) Islam: its meaning and message (London, Islamic Council of Europe), 1976; Development Strategy for the Sixth Plan (Islamabad), 1983; Islamic Approach to Development: some policy implications (Islamabad), 1994; Islamic Resurgence: challenges, directions and future perspectives, ed I. M. Abu-Rabi, 1995; The Crisis of the Political System in Pakistan and the Jamaat-e-Islami, 1996; *for Islamic Foundation, Leicester:* Islam: Basic Principles and Characteristics, 1974; Family Life in Islam, 1974; Islamic Perspectives: Studies in honour of Maulana Mawdudi, 1979; The Quran: Basic Teachings, 1979; Studies in Islamic Economics, 1980; contrib. The Third World's Dilemma of Development, Non-Aligned Third World Annual, (USA) 1970. *Recreations:* travelling, reading. *Address:* Islamic Foundation, Markfield Conference Centre, Ratby Lane, Markfield, Leics LE67 9SY. *T:* (01530) 244944; Institute of Policy Studies, Block 19, Markaz F-7, Islamabad, Pakistan. *T:* (51) 272590; *e-mail:* ips@isb.compol.com.

AHMADI, Hon. Aziz Mushabber; Chief Justice of India, 1994–97; *b* 25 March 1932; *s* of M. I. Ahmadi and Shirin I. Ahmadi; *m* 1960, Amena A. Muchhala; one *s* one *d.* *Educ:* Ahmedabad and Surat (LLB). Called to the Bar, Ahmedabad, 1954; Judge, City Civil and Sessions Court, Ahmedabad, 1964–74; Sec., Legal Dept, Govt of Gujarat, 1974–76; Judge, High Court of Gujarat, 1976–88; Judge, Supreme Court of India, 1988–94. Pres., Supreme Court Legal Aid Cttee, 1989; Exec. Chm., Cttee for Implementing Legal Aid Schemes in India, 1994. Chairman: Adv. Bd, Conservation of Foreign Exchange and Prevention of Smuggling Activities Act, 1974; Adv. Bd, Prevention of Black Marketing, Maintenance of Supplies of Essential Commodities Act, 1982–83; Gujarat Third Pay Commn, 1982–85. Mem., UN Commn of Inquiry, East Timor, 1999. Hon. Bencher, Middle Temple, 1996. Hon. LLD: Kurukshetra, 1994; Maharishi Dayanand, 1995; Kanpur, 1995; Sardar Patel, 1996; Cochin, 1997; Leicester, 1998. *Recreations:* reading, music. *Address:* C-3 Kant Enclave, near Dr Karni Singh Shooting Ranges, Anangpur, Haryana 121003, India. *T:* (129) 5251291, (129) 5251293, *Fax:* (129) 5251285, (11) 6966389; *e-mail:* ahmadi@bol.net.in. *Clubs:* Delhi Gymkhana, India International Centre (New Delhi).

AHMED, Baron *cr* 1998 (Life Peer), of Rotherham in the co. of South Yorkshire; **Nazir Ahmed;** JP; business development manager; *b* 24 April 1957; *s* of Haji Sain Mohammed and Rashim Bibi; *m* 1974, Sakina Bibi; two *s* one *d.* *Educ:* Thomas Rotherham Coll.; Sheffield Hallam Univ. Business development manager: mini-markets, 1979–82; fish and chip shops, 1979–; petrol station, 1982–84; marble mining, Azad, Kashmir, 1985–87; business park and property develt, 1990–. Mem. (Lab) Rotherham MBC, 1990–. Founder, British Muslim Councillors Forum. Chm., S Yorks Lab. Party, 1993–. Chm., All-Pty Parly Libya Gp, 1999–. Co-Chm., Govt's Forced Marriage Wkg Gp, 1999–; Mem., Channel 4 Hate Commn (on hate crime), 1999–. JP Rotherham, 1992. *Recreation:* volleyball. *Address:* 152 East Bawtry Road, Rotherham S60 4LG. *T:* (01709) 730140; House of Lords, SW1A 0PW.

AHMED, Prof. Haroon, ScD; FREng; Professor of Microelectronics, University of Cambridge, since 1992; Master of Corpus Christi College, Cambridge, since 2000 (Fellow, since 1967; Warden of Leckhampton, 1993–98); *b* 2 March 1936; *s* of Mohammad Nizam Ahmed and Bilquis Jehan Ahmed; *m* 1969, Evelyn Anne Travers Goodrich; one *s* two *d.* *Educ:* St Patrick's Sch., Karachi; Imperial College London; King's College, Cambridge (PhD 1963); ScD Cantab 1996. GEC and Hirst Research Centre, 1958–59; Turner and Newall Res. Fellow, 1962–63; University of Cambridge: Univ. Demonstrator, Engineering Dept, 1963–66; Lectr, Engineering Dept, 1966–84; Reader in Microelectronics, 1984–92. Syndic, CUP, 1996–. FREng (FEng 1990). *Publications:* (with A. H. W. Beck) Introduction to Physical Electronics, 1968; (with P. J. Spreadbury) Electronics for Engineers, 1973, 2nd edn 1984. *Recreations:* golf, tennis. *Address:* Corpus Christi College, Cambridge CB2 1RH.

AHMED, Shami; Chief Executive, Joe Bloggs Inc. Co., since 1997; *b* Pakistan, 7 July 1962; *s* of Nizam Ahmed and Saeeda Ahmed; *m* 1997, Samina. *Educ:* Barden High Sch., Burnley. Set up wholesale clothing business, Pennywise, with father, 1977; founded: Legendary Joe Bloggs Inc. Co., 1986; Legendary Property Co., 1993. Hon. Fellow, Lancashire Poly., 1991. *Recreation:* swimming. *Address:* (office) 18–24 Bury New Road, Manchester M8 8FR. *T:* (0161) 831 7550.

AHO, Esko Tapani; MP (Centre Party), Helsinki, Finland, since 1983; Prime Minister of Finland, 1991–95; *b* Veteli, 20 May 1954; *s* of Kauko Kaleva Aho and Laura Kyllikki Aho (*née* Harjupatana); *m* 1980, Kirsti Hannele Söderkultalahti; two *s* one *d.* *Educ:* Master of Pol Scis. Political Sec. to Minister for Foreign Affairs, Finland, 1979–80; Chm., Finnish Parlt, April 1991; Member: Traffic Commn, 1983–86; Finances Commn, 1987–90. Member: CSCE Cttee, 1984–90; Finnish Delegn, Nordic Council, 1983–89; Finnish Delegn, Council of Europe, 1989–91. Chairman: League, Centre Party Youth, 1974–80; Finnish Centre Party, 1990–. Member, Advisory Board: Outokumpu Oy (Metal Ind.), 1985–91; OKO (Bank), 1991; SOK (Diversified Co-op.), 1990–91. Grand Cross, Order of White Rose (Finland), 1992; Cavaliere di Gran Croce, Order of Merit (Italy), 1993. *Recreations:* tennis, literature. *Address:* Centre Party of Finland, Pursimiehenkatu 15, 00150 Helsinki, Finland.

AHRENDS, Peter; Founding Partner and Director, Ahrends Burton & Koralek, Architects, since 1961; *b* 30 April 1933; *s* of Steffen Bruno Ahrends and Margarete Marie Sophie Visino; *m* 1954, Elizabeth Robertson; two *d.* *Educ:* King Edward VII Sch., Johannesburg; Architectural Assoc. Sch. of Architecture (Dipl., Hons). RIBA 1959. Steffen Ahrends & Partners, Johannesburg, 1957–58; Denys Lasdun & Partners, 1959–60; Julian Keable & Partners; major-projects, 1961–, include: *public buildings:* Hampton Site, Nat. Gall. Extn, 1982–85 (comp. winning entry); St Mary's Hosp., Newport, IoW (nucleus low energy hosp.), 1990; White Cliffs Heritage Centre, Dover, 1991; Techniquest Science Centre, 1995 (RIBA Arch. Award); Dublin Dental Hosp., 1994–; Sculpture Court, Whitworth Art Gall., Manchester, 1995 (RIBA Arch. Award); Waterford Visitor Centre, 1998; *educational buildings:* New Liby, TCD, 1961 (internat. comp.); Templeton Coll., Oxford, phased completion over 25 years from 1969; residential bldg, Keble Coll., Oxford, 1976 (RIBA Arch. Award, 1978); Arts Faculty Bldg, TCD, 1979; Loughborough Univ. Business Sch., 1997; IT bldg and catering bldg, Inst. of Technology, Tralee, 1998; tourism and leisure bldg, Waterford Inst. of Technology, 1999; first phase bldgs, Inst. of Technology, Blanchardstown, 1999; *residential buildings:* Nebenzahl House, Jerusalem, 1972; Whitmore Court Housing, 1975 (RIBA Good Design in Housing Award, 1977); *commercial/industrial buildings:* warehouse, showroom and offices, Habitat, 1974 (Structural Steel Design Award, FT Industrial Arch. Award, 1976); factory, Cummins Engines (Struct. Steel Design Award, 1980); Sainsbury supermarket, Canterbury, 1984 (Struct. Steel Design Award, 1985); W. H. Smith offices, Swindon, 1985; British Embassy, Moscow, 1988–99; John Lewis dept store, Kingston-upon-Thames, 1990; office develt for Stanhope Trafalgar, 1990–; office building, Tel Aviv, 1998; *sports buildings:* Carrickmines Croquet and Lawn Tennis Club, Dublin, 1998; *transport:* Docklands Light Railway Beckton Extension stations, 1987–93; *development plans:* won internat. competition for Campus Develt Plan, Univ. of Grenoble, 1990–93; MBA Sch., Templeton Coll., Univ. of Oxford, 1992; Falmer Develt Plan, Univ. of Brighton, 1992; Cardiff Inner Harbour, 1993; Inst. of Technology, Tralee, 1998; Waterford Inst. of Technology, 1998; Inst. of Technology, Blanchardstown, 1999; City Block, Dublin, 2000. Chair, UK Architects Against Apartheid, 1988–93; Member: Design Council, 1988–93; Council, AA, 1965–67. Vis. Prof. of Architecture, Kingston Poly., 1983–84; Bartlett Prof. of Arch., Bartlett Sch. of Arch. and Planning, UCL, 1986–89; part-time teaching posts and workshops at AA Sch. of Arch., Canterbury Sch. of Art, Edinburgh Univ., Winter Sch. Edinburgh, Plymouth Poly., Kingston Poly., and Plymouth Sch. of Art; vis. critic and/or ext. examr at Kumasi Univ., AA Sch. of Arch., Nova Scotia Tech. Univ., Strathclyde Univ. Exhibitions of drawings and works: RIBA Heinz Gall., 1980; RIAI, 1981; Douglas Hyde Gall., Dublin, 1981; Braunschweig Tech. Univ., Tech. Univ. of Hanover, Museum of Finnish Arch., 1982; Univ. of Oulu, Alvar Aalto Museum, Finland, 1982; AA HQ, Oslo, 1983. *Publications:* (contrib.) Ahrends Burton & Koralek, Architects (monograph), 1991; papers and articles in RIBA Jl and other prof. jls. *Recreations:* architecture, France. *Address:* (home) 16 Rochester Road, NW1 9JH; (office) 7 Chalcot Road, NW1 8LH. *T:* (020) 7586 3311, *Fax:* (020) 7722 5445; *e-mail:* 100045.3147@compuserve.com.

AHTISAARI, Martti; President, Republic of Finland, 1994–2000; Chairman, International Crisis Group, since 2000; *b* 23 June 1937; *s* of Oiva and Tyyne Ahtisaari; *m* 1968, Eeva Irmeli Hyvärinen; one *s.* Finnish diplomat; UN envoy; head, operation monitoring Namibia's transition to independence, 1989–90; senior envoy in Yugoslavia, 1992–93; EU Special envoy in Kosovo, 1999; Mem., observer gp on Austrian govt human rights record, 2000; co-inspector, IRA arms dumps, 2000–. Co-Chm., EastWest Inst.; Chairman: War-torn Societies Project Internat.; Balkan Youth and Children Foundn.

Member: Internat. Advrs' Gp, Open Soc. Inst.; Exec. Bd, Internat. Inst. for Democracy and Electoral Assistance. *Address:* Erottajankatu 11A, 00130 Helsinki, Finland.

AIKEN, Joan Delano, (Mrs Julius Goldstein), MBE 1999; writer of historical, mystery and children's novels, plays and poetry; *b* 4 Sept. 1924; *d* of Conrad Potter Aiken and Jessie McDonald; *m* 1st, 1945, Ronald George Brown (*d* 1955); one *s* one *d*; 2nd, 1976, Julius Goldstein. *Educ:* Wychwood Sch., Oxford. Inf. Officer, subseq. Librarian, UN London Inf. Centre, 1943–49; Features Editor, Argosy magazine, 1955–60; Copy-writer, J. Walter Thompson London office, 1960–61; time thereafter devoted to writing. Mem., Soc. of Authors. Guardian Award for Children's Literature, 1969; Lewis Carroll Award, 1970. *Publications:* (most also published in USA and as paperbacks): The Silence of Herondale, 1964; The Fortune Hunters, 1965; Trouble with Product X, 1966 (Beware of the Bouquet, USA 1966); Hate Begins at Home, 1967 (Dark Interval, USA 1967); The Ribs of Death, 1967 (The Crystal Crow, USA 1968); The Windscreen Weepers (stories), 1969; The Embroidered Sunset, 1970; The Butterfly Picnic, 1970 (A Cluster of Separate Sparks, USA 1972); Died on a Rainy Sunday, 1972; Voices in an Empty House, 1975; Castle Barebane, 1976; Last Movement, 1977; The Five-Minute Marriage, 1977; The Smile of the Stranger, 1978; A Touch of Chill (horror stories), 1979; The Lightning Tree, 1980 (The Weeping Ash, USA); The Girl from Paris, 1982; The Way to Write for Children, 1982; A Whisper in the Night, 1982; Foul Matter, 1983; Mansfield Revisited, 1984; Deception, 1987; Jane Fairfax, 1990; The Youngest Miss Ward, 1998; *for children:* (many also published in USA): All You've Ever Wanted (stories), 1953; More Than You Bargained For (stories), 1955; The Kingdom and the Cave, 1960; The Wolves of Willoughby Chase, 1962; Black Hearts in Battersea, 1964; Night Birds on Nantucket, 1966; The Whispering Mountain, 1968; A Necklace of Raindrops (stories), 1968; A Small Pinch of Weather (stories), 1969; Night Fall, 1969; Armitage, Armitage, Fly Away Home (stories), USA 1970; Smoke From Cromwell's Time, USA 1970; The Cuckoo Tree, 1971; The Kingdom Under the Sea (folktales), 1971; The Green Flash (fantasy and horror stories), USA 1971; A Harp of Fishbones (stories), 1972; Winterthing (play), USA 1972; The Mooncusser's Daughter (play), USA 1973; Winterthing & The Mooncusser's Daughter, 1973; Midnight is a Place, 1974; Arabel's Raven, USA 1974; Tales of Arabel's Raven, 1974; Not What You Expected (stories), USA 1974; Tale of a One-Way Street (stories), 1976; The Skin Spinners (poems), USA 1976; A Bundle of Nerves (horror stories), 1976; The Angel Inn (trans. from French), 1976; The Faithless Lollybird (stories), 1977; Mice and Mendelson, 1978; Go Saddle the Sea, 1978; Street (play), USA 1978; Arabel and Mortimer, 1979; The Shadow Guests, 1980; The Stolen Lake, 1981; Mortimer's Cross, 1983; Bridle the Wind, 1983; Up the Chimney Down and Other Stories, 1984; Fog Hounds, Wind Cat, Sea Mice, 1984, 2nd edn 1997; The Kitchen Warriors, 1984; The Last Slice of Rainbow, 1985; Mortimer Says Nothing, 1985; Dido and Pa, 1986; Past Eight O'Clock, 1986; A Goose on Your Grave, 1987; Beware of the Moon, 1987; The Teeth of the Gale, 1988; The Erl King's Daughter, 1988; Blackground, 1989; Give Yourself a Fright, 1989; Voices, 1989; A Foot in the Grave, 1990; A Fit of Shivers (horror stories), 1990; Morningquest, 1992; (with Lizza Aiken) Mortimer and Arabel, 1992; A Creepy Company, 1993; The Midnight Moropus, 1993; The Shoemaker's Boy, 1993; Is, 1993; Eliza's Daughter, 1994; The Winter Sleepwalker, 1994; Cold Shoulder Road, 1995; A Handful of Gold, 1995; The Cockatrice Boys, 1996; Emma Watson, 1996; The Jewel Seed, 1997; Mooncake, 1998; Limbo Lodge, 1999; Lady Catherine's Necklace, 2000; In Thunder's Pocket, 2001; The Scream, 2001. *Recreations:* listening to music, looking at art, travel, reading, gardening, walking, talking to friends. *Address:* The Hermitage, East Street, Petworth, West Sussex GU28 0AB. *T:* (01798) 42279. *Clubs:* Society of Authors, Writers' Guild, Crime Writers' Association, PEN; Mystery Writers of America.

AIKEN, Air Chief Marshal Sir John (Alexander Carlisle), KCB 1973 (CB 1967); Director General of Intelligence, Ministry of Defence, 1978–81; *b* 22 Dec. 1921; *s* of Thomas Leonard and Margaret Aiken; *m* 1948, Pamela Jane (*née* Bartlett); one *s* one *d*. *Educ:* Birkenhead School. Joined RAF, 1941; Fighter Sqdns, Europe and Far East, 1942–45; Fighter Comd, 1946–47; CFS, 1948; Staff of RAF Coll., Cranwell, 1948–50; OC Univ. of Birmingham Air Sqdn, 1950–52; Staff Coll., 1953; HQ Fighter Comd, 1954–55; OC 29 Fighter Sqdn, 1956–57; jssc 1958; Headquarters AF North, 1958–60; Air Min., 1960–63; Station Comdr, RAF Finningley, 1963–64; Air Cdre Intelligence, Min. of Defence, 1965–67; idc 1968; Dep. Comdr, RAF, Germany, 1969–71; Dir-Gen. Training, RAF, 1971–72; Head of Economy Project Team (RAF), 1972–73; AOC-in-C, NEAF, Comdr British Forces Near East, and Administrator, Sovereign Base Areas, Cyprus, 1973–76; Air Member for Personnel, 1976–78. Pres., RAFA, 1984–85 and 1987–88 (Chm., Central Council, 1981–84); Member Council: RAF Benevolent Fund, 1988–; Chatham House, 1984–90. *Recreations:* walking, ski-ing, music. *Club:* Royal Air Force.

AIKENS, Hon. Sir Richard (John Pearson), Kt 1999; **Hon. Mr Justice Aikens;** a Judge of the High Court, Queen's Bench Division, since 1999; Presiding Judge, South Eastern Circuit, since 2001; *b* 28 Aug. 1948; *s* of late Basil Aikens and of Jean Eleanor Aikens; *m* 1979, Penelope Anne Hartley Rockley (*née* Baker); two *s* two step *d*. *Educ:* Norwich Sch.; St John's Coll., Cambridge (MA). Called to Bar, Middle Temple, 1973 (Harmsworth scholar, 1974; Bencher, 1994); in practice, 1974–99; a Junior Counsel to the Crown, Common Law, 1981–86; QC 1986; a Recorder, 1993–99. Mem., Supreme Court Rules Cttee, 1984–88. Dir, Bar Mutual Indemnity Fund Ltd, 1988–2000 (Chm., 1998–99). Dir, ENO, 1995–. Governor, Sedbergh Sch., 1988–97. *Publication:* (contributing editor) Bullen and Leake and Jacob, Precedents of Pleading, 13th edn 1990. *Recreations:* music, gardening, wine. *Address:* Royal Courts of Justice, Strand, WC2A 2LL. *Clubs:* Groucho; Leander.

AIKIN, Olga Lindholm, (Mrs J. M. Driver), CBE 1997; Partner, Aikin Driver Partnership, since 1988; Visiting Lecturer, London Business School, since 1985; Council Member, Advisory Conciliation and Arbitration Service, 1982–95; *b* 10 Sept. 1934; *d* of Sidney Richard Daly and Lilian May Daly (*née* Lindholm); *m* 1st, 1959, Ronald Sidney Aikin (marr. diss. 1979); one *d*; 2nd, 1982, John Michael Driver; one step *d*. *Educ:* London School of Economics (LLB); King's Coll., London. Called to Bar, Gray's Inn, 1956. Assistant Lecturer, King's Coll., London, 1956–59; Lecturer, London School of Economics, 1959–70; London Business School: Sloan Fellowship Programme, 1970–71; Vis. Lectr, 1971–79; Lectr in Law, 1979–85. Dir, Gen. Law Div., Lion Internat. (Keiser Enterprises Inc.), 1985–90; Chm. Bd of Mgt, Nat. Conciliation Service of Qualitas Furnishing Standards Ltd, 1992–94. *Publications:* (with Judith Reid) Employment, Welfare and Safety at Work, 1971; (with Sonia Pearson) Legal Problems of Employment Contracts, 1990; (ed) IPM Law and Employment series (Discipline; Industrial Tribunals; Redundancy), 1992; articles in Personnel Management. *Recreation:* collecting cookery books and pressed glass. *Address:* 22 St Luke's Road, W11 1DP. *T:* (office) (020) 7727 9791.

See also Hon. F. L. Daly.

AIKMAN, Colin Campbell, CBE 1990; PhD; consultant; *b* 24 Feb. 1919; *s* of Colin Campbell Aikman and Bertha Egmont Aikman (*née* Harwood); *m* 1952, Betty Alicia, *d* of R. Y. James; three *d* (one *s* decd). *Educ:* Palmerston North Boys' High Sch.; Victoria University Coll., Wellington, NZ (LLM); London Sch. of Economics (PhD). Law Clerk in Legal Offices, 1935–41; Barrister and Solicitor of High Court of New Zealand, 1940–41; Prime Minister's Dept and Dept of External Affairs (Legal Adviser, 1949–55), 1943–55; Mem. NZ Delgn to San Francisco Conf., 1945; Prof. of Jurisprudence and Constitutional Law, Victoria Univ. of Wellington (Dean of Law Faculty, 1957–59, 1962–67), 1955–68; Mem. Council, NZ Inst. of Internat. Affairs (Nat. Pres., 1960–63, Dir. 1979–84), 1955–; Advr to NZ Govt on Constitutional Develt of Cook Is, Western Samoa and Niue, 1956–68, 1975; Vice-Chancellor, The Univ. of the South Pacific, Suva, Fiji, 1968–74; NZ High Comr to India, accredited also to Bangladesh and Nepal, 1975–78. Member: Council of Volunteer Service Abroad (Inc.) (Chm. 1962–65), 1962–68; Adv. Cttee on External Aid and Develt, 1980–88. Consultant, NZ Law Commn, 1988–91. Trustee, Norman Kirk Meml Trust, 1979– (Chm., 1994–99). Mem. Council, Nat. Univ. of Samoa, 1985–98. Hon. LLD Victoria Univ. of Wellington, 1992; DU Univ. of South Pacific, 1992; DUniv Nat. Univ. of Samoa, 1996. Silver Jubilee Medal, 1977; Western Samoa Order of Tiafau, 1993. *Publications:* (co-author): A Report to Members of the Legislative Assembly of the Cook Islands on Constitutional Development, 1963; New Zealand, The Development of its Laws and Constitution (ed Robson), 1967 (2nd edn); New Zealand's Record in the Pacific Islands in the Twentieth Century (ed Angus Ross), 1969; contribs to NZ Internat. Review, Victoria Univ. of Wellington Law Review. *Recreations:* golf, cricket, carpentry. *Address:* 7A/186 The Terrace, Wellington, New Zealand. *T:* (4) 4711602, *Fax:* (4) 4711630; *e-mail:* aikman@attglobal.net. *Clubs:* Wellington; Wellington Golf (Heretaunga).

AILESBURY, 8th Marquess of, *cr* 1821; **Michael Sydney Cedric Brudenell-Bruce;** Bt 1611; Baron Brudenell 1628; Earl of Cardigan 1661; Baron Bruce 1746; Earl of Ailesbury 1776; Earl Bruce 1821; Viscount Savernake 1821; 30th Hereditary Warden of Savernake Forest; *b* 31 March 1926; *e s* of 7th Marquess of Ailesbury and Joan (*d* 1937), *d* of Stephen Salter, Ryde, Isle of Wight; *S* father, 1974; *m* 1st, 1952, Edwina Sylvia de Winton (from whom he obtained a divorce, 1961), *yr d* of Lt-Col Sir (Ernest) Edward de Winton Wills, 4th Bt; one *s* two *d*; 2nd, 1963, Juliet Adrienne (marr. diss. 1974), *d* of late Hilary Lethbridge Kingsford and Mrs Latham Hobrow, Marlborough; two *d*; 3rd, 1974, Mrs Caroline Elizabeth Romilly (marr. diss. 1990), *d* of late Commander O. F. M. Wethered, RN, DL, JP. *Educ:* Eton. Lt RHG, 1946. Mem., London Stock Exchange, 1954. *Heir: s* Earl of Cardigan, *qv*. *Address:* Luton Lye, Savernake Forest, near Marlborough, Wilts SN8 3HP.

AILSA, 8th Marquess of, *cr* 1831; **Archibald Angus Charles Kennedy;** Baron Kennedy 1452; Earl of Cassillis 1509; Baron Ailsa (UK) 1806; *b* 13 Sept. 1956; *er s* of 7th Marquess of Ailsa, OBE and of Mary, 7th *c* of John Burn; *S* father, 1994; *m* 1979, Dawn Leslie Anne Keen (marr. diss. 1989); two *d*. *Recreations:* shooting, ski-ing, cadets and youth-work. *Heir: b* Lord David Thomas Kennedy [*b* 3 July 1958; *m* 1991, Anne Kelly; one *s* one *d*]. *Address:* Cassillis House, Maybole, Ayrshire KA19 7JN. *T:* (01292) 560310. *Club:* New (Edinburgh).

AINGER, Nicholas Richard, (Nick); MP (Lab) Carmarthen West and Pembrokeshire South, since 1997 (Pembroke, 1992–97); a Lord Commissioner of HM Treasury (Government Whip), since 2001; *b* Sheffield, 24 Oct. 1949; *m* 1976, Sally Robinson; one *d*. *Educ:* Netherthorpe Grammar Sch., Staveley. Rigger, Marine and Port Services Ltd, Pembroke Dock, 1977–92. Mem. (Lab) Dyfed CC, 1981–93. Branch Sec., TGWU, 1978–92. PPS to Sec. of State for Wales, 1997–2001. *Address:* House of Commons, SW1A 0AA.

AINLEY, David Geoffrey, CEng, FIMechE, FRAeS; Deputy Director (Projects and Research), Military Vehicles and Engineering Establishment, Chertsey, 1978–84; *b* 5 July 1924; *s* of Cyril Edward and Constance Ainley; *m* 1st, 1948, Dorothy Emily (*née* Roberts); one *s* one *d*; 2nd, 1959, Diana Margery Hill (*née* Sayles); one *d*; 3rd, 1988, Joyce Dinah (*née* Jessett). *Educ:* Brentwood Sch., Essex; Queen Mary Coll., London Univ. (BSc, 1st Cl. Hons). Engine Dept, RAE, Farnborough, 1943–44; Power Jets (R&D) Ltd, 1944–46; National Gas Turbine Estabt, Pyestock, 1946–66; idc 1967; Dir of Engine Develt, MoD (Procurement Exec.), 1968–78. George Stephenson Research Prize, IMechE, 1953. *Publications:* contrib. books and learned jls on gas turbine technology. *Recreations:* painting, sketching, golf. *Address:* 20 Hampton Close, Church Crookham, Fleet, Hants GU52 8LB.

AINSCOW, Robert Morrison, CB 1989; independent consultant, since 1996; Deputy Secretary, Overseas Development Administration, Foreign and Commonwealth Office, 1986–96; *b* 3 June 1936; *s* of Robert M. Ainscow and Hilda Ainscow (*née* Cleminson); *m* 1965, Faye Bider; one *s* one *d*. *Educ:* Salford Grammar School; Liverpool Univ. (BA Econ Hons). Statistician: Govt of Rhodesia and Nyasaland, 1957–61; UN Secretariat, New York, 1961–65 and 1966–68; Dept of Economic Affairs, London, 1965–66. Ministry of Overseas Development: Economic Adviser, 1968–70; Senior Economic Adviser, 1971–76; Head, South Asia Dept, 1976–79; Under Secretary, FCO (ODA), 1979–86. Chm., OECD (DAC) Working Party on Financial Aspects of Develt Assistance, 1982–86; Member: World Bank/IMF Develt Cttee Task Force on Concessional Flows, 1983–85, on Multilateral Develt Banks, 1994–96; Asian Develt Bank Inspection Panel, 1996–. Consultant to UN, World Bank, OECD, DFID, Irish Aid, and Overseas Develt Council, Washington. Mem. Bd Trustees, BRCS, 2000–. *T:* and *Fax:* (020) 7435 2218.

AINSLEY, John Mark; tenor; *b* 9 July 1963; *s* of John Alwyn Ainsley and Dorothy Sylvia (*née* Anderson). *Educ:* Royal Grammar Sch., Worcester; Magdalen Coll., Oxford. Début in Stravinsky's Mass, RFH, 1984; subsequent débuts: USA, in NY and Boston, 1990; with Berlin Philharmonic Orch., 1992; Glyndebourne Fest., in Così fan Tutte, 1992; Aix-en-Provence, in Don Giovanni, 1993; San Francisco, in Don Giovanni, 1995; appears regularly with leading orchestras incl. LPO, LSO, Scottish Chamber Orch. and Orchestre de Paris. Has made numerous recordings. Grammy Award for best opera recording, 1995. *Recreation:* chocolate. *Address:* Askonas Holt Ltd, Lonsdale Chambers, 27 Chancery Lane, WC2A 1PF. *T:* (020) 7400 1700.

AINSLIE, Charles Benedict, (Ben), MBE 2001; professional yachtsman; *b* 5 Feb. 1977; *s* of Michael Roderick and Susan Linda Ainslie. *Educ:* Truro Sch.; Peter Symonds Coll., Winchester. Gold Medal, Laser Cl. Sailing, Sydney Olympics, 2000. Hon. MSc UC Chichester, 2001. *Recreations:* motor racing, cycling, flying. *Address:* Carne Vean, Manaccan, Helston, Cornwall TR12 6HD. *Clubs:* Royal Cornwall Yacht (Hon. Mem.), Stokes Bay Sailing (Gosport) (Hon. Mem.), Restronguet Sailing (Falmouth) (Hon. Mem.).

AINSWORTH, Sir Anthony (Thomas Hugh), 5th Bt *cr* 1916, of Ardanaiseig, co. Argyll; Director, Richard Glynn Consultants, since 2000; *b* 30 March 1962; *er s* of Sir David Ainsworth, 4th Bt and of Sarah Mary, *d* of Lt-Col H. C. Walford; *S* father, 1999. *Educ:* Harrow. *Heir: b* Charles David Ainsworth, *b* 24 Aug. 1966. *Address:* 208 Wireless Road, Lumpini, Bangkok 10330, Thailand.

AINSWORTH, James Bernard; Editor, Good Food Guide, since 1994; *b* 1 Feb. 1944; *s* of Henry Bernard Ainsworth and Margaret Ainsworth (*née* Fletcher). *Educ:* Duke St Primary Sch.; Chorley Grammar Sch.; Liverpool Univ. (BA Psychol.). Lectr in Psychol. and Educn, Chorley Coll. of Educn, 1970–78; Proprietor, Vineyard Restaurant, Northampton, 1979–84; drinks columnist, Punch, 1984–92; freelance wine writer and restaurant reviewer, 1984–. *Publications:* Mitchell Beazley Red Wine Guide, 1990; Mitchell Beazley White Wine Guide, 1990. *Recreations:* having turned my hobbies (eating and drinking) into my job, all I am left with is music: singing in the village choir and playing the hymns in church. *Address:* Good Food Guide, Consumers' Association, 2 Marylebone Road, NW1 4DF.

AINSWORTH, (Mervyn) John, FCIS, FInstAM; Chief Executive and Secretary, Institute of Chartered Secretaries and Administrators, since 1990; *b* 28 Jan. 1947; *s* of late Gordon John Ainsworth and Eileen Ainsworth; *m* 1973, Marta Christina Marmolak; two *s* one *d. Educ:* Stanfields Technical High Sch., Stoke-on-Trent; Goldsmiths' Coll., Univ. of London (DipEd). Asst Clerk to Govs and Bursar, Dulwich Coll., 1969–74; Principal Assistant, Sec. and Solicitors' Dept, CEGB, 1974–77; Secretarial Asst, BTDB, 1977–78; Sec., 1978–83, Sec. and Dir of Finance, 1983–84, BPIF; Sec. General, Inst. of Administrative Management, 1984–90. Director: ICSA Publishing, 1990–; ICSA Consultants, 1992–; ICSA Software, 1993–; Inst. of Business Administration, 1992–. Member: Bd, Nat. Examining Bd for Supervisory Management, 1984–99; Academic Bd, Greenwich Coll., 1984–97; Court, Cranfield Univ. (formerly Inst. of Technology), 1990–; Council for Admin (formerly Admin Lead Body), 1991–; Open and Distance Learning Quality Council (formerly Council for Certification of Correspondence Colls), 1994– (Chm., 1998–); City & Guilds Quality Standards Cttee, 1999–. Hon. Fellow, Canadian Inst. of Certified Administrative Managers, 1987. Liveryman, Worshipful Co. of Chartered Secs and Administrators. Hon. DBA Bournemouth, 1997. *Publications:* articles on management education and administrative systems. *Recreations:* golf, gardening, family life. *Address:* (office) 16 Park Crescent, W1N 4AH. *T:* (020) 7580 4741.

AINSWORTH, Peter Michael; MP (C) Surrey East, since 1992; *b* 16 Nov. 1956; *s* of late Lt-Comdr Michael Lionel Yeoward Ainsworth, RN and of Patricia Mary Ainsworth (*née* Bedford); *m* 1981, Claire Alison Burnett; one *s* two *d. Educ:* Ludgrove, Wokingham; Bradfield Coll.; Lincoln Coll., Oxford (MA Eng. Lit and Lang.). Res. Asst to Sir J. Stewart-Clark, MEP, 1979–81; Investment Analyst, Laing & Cruickshank, 1981–85; Sen. Investment Analyst, S. G. Warburg Securities, 1985–87; Asst Dir, 1987–89, Dir, 1989–92, S. G. Warburg Securities Corporate Finance. Mem., Wandsworth Borough Council, 1986–94 (Chm., Cons. Group, 1990–92). PPS to Chief Sec. to HM Treasury, 1994–95, to Sec. of State for Nat. Heritage, 1996; an Asst Govt Whip, 1996–97; Opposition Dep. Chief Whip, 1997–98; opposition front bench spokesman on culture, media and sport, 1998–2001; Shadow Sec. of State for Envmt, Food and Rural Affairs, 2001–. Member, Select Committee: on Envmt, 1993–94; on Public Affairs, 1996. Sec., All-Party Conservation Gp, 1994–97. Mem. Council, Bow Group, 1984–86. FRSA. *Recreations:* family, music, gardening. *Address:* House of Commons, SW1A 0AA. *Club:* MCC.

AINSWORTH, Robert William; MP (Lab) Coventry North East, since 1992; Parliamentary Under-Secretary of State, Home Office, since 2001; *b* 19 June 1952; *s* of late Stanley Ewart Ainsworth and Monica Pearl Ainsworth (later Mrs D. J. Scullion); *m* 1974, Gloria Jean Sandall; two *d. Educ:* Foxford Comprehensive School. Sheet metal worker and fitter, Jaguar, 1971–91 (Shop Steward, MSF, 1974–91; Sec., Joint Stewards, 1980–91). City Councillor, Coventry, 1984–93 (Dep. Leader, 1988–91; Chm., Finance, 1989–92). An Opposition Whip, 1995–97; a Lord Comr of HM Treasury (Govt Whip), 1997–2001; Parly Under-Sec. of State, DETR, 2001. Mem., Select Cttee on environmental affairs, 1993–95. Vice-Chm., W Midlands Gp of Labour MPs, 1995–97. *Recreations:* walking, reading, chess. *Address:* House of Commons, SW1A 0AA. *T:* (020) 7219 4047. *Clubs:* Bell Green Working Men's (Coventry); Broad Street Old Boy's RFC (Coventry).

AIPO RONGO, Bishop of; *see* Papua New Guinea, Archbishop of.

AIRD, Captain Sir Alastair (Sturgis), GCVO 1997 (KCVO 1984; CVO 1977; LVO 1969); Comptroller, since 1974 and Private Secretary and Equerry, since 1993, to Queen Elizabeth the Queen Mother; *b* 14 Jan. 1931; *s* of Col Malcolm Aird; *m* 1963, Fiona Violet Myddelton (*see* F. V. Aird); two *d. Educ:* Eton; RMA Sandhurst. Commnd 9th Queen's Royal Lancers, 1951; served in BAOR; Adjt 9th Lancers, 1956–59; retd from Army, 1964. Equerry to Queen Elizabeth the Queen Mother, 1960; Asst Private Sec. to the Queen Mother, 1964. Mem. Council, Feathers Assoc. of Youth Clubs, 1973–93; Trustee, RSAS Develt Trust, 1986–99. Hon. Bencher, Middle Temple, 1991. *Recreations:* shooting, fishing, golf. *Address:* 31B St James's Palace, SW1A 1BA. *T:* (020) 7839 6700. *Clubs:* Cavalry and Guards; Eton Ramblers; I Zingari.

AIRD, Fiona Violet, (Lady Aird), CVO 2001 (LVO 1980); Extra Lady-in-Waiting to HRH Princess Margaret, Countess of Snowdon, since 1963; *b* 24 Sept. 1934; *d* of late Lt Col Ririd Myddelton, LVO, and of Lady Margaret Myddelton; *m* 1963, Capt. Sir Alastair Sturgis Aird, *qv* ; two *d. Educ:* Westonbirt Sch.; in France. Lady-in-Waiting to HRH Princess Margaret, 1960–63. Mem. Council, UCL, 1987–97. Chm., Middx Hosp. League of Friends, 1987–; Vice-Pres., England, Nat. Assoc. of Hosp. and Community Friends, 2000–; Chm., Florence Nightingale Aid in Sickness Trust, 1994–. *Recreations:* reading, fishing. *Address:* 31B St James's Palace, SW1A 1BA. *T:* (020) 7839 6700.

AIRD, Sir (George) John, 4th Bt *cr* 1901; Chairman and Managing Director, Sir John Aird & Co. Ltd, 1969–96; Chairman, Matcon plc, since 1981; *b* 30 Jan. 1940; *e s* of Sir John Renton Aird, 3rd Bt, MVO, MC, and of Lady Priscilla Aird, *yr d* of 2nd Earl of Ancaster; *S* father, 1973; *m* 1968, Margaret, *yr d* of Sir John Muir, 3rd Bt; one *s* two *d. Educ:* Eton; Oxford Univ.; Harvard Business Sch. MICE. Trainee, Sir Alexander Gibb & Partners, 1961–65; Manager, John Laing & Son Ltd, 1967–69. Dir, Healthcare Development Services Ltd, 1994–. *Recreations:* skiing, tennis, hunting. *Heir: s* James John Aird, *b* 12 June 1978. *Address:* Grange Farm, Evenlode, Moreton-in-Marsh, Glos GL56 0NT. *T:* (01608) 650607, *Fax:* (01608) 652442; *e-mail:* johnaird@aol.com. *Club:* White's.

AIREY, David Lawrence; Managing Director, Bunge & Co. Ltd, 1987–90, retired; *b* 28 April 1935; *s* of Samuel Airey and Helena Florence Lever; *m* 1961, Joan Mary Stewart; three *d. Educ:* Oldershaw Grammar Sch., Wallasey. J. Bibby & Sons Ltd: Management trainee, various sales/commercial management positions, 1952–74; Chief Exec., Edible Oils Div., 1974–78; Man. Dir, J. Bibby Edible Oils Ltd, 1979–86; Dep. Man. Dir, Bunge & Co. Ltd, 1986. Chm., Seed Crushers & Oil Processors Assoc., 1980–82. Trustee, Wiltshire Community Foundn, 1996–. JP Liverpool, 1980–86. *Recreations:* Rugby Union football (Birkenhead Park FC, 1955–66, Cheshire, 1958–65, North West Counties, 1964, Barbarians, 1965), fishing, cooking, gardening, golf. *Address:* Darnley, Church Road, Woodborough, Pewsey, Wilts SN9 5PH. *T:* (01672) 851647. *Clubs:* Birkenhead Park FC; Upavon Golf.

AIREY, Dawn Elizabeth; Director of Programmes, since 1996, and Chief Executive, since 2000, Channel 5; *b* Preston, Lancs, 15 Nov. 1960. *Educ:* Kelly College; Girton College, Cambridge (MA Hons). Central TV: management trainee, 1985–86; Channel 4 Liaison Officer, 1987; Associate Producer, 1988; Controller, later Dir, Programme Planning, Central Broadcasting, 1988–93; Controller of Network Children's and Daytime Progs, ITV Network Centre, 1993–94; Controller of Arts and Entertainment, Channel 4, 1994–96. Mem., Film Council, 1999–. Patron, Birmingham Film and TV Festival, 1996–; Gov., Banff Fest., 1999–; Chm., Edinburgh Internat. Television Fest., 2000. Trustee, ActionAid, 2000–. FRSA 1996; FRTS 1999. *Recreations:* tennis, fine wines, cinema, TV, collecting antique maps. *Address:* Channel 5 Broadcasting Ltd, 22 Long Acre, WC2E 9LY.

AIRLIE, 13th Earl of, *cr* 1639 (*de facto* 10th Earl, 13th but for the Attainder); **David George Coke Patrick Ogilvy,** KT 1985; GCVO 1984; PC 1984; Royal Victorian Chain, 1997; JP; Baron Ogilvy of Airlie, 1491; Captain late Scots Guards; Lord Chamberlain of HM Household, 1984–97; Chancellor, Royal Victorian Order, 1984–97; Lord-Lieutenant of Angus, 1989–2001; a Permanent Lord-in-Waiting to the Queen, since 1997; *b* 17 May 1926; *e s* of 12th (*de facto* 9th) Earl of Airlie, KT, GCVO, MC, and Lady Alexandra Marie Bridget Coke (*d* 1984), *d* of 3rd Earl of Leicester, GCVO; *S* father, 1968; *m* 1952, Virginia Fortune Ryan (*see* Countess of Airlie); three *s* three *d. Educ:* Eton. Lieutenant Scots Guards, 1944; serving 2nd Battalion Germany, 1945; Captain, ADC to High Comr and C-in-C Austria, 1947–48; Malaya, 1948–49; resigned commission, 1950. Ensign, 1975–85, Lieutenant, 1985–, Queen's Body Guard for Scotland, Royal Company of Archers. Chairman: Schroders plc, 1977–84; Gen. Accident Fire & Life Assurance Corp., 1987–97 (Dir, 1962–97; Dep. Chm., 1975–87); Ashdown Investment Trust Ltd, 1968–82; Director: J. Henry Schroder Wagg & Co. Ltd, 1961–84 (Chm., 1973–77); Scottish & Newcastle Breweries plc, 1969–83; The Royal Bank of Scotland Gp, 1983–93; Baring Stratton Investment Trust (formerly Stratton Investment Trust), 1986–. Chm., Historic Royal Palaces, 1998–; Dep. Chm., Royal Collection Trust, 1992–97; Pres., NT for Scotland, 1998–. Treasurer, Scout Assoc., 1962–86; Hon. Pres., Scottish Council of Scout Assoc., 1988–. DL Angus, 1964; JP Angus, 1990. Governor, Nuffield Nursing Homes Trust, 1985–89; Chancellor, Univ. of Abertay Dundee, 1994–. Hon. LLD Dundee, 1990. *Heir: s* Lord Ogilvy, *qv. Address:* Cortachy Castle, Kirriemuir, Angus DD8 4LX. *T:* (01575) 540231; 36 Sloane Court West, SW3 4TB. *T:* (020) 7823 6246.

See also Rt Hon. Sir A. J. B. Ogilvy, Hon. J. D. D. Ogilvy, Sir H. Wake.

AIRLIE, Countess of; Virginia Fortune Ogilvy, DCVO 1995 (CVO 1983); Lady of the Bedchamber to the Queen since 1973; *b* 9 Feb. 1933; *d* of John Barry Ryan, Newport, RI, USA; *m* 1952, Lord Ogilvy (now Earl of Airlie, *qv*); three *s* three *d. Educ:* Brearley School, New York City. Founder Governor, Cobham School, Kent, 1958. Mem., Industrial Design Panel, British Rail, 1974–94; Comr, Royal Fine Arts Commn, 1975–88. Trustee: Tate Gallery, 1983–95 (Chm. Friends of Tate Gallery, 1978–83); Amer. Mus. in Britain, 1985–89 (Chm., 2001–); Nat. Gallery, 1989–95Nat. Galls of Scotland, 1995– (Chm., 1997–2000). Pres., Angus Br., BRCS, 1988. *Address:* Cortachy Castle, Kirriemuir, Angus DD8 4LX; 36 Sloane Court West, SW3 4TB.

AIRS, Dr Malcolm Russell, FSA; Fellow, Kellogg College (formerly Rewley House), Oxford, since 1991; Reader in Conservation and the Historic Environment, University of Oxford, since 1996; President, Institute of Historic Building Conservation, since 2001 (Chairman, 1998–2001); *b* 7 March 1941; *s* of George William Laurence Airs and Gwendoline Elizabeth Airs (*née* Little); partner, 1971, Megan Parry; one *s. Educ:* Bushey Grammar Sch.; Oriel Coll., Oxford (BA Hons Modern Hist. 1963, MA, DPhil 1970). FSA 1980; IHBC 1998. Historian, Historic Bldgs Div., GLC, 1966–73; Architectural Ed., Survey of London, 1973–74; Conservation Officer, S Oxfordshire DC, 1974–91; Lectr in Conservation and Historic Envmt, Univ. of Oxford, 1991–96. Mem., Historic Bldgs and Areas Adv. Cttee, English Heritage, 1988–; Comr, RCHM, 1993–99. Trustee: Oxford Preservation Trust, 1993–; Standing Conf. on Trng of Architects in Conservation, 1996–. *Publications:* The Making of the English Country House 1500–1640, 1975; The Buildings of Britain: Tudor and Jacobean, 1982; The Tudor and Jacobean Country House, 1995; numerous articles on architectural hist. and historic conservation. *Recreations:* visiting buildings, cultivating my allotment, following the lost cause of Oxford United. *Address:* Oxford University Department for Continuing Education, Rewley House, 1 Wellington Square, Oxford OX1 2JA. *Club:* Oxford United Supporters.

AIRY, Maj.-Gen. Sir Christopher (John), KCVO 1989; CBE 1984; Private Secretary and Treasurer to TRH The Prince and Princess of Wales, 1990–91; an Extra Equerry to the Prince of Wales, since 1991; *b* 8 March 1934; *m* 1959, Judith Stephenson; one *s* two *d. Educ:* Marlborough Coll.; RMA Sandhurst. 2nd Lieut, Grenadier Guards, 1954; Scots Guards, 1974. PMA to Sec. of State for War, 1960; sc 1966; DAAG, Regtl Adjt, 1967; Bde Major, 4th Guards Armoured Bde, 1971; ndc 1973; CO, 1st Bn Scots Guards, 1974; Mil. Asst (GSO1) to Master Gen. of the Ordnance, 1976; Comdr 5th Field Force, 1979; rcds 1981; ACOS, HQ UKLF, 1982–83; Sen. Army Mem., RCDS, 1984–85; GOC London District and Maj.-Gen. Comdg Household Div., 1986; retd 1989. Chairman: Not Forgotten Assoc., 1993–; Nat. Assoc. of Air Ambulance Services, 1999–; Comr, Royal Hosp., Chelsea, 1990–96; Mem., Prince of Wales's Council, 1990–91. Dir, Hedley Foundn, 1994–.

AITCHISON, Sir Charles (Walter de Lancey), 4th Bt *cr* 1938; *b* 27 May 1951; *er s* of Sir Stephen Charles de Lancey Aitchison, 3rd Bt, and (Elizabeth) Anne (Milburn), *er d* of late Lt-Col Edward Reed, Ghyllheugh, Longhorsley, Northumberland; *S* father, 1958; *m* 1984, Susan, *yr d* of late Edward Ellis; one *s* one *d.* Lieut, 15/19th The King's Royal Hussars, 1974; RARO, 1974–78. Chm., Lune Valley Housing Assoc., 1988–. ARICS. *Recreation:* fishing. *Heir: s* Rory Edward de Lancey Aitchison, *b* 7 March 1986.

AITCHISON, Craigie (Ronald John), CBE 1999; RA 1988 (ARA 1978); painter; *b* 13 Jan. 1926; *yr s* of late Rt Hon. Lord Aitchison, PC, KC, LLD. *Educ:* Scotland; Slade Sch. of Fine Art. British Council Italian Govt Scholarship for painting, 1955; Edwin Austin Abbey Premier Scholarship, 1965; Lorne Scholarship, 1974–75. One-man Exhibitions: Beaux Arts Gall., 1959, 1960, 1964; Marlborough Fine Art (London) Ltd, 1968; Compass Gall., Glasgow, 1970; Basil Jacobs Gall., 1971; Rutland Gall., 1975; Knoedler Gall., 1977; Kettle's Yard Gall., Cambridge, 1979; Serpentine Gall. (major retrospective, 1953–81), 1981–82; Artis, Monte Carlo, Monaco, 1986; Albemarle Gall., 1987, 1989; Castlefield Gall., Manchester, 1990; Thomas Gibson Fine Art, London, 1993; Harewood House, Leeds (retrospective, 1954–94); Gall. of Modern Art, Glasgow (retrospective, 1956–96), 1996; Timothy Taylor Gall., Waddington Gall., 1998. Exhibited: Calouste Gulbenkian Internat. Exhibn, 1964; Il Tempo del imagine, 2nd Internat. Biennale, Bologna, 1967; Modern British Painters, Tokyo, Japan, 1969; 23rd Salon Actualité de l'Esprit, Paris, 1975; The Proper Study, British Council Lalit Kala Akademi, Delhi, 1984; Hard Won Image, Tate Gall., 1985; British Council Exhibn, Picturing People, Hong Kong and Zimbabwe, 1990; The Journey, Lincoln Cathedral, 1990; Nine Contemporary Painters, City of Bristol Mus. and Art Gall., 1990; British Council Exhibn, British Figurative Painting of 20th Century, Israel Mus., Jerusalem, 1992. Pictures in public collections: Tate Gall., Arts Council, Contemp. Art Soc., Scottish National Gall. of Modern Art, Glasgow Mus. and

Art Gall., and Nat. Gall. of Melbourne, Australia; Truro Cathedral, Liverpool Cathedral and chapel of King's College, Cambridge. 1st Johnson Wax Prize, Royal Acad., 1982; Korn Ferry Internat. Award, Royal Acad., 1989 and 1991; 1st Jerwood Foundn Award, 1994. *Address:* c/o Royal Academy of Arts, Burlington House, Piccadilly, W1V 0DS.

AITCHISON, Prof. Jean Margaret; Rupert Murdoch Professor of Language and Communication, University of Oxford, since 1993; Fellow, Worcester College, Oxford, since 1993; *b* 3 July 1938; *d* of late John Frederick and Joan Eileen Aitchison; *m* 2000, John Robert Ayto. *Educ:* Wimbledon High Sch.; Girton Coll., Cambridge (BA 1st Cl. Hons Classics, MA); Radcliffe Coll., Harvard (AM Linguistics 1961). University of London: Asst Lectr in Ancient Greek, Bedford Coll., 1960–65; Lectr, 1965–82, Sen. Lectr, 1982–92, Reader, 1992, in Linguistics, LSE, 1965–92. Reith Lectr, BBC, 1996. *Publications:* Linguistics, 1972, 5th edn 1999; The Articulate Mammal: an introduction to psycholinguistics, 1976, 4th edn 1998; Language Change: progress or decay?, 1981, 3rd edn 2001; Words in the Mind: an introduction to the mental lexicon, 1987, 2nd edn 1994; The Seeds of Speech: language origin and evolution, 1996; The Language Web: the power and problem of words (Reith lectures), 1997. *Recreation:* gardening. *Address:* Worcester College, Oxford OX1 2HB. *T:* (01865) 278392.

AITCHISON, June Rosemary, (Mrs T. J. Aitchison); *see* Whitfield, J. R.

AITCHISON, Thomas Nisbet; Chief Executive, City of Edinburgh Council, since 1995; *b* 24 Feb. 1951; *s* of Thomas Aitchison and Mary (*née* Millar); *m* 1973, Kathleen Sadler; one *s* two *d*. *Educ:* Univ. of Glasgow (MA 1st Class Hons Geography); Heriot-Watt Univ. (MSc). Lothian Regional Council: Policy Planning, 1975–78; PA to Chief Exec., 1978–81; seconded to Chief Exec's Co-ordination Team, 1981–82; Co-ordination Unit, Dept of Manpower Services, 1982–85; Dept of Management and Inf. Services, 1985–87; Corporate Planning Manager and Depute Dir, 1987–91; Depute Chief Exec., 1991–94; Chief Exec., 1994–95. Mem. Court, Napier Univ., 1997–. Sec., Edinburgh Internat. Fest. Soc., 1996–. *Recreations:* hill-walking, football, music. *Address:* City of Edinburgh Council, Council Headquarters, Wellington Court, 10 Waterloo Place, Edinburgh EH1 3EG. *Fax:* (0131) 469 3010.

AITKEN, family name of **Baron Beaverbrook**.

AITKEN, Cairns; *see* Aitken, R. C. B.

AITKEN, Gillon Reid; literary agent; Chairman, Gillon Aitken Associates (formerly Aitken, Stone & Wylie, then Aitken & Stone) Ltd, since 1985; *b* 29 March 1938; *s* of James Aitken and Margaret Joane Aitken (*née* Simpson); *m* 1982, Cari Margareta Bengtsson (marr. diss. 2000); one *d*. *Educ:* Charterhouse Sch.; privately. Private schoolmaster, Surbiton, 1955–56; National Service, 1956–58: Somerset LI; Intelligence Corps; Jt Services Sch. for Linguists (Russian course); Royal Signal Corps, Berlin. Stuart's Advertising Agency Ltd, 1958–59; Editor: Chapman & Hall Ltd, 1959–66; Hodder & Stoughton Ltd, 1966–67; Dir, Anthony Sheil Associates Ltd, 1967–71; Man. Dir, Hamish Hamilton Ltd, 1971–74; Vice-Pres., Wallace, Aitken & Sheil, Inc. (NY), 1974–77; Chairman: Gillon Aitken Ltd, 1977–85; Christy & Moore Ltd, 1977–; Dir, Hughes Massie Ltd, 1985–; Vice-Pres., Wylie, Aitken & Stone, Inc. (New York), 1986–96. *Publications:* translations from Russian: The Captain's Daughter & Other Stories by Alexander Sergeyevitch Pushkin, 1962; The Complete Prose Tales of Pushkin, 1966; One Day in the Life of Ivan Denisovich by Alexander Solzhenitsyn, 1970. *Recreations:* crossword puzzles, ping-pong. *Address:* c/o Gillon Aitken Associates Ltd, 29 Fernshaw Road, SW10 0TG. *T:* (020) 7351 7561; The Garden Flat, 4 The Boltons, SW10 9TB. *T:* (020) 7373 7438. *Clubs:* Beefsteak, Brooks's.

AITKEN, Ian Levack; columnist: The Guardian, since 1992; Tribune, since 1998; *b* 19 Sept. 1927; *s* of George Aitken and Agnes Levack Aitken; *m* 1956, Dr Catherine Hay Mackie, *y d* of late Maitland Mackie, OBE; two *d*. *Educ:* King Alfred Sch., Hampstead; Regent Street Polytechnic; Lincoln Coll., Oxford (BA PPE; MA); LSE. Served Fleet Air Arm, 1945–48. HM Inspector of Factories, 1951; Res. Officer, CSEU, 1952; Industrial Reporter, Tribune, 1953–54; Industrial Reporter, subseq. Foreign Correspondent and Political Correspondent, Daily Express, 1954–64; political staff, The Guardian, 1964–92 (Political Editor, 1975–90; political columnist, 1990–92); columnist and contributing editor, New Statesman, 1993–96. Gerald Barry Award for journalism, 1984. *Recreation:* music. *Address:* 52A North Hill, N6 4RH. *T:* (020) 8340 5914. *Clubs:* Garrick, Wig and Pen.

See also Baron Mackie of Benshie.

AITKEN, Jonathan William Patrick; *b* 30 Aug. 1942; *s* of late Sir William Aitken, KBE and of Hon. Lady Aitken, MBE, JP; *m* 1979, Lolicia Olivera (marr. diss. 1998), *d* of Mr and Mrs O. Azucki, Zürich; one *s* twin *d*. *Educ:* Eton Coll.; Christ Church, Oxford (MA Hons Law); HMP Standford Hill; Wycliffe Hall, Oxford. Private Sec. to Selwyn Lloyd, 1964–66; Foreign Corresp., London Evening Standard, 1966–71; Man. Dir, Slater Walker (Middle East) Ltd, 1973–75; Dep. Chm., Aitken Hume Internat. PLC, 1990–92 (Co-founder, 1981; Chm., 1981–90); Dir, TV-am PLC, 1981–88. MP (C) Thanet East, Feb. 1974–83, Thanet South, 1983–97; contested (C) Thanet South, 1997. Minister of State for Defence Procurement, MoD, 1992–94; PC, 1994–97; Chief Sec. to HM Treasury, 1994–95. Mem., Select Cttee on Employment, 1979–82. *Publications:* A Short Walk on the Campus, 1966; The Young Meteors, 1967; Land of Fortune: A Study of Australia, 1969; Officially Secret, 1970; Richard Nixon: a life, 1993; Pride and Perjury, 2000; articles in Spectator, Sunday Telegraph, Sydney Morning Herald, Washington Post, The Independent, etc. *Address:* Wycliffe Hall, 54 Banbury Road, Oxford OX2 6PW.

See also M. P. K. Aitken.

AITKEN, Maria Penelope Katharine; actress; Director, Dramatis Personae Co.; *b* 12 Sept. 1945; *d* of Sir William Traven Aitken, KBE and Hon. Penelope Loader Maffey, MBE, JP; *m* 1st, 1968, Mark Durden-Smith (marr. diss.); 2nd, 1972, Arthur Nigel Davenport, *qv* (marr. diss.); one *s*; 3rd, 1992, Patrick McGrath. *Educ:* Riddlesworth Hall, Norfolk; Sherborne Girls' Sch.; St Anne's Coll., Oxford. Associate Prof., Yale Sch. of Drama, 1990; Faculty Member: Juilliard Sch., NY, 1991–97; Drama Dept, NY Univ., 1995–96. *Stage includes:* first professional appearance, Belgrade Th., Coventry, 1967; rep., Th. Royal, Northampton, 1970–71; Travesties, RSC, 1974; A Little Night Music, Adelphi, 1975; Blithe Spirit, NT, 1976; Bedroom Farce, NT, 1977; Private Lives, Duchess, 1980; Design for Living, Queen's, 1982; Sister Mary Ignatius (also dir.), Ambassadors, 1983; Happy Family (dir.), Duke of York's, 1983; Private Lives (also dir.), 1984; After the Ball (dir.), Old Vic, 1985; The Rivals (dir.), Court, Chicago, 1985; Waste, RSC, 1985; The Women, Old Vic, 1986; The Vortex, Garrick, 1989; Other People's Money, Lyric, 1990; The Mystery of Irma Vep (dir.), Ambassadors, 1990; As You Like It (dir.), Regent's Park Open Air Th., 1992; Hay Fever, Albery, 1992; The Picture of Dorian Gray, Lyric, Hammersmith, 1994; Sylvia, Lyric, 1997; Easy Virtue (dir.), Chichester, 1999; *films:* A Fish Called Wanda, 1988; Fierce Creatures, 1997; Jinnah, 1998; producer, director and actor for TV and radio. *Publications:* A Girdle Round the Earth, 1986; Style: acting in high comedy, 1996. *Address:* c/o Michael Whitehall, 125 Gloucester Road, SW7 4TE.

See also J. W. P. Aitken.

AITKEN, Prof. Martin Jim, FRS 1983; FSA, FRAS; Professor of Archaeometry, 1985–89, and Deputy Director, Research Laboratory for Archaeology, 1957–89, Oxford University; Fellow of Linacre College, Oxford, 1965–89; *b* 11 March 1922; *s* of Percy Aitken and Ethel Brittain; *m* Joan Killick; one *s* four *d*. *Educ:* Stamford Sch., Lincs; Wadham Coll. and Clarendon Lab., Oxford Univ. (MA, DPhil). Served War, RAF Radar Officer, 1942–46 (Burma Star, 1945). Mem., Former Physical Soc., 1951–; MRI, 1972–89. Editor, Archaeometry, 1958–89. *Publications:* Physics and Archaeology, 1961, 2nd edn 1974; Thermoluminescence Dating, 1985; Science-based dating in Archaeology, 1990; Introduction to Optical Dating, 1998. *Recreations:* sailing, dinghy-racing. *Address:* Le Garret, 63930 Augerolles, France.

AITKEN, Oonagh Melrose; Chief Executive, Convention of Scottish Local Authorities, since 1999; *b* 11 March 1956. *Educ:* Paisley Grammar Sch.; Glasgow University (MA Hons, MEd). Teacher of modern languages, Linwood High Sch., Braidfield High Sch., and Garrion Acad., Wishaw (also Asst Head Teacher), 1982–90; Strathclyde Regional Council: Educn Officer, 1990–93; Brussels Officer, 1993–95; Actg Asst Chief Exec., 1995–96; Hd, Social Policy, Glasgow CC, 1996; Corporate Manager (Social Strategy), Fife Council, 1996–99. *Recreations:* literature, cinema, current affairs. *Address:* (office) 9 Haymarket Terrace, Edinburgh EH12 5XZ. *T:* (0131) 474 9200. *Club:* Western Baths (Glasgow).

AITKEN, Prof. (Robert) Cairns (Brown), CBE 1998; MD; FRCPE, FRCPsych; Chairman, Royal Infirmary of Edinburgh NHS Trust, 1993–97; *b* 20 Dec. 1933; *s* of late John Goold Aitken and Margaret Johnstone (*née* Brown); *m* 1959, Audrey May Lunn; one *s* one *d* (and one *d* decd). *Educ:* Cargilfield Sch., Edinburgh; Sedbergh Sch., Yorks; Univ. of Glasgow (MB, ChB 1957; MD 1965). FRCPE 1971; FRCPsych 1974. Univ. of Glasgow–McGill Univ. Exchange Schol., Montreal, 1958–59; RAF Inst. of Aviation Medicine, 1960–62; Registrar in Medicine, Orpington Hosp., Kent, 1962–64; Registrar, then Sen. Registrar, Maudsley Hosp., 1964–66; University of Edinburgh: Lectr and Sen. Lectr, Dept of Psychiatry, 1966–74; Prof. of Rehabilitation Studies and Hon. Consultant Physician, 1974–94; Dir, Disability Mgt Res. Gp, Assoc. of British Insurers, 1980–94; Dean, Faculty of Medicine, 1990–91; Vice-Principal (Planning and Budgeting), 1991–94. Visiting Professor: Univ. of Pennsylvania, 1971; Saragossa Univ., 1976; Monash Univ., 1982; Univ. of Malaysia, 1993. Ed., Jl of Psychosomatic Res., 1979–86. Dir, Lothian Health Bd, 1991–93. Member: Council, RCPsych, 1972–74; Scottish Council on Disability, 1975–84; Council, Professions Supplementary to Medicine, 1983–90; Scottish Cttee for Hosp. Med. Services, 1985–87; GMC, 1991–96; Human Genetics Adv. Commn, 1996–99; Pres., Internat. Coll. of Psychosomatic Medicine, 1985–87. Associate Mem., Inst. of Medicine, Amer. Acad. of Sci., 1995. Hon. Fellow: Napier Poly. of Edinburgh, 1990; Internat. Coll. of Psychosomatic Medicine, 1994. Hon. DSc CNAA, 1992. Officers' Cross, Order of Merit (Poland), 1994. *Publications:* on stress in aircrew, measurement of mood and assessment and management of disability. *Recreations:* people, places and pleasures of Edinburgh, Scotland and beyond. *Address:* 11 Succoth Place, Edinburgh EH12 6BJ. *T:* (0131) 337 1550, *Fax:* (0131) 313 0735. *Club:* New (Edinburgh).

AITKEN, William Mackie; JP; DL; Member (C) Glasgow, Scottish Parliament, since 1999; *b* 15 April 1947; *s* of William Aitken and Nell Aitken. *Educ:* Allan Glen's Sch., Glasgow; Glasgow Coll. of Technol. ACII 1971. Underwriter and sales exec., insurance industry, 1965–98. Glasgow City Council: Mem. (C), 1976–99; Convenor, Licensing Cttee, 1977–80; Leader of Opposition, 1980–84 and 1992–96; Bailie of City, 1980–84, 1988–92 and 1996–99. JP 1985, DL 1992, Glasgow. *Publications:* contrib. articles to newspapers. *Recreations:* reading, walking, foreign travel, wining and dining with friends. *Address:* 35 Overnewton Square, Glasgow G3 8RW. *T:* (0141) 357 1284.

AITKIN, Prof. Donald Alexander, AO 1998; PhD; Vice-Chancellor, 1991–2002 and President, 1997–2002, University of Canberra; *b* 4 Aug. 1937; *e s* of late Alexander George Aitkin and Edna Irene (*née* Taylor); *m* 1st, 1958, Janice Wood (marr. diss. 1977); one *s* three *d*; 2nd, 1977, Susan Elderton (marr. diss. 1991); one *s*; 3rd, 1991, Beverley Benger. *Educ:* Univ. of New England (MA 1961); ANU (PhD 1964). Postdoctoral Travelling Fellow, Nuffield Coll., Oxford, 1964; Australian National University: Res. Fellow in Pol Sci., 1965–68; Sen. Res. Fellow, 1968–71; Prof. of Politics (Foundn Prof.), Macquarie Univ., 1971–80; Institute of Advanced Studies, Australian National University: Prof. of Pol Sci., 1980–88; Chm. Bd, 1986–88. Chairman: Aust. Res. Grants Cttee, 1986–87; Aust. Res. Council, 1988–90; ACT Schs Legislation Review, 1999–2000; Dep. Chm., ACT Sci. and Technol. Council, 1999–; Mem Aust. Sci. and Technol. Council, 1986–92. Vice-Pres., Australian Vice-Chancellors' Cttee, 1994–95. FASSA 1975; FACE 1995. *Publications:* The Colonel, 1969; The Country Party in New South Wales, 1972; Stability and Change in Australian Politics, 1977, 2nd edn 1982; The Second Chair (novel), 1977; (with B. Jinks) Australian Political Institutions, 1980 (trans. Japanese, 1985), 6th edn 1999; (ed) The Life of Politics, 1984; (ed) Surveys of Australian Political Science, 1985. *Recreations:* bushwalking, music, cooking. *Address:* University of Canberra, ACT 2601, Australia. *Club:* Commonwealth (Canberra).

AJAYI, Prof. (Jacob Festus) Ade, OFR 2000; Professor of History, University of Ibadan, 1963–89, now Emeritus; *b* 26 May 1929; *s* of late Chief E. Ade Ajayi and Mrs C. Bolajoko Ajayi; *m* 1956, Christie Aduke Martins; one *s* four *d*. *Educ:* University College, Ibadan; University College, Leicester; Univ. of London; BA, PhD (London). Research Fellow, Inst. of Historical Research, London, 1957–58; Lectr, Univ. of Ibadan, 1958–62, Sen. Lectr, 1962–63; Dean, Faculty of Arts, 1964–66; Asst to Vice-Chancellor, 1966–68. Fellow, Centre for Advanced Study in the Behavioural Sciences, Stanford, Calif, 1970–71; Vice-Chancellor, Univ. of Lagos, 1972–78; Pro-Chancellor, Ondo State Univ., Ado-Ekiti, 1984–88. Member: UN University Council, 1974–80 (Chm., 1975–77); Nat. Archives Cttee, Nigeria, 1961–72; Nat. Antiquities Commn, Nigeria, 1970–74; Exec. Council, Internat. African Inst. London, 1971– (Chm., 1975–87); Exec. Bd, Assoc. of African Univs, 1974–80; Admin. Bd, Internat. Assoc. of Univs, 1980–90; Pres., Historical Soc. of Nigeria, 1972–81; Pres., Internat. Congress of African Studies, 1978–85. Director: BCN plc, 1988–92; SOWSCO, 1994–. Chm., Jadeas Trust, 1989–. Mem. Governing Bd, Nigerian Nat. Order of Merit, 1996–2000. Hon. LLD Leicester, 1975; Hon. DLitt: Birmingham, 1984; Ondo State Univ., Ado-Ekiti, 1992. Hon. Fellow, SOAS, Univ. of London, 1994. Fellow, Hist. Soc. of Nigeria, 1980; Overseas FRHistS, 1982. Nigerian National Order of Merit, 1986. Traditional titles, Bobapitan of Ikole-Ekiti and Onikoyi of Ife, 1983. *Publications:* Milestones in Nigerian History, 1962; (ed, with Ian Espie) A Thousand Years of West African History, 1964; (with R. S. Smith) Yoruba Warfare in the Nineteenth Century, 1964; Christian Missions in Nigeria: the making of a new elite, 1965; (ed, with Michael Crowder) A History of West Africa, vol. I, 1972; vol. II, 1974; (ed jtly) The University of Ibadan, 1948–73, 1973; (ed with Bashir Ikara) Evolution of Political Culture in Nigeria, 1985; (ed with M. Crowder) A Historical Atlas of Africa, 1985; (ed) Africa in the Nineteenth Century until the 1880s, vol. VI of Unesco General History of

Africa, 1989; History and the Nation, and other Addresses, 1990; (with Peter Pugh) Cementing a Partnership: the story of WAPCO 1960–1990, 1990; A Patriot to the Core: Samuel Ajayi Crowther, 1992; History of the Nigerian Society of Engineers, 1995; (jtly) The African Experience with Higher Education, 1996; contribs to Jl Historical Soc. of Nigeria, Jl of African History, etc. *Recreations:* dancing, tennis. *Address:* 1 Ojobadan Avenue, Bodija, Ibadan, Nigeria; PO Box 14617 UI, Ibadan, Nigeria.

AJIBOLA, Prince Bola Adesumbo, Hon. KBE 1989; SAN 1986; High Commissioner for Nigeria in the United Kingdom, since 1999; *b* 22 March 1934; *s* of Oba A. S. Ajibola and Adikatu Ashakun Ajibola; *m* 1961, Olu Olugbemi; three *s* two *d*. *Educ:* Owu Baptist Day Sch., Abeokuto, Nigeria; Baptist Boys' High Sch., Abeokuto. Called to the Bar, Lincoln's Inn, London, 1962. Principal Partner, Bola Ajobola & Co., Nigeria, 1967–85 (specialising in commercial law and internat. arbitration); Hon. Attorney-Gen. and Minister of Justice, Nigeria, 1985–91; Judge: Internat. Court of Justice, The Hague, 1991–94; World Bank Admin. Tribunal, 1994; Constitutional Court, Fedn of Bosnia and Herzegovina, 1995; delegate to numerous internat. confs. President: Nigerian Bar Assoc., 1984–85 (Chm., Human Rights Cttee, 1980–84); Pan African Council, London Court of Internat. Arbitration, 1994; Pres. and Founder, African Concern, 1995–; Chairman: Gen. Council of the Bar, Nigeria, 1985–91; Body of Sen. Advocates of Nigeria, 1985–91; Adv. Cttee of Prerogative of Mercy, Nigeria, 1989–91; Task Force for Revision of Laws, Nigeria, 1990; Member: Privileges Cttee, Nigerian Bar, 1985–91; Nigerian Police Council, 1989–91; Internat. Bar Assoc.; Internat. Chamber of Commerce; World Arbitration Inst.; Perm. Court of Arbitration, The Hague (also Mem., Bd of Trustees); Governing Bd, Internat. Maritime Law Inst., IMO; Internat. Law Commn, UN, 1986–91; Internat. Court of Arbitration, ICC (Vice Chm., Commn; arbitrator, numerous internat. cases); Internat. Maritime Arbitration Commn; Governing Body, African Soc. of Internat. and Comparative Law. Fellow, Nigerian Inst. of Advanced Legal Studies; FCIArb. Editor: All Nigeria Law Reports, 1961–90; Nigeria's Treaties in Force, 1970–90; Ed.-in-Chief, Justice; Gen. Editor, Federal Min. of Justice Law Review Series. *Publications:* Law Development and Administration in Nigeria, 1987; Towards a Better Administration of Justice System in Nigeria, 1988; Narcotics, Law and Policy in Nigeria, 1989; Compensation and Remedies for Victims of Crime, 1989; Banking Frauds and Other Financial Malpractices in Nigeria, 1989; Unification and Reform of Criminal Laws and Procedure Codes of Nigeria, 1990; Women and Children under Nigerian Law, 1990; Customary Law in Nigeria, 1991; Democracy and the Law; Dispute Resolution by International Court of Justice; papers and articles in learned jls. *Address:* Nigeria High Commission, 9 Northumberland Avenue, WC2N 5BX. *T:* (020) 7839 1244. *Clubs:* Abeokuta (Abeokuta); Metropolitan (Lagos); Yoruba Tennis.

AKAM, Prof. Michael Edwin, DPhil; FRS 2000; FRES, FLS; Professor of Zoology, and Director, University Museum of Zoology, University of Cambridge, since 1997; *b* 19 June 1952; *s* of William Edwin Akam and Evelyn Warriner Akam (*née* Thorne); *m* 1979, Margaret Madeleine Bray; two *s*. *Educ:* King's Coll., Cambridge (BA Nat. Scis 1974); Magdalen Coll., Oxford (DPhil Genetics 1978). FRES 1985; FLS 1999. Australian Sci. Schol., Royal Instn, 1970. Coll. Lectr in Zoology, Magdalen Coll., Oxford, 1978; Res. Fellow, King's Coll., Cambridge, 1978–86; MRC Fellow, Lab. of Molecular Biology, Cambridge, 1978–79; Fellow, Dept of Biochemistry, Stanford Univ., 1979–81 (Damon-Runyan/Walter Winchell Fellow, 1979); Cambridge University: MRC Sen. Fellow, Dept of Genetics, 1982–90; Wellcome Principal Fellow, and Founding Mem., Wellcome/CRC Inst., 1990–97. Chm., British Soc. for Developmental Biology, 1989–94. Mem., EMBO, 1987. *Publications:* (ed jtly) The Evolution of Developmental Mechanisms, 1994; res. papers and reviews in jls, Proc. Royal Soc., etc. *Recreation:* the living world. *Address:* University Museum of Zoology, Downing Street, Cambridge CB2 3EJ. *T:* (01223) 336650.

'AKAU'OLA, 'Inoke Fotu Faletau, CVO 1993; Secretary for Fisheries, Tonga, since 1996; *b* 24 June 1937; 2nd *s* of 'Akau'ola (Sateki Faletau) and Celia Lyden; *S* brother, 1995; *m* 'Evelini Ma'ata Hurrell; three *s* three *d*. *Educ:* St Peter's, Cambridge, NZ; Tonga High Sch.; Auckland Grammar Sch.; UC Swansea (Hon. Fellow 1990); Manchester Univ. Joined Tonga Civil Service, 1958; Asst Sec., Prime Minister's Office, 1965; Sec. to Govt, 1969; seconded to Univ. of South Pacific, 1971; Sec. to Govt, 1972; High Comr, UK, 1972–82; Ambassador to: France, 1972–82; Germany, 1976–82; Belgium, Luxembourg, Netherlands, EEC, 1977–82; USA, 1979–82; USSR, 1980–82; Denmark, 1981–82; Director: Management Develt Programme, Commonwealth Secretariat, 1983–84; Commonwealth Foundn, 1985–93; Dep. Sec., Prime Minister's Office, Nuku'alofa, 1994–96. *Heir: s* Ahovaleamoemapa Faletau. *Recreations:* Rugby, tennis, reading, bridge, fishing. *Address:* Teu Folau, Fanga-ò-Pilolevu, Nuku'alofa, Tonga. *Clubs:* Royal Over-Seas League; Royal Nuku'alofa.

AKEHURST, Gen. Sir John (Bryan), KCB 1984; CBE 1976; Deputy Supreme Allied Commander, Europe, 1987–90; *b* 12 Feb. 1930; *s* of late Geoffrey and Doris Akehurst; *m* 1955, Shirley Ann, *er d* of late Major W. G. Webb, MBE, and Ethel Webb; one *s* one *d* decd. *Educ:* Cranbrook Sch.; RMA, Sandhurst. Commnd Northamptonshire Regt, 1949; Malay Regt (despatches), 1952–55; Adjt, 5th Northamptonshire Regt (TA), 1959–60; Staff Coll., Camberley, 1961; Brigade Major, 12 Infantry Bde Gp, 1962–64; Instructor, Staff Coll., Camberley, 1966–68; commanded 2nd Royal Anglian Regt, 1968–70; Directing Staff, IDC/RCDS, 1970–72; Comdt, Jun. Div., Staff Coll., 1972–74; Comdr, Dhofar Bde, Sultan of Oman's Armed Forces, 1974–76; Dep. Mil. Sec. (A), MoD (Army), 1976–79; GOC 4th Armoured Div., BAOR, 1979–81; Comdt, The Staff Coll., Camberley, 1982–83; Comdr, UK Field Army, and Inspector Gen., TA, 1984–87. Sen. Mil. Visitor to Saudi Arabia, 1985–87; Dep. Col, 1981–86, Col, 1986–91, Royal Anglian Regt. Comr, Commonwealth War Graves Commn, 1993–98. Chm., Council, TA&VRA, 1990–95; Mem. Council, RUSI, 1985–88; Pres., Reserve Forces Assoc., 1991–99. Chm., 1982–84, Pres., 1984–90, Army Golf Assoc.; Vice Patron, Army Officers' Golf Soc., 1986– (Pres., 1983–86). Gov., Royal Star and Garter Home, 1990–91. Governor: Harrow Sch., 1982–97 (Chm. of Govs, 1991–97); John Lyon Sch., 1989–91; Princecroft Primary Sch., Warminster, 1990–2000 (Chm. of Govs, 1995–2000). Pres., Warminster Civic Trust, 1998–. Liveryman, Poulters' Co., 1997–. Order of Oman, 3rd Class (mil.), 1976. *Publications:* We Won a War, 1982; Generally Speaking, 1999. *Recreations:* golf, trout fishing, travel. *Address:* c/o HSBC, Minehead, Somerset TA24 5LH. *Clubs:* Army and Navy; Woking Golf; Senior Golfers' Society.

AKENHEAD, Robert; QC 1989; a Recorder, since 1994; *b* 15 Sept. 1949; *s* of late Edmund and of Angela Akenhead; *m* 1972, Elizabeth Anne Jackson; one *s* three *d*. *Educ:* Rugby School; Exeter Univ. (LLB). Called to the Bar, Inner Temple, 1972, Bencher, 1997; in practice as barrister, 1973–; an Asst Recorder, 1991–94. Examiner, Dio. of Canterbury, 1991–. Ed., Building Law Reports. *Publication:* Site Investigation and the Law, 1984. *Recreations:* theatre, cricket, ski-ing. *Address:* 1 Atkin Building, Gray's Inn, WC1R 5BQ. *T:* (020) 7404 0102.

AKERLOF, Prof. George Arthur, PhD; teaching in Economics Department, University of California at Berkeley, since 1980; Cassel Professor of Economics, London School of Economics and Political Science, 1978–81; *b* 17 June 1940; *s* of Gosta C. Akerlof and Rosalie C. Akerlof; *m* 1978, Janet Yellen. *Educ:* Yale Univ. (BA 1962); MIT (PhD 1966). Fellowships: Woodrow Wilson, 1962–63; National Science Co-op., 1963–66; Fulbright, 1967–68; Guggenheim, 1973–74. Univ. of Calif, Berkeley: Asst Prof. of Econs, 1966–70; Associate Prof., 1970–77; Prof., 1977–78. Vis. Prof., Indian Statistical Inst., New Delhi, 1967–68. Sen. Economist, Council of Econ. Advisors, USA, 1973–74; Vis. Economist, Bd of Governors of Fed. Reserve System, USA, 1977–78. *Publications:* contrib. American Econ. Rev., Econ. Jl, Qly Jl Econs, Jl Polit. Econ., Rev. of Econ. Studies, Internat. Econ. Rev., Jl Econ. Theory, Indian Econ. Rev., and Rev. of Econs and Stats. *Address:* Economics Department, University of California, Berkeley, CA 94720, USA. *Club:* Piggy (Center Harbor, NH, USA).

AKERS, John Fellows; Chairman, International Business Machines Corp., 1986–93; *b* 1934; *m* 1960, Susan Davis; one *s* two *d*. *Educ:* Yale Univ. (BS). International Business Machines Corp., 1960–93: Pres., Data Processing Div., 1974–76; Vice Pres., Asst Gp Exec., plans and controls, Data Processing Product Gp, 1976–78; Vice Pres., Gp Exec., Data Processing Marketing Gp, 1978–81, Inf. Systems and Communications Gp, 1981–82, Sen. Vice Pres., 1982–83; Dir, 1983–93; Pres., 1983–89; Chief Exec. Officer, 1985–93. Dir, New York Times Co., 1985; formerly Dir, PepsiCo. Inc. Formerly Mem., President's Educn Policy Adv. Cttee. Trustee: MMA; CIT; Mem. Bd of Governors, United Way of America.

AKERS-DOUGLAS, family name of **Viscount Chilston**.

AKERS-JONES, Sir David, KBE 1985; CMG 1978; Chief Secretary, Hong Kong, 1985–86; Acting Governor, Hong Kong, Dec. 1986–April 1987; *b* 14 April 1927; *s* of Walter George and Dorothy Jones; *m* 1951, Jane Spickernell (MBE 1988); one *d* (one *s* decd). *Educ:* Worthing High Sch.; Brasenose Coll., Oxford (MA). British India Steam Navigation Co., 1945–49. Malayan Civil Service (studied Hokkien and Malay), 1954–57; Hong Kong Civil Service, 1957–86; Government Secretary: for New Territories, 1973–81; for City and New Territories, 1981–83; for Dist Admin, 1983–85; Advr to Gov., April-Sept. 1987. Chm., Hong Kong Housing Authy, 1988–93; Advr to China on Hong Kong Affairs, 1993–97; Hong Kong Chief Exec. Selection Cttee, 1996. Vice-Pres., WWF Hong Kong, 1995–. Hon. Pres., Outward Bound Trust, Hong Kong, 1996– (Pres., 1986–95); Vice-Patron, Hong Kong Football Assoc. Hon. Mem., RICS, 1991. Hon. DCL Kent, 1987; Hon. LLD Chinese Univ. of Hong Kong, 1988; Hon. DSSc City Polytechnic of Hong Kong, 1993. *Recreations:* painting, gardening, walking, music. *Address:* Villa Monte Rosa, Flat A-1, 1/F, 41A Stubbs Road, Hong Kong. *Clubs:* Royal Over-Seas League; Hong Kong, Kowloon, Dynasty, China, Gold Coast Country and Yacht (Hong Kong).

AKHTAR, Prof. Muhammad, FRS 1980; Professor of Biochemistry, University of Southampton, 1973–98, now Emeritus; *b* 23 Feb. 1933; *m* 1963, Monika E. Schurmann; two *s*. *Educ:* Punjab Univ., Pakistan (MSc 1st class 1954); Imperial College, London (PhD, DIC 1959). Research Scientist, Inst. for Medicine and Chemistry, Cambridge, Mass, USA, 1959–63; University of Southampton: Lecturer in Biochemistry, 1963–66; Senior Lectr, 1966–68; Reader, 1968–73; Hd of Dept of Biochemistry, 1978–93; Chm., Sch. of Biochem. and Physiol. Scis, 1983–87; Dir, SERC Centre for Molecular Recognition, 1990–94. Chm., Inst. of Biomolecular Scis, 1989–90. Member: Chemical Soc. of GB; American Chemical Soc.; Biochemical Soc. of GB; Council, Royal Soc., 1983–85; Founding Fellow, Third World Acad. of Sciences, 1983 (Mem. Council and Treas., 1993–98; Vice-Pres., 1998–; Medal, 1996). Flintoff Medal, RSC, 1993. Sitara-I-Imtiaz (Pakistan), 1981. *Publications:* numerous works on: enzyme mechanisms; synthesis and biosynthesis of steroids and porphyrins; biochemistry of vision; synthesis of anti-microbial compounds. *Address:* Department of Biochemistry, University of Southampton, Southampton SO16 7PX. *T:* (023) 8059 4338.

AKIHITO, HM the Emperor of Japan; Collar, Supreme Order of Chrysanthemum, 1989; KG 1998; *b* Tokyo, 23 Dec. 1933; *e s* of His late Majesty Emperor Hirohito (Showa) and HM Empress Dowager Nagako; *S* father, 1989; *m* 1959, Michiko Shoda; two *s* one *d*. *Educ:* Gakushuin Primary, Jun. and Sen. High Schs; Dept of Politics, Faculty of Politics and Econs, Gakushuin Univ. Official Investiture as Crown Prince of Japan, 1952. Res. Associate, Australian Mus.; Mem., Ichthyological Soc. of Japan; Hon. Member: Linnean Soc. of London; Zool Soc. of London, 1991. King Charles II Medal, Royal Soc., 1998. *Heir: er s* Crown Prince Naruhito [*b* Tokyo, 23 Feb. 1960; *m* 1993, Masako Owada]. *Publications:* (contrib. jtly) Fishes of the Japanese Archipelago, 1984; (jtly) The Fresh Water Fishes of Japan, 1987; 29 papers on gobies. *Recreation:* tennis. *Address:* Imperial Palace, 1-1 Chiyoda, Chiyoda-ku, Tokyo 100, Japan. *T:* (3) 32131111.

AKINKUGBE, Prof. Oladipo Olujimi, NNOM 1997; CON 1979; Officier de l'Ordre National de la République de Côte d'Ivoire, 1981; MD, DPhil; FRCP, FWACP, FAS; Professor of Medicine, University of Ibadan, Nigeria, 1968–95, now Emeritus; *b* 17 July 1933; *s* of late Chief David Akinbobola and of Chief (Mrs) Grace Akinkugbe; *m* 1965, Dr Folasade Modupeore Dina, *d* of late Chief I. O. Dina, CFR, OBE; two *s*. *Educ:* Univs of Ibadan (Hon. Fellow, 1998), London (MD), Liverpool (DTM&H) and Oxford (DPhil). FRCP 1968; FWACP 1975; FAS 1980. House Surg., London Hosp., 1958; House Phys., King's Coll. Hosp., London, 1959; Commonwealth Res. Fellow, Balliol Coll. and Regius Dept of Medicine, Oxford, 1962–64; Head of Dept of Medicine, 1972, Dean of Medicine, 1970–74, and Chm., Cttee of Deans, 1972–74, Univ. of Ibadan; Vice-Chancellor: Univ. of Ilorin, 1977–78 (Principal, 1975–77); Ahmadu Bello Univ., Zaria, 1978–79. Rockefeller Vis. Fellow, US Renal Centres, 1966; Vis. Fellow in Medicine, Univs of Manchester, Cambridge and London, 1969; Visiting Professor of Medicine: Harvard Univ., 1974–75; Univ. of Oxford (and Vis. Fellow, Balliol Coll.), 1981–82; Univ. of Cape Town, 1996. Adviser on Postgrad. Med. Educn to Fed. Govt of Nigeria, 1972–75; Chm., Nat. Implementation Commn on Rev. of Higher Educn in Nigeria, 1992; Member: Univ. Grants Commn, Uganda Govt; OAU Scientific Panels on Health Manpower Develt; Council, Internat. Soc. of Hypertension, 1982–90; Bd of Trustees, African Assoc. of Nephrology, 1986–94; Bd of Trustees, Nigerian Educare Trust, 1997–; internat. socs of hypertension, cardiology, and nephrology; Med. Res. Soc. of GB; Scientific Adv. Panel, Ciba Foundn, 1970–98; WHO Expert Adv. Panels on Cardiovascular Diseases, 1973–78, on Health Manpower 1979–; WHO Adv. Council on Health Res., 1990–95; Sec. to WHO 1984 Technical Discussions. Pro-Chancellor, and Chm. of Council, Univ. of Port-Harcourt, Nigeria, 1986–90; Chm. Bd of Mgt, UCH, Ibadan, 2000–; Member: Governing Council and Bd of Trustees, Obafemi Awolowo Foundn, 1992; Governing Council, Nigeria Heart (formerly Heartcare) Foundn, 1994– (Chm., Bd of Trustees, 2000–); Chm. Governing Council, Ajumogobia Science Foundn, 1997–; Exec. Council, World Innovation Foundn, 1998–; Bd of Trustees, Heritage Resources Conservation, 1999–. President: Nigerian Assoc. of Nephrology, 1987–90; Nigerian Hypertension Soc., 1994; African Heart Network, 2001. Member, Editorial Bd: Jl of Hypertension, 1984–90; Jl of Human Hypertension, 1988–; Kidney International, 1990–98; Blood Pressure, 1991–; News in Physiological Scis, 1992–98. Hon. DSc: Ilorin, 1982; Fed. Univ. of Technol., Akure, 1992; Port Harcourt, 1997; Ogun State, 1998. Searle Dist. Res. Award,

1989. Traditional title, Atobase of Ife, 1991; Babalofin of Ijebu-Igbo, 1994; Adengbua of Ondo, 1995; Ikolaba Balogun Basegun of Ibadan, 1997. *Publications:* High Blood Pressure in the African, 1972; (ed) Priorities in National Health Planning, 1974; (ed) Cardiovascular Disease in Africa, 1976; (ed) Nigeria and Education: the challenges ahead, 1994; (ed jtly) Nigeria's Health in the 90s, 1996; (ed) Non-Communicable Diseases in Nigeria: final report of a national survey, 1997; (ed jtly) A Compendium of Clinical Medicine, 1999; (ed jtly) Clinical Medicine in the Tropics Series, 1987–; papers on hypertension and renal disease in African, Eur. and Amer. med. jls, and papers on med. and higher educn. *Recreations:* music, gardening, birdwatching. *Address:* c/o Department of Medicine, University of Ibadan, Ibadan, Nigeria. *T:* 22317717; The Little Summit, Olubadan Aleshinloye Way, Iyaganku, Ibadan, Nigeria. *Clubs:* Dining (Ibadan); Oxford and Cambridge (Nigeria).

AKKER, John Richard; Executive Secretary, Council for Assisting Refugee Academics, since 1999; General Secretary, National Association of Teachers in Further and Higher Education, 1994–97; *b* 6 May 1943; *s* of Alec Louis Morris Akker and Ruby (*née* Bryant); *m* 1967, Jean-Anne Roxburgh (marr. diss. 1990); two *d*. *Educ:* SW Essex Tech. Coll.; Ruskin Coll., Oxford (L. C. White Schol.; Dip. Econ./Pol.); Univ. of York (BA Hons 1969); Cranfield Inst. of Technol. Mgt Sch. Clerical Officer, Ministry of Works, 1959–64; Asst Nat. Officer, 1969–71, Dep. Nat. Local Govt Officer, 1972–73, NALGO; Association of University Teachers: Asst Gen. Sec., 1973–77; Dep. Gen. Sec., 1978–94. Advr to EC, 1985–88. Exec. Dir, Network for Educn and Academic Rights, 2001–. Visiting Lecturer: CIT, 1970–74; Univ. of Wisconsin, 1977–78. Winston Churchill Fellowship, USA, 1976. *Recreations:* motor sport, sailing, football. *Address:* 38 King Street, WC2E 8JS. *T:* (020) 7836 8963. *Club:* National Liberal.

ALAGIAH, George Maxwell; News Presenter and journalist, BBC, since 1999; *b* 22 Nov. 1955; *s* of Donald and Therese Alagiah; *m* 1984, Frances Robathan; two *s*. *Educ:* St John's Coll., Southsea; Van Mildert Coll., Durham Univ. South Magazine, 1982–89; BBC Foreign Affairs Correspondent, 1989–99, Africa Correspondent, 1994–99. Monte Carlo TV Fest. Award; BAFTA commendation; awards as Journalist of the Year from: Amnesty Internat., 1994; BPG, 1994; James Cameron Meml Trust, 1995; Bayeux Award for War Reporting, 1996. *Recreations:* sport, tennis, music, hiking. *Address:* BBC Television Centre, Wood Lane, W12 7RJ.

ALAGNA, Roberto; French tenor; *b* 7 June 1963; *m* 1st, Florence (*d* 1994); one *d*; 2nd, 1996, Angela Gheorghiu, *qv*. Worked as accountant, electrician and cabaret singer; studied under Rafael Ruiz; Pavarotti Internat. Voice Competition Prize, 1988. Débuts: Alfredo in La Traviata, Glyndebourne Touring Opera, 1988; Royal Opera, Covent Garden, 1992; La Scala, Milan, 1994; Théâtre du Chatelet, Paris, 1996; Metropolitan Opera, NY, 1996. Rôles include: Roméo in Roméo et Juliette (Laurence Olivier Award, Covent Garden, 1995); title rôle in Don Carlos; Rodolpho in La Bohème; Nemorino in L'elisir d'amore; Edgard in Lucia di Lamermoor; Cavaradossi in Tosca. Numerous recordings. *Address:* c/o Royal Opera House, Covent Garden, WC2E 9DD; c/o M Levon Sayan, 76–78 avenue des Champs Elysées, 75008 Paris, France.

ALAIN, Marie-Claire Geneviève; organist; Lecturer, Conservatoire National de Région Rueil-Malmaison, Paris, 1978–98; *b* 10 Aug. 1926; *d* of Albert Alain and Magdeleine Alain (*née* Alberty); *m* 1950, Jacques Gommier (*d* 1992); one *s* one *d*. *Educ:* Institut Notre Dame, Saint-Germain-en-Laye; Conservatoire Nat. Supérieur de Musique, Paris. Lectr, Summer Acad. for Organists, Haarlem, Netherlands, 1956–72; Dir, Internat. Summer Acad. for Organists, Saint-Donat, 1978–92. Numerous concerts and recitals worldwide, 1955–; more than 250 recordings, incl. works of Jehan Alain, complete organ works of J. S. Bach, César Franck, Handel, Buxtehude and Mendelssohn. Prix Léonie Sonning, Copenhagen; Buxtehude Prize, Lübeck, 1976; Prix Franz Liszt, Budapest, 1987; 15 Grands Prix du Disque. Hon. doctorates: Colorado, 1972; Southern Methodist, Dallas, 1990; Sibelius Acad., 1997; Boston Conservatory, 1999. Commandeur: Légion d'honneur (France), 1997; Ordre Nat. du Mérite (France), 1998; Officier des Arts et des Lettres (France), 1999. *Address:* 4 rue Victor Hugo, 78230 Le Pecq, France.

ALANBROOKE, 3rd Viscount *cr* 1946; **Alan Victor Harold Brooke;** Baron Alanbrooke, 1945; *b* 24 Nov. 1932; *s* of 1st Viscount Alanbrooke, KG, GCB, OM, GCVO, DSO, and Benita Blanche (*d* 1968), *d* of Sir Harold Pelly, 4th Bt; *S* half-brother, 1972. *Educ:* Harrow; Bristol Univ. (BEd Hons 1976). Qualified teacher, 1975. Served Army, 1952–72; Captain RA, retired. *Heir:* none.

ALBEE, Edward; American dramatist; *b* 12 March 1928. Has directed prodns of own plays, 1961–, mainly at English Th., Vienna, and Alley Th., Houston. *Publications: plays:* The Zoo Story, 1958; The Death of Bessie Smith, 1959; The Sandbox, 1959; Fam and Yam, 1959; The American Dream, 1960; Who's Afraid of Virginia Woolf?, 1962; (adapted from Carson McCullers' novella) The Ballad of the Sad Café, 1963; Tiny Alice, 1964; (adapted from the novel by James Purdy) Malcolm, 1965; A Delicate Balance, 1966 (Pulitzer Prize, 1967); (adapted from the play by Giles Cooper) Everything in the Garden, 1967; Box and Quotations from Chairman Mao Tse-Tung, 1968; All Over, 1971; Seascape, 1974 (Pulitzer Prize, 1975); Listening, 1975; Counting the Ways, 1976; The Lady from Dubuque, 1978; Lolita (adapted from V. Nabakov), 1979; The Man Who Had Three Arms, 1981; Finding the Sun, 1982; Marriage Play, 1986; Three Tall Women, 1991 (Pulitzer Prize, 1994); The Lorca Play, 1992; Fragments, 1993; The Play About the Baby, 1996. *Address:* (office) 14 Harrison Street, New York, NY 10013, USA.

ALBEMARLE, 10th Earl of, *cr* 1696; **Rufus Arnold Alexis Keppel;** Baron Ashford, 1696; Viscount Bury, 1696; *b* 16 July 1965; *s* of Derek William Charles Keppel, Viscount Bury (*d* 1968), and Marina, *yr d* of late Count Serge Orloff-Davidoff; *S* grandfather, 1979; *m* 2001, Sally Claire Tadayon, *d* of Dr Jamal Tadion. *Educ:* Central Sch. of Art (BA (Hons) Industrial Design, 1990). *Heir: cousin* Crispian Walter John Keppel [*b* 29 Oct. 1948; *m* 1990, Tina Ammann; one *d*]. *Address:* Hurst Barns Farm, East Chiltington, Lewes, Sussex BN7 3QU.

ALBEMARLE, Countess of, (Diana Cicely), DBE 1956; Chairman: Development Commission, 1948–74; The Drama Board, 1964–78; *b* 6 Aug. 1909; *o c* of John Archibald Grove; *m* 1931, 9th Earl of Albemarle, MC (*d* 1979); one *d*. *Educ:* Sherborne Sch. for Girls. Norfolk County Organiser, WVS, 1939–44. Chairman: Exec. Cttee, Nat. Fedn of Women's Institutes, 1946–51; Departmental Cttee on Youth Service, 1958–60; Nat. Youth Employment Council, 1962–68. Vice-Chm., British Council, 1959–74. Member: Arts Council, 1951; Royal Commn on Civil Service, 1954; Harkness Fellowship Cttee of Award, 1963–69; UGC, 1956–70; Standing Commn on Museums and Galleries, 1958–71; English Local Govt Boundary Commn, 1971–77; Youth Develt Council, 1960–68; Council, Univ. of E Anglia, 1964–72. Life Trustee, Carnegie UK Trust (Chm., 1977–82); Trustee of: The Observer until 1977; Glyndebourne Arts Trust, 1968–80. RD Councillor, Wayland, Norfolk, 1935–46. Hon. DLitt Reading, 1959; Hon. DCL Oxon, 1960; Hon. LLD London, 1960. *Recreations:* gardening, reading. *Address:* Seymours, Melton, Woodbridge, Suffolk IP12 1LW. *T:* (01394) 382151.

See also Sir Hew Hamilton-Dalrymple.

ALBERTI, Sir (Kurt) George (Matthew Mayer), Kt 2000; DPhil; FRCP, FRCPE, FRCPath; Professor of Medicine, University of Newcastle upon Tyne, since 1985 (Dean of Medicine, 1995–97); Professor of Metabolic Medicine, Imperial College of Science, Technology and Medicine, University of London, since 2000; President, Royal College of Physicians, since 1997; *b* 27 Sept. 1937; *s* of William Peter Mathew Alberti and Edith Elizabeth Alberti; *m* 1st, 1964; three *s*; *m* 2nd, 1998, Prof. Stephanie A. Amiel. *Educ:* Balliol Coll., Oxford (MA; DPhil 1964; BM, BCh 1965; Hon. Fellow 1999). FRCP 1978; FRCPath 1985; FRCPE 1988. Res. Fellow, Harvard Univ., Boston, USA, 1966–69; Res. Officer, Dept of Medicine, Oxford Univ., 1969–73; Prof. of Chemical Pathology and Human Metabolism, 1973–78, Prof. of Clinical Biochemistry and Metabolic Medicine, 1978–85, Univ. of Southampton. Mem., WHO Expert Adv. Panel on Diabetes, 1979–. Pres., Internat. Diabetes Fedn, 2000– (Vice-Pres., 1988–94); Vice-Chm., British Diabetic Assoc., 1996–99; Vice Pres., Diabetes UK, 2000–. Founder FMedSci 1998 (Mem. Council, 1998–). Hon. FRCPGlas 1999; Hon. FRCPI 1999. Hon. Member: Hungarian Diabetes Assoc., 1986; Argentinian Diabetes Assoc., 1991. Hon. MD Aarhus, 1998; Hon. DM Southampton, 1999. *Publications:* edited more than 30 medical books, including: Diabetes Annual, Vols 1–6; Internat. Textbook of Diabetes Mellitus, 1992, 2nd edn 1997; author of more than 900 pubns in learned jls. *Recreations:* hill walking, jogging, crime fiction, opera.

ALBERTYN, Rt Rev. Charles Henry; a Bishop Suffragan, Diocese of Cape Town, 1983–93; *b* 24 Dec. 1928; *s* of Adam and Annie Albertyn; *m* 1965, Berenice Lategan; one *s* two *d*. *Educ:* Hewat Training College (Teacher's Diploma 1948); Diocesan Clergy School, Cape Town (LTh 1956). Teaching, 1948–52. Deacon 1955, priest 1956; Assistant, St Nicholas, Matroosfontein, 1955–60; Priest-in-charge, St Helena Bay, 1960–64; Assistant, St George's, Silvertown, 1965–70; Rector: Church of Holy Spirit, Heideveld, 1970–75; St Mary's, Kraaifontein, 1975–78; Church of Resurrection, Bonteheuwel, 1978–83; Canon of St George Cathedral, Cape Town, 1972–83; Archdeacon of Bellville, 1981–83. *Recreation:* watching soccer. *Address:* 7 Mynweg, Vanguard Estate, Athlone, Cape 7764, S Africa.

ALBERY, Ian Bronson; Chief Executive and Producer, Sadler's Wells, Peacock and Lilian Baylis Theatres; *b* 21 Sept. 1936; *s* of Sir Donald Albery and Rubina Albery (*née* McGilchrist); *m* Barbara Yu Ling Lee (marr. diss.; she *d* 1997); two *s*; one *d* by Jenny Beavan. *Educ:* Stowe; Lycée de Briançon, France. Stage, Production or Technical Manager for over 100 West End productions, 1958–70; Technical Dir, London Festival Ballet, 1964–68; Theatre Consultant, UK and overseas, 1968–; Producer or Co-Producer for over 50 West End prodns, 1978–; Managing Director: Wyndham Theatres, Piccadilly Theatre, Donmar Productions, Omega Stage, 1978–87; Theatre of Comedy, 1987–90; Dep. Chm., English Nat. Ballet, 1984–90; Dir, Ticketmaster (UK) Ltd, 1985–92. Consultant, Japan Satellite Broadcasting, 1991–92. Trustee, Theatres Trust, 1977–96; Chief Exec., Sadler's Wells Trust, 1994–. Pres., 1977–79, Vice-Pres., 1979–80, SWET. *Address:* Sadler's Wells Theatre, Rosebery Avenue, EC1R 4TN. *T:* (020) 7863 8034. *Club:* Garrick.

ALBERY, John; *see* Albery, W. J.

ALBERY, Tim; theatre and opera director; *b* 20 May 1952. *Theatre* productions include: War Crimes, ICA, 1981; Secret Gardens, Amsterdam and ICA, 1983; Venice Preserv'd, Almeida, 1983; Hedda Gabler, Almeida, 1984; The Princess of Cleves, ICA, 1985; Mary Stuart, Greenwich, 1988; As You Like It, Old Vic, 1989; Berenice, NT, 1990; Wallenstein, RSC, 1993; Macbeth, RSC, 1996; Attempts on her Life, Royal Court, 1997; *opera* productions include: for English National Opera: Billy Budd, 1988; Beatrice and Benedict, 1990; Peter Grimes, 1991; Lohengrin, 1993; From the House of the Dead, 1997; La Bohème, 2000; War and Peace, 2001; for Opera North: The Midsummer Marriage, 1985; The Trojans, 1986; La finta giardiniera, 1989; Don Giovanni, 1991; Don Carlos, 1992; Luisa Miller, 1995; Così fan Tutte, 1997; Katya Kabanova, 1999; for Royal Opera: Chérubin, 1994; for Welsh National Opera: The Trojans, 1987; La finta giardiniera, 1994; Nabucco, 1995; for Scottish Opera: The Midsummer Marriage, 1988; The Trojans, 1990; Fidelio, 1994; The Ring Cycle, 2000–; for Australian Opera: The Marriage of Figaro, 1992; for Netherlands Opera: Benvenuto Cellini, 1991; La Wally, 1993; Beatrice and Benedict, 2001; for Santa Fé Opera: Beatrice and Benedict, 1998; for Batignano Fest., Italy, The Turn of the Screw, 1983; for Bregenz Fest., Austria, La Wally, 1990; for Bayerische Staatsoper, Munich: Peter Grimes, 1991; Simon Boccanegra, 1995; Ariadne auf Naxos, 1996; for Metropolitan Opera, NY: A Midsummer Night's Dream, 1996; The Merry Widow, 2000. *Address:* c/o Harriet Cruickshank, Cruickshank Cazenove, 97 Old South Lambeth Road, SW8 1XU.

ALBERY, Prof. Wyndham John, FRS 1985; FRSC; Master, University College, Oxford, 1989–97; *b* 5 April 1936; *s* of late Michael James Albery, QC, and Mary Lawton Albery. *Educ:* Winchester Coll.; Balliol Coll., Oxford (MA, DPhil). Weir Jun. Research Fellow, 1962, Fellow, 1963–78, University Coll., Oxford; Lectr, Phys. Chem., Univ. of Oxford, 1964–78; Imperial College, London: Prof., Phys. Chemistry, 1978–89; Staff Orator, 1980–83; Dean, RCS, 1986–89. Vis. Fellow, Univ. of Minnesota, 1965; Vis. Prof., Harvard Univ., 1976. Tilden Lectr, RSC, 1979; Sherman Fairchild Schol., Calif. Inst. of Tech., 1985. Chairman: SERC Chemistry Cttee, 1982–85; Electrochem. Gp, RSC, 1985–89. Mem. Council, Royal Instn, 1985–88; Pres., Chemistry Section, British Assoc., 1992. Writer for television series That Was The Week That Was, 1963–64; also (with John Gould) two musicals, Who Was That Lady?, and On The Boil. Curator, Oxford Playhouse, 1974–78; Governor, Old Vic, 1979–89; Chm., Burton Taylor Theatre Management Cttee, 1990–93. Gov., Rugby Sch., 1987–. Fellow, Winchester Coll., 1989–. Hon. DSc Kent, 1990. *Publications:* Ring-Disc Electrodes, 1971; Electrode Kinetics, 1975; papers in jls: Faraday I, Nature, and Jls of Electrochemical Soc., Electroanalytical Chemistry, etc. *Recreations:* theatre, skiing. *Address:* 35 Falmouth House, Hyde Park Place, W2 2NT. *T:* (020) 7262 3909. *Club:* Garrick.

ALBRIGHT, Madeleine Korbel, PhD; Secretary of State, United States of America, 1997–2001; Member, National Security Council, USA, 1993–2001; *b* 15 May 1937; *m* Joseph Albright (marr. diss.); three *d*. *Educ:* Wellesley Coll. (BA Hons Pol Sci. 1959); Sch. of Advanced Internat. Studies, Johns Hopkins Univ.; Columbia Univ (BA 1968; PhD 1976). Chief Legislative Asst to Senator Edmund Muskie, 1976–78; Staff Mem., Nat. Security Council and Mem., White House Staff, 1978–81; Sen. Fellow in Soviet and E European Affairs, Center for Strategic and Internat. Studies; Fellow, Woodrow Wilson Internat. Center for Scholars, 1981–82; Res. Prof. of Internat. Affairs and Dir, Women in Foreign Service Program, Georgetown Univ. Sch. of Foreign Service, 1982–92; Pres., Center for Nat. Policy, 1989–92 (Mem., Bd of Dirs); US Perm. Rep. to UN, 1993–96. Member: Bd of Dirs, Atlantic Council of US; US Nat. Commn, UNESCO. Vice-Chm., Nat. Democratic Inst. for Internat. Affairs. *Publications:* Poland: the role of the press in political change, 1983; articles in professional jls and chapters in books.

ALBU, Sir George, 3rd Bt *cr* (UK) 1912, of Grosvenor Place, City of Westminster, and Johannesburg, Province of Transvaal, South Africa; farmer; *b* 5 June 1944; *o s* of Major Sir George Werner Albu, 2nd Bt, and Kathleen Betty (*d* 1956), *d* of Edward Charles Dicey,

Parktown, Johannesburg; *S* father, 1963; *m* 1969, Joan Valerie Millar, London; two *d.* *Recreation:* horse racing. *Heir:* none. *Address:* Glen Hamish Farm, PO Box 62, Richmond, Natal, 3780, South Africa. *T:* (33) 2122587. *Clubs:* Victoria Country (Pietermaritzburg); Durban Country; Richmond (Natal) Country (Richmond).

ALCOCK, Prof. Leslie, OBE 1991; Hon. Professorial Research Fellow, University of Glasgow, since 1990; *b* 24 April 1925; *o s* of Philip John Alcock and Mary Ethel (*née* Bagley); *m* 1950, Elizabeth A. Blair; one *s* one *d.* *Educ:* Manchester Grammar Sch.; Brasenose Coll., Oxford. BA 1949, MA 1950. Supt of Exploration, Dept of Archaeology, Govt of Pakistan, 1950; Curator, Abbey House Museum, Leeds, 1952; Asst Lectr, etc, UC Cardiff, 1953; Professor of Archaeology: UC Cardiff, 1973; Univ. of Glasgow, 1973–90. Member: Bd of Trustees, Nat. Mus. of Antiquities, Scotland, 1973–85; Ancient Monuments Bd, Scotland, 1974–90; Royal Commn on Ancient and Historical Monuments of Scotland, 1977–92; Royal Commn on Ancient and Historical Monuments in Wales, 1986–90. President: Cambrian Archaeological Assoc., 1982; Glasgow Archaeological Soc., 1984–85; Soc. of Antiquaries, Scotland, 1984–87. Lectures: Jarrow, 1988; Rhind, Soc. of Antiquaries, Scotland, 1988–89. FRHistS 1969. Hon. FSAScot, 1994. *Publications:* Dinas Powys, 1963; Arthur's Britain, 1971; Cadbury/Camelot, 1972; Economy, Society and Warfare, 1987; (co-ed) From the Baltic to the Black Sea, 1988; Cadbury Castle, Somerset, 1995; articles and reviews in British and Amer. jls. *Recreations:* mountain and coastal scenery, music. *Address:* 29 Hamilton Drive, Hillhead, Glasgow G12 8DN.

ALCOCK, Air Chief Marshal Sir (Robert James) Michael, GCB 1996 (CB 1989); KBE 1992; FREng; Royal Air Force, retired; aerospace consultant, since 1997; Director, Cygnae Ltd, since 1997; *b* 11 July 1936; *s* of late William George and Doris Alcock; *m* 1965, Pauline Mary Oades; two *d.* *Educ:* Victoria College, Jersey; Royal Aircraft Establishment. FIMechE; FRAeS. Commissioned, Engineer Branch, RAF, 1959; RAF Tech. Coll., Henlow, 1961; Goose Bay, Labrador, 1964; Units in Bomber Comd, 1959–69; RAF Staff Coll., Bracknell, 1970; PSO to DG Eng (RAF), 1971–73; OC Eng. Wing, RAF Coningsby, 1973–75; OC No 23 Maintenance Unit, RAF Aldergrove, 1975–77; Group Captain (Plans), HQ RAF Support Command, 1977–79; MoD, 1979–81; Dep. Comdt, RAF Staff Coll., Bracknell, 1981–84; RCDS, 1984; Dir Gen. of Communications, Inf. Systems and Orgn (RAF), 1985–88; AO Engrg, HQ Strike Comd, 1988–91; Chief Engr and Chief of Logistic Support, RAF, 1991–93; Air Mem. for Supply and Orgn, MoD, 1993–94; Air Member for Logistics and AOC-in-C, Logistics Comd, 1994–96. Trustee, RAF Benevolent Fund, 1996–. Chm., Bd of Mgt, Princess Marina Hse, 1996–. Pres., British Model Flyers' Assoc., 2000–. Governor, Victoria Coll., Jersey, 1995–. FREng (FEng 1995). Hon. DSc Cranfield, 1994. *Recreations:* golf, model aircraft, sailing. *Address:* c/o National Westminster Bank, PO Box 61, 2 Alexandra Road, Farnborough, Hants GU14 6YR. *Clubs:* Royal Air Force; Berkshire Golf, St Enodoc Golf.

ALDENHAM, 6th Baron *cr* 1896, of Aldenham, Co. Hertford, **AND HUNSDON OF HUNSDON,** 4th Baron *cr* 1923, of Briggens, Co. Hertford; **Vicary Tyser Gibbs;** *b* 9 June 1948; *s* of 5th Baron Aldenham and of Mary Elizabeth, *o d* of late Walter Parkyns Tyser; *S* father, 1986; *m* 1980, Josephine Nicola, *er d* of John Richmond Fell, Lower Bourne, Farnham, Surrey; three *s* one *d.* *Educ:* Eton; Oriel College, Oxford; RAC, Cirencester. Capel-Cure Myers Ltd, 1975–79; Dir, Montclare Shipping Co., 1986–. Chairman: Herts CLA, 1995–98; Watling Chase Community Forest, 1997–99. Freeman, City of London, 1979. *Heir:* *s* Hon. Humphrey William Fell Gibbs, *b* 31 Jan. 1989. *Address:* c/o Aldenham Estate Office, Home Farm, Aldenham Road, Elstree, Herts WD6 3AZ.

ALDER, Lucette, (Mrs Alan Alder); *see* Aldous, L.

ALDER, Michael; Controller, English Regional Television, British Broadcasting Corporation, 1977–86, retired; *b* 3 Nov. 1928; *s* of late Thomas Alder and Winifred Miller; *m* 1955, Freda, *d* of late John and Doris Hall; two *d.* *Educ:* Ranelagh Sch., Bracknell, Berks; Rutherford Coll., Newcastle-upon-Tyne. Newcastle Evening Chronicle, 1947–59; BBC North-East: Chief News Asst, Newcastle; Area News Editor, Newcastle; Representative, NE England, 1959–69; Head of Regional Television Development, BBC, 1969–77. Mem., Exec. Cttee, Relate (formerly Nat. Marriage Guidance Council), 1987–94 (Chm., S Warwicks, 1987–89; Chm., Appeals Cttee, 1988–94). Vice Chm., Tanworth Educnl Foundn, 1994–. Mem., Incorporated Co. of Butchers, 1948. Freeman, City of Newcastle upon Tyne. *Recreations:* gardening, fishing, walking, country pursuits. *Address:* Red Roofs, Bates Lane, Tanworth-in-Arden, Warwicks B94 5AR. *T:* (01564) 742403.

ALDERDICE, family name of **Baron Alderdice**.

ALDERDICE, Baron *cr* 1996 (Life Peer), of Knock, in the City of Belfast; **John Thomas Alderdice,** FRCPsych; Member (Alliance) Belfast East, and Speaker, Northern Ireland Assembly, since 1998; consultant psychotherapist, Eastern Health and Social Services Board, Belfast, since 1988; *b* 28 March 1955; *s* of Rev. David Alderdice and Helena Alderdice (*née* Shields); *m* 1977, Dr Joan Margaret Alderdice (*née* Hill), consultant pathologist; two *s* one *d.* *Educ:* Ballymena Acad.; Queen's Univ., Belfast (MB, BCh, BAO 1978). MRCPsych 1983; FRCPsych 1997; Jun. House Officer, Lagan Valley Hosp., 1978–79; Sen. House Officer, Belfast City Hosp., 1979–80; Registrar: Holywell and Whiteabbey Hosps, 1980–81; Shaftesbury Square Hosp., 1981–82; Lissue and Belfast City Hosps, 1982–83; Sen. Tutor and Sen. Registrar, Belfast City Hosp. and Queen's Univ., Belfast, 1983–87. Exec. Med. Dir, S and E Belfast Health and Social Services Trust, 1993–97. Hon. Lectr/Sen. Lectr, QUB, 1991–99; Hon. Prof., Univ. of San Marcos, Peru, 1999. Dir, NI Inst. of Human Relns, 1991–94. Contested (Alliance): Belfast E, 1987, 1992; NI, European Parly Election, 1989. Alliance Party of Northern Ireland: Mem., Exec. Cttee, 1984–98; Chm., Policy Cttee, 1985–87; Vice-Chm., March–Oct. 1987; Leader, 1987–98; Leader: delegn at Inter-Party and Inter-Governmental Talks on the future of NI, 1991–98; delegn at Forum for Peace and Reconciliation, Dublin Castle, 1994–96; Mem., NI Forum, 1996–98. European Liberal, Democrat and Reform Party (formerly Fedn of European Liberal, Democratic and Reform Parties): Mem., Exec. Cttee, 1987–; Treas., 1995–99; Vice-Pres., 1999–; Dep. Pres., Liberal International, 2000– (Mem. Bureau, 1996–; Vice Pres., 1992–99). Mem. (Vic. Area), Belfast City Council, 1989–97. Trustee, Ulster Museum, 1993–97. Hon. FRCPI 1997; Hon. FRCPsych 2001. Hon Mem., Peruvian Psychiatric Assoc., 2000. Silver Medal, Congress of Peru, 1999; Medal of Honour, Coll. of Medicine, Peru, 1999. *Publications:* professional articles on eating disorders, psychotherapy, ethics; political articles. *Recreations:* reading, music, gastronomy. *Address:* Parliament Buildings, Stormont, Belfast BT4 3XX. *T:* (028) 9079 3097, *Fax:* (028) 9022 5276; House of Lords, SW1A 0PW; *e-mail:* alderdicej@parliament.uk. *Clubs:* National Liberal; Ulster Reform (Belfast).

See also D. K. Alderdice.

ALDERDICE, David King, OBE 1999; Lord Mayor of Belfast, 1998–99; *b* 2 June 1966; *s* of Rev. David and Helena Alderdice; *m* 1989, Fiona Alison Johnston; one *s* two *d.* *Educ:* Queen's Univ., Belfast (MB BCh BAO 1989); Manchester Coll., Oxford (BA PPE 1994; MA 1998). MRCPI 1996. Jun., subseq. Sen., House Officer, Royal Victoria Hosp., Belfast, 1989–92; Specialist Registrar in Dermatology, Royal Victoria Hosp., Belfast and Belfast City Hosp., 1997–; Clin. Res. Fellow, Ulster Hosp., Dundonald, 1997–98. Contested (Alliance), N Antrim, Forum, 1996, parly elecns, 1997. Mem. (Alliance), Belfast CC, 1997–. *Publications:* articles in dermatology, genitourinary and psychol learned jls. *Recreation:* squash racquets. *Address:* 48 Wandsworth Road, Belfast BT4 3LT. *T:* (028) 9065 2216.

See also Baron Alderdice.

ALDERMAN, Richard John; Principal Assistant Solicitor of Inland Revenue, since 1996; *b* 5 Aug. 1952; *s* of John Edward Alderman and Patricia Eileen Alderman; *m* 1981, Joyce Sheelagh, *d* of Herrick Edwin and Joyce Hilda Wickens; one *d.* *Educ:* Woking Grammar Sch.; University College London (LLB). Called to the Bar, Gray's Inn, 1974; joined Solicitor's Office, Inland Revenue, 1975; seconded to Legal Secretariat to the Law Officers, 1991–93. *Recreations:* family life, horses. *Address:* Solicitor's Office, Inland Revenue, Somerset House, Strand, WC2R 1LB.

ALDERSLADE, Prof. Richard, FRCP, FFPHM; Special Professor of Health Policy, Nottingham University, since 1993; Regional Adviser, Evidence on Health Needs and Interventions, WHO Regional Office for Europe, Copenhagen, since 1995; *b* 11 Aug. 1947; *s* of Herbert Raymond Alderslade and Edna F. Alderslade; *m* 1st, 1974, Elizabeth Rose (marr. diss. 1999); two *s* one *d* (and one *d* decd); 2nd, 1999, Angela Hendriksen; one step *d.* *Educ:* Chichester High Sch. for Boys; Christ Church, Oxford (BM BCh; MA); St George's Hosp. FFPHM 1987; FRCP 1993. GP, 1974–76; Registrar in Community Medicine, 1976–78, Lectr, 1978–79; MO and SMO, DHSS, 1979–85; Specialist in Community Medicine, 1985–88 and Community Unit Gen. Manager, 1986–88, Hull HA; Regl Dir of Public Health and Regl MO, Trent RHA, 1988–94; Prof. of Community Care, Univ. of Sheffield, 1994–95. *Publications:* articles on public health, BMJ and other jls. *Recreations:* walking, railways, photography. *Address:* Strandagervej 9, 2900 Hellerup, Denmark. *T:* 39620741.

ALDERSON, Brian Wouldhave; freelance editor and writer; Children's Books Consultant, The Times, since 1995 (Children's Books Editor, 1967–95); *b* 19 Sept. 1930; *s* of John William Alderson and Helen Marjory (*née* Hogg); *m* 1953, Valerie Christine (*née* Wells); three *s* (and two *s* decd). *Educ:* Ackworth Sch.; University College of the South-West, Exeter (BA Hons). Work in the book trade, 1952–63; Tutor-librarian, East Herts Coll. of Further Educn, 1963–65; Sen. Lectr, (on Children's Literature and on the Book Trade), Polytechnic of N London, 1965–83. Visiting Professor: Univ. of Southern Mississippi, 1985; UCLA, 1986. Founder and first Chm., Children's Books Hist. Soc., 1969–78 and 1995–. Pres., Beatrix Potter Soc., 1995–. Exhibition organiser: (with descriptive notes): Early English Children's Books, BM, 1968; Looking at Picture Books, NBL, 1973; Grimm Tales in England, British Library, 1985–86; Be Merry and Wise: the early development of English children's books, Pierpont Morgan Library, NY, 1990–91; Randolph Caldecott and the Art of the English Picture Book, British Library, 1986–87; Childhood Re-Collected, Christ Church, Oxford, 1994. Eleanor Farjeon Award, 1968. *Publications:* Sing a Song for Sixpence, 1986; (with Iona and Robert Opie) Treasures of Childhood, 1989; The Arabian Nights, 1992; Ezra Jack Keats: artist and picture book maker, 1994; *translations:* Hürlimann: Three Centuries of Children's Books in Europe, 1967; Picture-book World, 1968; Grimm, Popular Folk Tales, 1978; Andersen, The Swan's Stories, 1997; *edited:* The Juvenile Library, 1966–74; The Colour Fairy Books, by Andrew Lang, 1975–82; Lear, A Book of Bosh, 1975; Children's Books in England, by F. J. Harvey Darton, 1982; Hans Christian Andersen and his Eventyr in England, 1982. *Recreations:* bibliography, dale-walking. *Address:* 28–30 Victoria Road, Richmond, North Yorks DL10 4AS. *T:* (01748) 823648.

ALDERSON, Daphne Elizabeth, (Mrs J. K. A. Alderson); *see* Wickham, D. E.

ALDERSON, Joanne Hazel; District Judge (Magistrates' Courts) (formerly Stipendiary Magistrate), Derbyshire, since 1997; *b* 18 March 1954; *d* of Colin and Joan Fleetwood; *m* 1983, Richard Alderson; two *s.* *Educ:* Wolverhampton Girls' High Sch.; Liverpool Univ. (LLB Hons); College of Law. Called to the Bar, Middle Temple, 1978. Legal Advr, W Midlands Prosecuting Solicitors' Dept, 1977–78; Court Clerk/Principal Asst, Wolverhampton Magistrates' Court, 1978–85; Deputy Clerk: to Warley Justices, 1985–86; to Wolverhampton Justices, 1986–97; Dep. Chief Exec., Wolverhampton Magistrates' Courts Cttee, 1995–97. *Recreations:* travel, bridge, swimming, reading. *Address:* The Court House, Derwent Street, Derby DE1 2EP. *T:* (01332) 292100.

ALDERSON, John Cottingham, CBE 1981; QPM 1974; writer and commentator on police and penal affairs; Chief Constable of Devon and Cornwall, 1973–82; *b* 28 May 1922; *e s* of late Ernest Cottingham Alderson and Elsie Lavinia Rose; *m* 1948, Irené Macmillan Stirling; one *s.* *Educ:* Barnsley Elem. Schs and Techn. College. Called to Bar, Middle Temple. British Meml Foundn Fellow, Australia, 1956; Extension Certif. in Criminology, Univ. of Leeds. Highland LI, 1938–41 (Corp.); Army Phys. Trng Corps, N Africa and Italy, 1941–46 (Warrant Officer). West Riding Constabulary as Constable, 1946; Police Coll., 1954; Inspector, 1955; Sub-Divisional Comd, 1960; Sen. Comd Course, Police Coll., 1963–64; Dep. Chief Constable, Dorset, 1964–66; Metropolitan Police, Dep. Comdr (Admin and Ops), 1966; 2nd-in-comd No 3 Police District, 1967; Dep. Asst Comr (Trng), 1968; Comdt, Police Coll., 1970; Asst Comr (Personnel and Trng), 1973. Consultant on Human Rights to Council of Europe, 1981–. Member: BBC Gen. Adv. Council, 1971–78; Royal Humane Soc. Cttee, 1973–81; Pres., Royal Life-Saving Soc., 1974–78. Vis. Prof. of Police Studies, Strathclyde Univ., 1983–89; Res. Fellow, Inst. of Police and Criminol Studies, Univ. of Portsmouth, 1994–. External Examiner, Leadership Studies, Univ. of Exeter, 1994–. Fellow Commoner, Corpus Christi Coll., Cambridge, 1982; Fellow, Inst. of Criminology, Cambridge, 1982; Gwilym Gibbon Res. Fellow, Nuffield Coll., Oxford, 1982–83; Australian Commonwealth Fellow, Australian Govt, 1987; Hon. Res. Fellow, Centre for Police Studies, Univ. of Exeter, 1987–95. Contested (L) Teignbridge, Devon, 1983. Hon. LLD Exeter, 1979; Hon. DLitt Bradford, 1982. *Publications:* (contrib.) Encyclopedia of Crime and Criminals, 1960; (ed jtly) The Police We Deserve, 1973; Policing Freedom, 1979; Law and Disorder, 1984; Human Rights and the Police, 1984; Principled Policing, 1998; articles in professional jls and newspapers. *Recreations:* reading, writing, keeping fit.

ALDERSON, Margaret Hanne, (Maggie); journalist; senior writer, Sydney Morning Herald, since 1996; *b* 31 July 1959; *d* of Douglas Arthur Alderson and Margaret Dura Alderson (*née* Mackay); *m* 1991, Geoffrey Francis Laurence (marr. diss. 1996). *Educ:* Alleyne's Sch., Stone, Staffs; Univ. of St Andrews (MA Hons History of Art). Features Editor: Look Now, 1983; Honey, 1984; Commng Editor, You, 1985; Metropolitan Features Editor, Evening Standard, 1986; Editor: ES Magazine, 1988; Elle, 1989–92; Dep. Editor, Cleo magazine, 1993–94; Editor, Mode, 1994–95. Editor of the Year, Colour Supplements, British Soc. of Magazine Eds, 1989. *Publications:* Shoe Money, 1998; Pants On Fire, 2000. *Recreations:* reading, travelling. *Address:* c/o Sydney Morning Herald, 201 Sussex Street, Sydney, NSW 2000, Australia. *Club:* Groucho.

ALDERSON, Martha, (Matti); international advisor on regulatory policy and strategy; Managing Director, FireHorses Ltd; Director General, Advertising Standards Authority, 1990–2000; *b* 20 Dec. 1951; *d* of Edward Connelly and Helen Connelly (*née* Peacock); *m* 1970, Alan Alderson. *Educ:* Bearsden Acad., Strathclyde; Open Univ. (BA 1994). Legal Exec., Scotland, 1970–72; Advertising Agency Poster Bureau, 1972–74; Advertising Standards Authority: Executive, 1975–80; Manager, 1980–89; Dep. Dir Gen., 1989–90. Vice Chm., European Advertising Standards Alliance, Brussels, 1991–2000. Member: Food Adv. Cttee, MAFF, 1997–; Better Regulation Task Force, 1998–; Doctors' and Dentists' Remuneration Review Body, 1998–2001 (Chm., Payroll Review, 1999–2000). FCAM 1993; FRSA 1993. *Publications:* columnist and contrib. numerous advertising and mktg textbooks, and jls in UK and EU. *Recreations:* design, cars, reading, studying. *Address:* Raglan House, Windsor Road, Gerrards Cross, Bucks SL9 7ND. *Clubs:* Arts, Royal Commonwealth Society.

ALDERTON, John; actor (stage, films, television); *b* Gainsborough, Lincs, 27 Nov. 1940; *s* of Gordon John Alderton and Ivy Handley; *m* 1st, 1964, Jill Browne (marr. diss. 1970; she *d* 1991); 2nd, Pauline Collins, *qv*; two *s* one *d*. *Educ:* Kingston High Sch., Hull. *Stage:* 1st appearance (Rep.) Theatre Royal, York, in Badger's Green, 1961; cont. Rep.; 1st London appearance, Spring and Port Wine, Mermaid (later Apollo), 1965; Dutch Uncle, RSC, Aldwych, 1969; The Night I chased the Women with an Eel, Comedy, 1969; Punch and Judy Stories, Howff, 1973; Judies, Comedy, 1974; The Birthday Party, Shaw, 1975; Confusions (4 parts), Apollo, 1976; Rattle of a Simple Man, Savoy, 1980; Special Occasions, Ambassadors, 1983; The Maintenance Man, Comedy, 1986; Waiting for Godot, NT, 1987; What the Butler Saw, RNT, 1995; *films:* (1962–): incl. Duffy, Hannibal Brooks, Zardoz, It Shouldn't Happen to a Vet, Please Sir, Clockwork Mice; *television:* series: Please Sir, No Honestly, My Wife Next Door, P. G. Wodehouse, The Upchat Line, Thomas and Sarah, Father's Day, Forever Green and various plays. *Address:* c/o Whitehall Artists, 125 Gloucester Road, SW7 4TE.

ALDINGTON, 2nd Baron *cr* 1962; **Charles Harold Stuart Low;** Managing Director, Investment Banking, Deutsche Bank, since 1996; *b* 22 June 1948; *s* of 1st Baron Aldington, KCMG, CBE, DSO, TD, PC and of Araminta Bowman, *d* of Sir Harold MacMichael, GCMG, DSO; *S* father, 2000; *m* 1989, Regine, *d* of Erwin von Csongrady-Schopf and Liselotte (*née* Horstmann); one *s* twin *d*. *Educ:* Winchester Coll.; New Coll., Oxford (BA Hons); INSEAD. Citibank NA (NY), Hong Kong and Dusseldorf, 1971–77; Head of Ship Finance, then Head of UK Corporate Lending, then Dir, Continental Europe, Grindlays Bank, 1978–86; Deutsche Bank AG: Dir, Duisburg Br., 1986–87; Man. Dir, London, 1988–96. Chairman: Eur. Vocational Coll., 1991–96; CENTEC, subseq. FOCUS Central London, Central London TEC, 1995–99; Mem. Council, British-German Chamber of Commerce and Industry, 1995–. Mem., Oxford Univ. Ct of Benefactors, 1990–. Trustee: English Internat., 1979–86; Whitechapel Art Gall. Foundn, 1991-96. *Heir: s* Hon. Philip Toby Augustus Low, *b* 1 Sept. 1990. *Address:* 59 Warwick Square, SW1V 2AL. *Clubs:* Brooks's; Hong Kong.

See also Hon. P. J. S. Roberts.

ALDISS, Brian Wilson; writer; critic; *b* 18 Aug. 1925; *s* of Stanley and Elizabeth May Aldiss; *m* 1965, Margaret Manson (*d* 1997); one *s* one *d*; and one *s* one *d* by previous *m*. *Educ:* Framlingham Coll.; West Buckland School. FRSL 1994. Royal Signals, 1943–47; book-selling, 1947–56; writer, 1956–; Literary Editor, Oxford Mail, 1958–69. Pres., British Science Fiction Assoc., 1960–64. Editor, SF Horizons, 1964–. Chairman, Oxford Branch Conservation Soc., 1968–69; Vice Pres., The Stapledon Soc., 1975–; Jt Pres., European SF Cttees, 1976–79; Society of Authors: Mem., Cttee of Management, 1976–78, Chm., 1978; Chm., Cultural Exchanges Cttee, 1979–; Member: Arts Council Literature Panel, 1978–80; Internat. PEN, 1983–; Pres., World SF, 1982–84; Vice-President: H. G. Wells Soc., 1983–; Soc. for Anglo-Chinese Understanding, 1987–91. Mem. Council, Council for Posterity, 1990–. Vice Pres., West Buckland Sch., 1996–. Hon. DLitt, 2000. Observer Book Award for Science Fiction, 1956; Ditmar Award for Best Contemporary Writer of Science Fiction, 1969; first James Blish Award, for SF criticism, 1977; Pilgrim Award, 1978; first Award for Distinguished Scholarship, Internat. Assoc. for the Fantastic in the Arts, Houston, 1986; Prix Utopie, France, 1999; Grand Master of Science Fiction, 2000. *Publications: science-fiction:* Space, Time and Nathaniel, 1957; Non-Stop, 1958 (Prix Jules Verne, 1977); Canopy of Time, 1959; The Male Response, 1961; Hothouse, 1962 (Hugo Award, 1961); Best Fantasy Stories, 1962; The Airs of Earth, 1963; The Dark Light Years, 1964; Introducing SF, 1964; Greybeard, 1964; Best SF Stories of Brian W. Aldiss, 1965; Earthworks, 1965; The Saliva Tree, 1966 (Nebula Award, 1965); An Age, 1967; Report on Probability A, 1968; Farewell, Fantastic Venus!, 1968; Intangibles Inc. and other Stories, 1969; A Brian Aldiss Omnibus, 1969; Barefoot in the Head, 1969; The Moment of Eclipse, 1971 (BSFA Award, 1972); Brian Aldiss Omnibus II, 1971; Frankenstein Unbound, 1973 (filmed, 1990); The Eighty-Minute Hour, 1974; (ed) Space Opera, 1974; (ed) Space Odysseys: an Anthology of Way-Back-When Futures, 1975; (ed) Hell's Cartographers, 1975; (ed) Evil Earths, 1975; Science Fiction Art: the fantasies of SF, 1975 (Ferrara Silver Comet, 1977); (ed with H. Harrison) Decade: the 1940s, 1976; (ed with H. Harrison) Decade: the 1950s, 1976; The Malacia Tapestry, 1976; (ed) Galactic Empires, vols 1 and 2, 1976; (ed with H. Harrison) The Year's Best Science Fiction No 9, 1976; Last Orders, 1977; (ed with H. Harrison) Decade: the 1960's, 1977; Enemies of the System, 1978; (ed) Perilous Planets, 1978; New Arrivals, Old Encounters, 1979; Moreau's Other Island, 1980; Helliconia Spring, 1982 (BSFA Award, John W. Campbell Meml Award); Helliconia Summer, 1983; Helliconia Winter, 1985; Helliconia Trilogy (boxed set of Helliconia Spring, Helliconia Summer, and Helliconia Winter), 1985; Cracken at Critical, 1987; Best SF Stories of Brian W. Aldiss, 1988; Science Fiction Blues, 1988; A Romance of the Equator, 1989; Dracula Unbound, 1991; A Tupolev Too Far, 1993; (with Roger Penrose) White Mars or, The Mind Set Free, 1999; *fiction:* The Brightfount Diaries, 1955 The Hand-Reared Boy, 1970; A Soldier Erect, 1971; Brothers of the Head, 1977; A Rude Awakening, 1978; Life in the West, 1980; Foreign Bodies, 1981; Seasons in Flight, 1984; The Horatio Stubbs Saga, 1985; Ruins, 1987; Forgotten Life, 1988; Remembrance Day, 1993; Somewhere East of Life, 1994; The Secret of This Book, 1995; The Squire Quartet, 1998; Supertoys Last All Summer Long, 2001; The Cretan Teat, 2002; *non-fiction:* Cities and Stones: A Traveller's Jugoslavia, 1966; The Shape of Further Things, 1970; Billion Year Spree: a history of science fiction, 1973 (Special BSFA Award, 1974; Eurocon Merit Award, 1976); This World and Nearer Ones, 1979; The Pale Shadow of Science, 1985; . . . And the Lurid Glare of the Comet, 1986; (with David Wingrove) Trillion Year Spree, 1986 (Hugo Award, 1987); Bury My Heart at W. H. Smith's, 1990; The Detached Retina, 1995; The Twinkling of an Eye, 1998; When the Feast is Finished, 1999; Art after Apogee, 2000; *verse:* Home Life with Cats, 1992; At the Caligula Hotel, 1995; Songs from the Steppes of Central Asia, 1996. *Recreations:* fame, obscurity, trances. *Address:* Hambleden, 39 St Andrews Road, Old Headington, Oxford OX3 9DL. *Clubs:* Groucho; Writers in Oxford.

ALDOUS, Charles; QC 1985; *b* 3 June 1943; *s* of Guy Travers Aldous, QC and Elizabeth Angela Aldous (*née* Paul); *m* 1969, Hermione Sara de Courcy-Ireland; one *s* two *d* (and one *d* decd). *Educ:* Harrow; University College London (LLB). Called to the Bar, Inner Temple, 1967 (Bencher, 1994), Lincoln's Inn *ad eund*, 1967 (Bencher). *Address:* Ravensfield Farm, Bures Hamlet, Suffolk CO8 5DP.

See also Rt Hon. Sir W. Aldous.

ALDOUS, Prof. David John, PhD; FRS 1994; Professor of Statistics, University of California, Berkeley, since 1986; *b* 13 July 1952; *s* of Kenneth George Aldous and Joyce Minnie Aldous (*née* Finch); *m* 1986, Katy Edwards; one *s*. *Educ:* St John's Coll., Cambridge (BA 1973; PhD 1977). Res. Fellow, St John's Coll., Cambridge, 1977–79; University of California, Berkeley: Asst Prof., 1979–82; Associate Prof., 1982–86. *Publication:* Probability Approximations via the Poisson Clumping Heuristic, 1989. *Recreations:* volleyball, science fiction. *Address:* Department of Statistics, University of California, Berkeley, CA 94720, USA. *T:* (510) 6422781.

ALDOUS, Hugh (Graham Cazalet), FCA; Partner, RSM Robson Rhodes (formerly Robson Rhodes), since 1976; Member, Competition Commission (formerly Monopolies and Mergers Commission), 1998–2001; *b* 1 June 1944; *s* of Maj. Hugh Francis Travers Aldous and Emily Aldous; *m* 1967, Christabel Marshall. *Educ:* Leeds Univ. (BCom). ACA 1970, FCA 1976. Robson Rhodes, then RSM Robson Rhodes, 1976–: on secondment to Depts of Transport and the Envmt, 1976–79; Man. Partner, 1987–97; DTI Inspector: House of Fraser Hldgs plc, 1987–88; TransTec plc, 2000–. Chairman: RSM Internat., 1997–2000; Protocol Associates NV, 2000–; Director: Freightliner Ltd, 1979–84; Sealink UK Ltd, 1981–84; British Waterways Bd, 1983–86; CILNTEC Ltd, 1991–96; Eastern European Trust plc (formerly First Russian Frontiers Trust plc), 1995– (Chm., 2000–); FOCUS Ltd, 1996–98; Elderstreet Millennium Venture Capital Trust (formerly Gartmore Venture Capital Trust plc), 1996–. *Publications:* Guide to Government Incentives to Industry, 1979; Study of Businesses Financed under the Small Business Loan Guarantee Scheme, 1984; (with H. Brooke) Report into the Affairs of House of Fraser Holdings plc, 1988; Review of the UK Financial and Professional Services Industry, 1992. *Recreation:* music. *Address:* RSM Robson Rhodes, 186 City Road, EC1V 2NU. *T:* (020) 7251 1644. *Club:* Royal Automobile.

ALDOUS, Lucette; Senior Lecturer in Classical Ballet, Edith Cowan University, since 1994; Head of Classical Dance, Dance Department, Western Australian Academy of Performing Arts, 1984–99, now Senior Lecturer; Senior Adjudicator, National Eisteddfods, since 1979; *b* 26 Sept. 1938; *d* of Charles Fellows Aldous and Marie (*née* Rutherford); *m* 1972, Alan Alder; one *d*. *Educ:* Toronto Public Sch., NSW; Brisbane Public Sch., Qld; Randwick Girls' High Sch., NSW. Awarded Frances Scully Meml Schol. (Aust.) to study at Royal Ballet Sch., London, 1955; joined Ballet Rambert, 1957, Ballerina, 1958–63; Ballerina with: London Fest. Ballet, 1963–66; Royal Ballet, 1966–71; Prima Ballerina, The Australian Ballet, 1971; Master Teacher, Australian Ballet Sch., 1979; Guest Teacher: Australian Ballet, 1988–; Royal NZ Ballet Co., 1988–; West Australian Ballet Co., 1988–. Rep. Australia, 1st Internat. Ballet Competition, Jackson, Miss, USA, 1979; Guest, Kirov Ballet and Ballet School, Leningrad, 1975–76. Guest appearances: Giselle, with John Gilpin, NY, 1968; Lisbon, 1969; with Rudolf Nureyev, in Don Quixote: Aust., 1970, NY, Hamburg and Marseilles, 1971; Carmen, Johannesburg, 1970; The Sleeping Beauty: E Berlin, 1970, Teheran, 1970, 1975; partnered Edward Villela at Expo '74, Spokane, USA. *Television:* title rôle, La Sylphide, with Fleming Flindt, BBC, 1960. *Films:* as Kitri, in Don Quixote, with Rudolf Nureyev and Robert Helpmann, Aust., 1972; The Turning Point, 1977. Mem., Australia Council for the Arts, 1996–98. Patron, Australian Cecchetti Soc., 1991–. Hon. DLitt Edith Cowan, 1999. *Recreations:* music, reading, gardening, breeding Burmese cats. *Address:* c/o Dance Department, Western Australian Academy of Performing Arts, 2 Bradford Street, Mount Lawley, Perth, WA 6050, Australia.

ALDOUS, Rt Hon. Sir William, Kt 1988; PC 1995; **Rt Hon. Lord Justice Aldous;** a Lord Justice of Appeal, since 1995; *b* 17 March 1936; *s* of Guy Travers Aldous, QC; *m* 1960, Gillian Frances Henson; one *s* two *d*. *Educ:* Harrow; Trinity Coll., Cambridge (MA). Barrister, Inner Temple, 1960, Bencher, 1985; Jun. Counsel, DTI, 1972–76; QC 1976; appointed to exercise appellate jurisdiction of BoT under Trade Marks Act, 1981–88; a Judge of the High Court, Chancery Div., 1988–95. Chm., Performing Rights Tribunal, 1986–88. *Address:* Royal Courts of Justice, Strand, WC2A 2LL.

See also C. Aldous.

ALDRED, Brian Gordon; Director of Resources, Lancashire County Council, since 2000; *b* 27 April 1951; *s* of late James Bernard Aldred and of Jean Margaret Layton Aldred; *m* 1973, Miriam Constance Shaw; one *s* one *d*. *Educ:* Queen Elizabeth's Grammar Sch., Blackburn; Jesus Coll., Oxford (BA Modern Hist.; MA); Liverpool Poly. CIPFA. Cheshire CC, 1972–82; Dep. Dir of Finance, Bolton MBC, 1982–85; Dep. County Treas., 1985–92, County Treas., 1992–2000, Lancs CC. *Address:* (office) PO Box 100, County Hall, Preston PR1 0LD. *T:* (01772) 264701.

ALDRED, Micheala Ann, PhD; Lecturer in Medical Molecular Genetics, University of Leicester, since 1996; *b* 16 Oct. 1966; *d* of Spencer and Barbara Aldred; *m* 1991, Keith Niven Mitchell. *Educ:* University Coll. London (BSc Hons); Open Univ. (PhD 1993); DipRCPath 1998. Postdoctoral Research Associate: MRC Human Genetics Unit, Edinburgh, 1991–94; Univ. of Cambridge, 1994–96. Mem., Human Genetics Adv. Commn, 1997–99. Trustee, Retinoblastoma Soc., 1992–. *Publications:* papers in jls on human genetics. *Recreations:* charity work, photography, hiking. *Address:* Division of Medical Genetics, Department of Genetics, University of Leicester, University Road, Leicester LE1 7RH.

ALDRIDGE, Frederick Jesse; Member, Public Health Laboratory Service Board, 1977–83; Under-Secretary and Controller of Supply, Department of Health and Social Security, 1968–75; *b* 13 Oct. 1915; *s* of late Jesse and Clara Amelia Aldridge; *m* 1940, Grace Hetty Palser (*d* 1999); two *d*. *Educ:* Westminster City Sch. Clerical Off., Air Min., 1933; Exec. Off., Min. of Health, 1935; RAF, 1940–46; Acct-General's Div., Min. of Health: Asst Acct-Gen., 1956; Dep. Acct-Gen., 1958; Asst Sec. for Finance and Dep. Acct-Gen., 1964; Asst Sec., Food, Health and Nutrition, also Civil Defence, 1966. *Recreation:* music. *Address:* 17 Tanglewood Close, Croydon CR0 5HX. *T:* (020) 8656 3623.

ALDRIDGE, (Harold Edward) James; author; *b* 10 July 1918; *s* of William Thomas Aldridge and Edith Quayle Aldridge; *m* 1942, Dina Mitchnik; two *s*. With Herald and Sun, Melbourne, 1937–38; Daily Sketch, and Sunday Dispatch, London, 1939; subsequently Australian Newspaper Service and North American Newspaper Alliance (war correspondent), Finland, Norway, Middle East, Greece, USSR, until 1945; also correspondent for Time and Life, Teheran, 1944. Rhys Meml Award, 1945; Lenin Peace Prize, 1972. *Play:* The 49th State, Lyric, Hammersmith, 1947. *Publications:* Signed With Their Honour, 1942; The Sea Eagle, 1944; Of Many Men, 1946; The Diplomat, 1950; The Hunter, 1951; Heroes of the Empty View, 1954; Underwater Hunting for Inexperienced Englishmen, 1955; I Wish He Would Not Die, 1958; Gold and Sand (short stories), 1960; The Last Exile, 1961; A Captive in the Land, 1962; The Statesman's Game, 1966; My Brother Tom, 1966; The Flying 19, 1966; (with Paul Strand) Living Egypt, 1969; Cairo: Biography of a City, 1970; A Sporting Proposition, 1973; The Marvellous

Mongolian, 1974; Mockery in Arms, 1974; The Untouchable Juli, 1975; One Last Glimpse, 1977 (adapted as stage play, Prague Vinohrady Th., 1981); Goodbye Un-America, 1979; The Broken Saddle, 1983; The True Story of Lilli Stubek, 1984 (Australian Children's Book of the Year, 1985); The True Story of Spit MacPhee, 1986 (Guardian Children's Fiction Prize; NSW Premier's Literary Award, 1986); The True Story of Lola MacKellar, 1993. *Recreations:* trout fishing, etc. *Address:* c/o Curtis Brown, 28/29 Haymarket, SW1Y 4SP.

ALDRIDGE, Dr John Frederick Lewis, OBE 1990, FRCP, FRCPEd, FFOM; consultant in occupational medicine, 1987–97; Civil Consultant in Occupational Medicine to the Royal Navy, 1983–92, Emeritus Consultant since 1992; *b* 28 Dec. 1926; *s* of Dr Frederick James Aldridge and Kathleen Marietta Micaela (*née* White); *m* 1955, Barbara Sheila Bolland; three *s* one *d*. *Educ:* Gresham's Sch.; St Thomas's Hosp. Med. Sch. (MB, BS 1951). DIH 1963; FRCPEd 1980; FFOM 1981; FRCP 1984. Served RAMC, 1953–60 (retd, Major). Indust. MO, Reed Paper Gp, 1960–63; CMO, IBM United Kingdom Ltd, 1963–87; part-time Hon. Clin. Asst, Dept of Psychol Medicine, UCH, 1970–76. Faculty of Occupational Medicine, Royal Coll. of Physicians: Vice-Dean, 1984–86; Dean, 1986–88; Chm., Ethics Cttee, 1991–96; Royal Soc. of Medicine: Fellow, 1964; Hon. Sec., 1970–72 and Vice-Pres., 1974–77, Occupl Medicine Section; Soc. of Occupational Medicine: Mem., 1960–; Hon. Meetings Sec., 1969–71. Member: Specialist Adv. Cttee on Occupl Medicine, Jt Cttee of Higher Med. Trng, 1970–74; Nat. Occupl Health and Safety Cttee, RoSPA, 1979–81; Standing Med. Adv. Cttee, DHSS, 1986–88; Defence Med. Emergency Steering Cttee, 1986–88; Indust. Soc. Med. Adv. Cttee, 1986–89 (Chm., 1987–89); CEGB Med. Adv. Cttee, 1988–89. Mem., Council and Cttee of Management, Shipwrecked Mariners' Royal Benevolent Soc., 1987–96; Dir, Shipwrecked Mariners' Trading Ltd, 1999–2001. Chm., W Sussex Assoc. for the Disabled, 1995–97 (Mem. Council and Mgt Cttee, 1991–; Vice-Pres., 1997–); Vice Chm., Chichester DFAS, 2000– (Librarian, 1999–); Trustee, Southampton and Wessex Med. Sch. Trust, 1978–82. Liveryman, Worshipful Soc. of Apothecaries, 1984–. *Publications:* papers on occupl med. topics and occupl mental health. *Recreations:* 18th century English porcelain, watercolours, walking, shooting. *Address:* East House, Charlton, Chichester, W Sussex PO18 0HU. *T:* (01243) 811392. *Clubs:* Lansdowne; Vintage Sports Car.

ALDRIDGE, Trevor Martin; solicitor; President: Special Educational Needs Tribunal, since 1994; Protection of Children Act Tribunal, since 1999; *b* 22 Dec. 1933; *s* of Dr Sidney and Isabel Aldridge; *m* 1966, Joanna, *d* of C. J. v. D. Edwards; one *s* one *d*. *Educ:* Frensham Heights School; Sorbonne; St John's College, Cambridge (MA). Partner in Bower Cotton & Bower, 1962–84; Law Comr, 1984–93. Chairman: Conveyancing Standing Cttee, 1989 (Mem., 1985–89); Commonhold Working Gp, reported 1987. Hon. Vis. Prof., City Univ., 1994–95. Pres., Frensham Heights School, 1996– (Chm. Govs, 1977–95). Hon. QC 1992; Hon. Life Mem., Law Soc., 1995. General editor, Property Law Bulletin, 1980–84. *Publications:* Boundaries, Walls and Fences, 1962, 7th edn 1997; Finding Your Facts, 1963; Directory of Registers and Records, 1963, (consulting ed.) 5th edn 1993; Service Agreements, 1964, 4th edn 1982; Rent Control and Leasehold Enfranchisement, 1965, 11th edn as Aldridge's Residential Lettings, 1998; Betterment Levy, 1967; Letting Business Premises, 1971, 7th edn 1998; Your Home and the Law, 1975, 2nd edn 1979; (jtly) Managing Business Property, 1978; Criminal Law Act 1977, 1978; Guide to Enquiries of Local Authorities, 1978, 2nd edn 1982; Guide to Enquiries Before Contract, 1978; Guide to National Conditions of Sale, 1979, 2nd edn 1981; Leasehold Law, 1980; Housing Act, 1980, and as amended 1984, 2nd edn 1984; (ed) Powers of Attorney, 6th edn 1986 to 9th edn 2000; Guide to Law Society's Conditions of Sale, 1981, 2nd edn 1984; Questions of Law: Homes, 1982; Law of Flats, 1982, 3rd edn 1994; Practical Conveyancing Precedents, 1984; Practical Lease Precedents, 1987; Companion to Standard Conditions of Sale, 1990, 2nd edn 1992; Companion to Property Information Forms, 1990; First Registration, 1991; Companion to Enquiries of Local Authorities, 1991; Companion to the Law Society Business Lease, 1991; Implied Covenants for Title, 1995; Privity of Contract: Landlord and Tenant (Covenants) Act, 1995. *Address:* Birkitt Hill House, Offley, Hitchin, Herts SG5 3DB. *T:* (01462) 768680, *Fax:* (01462) 769135; *e-mail:* tmaldridge@cwcom.net. *Club:* Oxford and Cambridge.

ALDRIN, Dr Buzz; President, Starcraft Enterprises International (research and development of space technology, manned flight to Mars), since 1988; *b* Montclair, NJ, USA, 20 Jan. 1930; *s* of late Col Edwin E. Aldrin, USAF retd, Brielle, NJ, and Marion Aldrin (*née* Moon); named Edwin Eugene, changed legally to Buzz; *m* 1988, Lois Driggs-Cannon; two *s* one *d* of former marriage. *Educ:* Montclair High Sch., Montclair, NJ (grad.); US Mil. Academy, West Point, NY (BSc); Mass Inst. of Technology (DSc in Astronautics). Received wings (USAF), 1952. Served in Korea (66 combat missions) with 51st Fighter Interceptor Wing. Aerial Gunnery Instr, Nellis Air Force Base, Nevada; attended Sqdn Officers Sch., Air Univ., Maxwell Air Force Base, Alabama; Aide to Dean of Faculty, USAF Academy; Flt Comdr with 36th Tactical Fighter Wing, Bitburg, Germany. Subseq. assigned to Gemini Target Office of Air Force Space Systems Div., Los Angeles, Calif; later transf. to USAF Field Office, Manned Spacecraft Center. One of 3rd group of astronauts named by NASA, Oct. 1963; served as back up pilot, Gemini 9 Mission and prime pilot, Gemini 12 Mission (launched into space, with James Lovell, 11 Nov. 1966), 4 day 59 revolution flight which brought Gemini Program to successful close; he established a new record for extravehicular activity and obtained first pictures taken from space of an eclipse of the sun; also made a rendezvous with the previously launched Agena; later assigned to 2nd manned Apollo flight, as back-up command module pilot; Lunar Module Pilot, Apollo 11 rocket flight to the Moon; first lunar landing with Neil Armstrong, July 1969; left NASA to return to USAF as Commandant, Aerospace Res. Pilots Sch., Edwards Air Force Base, Calif, 1971; retired USAF 1972. Mem., Soc. of Experimental Test Pilots; FAIAA; Tau Beta Pi, Sigma Xi. Further honours include Presidential Medal of Freedom, 1969; Air Force DSM with Oak Leaf Cluster; Legion of Merit; Air Force DFC with Oak Leaf Cluster; Air Medal with 2 Oak Leaf Clusters; and NASA DSM, Exceptional Service Medal, and Group Achievement Award. Various hon. memberships and hon. doctorates. *Publications:* Return to Earth (autobiography), 1973; Men From Earth: the Apollo Project, 1989; (jtly) Encounter with Tiber (science fiction), 1996; The Return (science fiction). *Recreations:* athletics, scuba diving, ski-ing, golf, etc. *Address:* 10380 Wilshire Boulevard #703, Los Angeles, CA 90024, USA.

ALEKSANDER, Prof. Igor, PhD; FREng; Professor of Neural Systems Engineering, and Head of Department of Electrical Engineering, Imperial College of Science, Technology and Medicine, University of London, 1988–97; *b* 26 Jan. 1937. *Educ:* Marist Brothers' Coll., S Africa; Univ. of the Witwatersrand (BSc Eng); Univ. of London (PhD). Section Head of STC, Footscray, 1958–61; Lectr, Queen Mary Coll., Univ. of London, 1961–65; Reader in Electronics, Univ. of Kent, 1965–74; Prof. of Electronics and Head of Electrical Engrg Dept, Brunel Univ., 1974–84; Prof. of Information Technology Management, Computing Dept, Imperial Coll., 1984–88. FREng (FEng 1989); FCGI 1994. *Publications:* An Introduction to Logic Circuit Theory, 1971; Automata Theory: an engineering approach, 1976; The Human Machine, 1978; Reinventing Man, 1983 (USA 1984); Designing Intelligent Systems, 1984; Thinking Machines, 1987; An Introduction to Neural Computing, 1990; Neurons and Symbols: the stuff that mind is made of, 1993; Impossible Minds: my neurons, my consciousness, 1996; How to Build a Mind, 2000; *c* 120 papers on computing and human modelling. *Recreations:* tennis, skiing, music, architecture. *Address:* Imperial College of Science, Technology and Medicine, Exhibition Road, SW7 2AZ. *T:* (020) 7594 9850.

ALEX; *see* Peattie, C. W. D. and Taylor, R. P.

ALEXANDER, family name of **Baron Alexander of Weedon,** of **Earl Alexander of Tunis,** and of **Earl of Caledon.**

ALEXANDER, Viscount; Frederick James Alexander; *b* 15 Oct. 1990; *s* and *heir* of Earl of Caledon, *qv*.

ALEXANDER OF TUNIS, 2nd Earl *cr* 1952; **Shane William Desmond Alexander;** Viscount, 1946; Baron Rideau, 1952; Lieutenant Irish Guards, retired, 1958; Director: International Hospitals Group and associated companies, since 1981; Pathfinder Financial Corporation, Toronto, since 1980; *b* 30 June 1935; *er s* of 1st Earl Alexander of Tunis, KG, PC, GCB, OM, GCMG, CSI, DSO, MC, and Lady Margaret Diana Bingham (Countess Alexander of Tunis), GBE, DStJ, DL (*d* 1977), *yr d* of 5th Earl of Lucan, PC, GCVO, KBE, CB; *S* father, 1969; *m* 1981, Hon. Davina Woodhouse (LVO 1991; Lady-in-Waiting to Princess Margaret, 1975–), *y d* of 4th Baron Terrington; two *d*. *Educ:* Ashbury Coll., Ottawa, Canada; Harrow. A Lord in Waiting (Govt Whip), 1974. Chm., Sterling Credit Guarantee Co. PLC, 1999–; Director: Marketform Ltd, 1996–; W. L. H. Ltd, 2000–. Trustee, 1987–, and Chm., 1989–, Canada Meml Foundn; Pres., British-American-Canadian Associates, 1989–94. Patron, British-Tunisian Soc., 1979–99. Freeman, City of London, 1964; Liveryman, Mercers Company. Freedom, City of New Orleans, 1993. Order of Republic of Tunisia, 1995. *Heir: b* Hon. Brian James Alexander [*b* 31 July 1939; *m* 1999, Mrs Johanna W. Morris]. *Address:* 59 Wandsworth Common, West Side, SW18 2ED. *Club:* MCC.

ALEXANDER OF WEEDON, Baron *cr* 1988 (Life Peer), of Newcastle-under-Lyme in the County of Staffordshire; **Robert Scott Alexander,** QC 1973; QC (NSW) 1983; Chairman, Royal Shakespeare Company, since 2000 (Governor, since 1995); *b* 5 Sept. 1936; *s* of late Samuel James and of Hannah May Alexander; *m*; two *s* two *d*; *m* 1985, Marie Anderson. *Educ:* Brighton Coll.; King's Coll., Cambridge (BA 1959; MA 1963). Called to Bar, Middle Temple, 1961, Bencher, 1979, Master Treasurer, 2001; Vice Chm., 1984–85, Chm., 1985–86, of the Bar Council. Chm., Nat. Westminster Bank, 1989–99. Chm., Panel on Takeovers and Mergers, 1987–89; Dep. Chm., SIB, 1994–96; Mem., Govt Panel on Sustainable Develt, 1994–. Chm., Delegated Powers and Deregulation Scrutiny Cttee, H of L, 1995–; Mem., Ind. Commn on Voting Reform, 1997–98. Non-executive Director: RTZ Corp., 1991–96; Internat. Stock Exchange of UK and Republic of Ireland, 1991–93. Chairman: Council, Justice, 1990–; Trustees, Crisis, 1990–96. Trustee: National Gall., 1987–93; The Economist, 1990–. Chancellor, Exeter Univ., 1998–. President: King's Coll. Assoc., 1980–81; Brighton Coll., 1993–; Mem., Council of Governors, Wycombe Abbey Sch., 1986–92. Presentation Fellow, KCL, 1995. FRSA 1991. Hon. LLD: Sheffield, 1991; Buckingham, 1992; Keele, 1993; Exeter, 1995. *Publication:* The Voice of the People: a constitution for tomorrow, 1997. *Recreations:* theatre, cricket, tennis, gardens, painting. *Address:* House of Lords, SW1A 0PW. *Clubs:* Garrick, MCC (Mem. Cttee; Pres., 2000–01).

ALEXANDER, Prof. Alan; Chairman designate, Scottish Water, since 2001; Professor of Local and Public Management, University of Strathclyde, 1993–2000, now Emeritus (Professor of Management in Local Government, 1987–93); *b* 13 Dec. 1943; *s* of Alexander Alexander and Rose (*née* Rein); *m* 1964, Morag MacInnes(*see* M. Alexander); one *s* one *d*. *Educ:* Possil Secondary Sch., Glasgow; Albert Secondary Sch., Glasgow; Univ. of Glasgow (MA 1965). Lectr/Asst Prof. of Political Sci., Lakehead Univ., Ontario, 1966–71; Lectr in Politics, Univ. of Reading, 1971–87; Dir, Scottish Local Authorities Management Centre, 1987–93, and Hd, Dept of Human Resource Mgt, 1993–96, Univ. of Strathclyde. Scholar-in-Residence, Rockefeller Foundn, Villa Serbelloni, Bellagio, Italy, Feb.–March 1984; Fulbright Vis. Prof. of Politics, Randolph-Macon Woman's Coll., Virginia, 1986. Member: Board, Housing Corp., 1977–80; Council, Quarrier's, 1995–2000; Ind. Commn on Relations between Local Govt and the Scottish Parlt, 1998–99. Chairman: Glasgow Regeneration Fund, 1998–; W of Scotland Water Authy, 1999–2002. Member: Reading BC, 1972–74; Berks CC, 1973–77. Mem., Standing Res. Cttee on Local and Central Govt Relns, Joseph Rowntree Foundn, 1988–92. Conducted independent inquiry into relations between Western Isles Islands Council and Bank of Credit and Commerce Internat., 1991. Contested (Lab) Henley, Feb. 1974. Pres., Raglan Housing Assoc., 1987– (Chm., 1975–87). *Publications:* Local Government in Britain since Reorganisation, 1982 (Italian edn, revised, 1984); The Politics of Local Government in the United Kingdom, 1982; Borough Government and Politics: Reading 1835–1985, 1985; Managing the Fragmented Authority, 1994; articles in Local Govt Studies, Public Admin, Brit. Jl Pol. Sci. and others. *Recreations:* walking, theatre, opera, cinema, avoiding gardening. *Address:* A'Chomraich, Dull, Aberfeldy, Perthshire PH15 2JQ. *T:* (01887) 820726.

ALEXANDER, Prof. Albert Geoffrey, FDSRCS; Professor of Conservative Dentistry, University of London, 1972–92, now Emeritus; *b* 22 Sept. 1932; *s* of William Francis Alexander and Muriel Katherine (*née* Boreham); *m* 1956, Dorothy Constance (*née* Johnson); one *d*. *Educ:* Bridlington Sch.; UCH Dental Sch., Univ. of London (BDS 1956; MDS 1968). LDSRCS 1955, FDSRCS 1961. Dental House Surgeon, Nat. Dental Hosp., 1955–56; Nat. Service, RADC, 1956–58; Clinical Asst, UCH Dental Dept, 1958; private dental practice, 1958–59; Lectr in Cons. Dentistry, 1959–62, Sen. Lectr in Cons. Dentistry and Periodontics, 1962–69, UCH Dental Sch.; Hon. Consultant, UCH Dental Hosp., 1967–92; Vice-Dean of Dental Studies, 1974–77, Dean, 1977–92, UCL Dental Sch., later UC and Middlesex Sch. of Dentistry; Vice-Dean, Faculty of Clinical Sciences, UCMSM, 1977–91; Prof. of Conservative Dentistry, Univ. of Hong Kong, 1992–94. Fellow, UCL, 1986; Member: Council, UCL, 1984–91; Senate, Univ. of London, 1987–91. Chm., Dental Educn Adv. Council, 1986–90; Member: GDC, 1986–92 (Treasurer, 1989–92); Bloomsbury HA, 1981–90. Fellow: Internat. Coll. of Dentists, 1975; Hong Kong Acad. of Medicine, 1993. *Publications:* (co-ed) The Prevention of Periodontal Disease, 1971; (jtly) Self-Assessment Manual, No 3, Clinical Dentistry, 1978; (co-ed) Companion to Dental Studies, Vol. 3, 1986, Vol. 2, 1988; scientific, technical and clinical articles on dentistry and dental research. *Recreations:* photography, blue and white Chinese ceramics.

ALEXANDER, Andrew Clive; columnist; City Editor, Daily Mail, 1984–2000; *b* 12 May 1935; *s* of Ronald and Doreen Alexander. *Educ:* Lancing College. Leader Writer, Yorkshire Post, 1960–65; Parly Sketch-Writer, Daily Telegraph, 1966–72; Parly Sketch-Writer and Columnist, Daily Mail, 1972–84. Director: Associated Newspapers plc, 1992–2000; Underoneroof Ltd, 2000–; OneStopCarShop Ltd, 2000–; Invest TV Ltd, 2000–. Contested (C) Colne Valley, March 1963, 1964. Specialist Writer of the Year, British Press Awards, 1976 and 1977; Political Journalist of the Year, What the Papers Say awards, 1977; Jt Financial Journalist of the Year, Baltic Trent Award, 1986; Sen. Financial Journalist of the Year, Wincott Foundn, 1991. *Publication:* (with Alan Watkins) The

Making of the Prime Minister, 1970. *Recreations:* music, gardening, history, weight training. *Address:* c/o Associated Newspapers plc, 141–143 Drury Lane, WC2B 5TS. *T:* (020) 7938 6000. *Clubs:* Reform, Espree.

ALEXANDER, Anthony George Laurence; Deputy Chairman, Imperial Tobacco Group, since 1996; *b* 4 April 1938; *s* of George and Margaret Alexander; *m* 1962, Frances, *d* of Cyril Burdett; one *s* two *d*. *Educ:* St Edward's School, Oxford. FCA. Hanson plc: Dir, 1976–96; UK Chief Operating Officer, 1986–96. Director: Inchcape Plc, 1993–; Misys plc, 1996–; Cookson Gp plc, 1996–; Laporte plc, 2000–. *Recreations:* tennis, golf. *Address:* Crafnant, Gregories Farm Lane, Beaconsfield, Bucks HP9 1HJ. *T:* (01494) 672882.

ALEXANDER, Bill, (William Alexander Paterson); Artistic Director, Birmingham Repertory Theatre, 1993–2000; Hon. Associate Director, Royal Shakespeare Company, since 1991 (Associate Director, 1984–91); *b* 23 Feb. 1948; *s* of Bill and Rosemary Paterson; *m* 1977, Juliet Harmer; two *d*. *Educ:* St Lawrence Coll., Ramsgate; Keele Univ. (BA Hons English/Politics). Seasons with The Other Company, Bristol Old Vic, Royal Court, 1972–78; Asst Dir, 1978–80, Resident Dir, 1980–84, RSC. Laurence Olivier award, Best Director, 1986. *Productions directed: Bristol Old Vic:* The Ride Across Lake Constance; Twelfth Night; Old Times; Butley; How the Other Half Loves; *Royal Court:* Sex and Kinship in a Savage Society, 1976; Amy and the Price of Cotton, 1977; Class Enemy, 1978; Sugar and Spice, 1979; *Royal Shakespeare Company:* Factory Birds, 1977; Shout Across the River, The Hang of the Gaol, Captain Swing, 1978; Men's Beano, 1979; Bastard Angel, Henry IV tour, 1980; Accrington Pals, 1981; Money, Clay, Molière, 1982; Tartuffe, Volpone, 1983; Richard III, Today, The Merry Wives of Windsor, 1984; Crimes in Hot Countries, Downchild (co-dir), 1985; Country Dancing, A Midsummer Night's Dream, 1986; Cymbeline, Twelfth Night, The Merchant of Venice, 1987; The Duchess of Malfi, Cymbeline, 1989; Much Ado About Nothing, The Taming of the Shrew (dir, regional tour), 1990; The Bright and Bold Design, 1991; The Taming of the Shrew, The School of Night, 1992; *Birmingham:* Othello, Volpone, Old Times, 1993; The Snowman, 1993, 1997; Awake and Sing, The Tempest, 1994; The Servant, Macbeth, The Way of the World, 1995; Divine Right, The Alchemist, 1996; The Merchant of Venice, 1997; Frozen, Hamlet, 1998; The Four Alice Bakers, Jumpers, Nativity, 1999; Quarantine, Twelfth Night, 2000; *other productions* include: Entertaining Mr Sloane, Nottingham Playhouse, 1977; The Gingerbread Lady, Ipswich, 1977; The Last of the Knuckle Men, Edin. Fest. Fringe, 1977; Julius Caesar, Newcastle upon Tyne, 1979; One White Day, Soho Poly, 1976; Mates, Leicester Square, 1976; Betrayal, 1980; Anna Christie, 1981, Cameri Th., Tel Aviv; Talk of the Devil, Watford Palace, 1986; Romeo and Juliet, Victory Theatre, NY, 1990; Troilus and Cressida, Shakespeare Theatre, Washington, 1992. *Recreation:* tennis. *Address:* Rose Cottage, Tunley, Glos GL7 6LP.

ALEXANDER, Sir Charles G(undry), 2nd Bt *cr* 1945; MA, AIMarE; Chairman, Alexander Shipping Co. Ltd, 1959–87; *b* 5 May 1923; *s* of Sir Frank Alexander, 1st Bt, and Elsa Mary (*d* 1959), *d* of Sir Charles Collett, 1st Bt; *S* father, 1959; *m* 1st, 1944, Mary Neale, *o c* of S. R. Richardson; one *s* one *d*; 2nd, 1979, Eileen Ann Stewart. *Educ:* Bishop's Stortford College; St John's College, Cambridge. Served War as Lieut (E), RN, 1943–46. Chm., Governors Care Ltd, 1975–86; formerly Dep. Chm., Houlder Bros and Co. Ltd; Director: Furness-Houlder Insurance Ltd, until 1988; Furness-Houlder (Reinsurance Services) Ltd, until 1988; Inner London Region, National Westminster Bank Ltd, until 1987; Chm., Hull, Blyth & Co. Ltd, 1972–75. Chm., Bd of Governors, Bishop's Stortford College, until 1986. Mem. Court of Common Council, 1969; Alderman (Bridge Ward), 1970–76. Master, Merchant Taylors' Co., 1981–82; Prime Warden, Shipwrights' Co., 1983–84. *Heir: s* Richard Alexander [*b* 1 Sept. 1947; *m* 1971, Lesley Jane, *d* of Frederick William Jordan, Bishop's Stortford; two *s*]. *Address:* Hollytree Farmhouse, North Cadbury, Yeovil, Somerset BA22 7DD. *T:* (01963) 440159. *Club:* Royal Automobile.

ALEXANDER of Ballochmyle, Sir Claud Hagart-, 3rd Bt *cr* 1886, of Ballochmyle; JP; DL; Vice Lord-Lieutenant, Ayr and Arran, 1983–98; *b* 6 Jan. 1927; *s* of late Wilfred Archibald Alexander (2nd *s* of 2nd Bt) and Mary Prudence, *d* of Guy Acheson; *S* grandfather, 1945; assumed additional surname of Hagart, 1949; *m* 1959, Hilda Etain, 2nd *d* of Miles Malcolm Acheson, Ganges, BC, Canada; two *s* two *d*. *Educ:* Sherborne; Corpus Christi Coll., Cambridge (BA 1948). MInstMC 1980. Hon. Sheriff, S Strathclyde, Dumfries and Galloway, 1997–. DL Ayrshire, 1973; JP Cumnock and Doon Valley, 1983. *Heir: s* Claud Hagart-Alexander [*b* 5 Nov. 1963; *m* 1994, Elaine Susan, *d* of Vincent Park, Winnipeg]. *Address:* Kingencleugh House, Mauchline, Ayrshire KA5 5JL. *T:* (01290) 550217. *Club:* New (Edinburgh).

ALEXANDER, David; *see* Alexander, J. D.

ALEXANDER, Maj.-Gen. David Crichton, CB 1976; Commandant, Scottish Police College, 1979–87, retired; *b* 28 Nov. 1926; *s* of James Alexander and Margaret (*née* Craig); *m* 1st, 1957, Diana Joyce (Jane) (*née* Fisher) (*d* 1995); one *s* two *d* and one step *s*; 2nd, 1996, Elizabeth Patricia (*née* Herrington). *Educ:* Edinburgh Academy. Joined RM, 1944; East Indies Fleet; 45 Commando, Malaya, Malta, Canal Zone, 1951–54; Parade Adjt, Lympstone, 1954–57; Equerry and Acting Treasurer to Duke of Edinburgh, 1957–60; psc 1960; Directing Staff, Staff Coll., Camberley, 1962–65; 45 Commando (2IC), Aden, 1965–66; Staff of Chief of Defence Staff, incl. service with Sec. of State, 1966–69; CO 40 Commando, Singapore, 1969–70; Col GS to CGRM, 1970–73; ADC to the Queen, 1973–75; RCDS 1974; Comdr, Training Gp RM, 1975–77. Dir-Gen., English-Speaking Union, 1977–79. Governor, Corps of Commissionaires, 1978–97 (Pres., 1994–97); Member: Civil Service Final Selection Bd, 1978–88; MoD Police Review Cttee, 1985; Transport Users' Consultative Cttee for Scotland, 1989–93. Dir, Edinburgh Acad., 1980–89 (Chm., 1985–89). Pres., SSAFA, Fife, 1990–94. Freeman, City of London; Liveryman, Painter Stainers' Co., 1978. *Recreations:* fishing, gardening, golf. *Address:* Baldinnie, Park Place, Elie, Fife KY9 1DH. *T:* (01333) 330882. *Club:* Army and Navy.

ALEXANDER, Sir Douglas, 3rd Bt *cr* 1921; with Cowen & Co.; *b* 9 Sept. 1936; *s* of Lt-Comdr Archibald Gillespie Alexander (*d* 1978) (2nd *s* of 1st Bt), and of Margery Isabel, *d* of Arthur Brown Griffith; *S* uncle, 1983; *m* 1958, Marylon, *d* of Leonidas Collins Scatterday; two *s*. *Educ:* Rice Univ., Houston, Texas (MA 1961). PhD 1967 (Univ. of N Carolina). Formerly Assoc. Prof. and Chairman, French, State Univ. of New York at Albany. *Heir: s* Douglas Gillespie Alexander, *b* 24 July 1962. *Address:* 2499 Windsor Way Court, Wellington, FL 33414, USA.

ALEXANDER, Douglas Garven; MP (Lab) Paisley South, since Nov. 1997; Minister of State (Minister for E-Commerce and Competitiveness), Department of Trade and Industry, since 2001; *b* 26 Oct. 1967; *s* of Rev. Douglas N. Alexander and Dr Joyce O. Alexander. *Educ:* Univ. of Edinburgh (MA 1st cl. Hons 1990; LLB (Dist.) 1993; DipLP 1994); Univ. of Pennsylvania. Admitted Solicitor, 1995; Brodies WS, 1994–96; Digby Brown, 1996–97. *Recreation:* fishing on the Isle of Mull. *Address:* c/o House of Commons, Westminster, SW1A 0AA.

See also W. C. Alexander.

ALEXANDER, Helen Anne; Chief Executive, Economist Group, since 1997; *b* 10 Feb. 1957; *d* of late Bernard Alexander and Tania Alexander (*née* Benckendorff); *m* 1985, Tim Suter; two *s* one *d*. *Educ:* Hertford Coll., Oxford (MA 1978); INSEAD, France (MBA 1984); CDipAF. Gerald Duckworth, 1978–79; Faber & Faber, 1979–83; Economist Gp, 1985–. Non-executive Director: Northern Foods plc, 1994–; British Telecom plc, 1998–. *Address:* The Economist Group, 25 St James's Street, SW1A 1HG. *T:* (020) 7830 7000.

ALEXANDER, Ian Douglas Gavin; QC 1989; a Recorder of the Crown Court, since 1982; *b* 10 April 1941; *s* of late Dr A. D. P. Alexander, MB ChB, and of Mrs D. Alexander; *m* 1969, Rosemary Kirkbride Richards; one *s* one *d*. *Educ:* Tonbridge; University College London (LLB). Called to Bar, Lincoln's Inn, 1964, Bencher, 1998; Recorder, Midland and Oxford Circuit, 1982–. A Pres., Mental Health Review Tribunal, 2000. Freemason. *Recreations:* horses, sailing, gardening, ski-ing, Church of England. *Address:* 5 Fountain Court, Steelhouse Lane, Birmingham B4 6DR. *T:* (0121) 606 0500. *Club:* Naval and Military.

ALEXANDER, Prof. (John) David, Hon. CBE 1998; DPhil; President Emeritus (formerly Trustees' Professor), Pomona College, since 1991 (President, 1969–91); *b* 18 Oct. 1932; *s* of John David Alexander, Sr and Mary Agnes McKinnon; *m* 1956, Catharine Coleman; one *s* two *d*. *Educ:* Southwestern at Memphis (BA); Louisville Presbyterian Theological Seminary; Oxford University (DPhil). Instructor to Associate Prof., San Francisco Theol Seminary, 1957–64; Pres., Southwestern at Memphis, 1965–69. Trustee, Teachers Insurance and Annuity Assoc., NY, 1970–; Director: Great Western Financial Corp., Beverly Hills, 1973–97; KCET (Community Supported TV of S Calif.), 1979–89; Amer. Council on Educn, Washington DC, 1981–84; National Assoc. of Indep. Colls and Univs, 1984–88; British Inst., 1979–87 (Mem., Bd of Advrs, 1987–); Member: Nat. Panel on Academic Tenure, 1971–72; Assoc. of Amer. Med. Colls Panel on Gen. Professional Preparation of Physicians, 1981–84; Bd of Overseers, Huntington Library, Art Collections and Botanical Gardens, 1991–. Amer. Sec., Rhodes Scholarship Trust, 1981–98. Ed., The American Oxonian, 1998–2000. Dir, Children's Hosp. of Los Angeles, 1993–. Trustee: Woodrow Wilson Nat. Fellowship Foundn, 1978–98; Seaver Inst., 1992–; Wenner-Gren Foundn for Anthropological Res., NY, 1995–. Hon. LLD: Univ. of S California, 1970; Occidental Coll., 1970; Centre Coll. of Kentucky, 1971; Pepperdine Univ., Calif, 1991; Albertson Coll. of Idaho, 1992; Pomona Coll., Calif., 1996; Hon. LHD Loyola Marymount Univ., 1983; Hon. LittD Rhodes Coll., Memphis, 1986. *Publications:* articles in Biblical studies; articles and chapters on higher educn in USA. *Recreations:* music, book collecting. *Address:* 807 North College Avenue, Claremont, CA 91711, USA. *T:* (909) 6247848. *Clubs:* Century Association (NY); California (Los Angeles); Bohemian (San Francisco).

ALEXANDER, Prof. John Malcolm; Emeritus Professor, University of Wales; *b* 14 Oct. 1921; *s* of Robert Henry Alexander and Gladys Irene Lightfoot Alexander (*née* Domville); *m* 1946, Margaret, *d* of F. A. Ingram; two *s*. *Educ:* Ipswich Sch.; City and Guilds Coll. DSc (Eng) London; PhD; FCGI; FICE; FIMechE; FIEE; FIM; FEng; FRSA. REME commn, 1942–47; Aluminium Labs Ltd, 1953–55; English Electric, 1955–57; London University: Reader in Plasticity, 1957–63; Prof. of Engrg Plasticity, 1963–69; Chm. Board of Studies in Civil and Mech. Engrg, 1966–68; Prof. of Applied Mechanics, Imp. Coll., 1969–78; Prof. and Head of Dept of Mech. Engrg, University Coll. of Swansea, 1978–83. Stocker Vis. Prof. in Engrg and Technol., 1985–87, Adjunct Prof., 1987–, Univ. of Ohio. Chm., Applied Mechanics Gp, IMechE, 1963–65; Mem., CIRP, 1965–; Vice-President. Inst. of Metals, 1968–71; Inst. of Sheet Metal Engrg, 1979–. Gov., Ipswich Sch., 1977–86. Chm., British Cold Forging Gp, 1973–79. Assessor, Sizewell 'B' Public Inquiry, 1983–85; Mem., Adv. Cttee on Safe Transport of Radioactive Materials, 1985–89. Series Editor, Ellis Horwood Ltd, 1970–91; Member Editorial Board: Internat. Jl Mech. Scis, 1968–91; Internat. Jl Machine Tool Design and Res., 1973–91. Liveryman, Blacksmiths' Co., 1976. Joseph Bramah Medal, IMechE, 1970. *Publications:* Advanced Mechanics of Materials, Manufacturing Properties of Materials, 1963; Hydrostatic Extrusion, 1971; Strength of Materials, 1980; Manufacturing Technology, 1987; papers to Royal Soc., IMechE, Iron and Steel Inst., Inst. Metals, Metals Soc. *Recreations:* music, gardening, golf. *Address:* Rowan Cottage, Furze Hill Road, Headley Down, Hants GU35 8NP. *Club:* Army and Navy.

ALEXANDER, Jonathan James Graham, DPhil; FBA 1985; FSA 1981; Professor of Fine Arts, Institute of Fine Arts, New York, since 1988; *b* 20 Aug. 1935; *s* of Arthur Ronald Brown and Frederica Emma Graham (who *m* 2nd, Boyd Alexander); *m* 1st, 1974, Mary Davey (marr. diss. 1995); one *s*; 2nd, 1996, Serita Winthrop. *Educ:* Magdalen Coll., Oxford (BA, MA, DPhil). Assistant, Dept of Western MSS, Bodleian Library, Oxford, 1963–71; Lecturer, 1971–73, Reader, 1973–87, History of Art Dept, Manchester Univ. Lyell Reader in Bibliography, Univ. of Oxford, 1982–83; Sen. Kress Fellow, Center for Adv. Study in Visual Arts, Nat. Gall. of Art, Washington DC, 1984–85; Sandars Reader in Bibliography, Cambridge Univ., 1984–85. Vis. Prof., UCL, 1991–93; John Simon Guggenheim Meml Fellow, 1995–96; Rio Tinto Distinguished Vis. Fellow, La Trobe Univ., Melbourne, 1997; Vis. Fellow, All Souls Coll., Oxford, 1998. Fellow, Medieval Acad. of America, 1999. Hon. Fellow, Pierpont Morgan Liby, NY, 1995. *Publications:* (with Otto Pächt) Illuminated Manuscripts in the Bodleian Library, Oxford, 3 vols, 1966, 1970, 1973; (with A. C. de la Mare) Italian Illuminated Manuscripts in the Library of Major J. R. Abbey, 1969; Norman Illumination at Mont St Michel *c* 966–1100, 1970; The Master of Mary of Burgundy, A Book of Hours, 1970; Italian Renaissance Illuminations, 1977; Insular Manuscripts 6th–9th Century, 1978; The Decorated Letter, 1978; (with E. Temple) Illuminated Manuscripts in Oxford College Libraries, 1986; (ed with Paul Binski) Age of Chivalry: Art in Plantagenet England 1200–1400, 1987; Medieval Illuminators and Their Methods of Work, 1993; (ed) The Painted Page: Italian Renaissance book illumination 1450–1550, 1994; The Towneley Lectionary illuminated for Cardinal Alessandro Farnese by Giulio Clovio, 1997; articles in Burlington Magazine, Arte Veneta, Pantheon, etc. *Recreation:* music. *Address:* Institute of Fine Arts, 1 East 78th Street, New York, NY 10021–0178, USA.

ALEXANDER, Rt Rev. Mervyn Alban Newman, DD; Bishop of Clifton, (RC), 1974–2001; Parish Priest, St Joseph, Weston-super-Mare, since 2001; *b* London, 29 June 1925; *s* of William Paul Alexander and Grace Evelyn Alexander (*née* Newman). *Educ:* Bishop Wordsworth School, Salisbury; Prior Park College, Bath; Gregorian University, Rome (DD 1951). Curate at Pro-Cathedral, Clifton, Bristol, 1951–63; RC Chaplain, Bristol University, 1953–67; Parish Priest, Our Lady of Lourdes, Weston-super Mare, 1967–72; Auxiliary Bishop of Clifton and Titular Bishop of Pinhel, 1972–74; Vicar Capitular of Clifton, 1974. Hon. LLD Bristol, 2001. *Address:* St Joseph, Camp Road, Weston-super-Mare BS23 2EN. *T:* (01934) 629865.

ALEXANDER, Michael Charles; writer; *b* 20 Nov. 1920; *s* of late Rear-Adm. Charles Otway Alexander and Antonia Geermans; *m* 1963, Sarah Wignall (marr. diss.); one *d*. *Educ:* Stowe; RMC, Sandhurst; Oflag IVC, Colditz. Served War: DCLI; 5 (Ski) Bn Scots Gds; 8 Commando (Layforce); HQ 70 Div. (Tobruk); HQ 13 Corps (GSO 3); SBS (POW, 1942–44); 2nd SAS Regt; War Office (Civil Affairs). Intergovtl Cttee on

Refugees, 1946; Capt., retd, 1946. Editorial Dir, Common Ground Ltd, 1946–50; OUP, 1950–51. Located Firuzkoh, Central Afghanistan, 1952; Himalayan Hovercraft Expedn, 1972; Yucatan Straits Hovercraft Expedn, 1975; Upper Ganges Hovercraft Expedn, 1980; Promoter, Scottish Highlands & Is Inflatable Boat Race; Founder and Hon. Pres., British Inflatable Boat Owners' Assoc., 1994. Dir, Adastra Productions. Founded: Woburn Safari Service, 1977; Chelsea Wharf Restaurant, 1983. FZS, FRGS; Fellow, Royal Soc. for Asian Affairs. Co-publisher, Wildlife magazine, 1982–86. *Publications:* The Privileged Nightmare (with Giles Romilly), 1952 (republ., as Hostages at Colditz, 1975); Offbeat in Asia, 1953; The Reluctant Legionnaire, 1955; The True Blue, 1957; Mrs Fraser on the Fatal Shore, 1972; Discovering the New World, 1976; Omai: Noble Savage, 1977; Queen Victoria's Maharajah, 1980; Delhi-Agra: a traveller's companion, 1987. *Address:* 48 Eaton Place, SW1X 8AL. *T:* (020) 7235 2724. *Clubs:* Beefsteak, Chelsea Arts.

ALEXANDER, Sir Michael (O'Donel Bjarne), GCMG 1992 (KCMG 1988; CMG 1982); HM Diplomatic Service, retired; Chairman, Royal United Services Institute for Defence Studies, since 1993; Director: Renaissance Capital (Moscow); RRC Bucharest, since 2000; *b* 19 June 1936; *s* of late Conel Hugh O'Donel Alexander, CMG, CBE, and Enid Constance Crichton Neate; *m* 1960, Traute Krohn; two *s* one *d*. *Educ:* Foyle Coll., Londonderry; Hall Sch., Hampstead; St Paul's Sch. (Schol.); King's Coll., Cambridge (Schol.); Harkness Fellow (Yale and Berkeley) 1960–62. MA (Cantab), AM (Yale). Royal Navy, 1955–57. Entered HM Foreign (later Diplomatic) Service, 1962; Moscow, 1963–65; Office of Political Adviser, Singapore, 1965–68; FCO, 1968–72; Asst Private Sec. to Secretary of State (Rt Hon. Sir Alec Douglas-Home, MP, and Rt Hon. James Callaghan, MP) 1972–74; Counsellor (Conf. on Security and Co-operation in Europe) and later Head of Chancery, UK Mission, Geneva, 1974–77; Dep. Head, 1977–78, Head, 1978–79, Personnel Operations Dept, FCO; Private Sec. (Overseas Affairs) to the Prime Minister (Rt Hon. Margaret Thatcher, MP), 1979–81; Ambassador, Vienna, 1982–86; concurrently Hd of UK Delegn to the Negotiations on Mutual and Balanced Reduction of Forces and Armaments in Central Europe, 1985–86; Ambassador and UK Permanent Rep. on North Atlantic Council, Brussels, 1986–92 (Dean of Council, 1991–92). Dep. Chm., Wasserstein Perella Eastern Europe, 1992–97; Chairman: KINTO Securities, Kiev, 1994–97; Capital SA, Bucharest, 1995–2000 (co-founder; Dep. Chm., 1993–95); Bi-Link Capital Markets Ltd, 1998–99; Dir (and co-founder) Sector Capital, Moscow, 1995–96. Sen. Advr, Bain & Co., 1994–99. Organised: Britain in Vienna Fest., 1986; Grosses Goldenes Ehrenzeichen (Wien), 1986. Vice-Pres., Atlantic Council of UK, 1993–; Mem., Exec. Cttee, Anglo-Austrian Soc., 1992–. Former Public Schools', British Universities' and National Junior Foil Champion; fenced for Cambridge Univ., 1957–60 (Captain, 1959–60); English Internat., 1958; Silver Medallist (Epée Team) Olympic Games, 1960; Gold Medallist, US Championships, 1961; Captained England, 1963. Represented Cambridge in Field Events Match with Oxford, 1959, 1960. *Publications:* articles on East/West relations and international security. *Recreations:* reading history; watching or participating in sport of any kind. *Address:* c/o Renaissance Capital, 1 Angel Court, Copthall Avenue, EC2R 7HJ. *Clubs:* Garrick, Epée, All England Fencing; Hawks (Cambridge).

ALEXANDER, Morag, OBE 2001; Convenor, Scottish Social Services Council, since 2001; *b* 10 Oct. 1943; *d* of Coll MacInnes and Sarah MacInnes (*née* Carberry); *m* 1964, Prof. Alan Alexander, *qv*; one *s* one *d*. *Educ:* Our Lady of Lourdes Sch., Glasgow; Glasgow Univ.; Lakehead Univ., Ont. (BA Hons). Res. Asst, ASTMS, 1971–73; editor and researcher, RIPA, 1973–82; freelance journalist and consultant, 1982–90; Founding Dir, TRAINING 2000 (Scotland) Ltd, Scottish Alliance for Women's Trng, 1990–92; Dir, EOC, Scotland, 1992–2001. Mem. Bd, Children in Scotland, 1995–2000 (Chm., Early Years Adv. Gp, 1995–). Member: Bd, Partnership for a Parliament, 1997; Scottish Senate, the Windsor Meetings, 1997–2000; Women's Adv. Gp to Scottish Exec. (formerly Scottish Office), 1997–2000; Expert Panel on Procedures and Standing Orders, Scottish Parlt, 1997–98; Bd, Turning Point Scotland, 1998–. Mem., Cttee of Inquiry into Student Finance, 1999–2000; Rep. of Scottish HEFC on Jt Equality Steering Gp, Equality Challenge UK, 2001–. Mem., Governing Body, Queen Margaret UC, 2001–. Founding Ed., Women in Europe, 1985–89; UK corresp., Women of Europe, 1987–92. *Recreations:* reading, walking, theatre, opera, spending time with family. *Address:* A'Chomraich, Dull, Aberfeldy, Perthshire PH15 2JQ.

ALEXANDER, Pamela Elizabeth; Chief Executive, Historic Buildings and Monuments Commission (English Heritage), 1997–2001; *b* 17 April 1954; *d* of Reginald William Purchase Alexander and Marion Elizabeth Alexander (*née* Ross); *m* 1994, Dr Roger Booker; two step *s* one step *d*. *Educ:* Lady Eleanor Holles Sch.; Newnham Coll., Cambridge (MA Geog.). Department of the Environment, 1975–94: Asst Private Sec. to Minister for Housing, 1978–81; seconded to UK Rep., EC, Brussels, 1981–82; Head of Publicity, 1987–90; Head, Finance, Deptl Services, 1990–92; Head, Housing Assocs Div., 1992–94; Dep. Chief Exec. (Ops), Housing Corp., 1995–97. Governor, Peabody Trust, 2000–. FRSA 1998. *Recreations:* choral singing, tennis, walking, talking. *Address:* 49 Westover Road, SW18 2RF.

ALEXANDER, Lt-Col Sir Patrick Desmond William C.; *see* Cable-Alexander.

ALEXANDER, Maj.-Gen. Paul Donald, CB 1989; MBE 1968; Policy Director (Army), Ministry of Defence, 1989–94; *b* 30 Nov. 1934; *s* of Donald Alexander and Alice Louisa Alexander (*née* Dunn); *m* 1958, Christine Winifred Marjorie Coakley; three *s*. *Educ:* Dudley Grammar Sch.; RMA Sandhurst; Staff Coll., Camberley; NDC; RCDS. Enlisted 1953; commissioned Royal Signals, 1955; served Hong Kong, E Africa, Germany; Comd 1st Div. Signal Regt, 1974–76; MoD, 1977–79; Comdr, Corps Royal Signals, 1st (Br) Corps, 1979–81; Dep. Mil. Sec. (B), 1982–85; Signal Officer in Chief (Army), 1985–89, retired. Col Comdt, RCS, 1989–95; Hon. Col, 35th Signal Regt, 1991–96. Chm., Royal Signals Assoc., 1990–95; Member: E Anglian TA&VRA, 1991– (County Chm., 1996–2000); ex-Service welfare cttees at local and nat. level. Chm., Lady Grover's Hosp. Fund, 1998–. *Publications:* occasional contribs to professional jls. *Recreations:* gardening, fly-fishing, unstructured hedonism. *Clubs:* Army and Navy; Royal Signals Yacht (Adm., 1989–93).

ALEXANDER, Richard Thain; *b* 29 June 1934; *s* of Richard Rennie Alexander and Gladys Alexander; *m* 1st, 1966, Valerie Ann Winn (marr. diss. 1985); one *s* one *d*; 2nd, 1987, Pat Hanson. *Educ:* Dewsbury Grammar Sch., Yorks; University Coll. London (LLB Hons). Articled with Sir Francis Hill, Messrs Andrew & Co., Lincoln, 1957–60; Asst Solicitor, Messrs McKinnell, Ervin & Holmes, Scunthorpe, 1960–64; Sen. Partner, Messrs Jones, Alexander & Co., Retford, 1964–85, Consultant, 1986–90. MP (C) Newark, 1979–97; contested (C) same seat, 1997. *Recreation:* golf. *Address:* 51 London Road, Newark, Notts NG24 1RZ. *Clubs:* Carlton; Newark Conservative, Newark Town and District.

ALEXANDER, Prof. (Robert) McNeill, CBE 2000; FRS 1987; FIBiol; Professor of Zoology, University of Leeds, 1969–99; *b* 7 July 1934; *s* of Robert Priestley Alexander and Janet McNeill; *m* 1961, Ann Elizabeth Coulton; one *s* one *d*. *Educ:* Tonbridge School; Trinity Hall, Cambridge (MA, PhD); DSc Wales. Asst Lectr in Zoology, University Coll. of North Wales, 1958, Lectr 1961, Sen. Lectr 1968; Head, Dept of Pure and Applied Zoology, Univ. of Leeds, 1969–78 and 1983–87. Visiting Professor: Harvard, 1973; Duke, 1975; Nairobi, 1976, 1977, 1978; Basle, 1986; St Francis Xavier Univ. (NS), 1990; Univ. of Calif, Davis, 1992. Mem., Biological Scis Cttee, SRC, 1974–77. Sec., Zool Soc. of London, 1992–99 (Mem. Council, 1988–91; Vice Pres., 1990–91); President: Soc. for Experimental Biology, 1995–97 (Vice Pres., 1993–95); Internat. Soc. for Vertebrate Morphology, 1997–. Ed., Royal Soc. Proc. B, 1998–. Hon. Mem., Amer. Soc. of Zoologists, 1986; Mem., Academia Europaea, 1996. Scientific Medal, Zoological Soc., 1969; Linnean Medal, Linnean Soc., 1979; Muybridge Medal, Internat. Soc. for Biomechanics, 1991. *Publications:* Functional Design in Fishes, 1967, 3rd edn 1974; Animal Mechanics, 1968, 2nd edn 1983; Size and Shape, 1971; The Chordates, 1975, 2nd edn 1981; Biomechanics, 1975; The Invertebrates, 1979; Locomotion of Animals, 1982; Optima for Animals, 1982, 2nd edn 1996; Elastic Mechanisms in Animal Movement, 1988; Dynamics of Dinosaurs and other Extinct Giants, 1989; Animals, 1990; The Human Machine, 1992; Exploring Biomechanics, 1992; Bones, 1994; Energy for Animal Life, 1999; papers on mechanics of human and animal movement. *Recreations:* history of natural history, local history. *Address:* 14 Moor Park Mount, Leeds LS6 4BU. *T:* (0113) 275 9218.

ALEXANDER, Rosemary Anne, (Mrs G. L. S. Dobry); Founder and Principal, English Gardening School, since 1983; *b* 15 Dec. 1937; *d* of late Charles Sleigh and of Violet Allison (*née* Petrie); *m* 1st, 1956, Walter Ronald Alexander, *qv* (marr. diss. 1975); two *s* two *d*; 2nd, 1982, His Honour George Leon Severyn Dobry, *qv*. *Educ:* Beacon Sch., Bridge of Allan, Stirlingshire. AIHort 1994. Trained as landscape architect; with Brian Clouston & Partners, Glasgow and London, 1973–79, then in private practice as garden designer. FRSA 1994; FSGD 1981. *Publications:* (with Tony Aldous) Landscape By Design, 1979; The English Gardening School, 1987; A Handbook for Garden Designers, 1994; Terraced, Town and Village Gardens, 1999; Garden Design, 2000; Caring for Your Garden, 2001. *Recreations:* opera, fishing, walking. *Address:* Sandhill Farm House, Rogate, Petersfield, Hants GU31 5HU. *T:* (01730) 818373.

ALEXANDER, Thomas John; Senior Research Fellow, Department of Educational Studies, University of Oxford; Director for Education, Employment, Labour and Social Affairs (formerly Social Affairs, Manpower and Education), OECD, Paris, 1989–2000; *b* 11 March 1940; *s* of late John Alexander and of Agnes Douglas Stewart (*née* Creedican); *m* 1961, Pamela Mason; two *s* one *d*. *Educ:* Royal High Sch., Edinburgh. Entered FO, 1958; MECAS, 1961; Third Sec. (Commercial), Kuwait, 1963; Asst Private Sec. to the Minister of State, FO, 1965; Second Sec. (Commercial), Tripoli, 1967; seconded to industry (ICI), 1970; Vice Consul (Commercial), Seattle, 1970; First Sec., FCO, 1974; special unpaid leave to act as Private Sec. to Sec.-Gen. of OECD, Paris, 1977–82; Counsellor and Head of Chancery, Khartoum, 1982–83; Dep. Head of Planning, 1984, Head of Private Office of Sec.-Gen., 1984–89, OECD. Member: Educn Bd, Open Soc. Inst., Budapest; Bd, Internat. Partnership Network. *Recreations:* squash, tennis. *Club:* Oriental.

ALEXANDER, Walter Ronald, CBE 1984; Chairman, Walter Alexander plc, 1979–90 (Managing Director, 1973–79); company director; *b* 6 April 1931; *s* of Walter Alexander and Katherine Mary Turnbull; *m* 1st, 1956, Rosemary Anne Sleigh (*see* R. A. Alexander) (marr. diss. 1975); two *s* two *d*; 2nd, 1979, Mrs Lorna Elwes, *d* of Lydia Duchess of Bedford. *Educ:* Loretto Sch.; Cambridge Univ. (MA Hons). Chm. and Man. Dir, Tayforth Ltd, 1961–71; Chm., Scottish Automobile Co. Ltd, 1971–73. Director: Scotcros plc, 1965–82 (Chm., 1972–82); Investors Capital Trust plc, 1967–99; Clydesdale Bank plc, 1971–96; RIT and Northern plc (formerly Great Northern Investment Trust plc), 1973–84; Dawson Internat. plc, 1979–96. Chm., Scottish Appeals Cttee, Police Dependants' Trust, 1974–81; Pres., Public Schs Golfing Soc., 1973–79; Chairman: PGA, 1982–85; Royal and Ancient Golf Club of St Andrews Trust, 1987–. Governor, Loretto Sch., 1961–89; Comr, Queen Victoria Sch., 1987–92. Scottish Free Enterprise Award, 1977. *Recreation:* golf. *Address:* Moonzie Mill, Balmullo, St Andrews, Fife KY16 0AH. *T:* (01334) 870990. *Clubs:* Royal and Ancient Golf (Captain, 1980–81); Hon. Company of Edinburgh Golfers; Prestwick Golf; Royal St George's Golf; Royal County Down Golf; Pine Valley Golf (USA).

ALEXANDER, Wendy Cowan; Member (Lab) Paisley North, Scottish Parliament, since 1999; Minister for Enterprise and Lifelong Learning, since 2000; *b* 27 June 1963; *d* of Rev. Douglas N. Alexander and Dr Joyce O. Alexander. *Educ:* Park Mains Sch., Erskine; Pearson Coll., Canada; Glasgow Univ. (MA Hons); Warwick Univ. (MA Econ); INSEAD, France (MBA). Research Officer, Scottish Lab. Party, 1988–92; with Booz Allen and Hamilton Internat., 1994–97; Advr to Sec. of State for Scotland, 1997–98; Minister for Communities, Scottish Parlt, 1999–2000. *Address:* Scottish Parliament, Edinburgh EH99 1SP.

See also D. G. Alexander.

ALEXANDER, William Gemmell, MBE 1945; *b* 19 Aug. 1918; *s* of Harold Gemmell Alexander and Winifred Ada Alexander (*née* Stott); *m* 1945, Janet Rona Page Alexander (*née* Elias); four *s* one *d*. *Educ:* Tre Arddur Bay Sch.; Sedbergh Sch.; Oxford Univ. (MA). Served War of 1939–45 (despatches, war stars and clasps): Driver Mechanic, 2nd Lieut, Lieut, Capt., Maj.; served in France, S Africa, Eritrea, Egypt, Middle East, Sicily, Italy, Algeria, NW Europe. HM Overseas Civil Service, 1946–59: Gilbert and Ellice Is, 1946–51; Mauritius, 1951–55; Cyprus, 1955–59; Man., Cooperative Wholesale Soc., Agricultural Dept, 1960–63; Dir, Internat. Cooperative Alliance, 1963–68; Dir-Gen., RoSPA, 1968–74; County Road Safety Officer, W Yorks MCC, 1974–78; Chm., W. H. Stott & Co. Ltd, 1979–83 (Dir, 1968–83). Mem., BSI Quality Assurance Council, 1975–83. Member: Bradford Dio. Bd of Finance, 1985–91; Ewecross Deanery Synod, 1985–99; Dent PCC, 1978–. Clerk, Dent Parish Council, 1980–86. Chm., Bd of Govs, Dent GS. AMBIM 1963. *Recreations:* all sports, long distance walking. *Address:* Flat 2, Seedsgill Barn, Deepdale Road, Dent, Sedbergh, Cumbria LA10 5QL. *T:* (01539) 625228. *Club:* Royal Commonwealth Society.

ALEXANDER, William John, FREng, FIMechE; Director, since 1994, Chief Executive, since 1997, Thames Water plc (Group Managing Director, 1996–97); *b* 15 Feb. 1947; *s* of John Fryer Alexander and Kathleen Mary (*née* Berry); *m* 1968, Dorothy Full; one *s* one *d*. FIMechE 1987; FREng (FEng 1996). British Coal: trng scheme, 1970; Chief Engr, Scottish Reg., 1982–86; Chief Mechanical Engr, 1986–87; Hd of Engrg, 1987–89; Thames Water Utilities: Engrg Dir, 1989–91; Technical Dir, 1991–92; Man. Dir, 1992–96. Dir, Laporte plc, 1999–. MInstD 1992. Freeman, City of London, 1994; Liveryman, Engineers' Co., 1997–. Hon. FIMM (Hon. FIMinE 1990). *Recreations:* classic cars, travel, swimming, walking. *Address:* (office) 14 Cavendish Place, W1G 9NU. *T:* (020) 7636 8686. *Clubs:* Mark's; Phyllis Court (Henley).

ALEXANDER-SINCLAIR of Freswick, Maj.-Gen. David Boyd, CB 1981; retired 1982; *b* 2 May 1927; *s* of late Comdr M. B. Alexander-Sinclair of Freswick, RN and late Avril N. Fergusson-Buchanan; *m* 1958, Ann Ruth, *d* of late Lt-Col Graeme Daglish; two *s* one *d*. *Educ:* Eton. Commnd into Rifle Bde, 1946, served in Germany, Kenya, Cyprus; ADC to GOC South Malaya District and Maj.-Gen. Bde of Gurkhas, 1950–51; psc 1958;

Bde Major, 6th Inf. Bde Gp, 1959–61; GSO2 (Dirg Staff) Staff Coll., 1963–65; comdg 3rd Bn Royal Green Jackets, 1967–69; MoD, 1965–67 and 1969–71; Comdr, 6th Armd Bde, 1971–73; Student, RCDS, 1974; GOC 1st Division, 1975–77; COS, UKLF, 1978–80; Comdt, Staff Coll., 1980–82.

AL FAYED, Mohamed; Chairman: Harrods Holdings plc, since 1994; Harrods Ltd, since 1985; Fulham Football Club, since 1997; Chairman and Owner, Ritz Hotel, Paris, since 1979; *b* Egypt, Jan. 1933; *m*; two *s* two *d* (and one *s* decd). *Educ:* Alexandria Univ. Hon. Mem., Emmanuel Coll., Cambridge, 1995. Officier, Légion d'Honneur, 1993 (Chevalier, 1985); La Grande Médaille de la Ville de Paris, 1985; Plaque de Paris, 1989; Commendatore, Order of Merit (Italy), 1990. *Address:* Harrods Ltd, Brompton Road, SW1 7XL.

ALFÖLDY, Tádé; Joint Chairman, Investor Holding Rt, since 1997; *b* 6 Aug. 1946; *s* of László Alföldy and Erzsébet (*née* Újvári); *m* 1968, Orsolya Baraczka; two *d. Educ:* Karl Marx Univ. of Economics, Budapest. Hungarian Shipping Agency, 1968–70; Hungarian Youth Union, 1970–74; Sec.-Gen., Internat. Cttee, Children's and Adolescents' Movements, 1974–79; joined Ministry of Foreign Affairs, Hungary, 1979–; Arab Desk Officer, 1979–80; 2nd, later 1st, Sec., Kuwait, 1980–85; British Desk Officer, 1985–89; Dir, N Atlantic Dept, 1989–90; Dep. State Sec., 1990–91; Ambassador: to Greece, 1991–94; to the UK, 1994–97. Vice Pres., Hungarian Atlantic Council, Budapest, 1997–. Mem., Foreign Policy Assoc., Budapest, 1991–. *Recreations:* family, tennis, gardening. *Address:* Investor Holding Rt, Budapest 1051, Szent István tér 11, Hungary.

ALFONSÍN, Dr Raúl Ricardo; President of Argentina, 1983–89; *b* 12 March 1927; *s* of Serafín Raúl Alfonsín and Ana María Foulkes; *m* 1949, María Lorenza Barreneche; three *s* three *d. Educ:* Regional Normal School, Chascomús; Gen. San Martín Mil. Acad.; Law Sch., Nat. Univ. of La Plata. Joined Radical Civic Union, 1945: Pres., 1983–91; Pres., Nat. Cttee, 1999–. Journalist, founder El Imparcial, Chascomús; Mem., Chascomús City Cttee, 1951, Mem. Council, 1954–55 (Pres., 1955 and 1959–61); Mem., Buenos Aires Provincial Legislature, 1952; Provincial Deputy, 1958–62; Deputy, Nat. Congress, 1963–66, 1973–76. Founder: Movimiento de Intransigencia y Renovación; Fundación Argentina para la Libre Información, 1992. Dr *hc:* New Mexico, New York, 1985; Bologna, Santiago de Compostela, Complutense de Madrid, 1988; Naples, 1990. Human Rights Prize (jtly), Council of Europe, 1986; numerous awards and foreign decorations. *Publications:* La Cuestión Argentina, 1980; Ahora, mi Propuesta Política, 1983; Que es el Radicalismo?, 1983; Alfonsín Responde, 1992; Democracia y Consenso, 1996. *Address:* Unión Cívica Radical, Alsina 1786, 1088 Buenos Aires, Argentina.

ALFORD, Richard Harding, OBE 1988; British Council Director, Italy, since 1996; *b* 28 Dec. 1943; *s* of Jack Harding Alford and Sylvia Alford; *m* 1968, Penelope Jane Wort; one *s* two *d. Educ:* Dulwich Coll.; Keble Coll., Oxford (BA; Diploma in History and Philosophy of Science). Asst Cultural Attaché, British Embassy, Prague, 1969–72; posts in ME Dept, Policy Res. Dept, and Educnl Contracts Dept, British Council, 1972–77; Project Planning Centre, Bradford Univ., 1977; Inst. of Educn, London Univ., 1978; British Council: Asst Rep., New Delhi, 1978–81; Dir, E Europe and N Asia Dept, 1982–85; Rep., Poland, 1985–89; Dir of Personnel, 1989–93; Regl Dir, Central Europe, 1993–96. Governor: Centre for Internat. Briefing, Farnham Castle, 1992–96; British Inst., Florence, 1996–. *Recreations:* tennis, theatre. *Address:* c/o The British Council, 10 Spring Gardens, SW1A 2BN. *T:* (020) 7930 8466. *Club:* Friends of Dulwich College Sports.

ALFRED, (Arnold) Montague; Deputy Chairman: Ward Lock Educational Co. Ltd, 1985–88; BLA Publishing Ltd, 1985–88; Ling Kee (UK) Ltd, 1985–88; retired; *b* 21 March 1925; *s* of Reuben Alfred and Bessie Alfred (*née* Arbesfield); *m* 1947, Sheila Jacqueline Gold; three *s. Educ:* Central Foundation Boys' Sch.; Imperial Coll., London; London Sch. of Economics. Head of Economics Dept, Courtaulds Ltd, 1953–69; Director, Nylon Div., Courtaulds Ltd, 1964–69; Dir, BPC Ltd, 1969–81; Chairman: BPC Publishing Ltd, 1971–81; Caxton Publishing Holdings Ltd, 1971–81; Second Permanent Sec., and Chief Exec., PSA, DoE, 1982–84. *Publications:* Discounted Cash Flow (jointly), 1965; Business Economics (jointly), 1968. Numerous articles in: Accountant, Textile Jl, Investment Analyst, etc. *Recreation:* active in Jewish community affairs. *Address:* c/o Institute of Directors, 168 Pall Mall, SW1Y 5ED.

ALGOMA, Bishop of, since 1995; **Rt Rev. Ronald Curry Ferris;** *b* 2 July 1945; *s* of Herald Bland Ferris and Marjorie May Ferris; *m* 1965, Janet Agnes (*née* Waller); two *s* four *d. Educ:* Toronto Teachers' Coll. (diploma); Univ. of W Ontario (BA); Huron Coll., London, Ont. (MDiv); Pacific Sch. of Religion (DMin 1995). Teacher, Pape Avenue Elem. School, Toronto, 1965; Principal Teacher, Carcross Elem. School, Yukon, 1966–68. Incumbent, St Luke's Church, Old Crow, Yukon, 1970–72; Rector, St Stephen's Memorial Church, London, Ont., 1973–81; Bishop of Yukon, 1981–95. Hon. DD Huron Coll., London, Ont, 1982; Hon. STD Thorneloe Univ., Ont, 1995. *Address:* (office) PO Box 1168, 619 Wellington Street E, Sault Ste Marie, ON P6A 5N7, Canada.

ALGOSAIBI, Dr Ghazi; Saudi Arabian Ambassador to the Court of St James's and to Ireland, since 1992; *b* 2 March 1940; *s* of Abdul Rahman and Fatma; *m* 1968, Sigrid Presser; three *s* one *d. Educ:* primary and secondary schs, Bahrain; Cairo Univ. (LLB 1961); Univ. of Southern California (MA Internat Relations 1964); Univ. of London (PhD 1970). King Saud University, Riyadh: Lectr, Faculty of Commerce, 1965–70, Asst Prof., 1970–74; Dean, Faculty of Commerce, and Hd, Pol Sci. Dept, 1971–73; Dir Gen., Saudi Railways, 1974–75; Minister: Industry and Electricity, 1975–82; Health, 1982–84; Ambassador to Bahrain, 1984–92. Numerous foreign awards. *Publications:* in Arabic: A Life in Poetry, 1980; From Here and There, 1981; Arabian Essays, 1982 (also in English); In My Humble Opinion, 1983; A Hundred Rose Petals, 1986; Development Face to Face, 1989; To Return to California as a Tourist, 1990; Cultural Invasion and Other Essays, 1991; Poems I Liked, 1992; The Gulf Crisis: an attempt to understand, 1992 (also in English); Poets Followed by Sinners: who are they?, 1994; An Apartment Called Freedom (novel), 1994 (trans. English 1996); The Dilemma of Development, 1995 (also in English); A Very Hot Political Dialogue, 1996; Al Asforiya, 1996; Conciliation, Fallacies and Other Issues, 1997; The Two of Them, 1997; The Myth, 1997; Voice from the Gulf, 1997; With Nagi and With Her, 1998; The Golden Cage (play), 1998; Yes, (Saudi) Minister!: a life in administration (autobiog.), 1999 (also in English); Seven (novel), 1999 (also in English); Thursday Break, 2000; Abu Shalaq, 2000; Dansko, 2000; *poetry:* Drops of Thirst; Battle Without Flag; Love Verses; You are Riyadh; Fever; Return to Old Places; The Complete Works of Poetry, 1960; Inside a Poet's Tent, 1988; Flowers in Sana's Braids, 1989; Necklace of Stones, 1991; Obituary of a Former Knight, 1992; Lyrics from Arabia, 1993 (also in English); From the Orient and the Desert, 1994; A Hundred Jasmine Flowers, 1995; Dusting the Colour from Roses, 1995 (also in English); Souhaim, 1996; Reading London's Face, 1997; Poems from the Pearl Islands; trans. Joseph Frankel, International Relations; anthologies. *Recreations:* swimming, fishing, table tennis. *Address:* Royal Embassy of Saudi Arabia, 30 Charles Street, W1X 7PM. *T:* (020) 7917 3000. *Clubs:* Brooks's, Travellers, Army and Navy (Hon. Mem.).

ALHAJI, Alhaji Abubakar, Hon. KBE 1989; High Commissioner for Nigeria in the United Kingdom, 1992–97; *b* 22 Nov. 1938; *m* Hajiya Amina Abubakar; three *s* three *d. Educ:* Univ. of Reading (BA Hons Political Economy); IMF Inst. course in public finance, 1974; Hague Inst. for Social Scis (course on industrialisation, 1970). Permanent Secretary, Ministries of: Trade, 1975–78; Industries, 1978–79; Finance, 1979–84; Nat. Planning, 1984–88; Hon. Minister, Ministries of: Budget and Planning, 1988–90; Finance and Economic Develt, 1990–92. Chm., Group 24 Cttee, 1991–92. Vice-Pres., Commonwealth Soc. for the Deaf. Sardauna of Sokoto, 1991. Hon. DSc Sokoto Univ., 1991. *Recreations:* horse riding, walking, reading. *Address:* c/o Ministry of Foreign Affairs, Abuja, Nigeria.

ALHEGELAN, Sheikh Faisal Al Abdul Aziz, Hon. GBE 1987; Grand Cross and Cordon, Order of King Abdul Aziz, Saudi Arabia; Saudi Arabian diplomat; Ambassador of Saudi Arabia to France, since 1996; *b* Jeddah, 7 Oct. 1929; *s* of Sheikh Abdulaziz Alhegelan and Fatima Al-Eissa; *m* 1961, Nouha Tarazi; three *s. Educ:* Faculty of Law, Fouad Univ., Cairo. Min. of Foreign Affairs, 1952–54; Saudi Arabian Embassy, Washington, USA, 1954–58; Chief of Protocol, Min. of Foreign Affairs, 1958–60; Polit. Adviser to King Sa'ud, 1960–61; Ambassador for Saudi Arabia to: Spain, 1961–68; Venezuela and Argentina (concurrently), 1968–75; Denmark, 1975–76; Court of St James's, 1976–79; USA, 1979–83; Minister of Health, Saudi Arabia, 1984–95. Chm. Bd of Dirs, Saudi Red Crescent Soc., 1984–. Order of Isabel la Católica, Spain; Gran Cordon, Orden del Libertador, Venezuela; Grande Official, Orden Rio Branco, Brazil; May Grand Decoration, Argentina. *Recreations:* golf, bridge, collecting selective books and objets d'art. *Address:* Ambassade du Royaume d'Arabie Saoudite, 5 avenue Hoche, 75008 Paris, France. *T:* 156794000, *Fax:* 156794002.

ALI, (Abul Hassan) Mahmood; High Commissioner for People's Republic of Bangladesh in London, 1996–2001; *b* 6 Feb. 1943; *s* of late Hassan Ali and Zubaida Ali; *m* 1968, Shaheen Khaliq; two *s. Educ:* Dhaka Univ. (BA Hons Econs 1962; MA 1963). Lectr in Econs, Dhaka Univ., 1964–66; joined Pakistan Foreign Service, 1966: New York, 1968–71; joined Bangladesh Liberation War in NY, 1971, served in NY, 1971–75; involved in organising Bangladesh Community in USA and Canada; served in New Delhi, 1977–79; Dir-Gen., Foreign Ministry, 1979–82; Beijing, 1983–86; Ambassador to Bhutan, 1986–90; Additional Foreign Sec., 1991–92; Ambassador to Germany, 1992–95; Sec. and A-Grade Ambassador, 1993; Ambassador to Kingdom of Nepal, Feb.–Oct. 1996. *Publication:* (contrib.) American Response to Bangladesh Liberation War, 1996. *Recreations:* tennis (playing), interest in sports, music, art and literature. *Address:* c/o Ministry of Foreign Affairs, Topkhana, Dhaka, Bangladesh. *Club:* Kurmitola Golf (Dhaka).

ALI, Rt Rev. Dr Michael N.; *see* Nazir-Ali.

ALISON, Rt Hon. Michael James Hugh; PC 1981; *b* 27 June 1926; *m* 1958, Sylvia Mary Haigh; two *s* one *d. Educ:* Eton; Wadham Coll., Oxford. Coldstream Guards, 1944–48; Wadham Coll., Oxford, 1948–51; Lazard Bros & Co. Ltd, 1951–53; London Municipal Soc., 1954–58; Conservative Research Dept, 1958–64. MP (C) Barkston Ash, 1964–83, Selby, 1983–97. Parly Under-Sec. of State, DHSS, 1970–74; Minister of State: Northern Ireland Office, 1979–81; Dept of Employment, 1981–83; PPS to Prime Minister, 1983–87; Second Church Estates Comr, 1987–97. *Publication:* (ed jtly) Christianity and Conservatism, 1990. *Club:* Cavalry and Guards.

See also T. J. S. Waterstone.

ALISON, William Andrew Greig, FLA; Director of Libraries, City of Glasgow, 1975–81; *b* 23 Oct. 1916; *m* 1942, Jessie Youngson Henderson; two *d. Educ:* Daniel Stewart's Coll., Edinburgh. Served War, Royal Air Force, 1940–46. Edinburgh Public Libraries, 1935–62: Assistant, 1935–46; Librarian, Fine Art Dept, 1946–55; Branch Librarian, 1955–61; Librarian, Scottish and Local History Depts, 1961–62; Glasgow City Libraries, 1962–81: Supt of District Libraries, 1962–64; Depute City Librarian, 1964–74; City Librarian, 1974–75. President: Scottish Library Assoc., 1975; Library Assoc., 1979 (also Mem. Council, 1979–82; Chm., Library Assoc. Publishing, 1981–82); Member: British Library Adv. Council, 1979–82; Nat. Library of Scotland Library Co-operation Cttee, 1974–81. British Council visits to: Zimbabwe, 1981; Bahrain, 1982; Syria, 1983. Church of Scotland elder. Silver Jubilee Medal, 1977. *Publication:* (assoc. ed.) New Library Buildings 1984–1989, 1990. *Recreations:* travel, philately. *Address:* St Mawgan, 103 Mossgiel Road, Glasgow G43 2BY. *T:* (0141) 632 6036.

ALIYEV, Heydar Alirza oglu; President, Republic of Azerbaijan, since 1993; *b* 10 May 1923; *s* of Alirza Aliyev and Izzat Aliyeva; *m* Zarifa Aliyeva (*d* 1985); one *s* one *d. Educ:* Azerbaijan Inst. of Industry (Dip.); Azerbaijan State Univ. (Dip.). Various positions, Azerbaijan State Security Orgns, 1941–69; First Sec., Azerbaijan Communist Party, 1969–82; Mem. Politburo, CPSU, 1976–87; First Dep. Chm., Council of Ministers, USSR, in Moscow, 1982–87; retd from Communist Party, 1991; Chairman: Supreme Mejlis (Parlt), Nakhichevan Autonomous Republic, 1991–93; Supreme Soviet (Parlt), Azerbaijan, 1993. Chm., New Azerbaijan Party, 1992–93. Hon. Dr: Baku State, 1994; Hojjat-Tapa, Turkey, 1994. Hero of Socialist Labour (USSR), 1979 and 1983. *Publications:* numerous articles on social, cultural, economic and political subjects published in foreign and domestic jls. *Recreations:* paintings, poetry, sport. *Address:* Office of the President, 19 Istiglaliyyat Strasse, Baku, Azerbaijan. *T:* (12) 988838, *Fax:* (12) 981414, 983328.

ALKER, Doug; freelance management consultant; Chief Executive, Royal National Institute for Deaf People, 1995–97; *b* 23 Nov. 1940. *Educ:* London Univ. (BSc (external) 1967); Birmingham Univ. (MBA 1993). Analytical Chemist, Pilkington Bros, 1959–64; Exptl Officer, ICI, 1964–85; Researcher, BBC, 1985–87; Royal National Institute for Deaf People: Principal Regl Officer, 1987; Dir, Community Services, 1987–90; Dir, Quality and Res., 1990–94. Member: Nat. Disability Council, 1995–2000; Exec. Cttee, RADAR, 1997–2000; Chair: E Lancs Deaf Soc., 1980–; Fedn of Deaf People, 1997–. Indep. Assessor for DETR, 1999–. Hon. Fellow, Univ. of Central Lancashire, 1995. *Address:* PO Box 11, Darwen, Lancs BB3 3GH.

AL KHALIFA, Shaikh Abdul Aziz bin Mubarak; Ministry of Foreign Affairs, Bahrain, since 2001; *b* 10 Oct. 1962; *m* 1988, Shaikha Lamees Daij Al Khalifa. *Educ:* Wellington Sch., Som; Newbury Coll. (HND); Amer. Univ. Sch. of Internat. Service, Washington (BA); Inst. for Social and Economic Policy in Middle East, Harvard. Prime Minister's Court: Researcher on Political and Economic Affairs, 1987–90; Asst Dir of Information, 1990–94; acting Dir of Admin and Public Relations, 1994–96; Ambassador for Bahrain to UK, Denmark, Ireland, Holland, Norway and Sweden, 1996–2001. *Address:* Ministry of Foreign Affairs, POB 547, Government House, Manama, Bahrain.

ALKIN, Lawrence Michael; Joint Chief Executive, Holmes Place plc, since 1997; *b* 16 June 1936; *s* of Henry and Phyllis Alkin. *Educ:* Mill Hill Sch.; University Coll. London (LLM). Sen. Partner, Alkin Colombotti and Partners, 1965–72; Managing Director: Filross Securities, 1972–; Holmes Place Ltd, 1979–96. *Recreations:* fishing (badly), cooking (moderately), dining out (well). *Address:* c/o Holmes Place plc, 17A Old Court Place, W8 4HP.

ALLAIN, Prof. Jean-Pierre Charles, MD, PhD; FRCPath, FMed Sci; Professor of Transfusion Medicine, University of Cambridge, since 1991; *b* 26 Jan. 1942; *s* of Jacques Louis Allain and Marthe Charlotte (*née* Petitjean); *m* 1st, 1962, DucDung Nguyen (marr. diss.); two *s* two *d*; 2nd, 1978, Helen Lee. *Educ:* Univ. of Paris (MD 1967; PhD 1986). FRCPath 1992. Asst Prof. of Haematol., Univ. of Paris, 1967–70; Dir, French Red Cross Haemophilia Centre, 1970–77; Head, Coagulation Res. Lab., Nat. Blood Transfusion Centre, Paris, 1977–81; Head, Dept of R&D Plasma Protein Derivatives, Nat. Blood Transfusion Centre, Paris, 1981–86; Dir of Med. Res., Diagnostic Div., Abbott Labs, Chicago, 1986–91; Dir, E Anglian Blood Transfusion Centre, 1991–94. FMed Sci 2000. *Publications:* 140 papers in learned jls incl. N Engl. Jl Med., Lancet, Jl of Clin. Invest., Jl Lab. Clin. Med., BMJ, Blood, Transfusion. *Recreations:* tennis, ceramics.

ALLAIRE, Paul Arthur; Chairman, 1991–2001, and Chief Executive Officer, 1990–99 and 2000–01, Xerox Corporation; *b* 21 July 1938; *s* of late Arthur E. Allaire and of Mrs G. P. Murphy; *m* 1963, Kathleen Buckley; one *s* one *d*. *Educ:* Worcester Polytechnic Inst., USA (BS Elect. Eng., 1960); Carnegie-Mellon Univ., USA (MS Industrial Admin, 1966). Engineer, Univac, 1960–62; Project Manager, General Electric, 1962–64; Manager Financial Planning and Pricing, Xerox Corp., 1966–70; Financial Controller, Rank Xerox Ltd, 1970–73; Xerox Corporation: Dir, Internat. Finance, 1973–74; Dir, Internat. Ops, 1974–75; Rank Xerox Ltd: Chief Staff Officer, 1975–79; Dep. Man. Dir, 1979–80; Man. Dir, 1980–83; Mem., Bd of Dirs; Sen. Vice-Pres., 1983–86, Pres., 1986–91, Xerox Corp. Member, Board of Directors: Fuji Xerox Co.; Sara Lee Corp.; SmithKline Beecham; Lucent Technologies; J. P. Morgan. Chm., Council on Competitiveness. Mem., Council on For. Relations. Member: Bd of Dirs, NY City Ballet; Bd, Catalyst. Member, Board of Trustees: Carnegie Mellon Univ. (Mem., Business Adv. Council, Grad. Sch. of Indust. Admin); Worcester Polytechnic Inst., Mass. Mem., Nat. Acad. of Engrg. *Recreations:* horse riding, tennis. *Address:* c/o Xerox Corporation, PO Box 1600, Stamford, CT 06904, USA.

ALLAIS, Prof. Maurice; Commandeur de la Légion d'honneur, 1989; Officier des Palmes académiques, 1949; Chevalier de l'économie nationale, 1962; Grand Officier de l'Ordre National du Mérite, 1993; French economist and engineer; *b* 31 May 1911; *s* of Maurice Allais and Louise (*née* Caubet); *m* 1960, Jacqueline Bouteloup; one *d*. *Educ:* Lycée Lakanal à Sceaux; Lycée Louis-le-Grand; Ecole Polytechnique; Ecole Nationale Supérieure des Mines de Paris. Engineer, Dept of Mines and Quarries, Nantes, 1937–43; Dir, Bureau de Documentation Minière, 1943–48; Prof. of Economic Analysis, Ecole Nationale Supérieure des Mines de Paris, 1944–88; Dir, Centre for Economic Analysis, 1946–; Prof. of Economic Theory, Inst. of Statistics, Univ. of Paris, 1947–68; research in economics, 1948–; Dir of Res., Centre National de la Recherche Scientifique, 1954–80; Prof., Graduate Inst. of Internat. Studies, Geneva, 1967–70; Dir, Clément Juglar Centre of Monetary Analysis, Univ of Paris, 1970–85. Fellow: Operations Res. Soc., 1958; Internat. Soc. of Econometrics, 1949. Mem. de l'Académie des Sciences Morales et Politiques, 1990; Hon. Mem., Amer. Econ. Assoc., 1976; Associate Foreign Member: US Nat. Acad. of Scis, 1989; Accademia Nazionale dei Lincei, Rome, 1991. Dr *hc*: Univ. of Groningen, 1964; Univ. of Mons, 1992; Amer. Univ. of Paris, 1992; Univ. of Lisbon, 1993; Ecole des Hautes Etudes Commerciales, 1993. Prizes from: L'Académie des Sciences, 1933; L'Académie des Sciences Morales et Politiques, 1954, 1959, 1983, 1984. Gravity Res. Foundn, 1959; also Lanchester Prize, Amer. Economic Assoc., 1958; Prix Galabert, 1959; Grand Prix André Arnoux, 1968; Gold Medal, Centre National de la Recherche Scientifique, 1978; Nobel Prize for Economics, 1988. *Publications* include: A la recherche d'une discipline économique, 1943, 2nd edn as Traité d'Economie Pure, 1952, 3rd edn 1994; Abondance ou misère, 1946; Economie et Intérêt, 1947, 2nd edn 1997; Les fondements comptables de la macroéconomique, 1954, 2nd edn 1992; Manifeste pour une société libre, 1959; L'Europe unie, route de la prosperité, 1960; The Role of Capital in Economic Development, 1963; Growth without Inflation, 1968; Les théories de l'équilibre économique général et de l'éfficacité maximale, 1971; Inequality and Civilization, 1973; L'impôt sur le capital et la réforme monétaire, 1977, 2nd edn 1988; La théorie générale des surplus, 1980, 2nd edn 1989; Frequency, Probability and Chance, 1982; Determination of Cardinal Utility, 1985; Les conditions monétaires d'une économie de marchés, 1987; Autoportraits, 1989; Pour l'indexation, 1990; Pour la réforme de la fiscalité, 1990; L'Europe face à son avenir, que faire, 1991; Erreurs et impasses de la construction européenne, 1992; Combats pour l'Europe, 1994; Cardinalism, 1994; L'Anisotropie de l'espace, 1997. *Address:* (office) 60 boulevard Saint Michel, 75006 Paris, France.

ALLAM, Peter John; Architect Principal in private practice of Peter Allam, Chartered Architect, Dollar, 1964–68, 1971–78 and since 1981; *b* 17 June 1927; *er s* of late Leslie Francis Allam and Annette Farquharson (*née* Lawson); *m* 1961, Pamela Mackie Haynes; two *d*. *Educ:* Royal High Sch., Edinburgh; Glasgow Sch. of Architecture. War service, 1944–48, Far East; commnd in Seaforth Highlanders, 1946. Architectural trng, 1948–53. Bahrain Petroleum Co., Engrg Div., 1954–55; Asst in private architectural practices, 1956–64; Partner in private practice of Haswell-Smith & Partners, Edinburgh, 1978–79; Director, Saltire Soc., 1968–70; Dir of Sales, Smith & Wellstood Ltd, Manfg Ironfounders, 1979–81. ARIBA 1964; FRIAS 1985 (Associate, 1964). Sen. Observer, IAM, 1994. VMSM 1999. *Recreations:* grandchildren, painting, caravanning, singing in the bath. *Address:* Seberham Flat, 1 Bridge Street, Dollar, Clackmannanshire FK14 7DF. *T:* (01259) 742973.

ALLAN; *see* Havelock-Allan.

ALLAN, Alexander Claud Stuart; Government e-envoy, 2000; *b* 9 Feb. 1951; *s* of Lord Allan of Kilmahew, DSO, OBE and of Maureen (*née* Stuart Clark); *m* 1978, Katie Christine Clemson. *Educ:* Harrow Sch.; Clare College, Cambridge; University College London (MSc). HM Customs and Excise, 1973–76; HM Treasury, 1976–92; secondments in Australia, 1983–84; Principal Private Sec. to Chancellor of the Exchequer, 1986–89; Under Sec. (Internat. Finance), 1989–90; Under Sec. (Gen. Expenditure Policy Gp), 1990–92; Principal Private Sec. to PM, 1992–97; High Comr, Australia, 1997–99. *Recreations:* Grateful Dead music, sailing, computers. *Address:* c/o Cabinet Office, 70 Whitehall, SW1A 2AS; *e-mail:* alex.allan@whitegum.com. *Club:* Royal Ocean Racing.

ALLAN, Andrew Norman; Chairman, Birmingham Repertory Theatre, since 2000; media consultant; *b* 26 Sept. 1943; *s* of Andrew Allan and Elizabeth (*née* Davison); *m* 1978, Joanna Forrest; two *s* one *d*, and two *d* of a former marriage. *Educ:* Birmingham Univ. (BA). Presenter, ABC Television, 1965–67; Producer: ITN, 1968; Thames Television, 1969–77; Head of News, Thames TV, 1977–78; Tyne Tees Television: Dir of Progs, 1978–82; Dep. Man. Dir, 1982–83; Man. Dir, 1983–84; Dir of Progs, Central Indep. TV, 1984–90; Managing Director: Central Broadcasting, 1990–93; Central Indep. TV, 1993–94; Chief Exec., 1994–95, Dir of Progs, 1996–98, Carlton TV. *Recreations:* reading, dining. *Address:* Wardington Lodge, Wardington, Banbury, Oxon OX17 1SE.

ALLAN, Christopher David; QC 1995; a Recorder, since 1993; *b* 5 April 1952; *s* of Herbert Roy Allan and Joan (*née* Womersly); *m* 1977, Lynne Margaret Hosking; one *s* three *d*. *Educ:* Teignmouth Grammar Sch.; Manchester Univ. (LLB). Called to the Bar, Gray's Inn, 1974; Mem., Northern Circuit, 1975–. *Recreations:* tennis, theatre, walking. *Address:* 12 Byrom Street, Manchester M3 4PF. *T:* (0161) 829 2100; 22 Old Buildings, WC2A 3UJ.

ALLAN, Colin Faulds, CB 1976; Chief Planning Inspector (Director of Planning Inspectorate), Department of the Environment, 1971–78, retired; *b* Newcastle upon Tyne, 1917; *s* of late Jack Stanley and Ruth Allan; *m* 1941, Aurea, 2nd *d* of Algernon Noble, Hexham; one *s* one *d*. *Educ:* Royal Grammar Sch., Newcastle upon Tyne; King's Coll. (Newcastle), Durham Univ. DipArch, ARIBA, DipTP (Distinction), FRTPI. Capt., RA, 1940–45; served in Iraq, India, Burma (despatches). Chief Asst to Dr Thomas Sharp, CBE, PPTPI, Planning Consultant, 1945–47; Area Planning Officer, Cumberland and Staffs CC, 1947–57; joined Housing and Planning Inspectorate, 1957; Chief Housing and Planning Inspector, DoE (formerly Min. of Housing and Local Govt), 1967–71. *Recreations:* painting, bird-watching, eighteenth-century wineglasses. *Address:* Fieldfares, Chinthurst Lane, Shalford, Guildford, Surrey GU4 8JR. *T:* (01483) 561528.

ALLAN, Diana Rosemary, (Mrs R. B. Allan); *see* Cotton, D. R.

ALLAN, Douglas; *see* Allan, J. D.

ALLAN, George Alexander, MA; Headmaster, Robert Gordon's College, Aberdeen, 1978–96; *b* 3 Feb. 1936; *s* of William Allan and Janet Peters (*née* Watt); *m* 1962, Anne Violet Veevers; two *s*. *Educ:* Daniel Stewart's Coll., Edinburgh; Edinburgh Univ. (MA 1st Cl. Hons Classics; Bruce of Grangehill Scholar, 1957). Classics Master, Glasgow Acad., 1958–60; Daniel Stewart's College: Classics Master, 1960–63; Head of Classics, 1963–73; Housemaster, 1966–73; Schoolmaster Fellow, Corpus Christi Coll., Cambridge, 1972; Dep. Headmaster, Robert Gordon's Coll., 1973–77. Headmasters' Conference: Sec., 1980–86, Chm., 1988, 1989, Scottish Div.; Mem. Cttee, 1982, 1983; Mem., ISIS Scotland Cttee, 1984–93; Council Mem., Scottish Council of Indep. Schs, 1988–96, 1997–. Dir, Edinburgh Acad., 1996–; Gov., Welbeck Coll., 1980–89. Mem., Scottish Adv. Cttee, ICRF, 1996–97. *Recreations:* golf, gardening, music. *Address:* Maxwiel, 5 Abbey View, Kelso TD5 8HX. *T:* (01573) 225128.

ALLAN, Rt Rev. Hugh James Pearson, DD; Assistant Bishop of Nova Scotia, 1991–94; *b* 7 Aug. 1928; *s* of Hugh Blomfield Allan and Agnes Dorothy (*née* Pearson); *m* 1955, Beverley Edith Baker; one *s* three *d*. *Educ:* St John's Coll., Univ. of Manitoba (LTh 1955, BA 1957). Deacon 1954, priest 1955; Assistant: St Aidan's, Winnipeg, 1954; All Saints, Winnipeg, 1955; Missionary, Peguis Indian Reserve, 1956–60; Rector, St Mark's, Winnipeg, 1960–68; Hon. Canon, Diocese of Rupert's Land, 1967; Rector, St Stephen's Swift Current, Sask., 1968–70; Rural Dean of Cypress, 1968–70; Dean of Qu'Appelle and Rector of St Paul's Cathedral, Regina, Sask., 1970–74; Bishop of Keewatin, 1974–91. Hon. DD, St John's Coll., Univ. of Manitoba, 1974. *Recreations:* ornithology, boating. *Address:* 26 Baldry Bay, Winnipeg, MB R3T 3C4, Canada.

ALLAN, Ian, OBE 1995; Chairman, Ian Allan Group Ltd, since 1962; *b* 29 June 1922; *s* of George A. T. Allan, OBE, and Mary Louise (*née* Barnes); *m* 1947, Mollie Eileen (*née* Franklin); two *s*. *Educ:* St Paul's Sch. Joined Southern Railway Co., 1939. Founded Ian Allan Ltd, Publishers, 1945; other cos co-ordinated into Ian Allan Group Ltd, 1962. Dir, Dart Valley Light Railway PLC, 1968– (Chm., 1976–87). Governor, Christ's Hosp., 1944–, Almoner, 1980–89; Chm., King Edward's Sch., Witley, 1983–95 (Governor, 1975–95); Treas., Bridewell Royal Hosp. 1983–95. Vice President: Transport Trust, 1979–; Assoc. of Indep. Rlys, 1997– (Chm., 1987–97); Heritage Rlys Assoc., 1996–; Mem., Transport Users Consultative Cttee for London, 1982–84. Pres., Main Line Steam Trust (Great Central Rly), 1995–. Patron, Mid Hants Rly plc, 1994–. Freeman, City of London, 1986. FCIT 1992. *Publications:* compiled and edited many books on railways and transport subjects, 1939–. *Recreations:* swimming, touring, miniature railways, Freemasonry. *Address:* Terminal House, Shepperton TW17 8AS. *T:* (01932) 255500; The Jetty, Middleton-on-Sea, Bognor Regis, W Sussex PO22 7TS. *T:* (01243) 593378.

ALLAN, James Nicholas, CMG 1989; CBE 1976; HM Diplomatic Service, retired; *b* 22 May 1932; *s* of late Morris Edward Allan and Joan Bach; *m* 1961, Helena Susara Crouse (*d* 2001); one *s* one *d*. *Educ:* Gresham's Sch.; London Sch. of Economics. HM Forces, 1950–53. Asst Principal, CRO, 1956–58; Third, later Second Sec., Cape Town/Pretoria, 1958–59; Private Sec. to Parly Under-Sec., 1959–61; First Secretary: Freetown, 1961–64; Nicosia, 1964; CRO, later FCO, 1964–68; Head of Chancery, Peking, 1969–71; Luxembourg, 1971–73; Counsellor, seconded to Northern Ireland Office, Belfast, 1973–75; Counsellor, FCO, 1976; Head of Overseas Inf. Dept., FCO, 1978–81 (Governor's Staff, Salisbury, Dec. 1979–March 1980); High Comr in Mauritius, 1981–85, concurrently Ambassador (non-resident) to the Comoros, 1984–85; Ambassador to Mozambique, 1986–89; Sen. Directing Staff, RCDS, 1989–92. Mem., Commonwealth Observer Gp, S African elecns, 1994. *Address:* 7 The Orchard, SE3 0QS. *Club:* Athenæum.

See also Baron Bach.

ALLAN, Prof. James Wilson, DPhil; Professor of Eastern Art, University of Oxford, since 1996; Keeper of Eastern Art, Ashmolean Museum, Oxford, since 1991; Fellow of St Cross College, Oxford, since 1990; *b* 5 May 1945; *s* of John Bellerby Allan and Evelyn Mary Allan; *m* 1970, Jennifer Robin Hawksworth; two *s* two *d*. *Educ:* Marlborough Coll.; St Edmund Hall, Oxford (MA 1966; DPhil 1976). Eastern Art Department, Ashmolean Museum: Asst Keeper, 1966–88; Sen. Asst Keeper, 1988–91. *Publications:* Medieval Middle Eastern Pottery, 1971; Persian Metal Technology 700–1300 AD, 1978; Islamic Metalwork: the Nuhad Es-Said Collection, 1982; Nishapur: metalwork of the early Islamic period, 1982; Metalwork of the Islamic World: the Aron Collection, 1986; (ed) Creswell: A Short Account of Early Muslim Architecture, 1989; (with B. Gilmour) Persian Steel: the Tanavoli Collection, 2000. *Recreations:* music, ornithology, walking, travel. *Address:* Ashmolean Museum, Oxford OX1 2PH. *T:* (01865) 278068.

ALLAN, (John) Douglas; Sheriff of Lothian and Borders at Edinburgh, since 2000; *b* 2 Oct. 1941; *s* of Robert Taylor Allan and late Christina Helen Blythe Reid or Allan; *m* 1966, Helen Elizabeth Jean Aiton or Allan; one *s* one *d*. *Educ:* George Watson's Coll.; Edinburgh Univ. (BL); Napier Coll., Edinburgh (DMS). Solicitor and Notary Public. Solicitor, 1963–67; Depute Procurator Fiscal, 1967–71; Sen. Legal Asst, Crown Office, 1971–76; Asst Procurator Fiscal, Glasgow, 1976–77; Sen. Asst Procurator Fiscal, Glasgow, 1978–79; Asst Solicitor, Crown Office, 1979–83; Regl Procurator Fiscal for Lothian and Borders and Procurator Fiscal for Edinburgh, 1983–88; Sheriff of South Strathclyde, Dumfries and Galloway at Lanark, 1988–2000. Chm., Judicial Commn, Gen. Assembly of C of S, 1998–. Bd Mem., Scottish Children's Reporter Admin, 1995–. Pres., Sheriffs' Assoc., 2000– (Vice Pres., 1997–2000; Sec., 1991–97). *Recreations:* youth work, church work, walking. *Address:* Sheriff Court, 27 Chambers Street, Edinburgh EH1 1LB; Minard, 80 Greenbank Crescent, Edinburgh EH10 5SW. *T:* (0131) 447 2593.

ALLAN, John Murray; Chief Executive, Exel (formerly Ocean Group) plc, since 1994; *b* 20 Aug. 1948; *s* of Archibald John and Anna Allan; *m*; two *d*. *Educ:* Edinburgh Univ. (BSc Hons Mathematical Sci.). Brand Manager, Lever Bros, 1970–73; Mkting Manager, Bristol Myers, 1973–77; Fine Fare: Mkting Dir, 1977–83; Dir, 1980; Mkting and Buying Dir, 1983–84; Dir and Gen. Manager, 1984–85; BET: Divl Chm., 1985–87; Dir, 1987–94. Mem., Southern Region Council, CBI, 1997–; Chm., CBI Transport Policy Cttee, 1998–. Chm., Mkting Soc. of GB, 1983–84. Trustee, Univ. of Edinburgh Develt Trusts, 1991–2000. FInstD 1986 (Mem. Council, 1991–99); CIMgt 1995. FRSA 1995. *Recreations:* reading, conversation, history. *Address:* Exel plc, Ocean House, The Ring, Bracknell, Berks RG12 1AN. *T:* (01344) 302000.

ALLAN, Richard Andrew; Director, Regional Policy, Department for Transport, Local Government and the Regions, since 2001; *b* 28 Feb. 1948; *s* of late Kenneth and of Mary Allan; *m* 1975, Katharine Mary Tait; one *s* one *d*. *Educ:* Bolton Sch.; Balliol Coll., Oxford (MA Mod. Hist.). VSO, Nigeria, 1970. Asst Principal, DTI, 1970; Asst British Trade Comr, Hong Kong, 1973; Department of Industry: Private Sec. to Perm. Sec., 1974–75; Principal, 1975–79; First Sec. (Civil Aviation and Shipping), Washington, 1980–84; Department of Transport: Asst Sec., 1984; Principal Private Sec. to Sec. of State for Transport, 1985–87; Under Sec., 1988; seconded to BRB, 1988–90; Dir of Personnel, 1990–94; Head, Urban and Local Transport Directorate, 1994–97; Dir, London Transport Directorate, DETR, 1997–98; Dir, New London Governance, Govt Office for London, 1998–2000; Dir, Regl Policy and Regeneration, DETR, 2000–01. *Recreations:* choral singing, theatre, walking. *Address:* Department for Transport, Local Government and the Regions, Eland House, Bressenden Place, SW1E 5DU.

ALLAN, Richard Beecroft; MP (Lib Dem) Sheffield, Hallam, since 1997; *b* 11 Feb. 1966; *s* of John and Elizabeth Allan; *m* 1991, Louise Maria Netley; one *d*. *Educ:* Pembroke Coll., Cambridge (BA Hons Archaeology and Anthropology); Bristol Polytechnic (MSc Information Technology). Archaeologist, 1988–90; NHS Computer Manager, 1991–97. *Recreation:* visiting sites of historical interest and natural beauty. *Address:* House of Commons, SW1A 0AA. *T:* (020) 7219 3000.

ALLAN, William Roderick Buchanan; formerly Arts Consultant to United Technologies Corporation, working with Tate Gallery, National Portrait Gallery and National Maritime Museum; *b* 11 Sept. 1945; *s* of James Buchanan Allan and Mildred Pattenden; *m* 1973, Gillian Gail Colgan; two *s*. *Educ:* Stowe; Trinity Coll., Cambridge (MA Hons History, 1970). Joined staff of The Connoisseur, 1972, Editor 1976–80; Editorial Consultant to Ommific, 1980–83. Author of seven radio plays with nineteenth century historical themes. *Publications:* contrib. to several books dealing with British history; contrib. to History Today, The Connoisseur, and Antique Collector. *Recreations:* military history, cooking. *Address:* 52 Jamieson House, Edgar Road, Hounslow, Middlesex TW4 5QH.

ALLANBRIDGE, Hon. Lord; William Ian Stewart; a Senator of the College of Justice in Scotland, 1977–95; *b* 8 Nov. 1925; *s* of late John Stewart, FRIBA, and Mrs Maysie Shepherd Service or Stewart, Drimfearn, Bridge of Allan; *m* 1955, Naomi Joan Douglas, *d* of late Sir James Boyd Douglas, CBE, and Lady Douglas, Barstibly, Castle Douglas; one *s* one *d*. *Educ:* Loretto; Glasgow and Edinburgh Univs. Sub-Lt, RNVR, 1944–46. Called to the Bar, 1951; QC (Scot.) 1965; Advocate-Depute, 1959–64; Mem., Criminal Injuries Compensation Bd, 1969–70; Home Advocate-Depute, 1970–72; Solicitor-General for Scotland, 1972–74; Temp. Sheriff-Principal of Dumfries and Galloway, Apr.-Dec. 1974; Justice of Appeal, Republic of Botswana, 1996–99. Mem., Criminal Injuries Compensation Bd, 1976–77. *Address:* 60 Northumberland Street, Edinburgh EH3 6JE. *T:* (0131) 556 2823. *Club:* New (Edinburgh).

ALLARDICE, His Honour William Arthur Llewellyn; DL; a Circuit Judge, 1972–96 (Midland and Oxford Circuit); *b* 18 Dec. 1924; *s* of late W. C. Allardice, MD, FRCSEd, JP, and late Constance Winifred Allardice; *m* 1956, Jennifer Ann, *d* of late G. H. Jackson; one *s* one *d*. *Educ:* Stonyhurst Coll.; University Coll., Oxford (MA). Open Schol., Classics, 1942; joined Rifle Bde, 1943, commnd 1944; served with 52nd LI, Europe and Palestine, 1945; Oxford, 1946–48; called to Bar, Lincoln's Inn, 1950; practised Oxford Circuit, 1950–71. Chm., Trustees, William Salt Liby, 1990–96. DL Staffs, 1980. *Recreations:* local history, matters equestrian. *Address:* c/o Stafford Crown and County Courts, Stafford ST18 2QQ. *T:* (01785) 255217.

See also H. O. Blacksell.

ALLASON, Lt-Col James Harry, OBE 1953; *b* 6 Sept. 1912; *s* of late Brigadier-General Walter Allason, DSO; *m* 1946, Nuala Elveen (marr. diss. 1974), *d* of late J. A. McArevey, Foxrock, Co. Dublin; two *s*. *Educ:* Haileybury; RMA, Woolwich. Commissioned RA, 1932; transferred 3rd DG, 1937; War Service India and Burma, 1939–44; retired 1953. Member Kensington Borough Council, 1956–65. Contested (C) Hackney Central, General Election, 1955; MP (C) Hemel Hempstead, 1959–Sept. 1974; PPS to Sec. of State for War, 1960–64. *Address:* 82 Ebury Mews, SW1W 9NX. *T:* (020) 7730 1576. *Clubs:* White's; Royal Yacht Squadron.

See also R. W. S. Allason.

ALLASON, Rupert William Simon; European Editor, World Intelligence Review (formerly Intelligence Quarterly), since 1985; *b* 8 Nov. 1951; *s* of Lt-Col J. H. Allason, *qv*; *m* 1979, Nicole Jane (marr. diss. 1996), *y d* of late M. L. Van Moppes; one *s* one *d*. *Educ:* Downside; Grenoble Univ.; London Univ. (external). Special Constable, 1975–82. BBC TV, 1978–82. Contested (C): Kettering, 1979; Battersea, 1983. MP (C) Torbay, 1987–97; contested (C) same seat, 1997. *Publications:* The Branch: A History of the Metropolitan Police Special Branch 1883–1983, 1983; *as Nigel West:* non-fiction: Spy! (with Richard Deacon), 1980; MI5: British Security Service Operations 1909–45, 1981; A Matter of Trust: MI5 1945–72, 1982; MI6: British Secret Intelligence Service Operations 1909–45, 1983; Unreliable Witnesses: espionage myths of World War II, 1984; Garbo (with Juan Pujol), 1985; GCHQ: The Secret Wireless War, 1986; Molehunt, 1987; The Friends: Britain's post-war secret intelligence operations, 1988; Games of Intelligence, 1989; Seven Spies Who Changed the World, 1991; Secret War, 1992; The Illegals, 1993; (ed) Faber Book of Espionage, 1993; (ed) Faber Book of Treachery, 1995; The Secret War for the Falklands, 1997; Counterfeit Spies, 1998; (with Oleg Tsarev) The Crown Jewels: the British secrets at the heart of the KGB archives, 1998; (ed) British Security Co-ordination: the secret history of British Intelligence in the Americas 1940–1945, 1998; Venona: the greatest secret of the Cold War, 1999; The Third Secret, 2000; fiction: The Blue List, 1989; Cuban Bluff, 1990; Murder in the Commons, 1992; Murder in the Lords, 1994. *Recreation:* sailing close to the wind. *Address:* 6 Burton Mews, SW1W 9EP. *Clubs:* White's, Special Forces; Royal Yacht Squadron (Cowes).

ALLAUN, Frank; *b* 27 Feb. 1913; *s* of Harry and Hannah Allaun; *m* 1st, 1941, Lilian Ball (*d* 1986); one *s* one *d*; 2nd, 1989, Millie Bobker. *Educ:* Manchester Grammar Sch. BA (Com); ACA. Town Hall Correspondent, and later Industrial Correspondent, Manchester Evening News; Northern Industrial Correspondent, Daily Herald; Editor, Labour's Northern Voice, 1951–67. Mem., NUJ; formerly Mem. AEU and Shop Assistants' Union; Vice President: Labour Action for Peace, 2001– (Pres., 1965–2001); Campaign for Nuclear Disarmament, 1983–; helped organise first Aldermaston march. MP (Lab) East Salford, 1955–83; PPS to the Secretary of State for the Colonies, Oct. 1964–March 1965, resigned. Mem., Labour Party National Executive, 1967–83, Dep. Chm., 1977–78, Chm., 1978–79. *Publications:* Stop the H Bomb Race, 1959; Heartbreak Housing, 1966; Your Trade Union and You, 1950; No Place Like Home, 1972; The Wasted '30 Billions, 1975; Questions and Answers on Nuclear Weapons, 1981; Spreading the News: a guide to media reform, 1989; The Struggle for Peace, 1992; numerous broadcasts. *Recreations:* walking, swimming. *Address:* 11 Eastleigh Road, Prestwich, Manchester M25 0BQ. *T:* (0161) 740 5085.

ALLAWAY, Percy Albert, CBE 1973; FREng; Director, EMI Ltd, 1965–81; Chairman, EMI Electronics Ltd, 1968–81; Member, Executive Management Board, THORN EMI Ltd, 1980–81, Consultant, 1981–82; *b* 22 Aug. 1915; *s* of Albert Edward Allaway and Frances Beatrice (*née* Rogers); *m* 1959, Margaret Lilian Petyt. *Educ:* Southall Technical College. FREng (FEng 1980); FIProdE, FIEE, FIQA. Trained EMI Ltd, 1930–35, returned 1940; Man. Dir, 1961–81, Chm., 1969–81, EMI Electronics Ltd; Chairman: EMI-Varian Ltd, 1969–81; EMI-MEC Ltd, 1968–81; Director: Nuclear Enterprises Ltd, 1961–81; SE Labs (EMI) Ltd, 1967–81. Pres., EEA, 1969–70 (former Mem. Council). Chm., Defence Industries Quality Assurance Panel, 1971–78; Past Chm. and Hon. Mem., NCQR; Member: Nat. Electronics Council, 1965–80; Raby Cttee, 1968–69; Parly and Scientific Cttee, 1976–82; Pres., IERE, 1975; a Vice-Pres., and Mem. Council, IQA; Member: Bd and Exec. Cttee, CEI, 1974–78 (Vice-Chm., 1979–80, Chm., 1980–81); Design Council, 1978–80; PO Engrg Adv. Cttee, 1977–81, British Telecom Engrg Adv. Cttee, 1981–82. Mem., Court and Council, Brunel Univ., 1976–82. Liveryman, 1978, and Mem. Court, 1981–86, Worshipful Co. of Scientific Instrument Makers. FRSA. DTech (hc) Brunel, 1973. *Address:* Kroller, 54 Howards Wood Drive, Gerrards Cross, Bucks SL9 7HW. *T:* (01753) 885028.

ALLCHIN, Rev. Canon Arthur Macdonald; Hon. Professor, University of Wales, Bangor, since 1992; *b* 20 April 1930; *s* of late Dr Frank Macdonald Allchin and Louise Maude Allchin. *Educ:* Westminster Sch.; Christ Church, Oxford (BLitt, MA); Cuddesdon Coll., Oxford. Curate, St Mary Abbots, Kensington, 1956–60; Librarian, Pusey House, Oxford, 1960–69; Warden, Community of Sisters of Love of God, Oxford, 1967–; Res. Canon of Canterbury, 1973–87, Hon. Canon, 1988–. Programme Dir, St Theosevia Centre for Christian Spirituality, Oxford, 1987–96. Visiting Lecturer: General Theological Seminary, NY, 1967 and 1968; Catholic Theological Faculty, Lyons, 1980; Trinity Inst., NY, 1983; Vis. Prof., Nashotah House, Wisconsin, 1984, 1995. Editor, Sobornost, 1960–77; Jt Editor, Christian, 1975–80. Hon. DD: Bucharest Theol Inst., 1977; Nashotah House, 1985; Aarhus, 1992; Wales, 1993. *Publications:* The Silent Rebellion, 1958; The Spirit and the Word, 1963; (with J. Coulson) The Rediscovery of Newman, 1967; Ann Griffiths, 1976; The World is a Wedding, 1978; The Kingdom of Love and Knowledge, 1979; The Dynamic of Tradition, 1981; A Taste of Liberty, 1982; The Joy of All Creation, 1984, 2nd edn 1993; (with E. de Waal) Threshold of Light, 1986; Participation in God, 1988; The Heart of Compassion, 1989; Landscapes of Glory, 1989; Praise Above All, 1991; (ed with D. Jasper and contrib.) Heritage and Prophecy, 1993; God's Presence Makes the World, 1997; N. F. S. Grundtvig: an introduction to his life and work, 1997; Resurrection's Children, 1998; (with D. Morgan and P. Thomas) Sensuous Glory: the poetic vision of D. Gwenallt Jones, 2000; (ed with S. Bradley and contrib.) Grundtvig in International Perspective, 2000; contrib. Studia Liturgica, Irenikon, Theology, Eastern Churches Review, Worship, One in Christ, Planet, Logos, Collectanea Cisterciensia. *Recreations:* music, poetry, enjoying hill country. *Address:* 1 Trem yr Wyddfa, Bangor LL57 2ER. *T:* (01248) 353744.

See also F. R. Allchin.

ALLCHIN, Frank Raymond, PhD; FBA 1981; Fellow of Churchill College, since 1963, and Reader in Indian Studies, 1972–90, University of Cambridge; Reader Emeritus, since 1990; *b* 9 July 1923; *s* of late Frank MacDonald Allchin and Louise Maude Wright; *m* 1951, Bridget Gordon; one *s* one *d*. *Educ:* Westminster Sch.; Regent Street Polytechnic; Sch. of Oriental and African Studies, London Univ. (BA, PhD 1954); MA Cantab. Lectr in Indian Archaeology, SOAS, 1954–59; Univ. Lectr in Indian Studies, Cambridge, 1959–72. Jt Dir, Cambridge Univ. (British) Archaeol Mission to Pakistan, 1975–92. Chm., Ancient India and Iran Trust, 1995– (Treas., 1978–); Vice Chm., British Assoc. for Conservation of Cultural Heritage of Sri Lanka, 1982–91; Dir, British Anuradhapura Project, Sri Lanka, 1989–93. Consultant: UNESCO, 1969, 1972, 1975; UNDP, 1971. *Publications:* Piklihal Excavations, 1960; Utnur Excavations, 1961; Neolithic Cattle Keepers of South India, 1963; Kavitāvalī, 1964; The Petition to Rām, 1966; (with B. Allchin) Birth of Indian Civilization, 1968; (with N. Hammond) The Archaeology of Afghanistan, 1978; (with D. K. Chakrabarti) Sourcebook of Indian Archaeology, vol. 1, 1979, vol 2, 1997; (with B. Allchin) The Rise of Civilization in India and Pakistan, 1982; (jtly) The Archaeology of Early Historic South Asia, 1995; (with B. Allchin) The Origins of a Civilisation, 1997; contribs to learned journals. *Recreations:* gardening, walking. *Address:* 2 Shepreth Road, Barrington, Cambridge CB2 5SB. *T:* (01223) 870494. *Clubs:* Royal Over-Seas League; India International Centre (New Delhi).

See also Rev. Canon A. M. Allchin.

ALLCOCK, Stephen James; QC 1993; *b* 29 Jan. 1952; *s* of James Allcock and Pamela Eve Allcock. *Educ:* Bristol Grammar Sch.; Jesus Coll., Cambridge (BA). Called to the Bar, Gray's Inn, 1975; private practice, 1977–. *Recreations:* motor cars, business, stock market, godfatherhood. *Address:* PricewaterhouseCoopers, 1 London Bridge, SE1 9QL. *Club:* Groucho.

ALLDAY, Coningsby, CBE 1971; BSc (Hons); Chairman and Chief Executive, British Nuclear Fuels plc, 1983–86 (Managing Director, 1971–83); *b* 21 Nov. 1920; *s* of late Esca and Margaret Allday; *m* 1st, 1945, Iris Helena, (Bobbin), Adams (*d* 1990); one *s* one *d*; 2nd, 1993, Rosalind Roberts. *Educ:* Solihull Sch.; BSc (Hons) Chemistry, London. CEng, FIChemE 1979; CIMgt (CBIM 1984). ICI, 1939–59; UKAEA, 1959–71: Chief Chemist, Technical Dir, Commercial Dir, Dep. Man. Dir; Mem. UKAEA, 1976–86. Chairman, NIMTECH NW, 1986–90; Director: North Region, National Westminster Bank, 1985–92; Sonomatic Ltd, 1988–90. FRSA. Hon. DSc Salford, 1985. Chevalier, Légion d'Honneur, 1983.

ALLDIS, Air Cdre Cecil Anderson, CBE 1962; DFC 1941; AFC 1956; RAF (retd); *b* 28 Sept. 1918; 2nd *s* of John Henry and Margaret Wright Alldis, Birkenhead; *m* 1942, Jeanette Claire Tarrant, *d* of Albert Edward Collingwood and Aida Mary Tarrant, Johannesburg; no *c*. *Educ:* Birkenhead Institute; Emmanuel Coll., Cambridge (MA). Served War, 1939–45 (despatches, DFC): Pilot, Wing Comdr, RAF, Bomber Command. Asst Air Attaché, Moscow, 1947–49; Flying and Staff appts, RAF, 1949–59; Dir of Administrative Plans, Air Ministry, 1959–62; Air Attaché, Bonn, 1963–66. Retd from RAF and entered Home Civil Service, 1966; MoD, 1966–69; seconded to HM Diplomatic Service, 1969; Counsellor (Defence Supply), HM Embassy, Bonn, 1969–80; retired from Home Civil Service, 1980. Sec. Gen., The Air League, 1982–90. *Recreations:*

walking, reading. *Address:* Tudor Cottage, Oxshott Way, Cobham, Surrey KT11 2RU. *T:* (01932) 866092.

ALLDIS, John; conductor; *b* 10 Aug. 1929; *s* of W. J. and N. Alldis; *m* 1960, Ursula Margaret Mason; two *s*. *Educ:* Felsted School; King's Coll., Cambridge (MA). ARCO. Formed John Alldis Choir, 1962; Founder and Conductor, London Symphony Chorus, 1966–69; Conductor, London Philharmonic Choir, 1969–82; Joint Chief Conductor, Radio Denmark, 1971–77; Conductor, Groupe Vocal de France, 1979–83; Chorus Master, Hallé Choir, 1992–93. Choral Prof., Guildhall Sch. of Music, 1966–79 (FGSM 1976); Music Consultant, Israel Chamber Choir (Cameran Singers), 1989–91. Mem., Vaughan Williams Trust, 1976–. Fellow, Westminster Choir Coll., Princeton, NJ, 1978. Chevalier des Arts et des Lettres (France), 1984. *Address:* 3 Wool Road, Wimbledon, SW20 0HN. *T:* (020) 8946 4168.

ALLEN, family name of **Baron Allen of Abbeydale** and **Baron Croham**.

ALLEN OF ABBEYDALE, Baron *cr* 1976 (Life Peer), of the City of Sheffield; **Philip Allen,** GCB 1970 (KCB 1964; CB 1954); *b* 8 July 1912; *yr s* of late Arthur Allen and Louie Tipper, Sheffield; *m* 1938, Marjorie Brenda Coe. *Educ:* King Edward VII Sch., Sheffield; Queens' Coll., Cambridge (Whewell Schol. in Internat. Law, 1934; Hon. Fellow 1974). Entered Home Office, 1934; Offices of War Cabinet, 1943–44; Commonwealth Fellowship in USA, 1948–49; Deputy Chm. of Prison Commn for England and Wales, 1950–52; Asst Under Sec. of State, Home Office, 1952–55; Deputy Sec., Min. of Housing and Local Govt, 1955–60; Deputy Under-Sec. of State, Home Office, 1960–62; Second Sec., HM Treasury, 1963–66; Permanent Under-Sec. of State, Home Office, 1966–72. Chairman: Occupational Pensions Bd, 1973–78; Nat. Council of Social Service, 1973–77; Gaming Bd for GB, 1977–85 (Mem., 1975); Mencap, 1982–88. Member Royal Commissions: on Standards of Conduct in Public Life, 1974–76; on Civil Liability and Compensation for Personal Injury, 1973–78; Member: Security Commn, 1973–91; tribunal of inquiry into Crown Agents, 1978–82. Chief Counting Officer, EEC Referendum, 1975. Chm. Council, RHBNC, London Univ., 1985–92 (Visitor, 1992–97). *Address:* Holly Lodge, Middle Hill, Englefield Green, Surrey TW20 0JP. *T:* (01784) 432291.

ALLEN, Anthony John, CBE 1994; Assistant Lay Inspector of Constabulary, since 1997; *b* 7 Oct. 1939; *s* of late Raymond Houghton Allen and Elsie Zillah Allen; *m* 1st, 1964, Suzanne Myfanwy Davies; two *s*; 2nd, 1987, Helen Leah Graney; two *s*. *Educ:* Battersea Grammar Sch.; Univ. of Exeter (LLB 1961). Admitted Solicitor, 1964. Asst Solicitor: Hendon Bor. Council, 1964–65; Barnet Bor. Council, 1965; Watford Bor. Council, 1966–68; Asst Town Clerk, Coventry CBC, 1968–71; Asst. Chief Exec., Lewisham Bor. Council, 1971–72; Solicitor to the Council and Dep. Town Clerk, Southwark Bor. Council, 1972–76; Chief Exec., Hammersmith and Fulham Bor. Council, 1976–86; Chief Exec., and Clerk to Lieutenancy, Royal Co. of Berks, 1986–93; Chief Exec., NHBC, 1994–96. Non-exec. Dir, BSI, 1992–95. Promoter and Dir, London Youth Games Ltd, 1979–. Chm., Working Party on Social and Psychol Aspects of Major Disasters (report published, 1990). CIMgt 1992. *Publications:* (contrib.) Practical Corporate Planning, ed John Skitt, 1975. *Recreations:* golf, travel. *Address:* Appledown, School Lane, Frilsham, Berks RG18 9XB. *T:* (01635) 201445.

ALLEN, His Honour Anthony Kenway, OBE 1946; a Circuit Judge, 1978–90; *b* 31 Oct. 1917; *s* of Charles Valentine Allen and Edith Kenway Allen; *m* 1975, Maureen Murtough. *Educ:* St George's Coll., Weybridge, Surrey; St John's Coll., Cambridge (BA Hons); Freiburg and Grenoble Univs. Served War, RAF Special Intelligence, 1939–45 (Wing Comdr). Called to the Bar, Inner Temple, 1947. *Recreations:* gardening, walking, music. *Address:* 73 Downswood, Epsom Downs, Surrey KT18 5UJ.

ALLEN, Arnold Millman, CBE 1977; Chairman, UKAEA, 1984–86; *b* 30 Dec. 1924; *s* of Wilfrid Millman and Edith Muriel Allen; *m* 1947, Beatrice Mary Whitaker; three *s* one *d*. *Educ:* Hackney Downs Sec. Sch.; Peterhouse, Cambridge (Scholar). Entered HM Treasury, 1945; Private Sec. to Financial Secretary, 1951–52; Principal, HM Treasury, 1953–55; Private Sec. to Chm. of UKAEA (Lord Plowden), 1956–57; HM Treasury, 1958; Dir of Personnel and Admin., Development and Engineering Group (subseq. Reactor Group), UKAEA, 1959–63; Gen. Manager, British Waterways Bd, 1963–68, and Mem. of Bd 1965–68; UKAEA: Personnel Officer, 1968–69; Personnel and Programmes Officer, 1970; Secretary and Mem. for Administration, 1971; Mem. for Finance and Admin, 1976–84; Dep. Chm., 1981–84; Chief Exec., 1982–84. *Address:* Duntish Cottage, Duntish, Dorchester, Dorset DT2 7DR. *T:* (01300) 345258.

ALLEN, Brian, PhD; FSA; Director of Studies, Paul Mellon Centre for Studies in British Art, since 1993; *b* 3 Oct, 1952; *s* of Herbert Allen and Mary Buckley; *m* 1978, Katina Michael; two *s*. *Educ:* Univ. of East Anglia (BA 1974); Courtauld Inst. of Art, Univ. of London (MA 1975; PhD 1984). Research Asst, Witt Library, Courtauld Inst. of Art, 1975–76; Paul Mellon Centre for Studies in British Art: Asst Dir and Librarian, 1977–85, Dep. Dir of Studies, 1985–92. Adjunct Prof. of History of Art, Yale Univ., 1993–; Vis. Prof. of History of Art, Birkbeck Coll., Univ. of London, 1999–July 2002. Hon. Sec. and Editor, 1977–85, Chm., 1996–, Walpole Soc.; Pres., Johnson Club, 1993–97; Member: Adv. Cttee, Yale Center for British Art, 1993–; Bd, Assoc. of Research Insts in Art History, 1993–; Council, Attingham Trust for Study of Country Houses and Collections, 1995–; Exec. Cttee, NACF, 1998–; Cttee, Friends of Strawberry Hill, 2000–; Trustee and Gov., Dr Johnson's House Trust, 1998; Trustee: Foundling Mus., 1998–; Holburne Mus., Bath, 2000–; Gov., Gainsborough's House Trust, 2000–. Chm. Judging Panel, Sunday Times/Singer and Friedlander Watercolour Competition, 1997–; Judge, Garrick/Milne Prize, 2000. Mem., Editorial Adv. Panel, Apollo, 1990–; Associate Editor, New DNB, 1997–; Member: Panel of Specialist Advrs, Architectural Heritage, 1998–; Internat. Adv. Bd, British Art Jl, 1999–; Adv. Bd, Visual Culture in Britain, 2000–. FSA 2000. Hon. DLitt Southampton Inst. (Nottingham Trent Univ.), 1999. *Publications:* Francis Hayman, 1987; (ed.) Towards a Modern Art World, 1995; (ed with L. Dukelskaya) British Art Treasures from Russian Imperial Collections in The Hermitage, 1996; numerous articles in Apollo, Burlington Mag., Jl RSA, etc. *Recreations:* watching association football, opera. *Address:* Paul Mellon Centre for Studies in British Art, 16 Bedford Square, WC1B 3JA. *T:* (020) 7580 0311; 7 Frances Road, Windsor, Berks SL4 3AE. *T:* (01753) 860452. *Club:* Garrick.

ALLEN, Charles Lamb, FCMA; Chairman, Granada plc (formerly Granada Media), since 2000; *b* 4 Jan. 1957. *Educ:* Bell Coll., Hamilton. FCMA 1989. Accountant, British Steel, 1974–79; Dep. Audit Manager, Galaghers plc, 1979–82; Dir, Management Services, Grandmet Internat. Services Ltd, 1982–85; Gp Man. Dir, Compass Vending, Grandmet Innovations Ltd, 1986–87; Man. Dir, Grandmet Internat. Services Ltd, 1987–88; Man. Dir, Compass Gp Ltd, 1988–91; Chief Exec., Leisure Div., Granada Gp, 1991–92; Chief Exec., 1992–96, Chm., 1996–, Granada TV; Chief Exec., 1994–96, Chm., 1996–, LWT; Chief Exec., Granada Gp, 1996–2000. Chairman: Granada Leisure and Services, 1993–2000; Granada Technology (formerly Rentals Div.), 1993–2000; Forte, 1997–2000; Tyne Tees TV, 1997–; Yorkshire TV, 1997–; Anglia TV, 2000–; Meridian, 2000–; OnDigital, 2000–; Dep. Chm., 1994–96, Chm., 1996–2000, GMTV; Jt Dep. Chm., Granada Compass, 2000–01; Dir, Boxclever, 2000–. Dir, British Digital Broadcasting, 1997–. Chm., Race for Opportunity, 1997–2000; Dep. Chm., BITC, 1997–. Vice-Pres., RTS, 1996–. Gov., RNCM, 1993–98 (Mem. Directorate, Internat. Council, 1996–). FRSA. Hon. DBA Manchester Metropolitan, 1999. *Recreations:* boating, swimming, travel. *Address:* (office) London Television Centre, Upper Ground, SE1 9LT. *T:* (020) 7620 1620.

ALLEN, Colin Mervyn Gordon, CBE 1978; General Manager, Covent Garden Market Authority, 1967–89; *b* 17 April 1929; *s* of late Cecil G. Allen and late Gwendoline L. Allen (*née* Hutchinson); *m* 1953, Patricia, *d* of late William and late Doris Seddon; two *s* one *d*. *Educ:* King Edward's Sch., Bath. BA Open, 1985; MA London, 1986; MA London (Dist.), 1991. FCIPS (FInstPS 1967). Naval Store Dept, Admiralty, 1948–56; National Coal Board: London HQ, 1956–59; Area Stores Officer, NE Div., 1959–64; Covent Garden Market Authority: Planning Officer, 1964–66; Asst Gen. Man., 1967. President: Assoc. of Wholesale Markets within Internat. Union of Local Authorities, 1972–78; IPS, 1982–83. Chm., Vauxhall Cross Amenity Trust, 1982–83. *Publications:* Transplanting the Garden: the story of the relocation of Covent Garden Market, 1998; various papers on horticultural marketing and allied topics, supply and logistics matters, and ancient history and archaeology. *Recreation:* archaeology. *Address:* Grassington, 142 Gidley Way, Horspath, Oxford OX33 1TD. *T:* (01865) 872388.

ALLEN, David Charles Keith, AO 1990; Chairman, Commonwealth Scientific and Industrial Research Organisation, since 1996; *b* 3 April 1936; *s* of G. Keith Allen and Dorothy M. Allen; *m* 1964, Angela Mary Evatt; two *s* one *d*. *Educ:* Oundle Sch.; Corpus Christi Coll., Cambridge (MA); Imperial Coll., London (MSc, DIC). Nat. Service, RE, Malaya, 1954–56. Joined Shell International, 1961: geophysicist, in Holland, NZ, Turkey and Nigeria, 1961–71; Chief Geophysicist, Shell Expro, London, 1971–74; Area Geologist, Shell Internat. Petroleum, The Hague, 1974–75; Western Division, Shell BP, Nigeria: Ops Manager, 1975–77; Divl Manager, 1977–79; Woodside Petroleum Ltd: Exec. Dir, 1980–82; Man. Dir, 1982–96. Director: Nat. Australia Bank, 1992–; Amcor Ltd, 1996–; AGL, 1996–; Air Liquide (Aust.), 1997–. Dir, Earthwatch Australia, 1994–. Hon. LLD Monash, 1994. *Recreations:* golf, travel. *Address:* 15 Stradbroke Avenue, Toorak, Vic 3142, Australia. *Clubs:* MCC; Grannies Cricket (UK); Australian, Melbourne (Melbourne).

ALLEN, David Kenneth; a Vice-President, Immigration Appeal Tribunal, since 2000; *b* 23 Feb. 1950; *yr s* of late P. H. Allen and of D. Allen; *m* 1974, Joan Rosalind, *d* of late Rev. E. N. O. Gray and of V. Gray; two *s* one *d*. *Educ:* Loughborough Grammar Sch.; Merton Coll., Oxford (BA Hons Juris; MA); McGill Univ., Montreal (LLM). Called to the Bar, Middle Temple, 1975; Lectr in Law, Inns of Court Sch. of Law, 1974–76; Department of Law, University of Leicester: Lectr, 1976–88; Sen. Lectr, 1988–99; Hd of Dept, 1993–96; Hon. Vis. Fellow, 1999–; Immigration Adjudicator, 1989–2000 (pt-time, 1989–99); in practice, Midland and Oxford Circuit, 1990–99. Vis. Prof., Dalhousie Univ., Halifax, NS, 1982–83. *Publications:* (jtly) Accident Compensation after Pearson, 1979; (jtly) Civil Liability for Defective Premises, 1982; (jtly) Fire, Safety and the Law, 1983, 2nd edn 1990; Misrepresentation, 1988; (jtly) Damages in Tort, 2000; essays; contrib. articles and notes in various jls. *Recreations:* golf, tennis, music. *Address:* Immigration Appeal Tribunal, Field House, 15–25 Bream's Buildings, EC4A 1DZ.

ALLEN, Prof. Deryck Norman de Garrs; Professor of Applied Mathematics in the University of Sheffield, 1955–80, now Emeritus; Warden of Ranmoor House, 1968–82; *b* 22 April 1918; *s* of Leonard Lincoln Allen and Dorothy Allen (*née* Asplin). *Educ:* King Edward VII School, Sheffield; Christ Church, Oxford. Messrs Rolls Royce, 1940; Research Asst to Sir Richard Southwell, FRS, 1941; Lectr in Applied Mathematics at Imperial Coll., London, 1945; Visiting Prof. in Dept of Mechanical Engineering, Massachusetts Inst. of Technology, 1949; Reader in Applied Mathematics at Imperial Coll. in Univ. of London, 1950. Pro-Vice-Chancellor, Sheffield Univ., 1966–70; Chm., Jt Matriculation Bd, 1973–76. *Publications:* Relaxation Methods, 1954 (US); papers on Applied Maths and Engineering Maths in: Proc. Royal Soc.; Philosophical Trans. of Royal Soc.; Quarterly Jl of Mechanics and Applied Maths; Jl of Instn of Civil Engineers. *Recreation:* travel. *Address:* 18 Storth Park, Fulwood Road, Sheffield S10 3QH. *T:* (0114) 230 8751.

ALLEN, Donald F.; Founder and Partner, Down Office Equipment Co., since 1975; Chairman, Sports Council for Northern Ireland, since 1990; *b* 23 Sept. 1938; *m* 1969, Rosaline; three *d*. *Educ:* by Christian Brothers. Completed optician's trng course, 1964; mgt posts with Olivetti Ltd, 1964–75. Mem., UK Sports Council, 1997–. Pres., Belfast East Rotary Club. FInstD. *Recreations:* golf (playing), all sport (watching), theatre. *Address:* 49 Demesne Road, Holywood, Co. Down, Northern Ireland BT18 9EX. *Clubs:* Holywood Golf (Capt.; Trustee, 1986–), Royal Belfast Golf.

ALLEN, Donald George, CMG 1981; Deputy Parliamentary Commissioner for Administration (Ombudsman), 1982–90; *b* 26 June 1930; *s* of Sidney George Allen and Doris Elsie (*née* Abercombie); *m* 1955, Sheila Isobel Bebbington; three *s*. *Educ:* Southall Grammar School. Foreign Office, 1948; HM Forces, 1949–51; FO, 1951–54; The Hague, 1954–57; 2nd Sec. (Commercial), La Paz, 1957–60; FO, 1961–65: 1st Sec. 1962; Asst Private Sec. to Lord Privy Seal, 1961–63 and to Minister without Portfolio, 1963–64; 1st Sec., Head of Chancery and Consul, Panama, 1966–69; FCO, 1969–72; Counsellor on secondment to NI Office, Belfast, 1972–74; Counsellor and Head of Chancery, UK Permanent Delegn to OECD, Paris, 1974–78; Inspector, 1978–80; Dir, Office of Parly Comr (Ombudsman), 1980–82, on secondment. Mem., Broadcasting Complaints Commn, 1990–97. *Recreations:* squash, tennis, golf. *Address:* 99 Parkland Grove, Ashford, Mddx TW15 2JF. *T:* (01784) 255617. *Club:* Royal Automobile.

ALLEN, Fergus Hamilton, CB 1969; ScD, MA, MAI; FRSL; First Civil Service Commissioner, Civil Service Department, 1974–81; *b* 3 Sept. 1921; *s* of late Charles Winckworth Allen and Marjorie Helen, *d* of F. J. S. Budge; *m* 1947, Margaret Joan, *d* of Prof. M. J. Gorman; two *d*. *Educ:* Newtown Sch., Waterford; Trinity Coll., Dublin. ScD 1966. Asst Engineer, Sir Cyril Kirkpatrick and Partners, 1943–48; Port of London Authority, 1949–52; Asst Director, Hydraulics Research Station, DSIR, 1952–58; Dir of Hydraulics Research, DSIR, 1958–65; Chief Scientific Officer, Cabinet Office, 1965–69; Civil Service Comr, 1969–74; Scientific and Technological Advr, CSD, 1969–72. Consultant, Boyden Internat. Ltd, 1982–86. Instn Civil Engrs: Mem., 1947–57; Fellow, 1957–86; Telford Gold Medal, 1958; Mem. Council, 1962–67, 1968–71. *Publications:* The Brown Parrots of Providencia (poems), 1993; Who Goes There? (poems), 1996; Mrs Power Looks Over the Bay (poems), 1999; papers in technical journals. *Address:* Dundrum, Wantage Road, Streatley, Berks RG8 9LB. *T:* (01491) 873234. *Club:* Athenæum.

See also M. Allen.

ALLEN, His Honour Francis Andrew Allen; a Circuit Judge, 1979–2001; *b* 7 Dec. 1933; *s* of Andrew Eric Allen and Joan Elizabeth Allen; *m* 1st, 1961, Marjorie Pearce; one *s* three *d*; 2nd, 1994, Sheila Baggaley. *Educ:* Solihull School; Merton College, Oxford. MA. 2nd Lieut, Highland Light Infantry, 1957; called to the Bar, Gray's Inn, 1958. A Recorder of the Crown Court, 1978–79. Chm., Magisterial Cttee, Judicial Studies Bd, 1990–95. *Recreation:* walking. *Club:* Mountain Bothies Association (Scottish Highlands).

ALLEN, Frank Graham, CB 1984; Clerk of the Journals, House of Commons, 1975–84; *b* 13 June 1920; *s* of Percy and Gertrude Allen; *m* 1947, Barbara Caulton; one *d* (one *s* decd). *Educ:* Shrewsbury Sch. (Schol.); Keble Coll., Oxford (Exhibr, BA). 7th Bn Worcs Regt, 1940–46, India, 1942–44; Allied Commn Austria, Vienna, 1945–46. Asst Clerk, House of Commons, 1946; Principal Clerk, 1973. Mem., House of Laity, Gen. Synod, 1970–80. Silver Jubilee Medal, 1977. *Recreation:* involvement in Chorleywood CARE and in St Andrew's old people's day centre. *Address:* 3 Badger's Walk, Cedars Village, Chorleywood, Herts WD3 5GA. *T:* (01923) 350054. *Club:* Rhinefield Owners (Brockenhurst).

ALLEN, Gary James, CBE 1991; DL; Chairman, IMI plc, since 2001 (Chief Executive, 1986–2001); *b* 30 Sept. 1944; *s* of Alfred and Alice Allen; *m* 1966, Judith Anne Nattrass; three *s*. *Educ:* King Edward VI Grammar School, Aston, Birmingham; Liverpool University (BCom). FCMA. Managing Dir, IMI Range, 1973–77; Dir, IMI, 1978–; Asst Man. Dir, IMI, 1985–86; Chairman: Optilon, 1979–84; Eley, 1981–85; (non-exec.) Nat. Exhibition Centre Ltd, 1989–; Dep. Chm., Marley, 1993–97 (Dir, 1989–97); Director: (non-exec.) NV Bekaert SA, Belgium, 1987–; Birmingham European Airways, 1989–91; London Stock Exchange, 1994–. Mem. Council, CBI, 1986–99 (Mem., W Midlands Regional Council, 1983–89); Mem. Council, Birmingham Chamber of Industry & Commerce, 1983–98 (Pres., 1991–92; Mem. Bd, 1994–96). Lord's Taverners: Pres., W Midlands Regl Cttee, 1994–; Trustee, 1995–; Mem., Nat. Council, 1992–. Trustee, Industry in Educn, 1998–. Mem. Council, Univ. of Birmingham, 1985–90 (Hon. Life Mem., Court, 1984–). Mem. Bd, Birmingham Royal Ballet, 1993–. Pres., Midlands Club Cricket Conf., 1995–96. Chm., Birmingham Children's Hosp. Appeal, 1995–2000. DL West Midlands, 1993. CIMgt; FRSA. Midland Businessman of the Year, 1989. *Recreations:* sport, reading, gardening. *Address:* IMI plc, PO Box 216, Birmingham B6 7BA. *T:* (0121) 356 4848. *Clubs:* Royal Automobile, Lord's Taverners.

ALLEN, Prof. Sir Geoffrey, Kt 1979; PhD; FRS 1976; FREng; FRSC; FInstP; FIM; Executive Adviser, Kobe Steel Ltd, 1990–2000; Head of Research, Unilever PLC, 1981–90 (Director, Unilever PLC and NV, 1982–90); *b* 29 Oct. 1928; *s* of John James and Marjorie Allen; *m* 1973, Valerie Frances Duckworth; one *d*. *Educ:* Clay Cross Tupton Hall Grammar Sch.; Univ. of Leeds (BSc, PhD). FInstP 1972; FPRI 1974; FIM 1991; FREng (FEng 1993). Postdoctoral Fellow, Nat. Res. Council, Canada, 1952–54; Lectr, Univ. of Manchester, 1955–65, Prof. of Chemical Physics, 1965–75; Prof. of Polymer Science, 1975–76, Prof. of Chemical Technology, 1976–81, Imperial Coll. of Science and Technology (Fellow, 1986); Vis. Fellow, Robinson Coll., Cambridge, 1980–. Non-exec. Dir, Courtaulds, 1987–93. Member: Science Research Council, 1976, Chm., 1977–81; Royal Commn on Envmtl Pollution, 1991–99; Nat. Consumer Council, 1993–96; Council, Foundn for Sci. and Technol., 1995–; President: PRI, 1990–92; Inst. of Materials, 1994–95. A Vice-Pres., Royal Soc., 1991–93. Chancellor, UEA, 1994–. Fellow, St Catherine's Coll., Oxford, 1992. Hon. FCGI 1990. Hon. FUMIST 1993. Hon. MSc Manchester; DUniv Open, 1981; Hon. DSc: Durham, East Anglia, 1984; Bath, Bradford, Loughborough, 1985; Essex, Keele, Leeds, 1986; Cranfield, 1988; Surrey, 1989; Sheffield, 1993. *Publications:* papers on chemical physics of polymers in Trans Faraday Soc., Polymer. *Recreations:* opera, walking, talking. *Address:* 18 Oxford House, 52 Parkside, Wimbledon, SW19 5NE.

ALLEN, Graham Leslie; Assistant Director (Museums and Arts), Birmingham City Council, since 1995; *b* 27 May 1949; *s* of William Leslie Allen and Doris Allen (*née* Fraser). *Educ:* Ladywood Comprehensive Sch., Birmingham. Joined Birmingham City Council, 1973; Assistant Director: Museums Services, 1990–94; Mgt Services, 1994–95; acting Head of Museums Services, 1995. Mem., Lunar Soc., 1999–. FRSA 2000. *Recreations:* the arts, museums, hill walking. *Address:* Birmingham Museum and Art Gallery, Chamberlain Square, Birmingham B3 3DH. *T:* (0121) 303 2833.

ALLEN, Graham William; MP (Lab) Nottingham North, since 1987; *b* 11 Jan. 1953; *s* of William and Edna Allen. *Educ:* Robert Shaw Primary Sch.; Forest Fields Grammar Sch.; City of London Polytechnic; Leeds Univ. Warehouseman, Nottingham, 1971–72; Labour Party Res. Officer, 1978–83; Local Govt Officer, GLC, 1983–84; Trades Union National Co-ordinator, Political Fund Ballots Campaign, 1984–86; Regional Res. and Educn Officer, GMBATU, 1986–87. Opposition front bench spokesman on social security, 1991–92, on democracy and the constitution, 1992–94, on the media, 1994, on transport, 1995; a Lord Comr of HM Treasury (Govt Whip), 1997–98; Vice Chamberlain of HM Household, 1998–2001. Member: Public Accounts Cttee, 1988–91; Procedure Cttee, 1989–91; 1990 Financial Bill Cttee. Chm., PLP Treasury Cttee, 1990–91. *Recreations:* cricket, football, golf, walking. *Address:* House of Commons, SW1A 0AA. *T:* (020) 7219 4343. *Clubs:* Long Eaton Labour, Strelley Social, Beechdale Community Centre, Bulwell Community Centre, Dunkirk Cricket (Nottingham).

ALLEN, Hamish McEwan, CB 1984; Head of Administration Department, House of Commons, 1981–85; *b* 7 Sept. 1920; *s* of late Ernest Frank Allen and Ada Florence Allen (*née* Weeks); *m* 1951, Peggy Joan Fifoot; one *s*. *Educ:* City of Bath Sch.; Portsmouth Southern Secondary Sch. Served RAF, 1941–46. Air Ministry: Clerical Officer, 1938; Exec. Officer, 1948; House of Commons: Asst Accountant, 1959; Dep. Accountant, 1962; Head of Estabs Office, 1968. *Address:* 124 Ridge Langley, South Croydon, Surrey CR2 0AS.

ALLEN, Dame Ingrid (Victoria), (Dame Ingrid Barnes Thompson), DBE 2001 (CBE 1993); DL; MD, DSc, FRCPath, FRCPI, FRCPSG, FRCPE; Director of Research and Development, Health and Personal Social Services, Northern Ireland, since 1997; Professor of Neuropathology, Queen's University of Belfast, 1979–97, now Emeritus; *b* 30 July 1932; *d* of Rev. Robert Allen, MA, PhD, DD and Doris V. Allen; *m* 1st, 1972, Alan Watson Barnes, MA, ARIBA, Past Pres., RSUA (*d* 1986); 2nd, 1996, Prof. John Thompson. *Educ:* Cheltenham Ladies College; QUB. House Officer, Royal Victoria Hosp., Belfast, 1957–58; Musgrave Res. Fellow, Tutor in Path., Calvert Res. Fellow, QUB, 1958–64; Sen. Registrar, RVH, 1964–65; Sen. Lectr and Consultant in Neuropath., QUB/RVH, 1966–78; Reader and Consultant, 1978–79; Head, NI Regional Neuropath. Service, RVH, Belfast, 1979–97. Vis. Prof., Univ. of Ulster. Mem., MRC, 1989 (Chm., Neuroscis Bd, 1989–92); President: British Neuropathological Soc., 1993–95; Irish Neurological Assoc., 1993–; Vice-President: Internat. Soc. of Neuropath., 1988–92; RCPath, 1993–96 (Mem. Council and Coll. Cttees, 1990–97). MRIA 1993 (Fellow, 1993). Founder FMedSci 1998. DL Belfast 1989. Mem. edtl bds of various scientific jls. *Publications:* (contrib.) Greenfield's Neuropathology, 1984; (contrib.) McAlpine's Multiple Sclerosis, 1990; contribs to jls on neuropathology, demyelinating diseases, neurovirology and neuro-oncology. *Recreations:* tennis, sailing, reading, history, architecture. *Address:* 95 Malone Road, Belfast BT9 6SP. *T:* (028) 9066 6662. *Clubs:* Royal Society of Medicine; Royal Ulster Yacht.

ALLEN, James Hendricuss; QC 1995; a Recorder, since 1995; *b* 19 Sept. 1949; *s* of James Ede Allen and Anna Catarina Allen; *m* 1st, 1974 (marr. diss. 1994); one *s* two *d*; 2nd, 1996, Melanie Jane Williamson. *Educ:* Morley Grammar Sch.; Newcastle upon Tyne Poly. (BA Hons Law). Called to the Bar, Gray's Inn, 1973. *Recreations:* theatre, opera, foreign travel, shooting, tennis, bridge. *Address:* 7 Lisbon Square, Leeds LS1 4LY. *T:* (0113) 244 6691.

ALLEN, Janet Rosemary; Headmistress of Benenden School, Kent, 1976–85; *b* 11 April 1936; *d* of John Algernon Allen and Edna Mary Allen (*née* Orton). *Educ:* Cheltenham Ladies' Coll.; University Coll., Leicester; Hughes Hall, Cambridge. BA London 1958; CertEd Cambridge 1959. Asst Mistress, Howell's Sch., Denbigh, North Wales, 1959: Head of History Dept, 1961; in charge of First Year Sixth Form, 1968; Housemistress, 1968 and 1973–75. Acting Headmistress: Sch. of St Mary and St Anne, Abbots Bromley, Sept.–Dec. 1988; Selwyn Sch., Gloucester, 1989–90. Member: E-SU Scholarship Selection Panel, 1977–85; South East ISIS Cttee, 1978–84; Boarding Schs Assoc. Cttee, 1980–83; GSA Educnl sub-cttee, 1983–85; Gloucester Diocesan Bd of Educn, 1992–97. Vice-Pres., Women's Career Foundn (formerly Girls of the Realm Guild), 1981–. Governor: St Catherine's Sch., Bramley, 1986–91; The King's Sch., Worcester, 1996–. *Recreations:* music, theatre, swimming, helping to preserve national heritage. *Address:* Bourne Rise, Queen's Square, Winchcombe, Cheltenham, Glos GL54 5LR. *Club:* Royal Over-Seas League.

ALLEN, Prof. John Anthony, PhD, DSc; FIBiol; FRSE; Professor of Marine Biology, University of London, and Director, University Marine Biological Station, Millport, Isle of Cumbrae, 1976–91, now Professor Emeritus; Hon. Research Fellow, University Marine Biological Station, since 1991; *b* 27 May 1926; *s* of George Leonard John Allen and Dorothy Mary Allen; *m* 1st, 1952, Marion Ferguson Crow (marr. diss. 1983); one *s* one *d*; 2nd, 1983, Margaret Porteous Aitken; one adopted step *s*. *Educ:* High Pavement Sch., Nottingham; London Univ. (PhD, DSc). FIBiol 1969; FRSE 1968 (Mem. Council, 1970–73). Served in Sherwood Foresters, 1945–46, and RAMC, 1946–48. Asst Lectr, Univ. of Glasgow, 1951–54; John Murray Student, Royal Soc., 1952–54; Lectr/Sen. Lectr in Zool., then Reader in Marine Biol., Univ. of Newcastle upon Tyne, 1954–76. Post Doctoral Fellow and Guest Investigator, Woods Hole Oceanographic Instn, USA, 1965–; Vis. Prof., Univ. of Washington, 1968, 1970, 1971; Royal Soc. Vis. Prof., Univ. of West Indies, 1976. Member: NERC, 1977–83 (Chm., Univ. Affairs Cttee, 1978–83); Council, Scottish Marine Biol Assoc., 1977–83; Council, Marine Biol Assoc. UK, 1981–83, 1990–93; Life Sciences Bd, CNAA, 1981–84; Nature Conservancy Council, 1982–90 (Chm., Adv. Cttee Sci., 1984–90); British Nat. Cttee for Oceanic Res., 1988–90. Pres., Malacological Soc. of London, 1982–84. *Publications:* many papers on decapod crustacea and molluscs, and deep sea benthos, in learned jls. *Recreations:* travel, appreciation of gardens, pub-lunching. *Address:* Drialstone, Millport, Isle of Cumbrae, Scotland KA28 0EP. *T:* (01475) 530479.

ALLEN, Sir John (Derek), Kt 1994; CBE 1987; FCIOB; Board Member, since 1998, and Vice Chairman,1998–2000, Welsh Development Agency; Member, Land Authority for Wales, 1976–98 (Deputy Chairman, 1988–98); *b* 6 Nov. 1928; *s* of late William Henry Allen and Lalla Dorothy Allen (*née* Bowen); *m* 1951, (Thelma) Jean Hooper; one *s*. *Educ:* Cardiff High Sch.; Cardiff Coll. of Technology (BA). FCIOB 1979. Civil Engr, then Chm. and Man. Dir, John Morgan Gp, Cardiff, 1947–79; Mgt Consultancy Practice, 1979–86. Dep. Chm., then Chm., Cwmbran Develt Corp., 1979–88; Chm., Housing for Wales, 1988–96. Pres., Nat. Fedn of Building Trade Employers, 1979 (Treas., 1980–83). FIMgt 1980. Hon. Fellow, UWIC, 2000. Freeman, City of London, 1980. *Recreations:* fly-fishing, golf, gardening. *Address:* 6 Egremont Road, Penylan, Cardiff, S Glam CF23 5LN. *T:* (029) 2045 2734. *Clubs:* Cardiff and County; Cardiff Golf.

ALLEN, Very Rev. John Edward; Provost of Wakefield, 1982–98; Chairman, Scarborough and North East Yorkshire Healthcare NHS Trust, since 1997; *b* 9 June 1932; *s* of Rev. Canon Ronald and Mrs Isabel Allen; *m* 1957, Eleanor (*née* Prynne); one *s* three *d*. *Educ:* Rugby; University Coll., Oxford (MA); Fitzwilliam Coll., Cambridge (MA); Westcott House. Colonial Service, Kenya, 1957–63; Sales and Marketing, Kimberly-Clark Ltd, 1963–66; Theological College, 1966–68; Curate, Deal, Kent, 1968–71; Senior Chaplain to Univ. of Bristol and Vicar of St Paul's, Clifton, 1971–78; Vicar of Chippenham, Wilts, 1978–82. Mem., Gen. Synod of C of E, 1985–97. Vice Chm., Partnership for World Mission, 1987–96. Dir, Wakefield HA, 1991–97; Chm., Local Research Ethics Cttee, 1992–97; Mem., Northern and Yorks Reg. Multi-Centre Res. Ethics Cttee, 1997– (Vice-Chm., 1997–99). Religious Advr, Yorkshire TV, 1994–96. Gov., Queen Elizabeth GS, Wakefield, 1983–97; Chm. of Govs, Cathedral High Sch., 1993–97. Trustee and Dir, Public Arts, 1997–99. *Recreations:* walking, fishing and people. *Address:* The Glebe Barn, Sawdon, near Scarborough, N Yorks YO13 9DY. *T:* (01723) 859854; *e-mail:* jeallen@globalnet.co.uk.

See also R. G. B. Allen.

ALLEN, Maj.-Gen. John Geoffrey Robyn, CB 1976; Lay Observer attached to Lord Chancellor's Department, 1979–85; *b* 19 Aug. 1923; *s* of R. A. Allen and Mrs Allen (*née* Youngman); *m* 1959, Ann Monica (*née* Morford); one *s* one *d*. *Educ:* Haileybury. Commissioned KRRC, 1942; trans. RTR, 1947; Bt Lt-Col, 1961; Lt-Col, CO 2 RTR, 1963; Mil. Asst (GSO1) to CGS, MoD, 1965; Brig., Comd 20 Armd Bde, 1967; IDC, 1970; Dir of Operational Requirements 3 (Army), MoD, 1971; Maj.-Gen., Dir-Gen., Fighting Vehicles and Engineer Equipment, MoD, 1973–74; Dir, RAC, 1974–76; Sen. Army Directing Staff, RCDS, 1976–78; retired 1979. Col Comdt, RTR, 1976–80; Hon. Colonel: Westminster Dragoons, 1982–87; Royal Yeomanry, 1982–87. Member: Adv. Cttee on Legal Aid, 1979–86; Booth Cttee on Procedure in Matrimonial Causes, 1982–85; Appeal Tribunals, FIMBRA, 1989–98; Membership and Disciplinary Tribunal, PIA, 1994–98. *Address:* Meadowleys, Charlton, Chichester, W Sussex PO18 0HU. *T:* (01243) 811638. *Club:* Army and Navy.

ALLEN, John Piers, OBE 1979; *b* 30 March 1912; *s* of Percy Allen and Marjorie Nash; *m* 1937; two *s*; *m* 1945; two *s* two *d*; *m* 1982. *Educ:* Aldenham Sch. Old Vic Theatre, 1933–35; Victor Gollancz Ltd, 1936–37; London Theatre Studio, 1937–39; RNVR, 1940–45; Dir, Glyndebourne Children's Theatre, 1945–51; writer-producer, BBC, 1951–61; Adjudicator, Dominion Drama Festival, Canada, 1956; UNESCO Drama Specialist, Australia, 1959, 1961; HM Inspector of Schs, 1961–72. Principal, Central School of Speech and Drama, 1972–78. Vis. Prof. of Drama, Westfield Coll., Univ. of London, 1979–83; Vis. Lectr, Centre for Arts, City Univ., 1979–83. Vice-Chm., British Theatre Assoc., 1978–83; Chairman: Accreditation Bd, Nat. Council of Drama Trng, 1979–83; Council of Dance Educn and Trng, 1982–95 (Chm., Accreditation Bd, 1979–82); Mem., CNAA Dance and Drama Panels, 1979–82; Vice-Pres., British Centre, Internat. Amateur Theatre Assoc., 1992–96. Chm., Old Meeting House Trust, Helmsley, 1993–. FGSM 1971; FRSAMD 1977; FRSA. *Publications:* Going to the Theatre, 1949; Great Moments in the Theatre, 1949; Masters of British Drama, 1957; Masters of European Drama, 1962; Drama in Schools, 1978; Theatre in Europe, 1981; A History of the Theatre in Europe, 1983; (ed) Three Medieval Plays, 1956. *Address:* Maple House, 2 Low Farm Close, Bolton Percy, York YO23 7HA. *T:* (01904) 744607.

ALLEN, Prof. John Robert Lawrence, DSc; FRS 1979; Research Professor, Postgraduate Research Institute for Sedimentology, University of Reading, since 1993 (Director, 1988–93); *b* 25 Oct. 1932; *s* of George Eustace Allen and Alice Josephine (*née* Formby); *m* 1959, Jean Mary (*née* Wood); four *s* one *d*. *Educ:* St Philip's Grammar Sch., Birmingham; Univ. of Sheffield (BSc; DSc 1972). Academic career in University of Reading, 1959–, Prof. of Geology, then of Sedimentology, 1972. Mem., NERC, 1992–94. FGS 1955; FSA 1991. Assoc. Mem., Royal Belgian Acad. of Scis, 1991. Hon. LLD Sheffield, 1994. Lyell Medal, Geolog. Soc., 1980; David Linton Award, British Geomorphological Research Group, 1983; Twenhofel Medal, Soc. of Economic Paleontologists and Mineralogists, 1987; G. K. Warren Prize, Nat. Acad. of Scis, USA, 1990; Sorby Medal, Internat. Assoc. of Sedimentologists, 1994; Penrose Medal, Geol Soc. of Amer., 1996. *Publications:* Current Ripples, 1968; Physical Processes of Sedimentation, 1970; Sedimentary Structures, 1982; Principles of Physical Sedimentology, 1985; numerous contribs to professional jls. *Recreations:* cooking, music, opera, pottery. *Address:* 17c Whiteknights Road, Reading RG6 7BY. *T:* (0118) 926 4621.

ALLEN, Joyce; *see* Moseley, J.

ALLEN, Katherine, (Kate); Director, Amnesty International UK, since 2000; *b* 25 Jan. 1955; *d* of William Allen and Patricia Allen (*née* Middleton). *Educ:* Brasenose Coll., Oxford (BA Hons PPE). Policy Officer, GLC, 1977–79; Scientific Officer, SSRC, 1979–80; Policy Officer, Haringey LBC, 1980 81; Sen. Policy Officer (Social Services), ACC, 1981–87; Dep. Chief Exec., Refugee Council, 1987–99.

ALLEN, Mark Echalaz, CMG 1966; CVO 1961; HM Diplomatic Service, retired; *b* 19 March 1917; *s* of late Lancelot John Allen and Eleanor Mary (*née* Carlisle); *m* 1948, Elizabeth Joan, *d* of late Richard Hope Bowdler and Elsie (*née* Bryning); two *s* one *d* (and one *d* decd). *Educ:* Charterhouse; Christ Church, Oxford (MA). Appointed Asst Principal, Dominions Office, 1939. Served War of 1939–45 in Western Desert, Sicily and Italy. Dublin, 1945; Bombay, 1948; United Nations, New York, 1953; Madras, 1960; New Delhi, 1961; Diplomatic Service Inspector, 1964; Dep. Chief of Administration, DSAO, 1966; Minister (Econ. and Social Affairs), UK Mission to UN, New York, 1968; Ambassador to Zaïre and Burundi, 1971, and to Congo Republic, 1973; Permanent UK Rep. to Disarmament Conf., Geneva, 1974–77, retired from Diplomatic Service, 1977. Mem., Jt Inspection Unit, UN, 1978–84. *Address:* 1 Pemberton Place, Esher, Surrey KT10 9HU. *T:* (01372) 466902.

ALLEN, Mary; Chief Executive, Royal Opera House, Covent Garden, 1997–98; *b* 22 Aug. 1951; *d* of Dr Fergus Hamilton Allen, *qv* and Joan Allen; *m* 1st, 1980, Robin Woodhead, *qv* (marr. diss.); 2nd, 1991, Nigel Pantling. *Educ:* School of St Helen and St Katherine; New Hall, Cambridge. Actress, West End and repertory, 1973–76; Agent, London Management, 1977–78; Arts, Sponsorship Manager, Mobil Oil Co., 1978–81; Assoc. for Business Sponsorship of the Arts, 1982–83; arts management consultant, 1983–90; Dir, Waterman's Arts Centre, 1990–92; Dir, Cheek by Jowl Theatre Co., 1989–92; Dep. Sec.-Gen., Arts Council of GB, 1992–94; Sec.-Gen., Arts Council of England, 1994–97. Public Art Develt Trust: Trustee, 1983–92; Chm., 1987–92. *Publications:* Sponsoring the Arts: new business strategies for the 1990s, 1990; A House Divided, 1998. *Recreations:* opera, theatre, collecting contemporary art, gardening.

ALLEN, Paul G.; Chairman, Vulcan Northwest Inc.; *b* 1953; *s* of late Kenneth Allen and of Faye Allen. *Educ:* Lakeside High Sch., Seattle; Washington State Univ. Programmer, Honeywell, Boston; Co-founder, Micro-Soft, later Microsoft Corp., 1975: Exec. Vice-Pres. of Res. and Product Develt, 1975–83; Dir, until 2000; Sen. Strategy Advr, 2000–. Founder: Asymetrix Corp., 1985; Vulcan Ventures, 1986; Starwave Corp., 1992; Interval Res., 1992; Paul Allen Group, 1994; Chm., Ticketmaster Hldgs Gp, 1993. Chairman: Portland Trailblazers, 1988–; Seattle Seahawks, 1997–. *Address:* Vulcan Northwest Inc., Suite 550, 110 110th Avenue North East, Bellevue, WA 98004, USA.

ALLEN, Prof. Percival, FRS 1973; Professor of Geology, and Head of Geology Department, University of Reading, 1952–82, now Emeritus Professor; Director, Sedimentology Research Laboratory, 1965–82; *b* 15 March 1917; *s* of late Norman Williams Allen and Mildred Kathleen Hoad; British; *m* 1941, Frances Margaret Hepworth, BSc; three *s* one *d*. *Educ:* Brede Council Sch.; Rye Grammar School; University of Reading. BSc 1939, PhD 1943, Hon. DSc, 1992, Reading; MA Cantab 1947. Univ. Demonstrator, 1942–45, Univ. Asst Lectr, 1945–46, Reading; University Demonstrator, 1946–47, Univ. Lectr, 1947–52, Cambridge; Dean of Science Faculty, Reading, 1963–66. Vis. Prof., Univ. of Kuwait, 1970. Served War of 1939–45. In Royal Air Force, 1941–42. Sedgwick Prize, Univ. of Cambridge, 1952; Daniel Pidgeon Fund, Geological Soc. of London, 1944; Leverhulme Fellowships Research Grant, 1948, 1949. Geological Soc. of London: Mem. Council, 1964–67; Lyell Medal, 1971; Pres., 1978–80; Royal Society: Mem. Council, 1977–79; a Vice-Pres., 1977–79; Chairman: Expeditions Cttee, 1974–; British Nat. Cttee for Geology, 1982–90; Sectional Cttee 5, 1983–88; Actg Chm., Earth Sciences Res. Priorities, 1987–89. Chm., Scottish Regional Cttee and Mem., Nat. and Eastern Reg. Cttees, UGC Earth Sciences Rev., 1987–90; Council Mem., NERC, 1971–74 and Royal Soc. Assessor, 1977–80; Chm., vis. group to Palaeont. Dept in British Mus. (Nat. Hist.), 1975, and Univ. of Strathclyde, 1982; External Appraiser (Geol. Depts): Meml Univ., Newfoundland, 1968; Jadavpur Univ., India, 1977; Univ. of Western Ontario, 1982; Univ. of London, 1982; Univ. of Malaya, 1983; Adv. Panel, UNDP Project on Nile Delta, 1972–; UNESCO/UNDP Geology Consultant, India, 1976–77. UK Editor, Sedimentology, 1961–67; Jt Editor, OUP Monographs in Geology and Geophysics series, 1980–87. Chm., Org. Cttees: VII Internat. Sedimentological Congress, 1967; first European Earth and Planetary Physics Colloquium, 1971; first Meeting European Geological Socs, 1975; UK Delegate to Internat. Union of Geol Sciences, Moscow, 1984; UK Corresp., IGCP Project 245, 1986–91. Sec.-Gen., Internat. Assoc. Sedimentologists, 1967–71; Pres., Reading Geol. Soc., 1976–78, 1987–88; Chm., British Inst. for Geological Conservation, 1987–91. Algerian Sahara Glacials Expedn, 1970; Sec., Philpots Quarry Ltd. Hon. Member: American Soc. of Economic Paleontologists and Mineralogists; Bulgarian Geological Soc.; Geologists' Assoc.; Internat. Assoc. of Sedimentologists; For. Fellow, Indian Nat. Sci. Acad., 1980. *Publications:* papers on Wealden (Lower Cretaceous) and Torridonian (Proterozoic) in various scientific journals. *Recreations:* chess, natural history, gardening, bicycling. *Address:* Orchard End, Hazeley Bottom, Hartley Wintney, Hook, Hants RG27 8LU. *T:* (01252) 842229; Postgraduate Research Institute for Sedimentology, University of Reading, Reading RG6 6AB. *T:* (0118) 931 6713.

ALLEN, Hon. Sir Peter (Austin Philip Jermyn); Kt 1987; High Court Judge, Lesotho, 1987–89; *b* 20 Oct. 1929; *yr s* of late Donovan Jermyn Allen and Edith Jane Bates. *Educ:* Headlands School, Swindon. LLB London. Army service, 1947–55, Lieut RA, 1952–55. HM Overseas Police Service, Asst Supt Uganda Police, 1955–62; ADC to Governor of Uganda, 1957; called to the Bar, Gray's Inn, 1964; Lectr, 1962–64, Principal, 1964–70, Uganda Law School; Judicial Adviser, Buganda Kingdom, 1964; Advocate, High Court of Uganda, 1965; Chief Magistrate, Uganda, 1970–73; Judge, Uganda High Court, 1973–85; Chief Justice (Head of Uganda Judiciary, Chm., Judicial Service Commn), 1985–86. Member: Uganda Law Reform Commn, 1964–68; Foundn Cttee, Uganda YMCA, 1959; Dir, Mbarara Branch, YMCA, 1970–73; Chairman: Presidential Commn of Inquiry into Kampala City Council, 1971; Judicial Review of Caribbean Dependent Territories (Allen Report for FCO), 1990; Commn of Inquiry into Grand Cayman New Hospital Contracts, 1993; Mem., Uganda Law Soc., 1964–70. Uganda Independence Medal, 1962. *Publications:* An Introduction to the Law of Uganda (co-author), 1968; Days of Judgment, 1987; Interesting Times—Uganda Diaries 1955–1986, 2000. *Address:* PO Box 38, Savannah, Grand Cayman, Cayman Islands, British West Indies. *Club:* Royal Commonwealth Society.

ALLEN, Peter William, FCA; *b* 22 July 1938; *s* of late Alfred William Allen, Sittingbourne, Kent, and Myra Nora (*née* Rogers); *m* 1965, Patricia Mary, *d* of late Joseph Frederick Dunk, FCA, Sheffield; three *d*. *Educ:* Cambridge Univ. (MA). Served RAF, 1957–59. Joined Coopers & Lybrand, 1963; qualified CA, 1966; Partner, 1973; Chm., Internat. Personnel Cttee, 1975–78; Partner in Charge, London Office, 1983; Man. Partner, 1984–90; Dep. Chm., 1990–94; Member: UK Bd, 1984–94; Internat. Exec. Cttee, 1988–90, 1992–94. Non-executive Director: Charter, 1994–2001; Schroder Ventures, 1994–; Bd Mem., Post Office, 1995–98. Bd Mem., BRCS, 1999–2000. Mem. Governing Body, Lister Inst. of Preventive Medicine, 1998–. CIMgt 1993. Freeman, City of London, 1988; Liveryman, Co. of Glaziers and Painters of Glass, 1989. *Recreations:* golf, painting. *Address:* John O'Gaddesden's House, Little Gaddesden, Berkhamsted, Herts HP4 1PF. *Club:* Reform.

ALLEN, (Philip) Richard (Hernaman); a Commissioner, since 1997, and Principal Executive Officer/Director Reorganisation Project, since 2001, HM Customs and Excise; *b* 26 Jan. 1949; *s* of late Philip Hernaman Allen and of Dorothy Allen (*née* Modral); *m* 1970, Vanessa (*née* Lampard); two *d*. *Educ:* Loughborough Grammar Sch.; Merton Coll., Oxford (BA (Hons) Mod. History). Asst Principal, HM Customs and Excise, 1970; Assistant Private Secretary: to Paymaster Gen., 1973; to Chancellor of the Duchy of Lancaster, 1974; HM Customs and Excise: Principal, 1975; Asst Sec., 1984; Comr of Customs and Excise, 1990; Director: Internal Taxes, 1990; Orgn, 1991; Dir, Policy, DSS, 1994; HM Customs and Excise: Director: Ops (Compliance), 1997–98; Personnel and Finance, 1998–2000; Human Resources, 2000–01. FRSA. *Recreations:* music, badminton, keeping fit. *Address:* HM Customs and Excise, New King's Beam House, 22 Upper Ground, SE1 9PJ. *T:* (020) 7865 5959.

ALLEN, Richard Ian Gordon; Senior Advisor on Governance, Asian Development Bank, since 2001; *b* 13 Dec. 1944; *s* of Reginald Arthur Hill Allen and Edith Alice Allen (*née* Manger); *m* 1988, Lynn Conroy. *Educ:* Edinburgh Academy; Edinburgh Univ. (MA); York Univ. (BPhil). Consultant, UN Economic Commn for Europe, Geneva, 1970; Research Officer, NIESR, 1971–75; Economic Adviser: Dept of Energy, 1975–78; HM Treasury, 1978–81; Senior Economic Adviser, later Asst Sec., HM Treasury, 1981–85; Counsellor (Economic), Washington, 1985–87; Press Sec. to Chancellor of the Exchequer, 1987–88; Under Sec., HM Treasury, 1988–95; Financial Advr, Govt of Bahrain, 1995–96; Sen. Counsellor, SIGMA prog., OECD, Paris, 1996–2001. Mem., Bd of Dirs, European Investment Bank, 1988–90. *Recreations:* collecting art, music, golf. *Address:* Asian Development Bank, 6 ADB Avenue, Mandaluyong City, 0401 Metro Manila, Philippines. *Club:* Royal Wimbledon Golf.

ALLEN, Robert Geoffrey Bruère, (Robin); QC 1995; a Recorder, since 2000; *b* 13 Feb. 1951; of Rev. Canon R. E. T. Allen and Isabel (*née* Otter-Barry); *m* 1977, Elizabeth Gay Moon; two *s*. *Educ:* Rugby; University Coll., Oxford (BA PPE 1972). Called to the Bar, Middle Temple, 1974; in practice, specialising in discrimination, employment and public law, and human rights, 1976–; an Asst Recorder, 1997–2000. Co-organiser and first Treas., Free Representation Unit, 1973. Employment Law Advr to Legal Action Gp, 1978–80; Legal Advr to Local Govt Gp, Inst. Public Relns, 1988–90; expert advr to EC on law affecting most disadvantaged, 1993. Founder Mem. Cttee, Employment Law Bar Assoc., 1994– (Chm., 1997–99); Chm., Bar Pro Bono Unit, 2000–; Mem., Bar Council, 1999–. Mem., Home Office Human Rights Task Force, 1999–2001. Sec., Lambeth Central CLP, 1977. Chm., London Youth Adv. Centre, 1984–90. Chairman: Bd of Govs, Eleanor Palmer Primary Sch., 1988–91; Brandon Centre for Psychotherapy, 1991–93. *Publications:* How to Prepare a Case for an Industrial Tribunal, 1987; contributed to: The Legal Framework and Social Consequences of Free Movement of Persons in the European Union, 1998; Women, Work and Inequality: the challenge of equal pay in a de-regulated labour market, 1999; Anti-Discrimination: the way forward, 1999; Race Discrimination: developing and using a new legal framework, 2000; Bullen and Leake and Jacob's Precedents of Pleadings, 2000; (ed) Home Office/Bar Council Study Guide to the Human Rights Act, 2000; The Legal Regulation of the Employment Relationship, 2001; A Practitioner's Guide to the Human Rights Act 1998, 2001. *Recreations:* family life, fishing. *Address:* Cloisters, 1 Pump Court, Temple, EC4Y 7AA. *T:* (020) 7827 4000, *Fax:* (020) 7827 4100. *Club:* Vincent's (Oxford).

See also Very Rev. J. E. Allen.

ALLEN, Sir Thomas, Kt 1999; CBE 1989; singer; *b* 10 Sept. 1944; *s* of Thomas Boaz Allen and Florence Allen; *m* 1st, 1968, Margaret Holley (marr. diss. 1986); one *s*; 2nd, 1988, Jeannie Gordon Lascelles. *Educ:* Robert Richardson Grammar Sch., Ryhope; Royal College of Music. ARCM; FRCM 1988. Welsh Nat. Opera, 1969–72; Principal Baritone, Royal Opera, Covent Garden, 1972–78; appearances include: Glyndebourne Fest. Opera; English Opera Group; Paris Opera; Florence; Teatro Colon, Buenos Aires; Met. Opera, NY; Hamburg; La Scala, Milan; BBC TV (The Gondoliers, The Marriage of Figaro); all major orchestras and various concert engagements abroad. Major rôles include: Figaro in Barber of Seville; Figaro and the Count in Marriage of Figaro; Papageno in The Magic Flute; Billy Budd; Marcello in La Bohême; Belcore in l'Elisir d'Amore; Sid in Albert Herring; Tarquinius in Rape of Lucretia; Guglielmo in Così fan Tutte; Demetrius in A Midsummer Night's Dream; Valentin in Faust; Dr Falke in Die Fledermaus; King Arthur; The Count in Voice of Ariadne; Silvio in Pagliacci; Pelléas in Pelléas and Mélisande; Germont in La Traviata; Don Giovanni; Mandryka in Arabella; Malatesta in Don Pasquale; title rôle in Il ritorno d'Ulisse; Beckmesser in Die Meistersinger; Prosdocimo in The Turk in Italy, and many others. Hambro Vis. Prof. of Opera, Oxford Univ., 2000–01. Hon. RAM, 1988. Hon. MA Newcastle, 1984; Hon. DMus Durham, 1988. *Publication:* Foreign Parts: a singer's journal, 1993. *Recreations:* gardening, golf, sailing, painting, ornithology. *Address:* c/o Askonas Holt Ltd, Lonsdale Chambers, 27 Chancery Lane, WC2A 1PF.

ALLEN, Twink; *see* Allen, W. R.

ALLEN, William Anthony; Deputy Director, Bank of England, since 1994 (Head of Foreign Exchange Division, 1990–94); *b* 13 May 1949; *s* of Derek William Allen and Margaret Winifred Allen (*née* Jones); *m* 1972, Rosemary Margaret Eminson; one *s* two *d*. *Educ:* King's College Sch., Wimbledon; Balliol College, Oxford (BA); LSE (MScEcon).

Joined Bank of England, 1972; Economic Intell. Dept, 1972–77; Gold and Foreign Exchange Office, 1977–78; seconded to Bank for Internat. Settlements, Basle, 1978–80; Asst Adviser, Economics Div., Bank of England (working on monetary policy), 1980–82; Manager, Gilt-Edged Div., 1982–86; Hd of Money Market Operations Div., 1986–90. Pt-time Advr, Nat. Bank of Poland, 1990–. *Publications:* articles in economics jls. *Recreations:* gardening, jazz. *Address:* Bank of England, Threadneedle Street, EC2R 8AH. *T:* (020) 7601 4444.

ALLEN, Sir William (Guilford); Kt 1981; Chairman, family group of companies; *b* 22 April 1932; *s* of Sir William Guilford Allen, CBE, and Mona Maree Allen; *m* 1959, Elaine Therese Doyle; two *s* one *d*. *Educ:* Downlands Coll., Toowoomba, Qld. In grazing industry, Merino sheep; Principal, Historic Malvern Hills Registered Merino Stud; stud Santa Gertrudis cattle breeder. Commercial broadcasting industry. Treasurer and Trustee, Nat. Party, Qld. Councillor, Longreach Shire. Chm., Qld Transport and Technology Centre, 1984–; Director: Qantas, 1981; Suncorp Building Soc., 1985–89; Power Brewing Co., 1989. Trustee, National Party, Qld, 1989–. Fellow, GAPAN. *Recreation:* aviation. *Clubs:* Brisbane, Tattersalls, Australian, Longreach, Queensland Turf, Brisbane Amateur Turf (Brisbane); Australian, Royal Sydney Golf (Sydney).

ALLEN, Maj.-Gen. William Maurice, CB 1983; FCIT, FIMI, FILDM, FIMgt; MInstPet; Senior Military Consultant to Mondial Defence Systems (formerly Mondial & Co.), since 1985; Regional Vice President and Senior Defence Adviser, Fortis Aviation Group, since 1995; *b* 29 May 1931; *s* of William James Allen and Elizabeth Jane Henrietta Allen; *m* 1st, 1955, Patricia Mary (*née* Fletcher) (*d* 1998); one *d* decd; 2nd, 1998, Elizabeth (*née* Irving). *Educ:* Dunstable Sch. FCIT 1972; FIMI 1982; FILDM (FIPDM 1982); FIMgt (FBIM 1983); MInstPet 1982. Commnd RASC, 1950; RCT, 1965; regtl and staff appts, Korea, Cyprus, Germany and UK; Student, Staff Coll., Camberley, 1961; Instructor, Staff Coll., Camberley and RMCS Shrivenham, 1968–70; Student, RCDS, 1976; Asst Comdt, RMA Sandhurst, 1979–81; Dir Gen. of Transport and Movements (Army), 1981–83. Dir of Educn and Trng, Burroughs Machines Ltd, 1983–85. Jt Man. Dir, Marina Moraira Yacht Brokers, 1989–92; Man. Dir, Fortis Internat. Ltd, 1991–92; Director: Govt Projects, Unisys Corp. (formerly Systems Develt Corp.), Heidelberg, 1985–86; Fortis Aviation Gp, Spain, 1988–89; European Management Information, 1989–. Member, Council: IAM, 1982–85; NDTA, 1983–. Chm., Milton Keynes Information Technol. Trng Centre, 1983–85. Associate, St George's House. Freeman, City of London, 1981; Hon. Liveryman, Worshipful Co. of Carmen, 1981. *Recreations:* economics, trout fishing, gardening, vigneron de Languedoc, ocean cruising. *Address:* c/o Royal Bank of Scotland, Holts Farnborough Branch, Lawrie House, 31–37 Victoria Road, Farnborough, Hants GU14 7NR. *Club:* Bristol Channel Yacht (Swansea).

ALLEN, Prof. William Richard, (Twink), PhD, ScD; Jim Joel Professor of Equine Reproduction, Department of Clinical Veterinary Medicine, University of Cambridge, since 1995; Director, Thoroughbred Breeders' Association Equine Fertility Unit, Newmarket, since 1989; *b* 29 Aug. 1940; *s* of Francis Cecil Allen and Rose St Ledger Allen (*née* Sinclair); *m* 1965, Diana Margaret Emms; one *s* two *d*. *Educ:* Auckland Grammar Sch.; Univ. of Auckland; Univ. of Sydney (BVSc 1965); Univ. of Cambridge (PhD in Equine Reproductive Physiology 1970). In vet. practice, Kaitaia, NZ, 1965; res. student, Dept of Clinical Vet. Medicine, Univ. of Cambridge, 1966–70; Post Doctoral Scientist, AFRC Unit of Reproductive Physiol. and Biochem., Cambridge, 1970–72; Prin. Vet. Res. Officer, Thoroughbred Breeders' Assoc. Equine Fertility Unit, Animal Res. Stn, Cambridge, 1972–89. *Publications:* (ed) Equine Reproduction, vols I–V, 1975–91; contrib. Proc. Internat. Symposia on Equine Reproduction; numerous papers in scientific jls and reference books. *Recreations:* fox hunting, horse racing, wildlife conservation. *Address:* Brunswick, Woodditton Road, Newmarket, Suffolk CB8 9BQ. *T:* (01638) 662507; TBA Equine Fertility Unit, Mertoun Paddocks, Woodditton Road, Newmarket, Suffolk CB8 9BH. *T:* (01638) 662491, *Fax:* (01638) 667207.

See also L. Dettori.

ALLEN, Prof. William Sidney, MA, PhD (Cantab); FBA 1971; Professor of Comparative Philology in the University of Cambridge, 1955–82; Fellow of Trinity College, since 1955; *b* 18 March 1918; *er s* of late W. P. Allen and Ethel (*née* Pearce); *m* 1955, Aenea, *yr d* of late Rev. D. McCallum and Mrs McCallum, Invergordon. *Educ:* Christ's Hosp.; Trinity Coll., Cambridge (Classical Scholar); Porson Scholarship, 1939. War of 1939–45: RAC and General Staff (Int) (despatches). Lecturer in Phonetics, 1948–51, and in Comparative Linguistics, 1951–55, School of Oriental and African Studies, Univ. of London. Dialect research in India, 1952; Fellow of Rockefeller Foundation, USA, 1953; Brit. Council visitor, Univ. of W Indies, 1959. Linguistic Soc. of America's Professor, 1961; Collitz Professor, Linguistic Institute, USA, 1962; Ida Beam Lectr, Univ. of Iowa, 1983. Pres., Philological Soc., 1965–67. Hon. Fellow, Soc. for Cycladic Studies (Athens), 1977. Chm. Editorial Bd, CUP linguistic series, 1969–82; Editor, Lingua, 1963–85. *Publications:* Phonetics in Ancient India, 1953; On the Linguistic Study of Languages (inaugural lecture), 1957; Sandhi, 1962; Vox Latina, 1965; Vox Graeca, 1968, 3rd edn 1987; Accent and Rhythm, 1973; articles on general and comparative linguistics, phonetics, metrics, classical, Indian and Caucasian languages, Icelandic, Aegean cartography. *Address:* Trinity College, Cambridge CB2 1TQ. *T:* (01223) 330871.

ALLEN, Woody, (Allen Stewart Konigsberg); writer, actor, director; *b* Brooklyn, 1 Dec. 1935; *s* of late Martin and of Nettie Konigsberg; *m* 1966, Louise Lasser (marr. diss.); one *s* by Mia Farrow, *qv*; *m* 1997, Soon-Yi Previn. TV script writer, 1953–64, and appeared as a comedian in nightclubs and on TV shows. Sylvania Award, 1957. *Plays:* (writer) Don't Drink the Water, 1966; (writer and actor) Play It Again Sam, 1969 (filmed 1972); The Floating Light Bulb, 1990. *Films:* (writer and actor) What's New Pussycat?, 1965; (actor): Casino Royale, 1967; Scenes from a Mall, 1991; (writer, actor and director): What's Up Tiger Lily?, 1966; Take the Money and Run, 1969; Bananas, 1971; Everything You Always Wanted to Know About Sex But Were Afraid to Ask, 1972; Sleeper, 1973; Love and Death, 1975; The Front, 1976; Annie Hall (Academy Award), 1977; Manhattan, 1979; Stardust Memories, 1980; A Midsummer Night's Sex Comedy, 1982; Zelig, 1983; Broadway Danny Rose, 1984; Hannah and her Sisters (Academy Award), 1986; New York Stories, 1989; Shadows and Fog, 1992; Husbands and Wives, 1992; Manhattan Murder Mystery, 1994; Mighty Aphrodite, 1995; Everyone Says I Love You, 1996; Deconstructing Harry, 1997; Small Time Crooks, 2000; The Curse of the Jade Scorpion, 2001; (writer and director): Interiors, 1978; The Purple Rose of Cairo, 1985; Radio Days, 1987; September, 1988; Another Woman, 1989; Crimes and Misdemeanours, 1989; Alice, 1990; Bullets over Broadway, 1995; Celebrity, 1999; Sweet and Lowdown, 1999. *Publications:* Getting Even, 1971; Without Feathers, 1975; Side Effects, 1981; contribs to New Yorker, etc.

ALLEN-JONES, Charles Martin; Senior Partner, Linklaters (formerly Linklaters & Paines), 1996–2001; Joint Chairman, Linklaters & Alliance, 1998–2001; *b* 7 Aug. 1939; *s* of late Air Vice-Marshal John Ernest Allen-Jones, CBE, and Margaret Allen-Jones (*née* Rix); *m* 1966, Caroline Beale; one *s* two *d*. *Educ:* Clifton Coll., Bristol. Admitted Solicitor, 1963. Articled Clerk: to the Clerk to the Justices, Uxbridge Magistrates Court, 1958–60; Vizard Oldman Crowder & Cash, London, 1960–63; Solicitor, Supreme Court, London, 1963; Linklaters & Paines, subseq. Linklaters: Solicitor, 1964; Partner, 1968–2001; Head, Hong Kong office, 1976–81; Head, Corporate Dept, 1985–91. Trustee, BM, 2000–; Mem., Barbican Adv. Council, 1997–. *Recreations:* gardening, tennis, travel, reading, golf. *Address:* 11 Campden Street, W8 7EP. *Clubs:* Athenæum, Oriental; Hong Kong (Hong Kong).

ALLENBY, family name of **Viscount Allenby**.

ALLENBY, 3rd Viscount *cr* 1919, of Megiddo and of Felixstowe; **Michael Jaffray Hynman Allenby;** Lieutenant-Colonel, The Royal Hussars, retired 1986; a Deputy Speaker, House of Lords, since 1993; *b* 20 April 1931; *s* of 2nd Viscount Allenby and of Mary Lethbridge Allenby (*d* 1988), *d* of Edward Champneys; *S* father, 1984; *m* 1965, Sara Margaret, *d* of Lt-Col Peter Milner Wiggin; one *s*. *Educ:* Eton; RMA Sandhurst. Commnd 2/Lieut 11th Hussars (PAO), 1951; served Malaya, 1953–56; ADC to Governor, Cyprus, 1957–58; Bde Major, 51 Brigade, Hong Kong, 1967–70; comd Royal Yeomanry (TA), 1974–77; GSO1 Instructor, Nigerian Staff Coll., Kaduna, 1977–79. Chm., Quickrest Ltd, 1987–90. Elected Mem., H of L, 1999. Chm., Internat. League for Protection of Horses, 1997–99. *Recreations:* horses, sailing. *Heir:* *s* Hon. Henry Jaffray Hynman Allenby [*b* 29 July 1968; *m* 1997, Louise, *yr d* of Michael Green; one *s*].

ALLENDALE, 3rd Viscount *cr* 1911; **Wentworth Hubert Charles Beaumont;** DL; Baron, 1906; *b* 12 Sept. 1922; *e s* of 2nd Viscount Allendale, KG, CB, CBE, MC, and Violet (*d* 1979), *d* of Sir Charles Seely, 2nd Bt; *S* father,1956; *m* 1948, Hon. Sarah Ismay (marr. diss.), 2nd *d* of 1st Baron Ismay, KG, PC, GCB, CH, DSO; three *s*. *Educ:* Eton. RAFVR, 1940; Flight-Lieutenant 1943; ADC to Viceroy of India, 1946–47. DL Northumberland, 1961. *Heir:* *s* Hon. Wentworth Peter Ismay Beaumont [*b* 13 Nov. 1948; *m* 1975, Theresa Mary, *d* of F. A. More O'Ferrall; one *s* three *d*]. *Address:* Bywell Hall, Stocksfield on Tyne, Northumberland NE43 7AE. *T:* (01661) 843169; Allenheads, Hexham, Northumberland. *T:* (01434) 685205.

See also Earl of Carlisle, Hon. Sir E. N. C. Beaumont.

ALLENDE, Isabel; writer; *b* 2 Aug. 1942; *d* of Tomás Allende Pesce and Francisca Llona Barros; *m* 1st, 1962, Miguel Frías (marr. diss. 1987); one *s* one *d*; 2nd, 1988, William C. Gordon. *Educ:* Ursulinas (German nuns), Chile; Dunalastaid Amer. Sch., La Paz; British Lebanese Trng Coll., Lebanon; La Maisonette, Chile. Journalist: Chile, 1964–74 (Paula (women's mag.), Mampato (children's mag.), TV programmes, film documentaries); El Nacional, Venezuela, 1975–84; Lecturer in Literature: Montclair Coll., USA; Univ. of Calif at Berkeley, 1988; Univ. of Virginia, 1988. Member: Academía de la Lengua, Chile, 1989; Academía de Artes y Ciencias, Puerto Rico, 1995. Hon. Prof. of Literature, Univ. of Chile, 1991. Lecture tours, N America and Europe. Work has been translated into more than 27 languages and has received numerous literary awards. Hon. DLitt: SUNY, 1991; Bates Coll., USA, 1994; Dominican Coll., USA, 1994; Columbia Coll., USA, 1996; Hon. DHL Florida Atlantic, 1996. Condecoración Gabriela Mistral (Chile), 1994; Chevalier, Ordre des Arts et des Lettres (France), 1994. *Plays:* El Embajador, 1971; La Balada del Medio Pelo, 1973; Los Siete Espejos, 1974. *Publications: novels:* La Casa de los Espíritus (The House of Spirits), 1982 (filmed; adapted for stage); De Amor y de Sombra (Of Love and Shadows), 1984 (filmed); Eva Luna, 1985 (adapted for stage); El Plan Infinito (The Infinite Plan), 1991; Paula, 1994 (adapted for stage); Hija de la Fortuna (Daughter of Fortune), 1999; Retrato en Sepia (Portrait in Sepia), 2000; *short stories:* La Gorda de Porcelana, 1983; Cuentos de Eva Luna (Stories of Eva Luna), 1989 (adapted for theatre, opera, and ballet); Afrodita (Aphrodite), 1997; articles in jls in N America and Europe. *Address:* 116 Caledonia Street, Sausalito, CA 94965, USA.

ALLERTON, Air Vice-Marshal Richard Christopher, CB 1989; DL; Director General of Supply, Royal Air Force, 1987–90, retired; Chairman, Sharpe's of Aberdeen, since 1995; *b* 7 Dec. 1935; *er s* of late Air Cdre Ord Denny Allerton, CB, CBE, and Kathleen Mary Allerton; *m* 1964, Marie Isobel Campbell Mackenzie, *er d* of Captain Sir Roderick Mackenzie, 11th Bt, CBE, DSC, RN, and Marie, Lady Mackenzie; two *s*. *Educ:* Stone House, Broadstairs; Stowe Sch. Commissioned RAF, 1954; served, 1955–78: RAF Hullavington, Oakington, Feltwell, Kinloss, RAF Unit HQ Coastal Command, Hereford, Little Rissington; Instructor, RAF Coll., Cranwell; Student, RAF Staff Coll., Bracknell; Staff, HQ RAF Germany; Chief Instructor, Supply and Secretarial Trng, RAF Coll., Cranwell; Student, Nat. Defence Coll., Latimer; MoD Harrogate; Dep. Dir, RAF Supply Policy, MoD, 1978–80; Station Comdr, RAF Stafford, 1980–82; RCDS 1983; Air Cdre, Supply and Movements, HQ Strike Comd, 1983–86. ADC to the Queen, 1980–82. Pres., RAF Cricket Assoc., 1987–89. Mem., St John Council for Cornwall, 1991–. DL Cornwall, 1995. *Recreations:* shooting, fishing, cricket. *Address:* c/o Lloyds TSB, 13 Broad Street, Launceston, Cornwall PL15 8AG. *Club:* Royal Air Force.

ALLEYNE, Sir George (Allanmore Ogarren), Kt 1990; MD, FRCP; Director, Pan American Health Organization, since 1995 (Assistant Director, 1990–95); *b* 7 Oct. 1932; *s* of Clinton O. Alleyne and Eileen A. Alleyne (*née* Gaskin); *m* 1958, Sylvan Ionie (*née* Chen); two *s* one *d*. *Educ:* Harrison College, Barbados; University College of the West Indies (MB BS London 1977, MD). Completed training as physician in Barbados and UCH, London, 1958–62; Sen. Med. Registrar, UCH, Jamaica, 1962–63; Res. Fellow, Sen. Res. Fellow, MRC Tropical Metabolism Res. Unit, 1963–72; Prof. of Medicine, Univ. of W Indies, 1972–81 (Chm., Dept of Medicine, 1976–81); Pan American Health Organization: Head of Res. Unit, 1981–83; Dir of Health Programs Develt, 1983–90. Sir Arthur Sims Travelling Prof., 1977. Hon. FACP. Hon. DSc Univ. of W Indies, 1989. Jamaica Assoc. of Scientists Award, 1979. Jamaica Centenary Medal, 1980. *Publications:* contribs to learned jls on medicine, renal physiology and biochemistry, health and develt issues. *Recreations:* reading, gardening. *Address:* Pan American Health Organization, 525 23rd Street NW, Washington, DC 20037, USA. *T:* (202) 9743408.

ALLEYNE, Rev. Sir John (Olpherts Campbell), 5th Bt *cr* 1769; Rector of Weeke, Diocese of Winchester, 1975–93; *b* 18 Jan. 1928; *s* of Captain Sir John Meynell Alleyne, 4th Bt, DSO, DSC, RN, and Alice Violet (*d* 1985), *d* of late James Campbell; *S* father, 1983; *m* 1968, Honor, *d* of late William Albert Irwin, Belfast; one *s* one *d*. *Educ:* Eton; Jesus Coll., Cambridge (BA 1950, MA 1955). Deacon 1955, priest 1956; Curate, Southampton, 1955–58; Chaplain: Coventry Cathedral, 1958–62; Clare Coll., Cambridge, 1962–66; to Bishop of Bristol, 1966–68; Toc H Area Sec., SW England, 1968–71; Vicar of Speke, 1971–73, Rector, 1973–75. *Heir:* *s* Richard Meynell Alleyne, *b* 23 June 1972. *Address:* 2 Ash Grove, Guildford, Surrey GU2 5UT.

ALLEYNE, Selwyn Eugene, CBE 1986; Hong Kong Commissioner in London, 1987–89, retired; *b* 4 Dec. 1930; *s* of Gilbert Sydney Alleyne and Dorothy Alleyne; *m* 1956, Ellie Lynn Wong, MBE. *Educ:* Queen's Royal Coll., Trinidad; Jesus Coll., Oxford (MA). Joined Hong Kong Govt, 1956; Dep. Dir of Urban Services, 1974; Dep. Sec. for Civil Service, 1979; Dir of Social Welfare, and MLC, 1980; Dep. Financial Sec., 1983–87. *Recreations:* tennis, chess, collecting Chinese ceramics. *Address:* 118 Whitehall Court, SW1A 2EL. *Club:* Royal Commonwealth Society.

ALLI, Baron *cr* 1998 (Life Peer), of Norbury in the London Borough of Croydon; **Waheed Alli;** Managing Director, Carlton Productions, 1999–2000; Director, Carlton Television, 1999–2000; *b* 16 Nov. 1964. *Educ:* Norbury Manor Sch. Formed televised production co., 24 Hour Productions, later Planet 24 Productions Ltd, with partner Charlie Parsons, Jt Man. Dir, 1992–99. Member: Teacher Trng Agency, 1997–98; Panel 2000; Creative Industry Taskforce. *Address:* House of Lords, SW1A 0PW.

ALLIANCE, Sir David, Kt 1989; CBE 1984; Chairman, N. Brown Group, since 1968; *b* June 1932. *Educ:* Iran. First acquisition, Thomas Hoghton (Oswaldtwistle), 1956; acquired Spirella, 1968, then Vantona Ltd, 1975, to form Vantona Group, 1975; acquired Carrington Viyella to form Vantona Viyella, 1983, Nottingham Manufacturing, 1985, Coats Patons to form Coats Viyella, 1986; Gp Chief Exec., 1975–90, Chm., 1989–99; Chm., Tootal Gp, 1991–99. Gov., Tel Aviv Univ., 1989–. CIMgt (CBIM 1985); CompTI 1984. FRSA 1988. Hon. Fellow: UMIST 1988; Shenkar Coll. of Textile Tech. and Fashion, Israel, 1990. Hon. FCGI 1991. Hon. LLD: Victoria Univ. of Manchester, 1989; Liverpool, 1996; Hon. DSc Heriot-Watt, 1991. *Address:* N. Brown Group, 53 Dale Street, Manchester M60 6ES.

ALLIBONE, Thomas Edward, CBE 1960; DSc Sheffield; FRS 1948; FREng; External Professor of Electrical Engineering, University of Leeds, 1967–79, now Emeritus; Visiting Professor of Physics, City University, since 1971; also Robert Kitchin (Saddlers) Research Professor, since 1983, and first Frank Poynton Professor, Physics Department, since 1984, City University; *b* 11 Nov. 1903; *s* of Henry J. Allibone; *m* 1931, Dorothy Margery, LRAM, ARCM (*d* 2001), *d* of Frederick Boulden, BSc, MEng, MIMechE; two *d*. *Educ:* Central Sch., Sheffield (Birley Scholar); Sheffield Univ. (Linley Scholar); Gonville and Caius Coll., Cambridge (Wollaston Scholar). PhD Sheffield; PhD Cantab. 1851 Exhibition Sen. Student, Cavendish Laboratory, Cambridge, 1926–30; i/c High-Voltage Laboratory, Metropolitan-Vickers Electrical Co., Manchester, 1930–46; Director: Res. Laboratory, AEI, Aldermaston, 1946–63; AEI (Woolwich) Ltd, 1948–63; Scientific Adviser, AEI, 1963; Chief Scientist, Central Electricity Generating Bd, 1963–70. Mem., British Mission on Atomic Energy, Berkeley, Calif, and Oakridge, Tenn, 1944–45; Visitor: BISRA, 1949–55; ASLIB, 1955–62. Lectures: Faraday, 1946, 1956; Royal Instn Christmas, 1959; Wm Menelaus, 1959; Bernard Price, 1959; Trotter Patterson, 1963; Fison Memorial, 1963; Royal Soc. Rutherford Memorial, 1964 and 1972; Baird Memorial, 1967; Melchett, 1970. President: Section A, British Assoc., 1958; EIBA, 1958–59; Inst. of Information Scientists, 1964–67. Vice-President: Inst. of Physics, 1948–52; Royal Instn, 1955–57, 1970–72. Chm., Res. Cttee, British Electrical and Allied Industries Res. Assoc., 1955–62. Member: Council, British Inst. of Radiology, 1935–38; Council, IEE, 1937–40, 1946–49, 1950–53; Cttee, Nat. Physical Laboratory, 1950–60; Govt Cttee on Copyright, 1951; DSIR (Mem., Industrial Grants Cttee, 1950–58); Council, Physical Soc., 1953–56; Council, Southern Electricity Bd, 1953–62; Adv. Council, Science Museum; Adv. Council, RMC; Adv. Court, AEA; Nuclear Safety Adv. Council, Min. of Power, 1959–88. Trustee, British Museum, 1968–74. Governor, Downe House, 1959–69; Chm. Governors, Reading Technical Coll., 1959–68. Lord of the Manor, Aldermaston, 1953–87. Mem. Court, Worshipful Co. of Broderers, 1985– (Liveryman, 1967). FInstP; FREng (Founder FEng 1976); Hon. FIEE; Fellow, Amer. Inst. of Electrical Engineers. Hon. DSc: Reading, 1960; City, 1970; Hon. DEng Sheffield, 1969. Röntgen Medal, British Inst. of Radiology; Thornton and Cooper Hill Medals, IEE; Melchett Medal, Inst. of Fuel. *Publications:* The Release and Use of Nuclear Energy, 1961; Rutherford: Father of Nuclear Energy (Rutherford Lecture 1972), 1973; The Royal Society and its Dining Clubs, 1975; Lightning: the long spark, 1977; Cockcroft and the Atom, 1983; Metropolitan-Vickers Electrical Co. and the Cavendish Laboratory, 1984; The Making of Physicists, 1987; papers on high voltage and transient electrical phenomena, fission and fusion. *Recreations:* photography, travel, gardening, philately. *Address:* York Cottage, Lovel Road, Winkfield, Windsor, Berks SL4 2ES. *T:* (01344) 884501.

ALLIES, Edgar Robin, (Bob); Partner, Allies and Morrison, architects, since 1983; *b* 5 Sept. 1953; *s* of Edgar Martyn Allies, MBE, DFC and Lily Maud Allies; *m* 1991, Jill Anne Franklin; one *s* one *d*. *Educ:* Reading Sch.; Univ. of Edinburgh (MA Hons 1976; DipArch 1977). Rome Schol. in Architecture, 1981–82; Lectr, Univ. of Cambridge, 1984–88; George Simpson Vis. Prof., Univ. of Edinburgh, 1995; Vis. Prof., Univ. of Bath, 1996–; Kea Dist. Vis. Prof., Univ. of Maryland, 1999. Mem., Faculty of Fine Arts, Brit. Sch. at Rome, 1998–. With G. Morrison, founded Allies and Morrison, 1983; *completed projects* include: Clove Bldg, London, 1990 (RIBA Award 1991); Pierhead, Liverpool, 1995; Sarum Hall Sch., London, 1995 (RIBA Award 1996); Nunnery Sq., Sheffield, 1995 (RIBA Award 1996); British Embassy, Dublin, 1995 (RIBA Award 1997); Rosalind Franklin Bldg, Newnham Coll., Cambridge, 1995 (RIBA Award 1996); Contemporary Applied Arts, London, 1996; Abbey Mills Pumping Station, Stratford (RIBA Award), 1997; Rutherford Inf. Services Bldg, Goldsmiths Coll., London, 1997 (RIBA Award 1998); Blackburn House, 1999 (RIBA Award 2000); *exhibitions* include: New British Architecture, Japan, 1994; Allies and Morrison Retrospective, USA Schools of Architecture, 1996–98, Helsinki, Delft, Strasbourg, 1999. Edinburgh Architectural Assoc. Medal for Architecture, 1977. *Publications:* Model Futures, 1983; Allies and Morrison, 1996. *Recreation:* contemporary music. *Address:* Allies and Morrison, 62 Newman Street, W1P 3PG; 46 Lady Somerset Road, Kentish Road, NW5 1TU. *T:* (020) 7485 9219.

ALLIN, George, RCNC; Director General Ship Refitting, Ministry of Defence, 1989–93, retired; *b* 21 June 1933; *s* of late Henry Richard Allin and Mary Elizabeth Allin (*née* Wyatt); *m* 1st, 1956, Barbara May Short (marr. diss.); two *s*; 2nd, 1977, Janice Annette Richardson-Sandell. *Educ:* Devonport High Sch.; Devonport Dockyard Tech. Coll.; RNEC Manadon; RNC Greenwich. WhSch, BSc, CEng, MIEE, FIIM; FBIM. Asst Elect. Engineer, 1957–59; HMS Belfast, 1959; Admiralty, Bath, 1959–62; Elect. Engineer, MoD (Navy), Bath, 1963–68; HM Dockyard, Devonport: Line Manager, 1968–70; Project Manager Frigates, 1970–71; Supt Elect. Engineer, Dep. Personnel Manager, 1971–74; Industrial Relations Manager, 1975; Org. and Develt. Div., Dockyard HQ, Bath, 1975–79; HM Dockyard, Rosyth: Project Manager, SSBN Refit, 1980–81; Production Dir, 1981–83; Dockyard HQ, Bath: Management Systems and Audit Div., 1984–85; Principal Dir, Policy and Plans, 1985–86; Principal Dir, Ship Refitting, MoD (Navy), Bath, 1986–87; Dir, Aldermaston Projects, Brown & Root (on secondment), 1987–89. *Recreations:* chess, music, bowls, snooker. *Address:* 3 Wild Orchard, Faulkland, Bath BA3 5XJ.

ALLINSON, Sir (Walter) Leonard, KCVO 1979 (MVO 1961); CMG 1976; HM Diplomatic Service, retired; *b* 1 May 1926; *o s* of Walter Allinson and Alice Frances Cassidy; *m* 1951, Margaret Patricia Watts; three *d* (of whom two are twins). *Educ:* Friern Barnet Grammar Sch.; Merton Coll., Oxford. First class in History, 1947; MA. Asst Principal, Ministry of Fuel and Power (Petroleum Div.), 1947–48; Asst Principal, later Principal, Min. of Education, 1948–58 (Asst Private Sec. to Minister, 1953–54); transf. CRO, 1958; First Sec. in Lahore and Karachi, 1960–62, Madras and New Delhi, 1963–66; Counsellor and Head of Political Affairs Dept, March 1968; Dep. Head, later Head, of Permanent Under Secretary's Dept, FCO, 1968–70; Counsellor and Head of Chancery, subsequently Deputy High Comr, Nairobi, 1970–73; RCDS, 1974; Diplomatic Service Inspectorate, 1975; Dep. High Comr and Minister, New Delhi, 1975–77; High Comr, Lusaka, 1978–80; Asst Under-Sec. of State (Africa), 1980–82; High Comr in Kenya and Ambassador to UN Environment Programme, 1982–86. Vice Pres., Royal African Soc., 1982–99; Mem. Council, East Africa Inst., 1986–92; Hon. Vice Chm., Kenya Soc., 1989–; Chm., Finance Cttee, Cornwall Red Cross, 1996–98. Gov., Wendron Voluntary Primary Sch., 1990–. *Address:* Tregarthen, Wendron, Helston, Cornwall TR13 0PY. *Club:* Oriental.

ALLIOTT, Sir John (Downes), Kt 1986; Judge of the High Court of Justice, Queen's Bench Division, 1986–2001; *b* 9 Jan. 1932; *er s* of late Alexander Clifford Alliott and Ena Kathleen Alliott (*née* Downes); *m* 1957, Patsy Jennifer, *d* of late Gordon Beckles Willson; two *s* one *d*. *Educ:* Charterhouse; Peterhouse, Cambridge (Schol., BA). Coldstream Guards, 1950–51; Peterhouse, 1951–54; called to Bar, Inner Temple, 1955, Bencher 1980; QC 1973. Dep. Chm., E Sussex QS, 1970–71; Recorder, 1972–86; Leader, 1983–86, Presiding Judge, 1989–92, SE Circuit. Member: Home Office Adv. Bd on Restricted Patients, 1983–86; Parole Bd, 1994–98 (Vice Chm., 1996–98). *Recreations:* rural pursuits, France and Italy, military history. *Address:* Park Stile, Love Hill Lane, Langley, Slough SL3 6DE.

ALLISON, Brian George; Chairman: Amtico Holdings Ltd, since 1996; Smith Group Holdings plc, since 1997; *b* 4 April 1933; *s* of late Donald Brian Allison and Edith Maud Allison (*née* Humphries); *m* 1st, 1958, Glennis Mary Taylor (*d* 1993); one *s* one *d*; 2nd, 1996, Joanne Valerie Norman. *Educ:* Hele's Sch., Exeter; University Coll. London (BSc Econ). FCIM 1981. Flying Officer, RAF, 1955–58. Economist Statistician, Shell-Mex & BP, 1958; Marketing Res. Manager, Spicers, 1958–64; Business Intelligence Services, subseq. The BIS Group: Dir, 1964–91; Gen. Manager, 1964–69; Man. Dir and Dep. Chm., 1969–74; Chm. and Man. Dir, 1974–81; Chm. and Chief Exec., 1981–85; Exec. Chm., 1985–87. Director: NYNEX Inf. Solutions Gp, 1987–90; NYNEX Network Systems Co. (Brussels) SA, 1991–93; non-executive Director: English China Clays plc, subseq. ECC Gp, 1984–92; Brammer plc, 1988–97; Electra Corporate Ventures Ltd, 1989–96; Microgen Holdings plc, 1992–98; Unitech plc, 1993–96; Flexible Management Systems Ltd, 1998–; Mem., London Bd, Halifax Building Soc., 1991–95; Chm., Holt Lloyd Gp, 1995–97. Vis. Prof., Univ. of Surrey, 1976–92, 1994–. Mem., ESRC, 1986–90. Chm., Industrial Adv. Panel, Sch. of Mechanical and Materials Engrg, Univ. of Surrey, 1998–. Distinguished Scholar, QUB, 1989. *Recreations:* tennis, travel, motoring, restoring historic properties. *Club:* Reform.

ALLISON, Air Vice-Marshal Dennis, CB 1987; Chief Executive, North Western Regional Health Authority, 1990–94 (General Manager, 1986–90); *b* 15 Oct. 1932; *m* 1964, Rachel Anne, *d* of Air Vice-Marshal J. G. Franks, CB, CBE; one *s* four *d*. *Educ:* RAF Halton; RAF Coll., Cranwell; Manchester Univ. (MA 1994). Commnd, 1954; No 87 Sqdn, 1955–58; cfs 1958; Flying Instructor and Coll. Adjt, RAF Coll., 1958–61; CO, RAF Sharjah, 1961–62; Indian Jt Services Staff Coll., 1965; HQ 224 Gp, 1965–68; MoD Central Staffs, 1968–70; ndc, 1973; MoD Central Staffs, 1973–74; CO, RAF Coningsby, 1974–76; Canadian Nat. Defence Coll., 1977; MoD Central Staffs, 1978–79; Comdt, Central Flying Sch., 1979–83; Dir of Training (Flying), MoD, 1983–84; Dir of Management and Support of Intelligence, MoD, 1985–86; retired 1987. Chm., Family Health Service Computer Unit, 1992–94; Member: NHS Trng Authority, 1988–91; Standing Cttee on Postgrad. Medical Educn, 1988–93; Steering Cttee on Pharmacist Postgrad. Educn, 1991–94; Adv. Bd, NHS Estates, 1991–95; Nat. Blood Authority, 1993–2001 (Vice Chm., 1994–2001). Gov., Salford Coll. of Technology, 1987–89. QCVSA 1959. *Recreation:* following professional ladies' golf. *Address:* The Old Forge, Castle Bytham, Grantham, Lincs NG33 4RU. *T:* (01780) 410372. *Club:* Royal Air Force.

ALLISON, John, CBE 1975; company director; *b* 4 Oct. 1919; *m* 1st, 1948, Elvira Gwendoline Lewis (*d* 1992); one *s* two *d*; 2nd, 1997, Barbara Mary Tarrant. *Educ:* Morriston Elementary Sch.; Glanmor Secondary Sch.; Swansea Tech. Coll. In family business of quarrying to 1968, and musical instrument retailing, 1957–89. Mem. (Lab) Swansea City Council, 1957–74, Leader, 1967–74 (Dep. Mayor, 1966–67 and 1972–73); Mem. (Lab) W Glamorgan County Council, 1974–89, Leader, 1977–89 (Chm., 1975–76); Chm., ACC, 1986–88. Contested (Lab) Barry, 1970. Chm., S Wales Police Authority, 1987–89. DL W Glam, subseq. Swansea, 1975; JP Swansea, 1966. *Recreations:* fishing, gardening. *Address:* 55 Pocketts Wharf, Maritime Quarter, Swansea SA1 3XL. *T:* (01792) 655882. *Club:* Morriston Golf.

ALLISON, John, PhD; Editor, Opera, since 2000; Music Critic, The Times, since 1995; *b* 20 May 1965; *s* of David Allison and Adele Myrtle Allison (*née* Kirby); *m* 1991, Nicole Galgut. *Educ:* Rondebosch Boys' High Sch., Cape Town; Univ. of Cape Town (BMus 1986, PhD 1989); ARCO. Asst Organist, St George's Cathedral, Cape Town, 1985–89; Music Master, Culford Sch., 1990–91; Asst Ed., 1991–97, Co-ed., 1998–99, Opera mag. *Publications:* Edward Elgar: sacred music, 1994; The Pocket Companion to Opera, 1994; (contrib.) New Grove Dictionary of Music and Musicians, 2nd edn 2001. *Recreations:* travel, art. *Address:* Opera Magazine, 36 Black Lion Lane, W6 9BE. *T:* (020) 8563 8893.

ALLISON, Air Chief Marshal Sir John (Shakespeare), KCB 1995; CBE 1986 (MBE 1971); Air Officer Commanding-in-Chief, Strike Command, 1997–99; Air Aide-de-Camp to the Queen, 1997–99; *b* 24 March 1943; *o s* of Walter Allison and Mollie Emmie Allison (*née* Poole); *m* 1966, Gillian Patricia Middleton; two *s* three *d*. *Educ:* Royal Grammar Sch., Guildford; RAF College, Cranwell; psc, rcds. Commissioned 1964; flying and staff appts include: 5 Sqn; 226 OCU; 310 TFTS (USAF), Arizona; OC 228 OCU; Station Comdr, RAF Wildenrath; Sec., Chiefs of Staff Cttee; Dir, Air Force Plans and Programmes, 1987–89; ACDS Operational Requirements (Air), MoD, 1989–91; AOC No 11 Gp, 1991–94; COS and Dep. C-in-C, Strike Command, 1994–96; Air Member for Logistics and AOC-in-C, Logistics Comd, 1996–97. Mem., Criminal Injuries Compensation Appeals Panel. FRAeS. *Recreations:* air display flying, gliding. *Address:* c/o National Westminster Bank, 24 Broadgate, Coventry CV1 1NB. *Club:* Royal Air Force.

ALLISON, Julia; General Secretary, Royal College of Midwives, 1994–97; *b* 26 Sept. 1939; *d* of Alfred Arthur Richley and Amelia (*née* Douglas); *m* 1960, Barrie Allison; one *s* one *d*. *Educ:* Lilley and Stone Foundn for Girls, Newark, Notts; Univ. of Nottingham (MA); Wolverhampton Poly. (CertEd (Dist.)). RM; ADM; MTD. Clerical officer, Civil Service, 1956–62; liby officer, Nottingham City Libraries, 1963–66; resident in Australia, 1966–68; liby officer, Nottingham City Libraries, 1968–79; direct entry pupil midwife, 1970–72; dist midwife, Nottingham Local Authy, 1972–76; midwifery sister, night duty, Nottingham AHA, 1976–77; registered foster mother, Nottingham Social Services, 1977–79; community midwife, Nottingham HA, 1979–86; midwife teacher, Kingsmill Hosp., 1986–89; Associate Researcher and Sen. Midwife Advr, Univ. of Nottingham, 1989–91; Head of Midwifery Educn, Norfolk Coll. of Nursing and Midwifery, 1991–94. Diocesan Pres., Mother's Union. Member: Parson Woodforde Soc.; Fine Arts Soc. *Publications:* Delivered at Home, 1996; The Organisation of Midwifery Care, 1998. *Recreations:* painting, piano, writing. *Address:* The Yews, 13 Friarscroft Lane, Wymondham, Norfolk NR18 0AT.

ALLISON, Roderick Stuart, CB 1996; Head of UK Delegation to Channel Tunnel Safety Authority, and Member, Inter-Governmental Commission, since 1997; Joint Chairman, Channel Tunnel Safety Authority, since 1997; *b* 28 Nov. 1936; *s* of Stuart Frew Allison and Poppy (*née* Hodges); *m* 1968, Anne Sergeant; one *s* one *d*. *Educ:* Manchester Grammar Sch.; Balliol Coll., Oxford. Entered Ministry of Labour, 1959; Private Sec. to Perm. Sec., 1963–64; Principal, 1964; Civil Service Dept, 1969–71; Asst Sec., 1971, Under Sec., 1977, Dept of Employment; Health and Safety Executive, 1989–96: Dir, Safety Policy Div., 1992–94; Chief Exec., Offshore Safety Div., 1994–96; Mem., 1995–96. Mem., Mgt Cttee, Homestart Camden, 1997–. *Recreations:* reading, music, languages. *Address:* c/o Health and Safety Executive, 2 Southwark Bridge, SE1 9HS.

ALLISON, Ronald William Paul, CVO 1978; journalist, author, broadcaster; television consultant; Chairman: Television Barter International, since 1990; Word and Wood IT, since 1998; Consultant, British Academy of Film and Television Arts, since 1999 (Director of Corporate Affairs, 1993–98); *b* 26 Jan. 1932; *o s* of Percy Allison and Dorothy (*née* Doyle); *m* 1st, 1956, Maureen Angela Macdonald (*d* 1992); two *d*; 2nd, 1993, Jennifer Loy Weider; one *s*. *Educ:* Weymouth Grammar Sch.; Taunton's Sch., Southampton. Reporter, Hampshire Chronicle, 1952–57; Reporter, BBC, 1957–67; freelance broadcaster, 1968–69; special correspondent, BBC, 1969–73; Press Sec. to Queen, 1973–78; regular presenter and commentator, Thames TV, 1978–90; Controller of Sport and Outside Broadcasts, 1980–85, Dir of Corporate Affairs, 1986–89, Thames TV; Chm. and Man. Dir, Grand Slam Sports, 1992–96; Dir, Corporate Affairs, API Gp, 1996–98. Consultant on Royal Family to ITN, 1991–. Editor, BAFTA News, 1993–99. *Publications:* Look Back in Wonder, 1968; The Queen, 1973; Charles, Prince of our Time, 1978; The Country Life Book of Britain in the Seventies, 1980; (ed with Sarah Riddell) The Royal Encyclopedia, 1991. *Recreations:* photography, watching football. *Clubs:* Royal Automobile, Lord's Taverners; Old Tauntonians (Southampton).

ALLISS, Peter; golfer; television commentator; *b* 28 Feb. 1931; *s* of Percy Alliss and Dorothy Alliss (*née* Rust); *m* 1st, 1953, Joan; one *s* one *d*; 2nd, 1969, Jacqueline Anne; two *s* one *d*. *Educ:* Queen Elizabeth's Grammar Sch., Wimborne; Crosby House, Bournemouth. Nat. Service, RAF Regt, 1949–51. Professional golfer, 1946; played in 8 Ryder Cup matches and 10 Canada Cup (now World Cup) matches; winner of 21 major events; open championships of Spain, Portugal, Italy, Brazil. Past Pres., Ladies' PGA and British Green Keepers' Assoc.; twice Captain, British PGA; golf course architect. Hon. Member, Golf Clubs: Royal Cinque Ports; Coombe Hill; Moor Allerton; Beaconsfield; Trevose; Parkstone; Ferndown; Stoke Poges; W Cornwall; Peel; Muirfield Village; Wentworth; Guildford; Rosses Point; Lahinch; Broadstone. *Publications:* Easier Golf (with Paul Trevillion), 1969; Bedside Golf, 1980; Shell Book of Golf, 1981; The Duke, 1983; Play Golf with Peter Alliss, 1983; The Who's Who of Golf, 1983; (with Michael Hobbs) The Open, 1984; Golfer's Logbook, 1984; Lasting the Course, 1984; More Bedside Golf, 1984; Peter Alliss' Most Memorable Golf, 1986; Peter Alliss' Supreme Champions of Golf, 1986; (ed) Winning Golf, 1986; Yet More Bedside Golf, 1986; Play Better Golf with Peter Alliss, 1989; (with Michael Hobbs) Peter Alliss' Best 100 Golfers, 1989; (with Bob Ferrier) The Best of Golf, 1989; The Lazy Golfers' Guide, 1995; *autobiography:* Alliss in Wonderland, 1964; Peter Alliss: an autobiography, 1981. *Recreation:* talking and taking wine with chums. *Address:* Bucklands, Hindhead, Surrey GU26 6HY. *Clubs:* Lansdowne, Crockfords, Ritz Casino.

ALLNUTT, Denis Edwin; former Director of Analytical Services, Department for Education and Employment; *b* 17 May 1946; *m* 1968, Patricia Livermore; one *s* one *d*. *Educ:* Hampton Sch., Middlesex; Univ. of Birmingham (BSc 1967). Statistician, Min. of Housing and Local Govt, DoE and Dept of Transport, 1967–82; Chief Statistician: Dept of Employment, 1982–88; DoE, 1988–90; Hd, subseq. Dir, Analytical Services, DES, then DFE, now DFEE, 1990–2000.

ALLNUTT, (Ian) Peter, OBE; MA; *b* 26 April 1917; *s* of Col E. B. Allnutt, CBE, MC, and Joan C. Gainsford; *m* 1st, 1946, Doreen Louise Lenagan (*d* 1995); four *d*; 2nd, 1997, Doreen Laven. *Educ:* Imperial Service Coll., Windsor; Sidney Sussex Coll., Cambridge. HM Colonial Service, 1939–46, Nigeria, with break, 1940–45, for service in World War II, Nigeria Regt, RWAFF (despatches). Service with the British Council in Peru, E Africa, Colombia, Argentina, Malta, London and Mexico, 1946–77. OBE 1976; Insignia of Aztec Eagle, 1975. *Recreations:* rowing, swimming, pre-Columbian America, the Hispanic world. *Club:* Leander (Henley-on-Thames).

ALLOTT, Prof. Antony Nicolas; Professor of African Law, University of London, 1964–86, now Professor Emeritus; *b* 30 June 1924; *s* of late Reginald William Allott and Dorothy Allott (*née* Dobson); *m* 1952, Anna Joan Sargant, OBE, *d* of late Tom Sargant, OBE, and Marie Cerny; two *s* two *d*. *Educ:* Downside Sch.; New Coll., Oxford. Lieut Royal Northumberland Fusiliers and King's African Rifles, 1944–46. BA Oxon (1st class Hons Jurisprudence), 1948; PhD London 1954. Lecturer in African Law, School of Oriental and African Studies, London, 1948–60; Reader in African Law, Univ. of London, 1960–64; Prof. of African and Comparative Law, Buckingham Univ., 1987–91. Vis. Prof., Université de Paris I, 1984. Hon. Director, Africa Centre, 1963–66; Pres., African Studies Assoc. of UK, 1969–70 (past Hon. Treas.); Vice-Pres., Internat. African Law Assoc., 1967. Académicien associé, Académie Internat. de Droit Comparé, 1982–; Hon. Corresponding Mem., Académie Royale des Sciences d'Outre-Mer, Belgium, 1980. Chm., Governing Body, Plater Coll., Oxford, 1993–98; formerly Gov., St Bartholomew's Hosp. Med. Sch. Member: Senate, Univ. of London, 1978–86; Council, Commonwealth Magistrates' and Judges' Assoc. (formerly Commonwealth Magistrates' Assoc.), 1972– (Hon. Life Vice-Pres., 1997); Chm., Mddx Magistrates' Cts Cttee, 1982–86. Chm., Barnet Petty Sessional Area, 1986; Dep. Chm., N Oxfordshire Magistrates' Court, 1993. JP: Middlesex 1969–86 (Chm., Gore Div., 1985–86); Oxfordshire 1987–94. KSG 1990. *Publications:* Essays in African Law, with special reference to the Law of Ghana, 1960; (ed) Judicial and Legal Systems in Africa, 1962, 2nd edn 1970; New Essays in African Law, 1970; The Limits of Law, 1980; (ed with G. Woodman) People's Law and State Law, 1985; articles in legal and other jls. *Recreations:* music, gardening. *Address:* Sorbrook Mill, Bodicote, Banbury, Oxon OX15 4AU.

See also R. M. Allott.

ALLOTT, Air Cdre Molly Greenwood; CB 1975; *b* 28 Dec. 1918; *d* of late Gerald William Allott. *Educ:* Sheffield High Sch. for Girls. Served War of 1939–45: joined WAAF, 1941; served in: Egypt, Singapore, Germany. Staff of AOC-in-C: RAF Germany, 1960–63; Fighter Command, 1963–66; Training Command, 1971–73; Dir, WRAF, 1973–76; ADC 1973–76. Nat. Chm., Girls' Venture Corps, 1977–82; Member: Council, Union Jack Club, 1977–91; Main Grants Cttee, RAF Benevolent Fund, 1977–82. FIMgt. *Recreations:* travel, fine and decorative arts. *Address:* 15 Camden Hurst, Milford-on-Sea, Lymington, Hants SO41 0WL. *Clubs:* Royal Air Force, Royal Lymington Yacht.

ALLOTT, Robin Michael; Under-Secretary, Departments of Industry and Trade, 1978–80; *b* 9 May 1926; *s* of Reginald William Allott and Dorothy (*née* Dobson). *Educ:* The Oratory Sch., Caversham; New Coll., Oxford; Sheffield Univ. Asst Principal, BoT, 1948; UK Delegn to OECD, Paris, 1952; Private Sec. to Sec. for Overseas Trade, 1953; Principal, Office for Scotland, Glasgow, 1954; UK Delegn to UN Conf. on Trade and Develt, Geneva, 1964; Asst Sec., BoT, 1965; Counsellor, UK Delegn to EEC, Brussels, 1971; sabbatical year, New Coll., Oxford, 1974–75; Dept of Industry (motor industry), 1975; Under-Sec., Dept of Trade, 1976. Member: European Sociobiol Soc., 1992; NY Acad. of Scis, 1995; AAAS, 1996. *Publications:* The Physical Foundation of Language, 1973; The Motor Theory of Language Origin, 1989; (ed) Studies in Language Origins 3, 1994; (ed jtly) Dorothy Dobson's Commonplace Book, 2000; The Natural Origin of Language, 2000; The Great Mosaic Eye, 2001; contrib. Jl of Social and Evolutionary Systems; contrib. collections on lang. and origin of semiosis, sound symbolism, syntax, etc. *Recreations:* studying the evolutionary relation of language, perception and action; computer programming. *Address:* 5 Fitzgerald Park, Seaford, East Sussex BN25 1AX. *T:* (01323) 896022.

See also A. N. Allott.

ALLPORT, Denis Ivor; Chairman, 1979–85 and Chief Executive, 1977–85, Metal Box Ltd (Director, 1973–85, Managing Director, 1977–79, Deputy Chairman, 1979); *b* 20 Nov. 1922; *s* of late A. R. Allport and late E. M. Allport (*née* Mashman); *m* 1949, Diana (*née* Marler); two *s* one *d*. *Educ:* Highgate School. Served War, Indian Army, 1941–46; joined Metal Box Ltd, 1946; various appts in UK, Singapore and Pakistan; Man. Dir, Metal Box Co. of India, 1969–70; Dir, Metal Box Overseas Ltd, 1970–74. Chairman: Castle Underwriting Agents Ltd, 1989–94 (Dir, 1988–94); Devonshire Underwriting Agents Ltd, 1991–93; Director: Beecham Gp plc, 1981–88; Marley plc, 1985–91. Member: Nat. Enterprise Bd, 1980–83; NRDC, 1981–83; Neill Cttee of Enquiry into Regulatory Arrangements at Lloyd's, 1986. Gov., Highgate Sch., 1981–94. CIMgt (FBIM 1977). *Recreation:* golf. *Address:* The Barn, Highmoor, Henley-on-Thames, Oxon RG9 5DH. *T:* (01491) 641283. *Clubs:* MCC, Oriental.

ALLSOP, Malcolm Vincent; Controller of Factual Entertainment, Formats and Daytime, LWT/United Productions, since 2001; Director, Anglia Television; *b* 9 Sept. 1950; *s* of Bernard and Irene Allsop; *m* 1975, Elaine Jessica Cox; one *s*. *Educ:* Highbury Grammar Sch., London. Reporter: Ormskirk Advertiser, Lancs, 1967–68; W Lancs Press Agency, 1968–70; and Producer, BBC Radio Merseyside, 1970–71; BBC TV Manchester, 1971–72; Anglia TV, Norwich, 1973; BBC TV East, Norwich, 1974–77; Anglia Television: Political Ed., 1978–84; Sen. Producer, Current Affairs, 1984–89; Controller, Current Affairs and Religion, 1990–94; Dep. Dir of Progs, 1994–96; Controller of Progs and Prodn, 1996–97; Dir of Progs and Prodn, 1998–2000. *Recreations:* painting, bird-watching, Victorian criminology, pipe-smoking. *Address:* Anglia TV, Anglia House, Norwich NR1 3JG. *T:* (01603) 615151.

ALLSOP, Peter Henry Bruce, CBE 1984; Publishing Consultant, Publishers' Management Advisers, since 1983; *b* 22 Aug. 1924; *s* of late Herbert Henry Allsop and Elsie Hilpern (*née* Whittaker); *m* 1950, Patricia Elizabeth Kingwell Bown; two *s* one *d*. *Educ:* Haileybury; Caius Coll., Cambridge (MA). Called to Bar, Lincoln's Inn, 1948, Bencher, 1989. Temp. Asst Principal, Air Min., 1944–48; Barrister in practice, 1948–50; Sweet & Maxwell: Editor, 1950–59; Dir, 1960–64; Man. Dir, 1965–73; Chm., 1974–80; Dir, Associated Book Publishers, 1963, Asst Man. Dir, 1965–67, Man. Dir, 1968–76, Chm., 1976–88. Chm., Teleordering Ltd, 1978–91; Trustee and Vice-Chm., Yale University Press, 1984–99 (Dir, 1981–84); Director: J. Whitaker & Sons, 1987–98; Lloyd's of London Press, 1991–95. Mem. Council, Publishers Assoc., 1969–81 (Treasurer, 1973–75, 1979–81; Pres., 1975–77; Vice-Pres., 1977–78; Trustee, 1982–95); Member: Printing and Publishing Industry Trng Bd, 1977–79; Publishers' Adv. Cttee, British Council, 1980–85; Chm., Management Cttee, Book House Training Centre, 1980–86. Chm., Social Security Appeal Tribunal, 1982–87 (Mem., 1979–82). Chm., Book Trade Benevolent Soc., 1986–92 (Trustee, 1976–85, 1994–98; Dir, 1985). Mem., St Albans City Council, 1955–58. Chm., DAC, Bath and Wells, 1985–94; Trustee, St Andrews Conservation Trust, Wells, 1987–99; Mem., Wells Cathedral Fabric Adv. Cttee, 1991–99. Chm. Council, King's Coll., Taunton, 1986–94 (Mem., 1983–86). Dir, Woodard Schools (Western Div.) Ltd, 1985–95. Editor, later Editor Emeritus: Current Law, 1952–90; Criminal Law Review, 1954–90. *Publications:* (ed) Bowstead's Law of Agency, 11th edn, 1951. *Recreations:* vegetable gardening, sculling, theatre. *Clubs:* Garrick, Farmers'; Leander (Henley-on-Thames); Avon County Rowing.

ALLSOPP, family name of **Baron Hindlip**.

ALLSOPP, Christopher John; Reader in Economic Policy, since 1997, and Fellow of New College, since 1967, Oxford University; Member, Monetary Policy Committee, Bank of England, since 2000; *b* 6 April 1941; twin *s* of late (Harold) Bruce Allsopp, FSA; *m* 1967, Marian Elizabeth Pearce. *Educ:* Balliol Coll., Oxford (MA 1967); Nuffield Coll., Oxford (BPhil Econs 1967). Econ. Asst, HM Treasury, 1966–67; Oxford University: Lectr in Econs, 1968–97; Tutor in Econs, New Coll., 1967–. Mem. Ct of Dirs, Bank of England, 1997–2000. *Address:* New College, Oxford OX1 3BN; Bank of England, Threadneedle Street, EC2R 8AH.

ALLTHORPE-GUYTON, Marjorie; Director of Visual Arts, Arts Council of England, since 1993; *b* 29 July 1948; *d* of Maurice Jack Allthorpe-Guyton and Edith Florence (*née* Clark); *m* 1st, 1970, Brian Collison (marr. diss.); 2nd, 1989, John Mullis (marr. diss.); one *s* one *d*; 3rd, 2000, Paul Dale. *Educ:* Univ. of East Anglia (BA Hons Fine Art); Courtauld Inst. AMA 1974. Asst Keeper, Norwich Castle Mus., 1969–79; Researcher, Norwich Sch. of Art, 1980–82; Selector, British Art Show, Arts Council, 1982–84; Associate Ed., 1988–91, Ed., 1990–92, Artscribe. External Assessor, Fine Art degrees, 1988–95, Mem. Council, 1997–, Goldsmiths' Coll., London Univ.; External Assessor, Fine Art, Oxford Brookes Univ., 1998–2000. FRSA 1994; FRCA 1999. *Publications:* A Happy Eye: history of Norwich Sch. of Art 1845–1982, 1982; catalogues: Henry Bright, 1973; John Sell Cotman, 1975; John Thirtle, 1977; Norwich Castle Museum, 1979; many essays and articles on contemporary art. *Recreations:* shopping, travel, yacht racing, film, theatre, family. *Address:* 1 Thornhill Road, N1 1HX. *Clubs:* Chelsea Arts, Blacks.

ALLUM, Sarah Elizabeth Royle, (Mrs R. G. Allum); *see* Walker, S. E. R.

ALLWEIS, Martin Peter; His Honour Judge Allweis; a Circuit Judge, since 1994; Designated Family Judge for Greater Manchester, since 1996; *b* 22 Dec. 1947; *s* of late Jack Allweis and of Iris Allweis (*née* Mosco); *m* 1984, Tracy Ruth, *d* of late Hyam Barr and of Bernice Barr; one *s* one *d*. *Educ:* Manchester Grammar Sch.; Sidney Sussex Coll., Cambridge (BA Hons 1969). Called to the Bar, Inner Temple, 1970; in practice on Northern Circuit, 1971–94; a Recorder, 1990–94. *Recreations:* family interests, football (Manchester City FC), squash. *Address:* c/o Manchester County Court, Courts of Justice, Crown Square, Manchester M3 3FL.

ALLWOOD; *see* Muirhead-Allwood.

ALMENT, Sir (Edward) Anthony (John), Kt 1980; FRCOG; Consultant Obstetrician and Gynaecologist, Northampton, 1960–85, retired; *b* 3 Feb. 1922; *s* of Edward and Alice Alment; *m* 1946, Elizabeth Innes Bacon. *Educ:* Marlborough Coll.; St Bartholomew's

Hosp. Med. Coll. MRCS, LRCP 1945; FRCOG 1967 (MRCOG 1951). Served RAFVR, 1947–48. Trng appointments: St Bartholomew's Hosp., 1945–46 and 1954–60; Norfolk and Norwich Hosp., 1948; Queen Charlotte's Hosp. and Chelsea Hosp. for Women, 1949–50; London Hosp., 1951–52. Royal Coll. of Obstetricians and Gynaecologists: Mem. Council, 1961–67, 1976–78; Hon. Sec., 1968–73; Pres., 1978–81. Chm., Cttee of Enquiry into Competence to Practise, 1973–76; Member: Oxford Reg. Hosp. Bd, 1968–74 (Chm., Med. Adv. Cttee, 1972–74); Oxford RHA, 1973–75; Central Midwives Bd, 1967–68; UK Central Council for Nursing, Midwifery and Health Visiting, 1980–83. Examiner: RCOG; Univs of Cambridge, Leeds and Dar-es-Salaam. Hon. Fellow, Amer. Assoc. of Obstetricians and Gynaecologists, 1973 (Joseph Price Oration, 1972); Hon. FRCPI 1979; Hon. FRCPE 1981; Hon. FRCGP 1982; Hon. FRACOG 1984; Hon. FRCPCH 1996. Hon. DSc Leicester, 1982. *Publications:* Competence to Practise, 1976; contrib. to med. jls; articles on wine-related subjects. *Recreations:* wine, fishing, engineering, church architecture. *Address:* Winston House, Boughton, Northampton NN2 8RR.

ALMOND, David John; novelist, short story writer and playwright for children and adults; *b* 15 May 1951; *s* of James Arthur Almond and Catherine Almond (*née* Barber); partner, Sara Jane Palmer; one *d. Educ:* St John's, Felling; St Aidan's, Sunderland; St Joseph's Hebburn; Univ. of E Anglia (BA Hons Eng. and American Lit.); Univ. of Newcastle upon Tyne (PGCE). Postman; teacher (primary, adults and special needs), Tyneside, 1976–98. Commune mem., 1982–83. Ed., Panurge (fiction mag.), 1987–93. *Play:* Wild Girl, Wild Boy, nat. tour, 2001. Hon. DLitt Sunderland, 2001. Silver Pencil (Holland), 2000; Silver Kiss (Holland), 2001; Michael L. Printz Award (USA), 2001. *Publications:* Sleepless Nights, 1985; A Kind of Heaven, 1997; Counting Stars (short stories), 2000; *for children:* Skellig (Library Assoc. Carnegie Medal, Whitbread Children's Book of the Year), 1998 (adapted for radio); Kit's Wilderness (Smarties Silver Award), 1999 (adapted for TV); Heaven Eyes, 2000 (adapted for radio); Secret Heart, 2001; Wild Girl, Wild Boy, 2002; books trans. into more than 20 langs. *Recreation:* walking (Yorkshire Dales, Northumbrian beaches). *Address:* c/o Maggie Noach, The Maggie Noach Literary Agency, 22 Dorville Crescent, W6 0HJ.

ALMOND, George Haylock, CBE 2001 (MBE 1993); DL; County Fire Officer and Chief Executive, Greater Manchester County Fire Service, since 1995; *b* 19 Jan. 1944; *s* of late Arthur Ernest Almond and of Mrs C. V. Almond; *m* 1968, Elizabeth Allcock; one *s* one *d. Educ:* Portsmouth Tech. High Sch.; Eastleigh Tech. Coll. Fireman, then Leading Fireman, and Sub-Officer, Hants Fire Service, 1962–70; Cheshire Fire Brigade: Station Officer, 1970–72; Asst Divl Officer, 1972–75; Divl Officer, Grade III, 1975–77; Divl Officer, Grade I, 1977–82 (Divl Comdr, 1978–82); Greater Manchester County Fire Service: Asst County Fire Officer, 1982–90; Dep. County Fire Officer, 1990–95. FIFireE 1988 (Internat. Pres., 1996–97); FRSH 1989; FIPD 1991. Fire Bde Long Service and Good Conduct Medal 1982. DL Greater Manchester, 1999. SBStJ 2001. *Publications:* Accidents, Injuries and Illnesses to Firemen in Great Britain, 1972; (contrib.) Fire Service Drill Book, 1985; Preliminary Certificate Students Handbook, 1994; contrib. papers to technical jls. *Recreations:* music, reading, walking. *Address:* Greater Manchester County Fire Service Headquarters, 146 Bolton Road, Swinton, Manchester M27 8US. *T:* (0161) 736 5866. *Club:* Rotary (Manchester).

ALMOND, Thomas Clive, OBE 1989; HM Diplomatic Service, retired; Consul-General, Bordeaux, 1992–98; *b* 30 Nov. 1939; *s* of late Thomas and Eveline Almond; *m* 1965, Auriol Gala Elizabeth Annette Hendry. *Educ:* Bristol Grammar Sch.; London Univ. Entered HM Diplomatic Service, 1967; Accra, 1968; Paris, 1971; FCO, 1975; Brussels, 1978; Jakarta, 1980; Brazzaville, 1983; Ambassador to People's Republic of the Congo, 1987–88; Asst Marshal of the Diplomatic Corps and Asst Head of Protocol Dept, 1988–92. *Recreations:* travelling, golf.

ALOTAU, Bishop of, (RC); *see* Moore, Most Rev. D. C.

ALPASS, John; Head of Fraud Strategy, Department for Work and Pensions (formerly Head of Fraud Intelligence, Department of Social Security), since 2000. Security Service, 1973–95; Intelligence Co-ordinator, Cabinet Office, 1996–99. *Address:* Department for Work and Pensions, The Adelphi, 1–11 John Adam Street, WC2N 6HT.

ALPHANDERY, Edmond Gérard; Member, General Council for Maine-et-Loire, since 1976; Mayor of Longué-Jumelles, since 1977; Chairman, Caisse Nationale de Prévoyance, since 1998; *b* 2 Sept. 1943; *m* 1972, Laurence Rivain; one *s. Educ:* Frédéric Mistral Lycée, Avignon; Inst. of Political Studies, Paris; Univs of Chicago and California at Berkeley. Asst Lectr, Univ. of Paris, IX, 1968–69; Lectr, Univ. of Aix-en-Provence, 1970–71; Sen. Lectr, and Dean, Faculty of Econ. Sci., Univ. of Nantes, 1971–74; Prof., Univ. of Angers, 1973; Associate Prof., Univ. of Pittsburgh, 1975; Prof. of Political Economy, Univ. of Paris II, 1974–92. Deputy (UDF-CDS) for Maine-et-Loire, French Nat. Assembly, 1978–93 (Mem., Finance Cttee, 1979–93); Minister of the Economy, France, 1993–95; Vice-Pres., 1991–94, Pres., 1994–95, Maine-et-Loire General Council. Vice-Pres., Centre des Démocrates Sociaux; numerous positions with economic and monetary bodies, incl. Mem., Supervisory Bd, Caisse des Dépôts et Consignations, 1988–93, and Mem., Consultative Cttee, Banque de France, 1998–. Chm., Supervisory Council, CNP Insurance SA, 1992–93; Chm., Electricité de France, 1995–98. Founder and Chm., Euro (50) Gp. Mem., Trilateral Commn, 1996–. *Publications:* Les Politiques de stabilisation (with G. Delsupehe), 1974; Cours d'analyse macroéconomique, 1976; Analyse monétaire approfondie, 1978; 1986: le piège, 1985; La Rupture: le liberalisme à l'épreuve des faits (with A. Fourçans), 1987; La Reforme obligée, sous le soleil de l'euro, 2000. *Address:* Caisse Nationale de Prévoyance, 4 Place Raoul Dautry, 75716 Paris Cedex 15, France.

AL-SABAH, Shaikh Saud Nasir; Minister of Oil, Kuwait; *b* 3 Oct. 1944; *m* 1962, Shaikha Awatif Al-Sabah; three *s* two *d.* Barrister-at-law, Gray's Inn. Entered Legal Dept, Min. of Foreign Affairs, Kuwait. Representative of Kuwait: to 6th Cttee of UN Gen. Assembly, 1969–74; to Seabed Cttee of UN, 1969–73; Vice-Chm., Delegn of Kuwait to Conf. of Law of the Sea, 1974–75; Rep. of Delegn to Conf. of Law of Treaties, 1969; Ambassador to: UK, to Norway, Sweden and Denmark, 1975–80; USA, 1981; Canada and Venezuela, 1981–92; Minister of Information, Kuwait. *Address:* Ministry of Oil, PO Box 5077, 13051 Safat, Fahd as-Salem Street, Kuwait.

AL SHAKAR, Karim Ebrahim; Director, International Directorate, Ministry of Foreign Affairs, Bahrain, since 1995; *b* 23 Dec. 1945; *m* 1979, Fatima Al Mansouri; three *d. Educ:* primary and secondary educn, Bahrain; Delhi Univ. (BA political science 1970). Attaché, Min. of Foreign Affairs, 1970; Mem., Perm. Mission to UN, later Min. of Foreign Affairs, 1972–76; First Sec., 1978; Counsellor, 1981; Perm. Rep. to UN, Geneva and Consul-Gen., 1982–87 (non-resident Ambassador to Germany and Austria and to UN, Vienna, 1984); Ambassador and Perm. Rep to UN, New York, 1987–90; Ambassador to UK, also to Republic of Ireland, the Netherlands and Denmark, 1992–95. *Recreation:* travelling. *Address:* Ministry of Foreign Affairs, POB 547, Government House, Government Road, Manama, Bahrain.

ALSOP, William Allen, OBE 1999; RA 2000; Principal, Alsop & Störmer, Architects, since 1979; *b* 12 Dec. 1947; *s* of Francis John Alsop and Brenda Hight; *m* 1972, Sheila E. Bean; two *s* one *d. Educ:* Architectural Association (DipAA). RIBA. Maxwell Fry, 1971; Cedric Price, 1973–77; Rodrick Ham, 1977–79. Prof. of Architecture, Technical Univ., Vienna, 1995–; Hon. Prof., Central St Martin's Coll. of Art and Design, 1997. Principal buildings: Hamburg Ferry Terminal; Cardiff Visitor Centre (RIBA Nat. Award, 1991); Cardiff Barrage; N Greenwich Underground station; Tottenham Hale Interchange station; Nat. Mus., Nuremberg; Govt HQ, Marseilles (RIBA Nat. Award, 1997). Hamburgische Architektenkammer, 1992; Mem., Russian Architectl Inst., 1995. SADG 1973; FRSA. Hon. LLD Leicester, 1996. *Publications:* City of Objects, 1992; William Alsop Buildings and Projects, 1992; William Alsop Architect, Four Projects, 1993; Will Alsop and Jan Störmer, Architects, 1993; Le Grand Bleu–Marseille, 1994. *Recreation:* fishing. *Address:* Parkgate Studio, 41 Parkgate Road, SW11 4NP. *T:* (020) 7978 7878.

ALSTON, David Ian; Galleries Director, The Lowry, since 1998; *b* 26 June 1952; *s* of Cyril Alston and Dorothy Alston; *m* 1975, Christine Bodin (marr. diss. 1987); two *d*; partner Lesley Webster; one *s* one *d. Educ:* Corpus Christi Coll., Oxford (Open Exhibn, MA; Postgrad. Dip. in History of Art (Dist.)). Asst Curator of Pictures, Christ Church, Oxford, 1978–82; Asst Keeper of Art (Ruskin Collection), Sheffield, 1982; Dep. Dir of Arts, Sheffield MDC, 1982–93; Sen. Principal Keeper, Sheffield Arts and Museums, 1993–94; Keeper of Art, Nat. Museums and Galls of Wales, 1994–98. Co-Founder Ed., Oxford Art Jl, 1978. *Publications:* Under the Cover of Darkness: Night Prints, 1986; Piranesi's Prisons: a perspective, 1987; sundry exhibn texts and articles. *Recreations:* listening, looking, cooking, talking, drinking, walking, playing, loving, musing and other 'ings. *Address:* c/o The Lowry, Pier 8, Salford Quays M5 2AZ. *T:* (0161) 876 2020, *Fax:* (0161) 876 2021; *e-mail:* david@thelowry.com.

ALSTON, John Alistair, CBE 1988; DL; Chairman, Norfolk Health Authority, since 1996; *b* 24 May 1937; *s* of late David Alston and Bathia Mary (*née* Davidson). *Educ:* Orwell Park, Sherborne; RAC, Cirencester. Norfolk County Council: Mem., 1973–97; Leader, 1981–87 and 1989–93; Vice-Chm., 1987–88; Chm., 1988–89. Chairman: Norwich, then E Norfolk HA, subseq. Norfolk Health Commn, 1994–96; Chm., Broads Bill Steering Cttee, 1984–87; Member: Broads Authority, 1988–95; Council, Morley Res. Station, 1981–97; Council, UEA, 1986– (Vice Chm., 1997–). Chm., Norfolk Connections, 2000–. Pres., Norfolk Athletics Assoc., 1997–. DL Norfolk, 1991. *Recreations:* gardening, shooting, fishing. *Address:* Besthorpe Hall, Attleborough, Norfolk NR17 2LJ. *T:* (01953) 452138.

ALSTON, Rt Rev. Mgr J(oseph) Leo; Parish Priest, Sacred Heart Church, Ainsdale, Southport, 1972–98; *b* 17 Dec. 1917; *s* of Benjamin Alston and Mary Elizabeth (*née* Moss). *Educ:* St Mary's School, Chorley; Upholland College, Wigan; English Coll., Rome; Christ's College, Cambridge. Priest, 1942; Licentiate in Theology, Gregorian Univ., Rome, 1942; BA (1st Cl. Hons Classics) Cantab 1945. Classics Master, Upholland Coll., Wigan, 1945–52, Headmaster, 1952–64; Rector, Venerable English Coll., Rome, 1964–71. Protonotary Apostolic, 1988. Mem., Cambridge Soc. *Recreation:* music. *Address:* St Marie's House, 27 Seabank Road, Southport, Merseyside PR9 0EJ. *T:* (01704) 501361.

ALSTON, Richard John William, CBE 2001; choreographer; Artistic Director, The Place, and Richard Alston Dance Company, since 1994; *b* 30 Oct. 1948; *s* of Gordon Walter Alston and late Margot Alston (*née* Whitworth). *Educ:* Eton; Croydon Coll. of Art. Choreographed for London Contemporary Dance Theatre, 1970–72; founded Strider, 1972; worked in USA, 1975–77; Resident Choreographer, 1980–86, Artistic Dir, 1986–92, Ballet Rambert, subseq. Rambert Dance Co. Principal Ballets: Nowhere Slowly; Tiger Balm; Blue Schubert Fragments; Soft Verges; Rainbow Bandit; Doublework; Soda Lake; for Ballet Rambert: Rainbow Ripples, 1980; The Rite of Spring, 1981; Apollo Distraught, 1982; Dangerous Liaisons, 1985; Zansa, 1986; Dutiful Ducks, 1986; Pulcinella, 1987; Strong Language, 1987; Hymnos, 1988; Roughcut, 1990; Cat's Eye, 1992. Created: The Kingdom of Pagodas, for Royal Danish Ballet, 1982; Midsummer, for Royal Ballet, 1983; Le Marteau Sans Maitre, for Compagnie Chopinot, 1992; Delicious Arbour, for Shobana Jeyasingh Dance Co., 1993; Movements from Petrushka, Lachrymae, Rumours Visions, for Aldeburgh Festival, 1994; for Richard Alston Dance Co.: Shadow Realm, Something in the City, 1994; Stardust, 1995; Orpheus Singing and Dreaming, Beyond Measure, Okho, 1996; Brisk Singing, Light Flooding into Darkened Rooms, 1997; Red Run, Waltzes in Disorder, Sophisticated Curiosities, 1998; Slow Airs Almost All, A Sudden Exit, 1999; The Signal of a Shake, Tremor, 2000; Fever, 2001. DUniv Surrey, 1993. Chevalier, Ordre des Arts et des Lettres (France), 1995. *Recreations:* music, reading. *Address:* The Place, 17 Duke's Road, WC1H 9AB.

ALSTON, Robert John, CMG 1987; HM Diplomatic Service, retired; High Commissioner to New Zealand, Governor (non-resident) of Pitcairn, Henderson, Ducie and Oeno Islands, and High Commissioner (non-resident) to Western Samoa, 1994–98; *b* 10 Feb. 1938; *s* of late Arthur William Alston and of Rita Alston; *m* 1969, Patricia Claire Essex; one *s* one *d. Educ:* Ardingly Coll.; New Coll., Oxford (BA Mod. Hist.). Third Sec., Kabul, 1963; Eastern Dept, FO, 1966; Head of Computer Study Team, FCO, 1969; First Sec. (Econ.), Paris, 1971; First Sec. and Head of Chancery, Tehran, 1974; Asst Head, Energy Science and Space Dept, FCO, 1977; Head, Joint Nuclear Unit, FCO, 1978; Political Counsellor, UK Delegn to NATO, 1981; Head, Defence Dept, FCO, 1984; Ambassador to Oman, 1986–90; seconded to Home Civil Service, 1990–92; Asst Under-Sec. of State (Public Depts), FCO, 1992–94. Chm., Link Foundn for UK–NZ Relations, 1999–; Advr, Internat. Trade & Investment Missions Ltd, 1999–; Dir, Romney Resource Centre 2000, 1999–. Consultant on Anglican Communion affairs to Archbishop of Canterbury, 1999–. Trustee, Antarctic Heritage Trust, 1998–. *Recreations:* gardening, travel, music. *Address:* 16 Carlisle Mansions, Carlisle Place, SW1P 1HX.

ALSTON, Prof. Robin Carfrae, OBE 1992; FSA; Professor of Library Studies, London University, 1990–98, now Professor Emeritus, University College London; Hon. Senior Research Fellow, English Studies, London University, since 1998; *b* 29 Jan. 1933; *s* of late Wilfred Louis Alston; *m* 1st, 1957, Joanna Ormiston (marr. diss. 1996); one *s* one *d* (and one *s* decd); 2nd, 1996, Janet Pedley-King (marr. diss. 1999). *Educ:* Rugby Sch.; Univs of British Columbia (BA), Oxford (MA), Toronto (MA) and London (PhD). Teaching Fellow, University Coll., Toronto, 1956–58; Lectr, New Brunswick Univ., 1958–60; Lectr in English Lit., Leeds Univ., 1964–76; Consultant to British Library, 1977–; Editor-in-Chief, 18th Century Short Title Catalogue, 1978–89; Advr to Develt and Systems Office, Humanities and Social Scis (formerly Ref. Div.), British Library, 1984–; Editl Dir, The Nineteenth Century, series of microfiche texts 1801–1900, 1985–. Dir, Sch. of Library, Archive and Information Studies, UCL, 1990–95; Course Dir, History of the Book, Sch. of Advanced Studies, London Univ., 1995–98. Hon. Res. Fellow, UCL, 1987–. Klein Vis. Prof., Univ of Texas, 1990; Vis. Prof., Univ. of Malta, 1994. David Murray Lectr, Univ. of Glasgow, 1983; Guest Lectr, Univ. of London, 1983, Sorbonne, 1984, Tokyo Symposium on micro-reproduction, 1984; Cecil Oldman Lectr, Leeds Univ., 1988, 1989; Morris Meml Lectr, Royal Instn, 1991. Jt Editor, Leeds Studies in English and Leeds Texts and Monographs, 1965–72; Editor, Studies in Early Modern

English, 1965–72; Jt Editor, The Direction Line, 1976–; Editor: Special Pubns, Bibliographical Soc., 1983–; Libraries and Archives (series), 1991–. Founder, Chm. and principal Editor, Scolar Press Ltd, 1966–72, Man. Dir, 1984–; Founder, Janus Press, devoted to original art prints, 1973. Member: Adv. Cttee, British Library, 1975–; Adv. Cttee, MLA of America for the Wing Project, 1980–; Adv. Panel, Aust. Research Grants Cttee, 1983–; Adv. Bd, Cambridge Hist. of the Book in Britain, 1989–. Member: Organising Cttee, 18th Century Short Title Catalogue, 1976–; Cttee, British Book Trade Index, 1984–. Mem. Council, Bibliographical Soc., 1967– (Vice-Pres., 1978–88, Pres., 1988–90); Founding Mem. Council, Ilkley Literature Festival, 1973–; Jt Founder, Frederic Madden Soc., 1989–. Consultant, Consortium of Univ. Research Libraries, 1985–86; Advr to Govt of Pakistan on estabt of Nat. Liby of Pakistan, 1988. FSA 1987; Hon. FLA, 1986. Samuel Pepys Gold Medal, Ephemera Soc., 1984; Smithsonian Instn award, 1985; Walford Medal, Library Assoc., 1993; Gold Medal, Bibliographical Soc., 1996. *Publications:* An Introduction to Old English, 1961 (rev. edn 1966); A Catalogue of Books relating to the English Language (1500–1800) in Swedish Libraries, 1965; English Language and Medieval English Literature: a Select Reading-List for Students, 1966; A Bibliography of the English Language from the Invention of Printing to the Year 1800: Vol. I, 1965; Vols V and VIII, 1966; Vols VII and IV, 1967; Vol. II, 1968; Vol. VI, 1969; Vol. III, 1970; Vol. IX, 1971; Vol. X, 1972; Vol. XI, 1978; Vol. XII part 1, 1987; Vol. XII part 2, 1988; Vol. XIII, 1999; Vol. XIV, 2000; Vol. XV, 2001; Alexander Gil's Logonomia Anglica (1619): a translation into Modern English, 1973; (jtly) The Works of William Bullokar, Vol. I, 1966; English Studies (rev. edn of Vol. III, Cambridge Bibl. Eng. Lit.), 1968; English Linguistics 1500–1800: a Collection of Texts in Facsimile (365 vols), 1967–72; European Linguistics 1500–1700: a Collection of Texts in Facsimile (12 vols), 1968–72; A Checklist of the works of Joseph Addison, 1976; Bibliography MARC and ESTC, 1978; Eighteenth-Century Subscription Lists, 1983; ESTC: the British Library Collections, 1983; The arrangement of books in the British Museum Library 1843–1973, and the British Library 1973–1985, 1987; The Nineteenth Century: subject scope and principles of selection, 1987; Index to Pressmarks in use in the British Museum Library and the British Library, 1987; Index to the Classification Schedules of the Map Collections in the British Library, 1987; Computers and Libraries, 1987; The British Library: past, present, future, 1989; Women Writers of Fiction, Verse and Drama: a checklist of works published between 1801 and 1900 in the collections of the British Library, 1990; Handlist of unpublished finding aids to the London Collections of the British Library, 1991; Handlist of catalogues and book lists in the Department of Manuscripts, British Library, 1991; Books with Manuscript: a catalogue, 1994; Books printed on vellum in The British Library, 1996; numerous articles, printed lectures, reviews, etc. *Recreations:* music, photography. *Address:* Dove Cottage, The Street, Brockford, Suffolk IP14 5PE; *e-mail:* r.alston@dircon.co.uk.

ALSTON-ROBERTS-WEST, Lt-Col George Arthur; *see* West.

ALT, Deborah; *see* Gribbon, D.

ALTHAUS, Sir Nigel (Frederick); Kt 1989; Senior Broker to the Commissioners for the Reduction of the National Debt (Government Broker), 1982–89; *b* 28 Sept. 1929; *er s* of late Frederick Rudolph Althaus, CBE and Margaret Frances (*née* Twist); *m* 1958, Anne, *d* of P. G. Cardew; three *s* one *d*. *Educ:* Eton; Magdalen Coll., Oxford (Roberts Gawen Scholar; 2nd Cl. Lit. Hum. 1954). National Service, 60th Rifles, 1948–50. Joined Pember and Boyle (Stockbrokers), 1954; Partner, 1955 75, Sen. Partner, 1975–82; Sen. Partner, Mullens and Co., 1982–86. Mem., Stock Exchange, 1955–89; Chm., Stock Exchange Benevolent Fund, 1975–82. Treas., ICRF, 1991–2000. Master, Skinners' Co., 1977–78; Chm. Governors, Skinners' Co. Sch. for Boys, Tunbridge Wells, 1982–89. Chm., British Library of Tape Recordings for Hosp. Patients, 1975–97. Comr, Royal Hosp., Chelsea, 1988–94. Queen Victoria's Rifles (TA), 1950–60; Hon. Col, 39 Signal Regt (TA), 1982–88. *Publication:* (ed) British Government Securities in the Twentieth Century, 1976. *Recreations:* golf, shooting, music. *Address:* c/o Bank of England, Threadneedle Street, EC2R 8AH. *Clubs:* Boodle's, Beefsteak; Swinley Forest Golf (Ascot).

ALTHORP, Viscount; Louis Frederick John Spencer; *b* 14 March 1994; *o s* and *heir* of Earl Spencer, *qv*.

ALTMAN, John; His Honour Judge Altman; a Circuit Judge since 1991; *b* 21 June 1944; *s* of Lionel and Vita Altman; *m* 1968, Elizabeth Brown; two *d*. *Educ:* Bootham Sch., York; Univ. of Bristol (LLB); Council of Legal Education. Called to the Bar, Middle Temple, 1967; part-time Chm., Industrial Tribunals, 1983; Asst Recorder, 1985; Chm., Industrial Tribunals, 1986; a Recorder, 1989. *Publications:* contribs to Law Guardian. *Recreations:* reading, photography, music, theatre. *Address:* c/o Luton Crown Court, 7 George Street, Luton, Beds LU1 2AA.

ALTMAN, Lionel Phillips, CBE 1979; special adviser to public bodies and private sector; Chairman: European Cleaning Services Group, 1991–94; Hydro-Lock Europe (formerly Hydro-Lock UK), 1992–96; Equity & General plc, 1978–91; Westminster Consultancy, since 1998; *s* of late Arnold Altman and Catherine Phillips; *m* Diana; one *s* two *d* by previous marriages. *Educ:* University Coll. and Business Sch., also in Paris. FIMI; FCIM; FMI; MIPR. Director: Carmo Holdings Ltd, 1947–63; Sears Holdings Motor Gp, 1963–72; Sears Finance, 1965–71; C. & W. Walker Holdings Ltd, 1974–77; H. P. Information plc, 1985–91; Motor Agents Assoc. Ltd, 1986–89 (Mem., Nat. Council, 1965–; Pres., 1975–77); Chm., Pre-Divisional Investments Ltd, 1972–95 (Chief Exec., 1972–94). Chairman: Motor Industry Educnl Consultative Council Industry Working Party, producing Altman Report on recruitment and training, 1968; Retail Motor Industry Working Party on Single European Market, 1988–92. Vice-Pres., and Mem. Council, Inst. of Motor Industry, 1970–78. Chairman: Publicity Club of London, 1961–62; Industry Taxation Panel, 1977–86; United Technologists Estabt, 1980–; Dep. Chm., Technology Transfer Assoc., 1984–90; Member: Council, CBI, 1977–88; CBI Industrial Policy Cttee, 1979–85; Dun & Bradstreet Industry Panel, 1982–86. Dep. Chm., Wallenberg Foundn, 1997–. Chairman: Automotive VIP Club, 1988–92; Barbican Assoc., 1995–98. Life Vice-Pres., Devon County Agricl Assoc., 1980. Gov., GSMD, 2000–. Various TV and radio broadcasts. Mem., Court of Common Council, Corp. of London, 1996– (Member: Policy and Resources Cttee; Finance Cttee; Deputy Chairman: Standards Cttee, 2001–; Libraries, Guildhall Art Gall. and Archives Cttee, 2001–); Freeman: City of London, 1973; City of Glasgow, 1974; Liveryman and former Hon. Treas., Coachmakers' and Coach Harness Makers' Co.; Burgess Guild Brother, Cordwainers' Co. *Publications:* articles. *Address:* (office) 405 Gilbert House, Barbican, EC2Y 8BD. *T:* and *Fax:* (020) 7638 3023.

ALTMAN, Robert; film director; *b* Kansas City, 20 Feb. 1925; *m* 3rd, Kathryn Altman; one *s* and one adopted *s* (and two *s* one *d* by previous marriages). *Educ:* Wentworth Mil. Acad. Served US Army, 1943–47. Industrial film maker, Calvin Co., Kansas City, 1950–57. Television writer, producer and director, 1957–65. *Films directed:* The Delinquents, 1957; (co-dir) The James Dean Story, 1957; Nightmare in Chicago, 1964; Countdown, 1968; That Cold Day in the Park, 1969; M*A*S*H*, 1970 (Grand Prix, Cannes, 1970); Brewster McCloud, 1971; McCabe and Mrs Miller, 1971; Images, 1972; The Long Goodbye, 1973; Thieves Like Us, 1974; Popeye, 1980; Come Back to the 5 & Dime Jimmy Dean, Jimmy Dean, 1982; OC & Stiggs, 1985; Fool for Love, 1986; Beyond Therapy, 1987; (jtly) Aria, 1987; Vincent & Theo, 1990; The Player, 1992 (Best Dir, Cannes Film Fest. 1992); Short Cuts, 1993; The Gingerbread Man, 1998; *directed and produced:* California Split, 1974; Nashville, 1975; Buffalo Bill and the Indians, 1976; 3 Women, 1977; A Wedding, 1978; Quintet, 1979; A Perfect Couple, 1979; Health, 1980; Streamers, 1983; Secret Honor, 1984; Tanner '88, 1988 (series); Prêt à Porter, 1994; Kansas City, 1996; Jazz '34: remembrances of Kansas City swing, 1997; Cookie's Fortune, 1999; Dr T and the Women, 2000; *produced:* Welcome to LA, 1977; The Late Show, 1977; Remember My Name, 1978; Rich Kids, 1979; Mrs Parker and the Vicious Circle, 1995; Afterglow, 1997; *also screenplay for:* The Delinquents; Images; 3 Women; (jointly): McCabe and Mrs Miller; Thieves Like Us; Buffalo Bill and the Indians; A Wedding; Quintet; A Perfect Couple; Health; Beyond Therapy; Short Cuts; Prêt à Porter; Kansas City. *Address:* c/o Sandcastle 5 Productions, Inc., 502 Park Avenue #15-G, New York City, NY 10022, USA.

ALTON, family name of **Baron Alton of Liverpool**.

ALTON OF LIVERPOOL, Baron *cr* 1997 (Life Peer), of Mossley Hill, in the Co. of Merseyside; **David Patrick Paul Alton;** *b* 15 March 1951; *s* of Frederick and Bridget Alton; *m* 1988, Dilys Elizabeth, *yr d* of Rev. Philip Bell; three *s* one *d*. *Educ:* Edmund Campion Sch., Hornchurch; Christ's College of Education, Liverpool. Elected to Liverpool City Council as Britain's youngest City Councillor, 1972; CC, 1972–80; Deputy Leader of the Council and Housing Chairman, 1978; Vice-Pres., AMA, 1979–. MP Liverpool, Edge Hill (by-election), March 1979–83, Liverpool, Mossley Hill, 1983–97 (L, 1979–88, Lib Dem, 1988–97). Liberal Party spokesman on: the environment and race relations, 1979–81; home affairs, 1981–82; NI, 1987–88 (Alliance spokesman on NI, 1987); Chief Whip, Liberal Party, 1985–87; Member: Select Cttee on the Environment, 1981–85; H of C Privileges Cttee, 1994–97; cross-bencher, 1997–. All Party Groups: Vice Chairman: Drugs Misuse, 1993–97; Mental Health, 1995–97; Treasurer: Pro-Life, 1993–; Landmines, 1996–; Friends of CAFOD; Chm., Street Children, 1992–97. Chm., Liberal Candidates Cttee, 1985. Nat. Pres., Nat. League of Young Liberals, 1979. Co-founder, Movement for Christian Democracy in Britain, 1990. Vis. Fellow, St Andrews Univ., 1996; Prof. of Citizenship, Liverpool John Moores Univ., 1997. Former Chm., Council for Educn in Commonwealth. Nat. Vice-Pres., Life; Pres., Liverpool Br., NSPCC; Vice-President: Liverpool YMCA; Crisis; Chairman: Forget-me-not Appeal (Royal Liverpool Hosp.); Merseyside CVS. Vice-Pres., Assoc. of Councillors. Patron: Jubilee Campaign for the release of prisoners of conscience, 1986–; Nat. Assoc. Child Contact Centres, 1997–. Mem., Catholic Writers' Guild; Trustee, Catholic Central Liby, 1998–. Columnist, The Universe, 1989–. *Publications:* What Kind of Country?, 1987; Whose Choice Anyway?, 1988; Faith in Britain, 1991; Signs of Contradiction, 1996; Life After Death, 1997; Citizen Virtues, 1999; Citizen 21, 2001; Pilgrim Ways, 2001. *Recreations:* gardening, reading, walking. *Address:* Jacob's Ladder, Lower Road, Knowle Green, Lancs PR3 2YN.

ALTON, Euan Beresford Seaton, MBE 1945; MC 1943; Under Secretary, Department of Health and Social Security, 1968–76; *b* 22 April 1919; *y s* of late William Lester St John Alton and Ellen Seaton Alton; *m* 1953, Diana Margaret Ede; one *s* one *d*. *Educ:* St Paul's Sch.; Magdalen Coll., Oxford (Exhibnr; MA). Served with Army, 1939–45; Major RA. Admin. Officer, Colonial Service and HM OCS, Gold Coast and Ghana, 1946–58; Admin. Officer, Class 1, 1957. Entered Civil Service as Asst Principal, Min. of Health, 1958; Principal, 1958; Asst Sec., 1961; Under Sec., 1968. *Recreations:* sailing, walking. *Address:* Spindlehurst, School Lane, Brantham, Manningtree, Essex CO11 1QE. *T:* (01206) 393419. *Club:* Stour Sailing (Manningtree).

ALTON, Roger; Editor, The Observer, since 1998; *b* 20 Dec. 1947; *s* of Reginald Ernest Alton and Jeanine Beatrice Alton (*née* Gentis); divorced; one *d*. *Educ:* Clifton Coll.; Exeter Coll., Oxford. Liverpool Post, 1969–74; The Guardian, 1974–98. Editor of the Year, What the Papers Say Awards, 2000. *Recreations:* sports, films, ski-ing, climbing. *Address:* The Observer, 119 Farringdon Road, EC1R 3ER. *Clubs:* Climbers', Soho House, Groucho.

ALTRINCHAM, Barony of, *cr* 1945, of Tormarton; title disclaimed by 2nd Baron. *Heir to barony:* Hon. Anthony Ulick David Dundas Grigg [*b* 12 Jan. 1934; *m* 1965, Eliane de Miramon; two *s* one *d*].

ALUN-JONES, Sir (John) Derek; Kt 1987; Director, Oyez Straker Group plc, since 1997, and several other private companies; *b* 6 June 1933; *s* of Thomas Alun-Jones, LLB and Madge Beatrice Edwards; *m* 1960, Gillian Palmer; two *s* three *d*. *Educ:* Lancing College; St Edmund Hall, Oxford (MA Hons Jurisp.). Philips Electrical, 1957–59; H. C. Stephens, 1959–60; Expandite, 1960–71 (Man. Dir, 1966–71); Man. Dir, Burmah Industrial Products, 1971–74; Man. Dir and Chief Exec., 1975–87, Chm., 1987–90, Ferranti, subseq. Ferranti Internat. Signal, then Ferranti Internat.; Director: Burmah Oil Trading, 1974–75; Royal Insurance Holdings plc (formerly Royal Insurance), 1981–96; Throgmorton Trust, 1978–84; SBAC, 1982–90; Reed International PLC, 1984–90; GKN plc, 1986–88; Consolidated Gold Fields PLC, 1988–89. Chm. of Govs, Lancing Coll., 1986–99. Fellow, Woodard Corp., 1986–. *Recreations:* shooting, fishing, golf. *Address:* The Willows, Effingham Common, Surrey KT24 5JE. *T:* (01372) 458158. *Clubs:* Effingham Golf, Swinley Forest Golf.

ALVAREZ, Alfred; poet and author; *b* London, 1929; *s* of late Bertie Alvarez and Katie Alvarez (*née* Levy); *m* 1st, 1956, Ursula Barr (marr. diss. 1961); one *s*; 2nd, 1966, Anne Adams; one *s* one *d*. *Educ:* Oundle Sch.; Corpus Christi Coll., Oxford. BA (Oxon) 1952, MA 1956. Research Schol., CCC, Oxon, and Research Schol. of Goldsmiths' Company, 1952–53, 1954–55. Procter Visiting Fellowship, Princeton, 1953–54; Vis. Fellow of Rockefeller Foundn, USA, 1955–56, 1958; gave Christian Gauss Seminars in Criticism, Princeton, and was Lectr in Creative Writing, 1957–58; D. H. Lawrence Fellowship, New Mexico Univ., 1958; Poetry Critic and Editor, The Observer, 1956–66. Visiting Professor: Brandeis Univ., 1960; New York State Univ., Buffalo, 1966. Adv. Ed., Penguin Modern European Poets in Translation, 1966–78. Hon. DLitt East London, 1998. Vachel Lindsay Prize for Poetry (from Poetry, Chicago), 1961. *Publications:* The Shaping Spirit (US title, Stewards of Excellence), 1958; The School of Donne, 1961; The New Poetry (ed and introd), 1962; Under Pressure, 1965; Beyond All This Fiddle, 1968; Lost (poems), 1968; Penguin Modern Poets, No 18, 1970; Apparition (poems, with paintings by Charles Blackman), 1971; The Savage God, 1971; Beckett, 1973; Hers (novel), 1974; Hunt (novel), 1978; Autumn to Autumn and Selected Poems 1953–76, 1978; Life After Marriage, 1982; The Biggest Game in Town, 1983; Offshore, 1986; Feeding the Rat, 1988; Rain Forest (with paintings by Charles Blackman), 1988; Day of Atonement (novel), 1991; The Faber Book of Modern European Poetry (ed and introd.), 1992; Night, 1995; Where Did It All Go Right? (autobiog.), 1999; Poker: bets, bluffs and bad beats, 2001. *Recreations:* poker, music, swimming. *Address:* c/o Gillon Aitken Associates, 29 Fernshaw Road, SW10 0TG. *Clubs:* Beefsteak, Climbers', Alpine.

ALVES, Colin, OBE 1990; General Secretary: General Synod Board of Education, 1984–90; National Society for Promoting Religious Education, 1984–90; *b* 19 April 1930; *s* of Donald Alexander Alves and Marjorie Alice (*née* Marsh); *m* 1953, Peggy (*née* Kember); two *s* one *d*. *Educ:* Christ's Hospital, Horsham; Worcester Coll., Oxford (MA). School teaching, 1952–59; Lectr, King Alfred's Coll., Winchester, 1959–68; Head of Dept, Brighton Coll. of Educn, 1968–74; Dir, RE Centre, St Gabriel's Coll., 1974–77; Colleges Officer, General Synod Bd of Educn, 1977–84. Mem., Durham Commn on RE, 1967–70; Chm., Schs Council RE Cttee, 1971–77; Sec., Assoc. of Voluntary Colls, 1978–84; Member: Adv. Cttee on Supply and Educn of Teachers, 1980–85; Nat. Adv. Body for Public Sector Higher Educn, 1983–88; Voluntary Sector Consultative Council, 1984–88. Review Officer, Churches Together in England, 1993–94. Governor: Christ Church Coll., Canterbury, 1981–95; Haywards Heath Coll., 1982–99; Digby Stuart Coll., 1990–96; Trustee: Shoei Coll., Winchester, 1982–94; St Gabriel's Trust, 1984–; St Pierre Internat. Youth Trust, 1990–96; St Gregory's Trust, 1991–99. MLitt Lambeth, 1989. *Publications:* Religion and the Secondary School, 1968; The Christian in Education, 1972; The Question of Jesus, 1987; Free to Choose, 1991; contrib. various symposia on RE. *Recreations:* music, walking, gardening. *Address:* 9 Park Road, Haywards Heath, Sussex RH16 4HY. *T:* (01444) 454496.

ALVEY, John, CB 1980; FREng; Chairman, SIRA Ltd, 1987–94; *b* 19 June 1925; *s* of George C. V. Alvey and Hilda E. Alvey (*née* Pellatt); *m* 1955, Celia Edmed Marson; three *s*. *Educ:* Reeds Sch.; London Univ.; BSc (Eng), DipNEC. FIEE. London Stock Exchange, to 1943. Royal Navy, 1943–46; Royal Naval Scientific Service, 1950; Head of Weapons Projects, Admiralty Surface Weapons Estabt, 1968–72; Dir-Gen. Electronics Radar, PE, MoD, 1972–73; Dir-Gen., Airborne Electronic Systems, PE, MoD, 1974–75; Dir, Admiralty Surface Weapons Estabt, 1976–77; Dep. Controller, R&D Estabts and Res. C, and Chief Scientist (RAF), MoD, 1977–80; Senior Dir, Technology, 1980–83, Man. Dir, Develt and Procurement, and Engr-in-Chief, 1983–86, British Telecom. Dir (non-exec.), LSI Logic Ltd, 1986–91. Member Council: Fellowship of Engrg, 1985–92 (Vice-Pres., 1989–92); Foundn for Sci. and Technology, 1986–90; City Univ., 1985–93. Fellow, Queen Mary and Westfield Coll. (formerly QMC), London, 1988. FREng (FEng 1984). FRSA 1983. Hon. DSc City, 1984; Hon. DTech CNAA, 1991. *Recreations:* reading, Rugby, ski-ing, theatre going. *Address:* 9 Western Parade, Emsworth, Hants PO10 7HS.

ALVINGHAM, 2nd Baron *cr* 1929, of Woodfold; **Maj.-Gen. Robert Guy Eardley Yerburgh,** CBE 1978 (OBE 1972); DL; *b* 16 Dec. 1926; *s* of 1st Baron and Dorothea Gertrude (*d* 1927), *d* of late J. Eardley Yerburgh; *S* father, 1955; *m* 1952, Beryl Elliott, *d* of late W. D. Williams; one *s* one *d*. *Educ:* Eton. Commissioned 1946, Coldstream Guards; served UK, Palestine, Tripolitania, BAOR, Farelf, British Guiana; Head of Staff, CDS, 1972–75; Dep. Dir, Army Staff Duties, 1975–78; Dir of Army Quartering, 1978–81, retired. Patron, Royal British Legion, Oxfordshire. DL Oxfordshire, 1996. *Heir: s* Captain Hon. Robert Richard Guy Yerburgh, 17th/21st Lancers, retired [*b* 10 Dec. 1956; *m* 1st, 1981, Vanessa, *yr d* of Captain Duncan Kirk (marr. diss. 1993); two *s*; 2nd, 1994, Karen, *er d* of Antony Baldwin; one *s* one *d*].

ALWARD, Peter Andrew Ulrich; Senior Vice President, Artists and Repertoire, EMI Classics, since 1997; *b* 20 Nov. 1950; *s* of Herbert Andrew Alward and Marion Evelyne (*née* Schreiber). *Educ:* Mowden Prep. Sch., Hove; Bryanston; Guildhall Sch. of Music and Drama. Simrock Music Publishers, London, 1968–70; with EMI, 1970–: EMI Records UK, London, 1970–74; Eur. Co-ordinator, EMI Classical Div., Munich, 1975–83; Exec. Producer, with Herbert von Karajan, for all EMI recordings, 1976–89; Artists and Repertoire, UK: Manager, 1983–84; Internat. Dir, 1985–88; Vice-Pres., 1989–97. Mem., Adv. Bd, Royal Opera House, Covent Garden, 1998–99. Dir, Young Concert Artists Trust, 1999–. *Recreations:* all classical music sectors, exhibitions of painting and sculpture, theatre, books, collecting stage designs and costume designs, cooking, travelling. *Address:* 24 Midway, Walton-on-Thames, Surrey KT12 3HZ. *T:* (01932) 248985; Reiteralpestrasse 19, 83395 Freilassing, Germany. *T:* (865) 43558; EMI Classics, 64 Baker Street, W1U 7DQ. *T:* (020) 7467 2203. *Club:* Arts.

AMANN, Prof. Ronald; PhD; Director-General, Centre for Management and Policy Studies, Cabinet Office, since 1999; Professor of Comparative Politics (formerly of Soviet Politics), University of Birmingham, since 1986 (on leave of absence); *b* 21 Aug. 1943; *s* of George James Amann and Elizabeth Clementson Amann (*née* Towell); *m* 1965, Susan Frances Peters; two *s* one *d*. *Educ:* Heaton Grammar Sch., Newcastle upon Tyne; Univ. of Birmingham (MSocSc, PhD). Consultant, OECD, and Res. Associate, 1965–68; University of Birmingham: Asst Lectr, then Lectr and Sen. Lectr, 1968–83; Dir, Centre for Russian and E European Studies, 1983–89; Dean, Faculty of Commerce and Soc. Sci., 1989–91; Pro-Vice-Chancellor, 1991–94; Chief Exec. and Dep. Chm., ESRC, 1994–99. Vis. Fellow, Osteuropa Inst., Munich, 1975. Special Advr, H of C Select Cttee on Sci. and Technol., 1976. Member: Technology Foresight Steering Cttee, 1995–2000; COPUS, 1996–1999. Mem. Council, SSEES, London Univ., 1986–89. Founder AcSS, 1999. FRSA. *Publications:* jointly: Science Policy in the USSR, 1969; The Technological Level of Soviet Industry, 1977; Industrial Innovation in the Soviet Union, 1982; Technical Progress and Soviet Economic Development, 1986. *Recreations:* modern jazz, walking. *Address:* 26 Spring Road, Edgbaston, Birmingham B15 2HA. *T:* (0121) 440 6186. *Club:* Athenæum.

AMARAL, Sergio Silva do, Hon. KBE 1997; Brazilian Ambassador to the Court of St James's, since 1999; *b* 1 June 1944; *s* of Pedro Augusto do Amaral and Maria Aparecida Silva do Amaral; *m* Rosario Jorge do Amaral; two *d*; one *s* one *d* from previous marriage. *Educ:* Univ. of Paris (Master in Pol Sci.); Rio Branco Inst.; Univ. of São Paulo (BSc Legal and Social Scis). Joined Brazilian Diplomatic Service, 1974; Paris, 1974–76; Bonn, 1977–80; Washington, 1984–87, 1992–93; Geneva, 1990–92; Sec. for Internat. Affairs, Min. of Finance, and Chief Debt Negotiator for Brazil, 1988–90; Dep. Rep. to GATT, Geneva, 1990–91; Vice-Minister for Envmt and the Amazon, 1993–94; COS to Minister of Finance, 1994; Exec. Sec., Federal Commn for Foreign Trade, 1995; Sec. of Social Communicn and Spokesman for Pres. of Brazil, 1995–99. Asst Prof. of Political Sci. and Internat. Relns, Univ. of Brasilia, 1981–. Grand Cross, Order of Rio Branco (Brazil), 1996; Officer, Dienst Kreuz (Germany), 1980; Grand Cross: Order of Prince Henry (Portugal), 1995; Order of Merit (Italy), 1996; Order of Sacred Treasure 1st Cl. (Japan), 1996; Order of Merit (Portugal), 1997; Grand Officer, Légion d'honneur (France), 1998. *Publications:* articles in jls, papers, and conf. proceedings. *Recreations:* cycling, tennis. *Address:* Brazilian Embassy, 32 Green Street, W1K 7AT. *T:* (020) 7399 9007.

AMARATUNGA, Prof. Gehan Anil Joseph; PhD; 1966 Professor of Engineering (Electrical), University of Cambridge, since 1998; Fellow, Churchill College, Cambridge, 1987–95 and since 1998; *b* 6 April 1956; *s* of Carl Hermen Joseph Amaratunga and Mallika Swarna (*née* Undugodage); *m* 1981, Praveen Dharshini Hitchcock; one *s* two *d*. *Educ:* Royal Coll., Colombo; Pelham Meml High Sch., NY; University Coll. Cardiff (BSc Hons); Wolfson Coll., Cambridge (PhD 1983). University of Southampton: Res. Fellow in Microelectronics, 1983; Lectr in Electronics, 1984–86; Lectr in Electrical Engrg, Univ. of Cambridge, 1987–95; Prof. of Electrical Engrg, Univ. of Liverpool, 1995–98. Royal Acad. Engrg Vis. Researcher, Stanford Univ., Calif, 1989. *Publications:* contrib. IEEE Trans, Physical Rev., Nature. *Recreations:* jazz, cricket, supporting Liverpool FC, classic cars, avant garde cinema. *Address:* Engineering Department, Cambridge University, Cambridge CB2 1PZ. *T:* (01223) 332648; *e-mail:* ga@eng.cam.ac.uk. *Club:* Royal Commonwealth Society.

AMBACHE, Jeremy Noel; Director of Social Services and Housing, London Borough of Bromley, since 2000; *b* 16 Dec. 1946; *s* of Nachman and Stella Ambache; *m* 1973, Ann Campbell; two *d*. *Educ:* Bedales Sch.; Sussex Univ. (BA); York Univ. (MPhil); Kingston Univ. (MA). Social worker, Birmingham Social Services, 1971–73; Team Manager, Hammersmith Social Services, 1974–80; Co-ordinator for Community Homes, Brent Social Services, 1981–84; Area Manager, Croydon Social Services, 1984–90; Divl Dir, Berks Social Services, 1990–91; Asst Dir, Bedfordshire Social Services, 1991–93; Dir of Social Services, Knowsley, 1993–2000. *Recreations:* tennis, yoga, travel, walking. *Address:* 17 Hazlewell Road, Putney, SW15 6LT. *T:* (020) 8785 9650. *Club:* Putney Lawn Tennis.

AMBERLEY, Viscount; Nicholas Lyulph Russell; *b* 12 Sept. 1968; *s* and *heir* of Earl Russell, *qv*.

AMBLER, John Doss; Vice-President, 1980–96, Vice-President, Human Resources, 1989–96, Texaco Inc.; *b* 24 July 1934; *m*; one *s* one *d*. *Educ:* Virginia Polytechnic Inst. (BSc Business Admin). Texaco Inc., USA: various assignments, Marketing Dept, Alexandra, Va, 1956–65; Dist Sales Manager, Harrisburg, Pa, 1965–67; Asst Divl Manager, Norfolk, Va, 1967–68; Staff Asst to Gen. Man. Marketing US, New York, 1968; various assignments, Chicago and New York, 1969–72; Gen. Man., Texaco Olie Maatschappij BV, Rotterdam, 1972–75; Man. Dir, Texaco Oil AB, Stockholm, 1975–77; Asst to Pres., 1977, Asst to Chm. of the Bd, 1980, Texaco Inc., USA; Pres., Texaco Europe, New York, 1981–82; Chm. and Chief Exec. Officer, Texaco Ltd, 1982–89. *Recreations:* hunting, fishing, tennis, photography.

AMBO, Rt Rev. George Somboba, KBE 1988 (OBE 1978); Archbishop of Papua New Guinea, 1983–89; Bishop of Popondota, 1977–89; Chairman, South Pacific Anglican Council, 1986–89; *b* Gona, Nov. 1925; *s* of late J. O. Ambo, Gona; *m* 1946, Marcella O., *d* of Karau; two *s* two *d*. *Educ:* St Aidan's College, Dogura; Newton Theological Coll., Dogura. Deacon, 1955; Priest, 1958. Curate of: Menapi, 1955–57; Dogura, 1957–58; Priest in charge of Boianai, Diocese of New Guinea, 1958–63; Missionary at Wamira, 1963–69; an Asst Bishop of Papua New Guinea, 1960 (first Papuan-born Anglican Bishop). *Publication:* St John's Gospel in Ewage. *Recreations:* reading, carpentry. *Address:* c/o Anglican Diocesan Office, PO Box 26, Popondetta, Papua New Guinea.

AMBRASEYS, Prof. Nicholas, FREng; FICE; Professor of Engineering Seismology, University of London, at Imperial College, since 1973; Senior Research Fellow, since 1995, and Senior Research Investigator, since 1996, Imperial College; *b* 19 Jan. 1929; *s* of Neocles Ambraseys, Athens, and Cleopatra Jambany; *m* 1955, Xeni, *d* of A. Stavrou. *Educ:* National Technical Univ. of Athens (DipEng); Univ. of London (DIC; PhD; DSc 1980). Lectr in Civil Engineering, Imperial Coll., 1958–62; Associate Prof. of Civil Engrg, Univ. of Illinois, 1963; Prof. of Hydrodynamics, Nat. Tech. Univ., Athens, 1964; Imperial College: Lectr, 1965–68; Univ. Reader in Engrg Seismology, 1969–72; Hd, Engrg Seismology Sect., 1969–95. Chm., British Nat. Cttee for Earthquake Eng., 1961–71; Dir, Internat. Assoc. for Earthquake Engrg, 1961–77; Vice-Pres., European Assoc. for Earthquake Engrg, 1964–75; Mem., 1969–78, Vice-Chm., 1979–81, Unesco Internat. Adv. Cttee of Earthquake Risk; leader, UN/Unesco earthquake reconnaisance missions to Pakistan, Iran, Turkey, Romania, Jugoslavia, Italy, Greece, Algeria, Nicaragua, East and Central Africa; Chm., Internat. Commn for earthquake protection of historical monuments, 1977–81; consultant to UN/Unesco. FREng (FEng 1985); FCGI 2000. Hon. Fellow, Internat. Assoc. for Earthquake Engrg, 1992; Hon. Mem., Earthquake Res. Inst., USA, 2001. Dr Eng *hc* Nat. Tech. Univ. of Athens, 1993. Decennial Award, European Assoc. for Earthquake Engrg, 1975; Busk Medal, RGS, 1975. Freedom of City of Skopje, 1999. *Publications:* (with C. Melville) A History of Persian Earthquakes, 1982; (with C. Melville) Seismicity of Arabia & Red Sea, 1994; (with C. Finkel) Seismicity of Turkey, 1995; papers on engrg seismology, soil mechanics, tectonics, historical seismicity. *Recreations:* history, philately. *Address:* Imperial College, SW7 2BU. *T:* (020) 7589 5111; 19 Bede House, Manor Fields, SW15 3LT. *T:* (020) 8788 4219.

AMBROZIC, Most Rev. Aloysius Matthew; *see* Toronto, Archbishop of, (RC).

AMERY, Colin Robert; architectural writer, critic and historian; *b* 29 May 1944; *yr s* of late Kenneth George Amery and Florence Ellen Amery (*née* Young). *Educ:* King's College London; Univ. of Sussex (BA Hons). Editor and Inf. Officer, TCPA, 1968–70; Asst Editor and Features Editor, Architectural Review, 1970–79; Architecture Corresp., Financial Times, 1979–99. Advr for Sainsbury Wing, Nat. Gall., 1985–91; Arch. consultant to J. Sainsbury plc, 1985–. Vis. Fellow, Jesus Coll., Cambridge, 1989. Member: Arts Panel, Arts Council, 1984–86; Exec. Cttee, Georgian Gp, 1985–93; Adv. Cttee, Geffrye Mus., 1985–87; Architecture Panel, NT, 1986–; London Adv. Cttee, English Heritage, 1987–90; Building Cttee, Nat. Gallery, 1988–92; British Council, Visual Art Adv. Cttee, 1989–93; Dir, Sir John Soane Soc., 1987–; Dir of Develt, Prince of Wales's Inst. of Architecture, 1993–96; Patron, 1993–, Pres., 1999–, Lutyens Trust (Chm., 1984–93); Chairman: Organising Cttee, Lutyens Exhibn, 1981–82; Duchy of Cornwall Commercial Property Develt Cttee, 1990–98; Perspectives on Architecture Ltd, 1994–98. Dir, World Monuments Fund in Britain, 1999– (Trustee, 1992–98); Trustee: Spitalfields Trust, 1977–85; Brooking Collection, 1985–94; Nat. Museums and Galls on Merseyside, 1988–97; Architectural Heritage Fund, 1998–; Heather Trust for the Arts; Gov., Museum of London, 1992–99. Hon. FRIBA 1998. *Publications:* Period Houses and Their Details, 1974; (jtly) The Rape of Britain, 1975; Three Centuries of Architectural Craftsmanship, 1977; (jtly) The Victorian Buildings of London 1837–1887, 1980; (compiled jtly) Lutyens 1869–1944, 1981; (contrib.) Architecture of the British Empire, 1986; Wren's London, 1988; A Celebration of Art and Architecture: the National Gallery Sainsbury Wing, 1991; Bracken House, 1992; Architecture, Industry and Innovation: the early work of Nicholas Grimshaw & Partners, 1995; articles in professional jls. *Address:* 15 York House, Upper Montagu Street, W1H 1FR. *Clubs:* Pratt's, Beefsteak.

AMESS, David Anthony Andrew; MP (C) Southend West, since 1997 (Basildon, 1983–97); *b* Plaistow, 26 March 1952; *s* of late James Henry Valentine Amess and of Maud Ethel Martin; *m* 1983, Julia Monica Margaret Arnold; one *s* four *d*. *Educ:* St Bonaventure's Grammar Sch.; Bournemouth Coll. of Technol. (BScEcon Hons 2.2., special subject Govt). Teacher, St John the Baptist Jun. Mixed Sch., Bethnal Green, 1970–71; Jun. Underwriter, Leslie & Godwin Agencies, 1974–77; Sen. Manager, Accountancy Personnel, 1977–80; Chm., Accountancy Aims, then Accountancy Ltd, 1990–96. Mem., Redbridge Council, 1982–86 (Vice Chm., Housing Cttee, 1982–85). Contested (C) Newham NW, 1979. Parliamentary Private Secretary: to Parly Under-Secs of State (Health), DHSS, 1987–88; to Minister of State and Parly Under-Sec. of State, Dept of Transport, 1988–90; to Minister of State, DoE, 1990–92; to Chief Sec. to the Treasury, 1992–94; to Sec. of State for Employment, 1994–95; to Sec. of State for Defence,

1995–97. Member: Health Select Cttee, 1998–; Chairman's Panel, 2001–. Chm., All-Party Solvent Abuse Gp, 2000–; Joint Chairman: All-Party Scouts Gp, 1997–; All-Party Fire Gp, later All-Party Fire Safety Gp, 1998–; Vice-Chairman: All-Party Guides Gp, 2000–; Cons. Back Bench Health Cttee, 1999–. Vice Pres., Nat. Lotteries Council, 1998. Dir, Parly Broadcasting Unit Ltd, 1997–99. Chm., 1912 Club, 1996–; Vice Chm., Assoc. of Cons. Clubs, 1997–. *Publications:* The Road to Basildon, 1993; Basildon Experience: Conservatives fight back, 1994; contrib. magazines and pamphlets. *Recreations:* gardening, music, sport, animals, theatre, travel. *Address:* c/o House of Commons, SW1A 0AA. *Clubs:* Carlton, St Stephen's; Kingswood Squash and Racketball (Basildon).

AMET, Hon. Sir Arnold (Karibone), Kt 1993; CBE 1987; **Hon. Mr Justice Amet;** Chief Justice, Papua New Guinea, since 1993; *b* 30 Oct. 1952; *m* 1972, Miaru; three *s* two *d*. *Educ:* Univ. of PNG (LLB 1975); Legal Trng Inst., PNG. Joined Public Solicitor's Office, PNG, 1976; qualified as barrister and solicitor, 1977; Legal Officer and Sec., Nat. Airline Commn, 1979–80; Dep. Public Solicitor, 1980–81; Public Solicitor, 1981–83; Judge of National Trial Court and Supreme Court of Appeal, 1983–93. Hon. LLD PNG, 1993. *Recreations:* Christian Ministry, watching Rugby and cricket. *Address:* Supreme Court, PO Box 7018, Boroko, Papua New Guinea.

AMHERST OF HACKNEY, 4th Baron *cr* 1892; **William Hugh Amherst Cecil;** Director, Short Sea Europe plc, since 1996; *b* 28 Dec. 1940; *s* of 3rd Baron Amherst of Hackney, CBE, and of Margaret Eirene Clifton Brown, *d* of late Brig.-Gen. Howard Clifton Brown; *S* father, 1980; *m* 1965, Elisabeth, *d* of Hugh Humphrey Merriman, DSO, MC, TD, DL; one *s* one *d*. *Educ:* Eton. Director: E. A. Gibson Shipbrokers Ltd, 1975–90; Seascope Sale and Purchase Ltd, 1994–97. Younger Brother, Trinity House, 1995–. Member Council: New Forest Assoc., 1997–2000; RYA, 1999–. Patron: St John-at-Hackney; St John of Jerusalem, S Hackney. *Heir: s* Hon. Hugh William Amherst Cecil [*b* 17 July 1968; *m* 1996, Nicola Jane, *d* of Major Timothy Michels; one *s* one *d*]. *Address:* 56 Hans Place, Knightsbridge, SW1X 0LA. *Clubs:* Royal Ocean Racing; Royal Yacht Squadron (Vice-Cdre, 1993–98), Royal Cruising.

AMIES, Sir (Edwin) Hardy, KCVO 1989 (CVO 1977); RDI 1964; FRSA 1965; Dressmaker by Appointment to HM The Queen, since 1955; Director, Hardy Amies Ltd, since 1946 (President, since 1996); Design Consultant to manufacturers in the UK, EEC, USA, Canada, Australia, New Zealand, Japan, and Korea; *b* 17 July 1909; *s* of late Herbert William Amies and Mary (*née* Hardy). *Educ:* Brentwood. Studied languages in France and Germany, 1927–30; trainee at W. & T. Avery Ltd, Birmingham, 1930–34; managing designer at Lachasse, Farm Street, W1, 1934–39. War Service, 1939–45: joined Intelligence Corps, 1939, becoming Lt-Col and head of Special Forces Mission to Belgium, 1944; founded dressmaking business, 1946. Chairman, Incorporated Society of London Fashion Designers, 1959–60 (Vice-Chm., 1954–56). Awards: Harper's Bazaar, 1962; Caswell-Massey, 1962, 1964, 1968; Ambassador Magazine, 1964; Sunday Times Special Award, 1965; Personnalité de l'Année (Haute Couture), Paris, 1986; Hall of Fame Award, British Fashion Council, 1989. Officier de l'Ordre de la Couronne (Belgium), 1946. *Publications:* Just So Far, 1954; ABC of Men's Fashion, 1964; Still Here, 1984; The Englishman's Suit, 1994. *Recreations:* gardening, opera, needlepoint. *Address:* The Old School, Langford, near Lechlade, Glos GL7 3LF; Hardy Amies Ltd, 14 Savile Row, W1X 2JN. *T:* (020) 7734 2436. *Clubs:* Queen's, Buck's.

AMIS, Martin Louis; author; special writer for The Observer, since 1980; *b* 25 Aug. 1949; *s* of Sir Kingsley Amis, CBE, and Hilary Bardwell; *m* 1984, Antonia Phillips (marr. diss. 1996); two *s*; *m* 1998, Isabel Fonseca; two *d*. *Educ:* various schools; Exeter Coll., Oxford (BA Hons 1st cl. in English). Fiction and Poetry Editor, TLS, 1974; Literary Editor, New Statesman, 1977–79. *Publications:* The Rachel Papers, 1973 (Somerset Maugham Award, 1974); Dead Babies, 1975; Success, 1978; Other People: a mystery story, 1981; Money, 1984; The Moronic Inferno and Other Visits to America, 1986; Einstein's Monsters (short stories), 1987; London Fields, 1989; Time's Arrow, 1991; Visiting Mrs Nabakov and Other Excursions, 1993; The Information, 1995; Night Train, 1997; Heavy Water and Other Stories, 1998; Experience (memoir), 2000 (James Tait Black Meml Prize); The War Against Cliché: essays and reviews 1971–2000, 2001. *Recreations:* tennis, chess, snooker. *Address:* c/o Wylie Agency (UK), 4–8 Rodney Street, N1 9JH; *e-mail:* mail@wylieagency.co.uk. *Club:* Oxford and Cambridge.

AMLOT, Roy Douglas, QC 1989; barrister; *b* 22 Sept. 1942; *s* of Douglas Lloyd Amlot and Ruby Luise Amlot; *m* 1969, Susan Margaret (*née* McDowell); two *s*. *Educ:* Dulwich Coll. Called to the Bar, Lincoln's Inn, 1963, Bencher, 1986. Second Prosecuting Counsel to the Inland Revenue, Central Criminal Court and London Crown Courts, 1974; First Prosecuting Counsel to the Crown, Inner London Crown Court, 1975; Jun. Prosecuting Counsel to the Crown, Central Criminal Court, 1977, Sen. Prosecuting Counsel, 1981; First Sen. Prosecuting Counsel, 1987. Chm., Bar Council, 2001. *Publication:* (ed) 11th edn, Phipson on Evidence. *Recreations:* skiing, squash, music. *Address:* 6 King's Bench Walk, Temple, EC4Y 7DR. *T:* (020) 7583 0410.

AMORY; *see* Heathcoat Amory and Heathcoat-Amory.

AMOS, Baroness *cr* 1997 (Life Peer), of Brondesbury in the London Borough of Brent; **Valerie Ann Amos;** Parliamentary Under-Secretary of State, Foreign and Commonwealth Office, since 2001; *b* 13 March 1954; *d* of E. Michael Amos and Eunice Amos. *Educ:* Univ. of Warwick (BA Sociol.); Univ. of Birmingham (MA Cultural Studies); Univ. of E Anglia (doctoral research). With London Boroughs: Lambeth, 1981–82; Camden, 1983–85; Hackney, 1985–89 (Head of Trng; Head of Management Services); Management Consultant, 1984–89; Chief Exec., Equal Opportunities Commn, 1989–94; Dir, Amos Fraser Bernard, 1995–98. A Baroness in Waiting (Govt Whip), 1998–2001. Chairman: Bd of Govs, RCN Inst., 1994–98; Afiya Trust (formerly Black Heath Foundn), 1995–98. Member: Adv. Cttee, Centre for Educnl Develt Appraisal and Res., Univ. of Warwick, 1991–98; Gen. Council, King's Fund, 1992–98; Council, Inst. of Employment Studies, 1993–98; Trustee, IPPR, 1994–98. External Examiner: (MA Equal Opportunities), Univ. of Northumbria, at Newcastle (formerly Newcastle Poly.), 1989–93; Liverpool Univ., 1992–97. Dir, UCL Hosps NHS Trust, 1995–98; Fellow, UCL Hosps, 2000. Dir, Hampstead Theatre, 1992–98; Dep. Chm., Runnymede Trust, 1990–98; Trustee: VSO, 1997–98; Project Hope, 1997–98. Hon. LLD: Warwick, 2000; Staffordshire, 2000; Manchester, 2001. *Publications:* various articles on race and gender issues. *Address:* House of Lords, SW1A 0PW. *T:* (020) 7219 4120, *Fax:* (020) 7219 6837.

AMOS, Alan Thomas; investigator with Local Government Ombudsman, since 1993; *b* 10 Nov. 1952; *s* of William Edmond Amos and Cynthia Florence Kathleen Amos. *Educ:* St Albans Sch.; St John's Coll., Oxford (MA(PPE) Hons); London Univ. Inst. of Educn (PGCE 1976). Pres., Oxford Univ. Cons. Assoc., 1974–75. Dir of Studies, Hd of Sixth Form, Hd of Econs and Politics Dept, Dame Alice Owen's Sch., Potters Bar, 1976–84; Hd of Agric. and Environment Sect., Cons. Res. Dept, 1984–86; Asst Prin., College of Further Educn, 1986–87. PA to Sec. of State for the Envmt, 1993. Councillor, 1978–90, Dep. Leader, and Chm. Educn Cttee, 1983–87, Enfield Bor. Council; Chm., London Boroughs Assoc. Educn Cttee, 1986–87; Mem. (Lab), Tower Hamlets LBC, 1998–. Contested (C): Tottenham, GLC, 1981; Walthamstow, 1983; MP (C) Hexham, 1987–92; contested (Lab) Hitchin and Harpenden, 2001. Mem., Agriculture Select Cttee, 1989–92; Chairman: Cons. backbench Forestry Cttee, 1987–92; Parly ASH Gp, 1991–92; Secretary: Cons. backbench Transport Cttee, 1988–92 (Vice Chm., 1991–92); Cons. backbench Educn Cttee, 1989–92; British-Bulgarian All Party Gp, 1991–92; Chm., Northern Gp of Cons. MPs, 1991–92. Joined Labour party, 1994; Mem. Exec. Cttee, Poplar and Canning Town Lab Party, 1996– (Treas., 1997–); Chm., Millwall Lab Party, 2000–; Prospective Parly Cand. (Lab) Hitchin and Harpenden, 2000–. Sec., Nat. Agricl and Countryside Forum, 1984–86. Lay Chm., NHS Indep. Review Panel, 1998–; Mem., Candidates Panel for appt to NHS Authorities, 1999–. A Vice-Pres., Gtr London YCs, 1981. Member: ESU, 1982–; ASH, 1987– (Mem. Council, 1991–); SPUC, 1987–. Hon. US Citizen, 1991. *Recreations:* travel, badminton, USA politics, bibliophilia.

AMOS, Air Comdt Barbara Mary D.; *see* Ducat-Amos.

AMOS, Francis John Clarke, CBE 1973; BSc(Soc); DipArch, SPDip, ARIBA, PPRTPI; international consultant on institutional development; Chief Executive, Birmingham City Council, 1973–77; Senior Fellow, University of Birmingham, since 1977; *b* 10 Sept. 1924; *s* of late Frank Amos, FALPA (Director, H. J. Furlong & Sons, Ltd, London), and Alice Mary Amos; *m* 1956, Geraldine Mercy Sutton, MBE, JP, BSc (Econ), MRTPI; one *s* one *d* (and one *d* decd). *Educ:* Alleyns Sch., and Dulwich Coll., London; Sch. of Architecture, The Polytechnic, London (DipArch); Sch. of Planning and Regional Research, London (SPDip); LSE and Birkbeck Coll., Univ. of London (BSc(Soc)). Served War: Royal Corps of Signals, 1942–44; RIASC, 1944–47. Harlow Devélt Corp, 1951; LCC, Planning Div., 1953–58; Min. of Housing and Local Govt, 1958–59 and 1962–63; Adviser to Imperial Ethiopian Govt, 1959–62; Liverpool Corp. City Planning Dept, 1962–74, Chief Planning Officer 1966–74; Chairman: Planning Sub-Cttee, Merseyside Area Land Use/Transportation Study, 1967–73; Working Gp, Educnl Objectives in Urban and Regional Planning, Centre for Environmental Studies, 1970–72; Examination in Public Buckinghamshire Structure Plan, 1981–82. Consultant, Halcrow Fox and Associates, 1984–. Member: Exec. Cttee, Internat. Centre for Regional Planning and Develt, 1954–59; various Cttees, Liverpool Council of Social Service, 1965–72; Exec. Cttee, Town and Country Planning Summer Sch., 1969–70; Planning, Architecture and Bldg Studies Sub-Cttee, UGC, 1968–74; Community Work Gp of Calouste Gulbenkian Foundn, 1970–82; Constitution Cttee, Liverpool Community Relations Council, 1970–73; Planning and Transport Res. Adv. Council, DoE, 1971–77; Town and Country Planning Council and Exec. Cttee, 1972–74; Adv. Cttee, Bldg Res. Estabt, 1972–77 (Chm., Planning Cttee, 1972–80); SSRC Planning and Human Geography and Planning Cttees, 1972–76; Social Studies Sub-Cttee, UGC, 1974–76; W Midlands Economic Planning Council, 1974–77; Environmental Bd, DoE, 1975–78; Trustee, Community Projects Foundn, 1978–88; Council of Management, Action Resource Centre, 1978–86; Study Commn on Family, 1978–83; Arts Council Regional Cttee, 1979–; Exec. Cttee, Watt Cttee on Energy, 1980–82; Planning Cttee, CNAA, 1980–83. Comr, London and Metropolitan Govt Staff Commn, 1984–87; Asst Comr, Local Govt Boundary Commn, 1986–. Chm., Birmingham Gp, Internat. Year for Shelter for the Homeless 1987. Special Prof. of Planning Practice and Management, Univ. of Nottingham, 1979–; Visiting Professor: Nottingham Univ., 1982–; QUB, 1991–. External Examiner in Planning: Univs of: Liverpool, 1967–70; Newcastle, 1968–71; Aston (Birmingham), 1970–71; Queen's (Belfast), 1972–74; Heriot Watt, 1972–74; Nottingham, 1973–76; UCL, 1975–77; Sheffield, 1979–82; Glasgow, 1979–82; Hong Kong, 1982–85; Polytechnics of: Leeds, 1967–68; Central London, 1967–70; Birmingham, 1975–79; Liverpool, 1977–82. Since 1977, has acted as adviser to govts in aid programmes: Bangladesh (UN); Barbados (IADB); Belize (World Bank); Bosnia (ODA); Dubai; Ghana (UN); Hong Kong (UK); Hungary; India (ODA); Iraq; Jordan; Laos; Latvia (EC); Poland; Tanzania (ODA); Trinidad and Tobago (UN); Turkey (OECD); Venezuela (IBRD); Kenya, Pakistan, Philippines, Romania and Zimbabwe (UN); Uganda (ODA); Ukraine (DFID); USSR (DFID); Zambia (British Council). Mem., County Exec. Cttee, Scout Assoc., 1977–85. Mem., Court, Univ. of Nottingham, 1975–. Chm., Sir Herbert Manzoni Scholarship Trust, 1975–95. Adviser to AMA Social Services Cttee, 1974–77; Chm., W Midlands Area, 1978–82, Mem. Nat. Exec., 1982–86, Nat. Assoc. of CAB. Member: Jt Land Requirements Cttee, 1983–; Nuffield Inquiry into Town and Country Planning, 1984–86. Pres., Royal Town Planning Inst., 1971–72 (AMTPI, 1955; Fellow 1967; Hon. Sec., 1979–90); Architect RIBA, 1951. FRSA 1977. Freeman of City of London, 1968. *Publications:* Education for Planning (CES Report), 1973; various reports on Liverpool incl.: Annual Reviews of Plans, Study of Social Malaise; RTPI Report on Future of Planning, 1971, 1977; (part) City Centre Redevelopment; (part) Low Income Housing in the Developing World; articles on Planning and Management in Local Govt in various professional jls. *Recreations:* travel; unsystematic philately and unskilled building. *Address:* Grindstones, 20 Westfield Road, Edgbaston, Birmingham B15 3QG. *T:* (0121) 454 5661, *Fax:* (0121) 454 8331; The Coach House, Ashton Gifford Lane, Codford St Peter, Warminster, Wilts BA12 0NX. *T:* (01985) 850610, *Fax:* (01985) 851170.

AMPLEFORTH, Abbot of; *see* Wright, Rt Rev. T. M.

AMPTHILL, 4th Baron *cr* 1881; **Geoffrey Denis Erskine Russell,** CBE 1986; PC 1995; Deputy Speaker, House of Lords, since 1983; Deputy Chairman: Express Newspapers, since 1989 (Director, since 1985); United Newspapers, 1991–96 (Director, 1981–96); *b* 15 Oct. 1921; *s* of 3rd Baron Ampthill, CBE, and Christabel, Lady Ampthill (*d* 1976); *S* father, 1973; *m* 1st, 1946, Susan Mary (marr. diss. 1971), *d* of late Hon. Charles John Frederic Winn; two *s* one *d* (and one *s* decd); 2nd, 1972, Elisabeth Anne Marie (marr. diss. 1987), *d* of late Claude Henri Gustave Mallon. *Educ:* Stowe. Irish Guards, 1941–46; 2nd Lt 1941, Captain 1944. Gen. Manager, Fortnum and Mason, 1947–51; Chairman, New Providence Hotel Co. Ltd, 1951–64; Dir, Dualvest plc, 1981–87. Managing Director of theatre owning and producing companies, 1953–81. Dep. Chm., 1980–92, Chm., 1992–94, of Cttees, H of L; Chairman: Select Cttee on Channel Tunnel Bill, 1987; Select Cttee on Channel Tunnel Rail Link Bill, 1996; elected Mem., H of L, 1999. Dir, Leeds Castle Foundn, 1980–82. *Heir: s* Hon. David Whitney Erskine Russell [*b* 27 May 1947; *m* 1980, April McKenzie Arbon, *y d* of Paul Arbon, New York; two *d*]. *Address:* 6 North Court, Great Peter Street, SW1P 3LL.

AMWELL, 3rd Baron *cr* 1947, of Islington; **Keith Norman Montague;** Development Director, Construction Industry Research and Information Association, since 1998; *b* 1 April 1943; *o s* of 2nd Baron Amwell and of Kathleen Elizabeth Montague (*née* Fountain); *S* father, 1990; *m* 1970, Mary, *d* of Frank Palfreyman; two *s*. *Educ:* Ealing Grammar Sch. for Boys; Nottingham Univ. BSc (Civil Engineering); CEng; FICE; CGeol, FGS; MIHT. Consulting civil engineer, 1965–96. Dir, Brian Colquhoun and Partners, then Thorburn Colquhoun Ltd, consulting engineers, 1994–96. *Publications:* papers to international construction confs. *Recreations:* gardening, walking, photography, badminton. *Heir: s* Hon. Ian Keith Montague, *b* 20 Sept. 1973.

AMY, Dennis Oldrieve, CMG 1992; OBE 1984; HM Diplomatic Service, retired; Ambassador to the Democratic Republic of Madagascar, 1990–92, and Ambassador (non-resident) to Federal Islamic Republic of the Comoros, 1991–92; *b* 21 Oct. 1932; *s* of late George Arthur Amy and Isabella Thompson (*née* Crosby); *m* 1956, Helen Rosamunde, *d* of late Wilfred Leslie Clemens; one *s* one *d*. *Educ:* Southall Grammar Sch. Served RM, 1951–53. Entered HM Foreign, later HM Diplomatic Service, 1949; FO, 1949–51 and 1953–58; Athens, 1958–61; Second Sec. and Vice Consul, Moscow, 1961–63; FO, 1963–65; DSAO, 1965; Second Sec. and Passport Officer, Canberra, 1966–70; First Sec., Ibadan, 1971–74; seconded to Dept of Trade, 1974–75; FCO, 1976–78; First Sec. (Commercial), Santiago, 1978–83 (Chargé d'Affaires, 1979); FCO, 1983–86 (Counsellor, 1985–86); Consul Gen., Bordeaux, 1986–89. *Recreation:* gardening. *Address:* Timbers, Hambledon Road, Godalming, Surrey GU7 1PJ.

AMY, Ronald John, OBE 1998; FFA; Chairman and Chief Executive, Aon Consulting, since 1998; *b* 17 June 1950; *s* of Ernest and Grace Amy; *m* 1st, 1975, Evelyn Morrison (marr. diss.); two *d*; 2nd, 1997, Patricia Groves. *Educ:* Glasgow Univ. (BSc Hons Pure Maths). FFA 1977. London Actuary, Scottish Mutual Assce Soc., 1978–80; UK Pensions Manager, Philips Electronics, 1980–84; Gp Pensions Dir, Metal Box Plc, 1984–86; Dir, New Business Develt, BZW Investment Mgt, 1986–87; Gp Pensions Dir, 1987–88, Gp Compensation and Benefits Dir, 1988–96, Grand Metropolitan PLC; Chm. and Chief Exec., Alexander Clay, 1996–97. Member: Occupational Pensions Bd, 1989–97; Bd, OPRA, 1996–. Chm., Nat. Assoc. of Pension Funds, 1993–95. *Recreation:* golf. *Address:* Aon Consulting, 15 Minories, EC3N 1NJ. *T:* (020) 7767 2000. *Clubs:* Royal Automobile, Caledonian; West Hill Golf (Woking).

AMYOT, Léopold Henri, CVO 1990; Secretary to Governor General of Canada and Secretary General of Order of Canada and of Order of Military Merit, 1985–90; Herald Chancellor of Canada, 1988–90; *b* 25 Aug. 1930; *s* of S. Eugène Amyot and Juliette Gagnon; *m* 1958, (Marie Jeanne) Andrée Jobin; one *s* two *d*. *Educ:* Laval Univ., Québec (BLSc, BScSoc); Ottawa Univ. (BA); Geneva Univ. (course on Internat. Instns). Joined External Affairs, 1957; Second Secretary: Canberra, 1960; New Delhi, 1961; Counsellor, Paris, 1968; Amb. to Lebanon (with accredn to Syria, Jordan, Iraq), 1974; Dep. Sec. Gen., Agence de Co-opération culturelle et technique, Paris, 1976; Chief of Protocol, Ext. Affairs, Ottawa, 1980; Exec. Dir, Task Force, on Pope's Visit to Canada, 1983; Amb. to Morocco, 1983. Chm., Official Residences Collections (formerly Official Residences Arts) Adv. Cttee, 1985–. Member: Professional Assoc. of For. Service Officers, Ottawa, 1957–; l'Inst. canadien des Affaires internat., Québec, 1985–. Prix d'honneur (Sect. de Québec) l'Inst. canadien des Affaires internat., 1985. *Recreations:* tennis, golf, swimming, contemporary art collector. *Address:* 140 Rideau Terrace #15, Ottawa, Ontario K1M 0Z2, Canada. *T:* (613) 7479077.

AMYOT, René; QC; barrister; Counsel, Jolin, Fournier, Morisset; *b* Quebec City, 1 Nov. 1926; *s* of Omer Amyot and Caroline L'Espérance (*née* Barry); *m* 1954, Monique, *d* of Fernand Boutin; two *s* two *d*. *Educ:* Collège des Jésuites de Québec (BA 1946); Laval Univ. Law Sch. (LLL 1949); Harvard Univ. Grad. Sch. of Business Admin (MBA 1951). Called to Bar of Québec, 1949; QC Canada 1965. Joined Procter & Gamble, Montreal, 1951; Bouffard & Associates, Quebec, 1952; Asst Prof., Faculty of Admin. Scis, Laval Univ., 1954–69; Asst Prof., Fiscal Law, Laval Univ. Law Sch., 1960–70; Consul for Belgium, 1966–82. Dir, and Mem. Exec. Cttee, Centre de Recherche Industrielle de Québec, 1971–76; Pres., Quebec Dist Chamber of Commerce, 1972; Founding Pres., Centre Internat. Recherches et Etudes en Management, 1972; Chairman, Air Canada, 1981–83; Director: Bank of Nova Scotia, 1972–81; Logistec Corp.; Rothmans Inc.; Palmar Inc.; Fidusco Ltd; Ferme Charlevoix Inc.; Expand Images Canada Inc.; Cedar Gp Inc.; Dominion Bridge Inc. Dir, Council for Business and the Arts in Canada. Member: Canadian Bar Assoc.; Québec Bar Assoc.; Canadian Tax Foundn; Cttee, Internat. Chamber; Assoc. des MBA du Québec. Gov., Faculty of Administrative Scis, Laval Univ. Chevalier de l'Ordre de Léopold (Belgium), 1985. *Recreations:* skiing, swimming, tennis, farming. *Address:* Jolin, Fournier, Morisset, Place Iberville 3, Suite 500, 2960 Boulevard Laurier, Sainte-Foy, Québec G1V 4S1, Canada. *Clubs:* Québec Garrison, Toronto.

ANCRAM, Earl of; Rt Hon. Michael Andrew Foster Jude Kerr, PC 1996; DL; QC (Scot.) 1996; MP (C) Devizes, since 1992; *b* 7 July 1945; *s* and *heir* of 12th Marquess of Lothian, *qv*; *m* 1975, Lady Jane Fitzalan-Howard, *y d* of 16th Duke of Norfolk, KG, PC, GCVO, GBE, TD, and Lavinia Duchess of Norfolk, LG, CBE; two *d*. *Educ:* Ampleforth; Christ Church, Oxford (BA); Edinburgh Univ. (LLB). Advocate, Scottish Bar, 1970. Contested (C) Edinburgh S, 1987. MP (C): Berwickshire and East Lothian, Feb.-Sept. 1974; Edinburgh S, 1979–87. Parly Under-Sec. of State, Scottish Office, 1983–87, NI Office, 1993–94; Minister of State, NI Office, 1994–97; Opposition front bench spokesman on constitutional affairs, 1997–98; Dep. Leader of the Opposition and Shadow Foreign Sec., 2001–. Mem., Select Cttee on Energy, 1979–83. Chairman: Cons. Party in Scotland, 1980–83 (Vice-Chm., 1975–80); Cons. Party, 1998–2001. Chm., Northern Corporate Communications, 1989–91; Dir, CSM Parly Consultants, 1988–92; Mem. Bd, Scottish Homes, 1988–90. DL Roxburgh, Ettrick and Lauderdale, 1990. *Recreations:* skiing, photography, folksinging. *Address:* House of Commons, SW1A 0AA.

ANDERSEN, Valdemar Jens, CMG 1965; OBE 1960 (MBE 1955); VRD 1962; Resident Commissioner, Gilbert and Ellice Islands Colony, 1962–70, retired; *b* 21 March 1919; 2nd *s* of Max Andersen, Maraenui, NZ; *m* 1946, Alison Leone, 2nd *d* of G. A. Edmonds, Remuera, Auckland, NZ; one *s* one *d*. *Educ:* Napier Boys High Sch. NZ; Auckland University Coll. (BSc). Lieut, RNZNVR, 1940–46; Lieut, RANVR, 1947–62. British Solomon Islands Protectorate: Administrative Officer, 1947; Class A, Administrative Officer, 1954; Secretary Protectorate Affairs, 1958. *Recreation:* gardening.

ANDERSON, family name of **Viscount Waverley**.

ANDERSON, Maj.-Gen. Alistair Andrew Gibson; CB 1980; *b* 26 Feb. 1927; *s* of Lt-Col John Gibson Anderson and Margaret Alice (*née* Scott); *m* 1953, Dr Margaret Grace Smith; one *s* two *d*. *Educ:* George Watson's Boys Coll., Edinburgh; University Coll. of SW of England, Exeter (Short Univ. Course, 1944); Staff Coll., Camberley; Jt Services Staff Coll., Latimer. Enlisted 1944; commnd Royal Corps of Signals, 1946; comd 18 Signal Regt, 1967–69; Defence Ops Centre, 1969–72; staff of Signal Officer-in-Chief, 1972–74; Comdt, Sch. of Signals, 1974–76; Signal Officer-in-Chief (Army), 1977–80, retired; Dir, Communications and Electronics Security Gp, GCHQ, 1980–85. Col Comdt, Royal Corps of Signals, 1980–86; Chm., Royal Signals Assoc., 1982–87. *Recreations:* hill walking, sailing, gardening. *Club:* Army and Navy.

See also Sir J. E. Anderson.

ANDERSON, Dr Alun Mark; Editor-in-Chief and Publishing Director, New Scientist, since 1999 (Editor 1992–99); *b* 27 May 1948; *s* of Peter Marchmont Anderson and Jane Watkin Anderson (*née* James). *Educ:* Univ. of Sussex (BSc 1968); Univ. of Edinburgh (PhD 1972). IBM Res. Fellow, 1972–74, Jun. Res. Fellow, Wolfson Coll., 1972–76, Oxford; Royal Soc. Res. Fellow, Kyoto Univ., 1977–79; Nature: News and Views Ed., 1980–83; Tokyo Bureau Chief, 1984–86; Washington Ed., 1986–90; Internat. Ed., Science, 1991–92. Dir, IPC Magazines Ltd, 1997–98. Mem., Royal Soc. COPUS, 1997–2000. Mem. Council, Univ. of Sussex, 1998–. Trustee, St Andrews Prize, 1999–. Editor of the Year (Special Interest Magazines), BSME, 1993, 1995, 1997; Editors' Editor of the Year, BSME, 1997. *Publications:* Science and Technology in Japan, 1984, 2nd edn 1991. *Recreations:* mountain walking, travel. *Address:* New Scientist, RBI Ltd, 151 Wardour Street, W1F 8WE. *T:* (020) 7331 2795.

ANDERSON, Anthony John, QC 1982; a Recorder, 1995–99; *b* 12 Sept. 1938; *s* of late A. Fraser Anderson and Margaret Anderson; *m* 1970, Fenja Ragnhild Gunn. *Educ:* Harrow; Magdalen Coll., Oxford. MA. 2nd Lieut, The Gordon Highlanders, 1957–59. Called to the Bar, Inner Temple, 1964, Bencher, 1992. Chm. of Tribunals, SFA (formerly The Securities Assoc.), 1988–. *Recreations:* golf, fishing. *Address:* 2 Mitre Court Buildings, Temple, EC4Y 7BX. *T:* (020) 7583 1380. *Clubs:* Garrick, MCC.

ANDERSON, Mrs Beverly Jean; Middle School Principal, Trinity School, New York, since 1999; *b* 9 Dec. 1940; *d* of Arthur Benjamin Phillpotts and Sylvia Tomlinson Phillpotts; *m* 1st, 1968, Angus Walker, *qv* (marr. diss. 1976); 2nd, 1976, Andrew Anderson (marr. diss. 1986); one *s*. *Educ:* Wellesley Coll., Mass (BA History, and Politics 1962); London Univ. (PGCE 1967). Jamaican Foreign Service, Kingston and Washington, 1963–66; primary sch. teacher, London, 1968–71, Oxfordshire primary schs, 1971–81; Headteacher, Berwood First Sch., Oxford, 1981–83; Sen. Lectr in Educn, Oxford Poly., 1985–89; Lectr in Educn, Warwick Univ., and educn consultant, 1989–93; Chief Exec., Book Trust, 1993–94; Head, Village Sch., Pacific Palisades, Calif, 1995–99. Dir, Railtrack, 1993–94. Chairman: Equal Opportunities Wkg Gp, NAB, 1987–88; CNAA Steering Cttee on Accesss Courses to HE Framework, 1988–89; Member: Nat. Curriculum Council, 1989–91; Council, ABSA, 1989–95; Arts Council, 1990–94; Governor: BFI, 1985–93; Oxford Stage Co. Bd, 1986–96; S Bank Bd, 1989–94. Mem., Nuffield Council on Bioethics, 1991–94; Chm. Council, Charter '88, 1989–93. Columnist, TES, 1989–93. Television includes: Presenter: Black on Black, 1982–83; Nothing but the Best; Sixty Minutes; After Dark, 1989–90; Behind the Headlines, 1990–91. FRSA 1991. Hon. Fellow, Leeds Metropolitan Univ., 1991. Hon. LLM Teesside, 1993. *Publications:* Learning with Logo: a teacher's guide, 1985; numerous articles on education, social issues and media education. *Recreations:* plays, paintings, poems, movies, dancing. *Address:* c/o Trinity School, 139 W 91st Street, New York, NY 10024, USA.

ANDERSON, Brian David Outram, AO 1993; PhD; FRS 1989; Professor of Systems Engineering, since 1981, and Director, Research School of Information Sciences and Engineering, since 1994, Australian National University; *b* 15 Jan. 1941; *s* of late David Outram Anderson and Nancy Anderson; *m* 1968, Dianne, *d* of M. Allen; three *d*. *Educ:* Sydney Univ.; Stanford Univ. (PhD 1966); California Univ. Res. Asst, Stanford Electronics Labs, 1964; Lectr in Electrical Engrg, Stanford Univ., 1965; Asst Prof. and Staff Consultant, Vidar Corp., Mount View, Calif., 1966; Hd of Dept, 1967–75, Prof., 1967–81, Dept of Electrical Engrg, Univ. of Newcastle. Mem., Scientific Adv. Bd, Rio Tinto (formerly CRA) Ltd, 1982–98; Director: Telectronics Hldgs Ltd, 1986–88; Nucleus Ltd, 1988–95; Cochlear Ltd, 1995–; Crasys Ltd, 1996–98; Anutech Pty Ltd, 1997–2000. Member: Aust. Res. Grants Cttee, 1972–77; Aust. Science and Technology Council, 1977–82; UNESCO Nat. Commn, 1982–83; Aust. Industrial Res. and Develt Incentives Bd, 1984–86; Prime Minister's Sci. and Engrg Council, 1989–93; Prime Minister's Sci., Engrg and Innovation Council, 1998–; Aust. Res. Council, 2000–. Pres., Australian Acad. of Sci., 1998–. FAA; FTS; FIEEE; Hon. FIE(Aust). Dr *hc*: Louvain, 1991; Swiss Federal Inst. of Technol., 1993; Hon. DEng: Sydney, 1995; Melbourne, 1997. *Publications* include: Linear Optimal Control, 1971; Network Analysis and Synthesis, 1975; Optimal Filtering, 1980; Optimal Control, 1990. *Address:* Research School of Information Sciences and Engineering, Australian National University, Canberra, ACT 0200, Australia.

ANDERSON, Campbell McCheyne; Managing Director, North Limited, 1994–98; *b* 17 Sept. 1941; *s* of Allen Taylor Anderson and Ethel Catherine Rundle; *m* 1965, Sandra Maclean Harper; two *s* one *d*. *Educ:* The Armidale Sch., NSW, Aust.; Univ. of Sydney (BEcon). AASA. Trainee and General Administration, Boral Ltd, Australia, 1962–69; Gen. Manager/Man. Dir, Reef Oil NL, Australia, 1969–71; Asst Chief Representative, Burmah Oil Australia Ltd, 1972; Corporate Development, Burmah Oil Incorporated, New York, 1973; Corporate Development, 1974; Finance Director and Group Planning, Burmah Oil Trading Ltd, UK, 1975; Special Projects Dir, 1976, Shipping Dir, 1978, Industrial Dir, 1979, Man. Dir, 1982–84, Burmah Oil Co.; Man. Dir, 1985–93, Chief Exec. Officer, 1986–93, Renison Goldfields Consolidated. Director: Consolidated Gold Fields, 1985–89; Ampolex Ltd, 1991–97 (Chm., 1991–96). Dir, Aust. Mines and Metals Assoc., 1985–93; Councillor: Aust. Mining Industry Council, 1985–98 (Pres., 1991–93); Business Council of Aust., 1986– (Pres., 1999–); Chm., Energy Resources Aust. Ltd, 1994–98. Pres., Australia–Japan Soc., Victoria, 1995–98. *Recreations:* golf, swimming, horse-racing, shooting. *Address:* 77 Drumalbyn Road, Bellevue Hill, NSW 2023, Australia. *Clubs:* Oil Industries; Frilford Heath Golf; Australian (Sydney); Australian (Melbourne); Royal Sydney Golf, Royal Melbourne Golf; Australian Jockey; Elanora Country (NSW).

ANDERSON, Rear-Adm. (Charles) Courtney, CB 1971; Flag Officer, Admiralty Interview Board, 1969–71, retired; *b* 8 Nov. 1916; *s* of late Lt-Col Charles Anderson, Australian Light Horse, and Mrs Constance Powell-Anderson, OBE, JP; *m* 1940, Pamela Ruth Miles; three *s*. *Educ:* RNC, Dartmouth. Joined RN, 1930. Served War of 1939–45: in command of Motor Torpedo Boats, Destroyers and Frigates. Naval Intelligence, 1946–49 and 1955–57; Commanded HMS Contest, 1949–51; Comdr, 1952; BJSM, Washington, 1953–55; Capt., 1959; Naval Attaché, Bonn, 1962–65; Director, Naval Recruiting, 1966–68; ADC to Queen, 1968; Rear-Adm., 1969. Editor, The Board Bulletin, 1971–78. *Publications:* The Drum Beats Still, 1951; Seagulls in my Belfry, 1997; numerous articles and short stories. *Recreations:* gardening, do-it-yourself. *Address:* Bybrook Cottage, Bustlers Hill, Sherston, Malmesbury, Wilts SN16 0ND.

ANDERSON, (Clarence) Eugene; business consultant; Chairman and Chief Executive, Ferranti International plc, 1990–94; *b* 31 Aug. 1938; *s* of Clarence Leslie Anderson and Wilda Faye Anderson; *m* 1977, Daniela Leopolda Proche; one *d*, and one *s* two *d* from a previous marriage. *Educ:* Univ. of Texas (BSc Chem. Engrg, 1961); Harvard Univ. (MBA 1963). Process Engr, New Orleans, 1961, Ops Analyst, Houston, 1963–66, Tenneco Oil Co.; Man. Dir, Globe Petroleum Sales Ltd, Lincs, 1966–69; Dir, Supply and Transportation, Houston, 1969–72, Dir, Operational Planning, Houston, 1972, Tenneco Oil Co.; Vice Pres., Tenneco International Co., Houston, 1973; Exec. Dir, Albright & Wilson Ltd, London, 1973–75; Vice Pres., Corporate Develt, Tenneco Inc., Houston, 1975–78; Dep. Man. Dir, Ops, Albright & Wilson Ltd, London, 1979–81; Pres., Celanese International Co., and Vice Pres., Celanese Corp., New York, 1981–85; Chief Exec., Johnson Matthey PLC, London, 1985–89. *Publication:* (jtly) report on microencapsulation. *Recreations:* music, literature, theatre, sailing, various sports.

ANDERSON, Clive Stuart; barrister; television presenter and writer; *b* 10 Dec. 1952; *s* of Gordon Menzies Randall Anderson and late Doris Elizabeth Anderson; *m* 1981, Dr Jane Hughes; one *s* two *d*. *Educ:* Harrow County Sch. for Boys; Selwyn Coll., Cambridge (MA). Called to the Bar, Middle Temple, 1976. *Radio:* Host, Cabaret Upstairs, 1986–88; Chm., Whose Line is it Anyway?, 1988; Presenter: Devil's Advocate, 1991–92; Unreliable Evidence, 1998–; *television:* Whose Line is it Anyway?, 1988–98; Clive Anderson Talks

Back, 1989–95; Notes & Queries, 1993; Our Man In, 1995, 1996; Clive Anderson All Talk, 1996–99; If I Ruled the World, 1998–99; Clive Anderson Now 2001–; various other progs. *Publications:* (jtly) Great Railway Journeys, 1994; (with Ian Brown) Patent Nonsense, 1994; Our Man In, 1995; Our Man in Heaven & Hell, 1996. *Recreations:* history, comedy, football. *Address:* London Management, 2–4 Noel Street, W1V 3RB. *T:* (020) 7287 9000; 4 King's Bench Walk, Temple, EC4Y 7DL. *T:* (020) 7822 8822.

ANDERSON, Courtney; *see* Anderson, (Charles) Courtney.

ANDERSON, Rev. David; Principal Lecturer in Religious Studies, Hertfordshire College of Higher Education (formerly Wall Hall College), Aldenham, Herts, 1974–84 (Senior Lecturer, 1970–74); *b* 30 Oct. 1919; *s* of William and Nancy Anderson, Newcastle upon Tyne; *m* 1953, Helen Finlay Robinson, 3rd *d* of Johnson and Eleanor Robinson, Whitley Bay, Northumberland; one *s* two *d.* *Educ:* Royal Grammar Sch. Newcastle upon Tyne; Selwyn Coll., Cambridge. Served in RA, 1940–42, Intelligence Corps, 1942–46, Lieut. Deacon, 1949, Priest, 1950; Curate of parish of St Gabriel, Sunderland, 1949–52; Tutor of St Aidan's Coll., Birkenhead, 1952–56; Warden of Melville Hall, Ibadan, Nigeria, 1956–58; Principal of: Immanuel Coll., Ibadan, Nigeria, 1958–62; Wycliffe Hall, Oxford, 1962–69. Examining Chaplain: to Bishop of Liverpool, 1969–75; to Bishop of St Albans, 1972–80. *Publications:* The Tragic Protest, 1969; Simone Weil, 1971; contrib: Religion and Modern Literature, 1975; William Golding: some critical considerations, 1978; The Passion of Man, 1980. *Recreations:* listening to music, hi-fi gramophones. *Address:* 6 Flassburn Road, Durham DH1 4LX. *T:* (0191) 3843063.

ANDERSON, David; Director, since 1990, and Chief Executive, since 1996, Yorkshire Building Society; *b* 23 Oct. 1955; *s* of Donald and Gweneth Anderson; *m* 1980, Fiona Ellen Hamilton; one *s* one *d.* *Educ:* Cheadle Hulme Sch.; St Edmund Hall, Oxford (MA PPE). Graduate trainee, Aveling Barford Ltd, construction equipment mfr, 1977–80; Dun and Bradstreet, 1980–83; PA Mgt Consultants, 1983–87; Dep. Gen. Manager (Mkting), Yorkshire Building Soc., 1987–90. *Recreations:* golf, sailing. *Address:* Yorkshire Building Society, Yorkshire Drive, Bradford BD5 8LJ. *T:* (01274) 740740. *Clubs:* Huddersfield Golf, Abersoch Golf; S Caernarvonshire Yacht.

ANDERSON, David Heywood, CMG 1982; Judge of the International Tribunal for the Law of the Sea, since 1996; Barrister-at-Law; *b* 14 Sept. 1937; *s* of late Harry Anderson; *m* 1961, Jennifer Ratcliffe; one *s* one *d.* *Educ:* King James' Grammar Sch., Almondbury. LLB (Leeds); LLM (London). Called to Bar, Gray's Inn, 1963. HM Diplomatic Service, 1960–96: Asst Legal Advisor, FCO 1960–69; Legal Adviser, British Embassy, Bonn, 1969–72; Legal Counsellor, FCO, 1972–79; Legal Adviser, UK Mission to UN, NY, 1979–82; Legal Counsellor, 1982–87, Dep. Legal Advr, 1987–89, Second Legal Advr, 1989–96, FCO. Visiting Professor: Durham Univ., 1995–; UCL, 1997–. Mem., Greenwich Forum, 1996–. *Publications:* (contrib.) International Maritime Boundaries, 1993–; contribs to British Yearbook of Internat. Law and learned jls. *Recreation:* gardening. *Address:* International Tribunal for the Law of the Sea, Am Internationalen Seegerichtshof 1, 22609 Hamburg, Germany. *T:* (40) 356070.

ANDERSON, David Munro; Chairman, Anderson Quantrend (formerly Allingham Anderson Roll Ross) Ltd, since 1990; *b* 15 Dec. 1937; *s* of Alexander Anderson and Jessica Anderson (*née* Vincent-Innes); *m* 1st, 1965, Veronica Jane (*née* Stevens) (marr. diss.); two *s* one *d*; 2nd, 1989, Ruth Lewis-Bowen. *Educ:* Morrison's Academy, Perthshire; Strathallan, Perthshire. Commissioned Black Watch; served W Africa; tea production with James Finlay & Co., India, 1959–62; London Chamber of Commerce and Industry, 1962–63; joined E. D. & F. Man Ltd, 1963; formed Anderson Man Ltd, 1981; formed E. D. & F. Man International Ltd, 1985, Chm., 1986–90; Man. Dir, Commodity Analysis Ltd, 1968; numerous directorships. Chairman, formation cttees: Internat. Petroleum Exchange; Baltic Internat. Freight Futures Exchange (jtly); former Vice-Chm., London Commodity Exchange; Dir, SIB, 1986–87. *Recreations:* ski-ing, shooting. *Address:* Clees Hall, Bures, Suffolk CO8 5DZ. *T:* (01787) 227271. *Club:* Caledonian.

ANDERSON, David William Kinloch; QC 1999; *b* 5 July 1961; *s* of (William) Eric (Kinloch) Anderson, *qv* and Poppy (*née* Mason); *m* 1989, Margaret Beeton; two *d.* *Educ:* Eton Coll. (King's Schol.); New Coll., Oxford (Open Schol.; MA Ancient and Modern Hist. 1982); Downing Coll., Cambridge (BA Law 1984); Inns of Court Sch. of Law. Called to the Bar, Middle Temple, 1985; Lawyer from Abroad, Covington & Burling, Washington, 1985–86; Stagiaire, Cabinet of Lord Cockfield, European Commn, 1987–88; in practice as barrister, Brick Court Chambers, 1988–. Vis. Lectr in European Law, 1989–95, Vis. Res. Fellow, 1995–99, Vis. Prof., 1999, KCL. *Publications:* References to the European Court, 1995, 2nd edn 2002; various articles in legal jls. *Recreations:* sailing, hill-walking, history. *Address:* Brick Court Chambers, 7–8 Essex Street, WC2R 3LD. *T:* (020) 7379 3550. *Club:* Royal Harwich Yacht.

ANDERSON, Prof. Declan John; Professor of Oral Biology, University of Bristol, 1966–85, now Professor Emeritus; Founder, The Oral and Dental Research Trust, 1989 (Director, 1989–92); *b* 20 June 1920; *s* of Arthur John Anderson and Katherine Mary Coffey; *m* 1947, Vivian Joy Dunkerton; four *s* three *d.* *Educ:* Christ's Hospital; Guy's Hospital Medical School, Univ. of London. BDS (London) 1942; LDSRCS 1943, BSc 1946, MSc 1947, PhD 1955. Prof. of Physiology, Univ. of Oregon, USA, 1957–58; Prof. of Physiology in Relation to Dentistry, Univ. of London, 1963–66. *Publications:* Physiology for Dental Students, 1952; (ed with R Buxton) How to Dissect and Understand Medical Terms, 1992; Introducing Silver, 2000; scientific papers in professional jls. *Recreations:* silversmithing, forging, music. *Address:* Little Dene, Stonequarry Road, Chelwood Gate, East Sussex RH17 7LS.

ANDERSON, Dr Digby Carter; Director, Social Affairs Unit, since 1980; *b* 25 May 1944; *s* of late Donald Anderson and Elizabeth Nance Ethel Anderson; *m* 1965, Judith Harris. *Educ:* St Lawrence Coll.; Univ. of Reading (BA Hons); Brunel Univ. (MPhil, PhD). Lectr, then Sen. Lectr, Luton Coll. of Higher Educn, 1965–77; Tutor, Brunel Univ. Youth Work Trng Unit, 1974–78; Res. Fellow, Univ. of Nottingham, 1977–80; Associate Lectr, Brunel Univ., 1977–78. Mem., ESRC, 1989–93. Mem., Health Studies Cttee, CNAA, 1987–92. Columnist: The Times, 1984–88; Sunday Telegraph, 1988–89; Sunday Times, 1989–90; Spectator, 1984–; National Review, 1991–. Ordained deacon 1985, priest 1986. Mem., Mont Pelerin Soc. *Publications:* (ed) Health Education in Practice, 1979; Evaluation by Classroom Experience, 1979; Evaluating Curriculum Proposals, 1980; (ed) The Ignorance of Social Intervention, 1980; Breaking the Spell of the Welfare State, 1981; (ed) The Kindness that Kills, 1984; (ed) A Diet of Reason, 1986; The Spectator Book of Imperative Cooking, 1987; (ed) Full Circle, 1988; (ed) Health, Lifestyle and Environment, 1992; (ed) The Loss of Virtue: moral confusion and social disorder in Britain and America, 1993; (ed) This Will Hurt: the restoration of civic order in America and Britain, 1995; (ed) Gentility Recalled: mere manners and the making of social order, 1996; (ed jtly) Faking It: the sentimentalisation of modern society, 1998; (compiler) The Dictionary of Dangerous Wars, 2000; contrib. Sociology, Jl Curriculum Studies, Econ. Affairs, Social Policy Rev. *Recreations:* non-Germanic music, the seaside, dinner. *Address:* 17 Hardwick Place, Woburn Sands, Bucks MK17 8QQ. *T:* (01908) 584526.

ANDERSON, Rt Hon. Donald; PC 2001; MP (Lab) Swansea East, since Oct. 1974; barrister-at-law; *b* 17 June 1939; *s* of David Robert Anderson and Eva (*née* Mathias); *m* 1963, Dr Dorothy Trotman, BSc, PhD; three *s.* *Educ:* Swansea Grammar Sch.; University Coll. of Swansea (Hon. Fellow, 1985). 1st cl. hons Modern History and Politics, Swansea, 1960. Barrister; called to Bar, Inner Temple, 1969. Member of HM Foreign Service, 1960–64: Foreign Office, 1960–63; 3rd Sec., British Embassy, Budapest, 1963–64; lectured in Dept of Political Theory and Govt, University Coll., Swansea, 1964–66. Councillor, Kensington and Chelsea, 1971–75. MP (Lab) Monmouth, 1966–70; Mem. Estimates Cttee, 1966–69; Vice-Chm., Welsh Labour Group, 1969–70, Chm., 1977–78; PPS to Minister of Defence (Administration), 1969–70; PPS to Attorney General, 1974–79; opposition front-bench spokesman on foreign affairs, 1983–92, on defence, 1993–94; Shadow Solicitor General, 1994–95. Member: Select Cttee on Welsh Affairs, 1980–83 (Chm., 1981–83); Select Cttee on Home Affairs, 1992–93; Home Affairs Cttee, 1994–95; Speaker's Panel of Chairmen, 1995–99; Chm., Foreign Affairs Cttee, 1997–. Chairman: Parly Lab. Party Environment Gp, 1974–79; Welsh Lab. Gp, 1977–78. Chm., British–French and British–S African Party Gp; Jt Chm., British–Norwegian Parly Gp; Vice Chm., British–German, –Spanish, –Netherlands, –Hungarian, Parly Gps; Mem. Exec., IPU, 1983– (Vice-Chm. Exec., 1985–88; Treas., 1988–90, 1992); Chm., UK Br., CPA, 1997– (Vice-Chm., 1986–97; Treas., 1990–93). Sen. Vice-Pres., Assoc. of European Parliamentarians for Africa (Southern), 1984–97; Member: North Atlantic Assembly, subseq. NATO Parly Assembly, 1992– (Ldr, UK Delegn, 1997–; Chm., Socialist Gp, 1997–); UK Delegn to OSCE, 1997–. Pres., Gower Soc., 1976–78. Chairman: Parly Christian Fellowship, 1990–93; Nat. Prayer Breakfast, 1989; President: Boys' Brigade of Wales, 1992–94; Swansea Male Choir. Local preacher. Freeman, City and County of Swansea, 2000. Commander's Cross, Order of Merit (FRG), 1986. *Recreations:* church work, walking and talking. *Address:* House of Commons, SW1A 0AA.

ANDERSON, Prof. Donald Thomas, AO 1986; PhD, DSc; FRS 1977; Challis Professor of Biology, University of Sydney, 1984–91, Professor Emeritus, since 1992 (Professor of Biology, 1972–84); *b* 29 Dec. 1931; *s* of Thomas and Flora Anderson; *m* 1960, Joanne Trevathan (*née* Claridge). *Educ:* King's Coll., London Univ. DSc London, 1966; DSc Sydney, 1983. Lectr in Zoology, Sydney Univ., 1958–61; Sen. Lectr, 1962–66; Reader in Biology, 1967–71. Clarke Medal, Royal Soc. of NSW, 1979. *Publication:* Embryology and Phylogeny, of Annelids and Arthropods, 1973; Barnacles: structure, function, development and evolution, 1993; Atlas of Invertebrate Anatomy, 1996; Invertebrate Zoology, 1998; papers in zool. jls. *Recreations:* gardening, photography. *Address:* 5 Angophora Close, Wamberal, NSW 2260, Australia. *T:* (2) 43846670.

ANDERSON, Dr Ephraim Saul, CBE 1976; FRCP; FRS 1968; Director, Enteric Reference Laboratory, Public Health Laboratory Service, 1954–78; *b* 1911; *e s* of Benjamin and Ada Anderson, Newcastle upon Tyne; *m* 1959, Carol Jean (*née* Thompson) (marr. diss.); three *s.* *Educ:* Rutherford Coll., and King's Coll. Med. Sch. (Univ. of Durham), Newcastle upon Tyne. MB, BS 1934; MD Durham, 1953; Dip.Bact. London, 1948; Founder Fellow, Royal Coll. of Pathologists, 1963. GP, 1935–39; RAMC, 1940–46; Pathologist, 1943–46; Registrar in Bacteriology, Postgrad. Med. Sch., 1946–47; Staff, Enteric Reference Lab., 1947–52, Dep. Dir, 1952–54. WHO Fellow, 1953; FIBiol 1973; FRCP 1975. Hon. Chm., Internat. Fedn for Enteric Phage Typing of Internat. Union of Microbiol. Socs, 1986– (Jt Chm., 1958–66; Chm., 1966–86); Dir, Internat. Ref. Lab. for Enteric Phage Typing of Internat. Fedn for Enteric Phage Typing, 1954–; Dir, Collab. Centre for Phage Typing and Resistance of Enterobacteria of WHO, 1960–; Mem., WHO Expert Adv. Panel for Enteric Diseases. Vis. Prof., Sch. of Biol Sciences, Brunel Univ., 1973–77; Royal Soc.–Israel Acad. Vis. Res. Prof., 1978–79. Lectures: Scientific Basis of Medicine, British Postgrad. Med. Fedn, 1966; Almroth Wright, Wright-Fleming Inst. of Microbiol., 1967; Holme, UCH, 1970; Cutter, Sch. of Public Health, Harvard, 1972; Marjory Stephenson Meml, Soc. for Gen. Microbiol., 1975. Hon. DSc Newcastle, 1975. *Publications:* contrib. to: The Bacteriophages (Mark Adams), 1959; The World Problem of Salmonellosis (Van Oye), 1964; Ciba Symposium: Bacterial Episomes and Plasmids, 1969; articles on bacteriophage typing and its genetic basis, microbial ecology, transferable drug resistance in bacteria, its evolution, and epidemiology, with special ref. to significance of bacterial plasmids. *Recreations:* music, photography. *Address:* 10 Rosecroft Avenue, NW3 7QB.

ANDERSON, Eric; *see* Anderson, W. E. K.

ANDERSON, Eugene; *see* Anderson, C. E.

ANDERSON, Rev. Prof. George Wishart, FRSE 1977; FBA 1972; Professor of Old Testament Literature and Theology, 1962–68, of Hebrew and Old Testament Studies, 1968–82, University of Edinburgh; *b* 25 Jan. 1913; *s* of George Anderson and Margaret Gordon Wishart; *m* 1st, 1941, Edith Joyce Marjorie Walter (decd); one *s* one *d*; 2nd, 1959, Anne Phyllis Walter (*d* 1999). *Educ:* Arbroath High Sch.; Univs of St Andrews, Cambridge, Lund. United Coll., St Andrews: Harkness Scholar; MA 1st Cl. Hons Classics, 1935. Fitzwilliam House and Wesley House, Cambridge: 1st Cl. Theol Tripos Part I, 1937; 2nd Cl. Theol Tripos Part II, 1938; BA 1937; MA 1946. Asst Tutor, Richmond Coll., 1939–41. Chaplain, RAF, 1941–46; Tutor in OT Lang. and Lit., Handsworth Coll., 1946–56; Lecturer in OT Lit. and Theol., Univ. of St Andrews, 1956–58; Prof. of OT Studies, Univ. of Durham, 1958–62. Hon. Sec., Internat. Organization of Old Testament Scholars, 1953–71 (Pres., 1971–74); Mem. Editorial Bd of Vetus Testamentum, 1950–75; Editor, Book List of Soc. for OT Study, 1957–66; President, Soc. for OT Study, 1963; Hon. Sec. (Foreign Correspondence), Soc. for OT Study, 1964–74; Charles Ryder Smith Meml Lectr, 1964; Fernley-Hartley Lectr, 1969; Speaker's Lectr in Biblical Studies, Univ. of Oxford, 1976–80; Henton Davies Lectr, 1977; A. S. Peake Meml Lectr, 1984. Hon. DD St Andrews, 1959; Hon. TeolD Lund, 1971. Burkitt Medal for Biblical Studies, British Acad., 1982. *Publications:* He That Cometh (trans. from Norwegian of S. Mowinckel), 1956; A Critical Introduction to the Old Testament, 1959, 2nd edn 1994; The Ras Shamra Discoveries and the Old Testament (trans. from Norwegian of A. S. Kapelrud, US 1963, UK 1965); The History and Religion of Israel, 1966 (trans. Chinese 1990); (ed) A Decade of Bible Bibliography, 1967; (ed) Tradition and Interpretation, 1979; articles in: The Old Testament and Modern Study (ed H. H. Rowley), 1951; The New Peake Commentary (ed M. Black and H. H. Rowley), 1962; The Cambridge History of the Bible, Vol. I (ed P. R. Ackroyd and C. F. Evans), 1970, and in various learned jls. *Recreations:* reading, music, walking. *Address:* 51 Fountainhall Road, Edinburgh EH9 2LH.

ANDERSON, Gerry, MBE 2001; film producer, director, and writer; Managing Director, Inimitable Ltd, since 1989; *b* 14 April 1929; *s* of Joseph and Deborah Anderson; *m* 1st, 1952, Betty Wrightman; two *d*; 2nd, 1961, Sylvia Thamm; one *s*; 3rd, 1981, Mary Robins; one *s.* *Educ:* Willesden County Secondary Sch. Entered film industry as Colonial Film Unit Trainee, 1943; Asst Editor, Gainsborough Pictures, 1945–47; dubbing editor, various indep. cos, 1949–53; Film Dir, Polytechnic Films, 1954–55; Co-Founder:

Pentagon Films, 1955; AP Films, 1956; AP Merchandising, 1961; Chm., Century 21 Orgn, 1966–75; Dir of TV Commercials, 1961, 1988–92. *Puppet films/series* include: director: The Adventures of Twizzle, 1956; Torchy the Battery Boy, 1957; producer: Four Feather Falls; Supercar, 1959–60; Fireball XL5, 1962; Stingray, 1963–65; Thunderbirds, 1966–67; Captain Scarlet and the Mysterons, 1967–68; Joe 90, 1968–69; The Secret Service, 1969; Terrahawks, 1981–85; *live action series* include: UFO, 1969; The Protectors, 1971; Space: 1999, 1973–75, 1977–78; Space Precinct, 1993–95; *stop motion series:* Dick Spanner, 1987; Lavender Castle, 1997; *feature films:* executive producer: Thunderbirds are Go (puppet); Thunderbird 6 (puppet); producer, Journey to the far side of the Sun (live action). Hon. Fellow, BKSTS. *Recreations:* gardening, walking, DIY.

ANDERSON, Gordon Alexander, CBE 2000; CA, FCMA; Chartered Accountant; *b* 9 Aug. 1931; *s* of Cecil Brown Anderson and Janet Davidson Bell; *m* 1958, Eirené Cochrane Howie Douglas; two *s* one *d. Educ:* High School of Glasgow. Qualified as Chartered Accountant, 1955; FCMA 1984. National Service, RN, 1955–57. Partner: Moores Carson & Watson, 1958 (subseq. McClelland Moores & Co., Arthur Young McClelland Moores & Co., Arthur Young (Chm., 1987–89), and Ernst & Young (Dep. Sen. Partner, 1989–90)); McLintock Moores & Murray, 1963–69. Chairman: Bitmac Ltd, 1990–96 (Dir, 1984–96); TSB Bank Scotland, 1994–99 (Dir, 1991–99); Director: Douglas Firebrick Co. Ltd, 1961–70; Lloyds TSB Group (formerly TSB Group), 1993–99; Merchants House of Glasgow, 1996–. Mem., Scottish Milk Marketing Bd, 1979–85. Mem., Council on Tribunals, 1990–96 (Mem., Scottish Cttee, 1990–96). Institute of Chartered Accountants of Scotland: Mem. Council, 1980–84; Vice-Pres., 1984–86; Pres., 1986–87. Chm. of Govs, High Sch. of Glasgow, 1992–. *Recreations:* golf, gardening, Rugby football. *Address:* Ardwell, 41 Manse Road, Bearsden, Glasgow G61 3PN. *T:* (0141) 942 2803. *Clubs:* Western (Glasgow); Glasgow Golf; Buchanan Castle Golf (Captain 1979–80).

ANDERSON, H(ector) John, FRCP; Physician: St Thomas' Hospital, 1948–80 (Special Trustee, 1972–81); Lambeth Hospital, 1960–80; South Western Hospital, 1948–80; French Hospital, 1950–80; *b* Central Provinces, India, 5 Jan. 1915; *s* of H. J. Anderson; *m* 1st, 1940, Frances Pearce (marr. diss.), *er d* of Rev. W. P. Putt; one *s* one *d*; 2nd, 1956, Pauline Mary, *d* of A. Hammond; one *d. Educ:* Exeter Sch.; St Catharine's Coll., Cambridge; St Thomas' Hospital. MA, MB (Cantab), FRCP 1950. Medical Registrar and Res. Asst Physician, St Thomas' Hospital, 1941 and 1942. Hon. Lt-Col RAMC; served MEF, 1944–47. Kitchener Scholar; Mead Prizeman, St Thomas' Hospital; Murchison Scholar, RCP, 1942; Goulstonian Lectr, RCP, 1951; Examiner: MB London; Medicine, Conjoint Bd, London and England; RCP. Mem. AHA, Lambeth, Southwark, Lewisham Area (T). Member: Assoc. of Physicians of Gt Britain; Thoracic Soc.; FRSoc.Med. *Publications:* Brim of Day, 1944; Poems, 1996; contrib. to medical literature. *Address:* 102 Lambeth Road, SE1 7PT. *T:* (020) 7928 1533.

ANDERSON, Rev. Prof. Hugh, MA, BD, PhD, DD, FRSE; Professor of New Testament Language, Literature and Theology, University of Edinburgh, 1966–85, now Professor Emeritus; *b* 18 May 1920; *s* of Hugh Anderson and Jeannie Muir; *m* 1945, Jean Goldie Torbit; one *s* one *d* (and one *s* decd). *Educ:* Galston Sch.; Kilmarnock Acad.; Univ. of Glasgow (MA (Hons Classics and Semitic Langs I), BD (Dist. New Testament); PhD); post-doctoral Fellow, Univs of Oxford and Heidelberg. FRSE 1987. Chaplain, Egypt and Palestine, 1945–46; Lectr in Old Testament, Univ. of Glasgow, 1946–51; Minister, Trinity Presb. Church, Glasgow, 1951–57; A. B. Bruce Lectr, Univ. of Glasgow, 1954–57; Prof. of Biblical Criticism, Duke Univ., N Carolina, 1957–66. Dir, Postgrad. Studies in Theology, Univ. of Edinburgh, 1968–72; Select Preacher, Oxford Univ., 1970; Haskell Lectr, Oberlin Coll., Ohio, 1971; McBride Vis. Prof. of Religion, Bryn Mawr Coll., Pa, 1974–75; Vis. Prof. of Religion, Meredith Coll., N Carolina, 1982; James A. Gray Lectr, 1982, Kenneth Willis Clark Meml Lectr, 1985, Duke Univ., N Carolina; Scholar-in-res., Florida Southern Coll., Lakeland, Fla, 1983; Warner Hall Lectr, St Andrews Presbyterian Coll., N Carolina, 1985; Bishop E. J. Pendergrass Prof. of Religion, Florida Southern Coll., 1986; J. Wallace Hamilton Lectr, Fla, 1988. Convener of Ch. of Scotland's Special Commn on Priorities of Mission in 70s and 80s, 1969–71; Chm., Internat. Selection Council for Albert Schweitzer Internat. Prizes, 1972–91. Hon. DD: Glasgow, 1970; Florida Southern Coll., 1986. *Publications:* Psalms I-XLV, 1951; Historians of Israel, 1957; Jesus and Christian Origins, 1964; The Inter-Testamental Period in The Bible and History (ed W. Barclay), 1965; (ed with W. Barclay) The New Testament in Historical and Contemporary Perspective, 1965; Jesus, 1967; The Gospel of Mark, 1976; Commentary on 3 and 4 Maccabees, Doubleday Pseudepigrapha Vol. 2, 1982; (with Walter Weaver) Perspectives on Christology, 1989; contribs to Religion in Life, Interpretation, Scottish Jl of Theology, Expos. Times, Anchor Bible Dictionary, Theologische Realenzyklopaedia. *Recreations:* golf, gardening, music. *Address:* Morningside Way, 23/13 Maxwell Street, Edinburgh EH10 5HT. *T:* (0131) 447 1401. *Clubs:* Greek (Edinburgh); Luffness Golf (E Lothian).

ANDERSON, James Frazer Gillan, CBE 1979; JP; DL; Member, Scottish Development Agency, 1986–89; *b* 25 March 1929; *m* 1956, May Harley; one *s* one *d. Educ:* Maddiston Primary Sch.; Graeme High Sch., Falkirk. Member: Stirling CC, 1958–75 (Convener, 1971–75); Central Regional Council, Scotland, 1974–96 (Convener, 1974–86). Mem., Health and Safety Commission, 1974–80. OStJ. DUniv Stirling, 1987. *Recreations:* gardening, walking.

ANDERSON, Janet; MP (Lab) Rossendale and Darwen, since 1992; *b* 6 Dec. 1949; *d* of late Thomas Anderson and Ethel Pearson; *m*; two *s* one *d. Educ:* Kingsfield Comprehensive Sch.; Polytechnic of Central London; Univ. of Nantes (Dip. Bi-lingual Business Studies). Asst to Rt Hon. Barbara Castle, 1974–81, to Jack Straw, MP, 1981–87; Campaign Officer, PLP, 1988–89; Regl Organiser, Shopping Hours Reform Council, 1991–92. Contested (Lab) Rossendale and Darwen, 1987. PPS to Dep. Leader of Labour Party, 1992–93; an Opposition Whip, 1995–97; Vice Chamberlain of HM Household, 1997–98; Parly Under-Sec. of State, DCMS, 1998–2001. Member: H of C Commn, 1993–94; Select Cttee on Home Affairs, 1994–95 (Home Affairs Campaigns Co-ordinator, 1994–95). Secretary: All Party Footwear Gp, 1992–97; Tribune Gp of Lab MPs, 1993–97. *Recreations:* playing the piano, listening to opera. *Address:* House of Commons, SW1A 0AA. *T:* (020) 7219 5375; (office) 23 Bolton Road, Darwen, Lancs BB3 1DF. *T:* (01254) 704201, *Fax:* (01254) 762077; (office) King George Chambers, St James's Square, Burnley Road, Bacup, Lancs OL13 9AA. *T:* (01706) 877010, *Fax:* (01706) 870010. *Club:* Rosemount Working Men's (Stacksteads, Rossendale).

ANDERSON, Dr Joan Mary, FRS 1996; FAA; Chief Research Scientist, Commonwealth Scientific and Industrial Research Organisation, since 1962; *b* 12 May 1932; *d* of William Arthur Anderson, OBE and Mary Anderson (*née* Lee). *Educ:* Univ. of Otago, NZ (BSc 1954; MSc 1st Cl. Hons 1956); Univ. of California, Berkeley (PhD 1959). Div. of Plant Industry, CSIRO, 1962–. Fellowships: King George VI Meml, NZ, 1956; Carnegie Inst., Stanford, 1966; Kettering, Dayton, Ohio, 1967; Harvard, 1973; Newnham Coll., Cambridge, 1973–74; Vis. Spring Prof., Univ. of California, Berkeley, 1982; Vis. Swedish Natural Sci. Res. Council Prof., Lund, 1986. Lemberg Medal, Aust. Soc. of Biochem., 1983. *Publications:* numerous articles on photosynthesis research. *Recreations:* music, art, water colour painting, bush walking. *Address:* Photobioenergetics Group, Research School of Biological Sciences, Australian National University, GPO Box 475, Canberra, ACT 2601, Australia. *T:* (2) 61255895, *Fax:* (2) 61258056; *e-mail:* anderson@rsbs.anu.edu.au.

ANDERSON, Prof. John, MD, FRCP; Professor of Medicine, King's College Hospital Medical School, 1964–86, now Emeritus; *b* 11 Sept. 1921; *s* of James and Margaret Anderson; *m* 1952, Beatrice May Venner; three *s. Educ:* Durham Univ. BA Hons, Dunelm (Mod. Hist.) 1942; MB, BS Hons, 1950; BSc Hons, 1952 (Physiology); MA (Mod. Hist.), MD. Served War, Lt, RA (Field) (Ayrshire Yeomanry), 1940–45. MRC Fellow in Clin. Med., Univ. Coll. Hosp., London, 1952–55; Rockefeller Travelling Fellowship, 1956–57; Reader in Medicine, King's Coll. Hosp. Med. Sch., Med. Unit, 1962–64. WHO Consultant, medical educn, 1968. Mem., Med. Research Soc. FRCP 1962; FBCS 1969; FIBiol 1977. *Publications:* A New Look at Medical Education, 1965; Information Processing of Medical Records, 1970; articles in Lancet and BMJ, on: neutron activation, medical computing, cancer, endocrinology, med. educn. *Recreation:* computing. *Address:* 14 Styles Way, Park Langley, Beckenham, Kent BR3 3AJ. *Club:* University (Durham).

ANDERSON, Prof. John, FRCP; FRCPGlas; FRCOG; Postgraduate Dean and Director, Postgraduate Institute for Medicine and Dentistry, and Professor of Medical Education, University of Newcastle upon Tyne, 1985–98, now Professor Emeritus; *b* 2 Feb. 1936; *s* of John and Norah Anderson, Newcastle upon Tyne; *m* Mary Bynon, Whitley Bay; one *s* one *d. Educ:* Royal Grammar Sch., Newcastle upon Tyne; Med. Sch., King's Coll., Univ. of Durham (MB, BS 2nd Cl. Hons). FRCP 1973 (MRCP 1961); FRCOG (*ad eundem*) 1983; FRCPGlas 1992. Med. Registrar, Royal Victoria Inf., Newcastle upon Tyne, 1962–64; Res. Fellow, Univ. of Virginia, Charlottesville, 1965–66; University of Newcastle upon Tyne: First Asst in Medicine 1967–68; Sen. Lectr in Medicine 1968–85; Academic Sub-Dean, Med. Sch., 1975–85. Hon. Cons. Phys., Royal Victoria Infirmary, 1968–. Mem. Council, RCP, 1974–77; Member: Assoc. of Phys of GB and Ire., 1976–; Exec. Cttee, ASME, 1979– (Hon. Treas., 1980–88; Gen. Sec., 1990–92; Chm. Council, 1992–95; Vice-Pres., 1996–); GMC, 1980–; GDC, 1986–99. *Publications:* The Multiple Choice Question in Medicine, 1976, 2nd edn 1982; numerous chapters in books, and papers in sci. jls on medicine, diabetes and med. educn. *Recreations:* listening to music, watching cricket, reading, thinking. *Address:* 6 Wilson Gardens, Newcastle upon Tyne NE3 4JA. *T:* (0191) 285 4745. *Clubs:* Yorkshire CC, Durham CC.

ANDERSON, Sir John (Anthony), KBE 1994; FCA; Chief Executive and Director: South Pacific Merchant Finance Ltd, since 1979; National Bank of New Zealand Ltd, since 1990; *b* 2 Aug. 1945; *s* of Donald Ian Mogine Anderson and Elizabeth Grace Anderson (*née* Plummer); *m* 1970, Carol Margaret Tuck; two *s* one *d. Educ:* Christ's Coll.; Victoria Univ. of Wellington. ACA 1967, FCA 1991. With Deloitte Ross Tohmatsu, Wellington, 1962–69; Guest & Bell, Melbourne, 1969–72. Director: NZ Steel, 1986–87; Lloyds Merchant Bank (London), 1986–92; Lloyds Bank NZA, 1989–96; Chm., Petroleum Corp. of NZ, 1986–88. Chairman: Adv. Bd, NZ Debt Mgt Office, 1989–; Prime Minister's NZ Employment Taskforce, 1994. Chairman: NZ Merchant Banks Assoc., 1982–89; NZ Bankers' Assoc., 1991–92 and 1999–2000; Pres., NZ Bankers' Inst., 1990. Bd Dir, ICC, 1997–; Chairman: NZ Cricket Bd, 1995–; NZ Sports Foundn, 1999–. NZ Commemoration Medal, 1990. *Recreations:* cricket, tennis, golf, bridge. *Address:* 5 Fancourt Street, Karori, Wellington, New Zealand. *T:* (4) 8022000. *Clubs:* Wellington, Wellesley (NZ).

ANDERSON, Hon. John (Duncan); MP (Nat.) Gwydir, NSW, since 1989; Deputy Prime Minister of Australia, since 1999; Leader, National Party of Australia, since 1999; *b* 14 Nov. 1956; *s* of Duncan Anderson and Beryl Anderson (*née* Mann); *m* 1987, Julia Gillian Robertson; one *s* three *d. Educ:* Univ. of Sydney (MA). Farmer and grazier. Minister: for Primary Industries and Energy, 1996–98; for Transport and Regl Services, 1998–99. Dep. Leader, Nat. Party of Australia, 1993–99. *Address:* Parliament House, Canberra, ACT 2600, Australia. *Club:* Australian (Sydney).

ANDERSON, Maj.-Gen. Sir John (Evelyn), KBE 1971 (CBE 1963); CEng, FIEE; CIMgt; Associate and Director, Space and Maritime Applications Inc., 1988–93; *b* 28 June 1916; *e s* of Lt-Col John Gibson Anderson, Christchurch, NZ, and Margaret (*née* Scott), Edinburgh; *m* 1944, Jean Isobel, *d* of Charles Tait, farmer, Aberdeenshire; one *s* one *d. Educ:* King's Sch., Rochester; RMA, Woolwich. Commissioned in Royal Signals, 1936; Lt-Col 1956; Col 1960; Brig. 1964; Maj.-Gen. 1967; Signal Officer in Chief (Army), MoD, 1967–69; ACDS (signals), 1969–72. Col Comdt, Royal Corps of Signals, 1969–74. Hon. Col 71st (Yeomanry) Signal Regt TAVR, 1969–76; Hon. Col Women's Transport Corps (FANY), 1970–76. Dir Gen., NATO Integrated Communications System Management Agency, 1977–81; Exec. Dir, Europe Gp, AFCEA, 1981–88. Pres., Piscatorial Soc., 1981–87. *Recreation:* fishing. *Address:* 23 Northfield Court, Aldeburgh, Suffolk IP15 5LU. *Club:* Flyfishers'.

See also Maj.-Gen. A. A. G. Anderson.

ANDERSON, John Ferguson; Chief Executive, Glasgow City Council, 1995–98; *b* 13 Dec. 1947; *s* of Charles and Isabella Anderson; *m* 1970, Sandra McFarlane; one *s* one *d. Educ:* Edinburgh Univ. (LLB Hons 1969). Legal Assistant, then Solicitor, later Asst Chief Solicitor, Glasgow Corp., 1969–75; Strathclyde Regional Council: Prin. Solicitor, 1975–78; Asst Dir of Admin, 1978–80; Sen. Exec. Officer, 1980–86; Prin. Exec. Officer, 1986–90; Dep. Chief Exec., 1990–95. *Recreations:* golf, watching football, transportation issues, church. *Address:* 6 Dumgoyne Avenue, Milngavie G62 7AL.

ANDERSON, John Graeme, CBE 1989; CEng, FInstE; Deputy Chairman, Northern Engineering Industries plc, 1986–89; Director, Team General Partner, since 1993; *b* 3 June 1927; *s* of John Anderson and Ella (*née* Pusey); *m* 1953, Nancy Clarice Taylor Johnson; one *s* twin *d. Educ:* Merchant Taylors' Sch., Sandy Lodge; London Univ. (BScEng Hons). MIMechE. Served RN, Fleet Air Arm, 1945–48. International Combustion Ltd: graduate apprentice, 1952; Dir, 1968; Dep. Chief Exec., 1969; Man. Dir, 1974; Northern Engineering Industries: Man. Dir, NEI-Internat. Combustion Ltd, 1977; Managing Director: Mechanical Gp, 1980; Power Gp, 1982; Internat. and Projects Gp, 1984; Chm., NEI Pacific, 1984–88. Chm., Internat. Combustion-HUD Hong Kong, 1978–82; Dir, British Nuclear Associates, 1985–88; Alternate Dir, Nat. Nuclear Corp., 1986–88; Director: Tyne and Wear Develt Corp., 1987–93; The Newcastle Initiative, 1988–90. Mem., Duke of Kent's BOTB mission to Turkey, 1984. Chairman: Solid Waste Assoc., 1972–74; Watertube Boilermakers' Assoc., 1976–80; Member: Process Plant Assoc., 1968–87; Process Plant, EDC, 1972–76; Heavy Electrical, EDC, 1976–80. Gov., Derby Coll. of Technology, 1969–74. Chm., Upstage, 1977–79. *Recreations:* shooting, painting, music, fell walking. *Address:* Trinity Barns, Corbridge, Northumberland NE45 5HP. *T:* (01434) 633228.

ANDERSON, John Huxley Fordyce, FCIOB; Managing Director: Bovis Construction Ltd, since 1993; Bovis Europe, since 1996; Joint Managing Director, Bovis Construction Group, since 1997 (Director, since 1988); Director, P&O Property Holdings, since 1985;

b 13 Jan. 1945; *s* of Alexander Robert Fordyce Anderson and Agnes Joan (*née* Huxley); *m* 1973, Tucker Lee Etherington; one *s* one *d*. *Educ:* Fan Court Sch.; Milton Abbey Sch.; Brixton Sch. of Building; Harvard Bus. Sch. (post-grad. PMD 1983). FCIOB 1988. Joined Higgs & Hill as indentured student, 1962; Project Planner on projects such as BBC TV Centre, RMA Sandhurst, 1966–69; Contract Manager, Sales and Marketing Manager then Dep. Man. Dir, Costains, Vale do Lobo, Portugal, 1969–74; with Town & City Properties in Holland, 1975–76; Develt Project Manager, Town & City Develts in London, 1976–83; Man. Dir, Town & City, then P&O, Develts, 1984–92; Dir, Chelsea Harbour, 1984–92. Man. Dir, PSA Building Management (on secondment to Govt), 1991–93. *Recreations:* parish council, local amenity society, golf, ski-ing, gardening, watching sport, theatre, ballet, eating and drinking with friends. *Address:* Bovis Construction Ltd, Bovis House, Northolt Road, Harrow, Middlesex HA2 0EE. *Club:* Royal Automobile.

ANDERSON, Prof. John Kinloch, FSA; Professor of Classical Archaeology, University of California, Berkeley, 1958–93, now Emeritus; *b* 3 Jan. 1924; *s* of late Sir James Anderson, KCIE, and Lady Anderson; *m* 1954, Esperance (*d* 2000), *d* of late Guy Batham, Dunedin, NZ; one *s* two *d*. *Educ:* Trinity Coll., Glenalmond; Christ Church, Oxford (MA). Served War, in Black Watch (RHR) and Intelligence Corps, 1942–46 (final rank, Lieut). Student, British Sch. at Athens, 1949–52; Lecturer in Classics, Univ. of Otago, NZ, 1953–58. FSA 1976. Award for Distinction in Teaching, Phi Beta Kappa (N Calif. Chapter), 1988. *Publications:* Greek Vases in the Otago Museum, 1955; Ancient Greek Horsemanship, 1961; Military Theory and Practice in the Age of Xenophon, 1970; Xenophon, 1974; Hunting in the Ancient World, 1985; articles and reviews in Annual of British Sch. at Athens; Jl of Hellenic Studies, etc. *Recreations:* gardening, riding (Qualified Riding Mem., Calif Dressage Soc.). *Address:* 1020 Middlefield Road, Berkeley, CA 94708, USA. *T:* (510) 8415335.

ANDERSON, John M., PhD; FBA 1991; Professor of English Language, University of Edinburgh, since 1988. *Educ:* Edinburgh Univ. (MA, PhD). Lectr until 1975, Reader, 1975–88, Edinburgh Univ. *Publications:* Grammar of Case: towards a localistic theory, 1971; (ed with C. Jones) Historical Linguistics, 2 vols, 1974; (with R. Lass) Old English Phonology, 1975; (with C. Jones) Phonological Structure and the History of English, 1977; (with C. J. Ewen) Principles of Dependency Phonology, 1987; Linguistic Representation: structural analogy and stratification, 1992; Notional Theory of Syntactic Categories, 1997. *Address:* Department of English Language, David Hume Tower, George Square, Edinburgh EH8 9JX.

ANDERSON, Sir John (Muir), Kt 1969; CMG 1957; Commissioner of State Savings Bank of Victoria, 1962–81, Chairman of Commissioners, 1967; *b* 14 Sept. 1914; *s* of John Weir Anderson; *m* 1949, Audrey Drayton Jamieson; one *s* one *d*. *Educ:* Brighton Grammar Sch.; Melbourne Univ. 2/6th Commando Co., 1941; Lieut, 1st Australian Parachute Bn, 1944; served SE Asia, 1941–45. Established John M. Anderson & Co. Pty Ltd, Manufacturers, Agents and Importers, 1951; Managing Director, King Oscar Fine Foods Pty Ltd, 1956–92. Pres. of Liberal and Country Party of Victoria, 1952–56 (Treasurer, 1957–61, 1978–80). Comr, Melbourne Harbour Trust, 1972–83. Trustee, Melbourne Exhibn, 1960, Chm. of Trustees, 1968. *Recreations:* swimming, fishing. *Address:* 25 Cosham Street, Brighton, Vic 3186, Australia.

ANDERSON, Professor John Neil; (first) Professor of Dental Prosthetics, 1964–82 (now Emeritus), (first) Dean of Dentistry, 1972–76, 1980–82, University of Dundee; *b* 11 Feb. 1922; *m* 1945, Mary G. Croll; one *s* one *d*. *Educ:* High Storrs Gram. Sch., Sheffield; Sheffield Univ. Asst Lectr, Sheffield Univ., 1945–46; Lectr, Durham Univ., 1946–48; Lectr, Birmingham Univ., 1948–52; Sen. Lectr, St Andrews Univ., 1952–64. External Examiner, Univs of Malaya, Baghdad, Newcastle upon Tyne, Bristol, Birmingham, Liverpool, RCSI. *Publications:* Applied Dental Materials, 1956; (with R. Storer) Immediate and Replacement Dentures, 1966, 3rd edn, 1981; contribs to leading dental jls. *Recreations:* music, gardening, carpentry. *Address:* Wyndham, Derwent Drive, Baslow, Bakewell, Derbyshire DE45 1RS.

ANDERSON, Prof. John Russell, CBE 1980; Professor of Pathology at the Western Infirmary, Glasgow University, 1967–83, retired; *b* 31 May 1918; *s* of William Gregg Anderson and Mary Gordon Adam; *m* 1956, Audrey Margaret Shaw Wilson; two *s* one *d* (and one *d* decd). *Educ:* Worksop Coll.; St Andrews Univ. BSc (St Andrews) 1939, MB, ChB (St Andrews) 1942, MD (St Andrews) 1955; MRCP 1961; FRCPGlas 1965; FRCPath 1966; FRSE 1968. RAMC, 1944–47 (Emergency Commn). Lecturer and Senior Lecturer in Pathology, Glasgow Univ., 1947–65; George Holt Prof. of Pathology, Liverpool Univ., 1965–67. Rockefeller travelling fellowship in Medicine, at Rochester, NY, 1953–54. Pres., RCPath, 1978–81 (Vice-Pres., 1975). Hon. FRCPI, 1981. Hon. LLD Dundee, 1981. *Publications:* Autoimmunity, Clinical and Experimental (jtly), 1967; (ed) Muir's Textbook of Pathology, 9th edn 1972 to 12th edn 1985; various papers on immunopathology in scientific jls. *Recreations:* golf, arboriculture, gardening. *Address:* 3 Connell Crescent, Milngavie, Glasgow G62 6AR.

ANDERSON, Dame Josephine; *see* Barstow, Dame J.

ANDERSON, Julian Anthony; Director General, Country Landowners' Association, since 1990; *b* 12 June 1938; *s* of Sir Kenneth Anderson, KBE, CB. *Educ:* King Alfred Sch.; Wadham Coll., Oxford (MA). Entered MAFF as Asst Principal, 1961; Asst Private Sec. to Minister of Agriculture, 1964–66; Principal, 1966; seconded to FCO, 1970–73; Asst Sec., 1973, Under Sec., 1982–90, MAFF; seconded as Minister (Food and Agriculture), UK Perm. Rep. to EEC, 1982–85. *Recreations:* music, sport, travel, photography, gardening, DIY. *Address:* c/o Country Landowners' Association, 16 Belgrave Square, SW1X 8PQ. *Clubs:* Oxford and Cambridge, Civil Service.

ANDERSON, Julian David; composer; *b* 6 April 1967. *Educ:* Royal Coll. of Music (BMus London 1st cl.); Gonville and Caius Coll., Cambridge, 1990–91; King's Coll., Cambridge, 1992–94 (MPhil Composition). Commissions from: London Sinfonietta, 1994 (Khorovod) and 1999; BBC Proms, 1998 (The Stations of the Sun); Cheltenham Festival, 1997 (The Crazed Moon). Works performed by numerous ensembles and orchestras in Europe and USA, incl. Cleveland Orch., Boston SO, Schoenberg and Asko Ensembles. Broadcast talks on music on BBC and Swiss Radio. *Publications:* articles on music in Musical Times, Tempo, The Independent. *Recreations:* films, reading, poetry, swimming. *Address:* c/o Faber Music, 3 Queen Square, WC1N 3AU.

ANDERSON, Hon. Sir Kevin (Victor); Kt 1980; Judge of the Supreme Court of Victoria, 1969–84; *b* 4 Sept. 1912; *s* of Robert Victor Anderson and Margaret Anderson (*née* Collins); *m* 1942, Claire Margaret Murphy; six *d*. *Educ:* Xavier Coll., Kew; Melbourne Univ. (LLB). Victorian Crown Law Dept, 1929–42: Courts Branch, 1929–35; Professional Asst, Crown Solicitor's Office, 1935–42; Lt, RAN, 1942–46; Victorian Bar, 1946–69; QC (Victoria) 1962. Chm., Bd of Inquiry into Scientology, 1963–65. Chm., Victorian Bar Council, 1966–67; Treasurer, Australian Law Council, 1966–68. Kt, Australian Assoc. of SMO of Malta, 1979. *Publications:* Stamp Duties in Victoria, 1949, 2nd edn 1968; joint author: Price Control, 1947; Landlord and Tenant Law, 1948, 3rd edn 1958; Victorian Licensing Law, 1952; Victoria Police Manual, 1956, 2nd edn 1969; Workers' Compensation, 1958, 2nd edn 1966; Fossil in the Sandstone: the Recollecting Judge, 1986; (ed) Victorian Law Reports, 1956–69. *Recreations:* yachting, woodworking. *Address:* PO Box 5081, Glenferrie South, Vic 3122, Australia. *Clubs:* Victoria Racing, Celtic, Essoign (Melbourne).

ANDERSON, Prof. Malcolm Grove; Professor of Physical Geography, University of Bristol, since 1989; Vice-Provost, Institute for Advanced Studies, Bristol, since 2000 (Director, 1997–2000); *b* 27 June 1949; *s* of Wilfred Roy Anderson and Frances Betty Anderson; *m* 1972, Elizabeth Ann Roger; one *d*. *Educ:* Univ. of Nottingham (BSc); Univ. of Cambridge (PhD); Univ. of Bristol (DSc). FICE 1996. Research Fellow, Sidney Sussex Coll., Cambridge, 1972; Lectr, 1973, Reader, 1985, Head of Dept of Geography, 1990–96, Univ. of Bristol. Res. Hydrologist, US Corps of Engrs, 1981–82; Sen. Res. Geotechnical Engr, Hong Kong Govt, 1982–83; Nuffield Foundn, Sen. Science Fellowship, 1988–89; Quater Centenary Vis. Fellowship, Emmanuel Coll., Cambridge, 1989. Mem., AAPS Cttee, 1990–93, Chm., Land-Ocean Interaction Study Steering Cttee, 1998–2001, NERC; Mem., Science Grants Panel, Nuffield Foundn, 1992–; Scholarship Assessor, ACU, 1993–. Editor-in-Chief, Hydrological Processes, 1986–. Life Fellow, Indian Assoc. of Hydrologists, 1995. Gill Meml Award, RGS, 1986; Trevithick Premium Award, ICE, 1996. *Publications:* (ed with T. P. Burt) Hydrological Forecasting, 1985; (ed with K. S. Richards) Slope Stability: geotechnical engineering and geomorphology, 1987; (ed) Modelling Geomorphological Systems, 1988; (ed with T. P. Burt) Process Studies in Hillslope Hydrology, 1990; (ed jtly) Floodplain Processes, 1996; (ed with S. Brooks) Advances in Hillslope Processes, 1996; (ed with P. D. Bates) Model Validation: perspectives in hydrological science, 2001. *Recreation:* France. *Address:* Institute for Advanced Studies, The Royal Fort, University of Bristol, Bristol BS8 1UJ. *T:* (0117) 928 9172.

ANDERSON, Brig. Hon. Dame Mary Mackenzie; *see* Pihl, Brig. Hon. Dame M. M.

ANDERSON, Mary Margaret, CBE 1996; FRCOG; Consultant Obstetrician and Gynaecologist, Lewisham Hospital, 1967–97; *b* 12 Feb. 1932; *d* of William Anderson and Lily Adams. *Educ:* Forres Acad.; Edinburgh Univ. (MB, ChB 1956). FRCOG 1974. Jun. hosp. posts in Scotland and England, including Hammersmith Hosp., and St Mary's Hosp., London (Sen. Registrar); Chm., Div. of Obst. and Gynaecol., Lewisham Hosp., 1984–87. Royal College of Obstetricians and Gynaecologists: Chm., Hosp. Recognition Cttee, 1987–89; Jun. Vice Pres., 1989–92. Chm., SE Thames RHA Specialist Sub Cttee, 1986–88; Member: Scientific Cttee, National Birthday Trust, 1990–; Council, Med. Defence Union, 1987–. *Publications:* Anatomy and Physiology of Obstetrics, 1979; Handbook of Obstetrics and Gynaecology, 1981; The Menopause, 1983; Pregnancy after Thirty, 1984; An A–Z of Gynaecology, 1986; Infertility, 1987; (contrib.) Ten Teachers in Obstetrics and Gynaecology, 1990. *Recreations:* reading, music, gardening. *Address:* Green Roof Cottage, 1 Heathway, Blackheath, SE3 7AN.

ANDERSON, Prof. Michael, OBE 1999; FRSE; FBA 1989; Professor of Economic History, University of Edinburgh, since 1979; *b* 21 Feb. 1942; *s* of Douglas Henry and Rose Lillian Anderson; *m* 1966, Rosemary Elizabeth Kitching; one *s* one *d*. *Educ:* Kingston Grammar Sch.; Queens' Coll., Cambridge (BA 1964; MA 1968; PhD 1969). FRSE 1990. University of Edinburgh: Department of Sociology: Asst Lectr, 1967; Lectr, 1969; Reader, 1975; Department of Economic and Social History, 1979; Dean, Faculty of Social Scis, 1985–89; Vice-Principal, 1989–93, 1997–; Acting Principal, April–Aug. 1994. Member: Economic and Social History Cttee, SSRC, 1974–78; Computing Cttee, SSRC, 1980–82; Scot. Records Adv. Council, 1984–93; ESRC, 1990–94 (Member: Res. Resources and Methods Cttee, 1982–84; Society and Politics Res. Develt Gp, 1989–92; Chm., Res. Resources Bd, 1992–94); History of Medicine Cttee, Wellcome Trust, 1988–92; BL Bd, 1994– (Dep. Chm., 2000–); Council, British Acad., 1995–98. Curator, RSE, 1997–99. Chm., Bd of Trustees, Nat. Library of Scotland, 2000– (Trustee, 1998–). *Publications:* Family Structure in Nineteenth Century Lancashire, 1971; (ed) Sociology of the Family, 1972; Approaches to the History of the Western Family 1500–1914, 1981; The 1851 Census: a national sample of the enumerators returns, 1987; Population Change in Northwestern Europe 1750–1850, 1988; (ed) Social and Political Economy of the Household, 1995; (ed) British Population History, 1996. *Recreations:* natural history, gardening, study of ancient civilizations.

ANDERSON, Vice Adm. Sir Neil (Dudley), KBE 1982 (CBE 1976); CB 1979; Chief of Defence Staff (NZ), 1980–83; *b* 5 April 1927; *s* of Eric Dudley Anderson and Margaret Evelyn (*née* Craig); *m* 1951, Barbara Lillias Romaine Wright; two *s*. *Educ:* Hastings High Sch.; BRNC. Joined RNZN, 1944; trng and sea service with RN, 1944–49; Korean War Service, 1950–51; qual. as navigation specialist; Navigator: HMS Vanguard, 1952–53; HMNZS Lachlan, 1954; HMS Saintes, 1958–59; Commanding Officer, HMNZS: Taranaki, 1961–62; Waikato, 1968–69; Philomel, 1969–70; Dep. Chief of Def. Staff, 1976–77; Chief of Naval Staff, 1977–80. Lieut 1949, Lt-Comdr 1957, Comdr 1960, Captain 1968, Cdre 1972, Rear Adm. 1977, Vice Adm. 1980. *Recreations:* golf, fishing. *Address:* 2/248 Oriental Parade, Wellington 6001, New Zealand. *T:* and *Fax:* (4) 3858494. *Club:* Wellington (Wellington, NZ).

ANDERSON, Paul James; journalist and author; *b* 3 Oct. 1959; *s* of James George Anderson and Marjorie Rosemary Anderson (*née* Thorpe). *Educ:* Ipswich Sch.; Balliol Coll., Oxford (BA Hons PPE 1981); London College of Printing. Dep. Ed., European Nuclear Disarmament Jl, 1984–87; Reviews Ed., 1986–91, Editor, 1991–93, Tribune; Dep. Ed., New Statesman, 1993–96; News Ed., Red Pepper, 1997–. Dir, People's Europe 98, 1998. *Publications:* (ed jtly) Mad Dogs: The US Raid on Libya, 1986; (with Nyta Mann) Safety First: the making of New Labour, 1997. *Address:* 46c Farleigh Road, N16 7TQ.

ANDERSON, Prof. Philip Warren; Joseph Henry Professor of Physics, Princeton University, New Jersey, 1975–96, now Emeritus; *b* 13 Dec. 1923; *s* of Prof. H. W. Anderson and Mrs Elsie O. Anderson; *m* 1947, Joyce Gothwaite; one *d*. *Educ:* Harvard Univ. BS 1943; MA 1947; PhD 1949, Harvard. Naval Res. Lab., Washington, DC, 1943–45 (Chief Petty Officer, USN). Mem., Technical Staff, 1949–76, Dir, 1976–84, Bell Telephone Labs. Fulbright Lectr, Tokyo Univ., 1952–53; Overseas Fellow, Churchill Coll., Cambridge, 1961–62; Vis. Prof. of Theoretical Physics, Univ. of Cambridge, 1967–75, and Fellow of Jesus College, Cambridge, 1969–75, Hon. Fellow, 1978–; Cherwell-Simon Meml Lectureship, 1979–80, George Eastman Prof., 1993–94, Oxford Univ. Member: Amer. Acad. of Arts and Sciences, 1966; Nat. Acad. of Sciences, US, 1967; Amer. Philosophical Soc., 1991; Foreign Member: Royal Society, London, 1980; Japan Acad., 1988; Indian Nat. Acad. of Scis, 1990; Russian Nat. Acad. of Sci., 1994; Foreign Associate: Accademia Lincei, Rome, 1985; Indian Acad. of Sci., 1996. Hon. FInstP, 1986. Hon. DSc: Illinois, 1978; Rutgers, 1991; Ecole Normale Supérieure, Paris, 1995; Gustavus Adolphus Coll., Minn, 1995; Sheffield, 1996. O. E. Buckley Prize, Amer. Phys. Soc., 1964; Dannie Heinemann Prize, Akad. Wiss. Göttingen, 1975; (jtly) Nobel Prize for Physics, 1977; Guthrie Medal, Inst. of Physics, 1978; Centennial Medal, Harvard, 1996; John Bardeen Prize, 1997. Nat. Medal of Science, US, 1984. *Publications:* Concepts in Solids, 1963; Basic Notions of Condensed Matter Physics, 1984; A Career in Theoretical Physics, 1994; The Theory of Superconductivity in the High Tc Cuprates, 1996; numerous articles in scholarly jls. *Recreations:* go (Japanese game), rank sho-dan, walking. *Address:* 74 Aunt Molly Road, Hopewell, NJ 08525, USA.

ANDERSON, Ray Thomas; Executive Director, Anglicare, since 1999; *b* 23 Nov. 1936; *s* of late Thomas James Anderson and Daisy Eva D'Arcy-Irvine (*née* Woodhouse); *m* 1962, Margaret, *d* of Ronald George Geach; one *s* three *d*. *Educ:* State Commercial High Sch., Brisbane; Univ. of Queensland (BCom Hons); Macquarie Univ. (BLegS). Public servant, Brisbane, 1956–60; RAAF Psychologist, Brisbane, 1961–62; Trainee Trade Comr, Canberra, 1963; First Sec. and Asst Trade Comr, Australian High Commn, Singapore, 1964–67; Trade Commissioner: Johannesburg, 1968; Cape Town, 1969–70; Counsellor (Commercial) and Sen. Trade Comr, Aust. High Commn, New Delhi, 1971–73; Regl Dir, DTI, Brisbane, 1974–76; Counsellor (Commercial) and Trade Comr (Mktg), Aust. Embassy, Tokyo, 1977–80; Asst Sec., Dept. of Trade, 1980–82; First Asst Sec., Depts of Foreign Affairs and Trade, Trade, Immigration and Ethnic Affairs, 1982–87; Manager, Nat. Ops, AUSTRADE, 1987–89; Minister (Marketing) and Sen. Trade Comr, London and Minister (Commercial), The Hague, 1990–91; Agent-Gen. for Qld in London, 1991–95; Exec. Dir, 1996, Asst Dir-Gen. 1997, Dept of Econ. Develt and Trade, Qld; Gen. Manager, Evans Deakin Industries, 1997–99. Admitted Barrister, Supreme Court, NSW and High Court of Australia, and Barrister and Solicitor, Supreme Court, ACT, 1989. Director: EPIC Inc., 2000–; EAC Ltd, 2000–. Freeman, City of London, 1991. Flying Officer, RAAF Reserve. Hon. FAIEx. *Recreations:* tennis, reading, travel, theatre. *Address:* 2 Silver Quays, 30 O'Connell Street, Kangaroo Point, Qld 4169, Australia. *T:* (7) 33921138. *Clubs:* Singapore Town; United Services, Queensland (Brisbane); Royal Queensland Golf.

ANDERSON, Reginald, CMG 1974; *b* 3 Nov. 1921; *s* of late Herbert Anderson and late Anne Mary (*née* Hicks); *m* 1945, Audrey Gabrielle Williams; two *d*. *Educ:* Palmers, Grays, Essex. Cabinet Office, 1938–40. Served War, RAF, Flt Lt, 1941–46. Ministry of: Supply, 1947–57; Supply Staff, Australia, 1957–59; Aviation, 1960–67; Counsellor, British Embassy, Washington, 1967–70; Asst Under-Sec. of State, 1970–76, Dep. Under-Sec. of State, 1976–81, MoD. *Address:* Reynosa, Heronway, Shenfield, Essex CM13 2LX. *T:* (01277) 213077. *Club:* Royal Air Force.

ANDERSON, Robert Geoffrey William; Director, British Museum, 1992–June 2002; *b* 2 May 1944; *er s* of Herbert Patrick Anderson and Kathleen Diana Anderson (*née* Burns); *m* 1973, Margaret Elizabeth Callis Lea; two *s*. *Educ:* Woodhouse Sch., London; St John's Coll., Oxford (Casberd exhibitioner; BSc, MA, DPhil; Hon. Fellow). FRSC 1984; FSA 1986; FRSE 1990. Assistant Keeper: Royal Scottish Museum, 1970–75; Science Museum, 1975–78; Dep. Keeper, Wellcome Museum of History of Medicine, and Sec., Adv. Council, Science Museum, 1978–80; Keeper, Dept of Chemistry, Science Mus., 1980–84; Director: Royal Scottish Mus., 1984–85; Nat. Museums of Scotland, 1985–92. Sec., Royal Scottish Soc. of Arts, 1973–75; Member Council: Soc. for History of Alchemy and Chemistry, 1978–; Gp for Scientific, Technological and Medical Collections, 1979–83; British Soc. History of Science, 1981–84 (Pres., 1988–90); Scottish Museums, 1984–91; Museums Assoc., 1988–92; Mem., British Nat. Cttee for Hist. of Science, 1985–89; Pres., Scientific Instrument Commn, IUHPS, 1982–97. Member Editorial Board: Annals of Science, 1981–; Annali di Storia della Scienza, 1986–. Trustee, Boerhaave Mus., Leiden, 1994–99. Hon. FSAScot 1991. Hon. DSc: Edinburgh, 1995; Durham, 1998. Dexter Prize, Amer. Chemical Soc., 1986. *Publications:* The Mariner's Astrolabe, 1972; Edinburgh and Medicine, 1976; (ed) The Early Years of the Edinburgh Medical School, 1976; The Playfair Collection and the Teaching of Chemistry at the University of Edinburgh, 1978; (contrib.) The History of Technology, Vol. VI, ed T. I. Williams, 1978; Science in India, 1982; (ed) Science, Medicine and Dissent: Joseph Priestley (1733–1804), 1987; Scientific Instrument Makers Trade Catalogues, 1990; (ed) A New Museum for Scotland, 1990; (with G. Fyffe) Joseph Black: a Bibliography, 1992; (ed) Making Instruments Count, 1993; The Great Court at the British Museum, 2000. *Recreation:* books. *Address:* British Museum, WC1B 3DG. *T:* (020) 7636 1555. *Club:* Athenæum.

ANDERSON, Prof. Robert Henry; Joseph Levy Professor of Paediatric Cardiac Morphology, Institute of Child Health, University College London, since 1999 (at National Heart and Lung Institute, Imperial College School of Medicine, 1979–99), University of London; *b* 4 April 1942; *s* of Henry Anderson and Doris Amy Anderson (*née* Callear); *m* 1966, Christine (*née* Ibbotson); one *s* one *d*. *Educ:* Wellington Grammar Sch., Shropshire; Manchester Univ. BSc (Hons); MD; FRCPath. House Officer, Professorial Surgical Unit, 1966, Medical Unit, 1967, Manchester Royal Infirmary; Asst Lectr in Anatomy, 1967–69, Lectr, 1969–73, Manchester Univ.; MRC Travelling Fellow, Dept of Cardiology, Univ. of Amsterdam, 1973–74; Cardiothoracic Institute, now National Heart and Lung Institute, University of London: British Heart Foundn Sen. Res. Fellow and Sen. Lectr in Paediatrics, 1974–77; Joseph Levy Reader, 1977–79, Joseph Levy Prof., 1979–, Paediatric Cardiac Morphology. Hon. Consultant: Royal Brompton & Harefield NHS Trust, 1974–99; Gt Ormond St Hosp., 1999–. Hon. Prof. of Surgery, Univ. of N Carolina, USA, 1984–; Visiting Professor: Univ. of Pittsburgh, Pa, 1985–; Liverpool Univ., 1989–; St George's Hosp. Med. Sch., 2000–. Excerpta Medica Travel Award, 1977; British Heart Foundn Prize for Cardiovascular Research, 1984. Associate Editor, Internat. Jl of Cardiology, 1985–91; Ed.-in-Chief, Cardiology in the Young, 1997– (Exec. Ed., 1992–97). *Publications:* (ed jtly) Paediatric Cardiology, 1977, vol. 3, 1981, vol. 5, 1983, vol. 6, 1986; (with A. E. Becker) Cardiac Anatomy, 1980; (with E. A. Shinebourne) Current Paediatric Cardiology, 1980; (with A. E. Becker) Pathology of Congenital Heart Disease, 1981; (with M. J. Davies and A. E. Becker) Pathology of the Conduction Tissues, 1983; (jtly) Morphology of Congenital Heart Disease, 1983; (with A. E. Becker) Cardiac Pathology, 1984; (with G. A. H. Miller and M. L. Rigby) The Diagnosis of Congenital Heart Disease, 1985; (with B. R. Wilcox) Surgical Anatomy of the Heart, 1985, 2nd edn 1992; (jtly) Paediatric Cardiology, 2 vols, 1987; (with P. J. Oldershaw and J. R. Dawson) Clinician's Illustrated Dictionary of Cardiology, 1988; (jtly) Atlas of the Heart, 1988; (jtly) Transesogophagal Echocardiography in Clinical Practice, 1991; (with A. E. Becker) The Heart Structure in Health and Disease, 1992; over 250 invited chapters in published books and over 500 papers in jls. *Recreations:* golf, tennis, music, wine. *Address:* 60 Earlsfield Road, SW18 3DN. *T:* (020) 8870 4368. *Clubs:* Saintsbury, Roehampton; Walton Heath Golf.

ANDERSON, Robert (Woodruff); playwright; *b* NYC, 28 April 1917; *s* of James Hewston Anderson and Myra Esther (*née* Grigg); *m* 1st, 1940, Phyllis Stohl (*d* 1956); 2nd, 1959, Teresa Wright (marr. diss. 1978). *Educ:* Phillips Exeter Acad.; Harvard Univ. AB (*magna cum laude*) 1939, MA 1940. Served USNR, 1942–46 (Lt); won prize (sponsored by War Dept) for best play written by a serviceman overseas, Come Marching Home, 1945, subseq. prod, Univ. of Iowa and Blackfriars Guild, NY. Rockefeller Fellowship, 1946; taught playwrighting, American Theatre Wing Professional Trng Prog., 1946–50; organized and taught Playwright's Unit, Actors Studio, 1955; Writer in Residence, Univ. of N Carolina, 1969; Faculty: Salzburg Seminar in Amer. Studies, 1968; Univ. of Iowa Writers' Workshop, 1976. Member: Playwrights Co., 1953–60; Bd of Governors, American Playwrights Theatre, 1963–; Council, Dramatists Guild, 1954– (Pres., 1971–73); New Dramatists Cttee, 1949– (Pres., 1955–57); Vice-Pres., Authors' League of America; Chm., Harvard Bd of Overseers' Cttee to visit the Performing Arts, 1970–76. Wrote and adapted plays for TV and Radio, 1948–53. Elected to Theater Hall of Fame, 1980. Connecticut Commn on the Arts Award, 1992. *Plays:* Eden Rose, 1948; Love Revisited, 1952; Tea and Sympathy, 1953; All Summer Long, 1954; Silent Night, Lonely Night, 1959; The Days Between, 1965; You Know I Can't Hear You When the Water's Running (four short plays), 1967; I Never Sang For My Father, 1968; Solitaire/Double Solitaire, 1971; Free and Clear, 1983; The Kissing was Always the Best, 1987; The Last Act is a Solo, 1989; *screenplays:* Tea and Sympathy, 1956; Until They Sail, 1957; The Nun's Story, 1959; The Sand Pebbles, 1965; I Never Sang For My Father, 1970 (Writers Guild Award for Best Screenplay, 1971); The Patricia Neal Story, TV, 1981; Absolute Strangers, TV, 1991; The Last Act is a Solo, TV, 1991 (ACE Award). *Publications: novels:* After, 1973; Getting Up and Going Home, 1978; *anthology:* (jtly) Elements of Literature, 6 vols, 1988. *Recreations:* photography, tennis. *Club:* Harvard (New York City).

ANDERSON, Rolande Jane Rita; Director, Competition Policy, Department of Trade and Industry, since 1999; *b* 10 Oct. 1955; *d* of late Arthur Ingham Anderson and of Rolande Marie Anderson; *m* 1981, Nicholas Michael Watts. *Educ:* Lycée Français de Londres; Newnham Coll., Cambridge (BA Hons Mod. and Mediaeval Langs, MA Mod. Langs). Fast Stream Admin Trainee, Depts of Industry and of Prices and Consumer Protection, 1976–79; HEO, Dept of Trade, 1979–83; Principal and Hd of Section, DTI, 1983–89; Grade 7, Eur. Secretariat, Cabinet Office, 1989–91; Hd (Asst Sec.), Policy and Planning, Insolvency Service Exec. Agency, 1991–92; Dir, Aerospace and Defence Industries Policy, 1992–96, Regl Eur. Funds, 1996–99, DTI. Mem., panel of assessors for Fast Stream recruitment, CSSB, 1988–91. *Address:* Department of Trade and Industry, 1 Victoria Street, SW1H 0ET. *T:* (020) 7215 5000.

ANDERSON, Roy Arnold; Chairman Emeritus, Lockheed Corporation, since 1986; Chairman and Chief Executive, Weingart Foundation, 1994–98; *b* Ripon, Calif, 15 Dec. 1920; *s* of Carl Gustav Anderson and Esther Marie Johnson; *m* 1948, Betty Leona Boehme; two *s* two *d*. *Educ:* Ripon Union High Sch.; Humphreys Sch. of Business; Stanford Univ. AB 1947; MBA 1949; Phi Beta Kappa; CPA. Served War, USNR, 1942–46 and 1950–52. Westinghouse Electric Corporation: Manager, Factory Accounting, 1952–56; Lockheed Missiles and Space Co.: Manager, Accounting and Finance, and Dir, Management Controls, 1956–65; Lockheed Georgia Co.: Dir of Finance, 1965–68; Lockheed Corporation: Asst Treas., 1968–69; Vice-Pres. and Controller, 1969–71; Sen. Vice-Pres., Finance, 1971–75; Vice-Chm. of Board, also Chief Financial and Admin. Officer, 1975–77; Chm. and Chief Exec. Officer, 1977–85; Chm., Exec. Cttee, Dir and Consultant, 1985–88. Director of cos in California. *Recreation:* golf. *Address:* c/o Lockheed-Martin Corporation, 606 South Olive Street, Los Angeles, CA 90014, USA. *T:* (213) 6898701.

ANDERSON, Prof. Roy Malcolm, FRS 1986; Professor and Head of Department of Infectious Disease Epidemiology, Imperial College School of Medicine, London University, since 2000; *b* 12 April 1947; *s* of James Anderson and Betty Watson-Weatherburn; *m* 1st, 1975, Dr Mary Joan Anderson (marr. diss. 1989); 2nd, 1990, Dr Claire Baron. *Educ:* Duncombe Sch., Bengeo; Richard Hale Sch., Hertford; Imperial Coll., London (BSc, ARCS, PhD, DIC). CBiol, FIBiol; FSS. IBM Research Fellow, Univ. of Oxford, 1971–73; Lectr, King's Coll., London, 1973–77; Lectr, 1977–80, Reader, 1980–82, Prof., 1982–93, Head of Dept of Biology, 1984–93, Imperial Coll., London Univ.; University of Oxford: Linacre Prof. of Zoology, and Hd, Zoology Dept, 1993–2000; Dir, Wellcome Trust Centre for Epidemiology of Infectious Diseases, 1994–2000; Fellow, Merton Coll., Oxford, 1993–2000. Vis. Prof., McGill Univ., 1982–; Alexander Langmuir Vis. Prof., Harvard, 1990–; Genentech Vis. Prof., Univ. of Washington, 1998; James McLaughlin Vis. Prof., Univ. of Texas, 1999. Member: NERC, 1988–91 (Chm., Services and Facilities Cttee, 1989–90); ACOST, 1989–93 (Chm., Standing Cttee on Envmt, 1990–93); Spongiform Encephalopathy Adv. Cttee, 1998–. Chm., Oxford Biologica Ltd. Member, Scientific Advisory Board: IMS, 1997–99; deCode, 1998–. Member, Council: Zoological Soc., 1988–90; Royal Soc., 1989–91; RSTM&H, 1989–92; RPMS, 1994–97; Mem. Ct, LSHTM. Gov., Wellcome Trust Ltd, 1992–2000 (Trustee, Wellcome Trust, 1991–92; Chairman: Infection and Immunity Grant Panel, 1990–92; Population Studies Panel). For. Mem., Inst. of Medicine, NAS, USA, 1999. Founder FMedSci 1998. Hon. FIA 2000; Hon. FRCPath 2000. Hon. Fellow, Linacre Coll., Oxford, 1993. Hon. DSc: East Anglia, 1997; Stirling, 1998. Zoological Soc. Scientific Medal, 1982; Huxley Meml Medal, Imperial Coll., London, 1983; Wright Meml Medal, British Soc. of Parasitology, 1986; David Starr Jordan Medal, Univs of Stanford, Cornell and Indiana, 1986; Chalmers Medal, RSTM&H, 1988; Weldon Medal, Oxford Univ., 1989; John Hill Grundy Medal, Royal Army Med. Coll., 1990; Frink Medal, Zoological Soc. of London, 1993; Joseph Smadel Medal, Infectious Diseases Soc. of Amer., 1994; Distinguished Statistical Ecologist Award, 1998; Dist. Parasitologists Award, Amer. Soc. of Parasitology, 1999. *Publications:* (ed) Population Dynamics of Infectious Disease Agents: theory and applications, 1982; (ed jtly) Population Biology of Infectious Diseases, 1982; (with R. M. May) Infectious Diseases of Humans: dynamics and control, 1991. *Recreations:* hill walking, croquet, natural history. *Address:* Imperial College School of Medicine, St Mary's Campus, Norfolk Place, W2 1PG. *Club:* Athenæum.

ANDERSON, Roy William; District Judge (Magistrates' Courts) (formerly Stipendiary Magistrate), West Yorkshire, since 1999; *b* 10 Feb. 1950; *s* of William Patterson Bruce Anderson and Thirza Elizabeth Anderson; *m* 1974, Pauline Mary Rylands; two *s*. *Educ:* King Edward VI Sch., Stratford-upon-Avon; University Coll. London (LLB). Articled clerk, City of Swansea, 1972–74; Prosecuting Solicitor, W Midlands CC, 1974–80; Solicitor, Jacobs Bird & Co., Birmingham, 1980–84; Sole Principal, Roy Anderson Solicitor, Birmingham, 1984–99. *Recreations:* reading, theatre, tennis. *Address:* Leeds District Magistrates' Court, PO Box 97, Westgate, Leeds LS1 3JP.

ANDERSON, Victor Frederick; Member (Green), London Assembly, Greater London Authority, since 2000; *b* 7 Feb. 1952; *s* of Tom and Iris Anderson; *m* 1987, Joan Rawlinson; one *s*. *Educ:* Whitgift Sch.; Brasenose Coll., Oxford (BA). Lectr, 1980–88, at Paddington Coll. of FE, 1982–88; Researcher: New Econs Foundn, 1987–92; Plaid Cymru Gp of MPs, 1992–2000. Mem. Bd, London Develt Agency, 2000–. *Publications:* Alternative Economic Indicators, 1991; Energy Efficiency Policies, 1993; Greens and the New Politics, 2001. *Recreations:* dancing, visiting museums. *Address:* Greater London Authority, Romney House, 43 Marsham Street, SW1P 3PY. *T:* (020) 7983 4406.

ANDERSON, (William) Eric (Kinloch), MA, MLitt, DLitt, FRSE; Provost of Eton College, since 2000; *b* 27 May 1936; *er s* of late W. J. Kinloch Anderson, Edinburgh; *m* 1960, Poppy, *d* of late W. M. Mason, Skipton; one *s* one *d*. *Educ:* George Watson's Coll.; Univ. of St Andrews (MA); Balliol Coll., Oxford (MLitt; Hon. Fellow, 1989). Asst Master: Fettes Coll., 1960–64; Gordonstoun, 1964–66; Asst Master, Fettes Coll., and Housemaster, Arniston House, 1967–70; Headmaster: Abingdon Sch., 1970–75; Shrewsbury Sch., 1975–80; Eton Coll., 1980–94; Rector, Lincoln Coll., Oxford,

1994–2000 (Hon. Fellow, 2000). Chairman: King George VI and Queen Elizabeth Foundn of St Catharine's, Cumberland Lodge, 1997–; Nat. Heritage Meml Fund, 1998–2001 (Trustee, 1996–). President: Edinburgh Sir Walter Scott Club, 1981; Johnson Soc., 1992; Member: Royal Shakespeare Theatre Trust, 1991–94; RSC Foundn Bd, 1994–97; Nat. Heritage Adv. Panel for Public Appointments, 1997–. Trustee: Karim Rida Said Foundn, 1994–98; Wordsworth Trust, 1996–97; Royal Collection, 2000–. Council Mem., Royal Holloway, London Univ. (formerly RHBNC), 1990–95; Gov., Shrewsbury Sch., 1994–2000. Chm. of Judges, Whitbread Book Awards, 2000. FRSE 1985. Hon. DLitt: St Andrews, 1981; Hull, 1994; Siena, 1999. *Publications:* The Written Word, 1964; (ed) The Journal of Sir Walter Scott, 1972, rev. edn 1998; (ed) The Percy Letters, vol IX, 1988; (ed) The Sayings of Sir Walter Scott, 1995; articles and reviews. *Recreations:* theatre, golf, fishing. *Address:* Provost's Lodge, Eton College, Windsor, Berks SL4 6DH.

See also D. W. K. Anderson.

ANDERTON, Prof. Brian Henry; PhD; Professor of Neuroscience, Institute of Psychiatry, since 1989, at King's College London; *b* 25 Dec. 1945; *s* of Henry Anderton and Mary Anderton (*née* Ashcroft); *m* 1969, Thérèse L. F. Loviny; one *s*. *Educ:* Allsop High Sch. for Boys, Liverpool; University College London (BSc 1967; PhD 1970). MRC Biophysics Unit, KCL, 1970–72; Lectr in Biochem., Poly. of Central London, 1972–77; Lectr in Biochem. and Immunology, Chelsea Coll., Univ. of London, 1977–79; St George's Hospital Medical School, University of London: Lectr in Immunology, 1979–81; Sen. Lectr in Immunology, 1981–86; Reader in Molecular Pathology, 1986–88. *Publications:* contribs to sci. jls on nervous system and molecular pathology of Alzheimer's disease and other neurodegenerative diseases. *Recreations:* hill walking, cycling, general reading, theatre, cinema, listening to music. *Address:* Department of Neuroscience, Institute of Psychiatry, King's College London, De Crespigny Park, SE5 8AF. *T:* (020) 7703 5411.

ANDERTON, Sir (Cyril) James, Kt 1991; CBE 1982; QPM 1977; DL; Chief Constable, Greater Manchester Police Force, 1976–91 (Deputy Chief Constable, 1975); *b* 24 May 1932; *o s* of late James Anderton and late Lucy Anderton (*née* Occleshaw); *m* 1955, Joan Baron; one *d*. *Educ:* St Matthew's Church Sch., Highfield; Wigan Grammar Sch. Certif. Criminology, Manchester Univ., 1960; Sen. Comd Course, Police Coll., 1967. Corps of Royal Mil. Police, 1950–53; Constable to Chief Inspector, Manchester City Police, 1953–67; Chief Supt, Cheshire Constab., 1967–68; Asst Chief Constable, Leicester and Rutland Constab., 1968–72; Asst to HM Chief Inspector of Constab. for England and Wales, Home Office, London, 1972–75; Dep. Chief Constable, Leics Constabulary, 1975. Mem., ACPO, 1968–91 (Pres., 1986–87). FCO lect. tour, FE and SE Asia, 1973. UK Govt deleg., UN Congress on Prevention of Crime, Budapest, 1974. British Institute of Management: Pres., Manchester Br., 1984–93; Chm., 1986–90, Mem., 1985–90, NW Regl Bd; Cert. of Merit, 1990. President: Manchester NSPCC Jun. League, 1979–93; Christian Police Assoc., 1979–81; Manchester and Dist RSPCA, 1984–2000 (Vice-Pres., 1981–84); Wigan and Dist RSPCA, 1999–2000 (Patron, 1986–99); Wythenshawe Hosp. League of Friends, 1991–; Altrincham Town Centre Partnership, 1994–; Disabled Living, Manchester, 1995– (Patron, 1991–); Bolton Outward Bound Assoc., 1995– (Vice-Pres., 1991–95); NW Reg., YMCA, 1996–; Manchester YMCA, 2000– (Vice-Pres., 1976–2000). Member: Manchester Adv. Bd, Salvation Army, 1977–2001 (Chm., 1993–2001; Hon. Life Mem., Salvation Army Adv. Bd, 2000); Salvation Army Territorial Adv. Bd, 1996–2001; Exec. Cttee, Manchester NSPCC, 1979–93; Bd, Henshaws Soc. for the Blind, 1991–95; Royal Soc. of St George, 1992–; CCJ, 1992–; Friends of Israel Assoc., 1992–; Broughton Catholic Charitable Soc., 1996–; Nat. Adv. Gp, YMCA, 1997– (Chm., Prisons Steering Gp, 1994–). Comdr, St John Amb., Greater Manchester, 1989–96 (County Dir, 1976–89); Vice-President: Manchester and District RLSS, 1976–2000; Adelphi Lads' Club, Salford, 1979–; Sharp Street Ragged Sch., Manchester, 1982–; Manchester Schools Football Assoc., 1976–91; Greater Manchester East Scout Council, 1977–91; Greater Manchester Fedn of Clubs for Young People, 1984–; 318 (Sale) Sqn, ATC, 1985–; Wigan Hospice, 1990–; Greater Manchester West Scout Council, 1992–; Manchester and Dist NSPCC, 1994–. Boys' Brigade: Pres., Leics Bn, 1972–76; Hon. Nat. Vice-Pres., 1983–. Patron: NW Counties Schs ABA, 1980–91; NW Campaign for Kidney Donors, 1983–; NW Eye Res. Trust, 1982–91; N Manchester Hosp. Broadcasting Service, 1983–; Internat. Spinal Res. Trust (Greater Manchester Cttee), 1983–91; Sale RNLI, 1986–; Stockport Canal Trust, 1989–; The British Trust, 1991–; Stockport ACROSS, 1993–; Trafford Multiple Sclerosis Soc., 1994–; Mottram and Hattersley ABC, 1994–; Rhodes Foundn Scholarship Trust, 1996–; Gtr Manchester LUPUS Gp, 1996–; Gtr Manchester Youth Field Gun Assoc., 1996– (Pres., 1992–96); Police Boxing Assoc. of England, 1997–; Manchester Stedfast Assoc., 1999–. British College of Accordionists: Chm., Governing Council, 1972–77; Vice-Pres., 1977–84; Pres., 1984–91; Patron, 1991–. Trustee, Manchester Olympic Bid Cttee, 1985–93; Chm., Trustees, S Manchester Accident Rescue Team, 1996–2001. Hon. FBCA 1976; Hon. RNCM 1984. Member: Catholic Union of GB; NT; Wigan Little Theatre; Royal Exchange Th., Manchester; Garrick Th., Altrincham; Corps of Royal Mil. Police Assoc.; Portico Library, Manchester. Mancunian of The Year, 1980. DL Greater Manchester, 1989. Freeman, City of London, 1990. KStJ 1989 (OStJ 1978; CStJ 1982; Mem., Chapter-Gen., 1993–99). KMLJ 1998; KHS 1999. Cross Pro Ecclesia et Pontifice, 1982. Chevalier de la Confrérie des Chevaliers du Tastevin, 1985. *Recreations:* opera, theatre, fell-walking; Rugby League supporter. *Address:* 9 The Avenue, Sale, Cheshire M33 4PB.

ANDERTON, Hon. James Patrick, (Jim); MP (Alliance) Wigram, New Zealand, since 1996 (MP Sydenham, 1984–96 (Lab 1984-89, NewLab, then Alliance, 1989-96); Deputy Prime Minister of New Zealand, since 1999; *b* 21 Jan. 1938; *m* 1st, Joan Caulfield (marr. diss.); three *s* one *d*; 2nd, Carole Anne. *Educ:* Seddon Meml Technical Coll.; Auckland Teachers' Trng Coll. Formerly: teacher; Child Welfare Officer, Educn Dept, Wanganui; Export Manager, UEB Textiles, 1969–70; Man. Dir, Anderton Hldgs, 1971. Member: Manukau CC, 1965–68; Auckland CC, 1974–77; Auckland Regl Authy, 1977–80. Labour Party, 1963–89: Pres., 1979–84; Mem., Policy Council, 1979–89; Leader, NewLabour Party, 1989–; Jt Founder, 1991, Leader, 1992–2001, Alliance. Organiser, Catholic Youth Movt, 1960–65; Sec., Catholic Diocesan Office, Auckland, 1967–69. *Address:* Parliament Buildings, Wellington, New Zealand; 286a Selwyn Street, Christchurch, New Zealand.

ANDO, Tadao; architect; *b* 13 Sept. 1941; *s* of Mitsugu Kitayama and Asako Kitayama; adopted by grandparents Hikoichi Ando and Kikue Ando; *m* 1970, Yumiko Kato. *Educ:* self-educated in architecture. Visiting Professor: Yale Univ., 1987; Columbia Univ., 1988; Harvard, 1990. *Works include:* Row House, Sumiyoshi (Azuma House), 1975; Rokko Housing I and II, 1978–89; Kidosaki House, 1982; Church of The Light, Osaka, 1987; Japanese Pavilion, Expo '92, Seville, 1989. *Exhibitions include:* Mus. of Modern Art, NY, 1991; Centre Georges Pompidou, Paris, 1993; Basilica Palladiana, Vicenza, 1994; RA, 1998. Hon. FAIA 1991; Hon. FRIBA 1993. Chevalier, Ordre des Arts et des Lettres (France), 1995. Alvar Aalto Medal, Finnish Assoc. Architects, 1986; Gold Medal of Architecture, French Acad. Architecture, 1989; Arnold W. Brunner Meml Prize, AAIL, 1991; Carlsberg Architectural Prize, 1992; Pritzker Architecture Prize, 1995; Royal Gold Medal, RIBA, 1997. *Publications:* Tadao Ando Monographies, 1982; Tadao Ando: buildings, projects, writings, 1984; Tadao Ando Complete Works, 1995; (with Richard Pare) The Colours of Light, 1996. *Address:* 5–23 Toyosaki 2–chome, Kita–ku, Osaka, Japan 531–0072. *T:* (6) 63751148.

ANDOVER, Viscount; Alexander Charles Michael Winston Robsahm Howard; Managing Director, Charlton Park OnLine Ltd (formerly Virtual Dimension), since 1997; *b* 17 Sept. 1974; *s* and *heir* of 21st Earl of Suffolk and Berkshire, *qv*. *Educ:* Eton Coll.; Bristol Univ. *Address:* Little Dene, Park Street, Charlton, Malmesbury, Wilts SN16 9DF; *e-mail:* andover@charltonpark.com. *Club:* Bluebird.

ANDRE, Carl; sculptor; *b* 16 Sept. 1935; *s* of George Hans Andre and Margaret Andre (*née* Johnson). First exhibn, 1964; represented in collections in: Tate Gall.; Mus. of Modern Art, NYC; Guggenheim Mus., NYC; La Jolla Mus. Contemporary Art; Mönchengladbach Mus., Germany; Kunstmuseum Basel, Switzerland; Stedelijk Mus., Amsterdam; Musée Nationale d'Art Moderne, Paris; Nat. Gall. of Canada, Ottawa; Seattle Art Mus.; Musèo de Arte Moderno, Bogotá; *solo exhibitions:* Tibor de Nagy Gall., NY, 1965; Konrad Fischer Gall., Düsseldorf, 1967; Guggenheim Mus., 1970; Univ. Art Mus., Berkeley, Calif, 1979; Paula Cooper Gall., NY, 1983; (retrospective) Whitechapel Art Gall., 2000. *Address:* c/o Konrad Fischer, Platanenstrasse 7, 40233 Düsseldorf, Germany; c/o Paula Cooper, 534 W 21 St, New York, NY 10011, USA.

ANDREAE, Sophie Clodagh Mary, (Mrs D. E. Blain); Member, Commission for Architecture and the Built Environment, since 1999; *b* 10 Nov. 1954; *d* of Herman Kleinwort (Sonny) Andreae and Clodagh Mary (*née* Alleyn); *m* 1984, Douglas Ellis Blain; three *s* one *d*. *Educ:* St Mary's, Ascot; Newnham Coll., Cambridge. SAVE Britain's Heritage: Sec., 1976–84; Chm., 1984–88; Head. London Div., English Heritage (Historic Bldgs and Monuments Commn for England), 1988–93. Mem., Royal Fine Art Commn, 1996–99. Trustee, Heritage of London Trust, 1985–; Member: London DAC, 1988–2001; St Paul's Cathedral Fabric Adv. Cttee, 1991–; Exec. Cttee, Georgian Gp, 1993–; Council, London Historic Parks and Gardens Trust, 1993–. Dir, Action for Mkt Towns, 1998–. *Publications:* (contrib.) Preserving the Past: the rise of heritage in modern Britain, 1996; ed and contrib. to numerous SAVE Britain's Heritage reports. *Address:* 23 Brompton Square, SW3 2AD.

ANDREAE-JONES, William Pearce; QC 1984; a Recorder of the Crown Court, since 1982; *b* 21 July 1942. *Educ:* Canford Sch.; Corpus Christi Coll., Cambridge (MA Hons). Called to the Bar, Inner Temple, 1965. *Address:* Coleridge Chambers, The Citadel, Corporation Street, Birmingham B4 6QD; 1 Sergeants' Inn, Fleet Street, EC4 1LL; King's Bench Chambers, Wellington House, 175 Holdenhurst Road, Bournemouth, Dorset BH8 8DQ.

ANDREOTTI, Giulio; Life Senator, Chamber of Deputies, since 1992; Prime Minister (President of the Council of Ministers) of Italy, 1972–73, 1976–79 and 1989–92; *b* 14 Jan. 1919; *s* of Filippo and Rosa Andreotti; *m* 1945, Livia Danese; two *s* two *d*. *Educ:* Univ. of Rome. Mem. for Rome Latina Viterbo Frosinone, Chamber of Deputies, 1946–92. Under Sec. of State, Council of Ministers, 1947–54; Minister of Interior, 1954; Minister of Finance, 1955–58; Minister of the Treasury, 1958–59; Minister of Defence, 1959–65; Minister of Industry and Commerce, 1966–68; Chm., Christian Democrats, 1968–72; Minister of Defence, March–Oct. 1974; Minister for Budget and Economic Planning, 1974–76; Minister of Foreign Affairs, 1983–89. Founder, and Editor, Concretezza (political weekly), 1955–76. Hon. Dr. Sorbonne; Loyola Univ., Chicago; Copernican Univ. of Torun, Poland; La Plata; Salamanca; St John's, NY; Warsaw; Univ. of Sci. and Technol., Beijing; New York; Jewish Theol Seminary, NY. Bancarella Prize, 1985. *Publications* include: Pranzo di magro per il cardinale, 1954; De Gasperi e il suo tempo, 1965; La Sciarada di Papa Mastai, 1967; Ore 13: il Ministro deve morire, 1975; Ad Ogni morte di Papa, 1980; Il diario 1976–79, 1981; De Gasperi visto da vicino, 1986; Visti da vicino (4 vols of profiles): Onorevole, stia zitto, 1987, vol II, 1992; L'URSS vista da vicino, 1988, Gli USA visti da vicino, 1989; Il potere logora … ma è meglio non perderlo, 1990; Governare con la crisi, 1991; The USA Up Close, 1992; Cosa Loro, 1995; De Prima Republica, 1996; many articles. *Address:* Senato della Repubblica, Palazzo Giustiniani, Via della Dogana Vecchia 29, 00816 Rome, Italy.

ANDRESKI, Prof. Stanislav Leonard; Professor of Sociology, University of Reading, 1964–84, now Emeritus; part-time Professor of Sociology, Polish University in London, 1969–99; *b* 18 May 1919; two *s* two *d*. *Educ:* Secondary sch. in Poznan, 1928–37; Univ. of Poznan (Faculty of Economics and Jurisprudence), 1938–39; London Sch. of Economics, 1942–43. Military service in Polish Army (with exception of academic year 1942–43), 1937–38 and 1939–47 (commissioned, 1944). Lectr in Sociology, Rhodes Univ., SA, 1947–53; Sen. Research Fellow in Anthropology, Manchester Univ., 1954–56; Lectr in Economics, Acton Technical Coll., London, 1956–57; Lectr in Management Studies, Brunel Coll. of Technology, London, 1957–60; Prof. of Sociology, Sch. of Social Sciences, Santiago, Chile, 1960–61; Sen. Res. Fellow, Nigerian Inst. of Social and Economic Research, Ibadan, Nigeria, 1962–64; Hd, Dept of Sociology, Univ. of Reading, 1964–82. Vis. Prof. of Sociology and Anthropology, City Coll., City Univ. of New York, 1968–69; Vis. Prof. of Sociology, Simon Frazer Univ., Vancouver, 1976–77; pt–time Prof. of Social Scis, Duxx Sch. of Business, Monterey, Mexico, 1995–98; pt-time Prof., Wyższa Szkoła Języków Obcych i Ekonomii, Czestochowa, Poland, 1998–. *Publications:* Military Organization and Society (Internat. Library of Sociology and Social Reconstruction), 1954 (2nd aug. edn, 1968, USA, 1968, paperback, 1969); Class Structure and Social Development (with Jan Ostaszewski and others), (London), 1964 (in Polish); Elements of Comparative Sociology (The Nature of Human Society Series), 1964, Spanish edn 1972; The Uses of Comparative Sociology (American edn of the foregoing), 1965, paperback 1969; Parasitism and Subversion: the case of Latin America, 1966 (NY, 1967, rev. edn 1968, etc; Buenos Aires (in Spanish with a postscript), 1968; paperback edn, London, 1970); The African Predicament: a study in pathology of modernisation, 1968 (USA, 1969); Social Sciences as Sorcery, 1972, Spanish edn 1973, German edn 1974, French edn 1975, Italian edn 1977, Japanese edn 1982; Prospects of a Revolution in the USA, 1973; The Essential Comte, 1974; Reflections on Inequality, 1975; Max Weber's Insights and Errors, 1984, Polish edn 1992, Chinese edn 2000; Syphilis, Puritanism and Witch-Hunts, 1989; Wars, Revolutions, Dictatorships, 1992; Editor: Herbert Spencer, Principles of Sociology, 1968; Herbert Spencer, Structure, Function and Evolution, 1970; Max Weber on Capitalism, Bureaucracy and Religion, 1983; contribs to: A Dictionary of the Social Sciences (UNESCO); A Dictionary of Sociology (ed D. Mitchell); Brit. Jl of Sociology; Japanese Jl of Sociology; The Nature of Fascism (ed S. Woolf); Science Jl, Man, European Jl of Sociology, Encounter, etc. *Recreations:* sailing, horse-riding. *Address:* Farriers, Village Green, Upper Basildon, Berkshire RG8 8LS. *T:* (01491) 671318.

ANDREW, Prof. Christopher Maurice, PhD; FRHistS; Professor of Modern and Contemporary History, University of Cambridge, since 1993; Fellow, Corpus Christi College, Cambridge, since 1967; *b* 23 July 1941; *s* of Maurice Viccars Andrew and Freda Mary (*née* Sandall); *m* 1962, Jennifer Ann Alicia Garratt; one *s* two *d*. *Educ:* Norwich Sch.; Corpus Christi Coll., Cambridge (MA, PhD). FRHistS 1976. Res. Fellow, Gonville and

Caius Coll., Cambridge, 1965–67; Dir of Studies in History, 1967–81 and 1988–, Sen. Tutor, 1981–87, Corpus Christi Coll., Cambridge; Univ. Lectr in History, 1972–89, Reader in Mod. and Contemp. Hist., 1989–93, Univ. of Cambridge. Ext. Examr in History, NUI, 1977–84. Specialist Adviser, H of C Select Cttee on Educn, Science and the Arts, 1982–83. Visiting Professor: Univ. of Toronto, 1991; Harvard Univ., 1992. Visiting Fellow: ANU, 1987; Wilson Center, Washington, 1987. TV Presenter: The Fatal Attraction of Adolf Hitler, 1989; Hess: an edge of conspiracy, 1990; The Cambridge Moles, 1990; All the King's Jews, 1990; A Cold War, 1991; BBC Radio Presenter (series): Tampering with the Past, 1990; What if?, 1990–94; Hindsight, 1993–95. Editor: The Historical Journal, 1976–85; Intelligence and National Security, 1986–. *Publications:* Théophile Delcasse and the making of the Entente Cordiale, 1968; The First World War: causes and consequences, 1970 (vol. 19 of Hamlyn History of the World); (with A. S. Kanya-Forstner) France Overseas: the First World War and the climax of French imperial expansion, 1981; (ed with Prof. D. Dilks) The Missing Dimension: governments and intelligence communities in the Twentieth Century, 1984; Secret Service: the making of the British Intelligence Community, 1985; Codebreaking and Signals Intelligence, 1986; (ed with Jeremy Noakes) Intelligence and International Relations 1900–1945, 1987; (with Oleg Gordievsky) KGB: the inside story of its foreign operations from Lenin to Gorbachev, 1990; (with Oleg Gordievsky) Instructions from The Centre: top secret files on KGB foreign operations, 1991; (with Oleg Gordievsky) More Instructions from The Centre, 1992; For The President's Eyes Only: secret intelligence and the American presidency from Washington to Bush, 1995; (with Vasili Mitrokhin) The Mitrokhin Archive: the KGB in Europe and the West, 1999; broadcasts and articles on mod. history, Association football, secret intelligence, internat. relations. *Address:* 67 Grantchester Meadows, Cambridge CB3 9JL. *T:* (01223) 353773.

ANDREW, Christopher Robert, (Rob), MBE 1995; Development Director, Newcastle Rugby Football Club, since 1995; *b* 18 Feb. 1963; *m* 1989, Sara; two *d.* *Educ:* Barnard Castle; St John's Coll., Cambridge (BA 1985; MA 1989; Rugby blue, cricket blue). ARICS 1988. Chartered surveyor with Debenham, Tewson & Chinnocks, until 1995. Played for: Nottingham RFC, 1984–87; Wasps FC, 1987–91, 1992–96; Toulouse RFC, 1991–92; Barbarians RFC, and Newcastle RFC, 1996–99; England, 1985–97 (over 50 caps); World Cup team 1987, 1991, 1995; Grand Slam side, 1991, 1992, 1995; British Lions tour, Australia, 1989, NZ 1993. Mem., UK Sports Council, 1996–. *Publications:* A Game and a Half, 1994; contrib. The Times. *Address:* c/o Newcastle Rugby Football Club, Newcastle upon Tyne NE3 2DT. *T:* (0191) 214 0422.

ANDREW, Prof. Colin, FIMechE; Professor of Manufacturing Engineering, 1986–94, and Chairman of Council, School of Technology, 1993–94, Cambridge University; Fellow, Christ's College, Cambridge, 1986–94; *b* 22 May 1934; *s* of Arnold Roy and Kathleen Andrew; *m* 1952, Ruth E. Probert; two *s* two *d.* *Educ:* Bristol Grammar Sch.; Christ's Coll., Cambridge Univ. MA; PhD. Res. Engr, Rolls-Royce, 1955–58; research, Cambridge, 1958–60; Develt Engr, James Archdale & Co., 1960–61; Bristol University: Lectr, 1961–68; Reader, 1968–71; Prof. of Applied Mechanics, 1971–82; Hon. Prof., 1982–86. Managing Director: Flamgard Ltd, 1982–85; Bristol Technical Develts Ltd, 1985–94. Chairman: Engrg Processes Cttee, SERC, 1981–83; Production Cttee, SERC, 1983–84; Main Engrg Panel, and Mech., Aeronautical and Manufacturing Panel, UFC Res. Assessment Exercise, 1992; Mech., Aeronautical and Manufacturing Panel, HEFCE Res. Assessment Exercise, 1996; Member: Technology Sub-Cttee, UGC, 1986–89; Engrg Council, 1990–94 (Chm., Bd of Engrs Registration, 1992–94). *Publications:* (jtly) Creep Feed Grinding, 1985; papers in scientific jls. *Address:* Hybank, Itton, Chepstow NP6 6BZ.

ANDREW, Douglas Robert; Board Member, and Group Director, Economic Regulation, Civil Aviation Authority, since 1997; *b* 14 June 1951; *s* of Douglas Robert Lawson Andrew and Patricia Eleanor (*née* Thorp). *Educ:* Princeton Univ. (MPA); Auckland Univ. (MCom Hons). Various posts in NZ Treasury, 1975–97 (Dep. Sec., 1995–97). *Recreation:* tennis. *Address:* Civil Aviation Authority, CAA House, 45–59 Kingsway, WC2B 6TE. *T:* (020) 7453 6200.

ANDREW, His Honour Herbert Henry; QC 1982; a Circuit Judge, 1984–99; *b* 26 July 1928; *s* of Herbert Henry Andrew and Nora Andrew (*née* Gough); *m* 1966, Annette Josephine Colbert; two *s* two *d.* *Educ:* Preston Grammar Sch.; Queens' Coll., Cambridge (BA). Called to the Bar, Gray's Inn, 1952; practised on Northern Circuit, 1953–84; a Recorder, 1978–84. *Recreation:* fell walking. *Club:* Liverpool Racquet.

ANDREW, Hon. (John) Neil; MP (L) Wakefield, SA, since 1983; Speaker, House of Representatives, Australia, since 1998; *b* 7 June 1944; *s* of Jack Clover Andrew and Elsie Mavis Andrew; *m* 1971, Carolyn Ann Ayles; two *s* one *d.* *Educ:* Waikerie High Sch.; Urrbrae Agricl Coll.; Australian Nuffield Schol. in Agric., UK, 1975. Horticulture (fruit and vineyards), 1964–83. Dep. Opposition Whip, 1985–89, 1990–93; Chief Govt Whip, House of Reps, 1997–98. *Recreations:* horticulture, camping, reading, aviation. *Address:* Parliament of Australia, Parliament House, Canberra, ACT 2600, Australia.

ANDREW, Rob; *see* Andrew, C. R.

ANDREW, Sir Robert (John), KCB 1986 (CB 1979); civil servant, retired; *b* 25 Oct. 1928; *s* of late Robert Young Andrew and Elsie (*née* Heritage); *m* 1963, Elizabeth Bayley (OBE 2000); two *s.* *Educ:* King's College Sch., Wimbledon; Merton Coll., Oxford (MA). Intelligence Corps, 1947–49. Joined Civil Service, 1952: Asst Principal, War Office, Principal, 1957; Min. of Defence, 1963; Asst Sec., 1965; Defence Counsellor, UK Delegn to NATO, 1967–70. Private Sec. to Sec. of State for Defence, 1971–73; Under-Sec., CSD, 1973–75; Asst Under-Sec. of State, MoD, 1975–76; Dep. Under-Sec. of State, Home Office, 1976–83; Perm. Under-Sec. of State, NI Office, 1984–88; Cabinet Office, Review of Govt Legal Services, 1988. Dir, Esmée Fairbairn Trust, 1989–94. Conservator of Wimbledon and Putney Commons, 1973–. Governor, King's College Sch., 1975–2000 (Chm., 1990–2000). Mem. Council, Royal Holloway, Univ. of London (formerly RHBNC), 1989–99 (Chm., 1992–99; Hon. Fellow, 2000). Trustee, BBC Children in Need Appeal, 1993–99. FRSA 1992. *Recreations:* walking, carpentry, canal boats. *Club:* Oxford and Cambridge.

ANDREW, Sandra Christine; Her Honour Judge Andrew; a Circuit Judge, since 1999; Designated Family Judge, Canterbury Combined Court, since 2000; *b* 5 Nov. 1941; *d* of Albert Hugh Dudley Tyas and Anne Florence (*née* Preston); *m* 1963, John Andrew; two *s.* *Educ:* various prep. schools; E Grinstead Co. Grammar Sch. Admitted Solicitor, 1964; in private practice, 1964–83; Registrar, SE Circuit, Bromley Co. Court, 1983, transf. to Maidstone, 1990; Trng Registrar, then Dist Judge, 1986–99; Care Dist Judge, 1991–99. Member: Lord Chancellor's Adv. Cttee on Ancillary Relief, 1993–; Family Proceedings Rules Cttee, 1993–97; Litigant Inf. Sub-Cttee, Civil Justice Council, 1998–; Tutor team for Dep. Dist Judges, Judicial Studies Bd, 1998–. Chm., SE Circuit Assoc. Dist Judges, 1992–95; SE Circuit (S) Rep., Nat. Cttee, Assoc. Dist Judges, 1996–99 (Co-opted Mem., Family Sub-Cttee, 1993–96). *Recreations:* music, bridge, travel, reading. *Address:* Canterbury Combined Court, Chaucer Road, Canterbury, Kent CT1 1ZA. *Club:* Army and Navy.

ANDREW, Sydney Percy Smith, FRS 1976; FREng, FIChemE, MIMechE; consultant chemical engineer; ICI Senior Research Associate, 1976–88; *b* 16 May 1926; *s* of Harold C. Andrew and Kathleen M. (*née* Smith); *m* 1986, Ruth Harrison Kenyon (*née* Treanor). *Educ:* Barnard Castl Sch.; King's Coll., Durham Univ. (Open Schol.; BSc); Trinity Hall, Cambridge (Schol. and Prizeman; MA). Joined ICI Billingham Div., 1950; Chemical Engrg Res., 1951; Plant Engr, 1953; Section Manager: Reactor Res., 1955; Process Design, 1959; Gp Man., Catalysts and Chemicals Res., 1963–76. Vis. Prof., Univ. of Bath, 1988–. Chm., Res. Cttee, IChemE. FREng (FEng 1976). Hon. DSc Leeds, 1979. Soc. of Chemical Industry Medal, 1989. *Publications:* Catalyst Handbook, 1970; various papers in chemical engrg, applied chemistry and plant physiology. *Recreations:* archaeology, ancient and medieval history. *Address:* 1 The Wynd, Stainton in Cleveland, Middlesbrough TS8 9BP. *T:* (01642) 596348.

ANDREWS, Baroness *cr* 2000 (Life Peer), of Southover in the co. of East Sussex; **Elizabeth Kay Andrews,** OBE 1998; DPhil; Director, Education Extra (national charity for out-of-school learning), since 1992; *b* 16 May 1943; *d* of Clifford and Louisa Andrews; *m* 1970, Prof. Roy MacLeod (marr. diss. 1992); one *s.* *Educ:* Univ. of Wales (BA 1964); Univ. of Sussex (MA 1970; DPhil 1975). Res. Fellow, Science Policy Res. Unit, Univ. of Sussex, 1968–70; Res. Clerk, then Sen. Res. Clerk, H of C, 1970–85; Special Advr, Rt Hon. Neil Kinnock, MP, Leader of the Opposition, 1985–92. *Publications:* (with J. B. Poole) The Government of Science, 1972; (with John Jacobs) Punishing the Poor, 1990; Good Practice & Policy for After School, 1997; articles in history, science policy and social policy jls. *Recreations:* opera, walking, friends. *Address:* Education Extra, 17 Old Ford Road, E2 9PF. *T:* (020) 8790 9900.

ANDREWS, Ann; *see* Beynon, A.

ANDREWS, Anthony Peter Hamilton; Director, British Council, Germany, since 2000; *b* 23 Dec. 1946; *s* of Col Peter Edward Clinton Andrews and Jean Margaret Hamilton (*née* Cooke); *m* 1973, Alison Margaret Dudley Morgan; one *s* two *d.* *Educ:* King's Sch., Worcester; Univ. of St Andrews (MA); UCNW, Bangor (Dip. TEFL). Served RM, 1964–71. Land agent, 1975–76; with British Council, 1976–: Kano, Nigeria, 1976–78; Belgrade, 1979–81; Muscat, Oman, 1981–85; Recife, Brazil, 1985–89; Director: Scotland, 1989–95; Russia, 1995–2000. *Recreations:* angling, river management, sailing, the arts. *Address:* Milton of Finavon House, by Forfar, Angus DD8 3PY. *T:* (01307) 850275. *Club:* New (Edinburgh).

ANDREWS, David; Member of the Dáil (TD) (FF) for Dún Laoghaire, since 1965; Minister for Foreign Affairs, Republic of Ireland, 1997–2000; *b* 15 March 1935; *s* of Christopher Andrews and Mary Coyle; *m* Annette Cusack; two *s* three *d.* *Educ:* Colaiste Mhuire, Christian Brothers' Sch.; Cistercian College, Roscrea; University College Dublin (BCL). Called to the Bar, King's Inns, 1962; Senior Counsel. Parly Sec. to Taoiseach, and Govt Chief Whip, 1970–73; opposition frontbench spokesman on justice and social welfare, 1973–77; Minister of State: Dept of Foreign Affairs, 1977–79; Dept of Justice, 1978–79; Minister: for Foreign Affairs, 1992–93; for Defence and the Marine, 1993–94; opposition spokesman on tourism and trade, 1995–97; Minister for Defence, 1997. Member: Cttee on the Constitution, 1967; New Ireland Forum, 1983–84. Mem., British–Irish Interparly Body, 1990–92. *Recreations:* fly fishing, walking, theatre. *Address:* Dáil Eireann, Leinster House, Dublin 2, Ireland. *T:* (1) 6789911.

ANDREWS, Prof. David John, PhD; FREng; FRINA; Professor of Engineering Design, Department of Mechanical Engineering, University College London, since 2000; *b* 9 Aug. 1947; *m* 1970, Philippa Vanette Whitehurst; one *s* one *d.* *Educ:* Stationers' Co. Sch.; University Coll. London (BSc Eng 1970; MSc 1971; PhD 1984). FRINA 1987; FREng 2000. RCNC Cadetship, 1965; Constructor Lieut, RN, 1971; Ministry of Defence: professional design on in-service and new build submarines, Submarine Design Section, Ship Dept, Bath, 1972–75; Constructor Grade, working on Invincible carrier design and subseq. Forward Design Gp, 1975–80; Lectr in Naval Architecture, UCL, 1980–84; Ministry of Defence: Hd, Trident Submarine Hull Design Section, Bath, 1984–86; Hd, Amphibious Gp (Chief Constructor), Replacement Amphibious Shipping Prog., 1986–90; Hd, Concept Design Div., Future Projects (Naval), Whitehall, 1990–93; Prof. of Naval Architecture, UCL, 1993–98; Dir, Frigates and Mine Countermeasures, Defence Procurement Agency, then Integrated Project Team Leader, Future Surface Combatant, MoD, Bristol, 1998–2000. Chm., Membership Cttee, 1993–2000, Chm., Future Directions Cttee, 2000–, RINA. FRSA 1996. *Publications:* Synthesis in Ship Design (thesis), 1984; (contrib.) Finite Element Methods Applied to Thin Walled Structures, 1987; (contrib.) Ship Design and Construction, 2001; contrib. numerous papers on ship design published by RINA, Royal Soc., etc, and in conf. proc. *Recreations:* painting and sketching, reading, cinema and theatre going, re-exploring London with my wife. *Address:* Department of Mechanical Engineering, University College London, Torrington Place, WC1E 7JE. *T:* (020) 7679 3874; *e-mail:* d_andrews@meng.ucl.ac.uk.

ANDREWS, David Roger Griffith, CBE 1981; Chairman, Gwion Ltd, 1986–95; *b* 27 March 1933; *s* of C. H. R. Andrews and G. M. Andrews; *m* 1963, Dorothy Ann Campbell; two *s* one *d.* *Educ:* Abingdon Sch.; Pembroke Coll., Oxford (MA). FCMA, CIMgt. Pirelli-General, 1956–59; Ford Motor Company, 1960–69: Controller: Product Engrg, 1965–66; Transmission and Chassis Div., 1967; European Sales Ops, 1967–69; Asst Controller, Ford of Europe, 1969; BLMC: Controller, 1970; Finance Dir, Austin Morris, 1971–72; Man. Dir, Power and Transmission Div., 1973–75; British Leyland Ltd: Man. Dir, Leyland International, 1975–77; Exec. Vice Chm., BL Ltd, 1977–82; Chm., Leyland Gp and Land Rover Gp, 1981–82; Chm. and Chief Exec., Land Rover-Leyland, 1982–86. Director: Clarges Pharmaceutical Trustees Ltd, 1983–91; Glaxo Trustees Ltd, 1983–91; Ex-Cell-O Ltd, 1987–88; Foundn for Sci. and Technology, 1990–95 (Mem. Council, 1990–95, and Hon. Treas., 1990–95; Foundn Medal, 1996). Member: CBI Council, 1981–86; Exec. Cttee, SMMT, 1981–86; Open Univ. Visiting Cttee, 1982–85. FRSA. *Recreations:* reading, golf. *Address:* Gainford, 36 Mill Lane, Gerrards Cross, Bucks SL9 8BA. *T:* (01753) 884310.

ANDREWS, Sir Derek (Henry), KCB 1991 (CB 1984); CBE 1970; Permanent Secretary, Ministry of Agriculture, Fisheries and Food, 1987–93, retired; Chairman, Residuary Milk Marketing Board, since 1994; *b* 17 Feb. 1933; *s* of late Henry Andrews and Emma Jane Andrews; *m* 1st, 1956, Catharine May (*née* Childe) (*d* 1982); two *s* one *d;* 2nd, 1991, Alison Margaret Blackburn, *d* of Sir William Nield, GCMG, KCB. *Educ:* LSE (BA (Hons) 1955). Ministry of Agriculture, Fisheries and Food: Asst Principal, 1957; Asst Private Sec. to Minister of Agriculture, Fisheries and Food, 1960–61; Principal, 1961; Asst Sec., 1968; Private Sec. to Prime Minister, 1966–70; Harvard Univ., USA, 1970–71; Under-Sec., 1973; Dep. Sec., 1981. FRGS. *Clubs:* Reform; Aldeburgh Yacht.

ANDREWS, Hon. Sir Dormer (George), Kt 1987; Chief Justice of Queensland, 1985–89; *b* 8 April 1919; *s* of Miles Dormer Andrews and Margaret Mary Andrews (*née* Robertson); *m* 1943, Joan Merle Tear; three *s.* *Educ:* University of Queensland (BA, LLB). Flying Officer, RAAF, served UK and ME, 1940–44. Admitted Queensland Bar, 1947; District Court Judge, Queensland, 1959; Chm., District Courts, 1965; Judge, 1971, Senior

Puisne Judge, 1982, Supreme Court of Queensland. Chm., Law Reform Commn, Queensland, 1973–82. *Recreations:* walking, reading. *Address:* 6 Jamieson Place, Brookfield, Brisbane, Qld 4069, Australia. *T:* (7) 33784298. *Clubs:* Queensland, Tattersalls, United Service (Brisbane).

ANDREWS, Geraldine Mary; QC 2001; a Recorder, since 2001; *b* 19 April 1959; *d* of Walter and Mary Andrews. *Educ:* King's Coll. London (LLB 1st Cl. Hons 1980, LLM 1982; AKC; Dip.). Called to the Bar, Gray's Inn, 1981; barrister, 1983–, specialising in commercial law, esp. banking; called to Irish Bar, 1993. *Publications:* (with S. Gee) Mareva Injunctions, 1988; (with R. Millett) The Law of Guarantees, 1992, 3rd edn 2001. *Recreations:* keen violinist, theatre, music, sport, reading, learning modern languages. *Address:* Essex Court Chambers, 24 Lincoln's Inn Fields, WC2A 3EG. *T:* (020) 7813 8000.

ANDREWS, Ian Charles Franklin, CBE 1992; TD 1989; Chief Executive, Defence Estates Agency, Ministry of Defence, since 1998; *b* 26 Nov. 1953; *s* of Peter Harry Andrews and Nancy Gwladys Andrews (*née* Franklin); *m* 1985, Moira Fraser McEwan; two *s* one *d*. *Educ:* Solihull Sch.; Univ. of Bristol (BSc Social Sci.). Joined Ministry of Defence, 1975: Private Sec. to 2nd Perm. Under Sec. of State, 1979–81; short service volunteer commn, RRF, 1981–82; Principal, 1982; NATO Defence Coll., 1984–85; Asst Private Sec. to Sec. of State for Defence, 1986–88; Head: Defence Lands, 1988–90; Resources and Prog. (Army), 1990–93; Civil Sec., British Forces Germany/BAOR, 1993–95; Man. Dir (Facilities), DERA, 1995–97. Served TA in rank of Major, 1972–93. FRGS 1996. *Recreations:* travel, ski-ing. *Address:* c/o Ministry of Defence, Whitehall, SW1A 2HB.

ANDREWS, His Honour James Roland Blake F.; *see* Fox-Andrews.

ANDREWS, Prof. John Albert, CBE 2000; Chief Executive, Further and Higher Education Funding Councils for Wales, 1992–2000; *b* 29 Jan. 1935; *s* of late Arthur George Andrews and Hilda May Andrews (*née* Banwell); *m* 1960, Elizabeth Ann Mary Wilkes; two *d*. *Educ:* Newport High Sch.; Wadham Coll., Oxford (MA, BCL). Called to the Bar, Gray's Inn, 1960, Bencher, 1991. Asst Lectr, Univ. of Manchester, 1957–58; Lectr in English Law, Univ. of Birmingham, 1958–67; University College of Wales, Aberystwyth: Prof. of Law, 1967–92; Hon. Prof., 1992–2000; Emeritus Prof., 2000–; Head of Dept of Law, 1970–92; Vice-Principal, 1985–88. Visiting Professor: Thessaloniki, 1974, 1990; Cracow, 1978; Maryland, 1983. Former chm. or mem., numerous educnl, police and adv. bodies; Member: Police Trng Council, 1987– (Academic Advr, 1997–); Lord Chancellor's Adv. Cttee on Legal Educn, 1987–90; Welsh Econ. Council, 1994–96; Adjudicator, Criminal Injuries Compensation Appeals Panel, 2000–; Chairman: Police Promotions Exams Bd, 1987–; Agricl Wages Bd, 1999–; Gen. Teaching Council for Wales, 2000–. Member Council: Cardiff Univ., 2000–; Univ. of Wales Coll. of Medicine, 2000–; Member, Court of Governors: Univ. of Wales, 1969–92, 2001–; Nat. Liby of Wales, 1979–92. Hon. Fellow, Univ. of Wales Coll., Newport, 2000. Trustee: SPTL, 1990– (Pres., 1988–89); Hamlyn Trust, 1969–2000. FRSA 1992. JP N Ceredigion, 1975–91. Editor, Legal Studies, 1981–93. *Publications:* (ed) Welsh Studies in Public Law, 1970; (ed) Human Rights in Criminal Procedure, 1982; (with L. G. Henshaw) The Welsh Language in the Courts, 1984; (with W. D. Hines) Keyguide to the International Protection of Human Rights, 1987; (with D. M. Hirst) Criminal Evidence, 1987, 3rd edn 1997; Criminal Evidence: statutes and materials, 1990; contribs to legal and educnl books and jls. *Recreations:* walking, theatre, food, opera. *Address:* 7 Maeshendre, Aberystwyth, Ceredigion SY23 3PR. *T:* (01970) 623921; 2 Androvan Court, Hollybush Road, Cyncoed, Cardiff CF23 6TF. *T:* (029) 2075 3980; Faculty of Law, University of Wales, Hugh Owen Building, Penglais, Aberystwyth, Ceredigion SY23 3DY. *T:* (01970) 622712. *Club:* Brynamlwg (Aberystwyth).

ANDREWS, John Hayward, CMG 1988; Director, Logan Motorway Group (formerly Logan Toll Motorway Group), 1988–95; *b* 9 Nov. 1919; *s* of James Andrews and Florence Elizabeth Andrews; *m* 1947; one *s* one *d* (and one *s* decd). *Educ:* Univ. of Queensland (BEc). FIE(Aust); FAIM; DipT&CP; DipCE. Served Royal Aust. Engineers, 1940–45. Local Govt City Engineer, Wagga Wagga and Tamworth, NSW, 1946–60; Deputy Commissioner, Main Roads Dept, Queensland, 1961–78; Administrator, Gold Coast City, 1978–79; private practice, 1979–81; Agent-Gen. for Qld, 1981–84; Chairman: Electoral Redistribution Commn for Qld, 1985–86; Sugar Bd (Qld), subseq. Qld Sugar Corp., 1986–92. Dir, White Industries Ltd, 1986–88. *Recreations:* golf, painting, walking. *Club:* Twin Towns Services.

ANDREWS, John Robert; Board Member, since 1994, and Treasurer, since 1996, Confédération Européenne des Cadres; *b* 15 June 1942; *s* of late John Henry Andrews, ERD, MA, FCCA, and of Marjorie Andrews (*née* Kirkman); *m* 1966, Minna D. L. Stevenson; two *d*. *Educ:* Nottingham High Sch.; Nottingham Coll. of Educn (CertEd 1963). ACP 1973; FCollP 1982; DipSMS 1982. Teacher in primary and secondary schs, 1963–72; Headteacher, Birmingham LEA, 1972–81; Professional Association of Teachers: Asst Gen. Sec., 1982–91; Gen. Sec., 1992–97; Mem. Council, 1972–81; Chairman: Educn Cttee, 1975–77; Pay and Conditions Cttee, 1977–81. Mem. Exec. Cttee, Council of Managerial and Professional Staffs, then Managerial and Professional Staffs Assoc., 1988–; Pres., Council of Managerial and Prof. Staffs, 1992–97 (Sec., Industrial Relns Cttee, 1990–92); Chm., Managerial and Professional Staffs Assoc., 1997–2000. Mem., Econ. and Social Cttee, EU, 1994–98. Chm., Indep. Unions Trng Council, 1989–96; Vice-Pres., European Confedn of Indep. Trade Unions, 1992–94; Bd Mem. and Treas., Eur. Managers Inst., 2000–. Mem., Schs Orgn Cttee for Staffordshire, 1999–. Dir, GTC (England & Wales) Trust, 1992–99. Member: Lichfield Deanery Synod, 1970–; Lichfield Diocesan Synod, 1979–; Exec. Cttee, Lichfield Diocesan Bd of Finance, 1987–; Lichfield Diocesan Bd of Educn, 1998– (Exec. Cttee, 2001–); Bishop's Council, 1999–; Reader, Lichfield Diocese (Gentleshaw and Farewell), 1967–. Mem., Parish Council, Longdon, Staffs, 1973– (Chm., 1991–93). Governor, Gentleshaw Sch., 1993–97, 1999– (Chm., 1996–97). FIMgt 1992 (MBIM 1982); FRSA 1992. *Publications:* contribs to various jls on multi-cultural educn, general educnl issues and educn law. *Recreations:* hill walking, horse riding, listening to music. *Address:* (office) Rue de la Loi 81a, 1040 Brussels, Belgium. *T:* (2) 4201051, *Fax:* (2) 4201292; *e-mail:* andrews@cec-managers.org; (home) 1 Chaseley Gardens, Burntwood, Staffs WS7 9DJ. *T:* (01543) 674354, *Fax:* (01543) 683985. *Club:* Royal Commonwealth Society.

ANDREWS, Dame Julie (Elizabeth), DBE 2000; actress; *b* 1 Oct. 1935; *m* 1st, Anthony J. Walton (marr. diss. 1968); one *d*; 2nd, 1969, Blake Edwards; one step *s* one step *d*, and two adopted *d*. *Educ:* Woodbrook Girls' Sch., Beckenham and private governess. Appeared in The Boy Friend, Broadway, New York, 1954; My Fair Lady: New York, 1956, London, 1958; Camelot, New York, 1960; Victor/Victoria, New York, 1995. *Films:* (Walt Disney) Mary Poppins, 1963 (Academy Award, 1964); Americanisation of Emily, 1964; Sound of Music, 1964; Hawaii, 1965; Torn Curtain, 1966; Thoroughly Modern Millie, 1966; Star, 1967; Darling Lili, 1970; The Tamarind Seed, 1973; "10", 1980; Little Miss Marker, 1980; S.O.B., 1981; Victor/Victoria, 1982; The Man Who Loved Women, 1983; Duet for One, 1987; That's Life, 1987; Relative Values, 2000; *television:* Julie & Carol at Carnegie Hall, 1961; An Evening with Julie Andrews and Harry Belafonte, 1969; Julie & Carol at Lincoln Center, 1971; The Julie Andrews Hour, 1972–73; Julie & Dick at Covent Garden, 1973–74; Julie & Jackie—How Sweet it is, 1973–74; Julie & Perry & The Muppets, 1973–74; My Favourite Things, 1975; The Puzzle Children, 1976; ABC's Silver Anniversary Celebration, 1978; Julie Andrews … One Step into Spring, 1978; The Sound of Christmas (Emmy Award), 1987; Julie & Carol Together Again, 1989; Great Performances Live in Concert, 1990; Our Sons, 1991; The Julie Show, 1992. *Publications:* (as Julie Andrews Edwards) Mandy, 1972; Last of the Really Great Whangdoodles, 1973. *Recreations:* boating, ski-ing, riding.

ANDREWS, Prof. Kenneth Raymond, FBA 1986; Professor of History, University of Hull, 1979–88 (part-time, 1986–88), now Emeritus; *b* 26 Aug. 1921; *s* of Arthur Walter and Marion Gertrude Andrews; *m* 1969, Ottilie Kalman, Olomouc, Czechoslovakia; two step *s*. *Educ:* Henry Thornton Sch., Clapham; King's College London (BA 1948, PhD 1951). Lectr, Univ. of Liverpool, 1963–64; Lectr and Sen. Lectr, Univ. of Hull, 1964–79; active research in English maritime history. *Publications:* English Privateering Voyages to the West Indies, 1959; Elizabethan Privateering, 1964; Drake's Voyages, 1967; The Last Voyage of Drake and Hawkins, 1972; The Spanish Caribbean, 1978; Trade, Plunder and Settlement, 1984; Ships, Money and Politics, 1991; articles in learned jls.

ANDREWS, Mark Björnsen; Deputy Chairman, Denton Wilde Sapte, solicitors, since 2000; *b* 12 July 1952; *s* of Harry Field Andrews and Ruth Margaret Andrews (*née* Legge). *Educ:* Reading Grammar Sch.; Hertford Coll., Oxford (BA Jurisp.). Articled Clerk, Clarks, solicitors, Reading, 1974–76; Wilde Sapte, subseq. Denton Wilde Sapte: Asst Solicitor, 1976–79; Partner, 1979–2000; Head of Insolvency Gp, 1989–2000; Sen. Partner, 1996–2000. Trustee, Pimlico Opera, 1991–. *Recreations:* music, history, ornithology, walking. *Address:* Denton Wilde Sapte, 1 Fleet Place, EC4M 7WS. *T:* (020) 7246 7000.

ANDREWS, Nigel John; Film Critic, Financial Times, since 1973; *b* 3 April 1947; *s* of Francis Yardley Andrews and Marguerite Joan Andrews. *Educ:* Lancing Coll., Sussex; Jesus Coll., Cambridge (MA English). Contributor and reviewer, Sight and Sound and Monthly Film Bulletin, 1969–73; Asst Ed., Cinema One books and Sight and Sound mag., 1972–73; regular broadcaster, BBC Radio; writer and presenter, Kaleidoscope, Radio 4, and other arts programmes, 1975–. Mem., BFI, 1971–. Critic of Year, British Press Awards, 1985. *Publications:* (contrib.) The Book of the Cinema, 1979; Horror Films, 1985; True Myths: the life and times of Arnold Schwarzenegger, 1995; Travolta: the life, 1998; Jaws, 1999. *Address:* c/o Michael Shaw, Curtis Brown, Haymarket House, 28–29 Haymarket, SW1Y 4SP.

ANDREWS, Peter John; QC 1991; a Recorder of the Crown Court, since 1990; a Deputy High Court Judge, Queen's Bench Division, since 1998; *b* 14 Nov. 1946; *s* of Reginald and Dora Andrews; *m* 1976, Ann Chavasse; two *d*. *Educ:* Bishop Vesey Grammar Sch.; Bristol Univ. (Undergraduate Scholar; LLB); Christ's Coll., Cambridge (Dip. Criminology). Called to the Bar, Lincoln's Inn (Hardwicke Scholar), 1970, Bencher, 1999; barrister specialising in catastrophic personal injury and clinical negligence litigation; Junior, Midland and Oxford Circuit, 1973–74; Asst Recorder, 1986–90. Chm., Fountain Court Chambers (Birmingham) Ltd, 1994–; Head of Chambers, 199 Strand, 1997–2000. Mem., Professional Conduct Cttee, GMC, 2001–. *Publications:* Catastrophic Injuries: a guide to compensation, 1997; (contrib.) Personal Injury Handbook, 1997, 2nd edn 2000; (contrib.) Kemp and Kemp, The Quantum of Damages, 1998, 2nd edn 2001. *Address:* 199 Strand, WC2R 1DR. *T:* (020) 7379 9779.

ANDREWS, Robert Graham M.; *see* Marshall-Andrews.

ANDREWS, Stuart Morrison; Head Master of Clifton College, 1975–90; *b* 23 June 1932; *s* of William Hannaford Andrews and Eileen Elizabeth Andrews; *m* 1962, Marie Elizabeth van Wyk; two *s*. *Educ:* Newton Abbot Grammar Sch.; St Dunstan's Coll.; Sidney Sussex Coll., Cambridge (MA). Nat. service with Parachute Bde, 1952–53. Sen. History Master and Librarian, St Dunstan's Coll., 1956–60; Chief History Master and Librarian, Repton Sch., 1961–67; Head Master, Norwich Sch., 1967–75. Chm., Direct-grant Sub-cttee, HMC, 1974–75; Dep. Chm., Assisted Places Cttee, 1982–91; Nat. Rep., HMC, 1986–87; HMC Lead Inspector of Schs, 1994–96. Trustee, Glastonbury Abbey Develt Trust, 1992–96; Chm. Trustees and Managers, Wells & Mendip Mus., 1999–. Chm., Emmott Foundn, 1999–. Editor, Conference, 1972–82. *Publications:* Eighteenth-century Europe, 1965; Enlightened Despotism, 1967; Methodism and Society, 1970; Rediscovery of America, 1998; British Periodical Press and the French Revolution, 2000; articles in various historical jls. *Recreations:* walking, writing. *Address:* 34 St Thomas Street, Wells, Somerset BA5 2UX.

ANDREWS, William Denys Cathcart, CBE 1980; WS; Partner, Shepherd & Wedderburn, WS, Edinburgh, 1962–91; *b* 3 June 1931; *s* of Eugene Andrews and Agnes Armstrong; *m* 1955, May O'Beirne; two *s* two *d*. *Educ:* Girvan High Sch.; Worksop Coll.; Edinburgh Univ. (BL). Served RASC, 1950–52. Law Society of Scotland: Mem. Council, 1972–81; Vice Pres., 1977–78; Pres., 1978–79. Examr in Conveyancing, Edinburgh Univ., 1974–77. Pt-time Mem., Lands Tribunal for Scotland, 1980–91. Fiscal to Soc. of Writers to HM Signet, 1987–91. *Recreation:* gardening. *Address:* Auchairne, Ballantrae, South Ayrshire KA26 0NX. *T:* (01465) 831344.

ANDRIESSEN, Prof. Frans, (Franciscus H. J. J.), Kt, Order of Dutch Lion; Grand Cross, Order of Orange-Nassau; LLD; Member, 1981–92, Vice-President, 1985–92, the European Commission (responsible for external relations); *b* Utrecht, 2 April 1929; *m*; four *c*. *Educ:* Univ. of Utrecht (LLD). Served at Catholic Housing Institute, latterly as Director, 1954–72. Member: Provincial States of Utrecht, 1958–67; Lower House of the States-General (Netherlands Parliament), initially as specialist in housing matters, 1967–77; Chairman, KVP party in Lower House, 1971–77; Minister of Finance, Netherlands, 1977–80; Member, Upper House of States-General (Senate), 1980. Prof. of European Integration, Rijksuniversiteit, Utrecht, 1989–99, now Emeritus. Grand Cross: Order of Leopold II (Belgium); Order of Isabel the Catholic (Spain); Order of Merit (Austria); Order of the Falcon (Iceland); Order of the Finnish Lion (Finland). *Address:* H. Vaesgaarde 1, 1950 Kraainem, Belgium.

ANDRUS, Francis Sedley, LVO 1982; Beaumont Herald of Arms Extraordinary, since 1982; *b* 26 Feb. 1915; *o s* of late Brig.-Gen. Thomas Alchin Andrus, CMG, JP, and Alice Loveday (*née* Parr); unmarried. *Educ:* Wellington Coll.; St Peter's Hall (now Coll.), Oxford (MA). Entered College of Arms as Member of Staff, 1938; Bluemantle Pursuivant of Arms, 1970–72; Lancaster Herald of Arms, 1972–82. Freeman, City of London, 1988. Lord of the Manor of Southfleet, Kent, 1952–. *Address:* 8 Oakwood Rise, Longfield, Kent DA3 7PA. *T:* (01474) 705424.

ANELAY OF ST JOHNS, Baroness *cr* 1996 (Life Peer), of St Johns in the county of Surrey; **Joyce Anne Anelay,** DBE 1995 (OBE 1990); JP; *b* 17 July 1947; *d* of late Stanley Charles Clarke and of Annette Marjorie Clarke; *m* 1970, Richard Alfred Anelay, *qv*. *Educ:* Merryhills Primary Sch., Enfield; Enfield Co. Sch.; Bristol Univ. (BA Hons Hist.); London Univ. Inst. of Educn (Cert Ed); Brunel Univ. (MA Public and Social Admin). Teacher, St

David's Sch., Ashford, Middx, 1969–74; Voluntary Advr, Woking CAB, 1976–85 (Chm., 1988–93; Pres., 1996–). Member: Social Security Appeal Tribunal, 1983–96; Social Security Adv. Cttee for GB and NI, 1989–96. Opposition spokesman on agriculture, 1997–98, on culture, media and sport, 1998–; an Opposition Whip, H of L, 1997–98. Mem., Procedure Cttee, 1997–2000. Conservative Women's Committee: Chm., SE Area, 1987–90; Vice-Chm., SE Area Exec. Cttee, 1990–93; Chm., Nat. Cttee, 1993–96; Member: Nat. Union of Cons. Party, 1987–97 (Vice-Pres., 1996–97); Women's Nat. Commission, 1990–93; Disability Partnership Funding Council, 2000–. Patron: Restaurant Assoc. of GB, 2000–; Tourism for All Consortium, 2000–. JP NW Surrey, 1985–97. Chm. Govs, Hermitage First and Middle Schs, 1981–88. FRSA 1991. Hon. DSocSc Brunel, 1997. *Recreations:* golf, reading. *Address:* House of Lords, SW1A 0PW. *Club:* Woking Golf.

ANELAY, Richard Alfred; QC 1993; a Recorder, since 1992; a Deputy High Court Judge, Family Division, since 1995; *b* 26 March 1946; *s* of late Maurice Alfred Anelay and of Bertha Anelay; *m* 1970, Joyce Anne Clarke (*see* Baroness Anelay of St Johns). *Educ:* Dodmire Primary Sch., Darlington; Queen Elizabeth Grammar Sch., Darlington; Bristol Univ. (BA Classics and Philosophy); Council of Legal Educn. Called to the Bar, Middle Temple, 1970; Asst Recorder, 1987. Consulting Ed, Encyclopedia of Financial Provision in Family Matters, 1998–. *Recreation:* golf. *Address:* 1 King's Bench Walk, Temple, EC4Y 7DB. *T:* (020) 7936 1500. *Club:* Woking Golf.

ANFOM, Emmanuel E.; *see* Evans-Anfom.

ANGEL, Anthony Lionel; Managing Partner, Linklaters, Solicitors, since 1998; *b* 3 Dec. 1952; *s* of William and Frances Angel; *m* 1975, Ruth Hartog; two *s*. *Educ:* Haberdashers' Aske's Sch., Elstree; Queens' Coll., Cambridge (MA). Admitted Solicitor, 1978. Linklaters: Articled Clerk, 1976; Partner, 1984–; Head of Tax, 1994–98. *Recreations:* skiing, tennis, theatre. *Address:* (office) One Silk Street, EC2Y 8HQ. *T:* (020) 7456 5636.

ANGEL, Gerald Bernard Nathaniel Aylmer; Senior District Judge, Family Division of the High Court, since 1991 (Registrar, 1980–90; District Judge, 1991); *b* 4 Nov. 1937; *s* of late Bernard Francis and Ethel Angel; *m* 1968, Lesley Susan Kemp; three *s* one *d* (and one *s* decd). *Educ:* St Mary's Sch., Nairobi. Served Kenya Regt, 1956–57. Called to Bar, Inner Temple, 1959, Bencher 1992; Advocate, Kenya, 1960–62; practice at Bar, 1962–80. Member: Judicial Studies Bd, 1989–90 (Mem., Civil and Family Cttee, 1985–90); Supreme Ct Procedure Cttee, 1990–95; Matrimonial Causes Rule Cttee, 1991; Family Proceedings Rule Cttee, 1991–. *Publications:* (ed) Industrial Tribunals Reports, 1966–78; (contrib.) Atkin's Court Forms (Adv. Editor), 1988. *Recreations:* reading, walking. *Address:* c/o Principal Registry of the Family Division, 42–49 High Holborn, WC1V 6NP. *T:* (020) 7947 6934.

ANGEL, Heather, FRPS, FBIPP; professional wildlife photographer, author and lecturer; *b* 21 July 1941; *d* of Stanley Paul Le Rougetel and Hazel Marie Le Rougetel (*née* Sherwood); *m* 1964, Martin Vivian Angel; one *s*. *Educ:* 14 schools in England and NZ; Bristol Univ. (BSc Hons (Zoology) 1962; MSc 1965). FRPS 1972; FBIPP 1974. One-man Exhibitions: The Natural History of Britain and Ireland, Sci. Mus., 1981; Nature in Focus, Natural Hist. Mus., 1987; The Art of Wildlife Photography, Gloucester, 1989; Natural Visions, UK tour, 2000–01. Television: demonstrating photographic techniques, Me and My Camera I, 1981; Me and My Camera II, 1983; Gardener's World, 1983; Nature, 1984; Nocon on Photography, 1988. Led British Photographic Delegn to China, 1985. Photos used worldwide in books, magazines, on TV, advertising, etc, 1972–. Special Prof., Dept of Life Sci., Nottingham Univ., 1994–. Hon. FRPS 1986 (Pres., 1984–86). Hon. DSc Bath, 1986. Hood Medal, RPS, 1975; Médaille de Salverte, Soc. Française de Photographie, 1984; Louis Schmidt Award, Biocommunications Assoc., 1998. *Publications:* Nature Photography: its art and techniques, 1972; All Colour Book of Ocean Life, 1975; Photographing Nature: Trees, 1975, Insects, 1975, Seashore, 1975, Flowers, 1975, Fungi, 1975; Seashore Life on Rocky Shores, 1975; Seashore Life on Sandy Beaches, 1975; Seashells of the Seashore, 1976; Wild Animals in the Garden, 1976; Life in the Oceans, 1977; Life in our Estuaries, 1977; Life in our Rivers, 1977; British Wild Orchids, 1977; The Countryside of the New Forest, 1977; The Countryside of South Wales, 1977; Seaweeds of the Seashore, 1977; Seashells of the Seashore, Book 1, 1978, Book 2, 1978; The Countryside of Devon, 1980; The Guinness Book of Seashore Life, 1981; The Natural History of Britain and Ireland, 1981; The Family Water Naturalist, 1982; The Book of Nature Photography, 1982; The Book of Close-up Photography, 1983; Heather Angel's Countryside, 1983; A Camera in the Garden, 1984; Close-up Photography, 1986; Kodak Calendar, The Thames, 1987; A View from a Window, 1988; Nature in Focus, 1988; Landscape Photography, 1989; Animal Photography, 1991; Kew: a world of plants, 1993; Photographing the Natural World, 1994; Outdoor Photography: 101 tips and hints, 1997; How to Photograph Flowers, 1998; Pandas, 1998; How to Photograph Water, 1999; Natural Visions, 2000; *for children:* Your Book of Fishes, 1972; The World of an Estuary, 1975; Fact Finder—Seashore, 1976; The World of a Stream, 1976; Fungi, 1979; Lichens, 1980; Mosses and Ferns, 1980. *Recreation:* travelling to remote parts of the world to photograph wilderness areas and unusual aspects of animal behaviour. *Address:* Highways, 6 Vicarage Hill, Farnham, Surrey GU9 8HJ. *T:* (01252) 716700, *Fax:* (01252) 727464.

ANGEL, Prof. James Roger Prior, FRS 1990; FRAS; Regents Professor of Astronomy, since 1990, Director, Steward Observatory Mirror Laboratory, since 1985, and Director, Center for Astronomical Adaptative Optics, since 1996, University of Arizona; *b* 7 Feb. 1941; *s* of James Lee Angel and Joan Angel; *m* 1965, Ellinor M. Goonan; one *s* one *d*. *Educ:* St Peter's Coll., Oxford (Hon. Schol.; BA 1963; Hon. Fellow, 1993); Calif. Inst. of Technology (MS 1966); DPhil Oxon 1967. FRAS 1993. Post Doctoral Assistant, then Asst Prof., later Associate Prof. of Physics, Columbia Univ., 1967–72; Alfred P. Sloan Res. Fellow, 1970–74; Associate Prof. and Prof. of Astronomy, Arizona Univ., 1973–90. MacArthur Fellow, John D. and Catherine T. MacArthur Foundn, 1996–2001. Vice-Pres., Amer. Astronomical Soc., 1987–90 (Pierce Prize, 1976); Fellow, Amer. Acad. of Arts and Scis, 1990. MNAS 2000. *Publications:* numerous papers on white dwarfs stars, quasars, the search for extra-solar planetary systems, astronomical mirrors, telescopes and their instruments, and adaptive optics. *Recreation:* planting trees. *Address:* Steward Observatory, University of Arizona, Tucson, AZ 85721–0065, USA. *T:* (520) 6216541.

ANGELES, Victoria de los; *see* de los Angeles.

ANGELL-JAMES, John, CBE 1967; MD, FRCP, FRCS; Hon. Consulting Surgeon in Otolaryngology, United Bristol Hospitals, 1966–87; *b* 23 Aug. 1901; *s* of Dr John Angell James, MRCS, LRCP and Emily Cornell (*née* Ashwin), Bristol; *m* 1930, Evelyn Miriam Everard (*d* 1998), *d* of Francis Over and Ada Miriam Everard, Birmingham; one *s* two *d*. *Educ:* Bristol Grammar Sch.; Univ. of Bristol; London Hosp.; Guy's Hosp. MB ChB 1st Cl. Hons 1924, Bristol; MBBS London (Hons) 1924; MD 1927; FRCS 1928; FRCP 1965. Res. appts, 1924–28, Bristol and London; Hon. ENT Registrar, Bristol Royal Infirmary, 1928–29; Hon. ENT Surg., Bristol Children's Hosp., 1928–48; Cons. ENT Surg., 1948–66; Hon. Asst ENT Surg., later Hon. ENT Surg., Bristol Royal Infirmary, 1929–48; Clin. Tutor, Univ. of Bristol, 1928–55, Lectr and Head of Dept of Otolaryngology, 1955–66; Cons. ENT Surg., United Bristol Hosps, 1948–66. Lt-Col RAMC, 1942–46; Adviser in Otorhinolaryngol., MEF, 1945. Hunterian Prof., RCS, 1962; Semon Lectr in Laryngol., Univ. of London, 1965; James Yearsley Lectr, 1966; Sir William Wilde Meml Lectr, Irish Otolaryngol. Soc., 1966; Vis. Lectr, Univs of Toronto, Vermont, Cornell, Baylor, Chicago and Johns Hopkins Hosp. Royal Soc. of Medicine: Former Fellow, Hon. FRSocMed 1976; Hon. Mem., Sections of Laryngol. (Pres., 1955) and otology. Member: SW Laryngolog. Assoc. (Chm. 1956); Brit. Medical Assoc. (Pres. Sect. of Otolaryngol., 1959; Chm. Bristol Div., 1966–67; Pres., Bath, Bristol and Som Br., 1968–69); Bristol Med.-Chirurg. Soc. (Pres. 1961); Visiting Assoc. of ENT Surgs of GB, 1948 (Pres. 1965–66); Brit. Assoc. of Otolaryngologists, 1942 (Pres. 1966–69); Collegium Oto-Rhino-Laryngologicum Amicitiae Sacrum, 1948 (Councillor, 1966–74; Pres., 1974); Barany Soc.; Pres., Otolaryngological Res. Soc., 1978. Extern. Examr, Univ. of Manchester, 1964. Hon. Member: Irish Otolaryngol. Soc.; S Africa Soc. of Otolaryngol.; Corresp. Mem., Deutsche Gesellschaft für Hals-Nasen-Ohren-Heilkunde Kopf-und Hals-Chirurgie. Hon. FRCSE 1971; Jobson Horne Prize, BMA, 1962; Colles Medal, RCSI, 1963; Dalby Prize, RSM, 1963; W. J. Harrison Prize in Laryngology, RSM, 1968. President: Gloucester Soc., 1977; Colston Soc., 1983–84. Chm. Editorial Cttee, Clinical Otolaryngology. *Publications:* Chapters in: British Surgical Practice, 1951; Diseases of the Ear, Nose and Throat, 1952 (2nd edn 1966); Ultrasound as a diagnostic and surgical tool, 1964; Clinical Surgery, 1966; Ménière's Disease, 1969; Family Medical Guide, 1980; articles in learned jls in Eng., USA, Canada, Germany and Sweden. *Recreations:* farming; shooting. *Address:* The Leaze, Sundayshill Lane, Falfield, Wotton-under-Edge, Glos GL12 8DQ.

ANGELOU, Marguerite Annie, (Maya); writer, singer and actress; *b* St Louis, 4 April 1928; *d* of Bailey Johnson and Vivian Baxter Johnson; one *s*. *Educ:* George Washington High Sch., San Francisco; California Labor Sch. Yale Univ. Fellowship, 1970; Rockefeller Foundn Scholar, 1975; Reynolds Prof. of Amer. Studies, Wake Forest Univ., 1981–. Writer, director, or actor: *stage:* Cabaret for Freedom, 1960; Medea, 1966; The Least of These, 1966; Gettin' Up Stayed On My Mind, 1967; Ajax, 1974; And Still I Rise, 1976; Look Away, 1975; Moon and Rainbow Shawl, 1988; *films:* Georgia, Georgia, 1972; All Day Long, 1974; Poetic Justice, 1993; How to Make an American Quilt, 1996; *television:* Black, Blue, Black, 1968; Roots, 1977; Sister, Sister, 1982. Awards include: Amer. Revolution Bicentennial, 1975; Woman of the Year in Communications, 1976; Horatio Alger, 1992. *Publications: autobiography:* I Know Why the Caged Bird Sings, 1970 (televised, 1979); Gather Together in My Name, 1974; Singin' and Swingin' and Gettin' Merry Like Christmas, 1976; The Heart of a Woman, 1981; All God's Children Need Travelling Shoes, 1986; Wouldn't Take Nothing for my Journey Now, 1993; (jtly) My Painted House, My Friendly Chicken and Me, 1994; *essays:* Lessons in Life, 1993; *poetry:* Just Give Me a Cool Drink of Water 'Fore I Diiie, 1971; Oh Pray My Wings are Gonna Fit Me Well, 1975; Shaker, Why Don't You Sing?, 1983; Now Sheba Sings the Song, 1987; I shall not be Moved, 1990; On the Pulse of Morning, 1993 (delivered personally at Presidential Inauguration); Complete Collected Poems of Maya Angelou, 1995; *fiction:* Even the Stars Look Lonesome, 1998; *short stories:* All Day Long. *Address:* c/o Dave La Camera Lordly and Dame Inc., 51 Church Street, Boston, MA 02116, USA.

ANGLESEY, 7th Marquess of, *cr* 1815; **George Charles Henry Victor Paget;** Baron Paget, of Beau Desert, 1549; Earl of Uxbridge, 1784; Bt 1730; Lord-Lieutenant of Gwynedd, 1983–89; *b* 8 Oct. 1922; *o s* of 6th Marquess of Anglesey, GCVO, and Lady Victoria Marjorie Harriet Manners (*d* 1946), *d* of 8th Duke of Rutland; *S* father, 1947; *m* 1948, Elizabeth Shirley Vaughan Morgan (*see* Marchioness of Anglesey); two *s* three *d*. *Educ:* Wixenford, Wokingham; Eton Coll. Major, RHG, 1946. Div. Dir, Wales, Nationwide Building Soc., 1973–89. President: Anglesey Conservative Assoc., 1948–83; Nat. Museum of Wales, 1962–68; Friends of Friendless Churches, 1966–84; Ancient Monuments Soc., 1979–84. Treasurer, Danilo Dolci Trust (Britain), 1964–86. Vice-Chm., Welsh Cttee, Nat. Trust, 1975–85; Member: Historic Buildings Council for Wales, 1953–92 (Chm., 1977–92); Royal Fine Art Commn, 1965–71; Redundant Churches Fund, 1969–78; Royal Commn on Historical Manuscripts, 1984–92; Council, Soc. of Army Historical Research; Trustee: Nat. Portrait Gall., 1979–91; Nat. Heritage Memorial Fund, 1980–92. Hon. Prof., UCW, 1986. FSA 1952; FRSL 1969; Hon. FRIBA, 1971; FRHistS, 1975. Anglesey: CC, 1951–67; JP, 1959–68, 1983–89; DL, 1960, Vice-Lieut, 1960. Hon. Fellow, Royal Cambrian Acad. Freeman of the City of London. Hon. DLitt Wales, 1984. CStJ 1984. *Publications:* (ed) The Capel Letters, 1814–1817, 1955; One-Leg: the Life and Letters of 1st Marquess of Anglesey, 1961, repr. 1996; (ed) Sergeant Pearman's Memoirs, 1968; (ed) Little Hodge, 1971; A History of the British Cavalry 1816–1919 (Chesney Gold Medal, RUSI, 1997): vol. I, 1816–1850, 1973; vol. II, 1851–1871, 1975; vol. III, 1872–1898, 1982 (Templer Medal, Nat. Army Mus., 1982); vol. IV, 1899–1913, 1986; vol. V, 1914–1919: Egypt, Palestine and Syria, 1995; vol. VI, 1914–1918: Mesopotamia, 1996; vol. VII, 1914: The Curragh Incident and the Western Front, 1996; vol. VIII, The Western Front, 1915–1918, and Epilogue, 1919–1939, 1997. *Recreations:* gardening, music. *Heir:* *s* Earl of Uxbridge, *qv*. *Address:* Plâs-Newydd, Llanfairpwll, Anglesey LL61 6DZ. *T:* (01248) 714330.

ANGLESEY, Marchioness of; (Elizabeth) Shirley Vaughan Paget, DBE 1983 (CBE 1977); LVO 1993; Member of Board, British Council, 1985–95 (Chairman, Drama and Dance Advisory Committee, 1981–91); Vice-Chairman, Museums and Galleries Commission, 1989–96 (Member, 1981–96); *b* 4 Dec. 1924; *d* of late Charles Morgan and Hilda Vaughan (both novelists); *m* 1948, Marquess of Anglesey, *qv*; two *s* three *d*. *Educ:* Francis Holland Sch., London; St James', West Malvern; Kent Place Sch., USA. Personal Secretary to Gladwyn Jebb, FO, until marriage. Chm., Broadcasting Complaints Commn, 1987–91. Dep. Chm., Prince of Wales Cttee, 1970–80. Member: Civic Trust for Wales, 1967–76; Arts Council, 1972–81 (Chm., Welsh Arts Council, 1975–81); Royal Commn on Environmental Pollution, 1973–79; IBA, 1976–82; Radioactive Waste Management Adv. Cttee, 1981–92; Vice-Chm., Govt Working Party on Methods of Sewage Disposal, 1969–70. Chm., NFWI, 1966–69. A Vice-Pres., C&G, 1998–. Mem., Theatres Trust, 1992–95. Trustee, Pilgrim Trust, 1982–. Hon. Fellow, UCNW, Bangor, 1990. Hon. LLD Wales, 1977. *Address:* Plâs-Newydd, Llanfairpwll, Gwynedd LL61 6DZ. *T:* (01248) 714330.

See also R. H. V. C. Morgan.

ANGLIN, Prof. Douglas (George); Professor of Political Science, Carleton University, Ottawa, Canada, 1958–89, Adjunct Professor, 1989–93, now Professor Emeritus; *b* Toronto, Canada, 16 Dec. 1923; *s* of George Chambers Anglin, MD, and Ruth Cecilia Cale, MD; *m* 1948, Mary Elizabeth Watson; two *d*. *Educ:* Toronto Univ.; Corpus Christi and Nuffield Colls, Oxford Univ. BA Toronto; MA, DPhil Oxon. Lieut, RCNVR, 1943–45. Asst (later Associate) Prof. of Polit. Sci. and Internat. Relations, Univ. of Manitoba, Winnipeg, 1951–58; Associate Prof. (later Prof.), Carleton Univ., 1958–89. Vice-Chancellor, Univ. of Zambia, Lusaka, Zambia, 1965–69; Associate Research Fellow, Nigerian Inst. of Social and Economic Research, Univ. of Ibadan, Ibadan, Nigeria, 1962–63; Research Associate, Center of Internat. Studies, Princeton Univ., 1969–70. Pres., Canadian Assoc. of African Studies, 1973–74. Consultant, Educn for Democracy

Prog., South African Council of Churches, Johannesburg, 1992–94. *Publications:* The St Pierre and Miquelon Affairs of 1941: a study in diplomacy in the North Atlantic quadrangle, 1966, repr. 1999; Zambia's Foreign Policy: studies in diplomacy and dependence, 1979; Zambian Crisis Behaviour: confronting Rhodesia's unilateral declaration of independence 1965–1966, 1994; edited jointly: Africa: Problems and Prospects 1961; Conflict and Change in Southern Africa, 1978; Canada, Scandinavia and Southern Africa, 1978; articles on Internat. and African affairs in a variety of learned jls. *Address:* Carleton University, Colonel By Drive, Ottawa, Ontario K1S 5B6, Canada.

ANGLO, Margaret Mary, (Mrs Sydney Anglo); *see* McGowan, M. M.

ANGUS, Rev. (James Alexander) Keith, LVO 1990; TD; Minister of Braemar and Crathie Parish Churches, 1979–95; an Extra Chaplain to the Queen, since 1996 (Domestic Chaplain, 1979–96); *b* 16 April 1929; *s* of late Rev. Walter C. S. Angus and late Margaret I. Stephen; *m* 1956, Alison Jane Daly; one *s* one *d.* *Educ:* High School of Dundee; Univ. of St Andrews (MA). National Service, Army, 1947–49; served with TA, 1950–76; Captain RA (TA), 1955; Chaplain to 5, KOSB (TA), 1957–67, to 154 Regt, RCT (V), 1967–76. Assistant Minister, The Cathedral, Glasgow, 1955–56; Minister: Hoddam Parish Church, 1956–67; Gourock Old Parish Church, 1967–79. Convener, Gen. Assembly's Cttee on Chaplains to HM Forces, 1981–85. *Recreations:* fishing, hill walking, golf. *Address:* Darroch Den, Hawthorn Place, Ballater, AB35 5QH. *T:* (01339) 756260. *Club:* New (Edinburgh).

ANGUS, Sir Michael (Richardson), Kt 1990; DL; Chairman, Whitbread PLC, 1992–2000 (Director, 1986–2000; Deputy Chairman, 1992); Deputy Chairman, The Boots Company PLC, 1998–2000 (Chairman, 1994–98); *b* 5 May 1930; *s* of William Richardson Angus and Doris Margaret Breach; *m* 1952, Eileen Isabel May Elliott; two *s* one *d.* *Educ:* Marling Sch., Stroud, Glos; Bristol Univ. (BSc Hons; Hon. Fellow, 1998). CIMgt (CBIM 1979). Served RAF, 1951–54. Unilever, 1954–92: Marketing Dir, Thibaud Gibbs, Paris, 1962–65; Man. Dir, Res. Bureau, 1965–67; Sales Dir, Lever Brothers UK, 1967–70; Toilet Preparations Co-ordinator, 1970–76; Chemicals Co-ordinator, 1976–80; Regional Dir, N America, 1979–84; Chairman and Chief Exec. Officer: Unilever United States, Inc., New York, 1980–84; Lever Brothers Co., New York, 1980–84; Chm., Unilever PLC, 1986–92 (Dir, 1970–92; Vice Chm., 1984–86); Vice Chm., Unilever NV, 1986–92 (Dir, 1970–92). Dir, Nat. Westminster Bank, 1991–2000 (a Dep. Chm., 1991–94); Chm., RAC Holdings Ltd, 1999; Jt Dep. Chm., 1989–93, Dep. Chm., 1993–2000, British Airways (Dir, 1988–2000); non-executive Director: Thorn EMI plc, 1988–93; Halcrow Gp Ltd, 2000–. Jt Chm., Netherlands-British Chamber of Commerce, 1984–89; Internat. Counsellor, The Conference Board, 1984–96, Emeritus, 1996. Pres., CBI, 1992–94 (Dep. Pres., 1991–92, 1994–95). Vis. Fellow, Nuffield Coll., Oxford, 1986–92. Dir, Ditchley Foundn, 1994–. Trustee, Leverhulme Trust, 1984– (Chm. Trustees, 1999–). Chairman of Governors: Ashridge Management Coll., 1991– (Governor, 1974–); RAC, Cirencester, 1992–; Mem. Court of Govs, LSE, 1985–95. DL Gloucestershire, 1997. Hon. DSc: Bristol, 1990; Buckingham, 1994; Hon. LLD Nottingham, 1996. Holland Trade Award, 1990. Comdr, Order of Oranje-Nassau (Netherlands), 1992. *Recreations:* countryside, wine, mathematical puzzles. *Address:* Cerney House, North Cerney, Cirencester, Glos GL7 7BX. *Clubs:* Athenæum, Brooks's; University (New York).

ANGUS, Robert James Campbell; Social Security and Child Support Commissioner, since 1995; *b* 7 Feb. 1935; *s* of James Angus and Jessie Macrae Angus; *m* 1968, Jean Anne Martin. *Educ:* Shawlands Acad.; Univ. of Glasgow (BL 1957). Nat. service, RA, 1958–60. Admitted solicitor, Scotland, 1960; in private practice, 1960–71; Legal Asst, Office of Solicitor to Sec. of State for Scotland, 1972–74, Sen. Legal Asst, 1974; on secondment as Administrator, SHHD, 1974–78; Solicitor's Office, 1978–82; Inquiry Reporter, Scottish Office, 1982–84; Chairman: Social Security, Medical and Vaccine Damage Appeal Tribunals, 1984–95; Child Support Appeal Tribunals, 1992–95. *Recreations:* history, music, history and mechanics of pianos, rough gardening. *Address:* Office of the Social Security and Child Support Commissioners, Harp House, 83 Farringdon Street, EC4A 4DH. *T:* (020) 7353 5145. *Club:* Glasgow Art (Glasgow).

ANNALY, 6th Baron *cr* 1863; **Luke Richard White;** a Lord in Waiting (Government Whip), 1994; *b* 29 June 1954; *o s* of 5th Baron Annaly and Lady Marye Isabel Pepys (*d* 1958), *d* of 7th Earl of Cottenham; *S* father, 1990; *m* 1983, Caroline Nina, *yr d* of Col Robert Garnett, MBE; one *s* three *d.* *Educ:* Eton; RMA Sandhurst. Commnd Royal Hussars, 1974–78, RARO, 1978–86. Freeman, Haberdashers' Co., 1997. *Heir: s* Hon. Luke Henry White, *b* 20 Sept. 1990.

ANNAN, Kofi Atta; Secretary-General, United Nations, since 1997; *b* 1938; *m*; one *s* two *d.* *Educ:* Univ. of Sci. and Technol., Kumasi, Ghana; Macalester Coll., St Paul, Minnesota, USA; Institut des Hautes Etudes Internationales, Geneva, Switzerland; MIT (Alfred P. Sloan Fellow, 1971–72). Various posts in UN, Addis Ababa and NY, and WHO, Geneva, 1962–71; Admin. Officer, UN, Geneva, 1972–74; Chief Civilian Personnel Officer, UNEF, Cairo, 1974; Man. Dir, Ghana Tourist Develt Co., 1974–76; Dep. Chief of Staff Services, 1976–80, Dep. Dir, Div. of Admin and Hd, Personnel Service, 1980–83, UNHCR, Geneva; UN, New York: Dir of Admin Mgt Services, then of Budget, 1984–87; Asst Sec.-Gen., Human Resources Mgt, 1987–90; Controller, Programme Planning, Budget and Finance, 1990–92; Under Sec.-Gen., 1993–95, Dept of Peace Keeping Ops; UN Special Envoy to former Yugoslavia, 1995–96. *Address:* United Nations, United Nations Plaza, New York, NY 10017, USA.

ANNAND, John Angus; Under Secretary, Welsh Office, 1975–85; *b* 13 May 1926; *s* of James Annand and Lilias Annand (*née* Smith); *m* 1971, Julia Dawn Hardman (marr. diss. 1986). *Educ:* Hillhead High Sch., Glasgow; Glasgow Univ. (MA, 1st Cl. Hons); Brasenose Coll., Oxford (MLitt). Lecturer: Univ. of Ceylon; Univ. of South Australia, 1951–53; Asst Dir, Civil Service Commn, 1953–57; Principal, 1957, Asst Sec., 1967, HM Treasury; Civil Service Dept, 1968; Welsh Office, 1971; Under Sec., Health and Social Work Dept, Welsh Office, 1975; Economic Policy Gp, 1978. Mem., GMC, 1986–90. *Address:* 21 Fairwater Road, Llandaff, Cardiff CF5 2LD.

ANNAND, Richard Wallace, VC 1940; ERD; DL; Personnel Officer at Finchale Abbey Training Centre for the Disabled, near Durham, 1948–79; late Captain Durham Light Infantry (RARO); *b* 5 Nov. 1914; *s* of Lt-Comdr Wallace Moir Annand, Royal Naval Division (killed Gallipoli 1915), and late Dora Elizabeth Chapman, South Shields; *m* 1940, Shirley Osborne, MBE 1978; JP 1957. *Educ:* Pocklington Sch., East Yorks. Staff of National Provincial Bank, 1933–37; commissioned in RNVR 1933 (Tyne and London Divisions), Midshipman, 1933, Sub-Lieut, 1936; transferred to Durham Light Infantry, Jan. 1938; served in France and Belgium, 1939–40 (wounded, VC (first Army VC of 2nd World War)). Invalided (severe deafness), Dec. 1948. Col in Chief, Europ. Legion of Frontiersmen. President: Durham and Cleveland Cos Br., Royal British Legion, 1992–97; N Eastern League of Hard of Hearing; Durham Co. Br., Normandy Veterans; Durham City Br., DLI Assoc.; St James's Art Soc. for Deafened, 1948–; Past Pres., Newcastle and Gateshead Br., Dunkirk Veterans' Assoc.; Founder Member: British Assoc. of Hard of Hearing, 1946; Durham Co. Assoc. for Disabled, 1956. Hon. Freeman Co. Borough of South Shields, 1940. DL Co. of Durham, 1956. *Recreation:* golf. *Address:* Springwell House, Whitesmocks, Durham DH1 4LL. *Clubs:* Royal Over-Seas League; County (Durham).

ANNANDALE AND HARTFELL, 11th Earl of, *cr* 1662 (S) with precedence to 1643; **Patrick Andrew Wentworth Hope Johnstone of Annandale and of that Ilk;** Earl of the territorial earldom of Annandale and Hartfell, and of the Lordship of Johnstone; Hereditary Steward of the Stewartry of Annandale; Hereditary Keeper of the Castle of Lochmaben; Chief of the Name and Arms of Johnstone; landowner; Vice-Lord Lieutenant, Dumfries and Galloway Region, districts of Nithsdale, Annandale and Eskdale, since 1992; *b* 19 April 1941; *s* of Major Percy Wentworth Hope Johnstone of Annandale and of that Ilk, TD (*d* 1983) (*de jure* 10th Earl) and Margaret Jane (*d* 1998), *d* of Herbert William Francis Hunter-Arundell; claim to earldom admitted by Committee for Privileges, House of Lords, 1985; *m* 1969, Susan Josephine, *d* of late Col Walter John Macdonald Ross, CB, OBE, MC, TD, Netherhall, Castle Douglas; one *s* one *d.* *Educ:* Stowe School; RAC, Cirencester. Member: Dumfries CC, 1970–75; Dumfries and Galloway Regional Council, 1974–86; Scottish Valuation Advisory Council, 1983–85. Director: Bowring Members Agency, 1985–88; Murray Lawrence Members Agency, 1988–92; Solway River Purification Bd, 1970–86; Chm., Royal Jubilee and Prince's Trusts for Dumfries and Galloway, 1984–88. Underwriting Member of Lloyds, 1976–. DL Nithsdale and Annandale and Eskdale, 1987. *Recreations:* golf, shooting. *Heir: s* Lord Johnstone, *qv.* *Address:* Annadale Estates Office, St Ann's, Lockerbie, Dumfriesshire DG11 1HQ. *Clubs:* Brooks's; Puffin's (Edinburgh).

ANNENBERG, Walter H., KBE (Hon.) 1976; US Ambassador to the Court of St James's, 1969–74; *b* 13 March 1908; *s* of M. L. Annenberg; *m* 1951, Leonore Cohn; one *d.* *Educ:* Peddie Sch.; Univ. of Pennsylvania. President 1940, and former Chm., Triangle Publications Inc., Philadelphia, Pa; former Publisher: Seventeen Magazine; TV Guide; Daily Racing Form. Dir, New American Schools Develt Corp. Hon. Chm., Bd of Trustees, Eisenhower Med. Center. Hon. Bencher, Middle Temple, 1969; Hon. Old Etonian, 1990; Trustee, Winston Churchill Traveling Fellowships. Medal of Freedom, 1986; holds foreign decorations. *Address:* Llanfair Road, Wynnewood, PA 19096, USA; Suite A200, St David's Center, 150 Radnor-Chester Road, St Davids, PA 19087, USA. *Clubs:* White's; Racquet (Philadelphia); Lyford Cay (Bahamas); Swinley Forest Golf.

ANNESLEY, family name of **Earl Annesley** and **Viscount Valentia**.

ANNESLEY, 10th Earl *cr* 1789; **Patrick Annesley;** Baron Annesley, 1758; Viscount Glerawly, 1766; *b* 12 August 1924; *e s* of 9th Earl Annesley, and of Nora, *y d* of late Walter Harrison; *S* father, 1979; *m* 1947, Catherine, *d* of John Burgess, Edinburgh; four *d.* *Heir: b* Hon. Philip Harrison Annesley [*b* 29 March 1927; *m* 1951, Florence Eileen (*d* 1995), *o d* of late John Arthur Johnston].

ANNESLEY, Sir Hugh (Norman), Kt 1992; QPM 1986; Chief Constable, Royal Ulster Constabulary, 1989–96; *b* 22 June 1939; *s* of late William Henry Annesley and of Agnes Annesley (*née* Redmond); *m* 1970, Elizabeth Ann (*née* MacPherson); one *s* one *d.* *Educ:* St Andrew's Prep. Sch., Dublin; Avoca Sch. for Boys, Blackrock. Joined Metropolitan Police, 1958; Chief Supt, 1974; Police Staff College: Special Course, 1963; Intermed. Command Course, 1971; Sen. Command Course, 1975; Asst Chief Constable, Personnel and Ops, Sussex Police, 1976; RCDS 1980; Metropolitan Police, Deputy Assistant Commissioner: Central and NW London, 1981; Personnel, 1983; Dir, Force Re-organisation Team, 1984; Assistant Commissioner: Personnel and Training, 1985; Specialist Ops, 1987. Graduate: Nat. Exec. Inst., FBI, 1986; Mem. Exec. Cttee, Interpol (British Rep.), 1987–90, and 1993–94. Bd of Govs, Burgess Hill Sch. for Girls, 1997 (Chm. Govs, 2000–). *Recreations:* hockey, sailing. *Address:* c/o Brooklyn, Knock Road, Belfast BT5 6LE.

ANNETT, David Maurice, MA; Headmaster of King's School, Worcester, 1959–79; *b* 27 April 1917; *s* of late M. W. Annett and Marguerite, *d* of Rev. W. M. Hobson; *m* 1953, Evelyn Rosemary (*d* 1996), *d* of late W. M. Gordon, Headmaster of Wrekin Coll., and *widow* of R. E. Upcott; one *d* (one step-*s* two step-*d*). *Educ:* Haileybury Coll.; Queens' Coll., Cambridge. Head of Classical Dept at Oundle Sch., 1939–53, and Housemaster, 1948–53; Headmaster of Marling Sch., Stroud, 1953–59. Served with 27th Field Regt, RA, in India and Burma (Capt.), 1941–45. *Address:* St Christopher, Beauchamp, Newland, Malvern, Worcs WR13 5AX. *T:* (01684) 565392.

ANNING, Raymon Harry, CBE 1982; QPM 1975; Commissioner of Police, The Royal Hong Kong Police Force, 1985–90; *b* 22 July 1930; *s* of Frederick Charles Anning and Doris Mabel Anning (*née* Wakefield); *m* 1949, Beryl Joan Boxall; one *s* one *d.* *Educ:* Richmond and East Sheen Grammar School. Army (East Surrey Regt and Royal Military Police), 1948–50. Metropolitan Police, 1952–79: Constable to Chief Supt, Divisions and Headquarters, 1952–69; Officer i/c Anguilla Police Unit, W Indies, 1969; Chief Supt i/c Discipline Office, New Scotland Yard, 1970–72; Commander i/c A 10 (Complaints Investigation) Branch, NSY, 1972–75; seconded to Hong Kong Govt, 1974; Dep. Asst Commissioner C (CID) Dept, 1975–78; Inspector of Metropolitan Police (Dep. Asst Comr), 1979; HM Inspector of Constabulary for England and Wales, 1979–83; Dep. Comr of Police, Hong Kong, 1983–85. Graduate of Nat. Exec. Inst., FBI Academy, Quantico, Virginia, USA, 1979. *Recreation:* walking. *Clubs:* Royal Automobile; Hong Kong Golf.

ANNIS, David, MD; FRCS; Senior Research Fellow, University of Liverpool, since 1981 (Science and Engineering Research Council Senior Research Fellow, Institute of Medical and Dental Engineering, 1981–86); *b* 28 Feb. 1921; *s* of Harold and Gertrude Annis; *m* 1948, Nesta Roberts; three *s* one *d.* *Educ:* Manchester Grammar Sch.; Univ. of Liverpool. ChM 1953, MD 1959; FRCS 1946. Res. Fellow in Exptl Surgery, Mayo Clinic, Minn., 1949–51. Liverpool University: Sen. Lectr in Surgery, 1951–54; Dir of Studies, Surg. Sci., 1964–69; Dir, Bioengineering Unit, Dept of Surgery, 1969–85; Consultant Gen. Surgeon, Royal Liverpool Hosp., 1954–81. Member: Biomaterials Sub-Cttee, SRC, 1978–80; Physiolog. Systems and Disorders Bd, MRC, 1980–. Mem. Ct of Examrs, RCS, 1963–69; Examiner in Surgery, Univs of Leeds, Glasgow, Cardiff, Dundee, Liverpool and Lagos. Member, Editorial Committee: Bioengineering Jl, 1980–; British Jl of Surgery, 1965–80. *Publications:* contribs to: Wells and Kyle, Scientific Foundations of Surgery, 1967, 3rd edn 1982; Cuschieri, Moosa and Giles, Companion to Surgical Practice, 1982; papers on surgical and med. bioengrg subjects in learned jls. *Recreation:* countryside. *Address:* Little Hey, Dibbinsdale Road, Bromborough, Merseyside L63 0HQ. *T:* (0151) 334 3422.

ANNIS, Francesca; actress; *b* 1945. *Theatre:* Royal Shakespeare Company: Romeo and Juliet, 1976; Troilus and Cressida, 1976; Luciana in Comedy of Errors, 1976; Natalya in A Month in the Country, Nat. Theatre, 1981; Masha in Three Sisters, Albery, 1987; Melitta in Mrs Klein, NT, 1988; Rosmersholm, Young Vic, 1992; Lady Windermere's Fan, Albery, 1994; Hamlet, Hackney Empire, 1995; Ghosts, Comedy, 2001. *Films* include: Penny Gold, 1972; Macbeth, 1973; Krull, 1983; Dune, 1984; The Golden River;

Under the Cherry Moon; The Debt Collector, 1999. *Television:* A Pin to see the Peepshow, 1973; Madame Bovary, 1975; Stronger than the Sun, 1977; The Ragazza, 1978; Lillie (series), 1978; Partners in Crime (series), 1983; Inside Story (series), 1986; Parnell and the Englishwoman, Absolute Hell, 1991; The Gravy Train Goes East (series), 1991; Between the Lines (series), 1993; Reckless (series), 1997; Deadly Summer, 1997; Wives and Daughters, Milk, 1999; Deceit, 2000. *Address:* c/o ICM, 76 Oxford Street, W1N 0AX.

ANSARI, Gholamreza; Departmental Chief Executive, Ministry of Foreign Affairs, Iran, since 2001; *b* 22 Nov. 1955; *m* 1981, Shahin K. Shirazi; four *d. Educ:* Allameh Tabatabaee Univ., Tehran (BSc Physics). Ministry of Interior, 1980–88: Gov. Gen., Piranshar City, 1980–81; Dep. Gov. Gen., 1981–87, Supt of Governor Generalship, 1987–88, Azerbaijan Province; Dep. Dir, Foreign Nationals and Refugees Dept, 1987–88; Ministry of Foreign Affairs, 1988–: Dep. Dir, Europe Dept, 1988–90; Dir, W Europe Dept, 1990–92; Chargé d'Affaires, London, 1992–99; Ambassador to UK, 1999–2000. *Recreations:* reading, walking, jogging, swimming, listening to Iranian traditional music, spending time with the family. *Address:* Ministry of Foreign Affairs, Tehran, Iran.

ANSBRO, David Anthony; Managing Partner, Eversheds, since 2000; *b* 3 April 1945; *s* of late David T. Ansbro and of Kathleen Mary Ansbro (*née* Mallett); *m* 1967, Veronica Mary (*née* Auton); two *d. Educ:* Xaverian Coll., Manchester; Leeds Univ. (LLB Hons). Articled to Town Clerk, Leeds, 1966–69; admitted Solicitor, 1969; Solicitor, Leeds City Council, 1969–73; Asst Dir of Admin, 1973–77, Dep. Dir of Admin, 1977–81, W Yorks County Council; Town Clerk and Chief Exec., York City Council, 1981–85; Chief Exec., Kirklees Council, 1985–87; Rees & Co., Solicitors, Huddersfield, 1987–88; Chief Exec., Leeds City Council, 1988–91; Partner, Hepworth & Chadwick, then Eversheds, 1991–; Managing Partner, Eversheds, Leeds and Manchester, 1995–2000. Mem., Local Govt Commn for England, 1992–95. Dir, Leeds TEC, 1990–99. Pro-Chancellor, Leeds Univ., 2000–. Papal Medal Pro Ecclesia et Pontifice, 1982. *Recreations:* family, friends, golf, watching Manchester City. *Address:* (office) Cloth Hall Court, Infirmary Street, Leeds LS1 2JB. *T:* (0113) 243 0391. *Clubs:* Honley Cricket; Skipton Golf; Wharfedale Rugby Union Football.

ANSELL, Anthony Ronald Louis; His Honour Judge Ansell; a Circuit Judge, since 1995; *b* 9 Sept. 1946; *s* of Samuel Ansell and Joan Ansell; *m* 1970, Karen Kaye; one *s* one *d. Educ:* Dulwich Coll.; University Coll. London (LLB). Called to the Bar, Gray's Inn, 1968; in practice at the Bar, 1968–80; admitted Solicitor, 1980; in practice as solicitor, 1980–95; Asst Recorder, 1987–91; Recorder, 1991–95. Vice-Pres., United Synagogue, 1992–97. *Publication:* (jtly) A Time for Change: the Kalms review of United Synagogue, 1992. *Recreations:* walking, opera, Chelsea Football Club. *Address:* c/o Watford County Court, Cassiobury House, 11/19 Station Road, Watford, Herts WD1 1EZ. *T:* (01923) 249666.

ANSELL, Maj.-Gen. Nicholas George Picton, CB 1992; OBE 1980; JP, DL; Clerk of the Course, Exeter Racecourse, since 1995; *b* 17 Aug. 1937; *s* of Col Sir Michael Ansell, CBE, DSO and late Victoria Jacintha Fleetwood Fuller; *m* 1961, Vivien, *e d* of Col Anthony Taylor, DSO, MC; two *s* one *d. Educ:* Wellington Coll.; Magdalene Coll., Cambridge (MA). Commnd into 5th Royal Inniskilling Dragoon Guards, 1956; served BAOR, Libya, Cyprus; sc Camberley, 1970; Bde Major RAC HQ 1 (BR) Corps, 1971–72; Instructor Staff Coll., 1976–77; CO 5th Royal Inniskilling Dragoon Guards, 1977–80; Col GS Staff Coll., 1980–81; comd 20 Armd Bde, 1982–83; RCDS, 1984; Dep. Chief of Staff HQ BAOR, 1985–86; Dir, RAC, 1987–89; Sen. DS, Army, RCDS, 1990–92. JP Bideford and Gt Torrington, 1994; DL Devon, 1996. *Recreations:* country pursuits. *Address:* Exeter Racecourse, Kennford, Exeter EX6 7XS.

ANSON, family name of **Earl of Lichfield.**

ANSON, Viscount; Thomas William Robert Hugh Anson; *b* 19 July 1978; *s* and *heir* of Earl of Lichfield, *qv.*

ANSON, Charles Vernon, CVO 1996 (LVO 1983); Director of Corporate Communications, Hilton Group plc, since 2000; *b* 11 March 1944; *s* of Philip Vernon Anson and Stella Anson (*née* Parish); *m* 1976, Clarissa Rosamund Denton; one *s* one *d. Educ:* Lancing College; Jesus College, Cambridge (BA History). Joined Diplomatic Service, 1966; Third, later Second Sec. (Commercial), Washington, 1968–71; FCO, 1971–74; Asst Private Sec. to Minister of State, 1974–76; Second Sec. (Commercial), Tehran, 1976–79; seconded to Press Office, 10 Downing St., 1979–81; First Sec. (Inf.), Washington, 1981–85; FCO, 1985–87; Dir of Public Relations, Kleinwort Benson, 1987–90; Press Sec. to the Queen, 1990–97; Gp Corporate Relns Dir, Grand Metropolitan, later Diageo plc, 1997–98; Hd of Communications, EBU, 1998–2000. *Address:* c/o Hilton Group plc, Reeds Crescent, Watford, Herts WD24 4QQ. *T:* (020) 7856 8107. *Club:* Hurlingham.

ANSON, Vice-Adm. Sir Edward (Rosebery), KCB 1984; FRAeS 1982; Senior Naval Adviser, British Aerospace plc, 1989–91, retired; Aerospace Consultant (part-time), I.A.D. Aerospace Ltd, Worthing, 1991–93; *b* 11 May 1929; *s* of Ross Rosebery Anson and Ethel Jane (*née* Green); *m* 1960, Rosemary Anne Radcliffe; one *s* one *d. Educ:* Prince of Wales Sch., Nairobi, Kenya; BRNC, Dartmouth; Empire Test Pilots Sch., Farnborough (grad. 1957). Served, 1952–64: Naval Air Sqdns, and 700X and 700Z Flts (Blackburn Aircraft Ltd, 1959–61); comd HMS Eskimo, 1964–66; Commander (Air): RNAS Lossiemouth, 1967–68; HMS Eagle, 1969–70; comd Inter Service Hovercraft Trials Unit, 1971; Naval and Air Attaché, Tokyo and Seoul, 1972–74; comd HMS Juno and Captain F4, 1974–76; comd HMS Ark Royal, 1976–78; Flag Officer, Naval Air Command, 1979–82 C of S to C-in-C Fleet, 1982–84, retired. Exec. Dir, Sales, BAe Bristol Div., 1985–86; Pres. and Chief Exec. Officer, BAe, Washington, 1986–89. *Recreations:* walking, golf, photography. *Address:* c/o Lloyds TSB, High Street, Yeovil, Somerset.

ANSON, Dame Elizabeth (Audrey), (Lady Anson), DBE 1995; JP, DL; Chairman, Independent Appeals Authority for School Examinations, 1990–99; Independent Monitor to Parliament on Entry Clearance Refusals, 1994–2000; *b* 9 Jan. 1931; *d* of late Rear-Adm. Sir Philip Clarke, KBE, CB, DSO, and Audrey (*née* White); *m* 1955, Rear-Adm. Sir Peter Anson, Bt, *qv*; two *s* two *d. Educ:* Weirfield Sch., Taunton; Royal Naval Sch., Haslemere; King's Coll., London (LLB). Called to Bar, Inner Temple, 1953; joined Western Circuit, 1953; practice at Bar, 1952–56; part-time Adjudicator, 1977–87, an Adjudicator, 1987–91, Immigration Appeals. Councillor, Waverley Bor. Council, 1974–95, Mayor, 1987–88. Association of District Councils of England and Wales: Mem., 1983–95; Vice-Chm., 1989–91; Chm., 1991–93; Dep. Chm., and Chm. Exec. Cttee, 1993–95; Chm., Housing and Environmental Health Cttee, 1987–89. Dep. Chm., Local Govt Management Bd, 1991–93; Member: Local Govt Audit Commn, 1987–90; Cons. Nat. Local Govt Adv. Cttee, 1991–95; Nat. Union Exec. Cttee, 1992–95; Local and Central Govt Relations Res. Cttee, Joseph Rowntree Meml Trust, 1992–96; EU Cttee of the Regions, 1993–98; Packaging Standards Council, 1992–96. Chm., County Sound Radio Network Ltd (formerly Surrey and NE Hampshire Radio Ltd), 1993–. Chm., Nat. Mobility Scheme, 1987–88. Vice President: Inst. of Envmtl Health Officers, 1989–; Assoc. of Drainage Authorities, 1995–. FRSA 1992. JP 1977, DL 1984, Surrey. *Recreations:* travel, needlecraft. *Address:* Rosefield, Rowledge, Farnham, Surrey GU10 4AT. *T:* (01252) 792724.

ANSON, Sir John, KCB 1990 (CB 1981); Second Permanent Secretary (Public Expenditure), HM Treasury, 1987–90; *b* 3 Aug. 1930; *yr s* of Sir Edward Anson, 6th Bt, and of Dowager Lady Anson; *m* 1957, Myrica Fergie-Woods; one *s* two *d* (and one *s* decd). *Educ:* Winchester, Magdalene Coll., Cambridge (MA; Smith's Prize). Served in HM Treasury, 1954–68; Financial Counsellor, British Embassy, Paris, 1968–71; Asst Sec., 1971–72, Under-Sec., 1972–74, Cabinet Office; Under-Sec., 1974–77, Dep. Sec., 1977–87, HM Treasury; Economic Minister, British Embassy, Washington, and UK Exec. Dir, IMF and World Bank, 1980–83. Chairman: Public Finance Foundn, 1991–94; Retirement Income Inquiry, 1994–96. Hon. Treas., Council of Churches for Britain and Ireland, 1990–92; Chair, House of Laity, Southwark Diocesan Synod, 1996–97.

See also Sir Peter Anson, Bt.

ANSON, Rear-Adm. Sir Peter, 7th Bt, *cr* 1831; CB 1974; DL; CEng, FIEE; Chairman, IGG Component Technology Ltd, 1992–97; *b* 31 July 1924; *er s* of Sir Edward R. Anson, 6th Bt, and Alison (*d* 1997), *o d* of late Hugh Pollock; *S* father 1951; *m* 1955, Elizabeth Audrey Clarke (*see* Dame Elizabeth Anson); two *s* two *d. Educ:* RNC, Dartmouth. Joined RN 1938; Lieut 1944. Served War of 1939–45, HMS Prince of Wales, HMS Exeter. Lieut-Comdr, 1952; Comdr 1956. Commanding Officer, HMS Alert, 1957–58; Staff of RN Tactical Sch., Woolwich, 1959–61; Commanding Officer, HMS Broadsword, 1961–62; Captain, 1963; Director Weapons, Radio (Naval), 1965–66 (Dep. Director, 1963–65); CO HMS Naiad and Captain (D) Londonderry Squadron, 1966–68; Captain, HM Signal School, 1968–70; Commodore, Commander Naval Forces Gulf, 1970–72; ACDS (Signals), 1972–74, retired 1975. Marconi Space and Defence Systems, later Marconi Space Systems: Divl Manager, Satellites, 1977–84; Man. Dir, 1984–85; Chm., 1985–91. Chm., UK Industrial Space Cttee, 1980–82. FIERE 1972. High Sheriff, Surrey, 1993. DL Surrey, 1993. *Heir: s* Philip Roland Anson, *b* 4 Oct. 1957. *Address:* Rosefield, Rowledge, Farnham, Surrey GU10 4AT. *T:* and *Fax:* (01252) 792724.

See also Sir John Anson.

ANSTEE, Dame Margaret (Joan), DCMG 1994; lecturer, writer and consultant; Adviser to: President and Government of Bolivia; United Nations (*ad honorem*), 1993–97; Under-Secretary-General of the United Nations, 1987–93; *b* 25 June 1926; *d* of Edward Curtis Anstee and Anne Adaliza (*née* Mills). *Educ:* Chelmsford County High Sch. for Girls; Newnham Coll., Cambridge (MA; 1st cl. Hons, Mod. and Med. Langs Tripos; Hon. Fellow, 1991); BSc(Econ) London. Lectr in Spanish, QUB, 1947–48; Third Sec., FO, 1948–52; Admin. Officer, UN Technical Assistance Bd, Manila, Philippines, 1952–54; Spanish Supervisor, Cambridge Univ., 1955–56; UN Technical Assistance Board: O i/c Bogotá, Colombia, 1956–57; Resident Rep., Uruguay, 1957–59; Resident Rep., UN Tech. Assistance Bd, Dir of Special Fund Progs, and Dir of UN Inf. Centre, Bolivia, 1960–65; Resident Rep., UNDP, Ethiopia, and UNDP Liaison Officer with UN Econ. Commn for Africa, 1965–67; Sen. Econ. Adviser, Prime Minister's Office, UK, 1967–68; Sen. Asst to Comr i/c Study of Capacity of UN Develt System, 1968–69; Resident Rep., UNDP, Morocco, 1969–72; Resident Rep., UNDP, Chile, and UNDP Liaison Officer with UN Econ. Commn for Latin America, 1972–74; Dep. to UN Under Sec.-Gen. i/c UN Relief Operation to Bangladesh, and Dep. Co-ordinator of UN Emergency Assistance to Zambia, June–Dec. 1973; United Nations Development Programme, New York: Dep. Asst Adminr, and Dep. Reg Dir for Latin America, 1974–76; Dir, Adminr's Unit for Special Assignments, Feb.–July 1976; Asst Dep. Adminr, July–Dec. 1976; Asst Adminr and Dir, Bureau for Prog. Policy and Evaluation, 1977–78; Asst Sec.-Gen. of UN (Dept of Technical Co-operation for Develt), NY, 1978–87; Dir-Gen., UN Office, Vienna, and Head, Centre for Social Develt and Humanitarian Affairs, 1987–92. Special Representative of Secretary-General: for Bolivia, 1982–92; for co-ordination of internat. assistance to Mexico following the earthquake, 1985–87; for UN Conf. for adoption of convention against illicit traffic in narcotic drugs and psychotropic substances, 1988; for Peru, 1991–92; Special Rep. of Sec.-Gen. for Angola, and Head, UN Angola Verification Mission (UNAVEM II), 1992–93; Sec.-Gen.'s Personal rep., to co-ordinate UN efforts, Kuwait (burning oil wells and envmtl impact of Gulf war in whole reg.), 1991–92. Chm., Adv. Gp on review of World Food Council, UN, 1985–86; Special Co-ordinator of UN Sec.-Gen. to ensure implementation of Gen. Assembly resolution on financial and admin. reform of UN, 1986–87; Co-ordinator for all UN Drug-Control-Related Activities, 1987–90; UN Co-ordinator of Internat. Co-operation for Chernobyl, 1991–92; Chm., Expert Adv. Gp to Lessons Learned Unit, UN Dept of Peacekeeping Ops, 1996–. Sec.-Gen., 8th UN Congress on Prevention of Crime and Treatment of Offenders, 1990. Member: Bd of Trustees, HelpAge Internat., 1993–96; Council of Advisers, Yale Univ. UN Studies, 1996–; Adv. Council, Oxford Res. Gp, 1997–; Adv. Bd, British-Angola Forum, 1998–; Internat. Adv. Council, UN Intellectual Hist. Project, 1999–. DU Essex, 1994; Hon. LLD Westminster, 1996; Hon. DSc (Econ) London, 1998. Reves Peace Prize, Coll. of William and Mary, Williamsburg, USA, 1993. Comdr, Order of Ouissam Alaouite, Morocco, 1972; Gran Cruz de Dama, Condor of the Andes, Bolivia, 1986; Grosse Goldene Ehrenzeichen am Bande, Austria, 1992. *Publications:* The Administration of International Development Aid, USA 1969; Gate of the Sun: a prospect of Bolivia, 1970 (USA 1971); (ed with R. K. A. Gardiner and C. Patterson) Africa and the World (Haile Selassie Prize Trust Symposium), 1970; Orphan of the Cold War; the inside story of the collapse of the Angolan peace process 1992–93, 1996 (USA 1996; Portugal, 1997); numerous articles and chapters in books on UN reform, peacekeeping, economic and social development. *Recreations:* writing, gardening, hill-walking (preferably in the Andes), bird-watching, swimming. *Address:* c/o PNUD, Casilla 9072, La Paz, Bolivia; c/o The Walled Garden, Knill, near Presteigne, Powys LD8 2PR. *T:* (01544) 267411. *Club:* Oxford and Cambridge.

ANSTEY, Edgar, MA, PhD; Deputy Chief Scientific Officer, Civil Service Department, and Head of Behavioural Sciences Research Division, 1969–77; *b* 5 March 1917; British; *s* of late Percy Lewis Anstey and Dr Vera Anstey; *m* 1939, Zoë Lilian Robertson (*d* 2000); one *s. Educ:* Winchester Coll.; King's Coll, Cambridge. Assistant Principal, Dominions Office, 1938; Private Sec. to Duke of Devonshire, 1939. 2nd Lieut Dorset Regt, 1940; Major, War Office (DSP), 1941. Founder-Head of Civil Service Commission Research Unit, 1945; Principal, Home Office, 1951; Senior Principal Psychologist, Min. of Defence, 1958; Chief Psychologist, Civil Service Commn, 1964–69. Pres., N Cornwall Liberal Democrat Assoc., 1988–90 (N Cornwall Liberal Assoc., 1985–88). *Publications:* Interviewing for the Selection of Staff (with Dr E. O. Mercer), 1956; Staff Reporting and Staff Development, 1961; Committees-How they work and how to work them, 1962; Psychological Tests, 1966; The Techniques of Interviewing, 1968; (with Dr C. A. Fletcher and Dr. J. Walker) Staff Appraisal and Development, 1976; An Introduction to Selection Interviewing, 1978; articles in Brit. Jl of Psychology, Occupational Psychology, etc. *Recreations:* fell-walking, surfing, bridge. *Address:* Sandrock, 3 Higher Tristram, Polzeath, Wadebridge, Cornwall PL27 6TF. *T:* (01208) 863324. *Club:* Royal Commonwealth Society.

ANSTRUTHER of that Ilk, Sir Ralph (Hugo), 7th Bt *cr* 1694 (S), of Balcaskie, and 12th Bt *cr* 1700 (S), of Anstruther; GCVO 1992 (KCVO 1976; CVO 1967); MC 1943; DL; Hereditary Carver to the Queen; Equerry to the Queen Mother, 1959–98, also Treasurer, 1961–98, now Treasurer Emeritus; *b* 13 June 1921; *o s* of Capt. Robert Edward Anstruther (*d* 1921), MC, The Black Watch, *o s* of 6th Bt, and Marguerite Blanche Lily (*d* 1992), *d* of Hugo de Burgh; *S* grandfather, 1934, and cousin, Sir Windham Eric Francis Carmichael-Anstruther, 11th Bt, 1980. *Educ:* Eton; Magdalene Coll., Cambridge (BA). Major (retd), Coldstream Gds. Served Malaya, 1950 (despatches). Mem. Queen's Body Guard for Scotland (Royal Co. of Archers). DL Fife, 1960–97, Caithness-shire, 1965. *Heir: cousin;* Ian Fife Campbell Anstruther, Capt. late Royal Corps of Signals [*b* 11 May 1922; *m* 1st, 1951, Honor (marr. diss. 1963), *er d* of late Capt. Gerald Blake, MC; one *d*; 2nd, 1963, Susan Margaret Walker, *e d* of H. St J. B. Paten; two *s* three *d*]. *Address:* Balcaskie, Pittenweem, Fife KY10 2RD; Watten Mains, Caithness KW1 5UH.
See also Sir T. D. Erskine.

ANSTRUTHER-GOUGH-CALTHORPE, Sir Euan (Hamilton), 3rd Bt *cr* 1929; property manager; *b* 22 June 1966; *s* of Niall Hamilton Anstruther-Gough-Calthorpe (*d* 1970) and of Martha Rodman (who *m* 2nd, 1975, Sir Charles C. Nicholson, Bt, *qv*), *d* of Stuart Warren Don; *S* grandfather, 1985. *Educ:* Hawtreys, Savernake Forest; Harrow School; Royal Agricultural Coll., Cirencester (Dip. in Estate Mgt). Pres., Birmingham Botanical Gdns, 1985–. *Clubs:* Brooks's; Edgbaston Priory (Pres., 1985–); Hartley Wintney Golf (Pres., 1985–99).

ANTALPÉTER, Tibor; Director: Hungarian Investment Company Ltd, since 1995; Mezőgép, Orosháza, since 1997; *b* 4 Feb. 1930; *s* of late István Antalpéter and Viktória Dobai; *m* 1956, Adél Máthé; two *d*. *Educ:* Univ. of Economics, Budapest; graduated 1954. Importtex, foreign trade co., 1954; Commercial Sec. in London, 1956–60; Department of International Commercial Relations, Ministry of Foreign Trade: Head of Section, 1960; Dir of Dept, 1964; Dep. Dir-Gen., 1968–73; Dir-Gen. of Dept, 1977–88; Commercial Counsellor, London, 1973–77, 1988–90; Ambassador to UK, 1990–94. Member, Supervisory Board: Danubius Hotels Gp, 2000– (Dir, 1996–2000); Weslin, Oroszlány, 2000–. Vice-Chm., CAB Internat., 1992–94. Internat. volley-ball player, 1947–56; Chm., Hungarian Volley-ball Assoc. and Mem., Hungarian Olympic Cttee, 1980–86. Hon. FRSA 1992. Order of Merit for Labour, Bronze 1966, Gold 1979; Order of Merit of Hungarian Republic, Middle Cross, 1995. Order of the Finnish Lion, 1st Cl., 1969; Comdr, Order of Prince Henry the Navigator (Portugal), 1979; Order of Merit, Grand Silver Grade (Austria), 1983. *Recreations:* sport, music. *Address:* Kavics u. 11, 1025 Budapest, Hungary.

ANTHONY, Metropolitan, of Sourozh; Head of the Russian Orthodox Patriarchal Church in Great Britain and Ireland (Diocese of Sourozh); *né* André Borisovich Bloom; *b* Lausanne, Switzerland, 19 June 1914; *o c* of Boris Edwardovich Bloom (Russian Imperial Diplomatic Service) and Xenia Nikolaevna Scriabin (sister of the composer Alexander Scriabin). *Educ:* Lycée Condorcet and Sorbonne, Paris. Dr of Med., Sorbonne, 1943. Army service, med. corps French Army and Resistance, 1939–45. Gen. Practitioner, 1945–49. Took monastic vows, 1943; Priest, Russian Orthodox Church in Paris, 1948; Chaplain to Fellowship of St Alban and St Sergius, London, 1949–50; Vicar, Russian Orthodox Church of St Philip, London, 1950; apptd Hegumen, 1953, Archimandrite, 1956; consecrated Bishop of Sergievo, Suffragan Bishop, Exarchate of Western Europe, 1957; Archbishop of Sourozh, 1960; acting Exarch, 1962–63, Metropolitan of Sourozh and Exarch of the Patriarch of Moscow and All Russia in Western Europe, 1965–74. Member: Ecumenical Commn of Russian Orthodox Church; Central Cttee and Christian Medical Commn of World Council of Churches, 1968. Hulsean Preacher, Cambridge, 1972–73; Preacher, Lambeth Conf., 1978; Firth Lectures, Nottingham Univ., 1982; Eliot Lectures, Kent Univ., 1982; Constantinople Lecture, 1982. Médaille de Bronze de la Société d'encouragement au bien (France), 1945; Browning Award (for spreading of the Christian gospel), USA, 1974. Orders of: St Vladimir 1st Cl. (Russia), 1962; St Andrew (Ecumenical Patriarchate), 1963; St Sergius (Russia), 1977. Lambeth Cross, 1975. Hon. DD (Aberdeen), 1973. *Publications:* Living Prayer, 1965; School for Prayer, 1970; God and Man, 1971; Meditations on a Theme, 1972; Courage to Pray, 1973; Essence of Prayer, 1986; Creative Prayer, 1987. *Address:* Russian Orthodox Cathedral, Ennismore Gardens, SW7 1NH. *T:* (020) 7584 0096.

ANTHONY, Rear Adm. Derek James, MBE 1983; Flag Officer Scotland, Northern England and Northern Ireland, since 2000; *b* 2 Nov. 1947; *s* of late James Kenwood Anthony and Nora Evelyn Anthony (*née* Honnor); *m* 1970, Denyse Irene Hopper Wright; two *d*. *Educ:* New Beacon Prep. Sch., Sevenoaks; Eastbourne Coll.; BRNC, Dartmouth. Joined Royal Navy, 1966: sea-going appts, HM Ships Opossum, Revenge, Andrew, Oxley, Oberon, Sovereign, 1970–80; CO, HMS Onslaught, 1981–82; Exchange Service, USN, 1982–84; jsdc, 1985; CO, HMS Warspite, 1986–88, Submarine Comd Course, 1988–90; Head, RN Seaman Officers Policy, MoD, 1990–91; CO, HMS Cumberland, 1991–93; Dir, Naval Service Conditions, 1993–96; hcsc, Camberley, 1996; Dep. Flag Officer Submarines, 1996–97; Naval Attaché, Asst Defence Attaché, Washington, and UK Nat. Liaison Rep. to SACLANT, 1997–2000. *Recreations:* golf, tennis, windsurfing, music, clarinet, history, family. *Address:* c/o Naval Secretary, Victory Building, HM Naval Base, Portsmouth PO1 3LS. *Clubs:* Army and Navy, Royal Navy of 1765 and 1785.

ANTHONY, Rt Hon. Douglas; *see* Anthony, Rt Hon. J. D.

ANTHONY, Evelyn Bridget Patricia, (Mrs Michael Ward-Thomas); DL; author; *b* 3 July 1928; *d* of Henry Christian Stephens, inventor of the Dome Trainer in World War II, and Elizabeth (*née* Sharkey); *g g d* of Henry Stephens of Cholderton, Wilts, inventor of Stephens Ink; *m* 1955, Michael Ward-Thomas; four *s* one *d* (and one *d* decd). *Educ:* Convent of Sacred Heart, Roehampton. Freeman, City of London, 1987; Liveryman, Needlemakers' Co., 1987. High Sheriff, Essex, 1994–95, DL Essex, 1995. *Publications:* Imperial Highness, 1953; Curse Not the King, 1954; Far Fly the Eagles, 1955; Anne Boleyn, 1956 (US Literary Guild Award); Victoria, 1957 (US Literary Guild Award); Elizabeth, 1959; Charles the King, 1961; Clandara, 1963; The Heiress, 1964; Valentina, 1965; The Rendezvous, 1967; Anne of Austria, 1968; The Legend, 1969; The Assassin, 1970; The Tamarind Seed, 1971; The Poellenberg Inheritance, 1972; The Occupying Power, 1973 (Yorkshire Post Fiction Prize); The Malaspiga Exit, 1974; The Persian Ransom, 1975; The Silver Falcon, 1977; The Return, 1978; The Grave of Truth, 1979; The Defector, 1980; The Avenue of the Dead, 1981; Albatross, 1982; The Company of Saints, 1983; Voices on the Wind, 1985; No Enemy But Time, 1987; The House of Vandekar, 1988; The Scarlet Thread, 1989; The Relic, 1991; The Dolls' House, 1992; Exposure, 1993; Bloodstones, 1994; The Legacy, 1997. *Recreations:* racing (National Hunt), gardening, going to sale rooms, preferably Christie's. *Address:* Horham Hall, Thaxted, Essex CM6 2NN.

ANTHONY, Graham George, CEng; Director, Industry and Regions, Engineering Council, 1983–90; *b* 25 Oct. 1931; *s* of George Alfred and Dorothy Anthony; *m* 1957, Thelma Jane Firmstone; two *s* one *d*. *Educ:* Fletton Grammar Sch.; King's College London (BSc Eng). Projects Manager, ICI Fibres, 1956; Works Engineer, ICI India, 1964; Chief Engineer, Ilford Ltd, 1968; Gen. Manager, Bonded Structures, 1975; Commercial Dir, Ciba-Geigy (UK) Ltd, 1979. FRSA. *Recreations:* offshore sailing, woodworking. *Address:* 11 North Terrace, Cambridge CB5 8DJ. *T:* (01223) 360553.

ANTHONY, Guy; *see* Anthony, M. G.

ANTHONY, Rt Hon. (John) Douglas, CH 1982; PC 1971; company director and farmer; Chairman: Resource Finance Corporation, since 1987; Commonwealth Regional Telecommunications Infrastructure Fund, since 1997; Director: John Swires & Sons Pty Ltd (Australia), since 1987; Clyde Agriculture Ltd, since 1988; *b* 31 Dec. 1929; *s* of late H. L. Anthony; *m* 1957, Margot Macdonald Budd; two *s* one *d*. *Educ:* Murwillumbah Primary and High Schs, The King's Sch., Parramatta; Queensland Agricultural Coll. (QDA). MP, Country Party, later National Party, Richmond, NSW, 1957–84, (Mem., Exec. Council, 1963–72, 1975–83). Minister for Interior, 1964–67; Minister for Primary Industry, 1967–71; Dep. Prime Minister and Minister for Trade and Industry, 1971–72; Minister for Overseas Trade, Minerals and Energy, Nov.–Dec. 1975; Dep. Prime Minister and Minister for Trade and Resources, 1975–83. Dep. Leader, Aust. Country Party, 1966–71; Leader, Nat. Country Party, later Nat. Party, 1971–84. Chm., Pan Australian Mining Ltd, then Mt Leyshon Gold Mines, 1986–92; Dir, Normandy Mining Ltd, 1992–2000. Chm. Governing Council, Old Parlt House, 1998–. Hon. Fellow, AATSE, 1990. Hon. LLD Victoria Univ. of Wellington, NZ, 1983; DUniv Sydney, 1997. Council Gold Medal, Qld Agricl Coll., 1985. Canberra Medal, 1989; NZ Commemorative Medal, 1990. *Recreations:* golf, tennis, fishing, swimming. *Address:* Sunnymeadows, Murwillumbah, NSW 2484, Australia. *Clubs:* Union, Royal Sydney Golf (Sydney); Queensland (Brisbane).

ANTHONY, (Michael) Guy; His Honour Judge Anthony; a Circuit Judge, since 1998; *b* 5 March 1950; *s* of Kenneth Anthony and June Anthony (*née* Gallifent); *m* 1974, Jane Farrer; one *s*. *Educ:* St Paul's Sch.; Magdalen Coll., Oxford (BA 1971; MA). Called to the Bar, Middle Temple, 1972; in practice at the Bar, 1972–98; an Asst Recorder, 1989–93; a Recorder, 1993–98; SE Circuit. *Recreations:* travel, reading, spending time with family, Rugby and other sports. *Address:* Lewes Combined Crown and County Court Centre, The Law Courts, High Street, Lewes, E Sussex BN7 1YB. *T:* (01273) 480400.

ANTHONY, Ronald Desmond; consultant in safety and engineering, since 1986; Chief Inspector of Nuclear Installations, Health and Safety Executive, 1981–85; *b* 21 Nov. 1925; *s* of William Arthur Anthony and Olive Frances Anthony (*née* Buck); *m* 1948, Betty Margaret Croft; four *d*. *Educ:* Chislehurst and Sidcup Grammar School; City and Guilds Coll., Imperial Coll. of Science and Technology (BSc, ACGI). CEng, FIMechE, MRAeS. Vickers Armstrongs (Supermarine), 1950; Nuclear Power Plant Co., 1957; Inspectorate of Nuclear Installations, 1960; Deputy Chief Inspector, 1973; Dir, Safety Policy Div., 1977, Hazardous Installations Gp, 1981–82, Health and Safety Exec. *Publications:* papers in technical journals. *Recreation:* golf. *Address:* 2 Perry House, Chislehurst Road, Sidcup, Kent DA14 6BE. *T:* (020) 8302 6090.

ANTHONY, Vivian Stanley; Training Co-ordinator, Headmasters' and Headmistresses' Conference, since 2000 (Secretary, 1990–2000); *b* 5 May 1938; *s* of Captain and Mrs A. S. Anthony; *m* 1969, Rosamund Anne MacDermot Byrn; one *s* one *d*. *Educ:* Cardiff High Sch.; LSE (1st Div. 2nd Cl. Hons BSc Econ); Fitzwilliam Coll., Cambridge (DipEd); Merton Coll., Oxford (schoolmaster student). Asst Master, Leeds Grammar Sch., 1960–64; Asst Master and Housemaster, Tonbridge Sch., 1964–69; Lectr in Educn, Univ. of Leeds, 1969–71; Dep. Headmaster, The King's Sch., Macclesfield, 1971–76; Headmaster, Colfe's Sch., London, 1976–90. Asst Examr, Econ. Hist., London Univ., 1964–71; Asst Examr, Econs, Oxford and Cambridge Bd, 1970–76, Chief Examr (Awarder), Econs, 1976–92; Ext. Examr, Educn, Univs of Manchester, 1972–75, Birmingham, 1975–78, and Lancaster, 1977–79. Chm., Econs Assoc., 1974–77; Member: Schools Council Social Science Cttee, 1976–83; London Univ. Schs Examinations Cttee, 1981–85; Secondary Examinations Council Economics Panel, 1984–89; CBI/Schools Panel, 1984–88; Court, Univ. Kent, 1985–90. Sabbatical tour, US indep. schools, 1983. Chm., London Area, 1988–89, Mem. Council, 1989–2000, SHA; elected Headmasters' Conf., 1980, Chm., Academic Policy Cttee, 1988–90 (Mem., 1983–2000), Member, Professional Develt Cttee, 1985–, Teacher Shortage Wkg Party, 1987–88, Assisted Places Cttee, 1987–89, Chm., Records of Achievement Wkg Party, 1987–90; Mem., DFEE Wkg Gp on Sch. Security, 1996–2000. Reporting Inspector of Ind. Schs, 1994–. Mem., Exec. Cttee, Nat. Professional Qualification for Headship (E Midlands), 1996–99. Mem., Admiralty Interview Bd, 1980–. Comr, Inland Revenue, 1989–90. Governor: Stamford Sch., 1992–; King's Sch., Macclesfield, 1993–96; Bromsgrove Sch., 1995–; Uppingham Sch., 1996–. Hon. Freeman, Leathersellers' Co., 1990. Hon. FCP 1991. Hon. DEd De Montfort, 1999. *Publications:* Monopoly, 1968, 3rd edn 1976; Overseas Trade, 1969, 4th edn 1981; Banks and Markets, 1970, 3rd edn 1979; Objective Tests in A Level Economics, 1971, 2nd edn 1974; Objective Tests in Introductory Economics, 1975, 3rd edn 1983; History of Rugby Football at Colfe's, 1980; US Independent Schools, 1984; 150 Years of Cricket at Colfe's, 1986; (ed) Head to Head, 1993; (ed) Manual of Guidance, 1995; (ed) Head to HoD, 1998; (ed) Head to House, 2000; *contributor:* The Teaching of Economics in Secondary Schools, 1970; Curriculum Development in Secondary Schools, 1973; Control of the Economy, 1974; Comparative Economics in Teaching Economics, 1984; The Search for Standards, 1992; Access and Affordability, 1994; articles in Economics. *Recreations:* choral singing (Chm., Leics Chorale, 1998–), Rugby football, tennis. *Address:* Bridge House, Allexton, Leics LE15 9AB. *T:* (01572) 717400, *Fax:* (01572) 717500. *Clubs:* East India, Devonshire, Sports and Public Schools, English-Speaking Union, Old Colfeians Association.

ANTICO, Sir Tristan, AC 1983; Kt 1973; President, Pioneer International Ltd (formerly Pioneer Concrete Services), since 1993 (Managing Director, 1949–88; Chairman, 1966–94); *b* 25 March 1923; *s* of Terribile Giovanni Antico and Erminia Bertin; *m* 1950, Dorothy Bridget Shields; three *s* four *d*. *Educ:* Sydney High Sch. Began career as Accountant; subseq. became Company Secretary, Melocco Bros; Founder of Pioneer Concrete Services Ltd. Chm., Tregoyd Holdings Pty Ltd, 1954; formerly Chairman: Ampol Ltd; Papuan Oil Search; formerly Director: Société Générale Australia Hldgs; Qantas Ltd. AC and Knighthood awarded for services to industry and the community. Comdr, Order of Star of Solidarity (Italy), 1967. *Recreations:* horse breeding and horse racing, swimming, yachting. *Clubs:* Tattersall's, Australian Jockey, Sydney Turf, American National, Royal Sydney Yacht Squadron (Sydney); Manly Golf.

ANTIGUA (diocese); *see* North-Eastern Caribbean and Aruba.

ANTON, Alexander Elder, CBE 1973; FBA 1972; *b* 1922; *m* 1949, Doris May Lawrence; one *s*. *Educ:* Aberdeen Univ. (MA, LLB with dist.; Hon. LLD 1993). Solicitor, 1949; Lectr, Aberdeen, 1953–59; Prof. of Jurisprudence, Univ. of Glasgow, 1959–73. Hon. Vis. Prof., 1982–84, Hon. Prof., 1984, Aberdeen Univ. Mem., Scottish Law Commission, 1966–82. Literary Dir, Stair Soc., 1960–66; Chm., Scottish Rights of Way Soc., 1988–92. *Publications:* Private International Law, 1967, 2nd edn (with P. R.

Beaumont), 1990; Civil Jurisdiction in Scotland, 1984; contribs to legal and historical jls. *Recreation:* hill walking. *Address:* 5 Seafield Drive West, Aberdeen AB15 7XA.

ANTONIONI, Michelangelo; film director; *b* Ferrara, Italy, 29 Sept. 1912; *s* of Ismaele and Elisabetta Roncagli; *m* Enrica Fico. *Educ:* Univ. of Bologna (degree in Econs); Centro Sperimentale di Cinematografia, Rome. Formerly an asst dir, film critic to newspapers (Corriere padano, Italia libera), and script writer. Films directed include: documentaries, etc (incl. Gente del Po), 1943–50; subseq. full-length films: Cronaca di un Amore, 1950; one episode in Amore in Città, 1951; I Vinti, 1952; La Signora Senza Camelie, 1953; Le Amiche, 1955; Il Grido, 1957; L'Avventura, 1960; La Notte, 1961; L'Eclisse, 1962; Il Deserto Rosso, 1964 (Golden Lion, Venice Film Fest., 1964); one episode in I Tre Volti, 1965; Blow-Up, 1967 (Palme d'Or, Cannes Film Fest., 1967); Zabriskie Point, 1969; Chung Kuo-China, 1972; The Passenger, 1974; Il Mistero di Oberwald, 1979; Identificazione di una Donna, 1981; Beyond the Clouds, 1995; documentaries include: Kumbha Mela, 1989; Roma, 1989. Academy Award, 1995. Kt Grand Cross, Order of Merit (Italian Republic), 1992; Comdr, Order of Arts and Letters (France), 1992; Legion of Honour (France), 1996. *Publication:* Quel Bowling sul Tevere, 1983. *Recreations:* collecting blown glass, tennis, ping-pong. *Address:* Via Vincenzo Tiberio 18, 00191 Rome, Italy; (office) Via Fleming III, 00191 Rome.

ANTRIM, 14th Earl of, *cr* 1620; **Alexander Randal Mark McDonnell;** Viscount Dunluce; Keeper of Conservation, 1975–95, and Director (formerly Head) of Collection Services, 1990–95, Tate Gallery; *b* 3 Feb. 1935; *er s* of 13th Earl of Antrim, KBE, and Angela Christina (*d* 1984), *d* of Sir Mark Sykes, 6th Bt; *S* father, 1977 (but continued to be known as Viscount Dunluce until 1995); *m* 1963, Sarah Elizabeth Anne (marr. diss. 1974), 2nd *d* of St John Harmsworth; one *s* two *d*; *m* 1977, Elizabeth, *d* of late Michael Moses Sacher; one *d*. *Educ:* Downside; Christ Church, Oxford; Ruskin Sch. of Art. Restorer: the Ulster Museum, 1969–71; Tate Gall., 1965–75. Dir, Ulster Television, 1982–2000; Chm., Northern Salmon Co. Ltd, 2000–. Mem., Exec. Cttee, City and Guilds Art School, 1983–. FRSA 1984. Prime Warden, Fishmongers' Co., 1995–96. *Recreations:* painting, vintage cars. *Heir: s* Viscount Dunluce, *qv*. *Address:* Deerpark Cottage, Castle Lane, Glenarm, Ballymena, Co. Antrim BT44 0BQ. *Club:* Beefsteak.

ANTROBUS, Sir Charles (James), GCMG 1996; OBE 1973; Governor-General, St Vincent and the Grenadines, since 1996; *b* 14 May 1933; *m* 1996, Gloria Janet Vena Ou Wai; one *s* two *d*. *Educ:* St Vincent Grammar Sch. Cable and Wireless: special assignment, Tortola, BVI, 1966–67; Relief Br. Manager, Montserrat, St Kitts and Dominica, 1967; Gen. Manager, St Vincent and the Grenadines, 1967–93. Mem. Bd, Duke of Edinburgh Award Scheme, St Vincent, 1972–. *Address:* Government House, Montrose, St Vincent and the Grenadines. *T:* 4561401. *Club:* St Vincent and the Grenadines Rotary (Past Pres.).

ANTROBUS, Sir Edward (Philip), 8th Bt *cr* 1815, of Antrobus, Cheshire; *b* 28 Sept. 1938; *er s* of Sir Philip Coutts Antrobus, 7th Bt and his 1st wife, Dorothy Margaret Mary (*d* 1973), *d* of Rev. W. G. Davis; *S* father, 1995; *m* 1st, 1966, Janet Sarah Elizabeth (*d* 1990), *d* of Philip Sceales, Johannesburg; one *s* two *d*; 2nd, 1996, Rozanne Penelope, *d* of Neville Simpson. *Educ:* Witwatersrand Univ. (BSc Mining Engrg); Magdalene Coll., Cambridge (MA). *Heir: s* Francis Edward Sceales Antrobus, BSc Eng Cape Town, *b* 24 Oct. 1972. *Address:* 54A 3rd Avenue, Parktown North, 2193 Johannesburg, South Africa.

ANWYL, Shirley Anne, QC 1979; **Her Honour Judge Anwyl;** a Circuit Judge, since 1995; *b* 10 Dec. 1940; *d* of James Ritchie and Helen Sutherland Ritchie; *m* 1969, Robin Hamilton Corson Anwyl; two *s*. *Educ:* St Mary's Diocesan Sch. for Girls, Pretoria; Rhodes Univ., S Africa (BA, LLB). Called to the South African Bar, 1963; called to the Bar, Inner Temple, 1966, Bencher, 1985. A Recorder, 1981–95. Member: Senate of Inns of Court and Bar, 1978–81; Gen. Council of the Bar, 1987; Criminal Injuries Compensation Bd, 1980–95; Mental Health Review Tribunal, 1983–99. Chm., Barristers' Benevolent Assoc., 1989–95. FRSA 1989. Freeman, City of London, 1994; Liveryman, Fruiterers' Co., 1996. *Recreations:* theatre, sailing. *Club:* Guild of Freemen of City of London.

ANWYL-DAVIES, His Honour Marcus John, MA; QC 1967; a Circuit Judge, 1972–93; *b* 11 July 1923; *s* of late Thomas Anwyl-Davies and Kathleen Beryl Anwyl-Davies (*née* Oakshott); *m* 1st, 1954, Eva Hilda Elisabeth Paulson (marr. diss. 1974); one *s* one *d*; 2nd, 1983, Myrna Dashoff. *Educ:* Harrow Sch.; Christ Church, Oxford. Royal Artillery, including service with Hong Kong and Singapore RA, 1942–47 (despatches 1945). Called to Bar, Inner Temple, 1949. Legal Assessor, GMC and GDC, 1969–72; Liaison Judge to Herts Magistrates, 1972–82; Resident Judge, St Albans Crown Court, 1972–82. Vice-Pres., Herts Magistrates' Assoc., 1975; Pres., Council of HM's Circuit Judges, 1989. Member: Panel, Amer. Arbitration Assoc., 1993–; London Court of Internat. Arbitration, 1994–; Bd of Dirs, Center for Internat. Commercial Arbitration, 1994–; Nat. Assoc. of Securities Dealers Bd of Arbitrators, 1994–; Indian Council of Arbitration, 1999–; Public Arbitrator, Pacific Stock Exchange, 1995–; Arbitrator, Korean Commercial Arbitration Bd, 1996–. FCIArb 1992 (Mem. Cttee, N Amer. Br., 1993–96). United Grand Lodge of England: Grand Sword Bearer, 1990; Pres., Bd of Grand Stewards, 1990–91. *Recreation:* photography. *Address:* 39 Essex Street, WC2R 3AT. *T:* (020) 7353 4741; 16624 Calle Arbolada, Pacific Palisades, CA 90272–1934, USA. *T:* (310) 4599234, *Fax:* (310) 4598220; *e-mail:* mjanwyldavies@cs.com. *Club:* Reform.

ANYAOKU, Eleazar Chukwuemeka, (Emeka), CON 1982; Ndichie Chief Adazie of Obosi; Ugwumba of Idemili; Secretary-General of the Commonwealth, 1990–2000; *b* 18 Jan. 1933; *e s* of late Emmanuel Chukwuemeka Anyaoku, Ononukpo of Okpuno Ire, Obosi, Nigeria, and Cecilia Adiba (*née* Ogbogu); *m* 1962, Ebunola Olubunmi, *yr d* of late barrister Olusola Akanbi Solanke, of Abeokuta, Nigeria; three *s* one *d*. *Educ:* Merchants of Light Sch., Oba; Univ. of Ibadan (Schol.), Nigeria; courses in England and France. Exec. Asst, Commonwealth Develt Corp., in London and Lagos, 1959–62. Joined Nigerian Diplomatic Service, 1962; Mem. Nigerian Permanent Mission to the UN, New York, 1963–66; seconded to Commonwealth Secretariat as Asst Dir, 1966–71, and Dir, 1971–75, Internat. Affairs Div.; Asst Sec.-Gen., 1975–77, Dep. Sec.-Gen. (Political), 1977–83 and 1984–90, of the Commonwealth. Minister of External Affairs, Nigeria, Nov.-Dec. 1983. Served as Secretary: Review Cttee on Commonwealth inter-governmental organisations, June-Aug., 1966; Commonwealth Observer Team for Gibraltar Referendum, Aug.-Sept., 1967; Anguilla Commn, WI, Jan.-Sept. 1970; Leader, Commonwealth Mission for Mozambique, 1975; Commonwealth Observer, Zimbabwe Talks, Geneva, 1976; accompanied Commonwealth Eminent Persons Gp, SA, 1986. Vice-Pres., Royal Commonwealth Society, London, 1975–; Mem. Council, Overseas Develt Inst., 1979–90. Mem., Governing Council: SCF, 1984–90; IISS, London, 1987; Hon. Mem., Club of Rome, 1992–. FRSA 1984. Hon. Fellow, Inst. of Educn, Univ. of London, 1994. Hon. DLitt: Ibadan, 1990; Buckingham, 1994; Bradford, 1995; Hon. DPhil Ahmadu Bello, 1991; Hon. LLD: Nigeria, 1991; Aberdeen, Reading, 1992; Bristol, Oxford Brookes, 1993; Leeds, South Bank, 1994; New Brunswick, North London, 1995; Liverpool, London, 1997; Nottingham. Livingstone Medal, RSGS, 1996. Freeman, City of London, 1998. *Publications:* essays in various pubns. *Recreations:* tennis, swimming, reading. *Address:* Orimili, Okpuno Ire, Obosi, Anambra State, Nigeria. *Clubs:* Royal Commonwealth Society, Africa Centre, Travellers; Metropolitan (Lagos).

AOTEAROA, Bishop of, since 1981; **Rt Rev. Whakahuihui Vercoe,** PCNZM 2000; MBE 1970; *b* 4 June 1928; *s* of Joseph and Wyness Vercoe; *m* 1951, Dorothy Eivers; three *s*. *Educ:* Torere Primary; Feilding Agricultural High School; College House Theological Coll.; Canterbury Univ. (Cert Soc. Studies, 1975); LTh 1985; DipSocServ Wellington, 1992. Curate, St John's Church, Feilding, 1951–53; Priest-in-Charge, Wellington Pastorate, 1953–54; Pastor: Wairarapa, 1954–57; Rangitikei, 1957–61; Chaplain: Armed Forces, Malaya, 1961–64; Papakura Military Camp, 1964–65; ANZAC Brigade, Vietnam, 1968–69; Burnham Mil. Camp, 1965–71; Principal, Te Waipounamu Girls' School, 1971–76; Vicar: Ohinemutu Pastorate, 1976–78; Ruatoki-Whakatane, 1978–81; Archdeacon of Tairawhiti and Vicar-General to Bishopric of Aotearoa, 1978–81. Mem., Central Cttee, WCC, Geneva, 1983–90. *Publications:* Te Aomarama series, 1993; (contrib.) Dictionary of New Zealand Biography, 1995. *Recreations:* Rugby, golf, reading, tennis, cricket, fishing. *Address:* PO Box 146, Rotorua, New Zealand. *T:* (home) (7) 3479241, (office) (7) 3486093, *Fax:* (7) 3486091.

APEL, Dr Hans Eberhard; Social-democratic Member of Bundestag, 1965–90 (Deputy-Chairman of Group, 1969–72); *b* Hamburg, 25 Feb. 1932; *m* 1956, Ingrid Schwingel; two *d*. *Educ:* Hamburg Univ. Diplom-Volkswirt, 1957, Dr.rer.pol, 1960. Apprentice in Hamburg export and import business, 1951–54; Sec., Socialist Group in European Parlt, 1958–61; Head of Economics, Finance and Transportation Dept of European Parlt, 1962–65. Chm., Bundestag Cttee on Transportation, 1969–72. Mem. Nat. Bd, Social-democratic Party (SPD), 1970–88; Parly Sec. of State, Min. for Foreign Affairs, 1972–74; Federal Minister of Finance, 1974–78, of Defence, 1978–82. Prof. in Econ. Dept, Rostock Univ. *Publications:* Edwin Cannan und seine Schüler (Doct. Thesis), 1961; Raumordnung der Bundesrepublik, in: Deutschland 1975, 1964; Europas neue Grenzen, 1964; Der deutsche Parlamentarismus, 1968; Bonn, den Tagebuch eines Bundestagsabgeordneten, 1972; Der Abstieg, 1990; Die deformierte Demokratie, 1991; Der kranke Koloss, 1994. *Recreations:* sailing, soccer. *Address:* Rögenfeld 42c, 22359 Hamburg, Germany.

APPEL, Karel Christian; Dutch artist (painter); *b* 25 April 1921; *s* of Jan Appel and Johanna Chevallier. *Educ:* Royal Academy of Art, Amsterdam. Began career as artist in 1938. Has had one-man exhibitions in Europe, America and Asia, including: Palais des Beaux-Arts, Brussels, 1953; Stedelijk Mus., Amsterdam, 1955, 1956, 1965; ICA, London, 1957; Palazzo dei Medici, Florence, 1985; travelling exhibitions: museums in Calif, 1961; museums in Canada and USA, 1972, 1973; museums in Brazil, Colombia, Mexico, 1978, 1981; 5 museums in Japan, 1989; Europe, 1990–92. UNESCO Prize, Venice Biennale, 1953; Lissone Prize, Italy, 1958; Acquisition Prize, São Paulo Biennale, Brazil, 1959; Graphique Internat. Prize, Ljubljana, Jugoslavia, 1959; Guggenheim National Prize, Holland, 1961; Guggenheim International Prize, 1961. *Publications:* Works on Paper, 1980; Street Art, 1985; Dupe of Being, 1989; Complete Sculptures 1936–1990, 1990; Karel Appel Sculpture: catalogue raisonné, 1994; *relevant publications:* Karel Appel, 1980; Karel Appel: the early years 1937–1957, 1988.

APPLEBY, Brian John, QC 1971; **His Honour Judge Appleby;** a Circuit Judge, since 1988; *b* 25 Feb. 1930; *s* of Ernest Joel and Gertrude Appleby; *m* 1st, 1958, Rosa Helena (*née* Flitterman) (*d* 1996); one *s* one *d*; 2nd, 1998, Lynda Jane Eaton. *Educ:* Uppingham; St John's Coll., Cambridge (BA). Called to Bar, Middle Temple, 1953; Bencher, 1980. Dep. Chm., Notts QS, 1970–71; a Recorder, 1972–88. Mem., Nottingham City Council, 1955–58 and 1960–63. District Referee, Nottinghamshire Wages Conciliation Board, NCB, 1980–88. Pres., Ct of Appeal, St Helena, 1998–. *Recreations:* watching good football (preferably Nottingham Forest: Mem. Club Cttee, 1965–82, Life Mem., 1982; Vice-Chm., 1972–75, Chm., 1975–78); swimming, reading and enjoying, when possible, company of wife and children. *Address:* The Briars, Old Melton Road, Normanton on the Wolds, Nottingham NG12 5NN.

APPLEBY, Douglas Edward Surtees; farmer; retired Managing Director, The Boots Co. Ltd; *b* 17 May 1929; *s* of Robert Appleby, MSc and Muriel (*née* Surtees); *m* 1952; one *s* one *d*. *Educ:* Durham Johnston Sch.; Univ. of London (BSc); Univ. of Nottingham (BSc). Chartered Accountant, 1957. Commissioned, RAF, Cranwell, 1950–54. Moore, Stephens & Co., Chartered Accountants, London, 1954–57; Distillers Co. Ltd, 1957–58; Corn Products Co., New York, 1959–63; Wilkinson Sword Ltd, 1964–68; The Boots Co Ltd, 1968–81 (Finance Dir, 1968–72, Man. Dir, 1973–81). Regional Dir, Nat. Westminster Bank, 1979–88; Chairman: John H. Mason Ltd, 1982–96; Meadow Farm Produce plc, 1984–86; Sims Food Gp plc, 1987–89. Member Council: Inst. Chartered Accountants, 1971–75; Loughborough Univ., 1973–75; CBI, 1977–81. *Address:* Burgh Island Causeway, Kingsbridge, Devon TQ7 4AS.

APPLEBY, Hazel Gillian; *see* Genn, H. G.

APPLEBY, (Lesley) Elizabeth, (Mrs Michael Kenneth Collins), QC 1979; barrister-at-law; a Deputy High Court Judge, since 1985; a Recorder, since 1989; *b* 12 Aug. 1942; *o d* of late Arthur Leslie Appleby and Dorothy Evelyn Appleby (*née* Edwards); *m* 1978, Michael Kenneth Collins, OBE, BSc, MICE; one *s* one *d*. *Educ:* Dominican Convent, Brewood, Staffs; Wolverhampton Girls' High Sch.; Manchester Univ. (LLB Hons). Called to Bar, Gray's Inn, 1965 (Richardson Schol.); *ad eundem* Lincoln's Inn, 1975, Bencher, 1986; in practice at Chancery Bar, 1966–; inspector of five cos, Dept of Trade, 1983; Chm., Inquiry into Lambeth BC, 1993. Member, Senate of Inns of Court and Bar, 1977–80, 1981–82. Chm., Ethics and Integrity Cttee, Cons. Party, 1998–. *Recreations:* swimming, gardening. *Address:* 4/5 Gray's Inn Square, Gray's Inn, WC1R 5AY. *T:* (020) 7404 5252; Glebe House, West Grinstead, Horsham, West Sussex RH13 8LR. *T:* (01403) 711228.

APPLEBY, Malcolm Arthur; engraver designer; *b* 6 Jan. 1946; *s* of James William and Marjory Appleby; *m* 2000, Philippa Swann; one *d*. *Educ:* Haws Down County Secondary Modern School for Boys; Beckenham Sch. of Art; Ravensbourne Coll. of Art and Design; Central Sch. of Arts and Crafts; Sir John Cass Sch. of Art; Royal Coll. of Art. Set up trade, 1968; bought Crathes station, 1970; moved workshop to Perthshire, 1996; developed fresh approaches to engraving on silver, forging after engraving; created first pure gold and pure silver pieces to bear Scottish hallmark, 1999; works designed and executed include: engraving on Prince of Wales coronet; model of moon (subseq. gift to first moon astronauts); steel and gold cylinder box for Goldsmiths' Co.; steel, gold, ivory and silver chess set, 1977; 500th anniv. silver for London Assay Office; King George VI Diamond Stakes trophy, 1978; seal for the Board of Trustees, V & A; silver condiment set for 10 Downing Street, commnd by Silver Trust; major silver commn for Royal Mus. of Scotland; silver table centre for new Scottish Parlt; gold Royal Medal for RSE, 2000; sporting guns (product designer, Holland & Holland, gunmakers, 1991–97), silver bowls, jewels, prints. Work in collections: Aberdeen Art Gallery; Royal Scottish Museum; Scottish Craft Collection; East Midlands Arts; Fitzwilliam Mus., Cambridge; BM; Goldsmiths' Co., V&A; Crafts Council; Contemporary Arts Soc.; Tower of London Royal Armouries; Nat. Mus. of Finland; Åland Maritime Mus.; S Australia Maritime Mus. One-man retrospective, Aberdeen Art Gall., 1998. Founder, British Art Postage Stamp Soc., 1986; Mem., British Art Medal Soc., 1987–. Chm., Crathes Drumoak Community Council, 1981. Life Member: NT for Scotland, 1971; SPAB, 1989. Member: Silver Soc.;

Butterfly Conservation Soc. Hon. Mem., Grandtully and Strathtay Br., Women's Rural Inst., 1997; Grandtully Hall Cttee, 1998– (Chm., 2000). Liveryman, Goldsmiths' Co. Hon. DLitt Heriot-Watt. *Recreations:* work, walking, garden design, drinking herbal tea with friends, acting in pantomime, conservation matters, breeding silver spangled Hamburg bantams, tree planting with Philippa Swann. *Address:* Aultbeag, Grandtully, by Aberfeldy, Perthshire PH15 2QU. *T:* (01887) 840484.

APPLEBY, Dom Raphael, OSB; Parish Priest, St Joseph's, Great Malvern, since 1996; *b* 18 July 1931; *s* of Harold Thompson Appleby and Margaret Morgan. *Educ:* Downside; Christ's Coll., Cambridge (MA). Downside novitiate, 1951; Housemaster at Downside, 1962–75, Head Master, 1975–80; Nat. Chaplain, Catholic Students' Council, 1974–94; Nat. Co-ordinator for RC Chaplains in Higher Educn, 1980–87. Diocesan Youth Chaplain, Clifton Dio., 1983–89. Sen. Cttee Mem., Cambridge Union Soc., 1959. Chaplain, British Assoc. of Knights of Malta, 1978–. *Publications:* Dear Church, What's the Point?, 1984; Glimpses of God, 1993. *Recreations:* books, music. *Address:* 125 Newtown Road, Malvern, Worcs WR14 1PF.

APPLEBY, Rt Rev. Richard Franklin; Bishop of the Northern Region and an Assistant Bishop, Diocese of Brisbane, since 1999; *b* 17 Nov. 1940; *s* of Julian Paul Leonard Appleby and Lilian Margaret Appleby (*née* Pragnell); *m* 1966, Elizabeth Clark; two *d. Educ:* Eltham High Sch.; Univ. of Melbourne (BSc); St John's Coll., Morpeth (ThL (Hons)). Curate of Glenroy, 1967–68; Curate of N Balwyn and Chaplain to Apprentices and Probation Hostels, 1969–70; Chaplain to Christchurch Grammar Sch., 1970–71; Warden of Wollaston Coll. and Chaplain to the Archbishop of Perth, 1972–75; Rector of Belmont, 1975–80; Dean of Bathurst and Examining Chaplain to the Bishop of Bathurst, 1980–83; Auxiliary Bishop of Newcastle, 1983–92; Bishop of the Northern Territory (Australia), 1992–99. Pres., NSW Ecumenical Council, 1987–89. *Recreations:* gardening, walking, listening to music. *Address:* GPO Box 421, Brisbane, Qld 4001, Australia; c/o Diocesan Office, 373 Ann Street, Brisbane, Qld 4000, Australia. *T:* (7) 38352213, *Fax:* (7) 38325030; *e-mail:* rappleby@anglicanbrisbane.org.au.

APPLEGARTH, Adam John; Chief Executive, Northern Rock plc, since 2000; *b* 3 Aug. 1962; *s* of John Speed Applegarth and Mary Applegarth; *m* 1984, Patricia Catherine Killeen; two *s. Educ:* Sedbergh Sch.; Grey Coll., Durham Univ. (BA). Gen. Manager, 1993–96, Exec. Dir, 1996–97, Northern Rock Building Soc.; Exec. Dir, Northern Rock plc, 1997–; Dir, Northern Rock (Guernsey) Ltd, 1996–. Trustee, Internat. Centre for Life Trust, 1997–. *Recreation:* cricket. *Address:* Northern Rock plc, Northern Rock House, Gosforth, Newcastle upon Tyne NE3 4PL. *T:* (0191) 285 7191. *Club:* Ashbrooke Sporting.

APPLETON, John Fortnam; His Honour Judge Appleton; a Circuit Judge, since 1992; Designated Civil Judge, Preston Group of Courts, since 1999; *b* 8 April 1946; *s* of George Fortnam Appleton, OBE, TD, JP, DL and Patricia Margaret Appleton; *m* 1983, Maureen Sellers; one *s. Educ:* Harrow; Bristol Univ. (LLB Hons). Called to the Bar, Middle Temple, 1969; a Recorder of the Crown Court, 1985. *Recreations:* salmon fishing, shooting, gardening. *Address:* The Court Service, Preston Group of Courts, Sessions House, Lancaster Road, Preston PR1 2PD. *T:* (01772) 821451, *Fax:* (01772) 884767.

APPLETON, Brig. John Roper, OBE 2000; CEng, FIMechE; Chairman, Smallpeice Trust, since 2001; *b* 29 April 1938; *s* of late John Jackson Appleton and of Ada Mary Appleton (*née* Roper); *m* 1st, 1959, Jenifer Jane Worman; one *s* one *d*; 2nd, 1978, Elizabeth Ann Cullen; two *d. Educ:* Liverpool Collegiate Sch.; Alun Grammar Sch., Mold; RMA Sandhurst; RMC Shrivenham. BScEng. Commnd REME, 1958; regtl and staff appts in UK, BAOR, Cyprus, Canada, 1961–78; MoD, 1978–79; Comdr REME, 1st Armd Div., BAOR, 1979–82; British Liaison Officer, HQ US Army, Pentagon, 1982–83; MoD, 1983–84; Asst Dir, Defence Commitments Staff, MoD, 1984–87, retired 1987. Fellowship, subseq. Royal Academy, of Engineering: Head of Engineering Affairs, 1987; Head of Corporate Affairs, 1991; Exec. Sec., 1993–2000; Hon. FREng 2000. Liveryman, Engineers' Co., 1996–. *Recreations:* gardening, garden construction. *Address:* Chatterton House, The Park, Great Bookham, Surrey KT23 3LN.

APPLEYARD, James; *see* Appleyard, W. J.

APPLEYARD, Joan Ena, (Lady Appleyard); Headmistress, St Swithun's School, Winchester, 1986–94; *b* 15 Aug. 1946; *d* of William Jefferson and Ruth Ena Leake; *m* 1994, Sir Leonard Appleyard, *qv. Educ:* Univ. of Newcastle (BA Hons History); Westminster Coll., Oxford (Dip Ed). Asst Mistress, 1968–70, Head of History, 1970–73, Scarborough Girls' High Sch.; Head of Humanities, Graham Sch., Scarborough, 1973–75; Dep. Head, 1975–79, Headmistress, 1979–86, Hunmanby Hall Sch., Filey. Pres., GSA, 1992–93. *Recreations:* drama, theatre, reading, cooking.

APPLEYARD, Sir Leonard (Vincent), KCMG 1994 (CMG 1986); HM Diplomatic Service, retired; Vice-Chairman, Barclays Capital, since 1999; *b* 2 Sept. 1938; *s* of Thomas William Appleyard; *m* 1st, 1964, Elizabeth Margaret West (marr. diss. 1994); two *d*; 2nd, 1994, Joan Ena Jefferson (*see* J. E. Appleyard). *Educ:* Read School, Drax, W Yorks; Queens' Coll., Cambridge (MA). Foreign Office, 1962; Third Secretary, Hong Kong, 1964; Second Secretary, Peking, 1966; Second, later First, Secretary, Foreign Office, 1969; First Secretary, Delhi, 1971, Moscow, 1975; HM Treasury, 1978; Financial Counsellor, Paris, 1979–82; Head of Economic Relations Dept, FCO, 1982–84; Principal Private Sec. to Sec. of State for Foreign and Commonwealth Affairs, 1984–86; Ambassador to Hungary, 1986–89; Dep. Sec., Cabinet Office, 1989–91 (on secondment); Political Dir and Dep. Under-Sec. of State, FCO, 1991–94; Ambassador to People's Republic of China, 1994–97; Barclays Capital, 1998–. *Recreations:* music, reading, golf. *Club:* Brooks's.

APPLEYARD, Sir Raymond (Kenelm), KBE 1986; PhD; Director-General for Information Market and Innovation, Commission of the European Communities, 1981–86; *b* 5 Oct. 1922; *s* of late Maj.-Gen. K. C. Appleyard, CBE, TD, DL, and Monica Mary Louis; *m* 1947, Joan Greenwood; one *s* two *d. Educ:* Rugby; Cambridge. BA 1943, MA 1948, PhD 1950. Instructor, Yale Univ., 1949–51; Fellow, Rockefeller Foundn, California Inst. of Technology, 1951–53; Research Officer, Atomic Energy of Canada Ltd, 1953–56; Sec., UN Scientific Cttee on effects of atomic radiation, 1956–61; Dir, Biology Services, Commn of European Atomic Energy Community, 1961–73; Dir-Gen. for Scientific and Tech. Information and Information Management, EEC Commn, 1973–80. Exec. Sec., European Molecular Biology Organisation, 1965–73; Sec., European Molecular Biology Conf., 1969–73; President: Inst. of Information Scientists, 1981–82; Inst. of Translation and Interpreting, 1989–94. Hon. Dr.med Ulm, 1977. *Publications:* contribs to: Nature, Jl Gen. Microbiol., Genetics. *Recreations:* bridge, tennis. *Clubs:* Athenæum; Fondation Universitaire (Brussels).

APPLEYARD, Dr (William) James, FRCP; Clinical Dean, Kigesi International School of Medicine, Uganda, since 2000; Consultant Paediatrician, 1971–98, Hon. Consultant Paediatrician, 1998–99, and Clinical Director, Paediatric Directorate, 1992–98, Kent and Canterbury Hospitals NHS Trust (formerly Canterbury and Thanet Health District); *b* 25 Oct. 1935; *s* of late E. R. Appleyard and Maud Oliver Collingwood (*née* Marshall); *m* 1964, Elizabeth Anne Ward; one *s* two *d. Educ:* Canford Sch.; Exeter College, Oxford (BM BCh, MA); Guy's Hosp. Med. Sch., Univ. of London. DObstRCOG; FRCP 1978; FRCPCH 1998. Junior paediat. posts, Guy's and Gt Ormond St; Resident in Pediat., Univ. of Louisville, 1964–65; Dyers' Co. Res. Registrar, St Thomas' Hosp., 1968–69. British Medical Association: Treas., 1996–July 2002; Member: Jt Consultants Cttee, 1976–95; Consultants Cttee, 1971– (Dep. Chm., 1979–83); Dep. Chm., 1989–91, Chm., 1992–95, Rep. Body. Treasurer, BPA, 1983–88; Mem., GMC, 1984– (Mem., Educn Cttee, 1993–96); Member Council: RCP, 1988–91 (Member: Standing Cttee, 1970–72; Res. Cttee, 1971–74; Paed. Cttee, 1987–91; Examng Bd, 1992–98); World Med. Assoc., 1995– (Chm., Med. Ethics Cttee, 1996–99); Member: Health Service Inf. Steering Gp, Korner Cttee, 1985; DoH Inf. Adv. Gp, 1986–90; Nat. Specialist Commissioning Adv. Gp, DoH, 1995–96; London Univ. Nominee, Kent AHA, 1974–78. Hon. Tutor in Paed., Guy's Hosp.; Hon. Lectr in Paed., St Thomas' Hosp.; Dean of Clin. Studies, (UK), St George's Univ. Sch. of Medicine, Grenada, 1995–97 (Associate Prof., 1985–90; Prof. of Paediatrics, 1991–95; Chm., Senate, 1991–93). Hon. Treas., Kent Postgrad. Med. Centre, Canterbury, 1998–2000. Patron, Dyspraxia Trust, 1988–. Liveryman, Apothecaries' Soc., 1983. Hon. DM Kent at Canterbury, 1999; Hon. DHL St George's, Grenada, 2000. Alumnus Award for Paed. Res., Univ. of Louisville, 1965. *Publications:* contribs to med. jls. *Recreations:* lawn tennis, photography, erstwhile allotment digger. *Address:* Thimble Hall, Blean Common, Blean, Kent CT2 9JJ. *T:* (01227) 781771. *Clubs:* Athenæum, Penn.

APSLEY, Lord; Allen Christopher Bertram Bathurst; *b* 11 March 1961; *s* and *heir* of 8th Earl Bathurst, *qv*; *m* 1986, Hilary (marr. diss. 1995), *d* of John F. George, Weston Lodge Albury, Guildford; one *s* one *d*; *m* 1996, Sara, *d* of Christopher Chapman. *Educ:* Harrow Sch.; Wye Coll., London Univ.; RAC, Cirencester. *Heir: s* Hon. Benjamin George Henry Bathurst, *b* 6 March 1990. *Address:* Cirencester Park, Cirencester, Glos GL7 2BT.

APTED, Michael David; director and producer of television and films; *b* 10 Feb. 1941; *m* (marr. diss.); two *s*; *m* Jo; one *s. Educ:* Downing Coll., Cambridge (BA 1963). With Granada TV, 1963-70: researcher, 1963; dir, episodes of Coronation Street; investigative reporter, World in Action, incl. research, 1964, on 7 Up, which became first of series (director: Seven Plus Seven, 1970; 21 Up, 1977; 28 Up, 1985; 35 Up, 1991; 42 Up, 1998). Director: *television:* series: Big Breadwinner Hog, 1969; The Lovers, 1970; Folly Foot (for children), 1972; My Life and Times, 1991; plays and films: Slattery's Mounted Foot, 1970; The Mosedale Horseshoe, 1971; The Reporters, 1972; Kisses at Fifty, 1972; Another Sunday and Sweet FA, 1972; The Collection, 1975; Stronger than the Sun, 1977; P'tang Yang Kipperbang, 1982; The Long Way Home, 1989; Always Outnumbered, 1998; Nathan Dixon, 1999; *films include*: Triple Echo, 1973; Stardust, 1975; The Squeeze, 1977; Agatha, 1979; Coal Miner's Daughter, 1980; Continental Divide, 1981; Gorky Park, 1983; Firstborn, 1984; Bring on the Night, 1985; Critical Condition, 1987; Gorillas in the Mist, 1988; Class Action, 1991; Incident at Oglala, 1992; Thunderheart, 1992; Blink, 1994; Moving the Mountain, 1994; Nell, 1995; Extreme Measures, 1997; (also prod) Inspirations (documentary), 1997; The World is Not Enough, 1999; Me and Isaac Newton, 1999; Enigma, 2001; *executive producer:* The River Rat, 1984; Dracula, 1992. *Publication:* 7 Up. *Address:* Michael Apted Film Co., 1901 Avenue of the Stars, Suite 1245, Los Angeles, CA 90067-6013, USA.

APTHORP, John Dorrington, OBE 1999; Chairman, Majestic Wine Warehouses (formerly Wizard Wine), since 1989; *b* 25 April 1935; *s* of late Eric and Mildred Apthorp, *m* 1959, Jane Frances Arnold; three *s* one *d. Educ:* Aldenham School. FBIM 1977; FInstD 1978; FIGD 1981. Sub-Lieut RNVR, 1953–55. Family business, Appypak, 1956–68; started Bejam Group, 1968, Exec. Chm., 1968–87, non-exec. Chm., 1987–88. Guardian Young Business Man of Year, 1974. Councillor, London Bor. of Barnet, 1968–74. Liveryman: Butchers' Co., 1974–; Vintners' Co., 1999–. Commandeur d'Honneur pour Commanderie du Bontemps de Medoc et des Graves, 1977. *Recreations:* shooting, wine. *Address:* The Field House, Newlands Avenue, Radlett, Herts WD7 8EL. *T:* (01923) 855201. *Clubs:* St Hubert's, Radlett Tennis and Squash.

AQUINO, Maria Corazón Cojuangco, (Cory Aquino); President of the Philippines, 1986–92; *b* 25 Jan. 1933; *d* of late José and Demetria Cojuangco; *m* 1954, Benigno S. Aquino (*d* 1983); one *s* four *d. Educ:* St Scholastica's Coll. and Assumption Convent, Manila; Ravenhill Acad., Philadelphia; Notre Dame Sch., NY; Mount St Vincent Coll., NY (BA); Far Eastern Univ., Manila. Numerous honours, awards and hon. degrees from Philippine and overseas bodies. *Address:* 25 Times Street, Quezon City, Philippines.

ARAFAT, Yasser; President, Palestinian National Authority, since 1996; *b* 4 Aug. 1929; *m* 1991, Suha Tawil; one *d. Educ:* Cairo Univ. Joined League of Palestinian Students, 1944, Mem. Exec. Cttee, 1950, Pres., 1952–56; formed jointly, Fatah, 1956; engineer in Egypt, 1956, in Kuwait, 1957–65; Pres., Exec. Cttee, Palestine Nat. Liberation Movt, and Chm., Exec. Cttee, Palestine Liberation Orgn, 1968–; Pres., Central Cttee and Head, Political Dept, PLO, 1973–; Comdr Palestinian Revolutionary Forces; signed Declaration of Principles on Interim Self-Government, 1993, with Yitzhak Rabin. Joliot-Curie Gold Medal, 1975; (jtly) Nobel Peace Prize, 1994. *Address:* c/o Palestinian Delegation, 5 Galena Road, W6 0LT. *T:* (020) 8563 0008, *Fax:* (0181) 563 0058; (office) Al-Muntada, Al-Rimal, Gaza City, via Israel.

ARAGONA, Giancarlo; Ambassador of the Republic of Italy to the Russian Federation, since 1999; *b* 14 Nov. 1942; *s* of late Giovanni Aragona and of Bianca Maria Aragona (*née* Vinci); *m* 1968, Sandra Pauline Jackson; two *d. Educ:* Messina Univ., Italy (degree in Internat. Law). Entered Italian Diplomatic Service, 1969: served in Vienna, Freiburg in Breisgau and Lagos, 1969–80; Foreign Ministry, Rome, 1980–84; First Counsellor (Political), London, 1984–87; First Counsellor, then Minister-Counsellor and Dep. Perm. Rep., Delegn to NATO, 1987–92; Diplomatic Advr to Defense Minister, Rome, 1992–95; Chief of Cabinet of Foreign Minister, 1995–96; Sec. Gen., OSCE, 1996–99. Kt Comdr, Order of Merit (Italy), 1992. *Address:* (office) Denezhny per. 5, 121002 Moscow, Russian Federation. *T:* 7969691.

ARAIN, Shafiq; Ugandan politician and diplomat; *b* 20 Nov. 1933; *s* of late Din Mohd Arain; *m* 1966, Maria Leana Godinho; one *s* two *d. Educ:* Government Sch., Kampala; Regent's Polytechnic, London; Nottingham Univ. MP (UPC), 1962–71; Member, E African Legislative Assembly, 1963–71; E African Minister for Common Market and Economic Affairs, later E African Minister for Communications, Research and Social Services; Chairman: Minimum Wages Commission, 1964; Statutory Commn on Cooperative Movement, 1967. Uganda's Delegate to UN General Assembly, 1965–66; Leader, Uganda Delegn to Canada and CPA Conf., Trinidad and Tobago, 1969. Member, Governing Council, Univ. of Dar es Salaam, 1967–68; Chm., Commonwealth Parly Assoc., Uganda Br., 1969–70. Pres., Uganda Cricket Assoc., 1968–69. Left for exile in London following coup in 1971; returned to Uganda, 1979; elections were held in Dec. 1980; Minister without Portfolio, President's Office, and High Comr for Uganda to London, 1980–85. Dir, Equatorial Bank, 1989–94. *Recreations:* golf, walking, reading. *Clubs:* Uganda, Royal Over-Seas League, Mark's.

ARBER, Prof. Werner; Professor of Molecular Microbiology, Basle University, 1971–96; President, International Council of Scientific Unions, 1996–99. Discovered restriction enzymes at Geneva in 1960's; Nobel Prize in Physiology or Medicine (jointly), 1978. *Address:* Department of Microbiology, Biozentrum der Universität Basel, 70 Klingelbergstrasse, 4056 Basel, Switzerland.

ARBIB, Martyn, DL; FCA; Founder, 1973, President, since 2000, Perpetual plc (Chairman 1973–2000); *b* 27 June 1939; *s* of late Richard Arbib and Denise Arbib; *m* 1969, Anne Hermione Parton; two *s* two *d*. *Educ:* Felsted Sch. FCA 1962. Trained with Spicer & Pegler, 1956–62; qualified Chartered Accountant, 1962; Kelsey Industries PLC, 1966–72 (non-exec. Dir, 1975–2000). Trustee, Arbib Foundn, 1987–; Dir, 1991–, Dep. Chm., 1994–, River and Rowing Mus. Foundn, Henley on Thames; Dir, 1993–, Jt Chm., 1994–, Henley Fest. of Music and the Arts. DL Oxon, 2001. *Recreations:* golf, dry fly fishing, flat racehorse owner and breeder. *Address:* Perpetual Park, Perpetual Drive, Henley-on-Thames RG9 1HH. *Clubs:* Huntercombe Golf, Oxfordshire Golf.

ARBOUR, Anthony Francis; JP; Member (C) South West, and Chairman, Planning Committee, London Assembly, Greater London Authority, since 2000; *b* 30 Aug. 1945; *s* of late Charles Foster Arbour and of Magdalen Arbour; *m* 1970, Caroline Anne Cooper; three *s* one *d*. *Educ:* St Andrew's Sch., Ham Common; Surbiton Co. Grammar Sch.; Kingston Coll. of Technol. (BSc Econ); City Univ. Business Sch. (MBA). Sen. Lectr, Kingston Univ. Business Sch., 1967–2000 (Vis. Fellow, 2000–). Mem., Employment Tribunals, London Central (formerly Industrial Tribunals, London North), 1993–. Member (C): Richmond upon Thames BC, 1968– (Chm., Planning Cttee, 1974–80; Leader, Cons. Gp, 1996–); Surbiton, GLC, 1983–87. Vice-Chm., Kingston and Richmond FHSA, 1990–96; Mem., Metropolitan Police Authy, 2000–. JP Richmond upon Thames, 1974. Chm., Hampton Wick United Charity, 1972–. Governor: Kingston Poly., 1988–90; Tiffin Sch., 1988–92. *Recreations:* book collecting, watching TV soap operas, car booting. *Address:* 3 Holmesdale Road, Teddington, Middx TW11 9LJ; Greater London Authority, Romney House, 43 Marsham Street, SW1P 3PY.

ARBUTHNOT, Rev. Andrew Robert Coghill; Missioner, London Healing Mission, 1983–95; Director, Sun Alliance and London Insurance Ltd, 1970–91; *b* 14 Jan. 1926; *s* of Robert Wemyss Muir Arbuthnot and Mary Arbuthnot (*née* Coghill); *m* 1952, Audrey Dutton-Barker; one *s* one *d*. *Educ:* Eton; Southwark Ordination Course. Served 1944–47, Captain, Scots Guards, wounded. Dir, Arbuthnot Latham & Co. Ltd, 1953–82; Chm. and Chief Exec., Arbuthnot Latham Holdings, 1974–81; Chm., Arbuthnot Insurance Services, 1968–83. Contested (C) Houghton-le-Spring, 1959. Ordained Deacon, 1974; Priest, 1975. *Publications:* (with Audrey Arbuthnot) Love that Heals, 1986; Christian Prayer and Healing, 1989; All You Need is More and More of Jesus, 1993. *Recreations:* water colour painting, operas. *Address:* Monksfield House, Tilford, Farnham, Surrey GU10 2AL. *T:* (01252) 782233.

ARBUTHNOT, Rt Hon. James (Norwich), PC 1998; MP (C) North East Hampshire, since 1997 (Wanstead and Woodford, 1987–97); *b* 4 Aug. 1952; 2nd *s* of Sir John Arbuthnot, 1st Bt, MBE, TD and of Margaret Jean, *yr d* of late Alexander G. Duff; *heir pres.* of Sir William Arbuthnot, Bt, *qv*; *m* 1984, Emma Louise Broadbent; one *s* three *d*. *Educ:* Wellesley House, Broadstairs; Eton Coll. (Captain of School); Trinity Coll., Cambridge (MA). Called to the Bar, 1975; practising barrister, 1977–92. Councillor, Royal Bor. of Kensington and Chelsea, 1978–87. Contested (C) Cynon Valley, 1983, May 1984. PPS to Minister of State for Armed Forces, 1988–90, to Sec. of State, DTI, 1990–92; an Asst Govt Whip, 1992–94; Parly Under-Sec. of State, DSS, 1994–95; Minister of State for Defence Procurement, MoD, 1995–97; Opposition Chief Whip, 1997–2001. Pres., Cynon Valley Cons. Assoc., 1983–92. *Recreations:* playing guitar, skiing, computers. *Address:* House of Commons, SW1A 0AA. *T:* (020) 7219 3000.

ARBUTHNOT, Sir Keith Robert Charles, 8th Bt *cr* 1823, of Edinburgh; *b* 23 Sept. 1951; *s* of Sir Hugh Fitz-Gerald Arbuthnot, 7th Bt and Elizabeth Kathleen (*d* 1972), *d* of late Sqdn-Ldr G. G. A. Williams; *S* father, 1983; *m* 1982, Anne, *yr d* of late Brig. Peter Moore; two *s* one *d*. *Educ:* Wellington; Univ. of Edinburgh. BSc (Soc. Sci.). *Heir: s* Robert Hugh Peter Arbuthnot, *b* 2 March 1986. *Address:* Mount Ulston, Jedburgh, Roxburghshire TD8 6TQ.

ARBUTHNOT, Sir William (Reierson), 2nd Bt *cr* 1964, of Kittybrewster, Aberdeen; *b* 2 Sept. 1950; *s* of Sir John Sinclair-Wemyss Arbuthnot, 1st Bt, MBE, TD, sometime MP (C) Dover Div. of Kent, and of (Margaret) Jean, *yr d* of late Alexander Gordon Duff; *S* father, 1992. *Educ:* Eton; Coll. of Law, London. Arbuthnot Latham Holdings, 1970–76; Joynson-Hicks & Co., solicitors, 1978–81. Member of Lloyd's, 1971–; Dir, Assoc. of Lloyd's Members, 1997–. Dep. Chm., High Premium Gp, 1994–. Liveryman, Grocers' Co., 1981. *Recreation:* genealogy. *Heir: b* Rt Hon. James Norwich Arbuthnot, *qv*. *Address:* 37 Cathcart Road, SW10 9JG. *T:* (020) 7823 3344; 14 Ashburn Gardens, SW7 4DG. *T:* and, *Fax:* (020) 7370 4907; *e-mail:* wra@arbuthnot.freeserve.co.uk.

ARBUTHNOTT, family name of **Viscount of Arbuthnott**.

ARBUTHNOTT, 16th Viscount of, *cr* 1641; **John Campbell Arbuthnott,** KT 1996; CBE 1986; DSC 1945; FRSE 1984; Lord-Lieutenant, Grampian Region (Kincardineshire), 1977–99; Her Majesty's Lord High Commissioner to General Assembly, Church of Scotland, 1986, 1987; *b* 26 Oct. 1924; *e s* of 15th Viscount of Arbuthnott, CB, CBE, DSO, MC, and Ursula Collingwood (*d* 1989); *S* father, 1966; *m* 1949, Mary Elizabeth Darley (*née* Oxley); one *s* one *d*. *Educ:* Fettes Coll.; Gonville and Caius Coll., Cambridge. Served RNVR (Fleet Air Arm), 1942–46; Near and Far East, British Pacific Fleet, 1945. Cambridge University, 1946–49 (Estate Management), MA 1967. Chartered Surveyor and Land Agent; Agricultural Land Service, 1949–55; Land Agent (Scotland), The Nature Conservancy, 1955–67. Chm., Aberdeen and Northern Marts, 1986–91 (Dir, 1973–91); Director: Scottish Widows' Fund and Life Assurance Soc., 1978–94 (Dep. Chm., 1982–84, 1987–88; Chm., 1984–87); Scottish Northern Investment Trust, 1979–85; Clydesdale Bank, 1985–92 (Northern Area, 1975–85); Britoil, 1988–90; Scottish Adv. Bd, BP, 1990–96. Member: Countryside Commn for Scotland, 1967–71; Aberdeen Univ. Court, 1978–84; Royal Commn on Historical MSS, 1987–94; Chm., Red Deer Commn, 1969–75; President: British Assoc. for Shooting and Conservation (formerly Wildfowlers Assoc. of GB and Ireland), 1973–92; The Scottish Landowners' Fedn, 1974–79 (Convener, 1971–74); Royal Zool Soc. of Scotland, 1976–96; Scottish Agricl Orgn Soc., 1980–83; RSGS, 1983–87; Fedn of Agricl Co-operatives (UK) Ltd, 1983–87; Dep. Chm., Nature Conservancy Council, 1980–85, Chm., Adv. Cttee for Scotland, 1980–85. Hon. Air Cdre, 612 Co. of Aberdeen Sqn, RAuxAF, 1998–. FRSA. Hon. LLD Aberdeen, 1995. GCStJ 1994; Prior of Scotland, OStJ, 1983–95. *Recreations:* countryside activities, historical research. *Heir: s* Master of Arbuthnott, *qv*. *Address:* Arbuthnott House, by Laurencekirk, Kincardineshire, Scotland AB30 1PA. *T:* (01561) 361226. *Clubs:* Army and Navy; New (Edinburgh).

ARBUTHNOTT, Master of; Hon. John Keith Oxley Arbuthnott, DL; *b* 18 July 1950; *s* and *heir* of 16th Viscount of Arbuthnott, *qv*; *m* 1974, Jill Mary, *er d* of Captain Colin Farquharson, *qv*; one *s* two *d*. *Educ:* Fettes College; Aberdeen Univ. Mem., Grampian Health Bd, 1993–97. DL Kincardineshire, 2000. *Address:* Kilternan, Arbuthnott, Laurencekirk, Kincardineshire AB30 1NA. *T:* (01561) 320417.

ARBUTHNOTT, Hugh James, CMG 1984; HM Diplomatic Service, retired; Chairman, Charities Evaluation Services, since 1997; *b* 27 Dec. 1936; *m*; two *s* (and one *s* decd). *Educ:* Ampleforth Coll., Yorks; New Coll., Oxford. Nat. Service, Black Watch, 1955–57. Joined Foreign (subseq. Diplomatic) Service, 1960; 3rd Sec., Tehran, 1962–64; 2nd, later 1st Sec., FO, 1964–66; Private Sec., Minister of State for Foreign Affairs, 1966–68; Lagos, 1968–71; 1st Sec. (Head of Chancery), Tehran, 1971–74; Asst, later Head of European Integration Dept (External), FCO, 1974–77; Counsellor (Agric. and Econ.), Paris, 1978–80; Head of Chancery, Paris, 1980–83; Under Sec., Internat. Div., ODA, 1983–85; Ambassador to Romania, 1986–89, to Portugal, 1989–93, to Denmark, 1993–96. Chm., Martin Currie European Investment Trust, 1997–. Trustee, Children at Risk Foundn (UK), 1997–. Hon. Prof. of Politics and Internat. Relns, Aberdeen Univ., 1996–99. *Publication:* Common Man's Guide to the Common Market (ed with G. Edwards), 1979, 2nd edn (co-author with G. Edwards), 1989. *Address:* 11 Bede House, Manor Fields, SW15 3LT. *T:* (020) 8785 1714.

ARBUTHNOTT, Sir John (Peebles), Kt 1998; PhD, ScD; FIBiol; FRSE; FRCPath; Secretary and Treasurer, Carnegie Trust for Universities of Scotland, since 2000; Board Member, Food Standards Agency and Chairman, Scottish Food Advisory Committee, since 2000; *b* 8 April 1939; *s* of James Anderson Arbuthnott and Jean (*née* Kelly); *m* 1962, Elinor Rutherford Smillie; one *s* two *d*. *Educ:* Univ. of Glasgow (BSc 1960; PhD 1964); Trinity Coll., Dublin (ScD 1984; Hon. FTCD 1992). FIBiol 1988; FRSE 1993; FIIB 1993; FRCPath 1995. University of Glasgow: Lectr, Dept of Bacteriology, 1963–67; Alan Johnston, Lawrence and Moseley Res. Fellow of Royal Soc., 1968–72; Sen. Lectr, Dept of Microbiol., 1972–73; Sen. Lectr, Dept of Bacteriol., 1973–75; Professor of Microbiology: TCD, 1976–88 (Bursar, 1983–86); Univ. of Nottingham, 1988–91; Prin. and Vice Chancellor, Strathclyde Univ., 1991–2000. Vis. Lectr, Dept of Microbiol., New York Univ. Med. Centre, 1966–67. Member: Bd, PHLS, 1991–97; Bd, Glasgow Development Agency, 1995–2000; Bd, British Council Educn Counselling Service, 1995–96; Cttee, DTI Multimedia Industry Adv. Gp, 1995–; Nat. Cttee of Inquiry into Higher Educn, 1996–97. Chm., Jt Inf. Systems Cttee, HEFC, 1994–98; Convenor, Cttee of Scottish Higher Educn Principals, 1994–96. Treasurer, Soc. for Gen. Microbiol., 1987–92. Chm., Nat. Review of allocation of health resources in Scotland, 1998–2000. Founder FMedSci 1998. Hon. FRCPSGlas 1997. MRIA 1985. Hon. DSc: Łódź, 1995; Univ. Teknologi, Malaysia, 1997; Glasgow, 1999; Hon. LLD: QUB, 1996; Aberdeen, 1998; Hon. DEd Queen Margaret's UC, 2000. *Publications:* edited: (jtly) Isoelectric Focusing, 1975; (jtly) The Determinants of Bacterial and Viral Pathogenicity, 1983; (jtly) Foodborne Illness: a Lancet review, 1991; more than 100 in prestigious scientific learned jls and books. *Recreations:* golf, birdwatching. *Address:* 9 Curlinghall, Broomfield Crescent, Largs KA30 8LB.

ARBUTHNOTT, Robert, CBE 1991; Minister (Cultural Affairs), India, British Council, 1988–93; *b* 28 Sept. 1936; *s* of late Archibald Arbuthnott, MBE, ED, and Barbara Joan (*née* Worters); *m* 1962, Sophie Robina (*née* Axford); one *s* two *d*. *Educ:* Sedbergh Sch. (scholar); Emmanuel Coll., Cambridge (exhibnr; BA Mod Langs, MA). Nat. service, 1955–57 (2nd Lieut The Black Watch RHR). British Council, 1960–94: Karachi, 1960–62; Lahore, 1962–64; London, 1964–67; Representative, Nepal, 1967–72; London Inst. of Education, 1972–73; Representative, Malaysia, 1973–76; Director, Educational Contracts Dept, 1976–77; Controller, Personnel and Staff Recruitment Div., 1978–81; Representative, Germany, 1981–85; RCDS, 1986; Controller, America, Pacific and S Asia Div., 1987. Member: Mgt Cttee, St Anthony's Cheshire Home, Wolverhampton, 1995–2000; English Haydn Fest. Cttee, Bridgnorth, 1995–2000; Internat. Cttee, Leonard Cheshire Foundn, 1997–; Adv. Panel, Nehru Centre, 1998–. FRAS 1995 (Mem. Council, 1996–2000). *Recreations:* music-making, the arts, historic buildings. *Club:* Oxford and Cambridge.

ARCAYA, Ignacio; Ambassador of Venezuela to the United States of America, since 2001; *b* Caracas, 3 June 1939; *s* of Ignacio Luis Arcaya and Antonieta (*née* Smith); *m* 1966, Lydia Vincenti; one *s* one *d*. *Educ:* Central Univ. of Venezuela (Internat. Affairs, 1964; Law, 1968). Third Sec., Perm. Mission of Venezuela in Geneva, 1966–68; Second Sec., Min. for Foreign Affairs, 1968–69; First Sec., Mission to OAS, Washington, 1969–72; Counsellor, Inst. of Foreign Trade, Min. for Foreign Affairs, 1972–75; Minister Counsellor of Econ. Affairs, Paris, 1975–78; Ambassador to Australia and non-resident Ambassador to NZ, Fiji and Philippines, 1978–84; Sec. Gen., Assoc. of Iron Ore Exporting Countries, 1984–88; Ambassador-at-large, Min. for Foreign Affairs, 1988; Ambassador: to Chile, 1989–92; to UK, 1992–95 and (non-resident) to Ireland, 1994–95; to Argentina, 1995–98; Perm. Rep. to UN, 1998–99 and 2000–01; Minister of Govt and Justice, 1999–2000; acting Pres. of Venezuela, Oct. 1999. Venezuelan orders: Order of Liberator, 1992; Orden Francisco de Miranda, 1995; Orden Andrés Bello, 1995; Orden al Merito en el Trabajo, 1998; Orden J. C. Falcón, 1999; numerous foreign orders. *Recreations:* polo, golf, tennis, fencing (sabre), ski-ing. *Address:* Embassy of Venezuela, 1099 30th Street NW, Washington, DC 20007, USA. *T:* (202) 3426804; *e-mail:* embajador@embavenezus.org; (residence) 2443 Massachusetts Avenue NW, Washington, DC 20007, USA. *T:* (202) 5183326; Avenida Principal del Caracas Country Club, Quinta Jamely, Caracas 1052, Venezuela. *Clubs:* Caracas Country; Royal Berkshire Polo; Royal & Ancient Golf (St Andrews); Chantilly Polo (Paris).

ARCHDALE, Sir Edward (Folmer), 3rd Bt *cr* 1928; DSC 1943; Captain, RN, retired; *b* 8 Sept. 1921; *s* of Vice-Adm. Sir Nicholas Edward Archdale, 2nd Bt, CBE, and Gerda (*d* 1969), 2nd *d* of late F. C. Sievers, Copenhagen; *S* father, 1955; *m* 1954, Elizabeth Ann Stewart (marr. diss. 1978), *d* of late Maj.-Gen. Wilfrid Boyd Fellowes Lukis, CBE; one *s* two *d*. *Educ:* Royal Naval Coll., Dartmouth. Joined Royal Navy, 1935; served War of 1939–45 (despatches, DSC). *Recreation:* civilization. *Heir: s* Nicholas Edward Archdale, *b* 2 Dec. 1965. *Address:* 16 Addison Crescent, W14 8JR.

ARCHER, family name of **Barons Archer of Sandwell** and **Archer of Weston-super-Mare**.

ARCHER OF SANDWELL, Baron *cr* 1992 (Life Peer), of Sandwell in the County of West Midlands; **Peter Kingsley Archer,** PC 1977; QC 1971; a Recorder of the Crown Court, 1982–98; *b* 20 Nov. 1926; *s* of Cyril Kingsley Archer and May (*née* Baker); *m* 1954, Margaret Irene (*née* Smith); one *s*. *Educ:* Wednesday Boys' High Sch.; LSE; University Coll., London (Fellow 1978). Called to Bar, Gray's Inn, 1952; Bencher, 1974; commenced practice, 1953. MP (Lab) Rowley Regis and Tipton, 1966–74, Warley West, 1974–92. PPS to Attorney-Gen., 1967–70; Solicitor General, 1974–79; chief Opposition spokesman on legal affairs, 1979–82, on trade, 1982–83, on N Ireland, 1983–87. UK Deleg. to UN Gen. Assembly (Third Cttee), 1969. Chairman: Council on Tribunals, 1992–99; Enemy Property Claims Assessment Panel, 1999–. Chairman: Amnesty International (British Section), 1971–74; Parly gp for World Govt, 1970–74; Soc. of Labour Lawyers, 1971–74, 1979–93 (Jt Pres., 1993–); Mem., Exec. Cttee, Fabian Soc.,

1974–86 (Chm., 1980–81; Pres., 1993–). Ombudsman for Mirror Group Newspapers, 1989–90. President: World Disarmament Campaign, 1993–; One World Trust, 1993–. Pres., Methodist Homes for the Aged, 1992–. *Publications:* the Queen's Courts, 1956; ed Social Welfare and the Citizen, 1957; Communism and the Law, 1963; (with Lord Reay) Freedom at Stake, 1966; Human Rights, 1969; (jtly) Purpose in Socialism, 1973; The Role of the Law Officers, 1978; contributions to: Trends in Social Welfare, 1965; Atkin's, Court Forms, 1965; The International Protection of Human Rights, 1967; Renewal, 1983; Fabian Centenary Essays, 1984; (ed) More Law Reform Now, 1984. *Recreations:* music, writing, talking. *Address:* House of Lords, SW1A 0PW.

ARCHER OF WESTON-SUPER-MARE, Baron *cr* 1992 (Life Peer), of Mark in the County of Somerset; **Jeffrey Howard Archer;** politician and author; *b* 15 April 1940; *s* of late William Archer and Lola Archer (*née* Cook); *m* 1966, Mary Weeden (*see* M. D. Archer); two *s*. *Educ:* by my wife since leaving Wellington Sch., Somerset; Brasenose Coll., Oxford. Athletics Blues, 1963–65, Gymnastics Blue, 1963, Pres. OUAC 1965; ran for Great Britain (never fast enough); Oxford 100 yards record (9.6 sec.), 1966. Mem. GLC for Havering, 1966–70; MP (C) Louth, Dec. 1969–Sept. 1974. Dep. Chm., Cons. Party, 1985–86. President: Somerset AAA, 1973; World Snooker Assoc. (formerly World Professional Billiards & Snooker Assoc.), 1997–99. Hon. Pres., Glasgow Univ. Dialectic Soc., 1984. Chm., Simple Truth Campaign, 1991. Patron, Small Business Bureau, 1995. FRSA 1973. *Plays:* Beyond Reasonable Doubt, Queen's, 1987; Exclusive, Strand, 1990; The Accused (and acted), Haymarket Theatre Royal, 2000. *Publications:* Not a Penny More, Not a Penny Less, 1975 (televised, 1990); Shall We Tell the President?, 1977; Kane and Abel, 1979 (televised, 1986); A Quiver Full of Arrows (short stories), 1980; The Prodigal Daughter, 1982; First Among Equals, 1984 (televised, 1986); A Matter of Honour, 1986; A Twist in the Tale (short stories), 1988; As the Crow Flies, 1991; Honour Among Thieves, 1993; Twelve Red Herrings (short stories), 1994; The Fourth Estate, 1996; The Collected Short Stories, 1997; The Eleventh Commandment, 1998; To Cut a Long Story Short (short stories), 2000. *Recreations:* theatre, watching Somerset play cricket (Pres., Somerset Wyverns, 1983), amateur auctioneer. *Address:* 93 Albert Embankment, SE1 7TY; The Old Vicarage, Grantchester CB3 9ND. *Club:* MCC.

ARCHER OF WESTON-SUPER-MARE, Lady; *see* Archer, M. D.

ARCHER, Albert, MBE 1980; Member, Royal Commission on Environmental Pollution, 1981–85; *b* 7 March 1915; *s* of Arthur Archer and Margaret Alice Norris; *m* 1st, 1939; two *s*; 2nd, 1975, Peggy, *widow* of John F. Marsh; two step *s*. *Educ:* Manchester Grammar Sch.; Manchester Coll. of Technology. Fellow, Instn of Environmental Health Officers, 1961. Chief Public Health Inspector, Bor. of Halesowen, 1943–73; City of Birmingham: Environmtl Protection Officer, 1973–75; Dep. City Environmtl Officer, 1975–76; City Environmtl Officer, 1976–80. Mem., govt working parties on air pollution. Pres., Inst. of Environmental Health Officers, 1979–83. *Publications:* articles on air pollution in technical jls. *Recreation:* watching cricket. *Address:* 8 Portland Drive, Stourbridge, West Midlands DY9 0SD. *T:* (01562) 883366.

ARCHER, Bruce; *see* Archer, L. B.

ARCHER, Graham Robertson, CMG 1997; HM Diplomatic Service, retired; High Commissioner to Malta, 1995–99; *b* 4 July 1939; *s* of late Henry Robertson Archer and Winifred Archer; *m* 1963, Pauline Cowan; two *d*. *Educ:* Judd School, Tonbridge. Joined Commonwealth Relations Office, 1962; British High Commission, New Delhi, 1964; Vice Consul, Kuwait, 1966; CRO (later FCO), 1967; Second Secretary (Commercial), Washington, 1970; First Secretary: FCO, 1972; Wellington, NZ, 1975; FCO, 1979; Counsellor: Pretoria, 1982; The Hague, 1986; FCO, 1990. *Recreations:* music, theatre, cultivating plants, walking.

ARCHER, Mrs Jean Mary; Under-Secretary, Ministry of Agriculture, Fisheries and Food, 1973–86; *b* 24 Aug. 1932; *e d* of late Reginald R. and D. Jane Harvey, Braiseworth Hall, Tannington, Suffolk; *m* 1954, G. Michéal D. Archer, MB, BChir, FFARCS, *er s* of Maj.-Gen. G. T. L. Archer, CB; two *d*. *Educ:* Fleet House, Felixstowe; St Felix Sch., Southwold; Newnham Coll., Cambridge. MA Econs 1954. Asst Principal, Min. of Agriculture, 1954; Private Sec. to successive Perm. Secs, MAFF, 1956–59; Principal 1960; Sec., Reorganisation Commn for Eggs, 1967; Asst Sec. 1968; Under-Sec. i/c Food Policy Gp, MAFF, 1973; Under-Sec., Dept of Prices and Consumer Protection, 1974–76; returned to MAFF, as Under-Sec., Milk and Marketing Group, 1976; Under-Sec., Meat, Poultry and Eggs Div., 1980. *Recreations:* travel, music, tennis, watching sport, swimming administration (Team Man., Chelsea/Kensington Swimming Club; Hon. Sec., Swimmers' Parents' and Supporters' Assoc.). *Address:* 118A St John's Hill, SW11 1SJ. *Club:* Hurlingham.

See also Rt Hon. Sir A. J. D. McCowan.

ARCHER, John Francis Ashweek, QC 1975; a Recorder of the Crown Court, 1974–97; *b* 9 July 1925; *s* of late George Eric Archer, FRCSE, and late Frances Archer (*née* Ashweek); *m* 1995, Vivienne Frances Weatherhead (*née* Ecclestone). *Educ:* Winchester Coll., 1938–43; New Coll., Oxford, 1947–49 (BA 1949). Served War of 1939–45, 1944–47; Lieut RA, 1948. Called to Bar, Inner Temple, 1950, Bencher, 1984. Mem., Criminal Injuries Compensation Bd, 1987–2000. *Recreations:* motoring, bridge. *Address:* The Cottage, 68 High Street, Wicken, Cambs CB7 5XR.

ARCHER, John Norman; Managing Director, International Tanker Owners Pollution Federation Ltd, 1979–86; *b* 27 Feb. 1921; *s* of late Clifford Banks Archer and Grace Archer; *m* 1st, 1952, Gladys Joy (*née* Barnes) (*d* 1985); one step *d*; 2nd, 1986, Mrs Anne L. M. Appleby (*née* Padwick). *Educ:* Wandsworth School. Served with RA, 1939–46 (Major). Entered Civil Service, Board of Educn, 1937; Asst Principal 1947, Principal 1949, Min. of Educn; attended Admin. Staff Coll., Henley, 1960; Asst Sec. (Joint Head, Architects and Buildings Br.), 1962; technical assistance assignments etc educn, Nigeria, Yugoslavia, Tunisia, 1961–63; Asst Sec., Treasury, O&M Div., 1964; Civil Service Department: Asst Sec., Management Services Development Div., 1968; Under-Sec., Management Services, 1970; Under-Sec., Marine Div., DTI, later Dept of Trade, 1972–79. Vice-Pres., Marine Soc. Freeman, City of London, 1985; Liveryman, Shipwrights' Co., 1986–. *Recreations:* lawn tennis, bridge, watching cricket. *Address:* 17 Sovereign House, Draxmont, Wimbledon Hill Road, SW19 7PG. *T:* (020) 8946 6429. *Clubs:* All England Lawn Tennis, Hurlingham, MCC; Kent CC; International Lawn Tennis of Great Britain.

ARCHER, Prof. John Stuart, PhD; FREng, FIMM, FInstE, FInstPet; FRSE; Principal and Vice-Chancellor, Heriot-Watt University, since 1997; *b* 15 June 1943; *s* of Stuart Leonard Archer and Joan (*née* Watkinson); *m* 1967, Lesley Oaksford; one *s* one *d*. *Educ:* County Grammar Sch., Chiswick; City Univ. (BSc Hons Ind. Chem.); Imperial Coll., London (DIC Advanced Chem. Engrg, PhD Combustion Engrg; FIC 1998). FInstE 1983; FInstPet 1984; FIMM 1986; FREng (FEng 1992); FRSE 1998. Sen. Res. Engr, Imperial Oil (Exxon), Canada, 1969–73; Sen. Petroleum Engr, British Gas Corp., 1973–74; Manager, Reservoir Engrg, D&S Petroleum Consultants, 1974–77; Energy Resource Consultants Ltd: Founder Dir, 1977; Dir of Reservoir Studies, 1977–81; Non-exec. Dir, 1982–90; Imperial College, London: Reader in Petroleum Engrg, 1980–86; Prof. of Petroleum Engrg, 1986–97; Hd, Petroleum Engrg, 1984–97; Hd, Dept of Mineral Resources Engrg, 1986–94; Dean, RSM, 1989–91; Pro Rector, then Dep. Rector, 1991–97. Vis. Prof., Univ. of Delft, 1990–93. Mem., EPSRC, 2000–. Director: IMPEL Ltd, 1989–97; MTD Ltd, 1993–; Clyde Petroleum, 1995–97; Scottish Enterprise, Edinburgh and Lothians (formerly Lothian Edinburgh Enterprise Ltd), 1998–. Convenor, Res. and Commercialisation Cttee, Cttee of Scottish Higher Educn Principals, 1999–; Member, Scottish Executive committees: Nat. Clusters Liaison Gp, 1999–; Foresight Steering Cttee, Scotland, 1999–; Science Strategy Review Gp, 1999–; Taskforce on the Knowledge Economy, 2000–; Manufg Image Gp, 2000–. Associate Editor: Jl Petroleum Sci. and Engrg, 1990–; Jls of Soc. Petroleum Engrs; Adv. Editor, Petroleum Engineering and Development Studies series, 1987–. Mem., Soc. Petroleum Engrs, 1973–. FRSA 1990; FCGI 1996. Distinguished Achievement Award, Soc. Petroleum Engrs, 1992. *Publications:* Petroleum Engineering: principles and practice, 1986; numerous papers in learned jls on petroleum reservoir engrg. *Recreations:* golf, gardening, theatre, music, the arts. *Address:* Heriot-Watt University, Edinburgh EH14 4AS. *T:* (0131) 449 5111. *Clubs:* Caledonian; New (Edinburgh).

ARCHER, Prof. (Leonard) Bruce, CBE 1976; DrRCA; CEng, MIMechE; Director of Research, Royal College of Art, 1985–88, now Emeritus Professor and Member of Court; Director and Secretary, Southwood House Estate Residents Co. Ltd, 1986–93; *b* 22 Nov. 1922; *s* of Leonard Castella Archer and Ivy Hilda Archer; *m* 1950, Joan Henrietta Allen; one *d*. *Educ:* Henry Thornton Sch., London; City Univ., London. MIED. Served, Scots Guards, 1941–44. City Univ., 1946–50. Various posts in manufacturing industry, 1950–57; Lectr, Central Sch. of Art and Design, London, 1957–60; Guest Prof., Hochschule für Gestaltung, Ulm, 1960–61; Research Fellow, later Prof., Royal Coll. of Art, 1961–88; Hd of Dept of Design Research, RCA, 1968–85. Examiner res. degrees, various univs, 1985–. Various public appointments in design, educn and industrial and scientific policy, 1968–; Member: Design Council, 1972–80; Internat. Science Policy Foundn, 1979–96; Council, Assoc. of Art Instns, 1980–90; Res. Adv. Council, Derby Univ., 1993–96; Court, Derby Univ., 1995–; Chairman: Confedn of Art and Design Assocs, 1981–88; Adv. Bd, Res. Inst. Consumer Ergonomics, 1996–. Pres., Design Res. Soc., 1994–. Director: Gore Projects Ltd, 1982–90; Design Research Innovation Centre Ltd, 1982–86. Hon. FRCA 1988. Hon. DSc City, 1986. *Publications:* varied, on the theory and practice of research, design, develt and educn. *Recreations:* music, the theatre. *Address:* 15 Church Vale, N2 9PB. *T:* (020) 8444 4363, *Fax:* (020) 8883 0351.

ARCHER, Malcolm David, FRCO; Organist and Master of the Choristers, Wells Cathedral, since 1996; *b* 29 April 1952; *s* of Gordon Austin Archer and Joan Eddleston Archer; *m* 1994, Alison Jane Robinson; one *s* one *d*. *Educ:* King Edward VII Sch., Lytham; Royal Coll. of Music (ARCM 1971); Jesus Coll., Cambridge (Organ Schol.; MA, CertEd). FRCO 1974. Asst Dir of Music, Magdalen Coll. Sch., Oxford, 1976 78; Asst Organist, Norwich Cathedral, 1978–83; Organist and Master of the Choristers, Bristol Cathedral, 1983–90; freelance organist, conductor and composer, 1990–96; music staff, 1990–96, Head of Chapel Music, 1994–96, Clifton Coll. Founder and Musical Dir, City of Bristol Choir, 1991–; Conductor, Wells Cathedral Oratorio Soc., 1996–. *Publications:* A Year of Praise, 1991; (ed jtly) Carols Old and New, 1991; After the Last Verse, 1995; (ed jtly) Advent for Choirs, 1999; over 200 compositions; major works include: Love Unknown, 1992; Requiem, 1993. *Recreations:* watercolour painting, cooking, classic cars, antique clocks. *Address:* 15 Vicars' Close, Wells, Somerset BA5 2UJ. *T:* (01749) 674483.

ARCHER, Dr Mary Doreen; scientist; *b* 22 Dec. 1944; *d* of late Harold Norman Weeden and Doreen Weeden (*née* Cox); *m* 1966, Jeffrey Howard Archer (*see* Baron Archer of Weston-super-Mare); two *s*. *Educ:* Cheltenham Ladies' College; St Anne's Coll., Oxford (Nuffield Schol.; MA 1972); Imperial Coll., London Univ. (PhD 1968); MA Cantab 1976. FRSC 1987. Junior Res. Fellow, St Hilda's Coll., Oxford, 1968–71; temp. Lectr in Chemistry, Somerville Coll., Oxford, 1971–72; Res. Fellow, Royal Instn of GB, 1972–76 (Dewar Fellow, 1975–76); Lector in Chemistry, Trinity Coll., Cambridge, 1976–86; Fellow and Coll. Lectr in Chem., Newnham Coll., Cambridge, 1976–86 (Bye-Fellow, 1987–). Sen. Academic Fellow, De Montfort Univ. (formerly Leicester Polytechnic), 1990–; Vis. Prof., Dept of Biochem., Imperial Coll., London, 1991–; Visitor, Univ. of Hertfordshire, 1993–. Member: Renewable Energy Adv. Gp, Dept of Energy/DTI, 1991–92; Energy Adv. Panel, DTI, 1992–; COPUS, 1995–. Trustee, Science Mus., 1990–. Mem. Council, Cheltenham Ladies' Coll., 1991–. Mem. Bd of Dirs, Internat. Solar Energy Soc., 1975–81 (Sec., UK Section, 1973–76); Manager, 1982–84, Mem. Council, 1984–85, Royal Instn; Chm., Nat. Energy Foundn, 1990–. Director: Anglia Television Gp, 1987–95; Mid Anglia Radio, 1988–94; Q103 (formerly Cambridge & Newmarket FM Radio), 1988–97; Addenbrooke's NHS Trust, 1992–. Mem. Council of Lloyd's, 1989–92. Pres., Guild of Church Musicians, 1989–. Hon. DSc Hertfordshire, 1994. *Publications:* Rupert Brooke and the Old Vicarage, Grantchester, 1989; contribs to chem. jls. *Recreations:* reading, writing, singing. *Address:* The Old Vicarage, Grantchester, Cambridge CB3 9ND. *T:* (01223) 840213.

ARCHER, Dr Mildred Agnes, (Mrs W. G. Archer), OBE 1979; in charge of Prints and Drawings Section, India Office Library, London, 1954–80; *b* 28 Dec. 1911; *d* of V. A. Bell, MBE; *m* 1934, William George Archer (*d* 1979); one *s* one *d*. *Educ:* St Hilda's College, Oxford (MA, DLitt 1978; Hon. Fellow 1978). Art historian (British period, India); resided India, 1934–47; revisited India (study tours), 1966, 1972, 1976, 1981–82, 1984, 1989. *Publications:* Patna Painting, 1947; (with W. G. Archer) Indian Painting for the British, 1955; Tippoo's Tiger, 1959; Natural History Drawings in the India Office Library, 1962; Indian Miniatures and Folk Paintings, 1967; Indian Architecture and the British, 1968; British Drawings in the India Office Library (2 vols), 1969; Indian Paintings from Court, Town and Village, 1970; Company Drawings in the India Office Library, 1972; Artist Adventurers in Eighteenth Century India, 1974; Indian Popular Painting, 1977; India and British Portraiture, 1770–1825, 1979; (with John Bastin) The Raffles Drawings in the India Office Library, 1979; Early Views of India, 1980; (with T. Falk) Indian Miniatures in the India Office Library, 1981; (with R. Lightbown) India Observed, 1982; Oil Paintings and Sculpture in the India Office Collection, 1986; Visions of India: the sketchbooks of William Simpson 1859–62, 1986; (with T. Falk) India Revealed: the art and adventures of James and William Fraser 1801–35, 1989; Company Drawings in the Victoria and Albert Museum, 1992; (with William Archer) India Served and Observed, 1994; articles in Country Life, Apollo, Connoisseur, History Today, Geographical Mag. *Recreations:* grandchildren, gardening, travel. *Address:* 5 Frog Meadow, Dedham, Colchester, Essex CO7 6AD. *T:* (01206) 323099.

ARCHER, Timothy John; Consultant, Richards Butler, since 2001 (Partner, 1973–2001; Senior Partner, 1991–2000); *b* 9 Feb. 1943; *s* of Jack Valentine Archer and Phyllis Emma Archer (*née* Cotton); *m* 1972, Gillian Karen Davies; one *s* one *d*. *Educ:* Sutton Valence Sch.; Merton Coll., Oxford (MA); Coll. of Law. Alfred Syrett Prizeman, Law Soc., 1966; admitted Solicitor, 1969. Richards Butler, Solicitors, 1965–. Director: Royal Philharmonic Orch., 1993–95; Philharmonia Orch. Trust, 1997–. Mem., Management

Cttee, Univ. of Exeter Centre for Legal Practice, 1993–96. *Publications:* (contrib.) International Handbook on Contracts of Employment, 1988, 2nd edn 1991; (jtly) Trade Unions, Employers and the Law, 1991; (jtly) Collective Labour Law, 2000. *Recreations:* sport, travel, music, art. *Address:* Richards Butler, Beaufort House, 15 St Botolph Street, EC3A 7EE. *T:* (020) 7247 6555.

ARCHIBALD, Liliana, OBE 1997; Chairman: Adam Brothers Contingency Ltd, 1991–92 (Director, 1957–73 and 1977–85); Wilton Park Academic Council, 1992–99; *b* 25 May 1928; *d* of late Noah and Sophie Barou; *m* 1951, George Christopher Archibald (marr. diss. 1965). *Educ:* Kingsley Sch.; Geneva University. Univ. Lectr, Otago Univ., 1952–55; Director: Const & Co. Ltd, 1955–73, 1977–83; Credit Consultants Ltd, 1957–73, 1977–85; Fenchurch Gp Internat., 1985–88; Holman Wade, 1989–92; CLM Insurance Fund, 1993–99. Head of Division (Credit Insurance and Export Credit), EEC, 1973–77; EEC Advr to Lloyd's and the British Insurance Brokers Assoc., 1978–85; Internat. Affairs Advr to Lloyd's, 1981–85; Advr to Internat. Gp of Protection & Indemnity Clubs, 1980–85. Frequent lecturer on insurance-related problems. Member: Liberalisation of Trade in Services Cttee, British Invisible Exports Council, 1981–95; British Export Finance Adv. Council, 1982–91; Action Resource Centre, 1986–91; Govt Inquiry into Shops Act—Sunday and Late-Night Trading, 1984–85; Review Cttee, Banking Law Services, 1987–88; Lord Chancellor's Adv. Cttee on Legal Educn and Conduct, 1991–94; Vice-Chm., ICC Insurance Commn, 1982–87; Chm., Insurance Cttee, British Nat. Cttee, ICC, 1983–87. Member of Lloyd's, 1973–94. *Publications:* (trans. and ed) Peter the Great, 1958; (trans. and ed) Rise of the Romanovs, 1970; contrib. Bankers Magazine. *Recreations:* driving fast cars, ski-ing, gardening. *Address:* 21 Langland Gardens, NW3 6QE.

ARCTIC, Bishop of The, since 1991; **Rt Rev. (John) Christopher (Richard) Williams;** *b* 22 May 1936; *s* of Frank Harold and Ceridwen Roberts Williams; *m* 1964, Rona Macrae (*née* Aitken); one *s* one *d*. *Educ:* Manchester Grammar Sch.; Univ. of Manchester (BA Comm); Univ. of Durham, Cranmer Hall (DipTh). Ordained: deacon, Stretford, England, 1960; priest, Sugluk, PQ, 1962; Missionary, diocese of The Arctic: Sugluk, PQ, 1961–72; Cape Dorset, NWT, 1972–75; Baker Lake, NWT, 1975–78; Archdeacon of The Keewatin, 1975–87; Rector, Yellowknife, NWT, 1978–87; Bp Suffragan, 1987–90, Coadjutor Bp, 1990, dio. of The Arctic. Hon. DD: Emmanuel and St Chad Coll., Saskatoon, 1997; Wycliffe Coll., Toronto Univ. *Recreations:* walking, cross country ski-ing. *Address:* 4916–44th Street, Yellowknife, NT X1A 1J8, Canada.

ARCULUS, David; *see* Arculus, T. D. G.

ARCULUS, Sir Ronald, KCMG 1979 (CMG 1968); KCVO 1980; HM Diplomatic Service, retired; *b* 11 Feb. 1923; *s* of late Cecil Arculus, MC and Ethel L. Arculus; *m* 1953, Sheila Mary Faux; one *s* one *d*. *Educ:* Solihull; Exeter Coll., Oxford (MA; Hon. Fellow, 1989). 4th Queen's Own Hussars (now Queen's Royal Hussars), 1942–45 (Captain). Joined HM Diplomatic Service, 1947; FO, 1947; San Francisco, 1948; La Paz, 1950; FO, 1951; Ankara, 1953; FO, 1957; Washington, 1961; Counsellor, 1965; New York, 1965–68; IDC, 1969; Head of Science and Technology Dept, FCO, 1970–72; Minister (Economic), Paris, 1973–77; Ambassador and Permt Leader, UK Delegn to UN Conf. on Law of the Sea, 1977–79; Ambassador to Italy, 1979–83. Dir, 1983–91, Trustee, 1986–93, Consultant, 1992–95, Glaxo Hldgs. Special Advr to Govt on Channel Tunnel trains, 1987–88. Consultant: Trusthouse Forte, 1983–86; London and Continental Bankers Ltd, 1985–90. Dir of Appeals, King's Med. Res. Trust, 1984–88. Pres., Kensington Soc., 2001– (Chm., 1999–2001). Governor, British Institute, Florence, 1983–94. FIMgt (FBIM 1984). Freeman, City of London, 1981. Kt Grand Cross, Order of Merit, Italy, 1980. *Recreations:* travel, music, fine arts, antiques. *Address:* 20 Kensington Court Gardens, W8 5QF. *Clubs:* Army and Navy, Hurlingham; Cowdray Park Polo.

ARCULUS, (Thomas) David (Guy); Chairman: Severn Trent plc, since 1998; ipc Group Ltd, since 1998; *b* 2 June 1946; *s* of Thomas Guy Arculus and Mary (*née* Barton); *m* 1973, Anne Murdoch Sleeman; two *s* one *d*. *Educ:* Bromsgrove Sch.; Oriel Coll., Oxford (MA 1968); London Graduate Sch. of Business Studies (MSc 1972). BBC Producer, 1968–70; EMAP plc: Publisher, 1972–84; Dep. Man. Dir, 1984–89; Gp Man. Dir, 1989–97; Chief Operating Officer, United News and Media plc, 1997–98. Non-executive Director: Barclays plc, 1997–; Guiton Gp, 2000–. Chairman: PPA, 1988–90; NCC, 1993–96. Deleg., Finance Cttee, OUP, 2000–; Chm., Investment Cttee, Oriel Coll., Oxford, 2000–. Industry and Parliament Trust Fellow, 1989. Freeman, City of London, 1990. Marcus Morris Award, PPA, 1993. *Recreations:* cricket, golf. *Address:* ipc media, King's Reach Tower, Stamford Street, SE1 9LS. *T:* (020) 7261 7253, *Fax:* (020) 7261 6391; *e-mail:* david_arculus@ipc.co.uk. *Clubs:* Oxford and Cambridge, Groucho, Thirty, MCC.

ARDAGH AND CLONMACNOISE, Bishop of, (RC), since 1983; **Most Rev. Colm O'Reilly;** *b* 11 Jan. 1935; *s* of John and Alicia O'Reilly. Ordained priest, 1960. *Address:* St Michael's, Longford, Ireland. *T:* (43) 46432.

ARDEE, Lord; Anthony Jaques Brabazon; *b* 30 Jan. 1977; *o s* of Earl of Meath, *qv*. *Educ:* Harrow Sch.

ARDEN, Andrew Paul Russel; QC 1991; *b* 20 April 1948; *m* 1991, Joanne Leahy; one *d*. *Educ:* Stowe; University College Sch.; University Coll. London (LLB). Called to the Bar, Gray's Inn, 1974; Dir, Small Heath Community Law Centre, Birmingham, 1976–78. Local government inquiries/reviews: for GLC, 1982–83; for Bristol CC, 1985; for Hackney LBC, 1985–87, 1993–94; for Camden LBC, 1992. General Editor: Encyclopaedia of Housing Law, 1978–; Housing Law Reports, 1981–; Jl of Housing Law, 1997–; Consultant Ed., Local Government Law Reports, 2000– (Gen. Ed., 1999–2000). *Publications:* Manual of Housing Law, 1978, 6th edn (with Caroline Hunter), 1997; Housing Act 1980 (annotations), 1980; (with Prof. M. Partington) Quiet Enjoyment, 1980, 2nd edn 1985; (with Prof. M. Partington) Housing Law, 1983, 2nd edn (also with C. Hunter), 1994; (with Prof. J. T. Farrand) Rent Acts & Regulations, amended and annotated, 1981; (with C. Cross) Housing & Building Control Act 1984 (annotations), 1984; Private Tenants Handbook, 1985, 2nd edn 1989; Public Tenants Handbook, 1985, 2nd edn 1989; (with S. McGrath) Landlord & Tenant Act 1985 (annotations), 1986; Housing Act 1985 (annotations), 1986; (with J. Ramage) Housing Associations Act 1985 (annotations), 1986; Homeless Persons Handbook, 1986, 2nd edn 1988; Housing Act 1988 (annotations), 1989; (with Sir Robert Megarry) Assured Tenancies, Vol. 3, The Rent Acts, 11th edn 1989; (with C. Hunter) Local Government & Housing Act 1989 (annotations), 1990; (with C. Hunter) Local Government Finance Law, 1994; (with C. Hunter) Housing Act 1996 (annotations), 1996; (with C. Hunter) Housing Grants, Construction and Renewal Act 1996 (annotations), 1996; Homeless Persons Act 1982, 5th edn (with C. Hunter) Homelessness and Allocations, 1997; (jtly) Local Government Constitutional and Administrative Law, 1999; *fiction:* The Motive Not The Deed, 1974; No Certain Roof, 1985; The Object Man, 1986; four thrillers under pseudonym Bernard Bannerman, 1990–91. *Recreations:* Southern Comfort, Hill Street Blues, Camel cigarettes, Manzi's Lunch Club. *Address:* Arden Chambers, 2 John Street, WC1N 2ES. *T:* (020) 7242 4244, *Fax:* (020) 7242 3224; *e-mail:* AndrewPRArden@cs.com.

ARDEN, Rt Rev. Donald Seymour, CBE 1981; Assistant Bishop of London, since 1981, and voluntary assistant priest, St Alban's, North Harrow, since 1986; *b* 12 April 1916; *s* of Stanley and Winifred Arden; *m* 1962, Jane Grace Riddle; two *s*. *Educ:* St Peter's Coll., Adelaide; University of Leeds (BA); College of the Resurrection, Mirfield. Deacon, 1939; Priest, 1940. Curate of: St Catherine's, Hatcham, 1939–40; Nettleden with Potten End, 1941–43; Asst Priest, Pretoria African Mission, 1944–51; Director of Usuthu Mission, Swaziland, 1951–61; Bishop of Nyasaland, 1961 (name of diocese changed, when Nyasaland was granted independence, July 1964); Bishop of Malaŵi, 1964–71, of Southern Malaŵi, 1971–81; Archbishop of Central Africa, 1971–80; Priest-in-charge of St Margaret's, Uxbridge, 1981–86. Commissary, dioceses of Southern Malaŵi and Lake Malaŵi, 1981, of Niassa, Mozambique, 1989–. *Publication:* Out of Africa Something New, 1976. *Recreation:* photography. *Address:* 6 Frobisher Close, Pinner, Mddx HA5 1NN. *T:* (020) 8866 6009, *Fax:* (020) 8868 8013; *e-mail:* dandjarden@cs.com.

ARDEN, John; novelist and playwright; *b* 26 Oct. 1930; *s* of C. A. Arden and A. E. Layland; *m* 1957, Margaretta Ruth D'Arcy; four *s* (and one *s* decd). *Educ:* Sedbergh Sch.; King's Coll., Cambridge; Edinburgh Coll. of Art. *Plays produced include:* All Fall Down, 1955; The Life of Man, 1956; The Waters of Babylon, 1957; Live Like Pigs, 1958; Serjeant Musgrave's Dance, 1959; Soldier, Soldier, 1960; Wet Fish, 1962; The Workhouse Donkey, 1963; Ironhand, 1963; Armstrong's Last Goodnight, 1964; Left-Handed Liberty, 1965; The True History of Squire Jonathan and his Unfortunate Treasure, 1968; The Bagman, 1970; Pearl, 1978; To Put It Frankly, 1979; Don Quixote, 1980; Garland for a Hoar Head, 1982; The Old Man Sleeps Alone, 1982; Little Novels of Wilkie Collins, 1997; Woe Alas, the Fatal Cashbox, 1999; *with Margaretta D'Arcy:* The Business of Good Government, 1960; The Happy Haven, 1960; Ars Longa Vita Brevis, 1964; Friday's Hiding, 1966; The Royal Pardon, 1966; The Hero Rises Up, 1968; Island of the Mighty, 1972; The Ballygombeen Bequest, 1972; The Non-Stop Connolly Cycle, 1975; Vandaleur's Folly, 1978; The Little Gray Home in the West, 1978; The Manchester Enthusiasts, 1984; Whose is the Kingdom?, 1988; A Suburban Suicide, 1994. *Publications:* (with Margaretta D'Arcy) To Present the Pretence (essays), 1977; Silence Among the Weapons (novel), 1982; Books of Bale (novel), 1988; (with Margaretta D'Arcy) Awkward Corners (essays, etc), 1988; Cogs Tyrannic (novellas), 1991; Jack Juggler and the Emperor's Whore (novel), 1995. *Recreations:* antiquarianism, mythology. *Address:* c/o Casarotto Ramsay Ltd, National House, 60–66 Wardour Street, W1V 3HP.

ARDEN, Rt Hon. Dame Mary (Howarth), (Rt Hon. Dame Mary Mance), DBE 1993; PC 2000; **Rt Hon. Lady Justice Arden;** a Lord Justice of Appeal, since 2000; *b* 23 Jan. 1947; *d* of late Lt-Col E. C. Arden, LLB, TD and M. M. Arden (*née* Smith); *m* 1973, Jonathan Hugh Mance (*see* Rt Hon. Sir J. H. Mance); one *s* two *d*. *Educ:* Huyton College; Girton College, Cambridge (MA, LLM); Harvard Law School (LLM). Called to the Bar, Gray's Inn, 1971 (Arden and Birkenhead Scholarships, 1971); admitted *ad eundem* to Lincoln's Inn, 1973 (Bencher, 1993); QC 1986; Attorney Gen., Duchy of Lancaster, 1991–93; a Judge of the High Ct of Justice, Chancery Div., 1993–2000. Chm., Law Commn, 1996–99. Bar Mem., Law Society's Standing Cttee on Company Law, 1976–; Member: Financial Law Panel, 1993–; Steering Gp, Company Law Review Project, 1998–2001. DTI Inspector, Rotaprint PLC, 1988–91. Acad. Trustee, Kennedy Meml Trust, 1995–. Pres., Assoc. of Women Barristers, 1994–98. DUniv Essex, 1997; Hon. LLD: Liverpool, 1998; Warwick, 1999; RHBNC, 1999. Editor, Chancery Guide, 1995, 1999. *Publications:* Negligence and the Public Accountant (contrib.), 1972; Legal Editor, Current Accounting Law and Practice, by Robert Willott, 1976; (with George Eccles) Tolley's Companies Act 1980, 1980; Legal Consultant Editor: Tolley's Companies Act 1981, 1981; Tolley's Accounting Problems of the Companies Acts, 1984; Accounting Provisions of the Companies Act 1985, 1985; Coopers & Lybrand Deloitte Manual of Accounting, vols 1 and 2, 1990, 1995; Jt Gen. Editor and Contributor, Buckley on the Companies Acts, 14th edn: Special Bulletin, 1990, 15th edn 2000; (contrib.) Accounting and the Law, 1992; (contrib.) Perspectives on Company Law, 1995; (contrib.) Law, Society and Economy, 1997; articles in legal jls. *Recreations:* family activities, reading, swimming. *Address:* Royal Courts of Justice, Strand, WC2A 2LL.

ARFIELD, John Alan; University Librarian, University of Western Australia, since 1996; *b* 15 March 1949; *s* of Donald Sidney Arfield and Barbara Winifred Arfield (*née* Alderton); *m* 1970, Paula May Perrin; one *s* two *d*. *Educ:* Kingston Grammar Sch.; Jesus Coll., Cambridge (BA 1971; MA 1975); Univ. of Sheffield (MA 1973). Cambridge University Library: Asst Liby Officer, 1973–78; Asst Under-Librarian, 1978–79; Under-Librarian, 1979–81; Sub-Librarian (Tech. Services), UC, Cardiff, 1981–88; Dep. Librarian, Reading Univ., 1988–92; University Librarian, Loughborough Univ., 1992–96. *Publications:* articles in librarianship. *Recreations:* squash, cricket, theatre, music. *Address:* University Library, University of Western Australia, Nedlands, Perth, WA 6907, Australia.

ARGENT, Eric William, FCA; FCIB; Director, Nationwide Anglia Building Society, 1987–88, retired (Joint General Manager, 1978–81, Director, 1978–87, Anglia Building Society); *b* 5 Sept. 1923; *s* of Eric George Argent and Florence Mary Argent; *m* 1949, Pauline Grant; two *d*. *Educ:* Chiswick Grammar Sch. FCA 1951. War Service, 1942–47. With City Chartered Accountants, 1940–42 and 1947–51; with London Banking House, Antony Gibbs & Sons Ltd, 1951–59; Hastings & Thanet Building Society, 1959–78: Sec. and Chief Accountant, 1962; Dep. Gen. Man., 1964; Gen. Man. and Sec., 1966; Dir and Gen. Man., 1976. *Recreations:* reading, gardening, travel. *Address:* Fairmount, 104 Longcliffe Road, Grantham, Lincs NG31 8DY. *T:* (01476) 591433.

ARGENT, Malcolm, CBE 1985; Deputy Chairman, Civil Aviation Authority, 1995–98; *b* 14 Aug. 1935; *s* of Leonard James and Winifred Hilda Argent; *m* 1st, 1961, Mary Patricia Addis Stimson (marr. diss. 1983); one *s* one *d*; 2nd, 1986, Thelma Hazel Eddleston. *Educ:* Palmer's Sch., Grays, Essex. General Post Office, London Telecommunications Region: Exec. Officer, 1953–62; Higher Exec. Officer, 1962–66; Principal, PO Headquarters, 1966–70; Private Sec., Man. Dir, Telecommunications, 1970–74; Personnel Controller, External Telecommun. Exec., 1974–75; Dir, Chairman's Office, PO Central Headquarters, 1975–77; Dir, Eastern Telecommun. Region, 1977; Secretary: of the Post Office, 1978–81; British Telecommunications Corp., 1981–94; British Telecommunications plc, 1984–94 (Dir, 1989–98); Chm., NATS, 1996–98. Trustee, British Telecommunications Staff Superannuation Fund, 1981–94. Director: McCaw Cellular Communications Inc., 1989–94; Westminster Health Care plc, 1992–99; Clerical, Medical & Gen. Assce Soc., 1994–; Clerical Medical Investment Gp, 1997–; Chm., Envision Licensing Ltd, 1999. Member: Council, CBI, 1994–95; Cttee, Essex Magistrates' Courts, 2000–. Freeman, City of London, 1987. CIMgt 1992 (CBIM 1991; FBIM 1980). *Recreation:* golf. *Address:* Chestnuts, Fryerning Lane, Ingatestone, Essex CM4 0GF.

ARGENTA, Nancy Maureen H.; *see* Herbison-Argenta.

ARGENTINA, Bishop of, since 1990; **Rt Rev. David Leake;** Presiding Bishop, Province of the Anglican Church of the Southern Cone of America, 1982–89; *b* 26 June 1935; *s* of Rev. Canon William Alfred Leake and Dorothy Violet Leake; *m* 1961, Rachel Yarham; two *s* one *d*. *Educ:* St Alban's Coll., Buenos Aires; London Coll. of Divinity. ALCD 1959 (LTh). Deacon 1959, priest 1960; Assistant Bishop: Paraguay and N Argentina, 1969–73; N Argentina, 1973–79; Bishop of Northern Argentina, 1979–89. *Recreations:* observing people's behaviour at airports, railway stations and bus terminals. *Address:* Casilla Correo 4293, 1000 Correo Central, Buenos Aires, Argentina.

ARGENTINA, Bishop Coadjutor of; *see* Venables, Rt Rev. G. J.

ARGYLL, 13th Duke of, *cr* 1701 (Scotland), 1892 (UK); **Torquhil Ian Campbell;** Marquess of Lorne and Kintyre; Earl of Campbell and Cowal; Viscount Lochow and Glenyla; Baron Inveraray, Mull, Morvern and Tiry, 1701; Baron Campbell, 1445; Earl of Argyll, 1457; Baron Lorne, 1470; Baron Kintyre, 1633 (Scotland); Baron Sundridge, 1766; Baron Hamilton of Hameldon, 1776; Bt 1627; 37th Baron and 47th Knight of Lochow; Celtic title, Mac Cailein Mhor, Chief of Clan Campbell; Hereditary Master of the Royal Household, Scotland; Hereditary High Sheriff of the County of Argyll; Admiral of the Western Coast and Isles; Keeper of the Great Seal of Scotland and of the Castles of Dunstaffnage, Dunoon, and Carrick and Tarbert; *b* 29 May 1968; *s* of 12th Duke of Argyll, and Iona Mary, *d* of Capt. Sir Ivar Colquhoun, *qv*; *S* father, 2001. *Educ:* Craigflower; Cargilfield; Glenalmond Coll. A Page of Honour to the Queen, 1981–83. *Heir: uncle* Lord Colin Ivar Campbell, *b* 14 May 1946. *Address:* Inveraray Castle, Inveraray, Argyll PA32 8XF.

ARGYLL AND THE ISLES, Bishop of, since 1993; **Rt Rev. Douglas Maclean Cameron;** *b* 23 March 1935; *s* of Andrew McIntyre Cameron and Helen Adam McKechnie; *m* 1969, Anne Patricia Purnell; two *d*. *Educ:* Eastwood Grammar Sch., Clarkston, Glasgow; Theol Coll., Edinburgh; Univ. of the South, Sewanee, Tennessee, USA. Bank of Scotland, 1951–59; RAF, 1953–55. Ordained: deacon, 1962; priest, 1963; curate, Christ Church, Falkirk, 1962–65; Anglican Church in Papua New Guinea: Mission Priest, 1966–67; priest in charge, Movi, 1967–72; Rector, St Francis, Goroka, 1972–74; Archdeacon of New Guinea Mainland, 1972–74; Priest in charge, St Fillan's, Edinburgh, 1974, Rector, 1978–88; Rector: St Hilda's, Edinburgh, 1977–88; St Mary's, Dalkeith and St Leonard's, Lasswade, 1988–93; Canon, St Mary's Cathedral, Edinburgh and Synod Clerk, 1990–91; Dean of Edinburgh, 1991–92. *Recreations:* hill-walking, listening to music. *Address:* The Pines, Ardconnel Road, Oban PA34 5DR. *T:* (01631) 566912.

See also Bishop of Aberdeen and Orkney.

ARGYLL AND THE ISLES, Bishop of, (RC), since 1999; **Rt Rev. Ian Murray;** *b* 15 Dec. 1932; *s* of John Murray and Margaret Murray (*née* Rodgers). *Educ:* Blairs Coll., Aberdeen; Royal Scots Coll., Valladolid, Spain; BA Hons Open Univ. 1991. Ordained priest, 1956; Curate: Lochore, Fife, 1956–61; St Columba, Edinburgh, 1961–63; Vice-Rector, Royal Scots Coll., Spain, 1963–70; Chaplain, Stirling Univ., 1970–78; Parish Priest: St Bride, Cowdenbeath, 1978–85; St Ninian, Edinburgh, 1985–87; Rector, Royal Scots Coll., Valladolid, 1987–88, Salamanca, 1988–94; Parish Priest: Galashiels, 1994–96; St Francis Xavier, Falkirk, 1996–99; VG, Archdio. of St Andrews and Edinburgh, 1996–99. Prelate of Honour, 1989. *Address:* Bishop's House, Esplanade, Oban PA34 5AB. *T:* (01631) 571395.

ARGYLL AND THE ISLES, Dean of; *see* Flatt, Very Rev. R. F. F.

ARGYLL AND THE ISLES, Provost in; *see* Maclean, Very Rev. A. M.

ARGYRIS, Prof. John, CBE 2000; DScEng, DE Munich; FRS 1986; FREng; FRAeS; Professor of Aeronautical Structures in the University of London, at Imperial College of Science and Technology, 1955–75, Visiting Professor 1975–78, now Emeritus Professor; Director, Institute for Computer Applications, Stuttgart, since 1984; *b* 19 Aug. 1916; *s* of Nicolas and Lucie Argyris; *m* 1953, Inga-Lisa (*née* Johansson); one *s*. *Educ:* 3rd Gymnasium, Athens; Technical Universities, Athens, Munich and Zurich. With J. Gollnow u. Son, Stettin, Research in Structures, 1937–39; Royal Aeronautical Soc., Research and Technical Officer, 1943–49; Univ. of London, Imperial Coll. of Science and Technology, Dept of Aeronautics: Senior Lecturer, 1949; Reader in Theory of Aeronautical Structures, 1950; Hon. FIC 1985. Dir, Inst. for Statics and Dynamics, Stuttgart, 1959–84. Principal Editor, Jl of Computer Methods in Applied Mechanics and Engineering, 1972–. Hon. Professor: Northwestern Polytech. Univ., Xian, China, 1980; Tech. Univ. of Beijing, 1983; Qinghua Univ., Beijing, 1984. Corresp. Mem., Acad. of Scis, Athens, 1973; Life Mem., ASME, 1981; Hon. Life Mem., NY Acad. of Scis, 1983; Foreign Associate, US Nat. Acad. of Engrg, 1986. FRAeS 1955; FAIAA 1983; FAAAS 1985; FREng (FEng 1990); FASCE 1991; Hon. Fellow, Groupe pour l'Avancement des Méthodes Numériques de l'Ingénieur, Paris, 1974; Hon. FCGI 1976; Hon. Fellow, Aeronautical Soc. of India, 1985; Hon. FRAeS 1986; Hon. Fellow, Romanian Acad., 1992; Hon. Mem., Greek Assoc. of Computational Mechs, 1994. Hon. Dott Ing Genoa, 1970; Hon. dr.tech Trondheim, 1972; Hon. Dr Ing Tech. Hanover, 1983; Hon. Tek. Dr Linköping, 1986; Hon. DSc (Maths) Athens, 1989; Hon. DSc (Mechs) Vilnius, 1991; Hon. DSc (Computer Mechs): Iasi, 1992; Tallinn, Estonia, 1993; Technical Univ., St Petersburg, 1993; Hon. DSc (phys, comput. and mechs) Tech. Univ. and Univ. of Timisoara, Romania, 1993; Hon. DSc (sci. of mechs) Technical Univ. of Athens, 1995; Hon. DSc (mechs and informatics) Univ. of Ioannina, 1995; Hon. DSc (engrg) Univ. of Thessaly in Volos, 1996. Silver Medal, RAeS, 1971; Von Kármán Medal, ASCE, 1975; Copernicus Medal, Polish Acad. of Scis, 1979; Timoshenko Medal, ASME, 1981; I. B. Laskowitz Award with Gold Medal in Aerospace Engrg, NY Acad. of Scis, 1982; World Prize in Culture, and election as Personality of the Year 1984, Centro Studi e Ricerce delle Nazione, Acad. Italia, 1983; Royal Medal, Royal Soc., 1985; Daidalus Gold Medal, Sir George Cayley Inst., 1988; Gold Medal, Bulgarian Acad. of Scis, 1991; Henri Coenda Medal in Gold, 1992. Gold Medal, Land Baden-Württemberg, 1980; Grand Cross of Merit, FRG, 1985; Grand Cross of Merit with Star, FRG, 1989; Grand Cross of the Phoenix, Greece, 1996; Gold Medal of Argonauts, Univ. of Thessaly in Volos, 1996. *Publications:* Handbook of Aeronautics, Vol. I, 1952: Energy Theorems and Structural Analysis, 1960; Modern Fuselage Analysis and the Elastic Aircraft, 1963; Recent Advances in Matrix Methods of Structural Analysis, 1964; Introduction into the Finite Element Method, vols I, II and III, 1986–88; Dynamics of Structures, 1991; An overview of aerolasticity, 1992; An Exploration of Chaos, 1994; articles and publications in Ingenieur Archiv, Reports and Memoranda of Aeronautical Research Council, Journal of Royal Aeronautical Society and Aircraft Engineering, CMAME, Jl of AIAA, etc; over 490 scientific publications. *Recreations:* reading, music, hiking, archæology. *Address:* Institute for Computer Applications, 27 Pfaffenwaldring, 70569 Stuttgart, Germany. *T:* (711) 6853594; c/o Department of Aeronautics, Imperial College, Prince Consort Road, SW7. *T:* (020) 7589 5111. *Club:* English-Speaking Union.

ARGYRIS, Nicholas John; Director, Communications Services: policy and regulatory framework (formerly Telecommunications Trans European Networks and Services and Postal Services), European Commission, since 1993; *b* 22 March 1943; *s* of late Costas Argyris and of Eileen Argyris (*née* Pollard); *m* 1st, 1966, Carol Bartlett (marr. diss. 1991); one *s* two *d*; 2nd, 1992, Danielle Canneel. *Educ:* St Paul's Sch.; Clare Coll., Cambridge (BA Hons Econs 1965; Cert. Ed. 1966). Schoolmaster, 1966–68; with Govt Econ. Service, in Depts of Econ. Affairs, Technol. and Trade and Ind., 1969–73; joined European Commission, 1973: worked in Directorate General for: Competition, 1973–84 (State Aids); Develt, 1985–86 (Trade and Private Investment Issues); Competition, 1987–91 (Head of Div., Transport and Tourist Industries); Dir for internal market, DG for Energy, 1991–93. Former Mem., England junior chess team (London junior champion, 1960). *Publications:* articles on air transport, energy and telecommunications policy. *Recreations:* reading, walking, the arts, traditional dancing.... *Address:* Commission of the European Communities, 200 rue de la Loi, 1049 Brussels, Belgium. *T:* (2) 2955899.

ARIAS-SALGADO Y MONTALVO, Fernando; Ambassador of Spain to Switzerland and concurrently (non-resident) to Liechtenstein, since 1996; Barrister-at-Law; *b* 3 May 1938; *s* of Gabriel Arias-Salgado y Cubas and Maria Montalvo Gutierrez; *m* 1969, Maria Isabel Garrigues Lopez-Chicheri; one *s* one *d*. *Educ:* Univ. of Madrid. Mem., Illustrious Coll. of Lawyers of Madrid. Entered Diplomatic Sch., 1963; Sec., Permanent Rep. of Spain to UN, 1966; Advr, UN Security Council, 1968–69; Asst Dir Gen., Promotion of Research, 1971, Asst Dir Gen., Internat. Co-operation, 1972, Min. of Educn and Science; Legal Advr (internat. matters), Legal Dept, Min. of Foreign Affairs, 1973; Counsellor, Spanish Delegn to Internat. Court of Justice, 1975; Tech. Sec. Gen., Min. of Foreign Affairs, 1976; Dir Gen., Radiotelevisión Española, 1977; Ambassador to the Court of St James's, 1981–83; Dir, Internat. Legal Dept, Min. of Foreign Affairs, 1983–85; Consul-Gen. for Spain in Zürich, 1985–90; Ambassador and Perm. Rep. of Spain to Internat. Orgns in Vienna, 1990–93; Ambassador to Tunisia, 1993–96. Comendador: Orden de Isabel la Católica; Orden del Merito Civil; Orden de San Raimundo de Peñafort; Caballero, Orden de Carlos III. *Address:* Kalcheggweg 24, Postfach 202, 3000 Bern 16, Switzerland.

ARIAS SÁNCHEZ, Oscar, PhD; President of Costa Rica, 1986–90; President, Arias Foundation for Peace, since 1990; *b* 13 Sept. 1940; *m* Margarita; one *s* one *d*. *Educ:* Univ. of Costa Rica; Univ. of Essex. Prof., Sch. of Political Sciences, Univ. of Costa Rica, 1969–72; Minister of Nat. Planning and Economic Policy, 1972–77; Gen. Sec., 1979–86, Liberación Nacional Party; Congressman, 1978–82. Formulated Central American Peace Agreement, 1986–87. Member: Stockholm Internat. Peace Res. Inst.; Carter Center; Inst. for Internat. Studies, Stanford Univ.; ILD Rockefeller Foundn; Internat. Centre for Human Rights and Democratic Develt; Inter Press Service; Bd of Dirs, WWF. Hon. PhD: Harvard, 1988; Essex, 1988; Dartmouth, 1992. Nobel Peace Prize, 1987; Martin Luther King Peace Prize, Martin Luther King Foundn, 1987; Prince of Asturias Prize, 1988; Nat. Audubon Soc. Prize, 1988; Liberty Medal, Univ. of Pennsylvania, 1991. *Publications:* Pressure Groups in Costa Rica, 1970; Who Governs in Costa Rica?, 1976; Latin American Democracy, Independence and Society, 1977; Roads for Costa Rica's Development, 1977; New Ways for Costa Rican Development, 1980. *Address:* c/o Arias Foundation/Center for Peace, PO Box 8–6410–1000, San José, Costa Rica. *T:* 2552955, *Fax:* 2552244.

ARIE, Prof. Thomas Harry David, CBE 1995; FRCPsych, FRCP, FFPHM; Foundation Professor of Health Care of the Elderly, University of Nottingham, 1977–95, and Hon. Consultant Psychiatrist, Nottingham Health Authority, 1977–95; *b* 9 Aug. 1933; *s* of late Dr O. M. Arie and Hedy (*née* Glaser); *m* 1963, Eleanor, FRCP, *yr d* of Sir Robert Aitken, FRCP, FRACP; two *d* one *s*. *Educ:* Reading Sch.; Balliol Coll., Oxford (Open Exhibnr in Classics; 1st cl. Hons, Classical Mods); MA, BM 1960; DPM. Training, Radcliffe Infirmary, Oxford, and Maudsley and London Hosps; Consultant Psychiatrist, Goodmayes Hosp., 1969–77; Sen. Lectr in Social Medicine, London Hosp. Med. Coll.; Hon. Sen. Lectr in Psychiatry, UCH Med. Sch. Royal College of Psychiatrists: Mem. Council, 1975–79, 1981–86, 1991–97; Vice-Pres., 1984–86; Chm., Specialist Section on Psychiatry of Old Age, 1981–86; Jt Cttee on Higher Psychiatric Training, 1978–84; Hon. FRCPsych 2001; Royal College of Physicians: Geriatrics Cttee, 1984–90; Examining Bd for Dipl. in Geriatric Medicine, 1983–92. Member: Central Council for Educn and Trng in Social Work, 1975–81; Standing Med. Adv. Cttee, DHSS, 1980–84; Cttee on Review of Medicines, 1981–90; Res. Adv. Council, Nat. Inst. for Social Work, 1982–90; Med. Adv. Cttee to Registrar General, 1990–93; Council, Royal Surgical Aid Soc. (RSAS-AgeCare), 1995– (Vice-Chm., 1998–). Fotheringham Lectr, Univ. of Toronto, 1979; Vis. Prof., NZ Geriatrics Soc., 1980; Dozor Vis. Prof., Univ. of the Negev, Israel, 1988; Fröhlich Vis. Prof., UCLA, 1991; Vis. Prof., Keele Univ., 1997. Chm., Geriatric Psych. Section, World Psych. Assoc., 1989–93. Governor, Centre for Policy on Ageing, 1992–98. *Publications:* (ed) Health Care of the Elderly, 1981; (ed) Recent Advances in Psychogeriatrics, Vol. 1 1985, Vol. 2 1992; articles in med. jls and chapters in other people's books. *Address:* Cromwell House, West Church Street, Kenninghall, Norfolk NR16 2EN. *T:* and *Fax:* (01953) 887375.

ARIS, Aung San Suu Kyi, (Mrs M. V. Aris); *see* Aung San Suu Kyi.

ARIS, John Bernard Benedict, TD 1967; with IMPACT Programme, 1990–99 (Director, 1990–95); *b* 6 June 1934; *s* of John (Jack) Woodbridge Aris and Joyce Mary (*née* Williams). *Educ:* Eton (King's Schol.); Magdalen Coll., Oxford (MA). FBCS; FInstD; FRSA. LEO Computers, 1958–63; English Electric Computers, 1963–69; ICL, 1969–75; Imperial Group, 1975–85 (Man., Gp Management Services, 1982–85); Dir, NCC, 1985–90. Non-exec. Dir, NCC, 1981–85; Chairman: FOCUS Private Sector Users Cttee (DTI), 1984–85; Alvey IT User Panel, 1985–88; Mem., IT 86 Cttee, 1986. Founder Freeman, Co. of Information Technologists, 1987 (Liveryman, 1992). *Publication:* (jtly) User Driven Innovation, 1996. *Recreations:* travel, music, art, scuba diving, gastronomy.

ARKELL, John Hardy, MA; Headmaster, Gresham's School, Holt, 1991–July 2002; *b* 10 July 1939; *s* of Hardy Arkell and Vivienne (*née* Le Sueur); *m* 1963, Jean Harding, JP; two *s* one *d*. *Educ:* Stowe Sch.; Selwyn Coll., Cambridge (BA Hons English Tripos; MA). National Service, HM Submarines, 1958–60 (Sub Lieut). Asst Master, Abingdon Sch., 1963–64; Head of VI form English, Framlingham Coll., 1964–70; Fettes College, 1970–83: Head of English Dept, 1971–73, 1976–78; Founder Headmaster, Fettes Jun. Sch., 1973–79; Housemaster, Glencorse House, 1979–83; Headmaster, Wrekin Coll., 1983–91. Chm., ISIS, Central England, 1989–91; Sec., HMC Midland Div., 1990–91; HMC Rep., ISC (formerly ISJC) Special Needs Cttee, 1991–. *Recreations:* tennis, sailing, motor cars, drama. *Address:* (until July 2002) Lockhart House, Gresham's School, Holt, Norfolk NR25 6DZ. *T:* (01263) 713739; (from July 2002) Church Farm House, Lower Bodham, Holt, Norfolk NR25 6PS. *T:* (01263) 712137.

ARLINGTON, Baroness (11th in line), *cr* 1664; **Jennifer Jane Forwood;** *b* 7 May 1939; *er d* of Maj.-Gen. Sir John Nelson, KCVO, CB, DSO, OBE, MC, and Lady Jane Nelson; *S* in 1999 to Barony of uncle, 9th Duke of Grafton, which had fallen into abeyance in 1936; *m* 1964, Rodney Forwood; two *s*. *Educ:* Downham. *Recreations:* horse racing, bridge, gardening. *Heir:* *s* Hon. Patrick John Dudley Forwood, *b* 23 April 1967.

ARMAGH, Archbishop of, and Primate of All Ireland, since 1986; **Most Rev. Dr Robert Henry Alexander Eames;** Baron Eames *cr* 1995 (Life Peer), of Armagh, in the County of Armagh; *b* 27 April 1937; *s* of William Edward and Mary Eleanor Thompson Eames; *m* 1966 Ann Christine Daly (*see* Lady Eames); two *s*. *Educ:* Belfast Royal Acad.; Methodist Coll., Belfast; Queen's Univ., Belfast (LLB (hons), PhD); Trinity Coll., Dublin. Research Scholar and Tutor, Faculty of Laws, QUB, 1960–63; Curate Assistant, Bangor Parish Church, 1963–66; Rector of St Dorothea's, Belfast, 1966–74; Examining Chaplain to Bishop of Down, 1973; Rector of St Mark's, Dundela, 1974–75; Bishop of Derry and Raphoe, 1975–80; Bishop of Down and Dromore, 1980–86. Select Preacher, Oxford Univ., 1987. Irish Rep., 1984, Mem. Standing Cttee, 1985, ACC; Chairman: Commn on Communion and Women in the Episcopate, 1988–; Commn on Inter-Anglican Relations, 1988–. Governor, Church Army, 1985–90. Hon. LLD: QUB, 1989; TCD, 1992; Lancaster, 1994; Hon. DD Cambridge, 1994. *Publications:* A Form of Worship for Teenagers, 1965; The Quiet Revolution—Irish Disestablishment, 1970; Through Suffering, 1973; Thinking through Lent, 1978; Through Lent, 1984; Chains to be Broken, 1992; contribs to New Divinity, Irish Legal Quarterly, Criminal Law Review. The Furrow. *Address:* The See House, Cathedral Close, Armagh, Co. Armagh BT61 7EE.

ARMAGH, Archbishop of, (RC), and Primate of All Ireland, since 1996; **Most Rev. Sean Brady;** *b* 16 Aug. 1939. *Educ:* St Patrick's Coll., Cavan; St Patrick's Coll., Maynooth (BA 1960; HDipEd 1967); Irish Coll., Rome; Lateran Univ., Rome (STB 1964; DCL 1967). Ordained priest, 1964; teacher, High Sch., St Patrick's Coll., Cavan, 1967–80; Vice Rector, 1980–87, Rector, 1987–93, Pontifical Irish Coll., Rome; Parish priest, Castletara, Co. Cavan, 1993–95; Coadjutor Archbishop of Armagh, 1995–96. *Address:* Ara Coeli, Armagh, Ireland BT61 7QY; *e-mail:* admin@aracoeli.com.

ARMAGH, Dean of; *see* Cassidy, Very Rev. H.

ARMANI, Giorgio; Italian fashion designer; *b* 11 July 1934; *s* of late Ugo Armani and of Maria Raimondi. *Educ:* Univ. of Milan. Mil. Service, 1957. La Rinascente, Milan, 1957–64; Designer and Product Developer, Nino Cerruti, 1964–70; freelance designer, 1970–; founded Giorgio Armani SpA, 1975 and created own-label ready-to-wear clothing; has since introduced other Armani lines, incl. accessories, fragrances and eyewear. Dr *hc* RCA, 1991. Numerous fashion awards. Gran Cavaliere dell'ordine al merito della Repubblica Italiana, 1987 (Commendatore, 1985; Grand'Ufficiale, 1986). *Address:* Giorgio Armani SpA, Via Borgonuovo 21, 20121 Milan, Italy. *T:* (02) 801481; Giorgio Armani Corporation, 114 Fifth Avenue, New York, NY 10011, USA.

ARME, Prof. Christopher, PhD, DSc; CBiol, FIBiol; Professor of Zoology, since 1979, and Dean of Natural Sciences, since 1998, University of Keele; *b* 10 Aug. 1939; *s* of Cyril Boddington and Monica Henrietta Arme; *m* 1962; three *s*. *Educ:* Heanor Grammar Sch.; Univ. of Leeds (BSc 1961; PhD 1964); Univ. of Keele (DSc 1985). FIBiol 1980; CBiol 1980. SRC/NATO Res. Fellow, Univ. of Leeds, 1964–66; Res. Associate, Rice Univ., Texas, 1966–68; Lectr, later Reader, QUB, 1968–76; Head of Biology Gp, N Staffs Polytechnic, 1976–79; Head, Dept of Biol Scis, Univ. of Keele, 1981–88; Dir of Terrestrial and Freshwater Scis, NERC, 1993–95 (on leave of absence from Keele Univ.). British Society for Parasitology: Hon. Gen. Sec., 1980–83; Silver Jubilee Lectr, 1987; Vice Pres., 1988–90; Pres., 1990–92; Hon. Mem., 1992. Chm., Heads of Zool. Depts of Univs Gp, 1981–82; Institute of Biology: Hon. Treas. and Chm., Finance Cttee, 1986–93; Chm., Staffing Cttee, 1993–; Treas., Europ. Fedn of Parasitologists, 1992–2000. Mem., Biol Scis Cttee, and Chm., Animal Scis and Psychol. Sub-Cttee, SERC, 1989–92; Chairman: Steering Cttee, NERC special topic prog. on wildlife diseases, 1992–93; Policy Adv. Cttee, Envmtl Res. Prog., DFID (formerly ODA), 1995–99; Molecular Genetics in Ecology Initiative, Aberdeen Univ./Inst. of Terrestrial Ecology, Banchory, 1995–99; Mem., Adv. Cttee, Centre for Ecology and Hydrology, NERC, 1998–. Mem. Bd of Govs, Harper Adams Agricl Coll., 1996–. Hon. Member: Czechoslovakian Parasitological Soc., 1989; All-Russia Soc. of Helminthologists, 1992; Bulgarian Soc. for Parasitology, 1995. Jt Editor, Parasitology, 1987–. Hon. DSc Slovak Acad. of Scis, 1995. K. I. Skryabin Medal, All-Russian Soc. of Helminthologists, 1994; Hovorka Medal, Slovak Acad. of Scis. 1995; Charter Award Medal, Inst. of Biology, 1995. *Publications:* (ed jtly) Biology of the Eucestoda, Vols I and II, 1983; (ed) Molecular Transfer across Parasite Membranes, 1988; (ed jtly) Toxic Reactions of the Liver, 1992; contribs to parasitological jls. *Address:* Department of Biological Sciences, University of Keele, Keele, Staffs ST5 5BG. *T:* (01782) 583025; *e-mail:* c.arme@biol.keele.ac.uk.

ARMFIELD, Diana Maxwell, (Mrs Bernard Dunstan), RA 1991 (ARA 1989); RWS 1983 (ARWS 1977); RWA; RCA 1991; NEAC; painter, since 1965; *b* 11 June 1920; *d* of Joseph Harold Armfield and Gertrude Mary Uttley; *m* 1949, Bernard Dunstan, *qv*; three *s*. *Educ:* Bedales; Bournemouth Art Sch.; Slade Sch.; Central School of Arts and Crafts. MCSD. Textile/wallpaper designer, 1949–65; work in Fest. of Britain, 1951, and Permanent Collection, V&A Mus. One woman exhibitions: Browse & Darby (London), regularly, 1979–, and 2000; RCA Conwy, and Cardiff, 2001; other exhibitions include: Friends' Room, RA, also Cardiff and Llanbedrog, 1995; Bala, 1996; Wassenaar, Holland, 1998; Nat. Mus. of Cardiff, 1998; Bedales Art & Design Centenary Exhibn, 1999. Artist in Residence: Perth, WA, 1985; Jackson, Wyoming, 1989. Work in Permanent Collections: Govt picture collection, RWA; Yale Center for British Art; Nat. Trust; Contemporary Art Soc. for Wales; Lancaster City Mus.; RWS collection, BM; Faringdon Trust; RWS Queen's birthday collection, 1996; Commissions: Reuters, Nat. Trust, 1989; Prince of Wales, 1989; Royal Acad. diploma collection. Hon. Mem., Pastel Soc., 1988. *Relevant publication:* The Art of Diana Armfield, by Julian Halsby, 1995. *Recreations:* music, gardening, travel. *Address:* 10 High Park Road, Kew, Richmond, Surrey TW9 4BH; Llwynhir, Parc, Bala, Gwynedd, North Wales LL23 7YU. *Club:* Arts.

ARMIDALE, Bishop of, since 2000; **Rt Rev. Peter Robert Brain,** DMin; *b* 2 April 1947; *s* of Paul W. and Doris J. Brain; *m* 1973, Christine Charlton; three *s* one *d*. *Educ:* North Sydney Tech. High Sch.; Moore Theol Coll. (ThL, DipA, DipRE); Fuller Seminary, Pasadena (DMin 1994). Worked in Accounts, and Investments, Australian Mutual Provident Soc., 1963–70. Ordained deacon and priest, 1975; Curate: Sans Souci, Sydney, 1975–76; Holy Trinity, Adelaide, 1977–80; Rector: Maddington, Perth, 1980–88; Wanneroo, Perth, 1988–99. *Recreations:* golf, walking, woodwork. *Address:* 206 Allingham Street, Armidale, NSW 2350, Australia. *T:* (2) 67724491.

ARMITAGE, Edward, CB 1974; Comptroller-General, Patent Office and Industrial Property and Copyright Department, Department of Trade (formerly Trade and Industry), 1969–77; *b* 16 July 1917; *s* of Harry and Florence Armitage; *m* 1940, Marjorie Pope (*d* 1997); one *s* two *d* ; *m* 1999 Marjorie Malby. *Educ:* Huddersfield Coll.; St Catharine's Coll., Cambridge. Patent Office, BoT: Asst Examr 1939; Examr 1944; Sen. Examr 1949; Principal Examr 1960; Suptg Examr 1962; Asst Comptroller 1966. Governor, Centre d'Etudes Internationales de la Propriété Industrielle, Strasbourg, 1975–85; Mem. Council, Common Law Inst. of Intellectual Property, 1981–97; Pres., Internat. Assoc. for Protection of Industrial Property, 1983–86. *Recreations:* bowls, bridge, gardening. *Address:* Richmond House, Plud Street, Wedmore, Somerset BS28 4BE. *T:* (01934) 712756.
See also P. Armitage.

ARMITAGE, (Ernest) Keith; QC 1994; **His Honour Judge Armitage;** a Circuit Judge, since 2001; *b* 15 May 1949; *s* of Selwyn and Marjorie Armitage; *m* 1972, Anita; one *s* one *d*. *Educ:* Trent Coll., Notts; Univ. of Liverpool (LLB Hons). Called to the Bar, Middle Temple, 1970; in practice, Northern Circuit, 1971–2001; a Recorder, 1989–2001. *Recreations:* travel, gliding (soaring).

ARMITAGE, Henry St John Basil, CBE 1978 (OBE 1968); HM Diplomatic Service, retired; Middle East consultant; Honorary Secretary to British/Saudi Arabian Parliamentary Group; *b* 5 May 1924; *s* of Henry John Armitage and late Amelia Eleanor Armitage; *m* 1956, Jennifer Gerda Bruford, *d* of Prof. W. H. Bruford, FBA; one *s* one *d*. *Educ:* St Bede's and Bradford Grammar Schs; Lincoln Christ's Hosp.; Trinity Coll., Cambridge. Served Army, 1943–49; Arab Legion, 1946; British Mil. Mission to Saudi Arabia, 1946–49. Mil. Adviser to Saudi Arabian Minister of Defence, 1949–51; Desert Locust Control, Kenya and Aden Protectorates, 1952; in mil. service of Sultan of Muscat and Oman in Oman and Dhofar, 1952–59; Resident Manager, Gen. Geophysical Co. (Houston), Libya, 1959–60; Oil Conslt, Astor Associates, Libya, 1960–61; Business conslt, Beirut, 1962; joined HM Diplomatic Service, 1962; First Secretary (Commercial): Baghdad, 1963–67; Beirut, 1967–68; First Sec., Jedda, 1968 and 1969–74; Chargé d'Affaires: Jedda, 1969 and 1973; Abu Dhabi, 1975, 1976 and 1977; Counsellor and Consul Gen. in charge British Embassy, Dubai, 1974–78. *Recreations:* reading, travel. *Address:* The Old Vicarage, East Horrington, Wells, Somerset BA5 3EA. *Club:* Travellers.

ARMITAGE, John Vernon, PhD; Principal, 1975–97, and Hon. Senior Fellow in Mathematical Sciences, since 1997, College of St Hild and St Bede, Durham; *b* 21 May 1932; *s* of Horace Armitage and Evelyn (*née* Hauton); *m* 1963, Sarah Catherine Clay; two *s*. *Educ:* Rothwell Grammar Sch., Yorks; UCL (BSc, PhD); Cuddesdon Coll., Oxford. Asst Master: Pontefract High Sch., 1956–58; Shrewsbury Sch., 1958–59; Lectr in Maths, Univ. of Durham, 1959–67; Sen. Lectr in Maths, King's Coll., London, 1967–70; Prof. of Mathematical Educn, Univ. of Nottingham, 1970–75; Special Prof., Nottingham Univ., 1976–79. Chm., Math. Instruction Sub-Cttee, Brit. Nat. Cttee for Maths, Royal Soc., 1975–78. *Publications:* A Companion to Advanced Mathematics (with H. B. Griffiths), 1969; papers on theory of numbers in various jls. *Recreations:* railways, cricket and most games inexpertly. *Address:* 7 Potters Close, Potters Bank, Durham DH1 3UB.

ARMITAGE, Keith; *see* Armitage, E. K.

ARMITAGE, Kenneth, CBE 1969; RA 1994; sculptor; *b* 18 July 1916; *m* 1940. Studied at Slade Sch., London, 1937–39. Served War of 1939–45 in the Army. Teacher of Sculpture, Bath Academy of Art, 1946–56. *One-man exhibitions:* Gimpel Fils, London, regularly 1952–; New York, 1954–58, the last at Paul Rosenberg & Co.; Marlborough Fine Art London, 1962, 1965; Arts Council Exhibn touring 10 English cities, 1972–73; Gall. Kasahara, Osaka, 1974, 1978 and Fuji Telecasting Gall., Tokyo, and Gal. Humanite, Nagoya; Stoke-on-Trent City Mus. and Art Gall., 1981; Sala Mendoza, Caracas, Venezuela, 1982; Taranman Gall., London, 1982; Retrospective Exhibn, Artcurial, Paris, 1985; Jonathan Clark Gall., London, 2001. Gregory Fellowship in sculpture, Leeds Univ., 1953–55; *Guest Artist:* Caracas, Venezuela, 1963; City of Berlin, 1967–69. *Work shown in:* Exhibn of Recent Sculpture in British Pavilion at 26th Venice Biennale, 1952; Internat. Open-Air Exhibns of sculpture in Antwerp, London, Sonsbeek, Varese, and Sydney; British Council Exhibns of sculpture since 1952, which have toured Denmark, Germany, Holland, Norway, Sweden, Switzerland, Canada, USA, and S America; New Decade Exhibn, Museum of Modern Art, New York, 1955; British Section of 4th Internat. São Paulo Biennial, Brazil, 1957; 5th Internat. Exhibn of Drawings and Engravings, Lugano, 1958 (prize-winner); British Pavilion at 29th Venice Biennale, 1958; Art since 1945, Kassel Exhibition, 1959; work in British Sculpture in the 'Sixties' exhibition, Tate Gallery, 1965; Internat. Open-air Exhibn, Hakone, Japan, 1969, 1971; 24 English Sculptors, Burlington House, 1971; Jubilee sculpture exhibn, Battersea Park, 1977; World Expo 88, Brisbane; Seoul Olympic sculpture exhibn, 1988; Twelve Stars, Europ. Parlt Art Collection, 1992; Chelsea Harbour Sculpture, 1993; Yorkshire Sculpture Park, 1996; Friend's Room, RA, 1996; Millennium Sculpture Exhibn, Holland Park, 2000; Le corps mis à nus, Donjon de Vez (Oise), 2001. Work represented in: Victoria and Albert Museum, Tate Gallery; Museum of Modern Art, New York; Musée d'Art Moderne, Paris; Galleria Nazionale d'Arti Moderne, Rome; Hakone Open-Air Sculpture Museum, Japan, and other galleries throughout the world. *Address:* c/o Director's Office, Tate Gallery, Millbank, SW1P 4RG.

ARMITAGE, Air Chief Marshal Sir Michael (John), KCB 1983; CBE 1975; Commandant, Royal College of Defence Studies, 1988–89; *b* 25 Aug. 1930; *m* 1st, 1955 (marr. diss. 1969); three *s*; 2nd, 1970, Gretl Renate Steinig. *Educ:* Newport Grammar Sch., IW; Halton Apprentice; RAF Coll., Cranwell. psc 1965, jssc 1970, rcds 1975. Commnd 1953; flying and staff appts, incl. 28 Sqn, Hong Kong, and No 4 and No 1 Flying Trng Schools; Personal Staff Officer to Comdr 2ATAF, 1966; OC 17 Sqdn, 1967–70; Stn Comdr, RAF Luqa, Malta, 1972–74; Dir Forward Policy, Ministry of Defence (Air Force Dept), 1976–78; Dep. Comdr, RAF Germany, 1978–80; Senior RAF Mem., RCDS, 1980–81; Dir of Service Intelligence, 1982; Dep. Chief of Defence Staff (Intelligence), 1983–84; Chief of Defence Intelligence, 1985–86; Air Mem. for Supply and Orgn, Air Force Dept, MoD, 1986–87. Mem. Council, RUSI, 1986. Chm., Mus. of E Asian Art, Bath, 1996–. Lectures on air power, defence and internat. affairs. *Publications:* (jtly) Air Power in the Nuclear Age, 1982; Unmanned Aircraft, 1988; The Royal Air Force: an illustrated history, 1993, 3rd edn 1999; (ed) Great Air Battles of the Royal Air Force, 1996; contrib. prof. jls. *Recreations:* military history, shooting, reading, writing, lecturing on cruise ships in the Far East. *Address:* c/o Lloyds TSB, Cox & King's Branch, 7 Pall Mall, SW1Y 5NA. *Club:* Royal Air Force.

ARMITAGE, Prof. Peter, CBE 1984; Professor of Applied Statistics (formerly of Biomathematics), 1976–90, now Emeritus, and Fellow, St Peter's College, University of Oxford, 1976–90, now Emeritus Fellow; *b* 15 June 1924; *s* of Harry and Florence Armitage, Huddersfield; *m* 1947, Phyllis Enid Perry, London (*d* 2001); one *s* two *d*. *Educ:* Huddersfield Coll.; Trinity Coll., Cambridge. Wrangler, 1947; MA Cambridge, 1952; PhD London, 1951; Ministry of Supply, 1943–45; National Physical Laboratory, 1945–46; Mem. Statistical Research Unit of Med. Research Council, London Sch. of Hygiene and Trop. Med., 1947–61; Prof. of Medical Statistics, Univ. of London, 1961–76. President: Biometric Soc., 1972–73 (Hon. Life Mem., 1998); Royal Statistical Soc., 1982–84 (Hon. Sec., 1958–64); Internat. Soc. for Clinical Biostatistics, 1990–91; Mem., International Statistical Institute, 1961. Hon. FFPM 1991. Hon. DSc De Montfort, 1998. (Jtly) J. Allyn Taylor Prize, John P. Robarts Res. Inst., London, Ont, 1987; Guy Medals in bronze, silver and gold, Royal Statistical Soc., 1962, 1978, 1990. Editor, Biometrics, 1980–84. *Publications:* Sequential Medical Trials, 1960, 2nd edn 1975; Statistical Methods in Medical Research, 1971, 4th edn (jtly), 2001; (ed with H. A. David) Advances in Biometry, 1996; (ed with T. Colton) Encyclopedia of Biostatistics, 1998; papers in statistical and medical journals. *Recreation:* music. *Address:* 2 Reading Road, Wallingford, Oxon OX10 9DP. *T:* (01491) 835840.
See also E. Armitage.

ARMITAGE, Simon Robert; poet; *b* 26 May 1963. *Publications: poetry:* Zoom!, 1989; Xanadu, 1992; Kid, 1992; Book of Matches, 1993; (with G. Maxwell) Moon Country, 1995; The Dead Sea Poems, 1996; CloudCuckooLand, 1997; Killing Time, 1999; Selected Poems, 2001; The Universal Home Doctor, 2002; *prose:* All Points North, 1998; *play:* Mister Heracles, 2000; Little Green Man (novel), 2001. *Address:* c/o Faber & Faber, 3 Queen Square, WC1N 3AU.

ARMITAGE, (William) Kenneth; *see* Armitage, K.

ARMITT, John Alexander, CBE 1996; FREng, FICE; Chief Executive, Costain Group PLC, 1997–2001; *b* 2 Feb. 1946; *s* of Alexander Walter Armitt and Lily Irene (*née* Dunce); *m* 1969, Mavis Dorothy Sage; one *s* one *d. Educ:* Portsmouth Northern Grammar Sch.; Portsmouth Coll. of Technology. FREng (FEng 1993); FICE 1989. John Laing Construction, 1966–93; Jt Man. Dir, 1988–93; Chairman: J. Laing Internat., 1988–93; Laing Civil Engrg, 1988–93; Chief Exec., Union Railways, 1993–97. Council Member: ICE, 1989–92 (Chm., Mgt Bd, 1989–92); FCEC, 1986–93 (Chm., European Affairs Cttee, 1989–92). Pres., Export Gp for Constructional Inds, 1992–93; Member: Overseas Project Bd, DTI, 1992–93; Export Guarantees Adv. Council, 2001–. Mem. Bd, Major Projects Assoc., 1994–. *Recreations:* sailing, golf, theatre, music. *Address: e-mail:* john_armitt@hotmail.com.

ARMOUR, Prof. Sir James, Kt 1995; CBE 1989; FRSE; FRCVS; FMedSci; Vice-Principal, 1990–95, and Professor of Veterinary Parasitology, 1976–95, now Emeritus, University of Glasgow; Chairman, Glasgow Dental Hospital and School NHS Trust, 1995–98; *b* 17 Sept. 1929; *s* of James Angus Armour and Margaret Brown Roy; *m* 1st, 1953, Irene Morris (*d* 1988); two *s* two *d*; 2nd, 1992, Christine Strickland. *Educ:* Marr Coll., Troon; Univ. of Glasgow (PhD 1967). MRCVS 1952, FRCVS 1995; FRSE 1991. Colonial Service, Nigeria: Vet. Officer, 1953–57; Vet. Parasitologist, 1957–60; Parasitologist, Cooper Technical Bureau, Berkhamsted, 1960–63; University of Glasgow: Research Fellow, 1963–67; Lectr, 1967–70; Sen. Lectr, 1970–73; Reader, 1973–76; Dean, Vet. Faculty, 1986–91. Chairman: Vet. Products Cttee, Medicines Commn, 1987–96; Governing Body, Inst. of Animal Health, Compton, 1991–97; Member: Adv. Bd, Inst. of Aquaculture, Univ. of Stirling, 1997–; Bd, Hannah Res. Inst., Ayr, 1999–. Chm., Moredun Foundn for Animal Health and Welfare, 2000–; Trustee, Scottish Sci. Trust, 1999–. Vice-Pres., RSE, 1998–2000. Founder FMedSci 1998. Hon. FIBiol 2001. Dr *hc* Utrecht 1981; DVM&S Edinburgh, 1995; DU Glasgow, 2001. *Publications:* (with Urquhart and Duncan) Veterinary Parasitology, 1988; numerous contribs to vet. and parasitology jls. *Recreations:* golf, watching soccer and Rugby. *Address:* Mokoia, 11 Crosbie Road, Troon KA10 6HE. *Clubs:* Royal Troon Golf (Captain, 1990–92), Turnberry Golf, Atlanta Athletic (USA).

ARMOUR, Mary Nicol Neill, RSA 1958 (ARSA 1940); RSW 1956; RGI 1977 (Vice-President, 1982; Hon. President, 1983); Teacher of Still Life, Glasgow School of Art, 1952–62 (Hon. Life President, 1982); *b* 27 March 1902; *d* of William Steel; *m* 1927, William Armour, RSA, RSW, RGI (*d* 1979). *Educ:* Glasgow Sch. of Art (Hon. Fellow 1993). Has exhibited at Royal Academy, Royal Scottish Academy, Soc. of Scottish Artists, and Royal Glasgow Institute. Work in permanent collections: Glasgow Municipal Gallery; Edinburgh Corporation; Art Galleries of Aberdeen, Perth, Dundee, Newport, Paisley, Greenock and Victoria (Australia). Fellow, Paisley Coll. of Technol., 1989; Hon. Life Vice Pres., Paisley Inst., 1983. Diploma, Paisley Art Inst., 1995. Hon. LLD Glasgow, 1980. *Recreations:* weaving, gardening. *Address:* Priory Park Private Residential Home, 19 Main Road, Castlehead, Paisley PA2 6AJ. *T:* (0141) 848 1718.

ARMOUR, Nicholas Hilary Stuart; HM Diplomatic Service; Head, North America Department, Foreign and Commonwealth Office, since 2000; *b* 12 June 1951; *s* of late Brig. William Stanley Gibson Armour and of Penelope Jean Armour; *m* 1982, Georgina Elizabeth Fortescue; two *d. Educ:* Ampleforth Coll.; Exeter Univ. (BA). FCO, 1974; MECAS, Lebanon, Beaconsfield, Jordan, 1975; Beirut, 1977; FCO, 1980; Head of Chancery, Athens, 1984; Asst Head of Dept, FCO, 1989; Counsellor, Muscat, 1991; on loan to DTI, 1994–97; Consul-Gen., Dubai and the Northern Emirates, 1997–99; on loan to Royal Mail ViaCode, 2000. Mem., Madrigal Soc., 1995–. *Recreations:* music, singing, sailing. *Address:* c/o Foreign and Commonwealth Office, King Charles Street, SW1A 2AH. *Club:* Helston River Sailing.

ARMSON, (Frederick) Simon (Arden); Chief Executive, The Samaritans, since 1990; *b* 11 Sept. 1948; *s* of late Frank Gerald Arden Armson and of Margaret Fenella Armson (*née* Newton); *m* 1975, Marion Albinia (*née* Hamilton-Russell); one *s* two *d. Educ:* Denstone Coll.; MSc (Mental Health Studies) Guy's Hosp. Med. Sch., London, 1996. Various administrative and managerial posts, NHS, 1970–84; Asst Gen. Sec. 1984–89, Gen. Sec. 1989, The Samaritans. Dir, The Samaritans Enterprises Ltd, 1996–. Chair: BBC Radio Helpline Adv. Gp, 1995–98; Telephone Helplines Gp, 1992–96; Develt Adv. Cttee, Cancer Bacup Service, 1998–. UK Rep., Internat. Assoc. for Suicide Prevention, 1996–; Member: Suicide Prevention Sub-Gp, DoH Wider Health Wkg Gp, 1995–97; RCN Men's Health Forum, 1995–97; Steering Cttee for Structure Review of British Red Cross, 1995; Adv. Cttee, Inst. of Volunteer Research, 1996–; Wkg Gp, Rev. of BACUP Cancer Counselling Service, 1997. Trustee, ChildLine, 1999–. Hon. Mem., Telephone Helplines Assoc., 1999. Chairman of Judges: Guardian Jerwood Award, 1995–99; Guardian Charity Award, 2000–. CIMgt 1995. FRSA 1993. *Publication:* (contrib.) International Handbook of Suicide and Attempted Suicide, 2000. *Recreations:* music, cycling (cross country), walking, sailing. *Address:* Broad Oak, Hurley, Maidenhead, Berkshire SL6 5LW. *T:* (01628) 824322. *Club:* Reform.

ARMSON, Rev. Canon John Moss, PhD; Member, Hengrave Ecumenical Community, since 2001; *b* 21 Dec. 1939; *s* of Arthur Eric Armson and Edith Isobel Moss. *Educ:* Wyggeston Sch.; Selwyn Coll., Cambridge (MA); St Andrews Univ. (PhD); College of the Resurrection, Mirfield. Curate, St John, Notting Hill, 1966; Chaplain and Fellow, Downing Coll., Cambridge, 1969; Chaplain, 1973–77, Vice-Principal, 1977–82, Westcott House, Cambridge; Principal, Edinburgh Theol Coll., 1982–89; Canon Residentiary, Rochester Cathedral, 1989–2001, Canon Emeritus, 2001–. *Recreations:* music, theatre, gardening, landscaping. *Address:* Hengrave Hall, Bury St Edmunds, Suffolk IP28 6LZ.

ARMSON, Simon; *see* Armson, F. S. A.

ARMSTRONG, family name of **Baron Armstrong of Ilminster**.

ARMSTRONG OF ILMINSTER, Baron *cr* 1988 (Life Peer), of Ashill in the county of Somerset; **Robert Temple Armstrong,** GCB 1983 (KCB 1978; CB 1974); CVO 1975; Secretary of the Cabinet, 1979–87, and Head of the Home Civil Service, 1983–87 (Joint Head, 1981–83), retired; Director, 3i Bioscience Investment Trust (formerly Biotechnology Investments Ltd), since 1989 (Chairman, 1989–2001); Chairman, Forensic Investigative Associates plc, since 1997; director of companies; *b* 30 March 1927; *o s* of Sir Thomas (Henry Wait) Armstrong, DMus, FRCM; *m* 1st, 1953, Serena Mary Benedicta (marr. diss. 1985), *er d* of Sir Roger Chance, 3rd Bt, MC; two *d*; 2nd, 1985, (Mary) Patricia, *d* of late C. C. Carlow. *Educ:* Dragon Sch., Oxford; Eton; Christ Church, Oxford (Hon. Student 1985). Asst Principal, Treasury, 1950–55; Private Secretary to: Rt Hon. Reginald Maudling, MP (when Economic Sec. to Treasury), 1953–54; Rt Hon. R. A. Butler, CH, MP (when Chancellor of the Exchequer), 1954–55; Principal, Treasury, 1955–57; Sec., Radcliffe Cttee on Working of Monetary System, 1957–59; returned to Treasury as Principal, 1959–64; Sec., Armitage Cttee on Pay of Postmen, 1964; Asst Sec., Cabinet Office, 1964–66; Sec. of Kindersley Review Body on Doctors' and Dentists' Remuneration and of Franks Cttee on Pay of Higher Civil Service, 1964–66; Asst Sec., Treasury, 1967–68; Jt Prin. Private Sec. to Rt Hon. Roy Jenkins, MP (Chancellor of the Exchequer), 1968; Under Secretary (Home Finance), Treasury, 1968–70; Principal Private Sec. to Prime Minister, 1970–75; Dep. Sec., 1973; Dep. Under-Sec. of State, Home Office, 1975–77, Permt Under Sec. of State, 1977–79. Director: BAT Industries, 1988–97; Inchcape, 1988–95; Bristol and West plc (formerly Bristol and West Building Soc.), 1988–97 (Chm., 1993–97); Lucas Industries, 1989–92; N. M. Rothschild & Sons, 1988–97; RTZ Corporation, 1988–97; Shell Transport & Trading Co., 1988–97; Carlton Television, 1991–95; IAM Gold Ltd, 1996–; Bank of Ireland, 1997–; Mem., Supervisory Bd, Robeco Gp, 1988–97. Chancellor, Univ. of Hull, 1994–. Chairman: Bd of Trustees, V & A Museum, 1988–98; Royal Acad. of Music Foundn, 1988–2000; Hestercombe Gardens Trust, 1996–; Bd of Govs, RNCM, 2000–; Trustee, Leeds Castle Foundn, 1988– (Chm., 2001–); Dir, RAM, 1975–98 (Hon. Fellow 1985); Member: Council of Management, Royal Philharmonic Soc., 1975–; Rhodes Trust, 1975–97; Bd of Dirs, Royal Opera House, Covent Garden, 1988–93 (Sec., 1968–88). Fellow of Eton Coll., 1979–94. Hon. Bencher, Inner Temple, 1986. *Recreation:* music. *Address:* House of Lords, SW1A 0PW.

ARMSTRONG, Alan Gordon; Senior Lecturer in Economics, University of Bristol, 1977–97; *b* 11 Feb. 1937; *s* of late Joseph Gordon Armstrong and Evelyn Armstrong (*née* Aird); *m* 1963, Margaret Louise Harwood; one *s* one *d. Educ:* Bede Grammar Sch., Sunderland; Queens' Coll., Cambridge (MA). Economist, Reed Paper Gp, 1960–62; Res. Officer, Dept of Applied Econs, Univ. of Cambridge, 1962–69; Fellow, Selwyn Coll., Cambridge, 1967–69; Lectr in Econs, Univ. of Bristol, 1970–77. Part-time Mem., Monopolies and Mergers Commn, 1989–95; Consultant on Economic Statistics to: UN Statistical Office, OECD, EEC, ONS, DTI, NEDO, various times, 1970–; Member: EC Adv. Cttee on Econ. and Social Statistics, 1992–97; UK Central Statistical Office (formerly Central Statistical Office Users') Adv. Cttee, 1992–96. *Publications:* Input–Output Tables and Analysis, 1973; Structural Change in UK, 1974; Review of DTI Statistics, 1989; res. papers and jl articles on input–output, nat. accounts and the motor industry. *Recreations:* gardening (by necessity), cricket, church affairs. *Address:* Rock House, King's Hill, Nailsea, Bristol BS48 2AU. *T:* (01275) 853197.

ARMSTRONG, Anne Legendre, (Mrs Tobin Armstrong); Member, Board of Directors: General Motors, 1977–99; Halliburton Company, 1977–2000; Boise Cascade Corporation, 1978–2000; American Express, 1975–76 and 1981–2000; *b* New Orleans, Louisiana, 27 Dec. 1927; *d* of Armant Legendre and Olive Martindale; *m* 1950, Tobin Armstrong; three *s* two *d. Educ:* Foxcroft Sch., Middleburg, Va; Vassar Coll., NY (BA). Deleg. Nat. Conventions, 1964, 1968, 1972, 1980, 1984; Mem. Republican Nat. Cttee, 1968–73 (Co-Chm., 1971–73); Counselor to the President, with Cabinet rank, 1973–74; Ambassador to the Court of St James's, 1976–77. Co Chm., Reagan/Bush Campaign, 1980; Chm., President's Foreign Intelligence Adv. Bd, 1981–90. Center for Strategic and International Studies: Chm., Bd of Trustees, 1987–99; Chm., Exec. Cttee, 1999–. Member: Council on Foreign Relations, 1977–; Chm. E-SU of the US, 1977–80. Trustee: Southern Methodist Univ., 1977–86; Economic Club of NY, 1978–81 (Mem., 1982–); Amer. Associates of the Royal Acad. (Vice Chm., 1984–). Citizen Regent, Smithsonian Instn, 1978–94, Emeritus, 1994–; Regent, Texas A & M Univ. System, 1997–. Hon. Mem., City of London Br., Royal Soc. of St George, 1978; Mem. and Governor, Ditchley Foundn, 1977–87. Pres., Blair House Restoration Fund, 1985–91. Hon. LLD: Bristol, 1976; Washington and Lee, 1976; Williams Coll., 1977; St Mary's Univ., 1978; Tulane, 1978; Hon. LHD: Mt Vernon Coll., 1978; Ripon Coll., 1986; Hamilton Coll., 1990. Gold Medal, Nat. Inst. Social Scis, 1977. Josephine Meredith Langstaff Award, Nat. Soc. Daughters of British Empire in US, 1978; Republican Woman of the Year Award, 1979; Texan of the Year Award, 1981; Texas Women's Hall of Fame, 1986; Presidential Medal of Freedom, 1987; Golden Plate Award, Amer. Acad. of Achievement, 1989. Phi Beta Kappa. *Address:* Armstrong Ranch, Armstrong, TX 78338, USA. *Clubs:* Pilgrims (New York); Alfalfa (Washington).

ARMSTRONG, Very Rev. Christopher John; Dean of Blackburn, since 2001; *b* 18 Dec. 1947; *s* of John Armstrong and Susan Elizabeth Armstrong; *m* 1976, Geraldine Anne Clementsen; two *s* one *d. Educ:* Dunstable Grammar Sch.; Bede Coll., Univ. of Durham (Cert Ed 1969); Kelham Theol Coll.; Univ. of Nottingham (BTh 1975). Ordained deacon, 1976, priest, 1976; Asst Curate, All Saints, Maidstone, 1976–79; Chaplain, Coll. of St Hild and St Bede, Univ. of Durham, 1979–85; Domestic Chaplain to Archbp of York and Diocesan Dir of Ordinands, Dio. York, 1985–91; Vicar, St Martin, Scarborough, 1991–2001. *Recreations:* sport, mountaineering, gardening, theatre and cinema, travel. *Address:* The Dean's House, Preston New Road, Blackburn, Lancs BB2 6PS. *T:* (01254) 52502.

ARMSTRONG, Lt-Col Sir Christopher (John Edmund Stuart), 7th Bt *cr* 1841, of Gallen Priory, King's County; MBE 1979; *b* 15 Jan. 1940; *s* of Sir Andrew Clarence Francis Armstrong, 6th Bt, CMG and Laurel May (*née* Stuart; *d* 1988); *S* father, 1997; *m* 1972, Georgina Elizabeth Carey, *d* of Lt-Col W. G. Lewis; three *s* one *d. Educ:* Ampleforth; RMA, Sandhurst. Lt-Col, RCT. *Heir: s* Charles Andrew Armstrong, *b* 21 Feb. 1973.

ARMSTRONG, Dr Ernest McAlpine, FRCPE, FRCPGlas, FRCGP; Chief Medical Officer, Scottish Executive Department of Health, since 2000; *b* 3 June 1945; *s* of Ernest Armstrong and Mary Brownlie McLean Armstrong (*née* McAlpine); *m* 1970, Dr Katherine Mary Dickson Young; two *s. Educ:* Hamilton Acad.; Glasgow Univ. (BSc (Hons) 1968; MB ChB (Hons) 1970). MRCP 1975; FRCGP 1987; FRCPGlas 1988; FRCPE 1996. Lectr in Pathology, Glasgow Univ., 1971–74; Trainee Assistant, Douglas, 1974–75; Principal in gen. practice, Argyll, 1975–93; Sec., BMA, 1993–2000. Chairman: Argyll and Clyde Area Med. Cttee, 1981–84; Scottish Gen. Med. Services Cttee, 1989–92; British Medical Association: Negotiator, Gen. Med. Services Cttee, 1990–93 (Dep. Chm., 1992–93); Chm., Scottish Council, 1992–93. *Publications:* articles on ultrastructure, clinical immunology and med. politics. *Recreations:* church music, opera, sailing, travelling. *Address:* (office) St Andrew's House, Regent Road, Edinburgh EH1 3DG. *Club:* Caledonian.

ARMSTRONG, Frank William, FREng; FIMechE; FRAeS; independent technical consultant, since 1991; *b* 26 March 1931; *s* of Frank Armstrong and Millicent L. Armstrong; *m* 1957, Diane T. Varley; three *d. Educ:* Stretford Grammar Sch.; Royal Technical Coll., Salford; Queen Mary Coll., Univ. of London (BSc Eng; MSc Eng 1956).

FIMechE 1981; FRAeS 1981; FREng (FEng 1991). Massey-Harris Ltd, 1947–51; De Havilland Engine Co., 1956–58; Admiralty Engineering Lab., 1958–59; NGTE, 1959–78; Engine Div., MoD (PE), 1978–81; Dep. Dir, R&D, NGTE, 1981–83; Royal Aircraft, later Royal Aerospace, Establishment: Head of Propulsion Dept, 1983–87; Dep. Dir (Aircraft), 1987–88; Dep. Dir (Aerospace Vehicles), 1988–90; Dir (Aerospace Vehicles), 1990–91. *Publications:* contribs on aeronautics research, gas turbines and aircraft propulsion to learned jls. *Recreations:* mountaineering, music, aviation history. *Address:* 6 Corringway, Church Crookham, Fleet, Hants GU52 6AN. *T:* (01252) 616526.

ARMSTRONG, Rt Hon. Hilary (Jane); PC 1999; MP (Lab) Durham North West, since 1987; Parliamentary Secretary to HM Treasury (Government Chief Whip), since 2001; *b* 30 Nov. 1945; *d* of Rt Hon. Ernest Armstrong, PC and of Hannah P. Lamb; *m* 1992, Dr Paul Corrigan. *Educ:* Monkwearmouth Comp. Sch., Sunderland; West Ham Coll. of Technology (BSc Sociology); Univ. of Birmingham (Dip in Social Work). VSO, Murray Girls' High Sch., Kenya, 1967–69; Social Worker, Newcastle City Social Services Dept, 1970–73; Community Worker, Southwick Neighbourhood Action Project, Sunderland, 1973–75; Lectr, Community and Youth Work, Sunderland Polytechnic, 1975–86. Frontbench spokesperson on education, 1988–92 (under-fives, primary, and special educn), on Treasury affairs, 1994–95; PPS to Leader of the Opposition, 1992–94; Minister of State, DETR, 1997–2001. *Recreations:* reading, knitting. *Address:* House of Commons, Westminster, SW1A 0AA. *T:* (020) 7219 5076; (constituency) (01388) 767065.

ARMSTRONG, Iain Gillies; QC (Scot.) 2000; *b* 26 May 1956; *s* of John Gillies Armstrong and June Bell Black; *m* 1977, Deirdre Elizabeth Mary Mackenzie; one *s* one *d*. *Educ:* Inverness Royal Acad., Glasgow Univ. Admitted Faculty of Advocates, 1986, Clerk of Faculty, 1995–99; Standing Jun. Counsel in Scotland, DSS, 1998–2000; Advocate Depute, 2000–. *Address:* 2 Ramsay Garden, Edinburgh EH1 2NA. *T:* (0131) 225 2292; Advocates' Library, Parliament House, Edinburgh EH1 1RF. *T:* (0131) 226 5071.

ARMSTRONG, Prof. Isobel Mair, PhD; Professor of English, Birkbeck College, University of London, since 1989; *b* 25 March 1937; *d* of Richard Aneurin Jones and Marjorie Jackson; *m* 1961, John Michael Armstrong; two *s* one *d*. *Educ:* Friends' Sch., Saffron Walden; Univ. of Leicester (BA 1959; PhD 1963). Asst Lectr and Lectr in English, UCL, 1963–70; Lectr and Sen. Lectr in English, Univ. of Leicester, 1971–79; Prof. of English, Univ. of Southampton, 1979–89. Vis. Prof., Princeton, 1983–84; Frank and Eleanor Griffiths Chair, Bread Loaf Sch. of English, Middlebury Coll., 1990; Vis. Prof., Harvard, 1995–96. FRSA. Jt Editor, Women: a cultural review, 1990–; Gen. Editor, Writers and their Work, British Council, 1992–. *Publications:* Victorian Scrutinies: reviews of poetry 1830–70, 1972; Language as Living Form in Nineteenth Century Poetry, 1982; Victorian Poetry, 1993; Nineteenth Century Women Poets, 1996; (ed with Virginia Blain) Women's Poetry in the Enlightenment, 1999; (ed with Virginia Blain) Women's Poetry, Late Romantic to Late Victorian, 1999; The Radical Aesthetic, 2000. *Recreation:* drawing in pen and ink. *Address:* Department of English, Birkbeck College, Malet Street, WC1E 7HX. *T:* (020) 7631 6078.

ARMSTRONG, Jack; *see* Armstrong, J. A.

ARMSTRONG, John Archibald, (Jack), OC 1983; retired; Chief Executive Officer, 1973–82, and Chairman, 1974–82, Imperial Oil Ltd; *b* Dauphin, Manitoba, 24 March 1917. *Educ:* Univ. of Manitoba (BSc Geol.); Queen's Univ. at Kingston (BSc Chem. Engrg). Worked for short time with Geol Survey of Canada and in mining industry; joined Imperial Oil Ltd as geologist, Regina, 1940; appts as: exploration geophysicist, western Canada, and with affiliated cos in USA and S America; Asst Reg. Manager, Producing Dept, 1949; Asst Co-ordinator, Producing Dept of Standard Oil Co. (NJ), New York; Gen. Man., Imperial's Producing Dept, Toronto, 1960; Dir, 1961; Dir resp. for Marketing Ops, 1963–65; Exec. Vice-Pres., 1966, Pres. 1970, Chief Exec. Officer, 1973, Chm., 1974. Chm., Commonwealth Study Conf. Assoc. Life Mem., Fraser Inst. Hon. LLD: Winnipeg, 1978; Calgary, 1980.

ARMSTRONG, Rear Adm. John Herbert Arthur James, (Louis); Chief Executive, Royal Institution of Chartered Surveyors, since 1998; *b* 4 Sept. 1946; *s* of John William Armstrong and Marie Helen (*née* Clark); *m* 1973, Marjorie Anne Corbett (separated); one *s* one *d*; partner, Sibley Pyne. *Educ:* King's Sch., Canterbury; BRNC Dartmouth; Magdalen Coll., Oxford (MA Law). Served in HM Ships Fife, Intrepid and Zulu, 1970–75; called to the Bar, Middle Temple, 1976; Staff Legal Advr to Flag Officer, Plymouth, 1977–79; HM Yacht Britannia, 1979–81; Comdr 1981; HMS Raleigh, 1981–83; Naval Secretary's Staff, 1983–85; HMS Illustrious, 1985–87; Capt. 1987; seconded to Cabinet Office, 1987–89; Asst Dir, Sea Systems' Operational Requirements, MoD, 1989–91; RCDS 1992; Director: Naval Manpower Planning, 1993; Cdre, 1994; Naval Personnel Plans and Progs, 1994; Comdt, RNSC, Greenwich, 1994–95; Rear Adm., 1996; Sen. Naval Directing Staff, RCDS, 1996–98. FRSA 1998. *Recreations:* the arts, ski-ing, tennis, parties. *Address:* Royal Institution of Chartered Surveyors, 12 Great George Street, Parliament Square, SW1P 3AD. *T:* (020) 7334 3707. *Club:* Reform.

ARMSTRONG, Neil A.; Chairman, AIL Systems Inc., since 1989; formerly NASA Astronaut (Commander, Apollo 11 Rocket Flight to the Moon, 1969); *b* Wapakoneta, Ohio, USA, 5 Aug. 1930; *s* of Stephen and Viola Armstrong, Wapakoneta; *m* 1956. *Educ:* High Sch., Wapakoneta, Ohio; Univ. of Southern California (MS); Purdue Univ. (BSc). Served in Korea (78 combat missions) being a naval aviator, 1949–52. He joined NASA's Lewis Research Center, 1955 (then NACA Lewis Flight Propulsion Lab.) and later transf. to NASA High Speed Flight Station at Edwards Air Force Base, Calif, as an aeronautical research pilot for NACA and NASA; in this capacity, he performed as an X-15 project pilot, flying that aircraft to over 200,000 feet and approximately 4,000 miles per hour; other flight test work included piloting the X-1 rocket airplane, the F-100, F-101, F-102, F-104, F5D, B-47, the paraglider, and others; as pilot of the B-29 "drop" aircraft, he participated in the launches of over 100 rocket airplane flights. Selected as an astronaut by NASA, Sept. 1962; served as backup Command Pilot for Gemini 5 flight; as Command Pilot for Gemini 8 mission, launched 16 March 1966; he performed the first successful docking of 2 vehicles in space; served as backup Command Pilot for Gemini 11 mission; assigned as backup Comdr for Apollo VIII Flight, 1969; Dep. Associate Administrator of Aeronautics, NASA HQ, Washington, 1970–71; University Prof. of Aerospace Engrg, Univ. of Cincinnati, 1971–79; Chm., Cardwell International Ltd, 1980–82. Mem., Nat. Acad. of Engrg. Fellow, Soc. of Experimental Test Pilots; FRAeS. Honours include NASA Exceptional Service Medal, and AIAA Astronautics Award for 1966; RGS Gold Medal, 1970. Presidential Medal for Freedom, 1969.

ARMSTRONG, Prof. Peter; Professor of Diagnostic Radiology, St Bartholomew's Hospital, since 1989; President, Royal College of Radiologists, 1998–2001; *b* 31 Aug. 1940; *s* of Alexander Armstrong and Ada Armstrong (*née* Lapidas); *m* 1967, Carole J. Gray; one *s* one *d* (and one *s* decd). *Educ:* Marylebone Grammar Sch.; Middlesex Hosp. Med. Sch. (MB BS 1963). Jun. hosp. posts, Middlesex Hosp. and Guy's Hosp., 1963–70; Consultant Radiologist, KCH, 1970–77; Prof. of Radiology and Dir, Diagnostic Radiology Dept, Univ. of Virginia, 1977–89. Ed., Clinical Radiology, 1990–94. Warden for Clinical Radiology, RCR, 1994–98. *Publications:* (with M. Wastie) Diagnostic Imaging, 1981, 4th edn 1998; (jtly) Imaging Diseases of the Chest, 1990, 3rd edn 2000; contrib. numerous articles on radiological topics to med. jls and books. *Recreations:* reading, theatre, opera. *Address:* Academic Department of Radiology, St Bartholomew's Hospital, Dominion House, 59 Bartholomew's Close, EC1A 7ED. *Club:* Shadows Radiology.

ARMSTRONG, Peter John Bowden; His Honour Judge Armstrong; a Circuit Judge, since 2000; *b* 19 Dec. 1951; *s* of late William David Armstrong and Kathleen Mary Armstrong; *m* 1976, Joanna Cox; two *d*. *Educ:* Durham Johnston Grammar Technical Sch.; Trinity Coll., Cambridge (MA). Called to the Bar, Middle Temple, 1974 (Benefactors Law Schol.); in practice at the Bar, Middlesbrough, 1976–2000; Asst Recorder, 1990–94; a Recorder, 1994–2000; North Eastern Circuit. *Recreations:* golf, cricket, Rugby, music. *Address:* c/o Bradford Court Centre, Exchange Square, Drake Street, Bradford BD1 1JA. *Clubs:* Bradford (Bradford); Eaglescliffe Golf (Stockton-on-Tees); Durham CC.

ARMSTRONG, Richard, CBE 1993; conductor; Music Director, Scottish Opera, since 1993; *b* 7 Jan. 1943. *Educ:* Wyggeston School, Leicester; Corpus Christi College, Cambridge (Hon. Fellow, 1994). Music staff, Royal Opera House, Covent Garden, 1966–68; Welsh National Opera: head of music staff, 1968–73; Musical Director, 1973–86; Principal Guest Conductor, Frankfurt Opera, 1987–90. Hon. DMus De Montfort, 1992. Janáček Medal, 1978. *Recreations:* walking, food. *Address:* c/o Ingpen & Williams, 26 Wadham Road, SW15 2LR.

ARMSTRONG, Robert George, CBE 1972; MC 1946; TD 1958; Deputy Director and Controller, Savings Bank, Department for National Savings, 1969–74, retired (Deputy Director and Controller, Post Office Savings Bank, 1964); *b* 26 Oct. 1913; *s* of late George William Armstrong; *m* 1947, Clara Christine Hyde; one *s* one *d*. *Educ:* Marylebone Grammar Sch.; University Coll., London. Post Office Engineering Dept, 1936–50. Served War of 1939–45, Royal Signals. Principal, PO Headquarters, 1950; Asst Sec., 1962; Dep. Dir of Savings, 1963; Under-Sec., 1972. *Address:* Barryleigh, Wheelers Lane, Brockham, Betchworth, Surrey RH3 7HJ. *T:* (01737) 843217.

ARMSTRONG, Sheila Ann; soprano; *b* 13 Aug. 1942; *m* 1980, Prof. D. E. Cooper, *qv* (marr. diss. 1998). *Educ:* Hirst Park Girls' Sch., Ashington, Northumberland; Royal Academy of Music, London. Debut Sadler's Wells, 1965 Glyndebourne, 1966, Covent Garden, 1973. Sings all over Europe, Far East, N and S America; has made many recordings. K. Ferrier and Mozart Prize, 1965; Hon. RAM 1970, FRAM 1973. Hon. MA Newcastle, 1979; Hon. DMus Durham, 1991. *Recreations:* interior decoration, collecting antique keys, gardening, flower arranging.

ARMSTRONG-JONES, family name of **Earl of Snowdon**.

ARMYTAGE, Captain David George, CBE 1981; Royal Navy, retired; Secretary General, British Diabetic Association, 1981–91; *b* 4 Sept. 1929; *e s* of late Rear-Adm. Reginald William Armytage, GC, CBE and Sylvia Beatrice Armytage; *heir* to Sir (John) Martin Armytage, Bt, *qv*; *m* 1954, Countess Cosima Antonia de Bosdari; two *s* one *d*. *Educ:* RNC, Dartmouth. Comd Motor Torpedo Boats, 1952–53; Direction Officer: 809 Sqn, 1956–58; HMS Chichester, 1958–59; Action Data Automation Project Team, 1959–64; Direction Officer, HMS Eagle, 1964–66; Directorate, Navigation and Tactical Control, 1966–68; comd HMS Minerva, 1968–70; Defence Policy Staff, 1970–72; Naval Asst to First Sea Lord, 1972–74; Internat. Mil. Staff, Brussels, 1975–76; comd, HMS Scylla, 1976 and HMS Jupiter, 1977–78. Capt., 7th Frigate Sqn, 1976–78; Dep. Dir, Naval Warfare, 1978–80; comd, NATO Standing Naval Force Atlantic, 1980–81. ADC to the Queen, 1981. *Recreations:* sailing, gardening, shooting. *Address:* Sharcott Manor, Pewsey, Wilts SN9 5PA. *T:* (01672) 563485. *Clubs:* Oriental, Royal Naval Sailing Association; Royal Channel Islands Yacht.

ARMYTAGE, Sir (John) Martin, 9th Bt *cr* 1738, of Kirklees, Yorkshire; *b* 26 Feb. 1933; *s* of Sir John Lionel Armytage, 8th Bt, and of Evelyn Mary Jessamine, *d* of Edward Herbert Fox, Adbury Park, Newbury; *S* father, 1983. *Educ:* Eton; Worcester Coll., Oxford. *Heir: cousin* Captain David George Armytage, *qv*. *Address:* 5 St James's Place, Cheltenham, Glos GL50 2EG. *T:* (01242) 525869.

ARNAULT, Bernard Jean Etienne; President, since 1989, and Chairman, since 1992, Louis Vuitton Moët Hennessy; *b* Roubaix, 5 March 1949; *s* of Jean Arnault and Marie-Jo (*née* Savinel); *m* 1991, Hélène Mercier; three *s*; one *s* one *d* by former marriage. *Educ:* Ecole Polytechnique, Paris. Qualified as engineer, 1971. President: Ferret Savinel, 1978–84; Financière Agache SA, 1984–89; Christian Dior, 1984–. Man of the Year, NY, 1991. Chevalier, Légion d'Honneur, 1995; Officier, Ordre des Arts et des Lettres, 1995. *Recreations:* music, piano, tennis. *Address:* Christian Dior Couture, 11 rue François 1er, 75008 Paris, France. *T:* 140735444.

ARNDT, Ulrich Wolfgang, MA, PhD; FRS 1982; Member, Scientific Staff of Medical Research Council Laboratory of Molecular Biology, Cambridge, since 1962; *b* 23 April 1924; *o s* of E. J. and C. M. Arndt; *m* 1958, Valerie Howard, *e d* of late Maj.-Gen. F. C. Hilton-Sergeant, CB, CBE, QHP; three *d*. *Educ:* Dulwich Coll.; King Edward VI High Sch., Birmingham; Emmanuel Coll., Cambridge (MA, PhD). Metallurgy Dept, Birmingham Univ., 1948–49; Davy-Faraday Laboratory of Royal Instn, 1950–63; Dewar Fellow of Royal Instn, 1957–61; Univ. of Wisconsin, Madison, 1956; Institut Laue-Langevin, Grenoble, 1972–73. *Publications:* (with B. T. M. Willis) Single Crystal Diffractometry, 1966; (with A. J. Wonacott) The Rotation Method in Crystallography, 1977; papers in scientific jls. *Recreations:* walking, reading. *Address:* 28 Barrow Road, Cambridge CB2 2AS. *T:* (01223) 350660.

ARNELL, Richard Anthony Sayer; Hon. FTCL; composer; conductor; poet; Principal Lecturer, Trinity College of Music, 1981–87 (Teacher of Composition, 1949–81); *b* 15 Sept. 1917; *s* of late Richard Sayer Arnell and of Helène Marie Scherf; *m* 1992, Joan Heycock; three *d* from former marriages. *Educ:* The Hall, Hampstead; University Coll. Sch., NW3; Royal Coll. of Music. Music Consultant, BBC North American Service, 1943–46; Lectr, Royal Ballet Sch., 1958–59. Editor, The Composer, 1961–64, 1991–93; Chairman: Composers' Guild of GB, 1965, 1974–75 (Vice-Pres., 1992–); Young Musicians' Symph. Orch. Soc., 1973–75. Vis. Lectr (Fulbright Exchange), Bowdoin Coll., Maine, 1967–68; Vis. Prof. Hofstra Univ., New York, 1968–70. Music Dir and Board Mem., London Internat. Film Sch., 1975–89 (Chm., Film Sch. Trust, 1981–87; Chm., Friends of LIFS, 1982–87, Vice-Pres., 1988–); Music Dir, Ram Filming Ltd, 1980–91; Director: Organic Sounds Ltd, 1982–87; A plus A Ltd, 1984–89. Chm., Friends of TCM Junior Dept, 1986–87 (Vice-Pres., 1987–). Chairman: Tadcaster Civic Soc. Music and Arts Cttee, 1988–91; Saxmundham Music and Arts, 1992–95 (Pres., 1995–). Composer of the Year 1966 (Music Teachers Assoc. Award); Tadcaster Town Council Merit Award, 1990. *Compositions include:* 7 symphonies; 2 concertos for violin; concerto for harpsichord; 2 concertos for piano; string trio; 6 string quartets; 2 quintets; piano trio; piano works;

songs; cantatas; organ works; music for string orchestra, wind ensembles, brass ensembles, song cycles; electronic music; *opera:* Love in Transit; Moonflowers; *ballet scores:* Punch and the Child, for Ballet Soc., NY, 1947; Harlequin in April, for Arts Council, 1951; The Great Detective, for Sadler's Wells Theatre Ballet, 1953; The Angels, for SWRB, 1957; Giselle (Adam) re-orchestrated, for Ballet Rambert, 1965; *film scores:* The Land, 1941; The Third Secret, 1963; The Visit, 1964; The Man Outside, 1966; Topsail Schooner, 1966; Bequest for a Village, 1969; Second Best, 1972; Stained Glass, 1973; Wires Over the Border, 1974; Black Panther, 1977; Antagonist, 1980; Dilemma, 1981; Doctor in the Sky, 1983; Toulouse Lautrec, 1984; Light of the World, 1990; *other works:* Symphonic Portrait, Lord Byron, for Sir Thomas Beecham, 1953; Landscapes and Figures, for Sir Thomas Beecham, 1956; Petrified Princess, puppet operetta (libretto by Bryan Guinness), for BBC, 1959; Robert Flaherty, Impression for Radio Eireann, 1960; Musica Pacifica for Edward Benjamin, 1963; Festival Flourish, for Salvation Army, 1965; 2nd piano concerto, for RPO, 1967; Overture, Food of Love, for Portland Symph. Orch., 1968; My Ladye Greene Sleeves, for Hofstra Univ., 1968; Life Boat Voluntary, for RNLI, 1974; Call, for LPO, 1980; Ode to Beecham, for RPO, 1986; War God II, 1987; Con Amore, 1990; Xanadu, 1993; Symphonic Statement (7), for Nelson Mandela, 1999; *mixed media:* Nocturne: Prague, 1968; I Think of all Soft Limbs, for Canadian Broadcasting Corp., 1971; Combat Zone, for Hofstra Univ., 1971; Astronaut One, 1973; Not Wanted on Voyage, 1990; 24 Hours in TR Scale, 1995; "B"-Queen Boudicca, 2000. *Address:* Benhall Lodge, Benhall, Saxmundham, Suffolk IP17 1JD. *Club:* Savage.

ARNISON, Maj.-Gen. Peter Maurice, AC 2001 (AO 1992); Governor of Queensland, Australia, since 1997; *b* 21 Oct. 1940; *s* of Frank and Norma Arnison; *m* 1964, Barbara Ruth Smith; one *s* one *d*. *Educ:* Lismore High Sch.; Royal Mil. Coll., Duntroon; Army Staff Coll., Queenscliff; Univ. of Queensland (BEc 1976); Securities Inst. of Australia (Grad. Dip. in Applied Finance and Investment 1993). CO 5th 7th Bn Royal Aust. Regt, 1981–82; JSSC 1983; COS HQ 1st Div., Brisbane, 1983–84; Comdt Land Warfare Centre, Canungra, Qld, 1985–86; Comdr 3rd Bde, Townsville, Qld, 1987–88; RCDS 1989; Dir-Gen. Jt Ops and Plans, HQ Aust. Defence Force, Canberra, 1990; Comdr 1st Div., Brisbane, Qld, 1991–94; Land Comdr Australia, Sydney, 1994–96. Exec. Dir, Allied Rubber Products (Qld), 1996–97. DUniv: Griffith, 1998; Qld Univ. of Technology, 1999. KStJ 1997. *Publication:* Australia's Security Arrangements in the South West Pacific, 1989. *Recreations:* golf, watching Rugby and cricket, theatre, reading, computing. *Address:* Government House, Fernberg Road, Paddington, Qld 4064, Australia. *T:* (7) 38585700. *Clubs:* Queensland, United Service (Brisbane); Royal Queensland Golf.

ARNOLD, Anne Mary; District Judge (Magistrates' Courts) (formerly Provincial Stipendiary Magistrate), East Sussex, since 1999; *b* 16 March 1958; *d* of late Lt Comdr Stanley Hugh Childs Plant, RNR, RD, and of Enid Edith Plant (*née* Morgan); *m* 1987, Peter Roderick Arnold. *Educ:* Talbot Heath, Bournemouth; Dorset Inst. Higher Educn and Université de Caen (BA Hons); Univ. of Birmingham (MBA Public Service); Homerton Coll., Cambridge (AdvDip Professional Trng and Develt). Called to the Bar, Inner Temple, 1981; Dorset Magistrates' Courts, 1979–99: Legal Advr, 1980–82; Principal Legal Advr, 1982–92; Dep. Justices' Trng Officer, 1991–94; Bench Legal Advr, 1992–94; Dir of Legal Services, 1994–99; Jt Staff Trng Officer, 1995–99; Associate Inspector, HM Magistrates' Courts Inspectorate, 1998; Actg Provincial Stipendiary Magistrate, E and W Sussex Commn Areas, 1997–99. *Publication:* (contrib.) Atkin's Court Forms. *Recreations:* sailing, ski ing, swimming, walking, gardening. *Address:* The Law Courts, Edward Street, Brighton, E Sussex BN2 2LG. *T:* (01273) 670888. *Club:* Bar Yacht.

ARNOLD, Rev. Duane Wade-Hampton, PhD; Principal, St Chad's College, University of Durham, 1994–97; *b* 5 Aug. 1953; *s* of Wade H. Arnold and Louise Elizabeth (*née* Hensley); *m* 1980, Janet Lee Drew. *Educ:* Univ. of State of New York (BA 1979); Concordia Seminary (MA 1981); St Chad's Coll., Durham (PhD 1989); STh (Lambeth Dip. in Theol.), 1984. Minister, First Church, Detroit, Michigan, 1985–87; Precentor, St Paul's Cathedral, Detroit, 1987; Chaplain, Wayne State Univ., Detroit, 1988–91; Curate, St Thomas Church, Fifth Ave, NY, 1991–93. Tutor, St Chad's Coll., Durham, 1983–85; Adjunct Lecturer: in Religious Studies, Univ. of Detroit, 1985–88; in Church History, Ashland Seminary, Ohio, 1987–91. ChStJ 1990. Governor's Award, Michigan, 1988. *Publications:* A Lutheran Reader, 1982; The Way, the Truth and the Life, 1982; Francis, A Call to Conversion, 1990; Prayers of the Martyrs, 1991; The Early Episcopal Career of Athanasius of Alexandria, 1991; Praying with John Donne and George Herbert, 1992; *De Doctrina Christiana*, Classic of Western Civilization, 1995; contribs to learned jls. *Recreations:* shooting, restoring college halls and churches.

ARNOLD, Eve; photographer and writer; *b* Philadelphia, 1925; *m* (marr. diss.); one *s*. Took a 6-week photography class with Alexei Brodovitch, at New Sch. for Social Research, NY, 1948, after receiving a $40 Rolleicord as her first camera; first photographs in Picture Post, followed by Ladies Home Jl, Life, Time, Look, Stern, Paris Match, Harpers, Queen, Sunday Times; joined Magnum Photos agency, 1951; works in USA, UK, Africa, China, Russia, Afghanistan, Arab countries; portrait photographs include Royalty, film stars and politicians. Exhibitions: Brooklyn Mus., NY, 1980; Nat. Portrait Gall., 1991; (retrospective) Barbican, 1996. *Films:* Behind the Veil, 1973; special production photographer on 31 films. *Publications:* The Unretouched Woman, 1976; Flashback!: the 50s, 1978; In China, 1980; In America, 1984; Marilyn Monroe: an appreciation, 1987; Private View: inside Baryshnikov's American Ballet Theatre, 1988; All in a Day's Work, 1989; Eve Arnold in Britain, 1991; Eve Arnold: in retrospect, 1996. *Address:* 26 Mount Street, W1Y 5RB.

ARNOLD, Glynis, (Mrs Elliott Arnold); *see* Johns, Glynis.

ARNOLD, Jacques Arnold; Adviser for Latin America, BAE Systems plc, since 2000; *b* London, 27 Aug. 1947; *s* of late Samuel Arnold and Eugenie (*née* Patentine); *m* 1976, Patricia Anne, *er d* of Dennis Maunder, of Windsor; one *s* two *d*. *Educ:* schools in Brazil and by correspondence; London School of Economics (BSc (Econ) 1972). Asst Gp Rep., Midland Bank, São Paulo, 1976–78; Regl Dir, Thomas Cook Gp, 1978–84; Asst Trade Finance Dir, Midland Bank, 1984–85; Dir, American Express Europe Ltd, 1985–87; Adviser for Latin America, GEC plc, 1998–2000; has travelled to over 90 countries on business. County Councillor for Oundle, Northants, 1981–85. Contested (C) Coventry SE, 1983. MP (C) Gravesham, 1987–97; contested (C) same seat, 1997, 2001. PPS to Minister of State: for Envmt and Countryside, 1992–93; Home Office, 1993–95. Member: Educn, Arts and Sci. Select Cttee, 1989–92; Treasury and CS Select Cttee, 1997; Sec., Cons. Backbench Cttee on Foreign and Commonwealth Affairs, 1990–92, 1995–97; Vice-Chm., 1995–96, Chm., 1996–97, Cons. Backbench Cttee on Constitutional Affairs. Secretary: British-Latin-American Parly Gp, 1987–97; Scout Assoc. Parly Gp, 1987–97; Chairman: British Brazilian Parly Gp, 1992–97; British Portuguese Parly Gp, 1995–97. Chm., LSE Cons. Soc., 1971–72; Treasurer, Nat. Assoc. of Cons. Graduates, 1974–76; Chm., Hyde Park Tories, 1975–76; Vice-Chairman: Croydon NE Cons. Assoc., 1974–76; Corby Cons. Assoc., 1983–85. Chm., Kent County Scout Council, 1998–2000. Trustee, Environment Foundn, 1989–. Grand Official, Order of Southern Cross (Brazil), 1993. *Publications:* on genealogy and constitutional affairs. *Recreations:* family life, gardening, genealogy. *Address:* Fairlawn, 243 London Road, West Malling, Kent ME19 5AD. *T:* and *Fax:* (01732) 848388. *Club:* Carlton.

ARNOLD, Jennette; Member (Lab) London Assembly, Greater London Authority, since July 2000. Formerly: nurse; health visitor; Regl Dir, RCN. Mem. (Lab) Islington BC, 1994– (formerly Deputy Mayor). Mem., Metropolitan Police Authy, 2000–. *Address:* Greater London Authority, Romney House, 43 Marsham Street, SW1P 3PY.

ARNOLD, Rt Hon. Sir John Lewis, Kt 1972; PC 1979; President of Family Division, 1979–88; a Judge in the Division, 1972–88; *b* 6 May 1915; *s* of late A. L. Arnold and E. K. Arnold; *m* 1940, Alice Margaret Dorothea (*née* Cookson) (marr. diss., 1963); one *s* one *d*; *m* 1963, Florence Elizabeth, *d* of H. M. Hague, Montreal; one *s* two *d*. *Educ:* Wellington Coll.; abroad. Called to Bar, Middle Temple, 1937; served War of 1939–45 in Army (despatches, 1945); resumed practice at Bar, 1946; QC 1958; Chm. Bar Council, 1970–72, Chm., Plant Variety Rights Tribunal for proceedings in England and Wales, 1969–72. Hon. DLitt Reading, 1982. *Recreations:* cricket, travel. *Address:* Villa La Pergola, Via B. Bonci 14, Vagliagli 53010, Siena, Italy.

ARNOLD, Very Rev. John Robert; Dean of Durham, since 1989; *b* 1 Nov. 1933; *s* of John Stanley and Ivy Arnold; *m* 1963, Livia Anneliese Franke; one *s* two *d*. *Educ:* Christ's Hospital; Sidney Sussex Coll., Cambridge (MA); Westcott House Theol College. Curate of Holy Trinity, Millhouses, Sheffield, 1960–63; Sir Henry Stephenson Fellow, Univ. of Sheffield, 1962–63; Chaplain and Lectr, Univ. of Southampton, 1963–72; Secretary, Board for Mission and Unity, General Synod of the Church of England, 1972–78; Dean of Rochester, 1978–89. Pt-time Lectr, Univ. of Durham, 1992–. Hon. Canon of Winchester Cathedral, 1974–78; Mem., General Synod, 1980–. Mem., European Ecumenical Commn for Church and Society, 1986–98; Pres., Conference of European Churches, 1986– (Vice-Chm., 1986–92; Chm., 1993–97). Pres., Anglican-Lutheran Soc., 1999–. DD Lambeth, 1999. Order of Saint Vladimir (Russian Orthodox Church), 1977. Officers' Cross, Order of Merit (Germany), 1991. *Publications:* (trans.) Eucharistic Liturgy of Taizé, 1962; (contrib.) Hewitt, Strategist for the Spirit, 1985; Rochester Cathedral, 1987; (contrib.) Cathedrals Now, 1996; (contrib.) Preaching from Cathedrals, 1998; contribs to Theology, Crucible, St Luke's Journal of Theology. *Recreations:* music, European languages and literature. *Address:* The Deanery, Durham DH1 3EQ. *T:* (0191) 384 7500. *Clubs:* Royal Commonwealth Society, Christ's Hospital.

ARNOLD, Rt Rev. Keith Appleby; Hon. Assistant Bishop, Diocese of Oxford, since 1996; *b* 1 Oct. 1926; *s* of Dr Frederick Arnold, Hale, Cheshire, and Alice Mary Appleby Arnold (*née* Holt); *m* 1955, Deborah Noreen Glenwright; one *s* one *d*. *Educ:* Winchester; Trinity Coll., Cambridge (MA); Westcott House, Cambridge. Served as Lieut, Coldstream Guards, 1944–48. Curate: Haltwhistle, Northumberland, 1952–55; St John's, Princes St, Edinburgh, 1955–61; Chaplain, TA, 1956–61; Rector of St John's, Edinburgh, 1961–69; Vicar of Kirkby Lonsdale, Cumbria, 1969–73; Team Rector of Hemel Hempstead, 1973–80; Bishop Suffragan of Warwick, 1980–90; Hon. Asst Bishop, dio. of Newcastle, 1991–96. Vice-Pres., Abbeyfield Soc., 1981–91; Chairman: Housing Assocs Charitable Trust, 1980–86; English Villages Housing Assoc., 1987–. Pres., S Warwicks Marriage Guidance Council, subseq. Relate, 1980–90. *Recreations:* 19th century history, gardening. *Address:* 9 Dingledерry, Olney, Bucks MK46 5ES. *T:* (01234) 713044.

ARNOLD, Hon. Lynn Maurice Ferguson; Chief Executive Officer, World Vision Australia, since 1997; *b* 27 Jan. 1949; *s* of Maurice and Jean Arnold; *m* 1978, Elaine Palmer; two *s* three *d*. *Educ:* Adelaide Boys' High Sch.; Univ. of Adelaide (BA, BEd). Dip. en la Alta Dirección de Empresas, ESADE, 1996. Teacher, Salisbury N High Sch., 1971–74; Adv. Teacher, Health Educn Project Team, 1975–76; Personal Assistant to MHR, 1977–79; MHA (ALP) Salisbury, 1979–87; MP (ALP) Ramsay, 1987–93, Taylor, 1993–94; Minister of: Education, 1982–85; Technology, 1982–87; Children's Services, 1985; Employment and Further Educn, and State Develt, 1985–89; Industry, Trade & Technol., also Agriculture, Fisheries, and Ethnic Affairs, 1989–92; Economic Develt, and Multicultural and Ethnic Affairs, 1992–93; Premier of S Australia, 1992–93; Leader of the Opposition and Shadow Minister of Econ. Develt and of Multicultural and Ethnic Affairs, 1993–94; Vis. Scholar, Univ. of Oviedo, Spain, 1994–95; student, Escuela Superior de Administación y Dirección de Empresas, Barcelona, 1995–96. Sec. and Pres., Campaign for Peace in Vietnam, 1970–73. Mem. Council, Univ. of Adelaide, 1979–82. Trustee, Cttee for the Economic Develt of Australia, 1997–. Mem., Australian Inst. of Co. Dirs, 1997–. *Publications:* Nigeria-Biafra Conflict, 1968; (jtly) Hoa Binh Third Force in Vietnam, 1970; (jtly) You and Me, 1975; (jtly) All Together, 1976. *Recreations:* sociolinguistics, history. *Address:* c/o 1 Vision Drive, East Burwood, Vic 3151, Australia.

ARNOLD, Sir Malcolm (Henry), Kt 1993; CBE 1970; FRCM; composer; *b* 21 Oct. 1921; *s* of William and Annie Arnold, Northampton; *m*; two *s* one *d*. *Educ:* Royal Coll. of Music, London (Schol., 1938). FRCM 1983; FTCL 1992; FRNCM 1997. Principal Trumpet, London Philharmonic Orchestra, 1941–44; served in the Army, 1944–45; Principal Trumpet, London Philharmonic Orchestra, 1945–48; Mendelssohn Schol. (study in Italy), 1948; Coronation Ballet, Homage to the Queen, performed Royal Opera House, 1953. Awarded Oscar for music for film Bridge on the River Kwai, 1957; Ivor Novello Award for outstanding services to British Music, 1985; Wavendon Allmusic Composer of the Year, 1987; Ivor Novello Award for Inn of Sixth Happiness, 1958. Bard of the Cornish Gorsedd, 1969. Hon. RAM; Hon. Mem., Schubert Soc., 1988. Hon. DMus: Exeter, 1970; Durham, 1982; Leicester, 1984; Hon. Dr Arts and Humane Letters, Miami Univ., Ohio, 1990. Hon. Freeman, Borough of Northampton, 1989. *Publications: symphonies:* No 1, 1949; No 2, 1953; No 3, 1957; No 4, 1960; No 5, 1961; No 6, 1967; No 7, 1973; No 8, 1978; No 9, 1986; Symphony for Brass Instruments, 1979; *other works:* Beckus the Dandipratt, overture, 1943; Tam O'Shanter, overture, 1955; Peterloo, overture, 1967; eighteen concertos; six ballets: Homage to the Queen, Electra, Rinaldo Armida, Flowers of the Forest, Solitaire, Sweeney Todd; two one-act operas; two string quartets; two brass quintets; vocal, choral and chamber music. *Recreations:* reading and foreign travel. *Address:* Music Unites, 26 Springfields, Attleborough, Norfolk NR17 2PA. *T:* and *Fax:* (01953) 455420. *Club:* Savile.

ARNOLD, Dr Richard Bentham; Executive Vice-President, International Federation of Pharmaceutical Manufacturers' Associations, 1984–96; *b* 29 Aug. 1932; *s* of George Benjamin and Alice Arnold; *m* 1956, Margaret Evelyn Racey; one *s* one *d*. *Educ:* Stamford Sch.; King Edward VII Sch., King's Lynn; Nottingham Univ. BSc, PhD. Joined May & Baker Ltd, 1959; Commercial Manager, Pharmaceuticals Div., 1974–76; Dir Designate, 1976, Dir, 1977–83, Assoc. of British Pharmaceutical Industry. *Recreations:* golf, fishing, bird watching.

ARNOLD, Richard David; QC 2000; *b* 23 June 1961; *s* of Francis Arnold and Ann Arnold (*née* Churchill); *m* 1990, Mary Elford; two *d*. *Educ:* Highgate Sch.; Magdalen Coll., Oxford (BA Nat. Sci. 1983, MA 1986); Univ. of Westminster (Dip. Law 1984). Called to the Bar, Middle Temple, 1985. Ed., Entertainment and Media Law Reports, 1993–. *Publications:* Performers' Rights, 1990, 2nd edn 1997; (jtly) Computer Software: legal protection in the UK, 2nd edn, 1992. *Recreations:* collecting contemporary British abstract paintings and ceramics, music, cinema, theatre, opera. *Address:* 11 South Square, Gray's Inn, WC1R 5EU. *T:* (020) 7405 1222. *Club:* MCC.

ARNOLD, Simon Rory; Deputy Chairman, Aon Group (formerly Bain Hogg Group) plc, since 1995; Chairman, Octavian Syndicate Management Services Ltd, since 1995; *b* 10 Sept. 1933; *s* of R. W. Arnold and R. A. Arnold; *m* 1960, (Janet) Linda May; one *s* one *d. Educ:* Diocesan Coll., Cape Town. J. H. Minet & Co. Ltd: S. Africa, 1952; London, 1955; Chm. and Chief Exec., 1979; Gp Man. Dir, Minet Holdings, 1983; Chief Exec., Bain Dawes Ltd, 1984; Chm. and Chief Exec., Bain Clarkson Ltd, 1986–95; Main Bd Dir, Inchcape plc, 1988–94. Member: Lloyd's Brokers Cttee, 1979–91 (Chm., 1986–91); Council, Lloyd's, 1991–94; Insurance Brokers' Registration Council, 1995– (Chm., 1998); Chm., BIIBA, 1994–. *Recreations:* ski-ing, walking, golf, tennis.

ARNOLD, Sir Thomas (Richard), Kt 1990; theatre producer; publisher; consultant; *b* 25 Jan. 1947; *s* of late Thomas Charles Arnold, OBE and Helen Breen; *m* 1984, Elizabeth Jane (marr. diss. 1993), *widow* of Robin Smithers; one *d. Educ:* Bedales Sch.; Le Rosey, Geneva; Pembroke Coll., Oxford (MA). Contested (C): Manchester Cheetham, 1970; Hazel Grove, Feb. 1974. MP (C) Hazel Grove, Oct. 1974–1997. PPS to Sec. of State for NI, 1979–81, to Lord Privy Seal, FCO, 1981–82; Chm., Treasury and CS Select Cttee, 1994–97 (Mem., 1992–94). Vice-Chm., Conservative Party, 1983–92. *Address:* 19 Ordnance Hill, NW8 6PR.

ARNOLD, Wallace; *see* Brown, C. E. M.

ARNOLD, William; Director, Regional Development Agency Policy, Finance and Sponsorship, Department of Trade and Industry, since 2001; *b* 13 May 1953; *s* of Rev. William and Mrs Ruth Arnold; *m* 1992, Elizabeth Anne McLellan; twin *s. Educ:* Bury Grammar Sch.; King's Coll., Cambridge (MA Classics). Joined Lord Chancellor's Department, 1974: Asst Private Sec. to Lord Chancellor, 1977–79; Principal, 1979; Head of Legal Services Div., 1987; Head of Remuneration and Competition Div., 1988; Head, Courts and Legal Services Bill Div., 1989; Dir of Corporate Services and Principal Estabt and Finance Officer, PRO, 1991–92; on loan to Dept of PM and Cabinet, Canberra, Australia, 1993–94; Hd, Family Policy Div., LCD, 1994–99; Hd of Govt Offices and Regl Policy, then Regl Policy and Regeneration, Div. 1, DETR, 1999–2001. Reader, St Margaret's Church, Putney, 1989–. *Recreations:* ski-ing, swimming, long-distance trekking, opera, ballet. *Address:* Department of Trade and Industry, 1 Victoria Street, SW1H 0ET.

ARNOLD-BAKER, Charles, OBE 1966; Chairman, Longcross Press, since 1968; Consultant Lecturer, 1978, and Visiting Professor, 1985–94, City University; *b* 25 June 1918; *s* of Baron Albrecht v. Blumenthal and Alice Wilhelmine (*née* Hainsworth); adopted surname of mother's second husband, Percival Richard Arnold Baker, 1938; *m* 1943, Edith (*née* Woods); one *s* one *d. Educ:* Winchester Coll.; Magdalen Coll., Oxford. BA 1940. Called to Bar, Inner Temple, 1948. Army (Private to Captain), 1940–46. Admty Bar, 1948–52; Sec., Nat. Assoc. of Local Councils, 1953–78; Dep. Eastern Traffic Comr, 1978–90. Editor, Road Law, 1992–96. Mem., Royal Commn on Common Lands, 1955–58; Mem. European Cttee, Internat. Union of Local Authorities, 1960–78; a Deleg. to European Local Govt Assembly, Strasbourg, 1960–78. Occasional broadcaster, Radio 4, 1987–92. Gwylim Gibbons Award, Nuffield Coll., Oxford, 1959. King Haakon's Medal of Freedom (Norway), 1945. *Publications:* Norway (pamphlet), 1946; Everyman's Dictionary of Dates, 1954; Parish Administration, 1958; New Law and Practice of Parish Administration, 1966; The 5000 and the Power Tangle, 1967; The Local Government Act 1972, 1973; Local Council Administration, 1975, 6th edn 2001; The Local Government, Planning and Land Act 1980, 1981; Practical Law for Arts Administrators, 1983, 3rd edn 1992; The Five Thousand and the Living Constitution, 1986; The Companion to British History, 1996, 2001; many contribs to British and European local govt and legal jls. *Recreations:* travel, history, writing, music, cooking, journalism, wine and doing nothing. *Address:* Top Floor, Mitre Court Buildings, Temple, EC4Y 7BX. *T:* (020) 7353 3490. *Club:* Union (Oxford).

ARNOLD-FORSTER, David Oakley, OBE 1994; TD 1992; Chief Executive and Council Member, English Nature, since 2000; *b* 13 Sept. 1956; *s* of Thomas Edward Oakley Arnold-Forster and Elsie Margaret Arnold-Forster (*née* Brooksbank); *m* 1988, Anita Irene Stimpson. *Educ:* Rugby Sch.; Wye Coll., London Univ. (BSc 1978). Ministry of Defence, 1978–85, 1990–94: Admin. Trainee, 1978; Overseas Service, Germany, 1979–80; Private Sec. to Parly Under-Sec. of State (Armed Forces), 1981–84; Head, Chem. and Biol Arms Control Br., Defence Arms Control Unit, 1990–92; Overseas Services, Bosnia and Croatia, 1992–93; Richard Ellis, Chartered Surveyors, 1985–88; Dir, Richmount Enterprise Zone Managers Ltd, 1988–90; PA to R. A. Clegg (sometime Chm. and CEO, Mountleigh Gp), 1988–90; Chief Exec., N Yorks Moors Nat. Park, 1994–2000. Chm., MAFF Task Force for the Hills, 2000–01. Territorial Army, 1978–94: Sandhurst, 1980; 100 Regt, RA; HQ, 201, and OC 307 Battery (Major). Pres., Scarborough Cavaliers Rotary Club, 1999. *Recreations:* environment, walking, fly fishing, ski-ing, riding, American Civil War history. *Address:* c/o English Nature, Northminster House, Peterborough PE1 1UA. *T:* (01733) 455344. *Club:* Cavalry and Guards.

ARNOTT, Sir Alexander John Maxwell; 6th Bt *cr* 1896, of Woodlands, Shandon, Co. Cork; *b* 18 Sept. 1975; *s* of Sir John Robert Alexander Arnott, 5th Bt, and of Ann Margaret, *d* of late T. A. Farrelly, Kilcar, Co. Cavan; *S* father, 1981. *Heir: b* Andrew John Eric Arnott, *b* 20 June 1978. *Address:* 11 Palmerston Road, Dublin 6, Ireland.

ARNOTT, Edward Ian W.; *see* Walker-Arnott.

ARNOTT, Geoffrey; *see* Arnott, W. G.

ARNOTT, Prof. Struther, CBE 1996; FRS 1985; Haddow Professor, Institute of Cancer Research, since 2000; Principal and Vice-Chancellor, University of St Andrews, 1986–2000; *b* 25 Sept. 1934; *s* of Charles McCann and Christina Struthers Arnott; *m* 1970, Greta Edwards (BA, DLitt); two *s. Educ:* Hamilton Academy, Lanarkshire; Glasgow Univ. (BSc, PhD). FRSC 1970; FRSE 1988. King's College London: scientist, MRC Biophysics Research Unit, 1960–70; demonstrator in Physics. 1960–67; dir of postgraduate studies in Biophysics, 1967–70; FKC 1997; Purdue University: Prof. of Molecular Biology, 1970–; Head, Dept of Biol Scis, 1975–80; Vice-Pres. for Research and Dean, Graduate Sch., 1980–86. Oxford University: Sen. Vis. Fellow, Jesus Coll., 1980–81; Nuffield Res. Fellow, Green Coll., 1985–86. Guggenheim Meml Foundn Fellow, 1985. Hon. ScD St Andrews, Laurinburg, USA, 1994; Hon. DSc Purdue, USA, 1998; Hon. LLD St Andrews, 1999. *Publications:* papers in learned jls on structures of fibrous biopolymers, especially nucleic acids and polysaccharides, and techniques for visualizing them. *Recreations:* bird watching, botanizing. *Address:* Institute for Cancer Research, Chester Beatty Laboratories, 237 Fulham Road, SW3 6JB. *Fax:* (020) 7352 8039; *e-mail:* essaie@icr.ac.uk. *Clubs:* Athenæum, Caledonian; Royal and Ancient (St Andrews).

ARNOTT, Prof. W(illiam) Geoffrey, PhD; FBA 1999; Professor of Greek Language and Literature, University of Leeds, 1968–91, now Emeritus; *b* 17 Sept. 1930; *s* of late Bertie Arnott and Edith May Arnott (*née* Smith); *m* 1955, Vera Hodson; three *d. Educ:* Bury Grammar Sch.; Pembroke Coll., Cambridge (Schol.; BA 1952; Porson Prize, 1952; MA 1956; PhD 1960). Asst Master, Bristol Grammar Sch., 1952–53; Carrington-Coe Res. Student, Univ. of Cambridge, 1953–54; Asst Lectr in Greek, Bedford Coll., London Univ., 1955–59; Asst Dir of Exams, Civil Service Commn, 1959–60; Asst Lectr in Classics, Univ. of Hull, 1950–61; Lectr in Classics, King's Coll., Univ. of Durham, 1960–63; Lectr in Classics, 1963–66, Sen. Lectr in Classics, 1966–67, Univ. of Newcastle upon Tyne. Vis. Mem., Inst. of Advanced Studies, Princeton, 1973; Vis. Schol., Univ. of British Columbia, 1982; Visiting Professor: Univ. of Wellington, 1982; Univ. of Alexandria, 1983; Univ. of Queensland, 1987; Univ. of Bologna, 1998; Vis. Fellow, Gonville and Caius Coll., Cambridge, 1987–88. Lectr, NADFAS, 1980–. Pres., Leeds Birdwatchers Club, 1981–84. Member: Classical Jls Bd, 1970–94; Editl Bd, Texts and Commentaries, Univs of London and Urbino, 1980–; Bd of Mgt, Greece & Rome, 1981–89. Fellow, Italian Soc. for Study of Classical Antiquity, 1981. *Publications:* Menander's Dyskolos: a translation, 1960; Menander, Plautus, Terence, 1975; Menander, vol. I, 1979, vol. II, 1996, vol. III, 2000; Alexis: a commentary, 1996; papers and reviews in classical jls, etc. *Recreations:* birds and 19th century bird painting, crosswords, photography, travel. *Address:* 35 Arncliffe Road, Leeds LS16 5AP. *T:* (0113) 275 2751.

ARON, Michael Douglas; HM Diplomatic Service; Counsellor and Deputy Head of Mission, Jordan, since 1999; *b* 22 March 1959; *s* of late Maurice Aron and of Sheila Aron (*née* Torrens); *m* 1986, Rachel Ann Golding Barker; two *s* two *d. Educ:* Exeter Sch.; Leeds Univ. (BA Hons Arabic and French); Poly. of Central London. English lang. teacher, Sudan, 1981–83; joined FCO, 1984: Conf. Support Officer, UK Mission to UN, NY, 1985; on secondment to EC, 1986; Second, later First Sec., FCO, 1986–88; First Secretary: (Commercial and Econ.), Brasilia, 1988–91; FCO, 1991–93; UK Mission to UN, 1993–96; Dep. Hd, ME Dept, FCO, 1996–97; Head: Comprehensive Spending Review Unit, FCO, 1997–98; Mgt Consultancy Services, FCO, 1998–99. *Recreations:* football, Arsenal, tennis, walking, France. *Address:* c/o Foreign and Commonwealth Office, King Charles Street, SW1A 2AH. *T:* (Amman) (6) 592 3100.

ARONSOHN, Lotte Therese; *see* Newman, L. T.

ARONSON, Hazel Josephine; *see* Cosgrove, Hon. Lady.

ARRAN, 9th Earl of, *cr* 1762, of the Arran Islands, Co. Galway; **Arthur Desmond Colquhoun Gore;** Bt 1662; Viscount Sudley, Baron Saunders, 1758; Baron Sudley (UK), 1884; *b* 14 July 1938; *er s* of 8th Earl of Arran and of Fiona Bryde, *er d* of Sir Iain Colquhoun of Luss, 7th Bt, KT, DSO; *S* father, 1983; *m* 1974, Eleanor, *er d* of Bernard van Cutsem and Lady Margaret Fortescue; two *d. Educ:* Eton; Balliol College, Oxford. 2nd Lieutenant, 1st Bn Grenadier Guards (National Service). Asst Manager, Daily Mail, 1972–73; Man. Dir, Clark Nelson, 1973–74; Asst Gen. Manager Daily and Sunday Express, June-Nov. 1974. Dir, Waterstone & Co. Ltd, 1984–87. A Lord in Waiting (Govt Whip), 1987–89; Parliamentary Under-Secretary of State: for the Armed Forces, MoD, 1989–92; NI Office, 1992–94; Parly Under-Sec. of State, DoE, 1994; Captain of the Yeomen of the Guard (Dep. Govt Chief Whip), 1994–95; elected Mem., H of L, 1999. Director: HMV, 1995–98; Bonham's, 1997–2000. Chm., Waste Mgt Industry NTO, 2000–. Co-Chm., Children's Country Holidays Fund. *Recreations:* tennis, shooting, gardening, croquet. *Address:* c/o House of Lords, SW1A 0PW. *Clubs:* White's, Pratt's, Turf, Beefsteak.

ARRAND, Ven. Geoffrey William; Archdeacon of Suffolk, since 1994; *b* 24 July 1944; *s* of Thomas Staniforth Arrand and Alice Ada Arrand; *m* 1968, Mary Marshall (marr. diss.); one *s* two *d. Educ:* King's Coll., London (BD 1966, AKC). Ordained deacon, 1967, priest, 1968; Assistant Curate: Washington, dio. of Durham, 1967–70; S Ormsby Gp, 1970–73; Team Vicar, Great Grimsby, 1973–79; Team Rector, Halesworth, 1979–85; Dean of Bocking and Rector of Hadleigh with Layham and Shelley, 1985–94; RD of Hadleigh, 1986–94. Hon. Canon, St Edmundsbury Cathedral, 1991–. OStJ 1994. *Recreation:* golf. *Address:* Glebe House, Ashfield cum Thorpe, Stowmarket, Suffolk IP14 6LX. *T:* (01728) 685497, *Fax:* (01728) 685969. *Club:* Ufford Park Golf.

ARRINDELL, Sir Clement Athelston, GCMG 1984; GCVO 1985; Kt 1982; QC; Governor-General, St Christopher and Nevis, 1983–95 (Governor, St Kitts-Nevis, 1981–83); *b* Basseterre, 19 April 1931. *Educ:* private school; Basseterre Boys' Elementary Sch.; St Kitts-Nevis Grammar Sch. (Island Scholar). Called to the Bar, Lincoln's Inn, 1958. Post-grad. studies; in practice as barrister and solicitor, 1959–66; Acting Magistrate, 1964–66; Magistrate, 1966–71; Chief Magistrate, 1972–78; Judge, WI Associated States Supreme Court, 1978–81. *Recreations:* piano-playing, classical music, gardening. *Address:* The Lark, Bird Rock, St Kitts, West Indies.

ARROW, Kenneth Joseph; Professor of Economics and Operations Research, Stanford University, 1979–91, Professor Emeritus, 1991; *b* 23 Aug. 1921; *s* of Harry I. and Lillian Arrow; *m* 1947, Selma Schweitzer; two *s. Educ:* City College (BS in Social Science 1940); Columbia Univ. (MA 1941, PhD 1951). Captain, US AAF, 1942–46. Research Associate, Cowles Commn for Research in Economics, Univ. of Chicago, 1947–49; Actg Asst Prof., Associate Prof. and Prof. of Economics, Statistics and Operations Research, Stanford Univ., 1949–68; Prof. of Econs, later University Prof., Harvard Univ., 1968–79. Staff Mem., US Council of Economic Advisers, 1962. Consultant, The Rand Corp., 1948–. Fellow, Churchill Coll., Cambridge, 1963–64, 1970, 1973, 1986. President: Internat. Economic Assoc., 1983–86; Internat. Soc. for Inventory Res., 1984–90; Member: Inst. of Management Sciences (Pres., 1963); Nat. Acad. of Sciences; Amer. Inst. of Medicine; Amer. Philosoph. Soc.; Pontifical Acad. of Social Scis; Fellow: Econometric Soc. (Pres., 1956); Amer. Acad. of Arts and Sciences (Vice Pres., 1979–80, 1991–94); Amer. Assoc. for Advancement of Science (Chm., Section K, 1982); Amer. Statistical Assoc.; Dist. Fellow: Amer. Econ. Assoc. (Pres., 1972); Western Econ. Assoc. (Pres., 1980–81); Corresp. Fellow, British Acad., 1976; Foreign Hon. Mem., Finnish Acad. of Sciences. John Bates Clark Medal, American Economic Assoc., 1957; Nobel Meml Prize in Economic Science, 1972; von Neumann Prize, Inst. of Management Scis and Ops Res. Soc. of America, 1986. Hon. LLD: Chicago, 1967; City Univ. of NY, 1972; Univ. of Pennsylvania, 1976; Washington Univ., St Louis, Missouri, 1989; Ben-Gurion Univ., 1989; Hon. Dr Soc. and Econ. Sciences, Vienna, 1971; Hon. ScD Columbia, 1973; Hon. DSocSci, Yale, 1974; Hon. Dr: Paris, 1974; Hebrew Univ. of Jerusalem, 1975; Helsinki, 1976; Aix-Marseille III, 1985; Sacro Cuore, Milan, 1994; Uppsala, 1995; Buenos Aires, 1999; Cyprus, 2000; Hon. LittD Cambridge, 1985. Order of the Rising Sun (2nd class), Japan, 1984. *Publications:* Social Choice and Individual Values, 1951, 2nd edn 1963; (with S. Karlin and H. Scarf) Studies in the Mathematical Theory of Inventory and Production, 1958; (with M. Hoffenberg) A Time Series Analysis of Interindustry Demands, 1959; (with L. Hurwicz and H. Uzawa) Studies in Linear and Nonlinear Programming, 1959; Aspects of the Theory of Risk Bearing, 1965; (with M. Kurz) Public Investment, the Rate of Return, and Optimal Fiscal Policy, 1971; Essays in the Theory of Risk-Bearing, 1971; (with F. Hahn) General Competitive Analysis, 1972; The Limits of Organization, 1974;

(with L. Hurwicz) Studies in Resource Allocation Processes, 1977; Collected Papers, Vols 1–6, 1984–86; (with H. Raynaud) Social Choice and Multicriterion Decision-Making, 1986; 200 articles in jls and collective vols. *Address:* Department of Economics, Stanford University, Stanford, CA 94305–6072, USA.

ARROWSMITH, Amanda Jane Elizabeth; Chair, Eastern Region Committee, Heritage Lottery Fund, since 2001; *b* 28 Dec. 1947; *d* of late Michael St George Arrowsmith and Elizabeth Arrowsmith (*née* Bartlett). *Educ:* Lady Margaret Hall, Oxford (MA); MBA Open Univ. Archive trng, Bodleian Liby, Oxford, 1971–72; asst, sen. asst and dep. archivist posts, Northumberland and Suffolk CCs, 1972–79; Co. Archivist, Berks, 1979–82, Suffolk, 1982–87; Dep. Dir of Arts and Libraries, 1987–90, Dir of Libraries and Heritage, 1990–2001, Suffolk. Comr, RCHME, 1994–98; Mem., Hist. Bldgs and Monuments Commn (Eng. Heritage), 1998–2001. Member: Adv. Council on Public Records, 1995–2000; Eastern Reg. Cttee, SE Museums Service, 1999–; Mem., Exec. Cttee, Friends of Nat. Libraries, 1993–96 and 1999–; Pres., Soc. of Archivists, 1996–99. Mem. Bd, Living East, 1999–. *Publications:* contrib. articles to Archives, Jl Soc. Archivists, New Liby World. *Recreations:* allotment gardening, sewing, learning Chinese. *Address:* 56 Bury Street, Stowmarket, Suffolk IP14 1HF.

ARROWSMITH, Pat; pacifist and socialist; on staff of Amnesty International, 1971–94, retired; *b* 2 March 1930; *d* of late George Ernest Arrowsmith and late Margaret Vera (*née* Kingham); *m* Mr Gardner, 11 Aug. 1979, separated 11 Aug. 1979; lesbian partnership with Wendy Butlin, 1962–76. *Educ:* Farringtons; Stover Sch.; Cheltenham Ladies' Coll.; Newnham Coll., Cambridge (BA history); Univ. of Ohio; Liverpool Univ. (Cert. in Social Science). Has held many jobs, incl.: Community Organizer in Chicago, 1952–53; Cinema Usher, 1953–54; Social Caseworker, Liverpool Family Service Unit, 1954; Child Care Officer, 1955 and 1964; Nursing Asst, Deva Psychiatric Hosp., 1956–57; Reporter for Peace News, 1965; Gardener for Camden BC, 1966–68; Researcher for Soc. of Friends Race Relations Cttee, 1969–71; Case Worker for NCCL, 1971; and on farms, as waiter in cafes, in factories, as a toy demonstrator, as a 'temp' in numerous offices, as asst in children's home, as newspaper deliverer and sales agent, as cleaner, as bartender, and in a holiday camp. Organizer for Direct Action Cttee against Nuclear War, Cttee of 100 and Campaign for Nuclear Disarmament, 1958–68; gaoled 11 times as political prisoner, 1958–85 (adopted twice as Prisoner of Conscience by Amnesty International); awarded: Holloway Prison Green Band, 1964; Girl Crusaders knighthood, 1940; Americans Removing Injustice, Suppression and Exploitation peace prize, 1991. Contested: Fulham, 1966 (Radical Alliance) and 1970 (Hammersmith Stop the SE Asia War Cttee), on peace issues; Cardiff South East (Independent Socialist), 1979. Member: War Resisters' Internat.; Campaign for Nuclear Disarmament; Ver Poets. *Publications:* Jericho (novel), 1965; Somewhere Like This (novel), 1970; To Asia in Peace, 1972; The Colour of Six Schools, 1972; Breakout (poems and drawings from prison), 1975; On the Brink (anti-war poems with pictures), 1981; The Prisoner (novel), 1982; Thin Ice (anti-nuclear poems), 1984; Nine Lives (poems and pictures), 1990; I Should Have Been a Hornby Train (fiction-cum-memoirs), 1995; Many are Called (novel), 1998; Drawing to Extinction (poems and pictures), 2000. *Recreations:* water colour painting (has held and contrib. exhibns), swimming, writing poetry. *Address:* 132c Middle Lane, N8 7JP. *T:* (020) 8340 2661.

ARSCOTT, Air Vice-Marshal John Robert Dare; Director, Airspace Policy, Civil Aviation Authority, since 1999; *b* 19 April 1947; *s* of Richard Arscott and Janet Arscott (*née* Knibbs); *m* 1971, Kyrle Margaret Bradley; one *d* and one *s* decd. *Educ:* Lindisfarne Coll. Command RAF, 1966; jsdc 1984; awc 1987; posts in NATS and Mil. Air Traffic Ops, 1990–95; AOC Mil. Air Traffic Ops, 1996–99. *Recreations:* aviation, railways, walking, DIY, 3-day eventing. *Address:* CAA House, 45-59 Kingsway, WC2B 6TE. *T:* (020) 7453 6500. *Club:* Royal Air Force.

ARTAZA, Mario; Director General of Foreign Policy, Ministry of Foreign Affairs, Chile, since 2000; *b* 2 Sept. 1937; *s* of Osvaldo Artaza and Guillermina Rouxel; *m* 1982, Anita Valsasnini; one *s* two *d*. *Educ:* Law Sch., Univ. of Chile; Univ. of Virginia (MA (Foreign Affairs) 1962); American Univ., Washington (Internat. Relations). Entered Foreign Service, 1958; Third Sec., Chilean Embassy, Washington, 1964; Second, subseq. First Sec., Chilean Mission to OAS, 1968–69; Dir, Inst. of Political Science, Catholic Univ. of Chile, 1970; Counsellor, Chilean Embassy, Peru, 1971–73; Chargé d'Affaires, Chilean Embassy, Washington, 1973; Prof., Univ. of the Pacific, Calif, 1973–74; World Bank: Public Affairs Officer, 1974–75; Loan Officer for Pakistan, 1976–82, for Argentina, Uruguay and Paraguay, 1982–87; Sen. Ops Officer, Infrastructure Projects, Latin Amer. Reg., 1988–90; Alternate Ambassador of Chile, Internat. Orgns, Geneva, 1990–92; Ministry of Foreign Affairs, Santiago: Director: Multilateral Affairs, 1992–93; Policy Planning, 1994–96; Ambassador of Chile: to UK, 1996–99; to USA, 1999–2000. Comendador, Orden del Sol (Peru), 1972; Grand Cross, Orden de Miranda (Venezuela), 1999. *Publications:* (contrib.) The Overall Development of Chile, ed M. Zañartu, 1968; (contrib.) America 70, ed A. Naudon, 1970. *Recreations:* music, theatre, reading, travel. *Address:* Ministry of Foreign Affairs, Catedral 1158, Santiago, Chile.

ARTHUIS, Jean Raymond Francis Marcel; Member for Mayenne, Senate, France; *b* 7 Oct. 1944; *m* 1971, Brigitte Lafont; one *s* one *d*. *Educ:* Ecole Supérieure de Commerce, Nantes; Institut d'Etudes Politiques, Paris. Sen. consultant in internat. auditing office; Founder of a soc. for accounting expertise and auditors. Senator, Mayenne, 1983–86, 1988–95 and 1997– (Pres., Gpe de l'Union Centriste, 1998–); Pres., Gen. Council of Mayenne, 1992– (Raporteur géneral of budget to Senate, 1992–95). Secretary of State: Ministry of Social Affairs and Employment, 1986–87; for competition and consumption, Ministry of Economy, Finance and Privatization, 1987–88; Minister of: Economic Development and Planning, May–Aug. 1995; the Economy, Finance and Planning, Aug.–Nov. 1995; the Economy and of Finance, 1995–97. Mayor, Château-Gontier, Mayenne, 1971–2001. *Publications:* (with H. Haenel) Justice Sinistrée: démocratie en danger, 1991; Les Délocalisations et l'emploi, 1993; Dans les coulisses de Bercy, 1998. *Recreation:* horse-riding. *Address:* Sénat, 15 rue de Vaugirard, 75006 Paris, France; 8 rue René Homo, 53200 Château-Gontier, France.

ARTHUR, family name of **Baron Glenarthur**.

ARTHUR, Adrian; Editor, The Courier, Dundee, since 1993; *b* 28 Sept. 1937; *s* of Alastair and Jean Arthur, Kirkcaldy; *m* 1962, Patricia Mill; one *s* two *d*. *Educ:* Harris Academy, Dundee; Univ. of St Andrews (BL). Sub-Editor, People's Journal, 1954–56; Nat. Service, RAF, 1956–58; The Courier: editorial staff, 1958–; Dep. Editor, 1978–93. *Recreations:* golf, reading, travel, Rotary. *Address:* The Courier, 80 Kingsway East, Dundee DD4 8SL. *T:* (01382) 223131. *Clubs:* Carnoustie; Dalhousie Golf.

ARTHUR, Gavyn Farr; barrister; Sheriff, City of London, 1998–99; *b* 13 Sept. 1951; *s* of late Maj. the Hon. Leonard Arthur, sometime Chm., Natal Provincial Assembly, and Raina Arthur (*née* Farr). *Educ:* Harrow Sch.; Christ Church, Oxford (MA Jurisprudence). Called to the Bar, Middle Temple, 1975 (Bencher, 2001); in practice as barrister, 1977–. Mem. Cttee, Western Circuit, 1985–88. Vice-President: British Red Cross, 1993–; Inst. of Export, 1999–. Common Councilman, Ward of Farringdon Without, 1988–91; Alderman, Cripplegate Ward, 1991–. Freeman, City of London, 1979; Liveryman: Co. of Gardeners, 1990–; Co. of Wax-Chandlers, 1996–. Mem., Co. of Public Relations Practitioners, 2000–. Trustee, Sir John Soane Mus., 1996–. Governor: Christ's Hosp., 1991–; King Edward's Sch., Witley, 1991–; City of London Sch. for Girls, 1991–; City of London Freemen's Sch., 1994–. *Recreations:* travel, Alpine walking, British India. *Address:* 2 Harcourt Buildings, Temple, EC4Y 9DB.

ARTHUR, Prof. Geoffrey Herbert; Emeritus Professor of Veterinary Surgery, University of Bristol, since 1980; *b* 6 March 1916; *s* of William Gwyn Arthur and Ethel Jessie Arthur; *m* 1948, Lorna Isabel Simpson; four *s* one *d*. *Educ:* Abersychan Secondary Sch.; Liverpool Univ. BVSc 1939; MRCVS 1939; MVSc 1945; DVSc 1957; FRCVS 1957. Lectr in Veterinary Medicine, Liverpool Univ., 1941–48; Reader in Veterinary Surgery, Royal Veterinary Coll., 1949–51; Reader in Veterinary Surgery and Obstetrics, Univ. of London, 1952–65; Prof. of Veterinary Obstetrics and Diseases of Reproduction, Univ. of London, 1965–73; Prof. and Head of Dept of Vet. Surgery, Bristol Univ., 1974–79. Regl Postgrad. Vet. Dean, W and SW England and S Wales, 1985–94. Examiner to Univs of Cambridge, Dublin, Edinburgh, Glasgow, Liverpool, London, Reading, Bristol and Ceylon. Visiting Professor: Univ. of Khartoum, 1964; Pahlavi Univ., 1976; Nairobi Univ., 1979; Clinical Prof., King Faisal Univ., Saudi Arabia, 1980–84. Chm., Soc. for Protection of Animals Abroad, 1992–94. *Publications:* Wright's Veterinary Obstetrics (including Diseases of Reproduction, 3rd edn), 1964, 5th edn, as Veterinary Reproduction and Obstetrics, 1982, 7th edn 1995; papers on medicine and reproduction in Veterinary Record, Veterinary Jl, Jl of Comparative Pathology, Jl Reprod. Fert., Equine Vet. Jl and Jl Small Animal Pract. (Editor). *Recreations:* observing natural phenomena and experimenting, North African and Middle Eastern travel. *Address:* Fallodene Farm, Stone Allerton, Axbridge, Som BS26 2NH.

ARTHUR, Prof. James Greig, FRS 1992; FRSC 1981; University Professor since 1987 and Professor of Mathematics since 1979, University of Toronto; *b* 18 May 1944; *s* of John Greig Arthur and Katherine Mary Patricia Scott; *m* 1972, Dorothy Pendleton Helm; two *s*. *Educ:* Upper Canada Coll.; Univ. of Toronto (BSc, MSc); Yale Univ. (PhD). Instructor, Princeton Univ., 1970–72; Asst Prof., Yale Univ., 1972–76; Prof., Duke Univ., 1976–79. Sloan Fellowship, 1976; E. W. R. Steacie Meml Fellowship, 1982. Synge Award, RSC, 1987. *Publication:* Simple Algebras, Base Change and the Advanced Theory of the Trace Formula (with Laurent Clozel), 1989. *Recreations:* tennis, golf. *Address:* 23 Woodlawn Avenue W, Toronto, Ontario M4V 1G6, Canada. *T:* (416) 9640975.

ARTHUR, James Stanley, CMG 1977; HM Diplomatic Service, retired; British High Commissioner in Bridgetown, 1978–82, also British High Commissioner (non-resident) to Dominica, 1978–82, to St Lucia and St Vincent, 1979–82, to Grenada, 1980–82, to Antigua and Barbuda, 1981–82, and concurrently British Government Representative to West Indies Associated State of St Kitts-Nevis; retired 1983; *b* 3 Feb. 1923; *s* of Laurence and Catherine Arthur, Lerwick, Shetland; *m* 1950, Marion North; two *s* two *d*. *Educ:* Trinity Academy, Edinburgh; Liverpool Univ. (BSc). Scientific Civil Service, 1944–46; Asst Principal, Scottish Educn Dept, 1946; Min. of Educn/Dept of Educn and Science, 1947–66: Private Sec. to Parly Sec., 1948–50; Principal Private Sec. to Minister, 1960–62; Counsellor, FO, 1966; Nairobi, 1967–70; Dep. High Comr, Malta, 1970–73; High Comr, Suva, 1974–78, and first High Comr (non-resident), Republic of Nauru, 1977–78. Mem. Court, Liverpool Univ., 1987–. *Recreations:* golf, music. *Address:* Moreton House, Longborough, Moreton-in-Marsh, Glos GL56 0QQ. *T:* (01451) 830774. *Club:* Royal Commonwealth Society.

ARTHUR, Lt-Gen. Sir (John) Norman (Stewart), KCB 1985; JP; Lord-Lieutenant, Stewartry of Kirkcudbright (Dumfries and Galloway Region), since 1996; General Officer Commanding Scotland and Governor of Edinburgh Castle, 1985–88, retired; *b* 6 March 1931; *s* of Col Evelyn Stewart Arthur and Mrs E. S. Arthur (*née* Burnett-Stuart); *m* 1960, Theresa Mary Hopkinson; one *s* one *d* (and one *s* decd). *Educ:* Eton Coll.; RMA, Sandhurst. rcds, jssc, psc. Commnd Royal Scots Greys, 1951; commanded: Royal Scots Dragoon Guards, 1972–74 (despatches, 1974); 7th Armoured Bde, 1976–77; Brig., Gen. Staff, Intelligence, MoD, 1979–90; GOC 3rd Armoured Div., 1980–82; Dir of Personal Services (Army), MoD, 1983–85. Col Comdt, Military Provost Staff Corps, 1985–88; Col, The Royal Scots Dragoon Gds (Carabiniers and Greys), 1984–92; Hon. Col, 205 (Scottish) Gen. Hosp., RAMC(V), 1988–93, The Scottish Yeomanry, 1993–97. Chm., Cavalry Colonels, 1987–92. Officer, Royal Co. of Archers, Queen's Body Guard for Scotland. Chairman: Scotland, Army Benevolent Fund, 1988–2000; Leonard Cheshire Services, SW Scotland, 1994–2000; Pres., Combined Cavalry Old Comrades Assoc., 1995–2000; Vice Pres., Edinburgh and Borders, Riding for the Disabled Assoc., 1988–94; Dir, Edinburgh Mil. Tattoo Co., 1988–91; Pres., Scottish Conservation Projects, 1989–94; Mem., Automobile Assoc. Cttee, 1990–98. Humanitarian aid work to Bosnia, 1992–. Mem., British Olympic Team, Equestrian Three-Day Event, 1960. DL Stewartry, 1989; JP 1996. *Recreations:* field and country sports and pursuits, horsemanship, military history. *Address:* Newbarns, Dalbeattie, Kirkcudbrightshire DG5 4PY. *T:* (01556) 630227.

ARTHUR, His Honour John Rhys, DFC 1944; JP; a Circuit Judge, 1975–93; *b* 29 April 1923; *s* of late John Morgan Arthur and Eleanor Arthur; *m* 1951, Joan Tremearne Pickering; two *s* one *d*. *Educ:* Mill Hill; Christ's Coll., Cambridge (MA). Commnd RAF, 1943, demobilised 1946. Cambridge, 1946–48; called to Bar, Inner Temple, 1949. Asst Recorder, Blackburn QS, 1970; Dep. Chm., Lancs County QS, 1970–71; a Recorder, 1972–75. JP Lancs 1970. *Address:* Orovales, Caldy, Wirral CH48 1LP. *T:* (0151) 625 8624. *Clubs:* MCC, Old Millhillians; Athenæum (Liverpool); Cardiff Athletic.

ARTHUR, Michael Anthony, CMG 1992; HM Diplomatic Service; Economic Director, Foreign and Commonwealth Office, since 2001; *b* 28 Aug. 1950; *s* of late John Richard Arthur and of Mary Deirdre (*née* Chaundy); *m* 1974, Plaxy Gillian Beatrice (*née* Corke); two *s* two *d*. *Educ:* Watford GS; Rugby; Balliol Coll., Oxford. Entered HM Diplomatic Service, 1972; UK Mission to UN, NY, 1972; FCO, 1973; 3rd, later 2nd Sec., UK Perm. Representation to Eur. Communities, 1974–76; 2nd Sec., Kinshasa, 1976–78; FCO, 1978–83; Private Secretary: to Lord Privy Seal, 1981; to Minister of State, FCO, 1982; 1st Sec., Bonn, 1984–88; Hd, EC Dept (Internal), FCO, 1988–93; Sen. Associate Mem., St Antony's Coll., Oxford, 1993; Counsellor and Hd of Chancery, Paris, 1993–97; Dir (Resources) and Chief Inspector, FCO, 1997–99; Minister and Dep. Hd of Mission, Washington, 1999–2001. *Recreations:* music, travel, books. *Address:* c/o Foreign and Commonwealth Office, King Charles Street, SW1A 2AH.

ARTHUR, Prof. Michael James Paul, DM; FRCP, FMedSci; Professor of Medicine, since 1992, and Director of Research, School of Medicine, since 2001, University of Southampton; *b* 3 Aug. 1954; *s* of Reginald Alfred John Arthur and Patricia Margaret Arthur; *m* 1979, Elizabeth Susan McCaughey; one *s* two *d*. *Educ:* Burnt Mill Comprehensive Sch., Harlow; Sch. of Medicine, Univ. of Southampton (BM 1977; DM 1986). FRCP 1993. Med. Registrar, Wessex Reg., 1980–82; University of Southampton: Lectr in Medicine, 1982–89; Sen. Lectr, 1989–92; Hd, Sch. of Medicine, 1998–2001. Fogarty Internat. Travelling Fellow, Liver Center Lab., Univ. of Calif, San Francisco, 1986–88. Mem., Adv. Gp on Hepatitis, DoH, 1998–. Vice-Chm., Molecular and Cell

Panel, Wellcome Trust, 2000–. Pres., British Assoc. for Study of the Liver, 2001–. FMedSci 1998. Res. Prize, Amer. Liver Foundn, 1987; Linacre Medal, RCP, 1994. *Publications:* (ed jtly) Wright's Liver and Biliary Disease, 3rd edn 1992; numerous contribs to biomed. jls relating to liver disease and the pathogenesis of liver fibrosis. *Recreations:* sailing and yacht racing in the Solent, amateur interest in St Emilion wines. *Address:* Level D, South Block (811), Southampton General Hospital, Tremona Road, Southampton SO16 6YD. *T:* (023) 8079 6886. *Club:* Royal Southern Yacht (Hamble).

ARTHUR, Lt-Gen. Sir Norman; *see* Arthur, Lt-Gen. Sir J. N. S.

ARTHUR, Rt Hon. Owen Seymour; PC 1995; MP (Lab) Barbados, since 1984; Prime Minister of Barbados, also Minister of Finance and Economic Affairs, Defence and Security and the Civil Service, since 1994; *b* 17 Oct. 1949; *m* 1978, Beverley Jeanne Batchelor. *Educ:* Harrison Coll., Barbados; Univ. of West Indies at Cave Hill (BA) and at Mona (MSc). Research Asst, UWI, Jamaica, 1973; Asst Economic Planner, then Chief Econ. Planner, Nat. Planning Agency, Jamaica, 1974–79; Dir of Econs, Jamaica Bauxite Inst., 1979–81; Chief Project Analyst, Min. of Finance, Barbados, 1981–83; Lectr, Dept of Management, UWI, Cave Hill, 1986, Res. Fellow, 1993. Mem., Barbados Senate, 1983–84; Parly Sec., Min. of Finance, 1985–86; Chm., Barbados Labour Party, 1993–96, 1998–99; Leader of Opposition, 1993–94. *Publications:* The Commercialisation of Technology in Jamaica, 1979; Energy and Mineral Resource Development in the Jamaica Bauxite Industry, 1981; The IMF and Economic Stabilisation Policies in Barbados, 1984. *Recreations:* cooking, gardening. *Address:* Prime Minister's Office, Government Headquarters, Bay Street, St Michael, Barbados. *T:* 4263179, *Fax:* 4369280; *e-mail:* info@primeminister.gov.bb.

ARTHUR, Richard Andrew; Member (Lab), Camden Borough Council, 1971–76 and since 1990; Member, Audit Commission, since 1995; *b* 24 March 1944; *s* of late Cyril Stuart Arthur and Cicely Arthur; *m* 1st, 1968, Diana Thompson (marr. diss.); one *s* one *d*; 2nd, 1986, Akiko Shindo; one step *s*. *Educ:* King's Sch., Canterbury; Christ's Coll., Cambridge (MA Econs); London Business Sch. (MSc Business). Commonwealth Development Finance Co.: Regl Dir, SE Asia, 1976–80; Chief Exec., Australia, 1981–82; Hd of Ops, 1982–86; Exec. Dir, Scimitar Develt Capital, 1986–93. Dir, 1998–, Chm., 1998–2000, Vice-Chm., 2000–, Public Private Partnerships Prog.; Vice-Chm., Central London Partnership, 1998–2000; Dir, Accord plc, 2000–; Mem. Bd, Housing Corp., 2000–. London Borough of Camden: Chm. of Staff, 1975–76; Chm., Social Services, 1991–93; Leader, 1993–2000. Mem., Mgt Exec., 1998–, Vice-Chm., 2000–, Chm., Community Safety and Policing Panels, 2000–, Assoc. of London Govt; Dir, Assoc. of London Govt Ltd, 2000–. Mem. Regl Exec., Greater London Lab Party, 2000–. Mem. Ct, Middlesex Univ., 1996–2000. *Recreations:* gardening, reading, travel. *Address:* 11d Highgate West Hill, N6 6JR. *T:* (020) 8341 9148. *Club:* Singapore Cricket.

ARTHUR, Sir Stephen (John), 6th Bt *cr* 1841, of Upper Canada; *b* 1 July 1953; *s* of Hon. Sir Basil Malcolm Arthur, 5th Bt, MP, and of Elizabeth Rita, *d* of late Alan Mervyn Wells; *S* father, 1985; *m* 1978, Carolyn Margaret (marr. diss.), *d* of Burney Lawrence Daimond, Cairns, Queensland; one *s* two *d*. *Educ:* Timaru Boys' High School. *Heir: s* Benjamin Nathan Arthur, *b* 27 March 1979.

ARTHURS, Prof. Harry William, OC 1989; OOnt 1995; FRSC 1982; University Professor, Osgoode Hall Law School, York University, Canada, since 1995 (Professor of Law, 1968–95); *b* 9 May 1935; *s* of Leon and Ellen Arthurs; *m* 1974, Penelope Geraldine Ann Milnes; two *s*. *Educ:* Univ. of Toronto (BA, LLB); Harvard Univ. (LLM). Barrister and Solicitor, 1961. York University: Asst Prof. 1961, Associate Prof. 1964, Associate Dean 1967, Dean 1972–77, Osgoode Hall Law Sch.; Pres., 1985–92, Pres. Emeritus, 1992–. Mem., Economic Council of Can., 1978–82; Bencher, Law Soc. of Upper Can., 1979–84; Chm., Consultative Gp on Res. and Educn in Law, 1981–84; Arbitrator, Mediator in Labour Disputes, 1962–84; Chair, Council of Ontario Univs, 1987–89; a Dir, Internat. Centre for Human Rights and Democratic Develt, 1999–. Visitor: Univs of Toronto, 1965, and McGill, 1967; Clare Hall, Cambridge, 1971; Inst. for Socio-Legal Res., Oxford, 1977–78; UCL, 1984. Hon. LLD: Sherbrooke, 1986; Brock, 1986; Law Soc. of Upper Can., 1987; McGill, 1995; Hon. DLitt Lethbridge, 1991. *Publications:* Law and Learning, 1983; (jtly) Industrial Relations and Labour Law in Canada, 1979, 3rd edn 1988; Without the Law, 1985. *Address:* Osgoode Hall Law School, York University, 4700 Keele Street, Toronto, Ontario M3J 1P3, Canada. *T:* (416) 7365407.

ARTIS, Prof. Michael John, FBA 1988; Professor of Economics, European University Institute, Florence, since 1995; Professor of Economics, Manchester University, 1975–1999, now Emeritus; *b* 29 June 1938; *s* of Cyril John and Violet Emily Artis; *m* 1st, 1961, Lilian Gregson (marr. diss. 1982); two *d*; 2nd, 1983, Shirley Knight. *Educ:* Baines Grammar Sch., Poulton-le-Fylde, Lancs; Magdalen Coll., Oxford. BA Hons (PPE) Oxon. Assistant Research Officer, Oxford Univ., 1959; Lectr in Economics, Adelaide Univ., 1964; Lectr and Sen. Lectr in Economics, Flinders Univ., 1966; Research Officer and Review Editor, Nat. Inst. of Economic and Social Research, London, 1967; Prof. of Applied Economics, Swansea Univ. Coll., 1972. *Publications:* Foundations of British Monetary Policy, 1964; (with M. K. Lewis) Monetary Control in the United Kingdom, 1981; Macroeconomics, 1984; (with S. Ostry) International Economic Policy Co-ordination, 1986; (with M. K. Lewis) Money in Britain, 1991; contribs on economics, economic policy to books and learned jls. *Recreation:* eating out. *Address:* Via dei Bosconi 16, Villa Il Poggiolo, Edificio 3, Monteloro, 50069 Pontassieve (FI), Italy. *Club:* Reform.

ARTON, Simon Nicholas B.; *see* Bourne-Arton.

ARTRO MORRIS, John Evan; District Judge, Principal Registry of the Family Division (formerly a Registrar of the Supreme Court, Family Division), 1977–95; *b* 17 Feb. 1925; *s* of Tudor and Mabel Artro Morris; *m* 1961, Karin Ilsa Alida Russell (*d* 1999); two *s*. *Educ:* Liverpool Coll.; The Queen's Coll., Oxford. MA Oxon. Served RN, 1943–47. Called to the Bar, Middle Temple, 1952. *Recreations:* D-I-Y, Alvis TA 21, fishing. *Address:* 69 Gowan Avenue, SW6 6RH. *T:* (020) 7736 6492. *Club:* London Welsh RFC.

ARUNDEL AND BRIGHTON, Bishop of, (RC), since 2001; **Rt Rev. Kieran Thomas Conry;** *b* 1 Feb. 1951. *Educ:* Cotton Coll., N Staffs; Ven. English Coll., Rome; Gregorian Univ., Rome (PhB, STB). Ordained 1975; Teacher, Cotton Coll., 1976–80; Private Sec. to Apostolic Delegate to the Court of St James's, 1980–88; Parish Priest, Leek, 1988; Administrator, St Chad's Cathedral, 1990; Dir, Catholic Media Office, 1994–2001; Parish Priest, St Austin's, Stafford, 2001. Mem., 1988–93, Vice-Chm., 1992–93, Nat. Conf. of Priests; Chm., Birmingham City Centre Churches, 1992–93. *Address:* St Joseph's Hall, Greyfriars Lane, Storrington, W Sussex RH20 4HE.

ARUNDEL AND SURREY, Earl of; Edward William Fitzalan-Howard; *b* 2 Dec. 1956; *s* and *heir* of 17th Duke of Norfolk, *qv*; *m* 1987, Georgina, *y d* of Jack and Serena Gore; three *s* two *d*. *Educ:* Ampleforth Coll., Yorks; Lincoln Coll., Oxford. Chairman: Sigas Ltd, 1979–88; Parkwood Group Ltd, 1989–. *Recreations:* ski-ing, motor-racing, shooting. *Heir: s* Lord Maltravers, *qv*. *Address:* Arundel Castle, West Sussex BN18 9AB. *T:* (01903) 883979; Scar House, Arkengarthdale, Reeth, N Yorks DL11 6RD. *T:* (01748) 884726. *Club:* British Racing Drivers (Silverstone).

ARUNDELL; *see* Monckton-Arundell, family name of Viscount Galway.

ARUNDELL, family name of **Baron Talbot of Malahide**.

ARVILL, Robert; *see* Boote, R. E.

ASANTE, Kwaku Baprui, GM 1976; MOV 1978; High Commissioner for Ghana in London, 1991–93; *b* 26 March 1924; *s* of Kweku Asante and Odorso Amoo; *m* 1958, Matilda Dzagbele Anteson; two *s* two *d*. *Educ:* Achimota Coll.; Durham Univ. (BSc); Final Exam., Inst. Statisticians (AIS), London. Sen. Maths Master, Achimota, 1954–56; joined Ghana Foreign Service, 1956; 2nd Sec., London, 1957–58; Chargé d'Affaires, Tel Aviv, 1958–60; Principal Sec., African Affairs Secretariat, Office of Pres., 1960–66; Head of Admin., OAU, 1966–67; Ambassador to Switzerland and Austria and Permanent Delegate to UN Office, Geneva, 1967–72; Principal Sec., Min. of Foreign Affairs, 1972; Sen. Principal Sec., Ministries of Trade and Tourism, and Economic Planning, 1973–76; Ambassador to Belgium, Luxembourg and EEC, 1976–79; Sec.-Gen., Social Democratic Front, 1979–81; Sec. (Minister) for Trade and Tourism, 1982; Private Consultant, 1982–88; Sec. (Minister) for Educn, 1988–91. Vice-Chm., La Community Bank. Chm., Achimota Sch. Bd, 1993–2000. Columnist, Daily Graphic. Hon. LLD Ghana, 1999. *Publications:* Foreign Policy Making in Ghana, 1997; articles in Ghanaian and foreign newspapers and jls. *Recreations:* music, cricket. *Address:* Asanteson, Palm Wine Junction, La, PO Box 6616, Accra, Ghana. *T:* (21) 774344.

ASBIL, Rt Rev. Walter Gordon; Bishop of Niagara, 1991–97; *b* 3 Oct. 1932; *m* 1957, Mavis Asbil; three *s* one *d*. *Educ:* Concordia Univ., Montreal (BA); McGill Univ. (BD, STM). Ordained deacon, 1957, priest, 1957; Rector: Aylwin River Desert, 1957–60; Montreal South Shore, 1960–65; St Stephen's, Montreal, 1965–67; St George, St Anne de Bellevue, 1967–70; St George, St Catharine's, 1970–86; Rector and Dean, Christ Church Cathedral, Ottawa, 1986–90; Co-adjutor Bishop of Niagara, 1990–91. Hon. DD Montreal Dio. Theol Coll., 1991. *Address:* 11 St Julien Drive, St Catherines, ON L2T 2G3, Canada.

ASCHERSON, (Charles) Neal; journalist and author; *b* 5 Oct. 1932; *s* of late Stephen Romer Ascherson and Evelyn Mabel Ascherson; *m* 1st, 1958, Corinna Adam (marr. diss. 1982); two *d*; 2nd, 1984, Isabel Hilton; one *s* one *d*. *Educ:* Eton College; King's College, Cambridge (MA; Hon. Fellow, 1993). Served RM, 1950–52. Reporter and leader writer, Manchester Guardian, 1956–58; Commonwealth corresp., Scotsman, 1959–60; The Observer: reporter, 1960–63; Central Europe corresp., 1963–68; Eastern Europe corresp., 1968–75; foreign writer, 1979–85; columnist, 1985–90; Associate Editor, 1985–89; columnist, The Independent on Sunday, 1990–98. Scottish politics corresp., Scotsman, 1975–79. Asst Lectr, Inst. of Archaeology, UCL, 1998–. Hon. DLitt Strathclyde, 1988; Hon. DSc(SocSci) Edinburgh, 1990; DUniv Open, 1991; Hon. LLD St Andrews, 1999. Reporter of the Year 1982, Journalist of the Year 1987, Granada Awards; James Cameron Award, 1989; David Watt Meml Prize, 1991; (jtly) George Orwell Award, Political Qly, 1993; Saltire Award for Literature, 1995. Golden Insignia, Order of Merit (Poland), 1992. *Publications:* The King Incorporated, 1963; The Polish August, 1981; The Struggles for Poland, 1987; Games with Shadows, 1988; Black Sea, 1995. *Address:* 27 Corsica Street, N5 1JT. *Club:* Ognisko Polskie (Polish Hearth Club).

ASH, Brian Maxwell; QC 1990; *b* 31 Jan. 1941; *s* of late Carl Ash and of Irene Ash (*née* Atkinson); *m* 1971, Barbara Anne Maxwell, creator and founding editor of BBC TV Question Time; two *s* one *d*. *Educ:* Mercers' Sch.; City of London Sch.; New Coll., Oxford (Open Exhibnr; BA). BBC TV Current Affairs Producer, Reporter and Programme Presenter, 1967–73; called to the Bar, Gray's Inn, 1975. Chm. of Panel, Examination in Public of First Alteration to Devon Structure Plan, 1986; Sec., Local Govt, Planning and Envmtl Bar Assoc., 1990–92. *Recreations:* golf, sailing, ski-ing, music. *Address:* 4/5 Gray's Inn Square, WC1R 5AY. *T:* (020) 7404 5252. *Clubs:* Royal Mid-Surrey Golf; Royal Norwich Golf.

ASH, Prof. Sir Eric (Albert), Kt 1990; CBE 1983; FRS 1977; FREng; Professor of Electrical Engineering, University College London, 1993–97, now Emeritus; Treasurer and Vice President, Royal Society, since 1997; *b* 31 Jan. 1928; *s* of Walter and Dorothea Ash; *m* 1954, Clare (*née* Babb); five *d*. *Educ:* University College Sch.; Imperial Coll. of Science and Technology. BSc(Eng), PhD, DSc; FCGI, DIC. FREng (FEng 1978); FIEE; FIEEE; FInstP. Research Fellow: Stanford Univ., Calif, 1952–54; QMC, 1954–55; Res. Engr, Standard Telecommunication Laboratories Ltd, 1955–63; Sen. Lectr, 1963–65, Reader, 1965–67, Prof., 1967–85, Pender Prof. and Head of Dept, 1980–85, Dept of Electronic and Electrical Engrg, UCL (Hon. Fellow, 1985); Rector, Imperial Coll., London Univ., 1985–93 (Hon. Fellow, 1995). Dir (non-exec.), BT (formerly British Telecom), 1987–93. Pres., IEE, 1987–88 (Vice-Pres., 1980–83; Dep. Pres., 1984–86); Mem., Exec. Bd, Fellowship of Engrg, 1981–84. Chm., BBC Science Advisory Cttee, 1987–. Trustee: Science Mus., 1987–; Wolfson Foundn, 1988–. Sec., Royal Instn, 1984–88 (Vice Pres., 1980–82, Manager, 1980–84; Vice Pres. and Chm. of Council, 1995–). NAE, US, 2001. Marconi International Fellowship, 1984. Dr *hc*: Aston, 1987; Leicester, 1987; Institut National Polytechnique de Grenoble, 1987; Edinburgh, 1988; Polytechnic Univ., NY, 1988; Westminster, 1992; Sussex, 1993; Glasgow, 1994; Chinese Univ. of Hong Kong, 1994; City Univ. of Hong Kong, 1998. Faraday Medal, IEE, 1980; Royal Medal, Royal Soc., 1986. National Order of Merit (France), 1990. *Publications:* patents; papers on topics in physical electronics in various engrg and physics jls. *Recreations:* music, skiing, swimming. *Address:* c/o Royal Society, 6 Carlton House Terrace, SW1Y 5AG.

ASH, Maurice Anthony, BSc (Econ); Vice President, Town and Country Planning Association, since 1987 (Chairman of Executive, 1969–83; Chairman of Council, 1983–87); *b* 31 Oct. 1917; *s* of Wilfred Cracroft and Beatrice Ash; *m* 1947, Ruth Whitney Elmhirst (*d* 1986); three *d* (one *s* decd). *Educ:* Gresham's Sch., Holt; LSE; Yale. Served War of 1939–45, armoured forces in Western Desert, Italy, Greece (despatches 1944). Mem., SW Regl Economic Planning Council, 1965–68; Chm., Green Alliance, 1978–83. Trustee, Dartington Hall, 1964– (Chm., 1972–84); Mem., Henry Moore Foundn, 1980–89. *Publications:* The Human Cloud, 1962; Who are the Progressives Now?, 1969; Regions of Tomorrow, 1969; A Guide to the Structure of London, 1972; Green Politics, 1980; New Renaissance, 1987; Journey into the Eye of a Needle, 1989; Fabric of the World, 1992; articles on land use, education and environment. *Recreation:* applying Wittgenstein. *Address:* Sharpham House, Ashprington, Totnes, Devon TQ9 7UT. *T:* (01803) 732216, *Fax:* (01803) 732037.

ASH, Raymond; former Director, Business Statistics Office, retired from Civil Service, 1986; Director, Business and Trade Statistics Ltd, since 1986; *b* 2 Jan. 1928; *s* of late Horace Ash and Gladys Ash; *m* 1947, Mavis (*née* Wootton); two *s* one *d*. *Educ:* Wolverhampton Grammar Sch. Civil Service, 1949–86: professional statistician and senior manager working on health, labour, overseas trade, and business statistics. *Publications:* contrib. learned jls. *Recreations:* country walks, tourism, historical studies. *Address:* 20 Taliesin Close, Rogerstone, Newport, Gwent NP10 0DD. *T:* (01633) 663814.

ASH, Timothy John G.; *see* Garton Ash.

ASH, Rear-Adm. William Noel, CB 1977; LVO 1959; *b* 6 March 1921; *s* of late H. Arnold Ash, MRCS, LRCP; *m* 1951, Pamela, *d* of late Harry C. Davies, Hawkes Bay, NZ; one *s* one *d*. *Educ:* Merchant Taylors' School. Joined RN, 1938; HM Yacht Britannia, 1955–58; Captain 1965; Canadian NDC, 1965–66; Staff of SACLANT (NATO), 1966–69; Cabinet Office, 1969–71; comd HMS Ganges, 1971–73; Rear-Adm. 1974; Dir of Service Intelligence, 1974–77. Sec. Defence Press and Broadcasting Cttee, 1980–84. *Address:* c/o National Bank of New Zealand, PO Box 25051, St Heliers, Auckland, New Zealand. *Club:* Royal Over-Seas League.

ASHBEE, Paul; Archaeologist, University of East Anglia, 1969–83; *b* 23 June 1918; *s* of Lewis Ashbee and Hannah Mary Elizabeth Ashbee (*née* Brett); *m* 1952, Richmal Crompton Lamburn Disher; one *s* one *d*. *Educ:* sch. in Maidstone, Kent; Univ. of London; Univ. of Leicester (MA; DLitt 1984). Post-grad. Dip. Prehistoric Archaeology, London. Royal W Kent Regt and REME, 1939–46; Control Commn for Germany, 1946–49; Univ. of London, Univ. of Bristol (Redland Coll.), 1949–54; Asst Master and Head of History, Forest Hill Sch., 1954–68. Excavation of prehistoric sites, mostly barrows both long and round for then Min. of Works, 1949–76; Co-dir with R. L. S. Bruce-Mitford of BM excavations at Sutton-Hoo, 1964–69; Mem., Sutton Hoo Research Cttee, 1982–. Mem. Council and Meetings Sec., Prehistoric Soc., 1960–74; Sec. (Wareham Earthwork), British Assoc. Sub-Cttee for Archaeological Field Experiment, 1961–; one-time Sec., Neolithic and Bronze Age Cttee, Council for British Archaeology; Mem. Royal Commn on Historical Monuments (England), 1975–85; Mem., Area Archaeological Adv. Cttee (DoE) for Norfolk and Suffolk, 1975–79. Pres., Cornwall Archæol Soc., 1976–80, Vice-Pres., 1980–84; Chm., Scole Cttee for E Anglian Archaeology, 1979–84. FSA 1958; FRSAI 1987. *Publications:* The Bronze Age Round Barrow in Britain, 1960; The Earthen Long Barrow in Britain, 1970, 2nd edn 1984; Ancient Scilly, 1974; The Ancient British, 1978; chapter in Sutton Hoo, Vol. I, 1976; Wilsford Shaft, 1989; Halangy Down, Isles of Scilly, 2000; numerous papers, articles and reviews in Archaeologia, Antiquaries Jl, Archaeological Jl, Proc. Prehistoric Soc., Antiquity, Cornish Archaeology, Arch. Cantiana, Proc. Dorset Arch. and Nat. Hist. Soc., Proc. Hants FC, Wilts Archaeol Magazine, Yorks Arch. Jl, etc. *Recreations:* East Anglia, historical architecture, bibliophilia, dog ownership. *Address:* The Old Rectory, Chedgrave, Norfolk NR14 6ND. *T:* (01508) 520595. *Club:* Norfolk (Norwich).

ASHBOURNE, 4th Baron *cr* 1885; **Edward Barry Greynville Gibson;** Lieut-Comdr RN, retired; *b* 28 Jan. 1933; *s* of 3rd Baron Ashbourne, CB, DSO, and Reta Frances Manning (*d* 1996), *e d* of E. M. Hazeland, Hong Kong; *S* father, 1983; *m* 1967, Yvonne Georgina, *d* of Mrs Flora Ham, of Malin, County Donegal; three *s*. *Educ:* Rugby. RN, 1951–72; Kitcat and Aitken, stockbrokers, 1972–73, 1976–79; Vickers, da Costa & Co., stockbrokers, 1973–76; Save & Prosper Gp, 1979–81; GT Management, 1981–88; MoD, 1989–93. Pres., Christian Broadcasting Council, 1998–. Pres., Petersfield Br., East Hants Cons. Assoc.; Pres., Hampshire Autistic Soc.; Chm., Joshua Christian Trust. *Heir: s* Hon. Edward Charles d'Olier Gibson, *b* 31 Dec. 1967. *Address:* Colebrook Barn, East Harting Farm, Petersfield, Hants GU31 5LU.

ASHBOURNE, (Kenneth) John (Turner); public sector consultant and company chairman; *b* 16 July 1938; *s* of Ernest John Ashbourne and Phyllis Ashbourne; *m* 1959, Valerie Anne Sado; one *s* one *d*. *Educ:* St Dunstan's Coll.; London Sch. of Econs (BSc Econs 1959). Teacher, then lectr, 1959–68; Mgt Develt Officer, BAC, 1968–71; Hd, Corporate Planning, London Borough of Lewisham, 1971–74; Asst Chief Exec., Suffolk CC, 1974–77; Chief Exec., Royal Borough of Kingston-upon-Thames, 1977–80; Dep. Man. Dir, Express Newspaper Gp, 1980–83; Sen. Consultant, Hay-MSL, 1983–85; Chief Executive: Cambridge HA, 1985–91; Addenbrooke's Hosp., then Addenbrooke's NHS Trust, 1991–98; E Anglian Ambulance NHS Trust, 1999. Chairman: Chapter Ltd, 1999–; Enterprise Cradle Ltd, 2001–. Sen. Mem., Hughes Hall, 1992–2000, and Associate Lectr, Clinical Sch., 1994–2000, Univ. of Cambridge. Chm., UK Univ. Hosps Forum, 1998–2000. Founder and Hon. Dir, Shelby Transplant Trust, 1994–2000. Mem. Nat. Council, British Falconers' Club, 1977–88; Mem., 1980–86, Vice-Chm., 1983–86, Hawk Bd. Gov., Anglia Poly. Univ., 1996–2000. *Recreations:* music, cars, birds of prey, wood. *Address:* Ruskview Ridge, RR#1, Creemore, ON L0M 1G0, Canada; Walnut Tree Cottage, 71 Billing Road, Brafield on the Green, Northampton NN7 1BL.

ASHBROOK, 11th Viscount *cr* 1751 (Ire.); **Michael Llowarch Warburton Flower;** JP; DL; Baron Castle Durrow 1733; landowner; Vice Lord-Lieutenant, Cheshire, since 1990; *b* 9 Dec. 1935; *s* of 10th Viscount Ashbrook and of Elizabeth, *er d* of Capt. John Egerton-Warburton and Hon. Mrs Waters; *S* father, 1995; *m* 1971, Zoë Mary Engleheart; two *s* one *d*. *Educ:* Eton; Worcester Coll., Oxford (MA Mod. Hist.). 2nd Lieut, Grenadier Guards, 1955. Solicitor, 1963; Partner, Farrer & Co., Solicitors, 1966–76; Partner, then Consultant, Pannone & Partners (formerly March Pearson & Skelton), 1985–96. Chm., Taxation Sub-Cttee, 1984–86, Pres., Cheshire Branch, 1990–, CLA. DL 1982, JP 1983, Cheshire. *Recreations:* gardening, the countryside, shooting. *Heir: s* Hon. Rowland Francis Warburton Flower, *b* 16 Jan. 1975. *Address:* The Old Parsonage, Arley Green, Northwich, Cheshire CW9 6LZ. *T:* (01565) 777277. *Club:* Brooks's.

ASHBROOK, Kate Jessie; General Secretary, Open Spaces Society, since 1984; *b* 1 Feb. 1955; *d* of John Ashbrook and Margaret Balfour; lives with Christopher Myles Hall, *qv*. *Educ:* Benenden Sch., Kent; Exeter Univ. (BSc). Member, Executive Committee: Open Spaces Soc., 1978–84; Ramblers' Assoc., 1982– (Vice-Chm., 1993–95; Chm., 1995–98; Chm., Access Cttee, 1997–; Footpath Sec., Bucks and W Middx, 1986–); Council for National Parks, 1983– (Vice-Chm., 1998–); Member: Common Land Forum, 1984–86; Countryside Agency, 1999–; Chm., Central Rights of Way Cttee, 1991–98; Sec., Countryside Link, 1989–92; Pres., Dartmoor Preservation Assoc., 1995– (Hon. Sec., 1981–84). Mem., Inst. of Public Rights of Way Officers, 1999–. Chm., Turville Sch. Trust, 1994–95. Editor, Open Space, 1984–. *Publications:* (contrib.) The Walks of South-East England, 1975; (contrib.) Severnside: a guide to family walks, 1976; pamphlets; contribs to The Countryman and various jls. *Recreations:* pedantry, finding illegally blocked footpaths. *Address:* Telfer's Cottage, Turville, Henley-on-Thames RG9 6QL. *T:* (01491) 638396.

ASHBURNER, Prof. Michael, PhD, ScD; FRS 1990; Professor of Biology, University of Cambridge, since 1991; Fellow, Churchill College, Cambridge, since 1980; *b* 23 May 1942; *s* of Geoffrey Staton Ashburner and Diane Ashburner (*née* Leff); *m* 1963, Francesca Ryan, *d* of Desmond Francis Ryan and Isabel Ryan; one *s* two *d*. *Educ:* Royal Grammar Sch., High Wycombe; Churchill Coll., Cambridge (BA 1964, PhD 1968, ScD 1978). FRES 1975. University of Cambridge: Asst in Research, 1966–68; Univ. Demonstrator, 1968–73; Univ. Lectr, 1973–80; Reader in Developmental Genetics, 1980–91. Gordon Ross Res. Fellow, Calif Inst. of Technology, 1968–69; Visiting Professor: Univ. of California Sch. of Medicine, San Francisco, 1977–78; Univ. of Crete, 1985; Univ. of Pavia, Italy, 1990–96; Miller Vis. Prof., Univ. of California at Berkeley, 1986. Lectures: Goldschmidt, Hebrew Univ., Jerusalem, 1985; Osborne, Edinburgh Univ., 1991; Dacre, Peterhouse, Cambridge, 1992. Res. Co-ordinator, EMBL, 1994–98; Jt Hd, EMBL-European Bioinformatics Inst., 1998–. Member: EMBO, 1977, Council, 1988–91; Governing Council, Internat. Centre for Insect Physiology and Ecology, Nairobi, 1991–96. Mem., Academia Europaea, 1989; Fellow, Japan Soc. for Promotion of Sci., 1992. Hon. Foreign Mem., Amer. Acad. of Arts and Scis, 1993. Pres., Genetical Soc., 1997–2000. *Publications:* (ed) The Genetics and Biology of Drosophila, 1976–86, 12 vols; (ed) Insect Cytogenetics, 1980; (ed) Heat Shock: from bacteria to man, 1982; Drosophila: a laboratory handbook and manual, 2 vols, 1989; contribs to scientific jls. *Recreations:* walking, watching birds. *Address:* 5 Bateman Street, Cambridge CB2 1NB. *T:* (01223) 364706; Department of Genetics, Downing Street, Cambridge CB2 3EH. *T:* (01223) 333969.

ASHBURNHAM, Sir James Fleetwood, 13th Bt *cr* 1661, of Broomham, Sussex; *b* 17 Dec. 1979; *s* of John Anchitel Fleetwood Ashburnham (*d* 1981) and of Corinne Ashburnham (*née* O'Brien, now Merricks); *S* grandfather, 1999. *Educ:* Sherborne; King's Coll., London. *Address:* The Manor, Icklesham, Winchelsea, East Sussex TN36 4BH.

ASHBURTON, 7th Baron *cr* 1835; **John Francis Harcourt Baring,** KG 1994; KCVO 1990 (CVO 1980); Kt 1983; DL; Chairman: Barings plc, 1985–89 (non-executive Director, 1989–94); Baring Brothers & Co. Ltd, 1974–89 (a Managing Director, 1955–74); Lord Warden of the Stannaries, Duchy of Cornwall, 1990–94 (Receiver-General, 1974–90); *b* 2 Nov. 1928; *er s* of 6th Baron Ashburton, KG, KCVO, DL and Hon. Doris Mary Thérèse Harcourt (*d* 1981), *e d* of 1st Viscount Harcourt; *S* father, 1991; *m* 1st, 1955, Susan Mary Renwick (marr. diss. 1984), *e d* of 1st Baron Renwick, KBE, and Mrs John Ormiston; two *s* two *d*; 2nd, 1987, Mrs Sarah Crewe, *d* of late J. G. Spencer Churchill. *Educ:* Eton (Fellow, 1982); Trinity Coll., Oxford (MA; Hon. Fellow 1989). Dep. Chm., Royal Insurance Co. Ltd, 1975–82 (Dir, 1964–82); Chairman: Outwich Investment Trust Ltd, 1968–86; Baring Stratton Investment Trust, 1986–97; BP Co. plc, 1992–95 (Dir, 1982–95); Director: Dunlop Holdings Ltd, 1981–84; Bank of England, 1983–91; Jaguar, 1989–91. Vice-Pres., British Bankers' Assoc., 1977–81; Pres., Overseas Bankers' Club, 1977–78. Chm., Accepting Houses Cttee, 1977–81; Chm., Cttee on Finance for Industry, NEDC, 1980–86. Member: British Transport Docks Bd, 1966–71; President's Cttee, CBI, 1976–79; Trustee and Hon. Treas., Police Foundn, 1989–; Member: Council, Baring Foundn, 1971–98 (Chm., 1987–98); Exec. Cttee, NACF, 1989–99. Trustee: Rhodes Trust, 1970–99 (Chm., 1987–99); Southampton Univ. Develt Trust, 1986–96 (Chm., 1989–96); Nat. Gall., 1981–87; Winchester Cathedral Trust, 1989– (Chm., 1993–). High Steward, Winchester Cathedral, 1991–. DL Hants, 1994. Hon. Fellow, Hertford Coll., Oxford, 1976. *Heir: s* Hon. Mark Francis Robert Baring [*b* 17 Aug. 1958; *m* 1983, Miranda Caroline, *d* of Captain Charles St John Graham Moncrieff; two *s* two *d*]. *Address:* Lake House, Northington, Alresford, Hants SO24 9TG; 3 Stanley House, 13 Stanley Crescent, W11 2NA. *Clubs:* Pratt's, Flyfishers', Beefsteak.

ASHBY, David Glynn; barrister; *b* 14 May 1940; *s* of Robert M. Ashby and Isobel A. Davidson; *m* 1965, Silvana Morena; one *d*. *Educ:* Royal Grammar Sch., High Wycombe; Bristol Univ. (LLB Hons). Called to the Bar, Gray's Inn, 1963; in practice on SE Circuit. Member: Hammersmith Bor. Council, 1968–71; for W Woolwich, GLC, 1977–81; ILEA, 1977–81. MP (C) NW Leics, 1983–97. *Recreations:* gardening, ski-ing, music. *Address:* 1 Middle Temple Lane, Temple, EC4Y 9AA.

ASHBY, Francis Dalton, OBE 1975; Director, National Counties Building Society, 1980–90; retired; *b* 20 Jan. 1920; *s* of late John Frederick Ashby and late Jessie Ashby; *m* 1948, Mollie Isabel Mitchell (*d* 1999); one *s* one *d* (and one *d* decd). *Educ:* Watford Grammar Sch. Diploma in Govt Admin. War Service, Royal Signals, 1940–46: POW, Far East, 1942–45. National Debt Office: Exec. Officer, 1938; Asst Comptroller and Estabt Officer, 1966–76; Comptroller-General, 1976–80. Hon. Treas., Cedars Village Residents' Assoc., 1998–2000. *Recreations:* listening to music, retirement village activities. *Address:* 21 Badgers Walk, Chorleywood, Herts WD3 5GA.

ASHBY, Rt Rev. Godfrey William Ernest Candler; Assistant Bishop of George, South Africa, since 1995; *b* 6 Nov. 1930; *s* of late William Candler Ashby and Vera Fane Ashby (*née* Hickey); *m* 1957, Sally Hawtree; four *s* two *d*. *Educ:* King's School, Chester; King's Coll., London (BD, AKC, PhD). Deacon 1955, priest 1956; Assistant Curate: St Peter, St Helier, Morden, 1955–57; Clydesdale Mission, 1958; Priest-in-charge, St Mark's Mission, 1958–60; Subwarden, St Paul's Coll., Grahamstown, 1960–65; Rector of Alice and Lectr, Federal Theological Seminary, 1966–68; Sen. Lecturer, Old Testament and Hebrew, Rhodes Univ., Grahamstown, 1969–75; Assoc. Professor, 1974–75; Overseas Visiting Scholar, St John's Coll., Cambridge, 1975; Dean and Archdeacon, Cathedral of St Michael and St George, Grahamstown, 1976–80; Bishop of St John's (Transkei and S Africa), 1980–84; Prof. of Divinity, Univ. of Witwatersrand, Johannesburg, 1985–88; Asst Bp of Leicester, 1988–95; Priest-in-Charge, Newtown Linford, 1992–95. Hon. Canon, Leicester Cathedral, 1994–. *Publications:* Theodoret of Cyrrhus as Exegete of the Old Testament, 1970; Sacrifice, 1988; Exodus (commentary), 1998; articles in theological jls. *Recreation:* ornithology. *Address:* 7 Graham Street, PO Box 2685, Knysna, 6570, S Africa.

ASHBY, Prof. Michael Farries, CBE 1997; FRS 1979; FREng; Royal Society Research Professor, Department of Engineering, University of Cambridge, since 1989 (Professor of Engineering Materials, 1973–89); *b* 20 Nov. 1935; *s* of Lord Ashby, FRS; *m* 1962, Maureen Stewart; two *s* one *d*. *Educ:* Campbell Coll., Belfast; Queens' Coll., Cambridge (BA, MA, PhD). Post-doctoral work, Cambridge, 1960–62; Asst, Univ. of Göttingen, 1962–65; Asst Prof., Harvard Univ., 1965–69; Prof. of Metallurgy, Harvard Univ., 1969–73. Mem., Akad. der Wissenschaften zu Göttingen, 1980–. FREng (FEng 1993). Hon. MA Harvard, 1969. Editor: Acta Metallurgica, 1974–96; Progress in Materials Science, 1995–. *Publications:* Deformation Mechanism Maps, 1982; Engineering Materials, pt 1 1986, pt 2 1996; Materials Selection in Design, 1992, 2nd edn 1999; Cellular Solids, 1997. *Recreations:* music, design. *Address:* 51 Maids Causeway, Cambridge CB5 8DE. *T:* (01223) 303015.

ASHCOMBE, 4th Baron *cr* 1892; **Henry Edward Cubitt;** late RAF; Chairman, Cubitt Estates Ltd; *b* 31 March 1924; *er s* of 3rd Baron Ashcombe; *S* father, 1962; *m* 1955, Ghislaine (marr. diss. 1968), *o d* of Cornelius Willem Dresselhuys, Long Island, New York; *m* 1973, Hon. Virginia Carington, *yr d* of Baron Carrington, *qv*; *m* 1979, Mrs Elizabeth Dent-Brocklehurst. *Educ:* Eton. Served War of 1939–45, RAF. Consul-General in London for the Principality of Monaco, 1961–68. *Heir: cousin* Mark Edward Cubitt [*b* 29 Feb. 1964; *m* 1992, Melissa Mary, *o d* of Maj. Charles Hay; two *s*]. *Address:* Sudeley Castle, Winchcombe, Cheltenham, Glos GL54 5JD. *Club:* White's.

See also Earl of Harrington.

ASHCROFT, Baron *cr* 2000 (Life Peer), of Chichester in the County of West Sussex; **Michael Anthony Ashcroft,** KCMG 2000; Chairman, Carlisle Holdings Ltd. Former Chairman: Hawley Group; ADT Group; Cope Allman International plc. Ambassador from Belize to the UN, 1998–2000. Sen. Party Treas., Conservative Party, 1998–2001. *Address:* House of Lords, SW1A 0PW.

ASHCROFT, David, TD 1957; MA Cantab; Headmaster, Cheltenham College, 1959–78; *b* 20 May 1920; *s* of late A. H. Ashcroft, DSO; *m* 1949, Joan Elizabeth Young; two *s* three *d*. *Educ:* Rugby Sch.; Gonville and Caius Coll., Cambridge. War Service, 1940–46 (despatches). Asst Master, Rossall Sch., 1946–50; Asst Master, Rugby Sch., 1950–59. *Address:* London House, Ashton Keynes, Swindon, Wilts SN6 6NL. *T:* (01285) 861319.

ASHCROFT, Prof. Frances Mary, PhD, ScD; FRS 1999; Professor of Physiology, University of Oxford, since 1996; Senior Research Fellow, Trinity College, Oxford, since 1992; *b* 15 Feb. 1952; *d* of John and Kathleen Ashcroft. *Educ:* Talbot Heath Sch., Bournemouth; Girton Coll., Cambridge (BA 1974; MA 1978; PhD 1979; ScD 1996). MRC Trng Fellow, Physiol., Leicester Univ., 1978–82; Oxford University: Demonstrator in Physiol., 1982–85; EPA Cephalosporin Jun. Res. Fellow, Linacre Coll., 1983–85; Royal Soc. 1983 Univ. Res. Fellow, Physiol., 1985–90; Lecturer in Physiology: Christ Church, 1986–87; Trinity Coll., 1988–89; Univ. Lectr in Physiol., 1990–96; Tutorial Fellow in Medicine, St Hilda's Coll., 1990–91. Grass Foundn Fellow, 1978; Muscular Dystrophy Assoc. Fellow, Physiol., UCLA, 1981–82. G. L. Brown Prize Lectr, 1997; Peter Curran Lectr, Yale Univ., 1999. FMedSci 1999. Frank Smart Prize, Cambridge Univ., 1974; Andrew Cudworth Meml Prize, 1990; G. B. Morgagni Young Investigator Award, 1991. *Publications:* (with S. J. H. Ashcroft) Insulin-Molecular Biology to Pathology, 1992; Ion Channels and Disease, 1999; Life at the Extremes: the science of survival, 2000; res. papers in Nature, Jl Physiology, etc. *Recreations:* reading, writing, walking. *Address:* University Laboratory of Physiology, Parks Road, Oxford OX1 3PT.

ASHCROFT, John Kevin, CBE 1990; Crabtree Consultancy Group Ltd, since 1990; *b* 24 Dec. 1948; *s* of Cumania Manion and late John Ashcroft; *m* 1972, Jennifer Ann (*née* King); two *s* one *d*. *Educ:* Upholland Grammar School; LSE (BSc Econ Hons); PhD Manchester Metropolitan Univ., 1996. Marketing Trainee, Tube Investments, 1970; Brand Manager, Crown Wallcoverings Internat. Div., 1974; Marketing Dir, Crown Wallcoverings French Subsidiary, 1976; Man. Dir, Coloroll, 1978–82, Dep. Chm. and Chief Exec., 1982–86, Chm., 1986–90. Young Business Man of the Year, The Guardian, 1987. *Recreations:* fine arts, opera, sports, wine.

ASHCROFT, Philip Giles; Solicitor, British Telecommunications, 1981–87; *b* 15 Nov. 1926; *s* of Edmund Samuel Ashcroft and Constance Ruth Ashcroft (*née* Giles); *m* 1st, 1968, Kathleen Margaret Senior (marr. diss. 1983); one *s*; 2nd, 1985, Valerie May Smith, *d* of late E. T. G. Smith. *Educ:* Royal Grammar Sch., Newcastle upon Tyne; Durham Univ. Admitted solicitor, 1951. Joined Treasury Solicitor's Dept, 1955; Asst Legal Adviser, Land Commn, 1967; Asst Treasury Solicitor, 1971; Under-Sec. (Legal), DTI, 1973; Legal Adviser, Dept of Energy, 1974–80; Dep. Solicitor to the Post Office, 1980–81. Legal Consultant, Registry of Friendly Socs and Building Socs Commn, 1988–96. *Recreations:* reading, listening to music, walking. *Address:* 24A Rudd's Lane, Haddenham, Aylesbury, Bucks HP17 8JP. *T:* (01844) 291921.

ASHDOWN, family name of **Baron Ashdown of Norton-sub-Hamdon**.

ASHDOWN OF NORTON-SUB-HAMDON, Baron *cr* 2001(Life Peer), of Norton-sub-Hamdon in the County of Somerset; **Jeremy John Durham Ashdown, (Paddy),** KBE 2000; PC 1989; *b* 27 Feb. 1941; *s* of late John W. R. D. Ashdown and Lois A. Ashdown; *m* 1962, Jane (*née* Courtenay); one *s* one *d*. *Educ:* Bedford Sch. Served RM, 1959–71: 41 and 42 Commando; commanded 2 Special Boat Section; Captain RM; HM Diplomatic Service, 1st Sec., UK Mission to UN, Geneva, 1971–76; Commercial Manager's Dept, Westlands Gp, 1976–78; Sen. Manager, Morlands Ltd, 1978–81; employed by Dorset CC, 1982–83. Contested (L) Yeovil, 1979; MP Yeovil, 1983–2001 (L 1983–88, Lib Dem 1988–2001); Leader, Liberal Democrats, 1988–99. L spokesman for Trade and Industry, 1983–86; Lib/SDP Alliance spokesman on education and science, 1987; Lib Dem spokesman on NI, 1988–97. *Publications:* Citizen's Britain, 1989; Beyond Westminster, 1994; Making Change our Ally, 1994; The Ashdown Diaries, vol. 1, 2000, vol. 2, 2001. *Recreations:* walking, gardening, wine making. *Address:* House of Lords, SW1A 0PW. *Club:* National Liberal.

ASHE, (Thomas) Michael; QC 1994; QC (NI) 1998; SC (Ire.) 2000; a Recorder, since 2000; *b* 10 March 1949; *s* of John Ashe and Nancy (*née* O'Connor); *m* 1977, Helen Morag Nicholson. *Educ:* Finchley Catholic Grammar Sch. Called to the Bar, Middle Temple, 1971, Bencher, 1998; called to Irish Bar, 1975, Northern Irish Bar, 1993. Estate Duty Office, CS, 1967–70; merchant banking, 1971–76; practice at the Bar, 1978–. Dep. Public Prosecutor, Min. of Finance, Singapore, 1988–90; an Asst Recorder, 1998–2000. Editor, Company Lawyer, 1983–. Hon. General Counsel to Brit. Inst. of Securities Laws, 1980–; Hon. Consultant to Commercial Crime Unit, Commonwealth Secretariat, 1980–84. Mem. Bd, Centre for Internat. Documentation on Organised and Economic Crime, Cambridge, 1990–; Guest Lectr, Fac. of Laws, Univ. of Cambridge, 1990–95. Auditor and Notary, Dio. of Brentwood, 1997–. *Publications:* (jtly) Insider Trading, 1990, 2nd edn 1994; (jtly) Insider Dealing (Ireland), 1992; (jtly) Insider Crime, 1994; contrib. Money, 1980, and (jtly) Injunctions, 1991, in Halsbury's Laws of England, 4th edn; articles in legal periodicals. *Recreations:* walking, railways, Gregorian Chant, classical music, Irish traditional music. *Address:* 9 Stone Buildings, Lincoln's Inn, WC2A 3NN. *T:* (020) 7404 5055.

ASHENHURST, Maj.-Gen. Francis Ernest; Director, Defence Dental Services, 1990–92, retired; *b* 1 April 1933; *s* of Charles Ashenhurst and Margaret Jane (*née* MacLaine); *m* 1959, Hilary Chapman; two *d*. *Educ:* Methodist Coll., Belfast; Queen's Univ., Belfast (BDS); London Univ. (MSc). Commnd RADC, 1963; OC Rhine Area Dental Unit, 1964–66; Instr and Chief Instr, Depot and Trng Estabt, RADC, 1967–71; Commanding Officer: Army Dental Centres, Hong Kong, 1971–73; 6 Dental Gp, UKLF, 1973–76; postgrad. studies, 1976–77; Asst Dir, Army Dental Service, 1977–78; CO 1 Dental Gp, BAOR, 1978–81; Dep. Dir, Army Dental Service, 1981–84; Comdt, HQ and Central Gp, RADC, 1984; Dep. Comdr, Med. (Dentistry), BAOR, 1984–86; Comdr, HQ and Tech. Services, RADC, BAOR, 1986–88; Dir, Army Dental Service, 1989–90. QHDS, 1989–92. OStJ 1974. *Recreations:* gardening, listening to music, cooking. *Club:* Norfolk (Norwich).

ASHER, Bernard Harry; Chairman (non-executive), Lonrho Africa, since 1998; *b* 9 March 1936; *s* of Samuel Asher and Rebecca (*née* Fisher); *m* 1961, Batia Sislin; one *s* two *d*. *Educ:* LSE (BSc). S. Japhet & Co., 1957–59; English Electric Co., 1960–67; ITT Inc., 1967–74 and 1978–80; on secondment to NEDO, 1974–78; Hong Kong Bank, 1980–92; Chairman: HSBC Investment Bank Ltd, 1993–98; James Capel & Co., 1991–98; Samuel Montagu, 1993–98. Non-executive Director: Rémy Cointreau SA, 1992–; The China Fund Inc., 1995–99; Randgold Resources Ltd, 1997–; Legal & General plc, 1998–; Morgan Sindall plc, 1998–. Investment Advr, RCP, 1998–. Trustee, PPP Med. Scheme, 1998–. Vice Chm. Governors, LSE, 1998–. *Recreations:* opera, walking. *Address:* Lonrho Africa, York House, Mercury Court, Tithebarn Street, Liverpool L2 2QP. *Clubs:* Reform; Hong Kong, Hong Kong Jockey.

ASHER, Jane; actress and writer; *b* 5 April 1946; *d* of late Richard A. J. Asher, MD, FRCP and of Margaret Asher (*née* Eliot); *m* Gerald Scarfe, *qv*; two *s* one *d*. *Educ:* North Bridge House; Miss Lambert's PNEU. *Stage:* Will You Walk a Little Faster, Duke of York's, 1960; Wendy in Peter Pan, Scala, 1961; Bristol Old Vic, 1965; Romeo and Juliet and Measure for Measure, NY, 1967; Look Back in Anger, Royal Court, 1969; The Philanthropist, Mayfair and NY, 1970; Treats, Royal Court, 1975; National Theatre, 1976; Whose Life is it Anyway?, Mermaid and Savoy, 1978; Before the Party, Queen's, 1978; Blithe Spirit, Vaudeville, 1986; Henceforward, Vaudeville, 1988; The School for Scandal, NT, 1990; Making it Better, Criterion, 1992; The Shallow End, Royal Court, 1997; Things We Do For Love, Gielgud, 1998; House, and Garden, RNT, 2000; What the Butler Saw, tour, 2001; *films include:* Mandy, 1951; Greengage Summer, 1961; Alfie, 1966; Deep End, 1970; Henry VIII and his Six Wives, 1970; Runners, 1984; Dream Child, 1985; Paris by Night, 1988; *television includes:* Brideshead Revisited, 1981; The Mistress, 1986; Wish Me Luck, 1987–89; Eats for Treats, 1990; Tonight at 8.30, Murder Most Horrid, 1991; Closing Numbers, 1993; The Choir, 1995; Good Living, 1997, 1998; numerous plays for radio; Radio Actress of the Year Award, 1986. Member: BBC Gen. Adv. Council, 1991–; BAFTA, 1985; Forum, 1993–. Pres., Nat. Autistic Soc., 1997– (Vice Pres., 1990–97); Trustee: WWF; Child Accident Prevention Trust; Ford Martin Trust for Cancer in Children; Children in Need. Governor, Molecule Theatre. Started business, Jane Asher Party Cakes, London, 1990; designer and consultant for Sainsbury's cakes, 1992–; Consultant, Debenhams, 1999–. Columnist: Today newspaper, 1994–95; The Express, 1998–2001. FRSA 1989. *Publications:* Jane Asher's Party Cakes, 1982; Jane Asher's Fancy Dress, 1983; Silent Nights for You and Your Baby, 1984; Jane Asher's Quick Party Cakes, 1986; The Moppy Stories, 1987; Easy Entertaining, 1987; Keep Your Baby Safe, 1988; Children's Parties, 1988; Calendar of Cakes, 1989; Eats for Treats, 1990; Jane Asher's Book of Cake Decorating Ideas, 1993; Round the World Cookbook, 1994; Time to Play, 1995; The Longing, 1996; 101 Things I wish I'd known before …, 1996; The Best of Good Living, 1998; The Question, 1998; Good Living at Christmas, 1998; Tricks of the Trade, 1999; Trying to Get Out, 2002; journalism for newspapers and magazines. *Recreations:* reading, ski-ing, The Times crossword. *Address:* c/o London Management, 2–4 Noel Street, W1V 3RB.

ASHFORD, Ronald, CBE 1992; CEng, FIMechE, FRAeS; aviation and safety consultant; *b* 24 Aug. 1932; *s* of Russell Sutcliffe Ashford and Dorothy Ashford (*née* Shorland); *m* 1955, Françoise Louisa Gabrielle Génestal du Chaumeil; two *s*. *Educ:* St Edward's Sch., Oxford; De Havilland Aeronautical Tech. Sch. Flight Develt Engr, De Havilland Aircraft Co., 1953–56; Pilot Officer, RAF, 1956–58; Flight Develt Engr and Sen. Aerodynamicist, De Havilland/Hawker Siddeley Aviation, 1958–68; Design Surveyor, Air Registration Bd, 1968–72; Civil Aviation Authority: Surveyor and Head, Flight Dept, 1972–83; Dir-Gen., Airworthiness, 1983–88; Group Dir, Safety Regulation, and Board Mem., 1988–92; Sec. Gen., Eur. Jt Aviation Authorities, 1992–94. Wakefield Gold Medal, 1989, Hodgson Prize, 1991, RAeS; Dist. Service Award, Flight Safety Foundn, 1992; Award for Dist. Service, US Fed. Aviation Admin, 1992; Cumberbatch Trophy, GAPAN, 1992; James Clayton Prize, IMechE, 1995. *Publications:* papers in Jl RAeS. *Recreations:* walking, gardening. *Address:* Sheeplands, 17 Granville Road, Limpsfield, Oxted, Surrey RH8 0BX. *T:* (01883) 382917. *Club:* Royal Air Force.

ASHFORD, Air Vice-Marshal Ronald Gordon, CBE 1978; *b* 2 May 1931; *s* of Richard Ashford and Phyllis Lancaster; *m* 1966, Patricia Ann Turner; two *d*. *Educ:* Ilfracombe Grammar Sch.; Bristol Univ. (LLB). Joined RAF, 1952; qualified as Navigator, 1953; OC No 115 Squadron, 1971–72; OC RAF Finningley, 1976–77; RCDS, 1978; Air Cdre Intelligence, 1979–83; Comdr, Southern Maritime Air Region, 1983–84; Dir Gen., Personal Services (RAF), MoD, 1984–85; retired. Chm., Metropolitan Traffic Comrs, 1985–91; Sen. Traffic Comr, Western Traffic Area and Licensing Authy, 1991–96. *Recreation:* golf. *Address:* Old Courthay, Church Lane, Brent Knoll, Som TA9 4DG. *Club:* Royal Air Force.

ASHFORD, William Stanton, OBE 1971; HM Diplomatic Service, retired; *b* 4 July 1924; *s* of Thomas and May Ashford; *m* 1957, Rosalind Anne Collett; two *s*. Served RAF, 1943–47; Air Ministry, 1948; Commonwealth Relations Office, 1961; Director of British Information Services, Sierra Leone, 1961, Ghana, 1962; Acting Consul-General, Tangier, 1965; Regional Information Officer, Bombay, 1966; Head of Chancery, British Government Office, Montreal, 1967; seconded to Northern Ireland Office, 1972; FCO, 1974; Consul-General, Adelaide, 1977; High Comr, Vanuatu, 1980–82. *Recreations:* 18th Century music, smallholder farming. *Address:* c/o Lloyds TSB, PO Box 770, St Helier, Jersey JE4 8ZZ. *T:* (01534) 59655.

ASHIOTIS, Costas; High Commissioner of Cyprus in London, 1966–79; Cyprus Ambassador to Denmark, Sweden, Norway and Malta, 1966–79; *b* 1908; *m*. *Educ:* Pancyprian Gymnasium, Nicosia; London Sch. of Economics. Journalist and editor; joined Govt Service, 1942; Asst Comr of Labour, 1948; Dir-Gen., Min. of Foreign Affairs, 1960. Mem. Cyprus delegns to UN and to internat. confs. Retired from Foreign Service, 1979. MBE 1952. *Publications:* Labour Conditions in Cyprus during the War Years, 1939–45; literary articles. *Address:* 10 Ev. Pallikarides Street, Nicosia, Cyprus.

ASHKEN, Kenneth Richard, CB 1996; JP; legal consultant; Director (Policy), Crown Prosecution Service, 1990–95; *b* 13 June 1945; *s* of Karol and Dulcinea Ashken; *m* 1st, 1969, Linda Salemink (marr. diss.); two *s* one *d*; partner, 1986; 2nd, 1996, Patricia Almond (*d* 1996); one *d*. *Educ:* Whitgift Sch., Croydon; London Univ. (LLB Hons); Cambridge Inst. of Criminology (DipCrim). Admitted solicitor, 1972. Office of Director of Public Prosecutions, 1972; Asst Dir of Public Prosecutions, 1984; Hd of Policy and Inf. Div., 1986, Dir, Policy and Communications Gp (Grade 3), 1990, Crown Prosecution Service. UK Govt consultant to S African Ministry of Justice, 1998–99. Lay Chm., indep. review panels, NHS, 1998–2001; non-exec. Dir, Bromley Primary Care NHS Trust, 2001–. Member: Cttee, SE London Probation Service, 1997–2001; London Area Bd, Nat. Probation Service, 2001–. Mem., Funding Panel, Victim Support, 1997–. FRSA 1990. JP 2000. *Recreation:* travel. *Club:* Royal Automobile.

ASHKENAZY, Vladimir; concert pianist; conductor; Music Director and Chief Conductor, Czech Philharmonic Orchestra, since 1998; *b* Gorky, Russia, 6 July 1937; *m* 1961, Thorunn Johannsdottir, *d* of Johann Tryggvason, Iceland; two *s* three *d*. *Educ:* Central Musical Sch., Moscow; Conservatoire, Moscow. Studied under Sumbatyan; Lev Oborin class, 1955: grad 1960. Internat. Chopin Comp., Warsaw, at age of 17 (gained 2nd prize); won Queen Elisabeth Internat. Piano Comp., Brussels, at age of 18 (gold medal). Joint winner (with John Ogdon) of Tchaikovsky Piano Comp., Moscow, 1962. London debut with London Symph. Orch. under George Hurst, and subseq. solo recital, Festival Hall, 1963. Music Dir, RPO, 1987–94; Chief Conductor, Berlin Radio SO, subseq. Deutsches Symphonie-Orchester Berlin, 1989–99. Has played in many countries. Makes recordings. Hon. RAM 1972. Icelandic Order of the Falcon, 1971. *Publication:* (with

Jasper Parrott) Beyond Frontiers, 1985. *Address:* Käppelistrasse 15, 6045 Meggen, Switzerland.

ASHLEY, family name of **Baron Ashley of Stoke**.

ASHLEY OF STOKE, Baron *cr* 1992 (Life Peer), of Widnes in the County of Cheshire; **Jack Ashley,** CH 1975; PC 1979; *b* 6 Dec. 1922; *s* of John Ashley and Isabella Bridge; *m* 1951, Pauline Kay Crispin; three *d. Educ:* St Patrick's Elem. Sch., Widnes, Lancs; Ruskin Coll., Oxford; Gonville and Caius Coll., Cambridge (Hon. Fellow). Labourer and cranedriver, 1936–46; Shop Steward Convenor and Nat. Exec. Mem., Chemical Workers' Union, 1946; Scholarship, Ruskin Coll., 1946–48 and Caius Coll., 1948–51 (Chm. Cambridge Labour Club, 1950; Pres. Cambridge Union, 1951); BBC Radio Producer, 1951–57; Commonwealth Fund Fellow, 1955; BBC Senior Television Producer, 1957–66; Mem., General Advisory Council, BBC, 1967–69, 1970–74. Councillor, Borough of Widnes, 1945. MP (Lab) Stoke-on-Trent, South, 1966–92. Parliamentary Private Secretary to: Sec. of State for Econ. Affairs, 1967–68; Sec. of State, DHSS, 1974–76. Mem., Lab. Party Nat. Exec. Cttee, 1976–78. Co-Chm., All-Party Disablement Gp. President: Hearing Research (formerly Hearing and Speech) Trust, 1985–; RNID, 1987–; Royal Coll. of Speech and Language Therapists, 1995–. Chancellor, Staffordshire Univ., 1993–. *Publications:* Journey into Silence (autobiog.), 1973; Acts of Defiance (autobiog.), 1992. *Address:* House of Lords, SW1A 0PW.

See also J. Ashley.

ASHLEY, Lord; Anthony Nils Christian Ashley-Cooper; *b* 24 June 1977; *s* and *heir* of Earl of Shaftesbury, *qv. Educ:* Marlborough Coll.; Studio Art Centers Internat.; Univ. of Bristol (BSc 1999). *Address:* St Giles, Wimborne, Dorset BH21 5NH.

ASHLEY, Sir Bernard (Albert), Kt 1987; Founder, Laura Ashley Holdings plc, 1993 (Chairman, 1985–93; non-executive Director, 1991–98); *b* 11 Aug. 1926; *s* of Albert Ashley and Hilda Maud Ashley; *m* 1st, 1949, Laura Mountney (*d* 1985); two *s* two *d*; 2nd, 1990, Mme Regine Burnell. *Educ:* Whitgift Middle Sch., Croydon, Surrey. Army commission, 1944; Royal Fusiliers, 1944–46, seconded 1 Gurkha Rifles, 1944–45. Incorporated Ashley, Mountney Ltd, 1954; Chm., Ashley, Mountney Ltd, later Laura Ashley Ltd, 1954–93. Hon. DScEcon Wales, 1986. *Recreations:* sailing, flying. *Clubs:* Garrick; Royal Thames Yacht (Southampton), Army Sailing Association; Lyford Cay (Bahamas).

ASHLEY, Cedric, CBE 1984; PhD; CEng, FIMechE; automotive engineering consultant; Chairman, Cedric Ashley and Associates, since 1989; Director, Euromotor, University of Birmingham, since 1992; Managing Director, Steyr Power Technology, since 1992; *b* 11 Nov. 1936; *s* of Ronald Ashley and Gladys Fincher; *m* 1st, 1960, Pamela Jane Turner (decd); one *s*; 2nd, 1965, (Marjorie) Vivien Gooch (marr. diss. 1991); one *s* one *d*; 3rd, 1991, Auriol Mary Keogh. *Educ:* King Edward's Sch., Birmingham; Mech. Engrg Dept, Univ. of Birmingham (BSc 1958, PhD 1964). CEng 1972; FIMechE 1978. Rolls-Royce Ltd, Derby, 1955–60; Univ. of Birmingham, 1960–73: ICI Res. Fellow, 1963; Lectr, 1966; Internat. Technical Dir, Bostrom Div., Universal Oil Products Ltd, 1973–77; Dir, Motor Industry Res. Assoc., 1977–87; Man. Dir, Lotus Engineering, 1987; Chief Exec., BICERI, 1989–91. Chairman: SEE, 1970–72; RAC Tech. Cttee, 1980–87; Member: SMMT Technical Bds, 1977–87; Board, Assoc. Ind. Contract Res. Orgns, 1977–86 (Pres., 1982–84); Coventry and District Engineering Employers Assoc., 1978–85; Board, Automobile Div., IMechE, 1978–93 (Chm., 1990–91); Court, Cranfield Inst. of Technol., 1977–87; Engine and Vehicles Cttee, DTI, 1980–88; Three-Dimensional Design Bd, CNAA, 1981–87. FRSA 1983. Cementation Muffelite Award, SEE, 1968; Design Council Award, 1974. TA, 1959–68. *Publications:* (contrib.) Infrasound and Low Frequency Vibration, ed Tempest, 1976; papers on electro-hydraulics, vehicle ride, and effect of vibration and shock on man and buildings, in learned jls. *Recreations:* travel, reading. *Address:* (office) Euromotor, Muirhead Tower, University of Birmingham, Birmingham B15 2TT. *T:* (0121) 414 7623; *e-mail:* c.ashley@bham.ac.uk.

ASHLEY, Jacqueline; Political Editor, New Statesman, since 2000; *b* 10 Sept. 1954; *d* of Lord Ashley of Stoke, *qv*; *m* 1987, Andrew William Stevenson Marr, *qv*; one *s* two *d. Educ:* Rosebery Grammar Sch., Epsom; St Anne's Coll., Oxford (MA PPE). Producer and Newsreader, Newsnight, BBC TV, 1980–83; Producer and Reporter, TV-am, 1983–84; Politics Producer, Channel 4 News, 1984–87; Editor, Their Lordships' House, Channel 4, 1987–88; Presenter, The Parliament Programme, Channel 4, 1988–89; Political Corresp., ITN, 1989–98; Presenter, People and Politics, BBC World Service, 1998–2000. *Recreations:* reading, swimming. *Address:* New Statesman, Victoria Station House, 191 Victoria Street, SW1E 5NE. *T:* (020) 7828 1232.

ASHLEY-COOPER, family name of **Earl of Shaftesbury**.

ASHLEY-MILLER, Dr Michael, CBE 1995; DPH; FFPHM; FRCPE; FRCP; Secretary, Nuffield Provincial Hospitals Trust, London, 1986–95; *b* 1 Dec. 1930; *s* of Cyril and Marjorie Ashley-Miller; *m* 1958, Yvonne Townend; three *d. Educ:* Charterhouse; Oxford Univ.; King's Coll. Hosp.; London Sch. of Hygiene and Tropical Med. MA Oxon; BM BCh; DObstRCOG. FFPHM (FFCM 1977); FRCPE 1985; FRCP 1990. Ho. Surg., Ho. Phys., King's Coll. Hosp., 1956–57; SMO, Dulwich Hosp., 1957; MO/SMO, RAF, 1958–61; SMO, IoW CC, 1961–64; MO/SMO, MRC (HQ Staff), 1964–74; PMO, SPMO, Scottish Home and Health Dept, 1974–86. Mem. Council, RSocMed, 1998– (Pres., Gen. Practice Sect., 1994–95). Mem. Council, Stroke Assoc., 1997–. Hon. MRCP 1986; Hon. FRCGP 1994. FRSA 1996. *Publications:* (invited contributor to) Vol. III, Textbook of Public Health, 1985; (jt ed) Screening for Risk of Coronary Heart Disease, 1987; contrib. to The Practitioner, Public Health, The Medical Officer, Health Bull., BMJ. *Recreations:* golf, reading, visiting cathedrals. *Address:* 28 Fitzwarren Gardens, N19 3TP. *T:* (020) 7272 7017. *Club:* Royal Society of Medicine.

ASHLEY-SMITH, Jonathan, PhD; FMA; Head of Conservation, Victoria and Albert Museum, since 1977; *b* 25 Aug. 1946; *s* of Ewart Trist and Marian Tanfield Ashley-Smith; *m* 1967, Diane Louise (*née* Wagland); one *s* one *d. Educ:* Sutton Valence Public Sch.; Bristol Univ. (BSc (Hons), PhD). FMA 1988. Post-doctoral research, Cambridge Univ., 1970–72; Victoria and Albert Museum, 1973–. Leverhulme Fellow, 1995; Sen. Mem., Wolfson Coll., Cambridge, 1995. Member: UKIC, 1974– (Accredited Mem., 1999; Mem., Exec Cttee, 1978–; Vice-Chm., 1980; Chm., 1983–84); Crafts Council, 1980–83 (Mem., Conservation Cttee, 1978–83); Council for Care of Churches Conservation Cttee, 1978–85; Board of Governors, London Coll. of Furniture, 1983–85. Vis. Prof., RCA, 1999. FRSC 1987; FIIC 1985; Hon. FRCA 1992; FRSA 2000. Scientific Editor, Science for Conservators (Crafts Council series), 1983–84. Plowden Medal, 2000. *Publications:* Risk Assessment for Object Conservation, 1999; articles in learned jls on organometallic chemistry, spectroscopy and scientific examination of art objects. *Recreations:* loud music, good beer. *Address:* Victoria and Albert Museum, Exhibition Road, SW7 2RL. *T:* (020) 7942 2132; *e-mail:* jonathan@vam.ac.uk.

ASHMOLE, (Harold) David; Senior Principal Dancer, 1984–93, Guest Artist, since 1994, Australian Ballet; Director, Australian Ballet Foundation, 1995–99; *b* 31 Oct. 1949; *s* of Richard Thomas Ashmole and Edith Ashmole. *Educ:* Sandye Place, Beds; Royal Ballet Sch; Grad. Dip Visual and Performing Arts, Melbourne Univ. Solo Seal, Royal Acad. of Dancing; ARAD. Joined Royal Ballet Co., 1968; Soloist, 1972; Principal, 1975; transf. to Sadler's Wells Royal Ballet, 1976, Sen. Principal, 1978–84. Lectr in Classical Dance, Victorian Coll. of the Arts, Univ. of Melbourne, 1998–; Guest Teacher: London Studio Centre, 1999–2000; K Ballet UK, 2000; Singapore Dance Theatre, 2000. Appeared in: Dame Alicia Markova's Master Classes, BBC Television, 1980; Maina Gielgud's Steps, Notes and Squeaks, Aberdeen Internat. Festival, 1981. Guest appearances with Scottish Ballet, 1981, with Bolshoi (for UNESCO Gala), 1986, with Sadler's Wells Royal Ballet at Royal Opera House, 1986 (season) and in Japan, Germany, S Africa and France. *Classical ballets include:* La Bayadère, Coppélia, Daphnis and Chloe, Giselle, Nutcracker, Raymonda, The Seasons, Sleeping Beauty, Swan Lake, La Sylphide; *other ballets include:* (choreography by Ashton): Cinderella, The Two Pigeons, La Fille Mal Gardée, Les Rendezvous, The Dream, Lament of the Waves, Symphonic Variations, Birthday Offering; (Balanchine): Apollo, Prodigal Son, Serenade, The Four Temperaments, Agon, Tchaikovsky Pas de Deux; (Béjart): Gaîté Parisienne, Webern Opus 5, Songs of a Wayfarer, Le Concours; (Bintley): Night Moves, Homage to Chopin, The Swan of Tuonela; (Cranko): Brouillards, Pineapple Poll, The Taming of the Shrew, Onegin; (Darrell): The Tales of Hoffmann; (de Valois): Checkmate, The Rake's Progress; (Fokine): Les Sylphides, Petrushka; (Hynd): Papillon; (Lander): Etudes; (Lifar): Suite en Blanc; (MacMillan): Concerto, Elite Syncopations, Romeo and Juliet, Quartet, Song of the Earth, Symphony; (Massine): La Boutique Fantasque; (Miller-Ashmole): Snugglepot-and-Cuddlepie; (Nijinska): Les Biches; (Nureyev): Don Quixote; (Robbins): Dances at a Gathering, Requiem Canticles, In the Night, Concert; (Seymour): Intimate Letters, Rashomon; (Samsova): Paquita; (Tetley): Gemini, Laborintus, Orpheus; (van Manen): Grosse Fugue, 5 Tangos; (Wright): Summertide; (Prokovsky): The Three Musketeers; (Seregei): Spartacus. *Recreations:* Moorcroft pottery collection, gardening, fishing. *Address:* c/o Australian Ballet, 2 Kavanagh Street, South Melbourne, Vic 3205, Australia.

ASHMORE, Dr Alick, CBE 1979; Director, Daresbury Laboratory, Science Research Council, 1970–81; *b* 7 Nov. 1920; *s* of Frank Owen Ashmore and Beatrice Maud Swindells; *m* 1947, Eileen Elsie Fuller; two *s* three *d. Educ:* King Edward VII Sch., Lytham; King's Coll., London. Experimental Officer, RRDE, Malvern, 1941–47; Lecturer in physics, University of Liverpool, 1947–59; Queen Mary Coll., London: Reader in experimental physics, 1960–64; Prof. of Nuclear Physics, 1964–70, also Head of Physics Dept, 1968–70. *Publications:* research publications on nuclear and elementary-particle physics in Proc. Phys. Soc., Nuclear Physics, Physical Review. *Recreations:* walking, travel. *Address:* Farnham House, Hesket Newmarket, Wigton, Cumbria CA7 8JG. *T:* (01697) 478414.

ASHMORE, Admiral of the Fleet Sir Edward (Beckwith), GCB 1974 (KCB 1971; CB 1966); DSC 1942; *b* 11 Dec. 1919; *er s* of late Vice-Admiral L. H. Ashmore, CB, DSO and late Tamara Vasilevna Schutt, St Petersburg; *m* 1942, Elizabeth Mary Doveton Sturdee, *d* of late Rear-Admiral Sir Lionel Sturdee, 2nd Bt, CBE; one *s* one *d* (and one *d* decd). *Educ:* RNC, Dartmouth. Served HMS Birmingham, Jupiter, Middleton, 1938–42; qualified in Signals, 1943; Staff of C-in-C Home Fleet, Flag Lieut, 4th Cruiser Sqdn, 1944–45; qualified Interpreter in Russian, 1946; Asst Naval Attaché, Moscow, 1946–47; Squadron Communications Officer, 3rd Aircraft Carrier Squadron, 1950; Commander 1950; comd HMS Alert, 1952–53; Captain 1955; Captain (F) 6th Frigate Sqdn, and CO HMS Blackpool, 1958; Director of Plans, Admiralty and Min. of Defence, 1960–62; Commander British Forces Caribbean Area, 1963–64; Rear-Adm., 1965; Asst Chief of the Defence Staff, Signals, 1965–67; Flag Officer, Second-in-Command, Far East Fleet, 1967–68; Vice-Adm. 1968; Vice-Chief, Naval Staff, 1969–71; Adm. 1970; C-in-C Western Fleet, Sept.-Oct. 1971; C-in-C, Fleet, 1971–74; Chief of Naval Staff and First Sea Lord, 1974–77; First and Principal Naval Aide-de-Camp to the Queen, 1974–77; CDS, Feb.-Aug. 1977. Gov., Suttons Hosp. in Charterhouse, 1976–2000. *Publication:* The Battle and the Breeze: the naval reminiscences of Admiral of the Fleet Sir Edward Ashmore, 1997. *Recreations:* usual.

See also Vice-Adm. Sir P. W. B. Ashmore, Sir John Sykes, Bt.

ASHMORE, Gillian Margaret; Principal, Mulberry Consulting, since 1999; *b* 14 Oct. 1949; *d* of John Oxenham and Joan Oxenham; *m* 1971, Frederick Scott Ashmore; two *s* two *d. Educ:* Walthamstow Hall, Sevenoaks; Winchester Co. High Sch. for Girls; Newnham Coll., Cambridge (BA Hons Hist.). Depts of the Envmt and Tspt, 1971–86; seconded to Housing Corp., 1974; Dep. Dir, Enterprise and Deregulation Unit, Dept of Employment, 1986–87, then DTI, 1987–89; Head, Central Finance Div., Dept of Transport, 1990–92; Dir, Privatisation Studies, BRB, 1992–94; Regl Dir, Govt Office for SE, 1994–98. Chairman: Kingston Victim Support, 1998–; Refugee Housing Assoc., 1999–; Trustee: Metropolitan Housing Assoc., 1999–; Victim Support London, 1999–. Gov., Richmond Adult and Community Coll., 2000–. Associate, Newnham Coll., Cambridge, 1998–. FRSA 1995. *Recreations:* children and all their doings, novels, eating and talking. *Address:* 47 Lower Teddington Road, Hampton Wick, Kingston, Surrey KT1 4HQ.

ASHMORE, Prof. Jonathan Felix, PhD; FRS 1996; Bernard Katz Professor of Biophysics, University College London, since 1996; *b* 16 April 1948; *s* of late Eric Peter Ashmore, theatre director, and Rosalie Sylvia Crutchley, actress; *m* 1974, Sonia Elizabeth Newby; one *s* one *d. Educ:* Westminster; Univ. of Sussex (BSc 1st cl. Mathematical Physics); Imperial Coll., London (PhD); University College London (MSc Physiology). Vis. Scientist, Internat. Centre for Theoretical Physics, Trieste, Italy, 1971–72; Nuffield Biological Scholar, 1972–74; Res. Asst, Dept of Biophysics, UCL, 1974–77; Fulbright Scholar, and Vis. Physiologist, Ophthalmology Dept, Univ. of California, San Francisco, 1977–80; Lectr, Univ. of Sussex, 1980–83; Lectr, 1983–88, Reader in Physiology, 1988–93, Prof. of Biophysics, 1993–96, Univ. of Bristol. G. L. Brown Lectr, Physiological Soc., 1992. Acted in film, A Kid for Two Farthings, 1955. *Publications:* contribs to learned jls on cellular basis of hearing. *Recreation:* travel. *Address:* Department of Physiology, University College London, Gower Street, WC1E 6BT. *T:* (020) 7679 6080, *Fax:* (020) 7387 6368; *e-mail:* j.ashmore@ucl.ac.uk.

ASHMORE, Vice-Adm. Sir Peter (William Beckwith), KCB 1972 (CB 1968); KCVO 1980 (MVO (4th Class) 1948); DSC 1942; Extra Equerry to the Queen, since 1952; *b* 4 Feb. 1921; *yr s* of late Vice-Adm. L. H. Ashmore, CB, DSO and late Tamara Vasilevna Schutt, St Petersburg; *m* 1952, Patricia Moray Buller, *o d* of late Admiral Sir Henry Buller, GCVO, CB and of Lady Hermione Stuart; one *s* three *d. Educ:* Yardley Court; RN Coll., Dartmouth. Midshipman, 1939. Served War of 1939–45, principally in destroyers (despatches); Lieut, 1941; Equerry (temp.) to King George VI, 1946–48; Extra Equerry, 1948; Comdr, 1951; Captain, 1957; Deputy Director, RN Staff Coll., Greenwich, 1957; Captain (F) Dartmouth Training Squadron, 1960–61; Imperial Defence Coll., 1962; Admiralty, Plans Division, 1963; Rear-Adm. 1966; Flag Officer, Admiralty Interview Board, 1966–67; Chief of Staff to C-in-C Western Fleet and to NATO C-in-

C Eastern Atlantic, 1967–69; Vice-Adm. 1969; Chief of Allied Staff, NATO Naval HQ, S Europe, 1970–72, retired 1972. Master of HM's Household, 1973–86. *Recreations:* fishing, golf. *Address:* Netherdowns, Sundridge, near Sevenoaks, Kent TN14 6AR.

See also Adm. of the Fleet Sir E. B. Ashmore.

ASHMORE, Prof. Philip George; Professor of Physical Chemistry, The University of Manchester Institute of Science and Technology, 1963–81, now Professor Emeritus; *b* 5 May 1916; *m* 1943, Ann Elizabeth Scott; three *s* one *d.* *Educ:* Emmanuel Coll., Cambridge. Fellow, Asst Tutor and Dir of Studies of Natural Sciences, Emmanuel Coll., Cambridge, 1949–59; Lecturer in Physical Chem., Univ. of Cambridge, 1953–63; Fellow and Tutor to Advanced Students, Churchill Coll., Cambridge, 1959–63. Vice-Principal Acad. Affairs, UMIST, 1973, 1974. Course Consultant, Open Univ., 1981–85. *Publications:* The Catalysis and Inhibition of Chemical Reactions, 1963; (ed) Reaction Kinetics, 1975; RIC Monographs for Teachers: No 5 and No 9; many papers in: TFS, International Symposium on Combustion, Jl of Catalysis. *Address:* 30 Queen Edith's Way, Cambridge CB1 4PN. *T:* (01223) 248225.

ASHRAWI, Hanan; Member, Palestinian Legislative Council, since 1996; *b* 1946; *m* Emile Ashrawi; two *d.* *Educ:* American Univ., Beirut; Univ. of Virginia. Prof. of English Literature, Chm. of English Dept, and Dean of Arts, Birzeit Univ., West Bank, 1973–90; Dir Gen., Human Rights Instn, Jerusalem. Joined Fatah, PLO; official spokesperson, Palestinian Delegn, 1991–93; Mem., and former Head, Palestinian Independent Commn for Palestinian Republic; Minister of Higher Educn, Palestinian Legislative Council, 1996–98. *Publications:* A Passion for Peace, 1994; This Side of Peace, 1995. *Address:* c/o Palestinian Legislative Council, Jerusalem, West Bank, via Israel.

ASHTON, family name of **Baron Ashton of Hyde**.

ASHTON OF HYDE, 3rd Baron *cr* 1911; **Thomas John Ashton,** TD; Director, Barclays Bank PLC and subsidiary companies, 1969–87; *b* 19 Nov. 1926; *s* of 2nd Baron Ashton of Hyde and Marjorie Nell (*d* 1993), *d* of late Hon. Marshall Jones Brooks; *S* father, 1983; *m* 1957, Pauline Trewlove, *er d* of late Lt-Col R. H. L. Brackenbury, OBE; two *s* two *d.* *Educ:* Eton; New Coll., Oxford (BA 1950, MA 1955). Sen. Exec. Local Dir, Barclays Bank, Manchester, 1968–81. Major retd, Royal Glos Hussars (TA). JP Oxon, 1965–68. *Heir: s* Hon. Thomas Henry Ashton [*b* 18 July 1958; *m* 1987, Emma, *d* of Colin Allinson; four *d*]. *Address:* Fir Farm, Upper Slaughter, Cheltenham GL54 2JR. *Club:* Boodle's.

ASHTON OF UPHOLLAND, Baroness *cr* 1999 (Life Peer), of St Albans in the county of Hertfordshire; **Catherine Margaret Ashton;** Parliamentary Under-Secretary of State, Department for Education and Skills, since 2001; *b* 20 March 1956; *d* of late Harold and Clare Margaret Ashton; *m* 1988, Peter Jon Kellner; one *s* one *d.* *Educ:* Upholland Grammar Sch.; Bedford Coll., Univ. of London (BSc 1977). Admin. Sec., CND, 1977–79; Business Manager, The Coverdale Orgn, 1979–81; Dir of Public Affairs, BITC, 1983–89; freelance policy advr, 1989–98; on secondment from London First to Home Office, 1998–99. Chm., E and N Herts, subseq. Herts, HA, 1998–2001. Vice Pres., Nat. Council for One-Parent Families. Trustee, Verulamium Mus. Chm. Governors, Spencer Jun. Sch., 1999–. *Recreations:* swimming, theatre, retail therapy. *Address:* House of Lords, SW1A 0PW. *Club:* Royal Commonwealth Society.

ASHTON, Anthony Southcliffe; *b* 5 July 1916; *s* of late Prof. Thomas Southcliffe Ashton, FBA, and of Mrs Marion Hague Ashton; *m* 1939, Katharine Marion Louise Vivian; two *d.* *Educ:* Manchester Grammar Sch.; Hertford Coll., Oxford (MA). Economist, Export Credits Guarantee Dept, 1937. Served War of 1939–45, as driver and Lt-Col, RASC. Asst Financial Editor, Manchester Guardian, 1945; Dep. Asst Dir of Marketing, NCB, 1947; Manager, various depts of Vacuum Oil Co. (later Mobil Oil Co.), 1949; attended Advanced Management Programme, Harvard Business Sch., 1961; Treasurer, 1961, Finance Director, 1967–69, Esso Petroleum Co.; Mem. Bd (Finance and Corporate Planning), Post Office Corp., 1970–73. Director: Tyzack and Partners Ltd, 1974–79; Provincial Insce Co., 1974–86. Member: Shipbuilding Industry Bd, 1967–71; Council of Manchester Business Sch., 1968–81; Dir, Oxford Univ. Business Summer Sch., 1974 (Mem., Steering Cttee, 1978–81). Trustee: PO Pension Fund, 1975–83; Tyzack Employee Trust, 1979–84; Dir, Exeter Trust, 1980–86 (Chm., 1982–86). Vice-Pres., Hertford Coll. Soc., 1977–. *Club:* Army and Navy.

ASHTON, Rt Rev. Cyril Guy; *see* Doncaster, Bishop of.

ASHTON, George Arthur, CEng; FIMechE; engineering and management consultant, retired; *b* 27 Nov. 1921; *s* of Lewis and Mary Ashton; *m* 1st, 1948, Joan Rutter (decd); one *s*; 2nd, 1978, Pauline Jennifer Margett. *Educ:* Llanidloes Grammar Sch.; Birmingham Central Tech. Coll. Student Engrg Apprentice, Austin Motor Co., 1939–42. HM Forces, 1943–47 (Major, REME). Works Dir, Tubes Ltd, 1958; Tech. Dir, 1962, Dep. Man. Dir, 1966, TI Steel Tube Div.; Dir, Tube Investments, 1969; Man. Dir, Machine Div., 1974, Technical Dir and Business Area Chm., 1978–84, TI Group plc; Chm., Seamless Tubes Ltd, 1983–86. Dir, A. Lee & Sons plc, 1981–91. Dep. Chm., Steering Cttee, WINTECH, Welsh Develt Agency, 1984–87. Pres., BISPA, 1974–75; Vice-Pres., AMTRI, 1986– (Chm. Council, 1982–86). FRSA 1981. *Recreations:* gardening, walking, theatre-going. *Address:* Barn Cottage, Longford, Ashbourne, Derbys DE6 3DT. *T:* (01335) 330561. *Club:* Royal Over-Seas League.

ASHTON, John; HM Diplomatic Service; Head of Environment Policy (formerly Environment, Science and Energy) Department, Foreign and Commonwealth Office, since 1998; *b* 7 Nov. 1956; *s* of Prof. John Ashton and Prof. Heather Ashton; *m* 1983, Kao Fengning, (Judy); one *s.* *Educ:* Royal Grammar Sch., Newcastle upon Tyne; St John's Coll., Cambridge (MA). Radio Astronomy Gp, New Cavendish Lab., Cambridge, 1977–78; FCO 1978; Science Officer, Peking, 1981–84; Head, China Section, FCO, 1984–86; Cabinet Office, 1986–88; Rome, 1988–93; Dep. Political Advr to Governor, Hong Kong, 1993–97; Vis. Fellow, Green Coll., Oxford, 1997–98. Member, Advisory Board: Climate Inst., Washington, 1998–; Tyndall Centre for Climate Change Res., 2000–. FRSA. *Recreations:* cricket, nature. *Address:* c/o Foreign and Commonwealth Office, SW1A 2AH. *Clubs:* Kew Cricket; Kowloon Cricket.

ASHTON, Prof. John Richard, CBE 2000; Professor of Public Health Policy and Strategy, University of Liverpool, since 1993; Regional Director of Public Health and Regional Medical Officer, North West Region, NHS Executive, Department of Health (formerly North West Regional Health Authority), since 1994; *b* Liverpool, 27 May 1947; *s* of Edward Ashton and Irene Ashton (*née* Pettit); *m* 1968, Pamela Scott; three *s.* *Educ:* Quarry Bank High Sch., Liverpool; Univ. of Newcastle upon Tyne (MB BS 1970); London Sch. of Hygiene and Trop. Medicine (MSc Soc. Med. 1978). House physician and surgeon, Newcastle Univ. Hosps, 1970–71; Registrar in Psychiatry and Family Practitioner, Newcastle, 1971–75; Lectr in Primary Care, Southampton Univ., 1975–76; Sen. Lectr in Preventive Medicine, LSHTM, 1980–82; Sen. Lectr in Public Health, Univ. of Liverpool, 1983–93; Regl Dir of Public Health and Regl MO, Mersey, 1993–94. Visiting Professor: Valencia Inst. Public Health, 1988; Liverpool John Moores Univ., 1998; Professorial Fellow, Liverpool Sch. of Trop. Medicine, 1994. Advr on Urban Health, Health Policy and Public Health Educn, WHO. Member: Liverpool Med. Instn, 1990–; Manchester Med. Soc., 1995–. Member: John Snow Soc.; Duncan Soc., 1998–. *Publications:* Everyday Psychiatry, 1980; The New Public Health, 1988; Esmedune 2000, 1988; Healthy Cities, 1992; (ed) The Epidemiological Imagination, 1994; The Pool of Life, 1997; contrib. articles on medical, public health and social issues. *Recreations:* Liverpool FC, walking, cycling, keeping chickens, dogs, contributing to regenerating Liverpool. *Address:* 15 Church Road, Much Woolton, Liverpool L25 5JE. *T:* (0151) 428 1563.

ASHTON, John Russell, CB 1988; retired engineer; *b* 28 Feb. 1925; *s* of Jessie Florence and John William Ashton; *m* 1951, Isobel Burbury; two *d.* *Educ:* Canberra Grammar School; Sydney University. BE (Civil Engineering). Hydro-Electric Commission, Tasmania: Engineer, 1947–54; System Development Engineer, 1954–71; Dep. Engineer for Civil Investigation, 1971–72; Asst to Comr, 1972–77; Commissioner, 1977–87. In-service training Fellowship with US Bureau of Reclamation, 1960. *Recreations:* golf, photography, carpentry, gardening. *Address:* 3 Lanrick Court, Lindisfarne, Tasmania 7015, Australia. *T:* (3) 62438758.

ASHTON, Joseph William; journalist; *b* 9 Oct. 1933; *s* of Arthur and Nellie Ashton, Sheffield; *m* 1957, Margaret Patricia Lee; one *d.* *Educ:* High Storrs Grammar Sch.; Rotherham Technical Coll. Engineering Apprentice, 1949–54; RAF National Service, 1954–56; Cost Control Design Engineer, 1956–68; Sheffield City Councillor, 1962–69. MP (Lab) Bassetlaw Div. of Notts, Nov. 1968–2001. PPS to Sec. of State for Energy, formerly Sec. of State for Industry, 1975–76; an Asst Govt Whip, 1976–77; Opposition Spokesman on Energy, 1979–81. Member, Select Committee: on Trade and Industry, 1987–92; on Home Affairs, 1989–92; on Nat. Heritage, 1992–97; on Modernising the House, 1997–98; Chm., Parly All-Party Football Cttee, 1992–2001. Dir, Sheffield Wednesday, 1990–99. Columnist for: Sheffield Star, 1970–75, 1979–80; Labour Weekly, 1971–82; Daily Star, 1979–87; Sunday People, 1987–88; Plus magazine, 1988–89. Columnist of the Year, What the Papers Say, Granada TV, 1984. *Publications:* Grass Roots, 1977; A Majority of One (stage play), 1981. *Recreations:* reading, do-it-yourself, motoring, travel, films, theatre. *Address:* 16 Ranmoor Park Road, Sheffield S10 3GX. *T:* (0114) 230 7175.

ASHTON, Kenneth Bruce; General Secretary, National Union of Journalists, 1977–85; *b* 9 Nov. 1925; *m* 1955, Amy Anne Sidebotham; four *s.* *Educ:* Latymer Upper School. Served Army, 1942–46. Reporter: Hampstead and Highgate Express, 1947–50; Devon and Somerset News, Mansfield Reporter, Sheffield Star, 1950–58; Sub-Editor, Sheffield Telegraph, Daily Express, London and Daily Mail, Manchester, 1958–75. Nat. Exec. Cttee Mem., NUJ, 1968–75, Pres., 1975, Regional Organiser, 1975–77. Member: TUC Printing Industries' Cttee, 1975–86; Printing and Publishers' Industry Training Bd, 1977–83; British Cttee, Journalists in Europe, 1980–86; Communications Adv. Cttee, UK Nat. Commn for Unesco, 1981–86; consultative Mem., Press Council, 1977–80; Pres., Internat. Fedn of Journalists, 1982–86.

ASHTON, Prof. Robert, PhD; Professor of English History, University of East Anglia, 1963–89, now Emeritus; *b* 21 July 1924; *s* of late Joseph and late Edith F. Ashton; *m* 1946, Margaret Alice Sedgwick; two *d.* *Educ:* Magdalen Coll. Sch., Oxford; University Coll., Southampton (1942–43, 1946–49); London Sch. of Economics (1949–52). BA 1st Cl. hons (London) 1949; PhD (London) 1953; Asst Lecturer in Economic History, Univ. of Nottingham, 1952; Lecturer, 1954; Senior Lecturer, 1961; Vis. Associate Prof. in History, Univ. of California, Berkeley, 1962–63; Prof. of English History, 1963, and Dean of Sch. of English Studies, 1964–67, Univ. of East Anglia. Vis. Fellow, All Souls Coll., Oxford, 1973–74 and 1987; James Ford Special Lectr in History, Oxford, 1982; Leverhulme Emeritus Fellow, 1989–91. FRHistS 1960 (Vice-Pres., 1983–86). *Publications:* The Crown and the Money Market, 1603–1640, 1960; Charles I and the City, in Essays in the Economic and Social History of Tudor and Stuart England in honour of R. H. Tawney (ed F. J. Fisher), 1961; James I by his Contemporaries, 1969; The Civil War and the Class Struggle, in The English Civil War and After 1642–1658 (ed R. H. Parry), 1970; The English Civil War: Conservatism and Revolution 1603–49, 1978, 2nd edn 1989; The City and the Court 1603–1643, 1979; Reformation and Revolution 1558–1660, 1984; Counter-Revolution: the second Civil War and its origins, 1646–8, 1994; articles in learned periodicals. *Recreations:* music, looking at old buildings, exploring Italy and things Italian, wine. *Address:* The Manor House, Brundall, Norwich NR13 5JY. *T:* (01603) 713368.

ASHTON, Prof. Rosemary Doreen, OBE 1999; FBA 2000; Professor of English, University College London, since 1991; *b* 11 April 1947; *d* of late David Thomson and of Doreen Sidley Thomson (*née* Rose); *m* 1971, Gerard Ashton (*d* 1999); two *s* one *d.* *Educ:* Univ. of Aberdeen (MA Hons English and German 1969); Newnham Coll., Cambridge (PhD 1974). Temp. Lectr, English Dept, Univ. of Birmingham, 1973–74; Lectr, 1974–86, Reader, 1986–91, English Dept, UCL. FRSL 1999; Founding Fellow, English Assoc., 1999. *Publications:* The German Idea: four English writers and the reception of German thought 1800–1860, 1980; Little Germany: exile and asylum in Victorian England, 1986; The Mill on the Floss: a natural history, 1990; G. H. Lewes: a life, 1991; The Life of Samuel Taylor Coleridge: a critical biography, 1996; George Eliot: a life, 1996; Thomas and Jane Carlyle: portrait of a marriage, 2002. *Recreations:* gardening, table tennis, listening to music. *Address:* English Department, University College London, Gower Street, WC1E 6BT. *T:* (020) 7419 3143.

ASHTON, Roy; a Recorder of the Crown Court, 1979–98; barrister-at-law; *b* 20 Oct. 1928; *s* of Charles and Lilian Ashton; *m* 1954, Brenda Alice Dales; one *s* one *d.* *Educ:* Boston Grammar Sch.; Nottingham Univ. (LLB Hons). National Service, Directorate of Legal Services, RAF, 1951–53. Called to the Bar, Lincoln's Inn, 1954. Dep. Chairman, Agricultural Land Tribunal, 1978–. Mem., Bishops Stortford UDC, 1961–64. *Recreations:* reading, horse racing, film collecting. *Address:* c/o 22 Albion Place, Northampton NN1 1UD. *Club:* Northampton and County.

ASHTON, Ruth Mary, (Mrs E. F. Henschel), OBE 1991; RN, RM, MTD; non-executive Director and Vice-Chairman, Bromley Primary Care NHS Trust, since 2001; management and health care consultant; *b* 27 March 1939; *d* of Leigh Perry Ashton and Marion Lucy Ashton (*née* Tryon); *m* 1984, E. Fred Henschel. *Educ:* Kenya High Sch. for Girls; Clarendon Sch. (lately Abergele). London Hosp. and Queen Mother's Hosp., Glasgow; High Coombe Midwife Teachers' Training College (RN 1964; RM 1967; MTD 1970). Staff Midwife and Midwifery Sister, Queen Mother's Hosp., Glasgow, 1967–69; Nursing Officer and Midwifery Tutor, King's College Hosp., 1971–75; Tutor, 1975–79, Professional Officer, 1979, Gen. Sec., 1980–94, Royal College of Midwives. Non-executive Director: Optimum Health Services NHS Trust, 1994–99; Community Health S London NHS Trust, 1999–2000. Temp. Advr on Midwifery, WHO, 1995. Treas., Internat. Confedn of Midwives, 1997–. Temp. Prof. March of Dimes, Los Angeles, 1982. ACIArb 1995. OStJ 1988. *Publications:* midwifery related articles. *Recreations:*

gardening, sailing, travel. *Address:* c/o National Westminster Bank, PO Box 192, 116 Fenchurch Street, EC3M 5AN. *T:* and *Fax:* (home) (020) 8851 7403; *e-mail:* rfhens.rafh@virgin.net. *Club:* Queenborough Yacht.

ASHTON, William Michael Allingham, MBE 1978; Musical Director, National Youth Jazz Orchestra of Great Britain, since 1968; *b* Blackpool, 6 Dec. 1936; *s* of Eric Sandiford Ashton and Zilla Dorothea (*née* Miles); *m* 1966, Kay Carol Watkins; two *s* one *d. Educ:* Rossall Sch., Fleetwood; St Peter's Coll., Oxford (BA Hons Mod. Langs 1961; DipEd 1962). Nat. Service, RAF, 1955–57. Professional musician, 1962–63; teacher of French in London schs, 1963–73. Founded London Schs Jazz Orch., 1965; became Nat. Youth Jazz Orch., 1968. Editor, News from NYJO, 1988–. Appeared in Royal Variety Perf., 1978; visits to America, Russia, Australasia, France, Poland, Portugal, Germany, Bulgaria, Turkey, Malta, Spain, Italy, etc; appearances at festivals, film premières, etc. Numerous recordings. Member: Arts Sub-cttee, Internat. Year of the Child, 1979; Cttee, Assoc. British Jazz Musicians, 1988–. Fellow, City of Leeds Coll. of Music, 1995. BP ABSA Award, 1991; Music Retailers Assoc. Annual Awards for Excellence, 1984, 1990; NYJO voted Best British Big Band, British Jazz Awards, 1993, 1995 and 1998; BBC R2 Award for services to British jazz, 1995; Silver Medal for Jazz, Musicians' Co., 1996. *Recreations:* song writing, swimming, reading. *Address:* 11 Victor Road, Harrow, Middx HA2 6PT. *T:* (020) 8863 2717, *Fax:* (020) 8863 8685; *e-mail:* bill.ashton@virgin.net.

ASHTOWN, 7th Baron *cr* 1800; **Nigel Clive Cosby Trench,** KCMG 1976 (CMG 1966); HM Diplomatic Service, retired; *b* 27 Oct. 1916; *s* of Clive Newcome Trench (*d* 1964), *g s* of 2nd Baron, and Kathleen (*d* 1979), 2nd *d* of Major Ivar MacIvor, CIE; *S* cousin, 1990; *m* 1st, 1939, Marcelle Catherine Clotterbooke Patyn (*d* 1994); one *s*; 2nd, 1997, Mary, Princess of Pless, *d* of late Lt Col and Mrs R. G. E. Minchin. *Educ:* Eton; Univ. of Cambridge. Served in KRRC, 1940–46 (despatches). Appointed a Member of the Foreign (subseq. Diplomatic) Service, 1946; Lisbon, 1946; First Secretary, 1948; returned Foreign Office, 1949; First Secretary (Commercial) Lima, 1952; transf. Foreign Office, 1955; Counsellor, Tokyo, 1961; Counsellor, Washington, 1963; Cabinet Office, 1967; HM Ambassador to Korea, 1969–71; CS Selection Board, 1971–73; Ambassador to Portugal, 1974–76. Mem., Police, Prison and Fire Service Selection Bds, 1977–86. Sungrye Medal, Order of Diplomatic Service Merit (Korea), 1984. *Heir: s* Hon. Roderick Nigel Godolphin Trench [*b* 17 Nov. 1944; *m* 1st, 1967, Janet (*d* 1971), *d* of Harold Hamilton-Faulkner; one *s*; 2nd, 1973, Susan Barbara, *d* of L. F. Day, FRCS, DLO; one *d*]. *Address:* 4 Kensington Court Gardens, Kensington Court Place, W8 5QE.

ASHURST, Kenneth William Stewart; Chief Executive and Clerk, Essex County Council, since 1995; *b* 19 May 1945; *s* of Kenneth Latham Ashurst, OBE and Helen Ferguson Ashurst (*née* Rae); *m* 1984, Catherine Mary Sample; two *s* one *d. Educ:* Royal Grammar Sch., Newcastle upon Tyne; King Edward VI Grammar Sch., Lichfield; Exeter Coll., Oxford Univ. (MA); Guildford Coll. of Law; Birmingham Univ. (MSocSc). Trainee solicitor, Leicester and Newcastle upon Tyne CBCs, 1967–68; Assistant Solicitor: Newcastle upon Tyne, 1968–71; Cumberland CC, 1972–73; Asst Co. Clerk, Cumbria CC, 1973–79; Dep. Co. Sec., 1979–81, Co. Solicitor and Dep. Co. Clerk, 1981–85, Suffolk CC; Dep. Chief Exec. and Clerk, Essex CC, 1985–94. Clerk to: Essex Police Authy, 1995–; Essex Fire Authy, 1998–; Essex Lieutenancy, 1995–; River Crouch Harbour Authy, 1995–; Secretary: Lord Chancellor's Adv. Cttee in Essex, 1995–; Stansted Airport Consultative Cttee, 1995–; Mem., Essex TEC Bd, 1995–. Law Society: Council Mem., 1989–97; Chm., Local Govt Gp, 1986–87. Mem. Council, Industrial Soc., 1997–, Dir, Year of Opera and Musical Theatre, 1996–97. FIMgt 1982; FRSA 1998. *Recreations:* family, wine tasting. *Address:* Essex County Council, PO Box 11, County Hall, Chelmsford CM1 1LX. *T:* (01245) 430015.

ASHWIN, Mary Christine; *see* Vitoria, M. C.

ASHWORTH, Prof. Andrew John, PhD, DCL; FBA 1993; Vinerian Professor of English Law, University of Oxford, since 1997; Fellow of All Souls College, Oxford, since 1997; *b* 11 Oct. 1947; *s* of late Clifford Ashworth and of Amy (*née* Ogden); *m* 1971, Gillian Frisby (separated); two *d. Educ:* London Sch. of Economics (LLB 1968); New Coll., Oxford (BCL 1970; DCL 1993); Manchester Univ. (PhD 1973). Lectr, then Sen. Lectr, in Law, Manchester Univ., 1970–78; Fellow and Tutor in Law, Worcester Coll., Oxford, 1978–88; Edmund-Davies Prof. of Criminal Law and Criminal Justice, KCL, 1988–97. Mem., Sentencing Adv. Panel, 1999–. Editor, Criminal Law Rev., 1975–99. Hon. QC 1997. Hon. LLD De Montfort, 1998. *Publications:* Sentencing and Penal Policy, 1983; Principles of Criminal Law, 1991, 3rd edn 1999; Sentencing and Criminal Justice, 1992, 3rd edn 2000; The Criminal Process, 1994, 2nd edn 1998; (with Ben Emmerson) Human Rights and Criminal Proceedings, 2001. *Recreations:* bridge, golf, travel. *Address:* All Souls College, Oxford OX1 4AL.

ASHWORTH, Prof. Graham William, CBE 1980; DL; Professor of Urban Environmental Studies, University of Salford, 1973–87, part-time Research Professor, since 1987; Chairman: Environmental Campaign Ltd, since 2000; Going for Green, since 1994 (Chief Executive, 1994–2000); *b* 14 July 1935; *s* of Frederick William Ashworth and Ivy Alice Ashworth; *m* 1960, Gwyneth Mai Morgan-Jones; three *d. Educ:* Devonport High Sch., Plymouth; Univ. of Liverpool (Master of Civic Design, BArch). RIBA, PPRTPI, FRSA, FInstEnvSci, FIMgt. LCC (Hook New Town Project), 1959–61; consultancy with Graeme Shankland, 1961–64; architect to Civic Trust, 1964–65; Dir, Civic Trust for North-West, 1965–73 (Chm., Exec. Cttee, 1973–87); Director: Univ. of Salford Environmental Inst., 1978–87; CAMPUS (Campaign to Promote Univ. of Salford), 1981–87; Dir Gen., Keep Britain Tidy, then Tidy Britain, Gp, 1987–2000. Member: Skeffington Cttee on Public Participation in Planning, 1969; North-West Adv. Council of BBC, 1970–75 (Chm.); NW Economic Planning Council (and Sub-gp Chm.), 1968–79; Countryside Commn, 1974–77; Merseyside Urban Develt Corp., 1981–92; (non-exec.) North Western Electricity Bd, 1985–88; Chm., Ravenhead Renaissance, 1988–. Governor, Northern Baptist Coll., 1966–82; President: RTPI, 1973–74; Foundn for Envmtl Educn in Europe, 1988–; Chm., Instn of Environmental Sciences, 1980–82. Member: Council, St George's House, Windsor, 1982–88; Council, Baptist Union, 1983– (Pres., 2000–01). Trustee, Manchester Mus. of Science and Industry, 1988–90. Editor, Internat. Jl of Environmental Educn, 1981–. DL Lancs 1991. *Publications:* An Encyclopædia of Planning, 1973; Britain in Bloom, 1991; The Role of Local Government in Environmental Protection, 1992. *Recreations:* gardening, painting, church and social work. *Address:* Manor Court Farm, Preston New Road, Samlesbury, Preston PR5 0UP. *Clubs:* Athenæum, National Liberal.

ASHWORTH, Ian Edward; Planning Inspector, Department of the Environment, 1987–95; *b* 3 March 1930; *s* of late William Holt and Cicely Ashworth, Rochdale; *m* Pauline, *er d* of late Maurice James Heddle, MBE, JP, and Gladys Heddle, Westcliff-on-Sea; two *s* one *d. Educ:* Manchester Grammar Sch.; The Queen's Coll., Oxford (BCL, MA). Admitted Solicitor, 1956; FGA 1983. Asst Solicitor, Rochdale, 1956–58; Dep. Town Clerk, Dep. Clerk of Peace, Canterbury, 1958–63; Town Clerk, Clerk of Peace, Deal, 1963–66; Town Clerk, Rugby, 1966–70; Circuit Administrator, Western Circuit, Lord Chancellor's Office (Under Sec.), 1970–87. *Recreations:* music, gemmology, gardening. *Address:* Westdale Edge, Beer Road, Seaton, Devon EX12 2PT. *T:* (01297) 21212. *Club:* Oxford and Cambridge.

ASHWORTH, James Louis, FIMechE, FIEE, ARTC (Salford); Full-Time Member for Operations, Central Electricity Generating Board, 1966–70, retired; *b* 7 March 1906; *s* of late James and late Janet Ashworth; *m* 1931, Clara Evelyn Arnold (*d* 1992); one *s* two *d. Educ:* Stockport Grammar Sch.; Salford Royal Coll. of Technology. Apprenticeship with Mirrlees, Bickerton & Day Ltd, Stockport (Diesel Oil Engine Manufrs), 1924–29; Metro-Vickers Electrical Co. Ltd, 1929; Manchester Corp. Elec. Dept, Stuart Street Gen. Stn, 1930–32; Hull Corp. Elec. Dept, 1932–35; Halifax Corp. Elec. Dept, 1935–40; Mersey Power Co. Ltd, Runcorn, 1940–48; British Elec. Authority, N West: Chief Generation Engr (O), 1948–57; Dep. Divisional Controller, 1957–58; Central Elec. Gen. Bd, N West, Merseyside and N Wales Region: Dep. Regional Dir, 1958–62; Regional Dir, 1962–66. *Recreations:* gardening, photography, travel, reading. *Address:* Chase Cottage, 23 The Chase, Reigate, Surrey RH2 7DJ. *T:* (01737) 61279.

ASHWORTH, Dr John Michael, FIBiol; Chairman, British Library Board, 1996–2001; *b* 27 Nov. 1938; *s* of late Jack Ashworth and late Constance Mary Ousman; *m* 1st, 1963, Ann Knight (*d* 1985); one *s* three *d*; 2nd, 1988, Auriol Stevens, *qv. Educ:* West Buckland Sch., N Devon; Exeter Coll., Oxford (MA, DSc; Hon. Fellow, 1983); Leicester Univ. (PhD). FIBiol 1974. Dept of Biochemistry, Univ. of Leicester: Res. Demonstr, 1961–63; Lectr, 1963–71; Reader, 1971–73; Prof. of Biology, Univ. of Essex, 1974–79 (on secondment to Cabinet Office, 1976–79); Under-Sec., Cabinet Office, 1979–81 and Chief Scientist, Central Policy Review Staff, 1976–81; Vice-Chancellor, Univ. of Salford, 1981–90; Dir, LSE, 1990–96. Harkness Fellow of Commonwealth Fund, NY, at Brandeis Univ. and Univ. of Calif, 1965–67. NEDO: Chm., Information Technology EDC, 1983–86; Mem., Electronics EDC, 1983–86. Chairman: Nat. Accreditation Council for Certification Bodies, BSI, 1984–88; NCC, 1983–92. Director: Granada TV, 1987–89; Granada Group, 1990–; J. Sainsbury, 1993–97; London First, 1993–98. Mem. Council, Inst. of Cancer Res., 2000–. Colworth Medal, Biochem. Soc., 1972. *Publications:* Cell Differentiation, 1972; (with J. Dee) The Slime Moulds, 1976; over 100 pubns in prof. jls on biochem., genet., cell biolog. and educnl topics. *Recreation:* sailing. *Address:* Garden House, Wivenhoe, Essex CO7 9BD. *Club:* Wivenhoe Sailing.

ASHWORTH, Peter Anthony Frank; Director, Leeds Permanent Building Society, 1971–92 (President, 1978); *b* 24 Aug. 1935; *s* of Peter Ormerod and Dorothy Christine Ashworth; *m* 1964, Elisabeth Crompton; one *s* one *d. Educ:* Leeds Grammar School. Articled to Hollis & Webb, Chartered Surveyors, Leeds (now Weatherall, Green & Smith), 1953–56; Partner, 1961–80. *Recreations:* golf, gardening. *Address:* 4 Bridge Paddock, Collingham, Wetherby LS22 5BN. *T:* (01937) 572953. *Club:* Alwoodley Golf (Leeds).

ASHWORTH, Piers; QC 1973; a Recorder of the Crown Court, 1974–96; *b* 27 May 1931; *s* of late Tom and Mollie Ashworth; *m* 1st, 1959, Iolene Jennifer (marr. diss. 1978), *yr d* of late W. G. Foxley; three *s* one *d*; 2nd, 1980, Elizabeth, *er d* of late A. J. S. Aston. *Educ:* Christ's Hospital; Pembroke Coll., Cambridge (scholar). Commnd Royal Signals, 1951. BA (Cantab) 1955; Harmsworth Law Scholar, 1956; called to Bar, Middle Temple, 1956, Bencher, 1984; Midland and Oxford circuit. Chm., Bar Mutual Indemnity Fund Ltd, 1987–98. Gov. and Almoner, Christ's Hosp, 1986–. *Recreations:* sailing, tennis, bridge. *Address:* 2 Harcourt Buildings, Temple, EC4Y 9DB. *T:* (020) 7583 9020.

ASKE, Sir Robert John Bingham, 3rd Bt *cr* 1922; *b* 12 March 1941; *s* of late Robert Edward Aske (*yr s* of Sir Robert Aske, 1st Bt) and of Joan, *o d* of late Capt. Eric Bingham Ackerley; *S* uncle, 2001. *Educ:* King's Sch., Canterbury. *Heir:* none. *Address:* 5 Bicton Place, Exeter EX1 2PF.

ASKEW, Barry Reginald William; journalist, broadcaster and public relations consultant; *b* 13 Dec. 1936; *s* of late Reginald Ewart Askew and Jane Elizabeth Askew; *m* 1st, 1958, June Roberts (marr. diss. 1978), *d* of late Vernon and Betty Roberts; one *s* one *d*; 2nd, 1980, Deborah Parker (marr. diss. 1989), *d* of Harold and Enid Parker. *Educ:* Lady Manners Grammar Sch., Bakewell, Derbys. Trainee reporter upwards, Derbyshire Times, 1952–57; Reporter and sub-ed., Sheffield Telegraph, 1957–59; reporter, feature writer and broadcaster, Raymonds News Agency, Derby, 1959–61; Editor, Matlock Mercury, 1961–63; Industrial Correspondent, Asst Ed., Dep. Ed., Sheffield Telegraph, later Morning Telegraph, Sheffield, 1964–68; Associate Ed., The Star, Sheffield, 1968; Editor, 1968–81, Dir, 1978–81, Lancashire Evening Post; Editor, News of the World, 1981. Presenter and anchor man: ITV, 1970–81; BBC Radio 4, 1971–72; BBC 1, 1972; BBC 2, 1972–76. Consultant in TV, radio, PR and commerce, 1982–95. Mem., Davies Cttee to reform hosp. complaints procedures in UK, 1971–73. Campaigning Journalist of 1971, IPC Nat. Press Awards; Journalist of 1977, British Press Awards; Crime Reporter of 1977, Witness Box Awards. *Recreations:* Rugby, chess, reading military history, golf. *Address:* 28A Redcar Avenue, Ingol, Preston, Lancs PR2 3YY. *T:* (01772) 731817.

ASKEW, Sir Bryan, Kt 1989; Personnel Director, Samuel Smith Old Brewery (Tadcaster), 1982–95; Chairman, Yorkshire Regional Health Authority, 1983–94; *b* 18 Aug. 1930; *s* of John Pinkney Askew and Matilda Askew; *m* 1955, Millicent Rose Holder; two *d. Educ:* Wellfield Grammar Sch., Wingate, Co. Durham; Fitzwilliam Coll., Cambridge (MA Hons History). ICI Ltd, 1952–59; Consett Iron Co. Ltd (later part of British Steel Corporation), 1959–71; own consultancy, 1971–74; Samuel Smith Old Brewery (Tadcaster), 1974–95. Chm., Advanced Digital Telecom Ltd, 1997–99. Member, Consett UDC, 1967–71; contested (C) General Elections: Penistone, 1964 and 1966; York, 1970. Mem., Duke of Edinburgh's Third Commonwealth Study Conf., Australia, 1968. Mem., Working Gp on Young People and Alcohol, Home Office Standing Conf. on Crime Prevention, 1987. Mem. Court, 1985–, Mem. Council, 1988–2000, Univ. of Leeds. FRSA 1986 (Chm., Yorks Region, 1997–99); FRSocMed 1988. Hon. LLD Hull, 1992. *Recreations:* listening to music, reading, writing to The Times. *Address:* 27 Golf Links Avenue, Tadcaster LS24 9HF. *T:* (01937) 833216; Flat 1, The Manor House, Alnmouth, Northumberland NE66 2RJ. *T:* (01665) 830047.

ASKEW, Rev. Canon Reginald James Albert; Dean of King's College, London, 1988–93; Canon Emeritus, Salisbury Cathedral, since 1988; *b* 16 May 1928; *s* of late Paul Askew and Amy Wainwright; *m* 1953, Kate, *yr d* of late Rev. Henry Townsend Wigley; one *s* two *d. Educ:* Harrow; Corpus Christi Coll., Cambridge (MA); Lincoln Theological College. Curate of Highgate, 1957–61; Tutor and Chaplain of Wells Theol Coll., 1961–65, Vice-Principal 1966–69; Priest Vicar of Wells Cath., 1961–69; Vicar of Christ Church, Lancaster Gate, London, 1969–73; Principal, Salisbury and Wells Theol Coll., 1973–87; Canon of Salisbury Cathedral and Prebendary of Grantham Borealis, 1975–87. Proctor in Convocation for London Univ., Gen. Synod of C of E, 1990–93. Chaplain, Merchant Taylors' Co., 1996–97. Trustee, Christian Evidence Soc., 1988–. Mem., Corrymeela Community, 1990–. Pres., Bath and Wells Clerical Soc., 1998–. *Publications:* The Tree of Noah, 1971; Muskets and Altars: Jeremy Taylor and the last of the Anglicans, 1997. *Recreations:* music, gardening, making wood-cuts and lino-cuts. *Address:* Carters

Cottage, North Wootton, Shepton Mallet, Somerset BA4 4AF. *T:* (01749) 890728. *Club:* Athenæum.

ASKONAS, Brigitte Alice, PhD; FRS 1973; with Institute of Molecular Medicine (Molecular Immunology), John Radcliffe Hospital, Oxford, since 1989 (part-time); Visiting Professor, Department of Biology, Imperial College of Science, Technology and Medicine, since 1995 (part-time); *b* 1 April 1923; *d* of late Charles F. Askonas and Rose Askonas. *Educ:* McGill Univ., Montreal (BSc, MSc); Cambridge Univ. (PhD; Hon. Fellow, New Hall and Girton Coll.). Research student, Sch. of Biochemistry, Univ. of Cambridge, 1949–52; Immunology Div., NIMR, 1953–89 (Head of Div., 1977–88); Dept of Bacteriology and Immunology, Harvard Med. Sch., Boston, 1961–62; Basel Inst. for Immunology, Basel, Switzerland, 1971–72. Vis. Prof., Dept of Medicine, St Mary's Hosp. Med. Sch., London, 1988–94. Mem. Council, Royal Soc., 1988–90 (Vice Pres., 1989–90). Founder FMedSci 1998; FIC 2000. Hon. Member: Amer. Soc. of Immunology; Soc. française d'Immunologie; German Ges. für Immunologie. Hon. DSc McGill, 1987. *Publications:* contrib. scientific papers to various biochemical and immunological jls and books. *Recreations:* art, travel. *Address:* 23 Hillside Gardens, N6 5SU. *T:* (020) 8348 6792; Department of Biology, Imperial College of Science, Technology and Medicine, Sir Alexander Fleming Building, Imperial College Road, SW7 2AZ. *T:* (020) 7594 5405, *Fax:* (020) 7584 2056.

ASLET, Clive William; Editor, Country Life, since 1993 (Deputy Editor, 1989–92); Editor in Chief, Country Life Books, since 1994; *b* 15 Feb. 1955; *s* of Kenneth and Monica Aslet; *m* 1980, Naomi Roth; two *s. Educ:* King's College Sch., Wimbledon; Peterhouse, Cambridge. Joined Country Life, 1977, Architectural Editor, 1984–88; Ed. in Chief, New Eden, 1999. Dir, Country and Leisure Media Ltd, 1999–. Founding Hon. Sec., Thirties Soc., 1979–87. Gov., St Peter's Eaton Sq. C of E Sch., 1999–. FRSA. *Publications:* The Last Country Houses, 1982; (with Alan Powers) The National Trust Book of the English House, 1985; Quinlan Terry, the Revival of Architecture, 1986; The American Country House, 1990; Countryblast, 1991; (introd.) The American Houses of Robert A. M. Stern, 1991; Anyone for England? a search for British identity, 1997; (with Derry Moore) The House of Lords, 1998; The Story of Greenwich, 1999; Greenwich Millennium, 2000. *Recreations:* the arts, books, hunting. *Address:* c/o Country Life, King's Reach Tower, Stamford Street, SE1 9LS. *T:* (020) 7261 6969. *Club:* Garrick.

ASPEL, Michael Terence, OBE 1993; broadcaster and writer; *b* 12 Jan. 1933; *s* of late Edward and of Violet Aspel; *m* 1st, 1957, Dian; one *s* (and one *s* decd); 2nd, 1962, Ann; twin *s* and *d;* 3rd 1977, Elizabeth; two *s. Educ:* Emanuel School. Tea boy, publishers, 1949–51. Nat. Service, KRRC and Para Regt, TA, 1951–53. Radio actor, 1954–57; television announcer, 1957–60, newsreader, 1960–68; freelance broadcaster, radio and TV, 1968–; presenter: Aspel and Company, 1984–93; This is Your Life, 1988–; Antiques Roadshow, 2000–; Going For a Song, 2001; occasional stage appearances. Pres., Stackpole Trust, 1985–; Vice-President: BLISS (Baby Life Support Systems), 1981–; ASBAH (Assoc. for Spina Bifida and Hydrocephalus), 1985–; Patron, Plan International, 1986–. Member: Equity, 1955–; Lord's Taverners; RYA. FZS. Mem., RTS Hall of Fame, 1996. *Publications:* Polly Wants a Zebra (autobiog.), 1974; Hang On! (for children), 1982; (with Richard Hearsey) Child's Play, 1985; regular contribs to magazines. *Recreations:* water sports, theatre, cinema, eating, travel. *Address:* c/o Shepherd & Ford Associates, 13 Radnor Walk, SW3 4BP.

ASPELL, Col Gerald Laycock, TD (2 clasps); DL, FCA; Vice Lord-Lieutenant of Leicestershire, 1984–90; *b* 10 April 1915; *s* of Samuel Frederick Aspell and Agnes Maude (*née* Laycock); *m* 1939, Mary Leeson Carroll (*d* 1998), *d* of Rev. Ion Carroll, Cork; one *s* two *d. Educ:* Uppingham Sch. FCA 1938. Commnd 2nd Lieut, 4th Bn Leicestershire Regt, TA, 1933; served War of 1939–45 in UK and Burma, RE, RA, RAF; commanded 579 Light Anti-Aircraft Regt, RA (TA), 1946–51. Partner, Coopers & Lybrand, 1952–78; mem. of various nat. and local cttees of Inst. of Chartered Accountants during that time. Dir, 1964–85, Chm., 1978–85, Leicester Building Soc.; Dep. Chm., Alliance and Leicester Building Soc., 1985; Local Dir, Eagle Star Insce Gp, 1949–84 (Chm., Midlands Bd, 1970–84). Chairman: Leicester and Dist Local Employment Cttee, then Leics Dist Manpower Cttee, 1971–79. Mem., Leicester Diocesan Bd of Finance, 1952–77. Civil Defence Controller, then Sub-Regl Dir CD, Leics, Rutland and Northants, 1956–65. Member: Leics and Rutland TAA, then E Midlands TAVRA, 1947–80 (Chm., Leics Cttee, 1969–80). Hon. Colonel: Royal Anglian Regt (Leics), 1972–79; Leics and Northants ACF, 1979–84. Grand Treasurer, United Grand Lodge of England, 1974–75. Trustee, Uppingham Sch., 1964–87 (Chm., 1977–87). DL Leics, 1952. *Recreations:* cricket, tennis, squash, fishing, charitable involvements. *Address:* Laburnum House, Great Dalby, Melton Mowbray, Leics LE14 2HA. *T:* (01664) 411513.

ASPIN, Norman, CMG 1968; HM Diplomatic Service, retired; Adviser and Secretary, East Africa Association, 1981–84; *b* 9 Nov. 1922; *s* of Thomas and Eleanor Aspin; *m* 1948, Elizabeth Irving, three *s. Educ:* Darwen Grammar Sch.; Durham Univ. (MA). War Service, 1942–45, Lieut RNVR. Demonstrator in Geography, Durham Univ., 1947–48; Asst Principal, Commonwealth Relations Office, 1948; served in India, 1948–51; Principal, Commonwealth Relations Office, 1952; served in Federation of Rhodesia and Nyasaland, 1954–57; HM Treasury, 1958–60; British Deputy High Commissioner in Sierra Leone, 1961–63; Commonwealth Relations Office, 1963–65; British Embassy, Tel Aviv, 1966–69; IDC 1970; Head of Personnel Policy Dept, FCO, 1971–73; Under-Sec., FCO, 1973–76; Comr, British Indian Ocean Territory, 1976; British High Comr in Malta, 1976–79; Asst Under-Sec. of State, FCO, 1979–80. *Recreations:* sailing, tennis. *Address:* Mounsey Bank, Dacre, Cumbria CA11 0HL.

ASPINALL, John Michael; QC 1995; a Recorder, 1990–98; *b* 19 Feb. 1948; *s* of Kenneth James Aspinall and Joan Mary Aspinall; *m* 1980, Frances Helen Parks. *Educ:* Kampala Kindergarten; Wigan and Dist Mining and Tech. Coll.; Liverpool Univ. (LLB Hons). Called to the Bar, Inner Temple, 1971; Asst Recorder, 1985–90. RAC Motor Sports Council: Mem., 1990, Chm., 1994, Judicial Cttee; Mem., 1994. Winner, Observer Mace Nat. Debating Comp., 1971. *Recreations:* motor sports, being with my wife and friends at the Drax Arms. *Address:* 3 Paper Buildings, 20 Lorne Park Road, Bournemouth BH1 1JN. *T:* (01202) 292102. *Club:* Savile.

ASPINALL, Rt Rev. Dr Phillip John; Assistant Bishop, Diocese of Adelaide, since 1998; *b* 17 Dec. 1959; *m* 1982, Christa Schmitt; two *s. Educ:* Univ. of Tasmania (BSc 1980); Brisbane Coll. of Advanced Educn (GradDipRE 1985); Ecumenical Inst., Geneva (Cert. 1987); Trinity Coll., Melbourne Coll. of Divinity (BD (Hons) 1988); Monash Univ. (PhD 1989); Deakin Univ. (MBA 1998). Field Officer, C of E Boys' Soc., 1980; Diocesan Youth and Educn Officer, 1981–84; Dep. Warden, Christ Coll., Dio. Tasmania, 1983–84; Dir, Parish Educn, St Stephen's, Mt Waverley, Dio. Melbourne, 1985–88; ordained deacon, 1988, priest, 1989; Asst Curate, St Mark-on-the-Hill, 1988–89; Asst Priest, Brighton, 1989–91; Priest in charge, Bridgewater-Gagebrook, 1991–94; Dir, Anglicare, Tasmania, 1994–98; Acting Archdeacon of Clarence, 1997; Archdeacon for Church and Society, Dio. Tasmania, 1997–98. *Address:* 19 Tennyson Street, Medindie, SA 5081, Australia. *T:* (8) 82695119.

ASPINALL, Wilfred; European Union policy and strategy adviser; Director: Aspinall & Associates, since 1988; Eversheds Financial Services Forum (Business Lawyers in Europe), since 1998; *b* 14 Sept. 1942; *s* of late Charles Aspinall and Elizabeth Aspinall; *m* 1973, Judith Mary, *d* of late Leonard James Pimlott and Kathleen Mary Pimlott; one *d. Educ:* Poynton Secondary Modern; Stockport Coll. for Further Educn. Staff, National Provincial Bank Ltd, 1960–69; Asst Gen. Sec., National Westminster Staff Assoc., 1969–75; Dep. Sec. (part-time), Council of Bank Staff Assocs, 1969–75; Mem., Banking Staff Council, 1970–77; Gen. Sec., Confedn of Bank Staff Assocs, 1975–79; Exec. Dir, Fedn of Managerial, Professional and Gen. Assocs, 1978–94. Mem., EU Economic and Social Consultative Assembly, 1986–99. Vice-Pres., Confédération Internat. des Cadres, 1979–94. Member: N Herts DHA, 1981–86; NW Thames RHA, 1986–88; Hammersmith and Queen Charlotte's SHA, 1981–90; Professions Allied to Medicine, Whitley Management Negotiating Cttee, 1983–87. *Recreations:* motoring, travel—particularly to places of historical interest, social affairs and political history. *Address:* The Croft, Shillington Road, Pirton, Hitchin, Herts SG5 3QJ. *T:* (01462) 712316; (Brussels private office) Rue de la Tourelle 23, 1040 Brussels. *T:* (2) 2308510, *Fax:* (2) 2307818; *e-mail:* wa@link4en.com.

ASPINWALL, Jack Heywood; author; company director; *b* 5 Feb. 1933; *m* 1954, Brenda Jean Aspinwall; one *s* two *d. Educ:* Prescot Grammar School, Lancs; Marconi College, Chelmsford. Served RAF, 1949–56. Director: family retail business, 1956–66; food distbn co., 1966–71; investment co., 1971–96. Mem., Avon CC, 1973–80. Contested (L) Kingswood, Feb. and Oct. 1974; MP (C) Kingswood, 1979–83, Wansdyke, 1983–97. *Publications:* (comp.) Kindly Sit Down!: best after-dinner stories from both Houses of Parliament, 1983; Hit Me Again, 1992; Tell Me Another, 1994. *Address:* 156 Bath Road, Willsbridge, Bristol BS30 6EF.

ASPRAY, Rodney George, FCA; Managing Director, Worthbase Ltd, since 1990; *b* 1934. Secretary, Manchester and Salford Cooperative Society, 1965–69; Chief Exec. Officer, Norwest Co-op Soc., 1969–91. Director: Co-operative Bank, 1980–89 (Chm., 1986–89); Co-operative Wholesale Soc. Ltd, 1980–89; Mersey Docks & Harbour Co., 1987–94; Piccadilly Radio Plc, 1989–90. Mem., Monopolies and Mergers Commn, 1975–81. FCA 1960. *Address:* Kambara, 4 Green Lane, Higher Poynton, Cheshire SK12 1TJ.

ASQUITH, family name of **Earl of Oxford and Asquith**.

ASQUITH, Viscount; Raymond Benedict Bartholomew Michael Asquith, OBE 1992; Director: Dessna Co. Ltd, since 1997; JKX Oil & Gas plc, since 1997; West Ukrainian Venture Partners, since 2001; *b* 24 Aug. 1952; *er s* and *heir* of 2nd Earl of Oxford and Asquith, *qv; m* 1978, Mary Clare, *e d* of Francis Pollen; one *s* four *d. Educ:* Ampleforth; Balliol College, Oxford. HM Diplomatic Service, 1980–97: FCO, 1980–83; First Sec., Moscow, 1983–85; Cabinet Office and FCO, 1985–92; Counsellor, Kiev, 1992–97. *Heir: s* Hon. Mark Julian Asquith, *b* 13 May 1979. *Address:* Branch Farm, Mells, Frome, Somerset BA11 3RE.

ASQUITH, Hon. Dominic Anthony Gerard; HM Diplomatic Service; Minister and Deputy Head of Mission, Argentina, since 1997; *b* 7 Feb. 1957; *y s* of 2nd Earl of Oxford and Asquith, *qv; m* 1988, Louise Cotton; one *d.* Joined HM Diplomatic Service, 1983; FCO, 1983–86; Second Sec., Damascus, 1986–87; First Secretary: Muscat, 1987–89; FCO, 1989–92; Washington, 1992–97. *Address:* c/o Foreign and Commonwealth Office, King Charles Street, SW1A 2AH.

See also Viscount Asquith.

ASSCHER, Sir (Adolf) William, Kt 1992; MD, FRCP; Principal (formerly Dean) and Professor of Medicine, St George's Hospital Medical School, London University, 1988–96; Consultant Physician, St George's Hospital; *b* 20 March 1931; *s* of William Benjamin Asscher and Roosje van der Molen; *m* 1st, 1959, Corrie van Welt (*d* 1961); 2nd, 1962, Dr Jennifer Lloyd, *d* of Wynne Llewelyn Lloyd, CB; two *d. Educ:* Maerlant Lyceum, The Hague; London Hosp. Med. Coll. BSc 1954; MB 1957; MD 1963; MRCP 1959, FRCP 1971; FFPM 1992. Nat. service, Lieut RE, 1949–51. Jun. appts, London Hosp., 1957–59; Lectr in Medicine, London Hosp. Med. Coll., 1959–64; Welsh National School of Medicine, later University of Wales College of Medicine: Sen. Lectr, 1964–70, and Hon. Cons. Physician, Royal Inf., Cardiff; Reader, 1970–76; Prof. of Medicine, 1976–80; Head of Dept of Renal Medicine, 1980–88. Chairman: Cttee on Review of Medicines, DHSS, 1985–87; Cttee on Safety of Medicines, Dept of Health (formerly DHSS), 1987–92 (Mem., 1984–87); Member: Medicines Commn, DHSS, 1981–84; SW Thames RHA, 1987–90; Jt Consultants Cttee, 1992–96; Med. Adv. Cttee, Royal Hosp. for Neuro-Rehabilitation, Putney, 1995–97; Welsh Arts Council, 1985–88. Chm., Morriston Hosp. NHS Trust, Swansea, 1996–99; non-executive Director: Wandsworth DHA, 1991–93; St George's Health Care Trust, 1993–96; Vanguard Media plc, 1996–; Cancer Research Ventures, 1999–2001. Consultant, Innovex plc, 1995–97. Chairman: Med. Benefit Risk Foundn UK, 1993–96; Welsh Med. Technology Forum, 1993–; BMA Bd of Sci. and Educn, 1998–; UK Co-ordinating Cttee on Cancer Res., 1998–; Working Party on Therapeutic Uses of Cannabinoids, RPharmS, 1998–. Royal College of Physicians: Regl Advr, 1976–79; Mem. Council, 1977–80; Pres., Faculty of Pharmaceutical Medicine, 1995–97. Examnr, Final MB, Wales, London, Bristol and Edinburgh. Pres., Renal Assoc., 1986–89. Hon. Fellow: St George's Hosp. Med. Sch., 1996; QMW, 1998. DUniv Kingston, 1996. *Publications:* (with W. Brumfitt) Urinary Tract Infection, 1973; The Challenge of Urinary Tract Infections, 1980; (with D. B. Moffat and E. Sanders) Nephrology Illustrated, 1982; (with D. B. Moffat) Nephro-Urology, 1983; (with W. Brumfitt) Microbial Diseases in Nephrology, 1986; (with S. R. Walker) Medicines and Risk-Benefit Decisions, 1986; (with J. D. Williams) Clinical Atlas of the Kidney, 1991; papers on nephrology and drug regulation in learned jls. *Recreation:* visual arts. *Address:* The Old Rectory, Llangan, near Bridgend, Vale of Glamorgan CF35 5DW. *T:* and *Fax:* (01656) 646351. *Clubs:* Reform; Cardiff and County (Cardiff).

ASSHETON, family name of **Baron Clitheroe**.

ASSHETON, Hon. Nicholas, FSA; Treasurer and Extra Equerry to the Queen Mother, since 1998; *b* 23 May 1934; *yr s* of 1st Baron Clitheroe, KCVO, PC, FSA and Sylvia Benita Frances, Lady Clitheroe, FRICS (*d* 1991), *d* of 6th Baron Hotham; *m* 1960, Jacqueline Jill, *d* of Marshal of the Royal Air Force Sir Arthur Harris, 1st Bt, GCB, OBE, AFC; one *s* two *d. Educ:* Eton; Christ Church, Oxford (MA). FSA 1984. 2nd Lieut, Life Guards, 1954; Lieut, Inns of Court Regt, 1954–57. Joined Montagu, Loebl, Stanley & Co. (Stockbrokers), 1957: Partner, 1960; Sen. Partner, 1978–86; Chm., 1986–87; Coutts & Co.: Dir, 1987–99; Dep. Chm., 1993–99; Chm., SG Hambros Bank & Trust Ltd, 2000–. Mem., Stock Exchange, 1960–92 (Mem. Council, 1969–87). Dir, United Services Trustee, 1981–, Chm., 1997–. Treas., Corp. of Church House, 1988–. Mem., Exec. Cttee, Heritage of London Trust, 1997–. Liveryman, Vintners' Co., 1955. Lord of the Manor and Liberty of Slaidburn, Grindleton and Bradford, 1977. *Address:* 15 Hammersmith Terrace, W6 9TS. *Clubs:* White's, Pratt's, Beefsteak.

ASSIRATI, Robert; Executive Director (Information Technology), Office of Government Commerce, HM Treasury, since 2001; *b* 27 May 1947; *s* of late Frederick Louis Assirati and Mary Violet Assirati (*née* Dillon); *m* 1968, Lynne Elizabeth Yeend; one *s* one *d*. *Educ:* Stationers' Company's Sch., London; Hertford Coll., Oxford (MA PPE). MCIPS, AFA. Nat. Coal Bd, 1968; Data Processing Manager, Eli Lilly & Co., 1972; Management Services Manager, British Carpets, 1976; Company Dir, C Squared, 1984; Commercial Dir, Inland Revenue IT Office, 1986; Chief Exec., CCTA, 1996–2001. Non-exec. Dir, Owner's Bd, Armed Forces Personnel Admin Agency, MoD, 1998–. Freeman: City of London, 1999; Co. of Information Technologists, 1999. MIMgt.; FRSA. Hon. FAPM. *Recreations:* bridge, tennis, travel, theatre. *Address:* The Alders, Capel, Tonbridge, Kent TN12 6SU. *T:* (01892) 836609.

ASTAIRE, Jarvis Joseph; Chairman, GRA (formerly Greyhound Racing Association), since 1993; *b* 6 Oct. 1923; *s* of late Max and Esther Astaire; *m* 1st, 1948, Phyllis Oppenheim (*d* 1974); one *s* one *d*; 2nd, 1981, Nadine Hyman (*d* 1986). *Educ:* Kilburn Grammar Sch., London. Dir, Lewis & Burrows Ltd, 1957–60; Managing Director: Mappin & Webb Ltd, 1958–60; Hurst Park Syndicate, 1962–71; Dep. Chm., Wembley Stadium, 1984–99; Director: Perthpoint Investments Ltd, 1959–70; Associated Suburban Properties Ltd, 1963–81; Anglo-Continental Investment & Finance Co. Ltd, 1964–75; William Hill Org., 1971–82; First Artists Prodns Inc. (USA), 1976–79; Wembley PLC (formerly GRA Gp), 1987–99; Revlon Group Ltd, 1991–98. Mem. Bd, British Greyhound Racing, 1991–. Introduced into UK showing of sporting events on large screen in cinemas, 1964. Pres., Royal Free Hosp. and Med. Sch. Appeal Trust, 1991–97 (Chm., 1974); Hon. Treas., 1976–, and Vice Pres., 1982–, Fedn of London Youth Clubs (formerly London Fedn of Boys' Clubs); Chm., Police Dependants' Trust Appeal, 1999–; Trustee, Bowles Outdoor Centre, 1985–; Patron, Nightingale House Home for Aged Jews, 1984–. Chm., Associated City Properties, 1981–. Chief Barker (Pres.), Variety Club of GB, 1983; Pres., Variety Clubs Internat. (Worldwide), 1991–93. Mem. Adv. Council, LSO, 1996–. Freeman, City of London, 1983. *Recreations:* playing tennis, watching cricket and football. *Address:* Broughton House, 6–8 Sackville Street, W1X 1DD. *T:* (020) 7287 4601. *Clubs:* East India, MCC, Queen's; Friars (USA).

ASTBURY, Prof. Alan, PhD; FRS 1993; FRS(Can) 1988; R. M. Pearce Professor of Physics, University of Victoria, British Columbia, 1983–2000, now Emeritus; Director, TRIUMF Laboratory, Vancouver, 1994–2001; *b* 27 Nov. 1934; *s* of Harold Astbury and Jane Astbury (*née* Horton); *m* 1964, Kathleen Ann Stratmeyer; two *d*. *Educ:* Nantwich and Acton Grammar Sch.; Univ. of Liverpool (BSc, PhD). Leverhulme Research Fellow, Univ. of Liverpool, 1959–61; Res. Associate, Lawrence Radiation Lab., Berkeley, Calif., 1961–63; Res. Physicist, Rutherford Appleton Lab., UK, 1963–83. Vis. Scientist, CERN, Geneva, 1970–74 and 1980–83. Rutherford Medal, Inst. Physics, 1986. *Publications:* numerous in learned jls. *Recreations:* ski-ing, jazz, playing piano. *Address:* Department of Physics and Astronomy, University of Victoria, PO Box 3055, Stn CSC, Victoria, BC V8W 3P6, Canada. *T:* (250) 7217736; 1383 St Patrick Street, Victoria, BC V8S 4Y5, Canada.

ASTILL, Hon. Sir Michael (John), Kt 1996; **Hon. Mr Justice Astill;** a Judge of the High Court of Justice, Queen's Bench Division, since 1996; *b* 31 Jan. 1938; *s* of Cyril Norman Astill and Winifred Astill; *m* 1968, Jean Elizabeth, *d* of Dr J. C. H. Mackenzie; three *s* one *d*. *Educ:* Blackfriars School, Laxton, Northants. Admitted solicitor, 1962; called to the Bar, Middle Temple, 1972, Bencher, 1996; a Recorder, 1980–84; a Circuit Judge, 1984–96; a Pres., Mental Health Tribunals, 1986–96; Presiding Judge, Midland and Oxford Circuit, 1999–. Mem., Judicial Studies Bd, 1995–99 (Chm., Magisterial Cttee, 1995–99). *Recreations:* music, reading, sport. *Address:* Royal Courts of Justice, Strand, WC2A 2LL.

ASTLEY, family name of **Baron Hastings**.

ASTLEY, Neil Philip; Editor and Managing Director, Bloodaxe Books Ltd, since 1978; *b* 12 May 1953; *s* of Philip Thomas Astley and late Margaret Ivy Astley (*née* Soleman); *m* 1st, 1976, Julie Callan (marr. diss. 1983); 2nd, 1988, Katharine Keens-Soper (marr. diss. 1999). *Educ:* Price's Sch., Fareham; Alliance Française, Paris; Univ. of Newcastle upon Tyne (BA 1st Cl. Hons). Journalist, England and Australia, 1972–74. Hon. DLitt Newcastle upon Tyne, 1996. Eric Gregory Award, Soc. of Authors, 1982. *Publications:* (ed) Ten North-East Poets, 1980; The Speechless Act, 1984; (ed) Bossy Parrot, 1987; Darwin Survivor (Recommendation, Poetry Book Soc., 1988), 1988; (ed) Poetry with an Edge, 1988, 2nd edn 1993; (ed) Dear Next Prime Minister, 1990; (ed) Tony Harrison (critical anthology), 1991; (ed) Wordworks, 1992; Biting My Tongue, 1995; (ed) New Blood, 1999. *Recreations:* reading, enjoying countryside, folklore, sheep. *Address:* Bloodaxe Books Ltd, Highgreen, Tarset, Northumberland NE48 1RP. *T:* (01434) 240500.

ASTLEY, Philip Sinton, CVO 1999 (LVO 1979); HM Diplomatic Service; Ambassador to Denmark, since 1999; *b* 18 Aug. 1943; *s* of Bernard Astley and Barbara Astley (*née* Sinton); *m* 1966, Susanne Poulsen; two *d*. *Educ:* St Albans Sch.; Magdalene Coll., Cambridge (BA 1965). Asst Representative, British Council, Madras, 1966–70; British Council, London, 1970–73; First Sec., FCO, 1973–76, Copenhagen, 1976–79; First Sec. and Head of Chancery, East Berlin, 1980–82; First Sec., FCO, 1982–84; Counsellor and Head of Management Review Staff, FCO, 1984–86; Econ. Counsellor and Consul Gen., Islamabad, 1986–90; Dep. Head of Mission, Copenhagen, 1990–94; Counsellor, and Hd of Human Rights Policy Dept, FCO, 1994–96; Asst Under-Sec. of State, FCO, and HM Vice-Marshal of the Diplomatic Corps, 1996–99. Grand Cross, Order of Dannebrog (Denmark), 2000. *Recreations:* oriental textiles, gardening. *Address:* c/o Foreign and Commonwealth Office, SW1A 2AH.

ASTLING, (Alistair) Vivian; Chairman, National Forest Co., since 1999; *b* 6 Sept. 1943; *s* of late Alec William Astling, MBE and Barbara Grace Astling; *m* 1967, Hazel Ruth Clarke. *Educ:* Glyn Grammar Sch., Epsom; Sheffield Univ. (LLB 1965; LLM 1967); Birmingham Univ. (MSocSci 1973). West Bromwich County Borough Council: articled clerk, 1967; Asst Solicitor, 1971; Asst Town Clerk, 1973; Walsall Metropolitan Borough Council: Corporate Planner, 1974; Chief Exec. and Town Clerk, 1982–88; Chief Exec., Dudley MBC, 1988–99. Clerk to W Midlands Police Authy, 1988–99; Sec. to Birmingham Internat. Airport Shareholders' Forum, 1988–97. Mem. Bd, Midlands Arts Centre, 1999–. Hon. MBA Wolverhampton, 1999. *Recreations:* squash, sculpture, theatre, music. *Address:* 16 Knighton Drive, Sutton Coldfield, W Midlands B74 4QP.

ASTON, Bishop Suffragan of, since 1992; **Rt Rev. John Michael Austin;** *b* 4 March 1939; *s* of John Fenner Austin and Margaret Austin; *m* 1971, Rosemary Joan Elizabeth King; two *s* one *d*. *Educ:* Worksop Coll.; St Edmund Hall, Oxford (BA 1963); St Stephen's House, Oxford. Ordained deacon, 1964, priest, 1965; Assistant Curate: St John the Evangelist, E Dulwich, 1964–68; St James Cathedral, Chicago, 1968–69; St Christopher's, Pembroke Coll. Mission, 1969–76; Social Responsibility Advr, St Alban's Dio., 1976–84; Dir, London Diocesan Bd for Social Responsibility, 1984–92. Prebendary, St Paul's Cathedral, 1982–87. Founding Chm., Church Action on Poverty, 1980–85; Mem., Follow-up Cttee for the Archbishop's Report, Faith in the City, 1986–92. Mem., Gen. Synod of C of E, 2000– (Chm., Inter-Faith Consultative Cttee, Bd for Mission). Chairman: Newtown/S Aston City Challenge Bd, Birmingham, 1993–99; St Basil's Young Homeless Provision in Birmingham, 2000–. Trustee, Church Urban Fund, 1999–. Hon. Dr UCE, 1996. *Recreations:* walking, cycling, playing the violin very badly! *Address:* Strensham House, 8 Strensham Hill, Birmingham B13 8AG. *T:* (0121) 449 0675.

ASTON, Archdeacon of; *see* Barton, Ven. C. J. G.

ASTON, Sir Harold (George), Kt 1983; CBE 1976; Chairman and Chief Executive, Bonds Coats Patons Ltd, 1981–87 (Deputy Chairman, 1970–80); Director, Central Sydney Area Health Service, 1988–92; *b* Sydney, 13 March 1923; *s* of Harold John Aston and Annie Dorothea McKeown; *m* 1947, Joyce Thelma Smith (decd); one *s* one *d*. *Educ:* Crown Street Boys' Sch., Sydney, Australia. Manager, Buckinghams Ltd, Sydney, 1948–55; Bonds Industries Ltd: Merchandising Manager, 1955–63; Gen. Man., 1963–67; Man. Dir, 1967–70; Director: Bonds Coats Patons Ltd (formerly Bonds Industries Ltd); Manufacturers Mutual Insurance, 1982– (Vice Chm., 1987–); Downard-Pickfords Pty Ltd, 1983–89 (Chm.); Australian Guarantee Corp. Ltd, 1983–88; Australian Manufacturing Life Assce Ltd, 1984–88; Rothmans Hldgs Ltd, 1986– (Dep. Chm., 1989–); Westpac Banking Corp., 1988–92; Chm., Television and Telecasters Ltd, 1991–92; Consultant, Pacific Dunlop Ltd, 1987–. President: Textile Council of Australia, 1973–80 (Life Mem., 1984); Confedn of Aust. Industry, 1980–82; Hon. Trustee, Cttee for Econ. Develt of Australia, 1988–; Governor: Aesop Foundn, 1988–; (Founding), Heart Inst. of Australia, 1986–93. CompTI 1984; FCFI 1986; CStJ 1993 (Dep. Receiver-Gen., Finance Cttee, 1985–). *Recreations:* walking, gardening, travelling. *Address:* 58/129 Surf Parade, Broadbeach, Qld 4218, Australia. *Clubs:* American, Australian, Royal Sydney Yacht Squadron (Sydney); Concord Golf.

ASTON, Dr Margaret Evelyn, (Hon. Mrs Buxton), FSA, FRHistS; FBA 1994; historian; *b* 9 Oct. 1932; *d* of 1st Baron Bridges, KG, GCB, GCVO, MC, PC, FRS and of late Katharine Dianthe, *d* of 2nd Baron Farrer; *m* 1st, 1954, Trevor Henry Aston (marr. diss. 1969; he *d* 1985); 2nd, 1971, Paul William Jex Buxton, *qv*; two *d*. *Educ:* Downe House; Lady Margaret Hall, Oxford (BA, MA; DPhil 1962). FRHistS 1962; FSA 1987. Lectr, St Anne's Coll., Oxford, 1956–59; Theodor Heuss Schol., W Germany, 1960–61; Res. Fellow, Newnham Coll., Cambridge, 1961–66; Res. Fellow, Folger Shakespeare Liby, and teaching post, Catholic Univ. of America, Washington, 1966–69; Hon. Sen. Res. Fellow, QUB, 1984–85. Pres., Ecclesiastical History Soc., 2000–01. *Publications:* Thomas Arundel: a study of church life in the reign of Richard II, 1967; The Fifteenth Century: the prospect of Europe, 1968, repr. 1994; Lollards and Reformers: images and literacy in late medieval religion, 1984; England's Iconoclasts: laws against images, 1988; Faith and Fire: popular and unpopular religion 1350–1600, 1993; The King's Bedpost: reformation and iconography in a Tudor group portrait, 1994; (ed) The Panorama of the Renaissance, 1996; (ed jtly) Lollardy and Gentry in the Later Middle Ages, 1997; contrib. learned jls, TLS etc. *Address:* Castle House, Chipping Ongar, Essex CM5 9JT. *T:* (01277) 362642.

ASTON, Prof. Peter George, DPhil; Professor and Head of Music, University of East Anglia, 1974–98, Professor Emeritus, since 2001; *b* 5 Oct. 1938; *s* of late George William Aston and Elizabeth Oliver (*née* Smith); *m* 1960, Elaine Veronica Neale; one *s*. *Educ:* Tettenhall Coll.; Birmingham Sch. of Music (GBSM); Univ of York (DPhil); FTCL, ARCM. Lectr in Music, 1964–72, Sen. Lectr, 1972–74, Univ. of York; Dean, Sch. of Fine Arts and Music, 1981–84, Professorial Fellow, 1998–2001, UEA. Dir, Tudor Consort, 1958–65; Conductor: English Baroque Ensemble, 1968–70; Aldeburgh Festival Singers, 1975–88; Principal Guest Conductor: Sacramento Bach Fest., USA, 1993–; Incontri Corali Internat. Choral Fest., Italy, 1996; Schola Cantorum Gedanensis, Poland, 1999; Jt Artistic Dir, Norwich Fest. of Contemporary Church Music, 1981–; Chorus Master, Norfolk and Norwich Triennial Fest., 1982–88. Chairman: Eastern Arts Assoc. Music Panel, 1976–81; Norfolk Assoc. for the Advancement of Music, 1990–93 (Pres., 1993–); Acad. Bd, Guild of Church Musicians, 1996–; Pres., Trianon Music Gp, 1984–96. Patron, Lowestoft Choral Soc., 1986–. Gen. Editor, UEA Recording Series, 1979–98. FRSA 1980; FRSCM 1999. Hon. Fellow, Curwen Inst., 1987; Hon. RCM 1991; Hon. FGCM 1995. *Compositions:* song cycles, chamber music, choral and orchestral works, church music, opera. *Publications:* George Jeffreys and the English Baroque, 1970; The Music of York Minster, 1972; Sound and Silence (jtly), 1970, German edn 1972, Italian edn 1979, Japanese edn 1982; (ed) The Collected Works of George Jeffreys, 3 vols, 1977; (jtly) Music Theory in Practice, vol. 1, 1992, vols 2 and 3, 1993; contrib. to internat. music jls. *Recreations:* Association football, cricket, bridge, chess. *Address:* University of East Anglia, Music Centre, School of Music, Norwich NR4 7TJ. *T:* (01603) 56161. *Clubs:* Athenæum; Norfolk (Norwich).

ASTOR, family name of **Viscount Astor** and **Baron Astor of Hever**.

ASTOR, 4th Viscount *cr* 1917, of Hever Castle; **William Waldorf Astor;** Baron 1916; *b* 27 Dec. 1951; *s* of 3rd Viscount Astor; *S* father, 1966; *m* 1976, Annabel Sheffield, *d* of T. Jones; two *s* one *d*. *Educ:* Eton Coll. A Lord in Waiting (Govt Whip), 1990–93. Parliamentary Under-Secretary of State: DSS, 1993–94; Dept of Nat. Heritage, 1994–95; an Opposition spokesman, H of L, 1996–; elected Mem., H of L, 1999; Director: Cliveden Hotel, 1985–90; Chorion plc, 1997–; ONdigital Ltd, 1998–. Trustee, Sir Stanley Spencer Gall., Cookham, 1975–. *Heir:* *s* Hon. William Waldorf Astor, *b* 18 Jan. 1979. *Address:* Ginge Manor, Wantage, Oxon OX12 8QT. *Clubs:* White's, Turf.

ASTOR OF HEVER, 3rd Baron *cr* 1956, of Hever Castle; **John Jacob Astor;** DL; *b* 16 June 1946; *s* of 2nd Baron Astor of Hever and Lady Irene Haig, *d* of Field Marshal 1st Earl Haig, KT, GCB, OM, GCVO, KCIE; *S* father, 1984; *m* 1st, 1970, Fiona Diana Lennox Harvey (marr. diss. 1990), *d* of Captain Roger Harvey; three *d*; 2nd, 1990, Hon. Elizabeth, *d* of 2nd Viscount Mackintosh of Halifax, OBE, BEM; one *s* one *d*. *Educ:* Eton College. Lieut Life Guards, 1966–70, Malaysia, Hong Kong, Ulster. Director: Terres Blanches Services Sarl, 1975–77; Valberg Plaza Sarl, 1977–82; Managing Director: Honon et Cie, 1982–; Astor France Sarl, 1989–; Pres., Astor Enterprises Inc., 1983–. An Opposition Whip, H of L, 1998–; elected Mem., H of L, 1999. Secretary: Anglo-Swiss Parly Assoc., 1992–; All Party Motor Gp; Joint Treasurer: British–S African Parly Assoc., 1994; Franco-British Parly Relations Cttee. Trustee: Rochester Cathedral Trust; Canterbury Cathedral Trust; Astor Foundn; Astor of Hever Trust; Patron: Edenbridge Music and Arts Trust; Bridge Trust, 1993–; Kent Assoc. of Youth Clubs, 1994–; President: Sevenoaks Westminster Patrons Club; Earl Haig Br., Royal British Legion; Motorsport Industry Assoc., 1995–; Kent Fedn of Amenity Socs, 1995–; RoSPA, 1996–99. Gov., Cobham Hall Sch., 1993–96. DL Kent, 1996. Chm., Council of St John, Kent, 1987–97; KStJ 1998. *Heir:* *s* Hon. Charles Gavin John Astor, *b* 10 Nov. 1990. *Address:* Frenchstreet House, Westerham, Kent TN16 1PW. *Clubs:* White's; Riviera Golf.

ASTOR, David Waldorf, CBE 1994; farmer, since 1973; Director, Priory Investments Ltd, since 1990; *b* 9 Aug. 1943; *s* of late Michael Langhorne Astor and Barbara Mary (*née* McNeill); *m* 1968, Clare Pamela St John; two *s* two *d*. *Educ:* Eton Coll.; Harvard Univ. Short service commn in Royal Scots Greys, 1962–65. United Newspapers, 1970–72;

Housing Corp., 1972–75; Head of Develt, National Th., 1978–79; Dir, Jupiter Tarbutt Merlin, 1985–91. Chairman: CPRE, 1983–93; Southern Arts Bd, 1998–. Trustee, Glyndebourne Arts Trust, 1995–. Contested (SDP/Alliance) Plymouth Drake, 1987. FRSA. *Recreations:* books, sport. *Address:* Bruern Grange, Milton under Wychwood, Oxford OX7 6HA. *T:* (01993) 830413. *Clubs:* Brook's, Beefsteak, MCC.

ASTOR, Hon. (Francis) David (Langhorne), CH 1994; Editor of The Observer, 1948–75; Director, The Observer, 1976–81; *b* 5 March 1912; *s* of 2nd Viscount Astor and Nancy, Viscountess Astor, CH, MP (*d* 1964); *m* 1st, 1945, Melanie Hauser; one *d*; 2nd, 1952, Bridget Aphra Wreford; two *s* three *d*. *Educ:* Eton; Balliol, Oxford. Yorkshire Post, 1936. Served War of 1939–45, with Royal Marines, 1940–45 (Croix de Guerre, 1944). Foreign Editor of The Observer, 1946–48. *Publication:* (with V. Yorke) Peace in the Middle East: super powers and security guarantees, 1978. *Address:* 24 St Ann's Terrace, NW8 6PJ. *T:* (020) 7586 8689; Manor House, Sutton Courtenay, Oxon OX14 4AD. *T:* (01235) 848221. *Clubs:* Athenæum, Reform.

ASTWOOD, Hon. Sir James (Rufus), KBE 1994; Kt 1982; JP; President, Court of Appeal: Bermuda, since 1994; Turks and Caicos Islands, since 1997; *b* 4 Oct. 1923; *s* of late James Rufus Astwood, Sr, and Mabel Winifred Astwood; *m* 1952, Gloria Preston Norton; one *s* two *d*. *Educ:* Berkeley Inst., Bermuda; Univ. of Toronto, Canada. Called to the Bar, Gray's Inn, London, Feb. 1956, Hon. Bencher, 1985; admitted to practice at Jamaican Bar, Oct. 1956; joined Jamaican Legal Service, 1957; Dep. Clerk of Courts, 1957–58; Clerk of Courts, Jamaica, 1958–63; Stipendiary Magistrate and Judge of Grand Court, Cayman Islands (on secondment from Jamaica), 1958–59; Resident Magistrate, Jamaica, 1963–74; Puisne Judge, Jamaica, during 1971 and 1973; retd from Jamaican Legal Service, 1974; Sen. Magistrate, Bermuda, 1974–76; Solicitor General, 1976–77; Acting Attorney General, during 1976 and 1977; Acting Dep. Governor for a period in 1977; Chief Justice, 1977–93, Justice of Appeal, 1993–94, Bermuda. Has served on several cttees, tribunals and bds of enquiry, both in Bermuda and Jamaica. *Recreations:* golf, cricket, photography, reading, bridge, travel, cycling. *Address:* The Pebble, 7 Astwood Walk, Warwick WK08, Bermuda; PO Box HM 1674, Hamilton HMGX, Bermuda. *Clubs:* Castle Harbour Golf, Bermuda Senior Golfers Society, Coral Beach and Tennis, Mid Ocean (Bermuda).

ATCHERLEY, Sir Harold Winter, Kt 1977; Chairman: Suffolk and North Essex Branch, European Movement, 1995–98 (President, since 1998); Aldeburgh Foundation, 1989–94 (Deputy Chairman, 1988–89); Toynbee Hall, 1985–90 (Member, Management Committee, 1979–90); *b* 30 Aug. 1918; *s* of L. W. Atcherley and Maude Lester (*née* Nash); *m* 1st, 1946, Anita Helen (*née* Leslie) (marr. diss. 1990); one *s* two *d*; 2nd, 1990, Mrs Elke Jessett, *d* of late Dr Carl Langbehn. *Educ:* Gresham's Sch.; Heidelberg and Geneva Univs. Joined Royal Dutch Shell Gp, 1937. Served War: Queen's Westminster Rifles, 1939; commissioned Intelligence Corps, 1940; served 18th Infty Div., Singapore; POW, 1942–45. Rejoined Royal Dutch Shell Gp, 1946: served Egypt, Lebanon, Syria, Argentina, Brazil, 1946–59. Personnel Co-ordinator, Royal Dutch Shell Group, 1964–70, retd. Recruitment Advisor to Ministry of Defence, 1970–71. Chm., Tyzack & Partners, 1979–85; Dir, British Home Stores Ltd, 1973–87. Chairman: Armed Forces Pay Review Body, 1971–82; Police Negotiating Bd, 1983–86 (Dep. Chm., 1982); Member: Top Salaries Review Body, 1971–87; Nat. Staff Cttee for Nurses and Midwives, 1973–77; Cttee of Inquiry into Pay and Related Conditions of Service of Nurses, 1974; Cttee of Inquiry into Remuneration of Members of Local Authorities, 1977. Vice-Chm., Suffolk Wildlife Trust, 1987–90; Mem. Management Cttee, Suffolk Rural Housing Assoc., 1984–87. Empress Leopoldina Medal (Brazil), 1958. *Recreations:* music, good food and wine with family and friends. *Address:* Conduit House, The Green, Long Melford, Suffolk CO10 9DU. *T:* (01787) 310897.

ATHA, Bernard Peter, OBE 1991; Principal Lecturer in Business Studies, Huddersfield Technical College, 1973–90; Lord Mayor, City of Leeds, 2000–01; *b* 27 Aug. 1928; *s* of Horace Michael Atha and Mary Quinlan; unmarried. *Educ:* Leeds Modern Sch.; Leeds Univ. (LLB Hons). Barrister-at-law, Gray's Inn. Commn, RAF, 1950–52. Variety artist on stage; Mem. Equity; films and TV plays. Elected Leeds City Council, 1957; Chm., Leeds Leisure Services Cttee, 1988–99; former Chairman: Watch Cttee; Social Services Cttee; Educn Cttee. Vice-Chm., W Leeds HA, 1988–90. Contested (Lab): Penrith and the Border, 1959; Pudsey, 1964. Pres., Leeds Co-op. Soc., 1976–96; Chairman: Leeds Playhouse and Leeds Grand Theatre; Northern Ballet Theatre, 1995–; Dir, Opera North. Member: Arts Council, 1979–82; Ministerial Working Party on Sport and Recreation, 1974, on Sport for the Disabled, 1989; EU (formerly EC) Sport for Disabled Cttee, 1992–99 (Vice- Chm., 1997–99); Internat. Paralympic Cttee, 1993–98; Sports Lottery Bd, 1995–; Vice-Chm., Sports Council, 1976–80; Chairman: Yorks and Humberside Reg. Sports Council, 1966–76; Nat. Water Sports Centre, 1978–84; UK Sports Assoc. for People with Mental Handicap, 1980– (Pres., INASFMH, 1993–); British Paralympics Assoc., 1989. Vice-Chm., St James' Univ. Hosp. NHS Trust, 1993–98 (Dir, 1990–98); Special Trustee, United Leeds Teaching Hosps NHS Trust. Chairman: Yorks Dance Centre Trust; British Paralympic Trust; Red Ladder Theatre Co.; English Fedn Disability Sport, 1999–; Craft Centre and Design Gall., Leeds, 1988–. Governor, Sports Aid Foundn. FRSA. *Recreations:* sport, the arts, travel. *Address:* 25 Moseley Wood Croft, Leeds, West Yorks LS16 7JJ. *T:* (0113) 267 2485.

ATHABASCA, Bishop of, since 1992; **Rt Rev. John Robert Clarke;** *b* 27 July 1938; *s* of Rt Rev. Neville and Alice Clarke; *m* 1964, Nadia Juliann Slusar; one *s* two *d*. *Educ:* Univ. of W Ontario (BA); Huron Coll., London, Ontario (LTh; DD *jure dignitatis*, 1992). Ordained: deacon, 1963; priest, 1964; Curate, St Michael and All Angels, Toronto, 1964–66; Priest-in-charge, Church of the Apostles, Moosonee, 1966–84; Exec. Archdeacon and Treas., Dio. of Athabasca, 1984–91. *Recreations:* woodworking, travelling, canoeing, gardening. *Address:* PO Box 6868, Peace River, Alberta T8S 1S6, Canada. *T:* (home) (780) 6241008; (office) (780) 6242767.

ATHERTON, Alan Royle, CB 1990; Director, The Argyll Consultancies PLC, since 1991 (Deputy Chairman, 1992–94; Chairman, 1994–99); *b* 25 April 1931; *s* of Harold Atherton and Hilda (*née* Royle); *m* 1959, Valerie Kemp (marr. diss. 1996); three *s* one *d*. *Educ:* Cowley Sch., St Helens; Sheffield Univ. (BSc (Hons Chem.)). ICI Ltd, 1955–58; Department of Scientific and Industrial Research: SSO, 1959–64; Private Sec. to Permanent Sec., 1960–64; PSO, Road Res. Lab., 1964–65; Principal, Min. of Housing and Local Govt, 1965–70; Asst Sec., Ordnance Survey, 1970–74; Under-Sec., 1975–87, Dep. Sec., 1987–91, DoE. Chm., Local Govt Staff Commn (Eng.), 1993–98. Vice Chm., CS Med. Assoc., then CS Healthcare, 1987–98. Chm., Queen Elizabeth II Conf. Centre Bd, 1990–93; Dir, Internat. Centre for Facilities, Canada, 1993–; Member: Letchworth Garden City Corp., 1991–94; Historic Royal Palaces Agency Adv. Gp, 1991–98. *Recreations:* walking, gardening, opera, ballet, Rugby. *Clubs:* Arts, Civil Service.

ATHERTON, Candice Kathleen, (Candy); MP (Lab) Falmouth and Camborne, since 1997; *b* 21 Sept. 1955; *d* of late Denis G. W. Atherton and of Pamela A. M. Osborne. *Educ:* Poly. of N London (BA Hons Applied Social Studies). Journalist, Portsmouth News, 1974; West Sussex Probation Service, 1975–76; Founder, Women's Aid Refuge, 1977; Co-Founder, Everywoman Magazine, 1984; freelance journalist, 1980–. Member: (Lab), Islington LBC, 1986–92 (Mayor, 1989–90); Islington HA, 1986–90. Contested (Lab), Chesham and Amersham, 1992. Mem., Select Cttee on Educn and Employment, 1997–2001. Chair, Associate Parly Water Gp, 1997–2001; Treas., Parly Waterways Gp, 1999–; Sec., All-Party Parly Objective 1 Areas Gp, 2000–. Freeman, City of London, 1989. *Recreations:* bird-watching, canal boats. *Address:* House of Commons, SW1A 0AA; (office) 4 Webber Hill, Falmouth, Cornwall TR11 2BU. *T:* (01326) 314440. *Club:* Falmouth Labour.

ATHERTON, David, OBE 1999; Founder and Artistic Director, Mainly Mozart Festival, Southern California and Northern Mexico, since 1989; Co-Founder, President and Artistic Director, Global Music Network, since 1998; Conductor Laureate, Hong Kong Philharmonic Orchestra, since 2000 (Music Director, 1989–2000); *b* 3 Jan. 1944; *s* of Robert and Lavinia Atherton; *m* 1970, Ann Gianetta Drake; one *s* two *d*. *Educ:* Cambridge Univ. (MA). LRAM, LTCL. Music Dir, London Sinfonietta, 1967–73 and 1989–91 (Co-Founder, 1967); Repetiteur, Royal Opera House, Covent Garden, 1967–68; Resident Conductor, Royal Opera House, 1968–79; Principal Conductor and Artistic Advr, 1980–83, Principal Guest Conductor, 1983–86, Royal Liverpool Philharmonic Orch.; Music Dir and Principal Conductor, San Diego Symphony Orch., 1980–87; Artistic Dir and Conductor: London Stravinsky Fest., 1979–82; Ravel/Varèse Fest., 1983–84; Principal Guest Conductor: BBC SO, 1985–89; BBC Nat. Orch. of Wales, 1994–97. Became youngest conductor in history of Henry Wood Promenade Concerts at Royal Albert Hall, and also at Royal Opera House, 1968; Royal Festival Hall debut, 1969; from 1970 performances in Europe, Middle East, Far East, Australasia, N America. Adapted and arranged Pandora by Roberto Gerhard for Royal Ballet, 1975. Conductor of the year award (Composers' Guild of GB), 1971; Edison award, 1973; Grand Prix du Disque award, 1977; Koussevitzky Award, 1981; Internat. Record Critics Award, 1982; Prix Caecilia, 1982. *Publications:* (ed) The Complete Instrumental and Chamber Music of Arnold Schoenberg and Roberto Gerhard, 1973; (ed) Pandora and Don Quixote Suites by Roberto Gerhard, 1973; contrib., The Musical Companion, 1978, The New Grove Dictionary, 1981. *Recreations:* travel, computers, theatre. *Address:* Askonas Holt Ltd, 27 Chancery Lane, WC2A 1PF. *T:* (020) 7400 1700, *Fax:* (020) 7400 1799.

ATHERTON, James Bernard; Secretary-General, British Bankers' Association, 1982–85; *b* 3 Dec. 1927; *s* of late James Atherton and Edith (*née* Atkinson); *m* 1953, Eileen Margaret Birch; two *s*. *Educ:* Alsop High Sch., Liverpool. Served RAF, 1946–48; Martins Bank, 1943–46 and 1948–69 (Asst Chief Accountant, 1966–69); Barclays Bank, 1969–82 (Chief Clearing Manager, 1969–73, Asst Gen. Manager, 1973–78, Divl Gen. Manager, 1978–82). *Recreations:* opera, gardening. *Address:* c/o Barclays Bank, 10 The Square, Petersfield, Hants GU32 3HW.

ATHERTON, Brig. Maurice Alan, CBE 1981; JP; Vice Lord-Lieutenant, Kent, since 2000; *b* 9 Oct. 1926; *s* of late Rev. Harold Atherton and Beatrice Atherton (*née* Shaw); *m* 1954, Guendolene Mary Upton; one *s* one *d*. *Educ:* St John's Sch., Leatherhead; Staff Coll., Camberley (psc). Commnd E Yorks Regt, 1946 (served in Egypt, Sudan, Malaya, Austria, Germany, UK); MA to Comdr British Forces, Hong Kong, 1959–62; coll. chief instructor, RMA Sandhurst, 1964–67; CO 1 Green Howards, 1967–69; GSO 1, NI, 1969–71; defence advr, Ghana, 1971–73; Comdr, Dover Shorncliffe Garrison and Dep. Constable, Dover Castle, 1976–81. Co. Pres., Kent, RBL, 1982–91; Chm., Kent Cttee, Army Benevolent Fund, 1984–96. Gov., Christ Church UC, Canterbury, 1985–99 (Chm. Govs, 1993–99); Comr, Duke of York's Royal Mil. Sch., 1992–. JP 1982–91, High Sheriff 1983–84, DL 1984, Kent. Hon. DCL Kent, 1996. *Recreations:* gardening, shooting. *Address:* Digges Place, Barham, Canterbury, Kent CT4 6PJ. *T:* (01227) 831420. *Club:* Lansdowne.

ATHERTON, Michael Andrew, OBE 1997; cricketer; *b* 23 March 1968; *s* of Alan and Wendy Atherton. *Educ:* Manchester Grammar Sch.; Downing Coll., Cambridge (BA Hons History; MA). 1st class début, Cambridge *v* Essex, 1987; played for Lancashire CCC, 1987–2001; Captain: Young England, Sri Lanka 1987, Australia 1988; Cambridge Univ., 1988–89; Combined Universities, 1989; Mem., England Test team, 115 matches, 1989–2001; captained 54 Test matches, 1993–98 and 2001; scored 16 Test centuries. Mem., Editl Board, Wisden Cricket Monthly, 1993–. *Recreations:* golf, reading; is cricket still a recreation?! *Address:* c/o Lancashire County Cricket Club, Old Trafford, Manchester M16 0PX. *Club:* Groucho.

ATHERTON, Rt Rev. Mgr Richard, OBE 1989; Chaplain to the Archbishop of Liverpool, since 1996; *b* 15 Feb. 1928; *s* of Richard Atherton and Winifred Mary Atherton (*née* Hurst). *Educ:* St Francis Xavier's Coll., Liverpool; Upholland Coll., Wigan; Dip. Criminology, London Univ., 1979; BA Hons Maryvale Inst., Birmingham, 1995; MA Durham, 1997. Ordained priest, 1954; Curate: St Cecilia's, Tuebrook, Liverpool, 1954–60; St Philip Neri's, Liverpool, 1960–65; Prison Chaplain: Walton, Liverpool, 1965–75; Appleton Thorne, Warrington, 1975–77; Principal RC Prison Chaplain, 1977–87; Parish Priest, St Joseph's, Leigh, Lancs, 1987–89; Pres., Ushaw Coll., 1991–96. *Publications:* Summons to Serve, 1987; New Light on the Psalms, 1993; Praying the Prayer of the Church, 1998; Praying the Sunday Psalms, 2001. *Recreations:* walking, reading. *Address:* Archbishop's House, Lowood, Carnatic Road, Mossley Hill, Liverpool L18 8BY. *T:* (0151) 724 6398.

ATHERTON, Robert Kenneth; His Honour Judge Atherton; a Circuit Judge, since 2000; *b* 22 June 1947; *s* of late John and Evelyn Atherton. *Educ:* Boteler Grammar Sch., Warrington; Univ. of Liverpool (LLB Hons). Called to the Bar, Gray's Inn, 1970; in practice at the Bar, 1971–2000; Asst Recorder, 1994–99; a Recorder, 1999–2000. Legal Mem., Mental Health Review Tribunal, 1989–2000. *Recreations:* travel, music, gardening. *Address:* Northern Circuit Secretariat, 15 Quay Street, Manchester M60 9FD.

ATHOLL, 11th Duke of *cr* 1703; **John Murray;** Lord Murray of Tullibardine 1604; Earl of Tullibardine 1606; Earl of Atholl 1629; Marquess of Atholl, Viscount of Balquhidder, Lord Murray, Balvenie and Gask, 1676; Marquess of Tullibardine, Earl of Strathtay and Strathardle, Viscount Glenalmond and Glenlyon, 1703 – all in the peerage of Scotland; professional land surveyor; *b* 19 Jan. 1929; *s* of Maj. George Murray (*d* 1940), and of Joan, *d* of William Eastwood; *S* cousin, 1996; *m* 1956, Margaret Yvonne, *o d* of Ronald Leonard Leach; two *s* one *d*. *Heir:* *s* Marquess of Tullibardine, *qv*. *Address:* PO Box 137, Haenertsburg 0730, South Africa.

ATIYAH, Sir Michael (Francis), OM 1992; Kt 1983; MA, PhD Cantab; FRS 1962; FRSE 1985; Master of Trinity College, Cambridge, 1990–97, Fellow since 1997; Director, Isaac Newton Institute for Mathematical Sciences, Cambridge, 1990–96; *b* 22 April 1929; *e s* of late Edward Atiyah and Jean Levens; *m* 1955, Lily Brown; three *s*. *Educ:* Victoria Coll., Egypt; Manchester Grammar Sch.; Trinity Coll., Cambridge. Research Fellow, Trinity Coll., Camb., 1954–58, Hon. Fellow, 1976–97; First Smith's Prize, 1954; Commonwealth Fund Fellow, 1955–56; Mem. Inst. for Advanced Study, Princeton, 1955–56, 1959–60, 1967–68, 1987; Asst Lectr in Mathematics, 1957–58, Lectr 1958–61, Univ. of Cambridge; Fellow, Pembroke Coll., Cambridge, 1958–61 (Hon. Fellow, 1983);

Reader in Mathematics, Univ. of Oxford, and Professorial Fellow of St Catherine's Coll., Oxford, 1961–63 (Hon. Fellow, 1992); Savilian Prof. of Geometry, and Fellow of New College, Oxford, 1963–69 (Hon. Fellow 1999); Prof. of Mathematics, Inst. for Advanced Study, Princeton, NJ, 1969–72; Royal Soc. Res. Prof., Mathematical Inst., Oxford, and Professorial Fellow, St Catherine's Coll., Oxford, 1973–90. Hon. Prof., Univ. of Edinburgh, 1997–. Visiting Lecturer, Harvard, 1962–63 and 1964–65. Member: Exec. Cttee, Internat. Mathematical Union, 1966–74; SERC, 1984–89; ACOST, 1991–93; President: London Mathematical Soc., 1975–77; Mathematical Assoc., 1981–82; Royal Soc., 1990–95; Chm., European Mathematical Council, 1978–90. Pres., Pugwash, 1997–. Chancellor, Univ. of Leicester, 1995–. Freeman, City of London, 1996. Fellow, Univ. of Wales Swansea, 1999. Founder FMedSci 1998. Hon. FREng (Hon. FEng 1993). Foreign Member: Amer. Acad. of Arts and Scis; Swedish Royal Acad.; Leopoldina Acad.; Nat. Acad. of Scis, USA; Acad. des Sciences, France; Royal Irish Acad.; Czechoslovak Union of Mathematicians and Physicists; Amer. Philos. Soc.; Indian Nat. Science Acad.; Australian Acad. of Scis; Ukrainian Acad. of Scis; Russian Acad. of Scis; Georgian Acad. of Scis; Venezuelan Acad. of Scis; Accad. Nazionale dei Lincei, Rome; Moscow Mathematical Soc. Hon. Prof., Chinese Acad. of Scis; Hon. Fellow, Darwin Coll., Cambridge, 1992. Hon. FFA 1999. Hon. DSc: Bonn, 1968; Warwick, 1969; Durham, 1979; St Andrew's, 1981; Dublin, Chicago, 1983; Edinburgh, 1984; Essex, London, 1985; Sussex, 1986; Ghent, 1987; Reading, Helsinki, 1990; Leicester, 1991; Salamanca, Rutgers, 1992; Wales, Montreal, Waterloo, 1993; Lebanese Univ., Birmingham, Keele, Queen's (Ontario), 1994; UMIST, Chinese Univ. of Hong Kong, 1996; Brown, 1997; Oxford, Prague, 1998; Heriot-Watt, 1999; Hon. ScD Cantab, 1984; DUniv Open, 1995. Fields Medal, Internat. Congress of Mathematicians, Moscow, 1966; Royal Medal, Royal Soc., 1968; De Morgan Medal, London Mathematical Soc., 1980; Antonio Feltrinelli Prize for mathematical sciences, Accademia Nazionale dei Lincei, Rome, 1981; King Faisal Foundn Internat. Prize for Science, Saudi Arabia, 1987; Copley Medal, Royal Soc., 1988; Gunning Victoria Jubilee Prize, RSE, 1990; Nehru Meml Medal, INSA, 1993; Franklin Medal, Amer. Phil. Soc., 1993. Commander, Order of Cedars (Lebanon), 1994; Mem. (1st Class), Order of Andrés Bello (Venezuela), 1997. *Publications:* Collected Works, 5 vols, 1988; The Geometry and Physics of Knots, 1990; papers in mathematical journals. *Recreation:* gardening. *Address:* 3/8 West Grange Gardens, Edinburgh EH9 2RA.

See also P. S. Atiyah.

ATIYAH, Prof. Patrick Selim, DCL; QC 1989; FBA 1978; Professor of English Law, and Fellow of St John's College, Oxford University, 1977–88, Hon. Fellow, 1988; *b* 5 March 1931; *s* of Edward Atiyah and D. J. C. Levens; *m* 1951, Christine Best; four *s*. *Educ:* Woking County Grammar Sch. for Boys; Magdalen Coll., Oxford (MA 1957, DCL 1974). Called to the Bar, Inner Temple, 1956. Asst Lectr, LSE, 1954–55; Lectr, Univ. of Khartoum, 1955–59; Legal Asst, BoT, 1961–64; Fellow, New Coll., Oxford, 1964–69; Professor of Law: ANU, 1970–73; Warwick Univ., 1973–77; Visiting Professor: Univ of Texas, 1979; Harvard Law Sch., 1982–83; Duke Univ., 1985. Lectures: Lionel Cohen, Hebrew Univ., Jerusalem, 1980; Oliver Wendell Holmes, Harvard Law Sch., 1981; Cecil Wright Meml, Univ. of Toronto, 1983; Viscount Bennett, Univ. of New Brunswick, 1984; Chorley, LSE, 1985; Hamlyn, Leeds Univ., 1987. Hon. LLD Warwick, 1989. General Editor, Oxford Jl of Legal Studies, 1981–86. *Publications:* The Sale of Goods, 1957, 8th edn 1990, 10th edn (ed John Adams), 2000; Introduction to the Law of Contract, 1961, 5th edn 1995; Vicarious Liability, 1967; Accidents, Compensation and the Law, 1970, 6th edn (ed Peter Cane), 1999; The Rise and Fall of Freedom of Contract, 1979; Promises, Morals and Law, 1981 (Swiney Prize, RSA/RSP, 1984); Law and Modern Society, 1983, 2nd edn 1995; Essays on Contract, 1987; Pragmatism and Theory in English Law, 1987; (with R. S. Summers) Form and Substance in Anglo-American Law, 1987; The Damages Lottery, 1997; articles in legal jls. *Recreations:* gardening, cooking. *Address:* 65 Seaview Road, Hayling Island, Hants PO11 9PD. *T:* (023) 9246 2474.

See also Sir M. F. Atiyah.

ATKIN, Alec Field, CBE 1978; FREng; FRAeS; Managing Director, Marketing, Aircraft Group, British Aerospace, 1981–82, retired; Director, AWA (Consultancy) Ltd, since 1983; *b* 26 April 1925; *s* of Alec and Grace Atkin; *m* 1948, Nora Helen Darby (marr. diss. 1982); two *s* one *d*; *m* 1982, Wendy Atkin (marr. diss. 1998). *Educ:* Riley High Sch.; Hull Technical Coll. (DipAe); Hull Univ. (BSc (Hons) Maths, ext. London). FIMechE 1945–2000; FRAeS 1952; FREng (FEng 1979). English Electric Co., Preston: Aerodynamicist, 1950; Dep. Chief Aerodyn., 1954; Head of Exper. Aerodyns, 1957; Asst Chief Engr, then Proj. Manager, 1959; Warton Div., British Aircraft Corporation Ltd: Special Dir, 1964; Dir, 1970; Asst Man. Dir, 1973–75; Dep. Man. Dir, 1975–76; Man. Dir, 1976–77; Man. Dir (Mil.), Aircraft Gp of British Aerospace, and Chm., Warton, Kingston-Brough and Manchester Divs, 1978–81. FRSA. Hon. DSc Hull, 1997. *Recreation:* sailing. *Address:* Les Fougères d'Icart, Icart Road, St Martin, Guernsey GY4 6JG.

ATKINS, Charlotte; MP (Lab) Staffordshire Moorlands, since 1997; *b* 24 Sept. 1950; *d* of Ronald and Jessie Atkins; *m* 1990, Gus Brain; one *d*. *Educ:* Colchester County High Sch.; LSE (BScEcon); MA London Univ. Asst Community Relations Officer, Luton CRC, 1974–76; Res. Officer, then Hd of Res., UCATT, 1976–80; Res. and Political Officer, AUEW (TASS), 1980–83; Press Officer, 1983–92, Parly Officer, 1992–97, COHSE, then UNISON. PPS to Minister of State for Trade, DTI, 2001–. Member: Select Cttee on Educn and Employment, 1997–2001; Cttee of Selection, 1997–2000. Mem., PLP Parly Cttee, 1997–2000. Contested (Lab) Eastbourne, Oct. 1990. *Address:* House of Commons, SW1A 0AA.

ATKINS, Dame Eileen, DBE 2001 (CBE 1990); actress and writer; *b* 16 June 1934; *d* of Arthur Thomas Atkins and late Annie Ellen (*née* Elkins); *m* Bill Shepherd. *Educ:* Latymer Grammar Sch., Edmonton; Guildhall Sch. of Music and Drama. *Stage appearances include:* Twelfth Night, Richard III, The Tempest, Old Vic, 1962; The Killing of Sister George (Best Actress, Standard Awards), Bristol Old Vic, transf. Duke of York's, 1965; The Cocktail Party, Wyndham's, transf. Haymarket, 1968; Vivat! Vivat Regina! (Variety Award), Piccadilly, 1970; Suzanne Andler, Aldwych, 1973; As You Like It, Stratford, 1973; St Joan, Old Vic, 1977; Passion Play, Aldwych, 1981; Medea, Young Vic, 1986; The Winter's Tale, and Cymbeline (Olivier Award), Mountain Language, NT, 1988; A Room of One's Own, Hampstead, 1989; Exclusive, Strand, 1989; Prin, NY, 1990; The Night of the Iguana, NT, 1992; Vita and Virginia, Ambassadors, 1993, NY, 1994; Indiscretions, NY, 1995; John Gabriel Borkman, NT, 1996; A Delicate Balance, Haymarket (Best Actress, Evening Standard Awards), 1997; The Unexpected Man, RSC, transf. Duchess (Best Actress, Olivier Awards), 1998; *films include:* Equus, 1974; The Dresser, 1984; Let Him Have It, 1990; Wolf, 1994; *TV appearances include:* The Duchess of Malfi; Sons and Lovers; Smiley's People; Nelly's Version; The Burston Rebellion; Breaking Up; The Vision; Mrs Pankhurst in In My Defence (series), 1990; A Room of One's Own, 1990; The Lost Language of Cranes, 1993; The Maitlands, 1993; Cold Comfort Farm, 1995 (film, 1997); Talking Heads 2, 1998; Madame Bovary, 2000. Co-created television series: Upstairs Downstairs; The House of Eliott; *screenplay:* Mrs Dalloway (Best Screenplay, Evening Standard British Film Awards), 1998. BAFTA Award, 1985. *Address:* c/o Paul Lyon Maris, ICM, Oxford House, 76 Oxford Street, W1N 0AX.

ATKINS, Rt Rev. Peter Geoffrey; Bishop of Waiapu, 1983–90; Dean, Theological College of St John the Evangelist, Auckland, 1991–96; *b* 29 April 1936; *s* of late Lt-Col Owen Ivan Atkins and Mrs Mary Atkins; *m* 1968, Rosemary Elizabeth (*née* Allen); one *d*. *Educ:* Merchant Taylors' School, Crosby, Liverpool; Sidney Sussex Coll., Cambridge; St John's Coll., Auckland, NZ. MA (Cantab), BD (Otago), LTh (NZ). Deacon 1962, priest 1963; Curate, Karori Parish, Wellington, 1962–66; Priest-Tutor, St Peter's Theological Coll., Siota, Solomon Is, 1966–67; Curate, Dannevirke Parish, dio. Waiapu, 1968–70; Vicar of Waipukurau Parish, 1970–73; Diocesan Sec. and Registrar, Diocese of Waiapu, 1973–79; Canon of St John's Cathedral, Napier, 1974–79; Vicar of Havelock North, 1979–83; Archdeacon of Hawkes Bay, 1979–83; Vicar-Gen., Diocese of Waiapu, 1980–83; Commissary to Archbishop of NZ, 1983; Lectr in Liturgy and Evangelism, Univ. of Auckland and Melbourne Coll. of Divinity, 1991–97. Hon. Sen. Res. Fellow, Univ. of Birmingham, 1996. *Publications:* Good News in Evangelism, 1992; (contrib.) Counselling Issues and South Pacific Communities, 1997; Worship 2000, 1999; Soul Time, 2000; (jtly) Personality Type and Scripture: exploring Luke's gospel, 2000, exploring Matthew's gospel, 2001; Soul Care, 2001; Ascension Now, 2001. *Recreations:* writing, gardening, music. *Address:* 9A Paunui Street, St Helier's Bay, Auckland 1005, New Zealand. *T:* (9) 5754775, *Fax:* (9) 5750477.

ATKINS, Prof. Peter William, PhD; Professor of Chemistry, University of Oxford, since 1998; Fellow and Tutor, Lincoln College, Oxford, since 1965; *b* 10 Aug. 1940; *s* of William Henry Atkins and Ellen Louise Atkins; *m* 1st, 1964, Judith Ann Kearton (marr. diss. 1983); one *d*; 2nd, 1991, Susan Adele Greenfield (*see* Baroness Greenfield). *Educ:* Dr Challoner's Sch., Amersham; Univ. of Leicester (BSc 1961; PhD 1964); MA Oxon 1965. Harkness Fellow, UCLA, 1964–65; Lectr, Univ. of Oxford, 1965–. Vis. Prof. in China, Japan, France, NZ and Israel. Nyholm Lectr, 1999. Chairman: Davy-Faraday Lab. Cttee, 1999–; Educn Strategy Develt Cttee, IUPAC, 2000. Mem. Council, Royal Instn, 1999–; Mem. Ct, Leicester Univ. Hon. Associate, Rationalist Press Assoc., 1993. Hon. DSc Utrecht, 1992. Meldola Medal, RSC, 1969. *Publications:* The Structure of Inorganic Radicals, 1967; Tables for Group Theory, 1970; Molecular Quantum Mechanics, 1970, 3rd edn 1997; Physical Chemistry, 1978, 7th edn 2002; Solutions Manual for Physical Chemistry, 1978, 7th edn 2002; Quanta: a handbook of concepts, 1974, 2nd edn 1991; Principles of Physical Chemistry, 1981; The Creation, 1981; Quantization, 1981; Solutions Manual for Molecular Quantum Mechanics, 1983, 2nd edn 1997; The Second Law, 1984; Molecules, 1987; General Chemistry, 1987, 2nd edn 1992; Chemistry: principles and applications, 1988; Inorganic Chemistry, 1990, 3rd edn 1999; Atoms, Electrons and Change, 1991; The Elements of Physical Chemistry, 1992, 3rd edn 2000; Creation Revisited, 1992; The Periodic Kingdom, 1995; Concepts of Physical Chemistry, 1995; Chemistry: molecules, matter, and change, 1997, 4th edn 1999; Chemical Principles, 1999, 2nd edn 2001. *Recreation:* working. *Address:* Lincoln College, Oxford OX1 3DR. *T:* (01865) 279797. *Club:* Athenæum.

ATKINS, Rt Hon. Sir Robert (James), Kt 1997; PC 1995; Member (C) North West Region, England, European Parliament, since 1999; *b* 5 Feb. 1946; *s* of late Reginald Alfred and of Winifred Margaret Atkins; *m* 1969, Dulcie Mary (*née* Chaplin); one *s* one *d*. *Educ:* Highgate School. Councillor, London Borough of Haringey, 1968–77; Vice-Chm., Greater London Young Conservatives, 1969–70, 1971–72. Contested (C) Luton West, Feb. 1974 and Oct. 1974 general elections. MP (C) Preston North, 1979–83, South Ribble, 1983–97; contested (C) South Ribble, 1997. PPS to Minister of State, DoI, then DTI, 1982–84, to Minister without Portfolio, 1984–85, to Sec. of State for Employment, 1985–87; Parly Under Sec. of State, DTI, 1987–89, Dept of Transport, 1989–90, DoE (Minister for Sport), 1990, DES (Minister for Sport), 1990–92; Minister of State, NI Office, 1992–94; Minister of State for the Environment and the Countryside, DoE, 1994–95. Vice-Chm., Cons. Aviation Cttee, 1979–82; Jt Sec., Cons. Defence Cttee, 1979–82. Pres., Cons. Trade Unionists, 1984–87; Chm., NW Cons. MPs, 1996–97. Member: Victorian Soc.; Sherlock Holmes Soc. of London; English Heritage; Historic Churches Preservation Trust; Nat. Trust. Freeman, City of London, 1989. *Publication:* (contrib.) Changing Gear, 1981. *Recreations:* cricket, ecclesiology, wine, Holmesiaria. *Address:* European Parliament, Rue Wiertz, 1047 Brussels, Belgium; Manor House, Lancaster Road, Garstang, Lancs PR3 1JA. *Clubs:* Carlton, MCC, Lord's Taverners'; Middlesex County Cricket, Lords and Commons Cricket, Lancashire County Cricket.

ATKINS, Ronald Henry; *b* Barry, Glam, 13 June 1916; *s* of Frank and Elizabeth Atkins; *m*; three *s* two *d*. *Educ:* Barry County Sch.; London Univ. (BA Hons). Teacher, 1949–66 (latterly Head, Eng. Dept, Halstead Sec. Sch.); Lectr, Accrington Coll. of Further Educn, 1970–74. Member: Braintree RDC, 1952–61; Preston Dist Council, 1974–76, 1980–. Contested (Lab) Lowestoft, 1964; MP (Lab) Preston North, 1966–70 and Feb. 1974–1979. *Recreations:* jazz, dancing, walking. *Address:* 38 James Street, Preston, Lancs PR1 4JU. *T:* (01772) 251910.

ATKINS, Rosemary Jean, (Rosie); Editor, Gardens Illustrated Magazine, since 1993; *b* 9 Oct. 1947; *m* 1973, Eric James Brown; one *s* one *d*. *Educ:* St Michael's Sch. for Girls, Limpsfield; Ravensbourne Sch. of Art. Sunday Times, 1968–82; freelance journalist and gardening writer, 1982; gardening corresp., Today. Produced jointly, In the Air, BBC Radio 4, 1983. Editor's Editor Award, BSME, 1996. *Publication:* (jtly) The Sunday Times Book of the Countryside. *Recreations:* gardening, painting, riding, walking, photography. *Address:* Gardens Illustrated, BBC Worldwide Ltd, Woodlands, Wood Lane, W12 0TT. *Club:* Chelsea Arts.

ATKINSON, Sir Alec; *see* Atkinson, Sir J. A.

ATKINSON, Sir Anthony Barnes, (Sir Tony), Kt 2000; FBA 1984; Warden of Nuffield College, Oxford, since 1994; *b* 4 Sept. 1944; *s* of Norman Joseph Atkinson and Esther Muriel Atkinson; *m* 1965, Judith Mary (*née* Mandeville); two *s* one *d*. *Educ:* Cranbrook Sch.; Churchill Coll., Cambridge (MA). Fellow, St John's Coll., Cambridge, 1967–71; Prof. of Econs, Univ. of Essex, 1971–76; Prof. and Hd of Dept of Political Economy, UCL, 1976–79; Prof. of Econs, LSE, 1980–92; Prof. of Political Economy, and Fellow, Churchill Coll., Cambridge, 1992–94. Vis. Prof. MIT, 1973. Member: Royal Commn on Distribution of Income and Wealth, 1978–79; Retail Prices Index Adv. Cttee, 1984–90; Pension Law Review Cttee, 1992–93; Social Justice Commn, 1992–94; Conseil d'Analyse Economique, France, 1997–. President: European Econ. Assoc., 1989 (Vice-Pres., 1986–88); Internat. Econ. Assoc., 1989–92; Vice-Pres., British Acad., 1988–90. Fellow, Econometric Soc., 1975 (Vice-Pres., 1986–87, Pres., 1988). Hon. Mem., Amer. Econ. Assoc., 1985. Fellow, Centre for Econ. Studies, Munich, 1995. Hon. Dr Rer. Pol. Univ. of Frankfurt, 1987; Hon. Dr en Sci. Econ., Univ. of Lausanne, 1988; Hon. Dr: Univ. of Liège, 1989; Athens Univ. of Econs, 1991; Stirling, 1992; Edinburgh, 1994; Essex, Bologna, and Ecole Normale Supérieure, Paris, 1995; South Bank and Univ. Catholique, Louvain, 1996; Nottingham, 2000. Scientific Prize, Union des Assurances de Paris, 1986; Frank E. Seidman Dist. Award in Pol. Econ., Rhodes Coll., Tenn, 1995. Editor, Jl of Public Economics, 1972–97. *Publications:* Poverty in Britain and the Reform of Social Security, 1969; Unequal Shares, 1972; The Tax Credit Scheme, 1973; Economics of Inequality, 1975; (with A. J. Harrison) Distribution of Personal Wealth in Britain, 1978; (with J. E. Stiglitz) Lectures on Public Economics, 1980; Social Justice and Public Policy, 1982; (jtly) Parents and Children, 1983; (with J. Micklewright) Unemployment Benefits and Unemployment Duration, 1985; Poverty and Social Security, 1989; (with J. Micklewright) Economic Transformation in Eastern Europe and the Distribution of Income, 1992; Public Economics in Action, 1995; Incomes and the Welfare State, 1996; The Economic Consequences of Rolling Back the Welfare State, 1999; articles in Rev. of Econ. Studies, Econ. Jl, Jl of Public Econs, Jl of Econ. Theory. *Address:* 39 Park Town, Oxford OX2 6SL. *T:* (01865) 556064; Nuffield College, Oxford OX1 1NF.

ATKINSON, Arthur Kingsley Hall, CB 1985; Chief Executive, Intervention Board for Agricultural Produce, 1980–86; *b* 24 Dec. 1926; *er s* of Arthur Hall Atkinson and Florence (*née* Gerrans). *Educ:* Priory Sch., Shrewsbury; Emmanuel Coll., Cambridge (MA). RAF, 1948; MAFF: Asst Principal 1950; Private Sec. 1953; Principal 1956; Asst Sec. 1965; Under Sec., 1973; Cabinet Office, 1976–78; MAFF, 1978–80. *Recreations:* travel, music, gardening.

ATKINSON, Prof. Bernard, OBE 2001; FREng, FIChemE; Director-General, BRF International (formerly Director, Brewing Research Foundation), 1981–96; *b* 17 March 1936; *s* of late Thomas Atkinson and of Elizabeth Ann (*née* Wilcox); *m* 1957, Kathleen Mary Richardson; two *s*. *Educ:* Farnworth Grammar Sch.; Univ. of Birmingham (BSc); Univ. of Manchester Inst. of Science and Technology; PhD Univ. of Manchester. FREng (FEng 1980). Post-Doctoral Fellow and Asst Prof., Rice Univ., Houston, Texas, 1960–63; Lectr, Sen. Lectr in Chem. Engrg, and latterly Reader in Biochem. Engrg, University Coll. of Swansea, 1963–74 (Hon. Fellow, 1991); Prof. and Head of Dept of Chem. Engrg, UMIST, 1974–81; Visiting Professor: UMIST, 1981–86; Swansea, 1986–; Heriot-Watt, 1991–96. European Brewery Convention: Mem., Management Cttee and Council, 1990–97; Vice Pres., 1991–97. Mem., BBSRC, 1996–2001. Editor, Biochemical Engineering Journal, 1983–93. Senior Moulton Medal, IChemE, 1976; Gairn EEC Medal, Soc. of Engrs, 1985; Presidential Award, Master Brewers' Assoc. of the Americas, 1988; Donald Medal, IChemE, 1996. *Publications:* Biochemical Reactors, 1974, trans. Japanese, Russian, Spanish; (with P. F. Cooper) Biological Fluidised Bed Treatment of Water and Waste Water, 1981; (with F. Mavituna) Biochemical Engineering and Biotechnology Handbook, 1982, 2nd edn 1991; (ed) Research and Innovation in the 1990s: the chemical engineering challenge, 1986; (with C. Webb and G. M. Black) Process Engineering Aspects of Immobilised Cell Systems, 1986; numerous contribs to chemical engrg and biochemical engrg jls. *Recreations:* cycling, sailing, walking. *Address:* Little Mieders, Borers Arms Road, Copthorne, Crawley, West Sussex RH10 3LJ. *T:* (01342) 713181.

ATKINSON, Prof. Bruce Wilson, PhD; Professor of Geography, Queen Mary and Westfield College (formerly at Queen Mary College), University of London, since 1983; *b* 28 Sept. 1941; *s* of J. and S. A. Atkinson. *Educ:* University Coll., London (BSc, PhD). Queen Mary, subseq. Queen Mary and Westfield College, University of London: Lectr, 1964–78; Reader, 1978–83; Hd, Dept of Geog., 1985–89; Dean of Social Scis, 1991–94; Mem., Senate and Acad. Council, Univ. of London, 1991–94. Natural Environment Research Council: Mem., 1982–85, Chm., 1988–91, Aquatic & Atmospheric Phys. Sci. Cttee; Mem., Atmos. Sci., Marine Sci., Terrestrial and Freshwater Sci. and Higher Educn Affairs Cttees, 1988–91. Member: Meteorol and Atmos. Phys. Sub-cttee, Nat. Cttee on Geodesy and Geophysics, 1988–90; Scientific Adv. Cttee, Meteorol Office, 1996–. Mem. Council and cttees, and Editor, Weather, RMetS, 1972–79; Chm., Pubns Cttee, 1992–98, Mem. Council, 1993–95, RGS–IBG (formerly RGS); Mem., Assoc. Brit. Climatologists, 1970– (Chm., 1976–78). Ed., Progress in Physical Geography, 1977–. Hugh Robert Mill Medal, RMetS, 1974; Back Award, RGS, 1981. *Publications:* Weather Business, 1968; (ed) Dynamical Meteorology, 1981; Meso-scale Atmospheric Circulations, 1981; Weather: Review of UK Statistical Sources, 1985; (ed jtly) Encyclopædic Dictionary of Physical Geography, 1986; (with A. Gadd) Weather: a modern guide to forecasting, 1986; articles in Qly Jl RMetS, Jl Applied Met., Boundary Layer Meteorol., Monthly Weather Rev., Revs of Geophysics, Jl of Geophysical Res., Trans IBG, Geog., Weather, Canadian Geog. *Recreations:* walking, music. *Address:* Department of Geography, Queen Mary and Westfield College, Mile End Road, E1 4NS. *T:* (020) 7882 5402. *Clubs:* Athenæum, Geographical.

ATKINSON, David Anthony; MP (C) Bournemouth East, since Nov. 1977; *b* 24 March 1940; *s* of late Arthur Joseph Atkinson and of Joan Margaret Atkinson (*née* Zink); *m* 1968, Susan Nicola Pilsworth; one *s* one *d*. *Educ:* St George's Coll., Weybridge; Coll. of Automobile and Aeronautical Engrg, Chelsea. Diplomas in Auto. Engrg and Motor Industry Management. Member: Southend County Borough Council, 1969–72; Essex CC, 1973–78. PPS, 1979–87, to Rt Hon. Paul Channon, MP (Minister of State, Civil Service Dept, 1979–81, Minister for the Arts, 1981–83, Minister of State, DTI, 1983–86, Sec. of State for Trade and Industry, 1986–87). Introduced Licensing (Occasional Permissions) Act 1983. Mem., Council of Europe and WEU, 1979–86, 1987– (Leader, Conservative delgn, 1997–; Chm., EDG, 1998–). Nat. Chm., Young Conservative Orgn, 1970–71; Life Vice Pres., Christian Solidarity Internat. (UK), 1996 (Chm., 1979–83; Pres., 1983–96). *Recreations:* mountaineering, art and architecture, travel. *Address:* House of Commons, SW1A 0AA.

ATKINSON, Rt Rev. David John; *see* Thetford, Bishop Suffragan of.

ATKINSON, David Rowland; Regional Chairman, British Gas East Midlands, 1987–92; *b* 18 June 1930; *s* of late Rowland Hodgson Atkinson and Nora Marian (*née* Coleman); *m* 1956, Marian Eileen Sales; one *d*. *Educ:* Wrekin College. FCA, CIMgt, CompIGasE. National Coal Board: NW Div., 1955; E Midlands Div., 1961; Chief Accountant, W Midlands Gas, 1969; Dir of Finance, E Midlands Gas, 1977; Dep. Chm., SE Gas, 1983; Dir of Finance, British Gas, 1985. *Recreations:* Rugby, gardening, ciné photography. *Address:* Russetts, 124 The Ridings, Rothley, Leics LE7 7SL.

ATKINSON, Air Marshal Sir David (William), KBE 1982; FFOM; FRCPE; FFPHM; Director-General, Stroke (formerly Chest, Heart and Stroke) Association, 1985–93; Director-General, RAF Medical Services, 1981–84; *b* 29 Sept. 1924; *s* of late David William Atkinson and Margaret Atkinson; *m* 1948, Mary (*née* Sowerby) (separated); one *s*. *Educ:* Edinburgh Univ. (MB, ChB 1948). DPH and DIH, London; FFPHM (FFCM 1976); MFOM 1978, FFOM 1983; FRCPE 1983. Joined RAF, 1949; med. officer appts, UK, Jordan and Egypt, 1949–63; Student, RAF Staff Coll., 1963–64; SMO, RAF Brüggen, Germany, 1964–67; Dep. PMO, HQ Air Support Comd, 1967–70; PMO, HQ Brit. Forces Gulf, Bahrain, 1970–71; OC RAF Hosp., Wegberg, Germany, 1971–73; Dir of Health and Research (RAF), 1974–78; QHP 1977–84; PMO, RAF Strike Command, 1978–81. Freeman, City of London, 1984; Liveryman, Soc. of Apothecaries. CStJ 1981. *Publication:* (jtly) Double Crew Continuous Flying Operations: a study of aircrew sleep patterns, 1970. *Recreations:* walking, gardening, reading, looking at pictures. *Address:* Rosedene, Woodside Lane, Lymington, Hants SO41 8FJ. *Club:* Royal Air Force.

ATKINSON, Frank, CBE 1995 (OBE 1980); FSA; FMA; Director, Beamish North of England Open Air Museum, 1970–87; *b* 13 April 1924; *s* of Ernest Atkinson and Elfrida (*née* Bedford); *m* 1953, Joan Peirson; three *s*. *Educ:* Holgate Grammar Sch., Barnsley; Sheffield Univ. (BSc). Director: Wakefield City Art Gall. and Mus., 1949; Halifax Museums, 1951; Bowes Mus. and Durham Co. Mus. Service, 1958. Member: Working Party on Preservation of Technolog. Material, 1970–71; Wright Cttee on Provincial Museums and Galls, 1971–73; Working Party of Standing Commn on Museums and Galls (Drew Report), 1975–78; Museums and Galleries Commn, 1987–94 (Chm., Registration Cttee, 1988–94). Chairman: Thomas Bewick Birthplace Trust, 1985–91; Northumbrian Tourism Co-ordination Gp, 1989–93; Thomas Bewick (Newcastle) Trust, 1996–2001; Juvenile Autism in the NE Wkg Gp, 1996–99; Friends of Beamish Mus. Ltd, 1996–. Pres., Museums Assoc., 1974–75. Hon. MA Newcastle upon Tyne, 1971; Hon. DCL Durham, 1987. *Publications:* Aspects of the 18th century Woollen and Worsted Trade, 1956; The Great Northern Coalfield, 1966, 3rd edn 1979; Industrial Archaeology of North East England, 1974; Life and Traditions in Northumberland and Durham, 1977, 3rd edn 2001; North East England: people at work 1860–1950, 1980; Victorian Britain: North East England, 1989; Northern Life, 1991; The Man Who Made Beamish: an autobiography, 1999; contribs to Trans Newcomen Soc., Procs of British Spel. Soc., Antiquaries Jl, Museums Jl, etc. *Recreations:* pot-holing (now only in retrospect), computer programming, village history. *Address:* The Old Vicarage, Ovingham, Prudhoe, Northumberland NE42 6BW. *T:* (01661) 835445.

ATKINSON, Sir Frederick John, (Sir Fred), KCB 1979 (CB 1971); Hon. Fellow of Jesus College, Oxford, since 1979; *b* 7 Dec. 1919; *s* of George Edward Atkinson and of late Elizabeth Sabina Cooper; *m* 1947, Margaret Grace Gibson; two *d*. *Educ:* Dulwich Coll.; Jesus Coll., Oxford. Lectr, Jesus and Trinity Colls, Oxford, 1947–49; Economic Section, Cabinet Office, 1949–51; British Embassy, Washington, 1952–54; HM Treasury, 1955–62; Economic Adviser, Foreign Office, 1962–63; HM Treasury, 1963–69 (Dep. Dir, Economic Section, Treasury, 1965–69); Controller, Economics and Statistics, Min. of Technology, 1970; Chief Econ. Adviser, DTI, 1970–73; an Asst Sec.-Gen., OECD, Paris, 1973–75; Dep. Sec. and Chief Econ. Advr, Dept of Energy, 1975–77; Chief Economic Adviser, HM Treasury, and Head of Govt Econ. Service, 1977–79. *Publication:* (with S. Hall) Oil and the British Economy, 1983. *Recreation:* reading. *Address:* 26 Lee Terrace, Blackheath, SE3 9TZ. *T:* (020) 8852 1040; Tickner Cottage, Aldington, Kent TN25 7EG. *T:* (01233) 720514.

ATKINSON, Brig. Geoffrey Arthur; Executive Secretary, Royal Academy of Engineering (formerly Fellowship of Engineering), 1990–93; *b* 17 March 1931; *s* of Arthur Vivian Atkinson and Flora Muriel Atkinson (*née* Lucas); *m* 1952, Joyce Eileen Pavey; one *s* one *d*. *Educ:* Berkhamsted Sch.; Royal Military College of Science (BScEng); Manchester Business Sch. CEng, FIMechE. Commnd REME, 1950; Regtl and technical employment, UK, Malaya, BAOR, 1950–60; EME, Queen's Own Hussars, 1960; Instr, RMA Sandhurst, 1962; Technical Staff trng, RMCS, 1963; BEME 20 Armd Bde, 1965; Weapons Staff, Army Sch. of Transport, 1967; CO 7 Armd Workshop, 1970; GSO1(W) DGFVE, 1972; ADEME 1/3 HQ DEME, 1975; Mil. Dir of Studies, Weapons and Vehicles, RMCS, 1977; CCREME HQ 1 BR Corps, BAOR, 1978; Dir of Equipment Engrg, HQ DGEME, 1981; Comdr HQ REME TA, 1983, retired 1984. Hon. Col REME Specialist Units TA, 1986–89. Dep. Sec., Fellowship of Engineering, 1984. Member: Council, Parly and Scientific Cttee, 1991–93; Cttee, Parly Gp for Engrg Develt, 1991–93. Freeman, City of London, 1990; Liveryman, Co. of Engineers, 1991. *Recreations:* sailing, antique furniture restoration.

ATKINSON, Harry Hindmarsh, PhD; consultant; Under Secretary, Director (Special Responsibilities), Science and Engineering Research Council, 1988–92; *b* 5 Aug. 1929; *s* of late Harry Temple Atkinson and Constance Hindmarsh Atkinson (*née* Shields); *m* 1958, Anne Judith Barrett; two *s* one *d*. *Educ:* Nelson Coll., Nelson, NZ; Canterbury University Coll., NZ (BSc, sen. schol.; MSc (1st cl. Hons)), 1948–52. Asst Lectr, Physics, CUC, 1952–53; Research Asst, Cornell Univ., USA, 1954–55; Corpus Christi Coll. and Cavendish Laboratory, Cambridge Univ., 1955–58 (PhD); Sen. Research Fellow, AERE, Harwell, 1958–61; Head, General Physics Group, Rutherford Laboratory, 1961–69; Staff Chief Scientific Adviser, Cabinet Office, 1969–72; Dep. Chief Scientific Officer and Head of Astronomy, Space and Radio Division, SRC, 1972–78; Dir (Astronomy, Space and Radio, and Nuclear Physics), SRC later SERC, 1979–83; Dir Science, SERC, 1983–88. Chm. Council, ESA, 1984–87 (Vice-Chm., 1981–84, UK Deleg., 1974–87); UK Member: EISCAT Council, 1976–86; Bd, Anglo-Aust. Telescope, 1979–88; Cttee, S African Astronomical Observatory, 1979–83; Council, European Synchrotron Radiation Facility, 1986–88; Chairman: Cttee on Netherlands/UK Astronomy Collaboration, 1981–88; Steering Cttee, Inst. Laue-Langevin, Grenoble, 1984 and 1987 (UK deleg., 1983–88); UK Govt Task Force on Potentially Hazardous Near-Earth Objects, 2000. Assessor, UGC, 1987–89; Member: NI Cttee, UFC, 1989–93; Working Gp on Internat. Collaboration (Cabinet Office), ACOST, 1989; Co-ordinator, UK, Australia, NZ sci. collaboration, 1989–94. Chief Scientist, Loss Prevention Council, 1990–98. *Publications:* papers on various branches of physics, science and higher education policy, international comparisons. *Address:* Bampton, Oxon. *Club:* Athenæum.

ATKINSON, Prof. James; Founder Director, Centre for Reformation Studies, Sheffield, since 1983; Professor of Biblical Studies, University of Sheffield, 1967–79, now Emeritus; *b* 27 April 1914; *s* of Nicholas Ridley Atkinson and Margaret (*née* Hindhaugh); *m* 1939, Laura Jean Nutley (decd); one *s* one *d*. *Educ:* Tynemouth High Sch.; Univ. of Durham. MA 1939, MLitt 1950 Durham; DrTheol, Münster, Germany, 1955. Curate, Newcastle upon Tyne, 1937; Precentor, Sheffield Cath., 1941; Vicar, Sheffield, 1944; Fellow, Univ. of Sheffield, 1951; Canon Theologian: Leicester, 1954–70; Sheffield, 1971–93; Reader in Theology, Univ. of Hull, 1956; Vis. Prof., Chicago, 1966; Public Orator, Univ. of Sheffield, 1972–79; Consultant Prof. with Evangelical Anglican Res. Centre, Latimer House, Oxford, 1981–84; Special Prof. in Reformation Theol., Univ. of Nottingham, 1993–. Examining Chaplain to: Bp of Leicester, 1968–79; Bp of Derby, 1978–95. Member: Anglican-Roman Catholic Preparatory Commission, 1967–; Gen. Synod of Church of England, 1975–80; Marriage Commn, 1976–78. Pres., Soc. for Study of Theology, 1978–80; Mem., Acad. Internat. des Sciences Religieuses, 1980–. Hon. DD Hull, 1997. *Publications:* Library of Christian Classics, Vol. XVI, 1962; Rome and Reformation, 1965; Luther's Works, Vol. 44, 1966; Luther and the Birth of Protestantism, 1968; (trans. Spanish 1971, Italian 1983); The Reformation, Paternoster Church History, Vol. 4, 1968; The Trial of Luther, 1971; Martin Luther: Prophet to the Church Catholic, 1983; The Darkness of Faith, 1987; (contrib.) The Bible, the Reformation and the Church, ed W. P. Stephens, 1994; contribs to learned jls, also essays and parts of books. *Recreations:* gardening, music. *Address:* Leach House, Hathersage, Derbyshire S32 1BA. *T:* (01433) 650570; Centre for Reformation Studies, St George's Hall, Portobello, Sheffield S1 4DP. *T:* (0114) 2227079.

See also Sir Robert Atkinson.

ATKINSON, James Oswald; HM Diplomatic Service; Ambassador to Democratic Republic of Congo and (non-resident) to Republic of Congo, since 2000; *b* 20 Oct. 1944;

s of James Edward Atkinson and Helen (*née* Liuta); *m* 1980, Annemiek van Werkum; one *d*. *Educ:* Woolverstone Hall, Suffolk. Joined HM Diplomatic Service, 1966: Third Secretary: Nicosia, 1969–72; Gabarone, 1972–76; Second Sec., Damascus, 1976–79; FCO, 1980–84; First Secretary: Athens, 1984–88; Jakarta, 1988–90; FCO, 1990–93; Dep. High Comr, Kampala, 1993–97; Dep. Hd of Consular Service, London, 1997–2000. *Recreations:* sailing, photography. *Address:* c/o Foreign and Commonwealth Office, King Charles Street, SW1A 2AH.

ATKINSON, Sir John Alexander, (Sir Alec), KCB 1978 (CB 1976); DFC 1943; Second Permanent Secretary, Department of Health and Social Security, 1977–79; *b* 9 June 1919; *yr s* of late Rev. R. F. Atkinson and late Harriet Harrold Atkinson, BSc (*née* Lowdon); *m* 1945, Marguerite Louise Pearson, MA; one *d*. *Educ:* Kingswood Sch.; Queen's Coll., Oxford. Served in RAF, 1939–45. Asst Prin., 1946, Prin., 1949, Min. of Nat. Insce; Cabinet Office, 1950–52; Prin. Private Sec. to Minister of Pensions and Nat. Insce, 1957–58; Asst Sec., 1958; Under-Sec., Min. of Social Security, later DHSS, 1966–73; Dep. Sec., DHSS, 1973–76. Member: Panel of Chairmen, CSSB, 1979–88; Occupational Pensions Bd, 1981–88. Chm., Working Gp on Pensions and Divorce, Pensions Management Inst. with Law Soc., 1992–93. Pres., Kingswood Assoc., 1983. *Address:* Bleak House, The Drive, Belmont, Sutton, Surrey SM2 7DH. *T:* (020) 8642 6479. *Club:* Oxford and Cambridge.

ATKINSON, Kenneth Neil, FCIPD; Managing Director, Travel Training Co. Ltd, 1995 (Dir, then Chief Executive, ABTA National Training Board, 1989–94); *b* 4 April 1931; *s* of William Atkinson and Alice Reid. *Educ:* Kingussie High Sch., Inverness-shire. ARCM 1961; FCIPD (FIPM 1986). Various appts, Min. of Labour and Dept of Employment, 1948–67; Dep. Chief Conciliation Officer, Dept of Employment, 1968–72; Dir, Industry Trng Bd Relations, MSC, 1973–78; Manpower Services Dir, Scotland, 1979–82; Dir of Youth Training, Training Agency (formerly Manpower Services/Training Commn), 1983–89. Chm., Prince's Trust Community Venture, 1989–92; Mem. Bd, Prince's Trust Volunteers, 1993–94. Mem., Council, CGLI, 1991–98. Musical Dir, Ruislip Operatic Soc., 1994–. *Recreations:* tennis, choral and solo singing, conducting. *Address:* 3 St Catherines Road, Ruislip, Middlesex HA4 7RX. *T:* (01895) 633945. *Club:* Royal Scottish Automobile (Glasgow).

ATKINSON, Kent; *see* Atkinson, M. K.

ATKINSON, Mary; *see under* Hardwick, Mollie.

ATKINSON, (Michael) Kent; Group Finance Director, Lloyds TSB Group plc, since 1997; *b* 19 May 1945; *s* of late Carl Kent Atkinson and Edith Atkinson (*née* Gilbert); *m* 1970, Eufemia Alexandra Alarcón; two *s*. *Educ:* Blundell's Sch. Entered Bank of London & South America Ltd, 1964: sen. appts, Bank of London/Lloyds Bank Internat. Ltd in Colombia, Ecuador, Panama, Bahrain, Dubai, Paraguay and Argentina, 1967–86; Gen. Manager, Argentina, Chile, Peru, Bolivia, Paraguay and Uruguay, 1987–89; Lloyds Bank plc: Regl Exec. Dir, 1989–94; Gen. Manager, Retail Ops, 1994–95; Gp Chief Financial Officer, Lloyds TSB Gp plc, 1995–96. Director: Lloyds Bank Subsidiaries Ltd, 1995–; Lloyds Commercial Properties Ltd, 1995–98; Lloyds Bank Financial Services (Hldgs) Ltd, 1995–; TSB Bank Ltd, 1995–99; Lloyds TSB Bank plc, 1995–; Three Copthall Avenue Ltd, 2000–, Non-exec. Dir, Coca-Cola HBC SA, 1998–. *Recreations:* tennis, golf, Rugby, soccer, opera, personal computers. *Address:* Lloyds TSB Group plc, 71 Lombard Street, EC3P 3BS. *T:* (020) 7356 1422. *Clubs:* Effingham Golf, Horsley Sports.

ATKINSON, Michael William, CMG 1985; MBE 1970; HM Diplomatic Service, retired; *b* 11 April 1932; *m* 1963, Veronica Bobrovsky; two *s* one *d*. *Educ:* Purley County Grammar School; Queen's College, Oxford (BA Hons). Served FO, Vientiane, Buenos Aires, British Honduras, Madrid; FCO 1975; NATO Defence Coll., 1976; Counsellor, Budapest, 1977–80, Peking, 1980–82; Hd of Consular Dept, FCO, 1982–85; Ambassador: to Ecuador, 1985–89; to Romania, 1989–92; Personnel Assessor, FCO, 1992–98.

ATKINSON, Norman; *b* 25 March 1923; *s* of George Atkinson, Manchester; *m* 1948, Irene Parry. *Educ:* elementary and technical schs. Served apprenticeship, Metropolitan Vickers Ltd, Trafford Park. Member of Manchester City Council, 1945–49. Chief Design Engineer, Manchester University, 1957–64. Contested (Lab) Wythenshawe, 1955, Altrincham and Sale, 1959. MP (Lab) Tottenham, 1964–87. Treasurer, Labour Party, 1976–81. Mem., Governing Body, Imperial Coll., London, 1975–. Hon. MA Manchester, 1997. *Publications:* Sir Joseph Whitworth: the world's best mechanician, 1996; political pamphlets. *Recreations:* walking, cricket, football, oil painting. *Address:* 4 Willow Court, 31 Willow Place, SW1P 1JJ. *Club:* Arts.

ATKINSON, Rev. Canon Peter Gordon; Canon Residentiary and Chancellor of Chichester Cathedral, since 1997; *b* 26 Aug. 1952; *m* 1983, Lynne Wilcock; two *s* one *d*. *Educ:* St John's Coll., Oxford (BA 1974; MA 1978); Westcott House, Cambridge. Ordained: deacon, 1979; priest, 1980; Asst Curate, Clapham Old Town Team Ministry, 1979–83; Priest-in-charge, St Mary, Tatsfield, 1983–90; Rector, Holy Trinity, Bath, 1990–91; Principal, Chichester Theol Coll., 1991–94; Rector, Lavant, 1994–97; Bursalis Preb., Chichester Cathedral, 1991–97. Mem., Gen. Synod of C of E, 2000–. *Publication:* (contrib.) Stepping Stones: joint essays on Anglican Catholic and Evangelical Unity, ed C. Baxter, 1987. *Recreations:* reading, travel. *Address:* The Residentiary, Canon Lane, Chichester, West Sussex PO19 1PX. *T:* (01243) 782961.

ATKINSON, Peter Landreth; MP (C) Hexham, since 1992; *b* 19 Jan. 1943; *s* of Major Douglas Wilson Atkinson, RTR (*d* Burma, 1945) and of Amy Landreth; *m* 1976, Brione, *d* of late Comdr Arthur Darley, RN and Elspeth Darley; two *d*. *Educ:* Cheltenham Coll. Journalist, 1961–87 (formerly News Editor, Evening Standard); Dep. Dir, British Field Sports Soc., 1987–92. Councillor: London Borough of Wandsworth, 1978–82; Suffolk County Council, 1989–92. PPS to Chm. of Cons. Pty, 1994–95, 1997–98; an Opposition Whip, 1999–2001. Mem., Select Cttee on Scottish Affairs, 1992–. *Recreations:* shooting, racing, gardening. *Address:* House of Commons, SW1A 0AA. *Clubs:* Turf; Albert Edward (Hexham); Northern Counties (Newcastle).

ATKINSON, Reay; *see* Atkinson, W. R.

ATKINSON, Sir Robert, Kt 1983; DSC 1941; RD 1947; FREng; Chairman, British Shipbuilders, 1980–84; *b* 7 March 1916; *s* of Nicholas and Margaret Atkinson; *m* 1st, 1941, Joyce Forster (*d* 1973); one *s* one *d*; 2nd, 1977, Margaret Hazel Walker. *Educ:* London Univ. (BSc(Eng) Hons). FIMechE, CEng, FREng (FEng 1983); FIMarE. Served War 1939–45 (DSC 1941 and two Bars, 1st, 1943, 2nd, 1944, mentioned in Despatches, 1943). Managing Director: Wm Doxford, 1957–61; Tube Investments (Eng), 1961–67; Unicorn Industries, 1967–72; Chm., Aurora Holdings, Sheffield, 1972–84; Dir, Stag Furniture Hldgs, 1973–92. Chm., Engrg and Shipbuilding Cttee, BSI, 1984–87. James Clayton Medal, NECInst, 1961. *Publications:* The Design and Operating Experience of an Ore Carrier Built Abroad, 1957; The Manufacture of Steel Crankshafts, 1960; Some Crankshaft Failures: Investigation into Causes and Remedies, 1960; The Development and Decline of British Shipbuilding, 1999; technical papers. *Recreations:* salmon fishing, walking, gardening. *Address:* Southwood House, Itchen Abbas, Winchester, Hants SO21 1AT. *Club:* Royal Thames Yacht.

See also Prof. James Atkinson.

ATKINSON, Rowan Sebastian; actor and writer; *b* 6 Jan. 1955; *s* of late Eric Atkinson and of Ella May Atkinson; *m* 1990, Sunetra Sastry; one *s* one *d*. *Educ:* Durham Cathedral Choristers' Sch.; St Bees Sch.; Newcastle Univ.; Oxford Univ. (BSc, MSc). *Stage:* Beyond a Joke, Hampstead, 1978; Oxford Univ. Revues at Edinburgh Festival Fringe; youngest person to have a one-man show in the West End of London, 1981; The Nerd, 1984; The New Revue, 1986; The Sneeze, 1988; *television:* Not the Nine O'clock News, 1979–82; The Black Adder, 1983; Blackadder II, 1985; Blackadder the Third, 1987; Blackadder goes Forth, 1989; Mr Bean, The Return of Mr Bean, The Curse of Mr Bean, 1990–94; The Thin Blue Line, 1995; *films:* The Tall Guy, 1989; The Appointment of Dennis Jennings, 1989; The Witches, 1990; Hot Shots—Part Deux, 1993; Four Weddings and a Funeral, 1994; The Lion King, 1994; Bean—The Ultimate Disaster Movie, 1997; Blackadder—Back and Forth, 2000; Maybe Baby, 2000; Rat Race, 2001; Scooby Doo, 2002. *Recreations:* motor cars, motor sport. *Address:* c/o PBJ Management Ltd, 7 Soho Street, W1D 3DQ. *T:* (020) 7287 1112; *e-mail:* general@pbjmgt.co.uk.

ATKINSON, Dr Susan, (Sue), FFPHM; Regional Director of Public Health/Medical Director, London Regional Office, NHS Executive, Department of Health, since 1999; *b* 10 Aug. 1946; *d* of Fredrick Booth Atkinson and Jay Atkinson (*née* Carruthers); *m*; one *d*. *Educ:* Merchant Taylors' Sch. for Girls; UCNW (BSc Zoology); New Hall, Cambridge (MA 1976; MB BChir 1975); Middlesex Hosp. Med. Sch. DCH 1977; FFPHM 1989. Res. Associate in animal behaviour/zool., Univ. of Cambridge, 1969–70; Registrar and SHO posts, Paediatrics, Bristol Children's Hosp. and Addenbrooke's Hosp., 1976–78; Registrar in Public Health Medicine, Avon Area HA, 1979–80; Res. Fellow, NH and MRC Perinatal Epidemiology Unit, Univ. of WA, 1980–81; GP, Bristol, 1981–82; Sen. Registrar in Public Health Medicine, Bristol and Weston HA, 1982–84; Public Health Consultant, Bristol HA, 1985–87; Dir, Public Health, and Chief Exec., SE London HA, 1987–93; Regional Director of Public Health: Wessex and SW (formerly Wessex) RHA, 1993–94; S Thames Regl Office, NHS Exec. (formerly S Thames RHA), 1994–99. Special Advr to Health Select Cttee, 1991–92. *Publications:* articles on spastic diplegia, vision screening and public health in UK. *Recreations:* cinema, art, music. *Address:* NHS Executive, 40 Eastbourne Terrace, W2 3QR. *T:* (020) 7725 5419.

ATKINSON, Prof. Thomas, PhD, DSc, DEng; FREng; Professor and Head of Department of Mining Engineering, Nottingham University, 1977–88, now Emeritus; Adjunct Professor, University of British Columbia, since 1997; *b* 23 Jan. 1924; *s* of Thomas Bell and Elizabeth Atkinson; *m* 1948, Dorothy; one *d*. *Educ:* Imperial Coll., London. DIC; PhD London, 1973; DSc Nottingham, 1988; DEng Witwatersrand, 1989. FREng (FEng 1987); FIMM, FIMinE, FIEE, FIMechE. Served RN, 1942–46. Charlaw and Sacriston Collieries Ltd, Durham, 1938–42; NCB, 1946–49; Andrew Yule, India, 1949–53; KWPR, Australia, 1953–56; Mining Engr, Powell Duffryn Technical Services Ltd, 1956–68; Sen. Lectr, Imperial Coll., 1968–73; Head of Coal Mining Div., Shell Internat. Petroleum Maatschappij BV, Holland, 1973–77. Dir, British Mining Consultants Ltd, 1969–88; Chm., Consolidated Coalfields Ltd, 1986–91. Chm., Nat. Awards Tribunal, British Coal (formerly NCB), 1984–92. FRSA. *Publications:* contribs to Mining Engrg, Mineral Econs, Mine Electrics, etc. *Recreation:* painting. *Address:* # 212, 5683 Hampton Place, Vancouver, BC V6T 2H3, Canada. *Club:* Chaps.

ATKINSON, (William) Reay, CB 1985; FBCS; Under Secretary, 1978–86, and Regional Director, North Eastern Region, 1981–86, Department of Industry; *b* 15 March 1926; *s* of William Edwin Atkinson and Lena Marion (*née* Haselhurst); *m*; one *s* two *d*; *m* 1983, Rita Katherine (*née* Bunn). *Educ:* Gosforth Grammar Sch., Newcastle upon Tyne; King's Coll., Durham Univ.; Worcester Coll., Oxford. Served RNVR, 1943–46. Entered Civil Service as Inspector of Taxes, 1950; Principal, 1958, Asst. Sec., 1965; Secretaries Office, Inland Revenue, 1958–61 and 1962–69; Asst Sec., Royal Commn on the Press, 1961–62; Civil Service Dept, 1969; Under Sec., and Dir, Central Computer Agency, CSD, 1973–78. Chm., Northern Development Co. Ltd, 1986–90; Director: English Estates Corp., 1986–94; Northern Rock Building Soc., 1987–96; Belasis Hall Technol. Park, 1989–98; Maryport Develt Co. Ltd, 1989–95. Chm., Northern Rock Foundn, 1997–2000. Chm. of Governors, Univ. of Northumbria at Newcastle (formerly Newcastle-upon-Tyne Polytechnic), 1989–96 (Hon. Fellow, 1987). Hon. DCL Northumbria at Newcastle, 1998. *Recreations:* gentle walking, reading, music. *Address:* High Dryburn, Garrigill, near Alston, Cumbria CA9 3EJ.

ATTALI, Jacques; Member, Conseil d'Etat, France, 1981–90 and since 1993; Président: Attali et Associés, since 1994; PlaNet Finance, since 1999; *b* 1 Nov. 1943. *Educ:* Ecole Polytechnique; Inst. d'Etudes Politiques de Paris; Ecole des Mines; Ecole Nat. d'Admin. Dr d'Etat en Sci. Econ. Conseil d'Etat: Auditeur, 1970; Maître des Requêtes, 1977; Conseiller, 1989; Special Advr to President of French Republic, 1981–91; Founding Pres., EBRD, 1991–93. *Publications:* Analyse économique de la vie politique, 1972; Modèles Politiques, 1973; (with Marc Guillaume) L'Anti-Economique, 1974; La Parole et l'outil, 1975; Bruits, 1976; La nouvelle Economie Française, 1977; L'Ordre Cannibale, 1979; Les Trois Mondes, 1981; Histoire du Temps, 1982; La figure de Fraser, 1984; Un homme d'influence, 1985; Au propre et au figuré, 1988; Lignes d'Horizon, 1990; 1492, 1991; Verbatim, 1993; Europe(s), 1994; L'Economie de l'Apocalypse, 1995; Verbatim II, 1995; Verbatim III, 1996; Chemins de Sagesse: traité du labyrinthe, 1996; Mémoire de Sabliers, 1997; Dictionnaire du XXIe siècle, 1998; *fiction:* La vie eternelle, 1989; Le premier Jour après moi, 1990; Il viendra, 1994; Manuel, l'Enfant Rêve (for children), 1994; Au-delà de nulle part, 1997; La femme du menteur, 1999; Fraternités, 1999; *play:* Les portes du Ciel, 1999. *Address:* 28 rue Bayard, 75008 Paris, France.

ATTALIDES, Michalis A.; Permanent Secretary, Ministry of Foreign Affairs, Cyprus, since 2000; *b* 15 Nov. 1941; *s* of Antonis Attalides and Katina Loizou; *m* 1991, Alexandra Alexandrou. *Educ:* London Sch. of Econs (BSc Econ); Princeton Univ. (PhD 1975). Lectr in Sociology, Univ. of Leicester, 1966–68; sociologist, Cyprus Town and Country Planning Project, 1968–70; Counterpart of UNESCO EXPERT, Social Research Centre, Cyprus, 1971 and 1973–74; mil. service, 1972; Guest Lectr, Otto Suhr Inst., Free Univ. of Berlin, 1974–75; journalist, 1975–76; Internat. Relns Service, House of Representatives of Cyprus, 1977–89 (Dir, 1979–89); Dir, Pol Affairs Div. B (Cyprus Question) (with rank of Ambassador), Min. of Foreign Affairs, 1989–91; Ambassador to France, also accredited to Morocco, Portugal and Spain, 1991–95; Perm. Delegate to EU, also accredited to Belgium and Luxembourg, 1995–98; High Comr in London, 1998–2000. *Publications:* Social Change and Urbanization in Cyprus: a study of Nicosia, 1971; Cyprus: nationalism and international politics, 1980. *Address:* Ministry of Foreign Affairs, Nicosia, Cyprus; *e-mail:* mattalides@hotmail.com.

ATTALLAH, Naim Ibrahim; Book Publisher and Proprietor: Quartet Books, since 1976; The Women's Press, since 1977; Robin Clark, since 1980; *b* 1 May 1931; *s* of Ibrahim and Genevieve Attallah; *m* 1957, Maria Attallah (*née* Nykolyn); one *s*. *Educ:* Battersea Polytechnic. Foreign Exchange Dealer, 1957; Financial Consultant, 1966; Dir of cos, 1969–; Financial Dir and Jt Man. Dir, Asprey of Bond Street, 1979–92; Gp Chief Exec., Asprey PLC, 1992–96; Managing Director: Mappin & Webb, 1990–95; Watches of Switzerland, 1990–95; Exec. Dir, Garrard, 1990–95; Magazine Proprietor: The Literary Review, 1981–2001; The Wire, 1984–; The Oldie, 1991–. Proprietor, Academy Club, 1989–96. Launched Parfums Namara, Avant l'Amour and Après l'Amour, 1985, Naïdor, 1987, l'Amour de Namara, 1990; launched Namara Fine Art, 1997. *Theatre:* co-presenter, Happy End, Lyric, 1975; presented and produced, The Beastly Beatitudes of Balthazar B, Duke of York's, 1981; co-prod, Trafford Tanzi, Mermaid, 1982; *films:* co-prod (with David Frost), The Slipper and the Rose, 1974–75; exec. producer, Brimstone and Treacle, 1982; also prod and presented TV docs. MUniv Surrey, 1993. *Publications:* Women, 1987; Singular Encounters, 1990; Of a Certain Age, 1992; More of a Certain Age, 1993; Speaking for the Oldie, 1995; A Timeless Passion (novel), 1995; Asking Questions, 1996; Tara & Claire (novel), 1996; A Woman a Week, 1998; In Conversation with Naim Attallah, 1998; Insights, 1999; Dialogues, 2000; contrib. Literary Review, Oldie, and most nat. newspapers. *Recreations:* classical music, opera, theatre, cinema, photography. *Address:* 25 Shepherd Market, W1J 7PP. *T:* (020) 7499 2901, *Fax:* (020) 7499 2914; *e-mail:* nattallah@aol.com.

ATTENBOROUGH, family name of **Baron Attenborough**.

ATTENBOROUGH, Baron *cr* 1993 (Life Peer), of Richmond upon Thames, in the London Borough of Richmond upon Thames; **Richard Samuel Attenborough,** Kt 1976; CBE 1967; actor, producer and director; Goodwill Ambassador for UNICEF, since 1987; Chancellor, University of Sussex, since 1998 (Pro-Chancellor, 1970–98); *b* 29 Aug. 1923; *s* of late Frederick L. Attenborough; *m* 1945, Sheila Beryl Grant Sim; one *s* two *d*. *Educ:* Wyggeston Grammar Sch., Leicester. Leverhulme Schol. to Royal Acad. of Dramatic Art, 1941 (Bancroft Medal). First stage appearance as Richard Miller in Ah Wilderness, Intimate Theatre, Palmers Green, 1941; Ralph Berger in Awake and Sing, Arts Theatre (West End début), 1942; Sebastian in Twelfth Night, Ba in Holy Isle, Murder in the Red Barn, Arts Theatre; The Little Foxes, Piccadilly Theatre, 1942; Brighton Rock, Garrick, 1943. Joined RAF 1943; seconded to RAF Film Unit for Journey Together, 1944; demobilised, 1946. Returned to stage in The Way Back (Home of the Brave), Westminster, 1949; To Dorothy, a Son, Savoy, 1950, Garrick, 1951; Sweet Madness, Vaudeville, 1952; The Mousetrap, Ambassadors, 1952–54; Double Image, Savoy, 1956–57, St James's, 1957; The Rape of the Belt, Piccadilly, 1957–58. *Film: appearances:* In Which We Serve (screen début), 1942; School for Secrets, The Man Within, Dancing With Crime, Brighton Rock, London Belongs to Me, The Guinea Pig, The Lost People, Boys in Brown, Morning Departure, Hell is Sold Out, The Magic Box, Gift Horse, Father's Doing Fine, Eight O'Clock Walk, The Ship That Died of Shame, Private's Progress, The Baby and the Battleship, Brothers in Law, The Scamp, Dunkirk, The Man Upstairs, Sea of Sand, Danger Within, I'm All Right Jack, Jet Storm, SOS Pacific; The Angry Silence (also co-prod), 1959; The League of Gentlemen, 1960; Only Two Can Play, All Night Long, 1961; The Dock Brief, The Great Escape, 1962; Séance On a Wet Afternoon (also prod; Best actor, San Sebastian Film Fest. and British Film Acad.), The Third Secret, 1963; Guns at Batasi (Best actor, British Film Acad.), 1964; The Flight of the Phœnix, 1965; The Sand Pebbles (Hollywood Golden Globe), 1966; Dr Dolittle (Hollywood Golden Globe), The Bliss of Mrs Blossom, 1967; Only When I Larf, 1968; The Last Grenade, A Severed Head, David Copperfield, Loot, 1969; 10 Rillington Place, 1970; And Then There Were None, Rosebud, Brannigan, Conduct Unbecoming, 1974; The Chess Players, 1977; The Human Factor, 1979; Jurassic Park, 1993; Miracle on 34th Street, 1994; The Lost World: Jurassic Park, 1997; Elizabeth, 1998; Puckoon, 2001; *produced:* Whistle Down the Wind, 1961; The L-Shaped Room, 1962; *directed:* Young Winston (Hollywood Golden Globe), 1972; A Bridge Too Far (Evening News Best Drama Award), 1976; Magic, 1978; A Chorus Line, 1985; In Love and War, 1997; *produced and directed:* Oh! What a Lovely War (16 Internat. Awards incl. Hollywood Golden Globe and SFTA UN Award), 1968; Gandhi (8 Oscars, 5 BAFTA Awards, 5 Hollywood Golden Globes, Dirs' Guild of America Award for Outstanding Directorial Achievement), 1980–81; Cry Freedom (Berlinale Kamera; BFI Award for Technical Achievement), 1987; Chaplin, 1992; Shadowlands, 1993 (Alexander Korda Award for Outstanding British Film of the Year, BAFTA); In Love and War, 1997; Grey Owl, 2000. Formed: Beaver Films with Bryan Forbes, 1959; Allied Film Makers, 1960. Chairman: Goldcrest Films & Television Ltd, 1982–87; Channel Four Television, 1987–92 (Dep. Chm., 1980–86); Capital Radio, 1972–92 (Life Pres., 1992–); Duke of York's Theatre, 1979–92. Dir, Chelsea Football Club, 1969–82 (Life Vice Pres., 1993–). Chairman: Actor's Charitable Trust, 1956–88 (Pres., 1988–); Combined Theatrical Charities Appeals Council, 1964–88 (Pres., 1988–); BAFTA (formerly SFTA), 1969–70 (Vice-Pres., 1971–94; Chm. Trustees, 1970–); RADA, 1972– (Mem. Council, 1963–); UK Trustees, Waterford-Kamhlaba Sch., Swaziland, 1976– (Gov., 1987–); BFI, 1981–92; Cttee of Inquiry into the Arts and Disabled People, 1983–85; British Screen Adv. Council, 1987–96 (Hon. Pres., 1996); European Script Fund, 1988–96 (Hon. Pres., 1996); Member: British Actors' Equity Assoc. Council, 1949–73; Cinematograph Films Council, 1967–73; Arts Council of GB, 1970–73. Trustee: Tate Gall., 1976–82 and 1994–96 (Tate Foundn, 1986–); Foundn for Sport and the Arts, 1991–. Pres., Nat. Film Sch., 1997– (Gov., 1970–81); Dir, Young Vic, 1974–84. Pres., Muscular Dystrophy Gp of GB, 1971– (Vice-Pres., 1962–71); Chm., Help a London Child; Gov., Motability, 1977–. Patron: Kingsley Hall Community Centre, 1982–; RA Centre for Disability and the Arts, Leicester, 1990–. President: The Gandhi Foundn, 1983–; Brighton Festival, 1984–95; British Film Year, 1984–86; Arts for Health, 1989–; Gardner Centre for the Arts, Sussex Univ., 1990– (Patron, 1969–90). Fleming Meml Lect., RTS, 1989; Cameron Mackintosh Vis. Prof. of Contemporary Theatre, Oxford Univ., 1996. Fellow: BAFTA, 1983; BFI, 1992. Freeman, City of Leicester, 1990. FKC 1993; Hon. Fellow: Univ. of Wales, 1997; Nat. Film and Television Sch., 2001. Hon. DLitt: Leicester, 1970; Kent, 1981; Sussex, 1987; Hon. DLit Amer. Internat. Univ., London, 1994; Hon. DCL Newcastle, 1974; Hon. LLD Dickinson, Penn., 1983. Evening Standard Film Award, 40 years service to British Cinema, 1983; Award of Merit for Humanitarianism in Film Making, European Film Awards, 1988; Shakespeare Prize, FVS Foundn, Hamburg, 1992; Praemium Imperiale, Japan Art Assoc., 1998. Martin Luther King, Jr Peace Prize, 1983. Padma Bhushan (India), 1983; Commandeur, Ordre des Arts et des Lettres (France), 1985; Chevalier, Légion d'Honneur (France), 1988. *Publications:* In Search of Gandhi, 1982; (with Diana Carter) Richard Attenborough's Chorus Line, 1986; Cry Freedom, A Pictorial Record, 1987. *Recreations:* collecting paintings and sculpture, listening to music, watching football. *Address:* Old Friars, Richmond Green, Surrey TW9 1NQ. *Clubs:* Garrick, Beefsteak.

See also Sir D. F. Attenborough, Hon. M. J. Attenborough.

ATTENBOROUGH, Sir David (Frederick), CH 1996; Kt 1985; CVO 1991; CBE 1974; FRS 1983; broadcaster and naturalist; *b* 8 May 1926; *s* of late Frederick Levi Attenborough; *m* 1950, Jane Elizabeth Ebsworth Oriel (*d* 1997); one *s* one *d*. *Educ:* Wyggeston Grammar Sch. for Boys, Leicester; Clare Coll., Cambridge (Hon. Fellow, 1980). Served in Royal Navy, 1947–49. Editorial Asst in an educational publishing house, 1949–52; joined BBC Television Service as trainee producer, 1952; undertook zoological and ethnographic filming expeditions to: Sierra Leone, 1954; British Guiana, 1955; Indonesia, 1956; New Guinea, 1957; Paraguay and Argentina, 1958; South West Pacific, 1959; Madagascar, 1960; Northern Territory of Australia, 1962; the Zambesi, 1964; Bali, 1969; Central New Guinea, 1971; Celebes, Borneo, Peru and Colombia, 1973; Mali, British Columbia, Iran, Solomon Islands, 1974; Nigeria, 1975; Controller, BBC-2, BBC Television Service, 1965–68; Dir of Programmes, Television, and Mem., Bd of Management, BBC, 1969–72. Writer and presenter, BBC series: Tribal Eye, 1976; Wildlife on One, annually 1977–; Life on Earth, 1979; The Living Planet, 1984; The First Eden, 1987; Lost Worlds, Vanished Lives, 1989; The Trials of Life, 1990; Life in the Freezer, 1993; The Private Life of Plants, 1995; The Life of Birds, 1998; State of the Planet, 2000; The Blue Planet, 2001. Huw Wheldon Meml Lecture, RTS, 1987. President: BAAS, 1990–91; RSNC, 1991–96; Mem., Nature Conservancy Council, 1973–82. Trustee: WWF UK, 1965–69, 1972–82, 1984–90; WWF Internat., 1979–86; British Museum, 1980–2001; Science Museum, 1984–87; Royal Botanic Gardens, Kew, 1986–92 (Kew Award, 1996). Corresp. Mem., Amer. Mus. Nat. Hist., 1985. Fellow, BAFTA 1980. Hon. Fellow: Manchester Polytechnic, 1976; UMIST, 1980; Hon. FRCP 1991; Hon FLS 1998; Hon. FIBiol 2000. Special Award, SFTA, 1961; Silver Medal, Zool Soc. of London, 1966; Silver Medal, RTS, 1966; Desmond Davis Award, SFTA, 1970; Cherry Kearton Medal, RGS, 1972; Kalinga Prize, UNESCO, 1981; Washburn Award, Boston Mus. of Sci., 1983; Hopper Day Medal, Acad. of Natural Scis, Philadelphia, 1983; Founder's Gold Medal, RGS, 1985; Internat. Emmy Award, 1985; Encyclopaedia Britannica Award, 1987; Livingstone Medal, RSGS, 1990; Franklin Medal, RSA, 1990; Gold Medal, RTS, 1991; Golden Kamera Award, Berlin, 1993; Edinburgh Medal, Edinburgh Sci. Fest., 1998; Internat. Cosmos Prize, 2000. Hon. DLitt: Leicester, 1970; City, 1972; London, 1980; Birmingham, 1982; Hon. DSc: Liverpool, 1974; Heriot-Watt, 1978; Sussex, 1979; Bath, 1981; Ulster, Durham, 1982; Keele, 1986; Oxford, 1988; Plymouth, 1992; Bradford, 1998; Nottingham, 1999; Hon. LLD: Bristol, 1977; Glasgow, 1980; DUniv: Open Univ., 1980; Essex, 1987; Antwerp, 1993; Hon. ScD Cambridge, 1984; Hon. DVetMed Edinburgh, 1994. Hon. Freeman, City of Leicester, 1990. Comdr of Golden Ark (Netherlands), 1983. *Publications:* Zoo Quest to Guiana, 1956; Zoo Quest for a Dragon, 1957; Zoo Quest in Paraguay, 1959; Quest in Paradise, 1960; Zoo Quest to Madagascar, 1961; Quest under Capricorn, 1963; The Tribal Eye, 1976; Life on Earth, 1979; The Living Planet, 1984, rev. edn 1985; The First Eden, 1987; The Trials of Life, 1990; The Private Life of Plants, 1994; The Life of Birds, 1998. *Recreations:* music, tribal art, natural history. *Address:* 5 Park Road, Richmond, Surrey TW10 6NS.

See also Baron Attenborough.

ATTENBOROUGH, John Philip, CMG 1958; CBE 1953 (OBE 1946); retired; *b* 6 Nov. 1901; *s* of late Frederick Samuel and Edith Attenborough; *m* 1947, Lucie Blanche Woods (*d* 1996), *y d* of late Rev. J. R. and Mrs Prenter and *widow* of late Dr P. P. Murphy; one step *s*. *Educ:* Manchester Grammar Sch.; Corpus Christi Coll., Oxford (MA). Superintendent of Education, Northern Nigeria, 1924–30; Lecturer and Senior Inspector, Education Dept, Palestine, 1930–37; Dir of Education, Aden, 1937–46; Deputy Dir of Education, Palestine, 1946–48; Asst Educational Adviser, Colonial Office, 1948; Dir of Education, Tanganyika, 1948–55; Mem. for Social Services, Tanganyika, 1955–57; Min. for Social Services, Tanganyika, 1957–58; Consultant: UNICEF, 1963–65; UNESCO, 1967; Devon, CC, 1961–68; Mem. SW Regional Hosp. Bd, 1965–71. Pres. Torbay Conservative Assoc., 1967–79. *Address:* 6 Erith House, Lower Erith Road, Torquay, Devon TQ1 2PX.

ATTENBOROUGH, (Hon.) Michael John; Principal Associate Director, Royal Shakespeare Company, since 1995; *b* 13 Feb. 1950; *s* of Baron Attenborough, *qv*; *m* 1st, 1971, Jane Seymour (*née* Joyce Frankenberg) (marr. diss. 1976); 2nd, 1984, Karen Lewis; two *s*. *Educ:* Westminster Sch.; Sussex Univ. (BA Hons English). Associate Director: Mercury Theatre, Colchester, 1972–74; Leeds Playhouse, 1974–79; Young Vic Theatre, 1979–80; Artistic Director: Palace Theatre, Watford, 1980–84; Hampstead Theatre, 1984–89; Turnstyle Gp, 1989–90; Exec. Producer, RSC, 1990–95. *Recreations:* music, football, reading, being with my family. *Address:* Royal Shakespeare Company, Royal Shakespeare Theatre, Stratford-upon-Avon, Warwicks CV37 6BB. *T:* (01789) 296655.

ATTENBOROUGH, Peter John; Director of Educational and Community Care Projects, The Rank Foundation, since 1994; Headmaster of Charterhouse, 1982–93; *b* 4 April 1938; *m* 1967, Alexandra Deidre Campbell Page; one *s* one *d*. *Educ:* Christ's Hospital; Peterhouse, Cambridge. BA Classics 1960, MA 1964. Asst Master, Uppingham Sch., 1960–75 (Housemaster, Senior Classics Master); Asst Master, Starehe Boys' Centre, Nairobi, 1966–67; Headmaster, Sedbergh Sch., 1975–81. Chairman: Common Entrance Cttee of Independent Schs, 1983–88; Schools Arabic Project, 1986–87; Mem., HMC Cttee, 1986–90. Almoner, Christ's Hosp., 1987–; Governor: Ashdown House, 1983–93; Haslemere Prep. Sch., 1986–93; St Edmund's Sch., 1986–94; Brambletye Sch., 1989–99; Caldicott Sch., 1990–93; Haberdashers' Monmouth Schs, 1996–; Trustee, Uppingham Sch., 1993–. Trustee: Inner City Young People's Project, 1989–98; Starehe Endowment Fund (UK), 1995–. Freeman, City of London, 1965; Liveryman, Skinners' Co., 1978. *Address:* Rawmarsh Cottage, Linton, near Ross-on-Wye, Herefords HR9 7RX.

ATTENBOROUGH, Philip John, CBE 1994; publisher; Deputy Chairman, Hodder Headline plc, 1993–96 (Chairman, Hodder & Stoughton Ltd and Hodder & Stoughton Holdings Ltd, 1975–93); *b* 3 June 1936; *er s* of late John Attenborough, CBE, and Barbara (*née* Sandle); *m* 1963, Rosemary, *y d* of late Dr (William) Brian Littler, CB, and Pearl Littler; one *s* one *d*. *Educ:* Rugby; Trinity Coll., Oxford. Christmas postman (parcels), 1952–54; Nat. Service, Sergeant 68th Regt RA, Oswestry, 1956; lumberjack, Blind River, Ont, 1957; joined Hodder & Stoughton, 1957: Export Manager, 1960; Dir, 1963–; Sales Dir, 1969. Chm., The Lancet Ltd, 1977–91; Dir, Book Tokens Ltd, 1985–96. Publishers Association: Mem. Council, 1976–92 (Treasurer, 1981–82; Vice-Pres., 1982–83, 1985–86; Pres., 1983–85); Leader, delegns of Brit. publishers to China, 1978, to Bangladesh, India and Pakistan, 1986, to India, 1990; Mem., Exec. Cttee, IPA, 1988–96 (Vice-Pres., 1992–96); Chairman: Book Develt Council, 1977–79; PA Freedom to Publish Cttee, 1987–92; Member: British Council Publishers Adv. Cttee, 1977–93 (Chm., 1989–93); British Library Adv. Council, 1986–89; UK Rep., Fédération des Editeurs Européens, 1986–93; Advr, UNESCO Publishing, 1992–95. Gov., Judd Sch., Tonbridge, 1987–. Mem. Governing Body, SPCK, 1999–. Liveryman, Skinners' Co., 1970 (Mem. Court, 1995–; Master, 2000–01). *Publication:* contrib. Book Research Qly. *Recreations:* trout fishing, dog and cat walking, watching cricket. *Address:* Coldhanger, Seal Chart, near Sevenoaks, Kent TN15 0EJ. *T:* (01732) 761516. *Clubs:* Garrick, MCC; Kent CC; Band of Brothers; Rye Golf, Senior Golfers' Society; Piscatorial Society.

ATTERTON, David Valentine, CBE 1981; PhD; FREng; FIM; Chairman, TriVen VCT plc, since 1999; *b* 13 Feb. 1927; *s* of Frank Arthur Shepherd Atterton and Ella Constance (*née* Collins); *m* 1948, Sheila Ann McMahon; two *s* one *d*. *Educ:* Bishop Wordsworth's Sch., Salisbury; Peterhouse, Cambridge (MA, PhD). Post-doctorate research, Cambridge, 1950–52; joined Foundry Services Ltd, 1952; Managing Director: Foseco Ltd, 1966; Foseco Minsep Ltd, 1969; Chm., Foseco Minsep plc, 1979–86. Dep. Chm., Associated Engineering plc, 1979–86 (Dir 1972–); Director: Investors in Industry plc (formerly Finance Corp. for Industry and FFI), 1974–92; IMI plc, 1976–89; Barclays Bank UK Ltd, 1982–84; Bank of England, 1984–92; Barclays Bank, 1984–92; (part-time) British Coal, 1986–95; Marks and Spencer plc, 1987–92; Rank Organisation, 1987–97; Dimex Ltd, 1988–89; Chairman: Peripheral Vision Ltd, 1992–98; Guinness Mahon Holdings, 1993–98. Chm., NEDO Iron and Steel Sector Working Party, 1977–82; Member: ACARD, 1982–85; British N Amer. Assoc., 1982–92; Member, Board of Governors: United World Coll. of the Atlantic, 1968–85 (Chm., 1973–79); Wells Cathedral Sch., 1990–. Pres., Birmingham Chamber of Commerce and Industry, 1974–75. Pres., Inst. of Metals, 1987–88. Master, Founders' Co., 1994–95. *Publications:* numerous scientific papers in learned jls. *Recreations:* cartography, Japanese language, photography. *Address:* Cathedral Green House, Wells, Somerset BA5 2UB. *T:* (01749) 74907.

ATTEWELL, Brian; HM Diplomatic Service, retired; *b* 29 May 1937; *s* of late William John Geldard Attewell and Marie Evelyn Attewell; *m* 1963, Mary Gillian Tandy (*d* 2000); two *s* one *d*. *Educ:* Dulwich Coll.; London School of Economics and Political Science (BScEcon 1961). BoT, 1956–58, 1961–66; Private Sec. to Parly Sec., 1964–66; transf. to Diplomatic Service, 1966: Washington, 1967–70; Buenos Aires, 1970–73; FCO, 1974–78; Canberra, 1978–80; FCO, 1980–83; Dubai, 1984–87; Brussels, 1988–92; High Comr, Bahamas, 1992–96. *Recreations:* golf, walking, listening to music (classical and jazz), watercolours, following fortunes of Charlton Athletic. *Address:* 86 Vineyard Hill Road, Wimbledon, SW19 7JJ. *Club:* Wimbledon Park Golf.

ATTLEE, family name of **Earl Attlee**.

ATTLEE, 3rd Earl *cr* 1955; **John Richard Attlee;** Viscount Prestwood, 1955; *b* 3 Oct. 1956; *s* of 2nd Earl Attlee and Anne Barbara, *er d* of late James Henderson, CBE; *S* father, 1991. *Educ:* Stowe. Engrg and automotive industries until 1993; British Direct Aid: Bosnia, 1993–94; Rwanda, 1995. TA officer, Maj. REME (V), Op. Lodestar, 1997–98, OC 150 Recovery Company, 1998–2000. Opposition Whip, H of L, 1997–99; spokesman, in H of L, for transport, 1997 and 1999–, for NI, 1997 and 1998–99, for energy, 1998, and for defence, 1998–; elected Mem., H of L, 1999. Pres., Heavy Transport Assoc., 1994–. *Address:* House of Lords, SW1A 0PW. *T:* (020) 7219 6071; *e-mail:* attleej@parliament.uk.

ATTLEE, Air Vice-Marshal Donald Laurence, CB 1978; LVO 1964; DL; fruit farmer, 1977–95, retired; *b* 2 Sept. 1922; *s* of Major Laurence Attlee; *m* 1952, Jane Hamilton Young; one *s* two *d*. *Educ:* Haileybury. Pilot trng in Canada, 1942–44; Flying Instructor, 1944–48; Staff, Trng Comd, 1949–52; 12 Sqdn, 1952–54; Air Ministry, Air Staff, 1954–55; RAF Staff Coll., 1956; 59 Sqdn, 1957–59; CO, The Queen's Flight (W/Cdr), 1960–63; HQ, RAF Germany, 1964–67; CO, RAF Brize Norton, 1968–69; IDC, 1970; MoD Policy Staff, 1971–72; Dir of RAF Recruiting, 1973–74; Air Cdre, Intell., 1974–75; AOA Trng Comd, 1975–77, retired. Chm., Mid-Devon Business Club, 1985–87; Mem. Bd, Mid-Devon Enterprise Agency, 1983–93. Mem., Mid-Devon DC, 1982– (Vice-Chm., 1987–89; Chm., 1989–91). DL Devon, 1991. *Recreations:* genealogy, Do-it-Yourself, gardening. *Address:* Jerwoods, Culmstock, Cullompton, Devon EX15 3JU. *T:* (01823) 680317. *Club:* Royal Air Force.

ATTRIDGE, Elizabeth Ann Johnston, (Mrs John Attridge); Senior Clerk/Adviser, European Legislation Committee, House of Commons, 1994–98; *b* 26 Jan. 1934; *d* of late Rev. John Worthington Johnston, MA, CF, and Mary Isabel Giraud (*née* McFadden); *m* 1956, John Attridge; one *s*. *Educ:* Richmond Lodge Sch., Belfast; St Andrews Univ., Fife. Assistant Principal, Min. of Education, NI, 1955, reappointed on marriage (marriage bar), MAFF, London, 1956; assisted on Agriculture Acts, 1957 and 1958; Head Plant Health Br., 1963–66, Finance, 1966–69, External Relations (GATT) Br., 1969–72; Assistant Secretary: Animal Health I, 1972–75; Marketing Policy and Potatoes, 1975–78; Tropical Foods Div., 1978–83; Under Secretary: European Community Group, 1983–85; Emergencies, Food Quality and Pest Control, 1985–89; Animal Health Gp, 1989–91; Agricl Inputs, Plant Protection and Emergencies Gp, 1991–94. Chairman, International Coffee Council, 1982–83. *Recreations:* collecting fabric, opera. *Address:* Croxley East, The Heath, Weybridge, Surrey KT13 0UA.

ATTWELL, Prof. David Ian, PhD; FMedSci; FRS 2001; Jodrell Professor of Physiology, University College London, since 1995; *b* 18 Feb. 1953; *s* of Arthur Attwell and Vera Eileen Attwell (*née* Slade); *m* 1988, Ulrike Schmidt; one *s*. *Educ:* Magdalen Coll., Oxford (BA 1st Cl. Physics 1974; BA 2nd Cl. Physiological Scis 1975; PhD Physiol. 1979). Fellow, Magdalen Coll., Oxford, 1977–79 and 1980–81; University College London: Lectr in Physiol., 1981–88; Reader, 1988–91; Prof. of Physiol., 1991–95. SRC Postdoctoral Fellow, Berkeley, Calif, 1979–80; Henry Head Fellow, Royal Soc., 1984–89. FMedSci 2000. *Publications:* contribs to learned jls on neuroscience. *Recreation:* travel. *Address:* Department of Physiology, University College London, Gower Street, WC1E 6BT. *T:* (020) 7679 7342.

ATTWOOD, Thomas Jaymril; management and marketing consultant; Chairman, Cargill, Attwood and Thomas Ltd, Management Consultancy Group, 1965–97; Associate Professor of Strategic Management, International Management Centres, since 1997; *b* 30 March 1931; *s* of George Frederick Attwood and Avril Sandys (*née* Cargill, NZ); *m* 1963, Lynette O. E. Lewis; one *s* one *d*. *Educ:* Haileybury and Imperial Service Coll.; RMA Sandhurst; Harvard Grad. Sch. of Business Admin; INSEAD, Fontainebleau. Pres., Internat. Consultants' Foundn, 1978–81. Conducted seminars for UN Secretariat, European Commn and World Council of Churches, 1970–80; presented papers to Eur. Top Management Symposium, Davos, Internat. Training Conf. and to World Public Relations Conf. Mem. Exec. Cttee, Brit. Management Training Export Council, 1978–85; Chm., Post Office Users National Council, 1982–83. Mem. Court, Worshipful Company of Marketors, 1985–93 (Liveryman, 1980). FCIM; FIMC; FIMgt; FInstD. Mem., Richmond upon Thames Borough Council, 1969–71. *Publications:* (jtly) Bow Group pubn on United Nations, 1961; contrib. to reference books, incl. Systems Thinking, Innovation in Global Consultation, Handbook of Management Development, and Helping Across Cultures; articles on marketing, management and business topics. *Recreations:* travel, music, chess, City of London, cricket. *Address:* 46 Rivermead Court, SW6 3RX. *T:* (020) 7736 3371, *Fax:* (020) 7751 0180; *e-mail:* Tom@twood.worldonline.co.uk. *Clubs:* City Livery, MCC, Lord's Taverners, Hurlingham.

ATTWOOLL, Elspeth Mary-Ann Muncy; Member (Lib Dem) Scotland, European Parliament, since 1999; *b* 1 Feb. 1943; *d* of Hugh Robert Rhind Attwooll and Joan Attwooll (*née* Fidler); *m* 1990, Donald Gordon Henry. *Educ:* Tiffin Girls' Sch., Kingston upon Thames; St Andrews Univ.; Queen's Coll., Dundee (LLB, MA Hons Politics and Philosophy). University of Glasgow: Asst Lectr, Lectr, Sen. Lectr in Jurisp., 1966–98; ILO, Geneva, 1968–69. *Publications:* The Tapestry of the Law, 1997; articles and essays on legal philosophy. *Recreation:* reading, particularly detective fiction. *Address:* 2A Whitton Street, Glasgow G20 0AN. *T:* (0141) 946 1370. *Club:* National Liberal.

ATTYGALLE, Gen. Don Sepala, Hon. LVO 1954; Chairman and Managing Director, Air Lanka Ltd, 1993–95; High Commissioner for Democratic Socialist Republic of Sri Lanka in London, 1990–93; *b* 14 Oct. 1921; *m* 1958, Ithali Mercia Attygalle; one *s*. *Educ:* Royal College, Colombo; psc 1953, idc 1966. Commissioned into Army, 1940; Ceylon Light Infantry; Extra ADC to Governor-General of Ceylon, 1952–65; CO, Ceylon Armoured Corps, 1955; Comdr, Sri Lanka Army, 1967–77; Chief Co-Ordinating Authority, 1977, Sec., 1983–90, Min. of Defence. Deshamanya, 1990. *Recreations:* sports. *Address:* 6 Fairfield Gardens, Colombo 8, Sri Lanka.

ATWELL, Very Rev. James Edgar; Dean (formerly Provost) of St Edmundsbury, since 1995; *b* 3 June 1946; *s* of Joseph Norman Edgar Atwell and Sybil Marion Atwell (*née* Burnett); *m* 1976, Lorna Goodwin; one *s* two *d*. *Educ:* Dauntsey's Sch.; Exeter Coll., Oxford (MA, BD); Harvard Univ. (ThM). Ordained deacon, 1970, priest, 1971; Assistant Curate: St John the Evangelist, E Dulwich, 1970–74; Great St Mary's, Cambridge, 1974–77; Chaplain, Jesus Coll., Cambridge, 1977–81; Vicar of Towcester, 1981–95; RD, Towcester, 1983–91. *Recreations:* countryside, walking, driving a Land Rover, travel, fairground organs, theology. *Address:* The Provost's House, Bury St Edmunds, Suffolk IP33 1RS. *T:* (home) (01284) 754852, (Cathedral office) (01284) 754933, *Fax:* (01284) 768655.

ATWOOD, Barry Thomas; public and European Community law consultant, since 1995; Principal Assistant Solicitor (Under Secretary), Ministry of Agriculture, Fisheries and Food, 1989–95; *b* 25 Feb. 1940; *s* of Percival Atwood and Vera Fanny Atwood (*née* Stoneham); *m* 1965, Jennifer Ann Burgess; two *s*. *Educ:* Bristol Grammar Sch.; Bristol Univ. (LLB); University College London. Solicitor. Articled John Robinson and Jarvis, Isle of Wight, 1961; Solicitor with Robert Smith & Co., Bristol, 1965; Legal Dept, Ministry of Agriculture, Fisheries and Food: conveyancing, 1966; food legislation, 1970; Common Agricultural Policy, 1977; i/c European Court litigation, 1982; Agricultural Commodities and Food Safety Bill, 1986; Legal Gp B (domestic and EC litigation and commercial work), 1989–92; Legal Gp A (legislation and adv. work), 1992–95. *Publications:* (contrib.) Law of the European Communities, 1999; Butterworth's Food Law, 2nd edn 2000. *Recreations:* family, music, swimming, walking, France. *Address:* 10 Box Ridge Avenue, Purley, Surrey CR8 3AP.

ATWOOD, Margaret, CC (Can.) 1981; FRSC 1987; writer; *b* Ottawa, 18 Nov. 1939; *m* Graeme Gibson; one *d*. *Educ:* Univ. of Toronto (BA 1961); Radcliffe Coll., Cambridge, Mass (AM 1962); Harvard Univ., Cambridge, Mass. Lectr in English, Univ. of BC, Vancouver, 1964–65; Instructor in English: Sir George Williams Univ., Montreal, 1967–68; Univ. of Alberta, 1969–70; Asst Prof. of English, York Univ., Toronto, 1971–72; Writer-in-Residence: Univ. of Toronto, 1972–73; Macquarie Univ., Australia, 1987; Hon. Chair, Univ. of Alabama, Tuscaloosa, 1985; Berg Prof., New York Univ., 1986. Holds hon. degrees from univs and colls; recipient of awards, medals and prizes for writing. TV scripts: The Servant Girl, 1974; Snowbird, 1981; (with Peter Pearson) Heaven on Earth, 1986; radio script, The Trumpets of Summer, 1964. *Publications: poetry:* The Circle Game, 1966; The Animals in That Country, 1969; The Journals of Susanna Moodie, 1970 (illus. edn, 1997); Procedures for Underground, 1970; Power Politics, 1971; You Are Happy, 1974; Selected Poems, 1976; Two-Headed Poems, 1978; True Stories, 1981; Notes Towards a Poem that Can Never be Written, 1981; (ed) The New Oxford Book of Canadian Verse in English, 1982; Snake Poems, 1983; Interlunar, 1984; Selected Poems II: poems selected and new 1976–1986, 1986; Selected Poems 1966–1984, 1990; Margaret Atwood Poems 1965–1975, 1991; Poems 1976–1986, 1992; Morning in the Burned House, 1995; also poetry in art and small press edns; *fiction:* The Edible Woman, 1969; Surfacing, 1972; Lady Oracle, 1976; Dancing Girls (short stories), 1977; Up in the Tree (for children), 1978; Anna's Pet (for children), 1980; Life Before Man, 1979; Bodily Harm, 1981; Encounters with the Element Man, 1982; Murder in the Dark (short stories), 1983; Bluebeard's Egg (short stories), 1983; Unearthing Suite, 1983; The Handmaid's Tale, 1985 (Governor General's Award, 1986; filmed 1990); (ed with Robert Weaver) The Oxford Book of Canadian Short Stories in English, 1986, new edn as The New Oxford Book of Canadian Short Stories in English, 1995; Cat's Eye, 1989; (ed with Shannon Ravenel) The Best American Short Stories, 1989; For the Birds (for children), 1990; Wilderness Tips (short stories), 1991; Good Bones (short stories), 1992; The Robber Bride, 1993; Princess Prunella and the Purple Peanut (for children), 1995; Alias Grace (Giller Prize, Giller Foundn, Canada; Canadian Booksellers Assoc. Author of the Year; Nat. Arts Club Medal of Honor for Literature), 1996; The Blind Assassin (Booker Prize), 2000; *non-fiction:* Survival: a thematic guide to Canadian literature, 1972; Days of the Rebels 1815–1840, 1977; Second Words: selected critical prose, 1982; Strange Things: the malevolent North in Canadian literature, 1995. *Address:* c/o McClelland & Stewart, 481 University Avenue, 9th Floor, Toronto, Ont M5G 2E9, Canada.

AUBREY, David John; QC 1996; a Recorder, since 1998; *b* 6 Jan. 1950; *s* of Raymond John Morgan Aubrey and Dorothy Mary (*née* Griffiths); *m* 1980, Julia Catherine Drew; one *d*. *Educ:* Cathays High Sch., Cardiff; University Coll., Cardiff (LLB Hons); Inns of Court Sch. of Law. Called to the Bar, Middle Temple, 1976; Head of Chambers, Temple Chambers, Cardiff and Newport. Member: Criminal Bar Assoc., 1988–; Bar Council, 1998–. *Recreations:* gardening, music, cricket, collecting Boys' Brigade memorabilia. *Address:* 32 Park Place, Cardiff CF1 3BA. *T:* (029) 2039 7364.

AUBREY-FLETCHER, family name of **Baroness Braye**.

AUBREY-FLETCHER, Sir Henry (Egerton), 8th Bt *cr* 1782, of Clea Hall, Cumberland; farmer and company director; Vice Lord-Lieutenant of Buckinghamshire, since 1997; *b* 27 Nov. 1945; *s* of Sir John Henry Lancelot Aubrey-Fletcher, 7th Bt and Diana Mary Fynvola (*d* 1996), *o c* of Lt-Col Arthur Egerton; *S* father, 1992; *m* 1976, Sara Roberta, *d* of late Major Robert Gilliam Buchanan and Mrs Margaret Ogden-White; three *s*. *Educ:* Eton. Chm., Chilton House Nursing Home, 1987–; Chm., Fox FM ILR, 1989–; Director: Mix 96 ILR, 1994–; FM 102 The Bear ILR, 1995–. Chm., Properties Cttee, NT, 2000–; Member: Landscape Adv. Cttee, Dept of Transport, 1990–94; Chm., Berks, Bucks and Oxon Wildlife (formerly Naturalist) Trust, 1995–; Trustee, Chequers Trust, 1997–. High Sheriff, Bucks, 1995–96. *Recreations:* IT, media and rural affairs. *Heir:* *s* John Robert Aubrey-Fletcher, *b* 20 June 1977. *Address:* Estate Office, Chilton, Aylesbury, Bucks HP18 9LR. *T:* (01844) 265201.

AUCHINCLOSS, Louis Stanton; author; Partner, Hawkins Delafield and Wood, NYC, 1957–86 (Associate, 1954–57); *b* NY, 27 Sept. 1917; *s* of J. H. Auchincloss and P. Stanton; *m* 1957, Adèle Lawrence; three *s*. *Educ:* Groton Sch.; Yale Univ.; Univ. of Virginia (LLB). Lieut USNR; served, 1941–45. Admitted to NY Bar, 1941; Associate Sullivan and Cromwell, 1941–51. Mem. Exec. Cttee, Assoc. of Bar of NY City. Pres., Museum of City of NY, 1967; Trustee, Josiah Macy Jr Foundn. Mem., Nat. Inst. of Arts and Letters. *Publications:* The Indifferent Children, 1947; The Injustice Collectors, 1950; Sybil, 1952; A Law for the Lion, 1953; The Romantic Egoists, 1954; The Great World and Timothy Colt, 1956; Venus in Sparta, 1958; Pursuit of the Prodigal, 1959; The House of Five Talents, 1960; Reflections of a Jacobite, 1961; Portrait in Brownstone, 1962; Powers of Attorney, 1963; The Rector of Justin, 1964; Pioneers and Caretakers, 1966; The

Embezzler, 1966; Tales of Manhattan, 1967; A World of Profit, 1969; Second Chance: tales to two generations, 1970; Edith Wharton, 1972; I Come as a Thief, 1972; Richelieu, 1972; The Partners, 1974; A Writer's Capital, 1974; Reading Henry James, 1975; The Winthrop Covenant, 1976; The Dark Lady, 1977; The Country Cousin, 1978; The House of the Prophet, 1980; The Cat and the King, 1981; Watch Fires, 1982; Honourable Men, 1986; Diary of a Yuppie, 1987; The Golden Calves, 1989; (ed) Hone and Strong Diaries of Old Manhattan, 1989; Fellow Passengers, 1990; J. P. Morgan, 1990; House of the Prophet, 1991; Lady of Situations, 1991; pamphlets on American writers. *Address:* 1111 Park Avenue, New York, NY 10128–1234, USA. *Club:* Century Association (NY).

AUCKLAND, 10th Baron *cr* 1789 (Ire.), 1793 (GB); **Robert Ian Burnard Eden;** *b* 25 July 1962; *s* of 9th Baron Auckland and Dorothy Margaret, *d* of H. J. Manser; *S* father, 1997; *m* 1986, Geraldine Caroll; one *d*. *Educ:* Blundell's Sch., Tiverton. *Heir: uncle* Hon. Ronald John Eden [*b* 5 March 1931; *m* 1957, Rosemary Dorothy Marion, *d* of Sir John Ellenborough Crowder; two *s*].

AUCKLAND (Dio. Durham), **Archdeacon of;** *see* Jagger, Ven. I.

AUCKLAND (NZ), Bishop of; *see* New Zealand, Primate and Archbishop of.

AUCKLAND (NZ), Bishop of, (RC), since 1994; **Most Rev. Patrick James Dunn;** *b* London, 5 Feb. 1950; *s* of Hugh Patrick Dunn and June Mary (*née* Grevatt). *Educ:* Sacred Heart Coll., Auckland; Canterbury Univ. (BA); Otago Univ. (BTheol); Melbourne Coll. of Divinity, Australia (MTheol 1989). Ordained priest, 1976; Catholic Maori Mission, Auckland, 1976–77; Assistant Priest: Mangere E, 1978–79; Takapuna, 1980–84; Co-Pastor, Pakuranga, 1985; Dir, First Year Formation House, Dio. of Auckland, 1986–87; Parish Priest, Northcote, 1990–92; Pastoral Asst to RC Bp of Auckland, and VG, 1993–94. *Publication:* Priesthood, 1990. *Address:* Pompallier Diocesan Centre, Private Bag 47904, Ponsonby, Auckland 1034, New Zealand. *T:* (9) 360 3002.

AUCKLAND, Mary Josephine; Director of Library and Learning Resources, London Institute, since 1998; *b* 22 Nov. 1950; *d* of Reginald George Auckland and Annie Auckland (*née* Sullivan). *Educ:* Poly of N London (LA Professional Exams 1971); University Coll. London (BSc Hons Anthropol. 1977); London Sch. of Econs (MSc Industrial Relns and Personnel Mgt 1986). ALA 1973. Res. Asst, Sch. of Librarianship and Inf. Studies, Poly. of N London, 1971–72; Res. Librarian, Liby and Learning Resources Service, City of London Poly., 1972–74; Asst Librarian, 1979–88, Sub-Librarian, 1988–89, British Liby of Pol and Econ. Sci., LSE; Dep. Librarian and Hd, User Services, Univ. of Southampton Liby, 1990–92; Librarian, SOAS, Univ. of London, 1992–98. Conf. Dir, Computers in Libraries Internat., 1993–95. Member: Cttee for Electronic Inf. of Jt Inf. Systems Cttee, 1996– (Chair, Content Wkg Gp, 1999–2000); Adv. Cttee, UK Interoperability Focus, 1999–; UK Office for Liby Networking Mgt Cttee, 1999–. Mem., Higher Educn, British Liby Task Force, 2000–01. Mem. Council, LA, 1991–99 (Chm. Council, 1997–99; Chm., Acad. and Res. Libraries Cttee, 1993–95). Acad. Gov., Ct of Govs, SOAS, 1996–98; Acad. Bd Gov., Ct of Govs, London Inst., 1999–. Cawthorne Prize, LA, 1970. *Publications:* contrib. various articles, chapters, etc, in professional pubns, and conf. papers. *Recreations:* good company, travel. *Address:* The London Institute, 65 Davies Street, W1K 5DA. *T:* (020) 7514 8072. *Club:* Reform.

AUDET, Daniel; Delegate General for Quebec in London, since 2000; *b* 6 April 1961; *s* of Marc Audet and Gisèle (*née* Bédard); *m* 1995, Nathalie Chalifour; one *d*. *Educ:* Univ. of Ottawa (philosophy); Univ. of Montreal (law); Montreal Bar school. Freelance journalist, Montreal, 1986–90; attorney, Lapointe Rosenstein, Montreal, 1990–94; COS for Quebec Dep. Premier and Minister of State for Economy and Finance, Quebec, 1994–97; Vice Pres., Corporate Affairs, Videotron Inc., Montreal, 1997–2000. Member Board: Canadian Customs and Revenue Agency, 1999–2000; Horizon Scis and Technologies Inc., 1999–2000. Chm. Bd, Fondation jeunesse du monde, 1998–2000; Mem. Exec., Montreal Internat. Ambassador Club, 1999–2000. *Recreations:* arts in general, economics and the digital revolution. *Address:* Quebec Government Office, 59 Pall Mall, SW1Y 5JH. *T:* (020) 7766 5917; *e-mail:* daniel.audet@mri.gouv.qc.ca.

AUDLAND, Sir Christopher (John), KCMG 1987 (CMG 1973); DL; HM Diplomatic Service and Commission of the European Communities, retired; *b* 7 July 1926; *s* of late Brig. Edward Gordon Audland, CB, CBE, MC, and Violet Mary, *d* of late Herbert Shepherd-Cross, MP; *m* 1955, Maura Daphne Sullivan; two *s* one *d*. *Educ:* Winchester Coll. RA, 1944–48 (Temp. Capt.). Entered Foreign (subseq. Diplomatic) Service, 1948; served in: Bonn; British Representation to Council of Europe, Strasbourg; Washington; UK Delegn to negotiations for British Membership of European Communities, Brussels, 1961–63; Buenos Aires; Head of Science and Technology Dept, FCO, 1968–70; Counsellor (Head of Chancery), Bonn, 1970–72; seconded to Commn of Eur. Communities, 1973: Dep. Sec.-Gen., 1973–81; Dir-Gen. for Energy, 1981–86. Head, UK Delegn to 1st UN Conf. on Seabed and Ocean Floor, 1968; Dep. Head, UK Delegn to Four-Power Negotiations on Berlin, 1970–72. Hon. Fellow, Faculty of Law, and Vis. Lectr on European Instns, Edinburgh Univ., 1986–. Vice President: Europa Nostra, 1988–91; Internat. Castles Inst., 1988–90 (Pres., 1990–91); Europa Nostra united with Internat. Castles Inst., 1991, 1993–96 (Exec. Pres., 1992; Hon. Pres., 1997–). Member: NW Regl Cttee, National Trust, 1987–95; European Strategy Bd, ICL, 1988–96; Lake District Nat. Park Authority, 1989–95; Pro-Chancellor, Lancaster Univ., 1990–97 (Mem., Council, 1988–97). Trustee: Peter Kirk Meml Fund, 1989–96; Ruskin Foundn, 1994–; European Opera Centre, 1996–. DL Cumbria, 1996. *Address:* The Old House, Ackenthwaite, Milnthorpe, Cumbria LA7 7DH. *T:* (015395) 62202, *Fax:* (015395) 64041. *Club:* Oxford and Cambridge.

AUDLEY, Barony *cr* 1312–13; in abeyance. *Co-heiresses:* Hon. Patricia Ann Mackinnon [*b* 10 Aug. 1946; *m* 1969, Carey Leigh Mackinnon; one *s* one *d*]; Hon. Jennifer Michelle Carrington [*b* 23 May 1948; *m* 1978, Michael William Carrington; two *s* one *d*]; Hon. Amanda Elizabeth Souter [*b* 5 May 1958; one *d*].

AUDLEY, Sir (George) Bernard, Kt 1985; Chairman: Caverswall Holdings, since 1990; Pergamon AGB plc, 1988–90; Founder, and Chairman, AGB Research PLC, 1973–88; *b* Stockton Brook, N Staffs, 24 April 1924; *s* of late Charles Bernard Audley and Millicent Claudia Audley; *m* 1950, Barbara, *d* of late Richard Arthur Heath; two *s* one *d*. *Educ:* Wolstanton Grammar Sch.; Corpus Christi Coll., Oxford (MA). Lieut, Kings Dragoon Guards, 1943–46. Asst Gen. Man., Hulton Press Ltd, 1949–57; Man. Dir, Television Audience Measurement Ltd, 1957–61; founded AGB Research, 1962. Chairman: Netherhall Trust, 1962–; Industry and Commerce Adv. Cttee, William and Mary Tercentenary Trust, 1985–89; Arts Access, 1986–98; Pres., EUROPANEL, 1966–70; Vice-Pres., Periodical Publishers Assoc., 1989– (Pres., 1985–89); Mem. Cttee, St Bride's World Wide Trust, 1991–. Vis. Prof. in Business and Management, Middlesex Univ. (formerly Poly.), 1989–. Governor, Hong Kong Coll., 1984–95. FRSA 1986. Freeman of City of London, 1978; Liveryman, Gold and Silver Wyre Drawers' Company, 1975–. *Recreations:* golf, reading, travel. *Address:* 56 River Court, SE1 9PE. *T:* (020) 7928 6576; Le Collet du Puits, Montauroux, 83440 Fayence, France. *T:* 494765287. *Clubs:* Cavalry and Guards, MCC; Rye Golf, Hadley Wood Golf.

AUDLEY, Prof. Robert John, PhD; FBPsS; Professor of Psychology, University College London, 1965–94, now Professor Emeritus and Consultant; *b* 15 Dec. 1928; *s* of Walter Audley and Agnes Lilian (*née* Baker); *m* 1st, 1952, Patricia Mary Bannister (marr. diss. 1977); two *s*; 2nd, 1990, Vera Elyashiv Bickerdike. *Educ:* Battersea Grammar Sch.; University Coll. London (BSc 1st Cl. Hons Psychology, 1952; PhD 1955). Fulbright Scholar and Res. Asst, Washington State Univ., 1952; University College London: Res. Worker, MRC Gp for Exptl Investigation of Behaviour, 1955–57; Lectr in Psychology, 1957–64; Reader in Psychology, 1964; Head, Psychology Dept, 1979–93; Dean, Faculty of Science, 1985–88; Vice-Provost, 1988–94; Fellow, 1989. Vis. Prof., Columbia Univ., NY, 1962; Vis. Miller Prof., Univ. of Calif, Berkeley, 1971; Vis Fellow, Inst. for Advanced Study, Princeton, 1970. Member: UGC Social Studies Sub-Cttee, 1975–82; UGC Equipment Sub-Cttee, 1982–89; Computer Bd for Univs and Res. Councils, 1986–90; MRC/RN Personnel Res. Cttee, 1984 (Chm., Psychology Sub-Cttee, 1984–95); Chm., Jt Wkg Gp, ESRC/HEFC Jt Inf. Systems Cttee, 1990–99 (Mem., New Technology Sub-Cttee, Jt Inf. Systems Cttee, 1993–95). President: British Psychological Soc., 1969–70; Exptl Psychology Soc., 1975–76. Editor, British Jl of Math. and Stat. Psychology, 1965–70. *Publications:* papers on choice, judgement, medical mishaps. *Recreations:* crosswords, cooking, the arts. *Address:* Psychology Department, University College London, Gower Street, WC1E 6BT. *T:* (020) 7391 1297; 22 Keats Grove, NW3 2RS. *T:* (020) 7435 6655.

AUDLEY-CHARLES, Prof. Michael Geoffrey, PhD; Yates-Goldsmid Professor of Geology, 1982–93, now Emeritus Professor, and Head of the Department of Geological Sciences, 1982–92, University College London; *b* 10 Jan. 1935; *s* of Lawrence Geoffrey Audley-Charles and Elsie Ada (*née* Ustonson); *m* 1965, Brenda Amy Cordeiro; one *s* one *d*. *Educ:* Royal Wanstead Sch.; Chelsea Polytechnic (BSc); Imperial Coll., London (PhD). Geologist with mining and petroleum cos, Canada and Australia, 1957–62; Imperial Coll. of Science and Technology, London: research in geology, 1962–67; Lectr in Geol., 1967–73; Reader in Geol., 1973–77; Prof. of Geol. and Head of Dept of Geol Sciences, Queen Mary Coll., London, 1977–82. Hon. Fellow, UCL, 1995. *Publications:* geological papers dealing with stratigraphy of British Triassic, regional geol. of Indonesia and Crete and evolution of Gondwanaland, in learned jls. *Recreation:* gardening. *Address:* La Serre, St Pantaléon, 46800 Montcuq, France. *T:* 565318067.

AUDU, Rev. Ishaya Shu'aibu, OFR 2000; FRCPE; Medical Director, Savannah Polyclinic, Zaria, since 1984; *b* 1 March 1927; *s* of Malam Bulus Audu and Malama Rakiya Audu; *m* 1958, Victoria Abosede Ohiorhenuan; two *s* five *d*. *Educ:* Ibadan and London Univs. House Officer, Sen. House Officer, Registrar in Surgery, Medicine, Obstetrics and Gynæcology and Pædiatrics, King's Coll. Hosp., London and Univ. Coll. Hosp., Ibadan, 1954–58; postgrad. studies, UK, 1959–60; Specialist Physician, Pædiatrician to Govt of Northern Nigeria and Personal Physician to Premier of North Region Govt, 1960–62; Lectr to Associate Professorship in Pæds, Univ. of Lagos Med. Sch., 1962–66; Vis. Res. Associate Prof., Univ. of Rochester Med. Sch., NY, 1964–65; Dep. Chm., Lagos Univ. Teaching Hosp. Man. Bd and Mem. Council, Univ. Lagos Med. Coll., 1962–66; Mem. Senate, Lagos Univ., 1963–66; Vice-Chancellor, Ahmadu Bello Univ., 1966–1975; Prof. of Medicine, 1967–77; Sen. Medical Officer, Ashaka Cement Co. Ltd, 1977–79; Minister of External Affairs, Fed. Republic of Nigeria, 1979–83; Ambassador and Perm. Rep. of Nigeria to UN, 1983–84. President: Christian Health Assoc. of Nigeria, 1986–93 (Trustee, 1993–); Leprosy Mission, Nigeria, 1998–; Chairman: Nat. Primary Health Care Develt Agency of Nigeria, 1992–94; Nat. Health Insurance Scheme, 2000–. Pro-Chancellor and Chairman of Council: Univ. of Nigeria, Nsukka, 1993–96; Univ. of Jos, 2000–. Ordained Minister, United Church of Christ in Nigeria, 1986. Hon. LHD Ohio, 1968; Hon DSc Nigeria, 1971; Hon. LLD Ibadan, 1973; FMC (Pæd) Nigerian Med. Council; FRSocMed. *Publications:* contribs to learned jls. *Recreations:* walking, table tennis. *Address:* (office) Basawa Road, Hayin Dogo, Samaru, Zaria, Nigeria; (home) 23a Circular Road, GRA, Zaria, Nigeria.

AUDUS, Prof. Leslie John, MA, PhD, ScD Cantab; FIBiol; Hildred Carlile Professor of Botany, Bedford College, University of London, 1948–79; *b* 9 Dec. 1911; English; *m* 1938, Rowena Mabel Ferguson (*d* 1987); two *d*. *Educ:* Downing Coll., Cambridge Univ. Downing Coll. Exhibitioner, 1929–31; Frank Smart Research Student (Cambridge Univ.), 1934–35; Lecturer in Botany, University Coll., Cardiff, 1935–40. Served War of 1939–45: RAFVR (Technical, Radar, Officer), 1940–46; PoW South Pacific, 1942–45. Scientific Officer, Agricultural Research Council, Unit of Soil Metabolism, Cardiff, 1946–47; Monsanto Lecturer in Plant Physiology, University Coll., Cardiff, 1948. Recorder, 1961–65, Pres., 1967–68, Section K, British Assoc. for the Advancement of Science. Vis. Prof. of Botany: Univ. of California, Berkeley, 1958; Univ. of Minnesota, Minneapolis, 1965. Vice-Pres. Linnean Soc. of London, 1959–60 (Hon. FLS 1995); Life Mem. New York Academy of Sciences, 1961. Editor, Journal Exp. Botany, 1965–74. *Publications:* Plant Growth Substances, 1953, 3rd edn 1972; (ed) The Physiology and Biochemistry of Herbicides, 1964; (ed) Herbicides: physiology, biochemistry and ecology, 1976; Spice Island Slaves, 1996; original research on plant respiration, hormones, responses to gravity, soil micro-biology in relation to pesticides, etc in Annals of Botany, New Phytologist, Nature, Journal of Experimental Botany, Weed Research, etc. *Recreations:* furniture construction and restoration, electronics, amateur radio. *Address:* Flat 14B, Langham Mansions, Earl's Court Square, SW5 9UH.

AUERBACH, Frank Helmuth; painter; *b* 29 April 1931; *s* of Max Auerbach, lawyer, and Charlotte Norah Auerbach; *m* 1958, Julia Wolstenholme; one *s*. *Educ:* privately; St Martin's Sch. of Art; Royal Coll. of Art. *One-man exhibitions:* Beaux Arts Gallery, 1956, 1959, 1961, 1962, 1963; Marlborough Fine Art, 1965, 1967, 1971, 1974, 1983, 1987, 1990, 1997; Marlborough Gall., New York, 1969, 1982, 1994, 1998; Villiers, Sydney, Australia, 1972; Bergamini, Milan, 1973; Univ. of Essex, 1973; Mun. Gall. of Modern Art, Dublin, 1975; Marlborough, Zurich, 1976; Anthony D'Offay, London, 1978; Arts Council Retrospective, Hayward Gall., 1978; Fruit Market Gall., Edinburgh, 1978; Jacobson, NY, 1979; Anne Berthoud, London, 1983; Venice Biennale, British Pavilion, 1986 (Golden Lion Prize); Kunstverein, Hamburg; Museum Folkwang, Essen; Centro de Arte Reina Sofia, Madrid, 1986–87; Rijksmuseum Vincent van Gogh, Amsterdam, 1989; Yale Center for British Art, New Haven, 1991; Nat. Gall., 1995; Campbell–Thiebaud Gall., San Francisco, 1995; Rex Irwin, Woollahra, 1996; Charlottenborg, Copenhagen, 2000; RA 2001. *Mixed exhibitions:* Carnegie International, Pittsburgh, 1958, 1961; Dunn International, Fredericton, 1963; Gulbenkian International, Tate Gallery, 1964; Peter Stuyvesant Foundn Collection, London, 1967; The Human Clay, Hayward Gall., 1976; European Painting in the Seventies, Los Angeles County Mus. and tour, 1976; Annual Exhbn, part I, Hayward Gall., 1977; Westkunst, Cologne, 1981; New Spirit in Painting, RA, 1981; Internat. Survey, Moma, NY, 1984; The Hard Won Image, Tate Gall., 1984; The British Show, Art Gall. of WA, Perth, and tour, 1985; British Art in the Twentieth Century, RA, 1987; Current Affairs, Mus. of Modern Art, Oxford, and tour, 1987; A School of London, Kunstnernes Hus., Oslo, and tour, 1987–88; Pursuit of the Real,

Manchester City Art Gall., 1990; British Figurative Painting of the Twentieth Century, Israel Mus., Jerusalem, 1992–93; From London, Scottish Nat. Gall. of Modern Art, Edinburgh, and tour, 1995–96; Fondation Dina Vierny, Musée Maillol, Paris, and tour, 1998–99; *public collections:* Arts Council; Brit. Council; Brit. Museum; Tate Gallery, London; Metropolitan Museum, NY; Mus. of Modern Art, NY; National Gallery of Victoria, Melbourne; Nat. Galls of Australia, W Australia and NSW; County Museum of LA, Calif; Cleveland Mus., Ohio; Art Inst., Chicago; Univ. of Cincinnati; St Louis Art Mus.; Yale Center for British Art, New Haven; Tamayo Mus., Mexico; Aberdeen, Bedford, Bolton, Cambridge, Edinburgh, Hartlepool, Huddersfield, Hull, Leeds, Leicester, Manchester, Nottingham, Oldham, Rochdale, Sheffield, Southampton Galls; Arts Council, British Council, Contemporary Art Soc., etc. *Address:* c/o Marlborough Fine Art, 6 Albemarle Street, W1S 4BY.

AUGIER, Sir Fitzroy (Richard), Kt 1996; Professor of History, University of the West Indies, 1989–95, now Professor Emeritus; *b* 17 Dec. 1924; *s* of Frank John Augier and Lucie Lastique; *m* 1959, Leila Yvette Gibbs; two *s* one *d. Educ:* St Mary's Coll., Castries; Univ. of St Andrews (MA 1949; PhD 1954); London Univ. Inst. of Educn (DipEd 1950); Inst. Commonwealth Studies. Served RAF, 1942–46. Pres., West Indian Students' Union, 1952–54; University of the West Indies: Jun. Res. Fellow, 1954; Lectr, Dept of Hist., 1955–65; Sen. Lectr, 1965–89; Dean, Faculty of Arts and Gen. Studies, 1967–72; Pro Vice Chancellor, 1972–90. Rockefeller Fellow, Inst. of Historical Res., London Univ., 1962. Chairman: Caribbean Exams Council, 1986–96; Drafting Cttee, UNESCO Gen. Hist. of Caribbean, 1981. Medal, Internat. Council on Archives, 1980; Musgrave Medal (Gold), Council, Inst. of Jamaica, 1996. Chevalier, Ordre des Arts et des Lettres (France), 1989. *Publications:* (jtly) The Making of the West Indies, 1960; (jtly) Sources of West Indian History: documents with commentary, 1962; contrib. to Caribbean Qly, New World Qly, Jl Caribbean Hist. *Recreation:* gardening. *Address:* Department of History, University of the West Indies, Mona, Kingston 7, Jamaica, West Indies. *T:* 9271922; *e-mail:* history@uwimona.edu.jm; 70 Donhead Close, Kingston 6, Jamaica, West Indies. *T:* 9275385.

AUKIN, David; Joint Chief Executive, HAL Films, since 1998; *b* 12 Feb. 1942; *s* of Charles and Regina Aukin; *m* 1969, Nancy Meckler, theatre director; two *s. Educ:* St Paul's Sch., London; St Edmund Hall, Oxford (BA). Admitted Solicitor, 1965. Literary Advr, Traverse Theatre Club, 1970–73; Administrator, Oxford Playhouse Co., 1974–75; Administrator, 1975–79, Dir, 1979–84, Hampstead Theatre; Dir, Leicester Haymarket Theatre, 1984–86; Exec. Dir, NT, 1986–90; Hd of Drama, 1990–97, Hd of Film, 1997–98, Channel 4 Television. Chm., Soho Theatre and Writers' Centre, 2000–. *Recreation:* golf. *Address:* c/o HAL Films, Elsley House, 24–30 Great Titchfield Street, W1P 7AD. *Club:* Groucho.

AULD, Alasdair Alpin, FMA; Director, Glasgow Museums and Art Galleries, 1979–88, retired; *b* 16 Nov. 1930; *s* of Herbert Bruce Auld and Janetta Isabel MacAlpine; *m* 1959, Mary Hendry Paul; one *s* one *d. Educ:* Shawlands Acad., Glasgow; Glasgow Sch. of Art (DA). FMA 1971. Glasgow Museums and Art Galleries: Asst Curator, 1956–72; Keeper of Fine Art, 1972–76; Depute Dir, 1976–79. Pres., Scottish Fedn of Museums and Art Galls, 1981–84. Hon. Curator, RCPSG. *Publications:* catalogues; articles on museum subjects. *Recreations:* golf, travel, painting. *Address:* 3 Dalziel Drive, Pollokshields, Glasgow G41 4JA. *T:* (0141) 427 1720.

AULD, Margaret Gibson, RGN, RM; FRCN; MPhil; Chief Nursing Officer, Scottish Home and Health Department, 1977–88, retired; *b* 11 July 1932; *d* of late Alexander John Sutton Auld and Eleanor Margaret Ingram. *Educ:* Glasgow; Cardiff High Sch. for Girls; Radcliffe Infirm., Oxford (SRN 1953); St David's Hosp., Cardiff; Queen's Park Hosp., Blackburn (SCM 1954). Midwife Teacher's Dipl., 1962; Certif. of Nursing Admin, 1966, MPhil 1974, Edinburgh. Queen's Park Hosp., Blackburn, 1953–54; Staff Midwife, Cardiff Maternity Hosp., 1955, Sister, 1957; Sister, Queen Mary Hosp., Dunedin, NZ, 1959–60; Deptl Sister, Cardiff Maternity Hosp., 1960–66; Asst Matron, Simpson Meml Maternity Pavilion, Edinburgh, 1966–68, Matron, 1968–73; Actg Chief Reg. Nursing Officer, S-Eastern Reg. Hosp. Bd, Edinburgh, 1973; Chief Area Nursing Off., Borders Health Bd, 1973–76. Life Vice Pres., Royal Coll. of Midwives of UK, 1988. Chm., CRAG/SCOTMEG Review of Maternity Services in Scotland, 1992–96; Member: GNC (Scotland), 1973–76; Central Midwives Bd (Scotland), 1972–76; Cttee on Nursing (Briggs), 1970–72; Maternity Services Cttee, Integration of Maternity Work (Tennent Report), 1972–73; Human Fertilization and Embryol. Authy, 1990–93; Cttee on Ethics of Gene Therapy, 1990–93; Nuffield Council on Bioethics, 1991–94. Mem., Eildon Housing Assoc., 1998–. Gov., Queen Margaret Univ. Coll. (formerly Queen Margaret Coll.), Edinburgh, 1989–2000 (Chm. Bd of Govs, 1997–2000; Patron, 1999–). FRCN 1981; CIMgt (CBIM 1983). Hon. DSc CNAA, 1987. *Recreations:* reading, music, entertaining. *Address:* Staddlestones, Neidpath Road, Peebles EH45 8NN. *T:* (01721) 729594.

AULD, Rt Hon. Sir Robin Ernest, Kt 1988; PC 1995; **Rt Hon. Lord Justice Auld;** a Lord Justice of Appeal, since 1995; *b* 19 July 1937; *s* of late Ernest Auld and Adelaide Mackie; *m* 1963, Catherine Eleanor Mary, *er d* of late David Henry Pritchard; one *s* one *d. Educ:* Brooklands Coll.; King's Coll., London (LLB 1st cl. Hons 1958; PhD 1963; FKC 1987). Called to Bar, Gray's Inn, 1959 (first in order of merit, Bar finals; Macaskie Schol., Lord Justice Holker Sen. Schol.), Bencher, 1984; SE Circuit; in practice at English Bar, 1959–87; admitted to Bar, State of NY, USA, 1984. Prosecuting Counsel to Dept of Trade, 1969–75; QC 1975; a Recorder, 1977–87; a Judge of the High Court of Justice, QBD, 1987–95; Presiding Judge, Western Circuit, 1991–94; Sen. Presiding Judge for England and Wales, 1995–98. Sen. Res. Scholar, Yale Law Sch., 2001. Legal Assessor, GMC and GDC, 1982–87. Mem., Judicial Studies Bd, 1989–91 (Chm., Criminal Cttee, 1989–91). Mem., Commn of Inquiry into Casino Gambling in the Bahamas, 1967; Chm., William Tyndale Schools' Inquiry, 1975–76; Dept of Trade Inspector, Ashbourne Investments Ltd, 1975–79; Counsel to Inquiry into Brixton Disorders, 1981; Chm., Home Office Cttee of Inquiry into Sunday Trading, 1983–84; conducted Criminal Courts Review, 1999–2001. Master, Woolmen's Co., 1984–85. *Address:* Royal Courts of Justice, Strand, WC2A 2LL. *Club:* Athenæum.

AUNG SAN SUU KYI; Co-Founder and General Secretary, National League for Democracy, Burma, since 1988; Burmese prisoner of conscience, 1989–95; *b* Rangoon, 19 June 1945; *d* of U Aung San (assassinated, 19 July 1947) and late Daw Khin Kyi; *m* 1972, Michael Vaillancourt Aris (*d* 1999); two *s. Educ:* St Francis Convent, Rangoon; Methodist English High Sch., Rangoon; Lady Shri Ram Coll., Delhi Univ.; St Hugh's Coll., Oxford (BA PPE 1967; MA; Hon. Fellow, 1990). Asst Sec., Adv. Cttee on Admin. and Budgetary Questions, UN Secretariat, NY, 1969–71; Res. Officer, Min. of Foreign Affairs, Bhutan, 1972. Vis. Schol., Centre for SE Asian Studies, Kyoto Univ., Japan, 1985–86. Fellow, Indian Inst. of Advanced Studies, Simla, 1987. Hon. Mem., World Commn on Culture and Develt, Unesco, 1992–95; Mem., Acad. Universelle des Cultures, Paris, 1993. Hon. Pres., LSE Students' Union, 1992; Hon. Life Mem., Univ. of London Union, 1992. Hon. doctorates: Thammasat Univ., Bangkok, 1992; Toronto Univ., 1993; Vrije Univ., Brussels, 1994; Queen's Univ., Kingston, 1995. Thorolf Rafto Award for Human Rights, Norway, 1990; Nobel Peace Prize, 1991; Sakharov Prize for Freedom of Thought, European Parlt, 1991; Annual Award, Internat. Human Rights Law Group, USA, 1992; Simón Bolívar Prize, Unesco, 1992; Prix Littéraire des Droits de l'Homme, Paris, 1992; Rose Prize, Internat. Forum of Danish Lab. Movement, 1993; Victor Jara Internat. Human Rights Award, Center for Human Rights and Constitutional Law, LA, 1993; Bremen Solidarity Prize, 1993; Liberal Internat. Prize for Freedom, 1995; Jawaharlal Nehru Award for Internat. Understanding, 1995; Freedom Award of Internat. Rescue Cttee, 1995. *Publications:* (ed with Michael Aris) Tibetan Studies in Honour of Hugh Richardson, 1980; Aung San, 1984, 2nd edn as Aung San of Burma: a biographical portrait by his daughter, 1990; (contrib.) Burma and Japan: basic studies on their cultural and social structure, 1987; Burma and India: some aspects of intellectual life under colonialism, 1990; Freedom from Fear and Other Writings, 1991, 2nd edn 1995; Towards a True Refuge (Joyce Pearce Meml Lect.), 1993; numerous speeches. *Address:* 54–6 University Avenue, Rangoon, Burma.

AUNG, U Win; Minister for Foreign Affairs, Myanmar, since 1998; *b* 28 Feb. 1944; *m* 1972, Daw San Yone; two *s* one *d. Educ:* Yangon Univ. (BSc). 2nd Lieut, 1964; Major 1978; joined Foreign Service, 1985; Chargé d'Affaires: Laos, 1986–88; Singapore, 1988–90; Ambassador to Germany, 1990–96; Ambassador to the Court of St James's, 1996–98. Naing Ngan Daw Sit Smu Htan Tazeik; Pyi Thu Wun Htan Gaung Tazeik. *Publications:* Nation of the Gold and Selected Articles, 1996; articles in periodicals in Myanmar. *Recreation:* music. *Address:* Ministry of Foreign Affairs, Pyay Road, Yangon, Union of Myanmar.

AUST, Anthony Ivall, CMG 1995; Deputy Legal Adviser, Foreign and Commonwealth Office, 2000–March 2002; *b* 9 March 1942; *s* of Ivall George Aust and Jessie Anne Salmon; *m* 1st, 1969, Jacqueline Antoinette Thérèse Paris (marr. diss. 1987); two *d*; 2nd, 1988, Dr Kirsten Kaarre Jensen. *Educ:* Wilson Central Sch., Reading; Stoneham Grammar Sch., Reading; London Sch. of Econs and Pol Science (LLB 1963, LLM 1967). Admitted Solicitor, 1967. Asst Legal Adviser, FCO (formerly CO), 1967–76; Legal Adviser, British Mil. Govt, Berlin, 1976–79; Asst Legal Adviser, FCO, 1979–84; Legal Counsellor, FCO, 1984–88 and 1991–2000; Counsellor (Legal Advr) UK Mission to UN, NY, 1988–91. *Publication:* Modern Treaty Law and Practice, 2000. *Recreations:* architecture, cinema, theatre, gardening, parlour games. *Address:* (until March 2002) c/o Foreign and Commonwealth Office, SW1A 2AH; c/o Cambridge University Press, Cambridge CB2 2RU.

AUSTEN, Patrick George; Chief Executive, Liberty plc, 1993–96; *b* 22 Sept. 1943; *m* 1968, Margaret; three *s* one *d. Educ:* Bristol Coll. of Commerce; Leicester Sch. of Textiles; Leicester Poly.; Centre d'Etudes Industrielles, Geneva. ICI Fibres, 1961–83: commercial apprentice, British Nylon Spinners (later ICI Fibres), 1961–65; mgt trainee, 1965–67; Trade Sales Manager, 1967–70; Fibres Manager, Republic of Ireland, 1970–73; Business Area Manager, 1974–79; Commercial Manager, Textile Fibres, 1979–83; BTR, 1983–93; Managing Director: Pretty Polly, 1983–85; Pretty Polly and Dunlopillo, 1985–87. *Recreations:* golf, motor-racing.

AUSTEN, Richard Bertram G.; *see* Godwin-Austen.

AUSTEN-SMITH, Air Marshal Sir Roy (David), KBE 1979; CB 1975; CVO 1994; DFC 1953; retired; a Gentleman Usher to HM the Queen, 1982–94, an Extra Gentleman Usher, since 1994; *b* 28 June 1924; *m* 1951, Ann (*née* Alderson); two *s. Educ:* Hurstpierpoint College. Pilot trng, Canada, 1943–44; 41 Sqn (2 TAF), 1945; 33 Sqdn, Malaya, 1950–53; Cranwell, 1953–56; 73 Sqdn, Cyprus, 1956–59; Air Min., 1960–63; 57 Sqdn, 1964–66; HQ 2 ATAF, 1966–68; CO, RAF Wattisham; MoD, 1970–72; AOC and Comdt, RAF Coll., Cranwell, 1972–75; SASO Near East Air Force, 1975–76; Comdr British Forces, Cyprus, AOC Air HQ Cyprus and Administrator, Sovereign Base Areas, Cyprus, 1976–78; Hd of British Defence Staff, Washington, and Defence Attaché, 1978–81. *Recreation:* golf. *Address:* c/o National Westminster Bank, Swanley, Kent BR8 7WL. *Club:* Royal Air Force.

AUSTIN, Sir Anthony Leonard, 6th Bt *cr* 1894, of Red Hill, Castleford, West Riding; *b* 30 Sept. 1930; *yr s* of Sir William Ronald Austin, 4th Bt (*d* 1989) and his 1st wife, Dorothy Mary (*d* 1957), *d* of L. A. Bidwell, FRCS; *S* brother, 1995; *m* 1st, 1956, Mary Annette (marr. diss. 1966), *d* of Richard Kelly; two *s* one *d*; 2nd, 1967, Aileen Morrison Hall, *d* of William Hall Stewart; one *d. Educ:* Downside. *Heir: s* Peter John Austin, *b* 29 July 1958. *Address:* Stanbury Manor, Morwenstow, Bude, Cornwall EX23 9JQ.

AUSTIN, Brian Patrick; HM Diplomatic Service, retired; Consul-General, Vancouver, 1993–98; *b* 18 March 1938; *s* of Edward William Austin and Winifred Alice Austin; *m* 1968, Augusta Francisca Maria Lina; one *s* one *d. Educ:* St Olave's Grammar Sch.; Clare Coll., Cambridge. National Service, 1956–58. Joined CRO, 1961; Central African Office, 1962; Lagos, 1963; The Hague, 1966; First Sec., FCO, 1969; Montreal, 1973; FCO, 1978; Dep. High Comr, Kaduna, 1981–84; Counsellor: FCO, 1984–88; Stockholm, 1989–93. *Recreation:* birdwatching. *Address:* Clinton, Nightingale Avenue, West Horsley, Surrey KT24 6PB.

AUSTIN, Prof. Colin François Lloyd, DPhil; FBA 1983; Director of Studies in Classics and Fellow, Trinity Hall, Cambridge, since 1965; Professor of Greek, University of Cambridge, since 1998; *b* Melbourne, Australia, 26 July 1941; *s* of Prof. Lloyd James Austin, FBA; *m* 1967, Mishtu Mazumdar, Calcutta, India; one *s* one *d. Educ:* Lycée Lakanal, Paris; Manchester Grammar Sch.; Jesus Coll., Cambridge (Scholar; MA 1965); Christ Church, Oxford (Sen. Scholar; MA, DPhil 1965); Freie Universität, West Berlin (Post-grad. Student). University of Cambridge: John Stewart of Rannoch Scholar in Greek and Latin, 1960; Battie Scholar, Henry Arthur Thomas Scholar and Hallam Prize, 1961; Sir William Browne Medal for a Latin Epigram, 1961; Porson Prize, 1962; Prendergast Greek Student, 1962; Res. Fellow, Trinity Hall, 1965–69; Asst Univ. Lectr in Classics, 1969–73, Lectr, 1973–88; Reader in Greek Lang. and Lit., 1988–98; Leverhulme Res. Fellow, 1979 and 1981. Treas., Cambridge Philological Soc., 1971–. *Publications:* De nouveaux fragments de l'Erechthée d'Euripide, 1967; Nova Fragmenta Euripidea, 1968; (with Prof. R. Kasser) Papyrus Bodmer XXV et XXVI, 2 vols, 1969; Menandri Aspis et Samia, 2 vols, 1969–70; Comicorum Graecorum Fragmenta in papyris reperta, 1973; (with Prof. R. Kassel) Poetae Comici Graeci: vol. IV, Aristophon–Crobylus, 1983, vol. III 2, Aristophanes, Testimonia et Fragmenta, 1984, vol. V, Damoxenus–Magnes, 1986, vol. VII, Menecrates–Xenophon, 1989, vol. II, Agathenor–Aristonymus, 1991, vol. VIII, Adespota, 1995, vol. VI 2, Menander, Testimonia et Fragmenta apud scriptores servata, 1998, vol. I, Comoedia Dorica, Mimi, Phlyaces, 2001; notes and reviews in classical periodicals. *Recreations:* cycling, philately, wine tasting. *Address:* 7 Park Terrace, Cambridge CB1 1JH. *T:* (01223) 362732; Trinity Hall, Cambridge CB2 1TJ.

AUSTIN, Prof. Colin Russell, FAA; Charles Darwin Professor of Animal Embryology, and Fellow of Fitzwilliam College, University of Cambridge, 1967–81, now Professor Emeritus; *b* 12 Sept. 1914; *s* of Ernest Russell Austin and Linda Mabel King; *m* 1941,

Patricia Constance Jack; two *s*. *Educ:* Univ. of Sydney, Australia (BVSc 1936; DSc 1954); MA Cantab 1967. FAA 1987; FAIBiol 1987. Mem. Research Staff, CSIRO, Australia, 1938–54; Mem. Scientific Staff of MRC, UK, 1954–64; Editor, Jl of Reproduction and Fertility, 1959–64; Head of Genetic and Developmental Disorders Research Program, Delta Regional Primate Research Center, and Prof. of Embryology, Tulane Univ., New Orleans, 1964–67. F. R. Lillie Meml Fellow, Marine Biol Lab, Woods Hole, Mass, 1961. Visiting Professor: Florida State Univ., 1962; Univ. of Palermo, 1969; Univ. of NSW, 1974; Murdoch Univ., 1979; Univ. of Auckland, 1980; Chulalongkorn Univ., Bangkok, 1985; Goding Lectr, Australian Soc. for Reproductive Biol., 1991. Editor: Reproduction in Mammals, 1972–86; Biological Reviews, 1981–84. Hon. Mem., Amer. Assoc. Anatomists, 1984; Hon. Member: Soc. Chilena Reprod. y Desarrollo, 1989; Eur. Soc. of Human Reproduction and Embryol., 1990. Medal and Citation, Istituto Sperimentale Italiano Lazzaro Spallanzani, 1972; Marshall Medal, Soc. for Study of Fertility, 1981; Pioneer Award, Internat. Embryo Transfer Soc., 1995. *Publications:* The Mammalian Egg, 1961; Fertilization, 1965; Ultrastructure of Fertilization, 1968; Human Embryos: the debate on assisted reproduction, 1989; numerous research papers. *Recreations:* gardening, swimming, tennis. *Address:* 79 Dixon Road, Buderim, Qld 4556, Australia.

AUSTIN, David Charles Henshaw; farmer, since 1943; Chairman, David Austin Roses Ltd, since 1970; *b* 16 Feb. 1926; *s* of Charles Frederick Austin and Lilian Austin; *m* 1956, Patricia Josephine Braithwaite; two *s* one *d*. *Educ:* Shrewsbury Sch. Non-professional rose breeder, 1946–70; nurseryman and professional rose breeder, developing new race, English Roses, 1970–. Hon. MSc East London, 1997. Veitch Meml Medal, RHS, 1994; Queen Mary Commemoration Medal, Royal Nat. Rose Soc., 1994; Landscape Gardening Award, Franco-British Soc., 1995. *Publications:* The Heritage of the Rose, 1988; Old Roses and English Roses, 1992; Shrub Roses and Climbing Roses, 1993; David Austin's English Roses, 1993 (Gardening Book of Year Award, Garden Writers' Guild, 1994); The English Rose, 1998. *Recreations:* reading and writing poetry, current affairs, swimming, gardens, the countryside. *Address:* David Austin Roses Ltd, Bowling Green Lane, Albrighton, Wolverhampton, W Midlands WV7 3HB. *T:* (01902) 376300; Bowling Green House, Bowling Green Lane, Albrighton, Wolverhampton, W Midlands WV7 3HB.

AUSTIN, Ven. George Bernard; Archdeacon of York, 1988–99, now Emeritus; broadcaster, writer; *b* 16 July 1931; *s* of Oswald Hulton Austin and Evelyn Austin; *m* 1962, Roberta Anise Thompson; one *s*. *Educ:* St David's Coll., Lampeter (BA); Chichester Theological Coll. Deacon 1955, priest 1956; Assistant Curate: St Peter's, Chorley, 1955–57; St Clement's, Notting Dale, 1957–59; Asst Chaplain, Univ. of London, 1960; Asst Curate, Dunstable Priory, 1961–64; Vicar: St Mary the Virgin, Eaton Bray, 1964–70; St Peter, Bushey Heath, 1970–88. Hon. Canon, St Albans, 1978–88; Canon, York, 1988–99, now Emeritus. Proctor in Convocation, 1970–95; a Church Commr, 1978–95. *Publications:* Life of our Lord, 1960; WCC Programme to Combat Racism, 1979; (contrib.) When will ye be Wise?, 1983; (contrib.) Building in Love, 1990; Journey to Faith, 1992; Affairs of State, 1995; (contrib.) Quo Vaditis, 1996; But This I Know, 1996; contrib. to national press. *Recreations:* cooking, theatre. *Address:* North Back House, Main Street, Wheldrake, York YO19 6AG. *T:* (01904) 448509; *e-mail:* george.austin@virgin.net.

AUSTIN, Hon. Jacob, (Jack); PC (Canada) 1981; QC (British Columbia) 1970; Member of the Senate, Canadian Parliament, since 1975; *b* 2 March 1932; *s* of Morris Austin and Clara Edith (*née* Chetner); *m* (marr. diss.); three *d*; *m* 1978, Natalie Veiner Freeman. *Educ:* Univ. of British Columbia (BA, LLB); Harvard Univ. (LLM). Barrister and Solicitor, BC and Yukon Territory. Asst Prof. of Law, Univ. of Brit. Columbia, 1955–58; practising lawyer, Vancouver, BC, 1958–63; Exec. Asst to Minister of Northern Affairs and Nat. Resources, 1963–65; contested (Liberal) Vancouver-Kingsway, Can. Federal Election, 1965; practising lawyer, Vancouver, BC, 1966–70; Dep. Minister, Dept of Energy, Mines and Resources, Ottawa, 1970–74; Principal Sec. to Prime Minister, Ottawa, May 1974–Aug. 1975; Minister of State, 1981–82; Minister of State for Social Develt, responsible for Canada Develt Investment Corp., and Minister for Expo '86, 1982–84; Chm., Ministerial Sub-Cttee on Broadcasting and Cultural Affairs, 1982–84. Pres., Internat. Div., Bank of British Columbia, 1985–86; Associate Counsel: Swinton & Co., 1986–92; Boughton Peterson & Co., 1992–; Chairman of Board and Director: Elite Insurance Management Ltd, 1986–90. Pres., Canada China Business Council, 1993–. Hon. DSocSc Univ. East Asia, 1987. *Publications:* articles on law and public affairs in Canadian Bar Rev., Amer. Soc. of Internat. Law and other publns. *Recreations:* sailing, tennis, reading, theatre. *Address:* Suite 304, 140 Wellington Street, The Senate, Ottawa, Ontario K1A 0A4, Canada. *T:* (613) 9921437. *Clubs:* Rideau (Ottawa); Vancouver (Vancouver, BC).

AUSTIN, John Eric; MP (Lab) Erith and Thamesmead, since 1997 (Woolwich, 1992–97); *b* 21 Aug. 1944; *s* of late Stanley George Austin and Ellen Elizabeth (*née* Day); adopted surname Austin-Walker, 1965, reverted to Austin, 1997; *m* 1965, Linda Margaret Walker (marr. diss. 1998); two *s* one *d*. *Educ:* Glyn Grammar Sch., Epsom; Goldsmiths' Coll., Univ. of London (Cert. Community and Youth Work 1972); Sch. for Advanced Urban Studies, Univ. of Bristol (MSc Policy Studies 1990). Hosp. lab. technician, 1961–63; Labour Party organiser, 1963–70; social worker/community worker, Bexley, 1972–74; Race Equality Officer (Dir, Bexley Council for Racial Equality), 1974–92. London Borough of Greenwich Council: Mem., 1970–94; Vice-Chm., 1971–74, Chm., 1974–78, Social Services; Dep. Leader, 1981–82; Leader, 1982–87; Mayor of Greenwich, 1987–88 and 1988–89. Vice-Chairman: ALA, 1983–87 (Envmt Spokesperson, 1989–92); London Strategic Policy Unit, 1986–88; Chaiman: London Ecology Unit, 1990–92; London Emergency Planning Inf. Centre, 1990–92. Chairman: British Youth Council, 1969–71; Assoc. CHCs for England and Wales, 1986–88. Contested (Lab) Woolwich, 1987. Mem., Select Cttee on Health, 1994–. Jt Chm., All Party Osteoporosis Gp, 1996–; Treasurer: Parly Human Rights Gp, 1997–98; Parly Gibraltar Gp, 1997–98; Secretary: Parly Western Sahara Gp, 1997–; British/Czech and Slovak Parly Gp, 1997–; Jt Sec., British/Hungary Parly Gp, 1997–; Chairman: British/Slovenia Parly Gp, 1997–; British/Albania Parly Gp, 1997–; All-Party UK Overseas Territories Parly Gp, 1998–; Vice-Chm., British Falkland Is Gp, 1997–. Vice Chm., London Gp of Labour MPs, 1992–; Chm., Socialist Campaign Gp of Labour MPs, 1992–98. Mem. Exec. Cttee, UK branches of CPA and IPU, 1997–. Hon. Chm., British Caribbean Assoc., 1997–. Director: London Marathon Charitable Trust; Adolescent & Children Trust. *Recreations:* cooking, gardening, marathon running, travel. *Address:* House of Commons, SW1A 0AA. *T:* (020) 7219 5195, *Fax:* (020) 7219 2706; (constituency office) *T:* (01322) 335464. *Clubs:* St Patrick's Social (Plumstead); Northumberland Heath Working Men's (Erith); Woolwich Catholic.

AUSTIN, Rt Rev. John Michael; *see* Aston, Bishop Suffragan of.

AUSTIN, Vice-Adm. Sir Peter (Murray), KCB 1976; Director, Mastiff Electronic Systems, since 1987 (Managing Director, 1990–91); *b* 16 April 1921; *er s* of late Vice-Adm. Sir Francis Austin, KBE, CB, and late Lady (Marjorie) Austin (*née* Barker); *m* 1959, Josephine Rhoda Ann Shutte-Smith; three *s* one *d*. *Educ:* RNC, Dartmouth. Cadet, Dartmouth, 1935. Served War of 1939–45: at sea in HMS Cornwall, 1939–40; destroyers, 1941–45. Qualif. as pilot in FAA, 1946; served in 807 Sqdn, 1947–49; CO 736 Sqdn, 1950–52; grad. from RAF Flying Coll., Manby, 1953; comd 850 Sqdn in HMAS Sydney, incl. Korea, 1953–54; Lt-Cmdr (Flying), HMS Bulwark, 1954–56; Comdr (Air), RNAS Brawdy, 1956–58; Comdr (Air), HMS Eagle, 1958–59; Captain, 1961; Captain F7 in HMS Lynx, 1963–65; CO, RNAS Brawdy, 1965–67; Staff of SACLANT, 1967–69; comd aircraft carrier, HMS Hermes, 1969–70; Rear-Adm., 1971; Asst Chief of Naval Staff (Ops and Air), 1971–73; Flag Officer, Naval Air Comd, 1973–76, retired; Vice-Adm., 1974. Operations Dir, Mersey Docks and Harbour Co., 1976–80; Dir, Avanova Internat. Consultants, 1980–89; Chm., Special Training Services, 1984–90. Vice-Chm. Council, Air League, 1987–95. Liveryman, GAPAN, 1987–. CIMgt. *Recreations:* bicycling, swimming. *Club:* Army and Navy.

AUSTIN, Sir Roger (Mark), KCB 1992; AFC 1973; aviation and defence consultant, since 1998; *b* 9 March 1940; *s* of Mark and Sylvia Joan Austin. *Educ:* King Alfred's Grammar Sch., Wantage. FRAeS. Commissioned in RAF, 1957; flying appts as Qualified Flying Instructor and with Nos 20 and 54 Sqns, 1960–68; commanded No 54 Sqn, 1969; flying appt with No 4 Sqn, 1970–72; Staff Coll., Camberley, 1973; commanded 233 OCU, 1974–77; PSO to AOC-in-C Strike Command, 1977–80; commanded RAF Chivenor, 1980–82; ADC to the Queen, 1980–82; Staff of HQ Strike Command, 1982–84; Dir of Op. Requirements, 1984–85; RCDS, 1986; AO i/c Central Tactics and Trials Orgn, 1987; DG Aircraft 1, MoD (PE), 1987–89; AOC and Comdt, RAF Coll., Cranwell, 1989–92; DCDS (Systems), MoD, 1992–94; Controller Aircraft, MoD, 1994–96; Dep. Chief of Defence Procurement (Ops), MoD (PE), 1995–96; Air Marshal, retd 1997. FO RAFVR (T), 1997. Chm., Victory Services Assoc., 1997–; Pres., RBL, 1997–2000. *Recreations:* flying, transport systems, photography. *Address:* 10 Cleveland Grove, Newbury, Berks RG14 1XF. *Club:* Royal Air Force.

AUSTIN-SMITH, Michael Gerard; QC 1990; a Recorder, since 1986; *b* 4 Sept. 1944; *s* of late Cyril John Austin-Smith and Joyce Austin-Smith; *m* 1971, Stephanie Maddocks; one *s* one *d*. *Educ:* Hampton Grammar Sch.; Exeter Univ. (LLB Hons). Called to the Bar, Inner Temple, 1969. DTI Inspector, 1988–89 and 1989–90. *Address:* 23 Essex Street, WC2R 3AS. *T:* (020) 7413 0353. *Clubs:* Rugby; Royal Corinthian Yacht, Island Sailing (Cowes).

AUSTIN-WALKER, John Eric; *see* Austin, J. E.

AUSTRALIA, Primate of; *see* Perth (Australia), Archbishop of.

AUSTRALIA, North-West, Bishop of, since 1992; **Rt Rev. Anthony Howard Nichols,** PhD; *b* 29 March 1938; *m* 1968, Judith Margaret Ross; two *s* two *d*. *Educ:* Univ. of Sydney (BA; MEd); Univ. of London (BD Hons); Macquarrie Univ. (MA Hons); Moore Coll., ACT (Theol. scholar); PhD Univ. of Sheffield 1997. Latin and history teacher, 1960–63. Assistant Curate: St Paul's Chatswood, 1966; St Bede's, Drummoyne, 1967; Lectr, Biblical Studies, Moore Coll., Sydney, 1968–72; Lectr, Biblical Studies and Educn, 1972–81, Dean of Faculty of Theology, 1977–81, Satya Wacana Christian Univ., Salatiga, Indonesia; Principal: Nungalinya Coll., Darwin (Training Coll. for Aboriginal theol students), 1982–87; St Andrew's Hall, Melbourne (CMS Training Coll.), 1988–91. Stephen Bayne Scholar, Univ. of Sheffield, 1985–86. *Publications:* jl articles on Bible translation, missiology, Indonesian religions, Aboriginal culture, and philosophy of educn. *Address:* Bishop's House, PO Box 140, Geraldton, WA 6530, Australia. *T:* (8) 99217277, *Fax:* (8) 99642220.

AUSTWICK, Prof. Kenneth; JP; Professor of Education, Bath University, 1966–91, now Emeritus; *b* 26 May 1927; *s* of Harry and Beatrice Austwick; *m* 1956, Gillian Griffin; one *s* one *d*. *Educ:* Morecambe Grammar Sch.; Sheffield Univ. BSc Maths, DipEd, MSc, PhD Sheffield. Fellow, Royal Statistical Soc.; FRSA. Schoolmaster, Bromsgrove, Frome and Nottingham, 1950–59; Lectr/Sen. Lectr, Sheffield Univ., 1959–65; Dep. Dir, Inst. of Educn, Reading Univ., 1965–66; Pro-Vice-Chancellor, Bath Univ., 1972–75. Vis. Lecturer: Univ. of BC, 1963; Univ. of Michigan, 1963; Univ. of Wits., 1967. Consultant, OECD, 1965; Adviser, Home Office, 1967–81; Chm., Nat. Savings SW Regional Educn, 1975–78. JP Bath 1970. *Publications:* Logarithms, 1962; Equations and Graphs, 1963; (ed) Teaching Machines and Programming, 1964; (ed) Aspects of Educational Technology, 1972; Maths at Work, 1985; Mathematics Connections, 1985; Level by Level Mathematics, 1991; (ed) Working Science, 1991; (ed) Working English, 1991; articles and contribs on maths teaching and educnl technology. *Recreations:* gardening, bridge. *Address:* Laundry Cottage, Combe Hay, Bath BA2 7EG. *T:* (01225) 832541. *Club:* Royal Commonwealth Society.

AVEBURY, 4th Baron *cr* 1900; **Eric Reginald Lubbock;** Bt 1806; *b* 29 Sept. 1928; *s* of Hon. Maurice Fox Pitt Lubbock (6th *s* of 1st Baron) (*d* 1957), and Hon. Mary Katherine Adelaide Stanley (*d* 1981), *d* of 5th Baron Stanley of Alderley; *S* cousin, 1971; *m* 1953, Kina Maria (marr. diss. 1983) (*see* Lady Avebury); two *s* one *d*; 2nd, 1985, Lindsay Stewart; one *s*. *Educ:* Upper Canada Coll.; Harrow Sch.; Balliol Coll., Oxford (BA Engineering; boxing blue). MIMechE, CEng; FBCS. Welsh Guards (Gdsman, 2nd Lieut), 1949–51; Rolls Royce Ltd, 1951–56; Grad. Apprentice; Export Sales Dept; Tech. Assistant to Foundry Manager. Management Consultant: Production Engineering Ltd, 1953–60; Charterhouse Group Ltd, 1960. MP (L) Orpington, 1962–70; Liberal Whip in House of Commons, 1963–70; elected Mem., H of L, 1999. Dir, C. L. Projects Ltd, 1966–; Consultant, Morgan-Grampian Ltd, 1970–. President: Data Processing Management Assoc., 1972–75; Fluoridation Soc., 1972–84; Conservation Soc., 1973–83. Member: Council, Inst. of Race Relations, 1972–74; Royal Commn on Standards of Conduct in Public Life, 1974–76; Chm., British Parly Human Rights Gp, 1976–97 (Vice Pres., 1997–). Vice Pres., London Bach Soc., 1998– (Pres., 1984–98); Pres., Steinitz Bach Players, 1984–. Patron, Buddhist Prison Chaplaincy, 1995–. *Recreations:* listening to music, reading. *Heir:* *s* Hon. Lyulph Ambrose Jonathan Lubbock [*b* 15 June 1954; *m* 1977, Susan (*née* MacDonald); one *s* one *d*]. *Address:* House of Lords, SW1A 0PW; 26 Flodden Road, SE5 9LH.

AVEBURY, Kina Lady; Kina-Maria Lubbock; consultant on health and social policy; *b* 2 Sept. 1934; *d* of late Count Joseph O'Kelly de Gallagh and Mrs M. Bruce; *m* 1953, 4th Baron Avebury, *qv* (marr. diss. 1983); two *s* one *d*. *Educ:* Convent of the Sacred Heart, Tunbridge Wells; Goldsmiths' College (BScSoc Hons) and LSE, Univ. of London. Lectr, Royal Coll. of Nursing, 1970–74; campaign organizer, European Movement, 1975; Asst Dir, Nat. Assoc. for Mental Health, 1976–82; Sociologist, Dept of Psychiatry, London Hosp. Med. Coll., 1983–85; Mental Health Planner, Tower Hamlets Social Services, 1986–94. Chairman: Nat. Marriage Guidance Council, 1975–82; Family Service Units, 1984–87; Avebury Working Party, 1982–84 (produced Code of Practice for Residential Care for DHSS); Working Party for A Better Home Life, 1996, Working Party on Nat. Required Standards for Long Term Care, 1998–99, Centre for Policy on Ageing; Mem., Central Council for Educn and Trng in Social Work, 1986–90. JP Kent, 1974–79. *Publications:* Volunteers in Mental Health, 1985; (with R. Williams) A Place in Mind,

1995; (jtly) The Substance of Young Needs, 1996; articles on mental health and related social policy. *Recreations:* painting, opera, cooking.

AVERY, Gillian Elise, (Mrs A. O. J. Cockshut); writer; *b* 1926; *d* of late Norman and Grace Avery; *m* 1952, A. O. J. Cockshut; one *d. Educ:* Dunottar Sch., Reigate. Chm., Children's Books History Soc., 1987–90; Mem., American Antiquarian Soc., 1988. *Publications: children's fiction:* The Warden's Niece, 1957; Trespassers at Charlcote, 1958; James without Thomas, 1959; The Elephant War, 1960; To Tame a Sister, 1961; The Greatest Gresham, 1962; The Peacock House, 1963; The Italian Spring, 1964; The Call of the Valley, 1966; A Likely Lad, 1971 (Guardian Award, 1972); Huck and her Time Machine, 1977; *adult fiction:* The Lost Railway, 1980; Onlookers, 1983; *non-fiction:* 19th Century Children: heroes and heroines in English children's stories (with Angela Bull), 1965; Victorian People in Life and Literature, 1970; The Echoing Green: memories of Regency and Victorian youth, 1974; Childhood's Pattern, 1975; Children and Their Books: a celebration of the work of Iona and Peter Opie (ed with Julia Briggs), 1989; The Best Type of Girl: a history of girls' independent schools, 1991; Behold the Child: a history of American children and their books 1622–1921, 1994; (ed with Kimberley Reynolds) Representations of Childhood Death, 2000; ed, Gollancz revivals of early children's books, 1967–70, and anthologies of stories and extracts from early children's books. *Recreations:* music, laughing. *Address:* 32 Charlbury Road, Oxford OX2 6UU.

AVERY, Graham John Lloyd; Chief Adviser, Directorate General for Enlargement, European Commission, Brussels, since 2000; *b* 29 Oct. 1943; *s* of Rev. Edward Avery and Alice Avery; *m* 1967, Susan Steele (separated 1982); two *s*; partner, 1989, Annalisa Cecchi; one *s. Educ:* Kingswood Sch., Bath; Balliol Coll., Oxford (MA). Fellow, Center for Internat. Affairs, Harvard Univ. Joined MAFF, 1965; Principal responsible for negotiations for British entry to European Communities, 1969–72; PPS to Ministers, Frederick Peart, John Silkin, 1976; Commission of the European Communities, subseq. European Commission, Brussels: Member of Cabinets: of President, Roy Jenkins, 1977–80; of Vice-Pres. for External Relns, Christopher Soames, 1973–76; of Comrs for Agric., Finn Gundelach 1981, Poul Dalsager 1981, Frans Andriessen 1985–86; a Dir, 1987–98; served in Directorate Gen. for Agric. as Hd of Div. for Econ. Affairs and Gen. Problems, 1981–84, as Dir for Agricl Structures, 1987–89, as Dir for Rural Develt, 1989–90; served: in Directorate Gen. for External Relations as Dir for relns with USA, Canada, Australia and NZ, 1990–92; as Dir for relns with Austria, Switzerland, Iceland, Norway, Sweden and Finland, 1992–93; in Task Force for Enlargement as Dir, 1993–94; in Directorate Gen. for External Political Relations, as Head of Policy Planning, 1995, as Chief Advr for Enlargement, 1996–98; Inspector Gen., 1998–2000. *Publications:* (with Fraser Cameron) The Enlargement of the European Union, 1998; articles in Internat. Affairs, World Today, Europ. Affairs, Oxford Internat. Rev., Jl of Agricl Econs, Europ. Environment Rev., etc. *Address:* European Commission, 1049 Brussels, Belgium. *T:* (2) 2992202.

AVERY, James Royle, (Roy); Headmaster, Bristol Grammar School, 1975–86; *b* 7 Dec. 1925; *s* of Charles James Avery and Dorothy May Avery; *m* 1954, Marjorie Louise (*née* Smith); one *s* one *d. Educ:* Queen Elizabeth's Hosp., Bristol; Magdalen Coll., Oxford; Bristol Univ. MA Oxon, CertifEd Bristol; FRSA. Asst History Master, Bristol Grammar Sch., 1951–59; Sen. History Master, Haberdashers' Aske's Sch. at Hampstead, then Elstree, 1960–65; Head Master, Harrow County Boys' Sch., 1965–75. Mem. Council, Bristol Univ., 1982–95. Hon. MLitt Bristol, 1996. *Publications:* The Story of Aldenham House, 1961; The Elstree Murder, 1962; The History of Queen Elizabeth's Hospital 1590–1990, 1990; John James, CBE, 1906–1996, Bristol's Philanthropist (biog.), 2001; contrib. Dictionary of World History, 1973; articles, reviews in educnl jls. *Recreations:* reading, walking, sport, music, the ecumenical movement, international studies. *Address:* First Floor Flat, 4 Rockleaze, Sneyd Park, Bristol BS9 1ND. *T:* (0117) 968 6805.

AVERY, John Ernest, CB 1997; Deputy Parliamentary Commissioner for Administration, 1990–2000; *b* 18 April 1940; *s* of Ernest Charles Avery and Pauline Margaret Avery; *m* 1966, Anna Meddings; two *d. Educ:* Plymouth Coll.; Leeds Univ. (BSc). Called to the Bar, Gray's Inn, 1972. Patent Examiner, Bd of Trade, 1964–72; Office of Fair Trading, 1972–76; Dept of Industry, later DTI, 1976–89; Dir of Investigations, Office of Parly Comr for Admin (Ombudsman), 1989–90. *Recreations:* squash, theatre.

AVERY, Roy; *see* Avery, J. R.

AVERY JONES, Dr John Francis, CBE 1987; FTII; Senior Partner, Speechly Bircham, since 1985; *b* 5 April 1940; *s* of Sir Francis Avery Jones, CBE, FRCP; *m* 1994, Catherine Susan Bobbett. *Educ:* Rugby Sch.; Trinity Coll., Cambridge (MA, LLM, PhD 1993). Solicitor, 1966; Partner in Bircham & Co., 1970. Member: Meade Cttee, 1975–77; Keith Cttee, 1980–84. Pres., Inst. of Taxation, 1980–82; Chm., Law Soc.'s Revenue Law Cttee, 1983–87; Member Council: Law Soc., 1986–90; Inst. for Fiscal Studies, 1988–; Exec. Cttee, Internat. Fiscal Assoc., 1988–94 (1st Vice-Pres., 1993–94; Chm., British Br., 1989–91); Mem., Bd of Trustees, Internat. Bureau of Fiscal Documentation, 1989– (Chm., 1991–). Vis. Prof. of Taxation, LSE, 1988–; Atax Cliffbrook Vis. Schol., Univ. of NSW, 1995. David R. Tillinghast Lectr on Internat. Taxation, New York Univ., 1997. Dep. Special Comr of Income Tax, 1991–; Chm., VAT and Duties Tribunals, 1991–. Mem., Steering Cttee, Tax Law Rewrite, 1996–; Chm., Tax Law Review Cttee, 1997–. Member, Board of Governors: Voluntary Hosp. of St Bartholomew, 1984–; LSE, 1995– (Chm., Audit Cttee, 1996–); Chm., Addington Soc., 1985–87. Master: Co. of Barbers, 1985–86; City of London Solicitors' Co., 1997–98. Consulting Ed., Encyclopedia of VAT, 1989–93 (Gen. Ed., 1972–89); Jt Editor, British Tax Review, 1974–97; Mem. Editl Bd, Simon's Taxes, 1977–. *Publications:* (ed) Tax Havens and Measures Against Tax Avoidance and Evasion in the EEC, 1974; numerous articles on tax. *Recreations:* music, particularly opera. *Address:* 4 Woodfield Road, W5 1SJ. *T:* (020) 8998 2143, *Fax:* (020) 8997 9736. *Club:* Athenæum.

AVIS, Rev. Preb. Dr Paul David Loup; General Secretary, Church of England Council for Christian Unity, since 1998; *b* 21 July 1947; *s* of Peter George Hobden Avis and Diana Joan (*née* Loup); *m* 1970, Susan Janet Haywood; three *s. Educ:* London Bible Coll. (BD Hons London Univ. (ext.) 1970; PhD 1976); Westcott House, Cambridge. Deacon 1975, priest 1976; Curate, South Molton, dio. Exeter, 1975–80; Vicar, Stoke Canon, Poltimore with Huxham, Rewe with Netherexe, 1980–98. Preb. of Exeter Cathedral, 1993–; Sub Dean of Exeter Cathedral, 1997–. Hon. Dir, Centre for Study of Christian Church, 1997–. *Publications:* The Church in the Theology of the Reformers, 1982; Ecumenical Theology, 1986; The Methods of Modern Theology, 1986; Foundations of Modern Historical Thought, 1986; Gore: Construction and Conflict, 1988; (ed and contrib.) The Threshold of Theology, 1988; Eros and the Sacred, 1989; Anglicanism and the Christian Church, 1989; Authority, Leadership and Conflict in the Church, 1992; (ed and contrib.) The Resurrection of Jesus Christ, 1993; (ed and contrib.) Divine Revelation, 1997; Faith in the Fires of Criticism, 1997; God and the Creative Imagination, 1999; The Anglican Understanding of the Church, 2000; Church, State and Establishment, 2001. *Recreations:* walking, literature, writing theology. *Address:* Church House, Great Smith Street, SW1P 3NZ. *T:* (020) 7898 1470; 48 Trinity Rise, SW2 2QR. *T:* (020) 8671 8450.

AVNER, Yehuda; Ambassador of Israel to Australia, 1992–96; *b* 30 Dec. 1928; *m* Miriam Avner; one *s* three *d. Educ:* High School, Manchester. Editor of publications, Jewish Agency, Jerusalem, 1956–64; Editor of Political Publications, Min. of Foreign Affairs, and Asst to Prime Minister Levi Eshkol, 1964–67; Consul, New York, 1967–68; First Sec. then Counsellor, Washington, 1968–72; Dir of Foreign Press Bureau, Foreign Ministry, and Asst to PM Golda Meir, 1972–74; seconded to PM's Bureau, and Adviser to PM Yitzhak Rabin, 1974–77; Adviser to PM Menachem Begin, 1977–83; Ambassador to UK, 1983–88; Dir Gen., Clore Foundn, Israel, 1989–90; Inspector General of Foreign Service, Israel, 1990–92. *Publication:* The Young Inheritors: a portrait of Israeli youth, 1982. *Address:* c/o Ministry of Foreign Affairs, Hakirya, Romena, Jerusalem 91950, Israel.

AVONSIDE, Lady; Janet Sutherland Shearer, OBE 1958; Scottish Governor, BBC, 1971–76; *b* 31 May 1917; *d* of William Murray, MB, ChB, and Janet Harley Watson; *m* 1954, Ian Hamilton Shearer, later Lord Avonside, PC (*d* 1996). *Educ:* St Columba's Sch., Kilmacolm; Erlenhaus, Baden Baden; Univ. of Edinburgh. LLB, Dip. of Social Science. Asst Labour Officer (Scot.), Min. of Supply, 1941–45; Sec. (Scot.), King George's Fund for Sailors, 1945–53; Hon. Sec. (Scot.), Federal Union and United Europe, 1945–64; Scottish Delegate: Congress of Europe, 1947; Council of Europe, Strasburg, 1949. Contested (C), elections: Maryhill, Glasgow, 1950; Dundee East, 1951; Leith, 1955. Lectr in Social Studies, Dept of Educational Studies, Univ. of Edinburgh, 1962–70. Governor, Queen Margaret Coll., Edinburgh, 1986–89. *Recreation:* gardening. *Address:* 4A Dirleton Avenue, North Berwick, East Lothian EH39 4AY. *Clubs:* Caledonian (Associate Mem.); New (Edinburgh).

AWDRY, Daniel (Edmund), TD; DL; *b* 10 Sept. 1924; *s* of late Col Edmund Portman Awdry, MC, TD, DL, Coters, Chippenham, Wilts, and Mrs Evelyn Daphne Alexandra Awdry, JP (formerly French); *m* 1950, Elizabeth Cattley; three *d. Educ:* Winchester Coll. RAC, OCTU, Sandhurst, 1943–44 (Belt of Honour). Served with 10th Hussars as Lieut, Italy, 1944–45; ADC to GOC 56th London Div., Italy, 1945; Royal Wilts Yeo., 1947–62; Major and Sqdn Comdr, 1955–62. Qualified Solicitor, 1950. Mayor of Chippenham, 1958–59; Pres., Southern Boroughs Assoc., 1959–60. MP (C) Chippenham, Wilts, Nov. 1962–1979; PPS to Minister of State, Board of Trade, Jan.–Oct. 1964; PPS to Solicitor-Gen., 1973–74. Director: BET Omnibus Services, 1966–80; Sheepbridge Engineering, 1968–79; Rediffusion Ltd, 1973–85; Colonial Mutual Life Assurance Ltd, 1974–89. DL Wilts, 1979. *Recreation:* chess. *Address:* Old Manor, Beanacre, near Melksham, Wilts SN12 7PT. *T:* (01225) 702315.

AX, Emanuel; concert pianist, since 1974; *b* 8 June 1949; *m* Yoko Nazaki; one *s* one *d. Educ:* Juilliard Sch. (studied with Mieczylaw Munz); Columbia Univ. Regular solo appearances with symphony orchs, incl. NY Philharmonic, Philadelphia Orch., Boston SO, Chicago SO, Cleveland Orch., Berlin Philharmonic, LPO, etc; recitals at Carnegie Hall, Concertgebouw, Amsterdam, Barbican Centre, Théâtre des Champs Elysées, etc; has played duo recitals with 'cellist Yo-Yo Ma annually since 1976; performed world premières of piano concertos by: Joseph Schwantner, 1988; Ezra Laderman, 1992; John Adams, 1997; Christopher Rouse, 1999; Bright Sheng, 2000. Numerous recordings; Grammy Awards, 1985–86, 1992–95. First Prize, Arthur Rubinstein Internat. Piano Competition, 1974; Michael's Award, Young Concert Artists, 1975; Avery Fisher Prize, 1979. *Address:* c/o ICM Artists Inc., 40 West 57th Street, New York, NY 10019, USA. *T:* (212) 5565600.

AXELROD, Julius, PhD; Guest Researcher, Laboratory of Cell Biology, since 1984, Chief, Section on Pharmacology, Laboratory of Clinical Science, 1955–84 (Acting Chief, Jan.–Oct. 1955), National Institute of Mental Health, USA; Scientist Emeritus, National Institutes of Health, 1996; *b* NYC, 30 May 1912; *s* of Isadore Axelrod, Michaliev, Poland, and Molly Liechtling, Striej, Poland (formerly Austria); *m* 1938, Sally (*née* Taub); two *s. Educ:* George Washington Univ., Wash., DC (PhD); New York Univ. (MA); New York City Coll. (BS). Lab. Asst. Dept Bacteriology, NY Univ. Med. Sch., 1933–35; Chemist, Lab. Industrial Hygiene, 1935–46; Res. Associate, Third NY Univ.; Research Div., Goldwater Memorial Hosp., 1946–49; Nat. Heart Inst., NIH: Associate Chemist, Section on Chem. Pharmacology, 1949–50; Chemist, 1950–53; Sen. Chemist, 1953–55. Jt Nobel Prize for Physiology-Medicine, 1970; Mem., Nat. Academy of Sciences, 1971; Fellow, Amer. Acad. of Arts and Sciences; Senior Mem., Amer. Inst. of Medicine, 1979. Thudicum Medal and Lecture, British Biochem Soc., 1989. Foreign Member: Royal Society, 1979; Deutsche Akademie der Naturforscher, 1984. Hon. LLD: George Washington, 1971; College City, NY, 1972; Hon. DSc: Chicago, 1966; Med. Coll., Wisconsin, 1971; New York, 1971; Pennsylvania Coll. of Med., 1973; Hahnemann Univ., 1987; McGill Univ., 1988; Doctor *hc* Panama, 1972; DPhil *hc*: Ripon Coll., 1984; Tel Aviv Univ., 1984. Winner of 15 awards; holds 23 hon. lectureships; Member: 13 editorial boards; 5 Sci. Adv. Cttees. *Publications:* (with Richard J. Wurtman and Douglas E. Kelly) The Pineal, 1968; numerous original papers and contribs to jls in Biochem., Pharmacol. and Physiology. *Recreations:* reading and listening to music. *Address:* 10401 Grosvenor Place, Rockville, MD 20852, USA. *T:* (301) 4936376.

AXFORD, David Norman, PhD; CMet, CEng, FIEE; international consultant meteorologist; Adviser to Earthwatch Europe, Oxford, 1996–2000; *b* 14 June 1934; *s* of Norman Axford and Joy Alicia Axford (*née* Williams); *m* 1st, 1962, Elizabeth Anne (*née* Stiles) (marr. diss. 1980); one *s* two *d*; 2nd, 1980, Diana Rosemary Joan (*née* Bufton); three step *s* one step *d. Educ:* Merchant Taylors' School, Sandy Lodge; Plymouth Coll.; St John's Coll., Cambridge (Baylis Open Scholarship in Maths; BA 1956, MA 1960, PhD (Met.) 1972); MSc (Electronics) Southampton 1963; FIEE 1982. Entered Met. Office, 1958; Flying Officer, RAF, 1958–60; Meteorological Office: Forecasting and Research, 1960–68; Met. Research Flight, and Radiosondes, 1968–76; Operational Instrumentation, 1976–80; Telecommunications, 1980–82; Dep. Dir, Observational Services, 1982–84; Dir of Services, 1984–89; Dep. Sec.-Gen., WMO, 1989–95; Special Exec. Advr to Sec.-Gen., WMO, 1995. Chm., Cttee on Operational World Weather Watch Systems Evaluation, N Atlantic (CONA), 1985–89. Pres., N Atlantic Observing Stations (NAOS) Bd, 1983–86; Vice Pres., RMetS, 1989–91 (Mem. Council and Hon. Gen. Sec., 1983–88; Mem., 1998–, Chm., 1999–, Accreditation Bd). Mem., Exec. Cttee, British Assoc. of Former UN Civil Service, 1996– (Vice Chm., 1998–99; Chm., 1999–). Chm. of Trustees, Stanford-in-the-Vale Public Purposes Charity, 2000–; Trustee, Thames Valley Hospice, 1996–98. L. G. Groves 2nd Meml Prize for Met., 1970. *Publications:* papers in learned jls on met. and aspects of met. instrumentation in GB and USA. *Recreations:* home and garden, music, travel, good food. *Address:* Honey End, 14 Ock Meadow, Stanford-in-the-Vale, Oxon SN7 8LN. *T:* (01367) 718480. *Club:* Phyllis Court (Henley-on-Thames).

AXFORD, Sir (William) Ian, Kt 1996; PhD; FRS 1986; Director, Max Planck Institut für Aeronomie, Katlenburg-Lindau, West Germany, 1974–82 and since 1985; *b* 2 Jan. 1933; *s* of John Edgar Axford and May Victoria Axford; *m* 1955, Catherine Joy; two *s* two *d. Educ:* Univ. of Canterbury, NZ (MSc Hons, ME Dist.); Univ. of Manchester (PhD); Univ. of Cambridge. NZ Defence Science Corps, 1957–63; seconded to Defence Res. Bd, Ottawa, 1960–62; Associate Prof. of Astronomy, 1963–66, Prof. of Astronomy, 1966–67, Cornell Univ., Ithaca, NY; Prof. of Physics and Applied Physics, Univ. of Calif at San Diego, 1967–74; Vice-Chancellor, Victoria Univ. of Wellington, NZ, 1982–85. Pres., COSPAR, 1986–94; Vice-Pres., Scientific Cttee on Solar-Terrestrial Physics, 1986–90. Hon. Prof., Göttingen Univ., 1978; Appleton Meml Lectr, URSI, 1969. Chm. Bd, NZ Foundn for Res., Sci. and Technol., 1992–95. Chm., Marsden Fund, 1994–98. Pres., European Geophysical Soc., 1990–92 (Hon. Mem., 1996). Fellow, Amer. Geophysical Union, 1971; ARAS 1981; For. Associate, US Nat. Acad. of Scis, 1983; Member: Internat. Acad. of Astronautics, 1985; Academia Europaea, 1989. Hon. FRSNZ 1993. Hon. DSc: Canterbury, 1996; Victoria Univ. of Wellington, 1999. Space Science Award, AIAA, 1970; John Adam Fleming Medal, Amer. Geophysical Union, 1972; Tsiolkovsky Medal, Kosmonautical Fedn, USSR, 1987; Chapman Medal, RAS, 1994; NZ Sci. and Technol. Gold Medal, 1994; NZ Scientist of the Year, New Zealander of the Year, We Care Foundn, 1995. Freedom, City of Napier, NZ, 1999. *Publications:* about 250 articles in scientific jls on aspects of space physics and astrophysics. *Address:* Max Planck Institut für Aeronomie, Max Planck Strasse 2, 37191 Katlenburg-Lindau, Germany. *T:* (5556) 979439, *Fax:* (5556) 979410; 2 Gladstone Road, Napier, New Zealand, *T:* (6) 8352188, *Fax:* (6) 8352176.

AXISA, John Francis, MOM 1995; MBE 1950; *b* 20 Nov. 1906; *s* of late Emmanuel Axisa and Vincenzina (*née* Micallef); *m* 1939, Ariadne Cachia; three *s* one *d. Educ:* St Paul's Sch., Malta and privately. Joined Malta Civil Service, 1927; Dir of Emigration, 1947–56; Dir of Technical Education, 1956–59; Dir of Emigration, Labour and Social Welfare, 1959–60; Under-Sec., 1960–61; Commissioner-Gen. for Malta in London, 1961–64; Malta's first High Commissioner on Malta's Independence, 1964–69; Ambassador of Malta to: France, 1966–69; Fed. Republic of Germany, 1967–69; Libya, 1966–68; Belgium, 1967–68; Netherlands, 1968–69. Chm., Bd of Govs, St Edward's Coll., Malta, 1988–90 (Trustee, 1988–93). *Recreations:* woodwork, fishing, reading. *Address:* 5/8 Tower Road, Sliema, Malta, GC. *Club:* Union (Malta).

AXON, Prof. Anthony Thomas Roger, MD; FRCP; Consultant Physician and Gastroenterologist, Leeds General Infirmary, since 1975; Hon. Professor of Gastroenterology, University of Leeds, since 1995; *b* 21 Nov. 1941; *s* of Robert and Ruth Axon; *m* 1965, Jill Coleman; two *s* one *d. Educ:* Woodhouse Grove Sch., W Yorks; St Bartholomew's Hosp. Med. Coll., London (MB BS Hons, Dist. in Medicine, MD 1973). FRCP 1980. Hse Physician and Resident in Pathology, St Bartholomew's Hosp., 1965–68; Registrar, 1968–70, Resident Registrar, 1970–71, Sen. Registrar, 1971–75, St Thomas' Hosp., London. Mem. Council, RCP, 1992–94. Vice-Pres. Endoscopy, British Soc. Gastroenterol., 1989–91; President: N of England Gastroenterol. Soc., 1999–2000; British Soc. of Gastroenterol., 2000–01; Eur. Soc. of Gastrointestinal Endoscopy, 2000–02; Mem., Educn Cttee, World Orgn of Gastroenterology, 1999–. *Publications:* contrib. numerous original papers on wide variety of gastrointestinal subjects, specifically inflammatory bowel disease, intestinal permeability, ERCP, safety in endoscopy, Helicobacter pylori, cancer surveillance, aetiology of gastric cancer, to peer review jls and other pubns. *Recreations:* travel, gardening. *Address:* Upwood, Woodlands Drive, Rawdon, Leeds LS19 6JZ. *T:* (0113) 250 3452; Leeds General Infirmary, Great George Street, Leeds LS1 3EX. *T:* (0113) 392 2125.

AXTON, Henry Stuart, (Harry), FCA; Chairman, Brixton Estate plc, 1983–93; *b* 6 May 1923; *s* of Wilfrid George Axton and Mary Louise Axton (*née* Laver); *m* 1947, Constance Mary Godefroy (*d* 1996); one *d. Educ:* Rock Ferry. RMC, Sandhurst, commissioned 1942; served: N Africa, Royal Tank Regt, NW Europe, Fife and Forfar Yeo.; wounded three times, invalided out, 1945. Articles, G. E. Holt & Son; Chartered Accountant 1948. Treas., United Sheffield Hosps and other hosp. appts, 1948–55; Company Sec., Midland Assurance, 1955–61; Brixton Estate, 1961–93: Man. Dir, 1964–83; Dep. Chm., 1971–83; Chm., Investment Cos in Australia and Switzerland. Pres., British Property Fedn, 1984–86 (Mem. Council, 1974–93; Vice-Pres., 1983–84; Hon. Life Mem., 1993). Dep. Chm., Audit Commn, 1987–91 (Mem., 1986–91). Chairman: Council, St George's Hosp. Med. Sch., 1977–92 (Mem., 1969–92; Dep. Chm. 1974–77; first Hon. Fellow 1992); St George's New Hosp. Bldg Cttee, 1972–92 (Mem., 1969–92); Nuffield Hosps, 1976–93 (Governor, 1968–93; Dep. Chm. 1975–76); BUPA Medical Centre, 1973–82 (Governor, 1970–82); Mem., Chichester HA, 1985–87; Governor: BUPA, 1969–80; St George's Hosp., 1970–74, Special Trustee, 1974–77. Chm., Chichester Festivities, 1989–98. Dir, Cathedral Works Organisation (Chichester), 1985–91. Mem., Archbp's Council for Church Urban Fund, 1990–94. Trustee, Chichester Fest. Theatre, 1995–. Chm., City of Chichester DFAS, 1999–2000 (Vice-Chm., 1995–99). Freeman, City of London, 1987. Lord of the Manor of Aldingbourne, 1993. *Recreations:* sailing, music. *Address:* Hook Place, Aldingbourne, near Chichester, Sussex PO20 6TS. *T:* (01243) 542291. *Clubs:* Royal Thames Yacht, Royal Ocean Racing; Sussex.

AXWORTHY, Hon. Lloyd; PC 1980; PhD; MP (L) Winnipeg South-Centre, since 1988; Minister for Foreign Affairs, Canada, since 1996; *b* 21 Dec. 1939; *s* of Norman Joseph and Gwen Anne Axworthy; *m* 1984, Denise Ommanney; one *s. Educ:* Univ. of Winnipeg (BA); Princeton Univ. (MA, PhD). MLA Manitoba, 1973–79; MP (L) Winnipeg-Fort Garry, 1979–88; Minister of State for Status of Women, Canada, 1980–81; Minister of Employment and Immigration, 1980–83; Minister of Transportation, 1983–84; Opposition spokesman on internat. trade, 1984–88; Liberal spokesman on external affairs, 1988–93; Minister of Human Resources Develt, and of Western Econ. Diversification, 1993–96. *Address:* Lester B. Pearson Building, 125 Sussex Drive, Ottawa, Ontario K1A 0G2, Canada.

AYALA, Jaime Z. de; *see* Zobel de Ayala.

AYALA-LASSO, José; Minister of Foreign Affairs, Ecuador, 1997–99; *b* 29 Jan. 1932; *m* Monique Wiets de Ayala-Lasso; one *s* three *d. Educ:* Catholic Univ. of Leuven, Belgium; Catholic Univ. of Ecuador; Central Univ. of Ecuador. Ministry of Foreign Affairs, Ecuador, 1955; served Tokyo, Lima, Rome and Min. of Foreign Affairs, to 1974; Ambassador of the Foreign Service, 1975; Under-Sec.-Gen., Min. of Foreign Affairs, 1975; Minister of Foreign Affairs, 1977; Ambassador to Belgium, Luxembourg and EC, 1979, to Peru, 1983; Ambassador and Perm. Rep. of Ecuador to UN, 1989–94; UN High Comr for Human Rights, 1994–97. Order Al Mérito (Ecuador); numerous orders from foreign counties. *Recreation:* classical music. *Address:* c/o Ministry of Foreign Affairs, Avenida 10 de Agosto y Carrión, Quito, Ecuador.

AYCKBOURN, Sir Alan, Kt 1997; CBE 1987; playwright; Artistic Director, Stephen Joseph Theatre, Scarborough; *b* 12 April 1939; *s* of Horace Ayckbourn and Irene Maude (*née* Worley); *m* 1st, 1959, Christine Helen (*née* Roland); two *s*; 2nd, 1997, Heather Stoney. *Educ:* Haileybury. Worked in repertory as Stage Manager/Actor at Edinburgh, Worthing, Leatherhead, Oxford, and with late Stephen Joseph's Theatre-in-the-Round Co., at Scarborough. Founder Mem., Victoria Theatre, Stoke-on-Trent, 1962. BBC Radio Drama Producer, Leeds, 1964–70; Co. Dir, NT, 1986–87. Vis. Prof. of Contemporary Theatre, and Fellow, St Catherine's Coll., Oxford, 1991–92. Has written numerous full-length plays. London productions: Mr Whatnot, Arts, 1964; Relatively Speaking, Duke of York's, 1967, Greenwich, 1986 (televised, 1969, 1989); How the Other Half Loves, Lyric, 1970, Duke of York's, 1988; Time and Time Again, Comedy, 1972 (televised, 1976); Absurd Person Singular, Criterion, 1973 (Evening Standard Drama Award, Best Comedy, 1973) (televised, 1985); The Norman Conquests (Trilogy), Globe, 1974 (Evening Standard Drama Award, Best Play; Variety Club of GB Award; Plays and Players Award) (televised, 1977); Jeeves (musical, with Andrew Lloyd Webber), Her Majesty's, 1975, reworked as By Jeeves, Duke of York's, transf. Lyric, 1996; Absent Friends, Garrick, 1975 (televised, 1985); Confusions, Apollo, 1976; Bedroom Farce, Nat. Theatre, 1977 (televised, 1980); Just Between Ourselves, Queen's, 1977 (Evening Standard Drama Award, Best Play) (televised, 1978); Ten Times Table (dir), Globe, 1978; Joking Apart, Globe, 1979 (Plays and Players Award); Sisterly Feelings, Nat. Theatre, 1980; Taking Steps, Lyric, 1980; Suburban Strains (musical with Paul Todd), Round House, 1981; Season's Greetings, Apollo, 1982; Way Upstream (dir), Nat. Theatre, 1982 (televised, 1988); Making Tracks (musical with Paul Todd), Greenwich, 1983; Intimate Exchanges, Ambassadors, 1984; A Chorus of Disapproval (dir), Nat. Theatre, 1985 (Standard Drama Award, Best Comedy; Olivier Award, Best Comedy; Drama Award, Best Comedy, 1985), transf. Lyric, 1986 (filmed, 1989); Woman in Mind (dir), Vaudeville, 1986; A Small Family Business (dir), Nat. Theatre, 1987 (Evening Standard Drama Award, Best Play); Henceforward … (dir), Vaudeville, 1988 (Evening Standard Drama Award, Best Comedy, 1989); Man of the Moment (dir), Globe, 1990 (Evening Standard Drama Award, Best Comedy, 1990); The Revengers' Comedies (dir), Strand, 1991; Time of My Life (dir), Vaudeville, 1993; Wildest Dreams (dir), Barbican, 1993; Communicating Doors (dir), Gielgud, 1995, transf. Savoy, 1996 (Writers' Guild of GB Award, Best West End Play, 1996); Things We Do For Love (dir), Gielgud, 1998; adapt. Ostrovsky's The Forest, RNT, 1999; Gizmo, RNT, 1999; Comic Potential (dir), Lyric, 1999; House, and Garden (dir), RNT, 2000; Scarborough: Body Language, 1990; Dreams from a Summer House (play with music by John Pattison), 1992; Haunting Julia, 1994; A Word from our Sponsor (musical with John Pattison), 1995; Callisto #7, 1999; Virtual Reality, 2000; Game Plan, 2001; Flat Spin, 2001; RolePlay, 2001; other plays directed: Tons of Money, Nat. Theatre, 1986; A View from the Bridge, Nat. Theatre, transf. Aldwych, 1987; 'Tis Pity she's a Whore, Nat. Theatre, 1988; Two Weeks with the Queen, Nat. Theatre, 1994; Conversations with my Father, Old Vic, 1995; Wild Honey, Scarborough, 1996; Love Songs for Shopkeepers, Scarborough, 1998. *Plays for children:* Callisto 5, 1990; My Very Own Story, 1991; This Is Where We Came In, 1991; Invisible Friends (dir), Nat. Theatre, 1991; Mr A's Amazing Maze Plays, Nat. Theatre, 1993; The Musical Jigsaw Play, 1994; The Champion of Paribanou, 1996; The Boy Who Fell into a Book, 1998; (with D. King) Whenever, 2000. Hon. DLitt: Hull, 1981; Keele, 1987; Leeds, 1987; York, 1992; Bradford, 1994; Univ. of Wales Coll. of Cardiff, 1995; DUniv Open, 1998. *Publications:* The Norman Conquests, 1975; Three Plays (Absurd Person Singular, Absent Friends, Bedroom Farce), 1977; Joking Apart and Other Plays (Just Between Ourselves, Ten Times Table), 1979; Sisterly Feelings, and Taking Steps, 1981; A Chorus of Disapproval, 1986; Woman in Mind, 1986; A Small Family Business, 1987; Henceforward . . ., 1988; Mr A's Amazing Maze Plays, 1989; Man of the Moment, 1990; Invisible Friends (play for children), 1991; The Revengers' Comedies, 1991; Time of My Life, 1993; Wildest Dreams, 1993; Callisto 5, This is Where We Came In, My Very Own Story, 1995; Communicating Doors, 1995; A Word from our Sponsor, 1998; Things We Do For Love, 1998; Alan Ayckbourn: Plays 2, 1998; The Forest, 1999; Comic Potential, 1999; House & Garden, 2000. *Recreations:* music, reading, cricket, films. *Address:* c/o Casarotto Ramsay & Associates Ltd, National House, 60–66 Wardour Street, W1V 4ND. *T:* (020) 7287 4450. *Club:* Garrick.

AYERS, John Gilbert; Keeper, Far Eastern Department, Victoria and Albert Museum, 1970–82; *b* 27 July 1922; *s* of H. W. Ayers, CB, CBE; *m* 1957, Bridget Elspeth Jacqualine Fanshawe; one *s* two *d. Educ:* St Paul's Sch.; St Edmund Hall, Oxford. Served in RAF, 1941–46 (Sgt). Asst Keeper, Dept of Ceramics, Victoria and Albert Museum, 1950, Dep. Keeper 1963. Pres., Oriental Ceramic Soc., 1984–87. *Publications:* The Seligman Collection of Oriental Art, II, 1964; The Baur Collection: Chinese Ceramics, I-IV, 1968–74, Japanese Ceramics, 1982; (with R. J. Charleston) The James A. de Rothschild Collection: Meissen and Oriental Porcelain, 1971; Oriental Ceramics, The World's Great Collections: Victoria and Albert Museum, 1975; (with J. Rawson) Chinese Jade throughout the Ages, exhbn catalogue, 1975; (with D. Howard) China for the West, 2 vols, 1978; (with D. Howard) Masterpieces of Chinese Export Porcelain, 1980; Oriental Art in the Victoria and Albert Museum, 1983; (ed) Chinese Ceramics in the Topkapi Saray Museum, Istanbul, 3 vols, 1986; (with O. Impey and J. V. G. Mallet) Porcelain for Palaces: the fashion for Japan in Europe 1650–1750, 1990; Chinese Ceramic Tea Vessels: the K. S. Lo Collection, Hong Kong, 1991; A Jade Menagerie: creatures real and imaginary from the Worrell Collection, 1993; Chinese Ceramics in the Baur Collection, Geneva, 2 vols, 1999. *Address:* 3 Bedford Gardens, W8 7ED. *T:* (020) 7229 5168.

AYERS, Prof. Michael Richard, PhD; FBA 2001; Professor of Philosophy, University of Oxford, since 1996; Fellow of Wadham College, Oxford, since 1965; *b* 27 June 1935; *s* of Dick Ayers and Sybil Kerr Ayers (*née* Rutherglen); *m* 1962, Delia Mary Bell; one *s* one *d. Educ:* Battersea Grammar Sch.; St John's Coll., Cambridge (BA 1959; MA, PhD 1965). Jun. Res. Fellow, St John's Coll., Cambridge, 1962–65; Tutor in Philosophy, Wadham Coll., Oxford, 1965; C. V. F. Lectr in Philosophy, 1965–94, Reader in Philosophy, 1994–. Univ. of Oxford. Vis. Lectr, 1964–65, Vis. Prof., 1979, Univ. of Calif, Berkeley; Vis. Prof., Univ. of Oregon, 1970–71; Vis. Fellow, Res. Sch. of Social Scis, ANU, 1993; Ida Beam Dist. Vis. Prof., Univ. of Iowa, 1995. *Publications:* The Refutation of Determinism, 1968; (with J. Ree and A. Westoby) Philosophy and its Past, 1978; Locke: vol. 1, Epistemology, vol. 2, Ontology, 1991; Locke: ideas and things, 1997; (ed with D. Garber) The Cambridge History of Seventeenth Century Philosophy, 2 vols, 1998; contrib. to jls, collections and works of reference. *Recreations:* walking, gardening, natural history, looking after a small piece of country. *Address:* Wadham College, Oxford OX1 3PN.

AYERST, Rev. Edward Richard; Chaplain to the Queen, 1987–95; *b* 21 Oct. 1925; *m* 1959, Pauline Clarke; one *s* two *d. Educ:* Coopers' Company's School; Leeds Univ. (BA Hons 1951); College of the Resurrection, Mirfield. Vicar of St Mary with St John, Edmonton, N18, 1960–66; Rector of East Cowes with Whippingham, IoW, 1966–77; Vicar of Bridgwater, 1977–90. Mem., Philosophical Soc., 1981. *Recreations:* sailing; helping the Sea Cadet Corps. *Address:* 56 Maple Drive, Burnham-on-Sea, Somerset TA8 1DH. *T:* (01278) 780701.

AYKROYD, Sir James (Alexander Frederic), 3rd Bt *cr* 1929, of Birstwith Hall, Hampsthwaite, co. York; Chairman, Speyside Distillery Co. Ltd, since 2001; *b* 6 Sept. 1943; *s* of Bertram Aykroyd (*d* 1983), *y s* of Sir Frederic Alfred Aykroyd, 1st Bt, and his 1st wife, Margot Aykroyd (*née* Graham Brown) (*see* Dame Margôt Smith); *S* uncle, 1993; *m* 1973, Jennifer Marshall; two *d. Educ:* Eton Coll.; Univ. of Aix en Provence; Univ. of Madrid. Sen. Export Dir, James Buchanan & Co. Ltd, 1965–83; Export Man. Dir, Martini & Rossi SpA, 1983–87; Chm., Alexander Muir & Son Ltd, 1993–2001. *Recreations:* active sports esp. tennis and golf. *Heir: half b* Toby Nigel Bertram Aykroyd, *b* 13 Nov. 1955. *Address:* Birstwith Hall, near Harrogate, Yorks HG3 2JW. *T:* (01423) 770250. *Club:* Alwoodley Golf.

AYKROYD, Sir William Miles, 3rd Bt *cr* 1920; MC 1944; *b* 24 Aug. 1923; *s* of Sir Alfred Hammond Aykroyd, 2nd Bt, and Sylvia Ambler Aykroyd (*née* Walker) (*d* 1992), *widow* of Lieut-Col Foster Newton Thorne; *S* father, 1965. *Educ:* Charterhouse. Served in 5th Royal Inniskilling Dragoon Guards, Lieut, 1943–47. Dir, Hardy Amies Ltd, 1950–69. *Heir: cousin* Michael David Aykroyd [*b* 14 June 1928; *m* 1952, Oenone Gillian Diana, *o d* of Donald George Cowling, MBE; one *s* three *d*]. *Address:* Buckland Newton Place, Dorchester, Dorset DT2 7BX. *T:* (01300) 345259. *Club:* Boodle's.

AYLARD, Richard John, CVO 1994; consultant on environmental issues and public affairs, since 1996; Extra Equerry to the Prince of Wales, since 1996; *b* 10 April 1952; *s* of John and Joy Aylard; *m* 1st, 1977, Sally Williams (marr. diss. 1984); 2nd, 1984, Suzanne Walker (marr. diss. 1998); two *d*; 3rd, 1998, Jennifer Jones; one *s* one *d*. *Educ:* Queen Elizabeth's Grammar Sch., Barnet; Reading Univ. (BSc Hons Applied Zoology with Maths). Joined RN as university cadet, 1972; served HM Ships Shavington, Ark Royal, Fox, 1974–77; Staff of Flag Officer Submarines, 1977–79; Flag Lieut to Dep. SACLANT, Norfolk, USA, 1979–81; Capt's Sec., HMS Invincible, 1981–83; Supply Officer, HMS Brazen, 1984–85; Equerry to the Princess of Wales, 1985–88; Comdr RN, 1987; Asst Private Sec. and Comptroller to the Prince and Princess of Wales, 1988–91; RN retd, 1989; Private Sec. and Treas. to the Prince of Wales, 1991–96. *Recreations:* sailing, fishing, gardening, ski-ing.

AYLEN, Rear-Adm. Ian Gerald, CB 1962; OBE 1946; DSC 1942; CEng, FIMechE; *b* 12 Oct. 1910; *s* of late Commander A. E. Aylen, RN and Mrs S. C. M. Aylen; *m* 1937, Alice Brough Maltby; one *s* two *d*. *Educ:* Blundell's, Tiverton. RNE Coll., Keyham, 1929–33; served in HMS Rodney; Curacoa; Galatea, 1939–40; Kelvin, 1940–42; 30 Assault Unit, 1945; Cossack; Fleet Engineer Officer, Home Fleet, 1957–58; CO HMS Thunderer, RNE Coll., 1958–60; Rear-Admiral, 1960; Admiral Superintendent, HM Dockyard, Rosyth, 1960–63; Dep. Sec., Instn Mechanical Engineers, 1963–65; Asst Sec., Council of Engineering Instns, 1966–71, retired 1971.

AYLEN, Walter Stafford; QC 1983; a Recorder, since 1985; *b* St Helena, 21 May 1937; *s* of late Rt Rev. Charles Arthur William Aylen and Elisabeth Margaret Anna (*née* Hills); *m* 1967, Peggy Elizabeth Lainé Woodford; three *d*. *Educ:* Summer Fields Sch.; Winchester Coll. (schol.); New Coll., Oxford (schol., sen. schol.; BCL; MA). Commnd 2nd Lieut KRRC, 1956–57. Called to the Bar, Middle Temple, 1962 (Bencher 1991); Asst Recorder, 1982; former Head of Chambers, Hardwicke Bldg; Mem., Internat. Panel, Alternative Dispute Resolution Gp, 2001. Mem., Bar Council, 1994–96 (Chm., Bar Services and IT Cttee, 1994; Vice-Chm., Finance Cttee, 1995–96). MCIArb 1999. FRSA 1989. *Recreations:* reading novels (especially his wife's), theatre, music. *Address:* 24 Fairmount Road, SW2 2BL. *T:* (020) 8671 7301; Hardwicke Building, New Square, Lincoln's Inn, WC2A 3SB. *T:* (020) 7242 2523.

AYLESFORD, 11th Earl of, *cr* 1714; **Charles Ian Finch-Knightley;** JP; Baron Guernsey, 1703; Lord-Lieutenant of West Midlands, 1974–93; *b* 2 Nov. 1918; *er s* of 10th Earl of Aylesford; *S* father, 1958; *m* 1946, Margaret Rosemary Tyer (*d* 1989); one *s* two *d*. *Educ:* Oundle. Lieut RSF, 1939; Captain Black Watch, 1947. Regional Dir, Birmingham and W Midlands Bd, Lloyds Bank, 1982–88. Mem., Water Space Amenity Commn, 1973–83. County Comr for Scouts, 1949–74, Patron 1974–. JP 1948, DL 1954, Vice-Lieutenant 1964–74, Warwicks. KStJ 1974. Hon. LLD Birmingham, 1989. *Recreations:* wild life and nature conservation. *Heir: s* Lord Guernsey, *qv*. *Address:* Packington Old Hall, Coventry, West Midlands CV7 7HG. *T:* (01676) 523273; (office) (01676) 523467. *Club:* Warwickshire CC (President, 1980–99).

AYLING, Peter William, OBE 1989; BSc, CEng, FRINA; Secretary, Royal Institution of Naval Architects, 1967–89; *b* 25 Sept. 1925; *s* of late William Frank and Edith Louise Ayling; *m* 1949, Sheila Bargery; two *s* two *d*. *Educ:* Royal Dockyard Sch., Portsmouth; King's Coll., Univ. of Durham (BSc). Shipwright apprentice, HM Dockyard, Portsmouth, 1942–47; King's Coll., Univ. of Durham, 1947–50; Research and Principal Research Officer, British Ship Research Assoc., London, 1950–65; Principal Scientific Officer, Ship Div., Nat. Physical Laboratory, Feltham (now British Maritime Technology Ltd), 1965–67. *Publications:* papers on ship strength and vibration, Trans RINA, NECInst and IESS. *Recreations:* music, gardening, walking, motoring. *Address:* Oakmead, School Road, Camelsdale, Haslemere, Surrey GU27 3RN. *T:* (01428) 644474.

AYLING, Robert John; Chief Executive, British Airways, 1996–2000; *b* 3 Aug. 1946; *m* 1972, Julia Crallan; two *s* one *d*. *Educ:* King's Coll. Sch., Wimbledon. Admitted solicitor, 1968; joined Elborne, Mitchell & Co., Solicitors, 1969, Partner, 1971; Department of Trade, later of Trade and Industry: Legal Advr, 1974 (work on UK accession to EEC, 1974–77); Asst Solicitor and Head, Aviation Law Br., 1979 (legislation to privatise British Airways Bd); UK deleg., UN Commn for Internat. Trade Law, 1979–83; Under Sec. (Legal), 1983; British Airways: Legal Dir, 1985; Company Sec., 1987; Human Resources Dir, 1988; Marketing and Ops Dir, 1991; Gp Man. Dir, 1993. Chm., New Millennium Experience Co., 1997–2000. Gov., King's Coll. Sch., 1996–. Hon. LLD Brunel, 1996. *Club:* Brooks's.

AYLMER, family name of **Baron Aylmer**.

AYLMER, 13th Baron *cr* 1718; **Michael Anthony Aylmer;** Bt 1662; *b* 27 March 1923; *s* of Christopher Aylmer (*d* 1955) and Marjorie (*d* 1981), *d* of Percival Ellison Barber, surgeon, Sheffield; *S* cousin, 1982; *m* 1950, Countess Maddalena Sofia, *d* of late Count Arbeno Attems, Aiello del Friuli, Italy; one *s* one *d*. *Educ:* privately and Trinity Hall, Cambridge (Exhibnr, MA, LLM). Admitted a solicitor, 1948. Employed in Legal Dept of Equity & Law Life Assurance Society plc, 1951 until retirement, 1983. *Recreations:* reading, music. *Heir: s* Hon. (Anthony) Julian Aylmer [*b* 10 Dec. 1951; *m* 1990, Belinda Rosemary, *d* of Maj. Peter Parker; one *s* one *d*]. *Address:* Dovecot House, Jesse's Lane, Long Crendon, Bucks HP18 9AG. *T:* (01844) 208464.

AYLMER, Sir Richard John, 16th Bt *cr* 1622, of Donadea, Co. Kildare; writer; *b* 23 April 1937; *s* of Sir Fenton Gerald Aylmer, 15th Bt and Rosalind Boultbee (*d* 1991), *d* of J. Percival Bell; *S* father, 1987; *m* 1962, Lise, *d* of Paul Demers; one *s* one *d*. *Educ:* Lower Canada Coll., Montreal; Western Ontario, London, Canada; Harvard Univ., Cambridge, Mass, USA. *Heir: s* Fenton Paul Aylmer, *b* 31 Oct. 1965.

AYLWARD, Adrian John Francis; Headmaster, Stonyhurst College, since 1996; *b* 12 Nov. 1957; *s* of John James and Cynthia Aylward; *m* 1990, Caroline Lesley; one *s* two *d*. *Educ:* Worth Sch., Sussex; Exeter Coll., Oxford (BA); King's Coll. London (PGCE). Formerly investment banker; Royal Sovereign Group (Chief Exec., 1986–91); Dir, EMESS plc, 1990–91; Housemaster and Head of Religious Studies, Downside Sch., 1992–96. Mem., Irish Assoc. Knight of Malta. *Recreations:* fishing, philosophy, sport, travel. *Address:* Stonyhurst College, near Clitheroe, Lancs BB7 9PZ. *T:* (01254) 826345, *Fax:* (01254) 826732; Lower Jud Falls, Stonyhurst, near Clitheroe, Lancs, *T:* (01254) 826711. *Club:* Brooks's.

AYLWARD, Dr Mansel; Chief Medical Officer, Department for Work and Pensions (formerly Department of Social Security), since 1995; Chief Medical Adviser, War Pensions Agency, Ministry of Defence, since 2001; *b* 29 Nov. 1942; *s* of John Aylward and Cora Doreen Aylward (*née* Evans); *m* 1963, Angela Bridget Besley; one *s* one *d*. *Educ:* Cyfarthfa Castle Grammar Sch., Merthyr Tydfil; London Hosp. Med. Coll., Univ. of London (BSc 1964; MB BS Hons 1967); FFPM 1991. MRC Clin. Res. Fellow in Exptl Surgery, London Hosp., 1968–70; Lectr in Surgery, London Hosp. Med. Coll., 1969; GP, Merthyr Tydfil, 1970–73; Clin. Assistant in Dermatol. and Minor Surgery, St Tydfil's Hosp., 1970–76; Res. Physician, Singleton Hosp., Swansea and Merthyr and Cynon Valleys, 1973–76; Chm. and Man. Dir, Simbec Research Ltd, 1974–84; Dir of Clin. Res., Berk Pharmaceuticals, 1974–76; Dir, Women's Health Concern, London, 1976–86; Pres., Simbec Research (USA) Inc., 1980–84; Dir of Clin. Res., Lyonaisse Industrielle Pharmaceutique, France, 1982–84; Regl MO, DHSS, Cardiff, 1985–88; SMO, DSS, London, 1988–90; Sec. to Attendance Allowance Bd, London, 1991; PMO and Dir of Med. Policy, R&D, Benefits Agency, London, 1991–95. Expert Agrée Medicine Interne, France, 1982. FRSocMed 1981 (Academic Dean (Wales), 2001–). *Publications:* Management of the Menopause and Post-Menopausal Years, 1975; The Disability Handbook, 1991, 2nd edn 1998; contribs on disability assessment, rehabilitation, and social security issues to learned jls. *Recreations:* military history, travel, theatre, video-making, grandchildren. *Address:* Office of the Chief Medical Adviser, Department for Work and Pensions, The Adelphi, John Adam Street, WC2N 6HT. *T:* (020) 7962 8702; (home) Cefn Cottage, Cefn Coed, Merthyr Tydfil CF48 2PH. *Club:* Blizard.

AYNSLEY-GREEN, Prof. Albert, DPhil; FRCP, FRCPE, FRCPCH, FMedSci; NHS National Director of Children's Healthcare Services, and Chair, NHS National Children's Taskforce, Department of Health, since 2001; Nuffield Professor of Child Health, since 1993, and Vice Dean for Clinical Research, since 1999, Institute of Child Health, University of London, at University College London; Director, Clinical Research and Development, Great Ormond Street Hospital for Children, since 1993; Hon. Consultant Paediatrician, Great Ormond Street Hospital and University College Hospital, since 1993; *b* 30 May 1943; *m* 1967, Rosemary Anne Boucher; two *d*. *Educ:* Glyn Grammar Sch., Epsom; Guy's Hosp. Med. Sch., Univ. of London (MB BS); Oriel Coll., Oxford (MA, DPhil). MRCS 1967; FRCP 1982; FRCPE 1987; FRCPCH 1997. House Officer posts at Guy's Hosp., London, St Luke's Hosp., Guildford, Radcliffe Infirmary, Oxford and RPMS, Hammersmith Hosp., London, 1967–70; Radcliffe Infirmary, Oxford: Wellcome Res. Fellow, 1970–72; Clinical Lectr in Internal Medicine, 1972–73; Sen. House Officer and Registrar posts in Paediatrics, Radcliffe Infirmary and John Radcliffe Hosp., Oxford, 1973–74; European Sci. Exchange Fellow, Royal Soc. and Swiss Nat. Res. Council, Univ. Children's Hosp., Zurich, 1974–75; University of Oxford: Clinical Lectr in Paediatrics, 1975–78; Univ. Lectr, 1978–83; Fellow, Green Coll., 1980–83; Hon. Consultant Paediatrician, Oxford AHA, 1978–83; University of Newcastle upon Tyne: James Spence Prof. of Child Health and Hd of Dept, 1984–93; Hd, Sch. of Clinical Med. Scis, 1991–93; Hon. Consultant Paediatrician, Royal Victoria Infirmary, Newcastle upon Tyne, 1984–93. Non-exec. Mem., Bd of Govs, Hosp. for Sick Children, Gt Ormond St, 1990–93; Exec. Mem., Trust Bd, Gt Ormond St Hosp. for Children NHS Trust, 1993–. Chm., Adv. Gp on NHS Priorities for R&D in Mother and Child Health, DoH, 1994–95; Mem., Central R&D Cttee, DoH, 1999–. Visiting Professor: Univ. of Ulm, FRG, 1986; Harvard Univ., 1987; Columbus Children's Hosp., Ohio State Univ., 1991; Vis. Paediatrician in Residence, Royal Children's Hosp., Univ. of Qld, 1989; Vis. Lectr, Children's Hosp., Camperdown, Sydney, 1992. Numerous lectures in Europe, USA and Australia including: Lockyer, RCP, 1988; Assoc. of Paediatric Anaesthetists of GB and Ire. (and Medal), 1990; Niilo Hallman, Univs of Helsinki and Tampere, Finland (and Medal), 1991. External Examiner in Paediatrics: Univ. of Malaya, 1990; Chinese Univ. of Hong Kong, 1994–98; Univ. of Kuwait, 1996. European Society for Paediatric Endocrinology: Sec., 1982–87; Pres., 1994–95; Pres., Assoc. of Clin. Profs of Paediatrics, 1999–. Founder FMedSci, 1998. Hon. Member: Hungarian Paediatric Assoc., 1988; S African Paediatric Assoc., 1998. Dr *hc* Pécs, 1998. Andrea Prader Prize and Medal, 1991, (jtly) Henning Andersen Prize, 1999, European Soc. for Paediatric Endocrinology. *Publications:* papers and articles on child health in general, and specifically on endocrinology and metabolism in infancy and childhood. *Recreations:* family, walking, music, photography. *Address:* Institute of Child Health, 30 Guilford Street, WC1N 1EH. *T:* (020) 7242 9789. *Club:* Royal Society of Medicine.

AYONG, Most Rev. James; *see* Papua New Guinea, Archbishop of.

AYOUB, Fouad; Ambassador of the Hashemite Kingdom of Jordan to Switzerland, since 1999; *b* 15 Aug. 1944; *m* 1974, Marie Vernazza; two *s* one *d*. *Educ:* California State Univ., San Francisco (BA; MA philosophy 1974). Press Secretary to King Hussein, 1977–91; Mem., Jordanian Delegn to Madrid Peace Conf., 1991; Ambassador of Jordan to UK, 1991–99, and (non-resident) to Iceland and Ireland, 1992–99. Fellow, Centre for Internat. Affairs, Harvard, 1983–84. Order of El Istiqlal (Jordan), 1991; numerous foreign orders. *Recreation:* reading. *Address:* Embassy of the Hashemite Kingdom of Jordan, Belpstrasse 11, 3007 Berne, Switzerland.

AYRES, Gillian, OBE 1986; RA; painter, artist; *b* 3 Feb. 1930; *d* of Stephen and Florence Ayres; *m* Henry Mundy (marr. diss.); two *s*. *Educ:* St Paul's Girls' Sch.; Camberwell Sch. of Art. Student, 1946–50; taught, 1959–81 (incl. Sen. Lectr, St Martin's Sch. of Art, and Head of Painting, Winchester Sch. of Art, 1978–81). ARA 1982, RA 1991–97 (resigned), rejoined 2000. One-woman Exhibitions include: Gallery One, 1956; Redfern Gall., 1958; Moulton Gall., 1960 and 1962; Kasmin Gall., 1965, 1966 and 1969; William Darby Gall., 1976; Women's Internat. Centre, New York, 1976; Knoedler Gall., 1979, 1982, 1987; Mus. of Mod. Art, Oxford, 1981; retrospective exhibitions: Serpentine Gall., 1983; RA Sackler Gall., Yale British Art Center, and Iowa Mus., 1997; also exhibited: Redfern Gall., 1957; 1st Paris Biennale, 1959; Hayward Gall., 1971; Silver Jubilee Exhibn, RA, 1977; Knoedler Gall., NY, 1985; Tate Gall., 1995. Works in public collections: Tate Gall.; Mus. of Mod. Art, NY; Olinda Mus., Brazil; Gulbenkian Foundn, Lisbon; V&A Mus.; British Council. Hon. DLit London, 1994. Prize winner: Tokyo Biennale, 1963; John Moores Prize, 1982; Indian Trienale, Gold Medal, 1991. *Address:* c/o Gimpel Fils Ltd, 30 Davies Street, W1Y 1LG.

AYRES, Pamela, (Mrs D. Russell); writer, broadcaster and entertainer; *b* 14 March 1947; *d* of Stanley William Ayres and Phyllis Evelyn Loder; *m* 1982, Dudley Russell; two *s*. *Educ:* Stanford-in-the-Vale Village Primary Sch., Berks, Faringdon Secondary Modern Sch., Berks. Served WRAF, 1965–69. Writer and performer: *television:* début on Opportunity Knocks, 1975; The World of Pam Ayres (series), 1977; TV specials in UK, Hong Kong and Canada, 1978–79; *radio:* Pam Ayres Radio Show (series), 1995; presenter: Pam Ayres on Sunday, 1996–99; Pam Ayres' Open Road, 2000–01; appeared in Royal Variety Show, Palladium, 1977; concert tours: annually to Australia, 1978–97; NZ, Canada, Ireland. *Publications:* Some of Me Poetry, 1976; Some More of Me Poetry, 1976; Thoughts of a Late-Night Knitter, 1978; All Pam's Poems, 1978; The Ballad of Bill Spinks' Bedstead and Other Poems, 1981; Dear Mum, 1985; Pam Ayres: The Works, 1992; With These Hands, 1997; *for children:* Bertha and the Racing Pigeon, 1979; Guess Who?, 1987;

Guess What?, 1987; When Dad Fills In The Garden Pond, 1988; When Dad Cuts Down The Chestnut Tree, 1988; Piggo and the Nosebag, 1990; Piggo has a Train Ride, 1990; Piggo and the Fork-lift Truck, 1991; The Bear Who Was Left Behind, 1991; Jack Crater, 1992; Guess Why?, 1994; Guess Where?, 1994; The Nubbler, 1997 (trans. Japanese, 1999). *Recreations:* gardening, bee-keeping, drawing, wildlife. *Address:* PO Box 64, Cirencester, Glos GL7 5YD. *T:* (01285) 644622. *Club:* Groucho.

AYRIS, Dr Paul; Director of Library Services, University College London, since 1997; *b* 27 April 1957; *s* of Walter Roy Ayris and Irene Ayris (*née* Ball). *Educ:* Selwyn Coll., Cambridge (BA, MA); Gonville and Caius Coll., Cambridge (PhD 1984); Univ. of Sheffield (MA). Sir Henry Stephenson Fellow, Univ. of Sheffield, 1982–84; Cambridge University Library: Asst Librarian, Scientific Periodicals Liby, 1985–89; Automation Div., 1989–96; Hd, IT Services, 1994–96; Dep. Librarian, UCL, Jan.–Sept. 1997. Exec. Ed., Reformation & Renaissance Rev., 1999–. *Publication:* (ed with D. Selwyn) Thomas Cranmer, Churchman and Scholar, 1993, 2nd edn 1999. *Recreations:* ecclesiastical architecture, visiting foreign cities, classical music, sailing. *Address:* Library Services, University College London, Gower Street, WC1E 6BT. *T:* (020) 7679 7834.

AYRTON, Norman Walter; international theatre and opera director; Dean, British American Drama Academy, London, 1986–96; *b* London, 25 Sept. 1924. Served War of 1939–45, RNVR. Trained as an actor at Old Vic Theatre School under Michael Saint Denis, 1947–48; joined Old Vic Company, 1948; repertory experience at Farnham and Oxford, 1949–50; on staff of Old Vic Sch., 1949–52; rejoined Old Vic Company for 1951 Festival Season; opened own teaching studio, 1952; began dramatic coaching for Royal Opera House, Covent Garden, 1953; apptd Asst Principal of London Academy of Music and Dramatic Art, 1954; taught at Shakespeare Festival, Stratford, Ont, and Royal Shakespeare Theatre, Stratford-upon-Avon, 1959–62; apptd GHQ Drama Adviser to Girl Guide Movement, 1960–74; Principal, LAMDA, 1966–72; Dean, World Shakespeare Study Centre, Bankside, 1972; Nat. Inst. of Dramatic Art, Sydney, 1973–74; Faculty, Juilliard Sch., NY, 1974–85; Dir of Opera, Royal Acad. of Music, 1986–90. *Director:* Artaxerxes, for Handel Opera Soc., Camden Festival, 1963; La Traviata, Covent Garden, 1963; Manon, Covent Garden, 1964; Sutherland-Williamson Grand Opera Season, in Australia, 1965; Twelfth Night at Dallas Theatre Center, Texas, 1967; The Way of the World, NY, 1976; Lakmé, Sydney Opera House, 1976; Der Rosenkavalier, Sydney Opera House, 1983; *Guest Director:* Australian Council for Arts, Sydney and Brisbane, 1973; Loeb Drama Center, Harvard (and teacher), 1974, 1976, 1978; Melbourne Theatre Co., 1974–; Vancouver Opera Assoc., 1975–83; Sydney Opera House, 1976–81, 1983; Williamstown Festival, USA, 1977; Hartford Stage Co. and Amer. Stage Fest., 1978–; Missouri Rep. Theatre, 1980–81; Nat. Opera Studio, London, 1980–81; Spoleto Fest., USA, 1984; Sarah Lawrence Coll., NY, 1993, 1997, 2001; Utah Shakespeare Fest., 1994; Resident Stage Director: Amer. Opera Center, NY, 1981–85; Vassar Coll., NY, 1990–2001; Cornell Univ., 1995, 1998; Florida State Univ., 1997–. Hon. RAM 1989. *Recreations:* reading, music, gardens, travel. *Address:* 40A Birchington Road, NW6 4LJ.

AZA, Alberto; Spanish Ambassador to the Court of St James's, 1992–99; *b* 22 May 1937; *s* of Alberto Aza and Marcela Arias; *m* 1963, María Eulalia Custodio Martí; two *s* four *d*. *Educ:* Univ. de Oviedo; Law Faculty of Madrid (Law Degree); BA, BSc. Joined Diplomatic Service, 1965; served Libreville, Algiers, Rome, Madrid; Dir, Cabinet of the Spanish Prime Minister, 1977–83; Chief Dir, OAS, Latin-America Dept, Min. of Foreign Affairs, 1983; Minister Counsellor, Lisbon, 1983–85; Ambassador: to OAS, Washington, 1985–89; to Belize (resident in Washington), 1985–89; to Mexico, 1990–92. Hon. DLitt Portsmouth, 1997. Gran Cruz del Mérito Civil (Spain), 1979; Gran Cruz del Mérito Naval (Spain), 1996. *Recreations:* fishing, golf, walking. *Address:* c/o Ministerio de Asuntos Exteriores, Plaza de la Provincia 1, 28012 Madrid, Spain. *Clubs:* Athenæum, White's, Travellers.

AZIZ, Suhail Ibne; international management consultant, since 1981; Chairman and Managing Director, Brettonwood Partnership Ltd, since 1990; Chairman, London Probation Board, National Probation Service, since 2001; *b* Bangladesh (then India), 3 Oct. 1937; permanently resident in England, since 1966; *s* of Azizur Rahman and Lutfunnessa Khatoon; *m* 1960, Elizabeth Ann Pyne, Dartmouth, Devon; two *d*. *Educ:* Govt High Sec. Sch., Sylhet; Murarichand Coll., Dacca Univ., Sylhet (Intermed. in Science, 1954); Jt Services Pre-Cadet Trng Sch., Quetta; Cadet Trng Sch., PNS Himalaya, Karachi; BRNC, Dartmouth (Actg Sub-Lieut 1958); (mature student) Kingston upon Thames Polytechnic and Trent Polytech., Nottingham (Dipl. in Man. Studies, 1970); (ext. student) London Univ. (BScEcon Hons 1972); (internal student) Birkbeck Coll., London Univ., (MScEcon 1976); Michigan Business Sch., USA (mgt courses, 1992). FIMgt 1981; FIMC 1991; CMC 1994. Sub-Lieut and Lieut, Pakistan Navy Destroyers/Mine Sweeper (Exec. Br.), 1954–61. Personnel and indust. relations: Unilever (Pakistan); Royal Air Force; Commn on Indust. Relations, London; Ford Motor Co. (GB); Mars Ltd, 1963–78; Dir of Gen. Services Div., CRE, 1978–81; Dep. Dir of Econ. Develt, London Borough of Lewisham, 1984–88; Management Consultant, Fullemploy Consultancy Ltd, 1989–90; Mem. Exec. Sub-Cttee, and Bd Mem., Tower Hamlets, Education Business Partnership, 1993–. Mem., London Electricity Consumer Cttee, 1991–95. Chairman: Lambeth Healthcare NHS Trust, 1998–99; S London Community Health NHS Trust, 1999–2000. Leading Mem., Bangladesh Movement in UK, 1971. Member: Exec., Standing Conf. of Asian Orgs in UK, 1972–90; N Metropol. Conciliation Cttee, Race Relations Bd, 1971–74; Exec., Post Conf. Constituent Cttee, Black People in Britain—the Way Forward, 1975–76; Adv. Cttee to Gulbenkian Foundn on Area Resource Centre and Community Support Forum, 1976–81; Exec., Nottingham and Dist Community Relations Council, 1975–78; Dept of Employment Race Relations Employment Adv. Gp, 1977–78; BBC Asian programme Adv. Cttee, 1977–81; Industrial Tribunals, 1977–95; Exec., Nat. Org. of African, Asian and Caribbean Peoples, 1976–77; Home Sec.'s Standing Adv. Council on Race Relations, 1976–78; Steering Cttee, Asian Support Forum, 1984–86; Steering Cttee, Develt Policy Forum, DFID, 1998–2000; Jt Consultative Cttee with Ethnic Minorities, Merton BC, 1985–; Plunkett Foundn for Co-operative Studies, 1985–; "One World", 1986–90; Adv. Gp, City of London Polytechnic Ethnic Minority Business Develt Unit, 1987–94; Res. Adv. Bd, QMW, London Univ., 1988–; (co-opted), Exec. Cttee, Tower Hamlets Assoc. for Racial Equality, 1988–91 (Mem., Action Tower Hamlets, 1987); Bangladeshis in Britain—a Response Forum, 1987–89; Tower Hamlets Consortium, 1994–; Exec. Mem. and Treas., Docklands Forum, 1991–; Chairman: Jalalabad Overseas Orgn in UK, 1983–; London Boroughs Bangladesh Assoc., 1984–; Founder Chm., East London Bangladeshi Enterprise Agency, 1985–. CRE Bursary to study Minority Business Develt initiatives in USA, 1986. Mem., Labour Econ. Finance Taxation Assoc., 1973–80; Institute of Management Consultants: Chm., Third World Specialist Gp, 1984–92; Treasurer, London Reg., 1985–87; Mem. Council, 1995–. Jt Trustee, United Action-Bangladesh Relief Fund, 1971–90; Trustee: Trust for Educn and Develt, 1992–; Global Partnership, 1992–; Community Develt Foundn, 1999–; Brixton Neighbourhood Assoc., 1979–82; Advr, SE London Community Foundn, 1996–. Comr, Commonwealth Scholarship Commn, 1996–. Governor: London Guildhall Univ., 1995–; Lambeth Coll., 1999–. Deeply interested in community and race relations and believes profoundly that future health of Brit. society depends on achieving good race relations. *Recreations:* travelling, seeing places of historical interest, meeting people, reading (*eg* political economy). *Address:* 126 St Julian's Farm Road, West Norwood, SE27 0RR. *Clubs:* Royal Air Force; Sudan (Khartoum).

AZNAR LÓPEZ, José María; Prime Minister of Spain, since 1996; *b* Madrid, 1953; *m* 1977, Ana Botella; two *s* one *d*. *Educ:* Univ. Complutense, Madrid (LLB). Tax Inspector, 1976. Mem., Cortes, 1982–; Chief Exec., Castile-León Reg.; Premier, Castilla y León Autonomous Reg., 1987. Joined Alianza Popular, later Partido Popular, 1978: Dep. Sec. Gen., 1982; Pres., 1990–; Vice-Pres., European Popular Party, 1993–. *Publications:* Libertad y solidaridad, 1991; La Segunda Transición, 1994; La España en que yo creo, 1995. *Recreations:* reading, sports, music. *Address:* Prime Minister's Office, Complejo La Moncloa, 28071 Madrid, Spain. *T:* (1) 3353535.

B

BABCOCK, Horace Welcome; astronomer; Director, Mount Wilson and Palomar Observatories, 1964–78; *b* 13 Sept. 1912; *s* of Harold D. Babcock and Mary G. (*née* Henderson); *m* 1st, 1940; one *s* one *d*; 2nd, 1958; one *s*. *Educ:* California Institute of Technology (BS); Univ. of California (PhD). Instructor, Yerkes and McDonald Observatories, 1939–41; Radiation Laboratory, Mass Inst. of Tech., 1941–42; Calif Inst. of Tech., 1942–45; Staff Mem., Mount Wilson Observatory, 1946–51; Astronomer, Mount Wilson and Palomar Observatories, 1951–80; Founding Dir, Las Campanas Observatory, Chile, of Carnegie Instn, Washington, 1968–78. Elected to: National Acad. of Sciences, 1954 (Councillor, 1973–76); American Acad. of Arts and Sciences, 1959; American Philosophical Soc., 1966; Corres. Mem., Société Royale des Sciences de Liège, 1968; Associate, Royal Astronomical Soc., 1969; Member: American Astronomical Soc.; Astronomical Soc. of the Pacific; Internat. Astronomical Union. Hon. DSc Univ. of Newcastle upon Tyne, 1965. US Navy Bureau of Ordnance Development Award, 1945; Eddington Gold Medal, RAS, 1958; Henry Draper Medal of the National Acad. of Sciences, 1957; Bruce Medal, Astronomical Soc. of the Pacific, 1969; Gold Medal, RAS, 1970; Hale Prize, Amer. Astronomical Soc., 1992; Rank Prize in Opto-electronics, 1993. *Publications:* scientific papers in Astrophysical Jl, Publications of the Astronomical Soc. of the Pacific, Jl of Optical Soc. of America, etc, primarily on magnetic fields of the stars and sun, astrophysics, diffraction gratings, adaptive optics, and astronomical instruments. *Address:* The Observatories, Carnegie Institution of Washington, 813 Santa Barbara Street, Pasadena, CA 91101–1292, USA. *T:* (818) 5771122.

BABINGTON, His Honour Anthony Patrick; a Circuit Judge, 1972–87; *b* 4 April 1920; 2nd *s* of late Oscar John Gilmore Babington, MAI, AMICE, Monkstown, Co. Cork. *Educ:* Reading Sch. Served with Royal Ulster Rifles and Dorset Regt, 1939–45 (wounded twice); Croix de Guerre with Gold Star (France), 1944. Called to the Bar, Middle Temple, 1948; Bencher, 1977, Autumn Reader, 1994; South Eastern Circuit; Prosecuting Counsel to Post Office, SE Circuit (South), 1959–64; Metropolitan Stipendiary Magistrate, 1964–72. Mem., Home Office Working Party on Bail, 1971–73. Mem., Nat. Exec. Cttee, Internat. PEN English Centre, 1979–82. Trustee: New Bridge, 1985–; PEN Literary Foundn, 1990–. Hon. Bencher, King's Inns, Dublin, 1995. *Publications:* No Memorial, 1954; The Power to Silence, 1968; A House in Bow Street, 1969; The English Bastille, 1971; The Only Liberty, 1975; For the Sake of Example, 1983; Military Intervention in Britain, 1990; The Devil to Pay, 1991; Shell-Shock, 1997; An Uncertain Voyage, 2000. *Recreations:* music, theatre, reading. *Address:* Thydon Cottage, Chilham, near Canterbury, Kent CT4 8BX. *T:* (01227) 730300. *Clubs:* Garrick, Special Forces.

BABINGTON, His Honour Robert John, DSC 1943; QC (NI) 1965. appointed County Court Judge for Fermanagh and Tyrone, 1978; *b* 9 April 1920; *s* of David Louis James Babington and Alice Marie (*née* McClintock); *m* 1952, Elizabeth Bryanna Marguerite Alton, *d* of Dr E. H. Alton, Provost of Trinity College, Dublin; two *s* one *d*. *Educ:* St Columba's Coll., Rathfarnham, Dublin; Trinity Coll., Dublin (BA). Called to the Bar, Inn of Court of NI, 1947. MP North Down, Stormont, 1968–72. *Recreations:* golf, bird-watching. *Address:* c/o Royal Courts of Justice, Chichester Street, Belfast BT1 3JF. *Clubs:* Special Forces; Tyrone County (Omagh); Fermanagh County (Enniskillen); Royal Belfast Golf.

BABINGTON, Roger Vincent, FREng; FRINA; Managing Director, BMT Defence Services Ltd (formerly Defence Services Ltd, British Maritime Technology), since 1999; *b* 6 April 1943; *s* of late George Cyril Babington and Rita Mary Babington (*née* Simpkins); *m* 1967, Susan Wendy Eaton; two *s* two *d*. *Educ:* King Edward's Sch., Bath; Univ. of Birmingham (BSc); University Coll. London (MSc). RCNC. MoD, 1967–76; Constructor, Principal Naval Overseer, Barrow-in-Furness, 1976–81; HM Dockyard, Rosyth: Constructor, 1981–82; Chief Constructor, 1982–86; Dir of Progs and Planning, 1986–87; Ministry of Defence, Bath: Dir, Surface Ships/D, 1987–89; Dir, SSN20, 1989–91; Dir, Submarines, 1991–93; Dir-Gen., Ship Refitting, 1993; Dir-Gen., Fleet Support (Ships), 1993–95; Dir-Gen. Ships, 1995–96; Chief Exec., Ships Support Agency, 1996–97; Man. Dir, Marine Procurement Ltd, British Maritime Technology, 1998–99. FREng (FEng 1995). *Recreations:* golf, house, garden and vehicle maintenance, watching sport, listening. *Address:* Shoscombe Lodge, Shoscombe, Bath BA2 8LU. *T:* (01761) 432436. *Club:* Bath and County (Bath).

BABINGTON-BROWNE, Gillian Brenda, (Mrs K. J. Wilson); a District Judge (Magistrates' Courts) (formerly Metropolitan Stipendiary Magistrate), since 1991; *b* 20 May 1949; *d* of Derek Keith Babington-Browne and Olive Maude (*née* Seymour); *m* 1983, Kenneth John Wilson. *Educ:* Rochester Girls' Grammar Sch.; Coll. of Law, London. Admitted Solicitor, 1973; Asst Solicitor with Arnold, Tuff & Grimwade, Rochester, 1973–74; Assistant with Ronald A. Prior, 1974, with Edward Lewis Possart, London, 1974–78; own practice, 1978–89; freelance advocate and consultant, 1989–91. Associate Mem., London Criminal Courts Solicitors' Assoc., 1991– (Pres., 1990–91). *Publications:* contribs to legal jls. *Recreations:* gardening, interior design/decorating, reading. *Address:* c/o Marylebone Magistrates' Court, 181 Marylebone Road, NW1 5QJ.

BACH, family name of **Baron Bach**.

BACH, Baron *cr* 1998 (Life Peer), of Lutterworth in the co. of Leicestershire; **William Stephen Goulden Bach;** barrister; Parliamentary Under-Secretary of State, Ministry of Defence, since 2001; *b* 25 Dec. 1946; *s* of late Stephen Craine Goulden Bach, CBE and Joan Bach; *m* 1984, Caroline Jones, *er d* of Eric and Cynthia Smeaton; one *d*, and one *s* one *d* from former marriage. *Educ:* Westminster Sch.; New Coll., Oxford (BA). Called to the Bar, Middle Temple, 1972; Midland and Oxford Circuit; Hd of Chambers. Member (Lab): Leicester City Council, 1976–87; Harborough DC, 1995–99; Mayor, Lutterworth, 1993–94. Labour Party: Treas., Leics W Const., 1974–87; Chm., Harborough Dist., 1989–95; Chm., Northants and Blaby Euro. Const., 1992–99. Member: Lab Party Econ. Commn, 1998–99; Lab Party Nat. Policy Forum, 1998–99. Govt spokesman, Home Office, DfEE, LCD, 1999–2000; a Lord in Waiting (Govt Whip), 1999–2000; Party Sec., LCD, 2000–01. Contested (Lab): Gainsborough, 1979; Sherwood, 1983 and 1987. Mem. Council, Leicester Univ., 1980–99. *Recreations:* playing and watching football and cricket, Leicester City FC supporter, music, reading hard-boiled American crime fiction. *Address:* House of Lords, SW1A 0PW; (chambers) 65–67 King Street, Leicester LE1 6RP.

See also J. N. Allan.

BACHE, Andrew Philip Foley, CMG 1992; JP; HM Diplomatic Service, retired; Ambassador to Denmark, 1996–99; *b* 29 Dec. 1939; *s* of late Robert Philip Sidney Bache, OBE and Jessie Bache; *m* 1963, Shân Headley; two *s* one *d*. *Educ:* Shrewsbury Sch.; Emmanuel Coll., Cambridge (MA). Joined HM Diplomatic Service, 1963; 3rd Sec., Nicosia, 1964–66; Treasury Centre for Admin. Studies, 1966; 2nd Sec., Sofia, 1966–68; FCO, 1968–71; 1st Sec., Lagos, 1971–74; FCO, 1974–78; 1st Sec. (Commercial), Vienna, 1978–81; Counsellor and Head of Chancery, Tokyo, 1981–85; Counsellor, Ankara, 1985–87; Hd of Personnel Services Dept, FCO, 1988–90; on secondment as Diplomatic Service Chm. to CSSB, 1990–91; Chief Exec., Westminster Foundn for Democracy, 1991–92; Ambassador, Romania, 1992–96. JP West London. Dr *hc*: Technical Univ., Cluj, 1994; Sibiu Univ., 1995. *Recreations:* diverse, including travel, history, ornithology, fine arts, squash, tennis, cricket, Real tennis. *Clubs:* Oxford and Cambridge, MCC.

BACHER, Dr Aron, (Ali); Managing Director, United Cricket Board of South Africa, 1991–2000; Director, 2003 Cricket World Cup, since 2000 (Executive, since 2001); *b* 24 May 1942; *s* of Rose and Koppel Bacher; *m* 1965, Shira Ruth Teeger; one *s* two *d*. *Educ:* Yeoville Boys' Primary Sch.; King Edward VII High Sch.; Witwatersrand Univ. (MB BCh). Junior appts, Baragwanath and Natalspruit Hosps, 1968–69; private practice, Rosebank, Johannesburg, 1970–79. Managing Director: Delta Distributors, 1979–81; Transvaal Cricket Council, 1981–86; South African Cricket Union, 1986–91; International Cricket Council: Mem. Exec. Bd, 1997–2000; Chm. Develt Cttee, 1996–2000. Cricket début for Transvaal, 1959–60; captained S Africa, 1970; played 12 Test matches, made 120 1st cl. appearances, 7,894 runs, 18 centuries, 110 catches, one stumping; retired, 1974; Transvaal and Nat. Selectors' Panels, 1976–83; Dir S African Cricket Develt Club, 1986. Numerous awards include Jack Cheetham Meml, 1990, for doing the most to normalise sport in S Africa. *Recreation:* jogging. *Address:* PO Box 55041, Northlands 2116, South Africa. *T:* (11) 7831263, (office) (11) 8802810.

BACK, Kenneth John Campbell, AO 1984; MSc, PhD; higher education consultant; *b* 13 Aug. 1925; *s* of J. L. Back; *m* 1950, Patricia, *d* of R. O. Cummings; two *d*. *Educ:* Sydney High Sch.; Sydney Univ. (MSc); Univ. of Queensland (PhD). Res. Bacteriologist, Davis Gelatine (Aust.) Pty Ltd, 1947–49; Queensland University: Lectr in Bacteriology, 1950–56; Sen. Lectr in Microbiology, 1957–61; Actg Prof. of Microbiology, 1962; Warden, University Coll. of Townsville, Queensland, 1963–70; Vice-Chancellor, James Cook Univ. of N Queensland, 1970–85, Prof. Emeritus, 1986–; Exec. Dir, Internat. Develt Program of Australian Univs and Colls Ltd, 1986–90. Vis. Fellow, ANU, 1996–2000. Chm., Standing Cttee, Australian Univs Internat. Develt Prog. (formerly Australian-Asian Univs Co-operation Scheme), 1977–85. Hon. DSc: Queensland, 1982; James Cook, 1995; DUniv: South Pacific, 1992; Nat. Univ. of Samoa, 1998. *Publications:* papers on microbiological metabolism, international education. *Recreations:* golf, bridge. *Address:* 11/41 Pethebridge Street, Pearce, ACT 2607, Australia. *T:* (2) 62865014. *Club:* Royal Canberra Golf (Canberra).

BACK, Patrick; QC 1970; a Recorder of the Crown Court, 1972–89; *b* 23 Aug. 1917; *s* of late Ivor Back, FRCS, and Barbara Back (*née* Nash); *m* 1971, Rosina Hare, QC. *Educ:* Marlborough; Trinity Hall, Cambridge. Captain, 14th Punjab Regt, 1941–46. Called to Bar, 1940; Bencher, Gray's Inn, 1978. Commenced practice, Western Circuit, 1948, Leader, 1984–89; Dep. Chm., Devon QS, 1968. *Recreation:* fly-fishing. *Address:* Paddock Edge, Broadwindsor, Dorset. *T:* (01308) 868644; 10 King's Bench Walk, EC4Y 7EB. *T:* (020) 7353 7742; Flat 71, 8 New Crane Place, Garnet Street, Wapping, E1 9TT. *T:* (020) 7488 4371.

BACKETT, Prof. (Edward) Maurice; Foundation Professor of Community Health, University of Nottingham, 1969–81, now Professor Emeritus; *b* 12 Jan. 1916; *o s* of late Frederick and Louisa Backett; *m* 1940, Shirley Paul-Thompson; one *s* two *d*. *Educ:* University Coll., London; Westminster Hospital. Operational Research with RAF; Nuffield Fellow in Social Medicine; Research Worker, Medical Research Council; Lecturer, Queen's Univ., Belfast; Senior Lecturer, Guy's Hospital and London Sch. of Hygiene and Tropical Medicine; Prof. and Head of Dept of Public Health and Social Medicine, Univ. of Aberdeen, 1958–69. Hon. Member: Internat. Epidemiol Assoc., 1984; Soc. for Social Medicine, 1986. *Publications:* The Risk Approach to Health Care, 1984; papers in scientific journals. *Recreations:* swimming, walking, sailing. *Address:* Harvey Cottage, Fore Street, Totnes, Devon TQ9 5NJ. *T:* (01803) 865241; *e-mail:* maurice.backett@btinternet.com.

BACKHOUSE, David Miles; Chairman, Leo Consult Ltd, since 1986; *b* 30 Jan. 1939; *s* of late Jonathan Backhouse and Alice Joan (*née* Woodroffe); *m* 1969, Sophia Ann (*née* Townsend); one *s* one *d*. *Educ:* Summerfields, Oxford; Eton Coll. Commenced career in banking with Schroders PLC, 1966; Chm., Henderson Admin Gp, 1990–92; Chm., Johnson Fry Hldgs, 1995–2000. Non-executive Director: TSB Group, 1985–92; Witan Investment Company, 1985–92; Royal Agricl Coll., 1987–; MktChoice, 2001–. *Recreations:* tennis, riding. *Address:* South Farm, Fairford, Glos GL7 3PN. *T:* (01285) 712225. *Clubs:* Turf; Vanderbilt.

BACKHOUSE, Sir Jonathan Roger, 4th Bt *cr* 1901; formerly Managing Director, W. H. Freeman & Co. Ltd, Publishers; *b* 30 Dec. 1939; *s* of Major Sir John Edmund Backhouse, 3rd Bt, MC, and Jean Marie Frances, *d* of Lieut-Col G. R. V. Hume-Gore, MC, The Gordon Highlanders; *S* father, 1944; *m* 1997, Sarah Ann, *o d* of James Stott, Cromer, Norfolk; one *d*. *Educ:* Oxford. *Heir: b* Oliver Richard Backhouse [*b* 18 July 1941; *m* 1970, Gillian Irene, *o d* of L; W. Lincoln, Northwood, Middx].

BACKHOUSE, Roger Bainbridge; QC 1984; *b* 8 March 1938; *s* of late Leslie Bainbridge Backhouse and of Jean Backhouse; *m* 1962, Elizabeth Constance, *d* of Comdr J. A. Lowe, DSO, DSC; two *s* one *d*. *Educ:* Liverpool Coll.; Trinity Hall, Cambridge (History Tripos parts I & II). Nat. Service, RAF, 1956–58 (Pilot Officer). Worked in family business, 1961–62; Schoolmaster, 1962–64; called to the Bar, Middle Temple, 1965. *Recreations:* shooting, golf, opera. *Address:* Preston House, Colebrook Street, Winchester, Hants SO23 9LH. *T:* (01962) 863053; (chambers) 1 Middle Temple Lane, EC4Y 9AA. *Clubs:* Royal Air Force; Hockley Golf.

BACKUS, Rear Adm. Alexander Kirkwood, OBE 1989; Flag Officer Surface Flotilla, since 2001; *b* 1 April 1948; *s* of late Jake Kirkwood Backus and of Jean Backus (*née* Stobie); *m* 1971, Margaret Joan Pocock; two s one d. *Educ:* Sevenoaks Sch., Kent; BRNC, Dartmouth. Joined RN, 1966; served HM Ships Fiskerton, Intrepid, Eastbourne, Cavalier, Bacchante, Blake, Arrow, Cleopatra, and Torquay, 1967-84; CO, Arethusa, 1984; JSDC Greenwich, 1986; Comdr Sea Training, 1988; Capt. 6th Frigate Sqn, HMS Hermione, 1990; Comdr British Forces Falkland Islands, 1995-96; ACOS (Policy) to C-in-C Fleet, 1996–99; Flag Officer Sea Trng, 1999–2001. Silver Jubilee Medal, 1977. *Recreations:* ornithology, photography, shooting, fishing, rural skills, tennis, ski-ing. *Address:* c/o Naval Secretary, Victory Building, HM Naval Base, Portsmouth PO1 3LS. *Club:* Western Isles Yacht.

BACON, Prof. George Edward, MA, ScD Cantab, PhD London; Professor of Physics, University of Sheffield, 1963–81, now Emeritus; *b* 5 Dec. 1917; *s* of late George H. Bacon and Lilian A. Bacon, Derby; *m* 1945, Enid Trigg; one *s* one *d*. *Educ:* Derby Sch.; Emmanuel Coll., Cambridge (Open and Sen. Schol.); CPhys. Air Ministry, Telecommunications Research Estabt, 1939–46. Dep. Chief Scientific Officer, AERE, Harwell, 1946–63; Dean, Faculty of Pure Science, Sheffield Univ., 1969–71. Leverhulme Emeritus Fellow, 1988. FInstP (Guthrie Medal, 1999). Hon. DSc Sheffield, 1998. *Publications:* Neutron Diffraction, 1955; Applications of Neutron Diffraction in Chemistry, 1963; X-ray and Neutron Diffraction, 1966; Neutron Physics, 1969; Neutron Scattering in Chemistry, 1977; The Architecture of Solids, 1981; Fifty Years of Neutron Diffraction, 1987; many scientific pubns on X-ray and neutron crystallographic studies in Proc. Royal Society, Acta Cryst., etc. *Recreations:* gardening, photography, genealogy. *Address:* Windrush Way, Guiting Power, Cheltenham GL54 5US. *T:* (01451) 850631.

BACON, Hon. James Alexander; MHA (Lab) Denison, Tasmania, since 1996; Premier of Tasmania, since 1998; *b* 15 May 1950. Union official, 1973–79, State Sec., Tasmanian Br., 1980–89, Builders' Labourers' Fedn; Sec., Tasmanian Trades and Labor Council, 1989–95. Dir, Tasmanian Develt Authy, 1989–95. Member: Council, Trade Unions Exec., 1989–95; Nat. Labour Consultative Council, 1991–95. Leader, Parly Labor Party, Tas, 1997–. Delegate to: ILO Regl Conf., Bangkok, 1991; ILO Internat. Labor Conf., Geneva, 1994. *Address:* Office of the Premier, 15 Murray Street, GPO Box 123B, Hobart, Tas 7001, Australia. *T:* (3) 62333464.

BACON, Jennifer Helen, CB 1995; Head, Animal Health and Environment Directorate, Department for Environment, Food and Rural Affairs (formerly Ministry of Agriculture, Fisheries and Food), 2000–01; *b* 16 April 1945; *d* of Dr Lionel James Bacon and Joyce Bacon (*née* Chapman). *Educ:* Bedales Sch., Petersfield; New Hall, Cambridge (BA Hons 1st cl.; Hon. Fellow, 1997). Joined Civil Service as Asst Principal, Min. of Labour, 1967; Private Sec. to Minister of State for Employment, 1971–72; Principal, 1972–78, worked on health and safety and industrial relations legislation; Principal Private Sec. to Sec. of State for Employment, 1977–78; Asst Sec., Controller of Trng Services, MSC, 1978–80; sabbatical, travelling in Latin America, 1980–81; Asst Sec., Machinery of Govt Div., CSD, later MPO, 1981–82; Under Sec., Dir of Adult (formerly Occupational) Trng, MSC, 1982–86; Under Sec., School Curriculum and Exams, DES, 1986–89; Department of Employment: Prin. Finance Officer (Grade 3), 1989–91; Dir of Resources and Strategy (Grade 2), 1991–92; Health and Safety Executive: Dep. Dir-Gen. (Policy), 1992–95; Dir-Gen., 1995–2000. Mem., Adv. Cttee on Degree Awarding Powers, QAA, 1998–. Mem. Bd, Sheffield Develt Corp., 1992–95. Vis. Fellow, Nuffield Coll., Oxford, 1989–97. Hon. DSc Aston, 2000. *Recreations:* classical music especially opera, travelling, walking.

BACON, Sir Nicholas (Hickman Ponsonby), 14th Bt of Redgrave, *cr* 1611, and 15th Bt of Mildenhall, *cr* 1627; Premier Baronet of England; DL; *b* 17 May 1953; *s* of Sir Edmund Castell Bacon, 13th and 14th Bt, KG, KBE, TD and Priscilla Dora, *d* of Col Sir Charles Edward Ponsonby, 1st Bt, TD; *S* father, 1982; *m* 1981, Susan, *d* of Raymond Dinnis, Edenbridge, Kent; four *s*. *Educ:* Eton; Dundee Univ. (MA). Barrister-at-law, Gray's Inn. A Page of Honour to the Queen, 1966–69. DL Norfolk, 1998. *Heir: s* Henry Hickman Bacon, *b* 23 April 1984. *Address:* Raveningham Hall, Norfolk NR14 6NS. *Club:* Pratt's.

BACON, Peter James; HM Diplomatic Service, retired; Consul–General, Houston, 1995–2001; *b* 17 Sept. 1941; *s* of Alfred J. Bacon and Mildred (*née* Randall); *m* 1963, Valerie Ann Colby; one *s* one *d*. *Educ:* Richard Huish Grammar Sch., Taunton. GPO, 1958–63; joined HM Diplomatic Service, 1963; CRO, 1963–64; Nicosia, 1964–66; Kota Kinabalu, 1967–70; Brussels, 1970–71; Beirut, 1971–75; Asst Private Sec. to Minister of State, FCO, 1975–78; Suva, 1978–80; First Sec. (Energy), Washington, 1980–84; Hd, Parly Relns Unit, FCO, 1984–88; Consul (Commercial), Johannesburg, 1988–92; Counsellor (Commercial and Develt), Jakarta, 1992–95. *Recreations:* golf, travel. *Address:* 47 Upper Selsdon Road, South Croydon CR2 8DG.

BACON, Richard Michael; MP (C) Norfolk South, since 2001; *b* 3 Dec. 1962; *s* of Michael Edward Bacon and Sheila Margaret Bacon (*née* Taylor, now Campbell). *Educ:* King's Sch., Worcester; LSE (BSc 1986); Goethe Inst., Berlin. Investment banker, Barclays de Zoete Wedd Ltd, 1986–89; financial journalist, principally with Euromoney Publications, 1993–94; Dep. Dir, Mgt Consultancies Assoc., 1994–96; Associate Partner, Brunswick Public Relations, 1996–99; Founder, English Word Factory, 1999–. Mem., Public Accounts Cttee, H of C, 2001–. Chm., Hammersmith Cons. Assoc., 1995–96. Co-founder, Geneva, Cons. Party's Gen. Election Vol. Agency, 2000. Contested (C) Vauxhall, 1997. *Recreation:* playing the bongos. *Address:* House of Commons, SW1A 0AA. *T:* (01379) 643728. *Club:* Ronnie Scott's.

BACON, Sir Sidney (Charles), Kt 1977; CB 1971; BSc(Eng); FREng, FIMechE, FIEE, FTP; Managing Director, Royal Ordnance Factories, 1972–79; Deputy Chairman, Royal Ordnance Factories Board, 1972–79; *b* 11 Feb. 1919; *s* of Charles and Alice Bacon. *Educ:* Woolwich Polytechnic; London Univ. Military Service, 1943–48, Capt. REME. Royal Arsenal, Woolwich, 1933–58; Regional Supt of Inspection, N Midland Region, 1958–60; Asst Dir, ROF, Nottingham, 1960–61; Director, ROF: Leeds, 1961–62; Woolwich, 1962–63; Birtley, 1965; idc, 1964; Dir of Ordnance Factories, Weapons and Fighting Vehicles, 1965–66; Dep. Controller, ROFs, 1966–69; Controller, ROFs, 1969–72. Dir, Short Brothers, 1980–89. Pres., IProdE, 1979; Mem. Council, CGLI, 1979–91. Hon. FCGI 1991. *Recreations:* golf, listening to music. *Address:* 228 Erith Road, Bexleyheath, Kent DA7 6HP. *Club:* Shooters Hill Golf.

BADCOCK, Maj.-Gen. John Michael Watson, CB 1976; MBE 1959; DL; Chairman, S. W. Mount & Sons, 1982–86; *b* 10 Nov. 1922; *s* of late R. D. Badcock, MC, JP and Mrs J. D. Badcock; *m* 1948, Gillian Pauline (*née* Attfield); one *s* two *d*. *Educ:* Sherborne Sch.; Worcester Coll., Oxford. Enlisted in ranks (Army), 1941; commnd Royal Corps of Signals, 1942; war service UK and BAOR; Ceylon, 1945–47; served in UK, Persian Gulf, BAOR and Cyprus; Comdr 2 Inf. Bde and Dep. Constable of Dover Castle, 1968–71; Dep. Mil. Sec., 1971–72; Dir of Manning (Army), 1972–74; Defence Advr and Head of British Defence Liaison Staff, Canberra, 1974–77; retired. psc, jssc, idc. Col Comdt, Royal Signals, 1974–80 and 1982–90; Master of Signals, 1982–90; Hon. Col, 31 (London) Signal Regt (Volunteers), 1978–83. Chm., SE TA&VRA, 1979–85. Chief Appeals Officer, CRC, 1978–82. DL Kent, 1980. *Recreations:* watching Rugby football, cricket, hockey, most field sports less horsemanship. *Address:* c/o RHQ Royal Signals, Blandford Camp, Blandford, Dorset DT11 8RH. *T:* (01258) 482076.

BADDELEY, Prof. Alan David, CBE 1999; PhD; FRS 1993; Professor of Psychology, University of Bristol, since 1995; *b* 23 March 1934; *s* of Donald and Nellie Baddeley; *m* 1964, Hilary Ann White; three *s*. *Educ:* University Coll., London (BA; Fellow, 1998); Princeton Univ. (MA). PhD Cantab, 1962. Walker Fellow, Princeton Univ., 1956–57; Scientist, MRC Applied Psychology Unit, Cambridge, 1958–67; Lectr then Reader, Sussex Univ., 1969–72; Prof. of Psychology, Stirling Univ., 1972–74; Dir, Applied Psychology Unit, MRC, Cambridge, 1974–95; Sen. Res. Fellow, Churchill Coll., Cambridge, 1988–95; Hon. Prof. of Cognitive Psychology, Cambridge Univ., 1991–95. Vis. Fellow, Univ. of California, San Diego, 1970–71; Visiting Professor: Harvard Univ., 1984; Univ. of Queensland, 1990; Univ. of Texas, Austin, 1991. President: Experimental Psychology Soc., 1984–86; European Soc. for Cognitive Psychology, 1986–90. Founder FMedSci 1998. Hon. FBPsS 1995. Mem., Academia Europaea, 1989; Hon. For. Mem., Amer. Acad. of Arts and Scis, 1996. Hon. DPhil Umeå, Sweden, 1991; DUniv: Stirling, 1996; Essex, 1999; Plymouth, 2000. *Publications:* The Psychology of Memory, 1976; Your Memory: a user's guide, 1982; Working Memory, 1986; Human Memory: theory and practice, 1990; Essentials of Human Memory, 1999. *Recreations:* walking, reading, travel. *Address:* Department of Psychology, University of Bristol, 8 Woodland Road, Bristol BS8 1TN. *T:* (0117) 928 8541.

BADDELEY, Sir John (Wolsey Beresford), 4th Bt *cr* 1922; *b* 27 Jan. 1938; *s* of Sir John Beresford Baddeley, 3rd Bt, and Nancy Winifred (*d* 1994), *d* of late Thomas Wolsey; *S* father, 1979; *m* 1st, 1962, Sara Rosalind Crofts (marr. diss. 1992); three *d*; 2nd, 1998, Mrs Carol Quinlan (*née* Greenham). *Educ:* Bradfield College, Berks. FCA. Qualified as Chartered Accountant, 1961. *Recreations:* inland waterways, tennis, squash, gardening. *Heir: cousin* Mark David Baddeley, *b* 10 May 1921. *Address:* Springwood, Sandgate Lane, Storrington, Sussex RH20 3HJ. *T:* (01903) 743054.

BADDELEY, Ven. Martin James; Archdeacon of Reigate, 1996–2000; *b* 10 Nov. 1936; *s* of Walter Hubert and Mary Katharine Baddeley; *m* 1962, Judith Clare Hill; two *s* one *d*. *Educ:* Keble Coll., Oxford (BA 1960; MA 1964); Lincoln Theol Coll. Ordained deacon, 1962, priest, 1963; Asst Curate, St Matthew, Stretford, 1962–64; staff, Lincoln Theol Coll., 1965–69; Chaplain, 1969–74, Fellow, 1972–74, Fitzwilliam Coll., Cambridge; Chaplain, New Hall, Cambridge, 1969–74; Canon Residentiary, Rochester Cathedral, 1974–80; Principal, Southwark Ordination Course, 1980–94; Jt Principal, SE Inst. for Theol Educn, 1994–96. *Recreations:* walking, reading. *Address:* 2 Glendower, Fossil Bank, Upper Colwall, Malvern, Worcs WR13 6PJ.

BADDELEY, Stephen John; Chief Executive, Badminton Association of England Ltd, since 1997; *b* 28 March 1961; *s* of William Baddeley and Barbara Isobel Baddeley (*née* Dufty); *m* 1984, Deirdre Ilene Sharman (marr. diss. 1997); one *s* one *d*. *Educ:* Chelsea Coll., Univ. of London (BSc 1982); Open Univ. (BA 1990). Professional badminton player, 1982–90; Dir of Coaching and Develt, Scottish Badminton Union, 1990–92; (pt-time) Manager, British Badminton Olympic Team, 1990–92; Head Coach, Nat. Badminton Centre, Lausanne, and Asst Nat. Coach for Switzerland, 1992–96; Dir of Elite Play, 1996–97, Performance Dir, 1997–99, Badminton Assoc. of England Ltd. *Publications:* Badminton in Action, 1988; Go and Play Badminton, 1992. *Recreation:* jogging. *Address:* Badminton Association of England, Bradwell Road, Loughton Lodge, Milton Keynes MK8 9LA. *T:* (01908) 268400. *Club:* National Badminton.

BADDILEY, Prof. Sir James, Kt 1977; PhD, DSc, ScD; FRS 1961; FRSE 1962; Professor of Chemical Microbiology, 1977–83, now Emeritus, and Director, Microbiological Chemistry Research Laboratory, 1975–83, University of Newcastle upon Tyne; SERC Senior Research Fellow, and Fellow of Pembroke College, University of Cambridge, 1981–85, now Emeritus; *b* 15 May 1918; *s* of late James Baddiley and Ivy Logan Cato; *m* 1944, Hazel Mary, *yr d* of Wesley Wilfrid Townsend and Ann Rayner Townsend (*née* Kilner); one *s*. *Educ:* Manchester Grammar Sch.; Manchester University (BSc 1941, PhD 1944, DSc 1953; Sir Clement Royds Meml Schol., 1942, Beyer Fellow, 1943–44); MA 1981, ScD 1986, Cantab. Imperial Chemical Industries Fellow, University of Cambridge, 1945–49; Swedish Medical Research Council Fellow, Wenner-Grens Institute for Cell Biology, Stockholm, 1947–49; Mem. of Staff, Dept of Biochemistry, Lister Institute of Preventive Medicine, London, 1949–55; Rockefeller Fellowship, Mass Gen. Hosp., Harvard Med. Sch., 1954; Prof. of Organic Chem., King's Coll., Univ. of Durham, 1955–77 (later Univ. of Newcastle upon Tyne); Head of Sch. of Chemistry, Newcastle upon Tyne Univ., 1968–78. Member: Council, Chemical Soc., 1962–65; Cttee, Biochemical Soc., 1964–67; Council, Soc. of Gen. Microbiol., 1973–75; Council, SERC (formerly SRC), 1979–81 (Mem., Enzyme Chem. and Technol Cttee, 1972–75, Biol Scis Cttee, 1976–79; Mem., Science Bd, 1979–81); Council, Royal Soc., 1977–79; Adv. Cttee, CIBA (later CIBA-GEIGY) Fellowships, 1966–88; Editorial Boards, Biochemical Preparations, 1960–70, Biochimica et Biophysica Acta, 1970–77, Cambridge Studies in Biotechnology, 1985–. Trustee, EPA Cephalosporin Fund, 1979–; Vice-Pres., Alzheimer's Res. Trust, 1993–. Karl Folkers Vis. Prof. in Biochem., Illinois Univ., 1962; Tilden Lectr, Chem. Soc., 1959; Special Vis. Lectr, Dept of Microbiology, Temple Univ., Pa, 1966; Leeuwenhoek Lectr, Royal Society, 1967; Pedler Lectr, Chem. Soc., 1978; Endowment Lectr, Bose Inst., Calcutta, 1980. Founder Mem., Interdisciplinary Cttee, Consejo Cultural Mundial. Hon. Mem., Amer. Soc. Biochem. and Molecular Biol. Hon. DSc Heriot Watt, 1979; Bath, 1986. Meldola Medal, RIC, 1947; Corday-Morgan Medal, Chem. Soc., 1952; Davy Medal, Royal Soc., 1974. Responsible for first chemical synthesis (structure definitive) of ADP and ATP; discovery of teichoic acids in bacterial cell walls and membranes. *Publications:* numerous contribs on chemistry and biochemistry of co-enzymes, bacterial cell walls and membranes in Journal of the Chemical Society, Nature, Biochemical Journal, etc; articles in various microbiological and biochemical reviews.

Recreations: mountaineering, swimming, photography, music, fine arts. *Address:* Hill Top Cottage, Hildersham, Cambridge CB1 6DA. *T:* (01223) 893055; Department of Biochemistry, University of Cambridge, Tennis Court Road, Cambridge CB2 1QW. *T:* (01223) 333600; *e-mail:* james@baddiley.fsnet.co.uk.

BADEN, (Edwin) John, CA; Director, 1987–98, and Deputy Chairman, 1989–90 and 1996–98, Girobank plc; *b* 18 Aug. 1928; *s* of Percy Baden and Jacoba (*née* de Blank); *m* 1952, Christine Irene (*née* Grose); two *s* three *d.* *Educ:* Winchester Coll.; Corpus Christi Coll., Cambridge (MA Econ and Law). Mem. Inst. of Taxation. Audit Clerk, Deloitte Haskins & Sells, CA, 1951–54; Financial Dir/Co. Sec., H. Parrot & Co., Wine Importer, 1954–61; Dir of various subsids, C & A Modes, 1961–63; a Man. Dir, Samuel Montagu & Co. Ltd, 1963–78; Man. Dir/Chief Exec., Italian International Bank Plc, 1978–89; Girobank: Chief Exec., 1989–91; Man. Dir, 1990–91; Chm., 1995–96. Dir, 1990–98, Dep. Chm., 1997–98, Alliance & Leicester Building Soc., then Alliance & Leicester PLC (Chm., Gp Credit Policy Cttee, 1998–). Member, Management Committee: Pan European Property Unit Trust, 1973–; N American Property Unit Trust, 1975–93 (Chm., 1980–93). Sec. Gen., Eurogiro (formerly European Post/Giro Dirs Gp), 1993–97 (Chm., 1990–92); Mem., EU Payment Systems Technical Develt Gp, 1990–97. Institute of Chartered Accountants of Scotland: Mem., Council, 1984–90; Mem., Res. Cttee, 1966–74, 1985–88, 1991–95. Trustee, Internat. Centre for Res. in Accounting, Univ. of Lancaster, 1975–96. Mem., Review Panel, Financial Reporting Council, 1990–95. Chm., Stammerham Amenity Assoc., 1998–; Dir, Rosebery Housing Assoc., 1999–. Liveryman, Co. of Information Technologists, 1992–. FRSA; CIMgt; FCIB. Cavaliere Ufficiale, Order of Merit, Italian Republic, 1986. *Publications:* (contrib.): Making Corporate Reports Valuable, 1988; Auditing into the 21st Century, 1993; Post Giro Banking in Europe, 1993; Internal Control and Financial Reporting, 1994; articles in professional magazines. *Recreations:* reading, sailing, shooting. *Address:* Lanaways Barn, Two Mile Ash, Horsham, W Sussex RH13 7LA. *T:* (01403) 733834, *Fax:* (01403) 732860.

BADEN-POWELL, family name of **Baron Baden-Powell**.

BADEN-POWELL, 3rd Baron *cr* 1929, of Gilwell; **Robert Crause Baden-Powell;** Bt 1922; Vice-President, Scout Association, since 1982; Chairman, Quarter Horse Racing UK, since 1985; *b* 15 Oct. 1936; *s* of 2nd Baron and Carine Crause Baden-Powell (*née* Boardman) (*d* 1993); *S* father, 1962; *m* 1963, Patience Hélène Mary Batty (*see* Lady Baden-Powell). *Educ:* Bryanston (Blandford). Money broker, 1964–84; Director: City Share Trust, 1964–70; Bolton Bldg Soc., 1974–88; Managing Director: Fieldguard Ltd, 1984–; Highline Estates Ltd, 1986–95. Chief Scouts Comr, 1965–82; Pres., West Yorks Scout Council, 1972–88; Mem., 1965–, Mem. Cttee, 1972–78, Council, Scout Assoc. Mem. Council, British Quarter Horse Assoc., 1984–90 (Chm., 1990); Chm., Quarter Horse Racing UK, 1985–88. Pres., Camping and Caravanning Club, 1992–. *Recreation:* breeding racing Quarter Horses. *Heir: b* Hon. David Michael Baden-Powell [*b* 11 Dec. 1940; *m* 1966, Joan Phillips, *d* of H. W. Berryman, Melbourne, Australia; three *s*]. *Address:* Weston Farmhouse, The Street, Albury, Surrey GU5 9AY. *T:* (01483) 205087.

BADEN-POWELL, Lady; Patience Hélène Mary Baden-Powell, CBE 1986; Vice President, The Girl Guides Association, 1990–2000; President, Commonwealth Youth Exchange Council, 1982–86; *b* 27 Oct. 1936; *d* of Mr and Mrs D. M. Batty, Zimbabwe; *m* 1963, Baron Baden-Powell, *qv*. *Educ:* St Peter's Diocesan Sch., Bulawayo. Internat. Comr, 1975–79, Chief Comr, 1980–85, Girl Guides Assoc. Director: Laurentian Financial Gp, 1981–94; Fieldguard Ltd, 1986–. President: Surrey Council for Voluntary Youth Services, 1986–; National Playbus Assoc., 1979–; Patron: Woodlarks Camp Site for the Disabled, 1978–; Surrey Antiques Fair, 1969–. *Address:* Weston Farmhouse, The Street, Albury, Surrey GU5 9AY. *T:* (01483) 205087.

BADENOCH, David Fraser, DM; FRCS; Consultant Urological Surgeon, St Bartholomew's and Royal London Hospitals, since 1988; Urological Surgeon, King Edward VII Hospital for Officers, since 1996; *b* 7 Feb. 1949; 3rd *s* of late Alec Badenoch, MD, ChM, FRCS and of Dr Jean Badenoch; *m* 1981, Michele Patricia Howard; two *s* two *d.* *Educ:* Marlborough Coll.; Lincoln Coll., Oxford (Rugby blue 1971; BA Animal Physiology 1970; BM BCh 1975; MA 1975; DM 1988; MCh 1988); Med. Coll., St Bartholomew's Hosp. FRCS 1979. House Surgeon, Registrar and Lectr in Surgery, St Bartholomew's Hosp., London, 1976–82; Sen. Registrar in Urology, London Hosp., 1982–87; Sen. Lectr in Urology, London Hosp. Med. Coll., London Univ., 1988–99. Surg. Lt Comdr, RNR, 1978–91. Hon. Surg., Royal Scottish Corp., 1993–. Vis. Prof. of Urology, Mayo Clinic, 2001. Member: British Assoc. of Urological Surgeons; Amer. Urological Assoc.; European Urological Assoc.; Société Internationale d'Urologie; British Fertility Soc.; RSocMed (Hon. Sec., 1997–99, Hon. Treas., 2000–, Section of Urology); British Prostate Gp; Hon. Sec., Chelsea Clin. Soc., 2001–. Fellow, Eur. Bd of Urology, 1995. Creevy Meml Lect., Minnesota Soc. of Urology, 2001. Surgitek Prize, British Assoc. of Urological Surgeons, 1987; Grand Prix, European Urological Assoc., 1988. *Publications:* Aids to Urology, 1987; contribs to textbooks and jls in urology and infertility. *Recreations:* reading, piano, Rugby, opera, company of good friends. *Address:* 123 Harley Street, W1G 6IA. *T:* (020) 7935 3881. *Clubs:* Lansdowne; Vincent's (Oxford).

BADENOCH, (Ian) James (Forster); QC 1989; a Recorder, since 1987; a Deputy High Court Judge, since 1994; *b* 24 July 1945; *s* of Sir John Badenoch and of Anne, *d* of Prof. Lancelot Forster; *m* 1979, Marie-Thérèse Victoria Cabourn-Smith; two *s* one *d.* *Educ:* Dragon Sch., Oxford; Rugby Sch.; Magdalen Coll., Oxford (MA). Called to the Bar, Lincoln's Inn, 1968 (Bencher, 2000); Mem., Inner Temple. Member: Medico-Legal Soc.; Harveian Soc.; London Common Law Bar Assoc.; Professional Negligence Bar Assoc. *Publication:* (contrib.) Medical Negligence, 1990, 3rd edn 2000. *Recreations:* family, tennis, travel. *Address:* 1 Crown Office Row, Temple, EC4Y 7HH. *T:* (020) 7797 7500.

BADER, Dr Alfred, Hon. CBE 1998;; President, Alfred Bader Fine Arts, since 1992; *b* Vienna, 28 April 1924; *s* of Alfred and Elisabeth Bader; *m* 1st, 1952, Helen Daniels (marr. diss.); two *s*; 2nd, 1982, Isabel Overton. *Educ:* Queen's Univ., Kingston, Ont. (BSc 1945, BA 1946, MSc 1947); Harvard Univ. (MA 1949, PhD 1950). *Publication:* Res. chemist, 1950-53, Gp Leader, 1953-54, Pittsburgh Plate Glass Co.; Aldrich Chemical Co.: Chief Chemist, 1954-55; Pres., 1955-81; Chm., 1981-91; Pres., 1975-80, Chm., 1980-91, Sigma-Aldrich Corp. (Chm. Emeritus, 1991-92). Guest Curator, Milwaukee Art Mus., 1976 and 1989. FRSA 1989. Hon. Fellow, RSC, 1990. Numerous hon. degrees, including: DSc: Wisconsin, Milwaukee, 1980; Purdue, 1984; Wisconsin-Madison, 1984; Northwestern, 1990; Edinburgh, 1998; Glasgow, 1999; Masaryk, 2000; LLD Queen's, Kingston, 1986; DUniv Sussex, 1989. Awards include: J. E. Purkyne Medal, Czech Acad. Scis, 1994; Charles Lathrop Parsons Award, 1995, Distinguished Contributors Award, 1998, ACS; Gold Medal, Amer. Inst. Chemists, 1997. *Publication:* Adventures of a Chemist Collector, 1995. *Address:* 2961 N Shepard Avenue, Milwaukee, WI 53211, USA. *T:* (414) 9625169. *Club:* University (Milwaukee).

BADGE, Sir Peter (Gilmour Noto), Kt 1998; Stipendiary Magistrate for Devon, since 1997; *b* 20 Nov. 1931; *s* of late Ernest Desmond Badge, LDS and Marie Benson Badge (*née* Clough); *m* 1956, Mary Rose Noble; four *d.* *Educ:* Univ. of Liverpool (LLB). National Service, 1956–58: RNVR, lower deck and commnd; UK, ME and FE; RNR, 1958–62. Solicitor, 1956; Mem., Solicitor's Dept, New Scotland Yard, 1958–61; Asst Solicitor and later Partner, 1961–75, Kidd, Rapinet, Badge & Co.; Notary Public; Metropolitan Stipendiary Magistrate, 1975–97 (Chief Metropolitan Stipendiary Magistrate, 1992–97); a Recorder, 1980–92, 1997–99; a Chm., Inner London Juvenile Panel, 1979–97; Pres., Mental Health Review Tribunals, 1997–. Member: Lord Chancellor's Adv. Cttee for Inner London, 1983–97; Magisterial Cttee, Judicial Studies Bd, 1985–90; Chm., Legal Cttee, Magistrates' Assoc., 1990–93. Mem., Basket Makers' Assoc., 1987–; Pres., Coracle Soc., 1997– (Chm., 1985–97); Chm., Binney Meml Awards Cttee, 1992–97. Mem. Bd of Green Cloth, Verge of the Palaces of St James's, Whitehall etc, 1992–. Liveryman, Co. of Basket Makers, 1995–. Contested (L) Windsor and Maidenhead, 1964. *Publications:* articles on coracles.

BADGE, Robin Howard L.; *see* Lovell-Badge.

BADGER, Prof. Anthony John, PhD; Paul Mellon Professor of American History, Cambridge University, since 1992; Fellow, Sidney Sussex College, Cambridge, since 1992; *b* 6 March 1947; *s* of Kenneth Badger and Iris G. (*née* Summerill); *m* 1979, Ruth Catherine Davis; two *s.* *Educ:* Cotham Grammar Sch.; Sidney Sussex Coll., Cambridge (BA, MA); Hull Univ. (PhD). Department of History, Newcastle University: Lectr, 1971–81; Sen. Lectr, 1981–91; Prof., 1991. Hon. DLitt Hull, 1999. *Publications:* Prosperity Road: the New Deal, North Carolina and tobacco, 1980; North Carolina and the New Deal, 1981; The New Deal: the Depression years, 1989; (ed jtly) The Making of Martin Luther King and the Civil Rights Movement, 1996; (ed jtly) Southern Landscapes, 1996; Race and War: Lyndon Johnson and William Fulbright, 2000; (ed jtly) Contesting Democracy: substance and structure in American political history 1775–2000, 2001. *Recreations:* walking, supporting Bristol Rovers. *Address:* Sidney Sussex College, Cambridge CB2 3HU. *T:* (01223) 335309; *e-mail:* ajb1001@cus.cam.ac.uk.

BADGER, Sir Geoffrey Malcolm, Kt 1979; AO 1975; PhD, DSc; FRSC, FRACI, FACE, FTSE, FAA; Chairman, Australian Science and Technology Council, 1977–82; *b* 10 Oct. 1916; *s* of J. McD. Badger; *m* 1941, Edith Maud, *d* of Henry Chevis. *Educ:* Geelong Coll.; Gordon Inst. of Technology; Univs of Melbourne, London (PhD), Glasgow (DSc). Instructor Lieut, RN, 1943–46. Finney-Howell Research Fellow, London, 1940–41; Research Chemist, ICI, 1941–43; Research Fellow, Glasgow, 1946–49. Univ. of Adelaide: Sen. Lectr, 1949–51; Reader, 1951–54; Prof. of Organic Chemistry, 1955–64, now Emeritus Professor; Dep. Vice-Chancellor, 1966–67; Vice-Chancellor, 1967–77; Res. Professor, 1977–79. Dir, Western Mining Corp., 1979–88. Mem. Executive, CSIRO, 1964–65. President: Aust. Acad. of Science, 1974–78; Aust. and NZ Assoc. for Advancement of Science, 1979–80; Chm., Order of Australia Assoc., 1989–92. DUniv Adelaide. H. G. Smith Medal, 1951, A. E. Leighton Medal, 1971, RACI; W. D. Chapman Medal, Instn of Engrs, Australia, 1974, ANZAAS Medal, 1981. *Publications:* Structures and Reactions of Aromatic Compounds, 1954; Chemistry of Heterocyclic Compounds, 1961; The Chemical Basis of Carcinogenic Activity, 1962; Aromatic Character and Aromaticity, 1969; (ed) Captain Cook, 1970; The Explorers of the Pacific, 1988; numerous papers in Jl Chem. Soc., etc. *Address:* 1 Anna Court, West Lakes, SA 5021, Australia. *T:* (8) 84494594. *Club:* Adelaide (Adelaide).

BADHAM, Douglas George, CBE 1975; JP; HM Lord-Lieutenant for Mid Glamorgan, 1985–89; company director; Chairman, Hamell (West) Ltd, since 1968; *b* 1 Dec. 1914; *s* of late David Badham, JP; *m* 1939, Doreen Spencer Phillips; two *d.* *Educ:* Leys Sch., Cambridge. CA. Exec. Director: Powell Duffryn Gp, 1938–69; Pascoe Hldgs, 1983–88; Alignrite, 1984–87; T. H. Couch, 1984–88; World Trade Centre Wales, 1984–; Chairman: Powell Duffryn Wagon Co., 1965–85; T. T. Pascoe, 1983–89; Economic Forestry Gp PLC, 1981–88 (Dir, 1978–88); Novastar Internat. Ltd, 1996–. Chm., Nat. Health Service Staff Commn, 1972–75; Mem., 1978–84, Dep. Chm., 1980–84, Welsh Develt Agency. Member: Wales and the Marches Telecommunications Bd, 1973–80; British Gas Corp., 1974–83; Forestry Commn, S Wales Reg. Adv. Cttee, 1946–76 (Chm., 1973–76); Western Region Adv. Bd, BR, 1977–82; Welsh Council (Chm., Industry and Planning Panel), 1971–80; Nature Conservancy Council Adv. Cttee for Wales; Council, UWIST, 1975–80; Develt Corp. for Wales, 1965–83 (Chm., 1971–80). JP Glamorgan, 1962; DL, 1975–82, High Sheriff, 1976, Lieut, 1982, Mid Glamorgan. KStJ 1991. *Recreations:* forestry, trout breeding. *Address:* Swyn-y-Coed, Watford Road, Caerphilly, Mid Glamorgan CF8 1NE. *T:* (029) 2088 2094. *Club:* Cardiff and County (Cardiff).

BADHAM, Prof. Paul Brian Leslie; Professor of Theology and Religious Studies, University of Wales, Lampeter, since 1991; *b* 26 Sept. 1942; *s* of Rev. Leslie Badham, QHC and Effie (*née* Garrett); *m* 1969, Linda Frances Elson; one *s.* *Educ:* Reading Sch.; Jesus Coll., Oxford (BA 1965; MA 1969); Jesus Coll., Cambridge (BA 1968; MA 1972); Univ. of Birmingham (PhD 1973). Divinity Master, Churcher's Coll., Petersfield, 1965–66; ordained deacon, 1968, priest, 1969; Curate: Edgbaston, 1968–69; Rubery, 1969–73; St David's University College, Lampeter, then University of Wales, Lampeter: Lectr, 1973–83; Sen. Lectr, 1983–88; Reader, 1988–91; Chm. of Church History, 1982–86; Chm. of Religion and Ethics, 1987–91; Dean, Faculty of Theology, 1991–97; Hd, Dept of Theology and Religious Studies, 1991–99; Hd, Sch. of Anthropology, Classics, Philosophy, Theology and Religious Studies, 1999–. Chm., Subject Panel for Theology and Religious Studies, Univ. of Wales, 1998–; Sec., Assoc. of Univ. Depts of Theology and Religious Studies, 1990–94. Member: Res. Panel for Philosophy, Law and Religious Studies, AHRB, 1999–; Benchmarking Panel for Theology and Religious Studies, QAA, 1999–2000. Trustee, Alister Hardy Centre for Study of Religious Experience, 1997–. Mem. Council, Modern Churchpeople's Union, 1974–95. Mem., Editl Bd, University of Wales Press, 1994–. *Publications:* Christian Beliefs about Life after Death, 1976; (with Linda Badham) Immortality or Extinction?, 1982; (ed jtly) Death and Immortality in the Religions of the World, 1987; (ed jtly) Perspectives on Death and Dying, 1987; (ed) Religious State and Society in Modern Britain, 1989; (ed) A John Hick Reader, 1990; (ed) Ethics on the Frontier of Human Existence, 1992; The Christian Understanding of God and Christ in Relation to True Pure-Land Buddhism, 1994; (ed jtly) Facing Death, 1996; The Contemporary Challenge of Modernist Theology, 1998; contribs to jls. *Address:* Department of Theology and Religious Studies, University of Wales, Lampeter, Ceredigion SA48 7ED. *T:* (01570) 424708.

BADIAN, Ernst, FBA 1965; Professor of History, 1971–82, John Moors Cabot Professor of History, 1982–98, Harvard University, now Emeritus; *b* 8 Aug. 1925; *s* of Joseph and Sally Badian, Vienna (later Christchurch, NZ); *m* 1950, Nathlie Anne (*née* Wimsett); one *s* one *d.* *Educ:* Christchurch Boys' High Sch.; Canterbury Univ. Coll., Christchurch, NZ; University Coll., Oxford (Hon. Fellow 1987). MA (1st cl. hons), NZ, 1946; LitD, Victoria, NZ, 1962. University of Oxford: Chancellor's Prize for Latin Prose, 1950; Craven Fellow, 1950; Conington Prize, 1959; BA (1st cl. hons Lit. Hum.) 1950; MA 1954; DPhil 1956. Asst Lectr in Classics, Victoria University Coll., Wellington, 1947–48; Rome Scholar in Classics, British Sch. at Rome, 1950–52; Asst Lectr in Classics and Ancient History, Univ. of Sheffield, 1952–54; Lectr in Classics, Univ. of Durham, 1954–65; Prof. of Ancient History, Univ. of Leeds, 1965–69; Prof. of Classics and History,

State Univ. of NY at Buffalo, 1969–71. Editor, Amer. Jl of Ancient History, 1976–2001. John Simon Guggenheim Fellow, 1985; Fellow, Nat. Humanities Center, 1988. Visiting Professor: Univs of Oregon, Washington and California (Los Angeles), 1961; Univ. of S Africa, 1965, 1973; Harvard, 1967; State Univ. of NY (Buffalo), 1967–68; Heidelberg, 1973; Univ. of California (Sather Prof.), 1976; Univ. of Colorado, 1978; Univ. of Tel-Aviv, 1981; Martin Classical Lectr, Oberlin Coll., 1978; lecturing visits to Australia, Canada, France, Germany, Holland, Israel, Italy, NZ, Rhodesia, Switzerland, and S Africa. Fellow: Amer. Acad. of Arts and Sciences, 1974; Amer. Numismatic Soc., 1987; Corresponding Member: Austrian Acad. of Scis, 1975; German Archaeol Inst., 1981; Foreign Mem., Finnish Acad. of Sci. and Letters, 1985. Hon. Mem., Soc. for Promotion of Roman Studies, 1983. Hon. LitD: Macquarie, 1993; Canterbury, NZ, 1999. Austrian Cross of Honour for Sci. and Art, 1999. *Publications:* Foreign Clientelae (264–70 BC), 1958; Studies in Greek and Roman History, 1964; (ed) Ancient Society and Institutions, 1966; Polybius (The Great Histories Series), 1966; Roman Imperialism in the Late Republic, 1967 (2nd edn 1968); Publicans and Sinners, 1972 (trans. German (updated) 1997); (ed) Sir Ronald Syme, Roman Papers, Vols 1–2, 1979; From Plataea to Potidaea, 1993; contribs to collections, dictionaries and encyclopaedias and to classical and historical journals. *Recreation:* parrots. *Address:* Department of History, Harvard University, Cambridge, MA 02138, USA.

BAER, Sir Jack (Mervyn Frank), Kt 1997; independent fine art consultant, since 2001; *b* 29 Aug. 1924; *yr s* of late Frank and Alix Baer; *m* 1st, 1952, Jean St Clair (marr. diss. 1969; she *d* 1973), *o c* of late L. F. St Clair and Evelyn Synnott; one *d*; 2nd, 1970, Diana Downes Baillieu, *yr d* of Aubrey Clare Robinson and late Mollie Panter-Downes; two step *d*. *Educ:* Bryanston; Slade Sch. of Fine Art, University Coll., London. Served RAF (Combined Ops), 1942–46. Proprietor, Hazlitt Gallery, 1948 until merger with Gooden & Fox, 1973; Man. Dir, 1973–92, Chm., 1992–94, Consultant, 1994–2001, Hazlitt, Gooden & Fox. Chm., Fine Arts and Antiques Export Adv. Cttee to Dept of Trade, 1971–73 (Vice-Chm., 1969–71). Member: Reviewing Cttee on Export of Works of Art, 1992–2001; Museums and Galls Commn, 1993–98 (Chm., Acceptance in Lieu of Tax Panel, 1993–2000). Pres., Fine Art Provident Institution, 1972–75. Chm., Soc. of London Art Dealers, 1977–80 (Vice Chm. 1974–77). Trustee: Burlington Magazine Foundn, 1991–; Nat. Mus and Galls on Merseyside Develt Trust, 1998–; Campaign for Museums, 1998–. *Publications:* numerous exhibition catalogues; articles in various jls. *Recreation:* drawing. *Address:* 9 Phillimore Terrace, W8 6BJ. *T:* (020) 7937 6899. *Clubs:* Brooks's, Beefsteak.

BAGGE, Sir (John) Jeremy (Picton), 7th Bt *cr* 1867, of Stradsett Hall, Norfolk; DL; *b* 21 June 1945; *s* of Sir John Bagge, 6th Bt, ED, DL and Elizabeth Helena (*d* 1996), *d* of late Daniel James Davies, CBE; *S* father, 1990; *m* 1979, Sarah Margaret Phipps, *d* of late Maj. James Shelley Phipps Armstrong; two *s* one *d*. *Educ:* Eton. FCA 1968. DL Norfolk, 1996. *Heir: s* Alfred James John Bagge, *b* 1 July 1980. *Address:* Stradsett Hall, King's Lynn, Norfolk PE33 9HA.

BAGIER, Gordon Alexander Thomas; DL; *b* 7 July 1924; *m* 1949, Violet Sinclair; two *s* two *d*. *Educ:* Pendower Secondary Technical Sch., Newcastle upon Tyne. Signals Inspector, British Railways; Pres., Yorks District Council, NUR, 1962–64. Mem. of Keighley Borough Council, 1956–60; Mem. of Sowerby Bridge Urban Council, 1962–65. MP (Lab) Sunderland South, 1964–87. PPS to Home Secretary, 1968–69. Chm., Select Cttee on Transport, 1985–87. DL Tyne and Wear, 1988. *Recreation:* golf. *Address:* Nesta, 89 Whaggs Lane, Whickham, Newcastle upon Tyne NE16 4PQ. *Club:* Westerhope Golf (Newcastle upon Tyne).

BAGLIN, Richard John; Chairman, Greenwich Healthcare NHS Trust, 1995–2000 (Director, since 1993); *b* 30 Oct. 1942; *s* of F. W. and C. C. Baglin; *m* 1964, Anne Christine; one *d*. *Educ:* Preston Manor County Grammar Sch.; St John's Coll., Cambridge (MA). Various posts with Abbey National BS, later Abbey National plc, 1964–93: Gen. Man., 1981–88; Dir, various subsidiaries, 1987–93; Man. Dir, New Businesses, 1988–92. Mem., SE London Probation Service Cttee, 1993–95. *Recreations:* theatre, the arts. *Address:* 2 Feathers Place, Greenwich, SE10 9NE. *T:* (020) 8858 9895.

BAGNALL, Air Chief Marshal Sir Anthony (John Crowther), KCB 1998 (CB 1994); OBE 1982; Vice-Chief of Defence Staff, since 2001; *b* 8 June 1945; *s* of Maurice Arthur Bagnall and Marjorie (*née* Crowther); *m* 1970, Pamela Diane Wilson; one *s* two *d*. *Educ:* Stretford Grammar Sch. RAF Coll., Cranwell, 1964; Flight Comdr, 5 Sqn, 1975; Advanced Staff College, 1978; Sqn Comdr, 43 Sqn, 1983, 23 Sqn, 1985; Dir, Air Staff Briefing and Co-ordination, 1985; Station Comdr, RAF Leuchars, 1987; RCDS 1990; Dir, Air Force Staff Duties, 1991; ACAS, 1992; AOC No 11 Gp, 1994; Dep. C-in-C, AFCENT, 1996–98; Air Mem. for Personnel, and AOC-in-C, Personnel and Trng Comd, 1998–2000; C-in-C Strike Comd, 2000–01; Air ADC to the Queen, 2000–01. Pres., RAF Rowing Club, 1996–. *Recreations:* golf, bridge, fell walking. *Address:* c/o Lloyds TSB, 53 King Street, Manchester M60 2ES. *Club:* Royal Air Force.

BAGNALL, Kenneth Reginald; QC 1973; QC (Hong Kong) 1983; Chairman, The New Law Publishing Co. plc, 1993; Editor-in-Chief, New Property Cases, 1986; *b* 26 Nov. 1927; *s* of Reginald and Elizabeth Bagnall; *m* 1st, 1955, Margaret Edith Wall; one *s* one *d*; 2nd, 1963, Rosemary Hearn; one *s* one *d*. *Educ:* King Edward VI Sch., Birmingham; Univ. of Birmingham (LLB Hons). Yardley Scholar. Served Royal Air Force; Pilot Officer, 1947, Flt Lt, 1948. Called to the Bar, Gray's Inn, 1950; a Dep. Judge of Crown Court, 1975–83. Co-founder, 1980, Chm., 1980–82, and Life Gov., 1983, Anglo-American Real Property Inst. Mem., Crafts Council, 1982–85; Co-founder, Bagnall Gall., Crafts Council, 1982. Founder, The New Law Fax Reporting Service, 1992; Founder and Designer, New Law Online, 1995; Co-founder and Consultant, Law Alert Ltd, 1999. Mem., Inst. of Dirs. Freeman, City and Corp. of London, 1972; Freeman and Liveryman, Barber-Surgeons' Co, 1972. *Publications:* Guide to Business Tenancies, 1956; Atkins Court Forms and Precedents (Town Planning), 1973; (with K. Lewison) Development Land Tax, 1978; Judicial Review, 1985. *Recreations:* yachting, motoring, travel. *Clubs:* 1900, United and Cecil.

BAGNALL, Field Marshal Sir Nigel (Thomas), GCB 1985 (KCB 1981); CVO 1978; MC 1950 and Bar 1953; Chief of the General Staff, 1985–88; *b* 10 Feb. 1927; *s* of Lt-Col Harry Stephen Bagnall and Marjory May Bagnall; *m* 1959, Anna Caroline Church; two *d*. *Educ:* Wellington Coll. Joined Army, 1945; commnd Green Howards, 1946; Palestine, 1946–48, 8 Para Bn, 6th Airborne Div.; Malaya, 1949–53, Canal Zone and Cyprus, 1954–56, Green Howards; sc 1957, jssc 1962; GSO1 (Intell.), Dir of Borneo Ops, 1966–67; comd 4/7 Royal Dragoon Guards, NI and BAOR, 1967–69; Sen. Directing Staff (Army), Jt Services Staff Coll., 1970; comd Royal Armoured Corps HQ 1 (Br.) Corps, 1970–72; Defence Fellow, Balliol Coll., Oxford, 1972–73; Sec., Chief of Staff Cttee, 1973–75; GOC 4th Div., 1975–77; ACDS (Policy), MoD, 1978–80; Comdr, 1 (Br.) Corps, 1980–83; C-in-C BAOR and Comdr, Northern Army Gp, 1983–85. Col Comdt, APTC, 1981–88, RAC, 1985–88; ADC Gen. to the Queen, 1985–88. Hon. Fellow, Balliol Coll., Oxford, 1986. Co-Pres., Anglo-German Officers' Assoc., 1992–98. Comdr's Cross, Order of Merit (Germany), 1993. *Publication:* The Punic Wars, 1991 (trans. German 1995). *Recreations:* writing, reading, gardening, breeding water fowl. *Address:* c/o Royal Bank of Scotland, 49 Charing Cross Road, SW1A 2DX.

BAGNALL, Peter Hill, CBE 1999; DL; Chairman, Oxford Radcliffe Hospitals NHS Trust, since 1993; *b* 8 Oct. 1931; *s* of Reginald Stuart Bagnall and Mary Adelaide (*née* Hill); *m* 1st, 1955, Edith Ann Wood (marr. diss. 1979); one *s* one *d* (and one *s* decd); 2nd, 1979, Diana Elizabeth Rayner. *Educ:* Newcastle-under-Lyme Sch.; St Catharine's Coll., Cambridge (MA). Nat. Service and TA Commns, N Staffs Regt. Dir, W. H. Smith & Son Ltd, 1968–88; Dir and Man. Dir, W. H. Smith PLC, 1974–88, retd; Chm., Book Club Associates, 1972–88; Director: Book Tokens Ltd, 1975–; W. H. Smith Pension Trustees Ltd, 1979–; TSB/Trustcard, 1986–89; The Book Trust, 1986–93 (Chm., 1989–91); Longman/Ladybird Books, 1987–90; British Museum Co., 1988–; Blackwell Ltd, Oxford, 1989–96. Dir, Oxon HA, 1989–93. Mem., Vis. Cttee, Open Univ., 1988–92; Chm. Govs and Pro-Chancellor, Oxford Brookes Univ., 1993–98 (Gov., 1988–98). Churchwarden, St Peter's, Alvescot. DL Oxfordshire, 1995. Hon. LLD Oxford Brookes, 1998. *Recreations:* fell-walking, book collecting, theatre, travel, local affairs. *Address:* Oxford Radcliffe Hospitals NHS Trust, The John Radcliffe, Headley Way, Headington, Oxford OX3 9DX. *T:* (01865) 741741; The Old Rectory, Alvescot, Bampton, Oxford OX18 2PS. *Clubs:* Garrick, Sloane.

BAGOT, family name of **Baron Bagot**.

BAGOT, 10th Baron *cr* 1780, of Bagot's Bromley, co. Stafford; **Charles Hugh Shaun Bagot;** Bt 1627; *b* 23 Feb. 1944; *s* of 9th Baron Bagot and of Muriel Patricia (*née* Moore-Boyle); *S* father, 2001; *m* 1986, Mrs Sally A. Stone, *d* of D. G. Blunden; one *d*. *Heir: kinsman* Richard Charles Villiers Bagot, *b* 26 April 1941. *Address:* 16 Barclay Road, SW6 1EH.

BAGRI, family name of **Baron Bagri**.

BAGRI, Baron *cr* 1997 (Life Peer), of Regent's Park in the City of Westminster; **Raj Kumar Bagri,** CBE 1995; Founder, and Chairman, since 1970, Metdist Ltd; *b* 24 Aug. 1930; *m* 1954, Usha Maheshwary; one *s* one *d*. Chairman: Metdist Trading Ltd, 1981–; Metdist International Ltd, 1981–; Minmetco Ltd, 1990–; Bagri Foundation, 1990–. Chm., London Metal Exchange, 1993– (Dir, 1983; Vice Chm., 1990). Mem., Governing Body, SOAS, 1997–. Chm. Trustees, Rajiv Gandhi (UK) Foundn, 1997–; Mem. Adv. Council, PYBT, 1996–. Hon. DSc: City, 1999; Nottingham, 2000. *Address:* Metdist Ltd, 80 Cannon Street, EC4N 6EJ.

BAGSHAW, (Charles) Kerry, CMG 1998; OBE 1992; General Manager, Group Security, De Beers, since 2000; *b* 5 Oct. 1943; *s* of Harry Bagshaw and Frances Bagshaw (*née* Mackay); *m* 1st, 1965, Janet Bond (marr. diss.); one *d*; 2nd, 1970, Pamela Georgina Slater; two *d*. *Educ:* White Fathers. Joined RM, 1961; commnd 1965; RM Commandos (43, 40 and 45), 1963–68; SBS, 1969–74. HM Diplomatic Service, 1974–99: First Secretary: Gaborone, 1977–79; FCO, 1979–82; UK Mission to UN, Geneva, 1982–86; FCO, 1986–87; Moscow, 1988–91; Counsellor, FCO, 1992–99. *Recreations:* mountains (winter and summer), music, wine and food, cycling. *Address:* De Beers Corporate Headquarters, Private Bag X01, Southdale, Johannesburg, 2135, South Africa. *Clubs:* Special Forces; Audax.

BAGSHAW, Dr Michael, FRAeS; Head of Medical Services, British Airways, since 1997; *b* 9 July 1946; *s* of Robert and Alice Bagshaw; *m* 1970, Penelope Isaac; two *d*. *Educ:* Welsh Nat. Sch. of Medicine, Cardiff (MB BCh 1973); MRCS, LRCP 1973; DipAvMed 1980; MFOM 1982; DFFP 1995; FRAeS 1995. Commercial Pilot's Licence; CAA Flying Examr. Clerical Asst, Architect's Dept, Swansea BC, 1966; Technical Photographer, Univ. of Swansea, 1967; medical student, Cardiff, 1967–70; RAF, 1970–86: Med. Br., 1970–75; Fast Jet Pilot (Hunter, Jaguar), 1975–78; Flying Instr, RAF Coll., Cranwell, 1978–80; Sen. Med. Officer Pilot, RAF Inst. of Aviation Medicine, 1980–86; Locum Consultant in Neuro-Otology, St George's Hosp., London, 1987; Principal, General Practice, Crowthorne, 1987–90; Estabt MO, DERA, Farnborough, 1990–92; Sen. Aviation Physician, British Airways, 1992–97. Technology lecture, Royal Society, 1996. Liveryman, GAPAN, 1992– (Award of Merit, 1997). Clarkson Trophy, RAF, 1978; Buchanan Barbour Award, RAeS, 1984. *Publications:* Human Performance and Limitations in Aviation, 1991; (contrib.) Oxford Textbook of Medicine; papers and articles on aviation medicine. *Recreations:* violinist, Crowthorne Chamber Orchestra; general aviation (flying instructor and examiner; corporate jet pilot). *Address:* Waterside (HMAG), PO Box 365, Harmondsworth, Middx UB7 0GB. *T:* (020) 8738 7705. *Club:* Royal Air Force.

BAGSHAWE, Prof. Kenneth Dawson, CBE 1990; MD; FRCP; FRCR; FRS 1989; Professor of Medical Oncology in the University of London at Charing Cross and Westminster Medical School (formerly Charing Cross Hospital Medical School), 1974–90, now Emeritus; Hon. Consultant Physician, Charing Cross Hospital, since 1990 (Consultant Physician, 1961–90); *b* 17 Aug. 1925; *s* of Harry Bagshawe and Gladys (*née* Dawson); *m* 1st, 1946, Ann Kelly (marr. diss. 1976; she *d* 2000); one *s* one *d*; 2nd, 1977, Sylvia Dorothy Lawler (*née* Corben) (*d* 1996); 3rd, 1998, Surinder Kanta Sharma. *Educ:* Harrow County Sch.; London Sch. of Econs and Pol Science; St Mary's Hosp. Med. Sch. (MB, BS 1952; MD 1964). FRCP 1969; FRCR 1983; FRCOG *ad eundem* 1978. Served RN, 1942–46. Fellow, Johns Hopkins Univ., Baltimore, USA, 1955–56; Sen. Registrar, St Mary's Hosp., 1956–60. Visiting Professor: Down State Univ., NY, 1977; Univ. of Hong Kong, 1982, 1994. Chm., DHSS Wkg Gp on Acute Cancer Services, 1980–84. Cancer Research Campaign: Chm., Scientific Cttee, 1983–88; Chm., Exec. Cttee, 1988–90; Vice Chm. Bd, 1988–. Chm., Aepact Ltd, 1996–. Hon. FRSocMed 1993. Hon. DSc Bradford, 1990. Galen Medal, London Soc. of Apothecaries, 1993. *Publications:* Choriocarcinoma, 1969; Medical Oncology, 1975; 300 papers on cancer chemotherapy, tumour markers, drug targeting, etc. *Recreations:* (passive) music, art; (active) demolition, conservation. *Address:* 115 George Street, W1H 5TA. *T:* (020) 7262 6033, (office) (020) 8846 7517. *Club:* Athenæum.

BAHL, Kamlesh, (Mrs N. Lakhani), CBE 1997; Vice-President, Law Society, 1999–2000; *b* 28 May 1956; *d* of Swinder Nath Bahl and Leela Wati Bahl; *m* 1986, Dr Nitin Lakhani. *Educ:* Univ. of Birmingham (LLB 1977). Admitted Solicitor, 1980. GLC, 1978–81; BSC, 1981–84; Texaco Ltd, 1984–87; Data Logic Ltd: Legal and Commercial Manager, 1987–89; Company Sec. and Manager, Legal Services, 1989–93. Chm., EOC, 1993–98. Mem., Barnet HA, 1989–90; non-exec. Dir, Parkside HA, 1990–93. Law Society: Chm., Commerce and Industry Gp, 1988–89; Mem. Council, 1990–2000. Member: Justice Sub-Cttee on Judiciary, 1991–92; Ethnic Minorities Adv. Cttee and Tribunals Cttee (Cttees of Lord Chancellor's Judicial Studies Bd), 1991–94; Council and Standing Cttee on HAs, NAHAT, 1993–94; Council, Justice, 1993–94. Indep. Mem., Diplomatic Service Appeal Bd, FCO, 1993–. EC Rep., EC Consultative Commn on Racism and Xenophobia, 1994–; Vice Pres., Eur. Adv. Cttee on Equal Opportunities, 1998. Mem. Council, Scout Assoc., 1996–99. FRSA. Hon. Fellow, Liverpool John Moores Univ., 1998. Hon. MA North London, 1997; Hon. LLD: De Montfort, 1998;

Birmingham, 1999; Hon. DCL Northumbria, 1999. *Publication:* (ed) Managing Legal Practice in Business, 1989. *Recreations:* swimming, dancing, travelling, theatre.

BAILES, Alyson Judith Kirtley, CMG 2001; HM Diplomatic Service; Ambassador to Finland, since 2000; *b* 6 April 1949; *d* of John-Lloyd Bailes and Barbara (*née* Martin). *Educ:* Belvedere Sch., Liverpool; Somerville Coll., Oxford (MA Modern Hist.). Entered Diplomatic Service, 1969; Budapest, 1970–74; UK Delgn to NATO, 1974–76; FCO, 1976–78; Asst to EC 'Cttee of Wise Men' (which reported on ways of improving functioning of EC instns), 1979; on loan to MoD, 1979–81; Bonn, 1981–84; Dep. Head of Planning Staff, FCO, 1984–86; Counsellor, Peking, 1987–89; on attachment to RIIA, 1990; Consul-Gen. and Dep. Head of Mission, Oslo, 1990–93; Head of Security Policy Dept, FCO, 1994–96; Vice-Pres., Inst. of East West Studies, NY, 1996–97 (on special leave); Political Dir, WEU, Brussels, 1997–2000. *Recreations:* music, nature, travel. *Address:* c/o Foreign and Commonwealth Office, King Charles Street, SW1A 2AH.

BAILEY, family name of **Baron Glanusk**.

BAILEY, Adrian Edward; MP (Lab and Co-op) West Bromwich West, since Nov. 2000; *b* 11 Dec. 1945; *s* of Edward Arthur Bailey and Sylvia Alice Bailey; *m* 1989, Jill Patricia Millard (*née* Hunscott); one step *s*. *Educ:* Cheltenham Grammar Sch.; Univ. of Exeter (BA Hons Econ. Hist.); Loughborough Coll. of Librarianship (Post Grad. DipLib). Librarian, Cheshire CC, 1971–82; Pol Organiser, Co-op Party, 1982–2000. Mem. (Lab), Sandwell MBC, 1991– (Dep. Leader, 1997–2000). Contested (Lab): S Worcs, 1970; Nantwich, Feb. and Oct. 1974; Wirral, March 1976; Cheshire W, EP, 1979. *Recreations:* supporting Cheltenham Town FC, cricket, dog walking. *Address:* House of Commons, SW1A 0AA; 181 Oakham Road, Tividale, Oldbury, W Midlands B69 1PZ.

BAILEY, Sir Alan (Marshall), KCB 1986 (CB 1982); Permanent Secretary, Department of Transport, 1986–91; *b* 26 June 1931; *s* of John Marshall Bailey and Muriel May Bailey; *m* 1st, 1959, Stella Mary Scott (marr. diss. 1981); three *s*; 2nd, 1981, Shirley Jane Barrett. *Educ:* Bedford Sch.; St John's and Merton Colls, Oxford (MA, BPhil; Hon. Fellow, St John's Coll., 1991). Harmsworth Senior Scholarship, 1954; Harkness Commonwealth Fellowship, USA, 1963–64. Principal Private Sec. to Chancellor of the Exchequer, 1971–73; Under-Sec., HM Treasury, 1973–78, Dep. Sec., 1978–83 (Central Policy Review Staff, Cabinet Office, 1981–82), 2nd Perm. Sec., 1983–85. Board Mem., London Transport, 1991–2000. Hon. Treas., Hist. of Parliament Trust, 1994–. Chm., Harkness Fellowship Assoc., 1998–. *Address:* 56 Greenfell Mansions, Glaisher Street, Victory Wharf, SE8 3LU.

BAILEY, Prof. Allen Jackson, FRSC; Professor of Biochemistry, University of Bristol, 1980–96, now Emeritus; *b* 31 Jan. 1931; *s* of late Horace Jackson Bailey and Mabel Bailey (*née* Young); *m* 1956, Beryl Lee; twin *s* two *d*. *Educ:* Eccles Grammar Sch. BSc London (Chem.) 1954; MSc (Physics) 1958, PhD (Chem.) 1960, Birmingham; MA 1967, ScD 1973, Cambridge. FIFST. Shell Chemicals, 1954–57; Low Temp. Res. Station, Univ. of Cambridge, 1960–67; Harkness Fellow, Commonwealth Fund, Biol. Dept, CIT, 1963–65; joined AFRC Meat Res. Inst., Bristol, 1967: SPSO (Special Merit), 1972; Head of Biochem. Dept, 1977–79; Director (DCSO), 1979–85; Hd of Lab., AFRC Inst. of Food Res., Bristol, 1985–90; Hd of Collagen Res. Gp, Bristol Univ., 1991–. Vis. Prof., São Paulo Univ., 1991. Scott Robertson Meml Lectr, QUB, 1986; Proctor Meml Lectr, Leeds, 1991. Hon. Fellow, British Connective Tissue Soc. Senior Medal Food Science, RSC, 1987; Internat. Lectureship Award, Amer. Meat Sci. Assoc., 1989. Mem. Editl Bds, sci. jls. *Publications:* Recent Advances in Meat Science, 1985; Collagen as a Food, 1987; Connective Tissue in Meat and Meat Products, 1989; sci. papers in learned jls. *Recreations:* travel, photography, painting. *Address:* Seasons, Bridgwater Road, Winscombe, Avon BS25 1NA. *T:* (01934) 843447. *Club:* Farmers'.

BAILEY, Sir Brian (Harry), Kt 1983; OBE 1976; JP; DL; Chairman, Television South West Ltd, 1980–93; Director: Channel Four Television, 1985–91 (Deputy Chairman, 1989–91); Oracle Teletext Ltd, 1983–93; *b* 25 March 1923; *s* of Harry Bailey and Lilian (*née* Pulfer); *m* 1948, Nina Olive Sylvia (*née* Saunders); two *d*. *Educ:* Lowestoft Grammar Sch. RAF, 1941–45. SW Dist Organisation Officer, NALGO, 1951–82; South Western Reg. Sec., TUC, 1968–81. Chairman: South Western RHA, 1975–82; Health Educn Council, 1983–87; Health Educn Authority, 1987–89; Member: Somerset CC, 1966–84; SW Econ. Planning Council, 1969–79; Central Health Services Council, 1978–80; MRC, 1978–86; Adv. Cttee on Severn Barrage, Dept of Energy, 1978–81; Business Educn Council, 1980–84; NHS Management Inquiry Team, 1983–84. Chm. Council, Indep. Television Assoc., 1991; Vice-Chm., BBC Radio Bristol Adv. Council, 1971–78; Member: BBC West Reg. Adv. Council, 1973–78; Council, ITCA, 1982–86; South and West Adv. Bd, Legal and General Assurance Soc. Ltd, 1985–87. Director: Independent Television Publications Ltd, 1985–90; Bournemouth Orchs (formerly Western Orchestral Soc. Ltd), 1982–96 (Vice Pres., 1996–). SW Regl Pres., MENCAP, 1984–90; Nat. Pres., Hosp. Caterers Assoc., 1987–. Trustee, EEC Chamber Orchestra, 1987–97. Gen. Governor, British Nutrition Foundn, 1987–91. Chm. of Govs, Dartington Coll. of Arts, 1992–. JP Somerset, 1964 (Chm., Taunton Deane Magistrates Bench, 1987–92); DL Somerset, 1988. *Recreations:* football, cricket and tennis (watching), music, golf (playing). *Address:* Runnerstones, 32 Stonegallows, Taunton, Somerset TA1 5JP. *T:* (01823) 461265. *Club:* Enmore Park Golf.

BAILEY, Colin Frederick, QPM 1993; Chief Constable, Nottinghamshire Constabulary, 1995–2000; *b* 17 Oct. 1943; *s* of late Fred Bailey and of Mary (*née* Sivill); *m* 1966, Christine Lound; one *s* one *d*. *Educ:* Queen Elizabeth's GS, Horncastle, Lincs; Univ. of Sheffield (LLB Hons). Lincolnshire Constab., 1960–86; Asst Chief Constable (Crime Ops), W Yorks Police, 1986–90; Dep. Chief Constable, Nottinghamshire Constab., 1990–95. Chairman: ACPO Race and Community Relns Sub Cttee, 1995–2000; ACPO Crime Prevention Sub Cttee, 1997–2000. Pres., Nottingham Br., RLSS, 1995–2000; Chm., E Midlands RLSS, 1998–2000. Chm., Police History Soc., 1998–. *Recreations:* antique porcelain, wildlife, gardening, wine, foreign travel. *Address:* c/o Nottinghamshire Constabulary Headquarters, Sherwood Lodge, Arnold, Notts NG5 8PP. *T:* (0115) 967 0999, *Fax:* (0115) 967 0900.

BAILEY, David, CBE 2001; FCSD; photographer, film maker; *b* 2 Jan. 1938; *s* of William Bailey and Agnes (*née* Green); *m* 1st, 1960, Rosemary Bramble; 2nd, 1967, Catherine Deneuve, *qv*; 3rd, 1975, Marie Helvin (marr. diss. 1985); 4th, 1986, Catherine Dyer; two *s* one *d*. *Educ:* self taught. FRPS 1972 (Hon. FRPS 1999); FSIAD 1975. Photographer for Vogue, 1959–, for Harpers & Queen, 1999–; dir of television commercials, 1966–, of documentaries, 1968–; director and producer: Who Dealt? (TV film), 1993; Models Close-Up (TV documentary), 1998; dir, The Intruder (film), 1999. Exhibitions: Nat. Portrait Gall., 1971; one-man retrospective, V&A, 1983; Internat. Centre of Photograph, NY, 1984; Photographs from the Sudan, ICA and tour, 1985; Bailey Now!, Nat. Centre of Photography, Bath, 1989; Hamilton's Gall., annually, 1995–; Camerawork, Berlin, 1997; Carla Sozzani Gall., Milan, 1997; Galerie Claire Fontaine, Luxembourg, 1997; A Gallery for Fine Photography, New Orleans; painting exhibn, Well Hung Gall., 1997; Barbican, 1999; Nat. Mus. of Photography, Film & TV, 1999; Modern a Museet, Stockholm, 2000; Helsinki City Art Mus., 2000. FRSA. Hon. FCGI. Hon. DLitt Bradford. D&AD President's Award, for outstanding contrib. to creativity, 1998; awards for commercials including Clios, D&AD Gold Award, Cannes Golden Lion and Emmy. *Publications:* Box of Pinups, 1964; Goodbye Baby and Amen, 1969; Warhol, 1974; Beady Minces, 1974; Papua New Guinea, 1975; Mixed Moments, 1976; Trouble and Strife, 1980; David Bailey's London NW1, 1982; Black and White Memories, 1983; Nudes 1981–84, 1984; Imagine, 1985; If We Shadows, 1992; The Lady is a Tramp, 1995 (TV film, 1995); Rock & Roll Heroes, 1997; Models Close-Up, 1998; Archive One, 1957–69, 1999; Chasing Rainbows, 2001. *Recreations:* aviculture, photography, travelling, painting.

BAILEY, D(avid) R(oy) Shackleton, LittD; FBA 1958; Pope Professor of the Latin Language and Literature, Harvard University, 1982–88, now Emeritus; Adjunct Professor, University of Michigan, since 1989; *b* 10 Dec. 1917; *y s* of late Rev. J. H. Shackleton Bailey, DD, and Rosamund Maud (*née* Giles); *m* 1st, 1967, Hilary Ann (marr. diss. 1974), *d* of Leonard Sidney and Margery Bardwell; *m* 2nd, 1994, Kristine Zvirbulis. *Educ:* Lancaster Royal Grammar Sch.; Gonville and Caius Coll., Cambridge (Hon. Fellow, 2000). Fellow of Gonville and Caius Coll., 1944–55, Praelector, 1954–55; Fellow and Dir of Studies in Classics, Jesus Coll., Cambridge, 1955–64; Visiting Lecturer in Classics, Harvard Coll., 1963; Fellow and Dep. Bursar, Gonville and Caius Coll., 1964; Senior Bursar 1965–68; Univ. Lectr in Tibetan, 1948–68; Prof. of Latin, Univ. of Michigan, 1968–74; Prof. of Greek and Latin, Harvard Univ., 1975–82. Andrew V. V. Raymond Vis. Prof., State Univ. of NY at Buffalo, 1973–74; Vis. Fellow of Peterhouse, Cambridge, 1980–81; Nat. Endowment of Humanities Fellowship, 1980–81. Mem., Amer. Philosophical Soc., 1977. Fellow, Amer. Acad. of Arts and Sciences, 1979. Hon. Mem., Soc. for Roman Studies, 1999. Editor, Harvard Studies in Classical Philology, 1978–84. Hon. LittD Dublin, 1984. Charles J. Goodwin Award of Merit, Amer. Philol Assoc., 1978; Kenyon Medal, British Acad., 1985. *Publications:* The Śatapañcāśatka of Mātrceta, 1951; Propertiana, 1956; Towards a Text of Cicero, *ad Atticum*; 1960; Ciceronis Epistulae ad Atticum IX–XVI, 1961; Cicero's Letters to Atticus, Vols I and II, 1965; Vol. V, 1966, Vol. VI, 1967, Vols III and IV, 1968, Vol. VII, 1970; Cicero, 1971; Two Studies in Roman Nomenclature, 1976; Cicero: *Epistulae ad Familiares*, 2 vols, 1977; (trans.) Cicero's Letters to Atticus, 1978; (trans.) Cicero's Letters to his Friends, 2 Vols, 1978; Towards a Text of *Anthologia Latina*, 1979; Selected Letters of Cicero, 1980; Cicero: *Epistulae ad Q. Fratrem et M. Brutum*, 1981; Profile of Horace, 1982; Anthologia Latina, I.1, 1982; Horatius, 1985; Cicero: Philippics, 1986; (trans.) Cicero, Selected Letters, 1986; Ciceronis Epistulae, 4 vols, 1987–88; Lucanus, 1988; Onomasticon to Cicero's speeches, 1988; Quintilianus: *Declamationes minores*, 1989; Martialis, 1990; Back from Exile, 1991; Martial, 3 vols, 1993; Homoeoteleuton in Latin dactylic verse, 1994; Onomasticon to Cicero's Letters, 1994; Onomasticon to Cicero's Treatises, 1996; Selected Classical Papers, 1997; Cicero's Letters to Atticus, 4 vols, 1999; Valerius Maximus, 2000; Cicero's Letters to Friends, 3 vols, 2001; articles in Classical and Orientalist periodicals. *Recreation:* cats. *Address:* 303 North Division, Ann Arbor, MI 48104, USA.

BAILEY, Dennis, RDI 1980; ARCA; graphic designer and illustrator; Partner, Bailey and Kenny, since 1988; *b* 20 Jan. 1931; *s* of Leonard Charles Bailey and Ethel Louise Funnell; *m* 1985, Nicola Anne Roberts; one *s* one *d*. *Educ:* West Sussex Sch. of Art, Worthing; Royal College of Art. Asst Editor, Graphis magazine, Zürich, 1956; free-lance design practice, London, 1957–87; Paris, 1961–64; Art Dir, Town magazine, London, 1964–66; Lectr in graphic design, Chelsea Sch. of Art, 1970–81, Middlesex Polytechnic, 1985–89. *Clients and work include:* Economist Newspaper: covers and typographic advisor, Economist Publications: The World in 1987–2000; Architectural Assoc.: art dir of magazine AA Files; Arts Council of GB: design of exhibn catalogues and posters for Dada and Surrealism Reviewed, 1978, Picasso's Picassos, 1981, Renoir, 1985, Torres-Garcia, 1985, Le Corbusier, 1987, Art in Latin America, 1989, Dali: the early years, 1994; Royal Academy: catalogue and graphics for Pompeii AD 79, 1977, graphics and publicity for The Genius of Venice, 1984, Inigo Jones, 1989, Frans Hals, 1990, Egon Schiele, 1990, Mantegna, 1992; Imperial War Museum: graphics for Cabinet War Rooms, Whitehall, 1984; RSA: housestyle, 1989; A. d'Offay Gallery: catalogues and housestyle, 1990–91; design of business print for Cons. Gold Fields, New Statesman, London Merchant Securities and N. M. Rothschild & Sons. Design of BMJ, 1997; illustrations for The Economist, Esquire, Harpers Bazaar (USA), Harpers and Queen, Illustrated London News, Listener, Nova, Observer, Olympia (Paris), Town; book jackets for Jonathan Cape, Penguin Books and Anglo-German Foundn. *Address:* Cunningham Place, NW8 8JU. *T:* (studio) (020) 7721 7705.

BAILEY, Sir Derrick Thomas Louis, 3rd Bt *cr* 1919; DFC; *b* 15 Aug. 1918; 2nd *s* of Sir Abe Bailey, 1st Bt, KCMG; *S* half-brother, 1946; *m* 1st, 1946, Katharine Nancy Stormonth Darling (marr. diss.; she *d* 1998); four *s* one *d*; 2nd, 1980, Mrs Jean Roscoe (marr. diss. 1990; she *d* 1996). *Educ:* Winchester. Engaged in farming. *Recreations:* all sports, all games. *Heir:* *s* John Richard Bailey [*b* 11 June 1947; *m* 1977, Jane, *o d* of John Pearson Gregory; two *s* one *d*]. *Address:* Bluestones, Alderney, CI. *Club:* Rand (Johannesburg).

BAILEY, Air Vice-Marshal Dudley Graham, CB 1979; CBE 1970; Deputy Managing Director, The Services Sound and Vision Corporation (formerly Services Kinema Corporation), 1980–93; Chairman, SSVC Pension Fund, 1993–99; *b* 12 Sept. 1924; *s* of P. J. Bailey and D. M. Bailey (*née* Taylor); *m* 1948, Dorothy Barbara Lovelace-Hunt; two *d*. Pilot trng, Canada, 1943–45; Intell. Officer, Air HQ Italy, 1946–47 and HQ 23 Gp, 1948–49; Berlin Airlift, 1949; Flt Comdr No 50 and 61 Sqdns, Lincolns, 1950–52; exchange duties, USAF, B-36 aircraft, 1952–54; Canberra Sqdn: Flt Comdr, 1955; Sqdn Comdr, 1956; Air Min., 1956–58; Army Staff Coll., Camberley, 1959; OC No 57 (Victor) Sqdn, 1960–62; Air Warfare course, Manby, 1962; Wing Comdr Ops, HQ Air Forces Middle East, 1963–65; MoD Central Staffs, 1965–66; MoD (Air) Directorate of Air Staff Plans, 1966–68; OC RAF Wildenrath, 1968–70; Sen. Personnel Staff Officer, HQ Strike Comd, 1970–71; Royal Coll. of Defence Studies, 1972; Dir of Personnel (Air), RAF, 1972–74; SASO, RAF Germany, 1974–75; Dep. Comdr, RAF Germany, 1975–76; Dir Gen., Personal Services (RAF), MoD, 1976–80, retired. Chm., Central Council, 1990–99, Life Vice Pres., 2000, RAFA. Gov., Piper's Corner Sch., Gt Kingshill, Bucks, 1991–. *Address:* Firs Corner, Abbotswood, Speen, Bucks HP27 0SR. *T:* (01494) 488462. *Club:* Royal Air Force.

BAILEY, Edward Henry; His Honour Judge Bailey; a Circuit Judge, since 2000; *b* 24 May 1949; *s* of Geoffrey Henry Bailey and Ninette Bailey; *m* 1983, Claire Dorothy Ann From; two *d*. *Educ:* King's Sch., Canterbury; Gonville and Caius Coll., Cambridge (MA, LLB). Called to the Bar, Middle Temple, 1970; Lectr, Inns of Court Sch. of Law, 1970–72; in practice as barrister, 1972–2000. *Publications:* Personal Insolvency: law and practice, 1987, 3rd edn 2001; Corporate Insolvency: law and practice, 1992, 2nd edn 2001; (contrib.) Halsbury's Laws of England, 4th edn 1989. *Recreations:* music, gardening.

BAILEY, Glenda Adrianne; Editor-in-Chief, Harper's Bazaar, since 2001; *b* 16 Nov. 1958; *d* of John Ernest Bailey and Constance Groome. *Educ:* Noel Baker Sch., Derby; Kingston Poly. (BA Fashion Design; Hon. MA). Editor: Honey Magazine, 1986; Folio Magazine, 1987; Marie Claire (UK edn), 1988–96; Editor-in-Chief, Marie Claire (US edn), 1996–2001. Women's Magazine Editor of the Year, BSME, 1989, 1992; Editor's Editor of the Year, BSME, 1992; Amnesty Internat. Award, 1997. Hon. PrD Derby, 2001. *Address:* (office) 1700 Broadway, 37th Floor, New York, NY 10019, USA.

BAILEY, Harold William; Chairman, Associated British Foods, since 2000; *b* 16 Nov. 1935; *s* of Harold Wilfred Bailey and Winifred Bailey (*née* Pollard); *m* 1955, Barbara Eileen Stringer (*d* 1999); two *s* one *d. Educ:* John Ruskin Grammar Sch., Croydon. CA 1959. With Thomson McLintock & Co., 1953–62; Associated British Foods plc, 1962–: Financial Dir, 1978–97; Dep. Chm., 1997–99. *Recreations:* sailing, diving, reading, gardening. *Address:* Associated British Foods plc, Weston Centre, Bowater House, 68 Knightsbridge, SW1X 7LQ. *Club:* Royal Automobile.

BAILEY, Jack Arthur; Secretary, MCC, 1974–87; Secretary, International Cricket Conference, 1974–87; *b* 22 June 1930; *s* of Horace Arthur and Elsie Winifred Bailey; *m* 1st, 1957, Julianne Mary Squier (marr. diss.); one *s* two *d*; 2nd, 1991, Vivian Mary Robins. *Educ:* Christ's Hospital; University Coll., Oxford (BA). Asst Master, Bedford Sch., 1958–60; Reed Paper Group, 1960–67; Rugby Football Correspondent, Sunday Telegraph, 1962–74; Asst Sec., MCC, 1967–74. Regular contributor to The Times, 1987–. Mem., Cricket Writers' Club. *Publications:* Conflicts in Cricket, 1989; Trevor Bailey: a life in cricket, 1993. *Recreations:* cricket (played for Essex and for Oxford Univ.), golf. *Address:* Wickets, Dippenhall Street, Crondall, Farnham, Surrey GU10 5NX. *T:* (01252) 851870. *Clubs:* Farmers', MCC; Harlequins Cricket (Pres., 1988–), XL (Pres., 1997–99); Vincent's (Oxford).

BAILEY, John; *see* Bailey, W. J. J.

BAILEY, Sir John Bilsland, KCB 1987 (CB 1982); Chief Adjudicator, 1989–2000, and Director, since 1998, Independent Committee for Supervision of Standards of Telephone Information Services; Chairman, Disciplinary Tribunal of Personal Investment Authority, since 1994; *b* 5 Nov. 1928; *o s* of late Walter Bailey and Ethel Edith Bailey, FRAM (who *m* 2nd, Sir Thomas George Spencer); *m* 1952, Marion Rosemary (*née* Carroll); two *s* one *d. Educ:* Eltham Coll.; University Coll., London (LLB). Solicitor of Supreme Court. Under-Sec. (Legal), Dept of HM Procurator General and Treasury Solicitor, 1973–77; Legal Dir, Office of Fair Trading, 1977–79; Dep. Treasury Solicitor, 1979–84; HM Procurator Gen. and Treasury Solicitor, 1984–88. Pres., Disciplinary Cttee, 1994, Public Interest Dir, 1993–94, LAUTRO; Dir, PIA, 1994–97. Gov., Anglo-European Coll. of Chiropractic, 1990–94. Chm., Westminster Soc., 1994–2000. *Recreations:* historical perambulations.

BAILEY, Rt Rev. Jonathan Sansbury; *see* Derby, Bishop of.

BAILEY, Mark David, PhD; Headmaster, Leeds Grammar School, since 1999; *b* 21 Nov. 1960; *s* of Ronald Bailey and Maureen Bailey (*née* Oates); *m* 1989, Julie Margaret Noy; one *s* one *d. Educ:* Univ. of Durham (BA Econ. Hist. 1982); Corpus Christi Coll., Cambridge (PhD History 1986; Rugby blue, 1982–85). Fellow, Gonville and Caius Coll., Cambridge, 1986–96; Lectr in Local History, Bd of Continuing Educn, Univ. of Cambridge, 1991–96; Fellow, Corpus Christi Coll., Cambridge, 1996–99. Mem. Council, RFU, 1994–98. Played Rugby Union for England, 1984–90 (7 caps); Captain, Suffolk CCC, 1988–90. FRHistS 1999. T. S. Ashton Award, British Econ. Hist. Soc., 1988, 1994. *Publications:* A Marginal Economy?: East Anglian Breckland in the later Middle Ages, 1989; (ed) The Bailiffs' Minute Book of Dunwich 1404–1430, 1992; (with J. Hatcher) Modelling the Middle Ages: the history and theory of England's Economic Development, 2001; various articles in learned jls and contribs to collections of essays on medieval England. *Recreations:* local history, walking, sport, food, music. *Address:* Leeds Grammar School, Alwoodley Gates, Leeds LS17 8GS. *T:* (0113) 229 1552. *Clubs:* East India (Hon. Mem.); Hawks (Cambridge).

BAILEY, Norman Stanley, CBE 1977; operatic and concert baritone; *b* Birmingham, 23 March 1933; *s* of late Stanley and Agnes Bailey; *m* 1st, 1957, Doreen Simpson (marr. diss. 1983); two *s* one *d*; 2nd, 1985, Kristine Ciesinski. *Educ:* Rhodes Univ., S Africa; Vienna State Academy. BMus; Performer's and Teacher's Licentiate in Singing; Diplomas, opera, lieder, oratorio. Principal baritone, Sadler's Wells Opera, 1967–71; regular engagements at world's major opera houses and festivals, including: La Scala, Milan; Royal Opera House, Covent Garden; Bayreuth Wagner Festival (first British Hans Sachs in Meistersinger, 1969); Vienna State Opera (first British Wanderer in Siegfried, 1976); Metropolitan Opera, NY; Chicago Opera; Paris Opera; Edinburgh Festival; Hamburg State Opera; Munich State Opera; Opera North; Glyndebourne Fest. BBC Television performances in Falstaff, La Traviata, The Flying Dutchman, Macbeth. Recordings include The Ring (Goodall); Meistersinger and Der Fliegende Holländer (Solti); Walküre (Klemperer), among others. Hon. RAM, 1981; Hon. DMus, Rhodes, 1986. *Recreations:* Mem., Baha'i world community; chess, notaphily, golf, microcomputing. *Address:* PO Box 655, Victor, ID 83455, USA.

BAILEY, Patrick Edward Robert; Director, Dan-Air Associated Services, 1985–92; *b* 16 Feb. 1925; *s* of late Edward Bailey and Mary Elizabeth Bailey; *m* 1947, Rowena Evelyn Nichols (*d* 1995); two *s* three *d. Educ:* Clapham Coll.; St Joseph's Coll., Mark Cross; LSE. BSc(Econ). MIPM; FCIT 1971 (Mem. Council, 1982–85 and 1987–89). RAPC and RAEC (Captain), 1943–48; Labour Management, Min. of Supply and Army Department: ROF Glascoed, 1951–54; RAE Farnborough, 1954–58; RSAF Enfield, 1958–59; ROF Radway Green, 1959–61; ROFs Woolwich, 1961–66. British Airports Authority: Dep. Personnel Dir, 1966; Personnel Dir, 1970; Airport Services Dir, 1974; Dir, Gatwick and Stansted Airports, 1977–85. Chm. Trustees, British Airports Authority Superannuation Scheme, 1975–86. Mem., Air Transport and Travel Industry Trng Bd, 1971–76; Mem. Bd, Internat. Civil Airports Assoc., 1974–77. Mem., Mid-Sussex DC, 1986–99 (Chm., 1991–93). *Address:* 17 Lucastes Lane, Haywards Heath, W Sussex RH16 1LE.

BAILEY, Paul, (christened **Peter Harry**); freelance writer, since 1967; radio broadcaster; *b* 16 Feb. 1937; *s* of Arthur Oswald Bailey and Helen Maud Burgess. *Educ:* Sir Walter St John's Sch., London; Central School of Speech and Drama. Actor, 1956–64: appeared in first productions of Ann Jellicoe's The Sport of My Mad Mother, 1958, and John Osborne's and Anthony Creighton's Epitaph for George Dillon, 1958. Literary Fellow at Univ. of Newcastle and Univ. of Durham, 1972–74; Bicentennial Fellowship, 1976; Visiting Lectr in English Literature, North Dakota State Univ., 1977–79. Frequent radio broadcaster, mainly on Radio 3; has written and presented programmes on Karen Blixen, Henry Green, I. B. Singer and Primo Levi, among others. FRSL, 1982–84. E. M. Forster Award, 1974; George Orwell Meml Prize, 1978, for broadcast essay The Limitations of Despair. *Publications:* At the Jerusalem, 1967 (Somerset Maugham Award, 1968; Arts Council Prize, 1968); Trespasses, 1970; A Distant Likeness, 1973; Peter Smart's Confessions, 1977; Old Soldiers, 1980; An English Madam, 1982; Gabriel's Lament, 1986; An Immaculate Mistake: scenes from childhood and beyond (autobiog.), 1990; Sugar Cane, 1993; (ed) The Oxford Book of London, 1995; (ed) First Love, 1997; Kitty and Virgil, 1998; (ed) The Stately Homo: a celebration of the life of Quentin Crisp, 2000; Three Queer Lives (Fred Barnes, Naomi Jacob and Arthur Marshall), 2001; contribs to Observer, TLS, Daily Telegraph, Guardian. *Recreations:* wandering in Eastern Europe, visiting churches, chamber music, watching tennis. *Address:* 79 Davisville Road, W12 9SH. *T:* (020) 8749 2279, *T:* and, *Fax:* (020) 8248 2127.

BAILEY, Sir Richard (John), Kt 1984; CBE 1977; Deputy Chairman, British Ceramic Research Limited, 1990–94 (Chairman, 1982–83 and 1987–90); Director, Central Independent Television plc, 1986–94; *b* 8 July 1923; *s* of Philip Bailey and Doris Margaret (*née* Freebody); *m* 1945, Marcia Rachel Cureton Webb; one *s* three *d. Educ:* Newcastle; Shrewsbury. FICeram 1955 (Founder Fellow). Served RNVR 1942–46 (Lieut). Doulton Fine China Ltd: Technical Dir, 1955–63; Man. Dir, 1963–72; Dir, Doulton & Co. Ltd, 1967–82; Man. Dir, Royal Doulton Tableware Ltd, 1972–80, Chm., 1980–83; Chairman: Royal Crown Derby Porcelain Co. Ltd, 1983–87; Royal Doulton Ltd, 1983–87. Member: Ceramics Industry Nat. Jt Council, 1961–84 (Jt Chm., 1969–84); Ceramic Industry Training Bd, 1967–70; Dir, W Midlands Industrial Develt Assoc., 1983–87; President: BCMF, 1973–74; British Ceramic Soc., 1980–81; Chm., North Staffs Business Initiative, 1981–91. Pres., North Staffs Med. Inst., 1987–99. Hon. Freeman, City of Stoke-on-Trent, 1987. Hon. Fellow, Staffordshire Univ. (formerly Poly.), 1988. MUniv Keele, 1983. FRSA 1977. *Recreations:* golf, walking, gardening. *Address:* Green Cottage, Vicarage Lane, Barlaston, Stoke-on-Trent ST12 9AG.

BAILEY, Ronald William, CMG 1961; HM Diplomatic Service, retired; *b* 14 June 1917; *o s* of William Staveley Bailey and May Eveline (*née* Cudlipp), Southampton; *m* 1946, Joan Hassall (*d* 2001), *d* of late A. E. Gray, JP, Stoke-on-Trent; one *s* one *d. Educ:* King Edward VI Sch., Southampton; Trinity Hall, Cambridge (Wootton Isaacson Scholar in Spanish). Probationer Vice-Consul, Beirut, 1939–41; HM Vice-Consul, Alexandria, 1941–45; Asst Oriental Sec., British Embassy, Cairo, 1945–48; 1st Sec., Foreign Office, 1948–49; British Legation, Beirut, 1949–52 (acted as Chargé d'Affaires, 1949, 1950 and 1951); British Embassy, Washington, 1952–55; Counsellor, Washington, 1955–57; Khartoum, 1957–60 (acted as Chargé d'Affaires in each of these years); Chargé d'Affaires, Taiz, 1960–62; Consul-Gen., Gothenburg, 1963–65; Minister, British Embassy, Baghdad, 1965–67; Ambassador to Bolivia, 1967–71; Ambassador to Morocco, 1971–75. Mem. Council, Anglo-Arab Assoc., 1978–85. Vice-Pres., 1975–87, Pres., 1987–89, Hon. Vice-Pres., 1989–2001, Soc. for Protection of Animals Abroad; Chm., Black Down Cttee, Nat. Trust, 1982–87; Founder, 1975, Hon. Pres., 1989–1998, British-Moroccan Soc. *Publication:* (ed) Records of Oman 1867–1960 (12 vols), 1989–92. *Recreations:* walking, photography, gardening. *Address:* Redwood, Tennyson's Lane, Haslemere, Surrey GU27 3AF. *T:* (01428) 642800. *Club:* Oriental.

BAILEY, Sir Stanley (Ernest), Kt 1986; CBE 1980; QPM 1975; DL; security consultant; *b* 30 Sept. 1926; *m* 1st, 1954, Marguerita Dorothea Whitbread (*d* 1997); 2nd, 1998, Maureen Shinwell. Joined Metropolitan Police, 1947; Asst Chief Constable, Staffs, 1966; Dir, Police Res., Home Office, 1970–72; Dep. Chief Constable, Staffs, 1973–75; Chief Constable, Northumbria, 1975–91; Regl Police Comdr, No 1 Home Defence Reg., 1981–91. Mem., IACP, 1970 (Chairman: Adv. Cttee on Internat. Policy, 1984–89; Europ. Sub-Cttee, 1984–89; Mem. Exec. Cttee, 1986–91; Life Mem., 1999); Rep., ICPO, 1986–88. Pres., ACPO, England, Wales & NI, 1985–86 (Vice-Pres., 1984–85; Immediate Past Pres., 1986–87; Chm., Crime Prevention Sub-cttee, 1986–91); Vice Pres., Police Mutual Assce Soc., 1986–94. Chairman: Cttee on Burglar Alarms, BSI, 1975–93; Cttee on Security Standards, BSI, 1976–93; Founder and Chm., 1st Internat. Police Exhibn and Conf., London, 1987; Founder and Jt Chm., Centre for Res. into Crime, Community and Policing, Univ. of Newcastle upon Tyne, 1989–92; Vice Chm., Crime Concern, 1989–93 (Mem., Adv. Bd, 1988–94); Member: Home Office Standing Conf. on Crime Prevention, 1977–91; Bd, Northumbria Coalition Against Crime, 1989–92; Chm. of cttees and working parties on crime prevention, intruder alarms, criminal intelligence, computer privacy, and physical stress in police work. Pres., Security Systems and Alarms Inspection Bd, 1995–. Observer, VIII UN Congress on Crime Prevention, Havana, 1990 (Organiser and Chm., First UN Meeting of Sen. Police Officials). Police Advr, AMA, 1987–91. President: Security Services Assoc., 1991–95; Security Services and Alarms Inspectorate Bd, 1995–; Ex Police in Commerce, 1998– (Vice Pres., 1992–98). Has presented papers etc in USA, Denmark, France, Hong Kong, NZ, Japan, Germany, Spain, Thailand, China, Holland, Portugal, Italy, Belgium and USSR on community crime prevention, measurement of effectiveness, and Private Security industry. Mem., NEI Associates, USA, 1984–. Trustee, Suzy Lamplugh Trust, 1991–93. Patron, Assoc. of Security Consultants, 1992–. Mem., Bd of Govs, Internat. Inst. of Security, 1990–. Grad., Nat. Exec. Inst., FBI Washington, 1984. Freeman, City of London, 1988. CIMgt (CBIM 1987). DL Tyne and Wear, 1986. ABIS—Ken Bolton Award for outstanding contribution to crime prevention, 1990. OStJ 1981. *Publications:* (jtly) Community Policing and Crime Prevention in America and England, 1993; articles in learned jls on policy issues. *Recreations:* gardening, travel. *Address:* 2 Hadrian Court, Darras Hall, Ponteland, Newcastle upon Tyne NE20 9JU.

BAILEY, Thomas Aubrey, MBE 1959; Senior Architect responsible for Ancient Monuments, Ministry of Public Building and Works, 1954–69; Director, Peter Cox Ltd, Building Restoration Specialists (Member of SGB Group of Cos), 1970–76; *b* 20 Jan. 1912; *o s* of late Thomas Edward Bailey and Emma Bailey; *m* 1944, Joan Woodman, *d* of late John Woodman Hooper; one *s. Educ:* Adams' Grammar Sch., Newport, Shropshire; Regent Street Polytechnic Sch. of Architecture. RIBA 1948. Entered HM Office of Works, Ancient Monuments Br., 1935; Asst Architect, 1945–49; Architect, London and E Anglia, 1949–54. Architectural Advr to Oxford Historic Bldgs Fund, 1963–69. Served on various cttees on stone decay and preservation; seconded to Sir Giles G. Scott, OM, RA, for Rebuilding of House of Commons, 1944–49. *Principal works:* Direction of MPBW Survey for Oxford Historic Bldg Appeal, 1957–62 and Cambridge Appeal, 1963; re-erection of fallen Trilithons at Stonehenge, 1958–64; Conservation of Claudian Aqueduct and Aurelian Wall, Brit. Embassy at Rome, 1957–69; etc. Resigned professional membership of RIBA and ARCUK, to enter specialised Bldg Industry, 1969. Mem. Conservation Cttee, for Council for Places of Worship, 1968; Mem. Council, 1970–, and Vice-Pres., Ancient Monuments Soc. FSA 1957; FRSA 1969; Fellow of Faculty of Bldg, 1970. Freeman of City of London, 1967; Freeman and Liveryman, Worshipful Company of Masons, 1973 (Hon. Court of Assts). Hon. MA Oxon, 1963. *Publications:* (jointly) The Claudian Aqueduct in the Grounds of the British Embassy, Rome, 1966; many technical reports on conservation of Historic Monuments. *Recreations:* music, photography, travel, motoring. *Address:* 32 Anne Boleyn's Walk, Cheam, Sutton, Surrey SM3 8DF. *T:* (020) 8642 3185. *Club:* City Livery.

BAILEY, (William) John (Joseph); journalist; Editor, Northern Cross, since 1981; *b* 11 June 1940; *s* of Ernest Robert Bailey and Josephine Smith; *m* 1963, Maureen Anne, *d* of James Gibbs Neenan and Marjorie Dorema Wrigglesworth; five *s* three *d. Educ:* St Joseph's, Stanford-le-Hope, Essex; Campion Hall, Jamaica; St George's Coll., Kingston, Jamaica; St Chad's Coll., Wolverhampton. Reporter: Southend Standard, Essex, and Essex and Thurrock Gazette, 1960–63; Northern Daily Mail, 1963–64; Chief Reporter, Billingham and Stockton Express, 1964–72; Sub-Editor, Mail, Hartlepool, 1972–75; Features Editor, Echo, Sunderland, 1975–97; Asst Media Officer, Sunderland City

Council, 1998–. Member: Press Council, 1974–80; Complaints Cttee, 1974–76, 1977–; Cttee for Evidence to Royal Commission on Press, 1975–76; Gen. Purposes Cttee, 1976–77; Secretariat Cttee, 1976–80. Nat. Union of Journalists: Mem., Nat. Exec. Council, 1966–82; Vice-Pres., 1972–73; Pres., 1973–74; Gen. Treasurer, 1975–83; Mem. of Honour, 1999. Sec., Hartlepool People Ltd, 1983–. Provincial Journalist of the Year (jtly with Carol Roberton), British Press Awards, 1977 (commended, 1979); Special award Northern Cross, Tom Cordner North East Press Awards, 1984–85, 1989, 1992, 1996, 1997. *Address:* 225 Park Road, Hartlepool TS26 9NG. *T:* (01429) 264577. *Clubs:* Press (Glasgow); Iona (Hartlepool).

BAILHACHE, Sir Philip (Martin), Kt 1996; Bailiff of Jersey, since 1995 (Deputy Bailiff, 1994–95); a Judge of the Court of Appeal, Jersey, since 1994, and Guernsey, since 1996; *b* 28 Feb. 1946; *s* of Jurat Lester Vivian Bailhache (Lieut-Bailiff of Jersey, 1980–82) and late Nanette Ross (*née* Ferguson); *m* 1st, 1967 (marr. diss. 1982); two *s* two *d*; 2nd, 1984, Linda (*née* Le Vavasseur dit Durell); one *s* one *d*. *Educ:* Charterhouse; Pembroke Coll., Oxford (Hon. Fellow, 1995). Called to the Bar, Middle Temple, 1968; called to the Jersey Bar, 1969; QC (Jersey) 1989. In private practice as Advocate, Jersey, 1969–74; States of Jersey Dep. for Grouville, 1972–74; Solicitor-Gen., Jersey, 1975–85; Attorney Gen. for Jersey, 1986–93. Chm., Jersey Arts Council, 1987–89. Editor, Jersey Law Review, 1997–. *Recreations:* books, wine, gardening, the arts. *Address:* L'Anquetinerie, Grouville, Jersey, Channel Islands JE3 9UX. *T:* (01534) 852533. *Clubs:* Reform; United (Jersey).
See also W. J. Bailhache.

BAILHACHE, William James; QC 2000; HM Attorney General for Jersey, since 2000; *b* 24 June 1953; *s* of Jurat Lester Vivian Bailhache, sometime Lieut Bailiff of Jersey, and late Nanette Ross Bailhache (*née* Ferguson); *m* 1975, Jennifer Laura Nudds; one *s* one *d*. *Educ:* Charterhouse; Merton Coll., Oxford (MA). Called to the Bar, Middle Temple, 1975; Advocate, Royal Court of Jersey, 1976; Partner, Bailhache & Bailhache, 1977–94, Bailhache Labesse, 1994–99. Chm., Barclays Bank Finance Co. (Jersey) Ltd, 1996–99 (Dir, 1982–99); Dir, Jersey Gas Co. Ltd, 1992–94. *Recreations:* golf, tennis, ski-ing, reading, opera. *Address:* Seymour House, La Rocque, Jersey JE3 9BB. *T:* (01534) 854708. *Clubs:* Oxford and Cambridge; Vincent's (Oxford); Royal Jersey Golf (Captain, 1995–96).
See also Sir P. M. Bailhache.

BAILIE, Robert Ernest, (Roy), OBE 1995; Chairman, W. & G. Baird (Holdings) Ltd, since 1982; *b* 2 June 1943; s of Robert and Rosetta Bailie; *m* 1971, Paddy Clark; two *s* one *d*. *Educ:* Belfast High Sch.; Queen's Univ., Belfast; Harvard Sch. of Business (grad. 1985). MSO Ltd, 1958–65; joined W. & G. Baird, 1965, Man. Dir, 1972, led mgt buy-out, 1977; Director: W. & G. Baird Ltd, 1977–; Graphic Plates Ltd, 1977–; MSO Ltd, 1984–; Textflow Services Ltd, 1987–; Biddles Ltd, 1989–; Blackstaff Press Ltd, 1995–; Thanet Press Ltd, 1995–; Court, Bank of Ireland, 1999– (Mem., NI Adv. Bd, 1994–98); Corporate Document Services Ltd, 2000–; non-executive Director: UTV, 1997–; Bank of England, 1998–. Pres., BPIF, 1999– (Mem., Exec. Bd of Mgt, 1978–80, Chm., 1980–84, NW Reg.; Vice-Pres., 1997–99). Member: NI Council for Higher Educn, 1985–90; IDB for NI, 1990–95; Adv. Council on Alcohol and Drug Educn, 1990–99; Chairman: CBI (NI), 1992–94; NI Tourist Bd, 1996–. *Recreations:* sailing, golf, walking. *Address:* 60 Ballymena Road, Doagh, Ballyclare, Co. Antrim BT39 0QR. *T:* (028) 9334 0383.

BAILIE, Rt Hon. Robin John; PC (NI) 1971; Solicitor of the Supreme Court of Judicature, Northern Ireland, since 1961; *b* 6 March 1937; *m* 1961, Margaret F. (*née* Boggs); one *s* three *d*. *Educ:* Rainey Endowed Sch. Magherafelt, Co. Londonderry; The Queen's Univ. of Belfast (LLB). MP (NI) for Newtonabbey, 1969–72; Minister of Commerce, Govt of NI, 1971–72. *Recreations:* wine drinking, ski-ing, squash, golf, tennis. *Address:* Calle del Cieruo 18, Los Monteros, Marbella 29600, Spain. *T:* (34) 52775568.

BAILIE, Roy; *see* Bailie, Robert E.

BAILLIE, family name of **Baron Burton**.

BAILLIE, Alastair Turner; HM Diplomatic Service, retired; Deputy High Commissioner in Calcutta, 1987–91; *b* 24 Dec. 1932; *s* of late Archibald Turner Baillie and Margaret Pinkerton Baillie; *m* 1st, 1965, Wilma Noreen Armstrong (marr. diss. 1974); one *s*; 2nd, 1977, Irena Maria Gregor; one step *s* one step *d*. *Educ:* Dame Allan's Sch., Newcastle upon Tyne; Christ's Coll., Cambridge (BA). National Service, commissioned Queen's Own Cameron Highlanders, 1951–53. HMOCS: North Borneo, subseq. Sabah, Malaysia, 1957–67; joined HM Diplomatic Service, 1967; FCO, 1967–73; Consul (Commercial), Karachi, 1973–77; First Sec. and Head of Chancery, Manila, 1977–80; Counsellor, Addis Ababa, 1980–81; Counsellor (Commercial), Caracas, 1981–83; Governor of Anguilla, 1983–87. *Recreations:* sport, reading, travelling.

BAILLIE, Alexander; 'cellist; *b* 1956; *m* Christel; one *s* two *d*. *Educ:* Royal Coll. of Music; Hochschule für Musik, Vienna; studied with Jacqueline du Pré. Soloist with LSO, BBC SO, CBSO and orchestras worldwide; premières of works include Colin Matthew's Cello Concerto, 1984, Penderecki's 2nd Cello Concerto, and concerti by H. K. Gruber and Andrew MacDonald; recitals include Bach's Cello Suites (unaccompanied), Wigmore Hall, 1997; also appears with chamber music ensembles; Member: Villiers Piano Quartet; Heveningham Hall Piano Trio; Alia Musica, Berlin; formerly Mem., The Fires of London. Vis. Prof., Royal Coll. of Music; Prof. of Cello, Bremen Hochschule. *Address:* c/o TransArt (UK) Ltd, 8 Bristol Gardens, W9 2JG.

BAILLIE, Andrew Bruce, QC 2001; a Recorder, since 1989; *b* 17 May 1948; *s* of Edward Oswald Baillie and Molly Eva (Renée) Baillie (*née* Andrews); *m* 1976, Mary Lou Meech Palmer (*d* 1988); one *s* two *d*. *Educ:* King's Coll. Sch., Wimbledon; Univ. de Besançon; Univ. of Kent at Canterbury (BA Social Scis 1969). called to the Bar, Inner Temple, 1970. *Recreations:* numerous. *Address:* 9 Gough Square, EC4A 3DE. *T:* (020) 7832 0500; *e-mail:* clerks@9goughsq.co.uk.

BAILLIE, Sir Gawaine George Hope, 7th Bt *cr* 1823, of Polkemmet, Linlithgowshire; *b* 8 March 1934; *s* of Sir Adrian Baillie, 6th Bt, and Hon. Olive Cecilia (*d* 1974), *d* of 1st Baron Queenborough, GBE; *S* father, 1947; *m* 1966, Margot, *d* of Senator Louis Beaubien, Montreal; one *s* one *d*. *Heir: s* Adrian Louis Baillie; *b* 26 March 1973. *Address:* Freechase, Warninglid, Sussex RH17 5SZ.

BAILLIE, Ian Fowler, CMG 1966; OBE 1962; Director, The Thistle Foundation, Edinburgh, 1970–81; *b* 16 Feb. 1921; *s* of late Very Rev. Principal John Baillie, CH, DLitt, DD, LLD and Florence Jewel (*née* Fowler); *m* 1951, Sheila Barbour (*née* Mathewson); two *s* one *d*. *Educ:* Edinburgh Acad.; Corpus Christi Coll., Oxford (MA). War service, British and Indian Armies, 1941–46. HM Overseas Civil Service (formerly Colonial Service), 1946–66: Admin. Officer (District Comr), Gold Coast, 1946–54; Registrar of Co-operative Socs and Chief Marketing Officer, Aden, 1955; Protectorate Financial Sec., Aden, 1959; Dep. British Agent, Aden, 1962; Brit. Agent and Asst High Comr, Aden, 1963; Dir, Aden Airways 1959–66; Sen. Research Associate and Administrative Officer, Agricultural Adjustment Unit, Dept of Agricultural Economics, Univ. of Newcastle upon Tyne, 1966–69. *Publication:* (ed with S. J. Sheehy) Irish Agriculture in a Changing World, 1971. *Recreation:* angling. *Address:* Flat 4, 61 Grange Loan, Edinburgh EH9 2EG. *T:* (0131) 667 2647.

BAILLIE, Jacqueline (Jackie); Member (Lab) Dumbarton, Scottish Parliament, since 1999; Minister for Social Justice, since 2000; *b* Hong Kong, 15 Jan. 1964; *d* of Frank and Sophie Barnes; *m* 1982, Stephen, *s* of James and Margaret Baillie; one *d*. Resource Centre Manager, Strathkelvin DC, 1990–96; Community Economic Develt Manager, E Dumbartonshire Council, 1996–99. A Dep. Minister for Communities, Scottish Parlt, 1999–2000. Chair, Scottish Labour Party, 1997–98 (Mem., Exec. Cttee, 1990–99). *Address:* Scottish Parliament, Edinburgh EH99 1SP.

BAILLIE, Prof. John, CA; Visiting Professor of Accountancy: Heriot-Watt University, since 1989; University of Glasgow, since 1996; Partner, Scott-Moncrieff, since 1993; *b* 7 Oct. 1944; *s* of Arthur and Agnes Baillie; *m* 1972, Annette Alexander; one *s* one *d*. *Educ:* Whitehill Sch. CA 1967 (Gold Medal and Distinction in final exams). Partner, Thomson McLintock & Co., later KPMG Peat Marwick, 1978–93. Johnstone-Smith Prof. of Accountancy, Univ. of Glasgow, 1983–88. Convenor, Res. Cttee, 1995–99, and Mem. various technical and professional affairs cttees, Inst. of Chartered Accountants of Scotland. FRSA 1996. Hon. MA Glasgow, 1983. *Publications:* Systems of Profit Measurement, 1985; Consolidated Accounts and the Seventh Directive, 1985; technical and professional papers; contribs to Accountants' Magazine and other professional jls. *Recreations:* keeping fit, reading, music, golf. *Address:* The Glen, Glencairn Road, Kilmacolm, Renfrewshire PA13 4PB. *T:* (01505) 873254. *Club:* Western (Glasgow).

BAILLIE, William James Laidlaw, CBE 1998; RSA 1979 (ARSA 1968); PPRSW (PRSW 1974 RSW 1963); painter; President, Royal Scottish Academy, 1990–98 (Treasurer, 1980–90); *b* 19 April 1923; *s* of James and Helen Baillie; *m* 1961, Helen Gillon; one *s* two *d*. *Educ:* Dunfermline High Sch.; Edinburgh College of Art (Andrew Grant Schol., 1941–50; Dip. Drawing and Painting 1950). Studies interrupted by war service with Royal Corps of Signals, mainly in Far East, 1942–47. Taught in Edinburgh schools, 1951–60; Mem., Teaching Staff, Edin. College of Art, 1960–88, Sen. Lectr, 1968–88; Visiting Tutor, National Gallery of Canada Summer Sch., near Ottawa, 1955. Exhibits at Thackeray Gall., London, but mostly in Scotland, mainly at Scottish Gall., Edinburgh; first retrospective exhibn in Kirkcaldy Art Gallery, 1977. *Recreations:* music, travel. *Address:* 6A Esslemont Road, Edinburgh EH16 5PX. *T:* (0131) 667 1538.

BAILLIE-HAMILTON, family name of **Earl of Haddington**.

BAILLIEU, family name of **Baron Baillieu**.

BAILLIEU, 3rd Baron *cr* 1953, of Sefton, Australia and Parkwood, Surrey; **James William Latham Baillieu;** Director: Anthony Baillieu and Associates (Hong Kong) Ltd, since 1992; CentreInvest Group, Moscow, since 1996; Managing Director, Bank NIKoil, since 2000; *b* 16 Nov. 1950; *s* of 2nd Baron Baillieu and Anne Bayliss, *d* of Leslie William Page, Southport, Queensland; *S* father, 1973; *m* 1st, 1974, Cornelia Masters Ladd (marr. diss. 1985), *d* of William Ladd; one *s*; 2nd, 1986, Clare Stephenson (marr. diss. 1995), *d* of Peter Stephenson. *Educ:* Radley College; Monash Univ., Melbourne (BEc 1977). Short Service Commission, Coldstream Guards, 1970–73. Banque Nationale de Paris, 1978–80; Asst Dir, Rothschild Australia Ltd, 1980–88; Dir, Manufacturers Hanover Australia Ltd, 1988–90; Dir, Standard Chartered Asia Ltd, 1990–92; Asst Dir, Credit Lyonnais Asia Ltd, 1992–94; Asst Dir, Nomura International (Hong Kong) Ltd, 1995; Gen. Dir, Regent European Securities, 1995–96. *Heir: s* Hon. Robert Latham Baillieu, *b* 2 Feb. 1979. *Address:* Post International Box 148, 2 Gales Gardens, Birbeck Street, E2 0EJ. *Clubs:* Boodle's; Hong Kong (Hong Kong); Australian (Melbourne).

BAILLIEU, Colin Clive; Lecturer: European Business School, London, since 1995; London College of Printing, since 1998; Member, Monopolies and Mergers Commission, 1984–93; *b* 2 July 1930; *s* of Ian Baillieu and Joanna Baillieu (*née* Brinton); *m* 1st, 1955, Diana Robinson (marr. diss. 1968); two *d*; 2nd, 1968, Renata Richter; two *s*. *Educ:* Dragon Sch.; Eton. Commissioned Coldstream Guards, 1949. Local newspaper, Evening Standard, 1951–52; British Metal Corp., 1952–58; British Aluminium, 1958–60; Monsanto Fibres, 1960–66; Arthur Sanderson, 1966–68; Ultrasonic Machines, 1968–76. Chm., Gresham Underwriting Agencies, 1990–92. Mem., Council of Lloyd's, 1983–88. Contested (C) Rossendale, Lancs, 1964 and 1966. Dir, Orchestra of St John's, Smith Square, 1999–2000. Dist Comr, Cowdray Pony Club, 1998–. *Publication:* The Lion and the Lamb, 1996. *Recreations:* ski-ing, teaching boys to play polo, 17th Century history. *Address:* Hoyle Farm, Heyshott, Midhurst, West Sussex GU29 0DY. *T:* (01798) 867230. *Clubs:* Travellers, Beefsteak, Shikar, MCC.

BAIN, Andrew David, OBE 1997; FRSE 1980; Visiting Professor of Political Economy, University of Glasgow, 1991–98, now Hon. Professor; *b* 21 March 1936; *s* of Hugh Bain and Kathleen (*née* Eadie); *m* 1st, 1960, Anneliese Minna Frieda Kroggel (marr. diss. 1988); three *s*; 2nd, 1989, Eleanor Riches. *Educ:* Glasgow Academy; Christ's Coll., Cambridge. PhD Cantab 1963. Junior Res. Officer, Dept of Applied Econs, Cambridge Univ., 1958–60; Res. Fellow, Christ's Coll., Cambridge, 1960; Instructor, Cowles Foundn, Yale Univ., 1960–61; Lectr, Cambridge, 1961–66; Fellow, Corpus Christi Coll., Cambridge, 1962; on secondment to Bank of England, 1965–67; Prof. of Econs, 1967–70, Esmee Fairbairn Prof. of Econs of Finance and Investment, 1970–77, Univ. of Stirling; Walton Prof. of Monetary and Financial Econs, Univ. of Strathclyde, 1977–84; Gp Econ. Advr, Midland Bank, 1984–90. Member: Cttee to Review the Functioning of Financial Institutions, 1977–80; (part-time) Monopolies and Mergers Commn, 1981–82; TEC Nat. Council, 1994–97; (part-time) Appeal Panel, Competition Commn, 2000–. Bd Mem., Scottish Enterprise, 1991–98. *Publications:* The Growth of Television Ownership in the United Kingdom (monograph), 1964; The Control of the Money Supply, 1970; Company Financing in the UK, 1975; The Economics of the Financial System, 1981, 2nd edn 1992; articles on demand analysis, monetary policy and other subjects. *Address:* 1 Stafford Street, Helensburgh, Dunbartonshire G84 9HU.

BAIN, Douglas John; Industrial Adviser to the Secretary of State for Scotland, 1983–85; *b* 9 July 1924; *s* of Alexander Gillan Bain and Fanny Heaford; *m* 1946, Jean Wallace Fairbairn; three *d*. *Educ:* Pollokshields Secondary School; Royal Technical Coll. (now Strathclyde Univ.), Glasgow (DRTC). ATI. Royal Tech. Coll., 1941–43 and 1948–51. RAF, 1943–48. J. & P. Coats Ltd, 1951–83: graduate trainee, 1951–55; overseas management, 1955–60; central management, 1960–68; Director, 1968–83; seconded to Scottish Office (Scottish Econ. Planning Dept) as Under Sec., 1979–82. *Recreations:* golf, walking, geology, flying. *Address:* 49 Bimbadeen Crescent, Yallambie, Melbourne, Vic 3085, Australia.

BAIN, Sir George Sayers, Kt 2001; DPhil; President and Vice-Chancellor, Queen's University of Belfast, since 1998; *b* 24 Feb. 1939; *s* of George Alexander Bain and Margaret Ioleen Bamford; *m* 1st, 1962, Carol Lynn Ogden White (marr. diss. 1987); one *s* one *d*; 2nd, 1988, Frances Gwynneth Rigby (*née* Vickers). *Educ:* Univ. of Manitoba (BA Hons

1961, MA 1964); Oxford Univ. (DPhil 1968). Lectr in Econs, Univ. of Manitoba, 1962–63; Res. Fellow, Nuffield Coll., Oxford, 1966–69; Frank Thomas Prof. of Indust. Relations, UMIST, 1969–70; University of Warwick: Dep. Dir, 1970–74, Dir, 1974–81, SSRC Industrial Relations Res. Unit; Pressed Steel Fisher Prof. of Industrial Relations, 1979–89; Chm., Sch. of Industrial and Business Studies, 1983–89; Principal, London Business Sch., 1989–97. Sec., British Univs Indust. Relations Assoc., 1971–74. Member: Mech. Engrg Econ. Develt Cttee, NEDO, 1974–76; Cttee of Inquiry on Indust. Democracy, Dept of Trade (Chm., Lord Bullock), 1975–76; Council: ESRC, 1986–91; Nat. Forum for Management Educn and Develt, 1987–90; Chm. Council, Univ. Management Schs, 1987–90. Member: Bd of Trustees, 1990–96, and Exec. Vice-Pres., 1991–95, European Foundn for Management Develt; Internat. Affairs Cttee, 1990–92, Bd of Dirs, 1992–94, Amer. Assembly of Collegiate Schs of Business; Council, Foundn for Management Educn, 1991–95; Council, IMgt (formerly BIM), 1991–93; Senior Salaries Review Body, 1993–96; Internat. Council, Amer. Management Assoc., 1993–95; Foundn for Canadian Studies in UK, 1993–; Exec. Cttee, Co-operation Ireland GB, 1994–97 (Dep. Chm., 1996–97); Bd of Dirs, Grad. Mgt Admission Council, 1996–97; Bd of Co-operation, Ireland, 1998–; Trustee: Navan at Armagh, 1999–; Scotch-Irish Trust, 1999–. Chairman: Food Sector Wkg Gp, NEDO, 1991–92; Commn on Public Policy and British Business, 1995–97; Low Pay Commn, 1997–2001; NI Meml Fund, 1998–; Conf. of Univ. Rectors in Ireland, 2000–01. Director: Blackwell Publishers Ltd (formerly Basil Blackwell Ltd), 1990–97; The Economist Gp, 1992–; Canada Life Gp (UK) Ltd, 1994–; Canada Life Assce Co., 1996–; Electra Investment Trust PLC, 1998–; Bombardier Aerospace Shorts Brothers Plc, 1998–; NI Sci. Park Foundn, 1999–; NI Adv. Bd, Bank of Ireland, 2000–. Consultant: Royal Commn on Trade Unions and Employers' Assocs (Donovan Commn), 1966–67; NBPI, 1967–69; Canadian Task Force on Labour Relns, 1968; acted as Consultant to Dept of Employment, and to the Manitoba and Canada Depts of Labour; arbitrator and mediator in indust. disputes. FRSA 1987; CIMgt 1991; Fellow: British Acad. of Mgt, 1994; London Business Sch., 1999; AcSS Hon. DBA De Montfort, 1994; Hon. LLD: NUI, 1998; Guelph, 1999; UC of Cape Breton, 1999. *Publications:* Trade Union Growth and Recognition, 1967; The Growth of White-Collar Unionism, 1970; (jtly) The Reform of Collective Bargaining at Plant and Company Level, 1971; (jtly) Social Stratification and Trade Unionism, 1973; (jtly) Union Growth and the Business Cycle, 1976; (jtly) A Bibliography of British Industrial Relations, 1979; (jtly) Profiles of Union Growth, 1980; (ed) Industrial Relations in Britain, 1983; (jtly) A Bibliography of British Industrial Relations 1971–1979, 1985; contrib. prof. and learned jls. *Recreations:* reading, genealogy, family history, Western riding. *Address:* Queen's University of Belfast, Belfast BT7 1NN. *T:* (028) 9033 5130. *Club:* Reform.

BAIN, Iain Andrew; Editor, Nairnshire Telegraph, since 1987; *b* 25 Feb. 1949; *s* of Alistair I. R. Bain and late Jean R. Forrest; *m* 1974, Maureen Beattie; three *d*. *Educ:* Nairn Acad.; Univ. of Aberdeen (MA). Research, Univ. of Durham, 1971–74; Sub-editor, 1974, Asst Editor, 1980, Editor, 1981–87, The Geographical Magazine. *Publications:* Mountains and People, 1982; Water on the Land, 1983; Mountains and Earth Movements, 1984; various articles. *Recreations:* reading, walking, photography, gardening. *Address:* Rosebank, Leopold Street, Nairn IV12 4BE. *Club:* Nairn Golf.

BAIN, Janet; *see* Rossant, J.

BAIN, John; *see* Bain, K. J.

BAIN, John Taylor, CBE 1975; Director of Education, Glasgow, 1968–75; Lay Observer (Solicitors Act) in Scotland, 1977–83; *b* 9 May 1912; *m*; one *s* two *d*. *Educ:* St Andrews Univ. (BSc, MA); Edinburgh Univ. (BEd). War Service, RAF (Technical Br.). Entered educational administration in 1947. JP Glasgow, 1971.

BAIN, (Kenneth) John, OBE 2000; MA; Headmaster, The Purcell School, 1983–99; *b* 8 July 1939; *s* of Allan John and Hetty Bain; *m* 1962, Cynthia Mary Spain; one *s* one *d*. *Educ:* Bancroft's School; St Peter's College, Oxford (MA). Assistant Master, Stanbridge Earls School, 1962–70; Assistant Master and Housemaster, Cranleigh School, 1970–83. Governor: The Abbey Sch., Tewkesbury, 1999–(Chm., 2001–); Arts Educnl Sch., Tring, 1999–. Dir, Endymion Ensemble, 1999–. FRSA 1992. Hon. RCM 1999. *Publications:* occasional articles in educational jls. *Recreations:* music, golf, walking, rough gardening. *Address:* Candida House, Whitechurch Canonicorum, Bridport, Dorset DT6 6RQ. *T:* (01297) 489629.

BAIN, Neville Clifford, FCA, FCIS; Chairman: Hogg Robinson Plc, since 1997; Post Office, since 1998; SHL Group, since 1998 (non-executive Director, since 1997); *b* 14 July 1940; *s* of Charles Alexander Bain and Gertrude Mae Bain; *m* 1987, Anne Patricia (*née* Kemp); one step *d*, and one *s* one *d* by previous marriage. *Educ:* King's High Sch., Dunedin, NZ; Otago Univ., Dunedin (BCom Acctcy 1964; BCom Econ 1966; MCom Hons 1968). CMA; ACA 1959, FCA 1989; FCIS 1962. Trainee Inspector, Inland Revenue, NZ, 1957–59; Manager, Anderson & Co., Chartered Accountants, NZ, 1960–62; Cadbury Schweppes Hudson: Cost Accountant, subseq. Financial Controller, and Co. Sec., NZ, 1963–68; Finance Dir, NZ, 1968–75; Cadbury Schweppes: Group Chief Exec., S Africa, 1975–80; Group Strategic Planning Dir, 1980–83 (apptd to Main Bd, 1981); Managing Director: Cadbury Ltd, 1983–86; Cadbury World Wide, 1986–89; Dep. Group Chief Exec. and Finance Dir, Cadbury Schweppes Plc, 1989–90; Gp Chief Exec., Coats Viyella PLC, 1990–97. Chm., Gartmore Split Capital Opportunities Trust, 1999–; Director: London Internat. Gp, 1988–93; Gartmore Scotland Investment Trust, 1992–; Safeway plc (formerly Argyll Group), 1993–2000; Scottish & Newcastle, 1997–. FInstD 1995 (Councillor, 1997–; Chm., Audit Cttee, 1999–). Hon. LLD Otago, NZ, 1993. *Publications:* Successful Management, 1995; (with D. Band) Winning Ways through Corporate Governance, 1996; (with Bill Mabey) The People Advantage, 1999. *Recreations:* sport, walking, music. *Address:* The Post Office, 148 Old Street, EC1V 9HQ. *T:* (020) 7250 2524, *Fax:* (020) 7250 2960; *e-mail:* nevillebain@postoffice.co.uk.

BAINBRIDGE, Dame Beryl, DBE 2000; FRSL; actress, writer; *b* 21 Nov. 1934; *d* of Richard Bainbridge and Winifred Baines; *m* 1954, Austin Davies (marr. diss.); one *s* one *d*; and one *d* by Alan Sharp. *Educ:* Merchant Taylors' Sch., Liverpool; Arts Educational Schools, Ltd, Tring. Weekly columnist, Evening Standard, 1987–. FRSL 1978; Fellow, Hunterian Soc., 1997. Hon. LittD Liverpool, 1986. *Plays:* Tiptoe Through the Tulips, 1976; The Warrior's Return, 1977; Its a Lovely Day Tomorrow, 1977; Journal of Bridget Hitler, 1981; Somewhere More Central (TV), 1981; Evensong (TV), 1986. *Publications:* A Weekend with Claud, 1967, rev. edn 1981; Another Part of the Wood, 1968, rev. edn 1979; Harriet Said. . . ., 1972; The Dressmaker, 1973 (film, 1989); The Bottle Factory Outing, 1974 (Guardian Fiction Award); Sweet William, 1975 (film, 1980); A Quiet Life, 1976, repr. 1999; Injury Time, 1977 (Whitbread Award); Young Adolf, 1978; Winter Garden, 1980; English Journey, 1984 (TV series, 1984); Watson's Apology, 1984; Mum and Mr Armitage, 1985; Forever England, 1986 (TV series, 1986); Filthy Lucre, 1986; An Awfully Big Adventure, 1989 (staged, 1992; filmed, 1995); The Birthday Boys, 1991; Something Happened Yesterday (essays), 1993; Every Man for Himself, 1996 (Whitbread Award); Master Georgie, 1998 (James Tait Black Meml Prize, W. H. Smith Award); According to Queeney, 2001. *Recreations:* painting, sleeping. *Address:* 42 Albert Street, NW1 7NU. *T:* (020) 7387 3113.

BAINBRIDGE, Cyril, FCIJ; author and journalist; *b* 15 Nov. 1928; *o s* of late Arthur Herman and Edith Bainbridge; *m* 1953, Barbara Hannah (*née* Crook); one *s* two *d*. *Educ:* privately (Negus Coll., Bradford). Served Army, staff of CGS, WO, 1947–49. Entered journalism as Reporter, Bingley Guardian, 1944–45; Telegraph and Argus, and Yorkshire Observer, Bradford, 1945–54; Press Assoc., 1954–63; joined The Times, 1963: Asst News Editor, 1967; Dep. News Editor, 1967–69; Regional News Editor, 1969–77; Managing News Editor, 1977–82; Asst Managing Editor, 1982–86; Editorial Data Manager, Times Newspapers, 1986–88. Vice-Pres., 1977–78, Pres., 1978–79, Fellow, 1986, Chartered Inst. of Journalists; Member: Press Council, 1980–90; Nat. Council for Trng of Journalists, 1983–86. *Publications:* Taught With Care: a Century of Church Schooling, 1974; The Brontës and their Country, 1978, 3rd edn 1993; Brass Triumphant, 1980; North Yorkshire and North Humberside, 1984, 2nd edn 1989; (ed) One Hundred Years of Journalism, 1984; Pavilions on the Sea, 1986; (jtly) The News of the World Story, 1993. *Recreations:* reading, brass bands, collecting old bookmarks. *Address:* 6 Lea Road, Hemingford Grey, Huntingdon, Cambs PE28 9ED.

BAINBRIDGE, Dr Janet Mary, OBE 2000; Chief Executive, European Process Industries Competitiveness Centre, since 2001; *b* 14 April 1947; *d* of Henry George Munn and Vera Doreen Munn; *m* 1st, 1970, Geoffrey Stathers Tuffnell (marr. diss. 1985); 2nd, 1987, Dr George Bainbridge; one *s* one *d*. *Educ:* Gravesend Girls' Grammar Sch.; Univ. of Newcastle upon Tyne (BSc Hons); Univ. of Leeds (PGCE); Univ. of Durham (PhD 1986). Microbiol. Res., Head Office, J. Sainsbury Ltd, 1968–70; NHS, 1970–71; secondary teaching, 1971–72; lectr, further educn, 1972–80; Teesside Polytechnic, then University: Lectr, then Sen. Lectr, 1980–85; Prin. Lectr, 1985–92; Divl Leader, 1992–98; Dir, Sch. of Sci. and Technol., 1998–2002; Tutor Counsellor, Sci. Foundn Degree, 1989–99, and Tutor, genetics, 1990–92, Open Univ. Mem., EPSRC, 2000–; Chair, Govt Adv. Cttee on novel foods and processes, 1997–; mem., other expert cttees and foresight panels. MSOFHT; MILT 2000; FRSA 1998. *Publications:* numerous contribs to learned jls; expert papers for parly cttees, enquiries, etc. *Recreations:* family, gardening, travel. *Address:* European Process Industries Competitiveness Centre, Cleveland Business Centre, Watson Street, Middlesbrough TS1 2RQ.

BAINBRIDGE, Simon; freelance composer, conductor and lecturer; *b* 30 Aug. 1952; *s* of John Bainbridge and Nan Knowles; *m* 1981, Lynda Richardson; one *d*. *Educ:* Central Tutorial Sch. for Young Musicians; Highgate Sch.; Royal Coll. of Music. Freelance composer, 1973–; Margaret Lee Crofts Fellowship (studying with Gunther Schuller), Berkshire Music Center, Tanglewood, USA, 1973; Leonard Bernstein Fellowship, 1974; Forman Fellow in Composition, Edinburgh Univ., 1976–78; US–UK Bicentennial Fellowship, 1978–79; Music Dir, Royal Nat. Theatre, 1980–82; Composer in residence, Southern Arts, 1982–86; Professor of Composition: RCM, 1989–; GSMD, 1991–; Composer in residence, Univ. of Wales Coll. of Cardiff, 1993–94. Gemini Prize in Composition, Musicians' Co., 1988. Numerous published works including: Viola Concerto, 1978; Fantasia for Double Orchestra, 1984; Ad ora Incerta: four orchestral songs from Primo Levi, 1994; (Grawemeyer Award for Music Composition, Univ. of Louisville, 1997); Landscape and Memory, 1995; Four Primo Levi settings, 1996. *Recreations:* films, reading, cooking, swimming, walking. *Address:* c/o Novello & Co. (Music Sales Ltd), 8/9 Frith Street, W1V 5TZ. *Club:* Royal Over-Seas League.

BAINES, Sir George G.; *see* Grenfell-Baines.

BAINES, Prof. John Robert, MA, DPhil; Professor of Egyptology, Oxford University and Fellow of Queen's College, Oxford, since 1976; *b* 17 March 1946; *o s* of late Edward Russell Baines and of Dora Margaret Jean (*née* O'Brien); *m* 1971, Jennifer Christine Ann, *e d* of S. T. Smith; one *s* one *d*. *Educ:* Winchester Coll.; New Coll., Linacre Coll., Worcester Coll., Oxford (BA 1967, MA, DPhil 1976). Lectr in Egyptology, Univ. of Durham, 1970–75; Laycock Student, Worcester Coll., Oxford, 1973–75. Visiting Professor: Univ. of Arizona, 1982, 1988; Univ. of Michigan, 1989; Ecole Pratique des Hautes Etudes, Paris, 1994; Harvard Univ., 1995–96, 1999–2000; Dist. Vis. Prof., Amer. Univ., Cairo, 1999; Fellow, Humboldt-Stiftung, 1982, 1989, 1996. Corresp. Mem., German Archaeol Inst., 1999. *Publications:* (trans. and ed) H. Schäfer, Principles of Egyptian Art, 1974, rev. edn 1986; (with J. Malek) Atlas of Ancient Egypt, 1980 (trans. 11 langs), 2nd edn 2000; (trans. and ed) E. Hornung, Conceptions of God in Ancient Egypt, 1982; Fecundity Figures, 1985; (ed jtly) Pyramid Studies and Other Essays presented to I. E. S. Edwards, 1988; (jtly) Religion in Ancient Egypt (ed B. Shafer), 1991; (ed) Stone Vessels, Pottery and Sealings from the Tomb of Tut'ankhamūn, 1993; (ed jtly) Civilizations of the Ancient Near East, 4 vols, 1995; (contrib.) Ancient Egyptian Kingship, 1995; articles in collections and in Acta Orientalia, American Anthropologist, Art History, Encyclopaedia Britannica, Jl Egypt. Archaeol., Man, Orientalia, Studien altägypt. Kultur, etc. *Address:* Oriental Institute, Pusey Lane, Oxford OX1 2LE.
See also P. J. Baines.

BAINES, Ven. Nicholas; Archdeacon of Lambeth, since 2000; *b* 13 Nov. 1957; *s* of Frank Baines and Beryl Amy Baines; *m* 1980, Linda Margaret Higgins; two *s* one *d*. *Educ:* Holt Comprehensive Sch., Liverpool; Univ. of Bradford (BA (Hons) Mod. Langs); Trinity Coll., Bristol (BA (Hons) Theol Studies). Linguist specialist, GCHQ, Cheltenham, 1980–84; ordained deacon, 1987, priest, 1988; Asst Curate, St Thomas, Kendal, 1987–91; Asst Priest, Holy Trinity with St John, Leicester, 1991–92; Vicar, St Mary and St John, Rothley, Leicester, 1992–2000. Mem., Gen. Synod of C of E, 1995–. *Publication:* Hungry for Hope, 1991. *Recreations:* music, reading, sport, travelling. *Address:* 7 Hoadly Road, Streatham, SW16 1AE. *T:* (020) 8769 4384.

BAINES, Priscilla Jean; Librarian, House of Commons, since 2000; *b* 5 Oct. 1942; *d* of late Edward Russell Baines and of (Dora Margaret) Jean Baines (*née* O'Brien). *Educ:* Tonbridge Girls' Grammar Sch.; Somerville Coll., Oxford (BA Agric. 1963; MA 1967); Linacre Coll., Oxford (BLitt 1969). Adminr, Chelsea Coll., Univ. of London, 1965–68; House of Commons: Library Clerk, 1968–77; Head: Economic Affairs Section, 1977–88; Science and Envmt Section, 1988–91; Parly Div., 1991–93; Dep. Librarian and Dir of Human Resources, 1993–99. *Publications:* (contrib.) New Select Committees, 1985, (contrib.) Westminster and Europe, 1996, and other pubns of Study of Parlt Gp. *Recreations:* food, travel, opera. *Address:* The Library, House of Commons, SW1A 0AA. *T:* (020) 7219 3635.
See also J. R. Baines.

BAINS, Lawrence Arthur, CBE 1983; DL; formerly Director: Bains Brothers Ltd; Crowland Leasings Ltd; Bains Finance Management Ltd; *b* 11 May 1920; *s* of late Arthur Bains and Mabel (*née* Payn); *m* 1954, Margaret, *d* of late Sir William and Lady Grimshaw; two *s* one *d*. *Educ:* Stationers' Company's School. Served War, 1939–46: Middlesex Yeomanry, 1939; N Africa, 1940; POW, 1942, escaped Italy, 1943. Hornsey Borough Council: Mem., 1949–65; Dep. Leader, 1958–64; Mayor, 1964–65; Council, London Borough of Haringey: Mem., 1964–74; Finance Chm., 1968–71; Greater London

Council: Chm., 1977–78; Mem. for Hornsey/Haringey, 1967–81; Chm., South Area Planning Bd, 1970–73; Dep. Leader, Housing Policy Cttee, 1979–81; Chm., GLC/Tower Hamlets Jt Housing Management Cttee, 1979–81; Mem., Lee Valley Regional Park Authority, 1968–81 (Chm., 1980–81); Chm., Haringey DHA, 1982–93. Chm., N London Coll. of Health Studies, 1991–95. Trustee, Help the Homeless, 1979–. Liveryman, Basketmakers' Co., 1978– (Mem., Ct of Assts, 1995–). DL Greater London, 1978 (Rep. DL for Borough of Barnet, 1983–95). Officer, Order of St Lazarus of Jerusalem. *Recreation:* being a grandfather. *Address:* Crowland Lodge, 100 Galley Lane, Arkley, Barnet EN5 4AL. *T:* (020) 8440 3499. *Club:* City Livery.

BAINS, Malcolm Arnold; JP, DL; Clerk of the Kent County Council and Clerk to the Lieutenancy of Kent, 1970–74; *b* 12 Sept. 1921; *s* of Herbert Bains, Newcastle-upon-Tyne; *m* 1st, 1942, Winifred Agnes Davies (marr. diss. 1961); three *s*; 2nd, 1968, Margaret Hunter. *Educ:* Hymers Coll.; Durham Univ. (LLB (Hons)); Solicitor. Commnd as Pilot in RAF, 1942–46. Solicitor with Taunton and Sunderland and with Notts and Hants County Councils, 1946–55; Dep. Clerk of Hants County Council and Dep. Clerk of the Peace, 1955–60; Dep. Clerk of Kent County Council, 1960–70; Chm., Working Group which advised Secretary of State for Environment on future management of Local Authorities, 1971–73. Chm., Local Govt Review Bd of Victoria, 1978–79. Fellow, ANU and Advr to NSW Govt, 1977–78. Head of Norfolk Island Public Service, 1979–82. FRSA 1976. DL Kent 1976; JP Norfolk Is, 1980. *Publications:* The Bains Report, 1972; Management Reform in English Local Government, 1978; Local Government in NSW, 1980. *Recreations:* swimming, tennis. *Address:* PO Box 244, Norfolk Island, NSW 2899, Australia.

BAIRD, Sir Andrew; *see* Baird, Sir J. A. G.

BAIRD, Anthony; *see* Baird, E. A. B.

BAIRD, Charles Fitz; Chairman and Chief Executive Officer, Inco Ltd, 1980–87, retired; *b* 4 Sept. 1922; *s* of George White and Julia (Fitz) Baird; *m* 1947, Norma Adele White; two *s* two *d*. *Educ:* Middlebury Coll. (BA); New York Univ. (Grad. Sch. of Bus. Admin); Harvard Univ. (Advanced Management Program). US Marine Corps, 1943–46, 1951–52 (Capt.). Standard Oil Co. (NJ), now Exxon, 1948–65: Dep. European Financial Rep., London, 1955–58; Asst Treas., 1958–62; Dir, Esso Standard SA Française, 1962–65; Asst Sec., Financial Man., US Navy, 1965–67, Under Secretary, 1967–69; Internat. Nickel Co. of Canada Ltd (Inco Ltd): Vice Pres. Finance, 1969–72, Sen. Vice Pres., 1972–76; Dir, 1974–93; Vice Chm., 1976–77; Pres., 1977–80. Director: Bank of Montreal, 1975–93; Aetna Life and Casualty Co., 1982–93. Nat. Advr, Council on Oceans and Atmosphere, 1972–74; Member: Presidential Commn on Marine Sci. Engrg and Resources, 1967–69; Council on Foreign Relations. Mem., Bd of Trustees, Bucknell Univ., 1969–95 (Chm., 1976–82); Trustee, Center for Naval Analyses, 1989– (Chm., 1992–97). Hon. LLD Bucknell Univ. 1976. US Navy Distinguished Civilian Service Award, 1969. *Recreations:* tennis, platform tennis, golf. *Clubs:* Chevy Chase (Washington, DC); Maidstone (E Hampton, NY); Bridgehampton (NY).

BAIRD, Sir Charles William Stuart, 6th Bt *cr* 1809, of Newbyth, Haddingtonshire; *b* 8 June 1939; *s* of Robert William Stuart Baird and Maxine Christine, *o c* of Rupert Darrell, NY; *S* uncle, 2000; *m* 1965, Jane Joanna, *e d* of late Brig. A. Darley Bridge; three *d*. *Educ:* Switzerland. *Heir:* none. *Address:* 12 Falstaff Street, Sunnybank Hills, Brisbane, Qld 4109, Australia.

BAIRD, Prof. David Tennent, CBE 2000; FRCP, FRCOG, FMedSci; Medical Research Council Clinical Research Professor of Reproductive Endocrinology, Edinburgh University, 1985–2000, now Emeritus; *b* 13 March 1935; *s* of Sir Dugald Baird, MD, FRCOG and Lady (May) Baird (*née* Tennent), CBE; *m* 1965, Frances Diana Lichtveld (marr. diss. 1995); two *s*; *m* 2000, Anna Frances Glasier. *Educ:* Aberdeen Grammar Sch., Aberdeen Univ.; Trinity Coll., Cambridge (BA); Edinburgh Univ. (MB, ChB; DSc). Junior med. posts, Royal Infirmary, Edinburgh, 1959–65; MRC Travelling Research Fellow, Worcester Foundn of Experimental Biology, USA, 1965–68; Lectr, later Sen. Lectr, Dept of Obstetrics, Univ. of Edinburgh, 1968–72; Dep. Dir, MRC Unit of Reproductive Biology, Edinburgh, 1972–77; Prof. of Obst. and Gyn., Univ. of Edinburgh, 1977–85. Consultant Gynaecologist, Royal Infirmary, Edinburgh, 1970–2000. FRSE 1990. Founder FMedSci 1998. *Publications:* Mechanism of Menstrual Bleeding, 1985; contribs in med. and sci. jls on reproductive endocrinology. *Recreations:* ski mountaineering, golf. *Address:* 22 India Street, Edinburgh EH3 6HB. *T:* (0131) 225 3962.

BAIRD, (Eric) Anthony (Bamber); Director, Institute for Complementary Medicine, since 1980; *b* 11 Dec. 1920; *s* of Oswald Baird and Marion Bamber; *m* 1st, 1952, Margareta Toss (marr. diss. 1957); 2nd, 1959, Inger Bohman (marr. diss. 1977); two *d*. *Educ:* LSE (BScEcon). Served RA, 1941–46. Swedish Broadcasting Corp., 1950–65; Public Relations Ltd, 1965–72; Civil Service, 1973–78; Inst. for Complementary Medicine, 1979–. Chm., British Council of Complementary Medicine, 1997–. FRSA 1992; FRSocMed 1999. *Publications:* Notes on Canada, 1962; (jtly) The Charm of Sweden, 1962. *Recreations:* writing children's stories, gardening. *Address:* 24 Backwoods Lane, Lindfield, Haywards Heath, West Sussex RH16 2ED. *T:* (01444) 482018. *Club:* Reform.

BAIRD, Guy Martin, FCA; Senior Adviser, European Investment Bank, Brussels, since 2001; *b* 3 Jan. 1948; *s* of late Thomas Herbert Mertens Baird and Kathleen Florence Baird (*née* Mapley, later Ballard); *m* 1969, Juliet Hope Mears (marr. diss. 1984); two *d*. *Educ:* Wellington Coll. ACA 1970, FCA 1975. Bland Fielden & Co., 1966–69; Cooper Brothers & Co., subseq. Coopers & Lybrand, 1970–72; Manager, Fidital, Coopers & Lybrand SpA, Rome, 1972–74; Vice Pres. Finance, Italicor Inc., Atlanta and Milan, 1975–77; Andrew Moore & Co., 1978–79; Luxembourg, 1980–83, Head of London Office, 1983–2001, EIB. *Recreations:* sailing, Wagner. *Address:* c/o European Investment Bank, 227 Rue de la Loi, Brussels 1040, Belgium. *Club:* East India.

BAIRD, Sir (James) Andrew (Gardiner), 11th Bt *cr* 1695 (NS), of Saughton Hall, Edinburgh; *b* 2 May 1946; *s* of Sir James Baird, 10th Bt, MC and of Mabel Ann, (Gay), *d* of A. Gill; *S* father, 1997; *m* 1984, Jean Margaret (marr. diss. 1988), *yr d* of Brig. Sir Ian Jardine, 4th Bt, OBE, MC; one *s*. *Educ:* Eton. *Heir:* *s* Alexander Baird, *b* 28 May 1986.

BAIRD, James Hewson; Chief Executive and Company Secretary, British Veterinary Association, since 1987; *b* 28 March 1944; *s* of James Baird, MBE, MRCVS and Ann Sarah Baird (*née* Hewson); *m* 1969, Clare Rosalind (*née* Langstaff); three *d*. *Educ:* Austin Friars; Creighton, Carlisle; Newcastle upon Tyne Univ. (BSc Hons Agric). Hydrologist, Essex River Authy, 1968–75; Policy Officer, Nat. Water Council, 1975–80. Institute of Civil Engineers: Asst Dir, 1980–81; Dir of Admin., 1981–86; Mem., Infrastructure Planning Gp, 1982–86; Dir, Assoc. of Municipal Engineers, 1984–86; Dir, External Affairs, Fedn of Civil Engineering Contractors, 1986–87. Dir, Vetsure, 1996–. Hon. Treas., Animal Welfare Foundn, 1993–. FRSocMed. *Recreations:* Rugby, gardening, farming, countryside. *Address:* British Veterinary Association, 7 Mansfield Street, W1M 0AT. *T:* (020) 7636 6541. *Clubs:* Farmers', Royal Society of Medicine.

BAIRD, Lt-Gen. Sir James (Parlane), KBE 1973; MD, FRCP, FRCPEd; Medical Adviser, National Advice Centre for Postgraduate Education, 1977–84; *b* 12 May 1915; *s* of Rev. David Baird and Sara Kathleen Black; *m* 1948, Anne Patricia Anderson; one *s* one *d*. *Educ:* Bathgate Academy; Univ. of Edinburgh. FRCPEd 1952, MD 1958, FRCP 1959. Commissioned, RAMC, 1939; Lt-Col 1956; Prof. of Military Medicine, Royal Army Medical Coll., 1965; Cons. Physician, BAOR, 1967; Dir of Medicine and Consulting Physician to the Army, 1969–71; Comdt and Dir of Studies, Royal Army Med. Coll., 1971–73; Dir Gen., Army Medical Services, 1973–77. QHP 1969. QHA (Pakistan), 1982. *Publications:* Tropical Diseases Supplement to Principles and Practice of Medicine, 1968; (contrib.) The Oxford Companion to Medicine, 1986. *Recreation:* golf. *Club:* West Sussex Golf.

BAIRD, Air Marshal Sir John (Alexander), KBE 1999; DL; Surgeon General to the Armed Forces, 1997–2000; *b* 25 July 1937; *s* of late Dr David Alexander Baird, CBE and Isobel T. Baird; *m* 1963, Mary Clews. *Educ:* Merchiston Castle Sch.; Edinburgh Univ. (MB ChB). FFOM; FRCPE 1998; FRCSE 1998; DipAvMed; FRAeS. Western Gen. Hosp., Edinburgh, 1961–62; MO Sarawak, 1962–63; commnd RAF, 1963; RAF Stations, UK and Singapore, 1963–80; exchange post, USA, 1970–73; HQ Strike Comd, 1980–83; MoD, 1983–86; OC Princess of Wales RAF Hosp., Ely, 1987–88; PMO, RAF Germany, 1988–91; PMO, HQ RAF Strike Comd, 1991–94; Dir Gen., RAF Med. Services, 1994–97. QHP 1991–2000. Mem., Internat. Acad. of Aviation and Space Medicine, 1993. FRSocMed 1983; Fellow, Aerospace Med. Assoc., 1992. DL Cambs, 1998. CStJ 1997. *Publications:* contribs to med. jls on aviation medicine subjects. *Recreations:* ornithology, wild-life conservation, cricket, music. *Address:* Braeburn, Barway, Ely, Cambs CB7 5UA. *Club:* Royal Air Force.

BAIRD, Joyce Elizabeth Leslie, OBE 1991; Joint General Secretary, Assistant Masters and Mistresses Association, 1978–90; *b* 8 Dec. 1929; *d* of Dr J. C. H. Baird and Mrs J. E. Baird. *Educ:* The Abbey School, Reading; Newnham College, Cambridge (MA); secretarial training. FEIS 1987. Sec. to Ernö Goldfinger, architect, 1952; Secretary to Sir Austin Robinson and editorial assistant, Royal Economic Soc., 1952–60; Senior Geography Mistress, Hertfordshire and Essex High School, Bishop's Stortford, 1961–77 (Dep. Head, 1973–75). President: Assoc. of Assistant Mistresses, 1976–77; Internat. Fedn of Secondary Teachers, 1981–85; Vice Pres., NFER, 1991–. Mem., Cambridge City Council, 1992–96. Trustee, Cambridge Preservation Soc., 1998–. *Recreations:* opera, thinking about gardening, travel. *Address:* 26 Fulbrooke Road, Cambridge CB3 9EE. *T:* (01223) 354909. *Club:* Royal Commonwealth Society.

BAIRD, Kenneth William; Project Director/Managing Director, European Opera Centre, since 1994; *b* 14 July 1950; *s* of William and Christine Baird. *Educ:* Uppingham School; St Andrews Univ. (MA); Royal College of Music; Royal Sch. of Church Music. LRAM, ARCM. English National Opera, 1974–82; Gen. Manager, Aldeburgh Foundn, 1982–88; Music Dir, Arts Council, 1988–94. Sec., New Opera Co., 1981–82. Member: NW Arts Bd, 1998– (Chm., Resources Cttee, 1999–); Bd, Huddersfield Contemporary Music Fest., 1997–; Birmingham Contemp. Music Gp, 2000–. Adv. Dir, Sonic Arts Network. Chairman: Snape Historical Trust, 1986–; British Arts Fests Assoc., 1988. Trustee, R. A. Vestey Meml Trust, 1991– . *Address:* 59 High Street, Wickham Market, Suffolk IP13 0HE. *Club:* Chelsea Arts.

BAIRD, Susan, CBE 1991; JP; Vice Lord-Lieutenant, City of Glasgow, since 1996; *b* 26 May 1940; *d* of Archie and Susan Reilly; *m* 1957, George Baird; three *s* one *d*. *Educ:* St Mark's Secondary School, Glasgow. Mem. Labour Party, 1969; City of Glasgow Council (formerly Glasgow District Council, then Glasgow City Council): Mem. (Lab), 1974–; Bailie of the City, 1980–84; Convener, Manpower Cttee, 1980–84; Vice-Convener, Parks and Recreation Cttee, 1984–88; Lord Provost and Lord-Lieutenant of Glasgow, 1988–92. JP 1977, DL 1992, Glasgow. DUniv Glasgow, 1990. St Mungo Prize, St Mungo Trust, 1991. OStJ. *Recreations:* reading, walking. *Address:* 138 Downfield Street, Parkhead, Glasgow G32 8RZ. *T:* (0141) 778 7641.

BAIRD, Vice-Adm. Sir Thomas (Henry Eustace), KCB 1980; DL; *b* Canterbury, Kent, 17 May 1924; *s* of Geoffrey Henry and Helen Jane Baird; *m* 1953, Angela Florence Ann Paul, Symington, Ayrshire; one *s* one *d*. *Educ:* RNC, Dartmouth. Served HM Ships: Trinidad, in support of convoys to Russia, 1941, Midshipman; Bermuda, Russian convoys and landings in N Africa, and Orwell, Russian convoys and Atlantic escort force, 1942; Howe, E Indies, 1943, Sub-Lt; Rapid, E Indies, 1944 until VJ Day, Lieut; St James, Home Fleet, 1946; Ganges, Ratings' New Entry Trng, 1948; Plucky, Exec. Officer, mine clearance in Mediterranean, 1950; Lt Comdr 1952; Veryan Bay, Exec. Officer, W Indies and Falkland Is., 1953; O-in-C, Petty Officers' Leadership Sch., Malta, 1954; Exec. Officer, HMS Whirlwind, Home Fleet and Med., for Suez Op., 1956; Comd, HMS Acute, Dartmouth Trng Sqdn, 1958; Comdr 1959; Comd, HMS Ulysses, Home Fleet, 1960; Staff, C-in-C, Home Fleet, Northwood, 1961; Exec. Officer, Jt Anti-Sub. Sch., Londonderry, 1963; EO, HMS Bulwark, Far East, 1965; Ch. Staff Officer to Cdre, Naval Drafting, 1966; Captain 1967; Dep. Dir, Naval Equipment, Adm., Bath, 1967; Captain: Mine Countermeasures; Fishery Protection and HMS Lochinvar (comd), 1969; Comd, HMS Glamorgan, Far East, W Indies, S Amer., Med., and UK Waters, 1971; Captain of the Fleet, 1973; Rear Adm. 1976; Chief of Staff to C-in-C Naval Home Comd, 1976–77; Dir Gen., Naval Personal Services, 1978–79; Vice-Adm. 1979; Flag Officer Scotland and NI, 1979–82. Chm. Exec. Cttee, Erskine Hosp., 1986–95. DL Ayr and Arran, 1982. *Recreations:* cricket, golf, shooting, fishing. *Address:* Craigrethill, Symington, Ayrshire KA1 5QN. *Club:* Prestwick Golf (Prestwick).

BAIRD, Vera; QC 2000; MP (Lab) Redcar, since 2001; *d* of Jack Thomas and Alice (*née* Marsland); *m* 1st, 1972, David John Taylor-Gooby (marr. diss. 1978); 2nd, 1978, Robert Brian Baird (*d* 1979); two step *s*. *Educ:* Newcastle Polytechnic (LLB Hons 1972); Open Univ. (BA 1982). Called to the Bar, Gray's Inn, 1975. Vis. Law Fellow, St Hilda's Coll., Oxford, 1999. *Publications:* Rape in Court, 1998; Defending Battered Women Who Kill, 2000. *Address:* 14 Tooks Court, Cursitor Street, EC4A 1LB.

BAIRD, William; Under Secretary, Scottish Home and Health Department, 1978–87; *b* 13 Oct. 1927; *s* of Peter and Christina Baird, Airdrie; *m* 1954, Anne Templeton Macfarlane; two *d*. *Educ:* Airdrie Academy; Glasgow Univ. Entered Scottish Home Dept, 1952; Private Sec. to Perm. Under-Sec. of State, Scottish Office, 1957; Principal, Scottish Educn Dept, 1958–63; Private Sec. to Minister of State and successive Secs of State for Scotland, 1963–65; Asst Sec., Scottish Educn Dept, 1965–66; Dept of Agriculture and Fisheries for Scotland, 1966–71; Scottish Office Finance Div., 1971–73; Registrar General for Scotland, 1973–78. *Address:* 8 Strathearn Road, North Berwick EH39 5BZ. *T:* (01620) 893190.

BAIRSTO, Air Marshal Sir Peter (Edward), KBE 1981 (CBE 1973); CB 1980; AFC 1957; DL; *b* 3 Aug. 1926; *s* of late Arthur Bairsto and Beatrice (*née* Lewis); *m* 1947,

Kathleen (*née* Clarbour); two *s* one *d*. *Educ:* Rhyl Grammar Sch. Pilot, FAA, 1944–46; 1946–62: FO RAF Regt, Palestine, Aden Protectorate; Flying Instr; Fighter Pilot, Fighter Comd and Near East; Flight Comdr, 43 Sqdn, and Leader, RAF Aerobatic Team; Sqdn Comdr, 66 Sqdn; RAF Staff Coll.; Wing Comdr, Flying, Nicosia, 1963–64; Op. Requirements, MoD, 1965–67; JSSC Latimer, 1967; Instr, RAF Staff Coll., 1968–70; Stn Comdr, RAF Honington, 1971–73; Dir, Op. Requirements, MoD, 1974–77; AOC Training Units, Support Command, 1977–79; Comdr, Northern Maritime Air Region, 1979–81; Dep. C-in-C, Strike Command, 1981–84. Vice-Chm. (Air), Highland TAVRA, 1984–90. Hon. Col, Northern Gp Field Sqns RE (Airfield Damage Repair) (Vol.), 1989–92. Mem., Scottish Sports Council, 1985–90. HM Comr, Queen Victoria Sch., Dunblane, 1984–93; Chm. Management Bd, RAF Benevolent Fund Home, Alastrean House, Tarland, 1984–94. Mem., St Andrews Links Trust, 1989–95 (Chm., 1993–95). Queen's Commendation for Valuable Services in the Air, 1955 and 1960. CIMgt. DL Fife, 1992. *Recreations:* golf, fishing, shooting, gardening. *Address:* Bearwood, Hepburn Gardens, St Andrews, Fife KY16 9LT. *T:* (01334) 475505. *Clubs:* Royal Air Force; Royal and Ancient Golf.

BAIRSTOW, John; Founder, 1968, Chairman, 1972–93, Queens Moat Houses PLC (formerly Queens Modern Hotels Ltd); *b* 25 Aug. 1930; *m*; four *d*. *Educ:* City of London Sch. FSVA. Founded Bairstow, Eves and Son, Valuers and Estate Agents, 1953. *Recreation:* salmon fishing.

BAKER, family name of **Baron Baker of Dorking**.

BAKER OF DORKING, Baron *cr* 1997 (Life Peer), of Iford in the Co. of East Sussex; **Kenneth Wilfred Baker,** CH 1992; PC 1984; *b* 3 Nov. 1934; *s* of late W. M. Baker, OBE and of Mrs Baker (*née* Harries); *m* 1963, Mary Elizabeth Gray-Muir; one *s* two *d*. *Educ:* St Paul's Sch.; Magdalen Coll., Oxford. Nat. Service, 1953–55: Lieut in Gunners, N Africa; Artillery Instructor to Libyan Army. Oxford, 1955–58 (Sec. of Union). Served Twickenham Borough Council, 1960–62. Contested (C): Poplar, 1964; Acton, 1966. MP (C): Acton, March 1968–1970; St Marylebone, Oct. 1970–1983; Mole Valley, 1983–97; Parly Sec., CSD, 1972–74; PPS to Leader of Opposition, 1974–75; Minister of State and Minister for Information Technology, DTI, 1981–84; Minister for Local Govt, DoE, 1984–85; Sec. of State for the Environment, 1985–86; Sec. of State for Educn and Sci., 1986–89; Chancellor of the Duchy of Lancaster, 1989–90; Chm., Conservative Party, 1989–90; Sec. of State for Home Dept, 1990–92. Mem., Public Accounts Cttee, 1969–70. Mem. Exec., 1922 Cttee, 1975–81. Chm., Hansard Soc., 1978–81. Sec. Gen., UN Conf. of Parliamentarians on World Population and Development, 1978. *Publications:* (ed) I Have No Gun But I Can Spit, 1980; (ed) London Lines, 1982; (ed) The Faber Book of English History in Verse, 1988; (ed) Unauthorized Versions: poems and their parodies, 1990; (ed) The Faber Book of Conservatism, 1993; The Turbulent Years: my life in politics, 1993; The Prime Ministers: an irreverent political history in cartoons, 1995; (ed) The Faber Book of War Poetry, 1996; The Kings and Queens: an irreverent cartoon history of the British monarchy, 1996; (ed) A Children's English History in Verse, 2000; (ed) The Faber Book of Landscape Poetry, 2000. *Recreation:* collecting books. *Address:* House of Lords, Westminster, SW1A 0PW. *Clubs:* Athenæum, Carlton, Garrick.

BAKER, Prof. Alan, FRS 1973; Professor of Pure Mathematics, University of Cambridge, since 1974; Fellow of Trinity College, Cambridge, since 1964; *b* 19 Aug. 1939; *o c* of Barnet and Bessie Baker. *Educ:* Stratford Grammar Sch.; University Coll. London; Trinity Coll., Cambridge. BSc (London); MA, PhD (Cantab). Mem., Dept of Mathematics, UCL, 1964–65 and Fellow, UCL, 1979; Research Fellow, 1964–68, and Dir of Studies in Mathematics, 1968–74, Trinity Coll., Cambridge; Mem., Dept of Pure Maths and Math. Statistics, Univ. of Cambridge, 1966–; Reader in Theory of Numbers, 1972–74. Visiting Professor: Univs of Michigan and Colorado, 1969; Stanford Univ., 1974; Royal Soc. Kan Tong Po Prof., Univ. of Hong Kong, 1988; ETH, Zürich, 1989; Mem., Inst. for Advanced Study, Princeton, 1970; Mathematical Scis Res. Inst., Berkeley, 1993; First Turán Lectr, J. Bolyai Math. Soc. Hungary, 1978. MAE 1998. Hon. Dr Univ. Louis Pasteur, Strasbourg, 1998. Foreign Fellow: Indian Nat. Sci. Acad., 1980; Nat. Acad. of Scis, India, 1993. Fields Medal, Internat. Congress of Mathematicians, Nice, 1970; Adams Prize of Univ. of Cambridge, 1971–72. *Publications:* Transcendental Number Theory, 1975; (ed jtly) Transcendence Theory: advances and applications, 1977; A Concise Introduction to the Theory of Numbers, 1984; (ed) New Advances in Transcendence Theory, 1988; papers in various mathematical jls. *Recreation:* travel. *Address:* Trinity College, Cambridge CB2 1TQ. *T:* (01223) 338400.

BAKER, Ann Maureen, (Mrs D. R. Baker); *see* Jenner, A. M.

BAKER, Anthony Baxter, CBE 1983; JP; Regional Administrator, Northern Regional Health Authority, 1973–83; *b* 12 June 1923; *s* of late Anthony Thurlbeck Baker and Robina Frances Jane (*née* Baxter); *m* 1st, 1946, Mary Margherita Patterson (*d* 1978); one *s* three *d*; 2nd, 1981, Judith Margaret Ayers, JP. *Educ:* Tynemouth High Sch.; Durham Univ. DPA; FHA. RAFVR, UK, Canada and Iceland, 1942–46. Admin. Asst, later Dep. Sec., SE Northumberland HMC, 1949–60; Asst Sec., later Principal Asst Sec., Newcastle Regional Hosp. Bd, 1960–73. JP Tynemouth 1965; former Chm., North Tyneside PSD. *Recreations:* Rugby football (PP Percy Park RFC; PP Northumberland RFU), golf. *Address:* 16 Dickson Drive, Highford Park, Hexham, Northumberland NE46 2RB.

BAKER, Anthony Castelli, LVO 1980; MBE 1975; HM Diplomatic Service, retired; *b* 27 Dec. 1921; *s* of late Alfred Guy Baker and Luciana (*née* Castelli). *Educ:* Merchant Taylors' Sch., Northwood, Mddx. Served War: munitions worker, 1940–41; volunteered for RAFVR and served in UK, ME and Italy, 1941–46 (Flt Lieut). Joined HM Diplomatic Service, 1946; served in Rome and Paris, 1946–50; Third Sec., Prague, 1951; Hamburg, 1953; Vice-Consul, Milan, 1954; Third, later Second Sec., Athens, 1959; Second Sec., Beirut, 1963; First Sec., Cairo, 1965; Naples, 1968; Turin, 1970; First Sec. Commercial, Calcutta, 1972; Consul, Montreal, 1975; First Sec. Commercial, Port of Spain, 1976; Consul, Genoa, 1979–81. Officer, Order of Merit (Italy), 1980. *Recreations:* tennis, watching cricket, travelling, jazz music. *Address:* Flat 16, Mourne House, 13 Maresfield Gardens, NW3 5SL. *Clubs:* Royal Air Force, MCC; Gloucestershire CC.

BAKER, Anthony Thomas; Director, International Aviation Negotiations, Department of the Environment, Transport and the Regions (formerly Department of the Environment), since 1996; *b* 13 March 1944; *s* of Charles Arthur Baker and Ivy Louvain Baker (*née* Rodgers); *m* 1969, Alicia Veronica Roberts; two *s* one *d*. *Educ:* Chatham House Grammar Sch., Ramsgate; Lincoln Coll., Oxford (BA Hons Modern History). Ministry of Transport: Asst Principal, 1965–70; Principal, 1970–75; Asst Sec., 1978–88, and 1991–96; Principal, HM Treasury, 1975–78; Dir, County NatWest Ltd, 1988–91. Freeman, City of London. *Recreations:* theatre, opera, reading. *Address:* 68 Talbot Road, N6 4RA. *T:* (020) 7944 4540.

BAKER, Arthur John, CBE 1981; Principal, Brockenhurst Tertiary College (formerly Brockenhurst Grammar School, then Brockenhurst Sixth Form College), 1969–88, retired; *b* 29 Nov. 1928; *s* of Arthur Reginald and Ruth Baker; *m* 1st, 1953, June Henrietta Dunham (*d* 1996); one *s* two *d*; 2nd, 1997, Maeve Mary Walker. *Educ:* Southampton Univ. (BSc; DipEd). Mathematics Master, Hampton Grammar Sch., 1952–55; Dep. Head, Sunbury Grammar Sch., 1955–61; Headmaster, Christchurch Grammar Sch., 1961–69. *Recreations:* walking, gardening, travel. *Address:* Honey Cottage, Crescent Drive, Barton-on-Sea, Hants BH25 7HS. *T:* (01425) 629049.

BAKER, Sir Bryan (William), Kt 1997; Chairman, West Midlands Region, NHS Executive, Department of Health, 1996–97 (Chairman, West Midlands Regional Health Authority, 1993–96); *b* 12 Dec. 1932; *m* 1954, Christine Margaret (*née* Hole); one *d*. Joined Tarmac, 1952; Gp Man. Dir, Tarmac plc, 1983–92. Non-executive Director: Volvo Truck & Bus Ltd, 1992–; Birse Group PLC, 1993–; Pemberstone PLC, 1995–; Benson Gp PLC, 1996–; Chm., Bruntcliffe Aggregates PLC, 1996–97.

BAKER, Cecil John; Director, Alliance & Leicester Building Society (formerly Alliance Building Society), 1970–92 (Chairman, 1981–91); *b* 2 Sept. 1915; *s* of late Frederick William Baker and Mildred Beatrice Palmer; *m* 1st, 1942, Kathleen Cecilia Henning (marr. diss. 1965); one *s*; 2nd, 1971, Joan Beatrice Barnes; one *d*. *Educ:* Whitgift Sch.; LSE (LLB 1939; BSc(Econ) 1949); Inst. of Actuaries. FIA 1948; ACII 1937. Sec., Insurance Inst. of London, 1945–49; Investment Manager, London Assurance, 1950–64; Investment Consultant, Hambros Bank Ltd, 1964–74; Chairman: Pension Fund Property Unit Trust, 1966–87; Charities Property Unit Trust, 1967–87; Agricl Property Unit Trust for Pension Funds and Charities, 1976–87; Victory Insurance Holdings Ltd, 1979–85; British American Property Unit Trust, 1982–87; United Real Property Trust plc, 1983–86 (Dir, 1982–86); Hunting Gate Group, 1980–90; Dir, Abbey Life Group plc, 1985–88. *Recreations:* golf, travel. *Address:* 3 Tennyson Court, 12 Dorset Square, NW1 6QB. *T:* (020) 7724 9716. *Club:* Savile.

BAKER, Charles A.; *see* Arnold-Baker.

BAKER, Air Vice-Marshal Christopher Paul, CB 1991; FCIPS; FIMgt; Chairman, Taylor Curnow Ltd, 1994; *b* 14 June 1938; *er s* of late Paul Hocking Baker, FCA and Kathleen Minnie Florence Baker; *m* 1st, 1961, Heather Ann Laity (decd), *d* of late Cecil Henry Laity and Eleanor Hocking Laity; three *s*; 2nd, 1981, Francesca R. Aghabi, *er d* of George Khalil Aghabi and Elizabeth Maria Regina Aghabi; two *s*. *Educ:* Bickley Hall, Kent; Tonbridge School. FCIPS (FInstPS 1989). Commnd RAF, 1958; served 1958–61: RAF Khormaksar (Air Movements), Aden; Supply Sqdn, RAF Coll., Cranwell; RAF Labuan, N Borneo; No 389 Maintenance Unit, RAF Seletar, Singapore; MoD Harrogate; student, RAF Staff Coll., Bracknell; OC Supply Sqdn, RAF Linton-on-Ouse; SHAPE, Two ATAF; ndc; Directing Staff, RAF Staff Coll., Bracknell; HQ RAF Support Comd; Dep. Dir, RAF Supply Systems, MoD; Comd Supply Movements Officer, HQ Strike Comd, RAF High Wycombe, 1982–84; RCDS, 1985; Dir, Supply Systems, MoD, 1986–87; Dir, Supply Policy and Logistics Plans, MoD, 1988–89; Dir Gen. of Support Management, RAF, 1989–93. Gen. Manager, Defence Sector Business Gp, TNT Express (UK) Ltd, 1993–94. FIMgt (FBIM 1979); MInstD 1993. Freeman, City of London; Liveryman, Bakers' Co. *Publications:* papers on the crisis of authority, oil potential of the Arctic Basin, and German reunification. *Recreations:* Rugby, rowing, ski-ing, modern history. *Address:* Lloyds TSB, Cox's & King's Branch, PO Box 1190, 7 Pall Mall, SW1Y 5NA. *T:* (020) 7839 1333. *Club:* Royal Air Force.

BAKER, David William; Chief Operating Officer, HSBC (formerly Midland) Bank plc, since 1998; *b* 1942. FCIB. Joined Midland Bank, 1962; posts incl. Exec. Dir, and Gen. Manager; Director: Griffin Factors Ltd; Forward Trust Business Finance Ltd. *Address:* HSBC Bank plc, 27-32 Poultry, EC2P 2BX.

BAKER, Derek; *see* Baker, L. G. D.

BAKER, Dick; *see* Baker, F. E.

BAKER, Douglas Robert Pelham, FCA; Treasurer, University of Sussex, since 1999; Chairman: Portman Building Society, 1990–99; Hardy Oil and Gas plc, 1989–98; *b* 21 May 1929. With Touche Ross & Co., Chartered Accountants, 1945–47 and 1949–89 (Chm., 1984–88). Dep. Chm., 1987–88, Chm., 1988–90, Regency and W of England Building Soc. (merged with Portman Wessex Building Soc., 1990); Dir, Merrett Hldgs, 1988–94; Dep. Chm., London Internat. Gp, 1989–96. Royal Naval Service, 1947–49. Chm., Brighton HA, 1988–91. *Address:* Hamsey Manor, Hamsey, E Sussex BN8 5TD.

BAKER, Elizabeth Margaret; Headmistress, Wimbledon High School, 1992–95, retired; *b* 13 Sept. 1945; *d* of Walter and Betty Gale; *m*; one *d*. *Educ:* University College of Wales, Swansea (BA, DipEd). Lectr, Derby Coll. of Further Educn, 1968–71; Classics Teacher: West Monmouth Sch., 1971–74; Cheltenham Bournside, 1974–81; Cheltenham Ladies' Coll., 1981–88; Headmistress, Ellerslie, Malvern, 1988–92. Editor, GSA Jl, 1996–. *Recreations:* wine, letter-writing, keeping the classics alive. *Address:* 33 Ashen Grove, SW19 8BW. *T:* (020) 8946 5023, *Fax:* (020) 8947 7205.

BAKER, Hon. Francis Edward N.; *see* Noel-Baker.

BAKER, Francis Eustace, (Dick), CBE 1984 (OBE 1979); business interests in property, farming and the automotive industry; Partner, Crossroads Motors, since 1988; *b* 19 April 1933; *s* of Stephen and Jessica Wilhelmina Baker; *m* 1957, Constance Anne Shilling; two *s* two *d*. *Educ:* Borden Grammar Sch.; New Coll., Oxford (MA). Nat. Service, RN, 1955–57 (Sub Lieut). Admin. Officer, HMOCS, 1957; Solomon Is, 1958–63; farming, 1963–67; Admin. Officer, Condominium of New Hebrides, 1967–79; Chief Sec. to Falkland Is Govt, 1979–83; Gov. and C-in-C, St Helena and Dependencies, 1984–88. Silver Jubilee Medal, 1977. *Recreations:* swimming, reading, farming, interesting motor cars. *Address:* Dark Orchard, Primrose Lane, Bredgar, near Sittingbourne, Kent ME9 8EH. *T:* (01622) 884295.

BAKER, Francis Raymond, OBE 1997; HM Diplomatic Service; Head, Africa Department (Equatorial), Foreign and Commonwealth Office, since 2000; *b* 27 Jan. 1961; *s* of late Raymond Albert Baker and Pamela Annis Baker; *m* 1983, Maria Pilar Fernandez; one *s* one *d*. *Educ:* Dartford Grammar Sch. Entered FCO, 1981: Third Sec., Panama City, 1983–86; Third, later Second Sec., Buenos Aires, 1986–91; Second Sec., FCO, 1991–93; First Secretary: Ankara, 1993–96; on secondment to US State Dept, Washington, 1996–97; FCO, 1997–98; Private Sec. to Minister of State, FCO, 1998–2000. *Recreations:* golf, cricket, watching football (Charlton Athletic FC), rock music, sailing, rallying. *Address:* c/o Foreign and Commonwealth Office, King Charles Street, SW1A 2AH. *T:* (020) 7270 2898.

BAKER, His Honour Geoffrey; QC 1970; a Circuit Judge, 1978–95, a Deputy Circuit Judge, 1995–98; *b* 5 April 1925; *er s* of late Sidney and Cecilia Baker, Bradford; *m* 1948, Sheila (*née* Hill); two *s* one *d*. *Educ:* Bradford Grammar Sch.; Leeds Univ.; LLB (Hons). Called to Bar, Inner Temple, 1947. Recorder: of Pontefract, 1967–71; of Sunderland, 1971; a Recorder of the Crown Court, 1972–78. Pres., Leeds and WR Medico-Legal Soc., 1984–85 (Mem. Cttee, 1980–94). Chm., Standing Cttee, Convocation of Leeds

Univ., 1986–90 (Mem. 1980–); Member: Adv. Cttee on Law, Leeds Univ., 1983–; Court, Leeds Univ., 1984–88, 1996–98; Pres., Leeds Univ. Law Graduates' Assoc., 1981–. *Recreations:* gardening, painting, photography. *Address:* c/o Court Service, Symons House, Belgrave Street, Leeds LS2 8DD.

BAKER, Gordon Meldrum; HM Diplomatic Service, retired; High Commissioner, Barbados and the Eastern Caribbean States, 1998–2001; *b* 4 July 1941; *o s* of Walter John Ralph Gordon Baker and Kathleen Margaret Henrietta Dawe Baker (*née* Meldrum); *m* 1978, Sheila Mary Megson. *Educ:* St Andrew's Sch., Bawdrip, near Bridgwater. MSc Bradford 1976. Lord Chancellor's Dept, 1959–66; transf. to HM Diplomatic Service, 1966; Commonwealth Office, 1966–68; FO (later FCO), 1968–69; Lagos, 1969–72; First Sec., FCO, 1973–75 (Resident Clerk, 1974–75); sabbatical at Postgrad. Sch. of Studies in Industrial Technol., Univ. of Bradford, 1975–76; FCO, 1976–78 (Res. Clerk, 1976–78); First Sec. (Chancery/Information), subseq. First Sec., Head of Chancery and Consul, Brasilia, 1978–81; Asst Head, Mexico and Central America Dept, FCO, 1982–84; Counsellor, 1984; on secondment to British Aerospace, 1984–86; Counsellor, Head of Chancery then Dep. Hd of Mission, and Consul-General, Santiago, 1986–89, Chargé d'Affaires, 1986, 1987 and 1989; RCDS, 1990–91; Head of W Indian and Atlantic Dept, FCO, 1991–94; High Comr, Belize, 1995–98. *Recreations:* walking, watching birds, browsing. *Address:* 78 Foyle Road, Blackheath, SE3 7RH.

BAKER, Howard Henry, Jr; Chief of Staff at the White House, 1987–88; lawyer; Senior Partner, Baker, Donelson, Bearman & Caldwell, Washington, since 1995; *b* 15 Nov. 1925; *s* of Howard H. Baker and Dora Ladd; *m* 1st, 1951, Joy Dirksen (*d* 1993); one *s* one *d*; 2nd, 1996, Hon. Nancy Landon Kassebaum. *Educ:* McCallie Sch.; Tulane Univ.; Univ. of Tennessee (LLB 1949). Served USN, 1943–46. Dir, Pennzoil; Chm. of Bd, Newstar Inc. US Senate: Senator from Tennessee 1967–85; Minority Leader, 1977–81; Majority Leader, 1981–85; former Co-Chm., Senate Select Cttee on Presidential Campaign Activities, and mem. other Senate cttees. Sen. Partner, Baker, Worthington, Crossley, Stansberry & Woolf, Knoxville, Tenn, 1985–87 and 1988–95. Mem., Bd of Regents, Smithsonian Instn. Mem., Amer. Bar Assoc. Presidential Medal of Freedom, 1984. *Address:* (office) 801 Pennsylvania Avenue NW, Suite 800, Washington, DC 20004, USA. *T:* (202) 5083400.

BAKER, Maj.-Gen. Ian Helstrip, CBE 1977 (MBE 1965); rcds, psc; General Officer Commanding, North East District, 1980–82; Secretary, University College London, 1982–91; *b* 26 Nov. 1927; *e s* of late Henry Hubert Baker and Mary Clare Baker (*née* Coles); *m* 1956, Susan Anne, *d* of late Major and Mrs Henry Osmond Lock; one *s* one *d* (and one *s* decd). *Educ:* St Peter's Sch., York; St Edmund Hall, Oxford; RMA, Sandhurst; Open Univ. (BA 1994). Commnd, 1948; 10th Fd Regt RA, 1949–51; 2nd Regt RHA, 1951–53; RAC Centre, 1953–55; transf. RTR, 1955; 4th Royal Tank Regt, 1955–57; HQ 10th Inf. Bde, 1957–58; Staff Coll., Camberley, 1959; DAAG HQ 17 Gurkha Div., Overseas Commonwealth Land Forces, Malaya and Singapore, 1960–62; OC Parachute Sqdn RAC (C Sqdn 2nd Royal Tank Regt), 1962–65; Instr Staff Coll., Camberley, and Bt Lt-Col, 1965; GSO1 and Asst Sec., Chiefs of Staff Cttee, MoD, 1966–67; Lt-Col 1966; CO, 1st Royal Tank Regt, UK and BAOR, 1967–69; Col 1970; Col, RTR, 1970–71; Brig. 1972; Comdr, 7th Armoured Bde, BAOR, 1972–74; RCDS, 1974; Brig. Gen. Staff, HQ UKLF, 1975–77; Services Fellow, St Catharine's Coll., Cambridge, 1977; Maj.-Gen. 1978; Asst Chief of the Gen. Staff, 1978–80. Col Comdt, Royal Tank Regt, 1981–86. Member: UK Conf. of Univ. Registrars and Secs, 1982–91; Organising Cttee for Internat. Confs of Univ. Administrators, 1983–91; Former UK Heads of Univ. Admin Soc., 1993– (Convener, 1998–2001). Mem., Univ. of London Mil. Educn Cttee, 1987–91. Elder, Crabtree Foundn, UCL, 1998– (Pres., 1995); Hon. President: Medical Students Soc., UCL, 1983–88; UCL Boat Club, 1986–93. Mem., RAC Benevolent Fund Cttee, 1985–89. Governor, Welbeck Coll., 1980–82. *Publications:* contribs to service and university papers and journals. *Recreations:* sailing, golf, outdoor pursuits, history, reading. *Address:* Owen's Farm, Hook, Hampshire RG27 9NG. *Club:* Sandford Springs Golf.

BAKER, Ian Michael; a District Judge (Magistrates' Courts) (formerly Metropolitan Stipendiary Magistrate), since 1990; *b* 8 May 1947; *s* of late David Ernest Baker and Phyllis Hinds; *m* 1st, 1976, Sue Joel (marr. diss. 1985); one *s*; 2nd, 1991, Jill Sack. *Educ:* Cynffig Grammar Sch., Mid Glam; St Catharine's Coll., Cambridge (MA). Articled, then Asst Solicitor to John Clitheroe, Kingsley Napley, 1972–76; Partner, Heninghem, Ambler & Gildener, York, 1976–79; Assistant Solicitor: Claude, Hornby & Cox, 1979; Seifert Sedley, 1980–83; Clinton Davis, 1984–87; Partner, T. V. Edwards, 1987–90. Trustee, Nat. Council for Welfare of Prisoners Abroad, 1986–99 (Chm., 1993–99). *Recreations:* playing classical clarinet and jazz saxophone, music, theatre. *Address:* Highbury Corner Magistrates' Court, 51 Holloway Road, N7 8JA. *Club:* Ronnie Scott's.

BAKER, James Addison, III; Senior Partner, Baker & Botts, since 1993; *b* 28 April 1930; *s* of James A. Baker, Jr and late Bonner Means Baker; *m* 1973, Susan Garrett; eight *c*. *Educ:* Princeton Univ. (BA); Univ. of Texas at Austin (law degree). Served US Marine Corps, 1952–54. Practised law, firm of Andrews, Kurth, Campbell and Jones, Houston, Texas, 1957–75, 1977–81. Under Sec. of Commerce, US Govt, 1975; National Chairman: President Ford's re-elecn campaign, 1976; George Bush for President Cttee, 1979–80; Dep. Dir, Reagan–Bush Transition and Sen. Advr to 1980 Reagan–Bush Cttee, 1980–Jan. 1981; Chief of Staff to US President, 1981–85; Sec. of US Treasury, 1985–88; Sec. of State, USA, 1989–92; COS and Sen. Counsellor to Pres. of USA, 1992–93. Personal Envoy of UN Sec. Gen. for Western Sahara, 1997. Numerous hon. degrees. *Recreations:* hunting, fishing, tennis, golf. *Address:* Baker & Botts, 1 Shell Plaza, 910 Louisiana, Houston, TX 77002–4995, USA. *Clubs:* numerous social, civic and paternal.

BAKER, Col James Henry, MBE 1999; Head of Conservation, Ministry of Defence, since 1986; *b* 15 Feb. 1938; *s* of late Lt-Col George Baker, TD, and Gwladys Joan Baker (*née* Russell), Dickhurst, Haslemere; *m* 1961, Lally Moss; one *s* one *d*. *Educ:* Harrow Sch. Commnd Irish Guards, 1957; served BAOR, Cyprus, Belize; ADC to Maj.-Gen. comdg Household Bde, 1965–67; CO, 1st Bn, Irish Guards, 1977–79; MA to QMG, 1979–81; Regtl Lt Col, Irish Guards, 1981–85. Harbinger, HM Body Guard of Hon. Corps of Gentlemen-at-Arms, 2000–. Chevalier, Order of Adolf-Nassau (Luxembourg), 1985. *Recreations:* fishing, shooting, archaeology. *Address:* Rovehurst, Chiddingfold, Surrey GU8 4SN. *T:* (01428) 644463. *Clubs:* White's, MCC.

BAKER, Dame Janet (Abbott), CH 1994; DBE 1976 (CBE 1970); professional singer; *b* 21 Aug. 1933; *d* of Robert Abbott Baker and May (*née* Pollard); *m* 1957, James Keith Shelley. *Educ:* The College for Girls, York; Wintringham, Grimsby. Mem., Munster Trust. Chancellor, Univ. of York, 1991–. Trustee, Foundn for Sport and the Arts, 1991–. Daily Mail Kathleen Ferrier Award, 1956; Queen's Prize, Royal College of Music, 1959; Shakespeare Prize, Hamburg, 1971; Copenhagen Sonning Prize, 1979. Hon. DMus: Birmingham, 1968; Leicester, 1974; London, 1974; Hull, 1975; Oxon, 1975; Leeds, 1980; Lancaster, 1983; York, 1984; Hon. MusD Cantab, 1984; Hon. LLD Aberdeen, 1980; Hon. DLitt Bradford, 1983. Hon. Fellow: St Anne's Coll., Oxford, 1975; Downing Coll., Cambridge, 1985. FRSA 1979. Gold Medal, Royal Philharmonic Soc., 1990. Comdr, Order of Arts and Letters (France), 1995. *Publication:* Full Circle (autobiog.), 1982. *Recreations:* reading, walking.

BAKER, Jeremy Russell; QC 1999; a Recorder, since 2000; *b* 9 Feb. 1958. Called to the Bar, Middle Temple, 1979. *Address:* Paradise Chambers, 26 Paradise Square, Sheffield S1 2DE.

BAKER, His Honour John Arnold; DL; a Circuit Judge, 1973–98; *b* Calcutta, 5 Nov. 1925; *s* of late William Sydney Baker, MC and Hilda Dora Baker (*née* Swiss); *m* 1954, Edith Muriel Joy Heward; two *d*. *Educ:* Plymouth Coll.; Wellington Sch., Somerset; Wadham Coll., Oxford (MA, BCL). Served RNVR, 1943–44. Treas., Oxford Union, 1948. Admitted Solicitor, 1951; called to Bar, Gray's Inn, 1960. A Recorder, 1972–73. Chm., Nat. League of Young Liberals, 1952–53; contested (L): Richmond, 1959 and 1964; Dorking, 1970; Vice-Pres., Liberal Party, 1968–69; Chm., Liberal Party Exec., 1969–70. Pres., Medico-Legal Soc., 1986–88. Mem., Guild of Sports Internationalists. Lay FRSocMed. DL Surrey, 1986. *Recreations:* music, watching sport. *Address:* c/o The Crown Court, 6–8 Penrhyn Road, Kingston upon Thames, Surrey KT1 2BB. *T:* (020) 8240 2500. *Clubs:* National Liberal (Trustee), MCC; Nothing (Richmond).

BAKER, Rt Rev. John Austin; Bishop of Salisbury, 1982–93; *b* 11 Jan. 1928; *s* of George Austin Baker and Grace Edna Baker; *m* 1974, Gillian Mary Leach (MBE 1997). *Educ:* Marlborough; Oriel Coll., Oxford (MA, MLitt). Asst Curate, All Saints', Cuddesdon, and Lectr in Old Testament, Cuddesdon Theol Coll., 1954–57; Priest 1955; Asst Curate, St Anselm's, Hatch End, and Asst Lectr in NT Greek, King's Coll., London, 1957–59; Official Fellow, Chaplain and Lectr in Divinity, Corpus Christi Coll., Oxford, 1959–73, Emeritus Fellow, 1977; Lectr in Theology, Brasenose and Lincoln Colls, Oxford, 1959–73; Hebrew Lectr, Exeter Coll., Oxford, 1969–73; Canon of Westminster, 1973–82; Treas., 1974–78; Sub-Dean and Lector Theologiae, 1978–82; Rector of St Margaret's, Westminster, and Speaker's Chaplain, 1978–82. Hon. Asst Bp, dio. Winchester, 1994–. Governor of Pusey House, Oxford, 1970–78; Exam. Chaplain to Bp of Oxford, 1960–78, to Bp of Southwark, 1973–78. Governor: Westminster Sch., 1974–81; Ripon Coll., Cuddesdon, 1974–80; Westminster City Sch., 1978–82; Dorset Inst. of Higher Educn, 1982–86; Bishop Wordsworth's Sch., 1982–93; Sherborne Sch., 1982–93; Salisbury & Wells Theological Coll., 1982–93; Pres. of Council, Marlborough Coll., 1982–93; Trustee, Harold Buxton Trust, 1973–79; Chm. Trustees, Bishop Morley Coll., Winchester, 1996–. Dorrance Vis. Prof., Trinity Coll., Hartford, Conn, USA, 1967; Vis. Prof., King's Coll., London, 1974–77; Hulsean Preacher, Univ. of Cambridge, 1979; Select Preacher, Univ. of Oxford, 1983; Stephenson Lectr, Univ. of Sheffield, 1994; Warburton Lectr, Inns of Court, 1994. Chairman: Defence Theol Working Party, C of E Bd for Social Responsibility, 1980–82; C of E Doctrine Commn, 1985–87 (Mem. 1967–76, 1977–81, 1984–87); House of Bps Working Party on Nature of Christian Belief, 1985–86, on Issues in Human Sexuality, 1990–91; Member: Faith and Order Advisory Gp, C of E Bd for Mission and Unity, 1976–81; Cttee for Theological Education, 1982–85; Standing Commn, WCC Faith and Order Commn, 1983–87; Exec. Cttee, CCJ, 1995–97; Vice-Pres., Nat. Family Mediation, 1993–. Chaplain, Playing Card Makers' Co., 1977. DD Lambeth, 1991. *Publications:* The Foolishness of God, 1970; Travels in Oudamovia, 1976; Prophecy in the Church, 1976; The Living Splendour of Westminster Abbey, 1977; The Whole Family of God, 1981; The Right Time, 1981; Evidence for the Resurrection, 1986; The Faith of a Christian, 1996; contrib. to: Man: Fallen and Free (ed Kemp), 1969; Thinking about the Eucharist (ed Ramsey), 1972; Church Membership and Intercommunion (ed Kent and Murray), 1973; What about the New Testament? (ed Hooker and Hickling), 1975; Man and Nature (ed Montefiore), 1975; Studia Biblica I, 1978; Religious Studies and Public Examinations (ed Hulmes and Watson), 1980; Believing in the Church, 1981; Hospice: the living Idea (ed Saunders, Summers and Teller), 1981; Darwin: a Commemoration (ed R. J. Berry), 1982; Unholy Warfare (ed D. Martin and P. Mullen), 1983; The Challenge of Northern Ireland, 1984; Lessons before Midnight (ed J. White), 1984; Feminine in the Church (ed M. Furlong), 1984; Dropping the Bomb (ed J. Gladwin), 1985; Theology and Racism, I (ed K. Leech), 1985; Peace Together (ed C. Barrett), 1986; Working for the Kingdom (ed J. Fuller), 1986; Faith and Renewal (ed T. F. Best), 1986; Women Priests? (ed A. Peberdy), 1988; For the Love of Animals (ed B. and M. Annett), 1989; Liberating Life (ed S. McFague *et al*), 1990; The Extended Circle (ed J. Wynne Tyson), 1990; Praying for Peace (ed M. Hare Duke), 1991; The Church, Medicine and the New Age (ed J. Watt), 1995; The Warburton Lectures 1985–94, 1995; Community-Unity-Communion: essays in honour of Mary Tanner (ed C. Podmore), 1998; Act of Synod—Act of Folly? (ed M. Furlong), 1998; *translations:* W. Eichrodt, Theology of the Old Testament, vol. 1 1961, vol. 2 1967; T. Bovet, That They May Have Life, 1964; J. Daniélou, Theology of Jewish Christianity, 1964; H. von Campenhausen, Ecclesiastical Authority and Spiritual Power, 1969; H. von Campenhausen, The Formation of the Christian Bible, 1972; J. Daniélou, Gospel Message and Hellenistic Culture, 1973; (with David Smith) J. Daniélou, The Origins of Latin Christianity, 1977. *Recreation:* music. *Address:* 4 Mede Villas, Kingsgate Road, Winchester, Hants SO23 9QQ. *T:* (01962) 861388.

BAKER, Prof. John Hamilton, LLD; FBA 1984; Downing Professor of the Laws of England, Cambridge University, since 1998; Fellow of St Catharine's College, since 1971; *b* 10 April 1944; *s* of Kenneth Lee Vincent Baker, QPM and Marjorie (*née* Bagshaw); *m* 1968, Veronica Margaret (marr. diss. 1997), *d* of Rev. W. S. Lloyd; two *d*. *Educ:* King Edward VI Grammar School, Chelmsford; UCL (LLB 1965 (Andrews Medal), PhD 1968; Fellow 1990); MA Cantab 1971, LLD 1984, Yorke Prize, 1975. FRHistS 1980. Called to the Bar, Inner Temple, 1966 (Hon. Bencher 1988), *aeg* Gray's Inn, 1978. Asst Lectr, Faculty of Laws, UCL, 1965–67, Lectr, 1967–71; Cambridge University: Librarian, Squire Law Library, 1971–73; Univ. Lectr in Law, 1973–83; Reader in English Legal History, 1983–88; Prof. of English Legal Hist., 1988–98; Junior Proctor, 1980–81; Chm., Faculty of Law, 1990–92. Visiting Professor: European Univ. Inst., Florence, 1979; Yale Law Sch., 1987; NY Univ. Sch. of Law, 1988–; Vis. Lectr, Harvard Law Sch., 1982; Mellon Senior Res. Fellow, H. E. Huntington Lib., San Marino, Calif., 1983; Ford Special Lectr, Oxford Univ., 1984; Vis. Fellow, All Souls Coll., Oxford, 1995. Corresp. Fellow, Amer. Soc. Legal History, 1993; Hon. Fellow, Soc. for Advanced Legal Studies, 1997. Literary Dir, Selden Soc., 1981– (Jt Dir, 1981–90). Hon. QC 1996. Hon. LLD Chicago, 1992. Ames Prize, Harvard, 1985. *Publications:* An Introduction to English Legal History, 1971, 3rd edn 1990; English Legal Manuscripts, vol. I, 1975, vol. II, 1978; The Reports of Sir John Spelman, 1977–78; (ed) Legal Records and the Historian, 1978; Manual of Law French, 1979, 2nd edn 1990; The Order of Serjeants at Law, 1984; English Legal Manuscripts in the USA, vol. I 1985, vol. II 1991; The Legal Profession and the Common Law, 1986; (with S. F. C. Milsom) Sources of English Legal History, 1986; The Notebook of Sir John Port, 1986; (ed) Judicial Records, Law Reports and the Growth of Case Law, 1989; Readings and Moots in the Inns of Court, vol. II, 1990; Cases from the lost notebooks of Sir James Dyer, 1994; Catalogue of English Legal MSS in Cambridge University Library, 1996; Spelman's Reading on Quo Warranto, 1997; Monuments of Endlesse Labours, 1998; The Reports of John Caryll, 1999; The Common Law Tradition, 2000; The Law's Two Bodies, 2001; Readers and Readings at the Inns of Court, 2001;

articles in legal and hist. jls. *Address:* St Catharine's College, Cambridge CB2 1RL. *T:* (01223) 338317.

BAKER, John William, CBE 2000; Deputy Chairman, Celltech Group, since 2000; *b* 5 Dec. 1937; *s* of Reginald and Wilhelmina Baker; *m* 1st, 1962, Pauline (*née* Moore); one *s*; 2nd, 1975, Gillian (*née* Bullen). *Educ:* Harrow Weald County Grammar Sch.; Oriel Coll., Oxford. Served Army, 1959–61. MoT, 1961–70; DoE, 1970–74; Dep. Chief Exec., Housing Corp., 1974–78; Sec., 1979–80, Bd Mem., 1980–89, Corporate Man. Dir, 1986–89, CEGB; Chief Exec., 1990–95, Chm., 1995–97, National Power; Chm., Medeva PLC, 1996–2000. Director: Royal and Sun Alliance Insce Gp (formerly Royal Insce), 1995–; The Maersk Co., 1996–; EIC, 1999–; Mem. Business Adv. Council, A. P. Moller Gp, 1996–. Chairman: ENO, 1996–2001; Associated Bd, Royal Schs of Music, 2000–. Chm., Exec. Assembly, World Energy Council, 1995–98. *Recreations:* tennis, bridge, music, theatre.

BAKER, Jonathan Leslie; QC 2001; a Recorder, since 2000; *b* 6 Aug. 1955; *s* of late Leslie Baker and of Isobel Baker; *m* 1980, Helen Sharrock; one *s* one *d*. *Educ:* St Albans Sch.; St John's Coll., Cambridge (MA). Called to the Bar, Middle Temple, 1978; barrister, specialising in Family Law, 1979–. Chm., Relate, Oxon, 1998–. *Recreations:* music, history, family life. *Address:* Harcourt Chambers, 2 Harcourt Buildings, Temple, EC4Y 9DB.

BAKER, Prof. (Leonard Graham) Derek, MA, BLitt; Director/Editor, Academia Publishing and Media, since 1991; Professor of History, 1986–95, Director, Institute for Medieval Renaissance and Hispanic Studies, 1989–95, Director, Centre for Undergraduate Study and Research, 1990–95, University of Texas; *b* 21 April 1931; *s* of Leonard and late Phoebe Caroline Baker; *m* 1970, Jean Dorothy Johnston; one *s* one *d*. *Educ:* Christ's Hospital; Oriel Coll., Oxford (1st Class Hons Modern History 1955, MA, BLitt). Captain, Royal Signals, 1950–52. Senior History Master, The Leys School, 1956–66; Lecturer in Medieval History, Univ. of Edinburgh, 1966–79; Headmaster, Christ's Hosp., 1979–85. Vis. Prof., Univ. of Houston, 1993–. Editor, Ecclesiastical History Soc., 1969–80; Pres., British Sub-Commission, Commission Internationale d'Histoire Ecclésiastique Comparée, 1971–80. Dir, Exec. Cttee, Haskins Soc., 1990– (Ed., 1995–). FRHistS 1969. *Publications:* Portraits and Documents, Vol. 1 1967, Vol. 2 1969; (ed) Studies in Church History, 7–17, 1970–80 (subsidia 1–2, 1978–79); Partnership in Excellence, 1974; Women of Power, vol. 1, 1993; Feminea Medievalia, vol. 1, 1993; numerous articles in historical jls. *Recreations:* singing; climbing, mountaineering, potholing, camping; good company; food and wine; travel. *Address:* New House, The Street, Nutbourne, Pulborough, W Sussex RH20 2HE. *T:* (01798) 813033; PO Box 2333, Denton, TX 76202–2333, USA. *T:* (940) 5659654. *Clubs:* National Liberal; Leander (Henley-on-Thames).

BAKER, Mark Alexander Wyndham, CBE 1998; Chairman, Magnox Electric plc, 1996–98; *b* 19 June 1940; *s* of late Lt-Comdr Alexander Arthur Wyndham Baker, RN and Renée Gavrelle Stenson (*née* Macnaghten); *m* 1964, Meriel, *yr d* of late Capt. Hugh Chetwynd-Talbot, MBE and of Cynthia Chetwynd-Talbot; one *s* one *d*. *Educ:* Prince Edward Sch., Salisbury, S Rhodesia; University Coll. of Rhodesia & Nyasaland (Beit Schol.; BA London); Christ Church, Oxford (Rhodes Schol.; MA). United Kingdom Atomic Energy Authority, 1964–89: Sec., 1976–78, Gen. Sec., 1978–81, AERE, Harwell; Dir of Personnel and Admin, Northern Div., 1981–84; Authority Personnel Officer, 1984–86; Authority Sec., 1986–89; Exec. Dir, Corporate Affairs and Personnel, Nuclear Electric plc, 1989–96. Chm., Electricity Pensions Ltd, 1996–; Dep. Chm., Police Negotiating Bd, 2000–; Police Adv. Bd, 2001–. Mem., Adv. Cttee, Envmtl Change Inst., Oxford Univ., 1999–. Mem. Bd of Trustees, SCF, 1998–. FInstE 1996 (Pres., 1998–99); FRSA 1992. *Recreations:* bridge, gardening, golf, walking, words. *Address:* The Old School, Fyfield, Abingdon OX13 5LR. *T:* (01865) 390724. *Clubs:* Oxford and Cambridge; Antrobus Dining (Cheshire).

BAKER, Martin John; Organist and Master of Music, Westminster Cathedral, since 2000; recitalist;; *b* 26 July 1967; *m* Anne Elise Smoot, organist. *Educ:* Royal Northern Coll. of Music Jun. Sch.; Chetham's Sch. of Music; Downing Coll., Cambridge (Organ Scholar; BA 1988). Organ Scholar, Westminster Cathedral, 1988–90; Assistant Organist: St Paul's Cathedral, 1990-92; Westminster Abbey, 1992-2000. Recitals include improvisations. *Address:* Clergy House, Westminster Cathedral, 42 Francis Street, SW1P 1QW.

BAKER, Martyn Murray; Director of Economic Development and Education, Corporation of London, since 1999; *b* 10 March 1944; *s* of late Norman and Constance Baker; *m* 1970, Rosemary Caroline Holdich. *Educ:* Dulwich Coll.; Pembroke Coll., Oxford (MA). Asst Principal, Min. of Aviation, 1965–67; Private Sec. to Ministers, Min. of Technology, Min. of Aviation Supply, and DTI, 1968–71; Principal, 1971; Principal Private Sec. to Sec. of State for Trade, 1977–78; Counsellor, Civil Aviation and Shipping, Washington, 1978–82; Department of Trade and Industry: Asst Sec., Air Div., 1982–85; Projects and Export Policy Div., 1985–86; Under Sec., 1986; Regl Dir, NW, 1986–88; Dir, Enterprise and Deregulation Unit, 1988–90; Head of Overseas Trade Div., 1990–93; Head of Exports to Asia, Africa and Australasia Div., 1993–96; Hd of Chemicals and Biotechnology Directorate, 1996–99, and Hd of Consumer Goods, Business and Postal Services Directorate, 1997–99. Member: Export Guarantees Advisory Council, 1985–86; Cttee for ME Trade, 1990–96; Council, China Britain Trade Gp, 1993–96; Asia Pacific Adv. Gp, 1993–96; BBSRC, 1996–99. Leader, Manchester-Salford City Action Team, 1986–88. FRSA 1988. *Address:* PO Box 270, Guildhall, EC2P 2EJ.

BAKER, Mary Geraldine, MBE 1995; National and International Development Consultant (formerly National Welfare Director), Parkinson's Disease Society; *b* 27 Oct. 1936; *d* of George and Emily Wheeler; *m* 1960, Robert William John Baker; three *s*. *Educ:* Bromley High Sch.; Leeds Univ. (BA); Inst. of Almoners. AIMSW. Almoner, St Thomas' Hosp., 1959–61; housewife and mother, 1961–75; Social Worker, 1975–82; Principal Med. Social Worker, Frimley Park Hosp., 1983; Parkinson's Disease Society: National Welfare Dir, 1984–91, 1992; Acting Chief Exec., 1991–92. Mem., Adv. Gp on Rehabilitation, DoH, 1992–94. Pres., European Parkinson's Disease Assoc., 1992–. Mem., Nat. Hosp. for Neurology and Neurosurgery SHA, 1994–. Member, Council: CSP, 1994–; Queen's Nursing Inst., 1994–. Chm., WHO Cttee of NGOs concerned with neurol disorders, 1998–. Mem., Med. Educn Res. Gp, World Fedn of Neurology, 1998–. Hon. FCSLT 1991. Paul Harris Fellow, Rotary Foundn, 1997. *Publications:* Speech Therapy in Practice, 1988; (with B. McCall) Care of the Elderly, 1990; (with P. Smith) The Role of the Social Worker in the Management of Parkinson's Disease, 1991; contribs to learned jls. *Recreations:* music, theatre, reading, bridge, caravanning. *Address:* Parkinson's Disease Society, 215 Vauxhall Bridge Road, SW1V 1EJ; Kailua, Maybourne Rise, Mayford, Woking, Surrey GU22 0SM. *T:* (01483) 763626. *Club:* Soroptimists'.

BAKER, Michael Findlay; QC 1990; **His Honour Judge Findlay Baker;** a Circuit Judge, since 1995; *b* 26 May 1943; *s* of Rt Hon. Sir George Baker, PC, OBE; *m* 1973, Sarah Hartley Overton; two *d*. *Educ:* Haileybury; Brasenose Coll., Oxford. Called to the Bar, Inner Temple, 1966; a Recorder, 1991–95. Sec., National Reference Tribunals for the Coal-mining Industry, 1973–95. *Recreations:* mountain climbing and walking, cross country running. *Address:* The Crown Court, Bricket Road, St Albans, Herts AL1 3HY. *Clubs:* Alpine; Thames Hare and Hounds.

See also Hon. Sir T. S. G. Baker.

BAKER, Prof. Michael John, TD 1971; Professor of Marketing, Strathclyde University, 1971–99, now Emeritus; Chairman, Westburn Publishers Ltd, since 1984; *b* 5 Nov. 1935; *s* of John Overend Baker and Constance Dorothy (*née* Smith); *m* 1959, Sheila (*née* Bell); one *s* two *d*. *Educ:* Worksop Coll.; Gosforth and Harvey Grammar Schs; Durham Univ. (BA); London Univ. (BScEcon); Harvard Univ. (CertITP, DBA); DipM. FRSE 1995; FCIM 1971; FCAM 1983; FScotvec 1988; FSQA 1997. 2nd Lieut, RA, 1956–57. Salesman, Richard Thomas & Baldwins (Sales) Ltd, 1958–64; Asst Lectr, Medway Coll. of Technology, 1964–66; Lectr, Hull Coll. of Technology, 1966–68; Foundn for Management Educn Fellow, 1968–71, Res. Associate, 1969–71, Harvard Business Sch.; Dean, Strathclyde Bus. Sch., 1978–84; Dep. Principal, 1984–91, Sen. Advr to Principal, 1991–94, Strathclyde Univ. Mem., Vice Chm. and Chm., Scottish Bus. Educn Council, 1973–85; Pres., Acad. of Marketing (formerly Marketing Educn Gp), 1986– (Chm., 1973–86); Member: Food and Drink, EDC, 1976–78; SSRC Management and Industrial Relns Cttee, 1976–80; Nat. Councillor, Inst. of Marketing, 1977, Vice Chm. 1984–86, Chm. 1987. Member: Scottish Hosps Endowment Res. Trust, 1983–96; Chief Scientist's Cttee, SHHD, 1985–96; Bus. and Management Sub-Cttee, UGC, 1985–89. Chairman: Scottish Marketing Projects Ltd, 1986–; IBEX Ltd, 1991–; Director: Stoddard Sekers International (formerly Stoddard Hldgs) PLC, 1983–97; Scottish Transport Gp, 1986–90; ARIS plc, 1990–94; Reid Gp, 1989–91; SGBS Ltd, 1990–97; STAMP Ltd, 1992–96. Dir, Scottish Med. Res. Fund, 1992–96. Visiting Professor: Univ. of Surrey, 1995–; Nottingham Trent Univ., 1999–2001; Nottingham Univ., 2001; Hon. Prof., Univ. of Wales, Aberystwyth, 1999–; Adjunct Prof., Monash Univ., 2000–. Governor, Lomond Sch., 1984–96. Dean, Senate, CIM, 1994–. FRSA 1986. Hon. Fellow, Acad. of Marketing, 1997. Founding Editor, Jl of Marketing Management, 1985. *Publications:* Marketing, 1971, 6th edn 1996; Marketing New Industrial Products, 1975; (with R. McTavish) Product Policy, 1976; (ed) Marketing in Adversity, 1976; (ed) Marketing Theory and Practice, 1976, 3rd edn 1995; (ed) Industrial Innovation, 1979; Market Development, 1983; (ed) Dictionary of Marketing, 1984, 3rd edn 1998; Marketing Strategy and Management, 1985, 3rd edn 2000; (with S. T. Parkinson) Organisational Buying Behaviour, 1986; (ed) The Marketing Book, 1987, 4th edn 1999; (with D. Ughanwa) The Role of Design in International Competitiveness, 1989; (with S. Hart) Marketing and Competitive Success, 1989; Research for Marketing, 1991; (ed) Perspectives on Marketing Management, vol. 1, 1991, vol. 2, 1992, vol. 3, 1993, vol. 4, 1994; Companion Encyclopedia of Marketing, 1995; The Marketing Manual, 1998; (with S. Hart) Product Strategy and Management, 1998; (ed) The Encyclopedia of Marketing, 1999; (ed) Marketing Theory, 2000. *Recreations:* hill walking, sailing, foreign travel. *Address:* Westburn, Helensburgh G84 9NH. *T:* (01436) 674686. *Clubs:* Royal Over-Seas League; Royal Scottish Motor Yacht.

BAKER, His Honour Michael John David; a Circuit Judge, 1988–99; *b* 17 April 1934; *s* of late Ernest Bowden Baker and Dulcie Baker; *m* 1958, Edna Harriet Lane; one *s* one *d*. *Educ:* Trinity Sch. of John Whitgift; Bristol Univ. (LLB Hons). Admitted solicitor, 1957. Flying Officer, RAF, 1957–60. Joined firm of Glanvilles, Solicitors, Portsmouth, 1960; Partner, 1963–88; a Recorder, 1980–88. Coroner, S Hampshire, 1973–88 (Asst Dep. Coroner, 1971; Dep. Coroner, 1972). Pres., Southern Coroners Soc., 1975–76; Mem. Council, Coroners Soc. of England and Wales, 1979–88 (Jun. Vice-Pres., 1987–88). *Recreations:* walking, tennis, the theatre, music (particularly choral singing), photography. *Address:* c/o 131 London Road, Waterlooville, Hants PO7 7SJ. *T:* (023) 9225 1414. *Clubs:* Law Society; Emsworth Sailing.

BAKER, Nigel Robert James; QC 1988; a Recorder, since 1985; a Deputy High Court Judge, Queen's Bench Division, since 1994; *b* 21 Dec. 1942; *s* of late Herbert James Baker and Amy Beatrice Baker; *m* 1973, Stephanie Joy Stephenson; one *s*. *Educ:* Norwich Sch.; Univ. of Southampton (BA Law); Queens' Coll., Cambridge (LLM). Lectr in Law, Univ. of Leicester, 1968–70; called to the Bar, Middle Temple, 1969, Bencher, 1997; practice in London and on Midland and Oxford Circuit. Mem., Bar Council, 1985. *Recreations:* football, fell walking, gardening. *Address:* 7 Bedford Row, WC1R 4BU. *T:* (020) 7242 3555.

BAKER, Norman John; MP (Lib Dem) Lewes, since 1997; *b* 26 July 1957. *Educ:* Royal Holloway Coll., London Univ. (BA Hons). Our Price Records, 1978–83; teacher, 1985–97. Member: Lewes DC, 1987–99 (Leader of Council, 1991–97); E Sussex CC, 1989–97. Contested (Lib Dem) Lewes, 1992. *Address:* House of Commons, SW1A 0AA.

BAKER, His Honour Paul Vivian; a Circuit Judge, 1983–96; *b* 27 March 1923; *er s* of Vivian Cyril Baker and Maud Lydia Baker; *m* 1957, Stella Paterson Eadie, *d* of William Eadie, MD; one *s* one *d*. *Educ:* City of London Sch.; University Coll., Oxford (BCL, MA). Called to Bar, Lincoln's Inn, 1950, Bencher, 1979; QC 1972. Editor, Law Quarterly Review, 1971–87. Chm., Incorporated Council of Law Reporting for England and Wales, 1992–2001. *Publication:* (ed) Black Books of Lincoln's Inn, vol. 6, 2001. *Recreations:* music, walking. *Address:* 9 Old Square, Lincoln's Inn, WC2A 3SR. *T:* (020) 7242 2633. *Clubs:* Athenæum, Authors'.

BAKER, Peter Maxwell, QC 1974; **His Honour Judge Peter Baker;** a Circuit Judge, since 1983; *b* 26 March 1930; *s* of late Harold Baker and of Rose Baker; *m* 1st, 1954, Jacqueline Mary Marshall (*d* 1986); three *d*; 2nd, 1988, Sandra Elizabeth Hughes. *Educ:* King Edward VII Sch., Sheffield; Exeter Coll., Oxford. MA Oxon. Called to Bar, Gray's Inn, 1956 (Holker Senior Exhibitioner); Junior, NE Circuit, 1960; a Recorder of the Crown Court, 1972–83. *Recreations:* fishing, shooting, yachting, music, watching others garden. *Address:* c/o Circuit Administrator, 17th Floor, West Riding House, Albion Street, Leeds LS1 5AA.

BAKER, Prof. Raymond, PhD; FRS 1994; Chief Executive, Biotechnology and Biological Sciences Research Council, since 1996; *b* 1 Nov. 1936; *s* of Alfred Baker and May (*née* Golds); *m* 1960, Marian Slater; one *s* two *d*. *Educ:* Ilkeston Grammar Sch.; Leicester Univ. (BSc, PhD). Postdoctoral Fellow, UCLA, 1962–64; University of Southampton: Lectr in Organic Chem., 1964–72; Sen. Lectr, 1972–74; Reader, 1974–77; Prof., 1977–84; Dir, Wolfson Unit of Chemical Entomology, 1976–84; Dir 1984–89, Exec. Dir, 1989–96, of Medicinal Chem., Merck Sharp & Dohme Res. Labs. *Publications:* Mechanism in Organic Chemistry, 1971; contrib. numerous articles to Jl Chemical Soc., Jl Medicinal Chem., and other scientific jls. *Recreations:* golf, gardening. *Address:* (office) Polaris House, North Star Avenue, Swindon SN2 1UH. *T:* (01793) 413208.

BAKER, Richard Douglas James, OBE 1976; RD 1979; broadcaster and author; Member, Broadcasting Standards Council, 1988–93; *b* Willesden, London, 15 June 1925; *s* of Albert and Jane Isobel Baker; *m* 1961, Margaret Celia Martin; two *s*. *Educ:* Kilburn Grammar Sch.; Peterhouse, Cambridge (MA). Served War, Royal Navy, 1943–46. Actor, 1948; Teacher, 1949; Third Programme Announcer, 1950–53; BBC TV Newsreader,

1954–82; Commentator for State Occasion Outside Broadcasts, 1967–70; TV Introductions to Promenade Concerts, 1960–95; Panellist on BBC2's Face the Music, 1966–79; Presenter, Omnibus, BBC TV, 1983; on Radio 4: presenter of Start the Week with Richard Baker, 1970–87; These You Have Loved, 1972–77; Baker's Dozen, 1978–87; Rollercoaster, 1984; Music in Mind, 1987–88; Richard Baker Compares Notes, 1987–95; The Musical Directors, 1998; on Radio 3: Mainly for Pleasure, 1986–92; In Tune, 1992–95; Rush Hour concerts, 1994–95; Sound Stories, 1998–99; on Radio 2: presenter of Melodies for You, 1986–95 and 1999–; Friday Night is Music Night, 1998–; on Classic FM: presenter, Classic Countdown, 1996; Evening Concerts, 1997–98; Baker's Choice, 1998–99. Columnist, Now! Magazine, 1979–80. Mem., Council, Friends of Covent Garden; Trustee, D'Oyly Carte Opera Co., 1985–98; Governor, NYO of GB, 1985–. TV Newscaster of the Year (Radio Industries Club), 1972, 1974, 1979; BBC Radio Personality of the Year (Variety Club of GB), 1984; Sony Gold Award for Lifetime Achievement in Radio, 1996. Hon. FLCM 1974; Hon. RCM 1988. Hon. LLD: Strathclyde, 1979; Aberdeen, 1983. *Publications:* Here is the News (broadcasts), 1966; The Terror of Tobermory, 1972; The Magic of Music, 1975; Dry Ginger, 1977; Richard Baker's Music Guide, 1979; Mozart, 1982, rev. edn 1991; London, a theme with variations, 1989; Richard Baker's Companion to Music, 1993; Schubert: an illustrated biography, 1997. *Address:* c/o Stephannie Williams Artists, 9 Central Chambers, Wood Street, Stratford upon Avon CV37 6JQ. *T:* (01789) 266272.

BAKER, Richard Hugh; HM Diplomatic Service, retired; *b* 22 Oct. 1935; *s* of late Hugh Cuthbert Baker and (Muriel) Lovenda Baker (*née* Owens); *m* 1963, Patricia Marianne Haigh Thomas; one *s* three *d*. *Educ:* Marlborough Coll.; New Coll., Oxford. Army (2nd Lieut RA), 1954–56. Plebiscite Officer, UN Plebiscite, S Cameroons, 1960–61; joined Diplomatic Service, 1962; 3rd, later 2nd, then 1st Sec., Addis Ababa, 1963–66; Foreign Office, 1967; Private Sec. to Permanent Under-Sec. of State, Foreign Office (later FCO), 1967–70; 1st Sec. and Head of Chancery, Warsaw, 1970–72; FCO, 1973–76; RCDS 1977; Econ. and Financial Counsellor, and Dep. Head, UK Perm. Delegn to OECD, Paris, 1978–82; Dep. High Comr, Ottawa, 1982–86; Asst Under-Sec. of State, and Civilian Mem., Sen. Directing Staff, RCDS, 1986–89. *Recreations:* music, painting, literature, pottery, printmaking, writing. *Address:* 1 The Thatched Cottages, Water Lane, Radwinter, Saffron Walden CB10 2TX.

BAKER, Sir Robert George Humphrey S.; *see* Sherston-Baker.

BAKER, Dr Robin William; Director, Europe, British Council, since 1999; *b* 4 Oct. 1953; *s* of late William John David Baker and of Brenda Olive Baker (*née* Hodges); *m* 1974, Miriam Joy Turpin (marr. diss. 1997); two *s*. *Educ:* Bishop Wordsworth's Sch., Salisbury; Sch. of Slavonic and East European Studies, Univ. of London (BA 1976); Univ. of East Anglia (PhD 1984). MoD, 1976–80; res. student, 1980–84; British Council: S Africa, 1984–89; Head of Recruitment, 1989; Hungary, 1990–93; Thessaloniki, Greece, 1994–96; Russia, 1996–99; Dir, W and S Europe, 1999. Sen. Vis. Fellow, Inst. for Balkan Studies, Thessaloniki, 1995–; Vis. Fellow, SSEES, 1995–97, 1999. Member, Advisory Council: Inst. of Romance Studies, Univ. of London, 1999–; SSEES, 2000–. FRSA 1998. *Publications:* The Development of the Komi Case System: a dialectological investigation, 1985; papers on history and languages of E Europe. *Recreations:* jazz, opera, Csángós, South-East Europe. *Address:* British Council, 10 Spring Gardens, SW1A 2BN. *T:* (020) 7389 4806. *Clubs:* Travellers, Ronnie Scott's.

BAKER, Scott; *see* Baker, T. S. G.

BAKER, Stephen, OBE 1987; consultant; Managing Director, British Electricity International Ltd, 1978–86; *b* 27 March 1926; *s* of late Arthur and Nancy Baker; *m* 1950, Margaret Julia Wright; one *s* two *d*. *Educ:* Epsom Coll.; Clare Coll., Cambridge (MA). FIMechE. Engr Officer, RN, 1944–47; Apprentice, Davy United Engineering Co. Ltd, 1947–49; Works Engr, John Baker & Bessemer Ltd, 1949–51; Davy United Engrg Co. Ltd, 1951: Dir of Prodn, 1960; Gen. Man., 1961; Dir, Davy Ashmore Ltd, 1963; Dir of Ops, Davy-Ashmore Engrg Ltd, 1964; Chm. and Chief Exec. of Davy United Engrg Co. Ltd, Ashmore Benson Pease Ltd and Loewy Robertson Engrg Co. Ltd, 1968; Man. Dir, Kearney & Trecker Ltd, 1970; Co-ordinator of Industrial Advrs, Depts of Trade and Industry, 1974–78. *Recreations:* fishing, gardening. *Address:* 75 Slayleigh Lane, Sheffield S10 3RG.

BAKER, Stuart William; His Honour Judge Stuart Baker; a Circuit Judge, since 1998; *b* 1 June 1952; *s* of Henry Baker and Elizabeth Baker (*née* Hooker); *m* 1975, Christine Elizabeth Bennett; one *s*. *Educ:* Univ. of Newcastle upon Tyne (LLB Hons 1973). Called to the Bar, Inner Temple, 1974; in practice at the Bar, 1975–98; Asst Recorder, 1991–94; a Recorder, 1994–98; Northern Circuit. Mem., Legal Aid Area Appeal Cttee, 1991–98; Legal Mem., Mental Health Review Tribunal, 1996–98. *Recreations:* fell walking, theatre. *Address:* Manchester Crown Court, Crown Square, Manchester M60 9DJ.

BAKER, Hon. Sir (Thomas) Scott (Gillespie), Kt 1988; **Hon. Mr Justice Scott Baker;** a Judge of the High Court of Justice, Queen's Bench Division, since 1993 (Family Division, 1988–92); Lead Judge of the Administrative Court, since 2000; *b* 10 Dec. 1937; *s* of late Rt Hon. Sir George Baker, PC, OBE and Jessie McCall Baker; *m* 1973, (Margaret) Joy Strange; two *s* one *d*. *Educ:* Haileybury; Brasenose Coll., Oxford. Called to the Bar, Middle Temple, 1961 (Astbury Schol.), Bencher 1985; a Recorder, 1976–88; QC 1978; Family Div. Liaison Judge (Wales and Chester Circuit), 1990–92; Presiding Judge, Wales and Chester Circuit, 1991–95. Member: Senate, Inns of Court, 1977–84; Bar Council, 1988. Member: Govt Cttee of Inquiry into Human Fertilisation (Warnock Cttee), 1982–84; Parole Bd, 1999– (Vice-Chm., 2000–). Mem., Chorleywood UDC, 1965–68. Dep. Chm., Cricket Council Appeals Cttee, 1986–88. Gov., Caldecott Sch., 1991– (Chm., 1996–). *Recreations:* golf, fishing, shooting. *Address:* Royal Courts of Justice, Strand, WC2A 2LL. *Clubs:* MCC; Denham Golf (Captain, 1992, Chm., 1995–2001).
See also M. F. Baker.

BAKER, Wallis James, CB 1989; Chairman, Land Administration Commission, Queensland, 1983–89, retired; *b* 19 March 1931; *s* of James Campbell Baker and Doris Isabel (*née* Nowland); *m* 1960, Eileen Merle Seeney; one *s* one *d*. *Educ:* Downlands Coll., Toowoomba, Qld. Admitted Solicitor, Supreme Court of Qld, 1954, re-admitted, 1990; called to the Bar, Qld, 1969. Practised as Solicitor, Monto, Qld, 1955–68; entered Qld Public Service as career public servant, 1968. *Recreations:* tennis, ancient history, rock collecting. *Address:* 40 Hughes Avenue, Main Beach, Qld 4217, Australia. *T:* (7) 55280885.

BAKER, Wilson, FRS 1946; FRSC; BSc, MSc, PhD, DSc (Manchester); MA (Oxon.); retired; Alfred Capper Pass Professor of Organic Chemistry, University of Bristol, 1945–65 (Dean of the Faculty of Science, 1948–51; Emeritus Professor, University of Bristol, 1965); *b* 24 Jan. 1900; *yr s* of Harry and Mary Baker, Runcorn, Cheshire; *m* 1927, Juliet Elizabeth, *d* of Henry and Julia R. Glaisyer, Birmingham; one *s* two *d*. *Educ:* Liverpool Coll. Upper Sch.; Victoria Univ. of Manchester (Mercer Schol., Baeyer Fellow and Dalton Scholar). Asst Lecturer in Chemistry, Univ. of Manchester, 1924–27; Tutor in Chemistry, Dalton Hall, Manchester, 1926–27; Univ. Lecturer and Demonstrator in Chemistry, Univ. of Oxford, 1927–44; Fellow and Praelector in Chemistry, The Queen's Coll., Oxford, 1937–44. Vice-Pres. of the Chemical Society, 1957–60. *Publications:* numerous original papers on organic chemistry, dealing chiefly with the synthesis of natural products, the development of synthetical processes, compounds of abnormal aromatic type, organic inclusion compounds, and the preparation of large-ring compounds, and the chemistry of penicillin, published mainly in Journal of the Chemical Society; (with T. W. J. Taylor) 2nd Edition of Professor N. V. Sidgwick's The Organic Chemistry of Nitrogen, 1937. *Recreations:* walking, gardening, music, mineralogy. *Address:* Lane's End, 54 Church Road, Winscombe, North Somerset BS25 1BJ. *T:* (01934) 843112.

BAKER-BATES, Merrick Stuart, CMG 1996; HM Diplomatic Service, retired; Consul-General, Los Angeles, 1992–97; *b* 22 July 1939; *s* of late E. T. Baker-Bates, MD, FRCP, and of Norah Stuart (*née* Kirkham); *m* 1963, Chrystal Jacqueline Goodacre; one *s* one *d*. *Educ:* Shrewsbury Sch.; Hertford Coll., Oxford (MA); College of Europe, Bruges. Journalist, Brussels, 1962–63; entered HM Diplomatic Service, 1963; 3rd, later 2nd Sec., Tokyo, 1963–68; 1st Secretary: FCO, 1968–73; (Inf.), Washington, 1973–76; (Commercial), Tokyo, 1976–79; Counsellor (Commercial), Tokyo, 1979–82. Dir, Cornes & Co., Tokyo, 1982–85; Representative Dir, Gestetner Ltd (Japan), 1982–85; Dep. High Comr and Counsellor (Commercial/Econ.), Kuala Lumpur, 1986–89; Hd of S Atlantic and Antarctic Dept, FCO, and Comr, British Antarctic Territory, 1989–92. Comdr, St John Ambulance (Northants), 1998–. Mem., Develt Council, 1998–, and Chm., Internat. Cttee, 1999–, Shakespeare's Globe Trust. OStJ 2000. *Recreations:* photography, golf, cycling. *Address:* The East House, Highfield Park, Creaton, Northants NN6 8NT. *Club:* Tokyo (Tokyo).
See also R. P. Baker-Bates.

BAKER-BATES, Rodney Pennington; Chief Executive, Prudential Financial Services, Prudential plc, since 2000; *b* 25 April 1944; *s* of Eric Tom Baker-Bates and Norah Stuart (*née* Kirkham); *m* 1972, Gail Elizabeth Roberts; one *s*. *Educ:* Shrewsbury Sch.; Hertford Coll., Oxford (MA History). FICA 1975; AIMC 1975; FCIB 1991. Glyn Mills & Co., 1966–68; Arthur Andersen & Co., 1968–77; Chase Manhattan Bank, 1977–84; Midland Bank, 1984–92; Dir of Finance and IT, BBC, 1993–98; Man. Dir, Corporate Pensions Business, Prudential Corp., 1998–99; Chief-Exec., Gp Pensions, Prudential plc, 1999–2000. Director: Dexia Municipal Bank, 1997–; Aspen Group, 1997–99; Lloyds Register of Shipping, 1998–; Prudential Assce Co. Ltd, 2000–; Chairman: Change Partnership Ltd, 1998–2001; Hydra Associates, 1999–2001; Coral Eurobet plc, 1999–. Dir, City of London Fest., 2001–. Governor, Bedales Sch., 1993–2001. Trustee, Royal Nat. Pension Fund for Nurses. *Recreations:* gardening, performing arts, country pursuits. *Address:* c/o Prudential plc, Laurence Pountney Hill, EC4R 0HH. *T:* (020) 7548 6150. *Clubs:* Brooks's; City of London.
See also M. S. Baker-Bates.

BAKER WILBRAHAM, Sir Richard, 8th Bt *cr* 1776; DL; Director, J. Henry Schroder Wagg & Co. Ltd, 1969–89; Chairman, Bibby Line Group, 1992–97 (Deputy Chairman, 1989–92); *b* 5 Feb. 1934; *s* of Sir Randle Baker Wilbraham, 7th Bt, and Betty Ann, CBE (*d* 1975), *d* of W. Matt Torrens; *S* father, 1980; *m* 1962, Anne Christine Peto, *d* of late Charles Peto Bennett, OBE; one *s* three *d*. *Educ:* Harrow. Welsh Guards, 1952–54. J. Henry Schroder Wagg & Co. Ltd, 1954–89. Director: Westpool Investment Trust, 1974–92; Brixton Estate, 1985–2001 (Dep. Chm., 1994–2001); The Really Useful Group plc, 1985–90; Charles Barker Group, 1986–89; Grosvenor Estates Hldgs, 1989–99 (Dep. Chm., 1989–99); Severn Trent, 1989–94; Majedie Investments, 1989–2001; Christie Hosp. NHS Trust, 1990–96. Mem., Gen. Council, King Edward's Hosp. Fund for London, 1986–98. Gov., Nuffield Hosps, 1990–2001. A Church Comr, 1994–. Trustee, Grosvenor Estate, 1981–99. Governor: Harrow Sch., 1982–92; The King's Sch., Macclesfield, 1986–; Manchester Metropolitan Univ., 1998–2001. Upper Bailiff, Weavers' Co., 1994–95. High Sheriff, Cheshire, 1991–92; DL Cheshire, 1992. *Recreations:* field sports. *Heir:* *s* Randle Baker Wilbraham [*b* 28 May 1963; *m* 1997, Amanda, *e d* of Robert Glossop; one *s*]. *Address:* Rode Hall, Scholar Green, Cheshire ST7 3QP. *T:* (01270) 882961. *Club:* Brooks's.

BAKEWELL, Joan Dawson, CBE 1999; broadcaster and writer; *b* 16 April; *d* of John Rowlands and Rose Bland; *m* 1st, 1955, Michael Bakewell (marr. diss. 1972); one *s* one *d*; 2nd, 1975, Jack Emery (marr. diss. 2001). *Educ:* Stockport High Sch. for Girls; Newnham Coll., Cambridge (BA History and Econs). Associate, 1980–91, Associate Fellow, 1984–87, Newnham Coll., Cambridge. Gov., BFI, 1994– (Dep. Chm., 1997–99; Chm., 1999–); Mem. Bd, RNT, 1996–. Pres., Soc. of Arts Publicists, 1984–90. Mem. Council, Aldeburgh Foundn, 1985–99. Hon. FRCA 1994; Hon. Fellow, RHBNC, 1997. *BBC Television incl:* Meeting Point, 1964; The Second Sex, 1964; Late Night Line Up, 1965–72; The Youthful Eye, 1968; Moviemakers at the National Film Theatre, 1971; Film 72, and Film 73, 1972–73; For the Sake of Appearance, Where is Your God?, Who Cares?, and The Affirmative Way (series), 1973; Holiday '74, '75, '76, '77 and '78 (series); What's it all About? (2 series) and Time Running Out (series), 1974; The Shakespeare Business, The Brontë Business, and Generation to Generation (series), 1976; My Day with the Children, 1977; The Moving Line, 1979; Arts UK: OK?, 1980; Arts Correspondent, 1981–87; The Heart of the Matter, 1988–2000; Travels with Pevsner: Derbyshire, 1998; My Generation, 2000; *ITV incl.* Sunday Break, 1962; Home at 4.30, 1964; (writer and producer) Thank You, Ron (documentary), 1974; Fairest Fortune and Edinburgh Festival Report, 1974; Reports Action (4 series), 1976–78. *Radio:* Away from it All, 1978–79; PM, 1979–81; Artist of the Week, 1998–; Chm., The Brains Trust, 1998–; plays: There and Back; Parish Magazine: 3 editions. *Theatre:* Brontës: The Private Faces, Edinburgh Fest., 1979. *Publications:* (with Nicholas Garnham) The New Priesthood: British television today, 1970; (with John Drummond) A Fine and Private Place, 1977; The Complete Traveller, 1977; The Heart of the Matter, 1996; journalism: Punch, Radio Times; Television Critic of The Times, 1978–81; columnist, Sunday Times, 1988–90. *Recreations:* theatre, travel, cinema. *Address:* Knight Ayton Management, 10 Argyll Street, W1V 1AB.

BALCHIN, John Alfred; General Manager, Stevenage Development Corporation, 1969–76, retired; *b* 8 Aug. 1914; *er s* of Alfred and Florence Balchin; *m* 1st, 1940, Elsie Dormer (*d* 1982); one *s* two *d*; 2nd, 1986, Edna Bilton (*née* Morgan). *Educ:* Sir Walter St John's Sch., Battersea; Sir John Cass Coll., City of London. DPA (London), DMA, FCIS, FCIH. LCC Clerk's Dept, 1932–38; civil defence co-ordination work, 1938–45; to Housing Dept, 1946–65; Principal Clerk, 1952; Asst Dir (Finance), 1960; Asst Dir (Housing Management), 1963; Sen. Asst Dir of Housing, GLC, 1965–69. Assoc. Sen. Lectr, for Housing Management and Administration, Brunel Univ., 1969–71. Member: Housing Services Adv. Gp, DoE, 1976–80; North British Housing Assoc., 1976–89; Auriol Housing Foundn, 1986–88. *Publications:* Housing: programming and development of estates, 1971, revd edn 1978; Housing Management: history, principles and practice, 1972; Housing Studies, 1st series, 1979, 2nd series, 1980, revd edn 1981; First New Town: an autobiography of the Stevenage Development Corporation, 1980; Sitting with Job: a

Biblical study, 1998. *Address:* Rhoswiel Lodge, Weston Rhyn, Oswestry, Shropshire SY10 7TG. *T:* (01691) 773139.

BALCHIN, Sir Robert (George Alexander), Kt 1993; DL; Chairman, The Grant-Maintained Schools Foundation and Centre, 1989–99; *b* 31 July 1942; *s* of late Leonard George Balchin and Elizabeth Balchin (*née* Skelton); *m* 1970, Jennifer, BA (Mus), DipEd, ACP, OStJ, *d* of late Bernard Kevin Kinlay, Cape Town; twin *s* (of whom one decd). *Educ:* Bec Sch.; Univ. of London; Univ. of Hull. Asst Master, Chinthurst Sch., 1964–68; Hd of English Dept, Ewell Sch., 1968–69; Res., Univ. of Hull Inst. of Educn, 1969–71; Headmaster, Hill Sch., Westerham, 1972–80; company chairman, 1980–; Chairman: Pardoe-Blacker (Publishing) Ltd, 1989–99; Grant-Maintained Schs Mutual Insce Ltd, 1992–95; Centre for Educn Mgt, 1994–. St John Ambulance: Nat. Schs Advr, 1978–82; Asst Dir-Gen., 1982–84; Dir-Gen., 1984–90; Mem. Chapter-Gen., Order of St John, 1984–99. Mem. Council, 1995–, Registrar, 1998–, Imperial Soc. of Kts Bachelor. Member: Standing Conf. on Sch. Sci. and Technol., 1976–79; FAS, 1994–97 (Chairman: New Schs Cttee, 1994–97; Schs Improvement Cttee, 1996–97); Jt Founder/Treas., Catch 'em Young Project Trust, 1984–; Chm./Founder, Campaign for a Gen. Teaching Council, 1981–85; Chairman: St John Nat. Schs Project, 1990–94; League of Mercy, 1999–; Pres., English Schs Orch., 1998–; Dep. Patron, Nat. Assoc. for Gifted Children, 1999–; Patron: Gateway Training Centre for Homeless, 1999–; Nat. Centre for Volunteering, 1999–. Mem. Editorial Bd, Education Today, 1981–87. Lecture Sec., Heraldry Soc., 1982–88; Chm., Balchin Family Soc., 1993–. Trustee, Adeline Genée Th., 1982–87. Mem., Surrey CC, 1981–85 (Mem., Educn and Social Services Cttees). Member: Court, Univ. of Leeds, 1995–2000; Council, Goldsmiths' Coll., London, 1997– (Dep. Chm. Council, 1999–); FCP 1971 (Hon. FCP 1987); Hon. FHS 1987; Hon. FCGI 1998 (Hon. MCGI 1983). Hon. DPhil Northland Open Univ., Canada, 1985. Freeman, 1980, Liveryman, 1987, Goldsmiths' Co. (Mem., Educn Cttee, 1995–). DL Greater London, 2001. KStJ 1984. Cross of Merit (Comdr), SMO Malta, 1987; Comdr, Order of Polonia Restituta, 1990. *Publications:* Emergency Aid in Schools, 1984; New Money, 1985, 2nd edn 1989; (jtly) Choosing a State School, 1989; (jtly) Emergency Aid at Work, 1990; numerous articles on educn/politics. *Address:* New Place, Lingfield, Surrey RH7 6EF. *T:* (01342) 834543, *Fax:* (01342) 835122; 88 Marsham Court, Westminster, SW1P 4LA. *Clubs:* Athenæum, Beefsteak.

BALCHIN, Prof. William George Victor, MA, PhD; FKC; FRGS, FRMetS, FBCartS; Emeritus Professor of Geography in the University of Wales (Swansea), 1978 (Professor of Geography, 1954–78); *b* 20 June 1916; *s* of Victor Balchin and Ellen Winifred Gertrude Chapple; *m* 1939, Lily Kettlewood (*d* 1999); one *s* one *d* (and one *d* decd). *Educ:* Aldershot County High Sch. (State Scholar and County Major Scholar, 1934); St Catharine's Coll., Cambridge (1st Cl. Pt I Geographical Tripos, 1936; College Prize for Geography, 1936; BA 1937; MA 1941). PhD KCL 1951; FKC 1984. FRGS 1937; FRMetS 1945; FBCartS, 1996. Jun. Demonstrator in Geog., Univ. of Cambridge, 1937–39 (Geomorphologist on Spitsbergen Expedn, 1938); Hydrographic Officer, Hydrographic Dept, Admiralty, 1939–45 (also part-time Lectr for Univ. of Bristol Regional Cttee on Educn and WEA Tutor and Lectr); Lectr in Geog., KCL, 1945–54 (Geomorphologist on US Sonora-Mohave Desert Expedn, 1952); University Coll. of Swansea, Univ. of Wales: Head, Dept of Geog., 1954–78; Dean, Faculty of Pure and Applied Science, 1959–61; Vice-Principal, 1964–66 and 1970–73. Leverhulme Emeritus Fellow, 1982. Royal Geographical Society: Open Essay Prize, 1936; Gill Meml Award, 1954; Mem. Council, 1962–65, 1975–82, 1984–88; Chm., Educn Cttee, 1975–88; Vice-Pres., 1978–82; Chm., Ordnance Survey Cons. Cttee for Educn, 1983–92. Geographical Association: Hon. Annual Conf. Organiser, 1950–54; Mem. Council, 1950–81; Trustee, 1954–77; Pres., 1971; Hon. Mem., 1980. Pres., Section E (Geog.), BAAS, 1972. Member: Met. Res. Cttee, MoD, 1963–69; British Nat. Cttee for Cartography, 1961–71 and 1976–79, for Geography, 1964–70 and 1976–78; Council, British Geography, 1988–92. Treasurer, Second Land Utilisation Survey of Britain, 1961–; Chm., Land Decade Educnl Council, 1978–83. Mem., Nature Conservancy Cttee for Wales, 1959–68; Vice-Pres., Glam Co. Naturalists' Trust, 1961–80. Pres., Balchin Family Hist. Soc., 1993–. Member: Hydrology Cttee, ICE, 1962–76; Bradford Univ. Disaster Prevention and Limitation Unit, 1989–97. Member, Court of Governors: Nat. Mus. of Wales, 1966–74; Univ. of Wales Swansea (formerly UC of Swansea), 1980–; Mem. Council, St David's UC, 1968–80. *Publications:* (ed) Geography and Man (3 vols), 1947; (with A. W. Richards) Climatic and Weather Exercises, 1949; (with A. W. Richards) Practical and Experimental Geography, 1952; Cornwall (The Making of the English Landscape Series), 1954; (ed and contrib.) Geography: an outline for the intending student, 1970; (ed and contrib.) Swansea and its Region, 1971; (ed and contrib.) Living History of Britain, 1981; Concern for Geography, 1981; The Cornish Landscape, 1983; The Geographical Association: the first hundred years, 1993; (ed and contrib.) The Joint School Story, 1997; over 150 res. papers, articles and contribs on geomorphology, climatology, hydrology, econ. geography and cartography in learned jls. *Recreations:* travel, writing. *Address:* 10 Low Wood Rise, Ben Rhydding, Ilkley, West Yorks LS29 8AZ. *T:* (01943) 600768. *Clubs:* Royal Commonwealth Society (Life Fellow, 1978), Geographical.

BALCON, Dr Raphael, MD; FRCP, FACC; Consultant Cardiologist, Bart's and the London NHS Trust; *b* 26 Aug. 1936; *s* of Henry and Rhoda Balcon; *m* 1959, Elizabeth Ann Henry; one *d*. *Educ:* King's Coll., London; King's Coll. Hosp. Med. Sch. (MB, BS 1960, MD 1969). LRCP, MRCS 1960, MRCP 1965, FRCP 1977; FACC 1973. House Phys., Med. Unit, KCH, 1960; House Surg., KCH, Dulwich, 1960; House Phys., London Chest Hosp., 1961; Sen. House Officer, St Stephen's Hosp., 1962; Public Health Fellow in Cardiology, Wayne State Univ. Med. Sch., USA, 1963; British Heart Foundn Fellow, Dept of Cardiol., KCH, 1964, Med. Registrar 1965; Registrar, then Sen. Registrar, National Heart Hosp., 1966–70; Consultant Cardiologist, Nat. Heart and Chest Hosps, London Chest Hosp., subseq. Royal Brompton and Nat. Heart and Lung Hosps, Victoria Park, then Royal Hosps, now Bart's and the London, NHS Trust, 1970–. Dean, Cardiothoracic Inst., 1976–80. Hon. Treasurer, 1981–86, Pres., 1995–97, British Cardiac Soc. *Publications:* contrib. books on cardiological subjects; papers in BMJ, Lancet, Brit. Heart Jl, Amer. Jl of Cardiol., Circulation, Eur. Jl of Cardiol., Acta Medica Scandinavica. *Recreations:* ski-ing, tennis, mountain walking.

BALDERSTONE, Sir James (Schofield), AC 1992; Kt 1983; company director, now retired, and grazier; Chairman: Australian Mutual Provident Society, 1990–93 (Director, 1979–93); Chase AMP Bank, 1990–91 (Director, 1985–91); Broken Hill Proprietary Co. Ltd, 1984–89 (Director, 1971–89); Stanbroke Pastoral Co., 1982–93 (Managing Director, 1964–81); *b* 2 May 1921; *s* of late James Schofield and Mary Essendon Balderstone; *m* 1946, Mary Henrietta Tyree; two *s* two *d*. *Educ:* Scotch College, Melbourne. Service with RANR, WWII, 1940–45. General Manager for Aust., Thos Borthwick & Sons, 1953–67; Dep. Chm., Westpac Banking Corp., 1992–93 (Dir, 1981–84); Director: NW Shelf Develt Pty, 1976–83; Woodside Petroleum, 1976–83; ICI (Australia), 1981–84. Founding Chm., Australian Meat Exporters' Fed. Council, 1963–64; Mem., Australian Meat Bd, 1964–67. Chairman: Commonwealth Govt Policy Discussion Gp on Agriculture, 1981–82; Scotch Coll. Council, 1991–95. Mem. Council, Aust. War Meml, 1994–99; Dir, Aust. War Meml Foundn, 1996–99. Pres., Inst. of Public Affairs (Vic.), 1981–84. DUniv Newcastle, NSW, 1985. Commander's Cross, Order of Merit (Germany), 1991. *Recreations:* farming, reading, sport. *Address:* 115 Mont Albert Road, Canterbury, Victoria 3126, Australia. *T:* (3) 98363137. *Clubs:* Australian, Melbourne (Melbourne); Union (Sydney); Queensland (Brisbane).

BALDING, Clare Victoria; sports presenter, BBC, since 1998; *b* 29 Jan. 1971; *d* of Ian Balding, LVO, and Lady Emma Balding, *sister* of Earl of Huntingdon, *qv*. *Educ:* Downe House; Newnham Coll., Cambridge (BA 2nd Cl. Hons English; Pres., Cambridge Union, 1992). Racing reporter, BBC Radio 5 Live, 1993–94; sports presenter, BBC Radio, 1994–; presenter: BBC horse-racing coverage, incl. Royal Ascot; Badminton, Burghley and Gatcombe Horse Trials; Sydney Olympics and Paralympics, 2000. Sports columnist, Evening Standard, 1997–. Judge, Whitbread Book Awards, 2001. *Recreations:* riding, tennis, ski-ing, theatre, cinema, travel. *Address:* c/o Jane Morgan Management, Café Royal, 68 Regent Street, W1R 6EL. *T:* (020) 7287 6045.

BALDOCK, Brian Ford, CBE 1997; Director, Marks & Spencer, since 1996 (Chairman, 1999–2000); Chairman, PIC International (formerly Dalgety), since 1998 (Director, since 1992); *b* 10 June 1934; *s* of Ernest A. and Florence F. Baldock; *m* 1st, 1956, Mary Lillian Bartolo (marr. diss. 1966); two *s*; 2nd, 1968, Carole Anthea Mason; one *s*. *Educ:* Clapham Coll., London. Army Officer, 1952–55. Procter & Gamble, 1956–61; Ted Bates Inc., 1961–63; Rank Orgn, 1963–66; Smith & Nephew, 1966–75; Revlon Inc., 1975–78; Imperial Group, 1978–86; Guinness PLC: Dir, 1986–96; Gp Man. Dir, 1989–96; Dep. Chm., 1992–96. Chm., Portman Group, 1989–96; Dir, Cornhill Insurance, 1996–. Chm., Mencap, 1998–. Freeman, City of London, 1989. CInstM 1991 (FInstM 1976); Fellow, Marketing Soc., 1988. FRSA 1987. *Recreations:* theatre (opera), cricket. *Address:* Michael House, Baker Street, W1U 8EP. *T:* (020) 7935 4422; *e-mail:* brian.baldock@marks-and-spenser.com. *Clubs:* Mark's, Lord's Taverners (Mem. Council; Chm., 1992–95).

BALDOCK, John Markham, MBE 2001; VRD 1949; Lieutenant Commander, RNVR, 1948; Chairman, Lenscrete Ltd, 1949–92; Director, CIBA-GEIGY (UK) Ltd, 1957–68; *b* 19 Nov. 1915; *s* of late Captain W. P. Baldock, and Mrs H. Chalcraft; *m* 1949, Pauline Ruth Gauntlett; two *s*. *Educ:* Rugby Sch.; Balliol Coll., Oxford. Agric. degree, 1937. Served War of 1939–45, with Royal Navy, Atlantic, Mediterranean, Indian Ocean; Russian convoys, 1942–43. Lloyds, EC3, 1945. Joined Board of Lenscrete, 1946. MP (C) Harborough Div. of Leics, 1950–Sept. 1959, retd, also as PPS to Rt Hon. D. Ormsby Gore (Minister of State, Foreign Office). Founder, Hollycombe steam collection. *Recreations:* country life, steam engines, industrial archæology. *Address:* The Old Stables, Hollycombe, Liphook, Hants GU30 7LR. *T:* (01428) 723233. *Club:* Farmers'.

BALDOCK, Lionel Trevor; Agent-General for Victoria, 1990–93; *b* 26 Nov. 1936; *s* of late Lionel Vernon Baldock and of Alice Thelma Baldock; *m* 1st, 1967, Carolynne Cutting (marr. diss.); one *s* one *d*; 2nd, 1993, Aude L. S. Jaffrézo; one *s* one *d*. *Educ:* Melbourne Univ. (BCom). Man. Dir, Evasoft Leather Co., 1958–73; General Manager: Tecnicast Pty Ltd, 1974–80; (also Dir) Centrifugal Castings Australia Pty Ltd, 1974–80; J. C. & Howard Wright Pty Ltd, 1983–84; Pacific Dunlop Ltd (NSW), 1984–85; Sen. Trade Comr, Australian Trade Commn, Paris, 1985–90. *Recreations:* swimming, ski-ing, sailing, walking. *Clubs:* Royal Automobile, Royal Over-Seas League (Mem. Council, 1995–); Royal Automobile, Royal South Yarra Lawn Tennis (Melbourne).

BALDOCK, (Richard) Stephen; High Master, St Paul's School, since 1992; *b* 19 Nov. 1944; *s* of John Allan Baldock and Marjorie Procter Baldock; *m* 1969, Dr Janet Elizabeth Cottrell; one *s* three *d*. *Educ:* St Paul's Sch.; King's Coll., Cambridge (John Stewart of Rannoch schol. in Greek and Latin 1964; BA 1967 Part I Classics, Part II Theology, MA 1970). St Paul's School: Asst Master, 1970–77; Housemaster, School House, 1977–84; Surmaster, 1984–92. Council Mem. and Educnl Advr, Overseas Missionary Fellowship, 1989–. Governor: Durston House Prep. Sch., Ealing, 1992–; Hall Sch., Hampstead, 1993–; Orley Farm Sch., Harrow, 1996–. *Recreations:* family, computers, sport. *Address:* St Paul's School, Lonsdale Road, Barnes, SW13 9JT. *T:* (020) 8748 8135. *Clubs:* East India, Devonshire, Sports and Public Schools, Naval, MCC.

BALDRY, Antony Brian, (Tony); MP (C) Banbury, since 1983; *b* 10 July 1950; *e s* of Peter Edward Baldry and Oina (*née* Paterson); *m* 1st, 1979, Catherine Elizabeth (marr. diss. 1996), 2nd *d* of Captain James Weir, RN and Elizabeth Weir; one *s* one *d*; 2nd, 2001, Pippa Isbell, *e d* of Col Penny Payne and Betty Payne. *Educ:* Leighton Park Sch., Reading; Univ. of Sussex (BA, LLB). Called to the Bar, Lincoln's Inn, 1975; barrister. Director: New Opportunity Press, 1975–90; Newpoint Publishing Gp, 1983–90; Camco Corp. plc, 1997–; XiMed Gp plc, 1997–; Tranmore Technologies plc, 1998–. Contested (C) Thurrock, 1979. PPS to Minister of State for Foreign and Commonwealth Affairs, 1986–87, to Lord Privy Seal and Leader of the House, 1987–89, to Sec. of State for Energy, 1989–90; Parliamentary Under-Secretary of State: Dept of Energy, 1990; DoE, 1990–94; FCO, 1994–95; Minister of State, MAFF, 1995–97. Mem., Parly Select Cttee on Employment, 1983–86; on Trade and Industry, 1997–2001; on Standards and Privileges, 2001–. Joined Sussex Yeomanry, 1971; TA Officer, resigned 1990; Hon. Col, RLC (TA), 1997–. Robert Schuman Silver Medal, Stiftung FVS Hamburg, 1978. *Recreations:* walking in the country, reading historical biography, gardening, cricket, beagling. *Address:* House of Commons, SW1A 0AA. *Clubs:* Carlton, Farmers', Brass Monkey; Banbury Conservative.

BALDRY, Jack Thomas; Director, Purchasing and Supplies, Post Office, 1969–72; *b* 5 Oct. 1911; *s* of late John and Ellen Baldry; *m* 1936, Ruby Berenice (*née* Frost); three *d*. *Educ:* Framlingham Coll. Post Office: Asst Traffic Supt, 1930; Asst Surveyor, 1935; Asst Princ., 1940; Princ., 1947 (Private Sec. to PMG, 1950–53); Asst Sec., 1953; Dep. Dir, External Telecommunications, 1960; Dir of Personnel, 1967. *Recreations:* farming, foreign travel, solving crossword puzzles, watching sport on TV. *Address:* Village End, Bruisyard Road, Badingham, Woodbridge IP13 8NA. *T:* (01728) 638331.

BALDRY, Tony; *see* Baldry, A. B.

BALDWIN, family name of **Earl Baldwin of Bewdley**.

BALDWIN OF BEWDLEY, 4th Earl *cr* 1937; **Edward Alfred Alexander Baldwin;** Viscount Corvedale, 1937; *b* 3 Jan. 1938; *o s* of 3rd Earl Baldwin of Bewdley and Joan Elspeth, *y d* of late C. Alexander Tomes, New York, USA; *S* father, 1976; *m* 1970, Sarah MacMurray (*d* 2001), *er d* of Evan James, *qv*; three *s*. *Educ:* Eton; Trinity Coll., Cambridge (MA, PGCE). Chm., British Acupuncture Accreditation Bd, 1990–98. Jt Chm., Parly Gp for Alternative and Complementary Medicine, 1992–; elected Mem., H of L, 1999; Mem., H of L Select Cttee inquiry into complementary and alternative medicine, 2000. *Heir:* *s* Viscount Corvedale, *qv*. *Address:* Manor Farm House, Godstow Road, Upper Wolvercote, Oxford OX2 8AJ. *T:* (01865) 552683. *Club:* MCC.

BALDWIN, Alan Charles; a District Judge (Magistrates' Court)(formerly Metropolitan Stipendiary Magistrate), since 1990; *b* 14 April 1948; *s* of Frederick Baldwin and Millicent Baldwin (*née* McCarthy); *m* 1974, Denise Maureen Jagger; two *s*. Admitted Solicitor, 1976. *Address:* Thames Magistrates' Court, 58 Bow Road, E3 4DJ.

BALDWIN, David Arthur, CBE 1990; CEng, FIEE; Director Emeritus, Hewlett-Packard Ltd, since 1996 (Chairman, 1988–96); *b* 1 Sept. 1936; *s* of late Isaac Arthur Baldwin and Edith Mary Baldwin (*née* Collins); *m* 1961, (Jacqueline) Anne Westcott; one *s* one *d*. *Educ:* Twickenham Technical Coll.; Wimbledon Technical Coll. (qualified electronic engineer). CEng; FIEE 1989. R&D Engineer, EMI, 1954–63; Sales Engineer, Solartron, 1963–65; Hewlett-Packard: Sales Engineer and Sales Manager, 1965–73; European Marketing Manager, 1973–78; Man. Dir, Hewlett-Packard Ltd, 1978–88. Man. Dir, Hewlett-Packard Europ. Multi-Country Region, 1990; Pres., Hewlett-Packard Belgium, 1991; Chm., Hewlett-Packard Spain, 1991; Director, Hewlett-Packard Finland, Sweden, Denmark, Netherlands and Austria, 1991–96. Mem., BOTB, 1994–98 (Chm., European Trade Cttee, 1994–98); Chm., Thames Action and Res. Gp for Educn and Trng Ltd, 1996–. Mem. Council, RSA, 1994–. Member, Court: Cranfield Univ. (formerly Inst. of Technol.), 1987–; Brunel Univ., 1988–. CIMgt; FInstD; FIMktg. Freeman City of London, 1988; Liveryman, Guild of Inf. Technologists, 1994. DUniv Strathclyde, 1990. *Recreations:* golf, ski-ing, photography, painting, sailing. *Address:* c/o Hewlett-Packard Ltd, Cain Road, Bracknell, Berks RG12 1HN. *T:* (01344) 360000.

BALDWIN, Captain George Clifton, CBE 1968; DSC 1941 and Bar 1944; RN (retd); Member: Press Council, 1973–78; Press Council Appointments Commission, 1978–90; *b* 17 Jan. 1921; *s* of late George and late Louisa Baldwin; *m* 1947, Hasle Mary McMahon; three *s*. *Educ:* Sleaford Grammar Sch., Lincs; Hitchin Grammar Sch., Herts. Served War: joined RN, 1939, Pilot in Fleet Air Arm; in comd: 807 Sqdn, 1943; No 4 Naval Fighter Wing, 1944–45. Qual. at Empire Test Pilots' Sch., 1946; in comd, 800 Sqdn, 1952; in comd, RN Air Station, Lossiemouth, 1961–62; Dir, Naval Air Warfare, MoD, 1964–66; in comd, RN Air Station, Yeovilton, 1966–68; ADC, 1967; retd, 1968. Chm., Fleet Air Arm Officers' Assoc., 1973–78 (Vice Pres., 1978–). *Address:* Applegarth, Church Lane, Lodsworth, Petworth, West Sussex GU28 9DD. *T:* (01798) 861236.

BALDWIN, Sir Jack (Edward), Kt 1997; PhD; FRS 1978; Waynflete Professor of Chemistry and Fellow of Magdalen College, University of Oxford, since 1978; *b* 8 Aug. 1938; *s* of Frederick Charles Baldwin and Olive Frances Headland; *m* 1977, Christine Louise, *d* of William B. Franchi. *Educ:* Lewes County Grammar Sch.; Imperial Coll., London Univ. (BSc, DIC, PhD). ARCS. Asst Lectr in Chem., Imperial Coll., 1963, Lectr, 1966; Asst Prof. of Chem., Pa State Univ., 1967, Associate Prof., 1969; Alfred P. Sloan Fellow, 1969–70, Associate Prof. of Chem., 1970, Prof., 1972, MIT; Daniell Prof. of Chem., King's Coll., London, 1972; Prof. of Chem., MIT, 1972–78. Dir, Oxford Centre for Molecular Sciences, 1988–98. Mem., BBSRC, 1994–97. Lectures: Tilden, RSC, 1979; Simonsen, RSC, 1982. Corresp. Mem., Academia Scientiarum Gottingensis, Göttingen, 1988; For. Mem., Amer. Acad. of Arts and Scis, 1993. Hon. DSc: Warwick, 1988, Strathclyde, 1989. Corday Morgan Medal and Prize, Chem. Soc., 1975; Medal and Prize for Synthetic Organic Chemistry, RSC, 1980; Paul Karrer Medal and Prize, Zurich Univ., 1984; Medal and Prize for Natural Product Chemistry, RSC, 1984; Hugo Müller Medal, RSC, 1987; Max Tischler Award, Harvard Univ., 1987; Dr Paul Jansen Prize for Creativity in Organic Synthesis, Belgium, 1988; Davy Medal, 1994, Leverhulme Medal, 1999, Royal Soc. *Publications:* res. pubns in Jl of Amer. Chem. Soc., Jl of Chem. Soc., Tetrahedron. *Address:* Dyson Perrins Laboratory, South Parks Road, Oxford OX1 3QY.

BALDWIN, John, OBE 1978; National Secretary, Amalgamated Engineering Union (formerly Amalgamated Union of Engineering Workers) Workers/Construction Section, 1976–88; *b* 16 Aug. 1923; *s* of Stephen John Baldwin and Elizabeth (*née* Hutchinson); *m* 1945, Grace May Florence (*née* Wilson); two *d*. *Educ:* Laindon High Road Sen. Sch., Essex. Boy service, RN, HMS Ganges, 1938; returned to civilian life, 1948; Steel Erector, CEU, 1950; played active part as Shop Steward and Site Convenor; elected full-time official, 1957; Asst Gen. Sec., AUEW/Construction Sect., 1969–76. Chm., Mechanical Handling Sector Working Party of NEDO; Member: Engrg Construction EDC, 1975; Construction Equipment and Mobile Cranes Sector Working Party of NEDO; National Jt Council for the Engrg Construction Industry. Mem., Labour Party, 1962–. *Recreations:* most sports. *Address:* 7 Ridge Langley, Sanderstead, South Croydon, Surrey CR2 0AP. *T:* (020) 8651 1643.

BALDWIN, Prof. John Evan, PhD; FRS 1991; Professor of Radioastronomy, 1989–99, now Emeritus, and Fellow of Queens' College, since 1989, University of Cambridge; Head of Mullard Radio Astronomy Observatory, Cavendish Laboratory, 1987–97; *b* 6 Dec. 1931; *s* of Evan Baldwin and Mary Wild; *m* 1969, Joyce Cox. *Educ:* Merchant Taylors', Crosby; Queens' Coll., Cambridge (MA; Clerk Maxwell Student, 1955–57; PhD 1956). FInstP 1997. Cambridge University: Research Fellow, later Fellow, Queens' Coll., 1956–74; Univ. Demonstrator in Physics, 1957–62; Asst Dir of Research, 1962–81; Reader, 1981–89. Guthrie Medal, Inst. of Physics, 1997; Hopkins Prize, Cambridge Philosophical Soc., 1997; Jackson Gwilt Medal, RAS, 2001. *Publications:* contribs to scientific jls. *Recreations:* gardening, mountain walking. *Address:* Cavendish Laboratory, Madingley Road, Cambridge CB3 0HE. *T:* (01223) 337294.

BALDWIN, Dr John Paul; QC 1991; *b* 15 Aug. 1947; *s* of Frank Baldwin and of late Marjorie Baldwin (*née* Jay); *m* 1981, Julie Campbell; two *d*. *Educ:* Nelson Grammar Sch.; Univ. of Leeds (BSc 1st Cl. Hons 1968); St John's Coll., Oxford (DPhil 1972). Res. Fellow, Univ. of Oxford, 1972–75; called to the Bar, Gray's Inn, 1977, Bencher, 2000. *Publications:* numerous scientific pubns, 1969–75. *Recreations:* tennis, gardening. *Address:* 8 New Square, Lincoln's Inn, WC2A 3QP. *T:* (020) 7405 4321. *Clubs:* Harbour, Campden Hill Lawn Tennis.

BALDWIN, Nicholas Peter, CEng, FIMechE; Chief Executive, PowerGen UK plc, since 2001; *b* 17 Dec. 1952; *s* of Desmond Stanley Frederick Baldwin and Beatrix Marie Baldwin (*née* Walker); partner, Adrienne Ann Plunkett; one *s* one *d*. *Educ:* City Univ. (BSc Mechanical Engrg); Birkbeck Coll., Univ. of London (MSc Econs). CEng 1979; FIMechE 1996. Metropolitan Water Bd, 1971–74; Thames Water Authy, 1974–80; CEGB, 1980–89, Sen. Energy Analyst, 1986–89; PowerGen plc, 1989–: Econ. Studies Manager, 1989–90; Business Planning Manager, 1990–92; Head of Strategic Planning, 1992–94; Director: Strategy, 1994–95; Generation, 1995–96; Man. Dir, UK Electricity Prodn, 1996–98; Exec. Dir, UK Ops, 1998–2001. FRSA 1998. *Publications:* articles in Energy Policy and Energy Economics. *Recreations:* hill-walking, jazz and rock music, reading, family activities. *Address:* PowerGen plc, Westwood Way, Westwood Business Park, Coventry CV4 8LG. *Club:* Worcester County Cricket.

BALDWIN, Air Vice-Marshal Nigel Bruce, CB 1996; CBE 1992; Assistant Chief of Defence Staff (Overseas), 1993–96; *b* 20 Sept. 1941; *s* of Peter William Baldwin and Doris Baldwin; *m* 1963, Jennifer; one *d* (and one *d* decd). *Educ:* Peter Symonds' Sch., Winchester; RAF Coll., Cranwell. Pilot, Vulcans, 9/35 Sqns, 1963–68; ADC to AOC 11 Gp, 1968–70; Sqn Ldr, Vulcans, 35 Sqn, Cyprus, 1970–73; Staff Coll., Bracknell, 1974; HQ Strike Command, 1975–76; OC 50 Sqn, Vulcans, 1977–79; US Air War Coll. and Faculty, US Air Command and Staff Coll., 1979–82; Gp Captain and Station Comdr, Wyton, 1983–85; Internat. Fellow, Nat. Defense Univ., Washington, 1986; Asst Dir of Defence Policy, MoD, 1986–88; Air Cdre Plans, HQ Strike Command, 1989–92. Chairman: Ex-Services Mental Welfare Soc., 1997–; RAF Historical Soc., 1997–. FRSA 1995; FRAeS 1997. *Recreations:* hill walking, Schubert, Nelson. *Club:* Royal Air Force.

BALDWIN, Maj.-Gen. Peter Alan Charles, CBE 1994; Company Secretary, Television Corporation, since 1997 (Consultant, 1996); *b* 19 Feb. 1927; *s* of Alec Baldwin and Anne Dance; *m* 1st, 1953, Judith Elizabeth Mace; 2nd, 1982, Gail J. Roberts. *Educ:* King Edward VI Grammar Sch., Chelmsford. Enlisted 1942; commnd R Signals 1947; early service included Berlin, 1948–49 (during airlift), and Korean War, 1950; Staff Coll., 1960; JSSC, 1964; Borneo operations (despatches, 1967); Directing Staff, Staff Coll., 1967–69; Comdr, 13 Signal Regt, BAOR, 1969–71; Sec. for Studies, NATO Defence Coll., 1971–74; Comdr, 2 Signal Group, 1974–76; ACOS Jt Exercises Div., Allied Forces Central Europe, 1976–77; Maj.-Gen. and Chief Signal Officer, BAOR, 1977–79. Dep. Dir of Radio, 1979–87, Dir of Radio, 1987–90, IBA; Chief Exec., Radio Authy, 1991–95. Mem., Media/Events Cttee, RCM, 1995–. Trustee: Eyeless Trust, 1996–; CSV, 1997–; D'Oyly Carte Opera Co., 2000–. Fellow, Radio Acad., 1992; FRSA 1993. *Recreations:* cricket, music, theatre. *Address:* c/o Lloyds TSB, 7 Pall Mall, SW1Y 5NA. *Clubs:* Army and Navy, MCC.

BALDWIN, Sir Peter (Robert), KCB 1977 (CB 1973); MA; President, Charities Aid Foundation, since 1999 (Member of the Board, 1988–98; Vice-Chairman, 1993; Chairman, 1994–98); *b* 10 Nov. 1922; *s* of Charles Baldwin and Katie Baldwin (*née* Field); *m* 1951, Margaret Helen Moar; two *s*. *Educ:* City of London Sch.; Corpus Christi Coll., Oxford (Hon. Fellow, 1980). Foreign Office, 1942–45; Gen. Register Office, 1948–54; HM Treasury, 1954–62; Cabinet Office, 1962–64; HM Treasury, 1964–76; Principal Private Sec. to Chancellor of Exchequer, July 1966–Jan. 1968; Under-Sec., HM Treasury, 1968–72; Dep. Sec., HM Treasury, 1972–76; Second Permanent Sec., DoE, 1976; Permanent Sec., Dept of Transport, 1976–82. Dir, Mitchell Cotts, 1983–87; Chairman: SE Thames RHA, 1983–91; Rural Village Devolt Foundn, 1983–85 (Vice-Chm., 1985–90); Brent Dial-a-Ride, 1983–85; Westminster Dial-a-Ride, 1984–87; Community Transport, 1985–87; Tripscope, 1986–94 (Pres., 1994–); Disabled Persons Transport Adv. Cttee, 1986–93; Kent Air Ambulance Appeal, 1992–94; President: Readibus, 1981–84; Disability Action Westminster, 1986–95 (Chm., 1983–86); AFASIC, 1995–; Vice-President: RNID, 1983–91; Disabled Drivers Motoring Club, 1985–; Hearing Dogs for the Deaf, 1986– (Chm., 1983–86); PHAB, 1988– (Vice-Chm., 1981, Chm., 1982–88; Vice-Pres., N Ireland, 1990–); RADAR, 1998– (Mem., 1983–96, Chm., 1992–96, Exec. Cttee); Chm. Trustees, Pets as Therapy, 1997– (Trustee, 1990–). Automobile Association: Vice-Pres., 1993–; Mem. Cttee, 1983–93, Vice-Chm. Cttee, 1990–93; Mem., Chm.'s Res. Adv. Gp, AA Road Safety Res. Foundn, 1994–. Member: Nat. Railway Mus. Cttee, 1983–87; Bd, Public Finance Foundn, 1984–98; Bd, RSA Exams, 1989–94; Bd, City Lit. Inst., 1990–95; Council, KCL, 1992–; Chairman: Council, Royal Soc. of Arts, 1985–87 (Vice Pres., 1987–; FRSA); Delegacy, KCH Med. and Dental Sch., 1991–98; Mem. Bd of Govs, UMDS of Guy's and St Thomas's Hosp., 1993–98. Life Vice-Pres., Civil Service Sports Council, 1982– (Chm., 1978–82; Vice-Chm., 1974–78). Chm., St Catherine's Home and Sch., Ventnor, 1961–78; Governor, Eltham Coll., 1984–85. FKC; FCIT; Hon. FIHT; CIMgt. Freeman, City of London, 1992. *Recreations:* painting, watching cricket. *Address:* 123 Alderney Street, SW1V 4HE. *T:* (020) 7821 7157. *Club:* Reform.

BALES, Kenneth Frederick, CBE 1990; Regional Managing Director, West Midlands Regional Health Authority, 1984–92; *b* 2 March 1931; *s* of Frederick Charles Bales and Deborah Alice Bales; *m* 1958, Margaret Hazel Austin; two *s* one *d*. *Educ:* Buckhurst Hill Grammar Sch.; LSE; Univ. of Manchester. BScSoc; DipSocAdmin; AHSM. Hosp. Sec., Newhall & Hesketh Park Hosps, 1958–62; Regional Trng Officer, Birmingham Regional Hosp. Bd, 1962–65; Regional Staff Officer, Birmingham Regional Staff Cttee, 1965–68; Group Sec., W Birmingham HMC, 1968–73; Regional Administrator, W Midlands RHA, 1973–84. Vice Pres., Disability W Midlands, 1999– (Chm., 1996–98). *Recreations:* painting, sport, bridge. *Address:* Stronefield, 4 St Catherine's Close, Blackwell, near Bromsgrove, Worcestershire B60 1BG. *T:* (0121) 445 1424.

BALFE, Richard Andrew; Member (Lab) London Region, European Parliament, since 1999 (London South Inner, 1979–99); *b* 14 May 1944; *s* of Dr Richard J. Balfe and Mrs Dorothy L. Balfe (*née* de Cann); *m* 1986, Susan Jane Honeyford; one *s* one *d*, and one *s* by a previous marriage. *Educ:* Brook Secondary Sch., Sheffield; LSE (BSc Hons 1971). Fellow Royal Statistical Soc., 1972. HM Diplomatic Service, 1965–70; Res. Officer, Finer Cttee on One Parent Families, 1970–73; Political Sec., RACS, 1973–79; Dir, RACS and associated cos, 1978–85. European Parliament: Quaestor, 1994–; Member: Foreign Affairs Cttee, 1981–99; Security Cttee, 1989–99; Econ. and Monetary Cttee, 1999–; Lab. spokesman on defence, 1989–99, on Treasury matters, 1999–; Lab. Mem. responsible for liaison with HM Treasury. Parly Candidate (Labour), Paddington South, 1970; contested (Lab) Southwark and Bermondsey, 1992. Mem., GLC for Southwark/Dulwich, 1973–77; Chairman: Thamesmead New Town Cttee, 1973–75; GLC Housing Cttee, 1975–77. Member: Exec. Cttee, Fabian Soc., 1981–82; London Labour Party Exec., 1973–95 (Chair, Policy Cttee, 1983–85); Chair, Political Cttee, CWS, 1984–95. Mem., Ct of Governors, LSE, 1973–91. *Publications:* Housing: a new Socialist perspective, 1976; Role and Problems of the Co-operative Movement in the 1980s (with Tony Banks), 1977. *Recreations:* collecting books and pamphlets on political and social history topics, opera, Wagner, walking. *Address:* European Parliament, Rue Wiertz,1047 Brussels, Belgium. *T:* (2) 2845406, *Fax:* (2) 2849406; *e-mail:* rbalfe@europarl.eu.int. *Club:* Reform.

BALFOUR, family name of **Earl of Balfour** and **Barons Balfour of Inchrye, Kinross** and **Riverdale**.

BALFOUR, 4th Earl of, *cr* 1922; **Gerald Arthur James Balfour;** Viscount Traprain 1922; JP; farmer; *b* 23 Dec. 1925; *er s* of 3rd Earl of Balfour and Jean (*d* 1981), 4th *d* of late Rev. Canon J. J. Cooke-Yarborough; *S* father, 1968; *m* 1956, Natasha Georgina (*d* 1994), *d* of late Captain George Anton. *Educ:* Eton; HMS Conway. Holds Master Mariner's certificate. Mem., E Lothian CC, 1960–75. JP East Lothian, 1970. *Heir: cousin* Roderick Francis Arthur Balfour [*b* 9 Dec. 1948; *m* 1971, Lady Tessa Mary Isabel Fitzalan-Howard, *e d* of 17th Duke of Norfolk, *qv*; four *d*]. *Address:* The Tower, Whittingehame, Haddington, Scotland EH41 4QA. *Clubs:* English-Speaking Union; International Association of Cape Horners.

BALFOUR OF BURLEIGH, Lord *cr* 1607 (*de facto* 8th Lord, 12th but for the Attainder); **Robert Bruce,** CEng, FIEE; FRSE; Chancellor, Stirling University, 1988–98; Vice Lord-Lieutenant, Clackmannan, since 1995; *b* 6 Jan. 1927; *e s* of 11th Lord Balfour of Burleigh and Dorothy (*d* 1976), *d* of late R. H. Done; *S* father, 1967; *m* 1st, 1971, Mrs Jennifer Brittain-Catlin (marr. diss. 1993), *d* of late E. S. Manasseh; two *d*; 2nd, 1993, Janet Morgan (*see* Lady Balfour of Burleigh). *Educ:* Westminster Sch. Served RN, 1945–48, as Ldg Radio Electrician's Mate. Joined English Electric Co. Ltd, 1951; graduate apprentice, 1951–52; Asst Foreman, Heavy Electrical Plant Dept, Stafford Works, 1952–54; Asst Superintendent, Heavy Electrical Plant Dept, Netherton Works, Liverpool, 1954–57; Manager, English Electric Co. of India (Pvt) Ltd, Madras, 1957–60; Dir and Gen. Manager, English Electric Co. India Ltd, 1960–64; Dep. Gen. Manager, English Electric Co. Ltd, Netherton, Liverpool, 1964–65, Gen. Manager 1965–66; Dir and Gen. Manager,

D. Napier & Son Ltd, 1966–68; Dep. Gov., Bank of Scotland, 1977–91 (Dir, 1968–91). Chairman: Viking Oil, 1971–80; NWS Bank (formerly North West Securities), 1978–91; Capella Nova, 1988–; Canongate Press, 1991–93; United Artists Communications (Scotland), 1993–96; Director: Scottish Investment Trust, 1971–97; Tarmac, 1981–90; William Lawson Distillers Ltd, 1984–97; Television Educnl Network, 1990–96; UAPT Infolink, 1991–94; Member: British Railways (Scottish) Board, 1982–93; Forestry Commn, 1971–74. Chm., Fedn of Scottish Bank Employers, 1977–86. Chairman: Scottish Arts Council, 1971–80; NBL Scotland, 1981–85; Turing Inst., 1983–91; Scottish Cttee, ABSA, 1990–94 (Mem. Council, 1976–94); Dir, Edinburgh Book Fest., 1981–97 (Chm., 1981–87). Pres., Friends of Vellore, 1973–. Vice-Pres., RNID, 1987–; Treasurer: Royal Scottish Corp., 1967–; RSE, 1989–94; Trustee: John Muir Trust, 1989–96; Bletchley Park Trust, 2000–. Hon. FRIAS, 1982. DUniv Stirling, 1988; Hon. DLitt Robert Gordon, 1995. *Recreations:* music, climbing, woodwork, open air ice-skating. *Heir:* d Hon. Victoria Bruce, *b* 7 May 1973. *Address:* Brucefield, Clackmannanshire FK10 3QF.
See also G. J. D. Bruce.

BALFOUR OF BURLEIGH, Lady; Janet Bruce; writer and consultant; *b* 5 Dec. 1945; *e d* of Frank Morgan and Shiela Sadler; *m* 1993, Lord Balfour of Burleigh, *qv*. *Educ:* Newbury Co. Girls Grammar Sch.; St Hugh's Coll., Oxford. MA, DPhil Oxon, MA Sussex. FSAScot 1992; FRSE 1999. Kennedy Meml Scholar, Harvard Univ., 1968–69; Student, Nuffield Coll., Oxford, 1969–71; Res. Fellow, Wolfson Coll., Oxford and Res. Officer, Univ. of Essex, 1971–72; Res. Fellow, Nuffield Coll., Oxford, 1972–74; Lectr in Politics, Exeter Coll., Oxford, 1974–76; Dir of Studies, St Hugh's Coll., Oxford, 1975–76 and Lectr in Politics, 1976–78; Mem., Central Policy Rev. Staff, Cabinet Office, 1978–81. Mem. Bd, British Council, 1989–99. Vis. Fellow, All Souls Coll., Oxford, 1983. Dir, Satellite Television PLC, 1981–83; Special Advr to Dir-Gen., BBC, 1983–86; Advr to Bd, Granada Gp, 1986–89; Mem., London Adv. Bd, Nat. and Provincial Bldg Soc., 1988–89; Chm., Cable & Wireless Flexible Resource Ltd, 1993–97; non-executive Director: Cable & Wireless, 1988–; W. H. Smith, 1989–95; Midlands Electricity, 1990–96; Pitney Bowes, 1991–93; Scottish American Investment Trust, 1991–; Scottish Med. Res. Fund, 1993–96; Scottish Life, 1995–2001; Scottish Oriental Smaller Cos Investment Trust, 1995–; Nuclear Generation Decommissioning Co. Ltd, 1996–; NMT Group plc, 1997–; BPB plc, 2000–; Stagecoach Gp, 2001–. Vice-Pres., Videotext Industries Assoc., 1985–91; Dir, Hulton Deutsch Collection, 1988–90. Member: Lord Chancellor's Adv. Council on Public Records, 1982–86; Scottish Museums Council Develt Resource, 1988–96; Adv. Council, Inst. for Advanced Studies in the Humanities, Univ. of Edinburgh, 1988–96; Ancient Monuments Bd for Scotland, 1990–97; Book Trust (Scotland), 1992–99; Scottish Econ. Council, 1993–96; Chairman: Scotland's Book Campaign, 1994–96; Readiscovery Touring Ltd, 1996–99. Trustee: Amer. Sch. in London, 1985–88; Fairground Heritage Trust, 1987–90; Cyclotron Trust, 1988–90; Scottish Hosp. Endowments Res. Trust, 1992–; Carnegie Endowment for Univs of Scotland, 1994–; Nuclear Trust, 1996–; Scottish Science Trust, 1997–99; Chairman: Dorothy Burns Charitable Trust, 1992–; Scottish Cultural Resources Access Network Ltd, 1996–; Scottish Mus. of Year Awards, 1999–. Mem., Editorial Bd, Political Quarterly, 1980–90. Hon. LLD Strathclyde, 1999; Hon. DLitt Napier, 1999. *Publications* (as Janet Morgan): The House of Lords and the Labour Government 1964–70, 1975; Reinforcing Parliament, 1976; (ed) The Diaries of a Cabinet Minister 1964–70 by Richard Crossman, 3 vols 1975, 1976, 1977; (ed) Backbench Diaries 1951–63 by Richard Crossman, 1980; (ed with Richard Hoggart) The Future of Broadcasting, 1982; Agatha Christie: a biography, 1984; Edwina Mountbatten: a life of her own, 1991. *Recreations:* music of Handel, sea-bathing, ice-skating out of doors, pruning. *Address:* Brucefield, Clackmannanshire FK10 3QF. *T:* (01259) 730228.

BALFOUR OF INCHRYE, 2nd Baron *cr* 1945, of Shefford; **Ian Balfour;** *b* 21 Dec. 1924; *s* of 1st Baron Balfour of Inchrye, PC, MC and Diana Blanche (*d* 1982), *d* of Sir Robert Grenville Harvey, 2nd Bt; *S* father, 1988; *m* 1953, Josephine Maria Jane, *d* of late Morogh Percy Wyndham Bernard and of the Hon. Mrs Bernard; one *d*. *Educ:* Eton, spasmodically, and Magdalen College, Oxford (MA). Business consultant, author and composer of 8 operas, and numerous orchestral and instrumental works. Performances include: In Memoriam II (oboe, harp, percussion and strings), Dublin, 1982; Suite No 1 for 'Cello, Edinburgh, 1984, London, 1986; Oxford Memories (orch.), Oxford, London, 1996; Millennium Surprise (orch.), Esterhazy, Leipzig, Moscow, Prague, 2000. *Publication:* Famous Diamonds, 1987, 4th edn 2000. *Recreations:* watching cricket and Association football, walking, writing, thinking, drinking, dreaming. *Address:* 4 Marsh End, Ferry Road, Walberswick, Suffolk IP18 6TH.

BALFOUR, Comdr Colin James, RN; farmer; Vice Lord-Lieutenant of Hampshire, 1996–99; *b* 12 June 1924; *s* of late Maj. Melville Balfour, MC, Wintershill Hall, Hants and Margaret, (Daisy), Mary Balfour (*née* Lascelles); *m* 1949, Prudence Elizabeth, JP, *d* of Adm. Sir Ragnar Colvin, KBE, CB; one *s* one *d*. *Educ:* Eton. Joined RN, 1942: served HMS Nelson, Mediterranean, 1943; D-Day and N Russia Convoys, 1944–45; HMS Cossack, Korean War, 1950–52; RNSC, 1955; 1st Lt, HM Yacht Britannia, 1956–57; Comdr 1957; Capt., HMS Finisterre, 1960–62; resigned 1965. Mem., Hants Local Valuation Panel, 1971–81 (Chm., 1977–81). Country Landowners' Association: Chm., 1980–81, Pres., 1987–94, Hants Br.; Chm., Legal and Parly Sub-cttee and Mem., Nat. Exec. Cttee, 1982–87; Chm., Charitable Trust, 1988–96. Pres., Hants Fedn of Young Farmers' Clubs, 1982. Liaison Officer (Hants), Duke of Edinburgh's Award Scheme, 1966–76. Governor: and Vice-Chm., Larkhills Special Sch., Winchester, 1975–80; Durley C of E Primary Sch., 1966–97 (Chm., 1980–96). High Sheriff 1972, DL 1973, Hants. Freeman, City of London, 1982; Liveryman, Farmers' Co., 1983–. *Recreations:* shooting, small woodland management. *Address:* Wintershill Farmhouse, Durley, Hants SO32 2AH; Flat 4, Cygnet House, 188 Kings Road, SW3 5XR. *Clubs:* Brooks's, Pratt's.

BALFOUR, (Elizabeth) Jean, CBE 1981; FRSE 1980; FRSA; FICFor; FIBiol; JP; Chairman, Countryside Commission for Scotland, 1972–82; *b* 4 Nov. 1927; 2nd *d* of late Maj.-Gen. Sir James Syme Drew, KBE, CB, DSO, MC, and late Victoria Maxwell of Munches; *m* 1950, John Charles Balfour, *qv*; three *s*. *Educ:* Edinburgh Univ. (BSc). Partner/Owner, Balbirnie Home Farms; Dir, A. & J. Bowen & Co. Ltd; Chm., Loch Duart Ltd, 1999–. Pres., Royal Scottish Forestry Soc., 1969–71; Mem., Fife CC, 1958–70; Chm., Fife County and City and Royal Burgh of Dunfermline Joint Probation Cttee, 1967–69; Governor, East of Scotland Coll. of Agriculture, 1958–88, Vice Pres. 1982–88; Dir, Scottish Agricl Colls, 1987–88, Dir, Council, 1974–87; Member: Scottish Agric. Develt Council, 1972–77; Verney Working Party on Natural Resources, 1971–72; Nature Conservancy Council, 1973–80; Oil Develt Council, 1973–78; Scottish Economic Council, 1978–83; Forth River Purification Bd, 1992–96; Council, SLF (Chm., Forestry Cttee, 1997–99); Chairman: Regional Adv. Cttee, East (Scotland) Forestry Commn, 1976–85; Regional Adv. Cttee, Mid (Scotland) Forestry Commn, 1987–2000; Food and Farming Adv. Cttee, Scottish Cons. and Unionist Assoc., 1985–88; Crarae Gardens Charitable Trust, 1986–93; W Sutherland Fisheries Trust, 1996–99; Hon. Vice Pres., Scottish Wildlife Trust (Vice-Chm., 1968–72; Founder Council Mem.). Deputy Chairman: Seafish Industry Authority, 1987–90; Cttee on Women in Science, Engrg and Technol., OST, Cabinet Office, 1993–94. Mem., Cttee of Enquiry on handling of geographical information, 1985–87. Trustee: Buckland Foundn, 1989–94; Royal Botanic Gdns, Edinburgh, 1992–98. Mem. Council, RSE, 1983–86; Mem. Council and Chm., Policy and Legislation Cttee, Inst. of Chartered Foresters, 1986–88; Council Mem. and Chm., Mid Scotland TGA. Hon. Vice-Pres., Scottish YHA, 1983–. Mem. Court, St Andrews Univ., 1983–87 (Chm. Ct Cttee, Estates and Buildings, 1983–87); Gov., Duncan of Jordanstone Coll. of Art, 1992–96. JP Fife, 1963. FRSA 1981; FRZSScot 1983; FIBiol 1988; FRSGS 1997. Hon. DSc St Andrews, 1977; DUniv Stirling, 1991. Forestry Medal, Inst. of Chartered Foresters, 1996. Order of the Falcon (Iceland), 1994. Report to Government, A New Look at the Northern Ireland Countryside, 1984–85. *Recreations:* hill walking, fishing, painting, exploring arctic vegetation, shooting. *Address:* Kirkforthar House, Markinch, Fife KY7 6LS. *T:* (01592) 752233; Scourie, by Lairg, Sutherland IV27 4TH. *Clubs:* Farmers'; (Assoc. Mem.) New (Edinburgh).

BALFOUR, Jean; *see* Balfour, E. J.

BALFOUR, John Charles, OBE 1978; MC 1943; JP; Vice Lord-Lieutenant for Fife, 1988–96; Chairman, Fife Area Health Board, 1983–87 (Member, 1981–87); *b* 28 July 1919; *s* of late Brig. E. W. S. Balfour, CVO, DSO, OBE, MC, and Lady Ruth Balfour, CBE; *m* 1950, (Elizabeth) Jean Drew (*see* (Elizabeth) Jean Balfour); three *s*. *Educ:* Eton Coll.; Trinity Coll., Cambridge (BA). Served war, Royal Artillery, 1939–45 (Major), N Africa and Europe. Member, Royal Company of Archers, Queen's Body Guard for Scotland, 1949–. Member: Inter-departmental Cttee on Children and Young Persons, Scotland (Chm., Lord Kilbrandon), 1961–64; Scottish Council on Crime, 1972–75; Chairman: Children's Panel, Fife County, 1970–75, Fife Region 1975–77; Scottish Assoc. of Youth Clubs, 1968–79. JP 1957, DL 1958, Fife. *Address:* Kirkforthar House, Markinch, Glenrothes, Fife KY7 6LS. *T:* (01592) 752233, *Fax:* (01592) 610314. *Club:* New (Edinburgh).
See also P. E. G. Balfour.

BALFOUR, Michael John; JP; Director, IMI Bank (International), since 1987 (Deputy Chairman, 1987–92); *b* 17 Oct. 1925; *s* of Duncan and Jeanne Germaine Balfour; *m* 1951, Mary Campbell Penney, *d* of Maj.-Gen. Sir (William) Ronald Campbell Penney, KBE, CB, DSO, MC; two *s* one *d* (and *e s* decd). *Educ:* Eton Coll.; Christ Church, Oxford (MA Hons Modern Languages 1949). War service, RAF, 1944–47. Entered Bank of England, 1950: Senior Adviser, European affairs, 1973, Chief Adviser, 1976; Asst Dir, 1980–85. Alternate Director, Bank for International Settlements, 1972–85; Member, EEC Monetary Cttee, 1974–85. Director, Balgonie Estates Ltd, 1955–; Chairman: IMI Capital Markets, later SIGECO (UK), Ltd, 1987–92 (Dir, 1987–95); IMI Securities Ltd, 1988–94. JP Roxburgh, 1988. *Recreations:* music, fishing, boating, etc. *Address:* Harrietfield, Kelso, Roxburghshire TD5 7SY. *T:* (01573) 224825.

BALFOUR, Neil Roxburgh; Chairman: York Trust Ltd, since 1983; Mermaid Overseas Ltd, since 1991; *b* 12 Aug. 1944; *s* of Archibald Roxburgh Balfour and Lilian Helen Cooper; *m* 1st, 1969, HRH Princess Elizabeth of Yugoslavia; one *s*; 2nd, 1978, Serena Mary Churchill Russell; one *s* one *d*. *Educ:* Ampleforth Coll., Yorks; University Coll., Oxford Univ. (BA History); called to the Bar, Middle Temple, 1969. Baring Brothers & Co., 1968–74; European Banking Co. Ltd, 1974–83 (Exec. Dir, 1980–83). Chm., York Trust Group plc, 1986–91. Mem. (C) N Yorks, European Parlt, 1979–84. *Publication:* Paul of Yugoslavia (biography), 1980. *Recreations:* bridge, golf, tennis, shooting, fishing. *Address:* (office) 155 Bishopsgate, 2nd Floor, EC2N 3DA. *T:* (020) 7200 7081, *Fax:* (020) 7200 7182; 55 Warwick Square, SW1V 2AJ. *Clubs:* Turf, Pratt's, White's; Harbour; Royal St George's (Sandwich).

BALFOUR, Peter Edward Gerald, CBE 1984; Chairman, Charterhouse plc, 1985–90; a Vice-Chairman, Royal Bank of Scotland, 1985–90 (Director, 1971–90); Director, 1978–91, Vice-Chairman, 1981–91, Royal Bank of Scotland Group; *b* 9 July 1921; *y s* of late Brig. Edward William Sturgis Balfour, CVO, DSO, OBE, MC and Lady Ruth Balfour, CBE, MB; *m* 1st, 1948, Grizelda Davina Roberta Ogilvy (marr. diss. 1967); two *s* one *d*; 2nd, 1968, Diana Rosemary Wainman; one *s* one *d*. *Educ:* Eton College. Scots Guards, 1940–54. Joined Wm McEwan & Co. Ltd, 1954; Chm. and Chief Exec., Scottish & Newcastle Breweries, 1970–83. Director: British Assets Trust Ltd, 1962–91; Selective Assets Trust (formerly Edinburgh American Assets Trust), 1962–92 (Chm., 1978–92); First Charlotte Assets Trust, 1980–92 (Chm., 1981–92). Chm., Scottish Council for Develt and Industry, 1978–85. Mem., Hansard Soc. Commn on Electoral Reform, 1975–76. *Address:* Scadlaw House, Humbie, East Lothian EH36 5PH. *T:* (01875) 833252. *Club:* Cavalry and Guards.
See also J. C. Balfour.

BALFOUR, Raymond Lewis, LVO 1965; HM Diplomatic Service, retired; Counsellor, Kuwait, 1979–83; *b* 23 April 1923; *s* of Henry James Balfour and Vera Alice (*née* Dunford); *m* 1975, Vanda Gaye Crompton. RMA Sandhurst, 1942; commnd RAC; served with IV Queen's Own Hussars, 1942–47. Diplomatic Service, 1947–87; served at Munich, Beirut, Gdansk (Poland), Baghdad, Khartoum, Geneva, Damascus; Counsellor, Tripoli, 1976–79. Order of the Blue Nile, Sudan, 1965. *Recreations:* travel, gardening. *Address:* 25 Chenery Drive, Sprowston, Norwich, Norfolk NR7 8RR.

BALFOUR, Richard Creighton, MBE 1945; retired; *b* 3 Feb. 1916; *s* of Donald Creighton Balfour and Muriel Fonçeca; *m* 1943, Adela Rosemary Welch; two *s*. *Educ:* St Edward's Sch., Oxford (Pres., Sch. Soc., 1985–86). FIB. Joined Bank of England, 1935; Agent, Leeds, 1961–65; Deputy Chief Cashier, 1965–70; Chief Accountant, 1970–75. Dir, Datasaab Ltd, 1975–81. Naval Service, Lt-Comdr RNVR, 1939–46. President: Royal National Rose Soc., 1973 and 1974; World Fedn of Rose Socs, 1983–85 (Vice-Pres. for Europe, 1981–83; Chm., Classification Cttee, 1981–88); Chairman: 1976—The Year of the Rose; Internat. Rose Conf., Oxford, 1976; organiser and designer of the British Garden at Montreal Floralies, 1980. Master, Worshipful Co. of Gardeners, 1991–92; Freeman, City of London. DHM 1974. Gold Medal, World Fedn of Rose Socs, 1985; Australian Rose Award, 1989. *Publications:* articles in many horticultural magazines and photographs in many publications. *Recreations:* roses, gardening, photography, dancing, sea floating, collecting rocks and hat pins, travel, watching sport. *Address:* Albion House, Little Waltham, Chelmsford, Essex CM3 3LA. *T:* (01245) 360410.

BALFOUR-PAUL, (Hugh) Glencairn, CMG 1968; HM Diplomatic Service, retired; Director General, Middle East Association, 1978–79; Research Fellow, University of Exeter, since 1979; *b* 23 Sept. 1917; *s* of late Lt-Col J. W. Balfour Paul, DSO; *m* 1st, 1950, Margaret Clare Ogilvy (*d* 1971); one *s* three *d*; 2nd, 1974, Janet Alison Scott; one *s* one *d*. *Educ:* Sedbergh; Magdalen Coll., Oxford. Served War of 1939–45, Sudan Defence Force. Sudan Political Service, Blue Nile and Darfur, 1946–54; joined Foreign Office, 1955; Santiago, 1957; Beirut, 1960; Counsellor, Dubai, 1964; Dep. Political Resident, Persian Gulf, 1966; Counsellor, FO, attached St Antony's Coll., Oxford, 1968; Ambassador to Iraq, 1969–71; Ambassador to Jordan, 1972–75; Ambassador to Tunisia, 1975–77. *Publications:* The End of Empire in the Middle East, 1991; (poems) A Kind of Kindness, 2000. *Recreations:* archaeology, poetry, pew ends. *Address:* Uppincott Barton, Shobrooke, Crediton, Devon EX17 1BE. *T:* (01363) 772104.

BALGONIE, Lord; David Alexander Leslie Melville; DL; Director, Amerind Ltd (formerly Wood Conversion Ltd), since 1984; *b* 26 Jan. 1954; *s* and *heir* of Earl of Leven and Melville, *qv*; *m* 1981, Julia Clare, *yr d* of Col I. R. Critchley, Lindores, Muthill, Perthshire; one *s* one *d*. *Educ:* Eton. Lieut (acting Captain), Queen's Own Highlanders (GSM for N Ireland); RARO 1979–89. DL Nairn, 1998. *Heir: s* Hon. Alexander Ian Leslie Melville, *b* 29 Nov. 1984. *Address:* Glenferness House, Nairn IV12 5UP.

BALKWILL, Bryan Havell; conductor; Professor of Conducting, Indiana University, Bloomington, 1977–92; *b* 2 July 1922; *s* of Arthur William Balkwill and Dorothy Silver Balkwill (*née* Wright); *m* 1949, Susan Elizabeth Roberts; one *s* one *d*. *Educ:* Merchant Taylors' Sch.; Royal Academy of Music. Asst Conductor, New London Opera Co., 1947–48; Associate Conductor, Internat. Ballet, 1948–49; Musical Director and Principal Conductor, London Festival Ballet, 1950–52; Music staff and subseq. Associate Conductor, Glyndebourne Opera, 1950–58; Musical Dir, Arts Council 'Opera For All', 1953–63; Resident Conductor, Royal Opera House, Covent Garden, 1959–65; Musical Director: Welsh Nat. Opera Company, 1963–67; Sadler's Wells Opera, 1966–69; freelance opera and concert conducting in N America, Europe and GB, 1970–. Guest Conductor: Royal Opera House, Covent Garden, English Nat. Opera, Glyndebourne, Wexford Festival, Aldeburgh, RPO, LPO, BBC. Life Mem. Royal Philharmonic Society; FRAM. *Address:* 8 The Green, Wimbledon Common, SW19 5AZ. *T:* (020) 8947 4250.

BALL, Air Marshal Sir Alfred (Henry Wynne), KCB 1976 (CB 1967); DSO 1943; DFC 1942; Vice-Chairman (Air), Council of Territorial, Auxiliary and Volunteer Reserve Associations, 1979–84; *b* 18 Jan. 1921; *s* of Captain J. A. E. Ball, MC, BA, BE, Chief Engineer, Bengal Nagpur Railway, 1937; *m* 1942, Nan McDonald; three *s* one *d*. *Educ:* Campbell Coll., Belfast; RAF Coll., Cranwell; idc, jssc, psc, pfc. Served War of 1939–45 (despatches twice; US Air Medal 1943); Sqdn Ldr 1942; Wing Comdr 1944; air operations, Lysanders, Spitfires, Mosquitoes; commanded: 4 Photo. Reconn. Unit; 682, 542, 540 and 13 Photo. Reconn. Sqdns in N Africa, UK, France and Middle East; E Africa, 1947; RAF Staff Coll., 1952; Canberras, RAF Wyton, 1953; RAF Flying Coll., Bomber Comd, 1956; jssc 1959; BJSM, Washington, 1959; Comdr, Honington V Bomber Base, 1963–64; Air Officer, Administration, Aden, 1965; IDC, 1967; Dir of Operations, (RAF), MoD, 1967–68; Air Vice-Marshal, 1968; ACOS, Automatic Data Processing Div., SHAPE, 1968–71; Dir-Gen. Organisation (RAF), 1971–75; Air Marshal, 1975; UK Rep., Perm. Mil. Deputies Gp, Cento, 1975–77; Dep. C-in-C, RAF Strike Command, 1977–79, retired 1979. Mil. Affairs Advr, Internat. Computers Ltd, 1979–83. Hon. Air Cdre, No 2624 (Co. of Oxford) RAuxAF Regt Sqdn, 1984–90. Hon. FBCS 1974. *Recreations:* golf, bridge. *Clubs:* Royal Air Force; Phyllis Court; Huntercombe.

BALL, Alison; QC 1995; a Recorder, since 1998; *b* 12 Jan. 1948; *d* of Winifred Alice Ball and Hilary Noble Ball; *m* 1980, Richard; two *d*. *Educ:* Bedales Sch.; King's Coll., London (LLB Hons). Called to the Bar, Middle Temple, 1972; founded Specialist Family Law Chambers, 1989, Joint Head, 1990–. *Recreations:* my family and other animals. *Address:* 1 Garden Court, Temple, EC4Y 9BJ. *T:* (020) 7797 7900.

BALL, Anthony; Chief Executive and Managing Director, British Sky Broadcasting, since 1999; *b* 18 Dec. 1955. *Educ:* Kingston Univ. (MBA). Thames TV, 1976–88; BSB Sport, 1988–91; International Management Gp, 1991–93; BSkyB, 1993–95; Fox/Liberty Network, 1995–99. *Recreation:* ski-ing. *Address:* BSkyB, Grant Way, Isleworth TW7 5QD.

BALL, Anthony George, (Tony), MBE 1986; FCIM; FIMI; FCGI; Chairman, Tony Ball Associates plc, since 1983; *b* 14 Nov. 1934; *s* of Harry Ball and Mary Irene Ball, Bridgwater; *m* 1st, 1957, Ruth Parry Davies (marr. diss. 1997); two *s* one *d*; 2nd, 2000, Ms Jan Kennedy. *Educ:* Grammar Sch., Bridgwater. Indentured engineering apprentice, Austin Motor Co., 1951–55; responsible for launch of Mini, 1959; UK Car Sales Manager, 1962–66, Austin Motor Co.; Sales and Marketing Exec., British Motor Corp., 1966–67; Chm. and Man. Dir, Barlow Rand UK Motor Gp, 1967–78; Managing Director: Barlow Rand Ford, S Africa, 1971–73; Barlow Rand European Operations, 1973–78; returned to British Leyland as Man. Dir, Overseas Trading Operations, 1978; Dep. Man. Dir, Austin Morris Ltd, 1979; Chm. and Man. Dir, British Leyland Europe & Overseas, 1979–82; Director, 1979–82: BL Cars Ltd (World Sales Chief, 1979–82; responsible for launch of the Austin Metro in 1980); Austin Morris Ltd; Rover Triumph Ltd; Jaguar Rover Triumph Inc. (USA); Dir, Jaguar Cars Ltd, 1980–82; Chief Exec., Henlys plc, 1981–83, 1994. Dep. Chm., Lumley Insce Gp, 1983–95; Director: Jetmaster UK, 1989–97; Theatrical Agents Billy Marsh Associates Ltd, 1993–; Royal Carlton Hotel, Blackpool, 1998–. Dir, producer and stager of 'Industrial Theatre' Motivational confs, sponsorship, marketing, promotions and new product launches, 1983–. Responsible for: staging new product launches for General Motors, Vauxhall, Proton, Mercedes-Benz, Daihatsu, LDV, Land Rover, Pioneer-UK, Fiat and Gillette; production and staging of opening ceremony of Rugby World Cup, Twickenham, 1991; DoH European drug abuse prevention campaign, 1992. Apptd Marketing Adviser: to Sec. of State for Energy, 1984–87; to Sec. of State for Wales, 1988–91; to SMMT for producing and promoting: British Internat. Motor Show, 1992–96; Scottish Motor Show, 1997, 1999, 2001; to FA for producing opening and closing ceremonies of European Football Championships, Wembley, 1996, FA Cup Finals, 1996–2000 and promotional and presentation work for England World Cup Bid, 2006; to RFU for 125th Anniversary celebrations, 1996, for 5 Nations Championship activities, Twickenham, 1997–; to Welsh RU for producing opening and closing ceremonies, Rugby World Cup, Millennium Stadium, Cardiff Arms Park, 1999; to ECB for producing opening ceremony, Cricket World Cup, Lord's, 1999; responsible for: promoting London Zoo relaunch, 1993; creating and producing Lloyds Bank's Playwright of the Year Award, annually 1994–. Lectr, public and after dinner speaker; TV and radio broadcasts on motoring, marketing, public speaking and industrial subjects; producer, The Birth of Rugby (TV); panellist, Any Questions (TV and radio). Mason Meml Lecture, Birmingham Univ., 1983. Governor, N Worcs Coll., 1984–91. Freeman of City of London, 1980; Liveryman: Worshipful Co. of Coach Makers and Coach Harness Makers, 1980; Worshipful Co. of Carmen, 1982. Fellowship of Inst. of Marketing awarded 1981, for services to Brit. Motor Industry; FCGI 1999; Hon. Mem. CGLI, 1982, for services to technical and vocational educn; Prince Philip Medal, CGLI, 1984, for outstanding lifetime contribution to British marketing; Benedictine Business After-Dinner Speaker of the Year Award, 1992, 1993. *Publications:* (contrib.) Metro: the book of the car, 1981; (contrib.) Tales out of School, 1983; A Marketing Study of the Welsh Craft Industry (Welsh Office report, 1988); (contrib.) Making Better Business Presentations, 1988; (contrib.) Men and Motors of 'The Austin', 2000; contribs to numerous industrial, management, marketing and public speaking books and jls. *Recreations:* theatre, British military history, sharing good humour. *Address:* Tony Ball Associates plc, 174–178 North Gower Street, NW1 2NB. *T:* (020) 7380 0953; Silverhowe, Red Bank Road, Grasmere, Cumbria LA22 9PX. *Club:* Lord's Taverners.

BALL, Arthur Beresford, OBE 1973; HM Diplomatic Service, retired; history teacher, 1989–91, language teacher, 1991–97, Gresham's School; *b* 15 Aug. 1923; *s* of Charles Henry and Lilian Ball; *m* 1961, June Stella Luckett; one *s* two *d*. *Educ:* Bede Collegiate Boys' Sch., Sunderland; Univ. of E Anglia (BA Hons 1987; MA 1989). Joined HM Diplomatic Service, 1949: Bahrain, 1949; Tripoli, 1950; Middle East Centre for Arab Studies, 1952; Ramullah, 1953; Damascus, 1954; Foreign Office, 1957; Kuwait, 1959; HM Consul, New Orleans, 1963; Jedda, 1965; FO, 1967; São Paulo, 1969; Lisbon, 1972; Ankara, 1975; Consul-Gen., Perth, WA, 1978–80. *Recreations:* bookbinding, historical studies. *Address:* 15 Eccles Road, Holt, Norfolk NR25 6HJ.

BALL, Sir Charles (Irwin), 4th Bt *cr* 1911; Deputy Chairman, Associated British Ports Holdings, 1982–98; *b* 12 Jan. 1924; *s* of Sir Nigel Gresley Ball, 3rd Bt, and Florine Isabel (*d* 1992), *d* of late Col Herbert Edwardes Irwin; *S* father, 1978; *m* 1st, 1950, Alison Mary Bentley (marr. diss. 1983); one *s* one *d*; 2nd, 1994, Christine Trilby Knowles (*d* 2001), *d* of William Bedo Hobbs. *Educ:* Sherborne Sch. FCA 1960. Served RA, 1942–47. Chartered Accountant, 1950; Peat, Marwick, Mitchell & Co., 1950–54; joined Robert, Benson, Lonsdale & Co. Ltd (later Kleinwort, Benson Ltd), 1954; Director: Kleinwort, Benson Ltd, 1964–76 (Vice-Chm., 1974–76); Kleinwort, Benson, Lonsdale Ltd, 1974–76; Cadbury Schweppes Ltd, 1971–76; Chubb & Son Ltd, 1971–76; Sun Alliance and London Insurance Ltd, 1971–83; Telephone Rentals plc, 1971–89 (Vice-Chm., 1978–81, Chm., 1981–89); Tunnel Holdings Ltd, 1976–82; Barclays Bank Ltd, 1976–77 (Chm., Barclays Merchant Bank Ltd, 1976–77); Rockware Group plc, 1978–84; Peachey Property Corporation plc, 1978–88 (Chm., 1981–88); British Transport Docks Bd, 1971–82; Chm., Silkolene plc, 1989–94; Dep. Chm., Century Oils Group plc, 1991–94. Liveryman, 1960, Mem. Ct of Assts, 1979–87, Master, 1985, Clockmakers' Co. *Heir: s* Richard Bentley Ball, *b* 29 Jan. 1953. *Address:* Killybegs, Eddystone Road, Thurlestone, Kingsbridge, Devon TQ7 3NU. *T:* (01548) 560062.

BALL, Sir Christopher (John Elinger), Kt 1988; MA; Chancellor, University of Derby, since 1995; *b* 22 April 1935; *er s* of late Laurence Elinger Ball, OBE, and Christine Florence Mary Ball (*née* Howe); *m* 1958, Wendy Ruth Colyer, *d* of late Cecil Frederick Colyer and of Ruth Colyer (*née* Reddaway); three *s* three *d*. *Educ:* St George's School, Harpenden; Merton College, Oxford (Harmsworth Scholar 1959; Hon. Fellow, 1987); 1st Cl. English Language and Literature, 1959; Dipl. in Comparative Philology, 1962; MA Oxon, 1963. 2nd Lieut, Parachute Regt, 1955–56. Lectr in English Language, Merton Coll., Oxford, 1960–61; Lectr in Comparative Linguistics, Sch. of Oriental and African Studies (Univ. of London), 1961–64; Fellow and Tutor in English Language, Lincoln Coll., Oxford, 1964–79 (Bursar, 1972–79; Hon. Fellow, 1981); Warden, Keble College, Oxford, 1980–88 (Hon. Fellow, 1989). Founding Fellow, Kellogg Forum for Continuing Educn, Univ. of Oxford, 1988–89; Vis. Prof. in Higher Educn, Leeds Poly., 1989–91; Fellow in Continuing Educn, 1989–92, Dir of Learning, 1992–97, RSA. Sec., Linguistics Assoc. of GB, 1964–67; Pres., Oxford Assoc. of University Teachers, 1968–71; Publications Sec., Philological Soc., 1969–75; Chairman: Oxford Univ. English Bd, 1977–79; Bd of NAB, 1982–88; Higher Educn Inf. Services Trust, 1987–90; Member: General Bd of the Faculties, 1979–82; Hebdomadal Council, 1985–89; CNAA, 1982–88 (Chm., English Studies Bd, 1973–80, Linguistics Bd, 1977–82); BTEC, 1984–89 (Chm., Quality Assurance & Control Cttee, 1989–90); IT Skills Shortages Cttee (Butcher Cttee), 1984–85; CBI IT Skills Agency, 1985–88; CBI Task Force, 1988–89. Chairman: NICEC, 1989–93; Pegasus, 1989–92; Strategic Educn Fora for Kent, 1992–97, Oxfordshire, 1992–97, and Gtr Peterborough, 1992–95; Educn Policy Cttee, RSA Exams Bd, 1993–96; Patron, Campaign for Learning, RSA, 1998– (Pres., 1996–98). Vice-Chm., Jigsaw Gp, 1998–; founding Chm., The Talent Foundn, 1999–; Chm., Global Univ. Alliance, 2000–. Member: Council and Exec., Templeton Coll., Oxford, 1981–92; Centre for Medieval and Renaissance Studies, Oxford, 1987–90; Brathay Hall Trust 1988–91 (Chm, 1990–91); Manchester Polytechnic, 1989–91 (Hon. Fellow, 1988). Pres., ACFHE, 1990–92. Gov., St George's Sch., Harpenden, 1985–89. Jt Founding Editor (with late Angus Cameron), Toronto Dictionary of Old English, 1970; Member Editorial Board: Oxford Rev. of Education, 1984–96; Science and Public Affairs, 1989–94. FRSA 1987. Hon. Fellow: Univ. of Westminster (formerly Poly. of Central London), 1991; Auckland Inst. of Technol., NZ, 1992; NE Wales Inst., Wrexham, 1996. Hon. DLitt CNAA, 1989; DUniv N London, 1993; Hon. DEd Greenwich, 1994. *Publications:* Fitness for Purpose, 1985; Aim Higher, 1989; (ed jtly) Higher Education in the 1990s, 1989; More Means Different, 1990; Learning Pays, 1991; Sharks and Splashes, 1991; Profitable Learning, 1992; Start Right, 1994; pamphlets and various contributions to philological, linguistic and educational jls. *Address:* 45 Richmond Road, Oxford OX1 2JJ. *T:* and *Fax:* (01865) 310800.

BALL, Christopher John Watkins; Deputy Chairman, PG Bison Ltd, since 1999; Director, BOE (formerly The Board of Executors) Ltd, since 1995; *b* 2 Nov. 1939; *s* of late Clifford George and of Cynthia Lindsay Watkins-Ball; *m* 1968, Susan Anne Nellist; one *s* two *d*. *Educ:* St John's Coll., Johannesburg; Univ. of the Witwatersrand (Dipl. Iuris 1963); Jesus Coll., Cambridge (MA Econs 1967). Outwich South Africa Ltd, 1968–72, Dir 1970; Barclays Group, 1972–89: Barclays Nat. Merchant Bank, S Africa, 1972–78; Manager, Corporate Finance, 1972–75; Gen. Manager, 1975–78; Man. Dir, Barclays Nat. Western Bank, S Africa, 1978–80; Regional Gen. Manager, London, Barclays Bank, 1980–83; Barclays Nat. Bank Ltd (now First Nat. Bank of Southern Africa), S Africa, 1983, Man. Dir, 1984–89; Chief Exec., Pvte Bank & Trust Co., 1989–93; Chm., SA Housing Trust, 1994–95; CEO, Cape Town 2004 Olympic Bid, 1995–97. Pres., Clearing Bankers' Assoc. of S Africa, 1985. *Recreations:* golf, tennis. *Address:* Buitensig, 4 Gardenia Lane, Constantia, Cape Town, 7806, South Africa. *T:* (21) 7941422, *Fax:* (21) 7944294; *e-mail:* buitcon@iafrica.com. *Club:* Leander.

BALL, Colin George; Director, Commonwealth Foundation, since 2000; *b* 22 July 1943; *s* of George Heyward Ball and Bessie Margaret Ball (*née* Henry); *m* 1st, 1968, Maureen Sheelagh Bryan (marr. diss. 1996); one *s* one *d*; 2nd, 1998, Susan Helen Armstrong. *Educ:* Sevenoaks Sch.; Univ. of Keele (BA (Hons)). Teaching, Malaysia, Ghana, Nigeria, UK, 1961–62, 1966–70; Dir Schs Adv. Service, CSV, 1970–72; Asst Principal, Birstall Community Coll., 1973–74; Principal, Home Office and MSC, 1975–79; Founder, Chm. and CEO, Centre for Employment Initiatives, 1980–88; Chm., Commonwealth Assoc. for Local Action and Econ. Develt, 1990–96; Dep. Dir, Commonwealth Foundn, 1998–99. *Publications:* Education for a Change, 1973; Community Service and the Young Unemployed, 1977; Fit for Work?, 1979; Whose Business is Business, 1980; Locally Based Responses to Long-term Unemployment, 1988; Towards an Enterprising Culture, 1989; Non-governmental Organisations: guidelines for good policy and practice, 1995. *Recreations:* music, reading, writing, Italy. *Address:* Commonwealth Foundation, Marlborough House, Pall Mall, SW1Y 5HY. *T:* (020) 7930 3783. *Club:* Royal Commonwealth Society.

BALL, Denis William, MBE 1971; industrial and financial consultant; *b* 20 Oct. 1928; *er s* of late William Charles Thomas and Dora Adelaide Ball, Eastbourne; *m* 1972, Marja Tellervo Lumijärvi (*d* 1987), *er d* of Osmo Kullervo and Leila Tellervo Lumijärvi, Toijala, Finland; two *s* one *d*. *Educ:* Brunswick Sch.; Tonbridge Sch. (Scholar); Brasenose Coll., Oxford (MA). Sub-Lt, RNR, 1953; Lieut 1954; Lt-Comdr 1958. Asst Master, 1953–72, Housemaster, 1954–72, The King's Sch., Canterbury; Headmaster, Kelly Coll., 1972–85 (Governor, 1997–). Director: Perkins Foods, 1987–96 (founder Dir); James Wilkes,

1987–88; Western Bloodstock, 1987–92; Redbridge Properties, 1990–96; Kelly Enterprises, 1997–; Cons., Throgmorton Investment Management, 1977–78. Trustee, Tavistock Sch., 1972–85; Vice-Chm. of Governors, St Michael's Sch., Tawstock Court, 1974–93 (Hon. Gov., 1993–; Headmaster during interregnum, 1986); Mem., Political and PR Sub-Cttee, HMC, 1979–84. Hon. Treas., Ickham PCC, 1990–. Mem., Johnson Club, 1987–98. *Recreations:* Elizabethan history, cryptography, literary and mathematical puzzles, cricket, Real tennis (played for MCC and Jesters), squash (played for Oxford Univ. and Kent), golf. *Address:* Ickham Hall, Ickham, Canterbury, Kent CT3 1QT. *Clubs:* East India, Devonshire, Sports and Public Schools, MCC; Jesters.

BALL, Dr Harold William; Keeper of Palæontology, British Museum (Natural History), 1966–86; *b* 11 July 1926; *s* of Harold Ball and Florence (*née* Harris); *m* 1955, Patricia Mary (*née* Silvester); two *s* two *d*. *Educ:* Yardley Gram. Sch.; Birmingham Univ. BSc 1947, PhD 1949, Birmingham. Geologist, Nyasaland Geological Survey, 1949–51; Asst Lectr in Geology, King's Coll., London, 1951–54; Dept of Palæontology, British Museum (Nat. Hist.), 1954–86: Dep. Keeper, 1965; Keeper, 1966. Adrian Vis. Fellow, Univ. of Leicester, 1972–77. Sec., 1968–72, Vice-Pres., 1972–73, 1984–86, Geological Soc. of London; Pres., 1981–84, Vice-Pres., 1984–86, Soc. for the History of Natural History. Wollaston Fund, Geological Soc. of London, 1965. *Publications:* papers on the stratigraphy of the Old Red Sandstone and on the palæontology of the Antarctic in several scientific jls. *Recreations:* music, wine, gardening. *Address:* Wilderbrook, Dormans Park, East Grinstead, West Sussex RH19 2LT. *T:* (01342) 870426.

BALL, Sir James; *see* Ball, Sir R. J.

BALL, Prof. John Geoffrey, CEng; consultant metallurgist; Professor of Physical Metallurgy, Imperial College, University of London, 1956–80, now Emeritus (Head of Metallurgy Department, 1957–79; Senior Research Fellow, 1980–86); *b* 27 Sept. 1916; *s* of late I. H. Ball and late Mrs E. M. Ball; *m* 1941, Joan C. M., *d* of late Arthur Wiltshire, JP, Bournemouth. *Educ:* Wellington (Salop) High Sch.; Univ. of Birmingham. British Welding Res. Assoc., 1941–49; Sen. Metallurgist, 1945–49; AERE, Harwell, 1949–56; Head of Reactor Metallurgy, 1953–56. Min. of Tech. Visitor to British Non-Ferrous Metals Res. Assoc., 1962–72. Dean, Royal Sch. of Mines, Imperial Coll., 1962–65 and 1971–74; Dean, Faculty of Engineering, Univ. of London, 1970–74. Chairman: Res. Bd, 1964–74, and Mem. of Council Br. Welding Res. Assoc., 1964–81; Engrg Physics Sub-Cttee, Aeronautical Res. Council, 1964–68; Metallurgy Bd, CNAA, 1965–71; Metallurgy and Materials Cttee and Univ. Science and Technology Bd, SRC, 1967–70; Engrg Bd, SRC, 1969–71; Manpower Utilisation Working Party, 1967–69; Mem., Light Water Reactor Pressure Vessel Study Gp, Dept of Energy, 1974–77. Consultant on Materials, SERC, 1983–84. President: Inst. of Welding, 1965–66; Instn of Metallurgists, 1966–67 (Mem. Council 1951–56, 1958–70); Member: Council, Br. Nuclear Forum, 1964–71; Manpower Resources Cttee, 1965–68; Council, Inst. of Metals, 1965; Council, Iron and Steel Inst., 1965; Council, City Univ., 1966–90; Brain Drain Cttee, 1966–67; Public Enquiry into loss of "Sea Gem", 1967; Materials and Structures Cttee, 1967–70; Technology Sub-Cttee of UGC, 1968–73; Chartered Engineer Section Bd, CEI, 1978–83; Mem., Group IV Exec. Cttee, Engineering Council, 1983–94. Governor, Sir John Cass Coll., 1958–67. Hon. ARSM 1961. Brooker Medal, Welding Inst., 1979; Freedom of Inst. and Distinguished Service Award, Indian Inst. of Technology, Delhi, 1985. *Recreation:* painting. *Address:* 3 Sylvan Close, Limpsfield, Surrey RH8 0DX. *T:* (01883) 713511.

BALL, Prof. John Macleod, DPhil; FRS 1989; FRSE; Sedleian Professor of Natural Philosophy, University of Oxford and Fellow, Queen's College, Oxford, since 1996; *b* 19 May 1948; *s* of Ernest Frederick Ball and Dorothy Forbes Ball; *m* 1st, 1973, Mary Judith Hodges (marr. diss. 1977); 2nd, 1992, Sedhar Chozam; two *s* one *d*. *Educ:* Mill Hill Sch.; St John's Coll., Cambridge (BA Maths, 1969); Univ. of Sussex (DPhil 1972). FRSE 1980. SRC Postdoctoral Res. Fellow, Dept of Maths, Heriot-Watt Univ., and Lefschetz Center for Dynamical Systems, Brown Univ., USA, 1972–74; Lectr in Maths, 1974–78, Reader in Maths, 1978–82, SERC Sen. Fellow, 1980–85, Prof. of Applied Analysis, 1982–96, Heriot-Watt Univ. Visiting Professor: Dept of Maths, Univ. of Calif, Berkeley, 1979–80; Laboratoire d'Analyse Numérique, Université Pierre et Marie Curie, Paris, 1987–88, 1994; Inst. for Advanced Study, Princeton, 1993–94; Hon. Prof., Heriot-Watt Univ., 1998–. Member Council: EPSRC, 1994–99; Edinburgh Mathematical Soc., 1972– (Pres., 1989–90); London Math. Soc., 1982– (Pres., 1996–98); Amer. Math. Soc., 1987–; Soc. for Nat. Phil., 1978–. Member: Steering Cttee, Internat. Centre for Mathematical Scis, Edinburgh, 1996– (Mem. Exec. Cttee, 1991–96, Chm., 1991–93); Scientific Bd, Hewlett-Packard Basic Res. Inst. in Math. Scis, 1994–; Bd of Govs, Weizmann Inst., 1998–. Delegate, OUP, 1998–. Associé Etranger, Acad. des Sciences, 2000. Hon. DSc: Ecole Polytechnique Fédérale, Lausanne, 1992; Heriot-Watt, 1998; Sussex, 2000. Whittaker Prize, Edinburgh Math. Soc., 1981; Jun. Whitehead Prize, 1982, Naylor Prize, 1994, London Math. Soc.; Keith Prize, RSE, 1990; Theodore von Karman Prize, SIAM, 1999. Mem. Editorial Boards of various math. and scientific jls and book series. *Publications:* articles in math. and scientific jls. *Recreations:* travel, music, chess. *Address:* Mathematical Institute, 24–29 St Giles, Oxford OX1 3LB. *T:* (01865) 273577.

BALL, Rt Rev. Michael Thomas, CGA; Bishop of Truro, 1990–97; *b* 14 Feb. 1932; *s* of Thomas James Ball and Kathleen Bradley Ball. *Educ:* Lancing Coll., Sussex; Queens' Coll., Cambridge (BA 1955; MA 1959). Schoolmastering, 1955–76; Co-Founder, Community of the Glorious Ascension, 1960; Prior at Stroud Priory, 1963–76; Curate, Whitehall, Stroud, Glos, 1971–76; Priest-in-charge of Stanmer with Falmer, and Senior Anglican Chaplain to Higher Education in Brighton, including Sussex Univ., 1976–80; Bishop Suffragan of Jarrow, 1980–90. Mem., H of L, 1996–97. Mem. Council, St Luke's Hosp. for the Clergy, 1994–. *Recreations:* music, Boxers, housework. *Address:* Manor Lodge, Aller, Langport, Somerset TA10 0QN.
See also Rt Rev. P. J. Ball.

BALL, Rt Rev. Peter John, CGA; Bishop of Gloucester, 1992–93; *b* 14 Feb. 1932; *s* of Thomas James and Kathleen Obena Bradley Ball. *Educ:* Lancing; Queens' Coll., Cambridge; Wells Theological College. MA (Nat. Sci.). Ordained, 1956; Curate of Rottingdean, 1956–58; Co-founder and Brother of Monastic Community of the Glorious Ascension, 1960 (Prior, 1960–77); Suffragan Bishop of Lewes, 1977–92; Prebendary, Chichester Cathedral, 1978, Canon Emeritus, 2000. Fellow of Woodard Corporation, 1962–71; Member: Archbishops' Council of Evangelism, 1965–68; Midlands Religious Broadcasting Council of the BBC, 1967–69; Admin. Council, Royal Jubilee Trusts, 1986–88. Archbishop of Canterbury's Adviser to HMC, 1985–90. Governor: Wellington Coll., 1985–93; Radley Coll., 1986–93; Lancing Coll., 1972–82, 1990–. Freeman, Bor. of Eastbourne, 1992. DUniv Sussex, 1992. *Recreations:* squash (Cambridge Blue, 1953) and music. *Address:* Manor Lodge, Aller, Langport, Somerset TA10 0QN.
See also Rt Rev. M. T. Ball.

BALL, Rev. Canon Peter William; Canon Emeritus, St Paul's Cathedral, since 1990 (Residentiary Canon, 1984–90); Public Preacher, diocese of Salisbury, since 1990; *b* 17 Jan. 1930; *s* of Leonard Wevell Ball and Dorothy Mary Ball; *m* 1956, Angela Jane Dunlop; one *s* two *d*. *Educ:* Aldenham School; Worcester Coll., Oxford (MA); Cuddesdon Coll., Oxford. Asst Curate, All Saints, Poplar, 1955; Vicar, The Ascension, Wembley, 1961; Rector, St Nicholas, Shepperton, 1968; Area Dean of Spelthorne, 1972–83; Prebendary of St Paul's Cathedral, 1976. Dir, Post Ordination Trng and Continuing Ministerial Educn, Kensington Episcopal Area, 1984–87. Chaplain: Rediffusion Television, 1961–68; Thames Television, 1970–93. First Dir, Brent Samaritans, 1965–68; Dep. Dir, NW Surrey Samaritans, 1973–79. Mem., European Conf. on the Catechumenate, 1975– (Chm., 1983). *Publications:* Journey into Faith, 1984; Adult Believing, 1988; Adult Way to Faith, 1992; Journey into Truth, 1996; Anglican Spiritual Direction, 1998; (with Ven. Malcolm Grundy) Faith on the Way, 2000. *Recreations:* gardening, walking, music. *Address:* Whittonedge, Whittonditch Road, Ramsbury, Marlborough, Wilts SN8 2PX.

BALL, Prof. Sir (Robert) James, Kt 1984; MA, PhD; Professor of Economics, 1965–97, now Emeritus, Principal, 1972–84, London Business School; Chairman, Legal and General Group Plc, 1980–94 (Director, 1978–94); *b* 15 July 1933; *s* of Arnold James Hector Ball; *m* 1st, 1954, Patricia Mary Hart Davies (marr. diss. 1970); three *d* (and one *s* one *d* decd); 2nd, 1970, Lindsay Jackson (*née* Wonnacott); one step *s*. *Educ:* St Marylebone Grammar Sch.; The Queen's College, Oxford; Styring Schol.; George Webb Medley Junior Schol. (Univ. Prizeman), 1956. BA 1957 (First cl. Hons PPE), MA 1960; PhD Univ. of Pennsylvania, 1973. RAF 1952–54 (Pilot-Officer, Navigator). Research Officer, Oxford University Inst. of Statistics, 1957–58; IBM Fellow, Univ. of Pennsylvania, 1958–60; Lectr, Manchester Univ., 1960, Sen. Lectr, 1963–65; London Business School: Governor, 1969–84; Dep. Principal, 1971–72; Fellow, 1998. Chm., Royal Bank of Canada Holdings (UK) Ltd, 1995–98; Director: Ogilvy and Mather Ltd, 1969–71; Economic Models Ltd, 1971–72; Barclays Bank Trust Co., 1973–86; Tube Investments, 1974–84; IBM UK Hldgs Ltd, 1979–95; LASMO plc, 1988–94; Royal Bank of Canada, 1990–98; IBM UK Pensions Trust Ltd, 1994–; Part-time Mem., NFC, 1973–77. Economic Advr, Touche Ross & Co., 1984–95; Mem., Adv. Bd, IBM UK Ltd, 1995–98. Member: Cttee to Review National Savings (Page Cttee), 1971–73; Economics Cttee of SSRC, 1971–74; Cttee on Social Forecasting, SSRC, 1971–72; Cttee of Enquiry into Electricity Supply Industry (Plowden Cttee), 1974–75; Chm., Treasury Cttee on Policy Optimisation, 1976–78. Marshall Aid Commemoration Comr, 1987–94. Governor, NIESR, 1973–. Vice-Pres., Chartered Inst. of Marketing, 1991–94; Member Council: REconS, 1973–79; BIM, 1974–82 (Chm., Economic and Social Affairs Cttee, 1979–82); British–N American Cttee, 1985–98. Pres., Sect. F, BAAS, 1990–91. Vice-Pres., CAM Foundn, 1983–92; Trustee: Foulkes Foundn, 1984–; Civic Trust, 1986–91; The Economist, 1987–99; Re Action Trust, 1991–93. Fellow, Econometric Soc., 1973; CIMgt (CBIM 1974); FIAM 1985. Freeman, City of London, 1987. Hon. DSc Aston, 1987; Hon. DSocSc Manchester, 1988. *Publications:* An Econometric Model of the United Kingdom, 1961; Inflation and the Theory of Money, 1964; (ed) Inflation, 1969; (ed) The International Linkage of National Economic Models, 1972; Money and Employment, 1982; (with M. Albert) Toward European Economic Recovery in the 1980s (report to European Parliament), 1984; (ed) The Economics of Wealth Creation, 1992; The British Economy at the Crossroads, 1998; articles in professional jls. *Recreations:* gardening, chess. *Address:* London Business School, Sussex Place, Regent's Park, NW1 4SA. *T:* (020) 7262 5050. *Club:* Royal Automobile.

BALL, Tessa; *see* Hilton, T.

BALLADUR, Edouard; Chevalier, Légion d'Honneur; elected Deputy (RPR) for Paris, French National Assembly, 1986, 1988, 1993 and 1995; Prime Minister of France, 1993–95; *b* 2 May 1929; *s* of Pierre Balladur and Emilie Latour; *m* 1957, Marie-Josèphe Delacour; four *s*. *Educ:* Lycée Thiers, Marseilles; Faculté de Droit, Aix-en-Provence; Inst. d'etudes Politiques; Ecole Nat. d'Admin. Jun. Auditeur, 1957, Maître des Requêtes, 1963, Conseil d'Etat; Adviser to Dir-Gen., ORTF, 1962–63 (Mem. Admin Council, 1967–68); Tech. Adviser, Office of Prime Minister Pompidou, 1966–68; Pres., French Co. for routier tunnel under Mont Blanc, 1968–81; Mem., Admin Council, Nat. Forestry Office, 1968–73; Asst Sec. Gen., later Sec. Gen., French President's Office, 1969–74; Chm. and Chief Exec., Générale de Service Informatique, 1977–86; Chm. and Chief Exec., Co. européene d'accumulateurs, 1980–86; Mem., Conseil d'Etat, 1984–; Minister for Economy, Finance and Privatization, 1986–88; Mem., Paris City Council, 1989–. Numerous medals and awards, incl. Jacques Rueff Prize, NY, 1986; Euromoney Prize, IMF, 1987; Gold Medal for patronage, French Acad., 1988; Louise Michel Prize, 1993. *Publications:* l'Arbre de mai, 1979; Je crois en l'homme plus qu'en l'Etat, 1987; (jtly) Passion et longueur de temps, 1989; Douze lettres aux Français trop tranquilles, 1990; Des modes et des convictions, 1992; Le dictionnaire de la réforme, 1992; Deux ans à Matignon, 1995; Caractère de la France, 1997; Avenir de la différence, 1999. *Address:* Assemblée nationale, 126 rue de l'Université, 75355 Paris, France.

BALLANTINE, (David) Grant, FFA; Directing Actuary, Government Actuary's Department, since 1991; *b* 24 March 1941; *s* of James Williamson Ballantine and Robertha (*née* Fairley); *m* 1969, Marjorie Campbell Brown; one *s* one *d*. *Educ:* Daniel Stewart's Coll.; Edinburgh Univ. (BSc 1st Cl.). Scottish Widows' Fund, 1963–68; Asst Vice-Pres., Amer. Insce Gp (Far East), 1968–73; Government Actuary's Department, 1973–: Actuary, 1973–82; Chief Actuary, 1983–90. Mem. Council, Faculty of Actuaries, 1991–94. *Publications:* articles in trade and professional jls. *Address:* Government Actuary's Department, 22 Upper Ground, SE1 9RJ. *T:* (020) 7211 2623.

BALLARAT, Bishop of, since 1994; **Rt Rev. (Robert) David Silk;** *b* 23 Aug. 1936; *s* of Robert Reeve Silk and Winifred Patience Silk; *m* 1957, Joyce Irene Bracey; one *s* one *d*. *Educ:* Gillingham Grammar School; Univ. of Exeter (BA Hons Theology 1958); St Stephen's House, Oxford. Deacon 1959, priest 1960, Rochester; Curate: St Barnabas, Gillingham, 1959–63; Holy Redeemer, Lamorbey, 1963–69; Priest-in-Charge of the Good Shepherd, Blackfen, 1967–69; Rector of Swanscombe, 1969–75; Rector of Beckenham, St George, 1975–80; Team Rector, Holy Spirit, Leicester, 1982–88; Archdeacon of Leicester, 1980–94. Proctor in Convocation, 1970–94; Prolocutor of Lower House of Convocation of Canterbury, 1980–94; Member of Liturgical Commn, 1976–91; Chm., Leicester Council of Faiths, 1986–93; Moderator, Churches Commn for Inter-Faith Relations (formerly Cttee for Relations with Peoples of Other Faiths), 1990–93; Pres., Victorian Council of Churches, 1995–97; Member: Anglican-Lutheran Dialogue in Australia (formerly Anglican-Lutheran Commn), 1995–; Liturgy Panel (formerly Liturgical Commn), 1996–; Chm., Leaders of Faith Communities Forum, Victoria, 1996–. *Publications:* Prayers for Use at the Alternative Services, 1980; Compline—an Alternative Order, 1980; In Penitence and Faith, 1988. *Recreations:* Richard III Society, Leicester FC, theatre. *Address:* Bishop's Lodge, 6 Banyule Drive, Delacombe, Ballarat, Vic 3356, Australia. *Club:* Athenæum.

BALLARD, Ven. Andrew Edgar; Archdeacon of Rochdale, since 2000; *b* 14 Jan. 1944; *s* of Arthur Henry and Phyllis Marian Ballard; *m* 1970, Marian Caroline Conolly; one *s* two *d*. *Educ:* Rossall Sch.; St John's Coll., Durham Univ. (BA Hons Theol. 1966); Westcott House, Cambridge. Ordained deacon 1968, priest 1969; Asst Curate, St Mary, Bryanston Sq., and Asst Chaplain, Middlesex Hosp., London, 1968–72; Sen. Asst Curate,

St Mary, Portsea, 1972–76; Vicar: St James, Haslingden with St Stephen, Haslingden Grane, 1976–82; St Paul, Walkden, 1982–93; Team Rector, St Paul, Walkden with St John the Baptist, Little Hulton, 1993–98; Area Dean, Farnworth, 1990–98; Priest in charge, 1998–2000, Team Rector, 2000, Rochdale Team Ministry. Hon. Canon, Manchester Cathedral, 1998–2000. *Recreations:* church music, playing the organ. *Address:* 57 Melling Road, Oldham OL4 1PN. *T:* (0161) 678 1454.

BALLARD, Jacqueline Margaret, (Jackie); *b* 4 Jan 1953; *d* of late Alexander Mackenzie and of Daisy Mackenzie (*née* Macdonald); *m* 1975, Derek Ballard (marr. diss. 1989); one *d*. *Educ:* Monmouth Sch. for Girls; London Sch. of Economics (BSc Social Psychology). Social Worker, Waltham Forest, 1974–76; Further Educn Lectr, Yeovil Coll., 1980–92; Council Support Officer, Assoc. of Lib Dem Councillors, 1993–97. MP (Lib Dem) Taunton, 1997–2001. Contested (Lib Dem) Taunton, 2001. *Recreations:* swimming at least one km a day, listening to Celtic rock music.

BALLARD, James Graham; novelist and short story writer; *b* 15 Nov. 1930; *s* of late James Ballard and Edna Ballard (*née* Johnstone); *m* 1954, Helen Mary Matthews (*d* 1964); one *s* two *d*. *Educ:* Leys School, Cambridge; King's College, Cambridge. *Publications:* The Drowned World, 1963; The 4-Dimensional Nightmare, 1963 (re-issued as The Voices of Time, 1985); The Terminal Beach, 1964; The Drought, 1965; The Crystal World, 1966; The Disaster Area, 1967; The Atrocity Exhibition, 1970; Crash, 1973 (filmed 1997); Vermilion Sands, 1973; Concrete Island, 1974; High Rise, 1975; Low-Flying Aircraft, 1976; The Unlimited Dream Company, 1979; Myths of the Near Future, 1982; Empire of the Sun, 1984 (filmed, 1988); The Venus Hunters, 1986; The Day of Creation, 1987; Running Wild, 1988; War Fever, 1990; The Kindness of Women, 1991; Rushing to Paradise, 1994; A User's Guide to the Millennium, 1996; Cocaine Nights, 1996; Super-Cannes, 2000. *Address:* 36 Old Charlton Road, Shepperton, Middlesex TW17 8AT. *T:* (01932) 225692.
See also M.A. Richardson.

BALLARD, John Frederick, CB 2001; Director, Water and Land, Department for Environment, Food and Rural Affairs (formerly Department of the Environment, Transport and the Regions), since 2001; *b* 8 Aug. 1943; *s* of Frederick and Margaret Ballard; *m* 1st, 1975, Ann Helm (marr. diss. 1999); one *s* two *d*; 2nd, 2000, Helena (*née* Rose). *Educ:* Roundhay Grammar Sch., Leeds; Ifield Grammar Sch., W Sussex; Southampton Univ. (BA); Exeter Univ. (CertEd). Academic Registrar's Dept, Univ. of Surrey, 1965–69; Asst Principal, MoT, 1969; Principal, DoE, 1972; Treasury, 1976; Asst Sec. 1978, Sec., Top Salaries Review Body and Police Negotiating Bd; DoE, 1979; Prin. Private Sec. to Sec. of State for the Environment, 1983–85; Under Sec., DoE and Dept of Transport, and Regl Dir, Yorks and Humberside Region, 1986; Dir, Housing Assocs and the Private Sector, DoE, 1990–92; Dir, Maxwell Pensions Unit, DSS, 1992–93 (on secondment); Dir, Town and Country Planning, DoE, 1993–97; Dir Finance, and Principal Finance Officer, DoE, subseq. DETR, 1997–2001. Trustee, Maxwell Pensioners Trust, 1993–97; Associate Special Trustee, Gt Ormond St Hosp. for Sick Children, 1992–99. *Recreations:* squash, singing, reading. *Address:* Department for Environment, Food and Rural Affairs, Ashdown House, 123 Victoria Street, SW1E 6DE. *T:* (020) 7890 6970.

BALLARD, Dr Robert Duane; oceanographer and marine explorer; Founder and President, Institute for Exploration, since 1995; *b* 30 June 1942; *s* of Chester P. Ballard and Harriett N. Ballard; *m* 1991, Barbara Earle; two *s* one *d*. *Educ:* Univ. of California, Santa Barbara (BS 1965); Univ. of Hawaii; Univ. of Southern California; Univ. of Rhode Island (PhD 1974). 2nd Lieut, US Army Intelligence, 1965–67; USN, 1967–70, served Vietnam War; Comdr, USNR, 1987–. Woods Hole Oceanographic Institution: Res. Associate, 1969–74; Asst Scientist, 1974–76; Associate Scientist, 1976–83; Founder, Deep Submergence Lab., and Sen. Scientist, Dept of Applied Ocean Physics and Engrg, 1983–; Dir, Center for Marine Exploration, 1989–95; Scientist Emeritus, 1997–. Founder, Jason Project (use of remotely operated vehicles for deep-sea exploration), 1989; Founder and Chm. of Bd, Jason Foundn for Educn, 1989–. Expeditions include: exploration of Mid-ocean Ridge, 1974, of Galapagos Rift, 1977; discovery of polymetallic sulphides, 1979; Titanic, 1985; German battleship Bismarck, 1989; warships from lost fleet of Guadalcanal, 1992; Lusitania, 1994; Roman ships off coast of Tunisia, 1997; USS Yorktown, 1998; Black Sea, 2000. Presenter, Nat. Geographic Explorer TV prog., 1989–91; award-winning films for television incl. Secrets of the Titanic, 1985, and Last Voyage of the Lusitania, 1994. Many scientific, academic and multi-media awards and honours. *Publications:* Photographic Atlas of the Mid-Atlantic Ridge Rift Valley, 1977; (jtly) The Discovery of the Titanic, 1987 (trans. 10 langs); The Discovery of the Bismarck, 1990 (trans. 8 langs); Bright Shark (novel), 1992 (trans. 6 langs); The Lost Ships of Guadalcanal, 1993 (trans. 5 langs); (jtly) Exploring the Lusitania, 1995 (trans. 2 langs); Explorations (autobiog.), 1995 (trans. 2 langs); Lost Liners, 1997 (trans. 5 langs); History of Deep Submergence Science and Technology, 1998; At the Water's Edge: coastal images of America, 1998; Return to Midway, 1999; The Eternal Darkness: a personal history of deep-sea exploration, 2000; *for children:* Exploring the Titanic, 1988 (trans. 7 langs); The Lost Wreck of the Isis, 1990 (trans. 5 langs); Exploring the Bismarck, 1991 (trans. 2 langs); Explorer, 1992; Ghost Liners, 1998; contrib. many learned jls. *Address:* Institute for Exploration, 55 Coogan Blvd, Mystic, CT 06355, USA.

BALLARD, Ronald Alfred; Head of Technical Services of the Central Computers and Telecommunications Agency, HM Treasury (formerly Civil Service Department), 1980–85; consultant, 1985–95; voluntary work, Help the Aged, since 1989; *b* 17 Feb. 1925; *s* of Joseph William and Ivy Amy Ballard; *m* 1948, Eileen Margaret Edwards; one *d*. *Educ:* Univ. of Birmingham (BSc (Hons) Physics). National Service, RN, 1945–47. Admiralty Surface Weapons Establishment, Portsmouth: Scientific Officer, then Sen. Scientific Officer, Research and Development Seaborne Radar Systems, 1948–55; Application of Computers to Naval Comd and Control Systems, 1955–69; PSO, 1960, responsibilities for Action Data Automation (ADA), on HMS Eagle and destroyers; SPSO, to Head Computer Systems and Techniques in Civil Service Dept (Central Computers Agency in 1972), 1969; Head of Central Computers Facility, 1972–76; DCSO, to Head Technical Services Div. of Central Computers Agency, 1977; CSO(B), 1980–85. Treas., Sutton Assoc. for the Blind, 1985–98; Asst Treas., League of Friends, Queen Mary's Hosp., Carshalton, 1986–95.

BALLENTYNE, Donald Francis, CMG 1985; HM Diplomatic Service, retired; Consul-General, Los Angeles, 1985–89; *b* 5 May 1929; *s* of late Henry Q. Ballentyne and Frances R. MacLaren; *m* 1950, Elizabeth Heywood, *d* of late Leslie A. Heywood; one *s* one *d*. *Educ:* Haberdashers' Aske's Hatcham Sch. FO, 1950–53; Berne and Ankara, 1953–56; Consul: Munich, 1957; Stanleyville, 1961; Cape Town, 1962; First Secretary: Luxembourg, 1965–69, Havana, 1969–72; FCO, 1972–74; Counsellor (Commercial), The Hague, 1974–78, Bonn, 1978–81; Counsellor, E Berlin, 1982–84. *Recreations:* sailing, riding. *Address:* Orford, Suffolk.

BALLESTEROS, Severiano; golfer; *b* Santander, Spain, 9 April 1957; *s* of Baldomero Ballesteros; *m* 1988, Carmen Botin; two *s* one *d*. Professional golfer, 1974–; won Spanish Young Professional title, 1975, 1978; French Open, 1977, 1982, 1985, 1986; Japan Open, 1977, 1978; Swiss Open, 1977, 1978, 1989; German Open, 1978, 1988; Open Champion, Lytham St Anne's, 1979 and 1988, St Andrews, 1984; won US Masters, 1980, 1983; World Matchplay Champion, Wentworth, 1981, 1982, 1984, 1985; Australian PGA Championship, 1981; Spanish Open, 1985, 1995; Dutch Open, 1986; British Masters, 1991; PGA Championship, 1991; Internat. Open, 1994; numerous other titles in Europe, USA, Australasia; Mem. Ryder Cup team, 1979, 1983, 1985, 1987, 1989, Captain, 1997. Prince of Asturias prize for sport, 1989. *Publication:* (with Robert Green) Trouble-shooting, 1996. *Address:* c/o Fairway SA, C1 Pasaje de Peña, 2–4ª Planta, 39008 Santander, Spain.

BALLIN, Dame (Reubina) Ann, DBE 1993 (CBE 1981); Chairman (New Zealand), Australia New Zealand Council for the Care of Animals in Research and Teaching, 1993–97; *b* 20 Feb. 1932; *d* of late Jack Ballin and of Thelma Joyce (*née* Penberthy). *Educ:* St Hilda's Collegiate Sch.; Waikato Diocesan Sch.; Univ. of Auckland; Univ. of Canterbury (MA 1964). Vis. Psychologist, Princess Margaret Hosp., 1964–69; private Psychologist, Calvary Psychiatric Clinic, 1964–73; Student Counsellor, Univ. of Canterbury, 1974–86. Mem., Royal Commn on Social Policy, 1987–88; Nat. Chm., Internat. Year of Disabled People, 1979–82; Chm., NZ Council of Recreation and Sport, 1985–86; Mem., Hillary Commn for Sport and Recreation, 1986–88; Chm., Victims' Task Force, 1988–93. Pres., NZ Psychological Soc., 1978–79. Mem., Cambodia Trust, 1993–. Patron, Family Help Trust, 1993–. Hon. DLitt Canterbury, 2001. Sesquicentennial Medal, NZ, 1990. *Recreations:* sport, literature, food, embroidery, all broadcast media, gardens. *Address:* 3 Marblewood Drive, Papanui, Christchurch 8005, New Zealand. *T:* (3) 3521867; *e-mail:* aballin@clear.net.nz.

BALLINGER, Martin Stanley Andrew, FCIT; Chief Executive (formerly Managing Director), Go-Ahead Group plc, since 1987; *b* 19 Nov. 1943; *s* of Cyril Herbert Ballinger and Sylvia May Ballinger; *m* 1968, Diana Susan Edgoose; one *s* one *d*. *Educ:* Salesians, Chertsey; University College London. ACMA; FCIT 1991. Accountant, 1972–82, Gen. Manager, 1982–87, National Bus Co. *Recreations:* golf, private pilot. *Address:* Bolam Hall (East), Morpeth NE61 3UA. *T:* (01661) 881620. *Clubs:* Northern Counties (Newcastle upon Tyne); Newcastle upon Tyne Aero; Stocksfield Golf.

BALLS, Alastair Gordon, CB 1995; Chief Executive, The International Centre for Life, since 1998; *b* 18 March 1944; *s* of late Dr Ernest George Balls and of Mrs Elspeth Russell Balls; *m* 1978, Beryl May Nichol; one *s* one *d*. *Educ:* Hamilton Acad.; Univ. of St Andrews (MA); Univ. of Manchester (MA). Economist: Treasury, Govt of Tanzania, 1966–68; Min. of Transport, UK, 1969–74; Sec., Adv. Cttee on Channel Tunnel, 1974–75; Sen. Econ. Adviser, HM Treasury, 1976–79; Asst Sec., Dept of Environment, 1979–83; Regl Dir, Depts of Environment and Transport (Northern Region), 1984–87; Chief Exec., Tyne and Wear Develt Corp., 1987–98. Mem., ITC, 1998–. Vice-Chm., Council, Univ. of Newcastle upon Tyne, 1994–2000. *Recreations:* sailing, cycling, walking, camping in the company of my family. *Address:* The International Centre for Life Trust, Times Square, Newcastle upon Tyne NE4 7BD.

BALLS, Edward Michael; Chief Economic Adviser to HM Treasury, since 1999; *b* 25 Feb. 1967; *s* of Prof. Michael Balls and Carolyn Janet Balls; *m* 1998, Yvette Cooper, *qv*; one *d*. *Educ:* Keble Coll., Oxford (BA 1st Cl. Hons PPE); John F. Kennedy Sch. of Govt, Harvard Univ. (MPA). Teaching Fellow, Dept of Econs, Harvard Univ. and Nat. Bureau of Econ. Res., 1989–90; econs leader writer and columnist, Financial Times, 1990–94; Econ. Advr to Shadow Chancellor, 1994–97; Sec., Labour Party Econ. Policy Commn, 1994–97; Econ. Advr to Chancellor of the Exchequer, HM Treasury, 1997–99. Mem. Council, REconS, 1997–. *Publications:* (Principal Ed.) World Bank Development Report, 1995; contribs to learned jls, incl. Scottish Jl Pol. Econ., and to reports published by Fabian Soc. and Social Justice Commn. *Recreations:* playing football, the violin and with daughter Ellie. *Address:* 3 Redhill Mount, Castleford WF10 3AE. *T:* (01977) 551113.

BALLS, Yvette; *see* Cooper, Y.

BALMER, Colin Victor, CB 2001; Principal Finance Officer, Ministry of Defence, since 1998; *b* 22 Aug. 1946; *s* of Peter Lionel Balmer and Adelaide Currie Balmer; *m* 1978, Frances Mary Montrésor; two *s* one *d*. *Educ:* Liverpool Inst. High Sch. War Office, 1963, later Ministry of Defence: Asst Private Sec. to Minister of State, 1972; Private Sec. to Parly Under-Sec. of State (RAF), 1973; Civil Advr to GOC N Ireland, 1973; Cabinet Office, 1977; Private Sec. to Minister of State (Defence Procurement), 1980; UK Delegn to NATO, 1982; MoD 1984; Minister (Defence Materiel), Washington, 1990; Asst Under-Sec. of State, 1992–96, Dep. Under-Sec. of State (Resources, Programmes and Finance), 1996–98, MoD. *Recreations:* golf, tennis, gardening, bridge, rock and roll music, playing guitar (badly). *Address:* 36 Pensford Avenue, Richmond, Surrey TW9 4HP. *T:* (020) 8878 2224.

BALMER, Derek Rigby, RWA 1970; painter and photographer; President, Royal West of England Academy, since 2001; *b* 28 Dec. 1934; *s* of Geoffrey Johnstone Balmer and Barbara Winifred Balmer (*née* Rigby); *m* 1962, Elizabeth Mary Rose Hawkins; one *s* one *d*. *Educ:* Waterloo House Sch.; Sefton Park Sch.; West of England Coll. of Art. *One-man exhibitions* include: Fimbarrus Gall., Bath, 1960; Arnolfini Gall., Bristol, 1966, 1968; City Art Gall., Bristol, 1975; Sharples Gall., RWA, 1980; Anthony Hepworth Fine Art, Bath, 1992, 1994, London, 1994, 2000; Gisela van Beers, London, 1992; Montpelier Sandelson, London, 1995; Smelik and Stokking Galls, Holland, 1996, 1998, 2000, 2001; *group exhibitions* include: Arnolfini Gall., Bristol, 1963, 1964, 1983; Arts Council Touring Exhibn, 1967; Leicester Galls, London, 1968, 1969, 1970; Victoria Art Gall., Bath, 1970; New Art Centre, London, 1982; Louise Hallet Gall., London, 1985; London Contemp. Art Fair, annually 1990–2001. Chm., RWA, 1997–2000. *Recreations:* art history, reading, cricket, walking Newfoundland dogs. *Address:* Mulberry House, 12 Avon Grove, Sneyd Park, Bristol BS9 1PJ. *T:* (0117) 968 2953. *Club:* Chelsea Arts.

BALMFORTH, Ven. Anthony James; Archdeacon of Bristol, 1979–90, now Archdeacon Emeritus; *b* 3 Sept. 1926; *s* of Joseph Henry and Daisy Florence Balmforth; *m* 1952, Eileen Julia, *d* of James Raymond and Kitty Anne Evans; one *s* two *d*. *Educ:* Sebright School, Wolverley; Brasenose Coll., Oxford (BA 1950, MA 1951); Lincoln Theological Coll. Army service, 1944–48. Deacon 1952, priest 1953, dio. Southwell; Curate of Mansfield, 1952–55; Vicar of Skegby, Notts, 1955–61; Vicar of St John's, Kidderminster, Worcs, 1961–65; Rector of St Nicolas, King's Norton, Birmingham, 1965–79; Hon. Canon of Birmingham Cathedral, 1975–79; RD of King's Norton, 1973–79; Examining Chaplain to: Bishop of Birmingham, 1978–79; Bishop of Bristol, 1981–90. Hon. Canon of Bristol Cathedral, 1979–. Mem., Gen. Synod of C of E, 1982–90. *Recreations:* cricket, gardening. *Address:* Slipper Cottage, Stag Hill, Yorkley, near Lydney, Glos GL15 4TB. *T:* (01594) 564016.

BALNIEL, Lord; Anthony Robert Lindsay; Director, J. O. Hambro Investment Management, since 1987; *b* 24 Nov. 1958; *s* and *heir* of Earl of Crawford and Balcarres, *qv*; *m* 1989, Nicola A., *y d* of Antony Bicket; two *s* one *d*. *Educ:* Eton Coll.; Univ. of

Edinburgh. *Heir:* *s* Master of Lindsay, *qv.* *Address:* 6 Pembridge Place, W2 4XB. *Clubs:* New (Edinburgh); XII.

BALSTON, Antony Francis; His Honour Judge Balston; a Circuit Judge, since 1985; *b* 18 Jan. 1939; *s* of late Comdr E. F. Balston, DSO, RN, and D. B. L. Balston (*née* Ferrers); *m* 1966, Anne Marie Judith Ball; two *s* one *d.* *Educ:* Downside; Christ's Coll., Cambridge (MA). Served Royal Navy, 1957–59; Univ. of Cambridge, 1959–62; admitted Solicitor, 1966. Partner, Herington Willings & Penry Davey, Solicitors, Hastings, 1967–85; a Recorder of the Crown Court, 1980–85; Hon. Recorder, Hastings, 1984–. *Recreation:* gardening. *Club:* Farmers.

BALTIMORE, David, PhD; President, California Institute of Technology, since 1997; *b* New York, 7 March 1938; *s* of Richard and Gertrude Baltimore; *m* 1968, Alice Huang; one *d.* *Educ:* Swarthmore Coll. (BA 1960); Rockefeller Univ. (PhD 1964). Postdoctoral Fellow, MIT, 1963–64; Albert Einstein Coll. of Med., NY, 1964–65; Research Associate, Salk Inst., La Jolla, Calif, 1965–68; Massachusetts Institute of Technology: Associate Prof., 1968–72; Amer. Cancer Soc. Prof. of Microbiol., 1973–83; Prof. of Biology, 1972–90; Dir, Whitehead Inst., 1982–90; Prof., 1990–94, Pres., 1990–91, Rockefeller Univ.; Ivan R. Cottrell Prof. of Molecular Biol. and Immunol., MIT, 1994–97. FAAAS 1980. Chm., AIDS Vaccine Adv. Cttee, NIH, 1997–. Member: Nat. Acad. of Scis, 1974; Amer. Acad. of Arts and Scis, 1974; Pontifical Acad. of Scis, 1978; Foreign Mem., Royal Soc., 1987. Eli Lilly Award in Microbiology and Immunology, 1971; US Steel Foundn Award in Molecular Biology, 1974; (jtly) Nobel Prize for Physiology or Medicine, 1975. *Address:* California Institute of Technology, 204–31, 1200 E California Boulevard, Pasadena, CA 91125, USA.

BAMBERG, Harold Rolf, CBE 1968; Chairman: Glos Air Cos, since 1985; Via Nova Properties Ltd, since 1985; Bamberg Organisation, Bamberg Farms Ltd, since 1996; *b* 17 Nov. 1923; *m* 1957 (marr. diss. 1990); one *s* two *d* (and one *s* one *d* of a former marriage). *Educ:* Hampstead. Former Chairman: British Independent Air Transport Assoc.; GAMTA; former Director: Cunard Steamship Co.; BOAC Cunard, etc; Founder: British Eagle International Airlines, 1948; Lunn Poly Ltd, 1956. FRAeS 1993. Kt, Order of Merit, Italian Republic, 1960. *Recreations:* horses, agriculture, golf. *Address:* 41 Windmill Field, Windlesham, Surrey GU20 6QD. *T:* (01276) 479816, *Fax:* (01276) 489302. *Club:* Guards' Polo.

BAMBOROUGH, John Bernard; Principal of Linacre College, Oxford, 1962–88; Pro-Vice-Chancellor, Oxford University, 1966–88; *b* 3 Jan. 1921; *s* of John George Bamborough; *m* 1947, Anne, *d* of Olav Indrehus, Indrehus, Norway; one *s* one *d.* *Educ:* Haberdashers' Aske's Hampstead Sch. (Scholar); New College, Oxford (Scholar). 1st Class, English Language and Literature, 1941; MA 1946. Service in RN, 1941–46 (in Coastal Forces as Lieut RNVR; afterwards as Educ. Officer with rank of Instructor Lieut, RN). Junior Lectr, New Coll., Oxford, 1946; Fellow and Tutor, Wadham Coll., Oxford, 1947–62 (Dean, 1947–54; Domestic Bursar, 1954–56; Sen. Tutor, 1957–61); Univ. Lectr in English, 1951–62; Mem. Hebdomadal Council, Oxford Univ., 1961–79. Hon. Fellow: New Coll., Oxford, 1967; Linacre Coll., Oxford, 1988; Wadham Coll., Oxford, 1988. Clerk of the Market, Oxford Univ., 1997–. Editor, Review of English Studies, 1964–78. Cavaliere Ufficiale, Order of Merit (Italy), 1991. *Publications:* The Little World of Man, 1952; Ben Jonson, 1959; (ed) Pope's Life of Ward, 1961; Jonson's Volpone, 1963; The Alchemist, 1967; Ben Jonson, 1970; (ed) Burton's Anatomy of Melancholy, vols iv–vi, 1998–2000. *Address:* 18 Winchester Road, Oxford OX2 6NA. *T:* (01865) 559886.

BAMERT, Matthias; conductor; Music Director, London Mozart Players, 1993–2000; *b* Switzerland, 5 July 1942; *m* 1969, Susan Exline; one *s* one *d.* Asst conductor to Leopold Stokowski, 1970–71; Resident Conductor, Cleveland Orch., USA, 1971–78; Music Dir, Swiss Radio Orch., Basel, 1977–83; Principal Guest Conductor, Scottish Nat. Orch., 1985–90. Director: Musica Nova fest., Glasgow, 1985–90; Lucerne Fest., 1992–98. Has worked with orchestras incl. LPO, RPO, BBC Philharmonic, BBC SO, CBSO, Orchestre de Paris, Rotterdam Philharmonic, Cleveland Orchestra, Pittsburgh Symphony, Houston Symphony, Montreal Symphony, and appears regularly at Promenade concerts; tours each season in Europe, N America, Australia and Japan and has made numerous recordings. *Address:* Intermusica Artists' Management Ltd, 16 Duncan Terrace, N1 8BZ.

BAMFIELD, Clifford, CB 1981; Under Secretary, Civil Service Department, 1974–80; *b* 21 March 1922; *s* of G. H. Bamfield. *Educ:* Wintringham Grammar Sch., Grimsby; Manchester Business Sch., 1966. Served War, RNVR, 1941–46. Customs and Excise: Exec. Officer, 1946; Private Sec. to Chm., 1959–61; Principal, 1961; Asst Sec., 1967; Under Sec., Comr and Dir of Estabs, 1973. Mem., 1982–91, Dep. Chm., 1989–91, CSAB; Civil Service Commn Panel of Selection Bd Chairmen, 1982–93. *Address:* 15 The Linkway, Sutton, Surrey SM2 5SE. *T:* (020) 8642 5377. *Club:* Army and Navy.

BAMFORD, Alan George, CBE 1985; Principal, Homerton College, Cambridge, 1985–91; *b* 12 July 1930; *s* of James Ross and Margaret Emily Bamford; *m* 1954, Joan Margaret, *e d* of Arthur W. Vint; four *s.* *Educ:* Prescot Grammar School; Borough Road College, London; Liverpool University (DipEd, MEd); MA Cantab; Cert. Ed. London. Teacher and Dep. Headmaster, Lancashire primary schs, 1952–62; Lectr in Primary Educn, Liverpool Univ., 1962–63; Sen. Lectr in Educn, Chester Coll., 1963–66; Principal Lectr and Head of Educn Dept, S Katharine's Coll., Liverpool, 1966–71; Principal, Westhill Coll., Birmingham, 1971–85. Pres., Birmingham Council of Christian Educn, 1972–74, Vice-Pres., 1974–91; Vice-Pres., Colls of Educn Christian Union, 1965–86, Pres., 1966–67, 1972–73; Chm., Birmingham Assoc. of Youth Clubs, 1972–85, Vice-Pres., 1985–; Member: Standing Conf. on Studies in Educn, 1974–91 (Exec. Cttee and Edtl Bd, 1978–87, Sec., 1982–84); Council of Nat. Youth Bureau, 1974–80 (Exec. Cttee, 1978–80); Adv. Cttee on religious broadcasts, BBC Radio Birmingham, 1972–80; Educn Cttee, Free Church Fed. Council, 1978–89; BCC Standing Cttee on Theol Educn, 1979–82; Council, British and Foreign School Soc., 1979–85; Exec. Cttee, Assoc. of Voluntary Colls, 1979–86; Standing Cttee on Educn and Training of Teachers, 1985–91 (Vice-Chm., 1988; Chm. , 1989); Cttee, Standing Conf. of Principals and Dirs of Colls and Insts of Higher Educn, 1986–91; Voluntary Sector Consultative Council, 1987–88; Cambridge HA, 1987–90 (Trustee, 1988–90); Chairman: Colls Cttee, NATFHE, 1981–82; Central Register and Clearing House Cttee, 1981–82 (Mem. Council of Management, 1982–92). Gov., London Bible Coll., 1981–89. JP Birmingham 1977–85. Hon. MA Birmingham, 1981. *Publications:* articles on educn and church-related subjects. *Recreations:* travel, photography. *Address:* Shiloh, 2 Bayham Road, Tunbridge Wells, Kent TN2 5HP.

BAMFORD, Sir Anthony (Paul), Kt 1990; DL; Chairman and Managing Director, J. C. Bamford Group, since 1975; *b* 23 Oct. 1945; *s* of late Joseph Cyril Bamford, CBE; *m* 1974, Carole Gray Whitt; two *s* one *d.* *Educ:* Ampleforth Coll.; Grenoble Univ. Joined JCB, 1962. Dir, Tarmac, 1987–95. Member: Design Council, 1987–89; President's Cttee, CBI, 1986–88. Pres., Staffs Agricl Soc., 1987–88. Pres., Burton on Trent Cons. Assoc., 1987–90. High Sheriff, Staffs, 1985–86. DL Staffs, 1989. Hon. MEng Birmingham, 1987; DUniv Keele, 1988; Hon. DSc Cranfield, 1994; Hon. DTec Staffordshire, 1998. Young Exporter of the Year, 1972; Young Businessman of the Year, 1979; Top Exporter of the Year, 1995. Chevalier, l'Ordre National du Mérite (France), 1989; Commendatore al merito della Repubblica Italiana, 1995. *Recreations:* farming, gardening. *Address:* c/o J. C. Bamford Excavators Ltd, Rocester, Uttoxeter, Staffs ST14 5JP. *Clubs:* Pratt's, White's, British Racing Drivers'.

BAMFORD, Louis Neville Jules; Legal Executive with Margetts & Ritchie, Solicitors, Birmingham, since 1960; *b* 2 July 1932; *s* of Neville Barnes Bamford and Elise Marie Bamford; unmarried. *Educ:* local schools in Birmingham. Member (Lab): Birmingham CC, 1971–74; W Midlands CC, 1974–86 (Chm., 1981–82; Chm., Legal and Parly Cttee, 1974–77; Mem. of various cttees); Birmingham CC, 1986–94 (Mem. various cttees incl. Policy and Resources, Gen. Purposes (Vice-Chm.), and Leisure; Chief Whip, Lab Gp). Chm., Birmingham Convention and Visitors Bureau. *Recreations:* sport, music. *Address:* 15 Chilton Court, Park Approach, Erdington, Birmingham B23 7XY; (office) Coleridge Chambers, 177 Corporation Street, Birmingham B4 6RL.

BAMPFYLDE, family name of **Baron Poltimore**.

BANANA, Rev. Dr Canaan Sodindo; President of Zimbabwe, 1980–87; *b* Esiphezini, Matabeleland, 5 March 1936; *s* of Aaron and Jese Banana; *m* 1961, Janet Mbuyazwe; three *s* one *d.* *Educ:* Mzinyati Mission; Tegwani Trng Inst.; Epworth Theol Coll., Salisbury; Kansai Industrial Centre, Japan; Wesley Theol Seminary, Washington, DC; Univ. of S Africa. Dip. in Urban and Industrial Mission, Kansai, 1970; MTS Hons, Wesley Theol Seminary, 1974; BA Hons Univ. of SA, 1980. Methodist Minister and Manager of Schools: Wankie Area, 1963–64; Plumtree Area, 1965–66 (Sch. Chaplain, Tegwani High Sch.); Methodist Minister, Fort Viet Area, 1967–68; Methodist Minister, Bulawayo and Chm., Bulaway Council of Churches, 1969–70; with Mambo Press as Promotion Officer for Moto, Catholic newspaper, 1971; Founder Mem. and first Vice Pres., ANC, Zimbabwe, 1971–73; ANC Rep. in N America and UN, 1973–75; Chaplain, American Univ., 1974–75; Publicity Sec., People's Movement Internal Co-ordinating Cttee (ZANU-PF), 1976–77; Reg. Co-ordinator, Matabeleland N and S Provinces, 1979–80. Chm., Southern Africa Contact Gp, 1970–73; Mem., Adv. Cttee, WCC, 1970–80. Hon. LLD: Amer. Univ., 1981; Univ. of Zimbabwe, 1983. *Publications:* The Zimbabwe Exodus, 1974; The Gospel According to the Ghetto, 1974, 3rd edn 1980; The Woman of my Imagination, 1980 (also in Ndebele and Shona versions); Theology of Promise, 1982; The Ethos of Socialism, 1988; various articles. *Recreations:* tennis, table tennis; soccer (player, referee and coach); volley ball (umpire); music. *Address:* c/o State House, Box 368, Harare, Zimbabwe. *T:* Harare (4) 26666.

BANATVALA, Prof. Jehangir Edalji, CBE 1999; MD; FRCP, FRCPath; Professor of Clinical Virology, Guy's, King's College and St Thomas' Hospitals Medical and Dental School, 1975–99, now Emeritus; Hon. Consultant Virologist, Guy's and St Thomas' Hospital Trust, 1975–99; *b* 7 Jan. 1934; *s* of Dr Edal Banatvala and Ratti Banatvala (*née* Shroff); *m* 1959, Roshan (*née* Mugaseth); three *s* (one *d* decd). *Educ:* Forest Sch., London; Gonville and Caius Coll., Cambridge (MA, MB BChir 1958; MD (Whitby Medal) 1964); London Hosp. Med. Coll. DPH London 1961; DCH 1961; MRCPath 1965, FRCPath 1977; MRCP 1986, FRCP 1995. Polio Fund Res. Fellow, Univ. of Cambridge, 1961–64; Fulbright Schol. and Amer. Thoracic Soc. Fellow, Yale Univ., 1964–65; Sen. Lectr, 1965–71, Reader, 1971–75, St Thomas' Hosp. Med. Sch., then UMDS of Guy's and St Thomas' Hosp.; Chm., St Thomas' Hosp. Mgt Team and Med. Adv. Cttee, 1983–84. Royal College of Pathologists: Registrar, 1985–87; Vice Pres., 1987–90; Mem. Council, 1993–96; Member: Council, Med. Defence Union, 1987–; Jt Cttee on Vaccination and Immunisation, DoH, 1986–95; PHLS Bd, 1995–; Chairman: Adv. Gp on Hepatitis, DoH, 1990–98; Mem., European Soc. of Clin. Virology, 1997–; Pres., European Assoc. Against Virus Disease, 1981–83. Hon. Cons. Microbiologist to the Army, 1992–97. Dir, Clinical Pathology Accreditation (UK) Ltd, 1997–. Governor, Forest Sch., E17, 2000–. Founder FMedSci 1998. Freeman, City of London, 1987; Liveryman, Co. of Apothecaries, 1986. *Publications:* (ed) Current Problems in Clinical Virology, 1971; (ed jtly) Principles and Practice of Clinical Virology, 1987, 4th edn 2000; (ed) Viral Infections of the Heart, 1993; papers in gen. and specialised med. jls on intrauterine and perinatal infections, blood-borne virus infections, viral vaccines, etc. *Recreations:* watching sports in which one no longer performs (rowing, cricket), playing tennis, music, good company in good restaurants. *Address:* Little Acre, Church End, Henham, Bishop's Stortford, Herts CM22 6AN. *T:* (01279) 850386. *Clubs:* Athenæum, MCC; Leander (Henley-on-Thames); Hawks (Hon. Mem.) (Cambridge).

BANBURY, family name of **Baron Banbury of Southam**.

BANBURY OF SOUTHAM, 3rd Baron *cr* 1924, of Southam; **Charles William Banbury;** Bt 1902; *b* 29 July 1953; *s* of 2nd Baron Banbury of Southam and of Hilda Ruth, *d* of late A. H. R. Carr; *S* father, 1981; *m* 1st, 1984, Lucinda Trehearne (marr. diss. 1986); 2nd, 1989, Inger Marianne Norton; two *d.* *Educ:* Eton College. *Heir:* none. *Address:* The Mill, Fossebridge, Glos GL54 3JN.

BANBURY, (Frederick Harold) Frith; theatrical director, producer and actor; *b* 4 May 1912; *s* of Rear-Adm. Frederick Arthur Frith Banbury and Winifred (*née* Fink); unmarried. *Educ:* Stowe Sch.; Hertford Coll., Oxford; Royal Academy of Dramatic Art. First stage appearance in "If I Were You", Shaftesbury Theatre, 1933; for next 14 years appeared both in London and Provinces in every branch of theatre from Shakespeare to revue. Appearances included: Hamlet, New Theatre, 1934; Goodness How Sad, Vaudeville, 1938; (revue) New Faces, Comedy, 1939; Uncle Vanya, Westminster, 1943; Jacobowsky and the Colonel, Piccadilly, 1945; Caste, Duke of York's, 1947. During this time he also appeared in numerous films including The Life and Death of Colonel Blimp and The History of Mr Polly, and also on the television screen. Since 1947 he has devoted his time to production and direction, starting with Dark Summer at Lyric, Hammersmith (later transferred St Martin's), 1947; subseq. many, in both London and New York, including The Holly and the Ivy, Duchess, 1950; Waters of the Moon, Haymarket, 1951; The Deep Blue Sea, Duchess, 1951, and Morosco, New York, 1952; A Question of Fact, Piccadilly, 1953; Marching Song, St Martin's, 1954; Love's Labour's Lost, Old Vic, 1954; The Diary of Anne Frank, Phoenix, 1956; A Dead Secret, Piccadilly, 1957; Flowering Cherry, Haymarket, 1957, and Lyceum, New York, 1959; A Touch of the Sun, Saville, 1958; The Ring of Truth, Savoy, 1959; The Tiger and the Horse, Queen's, 1960; The Wings of the Dove, Lyric, 1963; The Right Honourable Gentleman, Billy Rose, New York, 1965; Howards End, New, 1967; Dear Octopus, Haymarket, 1967; Enter A Free Man, St Martin's, 1968; A Day In the Death of Joe Egg, Cameri Theatre, Tel Aviv, 1968; Le Valet, Théâtre de la Renaissance, Paris, 1968; On the Rocks, Dublin Theatre Festival, 1969; My Darling Daisy, Lyric, 1970; The Winslow Boy, New, 1970; Captain Brassbound's Conversion, Cambridge, 1971; Reunion in Vienna, Chichester Festival, 1971, Piccadilly, 1972; The Day After the Fair, Lyric, 1972, Shubert, Los Angeles, 1973; Glasstown, Westminster, 1973; Ardèle, Queen's, 1975; On Approval, Canada and SA, 1976, Vaudeville, 1977; directed in Australia, Kenya, USA, 1978–79; Motherdear, Ambassadors, 1980; Dear Liar, Mermaid, 1982; The Aspern Papers, Haymarket, 1984;

The Corn is Green, Old Vic, 1985; The Admirable Crichton, Haymarket, 1988; Screamers, Arts, 1989; The Gin Game, Savoy, 1999. *Recreation:* playing the piano.

BAND, Vice Adm. Jonathon; Deputy Commander-in-Chief Fleet, since 2001; *b* 2 Feb. 1950; *s* of Victor and Muriel Band; *m* 1979, Sarah Asbury; two *d*. *Educ:* Brambletye Sch.; Haileybury Coll.; Exeter Univ. (BA 1972). Served: HMS Soberton, 1979–81; Fleet HQ, 1981–83; HMS Phoebe, 1983–85; MoD, 1986–89; HMS Norfolk and Ninth Frigate Sqn, 1989–91; MoD, 1991–95; HMS Illustrious, 1995–97; ACNS, MoD, 1997–99; Team Leader, Defence Trng and Educn Study, MoD, 2000–01. Pres., RNRU. Younger Brother, Trinity House, 1998–. *Recreations:* family dominated, including sailing, tennis. *Address:* Maritime Headquarters, Northwood, Middx HA6 3HP. *Club:* Royal Naval and Royal Albert Yacht (Portsmouth).

BAND, His Honour Robert Murray Niven, MC 1944; QC 1974; a Circuit Judge, 1978–91; *b* 23 Nov. 1919; *s* of Robert Niven Band and Agnes Jane Band; *m* 1948, Nancy Margery Redhead; two *d*. *Educ:* Trinity Coll., Glenalmond; Hertford Coll., Oxford (MA). Served in Royal Artillery, 1940–46. Called to the Bar, Inner Temple, 1947; Junior Treasury Counsel in Probate Matters, 1972–74; Chm. Family Law Bar Assoc., 1972–74; a Recorder of the Crown Court, 1977–78. Chm., St Teresa's Hosp., Wimbledon, 1969–83. *Recreations:* the countryside, gardens, old buildings, treen.

BAND, Thomas Mollison, FSAScot; FTS; Chairman, Perth Repertory Theatre Ltd, since 1995 (Director, since 1994); *b* 28 March 1934; *s* of late Robert Boyce Band and Elizabeth Band; *m* 1959, Jean McKenzie Brien; one *s* two *d*. *Educ:* Perth Academy. National Service, RAF, 1952–54. Joined Civil Service, 1954; Principal, BoT, 1969; Sen. Principal, Dept of Industry, 1973; Scottish Econ. Planning Dept, 1975, Asst Sec., 1976; Scottish Development Dept, 1978; Scottish Office, Finance, 1981; Dir, Historic Bldgs and Monuments, Scottish Develt Dept, 1984–87; Chief Exec., Scottish Tourist Bd, 1987–94. Chairman: Made in Scotland Ltd, 1994–95; Anderson Enterprises Ltd, 1994–98; Edinburgh Europa Ltd, 1994–98. Dir, Edinburgh Telford Coll., 1989–98. Chm., Industrial Cttee, Napier Univ. (formerly Napier Poly. of Edinburgh), 1989–95. Gov., Queen Margaret UC, Edinburgh, 1995–. Vice Chm., Perth Housing Assoc., 1998–. FRSA 1993. *Recreations:* ski-ing, gardening. *Address:* Heathfield, Pitcairngreen, Perthshire PH1 3LT. *T:* (01738) 583403, *Fax:* (01738) 583063.

BANDA, Prof. Enric, DSc; Secretary General, European Science Foundation, since 1998; *b* 21 June 1948; *s* of Emilio and Maria Banda; *m* 1st, 1973 (marr. diss. 1982); 2nd, 1983, Gemma Lienas. *Educ:* Univ. of Barcelona (BSc Physics 1974; DSc Physics 1979). Researcher, ETH-Zürich, 1980–83; Head, Geophysical Survey, Catalan Govt, 1983–87; Res. Prof., Consejo Superior de Investigaciones Científicas, 1987; Head, Inst. of Earth Sciences, Barcelona, 1988–91; Sec. Gen., Nat. Plan R&D, Spain, 1994; Sec. of State for Universities and Research, Spain, 1995–96. Chevalier de la Légion d'Honneur (France), 1997. *Publications:* more than 150 scientific papers. *Address:* European Science Foundation, 1 quai Lezay-Marnésia, 67080 Strasbourg, France. *T:* (3) 88767117.

BANFIELD, Ven. David John; Archdeacon of Bristol, 1990–98; *b* 25 June 1933; *s* of Norman Charles Banfield and Muriel Gladys Honor Banfield (*née* Pippard); *m* 1967, Rita (*née* Woolhouse); three *d*. *Educ:* Yeovil Sch.; London Coll. of Divinity, London Univ. (ALCD). RAF, 1951–53. Deacon 1957, priest 1958; Curate, Middleton, Manchester, 1957–62; Chaplain and Asst Warden, Scargill House, Yorks, 1962–67; Vicar of Addiscombe, Croydon, 1967–80; Vicar of Luton, Beds, 1980–90; RD, Luton, 1989–90; Hon. Canon, St Alban's, 1989–90. *Recreations:* travel, walking, music, gardening. *Address:* 47 Avon Way, Stoke Bishop, Bristol BS9 1SL. *T:* (0117) 968 4227.

BANFIELD, John Martin; FInstP; Director, Mobil Europe, 1996–2001; *b* 15 Nov. 1947; *s* of Jack Banfield and Peggy Winifred Banfield (*née* Parker); *m* 1978, Mary Gerrey Morton; one *s* one *d*. *Educ:* Haberdashers' Aske's; St John's Coll., Cambridge (MA Geography). Joined Mobil Oil Co., 1969; Man. Dir, Mobil Cyprus, 1986–87; Director: Mobil Benelux, 1988–89; Mobil Oil Co., 1990–91; Pres., Mobil Benelux, 1992; Dir, Mobil Germany, 1993; Chm., Mobil Oil Co., 1994–96. Vice-Pres., Inst. of Petroleum, 1996–99; Pres., Oil Industries Club, 1997–98. *Recreations:* music, sailing, travel. *Address:* Garden Corner, Old London Road, Mickleham, Surrey RH5 6DL. *Club:* MCC.

BANGEMANN, Dr Martin; a Member, European Commission (formerly Commission of the European Community), 1989–99 (a Vice-President, 1989–93); *b* 15 Nov. 1934; *s* of Martin Bangemann and Lotte Telge; *m* 1962, Renate Bauer; three *s* two *d*. *Educ:* Univ. of Tübingen; Univ. of Munich (DJur). Lawyer, 1964–. Mem., Bundestag, 1972–80 and 1986–89; Mem., European Parliament, 1973–84; Minister of Econs, FRG, 1984–88. Freie Demokratische Partei: Mem., 1963–; Chm., 1985–88. Dir, Telefónica, 2000–. Fed. Cross of Merit with star (Germany); Bavarian Order of Merit.

BANGHAM, Alec Douglas, MD; FRCP; FRS 1977; retired; Research Worker, Agricultural Research Council, Institute of Animal Physiology, Babraham, 1952–82 and Head, Biophysics Unit, 1971–82; *b* 10 Nov. 1921; *s* of Dr Donald Hugh and Edith Bangham; *m* 1943, Rosalind Barbara Reiss; three *s* one *d*. *Educ:* Bryanston Sch.; UCL and UCH Med. Sch. (MD). FRCP 1997. Captain, RAMC, 1946–48. Lectr, Dept of Exper. Pathology, UCH, 1949–52; Principal Scientific Officer, 1952–63, Senior Principal Scientific Officer (Merit Award), 1963–82, ARC, Babraham. Fellow, UCL, 1981–. *Publications:* contrib. Nature, Biochim. Biophys. Acta, and Methods in Membrane Biol. *Recreations:* horticulture, photographic arts, sailing. *Address:* 17 High Green, Great Shelford, Cambridge CB2 5EG. *T:* (01223) 843192, *Fax:* (01223) 844683; *e-mail:* alec.bangham@wwr.co.uk.

BANGOR, 8th Viscount *cr* 1781 (Ire.); **William Maxwell David Ward;** Baron 1770 (Ire.); antiquarian bookseller; *b* 9 Aug. 1948; *s* of 7th Viscount Bangor and his 3rd wife, Leila Mary Heaton (*d* 1959); *S* father, 1993; *m* 1976, Sarah Mary Malet Bradford (*née* Hayes). *Educ:* University Coll., London. *Recreations:* history, music, antiquity, Bolton Wanderers. *Heir presumptive: b* Hon. (Edward) Nicholas Ward [; *b* 16 Jan. 1953; *m* 1985, Rachel Mary, *d* of Hon. Hugh Waldorf Astor, *qv*; two *d*]. *Address:* 31 Britannia Road, SW6 2HJ. *Club:* Chelsea Arts.

BANGOR, Bishop of, since 2000; **Rt Rev. (Francis James) Saunders Davies;** *b* 30 Dec. 1937; *s* of Tom and Clara Davies; *m* 1963, (Marianne) Cynthia Young; one *s* one *d*. *Educ:* UCNW Bangor (BA Hons Welsh and accessory Hebrew 1960); Selwyn Coll., Cambridge (MA Theol. 1966); St Michael's Coll., Llandaff; Bonn Univ., Germany. Ordained deacon, 1963, priest, 1964; Curate, Holyhead, 1963–67; Minor Canon, Bangor Cathedral and Hon. Staff Mem., SCM, 1967–69; Rector, Llanllyfni, 1969–75; Canon Missioner, Bangor Dio., 1975–78; Vicar, Gorseinon, 1978–86; Rural Dean, Llwchwr, 1983–86; Vicar, Eglwys Dewi Sant, Cardiff, 1986–93; Rector, Cricieth with Treflys and Archdeacon of Meirionnydd, 1993–2000. Tutor: NSM Course, Llandaff Dio., 1987–93; for Continuing Educn, UC Cardiff, 1988–93. Vice-Chm., Cardiff Christian Adult Educn Centre, 1990–93. *Publications:* (ed jtly) Euros Bowen Poet-Priest/Bardd Offeiriad, 1993; Y Daith Anorfod: a commentary on St Luke's Gospel, 1993. *Recreations:* reading, walking, listening to classical music, going to the theatre and the Nat. Eisteddfod of Wales. *Address:* Tŷ'r Esgob, Bangor, Gwynedd LL57 2SS. *T:* (01248) 362895.

BANGOR, Dean of; *see* Evans, Very Rev. T. O.

BANHAM, Mrs Belinda Joan, CBE 1977; JP; Lay Chairman, NHS Complaints Procedure, London Region, since 1999; independent consultant, health care services, since 1996; *d* of late Col Charles Unwin and Winifred Unwin; *m* 1939, Terence Middlecott Banham (*d* 1995); two *s* two *d*. *Educ:* privately; West Bank Sch.; Brussels. BSc (Hons) London; Dip. Social Studies London. RGN. Work in health services, 1937–; work in theory and practice on aspects of social deviance and deprivation, Cornwall CC, 1954–67; Mem., SW RHB, 1965–74; Chairman: Cornwall and Isles of Scilly HMC, 1967–74 (Mem., 1964–77); Cornwall and Isles of Scilly AHA, 1974–77; Kensington, Chelsea and Westminster FPC, 1979–85 (Mem. 1977–79); Paddington and N Kensington DHA, 1981–86; Mem., Lambeth, Southwark and Lewisham FPC, 1987–90; Chm., Lambeth, Southwark and Lewisham FHSA, 1993–96 (Vice-Chm., 1990–93); Vice-Chm., Lambeth, Southwark and Lewisham Health Commn, 1993–96. Mem., MRC, 1980–87 (Chm., Standing Cttee on Use of Medical Inf. in Research, 1980–87). Mem., Industrial Tribunals, 1974–87. Marriage Guidance Councillor, 1960–72. A Vice-Chm., Disabled Living Foundn, 1984–91 (Dir, then Hon. Dir, 1977–83); Pres., Friends of St Mary's Hosp., Paddington, 1983–; Vice-President: KIDS, 1987– (Chm., 1982–87); AFASIC, 1990–. Mem. Delegacy, KCH Med. Sch., 1996–99. Trustee, Wytham Hall, 1985– (Vice Chm., 1990–). JP Cornwall, 1972. Special interests: social deprivation and deviance, Health Service management and use of resources. *Publications:* Snapshots in Time: some experiences in health care 1936–1991, 1991; General Practice in the NHS: or, football round the mulberry bush 1918–1995, 1995; (jtly) (paper) Systems Science in Health Care (NATO Conf., Paris, 1977); (jtly) (report) Partnership in Action: a study of healthcare services for elderly and physically handicapped in Newcastle, 1989. *Recreations:* gardening, plant biology, theatre. *Address:* 73 Vandon Court, Petty France, SW1H 9HG. *T:* (020) 7222 3676.

See also Sir J. M. M. Banham.

BANHAM, Sir John (Michael Middlecott), Kt 1992; DL; Chairman: ECI Ventures Ltd, since 1992; Tarmac, since 1994 (Director, since 1992); Whitbread, since 2000 (Director, since 1999); *b* 22 Aug. 1940; *s* of late Terence Middlecott Banham, FRCS and of Belinda Joan Banham, *qv*; *m* 1965, Frances Barbara Molyneux Favell; one *s* two *d*. *Educ:* Charterhouse; Queens' Coll., Cambridge (Foundn Schol.; BA 1st cl. in Natural Scis, 1962; Hon. Fellow, 1989). Asst Principal, HM Foreign Service, 1962–64; Dir of Marketing, Wallcoverings Div., Reed International, 1965–69; McKinsey & Co. Inc.: Associate, 1969–75; Principal, 1975–80; Dir, 1980–83. Controller, Audit Commn, 1983–87; Dir-Gen., CBI, 1987–92; Chm., Local Govt Commn for England, 1992–95. Chm., Retail and Consumer Affairs Foresight Panel, 1997–. Chairman: John Labatt (Europe), subseq. Labatt Breweries of Europe, 1992–95; Westcountry Television Ltd, 1992–95; Kingfisher, 1996–2001; Director: National Westminster Bank, 1992–98; National Power, 1992–98; (non-exec.) Amvescap plc, 1999–; John Labatt; Merchants Trust. Mem., BOTB, 1989–92; Dir and Mem. Bd, Business in the Community, 1989–92. Member Council: PSI, 1986–92; Forum for Management Educn and Develt, 1988–93; BESO, 1991–92. Member: Council of Management, PDSA, 1982–93; Governing Body, London Business Sch., 1987–92; Managing Trustee, Nuffield Foundn, 1988–97; Hon. Treas., Cancer Res. Campaign, 1991–. DL Cornwall, 1999. Hon. LLD Bath, 1987; Hon. DSc: Loughborough, 1989; Exeter, 1993; Strathclyde, 1995. *Publications:* Future of the British Car Industry, 1975; Realizing the Promise of a National Health Service, 1977; The Anatomy of Change: blueprint for a new era, 1994; numerous reports for Audit Commn on education, housing, social services and local government finance, 1984–87, and for CBI on UK economy, skills, transport, the infrastructure, urban regeneration and manufacturing. *Recreations:* walking, gardening, music. *Address:* c/o Westcountry Management, 64A Neal Street, Covent Garden, WC2H 9PA. *T:* (020) 7379 1697, *Fax:* (020) 7379 1659. *Clubs:* Travellers, Oriental.

BANISTER, Prof. David John, PhD; Professor of Transport Planning, University of London, at University College London, since 1995; *b* 10 July 1950; *s* of Stephen Michael Alvin Banister, *qv*; *m* 1985, Elizabeth Dawn Bucknell; three *d*. *Educ:* Royal Grammar Sch., Guildford; Nottingham Univ. (BA 1st Cl. Hons Geog.); Leeds Univ. (PhD Transport Studies 1976). MCIT 1976; MILT 1999. Lectr in Geog., Univ. of Reading, 1975–78; Lectr in Transport Policy, 1979–88, Sen. Lectr, 1988–90, Reader in Transport Planning, 1990–95, UCL. Vis. VSB Prof., Tinbergen Inst., Amsterdam, 1994–97. Jt Ed., Built Envmt, 1992–; Ed., Transport Reviews, 2001–; Mem., editl bds of several jls. Non-exec. Dir, Taylor and Francis Gp PLC, 1990–. Dir, Res. Prog. on Transport and Envmt, ESRC, 1992–96; Member: Adv. Gps on Future Integrated Transport, Inland Surface Transport, Cities and Sustainability, EPSRC, 1994–; Team for Town and Country Planning, RAE 2001, HEFCE; Chm., Econ. Commn for Europe's Task Force on Urban Transport Patterns and Land Use Planning, UN, 2000–. FRSA 1988. Trustee, Ferguson Charitable Trust, 1979–. Editor, Spon series on Transport, Development and Sustainability, 1999–. *Publications:* Transport Mobility and Deprivation in Inter-Urban Areas, 1980; (jtly) Transport and Public Policy Planning, 1981; Rural Transport and Planning, 1985; (jtly) Urban Transport and Planning, 1989; (jtly) Transport in a Free Market Economy, 1991; (jtly) Transport in Unified Europe: policies and challenges, 1993; (jtly) Transport, the Environment and Sustainable Development, 1993; Transport Planning, 1994, rev. edn, 2001; (jtly) Transport and Urban Development, 1995; European Transport and Communications Networks: policy evolution and change, 1995; (jtly) Telematics and Transport Behaviour, 1996; Transport Policy and the Environment, 1998; (jtly) Environment, Land Use and Urban Policy, 1999; (jtly) European Transport Policy and Sustainable Mobility, 2000; (jtly) Encouraging Transport Alternatives: good practice in reducing travel, 2000; (jtly) Transport Investment and Economic Development, 2000; contrib. books and internat. jls. *Recreations:* gardening, farming, walking, good company and conversation. *Address:* Bartlett School of Planning, University College London, Wates House, 22 Gordon Street, WC1H 0QB. *T:* (020) 7679 4891.

BANISTER, Stephen Michael Alvin; Secretary, British and Foreign School Society, 1978–96; Founder Editor, Transport Reviews, since 1981; *b* 7 Oct. 1918; *s* of late Harry Banister and Idwen Banister (*née* Thomas); *m* 1944, Rachel Joan Rawlence; four *s*. *Educ:* Eton; King's Coll., Cambridge (MA). With Foreign Office, 1939–45; Home Guard (Major, 1944). Asst Principal, Min. of Civil Aviation, 1946; Principal, 1947; Private Sec. to six successive Ministers of Transport and Civil Aviation, 1950–56; Asst Sec., Min. of Transport and BoT, 1956–70; Under Sec., DoE, 1970–76, Dept of Transport, 1976–78. UK Shipping Delegate, UNCTAD, 1964; UK Dep., European Conf. of Ministers of Transport, 1976–78. Dir, Taylor and Francis, 1978–91. Mem., Nat. Insurance Tribunal, Kingston upon Thames, 1979–85. MCIT 1994; MILT 1999. *Compositions:* (amateur) for singers, including Bluebeard. *Recreations:* countryside, walking, singing (formerly in opera, now in choirs); formerly cricket (Cambridge Crusader); played for CU *v* Australians, 1938. *Address:* Bramshaw, Lower Farm Road, Effingham, Surrey KT24 5JJ. *T:* (01372) 452778.

See also D. J. Banister.

BANKS, Anthony Louis, (Tony); MP (Lab) West Ham, since 1997 (Newham North West, 1983–97). *Educ:* St John's Primary Sch., Brixton; Archbishop Tenison's Grammar Sch., Kennington; York Univ. (BA); London School of Economics. Former trade union research worker; Head of Research, AUEW, 1969–75; an Asst Gen. Sec., Assoc. of Broadcasting and Allied Staffs, 1976–83. Political Advr to Minister for Overseas Develt, 1975. Joined Labour Party, 1964; Greater London Council: Mem. for Hammersmith, 1970–77, for Tooting, 1981–86; Chairman: Gen. Purposes Cttee, 1975–77; Arts and Recreation Cttee, 1981–83; GLC, 1985–86. Contested (Lab): E Grinstead, 1970; Newcastle upon Tyne N, Oct. 1974; Watford, 1979. Parly Under-Sec. of State, DCMS, 1997–99. Member: Select Cttee, HM Treasury, 1986–87; Select Cttee on Procedure, 1987–97; Jt Lords/Commons Cttee on Private Bill Procedure, 1987–88; Council of Europe Parly Assembly and WEU, 1989–. Chm., London Gp, Labour MP's, 1987–91. Member: ENO Bd, 1981–83; London Festival Ballet Bd, 1981–83; Nat. Theatre Bd, 1981–85. *Publication:* (jtly) Out of Order, 1993. *Address:* 306 High Street, Stratford, E15 1AJ. *T:* (020) 8555 0036.

BANKS, (Arthur) David; journalist and broadcaster; *b* 13 Feb. 1948; *s* of Arthur Banks and Helen (*née* Renton); *m* 1975, Gemma Newton; one *s* one *d*. *Educ:* Boteler Grammar Sch., Warrington. Asst Man. Editor, NY Post, 1979–81; Night Editor, then Asst Editor, The Sun, 1981–86; Dep. Man. Editor, NY Daily News, 1986–87; Dep. Editor, The Australian, 1987–89; Editor: Daily Telegraph Mirror (Sydney), 1989–92; Daily Mirror, 1992–94; Editl Dir, Mirror Gp Newspapers, 1994–97; Consultant Ed., Sunday Mirror, 1997–98; Dir of Information, Mirror Gp, 1998–99. Presenter, Breakfast Show, Talk Radio, 1999–2000. *Recreations:* dining, dieting. *Address:* c/o The Roseman Organisation, Suite 9, Power House, 70 Chiswick High Road, W4 1SY.

BANKS, Caroline; Director, Consumer Affairs, Office of Fair Trading, since 1998; *b* 24 April 1950; *d* of Geoffrey Banks and Pamela Dane Banks. *Educ:* Kitwe Girls' High Sch., Zambia; Middlesex Poly. (BA Hons). Office of Fair Trading: EO, Competition Policy Cartel Investigations, 1975–79; HEO, Consumer Affairs Policy, 1979–82; Head, Consumer Credit Licensing Bureau, 1982–88; Principal Estabt and Finance Officer, 1988–97. *Recreations:* gardening, tapestry. *Address:* Office of Fair Trading, Fleetbank House, 2–6 Salisbury Square, EC4Y 8JX. *T:* (020) 7211 8821.

BANKS, Colin; Founder Partner, Banks and Miles, graphic designers, London, 1958–98 (Amsterdam, 1969–74, Hamburg, 1990–93, and Brussels, 1991–93); *b* 16 Jan. 1932; *s* of late William Banks and Ida Jenny; *m* 1961, Caroline Grigson, PhD; one *s* (one *d* decd). Prodn Editor (with John Miles) of Which? and other Consumers' Assoc. magazines, 1964–93. Design Consultant to: Zool Soc., 1962–82; British Council, 1968–83; English National Opera, 1975–76; Direct Election Campaign, European Parlt, 1978, 1984; (new visual identity for) Post Office: Royal Mail, Telecommunications, etc, 1972–; British Telecom., 1980; Open Univ., 1980; US Govt Social Marketing Project, Family Planning, Indonesia, 1985; NERC, 1986; City Univ., 1987; CNAA, 1988; IMechE, 1988; Fondation Roi Baudouin, 1988–89; SERC, 1989. Designer/Design Adviser to: City and Guilds; Commn for Racial Equality; UN Univ., Japan, 1991–93; UNHCR, 1995–; other instns and commercial cos; Graphic Consultant to: London Transport, 1964–95; Mott MacDonald, 1989–; OUP, 1996–. Exhibitions: London, Paris, Amsterdam, Glasgow, Brussels, Kyoto, Hamburg; True To Type, Crafts Council, UK and Copenhagen, 1994–96. Vice-Pres., SIAD, 1974–76. Pres., Soc. of Typographic Designers, 1988–93 and 2000–; Design and Industries Assoc. Manager, Blackheath Sch. of Art, 1981–89; Gov., Bournemouth Coll. of Art, 1990–97; Mem. Bd, Internat. Inst. for Information Design, 1996–. Treas., Project Mala for children's educn and welfare, India, 1989–92. Vis. Prof., Royal Danish Acad., 1998–99. Lectured Europe, Asia, USA. FZS. Fifty Best German Printed Books, W Germany, 1989; Internationalen Buchkunst Ausstellung Medal, Leipzig, 1971, 1989; Gold Medal, Brno Biennale, 1986; RSA Green Award, 1989; BBC Envmtl Design Prize, 1990; Technol. and Creation Prize, Paris Cité, 1991; Internat. Award, Soc. of Typographic Designers, 1996; Ærespris, Danish Soc. for the Book, 1996. *Publications:* Social Communication, 1979; (with E. Schumacher Gebler) 26 Letters, Vol. I 1989, Vol. II 1992; London's Handwriting, 1995; contrib. jls, London, Budapest, Copenhagen, USA etc. *Recreation:* heuristics (productive laziness). *Address:* 29 Langton Way, SE3 7TJ. *Clubs:* Arts; Double Crown (Pres., 1989–90), Wynkyn de Worde (Chm., 1984–85); Rencontres Internationales de Lure.

BANKS, David; *see* Banks, A. D.

BANKS, Frank David, FCA; Chairman, H. Berkeley (Holdings) Ltd, 1984–90; *b* 11 April 1933; *s* of Samuel and Elizabeth Banks; *m* 1st, 1955, Catherine Jacob; one *s* two *d*; 2nd, 1967, Sonia Gay Coleman; one *d*. *Educ:* Liverpool Collegiate Sch.; Carnegie Mellon Univ. (PFE); Open Univ. (BA 1988); Univ. of Sussex (MA 1992). British Oxygen Co. Ltd, 1957–58; Imperial Chemical Industries Ltd, 1959–62; English Electric Co. Ltd, 1963–68; Finance Dir, Platt International Ltd, 1969–71; Industrial Advr, DTI, 1972–73; Constructors John Brown Ltd, 1974–80; Man. Dir, Agribusiness Div., Tate & Lyle Ltd, 1981–83. *Recreations:* music, history. *Address:* 117 Village Road, Bromham, Bedford MK43 8HU.

BANKS, Mrs Gillian Theresa, CB 1990; *b* 7 Feb. 1933; *d* of Percy and Enid Brimblecombe; *m* 1960, John Anthony Gorst Banks (marr. diss. 1993); one *s* two *d*. *Educ:* Walthamstow Hall Sch., Sevenoaks; Lady Margaret Hall, Oxford (BA). Asst Principal, Colonial Office, 1955; Principal, Treasury, 1966; Department of Health and Social Security: Asst Sec., 1972; Under Sec. 1981; Dir, Health Authy Finance, 1985; Dir, OPCS and Registrar Gen. for Eng. and Wales, 1986; Dir, Carnegie Inquiry into the Third Age, 1990; led Functions, Manpower and Sen. Management Review of Wider DoH, 1994; Dir, Retirement Income Inquiry, 1994; Mem., Camden and Islington HA, 1995; Vice Chm., Royal Free Hampstead NHS Trust, 1998–. Policy Consultant, Age Concern, England, 1996. Hon. Treas., Camden Age Concern, 1997–. Lay Mem., Council, RPSGB, 1996–. *Recreation:* hill walking. *Address:* 16 Chalcot Square, NW1 8YA. *T:* (020) 7722 3962.

BANKS, John, FREng, FIEE; Chairman, Adacom 3270 Communications Ltd, 1986–90; *b* 2 Dec. 1920; *s* of John Banks and Jane Dewhurst; *m* 1943, Nancy Olive Yates; two *s*. *Educ:* Univ. of Liverpool (BEng Hons; MEng). FREng (FEng 1983); FIEE 1959. Chief Engr, Power Cables Div., BICC, 1956–67; Divl Dir and Gen Man., Supertension Cables Div., BICC, 1968–74; Exec. Dir, 1975–78, Chm., 1978–84, BICC Research and Engineering Ltd; Exec. Dir, BICC, 1979–84. Vis. Prof., Liverpool Univ., 1987–. Pres., IEE, 1982–83. *Recreations:* golf, swimming, music and the arts. *Address:* Flat B1 Marine Gate, Marine Drive, Brighton BN2 5TQ. *T:* (01273) 690756. *Club:* Seaford Golf.

BANKS, Lynne Reid; writer; *b* 1929; *d* of Dr James Reid-Banks and Muriel (Pat) (*née* Marsh); *m* 1965, Chaim Stephenson, sculptor; three *s*. *Educ:* schooling mainly in Canada; RADA. Actress, 1949–54; reporter for ITN, 1955–62; English teacher in kibbutz in Western Galilee, Israel, 1963–71; full-time writer, 1971–; writing includes plays for stage, television and radio. *Publications: plays:* It Never Rains, 1954; All in a Row, 1956; The Killer Dies Twice, 1956; Already, It's Tomorrow, 1962; (for children) Travels of Yoshi and the Tea-Kettle, 1993; *fiction:* The L-Shaped Room, 1960 (trans. 10 langs; filmed 1962); An End to Running, 1962 (trans. 2 langs); Children at the Gate, 1968; The Backward Shadow, 1970; Two is Lonely, 1974; Defy the Wilderness, 1981; The Warning Bell, 1984; Casualties, 1986; Fair Exchange, 1998; *biographical fiction:* Dark Quartet: the story of the Brontes, 1976 (Yorks Arts Lit. Award, 1977); Path to the Silent Country: Charlotte Bronte's years of fame, 1977; *history:* Letters to my Israeli Sons, 1979; Torn Country, USA 1982; *for young adults:* One More River, 1973; Sarah and After, 1975; My Darling Villain, 1977 (trans. 3 langs); The Writing on the Wall, 1981; Melusine, 1988 (trans. 3 langs); *for children:* The Adventures of King Midas, 1976 (trans. 4 langs); The Farthest-Away Mountain, 1977; I, Houdini, 1978 (trans. 4 langs); The Indian in the Cupboard, 1980 (trans. 20 langs) (Pacific NW Choice Award, 1984; Calif. Young Readers Medal, 1985; Va Children's Choice, 1988; Mass. Children's Choice, 1988; Rebecca Caudill Award, Ill, 1989; Arizona Children's Choice, 1989; filmed, 1995); Maura's Angel, 1984 (trans. 2 langs); The Fairy Rebel, 1985 (trans. 3 langs); Return of the Indian, 1986 (trans. 5 langs); The Secret of the Indian, 1989 (trans. 4 langs); The Magic Hare, 1992; Mystery of the Cupboard, 1993 (trans. 3 langs); Broken Bridge, 1994 (trans. 2 langs); Harry the Poisonous Centipede, 1996; Angela and Diabola, 1997 (trans. 2 langs); The Key to the Indian, 1999; Moses in Egypt, 1998 (trans. 3 langs); Alice-by-Accident, 2000; Harry the Poisonous Centipede's Big Adventure, 2000; short stories; articles in The Times, The Guardian, Sunday Telegraph, Observer, TES, TLS, Independent on Sunday, Sunday Times, Spectator, Saga Magazine, and in overseas periodicals. *Recreations:* theatre, gardening, teaching EFL abroad. *Address:* c/o Watson, Little Ltd, Capo di Monte, Windmill Hill, NW3 6RJ. *T:* (020) 7431 0770.

BANKS, Matthew Richard William; *see* Gordon-Banks, M. R. W.

BANKS, Richard Lee; Director, since 1998, Distribution Operations Director, since 2000, Alliance & Leicester plc; *b* 15 June 1951; *s* of Richard Cyril Banks and Mary Banks; *m* 1978, Elaine Helena Kret; two *s*. *Educ:* Stockport Secondary Technical High Sch.; Manchester Poly. (BA Hons Business Studies). Joined Midland Bank, 1974, various mgt posts, 1978–87; Girobank: Gen. Manager, 1987–91; Sen. Gen. Manager, 1991–94; Dir, Corporate Banking, 1994–96; Man. Dir, 1996–2000. *Recreations:* reading, cottage renovation.

BANKS, Robert George; Director: CMR Insurance Services (formerly CMR Intrum Justitia) Ltd, since 1996; Trade Risk & Surety Ltd, since 1999; Chairman, H. Balcazar Ltd, since 1998; *b* 18 Jan. 1937; *s* of late George Walmsley Banks, MBE, and of Olive Beryl Banks (*née* Tyler); *m* 1967, Diana Margaret Payne Crawfurd; four *s* one *d* (of whom one *s* one *d* are twins). *Educ:* Haileybury. Lt-Comdr RNR. Jt Founder Dir, Antocks Lairn Ltd, 1963–67. Mem., Alcohol Educn and Res. Council, 1982–88. Mem., Paddington BC, 1959–65. MP (C) Harrogate, Feb. 1974–97. PPS to Minister of State and to Under-Sec. of State, FCO, 1979–82. Member: Select Cttee on Foreign Affairs (and its Overseas Develt Sub-Cttee), 1982; Select Cttee on Trade and Industry, 1994–97; Jt Sec., Cons. Defence Cttee, 1976–79; Chairman: British-Sudan All Party Parly Gp, 1984–97; All-Party Tourism Gp, 1992–97 (Sec., 1973–79; Vice-Chm., 1979–92); Vice-Chm., Yorks Cons. Mems' Cttee, 1983–97. Member: Council of Europe, 1977–81; WEU, 1977–81; N Atlantic Assembly, 1981–95. Introd Licensing (Alcohol Educn and Res.) Act, 1981; sponsored Licensing (Restaurants Meals) Act, 1987. Reports: for Mil. Cttee of WEU, Report on Nuclear, Biol. and Chem. Protection, adopted by WEU Assembly April 1980; North Atlantic Assembly document, The Technology of Military Space Systems, 1982. Consultant, Amies Mergers. *Publications:* (jtly) Britain's Home Defence Gamble (pamphlet), 1979; New Jobs from Pleasure, report on tourism, 1985; Tories for Tourism, 1995. *Recreations:* travel, farming, architecture, contemporary art. *Address:* Bretteston Hall, near Sudbury, Suffolk.

BANN, Prof. Stephen, PhD; FBA 1998; Professor of History of Art, University of Bristol, since 2000; *b* 1 Aug. 1942; *s* of Harry Bann, OBE and Edna Bann (*née* Pailin). *Educ:* Winchester Coll. (schol.); King's Coll., Cambridge (schol.; BA Hist. 1963; MA; PhD 1967). State Res. Studentship, 1963–66, in Paris, 1964–65; University of Kent: Lectr, 1967–75, Sen. Lectr, 1975–80, in History; Reader in Modern Cultural Studies, 1980–88; Prof. of Modern Cultural Studies, 1988–2000. Visiting Professor: Rennes Univ., 1994; Johns Hopkins Univ., 1996–98; Bologna Univ., 1998, etc. Member: Art Panel, Arts Council of GB, 1975–78; Humanities Res. Bd, British Acad., 1997–98; Chm. Res. Cttee, AHRB, 1998–2000; Res. Awards Adv. Cttee, Leverhulme Trust, 1998–. Pres., Comité Internat. d'Histoire de l'Art, 2000–. Mem. Council, Friends of Canterbury Cathedral, 1990–2000. Dep. Ed., then Ed., 20th Century Studies, 1969–76; Adv. Ed., Reaktion Books, 1985–. *Publications:* Experimental Painting, 1970; (ed) The Tradition of Constructivism, 1974; The Clothing of Clio, 1984; The True Vine: on visual representation and the Western tradition, 1989; The Inventions of History, 1990; Under the Sign: John Bargrave as collector, traveler and witness, 1994; Romanticism and the Rise of History, 1995; Paul Delaroche: history painted, 1997; Parallel Lines: printmakers, painters and photographers in nineteenth-century France, 2001. *Recreations:* travel, collecting. *Address:* 2 New Street, St Dunstan's, Canterbury, Kent CT2 8AU. *T:* (01227) 761135; Department of History of Art, University of Bristol, Bristol BS8 1TH. *Club:* Savile.

BANNENBERG, Jon, RDI 1978; AMRINA; *b* Australia, 8 July 1929; *s* of Henryk and Kay Bannenberg; *m* 1960, Beaupré Robinson; two *s*. *Educ:* Canterbury High Sch., Sydney; Sydney Conservatorium of Music. RDI (Motor Yacht Design) 1978. Designed: 'Siècle d'Elégance' Exhibn, Louvre, Paris, 1959; CINOA Exhibn, V&A Museum, London, 1960; Eskenazi Gall., London, 1993; motor and sail boat designs include: Queen Elizabeth 2, 1967; Tiawana, Tamahine, 1968; Carinthia V, Anemos II, 1969; Benedic, 1970; Carinthia VI, Arjuna, Aetos, 1971; Blue Lady, Yellowbird, Firebird, Heron 21, 1972; Stilvi, Pegasus III, 1973; My Gail, Xiphas, Mediterranean Sky, 1974; Boule Dogue, Southern Breeze, 1975; Solitaire, 1976; Majestic, 1977; Rodis Island, Nabila, Cimba, 1979; My Gail II, Nahema, 1981; Acajou, Azteca, Paraiso, Bobbara, Three Y's, 1983; My Gail III, Cedar Sea, Shirley B, Highlander, Sterling One, Never Say Never, Garuda, 1985; Southern Cross III, Lady Ghislaine, 1987; Acharné, Starlight, 1988; Beaupré, Stefaren, G. Whiz, Mercedes, Mystique, 1989; Gee. Dee, Oceana, Opal C, 1991; Siran, Moecca, 1992; Coral Island, Kremlin Princess, 1994; Limitless, 1997; Thunder, 1998; Millennium, 1999. Member, RYA. *Recreations:* running, swimming, sailing, music, Polynesian and Pacific history. *Address:* 35 Carlyle Square, Chelsea, SW3 6HA. *T:* (020) 7352 6129; 6 Burnsall Street, SW3 3ST. *T:* (020) 7352 4851, *Fax:* (020) 7352 8444.

BANNER, Josephina, (Mrs Delmar Banner); *see* Vasconcellos, J. de.

BANNER, Rev. Prof. Michael Charles, DPhil; F. D. Maurice Professor of Moral and Social Theology, King's College, London, since 1994; *b* 19 April 1961; *s* of Maurice Banner and Maureen (*née* Ince); *m* 1983, Elizabeth Jane Wheare; two *d*. *Educ:* Bromsgrove Sch.; Balliol Coll., Oxford (BA Philos. and Theol. 1st cl. 1983; MA 1985; DPhil 1986). Ordained Deacon 1986; Priest 1987. Bampton Res. Fellow, St Peter's Coll., Oxford, 1985–88; Dean, Chaplain, Fellow and Dir of Studies in Philosophy and Theol., 1988–94, Tutor 1989–94, Peterhouse, Cambridge. Vis. Res. Fellow, Merton Coll., Oxford, 1993.

Chairman: HM Govt Cttee of Enquiry on Ethics of Emerging Technologies in Breeding of Farm Animals, 1993–95; Home Office Animal Procedures Cttee, 1998–; CJD Incidents Panel, DoH, 2000–. Member: Royal Commn on Envmtl Pollution, 1996–; Agric. and Envmt Biotech. Commn, 2000–. Member: C of E Bd for Social Responsibility, 1995–2001; C of E Doctrine Commn, 1996–99. Trustee, Scott Holland Fund, 1996–99. Baron de Lancey Lectr, Cambridge Univ., 1998. Consultant Editor, Studies in Christian Ethics, 1996–; Corresp. Editor, Jl of Ethical Theory and Moral Practice, 1997–; Mem. Editl Bd, Internat Jl of Systematic Theology, 1998–. *Publications:* The Justification of Science and the Rationality of Religious Belief, 1990; The Practice of Abortion: a critique, 1999; Christian Ethics and Contemporary Moral Problems, 1999; various articles in learned jls. *Recreations:* walking, gardening, reading, galleries, tennis. *Address:* Department of Theology and Religious Studies, King's College, Strand, WC2R 2LS. *T:* (020) 7848 2073. *Club:* National.

BANNERMAN, Bernard; *see* Arden, A. P. R.

BANNERMAN, Sir David (Gordon), 15th Bt *cr* 1682 (NS), of Elsick, Kincardineshire; OBE 1977; Ministry of Defence, 1963–97; *b* 18 Aug. 1935; *s* of Lt-Col Sir Donald Arthur Gordon Bannerman, 13th Bt and of Barbara Charlotte, *d* of late Lt-Col Alexander Cameron, OBE, IMS; *S* brother, Sir Alexander Patrick Bannerman, 14th Bt, 1989; *m* 1960, Mary Prudence, *d* of Rev. Philip Frank Ardagh-Walter; four *d*. *Educ:* Gordonstoun; New Coll., Oxford (MA); University Coll. London (MSc 1999). Lieut Queen's Own Cameron Highlanders, 1954–56. HMOCS (Tanzania), 1960–63. Chm., Gordonstoun Assoc., 1997–2000. *Recreations:* painting, ornithology, architecture. *Address:* 3 St George's Road, St Margaret's, Twickenham, Middlesex TW1 1QS.

BANNISTER, (Richard) Matthew; Chairman and Chief Executive, Trust the DJ, since 2001; *b* 16 March 1957; *s* of Richard Neville Bannister and Olga Margaret Bannister; *m* 1st, 1984, Amanda Gerrard Walker (*d* 1988); one *d*; 2nd, 1989, Shelagh Margaret Macleod; one *s*. *Educ:* King Edward VII Sch., Sheffield; Nottingham Univ. (LLB Hons). Presenter, BBC Radio Nottingham, 1978–81; Reporter/Presenter: Capital Radio, 1981–83; Newsbeat, Radio 1, 1983–85; Dep. Head, 1985–87, Head, 1987–88, News and Talks, Capital Radio; BBC 1988–2000: Man. Ed., Gtr London Radio, 1988–91; Project Co-ordinator: Charter Renewal, 1991–93; Prog. Strategy Review, 1993; Controller, BBC Radio 1, 1993–98; Dir, BBC Radio, 1996–98; Chief Exec., BBC Prodn, 1999–2000; Dir of Mkting and Communications, BBC, 2000. Mem. Bd, Chichester Fest. Theatres Prodns Co., 1999–. Fellow, Radio Acad., 1998. *Recreations:* rock music, collecting P. G. Wodehouse first editions. *Address:* 9th Floor, 10 Wardour Street, W1D 6QF.

BANNISTER, Sir Roger (Gilbert), Kt 1975; CBE 1955; DM (Oxon); FRCP; Master of Pembroke College, Oxford, 1985–93; Hon. Consultant Physician, National Hospital for Neurology and Neurosurgery, Queen Square, WC1 (non-executive Director, 1992–96; formerly Consultant Physician, National Hospital for Nervous Diseases); Hon. Consultant Neurologist: St Mary's Hospital, W2 (formerly Consultant Neurologist); Oxford Regional and District Health Authorities, 1985–95; *b* 23 March 1929; *s* of late Ralph and of Alice Bannister, Harrow; *m* 1955, Moyra Elver, *d* of late Per Jacobsson, Chairman IMF; two *s* two *d*. *Educ:* City of Bath Boys' Sch.; University Coll. Sch., London; Exeter and Merton Colls, Oxford; St Mary's Hospital Medical Sch., London. Amelia Jackson Studentship, Exeter Coll., Oxford, 1947; BA (hons) Physiology, Junior Demonstrator in Physiology, Harmsworth Senior Scholar, Merton Coll., Oxford, 1950; Open and State Schol., St Mary's Hosp., 1951; MSc Thesis in Physiology, 1952; MRCS, LRCP, 1954; BM, BCh Oxford, 1954; DM Oxford, 1963. William Hyde Award for research relating physical education to medicine; MRCP 1957. Junior Medical Specialist, RAMC, 1958; Radcliffe Travelling Fellowship from Oxford Univ., at Harvard, USA, 1962–63. Correspondent, Sunday Times, 1955–62. Consultant Neurologist, Western Ophthalmic Hosp., 1963–85. Chm., Hon. Consultants, King Edward VII Convalescent Home for Officers, Osborne, 1979–87. Chm., Medical Cttee, St Mary's Hosp., 1983–85; Deleg., Imperial Coll., representing St Mary's Hosp. Med. Sch., 1988–92; Trustee, St Mary's Hosp. Med. Sch. Develt Trust, 1994– 98(Chm. Trustees, 1998–). President: National Fitness Panel, NABC, 1956–59; Alzheimer's Disease Soc., 1982–84; Sports Medicine Sect., RSM, 1994–95; Gen. Sect., BAAS, 1995; Founder and Chm., Clinical Autonomic Res. Soc., 1982–84. Mem. Council, King George's Jubilee Trust, 1961–67; Pres., Sussex Assoc. of Youth Clubs, 1972–79; Chm., Res. Cttee, Adv. Sports Council, 1965–71; Mem., Min. of Health Adv. Cttee on Drug Dependence, 1967–70; Chm., Sports Council, 1971–74; Pres., Internat. Council for Sport and Physical Recreation, 1976–83. Mem., Management Cttee, 1979–84, Council, 1984–, King Edward's Hosp. Fund for London; Trustee: King George VI and Queen Elizabeth Foundn of St Catharine's, Cumberland Lodge, Windsor, 1985–; Leeds Castle, 1989–; Henry and Proctor Amer. Fellowships, 1987–99; Winston Churchill Fellowships, 1988–; Med. Commn on Accident Prevention, 1994–99; Mem. of Commn, Marshall Fellowships, 1986–94; Steering Cttee, Fulbright Fellowships, 1996–97. Patron, British Assoc. of Sport and Medicine, 1996–. Pres., Bath Inst. of Biomedical Engrg, 1990–; Governor: Atlantic Coll., 1985–93; Sherborne Sch., 1989–93. Winner Oxford *v* Cambridge Mile, 1947–50; Pres. OUAC, 1948; Capt. Oxford & Cambridge Combined American Team, 1949; Finalist, Olympic Games, Helsinki, 1952; British Mile Champion, 1951, 1953, 1954; World Record for One Mile, 1954; British Empire Mile title and record, 1954; European 1500 metres title and record, 1954. FIC 1992. Hon. FUMIST, 1974; Hon. Fellow: Exeter Coll., Oxford, 1979; Merton Coll., Oxford, 1986; Pembroke Coll., Oxford, 1993. Hon. LLD Liverpool, 1972; Hon. DLitt Sheffield, 1978; hon. doctorates: Univ. of Jyvaskyla, Finland; Univ. of Bath, Univ. of Grinnell, 1984; Univ. Rochester, NY, 1985; Univ. of Pavia, Italy, 1986; Williams Coll., USA, 1987; Victoria Univ., Canada, 1993; Univ. of Wales, Cardiff, 1995; Univ. of Loughborough, 1996; UEA, 1997. Hans-Heinrich Siegbert Prize, 1977. Chm. Editorial Bd, Clinical Autonomic Res., 1991–97; Mem., Editorial Bd, Jl of the Autonomic Nervous System, 1980–95; Associate Editor, Jl Neurol Sci., 1985–95. *Publications:* First Four Minutes, 1955; (ed) Brain's Clinical Neurology, 3rd edn 1969 to 6th edn 1985, 7th edn 1992 (as Brain and Bannister's Clinical Neurology); (ed) Autonomic Failure, 1983 to 3rd edn 1992 (ed with C. J. Mathias); papers on physiology of exercise, heat illness and neurological subjects. *Address:* 21 Bardwell Road, Oxford OX2 6SU. *T:* (01865) 511413; 7 Pembroke Court, South Edwardes Square, W8 6HN. *T:* (020) 7938 1980. *Clubs:* Athenæum, Oxford and Cambridge; Vincent's (Oxford).

BANNON, John Kernan, ISO 1969; Director of Services, Meteorological Office, 1973–76; *b* 26 April 1916; *s* of Frederick J. Bannon, Clerk in Holy Orders and Eveline Bannon, Muckamore, NI; *m* 1947, Pauline Mary Roch Thomas, Pembroke; one *s* one *d*. *Educ:* Royal Sch., Armagh; Emmanuel Coll., Cambridge (Braithwaite Batty Scholar). BA (Wrangler) 1938. Technical Officer, Meteorological Office, 1938; commnd RAFVR, 1943–46 (Temp. Sqdn Ldr); Met. Office, 1946–76; idc 1963. *Publications:* some official scientific works; articles in meteorological jls. *Recreations:* walking, gardening. *Address:* 18 Courtenay Drive, Emmer Green, Reading RG4 8XH. *T:* (0118) 947 3696.

BANNON, Yvonne Helen; *see* Carter, Y. H.

BANO, (Ernest) Andrew (Louis); Social Security and Child Support Commissioner, since 2000; *b* 7 May 1944; *s* of late Imre Bano and Susanne Bano; *m* 1985, Elizabeth Anne Sheehy; three *s* one *d*. *Educ:* Cardinal Vaughan Meml Sch.; Inns of Court Sch. of Law. Trng Consultant, 1966–69; Trng Develt Officer, BEA, 1969–72; called to the Bar, Gray's Inn, 1973; in practice at Common Law Bar, 1973–88; Head of Chambers, 1986–88; Chm. (part-time), Industrial Tribunals, 1984–88; Chm., Employment Tribunals, 1988–2000; Dep. Social Security Comr, 1996–2000. Sec., Industrial Tribunals Adv. Cttee on Legislation and Rules, 1992–95. *Recreations:* opera, private flying, woodwork. *Address:* Office of the Social Security and Child Support Commissioners, 83 Farringdon Street, EC4A 4DH. *T:* (020) 7353 5145.

BANTING, Ven. (Kenneth) Mervyn (Lancelot Hadfield); Archdeacon of the Isle of Wight, since 1996; *b* 8 Sept. 1937; *s* of late Rev. Canon H. M. J. Banting and P. M. Banting; *m* 1970, Linda (*née* Gick); four *d*. *Educ:* Pembroke Coll., Cambridge (MA, 1965); Cuddesdon Coll., Oxford. Ordained deacon, 1965, priest, 1966; Chaplain, Winchester Coll., 1965–70; Asst Curate, St Francis, Leigh Park, Portsmouth, 1970–73; Team Vicar, Highfield, Hemel Hempstead, 1973–79; Vicar, Goldington, Bedford, 1979–88; Priest-in-charge, Renhold, 1980–82; RD, Bedford, 1984–87; Vicar, St Cuthbert's, Portsmouth, 1988–96; RD, Portsmouth, 1994–96. *Recreations:* sailing, battery electric vehicles, horology. *Address:* The Archdeacon's House, 5 The Boltons, Wootton Bridge, Ryde, Isle of Wight PO33 4PB. *T:* (01983) 884812, (office) (01983) 884432.

BANTOCK, John Leonard; Assistant Under Secretary of State, Home Office Police Department, 1980–84; *b* 21 Oct. 1927; *s* of Edward Bantock and Agnes Bantock; *m* 1947, Maureen McKinney; two *s*. *Educ:* Colfe's Sch., SE13; King George V Sch., Southport, Lancs; LSE, London Univ. (LLB 1951). Unilever Ltd, 1943–45; Army, 1945–48 (Staff Captain, UK, India and Cyprus); Colonial Office, 1951–52; Inland Revenue, 1952–69; Secretariat, Royal Commn on Constitution, 1969–73; Cabinet Office, 1973–76; Sec., Cttee of Privy Counsellors on Recruitment of Mercenaries, 1976; Asst Under Sec. of State, Home Office Radio Regulatory Dept, 1976–79 (Head, UK Delegn, World Admin. Radio Conf., 1979). *Club:* MCC.

BANTON, Prof. Michael Parker, CMG 2001; JP; PhD, DSc; Professor of Sociology, 1965–92, now Emeritus, and Pro-Vice-Chancellor, 1985–88, University of Bristol; *b* 8 Sept. 1926; *s* of Francis Clive Banton and Kathleen Blanche (*née* Parkes); *m* 1952, Rut Marianne (*née* Jacobson), Luleå; one *s* two *d* (and one *s* decd). *Educ:* King Edward's Sch., Birmingham; London Sch. of Economics. BSc Econ. 1950; PhD 1954; DSc 1964. Midn, then Sub-Lieut RNVR, 1945–47. Asst, then Lecturer, then Reader, in Social Anthropology, University of Edinburgh, 1950–65. Dir, SSRC Res. Unit on Ethnic Relations, 1970–78. Visiting Professor: MIT, 1962–63; Wayne State Univ., Detroit, 1971; Univ. of Delaware, 1976; ANU, 1981; Duke Univ., 1982. Editor, Sociology, 1966–69. President: Section N, 1969–70 and Section H, 1985–86, BAAS; Royal Anthropological Inst., 1987–89; Mem., Vetenskapssocieteten, Lund, Sweden, 1972; Member: Royal Commn on Criminal Procedure, 1978–80; Royal Commn on Bermuda, 1978; UK National Commn for UNESCO, 1963–66 and 1980–85; UN Cttee for the Elimination of Racial Discrimination, 1986– (Chm., 1996–98); Ethnic Minorities Adv. Cttee, Judicial Studies Bd, 1993–96; SW Regl Hosp. Board, 1966–70. JP Bristol, 1966. FRSA 1981. FilDr *hr* Stockholm, 2000. *Publications:* The Coloured Quarter, 1955; West African City, 1957; White and Coloured, 1959; The Policeman in the Community, 1964; Roles, 1965; Race Relations, 1967; Racial Minorities, 1972; Police-Community Relations, 1973, (with J. Harwood) The Race Concept, 1975; The Idea of Race, 1977; Racial and Ethnic Competition, 1983; Promoting Racial Harmony, 1985; Investigating Robbery, 1985; Racial Theories, 1987, 2nd edn 1998; Racial Consciousness, 1988; Discrimination, 1994; International Action Against Racial Discrimination, 1996; Ethnic and Racial Consciousness, 1997. *Address:* The Court House, Llanvair Discoed, Chepstow NP16 6LX. *T:* (01633) 400208; *e-mail:* michael@banton.demon.co.uk.

BANWELL, Derick Frank, CBE 1978; retired 1995 as Member: Refugee Housing Association Ltd (formerly BCAR (Housing) Ltd), 1978–95 (Chairman, 1979–89); Refugee Housing Society Ltd (formerly BCAR (Homes) Ltd), 1978–95 (Chairman, 1979–86); *b* 19 July 1919; *s* of Frank Edward Banwell; *m* 1945, Rose Kathleen Worby; two *s* one *d*. *Educ:* Kent Coll., Canterbury. RA, 1939–46. Admitted as Solicitor, 1947; Asst Solicitor, Southend-on-Sea Co. Borough Coun., 1947–48; Sen. Asst Solicitor, Rochdale Co. Borough Coun., 1948–51; Chief Common Law Solicitor, City of Sheffield, 1951–56; Sen. Asst Solicitor, 1956–59, Asst Town Clerk, 1959–60, Southend-on-Sea Co. Borough Coun.; Dep. Town Clerk and Dep. Clerk of the Peace, Swansea Co. Borough Council, 1960–64; Gen. Manager, Runcorn Develt Corp., 1964–78. Sec., Church Bldgs Cttee, United Reformed Church, 1978–85. *Recreations:* history, music, model railways. *Address:* 57 Broad Street, Canterbury, Kent CT1 2LS.

BAPTISTA DA SILVA, Dr Carlos Boaventura; Secretary, Board of Trustees, Calouste Gulbenkian Foundation, since 1974; *b* 13 Feb. 1935; *s* of Fernando Baptista da Silva and Virginia Boaventura Baptista da Silva; *m* 1961, Emilia de Almeida Nadal; two *s* one *d*. *Educ:* Univ. of Lisbon (Lic. in Law). Lawyer, 1968–74. Counsellor, Lisbon Mint Consulting Cttee. Pres., FIDEM, 2000. Comdr, Order of Public Instruction (Portugal), 1968. *Publications:* several texts on medal art. *Recreations:* collector of medals and modern art, music, reading. *Address:* (office) Av. de Berna 45A, 1067-001 Lisbon, Portugal. *T:* (1) 782 3301, *Fax:* (1) 782 3035; (home) Rua dos Navegantes 53–5° DT°, 1200-730 Lisbon, Portugal. *T:* and *Fax:* 3974242.

BAR-HILLEL, Mira; Property and Planning Correspondent, Evening Standard, since 1986; *b* 30 Sept. 1946; *d* of late Prof. Yehoshua Bar-Hillel and Shulamit (*née* Aschkenazy); *m* 1976, Geoffrey Addison. *Educ:* Hebrew Gymnasia, Jerusalem; Hebrew Univ., Jerusalem (BA Soviet Studies 1972). Military Service, Israel Defence Forces, 1963–65. News reporter: Voice of Israel, 1965–72; Building mag., 1973–82 (News Editor, 1978–82); freelance writer on property and also architecture and planning, 1982–. LBC Radio Property Expert, 1993–94. Internat. Bldg Press Award, 1979, 1980, 1983, 1988, 1994, 1995, 1996; RICS Award, 1985; Incorporated Soc. Valuers and Auctioneers Award, 1986, 1996; Laing Homes Award, 1989, 1991, 1993. Consultant to Which on residential property. *Publication:* Goldfish Guide to Buying, Selling and Moving Home. *Recreations:* cats, shopping abroad, fighting Modernism, science fiction. *Address:* Evening Standard, Northcliffe House, 2 Derry Street, High Street, Kensington, W8 5TT. *T:* (office) (020) 7938 6000, ext. 1053.

BARBACK, Ronald Henry; Professor of Economics, University of Hull, 1965–76 (Dean, Faculty of Social Sciences and Law, 1966–69); *b* 31 Oct. 1919; *s* of late Harry Barback and Winifred Florence (*née* Norris); *m* 1950, Sylvia Chambers; one *s* one *d*. *Educ:* Woodside Sch., Glasgow; Univ. Coll., Nottingham (BScEcon); Queen's and Nuffield Colls, Oxford (MLitt). Asst Lectr in Econs, Univ. of Nottingham, 1946–48; Lectr in Econs, subseq. Sen. Lectr, Canberra University Coll., Australia, 1949–56; Univ. of Ibadan (formerly University Coll., Ibadan): Prof. of Econs and Social Studies, 1956–63; Dean, Faculty of Arts, 1958–59; Dean, Faculty of Econs and Social Studies, 1959–63; Dir, Nigerian (formerly W African) Inst. of Social and Econ. Res., 1956–63; Sen. Res. Fellow,

Econ. Res. Inst., Dublin, 1963–64; Prof. of Econs, TCD, 1964–65; Vis. Prof., Brunel Univ., 1984–86. Dep. Econ. Dir and Head, Econ. Res., CBI, 1977–81, Consultant, 1981–82. Nigeria: Mem., Ibadan Univ. Hosp. Bd of Management, 1958–63; Mem., Jt Econ. Planning Cttee, Fedn of Nigeria, 1959–61; Sole Arbitrator, Trade Disputes in Ports and Railways, 1958; Chm., Fed. Govt Cttee to advise on fostering a share market, 1959. UK Official Delegate, FAO meeting on investment in fisheries, 1970; Mem., FAO mission to Sri Lanka, 1975. Consultant, Div. of Fisheries, Europ. Commn Directorate-Gen. of Agriculture, 1974; Specialist Advr, H of L Select Cttee on Eur. Communities, 1980–83; Commonwealth Scholarships Commn Adviser on Econs, 1971–76. Mem., Schools Council Social Sciences Cttee, 1971–80; Chm., Schs Council Econs and Business Studies Syllabus Steering Gp, 1975–77. Member: Hull and Dist Local Employment Cttee, 1966–73; N Humberside Dist Manpower Cttee, 1973–76; CNAA Business and Management Studies Bd, 1978–81, Economics Bd, 1982–86; Ct, Brunel Univ., 1979–83; Gov., Tunbridge Wells Girls' GS, 1996–98. Chm., Royal Tunbridge Wells Civic Soc., 1991–93 (Vice-Pres., 1994–96). Member: Editorial Bd, Bull. of Economic Research (formerly Yorks Bull. of Social and Economic Research), 1965–76 (Jt Editor, 1966–67); Editorial Adv. Bd, Applied Economics, 1969–80; Editor, Humberside Statistical Bull., nos 1–3, 1974, 1975, 1977. *Publications:* (contrib.) The Commonwealth in the World Today, ed J. Eppstein, 1956; (ed with Prof. Sir Douglas Copland) The Conflict of Expansion and Stability, 1957; (contrib.) The Commonwealth and Europe (EIU), 1960; The Pricing of Manufactures, 1964; (contrib.) Insurance Markets of the World, ed M. Grossmann 1964; (contrib.) Webster's New World Companion to English and American Literature, 1973; Forms of Co-operation in the British Fishing Industry, 1976; (with M. Breimer and A. F. Haug) Development of the East Coast Fisheries of Sri Lanka, 1976; The Firm and its Environment, 1984; contrib. New Internat. Encyc., FAO Fisheries Reports, and jls. *Recreations:* walking, music. *Address:* Amberley House, Back Lane, Goudhurst, Kent TN17 1AN. *T:* (01580) 212571. *Club:* Royal Commonwealth Society.

BARBARA, Agatha, KUOM 1990; social/welfare worker; President of the Republic of Malta, 1982–87; Chairperson, The Samaritans – Malta, since 1988; *b* Zabbar, 11 March 1923. *Educ:* Government Grammar School. ARP, 1940; Supervisor, Main Ammunition Depot, 1941–43. School teacher, 1944–46; entered politics, 1946; first woman Member of Parliament, 1947; became first woman Minister, in Labour Govt, 1955, as Minister of Education; also Minister of Educn, 1971–74; Minister of Labour, Culture, and Welfare, 1974–81. Was Acting Prime Minister of Malta on various occasions, and elected President of the Republic, 16 Feb. 1982. Patron: Ad Vitam St Michael's Band Club, Zabbar; Malta-China Friendship and Cultural Soc.; Boy Scouts Assoc., Malta, 1982 (Thanks Badge, 1986). Hon. Life Mem., Council of Women, Malta, 1986. Official Rep., World Inst. of Achievement, USA, 1992. Hon. Mem., European Community of Journalists, 1979. Hon. Academician: Accademia Universale A. Magno, Prato, Italy; Eur. Acad. of Lit., Sci. and Arts, Naples. Hon. PhD Univ. of Beijing, China, 1984. Keys and Freedom of: Lahore, Buenos Aires, Lima, San José, Bogotà and Montevideo, 1986; Aden, 1987. GCStJ 1996. Coronation Medal, 1953; Malta GC 50th anniv. medal for service in civil defence, 1992; 75th anniv. medal of re-introduction of self-govt in Malta, 1996. Stara Planina, 1st cl. with ribbon (Bulgaria), 1983; Order of National Flag 1st Class (Democratic People's Republic of Korea), 1985; Hishan-e-Pakistan (Islamic Republic of Pakistan), 1986; Sceptre of Authority of the Incas (Peru), 1986. *Recreations:* philately, classical and modern music. *Address:* Kenn Taghna, Wied Il-Ghajn Street, Zabbar, Republic of Malta.

BARBARITO, Most Rev. Luigi, Hon. GCVO 1996; DD, JCD; Titular Archbishop of Fiorentino; Apostolic Nuncio (formerly Pro-Nuncio) to the Court of St James's, 1986–97; *b* Atripalda, Avellino, Italy, 19 April 1922; *s* of Vincenzo Barbarito and Alfonsina Armerini. *Educ:* Pontifical Seminary, Benevento, Italy; Gregorian Univ., Rome (JCD); Papal Diplomatic Academy, Rome (Diploma). Priest, 1944; served Diocese of Avellino, 1944–52; entered Diplomatic Service of Holy See, 1953; Sec., Apostolic Delegn, Australia, 1953–59; Secretariat of State of Vatican (Council for Public Affairs of the Church), 1959–67; Counsellor, Apostolic Nunciature, Paris, 1967–69; Archbishop and Papal Nuncio to Haiti and Delegate to the Antilles, 1969–75; Pro-Nuncio to Senegal, Bourkina Fasso, Niger, Mali, Mauretania, Cape Verde Is and Guinea Bissau, 1975–78; Apostolic Pro-Nuncio to Australia, 1978–86. Mem., Mexican Acad. of Internat. Law. Grand Cross, National Order of Haiti, 1975; Grand Cross, Order of the Lion (Senegal), 1978; Knight Commander, Order of Merit (Italy), 1966, (Portugal), 1967. *Recreations:* music, walking. *Address:* via Bravetta 518, 00164 Rome, Italy.

BARBER, family name of **Baron Barber**.

BARBER, Baron *cr* 1974 (Life Peer), of Wentbridge; **Anthony Perrinott Lysberg Barber,** PC 1963; TD; DL; Chairman, Standard Chartered Bank plc, 1974–87; *b* 4 July 1920; *s* of John Barber, CBE, Doncaster; *m* 1st, 1950, Jean Patricia (*d* 1983), *d* of Milton Asquith, Wentbridge, Yorks; two *d*; 2nd, 1989, Mrs Rosemary Youens, *d* of Rev. Canon Fearnly Youens. *Educ:* Retford Grammar Sch.; Oriel Coll., Oxford Univ. (PPE, MA) (Hon. Fellow 1971). Served War of 1939–45: commnd in Army (Dunkirk); seconded to RAF as pilot, 1940–45 (despatches; prisoner of war, 1942–45, took Law Degree with 1st Class Hons while POW, escaped from Poland, prisoner of the Russians). Barrister-at-law, Inner Temple, 1948 (Inner Temple Scholarship). MP (C): Doncaster, 1951–64; Altrincham and Sale, Feb. 1965–Sept. 1974; PPS to the Under-Sec. of State for Air, 1952–55; Asst Whip, 1955–57; a Lord Comr of the Treasury, 1957–58; PPS to the Prime Minister, 1958–59; Economic Sec. to the Treasury, 1959–62; Financial Sec. to the Treasury, 1962–63; Minister of Health and Mem. of the Cabinet, 1963–64; Chancellor of the Duchy of Lancaster, June–July 1970; Chancellor of the Exchequer, 1970–74. Chm., Conservative Party Organisation, 1967–70; Pres., Nat. Union of Cons. & Unionist Assocs, 1973. Dir, BP, 1979–88. Mem., Falkland Islands Inquiry (Franks Cttee), 1982. British Mem., Eminent Persons Gp on S Africa, 1986. Vice-Chm. Council, Charing Cross and Westminster Med. Sch., 1984–96 (Chm. Council, Westminster Med. Sch., 1975–84). Chm., RAF Benevolent Fund, 1991–95. DL W Yorks, 1987. *Address:* House of Lords, SW1A 0PW. *Clubs:* Carlton, Royal Air Force.

BARBER OF TEWKESBURY, Baron *cr* 1992 (Life Peer), of Gotherington in the County of Gloucestershire; **Derek Coates Barber,** Kt 1984; Chairman: Booker Countryside Advisory Board, 1990–96; Countryside Commission, 1981–91; *s* of Thomas Smith-Barber and Elsie Coates; 1st marr. diss. 1981; *m* 2nd, 1983, Rosemary Jennifer Brougham, *o d* of late Lt-Comdr Randolph Brougham Pearson, RN, and Hilary Diana Mackinlay Pearson (*née* Bennett). *Educ:* Royal Agricl Coll., Cirencester (MRAC; Gold Medal, Practical Agriculture; FRAC 1999). Served War: invalided, Armed Forces, 1942. Farmed in Glos Cotswolds; Mem., Cheltenham Rural District Council, 1948–52; Dist Adv. Officer, National Agricl Adv. Service, MAFF, 1946–57; County Agricl Advisor, Glos, 1957–72; Environment Consultant to Humberts, Chartered Surveyors, 1972–93; MAFF Assessor: Pilkington Cttee on Agric. Educ., 1966; Agric. and Hort. Trng Bd, 1968. Member: H of L Sub-Cttee D (Food and Agric.), 1992–96; H of L Select Cttee on Sustainable Devclt, 1994–95. Chairman: BBC's Central Agricl Adv. Cttee, 1974–80 (*ex officio* Mem., BBC's Gen. Adv. Council, 1972–80); New National Forest Adv. Bd, 1991–95. Royal Soc. for Protection of Birds: Mem., 1970–75, Chm., 1976–81, Council; Chm., Educn Cttee, 1972–75; Vice-Pres., 1982; Pres., 1990–91. President: RASE, 1991–92; Rare Breeds Survival Trust, 1991–95, 1997–99 (Mem. Council, 1987–99); Hawk and Owl Trust, 1992–96; British Pig Assoc., 1995–96 (Vice-Pres., 1997–99); Glos Naturalists' Soc., 1981–; Vice-Pres., Ornithol Soc. of Mid-East, 1987–97; Mem. Council, British Trust for Ornithology, 1987–90; Founder Mem., 1969, Farming and Wildlife Adv. Gp of landowning, farming and wildlife conservation bodies; Member: Ordnance Survey Adv. Bd, 1982–85; Bd, RURAL Council, 1983–94; Bd, CEED, 1984–98; Centre for Agricl Strategy, 1985–91; Arable Res. Insts Assoc., 1991–95; Long Ashton Res. Stn Cttee, 1991–95. Dep. Chm., Bd, Groundwork Foundn, 1985–91; Patron, Woodland Trust, 1991–. FRAgS 1992; FIAgrM 1992. Hon. FRASE 1986. Hon. DSc Bradford, 1986. First Recipient, Summers Trophy for services to agric. in practice or science, 1955; Bledisloe Gold Medal for distinguished service to UK agriculture, 1967; RSPB Gold Medal for services to bird protection, 1982; Massey-Ferguson Award for services to agric., 1989; RASE Gold Medal, for distinguished service to UK agric., 1991. Silver Jubilee Medal, 1977. Editor, Humberts Commentary, 1973–88; columnist, Power Farming, 1973–91; Spec. Correspondent, Waitaki NZR Times, 1982–88. *Publications:* (with Keith Dexter) Farming for Profits, 1961, 2nd edn 1967; (with J. G. S. and Frances Donaldson) Farming in Britain Today, 1969, 2nd edn 1972; (ed) Farming with Wildlife, 1971; A History of Humberts, 1980; contrib. farming and wildlife conservation jls. *Recreations:* birds, wildlife conservation, farming. *Address:* House of Lords, SW1A 0PW. *Club:* Farmers'.

BARBER, Chris; *see* Barber, D. C.

BARBER, Sir David; *see* Barber, Sir T. D.

BARBER, (Donald) Chris(topher), OBE 1991; band leader, Chris Barber's Jazz and Blues Band; *b* 17 April 1930; *s* of Henrietta Mary Evelyn Barber, MA Cantab and Donald Barber, CBE, BA Cantab; *m*; one *s* one *d*. *Educ:* King Alfred School; St Paul's School. Formed first amateur band, 1949; present band commenced on professional basis, 1954; plays trombone, trumpet, baritone horn, contra bass. Hon. Citizen, New Orleans. Numerous recordings, including over 150 LPs and 100 CDs, with records in the hit parade of over 40 countries world wide. *Recreations:* motor racing, snooker, antique collecting. *Address:* c/o Cromwell Management, 4 & 5 High Street, Huntingdon, Cambs PE18 6TE. *T:* (01480) 435600, *Fax:* (01480) 356250; *e-mail:* tricvic@lineone.net.

BARBER, Frank; Senior Partner, Morgan, Fentiman & Barber, 1993–97; Deputy Chairman of Lloyd's, 1983, 1984; *b* 5 July 1923; *s* of Sidney Barber and Florence (*née* Seath); *m* 1st, 1945, Gertrude Kathleen Carson (decd); one *s* one *d* (and one *s* decd); 2nd, 1994, Elizabeth Joan Charvet. *Educ:* West Norwood Central School. RAFVR, 1942–46. Entered Lloyd's, 1939; Underwriter, Lloyd's syndicate, Frank Barber & others, 1962–81; Member: Cttee of Lloyd's, 1977–80, 1982–85 and 1987; Council of Lloyd's, 1983–85 and 1987; Dep. Chm., Lloyd's Underwriters' Non-Marine Assoc., 1971, Chm., 1972; Dep. Chm., British Insurers' European Cttee, 1983. Partner: Morgan, Fentiman & Barber, 1968–97; G. S. Christanson & Partners, 1985–; Chairman: A. E. Grant (Underwriting Agencies) Ltd, 1991–96; Frank Barber Underwriting Ltd, 2000–. *Recreations:* music, walking, sailing. *Address:* Doiley Hill House, Hurstbourne Tarrant, Andover, Hants SP11 0ER. *T:* (01264) 736595; *e-mail:* frankbarber@limestreet.freeserve.co.uk.

BARBER, Giles Gaudard; Librarian, Taylor Institution, University of Oxford, 1970–96; Fellow, Linacre College, Oxford, 1963–96, now Emeritus (Vice-Principal, 1988–90); *b* 15 Aug. 1930; *s* of Eric Arthur Barber and Madeleine Barber (*née* Gaudard); *m* 1st, 1958, Monique Fluchère (*d* 1969); one *d*; 2nd, 1970, Gemma Miani (marr. diss. 1997); two *s* one *d*; 3rd, 1997, Lisa Jefferson; one step *d*. *Educ:* Dragon Sch., Oxford; Leighton Park Sch.; St John's Coll., Oxford (MA, BLitt). Asst, Bodleian Library, 1954–70; Univ. Lectr in Continental Bibliography, Oxford, 1969–96. Pres., Oxford Bibliographical Soc., 1992–96 and 1999–2000; Vice-Pres., Bibliographical Soc., 1983–93; Chm., Voltaire Foundn, 1987–89; Mem. Council, Internat. Soc. for 18th Century Studies, 1979–83. Vis. Lectr, Univ. of Paris IV (Sorbonne), 1980; Lectures: 1st Graham Pollard Meml, 1984; Moses Tyson Meml, Manchester Univ., 1985; Panizzi, British Library, 1988; First Founders' Library Lectr, Univ. of Wales, Lampeter, 1996; Sandars Reader in Bibliography, Cambridge Univ., 1997–98. Gordon Duff Prize in Bibliography, 1962. Officier, Ordre des Arts et des Lettres (France), 1992. *Publications:* Fine Bindings 1500–1700, 1968 (ed jtly); A checklist of French printing manuals, 1969; Textile and embroidered bookbindings, 1971; (ed) Book making in Diderot's Encyclopédie, 1973; (ed) Contat, Anecdotes typographiques, 1980; (ed jtly) Buch und Buchhandel in Europa im achtzehnten Jahrhundert, 1981; Daphnis and Chloe, 1989; Studies in the booktrade of the European Enlightenment, 1994; Arks for Learning, 1995; articles in learned jls. *Recreations:* book-collecting, gardening, walking. *Address:* Galliards, Hixet Wood, Charlbury, Oxon OX7 3SB. *T:* (01608) 810747.

BARBER, Prof. James, PhD; FRSC; Ernst Chain Professor of Biochemistry, Imperial College of Science, Technology and Medicine, since 1989 (Head of Department of Biochemistry, 1989–99); *b* 16 July 1940; *s* of Stanley William George Barber and Sophia Helen Barber; *m* 1965, Marilyn Jane Emily Tyrrell; one *s* one *d*. *Educ:* Portsmouth Southern Grammar Sch.; Univ. of Wales (BSc Hons Chem.); Univ. of East Anglia (MSc, PhD Biophys.). FRSC 1983. Unilever Biochem. Soc. European Fellow, Univ. of Leiden, 1967–68; Imperial College: Lectr, Dept of Botany, 1968–74; Reader in Plant Physiology, 1974–79, Prof., 1979–89; Dean, Royal Coll. of Science, 1989–91. Miller Prof., Univ. of Calif at Berkeley, 1989–90, 2001; Burroughs Wellcome Fund Prof., Univ. of Calif, 2000. Selby Fellow, Australian Acad. of Scis, 1996. Mem., Academia Europaea, 1989. Hon. Dr Univ. of Stockholm, 1992. *Publications:* The Intact Chloroplast, 1976; Primary Processes in Photosynthesis, 1977; Photosynthesis in Relation to Model Systems, 1979; Electron Transport and Photophosphorylation, 1982; Chloroplast Biogenesis, 1984; Photosynthetic Mechanisms and the Environment, 1986; The Light Reactions, 1987; The Photosystems: structure, function and molecular biology, 1992; articles and reviews. *Recreations:* running, sailing, gardening. *Address:* Wolfson Laboratories, Biochemistry Department, Imperial College of Science, Technology and Medicine, SW7 2AY. *T:* (020) 7594 5266; *e-mail:* j.barber@ic.ac.uk.

BARBER, Prof. James Peden, PhD; Master, Hatfield College, Durham, 1980–96; Professor of Politics, Durham University, 1992–96, now Emeritus; Associate Fellow, Centre of International Studies, Cambridge University, since 1996; Rsearch Fellow, South African Institute of International Affairs, since 1996; *b* 6 Nov. 1931; *s* of John and Carrie Barber; *m* 1955, Margaret June (*née* McCormac); three *s* one *d*. *Educ:* Liverpool Inst. High Sch.; Pembroke Coll., Cambridge (MA, PhD); The Queen's Coll., Oxford. Served RAF, 1950–52 (Pilot Officer). Colonial Service, Uganda: Dist Officer, subseq. Asst Sec. to Prime Minister and Clerk to the Cabinet, 1956–63; Lectr, Univ. of NSW, Australia, 1963–65; Lectr in Govt, Univ. of Exeter, 1965–69 (seconded to University Coll. of Rhodesia, 1965–67); Prof. of Political Science, Open Univ., 1969–80; Pro-Vice-Chancellor, 1987–92 and Sub-Warden, 1990–92, Durham Univ. Advr, Commons Select Cttee on Foreign Affairs, 1990–91. Mem. RIIA; Part-time Dir, Chatham House study, Southern Africa in Conflict, 1979–81. Mem., Amnesty International. President: Durham Univ. Soc. of Fellows, 1988; Durham Univ. Hockey Club, 1981–96. JP Bedford,

1977–80. *Publications:* Rhodesia: the road to rebellion, 1967; Imperial Frontier, 1968; South Africa's Foreign Policy, 1973; European Community: vision and reality, 1974; The Nature of Foreign Policy, 1975; Who Makes British Foreign Policy?, 1977; The West and South Africa, 1982; The Uneasy Relationship: Britain and South Africa, 1983; South Africa: the search for status and security, 1990; The Prime Minister since 1945, 1991; Forging the New South Africa, 1994; South Africa in the Twentieth Century: a political history, 1999. *Recreations:* choral music, all kinds of sport, walking. *Address:* 14 North Terrace, Midsummer Common, Cambridge CB5 8DJ. *T:* (01223) 313453.

BARBER, John Norman Romney; company director and business consultant; *s* of George Ernest and Gladys Eleanor Barber; *m* 1941, Babette Chalu; one *s*. *Educ:* Westcliff. Served with Army, 1939–46 (Capt.). Min. of Supply, 1946–55 (Princ.). Joined Ford Motor Co. Ltd, 1955, Finance Dir, 1962; Chm., Ford Motor Credit Co. Ltd, 1963; Dir, Henry Ford & Son Ltd, Cork, 1963; Dir Autolite Motor Products Ltd, 1963; Finance Dir, AEI Ltd, 1965; Chm., Telephone Cables Ltd, 1967; Dir of Finance and Planning, 1968–71, Dep. Man. Dir, 1971–73, Dep. Chm. and Man. Dir, 1973–75, British Leyland Motor Corp. Ltd; Chairman, 1973–75: British Leyland International Ltd; Leyland Innocenti, SpA; Leyland Motor Corp. of Australia Ltd; Director: Leyland España SA; Automóviles de Turismo Hispano Ingleses SA; NZ Motor Corp. Ltd; British Leyland Motors Inc.; Metalurgica de Santa Ana SA; Chairman: Pullmaflex International Ltd, 1976–79; Aberhurst Ltd, 1976–88; A. C. Edwards Engineering Ltd, 1976–81; Cox & Kings Financial Services Ltd, 1980–85; C & K Executive Search Ltd, 1980–85; C & K Consulting Group Ltd, 1982–88; Director: Acrow plc, 1977–84; Good Relations Group plc, 1979–86; Amalgamated Metal Corp. Ltd, 1980–81; Spear & Jackson International plc, 1980–85; Economists Advisory Group Ltd, 1981–98; UK Investments Ltd, 1985–; The Communications Group Hldgs plc, 1990–; Deputy Chairman: Cox & Kings Ltd, 1980–81; John E. Wiltshier Group plc, 1980–88 (Dir, 1979–88). Mem., Royal Commn on Medical Educn, 1965–68; Chm., Adv. Cttee to BoT on Investment Grants, 1967–68; Mem., Adv. Council for Energy Conservation, 1974–75. Vice Pres., SMMT, 1974–76. CIMgt (Mem. Council BIM, 1967–71). *Publications:* papers on management subjects in various jls. *Recreations:* motor sport, forestry, photography. *Address:* Woodpecker Lodge, Romsey Road, Ower, Romsey, Hants SO51 6AE. *Club:* British Automobile Racing.

BARBER, Prof. Michael Bayldon; Chief Adviser to Prime Minister on Delivery, and Head of Prime Minister's Delivery Unit, since 2001; *b* 24 Nov. 1955; *s* of Christopher and Anne Barber; *m* 1982, Karen Alderman; three *d*. *Educ:* Bootham Sch., York; Queen's Coll., Oxford (BA Hons 1977); Georg-August Univ., Göttingen; Westminster Coll., Oxford (PGCE 1979); Inst. of Educn, London Univ. (MA 1991). History Teacher: Watford, 1979–83; Zimbabwe, 1983–85; Policy and Res. Officer, 1985–89, Education Officer, 1989–93, NUT; Professor of Education: Keele Univ., 1993–95; Inst. of Educn, London Univ., 1995–97; Dir, Standards and Effectiveness Unit, and Chief Advr to Sec. of State on Sch. Standards, DFEE, 1997–2001. Vis. Prof., Univ. of London; Special Prof., Univ. of Nottingham, 2001–. Mem. (Lab), Hackney LBC, 1986–90 (Chair, Educn Cttee, 1988–89). Contested (Lab) Henley-on-Thames, 1987. FRSA 1993. *Publications:* Education and the Teacher Unions, 1992; The Making of 1944 Education Act, 1994; The National Curriculum: a study in policy, 1996; The Learning Game: arguments for an education revolution, 1996, revd edn 1997; High Standards and High Expectations for All No matter What: creating a world class eduacation service in England, 2000. *Recreations:* mountain walking, Liverpool Football Club, chess, reading history books. *Address:* 62 Lawford Road, N1 5BL. *T:* (020) 7249 7689.

BARBER, Nicholas Charles Faithorn; Chairman, Bolero International Ltd, since 1998; *b* 7 Sept. 1940; *s* of Bertram Harold and Nancy Lorraine Barber; *m* 1966, Sheena Macrae Graham; two *s* one *d*. *Educ:* Ludgrove Sch.; Shrewsbury Sch.; Wadham Coll., Oxford (MA); Columbia Univ., New York, 1969–71 (MBA). Lectr, Marlboro Coll., Vermont, USA, 1963–64; joined Ocean Steam Ship, subseq. Ocean Transport and Trading, later Ocean Group, 1964; Dir, 1980–94; Chief Exec., 1986–94. Divl Dir, NEB, 1977–79. Chairman: IEC Gp plc, 1996–99; Orion Publishing Gp, 1997–98; Kappa IT Ventures, 1998–; Director: Costain Gp, 1990–93; Royal Insurance Hldgs plc, 1991–96 (Dep. Chm., 1994–96); Royal & Sun Alliance Insurance Gp plc, 1996–; Barings plc, 1994–95; Bristol and West plc (formerly Bristol & West Bldg Soc.), 1994–; Albright & Wilson plc, 1995–99; Fidelity Japanese Values PLC, 2000–. Mem., NW Industrial Develt Bd, 1982–85; Gov., NIESR, 1991–. Dir, Liverpool Playhouse, 1982–87; Mem., Adv. Cttee, Tate Gall., Liverpool, 1988–92; Trustee: Nat. Museums and Galls on Merseyside, 1986–94; British Mus., 1993–; Chairman: British Mus. Friends, 1992–; British Mus. Co. Ltd, 1996–. Governor: Shrewsbury Sch., 1983–; London Business Sch., 1993–; Vice-Pres., Liverpool Sch. of Tropical Medicine, 1988–; Chm., Huron Univ. USA in London Ltd, 1998–; Member Council: Liverpool Univ., 1985–88; Industrial Soc., 1993–99. *Recreations:* mountainwalking, cricket, destructive gardening. *Address:* 4 Lytton Court, 14 Barter Street, WC1A 2AH. *Clubs:* Oxford and Cambridge, MCC.

BARBER, Rt Rev. Paul Everard; Bishop Suffragan of Brixworth, 1989–2001; *b* 16 Sept. 1935; *s* of Cecil Arthur and Mollie Barber; *m* 1959, Patricia Jayne Walford; two *s* two *d* (and one *s* decd). *Educ:* Sherborne School; St John's Coll., Cambridge (BA 1958, MA 1966); Wells Theological College. Deacon 1960, priest 1961, dio. Guildford; Curate of St Francis, Westborough, 1960–66; Vicar: Camberley with Yorktown, 1966–73; St Thomas-on-The Bourne, Farnham, 1973–80; Rural Dean of Farnham, 1974–79; Archdeacon of Surrey, 1980–89; Hon. Canon: of Guildford, 1980–89; of Peterborough, 1997–. General Synod, 1979–85; Member, Council of College of Preachers, 1969–98. Archbp of Canterbury's Advr to HMC, 1993–2001. *Recreations:* diocesan clergy cricket, theatre. *Address:* 41 Somerton Road, Street, Somerset BA16 0DR.

BARBER, Stephen James; Chief Children's Officer, and Director of Social Services, London Borough of Barnet, 1999–2000; *b* 15 Nov. 1946; *s* of John Barber and Jenny Barber (née Roshan Mirza); *m* 1972, Mary Margaret Hoffman; three *d*. *Educ:* Hall Sch., Hampstead; Uppingham Sch., Rutland; Trinity Coll., Cambridge (BA, MA); Brunel Univ. (MA, CQSW). Res. student, 1970–73; nursing asst, Cassell Hosp., 1973–74; social worker, 1974–79, Team Leader, 1979–85, Principal Officer, 1985–88, RBK&C; Asst Dir (Children and Families), London Borough of Ealing, 1988–93; Controller of Community Services, London Borough of Barnet, 1993–99. Mem. Bd, S Barnet Primary Care Gp, 1998–2000. Trustee, British Agencies for Adoption and Fostering, 1999–2000. *Publications:* contrib. reviews and articles to TES, Community Care, Adoption and Fostering, etc. *Recreations:* playing the piano, collecting books and CDs, pottering around old towns. *Address:* Greystones, Lawton Avenue, Carterton, Oxon OX18 3JY.

BARBER, Sir (Thomas) David, 3rd Bt *cr* 1960, of Greasley, Nottingham; self-employed philatelist; *b* 18 Nov. 1937; *o s* of Col Sir William Francis Barber, 2nd Bt and his 1st wife, Diana Constance Barber (*née* Lloyd) (*d* 1984); *S* father, 1995; *m* 1st, 1971, Amanda Mary Healing (*née* Rabone) (marr. diss. 1976); one *s*; 2nd, 1978 Jeannine Mary Boyle (*née* Gurney); one *s* one *d*. *Educ:* Eton; Trinity Coll., Cambridge (MA). 2nd Lieut, RA, 1958–61. *Heir:* *s* Thomas Edward Barber, *b* 14 March 1973. *Address:* Windrush House, Inkpen, Hungerford, Berks RG17 9QY. *Clubs:* Free Foresters.

BARBER, Trevor Wing; His Honour Judge Barber; a Circuit Judge, since 1992; *b* 10 June 1943; *s* of Robert and Margaret Barber; *m* 1967, Judith Penelope Downey; one *s* one *d*. *Educ:* Worksop Coll.; Newcastle Univ. (LLB). Called to the Bar, Inner Temple, 1967; practice in Sheffield, 1967–92. *Recreations:* gardening, golf, reading. *Address:* Juniper Lodge, Hillfoot Road, Totley, Sheffield S17 2AY.

BARBER, Prof. William Joseph, Hon. OBE 1981; Professor of Economics, Wesleyan University, Middletown, Conn, USA, 1965–93; *b* 13 Jan. 1925; *s* of Ward Barber; *m* 1955, Sheila Mary Marr; three *s*. *Educ:* Harvard Univ. (AB); Balliol Coll., Oxford. BA, 1st Cl. Hons, 1951, MA 1955; DPhil (Nuffield Coll.) 1958. Served War, US Army, 1943–46. Lectr in Econs, Balliol Coll., Oxford, 1956; Wesleyan University: Dept of Economics, 1957–93; Asst Prof., 1957–61; Associate Prof., 1961–65; Prof., 1965–93; Andrews Prof., 1972–93; Andrews Prof. Emeritus, 1994–; Acting Pres., Aug.–Oct. 1988. Research Associate: Oxford Univ. Inst. of Economics and Statistics, 1962–63; Twentieth Century Fund, South Asian Study, 1961–62. Amer. Sec., Rhodes Scholarship Trust, 1970–80. Pres., Hist. of Econs Soc., 1989–90. *Publications:* The Economy of British Central Africa, 1961; A History of Economic Thought, 1967; contributor to Asian Drama: an inquiry into the poverty of nations (with Gunnar Myrdal and others), 1968; British Economic Thought and India 1600–1858, 1975; (jtly) Exhortation and Controls: the search for a wage-price policy, 1975; Energy Policy in Perspective, 1981; From New Era to New Deal: Herbert Hoover, the economists, and American economic policy 1921–1933, 1985; (ed, and jt author) Breaking the Academic Mould: economists and American higher learning in the nineteenth century, 1988; (ed) Perspectives on the History of Economic Thought, vols V and VI, 1991; Designs within Disorder: Franklin D. Roosevelt, the economists, and the shaping of American economic policy 1933–1945, 1996; (ed) Works of Irving Fisher, 14 vols, 1997; contribs to professional jls. *Address:* 306 Pine Street, Middletown, CT 06457, USA. *T:* (860) 3462612.

BARBIERI, Margaret Elizabeth, (Mrs M. E. Barbieri-Webb); freelance ballet teacher and coach, since 1990; Artistic Director, Images of Dance, since 1990; *b* 2 March 1947; *d* of Ettore Barbieri and Lea Barbieri; *m* 1982, Iain Webb, soloist SWRB; one *s*. *Educ:* Convent High Sch., Durban, S Africa. Trained with Iris Manning and Brownie Sutton, S Africa; Royal Ballet Sen. Sch., 1963; joined Royal Ballet, 1965; Principal, 1970; Sen. Principal, SWRB, 1974–89. Dir, Classical Graduate Course, London Studio Centre, 1990–; guest teacher, Royal Ballet Sch., 1990–94. Gypsy Girl, Two Pigeons, 1966; 1st Giselle, Covent Garden, 1968; 1st Sleeping Beauty, Leeds, 1969; 1st Swan Lake, Frankfurt, 1977, Covent Garden, 1983; 1st Romeo and Juliet, Covent Garden, 1979; 1st Sleeping Beauty, Covent Garden, 1985. Other roles with Royal Ballet: La Fille mal Gardée, Two Pigeons, The Dream, Façade, Wedding Bouquet, Rendezvous (Ashton); Lady and the Fool, Card Game, Pineapple Poll (Cranko); The Invitation, Solitaire, (Summer) The Four Seasons (MacMillan); Checkmate, The Rake's Progress (de Valois); Grosse Fugue, Tilt (van Manen); Lilac Garden (Tudor); Fête Etrange (Howard); Grand Tour (Layton); Summer Garden (Hynd); Game Piano (Thorpe), 1978; Cinderella (Killar), 1978; Cinderella (Rodrigues), 1979; Papillon, The Taming of the Shrew, 1980; Coppélia, Les Sylphides, Raymonda Act III, Spectre de la Rose; La Vivandière, 1982; Petrushka, 1984. Roles created: Knight Errant (Tudor), 1968; From Waking Sleep (Drew), 1970; Ante-Room (Cauley), 1971; Oscar Wilde (Layton), 1972; Sacred Circles and The Sword (Drew), 1973; The Entertainers (Killar), 1974; Charlotte Brontë (Hynd), 1974; Summertide (Wright), 1977; Metamorphosis (Bintley), 1984; Flowers of the Forest (Bintley), 1985; The Wand of Youth (Cordor), 1985. Recreated: Pavlova's Dragonfly Solo, 1977; The Dying Swan, produced by Dame Alicia Markova after Fokine, 1985. Guest artist, 1990–92, guest teacher, 1991–92, Birmingham Royal Ballet. Staged for Images of Dance: Les Sylphides, Façade, 1991; Rake's Progress, 1992; Pineapple Poll, La Bayadère, 1993; Raymonda, 1994; Swan Lake, 1995; Paquita, 1996. Travelled with Royal Ballet to Australia, Canada, China, Egypt, Far East, France, Germany, Greece, Holland, Israel, Italy, Japan, New Zealand, Portugal, Spain, Switzerland, Yugoslavia, India and North and South America; guest appearances, USA, Germany, S Africa, France, Norway, Czechoslovakia. TV Appearances in: Spectre de la Rose; Grosse Fugue; Giselle; Coppelia; Checkmate; Metamorphosis; Markova master classes. Gov., Royal Ballet, 1991–. *Recreations:* music (classical), theatre, gardening. *Address:* Chiswick.

BARBOSA, Rubens Antonio, Hon. GCVO 1997 (Hon. LVO 1969); Brazilian Ambassador to the United States of America, since 1999; *b* 13 June 1938; *s* of José Orlando Barbosa and Lice Farina Barbosa; *m* 1969, Maria Ignez Correa da Costa Barbosa; one *s* one *d*. *Educ:* Univ. of São Paulo, Brazil (Law graduate); LSE (MA); other degrees in economics, finance and politics. Exec. Sec., Brazilian Trade Commn with socialist countries of Eastern Europe, 1976–84; Head of Staff, Min. of External Relations, 1985–86; Under-Sec. Gen., Multilateral and Special Pol Affairs, 1986; Head, Internat. Affairs, Min. of Economy, 1987–88; Ambassador and Perm. Rep. to Latin-Amer. Integration Assoc., 1988–91; Under-Sec. Gen., Regl Integration, Econ. Affairs and Foreign Trade, Min. of External Relations, and Co-ordinator for Mercosur, Brazil, 1991–93; Ambassador to UK, 1994–99. Pres., Assoc. of Coffee Producing Countries, 1993–99. Grand Cross, Order of Rio Branco (Brazil); French Legion of Honour; orders from Argentina and Mexico; honours from Germany, Belgium, Italy, Iran, Portugal. *Publications:* America Latina em Perspectiva: a integração regional da retórica à realidade, 1991; The Mercosur Codes, 2000; articles in newspapers and learned jls. *Recreations:* tennis, classical music. *Address:* Brazilian Embassy, 3006 Massachusetts Avenue NW, Washington, DC 20008–3699, USA. *T:* (202) 2382712, *Fax:* (202) 2382827.

BARBOUR, James Jack, OBE 1992; Chief Executive, Sheffield Health Authority, since 1998; *b* 16 Jan. 1953; *s* of late Thomas Jack Barbour and Flora Jean Barbour (*née* Murray); partner, Rosalind Marjorie Doig; one *s* two *d*. *Educ:* Madras Coll., St Andrews; Univ. of Strathclyde (BA Jt Hons Politics, Sociol., Econs). MHSM 1983. Grad. Mgt Trainee, NHS in Scotland, 1977–79; Administrator, Gtr Glasgow Health Bd, 1979–83; EEC Exchange scholarship in Germany, 1981; Unit Administration, Gt Ormond St Gp of Hosps, 1983–86; General Manager: Royal Manchester Children's Hosp., 1986–87; Aberdeen Royal Infirmary, 1987–92; Chief Executive: Aberdeen Royal Hosps NHS Trust, 1992–94; Central Manchester Healthcare NHS Trust, 1994–98. Mem. Council, Univ. of Sheffield, 1998–. Alumnus, London Business Sch. Develt Prog., 1989. FRSA 1993. Hon. Sen. Fellow, Univ. of Manchester, 1996. Burgess, City of Aberdeen, 1992. *Recreations:* spoiling my children, trying to stay fit! *Address:* Sheffield Health Authority, 5 Old Fulwood Road, Sheffield S10 3TG. *T:* (0114) 271 1132. *Club:* Royal Northern (Aberdeen).

BARBOUR, Very Rev. Prof. Robert Alexander Stewart, KCVO 1991; MC 1945; Professor of New Testament Exegesis, University of Aberdeen, 1971–82; Master of Christ's College, Aberdeen, 1977–82; an Extra Chaplain to the Queen in Scotland since 1991 (Chaplain-in-Ordinary to the Queen, 1976–91); Dean of the Chapel Royal in Scotland, 1981–91; Prelate of the Priory of Scotland of the Order of St John, 1977–93; *b* 11 May 1921; *s* of George Freeland Barbour and Helen Victoria (*née* Hepburne-Scott); *m* 1950, Margaret Isobel Pigot; three *s* one *d*. *Educ:* Rugby Sch.; Balliol Coll., Oxford (MA 1946); Univ. of St Andrews (BD 1952); Yale Univ. (STM 1953). Sec., Edinburgh Christian Council for Overseas Students, 1953–55; Lectr and Sen. Lectr in NT Lang., Lit.

and Theol., Univ. of Edinburgh, 1955–71. Hensley Henson Lectr, Univ. of Oxford, 1983–84. Moderator, Gen. Assembly of Church of Scotland, 1979–80. Chm., Scottish Churches' Council, 1982–86. Hon. Sec., Studiorum Novi Testamenti Societas, 1970–77. Chm. Governors, Rannoch Sch., 1973–79. Hon. DD St Andrews, 1979. *Publications:* The Scottish Horse 1939–45, 1950; Traditio-Historical Criticism of the Gospels, 1972; What is the Church for?, 1973; articles in various jls. *Recreations:* music, walking, forestry. *Address:* Old Fincastle, Pitlochry, Perthshire PH16 5RJ. *T:* (01796) 473209. *Club:* New (Edinburgh).

BARBOZA, Mario G.; *see* Gibson-Barboza.

BARCLAY, Prof. (Alan) Neil, DPhil; Scientific Staff, Medical Research Council, Sir William Dunn School of Pathology, University of Oxford, since 1978; Titular Professor of Molecular Immunology, University of Oxford, since 1998; *b* 12 March 1950; *s* of Frank Rodney Barclay and late Betty Cowie Barclay (*née* Watson); *m* 1975, Ella Geraldine Quinn; two *s* one *d. Educ:* Hardye's Sch., Dorchester; Oriel Coll., Oxford (DPhil Biochem 1976). Res. Fellow, Inst. of Neurobiology, Univ. of Göteborg, Sweden, 1976–78; Scientific Staff, MRC Cellular Immunol. Unit, Oxford, 1978–99. Academic Advr, Oxford Univ. Bioinformatics Centre, 1990–2000. Dir, Everest Biotech Ltd, 1999–. Hon. Mem., Scandinavian Soc. of Immunology, 1993. *Publications:* (jtly) The Leucocyte Antigen Factsbook, 1993, 2nd edn 1997; contribs to scientific jls. *Recreations:* literature, listening to music, writing stories (unpublished). *Address:* Sir William Dunn School of Pathology, Oxford University, Oxford OX1 3RE. *T:* (01865) 275598.

BARCLAY, Christopher Francis Robert, CMG 1967; Secretary, Government Hospitality Fund, 1976–80; *b* 8 June 1919; *s* of late Captain Robert Barclay, RA (retired) and late Annie Douglas Dowdeswell Barclay (*née* Davidson); *m* 1st, 1950, Clare Justice Troutbeck (marr. diss., 1962); two *s* one *d*; 2nd, 1962, Diana Elizabeth Goodman; one *s* one *d. Educ:* Eton Coll.; Magdalen Coll., Oxford (MA). 2nd Lieut The Rifle Bde, 1940; Capt. 1942; Major 1943; served in Middle East; Political Officer, Northern Iraq, 1945; Brit. Embassy, Baghdad, 1946. Foreign Office, 1946; Second Sec., British Embassy, Cairo, 1947; First Sec., Foreign Office, 1950; Brit. Embassy, Bonn, 1953; FO, 1956; Regional Information Officer, Beirut, 1960; FO, 1961; Counsellor and Head of Information Research Dept, 1962–66; Head of Personnel Dept (Training and General), FCO, 1967–69; Asst Sec., CSD, 1969–73, DoE, 1973–76. Chm., Jt Nat. Horse Educn and Trng Council, 1988–90. Mem. Council, City Univ., 1976–84. Master, Saddlers' Co., 1983–84. FRSA 1984. *Recreations:* fishing, gardening. *Address:* Croft Edge, Painswick, Glos GL6 6XH. *T:* (01452) 812332. *Club:* Army and Navy.

BARCLAY, Sir Colville Herbert Sanford, 14th Bt *cr* 1668; painter; *b* 7 May 1913; *s* of late Rt Hon. Sir Colville Adrian de Rune Barclay, 3rd *s* of 11th Bt, and Sarita Enriqueta, *d* of late Herbert Ward; *S* uncle, 1930; *m* 1949, Rosamond Grant Renton Elliott; three *s. Educ:* Eton, Trinity Coll., Oxford. Third Sec., Diplomatic Service, 1937–41; enlisted in Navy, Nov. 1941; Sub-Lieut RNVR 1942; Lieut 1943; Lieut Commander 1945; demobilised, 1946. Exhibitor: Royal Academy, RBA, London Group, Bradford City and Brighton Art Galleries. Chm. Royal London Homoeopathic Hospital, 1970–74 (Vice-Chm., 1961–65; Chm., League of Friends, 1974–84). Plant-hunting expedns to Crete, Turkey, Cyprus, Réunion, Mauritius and Nepal, 1966–81. *Publications:* Crete: checklist of the vascular plants, 1986; articles in botanical jls. *Recreation:* gardening. *Heir: s* Robert Colraine Barclay [*b* 12 Feb. 1950; *m* 1980, Lucilia Saboia, *y d* of Carlos Saboia de Albuquerque, Rio de Janeiro; one *s* one *d*]. *Address:* 23 High Street, Broughton, near Stockbridge, Hants SO20 8AE.

BARCLAY, Sir David (Rowat), Kt 2000; Joint Proprietor, Scotsman Publications, since 1995. Former estate agent. Joint Proprietor: Howard Hotel, 1975–2000; The European, 1992–98; Ritz Hotel, 1995–. Mem., Chief Pleas, Sark, 1993–. Jt Founder and Trustee, David and Frederick Barclay Foundn. Hon. Dr Glasgow, 1998. Officier, Ordre de Saint Charles (Monaco), 2000. *Address:* c/o Le Montaigne, 7 avenue de Grande Bretagne, Monte Carlo, MC 98000, Monaco.

See also Sir F. H. Barclay.

BARCLAY, Sir Frederick (Hugh), Kt 2000; Joint Proprietor, Scotsman Publications, since 1995. Former estate agent. Joint Proprietor: Howard Hotel, 1975–2000; The European, 1992–98; Ritz Hotel, 1995–. Jt Founder and Trustee, David and Frederick Barclay Foundn. Hon. Dr Glasgow, 1998. Officier, Ordre de Saint Charles (Monaco), 2000. *Address:* c/o Le Montaigne, 7 avenue de Grande Bretagne, Monte Carlo, MC 98000, Monaco.

See also Sir D. R. Barclay.

BARCLAY, Hugh Maben, CB 1992; Clerk of Public Bills, House of Commons, 1988–91; *b* 20 Feb. 1927; *s* of late William Barclay, FRCS, and late Mary Barclay; *m* 1956, Hilda Johnston; one *s* one *d. Educ:* Fettes Coll., Edinburgh (exhbnr); Gonville and Caius Coll., Cambridge (schol.). Served Royal Artillery, 1948. House of Commons: Asst Clerk, 1950; Sen. Clerk, 1955; Dep. Principal Clerk, 1967; Principal Clerk, 1976; Clerk of Standing Cttees, 1976; Clerk of Private Bills, 1982. *Address:* 2 Empress Mansions, 130 Stonhouse Street, SW4 6AL. *T:* (020) 7622 1633.

BARCLAY, James Christopher; Chairman: M & G Equity Investment Trust PLC, since 1998 (Director, since 1996); LTP Trade Limited, since 2000; *b* 7 July 1945; *s* of late Theodore David Barclay and Anne Barclay; *m* 1974, Rolleen Anne, *d* of late Lt-Col Arthur Forbes and Joan Forbes; one *s* one *d. Educ:* Harrow. Served 15th/19th The King's Royal Hussars, 1964–67. Dep. Chm., 1981–85, Chm., 1985–98, Cater Allen Hldgs PLC; Chm., Cater Ryder & Co. Ltd, 1981. Director: Abbey National Treasury Services plc, 1997–98; Abbey National Offshore Hldgs Ltd, 1998–; Thos Agnew & Sons Ltd, 1998–; New Fulcrum Investment Trust plc, 1999–; Liontrust Knowledge Economy Trust PLC, 2001–. Dir, UK Debt Mgt Office, 2000–. Chm., London Discount Market Assoc., 1988–90. *Recreations:* fresh air pursuits. *Address:* Rivers Hall, Waldringfield, Woodbridge, Suffolk IP12 4QX. *Clubs:* Boodle's, Pratt's, City of London.

BARCLAY, John Alistair; Executive Director, Royal Bank of Scotland Group plc, retired; *b* 5 Dec. 1933; *m* 1963, Mary Tierney (*née* Brown); three *d. Educ:* Banff Academy. FCIBS. Joined Royal Bank of Scotland, 1949; Chief City Manager, 1982–84; seconded to Williams & Glyn's Bank (Asst Gen. Manager), 1984–85; Exec. Vice-Pres., NY, 1985–88; Sen. Gen. Manager, UK Banking, 1988–89; Exec. Dir, International, 1989–90; Man. Dir, Corporate and Institutional Banking, 1990–92; Dep. Gp Chief Exec., 1992–94. *Recreations:* travel, golf, reading, gardening, curling, photography, good food and wine.

BARCLAY, Neil; *see* Barclay, A. N.

BARCLAY, Patrick; football writer, Sunday Telegraph, since 1996; *b* 15 Aug. 1947; *s* of Guy Deghy and Patricia Wighton; one *s* one *d. Educ:* Dundee High Sch. Sub-editor, 1966–77, football writer, 1977–86, The Guardian; football writer: Today, 1986; The Independent, 1986–91; The Observer, 1991–96. *Recreations:* reading, travel. *Address:* c/o The Sunday Telegraph, 1 Canada Square, Canary Wharf, E14 5DT.

BARCLAY, Paul Robert; His Honour Judge Barclay; a Circuit Judge, since 1998; *s* of late John Alexander Barclay and of Mabel Elizabeth Barclay; *m* 1972, Sarah Louise Jones; two *s* two *d. Educ:* Nottingham High Sch.; St John's Coll., Cambridge (MA 1971). Called to the Bar, Middle Temple, 1972; in practice at the Bar, 1972–98; an Asst Recorder, 1992–96; a Recorder, 1996–98. *Recreation:* village cricket. *Address:* Swindon Combined Court, Islington Street, Swindon SN1 2HG. *T:* (01793) 614848.

BARCLAY, Sir Peter (Maurice), Kt 1992; CBE 1984; Chairman, 1996–2001, Trustee, 1972–2001, Joseph Rowntree Foundation (formerly Joseph Rowntree Memorial Trust); *b* 6 March 1926; *s* of George Ronald Barclay and Josephine (*née* Lambert); *m* 1953, Elizabeth Mary Wright; one *s* two *d. Educ:* Bryanston Sch.; Magdalene Coll., Cambridge (MA). Served RNVR, 1944–46. Admitted Solicitor, 1952; Senior Partner, 1964–74, Partner, 1974–88, Beachcroft & Co. Chm., The Family Fund Trust, 1973–97. Chairman: Cttee on Roles and Tasks of Social Workers, 1981–82; Social Security Adv. Cttee, 1984–93; Nat. Family Mediation, 1994–96. Non-exec. Mem., DSS Deptl Bd, 1994–97. Pres., National Inst. for Social Work, 1988 (Chm., 1973–85); Chm., Horticultural Therapy, 1989–94; Pres., St Pancras and Humanist Housing Assoc., 2000– (Vice Pres., St Pancras Housing Assoc., 1994–2000; Mem., 1971–93, Chm., 1983–91, Management Cttee). Governor, Bryanston Sch., 1972–88; Council Mem., PSI, 1989–95; Trustee, Nat. Family and Parenting Inst., 1999–. DUniv: Stirling, 1994; York, 1996. *Recreations:* gardening, painting. *Address:* 4/43 Ladbroke Grove, W11 3AR. *T:* (020) 7727 4613, *Fax:* (020) 7243 8969.

BARCLAY, Yvonne Fay, (Mrs William Barclay); *see* Minton, Y. F.

BARD, Dr Basil Joseph Asher, CBE 1968; Innovation consultant, retired; Director, Scanning Technology Ltd, 1984–95; *b* London, 20 Aug. 1914; *s* of late Abram Isaac Bard and Anita Bard; *m* 1942, Ena Dora Birk; three *s. Educ:* Owen's Sch.; RCS (Imperial Coll.). BSc(Chem.), ARCS 1934, DIC (Chem. Engrg and Fuel Technology) 1935, PhD (Chem. Constitution of Coal) 1936, London; Bar Finals (1st cl. hons) and Studentship, Coun. of Legal Educn, 1937; called to Bar, Gray's Inn (Birkenhead and William Shaw Schol.), 1938. Practised at Bar, 1938–39; Legal Dept, Coal Commn, 1939–41; Explosives Prodn Dept, Min. of Supply, 1941–43; Materials Dept, Min. of Aircraft Production, 1943–45; Depts of Industrial Res., Educn, Design, etc, FBI, 1945–49; NRDC, 1950–74; in turn, Commercial Man., Techn. Dir and Exec. Dir, Dept of Applied Science; Mem., NRDC, 1956–73, Man. Dir, 1971–73; Exec. Dir, First National Finance Corp., 1974–76; Chm., Birmingham Mint Ltd, 1977–81. Director: Allied Insulators Ltd, 1975–77; Interflex Group, 1984–89; Chairman: NPM Gp, 1977–83; Xtec Ltd, 1983–86 (Dir, 1981–86); ProMicro Ltd, 1985–91. Founder and Chm., 1968–70, subsequently Vice-Pres., UK Licensing Execs Soc. (awarded Gold Medal 1973; Hon. Life Member, 1989). Consultant to UNIDO, 1972–74; Hon. Mem., Foundn for Sci. and Technol., 1990– (Hon. Treasurer, 1984–90); has served on various Govt Cttees. Pres., Jewish Meml Council, 1982–89; Vice-Pres., Anglo-Jewish Assoc., 1983– (Pres., 1977–83); Chm., Administration Cttee, UK Friends of Hebrew Univ. of Jerusalem, 1991– (Hon. Fellow, 1993; Life Gov., 1996). *Publications:* (ed) Industry and Research, 1947; (ed) The Patent System, 1975; various articles on science, technology, patents, industry, commerce and their inter-relationships. *Recreations:* music, bridge, chess, social life. *Address:* 23 Mourne House, Maresfield Gardens, Hampstead, NW3 5SL. *T:* (020) 7435 5340. *Club:* Athenæum.

BARDEN, Prof. Laing, CBE 1990; PhD, DSc; Vice-Chancellor, University of Northumbria at Newcastle, 1992–96 (Director, Newcastle upon Tyne Polytechnic, 1978–92); *b* 29 Aug. 1931; *s* of Alfred Eversfield Barden and Edna (*née* Laing); *m* 1956, Nancy Carr; two *s* one *d. Educ:* Washington Grammar Sch.; Durham Univ. (BSc, MSc). R. T. James & Partners, 1954–59. Liverpool Univ., 1959–62 (PhD); Manchester Univ., 1962–69 (DSc); Strathclyde Univ., 1969–74; Newcastle upon Tyne Polytechnic, subseq. Univ. of Northumbria at Newcastle, 1974–96. Director: Microelectronics Applications Res. Inst. Ltd, 1980–90; Tyne and Wear Enterprise Trust Ltd, 1982–96; Newcastle Technology Centre Ltd, 1985–90; Newcastle Initiative, 1988–96. Mem., Council for Industry and Higher Educn, 1987–96. *Publications:* contribs to Geotechnique, Proc. ICE, Jl Amer. Soc. CE, Qly Jl Eng. Geol. *Recreations:* cricket, soccer, snooker. *Address:* 7 Westfarm Road, Cleadon, Tyne and Wear SR6 7UG. *T:* (0191) 536 2317. *Clubs:* National Liberal; Mid Boldon (Boldon).

BARDER, Sir Brian (Leon), KCMG 1992; HM Diplomatic Service, retired; High Commissioner to Australia, 1991–94; *b* 20 June 1934; *s* of Harry and Vivien Barder; *m* 1958, Jane Maureen Cornwell; two *d* one *s. Educ:* Sherborne; St Catharine's Coll., Cambridge (BA). 2nd Lieut, 7 Royal Tank Regt, 1952–54. Colonial Office, 1957; Private Sec. to Permanent Under-Sec., 1960–61; HM Diplomatic Service, 1965; First Secretary, UK Mission to UN, 1964–68; FCO, 1968–70; First Sec. and Press Attaché, Moscow, 1971–73; Counsellor and Head of Chancery, British High Commn, Canberra, 1973–77; Canadian Nat. Defence Coll., Kingston, Ontario, 1977–78; Head of Central and Southern, later Southern African Dept, FCO, 1978–82; Ambassador to Ethiopia, 1982–86; Ambassador to Poland, 1986–88; High Comr to Nigeria, and concurrently Ambassador to Benin, 1988–91. Mem., Commonwealth Observer Mission for Namibian elections, 1994. ODA Consultant on Diplomatic Trng, Eastern and Central Europe, 1996. Panel of Chairs, CSSB, 1995–96. Member: Bd of Management, Royal Hosp. for Neuro-disability, 1996–; Cttee, ESU Centre for Speech and Debate (formerly Internat. Debate and Communication Trng), 1996–; Special Immigration Appeals Commn, 1998–. CON 1989. *Recreations:* computer, music, cycling, writing letters to the newspapers. *Address:* 10 Melrose Road, SW18 1NE; *e-mail:* brianbarder@compuserve.com. *Club:* Oxford and Cambridge.

See also E. L. Wen.

BARDSLEY, Andrew Tromlow; JP; General Manager and Chief Executive, Harlow Development Corporation, 1973–80; *b* 7 Dec. 1927; *o s* of Andrew and Gladys Ada Bardsley; *m* 1954, June Patricia (*née* Ford); one *s* one *d. Educ:* Ashton-under-Lyne Grammar Sch.; Manchester Coll. of Art. CEng, FICE. Royal Navy, 1947–49. Entered Local Govt (Municipal Engrg), 1950; various appts leading to Borough Engr and Surveyor, Worksop MB, 1962–69; Director of Technical Services: Corby New Town, 1969–71; Luton CBC, 1971–73; Principal, Westgate Develt Consultancy, 1981–93. Gen. Comr. of Taxes in England and Wales, 1987–92. JP Essex, 1975 (Dep. Chm., Harlow Bench, 1987–92). *Recreations:* golf, music, gardening, most spectator sports. *Address:* 2 Carrbridge Gardens, Talbot Woods, Bournemouth, Dorset BH3 7EL. *T:* (01202) 537954. *Clubs:* Ferndown Golf; Bournemouth Bowling (Past Pres.).

BAREAU, Peter John; Chief Executive, National Savings, since 1996; *b* 1 June 1942; *s* of late Paul Bareau, OBE and Kitty Bareau (*née* Gibson); *m* 1st, 1967, Irene Nelson (marr. diss.); one *s* one *d*; 2nd, 1976, Karen Giesemann (*d* 2001); one *s* two *d. Educ:* Eton Coll.; Queens' Coll., Cambridge (MA). With Bank of London & S America in UK, USA, Paraguay and Spain, 1966–72; with Lloyds Bank Internat. in UK and Brazil, 1973–84; Lloyds Bank PLC: General Manager: Strategic Planning, 1985–86; Europe, ME and Internat. Pvte Banking, 1987–91; Personnel, 1992–96. Non exec. Dir, Inst. of Mgt Consultancy, 1999–; Mem., UK Regl Adv. Bd, London Business Sch., 2000–. *Recreations:*

music, tennis, travel. *Address:* Old Coach House, Alldens Lane, Munstead, Godalming, Surrey GU8 4AP. *T:* (01483) 415010.

BARENBLATT, Prof. Grigory Isaakovich, PhD; ScD; Professor of Mathematics, University of California at Berkeley, since 1997; G. I. Taylor Professor of Fluid Mechanics, University of Cambridge, 1992–94, now Emeritus, and Hon. Fellow, Gonville and Caius College, Cambridge, 1999 (Fellow, 1994–99); *b* 10 July 1927; *s* of Isaak Grigorievich Barenblatt and Nadezhda Veniaminovna (*née* Kagan); *m* 1952, Iraida Nikolaevna Kochina; two *d.* *Educ:* Moscow Univ. (MSc 1950; PhD 1953; ScD 1957); Univ. of Cambridge (MA 1993). Res. Scientist, Inst. of Petroleum, USSR Acad. of Sci., Moscow, 1953–61; Prof. and Hd, Dept of Mechanics of Solids, Inst. of Mechanics, Moscow Univ., 1961–75; Hd, Theoretical Dept, Inst. of Oceanology, USSR Acad. of Sci., Moscow, 1975–92. Foreign Member: Amer. Acad. of Arts and Scis, 1975; Royal Soc., 2000; Foreign Associate: US Nat. Acad. of Engrg, 1992; US Nat. Acad. of Sci., 1997; MAE, 1993. Hon. DTech Royal Inst. of Technol., Stockholm, 1989. Laureate, Panetti Medal and Prize, 1995; G. I. Taylor Medal, Amer. Soc. of Engrg Sci., 1999; J. C. Maxwell Prize, Internat. Congress on Industrial and Applied Maths, 1999. *Publications:* Similarity, Self-Similarity, and Intermediate Asymptotics, 1979; Dimensional Analysis, 1987; (jtly) Theory of Fluid Flows in Porous Media, 1990; Scaling, Self-Similarity, and Intermediate Asymptotics, 1996; contrib. Jl Applied Maths and Mechanics, Physics of Atmosphere and Ocean, Jl Fluid Mechanics. *Recreation:* historical reading. *Address:* Department of Mathematics, University of California, Berkeley, CA 94720–3840, USA.

BARENBOIM, Daniel; pianist and conductor; Musical Director: Chicago Symphony Orchestra, since 1991; Berlin State Opera, since 1992; *b* Buenos Aires, 15 Nov. 1942; *s* of Enrique Barenboim and late Aida Barenboim (*née* Schuster); *m* 1st, 1967, Jacqueline du Pré (*d* 1987); 2nd, 1988, Elena Bashkirova; two *s.* *Educ:* Santa Cecilia Acad., Rome; studied with his father; coached by Edwin Fischer, Nadia Boulanger, and Igor Markevitch. Debut as pianist with: Israel Philharmonic Orchestra, 1953; Royal Philharmonic Orchestra, 1956; Berlin Philharmonic Orchestra, 1963; NY Philharmonic Orchestra, 1964; Musical Dir, Orchestre de Paris, 1975–88; tours include: Australia, North and South America, Far East; regular appearances at Bayreuth, Edinburgh, Lucerne, Prague and Salzburg Festivals. Many recordings as conductor and pianist. Beethoven Medal, 1958; Paderewski Medal, 1963; subsequently other awards. Legion of Honour (France), 1987. *Publication:* A Life in Music, 1991. *Address:* c/o Daniel Barenboim Secretariat, 29 rue de la Coulouvrenière, 1204 Genève, Switzerland.

BARHAM, Geoffrey Simon; His Honour Judge Barham; a Circuit Judge, since 1993; *b* 23 Dec. 1945; *s* of Denis Patrick Barham and Pleasance (*née* Brooke); *m* 1976, Sarah Seebold; one *s* one *d.* *Educ:* Malvern Coll.; Christ's Coll., Cambridge (MA). Called to the Bar, Lincoln's Inn, 1968; Asst Recorder, 1983; Recorder, 1987. *Recreation:* golf. *Address:* c/o SE Circuit Office, New Cavendish House, 18 Maltravers Street, WC2R 3EU. *Club:* Norfolk (Norwich).

BARING, family name of **Baron Ashburton,** of **Earl of Cromer,** of **Baron Howick of Glendale,** of **Baron Northbrook,** and of **Baron Revelstoke**.

BARING, Sir John (Francis), 3rd Bt *cr* 1911, of Nubia House, Isle of Wight; Managing Partner, Mercator Capital LLC, since 1999; Mercator Management LLC, since 1999; *b* 21 May 1947; *s* of Raymond Alexander Baring (*d* 1967) (2nd *s* of 1st Bt) and Margaret Fleetwood Baring (who *m* 1991, 6th Earl of Malmesbury, TD; she *d* 1994), *d* of late Col R. W. P. C. Campbell-Preston; *S* uncle, 1990; *m* 1971, Elizabeth Anne, MS, ATR (BC), *yr d* of Robert D. H. Pillitz; two *s* one *d.* Citibank NA, 1971–72; Chemical Bank, 1972–84; Kidder, Peabody & Co. Inc., 1984–89; GPA Group Ltd, 1989; Partner, 1991–94, Chm., 1994–97, Hackman, Baring & Co.; Man. Dir, PricewaterhouseCoopers Securities LLC, 1997–99. *Recreations:* gardening, fishing. *Heir:* *s* Julian Alexander David Baring, *b* 10 Feb. 1975. *Address:* 2500 Virginia Avenue NW, Washington, DC 20037, USA.

BARING, Nicholas Hugo; Chairman, Council of Management, Baring Foundation, since 1998 (Member, since 1969); *b* 2 Jan. 1934; *er s* of Francis Anthony Baring (killed in action, 1940) and Lady Rose Baring, DCVO; *m* 1972, (Elizabeth) Diana, *d* of late Brig. Charles Crawfurd; three *s.* *Educ:* Eton (King's Schol.); Magdalene Coll., Cambridge (exhibnr, BA). Nat. service, 2nd Lieut Coldstream Guards, 1952–54. ADC to Governor of Kenya, 1957–58; joined Baring Brothers, 1958; Man. Dir, Baring Brothers & Co., 1963–86; Dir, Barings plc, 1985–94 (Dep. Chm., 1986–89). Dir, Commercial Union plc, 1968–98 (Chm., 1990–98). Mem., City Capital Markets Cttee, 1983–89 (Chm., 1983–87). Vice Pres., Liverpool Sch. of Tropical Medicine, 1982–89, 1996– (Pres., 1989–96); Chm., Bd of Trustees, Nat. Gall., 1992–96 (Trustee, 1989–96); Trustee, Fitzwilliam Museum Trust, 1997–. National Trust: Mem. Exec. Cttee, 1965–69 and 1979–; Mem. Council, 1978–; Chm., Finance Cttee, 1980–91. Mem. Council of Management, Architectl Heritage Fund, 1987–. Hon. LLD Liverpool, 1995; Hon. DCL Kent, 1998. *Address:* Baring Foundation, 60 London Wall, EC2M 5TQ. *T:* (020) 7767 1136. *Club:* Brooks's.
See also P. Baring.

BARING, Peter; *b* 28 Oct. 1935; *yr s* of Francis Anthony Baring (killed in action, 1940) and Lady Rose Baring, DCVO; *m* 1960, Teresa Anne Bridgeman (CBE 1998); three *s.* *Educ:* Magdalene College, Cambridge (MA English). Joined Baring Brothers & Co., 1959, Director, 1967; Chairman: Barings plc, 1989–95; Baring Asset Management, 1993–95. Dir, Inchcape, 1978–96. Dep. Chm., Provident Mutual Life Assurance Assoc., 1989–95. Chm., London Investment Banking Assoc., 1991–94. Gov., London Business Sch., 1991–95. Chm., Glyndebourne Arts Trust, 1994–96.
See also N. H. Baring.

BARKER, family name of **Baroness Trumpington**.

BARKER, Baroness *cr* 1999 (Life Peer), of Anagach in Highland; **Elizabeth Jean Barker;** Field Officer, Age Concern England, since 1992; *b* Outwood, W Yorks, 31 Jan. 1961. *Educ:* Dalziel High Sch., Motherwell; Broadway Sch., Oldham; Univ. of Southampton (BSc(SocSci) Hons Psychology). Pres., Union of Liberal Students, 1982–83. Age Concern England: Project Co-Ordinator, Opportunities for Volunteering Programme, 1983–88; Grants Officer, 1988–92. Member: Liberal Party Nat. Exec., 1982–83; Liberal Assembly Cttee, 1984–88; Lib Dem Federal Conf. Cttee, 1988– (Chm., 1997); Lib Dem Federal Policy Cttee, 1997–. Mem., T&GWU (ACTSS). Trustee, Andy Lawson Meml Fund. *Address:* House of Lords, SW1A 0PW.

BARKER, Hon. Dame Anne Judith; *see* Rafferty, Dame A. J.

BARKER, Anthony; QC 1985; a Recorder, since 1985; *b* 10 Jan. 1944; *s* of Robert Herbert Barker and Ellen Doreen Barker; *m* 1st, 1969 (marr. diss. 1980); two *d*; 2nd, 1983 (marr. diss. 1998); one step *s.* *Educ:* Newcastle-under-Lyme High Sch.; Clare Coll., Cambridge (BA Hons). Called to the Bar, Middle Temple, 1966, Bencher, 1997. Asst Recorder, 1981. *Recreations:* gardening, walking, music. *Address:* Hilderstone House, Hilderstone, near Stone, Staffs ST15 8SF. *T:* (01889) 505331.

BARKER, Audrey Lilian; writer; *b* 13 April 1918; *d* of Harry and Elsie Barker. *Educ:* County secondary schools in Beckenham, Kent and Wallington, Surrey. Editorial office, Amalgamated Press, 1936; Publisher's reader, Cresset Press, 1947; BBC, 1949–78. Atlantic Award in Literature, 1946; Somerset Maugham Award, 1947; Cheltenham Festival of Literature Award, 1963; SE Arts Creative Book Award, 1981. FRSL 1970; Mem. Exec. Cttee, PEN, 1981–85; Member Panel of Judges: Katherine Mansfield Prize, 1984; Macmillan Silver Pen Award for Fiction, 1986 and 1989. *Publications: collected stories:* Innocents, 1947; Novelette, 1951; Lost Upon the Roundabouts, 1964; Femina Real, 1971; Life Stories, 1981; No Word of Love, 1985; Any Excuse for a Party, 1991; Element of Doubt: ghost stories, 1992; *novels:* Apology for a Hero, 1950; The Joy-Ride (three novellas), 1963; A Case Examined, 1965; The Middling, 1967; John Brown's Body, 1969 (shortlisted for Booker Prize, 1969); A Source of Embarrassment, 1974; A Heavy Feather, 1978; Relative Successes, 1984; The Gooseboy, 1987; The Woman Who Talked to Herself, 1989; Zeph, 1992; The Haunt, 1999. *Address:* Carshalton, Surrey.

BARKER, Barry, MBE 1960; FCIS; Secretary and Chief Executive, Institute of Chartered Secretaries and Administrators (formerly Chartered Institute of Secretaries), 1976–89; *b* 1929; *s* of late Francis Walter Barker and Amy Barker; *m* 1954, Dr Vira Dubash; two *s.* *Educ:* Ipswich Sch.; Trinity Coll., Oxford (MA Class. Greats). Secretary: Bombay Chamber of Commerce and Industry, 1956–62; The Metal Box Co. of India Ltd, 1962–67. Dir, Shipbuilding Industry Bd, 1967–71; Consultant at Dept of Industry, 1972; Sec., Pye Holdings Ltd, 1972–76. Chairman: Consultative Council of Professional Management Orgns, 1981–90; Nat. Endorsement Bd, Management Charter Initiative, 1990–94. Member: BTEC, 1985–94; RSA Exams Bd, 1987–94; NCVQ, 1989–92; Bd of Management, Young Vic Co., 1984–90. *Recreations:* the theatre and the arts. *Address:* 82 Darwin Court, Gloucester Avenue, NW1 7BQ. *T:* (020) 7911 0570.

BARKER, Brian John; QC 1990; **His Honour Judge Barker;** a Circuit Judge, since 2000; *b* 15 Jan. 1945; *s* of William Barker and Irene Barker (*née* Gillow); *m* 1977, Anne Judith Rafferty (*see* Dame A. J. Rafferty); three *d* (and one *d* decd). *Educ:* Strode's School, Egham; Univ. of Birmingham (LLB); Univ. of Kansas (MA). Called to the Bar, Gray's Inn, 1969, Bencher, 1999. A Recorder, 1985–2000. Mem., Senate and Bar Council, 1976–79. A Pres., Mental Health Review Tribunals, 1993–. Chm., Criminal Bar Assoc., 1998–2000. Gov., Strode's Coll., Egham. Freeman, City of London; Liveryman, Coopers' Co., 1989– (Mem., Ct of Assts, 1995–). *Recreations:* sheep rearing, golf. *Address:* Central Criminal Court, Old Bailey, EC4M 7EH. *Clubs:* City Livery, Bishopsgate Ward; Royal Mid-Surrey Golf, Rye Golf.

BARKER, Rt Rev. Clifford Conder, TD 1970; Bishop Suffragan of Selby, 1983–91; Hon. Assistant Bishop of York, since 1991; *b* 22 April 1926; *s* of Sidney and Kathleen Alice Barker; *m* 1952, Marie Edwards (*d* 1982); one *s* two *d*; 2nd, 1983, Mrs Audrey Gregson; two step *s* one step *d.* *Educ:* Oriel Coll., Oxford (BA 1950, MA 1955); St Chad's Coll., Durham (Dip. in Theol. 1952). Emergency Commun, The Green Howards, 1944–48; deacon 1952, priest 1953; Curate: All Saints', Scarborough, 1952–55; Redcar, 1955–57; Vicar: All Saints', Sculcoates, Hull, 1957–63; Rudby-in-Cleveland, 1963–70; RD of Stokesley, 1965–70; Vicar, St Olave with St Giles, York, 1970–76; RD of York, 1971–76; Canon of York, 1973–76; Bishop Suffragan of Whitby, 1976–83. CF (TA), 1958–74. *Recreations:* travel, reading, crosswords, gardening, music. *Address:* Wylde Green, 15 Oak Tree Close, Strensall, York YO32 5TE. *T:* (01904) 490406.

BARKER, Sir Colin, Kt 1991; Chairman, British Technology Group Ltd, 1983–93 (Chief Executive, 1983–85); *b* 20 Oct. 1926; *m* 1951, Beryl; three *s* one *d.* *Educ:* Hull Grammar Sch.; London and Edinburgh Univs. Ford UK, 1960–67 (Finance Dir, 1967); Finance Director: Blue Circle, 1968–70; STC, 1970–80; British Steel Corp., 1980–83. Chairman: CIN Management, 1985–93; British Investment Trust, 1985–93; MCD (UK), 1990–95; Anglian Group (formerly Anglian Windows), 1991–95; Director: Reed Internat., 1983–92; British Coal Corp., 1984–91; Edinburgh Fund Managers, 1988–93. *Address:* 12 Clune Court, Hutton Road, Shenfield, Essex CM15 8NQ.

BARKER, David; QC 1976; a Recorder of the Crown Court, 1974–98; *b* 13 April 1932; *s* of late Frederick Barker and of Amy Evelyn Barker; *m* 1957, Diana Mary Vinson Barker (*née* Duckworth); one *s* three *d.* *Educ:* Sir John Deane's Grammar Sch., Northwich; University Coll., London; Univ. of Michigan. 1st cl. hons LLB London; LLM Michigan. RAF, 1956–59. Called to Bar, Inner Temple, 1954, Bencher, 1985; practised Midland and Oxford Circuit; a Dep. High Court Judge, 1993–98. Mem., Senate of Inns of Court and the Bar, 1981–84. Member: Criminal Injuries Compensation Bd, 1990–2000; Criminal Injuries Compensation Appeals Panel, 1997–. Contested (Lab) Runcorn, 1955. *Recreations:* gardening, walking, sailing. *Address:* Nanhill, Woodhouse Eaves, Leics LE12 8TL. *T:* (01509) 890224; 65–67 King Street, Leicester LE1 6RP. *T:* (0116) 254 7710. *Club:* Western (Glasgow).

BARKER, Prof. David (Faubert), MA, DPhil, DSc; Professor of Zoology, University of Durham, 1962–87, now Professor Emeritus; *b* 18 Feb. 1922; *s* of Faubert and Doreen Barker; *m* 1st, 1945, Kathleen Mary Frances Pocock; three *s* two *d*; 2nd, 1978, Patricia Margaret Drake (*see* P. M. Barker); one *s* one *d.* *Educ:* Bryanston Sch.; Magdalen Coll., Oxford. DSc 1972. Senior Demy of Magdalen Coll., 1946; Leverhulme Research Scholar, Royal Coll. of Surgeons, 1946; Demonstrator in Zoology and Comparative Anatomy, Oxford, 1947; DPhil 1948; Rolleston Prizeman, 1948; Prof. of Zoology, Univ. of Hong Kong, 1950–62; led scientific expeditions to Tunisia, 1950, North Borneo, 1952; Dean of Faculty of Science, Hong Kong, 1959–60; Public Orator, Hong Kong, 1961; Sir Derman Christopherson Fellow, Durham Univ. Research Foundn, 1984–85. Emeritus Fellow, Leverhulme Trust, 1989–92. *Publications:* (Founder) Editor, Hong Kong Univ. Fisheries Journal, 1954–60; Editor, Symposium on Muscle Receptors, 1962; scientific papers, mostly on muscle innervation. *Address:* Department of Biological Sciences, Science Laboratories, Mountjoy, Durham DH1 3LE. *T:* (0191) 3743342.

BARKER, Prof. David James Purslove, MD, PhD; FRCP; FRS 1998; Professor of Clinical Epidemiology, since 1979 and Director, Medical Research Council Environmental Epidemiology Unit, since 1984, University of Southampton; *b* 29 June 1938; *s* of Hugh Purslove and Joye Frances Barker; *m* 1st, 1960, Angela Beatrice Coddington (*d* 1980); three *s* two *d*; 2nd, 1983, Janet Elizabeth Franklin; one step *s* two step *d.* *Educ:* Oundle Sch.; Guy's Hosp. Med. Sch., London Univ. (BSc 1st Cl. Hons, 1959; MB BS 1962; PhD 1966; MD 1973). FRCP 1979. University of Birmingham: Research Fellow in Social Medicine, 1963–66; Lectr in Medicine, 1966–69; Lectr in Preventive Medicine, Makerere Univ., Uganda, 1969–72; Sen. Lectr in Clinical Epidemiology and Consultant Physician, Univ. of Southampton, 1972–79. Founder FMedSci 1998. Hon. FRCOG, 1993. Royal Soc. Wellcome Gold Medal, 1994. *Publications:* Practical Epidemiology, 1973, 4th edn 1992; (with G. Rose) Epidemiology in Medical Practice, 1976, 5th edn (with C. Cooper and G. Rose) 1998; (with G. Rose) Epidemiology for the Uninitiated, 1979, 3rd edn 1993; Fetal and infant origins of adult disease, 1992; Mothers, babies and disease in later life, 1994, 2nd edn 1998. *Recreations:* writing, drawing, golf, fishing, craic. *Address:* Manor Farm, East Dean, near Salisbury, Wilts SP5 1HB. *T:* (01794) 340016.

BARKER, Prof. Eileen Vartan, OBE 2000; PhD; FBA 1998; Professor of Sociology with Special Reference to the Study of Religion, London School of Economics, since 1992; *b* 21 April 1938; *d* of Calman MacLennan and Mary Helen MacLennan (*née* Muir); *m* 1958, Peter Johnson Barker, MBE; two *d.* *Educ:* Cheltenham Ladies' Coll.; Webber Douglas Sch. of Singing and Dramatic Art; London Sch. of Econs (BSc 1st Cl. Hons Sociol. 1970; PhD 1984). London School of Economics: Lectr, 1970–85; Sen. Lectr, 1985–90; Reader, 1990–92; Dean, Undergrad. Studies, 1982–86. Leonard Greenberg Distinguished Vis. Fellow, Trinity Coll., Hertford, USA, 2000. Founder and Chm., INFORM, 1988–. Pres., Soc. for Scientific Study of Religion, 1991–93. Phd *hc* Copenhagen, 2000. Martin E. Marty Award for Public Understanding of Religion, 2000. *Publications:* (ed) Of Gods and Men, 1982; (ed) New Religious Movements: a perspective for understanding society, 1982; The Making of a Moonie: brainwashing or choice?, 1984 (SSSR Dist. Book Award 1985); New Religious Movements: a practical introduction, 1989, 2nd edn 2001; (ed jtly) Secularization, Rationalism and Sectarianism, 1993; (ed jtly) Twenty Years On: changes in new religious movements, 1995; (ed) LSE on Freedom, 1995; (ed jtly) New Religions and New Religiosity, 1998; numerous contribs to scholarly jls and books. *Address:* London School of Economics, Department of Sociology, Houghton Street, WC2A 2AE. *T:* (020) 7955 7289.

BARKER, Prof. Graeme William Walter, FSA; FBA 1999; Dean, University of Leicester Graduate School, since 2000; *b* 23 Oct. 1946; *s* of Reginald Walter Barker and Kathleen (*née* Walton); *m* 1976, Sarah Miranda Buchanan (marr. diss. 1991); one *s* one *d.* *Educ:* Alleyn's Sch., Dulwich; St John's Coll., Cambridge (Henry Arthur Thomas Schol., 1965–67; MA; PhD 1973). FSA 1979. Rome Schol. in Classical Studies, British Sch. at Rome, 1969–71; Lectr, 1972–81, Sen. Lectr, 1981–88, in Prehist. and Archaeol., Sheffield Univ.; Dir., British Sch. at Rome, 1984–88; Prof. and Hd, Sch. of Archaeol Studies, Leicester Univ., 1988–2000. *Publications:* Landscape and Society: Prehistoric Central Italy, 1981, Italian edn 1984; (with R. Hodges) Archaeology and Italian Society, 1981; Prehistoric Communities in Northern England, 1981; (jtly) La Casatico di Marcaria, 1983; (jtly) Cyrenaica in Classical Antiquity, 1984; Prehistoric Farming in Europe, 1985; (with C. S. Gamble) Beyond Domestication in Prehistoric Europe: Investigations in Subsistence Archaeology and Social Complexity, 1985; (with J. A. Lloyd) Roman Landscapes, 1991; (with R. Maggi and R. Nisbet) Archeologia della Pastorizia nell'Europa Meridionale, 1993; A Mediterranean Valley: landscape archaeology and *Annales* history in the Biferno Valley, 1995; The Biferno Valley Survey: the archaeological and geomorphological record, 1995; (jtly) Farming the Desert: the UNESCO Libyan valleys survey, 2 vols, 1996; (with T. Rasmussen) The Etruscans, 1998; (ed) The Companion Encyclopedia of Archaeology, 2 vols, 1999; (with D. Gilbertson) The Archaeology of Drylands: living at the margin, 2000; contribs, esp. on landscape archaeol. and ancient agric., to learned jls. *Address:* University Graduate School, University of Leicester, University Road, Leicester LE1 7RH. *T:* (0116) 252 2611.

BARKER, Gregory; MP (C) Bexhill and Battle, since 2001; *b* Sussex, 8 March 1966; *m* 1992, Celeste Harrison; two *s* one *d.* *Educ:* Steyning Grammar Sch.; Lancing Coll.; RHBNC (BA 1987). Researcher, Centre for Policy Studies, 1987–89 (Associate, 1988–); Equity Analyst, Gerrard Vivian Gray, 1988–90; Dir, Internat. Pacific Securities, 1990–97; Associate Partner, Brunswick Gp Ltd, 1997–98; Hd, Investor Communications, Siberian Oil Co., 1998–2000. Dir, Daric plc, 1998–. Contested (C) Eccles, 1997. *Address:* c/o House of Commons, SW1A 0AA.

BARKER, Harold; retired; Keeper, Department of Conservation and Technical Services, British Museum, 1975–79; Member: Council for Care of Churches, 1976–81; Crafts Council, 1979–80; *b* 15 Feb. 1919; *s* of William Frampton Barker and Lily (*née* Pack); *m* 1942, Everilda Alice Whittle; one *s* one *d.* *Educ:* City Secondary Sch., Sheffield; Sheffield Univ. (BSc). Experimental Asst, 1940, Experimental Officer, 1942, Chemical Inspectorate, Min. of Supply; British Museum: Experimental Officer, Research Lab., 1947; Sen. Experimental Officer, 1953; Chief Experimental Officer, 1960; Principal Scientific Officer, 1966; Acting Keeper, 1975. *Publications:* papers on radiocarbon dating and scientific examination of antiquities in various jls. *Recreations:* music, walking, videography. *Address:* 27 Westbourne Park, Falsgrave, Scarborough, N Yorks YO12 4AS. *T:* (01723) 353273.

BARKER, Howard; playwright and poet; *b* 28 June 1946. *Educ:* Univ. of Sussex (MA). Theatre productions, 1970–, include: *Royal Court:* No End of Blame, 1981; Victory, 1983; version of Thomas Middleton's Women Beware Women, 1986; The Last Supper, 1988; Golgo, 1990; Hated Nightfall, 1995; *RSC* at The Pit: The Castle, 1985; Downchild: a fantasy, 1985; The Bite of the Night, 1988; *Leicester:* The Last Supper, 1989; Seven Lears, 1990; Judith, 1995; (Uncle) Vanya, 1996; other productions: A Passion in Six Days, Crucible, Sheffield, 1983; The Power of the Dog, Hampstead, 1985; Possibilities, Almeida, 1988. TV and radio plays include: Scenes from an Execution, Radio 3, 1984 (Best Drama Script, Sony Radio Awards, 1985; Prix Italia, 1985; perf. Almeida, 1990); Pity in History, BBC 2, 1985; A Hard Heart, Radio 3, 1992 (perf. Almeida, 1992); The Early Hours of a Reviled Man, Radio 3, 1992; A House of Correction, Albertina, Radio 3, 1999; Knowledge and a Girl, Radio 4, 2001. Opera (with Nigel Osborne) Terrible Mouth, ENO, Almeida, 1992. Formed The Wrestling School (company to perform own work), 1989: Wounds to the Face, 1997; Ursula, 1998; Und, 1999; The Ecstatic Bible, 2000; He Stumbled, 2000. *Publications: plays:* Stripwell, and Claw, 1977; Fair Slaughter, 1978; Love of a Good Man, and All Bleeding, 1981; That Good Between Us, and Credentials of a Sympathiser, 1981; No End of Blame: scenes of overcoming, 1981; Two Plays for the Right: Birth on a Hard Shouder, and The Loud Boy's Life, 1982; Hang of the Gaol, 1982; Victory: choices in reaction, 1983; The Castle, and Scenes from an Execution, 1984; Crimes in Hot Countries, and Fair Slaughter, 1984; Power of the Dog, 1985; A Passion in Six Days, and Downchild, 1985; The Last Supper: a New Testament, 1988; Lullabies for the Impatient, 1988; Possibilities, 1988; Pity in History, 1989; Seven Lears, and Golgo, 1990; Europeans, and Judith, 1990; Collected Plays, vol. I, 1990, vol II, 1993, vol. III, 1996, vol. IV, 1997, vol. V, 1999; A Hard Heart, 1992; The Early Hours of a Reviled Man, 1992; *poetry:* Don't Exaggerate (Desire and Abuse), 1985; Breath of the Crowd, 1986; Gary the Thief/Gary Upright, 1987; The Ascent of Monte Grappa, 1991; The Tortmann Diaries, 1996; *essays:* Arguments for a Theatre, 1989. *Address:* c/o Judy Daish Associates, 2 St Charles Place, W10 6EG.

BARKER, Hon. Sir Ian; *see* Barker, Hon. Sir R. I.

BARKER, John Francis Holroyd, CB 1984; Consultant, Cabinet Office, 1985–93; *b* 3 Feb. 1925; *s* of Rev. C.H. Barker and B.A. Barker (*née* Bullivant); *m* 1954, Felicity Ann (*née* Martindale); three *d.* *Educ:* King Edward's School, Stourbridge; Oriel College, Oxford. RNVR, 1943–46. Director of Music, Abingdon School, 1950–54; War Office/Ministry of Defence, 1954–85. *Recreation:* music. *Address:* c/o Coutts & Co., 440 Strand, WC2R 0QS. *Club:* Athenæum.

BARKER, Air Vice-Marshal John Lindsay, CB 1963; CBE 1946; DFC 1945; RAF (retired); *b* 12 Nov. 1910; *s* of Abraham Cockroft Barker and Lilian Alice (*née* Woods); *m* 1948, Eleanor Margaret Hannah (*d* 2001); one *s.* *Educ:* Trent Coll., Derbys; Brasenose Coll., Oxford. Called to the Bar, Middle Temple, 1947. RAFO, 1930, RAF, 1933. Served War of 1939–45: France, 1939–40; N Africa, 1942–44; Bomber Command, 1944–45; Far East, 1945–46; Palestine, 1946–48; Egypt, 1950–53; Air Attaché, Rome, 1955–58; Cmdr Royal Ceylon Air Force, 1958–63. Air Vice-Marshal, 1959. Retd, 1963. Order of Merit, Italy, 1958. *Recreations:* golf, photography, sailing. *Address:* Wreyland Barn, Wreyland Way, Lustleigh, Devon TQ13 9TS. *T:* (01647) 277556. *Club:* Royal Air Force.

BARKER, Rear-Adm. John Perronet, CB 1985; RN retired, 1986. Administration Secretary, Missions to Seamen, 1987–93; *b* 24 June 1930; *s* of late Gilbert Barker and Dorothy G. Barker (*née* Moore); *m* 1955, Priscilla, *d* of late Sir William Christie, KCIE, CSI, MC; two *s.* *Educ:* Edgbaston Prep. Sch., Birmingham; Nautical Coll., Pangbourne; BRNC, Dartmouth. Entered RN, 1948; served, 1949–72: HMS King George V, Glory, Condor, Ceres, Lagos, Hampshire and Centurion; staff of C-in-C Home Fleet, of C-in-C Nore and of Comdr British Navy Staff, Washington; Sec. to ACNS (OR), MoD (Navy), to Flag Officer 2FEF, and to Flag Officer Plymouth; Sec. to Controller of the Navy, 1972–76; Student, RCDS, 1977; Dir, Fleet Supply Duties, MoD (Navy), 1978–80; Cdre, HMS Centurion, 1980–83; Chief of Staff to C-in-C, Naval Home Command, 1983–85. Member: IYRU World Youth Sailing, 1986–; Assoc. of RN Officers, 1987–; Sea Cadet Assoc., 1986–95; Life Rear Cdre, RNSA, 1986; Chm. Mgt Cttee, YMCA Fairthorne Manor, 1997–; Trustee, Whitby Mission and Seafarers' Trust, 1993–. Freeman, Co. of Shipwrights, 1983. *Recreations:* sailing, gardening, DIY. *Address:* 25 Cambridge Road, Lee-on-the-Solent, Hants PO13 9DH. *Clubs:* Royal Yacht Squadron (Cowes); Royal Naval Sailing Association (Portsmouth); Midland Sailing (Birmingham).

BARKER, Katharine Mary, (Mrs P. R. Donovan); Chief Economic Advisor, Confederation of British Industry, since 1994; Member, Monetary Policy Committee, Bank of England, since 2001; *b* 29 Nov. 1957; *d* of Wilfred Barker and Eileen May (*née* Pinhorn); *m* 1982, Peter Richard Donovan; two *s.* *Educ:* St Hilda's Coll., Oxford (BA Hons PPE). Investment analyst, PO Pension Fund, 1979–81; Res. Officer, NIESR, 1981–85; Chief Economist, Ford of Europe, 1985–94. Mem., Panel of Independent Advrs, HM Treasury, 1996–97. Non-exec. Dir, Yorkshire Bldg Soc., 1999–. Mem., Bd of Govs, Anglia Poly. Univ., 1999–. *Publications:* contribs to jls. *Recreation:* bell-ringing. *Address:* Confederation of British Industry, Centre Point, 103 New Oxford Street, WC1A 1DU. *T:* (020) 7395 8099.

BARKER, Prof. Kenneth, CBE 1994; Vice-Chancellor, Thames Valley University, since 1999; *b* 26 June 1934; *s* of Thomas William and Lillian Barker; *m* 1958, Jean Ivy Pearl; one *s* one *d.* *Educ:* Royal Coll. of Music (ARCM); King's Coll., London (BMus); Sussex Univ. (MA). GRSM, FTCL, FLCM. Schoolmaster, 1958–62; lectr and university teacher, 1962–75; Principal, Gipsy Hill Coll., 1975; Pro-Dir, Kingston Polytechnic, 1975–86; Dep. Dir/Dir Designate, 1986–87, Dir, 1987–92, Leicester Poly., then Chief Exec. and Vice-Chancellor, De Montfort Univ., 1992–99. FRSA; CIMgt. Hon. DSc Moscow State Tech. Univ., 1995; DUniv: St Petersburg Univ. of Design and Technology, 1997; De Montfort, 1999. *Publications:* contribs to jls. *Recreations:* music, theatre, watching Rugby. *Address:* Bramshott, Church Road, Surbiton, Surrey KT6 5HH. *T:* (020) 8398 4700. *Clubs:* Athenæum, Reform, Institute of Directors.

BARKER, Nicolas John, FBA 1998; Editor, Book Collector, since 1965; *b* 6 Dec. 1932; *s* of Sir Ernest Barker, FBA, and Olivia Stuart Horner; *m* 1962, Joanna Mary Sophia Nyda Cotton; two *s* three *d.* *Educ:* Westminster Sch.; New Coll., Oxford (MA). With Bailliere, Tindall & Cox, 1958 and Rupert Hart-Davis, 1959; Asst Keeper, National Portrait Gallery, 1964; with Macmillan & Co. Ltd, 1965; with OUP, 1971; Dep. Keeper, British Library, 1976–92. William Andrews Clark Vis. Prof., UCLA, 1986–87; Scholar, Getty Center for History of Art and the Humanities, 1996; Sandars Reader in Bibliography, Cambridge Univ., 1999–2000. President: Amici Thomae Mori, 1978–89; Double Crown Club, 1980–81; Bibliographical Soc., 1981–85; Chairman: London Liby, 1994– (Mem. Cttee, 1971–); Liby Cttee, RHS, 1996–; Member: Publication Bd of Dirs, RNIB, 1969–92; BBC and ITV Appeals Adv. Cttee, 1977–86; Nat. Trust Arts Panel, 1979–91 (Libraries Advr, 1991–); Trustee, The Pilgrim Trust, 1977–; Chm., Laurence Sterne Trust, 1984–; Chm. Trustees, Type Mus., 1995–. DUniv York, 1994. *Publications:* The Publications of the Roxburghe Club, 1962; The Printer and the Poet, 1970; Stanley Morison, 1972; (ed) Essays and Papers of A. N. L. Munby, 1977; (ed) The Early Life of James McBey: an autobiography, 1883–1911, 1977; Bibliotheca Lindesiana, 1977; The Oxford University Press and the Spread of Learning 1478–1978, 1978; (with John Collins) A Sequel to an Enquiry,1983; Aldus Manutius and the Development of Greek Script and Type, 1985; The Butterfly Books, 1987; Two East Anglian Picture Books, 1988; (ed) Treasures of the British Library, 1989; (ed) S. Morison, Early Italian Writing-Books, 1990; (with Sir Anthony Wagner and A. Payne) Medieval Pageant, 1993; Hortus Eystettensis: the Bishop's Garden and Besler's Magnificent Book, 1994; The Great Book of Thomas Trevilian, 2000. *Address:* 22 Clarendon Road, W11 3AB. *T:* (020) 7727 4340. *Clubs:* Garrick, Beefsteak, Roxburghe; Roxburghe (San Francisco); Zamorano (Los Angeles).

BARKER, Patricia Margaret, CBE 2000; novelist, since 1982; *b* 8 May 1943; *d* of Moyra Drake; *m* 1978, David Faubert Barker, *qv*; one *s* one *d.* *Educ:* Grangefield GS; London School of Economics (BScEcon; Hon. Fellow, 1998); Durham Univ. (DipEd). Teacher, until 1982. Hon. MLitt Teesside, 1994; Hon. DLitt: Napier, 1996; Durham, 1998; Hertfordshire, 1998; DUniv Open, 1997. Author of the Year Award, Booksellers' Assoc., 1996. *Publications:* Union Street (Fawcett Prize), 1982; Blow Your House Down, 1984; The Century's Daughter, 1986 (retitled Liza's England, 1996); The Man Who Wasn't There, 1989; The Regeneration Trilogy: Regeneration, 1991 (filmed 1997); The Eye in the Door, 1993 (Guardian Fiction Prize, Northern Electric Special Arts Award, 1994); The Ghost Road (Booker Prize), 1995; Another World, 1998; Border Crossing, 2001. *Address:* c/o Gillon Aitken Associates, 29 Fernshaw Road, SW10 0TG. *T:* (020) 7351 7561.

BARKER, Paul; writer and broadcaster; *b* 24 Aug. 1935; *s* of Donald and Marion Barker; *m* 1960, Sally, *e d* of James and Marion Huddleston; three *s* one *d.* *Educ:* Hebden Bridge Grammar Sch.; Calder High Sch.; Brasenose Coll., Oxford (Hulme Exhibr), MA. Intell. Corps (commn), 1953–55. Lecteur, Ecole Normale Supérieure, Paris, 1958–59; The Times, 1959–63; New Society, staff writer, 1964; The Economist, 1964–65; New Society: Dep. Editor, 1965–68; Editor, 1968–86; Social Policy Ed., Sunday Telegraph, 1986–88; Associate Ed., The Independent Magazine, 1988–90. Evening Standard: townscape and arts columnist, 1987–92; social commentary, 1992–; social and political columnist, Sunday Times, 1990–91; columnist, New Statesman, 1996–99. Dir and Adv. Editor, The Fiction Magazine, 1982–87. Dir, Pennine Heritage, 1978–86. Vis. Fellow, Centre for Analysis of Social Policy, Univ. of Bath, 1986–2000; Leverhulme Res. Fellow, 1993–95; Res. Fellow in Architecture, Royal Commn for Exhibn of 1851, 2000–April 2002. Institute of Community Studies: Chm., 2000–01 (Trustee, 1991–2001); Fellow, 1992, Sen. Fellow,

1995, Sen. Res. Fellow, 2000. FRSA 1990. (Jtly) BPG Award for outstanding radio prog., My Country, Right or Wrong, 1988. *Publications:* (contrib.) Youth in New Society, 1966; (contrib.) Your Sunday Paper, 1967; (contrib. and ed) One for Sorrow, Two for Joy, 1972; (ed) A Sociological Portrait, 1972; (ed) The Social Sciences Today, 1975; (contrib. and ed) Arts in Society, 1977; (contrib. and ed) The Other Britain, 1982; (ed) Founders of the Welfare State, 1985; (contrib.) Britain in the Eighties, 1989; (contrib.) Towards a New Landscape, 1993; (contrib.) Young at Eighty, 1995; (contrib. and ed) Gulliver and Beyond, 1996; (contrib. and ed) Living as Equals, 1996; (ed jtly) A Critic Writes, 1997; (contrib.) Town and Country, 1998; (contrib.) Non-Plan, 2000. *Recreation:* driving along the motorway to a baroque church, with the radio on. *Address:* 15 Dartmouth Park Avenue, NW5 1JL. *T:* (020) 7485 8861.

BARKER, Peter William, CBE 1988; DL; Chairman, Fenner (formerly J. H. Fenner (Holdings)) PLC, 1982–93; *b* 24 Aug. 1928; *s* of William Henry George and Mabel Irene Barker; *m* 1961, Mary Rose Hainsworth, JP, DL; one *s* one *d*. *Educ:* Royal Liberty Sch., Romford; Dorking County High Sch.; South London Polytechnic. CIMgt; FInstD; FCIM. J. H. Fenner & Co., 1953–67; Jt Managing Dir, Fenner International, 1967–71; Chief Exec., J. H. Fenner (Holdings), 1971–82. Dir, Neepsend plc, 1984–93; Chm., Hartingdon Ltd, 1997–99. Member: Yorks and Humberside Regional Council, CBI, 1981–94 (Chm., 1991–93); National Council, CBI, 1985–95; Yorks and Humberside Regional Indust. Develt Bd, 1981–95 (Chm., 1992–95). Pro-Chancellor, Univ. of Hull, 1993–. Hon. DSc (Econ) Hull, 1992. FRSA. DL E Yorks (formerly Humberside), 1990; High Sheriff, Humberside, 1993–94. *Recreations:* sailing, ski-ing, tennis, music. *Address:* Swanland Rise, West Ella, East Yorks HU10 7SF. *T:* (01482) 653050. *Clubs:* Royal Yorkshire Yacht, Royal Thames Yacht.

BARKER, Hon. Sir (Richard) Ian, Kt 1994; arbitrator and mediator; Senior Judge, High Court of New Zealand, 1991–97; Chairman, Banking Ombudsman Commission, New Zealand, since 1997; *b* 17 March 1934; *s* of Archibald Henry Barker and Kate Dorothy Barker (*née* Humphrys); *m* 1965, Mary Christine Allardyce; two *s* three *d*. *Educ:* Auckland Univ. (BA, LLB, 1958). FCIArb; FInstArb (NZ). Called to the Bar, NZ, 1958; Partner, Morpeth, Gould & Co., solicitors, Auckland, 1968–80; Barrister, 1968–76; QC (NZ) 1973; Judge, High Court of NZ, 1976–97; Member, Court of Appeal: Cook Is, 1990–; Fiji, 1997–; Samoa, and Vanuatu, 1998–. Chancellor, Univ. of Auckland, 1991–99. President: Legal Res. Foundn of NZ, 1981–90; Arbitrators' and Mediators' Inst. of NZ, 2000–. Chartered Arbitrator (UK). Hon. LLD Auckland Univ., 1999. *Publications:* contrib. articles to NZ and Australian jls. *Recreations:* walking, reading, music, railways. *Address:* 18 Mahoe Avenue, Auckland 5, New Zealand. *Club:* Northern (Auckland).

BARKER, Richard Philip; Headmaster, Sevenoaks School, 1981–96; *b* 17 July 1939; *s* of late Philip Watson Barker and Helen May Barker; *m* 1966, Imogen Margaret Harris; two *s* one *d*. *Educ:* Repton; Trinity Coll., Cambridge (MA 1962); Bristol Univ. (Cert. Ed. 1963). Head of Geography, Bedales Sch., 1963–65; Founder Dir, A level business studies project, 1966–73; Lectr, Inst. of Education, London Univ., 1973–74; Housemaster, Marlborough Coll., 1973–81. Resident Gov., British Sch., Colombo, Sri Lanka, 1996–97; Governor: Epsom Coll., 1996– (Chm.); Worth Sch., 1999–. Chm., Friends of Yehudi Menuhin Sch., 1996–. Mem., RSA. *Publications:* (ed) Understanding Business Series, (annually) 1976–. *Recreations:* educational interests, beekeeping, fishing, repairing buildings, travelling. *Address:* Oldfield Farm House, Stoke D'Abernon, Cobham, Surrey KT11 3QE. *T:* (01932) 862634; *e-mail:* barker@totalise.co.uk.

BARKER, Ronald Hugh, PhD; BSc; CEng, FIEE, FIMechE; Deputy Director, Royal Armament Research and Development Establishment, 1965–75, retired; *b* 28 Oct. 1915; *s* of E. W. Barker and L. A. Taylor; *m* 1943, W. E. Hunt; two *s*. *Educ:* University of Hull. Physicist, Standard Telephones and Cables, 1938–41; Ministry of Supply, 1941–59; Dep. Dir, Central Electricity Research Laboratories, 1959–62; Technical Dir, The Pullin Group Ltd, 1962–65. *Publications:* various, on servomechanisms and control systems. *Address:* Cramond, 17 Dewlands Way, Verwood, Dorset BH31 6JN.

BARKER, Ronnie, (Ronald William George Barker), OBE 1978; actor, retired 1987; *b* 25 Sept. 1929; *s* of Leonard and Edith Barker; *m* 1957, Joy Tubb; two *s* one *d*. *Educ:* Oxford High Sch. Started acting career, Aylesbury Rep. Co., 1948. *Plays (West End):* Mourning Becomes Electra, 1955; Summertime, 1955; Listen to the Wind, 1955; Double Image, 1956; Camino Real, 1957; Lysistrata, 1958; Irma la Douce, 1958; Platanov, 1960; On the Brighter Side, 1961; Midsummer Night's Dream, 1962; Real Inspector Hound, 1968; The Two Ronnies, Palladium, 1978. *Films include:* Robin and Marian, 1975; Picnic, 1975; Porridge, 1979. *Television: series:* Seven Faces of Jim, 1965; Frost Report, 1966–67; Hark at Barker, 1968–69; Six Dates with Barker, 1970; The Two Ronnies, 10 series, 1971–86; Twenty Years of the Two Ronnies, 1986; Porridge, 1974, 1975, 1976, 1977; Open All Hours, 1976, 1981, 1982; Going Straight, 1978; Clarence, 1987. Awards: Variety Club, 1969, 1974, 1980; SFTA, 1971; Radio Industries Club, 1973, 1974, 1977, 1981; Water Rats, 1975; British Acad. Award, 1975, 1977, 1978; Royal Television Society's award for outstanding creative achievement, 1975; British Comedy Award for lifetime achievement, 1990; Lifetime Achievement Award, BBC, 1996. *Publications:* Book of Bathing Beauties, 1974; Book of Boudoir Beauties, 1975; It's Goodnight From Him, 1976; Sauce, 1977; Gentlemen's Relish, 1979; Sugar and Spice, 1981; Ooh-la-la!, 1983; Pebbles on the Beach, 1985; A Pennyworth of Art, 1986; Dancing in the Moonlight (autobiog.), 1993; All I Ever Wrote, 1999. *Recreations:* writing song lyrics, collecting postcards.

BARKER, Prof. Theodore Cardwell, PhD; FRHistS; Professor of Economic History, University of London, 1976–83, now Emeritus and engaged in research; *b* 19 July 1923; *s* of Norman Humphrey Barker and Louie Nettleton Barker (*née* Cardwell); *m* 1955, Joy Marie (Judith) Pierce. *Educ:* Cowley Sch., St Helens; Jesus Coll., Oxford (MA); Manchester Univ. (PhD). FRHistS 1963. Econ. History staff, LSE, 1953–64; first Prof. of Econ. and Social Hist., Univ. of Kent at Canterbury, 1964–76. President: Internat. Historical Congress, 1990–95 (Chm., British Nat. Cttee, 1978–93; Mem. Bureau, 1995–); Econ. Hist. Soc., 1986–89 (Hon. Sec., 1960–86); Railway and Canal Hist. Soc., 1986–88; Chairman: Management Cttee, Inst. of Historical Res., London Univ., 1977–88; Hist. Bd, CNAA, 1977–81; Management Cttee, London Univ. Business History Unit, 1979–86; Debrett's Business History Research Ltd, 1984–89; Athlone Press Adv. Cttee, 1988–. Chairman: Oral Hist. Soc., 1973–76; Transport History Res. Trust, 1991–97. Mem. Council, RHistS, 1967–70 and 1974–77. Hon. DLitt Manchester Metropolitan, 1998. *Publications:* A Merseyside Town in the Industrial Revolution (with J. R. Harris), 1954, repr. 1993; A History of the Girdlers Company, 1957; Pilkington Brothers and the Glass Industry, 1960; (with R. H. Campbell, Peter Mathias and B. S. Yamey) Business History, 1960, 2nd edn 1970; (with R. M. Robbins) A History of London Transport: Vol. I, 1963, Vol. II, 1974; (ed with J. C. McKenzie and John Yudkin) Our Changing Fare: two hundred years of British food habits, 1966; (with B. W. E. Alford) A History of the Worshipful Company of Carpenters, 1968; (ed) The Long March of Everyman, 1974; (with M. J. Hatcher) A History of British Pewter, 1974; (with C. I. Savage) An Economic History of Transport, 1975; The Glassmakers, 1977; The Transport Contractors of Rye, 1982; (ed with Michael Drake) The Population Factor, 1982; (ed) The Economic and Social Effects of the Spread of Motor Vehicles, 1987; Moving Millions, 1990; (with Dorian Gerhold) The Rise and Rise of Road Transport 1700–1990, 1993; (ed with Anthony Sutcliffe) Megalopolis: the giant city in history, 1993; A Short, Illustrated and Updated History of Pilkington, 1994. *Recreations:* walking, motoring, visiting parts of Europe which many others do not reach. *Address:* Minsen Dane, Brogdale Road, Faversham, Kent ME13 8YA. *T:* (01795) 533523. *Club:* Reform (Mem., Gen. Cttee, 1997–).

BARKER, Thomas Christopher; HM Diplomatic Service, retired; *b* 28 June 1928; *m* 1960, Griselda Helen Cormack; two *s* one *d*. *Educ:* Uppingham (Schol.); New Coll., Oxford (Schol.). MA, Lit Hum, 1952; Gaisford Prize for Greek Verse. 2nd Lt, 1st Bn, The Worcestershire Regt, 1947–48. HM Foreign Service, 1952; Third Sec., Paris, 1953–55; Second Sec., Baghdad, 1955–58; FO, 1958–62; First Sec., Head of Chancery and Consul, Mexico City, 1962–67; FO, 1967–69; Counsellor and Head of Chancery, Caracas, 1969–71; FCO, 1971–75; seconded as Under Sec., NI Office, Belfast, 1976. Curator, 1978–87, Secretary to Trustees, 1987–93, Scottish Nat. War Meml, Edinburgh.

BARKER, Timothy Gwynne; Vice Chairman, Dresdner Kleinwort Benson (formerly Kleinwort Benson Group plc), since 1993 (Director, since 1988; Deputy Chief Executive, 1990–93); Director, Kleinwort Benson Ltd, since 1973 (Vice-Chairman, since 1989); *b* 8 April 1940; *s* of late Frank Richard Peter Barker and Hon. Olwen Gwynne (*née* Philipps); *m* 1964, Philippa Rachel Mary Thursby-Pelham; one *s* one *d*. *Educ:* Eton Coll.; McGill Univ., Montreal; Jesus Coll., Cambridge (MA). Director-General: City Panel on Take-overs and Mergers, 1984–85; Council for the Securities Industry, 1984–85; Hd of Corporate Finance, Kleinwort Benson Ltd, 1986–90. Mem., CBI Econ. Affairs Cttee, 1997–. *Address:* 20 Fenchurch Street, EC3P 3DB. *T:* (020) 7623 8000.

BARKER, Trevor; Chairman, Alpha Consolidated Holdings Ltd, since 1988; *b* 24 March 1935; *s* of Samuel Lawrence Barker and Lilian Barker (*née* Dawson); *m* 1957, Joan Elizabeth Cross; one *s* one *d*. *Educ:* Acklam Hall Grammar School. FCA. Price Waterhouse & Co., 1957–58; Cooper Brothers, 1958–62; sole practitioner, 1962–70; Chm. and Chief Exec., Gold Case Travel, 1964–77; Dir, Ellerman Wilson Lines, 1977–80; Chairman: John Crowther Gp, 1980–88; William Morris Fine Arts, 1981–88; Micklegate Gp, 1989–95; Drew Scientific Gp, 1993–95; Dep. Chm., Blanchards, 1988–94; Dir, Darlington Bldg Soc., 1994–2000. FRSA 1989. Liveryman, Co. of Woolmen, 1986. *Recreations:* grandchildren, breeding and racing thoroughbred horses, opera, music, literature, the arts. *Address:* Windholme, 327 Coniscliffe Road, Darlington, Co. Durham DL3 8AH. *T:* (01325) 350436.

BARKING, Area Bishop of, since 1991; **Rt Rev. Roger Frederick Sainsbury;** *b* 2 Oct. 1936; *s* of Frederick William Sainsbury and Lillian Maude Sainsbury; *m* 1960, Jennifer Marguerite Carey. *Educ:* High Wycombe Royal Grammar School; Jesus Coll., Cambridge (MA); Clifton Theological Coll., Curate, Christ Church, Spitalfields, 1960–63; Missioner, Shrewsbury House, Liverpool, 1963–74; Warden, Mayflower Family Centre, Canning Town, 1974–81; Priest-in-Charge, St Luke, Victoria Dock, 1978–81; Vicar of Walsall, 1981–87; Rector, Walsall Team Ministry, 1987–88; Archdeacon of West Ham, 1988–91. Alderman, London Borough of Newham, 1976–78. Moderator, Churches' Commn for Racial Justice, 1999–; Chairman: Frontier Youth Trustees, 1987–92; Barking Area Church Leaders Gp, 1994–; Urban Bishops Panel, 1996–; London Churches Gp, 1998–; Trustees, Children in Distress, 1998–. *Publications:* From a Mersey Wall, 1970; Justice on the Agenda, 1985; Lifestyle, 1986; Rooted and Grounded in Love, 1988; God of New Beginnings, 1990; Barking Mad Letters, 1999. *Recreations:* cricket, football supporting, stone polishing. *Address:* Barking Lodge, 110 Capel Road, Forest Gate, E7 0JS. *T:* (020) 8478 2456.

BARKSHIRE, John; *see* Barkshire, R. R. St J.

BARKSHIRE, Robert Hugh, CBE 1968; *b* 24 Oct. 1909; *yr s* of late Lt-Col Charles Robert Barkshire, OBE; *m* 1934, Sally Blunt (*d* 1992); one *s*. *Educ:* King's Sch., Bruton. Bank of England, 1927–55: Private Sec. to the Governor (C. F. Cobbold, later Lord Cobbold), 1949–53; Sec. to Cttee of London Clearing Bankers, British Bankers' Assoc., Bankers' Clearing House, and Mem., various inter-Bank Cttees, 1955–70; Hon. Sec., Meetings of Officers of European Bankers' Assocs, 1959–72; Gen. Comr of Income Tax for City of London, 1969–78; Governor, NIESR, 1970–78. FCIB (FIB 1960). Freeman, City of London. *Address:* The Dower House, Headbourne Worthy, Winchester, Hants SO23 7JG. *Club:* Royal Thames Yacht.

See also R. R. St J. Barkshire.

BARKSHIRE, Robert Renny St John, (John), CBE 1990; TD; JP; DL; banker; *b* 31 Aug. 1935; *s* of Robert Hugh Barkshire, *qv*; *m* 1st, 1960, Margaret Elizabeth Robinson (marr. diss. 1990); two *s* one *d*; 2nd, 1990, Audrey Mary Anne Witham. *Educ:* Bedford School. ACIB. Served Duke of Wellington's Regt, 2nd Lieut, 1953–55; HAC, 1955–74 (CO, 1970–72; Regtl Col, 1972–74). Joined Cater Ryder & Co., 1955, Jt Man. Dir, 1963–72; Chm., Mercantile House Holdings plc, 1972–87; Non-exec. Dir, Extel Gp PLC, 1979–87 (Dep. Chm., 1986–87); Chairman: CL-Alexanders Laing & Cruickshank Hldgs Ltd, 1984–88; Internat. Commodities Clearing House Ltd, 1986–90. Chm., Financial Futures Wkg Pty, 1980, later LIFFE Steering Cttee, 1981–82; Dir, LIFFE, 1982–91 (Chm., 1982–85); Member: Adv. Bd, Internat. Monetary Market Div., Chicago Mercantile Exchange, 1981–84; London Adv. Bd, Bank Julius Baer, 1988–91. Chairman: Uplink Ltd (EPN Satellite Service), 1988–90; Chaco Investments Ltd, 1994–2001; non-executive Director: Household Mortgage Corp., 1985–94; Savills, 1988–95; Sun Life and Provincial Holdings plc, 1988–99; TR Property Investment Trust plc, 1993–. Chm., Eastbourne Hosps NHS Trust, 1993–99. Chm., Cttee on Market in Single Properties, 1985–2000. Gen. Comr for Income Tax, City of London, 1981–. Chairman: Reserve Forces Assoc., 1983–87; Sussex TA Cttee, 1983–85; SE TAVRA, 1985–91; Dep. Chm., TA Sport Bd, 1983–95 (Mem., 1979–95). Financial Advisor: Victory Services Assoc. (formerly Club), 1981–95; RE Central Mgt Investments Policy Cttee, 1988–; RBL Mgt Bd, 1991–; Army Central Fund, 1995–; Royal Signals Trustees Ltd, 1996–; Dir, Officers' Pensions Soc. Investment Co. Ltd, 1982–95; Member: Regular Forces Employment Assoc. Council, 1986–95; SSAFA Council (Trustee and Mem. Exec. and Finance Cttee), 1996–; Man. Trustee, Regtl Assoc., Duke of Wellington's Regt, 1990–; Trustee, Army Benevolent Fund (Pres., E Sussex Br., 1999–). Chairman: E Sussex Br., Magistrates' Assoc., 1986–91; E Sussex Magistrates' Courts Cttee, 1993–97 and 1999–2001; Sussex Magistrates' Courts Cttee, 2001–. Mem., Chiddingly Parish Council, 1979–86; Treas., Burwash PCC, 1999–. Chm., Chiddingly and Dist RBL, 1982–87; Vice Pres., St James Br., RBL, 1991–; Mem., Burwash RBL, 1994–. Governor: Harpur Trust, 1984–89 (Chm., Bedford Sch. Cttee, 1984–89); Eastbourne Coll., 1980–95 (Vice Chm., 1983–92); Roedean Sch., 1984–89; Burwash Primary C of E Sch., 1999–; Comr, Duke of York's Royal Military Sch., 1986–95. Freeman, City of London, 1973; Liveryman, Worshipful Co. of Farmers, 1981. JP Lewes, 1980; DL E Sussex, 1986. *Recreations:* sailing, shooting. *Address:* Denes House, High Street, Burwash, East Sussex TN19 7EH. *T:* (01435) 882646. *Clubs:* City of London, Cavalry and Guards, MCC; Royal Fowey Yacht (Cornwall).

BARKWORTH, Peter Wynn; actor, since 1948; director, since 1980; *b* 14 Jan. 1929; *s* of Walter Wynn Barkworth and Irene May Barkworth. *Educ:* Stockport Sch.; Royal Academy of Dramatic Art. Folkestone and Sheffield Repertory Cos, 1948–51. West End plays include: A Woman of No Importance, Savoy, 1953; Roar Like a Dove, Phoenix, 1957–60; The School for Scandal, Haymarket, 1962; Crown Matrimonial, Haymarket, 1972; Donkeys' Years, Globe, 1976; Can You Hear Me at the Back?, Piccadilly, 1979; A Coat of Varnish, Haymarket, 1982; Siegfried Sassoon, Apollo, 1987; Hidden Laughter, Vaudeville, 1990; The Winslow Boy, Globe, 1994. Director: Night and Day, Leatherhead, 1980; Sisterly Feelings, nat. tour, 1982; The Eight O'Clock Muse, Riverside Studios, 1989. Television serials: The Power Game, 1966; Manhunt, 1969; Telford's Change, 1979; Winston Churchill: the wilderness years, 1981; The Price, 1985; Late Starter, 1985; The Gospel According to St Matthew, 1986. Film: Champions, 1984. Awards: Best Actor, BAFTA, 1974 and 1977; Royal TV Soc. and Broadcasting Press Guild, 1977 (both 1977 awards for Professional Foul). *Publications:* About Acting, 1980; First Houses, 1983; More About Acting, 1984; The Complete About Acting, 1991; For All Occasions, 1997. *Recreations:* walking, gardening, music, looking at paintings. *Address:* 47 Flask Walk, NW3 1HH. *T:* (020) 7794 4591. *Club:* British Academy of Film and Television Arts.

BARLING, Gerald Edward; QC 1991; practising in EC Law, London and Brussels, since 1981; a Recorder, since 1993; *b* 18 Sept. 1949; *s* of Banks Hubert Barling and Barbara Margarita (*née* Myerscough); *m* 1983, Myriam Frances (*née* Ponsford); three *d*. *Educ:* St Mary's Coll., Blackburn; New Coll., Oxford (Burnett Open Exhibnr in Classics, 1968; Hons Sch. of Jurisprudence (1st Cl.), 1971; MA). Called to the Bar, Middle Temple, 1972 (Harmsworth Entrance Exhibnr, 1971; Astbury Law Scholar, 1973; Bencher, 2001). Practised at Common Law Bar, Manchester, 1973–81; an Asst Recorder, 1990–93. Lectr in Law, New Coll., Oxford, 1972–77. Chairman: Western European Sub-Cttee, Bar Council, 1991–92; Bar European Gp, 1994–96 (Vice-Chm., 1992–94). *Publications:* (contrib.) Butterworth's European Court Practice, 1991; (co-ed) Practitioner's Handbook of EC Law, 1998; papers on different aspects of EC Law. *Recreations:* fishing, forestry, family. *Address:* Brick Court Chambers, 7–8 Essex Street, WC2R 3LD. *T:* (020) 7379 3550; avenue d'Auderghem 36, 1040 Brussels, Belgium.

BARLOW, Sir Christopher Hilaro, 7th Bt *cr* 1803; architect; *b* 1 Dec. 1929; *s* of Sir Richard Barlow, 6th Bt, AFC, and Rosamund Sylvia, *d* of late F. S. Anderton (she; *m* 2nd, 1950, Rev. Leonard Haslet Morrison, MA); *S* father, 1946; *m* 1952, J. C. de M. Audley, *e d* of late J. E. Audley, Cheshire; one *s* two *d* (and one *s* decd). *Educ:* Eton; McGill Univ., Montreal. BArch. MRAIC. Past Pres., Newfoundland Architects' Assoc. Lt Governor's Silver Medal, 1953. *Heir: s* Crispian John Edmund Audley Barlow, Chief Ranger, Ibhubesi Wildlife Service, S Africa, [*b* 20 April 1958; *m* 1981, Anne Waiching Siu; one *d*]. *Address:* 18 Winter Avenue, St John's, Newfoundland A1A 1T3, Canada.

BARLOW, Prof. David Hearnshaw, MD; Nuffield Professor of Obstetrics and Gynaecology, University of Oxford, since 1990; Fellow, Oriel College, Oxford, since 1990; *b* 26 Dec. 1949; *s* of Archibald and Anne Barlow; *m* 1973, Norma Christie Woodrow; one *s* one *d*. *Educ:* Clydebank High Sch.; Univ. of Glasgow (BSc Hons Biochem. 1971; MB ChB 1975; MD 1982); MA Oxon 1985. FRCOG 1993. MRC Trng Fellowship, 1977–78; Hall Tutorial Fellow, Univ. of Glasgow, 1979–81; Sen. Registrar, Queen Mother's Hosp., Glasgow, 1981–84; Clinical Reader in Obstetrics and Gynaecology, Univ. of Oxford, 1984–90; Fellow, Green Coll., Oxford, 1984–90, Hon. Sen. Associate Mem., 1990; Hon. Consultant Obstetrician and Gynaecologist, The Women's Centre, Oxford Radcliffe (formerly John Radcliffe) Hosp., Oxford, 1984–. Chm., DoH Adv. Gp on Osteoporosis (report published, 1995); Mem., HFEA, 1998–. Mem. Council, RCOG, 1996–. Mem., Nat. Osteoporosis Soc., 1995–; Trustee, Nat. Endometriosis Soc., 1997–; Treas., British Menopause Soc. Blair Bell Meml Lectr, RCOG, 1985. Founder FMedSci 1998. *Publications:* scientific publications in field of reproduction, particularly on endometriosis, the menopause and IVF. *Recreations:* wide-ranging interest in music, painting. *Address:* Nuffield Department of Obstetrics and Gynaecology, Oxford Radcliffe Hospital, Headington, Oxford OX3 9DU. *T:* (01865) 221008.

BARLOW, David John; broadcasting consultant; Adviser on International Relations, BBC, since 1993; *b* 20 Oct. 1937; *s* of Ralph and Joan Barlow; *m* 1981, Sanchia Béatrice Oppenheimer (marr. diss. 1998); two *s* one *d*, and three *s* of previous marr. *Educ:* Leighton Park Sch.; The Queen's Coll., Oxford; Leeds Univ. MA, DipEd (Oxon); DipESL (Leeds). British Council, 1962–63; BBC, 1963–: Producer, African Service; Schools Broadcasting, 1965–67; Programme Organiser, Hindi, Tamil, Nepali and Bengali Service, 1967–70; Further Educn Radio, 1970–71; UNESCO, British Council Consultancies, 1970–73; Head of Liaison Internat. Relations, 1974–76; Chief Asst Regions, 1977–79; Gen. Sec., ITCA, 1980–81; BBC: Sec., 1981–84; Controller: Public Affairs and Internat. Relations, 1984–86; Public Affairs, 1986–87; Regional Broadcasting, 1987–90; seconded to EBU as Co-ordinator for Audio Visual Eureka Project, 1990–91; Controller, Information Services and Internat. Relns, 1991–92. Mem., RTS, 1980–. *Recreations:* bird watching, mountains, books. *Address:* 7 Priory Close, Harrold, Beds MK43 7DL. *T:* (01234) 720584. *Club:* English-Speaking Union.

BARLOW, David Michael Rigby, CB 1996; Under Secretary, Government Legal Service, 1989–96; *b* 8 June 1936; *s* of late Samuel Gordon Barlow and Eunice Hodson Barlow; *m* 1973, Valeree Elizabeth Rush-Smith; one *s*; one *d* by previous marr. *Educ:* Shrewsbury Sch.; Christ Church, Oxford (MA Law). National Service: Midshipman RNVR in Submarine Br. of RN, 1954–56; Sub-Lieut and Lieut in permanent RNR, 1956–61. Solicitor, England and Wales, 1965, NI, 1991. Appointments as a lawyer in the public service, 1965–73; Asst Sec. in Govt Legal Service, 1973–89. *Recreations:* Spanish language and culture, ski-ing, cinema.

BARLOW, Prof. Frank, CBE 1989; MA, DPhil; FBA 1970; FRSL 1971; Professor of History and Head of Department, University of Exeter, 1953–76, now Emeritus Professor; *b* 19 April 1911; *e s* of Percy Hawthorn and Margaret Julia Barlow; *m* 1936, Moira Stella Brigid Garvey; two *s*. *Educ:* Newcastle High Sch.; St John's Coll., Oxford. Open Schol., St John's Coll., Oxford, 1929; 1st Cl. Hons Sch. of Modern History, 1933; Bryce Student, 1933; Oxford Senior Student, 1934.; BLitt, 1934; Fereday Fellow, St John's Coll., Oxford, 1935–38; DPhil 1937. Asst Lecturer, University Coll., London, 1936–40; War service in the Army, 1941–46, commissioned into Intelligence Corps, demobilised as Major; Lecturer 1946, Reader 1949, Dep. Vice-Chancellor, 1961–63, Public Orator, 1974–76, University of Exeter. Hon. DLitt Exon, 1981. *Publications:* The Letters of Arnulf of Lisieux, 1939; Durham Annals and Documents of the Thirteenth Century, 1945; Durham Jurisdictional Peculiars, 1950; The Feudal Kingdom of England, 1955; (ed and trans.) The Life of King Edward the Confessor, 1962; The English Church, 1000–1066, 1963; William I and the Norman Conquest, 1965; Edward the Confessor, 1970; (with Martin Biddle, Olof von Feilitzen and D. J. Keene) Winchester in the Early Middle Ages, 1976; The English Church 1066–1154, 1979; The Norman Conquest and Beyond (selected papers), 1983; William Rufus, 1983; Thomas Becket, 1986; Introduction to Devonshire Domesday Book, 1991; English Episcopal Acta, xi–xii (Exeter 1046–1257), 1996; (ed and trans.) Carmen de Hastingae Proelio, 1999. *Recreation:* gardening. *Address:* Middle Court Hall, Kenton, Exeter EX6 8NA. *T:* (01626) 890438.

BARLOW, Sir Frank, Kt 1998; CBE 1993; Chairman, Logica, since 1995; *b* 25 March 1930; *s* of John and Isabella Barlow; *m* 1950, Constance Patricia Ginns (*d* 2000); one *s* two *d*. *Educ:* Barrow Grammar Sch., Cumbria. Nigerian Electricity Supply Corp., 1952–59; Daily Times, Nigeria, 1960–62; Managing Director: Ghana Graphic, 1962–63; Barbados Advocate, 1963; Trinidad Mirror Newspapers, 1963–64; Gen. Manager, Daily Mirror, 1964–67; Man. Dir, King & Hutchings, 1967–75; Dir and Gen. Manager, Westminster Press, 1975–83; Dir, Economist, 1983–99; Chief Executive: Financial Times Group, 1983–90 (Chm., 1993–96); Westminster Press Group, 1985–90; Man. Dir, Pearson plc, 1990–96; Chm., BSkyB, 1991–95. Pres., Les Echos, Paris, 1988–90; Director: Elsevier (UK), 1991–94; Soc. Européene des Satellites SA, 2000–; Chm., Lottery Products Ltd, 1997–. Dir, Press Assoc., 1985–93. Chm., Printers' Charitable Corp., 1995–. Dir, Royal Philharmonic Orch., 1988–93. *Recreations:* golf, fell walking, angling. *Address:* Stephenson House, 75 Hampstead Road, NW1 2PL; Tremarne, Marsham Way, Gerrards Cross, Bucks SL9 8AW. *Club:* Carlton.

BARLOW, George Francis, OBE 1998; FRICS; Chairman, London Development Agency, since 2000; Chief Executive (formerly Director), Peabody Trust, 1987–99; *b* 26 May 1939; *s* of late George and Agnes Barlow; *m* 1969, Judith Alice Newton; one *s* two *d*. *Educ:* Wimbledon Coll.; Hammersmith Sch. of Art and Building; Polytechnic of Central London. Surveyor, Building Design Partnership, 1962–67; Develt Surveyor, GLC Housing Dept, 1967–70; The Housing Develt Officer, London Borough of Camden, 1970–76; Dir/Sec., Metropolitan Housing Trust, 1976–87. External Examiner, Polytechnic of Central London, 1989–90. Mem., Housing Cttee, 1986–91, Chm., Housing Policy Panel, 1996–99, RICS; Chm., London Housing Assocs Council, 1978–82; Dep. Chm., London Develt Partnership, 1998–2000; Member: Central YMCA Housing Assoc., 1982–85; Council, Nat. Fedn of Housing Assocs, 1985–89; Cttee, Community Self Build Agency, 1989–94; Cttee, Broomleigh Housing Assoc., 1989–95; Trustee, Kent Community Housing Trust, 1989–92; Mem. Bd, East London Partnership, 1991–99. Chm., Youth Homelessness Cttee, Prince's Trust/BITC, 1994–98. Gov., Univ. of E London, 1996–2000. Sen. Associate, King's Fund, 1999–. FRSA 2000. *Publications:* articles in Housing Review and Voluntary Housing. *Recreations:* theatre, travel, supporter of Crystal Palace FC. *Address:* London Development Agency, Romney House, Massham Street, SW1P 3PY.

BARLOW, Sir (George) William, Kt 1977; BSc Tech, FREng, FIMechE, FIEE; President, Royal Academy of Engineering (formerly Fellowship of Engineering), 1991–96; Chairman, Parsons Brinckerhoff (formerly Kennedy and Donkin) Holdings, since 1997; *b* 8 June 1924; *s* of Albert Edward and Annice Barlow; *m* 1948, Elaine Mary Atherton (*née* Adamson); one *s* one *d*. *Educ:* Manchester Grammar Sch.; Manchester Univ. (Kitchener Schol., Louis Atkinson Schol.; BSc Tech. 1st cl. Hons Elec. Engrg, 1944). Served as Elec. Lt, RNVR, 1944–47. Various appts, The English Electric Co. Ltd (in Spain, 1952–55, Canada, 1958–62); Gen. Manager, Liverpool and Netherton, 1964–67; Managing Director: English Electric Domestic Appliance Co. Ltd, 1965–67; English Electric Computers Ltd, 1967–68; Gp Chief Exec., 1969–77, Chm., 1971–77, Ransome Hoffman Pollard Ltd; Chm., Post Office, 1977–80, organized separation of Post Office and British Telecom, 1980; Chairman: Thorn EMI Engrg Gp, 1980–84; Ericsson, 1981–94; BICC, 1984–91 (Dir, 1980–91); SKF (UK), 1990–92; Barking Power Ltd, 1992–93; Director: Vodafone Group, 1988–98; Waste Management International, 1992–98; Chemring Gp, 1994–97. Chm., NICG, 1980. Member: Industrial Develt Adv. Bd, 1972–79; Electronics EDC, 1981–83; Council, IEE, 1969–72 (Vice-Pres., 1978–80, Dep. Pres., 1983–84; Hon. Fellow, 1990); Council, IMechE, 1971–74; National Electronics Council, 1982–94; President: BEAMA, 1986–87; ORGALIME, 1990–92; Chm., Ferrous Foundries Adv. Cttee, 1975–78; Vice Pres., City and Guilds of London Inst., 1982–92. Chairman: Design Council, 1980–86; Engineering Council, 1988–90. Pres., Assoc. of Lancastrians in London, 1981 and 1992. Trustee, Brain Res. Trust, 1987–99. Governor, London Business Sch., 1979–92 (Hon. Fellow, 1991). Master, Worshipful Company of Engineers, 1986–87. CIMgt (CBIM 1971). Hon. FUMIST 1978; Hon. FIEE 1990; Hon. FICE 1991; Hon. FIMechE 1993; Hon. FCGI 1996. Hon. DSc: Cranfield, 1979; Bath, 1986; Aston, 1988; City, 1989; Hon. DTech: CNAA, 1988; Loughborough, 1993; Hon DEng UMIST, 1996. *Recreations:* golf, racing. *Address:* 4 Parkside, Henley-on-Thames, Oxon RG9 1TX. *T:* (01491) 411101. *Clubs:* Army and Navy, Brooks's; Leander (Henley-on-Thames); Huntercombe Golf.

BARLOW, Dr Horace Basil, FRS 1969; Royal Society Research Professor, Physiological Laboratory, Cambridge University, 1973–87; *b* 8 Dec. 1921; *s* of Sir (James) Alan (Noel) Barlow, 2nd Bt, GCB, KBE and Nora Barlow (*née* Darwin); *m* 1st, 1954, Ruthala (marr. diss., 1970), *d* of late Dr M. H. Salaman; four *d*; 2nd, 1980, Miranda, *d* of John Weston Smith; one *s* three *d*. *Educ:* Winchester; Trinity Coll., Cambridge. Research Fellow, Trinity Coll., 1950–54, Lectr, King's Coll., Cambridge, 1954–64. Demonstrator and Asst Dir of Research, Physiological Lab., Cambridge, 1954–64; Prof. of Physiological Optics and Physiology, Univ. of Calif, Berkeley, 1964–73. Australia Prize, 1993; Royal Medal, Royal Soc., 1993. *Publications:* several, on neurophysiology of vision in Jl of Physiology, and elsewhere. *Address:* Trinity College, Cambridge CB2 1TQ.

See also Sir T. E. Barlow, Bt.

BARLOW, Sir John (Kemp), 3rd Bt *cr* 1907, of Bradwall Hall, Sandbach; merchant banker and farmer; Chairman: Thomas Barlow and Bro. Ltd; Barlow Services Ltd; Majedie Investments plc, since 1978; Director of other companies; *b* 22 April 1934; *s* of Sir John Denman Barlow, 2nd Bt and Hon. Diana Helen (*d* 1986), *d* of 1st Baron Rochdale, CB and *sister* of 1st Viscount Rochdale, OBE, TD; *S* father, 1986; *m* 1st, 1962, Susan (marr. diss. 1998), *er d* of Col Sir Andrew Horsbrugh-Porter, 3rd Bt, DSO; four *s*; 2nd, 1998, Mrs Pauline Windsor. *Educ:* Winchester; Trinity Coll., Cambridge (MA 1958). Chm., Rubber Growers' Assoc., 1974. Steward of the Jockey Club, 1988–90. High Sheriff, Cheshire, 1979. *Recreations:* steeplechasing, hunting, shooting. *Heir: s* John William Marshall Barlow [*b* 12 March 1964; *m* 1991, Sarah Nobes; three *s*]. *Clubs:* Brooks's, City of London, Jockey.

BARLOW, Patrick; actor, writer, director; *b* 18 March 1947; *s* of Edward Morgan and Sheila Maud Barlow; two *s* one *d*. *Educ:* Uppingham Sch.; Birmingham Univ. (BA 1968). Founder mem., Inter-Action Community Arts, 1968–72; Dir, Lancaster Young People's Theatre, 1972–74; Founder Dir, Solent People's Theatre, 1974–76; created Henrietta Sluggett and appeared nationwide in clubs, streets, theatres, incl. Crucible, Sheffield, Haymarket, Leicester and NT, 1976–79; created *National Theatre of Brent*, 1980, appeared in and wrote jointly: stage: Charge of the Light Brigade, 1980; Zulu!, 1981; Black Hole of Calcutta, 1982; Götterdämmerung, 1982; The Messiah, 1983, (up-dated) 2000; Complete Guide to Sex, 1984; Greatest Story Ever Told, 1987; Mysteries of Sex, 1997; Love Upon the Throne, 1998; television: Messiah, 1983; Mighty Moments from World History, Lawrence of Arabia, Dawn of Man, Boadicea, Arthur and Guinevere, 1985;

Revolution!!, 1989; created Royal Dingle Co. for Oh Dear Purcell!, 1995; Massive Landmarks of the Twentieth Century, 1999; *other stage appearances* incl.: Truscott, in Loot, Manchester Royal Exchange, 1987; Humphry, in Common Pursuit, Phoenix, 1988; Pseudolus, in A Funny Thing Happened on the Way to the Forum, Manchester Liby Th., 1988; Sidney, in Silly Cow, Haymarket, 1991; Toad, in Wind in the Willows, RNT, 1994; *television* incl.: Talk to Me, 1983; All Passion Spent, 1986; Thank You Miss Jones, 1987; Aristophanes, 1995; Is It Legal?, 1995, 1996, 1998; Cows, 1996; *films* incl.: Shakespeare in Love, 1999; Notting Hill, 1999; That Girl from Rio, 2001; The Diary of Bridget Jones, 2001; *radio* incl.: All the World's a Globe, Midsummer Wedding, 1990; Noah, 1991; Looking Forward to the Past, 1991–93; Desmond Dingle's Compleat Life and Works of William Shakespeare, 1995; Rent, 1996, 1997, 1998; The Patrick and Maureen Maybe Music Experience, 1998; Writer for television: The Ghost of Faffner Hall (jtly), 1989; adaptation, The Growing Pains of Adrian Mole, 1986; screenplay, Van Gogh (Prix Futura, Berlin Film Fest.), 1990; Scarfe on Sex, 1991; The True Adventures of Christopher Columbus (also actor and dir), 1992; Queen of the East, 1994 (also actor); also libretto, Judgement of Paris, Garden Venture, Royal Opera, 1991. *Publications:* All the World's a Globe, 1987 (adapted for radio) (Sony Radio award), 1990; Premier Ondas award, 1991); Shakespeare: The Truth, 1993; Love Upon the Throne, 1998; The Messiah, 2001. *Address:* Casarotto Company, National House, 60–66 Wardour Street, W1V 4ND. *Clubs:* Groucho, Two Brydges, Cobden.

BARLOW, Roy Oxspring; solicitor; a Recorder of the Crown Court, 1975–97; *b* 13 Feb. 1927; *s* of George and Clarice Barlow; *m* 1957, Kathleen Mary Roberts; two *s* one *d. Educ:* King Edward VII Sch., Sheffield; Queen's Coll., Oxford; Sheffield Univ. (LLB). Local Government, 1952–62; solicitor in private practice, 1962–. Asst Comr, Parly Boundary Commn, 1992–95. *Recreations:* farming, walking, reading. *Address:* The Cottage, Oxton Rakes, Barlow Dronfield, NE Derbys S18 7TH. *T:* (0114) 289 0652.

BARLOW, Sir Thomas (Erasmus), 3rd Bt *cr* 1902; DSC 1945; DL; *b* 23 Jan. 1914; *s* of Sir Alan Barlow, 2nd Bt, GCB, KBE, and Nora (*d* 1989), *d* of late Sir Horace Darwin, KBE; *S* father, 1968; *m* 1955, Isabel, *d* of late Dr T. M. Body, Middlesbrough, Yorks; two *s* two *d. Educ:* Winchester College. Entered RN as cadet, 1932; qualified Submarines, 1937; served in Submarines in Atlantic, Mediterranean, Indian Ocean and Far East during War of 1939–45; Naval Staff Course, 1946; Joint Services Staff Course, 1947, Commander, 1950. British Joint Services Mission, Washington, 1950–53; Captain 1954; Imperial Defence Coll., 1957; Chief Staff Officer to Flag Officer Submarines, 1960–62; Commodore, HMS Drake, Devonport, 1962–64; retired, 1964. Actively concerned in Wildlife and Countryside Conservation: Berks, Bucks and Oxfordshire Wildlife Trust; Galapogos Conservation Trust. DL Bucks, 1977. Hon. DLitt Sussex, 1997. *Recreations:* bird watching, the countryside. *Heir: s* James Alan Barlow, *b* 10 July 1956. *Address:* 45 Shepherds Hill, Highgate, N6 5QJ. *T:* (020) 8340 9653. *Clubs:* Athenæum, Savile.
See also H. B. Barlow.

BARLOW, Sir William; *see* Barlow, Sir G. W.

BARLTROP, Roger Arnold Rowlandson, CMG 1987; CVO 1982; HM Diplomatic Service, retired; Ambassador to Fiji, 1988–89 (High Commissioner, 1982–88) and High Commissioner (non-resident) to Republic of Nauru and to Tuvalu, 1982–89; *b* 19 Jan. 1930; *s* of late Ernest William Barltrop, CMG, CBE, DSO, and Ethel Alice Lucy Barltrop (*née* Baker); *m* 1st, 1962, Penelope Pierrepont Dalton (marr. diss.); two *s* two *d*; 2nd, 1998, Bojana Komadina (*née* Jovanovic). *Educ:* Solihull Sch.; Leeds Grammar Sch.; Exeter Coll., Oxford. MA. Served RN, 1949–50, RNVR/RNR, 1950–64 (Lt-Comdr 1962). Asst Principal, CRO, 1954–56; Second Sec., New Delhi, 1956–57; Private Sec. to Parly Under-Sec. of State and Minister of State, CRO, 1957–60; First Sec., E Nigeria, 1960–62; Actg Dep. High Comr, W Nigeria, 1962; First Sec., Salisbury, Rhodesia, 1962–65; CRO, Commonwealth Office and FO, later FCO, 1965–69; First Sec. and Head of Chancery, Ankara, 1969–70; Dep. British Govt Rep., WI Associated States, 1971–73; Counsellor and Head of Chancery, Addis Ababa, 1973–77; Head of Commonwealth Coordination Dept, FCO, 1978–82. Mem., Commonwealth Observer Gp for elections in Bangladesh, Feb. 1991, and in St Kitts/Nevis, 1995; Mem., UK/OSCE Observer Gp for elections in Bosnia, 1996; Foreign Affairs Trng Advr, Solomon Is, 1994. Chm., Pacific Is Soc. of UK and Ireland, 1992–98. *Publications:* contribs to Round Table (Commonwealth jl of internat. affairs). *Recreations:* sailing, genealogy, opera. *Address:* 35 Highfield Drive, Hurstpierpoint, West Sussex BN6 9AU. *Club:* Royal Commonwealth Society.

BARNA, Prof. Tibor, CBE 1974; Professor of Economics, University of Sussex, 1962–82, Professor Emeritus 1984; Member, Monopolies and Mergers Commission, 1963–78; *b* 1919. *Educ:* London School of Economics. Lecturer, London School of Economics, 1944; Official Fellow, Nuffield College, Oxford, 1947; senior posts in UN Economic Commission for Europe, 1949; Assistant Director, National Institute of Economic and Social Research, London, 1955. *Publications:* Redistribution of Income through Public Finance in 1937, 1945; Investment and Growth Policies in British Industrial Firms, 1962; Agriculture towards the Year 2000, 1979; European Process Plant Industry, 1981; papers in Jl Royal Statistical Soc., Economic Jl, European Econ. Review. *Address:* Beanacre, Westmeston, Hassocks, West Sussex BN6 8XE. *T:* (01273) 842384.

BARNARD, 11th Baron, *cr* 1698; **Harry John Neville Vane,** TD 1960; landowner; Lord-Lieutenant and Custos Rotulorum of County Durham, 1970–88; a Vice-Chairman, Council, British Red Cross Society, 1987–93 (Member Council 1982–85; Hon. Vice President, since 1999); *b* 21 Sept. 1923; *er s* of 10th Baron Barnard, CMG, OBE, MC, TD, and Sylvia Mary (*d* 1993), *d* of Herbert Straker; *S* father, 1964; *m* 1952, Lady Davina Mary Cecil, DStJ (marr. diss. 1992), *e d* of 6th Marquess of Exeter, KCMG; one *s* four *d. Educ:* Eton. MSc Durham, 1986. Served War of 1939–45, RAFVR, 1942–46 (Flying Officer, 1945). Northumberland Hussars (TA), 1948–66; Lt-Col Commanding, 1964–66. Vice-Pres., N of England TA&VRA, 1970 and 1977–88, Pres., 1974–77. Hon. Col, 7 (Durham) Bn The Light Infantry, 1979–89. County Councillor, Durham, 1952–61. Member: Durham Co. AEC, 1953–72 (Chm., 1970–72); N Regional Panel, MAFF, 1972–76; CLA Council, 1950–80; Dir, NE Housing Assoc., 1964–77. President: Farmway Ltd, 1965–; Durham Co. Br., CLA, 1965–89; Durham Co. St John Council, 1971–88; Durham Co. Scouts Assoc., 1972–88; Durham and Cleveland Co. Br. RBL, 1973–92; Durham Wildlife Trust (formerly Durham Co. Conservation Trust), 1984–95; Durham Co. Fedn of Young Farmers Clubs, 1991–92; Vice-Pres., Game Conservancy Trust, 1997–. Patron: Durham Co. Br., BRCS, 1993– (Pres., 1969–87); Durham Co. RBL, 2001–. DL Durham, 1956, Vice-Lieutenant, 1969–70; JP Durham, 1961. Joint Master of Zetland Hounds, 1963–65. Sen. Grand Warden, United Grand Lodge of England, 1970–71; Provincial Grand Master for Durham, 1969–98. Queen's Badge of Honour, BRCS, 1991. KStJ 1971. *Heir: s* Hon. Henry Francis Cecil Vane [*b* 11 March 1959; *m* 1998, Kate, *yr d* of Christopher Robson; one *d*]. *Address:* Raby Castle, PO Box 50, Staindrop, Darlington, Co. Durham DL2 3AY. *T:* (01833) 660751. *Clubs:* Brooks's; Durham County (Durham); Northern Counties (Newcastle upon Tyne).

BARNARD, David; *see* Barnard, J. D. W.

BARNARD, Prof. Eric Albert, PhD; FRS 1981; Director, Molecular Neurobiology Unit, and Professor of Neurobiology, Royal Free and University College Medical School (formerly Royal Free Hospital School of Medicine), London University, 1992–98, now Emeritus Professor; Visiting Professor, Department of Pharmacology, University of Cambridge; *m* 1956, Penelope J. Hennessy; two *s* two *d. Educ:* Davenant Foundn Sch.; King's Coll., London. BSc, PhD 1956. King's College, London: Nuffield Foundn Fellow, 1956–59; Asst Lectr, 1959–60; Lectr, 1960–64. State University of New York at Buffalo: Associate Prof. of Biochemical Pharmacol., 1964–65; Prof. of Biochemistry, 1965–76; Head of Biochemistry Dept, 1969–76; Imperial College of Science and Technology, London: Rank Prof. of Physiol Biochemistry, 1976–85; Chm., Div. of Life Sciences, 1977–85; Head, Dept of Biochem., 1979–85; Dir, MRC Molecular Neurobiol. Unit, Cambridge, 1985–92. Rockefeller Fellow, Univ. of Calif, Berkeley, 1960–61; Guggenheim Fellow, MRC Lab. of Molecular Biol., Cambridge, 1971. Visiting Professor: Univ. of Marburg, Germany, 1965; Tokyo Univ., 1993; Vis. Scientist, Inst. Pasteur, France, 1973. Member: Internat. Soc. Neurochem; EMBO; IBRO; Cttee, Internat. Union of Pharmacology, 1991–2000; Cttee Mem., CNRS, France. UK rep., EC Cttee on Decade of the Brain. Foreign Mem., Polish Acad. of Scis, 2000. Josiah Macy Faculty Scholar Award, USA, 1975; Medal of Polish Acad. of Scis, 1980; Ciba Medal and Prize, 1985; Eastman Kodak Award, USA, 1988; Erspamer Internat. Award for Neuroscience, 1991; ECNP-Synthélabo Award for Neuroscience Res., 1996; Eli Lilly Prize for European Neuroscience, 1998. Editor-in-Chief, Receptors and Channels, 1993–2000; mem. editl bd, three other scientific jls. *Publications:* editor of eight scientific books; several hundred papers in learned jls. *Recreation:* the pursuit of good claret. *Address:* Department of Pharmacology, University of Cambridge, Tennis Court Road, Cambridge CB2 1QJ. *T:* (01223) 847876, 334078, *Fax:* (01223) 334178; *e-mail:* eb247@cam.ac.uk.

BARNARD, Surg. Rear Adm. Ernest Edward Peter, DPhil; FFCM; Surgeon Rear Admiral, Operational Medical Services, 1982–84; retired 1984; *b* 22 Feb. 1927; *s* of Lionel Edward Barnard and Ernestine (*née* Lethbridge); *m* 1955, Dr Joan Barnard (*née* Gunn); one *s* one *d. Educ:* schools in England and Australia; Univ. of Adelaide; St Mary's Hosp., Univ. of London (MB, BS 1955); St John's Coll., Univ. of Oxford (student, 1966–68; DPhil 1969). MRCS, LRCP 1955; MFOM 1979; FFCM 1980. After house appts, joined RN, 1956; served, 1957–76: HMS Bulwark, Reclaim and Dolphin; RN Physiol Lab.; RN Med. Sch.; Inst. of Naval Medicine; Dept of Med. Dir Gen. (Naval); exchange service with US Navy at Naval Med. Res. Inst., Bethesda, Md, 1976–78; Inst. of Naval Medicine, 1978–80; QHP 1980–84; Dep. Med. Dir Gen. (Naval), 1980–82; Surgeon Rear-Adm., Inst. of Naval Medicine, and Dean of Naval Medicine, 1982. FRSocMed 1962. *Publications:* papers on underwater medicine and physiology. *Recreations:* gardening, genealogy, photography. *Address:* c/o Barclays Bank, PO Box 6, Portsmouth PO6 3DH.

BARNARD, Prof. George Alfred, MA, DSc; Emeritus Professor of Mathematics, University of Essex; *b* 23 Sept. 1915; *s* of Frederick C. and Ethel C. Barnard; *m* 1st, 1942, Helen J. B. Davies; three *s*; 2nd, 1949, Mary M. L. Jones; one *s. Educ:* Sir George Monoux Grammar Sch., Walthamstow; St John's Coll., Cambridge. Math. Trip., Pt III, 1936, Res. Studentship, St John's Coll., spent at Grad. Sch. Princeton, NJ, USA, 1937–39. Plessey Co., Ilford, as Math. Consultant, 1940–42; Ministry of Supply Adv. Unit, 1942–45; Maths Dept, Imperial Coll., London: Lectr, 1945–47; Reader in Math. Statistics, 1948–54, Professor, 1954–66; Prof. of Mathematics, Univ. of Essex, 1966–75; Prof. of Statistics, Univ. of Waterloo, 1975–81. Visiting Professor: Yale, 1966, Univ. of Waterloo, 1972–73, Univ. of Nottingham, 1975–77. Member: UGC, 1967–72; Computer Bd, 1970–72; SSRC, 1971–74. Royal Statistical Society: Council Mem. and Vice-Pres., 1952, 1962, Pres. 1971–72 (Chm. Res. Sect., 1958; Guy Medal in Silver, 1958, in Gold, 1975); Hon. Fellow, 1993. Mem. Internat. Statistical Inst., 1952 (Hon. Mem. 1996); Statistical Adviser, Brit. Standards Instn (with Prof. E. S. Pearson), 1954; Chm. Inst. of Statisticians, 1960–62; President: Operational Res. Soc., 1962–64; Inst. of Mathematics and its Applications, 1970–71 (Gold Medal, 1986); Fellow: Amer. Statistical Assoc.; Inst. of Mathematical Statistics; Amer. Assoc. for Advancement of Science. Hon. Dr Math. Waterloo, 1983; DUniv: Open, 1986; Essex, 1994; Hon. DSc City, 1991. Deming Medal, Amer. Soc. for Quality Control, 1991. *Publications:* (ed) The Foundations of Statistical Inference, 1962; papers in Jl Royal Statistical Society; Technometrics; Biometrika. *Recreation:* viola playing. *Address:* Mill House, Hurst Green, Brightlingsea, Essex CO7 0EH. *T:* (01206) 302388.
See also D. E. C. Wedderburn.

BARNARD, Hermione; *see* Lee, H.

BARNARD, (John) David (William), CBE 2000; FRCS, FDSRCS; Consultant Oral and Maxillofacial Surgeon, Portsmouth Hospitals NHS Trust (formerly Queen Alexandra Hospital, Portsmouth), since 1979; *b* 5 March 1943; *s* of Dr George Edward Barnard and Gwenllian Mary Barnard (*née* Thomas); *m* 1980, Cheryl Barlow. *Educ:* St Marylebone Grammar Sch.; Guy's Hosp. Dental Sch. (BDS London 1966). FDSRCS 1974; FDSRCPSGlas 1974. Hse surgeon, Guy's Hosp., 1967; RN Dental Service, 1967-72; Asst Dental Surgeon, Queen Victoria Hosp., E Grinstead, 1973-75; Sen. Registrar, Oxford Hosps, 1975-79. Consultant Advr in Oral and Maxillofacial Surgery, RN, 2002-. Hunterian Prof., RCS, 1978. Mem., GDC, 1998-2001(Mem., Standing Dental Adv. Cttee, 1998-2002); Hosps Gp Pres., 1985, Chm., Gp Cttee, 1988-99, BDA; Mem., Central Cttee, Hosp. Dental Services, 1988-99 (Chm., 1995-98). Mem. Council, 1987-92, Hon. Treas., 1989-92, Pres. designate, 2002, BAOMS; Odontological Section, Royal Society of Medicine: Mem. Council, 1990-99; Hon. Treas., 1993-96; Vice-Pres., 1996-99; Royal College of Surgeons of England: Bd Mem., 1995-2002, Dean, 1998-2001, Faculty of Dental Surgery; Mem. Council, 1998-2002. FDSRCSE (*ad hominem*) 1998; FRCS (by election) 2000. *Publications:* contrib. chapters in books and articles to learned jls. *Recreations:* motor sport (sports car racing), my dogs, choral music, reading. *Address:* Forbury, 41 Havant Road, Emsworth, Hants PO10 7JD. *T:* (01243) 372987.

BARNARD, Prof. John Michael; Professor of English Literature, School of English, University of Leeds, since 1978; *b* Folkestone, 13 Feb. 1936; *s* of John Claude Southard Barnard and Dora Grace Barnard; *m* 1st, 1961, Katherine Duckham (marr. diss. 1975); one *s* two *d*; partner, 1975, *m* 2nd, 1991, Hermione Lee, *qv. Educ:* Wadham Coll., Oxford (BA (Hons) Eng. Lang. and Lit.; BLitt; MA). Res. Asst, English Dept, Yale Univ., 1961–64; Vis. Lectr, English Dept, Univ. of California at Santa Barbara, 1964–65; Post-doctoral Fellow, William Andrews Clark Meml Liby, UCLA, 1965; Leeds University: Lectr and Sen. Lectr, Sch. of English, 1965–78; Dir, Inst. of Bibliography and Textual Criticism, Sch. of English, 1996– (Actg Dir, 1982–96). Res. Fellow, William Andrews Clark Meml Liby, UCLA, and Huntington Liby, 1994. Mem., British Cttee, Eighteenth Century Short Title Catalogue, 1983–89; Vice-Pres., Bibliographical Soc., 1998– (Mem. Council, 1989–94). Mem., English Panel, 1996 RAE, Chm., English Panel, 2001 RAE, HEFCE. British Academy Warton Lecture, 1989. Internat. expert Verkenningscommissie Moderne Letteren, Netherlands, 1992–93. FEA 2000. Gen. Editor, Longman Annotated Poets, 1976–; Member, Editorial Board: English Poetry Full Text Database, 1991–93; English Verse Drama Full Text Database, 1993–95; English Prose Drama Full Text Database, 1994–96. *Publications:* (ed) William Congreve, The Way of the World, 1972; (ed) Pope: The Critical Heritage, 1973; (ed) John Keats: the complete poems, 1973, 3rd edn 1988;

(ed) Etherege: The Man of Mode, 1979; John Keats, 1987; (ed) John Keats: selected poems, 1988; (jtly) The Early Seventeenth-Century York Book Trade and John Foster's Inventory of 1616, 1994; (ed) The Folio Society John Keats, 2001; articles in Brit. and Amer. learned jls, occasional reviews, etc. *Recreations:* travel, walking. *Address:* School of English, University of Leeds, Leeds LS2 9JT. *Club:* Johnson.

BARNARD, Sir Joseph (Brian), Kt 1986; DL; *b* 22 Jan. 1928; *s* of Joseph Ernest Barnard and Elizabeth Loudon (*née* Constantine); *m* 1959, Suzanne Hamilton Bray; three *s* (incl. twins). *Educ:* Bramcote School, Scarborough; Sedbergh School. Served Army, 1946–48, commissioned KRRC. Director: Joseph Constantine Steamship Line, 1952–66; Teesside Warehousing Co., 1966–97; Indeck Energy Services, 1991–; Lustrum Warehousing Co., 1997–; Financial Consultancy Centre Ltd, 2000–. Farms at East Harlsey. Dir, Northern Electric (formerly NE Electricity Bd), 1986–90; Chm., NE Electricity Cons. Council, 1986–90; Mem., Electricity Consumers' Council, 1986–90. Vice-Chm., 1988–91, Chm., 1991–92, Nat. Union of Cons. and Unionist Assocs (Chm., Yorks Area, 1983–88); Chm., Cons. Assoc. for Cleveland and Yorks N Euro Constituency, 1993–94. Life Vice President: Yorkshire Conservative Clubs, 1994; Conservatives at Work, 1994. Chm. Governors, Ingleby Arncliffe C of E Primary School, 1979–91; Patron, St Oswald's, E Harlsey. JP Northallerton, 1973–94; Chm., Northallerton (formerly Allertonshire PSD), 1981–93; Mem., N Yorks Magistrates' Courts Cttee, 1981–93. DL N Yorks, 1988. *Recreations:* walking, shooting, gardening. *Address:* Harlsey Hall, Northallerton, N Yorks DL6 2BL. *T:* (01609) 882203. *Club:* Carlton.

BARNE, Major Nicholas Michael Lancelot, LVO 1996; Private Secretary, Comptroller and Equerry to Princess Alice, Duchess of Gloucester, and to the Duke and Duchess of Gloucester, since 1989; *b* 25 Nov. 1943; *m* 1974, Hon. Janet Elizabeth, *d* of Baron Maclean, KT, GCVO, KBE, PC; two *s. Educ:* Eton Coll. Regular officer, Scots Guards, 1965–79; fruit farming, 1979–84; Co. Comdt, Norfolk Army Cadet Force, 1985–89. *Recreations:* golf, ski-ing, shooting. *Address:* Blofield House, Blofield, Norwich, Norfolk NR13 4RW; Tower Flat, Kensington Palace, W8 4PU.

BARNEBY, Col Michael Paul; Clerk to the Salters' Company, since 1990; *b* 29 March 1939; *m* 1973, Bridget, *d* of Col A. G. Roberts, DSO, Crickhowell; three *d. Educ:* Radley Coll. Commissioned into 15th/19th King's Royal Hussars, 1958; served Germany, NI, Hong Kong; commanded Royal Hong Kong Regt (Volunteers), 1981–83; retired from Army, 1988; Dir of Planning and Admin, Clark Whitehill, 1988–89. *Recreations:* hunting, shooting, racing. *Address:* Fairfield House, Godsfield, near Old Alresford, Hants SO24 9RQ. *Club:* Cavalry and Guards.

BARNES; *see* Oppenheim-Barnes.

BARNES, family name of **Baron Gorell**.

BARNES, Adrian Francis Patrick, CVO 1996; Remembrancer of the City of London, since 1986; *b* 25 Jan. 1943; *s* of late Francis Walter Ibbetson Barnes and of Heather Katherine (*née* Tamplin); *m* 1980, Sally Eve Whatley; one *s* one *d. Educ:* St Paul's School; MA City of London Polytechnic 1981. Called to the Bar, Gray's Inn, 1973 (Doyen, Seniors in Hall, 1992–2000; Bencher, 2000); Solicitor's Dept, DTI, 1975; Dep. Remembrancer, Corp. of London, 1982. Wimbledon Civic Forum: Founder, Mem. Exec. and Adv. Council, 1999–; Chm., Gen. Meetings on Constitution, 1999, and on Strategy, 2000–. Chm. Govs, The Music Therapy Charity, 1997– (Gov., 1995–). Freeman, City of London, 1982. Liveryman, Merchant Taylors' Co., 1989–. *Recreations:* music, chess, cricket, biography, circuit training, City lore. *Address:* Guildhall, EC2P 2EJ. *T:* (020) 7332 1200, *Fax:* (020) 7332 1895. *Clubs:* Brooks's, Guildhall.

BARNES, Alan Robert, CBE 1976; JP; Headmaster, Ruffwood School, Kirkby, Liverpool, 1959–87; Consultant, Secondary Heads Association, since 1997 (Field Officer, 1987–97); *b* 9 Aug. 1927; *s* of Arthur Barnes and Ida Barnes; *m* 1951, Pearl Muriel Boughton; (two *s* decd). *Educ:* Enfield Grammar Sch.; Queens' Coll., Cambridge (MA). National Service, RAEC. Wallington County Grammar Sch., 1951–55; Churchfields Sch., West Bromwich, 1955–59. Pres., Headmasters' Assoc., 1974, Treas., 1975–77; Chm., Jt Four Secondary Assocs, 1978; Treas., Secondary Heads Assoc., 1978–82; Vice-Chm., British Educn Management and Admin Soc., 1980–82, Chm. 1982–84. Schools Liaison Officer, Univ. of Essex, 1988–92. Chm., HMA Benevolent Fund, 1975–. JP Knowsley, Merseyside, 1967. *Publications:* (contrib.) Going Comprehensive (ed Halsall), 1970; (contrib.) Management and Headship in the Secondary School (ed Jennings), 1978; contrib. to: Education, BEMAS Jl, SHA publications. *Recreation:* bridge. *Address:* 2 Lark Valley Drive, Fornham St Martin, Bury St Edmunds, Suffolk IP28 6UF; *e-mail:* AlanBarnes@Larkvalley.fsnet.co.uk.

BARNES, Anthony Hugh; Director, Redundant Churches Fund, 1984–92; *b* 16 June 1931; *s* of Sir George Barnes and Anne Barnes; *m* 1st, 1956, Susan Dempsey; two *s* one *d*; 2nd, 1984, Jennifer Carey. *Educ:* King's Coll., Cambridge (MA). FCIPD. Schweppes Ltd, 1954–66; Royal Opera House, 1966–70; ICI, 1970–82; self-employed, 1982–84. Trustee, Norfolk Churches Trust, 1995– (Sec., 1992–95). Vice-Pres., Norwich Labour Party, 2000–01. *Address:* 1 Dixon's Court, 52 Bethel Street, Norwich NR2 1NR. *T:* (01603) 666783.

BARNES, Christopher John Andrew, CB 1996; Chairman, Assured Food Standards Ltd, since 2000; *b* 11 Oct. 1944; *s* of late Eric Vernon Barnes and of Joan Mary Barnes; *m* 1st, 1978, Carolyn Elizabeth Douglass Johnston (*d* 1990); two *s*; 2nd, 1990, Susan Elizabeth Bird; two *s. Educ:* City of London Sch.; London School of Economics (BScEcon). Ministry of Agriculture, Fisheries and Food: Exec. Officer, 1962; Asst Principal, 1967; Private Sec. to Parly Sec., 1969–71; Principal, 1971; Sec. to Northfield Cttee on Agricultural Land Ownership and Occupancy, 1977–79; Asst Sec., 1980; Chief Reg. Officer, Nottingham and Reading, 1980–83; Hd of Personnel and R&D Requirements Divs, 1983–90; 'Barnes Review' of near market R&D, 1988; Under Sec. (Grade 3), 1990–96; Arable Crops and Hortic., later Arable Crops and Alcoholic Drinks Gp, 1990–95; Dir of Estabs, 1995–96, retired. A Chm., CSSB, 1995–97. Sen. Consultant, Andersons, 1996–98; Associate Dir, Andersons Chamberlain Recruitment, 1996–98; Dir, Drew Associates Ltd, 1996–98; Chairman: Assured Produce Ltd, 1999–; Modernising Skills Ltd, 1999–; non-exec. Dir, Booker Food Services, 1987–90. Mem. Management Cttee, CS Healthcare, 1992– (Vice-Chm., 1997–99); Chm., Bucks HA, 1999–2000 (non-exec. Dir, 1996). FRSA 1999. *Recreations:* off-road vehicles, country living, France. *Club:* Farmers'.

BARNES, Clive Alexander, CBE 1975; Associate Editor and Chief Drama and Dance Critic, New York Post, since 1977; *b* London, 13 May 1927; *s* of Arthur Lionel Barnes and Freda Marguerite Garratt; *m* 1958, Patricia Winckley; one *s* one *d. Educ:* King's Coll., London; St Catherine's Coll., Oxford. Served RAF, 1946–48. Admin. Officer, Town Planning Dept, LCC, 1952–61; concurrently freelance journalist; Chief Dance Critic, The Times, 1961–65; Exec. Editor, Dance and Dancers, Music and Musicians, and Plays and Players, 1961–65; a London Correspondent, New York Times, 1963–65, Dance Critic, 1965–77, Drama Critic (weekdays only), 1967–77; a NY correspondent, The Times, 1970–. Knight of the Order of Dannebrog (Denmark), 1972. *Publications:* Ballet in Britain since the War, 1953; (ed, with others) Ballet Here and Now, 1961; Frederick Ashton and his Ballets, 1961; Dance Scene, USA (commentary), 1967; (ed with J. Gassner) Best American Plays, 6th series, 1963–67, 1971, and 7th series, 1974; (ed) New York Times Directory of the Theatre, 1973; Nureyev, 1983; contribs to jls, inc. Punch, The New Statesman, The Spectator, The New Republic. *Recreations:* eating, drinking, walking, theatregoing. *Address:* c/o New York Post, 210 South Street, New York, NY 10002, USA. *Club:* Century (NY).

BARNES, Rev. Cyril Arthur; Dean of Moray, Ross and Caithness, 1980–84; *b* 10 Jan. 1926; *s* of Reginald William and Mary Adeline Barnes; *m* 1951, Patricia Patience Allen. *Educ:* Penistone Grammar School; Edinburgh Theological Coll. (GOE 1950). King's Own Scottish Borderers and RAEC, 1944–47. Curate, St John's, Aberdeen, 1950–53; Rector, St John's, Forres, 1953–55; Priest-in-Charge, Wentbridge, Yorks, 1955–58; Vicar, St Bartholomew's, Ripponden with St John's, Rishworth, 1958–67, also St John's, Thorpe, 1966–67; Rector, Christ Church, Huntly with St Marnan's, Aberchirder, 1967–84, also Holy Trinity, Keith, 1974–84; Canon of Inverness Cathedral, 1971–80; Synod Clerk, 1977–80. Editor: Huntly Express, 1985–91; Northern See, 1990–96; Newscan, 1991–93. *Recreations:* gardening, do-it-yourself. *Address:* Tillytarmont Cottage, Bridge of Isla, Huntly, Aberdeenshire AB54 4SP.

BARNES, Sir David; *see* Barnes, Sir J. D. F.

BARNES, David John; Head Master, Pate's Grammar School, Cheltenham, 1986–2000; *b* 6 Nov. 1939; *s* of David Alan Barnes and Norah Barnes (*née* Fleming); *m* 1961, Jan Crofts; one *s* one *d. Educ:* The Grammar Sch., Wolstanton, Staffs; Queen's Coll., Oxford (Open Schol.; MA); DipEd London. Assistant Master: Pocklington Sch., York, 1962–66; Nottingham High Sch., 1966–68; Vice-Principal, Newcastle-under-Lyme Sch., 1968–86. *Publications:* A Parent's Guide to GCSE, 1988; various check-lists and guides to students' reading, 1991. *Recreations:* fly-fishing, Homer, digging holes and other honest labour. *Address:* 32 Gretton Road, Gotherington, Cheltenham, Glos GL52 9QU.

BARNES, (David) Michael (William); QC 1981; a Recorder, since 1985; *b* 16 July 1943; *s* of David Charles Barnes and Florence Maud Barnes; *m* 1970, Susan Dorothy Turner; three *s. Educ:* Monmouth Sch.; Wadham Coll., Oxford. Called to Bar, Middle Temple, 1965, Bencher, 1989. Hon. Research Fellow, Lady Margaret Hall, Oxford, 1979; Vis. Fellow, Univ. of Auckland, NZ, 1995. Chm., Hinckley Point 'C' Public Inquiry, 1988. *Publications:* Leasehold Reform Act 1967, 1967; Hill and Redman's Law of Landlord and Tenant, 15th edn 1970 – 18th edn 1988. *Recreations:* walking, crime fiction. *Address:* 4 Breams Buildings, EC4A 1AQ. *Club:* Beefsteak.

BARNES, Edward Campbell; independent television producer/director and television consultant, since 1986; Head of Children's Programmes, BBC Television, 1978–86; *b* 8 Oct. 1928; *s* of Hubert Turnbull Barnes and Annie Mabel Barnes; *m* 1950, Dorothy Smith (*d* 1992); one *s* two *d. Educ:* Wigan Coll. British Forces Network, Vienna, 1946–49; stage management, provincial and West End theatre, 1949–55; BBC Television: studio management, 1955–62; Producer, Blue Peter, 1962–70; Dep. Head of Children's Progs, 1970–78, incl.: original Editor, John Craven's Newsround; Producer: Blue Peter Royal Safari with Princess Anne; 6 series of Blue Peter Special Assignments; Producer and Director: Treasure Houses, 1986; All Our Children, 1987–90; Boxpops, 1992; The Lowdown, 1992. Mem. Bd, Children's Film and Television Foundn Ltd, 1983–97; Dir, Christian Children's Fund, 1995–. Consultant, St Paul's Multi-media, 1995–96. Mem., RTS (Mem., Awards Cttee, 1989–91). SFTA Award, 1969; RTS Silver Medal, 1986; Pye Television Award, 1986. *Publications:* 25 Blue Peter Books and 8 Blue Peter Mini Books, 1964–; 6 Blue Peter Special Assignment Books, 1973–75; Blue Peter Royal Safari, 1971; Petra: a dog for everyone, 1977; Blue Peter: the inside story, 1989; numerous articles for nat. press. *Recreations:* cricket, music, birding, walking, Venice, Bali.
See also S. J. C. Barnes.

BARNES, Rt Rev. Edwin Ronald; Bishop Suffragan of Richborough, Episcopal Visitor for the Province of Canterbury, 1995–2001; *b* 6 Feb. 1935; *s* of Edwin and Dorothy Barnes; m 1963, Jane Elizabeth (*née* Green); one *s* one *d. Educ:* Plymouth College; Pembroke Coll., Oxford (MA). Rector of Farncombe, Surrey, 1967–78; Vicar of Hessle, dio. York, 1978–87; Principal, St Stephen's House, Oxford, 1987–95. Proctor in Convocation, Canterbury 1975–78, York 1985–87; Mem., General Synod of C of E, 1990–95 (Mem. Standing Cttee, 1992–95). Hon. Canon: Christ Church, Oxford, 1994; St Albans Cathedral, 1997–. *Address:* 1 Queen Elizabeth Avenue, Lymington, Hants SO41 9HN.

BARNES, Eric Charles, CBE 1992; High Court Judge, Hong Kong, 1981–91; *b* 12 Sept. 1924; *m* 1st, Estelle Fay Barnes (*née* Darnell); four *s* one *d*; 2nd, 1978, Judianna Wai Ling Barnes (*née* Chang); one *s* one *d. Educ:* Univ. of Queensland (LLB). Chief Adjudicator, Immigration Tribunal, Hong Kong, 1993–; Chm., Appeal Bd on Public Meetings and Demonstrations, Hong Kong, 1995–. Mem., Australian Assoc., Hong Kong, 1994–. *Recreations:* tennis, racing (horse), sports. *Address:* Flat 8 Block D, Government Quarters, 122 Pokfulam Road, Hong Kong. *Clubs:* United Services Recreation, Kowloon Cricket, Hong Kong Jockey (Hong Kong); Tattersall's (Brisbane).

BARNES, Geoffrey Thomas, CBE 1989; HM Overseas Civil Service, retired; *b* 18 Aug. 1932; *s* of late Thomas Arthur Barnes and Ethel Maud (*née* Walker); *m* 1962, Agnete Scot Madsen; three *s* one *d. Educ:* Dover College; St Catharine's College, Cambridge (MA). Nat. Service, 2nd Lieut QO Royal West Kent Regt; served Malaya, 1951–52; Lieut, Royal Warwickshire Regt, TA, 1952–55. Admin Officer, HMOCS Sarawak, 1956–68; City and Guilds of London, 1968–70; HMOCS Hong Kong: Asst Defence Sec., 1970–72; Police Civil Sec., 1972–76; Asst Dir, Commerce and Industry Dept, 1976–77; Dep. Sec. for Security, 1977–81, for Health and Welfare, 1981–84; Comr, Indep. Commn Against Corruption, 1985–88; Sec. for Security, Hong Kong Govt, and Official Mem., Legislative Council, 1988–90. Consultant to FCO on anti-corruption measures in Jamaica, 1990, Peru, 1991, Venezuela, 1992 and Ecuador, 1993. Pres., ICAC Assoc., 1993–98. JP Hong Kong, 1980. *Publications:* Mostly Memories (autobiog.), 1996, rev. edn 1999; With the Dirty Half-Hundred in Malaya (autobiog.), 2001. *Recreations:* sailing, painting, golf, gardening. *Address:* Alloways, Cranleigh Road, Ewhurst, Surrey GU6 7RJ. *T:* (01483) 276490. *Clubs:* Royal Over-Seas League; Hong Kong (Hong Kong) (Life Mem.); Chichester Yacht.
See also K. J. Barnes.

BARNES, Harold, (Harry); MP (Lab) Derbyshire North East, since 1987; *b* 22 July 1936; *s* of late Joseph and Betsy Barnes; *m* 1963, Elizabeth Ann Stephenson; one *s* one *d. Educ:* Ruskin Coll., Oxford (Dip. Econs and Political Science); Hull Univ. (BA Philosophy and Political Studies). National Service, 1954–56. Railway clerk, 1952–54 and 1956–60; adult student, 1960–65; further educn lectr, 1965–66; Lectr, Sheffield Univ., 1966–87. Jt Pres., New Dialogue (Britain), 1992– (Chm., 1990–92). Mem., National Admin. Council, Ind.

Labour Publications, 1977–80 and 1982–85. *Publications:* pamphlets on local govt and on the public face of Militant; articles and reviews in Labour Leader, London Labour Briefing, Tribune, Morning Star, Local Socialism, New Socialist, Derbyshire Miner, Leeds Weekly Citizen, Sheffield Forward, Industrial Tutor, Political Studies. *Address:* House of Commons, SW1A 0AA. *T:* (020) 7219 4521. *Clubs:* Dronfield Contact; Chesterfield Labour.

BARNES, Jack Henry; Director of Research and Policy, National Asthma Campaign, since 2000; *b* 11 Dec. 1943; *s* of James Barnes and Joan Ivy (*née* Sears); *m* 1966, Nicola Pearse; two *d*. *Educ:* Hatfield Sch., Herts; Univ. of Sussex (BA); LSE (MSc). Dep. Chief Inspector, Social Services Inspectorate, DHSS, 1983–88; Department of Health: Dep. Chief Scientist and Dir, Res. Management, 1988–91; Under Sec. 1991–99; Head: Primary Care Div., NHS Exec., 1991–95; Internat. and Industry Div., 1995–99. Trustee, Mental Health Foundn, 1997–. *Address:* (Office) Providence House, Providence Place, N1 0NT.

BARNES, Sir (James) David (Francis), Kt 1996; CBE 1987; Deputy Chairman, AstraZeneca PLC, 1999–2001; *b* 4 March 1936; *s* of Eric Cecil Barnes, CMG, and of Jean Margaret Barnes; *m* 1963, Wendy Fiona Mary (*née* Riddell); one *s* one *d*. *Educ:* Shrewsbury Sch.; Liverpool Univ. National Service, commnd 'N' Battery (Eagle Troop), 2nd Regt RA, 1958–60 (Malaya). ICI Pharmaceuticals Division: Overseas Dir 1971–77, Dep. Chm. 1977–83; Chm., ICI Paints Div., 1983–86; Exec. Dir, ICI, 1986–93; CEO, Zeneca Group PLC, 1993–99. Non-executive Director: Thorn EMI, 1987–94; Redland, 1994–98; Prudential, 1999–; non-exec. Chm., Imperial Cancer Res. Technol., 1999–; Dep. Chm., Syngenta AG, 2000–. Chairman: Pharmaceuticals EDC, NEDO, 1983–92; Biotechnology Industries Working Party, NEDO, 1989–91. Vice-Pres., Thames Valley Hospice, 1986–. Mem. Council, VSO, 1996–99; a Dep. Chm., BITC, 1996–2000 (Chm., Economic Regeneration Leadership Team, 1996–2000). Mem. Bd of Governors, Ashridge (Bonar Law Meml) Trust, 1993–; Gov. and Bd Mem., Intellectual Property Inst., 1994–2000; Member: Governing Body, Shrewsbury Sch., 1997–; Bd of Trustees, BRCS, 1998–. FInstD; CIMgt; FRSA 1988; Hon. Associate, BVA, 1995 (Wooldridge Meml Medal, 1995). Hon. LLD Liverpool, 1996; Hon. DSc UMIST, 1998. Centenary Medal, SCI, 2000. *Recreations:* fishing, shooting, walking.

BARNES, James Frederick, CB 1982; Deputy Chief Scientific Adviser, and Head of Profession for the Science Group, Ministry of Defence, 1987–89; *b* 8 March 1932; *s* of Wilfred and Doris M. Barnes; *m* 1957, Dorothy Jean Drew; one *s* two *d*. *Educ:* Taunton's Sch., Southampton; Queen's Coll., Oxford. BA 1953, MA 1957; CEng, FRAeS. Bristol Aeroplane Co. (Engine Div.), 1953; Min. of Supply, Nat. Gas Turbine Estabt: Sci. Officer 1955; Sen. Sci. Off. 1957; Principal Sci. Off. 1962; Sen. Principal Sci. Off. (Individual Merit) 1965; Min. of Aviation Supply, Asst Dir, Engine R&D, 1970; seconded to HM Diplomatic Service, Counsellor (Science and Technology), British Embassy, Washington, 1972; Under-Sec., MoD, 1974; Dir Gen. Res. (C), MoD (Procurement Exec.), 1974–77; Dep. Dir (Weapons), RAE, 1978–79; Dep. Chief Scientific Adviser (Projs), MoD, 1979–82; Dep. Controller, Establishments Resources and Personnel, MoD, 1982–84; Dep. Controller, Estabts and Res., MoD, 1984–86. Chm., MoD Individual Merit Promotion Panel, 1990–98. Stewardship Advr, dio. of Monmouth, 1989–96; Dir, Monmouth Diocesan Bd of Finance, 1999–; Sec., Monmouth DAC for Care of Churches, 1994–96; Chm., CCBI Stewardship Network, 1993–96; Member: Council on Christian Approaches to Defence and Disarmament, 1980–; Member, Church in Wales Working Gps on Ecclesiastical Exemption, Charities Act 1993 and status of PCCs, 1995–96. Lay Member: Guildford Diocesan Synod, 1978–84; Winchester Diocesan Synod, 1985–89; Chm., Deanery Finance Cttee, Alton, Hants, 1987–89; Bishop's Nominee, Monmouth Diocesan Conf.; Churchwarden, All Saints', Farringdon, 1985–89; Sec. and Sub-Warden, Trellech PCC, 1997–. Chm., Tymawr Convent Appeals Gp, 1997–. Member: Monmouth & Llandaff Housing Assoc., 1991–93; Gwerin (Cymru) Housing Assoc., 1993–94; Trustee: Roger Williams & Queen Victoria Almshouses, Newport, 1990–99; Babington Educnl Trust, 1997–. Chm. of Govs, Yateley Manor Prep. Sch., 1981–89. James Clayton Fund Prize, IMechE, 1964. *Publications:* (contrib.) Trellech Millennium book; contrib. books and learned jls on mech. engrg, esp. gas turbine technology, heat transfer and stress analysis. *Recreation:* making things. *Address:* Richmond House, 1 Tintern Heights, Catbrook, Chepstow, Monmouthshire NP16 6NH.

BARNES, Janet; Director, Crafts Council, since 1999; *b* 23 April 1952; *d* of Frederick George Hagan and Margaret Hagan (*née* Wilson); *m* 1970, Philip Barnes. *Educ:* Sheffield Univ. (BA Hons English Lit.); Manchester Univ. (Postgrad. Dip. Mus and Art Gall. Studies). Keeper, Ruskin Gall. and Ruskin Craft Gall., 1985–94; Sen. Curator, Sheffield Galls and Museums, 1995–99. Hon. Curator, Turner Mus. of Glass, Univ. of Sheffield, 1979–99. Dir, Guild of St George, 1994–. Hon. LLD Sheffield, 2000; Hon. Dr Sheffield Hallam, 2001. *Publications:* Percy Horton: 1897–1970 Artist and Absolutist, 1982; Ruskin and Sheffield, 1985, 2nd edn 1996; Catalogue of the Turner Museum of Glass, 1993. *Recreations:* husband, walking. *Address:* c/o Crafts Council, 44a Pentonville Road, N1 9BY. *T:* (020) 7806 2523.

BARNES, John; a Vice-President, Immigration Appeal Tribunal, since 2000; *b* 13 March 1938; *s* of Frederick Walter John Barnes, MBE, LLB and Phyllis Edna Barnes (*née* Brooks); *m* 1992, Frances (*née* Broadrick); three *s* by a previous marriage. *Educ:* Brentwood Sch., Essex; Univ. of London (LLB Hons ext.). Admitted solicitor, 1961; engaged in private practice, 1961–97. Part-time Chm., Industrial Tribunals, 1993–99; Immigration Adjudicator, part-time, 1995–97, full-time, 1997–2000. *Recreations:* theatre, history, art, golf. *Address:* c/o Immigration Appeal Tribunal, Field House, 15 Breams Buildings, EC4A 1DZ. *T:* (020) 7073 4009.

BARNES, John Alfred, CBE 1993; Director-General, City and Guilds of London Institute, 1985–93; *b* 29 April 1930; *s* of John Joseph and Margaret Carr Barnes; *m* 1954, Ivy May (*née* Walker); two *d*. *Educ:* Bede Boys Grammar Sch., Sunderland; Durham Univ. (MA, BSc, MEd). Teacher, Grangefield Grammar Sch., Stockton-on-Tees, 1953–57; Asst Educn Officer, Barnsley, 1957–61; Dep. Dir, then Dir of Educn, City of Wakefield, 1963–68; Chief Educn Officer, City of Salford, 1968–84. Mem. Council, Assoc. of Colls of Further and Higher Educn, 1976–82 (Chm. 1980–81); Chairman: Northern Examining Assoc., 1979–82; Associated Lancs Schs Examg Bd, 1972–84; Member: Associated Examg Bd, Nat. Exams Bd for Supervisory Studies, 1985–93; Further Educn Unit Management Bd, 1986–89; YTS Certification Bd, 1986–89; various ind. trng bds, 1969–78, and MSC cttees, 1978–84; Review of Vocational Qualifications Working Gp, 1985–86; Task Gp on Assessment and Testing, 1987–88; Exec. Mem., Standing Conf. on Sch. Sci. and Technol., 1985–89 (Chm., Exec. Cttee, 1988–89). Mem., Nat. Exec. Cttee, Soc. of Educn Officers, 1979–84; Sec., Assoc. of Educn Officers, 1977–84; Treas., NFER, 1979–84; Pres., Educnl Develt Assoc., 1980–85. Chm., Sir Isaac Pitman Ltd, 1990–93; Sec., UK Skills, 1990–93. Mem. Council, City Technology Colls Trust, 1990–93; Gov., Imperial Coll., 1987–93; Mem. Court, Reading Univ., 1994–97. Mem. (C), Bucks CC, 1993–97 (Chm., Personnel Cttee, 1994–97; Vice-Chm., 1994–96, Chm., 1996–97, Educn Cttee). Mem., Thames Valley Valuation Tribunals Gp, 1997–. Trustee, City Parochial Foundn and Trust for London, 1993–. FRSA 1973; FITD 1986 (Hon. FITD 1993); FCollP 1991; Hon. FCGI 1993; Hon. CIPD 1994. *Publications:* occasional papers in educnl press. *Recreations:* cultural activities, foreign travel. *Address:* 37 Woodfield Park, Amersham, Bucks HP6 5QH. *T:* (01494) 726120. *Club:* Athenæum.

BARNES, Prof. John Arundel, DSC 1944; FBA 1981; Professor of Sociology, University of Cambridge, 1969–82, now Emeritus; Fellow of Churchill College, Cambridge, since 1969; *b* Reading, 9 Sept. 1918; *s* of T. D. and M. G. Barnes, Bath; *m* 1942, Helen Frances, *d* of Charles Bastable; three *s* one *d*. *Educ:* Christ's Hosp.; St John's Coll., Cambridge; Sch. of African Studies, Univ. of Cape Town; Balliol Coll., Oxford. Fellow, St John's Coll., Cambridge, 1950–53; Simon Research Fellow, Manchester Univ., 1951–53; Reader in Anthropology, London Univ., 1954–56; Prof. of Anthropology, Sydney Univ., 1956–58; Prof. of Anthropology, Inst. of Advanced Studies, ANU, Canberra, 1958–69; Overseas Fellow, Churchill Coll., Cambridge, 1965–66. Australian National University: Vis. Fellow, 1978–79, 1985–92; Program Visitor, Sociology, Res. Sch. of Social Scis, 1992–98. *Publications:* Marriage in a Changing Society, 1951; Politics in a Changing Society, 1954; Inquest on the Murngin, 1967; Sociology in Cambridge, 1970; Three Styles in the Study of Kinship, 1971; Social Networks, 1972; The Ethics of Inquiry in Social Science, 1977; Who Should Know What?, 1979; Models and interpretations, 1990; A Pack of Lies, 1994. *Address:* Churchill College, Cambridge CB3 0DS.

BARNES, Prof. Jonathan, FBA 1987; Professor of Ancient Philosophy, University of Geneva, since 1994; *b* 26 Dec. 1942; *s* of late A. L. Barnes and K. M. Barnes; *m* 1965, Jennifer Postgate; two *d*. *Educ:* City of London Sch.; Balliol Coll., Oxford. Fellow, Oriel Coll., Oxford, 1968–78; Fellow of Balliol Coll., 1978–94, Emeritus Fellow, 1994–, Prof. of Ancient Philosophy, 1989–94, Oxford Univ. Visiting posts at: Inst. for Advanced Study, Princeton, 1972; Univ. of Texas, 1981; Wissenschaftskolleg zu Berlin, 1985; Univ. of Alberta, 1986; Univ. of Zurich, 1987; Istituto Italiano per gli studi filosofici, 1988, 1998; Ecole Normale Supérieure, Paris, 1996. *Publications:* The Ontological Argument, 1972; Aristotle's Posterior Analytics, 1975; The Presocratic Philosophers, 1979; Aristotle, 1982; Early Greek Philosophy, 1987; The Toils of Scepticism, 1991; The Cambridge Companion to Aristotle, 1995; Logic and the Imperial Stoa, 1997. *Address:* Les Charmilles, 36200 Ceaulmont, France.

See also J. P. Barnes.

BARNES, Joseph Harry George; Chairman, Baxters of Speyside, 1994–98; Director, 1969–93, Joint Managing Director, 1988–90, J. Sainsbury plc; *b* 24 July 1930; *s* of William Henry Joseph Barnes and Dorothy Eleanor Barnes; *m* 1958, Rosemary Gander; two *s*. *Educ:* John Ruskin Grammar Sch., Croydon. FCA 1963. Articled clerk, Lever Honeyman & Co., 1946–52. National Service, 2nd Lieut RAPC, 1953–55. Joined J. Sainsbury plc, 1956. *Recreations:* tennis, fishing. *Address:* Tudor Court, 29 Grimwade Avenue, Croydon, Surrey CR0 5DJ. *T:* (020) 8654 5696.

BARNES, Julian Patrick; writer; *b* 19 Jan. 1946; *m* Pat Kavanagh. *Educ:* City of London Sch.; Magdalen Coll., Oxford. Lexicographer, OED Supplement, 1969–72; freelance journalist; Contributing Ed., New Review, 1977; Asst Literary Ed., 1977–79, TV Critic, 1977–81, New Statesman; Dep. Literary Ed., Sunday Times, 1980–82; TV Critic, Observer, 1982–86; London correspondent, The New Yorker, 1990–95. E. M. Forster Award, US Acad. of Arts and Letters, 1986; Shakespeare Prize, Germany, 1993. Officier de l'Ordre des Arts et des Lettres (France), 1995. *Publications:* Metroland, 1980 (Somerset Maugham Award, 1981); Before She Met Me, 1982; Flaubert's Parrot, 1984 (Geoffrey Faber Meml Prize, 1985; Prix Médicis, 1986; Grinzane Cavour Prize (Italy), 1988); Staring at the Sun, 1986; A History of the World in 10½ Chapters, 1989; Talking it Over, 1991 (Prix Femina, 1992); The Porcupine, 1992; Letters from London (essays), 1995; Cross Channel (short stories), 1996; England, England, 1998; Love, etc, 2000; (as Dan Kavanagh): Duffy, 1980; Fiddle City, 1981; Putting the Boot In, 1985; Going to the Dogs, 1987. *Address:* c/o Peters, Fraser & Dunlop, Drury House, 34–43 Russell Street, WC2B 5HA.

See also Jonathan Barnes.

BARNES, Sir Kenneth, KCB 1977 (CB 1970); Permanent Secretary, Department of Employment, 1976–82; *b* 26 Aug. 1922; *s* of Arthur and Doris Barnes, Accrington, Lancs; *m* 1948, Barbara Ainsworth; one *s* two *d*. *Educ:* Accrington Grammar Sch.; Balliol Coll., Oxford. Lancs Fusiliers, 1942–45. Entered Ministry of Labour, 1948; Under-Sec., Cabinet Office, 1966–68; Dep. Sec., Dept of Employment, 1968–75. *Address:* South Sandhills, Sandy Lane, Betchworth, Surrey RH3 7AA. *T:* (01737) 842445.

BARNES, Kenneth James, CBE 1969 (MBE 1964); Advisor (Finance), Directorate General for Development, Commission of the European Communities, 1982–87; *b* 8 May 1930; *s* of late Thomas Arthur Barnes and Ethel Maud Barnes; *m* 1st, 1953, Lesley Dawn Grummett Wright (*d* 1976); two *s* one *d*; 2nd, 1981, Anna Elisabeth Gustaf Maria Vanoorlé (marr. diss. 1988). *Educ:* Guilford and Hale Schs, Perth, WA; Dover Coll.; St Catharine's Coll., Cambridge (Crabtree exhibnr; MA); London Univ. Pilot Officer, RAF, 1949–50; Flying Officer, RAFVR, 1950–53. Administrative Officer, HMOCS Eastern Nigeria, 1954–60; Asst Sec., Min. of Finance, Malawi, 1960–64, Sen. Asst Sec., 1965, Dep. Sec., 1966, Permanent Sec., 1967–71; Asst Sec., British Steel Corp., 1971–73; EEC: Principal Administrator, Directorate-Gen. for Develt, 1973–75; Head of Div. for Ind. Co-operation, Trade Promotion and Regional Co-operation, 1976–78; Hd of Div. for Caribbean, Indian and Pacific Oceans, 1979–80; Advr (Political), 1981–82; Advr (Finance), 1983–87. Chm., Newbury Dist Liaison Group on Disablement, 1990–; Member: Council, Anti-Slavery Internat., 1991–98 (Jt Treas., 1992–97); Internat Cttee, RADAR, 1993– (Chm. Cttee, 1994–). Council, John Grooms Assoc. for Disabled, 1994–97; UK Disability Forum for Europe (formerly HELIOS Forum), 1994– (Treas., 1997–98); W Berks Liaison Gp on Disability, 1990– (successively Vice Chm., Chm., Treas.). *Publications:* Polio and ME in Nigeria, Malawi, Belgium, England and Other Places, 1998; contrib. Palm Wine & Leopard's Whiskers, 1999. *Recreations:* reading, esp. history, listening to music, mediaeval fortifications, strengthening European Community links, charities for the disabled. *Address:* 29 Bearwater, Charnham Street, Hungerford, Berks RG17 0NN. *T:* (01488) 684329, *Fax:* (01488) 681733; *e-mail:* KJBarnes@29bearwater.freeserve.co.uk. *Club:* Royal Over-Seas League.

See also G. T. Barnes.

BARNES, Mark Richard Purcell, QC 1992; called to the Bar, Lincoln's Inn, 1974. *Address:* 1 Essex Court, Temple, EC4Y 9AR. *T:* (020) 7583 2000; *e-mail:* mbarnes@oeclaw.co.uk.

BARNES, Melvyn Peter Keith, OBE 1990; ALA; Guildhall Librarian and Director of Libraries and Art Galleries, Corporation of London, since 1984; *b* 26 Sept. 1942; *s* of Harry and Doris Barnes; *m* 1965, Judith Anne Leicester; two *s*. *Educ:* Chatham House Sch., Ramsgate; North-Western Polytechnic, London. ALA 1965; DMA 1972; FIMgt (FBIM 1980); FRSA 1983. Public library posts in Kent, Herts and Manchester, 1958–68; Dep. Bor. Librarian, Newcastle-under-Lyme, 1968–72; Chief Librarian, Ipswich, 1972–74; Bor. Librarian and Arts Officer, Kensington and Chelsea, 1974–80; City Librarian,

Westminster, 1980–84. Hon. Librarian to Clockmakers' Co., Gardeners' Co. Member: LA Council, 1974–98 (Chm. Exec. Cttee, 1987–92; Vice-Pres., 1991–93; Pres., 1995); Liby and Inf. Services Council, 1984–89; Brit. Liby Adv. Council, 1986–91; Brit. Liby SRIS Adv. Cttee, 1986–91. Pres., Internat. Assoc. of Metropolitan City Libraries, 1989–92; Dep. Chm., Liby Services Trust and Liby Services Ltd, 1983–93. Hon. Treas., Victoria County History of Inner Middlesex, 1979–90. Gov., St Bride Inst., 1984–. Liveryman, Clockmakers' Co., 1990–; Hon. Freeman, Gardeners' Co., 1995. Editorial Cons., Journal of Librarianship, 1980–94; Editorial Advr, Librarianship & Information Work Worldwide, 1991–99. *Publications:* Youth Library Work, 1968, 2nd edn 1976; Best Detective Fiction, 1975; Murder in Print, 1986; Dick Francis, 1986; Root and Branch: a history of the Worshipful Company of Gardeners of London, 1994; (ed) Deerstalker series of classic crime fiction reprints, 1977–82; contributor to numerous books and jls in fields of librarianship and crime fiction criticism. *Recreations:* reading and writing, going to the theatre, studying the history of the movies and stage musicals, performing amateur operatics. *Address:* Guildhall Library, Aldermanbury, EC2P 2EJ. *T:* (020) 7332 1850.

BARNES, Michael; *see* Barnes, D. M. W.

BARNES, Michael Cecil John, CBE 1998; Legal Services Ombudsman for England and Wales, 1991–97; *b* 22 Sept. 1932; *s* of late Major C. H. R. Barnes, OBE and of Katherine Louise (*née* Kennedy); *m* 1962, Anne Mason; one *s* one *d*. *Educ:* Malvern; Corpus Christi Coll., Oxford. Nat. Service, 2nd Lieut, Wilts Regt, served in Hong Kong, 1952–53. MP (Lab) Brentford and Chiswick, 1966–Feb. 1974; an Opposition Spokesman on food and food prices, 1970–71; Chairman: Parly Labour Party Social Security Group, 1969–70; ASTMS Parly Cttee, 1970–71; Jt Hon. Sec., Labour Cttee for Europe, 1969–71; Mem., Public Accounts Cttee, 1967–74. Contested (Lab): Wycombe, 1964; Brentford and Isleworth, Feb. 1974; Mem. Labour Party, 1957–79; helped form SDP, 1981; rejoined Labour Party, 1983–. Chm., Electricity Consumers' Council, 1977–83; Dir, UKIAS, 1984–90. Member: Council of Management, War on Want, 1972–77; Nat. Consumer Council, 1975–80; Arts Council Trng Cttee, 1977–83; Energy Commn, 1977–79; Internat. Cttee of Nat. Council for Voluntary Organisations, 1977–83; Advertising Standards Authority, 1979–85; Direct Mail Services Standards Bd, 1983–86; Data Protection Tribunal, 1985–90; Investigation Cttee, Solicitors' Complaints Bureau, 1987–90; Legal Services Commn (formerly Legal Aid Bd), 1998–; Financial Services Ombudsman Bd, 1999–. Chm., British and Irish Ombudsman Assoc., 1995–98. Chairman: UK Adv. Cttee on EEC Action Against Poverty Programme, 1975–76; Notting Hill Social Council, 1976–79; West London Fair Housing Gp Ltd, 1980–87; Vice Chm., Bangabandhu Soc., 1980–90; Organising Secretary: Gulbenkian Foundn Drama Trng Inquiry, 1974–75; Music Trng Inquiry, 1976–77; Sec., Nat. Council for Drama Trng, 1976–84; Chm., Hounslow Arts Trust, 1974–82; Trustee, Project Hand Trust, 1974–77; Governor, Internat. Musicians Seminar, Prussia Cove, 1978–81. *Recreations:* walking, reading. *Address:* 45 Ladbroke Grove, W11 3AR. *T:* (020) 7727 2533.

BARNES, Prof. Michael Patrick; Professor of Scandinavian Studies, University College London, since 1995 (Professor of Scandinavian Philology, 1983–94); *b* 28 June 1940; *s* of William Edward Clement Barnes and Gladys Constance Barnes (*née* Hooper); *m* 1970, Kirsten Heiberg (*née* Røer); one *s* three *d*. *Educ:* University College London (BA, MA); Univ. of Oslo. Asst Lectr, Lectr and Reader in Scandinavian Philology, UCL, 1964–83. Visiting Professor: Tórshavn, Faroe Islands, 1979 and 1990; Uppsala Univ., 1984. Member: Gustav Adolfs Akademien, Uppsala, 1984 (Corresp. Mem., 1977); Det norske Videnskaps-Akademi, Oslo, 1997. Jt Ed., North-Western European Language Evolution, 1989– (Mem. Adv. Bd, 1981–88); Member, Editorial Board: Fróðskaparrit, 1995–; Maal og Minne, 1996–; Norsk lingvistisk tidsskrift, 1997–; Nordic Jl of Linguistics, 2000–; Beiträge sur nordischen Philologie, 2000–; Jt Hon. Sec., Viking Soc. for Northern Research, 1982– (Mem. Editl Bd, 1970–76, Chief Editor, 1977–83, Saga Book of the Viking Soc.). Knight, Order of the Falcon (Iceland), 1992. *Publications:* Draumkvæde: an edition and study, 1974; The Runic Inscriptions of Maeshowe, Orkney, 1994; (jtly) The Runic Inscriptions of Viking Age Dublin, 1997; The Norn Language of Orkney and Shetland, 1998; A New Introduction to Old Norse, vol. I: Grammar, 1999; articles in learned jls. *Recreations:* badminton, being with family, walking disused railways. *Address:* 93 Longland Drive, N20 8HN. *T:* (020) 8445 4697.

BARNES, Peter; dramatist; *b* 10 Jan. 1931; *s* of Frederick and Martha Barnes; *m* 1958, Charlotte (*née* Beck); *m* 1995, Christie (*née* Horn); one *d*. *Educ:* Stroud Grammar Sch. 1st Play, Sclerosis, 1965. Adapted and co-directed: Wedekind's Lulu, 1972; The Bewitched, 1974; adapted and dir., Feydeau's The Purging, 1976; directed: Wedekind's The Singer, 1976; Jonson's Bartholomew Fair, 1978, 1987; Marston's Antonio, 1979; Wedekind's The Devil Himself, 1980; adapted Jonson's The Devil is an Ass, 1977; directed: For All Those Who Get Despondent, 1977; Laughter!, 1978; Somersaults, 1981; Red Noses (Laurence Olivier Award for Best Play), 1985; adapted Feydeau's Scenes from a Marriage, 1986; directed: The Spirit of Man (TV plays), 1989; Nobody Here But Us Chickens (TV plays) (RTS Award for Best TV Play), 1990; Sunsets and Glories, 1990; adapted Ninagawa's Tango at the End of Winter, 1991; dir, Bye Bye Columbus (TV play), 1992; adapted Enchanted April (film), 1993; adapted and dir., Hard Times (TV play), 1994; writer and dir, Dreaming, 1999; writer, Jubilee (play), 2001. *Radio plays include:* My Ben Jonson, 1973; The Two Hangmen, from Wedekind and Brecht, 1979; Barnes' People One, 1981; The Jumping Minuses of Byzantinium, 1981 (Giles Cooper Radio Award); A Mad World My Masters, from Middleton, 1983; Barnes' People Two, 1983; The Primrose Path, from Feydeau, 1984; The Old Law, from Middleton, Rowley and Massinger, 1986; Barnes' People Three, 1986; Don Juan and Faust, from Grabbe, 1987; The Magnetic Lady, from Jonson, 1987; More Barnes' People, 1989. *Publications:* The Ruling Class, 1969 (John Whiting Award; Evening Standard Award); Leonardo's Last Supper, 1970; Noonday Demons, 1970; Lulu, 1971; The Bewitched, 1974; The Frontiers of Farce, 1976; Laughter!, 1978; The Collected Plays, 1981; Barnes' People Two, 1984; Red Noses, 1985; The Real Long John Silver (Barnes' People Three), 1986; The Collected Plays, 1989, vol. II, 1993, vol. III, 1996; The Spirit of Man, 1990; Nobody Here But Us Chickens, 1990; Sunsets and Glories, 1991; Dreaming, 1999. *Address:* 7 Archery Close, Connaught Street, W2 2BE. *T:* (020) 7262 9205; (agent) Jeanne Casarotto, Casarotto Ramsay Ltd, National House, 60–66 Wardour Street, W1V 3HP. *T:* (020) 7287 4450.

BARNES, Prof. Peter John, DM, DSc; FRCP, FMedSci; Professor of Thoracic Medicine, Imperial College, London (National Heart and Lung Institute) and Hon. Consultant Physician, Royal Brompton Hospital, since 1987; Chairman of Respiratory Science, Imperial College, London, since 1997; *b* 29 Oct. 1946; *s* of late John Barnes and Eileen Gertrude Barnes (*née* Thurman); *m* 1976, Olivia Harvard-Watts; three *s*. *Educ:* Leamington Coll.; St Catharine's Coll., Cambridge (open schol., BA (1st class); MA); Worcester Coll., Oxford (DM, DSc). FRCP 1985. Jun. med. posts, then Registrar, Oxford and UCH, London; MRC fellowships, Univ. of Calif, San Francisco, and RPMS, London; Hammersmith Hospital, London: Sen. Registrar, 1979–82; Sen. Lectr and Consultant Physician, RPMS, 1982–85; Prof. of Clinical Pharmacol., Cardiothoracic Inst., London, 1985–87. Vis. Prof., RSocMed, 1993. Lectures: Linacre, RCP, 1994; Amberson (and Prize), Amer. Thoracic Soc., 1996; Sadoul, Eur. Respiratory Soc., 1999. Founder FMedSci 1998. Hon. MD Ferarra, Italy, 1997. Dutch Med. Fedn Prize, 1995. *Publications:* New Drugs for Asthma, 1982, 3rd edn 1998; Asthma: basic mechanisms and clinical management, 1989, 3rd edn 1998; (ed jtly) The Lung: scientific foundations, 1991, 3rd edn 1998; Recent Advances in Respiratory Medicine, 1993; (jtly) Conquering Asthma, 1994; (jtly) Molecular Biology of Lung Disease, 1994; Asthma (2 vols), 1997; (ed jtly) Antonomic Control of the Respiratory System, 1997; (jtly) Asthma Therapy, 1998; Managing Chronic Obstructive Pulmonary Disease, 1999; over 700 pubns on lung pharmacol. and asthma. *Recreations:* travel, ethnic art collecting, gardening, film and theatre going. *Address:* Department of Thoracic Medicine, National Heart and Lung Institute (Imperial College), Dovehouse Street, SW3 6LY. *T:* (020) 7351 8174.

BARNES, Richard Michael; Member (C) Ealing and Hillingdon, London Assembly, Greater London Authority, since 2000; *b* 1 Dec. 1947; *s* of late John William Barnes and of Kate (Kitty) Barnes (*née* Harper). *Educ:* UWIST, Cardiff (BSc Hons Econs). Mem. (C) Hillingdon BC, 1982– (Leader, Cons. Gp, 1992–2000; Leader, 1998–2000). Mem., Metropolitan Police Authority, 2000–. *Recreations:* gardening, chelonia, opera, bibliophile. *Address:* 280 Northwood Road, Harefield, Middx UB9 6PU. *T:* (020) 7983 4387. *Club:* Hayes and Harlington Conservative.

BARNES, Dr Robert Sandford; Chairman, Robert S. Barnes Consultants, since 1978; Principal, Queen Elizabeth College, Kensington, London University, 1978–85, Fellow, 1985; *b* 8 July 1924; *s* of William Edward and Ada Elsie Barnes (*née* Sutherst); *m* 1952, Julia Frances Marriott Grant; one *s* three *d*. *Educ:* Univ. of Manchester. BSc Hons 1948, MSc 1959, DSc 1962. Radar Research, Admiralty Signals Estab., Witley, Surrey, 1944–47; AERE, Harwell: Metallurgical Research, 1948–62; Head of Irradiation Branch, 1962–65; Vis. Scientist, The Science Center, N Amer. Aviation Co., Calif, 1965; Head of Metallurgy Div., AERE, Harwell, 1966–68; Dep. Dir, BISRA, 1968–69; Dir, BISRA, 1969–70; Dir R&D, British Steel Corp., 1970–75; Chief Scientist, BSC, 1975–78. Technical Adviser: Bd of BOC Ltd, 1978–79; Bd of BOC International Ltd, 1979–81; Bd of New Ventures Secretariat, 1978–80. Chm., Ruthner Continuous Crop Systems Ltd, 1976–78. Member: CBI Res. and Technol. Cttee, 1968–75; Adv. Council on R&D for Iron and Steel, 1970–75; Materials Science and Technol. Cttee, SRC, 1975–79; European Industrial Res. Management Assoc., 1970 (Vice-Pres., 1974–78); Parly and Scientific Cttee, 1970–80, 1983–85; Foundn for Science and Technology, 1984– (Mem., Membership Cttee, 1987–98); Chm., Materials Technology Panel, Internat. Tin Res. Inst., 1988–94. Member: Council, Welding Inst., 1970–75; Council, Instn of Metallurgists, 1970–75 and 1979–85 (Vice Pres., 1979; Sen. Vice Pres., 1982; Pres., 1983–85); Council, Metals Soc., 1974–80, 1982–85 (Chm., Coordinating Cttee, 1976–78; Mem., Executive Cttee, 1976–80). Institute of Metals: Mem., Steering Gp, 1983–84; Mem. Council, 1985–92; Mem. Exec. Cttee, 1985–92; Past Pres., 1985–; Chm., Professional Bd, 1985–92; Institute of Materials Members Trust: Trustee, 1984–; Mem., 1986–; Chm., 1992–99. Chairman: Combined Operations Working Party, 1980–81; European Nuclear Steel-making Club, 1973–76; UK Representative: Commn de la Recherche Technique Sidérurgique, 1972–78; Conseil d'Association Européenne pour la Promotion de la Recherche Technique en Sidérurgie, 1972–78; Adv. Council on Energy Conservation, Industry Group, 1977–78; Council, Nat. Backpain Assoc., 1979–98. Hon. Mem. Council, Iron and Steel Inst., 1969–73. Governor, Sheffield Polytechnic, 1968–72; Member: Court of Univ. of Surrey, 1968–80; Collegiate Council, Univ. of London, 1978–85; Jt Finance and Gen. Purposes Cttee, Univ. of London, 1978–85; Senate, Univ. of London, 1980–85; Member Council: King's Coll. London, 1982–85; Chelsea Coll., 1983–85; Bd Mem., CSTI, 1984–88. Lectures: Hatfield Meml, Iron and Steel Inst., 1973; John Player, IMechE, 1976. Freeman, City of London, 1984; Liveryman, Worshipful Co. of Engrs, 1985. Rosenhain Medallist, Inst. of Metals, 1964. FInstP 1961; FIM 1965; FRSA 1976; FKC 1985; Life Member: Royal Instn, 1986; RYA 1990 (Mem., 1976–); Nat. Trust, 1986. CEng 1977; CPhys 1985. *Publications:* chapters in specialist books of science; scientific papers in various learned jls on the effects of atomic radiation on materials, also on the rôle of energy in the production of engineering materials, steel in particular. *Recreations:* cruising in the Mediterranean (sailing yacht Bombero), archaeology. *Address:* One The Mansion, Ashwood Place, Woking, Surrey GU22 7JR. *T:* (01483) 761529. *Clubs:* Athenæum, Cruising Association.

BARNES, Roger Anthony; Director, Hambros Bank Ltd, 1993–97; Assistant Director, Bank of England and Head of Banking Supervision Division, 1988–93; *b* 29 May 1937; *s* of Kenneth Ernest Barnes and Lilian Agnes (*née* King); *m* 1961, Tessa Margaret Soundy; two *s* two *d*. *Educ:* Malvern College; St John's College, Oxford (BA). Bank of England, 1961–93. Mem. Council of Management, European Sch. of Management, 1994–. Trustee, CAF, 1999–. *Recreations:* golf, music, English folk dancing. *Address:* 40 Battlefield Road, St Albans, Herts AL1 4DD. *T:* (01727) 851987. *Clubs:* Bankers', City of London.

BARNES, Rosemary Susan, (Rosie); Chief Executive, Cystic Fibrosis Trust, since 1996; *b* 16 May 1946; *d* of Alan Allen and Kathleen (*née* Brown); *m* 1967, Graham Barnes; two *s* one *d*. *Educ:* Bilborough Grammar Sch.; Birmingham Univ. (BSocSci Hons). Management Trainee, Research Bureau Ltd, 1967–69; Product Manager, Yardley of London Ltd, 1969–72; primary teacher (briefly), 1972; freelance market researcher, 1973–87. MP Greenwich, Feb. 1987–1992 (SDP, 1987–90, Social Democrat, 1990–92); contested (Soc. Dem.) Greenwich, 1992. Dir, Birthright, subseq. WellBeing, 1992–96. *Recreations:* gardening, cooking, reading, travelling, walking, yoga, my dog. *Address:* (office) 11 London Road, Bromley, Kent BR1 1BY.

BARNES, Simon John Campbell; writer; sports columnist: The Times, since 1982; The Spectator, since 1995; Horse and Rider, since 1999; *b* 22 July 1951; *s* of Edward Campbell Barnes, *qv* and of late Dorothy Elsie Barnes (*née* Smith); *m* 1983, Cindy Lee Wright; one *s*. *Educ:* Emanuel Sch.; Bristol Univ. (BA Hons). Surrey and S London Newspapers, 1974–78; contributor to S China Morning Post, Asian Business and Asian Finance, based in Asia, 1978–82; wildlife writer, RSPB Birds magazine, 1994–. Sports Writer of Year, British Press Awards, 1987; Sports Feature Writer of Year, Sports Council, 1988 and 1998; Football Writer of Year, Football Supporters' Assoc., 1991. *Publications:* Phil Edmonds: a singular man, 1986; Horsesweat and Tears, 1988; A Sportswriter's Year, 1989; A la Recherche du Cricket Perdu, 1989; Sportswriter's Eye, 1989; Flying in the Face of Nature, 1991; Tiger!, 1994; Planet Zoo, 2000; On Horseback, 2000; *novels:* Rogue Lion Safaris, 1997; Hong Kong Belongers, 1999; Miss Chance, 2000. *Recreations:* Africa, horses, birdsong, Bach. *Address:* c/o The Times, 1 Pennington Street, E1 9XN. *T:* (020) 7782 5000, *Fax:* (020) 7782 5211. *Club:* Tewin Irregulars Cricket.

BARNES, Timothy Paul; QC 1986; a Recorder, since 1987; *b* 23 April 1944; *s* of late Arthur Morley Barnes and Valerie Enid Mary Barnes; *m* 1969, Patricia Margaret Gale; one *s* three *d*. *Educ:* Bradfield Coll., Berkshire; Christ's Coll., Cambridge (MA). Called to Bar, Gray's Inn, 1968, Hilbery Exhibn; practises Midland and Oxford Circuit; Asst Recorder, 1983. *Recreations:* gardening, theatre. *Address:* The White House, Crooms Hill, SE10 8HH. *T:* (020) 8858 1185, *Fax:* (020) 8858 0788. *Club:* MCC.

BARNES THOMPSON, Dame Ingrid Victoria; *see* Allen, Dame I. V.

BARNETT, family name of **Baron Barnett**.

BARNETT, Baron *cr* 1983 (Life Peer), of Heywood and Royton in Greater Manchester; **Joel Barnett;** PC 1975; JP; chairman and director of a number of companies; Vice-Chairman, Board of Governors, BBC, 1986–93; *b* 14 Oct. 1923; *s* of Louis and Ettie Barnett, both of Manchester; *m* 1949, Lilian Goldstone; one *d. Educ:* Derby Street Jewish Sch.; Manchester Central High Sch. Certified accountant. Served RASC and British Military Govt in Germany. Mem. of Prestwich, Lancs, Borough Council, 1956–59; Hon. Treas. Manchester Fabian Society, 1953–65. Contested (Lab) Runcorn Div. of Cheshire, Oct. 1959; MP (Lab) Heywood and Royton Div., Lancs, 1964–83. Member: Public Accounts Cttee, 1965–71 (Chm., 1979–83); Public Expenditure Cttee, 1971–74; Select Cttee on Tax Credits, 1973–74; Chm. Parly Labour Party Economic and Finance Group, 1967–70 and 1972–74 (Vice-Chm., 1966–67); Opposition Spokesman on Treasury matters, 1970–74; Chief Sec. to the Treasury, 1974–79 (Cabinet Mem., 1977–79); Opposition spokesman on the Treasury in House of Lords, 1983–86. Hon. Visiting Fellow, Univ. of Strathclyde, 1980–. Chm., British Screen Finance Ltd (formerly British Screen Finance Consortium), 1985–97. Mem., Internat. Adv. Bd, Unisys, 1989–96. Chm., Building Societies' Ombudsman Council, 1987–96. Trustee, V&A Museum, 1984–97. Mem., Hallé Cttee, 1982–93. Chm., Birkbeck Coll. Appeal Cttee, 1990–96; Trustee, Open Univ. Foundn, 1994–. Chm., Hansard Soc. for Parly Govt, 1984–90. Pres., RIPA, 1989–92. Hon. Fellow, Birkbeck Coll., London, 1992. JP Lancs 1960. Hon. LLD Strathclyde, 1983. *Publication:* Inside the Treasury, 1982. *Recreations:* walking, conversation and reading; good food. *Address:* Flat 92, 24 John Islip Street, SW1P 4LG; 7 Hillingdon Road, Whitefield, Manchester M45 7QQ.

BARNETT, Charles Henry; Managing Directror, Aintree Racecourse Co. Ltd, since 1993; *b* 15 July 1948; *s* of late Major B. G. Barnett and of D. Barnett; *m* 1978, Georgina Greig; one *s* two *d. Educ:* Eton Coll.; Christ Church, Oxford (BA 2nd Cl. Hons Jurisprudence; MA). Chief Executive Haydock Park Racecourse, 1984–93; Chester Race Co. Ltd, 1996–2000. *Recreation:* country pursuits. *Address:* Aintree Racecourse, Aintree, Liverpool L9 5AS. *T:* (0151) 523 2600.

BARNETT, Dr Christopher Andrew; Headmaster, Whitgift School, Croydon, since 1991; *b* 1 Feb. 1953; *s* of Peter Alan Barnett and Joan Barnett (*née* Cullis); *m* 1976, Hon. Laura Miriam Elizabeth, *o c* of Baron Weidenfeld, *qv*; three *s* one *d. Educ:* Cedars Sch., Leighton Buzzard; Oriel Coll., Oxford (Exhibnr; BA Hons History 1974; MA 1978; DPhil 1981). Lectr in Econs, Brunel Univ., 1975–77; Head of History Dept, Bradfield Coll., Berks, 1978–87; Second Master, Dauntsey's Sch., Wilts, 1987–91. Fellow Commoner, Downing Coll., Cambridge, 1987; Evelyn Wrench Scholar, ESU, 1990. Chm., Whitgift Racing Ltd, 1999–. Pres., Croydon Music Fest., 1992–. Trustee, Warlingham Park Sch., 1994–. *Recreations:* opera, political Victoriana, hill-walking, travel, horse-racing. *Address:* Whitgift School, Haling Park, South Croydon CR2 6YT. *T:* (020) 8688 9222. *Club:* Athenæum.

BARNETT, Christopher John Anthony, QC 1983; **His Honour Judge Barnett;** a Circuit Judge, since 1988; Designated Family Judge, Suffolk, since 1991; *b* 18 May 1936; *s* of Richard Adrian Barnett and Phyllis Barnett (*née* Cartwright); *m* 1959, Sylvia Marieliese (*née* Pritt); two *s* one *d. Educ:* Repton Sch., Derbyshire; College of Law, London. Called to the Bar, Gray's Inn, 1965. District Officer (Kikuyu Guard) and Kenya Government Service, 1955–60; a District Officer in HM Overseas Civil Service, serving in Kenya, 1960–62; in practice as barrister, 1965–88; a Recorder, 1982–88. Mem., Wine Cttee, SE Circuit, 1984–88; Chm., SE Circuit Area Liaison Cttee, 1985–88. Chm., Suffolk Community Alcohol Services, 1993–95; Patron, Relate, W Suffolk, 1998–. Mem., Court of Essex Univ., 1983–. *Recreations:* cricket, tennis, walking. *Address:* 9–12 Bell Yard, WC2A 2LF. *Club:* Kenya Kongonis Cricket.

BARNETT, Clive Durac, MA; Headmaster, Bishop Wordsworth's School, Salisbury, since 1992; *b* 22 July 1949; *s* of Edgar Thomas Barnett and Betty Marian Barnett; *m* 1981, Patricia Michelle Morrissey. *Educ:* King's Coll. Sch., Wimbledon; Magdalen Coll., Oxford (BA Hons, MA, PGCE). Asst Teacher of History, Kingston GS, 1971–79; Head, History and Politics Depts, Watford Boys' GS, 1979–86; Dep. Headmaster, Portsmouth GS, 1986–92. Chm. Trustees, Trade Aid, 1996–. *Publication:* (jtly) Smike (a musical), 1973 (televised 1974). *Recreations:* cricket, cycling, listening to most forms of music, travelling, spending time with my wife! *Address:* Bishop Wordsworth's School, 11 The Close, Salisbury, Wilts SP1 2EB. *T:* (01722) 333851. *Clubs:* East India, MCC.

BARNETT, Colin Michael; international business consultant, since 1990; Regional Secretary, North-West Regional Council of the Trades Union Congress, 1976–85; Divisional Officer, North-West Division of the National Union of Public Employees, 1971–84; *b* 27 Aug. 1929; *s* of Arthur Barnett and Kathleen Mary Barnett; *m* 1st, 1953, Margaret Barnett (marr. diss. 1980); one *s* one *d*; 2nd, 1982, Hilary Carolyn Hodge, PhD; one *s* one *d. Educ:* St Michael's Elem. Sch., Southfields; Wandsworth Grammar Sch.; London Sch. of Econs and Polit. Science; WEA classes. Area Officer, NUPE, 1959, Asst Divl Officer 1961. Chm. Gp H, Duke of Edinburgh Conf. on Industry and Society, 1974. Secretary: NW Peace Council, 1979–; NW Cttee Against Racism, 1980–. Chm., MSC Area Bd, Gtr Manchester and Lancashire, 1978–83. Member: Merseyside District Manpower Bd, 1983–86; Industrial Tribunal, Manchester, 1974–99; Liverpool Social Security Appeal Tribunal, 1986–99. Dir, AT4 Community Prog. Agency, 1986–89. Debt and Industrial Advr, St Helens CAB, 1984–92; Marriage Guidance Counsellor, 1984–92. Organised: People's March for Jobs, 1981; (jtly) People's March for Jobs, 1983. British Representative: NW Russia Agency for Internat. Co-operation and Develt; St Petersburg British-Russia Soc.; Co-ordinator, UK projects for St Petersburg Health Dept. Employment Advr, This is Your Right, Granada TV, 1970–89. Governor, William Temple Foundn, 1980–87; Chm. Governors, Broadway Community High Sch., St Helens, 1999–. Chm. Trustees, Prescot and St Helens Victim Support Service. *Recreations:* reading, promoting values of socialist ethics. *Address:* 14 Elm Grove, Eccleston Park, Prescot, Merseyside L34 2RX. *T:* (0151) 426 4045, *Fax:* (0151) 426 0100; *e-mail:* colin_barnett@virgin.net.

BARNETT, Correlli (Douglas), CBE 1997; author; Fellow, Churchill College, Cambridge, since 1977; Keeper of the Churchill Archives Centre, 1977–95; *b* 28 June 1927; *s* of D. A. Barnett; *m* 1950, Ruth Murby; two *d. Educ:* Trinity Sch., Croydon; Exeter Coll., Oxford. Second class hons, Mod. Hist. with Mil. Hist. and the Theory of War as a special subject; MA 1954. Intell. Corps, 1945–48. North Thames Gas Bd, 1952–57; Public Relations, 1957–63. Vice-Pres., E Arts Assoc., 1978–91 (Chm. Literature Panel, and Mem. Exec. Cttee, 1972–78); Pres., East Anglian Writers, 1969–88; Member: Council, Royal Utd Services Inst. for Defence Studies, 1973–85; Cttee, London Library, 1977–79 and 1982–84. Leverhulme Res. Fellowship, 1976; apptd Lectr in Defence Studies, Univ. of Cambridge, 1980; resigned in order to devote more time to writing, 1983. Winston Churchill Meml Lectr, Switzerland, 1982. Hon. Pres., Western Front Assoc., 1998–. FRSL; FRHistS; FRSA. Hon. DSc Cranfield, 1993. Chesney Gold Medal, RUSI, 1991. *Publications:* The Hump Organisation, 1957; The Channel Tunnel (with Humphrey Slater), 1958; The Desert Generals, 1960, new enlarged edn, 1983; The Swordbearers, 1963; Britain and Her Army, 1970 (RSL award, 1971); The Collapse of British Power, 1972; Marlborough, 1974; Bonaparte, 1978; The Great War, 1979; The Audit of War, 1986 (US edn as The Pride and the Fall, 1987); Engage the Enemy More Closely: the Royal Navy in the Second World War, 1991 (Yorkshire Post Book of the Year Award, 1991); The Lost Victory: British Dreams, British Realities 1945–1950, 1995; The Verdict of Peace: Britain between her yesterday and the future, 2001; (historical consultant and writer to) BBC Television series: The Great War, 1963–64; The Lost Peace, 1965–66; The Commanders, 1972–73; reviews Mil. Hist. for The Spectator and The Sunday Telegraph; contrib. to: The Promise of Greatness (a symposium on the Great War), 1968; Governing Elites (a symposium), 1969; Decisive Battles of the Twentieth Century, 1976; The War Lords, 1976; The Economic System in the UK, 1985; Education for Capability, 1986; (ed) Hitler's Generals, 1989. *Recreations:* gardening, interior decorating, idling, eating, mole-hunting, travelling through France. *Address:* Catbridge House, East Carleton, Norwich NR14 8JX. *T:* (01508) 570410. *Club:* Beefsteak.

BARNETT, Prof. David Braham, MD; FRCP; Professor of Clinical Pharmacology, since 1984, and Head, Department of Medicine, since 1999, University of Leicester Medical School; *b* 17 July 1944; *s* of Joseph and Jeanne Barnett; *m* 1967, Sharon Diane Solomons; one *d. Educ:* Sheffield Univ. Med. Sch. (MB ChB Hons 1967; MD 1979). FRCP 1981. Merck Internat. Travelling Fellow, 1975–76; Sen. Lectr, Univ. of Leicester, 1976–84; Hon. Consultant Physician, Leicester Royal Infirmary, 1976–. Non-exec. Dir, Leicester Royal Infirmary NHS Trust, 1993–2000. Chairman: Appraisals Cttee, NICE, 1999–. *Publications:* original research, rev. articles and book chapters in fields of molecular pharmacology and general cardiovascular clinical pharmacology, with specialist interest in ischaemic heart disease. *Recreations:* golf, reading, theatre. *Address:* Division of Medicine and Therapeutics, Level 4, Robert Kilpatrick Clinical Sciences Building, Leicester Royal Infirmary, Leicester LE2 7LX. *T:* (0116) 252 3126.

BARNETT, Geoffrey Grant Fulton, OBE 2001; director of and consultant to businesses and charities; *b* 9 March 1943; *s* of Air Chief Marshal Sir Denis H. F. Barnett, GCB, CBE, DFC; *m* 1968, Fiona Katharine Milligan; two *s* two *d. Educ:* Winchester; Clare Coll., Cambridge (MA). Courtaulds Ltd, 1964–67; The Economist Intelligence Unit, 1967–70; British Printing Corp., 1970–71; Baring Brothers & Co. Ltd, 1971–95 (Dir, 1979–95); Man. Dir, Baring Brothers Asia, Hong Kong, 1979–83; seconded as Dir Gen., Panel on Takeovers and Mergers, 1989–92. Director: Language Line Ltd, 1996–99; StartHere, 2000–. Hon. Treas., VSO, 1984–2000; Member Governing Bd, London and Quadrant Housing Trust, 1985–2000; Council, Barnardo's, 2001–. FRSA 1992. *Recreations:* Scotland, walking, music, bird watching. *Address:* 2 Mill Hill Road, SW13 0HR. *T:* (020) 8878 6975.

BARNETT, Jenifer W.; *see* Wilson-Barnett.

BARNETT, Jeremy John, OBE 1982; independent tour consultant, since 1999; *b* 26 Jan. 1941; *s* of late Audrey Wickham Barnett and Lt-Comdr Charles Richard Barnett, RN; *m* 1968, Maureen Janet Cullum; one *s* one *d. Educ:* St Edward's Sch., Oxford; St Andrews Univ. (MA); Leeds Univ. (Dip TEFL); SOAS, London Univ. (MA 1994). Joined British Council, 1964; teaching, Victory Coll., Cairo, 1965–67; Lectr, Inst. of Educn, Istanbul, 1967–69; MECAS, Lebanon, 1969–70; Dir of Studies, Turco-British Assoc., Ankara, 1970–72; British Council Rep., Riyadh, 1972–75; Dir, ME Dept, 1975–78; Counsellor for British Council and Cultural Affairs, Ankara, 1978–82; British Council Rep., Warsaw, 1982–85; Dir, E Europe and N Asia Dept, 1985–88; Controller, S and W Asia Div., 1988–89; British Council Rep., later Dir, and Cultural Counsellor, British Embassy, Cairo, 1989–93. Westminster Classic Tours, 1995–98 (Man. Dir, 1998–99). *Recreation:* hill walking. *Address:* Oakdene Station Road, Groombridge, Tunbridge Wells, Kent TN3 9NB. *T:* and *Fax:* (01892) 864626.

BARNETT, Joseph Anthony, CBE 1983 (OBE 1975); Director (formerly Representative), British Council, Tokyo, 1983–91, retired; *b* 19 Dec. 1931; *s* of Joseph Edward Barnett and Helen Johnson; *m* 1960, Carolina Johnson Rice (*d* 1998); one *s* one *d. Educ:* St Albans Sch.; Pembroke Coll., Cambridge (BA (Hons) English and Psychology); Edinburgh Univ. (Diploma in Applied Linguistics). Served Army, 1950–51 (2nd Lieut). Teaching, Aylesford House, St Albans, 1954–55; Unilever Ltd, 1955–58; apptd British Council, 1958; Asst Educn Officer, Dacca, Pakistan, 1958; trng at Sch. of Applied Linguistics, Edinburgh Univ., 1960; Educn Officer, Dacca, 1961; seconded to Inst. of Educn, London Univ., 1963; Head, English Language Teaching Inst., London, 1964; Dir of Studies, Regional Inst. of English, Bangalore, India, 1968; Representative, Ethiopia, 1971; Controller, English Language Teaching Div., 1975; Representative, Brazil, 1978–82. *Publications:* (jtly) Getting on in English, 1960; Success with English (language laboratory materials), Books 1–3, 1966–69. *Recreation:* sport (tennis, cricket, riding). *Address:* The Thatch, Stebbing Green, Dunmow, Essex CM6 3TE. *T:* (01371) 856014. *Club:* Athenæum.

BARNETT, Kenneth Thomas, CB 1979; Director, Abbey Data Systems Ltd, since 1984; *b* 12 Jan. 1921; *yr s* of late Frederick Charles Barnett and Ethel Barnett (*née* Powell); *m* 1943, Emily May Lovering; one *d. Educ:* Howard Gardens High Sch., Cardiff. Entered Civil Service (Min. of Transport), 1937; Sea Transport Office, Port Said, 1951–54; Asst Sec., 1965; Under-Sec., Cabinet Office (on secondment), 1971–73; Under-Sec., DoE, 1970–76, Dep. Sec., 1976–80. *Recreations:* gardening, watching Rugby football. *Address:* 5 Redan Close, Highcliffe-on-Sea, Christchurch, Dorset BH23 5DJ. *T:* (01425) 276945.

BARNETT, Kevin Edward; His Honour Judge Kevin Barnett; a Circuit Judge, since 1996; *b* 2 Jan. 1948; *s* of Arthur and Winifred Barnett; *m* 1972, Patricia Margaret Smith; one *d. Educ:* Wellesbourne Sch.; Tudor Grange Grammar Sch.; London Univ. (LLB Hons ext.). Called to the Bar, Gray's Inn, 1971; Wales and Chester Circuit. *Recreations:* painting, photography, cooking. *Address:* Court Service, Wales and Chester Circuit, 2nd Floor, Churchill House, Churchill Way, Cardiff CF1 4HH. *Club:* Lansdowne.

BARNETT, Rt Rev. Paul William, PhD; Bishop of North Sydney, and an Assistant Bishop, Diocese of Sydney, since 1990; *b* 23 Sept. 1935; *s* of William and Edna Barnett; *m* 1963, Anita Janet Simpson; two *s* two *d. Educ:* Univ. of London (BD Hons 1963, PhD 1978); Univ. of Sydney (MA Hons 1975). Deacon, 1963; priest, 1965; Lectr, Moore Theol Coll., 1964–67; Rector, St Barnabas, Broadway, 1967–73; Rector, Holy Trinity, Adelaide, 1973–79; Master, Robert Menzies Coll., Macquarie Univ., 1980–90. Lecturer, part time: Macquarie Univ., 1980–86; Univ. of Sydney, 1982–. Vis. Prof., 1987, 1991, 1993, 1995, Res. Prof., 1996–, Regent Coll., Vancouver. Vis. Fellow in History, Macquarie Univ., 1987–. Kingham Fellow, Oak Hill Theol Coll., 1996. Highly commended author, Christian Booksellers Conf., 1990. *Publications:* Is the New Testament History?, 1986; The Message of 2 Corinthians, 1988; Bethlehem to Patmos, 1989; Apocalypse Now and Then, 1990; The Two Faces of Jesus, 1990; The Servant King, 1991; The Truth About Jesus, 1994; Jesus and the Logic of History, 1997; Commentary on 2 Corinthians, 1997; Jesus and the Rise of Early Christianity, 1999; Commentary on 1 Corinthians. *Recreations:* tennis, swimming, fishing, fine music. *Address:*

Diocese of Sydney, St Andrew's House, Sydney Square, Sydney, NSW 2001, Australia. *T:* (2) 4196761.

BARNETT, Robert William, OBE 1993; HM Diplomatic Service; Counsellor, Review of Overseas Science and Technology Work, Foreign and Commonwealth Office, since 1999; *b* 25 May 1954; *s* of late Harry Frederick Barnett, Wells-next-the-Sea, Norfolk and Dorothy Anne Barnett (*née* Williamson); *m* 1979, Caroline Sara Weale; two *s*. *Educ:* Wymondham Coll., Norfolk; St Catharine's Coll., Cambridge (BA Hons Mod. & Med. Langs 1977; MA 1979). Joined FCO, 1977: Japanese lang. trng, 1979; Third Sec., Tokyo, 1980–83; Policy Planning Staff, FCO, 1984; Asst Private Sec. to Minister of State, 1984–86; First Secretary: Western European Dept, FCO, 1986–88; Bonn, 1988–91; seconded to Saxony State Govt as Inward Investment Advr, 1992; Asst Hd, Eastern Adriatic Unit, FCO, 1993–94; Ambassador to Bosnia-Herzegovina, 1994–95; Counsellor (Sci., Technol. and Envmt), Bonn, 1995–99. *Recreations:* walking, photography, gardening. *Address:* c/o Foreign and Commonwealth Office, King Charles Street, SW1A 2AH.

BARNETT, Robin Anthony; HM Diplomatic Service; Foreign and Commonwealth Office, since 2001; *b* 8 March 1958; *s* of Bryan Anderson Barnett and Marion Barnett; *m* 1st, 1989, Debra Marianne Bunt (marr. diss. 1999); one *s*, and one step *s*; 2nd, 1999, Tesca Marie Osman; one step *s* one step *d*. *Educ:* Birmingham Univ. (LLB Hons 1979). Joined FCO, 1980: Second Secretary: Warsaw, 1982–85; FCO, 1985–90; First Secretary: UK Delegn to conventional forces in Europe negotiations, Vienna, 1990–91; UK Mission to UN, NY, 1991–95; FCO, 1996–98; Counsellor and Dep. Hd of Mission, Warsaw, 1998–2001. *Recreations:* travel, football (Manchester United), reading, film, cooking. *Address:* c/o Foreign and Commonwealth Office, King Charles Street, SW1A 2AH.

BARNETT, William Evans, QC 1984; **His Honour Judge William Barnett;** a Circuit Judge, since 1994; *b* 10 March 1937; *s* of late Alec Barnett and Esmé (*née* Leon); *m* 1976, Lucinda Jane Gilbert, JP, MA, ARCM; two *s*. *Educ:* Repton; Keble Coll., Oxford (BA Jurisprudence, 1961; MA 1965). National Service, RCS, 1956–58. Called to the Bar, Inner Temple, 1962; Major Scholarship, Inner Temple, 1962. A Recorder, 1981–94. Mem., Personal Injuries Litigation Procedure Wkg Pty, 1976–78; Judicial Mem., Mental Health Rev. Tribunal, 1993–. Mem., Whitgift Sch. Cttee, 1996–. *Recreations:* golf, photography, gardening. *Address:* c/o Croydon Combined Court Centre, The Law Courts, Altyre Road, Croydon, Surrey CR9 5AB. *T:* (020) 8410 4700. *Club:* Royal Automobile.

BARNEVIK, Percy; Chairman of the Board: ABB (formerly ABB Asea Brown Boveri) Ltd, Zürich, Switzerland, since 1996 (President and Chief Executive Officer, 1988–96); AstraZeneca PLC, since 1999; *b* Simrishamn, Sweden, 1941. *Educ:* Sch. of Econs, Gothenburg, Sweden (MBA 1964); Stanford Univ. Johnson Group, 1966–69; Sandvik AB: Group Controller, 1969–75; Pres. of Sandvik, USA, 1975–79; Exec. Vice Pres., Sandvik AB Sweden, 1979–80; Chm., 1983–; Pres. and Chief Exec. Officer, Asea, 1980–87. Chm. Bd, Investor AB, 1997– (Bd Mem., Providentia, subseq. Investor, 1987–); Bd Mem., General Motors, 1996–. Hon. DTech Linköping, Sweden, 1989; Hon. DEcons Gothenburg, 1991; Hon. DLaws Babson Coll., Mass, USA, 1995; Hon. DSc Cranfield, 1997; Hon. Dr UMIST with Manchester, 1999. *Address:* ABB Ltd, PO Box 8131, 8050 Zürich, Switzerland.

BARNEWALL, family name of **Baron Trimlestown**.

BARNEWALL, Sir Reginald Robert, 13th Bt *cr* 1622; cattle breeder and orchardist at Mount Tamborine; *b* 1 Oct 1924; *o s* of Sir Reginald J. Barnewall, 12th Bt and of Jessie Ellen, *d* of John Fry; *S* father, 1961; *m* 1st, 1946, Elsie Muriel (*d* 1962), *d* of Thomas Matthews-Frederick, Brisbane; three *d* (one *s* decd); 2nd, 1962, Maureen Ellen, *d* of William Joseph Daly, South Caulfield, Vic; one *s*. *Educ:* Xavier Coll., Melbourne. Served War of 1939–45, overseas with RAE, AIF. Served with Citizen Military Forces Unit, 8/13 Victorian Mounted Rifles, Royal Australian Armoured Corps, 1948–58 (Lieut, acting Major). Managing Dir, Southern Airlines Ltd of Melbourne, 1953–58; Founder, and Operations Manager, Polynesian Airlines, Apia, Western Samoa, 1958–62; Managing Dir, Orchid Beach (Fraser Island) Pty Ltd, 1962–71; Dir, Island Airways Pty Ltd, Pialba, Qld, 1964–68; owner and operator, Coastal-Air Co. (Qld), 1971–76; Dir and Vice-Chm., J. Roy Stevens Pty Ltd, to 1975. *Heir: s* Peter Joseph Barnewall [*b* 26 Oct. 1963; *m* 1988, Kathryn Jane, *d* of Hugh Carroll; two *s* one *d*]. *Address:* Innisfree House, Normandie Court, Mount Tamborine, Queensland 4272, Australia. *Clubs:* United Service (Brisbane); RSL (Surfers Paradise); Royal Automobile (Queensland).

BARNIER, Michel Jean; Member of the European Commission, since 1999; *b* 9 Jan. 1951; *m* 1982, Isabelle Altmayer; two *s* one *d*. *Educ:* Ecole Supérieure de Commerce de Paris (Dip. 1972). Govt service, 1973–78. Mem. (RPR) for Savoie, Nat. Assembly, 1978–93; Minister of the Environment, France, 1993–95; Minister of State for European Affairs, 1995–97. Mem., 1973–, Chm., 1982–, Deptl Council of Savoie; Senator for Savoie, 1997–; Pres., Senate Delegn for EU, 1998. Jt Pres., Organising Cttee, Olympic Games, Albertville and Savoie, 1987–92. *Publications:* Vive la politique, 1985; Chacun pour tous: le défi écologique, 1990; Atlas des risques majeurs, 1992; Vers une mer inconnue, 1994. *Address:* European Commission, 200 rue de la Loi, 1049 Brussels, Belgium; 19 chemin des Jardins, 73200 Albertville, France.

BARNISH, Alan Joseph; Chief Executive, Cambridgeshire County Council, since 1997; *b* 13 Oct. 1949; *s* of Sydney and Dora Barnish; *m* 1972, Elizabeth Sanders; one *s* one *d*. *Educ:* Leeds Univ. (BCom); IPFA. Mid Glam CC, 1975–90; Chief Exec. and Co. Treas., Powys CC, 1990–93; Chief Exec., Shropshire CC, 1993–97. *Address:* (office) Shire Hall, Cambridge CB3 0AP. *T:* (01223) 717090.

BARNSLEY, John Corbitt; Global Leader, Business Process Outsourcing, PricewaterhouseCoopers, since 1998; *b* 25 May 1948; *s* of William C. Barnsley, consultant thoracic surgeon, and Hilda C. Barnsley (*née* Robson); *m* 1971, Denise Roberts (marr. diss. 1997); one *s* one *d* (and one *d* decd). *Educ:* Heaton Grammar Sch., Newcastle upon Tyne; Newcastle upon Tyne Univ. (LLB 1st Cl. Hons 1969; Reynoldson Meml Prize). Joined Price Waterhouse, Newcastle, 1970: Partner, 1979–95; Regl Sen. Tax Partner, 1988–90; Sen. Tax Partner, UK, 1990–95; European Leader for Audit and Business Services, 1993–95; Man. Partner, UK, 1995–98; company merged with Coopers & Lybrand, 1998. Non-exec. Dir, Tyne & Wear Develt Corp., 1988–98. Chairman: Newcastle Hosps Special Trustees, 1988–97; London (formerly N Thames) R & D Cttee, NHS Exec., 1997–. *Recreation:* Chinese porcelain. *Address:* PricewaterhouseCoopers, 1 London Bridge, SE1 9QL; Montpelier Terrace, Knightsbridge, SW7 1JP. *Club:* Reform.

BARNSLEY, Victoria, (Hon. Mrs Nicholas Howard); Chief Executive and Publisher, HarperCollins UK, since 2000; *b* 4 March 1954; *d* of late T. E. Barnsley, OBE and Margaret Gwyneth Barnsley (*née* Llewellin); *m* 1992, Hon. Nicholas Howard; one *d*, and one step *s*. *Educ:* University Coll. London (BA Hons English); Univ. of York (MA French and English 19th Century Novel). Founder, and Chm. and Chief Exec., Fourth Estate Ltd, 1984–2000. Trustee, Tate Gall., 1998–; Dir, Tate Gall. Publications Ltd, 1998–. *Address:* HarperCollins, 77–85 Fulham Palace Road, Hammersmith, W6 8JB. *Club:* Groucho.

BARNSTAPLE, Archdeacon of; *see* Lloyd, Ven. B. T.

BARON, Florence Jacqueline, QC 1995; a Recorder, since 1999; a Deputy High Court Judge, since 2000; *b* 7 Oct. 1952; *d* of Jose Baron and Ellen Elizabeth Jane Baron (*née* McLennan). *Educ:* Jersey Coll. for Girls; St Hugh's Coll., Oxford (BA Juris.). Called to the Bar, Middle Temple, 1976. *Recreation:* relaxing. *Address:* Queen Elizabeth Building, Temple, EC4Y 9BS.

BARON, Franklin Andrew Merrifield; Permanent Representative of Commonwealth of Dominica to United Nations and to Organisation of American States, 1982–95; Dominican High Commissioner to London, 1986–92; *b* 19 Jan. 1923; *m* 1973, Sybil Eva Francisca McIntyre. *Educ:* Portsmouth Govt Sch., St Mary's Acad., Dominica Grammar Sch. A. A. Baron & Co.: entered firm, 1939; Partner, 1945; sole owner, 1978–. Member: Roseau Town Council, 1945–47 and 1956–58; Legislative and Exec. Councils, 1954–61; Founder and Leader, United People's Party, 1954–56; Minister of Trade and Production, 1956–60; Chief Minister and Minister of Finance, 1960–61. Ambassador to USA, 1982–86. Chairman: National Commercial Bank, 1986–90; Fort Young Hotel Co., 1986–89; The New Chronicle, 1989–96 (Dir, 1984–96); Proprietor: Paramount Printers Ltd, 1992–; The Chronicle, 1996–. Member: Public Service Commn, 1976–78; Electoral Commn, 1979–90; Dominica Boundaries Commn, 1979–90; Bd, Dominica Electricity Services, 1981–91 (Chm., 1983–91); Bd, Industrial Develt Corp., 1984–89; Chm., Dominica Public Library, 1985–89. *Recreations:* horticulture, reading, travel. *Address:* 14 Cork Street, Roseau, Dominica. *T:* 4488151, 4480415.

BARON, Prof. Jean-Claude, MD; Professor of Stroke Medicine, Departments of Medicine and Neurology, University of Cambridge, since 2000; *b* 25 March 1949; *s* of Marcel and Yolaine Baron (*née* Bonan); *m* 1974, Annik Arnette de la Charlonny; one *s* two *d*. *Educ:* Univ. of Paris (MD). Asst Lectr in Biophysics, 1979-82, then in Neurol., 1982-86, Univ. of Paris; Sen. Registrar in Nuclear Medicine, 1979-82, then in Neurol., 1982-86, Salpêtrière Hosp., Paris; Director: of Res., INSERM, France, 1986-2000; INSERM Res. Unit # 320, Caen, 1989-2000; Scientific Dir, CYCERON Neuroimaging Res. Centre, Univ. of Caen, 1987-2000; Hon. Consultant in Neurol., Addenbrooke's Hosp., Cambridge, 2000-. *Publications:* contrib. numerous peer-reviewed articles to learned jls, incl. Lancet, Brain, Annals of Neurol., Stroke; numerous book chapters and refereed abstracts. *Recreations:* music (playing the guitar), classic blues, J. S. Bach, Mozart, sport (running, swimming, ski-ing). *Address:* Department of Neurology, Box 165, Addenbrooke's Hospital, Cambridge CB2 2QQ. *T:* (01223) 216073.

BARON, John Charles; MP (C) Billericay, since 2001; *b* 21 June 1959; *s* of Raymond Arthur Ernest Baron and Kathleen Ruby Baron; *m* 1992, Thalia Anne Mayson Laird; two *d*. *Educ:* Jesus Coll., Cambridge (MA). MSI 1978–82. Capt., RRF, 1984–88. Director: Henderson Private Investors, 1988–99; Rothschild Asset Mgt, 1999–2001. *Recreations:* tennis, walking, cycling, family. *Address:* c/o House of Commons, SW1A 0AA; The Mallards, 125 Bramble Tye, Noak Bridge, Laindon, Essex SS15 5GR. *T:* (01268) 520765.

BARON, Dr (Ora) Wendy, OBE 1992; Director (formerly Curator), Government Art Collection, 1978–97; *b* 20 March 1937; *d* of late Dr S. B. Dimson and Gladys Felicia Dimson, CBE; *m* 1st, 1960, Jeremy Hugh Baron (marr. diss.); one *s* one *d*; 2nd, 1990, David Joseph Wyatt, *qv*. *Educ:* St Paul's Girls' Sch.; Courtauld Institute of Art (BA, PhD). Trustee: Contemporary Art Soc., 1997–; Arts Res. Ltd, 1998–; Mem., Cttee, NACF, 1998–. Has selected, researched and catalogued exhibitions, including: Sickert, Fine Art Soc., 1973; Camden Town Recalled, Fine Art Soc., 1976; The Camden Town Group, New Haven, USA, 1980; Late Sickert, Hayward Gall., 1981; Sickert, Royal Acad., 1992, Amsterdam, 1993. FRSA 1993. *Publications:* Sickert, 1973; Miss Ethel Sands and her Circle, 1977; The Camden Town Group, 1979; Perfect Moderns, 2000; articles and reviews in professional jls in the field of modern British art. *Club:* Chelsea Arts.

BARON, Sir Thomas, Kt 1992; CBE 1983. FRICS 1948. *Address:* Lightoaks Hall Farm, Glazebury, near Warrington WA3 5PX.

BARÓN CRESPO, Enrique Carlos; lawyer; Member, European Parliament, since 1986 (President, 1989–91); *b* Madrid, 27 March 1944; *m*; one *s*. *Educ:* Univ. of Madrid (LLL); Inst. Católico de Dirección de Empresas (Lic. en Ciencias Empresariales); Ecole Supérieure des Scis Econ. et Commerciales, Paris (Dip.). Lectr in Agricl Econs, Inst. Nacional de Estudios Agrarios, Valladolid, and in Structural Econs, Univ. of Madrid, 1966–70; lawyer in private practice, 1970–77. Mem. (PSOE), Congress of Deputies, Spain, 1977–87; spokesman on econ. and budgetary affairs, 1977–82; Minister of Transport, Tourism and Communications, 1982–85. European Parliament: a Vice-Pres., 1987–89; Pres., Spanish Socialist Gp.; Pres., PSE, 1999–. Pres., Internat. European Movt, 1987–89. *Publications:* Población y Hambre en el Mundo; El Final del Campesinado; La Civilización del Automóvil; Europa 92: el rapto del futuro; Europe at the Dawn of the Millennium, 1997; contribs on economic and social questions to major Spanish periodicals. *Address:* European Parliament, Rue Wiertz 60, 1047 Brussels, Belgium; Oficina Parlamento Europeo, Paseo de la Castellana 46, 28046 Madrid, Spain.

BARR, Danielle; Member, Broadcasting Standards Commission, 1994–99; *b* 7 Aug. 1940; *d* of Michael and Helen Brachfeld; *m* 1966, Marvin Stein; one *d*, and one step *s*. *Educ:* Tichon Hadash High Sch., Tel Aviv. Nat. Service, Israeli Army, 1958–60; Account Exec., Crane Advertising, 1961–64; Asst Advertising Manager, Goya, 1964–67; Brand Manager, 1967–76, Mktg Manager, 1976–80, Elida Gibbs; Dir, Geers Gross Advertising, 1980–84; Head of Advertising, Natwest Bank, 1984–87; Man. Dir, 1987–89, Chm., 1989–91, Publicis; Man. Dir, Third Age Mktg, 1993–95. Mem., Mktg Gp of GB, 1986–. *Recreations:* theatre, music, quilting. *Address:* 20 Jameson Street, W8 7SH. *T:* (020) 7221 2632. *Club:* Women's Advertising of London (Pres., 1985–86).

BARR, David; a Metropolitan Stipendiary Magistrate, 1976–96; *b* Glasgow, 15 Oct. 1925; *s* of late Walter and Betty Barr; *m* 1960, Ruth Weitzman; one *s* one *d*. *Educ:* Haberdashers' Aske's Hampstead Sch.; Largs Higher Grade Sch.; Brookline High Sch., Boston, USA; Edinburgh Univ.; University Coll., London (LLB). Royal Navy, 1943–47. Solicitor, 1953; private practice, 1953–76 (Partner, Pritchard Englefield & Tobin). JP Inner London Area, 1963–76; Chm., Inner London Juvenile Panel, 1969–76; Dep. Chm., N Westminster PSD, 1968–76. Manager, Finnart House Sch., Weybridge, 1955–73 (Trustee, 1973–96, Chm., 1985–96). Pres., David Isaacs Fund, 1986–94. *Recreations:* collecting 'Alice', bridge. *Address:* 19 St Mark's Crescent, NW1 7TU. *Clubs:* Garrick, MCC.

BARR, Prof. James, MA, BD, DD; FBA 1969; Professor of Hebrew Bible, Vanderbilt University, Nashville, Tennessee, 1989–98, Distinguished Professor, 1994–98, now Emeritus; *b* 20 March 1924; *s* of Rev. Prof. Allan Barr, DD; *m* 1950, Jane J. S. Hepburn, MA; two *s* one *d*. *Educ:* Daniel Stewart's Coll., Edinburgh; Edinburgh Univ. (MA 1948, BD 1951); MA 1976, BD, DD 1981, Oxon. Served War of 1939–45 as pilot in RNVR

(Fleet Air Arm), 1942–45. Minister of Church of Scotland, Tiberias, Israel, 1951–53; Prof. of New Testament Literature and Exegesis, Presbyterian Coll., Montreal, 1953–55; Prof. of Old Testament Literature and Theology, Edinburgh Univ., 1955–61; Prof. of Old Testament Literature and Theology, Princeton Theological Seminary, 1961–65; Prof. of Semitic Languages and Literatures, Manchester Univ., 1965–76; Oriel Prof. of the Interpretation of Holy Scripture, and Fellow of Oriel Coll., Oxford Univ., 1976–78 (Hon. Fellow, 1980); Regius Prof. of Hebrew, Oxford Univ., and Student of Christ Church, 1978–89, Prof. Emeritus, 1989. Visiting Professor: Hebrew Univ., Jerusalem, 1973; Chicago Univ., 1975, 1981; Strasbourg Univ., 1975–76; Brown Univ., Providence, RI, 1985, 1994; Univ. of Otago, NZ, 1986; Univ. of South Africa, 1986; Vanderbilt Univ., Nashville, Tenn, 1987–88; Heidelberg Univ., 1993; lectured: in Princeton Univ., 1962–63; in Union Theol Seminary, New York, 1963; in Pittsburgh Theol Seminary, 2000; Lectures: Currie, Austin Theol Seminary, Texas, 1964; Cadbury, Birmingham Univ., 1969; Croall, Edinburgh Univ., 1970; Grinfield, on the Septuagint, Oxford Univ., 1974–78; Firth, Nottingham Univ., 1978; Sprunt, Richmond, Va, 1982; Sanderson, Ormond Coll., Melbourne, 1982; Faculty, Cardiff, 1986; Schweich, British Acad., 1986; Cole, Vanderbilt, 1988; Sarum, Oxford, 1989; Read-Tuckwell, Bristol, 1990; Gifford, Edinburgh, 1991; Hensley Henson, Oxford, 1997; Alexander Robertson, Glasgow Univ., 1999; Guggenheim Memorial Fellowship for study in biblical semantics, 1965. Mem., Inst. for Advanced Study, Princeton, NJ, 1985. Editor: Jl of Semitic Studies, 1965–76; Oxford Hebrew Dictionary, 1974–80. President: SOTS, 1973; British Assoc. for Jewish Studies, 1978. FRAS 1969; Fellow, Amer. Acad. of Arts and Scis, 1993. Corresp. Mem., Göttingen Acad. of Sciences, 1976; Member: Norwegian Acad. of Science and Letters, 1977; Royal Soc. of Scis, Uppsala, 1991; Amer. Philosophical Soc., 1993; Hon. Mem., Soc. of Biblical Lit. (USA), 1983. Hon. Fellow, SOAS, 1975. Hon. DD: Knox Coll., Toronto, 1964; Dubuque, 1974; St Andrews, 1974; Edinburgh, 1983; Victoria Univ., Toronto, 1988; Hon. DTheol: Univ. of South Africa, 1986; Protestant Theol Faculty, Paris, 1988; Oslo, 1991; Helsinki, 1997; Hon. MA Manchester, 1969. *Publications:* The Semantics of Biblical Language, 1961; Biblical Words for Time, 1962; Old and New in Interpretation, 1966; Comparative Philology and the Text of the Old Testament, 1968; The Bible in the Modern World, 1973; Fundamentalism, 1977; The Typology of Literalism, 1979; Explorations in Theology 7: The Scope and Authority of the Bible, 1980; Holy Scripture: Canon, Authority, Criticism, 1983; Escaping from Fundamentalism, 1984; The Variable Spellings of the Hebrew Bible, 1988; The Garden of Eden and the Hope of Immortality, 1992; Biblical Faith and Natural Theology, 1993; The Concept of Biblical Theology, 1999; History and Ideology in the Old Testament, 2000; articles in Semitic and biblical journals. *Recreation:* bird watching. *Address:* 1432 Sitka Court, Claremont, CA 91711–2734, USA; 6 Fitzherbert Close, Iffley, Oxford OX4 4EN. *T:* (01865) 772741.

BARR, Maj.-Gen. John Alexander James Pooler, CB 1993; CBE 1989; Engineer in-Chief (Army), 1991–93; *b* 29 Jan. 1939. 2nd Lieut, RE, 1960; Lt-Col, 1978; GSO1 (DS) SC, 1978; Brig. 1983; Comdt, Royal Sch. of Mil. Engrg, Chatham, 1983–87; Dir of Army Staff Duties, MoD, 1987–89; DCS (Support), HQ Allied Forces Northern Europe, 1989–91; Maj.-Gen., 1991. Col Comdt, RE, 1993–. CompICE 1992. *Address:* c/o Lloyds TSB, Cox's & King's Branch, PO Box 1190, 7 Pall Mall, SW1Y 5NA.

BARR, Kenneth Glen; Sheriff of South Strathclyde, Dumfries and Galloway at Dumfries, since 1978; *b* 20 Jan. 1941; *s* of late Rev. Gavin Barr and Catherine McLellan Barr (*née* McGhie); *m* 1970, Susanne Crichton Keir (*d* 1996). *Educ:* Ardrossan Acad.; Royal High Sch.; Edinburgh Univ. (MA, LLB). Admitted to Faculty of Advocates, 1964. *Address:* Sheriff Court House, Dumfries DG1 2AN.

BARR, His Honour Reginald Alfred; a Circuit Judge (formerly Judge of County Courts), 1970–92; *b* 21 Nov. 1920; *s* of Alfred Charles Barr; *m* 1946, Elaine, 2nd *d* of James William Charles O'Bala Morris, Llanstephan, Carmarthenshire. *Educ:* Christ's Hospital; Trinity Coll., Oxford (MA). Served War, 1941–46, Middle East and Burma. Called to Bar, Middle Temple, 1954; Standing Counsel to Registrar of Restrictive Trading Agreements, 1962–70. Mem. Review Bd for Govt Contracts, 1969–70. *Address:* Gosfield Hall, Halstead, Essex CO9 1SF.

BARR, William Greig; DL; Rector, Exeter College, Oxford, 1972–82; *b* 10 June 1917; *s* of late William S. Barr, Glasgow; *m* 1st, 1954, Helen Georgopoulos (*d* 1988); two *s*; 2nd, 1991, Valerie Bowman (*née* Tatham). *Educ:* Sedbergh Sch.; Magdalen Coll., Oxford. Stanhope Prize, 1938; 1st cl., Hon. Sch. of Modern History, 1939. Served War, 1939–45: Lt-Col, Royal Devon Yeomanry. Exeter College, Oxford: Fellow, 1945–72; Sub-Rector, 1947–54; Sen. Tutor, 1960–66; Hon. Fellow, 1982; Oxford University: Lectr in Modern History, 1949–72; Jun. Proctor, 1951–52; Pro-Vice-Chancellor, 1980–82. Hon. Treas., Oxford Univ. Rugby Football Club, 1948–73. A Rhodes Trustee, 1975–87. Visiting Prof. of Hist., Univ. of South Carolina, 1968. DL Oxon 1974. *Address:* 24 Northmoor Road, Oxford OX2 6UR. *T:* (01865) 558253.

BARR YOUNG, Gavin Neil; His Honour Judge Barr Young; a Circuit Judge, since 1988; *b* 14 Aug. 1939; *s* of Dr James Barr Young and Elsie Barr Young (*née* Hodgkinson); *m* 1969, Barbara Elizabeth Breckon; two *d*. *Educ:* Loretto Sch., Musselburgh; Leeds Univ. (LLB). Called to the Bar, Gray's Inn, 1963; Member, North Eastern Circuit, 1964–88 (North Eastern Circuit Junior, 1968); a Recorder of the Crown Court, 1979–88. *Recreations:* gardening, music. *Address:* Flaxbourne House, Great Ouseburn, York YO26 9RG.

BARRACK, William Sample, Jr; Senior Vice-President, Texaco Inc., NY, 1983–92; *b* 26 July 1929; *s* of William Sample Barrack and Edna Mae Henderson; *m* 1953, Evelyn Irene Ball; one *s* one *d*. *Educ:* Pittsburgh Univ. BSc (Eng) 1950. Comdr, USN, 1950–53. Joined Texaco Inc., 1953; marketing and management positions in USA, 1953–67; in Europe, 1967–71; Vice-President: in NY, 1971–80; Marketing Dept, Europe, 1971–76; Producing Dept, Eastern Hemisphere, 1976–77; Personnel and Corporate Services Dept, 1977–80; Chm. and Chief Exec., Texaco Ltd, London, 1980–82. Director: Caltex Petroleum Corp.; Texaco Foundn Inc.; Standard Commercial Corp.; Consolidated Natural Gas Corp. Governor, Foreign Policy Assoc.; Member: US Naval War College Foundn; Bd of Visitors, Univ. of Pittsburgh. Trustee, Manhattanville College. *Clubs:* Woodway Country; Ox Ridge Hunt; Ida Lewis Yacht; North Sea Yacht (Belgium); Clambake (Newport, RI); New York Yacht.

BARRACLOUGH, Air Chief Marshal Sir John, KCB 1970 (CB 1969); CBE 1961; DFC 1942; AFC 1941 (despatches twice); FRAeS; Gentleman Usher to the Sword of State, 1980–88; Vice-Chairman, Commonwealth War Graves Commission, 1981–86 (Commissioner 1974–86); Director, Data-Track Fuel Services Ltd, since 1996; *b* 2 May 1918; *s* of late Horatio and Marguerite Maude Barraclough; *m* 1946, Maureen (*née* McCormack) (*d* 2001), *niece* of George Noble, Count Plunkett; one *d*. *Educ:* Cranbrook Sch. Mem., Artists' Rifles, 1935–38. Commissioned RAF, 1938. Air Vice-Marshal, 1964; Air Marshal, 1970; Air Chief Marshal, 1973. Served Near, Middle and Far East; commanded RAF Mogadishu, 1943; first single-engined jet flight to S Africa, 1951. Examining Wing, Central Flying Sch., 1948–51; Staff of IDC, 1952–54; Station Commander, RAF Biggin Hill, 1954–56 and Middleton St George, 1956–58; GC Ops, FEAF, 1958–61; Dir of Public Relations, Air Ministry, 1961–64; AOC No 19 Group, and NATO Air Comdr, Central Sub-Area, Eastern Atlantic Comd, 1964–67; Harvard Business Sch., AMP, 1967; AOA, Bomber Command, 1967–68; AOA, Strike Comd, 1968–70; Vice-Chief of Defence Staff, 1970–72; Air Secretary, 1972–74; Comdt, Royal Coll. of Defence Studies, 1974–76, retired. Underwriting Mem. of Lloyd's, 1979–. Hon. Air Cdre, No 3 (County of Devon) Maritime HQ Unit, RAuxAF, 1979–90; Hon. Inspector Gen., RAuxAF, 1984–89. Mem., RAF Training and Educn Adv. Bd, 1976–79; Vice Chairman: Air League Council, 1977–81; British Export Finance Adv. Council, 1982–89; Chm., Council, 1977–80, Vice-Pres., 1980–90, Vice-Patron, 1990–, RUSI; President: Air Public Relations Assoc., 1976–99 (Vice-Patron, 1999–); West Devon Area, St John Ambulance, 1977–85; Royal Crescent Soc., Bath, 1990–; Coastal Comd and Maritime Air Assoc. Special Advr, Air League, 1994–97. OStJ 1985. Past President: RAF Modern Pentathlon Assoc.; Combined Services Equitation Assoc. Editl Dir, 1978–81, Vice-Chm. of Editl Bd, 1981–86, NATO's Sixteen Nations. Freeman, City of London, 2001; Freeman, 1970, Liveryman, 2001, GAPAN. FRSA, FIMgt, MIPR. Air League Gold Medal, 1999. *Publications:* (jtly) The Third World War, 1978; contrib. to The Third World War: The Untold Story, 1982; contribs to professional jls. *Recreations:* country pursuits, sailing (Irish Admiral's Cup Team, 1973), classic cars, stilt-walking. *Address:* 28 The Royal Crescent, Bath BA1 2LT. *Clubs:* Boodle's, Royal Air Force, Royal Anglo-Belgian; Bath and County; Royal Western Yacht.

BARRAN, Sir David Haven, Kt 1971; Chairman, Midland Bank Ltd, 1980–82 (Deputy Chairman, 1975–80); *b* 23 May 1912; *s* of Sir John Barran, 2nd Bt and Alice Margarita (*née* Parks); *m* 1944, Jane Lechmere Macaskie; three *s* three *d* (and one *s* decd). *Educ:* Winchester; Trinity Coll., Cambridge. BA 1934. Joined Asiatic Petroleum Co., 1934; served in Egypt, Palestine, Sudan, India, 1935–46. Pres., Asiatic Petroleum Corp., New York, 1958; Managing Dir, Royal Dutch/Shell Group, 1961–72; Chm., Shell Oil Co., 1970–72; Director: Shell Transport and Trading Co. Ltd, 1961–83 (Dep. Chm., 1964–67; Chm., 1967–72; Man. Dir, 1964–73); General Accident Insurance; BICC; Glaxo Hldgs. Chairman: CBI Cttee on Inflation Accounting, 1973–74; Adv. Cttee on Appt of Advertising Agents, 1975–78 (Mem., 1973–78); Ct of Governors, Administrative Staff Coll., 1971–76; Governor, Centre for Environmental Studies, 1972–75. Comdr, Order of Oranje Nassau, 1971; Comdr, Order of Merit, Fed. Repub. of Germany, 1980. *Recreations:* gardening, shooting, embroidery (Pres., Embroiderers' Guild, 1982–87). *Address:* 36 Kensington Square, W8 5HP. *T:* (020) 7937 5664; Brent Eleigh Hall, Suffolk CO10 9NP. *T:* (01787) 247202.

BARRAN, Sir John (Napoleon Ruthven), 4th Bt *cr* 1895; Head of Information Technology, Central Office of Information, 1985–87, retired; *b* 14 Feb. 1934; *s* of Sir John Leighton Barran, 3rd Bt, and Hon. Alison Mary (*d* 1973), 3rd *d* of 9th Baron Ruthven, CB, CMG, DSO; *S* father, 1974; *m* 1965, Jane Margaret, *d* of Sir Stanley Hooker, CBE, FRS; one *s* one *d*. *Educ:* Heatherdown Sch., Ascot; Winchester Coll.; University Coll., London (BA 1994). National Service, 1952–54, Lieut, 5th Roy. Inniskilling Dragoon Guards; served Canal Zone. Asst Account Executive: Dorland Advertising Ltd, 1956–58; Masius & Fergusson Advertising Ltd, 1958–61; Account Executive, Ogilvy, Benson & Mather (New York) Inc., 1961–63; Overseas TV News Service, COI, 1964; First Sec. (Information), British High Commission, Ottawa, 1965–67; Central Office of Information: Home Documentary Film Section, 1967–72; Overseas TV and Film News Services, 1972–75; TV Commercials and Fillers Unit, 1975–78; Head of Viewdata Unit, 1978–85. Founded Video History to make documentaries, 1986. *Recreations:* entertaining, gardening, shooting. *Heir:* *s* John Ruthven Barran, *b* 10 Nov. 1971. *Address:* 17 St Leonard's Terrace, SW3 4QG. *T:* (020) 7730 2801; The Hermitage, East Bergholt, Suffolk CO7 6RB; Middle Rigg Farm, Sawley, North Yorks HG4 3HA.

BARRASS, Gordon Stephen, CMG 1992; HM Diplomatic Service, retired; Adviser, International Affairs, PricewaterhouseCoopers (formerly Coopers & Lybrand), since 1993; *b* 5 Aug. 1940; *s* of James and Mary Barrass; *m* 1st, 1965, Alice Cecile Oberg (*d* 1984); 2nd, 1992, Dr Kristen Clarke Lippincott, *qv*. *Educ:* Hertford Grammar Sch.; LSE (BSc (Econs)); SOAS (postgrad.). FCO, 1965–67; Chinese Language student, Hong Kong Univ., 1967–69; in Office of HM Chargé d'Affaires, Peking, 1970–72; Cultural Exchange Dept, FCO, 1972–74; UKMIS Geneva, 1974–78; Planning Staff, FCO, 1979–82; RCDS, 1983; seconded to MoD, 1984, Cabinet Office, 1987; Under Sec., 1991–93. *Recreations:* Chinese and Western art, classical archaeology, opera, travel, books. *Address:* PricewaterhouseCoopers, Southwark Towers, 32 London Bridge Street, SE1 9SY.

BARRASS, Kristen Clarke; *see* Lippincott, K. C.

BARRATT, Francis Russell, CB 1975; Deputy Secretary, HM Treasury, 1973–82; *b* 16 Nov. 1924; *s* of Frederick Russell Barratt; *m* 1st, 1949, Janet Mary Sherborne (marr. diss. 1978); three *s*; 2nd, 1979, Josephine Norah Harrison (*née* McCririck). *Educ:* Durban High Sch., SA; Clifton; University Coll., Oxford. War Service, 1943–46; Captain, Intelligence Corps, 1946. Asst Principal, HM Treasury, 1949; Principal, 1953; First Sec., UK High Commission, Karachi, 1956–58; Asst Sec., 1962, Under Sec., 1968, HM Treasury. Dir, Amdahl (UK), 1983–93; Trustee, Amdahl (UK) Pension Fund, 1984–95. Mem., Rev. Bd for Govt Contracts, 1984–93. *Address:* Little Paddocks, Smallhythe Road, Tenterden, Kent TN30 7LY. *T:* (01580) 763734. *Club:* Athenæum.

BARRATT, Gilbert Alexander; Master of the Supreme Court, Chancery Division, 1980–97; *b* 7 Aug. 1930; *s* of Arthur Walter Barratt and Frances Erskine Barratt (*née* Scott); *m* 1964, Fiona MacDermott; one *s* one *d*. *Educ:* Winchester; New Coll., Oxford. BA Modern History. Qualified as Solicitor, 1957; Partner: Stitt & Co., 1960–63; Thicknesse & Hull, 1963–67; Lee Bolton & Lee, 1967–78; Winckworth & Pemberton, 1978–80. *Recreation:* travel. *Address:* The Old School, Clungunford, Craven Arms, Shropshire SY7 0QE. *Club:* Travellers.

BARRATT, Sir Lawrence Arthur, (Sir Lawrie), Kt 1982; FCIS; Life President, Barratt Developments PLC, and subsidiary companies, 1989–91 and since 1997 (Managing Director, 1962–88; Chairman, 1962–88 and 1991–97); *b* Newcastle, 14 Nov. 1927; *m* 1st, 1951 (marr. diss. 1984); two *s*; 2nd, 1984, Mary Sheila (*née* Brierley). Founded Barratt Developments, as a private co., 1958. *Recreations:* golf, shooting, sailing. *Address:* Barratt Developments, Wingrove House, Ponteland Road, Newcastle upon Tyne NE5 3DP.

BARRATT, Michael Fieldhouse; communications consultant; broadcaster on radio and television; Chairman: Michael Barratt Ltd, 1977–97; Commercial Video Ltd, since 1981; *b* 3 Jan. 1928; *s* of late Wallace Milner Barratt and Doris Barratt; *m* 1st, 1952, Joan Francesca Warner (marr. diss.; she *d* 1995); three *s* three *d*; 2nd, 1977, Dilys Jane Morgan; two *s* one *d*. *Educ:* Rossall and Paisley Grammar Sch. Entered journalism, Kemsley Newspapers, 1944; Editor, Nigerian Citizen, 1956; *television:* Reporter, Panorama, 1963; Presenter: 24 Hours, 1965–69; Nationwide, 1969–77; Songs of Praise, 1977–82; Reporting London, 1983–88; *radio:* Question-Master, Gardeners' Question Time, 1973–79. Dir, Career Best Ltd, 1995–97. Chm. of Trustees, People to Places, 1996–; Trustee, Temple Holdings, 1992–96. Rector, Aberdeen Univ., 1973. Mem., RTS;

FRSA; FInstD. Hon. LLD Aberdeen, 1975. *Publications:* Michael Barratt, 1973; Michael Barratt's Down-to-Earth Gardening Book, 1974; Michael Barratt's Complete Gardening Book, 1977; Golf with Tony Jacklin, 1978; Making the Most of the Media, 1996; Making the Most of Retirement, 1999. *Recreations:* golf, cricket, listening. *Address:* Field House, Ascot Road, Maidenhead, Berks SL6 3LD. *T:* (01628) 770800; *e-mail:* mbarratt@compuserve.com.

BARRATT, Prof. Michael George; Professor of Mathematics, Northwestern University, Illinois, since 1974; *b* 26 Jan. 1927; *e s* of George Bernard Barratt and Marjorie Holloway Barratt (*née* Oldham); *m* 1952, Jenepher Hudson; one *s* four *d. Educ:* Stationers' Company's Sch.; Magdalen Coll., Oxford. Junior Lecturer, Oxford Univ., 1950–52; Fellow, Magdalen Coll., Oxford, 1952–56; Lectr, Brasenose Coll., Oxford, 1955–59; Sen. Lectr and Reader, 1959–63, Prof. of Pure Maths, 1964–74, Manchester Univ. Vis. Prof., Chicago Univ., 1963–64. *Publications:* papers in mathematical jls. *Address:* Department of Mathematics, Northwestern University, Lunt Building, Evanston, Ill 60201, USA.

BARRATT, Sir Richard (Stanley), Kt 1988; CBE 1981; QPM 1974; HM Chief Inspector of Constabulary, 1987–90; *b* 11 Aug. 1928; *s* of Richard Barratt and Mona Barratt; *m* 1952, Sarah Elizabeth Hale; one *s* two *d. Educ:* Saltley Grammar Sch., Birmingham. CIMgt. Birmingham City Police (Constable to Chief Inspector), 1949–65; Dir, Home Office Crime Prevention Centre, Stafford, 1963; seconded to Home Office (Res. and Develt), 1964; Sen. Comd Course, Police Coll., 1964; Supt, Cheshire Constab., 1965, Chief Supt, 1966; Asst Chief Constable, Manchester City Police, 1967; Asst Chief Constable, Manchester and Salford Police, 1968, Dep. Chief Constable, 1972; Dep. Chief Constable, Greater Manchester Police, 1974; Chief Constable, S Yorks Police, 1975–78; HM Inspector of Constabulary, 1978–87. Review of the Royal Bahamas Police, 1985. Led Police delegns to China, 1987, Pakistan, 1990. Assessor, Guildford and Woolwich Inquiry, 1990–94. Mem., Gaming Bd for GB, 1991–95. CStJ 1996. *Recreations:* reading, gardening, golf. *Address:* c/o Home Office, Room 565, Queen Anne's Gate, SW1H 9AT.

BARRATT, Robin Alexander, QC 1989; **His Honour Judge Barratt;** a Circuit Judge, since 1998; *b* 24 April 1945; *s* of Harold and Phyllis Barratt; *m* 1972, Gillian Anne Ellis (marr. diss. 1999); one *s* three *d. Educ:* Charterhouse; Worcester Coll., Oxford (Exhibnr; BA Hons, MA). Harmsworth Entrance Exhibnr, 1965, Schol. 1969; called to the Bar, Middle Temple, 1970. Lectr in Law, Kingston Polytechnic, 1968–71; Western Circuit, 1971; Asst Recorder, 1990; a Recorder, 1993–98. Councillor (C), London Bor. of Merton, 1978–86. *Recreations:* squash, fell walking, music.

BARRATT-BOYES, Sir Brian (Gerald), KBE 1971 (CBE 1966); Surgeon-in-Charge, Cardio-Thoracic Surgical Unit, Greenlane Hospital, Auckland, 1964–88, now Hon. Consultant; Hon. Senior Cardio-Thoracic Surgeon, Mercy (formerly Mater Misericordiae) Hospital, Auckland, 1966–89; *b* 13 Jan. 1924; *s* of Gerald Cave Boyes and Edna Myrtle Boyes (*née* Barratt); *m* 1st, 1949, Norma Margaret Thompson (marr. diss. 1986); five *s*; 2nd, 1986, Sara Rose Monester. *Educ:* Wellington Coll.; Univ. of Otago. MB, ChB 1946; FRACS 1952; FACS 1960; ChM 1962. Lectr in Anatomy, Otago Univ. Med. Sch., 1947; House Surg. and Registrar, Wellington Hosp., 1948–50; Surgical Registrar and Pathology Registrar, Palmerston North Hosp., 1950–52; Fellow in Cardio-Thoracic Surgery, Mayo Clinic, USA, 1953–55; Nuffield Trav. Fellowship UK (Bristol Univ.), 1956; Sen. Cardio-Thoracic Surg., Greenlane Hosp., 1957. Hon. Prof. of Surgery, Auckland Univ., 1971; Sir Arthur Sims Commonwealth Travelling Prof., 1982. FRSNZ 1970. Hon. FACS 1977; Hon. FRCS 1985; Hon. Fellow, Royal Coll. of Surgeons of Thailand, 1987; Hon. FACC 1988; Hon. FRACP 1995. Hon. DSc, 1985. R. T. Hall Prize for Disting. Cardiac Surgery in Austr. and NZ, 1966; René Leriche Prize, Société Internationale de Chirurgie, 1987; Award for Excellence in Surgery, RACS, 1994. Depicted on special stamp issued by NZ Post (Famous New Zealanders series, science, medicine and education category), 1995. *Publications:* Heart Disease in Infancy: diagnosis and surgical treatment, 1973; (jtly) Cardiac Surgery, 1986, 2nd edn 1993; numerous in med. jls throughout the world. *Recreations:* farming, trout fishing, tennis. *Address:* Greenhills, 982 Hibiscus Coast Highway, PO Box 51, Waiwera, Auckland 1240, New Zealand. *Club:* Northern (Auckland).

BARRE, Raymond; Chevalier de la Légion d'Honneur, Chevalier de l'Ordre National du Mérite agricole, Officier des Palmes Académiques; Grand Croix de l'Ordre National du Mérite, 1977; Député, Rhône, French National Assembly; Mayor of Lyon, since 1995; *b* Saint-Denis, Réunion, 12 April 1924; *s* of René Barre and Charlotte Déramond; *m* 1954, Eve Hegedüs; two *s. Educ:* Lycée Leconte-de-Lisle, Saint-Denis-de-la-Réunion; Faculté de Droit, Paris; Institut d'Etudes Politiques, Paris. Professor at Faculté de Droit et des Sciences Economiques: Caen, 1950; Paris (Chair of Political Economy), 1963; Econs Res. Dir Foundation Nat. des Scis Politiques, 1958; Professor at Institut d'Etudes Politiques, Paris, 1961, 1982–. Director of Cabinet of Mr J.-M. Jeanneney (Minister of Industry), 1959–62; Member: Cttee of Experts (Comité Lorain) studying financing of investments in France, 1963–64; Gen. Cttee on Economy and Financing of Fifth Plan, 1966; Vice-Chm., Commn of European Communities (responsible for Economic and Financial Affairs), 1967–72; Minister of Foreign Trade, Jan.–Aug. 1976; Prime Minister of France, 1976–81, and Minister of Economics and Finance, 1976–78; elected to National Assembly, from Rhône, 1978. Mem. Gen. Council, Banque de France, 1973; Chm. Cttee for studying Housing Financing Reform, 1975–76. *Publications:* Economie Politique, vol. 1, 1961, vol. 2, 1965; Une Politique pour l'Avenir, 1981; Refléxions pour Demain, 1984; Question de Confiance, 1987; Au Tournant du Siècle, 1988. *Address:* 4–6 avenue Emile-Acollas, 75007 Paris, France; (office) 2 rue de Viller Sexel, 75007 Paris, France.

BARRELL, Dr Anthony Charles, CB 1994; FREng; Chief Executive, North Sea Safety, Health and Safety Executive, 1991–94; *b* 4 June 1933; *s* of William Frederick Barrell and Ruth Eleanor Barrell (*née* Painter); *m* 1963, Jean, *d* of Francis Henry Hawkes and Clarice Jean (*née* Silke); one *s* one *d. Educ:* Friars Sch., Bangor; Kingston Grammar Sch.; Birmingham Univ.; Imperial Coll. BSc Hons chem. eng. CEng; FREng (FEng 1990); FIChemE 1984; Eur Ing 1988. Chemist, Ministry of Supply, later War Dept, 1959–64; Commissioning Engineer, African Explosives and Chemical Industries, 1964–65; Shift Manager, MoD, 1965–66; Chemical Inspector, then Supt. Specialist Inspector, HM Factory Inspectorate, 1966–78; Head of Major Hazards Assessment Unit, HSE, 1978–85; Dir, Technology, HSE, 1985–90; Chief Exec., N Sea Safety, Dept of Energy, 1990–91. Non-executive Director: BAA, 1994–; Lloyd's Register of Shipping, 1998–; Partner, TBP, 1994–. Member, Council: IChemE, 1989–94 (Pres., 1993–94); Royal Acad. of Engrg, 1994–97. Hon. DEng Birmingham, 1995. *Publications:* papers on assessment and control of major hazards, on offshore safety and on fire and explosion risks. *Recreations:* offshore sailing, golf. *Address:* Sanderling, Ridley Hill, Kingswear, Devon TQ6 0BY. *T:* (01803) 752266; *e-mail:* tonybarrell@tbpa.freeserve.co.uk. *Clubs:* Royal Dart Yacht (Cdre, 2000–); Churston Golf.

BARRELL, Prof. John Charles, PhD; FBA 2001; Professor of English, University of York, since 1993; *b* 3 Feb. 1943; *s* of John Ellis Barrell and Beatrice Mary Barrell; *m* 1st, 1965, Audrey Jones (marr. diss. 1975); two *s*; 2nd, 1975, Jania Miller (marr. diss. 1978); 3rd, 1992, Prof. Harriet Guest; one *d. Educ:* Trinity Coll., Cambridge (BA 1964; MA 1967); Univ. of Essex (PhD 1971). Lectr, Dept of Lit., Univ. of Essex, 1968–72; University of Cambridge: Lectr in English, and Fellow, King's Coll., 1972–85; Lectr, Newnham Coll., 1972–84; Prof. of English, Univ. of Sussex, 1986–93. British Acad. Reader, 1991–93. *Publications:* The Idea of Landscape and the Sense of Place 1730–1840: an approach to the poetry of John Clare, 1972; The Dark Side of the Landscape: the rural poor in English painting 1730–1840, 1980; English Literature in History 1730–1780: an equal, wide survey, 1983; The Political Theory of Painting from Reynolds to Hazlitt, 1986; Poetry, Language and Politics, 1988; The Infection of Thomas De Quincey: a psychopathology of Imperialism, 1991; The Birth of Pandora and the Division of Knowledge, 1992; Imagining the King's Death: figurative treason, fantasies of regicide 1793–1796, 2000. *Recreations:* gardening, playing cricket, book-collecting. *Address:* Centre for Eighteenth Century Studies, University of York, King's Manor, York Y01 7EP. *T:* (01904) 433352.

BARRETT, Prof. Ann, MD; FRCP, FRCR; FMedSci; Professor of Radiation Oncology, University of Glasgow, since 1986; *b* 27 Feb. 1943; *d* of Robert Douglas and Elsie Mary Brown; *m* 1989, Adrian Bell. *Educ:* St Bartholomew's Hosp. (MD). Junior posts, St Bartholomew's, UCH, Middlesex, Mount Vernon and Westminster Hosps, 1968–76; Chef de Clinique, Hôpital Tenon, Paris, 1976; Sen. Lectr and Consultant, Royal Marsden Hosp., 1977–86. Dir, Beatson Oncology Centre, Glasgow, 1987–91. Member: Cttee on Med. Aspects of Radiation in the Envmt, NRPB, 1988–93; Molecular and Cellular Med. Bd, MRC, 1991–94. Chm., Standing Scottish Cttee, 1992–95, Registrar, Faculty of Clin. Oncology, RCR; Pres., Scottish Radiological Soc., 1995–97; Pres., Eur. Soc. for Therapeutic Radiation Oncology, 1997–99. Founder FMedSci 1998. *Publications:* Practical Radiotherapy Planning, 1985, 3rd edn 1999; Cancer in Children, 1986, 4th edn 1998. *Recreations:* hill walking, the Arts. *Address:* Beatson Oncology Centre, Western Infirmary, Glasgow G11 6NT. *T:* (0141) 211 2123.

BARRETT, Prof. Anthony Gerard Martin, FRS 1999; Glaxo Professor of Organic Chemistry, and Director, Wolfson Centre for Organic Chemistry in Medical Science, since 1993, and Sir Derek Barton Professor of Synthetic Chemistry, since 1999, Imperial College of Science, Technology and Medicine; *b* Exeter, Devon, 2 March 1952; *s* of Claude E. V. Barrett and Margaret Teresa Barrett (*née* Bannon); naturalised US citizen. *Educ:* Imperial Coll. of Science and Technology (BSc 1st Cl. Hons Chemistry 1973; PhD 1975; DIC 1975; SRC Student, 1973–75). Lectr, 1975–82, Sen. Lectr, 1982–83, Imperial Coll. of Science and Technology; Professor of Chemistry: Northwestern Univ., 1983–90; Colorado State Univ., 1990–93. Consultant: Roche Products Ltd, 1993–; Unilever, 1996–; Dir of Chemistry, Argenta Discovery (formerly ChemMedICa), 1998–. Fellow, Japan Soc. for Promotion of Science, 1989. Mem., Chemicals Panel, Technology Foresight Prog., Office of Sci. and Technology, 1994. Lectureships: Tilden, RSC, 1994; Backer, Univ. of Groningen, 1996; Glaxo Wellcome, E Carolina Univ., 1998; Organic Divl Interim, Royal Aust. Chem. Inst., 1999; Eaborn-Cornforth, Sussex Univ., 1999; Allelix Dist., Queens Univ., Ont., 1999; Sir Robert Price, CSIRD, 1999; Novo Nordisk, Tech. Univ. of Denmark, 2000; Upper Rhine, 2001. Meldola Medal, 1980, Harrison Medal, 1982, Corday-Morgan Medal, 1986, RSC; Armstrong Medal, Imperial Coll., 1981; Glaxo Wellcome Award, 2000. *Address:* Department of Chemistry, Imperial College of Science, Technology and Medicine, SW7 2AY. *T:* (020) 7594 5766, *Fax:* (020) 7594 5805; *e-mail:* agmb@ic.ac.uk.

BARRETT, Rev. Prof. Charles Kingsley, DD; FBA 1961; Professor of Divinity, Durham University, 1958–82; *b* 4 May 1917; *s* of Rev. F. Barrett and Clara (*née* Seed); *m* 1944, Margaret E. Heap, Calverley, Yorks; one *s* one *d. Educ:* Shebbear Coll.; Pembroke Coll., Cambridge (Hon. Fellow, 1995); Wesley House, Cambridge. DD Cantab, 1956. Asst Tutor, Wesley Coll., Headingley, 1942; Methodist Minister, Darlington, 1943; Lecturer in Theology, Durham Univ., 1945. Lectures: Hewett, USA, 1961; Shaffer, Yale, 1965; Delitzsch, Münster, 1967; Cato, Australia, 1969; Tate-Willson, Dallas, 1975; McMartin, Ottawa, 1976; Sanderson, Melbourne, and West-Watson, Christchurch, NZ, 1983; Alexander Robertson, Univ. of Glasgow, 1984; K. W. Clark, Duke, USA, 1987; Ryan, Asbury Seminary, Kentucky, 1988; Dominion-Chalmers, Ottawa, 1990; Woodruff Vis. Prof., Emory Univ., Atlanta, 1986; Gunning Fellow, Edinburgh Univ., 1994. Vice-Pres., British and Foreign Bible Soc.; Pres., Studiorum Novi Testamenti Societas, 1973; Mem., Royal Norwegian Soc. of Scis and Letters, 1991; Hon. Mem., Soc. of Biblical Literature, USA. Hon. DD: Hull, 1970; Aberdeen, 1972; Hon. DrTheol Hamburg, 1981. Burkitt Medal for Biblical Studies, 1966; von Humboldt Forschungspreis, 1988. *Publications:* The Holy Spirit and the Gospel Tradition, 1947; The Gospel according to St John, 1955, 2nd edn 1978; The New Testament Background: Selected Documents, 1956, 2nd edn 1987; Biblical Preaching and Biblical Scholarship, 1957; The Epistle to the Romans, 1957, 2nd edn 1991; Westcott as Commentator, 1959; Yesterday, Today and Forever: The New Testament Problem, 1959; Luke the Historian in Recent Study, 1961; From First Adam to Last, 1962; The Pastoral Epistles, 1963; Reading Through Romans, 1963; History and Faith: the Story of the Passion, 1967; Jesus and the Gospel Tradition, 1967; The First Epistle to the Corinthians, 1968; The Signs of an Apostle, 1970; Das Johannesevangelium und das Judentum, 1970; The Prologue of St John's Gospel, 1971; New Testament Essays, 1972; The Second Epistle to the Corinthians, 1973; The Fourth Gospel and Judaism, 1975; (ed) Donum Gentilicium, 1978; Essays on Paul, 1982; Essays on John, 1982; Freedom and Obligation, 1985; Church, Ministry and Sacraments in the New Testament, 1985; The Acts of the Apostles, vol. I (Internat. Critical Commentary series), 1994, vol. II, 1998; Paul: an introduction to his thought, 1994; Jesus and The Word, 1995; (jointly) Jesus, Paul and John, 1999; (jtly) Conflicts and Challenges in Early Christianity, 1999; contributions to learned journals and symposia in Britain, the Continent, Australia and USA. *Address:* 22 Rosemount, Plawsworth Road, Pity Me, Durham DH1 5GA. *T:* (0191) 386 1340.

BARRETT, David; broadcaster, writer and political commentator on national and provincial media, since 1985; Premier and Minister of Finance, Province of British Columbia, Canada, 1972–75; *b* Vancouver, 2 Oct. 1930; *s* of Samuel Barrett and Rose (*née* Hyatt); father a business man in East Vancouver, after war service; *m* 1953, Shirley Hackman, West Vancouver; two *s* one *d. Educ:* Britannia High Sch., Vancouver; Seattle Univ. (BA(Phil) 1953); St Louis Univ. (Master of Social Work 1956). Personnel and Staff Trng Officer, Haney Correctional Inst., 1957–59; also gained experience in a variety of jobs. Fellow, Inst. of Politics, Harvard Univ., 1987; Adjunct Prof., Simon Fraser Univ.; Visiting Scholar: McGill Univ., 1988; Western Washington Univ. Elected: MLA for Dewdney, Sept. 1960 and 1963; to re-distributed riding of Coquitlam 1966, 1969 and 1972; Vancouver East, by-election 1976, 1979; New Democratic Party Leader, June 1970–1984 (first Social Democratic Govt in history of Province); Leader, Official Opposition, British Columbia, 1970–72 and 1975–84; MP (NDP) Esquimalt-Juan de Fuca, 1988–93. Dr of Laws, *hc*, St Louis Univ., 1974; Hon. DPhil Simon Fraser Univ., BC, 1986. *Publication:* Barrett (memoirs), 1995. *Address:* 1179 Monro Street, Victoria, British Columbia V9A 5P5, Canada.

BARRETT, Lt-Gen. Sir David William S.; *see* Scott-Barrett.

BARRETT, Edmond Fox, OBE 1981; HM Diplomatic Service, retired; First Secretary, Foreign and Commonwealth Office, 1986–88; *b* 24 Aug. 1928; *s* of late Edmond Henry Barrett and Ellen Mary Barrett (*née* Fox); *m* 1959, Catherine Wendy Howard (*née* Slater). *Educ:* St Brendan's Coll., Bristol. Dominions Office, 1946; Royal Navy, 1947–49; CRO, 1949–50; Karachi, 1950–52; New Delhi, 1952–54; CRO, 1954–55; Admiralty, 1955–60; Foreign Office, 1960–63; Bucharest, 1963–65; Rio de Janeiro, 1965–68; Boston, 1968–70; Mexico City, 1971–73; FCO, 1973–76; Santo Domingo, 1976–79; Tehran, 1979–81; Consul Gen., Bilbao, 1981–86. *Recreations:* reading, golf, gardening. *Address:* 10 Greenheys Place, Woking, Surrey GU22 7JD.

BARRETT, John; MP (Lib Dem) Edinburgh West, since 2001; *b* 11 Feb. 1954; *s* of Andrew Barrett and Elizabeth Mary Benert; *m* 1975, Carol Pearson; one *d*. *Educ:* Forrester High Sch., Edinburgh; Napier Poly., Edinburgh. Director: ABC Productions, 1985–; Edinburgh Internat. Film Fest., 1995–2001; EDI Group, 1997–99; Edinburgh and Borders Screen Industries, 1997–; Edinburgh Film House, 1997–2001. Mem. (Lib Dem) Edinburgh CC, 1995–. *Recreations:* travel, film, theatre, music (playing and listening). *Address:* House of Commons, SW1A 0AA. *T:* (020) 7219 8224. *Club:* National Liberal.

BARRETT, Rev. John Charles Allanson; Headmaster, The Leys School, Cambridge, since 1990; *b* 8 June 1943; *s* of Leonard Wilfred Allanson Barrett and Marjorie Joyce Barrett; *m* 1967, Sally Elisabeth Hatley; one *s* one *d*. *Educ:* Culford Sch.; Univ. of Newcastle upon Tyne (BA Hons); Fitzwilliam Coll., Cambridge; Wesley House, Cambridge. MA Cantab. Ordained Methodist Minister. Chaplain and Lectr in Divinity, Westminster Coll., Oxford, 1968–69; Asst Tutor, Wesley Coll., Bristol, 1969–71; Circuit Minister, Hanley Trinity Circuit, Stoke on Trent, and actg Hd of Religious Studies, Birches High Sch., Hanley, 1971–73; Chaplain and Hd of Religious and Gen. Studies, Kingswood Sch., Bath, 1973–83; Headmaster, Kent Coll., Pembury, 1983–90. Mem., HMC Cttee, 1997–98 (Sec., 1997, Chm., 1998, Eastern Div., HMC; Chm., HMC Working Party on Alcohol and Drug Abuse, 1996–99). World Methodist Council: Mem. Exec. Cttee, 1981–; Sec., Brit. Cttee, 1986–97; Chairman: Educn Cttee, 1991–; Prog. Cttee, 1992–96; Mem., Presidium, 1996–. Vice-Pres., Internat. Assoc. of Methodist Schs, Colls and Univs, 1998–. Mem. Steering Cttee, Bloxham Project, 1986–92. Governor, Queenswood Sch., 1997–. FRSA 1996. Hon. DD Florida Southern, 1992. *Publications:* What is a Christian School?, 1981; Family Worship in Theory and Practice, 1983; Methodist Education in Britain, 1990; Methodists and Education: from roots to fulfilment, 2000; sections on Methodism in Encyc. Britannica Year Books, 1988–98. *Address:* The Leys School, Cambridge CB2 2AD. *T:* (01223) 355327. *Club:* East India.

BARRETT, John Edward; tennis commentator and journalist; *b* 17 April 1931; *s* of Alfred Edward Barrett and Margaret Helen Barrett (*née* Walker); *m* 1967, (Florence) Angela (Margaret) Mortimer; one *s* one *d*. *Educ:* University College Sch., Hampstead; St John's Coll., Cambridge (MA History). Joined Slazengers as management trainee, 1957; Tournament Dir, 1975; Dir, 1978; Consultant, 1981–95 (latterly Dunlop Slazenger International). Tennis career: RAF champion, 1950, 1951; Captain of Cambridge, 1954; Nat. Indoor Doubles champion (with D. Black), 1953; Davis Cup, 1956–57, non-playing Captain, 1959–62; Dir, LTA Trng Squad (Barrett Boys), 1965–68; qualified LTA coach, 1969; Founded: BP Internat Tennis Fellowship, 1968–80 (and directed); BP Cup (21-and-under), 1973–80; Junior Internat. Series, 1975–79. Financial Times: tennis corresp., 1963–, crossword contribs, 1986–. TV tennis commentator: BBC, 1971–; Australian networks, 1981–; USA. *Publications:* Tennis and Racket Games, 1975; Play Tennis with Rosewall, 1975; 100 Wimbledon Championships, 1986; (with Dan Maskell) From Where I Sit, 1988; (with Dan Maskell) Oh, I Say, 1989; Wimbledon: the official history of The Championships, 2001; (ed and contrib.) World of Tennis, annually, 1969–2001. *Recreations:* music, theatre, reading. *Address:* All England Lawn Tennis Club, Church Road, Wimbledon, SW19 5AE. *Clubs:* Oxford and Cambridge, All England Lawn Tennis (Mem. Cttee), International Lawn Tennis (Dep. Pres.), Queen's.

BARRETT, Lorraine Jayne; Member (Lab) Cardiff South and Penarth, National Assembly for Wales, since 1999; *b* 18 March 1950; *m* 1972, Paul Franklyn Barrett; one *s* one *d*. *Educ:* Porth County Sch. for Girls. Nursing, 1966–70; secretarial work, 1970–74; Personal and Political asst to Alun Michael, MP, 1987–99. Mem. (Lab), Vale of Glamorgan UA, 1995–99. *Recreations:* reading horror and thriller books, walking, cinema. *Address:* National Assembly for Wales, Cardiff CF99 1NA. *T:* (029) 2089 8376.

BARRETT, Matthew W., OC 1995; Group Chief Executive, Barclays PLC, since 1999; *b* Co. Kerry, 20 Sept. 1944. *Educ:* Christian Brothers Sch., Kells; Harvard Univ. (AMP 1981). Joined Bank of Montreal, 1962; Chief Operating Officer, 1987–89; Chief Exec. Officer, 1989–99; Chm., 1990–99. *Address:* Barclays PLC, 54 Lombard Street, EC3P 3AH.

BARRETT, Michael Paul, OBE 1987; Chief Executive Officer, Great Britain Sasakawa Foundation, since 2000; *b* 30 July 1941; *s* of William James Barrett and Irene (*née* Beynon); *m* 1966, Marie-Thérèse Françoise Juliette Lombard; two *s*. *Educ:* Westminster City Sch; Univ. of Durham (BA Hons Classics). Asst Tutor in English to Overseas Students, Univ. of Birmingham, 1963–64; British Council: Asst Dir, Port Harcourt, 1964–65; Asst Rep., Addis Ababa, 1966–69; Educnl Television Officer, Tokyo, 1970–72; Dir, Films Dept, 1972–75; Educnl Technologist, Media Dept, 1975–77; Non-Formal Educn Specialist, Nairobi, 1977–80; Dep. Rep., Japan, 1980–84; Cultural Attaché, Washington, 1984–87; Dir, PR, 1987–88; Consultant, Goddard Kay Rogers & Associates Ltd, 1989; Man. Dir, GKR Japan Ltd, 1989–93; Dir, British Council, Japan, 1993–99. Vice-Pres., British Chamber of Commerce in Japan, 1992–99. Non-exec. Dir, S London & Maudsley NHS Trust, 2001–. Mem. Council, Japan Soc., 2000–; Mem. Culture Cttee, Asia House, 2001–. Trustee, British Sch. in Tokyo, 1992–99 (Chm., 1992–95). FRGS 1989. *Recreations:* contemporary art and music, fishing, sailing, Celtic culture. *Address:* 25 Offerton Road, SW4 0DJ; Rosalbert, Roullens 11290, Montréal, France. *Club:* Chelsea Arts.

BARRETT, Sir Stephen (Jeremy), KCMG 1991 (CMG 1982); HM Diplomatic Service, retired; Ambassador to Poland, 1988–91; *b* 4 Dec. 1931; *s* of late W. P. Barrett and Dorothy Barrett; *m* 1958, Alison Mary Irvine; three *s*. *Educ:* Westminster Sch.; Christ Church, Oxford (MA). FO, 1955–57; 3rd, later 2nd Sec., Political Office with Middle East Forces, Cyprus, 1957–59; Berlin, 1959–62; 1st Sec., FO, 1962–65; Head of Chancery, Helsinki, 1965–68; 1st Sec., FCO, 1968–72; Counsellor and Head of Chancery, Prague, 1972–74; Head of SW European Dept, FCO, later Principal Private Sec. to Foreign and Commonwealth Sec., 1975; Head of Science and Technology Dept, FCO, 1976–77; Fellow, Center for Internat. Affairs, Harvard, 1977–78; Counsellor, Ankara, 1978–81; Head of British Interests Section, Tehran, 1981; Asst Under-Sec. of State, FCO, 1981–84; Ambassador to Czechoslovakia, 1985–88. *Recreations:* climbing small mountains, reading. *Club:* Ausable (St Huberts, NY).

BARRETT-LENNARD, Rev. Sir Hugh (Dacre), 6th Bt *cr* 1801; Priest, London Oratory; *b* 27 June 1917; *s* of Sir Fiennes Cecil Arthur Barrett-Lennard (*d* 1963) and Winifrede Mignon (*d* 1969), *d* of Alfred Berlyn; *S* cousin, 1977. *Educ:* Radley College, Berks; Pontifical Beda College, Rome. Teaching, 1936. Served War of 1939–45, NW Europe (despatches); enlisted London Scottish, Jan. 1940; commissioned 2nd Lt, Oct. 1940; Captain Essex Regt, 1945. Entered Brompton Oratory, 1946; ordained Priest in Rome, 1950. *Recreations:* on Isle of Eigg, Hebrides. *Heir: cousin* Richard Fynes Barrett-Lennard, *b* 6 April 1941. *Address:* The Oratory, South Kensington, SW7 2RW. *T:* (020) 7589 4811.

BARRIE, (Charles) David (Ogilvy); Director, National Art Collections Fund, since 1992; *b* 9 Nov. 1953; *s* of late Alexander Ogilvy Barrie and Patricia Mary Tucker; *m* 1978, Mary Emily, *d* of Rt Hon. Sir Ralph Gibson, *qv*; two *d*. *Educ:* Bryanston Sch.; Brasenose Coll., Oxford (Phil and Exp. Psych.). HM Diplomatic Service, 1975; served FCO 1975–76; Dublin, 1976–80; seconded to Cabinet Office, 1980–81; FCO, 1981–87; transf. Cabinet Office, 1988; seconded to Japan Festival 1991, as Exec. Dir, 1989–92; resigned from Cabinet Office, 1992. Bd Mem., Resource: Council for Mus, Archives, and Libraries, 2000–. Companion and Dir, Guild of St George, 1992–. Trustee: Civitella Ranieri Foundn, 1995–99; Ruskin Foundn, 1996–; Chm., Ruskin To-Day (Ruskin centenary prog., 2000). *Publications:* (ed) John Ruskin's Modern Painters, 1987, 2nd edn 2000; numerous articles and reviews. *Recreations:* sailing, collecting paintings and drawings. *Address:* National Art Collections Fund, Millais House, 7 Cromwell Place, SW7 2JN. *T:* (020) 7225 4800. *Clubs:* Arts; Royal Cruising; Emsworth Sailing.

BARRIE, Herbert, MD, FRCP, FRCPCH; Consultant Paediatrician, Charing Cross Hospital, 1966–84 (Physician in charge, 1984–86); *b* 9 Oct. 1927; *m* 1963, Dinah Barrie, MB, BS, FRCPath; one *s* one *d*. *Educ:* Wallington County Grammar School; University College and Med. Sch., London. MB, BS 1950; MD 1952; MRCP 1957, FRCP 1972; FRCPCH 1997. Registrar, Hosp. for Sick Children, Gt Ormond St, 1955–57; Research Fellow, Harvard Univ., Children's Med. Center, 1957; Sen. Registrar and Sen. Lectr, Dept of Paediatrics, St Thomas' Hosp., 1959–65; Consultant Paediatrician: Moor House Sch. for Speech Disorders, 1968–74; Ashtead Hosp., Surrey, 1986; New Victoria Hosp., Kingston, 1993. Vis. Prof., Downstate Univ. Med. Center, NY, 1976. Member: British Assoc. of Perinatal Paediatrics; Vaccine Damage Tribunal Panel. *Publications:* numerous contribs to books and jls on paediatric and neonatal topics, esp. resuscitation of newborn and neonatal special care. *Recreations:* tennis, writing, wishful thinking. *Address:* 3 Burghley Avenue, New Malden, Surrey KT3 4SW. *T:* (020) 8942 2836.

BARRIE, Lesley; General Manager, Tayside Health Board, 1993–97, retired; *b* 28 Sept. 1944. *Educ:* Glasgow High Sch. for Girls; Univ. of Glasgow (DPA). MHSM; DipHSM. NHS admin. trainee, 1963–66; hosp. mgt, 1966–77; District General Manager: Inverclyde Dist, 1977–81; Glasgow SE, 1981–83; Dir, Admin Services, Glasgow Royal Infirmary, Royal Maternity Hosp. and Glasgow Dental Hosp., 1983–87; Unit Gen. Manager, Stirling Royal Infirmary, 1987–91; Gen. Manager, Forth Valley Health Bd, 1991–93. Chm., Social Security Appeal Tribunals, 1978–90; Mem., Industrial Tribunal, 1992–98. Hon. Sen. Lectr, Dept of Epidemiology and Public Health, Dundee Univ., 1994–97. MIMgt. *Recreations:* table tennis (Scottish International, 1963–70), badminton, reading.

BARRIE, (Thomas) Scott; Member (Lab) Dunfermline West, Scottish Parliament, since 1999; *b* 10 March 1962; *s* of William Barrie and Helen McBain Barrie (*née* Scott). *Educ:* Auchmuty High Sch., Glenrothes; Edinburgh Univ. (MA Hons 1983); Stirling Univ. (CQSW 1986). Fife Regional Council: Social Worker, 1986–90; Sen. Social Worker, 1990–91; Team Manager, Social Work Dept, 1991–96; Team Leader, Social Work Service, Fife Council, 1996–99. Mem. (Lab), Dunfermline DC, 1988–92. *Recreations:* hill walking, supporter of Dunfermline Athletic. *Address:* Scottish Parliament, Edinburgh EH99 1SP.

BARRINGTON, Sir Alexander (Fitzwilliam Croker), 7th Bt *cr* 1831; retired; *b* 19 Nov. 1909; *s* of Sir Charles Burton Barrington, 5th Bt, and Mary Rose (*d* 1943), *d* of Sir Henry Hickman Bacon, 10th and 11th Bt; *S* brother, 1980. *Educ:* Castle Park, Dalkey, Co. Dublin; Shrewsbury School; Christ Church, Oxford. Director of various private companies, 1932–39. Served in Army as Captain, Intelligence Corps, 1939–42; prisoner of war, Singapore and Thailand, 1942–45. Book publishers' executive, editor and production manager, 1946–72. *Recreations:* gardening, travel. *Heir: cousin* Benjamin Barrington [*b* 23 Jan. 1950; *m* 1980, Carola Christel Mogck; one *s* one *d*]. *Address:* Rush Court, Shillingford Road, Wallingford, Oxon OX10 8LL.

BARRINGTON, Donal; Judge of the Supreme Court of Ireland, 1996–2000; President, Irish Commission on Human Rights, since 2000; *b* 28 Feb. 1928; *s* of Thomas Barrington and Eileen Barrington (*née* Bracken); *m* 1959, Eileen O'Donovan; two *s* two *d*. *Educ:* Belvedere Coll.; University Coll., Dublin (MA, LLB). Called to the Bar, King's Inns, 1951, Bencher, 1978; called to Inner Bar, 1968; Judge, High Court of Ireland, 1979–89; Judge, Court of First Instance of European Communities, 1989–96. Chairman: Commn on Safety at Work, 1983–84; Stardust Compensation Tribunal, 1985–86. Chm., Gen. Council of the Bar, Ireland, 1977–79. Pres., Irish Centre for European Law, 1996–2000. *Publications:* contribs to learned jls. *Recreations:* music, gardening. *Address:* 8 St John's Park, Dun Laoghaire, Co. Dublin, Republic of Ireland. *T:* (1) 2841817.

BARRINGTON, Edward John, (Ted); Irish Ambassador to the Court of St James's, 1995–2001; *b* 26 July 1949; *s* of Edward Barrington and Sarah Barrington (*née* Byrne); *m* 1972, Clare O'Brien; one *s*. *Educ:* University College Dublin (BA). Entered Irish Diplomatic Service, 1971; 3rd Sec., 1971, 1st Sec., 1973; Perm. Rep. to EEC, 1975–80; 1st Sec., Press and Information, 1980; Counsellor, Political, 1980–85; Assistant Secretary: Admin, 1985–89; EC Div., 1989–91; Political Div. and Political Dir, 1991–95; Dep. Sec., 1995. *Recreations:* bird-watching, cinema, hiking, theatre, jazz. *Address:* Sun Villa, Mauritiustown, Rosslare Strand, Co. Wexford, Ireland. *T:* (53) 32880.

BARRINGTON, Jonah; Consultant, Squash Rackets Association, since 1996; *b* 29 April 1941; *m* 1973, Madeline Ibbotson (*née* Wooller); two *s*. *Educ:* Cheltenham Coll.; Trinity Coll., Dublin. Professional squash rackets player, 1969–83; winner: British Open, 1967–68, 1970–73; Egyptian Open, 1968; Canadian Open, 1983. Coach, English Squash Rackets Team; Dir of Excellence, 1988–93, Pres., 1994, Squash Rackets Assoc. *Publications:* On Squash, 1973; (jtly) Tackle Squash, 1977; Murder in the Squash Court, 1982. *Address:* c/o Squash Rackets Association, PO Box 1106, W3 0ZD.

BARRINGTON, Sir Nicholas (John), KCMG 1990 (CMG 1982); CVO 1975; HM Diplomatic Service, retired; High Commissioner to Pakistan, 1989–94 (Ambassador, 1987–89); non-resident Ambassador to Afghanistan, 1994; *b* 23 July 1934; *s* of late Eric Alan Barrington and Mildred (*née* Bill). *Educ:* Repton (Pres., Old Reptonian Soc., 1995–96); Clare Coll., Cambridge (MA 1957; Hon. Fellow 1992). HM Forces, RA, 1952–54. Joined Diplomatic Service, 1957; Tehran (language student), 1958; Oriental Sec., Kabul, 1959; FO, 1961; 2nd Sec., UK Delegn to European Communities, Brussels, 1963; 1st Sec., Rawalpindi, 1965; FO, 1967; Private Sec. to Permanent Under Sec., Commonwealth Office, April 1968; Asst Private Sec. to Foreign and Commonwealth Sec., Oct. 1968; Head of Chancery, Tokyo, 1972–75 (promoted Counsellor and for a period apptd Chargé d'Affaires, Hanoi, 1973); Head of Guidance and Information Policy (subsequently Information Policy) Dept, FCO, 1976–78; Counsellor, Cairo, 1978–81; Minister and Head of British Interests Section, Tehran, 1981–83; Supernumary Ambassador attached to UK Mission to UN, NY, for Gen. Assembly, autumn 1983; Co-ordinator for London Econ. Summit, 1984; Asst Under-Sec. of State (Public Depts), FCO, 1984–87. Chm., Management Cttee, Southwold Summer Theatre, 1995–; Co-Pres., Clare Coll. Develt Prog., 1995–; Member: Develt Cttee, Cambridge Univ. Divinity Faculty, 1994–97; Standing Cttee on Schs and Insts, British Acad., 1995–96; Special Projs Cttee, Sadler's Wells Th., 1996–; Friends of New River Walk, Islington, 1995–. Member: Exec. Cttee, Asia House, 1994–2000; Pakistan Soc., 1995– (originator and Exhibn Comr, 50 Years of Painting and Sculpture in Pakistan, 2000); Council: Royal Soc. for Asian Affairs, 1995–2000; British Inst. of Persian Studies, 1996–; British Assoc. for Cemeteries in S Asia, 1996–. Trustee, Ancient India and Iran Trust, 1993–; Trustee and Pres., Friends of Mus. of Empire and Commonwealth, Bristol, 1996–; Patron, Hindu Kush Conservation Assoc., 1995–2000. FRSA 1984. 3rd Cl., Order of the Sacred Treasure, Japan, 1975. *Publication:* (foreword and asst ed.) Old Roads, new Highways: 50 years of Pakistan, 1997. *Recreations:* theatre, drawing, prosopography, Persian poetry. *Address:* 20 Canonbury Grove, N1 2HR. *Clubs:* Athenæum, Royal Commonwealth Society, Nikaean.

BARRINGTON, Ted; *see* Barrington, E. J.

BARRINGTON-WARD, Rt Rev. Simon, KCMG 2001; Bishop of Coventry, 1985–97; Hon. Assistant Bishop, Diocese of Ely, since 1998; Prelate of the Most Distinguished Order of St Michael and St George, since 1989; *b* 27 May 1930; *s* of Robert McGowan Barrington-Ward and Margaret Adele Barrington-Ward; *m* 1963, Jean Caverhill Taylor; two *d*. *Educ:* Eton; Magdalene Coll., Cambridge (MA; Hon. Fellow, 1987). Lektor, Free Univ., Berlin, 1953–54; Westcott House, Cambridge, 1954–56; Chaplain, Magdalene Coll., Cambridge, 1956–60; Asst Lectr in Religious Studies, Univ. of Ibadan, 1960–63; Fellow and Dean of Chapel, Magdalene Coll., Cambridge, 1963–69; Principal, Crowther Hall, Selly Oak Colls, Birmingham, 1969–74; Gen. Sec., CMS, 1975–85; Hon. Canon of Derby Cathedral, 1975–85; a Chaplain to the Queen, 1984–85. Chairman: Partnership for World Mission, 1987–91; Internat. Affairs Cttee, Bd for Social Responsibility of Gen. Synod, 1986–96. Pres., St John's Coll., Nottingham, 1987. FRAI. Hon. DD Wycliffe Coll., Toronto, 1984; Hon. DLitt Warwick, 1998. *Publications:* CMS Newsletter, 1975–85; Love Will Out (anthology of news letters), 1988; Why God?, 1993; The Jesus Prayer, 1996; *contributor to:* Christianity in Independent Africa (ed Fasholé Luke and others), 1978; Today's Anglican Worship (ed C. Buchanan), 1980; Renewal—An Emerging Pattern, by Graham Pulkingham and others, 1980; A New Dictionary of Christian Theology (ed Alan Richardson and John Bowden), 1983; Christianity Today, 1988; The World's Religions, 1988; The Weight of Glory (ed D. W. Hardy and P. H. Sedgwick), 1991. *Address:* 4 Searle Street, Cambridge CB4 3DB.

BARRITT, Rev. Dr Gordon Emerson, OBE 1979; Principal, National Children's Home, 1969–86; President of the Methodist Conference, 1984–85; *b* 30 Sept. 1920; *s* of Norman and Doris Barritt; *m* 1st, 1947, Joan Mary Alway (*d* 1984); two *s* one *d*; 2nd, 1993, Karen Lesley Windle (marr. diss. 1999). *Educ:* William Hulme's Grammar Sch., Manchester; Manchester Univ.; Cambridge Univ. (Wesley House and Fitzwilliam Coll.). Served War, RAF, 1942–45 (despatches). Methodist Minister: Kempston Methodist Church, Bedford, 1947–52; Westlands Methodist Church, Newcastle-under-Lyme, 1952–57; Chaplain, Univ. of Keele, 1953–57. Dir, Enfield Counselling Service, 1986–89; Treasurer, 1969–86, Chm., 1970–72, Nat. Council of Voluntary Child Care Organisations; Member: Home Office Adv. Council on Child Care, 1968–71; Brit. Assoc. of Social Workers, 1960–95; Nat. Children's Bureau, 1963–2000 (Treasurer, 1989–95; Vice Pres., 1997–); Internat. Union for Child Welfare, 1969–86; Chm., Kids, 1986–93; Gov., CAF, 1996–2000. Vice Chm. of Council, Selly Oak Colls, Birmingham, 1991–2000 (Fellow, 1987); Governor: Farringtons Sch., 1986–94 (Chm. of Govs, 1986–93); Queenswood Sch., 1986–93. DUniv Keele, 1985. *Publications:* The Edgworth Story, 1972; (ed) Many Pieces—One Aim, 1975; (ed) Family Life, 1979; Residential Care, 1979; contrib.: Caring for Children, 1969; Giving Our Best, 1982; Thomas Bowman Stephenson, 1996. *Recreations:* music, do-it-yourself. *Address:* 10 Cadogan Gardens, Grange Park, N21 1ER. *T:* and *Fax:* (020) 8360 8687.

BARRON, Brian Munro; Rome Correspondent, BBC Television News and Current Affairs, since 2000; *b* 28 April 1940; *s* of Albert and Norah Barron; *m* 1974, Angela Lee, MA; one *d*. *Educ:* Bristol Grammar School. Junior Reporter, Western Daily Press, Bristol, 1956–60; Dep. Chief Sub-editor, Evening World, Bristol, 1960–61; Sub-editor, Daily Mirror, 1961–63; Dep. Chief Sub-editor, Evening Post, Bristol, 1963–65; Sub-editor, BBC External Services, London, 1965–67; Correspondent, BBC Radio: Aden, 1967–68; ME, Cairo, 1968–69; SE Asia, Singapore, 1969–71; Reporter, BBC TV News, 1971–73; Correspondent, BBC TV: Far East, Hong Kong, 1973–76; Africa, Nairobi, 1976–81; Ireland, 1981–83; Washington, 1983–86; Asia, 1986–94; NY, 1994–2000. Royal Television Society: Journalist of the Year, 1979–80; Internat. Reporting Award, 1985. *Recreations:* opera, cinema, running, tennis. *Address:* British Broadcasting Corporation, Piazza del Collegio Romano 1/A, 00186 Rome, Italy. *Club:* Oriental.

BARRON, Prof. Caroline Mary, PhD; FRHistS, FSA; Professor of the History of London and Dean of the Graduate School, Royal Holloway, University of London, since 1999; *b* 7 Dec. 1939; *d* of late William David Hogarth, OBE and Grace Allen Hogarth; *m* 1962, Prof. John Penrose Barron, *qv*; two *d*. *Educ:* North London Collegiate Sch.; Somerville Coll., Oxford (Exhibnr; MA Mod. Hist. 1966); Westfield Coll., London (PhD 1970). Bedford College, subseq. Royal Holloway and Bedford New College, University of London: Asst Lectr, 1967, Lectr, 1968–83, Sen. Lectr, 1983–91, in Hist.; Dean, Faculty of Arts, 1983–85; Reader in Hist. of London, 1991–99; Mem. Council, 1984–87. Reader, British Academy, 1988–90. Member: Cttee, Victoria County Hist., 1970–95; Council, London Record Soc., 1973–76, 1996–; Royal Commn on Historical Manuscripts, 1999–. Chm., Hilda Martindale Trust, 1984–87; Mem. Council, GPDST, 1979–84 (Chm. Educn Cttee, 1992–94); Chm. Govs, Wimbledon High Sch., 1985–88; Gov., NLCS, 1985–91; Mem., Mgt Cttee, Inst. Histl Res., 1982–85. Pres., Assoc. of Senior Mems, Somerville Coll., 1994–99; Chm. Friends, PRO, 1999–. Mem. Editorial Bd, Hist. of Parliament, 1988–. FRHistS (Mem. Council, 1989–94). *Publications:* (ed and contrib.) The Reign of Richard II, 1971; The Medieval Guildhall of London, 1974; The Parish of St Andrew Holborn, 1979; Revolt in London 11th to 15th June 1381, 1981; (ed and contrib.) The Church in the Century before the Reformation, 1985; Hugh Alley's Caveat: markets of London in 1598, 1988; (ed and contrib.) Widows of Medieval London, 1994; (ed and contrib.) England and the Low Countries in the Late Middle Ages, 1995; (ed and contrib.) The Church and Learning in Later Medieval Society, 2001; *contributions to:* Dictionary of the Middle Ages, 1986; British Atlas of Historic Towns, 1990; New Cambridge Medieval History, 1999; Cambridge Urban History of England, 2000. *Recreations:* travel, people. *Address:* Department of History, Royal Holloway, University of London, Egham, Surrey TW20 0EX. *T:* (01784) 434455. *Club:* University Women's.

BARRON, Derek Donald; Chairman and Chief Executive, Ford Motor Co. Ltd, 1986–91; Chairman, Ford Motor Credit Co., 1986–91; *b* 7 June 1929; *s* of Donald Frederick James Barron and Hettie Barbara Barron; *m* 1963, Rosemary Ingrid Brian; two *s*. *Educ:* Beckenham Grammar School; University College London. Joined Ford Motor Co. Sales, 1951; Tractor Group, 1961; Tractor Manager, Ford Italiana 1963; Marketing Associate, Ford Motor Co. USA, 1970; Gen. Sales Manager, Overseas Markets, 1971; Man. Dir, Ford Italiana, 1973; Group Dir, Southern European Sales, Ford of Europe, 1977; Sales and Marketing Dir, Ford Brazil, 1979; Vice-Pres., Ford Motor de Venezuela, 1982; Dir-Vice-Pres., Operations, Ford Brazil, 1985. DUniv Essex, 1989.

BARRON, Sir Donald (James), Kt 1972; DL; Chairman, Joseph Rowntree Foundation, 1981–96; *b* 17 March 1921; *o s* of Albert Gibson Barron and Elizabeth Macdonald, Edinburgh; *m* 1956, Gillian Mary, *o d* of John Saville, York; three *s* two *d*. *Educ:* George Heriot's Sch., Edinburgh; Edinburgh Univ. (BCom). Member, Inst. Chartered Accountants of Scotland. Joined Rowntree Mackintosh Ltd, 1952; Dir, 1961; Vice-Chm., 1965; Chm., 1966–81. Dir, 1972, Vice-Chm., 1981–82, Chm., 1982–87, Midland Bank plc. Dep. Chm., CLCB, 1983–85; Chm., Cttee of London and Scottish Bankers, 1985–87. Director: Investors in Industry, subseq. 3i, Gp, 1980–91; Canada Life Assurance Co. of GB Ltd, 1980–96 (Chm., 1991–94; Dep. Chm., 1994–96); Canada Life Unit Trust Managers Ltd, 1980–96 (Chm., 1982–96); Canada Life Assurance Co., Toronto, 1980–96; Canada Life Assce (Ireland), 1992–96; Clydesdale Bank, 1986–87. Mem., Bd of Banking Supervision, 1987–89. Dir, BIM Foundn, 1977–80 and Mem. Council, BIM, 1978–80; Trustee, Joseph Rowntree Foundn (formerly Meml Trust), 1966–73, 1975–96 (Chm., 1981–96); Treasurer, 1966–72, a Pro-Chancellor, 1982–95, York Univ.; Member: Council of CBI, 1966–81 (Chm., CBI Educn Foundn, 1981–85); SSRC, 1971–72; UGC, 1972–81; Council, PSI, 1978–85; Council, Inst. of Chartered Accountants of Scotland, 1980–81; NEDC, 1983–85. Governor, London Business Sch., 1982–88. Chm., York Millennium Bridge Trust, 1997–. DL N Yorks (formerly WR Yorks and City of York), 1971–96. Hon. doctorates: Loughborough, 1982; Heriot-Watt, 1983; CNAA, 1983; Edinburgh, 1984; Nottingham, 1985; York, 1986. *Recreations:* travelling, golf, tennis, gardening. *Address:* Greenfield, Sim Balk Lane, Bishopthorpe, York YO23 2QH. *T:* and *Fax:* (01904) 705675. *Club:* Athenæum.

BARRON, Henry Denis; Judge of the Supreme Court, Ireland, 1997–2000; *b* 25 May 1928; *s* of Harrie and Lena Barron; *m* 1958, Rosalind Scheps (*d* 1997); two *s* two *d*. *Educ:* Castle Park Sch., Dalkey; Coll. of St Columba, Rathfarnham, Dublin; Trinity Coll., Dublin (BA, LLB); King's Inns, Dublin (BL). Called to the Irish Bar, 1951, Sen. Bar, 1970; called to the Bar, Middle Temple, 1953; Judge of the High Court, Ireland, 1982–97. Mem., Commn of Inquiry into bombings in Dublin, Monaghan, 1974, and Dundalk, 1975, 2000–. Visitor, Univ. of Dublin, 1983–. *Recreations:* bridge, travel. *Address:* 8 Burleigh Court, Burlington Road, Dublin 4, Ireland. *T:* (1) 6686884. *Club:* Kildare Street and University (Dublin).

BARRON, Iann Marchant, CBE 1994; Chairman, Division Group plc, 1990–99; *b* 16 June 1936; *s* of William Barron; *m* 1962, Jacqueline Almond (marr. diss. 1989); two *s* two *d*; one *s*. *Educ:* University College School; Christ's College, Cambridge (exhibitioner; MA). Elliott Automation, 1961–65; Managing Director: Computer Technology Ltd, 1965–72; Microcomputer Analysis Ltd, 1973–78; Exec. Dir, 1978–89, Chief Strategic Officer, 1984–89, INMOS International; Man. Dir, INMOS, 1981–88. Vis. Prof., Westfield Coll., London, 1976–78; Vis. Indust. Prof., Bristol Univ., 1985–; Vis. Fellow: QMC, 1976; Science Policy Res. Unit, 1977–78. Exec. Trustee, The Exploratory, 1992–98; Dir, Bristol 2000, 1995–2000. Mem. Council, UCS, 1983–. Distinguished FBCS, 1986. FIEE 1994. Hon. DSc: Bristol Polytechnic, 1988; Hull, 1989. R. W. Mitchell Medal, 1983; J. J. Thompson Medal, IEE, 1986; IEE Achievement Medal for computing and control, 1996. *Publications:* The Future with Microelectronics (with Ray Curnow), 1977; technical papers. *Address:* Barrow Court, Barrow Gurney, Somerset BS48 3RW.

BARRON, Prof. John Penrose, MA, DPhil, FSA; Master of St Peter's College, Oxford, since 1991; *b* 27 April 1934; *s* of George Barron and Minnie Leslie Marks; *m* 1962, Caroline Mary Hogarth (*see* C. M. Barron); two *d*. *Educ:* Clifton Coll.; Balliol Coll., Oxford (Hon. Exhibnr). 1st Cl., Class. Hon. Mods, 1955; Lit. Hum., 1957; MA 1960, DPhil 1961; Thomas Whitcombe Greene Prize, 1955, and Scholar, 1957; Barclay Head Prize, 1959; Cromer Prize, British Academy, 1965. London University: Asst Lectr in Latin, Bedford Coll., 1959–61, and Lectr, 1961–64; Lectr in Archaeology, UCL, 1964–67; Reader in Archaeology and Numismatics, 1967–71; Prof. of Greek Lang. and Lit., 1971–91, and Head of Dept of Classics, 1972–84, KCL; Dean, Faculty of Arts, 1976–80; Dir, Inst. of Classical Studies, 1984–91; Dean, Insts for Advanced Study, 1989–91; Mem. Senate, 1977–81, 1987–91; Mem. Academic Council, 1977–81, 1985–89; Public Orator, 1978–81, 1986–88; Pro-Vice-Chancellor, 1987–89; Oxford University: Chairman: Conf. of Colls, 1993–95; Ashmolean Mus. Review, 1993–95; Admissions Cttee, 1997–2000. Mem., UFC, 1989–93. FKC 1988. Vis. Mem., Inst. for Advanced Study, Princeton, 1973. Blegen Distinguished Vis. Res. Prof., Vassar Coll., NY, 1981; T. B. L. Webster Vis. Prof., Stanford Univ., 1986; Vis. Prof., Aust. Archaeol Inst., Athens, 1994. Lectures: Eberhard L. Faber, Princeton, 1985; Woodward, Yale, 1985; Sotheby, Edinburgh, 1986; Dill, QUB, 1986; Batchelor, UEA, 1992; Dabis, Royal Holloway, 1996. Pres., Soc. for Promotion of Hellenic Studies, 1990–93 (Trustee, 1970–2000; Hon. Sec., 1981–90); Mem., Academia Europaea, 1990. Trustee, Prince of Wales Inst. of Architecture, 1990–96. Chm., Lambeth Palace Library Cttee, 1998–. Governor: SOAS, 1989–99 (Vice-Chm., 1992–99); St Paul's Schools, London, 1991–; Clifton Coll., Bristol, 1996– (Pres., 1999–); Almoner, Christ's Hosp., 1975–80. *Publications:* Greek Sculpture, 1965 (new and rev. edn 1981); Silver Coins of Samos, 1966; articles in Classical Quarterly, Jl of Hellenic Studies, Bulletin of Inst. of Classical Studies, etc. *Recreations:* travel, gardens. *Address:* St Peter's College, Oxford OX1 2DL. *Clubs:* Athenæum, Oxford and Cambridge.

BARRON, Kevin John; MP (Lab) Rother Valley, since 1983; *b* 26 Oct. 1946; *s* of Richard Barron; *m* 1969; one *s* two *d*. *Educ:* Maltby Hall Secondary Modern Sch.; Ruskin Coll., Oxford. NCB, 1962–83. PPS to Leader of the Opposition, 1985–87; Opposition spokesman on energy, 1988–92, on employment, 1993–95, on health, 1995–97. Member: Select Cttee on Energy, 1983–85; Select Cttee on Environmental Affairs, 1992–93; Parly Intelligence and Security Cttee, 1997–. Chm., Yorkshire Lab. MPs, 1987–. Pres., Rotherham and Dist TUC, 1982–83. *Address:* House of Commons, SW1A 0AA.

BARRON, Maj.-Gen. Richard Edward, CB 1993; *b* 22 Nov. 1940; *s* of John Barron and Lorna Frances Barron; *m* 1968, Margaret Ann Eggar; one *s* one *d*. *Educ:* Oundle; RMA. Commissioned Queen's Royal Irish Hussars, 1962; Staff College, 1973; DAA&QMG 7th Armoured Brigade, 1974–76; Instructor, Staff Coll., 1978–81; CO, QRIH, 1981–84; Comdr, 7th Armoured Brigade, 1984–86; RCDS 1987; QMG's Staff, 1988–89; Dir, RAC, 1989–92. Col, Queen's Royal Hussars, 1993–99. *Recreations:* restoration, gardening, fishing. *Address:* Middle Burrow, Timberscombe, Som TA24 7UD. *Clubs:* Cavalry and Guards, MCC.

BARRON, (Thomas) Robert, CBE 1980; Member, British Railways Board, 1978–81; *b* 27 Dec. 1918; *s* of late Robert and Florence May Barron; *m* 1st, 1942, Constance Lilian Bolter (*d* 1997); one *s* three *d*; 2nd, 1997, Kathleen Lucy Corcoran. *Educ:* Dame Allan's Sch., Newcastle upon Tyne; King's Coll., Durham Univ. BA 1st class Hons (Econ.). Served RA and 1st Airborne Div., 1940–46. Joined LNER as Traffic Apprentice, 1946; Asst Gen. Manager, London Midland Region, 1966, Western Region, 1967; British Railways Board: Dir Management Staff, 1970; Controller of Corporate Planning, 1972; Dir of Planning and Investment, 1977. Exec. Dir, Channel Tunnel, 1981–82. Mem., NW Economic Planning Council, 1965–67. *Recreations:* music, fishing, watching sport. *Address:* 25 Shotford Road, Harleston, Norfolk IP20 9JN. *T:* (01379) 853625.

BARRONS, John Lawson; Director, Century Newspapers Ltd, Belfast, 1989–98 (Chief Executive, 1989–97); *b* 10 Oct. 1932; *s* of late William Cowper Barrons, MBE and Amy Marie Barrons (*née* Lawson); *m* 1st, 1957, Caroline Anne (marr. diss. 1986), *d* of late George Edward Foster; three *s*; 2nd, 1987, Lauren Ruth, *d* of late Robert Z. Friedman. *Educ:* Caterham Sch. Nat. Service, 1st Bn Northamptonshire Regt, 1952–54. Journalist, UK and USA, 1950–57; Gen. Manager, Nuneaton Observer, 1957; Managing Editor, Northampton Chronicle & Echo, 1959; Gen. Manager, Edinburgh Evening News, 1961; Gen. Manager, 1965–76, Man. Dir, 1976–85, Westminster Press. Director: Pearson Longman, 1979–83; Stephen Austin Newspapers, 1986–91; Northern Press, 1986–91; Lincolnshire Standard Gp plc, 1987–88; President: Westminster (Florida) Inc., 1980–85; Westminster (Jacksonville) Inc., 1982–85. Dir, Evening Newspaper Advertising Bureau, 1978–81 (Chm. 1979–80); Dir, The Press Association Ltd, 1985–86; Chm., Printing Industry Res. Assoc., 1983–85 (Mem. Council, 1978, a Vice-Chm., 1979–83); Mem. Bd of Management, Internat. Electronic Publishing Res. Centre, 1981–85. Member, Council: Newspaper Soc., 1975–87 (Pres., 1981–82; Hon. Vice-Pres., 1983–); CPU, 1970–86. Director: BITC, NI, 1994–; City West Action Ltd, Belfast, 1995–. *Recreations:* walking, fishing. *Address:* 8 Harberton Avenue, Belfast BT9 6PH. *Clubs:* Flyfishers', MCC.

BARROS MELET, Cristián; Ambassador of Chile to the Court of St James's, since 2000; *b* 19 Oct. 1952; *s* of Diego Barros and Tencha Melet; *m* 1976, Mary Florence Michell Nielsen; one *s*. *Educ:* St Gabriel's Sch.; Sagrados Corazones Padres Franceses; Sch. of Law, Univ. of Chile; Diplomatic Acad. Andrés Bello; Catholic Univ., Santiago. Entered Diplomatic Service, Consular Div., Chile, 1974; Legal Dept, 1975–78; Protocol Dept, 1978; Admin. Dept, 1978–79; Consul: Mendoza, Argentina, 1979; Bariloche, Argentina, 1980–83; Bilateral Policy Dept, America Div., 1983–85; Consul and Consul Gen., Chicago, 1985–88; First Sec., Canada, 1989–90; Hd of Cabinet for Dir Gen. of Foreign Policy, 1990; Dir of Personnel, 1990–91; Ambassador, Dir Gen., Admin. Dept, 1991–93; Ambassador to Denmark, 1993–96; Dir Gen., Admin. Dept, 1996–98; Dir Gen., Foreign Policy, 1998–99. Grand Cross: Order of Merit (Portugal), 1993, Order of Dannebrog (Denmark), 1996; Order of May (Argentina), 1998; Order of El Sol (Peru), 1999; Grand Order, Order of Merit (Brazil), 1999. *Address:* Embassy of Chile, 12 Devonshire Street, W1N 2DS; 92 Eaton Place, SW1X 8LW. *T:* (020) 7235 1047.

BARROW, Prof. Geoffrey Wallis Steuart, FBA 1976; Sir William Fraser Professor of Scottish History and Palæography, University of Edinburgh, 1979–92, now Professor Emeritus; *b* Headingley, Leeds, 28 Nov. 1924; *s* of late Charles Embleton Barrow and Marjorie, *d* of Donald Stuart; *m* 1951, Heather Elizabeth, *d* of James McLeish Lownie; one *s* one *d*. *Educ:* St Edward's Sch., Oxford; Inverness Royal Acad.; St Andrews Univ.; Pembroke Coll., Oxford. FRSE 1977. Lecturer in History, University Coll., London, 1950–61; Prof. of Mediaeval Hist., King's Coll., Univ. of Durham, later Univ. of Newcastle upon Tyne, 1961–74; Prof. of Scottish History, Univ. of St Andrews, 1974–79. Mem., Royal Commn on Historical MSS, 1984–90. Ford's Lectr, Univ. of Oxford, 1977; Rhind Lectr, Soc. of Antiquaries of Scotland, 1985. Vice Pres., Commn Internationale de Diplomatique, 1994–. Hon. DLitt: Glasgow, 1988; Newcastle, 1994. *Publications:* Feudal Britain, 1956; Acts of Malcolm IV, King of Scots, 1960; Robert Bruce and the Community of the Realm of Scotland, 1965; Acts of William I, King of Scots, 1971; Kingdom of the Scots, 1973; (ed) The Scottish Tradition, 1974; The Anglo-Norman Era in Scottish History, 1980; Kingship and Unity, 1981; Scotland and its Neighbours, 1992; The Charters of David I, 1999; contrib. Scottish Historical Review, etc. *Recreation:* hill walking. *Address:* 12A Lauder Road, Edinburgh EH9 2EL.

BARROW, Jill Helen; Chief Executive, South West of England Regional Development Agency, 1999–2001; *b* 26 April 1951; *d* of Philip Eric Horwood and Mavis Mary (*née* Handscombe); *m* (marr. diss.); two *d*. *Educ:* Durham Univ. (Cert Ed 1972; MA Ed 1983); Open Univ. (BA 1980). Teaching in secondary, special and further educn, 1972–86; educn mgt and inspection, 1986–90; Dep. Dir of Educn, Essex CC, 1990–93; Dir of Educn, Surrey CC, 1993–95; Chief Exec., Lincs CC, 1995–98. *Recreations:* walking, outdoor activities, travelling, reading.

BARROW, Dame Jocelyn (Anita), DBE 1992 (OBE 1972); Development Director, Focus Consultancy Ltd, since 1996; Deputy Chairman, Broadcasting Standards Council, 1989–95; *b* 15 April 1929; *d* of Charles Newton Barrow and Olive Irene Barrow (*née* Pierre); *m* 1970, Henderson Downer. *Educ:* Univ. of London. Mem., Taylor Cttee on School Governors; Gen. Sec., later Vice-Chm., Campaign Against Racial Discrimination, 1964–69; Vice-Chm., Internat. Human Rights Year Cttee, 1968; Member: CRC, 1968–72; Parole Bd, 1983–87. A Governor, BBC, 1981–88. Chairman: Independent Cttee of Management, Optical Consumer Complaints Service, 1992–; Independent Equal Opportunities Inquiry into Ethnicity and Trng and Assessment on Bar Vocational Course, 1993–94; Non-exec. Dir, Whittington Hosp. NHS Trust, 1993–. Mem., Econ. and Social Cttee, EC, 1990–. Nat. Vice-Pres., Nat. Towns-women's Guilds, 1978–80, 1987–; Pres. and Founder, Community Housing Assoc.; Governor: Farnham Castle, 1977–93; BFI, 1991–97. FRSA. Hon. DLitt E London, 1992. *Recreations:* theatre, music, cooking, reading. *Address:* c/o Focus Consultancy Ltd, 38 Grosvenor Gardens, SW1W 0EB. *Club:* Reform.

BARROW, John Frederick; HM Diplomatic Service, retired; *b* 28 Dec. 1918; *s* of Frederick William and Caroline Barrow; *m* 1947, Mary Roberta Young; two *d*. *Educ:* King Edward VII Sch., King's Lynn. Home Civil Service, 1936–39; war service in British and Indian Armies, 1939–46 (Major); rejoined Home Civil Service, 1946; Treasury, 1952–62; FCO, 1962; service overseas at Delhi, Kuala Lumpur, Jesselton, Prague, Washington, Hong Kong; retired as Counsellor, 1977. *Address:* 55 Chancellor House, Mount Ephraim, Tunbridge Wells, Kent TN4 8BT.

BARROW, Captain Michael Ernest, DSO 1982; RN; *b* 21 May 1932; *s* of late Captain Guy Runciman Barrow, OBE, RN and late Barbara Barrow (*née* Heinekey); *m* 1962, Judith Ann (*née* Cooper); two *s* one *d*. *Educ:* Wellesley House; RNC, Dartmouth. Served in HM Ships: Devonshire, Liverpool (trng, 1950–52); Agincourt, Euryalus, 1952–53; HM Yacht Britannia, 1954–56; Camperdown, 1958–59; Flag Lt to Cdre Hong Kong, 1956–58; commanded: Caunton, 1960; Laleston, 1961–62; Mohawk, 1963–64; Torquay, 1967–69; Diomede, 1973–75; Glamorgan, 1980–83 (served in Falkland Is conflict); RN Staff Course, 1966; Staff Flag Officer, Malta, 1970–71; Comdr RNC, Dartmouth, 1971–73; Dep. Dir, Recruiting, 1975–77; Asst Chief of Staff (Ops) to Comdr, Allied Naval Forces Southern Europe, Naples, 1978–80; ADC to the Queen, 1982–83; retired RN 1983. Clerk to the Worshipful Co. of Haberdashers, 1983–95, Hon. Assistant, 1995–. Gentleman Usher to Her Majesty, 1984–. Trustee: RN Benevolent Soc. for Officers, 1985–; Falkland Is Meml Chapel, 1992–; Union Jack Club, 1996–. *Recreations:* sailing, skiing, gardening. *Address:* Heathfield, Shear Hill, Petersfield, Hampshire GU31 4BB. *T:* (01730) 264198. *Clubs:* Army and Navy; Royal Naval Sailing; Royal Naval Ski.

BARROW, Captain Sir Richard John Uniacke, 6th Bt *cr* 1835; *b* 2 Aug. 1933; *s* of Sir Wilfrid John Wilson Croker Barrow, 5th Bt and (Gwladys) Patricia (*née* Uniacke); *S* father, 1960; *m* 1961, Alison Kate (marr. diss. 1974), *yr d* of late Capt. Russell Grenfell, RN, and of Mrs Lindsay-Young; one *s* two *d*. *Educ:* Abbey Sch., Ramsgate; Beaumont Coll., Old Windsor. Commnd 2nd Lieut Irish Guards, 1952; served: Germany, 1952–53; Egypt, 1953–56; Cyprus, 1958; Germany, 1959–60; retired, 1960; joined International Computers and Tabulators Ltd; resigned 1973. *Heir:* *s* Anthony John Grenfell Barrow [*b* 24 May 1962; *m* 1990, Rebecca Mary Long (marr. diss. 1996); one *d*].

BARROW, Simon William; Headmaster, The Oratory School, 1992–2000; *b* 17 Jan. 1942; *s* of Alfred Francis Lendon Barrow and Ruth Mary Barrow; *m* 1977, Brenda Cora Mary Kelly; one *s* one *d*. *Educ:* Stonyhurst; Reading Univ. (BA Mod Hist). Asst Master, Caldicott Sch., Farnham Royal, 1963–69; The Oratory Sch., Woodcote, 1969–2000 (Housemaster, 1971; Dep. Head, 1982). *Recreations:* Rugby refereeing, walking, gardening, giving others good advice. *Address:* 19 Treforgan, Hunters Chase, Caversham, Reading RG4 7XG.

BARROW, Ursula Helen, (Viscountess Waverley), PhD; High Commissioner for Belize in London, 1993–98, also Ambassador to the European Union, Belgium, France, Germany and the Holy See; *b* 31 Oct. 1955; *d* of Raymond Hugh and Rita Helen Barrow; *m* 1994, Viscount Waverley, *qv*; one *s*. *Educ:* Newnham Coll., Cambridge (BA 1977; MA 1981; LLM; PhD 1988). Econ. Develt Planner, Planning Unit, Govt of Belize, 1978; consultant for small business affairs, urban planning and marketing, Frazier & Assocs, 1979–85; Counsellor and Dep. High Comr, London, 1988–89; Perm. Rep. to UN, 1989–91; Asst Dir (Pol), Commonwealth Secretariat, 1991–93. *Address:* c/o Belize High Commission, 22 Harcourt House, 19 Cavendish Square, W1M 9AD.

BARROWCLOUGH, Sir Anthony (Richard), Kt 1988; QC 1974; Parliamentary Commissioner for Administration, and Health Service Commissioner for England, Wales and Scotland, 1985–90; *b* 24 June 1924; *m* 1949, Mary Agnes Pery-Knox-Gore; one *s* one *d*. *Educ:* Stowe; New Coll., Oxford. Served RNVR, 1943–46 (Sub-Lieut and later Lieut). Called to the Bar, Inner Temple, 1949, Bencher 1982; Recorder, 1972–84. Part-time Member, Monopolies Commn, 1966–69; Mem., Council on Tribunals (and Mem., Scottish Cttee), 1985–90; Indep. Mem. Council, FIMBRA, 1991–94. Chm., Dartmoor Steering Gp, 1990–99. *Recreation:* country pursuits. *Address:* The Old Vicarage, Winsford, near Minehead, Somerset TA24 7JF.

BARRY, Prof. Brian Michael, FBA 1988; Professor of Political Science, London School of Economics and Political Science, since 1987; *b* 7 Aug. 1936; *s* of James Frederick and Doris Rose Barry; *m* 1st, 1960, Joanna Hill Scroggs (marr. diss. 1988); one *s*; 2nd, 1991, Anni Parker. *Educ:* Taunton's Sch., Southampton; Queen's Coll., Oxford (MA; DPhil 1965). Lloyd Muirhead Res. Fellow, Univ. of Birmingham, 1960–61; Rockefeller Fellow in Legal and Political Philosophy, and Fellow of Harvard College, 1961–62; Asst Lectr, Keele Univ., 1962–63; Lectr, Univ. of Southampton, 1963–65; Tutorial Fellow, University Coll., Oxford, 1965–66; Official Fellow, Nuffield Coll., Oxford, 1966–69 and 1972–75; Prof., Univ. of Essex, 1969–72 (Dean of Social Studies, 1971–72); Prof., Univ. of British Columbia, 1975–76; Fellow, Center for Advanced Study in the Behavioral Scis, 1976–77; Professor: Univ. of Chicago, 1977–82; California Inst. of Technology, 1982–86; European Univ. Inst., Florence, 1986–87. Fellow, Amer. Acad. of Arts and Scis, 1978. Founding Editor, British Jl of Political Science, 1971–72; Editor, Ethics, 1979–82. *Publications:* Political Argument, 1965; Sociologists, Economics and Democracy, 1970; The Liberal Theory of Justice, 1973; (with Russell Hardin) Rational Man and Irrational Society?, 1982; A Treatise on Social Justice: vol. 1, Theories of Justice, 1989, vol. 2, Justice as Impartiality, 1995; Democracy, Power and Justice: collected essays, 1989, rev. edn 1991; articles in learned jls. *Recreations:* music, theatre, cooking. *Address:* London School of Economics, Houghton Street, WC2A 2AE. *T:* (020) 7955 7175.

BARRY, Daniel, CB 1988; Permanent Secretary, Department of the Environment for Northern Ireland, 1983–88; *b* 4 March 1928; *s* of William John Graham Barry and Sarah (*née* Wilkinson); *m* 1951, Florence (*née* Matier); two *s* one *d*. *Educ:* Belfast Mercantile Coll. FCIS, FSCA, FIHT. Local Government Officer with various NI Councils, 1944–68; Town Clerk, Carrickfergus Borough Council, 1968–73; Asst Sec. (Roads), Dept of the Environment for NI, 1973–76, Dep. Sec., 1976–80; Dep. Sec., Dept of Educn for NI, 1980–83. *Recreations:* golf, gardening, tobacco producing, wine making.

BARRY, Sir Edward; *see* Barry, Sir L. E. A. T.

BARRY, Edward Norman, CB 1981; Under Secretary, Northern Ireland Office, 1979–81, retired 1981; *b* 22 Feb. 1920; *s* of Samuel and Matilda (*née* Legge); *m* 1952, Inez Anna (*née* Elliott); one *s* two *d*. *Educ:* Bangor Grammar Sch. Northern Ireland Civil Service: Department of Finance: Establishment Div., 1940–51; Works Div., 1951–60; Treasury Div., 1960–67; Establishment Officer, 1967–72; Min. of Home Affairs, 1972–74; Asst Sec., N Ireland Office, 1974–79. *Recreations:* golf, football (Hon. Treas., 1977–96, and Life Mem., Irish Football Association).

BARRY, James Edward; His Honour Judge Barry; a Circuit Judge, since 1994; *b* 27 May 1938; *s* of James Douglas Barry and Margaret (*née* Thornton); *m* 1963, Pauline Pratt; three *s*. *Educ:* Merchant Taylors' Sch., Crosby; Brasenose Coll., Oxford (schol.; MA Jurisp.). Called to the Bar, Inner Temple, 1963; in practice, NE Circuit, 1963–85; Stipendiary Magistrate for S Yorks, 1985–94; a Recorder, 1985–94. Part-time Chm., Industrial Tribunals, 1983–85. *Recreations:* binding the Rings of the Legal Nibelungs, studying the New Musical Express. *Address:* Leeds Combined Court Centre, 1 Oxford Place, Leeds LS1 3BG.

BARRY, Sir (Lawrence) Edward (Anthony Tress), 5th Bt *cr* 1899; Baron de Barry in Portugal *cr* 1876; *b* 1 Nov. 1939; *s* of Sir Rupert Rodney Francis Tress Barry, 4th Bt, MBE, and Diana Madeline (*d* 1948), *o d* of R. O'Brien Thompson; *S* father, 1977; *m* 1st, 1968, Fenella Hoult (marr. diss. 1991); one *s* one *d*; 2nd, 1992, (Elizabeth) Jill Dawe, *d* of G. Bradley, Fishtoft. *Educ:* Haileybury. Formerly Captain, Grenadier Guards. *Heir:* *s* William Rupert Philip Tress Barry, *b* 13 Dec. 1973. *Address:* 4 The Gables, Argos Hill, Rotherfield, East Sussex TN6 3QJ. *T:* (01892) 852322.

BARRY, Michael; *see* Bukht, M. M. J.

BARRY, Rt Rev. (Noel) Patrick, OSB; Abbot of Ampleforth, 1984–97; *b* 6 Dec. 1917; 2nd *s* of Dr T. St J. Barry, Wallasey, Cheshire. *Educ:* Ampleforth Coll.; St Benet's Hall,

Oxford. Housemaster, Ampleforth Coll., 1954–64, Headmaster 1964–79. First Asst to Abbot Pres. of English Benedictine Congregation, 1985–97. Chairman: Conference of Catholic Colleges, 1973–75; HMC, 1975; Union of Monastic Superiors, 1989–95. *Address:* St Louis Abbey, 500 South Mason Road, St Louis, MO 63141, USA; Ampleforth Abbey, York YO6 4EN.

BARRY, Peter; *b* Cork, 10 Aug. 1928; *s* of Anthony Barry and Rita Costello; *m* 1958, Margaret O'Mullane; four *s* two *d.* *Educ:* Christian Brothers' Coll., Cork. Alderman of Cork Corp., 1967–73; Lord Mayor of Cork, 1970–71. TD: Cork City SE, 1969–82; Cork South Central, 1982–97; opposition spokesman on labour and public services, 1972–73; Minister for: Transport and Power, 1973–76; Education, 1976–77; opposition spokesman on finance and economic affairs, 1977–81; Minister for the Environment, 1981–82; opposition spokesman on the environment, 1982; Minister for Foreign Affairs, 1982–87; opposition spokesman on foreign affairs, 1987–91, on industry and commerce, 1991–92. Dep. Leader of Fine Gael Party, 1979–87, 1991; Chm., Nat. Exec., 1982–84. Co-Chm., Anglo-Irish Conf., 1982–87. *Address:* Sherwood, Blackrock, Co. Cork.

BARSTOW, Dame Josephine (Clare), DBE 1995 (CBE 1985); opera singer, free-lance since 1971; *b* Sheffield, 27 Sept. 1940; *m* 1969, Ande Anderson (*d* 1996); no *c.* *Educ:* Birmingham Univ. (BA). Debut with Opera for All, 1964; studied at London Opera Centre, 1965–66; Opera for All, 1966; Glyndebourne Chorus, 1967; Sadler's Wells Contract Principal, 1967–68, sang Cherubino, Euridice, Violetta; *Welsh National Opera:* Contract Principal, 1968–70, sang Violetta, Countess, Fiordiligi, Mimi, Amelia, Simon Boccanegra; Don Carlos, 1973; Jenufa, 1975; Peter Grimes, 1978, 1983; Tatyana in Onegin, 1980; Tosca, 1985; Un Ballo in Maschera, 1986; The Makropoulos Case, 1994; *Covent Garden:* Denise, world première, Tippett's The Knot Garden, 1970 (recorded 1974); Falstaff, 1975; Salome, 1982; Santuzza, 1982; Peter Grimes, 1988 and 1995; Attila, 1990; Fidelio, 1993; Katya Kabanova, 2000; Queen of Spades, 2001; *Glyndebourne:* Lady Macbeth (for TV), 1972; Idomeneo, 1974; Fidelio, 1981; *English National Opera:* has sung all parts in Hoffman, Emilia Marty (Makropulos Case), Natasha (War and Peace) and Traviata; Der Rosenkavalier, 1975, 1984; Salome, 1975; Don Carlos, 1976, 1986; Tosca, 1976, 1987; Forza del Destino, 1978, 1992; Aida, 1979; Fidelio, Arabella, 1980; The Flying Dutchman, La Bohème, 1982; The Valkyrie, 1983; Don Giovanni, 1986; Lady Macbeth of Mtsensk, 1987, 1991; Street Scene, 1993; Jenufa, 1994; The Carmelites, 1999; *Opera North:* Gloriana, 1993, 1997; Jenufa, 1995; Medea, Wozzeck, 1996; Aida, 1997; Falstaff, 2000. Other appearances include: Alice in Falstaff, Aix-en-Provence Festival, 1971; Nitocris in Belshazzar, Geneva, 1972; Jeanne, British première, Penderecki's The Devils, 1973; Marguerite, world première, Crosse's The Story of Vasco, 1974; Fidelio, Jenufa, Scottish Opera, 1977; Gayle, world première, Tippett's The Ice Break, 1977; US début as Lady Macbeth, Miami, 1977; Musetta in La Bohème, NY Met., 1977; Salome, East Berlin, 1979 (Critics Prize), San Francisco, 1982; Abigaille in Nabucco, Miami, 1981; début in Chicago as Lady Macbeth, 1981; new prod. of Jenufa, Cologne, 1981; La Voix Humaine and Pagliacci, Chicago, 1982; The Makropulos Case (in Italian), Florence, 1983; Gutrune, Göterdämmerung, Bayreuth, 1983; Die Fledermaus, San Francisco, 1984; Peter Grimes, 1984, La Traviata, 1985, Salome, 1987, Der Rosenkavalier, 1990, Houston; Benigna, world première, Penderecki's Die Schwarze Maske, Salzburg, 1986, Vienna Staatsoper, 1986; Manon Lescaut, USA, 1986; Tosca, Bolshoi, Tiblisi, 1986; Tosca, and Macbeth, Bolshoi, Riga, 1986; Macbeth, Zurich, 1986, Munich, 1987; Medea, Boston, 1988; Prokofiev's The Fiery Angel, Adelaide, 1988; Un Ballo in Maschera, Salzburg, 1989, 1990; Fanciulla del West, Toulouse, 1991; Chrysothemis, Houston, 1993; Fidelio, 1992, Salome, 1994, Amsterdam; Peter Grimes, Tokyo, 1998; first Jenufa in Czech, Antwerp, 1999. Sings in other opera houses in USA, Canada and Europe. Recordings include: Un Ballo in Maschera; Verdi arias; scenes from Salome, Medée, Makropulos Case and Turandot; Kiss Me Kate; Kurt Weill's Street Scene, Gloriana; Albert Herring. Fidelio medal, Assoc. of Internat. Opera Directors, 1985. *Recreation:* farm which she runs (she breeds pure-bred Arabian horses and Sussex cattle). *Address:* c/o Askonas Holt Ltd, Lonsdale Chambers, 27 Chancery Lane, WC2A 1PF.

BARSTOW, Stan, FRSL; writer; *b* 28 June 1928; *s* of Wilfred Barstow and Elsie Gosnay; *m* 1951, Constance Mary Kershaw; one *s* one *d.* *Educ:* Ossett Grammar Sch. Employed in Engineering Industry, 1944–62, mainly as Draughtsman. Best British Dramatisation, Writers' Guild of GB, 1974; Royal TV Soc. Writers' Award, 1975. FRSL 1999. Hon. Fellow, Bretton Coll., 1985. Hon. MA Open Univ., 1982. *Radio: dramatisations:* A Kind of Loving, 1964; The Pity of it All, 1967; Bright Day, 1968; The Watchers on the Shore, 1971; We could always fit a sidecar, 1974; The Right True End, 1978; The Apples of Paradise, 1988; Foreign Parts, 1990; My Son, my Son, 1993. *Television: dramatisations:* A Raging Calm, 1974; South Riding, 1974; Joby, 1975; The Cost of Loving, 1977; Travellers, 1978; A Kind of Loving (from A Kind of Loving, The Watchers on the Shore, The Right True End), 1982; A Brother's Tale, 1983; The Man Who Cried, 1993. *Publications:* A Kind of Loving, 1960; The Desperadoes, 1961; Ask Me Tomorrow, 1962; Joby, 1964; The Watchers on the Shore, 1966; A Raging Calm, 1968; A Season with Eros, 1971; The Right True End, 1976; A Brother's Tale, 1980; A Kind of Loving: The Vic Brown Trilogy, 1982; The Glad Eye, 1984; Just You Wait and See, 1986; B-Movie, 1987; Give Us This Day, 1989; Next of Kin, 1991; In My Own Good Time, 2001; *plays:* Listen for the Trains, Love, 1970; Joby (TV script), 1977; An Enemy of the People (ad. Ibsen), 1978; The Human Element, and Albert's Part (TV scripts), 1984; (with Alfred Bradley): Ask Me Tomorrow, 1966; A Kind of Loving, 1970; Stringer's Last Stand, 1972. *Address:* c/o The Agency, 24 Pottery Lane, W11 4LZ.

BART, André S.; *see* Schwarz-Bart.

BARTELL, family name of **Baroness Gibson of Market Rasen.**

BARTER, Nicholas Arthur Beamish; Principal, Royal Academy of Dramatic Art, since 1993; *b* 12 Sept. 1940; *s* of Paul André Valentine Spencer and Sylvia Theadora Essex Barter; *m* 1961, Brigid Alice Panet (marr. diss. 1981); one *s* one *d*; *m* 1998, Noriko Sasaki. *Educ:* Cheltenham Coll.; Pembroke Coll., Cambridge (BA Hons, MA). ABC TV Trainee Directors Award, 1963; Asst Dir, Phoenix Th., Leicester, 1963–65; Dir of Prodns, Lincoln Theatre Royal, 1965–68; Dep. Artistic Dir, RSC Theatregoround, 1968; Dir, Ipswich Arts Th., 1968–71; Asst Drama Dir, Arts Council of GB, 1971–75; Artistic Dir, Unicorn Th., 1977–86 (Best Prodn for Young People Award, Drama mag., 1982, for Beowulf); Children's Th. Consultant, Los Angeles, 1986–; Course Dir, and Dep. Principal, RADA, 1988–93. Chm., Dharma Trust, 1990–97. *Publications:* Playing with Plays, 1979; contrib. Theatre Qly, Theatre Internat. *Recreation:* pottery. *Address:* c/o Royal Academy of Dramatic Art, 62–64 Gower Street, WC1E 6ED. *T:* (020) 7636 7076.

BARTER, Sir Peter (Leslie Charles), Kt 2001; OBE 1986; *b* Sydney, Australia, 26 March 1940; *s* of late John Frank Barter and of Wyn Emily Barter; *m* 1970 Janet Ellen Carter; one *s.* *Educ:* Newington Coll.; Wellington Coll., Sydney. Former Minister for Health, PNG; First Provincial Gov., Madang Province. Work in aviation and tourism develt in Papua New Guinea: Chairman: PNG Tourist Promotion Authy; PNG Nat. Events Council; PNG Incentive Fund; Melanesian Foundn; MTS Ltd. *Recreation:* sailing. *Address:* PO Box 707, Madang, Papua New Guinea. *T:* 8522766, *Fax:* 8523543.

BARTFIELD, Robert; His Honour Judge Bartfield; a Circuit Judge, since 1996; *b* 30 Dec. 1949; *s* of Isaac and Emily Bartfield; *m* 1977, Susan Eleanor Griffin; one *s* one *d.* *Educ:* Leeds Grammar Sch.; Queen Mary Coll., London (LLB). Called to the Bar, Middle Temple, 1971; in practice as barrister, 1971–96; a Recorder, 1993–96. *Recreations:* tennis, football. *Address:* 2 Littleway, Leeds LS17 6JN. *T:* (0113) 294 3408.

BARTHOLOMEW, Prof. David John, PhD; FBA 1987; Professor of Statistics, London School of Economics, 1973–96, then Emeritus (Pro-Director, 1988–91); *b* 6 Aug. 1931; *s* of Albert and Joyce Bartholomew; *m* 1955, Marian Elsie Lake; two *d.* *Educ:* University College London (BSc, PhD). Scientist, NCB, 1955–57; Lectr in Stats, Univ. of Keele, 1957–60; Lectr, then Sen. Lectr, UCW, Aberystwyth, 1960–67; Prof. of Stats, Univ. of Kent, 1967–73. Pres., Royal Statistical Soc., 1993–95 (Hon. Sec., 1976–82; Treas., 1989–93); Vice-Pres., Manpower Soc., 1987–95. Chm., Science and Religion Forum, 1997–2000. *Publications:* (jtly) Backbench Opinion in the House of Commons 1955–1959, 1961; Stochastic Models for Social Processes, 1967, 3rd edn 1982; (jtly) Let's Look at the Figures: the quantitative approach to human affairs, 1971; (jtly) Statistical Inference Under Order Restrictions, 1972; (jtly) Statistical Techniques for Manpower Planning, 1979, 2nd edn 1991; Mathematical Methods in Social Science, 1981; God of Chance, 1984; Latent Variable Models and Factor Analysis, 1987, 2nd edn (jtly) 1999; Uncertain Belief, 1996; The Statistical Approach to Social Measurement, 1996; papers in statistical, theological and social science jls. *Recreations:* gardening, steam railways, theology. *Address:* The Old Manse, Stoke Ash, Eye, Suffolk IP23 7EN. *T:* (01379) 678197.

BARTLE, Ronald David; a Metropolitan Stipendiary Magistrate, 1972–99; Deputy to Chief Magistrate, 1992–99; *b* 14 April 1929; *s* of late Rev. George Clement Bartle and Winifred Marie Bartle; *m* 1st, 1963; one *s* one *d*; 2nd, 1981, Hisako (*née* Yagi). *Educ:* St John's Sch., Leatherhead; Jesus Coll., Cambridge (MA). Nat. Service, 1947–49 (Army Athletic Colours). Called to Bar, Lincoln's Inn, 1954; practised at Criminal Bar, 1954–72; a Dep. Circuit Judge, 1975–79; a Chm., Inner London Juvenile Courts, 1975–79. Member: Home Office Council on Drug Abuse, 1987–; Home Office Cttee on Magistrates' Court Procedure, 1989–. Lectr on Advocacy, Council of Legal Educn, 1984–89. Contested (C) Islington N, 1958, 1959; Mem., Essex CC, 1963–66. Freeman, City of London, 1976; Liveryman, Basketmakers' Co., 1976– (Steward, 1990; Mem. Ct, 1997–). Patron, Pathway to Recovery Trust. Governor: Corp. of Sons of the Clergy, 1995–; RNLI, 1997–. Church Warden, St Mary the Boltons, Kensington, 1992–95; Church Warden and Trustee, St Margaret Pattens, 1999–. *Publications:* Introduction to Shipping Law, 1958; The Police Officer in Court, 1984; Crime and the New Magistrate, 1985; The Law and the Lawless, 1987; Bow Street Beak, 1999; (contrib.) Atkin's Court Forms and Precedents; contrib. to legal jls. *Recreations:* music, reading, swimming. *Clubs:* Garrick, Lansdowne.

BARTLEET, Rt Rev. David Henry; Bishop Suffragan of Tonbridge, 1982–93; *b* 11 April 1929; *s* of Edmund Arthur Bartleet and Helen Bartleet (*née* Holford); *m* 1956, Jean Mary (*née* Rees); one *s* two *d.* *Educ:* St Edward's School, Oxford; AA School of Architecture, London; St Peter's Hall, Oxford; Westcott House, Cambridge. Curate: St Mary-le-Tower, Ipswich, 1957–60; St George's, Doncaster (in charge of St Edmund's), 1960–64; Vicar: Edenbridge, Kent, 1964–73; Bromley, Kent, 1973–82. *Recreations:* music, architecture, icons. *Address:* 21 Lee Road, Aldeburgh, Suffolk IP15 5EY. *T:* (01728) 452724.

BARTLES-SMITH, Ven. Douglas Leslie; Archdeacon of Southwark, since 1985; Chaplain to the Queen, since 1996; *b* 3 June 1937; *s* of late Leslie Charles and Muriel Rose Bartles-Smith; *m* 1967, Patricia Ann Coburn; two *s* one *d.* *Educ:* Shrewsbury School; St Edmund Hall, Oxford (MA); Wells Theol Coll. Nat. Service (2nd Lieut, RASC), 1956–58. Curate of St Stephen's, Rochester Row, SW1, 1963–68; Curate-in-charge, St Michael and All Angels with Emmanuel and All Souls, Camberwell, 1968–72; Vicar, 1972–75; Vicar of St Luke, Battersea, 1975–85; RD of Battersea, 1981–85. *Publications:* (co-author) Urban Ghetto, 1976; Opportunities for a Strong Church, 1993. *Recreations:* Shrewsbury Town Football Club, reading, walking, travel. *Address:* 1a Dog Kennel Hill, East Dulwich, SE22 8AA. *T:* (020) 7274 6767.

BARTLETT, Sir Andrew (Alan), 5th Bt *cr* 1913, of Hardington Mandeville, Somerset; *b* 26 May 1973; *er s* of Sir John Hardington David Bartlett, 4th Bt and of his 2nd wife, Elizabeth Joyce (*née* Raine); *S* father, 1998. *Heir:* *b* Stephen Bartlett, *b* 5 July 1975.

BARTLETT, Andrew Vincent Bramwell; QC 1993; *b* 7 Oct. 1952; *s* of John Samuel Bartlett and Doris Jean Bartlett; *m* 1974, Elisabeth Jefferis. *Educ:* Jesus Coll., Oxford (BA). Called to the Bar, Middle Temple, 1974. FCIArb. *Address:* 1 Paper Buildings, Temple, EC4Y 7EP. *T:* (020) 7797 8100.

BARTLETT, Charles; *see* Bartlett, H. C.

BARTLETT, Dr Christopher Leslie Reginald, FRCP, FFPHM; Director, Public Health Laboratory Service Communicable Disease Surveillance Centre, 1988–2000; *b* 20 Dec. 1940; *s* of Reginald James Bartlett and Dorothea Amelia Bartlett; *m* 1979, Alicia Teresa Tower; one *s* two *d.* *Educ:* Milton Sch., Bulawayo, Southern Rhodesia; Lysses Sch., Hants; St Bartholomew's Hosp. Med. Coll. (MB, BS 1965); MSc LSHTM 1977. MRCS 1965; LRCP 1965, FRCP 1991; MFCM 1978, FFPHM 1983. RAF SSC, 1967–72. Registrar, Wessex RHA, seconded to LSHTM, 1975–77; Public Health Laboratory Service: Sen. Registrar, 1977–79; Consultant Epidemiologist, 1979–88. Consultant Med. Epidemiologist, Caribbean Epidemiol. Centre, 1984–85. Hon. Lectr, Dept of Envmtl and Preventative Medicine, St Bartholomew's Hosp. Med. Coll., 1980; Hon. Sen. Lectr, Dept of Epidemiol. and Med. Stats, Royal London Hosp., 1990; Vis. Prof., LSHTM, 1997–. Chm., PHLS Cttee on Legionnaire's Disease, 1989; Member: DHSS Cttee on Aspects and Use of Biocides, 1986; Registrar-Gen's Med. Adv. Cttee, DoH, 1988–90; Expert Gp on Cryptosporidium in Water Supplies, DoE and DoH, 1989–90; Steering Gp on Microbiol Safety of Food, MAFF and DoH, 1991–95; CMO's Health of Nation Cttee, DoH, 1992–2000. Faculty of Public Health Medicine: Member: Bd, 1988–91; Educn Cttee, 1988–94; Pres., Sect. of Epidemiol. and Public Health, RSocMed. 1996 (Mem., Council, 1990–94); Mem. Council, RIPH&H, 1991–94. Member: Scientific Steering Cttee, Réseau Nat. de Santé Publique, France, 1992; Steering Gp, European Prog. for Intervention Epidemiol. Trng, 1994; PROMED Steering Cttee, Fedn of Amer. Scientists, 1995; Communicable Diseases Wkg Gp, G7 Nations Global Healthcare Applications Project, 1995; MRC CJD Epidemiol. Subcttee, 1996; EU/USA Task Force on Communicable Diseases, 1996 (Co-Chm., Surveillance and Response Wkg Gp, 1996); Project Leader, European Surveillance of Travel Associated Legionnaire's Disease, 1993; Jt Project Leader, SALMNET (EU Surveillance of Salmonella Infections), 1994; Chm., Charter Gp of Heads of Instns with responsibilities in nat. surveillance of disease in EU countries, 1994. Specialist Advr, Editl Bd, Jl Infection, 1991–. *Publications:* chapters, articles and papers in med. and scientific texts on aspects of epidemiology and prevention of infectious diseases. *Recreations:* family, walking, ski-ing, travelling. *Address:* 43A Oakridge Avenue, Radlett, Herts WD7 8EW. *Club:* Royal Society of Medicine.

BARTLETT, George Robert, QC 1986; President of the Lands Tribunal, since 1998; a Deputy High Court Judge, since 1994; *b* 22 Oct. 1944; *s* of late Commander H. V. Bartlett, RN and of Angela (*née* Webster); *m* 1972, Dr Clare Virginia, *y d* of G. C. Fortin; three *s*. *Educ:* Tonbridge Sch.; Trinity Coll., Oxford (MA). Called to the Bar, Middle Temple, 1966, Bencher, 1995. A Recorder, 1990–2000; An Asst Parly Boundary Comr, 1992–98. *Address:* Lands Tribunal, 48–49 Chancery Lane, WC2A 1JR.

BARTLETT, (Harold) Charles, RE 1961 (ARE 1950); RWS 1970 (ARWS 1959); President, Royal Society of Painters in Water Colours, 1987–92; painter and printmaker; *b* Grimsby, 23 Sept. 1921; *s* of Charles Henry and Frances Kate Bartlett; *m*; one *s*; *m* 1970, Olwen Jones, RE, RWS. *Educ:* Eastbourne Grammar Sch.; Eastbourne Sch. of Art; Royal College of Art (ARCA 1949). First one man exhibition in London, 1960; major retrospective, Bankside Gall., London, 1997. *Recreations:* music, sailing. *Address:* St Andrews, Fingringhoe, near Colchester, Essex CO5 7BG. *T:* (01206) 729406.

BARTLETT, Henry Francis, CMG 1975; OBE 1964; HM Diplomatic Service, retired; *b* 8 March 1916; *s* of F. V. S. and A. G. Bartlett, London; *m* 1940, A. D. Roy. *Educ:* St Paul's Sch.; Queen's Coll., Oxford; Ruskin Sch. of Drawing; Univ. of California (Commonwealth Fellow). Min. of Inf., 1940–45; Paris, 1944–47; Vice-Consul Lyons, 1948–49; FO, 1949–50; Vice-Consul, Szczecin, 1950; Second, later First, Sec., Warsaw, 1951–53; FO, 1953–55; First Sec. (Commercial), Caracas, 1955–60; First Sec. (Inf.), Mexico City, 1960–63; Consul, Khorramshahr, 1964–67; Dep. High Comr, Brisbane, 1967–69; Counsellor, Manila, 1969–72 (Chargé d'Affaires, 1971); Ambassador to Paraguay, 1972–75. Hon. Prof., Nat. Univ. of Asunción, 1975. Exec. Officer, Utah Foundation, Brisbane, 1976–89. Exhibitions of painting: Paris, 1947; London, 1950; Caracas, 1957, 1959; Mexico City, 1962; Brisbane, 1969, 1978, 1981, 1983, 1985, 1988, 1990, 1992, 1994, 1996. Represented: Commonwealth Art Bank; Queensland and S Aust. State Galleries; Queensland Univ. of Technol.; Brisbane Civic Art Gall.; Bendigo Art Gall. Trustee: Queensland Art Gallery, 1977–87; Qld Cultural Centre Trust, 1980–87. *Recreation:* painting. *Address:* 14 Bowen Place, 341 Bowen Terrace, New Farm, Brisbane, Qld 4005, Australia.

BARTLETT, Maj.-Gen. John Leonard, CB 1985; Paymaster-in-Chief and Inspector of Army Pay Services, 1983–86, retired; *b* 17 Aug. 1926; *s* of late F. Bartlett and E. Bartlett; *m* 1952, Pauline (*née* Waite); two *s*. *Educ:* Holt Grammar Sch., Liverpool. MBCS, FIMgt, jssc, psc, pfc. Commissioned Royal Army Pay Corps, 1946; served Hong Kong, Singapore, BAOR, War Office, Washington, Malta, Libya, HQ MELF, 1966–67 (despatches 1968); Staff Pmr and O i/c FBPO Berlin, 1968–69; GSO1 (Secretary) NATO Mil. Agency for Standardisation, 1969–71; Comd Pmr, Hong Kong, 1972–74; Col GS, MoD (ADP Coord.), 1974–76; Chief Pmr ADP and Station Comdr, Worthy Down, 1976–79; Chief Pmr, BAOR, 1980–82. Col Comdt, RAPC, 1987–90. Freeman, City of London, 1984. *Recreation:* golf. *Address:* c/o Lloyds TSB, The Square, Wickham, Hants PO17 5JQ.

BARTLETT, John Vernon, CBE 1976; MA; FREng, FICE; consulting engineer, retired; *b* 18 June 1927; *s* of late Vernon F. Bartlett and Olga Bartlett (*née* Testrup); *m* 1951, Gillian, *d* of late Philip Hoffmann, Sturmer Hall, Essex; four *s*. *Educ:* Stowe; Trinity Coll., Cambridge. Served 9th Airborne Squadron, RE, 1946–48; Engineer and Railway Staff Corps, TA, 1978; Col 1986. Engineer with John Mowlem & Co. Ltd, 1951–57; joined staff of Mott, Hay & Anderson, 1957; Partner, 1966–88; Chm., 1973–88. Pres., ICE, 1983–84 (Vice-Pres., 1979–82; Mem. Council, 1974–77); Chm., British Tunnelling Soc., 1977–79. Gov., Imperial Coll., 1991–95. FRSA 1975. Mem. Council, Fellowship of Engrg, 1982–86. Master, Engineers' Co., 1992–93 (Mem., Court of Assts, 1986–). Telford Gold Medal, (jointly) 1971, 1973; S. G. Brown Medal, Royal Soc., 1973. *Publications:* Tunnels: Planning Design and Construction (with T. M. Megaw), vol. 1, 1981, vol. 2, 1982; Ships of North Cornwall, 1996; contrib. various papers to ICE, ASCE, etc. *Recreations:* sailing, maritime history. *Address:* 6 Cottenham Park Road, SW20 0RZ. *T:* (020) 8946 9576. *Clubs:* Hawks (Cambridge); Harlequin Football; Royal Engineers Yacht.

BARTLETT, Prof. Maurice Stevenson, FRS 1961; MA Cambridge, DSc London; Professor of Bio-mathematics in the University of Oxford, 1967–75, now Emeritus; *b* 18 June 1910; *s* of W. S. Bartlett, Scrooby; *m* 1957, Sheila (*d* 1998), *d* of C. E. Chapman; one *d*. *Educ:* Latymer Upper Sch.; Queens' Coll., Cambridge. Wrangler, 1932; Rayleigh Prize, 1934. Asst Lectr in Statistics, University Coll., London, 1933–34; Statistician, Imperial Chemical Industries, Ltd, 1934–38; Lectr in Mathematics, Univ. of Cambridge, 1938–47. National Service, Min. of Supply, 1940–45. Visiting Prof. of Mathematical Statistics, Univ. of North Carolina, 1946; Prof. of Mathematical Statistics, Univ. of Manchester, 1947–60; Prof. of Statistics, Univ. of London (University Coll.), 1960–67. Mem. Internat. Statistical Institute, 1949, Hon. Mem., 1980; President: Manchester Statistical Soc., 1959–60; Biometric Soc. (Brit. Reg.), 1964–66; Internat. Assoc. Statistics Phys. Sci., 1965–67; Royal Statistical Society, 1966–67. Foreign Asociate, Nat. Acad. of Scis, USA, 1993. Hon. DSc: Chicago, 1966; Hull, 1976. Gold Medal, Royal Statistical Soc., 1969; Weldon Prize and Medal, Oxford, 1971. *Publications:* An Introduction to Stochastic Processes, 1955; Stochastic Population Models in Ecology and Epidemiology, 1960; Essays in Probability and Statistics, 1962; Probability, Statistics and Time, 1975; Statistical Analysis of Spatial Pattern, 1976; Selected Papers, 3 vols, 1988; papers on statistical and biometrical theory and methodology. *Address:* Overcliff, 4 Trefusis Terrace, Exmouth, Devon EX8 2AX.

BARTLETT, Prof. Neil, FRS 1973; Professor of Chemistry, University of California, Berkeley, 1969–93, now Professor Emeritus; Principal Investigator, Chemical Sciences Division, Lawrence Berkeley Laboratory, 1969–99; *b* Newcastle upon Tyne, 15 Sept. 1932; *s* of Norman Bartlett and Ann Willins Bartlett (*née* Vock), both of Newcastle upon Tyne; *m* 1957, Christina I., *d* of J. W. F. Cross, Guisborough, Yorks; three *s* one *d*. *Educ:* Heaton Grammar Sch., Newcastle upon Tyne; King's Coll., Univ. of Durham, Newcastle upon Tyne. BSc 1954, PhD 1958. Senior Chemistry Master, The Duke's Sch., Alnwick, Northumberland, 1957–58; Mem. Faculty (Dept of Chemistry), Univ. of British Columbia, 1958–66; Prof. of Chemistry, Princeton Univ., and Scientist, Bell Telephone Laboratories, Murray Hill, NJ, USA, 1966–69. Visiting Miller Prof., Univ. of Calif, Berkeley, 1967–68; Brotherton Vis. Prof., Univ. of Leeds, 1981; Erskine Fellow, Univ. of Canterbury, NZ, 1983; Vis. Fellow, All Souls, Oxford, 1984, etc. Foreign Associate: Nat. Acad. of Sciences, USA, 1979; Acad. des Scis, France, 1989; For. MAE, 1998; Member: Deutsche Akademie der Naturforscher Leopoldina, 1969; Der Akademie der Wissenschaften in Göttingen, 1977; Amer. Chem. Soc., etc; Fellow: Amer. Acad. of Arts and Scis, 1977; Chem. Inst. of Canada; Chem. Soc. (London). Sigma Xi. Hon. DSc: Waterloo, Canada, 1968; Colby Coll., Maine, USA, 1972; Newcastle, 1981; McMaster, 1992; Dr *hc* Bordeaux, 1976; Ljubljana, 1989; Nantes, 1990; Hon. LLD Simon Fraser, 1993; Hon. Dr rer. nat. Freie Univ., Berlin, 1998. Corday-Morgan Medal and Prize of Chem. Soc., 1962; Res. Corp. Plaque and Prize, 1965; E. W. R. Steacie Prize, 1965; Robert A. Welch Award, 1976; Medal of Inst. Jožef Stefan, Ljubljana, 1980; W. H. Nichols Medal, NY Section, ACS, 1983; Prix Moissan, 1988; Amer. Chem. Soc. Award for Distinguished Service to Inorganic Chemistry, 1989, for Creative Work in Fluorine Chemistry, 1992; Pauling Medal, 1989; Bonner Chemiepreis, Bonn, 1992. *Publications:* The Chemistry of the Monatomic Gases, 1975; scientific papers to: Jl of Chem. Soc., Inorganic Chem., etc; Mem. various editorial advisory bds in Gt Britain, France and USA. *Recreations:* water colour painting; walking in high country; gardening. *Address:* 6 Oak Drive, Orinda, CA 94563, USA; Chemistry Department, University of California, Berkeley, CA 94720, USA. *T:* (business) (510) 642–7259.

BARTLETT, Neil Vivian, OBE 2000; Artistic Director, Lyric Theatre, Hammersmith, since 1994; *b* 23 Aug. 1958; *s* of Trevor and Pam Bartlett; partner, James Gardiner. *Educ:* Magdalen Coll., Oxford (BA Hons Eng. Lit.). Works written, adapted and directed include: *theatre:* More Bigger Snacks Now, 1985; A Vision of Love Revealed in Sleep, 1987; Sarrasine, 1990; A Judgement in Stone, 1992; Night After Night, 1993; The Picture of Dorian Gray, 1994; Lady into Fox, 1996; The Seven Sacraments of Nicholas Poussin, 1997; *television:* That's What Friends are For, 1987; Where is Love?, 1988; Pedagogue, 1989; That's How Strong My Love Is, 1990; *film:* Now That It's Morning, 1992; major productions directed: Romeo and Juliet, 1994; The Letter, 1995; Mrs Warren's Profession, A Christmas Carol, 1996; Then Again, Treasure Island, 1997; Cause Célèbre, Seven Sonnets of Michaelangelo, Cinderella, 1998; The Dispute, 1999; The Servant, 2001; has performed at RNT, Royal Court, Blackpool Grand and Vauxhall Tavern. *Publications:* Who Was That Man?, 1988; Ready to Catch Him Should He Fall, 1989; A Vision of Love Revealed in Sleep, 1990; (trans.) Berenice/ The Misanthrope/ School for Wives, 1991; (trans.) The Game of Love and Chance, 1992; Night After Night, 1993; Mr Clive and Mr Page, 1995; (trans.) Splendid's, 1995; (trans.) The Dispute, 1999; (trans.) The Threesome, 2000; In Extremis, 2000. *Recreations:* weight training, bull terriers, tree peonies, HIV and breast cancer charity work. *Address:* c/o Lyric Theatre, Hammersmith, King Street, W6 0QL. *T:* (020) 8741 0824.

BARTLETT, Prof. Robert John, FBA 1997; FRSE, FSA, FRHistS; Professor of Mediaeval History, University of St Andrews, since 1992; *b* 27 Nov. 1950; *s* of Leonard Frederick Bartlett and Mabel Emily Adams; *m* 1979, Honora Elaine Hickey; one *s* one *d*. *Educ:* Peterhouse, Cambridge (BA 1972; MA 1976); St John's Coll., Oxford (DPhil 1978). Lectr in History, Edinburgh Univ., 1980–86; Prof. of Medieval History, Univ. of Chicago, 1986–92; British Acad. Reader, 1995–97. Junior Fellow, Univ. of Michigan Soc. of Fellows, 1979–80; Mem., Inst. for Advanced Study and Fellow, Davis Center, Princeton, 1983–84; von Humboldt Fellow, Göttingen, 1988–89. *Publications:* Gerald of Wales 1146–1223, 1982; Trial by Fire and Water, 1986; The Making of Europe, 1993; England under the Norman and Angevin Kings, 2000; contribs to learned jls. *Address:* Department of Mediaeval History, University of St Andrews, St Andrews, Fife KY16 9AL. *T:* (01334) 463308.

BARTLETT, Timothy Conn; Chief Executive, British Association of Leisure Parks, Piers and Attractions, since 1999; Director, Tourism Division, TRI Hospitality Consulting, since 1999; *b* 15 Dec. 1944; *s* of Gordon Thomas Bartlett and Margaret Decima Bartlett; *m* 1st, 1970, Deira Janis Vacher (marr. diss.); one *s* one *d*; 2nd, 1988, Xochitl Alicia Quintanilla; two *d*. *Educ:* Cranleigh Sch.; Pembroke Coll., Oxford (Hons French and Spanish). Morgan Grampian Books, 1967–68; British Tourist Authority: London, 1968–70 and 1974–77; Sydney, 1970–74; Manager: Mexico, 1977–82; Western USA, based in LA, 1982–87; France, 1987–88; General Manager: S Europe, 1988–91; Asia Pacific, 1991–94; Europe, based in Brussels, 1994–95; Acting Chief Exec., 1995–96, Chief Exec., 1996–99, English Tourist Bd. *Recreations:* tennis, reading, music, travel. *Address:* (office) 25 King's Terrace, NW1 0JP.

BARTOLI, Cecilia; mezzo soprano; *b* Rome, 4 June 1966; *d* of Pietro Angelo Bartoli and Silvana Bartoli (*née* Bazzoni). *Educ:* Acad. of Santa Cecilia, Rome. Début, Barber of Seville, Teatro dell'opera, Rome, 1986; has performed at La Scala, Milan, Opéra Bastille, Carnegie Hall, Maggio Musicale Fest., Florence, Salzburg Fest., Wigmore Hall, Aix-en-Provence Fest., NY Metropolitan Opera, Royal Opera House, Covent Garden; also with major orchs, incl. Philadelphia Orch., Chicago SO, Montreal SO. Numerous recordings. *Address:* c/o Columbia Artists Management Inc., 165 W 57th Street, New York, NY 10019, USA.

BARTON, Alan Burnell; Head of Resource Management and Finance Division (formerly Under Secretary), Department of Health, 1993–98; *b* 2 May 1943; *s* of Charles Henry Barton and Rose Edith Barton; *m* 1969, Jirina Klapstova; one *s* one *d*. *Educ:* Glyn Grammar Sch., Ewell; Bristol Univ. (BSc Chem.). Operational Research Exec., NCB, 1966–73; Department of Health and Social Security: Principal, 1973–78; Asst Sec., 1979–90; Dir, Medical Devices Directorate, DoH, 1990–93. Advr, Rickmansworth CAB, 2000–; Social Policy Advr, NACAB, 2000–. *Recreations:* jazz, theatre, country houses. *Address:* 67 Heronsgate Road, Chorleywood, Rickmansworth, Herts WD3 5PA.

BARTON, Anne; *see* Barton, B. A.

BARTON, Prof. (Barbara) Anne, PhD; FBA 1991; Professor of English, Cambridge University, 1984–2000; Fellow of Trinity College, Cambridge, since 1986; *b* 9 May 1933; *d* of Oscar Charles Roesen and Blanche Godfrey Williams; *m* 1st, 1957, William Harvey Righter; 2nd, 1969, John Bernard Adie Barton, *qv*. *Educ:* Bryn Mawr College, USA. BA 1954 (*summa cum laude*); PhD Cantab 1960. Lectr in History of Art, Ithaca Coll., NY, 1958–59; Girton College, Cambridge: Rosalind Lady Carlisle Research Fellow, 1960–62; Official Fellow in English, 1962–72; Dir of Studies in English, 1963–72; Univ. Asst Lectr, later Univ. Lectr in English, Cambridge, 1962–72; Hildred Carlile Prof. of English and Head of Dept, Bedford Coll., London, 1972–74; Fellow and Tutor in English, New Coll., Oxford and CUF Lectr, 1974–84. Lectures: British Acad. Chatterton, 1967; Alexander Meml, Univ. Coll., Toronto, 1983; British Acad. Shakespeare, 1991; Northcliffe, UCL, 1994. MAE 1995. Hon. Fellow: Shakespeare Inst., Univ. of Birmingham, 1982; New Coll., Oxford, 1989. Member Editorial Advisory Boards: Shakespeare Survey, 1972–99; Shakespeare Quarterly, 1981–; Studies in English Literature, 1976–; Romanticism, 1995–. *Publications:* Shakespeare and the Idea of the Play, 1962, 4th edn 1977, trans. Japanese 1982; Ben Jonson, Dramatist, 1984; The Names of Comedy, 1990; Byron: Don Juan, 1992; Essays, Mainly Shakespearean, 1994; essays and studies in learned jls. *Recreations:* opera, fine arts. *Address:* Trinity College, Cambridge CB2 1TQ. *T:* (01223) 338466.

BARTON, Ven. (Charles) John Greenwood; Archdeacon of Aston, since 1990; *b* 5 June 1936; *s* of Charles William Greenwood Barton and Doris Lilian Leach. *Educ:* Battersea Grammar Sch.; London Coll. of Divinity (ALCD). Asst Curate, St Mary Bredin, Canterbury, 1963–66; Vicar, Whitfield with West Langdon, dio. Canterbury, 1966–75; Vicar, St Luke, South Kensington, 1975–83; Area Dean, Chelsea, 1980–83; Chief Broadcasting Officer, Church of England, 1983–90. Mem., Gen. Synod of C of E, 2000–. Chm., BBC W Midlands Regl Adv. Council, 1995–98; Mem., English Nat. Forum, 1995–98. Member, Council: Corp. of Church House, 1989; St Luke's Hosp. for Clergy, 2000–. Chm., Midlands Ethnic Albanian Foundn, 2000–. *Address:* 26 George Road, Edgbaston, Birmingham B15 1PJ. *T:* (0121) 454 5525, *Fax:* (0121) 455 6085; *e-mail:* venjb@globalnet.co.uk. *Club:* National Liberal.

BARTON, Maj.-Gen. Eric Walter, CB 1983; MBE 1966; BSc; FIMgt, FRGS; Director, Caravan Club Ltd, 1984–93; *b* 27 April 1928; *s* of Reginald John Barton and Dorothy (*née* Bradfield); *m* 1963 (marr. diss. 1983); two *s*; *m* 1984, Mrs Pamela Clare Frimann, *d* of late Reginald D. Mason and of Doris Mason, Winchelsea. *Educ:* St Clement Danes Sch., London; Royal Military Coll. of Science (BScEng 1955). Dip. in Photogrammetry, UCL, 1960. FIMgt (FBIM 1979); FRGS 1979. Commnd RE, 1948; served Mid East, 1948–50; Arab Legion, 1951–52; seconded to Dir, Overseas Surveys, E Africa, 1957–59; Sen. Instr, Sch. of Mil. Survey, 1961–63; OC 13 Fd Survey Sqn, Aden, 1965–67; Dir, Surveys and Prodn, Ordnance Survey, 1977–80; Dir of Mil. Survey, 1980–84. Major 1961, Lt-Col 1967, Col 1972, Brig. 1976, Maj.-Gen. 1980. Col Comdt, RE, 1982–87; Hon. Col, Field Survey Sqn, later 135 Indep. Topographic Sqn RE (V) TA, 1984–89. Pres., Defence Surveyors' Assoc. (formerly Field Survey Assoc.), 1991– (Chm., 1984–86); Member: Council, Photogrammetric Soc., 1979–82; Nat. Cttee for Photogrammetry, 1979–84; Council, RGS, 1980–83; Council, British Schs Exploring Soc., 1980–84; Nat. Cttee for Geography, 1981–84. *Recreations:* swimming, water sports, numismatics. *Address:* c/o Barclays Bank, Haywards Heath, W Sussex.

BARTON, Rev. Prof. John, DPhil, DLitt; Oriel and Laing Professor of the Interpretation of Holy Scripture, University of Oxford, since 1991; Fellow of Oriel College, Oxford, since 1991; *b* 17 June 1948; *s* of Bernard Arthur Barton and Gwendolyn Harriet Barton; *m* 1973, Mary Burn; one *d*. *Educ:* Latymer Upper Sch., Hammersmith; Keble Coll., Oxford (MA; DPhil 1974; DLitt 1988). Deacon and priest, 1973. University of Oxford: Jun. Res. Fellow, Merton Coll., 1973–74; Official Fellow, St Cross Coll., 1974–91; University Lectr in Theology (OT), 1974–89; Reader in Biblical Studies, 1989–91; Chaplain, St Cross Coll., 1979–91. Canon Theologian, Winchester Cathedral, 1991–. Hon. Dr theol. Bonn, 1998. *Publications:* Amos's Oracles against the Nations, 1980; Reading the Old Testament: method in biblical study, 1984, 2nd edn 1996; Oracles of God: perceptions of ancient prophecy in Israel after the Exile, 1986; People of the Book?—the authority of the Bible in Christianity, 1988, 2nd edn 1993; Love Unknown: meditations on the Death and Resurrection of Jesus, 1990; What is the Bible?, 1991, 2nd edn 1997; Isaiah 1–39, 1995; The Spirit and the Letter: studies in the biblical canon, 1997; Making the Christian Bible, 1997; Ethics and the Old Testament, 1998; (ed) The Cambridge Companion to Biblical Interpretation, 1998; (ed jtly) The Oxford Bible Commentary, 2001. *Address:* Oriel College, Oxford OX1 4EW.

BARTON, John Bernard Adie, CBE 1981; Advisory Director, Royal Shakespeare Company, since 1991 (Associate Director, 1964–91); *b* 26 Nov. 1928; *s* of late Sir Harold Montague Barton and Joyce Wale; *m* 1968, Anne Righter (*see* B. A. Barton). *Educ:* Eton Coll.; King's Coll., Cambridge (BA, MA). Fellow, King's Coll., Cambridge, 1954–60 (Lay Dean, 1956–59). Joined Royal Shakespeare Company, 1960; Associate Dir, 1964. Has adapted texts and directed or co-directed many plays for Royal Shakespeare Company, including: The Taming of the Shrew, 1960; The Hollow Crown, 1961; The Art of Seduction, 1962; The Wars of the Roses, 1963–64; Henry IV, Parts I and II, and Henry V, 1964–66; Love's Labour's Lost, 1965; Coriolanus and All's Well That Ends Well, 1967; Julius Caesar and Troilus and Cressida, 1968; Twelfth Night and When Thou Art King, 1969; Measure for Measure and The Tempest, 1970; Richard II, Henry V, and Othello, 1971; Richard II, 1973; King John, Cymbeline, and Dr Faustus, 1974; Perkin Warbeck, 1975; Much Ado About Nothing, The Winter's Tale, and Troilus and Cressida, 1976; A Midsummer Night's Dream, Pillars of the Community, 1977; The Way of the World, The Merchant of Venice, Love's Labour's Lost, 1978; The Greeks, 1979; Hamlet, 1980; The Merchant of Venice, Titus Andronicus and The Two Gentlemen of Verona, 1981; La Ronde, 1982; Life's a Dream, 1983; The Devils, 1984; Waste, Dream Play, 1985; The Rover, 1986; Three Sisters, 1988; Coriolanus, 1989; Peer Gynt, 1994; Cain, 1995. Directed: The School for Scandal, Haymarket, 1983, Duke of York's, 1983; The Vikings at Helgeland, Den Nationale Scene, Bergen, 1983; Peer Gynt, 1990, Measure for Measure, As You Like It, 1991, Oslo. Wrote and presented Playing Shakespeare, LWT, 1982, Channel 4, 1984; narrated Morte d'Arthur, BBC2, 1984; wrote: The War that Never Ends, BBC2, 1990; Tantalus, 2000. *Publications:* The Hollow Crown, 1962 (and 1971); The Wars of the Roses, 1970; The Greeks, 1981; Playing Shakespeare, 1982. *Recreations:* travel, chess, work. *Address:* 14 de Walden Court, 85 New Cavendish Street, W1W 6XD.

BARTON, Ven. John Greenwood; *see* Barton, Ven. C. J. G.

BARTON, Prof. Leonard Francis; Professor of Inclusive Education, Institute of Education, London University, since 2001; *b* 20 April 1941; *m* 1968, Joan Bennett; two *d*. *Educ:* Liverpool Univ. (BA Hons); Manchester Univ. (MEd). Prof. of Educn, Bristol Poly., 1986–90; Sheffield University: Head of Res. Degrees, and Dir of Inclusive Educn Res. Centre; Prof. of Educn, 1990–2001. Sir Allan Sewell Fellow, Griffiths Univ., Australia, 1995–96. Founder and Editor, Disability and Society, 1985–. *Publication:* (ed) Disability and Society: emerging issues and insights, 1996. *Recreations:* swimming, walking, listening to music. *Address:* c/o Institute of Education, 20 Bedford Way, WC1H 0AL.

BARTON, Prof. Nicholas Hamilton, PhD; FRS 1994; Professor, Institute of Cell, Animal and Population Biology, University of Edinburgh, since 1994. *Educ:* Peterhouse, Cambridge (BA 1976; MA 1980); Univ. of E Anglia (PhD). Cambridge University: Res. Fellow, Girton Coll., 1980; Demonstrator, Dept of Genetics, 1980–82; Lectr, then Reader, Dept of Genetics and Biometry, UCL, 1982–90; Darwin Trust Fellow, Inst. of Cell, Animal and Population Biol., Edinburgh Univ., 1990–. FRSE 1995. *Address:* Institute of Cell, Animal and Population Biology, Ashworth Laboratories, University of Edinburgh, West Mains Road, Edinburgh EH9 3JT. *T:* (0131) 650 5509, *Fax:* (0131) 667 3210.

BARTON, Philip Robert, OBE 1997; HM Diplomatic Service; Deputy High Commissioner, Cyprus, since 2000; *b* 18 Aug. 1963; *s* of late Geoffrey Howard Barton and of Katharine Anne (*née* Stubbings); *m* 1999, Amanda Joy Bowen. *Educ:* Warwick Univ. (BA Econs and Politics); London Sch. of Econs (MSc Econs). Joined FCO, 1986: Third, then Second, Sec., Caracas, 1987–91; Cabinet Office (on secondment), 1991–93; First Secretary: FCO, 1993–94; New Delhi, 1994–96; Private Sec. to Prime Minister (on secondment), 1997–2000. *Recreations:* football, tennis, hiking, travel, reading. *Address:* c/o Foreign and Commonwealth Office, King Charles Street, SW1A 2AH; British High Commission, Nicosia, BFPO 567. *T:* (Cyprus) (2) 861100.

BARTON, Roger; Director, Insight Dynamics; *b* 6 Jan. 1945; *s* of late Joseph and Doreen Barton; *m* 1965; two *s*. *Educ:* Burngreave Secondary Modern Sch.; Granville Coll. (Engrg Technician's Cert.). Fitter, 1961–81; Sheffield TUC and Labour Party Sec., 1981–89. Mem., Sheffield CC, 1971–90. Mem. (Lab) Sheffield, Eur. Parlt, 1989–99; contested (Lab) Yorkshire and the Humber Region, 1999. *Recreations:* walking, gentle cycling, water sports. *Address:* 50 Hartley Brook Avenue, Sheffield S5 0HN. *Clubs:* Trades and Labour, Wortley Hall Labour (Sheffield).

BARTOSIK, Rear-Adm. Josef C., CB 1968; DSC 1943; *b* 20 July 1917; *m* 1st, 1943, Cynthia Pamela Bowman; three *s* one *d*; 2nd, 1969, Jeannine Scott (*née* Bridgeman). Joined Polish Navy, 1935; served War 1939–45 as gunnery officer in destroyers in Norwegian campaign, E Mediterranean, Western Approaches, convoys to Malta, Murmansk and Atlantic, Normandy operation; transf. to RN, 1948; commanded: HMS Comus, 1955–56; HMS Scarborough and 5th Frigate Sqn, 1960–61; HMS Seahawk (RN Air Station Culdrose), 1962–63, HMS London, 1964–65; Rear-Adm. 1966; Asst Chief of Naval Staff (Ops), 1966–68; retired 1968. Coordinating Dir, European Jt Org., Australia Europe Container Service and Australia NZ Europe Container Service, 1969–81, retired 1981. *Recreation:* computers. *Address:* 33 Cheval Place, SW7 1EW.

BARTRAM, George Christopher, TD 1960; Vice Lord-Lieutenant of Co. Durham, since 1997; *b* 23 Aug. 1927; *s* of Robert Appleby Bartram and Winifred Hannah (*née* Murray); *m* 1969, Josephine Anne Ker Staveley; two *s*. *Educ:* Rugby Sch.; St Catharine's Coll., Cambridge (MA). Served DLI, 1945–48; TA service, DLI, 1948–64; Hon. Col, 7th Bn (Durham) LI, 1989–94. Bartram & Sons Ltd, Ship Builders, 1952–63; Colvilles Ltd, Steel Mfrs, 1964–72; trainee, Paddington Churches Housing Assoc., 1974; Chief Exec., Endeavour Housing Assoc., 1975–92. Pres., Co. Durham SSAFA Forces Help, 1987–. High Sheriff, 1982, DL 1990, Co. Durham. *Recreations:* unskilled gardening, high handicap golf, family history research. *Address:* Eldon House, Heighington, Newton Aycliffe, Co. Durham DL5 6PP. *T:* (01325) 312270. *Club:* Victory Services.

BARTTELOT, Col Sir Brian Walter de Stopham, 5th Bt *cr* 1875; OBE 1983; psc; Vice Lord-Lieutenant for West Sussex, since 1994; Member, HM Body Guard of the Honourable Corps of Gentlemen at Arms, since 1993; *b* 17 July 1941; *s* of Lt-Col Sir Walter de Stopham Barttelot, 4th Bt, and Sara Patricia (who *m* 2nd, 1965, Comdr James Barttelot, RN retd; she *d* 1998), *d* of late Lieut-Col H. V. Ravenscroft; *S* father, 1944; *m* 1969, Hon. Mary Angela Fiona Weld Forester, (MBE 2001; DL, DStJ), *y d* of 7th Baron Forester, and of Marie Louise Priscilla, CStJ, *d* of Sir Herbert Perrott, 6th Bt, CH, CB; four *d*. *Educ:* Eton; RMA, Sandhurst. Commnd Coldstream Guards, 1961; Temp. Equerry to HM the Queen, 1970–71. Camberley Staff Coll., 1974; GSO2, Army Staff Duties Directorate, MoD, 1975–76; Second in comd, 2nd Bn, Coldstream Guards, 1977–78; Mil. Sec. to Maj.-Gen. comdg London Dist and Household Div., 1978–81; GSO1, MoD, 1981–82; CO 1st Bn Coldstream Gds, 1982–85; GSO1, HQ BAOR, 1985–86; Regtl Lt-Col Comdg Coldstream Guards, 1986–92. Col, Foot Guards, 1989–92; Hon. Col, Sussex ACF, 1996–. President: W Sussex Scout Council, 1993–; S of England Agricl Soc., 2001. Chm. Exec. Cttee, Standing Council of the Baronetage, 1996–. Liveryman, Gunmakers' Co., 1981. DL W Sussex, 1988, High Sheriff, W Sussex, 1997–98. *Heir:* *b* Robin Ravenscroft Barttelot [*b* 15 Dec. 1943; *m* 1987, Theresa, *er d* of late Kenneth Greenlees; one *s* one *d*]. *Address:* Stopham Park, Pulborough, W Sussex RH20 1DY. *Clubs:* Cavalry and Guards, Pratt's, Farmers'.

BARTY-KING, Mark Baxter, MC 1958; Chairman, Transworld Publishers, since 2001; *b* 3 March 1938; *s* of George Ingram, (Tom), Barty-King and Barbara (*née* Baxter); *m* 1st, 1963, Margild Bolten (marr. diss. 1975); two *s*; 2nd, 1976, Marilyn Scott Barrett; two *s*. *Educ:* Winchester Coll. Nat. Service, 13th/18th Royal Hussars (QMO), Aden, Oman, Malaya, 1957–61 (Capt.). Abelard Schuman, NY, 1962–63; John Howell Books, San Francisco, 1964–65; Heinemann Gp, 1966–74 (Director: Peter Davies Ltd, 1969; William Heinemann Ltd, 1971); Editorial Dir, 1974–81, Man. Dir, Hardback Div., 1981–83, Granada Publishing; William Collins Ltd, 1983–84; Transworld Publishers Ltd, 1984– (part of Random House Group, 1998–): Dep. Man. Dir, Publishing, 1992; Man. Dir and CEO, 1995–2000. Founder, Bantam Press, 1985. Mem. Council, Publishers Assoc., 1999–. Chm. of Govs, St John's Sch., Northwood, 1997–. FRSA. Mem., Ct of Assts, Merchant Taylors' Co., 1992–. *Recreation:* countryside. *Address:* 46 Elms Road, SW4 9EX. *T:* (020) 7622 1544. *Clubs:* Groucho, Lansdowne.

BARWELL, David John Frank; international business consultant with Control Risks Gp Ltd, since 1994; *b* 12 Oct. 1938; *s* of James Howard and Helen Mary Barwell; *m* 1968, Christine Sarah Carter; one *s*. *Educ:* Lancing College; Trinity College, Oxford; Institut des Hautes Etudes Internationales, Geneva. FCO, 1965; served: Aden, 1967; Baghdad, 1968; Bahrain, 1971; Cairo, 1973; FCO, 1976; Nicosia, 1982; Paris, 1985; FCO, 1989–92. *Recreations:* gardening, singing. *Address:* Duckyls Clock House, West Hoathly, Sussex RH19 4LP. *Club:* Athenæum.

BARWICK, Brian Robert; Controller, ITV Sport, and Director of Programming, ITV2, since 1998; *b* 21 June 1954; *s* of John Leonard Barwick and Jean Ellen Barwick; *m* 1982, Geraldine Lynch; two *s*. *Educ:* Rudston Rd Co. Primary Sch.; Quarry Bank Comprehensive Sch.; Liverpool Univ. (BA Hons Econs). Journalist/sub-editor, North Western Evening Mail, Barrow-in-Furness, 1976–79; BBC Television (Sport): Asst Producer, 1979–84; Producer, Football Focus, 1982–84; Asst Ed., Grandstand, 1984–88; Editor: Match of the Day, 1988–95; Sportsnight, 1990–94; World Cup coverage, 1990 and 1994; Olympics, 1992 and 1996; Sports Rev. of the Year, 1991–95; Hd, Sport (Prodn), 1995–97. *Publication:* (with G. Sinstadt) The Great Derbies: Everton *v* Liverpool, 1988. *Recreations:* watching sport, football, boxing and cricket; British TV comedy, sports and comedy memorabilia collecting, contemporary music, holidaying with family. *Address:* ITV Network Ltd, 200 Gray's Inn Road, WC1X 8HF.

BARYSHNIKOV, Mikhail; ballet dancer and company director; with Mark Morris formed White Oak Dance Project, 1990; *b* 28 Jan. 1948; *s* of Nicolai Baryshnikov and Alexandra (*née* Kisselov). *Educ:* Ballet Sch. of Riga, Latvia; Kirov Ballet Sch., Leningrad. Soloist, Kirov Ballet Co., 1969–74; Principal Dancer, NY City Ballet, 1978–79; Artistic Dir, 1980–89, Principal Dancer, 1974–78 and 1980–89, American Ballet Theater. Guest Artist, 1974–, with: Royal Ballet; National Ballet of Canada; Hamburg Ballet; Ballet Victoria, Aust.; Stuttgart Ballet; Alvin Ailey Dance Co., and Eliot Feld Ballet, New York; Spoleto Festival. Repertoire includes: Shadowplay (Tudor); Le Jeune Homme et la Morte (Petit); Sacré du Printemps (Tetley); Prodigal Son, Apollo, Theme and Variations (Balanchine); Afternoon of a Faun (Robbins); Romeo and Juliet, Wild Boy (MacMillan); Configurations (Choo San Goh); Les Patineurs, A Month in the Country (Ashton); Spectre de la Rose, Le Pavillon d'Armide, Petrouchka (Fokine); Santa Fe Saga (Feld); La Sylphide, La Bayadère, Coppélia, La Fille mal gardée (Bournonville); Swan Lake (Sergeyev and Bruhn); The Nutcracker, Don Quixote (own choreography). Works created: Medea (Butler), 1975; Push Comes to Shove, and, Once More Frank (Tharp), Connotations on Hamlet (Neumeier), Pas de Duke (Ailey), Other Dances (Robbins), 1976; Variations on America (Feld), 1977; Rubies (Balanchine), Opus Nineteen (Robbins), 1979; Rhapsody (Ashton), 1980. Gold Medal: Varna Competition, Bulgaria, 1966; 1st Internat. Ballet Comp., Moscow, 1968 (also awarded Nijinsky Prize by Paris Acad. of Dance); Dance Magazine Award, NYC, 1978. *Films:* The Turning Point, 1978; White Nights, 1986; Dancers, 1987. *Publication:* (with Charles Engell France, photographs by Martha Swope) Baryshnikov at Work, 1976. *Recreation:* fishing. *Address:* c/o Vincent and Farrell Associates, 157 West 57th Street, #502, New York, NY 10019, USA.

BARZEL, Dr Rainer C.; Member of the Bundestag, Federal Republic of Germany, 1957–87; *b* 20 June 1924; *s* of Dr Candidus Barzel, Senior Asst Master, and Maria Barzel. *Educ:* studied Jurisprudence and Political Economy, Univ. of Cologne (Referendar, Dr jur.). With Govt of North Rhine-Westphalia, 1949–56; Federal Minister in the Adenauer

Govt, for all-German affairs, Dec. 1962–Oct. 1963; Chairman: Cttee on Economic Affairs, German Fed. Parlt, 1977–79; Cttee on Foreign Affairs, 1980–82; Fed. Minister for Inter-German Affairs, 1982–83; Pres. of Bundestag, 1983–84. Coordinator for German-French cooperation, Feb.-Dec. 1980, 1986–90. Chm., CDU, 1971–73 and Chm., CDU/CSU Group in German Federal Parlt, 1964–73. Pres., German-French Inst., 1980–83. *Publications:* (all publ. in Germany): Die geistigen Grundlagen der politischen Parteien, 1947; Die deutschen Parteien, 1952; Gesichtspunkte eines Deutschen, 1968; Es ist noch nicht zu spät, 1976; Auf dem Drahtseil, 1978; Das Formular, 1979; Unterwegs—Woher und wohin, 1982; Im Streit und umstritten, 1986; Geschichten aus der Politik, 1987; Ermland und Masuren—Zu Besuch, aber nicht als ein Fremder, 1988; Plädoyer für Deutschland, 1989; (ed) Sternstunden des Parlaments, 1989; So Nicht, 1993. *Recreation:* skating.

BARZUN, Jacques; University Professor Emeritus, Columbia University; *b* 30 Nov. 1907; *s* of Henri Barzun and Anna-Rose Martin; *m* 1936, Mariana Lowell (*d* 1979); two *s* one *d*; *m* 1980, Marguerite Davenport. *Educ:* Lycée Janson de Sailly; Columbia Univ. Instructor in History, Columbia Univ., 1929; Research Fellow, American Council of Learned Socs, 1933–34; Columbia University: Asst Prof., 1938; Associate Prof., 1942; Prof. of History, 1945–75; University Prof., 1967; Dean of Grad. Faculties, 1955–58; Dean of Faculties and Provost, 1958–67. Dir Emeritus, Council for Basic Educn; Dir, NY Soc. Library; Mem. Adv. Council, Univ. Coll. at Buckingham. Membre Associé de l'Académie Delphinale, Grenoble, 1952; Member: Amer. Acad. of Arts and Letters, USA (President, 1972–75, 1977–79); Amer. Acad. of Arts and Sciences; American Historical Assoc.; Amer. Philos. Soc.; FRSA, USA (Benjamin Franklin Fellow); FRSL. Seth Low Prof. of History, Columbia Univ., 1960; Extraordinary Fellow, Churchill Coll., Cambridge, 1961–. Literary Advisor, Charles Scribner's Sons Ltd, 1975–93; Mem. Bd of Editors, Encyclopaedia Britannica, 1962–. Chevalier de la Légion d'Honneur. *Publications:* The French Race: Theories of its Origins, 1932; Race: A Study in Superstition, 1937 (revd, 1965); Of Human Freedom, 1939 (revd, 1964); Darwin, Marx, Wagner, 1941 (revd, 1958); Teacher in America, 1945 (revd, 1981); Berlioz and the Romantic Century, 1950, 4th edn 1982; Pleasures of Music, 1951, rev. edn 1977; Selected Letters of Byron, 1953, 2nd edn 1957; Nouvelles Lettres de Berlioz, 1954, 2nd edn 1974; God's Country and Mine, 1954; Music in American Life, 1956; The Energies of Art, 1956; The Modern Researcher (with Henry F. Graff), 1957, 5th edn 1993; The House of Intellect, 1959, 2nd edn 1961; Classic, Romantic and Modern, 1961; Science: The Glorious Entertainment, 1964; (ed) Follett's Modern American Usage, 1967; The American University, 1968, 3rd edn 1992; (with W. H. Taylor) A Catalogue of Crime, 1971, rev. edn 1989; On Writing, Editing and Publishing, 1971; Berlioz's Evenings with the Orchestra, 1956, 2nd edn 1973; The Use and Abuse of Art, 1974; Clio and the Doctors, 1974; Simple and Direct, 1975; Critical Questions, 1982; A Stroll with William James, 1983; A Word Or Two Before You Go, 1986; The Culture We Deserve, 1989; Begin Here, 1991; An Essay on French Verse for Readers of English Poetry, 1991; From Dawn to Decadence, 2001; contrib. to leading US journals. *Address:* 18 Wolfeton Way, San Antonio, TX 78218–6045, USA. *Club:* Century (New York).

BASHAM, Brian Arthur; Founder, 1994, and Deputy Chairman, since 1999, Equity Development Ltd; *b* 30 July 1943; *s* of late Arthur Edgar Basham and Gladys Florence Alice (*née* Turner); *m* 1st, 1968, Charlotte Blackman; two *d*; 2nd, 1988, Eileen Wise (marr. diss. 1996); 3rd, 1998, Lynne Goodson. *Educ:* Brownhill Road Primary Sch., Catford, Catford Secondary Sch. GEC Export Clerk, 1961; Daily Mail City Office: Stock Exchange prices collector, 1962; City Press reporter, then chief sub-editor, 1963; Prodn Editor, Daily Mail City Page, 1964; Financial Journalist: Daily Telegraph, 1966; The Times, 1968; Fund Man., Regent Fund Managers, 1971; Associate Dir, John Addey Associates, 1973; Founder, 1976, subseq. Dep. Chm., Broad Street Gp; Co-Founder and Dep. Chm., Primrose Care, 1993–; Chairman: Intershare, 1995–; Basham & Coyle Partnership, 1996–. *Recreations:* reading, constitutional reform, motorcycling, gardening, walking. *Address:* 14 Elsworthy Rise, NW3 3SH. *T:* (office) (020) 7253 3300.

BASHFORD, Humphrey John Charles, MA; Headmaster, Hessle High School, 1964–81, retired; *b* 5 Oct. 1920; *s* of late Sir Henry Bashford, MD, FRCP, and late Margaret Eveline Sutton; *m* 1942, Alyson Margaret Liddle; one *s* three *d* (and one *s* decd). *Educ:* Sherborne Sch.; Clare Coll., Cambridge. MA Cambridge 1950. Served War of 1939–45: commissioned 2nd Bn Oxford Bucks LI, 1941; GSO3 HQ Airborne Corps 1944–46. Senior History Master, Leys Sch., Cambridge, 1947; Part-time Tutor, WEA, 1950; Headmaster, Wellingborough Sch., 1956–64. *Recreations:* gardening, fly-fishing. *Address:* 11 Cowgate, Welton, Brough, N Humberside HU15 1NB.

BASHMET, Yuri Abramovich; viola player; *b* 24 Jan. 1953; *m* Natalia Timofeevna; one *s* one *d*. *Educ:* Moscow State Conservatory. Winner, Munich International Viola Competititon, 1976; Founder and Dir, Chamber Orchestra Moscow Soloists,1989–. Has performed with many orchestras including: Berlin Philharmonic; Boston Symphony; Concertgebouw; LSO; Los Angeles Philharmonic; Montreal Symphony; first performance of viola concerti by Alfred Schnittke, Aleksander Tchaikovsky, Poul Ruders and Sofia Gubaidulina. *Address:* c/o Van Walsum Management, 4 Addison Bridge Place, W14 8XP. *T:* (020) 7371 4343; Apartment 16, Nezhdanovoy str. 7, 103009, Moscow, Russia.

BASIL OF SERGIEVO, Bishop; *see* Sergievo, Bishop of.

BASING, 5th Baron *cr* 1887; **Neil Lutley Sclater-Booth;** *b* 16 Jan. 1939; *s* of 4th Baron Basing and Jeannette (*d* 1957), *d* of late Neil Bruce MacKelvie, New York; *S* father, 1983; *m* 1967, Patricia Ann, *d* of late George Bryan Whitfield, New Haven, Conn; two *s*. *Educ:* Eton; Harvard Univ. (BA). *Heir:* *s* Hon. Stuart Anthony Whitfield Sclater-Booth [*b* 18 Dec. 1969; *m* 1997, Kirsten Erica Oxboel].

BASINGSTOKE, Bishop Suffragan of; *no new appointment at the time of going to press.*

BASKER, Prof. Robin Michael, OBE 2001; DDS; Professor of Dental Prosthetics, University of Leeds, 1978–2000, now Emeritus; Consultant in Restorative Dentistry, United Leeds Teaching Hospitals NHS Trust (formerly Leeds Western Health Authority), 1978–2000; *b* 26 Dec. 1936; *s* of Caryl Ashbourne Basker and Edna Crowden (*née* Russell); *m* 1961, Jacqueline Mary Bowles; two *d*. *Educ:* Wellingborough Sch.; London Hosp. Med. Coll., Univ. of London (BDS 1961); Birmingham Univ. (DDS 1969). LDSRCS 1961, MGDSRCS 1979; FDSRCSE 2000. General dental practice, 1961–63; Lectr and Sen. Lectr, Univ. of Birmingham, 1963–78; Leeds University: Dean, Sch. of Dentistry, 1985–90; Chm., Bd of Faculty of Medicine and Dentistry, 1990–93. Hon. Scientific Advr, British Dental Jl, 1980–96; British Standards Expert Advr, ISO TC/106, 1982–. Mem., Nuffield Foundn Inquiry into trng and educn of personnel auxiliary to dentistry, 1992–93. Member: Dental Cttee, Med. Defence Union, 1985–95; GDC, 1986–99 (Treas., 1992–94; Chm., Registration Sub-Cttee, 1994; Chm., Educn Cttee, 1994–99); President: British Soc. for Study of Prosthetic Dentistry, 1988 (Mem. Council and Sec., 1978–81); Yorks Br., BDA, 1991–92; British Soc. of Gerodontology, 1999. Ext. Examr in Dental Subjects, Univs of Birmingham, Bristol, Dundee, London, Manchester, Malaya, Newcastle upon Tyne, Sheffield, Wales and UC, Cork; Examr for Membership of Gen. Dental Surgery, RCS, 1979–84 (Chm. Examrs, 1987–92). FRSocMed. John Tomes Medal, BDA, 2000. *Publications:* Prosthetic Treatment of the Edentulous Patient, 1976, 3rd edn 1992; Overdentures in General Dental Practice, 1983, 3rd edn 1993; A Colour Atlas of Removable Partial Dentures, 1987; Clinical Guide to Removable Partial Dentures, 2000; Clinical Guide to Removable Partial Denture Design, 2000. *Recreations:* choral singing, walking.

BASKERVYLE-GLEGG, Maj.-Gen. John, MBE 1974; Senior British Loan Service Officer, Oman, 1990–93; *b* 10 Nov. 1940; *s* of late Lt-Col John Baskervyle-Glegg and Ethne Baskervyle-Glegg (*née* Woollan); *m* 1974, Jane Van der Noot. *Educ:* Eton; rcds, psc, osc. Grenadier Guards, 1960; served UK, Germany, Cyprus, Far East, Africa; Staff College, 1974; Comd 1st Bn Grenadier Guards, Berlin and UK, 1980–82; RCDS, 1982–84; Comdr 24 Inf. Bde, Catterick, 1984–86; Comdr British Mil. Adv. Training Team, Zimbabwe, 1987–89. *Recreations:* music, gardening, all sports, travel. *Address:* c/o National Westminster Bank, PO Box 11, 16 Library Place, St Helier, Jersey JE4 8PD. *Clubs:* Cavalry and Guards, MCC; I Zingari, Free Foresters.

BASS; *see* Hastings Bass, family name of Earl of Huntingdon.

BASS, Bryan Geoffrey; Headmaster, City of London School, 1990–95; *b* 23 March 1934; *s* of Leslie Horace Bass and Mary Joyce Light; *m* 1956, Cecilia Manning; one *s* two *d*. *Educ:* Wells Cathedral School; Christ Church, Oxford (BA Hons English 1956; MA 1983). Teacher, Manchester Grammar School; Headmaster, Hymers College, Hull, 1983–90. Mem., NE London Educn Assoc., 1995–96. *Recreations:* making music, cooking with friends. *Address:* 32 Newland Park, Hull HU5 2DW.

BASS, Harry Godfrey Mitchell, CMG 1972; HM Diplomatic Service, retired; *b* 26 Aug. 1914; *s* of late Rev. Arthur Edward Bass and Mildred Bass; *m* 1948, Monica Mary, *d* of late Rev. H. F. Burroughs (and eponym of the orchid *Oncidium flexuosum* x *Rodriguezia fragrans*); two *s* one *d*. *Educ:* Marlborough Coll.; Gonville and Caius Coll., Cambridge; St John's Coll., Oxford (BA (Oxon) 1937, MA (Cantab) 1940). British Museum, Dept of Egyptian and Assyrian Antiquities, 1939; Admiralty, 1940; Dominions Office, 1946; Asst Sec., Office of UK High Commissioner, Australia, 1948–51; Mem. of Secretariat, Commonwealth Economic Conference, 1952 and Meeting of Commonwealth Prime Ministers, 1953; Counsellor, Office of UK High Commissioner, Calcutta, 1954–57; Dep. UK High Commissioner, Federation of Rhodesia and Nyasaland, 1959–61; British Minister (Pretoria and Cape Town) in the Republic of S Africa, 1961–62; seconded to Central African Office, 1963–64; British Dep. High Commissioner, Ibadan, 1965–67; Head of Consular Dept, FCO, 1967–70; High Comr in Lesotho, 1970–73. Chapter Clerk, St George's Chapel, Windsor, 1974–77. Compiled index of hatchment mottoes, 1998. Silver Jubilee Medal, 1977. *Recreation:* birdwatching. *Address:* Tyler's Mead, Reepham, Norfolk NR10 4LA.

See also Baron Crofton.

BASS, Rear-Adm. Paul Eric, CB 1981; CEng, FIMechE, MIMarE; *b* 7 March 1925; *s* of C. H. P. Bass, Ipswich; *m* 1948, Audrey Bruce Tomlinson; one *s*. *Educ:* Northgate School, Ipswich; Royal Naval Engineering Coll., Keyham. Served as Midshipman in HM Ships Cambrian, Mauritius, Premier and Rodney; Lieut in Belfast, Phoebe and Implacable; Lt Comdr in Ulysses; Comdr in Lion and Tiger; Naval Staff Course, 1962; Captain, Weapons Trials, 1969–72; NATO Defence Course, 1972–73; Asst Chief of Staff (Intelligence), SACLANT, 1973–75; Dir, Naval Manning and Training (Engineering), 1975–78; Flag Officer, Portsmouth and Port Admiral, Portsmouth, 1979–81, retired 1981. *Recreation:* sailing. *Clubs:* Royal Yacht Squadron; Royal Naval Sailing Association; Royal Naval and Royal Albert Yacht (Portsmouth).

BASSAM OF BRIGHTON, Baron *cr* 1997 (Life Peer), of Brighton in the co. of East Sussex; **John Steven Bassam;** a Lord in Waiting (Government Whip), since 2001; *b* 11 June 1953; *s* of late Sydney Stevens and Enid Bassam; partner, Jill Whittaker; one *s* two *d* (and one *s* decd). *Educ:* Univ. of Sussex (BA Hons History 1975; Hon. Fellow, 2001); Univ. of Kent (MA Social Work 1979). Social Worker, E Sussex CC, 1976–77; Legal Advr, N Lewisham Law Centre, 1979–83; Policy Adviser: LB Camden, 1983–84; GLC (Police Cttee), 1984–86; London Strategic Policy Unit (Policing), 1986–87; Asst Sec., Police, Fire, Envmntl Health and Consumer Affairs, AMA, 1988–97; Consultant Advr, KPMG, 1997–99. Parly Under-Sec. of State, Home Office, 1999–2001. Member (Lab): Brighton BC, 1983–97 (Leader, 1987–97); Brighton & Hove Unitary Council, 1996–99 (Leader, 1996–99). *Publications:* articles for local govt pubns. *Recreations:* cricket (plays for Preston Village CC), walking, watching football, reading, history of churches. *Address:* Longstone, 25 Church Place, Brighton BN2 5JN. *T:* (01273) 609473.

BASSET, Bryan Ronald, CBE 1988; Chairman, Royal Ordnance plc, 1985–87; *b* 29 Oct. 1932; *s* of late Ronald Lambart Basset and Lady Elizabeth Basset, DCVO; *m* 1960, Lady Carey Elizabeth Coke, *d* of 5th Earl of Leicester; three *s*. *Educ:* Eton; RMA Sandhurst. Captain, Scots Guards, 1952–57. Stockbroker, Toronto, Canada, 1957–59; Panmure Gordon & Co., Stockbrokers, 1959–72; Managing Director, Philip Hill Investment Trust, 1972–85. *Recreations:* shooting, fishing. *Address:* Quarles, Wells-next-the-Sea, Norfolk NR23 1RY. *T:* (01328) 738105. *Club:* White's.

BASSETT, Douglas Anthony; Director, National Museum of Wales, 1977–86, now Senior Research Fellow; *b* 11 Aug. 1927; *s* of Hugh Bassett and Annie Jane Bassett; *m* 1955, Elizabeth Menna Roberts; three *d*. *Educ:* Llanelli Boys' Grammar Sch.; University Coll. of Wales, Aberystwyth. Asst Lectr and Lectr, Dept of Geology, Glasgow Univ., 1952–59; Keeper, Dept of Geology, Nat. Museum of Wales, 1959–77. Member: Water Resources Bd, 1965–73; Nature Conservancy Council (and Chm., Adv. Cttee for Wales), 1973–85; Secretary of State for Wales' Celtic Sea Adv. Cttee, 1974–79; Ordnance Survey Rev. Cttee, 1978–79; Adv. Cttee for Wales, British Council, 1983–90; Founder Mem. and first Chm., Assoc. of Teachers of Geology, 1967–68; Chm., Royal Soc. Cttee on History of Geology, 1972–82. Dir, Nat. Welsh-American Foundn, 1980– (Vice-Pres., 1996–99). Prince of Wales' Cttee, 1977–86. Hon. Professorial Fellow, University Coll., Cardiff, 1977. Editor: Nature in Wales, 1982–87; Manual of Curatorship, Museums Assoc., 1983–. Aberconway Medal, Instn of Geologists, 1985; Silver Medal, Czechoslavakian Soc. for Internat. Relns, 1985. Mem. White Order of Bards of GB, 1979; Officier de l'Ordre des Arts et des Lettres (received from Min. of Culture, Paris), 1983. *Publications:* Bibliography and Index of Geology and Allied Sciences for Wales and the Welsh Borders, 1897–1958, 1961; A Source-book of Geological, Geomorphological and Soil Maps for Wales and the Welsh Borders (1800–1966), 1967; Wales in miniature, 1993; contribs to various geological, museum and historical jls. *Recreations:* bibliography, chronology. *Address:* 4 Romilly Road, Cardiff CF5 1FH.

BASSETT, John Anthony Seward, FRICS; Consultant, Jones Lang LaSalle (formerly Jones, Lang, Wootton), since 1997 (Senior Partner, 1991–97); *b* 8 Sept. 1936; *s* of Roger Seward and Marjorie Bassett; *m* 1st, 1960, Jean Margaret Cooper (marr. diss. 1993); one *s* one *d*; 2nd, 1994, Jennifer David. *Educ:* Blundell's Sch.; Coll. of Estate Management, London Univ. FRICS 1972. Joined Folkard & Hayward, 1957; Donaldson & Sons,

1960–63; joined Jones, Lang, Wootton, 1963, Partner 1967–97. Chm., MWB Leisure Funds, 1996–. Hon. Treas., Westminster Property Owners' Assoc., 1989–98. Trustee, Chatham Historic Dockyard Trust, 1997–. *Recreations:* ocean racing, ski-ing, travel, fly fishing. *Address:* 16 Pelham Place, SW7 2NH. *Clubs:* Pilgrims; Royal Thames Yacht, Royal Ocean Racing.

BASSETT, Nigel F.; *see* Fox Bassett.

BASSETT CROSS, Alistair Robert Sinclair; District Judge, Principal Registry, Family Division, High Court of Justice, since 1991; *b* 25 Aug. 1944; *s* of late Edward Bassett Cross and Marguerite Sinclair Bassett Cross (*née* Mitchell); *m* 1977, Margaret Victoria Janes; one *s* one *d*. *Educ:* Bishop Challoner Sch., Shortlands; Coll. of Law, Lancaster Gate. FInstLEx 1971. Legal Exec. with Lawrence Graham, 1964–77; solicitor, 1980; Legal Exec. and Solicitor, Payne Hicks Beach, 1977–91 (Partner, 1988–91); Dep. County Court and Dist Registrar, 1990. Mem., Solicitors' Family Law Assoc., 1984; Mem., Family Mediators' Assoc., 1989; Accredited Family Mediator, 1990; Mem., Adv. Bd of Mediation Service, Inst. of Family Therapy, 1995–98; Trustee, Mediation for Families (London E and City), 1999–. HAC, 1965, commnd, 1969. Freeman, City of London, 1993; Liveryman, Poulters' Co., 1996. *Publications:* (ed) Supreme Court Practice, 1994–99; Civil Procedure, 2000–. *Recreations:* family, anything and everything. *Address:* Principal Registry (Family Division), First Avenue House, 42–49 High Holborn, WC1V 6NP. *Club:* Naval and Military.

BASSEY, Dame Shirley (Veronica), DBE 2000 (CBE 1994); singer; *b* Tiger Bay, Cardiff, 8 Jan. 1937; *d* of late Henry and Eliza Jane Bassey; one *d*; *m* 1st, 1961, Kenneth Hume (marr. diss. 1965; decd); 2nd, 1971, Sergio Novak (marr. diss. 1981); one adopted *s* (one *d* decd). Appeared in Such is Life, 1955; *recordings* include: *singles:* Burn My Candle; Banana Boat Song, 1957; As I Love You, 1959; Kiss Me Honey; Reach for the Stars/Climb Every Mountain, 1961; What Now My Love; I Am What I Am; I (Who Have Nothing); Goldfinger, 1964; Diamonds Are Forever, 1971; Something; For All We Know; Never Never Never; Moonraker, 1979; *albums:* Born to Sing the Blues, 1958; And I Love You So, 1972; Live at Carnegie Hall, 1973; Magic Is You, 1978; Sassy Bassey, 1985; La Mujer, 1989; New York, New York, 1991; Great Shirley Bassey, 1999; numerous concerts and tours; series, BBC TV; appeared in film, La Passione, 1996. Britannia Award for Best Female Singer, 1977; Artist for Peace, UNESCO, 2000; Internat. Ambassador, Variety Club, 2001.

BASSINGTHWAIGHTE, Keith; His Honour Judge Bassingthwaighte; a Circuit Judge, since 1991; *b* 19 Jan. 1943; *s* of Reginald and Barbara Bassingthwaighte; *m* 1966, Olwyn Burn. *Educ:* Ashford (Middx) County Grammar Sch. Admitted solicitor, 1967. Served RAF Legal Branch as Flt Lt, 1968, Sqdn Ldr 1973, Wing Comdr 1978 and Gp Capt. 1981; retired 1984. Chm., Industrial Tribunals (London Central and S regions), part-time 1984–85, full-time 1985–91; a Recorder of the Crown Court, 1987–91. Pres., Social Security Appeal, Medical Appeal, Disability Appeal, Child Support Appeal and Vaccine Damage Tribunals, 1994–98; a Judge, Employment Appeal Tribunal, 1996. *Recreations:* golf, tennis, scuba diving, bridge, opera. *Address:* Guildford Crown Court, Bedford Road, Guildford, Surrey GU1 4ST. *Clubs:* Royal Air Force; Worplesdon Golf (Woking).

BASTIN, Prof. John Andrew, MA, PhD; FRAS; Professor, 1971–84, now Emeritus, and Head of Department of Physics, 1975–80, Queen Mary College, London University; *b* 3 Jan. 1929; *s* of Lucy and Arthur Bastin; *m*; one *s* one *d*; *m* 1985, Aida Baterina Delfino. *Educ:* George Monoux Grammar Sch., London; Corpus Christi Coll., Oxford (MA, PhD). Univ. of Ibadan, Nigeria, 1952–56; Univ. of Reading, 1956–59; Queen Mary Coll., Univ. of London, 1959–84. Initiated a group in far infrared astronomy at Queen Mary College, 1960–70. *Publications:* papers on far infrared astronomy and lunar evolution. *Recreations:* English water colours, architecture, Renaissance and Baroque music. *Address:* 5 The Clockhouse, Redlynch Park, Bruton, Somerset BA10 0NH.

BATCHELOR, Sir Ivor (Ralph Campbell), Kt 1981; CBE 1976; FRCPE, DPM, FRCPsych; FRSE; Professor of Psychiatry, University of Dundee, 1967–82, now Emeritus Professor; *b* 29 Nov. 1916; *s* of Ralph C. L. Batchelor, FRCSE, FRCPE, and Muriel (*née* Shaw); *m* 1941, Honor Wallace Williamson; one *s* three *d*. *Educ:* Edinburgh Academy; Edinburgh Univ. MB ChB. FRCPsych 1971 (Hon. 1984). RAFVR, 1941–46; Sqdn Ldr, Comd Neuro-psychiatrist, CMF. Asst Phys. and Dep. Phys. Supt, Royal Edinburgh Hosp., and Sen. Lectr in Psychiatry, Univ. of Edinburgh, 1947–56; Phys. Supt, Dundee Royal Mental Hosp., 1956–62; Prof. of Psychiatry, Univ. of St Andrews, 1962–67. Member: Gen. Nursing Council for Scotland (Chm. Educn Cttee), 1964–71; Standing Med. Adv. Cttee, Scot., 1967–74; Adv. Cttee on Med. Research, Scotland, 1969–73; Scottish Council for Postgraduate Med. Educn, 1970–79; Chief Scientist Cttee, Scotland, 1973–82. Mem., Med. Services Review (Porritt) Cttee, 1958–62; Chm., Cttee on Staffing Mental Deficiency Hosps, 1967–70; Member: Cttee on Nursing (Briggs Cttee), 1970–72; Cttee on the Working of the Abortion Act (Lane Cttee), 1971–74; MRC (Chm. Clinical Research Bd, 1973–74, Chm. Neuro-Sciences Bd, 1974–75), 1972–76; MRC Health Services Res. Panel, 1981–82; Royal Commn on the Nat. Health Service, 1976–79; Indep. Sci. Cttee on Smoking and Health, 1980–86; UK Central Council for Nursing, Midwifery and Health Visiting, 1980–83; Scottish Hosp. Endowments Res. Trust, 1984–90; Trustee, Tobacco Products Res. Trust, 1981–96. Chm. Trustees, Orchar Art Gall., Dundee, 1980–87. *Publications:* (with R. N. Ironside) Aviation Neuro-Psychiatry, 1945; Henderson and Gillespie's Textbook of Psychiatry, 8th edn 1956 and subseq. edns to 10th edn 1969; papers on clinical psychiatry and health services. *Recreation:* rural rambles and natural history. *Address:* 55 Hepburn Gardens, St Andrews, Fife KY16 9LS. *T:* (01334) 473130. *Clubs:* Athenæum; Royal and Ancient Golf (St Andrews).

BATCHELOR, Prof. (John) Richard; Professor of Immunology, Royal Postgraduate Medical School, Hammersmith Hospital, 1979–94, now Professor Emeritus; *b* 4 Oct. 1931; *s* of B. W. Batchelor, CBE and Mrs C. E. Batchelor; *m* 1955, Moira Ann (*née* McLellan); two *s* two *d*. *Educ:* Marlborough Coll.; Emmanuel Coll., Cambridge; Guy's Hospital, London. MB, BChir Cantab, 1955; MD Cantab 1965. FRCPath 1991; FRCP 1995. Nat. Service, RAMC, 1957–59; Dept of Pathology, Guy's Hospital: Res. Fellow, 1959–61; Lectr and Sen. Lectr, 1961–67; Prof. of Transplantation Research, RCS, 1967; Dir, McIndoe Res. Unit, Queen Victoria Hosp., East Grinstead, 1967–78. Pres., Transplantation Soc., 1988–90 (Hon. Sec., then Vice-Pres. (E Hemisphere), 1976–80); Member Council, Nat. Kidney Res. Fund, 1979–86; Chm., Scientific Co-ord. Cttee, Arthritis and Rheumatism Council, 1988–96. MRSocMed. Mem. Court, Skinners' Company. European Editor, Transplantation, 1964–97. *Publications:* scientific articles upon tissue transplantation research in various special jls. *Recreations:* sailing; tennis; walking. *Address:* Little Ambrook, Nursery Road, Walton-on-the-Hill, Tadworth, Surrey KT20 7TU. *T:* (01737) 812028. *Clubs:* Brooks's, Queen's.

BATE, Prof. (Andrew) Jonathan, PhD; FBA 1999; King Alfred Professor of English Literature, since 1991, and Leverhulme Personal Research Professor, since 1999, University of Liverpool; *b* 26 June 1958; *s* of Ronald Montagu Bate and Sylvia Helen Bate; *m* 1st, 1984, Hilary Gaskin (marr. diss. 1995); 2nd, 1996, Paula Jayne Byrne; one *s* one *d*. *Educ:* Sevenoaks Sch., Kent; St Catharine's Coll., Cambridge (MA; PhD 1984; Hon. Fellow, 2000). Harkness Fellow, Harvard Univ., 1980–81; Research Fellow, St Catharine's Coll., Cambridge, 1983–85; Fellow, Trinity Hall, Cambridge and Lectr, Trinity Hall and Girton Coll., 1985–90; Research Reader, British Acad., 1994–96. Vis. Prof., UCLA, 1989, 1996. FRSA 1997. *Publications:* Shakespeare and the English Romantic Imagination, 1986; (ed) Lamb, Essays of Elia, 1987; Shakespearean Constitutions, 1989; Romantic Ecology, 1991; (ed) The Romantics on Shakespeare, 1992; Shakespeare and Ovid, 1993; The Arden Shakespeare: Titus Andronicus, 1995; (ed) Shakespeare: an illustrated stage history, 1996; The Genius of Shakespeare, 1997; The Cure for Love (novel), 1998; The Song of the Earth, 2000. *Recreations:* cricket, tennis, opera, walking. *Address:* Department of English, University of Liverpool, PO Box 147, Liverpool L69 3BX. *T:* (0151) 794 2704.

BATE, Prof. Christopher Michael, PhD; FRS 1997; Professor of Developmental Neurobiology, since 1998, and Fellow of King's College, since 1992, University of Cambridge. *Educ:* Trinity Coll., Oxford (BA 1966); PhD Cantab 1976. Cambridge University: Lectr in Zoology, until 1994; Reader in Develtl Biol., 1994–98. *Address:* Department of Zoology, Downing Street, Cambridge CB2 3EJ. *T:* (01223) 336639, *Fax:* (01223) 336676; King's College, Cambridge CB2 1ST.

BATE, David Christopher; QC 1994; a Recorder, since 1991; *b* 2 May 1945; *s* of late Robert Leslie Bate and Brenda Mabel Bate (*née* Price); *m* 1973, Patricia Joan Bailey; three *s* one *d*. *Educ:* Hendon Co. Grammar Sch.; Manchester Univ. (LLB Hons). Called to the Bar, Gray's Inn, 1969; VSO (UNA) with Melanesian Mission, 1969–70; Crown Counsel, British Solomon Is Protectorate, 1971. *Recreations:* trying to sing in tune, running, tennis. *Address:* Hollis Whiteman Chambers, Queen Elizabeth Building, Temple, EC4Y 9BS. *T:* (020) 7583 5766.

BATE, Sir David (Lindsay), KBE 1978 (CBE 1968); Chief Judge, Benue and Plateau States of Nigeria, 1975–77; Senior Puisne Judge, High Court of Justice, Northern States of Nigeria, 1968–75 (Puisne Judge, 1957–68); *b* 3 March 1916; *m* 1948, Thadeen June, *d* of late R. F. O'Donnell Peet; two *s*. *Educ:* Marlborough; Trinity Coll., Cambridge. Called to Bar, Inner Temple, 1938. Commissioned, Royal Artillery, 1939 and served, Royal Artillery, 1939–46. Entered Colonial Legal Service, 1947; Crown Counsel, Nigeria, 1947–52; Senior Crown Counsel, Nigeria, 1952–54; Senior Crown Counsel, Northern Nigeria, 1954–56; Solicitor-Gen., Northern Nigeria, 1956. *Recreations:* shooting, fishing. *Address:* PO Box 1339, Howick 3290, Natal, South Africa.

BATE, Jonathan; *see* Bate, A. J.

BATE, Maj.-Gen. William, CB 1974; OBE 1963; DL; Secretary to the Council of TAVR Associations, 1975–86 (Deputy Secretary, 1973–75); *b* 6 June 1920; *s* of S. Bate, Warrington; *m* 1946, Veronica Mary Josephine (*née* Quinn); two *s* two *d*. Commnd, 1941; war service in Burma, 1941–46 (despatches); Senior Instructor, RASC Officers Sch., 1947–50; Co. Comd 7th and 11th Armoured Divs, 1951–53; psc 1954; DAA&QMG Q (Ops), WO, 1955–57; jssc 1957; Admin. Staff Coll., Henley, 1958; Directing Staff, Staff Coll., Camberley, 1958–60; AA&QMG, Ops and Plans, HQ BAOR, 1961–63; CO, 2 Div. Column, BAOR, 1963–65; Col GS, Staff Coll., Camberley, 1965–67; Brig. Q (Maint.), MoD, 1967–68; ADC to the Queen, 1969; idc 1969; Dir of Admin. Planning (Army), 1970; Dir of Movements (Army), MoD, 1971–73. Col Comdt, 1974–86, Rep. Col Comdt, RCT, 1975, 1977, 1982, 1986. Hon. Col, 163 Movement Control Regt, RCT(V), TAVR, 1974–79. President: RASC/RCT Benevolent Fund; Waggon Club. DL Surrey, 1980. *Recreations:* cricket, tennis. *Address:* Netherbury, 14 Belton Road, Camberley, Surrey GU15 2DE. *T:* (01276) 63529. *Clubs:* East India, Devonshire, Sports and Public Schools, MCC.

BATELY, Prof. Janet Margaret, (Mrs L. J. Summers), CBE 2000; FBA 1990; Sir Israel Gollancz Professor of English Language and Medieval Literature, King's College, University of London, 1995–97, now Emeritus (Professor of English Language and Medieval Literature, 1977–95); *b* 3 April 1932; *d* of late Alfred William Bately and Dorothy Maud Bately (*née* Willis); *m* 1964, Leslie John Summers, sculptor; one *s*. *Educ:* Greenhead High Sch., Huddersfield; Westcliff High Sch. for Girls; Somerville Coll., Oxford (Shaw Lefevre Scholar; Eileen Gonner Meml Prize, 1953; BA 1st cl. hons English 1954, Dip. in Comparative Philology (with distinction) 1956, MA 1958; Hon. Fellow, 1997); FKC 1986. Asst Lectr in English, Birkbeck Coll., Univ. of London, 1955–58, Lectr, 1958–69, Reader, 1970–76. Lectures: Sir Israel Gollancz Meml, British Acad., 1978; Toller Meml, Manchester Univ., 1987; Dark Age, Univ. of Kent, 1991. Chm., Scholarships Cttee, Univ. of London, 1988–91. Member: Council, EETS, 1981–; Exec. Cttee, Fontes Anglo-Saxonici, 1985–; Adv. Cttee, Internat. Soc. of Anglo-Saxonists, 1986–91; Adv. Cttee, Sources of Anglo-Saxon Lit. and Culture, 1987–; Humanities Res. Bd, British Acad., 1994–95; Adv. Bd, Inst. for Histl Study of Lang., Glasgow Univ., 1998–. Governor: Cranleigh Sch., 1982–88; King's Coll. Sch., Wimbledon, 1991–94; Notting Hill and Ealing High Sch., 1998–. FRSA 2000. Gen. Ed., King's Coll. London Medieval Studies, 1987–. *Publications:* The Old English Orosius, 1980; The Literary Prose of King Alfred's Reign: Translation or Transformation, 1980; (ed) The Anglo-Saxon Chronicle: MS.A, 1986; The Anglo-Saxon Chronicle: texts and textual relationships, 1991; The Tanner Bede, 1992; Anonymous Old English Homilies: a preliminary bibliography, 1993; contribs to: England Before the Conquest, 1971; Saints, Scholars and Heroes (ed M. H. King and W. M. Stevens), 1979; Five Hundred Years of Words and Sounds (ed E. G. Stanley and Douglas Grey), 1983; Learning and Literature in Anglo-Saxon England (ed M. Lapidge and H. Gneuss), 1985; Medieval English Studies (ed D. Kennedy, R. Waldron and J. Wittig), 1988; Words for Robert Burchfield's Sixty-Fifth Birthday (ed E. G. Stanley and T. F. Hoad), 1988; From Anglo-Saxon to Early Middle English (ed M. Godden *et al.*), 1994; Leeds Studies in English, Reading Medieval Studies, Eichstätter Beiträge, Medium Aevum, Rev. of English Studies, Anglia, English Studies, Essays and Studies, Classica et Mediaevalia, Scriptorium, Studies in Philology, Mediev. Arch., Notes and Queries, Archaeologia, Anglo-Saxon England, The Dickensian, Jl Soc. of Archivists, Bull. John Rylands Library, etc. *Recreations:* music, gardening. *Address:* 86 Cawdor Crescent, W7 2DD. *T:* (020) 8567 0486.

BATEMAN, Leslie Clifford, CMG 1965; FRS 1968; Secretary-General, International Rubber Study Group, 1976–83; *b* 21 March 1915; *s* of Charles Samuel Bateman; *m* 1st, 1945, Marie Louise Pakes (*d* 1967); two *s*; 2nd, 1973, Mrs Eileen Joyce Jones (*née* Henwood); one step *s* one step *d*. *Educ:* Bishopshalt Sch., Uxbridge; University Coll., London. BSc, 1st cl. Hons Chem., 1935; PhD and Ramsey Memorial Medal, 1938; DSc 1955; Fellow, 1974. Oriel Coll., 1940–41; Chemist, Natural Rubber Producers Research Assoc., 1941–53; Dir of Research, 1953–62; Controller of Rubber Res., Malaysia, 1962–74; Chm., Internat. Rubber R&D Board, 1962–74. Mem., Malaysian Govt Task Force on Rubber Industry, 1983. Hon. DSc: Malaya, 1968; Aston, 1972. Colwyn Medal, 1963, and Jubilee Foundn Lectr, 1971, Inst. of Rubber Industry. Hon. PSM, Malaysia, 1974. *Publications:* (ed and contrib.) The Chemistry and Physics of Rubber-like

Substances, 1963; numerous scientific papers in Jl Chem. Soc., etc, and articles on technical-economic status of natural rubber and its developments. *Recreations:* cricket, golf and other outdoor activities. *Address:* 3 Palmerston Close, Welwyn Garden City, Herts AL8 7DL. *T:* (01707) 322391.

BATEMAN, Mary-Rose Christine, (Mrs R. D. Farley), MA; Headmistress, Perse School for Girls, Cambridge, 1980–89; *b* 16 March 1935; *d* of Comdr G. A. Bateman, RN, and Mrs G. A. Bateman; *m* 1990, Richard Dashwood Farley (*d* 1996). *Educ:* The Abbey, Malvern Wells, Worcs; St Anne's Coll., Oxford (MA); CertEd Cambridge. Assistant English Mistress: Westonbirt Sch., Tetbury, Glos, 1957–60; Ashford Sch., Kent, 1960–61; Lady Eleanor Holles Sch., Mddx, 1961–64; Head of English Department: Westonbirt Sch., Glos, 1964–69; Brighton and Hove High Sch., GPDST, 1969–71; Headmistress, Berkhamsted School for Girls, Herts, 1971–80. Administrator, Women's Nat. Cancer Control Campaign, 1989. *Address:* Harrow Hill Cottage, Long Compton, Shipston on Stour, Warwickshire CV36 5JJ. *T:* (01608) 684231.

BATEMAN, Paul Terence; Head, Asset Management for Europe, Asia and Japan, JP Morgan Fleming Asset Management, since 2001; *b* 28 April 1946; *s* of Nelson John Bateman and Frances Ellen (*née* Johnston); *m* 1970, Moira (*née* Burdis); two *s*. *Educ:* Westcliff High Sch. for Boys; Univ. of Leicester (BSc). Save and Prosper Gp Ltd, 1967: graduate, secretarial dept, 1967–68; asst to Gp Actuary, 1968–73; Marketing Manager, 1973–75; Gp Marketing Manager, 1975–80; Gp Marketing and Develt Manager, 1980–81; Exec. Dir, Marketing and Develt, 1981–88; Chief Exec., 1988–95; Chm., Robert Fleming Asset Management, 1995–2001. *Recreation:* yachting. *Address:* JP Morgan Fleming Asset Management, 10 Aldermanbury, EC2V 7RF. *T:* (020) 7742 6000. *Club:* Royal Burnham Yacht.

BATEMAN, Peter; HM Diplomatic Service; Commercial Counsellor, Tokyo, since 1998; *b* 23 Dec. 1955; *s* of Sqdn Ldr Ralph Edwin Bateman, MBE and Alma Bateman (*née* Laws); *m* 1985, Andrea Henriette Subercaseaux; two *s* one *d*. *Educ:* Carre's Grammar Sch., Sleaford, Lincs; St Peter's Coll., Oxford (MA). Conf. interpreter, EC, 1979–84; joined HM Diplomatic Service, 1984: First Secretary: Tokyo, 1986–90; FCO, 1991–93; (Commercial), Berlin, 1993–97; FCO, 1997–98. *Recreations:* family life, golf, travel. *Address:* c/o Foreign and Commonwealth Office, King Charles Street, SW1A 2AH. *Club:* Queen's.

BATEMAN, Richard George Saumarez La T.; *see* La Trobe-Bateman.

BATEMAN, Richard Mark, PhD, DSc; Keeper of Botany, Natural History Museum, since 1999; *b* Bradford, 27 May 1958; *s* of William Horace Roy Bateman and Joan Mary Lund (*née* Laban); separated. *Educ:* Luton Coll. of Higher Educn (BSc (Commendation) 1982); Birkbeck Coll., London (BSc 1st Cl. Hons 1984); PhD (Palaeozoic Palaeobotany) London 1988; DSc (Systematic Botany) London 2001. Asst SO, Sect. for Quaternary Studies, Rothamsted Exptl Station, 1977–84; Lindemann Res. Fellow and Vis. Scientist, Dept of Paleobiol., Smithsonian Instn, Washington, 1988–91; Sen. NERC Res. Fellow (Palaeobotany), Depts of Earth and Plant Scis, Oxford Univ., 1991–94; PSO, Royal Botanic Gdn, Edinburgh, and Nat. Museums of Scotland, 1994–96; Dir of Sci. and SPSO, Royal Botanic Gdn, Edinburgh, 1996–99. Hon. Res. Fellow, Edinburgh Univ., 1997; Vis. Prof., Reading Univ., 2000. Member Council: Systematics Assoc., 1992–; UK Systematics Forum, 1997–; Linnean Soc., 1999–. President's Award, Geol Soc. of GB, 1988; Bicentenary Medal, Linnean Soc., 1994. *Publications:* (jtly) Molecular Systematics and Plant Evolution, 1999; (jtly) Developmental Genetics and Plant Evolution, 2001; contrib. numerous papers to scientific jls. *Recreations:* natural history, travel, film, pontificating while drinking decent beer. *Address:* c/o Department of Botany, Natural History Museum, Cromwell Road, SW7 5BD. *T:* (020) 7942 5282.

BATEMAN, Richard Montague; Executive Secretary, Geological Society, 1980–97; *b* 27 Nov. 1943; *s* of late Gordon Montague Bateman and Joan Rhoda Bateman (*née* Puddifoot); *m* 1970, Gillian Elizabeth, *er d* of Noel Leslie Costain, *qv*; one *d*. *Educ:* Lyme Regis Grammar Sch. Entered Civil Service, 1964, MoD (Air), 1965–69; Chamber of Shipping of UK, 1969–75, Asst Sec., 1973–75; Gen. Council of British Shipping, 1975–80. Sec., Assoc. of European Geol Socs, 1987–92. Mem., Envmt Council, 1994–97. Mem. Council, Haslemere Educnl Mus., 1998–. Member: Ocean Liner Soc., 1992; Sci., Technol., Engrg and Med. PR Assoc., 1993; Geologists' Assoc., 1997; Soc. for Nautical Res., 1997; British Titanic Soc., 1998; Steamship Historical Soc. of America, 1999. Associate Mem., Inst. of Dirs, 1989; Associate, ACEVO, 1998–2001. *Recreations:* maritime history, classical music. *Address:* Grayswood Place Cottage, Three Gates Lane, Haslemere, Surrey GU27 2ET. *Club:* Anchorites.

BATES; *see* Baker-Bates.

BATES, Alan (Arthur), CBE 1995; actor; *b* 17 Feb. 1934; *m* 1970, Victoria Ward (*d* 1992); one *s* (one twin *s* decd). *Educ:* Herbert Strutt Grammar Sch., Belper, Derbyshire; RADA. *Theatre:* English Stage Co. (Royal Court Theatre, London): The Mulberry Bush; Cards of Identity; Look Back in Anger; The Country Wife; In Celebration; London (West End): Long Day's Journey into Night; The Caretaker; The Four Seasons; Hamlet; Butley, London and NY (Evening Standard Best Actor award, 1972; Antoinette Perry Best Actor award, 1973); Poor Richard, NY; Richard III and The Merry Wives of Windsor, Stratford, Ont.; Venice Preserved, Bristol Old Vic; Taming of the Shrew, Stratford-on-Avon, 1973; Life Class, 1974; Otherwise Engaged, Queen's, 1975 (Variety Club of GB Best Stage Actor award, 1975); The Seagull, Duke of York's, 1976; Stage Struck, Vaudeville, 1979; A Patriot for Me, Chichester, Haymarket, 1983, transf. Ahmanson, LA (Variety Club of GB Best Stage Actor award, 1983); Victoria Station, and One for the Road, Lyric Studio, 1984; The Dance of Death, Riverside Studios, Hammersmith, 1985; Yonadab, NT, 1985; Melon, Haymarket, 1987; Ivanov, and Much Ado About Nothing, Strand, 1989; Stages, NT, 1992; The Showman, Almeida, 1993; The Master Builder, Haymarket, 1995, Toronto, 1996; Simply Disconnected, and Fortune's Fool, Chichester, 1996; Life Support, Aldwych, 1997; Antony and Cleopatra, Timon of Athens, RSC, 1999. *Films:* The Entertainer, 1960; Whistle Down the Wind, 1961; A Kind of Loving, 1962; The Running Man, The Caretaker, 1963; Zorba the Greek, Nothing but the Best, 1964; Georgie Girl, 1965; King of Hearts, Far from the Madding Crowd, 1967; The Fixer (Oscar nomination), 1968; Women in Love, 1969; The Three Sisters (National Theatre Co.), 1970; A Day in the Death of Joe Egg, The Go-Between, 1971; Second Best (also prod.), 1972; Impossible Object, 1973; Butley, 1974; In Celebration, Royal Flash, 1975; An Unmarried Woman, 1977; The Shout, 1978; The Rose, 1979; Nijinsky, 1981; Quartet, 1982; The Return of the Soldier, 1983; The Wicked Lady, 1984; Duet for One, 1986; Prayer for the Dying, 1987; We Think the World of You, 1989; Mr Frost, Dr M, 1990; Hamlet, 1991; Losing Track, Secret Friends, 1992; Shuttlecock, 1994; Silent Tongue, 1994; The Grotesque, 1996; The Cherry Orchard, 2000. *Television:* various plays; Plaintiff and Defendant, Two Sundays, The Collection, 1977; The Mayor of Casterbridge, 1978; Very Like a Whale, The Trespasser, 1980; A Voyage Round my Father, Separate Tables, An Englishman Abroad, 1983 (BAFTA Best TV Actor award, 1984); Dr Fisher of Geneva, 1984; One for the Road, 1985; Pack of Lies, 1988; The Dog It Was that Died, 1988; 102 Boulevard Haussmann, 1991; Unnatural Pursuits, 1992; Hard Times, 1994; Oliver's Travels, 1995; Arabian Nights, In the Beginning, 2000; Love in a Cold Climate, Prince and the Pauper, 2001. *Recreations:* swimming, driving, riding, reading. *Address:* c/o Chatto & Linnit, 123A Kings Road, SW3 4PL. *T:* (020) 7352 7722, *Fax:* (020) 7352 3450.

BATES, Alfred; Research Assistant, Union of Shop, Distributive and Allied Workers, 1991–2000; *b* 8 June 1944; *s* of Norman and Alice Bates; single. *Educ:* Stretford Grammar Sch. for Boys; Manchester Univ. (BSc); Corpus Christi Coll., Cambridge. Lectr in Maths, De La Salle Coll. of Educn, Middleton, 1967–74. MP (Lab) Bebington and Ellesmere Port, Feb. 1974–1979; PPS to Minister of State for Social Security, 1974–76; Asst Govt Whip, 1976–79; a Lord Comr, HM Treasury, 1979. Researcher and presenter, 1980–87, and an assistant producer, 1983–87, BBC TV; freelance media consultant, 1987–91. Mem., Trafford MBC, 1992– (Chm., Licensing Cttee, 1996–97, 1998–; Chm., Public Protection Cttee, 1997–98). Mem. Bd of Dirs, Hallé Concerts Soc., 1996–98. *Recreation:* cricket umpiring. *Address:* 116 Jackson Street, Stretford, Manchester M32 8BB.

BATES, Clive David Nicholas; Director, Action on Smoking and Health, since 1997; *b* 16 Feb. 1961; *s* of David and Patricia Bates. *Educ:* Wilmslow Grammar Sch., Cheshire; Emmanuel Coll., Cambridge (BA Hons Engrg 1983); Imperial Coll., London (MSc Envmtl Technol. 1992). Marketing computers for IBM (UK) Ltd, 1983–91; envmtl campaigner, Greenpeace, 1992–95; Programme Manager, Internat. Inst. for Energy Conservation, 1996–97. FRSA 1998. *Publications:* reports and papers for campaigning groups. *Recreations:* cycling, mountains. *Address:* (office) 102–108 Clifton Street, EC2A 4HT; 42 Allerton Road, N16 5UF.

BATES, Air Vice-Marshal David Frank, CB 1983; RAF retired; *b* 10 April 1928; *s* of late S. F. Bates, MusB, FRCO, and N. A. Bates (*née* Story); *m* 1954, Margaret Winifred (*née* Biles); one *s* one *d*. *Educ:* Warwick Sch.; RAF Coll., Cranwell. Commnd, 1950; served Egypt, Innsworth, UKSLS Australia, HQ Transport Comd, RAF Technical Coll., Staff Coll., Lyneham, El Adem, Staff Coll., Jt Services Staff Coll., Innsworth, and RCDS, 1950–73; Stn Comdr, Uxbridge, 1974–75; Dir of Personnel Ground, 1975–76; Dir of Personnel Management (ADP), 1976–79; AOA, RAF Support Comd, 1979–82. Bursar, Warwick Sch., 1983–85. Pres., Adastrian Cricket Club, 1977–82. *Recreations:* cricket, most sports, gardening, model railways. *Address:* The Long House, Calf Lane, Chipping Campden, Glos GL55 6JQ. *Clubs:* Royal Air Force, MCC.

BATES, Sir Geoffrey Voltelin, 5th Bt *cr* 1880; MC 1942; *b* 2 Oct. 1921; *s* of Major Cecil Robert Bates, DSO, MC (3rd *s* of 2nd Bt) and Hylda, *d* of Sir James Heath, 1st Bt; *S* uncle, 1946; *m* 1st, 1945, Kitty Kendall Lane (*d* 1956); two *s*; 2nd, 1957, Olivia Gwyneth Zoë (*d* 1969) *d* of Capt. Hon. R. O. FitzRoy (later 2nd Viscount Daventry); one *d* (and one *d* decd); 3rd, 1971, Mrs Juliet Eleanor Hugolyn Whitelocke-Winter, *widow* of Edward Colin Winter and *d* of late Comdr G. C. A. Whitelocke, RN retd, and Mrs S. H. Whitelocke. *Educ:* Radley. High Sheriff, Flintshire, 1969. *Recreations:* hunting, shooting, fishing. *Heir:* *s* Edward Robert Bates, *b* 4 July 1946. *Address:* Gyrn Castle, Llanasa, near Holywell, Clwyd CH8 9BG. *T:* (01745) 853500.

BATES, Prof. Gillian Patricia, PhD; Professor of Neurogenetics, Guy's, King's College and St Thomas' Hospitals School of Medicine, since 1998; *b* 19 May 1956; *d* of Alan Richard Bates and Joan Mabel Bates. *Educ:* Kenilworth Grammar Sch.; Sheffield Univ. (BSc 1979); Birkbeck Coll., London (MSc 1984); St Mary's Hosp. Med. Sch., Univ. of London (PhD 1987). Postdoctoral Fellow, ICRF, 1987–93; Sen. Lectr in Molecular Biology, UMDS of Guy's and St Thomas' Hosps, 1994–98. FMedSci 1999. Nat. Med. Res. Award, Nat. Health Council, USA, 1993; Milton Wexler Award for Res. into Huntington's Disease, Huntington's Disease Soc. of America, 1998; Glaxo Wellcome Gold Medal, Royal Soc., 1998. *Publications:* papers in genetics, molecular biology, and neurosci. jls; contribs to scientific and med. reference books. *Recreations:* reading, contemporary arts and design. *Address:* Division of Medical and Molecular Genetics, Guy's, King's College and St Thomas' Hospitals School of Medicine, 8th Floor, Guy's Tower, Guy's Hospital, SE1 9RT. *T:* (020) 7955 4485.

BATES, Rt Rev. Gordon; Bishop Suffragan of Whitby, 1983–99; *b* 16 March 1934; *s* of Ernest and Kathleen Bates; *m* 1960, Betty (*née* Vaux); two *d*. *Educ:* Kelham Theological Coll. (SSM). Curate of All Saints, New Eltham, 1958–62; Youth Chaplain in Gloucester Diocese, 1962–64; Diocesan Youth Officer and Chaplain of Liverpool Cathedral, 1965–69; Vicar of Huyton, 1969–73; Canon Residentiary and Precentor of Liverpool Cathedral and Diocesan Director of Ordinands, 1973–83. Mem., House of Bishops, Gen. Synod, 1988–99. Mem., Central Religious Adv. Council to BBC and ITV, 1990–93. Trustee, Sandford St Martin Trust, 1990–93. *Recreations:* golf, music, writing. *Address:* Caedmon House, 2 Loyne Park, Whittington, via Carnforth, Lancs LA6 2NL. *T:* (01524) 272010. *Club:* Royal Over-Seas League.

BATES, James Patrick M.; *see* Martin-Bates.

BATES, John Gerald Higgs; Solicitor, Office of Inland Revenue, 1990–96; *b* 28 July 1936; *o s* of Thomas William Bates and Winifred Alice Higgs; *m* 1971, Antoinette Lotery (*d* 1984); two *s*; *m* 1992, Alba Heather Phyllida Whicher. *Educ:* Kettering Grammar Sch.; St Catharine's Coll., Cambridge (MA); Harvard Law Sch. (LLM). Called to the Bar, Middle Temple, 1959. Practised at the Bar, 1962–66; Office of Solicitor of Inland Revenue, 1966–96: Under Sec. (Legal), 1990. *Recreations:* cooking, wine, music.

BATES, Sir Malcolm (Rowland), Kt 1998; Chairman: Pearl Assurance (formerly Pearl Group plc), since 1996; Premier Farnell, since 1997; *b* 23 Sept. 1934; *s* of late Rowland Bates and Ivy Bates (*née* Hope); *m* 1960, Lynda Margaret Price; three *d*. *Educ:* Portsmouth Grammar Sch.; Univ. of Warwick (MSc); Harvard Business Sch. FCIS 1963; FRAeS 1993; CIMgt 1983. Flying Officer, RAF, 1956–58. Delta Group plc, 1959–68 (Man. Dir, Elkington & Co. plc, 1966–68); Adwest Gp plc, 1968–69; Industrial Reorgn Corp., 1969–70; Man. Dir, Spey Investments, 1970–72; Jt Man. Dir, Wm Brandt & Sons Ltd, 1972–75; General Electric Co. plc: Sen. Commercial Dir, 1976–80; Dir, 1980–97; Dep. Man. Dir, 1985–97. Chm., LRT, 1999–2001. Special Advr to Paymaster General, HM Treasury, 1997–99. Non-executive Director: Enterprise Oil, 1991–95; AMP (UK) plc, 1996–; BICC plc, 1997–99; Wavetek, Wandel & Goltermann Inc. (formerly Wavetek Corp.) (USA), 1997–99; AMP Ltd (Australia), 1998–; Grass Valley Group (USA), 1999–; The New Theatre Royal Trustees (Portsmouth) Ltd, 1999–; NPI Ltd, 1999. Advr, DLJ Phoenix Equity Partners II, 1997–. Chm., Engrg Deregulation Task Force, 1993–94; Member: Industrial Develt Adv. Bd, 1993–99; Private Finance Panel, 1993–96; IMRO, 1995–96; Finance Bd, RAeS, 1997–99. Chm., Business in the Arts, 1996–99; Mem. Council, ABSA, 1996–99. Gov., Univ. of Westminster, 1995– (Dep. Chm., 1999–). FRSA 1993. Freeman: City of London, 1985; Painter-Stainers' Co., 1985. *Recreations:* classical music, reading. *Address:* Mulberry Close, Croft Road, Goring-on-Thames, Oxon RG8 9ES. *T:* (01491) 872214. *Club:* Royal Air Force.

BATES, Margaret Patricia; *see* Munn, M. P.

BATES, Michael, (Mick); Member (Lib Dem) Montgomeryshire, National Assembly for Wales, since 1999; *b* 24 Sept. 1947; *s* of George William Bates and Lilly (*née* Stevens); *m* 1972, Buddug Thomas; one *s* one *d*. *Educ:* Open Univ. (BA Educn and Sci. 1970). Science teacher, Humphrey Perkins Jun. High Sch., Barrow on Soar, and Belvidere Secondary Sch., Shrewsbury, 1970–75; Head of Gen. Sci., Grove Sch., Market Drayton, 1975–77; farmer, 1977–99. Mem. (Lib Dem) Powys CC, 1994–95. National Farmers' Union: Chm., Llanfair Caereinion Br., 1983–85; Chm., Co. Livestock Cttee, 1988–91; Mem., Co. Public Affairs Cttee, 1990–; County Chm., Powys, 1991; NFU delegate, 1995. Lib Dem Br. Sec., 1988, Election Sub Agent, 1992. Mem., Eisteddfod Finance Cttee, 1989. Gov., Llanfair Co. Primary Sch., 1994–95. Chm., Llanfair Forum Community Regeneration Project. *Recreations:* all sports, especially Rugby, charity work, painting, walking, music. *Address:* National Assembly for Wales, Cardiff Bay, Cardiff CF99 1NA. *T:* (029) 2089 8340.

BATES, Michael Charles, OBE 1994; HM Diplomatic Service; Consul-General, Atlanta, since 2001; *b* 9 April 1948; *s* of late Stanley Herbert Bates and of Winifred (*née* Watkinson); *m* 1971, Janice Kwan Foh Yin; one *s* one *d*. *Educ:* Stratton Grammar Sch. Joined HM Diplomatic Service, 1966: Attaché, New Delhi, 1971–74; Third Sec., Moscow, 1974–77; FCO, 1977–79; Second, later First Sec., Singapore, 1979–83; First Sec., Brussels, 1983–87; Press Officer to Prime Minister, 1987–89; Head, Parly Relns Unit, FCO, 1989–91; Dep. Head of Mission, Riga, 1991–92; Chargé d'Affaires, Bratislava, 1993–94; Ambassador, Slovak Republic, 1994–95; Dep. Head, News Dept, FCO, 1995–96; Dep. High Comr, Bombay, 1996–2001. *Recreations:* music, reading, travel. *Address:* c/o Foreign and Commonwealth Office, King Charles Street, SW1A 2AH.

BATES, Michael Walton; Director of Consultancy and Research, Oxford Analytica Inc., since 1998; *b* 26 May 1961; *s* of John Bates and Ruth Walton; *m* 1983, Carole Whitfield, *d* of Sydney and late Irene Whitfield; two *s*. *Educ:* Heathfield Sen. High Sch.; Gateshead Coll.; Wadham Coll., Oxford (MBA 1998). Young Conservatives: Mem., Nat. Adv. Cttee, 1984–87; Chm., Northern Area, 1984–87. Director: estandardsforum.com Inc., 2001–; Financial Standards Foundn (Bermuda) Ltd, 2001–. Assoc. Chm., Northern Area Develt Initiative, 1990–92. Contested (C): Tyne Bridge, 1987; Langbaurgh, Nov. 1991. MP (C) Langbaurgh, 1992–97; contested (C) Middlesbrough South and Cleveland East, 1997. PPS to Minister of State, DSS, 1992–93, NI Office, 1994; an Asst Govt Whip, 1994–95; a Lord Comr, HM Treasury, 1995–96; HM Paymaster Gen., 1996–97. Member: Select Cttee on Social Security, 1992; Select Cttee on Health, 1994. Shell Fellow, Industry and Parlt Trust, 1997–. Mem., RIIA, 1998–. Mem. Council, Sch. of Mgt Studies, Oxford Univ., 2000–. *Address:* 1 Church Green, Witney, Oxon OX8 6AZ. *Club:* Carlton.

BATES, Paul Spencer; independent consultant; *b* 1 Jan. 1940; *s* of Rev. John Spencer Bates and Margaret Annie Bates (*née* Harwood); *m* 1964, Freda Ann Spillard (marr. diss. 1998); two *s*. *Educ:* St Edmund's Sch., Canterbury; Corpus Christi Coll., Cambridge (MA); Lincoln Theol Coll. Deacon 1965, priest 1966; Asst Curate, Hartcliffe, Bristol, 1965–69; Chaplain, Winchester Coll., 1970–80; Dir of Training, dio. of Winchester, 1980–90; Residentiary Canon, Westminster Abbey, 1990–94; Consultant, Alexander Corp., then Alexander, subseq. Sibson & Co., 1994–2000. *Publications:* contrib. SPCK Taleteller series. *Recreations:* cricket, modern novels, gardening. *Address:* 56 Coopers Close, E1 4BB. *T:* (020) 7790 0031; 15 Rue de l'Avenir, 1950 Brussels, Belgium. *T:* (2) 7822256.

BATES, Peter Edward Gascoigne, CBE 1987; Deputy Chairman, Plessey Electronic Systems Ltd, 1976–86; *b* 6 Aug. 1924; *s* of James Edward Bates and Esmé Grace Gascoigne Bates (*née* Roy); *m* 1947, Jean Irene Hearn, *d* of late Brig. W. Campbell Grant; two *s* one *d*. *Educ:* Kingston Grammar Sch.; School of Oriental and African Studies, Univ. of London; Lincoln Coll., Oxford. Served War, Intelligence Corps, SEAC and Japan, 1943–46; Captain 1945. Malayan CS, 1947–55; Rolls-Royce, Aero Engine Div., 1955–57; Bristol Aircraft (later British Aircraft Corp.), 1957–64, Special Director, 1963; joined Plessey Co., 1964: Gen. Man., Plessey Radar, 1967–71; Man. Dir, Radar Div., 1971–76. Mem., Adv. Cttee, Mitsubishi Electric Europe, 1991–99. Member: CBI Overseas Cttee, 1981–86; BOTB, 1984–87. Member: Council, Electronic Engrg Assoc., 1973–86 (Pres. 1976); Council, SBAC, 1978–86 (Pres. 1983–84); Pres., AECMA, 1985–86. *Publication:* Japan and the British Commonwealth Occupation Force 1946–1952, 1993. *Recreations:* golf, theatre, reading history and biography. *Address:* 22 Haygarth Place, Wimbledon, SW19 5BX. *T:* (020) 8946 0345. *Clubs:* Travellers; Royal Wimbledon Golf.

BATES, Sir Richard (Dawson Hoult), 3rd Bt *cr* 1937, of Magherabuoy, co. Londonderry; *b* 12 May 1956; *er s* of Sir Dawson Bates, 2nd Bt, MC and of Mary Murray (*née* Hoult); *S* father, 1998; *m* 2001, Harriet Domenique, *yr d* of Domenico Scaramella. *Heir:* *b* Charles Joseph Dill Bates [*b* 25 April 1959; *m* 1984, Suzanne C. Beaumont; two *s* one *d*].

BATES, Wendy Elizabeth; *see* Sudbury, W. E.

BATESON; *see* de Yarburgh-Bateson, family name of Baron Deramore.

BATESON, John Swinburne, FIHT; Chairman: Bateson's Hotels (1958) Ltd, since 1986; Merewood Group Ltd, since 1997; Group Chief Executive, AMEC plc, 1988–95; *b* 11 Jan. 1942; *s* of William Swinburne Bateson and Katherine Urquart (*née* Lyttle); *m* Jean Vivien Forsyth; one *s* two *d*. *Educ:* Appleby Grammar Sch.; Lancaster Royal Grammar Sch. FIHT 1986. Family business and associated activities, 1959–61; Harbour & General Works Ltd: Trainee Quantity Surveyor, 1961; Quantity Surveyor, 1966; Site Quantity Surveyor, Marples Ridgway Ltd, 1966–68; Leonard Fairclough Ltd: Site Quantity Surveyor, 1969; Contracts Surveyor, 1971; Chief Quantity Surveyor, Scotland, 1974; Fairclough Civil Engineering Ltd: Asst to Chief Exec., 1977; Man. Dir, Southern Div., 1979; Fairclough Construction Group Ltd: Asst to Chief Exec., 1980; Dir, 1981–95; AMEC plc: Dir, 1982–86; Dep. Chief Exec., 1986–88. Chm., Indep. Radio Gp, 1995–99. *Recreations:* gardening, aviation, reading, photography, chess, bridge, antiques. *Address:* Clayton Croft, Ribchester Road, Clayton-le-Dale, Blackburn, Lancs BB1 9EE.

BATESON, Prof. (Paul) Patrick (Gordon), FRS 1983; Professor of Ethology, University of Cambridge, since 1984; Provost of King's College, Cambridge, since 1988 (Fellow, 1964–84; Professorial Fellow, 1984–88); *b* 31 March 1938; *s* of Richard Gordon Bateson and Sölvi Helene Berg; *m* 1963, Dusha Matthews; two *d*. *Educ:* Westminster Sch.; King's Coll., Cambridge (BA 1960, PhD 1963, MA 1965, ScD 1977). Harkness Fellow, Stanford Univ. Medical Centre, Calif, 1963–65; Sen. Asst in Res., Sub-Dept of Animal Behaviour, Univ. of Cambridge, 1965–69; Lectr in Zoology, Univ. of Cambridge, 1969–78; Dir, Sub-Dept of Animal Behaviour, 1976–88; Reader in Animal Behaviour, 1978–84. Pres., Assoc. for the Study of Animal Behaviour, 1977–80; Member: Council for Sci. and Soc., 1989–92; Council, Zool Soc. of London, 1989–92; Museums and Galls Commn, 1995–2000 (Vice-Chm., 1998–2000). Biological Sec., Royal Soc., 1998–. Trustee, Inst. for Public Policy Research, 1988–95. Hon. Fellow, QMW. Scientific Medal, Zool Soc. of London, 1976; Medal Assoc. for Study of Animal Behaviour, 2001. *Publications:* (ed with P. H. Klopfer) Perspectives in Ethology, Vols 1–8, 1973–89; (ed with R. A. Hinde) Growing Points in Ethology, 1976; (ed) Mate Choice, 1983; (contrib.) Defended to Death, 1983; (with Paul Martin) Measuring Behaviour, 1986, 2nd edn 1993; (ed with D. S. Turner) The Domestic Cat: the biology of its behaviour, 1988, 2nd edn 2000; (ed) The Development and Integration of Behaviour, 1991; (with P. Martin) Design for a Life: how behaviour develops, 1999. *Address:* Provost's Lodge, King's College, Cambridge CB2 1ST. *T:* (01223) 355949.

BATEY, Mavis Lilian, MBE 1986; President, Garden History Society, 1985–2000; *b* 5 May 1921; *d* of Frederick Lever and Lily Lever; *m* 1942, Keith Batey; one *s* two *d*. *Educ:* Convent of Ladies of Mary, Croydon; University Coll. London. Worked at Bletchley Park, breaking German Enigma codes, 1940–45. Tutor (part time), Oxford Dept of External Studies, 1970–92. Mem., Historic Parks and Gardens Panel, English Heritage, 1984–94. Hon. Sec., Garden History Soc., 1971–85. Veitch Meml Medal, RHS, 1985. *Publications:* Alice's Adventures in Oxford, 1980; Oxford Gardens, 1982; Historic Gardens of Oxford and Cambridge, 1989; (with D. Lambert) The English Garden Tour, 1990; Arcadian Thames, 1994; Privy Garden at Hampton Court, 1995; Regency Gardens, 1995; Jane Austen and the English Landscape, 1996; Alexander Pope: the poet and the landscape, 1999. *Recreations:* walking, bird-watching, reading.

BATH, 7th Marquess of, *cr* 1789; **Alexander George Thynn,** Bt 1641; Viscount Weymouth and Baron Thynne, 1682; Director: Cheddar Caves, since 1956; Longleat Enterprises, since 1964; *b* 6 May 1932; *s* of 6th Marquess of Bath and his 1st wife, Hon. Daphne Winifred Louise (*d* 1997), *d* of 4th Baron Vivian; *S* father, 1992; *m* 1969, Anna Gael Gyarmathy; one *s* one *d*. *Educ:* Eton College; Christ Church, Oxford (BA, MA). Lieutenant in the Life Guards, 1951–52, and in Royal Wilts Yeomanry, 1953–57. Contested (Wessex Regionalist): Westbury, Feb. 1974; Wells, 1979; contested (Wessex Regionalist and European Federal Party) Wessex, European Election 1979. Permanent exhibn of paintings since 1949 and murals since 1964, first opened to the public in 1962 in private apartments at Longleat House. Record, I Play the Host, singing own compositions, 1974. *Publications:* (as Alexander Thynn) (before 1976 Alexander Thynne) The Carry-cot, 1972; Lord Weymouth's Murals, 1974; A Regionalist Manifesto, 1975; The King is Dead, 1976; Pillars of the Establishment, 1980; The New World Order of Alexander Thynn, 2000. *Heir:* *s* Viscount Weymouth, *qv*. *Address:* Longleat, Warminster, Wilts BA12 7NN. *T:* (01985) 844300.

BATH and WELLS, Bishop of; *no new appointment at time of going to press.*

BATH, Archdeacon of; *see* Evens, Ven. R. J. S.

BATHER, John Knollys; Lord-Lieutenant of Derbyshire, since 1994; Deputy Chairman, Chamberlin & Hill plc, since 1995; *b* 5 May 1934; *m* 1960, Elizabeth Barbara Longstaff; one *s* two *d*. *Educ:* Shrewsbury Sch.; Nat. Foundry Coll. MIBF. High Sheriff, Derbys, 1990–91. Freeman, City of London; Liveryman, Founders' Co. *Recreations:* gardening, shooting, watercolours. *Address:* Longford Grange, Longford, Ashbourne, Derbys DE6 3AH. *T:* (01335) 330429. *Club:* Boodle's.

BATHERSBY, Most Rev. John Alexius; *see* Brisbane, Archbishop of, (RC).

BATHO, James; *see* Batho, W. J. S.

BATHO, Sir Peter (Ghislain), 3rd Bt *cr* 1928, of Frinton, Essex; *b* 9 Dec. 1939; *s* of Sir Maurice Benjamin Batho, 2nd Bt and Antoinette Marie (*d* 1994), *d* of Baron d'Udekem d'Acoz; *S* father, 1990; *m* 1966, Lucille Mary, *d* of Wilfrid F. Williamson; three *s*. *Educ:* Ampleforth Coll.; Writtle Agricl Coll. Career in agriculture. Mem., Suffolk CC, 1989–93. *Heir:* *s* Rupert Sebastian Ghislain Batho, *b* 26 Oct. 1967. *Address:* Park Farm, Saxmundham, Suffolk IP17 1DQ. *T:* (01728) 602132.

BATHO, (Walter) James (Scott), CBE 1998; Chairman: London and Quadrant Housing Trust, 1989–98; Crown Housing Association, since 1996; *b* 13 Nov. 1925; *er s* of Walter Scott Batho and Isabella Laidlaw Batho (*née* Common); *m* 1951, Barbara Kingsford; two *s* two *d*. *Educ:* Epsom County Grammar Sch.; Univ. of Edinburgh (MA Eng. Lit. and Lang.). Served War, RNVR, 1943–46. Air Min., 1950–53; WO, 1953–63 (Private Sec. to Perm. Under Sec. of State, 1956–57); MPBW, 1963–70; DoE, 1970–85, Under Sec., 1979–85 (Regl Dir and Chm., Regl Bd for Eastern Region, DoE and Dept of Transport, 1983–85). Chm., Noise Review Wkg Party, DoE, 1990. Pres., Ashtead Choral Soc., 1990–. *Recreations:* singing, reading, gardening. *Address:* Bushpease, 16 Grays Lane, Ashtead, Surrey KT21 1BU. *T:* (01372) 273471. *Clubs:* Naval, MCC.

BATHURST, family name of **Earl Bathurst** and **Viscount Bledisloe**.

BATHURST, 8th Earl *cr* 1772; **Henry Allen John Bathurst,** DL; Baron Bathurst of Battlesden, Bedfordshire, 1712; Baron Apsley of Apsley, Sussex, 1771; Earl Bathurst of Bathurst, Sussex, 1772; Capt. Royal Gloucestershire Hussars (TA); TARO, 1959; *b* 1 May 1927; *s* of Lord Apsley, DSO, MC, MP (killed on active service, 1942) and Lady Apsley, CBE, MP for Bristol Central 1943–45 (*d* 1966); *g s* of 7th Earl; *S* grandfather, 1943; *m* 1st, 1959, Judith Mary (marr. diss. 1977; she *d* 2001), *d* of Mr and Mrs A. C. Nelson, Springfield House, Foulridge, Lancs; two *s* one *d*; 2nd, 1978, Gloria, *widow* of David Rutherston and *o d* of Harold Edward Clarry, Vancouver, BC. *Educ:* Ridley Coll., Canada; Eton; Christ Church, Oxford, 1948–49. Lieut 10th Royal Hussars (PWO), 1946–48. Capt., Royal Glos. Hussars, TA, 1949–57. Hon. Sec. Agricultural Cttee (Conservative), House of Lords, 1957; a Lord-in-Waiting, 1957–61; Joint Parliamentary Under-Sec. of State, Home Office, 1961–July 1962. Governor, Royal Agricultural Coll.; Pres. Glos Branch CPRE. Chancellor, Primrose League, 1959–61. Dir, Forestor Gp, 1986–92. Member: CLA Council, 1965 (Chm., Glos Branch of CLA, 1968–71); Timber Growers' Organisation (TGO) Council, 1966; President: Royal Forestry Soc., 1976–78; InstSMM, 1982–92; Assoc. of Professional Foresters, 1983–87, 1995–98. Master, 1950–64, Jt Master, 1964–66, Vale of White Horse (Earl Bathurst's) Hounds. DL County of Gloucester, 1960. *Heir:* *s* Lord Apsley, *qv*. *Clubs:* White's, Cavalry and Guards.

BATHURST, Admiral of the Fleet Sir (David) Benjamin, GCB 1991 (KCB 1987); First Sea Lord and Chief of Naval Staff, and First and Principal Naval Aide-de-Camp to the Queen, 1993–95; Vice Lord-Lieutenant, Somerset, since 1999; *b* 27 May 1936; *s* of late Group Captain Peter Bathurst, RAF and Lady Ann Bathurst; *m* 1959, Sarah Peto; one *s* three *d*. *Educ:* Eton College; Britannia RN College, Dartmouth. Joined RN, 1953; qualified as Pilot, 1960, as Helicopter Instructor, 1964; Fleet Air Arm appts incl. 2 years' exchange with RAN, 723 and 725 Sqdns; Senior Pilot, 820 Naval Air Sqdn; CO 819 Naval Air Sqdn; HMS Norfolk, 1971; Naval Staff, 1973; CO, HMS Ariadne, 1975; Naval Asst to First Sea Lord, 1976; Captain, 5th Frigate Sqdn, HMS Minerva, 1978; RCDS 1981; Dir of Naval Air Warfare, 1982; Flag Officer, Second Flotilla, 1983–85; Dir.-Gen., Naval Manpower and Training, 1985–86; Chief of Fleet Support, 1986–89; C-in-C Fleet, Allied C-in-C Channel, and C-in-C Eastern Atlantic Area, 1989–91; Vice Chief of Defence Staff, 1991–93. FRAeS. Younger Brother, Trinity House. Liveryman, GAPAN.

DL Somerset, 1996. *Recreations:* gardening, shooting, fishing. *Address:* c/o Coutts and Co., 440 Strand, WC2R 0QS. *Clubs:* Boodle's, Army and Navy, MCC.

BATHURST, Sir (Frederick) John (Charles Gordon) Hervey-, 7th Bt *cr* 1818, of Lainston, Hants; *b* 23 April 1934; *o s* of Sir Frederick Peter Methuen Hervey-Bathurst, 6th Bt and of Maureen Eley (*née* Gordon); *S* father, 1995; *m* 1957, Caroline, *d* of Lt-Col Sir William Starkey, 2nd Bt; one *s* two *d*. *Educ:* Eton; Trinity Coll., Cambridge (MA). Grenadier Guards, 1952–54. Lazard Brothers & Co. Ltd, 1957–91. *Heir: s* Frederick William John Hervey-Bathurst [*b* 18 Sept. 1965; *m* 1991, Annabel Warburg; one *s* one *d*]. *Address:* Somborne Park, Stockbridge, Hants SO20 6QT. *T:* (01794) 388322.

See also Sir J. F. Portal, Bt.

BATHURST, Sir Maurice (Edward), Kt 1984; CMG 1953; CBE 1947; QC 1964; *b* 2 Dec. 1913; *o s* of late Edward John James Bathurst and Annie Mary Bathurst; *m* 1941, Dorothy (marr. diss. 1963), *d* of late W. S. Stevens, LDS, RCS; one *s*; *m* 1968, Joan Caroline Petrie (*d* 1999). *Educ:* Haberdashers' Aske's, Hatcham; King's Coll., London; Gonville and Caius Coll., Cambridge; Columbia Univ. LLB, First Class Hons. (London), 1937; University Law Schol. (London), 1937; Post-Grad. Research Studentship (London), 1938; Bartle Frere Exhibitioner (Camb.), 1939; Tutorial Fellow (Chicago), 1939; Special Fellow (Columbia), 1940; LLM (Columbia), 1941; Hon. DCL (Sacred Heart, NB), 1946; PhD (Camb.), 1949; LLD (London), 1966. Solicitor of Supreme Court, 1938–56. Called to Bar, Gray's Inn, 1957; Master of the Bench, 1970; Master of the Library, 1978–81. Legal Adviser, British Information Services, USA, 1941–43; Legal Adviser, British Embassy, Washington, 1943–46 (First Sec., 1944; Counsellor, 1946); Legal Member, UK Delegation to United Nations, 1946–48; UK Representative, Legal Advisory Cttee, Atomic Energy Commission, 1946–48; Legal Adviser to British Chm., Bipartite Control Office, Frankfurt, 1949; Dep. Legal Adviser, CCG, 1949–51; Legal Adviser, UK High Commn, Germany, 1951–55; Judge, Supreme Court, British Zone, Germany, 1953–55; Legal Adviser, British Embassy, Bonn, 1955–57; British Judge, Arbitral Commn, Germany, 1968–69; Mem., Panel of Arbitrators, Internat. Centre for Settlement of Investment Disputes, 1968–87; a Pres., Arbitral Tribunals, Internat. Telecommunication's Satellite Orgn, 1974–78; Judge, Arbitral Tribunal and Mixed Commn for Agreement on German External Debts, 1977–88. Mem. UK Delegations to UNRRA; United Nations San Francisco Conference; Bermuda Civil Aviation Conference; PICAO; Washington Financial Talks; UN Gen. Assembly; FAO; WHO; Internat. Tin Study Group; UK-US Double Taxation Treaty Negotiations; London Nine-Power Conf.; Paris Conf. on W Eur. Union; NATO Status of Forces Conf., Bonn. Internat. Vice-Pres. UN League of Lawyers; Vice President: Brit. Inst. of International and Comparative Law; Acad. of Experts, 1988–92 (Hon. Fellow, 1992). Member: UK Cttee, UNICEF, 1959–84; Ct of Assistants, Haberdashers' Co. (Fourth Warden, 1973–74; Second Warden, 1978–79; First Warden, 1979–80; Master, 1980–81); Editorial Cttee, British Yearbook of International Law; *ad eundem*, Inner Temple; Gen. Council of the Bar, 1970–71; Senate of Inns of Court, 1971–73; Council of Legal Educn, 1971–79; Senate of the Inns of Court and the Bar, 1974–77. Hon. Vis. Prof. in Internat. Law, King's Coll., London, 1967–77; Hon. Fellow, King's Coll., London. Chm. Governors, Haberdashers' Aske's Hatcham Schools, 1973–80. Pres., British Insurance Law Assoc., 1971–75. Freeman of the City of London and of the City of Bathurst, NB. *Publications:* Germany and the North Atlantic Community: A Legal Survey (with J. L. Simpson), 1956; (ed, jtly) Legal Problems of an Enlarged European Community, 1972, notes and articles in legal jls, etc., British and American. *Recreation:* theatre. *Address:* Airlie, The Highlands, East Horsley, Surrey KT24 5BG. *T:* (01483) 283269. *Club:* Garrick.

BATHURST NORMAN, George Alfred; His Honour Judge Bathurst Norman; a Senior Circuit Judge, since 1997 (a Circuit Judge, since 1986); *b* 15 Jan. 1939; *s* of Charles Phipps Bathurst Norman and Hon. Doreen Albinia de Burgh Norman (*née* Gibbs); *m* 1973, Susan Elizabeth Ball; one *s* one *d*. *Educ:* Harrow Sch.; Magdalen Coll., Oxford (BA). Called to the Bar, Inner Temple, 1961; SE Circuit, 1962; Dep. Circuit Judge, 1975; a Metropolitan Stipendiary Magistrate, 1981–86; a Recorder, 1986. Mem., Home Office Working Party on Coroners Rules, 1976–81. Mem., Gen. Council of the Bar, 1968–70. Mem., Middlesex Probation Cttee, 1994–99. Chm., Lord Chancellor's Adv. Cttee on JPs for Middlesex, 1996– (Dep. Chm., 1994–96). *Publications:* research papers on drugs and drug smuggling. *Recreations:* wildlife, ornithology, cricket, travel. *Address:* Southwark Crown Court, 1 English Grounds, SE1 2HU. *Club:* MCC.

BATISTE, Spencer Lee; solicitor since 1970; Immigration Adjudicator, since 1997; *b* 5 June 1945; *m* 1969, Susan Elizabeth (*née* Atkin); one *s* one *d*. *Educ:* Carmel Coll.; Sorbonne, Paris; Cambridge Univ. (MA). MP (C) Elmet, 1983–97; contested (C) same seat, 1997. PPS to Minister of State for Industry and IT, 1985–87, to Minister of State for Defence Procurement, 1987–89, to Sir Leon Brittan, Vice-Pres. of EC Commn, 1989–97. Member: Select Cttee on Energy, 1985; Select Cttee on Information, 1991–97; Select Cttee on Sci. and Technology, 1992–97; Vice-Chairman: Cons. Space Cttee, 1986–97 (Sec., 1983–85); Cons. Trade and Industry Cttee, 1989–97. Pres., Yorks Cons. Trade Unionists, 1984–87 (Nat. Pres., 1990). Vice-Chm., Small Business Bureau, 1983–92. Law Clerk to Sheffield Assay Office, 1974–2000. Mem., British Hallmarking Council, 1988–2000. *Recreations:* gardening, reading, photography. *Address:* c/o Immigration Appellate Authorities, Field House, 15–25 Bream's Buildings, EC4A 1DZ.

BATLEY, John Geoffrey, OBE 1987; CEng; Consultant, Dan-Rail, Copenhagen, 1988–92; Transport Consultant, Carl Bro (UK), 1993–96; *b* 21 May 1930; *s* of John William and Doris Batley; *m* 1953, Cicely Anne Pindar; one *s* one *d*. *Educ:* Keighley Grammar School. MICE. British Rail: trained and qualified as a chartered engineer in NE Region, 1947–53; Asst Divl Engr, Leeds, 1962; Management Services Officer, BR HQ, London, 1965; Dep. Principal, British Transport Staff Coll., Woking, 1970; Divl Manager, Leeds, 1976; Dep. Chief Secretary, BRB, London, 1982; Sec., BRB, 1984–87; Project Co-ordinator, World Bank/Tanzanian Railway Corp., 1988–92. *Recreations:* walking, golf, gardening. *Address:* Wentworth Cottage, Old Lodge Hill, Ilkley, West Yorkshire LS29 0BB. *T:* (01943) 601396. *Clubs:* Farmers', Savile.

BATTEN, Sir John (Charles), KCVO 1987; MD, FRCP; Physician to the Queen, 1974–89 (Physician to HM Royal Household, 1970–74), and Head of HM Medical Household, 1982–89; Physician: King Edward VII Hospital for Officers, 1968–89; King Edward VII Hospital, Midhurst, 1969–89; Hon. Physician to: St George's Hospital, since 1980; Royal Brompton Hospital (formerly Brompton Hospital), since 1986; *b* 11 March 1924; *s* of late Raymond Wallis Batten, JP and Gladys (*née* Charles); *m* 1950, Anne Mary Margaret, *d* of late John Oriel, CBE, MC; one *s* two *d* (and one *d* decd). *Educ:* Mill Hill School; St Bartholomew's Medical School. MB, BS 1946 London Univ.; MRCP 1950; MD London 1951; FRCP 1964. Junior appts, St George's Hosp. and Brompton Hosp., 1946–58. Surgeon Captain, Royal Horse Guards, 1947–49. Physician: St George's Hospital, 1958–79; Brompton Hosp., 1959–86. Dep. Chief Med. Referee, 1958–74, CMO, 1974–95, Confederation Life. Dorothy Temple Cross Research Fellow, Cornell Univ. Medical Coll., New York, 1954–55. Examiner in Medicine, London Univ., 1968; Marc Daniels Lectr, RCP, 1969; Croonian Lectr, RCP, 1983. Member: Board of Governors, Brompton Hosp., 1966–69; St George's Hosp. Medical School Council, 1969; Council, RSocMed, 1970; Royal College of Physicians: Censor, 1977–78; Senior Censor, 1980–81; Vice-Pres., 1980–81. President: Cystic Fibrosis Trust, 1986–; British Lung Foundn, 1987–95; Medical Protection Soc., 1988–97. Life Vice-Pres., RNLI, 2000. *Publications:* contributions to medical books and journals. *Recreations:* music and sailing. *Address:* 7 Lion Gate Gardens, Richmond, Surrey TW9 2DF. *T:* (020) 8940 3282.

BATTEN, Stephen Duval; QC 1989; barrister; a Recorder, since 1988; *b* 2 April 1945; *s* of Brig. Stephen Alexander Holgate Batten, CBE and of Alice Joan Batten, MBE, *d* of Sir Ernest Royden, 3rd Bt; *m* 1976, Valerie Jean Trim; one *s* one *d*. *Educ:* Uppingham; Pembroke Coll., Oxford (BA). Called to the Bar, Middle Temple, 1968, Bencher 1998. *Recreations:* golf, equestrianism. *Address:* 3 Raymond Buildings, Gray's Inn, WC1R 5BH. *T:* (020) 7831 3833.

BATTERBURY, His Honour Paul Tracy Shepherd, TD 1972 (2 bars); DL; a Circuit Judge, 1983–99; *b* 25 Jan. 1934; only *s* of late Hugh Basil John Batterbury and of Inez Batterbury; *m* 1962, Sheila Margaret, *d* of John Watson; one *s* one *d*. *Educ:* St Olave's Grammar Sch., Southwark; Univ. of Bristol (LLB). Served RAF, 1952–55, TA, 1959–85 (Major, RA). Called to Bar, Inner Temple, 1959; practising barrister, 1959–83. Councillor: Chislehurst and Sidcup UDC, 1960–62; London Borough of Greenwich, 1968–71 (Chm., Housing Cttee, 1970–71). Founder Trustee, St Olave's Sch., SE9, 1970–2001; Founder Chm., Gallipoli Meml Lects, 1986–89. Vice-Pres., SE London, SJAB, 1988–91. DL Greater London, 1986–2001; rep. DL, London Borough of Havering, 1989–95. *Recreations:* photography, walking, caravanning. *Address:* 5 Paper Buildings, Temple, EC4Y 9HB. *T:* (020) 7583 9275.

BATTERSBY, Sir Alan (Rushton), Kt 1992; MSc, PhD, DSc, ScD; FRS 1966; Professor of Organic Chemistry, Cambridge University, 1969–92, now Emeritus; Fellow of St Catharine's College, Cambridge, 1969–92, Emeritus Fellow, 1992, Hon. Fellow, 2000; Director, Schering Agrochemicals Ltd; *b* Leigh, 4 March 1925; *s* of William and Hilda Battersby; *m* 1949, Margaret Ruth (*d* 1997), *d* of Thomas and Annie Hart, Whaley Bridge, Cheshire; two *s*. *Educ:* Grammar Sch., Leigh; Univ. of Manchester (Mercer and Woodiwis Schol.; MSc); Univ. of St Andrews (PhD); DSc Bristol; ScD Cantab. Asst Lectr in Chemistry, Univ. of St Andrews, 1948–53; Commonwealth Fund Fellow at Rockefeller Inst., NY, 1950–51 and at Univ. of Illinois, 1951–52; Lectr in Chemistry, Univ. of Bristol, 1954–62; Prof. of Organic Chemistry, Univ. of Liverpool, 1962–69. Mem. Council, Royal Soc., 1973–75. Mem. Deutsche Akademie der Naturforscher Leopoldina, 1967; MAE 1990. Pres., Bürgenstock Conf., 1976. Chm., Exec. Council, 1983–90, Trustee, 1993–, Novartis (formerly Ciba) Foundn. Foreign Fellow: Nat. Acad. of Scis, India, 1990; Indian Nat. Science Acad., 1993. Honorary Member: Soc. Royale de Chimie, Belgium, 1987; Amer. Acad. of Arts and Scis, 1988; Soc. Argentina de Investigaciones en Quimica Organica, 1997. Lectures: Treat Johnson, Yale, 1969; Pacific Coast, USA, 1971; Karl Folkers, Wisconsin, 1972; N-E Coast, USA, 1974; Andrews, NSW, 1975; Middle Rhine, 1976; Tishler, Harvard, 1978; August Wilhelm von Hoffmann, Ges. Deutscher Chem., 1979; Pedler, Chem. Soc., 1980–81; Rennebohm, Wisconsin, 1981; Kharasch, Chicago, 1982; Bakerian, Royal Soc., 1984; Baker, Cornell, 1984; Lady Masson Meml, Melbourne, 1987; Atlantic Coast, USA, 1988; Nehru Centenary, Seshadri Meml and Zaheer Meml, India, 1989; Marvel, Illinois, 1989; Gilman, Iowa, 1989; Alder, Cologne, 1991; Dauben, Berkeley, 1994; Alexander Cruickshank, Gordon Confs, 1994; Linus Pauling, Oregon, 1996; IAP, Columbia, 1999; Univ. Lectr, Ottawa, 1993; Visiting Professor: Cornell Univ., 1969; Virginia Univ., 1971; Tohoku Univ., Japan, 1974; ANU, 1975; Technion, Israel, 1977; Univ. of Canterbury, NZ, 1980; Melbourne Univ., 1987; Univ. of Auckland, NZ, 1989, 1993; Univ. of NSW, 1990. Chemical Society: Corday-Morgan Medal, 1959; Tilden Medal and Lectr, 1963; Hügo Müller Medal and Lectr, 1972; Flintoff Medal, 1975; Award in Natural Product Chemistry, 1978; Longstaff Medal, 1984; Robert Robinson Lectr and Medal, 1986. Paul Karrer Medal and Lectr, Univ. Zürich, 1977; Davy Medal, 1977, Royal Medal, 1984, Copley Medal, 2000, Royal Soc.; Roger Adams Award in Organic Chemistry, ACS, 1983; Havinga Medal, Holland, 1984; Antoni Feltrinelli Internat. Prize for Chemistry, Rome, 1986; Varro Tyler Lect. and Award, Purdue, 1987; Adolf Windaus Medal, Göttingen, 1987; Wolf Prize, Israel, 1989; Arun Guthikonda Meml Award, Columbia, 1991; Hofmann Meml Medal, Ges. Deutscher Chem., 1992; Tetrahedron Prize for creativity in org. chem., 1995; Hans Herloff Inhoffen Medal, Univ. Braunschweig, 1997; Robert A. Welch Award in Chemistry, USA, 2000. Hon. LLD St Andrews, 1977; Hon. DSc: Rockefeller Univ., USA, 1977; Sheffield, 1986; Heriot-Watt, 1987; Bristol, 1994; Liverpool, 1996. *Publications:* papers in chemical jls, particularly Jl Chem. Soc. *Recreations:* music, hiking, camping, sailing, fly fishing, gardening. *Address:* University Chemical Laboratory, Lensfield Road, Cambridge CB2 1EW. *T:* (01223) 336400.

BATTERSBY, Robert Christopher, CBE 1990 (MBE 1971); *b* 14 Dec. 1924; *s* of late Major Robert Luther Battersby, MM, RFA, late Indian Army, and Dorothea Gladys (*née* Middleton); *m* 1st, 1949, June Scriven (marr. diss.); one *d*; 2nd, 1955, Marjorie Bispham; two *s* one *d*. *Educ:* Firth Park Grammar Sch., Sheffield; Edinburgh Univ. (Gen. Sciences); Fitzwilliam House, Cambridge; Sorbonne; Toulouse Univ. BA Cantab (Hons Russian and Modern Greek) 1950; Cert. of Educn 1952; MA Cantab 1954; Cert. de Langue française, Toulouse, 1953; FIL 1958. Served Royal Artillery (Field) and Intelligence Corps, 1942–47 (Italian Campaign, Greece and Crete 1944, Central and Western Macedonia 1945–47); TA to 1952; Lieut RARO. Manager: Dowsett Gp of shipbuilding and civil engrg cos on major distant water trawler and pre-stressed concrete plant export contracts, 1953–63; Eastern Trade Dept, Glacier Metal Co. Ltd, 1963–66; Sales Dir, Associated Engrg Export Services Ltd, 1966–71; Sales Dir, GKN Contractors Ltd, 1971–73. Responsible for negotiating and installing USSR, Polish, Czechoslovak and Romanian plain bearing industries, Polish diesel engine component industry, and several other metallurgical and machining plants in E Europe; Export, Financial and Commercial Adviser to various UK and USA cos. Mem. CBI and Soc. of British Engrs delegns to China, Poland, Yugoslavia and Singapore. Mem. Exec. Council, Russo-British Chamber of Commerce, and of London Chamber of Commerce Russian and Polish sections, 1968–73; Adviser to E European Trade Council, 1969–71. Principal Administrator: Credit and Investments Directorate-Gen., EEC Commn, Luxembourg, 1973–75; Agriculture Directorate-Gen., 1975–76; Fisheries Directorate-Gen., Brussels, 1976–79; Mem., first EEC Vice-Presidential delegn to Poland, 1977. MEP (C) Humberside, 1979–89; Mem., Agriculture and Budgetary Control Cttees, 1979; Chm., Fisheries Working Gp, 1979–84; Vice-Chairman: Fisheries Sub-Cttee, 1984–87; Budgetary Control, 1984–89; Vice-Pres., Eur. Parlt Delegn to China, 1981, 1984, and 1987, Eur. Parlt Delegn to USSR, 1987–89; Chief Whip, EDG, 1987–89. Contested (C) Humberside, Eur. Parly Elecn, 1989. Consultant on E Europe, 1990–; Special Advr on E Europe, Cons. Party, and Consultant to internat. orgns on E Europe, Russia and Central Asia, 1990–. Vice Pres., Yorkshire and Humberside Develt Assoc., 1980–87. Chm., Friends of Poland Assoc., Eur. Parlt, 1982–93. Occasional lectr at Farnham Castle and at American univs on East/West trade, and in Poland and USSR on automotive component manufg technology; broadcaster. Member: RIIA; Anglo-Hellenic Soc. FIMgt (FBIM 1982). Order of European Merit, Luxembourg, 1981. KSG 1990. *Publications:* articles on fishing technology, shipbuilding and East/West trade; translations from Greek, Russian and other languages. *Recreations:* politics, European and Oriental languages, history, opera, music, travel. *Address:* 3 Ridgemount Way, Redhill, Surrey RH1 6JT. *T:* (01737) 213549, *Fax:* (01737) 213263.

BATTISCOMBE, Christopher Charles Richard, CMG 1992; HM Diplomatic Service; retired; *b* 27 April 1940; *s* of late Lt-Col Christopher Robert Battiscombe and Karin Sigrid (*née* Timberg); *m* 1972, Brigid Melita Theresa Lunn; one *s* one *d*. *Educ:* Wellington Coll.; New Coll., Oxford (BA Greats). Entered FO, 1963; ME Centre for Arabic Studies, Shemlan, Lebanon, 1963–65; Third/Second Sec., Kuwait, 1965–68; FCO, 1968–71; First Secretary: UK Delegn, OECD, Paris, 1971–74; UK Mission to UN, New York, 1974–78; Asst Head, Eastern European and Soviet Dept, FCO, 1978–80; Commercial Counsellor: Cairo, 1981–84; Paris, 1984–86; Counsellor, FCO, 1986–90; Ambassador to Algeria, 1990–94; Asst Under-Sec. of State, then Dir (Public Depts), FCO, 1994–97; Ambassador to Jordan, 1997–2000. *Recreations:* golf, ski-ing, tennis. *Clubs:* Kandahar; Temple Golf.

BATTISCOMBE, Mrs (Esther) Georgina, BA; FRSL 1964; author; *b* 21 Nov. 1905; *d* of late George Harwood, MP, Master Cotton Spinner, Bolton, Lancs, and Ellen Hopkinson, *d* of Sir Alfred Hopkinson, KC, MP, First Vice-Chancellor of Manchester Univ.; *m* 1932, Lt-Col Christopher Francis Battiscombe, OBE, FSA (*d* 1964), Grenadier Guards; one *d*. *Educ:* St Michael's Sch., Oxford; Lady Margaret Hall, Oxford. *Publications:* Charlotte Mary Yonge, 1943; Two on Safari, 1946; English Picnics, 1949; Mrs Gladstone, 1956; John Keble (James Tait Black Memorial Prize for best biography of year), 1963; Christina Rossetti, 1965; ed, with M. Laski, A Chaplet for Charlotte Yonge, 1965; Queen Alexandra, 1969; Shaftesbury, 1974; Reluctant Pioneer: The Life of Elizabeth Wordsworth, 1978; Christina Rossetti: a divided life, 1981; The Spencers of Althorp, 1984; Winter Song, 1992. *Recreation:* looking at churches. *Address:* Thamesfield, Wargrave Road, Henley-on-Thames, Oxfordshire RG9 2LX. *T:* (01491) 575760.

BATTISHILL, Sir Anthony (Michael William), GCB 1997 (KCB 1989); Chairman, Student Loans Co. Ltd, since 1998; Chairman, Board of Inland Revenue, 1986–97 (Deputy Chairman, 1985); *b* 5 July 1937; *s* of William George Battishill and Kathleen Rose Bishop; *m* 1961, Heather Frances Lawes; one *d*. *Educ:* Taunton Sch.; Hele's Sch., Exeter; London Sch. of Economics. BSc (Econ). 2nd Lieut, RAEC, 1958–60. Inland Revenue, 1960–63; HM Treasury, 1963–65; Inland Revenue, 1965–76, Asst Sec., 1970; Central Policy Review Staff, 1976–77; Principal Private Sec. to Chancellor of the Exchequer, HM Treasury, 1977–80; Under Sec., HM Treasury, 1980–82, 1983–85, Inland Revenue, 1982–83. Mem. Ct of Governors, LSE, 1987–. CIMgt. *Recreations:* gardening, old maps. *Address:* 4 Highfield Close, West Byfleet, Surrey KT14 6QR.

BATTLE, Dennis Frank Orlando; Commissioner, 1990–98, and Director of Personnel and Finance, 1994–98, HM Customs and Excise; *b* 17 Dec. 1942; *s* of Frank William Orlando and Marion Kathleen Battle; *m* 1965, Sandra Moule; one *s* one *d*. *Educ:* Bedford Modern School. Joined Customs and Excise as Exec. Officer, 1962; Higher Exec. Officer, NBPI, 1967; Sen. Exec. Officer, CS Coll., 1972; returned to Customs and Excise, 1975, Grade 7 1978, Asst Sec. 1985; Dir of Personnel, 1990–94. Non-executive Director: Customs Annuity and Benevolent Fund, 1995–; Sayers Publishing Gp, 1998–; Sentinel Housing Gp, 1998–; consultant on human resources and public sector reform, 1998–. FIPD 1998. *Address:* 96 Prospect Road, Farnborough, Hants GU14 8NS.

BATTLE, John Dominic; MP (Lab) Leeds West, since 1987; *b* 26 April 1951; *s* of John and late Audrey Battle; *m* 1977, Mary Meenan; one *s* two *d*. *Educ:* Leeds Univ. (BA Hons (1st cl.) 1976). Training for RC Priesthood, Upholland Coll., 1969–72; Leeds Univ., 1973–77; Res. Officer to Derek Enright, MEP, 1979–83; Nat. Co-ordinator, Church Action on Poverty, 1983–87. Opposition front-bench spokesman on housing, 1992–94, on science and technology, 1994–95, on energy, 1995–97; Minister of State: (Minister for Energy and Industry), DTI, 1997–99; FCO, 1999–2001. Chm., All Party Gp on Epilepsy, 1993–97; Vice-Chm., All Party Gp on Overseas Develt, 1992–97; Mem., All Party Gp on Homelessness, 1993. *Recreations:* walking, poetry, supporting Leeds United FC. *Address:* House of Commons, SW1A 0AA. *T:* (020) 7219 4201.

BATTLE, Susan, (Sue), OBE 1995; Chief Executive, Birmingham Chamber of Commerce and Industry, since 1999; *b* 7 Aug. 1946; *d* of Harry and Beryl Sagar; *m* 1969, George Henry Battle. *Educ:* Old Hall Sch., Norfolk; Newcastle upon Tyne Coll. of Commerce (HND Business Studies). Statistical Asst to Sales Dir, Procter & Gamble Ltd, 1967–72; Adminr, M & R Internat., Riyadh, 1972–75; Birmingham Chamber of Commerce and Industry: Asst Sec., 1977–80; Head of Home and Economic Dept, 1980–84; Asst Dir, 1984–88; Dep. Chief Exec., 1989–99. *Recreations:* ornithology, the countryside, Islamic history and culture. *Address:* (office) 75 Harborne Road, Edgbaston B15 3DH. *T:* (0121) 454 6171; Apartment 8, Brookfield House, Hackmans Gate Lane, Belbroughton, near Stourbridge, Worcs DY9 2PR.

BATTY, Prof. (John) Michael, PhD; FBA 2001; FRTPI, FCIT; Professor of Spatial Analysis and Planning, and Director, Centre for Advanced Spatial Analysis, University College London, since 1995; *b* 11 Jan. 1945; *s* of Jack Batty and Nell Batty (*née* Marsden); *m* 1969, Susan Elizabeth Howell; one *s*. *Educ:* Quarry Bank Grammar Sch., Liverpool; Univ. of Manchester (BA 1966); UWIST (PhD 1984). FRTPI 1983; FCIT 1990. Asst Lectr, Univ. of Manchester, 1966–69; University of Reading: Res. Asst, 1969–72; Lectr, 1972–74 and 1975–76; Reader, 1976–79; Prof. of City and Regl Planning, 1979–90, Dean, Sch. of Envmtl Design, 1983–86, UC Cardiff; Prof. of Geog., 1990–95, Dir, Nat. Center for Geographic Inf. and Analysis, 1990–95, SUNY, Buffalo. Vis. Asst Prof., Univ. of Waterloo, Ont, 1974; Vis. Fellow, Univ. of Melbourne, 1982; Croucher Fellow, Univ. of Hong Kong, 1986; Vis. Prof., Univ. of Illinois at Urbana-Champaign, 1986; Sir Edward Youde Meml Foundn Vis. Prof., Univ. of Hong Kong, 2001. Ed., Envmt and Planning B, 1981–. Chm., British Section, Regl Sci. Assoc., 1979–81; Mem., Res. Bd, 1980–82, Chm., Planning Cttee, 1980–82, SSRC; Vice-Chm., Envmt and Planning Cttee, ESRC, 1982–84; Mem., Jt Transport Cttee, 1982–85, Mem., Scientific Computing Adv. Panel, 1989–90, SERC; Mem., Cttee on Scientific Computing, NERC, 1988–90; Mem., Computer Bd for Univs and Res. Councils, 1988–90. Mem., Res. Bd, 1979–85, Mem., Exec. Cttee, S Wales Br., 1986–90, RTPI. Member: Univ. Cttee on Integrated Sandwich Courses, 1984–89; Adv. Gp on Computer Graphics, Jt Inf. Systems Cttee, 1996–98. Mem., Res. Quality Assessment Cttee, Assoc. of Univs of Netherlands, 1997–99. FRSA 1983. Award for Technol Progress, Assoc. Geographic Inf., 1998; Back Award, RGS, 1999. *Publications:* Urban Modelling, 1976; (ed) Systems Analysis in Urban Policy-Making and Planning, 1983; (ed) Optimization and Discrete Choice in Urban Systems, 1985; (ed) Advances in Urban Systems Modelling, 1986; Microcomputer Graphics, 1987; (ed) Cities of the 21st Century, 1991; Fractal Cities, 1994; (ed) Cities in Competition, 1995; (ed) Spatial Analysis, 1996. *Recreations:* discovering America, reading, Indian food, Georgian architecture. *Address:* Centre for Advanced Spatial Analysis, University College London, 1-19 Torrington Place, WC1E 6BT. *T:* (020) 7679 1781; 9 White Horse House, 1 Little Britain, EC1A 7BX. *T:* (020) 7600 8186.

BATTY, Paul Daniel; QC 1995; a Recorder, since 1994; *b* 13 June 1953; *s* of late Vincent Batty and of Catherine Batty; *m* 1986, Angela Jane Palmer; one *d*. *Educ:* St Aidan's Grammar Sch., Sunderland; Newcastle upon Tyne Univ. (LLB). Called to the Bar, Lincoln's Inn, 1975; Junior, NE Circuit, 1985; Bar Mess Junior, 1982–85; Asst Recorder, 1991. *Recreations:* boating, angling. *Address:* 33 Broad Chare, Quayside, Newcastle upon Tyne NE1 3DQ. *T:* (0191) 232 0541.

BATTY, Peter Wright; television and film producer, director and writer; Chief Executive, Peter Batty Productions, since 1970; *b* 18 June 1931; *s* of late Ernest Faulkner Batty and Gladys Victoria Wright; *m* 1959, Anne Elizabeth Stringer (*d* 2000); two *s* one *d*. *Educ:* Bede Grammar Sch., Sunderland; Queen's Coll., Oxford. Feature-writer, Financial Times, 1954–56; freelance journalist, 1956–58; Producer, BBC TV, 1958–64: mem. original Tonight team, other prodns incl. The Quiet Revolution, The Big Freeze, The Katanga Affair, Sons of the Navvy Man; Editor, Tonight, 1963–64; Exec. Producer and Associate Head of Factual Programming, ATV, 1964–68: prodns incl. The Fall and Rise of the House of Krupp (Grand Prix for Documentary, Venice Film Fest., 1965; Silver Dove, Leipzig Film Fest., 1965), The Road to Suez, The Suez Affair, Vietnam Fly-in, Battle for the Desert; freelance work for BBC TV, ITV and Channel 4, 1968–. Progs dir., prod and scripted incl. The Plutocrats, The Aristocrats, Battle for Cassino, Battle for the Bulge, Birth of the Bomb, Farouk: last of the Pharaohs, Operation Barbarossa, Superspy, Sunderland's Pride and Passion, A Rothschild and his Red Gold, Search for the Super, Spy Extraordinary, Story of Wine, World of Television, The Rise and Rise of Laura Ashley, The Gospel According to St Michael, Battle for Warsaw, Battle for Dien Bien Phu, Nuclear Nightmares, A Turn Up in a Million, Il Poverello, Swindle!, The Algerian War, Fonteyn and Nureyev: the perfect partnership, The Divided Union, A Time for Remembrance, Swastika over British Soil; prod and scripted 6 episodes World at War series. *Publications:* The House of Krupp, 1966; (with Peter Parish) The Divided Union, 1987; La Guerre d'Algérie, 1989. *Recreations:* walking, reading, listening to music. *Address:* Claremont House, Renfrew Road, Kingston, Surrey KT2 7NT. *T:* (020) 8942 6304. *Club:* Garrick.

BATTY, Sir William (Bradshaw), Kt 1973; TD 1946; Chairman, Ford Motor Co. Ltd, 1972–75, retired (Managing Director, 1968–73); *b* 15 May 1913; *s* of Rowland and Nellie Batty; *m* 1946, Jean Ella Brice; one *s* one *d* (and one *s* decd). *Educ:* Hulme Grammar Sch., Manchester. Served War of 1939–45, RASC (Lt-Col). Apprentice toolmaker, Ford Motor Co. Ltd, Trafford Park, Manchester, 1930; Co. trainee, 1933; Press liaison, Advertising Dept, 1936; Service Dept, 1937; Tractor Sales Dept, 1945; Asst Man., Tractor Dept, 1948; Man., Tractor and Implement Product Planning, 1953; Man., Tractor Div., 1955; Gen. Man., Tractor Gp, 1961; Dir, Tractor Gp, 1963; Dir, Car and Truck Gp, 1964; Exec. Dir, 1963–75. Chairman: Ford Motor Credit Co. Ltd, 1968 (Dir, 1963–); Automotive Finance Ltd, 1970–75; Director: Henry Ford & Son Ltd, Cork, 1965–75; Ford Lusitana SARL, Portugal, 1973–75. Mem., Engineering Industries Council, 1975–76. Pres., SMMT, 1975–76. Hon. LLD Manchester, 1976. FIMgt. *Recreations:* golf, sailing, gardening. *Address:* Glenhaven Cottage, Riverside Road West, Newton Ferrers, South Devon PL8 1AD. *Club:* Royal Western Yacht.

BAUCKHAM, Prof. Richard John, PhD; FBA 1998; Professor of New Testament Studies, St Mary's College, University of St Andrews, since 1992; *b* 22 Sept. 1946; *s* of John Robert Bauckham and Stephania Lilian Bauckham (*née* Wells). *Educ:* Enfield GS; Clare Coll., Cambridge (BA Hons Hist. 1st cl. 1969; MA 1972; PhD 1973). Fellow, St John's Coll., Cambridge, 1972–75; Lectr in Theol., Leeds Univ., 1976–77; Lectr, 1977–87, Reader, 1987–92, in Hist. of Christian Thought, Manchester Univ. Member: Doctrine Commn, C of E, 1990–; Doctrine Cttee, Scottish Episcopal Ch, 1997–. *Publications:* Tudor Apocalypse, 1978; Jude, 2 Peter (commentary), 1983; Moltmann: Messianic theology in the making, 1987; The Bible in Politics, 1989; Word Biblical Themes: Jude, 2 Peter, 1990; Jude and the Relatives of Jesus in the Early Church, 1990; The Theology of the Book of Revelation, 1993; The Climax of Prophecy, 1993; The Theology of Jürgen Moltmann, 1995; The Fate of the Dead, 1998; James: Wisdom of James, Disciple of Jesus the Sage, 1999; God Crucified: monotheism and Christology in the New Testament, 1999; (with Trevor Hart) Hope Against Hope: Christian eschatology in contemporary context, 1999; *edited:* (jtly) Scripture, Tradition and Reason, 1988; (jtly) The Nuclear Weapons Debate: theological and ethical issues, 1989; The Book of Acts in its Palestinian Setting, 1995; The Gospels for All Christians, 1997; God will be All in All: the eschatology of Jürgen Moltmann, 1999; many articles in books and learned jls. *Recreations:* gardening, walking, novels. *Address:* St Mary's College, St Andrews KY16 9JU. *T:* (01334) 462830.

BAUER, family name of **Baron Bauer**.

BAUER, Baron *cr* 1982 (Life Peer), of Market Ward in the City of Cambridge; **Peter Thomas Bauer,** MA; DSc; FBA; Professor of Economics, University of London, at the London School of Economics, 1960–83, now Emeritus Professor of Economics; Fellow of Gonville and Caius College, Cambridge, 1946–60, and since 1968; unmarried. *Educ:* Scholae Piae, Budapest; Gonville and Caius Coll., Cambridge. Reader in Agricultural Economics, University of London, 1947–48; University Lecturer in Economics, Cambridge Univ., 1948–56; Smuts Reader in Commonwealth Studies, Cambridge Univ., 1956–60. Hon. Fellow, LSE, 1997. *Publications:* books and articles on applied economics. *Address:* House of Lords, Westminster, SW1A 0PW. *Clubs:* Garrick, Beefsteak.

BAUGH, John Trevor; Director General of Supplies and Transport (Naval), Ministry of Defence, 1986–93; *b* 24 Sept. 1932; *s* of late Thomas Harold Baugh and of Nellie Baugh (*née* Machin); *m* 1st, 1956, Pauline Andrews (decd); three *s*; 2nd, 1981, Noreen Rita Rosemary Sykes; two step *s*. *Educ:* Queen Elizabeth's Hospital, Bristol. MCIT 1956. Asst Naval Store Officer, Devonport, 1953; Dep. Naval Store Officer, Admiralty, 1959; Armament Supply Officer, Alexandria, 1966; Principal, MoD, Bath, 1970; Supt, RN Store Depot, Copenacre, 1974; Asst Sec., MoD (Navy), 1976, Exec. Dir, 1979; MoD (Army), 1983, Asst Under Sec. of State 1985. *Recreations:* bridge, golf. *Address:* Wonham, Lansdown Road, Bath, Avon BA1 5RB. *Clubs:* Athenæum; Bath Golf.

BAUGHAN, Julian James; QC 1990; a Recorder, since 1985; *b* 8 Feb. 1944; *s* of late Prof. E. C. Baughan, CBE, and Mrs E. C. Baughan. *Educ:* Eton Coll. (King's Schol.); Balliol Coll., Oxford (Brassey Italian Schol.; BA History). Called to Bar, Inner Temple, 1967 (Profumo Schol., Philip Teichman Schol., Major Schol.); Prosecuting Counsel to DTI, 1983–90. *Address:* 13 King's Bench Walk, Temple, EC4Y 7EN.

BAUGHEN, Rt Rev. Michael Alfred; Bishop of Chester, 1982–96; Assistant Bishop, diocese of London, since 1996; *b* 7 June 1930; *s* of Alfred Henry and Clarice Adelaide Baughen; *m* 1956, Myrtle Newcomb Phillips; two *s* one *d*. *Educ:* Bromley County Grammar Sch.; Univ. of London; Oak Hill Theol Coll. BD (London). With Martins Bank, 1946–48, 1950–51. Army, Royal Signals, 1948–50. Degree Course and Ordination Trng, 1951–56; Curate: St Paul's, Hyson Green, Nottingham, 1956–59; Reigate Parish Ch., 1959–61; Candidates Sec., Church Pastoral Aid Soc., 1961–64; Rector of Holy Trinity (Platt), Rusholme, Manchester, 1964–70; Vicar of All Souls, Langham Place, W1,

1970–75; Rector, 1975–82; Area Dean of St Marylebone, 1978–82; a Prebendary of St Paul's Cathedral, 1979–82; Priest-in-charge, St James's, Clerkenwell, 1997–98. Hon. LLD Liverpool, 1994. *Publications:* Moses and the Venture of Faith, 1979; The Prayer Principle, 1981; II Corinthians: a spiritual health-warning to the Church, 1982; Chained to the Gospel, 1986; Evidence for Christ, 1986; Getting through to God, 1992; (with Myrtle Baughen) Your Marriage, 1994; Editor: Youth Praise, 1966; Youth Praise II, 1969; Psalm Praise, 1973; consultant editor, Hymns for Today's Church, 1982; gen. ed, Sing Glory, 1999. *Recreations:* music, railways, touring. *Address:* 99 Brunswick Quay, SE16 7PX.

BAULCOMBE, David Charles, PhD; FRS 2001; Senior Scientist, Sainsbury Laboratory, John Innes Centre, Norwich, since 1988; *b* 7 April 1952; *s* of William (Jim) and Joan Baulcombe; *m* 1976, Rose Eden; one *s* three *d*. *Educ:* Leamington Coll., Leamington Spa; Leeds Univ. (BSc Botany); Edinburgh Univ. (PhD 1977). Postdoctoral Fellow: McGill Univ., Montreal, 1977–78; Univ. of Georgia, Athens, 1979–80; res. scientist, Plant Breeding Inst., Cambridge, 1981–88. Hon. Prof., UEA. Mem., EMBO, 1998. Mem., Norwich Labour Party. Prix des Céréalières de France, 1990. *Publications:* contrib. res. papers and articles on plant genetics, virology and genetic engrg in Nature, Science, Cell, and specialist jls. *Recreations:* sailing, hill-walking, music. *Address:* Sainsbury Laboratory, John Innes Centre, Norwich, Norfolk NR4 7UH. *T:* (01603) 450420. *Club:* Norfolk Punt (Barton, Norfolk).

BAUM, Prof. Michael, ChM; FRCS; Professor of Surgery, 1996–2000, now Emeritus, and Visiting Professor of Medical Humanities, since 2000, University College London; Consultant Surgeon, UCL Hospitals NHS Trust, since 1996; *b* 31 May 1937; *s* of Isidor and Mary Baum; *m* 1965, Judith (*née* Marcus); one *s* two *d*. *Educ:* Univ. of Birmingham (MB, ChB; ChM). FRCS 1965. Lecturer in Surgery, King's College Hosp., 1969–72; Research Fellow, Univ. of Pittsburgh, USA, 1971–72; Reader in Surgery, Welsh National Sch. of Medicine, Cardiff, 1972–78; Hon. Cons. Surgeon, King's College Hosp., 1978–80; Professor of Surgery: KCH Med. Sch., London, 1980–90; Inst. of Cancer Res., Royal Marsden Hosp., 1990–96, Prof. Emeritus, 1996–; Vis. Prof., UCL, 1995–96. Chairman: SE Thames Regional Cancer Organisation, 1988–90; British Breast Gp, 1989–91; Breast Cancer Cttee, UK Co-ordinating Cttee for Cancer Research, 1989–96. Mem., Adv. Cttee on Breast Cancer Screening, DHSS, 1987–95; Specialist Advr, Select Cttee on Health, 1996–98. President: British Oncological Assoc., 1996–98; Eur. Breast Cancer Conf., 2000–02. FRSA 1998. Hon. FRCR 1998. Hon. MD Göteborg, 1986. Celebrating Survival award, 2000. *Publications:* Breast Cancer—The Facts, 1981, 3rd edn 1994; multiple pubns on breast cancer, cancer therapy, cancer biology and the philosophy of science. *Recreations:* painting, sculpting, theatre, reading, philosophizing. *Address:* 2 Cotman Close, NW11 6PT. *T:* (020) 8905 5069. *Clubs:* Royal Society of Medicine, Chelsea Arts.

BAUMAN, Robert Patten; Chairman, BTR, 1998–99 (Deputy Chairman, 1997–98); *b* 27 March 1931; *s* of John Nevan Bauman Jr and Lucille Miller Patten; *m* 1961, Patricia Hughes Jones; one *s* one *d*. *Educ:* Ohio Wesleyan Univ. (BA); Harvard Sch. of Business (MBA). Served USAF, 1955–57. General Foods Corp., 1958–81: Corp. Vice-Pres., 1968; Group Vice-Pres., 1970; Exec. Vice-Pres. and Corp. Dir, 1972–81; Pres., Internat. Ops, 1974–81; Dir, Avco Corp., 1980, Chm. and Chief Exec., 1981–85; Vice-Chm. and Dir, Textron Inc., 1985–86; Chm. and Chief Exec., Beecham Gp, 1986–89; Chief Exec., SmithKline Beecham, 1989–94; Chm., BAe, 1994–98. Director: Cap Cities/ABC Inc., 1986–96; Union Pacific Corp., 1987–2001; CIGNA Corp., 1990–2001; Reuters Holdings, 1993–2000; Russell Reynolds Associates Inc., 1994–; Morgan Stanley Gp Inc., 1996–; Hathaway Holdings Inc., 1996–; Invensys, 1999–. Mem., MRC, 1991–95. Trustee: Ohio Wesleyan Univ., 1982–; Royal Botanic Gardens, Kew, 1990–2000. *Publications:* Plants as Pets, 1982; (jtly) From Promise to Performance, 1996. *Recreations:* growing orchids, tennis, photography, golf. *Clubs:* Queen's; Blind Brook (New York); Walton Heath Golf; Wisley Golf.

BAUMBERG, Prof. Simon, DPhil; Professor of Bacterial Genetics, University of Leeds, since 1996; *b* 5 March 1940; *s* of Pincus and Esther Baumberg; *m* 1963, Ruth Elizabeth Geiger; three *s* (and one *s* decd). *Educ:* St Paul's Sch.; Merton Coll., Oxford (MA; DPhil 1964). University of Leeds: Lectr, 1966–76; Sen. Lectr, 1976–92; Reader, 1992–96. EMBO Long-Term Fellow, Univ. of Wisconsin-Madison, 1975–76. Ed., Jl Gen. Microbiol., 1986–91. Medical Research Council: Chairman: Molecular and Cellular Medicine Bd Grants Cttee B, and Mem., Molecular and Cellular Medicine Bd, 1993–97; Non-Clinical Trng Fellowships and Career Develt Awards Panel, 1997–99; Adv. Bd, 1997–. Genetical Society: Sec., 1978–84; Vice-Pres., 1984–87 and 1996–99; Society for General Microbiology: Mem. Council, 1986–90; Convener, Physiol., Biochem. and Molecular Genetics Gp, 1992–97. *Publications:* (ed jtly) Microbial Products: new approaches, 1989; (ed jtly) Population Genetics of Bacteria, 1995; (ed jtly) Microbial Responses to Light and Time, 1998; (ed jtly) Transport of Molecules across Microbial Membranes, 1999; (ed) Prokaryotic Gene Expression, 1999; contrib. papers to scientific jls. *Recreations:* listening to classical music, playing the piano badly, hill walking, reading. *Address:* School of Biology, University of Leeds, Leeds LS2 9JT. *T:* (0113) 233 3080.

BAUME, Jonathan Edward; General Secretary, Association of First Division Civil Servants, since 1997; *b* 14 July 1953; *s* of late George Frederick Baume and Mary Louisa Baume (*née* Hardwick). *Educ:* Queen Elizabeth Grammar Sch., Wakefield; Keble Coll., Oxford (BA Hons 1974; MA). Oxfordshire CC, 1974–76; Dept of Employment Gp, 1977–87; Orgn and Indust. Relns Dept, TUC, 1987–89; Asst Gen. Sec., 1989–94, Dep. Gen. Sec., 1994–97, FDA. *Recreations:* yoga, post-war jazz, world music, rambling. *Address:* Association of First Division Civil Servants, 2 Caxton Street, SW1H 0QH. *T:* (020) 7343 1111. *Clubs:* Ronnie Scott's; Surrey CC.

BAUR, Christopher Frank; writer and broadcaster; Managing Director, Insider Custom Publishing, since 1997; Director, Insider Group, since 1994; *b* 28 May 1942; *s* of Mrs Marty Stewart (*née* Sigg) and Frank Baur; *m* 1965, Jaqueline Gilchrist; four *s*. *Educ:* Dalhousie Prep. Sch.; Strathallan Sch., Perthshire. Joined Scotsman as copy boy, 1960; trained as journalist; Scotsman's Industrial Reporter, 1963, additionally Scottish Politics, 1972; Financial Times, Scottish corresp., 1973; Scottish political corresp., BBC, 1976; The Scotsman: Asst Editor, 1978, writing on politics and economic affairs; Dep. Editor, 1983–85; Editor, 1985–87; Editor, Scottish Business Insider, 1990–94. *Recreation:* creating. *Address:* 29 Edgehead Village, near Pathhead, Midlothian EH37 5RL. *T:* (01875) 320476.

BAVIN, Alfred Robert Walter, CB 1966; Deputy Secretary, Department of Health and Social Security, 1968–73 (Ministry of Health, 1966–68); *b* 4 April 1917; *s* of late Alfred and late Annie Bavin; *m* 1947, Helen Mansfield (*d* 1987); one *s* three *d*. *Educ:* Christ's Hosp.; Balliol Coll., Oxford. 1st cl. Hon. Mods 1937; 1st cl. Lit. Hum. 1939. Min. of Health, Asst Principal, 1939, Principal, 1946; Cabinet Office, 1948–50; Min. of Health, Principal Private Sec. to Minister, 1951; Asst Sec. 1952; Under-Sec. 1960. Nuffield Home Civil Service Travelling Fellowship, 1956. *Address:* Oakland Court Hotel, Admiralty Road, Felpham, Bognor Regis, West Sussex PO22 7DW. *Clubs:* Athenæum, MCC.

BAVIN, Rt Rev. Timothy John, FRSCM; OSB; *b* 17 Sept. 1935; *s* of Edward Sydney Durrance and Marjorie Gwendoline Bavin. *Educ:* Brighton Coll.; Worcester Coll., Oxford (2nd Cl. Theol., MA); Cuddesdon Coll. Curate, St Alban's Cathedral Pretoria, 1961–64; Chaplain, St Alban's Coll., Pretoria, 1965–68; Curate of Uckfield, Sussex, 1969–71; Vicar of Good Shepherd, Brighton, 1971–73; Dean and Rector of Cathedral of St Mary the Virgin, Johannesburg, 1973–74; Bishop of Johannesburg, 1974–84; Bishop of Portsmouth, 1985–95; monk, OSB, 1996–. Mem., OGS, 1987–97; FRSCM 1991. ChStJ 1975. *Publication:* Deacons in the Ministry of the Church, 1987. *Recreations:* music, gardening. *Address:* Alton Abbey, Alton, Hants GU34 4AP.

BAWDEN, Prof. Charles Roskelly, FBA; Professor of Mongolian, University of London, 1970–84, now Emeritus Professor; *b* 22 April 1924; *s* of George Charles Bawden and Eleanor Alice Adelaide Bawden (*née* Russell); *m* 1949, Jean Barham Johnson; three *s* one *d*. *Educ:* Weymouth Grammar School; Peterhouse, Cambridge (MA, PhD, Dipl. in Oriental Languages). War Service, RNVR, 1943–46. Asst Principal, German Section, Foreign Office, 1948–49; Lectr in Mongolian, SOAS, 1955; Reader in Mongolian, 1962, and Prof., 1970, Univ. of London; Head of Dept of Far East, SOAS, 1970–84; Pro-Director, SOAS, 1982–84. FBA 1971–80, 1985; Mem. corresp., Soc. Finno-Ougrienne 1975. Friendship Medal, Mongolia, 1997. *Publications:* The Mongol Chronicle Altan Tobči, 1955; The Jebtsundamba Khutukhtus of Urga, 1961; The Modern History of Mongolia, 1968, 2nd edn 1989; The Chester Beatty Library: a catalogue of the Mongolian Collection, 1969; Shamans Lamas and Evangelicals: the English missionaries in Siberia, 1985; Mongolian–English Dictionary, 1997; Tales of an Old Lama, 1997; articles and reviews in SOAS Bull., Central Asiatic Jl, Zentralasiatische Studien and other periodicals. *Address:* 19 Richings Way, Iver, Bucks SL0 9DA.

BAWDEN, Nina Mary, (Mrs A. S. Kark), CBE 1995; MA; FRSL; JP; novelist; *b* 19 Jan. 1925; *d* of Charles and Ellalaine Ursula May Mabey; *m* 1st, 1946, Henry Walton Bawden; one *s* (and one *s* decd); 2nd, 1954, Austen Steven Kark, *qv*; one *d*. *Educ:* Ilford County High Sch.; Somerville Coll., Oxford (BA). Asst, Town and Country Planning Assoc., 1946–47. JP Surrey, 1968. Mem., ALCS. Pres., Soc. of Women Writers and Journalists. *Publications: novels:* Who Calls the Tune, 1953; The Odd Flamingo, 1954; Change Here for Babylon, 1955; The Solitary Child, 1956; Devil by the Sea, 1958, 2nd edn 1972 (abridged for children, 1976); Just Like a Lady, 1960; In Honour Bound, 1961; Tortoise by Candlelight, 1963; Under the Skin, 1964; A Little Love, a Little Learning, 1965; A Woman of My Age, 1967; The Grain of Truth, 1969; The Birds on the Trees, 1970; Anna Apparent, 1972; George beneath a Paper Moon, 1974; Afternoon of a Good Woman, 1976 (Yorkshire Post Novel of the Year, 1976); Familiar Passions, 1979; Walking Naked, 1981; The Ice House, 1983; Circles of Deceit, 1987 (televised, 1990); Family Money, 1991 (televised, 1997); A Nice Change, 1997; Ruffian on the Stair, 2001; *for children:* The Secret Passage, 1963; On the Run, 1964; The White Horse Gang, 1966; Squib, 1966; A Handful of Thieves, 1967; The Witch's Daughter, 1968; The Runaway Summer, 1969; Carrie's War, 1975 (Phoenix Award, 1995); The Peppermint Pig, 1975 (Guardian award, 1976); Rebel on a Rock, 1978; The Robbers, 1978; Kept in the Dark, 1982; The Finding, 1985; Princess Alice, 1985; Keeping Henry, 1987; The Outside Child, 1989; Humbug, 1992; The Real Plato Jones, 1993; Granny the Pag, 1995; Off the Road, 1998; *autobiography:* In My Own Time, 1994. *Recreations:* travelling, reading, politics, friends. *Address:* 22 Noel Road, N1 8HA. *T:* (020) 7226 2839; 19 Kapodistriou, Nauplion, Greece 21100. *Clubs:* Oriental, PEN, Society of Authors.

BAWN, Cecil Edwin Henry, CBE 1956; FRS 1952; BSc, PhD; Brunner Professor of Physical Chemistry in the University of Liverpool, 1969–Dec. 1973, now Emeritus (Grant-Brunner Professor of Inorganic and Physical Chemistry, 1948–69); *b* 6 Nov. 1908; British; *m* 1934, Winifred Mabel Jackson; two *s* one *d*. *Educ:* Cotham Grammar Sch., Bristol. Graduated, Univ. of Bristol, 1929; PhD in Chemistry (Bristol), 1932; Asst Lectr in Chemistry, Univ. of Manchester, 1931–34; Lectr in Chemistry, 1934–38; Lectr in Physical Chemistry, Univ. of Bristol, 1938–45; Reader in Physical Chemistry, 1945–49. During War of 1939–45 was in charge of a Physico-Chemical Section in Armament Research Dept, Min. of Supply. Mem., Univ. Grants Cttee, 1965–74. Swinburne Gold Medal, 1966. Hon. DSc: Bradford, 1966; Birmingham, 1968; Bristol, 1974. *Publications:* The Chemistry of High Polymers, 1948; papers in chemical journals. *Address:* Springfields, Stoodleigh, near Tiverton, Devon EX16 9PT. *T:* (01398) 351220.

BAWTREE, Rear Adm. David Kenneth, CB 1993; DL; EurIng, CEng, FIMechE, FIEE; Adviser in Civil Emergencies, Visor Consultants, since 1998; *b* 1 Oct. 1937; *s* of Kenneth Alfred Bawtree and Dorothy Constance Bawtree (*née* Allen); *m* 1962, Ann Cummins; one *s* one *d*. *Educ:* Christ's Hospital; Royal Naval Engineering College. BSc(Eng). Served in HM Ships Maidstone, Jutland, Diamond, Defender, Rothesay, Bristol, and MoD, 1965–76; Staff of C-in-C Fleet, 1979, of DG Weapons, 1981; Dep. Dir, Naval Analysis, 1983; RCDS 1985; Dep. Dir, Op. Requirements (Navy), 1986; Dir, Naval Engrg Training, 1987–90; Flag Officer, and Naval Base Comdr, Portsmouth, 1990–93; Civil Emergencies Advr, Home Office, 1993–97. Dir, Flagship Portsmouth, 1997 (Chm., 2000). Dir, Portsmouth Healthcare NHS Trust, 1993–96; Chm., Portsmouth Hosps NHS Trust, 1996–2001. Pres., Portsmouth Model Boats Display Team., 1992–. Past President: Royal Naval and Royal Albert Yacht Club, Portsmouth; Naval Home Club; RN & RM Children's Home; Royal Naval Squash Rackets Assoc.; Chm., Portsmouth Dockyard Industries, 1997; Past Member: Victory Technical Adv. Cttee; Mary Rose Trust; Portsmouth Naval Base Heritage Trust; Royal Naval Mus.; Trustee: St Mary's Music Foundn, 1990–2001 (Chm., 1990–2001); Portsmouth News Snowball Appeal, 1992–94; HMS Warrior 1860, 1993– (Chm., 1997–); Chm., Hants Foundn for Young Musicians, 1993–. Former Patron, Portsmouth MacMillan Appeal. Almoner, Christ's Hospital, 1998–. Governor: Portsmouth Grammar Sch., 1990– (Chm., 1993–); Penhale First Sch., 1991–. Guildsman, St Bride's, Fleet St, 1997–; Freeman, City of London; Liveryman, Engineers' Co. DL Hants, 1997. *Recreations:* squash, organs and their music, miniature furniture.

BAX, Martin Charles Owen, DM; FRCP; Senior Editor, Mac Keith Press, since 1978; Senior Lecturer, Imperial College School of Medicine, since 1997; *b* 13 Aug. 1933; *s* of Cyril E. O. Bax and E. C. M. Bayne; *m* 1956, Judith Mary Osborne; three *s*. *Educ:* Dauntsey's Sch., Wilts; New Coll., Oxford (MA, BM BCh, DM); Guy's Hosp., London. Lectr, Guy's Med. Sch., 1961–74; Res. Paediatrician, Thomas Coram Res. Unit, St Mary's Hosp., London, 1974–82; Dir, Community Paediatric Res. Unit, St Mary's Hosp. Med. Sch., 1982–85; Med. Dir, Community Paediatric Res. Unit, Westminster Hosp. Med. Sch., later Charing Cross and Westminster Med. Sch., subseq. Imperial Coll. Sch. of Medicine, 1985–. Editor, Ambit Literary & Arts Magazine, 1959–. Folke Bernadette Lectr, Sweden, 1984. Anderson-Aldrich Award, Amer. Acad. of Paediatrics, 1990; Dist. Service Award, Amer. Acad. for Cerebral Palsy & Develt Paediatrics, 1994. *Publications:* The Hospital Ship (novel), 1975; Edmond Went Far Away (for children), 1990; (jtly) Child Development and Child Health, 1990. *Recreations:* tennis, walking. *Address:* 17 Priory Gardens, Highgate, N6 5QY. *T:* (020) 8340 3566. *Clubs:* Chelsea Arts, Royal Society of Medicine.

BAXANDALL, Prof. Michael David Kighley, FBA 1982; Professor of the History of Art, University of California, Berkeley, 1987–96, then Emeritus; *b* 18 Aug. 1933; *o s* of late David Baxandall, CBE; *m* 1963, Katharina Simon; one *s* one *d*. *Educ:* Manchester Grammar Sch.; Downing Coll., Cambridge (MA); Univs of Pavia and Munich. Jun. Res. Fellow, Warburg Inst., 1959–61; Asst Keeper, Dept of Architecture and Sculpture, Victoria and Albert Museum, 1961–65; Warburg Institute, University of London: Lectr in Renaissance Studies, 1965–73; Reader, 1973–81; Prof., History of the Classical Tradition, 1981–88. Slade Prof. of Fine Art, Univ. of Oxford, 1974–75; A. D. White Prof.-at-Large, Cornell Univ., 1982–88. *Publications:* Giotto and the Orators, 1971; Painting and Experience in Fifteenth-Century Italy, 1972; South German Sculpture 1480–1530 in the Victoria and Albert Museum, 1974; The Limewood Sculptors of Renaissance Germany, 1980; Patterns of Intention, 1985; (jtly) Tiepolo and the Pictorial Intelligence, 1994; Shadows and Enlightenment, 1995.

BAXENDALE, Presiley Lamorna, (Mrs R. K. FitzGerald); QC 1992; *b* 31 Jan. 1951; *d* of Geoffrey Arthur Baxendale and late Elizabeth (*née* Stevenson); *m* 1978, Richard Kieran FitzGerald; one *s* one *d*. *Educ:* St Mary's Sch., Wantage; St Anne's Coll., Oxford (BA). Called to the Bar, Lincoln's Inn, 1974, Bencher, 1999; Jun. Counsel to Crown, Common Law, 1991. Member: ICSTIS, 1986–90; Council, Justice, 1994– (Vice Chm. Exec. Cttee, 1994–96). Mem., Ct of Govs, LSE, 1988–. Counsel to Scott Inquiry, 1992–95. *Address:* Blackstone Chambers, Blackstone House, Temple, EC4Y 9BW. *T:* (020) 7583 1770, *Fax:* (020) 7822 7350. *Club:* CWIL.

BAXENDELL, Sir Peter (Brian), Kt 1981; CBE 1972; FREng; FIC; Director, Shell Transport and Trading Co., 1973–95 (Chairman, 1979–85); *b* 28 Feb. 1925; *s* of Lesley Wilfred Edward Baxendell and Evelyn Mary Baxendell (*née* Gaskin); *m* 1949, Rosemary (*née* Lacey); two *s* two *d*. *Educ:* St Francis Xavier's, Liverpool; Royal School of Mines, London (ARSM, BSc; FIC 1983). FREng (FEng 1978). Joined Royal Dutch/Shell Group, 1946; Petroleum Engr in Egypt, 1947, and Venezuela, 1950; Techn. Dir, Shell-BP Nigeria, 1963; Head of SE Asia Div., London, 1966; Man. Dir, Shell-BP Nigeria, 1969; Chm., Shell UK, 1974–79; Man. Dir, 1973, Chm., Cttee of Man. Dirs, 1982–85, Royal Dutch/Shell Gp of Cos; Chm., Shell Canada Ltd, 1980–85; Dir, Shell Oil Co., USA, 1982–85; Chm., Hawker Siddeley Gp, 1986–91 (Dir, 1984–91; Dep. Chm., Jan.–April 1986); Director: Sun Life Assurance Co. of Canada, 1986–97; Inchcape, 1986–93. Mem., UGC, 1983–89. Mem., Governing Body, Imperial Coll., London, 1983–99 (Vice Chm., 1991–99). Hon. DSc: Heriot-Watt, 1982; QUB, 1986; London, 1986; Loughborough, 1987. Commander, Order of Orange-Nassau, 1985. *Publications:* articles on petroleum engrg subjects in scientific jls. *Recreations:* tennis, fishing. *Address:* c/o Shell Centre, SE1 7NA. *T:* (020) 7934 2772.

BAXTER, Canon Dr Christina Ann; Principal, St John's College, Nottingham, since 1997 (Dean, 1988–97); Canon Theologian, Coventry Cathedral, since 1996; Chairman of House of Laity, General Synod of Church of England, since 1995 (Vice-Chairman, 1990–95); *b* 8 March 1947; *d* of Leslie John David and Madge Adeline Baxter. *Educ:* Walthamstow Hall, Sevenoaks, Kent; Durham Univ. (BA, PhD); Bristol Univ. (Cert Ed). Asst Teacher, 1969–73, Head of Religious Educn, 1973–76, John Leggott Sixth Form Coll., Scunthorpe; part-time tutor, St John's Coll., Durham, and Durham research student, 1976–79; Lectr in Christian Doctrine, St John's Coll., Nottingham, 1979–. Lay Canon, Southwell Minster, 2000–. Mem., Archbishops' Council, 1998–. *Recreation:* swimming. *Address:* St John's College, Chilwell Lane, Bramcote, Nottingham NG9 3DS. *T:* (0115) 925 1114; 18 St Michael's Square, Bramcote, Nottingham NG9 3HG. *T:* (0115) 922 4087.

BAXTER, Glen; artist; *b* 4 March 1944; *s* of Charles Baxter and Florence Baxter; *m* 1991, Carole Suzanne Elsa Agis; one *s* one *d*. *Educ:* Leeds Coll. of Art. *Exhibitions:* Gotham Book Mart, NYC, 1974, 1976, 1979; Anthony Stokes Gall., London, 1978, 1980; ICA, 1981; Mus. of Modern Art, Oxford, 1981; Nigel Greenwood Gall., London, 1983, 1985, 1990; Holly Solomon Gall., NY, 1985; Sydney Biennale, Australia, 1986; Samia Saouma, Paris, 1987, 1991; Musée de l'Abbaye Sainte-Croix, Les Sables d'Olonne, France, 1987; Seita Mus., Paris, 1990; Adelaide Fest., 1992; Tanya Rumpff Galerie, Haarlem, 1992; Ginza Art Space, Tokyo, 1994; Wilkinson Fine Art, London, 1994; Les Entrepôts Laydet, Paris, 1995; Nagy Fine Art, Sydney, 1996; Modernism, San Francisco, Gal. de la Châme, Paris, 1998; Artothèque Gal., Angoulême, and Gal. de la Châtre, Palais de Congrès, Paris, Chris Beetles Gall., and Anthony Wilkinson Gall., London, 1999; Lombard Freid Fine Arts, NY, 2001; Galerie Daniel Blau, Munich, 2001. *Publications:* The Works, 1977; Atlas, 1979; The Impending Gleam, 1981; Glen Baxter: his life, 1983; Jodhpurs in the Quantocks, 1986; The Billiard Table Murders, 1990; Returns to Normal, 1992; The Wonder Book of Sex, 1995; 1936 at the Hotel Furkablick, 1997; Glen Baxter's Gourmet Guide, 1997; Blizzards of Tweed, 1999. *Recreations:* marquetry, snood retrieval. *Clubs:* Groucho, Chelsea Arts; Ale and Quail (New York).

BAXTER, Maj.-Gen. Ian Stuart, CBE 1982 (MBE 1973); antiques dealer, since 1990; *b* 20 July 1937; *s* of Charles Baxter and Edith (*née* Trinder); *m* 1961, Meg Bullock; three *d*. *Educ:* Ottershaw Sch. Commissioned RASC, 1958; RCT, 1965; regtl and staff appts UK, NI, Kenya, India, Germany and Falkland Is; sc, Camberley, 1970; ndc, Latimer, 1974; DS, Staff Coll., Camberley, 1975–78; CO, 2nd Armoured Div., Regt RCT, 1978–80; Col AQ Commando Forces, RM, 1980–83 (incl. Falklands Campaign); RCDS, 1984; Dir, Army Recruiting, 1985–87; ACDS (Logistics), 1987–90, retd. Col Comdt, RCT, 1989–93. Dir (non-exec.), Cornwall Community Healthcare NHS Trust, 1990–93; Vice-Chm. (non-exec.), Cornwall HealthCare NHS Trust, 1993–95. Dir (non-exec.), Curnow Care, 1995–. Pres., RCT/RASC Instn, 1993–98. *Recreations:* antique restoration, Rugby. *Address:* c/o Barclays Bank, 50 Fore Street, Callington, Cornwall PL17 7AQ.

BAXTER, John Lawson; DL; *b* 25 Nov. 1939; *s* of John Lawson Baxter and Enid Maud Taggart; *m* 1967; three *s*. *Educ:* Trinity Coll., Dublin; Queen's Univ., Belfast; BA, BComm, LLB; LLM Tulane Univ., New Orleans. Solicitor. Mem. (U) N Ireland Assembly, for N Antrim, 1973–75; Minister of Information, N Ireland Executive, 1974. Chm. (part-time), Industrial Tribunals (NI), 1980–83; Mem., Northern Health and Social Services Board, 1982–. DL Co Londonderry, 1988. *Recreations:* golf, fishing. *Address:* Beardiville, Cloyfin, Coleraine, N Ireland. *T:* (028) 7033 1552.

BAXTER, John Stephen; Head Master, Wells Cathedral School, 1986–2000; *b* 7 Sept. 1939; *s* of George Baxter and Muriel (*née* Firman); *m* 1965, Priscilla Candy; two *s*. *Educ:* Magdalen Coll. Sch., Oxford; Merton Coll., Oxford; Grey Coll., Durham. BA Modern History, Durham; DipEd Oxford. Assistant Master: Cranleigh Sch., 1964–67; Christ's Coll., NZ, 1967–70; Westminster Sch., 1971–86 (Hd of Hist., 1974–79; Hse Master, 1979–81). Educn Consultant, Breakthrough Technologies, 2000–. Ecclesiastical Insce Gp Scholar, 1993; Korea Foundn Fellow, 1993. Res. Asst, H of C, 1971–79; Reader, Edward Arnold, 1980–83. Mem., Admiralty Interview Bd, 1988–. Chairman: SW Div., HMC, 1991; Choir Schs Assoc., 1995–97; Nat. Assoc. of Music and Ballet Schs, 1998–2000. Governor: St Aubyn's Sch., 1978–95; Truro Sch., 2000–; Trustee, Commonwealth Linking Trust, 1972–95; Member, Board of Management: MusicSpace, 1988–; British Sch. of Brussels, 2000–. Mem., NYO, 1986–2000. Page Schol., ESU, 1998. MIMgt 1991; FRSA 1990. Freeman, City of London, 1991; Liveryman, Musicians' Co., 1991–. *Publications:* (contrib.) History of Lords and Commons Cricket, 1989; papers and articles in educn jls. *Recreations:* music, Cornish history, golf, sport (GB Olympic Hockey Squad, Oxon; Capt., Oxon U19 Rugby; Minor Counties Cricket, Cornwall Veterans Cricket). *Address:* Lowerdale, Daymer Lane, Trebetherick, Cornwall PL27 6SA. *T:* (01208) 863613. *Clubs:* MCC (Mem., Indoor Sch. Cttee, 1976–86); Vincent's (Oxford); Cornish Choughs, St Minver Cricket, St Enodoc Golf, (Cornwall).

BAXTER, John Walter, CBE 1974; Consultant, G. Maunsell & Partners (Partner, 1955, Senior Partner, 1959–80); *b* 4 June 1917; *s* of late J. G. Baxter and late D. L. Baxter (*née* Phelps); *m* 1941, Jessie, *d* of late T. Pimblott; one *d*. *Educ:* Westminster City Sch.; City and Guilds Engrg College. BSc(Eng), FCGI, FEng, FICE, FRSA. Civil Engineer: Trussed Concrete Steel Co. Ltd, 1936–41; Shell Refining Co. Ltd, 1941–52; Maunsell Posford & Pavry, 1952–55. President: ICE, 1976–77 (Vice-Pres., 1973–76, Mem. Council, 1963–68 and 1970–79); Smeatonian Soc. of Civil Engrs, 1986; Vice-Chm., ACE, 1979–80, Chm., 1980–81. *Publications:* contrib. Proc. ICE. *Address:* 27 Govers Meadow, Colyton, Devon EX24 6PG. *T:* (01297) 552914.

BAXTER, Kenneth Peter; Director, KPMG, since 1996; *b* 23 Oct. 1943; *s* of P. F. Baxter; *m* 1973, Pamela Annabel Marr; two *s* one *d*. *Educ:* Fort St Boys' High Sch.; Univ. of Sydney (BEc). Farming columnist and press sec., 1972–80; Dir, Corporate Affairs, Philip Morris Ltd and Asst Man. Dir, Philip Morris Aust. Ltd, 1981–82; Cllr, Aust. Rural Adjustment Unit, 1982–87; Mem., Aust. Egg Bd, 1983–85; Man. Dir, NSW Egg Corp., 1983–88; Dir, Grain Handling Authy, NSW, 1986–89; Chairman: Good Food Products Aust. Pty Ltd, 1986–88; Aust. Dairy Res. Council, 1986–; Darling Harbour Authy, 1989–90; Dairy R&D Corp., 1990–92; Aust. Dairy Ltd, 1992–; Aust. Dairy Corp., 1992–98; Director: Thai Dairy Ind. Co. Ltd, 1992–98; Hydro Electric Corp. of Tasmania, 1996–. Dep. Dir-Gen., Premier's Dept, NSW, 1988–92; Sec., Dept of the Premier and Cabinet, Vic, 1992–95; Dir-Gen., Premier's Dept, NSW, 1995–96. Mem., Sydney Orgng Cttee for Olympic Games, 1995–96. Comr, Aust. Nat. Rlys Commn, 1997–98. Dir, Baker Med. Res. Foundn, 1996–98. FAICD 1980; FAIM 1985. *Publications:* Wool Marketing in New Zealand, 1967, 2nd edn 1972; Statutory Marketing Authorities, 1988. *Recreations:* rowing, sailing, surf life-saving, reading. *Address:* KPMG, 45 Clarence Street, Sydney, NSW 2000, Australia. *T:* (2) 93357513. *Clubs:* Melbourne (Victoria); Royal Sydney Yacht Squadron (Sydney); Mosman Rowing.

BAXTER, Prof. Murdoch Scott, PhD, CChem, FRSC; FRSE; scientific consultant; Founder and Chief Editor, Journal of Environmental Radioactivity, since 1983; *b* 12 March 1944; *s* of John Sawyer Napier Baxter and Margaret Hastie Baxter (*née* Murdoch); *m* 1968, Janice Henderson; one *s*. *Educ:* Univ. of Glasgow. BSc Hons Chem. 1966, PhD Geochem. 1969. Research Fellow, State Univ. of NY (Noble gas history of lunar rocks and meteorites), 1969–70; Lectr, Dept of Chemistry, Univ. of Glasgow (geochem., radiochem. and envtl radioactivity), 1970–85; Vis. Consultant, IAEA (nuclear waste disposal), 1981–82; Dir, Scottish Univs Res. and Reactor Centre, 1985–90; Dir, Marine Envmnt Lab. (formerly Internat. Lab. of Marine Radioactivity), IAEA, 1990–97; Personal Chair, Univ. of Glasgow, 1985–95. Member: Challenger Soc. for Marine Sci., 1975–; Scottish Assoc. for Marine Sci., 1975–. FRSE 1989; Fellow, Internat. Union of Eco-Ethics, 1998; Hon. Mem. and Advr, Internat. Union of Radioecol., 1999–; Advr, Inst. Nuclear Technol., Portugal, 2000–. Mem., Scotch Malt Whisky Soc. Ed., Radioactivity in the Environment series, 1999–; Associate Ed., TheScientificWorld, virtual jl. Chevalier, Order of St Charles (Monaco), 1997. *Publications:* numerous papers to professional jls. *Recreations:* hill walking, golf, sailing, sport watching, Queen's Park FC. *Address:* Ampfield House, Clachan Seil, Argyll PA34 4TL. *T:* and *Fax:* (01852) 300351; *e-mail:* baxter@j-e-r.demon.co.uk.

BAXTER, Raymond Frederic, FRSA; broadcaster and writer; *b* 25 Jan. 1922; *s* of Frederick Garfield Baxter and Rosina Baxter (*née* Rivers); *m* 1945, Sylvia Kathryn (*née* Johnson) (*d* 1996), Boston, Mass; one *s* one *d*. *Educ:* Ilford County High Sch. Joined RAF, 1940; flew Spitfires with 65, 93 and 602 Sqdns, in UK, Med. and Europe. Entered Forces Broadcasting in Cairo, still as serving officer, 1945; civilian deputy Dir BFN BBC, 1947–49; subseq. short attachment West Region and finally joined Outside Broadcast Dept, London; with BBC until 1966; Dir, Motoring Publicity, BMC, 1967–68. Member Cttee of Management: RNLI, 1979–97 (Vice Pres., 1987–97; Life Vice Pres., 1997); Air League, 1980–85. Hon. Freeman, City of London, 1978; Liveryman, GAPAN, 1983 (Award of Merit, 1994–95). Hon. Admiral, Assoc. of Dunkirk Little Ships, 1982–. CRAeS 1991. *Publications:* (with James Burke and Michael Latham) Tomorrow's World, Vol. 1, 1970, Vol. 2, 1971; Farnborough Commentary, 1980; film commentaries, articles and reports on motoring and aviation subjects, etc. *Recreations:* motoring, boating. *Address:* The Green Cottage, Wargrave Road, Henley-on-Thames, Oxon RG9 3HX. *T:* (01491) 571081. *Clubs:* Royal Air Force, British Racing Drivers, etc.

BAXTER, Prof. Rodney James, FRS 1982; FAA 1977; Professor in the Department of Theoretical Physics, Institute of Advanced Studies, and in the School of Mathematical Sciences, Australian National University, since 1981; *b* 8 Feb. 1940; *s* of Thomas James Baxter and Florence A. Baxter; *m* 1968, Elizabeth Phillips; one *s* one *d*. *Educ:* Bancroft's Sch., Essex; Trinity Coll., Cambridge; Australian National Univ. Reservoir Engineer, Iraq Petroleum Co., 1964–65; Research Fellow, ANU, 1965–68; Asst Prof., Mathematics Dept, Massachusetts Inst. of Technology, 1968–70; Fellow, ANU, 1970–81; Royal Soc. Res. Prof., 1992, Sen. Fellow, 1992–, Isaac Newton Inst. for Mathematical Scis, Cambridge Univ. Pawsey Medal, Aust. Acad. of Science, 1975; Boltzmann Medal, IUPAP, 1980; Heineman Prize, Amer. Inst. of Physics, 1987; Harrie Massey Medal, Inst. of Physics, 1994. *Publications:* Exactly Solved Models in Statistical Mechanics, 1982; contribs to Proc. Royal Soc., Jl of Physics A, Physical Rev., Statistical Physics, Annals of Physics. *Recreation:* theatre. *Address:* Theoretical Physics IAS, Australian National University, Canberra, ACT 0200, Australia. *T:* (2) 62492968.

BAXTER, Roger George, PhD; FRAS; UK boarding school consultant; Partner, Select Education (formerly Select Education and Select Consultants), since 1995; *b* 21 April 1940; *s* of late Rev. Benjamin George Baxter and Gweneth Muriel Baxter (*née* Causer); *m* 1967, Dorothy Ann Cook; one *s* one *d*. *Educ:* Handsworth Grammar Sch., Birmingham; Univ. of Sheffield (BSc, PhD). Junior Research Fellow, Univ. of Sheffield, 1965–66, Lectr, Dept of Applied Mathematics, 1966–70; Asst Mathematics Master, Winchester Coll., 1970–81, Under Master, 1976–81; Headmaster, Sedbergh Sch., 1982–95. Governor: Bramcote Sch., Scarborough, 1982–95; Hurworth Hse Sch., Darlington, 1982–95; Cathedral Choir Sch., Ripon, 1984–95; Mowden Hall Sch., Northumberland, 1984–96; Cundall Manor Sch., York, 1988–98; Durham Sch., 1995–; Bow Sch., Durham, 1995–. Member: HMC Academic Policy Cttee, 1985–90; Common Entrance Board, 1989–94. Mem. Ct, Univ. of Lancaster, 1994–95. Overseas Mem., British Business Gp Dubai & Northern Emirates, 1999–. Church Warden, Cartmel Priory, 1997–. Freeman, City of London, 1992; Liveryman, Gunmakers' Co., 1992–. *Publications:* various papers on numerical studies in magnetoplasma diffusion with applications to the F-2 layer of the ionosphere. *Recreations:* opera, music, cooking, wine. *Address:* The Rivelin, Lindale, Grange-over-Sands, Cumbria LA11 6LJ. *T:* and *Fax:* (01539) 535129; *e-mail:* baxterrg@aol.com.

BAXTER, William T., BCom Edinburgh; Professor of Accounting, London School of Economics, 1947–73, Hon. Fellow 1978; *b* 27 July 1906; *s* of W. M. Baxter and Margaret Threipland; *m* 1st, 1940, Marjorie Allanson (*d* 1971); one *s* one *d*; 2nd, 1973, Leena-Kaisa Laitakari-Kaila. *Educ:* George Watson's Coll.; Univ. of Edinburgh (Hon. Fellow, 1994). Chartered Accountant (Edinburgh), 1930; Commonwealth Fund Fellow, 1931, at Harvard Univ.; Lectr in Accounting, Univ. of Edinburgh, 1934; Prof. of Accounting, Univ. of Cape Town, 1937. Visiting Professor: Columbia, 1958–59; Baruch, 1978–79, 1982–83. Hon. DLitt: Kent at Canterbury, 1974; Heriot-Watt, 1976; Hon. DSc Buckingham, 1983; Hon. DSc(Econ) Hull, 1977. *Publications:* Income Tax for Professional Students, 1936; The House of Hancock, 1945; Depreciation, 1971; Accounting Values and Inflation, 1975; Collected Papers on Accounting, 1979; Inflation Accounting, 1984; Accounting Theory, 1996. *Address:* 1 The Ridgeway, NW11 8TD. *T:* (020) 8455 6810.

BAYCROFT, Rt Rev. John Arthur; Director of the Anglican Centre in Rome, and Archbishop of Canterbury's Representative to the Holy See, 1999–2001; *b* 2 June 1933; *s* of Robert Baycroft and Mary Alice (*née* Williams); *m* 1955, Joan, *d* of V. Lake; one *s* two *d*. *Educ:* Sir William Turner Sch.; Christ's Coll., Cambridge (Synge Schol.) (BA 1954; MA 1958); Ripon Hall, Oxford; Trinity Coll., Toronto (BD 1959). Ordained deacon, 1955, priest, 1956; Rector, Loughborough, Ont, 1955–57; Asst Rector, St Matthew's, Ottawa, 1957–62; Rector: Perth, Ont, 1962–67; St Matthias, Ottawa, 1967–84; Christchurch Cathedral, and Dean of Ottawa, 1984–86; Suffragan Bishop of Ottawa, 1985–93; Bishop of Ottawa, 1993–99. Hon. DD: Montreal Diocesan Theol Coll., 1988; Huron Coll., 1997; DSLitt (*jur. dig.*) Thornloe Univ., 1991. *Publications:* The Anglican Way, 1980; The Eucharistic Way, 1982; The Way of Prayer, 1983; numerous articles in jls. *Recreations:* theatre, art, ballet. *Clubs:* National Press, Rideau (Ottawa).

BAYDA, Hon. Edward Dmytro; Chief Justice of Saskatchewan, since 1981; *b* 9 Sept. 1931; *s* of Dmytro Andrew Bayda and Mary Bilinski; *m* 1953, Marie-Thérèse Yvonne Gagné; one *s* five *d*. *Educ:* Univ. of Saskatchewan (BA 1951, LLB 1953). Called to the Bar, Saskatchewan, 1954; QC (Sask) 1966. Senior Partner, Bayda, Halvorson, Scheibel & Thompson, 1966–72. Judge, Court of Queen's Bench, 1972; Justice, Court of Appeal, 1974. Hon. LLD Saskatchewan, 1989. KM 1975. *Address:* (home) 3000 Albert Street, Regina, SK S4S 3N7, Canada. *T:* (306) 5862126; (chambers) Court House, 2425 Victoria Avenue, Regina, SK S4P 3V7. *T:* (306) 7875415.

BAYFIELD, Rabbi Anthony Michael; Chief Executive, Reform Movement and Reform Synagogues of Great Britain, since 1994; *b* 4 July 1946; *s* of Ronald Bayfield and Sheila (*née* Mann); *m* 1969, Linda Gavinia (*née* Rose); one *s* two *d*. *Educ:* Royal Liberty Sch., Gidea Park; Magdalene Coll., Cambridge (MA (Hons) Law); Leo Baeck Coll., London (Rabbinic degree). Rabbi, NW Surrey Synagogue, 1972–82; Dir, Sternberg Centre for Judaism (Manor House Trust), 1983–. Dir, Advancement of Jewish Educn Trust, 1987–93; Co-ordinator of Supervisors, 1987–93, Lectr in Homiletics, Leo Baeck Coll., 1992–96. Chairman: Assembly of Rabbis, Reform Synagogues of GB, 1980–82; Council of Reform and Liberal Rabbis, 1984–86. Founder Editor, Manna (Qly Jl of Progressive Judaism), 1983–. *Publications:* Churban: the murder of the Jews of Europe, 1981; (ed) Dialogue with a Difference, 1992; Sinai, Law and Responsible Autonomy: Reform Judaism and the Halakhic tradition, 1993; articles in European Judaism, Brit. Jl of Religious Educn, Church Times. *Recreations:* family life, reading, walking, Essex CCC, suffering with West Ham United FC. *Address:* Reform Synagogues of Great Britain, Sternberg Centre for Judaism, 80 East End Road, Finchley, N3 2SY. *T:* (020) 8349 4731, (020) 8346 2288.

BAYLEY, Gordon Vernon, CBE 1976; FIA, FIMA, FSS; General Manager and Actuary, National Provident Institution, 1964–85; *b* 25 July 1920; *s* of late Capt. Vernon Bayley, King's Regt, and Mrs Gladys Maud Bayley; *m* 1945, Miriam Allenby, *d* of late Frederick Walter Ellis and Miriam Ellis, Eastbourne; one *s* two *d*. *Educ:* Abingdon. Joined HM Forces, 1940; commissioned Royal Artillery, Major 1945. Asst Actuary, Equitable Life Assurance Soc., 1949; Partner, Duncan C. Fraser and Co. (Actuaries), 1954–57; National Provident Institution: Assistant Sec., 1957, Joint Sec., 1959; Dir, 1970–94. Chm., Swiss Reinsurance Co. (UK), 1985–92; Dir, TR Industrial and Gen. Trust PLC, 1983–88. Mem., Occupational Pensions Bd, 1973–74. Member: Cttee to Review the Functioning of Financial Institutions, 1977–80; Companies House Steering Bd, 1988–90. Institute of Actuaries: Fellow, 1946; Hon. Sec., 1960–62; Vice-Pres., 1964–67; Pres., 1974–76; Chm., Life Offices Assoc., 1969–70 (Dep. Chm., 1967–68); Gold Medal, 1985. Chm., Bd of Governors, Abingdon Sch., 1979–83. *Publications:* contribs to Jl Inst. Actuaries, Jl Royal Statistical Soc. *Recreation:* sailing. *Address:* The Old Manor, Witley, Surrey GU8 5QW. *T:* (01428) 682301. *Clubs:* Athenæum, English Speaking Union; Sea View Yacht.

BAYLEY, Hugh; MP (Lab) City of York, since 1997 (York, 1992–97); *b* 9 Jan. 1952; *s* of Michael and Pauline Bayley; *m* 1984, Fenella Jeffers; one *s* one *d*. *Educ:* Haileybury Sch.; Univ. of Bristol (BSc); Univ. of York (BPhil). Dist Officer, 1975–77, Nat. Officer, 1977–82, NALGO; Gen. Sec., Internat. Broadcasting Trust, 1982–86; Lectr in Social Policy, 1986–87, Res. Fellow in Health Econs, 1987–92, Univ. of York. Councillor, London Bor. of Camden, 1980–86. Mem., York HA, 1988–90. PPS to Sec. of State for Health, 1997–98; Parly Under-Sec. of State, DSS, 1999–2001. Mem., Select Cttee on Health, 1992–97, on Internat. Develt, 2001–. UK delegate to N Atlantic Assembly, 1997–99. Chm., Yorks Region, Fabian Soc., 1988–97. *Publication:* The Nation's Health, 1995. *Address:* 59 Holgate Road, York YO24 4AA. *T:* (01904) 623713.

BAYLEY, Prof. John Oliver, CBE 1999; FBA 1990; Warton Professor of English Literature, and Fellow of St Catherine's College, University of Oxford, 1974–92; *b* 27 March 1925; *s* of F. J. Bayley; *m* 1st, 1956, Dame Jean Iris Murdoch, DBE, CLit (*d* 1999); 2nd, 2000, Audhild Villers. *Educ:* Eton; New Coll., Oxford. 1st cl. hons English Oxon 1950. Served in Army, 1943–47. Mem., St Antony's and Magdalen Colls, Oxford, 1951–55; Fellow and Tutor in English, New Coll., Oxford, 1955–74. *Publications:* The Romantic Survival: A Study in Poetic Evolution, 1956; The Characters of Love, 1961; Tolstoy and the Novel, 1966; Pushkin: A Comparative Commentary, 1971; The Uses of Division: unity and disharmony in literature, 1976; An Essay on Hardy, 1978; Shakespeare and Tragedy, 1981; The Order of Battle at Trafalgar, 1987; The Short Story: Henry James to Elizabeth Bowen, 1988; Housman's Poems, 1992; Iris: a memoir of Iris Murdoch, 1998; Iris and the Friends: a year of memories, 1999; Widower's House, 2001; Hand Luggage (anthology), 2001; *fiction:* In Another Country, 1954; trilogy: Alice, 1994; The Queer Captain, 1995; George's Lair, 1996; The Red Hat, 1997.

BAYLEY, Nicola Mary; writer, artist and illustrator; *b* 18 Aug. 1949; *d* of Percy Harold Bayley and Ann Barbara Crowder; *m* 1978, Alan John Howard Hilton, *qv*; one *s*. *Educ:* Farnborough Hill Convent College; St Martin's Sch. of Art (DipAD); Royal College of Art (MA Illus.). *Publications: written and illustrated:* Nicola Bayley's Book of Nursery Rhymes, 1975; One Old Oxford Ox, 1977; Copy Cats (5 books), 1984; As I was Going Up and Down, 1985; Hush-a-bye Baby, 1985; *compiled and illustrated:* The Necessary Cat, 1998; *illustrated:* Tyger Voyage, 1976; Puss in Boots, 1976; La Corona and the Tin Frog, 1979; The Patchwork Cat, 1981; The Mouldy, 1983; Merry Go Rhymes (4 books), 1987; The Mousehole Cat, 1990; (with Jan Mark) Fun with Mrs Thumb, 1993. *Recreations:* watching the garden, opera, sleeping, cats. *Address:* c/o Walker Books, 87 Vauxhall Walk, SE11 5HJ. *Club:* Art Workers Guild.

BAYLEY, Lt-Comdr Oscar Stewart Morris; RN retd; *b* 15 April 1926; *s* of late Rev. J. H. S. Bayley; *m* Pamela Margaret Harrison (one *s* one *d* by a former marriage). *Educ:* St John's Sch., Leatherhead; King James's Grammar Sch., Knaresborough. Called to Bar, Lincoln's Inn, 1959. Entered RN, 1944: Ceylon, 1956–58; Supply Off., HMS Narvik and Sqdn Supply Off., 5th Submarine Div., 1960–62; Sec. to Comdr British Forces Caribbean Area, 1962–65; retd from RN at own request, 1966. Legal Asst (Unfair Competition), The Distillers Co. Ltd, 1966–68; Clerk, Fishmongers' Co., 1968–73; Accountant, Hawker Siddeley Gp, 1978–81, John Lewis Partnership, 1981–82. Dir, Seed Oysters (UK) Ltd. Clerk to Governors of Gresham's Sch., Holt; Hon. Sec., Salmon and Trout Assoc. and of Shellfish Assoc. of Great Britain; Vice-Chm., National Anglers' Council; Secretary: Atlantic Salmon Research Trust; City and Guilds of London Art Sch. Ltd, 1968–73; Nat. Assoc. of Pension Funds Investment Protection Cttee, 1974–75. Dir and Chief Sec., The Royal Life Saving Soc., 1976–78: Reader: All Saints Church, Footscray, 1989; St Andrew's Church, Orpington, Kent, 1994; St Botolph's Ch, Lullingstone, Kent, 1999; Chm., Sidcup Council of Churches, 1990–92. *Address:* 244 Bexley Lane, Sidcup, Kent DA14 4JG.

BAYLEY, Peter Charles; Emeritus Professor, University of St Andrews; Emeritus Fellow, University College, Oxford; *b* 25 Jan. 1921; *y s* of late William Charles Abell Bayley and Irene Evelyn Beatrice (*née* Heath); *m* 1951, Patience (marr. diss. 1980), *d* of late Sir George (Norman) Clark and Lady Clark; one *s* two *d*. *Educ:* Crypt Sch., Gloucester; University Coll., Oxford (Sidgwick Exhibnr; MA 1st Cl. Hons English, 1947). Served RA and Intell. Corps (India), 1941–45. Jun. Fellow, University Coll., Oxon, 1947; Fellow and Praelector in English, 1949–72 (at various times Keeper of Coll. Buildings, Domestic Bursar, Tutor for Admissions, Librarian, Editor of University Coll. Record); Univ. Lectr in English, 1952–72; Proctor, 1957–58; Master of Collingwood Coll. and Lectr, Dept of English, Univ. of Durham, 1971–78; Berry Prof. and Head of Dept of English, Univ. of St Andrews, 1978–85. Vis. Reader, Birla Inst., Pilani, Rajasthan, India, 1966; Vis. Lectr, Yale Univ., and Robert Bates Vis. Fellow, Jonathan Edwards Coll., 1970; Brown Distinguished Vis. Prof., Univ. of the South, Sewanee, Tenn, 1978; Brown Distinguished Vis. Lectr in British Studies, Vanderbilt Univ., Univ. of the South, Sewanee, etc, 1985. Oxford Univ. Corresp., The Times, 1960–63. Chairman: Oxford Univ. Theatre Fund, 1959–61; Oxford Playhouse Mgt Cttee, 1961–65; Founder Mem., Cherwell Family Housing Trust, later Cherwell Housing Trust, Oxford, 1967. *Publications:* Edmund Spenser, Prince of Poets, 1971; 'Casebook' on Spenser's The Faerie Queene, 1977; Poems of Milton, 1982; An ABC of Shakespeare, 1985; University College, Oxford: a guide and brief history, 1992; edited: Spenser, The Faerie Queene: Book II, 1965; Book I, 1966; Loves and Deaths: short stories by 19th century novelists, 1972; contributed to: Patterns of Love and Courtesy, 1966; Oxford Bibliographical Guides, 1971; C. S. Lewis at the Breakfast Table, 1979; Encyclopaedia of Oxford, 1988; Literature East and West, 1995; Sir William Jones 1746–94, 1998; articles in TLS, Rev. of English Studies, Essays in Criticism, Critical Qly. *Recreations:* nature, art. *Address:* 63 Oxford Street, Woodstock, Oxford OX20 1TJ.

BAYLEY, Prof. Peter James; Drapers Professor of French, since 1985, and Fellow of Gonville and Caius College, since 1971, Cambridge University; *b* 20 Nov. 1944; *s* of John Henry Bayley and Margaret Burness, Portreath, Cornwall. *Educ:* Redruth County Grammar Sch.; Emmanuel Coll., Cambridge (Kitchener Schol., 1963–66; 1st cl. Hons Mod. and Med. Langs Tripos, 1964 and 1966; MA 1970; PhD 1971); Ecole Normale Supérieure, Paris (French Govt Schol., 1967–68). Cambridge University: Fellow of Emmanuel Coll., 1969–71; Coll. Lectr, Gonville and Caius Coll., 1971–85; Tutor, 1973–79; Praelector Rhetoricus, 1980–86; Univ. Asst Lectr in French, 1974–78; Univ. Lectr, 1978–85; Head, Dept of French, 1983–96. Hon. Sen. Res. Fellow, Inst. of Romance Studies, London Univ., 1990. Vice-Pres., Assoc. of Univ. Profs of French, 1989–97. Pres., Soc. for French Studies, 1990–92; deleg., and Mem. Exec., Univ. Council for Modern Langs, 1994–96. Officier des Palmes Académiques, 1988. *Publications:* French Pulpit Oratory 1598–1650, 1980; (ed with D. Coleman) The Equilibrium of Wit: essays for Odette de Mourgues, 1982; (ed) Selected Sermons of the French Baroque, 1983; contributions to: Critique et création littéraires en France (ed Fumaroli), 1977; Bossuet: la Prédication au XVIIe siècle (ed Collinet and Goyet), 1980; Catholicism in Early Modern History: a guide to research (ed O'Malley), 1988; Convergences: rhetoric and poetic in Seventeenth-Century France (ed Rubin and McKinley), 1989; New Oxford Companion to Literature in French (ed France), 1995; Cambridge Rev., Dix-Septième Siècle, French Studies, Mod. Lang. Rev., Studies on Voltaire and the Eighteenth Century, etc. *Recreations:* Spain, food and wine, gardening, English ecclesiastical history. *Address:* Gonville and Caius College, Cambridge CB2 1TA. *T:* (01223) 332439; (vacations) The White House, Hackleton, Northants NN7 2AD. *T:* (01604) 870059.

BAYLEY, Stephen Paul; design consultant and writer; Principal, EYE-Q Ltd, since 1990; *b* 13 Oct. 1951; *s* of Donald and Anne Bayley; *m* 1981, Flo Fothergill; one *s* one *d*. *Educ:* Quarry Bank Sch., Liverpool; Manchester Univ.; Liverpool Univ. Sch. of Architecture. Lecturer: Hist. of Art, Open Univ., 1974–76; Hist. and Theory of Art, Univ. of Kent, 1976–80; Dir, Conran Foundn, 1981–89; Dir, Boilerhouse Project, in V&A Mus., 1982–86; Founding Dir, later Chief Exec., Design Mus., 1986–89. A Contributing Editor: GQ, 1991–; Management Today, 1999–. Mem., Design Cttee, LRT, 1989–91. Has lectured at: Nat. Inst. of Design, Ahmedabad; India Inst. of Technol., Bombay; Art Gall. of WA, Perth; Nat. Gall. of Victoria, Melbourne; Salon de l'Automobile, Geneva; Sony Design Center, Tokyo; Internat. Expo, Nagoya; Art Coll. Center of Design (Europe), La Tour-de-Peilz, Switzerland; RIBA; RSA; RCA; and at univs, colls and museums throughout Britain and Europe. Magazine Columnist of the Year, PPA, 1995. Chevalier de l'Ordre des Arts et des Lettres (France), 1989. *Publications:* In Good Shape, 1979; The Albert Memorial, 1981; Harley Earl and the Dream Machine, 1983; The Conran Directory of Design, 1985; Sex, Drink and Fast Cars, 1986; Twentieth Century Style and Design, 1986; Commerce and Culture, 1989; Taste, 1991; Beefeater 2-Day Guide to London, 1993; Labour Camp: the failure of style over substance, 1998; Moving Objects, 1999; General Knowledge, 2000; numerous Open Univ. books, and Boilerhouse/Design Mus. catalogues inc. Art and Industry, 1982; Sony Design, 1982; Taste, 1983; Robots, 1984; National Characteristics, 1985; Coke, 1986. *Recreations:* indistinguishable from work, but both involve words, pictures, food, drink, sport and travel. *Address:* (office) 176 Kennington Park Road, SE11 4BT. *T:* (020) 7820 8899. *Clubs:* Savile, Hurlingham.

BAYLIS, Prof. Peter Howard, MD; FRCP, FMedSci; Dean of Medicine, University of Newcastle upon Tyne, since 1997; *b* 9 Sept. 1943; *s* of late Derek Baylis and of Lore Baylis; *m* 1968, Dr Susan Mary While; one *s* two *d*. *Educ:* Wallington Grammar Sch.; Univ. of Bristol (BSc, MB ChB, MD). FRCP 1983. Trng in medicine, endocrinology and research, Queen Elizabeth Hosp., Birmingham, 1970–76; Clinical Endocrinology Fellow, Univ. of

Indiana, 1976–78; Lectr in Medicine, Univ. of Birmingham, 1978–80; Consultant Physician and Sen. Lectr in Medicine, Royal Victoria Infirmary, Newcastle, 1980–90; Prof. of Exptl Medicine and Clinical Sub-Dean, Med. Sch., Univ. of Newcastle upon Tyne, 1990–97. Founder FMedSci, 1998. *Publications:* (with P. Padfield) The Posterior Pituitary; hormone secretion in health and disease, 1985; (jtly) Case Presentations in Endocrinology and Diabetes, 1988; Salt and Water Homeostasis in Health and Disease, 1989; numerous original res. articles and book chapters on salt water balance. *Recreations:* long-distance running, classical music, reading. *Address:* The Medical School, University of Newcastle upon Tyne, Framlington Place, Newcastle upon Tyne NE2 4HH. *T:* (0191) 222 7003.

BAYLIS, Rear-Adm. Robert Goodwin, CB 1984; OBE 1963; CEng; FIEE; Chief Executive, R. G. Baylis & Associates, since 1984; *b* 29 Nov. 1925; *s* of Harold Goodwin Baylis and Evelyn May (*née* Whitworth); *m* 1949, Joyce Rosemary Churchill (*d* 1995); two *s* one *d*. *Educ:* Highgate Sch.; Edinburgh Univ.; Loughborough Coll.; RN Engrg Coll.; Trinity Coll., Cambridge. MA Cantab. MRAeS. Joined Royal Navy, 1943; various appts at sea in Far East and Home Fleet and ashore in research and develt and trng establishments; Staff of C-in-C, S Atlantic and S America, 1958; British Navy Staff, Washington, and Special Projects (Polaris), 1964; Defence Fellow, Southampton Univ., 1969; Naval ADC to HM the Queen, 1978; Staff of Vice Chief of Defence Staff, 1979; President, Ordnance Board, 1981–84. Comdr 1961, Captain 1970, Rear-Adm. 1979. Dir, 1988–2000, Associate, 2000–, British Maritime Technol. Reliability Consultants. Mem., Nuffield Theatre Bd, 1988– (Chm., 1989–93, 1995–97). Mem. (Emeritus), Australian Ordnance Council; Mem. Council, IEE, 1984–86. *Recreations:* tennis, sailing, painting, playwriting. *Address:* Broadwaters, 4 Cliff Road, Hill Head, Fareham, Hants PO14 3JS. *Clubs:* Lansdowne; Owls (Cape Town).

BAYLIS, Trevor Graham, OBE 1997; inventor; *b* 13 May 1937; *s* of Cecil Archibald Walter Baylis and Gladys Jane Brown. *Educ:* Dormer's Wells Secondary Modern Sch. Represented Britain in swimming competitions at age of 15; Soil Mechanics Lab., 1953–59; Phys. Trng Instr, NS, 1959–61; Technical Salesman, Purley Pools, 1961 (also designed 50 products for swimming pools); professional swimmer and stuntman; founded Shotline Displays, 1970 (appeared on TV with Peter Cook and Dudley Moore, Dave Allen, and David Nixon); underwater escape artiste, Berlin Circus, Dec. 1970; founded Shotline Steel Swimming Pools, 1971 (built over 300 pools in schs in UK); developed 200 products for the disabled, Orange Aids, 1985; invented clockwork radio, 1992; jt Founder, Baygen, 1995; Dir, Baylis Generators Ltd, 1994–; Co-founded The Electric Shoe Co. and The Personal Power Co. (to power mobile 'phone batteries through walking), 1999. Vis. Prof., Buckingham Univ., 1998–. Vice-Pres., Techknowlogy charity. Hon. Fellow: Univ. of Wolverhampton, UWIST. Hon. MSc: Brunel, 1997; UEA, 1997; Teesside, 1998; Hon. DTech: Nottingham Trent; Southampton Inst.; DUniv Open, 2001. Presidential Gold and Silver Medals, IMechE, 1997; Paul Harris Fellow, Rotary Club. *Publication:* Clock This: my life as an inventor, 1999. *Recreations:* swimming, diving, underwater swimming, boating, after dinner speaking. *Address:* Haven Studio, Eel Pie Island, Twickenham TW1 3DY.

BAYLISS, David, OBE 1992; FREng; Eur Ing; Director, Halcrow Fox, since 1999; *b* 9 July 1938; *s* of Herbert and Annie Esther Bayliss; *m* 1961, Dorothy Christine Crohill; two *s* one *d*. *Educ:* Arnold Sch., Blackpool; UMIST (BSc Tech 1961); Manchester Univ. (Dip TP 1966). CEng, FICE, 1980; FITE 1984; FIHT 1972; FCIT 1977; FRTPI 1972; FREng (FEng 1993); Eur Ing 1991. Manchester Corp., 1961–66; GLC, 1966–68; Centre for Environmental Studies, 1968–69; GLC, 1969–84 (Asst Divl Engr; Head, Transport Studies; Chief Transport Planner); Dir of Planning, London Transport, 1984–99. Chairman: SERC/DoT LINK Transport Infrastructure and Ops Steering Gp, 1991–96, Inland Surface Transport Prog. Adv. Gp, 1996–; UITP Internat. Commn on Transport Econs, 1996–98; Fifth Framework Expert Adv. Gp on Sustainable Mobility and Intermodality, EC, 1998–. Vis. Prof., ICSTM, 1999–. Chm., Regional Studies Assoc., 1978–81; Member Council: CIT, 1978–82; IHT, 1992–94; ICE, 1996–98; President: British Parking Assoc., 1987–89; Transport Studies Soc., 1989–90; UK Vice Pres., Internat. Union of Public Transport, 1997–98. FRSA 1994. *Recreations:* writing, travel, wine. *Address:* 37 Ledborough Lane, Beaconsfield, Bucks HP9 2DB. *T:* (01494) 673313.

BAYLISS, Frederic Joseph; Special Professor, Department of Continuing Education (formerly Adult Education), University of Nottingham, 1988–97; *b* 15 April 1926; *s* of Gordon and Gertrude Bayliss; *m* 1948, Mary Provost; two *d*. *Educ:* Ashby de la Zouch Grammar Sch.; Hertford Coll., Oxford. PhD Nottingham 1960. RAF, 1944–47. Tutor in Economics, Oxford Univ. Tutorial Classes Cttee, 1950–57; Lectr in Industrial Relations, Dept of Adult Education, Univ. of Nottingham, 1957–65; Industrial Relations Advr, NBPI, 1965–69; Asst Sec., CIR, 1969–71; Sen. Economic Advr, Dept of Employment, 1971–73; Under Sec., Pay Board, 1973–74; Sec., Royal Commn on the Distribution of Income and Wealth, 1974–77; Acct Gen., Dept of Employment, 1977–86. Chairman: Campaign for Work, 1988–92; Employment Policy Inst., 1992–95. *Publications:* British Wages Councils, 1962; The Standard of Living, 1965; Making a Minimum Wage Work, 1991; (with S. Kessler) Contemporary British Industrial Relations, 1992, 3rd edn 1998; Does Britain still have a Pay Problem?, 1993. *Recreations:* gardening, walking. *Address:* 37 Rufus Close, Lewes, East Sussex BN7 1BG. *T:* (01273) 474317, *Fax:* (01273) 474542. *Club:* Reform.

BAYLISS, Jeremy David Bagot, FRICS; Chief Executive, The Foundation, Royal Botanic Gardens, Kew, since 1997; President, Royal Institution of Chartered Surveyors, 1996–97; *b* 27 March 1937; *s* of Edmund Bayliss and Marjorie Clare (*née* Thompson); *m* 1962, Hon. Mary Selina, *y d* of 2nd Viscount Bridgeman, KBE, CB, DSO, MC; three *s*. *Educ:* Harrow; Sidney Sussex Coll., Cambridge (MA). ARICS 1962, FRICS 1971. 2nd Lieut, Coldstream Guards, 1956–57. Partner, Gerald Eve, Chartered Surveyors, 1967–97 (Sen. Partner, 1988–97); Chm., Gerald Eve Financial Services, 1989–96. Royal Institution of Chartered Surveyors: Chm., various cttees, 1983–; Mem., Gen. Council, 1987–; Pres., Planning and Develt Div., 1989–90. Chm., CBI Land Use Panel, 1992–95. Mem., Adv. Panel to Secs of State for the Envmt and for Wales on Standards for Planning Inspectorate, 1993–96. *Recreations:* gardening, country pursuits, tapestry work. *Address:* Sheepbridge Court, Swallowfield, near Reading, Berks RG7 1PT. *T:* (0118) 988 3218. *Club:* Boodle's.

BAYLISS, John; Chairman, Broomleigh Charitable Trust, since 1999; *b* 22 Jan. 1934; *s* of late Athol Thomas Bayliss and Elizabeth Rose Bayliss; *m* 1954, Maureen (*née* Smith); one *d*. *Educ:* Haberdashers' Aske's, Hatcham. Westminster Bank, 1950; Abbey National Building Society, then Abbey National plc, 1957–93: Regional Man., 1969; Personnel Man., 1972; Asst Gen. Man., 1974; General Manager: Field Operations, 1976; Housing, 1981; Marketing, 1983; Man. Dir (Retail Ops), 1988; Dep. Chm., 1991–93. Chairman: Broomleigh Housing Assoc. Ltd, 1990–96; Richmount Mgt Ltd, 1994–2000. *Recreation:* France. *Address:* Gun Green Oast, Water Lane, Hawkhurst, Kent TN18 5BA.

BAYLISS, John Francis Temple; an Assistant Judge Advocate General, since 1996; a Recorder, since 1999; *b* 11 Aug. 1942; *s* of Capt. Horace Temple Taylor Bayliss, DSO, RN and Patricia Bayliss (*née* Loftus); *m* 1981, Annelize Kors; one *s* one *d*. *Educ:* Ampleforth Coll.; BRNC, Dartmouth. Joined Royal Navy, 1960; called to the Bar, Gray's Inn, 1974, NSW, 1981; Comd Legal Officer, Sydney, RAN, 1980–82; Captain, 1986; Sec. to C-in-C Fleet, 1986–88; IMS, Brussels, 1988–92; Chief Naval Judge Advocate, 1992–95; an Asst Recorder, 1994–99. *Recreation:* golf. *Address:* Office of the Judge Advocate General, 22 Kingsway, WC2B 6LE. *T:* (020) 7218 8078.

BAYLISS, Sir Richard (Ian Samuel), KCVO 1978; MD, FRCP; FMedSci; consulting physician, Lister Hospital, London; Physician to the Queen, 1970–81, and Head of HM Medical Household, 1973–81; Consultant Physician, King Edward VII's Hospital for Officers, 1964–87; Vice-President, Private Patients Plan, 1989–98 (Director, 1979–89); *b* 2 Jan. 1917; *o s* of late Frederick William Bayliss, Tettenhall, and late Muryel Anne Bayliss; *m* 1st, 1941, Margaret Joan Lawson (marr. diss. 1956); one *s* one *d*; 2nd, 1957, Constance Ellen, *d* of Wilbur J. Frey, Connecticut; two *d*; 3rd, 1979, Marina de Borchgrave d'Altena, *widow* of Charles Rankin. *Educ:* Rugby; Clare Coll., Cambridge (Hon. Fellow, 1983); St Thomas' Hosp., London. MB, BChir Cambridge 1941; MRCS, LRCP 1941; MRCP 1942; MD Cambridge 1946; FRCP 1956. Casualty Officer, Ho.-Phys., Registrar, Resident Asst Phys., St Thomas' Hosp.; Off. i/c Med. Div., RAMC, India; Sen. Med. Registrar and Tutor, Hammersmith Hosp.; Rockefeller Fellow in Medicine, Columbia Univ., New York, 1950–51; Lectr in Medicine and Physician, Postgrad. Med. Sch. of London; Dean, Westminster Med. Sch., 1960–64; Physician to HM Household, 1964–70; Consulting Physician: Westminster Hosp., 1954–81; King Edward VII Hosp., Midhurst, 1973–82; Civilian Consultant in Medicine, RN, 1975–82. Asst Dir, RCP Res. Unit, 1982–88. Hon. Sec., Assoc. of Physicians, 1958–63, Cttee 1965–68, Pres., 1980–81; Pres., Section of Endocrinology, RSM, 1966–68; Examr in Medicine, Cambridge and Oxford Univs; Examr, MRCP. Chm., Med. Adv. Panel, ITC, 1980–. Member: Bd of Governors, Westminster Hosp., 1960–64, 1967–74; Council, Westminster Med. Sch., 1960–75; Soc. for Endocrinology (Council, 1956–60); Brit. Cardiac Soc., 1952; Council, RCP, 1968–71 (Second Vice-Pres., 1983–84); Bd of Advrs, Merck Inst. of Therapeutic Res., 1972–76. Med. Dir, Swiss Reinsurance Co. (UK), 1968–85; Dir, JS Pathology plc, 1984–90; Hon. Med. Adviser, Nuffield Nursing Home Trust, 1981–88; Consultant: Biotechnology Investments Ltd, 1984–; Internat. Biotechnology Trust plc. Harveian Orator, RCP, 1983. Founder FMedSci 1998. Hon. FRCPath 1994. *Publications:* Thyroid Disease: the facts, 1982, 3rd edn 1998; Practical Procedures in Clinical Medicine, 3rd edn; various, in med. jls and textbooks, on endocrine, metabolic and cardiac diseases. *Recreations:* ski-ing, music. *Address:* Flat 7, 61 Onslow Square, SW7 3LS. *T:* (020) 7589 3087, *Fax:* (020) 7581 5937; *e-mail:* ricbayliss@.pipex.com. *Club:* Garrick.

BAYLISS, Rev. Roger Owen; Principal Chaplain, Church of Scotland and Free Churches, and Director, Chaplaincy Services, Royal Air Force, 1998–2001; *b* 21 July 1944; *s* of Stanley John Bayliss and Joyce Audrey Bayliss; *m* 1976, Pauline Jones; two *s*. *Educ:* Westminster Coll., Oxford (DTh 1999). RMN 1966; SRN 1969; SRN for Mentally Subnormal, 1975; Dip. Counselling. Nurse training: Saxondale Hosp., 1963–66; Nottingham Gen. Hosp., 1966–69; Lea Castle Inst., 1973–75; ordained, 1981; entered Chaplains' Branch, RAF, 1981: served at stations: Lyneham, Marham, Stanley (Falkland Is), Bruggen, N Luffenham, Cottesmore, Leeming, Coningsby; HQ RAF Germany; 2 Gp HQ; RAF Support Comd; HQ PTC. QHC, 1998–2001. *Recreations:* classic cars, fly fishing, squash, music (rock and blues), reading. *Address:* Dorreg, Crown Cottages, Park End, Stroud, Glos GL5 4AZ. *T:* (01452) 712612. *Club:* Royal Air Force.

BAYLISS, Valerie June, CB 1996; education and training consultant; Associate Professor of Education, University of Sheffield, 1996–2001; *b* 10 June 1944; *d* of George and Ellen Russell; *m* 1971, Derek Andrew Bayliss; one *s*. *Educ:* Wallington County Grammar Sch. for Girls; Univ. of Wales (1st cl. hons History, BA 1965; MA 1967). Research Student, LSE, 1966–68; Dept of Employment, 1968; Manpower Services Commission, subseq. Training Agency: Head of Job Centre Services, 1978–82; Head, YTS Policy, 1982–85; Dir, Field Ops, 1985–87; Dir, Resources and Personnel, 1987–90; Under Sec., and Dir of Educn Progs, later of Youth and Educn Policy, Dept of Employment, subseq. Dept for Educn and Employment, 1991–95. Sheffield University: Mem. Council, 1988–95; Dir, Management Sch., 1991–96. Dir, Sheffield Careers Guidance Services Ltd, 1997– (Chm., 1999–). Mem. Bd, Sheffield Develt Corp., 1996–97. Dep. Chm., Nat. Adv. Council for Careers and Educnl Guidance, 1996–2000. Director, RSA projects: Redefining Work, 1996–98; Redefining Schooling, 1998–. Mem. Council, 1996–, Exec., 1999–, C&G; Gov., Barnsley Coll., 1996–. Chm., S Yorks Reg., Victorian Soc., 1997–. Patron, Nat. Youth Agency, 1996–. Hon. Fellow, Inst. of Careers Guidance, 1996. FRSA 1990. *Publications:* Key Views on the Future of Work, 1997; Redefining Work, 1998; Redefining Schooling, 1998; Redefining the Curriculum, 1999; Opening Minds: education for the 21st Century, 1999; What Should Our Children Learn?, 2000. *Recreations:* walking, reading, listening to music. *T:* (0114) 230 7693.

BAYLY, Prof. Christopher Alan, LittD; FRHistS; FBA 1990; Vere Harmsworth Professor of Imperial and Naval History, since 1992 and Fellow of St Catharine's College, since 1970, Cambridge University; *b* 18 May 1945; *s* of Roy Ernest and Elfreda Madeleine Bayly; *m* 1981, Susan Banks Kaufmann. *Educ:* Skinners School, Tunbridge Wells; Balliol College, Oxford (MA); St Antony's, Oxford (DPhil 1970); LittD Cantab. Stanhope Prize, Oxford, 1965. Cambridge University: Dir of Studies in History, St Catharine's Coll., 1970–92 (Tutor, 1977–80); Smuts Reader in Commonwealth Studies, 1981–87; Reader in Modern Indian History, 1988–91; Prof. of Modern Indian Hist., 1991–92. Directeur d'Etudes associé, CNRS, Ecole des Hautes Etudes, Paris, 1986. Vis. Prof., Univ. of Virginia, Charlottesville, 1975. MAE. *Publications:* The Local Roots of Indian Politics: Allahabad 1880–1920, 1975; Rulers, Townsmen and Bazaars: North Indian society in the age of British Expansion 1770–1870, 1983, 2nd edn 1988; Indian Society and the Making of the British Empire, 1988; Imperial Meridian: the British Empire and the world 1780–1830, 1989; (ed) The Raj: India and the British 1600–1947, 1990; Empire and Information: intelligence gathering and social communication in India 1780–1870, 1996; Origins of Nationality in South Asia, 1998; contribs to jls. *Recreation:* travelling. *Address:* St Catharine's College, Cambridge CB2 1RL. *T:* (01223) 338321. *Club:* Reform.

BAYLY, Richard Dion; Director, Devon and Cornwall, Government Office for the South West, since 1999; *b* 25 Feb. 1951; *s* of Edward Hugh Bayly and Denise Bayly (*née* Dudley); *m* 1986, Dr Lea Diane Jones; two *d*. *Educ:* Rugby Sch.; Bristol Univ. (BScEcon). Entered Civil Service, 1974: DoE, 1974–79; Dept of Transport, 1979–97 (on secondment to BRB, as Dir, Privatisation Studies, 1990–91); DETR, 1997– (on secondment to Cabinet Office, 1997–99; Acting Chief Exec., CS Coll., 1998–99). *Address:* (office) Mast House, Shepherds Wharf, 24 Sutton Road, Plymouth PL4 0HJ. *T:* (01752) 635050.

BAYNE, Prof. Brian Leicester, OBE 1998; PhD; FIBiol; Research Professor, Centre for Research on Ecological Impacts of Coastal Cities, University of Sydney, since 1997; *b* 24 July 1938; *s* of John Leonard and Jean Leicester Bayne; *m* 1961, Marianne Middleton; two *d*. *Educ:* Ardingly Coll.; Univ. of Wales (BSc, PhD). Post-doctoral res., Univ. of Copenhagen and Fisheries Laboratory, Conwy, 1963–68; Lectr, Sch. of Biology, Univ. of Leicester, 1968–73; Institute for Marine Environmental Research, Plymouth: Res. Scientist, 1973–83; Dir, 1983–88; Plymouth Marine Laboratory, NERC: Dir, 1988–94;

Dir, Centre for Coastal and Marine Scis, 1995–97. Hon. Professorial Fellow, Sheffield Univ., 1987; Hon. Prof., Univ. of Wales, 1989. *Publications:* Marine Mussels: ecology and physiology, 1976; res. papers in marine sci. jls, *eg* Jl of Experimental Marine Biol. and Ecol. *Recreation:* sailing. *Address:* Centre for Research on Ecological Impacts of Coastal Cities, Marine Ecology Labs A11, University of Sydney, NSW 2006, Australia.

BAYNE, Sir Nicholas (Peter), KCMG 1992 (CMG 1984); HM Diplomatic Service, retired; High Commissioner to Canada, 1992–96; *b* 15 Feb. 1937; *s* of late Captain Ronald Bayne, RN and Elisabeth Ashcroft; *m* 1961, Diana Wilde; two *s* (and one *s* decd). *Educ:* Eton Coll.; Christ Church, Oxford (MA, DPhil). Entered Diplomatic Service, 1961; served at British Embassies in Manila, 1963–66, and Bonn, 1969–72, seconded to HM Treasury, 1974–75; Financial Counsellor, Paris, 1975–79; Head of Financial, later Economic Relations, Dept, FCO, 1979–82; attached to RIIA, 1982–83; Ambassador to Zaire, 1983–84, also accredited to the Congo, Rwanda and Burundi, 1984; seconded to CSSB, 1985; Ambassador and UK Perm. Rep. to OECD, Paris, 1985–88; Dep. Under-Sec. of State, FCO, 1988–92. Chm., Liberalisation of Trade in Services Cttee, British Invisibles, 1996–2000. Vis. Fellow, Internat. Relns Dept, LSE, 1997–. *Publications:* (with R. D. Putnam) Hanging Together: the Seven-Power Summits, 1984, rev. edn 1987 (trans. German, Japanese, Italian); Hanging in There: the G7 and G8 summit in maturity and renewal, 2000; The Grey Wares of North-West Anatolia and their Relation to the Early Greek Settlements, 2000. *Recreations:* reading, sightseeing. *Address:* 2 Chetwynd House, Hampton Court Green, East Molesey, Surrey KT8 9BS. *Club:* Travellers.

BAYNES, Sir John (Christopher Malcolm), 7th Bt *cr* 1801; Lieutenant-Colonel, retired; *b* 24 April 1928; *s* of Sir Rory Malcolm Stuart Baynes, 6th Bt and Ethel Audrey (*d* 1947), *d* of late Edward Giles, CIE; *S* father, 1979; *m* 1955, Shirley Maxwell, *o d* of late Robert Allan Dodds; four *s*. *Educ:* Sedbergh School; RMA Sandhurst; Edinburgh Univ. (MSc). Commissioned Cameronians (Scottish Rifles), 1949; served Malaya, 1950–53 (despatches); Aden, 1966; Defence Fellow, Edinburgh Univ., 1968–69; comd 52 Lowland Volunteers (TAVR), 1969–72; retired, 1972. Order of the Sword, 1st Class (Sweden), 1965. *Publications:* Morale, 1967, new edn 1987; The Jacobite Rising of 1715, 1970; History of the Cameronians, Vol. IV, 1971; The Soldier in Modern Society, 1971; Soldiers of Scotland, 1988; The Forgotten Victor, 1989; (ed jtly) A Tale of Two Captains, 1990; No Reward but Honour?, 1991; Urquhart of Arnhem, 1993; Far from a Donkey: Gen. Sir Ivor Maxse, 1995; For Love of Justice, 1997; contribs to military and sporting jls. *Recreations:* shooting, fishing, golf. *Heir: s* Christopher Rory Baynes, *b* 11 May 1956. *Address:* Talwrn Bach, Llanfyllin, Powys SY22 5LQ. *T:* (01691) 648576. *Club:* Army and Navy.

BAYNES, Pauline Diana, (Mrs F. O. Gasch); designer and book illustrator; *b* 9 Sept 1922; *d* of Frederick William Wilberforce Baynes, CIE and Jessie Harriet Maud Cunningham; *m* 1961, Fritz Otto Gasch (*d* 1988). *Educ:* Beaufront Sch., Camberley; Farnham Sch. of Art; Slade Sch. of Art. MSIA 1951. Mem., Women's Internat. Art Club, 1938. Voluntary worker, Camouflage Develt and Trng Centre, RE, 1940–42; Hydrographic Dept, Admty, 1942–45. Designed world's largest crewel embroidery, Plymouth Congregational Church, Minneapolis, 1970. Kate Greenaway Medal, Library Assoc., 1968. *Publications: illustrated:* Farmer Giles of Ham, and subseq. books and posters by J. R. R. Tolkien, 1949; The Lion, the Witch and the Wardrobe, and subseq. Narnia books by C. S. Lewis, 1950; The Arabian Nights, 1957; The Puffin Book of Nursery Rhymes by Iona and Peter Opie, 1963; Recipes from an Old Farmhouse by Alison Uttley, 1966; Dictionary of Chivalry, 1968; Snail and Caterpillar, 1972; A Companion to World Mythology, 1979; The Enchanted Horse, 1981; Frog and Shrew, 1981; All Things Bright and Beautiful, 1986; The Story of Daniel by George MacBeth, 1986; Noah and the Ark, 1988; Bilbo's Last Song, 1990; The Naming by Margaret Greaves, 1992; The Lion, the Witch and the others: a book of Narnians, 1994; numerous other children's books, etc.; *written and illustrated:* Victoria and the Golden Bird, 1948; How Dog Began, 1985; King Wenceslas, 1987; In the beginning, 1990; A book of Narnians, 1994. *Recreation:* going for walks with dogs. *Address:* Rock Barn Cottage, Dockenfield, Farnham, Surrey GU10 4HH. *T:* (01428) 713306.

BAYNHAM, Prof. Alexander Christopher; strategic technical consultant, since 1996; Principal, Cranfield University (formerly Cranfield Institute of Technology) (Shrivenham Campus), 1989–96, now Emeritus Professor; *b* 22 Dec. 1935; *s* of Alexander Baynham and Dulcie Rowena Rees; *m* 1961, Eileen May Wilson; two *s* one *d*. *Educ:* Marling Sch.; Reading Univ. (BSc); Warwick Univ. (PhD); Royal Coll. of Defence Studies (rcds). Joined Royal Signals and Radar Estab., Malvern, 1955; rejoined, 1961 (univ. studies, 1958–61); Head, Optics and Electronics Gp, 1976; RCDS, 1978; Scientific Adviser to Asst Chief Adviser on Projects, 1979; Dep. Dir, 1980–83, Dir, 1984–86, RSRE; Dir, RARDE, 1986–89. *Publications:* Plasma Effects in Semi-conductors, 1971; assorted papers in Jl of Physics, Jl of Applied Physics and in Proc. Phys. Soc. *Recreations:* church activities, music. *Address:* c/o Cranfield University, Shrivenham Campus, Swindon, Wilts SN6 8LA.

BAYNHAM, Dr John William, CBE 1994; Chairman, Lothian Health Board, 1990–97; *b* 20 Jan. 1929; *s* of Rev. Albert J. Baynham and Euphemia Baynham; *m* 1959, Marcella Bridget (Marié) Friel; one *d*. *Educ:* Bathgate Academy; Aberdeen Univ. (BSc, PhD); Imperial College London (DIC). Scottish Agricultural Industries: res. develt chemist, 1955–62; Production Planning/ Techno Commercial, 1962–70; Trade Union negotiating and gen. management, 1970–80; Dir, Sales and Marketing, 1980–84; overall Agribusiness Dir, 1984–87. Founder Dir, Leith Enterprise Trust, 1984 (Chm., 1987–90). Chm., Salary Cttee, Conf. of Scottish Centrally Funded Colls, 1997–99. Chm., Bd of Govs, Moray House Inst. of Educn, Heriot-Watt Univ., 1991–95; Gov., Queen Margaret Coll., Edinburgh, 1995–99. Dr *hc:* Edinburgh, 1995; Queen Margaret UC, 1999. *Publications:* contribs to learned jls and seminars. *Recreations:* golf, good food and wine, grandchildren. *Address:* 2/18 Succoth Court, Succoth Park, Edinburgh EH12 6BZ. *T:* and *Fax:* (0131) 337 2813. *Club:* Royal Burgess Golfing Society (Edinburgh).

BAYS, Rt Rev. Eric; Bishop of Qu'Appelle, 1986–97; *b* 10 Aug. 1932; *s* of Rev. Canon P. C. Bays and Hilda (*née* Harper); *m* 1967, Patricia Ann Earle; one *s* one *d*. *Educ:* Univ. of Manitoba (BSc 1955); Univ. of Saskatchewan (BA 1959): Univ. of Emmanuel College (LTh 1959); Christian Theological Seminary (MMin 1974). Flight Lieut, RCAF (Reserve), 1955. Asst Curate, All Saints', Winnipeg, 1959–61; Lecturer, Emmanuel Coll., 1961–62; Priest-in-charge: Burns Lake, BC, 1962–63; Masset, BC, 1963–64; Novice, Community of the Resurrection, Mirfield, 1964–65; Vicar, St Saviour's, Winnipeg with Bird's Hill, 1965–68; Rector, All Saints', Winnipeg, 1968–76; Professor, Coll. of Emmanuel and St Chad, 1976–86, Vice-Principal, 1981–86. Canon of St John's Cathedral, Winnipeg, 1971–86. Hon. DD Coll. of Emmanuel and St Chad, 1987. *Recreations:* golf, curling. *Address:* 700 Roosevelt Avenue, Ottawa, ON K2A 2A7, Canada.

BAYTON, Rt Rev. John, AM 1983; Master Iconographer, St Peter's Icon School, since 1999; *b* 24 March 1930; *s* of Ernest Bayton and Jean Bayton (*née* Edwards); *m* 1959, Elizabeth Anne, *d* of Rt Rev. J. A. G. Housden; one *s* two *d*. *Educ:* Aust. Coll. of Theology, ACT (ThL (Hons)); St Francis Theol Coll., Brisbane. Ordained deacon 1956, priest 1957; Rector, Longreach, Qld, 1958–63; Rector and Sub-dean, Thursday Island (Canon in Residence), 1963–65; Rector, Auchenflower, 1965–68; Dean of St Paul's Cathedral, Rockhampton, 1968–79; Vicar, St Peter's, Eastern Hill, 1980–89; Archdeacon of Malvern, 1986–89; Bishop of Geelong (Asst Bishop, dio. of Melbourne), 1989–95; Episcopal Chaplain, St George's Coll., Jerusalem, 1995–96, 1998; Assisting Bishop in Chicago, Chaplain-in-Residence and Vis. Prof., Seabury-Western Seminary, Evanston, 1997; Adminr, St John's Cathedral, Brisbane, 1998–99. Founder, 1981, Patron, 1993–, Inst. for Spiritual Studies, Melbourne. Solo Art Exhibitions: Brisbane 1967, 1976, 1978, 1998; Rockhampton 1975, 1976; Melbourne 1981, 1984, 1986, 1987; Jerusalem, 1995, 1996; Chicago, 1997. Represented in public and private collections Australia, Chicago, USA, Jerusalem and UK. Prelate, Aust. Priory, Order of St John of Jerusalem and Knights Hospitaler, 1990; GCSJ 1995; ChLJ 2000. *Publications:* Cross over Carpentaria, 1965; Coming of the Light, 1971; The Icon, 1980; (ed) Anglican Spirituality, 1982. *Recreations:* painting, sketching, sculpting, reading, walking. *Address:* 219 Canterbury Road, Blackburn, Vic 3130, Australia. *Club:* Melbourne (Melbourne).

BAYÜLKEN, Ümit Halûk, Hon. GCVO 1967; President: Turkish Atlantic Treaty Association, since 1984; Turkish Parliamentarians' Union, since 1992; Atlantic Treaty Association, Paris, since 1994; *b* 7 July 1921; *s* of Staff Officer H. Hüsnü Bayülken and Mrs Melek Bayülken; *m* 1952, Mrs Valihe Salci; one *s* one *d*. *Educ:* Lycée of Haydarpasa, Istanbul; Faculty of Political Science (Diplomatic Sect.), Univ. of Ankara. Joined Min. of For. Affairs, 1944; 3rd Sec., 2nd Political Dept; served in Private Cabinet of Sec.-Gen.; mil. service as reserve Officer, 1945–47; Vice-Consul, Frankfurt-on-Main, 1947–49; 1st Sec., Bonn, 1950–51; Dir of Middle East Sect., Ankara, 1951–53; Mem. Turkish Delegn to UN 7th Gen. Assembly, 1952; Political Adviser, 1953–56, Counsellor, 1956–59, Turkish Perm. Mission to UN; rep. Turkey at London Jt Cttee on Cyprus, 1959–60; Dir-Gen., Policy Planning Gp, Min. of Foreign Affairs, 1960–63; Minister Plenipotentiary, 1963; Dep. Sec.-Gen. for Polit. Affairs, 1963–64; Sec.-Gen. with rank of Ambassador, 1964–66; Ambassador to London, 1966–69, to United Nations, 1969–71; Minister of Foreign Affairs, 1971–74; Secretary-General, Cento, 1975–77; Sec.-Gen., Presidency of Turkish Republic, 1977–80; Senator, 1980; Minister of Defence, 1980–83; MP, Antalya, 1983–87. Mem., Turkish Delegns to 8th-13th, 16th-20th Gen. Assemblies of UN; rep. Turkey at internat. confrs, 1953–66; Leader of Turkish Delegn: at meeting of For. Ministers, 2nd Afro-Asian Conf., Algiers, 1965; to Ministerial Councils of NATO, OECD, Cento and Regl Co-operation for Develt, 1971–74; Turkey and EEC Jt Assoc., 1971–74; to Cttee of Ministers, Council of Europe, 1972; at Conf. on European Security and Co-operation, 1973; Mem., Parly Assembly of European Council, 1984–87. Univ. of Ankara: Mem., Inst. of Internat. Relations; Lectr, Faculty of Polit. Scis, 1963–66. Hon. Gov., Sch. of Oriental and African Studies, London; Hon. Mem., Mexican Acad. of Internat. Law. Isabel la Católica (Spain), 1964; Grand Cross of Merit (Germany), 1965; Sitara-i-Pakistan (Pakistan), 1970; Star, Order One (Jordan), 1972; Sirdar-i-Ali (Afghanistan), 1972. Tunisia, 1973; UAR, 1973; UN, 1975; Turkish Pres., 1980. *Publications:* lectures, articles, studies and essays on subject of minorities, Cyprus, principles of foreign policy, internat. relations and disputes. *Recreations:* music, painting, reading. *Address:* Nergiz, Sokak no 15/20, Çankaya, Ankara 06680, Turkey.

BAZALGETTE, Rear-Adm. Derek Willoughby; CB 1976; *b* 22 July 1924; *yr s* of late H. L. Bazalgette; *m* 1st, 1947, Angela Hilda Vera (*d* 1991), *d* of late Sir Henry Hinchliffe, JP, DL; four *d*; 2nd, 1994, Ann, *widow* of Adm. Sir Peter Stanford, GCB, LVO. *Educ:* RNC Dartmouth. Served War of 1939–45; specialised in Gunnery, 1949; HMS Centaur, 1952–54; HMS Birmingham, 1956–58; SO 108th Minesweeping Sqdn and in comd HMS Houghton, 1958–59; HMS Centaur, 1963–65; Dep. Dir Naval Ops, 1965–67; comd HMS Aurora, 1967–68; idc 1969; Chief Staff Officer to Comdr British Forces Hong Kong, 1970–72; comd HMS Bulwark, 1972–74; Admiral President, RNC Greenwich, 1974–76; Comdr 1958; Captain 1965; Rear-Adm. 1974. ADC 1974. HQ Comr for Water Activities, Scout Assoc., 1976–87; Principal, Netley Waterside House, 1977–83; Indep. Inquiry Inspector, 1983–92. Lay Canon, Portsmouth Cathedral, 1984–; Mem., General Synod, 1985–90. Sen. Treas., Corp. of Sons of the Clergy, 1992–94. Chm., Portsmouth Housing Trust, 1989–95. Liveryman, Shipwrights' Co., 1986. Freeman, City of London, 1976. FIMgt (FBIM 1976). *Address:* Park House, Hambledon, Waterlooville, Hants PO7 4SB. *Club:* Lansdowne.

BAZALGETTE, Peter Lytton; Creative Director, GMG Endemol Entertainment, since 1998; *b* 22 May 1953; *s* of late Paul Bazalgette and Diana (*née* Coffin); *m* 1985, Hilary Jane Newiss; one *s* one *d*. *Educ:* Dulwich Coll.; Fitzwilliam Coll., Cambridge (Pres., Cambridge Union, 1975; BA Hons Law 1976; MA 1978). BBC News Trainee, 1977; Man. Dir, Bazal, 1987–98. Non-executive Director: Channel 4, 2001–; Victoria Real; Zeppotron. TV formats created, 1984–, incl. Food and Drink, Ready Steady Cook, Can't Cook Won't Cook, Changing Rooms, Ground Force, Dishes; formats sold to 30 countries; UK producer, Big Brother, 2000. MacTaggart Lectr, Edinburgh TV Fest., 1998. Mem., Creative Industries Task Force Enquiry into TV Exports, 1999; Mem. Cttee, ESU Centre for Internat. Debate, 1996–; Chm., British Acad. of Gastronomes, 1993–. Trustee, Crossness Engines Trust, 1994– (Chm., 1999); Pres., Caroline Walker Trust, 1997–. Fellow, BAFTA, 2000. Independent Producer of the Year, Broadcast TV Awards, 1997; Hat Trick Pioneer, Indie Awards, 1998; Indie-Vidual Award for Outstanding Personal Contribn to Ind. Sector, Indie Awards, 2000, 2001. *Publications:* jointly: BBC Food Check, 1989; The Food Revolution, 1991; The Big Food & Drink Book, 1993; You Don't Have to Diet, 1994; contribs to newspapers, incl. Guardian. *Recreations:* cricket, gluttony. *Address:* (office) Shepherd's Central, Shepherd's Building, Charecroft Way, Shepherd's Bush, W14 0EH. *T:* (0870) 333 1700, *Fax:* (0870) 333 1800.

BAZLEY, Rt Rev. Colin Frederick; Bishop of Chile, 1977–2000; Hon. Assistant Bishop, diocese of Chester, since 2000; *b* 27 June 1935; *s* of Reginald Samuel Bazley and Isabella Davies; *m* 1960, Barbara Helen Griffiths; three *d*. *Educ:* Birkenhead School; St Peter's Hall, Oxford (MA); Tyndale Hall, Bristol. Deacon 1959, priest 1960; Assistant Curate, St Leonard's, Bootle, 1959–62; Missionary of S American Missionary Society in Chile, 1962–69; Rural Dean of Chol-Chol, 1962–66; Archdeacon of Temuco, 1966–69; Assistant Bishop for Cautin and Malleco, Dio. Chile, Bolivia and Peru, 1969–75; Assistant Bishop for Santiago, 1975–77; Bishop of Chile, Bolivia and Peru, 1977; diocese divided, Oct. 1977; Bishop of Chile and Bolivia until Oct. 1981, when diocese again divided; Presiding Bishop of the Anglican Council for South America, 1977–83; Primate, Province of S Cone of America, 1989–95. Warden of Readers, dio. of Chester, 2000–. Mem., Inter-Anglican Theol and Doctrinal Commn, 1994–97. *Recreations:* football (Liverpool supporter) and fishing on camping holidays. *Address:* 121 Brackenwood Road, Higher Bebington, Wirral CH63 2LU.

BAZLEY, Dame Margaret (Clara), DNZM 1999; Chairman, New Zealand Fire Commission, since 1999; *b* 23 Jan. 1938. Registered Comprehensive Nurse; Dip. Nursing, DoH and Victoria Univ.; Dip. Health Admin., Massey Univ. Nursing, 1956–78, including: Matron, Sunnyside Psych. Hosp., Christchurch, 1965–73; Dep. Matron in Chief, Auckland Hosp. Bd, 1974–75; Chief Nursing Officer, Waikato Hosp. Bd, 1975–78; Dir, Div. of Nursing, NZ Dept of Health, 1978–84; State Services Commission: Comr, 1984–87; Dep. Chm., 1987–88; Sec. for Transport, 1988–93; Dir-Gen., Dept of

Social Welfare, 1993–99; Chief Exec., Min. of Social Policy, NZ, 1999–2001. Mem., NZ delegns to OECD, ISSA, WHO, Internat. Council of Nursing, etc, in Australia, USA and Europe. Business Woman of the Year, More/AirNZ, 1987. *Recreations:* gardening, reading, cooking, music. *Address:* (office) PO Box 2133, Wellington, New Zealand.

BAZLEY, Sir (Thomas John) Sebastian, 4th Bt *cr* 1869, of Hatherop, co. Gloucester; *b* 31 Aug. 1948; *s* of Sir Thomas Bazley, 3rd Bt and of Carmen, *o d* of James Tulla; *S* father, 1997. *Educ:* St Christopher Sch., Letchworth; Magdalen Coll., Oxford (BA Hons Maths). *Heir: b* Anthony Martin Christopher Bazley [*b* 23 Feb. 1958; *m* 1996, Claudia Patricia Montoya Cano; one *s* one *d*].

BEACH; *see* Hicks-Beach, family name of Earl St Aldwyn.

BEACH, David Hugh, PhD; FRS 1996; Founder and President, Genetica Inc., since 1996; Hugh and Catherine Stevenson Professor of Cancer Biology, University College London, since 1997; *b* 18 May 1954; *s* of Gen. Sir Hugh Beach, *qv*. *Educ:* Peterhouse, Cambridge (BA); Univ. of Miami (PhD 1977). Postdoctoral Fellow, Univ. of Sussex, 1978–82; Cold Spring Harbor Laboratory: Postdoctoral Fellow, 1982–83; Jun. Staff Investigator, then Sen. Staff Investigator, 1984–89; Tenured Scientist, 1992–; Sen. Staff Scientist, 1989–97; Investigator, Howard Hughes Med. Inst., 1990–97; Adjunct Investigator, Cold Spring Harbour Lab., 1997–2000. Adjunct Associate Prof., SUNY, Stony, 1990–97. Founder, Mitotix Inc., 1992. Eli Lilly Research Award, 1994; Bristol-Myers Squibb Award, 2000; Raymond Bourgine Award, 2001. *Publications:* numerous papers in reviewed jls, incl. Nature and Cell and Science. *Recreations:* flying, scuba diving. *Address:* Wolfson Institute for Biomedical Research, Cruciform Building, University College London, Gower Street, WC1E 6AE. *T:* (020) 7679 6762. *Club:* Royal Lymington Yacht.

BEACH, Gen. Sir (William Gerald) Hugh, GBE 1980 (OBE 1966); KCB 1976; MC 1944; *b* 20 May 1923; *s* of late Maj.-Gen. W. H. Beach, CB, CMG, DSO; *m* 1951, Estelle Mary Henry (*d* 1989); three *s* one *d*. *Educ:* Winchester; Peterhouse, Cambridge (MA; Hon. Fellow 1982). Active service in France, 1944 and Java, 1946; comd: 4 Field Sqn, 1956–57; Cambridge Univ. OTC, 1961–63; 2 Div. RE, 1965–67; 12 Inf. Bde, 1969–70; Defence Fellow, Edinburgh Univ. (MSc), 1971; Dir, Army Staff Duties, MoD, 1971–74; Comdt, Staff Coll., Camberley, 1974–75; Dep. C-in-C, UKLF, 1976–77; Master-Gen. of the Ordnance, 1977–81; Chief Royal Engr, 1982–87; Warden, St George's House, Windsor Castle, 1981–86. Dir, Council for Arms Control, 1986–89. Vice Lord-Lieut for Greater London, 1981–87. Kermit Roosevelt Vis. Lectr to US Armed Forces, 1977; Mountbatten Lectr, Edinburgh Univ., 1981; Gallipoli Meml Lectr, 1985; Wilfred Fish Meml Lectr, GDC, 1986. Colonel Commandant: REME, 1976–81; RPC, 1976–80; RE, 1977–87; Hon. Colonel, Cambridge Univ. OTC, TAVR, 1977–87; Chm., CCF Assoc., 1981–87; Chm., MoD Study Gp on Censorship, 1983. Mem., Security Commn, 1982–91. Chairman: Rochester Cathedral Develt Trust, 1986–99; Winchester DAC for Care of Churches, 1988–97; Hampshire and the Islands Historic Churches Trust, 1993–; Winchester Cathedral Fabric Adv. Cttee, 1996–; Member: Peace Forum, CTBI (formerly CCBI), 1986–; Cttee of Mgt, Council for Christian Approaches to Defence and Disarmament, 1988–; Vice-Chm., Council for Arms Control, 1989–99. Chairman: SPCK, 1994–99; Foundation Trustees, Church Army, 1996–. Chm. Govs, Bedales Sch., 1989–96. Patron, Venturers Search and Rescue, 1985–99. CIMgt; FRSA. Hon. Fellow CIBSE, 1988. Hon. DCL Kent, 1990. *Publications:* numerous articles, reviews and chapters in books on military matters and arms control. *Recreation:* ski-ing. *Address:* Flat 12, Roberts Court, 45 Barkston Gardens, SW5 0ES. *T:* (020) 7835 1219. *Clubs:* Farmers'; Royal Lymington Yacht.
See also D. H. Beach.

BEACHAM, Prof. Arthur, OBE 1961; MA, PhD; Deputy Vice-Chancellor, Murdoch University, Western Australia, 1976–79 (Acting Vice-Chancellor, 1977–78); *b* 27 July 1913; *s* of William Walter and Maud Elizabeth Beacham; *m* 1938, Margaret Doreen Moseley (*d* 1979); one *s* one *d*. *Educ:* Pontywaun Grammar Sch.; University Coll. of Wales (BA 1935); Univ. of Liverpool (MA 1937); PhD Belfast 1941. Jevons Res. Student, Univ. of Liverpool, 1935–36; Leon Res. Fellow, Univ. of London, 1942–43; Lectr in Economics, Queen's Univ. of Belfast, 1938–45; Sen. Lectr, University Coll. of Wales, 1945–47; Prof. of Indust. Relations, University Coll., Cardiff, 1947–51; Prof. of Economics, University Coll. of Wales, Aberystwyth, 1951–63; Vice-Chancellor, Univ. of Otago, Dunedin, New Zealand, 1964–66; Gonner Prof. of Applied Econs, Liverpool Univ., 1966–75. Chairman: Mid-Wales Industrial Develt Assoc., 1957–63; Post Office Arbitration Tribunal, 1972–73; Member: Advisory Council for Education (Wales), 1949–52; Transp. Consultative Cttee for Wales, 1948–63 (Chm. 1961–63); Central Transp. Consultative Cttee, 1961–63; Economics Cttee of DSIR, 1961–63; North West Economic Planning Council, 1966–74; Merseyside Passenger Transport Authority, 1969–71; Council, Royal Economic Soc., 1970–74. Chm., Cttees on Care of Intellectually Handicapped, Australia, 1982–85; Dir, Superannuation Scheme for Aust. Univs, 1982–83. Hon. LLD Otago, 1969; Hon. DUniv Murdoch, 1982. *Publications:* Economics of Industrial Organisation, 1948 (5th edn 1970); Industries in Welsh Country Towns, 1950. Articles in Econ. Jl, Quarterly Jl of Economics, Oxford Econ. Papers, etc. *Recreations:* golf, gardening. *Address:* 10 Mannersley Street, Carindale, Qld 4152, Australia. *T:* (7) 33986630. *Clubs:* Dunedin (Dunedin, NZ); Cricketers' (Qld).

BEADLES, Anthony Hugh, MA; Headmaster of Epsom College, 1993–2000; *b* 18 Sept. 1940; *s* of O. H. R. Beadles, OBE and N. K. Beadles; *m* 1970, Heather Iona McFerran; two *s* one *d*. *Educ:* Epsom Coll.; Christ Church, Oxford (MA). Head of History, Ellesmere Coll., 1963–67; Head of History and Asst Housemaster, Harrow Sch., 1967–85; Headmaster, King's Sch., Bruton, 1985–93. *Recreations:* cricket, mountains, golf. *Address:* Chaff Barn, Downyard, Compton Pauncefoot, Yeovil, Somerset BA22 7EL. *Clubs:* MCC; Vincent's (Oxford).

BEAL, Anthony Ridley; publishing consultant; Chairman: Heinemann Educational Books, 1979–84; Heinemann International, 1984–85; Managing Director, Heinemann Educational Books (International), 1979–84; *b* 28 Feb. 1925; *s* of Harold and Nesta Beal; *m* 1st, 1958, Rosemary Jean Howarth (*d* 1989); three *d*; 2nd, 1990, Carmen Dolores Carter (*née* Martinez). *Educ:* Haberdashers' Aske's Hampstead School; Downing College, Cambridge (scholar); 1st class English Tripos 1948. RNVR, 1943–46; Lectr in English, Eastbourne Training Coll., 1949; joined William Heinemann, 1949; Dep. Man. Dir, Heinemann Educational Books, 1962–73, Man. Dir, 1973–79; Dir, Heinemann Group of Publishers, 1973–85; Chairman: Heinemann Publishers (NZ), 1980–85; Heinemann Publishers Australia Pty, 1981–85; Ginn & Co., 1979–84. Chm., Educational Publishers' Council, 1980–83 (Vice-Chm., 1978–80); Mem. Council, Publishers' Assoc., 1982–86. *Publications:* D. H. Lawrence: Selected Literary Criticism, 1956; D. H. Lawrence, 1961; contribs to books on literature, education and publishing. *Recreations:* reading maps, travelling, thinking while gardening. *Address:* 19 Homefield Road, Radlett, Herts WD7 8PX. *T:* (01923) 854567.

BEAL, Peter George, PhD; FBA 1993; Manuscript Expert, since 1980, Director, since 1996, Department of Printed Books and Manuscripts, Sotheby's, London (Deputy Director, 1990–95); *b* Coventry, 16 April 1944; *s* of William George Beal and Marjorie Ena Owen; *m* 1st, 1974, Gwyneth Morgan (marr. diss. 1980); 2nd, 1982, Sally Josephine Taylor (marr. diss. 1994); one step *s*; 3rd, 1998, Grace Janette Ioppolo. *Educ:* King Henry VIII Grammar Sch., Coventry; Leeds Univ (BA Hons English, 1966; PhD 1974). Res. editor, Bowker/Mansell Publishing, 1974–79. Lyell Reader in Bibliography, Oxford Univ., 1995–96. Vis. Prof., Dept of English, Reading Univ., 2000. *Publications:* Index of English Literary Manuscripts, vol. I, parts 1 and 2, 1450–1625 (2 vols), 1980, vol. II, parts 1 and 2, 1625–1700 (2 vols), 1987, 1993; (gen. ed.) English Verse Miscellanies of the Seventeenth Century (5 vols), 1990; In Praise of Scribes: manuscripts and their makers in 17th century England, 1998; (co-founded and co-ed) English Manuscript Studies 1100–1700, annually, 1989–; contribs, mainly on 16th and 17th century literary MSS, to learned jls. *Recreations:* reading, films, travel. *Address:* Department of Printed Books and Manuscripts, Sotheby's, 34–35 New Bond Street, W1A 2AA. *T:* (020) 7293 5298; *e-mail:* peter.beal@sothebys.com.

BEAL, Rt Rev. Robert George; Bishop of Wangaratta, 1985–94; *b* 17 Aug. 1929; *s* of Samuel and Phyllis Beal; *m* 1956, Valerie Francis Illich; two *s* four *d*. *Educ:* Sydney Grammar School; St Francis' College, Brisbane, Qld; Newcastle Univ., NSW (BA, ThL). Ordained, 1953; Priest, Asst Curate, St Francis', Nundah, Brisbane, 1953–55; Rector: South Townsville, 1955–59; Auchenflower, Brisbane, 1959–65; Dean of Wangaratta, 1965–72; Rector of Ipswich, Brisbane, and Residentiary Canon of St John's Cathedral, 1974–75; Dean of Newcastle, NSW, 1975–83; Archdeacon of Albury, 1983–85. *Recreations:* tennis, gardening. *Address:* 1 Pangari Place, New Lambton Gardens, Newcastle, NSW 2299, Australia.

BEALE, Anthony John; Solicitor and Legal Adviser, Welsh Office, 1980–91; Under Secretary (Legal), Welsh Office, 1983–91; *b* 16 March 1932; *o s* of late Edgar Beale and Victoria Beale; *m* 1969, Helen Margaret Owen-Jones; one *s* one *d*. *Educ:* Hitchin Grammar Sch.; King's Coll. London (LLB; AKC); BA Hons Open 1999. Solicitor of the Supreme Court, 1956. Legal Asst, 1960, Sen. Legal Asst, 1966, Min. of Housing and Local Govt and Min. of Health; Consultant, Council of Europe, 1973; Asst Solicitor, DoE 1974. ARPS. *Recreations:* photography, golf, collecting old cheques.

BEALE, Prof. Geoffrey Herbert, MBE 1947; FRS 1959; FRSE; PhD; Royal Society Research Professor, Edinburgh University, 1963–78; *b* 11 June 1913; *s* of Herbert Walter and Elsie Beale; *m* 1949, Betty Brydon McCallum (marr. diss. 1969); three *s*. *Educ:* Sutton County Sch.; Imperial Coll. of Science, London. Scientific Research Worker, John Innes Horticultural Institution, London, 1935–40. Served in HM Forces (1941–46). Research worker, Department of Genetics, Carnegie Institute, Cold Spring Harbor, New York, 1947; Rockefeller Fellow, Indiana Univ., 1947–48; Lecturer, Dept of Animal Genetics, 1948–59, Reader in Animal Genetics, 1959–63, Edinburgh Univ. Research Worker (part-time), Chulalongkorn Univ., Bangkok, 1976–. FRSE 1966. Hon. DSc Chulalongkorn, 1996. *Publications:* The Genetics of Paramecium aurelia, 1954; (with Jonathan Knowles) Extranuclear Genetics, 1978; (with S. Thaithong) Malaria Parasites, 1992. *Address:* 23 Royal Terrace, Edinburgh EH7 5AH. *T:* (0131) 557 1329.

BEALE, Prof. Hugh Gurney; a Law Commissioner, since 2000; Professor of Law, University of Warwick, since 1987; *b* 4 May 1948; *s* of Charles Beale and Anne Freeland Beale (*née* Gurney-Dixon); *m* 1970, Jane Wilson Cox; two *s* one *d*. *Educ:* Leys Sch., Cambridge; Exeter Coll., Oxford (BA Jurisp. 1969). Called to the Bar, Lincoln's Inn, 1971 (Hon. Bencher, 1999). Lecturer in Law: Univ. of Connecticut, 1969–71; UCW, Aberystwyth, 1971–73; Univ. of Bristol, 1973–86; Reader, Univ. of Bristol, 1986–87. Visiting Professor: Univ. of N Carolina, 1982–83; Univ. of Paris I, 1995; Univ. of Utrecht, 1996. Hon. LLD Miskolc, 1995. *Publications:* Remedies for Breach of Contract, 1980; (jtly) Contract Cases and Materials, 1985, 3rd edn 1995; (ed jtly) Principles of European Contract Law, Part I, 1995, Parts I and II, 2000; (Gen. Ed.) Chitty on Contracts, 28th edn 1999. *Recreations:* fishing, music, walking. *Address:* Law Commission, Conquest House, 37/38 John Street, WC1N 2BQ. *T:* (020) 7453 1203.

BEALE, James Patrick; Chief Executive, Ockenden International (formerly Ockenden Venture), since 1995; *b* 14 Nov. 1959; *s* of Patrick Ashton Beale and Janet Margaret Beale; *m* 1991, Mary Elizabeth Wilson; two *d*. *Educ:* Sch. of Oriental and African Studies, Univ. of London (BA Hons Geog.); Univ. of Reading (MSc Agricl Econs 1986). Data analyst, Kestrel Gp, Tripoli, Libya, 1982–84; Project Manager, Agric. and Fisheries Div., Crown Agents, 1986–88; Sight Savers International: Programme Manager, E Asia and Pacific, 1988–93; Regl Dir, Thailand and Bangladesh, 1993–95. *Address:* c/o Ockenden International, Constitution Hill, Woking, Surrey GU22 7UU. *T:* (01483) 772012.

BEALE, (Josiah Edward) Michael; lately Assistant Secretary, Department of Trade and Industry; *b* 29 Sept. 1928; *s* of late Mr and Mrs J. E. Beale, Upminster, Essex; *m* 1958, Jean Margaret McDonald; two *d* (and one *d* decd). *Educ:* Brentwood Sch.; Jesus Coll., Cambridge. UK Shipping Adviser, Singapore, 1968–71. Assistant Secretary, Monopolies and Mergers Commission, 1978–81. Vice-Chm., Friends of Historic Essex, 2000– (Hon. Sec., 1987–2000). *Publication:* (contrib.) Essex, full of Profitable Thinges, 1996. *Address:* The Laurels, The Street, Great Waltham, Chelmsford, Essex CM3 1DE.

BEALE, Lt-Gen. Sir Peter (John), KBE 1992; FRCP; Hon. Consultant, British Red Cross, since 2000 (Chief Medical Adviser, 1994–2000); *b* 18 March 1934; *s* of Basil and Eileen Beale; *m* 1959, Julia Mary Winter, MB BS (*d* 2000); four *s* one *d* (and one *d* decd). *Educ:* St Paul's Cathedral Choir Sch.; Felsted Sch. (Music Schol.); Gonville and Caius Coll., Cambridge (Choral Schol.; BA); Westminster Hosp. MB BChir 1958. DTM&H; FFCM; FFOM. Commissioned RAMC, 1960; medical training, 1964–71; Consultant Physician, Army, 1971; served Far East, Middle East, BAOR; Community Physician, Army, 1981; served BAOR and UK; Comdr Medical, HQ UKLF, 1987–90; DGAMS, 1990–93; Surg. Gen., MoD, 1991–94. QHP 1987–94. Pres., Old Felstedian Soc., 1998–. Gov., Yehudi Menuhin Sch., 1995–. OStJ. *Publications:* contribs to professional jls on tropical and military medicine. *Recreations:* music (conductor, tenor, pianist, French Horn player), sport (golf, squash, tennis), bridge. *Address:* The Old Bakery, Avebury, Marlborough, Wilts SN8 1RF. *T:* (01672) 539315. *Club:* Tidworth Garrison Golf (Pres., 1989–).
See also S. R. Beale.

BEALE, Simon Russell, (Simon Russell Beale); actor; *b* 12 Jan. 1961; *s* of Lt Gen. Sir Peter Beale, *qv*. *Educ:* St Paul's Cathedral Choir Sch.; Clifton Coll., Bristol; Gonville and Caius Coll., Cambridge (BA 1st Cl. Hons English 1982); Guildhall Sch. of Music and Drama. Royal Shakespeare Co., 1985–93 (Associate Artist); Royal National Theatre, 1995–98. *Theatre:* Look to the Rainbow, Apollo, 1983; Women Beware Women, Royal Court, 1985; Royal Shakespeare Company: A Winter's Tale, The Fair Maid of the West, 1985; Restoration, Man of Mode, 1987; Troilus and Cressida, The Seagull, Edward II, 1989; Richard III, 1990; Ghosts, 1993; The Tempest, 1993–94; Royal National Theatre: Volpone, 1995 (best supporting actor, Olivier Award, 1996); Rosencrantz and

Guildenstern are Dead, 1995; Othello, 1997; Candide (best actor in a musical, Olivier Award, 2000), Money, Summerfolk, Battle Royal, 1999; Hamlet (best actor, Evening Standard Award, best Shakespearean perf., Critics' Circle Award), 2000; Humble Boy, 2001; *television:* Persuasion, 1995; A Dance to the Music of Time, 1997 (best actor, RTS Award, 1997, BAFTA Award, 1998); *films:* Hamlet, 1997; The Temptation of Franz Schubert, 1997; An Ideal Husband, 1999; performances on radio. *Recreations:* music, history, history of religion. *Address:* Richard Stone Partnership, 25 Whitehall, SW1A 2BS. *T:* (020) 7839 6421.

BEALES, Prof. Derek Edward Dawson, PhD, LittD; FRHistS; FBA 1989; Professor of Modern History, University of Cambridge, 1980–97, now Emeritus; Fellow of Sidney Sussex College, Cambridge, since 1958; *b* 12 June 1931; *s* of late Edward Beales and Dorothy Kathleen Beales (*née* Dawson); *m* 1964, Sara Jean (*née* Ledbury); one *s* one *d*. *Educ:* Bishop's Stortford Coll.; Sidney Sussex Coll., Cambridge (MA, PhD, LittD). Sidney Sussex College, Cambridge: Research Fellow, 1955–58; Tutor, 1961–70; Vice-Master, 1973–75; Cambridge University: Asst Lectr, 1962–65, Lectr, 1965–80; Chairman: Faculty Board of History, 1979–81; Mgt Cttee, Internat. Studies, 1992–95; Member: Liby Syndicate, 1982–88; Gen. Bd of Faculties, 1987–89. Vis. Lectr, Harvard Univ., 1965; Lectures: Founder's Meml, St Deiniol's Liby, Hawarden, 1990; Stenton, Univ. of Reading, 1992; Birkbeck, Trinity Coll., Cambridge, 1993. Vis. Prof., Central Eur. Univ., Budapest, 1995–. Fellow, Collegium Budapest, 1995; Leverhulme Emeritus Fellowship, 2000. British rep., Humanities Standing Cttee, ESF, 1994–99. Mem. Council, RHistS, 1984–88. Editor, 1971–75, Mem. Editl Bd, Historical Jl, 1976–2002 (Chm., 1990–97). *Publications:* England and Italy 1859–60, 1961; From Castlereagh to Gladstone, 1969; The Risorgimento and the Unification of Italy, 1971; History and Biography, 1981; (ed with Geoffrey Best) History, Society and the Churches, 1985; Joseph II: in the shadow of Maria Theresa 1741–80, 1987; Mozart and the Habsburgs, 1993; (ed with H. B. Nisbet) Sidney Sussex Quatercentenary Essays, 1996; articles in learned jls. *Recreations:* playing keyboard instruments and bridge, walking, not gardening. *Address:* Sidney Sussex College, Cambridge CB2 3HU. *T:* (01223) 338833.

BEALES, Peter Leslie; Chairman and Managing Director, Peter Beales Roses, since 1967; *b* 22 July 1936; *s* of E. M. Howes; *m* 1961, Joan Elizabeth Allington; one *s* one *d*. *Educ:* Aldborough School, Norfolk; Norwich City Tech. Coll. FIHort. Apprenticed E. B. LeGrice Roses (1st apprentice, Horticultural Apprentice Scheme), 1952–57; Nat. Service, RA, 1957–59; Manager, Rose Dept, Hillings Nurseries, Chobham, 1959–66; founded Peter Beales Roses, 1967. Lecturer, UK and overseas, 1985–. Chm., Attleborough Chamber of Commerce, 1988–89. Chm., Norfolk and Norwich Horticultural Soc., 1998–2001 (Pres., 1997–98); Vice Pres., Norfolk Br., Gardening with Disabilities, 1999–; Pres., Attleborough Horticl Soc., 2000–. Hon. Life Mem., Bermuda Rose Soc., 1987; Life Mem., N Ireland Rose Soc., 1985. Freeman, City of London; Liveryman, Gardeners' Co. Lester E. Harrell Award for significant contrib. to heritage roses, USA, 1988; DHM, Royal Nat. Rose Soc., 1997. *Publications:* Georgian and Regency Roses, 1981; Early Victorian Roses, 1981; Late Victorian Roses, 1981; Edwardian Roses, 1981; Classic Roses, 1985; Twentieth-Century Roses, 1988; Roses, 1992; Visions of Roses, 1996; New Classic Roses, 1997. *Recreations:* photography, rose breeding, travelling, sport, book collecting. *Address:* Peter Beales Roses, London Road, Attleborough, Norfolk NR17 1AY. *T:* (01953) 454707.

BEALEY, Prof. Frank William; Professor of Politics, University of Aberdeen, 1964–90, now Emeritus; *b* Bilston, Staffs, 31 Aug. 1922; *er s* of Ernest Bealey and Nora (*née* Hampton), both of Netherton, Dudley; *m* 1960, Sheila Hurst; one *s* two *d*. *Educ:* Hill Street Elem. Sch.; King Edward VI Grammar Sch., Stourbridge; London Sch. of Economics (BSc Econ 1948); DSc Econ London, 1990. Seaman in RN, 1941–46; student, LSE, 1946–48; Finnish Govt Scholar, 1948–49; Research Asst for Passfield Trust, 1950–51; Extra-Mural Lectr, University of Manchester (Burnley Area), 1951–52; Lectr, then Sen. Lectr, University of Keele, 1952–64. Vis. Fellow, Yale, 1980. Treas., Soc. for Study of Labour Hist., 1960–63. Organiser, Parly All-Party Gp, Social Sci. and Policy, 1984–89. Trustee, Jan Hus Educnl Foundn, 1981–2001; Co-ordinator of Jt European Project 0276 (Political Sci. in Czechoslovakia), 1991–93. FRHistS 1974. *Publications:* (with Henry Pelling) Labour and Politics, 1958, 2nd edn 1982; (with J. Blondel and W. P. McCann) Constituency Politics, 1965; The Social and Political Thought of the British Labour Party, 1970; The Post Office Engineering Union, 1976; (with John Sewel) The Politics of Independence, 1981; Democracy in the Contemporary State, 1988; (jtly) Elements in Political Science, 1999; The Blackwell Dictionary of Political Science, 1999; Power in Business and the State, 2001; articles in academic jls. *Recreations:* reading poetry, eating and drinking, watching football and cricket, darts. *Address:* 11 Viewforth Terrace, Edinburgh EH10 4LH. *T:* (0131) 229 8313. *Club:* Economicals Association Football and Cricket.

BEAMENT, Sir James (William Longman), Kt 1980; ScD; FRS 1964; Drapers Professor of Agriculture, University of Cambridge, 1969–89, now Emeritus; Life Fellow, Queens' College, Cambridge, since 1989; *b* 17 Nov. 1921; *o c* of late T. Beament, Crewkerne, Somerset; *m* 1962, Juliet, *y d* of late Prof. Sir Ernest Barker, Cambridge; two *s*. *Educ:* Crewkerne Grammar Sch.; Queens' Coll., Cambridge; London Sch. of Tropical Medicine. Exhibitioner, Queens' Coll., 1941; BA 1943; MA 1946; PhD London 1945; ScD Cantab 1960. Research Officer with Agricultural Research Council, Cambridge, 1946; Cambridge University: Univ. Lectr, 1961; Reader in Insect Physiology, 1966; Hd of Dept of Applied Biol., 1969–89; Queens' College, Cambridge: Fellow and Tutor, 1961; Vice-Pres., 1981–86. Member: Adv. Bd for the Res. Councils, 1977; NERC, 1970–83 (Chm., 1977–80). Mem., Composers' Guild of Great Britain, 1967. Scientific Medal of Zoological Soc., 1963. *Publications:* The Violin Explained, 1997; How We Hear Music, 2001; many papers on physiology in scientific journals; Editor of several review volumes; *music:* String Sextet, 1999. *Recreation:* exposing musical fallacies. *Address:* 19 Sedley Taylor Road, Cambridge CB2 2PW. *T:* (01223) 562433; Queens' College, Cambridge CB3 9ET. *T:* (01223) 335511.

BEAMISH, Sir Adrian (John), KCMG 1999 (CMG 1988); HM Diplomatic Service, retired; International Adviser to BOC Group, since 1999; Lecturer, History Department, University College, Cork, since 1999; *b* 21 Jan. 1939; *s* of Thomas Charles Constantine Beamish and Josephine Mary (*née* Lee); *m* 1965, Caroline Lipscomb (marr. diss. 1991); two *d*; *m* 1994, Antonia Cavanagh; one *d*, and one step *s* one step *d*. *Educ:* Christian Brothers' Coll., Cork; Prior Park Coll., Bath; Christ's Coll., Cambridge (MA); Università per gli Stranieri, Perugia. Third, later Second Secretary, Tehran, 1963–66; Foreign Office, 1966–69; First Sec., UK Delegn, OECD, Paris, 1970–73; New Delhi, 1973–76; FCO, 1976–78; Counsellor, Dep. Head, Personnel Operations Dept, FCO, 1978–80; Counsellor (Economic), Bonn, 1981–85; Hd, Falkland Is Dept, FCO, 1985–87; Ambassador to Peru, 1987–89; Asst Under-Sec. of State (Americas), FCO, 1989–94; Ambassador to Mexico, 1994–99. *Recreations:* books, plants. *Address:* The Parochial House, Inniscarra, Co. Cork, Ireland. *T:* (21) 871239.

BEAMISH, Sarah Frances, (Sally); composer; *b* 26 Aug. 1956; *d* of William Anthony Alten Beamish and Ursula Mary (*née* Snow); *m* 1988, Robert Irvine; two *s* one *d*. *Educ:* Camden Sch. for Girls; Nat. Youth Orch.; Royal Northern Coll. of Music (GRNCM); Staatliche Hochschule für Musik, Detmold. Viola player, Raphael Ensemble, Acad. of St Martin-in-the-Fields, London Sinfonietta, Lontano, 1979–90; Composer's Bursary, Arts Council, 1989; Composer-in-Residence: Swedish Chamber Orch., 1998–Dec. 2002; Scottish Chamber Orch., 1998–Dec. 2002. Recordings: River ('Cello, Viola and Oboe Concertos); Sun on Stone (Saxophone Concerto, etc). *Compositions include:* 1st Symphony (first perf., Iceland SO, 1993); Viola Concerto (first perf., BBC Proms, 1995); Knotgrass Elegy (oratorio), 2001; Monster (opera), 2001. Hon. DMus Glasgow, 2001. *Recreations:* painting, gardening. *Address:* Scottish Music Information Centre, 1 Bowmont Gardens, Glasgow G12 9LR. *T:* (0141) 334 6393.

BEAMONT, Wing Comdr Roland Prosper, CBE 1969 (OBE 1953); DSO 1943, Bar 1944; DFC 1941, Bar 1943; DFC (US) 1946; FRAeS; author; *b* 10 Aug. 1920; *s* of Lieut-Col E. C. Beamont and Dorothy Mary (*née* Haynes); *m* 1st, 1942, Shirley Adams (*d* 1945); one *d*; 2nd, 1946, Patricia Raworth; two *d*. *Educ:* Eastbourne Coll. Commissioned in RAF, 1939; served War of 1939–45, Fighter Command, RAF, BEF, Battle of Britain (despatches), Battle of France and Germany. Attached as Test Pilot to Hawker Aircraft Ltd during rest periods, in 1941 and 1943; Experimental Test Pilot, Gloster Aircraft Co. Ltd, 1946; Chief Test Pilot, English Electric Co., 1947–61; Special Dir and Dep. Chief Test Pilot, BAC, 1961–64; Director, Flight Operations, BAC Preston, later British Aerospace, Warton Division, 1965–78; Dir of Flight Operations, Panavia (Tornado testing), 1971–79. Events while Chief Test Pilot, English Electric Co. Ltd: 1st British pilot to fly at speed of sound (in USA), May 1948; 1st Flight of Britain's 1st jet bomber (the Canberra), May 1949; holder of Atlantic Record, Belfast-Gander, 4 hours 18 mins. Aug. 1951 and 1st two-way Atlantic Record, Belfast-Gander-Belfast, 10 hrs 4 mins Aug. 1952 (in a Canberra); first flight of P1, 1954 (Britain's first fully supersonic fighter); first British pilot in British aircraft to fly faster than sound in level flight, 1954, and first to fly at twice the speed of sound, Nov. 1958; first flight of Lightning supersonic all-weather fighter, 1957; first flight of TSR2, Sept. 1964 (Britain's first supersonic bomber). Britannia Trophy for 1953; Derry and Richards Memorial Medal, 1955; R. P. Alston Memorial Medal, RAeS, 1960; British Silver Medal for Aeronautics, 1965. Pres., Popular Flying Assoc., 1979–84. Master Pilot and Liveryman, Guild of Air Pilots. Hon. Fellow, Soc. of Experimental Testpilots, USA, 1985. DL Lancashire 1977–81. *Publications:* Phoenix into Ashes, 1968; Typhoon and Tempest at War, 1975; Testing Years, 1980; English Electric Canberra, 1984; English Electric P1 Lightning, 1985; Fighter Test Pilot, 1986; My Part of the Sky, 1989; Testing Early Jets, 1990; Tempest over Europe, 1994; Flying to the Limit, 1996; The Years Flew Past, 2001. *Recreation:* fly-fishing. *Address:* 5 Earls Manor Court, Winterbourne Earls, Salisbury, Wilts SP4 6EJ. *Club:* Royal Air Force.

BEAN, Basil, CBE 1985; Vice Chairman, Barratt Developments Plc, since 1997; Vice President, National House Building Council, since 1994 (Director General, then Chief Executive, 1985–94 and 1996–97); *b* 2 July 1931; *s* of Walter Bean and Alice Louise Bean; *m* 1956, Janet Mary Brown; one *d*. *Educ:* Archbishop Holgate Sch., York. Mem. CIPFA. York City, 1948–53; West Bromwich Borough, 1953–56; Sutton London Bor., 1957–62; Skelmersdale Develt Corp., 1962–66; Havering London Bor., 1967–69; Northampton Develt Corp., 1969–80 (Gen. Manager, 1977–80); Chief Exec., Merseyside Develt Corp., 1980–85; overseas consultancies. Chm., Admiral Homes Ltd, 1996–97. Mem., British Waterways Bd, 1985–88. Hon. FABE 1980. *Publications:* financial and technical papers. *Recreations:* reading, walking, travel. *Address:* 4 Paget Close, Great Houghton, Northampton NN4 7EF. *T:* (01604) 765135. *Club:* Northampton and County (Northampton).

BEAN, Dr Charles Richard; Chief Economist and Executive Director, Bank of England, since 2000; *b* 16 Sept. 1953; *s* of Charles Ernest Bean and Mary (*née* Welsh). *Educ:* Emmanuel Coll., Cambridge (BA 1975); MIT (PhD 1981). Economist, HM Treasury, 1975–79 and 1981–82; London School of Economics: Lectr, 1982–86; Reader, 1986–90; Prof., 1990–2000. Visiting Professor: Stanford Univ., 1990; Reserve Bank of Australia, 1999. *Publications:* contrib. learned jls. *Recreations:* cricket, opera. *Address:* Bank of England, Threadneedle Street, EC2R 8AH. *T:* (020) 7601 4999.

BEAN, David Michael; QC 1997; a Recorder, since 1996; *b* 25 March 1954; *s* of late George Joseph Bean and of Zdenka White; two *s*. *Educ:* St Paul's Sch., Barnes; Trinity Hall, Cambridge (1st Cl. Hons Law). Called to the Bar, Middle Temple, 1976, Bencher, 2001. Mem., Gen. Council of the Bar, 1995– (Chm., 2002); Chm., Employment Law Bar Assoc., 1999–2001. Chm., Fabian Soc., 1989–90; Dep. Chm., Soc. of Labour Lawyers, 1995–99. *Publications:* Injunctions, 1979, 7th edn 1997; (with Anthony Nigel Fricker) Enforcement of Injunctions and Undertakings, 1991; (ed) Law Reform for All, 1996. *Recreations:* opera, hill-walking, books. *Address:* Matrix Chambers, Gray's Inn, WC1R 5LN. *Club:* Reform.

BEAN, Hugh (Cecil), CBE 1970; violinist (freelance); Professor of Violin, Royal College of Music, since 1954; *b* 22 Sept. 1929; *s* of Cecil Walter Claude Bean and Gertrude Alice Chapman; *m* 1963, Mary Dorothy Harrow; one *d*. *Educ:* Beckenham Grammar Sch. Studied privately, and at RCM, London (principal prize for violin) with Albert Sammons, 1938–57; Boise Trav. Schol., 1952; at Brussels Conservatoire with André Gertler (double premier prix for solo and chamber music playing), 1952–53. National Service, Gren. Gds, 1949–51. Formerly Leader of Harvey Phillips String Orch. and Dennis Brain Chamber Orch.; Leader of Philharmonia and New Philharmonia Orch., 1957–67; Associate Leader, BBC Symph. Orch., 1967–69; Co-Leader, Philharmonia Orch., 1990–94, Leader Emeritus, 1994–. Formerly Member: Bean-Parkhouse Duo; Music Gp of London. Has made solo commercial records, and has performed as soloist with many major orchestras. Hon. ARCM 1961, FRCM 1968. *Recreations:* design and construction of flying model aircraft; steam-driven passenger hauling model railways; gramophone record collection. *Address:* Rosemary Cottage, 30 Stone Park Avenue, Beckenham, Kent BR3 3LX. *T:* (020) 8650 8774.

BEAN, Rev. Canon John Victor; Vicar, St Mary, Cowes, Isle of Wight, 1966–91, and Priest-in-charge, All Saints, Gurnard, IoW, 1978–91; Chaplain to the Queen, 1980–95; *b* 1 Dec. 1925; *s* of Albert Victor and Eleanor Ethel Bean; *m* 1955, Nancy Evelyn Evans; two *s* one *d* (and one *d* died in infancy). *Educ:* local schools; Grammar Sch., Gt Yarmouth; Downing Coll., Cambridge (MA); Salisbury Theological Coll., 1948. Served War, RNVR, 1944–46; returned to Cambridge, 1946–48. Assistant Curate: St James, Milton, Portsmouth, 1950–55; St Peter and St Paul, Fareham, 1955–59; Vicar, St Helen's, IoW, 1959–66. Rural Dean of West Wight, 1968–73; Clergy Proctor for Diocese of Portsmouth, 1973–80; Hon. Canon, Portsmouth Cathedral, 1970–91, Canon Emeritus, 1991. *Recreations:* photography, boat-watching, tidying up. *Address:* 23 Seldon Avenue, Ryde, Isle of Wight PO33 1NS. *Club:* Gurnard Sailing (Gurnard).

BEAN, Leonard, CMG 1964; MBE (mil.) 1945; MA; Secretary, Southern Gas Region, 1966–79, retired; *b* 19 Sept. 1914; *s* of late Harry Bean, Bradford, Yorks, and late Agnes Sherwood Beattie, Worcester; *m* 1938, Nancy Winifred (*d* 1990), *d* of Robert John

Neilson, Dunedin, NZ; one *d.* *Educ:* Canterbury Coll., NZ; Queens' Coll., Cambridge. Served War of 1939–45: Major, 2nd NZ Div. (despatches, MBE). Entered Colonial Service, N Rhodesia, 1945; Provincial Comr, 1959; Perm. Sec. (Native Affairs), 1961; acted as Minister for Native Affairs and Natural Resources in periods, 1961–64; Permanent Secretary: to Prime Minister, 1964; also to President, 1964. Adviser to President, Zambia, 1964–66. *Recreations:* golf, gardening. *Address:* Squirrels Gate, 20 Ashley Park, Ringwood, Hants BH24 2HA. *T:* (01425) 475262. *Clubs:* MCC; Bramshaw Golf.

BEAN, Marisa; *see* Robles, M.

BEAN, Prof. Philip Thomas, PhD; Professor of Criminology and Director, Midlands Centre for Criminology and Criminal Justice, Department of Social Sciences, Loughborough University, since 1990; *b* 24 Sept. 1936; *s* of Thomas William Bean and Amy Bean; *m* 1st, 1964, Anne Elizabeth Sellar (marr. diss. 1968); 2nd, 1969, Valerie Winifred Davis (*d* 1999); two *s*. *Educ:* Bedford Modern Sch.; Univ. of London (BSc Soc (ext.), MSc Econ); Univ. of Nottingham (PhD). Probation Officer, Inner London Probation Service, 1963–69; Res. Officer, MRC, 1969–72; Lectr and Sen. Lectr in Social Sci., Univ. of Nottingham, 1972–90; Reader in Criminology, Univ. of Loughborough, 1990. Vis. Prof. at American, Canadian and Australian univs. Pres., British Soc. of Criminology, 1996–99; Mem., GMC, 2000–. *Publications* include: The Social Control of Drugs, 1974; Rehabilitation and Deviance, 1976; Compulsory Admissions to Mental Hospitals, 1980; Punishment, 1981; Mental Disorder and Legal Control, 1987; Mental Disorder and Community Safety, 2000; numerous contribs to learned jls. *Recreations:* poetry, music, esp. New Orleans jazz and opera. *Address:* 41 Trevor Road, West Bridgford, Notts NG2 6FT. *T:* (0115) 923 3895.

BEARD, Allan Geoffrey, CB 1979; CBE 1994; Under Secretary, Department of Health and Social Security, 1968–79 (Ministry of Social Security 1966–68); *b* 18 Oct. 1919; *s* of late Major Henry Thomas Beard and Florence Mercy Beard; *m* 1945, Helen McDonagh; one *d*. *Educ:* Ormskirk Grammar Sch. Clerical Officer, Air Min., 1936; Exec. Off., Higher Exec. Off., Asst Principal, Assistance Board, 1938–47; Army Service, 1940–46 (Capt., RE); Principal, Nat. Assistance Board, 1950; Asst Sec., 1962. Governor, 1981–99, Hon. Treasurer, 1985–98, Motability. *Publication:* Motability: the road to freedom, 1998. *Recreation:* gardening. *Address:* 51 Rectory Park, Sanderstead, Surrey CR2 9JR. *T:* (020) 8657 4197. *Club:* Royal Automobile.

BEARD, (Christopher) Nigel; MP (Lab) Bexleyheath and Crayford, since 1997; *b* 10 Oct. 1936; *o s* of Albert Leonard Beard, Castleford, Yorks, and Irene (*née* Bowes); *m* 1969, Jennifer Anne, *d* of T. B. Cotton, Guildford, Surrey; one *s* one *d*. *Educ:* Castleford Grammar Sch., Yorks; University Coll. London. BSc Hons, Special Physics. Asst Mathematics Master, Tadcaster Grammar Sch., Yorks, 1958–59; Physicist with English Electric Atomic Power Div., working on design of Hinckley Point Nuclear Power Station, 1959–61; Market Researcher, Esso Petroleum Co., assessing future UK Energy demands and market for oil, 1961; Ministry of Defence: Scientific Officer, later Principal Scientific Officer, in Defence Operational Analysis Estabt (engaged in analysis of central defence policy and investment issues), 1961–68, and Supt of Studies pertaining to Land Ops; responsible for policy and investment studies related to Defence of Europe and strategic movement of the Army, Dec. 1968–72; Chief Planner, Strategy, GLC, 1973–74; Dir, London Docklands Develt Team, 1974–79; Sen. Consultant, ICI, 1979–93; Sen. Man., ICI-Zeneca Ltd, 1993–97. Mem., SW Thames RHA, 1978–86; Mem. Bd, Royal Marsden Hosp., 1982–90. Mem., Lab. Pty Nat. Constitutional Cttee, 1995–98. Member: Select Cttee on Science and Technol., 1997–2000; Ecclesiastical Cttee, 1997–; Treasury Select Cttee, 2000–. Contested (Lab): Woking, 1979; Portsmouth N, 1983; Erith and Crayford, 1992. FRSA. *Publication:* The Practical Use of Linear Programming in Planning and Analysis, 1974 (HMSO). *Recreations:* reading, walking, the theatre. *Address:* House of Commons, SW1A 0AA. *T:* (020) 7219 5061. *Club:* Athenæum.

BEARD, Nigel; *see* Beard, C. N.

BEARD, Peter Hill; American photographer; *b* 22 Jan. 1938; *s* of Anson Beard; *m* 1st, 1967, Minnie Cushing (marr. diss. 1971); 2nd, 1978, Cheryl Tiegs (marr. diss. 1984); 3rd, 1986, Najma Khanum; one *d*. *Educ:* Yale Univ. (grad 1961). Career of escapism through collage, books, diaries and anthropology. Major exhibns include: Carnets Africains, Paris, 1996–97; Pettiness and Futility, LA. *Publications:* The End of the Game, 1965; Eyelids of Morning: the mingled destinies of crocodyles and men, 1973; Longing for Darkness: Kamante's tales from Out of Africa, 1975; Zara's Tales from Hog Ranch, 2001; exhibition catalogues: Peter Beard: 50 Years of Portraits, 1999; Stress and Density, 2002. *Address:* Driftwood Cove, Box 603, Montauk Point, Long Island, NY 11954, USA. *Club:* White Rhino (Nyeri, Kenya).

BEARD, Prof. Richard William, MD 1971; FRCOG 1972; Professor and Head of Department of Obstetrics and Gynaecology, St Mary's Hospital Medical School, 1972–96; *b* 4 May 1931; *s* of late William and Irene Beard; *m* 1st, 1957, Jane; two *s*; 2nd, 1979, Irène Victoire Marie de Marotte de Montigny; one *s*. *Educ:* Westminster Sch.; Christ's Coll., Cambridge (MA, MB BChir); St Bartholomew's Hosp. Obstetrician and Gynaecologist, RAF Changi, Singapore, 1957–60; Chelsea Hosp. for Women, 1961–62; UCH, 1962–63; Senior Lecturer/Hon. Consultant: Queen Charlotte's and Chelsea Hosps, 1964–68; King's Coll. Hosp., 1968–72. Dir, Pelvic Pain Clinic, Northwick Park Hosp., 1996–2000. Advr to Social Services Select Cttee, H of C (2nd Report on Perinatal and Neonatal Mortality), 1978–80; Civilian Consultant in Obstetrics and Gynaecology to RAF, 1983–; Consultant Advr in Obst. and Gyn. to DoH (formerly DHSS), 1985–91. Pres., Eur. Bd and Coll. of Obsts and Gynaecol., 1996–99. Mem., Acad. Royale de Medécine de Belgique, 1983. *Publications:* Fetal Physiology and Medicine, 1976, 2nd edn 1983; contribs to learned jls. *Recreations:* tennis, sailing, Chinese history. *Address:* 64 Elgin Crescent, W11 2JJ. *T:* (020) 7727 3129. *Club:* Garrick.

BEARDMORE, Alexander Francis, OBE 1987; FREng, FIMechE, FIEE; Engineer in Chief, Post Office, 1981–91, retired; *b* 20 Feb. 1931; *s* of Alexander Beardmore and Alice Beardmore (*née* Turner); *m* 1959, Pamela Anne Cozens; two *d*. *Educ:* Mitcham County Grammar School; London Univ. (BScEng, MSc). Nat. Service, Royal Signals, 1954–56. Post Office, 1948–91: Research Engineer, 1948–68; Controller Marketing, London Postal Region, 1972–77; Asst Dir, equipment provision, 1977–81. Chm., Unit Load Tech. Cttee, British Materials Handling Board, 1981–91. FIMgt. *Recreations:* Lions International, gardening, DIY, walking. *Address:* Three Gables, Cheltenham Road, Baunton, Cirencester, Glos GL7 7BE. *T:* (01285) 654361.

BEARDMORE, Prof. John Alec, CBiol, FIBiol; Professorial Fellow in Genetics, University of Wales, Swansea, since 1997; *b* 1 May 1930; *s* of George Edward Beardmore and Anne Jean (*née* Warrington); *m* 1953, Anne Patricia Wallace; three *s* one *d* (and one *s* decd). *Educ:* Burton on Trent Grammar Sch.; Birmingham Central Tech. Coll.; Univ. of Sheffield. BSc (1st Cl. Botany) 1953, PhD (Genetics) 1956. Research Demonstrator, Dept of Botany, Univ. of Sheffield, 1954–56; Commonwealth Fund Fellow, Columbia Univ., 1956–58; Vis. Asst Prof. in Plant Breeding, Cornell Univ., 1958; Lectr in Genetics, Univ. of Sheffield, 1958–61; Prof. of Genetics and Dir, Genetics Inst., Univ. of Groningen, 1961–66; Nat. Science Foundn Senior Foreign Fellow, Pennsylvania State Univ., 1966; University College of Swansea, subseq. University of Wales, Swansea: Prof. of Genetics, 1966–97; Dean of Science, 1974–76; Vice-Principal, 1977–80; Dir, Inst. of Marine Studies, 1983–87; Hd, Sch. of Biol Scis, 1988–95. Manager, DFID (formerly ODA) Fish Genetics Res. Prog., 1990–2001; Man. Dir, Fishgen Ltd, 1995–. Chm., Univ. of Wales Validation Bd, 1994–97; Mem., Univ. of Wales Vice Chancellors' Bd, 1993–96. Vis. Prof., Univ. of Ghent, 1992–. Member: NERC Aquatic Life Scis Cttee, 1982–87 (Chm., 1984–87); CNAA: Life Scis Cttee, 1979–85; Cttee for Science, 1985–87; Bd, Council of Sci. and Technology Insts, 1983–85 (Chm., 1984–85); Council, Galton Inst. (formerly Eugenics Soc.), 1980–96 (Chm., Res. Cttee, 1979–87); British Nat. Cttee for Biology, 1983–87; Council, Linnean Soc., 1989–93; Cttee, Heads of Univ. Biol Scis (Treas., 1989–91, Chm., 1991–94); Adv. Bd, Internat. Foundn for Sci., 1992–; Vice-Pres., Inst. of Biol., 1985–87 (Mem. Council, 1976–79; Hon. Sec., 1980–85); UK rep., Council of European Communities Biologists Assoc., 1980–87. FRSA; FAAAS. Darwin Lectr, Inst. of Biol. and Eugenics Soc, 1984. Univ. of Helsinki Medal, 1980. *Publications:* (ed with B. Battaglia) Marine Organisms: genetics ecology and evolution, 1977; articles on evolutionary genetics, human genetics and applications of genetics to aquaculture. *Recreations:* bridge, walking. *Address:* 153 Derwen Fawr Road, Swansea SA2 8ED. *T:* (01792) 206232.

BEARDSWORTH, Maj.-Gen. Simon John, CB 1984; *b* 18 April 1929; *s* of late Paymaster-Captain Stanley Thomas Beardsworth, RN and Pearl Sylvia Emma (Biddy) Beardsworth (*née* Blake); *m* 1954, Barbara Bingham Turner; three *s*. *Educ:* RC Sch. of St Edmund's Coll., Ware; RMA Sandhurst; RMCS. BSc. Commissioned Royal Tank Regt, 1949; Regtl service, staff training and staff appts, 1950–69; CO 1st RTR, 1970–72; Project Manager, Future Main Battle Tank, 1973–77; Student, Royal Naval War College, 1977; Dir of Projects, Armoured Fighting Vehicles, 1977–80; Dep. Comdt, RMCS, 1980–81; Vice Master Gen. of the Ordnance, 1981–84; consultant in defence procurement, 1984–97. *Recreations:* game shooting, travel, support to equestrian events, authorship. *Address:* c/o Lloyds TSB, Crewkerne, Somerset TA18 7LR. *Club:* Army and Navy.

BEARE, Robin Lyell Blin, MB, BS; FRCS; Hon. Consultant Plastic Surgeon: Queen Victoria Hospital, East Grinstead, since 1960; Brighton General Hospital and Brighton and Lewes Group of Hospitals, since 1960; Hon. Consulting Plastic Surgeon, St Mary's Hospital, London, since 1976 (Consultant Plastic Surgeon, 1959–76); *b* 31 July 1922; *s* of late Stanley Samuel Beare, OBE, FRCS, and late Cecil Mary Guise Beare (*née* Lyell); *m* 1947, Iris Bick; two *s* two *d*. *Educ:* Radley (scholar). Middlesex Hosp. Medical Sch. MB, BS (Hons) 1952 (dist. Surg.); FRCS 1955. Served with RAF Bomber Command (Aircrew) 1940–46. Formerly Ho. Surg., Casualty Officer, Asst Pathologist and Surgical Registrar, The Middlesex Hosp., 1952–56. Surg. Registrar, Plastic Surgery and Jaw Injuries Centre, Queen Victoria Hosp., East Grinstead, 1957–60. Examr in gen. surgery for FRCS, 1972–78. Fellow Assoc. of Surgeons of Gt Britain and Ireland; Fellow Royal Society Med.; Mem. Brit. Assoc. of Plastic Surgeons; Mem. of Bd of Trustees, McIndoe Memorial Research Unit, E Grinstead; Hon. Mem. Société Française de Chirurgie Plastique et Reconstructive. *Publications:* various on surgical problems in BMJ, Amer. Jl of Surgery, etc. *Recreations:* fishing, shooting. *Address:* Scraggs Farm, Cowden, Kent TN8 7EB. *T:* (01342) 850386.

BEARE, Stuart Newton; Consultant, Richards Butler, Solicitors, since 1996 (Partner, 1969–96, Senior Partner, 1988–91); *b* 6 Oct. 1936; *s* of Newton Beare and Joyce (*née* Atkinson); *m* 1974, Cheryl Wells. *Educ:* Clifton Coll.; Clare Coll., Cambridge (MA, LLB). Nat. Service, commnd Royal Signals, attached RWAFF, 1956–57. Plebiscite Supervisory Officer, N Cameroons, 1960–61; admitted solicitor, 1964. Clerk, Ward of Portsoken, 1993–96 (Hon. Ward Clerk, 1996–). Master, City of London Solicitors' Co. and Pres., City of London Law Soc., 1995–96. *Recreations:* mountain walking, ski-ing. *Addresses:* 24 Ripplevale Grove, N1 1HU. *T:* (020) 7609 0766. *Clubs:* Alpine, City of London, Oriental.

BEARMAN, Prof. Peter William, FREng; Professor of Experimental Aerodynamics, since 1986, and Pro-Rector, Projects, since 1999, Imperial College of Science, Technology and Medicine; *b* 8 Oct. 1938; *s* of William Stanley Bearman and Nana Joan Bearman; *m* 1969, Marietta Neubauer; one *s* one *d*. *Educ:* Jesus Coll., Cambridge (MA 1962; PhD 1965). SSO, Nat. Phys. Lab., 1965–69; Department of Aeronautics, Imperial College, London: Lectr, 1969–81; Reader, 1981–86; Head of Dept, 1989–98. FRAeS 1990; FCGI 1997; FREng (FEng 1997). *Publications:* (ed) Flow-induced Vibration, 1995; around 150 sci. papers. *Recreations:* cycling, gardening, DIY. *Address:* Department of Aeronautics, Imperial College, SW7 2BY. *T:* (020) 7594 5055.

BEARN, Prof. Alexander Gordon, MD; FRCP, FRCPEd, FACP; Executive Officer, American Philosophical Society, since 1997; Professor of Medicine, Cornell University Medical College, 1966–79, now Professor Emeritus (Stanton Griffis Distinguished Medical Professor, 1977–79); Attending Physician, The New York Hospital, since 1966; *b* 29 March 1923; *s* of E. G. Bearn, CB, CBE; *m* 1952, Margaret, *d* of Clarence Slocum, Fanwood, NJ, USA; one *s* one *d*. *Educ:* Epsom Coll.; Guy's Hosp., London. Postgraduate Medical Sch. of London, 1949–51. Rockefeller Univ., 1951–66; Hon. Research Asst, University Coll. (Galton Laboratory), 1958–59; Prof. and Sen. Physician, Rockefeller Univ., 1964–66; Chm., Dept of Medicine, Cornell Univ. Med. Coll., 1966–77; Physician-in-Chief, NY Hosp., 1966–77; Sen. Vice Pres., Medical and Scientific Affairs, Merck Sharp and Dohme Internat., 1979–88. Woodrow Wilson Foundn Vis. Fellow, 1979–80; Dist. Vis. Fellow, 1996–97, Fellow Commoner, 1997–, Christ's Coll., Cambridge; Adjunct and Vis. Prof., Rockefeller Univ., 1966– (Hon. Physician, 1988–); Adjunct Prof., Univ. of Pennsylvania Sch. of Medicine, 1998–. Trustee: Rockefeller Univ., 1970–98; Howard Hughes Medical Inst., 1987–; Dir, Josiah Macy Jr Foundn, 1981–98. Mem. Editorial Bd, several scientific and med. jls. Lectures: Lowell, Harvard, 1958; Medical Research Soc., 1969; Lilly, RCP, 1973; Harvey, 1975; Lettsomian, Med. Soc., 1976. Macy Faculty Scholar Award, 1974–75. Alfred Benzon Prize, Denmark, 1979. Member: Nat. Acad. Science; Amer. Philosophical Soc. (Exec. Officer, 1997–); Foreign Mem., Norwegian Acad. Science and Letters. Hon. MD Catholic Univ., Korea, 1968; Docteur *hc* Paris, 1975. *Publications:* Archibald Garrod and the individuality of man, 1993; articles on human genetics and liver disease, 1950–; (Co-Editor) Progress in Medical Genetics, annually, 1962–85; (Associate Editor) Cecil and Loeb: Textbook of Medicine. *Recreations:* biography, collecting snuff-mulls, aristology. *Address:* 241 South 6th Street, Philadelphia, PA 19106, USA. *T:* (215) 9252666; 31 Clarendon Street, Cambridge CB1 1JX; 41 Shoregate, Crail, Fife KY10 3SU. *Clubs:* Philadelphia (Pa); Knickerbocker, Century (NY); Hawks (Cambridge); Crail Golf (Scotland).

BEARNE, Air Vice-Marshal Guy, CB 1956; *b* 5 Nov. 1908; *y s* of late Lieut-Col L. C. Bearne, DSO, AM; *m* 1933, Aileen Cartwright, *e d* of late H. J. Randall, Hove; one *s* two *d*. Commissioned RAF, 1929; served in various Bomber Sqdns, 1930–33; specialist armament course, 1933; armament duties, 1934–44; Bomber Command, 1944–45 (despatches twice); Staff Officer i/c Administration, RAF Malaya, 1946; Joint Services Staff Coll., 1947; Dep. Dir Organisation (Projects), 1947–49; Command of Central Gunnery Sch., 1949–51; SASO, Rhodesian Air Training Gp, 1951–52; AOC Rhodesian Air Training Gp, 1953; Dir of Organisation (Establishments), Air Ministry, 1954–56; Air Officer in Charge of Administration, Technical Training Command, 1956–61; retd, 1961. *Address:* The Hollies, 6 Bradford Road, Corsham SN13 0QR. *T:* (01249) 713539.

BEARSTED, 5th Viscount *cr* 1925, of Maidstone, Kent; **Nicholas Alan Samuel;** Bt 1903; Baron 1921; *b* 22 Jan. 1950; *s* of 4th Viscount Bearsted, MC, TD and Hon. Elizabeth Adelaide (*d* 1983), *d* of Baron Cohen, PC; *S* father, 1966; *m* 1975, Caroline Jane, *d* of Dr David Sacks; one *s* four *d*. *Educ:* Eton; New Coll., Oxford. *Heir: s* Hon. Harry Richard Samuel, *b* 23 May 1988. *Address:* 9 Acacia Road, NW8 6AB.

BEASHEL, John Francis; His Honour Judge Beashel; a Circuit Judge, since 1993; *b* 3 Aug. 1942; *s* of late Nicholas Beashel and of Margaret Rita Beashel, JP; *m* 1966, Kay Dunning; three *s* one *d*. *Educ:* Coll. of Law. Called to the Bar, Gray's Inn, 1970; Asst Recorder, 1983–89; Recorder, 1989–93; Called to the Bar, NSW, 1989; Liaison Judge to Dorset Justices, 1994–. Pres., Dorset Br., Magistrates' Assoc., 1998–. *Recreations:* golf, travel, reading, walking, cooking. *Address:* Courts of Justice, Deansleigh Road, Bournemouth, Dorset BH7 7DS. *T:* (01202) 502800. *Club:* Ferndown Golf.

BEASLEY, Michael Charles, IPFA, FCA, FCCA; County Treasurer, Royal County of Berkshire, 1970–88; *b* 20 July 1924; *y s* of late William Isaac Beasley and Mary Gladys (*née* Williams), Ipswich, Suffolk; *m* 1955, Jean Anita Mary, *o d* of late Reginald John Shedrick Webber and Margaret Dorothy (*née* Rees), Penarth, S Glamorgan; one *s*. *Educ:* Northgate Grammar Sch., Ipswich. BScEcon London. Treasurer's Dept, East Suffolk County Council, 1940–48; served Royal Navy, 1943–46; Treasurer's Dept, Staffordshire CC, 1948–51; Educn Accountant, Glamorgan CC, 1951–54; Asst County Treasurer, Nottinghamshire CC, 1954–61; Dep. County Treasurer, Royal County of Berkshire, 1961–70, Acting Chief Exec., 1986. Examiner, CIPFA, 1963–66; Financial Adviser, Assoc. of County Councils and former County Councils Assoc., 1971–87; Hon. Treasurer, Soc. of County Treasurers, 1984–88 (Hon. Sec., 1972–80, Vice-Pres., 1980–81, Pres., 1981–82); Mem., Treasury Cttee on Local Authority Borrowing, 1972–87; Member Council: Local Authorities Mutual Investment Trust, 1974–75; RIPA, 1976–82. *Publications:* contribs to jls on local govt finance and computers. *Recreations:* cultivating indolence, pottering and pondering. *Address:* 239 Hyde End Road, Spencers Wood, Berkshire RG7 1BU. *T:* (0118) 988 3868.

BEASLEY, Prof. William Gerald, CBE 1980; BA, PhD; FRHistS; FBA 1967; Professor of the History of the Far East, University of London, 1954–83; Head of Japan Research Centre, School of Oriental and African Studies, 1978–83; *b* 22 Dec. 1919; *m* 1955, Hazel Polwin; one *s*. *Educ:* Magdalen Coll. Sch., Brackley; University Coll., London. Served War, 1940–46, RNVR. Lecturer, Sch. of Oriental and African Studies, University of London, 1947. Mem., 1961–68, British Chm., 1964–68, Anglo-Japanese Mixed Cultural Commn. Vice-Pres., British Acad., 1974–75, Treasurer, 1975–79. Lectures: Raleigh, British Acad., 1969; Creighton, Univ. of London, 1984. Hon. Mem., Japan Acad., 1984. Hon. Fellow, SOAS, 1991. Hon. DLitt Hong Kong, 1978. Order of the Rising Sun (Third Class), Japan, 1983. *Publications:* Great Britain and the opening of Japan, 1951; Select Documents on Japanese foreign policy, 1853–1868, 1955; The Modern History of Japan, 1963; The Meiji Restoration, 1972; Japanese Imperialism 1894–1945, 1987; The Rise of Modern Japan, 1990; Japan Encounters the Barbarian: Japanese travellers in America and Europe, 1995; The Japanese Experience: a short history of Japan, 1999. *Address:* 172 Hampton Road, Twickenham TW2 5NJ.

BEASLEY-MURRAY, Rev. Dr Paul; Senior Minister, Baptist Church, Victoria Road South, Chelmsford, since 1993; *b* 14 March 1944; *s* of late Rev. Dr George R. Beasley-Murray; *m* 1967, Caroline (*née* Griffiths); three *s* one *d*. *Educ:* Trinity School of John Whitgift; Jesus Coll., Cambridge (MA); Northern Baptist Coll. and Manchester Univ. (PhD); Baptist Theol Seminary, Rüschlikon and Zürich Univ. Baptist Missionary Soc., Zaire (Professor at National Univ., Theol. Faculty), 1970–72; Pastor of Altrincham Baptist Church, Cheshire, 1973–86; Principal, Spurgeon's Coll., 1986–92. Chm., Richard Baxter Inst. for Ministry, 1994–. Editor, Ministry Today, 1994–. *Publications:* (with A. Wilkinson) Turning the Tide, 1981; Pastors Under Pressure, 1989; Dynamic Leadership, 1990; (ed) Mission to the World, 1991; Faith and Festivity, 1991; Radical Believers, 1992; (ed) Anyone for Ordination?, 1993; A Call to Excellence, 1995; Radical Disciples, 1996; Happy Every After?: a guide to the marriage adventure, 1996; Radical Leaders, 1997; Power for God's Sake, 1998; The Message of the Resurrection, 2000. *Recreations:* music, walking, cooking. *Address:* The Old Manse, 3 Roxwell Road, Chelmsford, Essex CM1 2LY. *T:* (01245) 352996, *Fax:* (01245) 267203; *e-mail:* beasleymurray@compuserve.com.

BEASTALL, John Sale, CB 1995; Head of Local Government Group, HM Treasury, 1993–95; *b* 2 July 1941; *s* of Howard and Marjorie Betty Beastall (*née* Sale). *Educ:* St Paul's School; Balliol College, Oxford (BA 1963). Asst Principal, HM Treasury, 1963–67 (Asst Private Sec. to Chancellor of the Exchequer, 1966–67); Principal: HM Treasury, 1967–68 and 1971–75 (Private Sec. to Paymaster General, 1974–75); CSD, 1968–71; Assistant Secretary: HM Treasury, 1975–79 and 1981–85; CSD, 1979–81; DES, 1985–87; Treasury Officer of Accounts, 1987–93. Receiver, Met. Police Dist, 1995; Develt Dir, St Paul's Sch., 1996–2000. *Recreation:* Christian youth work. *Club:* Oxford and Cambridge.

BEATON, James Wallace, GC 1974; CVO 1992 (LVO 1987); security manager, now retired; Chief Superintendent, Metropolitan Police, 1985–92; *b* St Fergus, Aberdeenshire, 16 Feb. 1943; *s* of J. A. Beaton and B. McDonald; *m* 1965, Anne C. Ballantyne; two *d*. *Educ:* Peterhead Acad., Aberdeenshire. Joined Metropolitan Police, 1962: Notting Hill, 1962–66; Sergeant, Harrow Road, 1966–71; Station Sergeant, Wembley, 1971–73; Royalty Protection Officer, 'A' Division, 1973; Police Officer to The Princess Anne, 1973–79; Police Inspector, 1974; Chief Inspector, 1979; Superintendent, 1983. Director's Honor Award, US Secret Service, 1974. *Recreations:* reading, keeping fit, golf, hill walking. *Address:* 57 Carter Drive, Beverley, East Yorkshire HU17 9GL.

BEATSON, Prof. Jack; QC 1998; FBA 2001; Rouse Ball Professor of English Law, since 1993, and Director, Centre for Public Law, since 1997, University of Cambridge; Fellow of St John's College, Cambridge, since 1994; a Recorder, since 1994; a Deputy High Court Judge, since 2000; *b* 3 Nov. 1948; *s* of late John James Beatson and Miriam Beatson (*née* White); *m* 1973, Charlotte, *y d* of Lt-Col J. A. Christie-Miller; one *s* one *d*. *Educ:* Whittingehame Coll., Brighton; Brasenose Coll., Oxford (BCL, MA; DCL 2000); LLD Cantab 2001. Called to the Bar, Inner Temple, 1972, Hon. Bencher, 1993; Lectr in Law, Univ. of Bristol, 1972–73; Fellow and Tutor in Law, Merton Coll., Oxford, 1973–94 (Hon. Fellow, 1995). A Law Comr, 1989–94. Visiting Professor: Osgoode Hall Law Sch., Toronto, 1979; Univ. of Virginia Law Sch., 1980, 1983; Vis. Sen. Teaching Fellow, Nat Univ. of Singapore, 1987; Vis. Fellow, Univ. of WA, 1988; Dist. Vis. Prof., Univ. of Toronto, 2000. Mem., Competition (formerly Monopolies and Mergers) Commn, 1995–2000. *Publications:* (ed jtly) Chitty on Contract, 25th edn 1982 to 28th edn 1999; (with M. H. Matthews) Administrative Law: Cases and Materials, 1983, 2nd edn 1989; The Use and Abuse of Unjust Enrichment, 1991; (ed jtly) Good Faith and Fault in Contract Law, 1995; (ed jtly) European Public Law, 1998; (ed) Anson's Law of Contract, 27th edn 1998; (jtly) Human Rights: the 1998 Act and the European Convention, 2000; articles on administrative law, contract, and restitution in legal jls. *Recreations:* gardening, travelling. *Address:* St John's College, Cambridge CB2 1TP.

BEATTIE, Anthony; *see* Beattie, G. A.

BEATTIE, David, CMG 1989; HM Diplomatic Service, retired; Personnel Assessor, Foreign and Commonwealth Office, since 1998; *b* 5 March 1938; *s* of late George William David Beattie and of Norna Alice (*née* Nicolson); *m* 1966, Ulla Marita Alha, *d* of late Allan Alha and of Brita-Maja (*née* Tuominen), Helsinki, Finland; two *d*. *Educ:* Merchant Taylors' Sch., Crosby; Lincoln Coll., Oxford (BA 1964, MA 1967). National Service, Royal Navy, 1957–59; Sub-Lieut RNR, 1959; Lieut RNR 1962–67. Entered HM Foreign (now Diplomatic) Service, 1963; FO, 1963–64; Moscow, 1964–66; FO, 1966–70; Nicosia, 1970–74; FCO, 1974–78; Counsellor, later Dep. Head, UK Delegn to Negotiations on Mutual Reduction of Forces and Armaments and Associated Measures in Central Europe, Vienna, 1978–82; Counsellor (Commercial), Moscow, 1982–85; Head of Energy, Science and Space Dept, FCO, 1985–87; Min. and Dep. UK Perm. Rep. to NATO, Brussels, 1987–92; Ambassador to Swiss Confedn, and concurrently (non-resident) to Principality of Liechtenstein, 1992–97. Principal Sec., Royal Stuart Soc., 1997–; Vice-Pres., Anglo-Swiss Soc., 2000–. Hon. Life Mem., British-Swiss Chamber of Commerce, 2000. Trustee, Chiswick House Friends, 1998–. Freeman, City of London, 1989; Mem. Ct Assts, Masons' Co., 2000–. *Recreations:* bridge, walking, history. *Address:* PO Box 13609, W4 4GU. *Club:* Travellers.

BEATTIE, (George) Anthony; UK Permanent Representative to the UN Food and Agriculture Agencies in Rome, since 1997; *b* 17 April 1944; *s* of James Ellison Beattie and Christine Beattie; *m* 1973, Janet Frances Dring; one *s*. *Educ:* Stationers' Company's Sch., London; Trinity Coll., Cambridge (MA). Economic Planning Div., Office of the President, Malawi, 1966–69; Overseas Development Administration: Economic Planning Staff, 1969–78; Admin. Group, 1978; Dir, Tropical Develt and Res. Inst., 1986; Dir, Overseas Develt Natural Resources Inst., 1987–90; Chief Exec., Natural Resources Inst., 1990–96; seconded to Efficiency and Effectiveness Gp, OPS, Cabinet Office, 1996–97; Internat. Div., Dept for Internat. Develt, 1997; Minister (UN Agencies and Aid Affairs), Rome, 1997 (on secondment). *Recreations:* music, pottering in the country, Border terriers. *Address:* c/o Foreign and Commonwealth Office, King Charles Street, SW1A 2AH.

BEATTIE, Hon. Dame Heather; *see* Steel, Hon. Dame A. H.

BEATTIE, Hon. Peter (Douglas); MLA (ALP) Brisbane Central, since 1989; Premier of Queensland, since 1998; *b* 18 Nov. 1952; *s* of Arthur and Edna Beattie; *m* 1975, Heather Scott-Halliday; twin *s* one *d*. *Educ:* Atherton High Sch.; Univ. of Queensland (BA, LLB); Qld Univ. of Technol. (MA). Admitted Solicitor, Supreme Court of Qld, 1978. Minister for Health, 1995–96; Leader, State Opposition, 1996–98. *Publications:* In the Arena, 1990; The Year of the Dangerous Ones, 1994. *Recreations:* walking, biotechnology history, reading, swimming. *Address:* Level 15, Executive Building, 100 George Street, Brisbane, Qld 4000, Australia. *T:* (7) 32244500.

BEATTY, 3rd Earl *cr* 1919; **David Beatty;** Viscount Borodale of Wexford, Baron Beatty of the North Sea and of Brooksby, 1919; *b* 21 Nov. 1946; *s* of 2nd Earl Beatty, DSC, and Dorothy Rita, *d* of late M. J. Furey, New Orleans, USA; *S* father, 1972; *m* 1971, Anne (marr. diss. 1983), *d* of A. Please, Wokingham; two *s*; *m* 1984, Anoma Corinne Wijewardene. *Educ:* Eton. *Heir: s* Viscount Borodale, *qv*.

BEATTY, Hon. (Henry) Perrin; PC (Can) 1979; President and Chief Executive Officer, Canadian Broadcasting Corporation, since 1995; *b* 1 June 1950; *m* 1974, Julia Kenny; two *s*. *Educ:* Upper Canada College; Univ. of Western Ontario (BA 1971). MP (Progressive C) Wellington–Grey–Dufferin–Simcoe, Canada, 1972–93; Minister of State for Treasury Bd, 1979; Minister of Nat. Revenue and for Canada Post Corp., 1984; Solicitor General, 1985; Minister of Nat. Defence, 1986–89; Minister of Nat. Health and Welfare, 1989–91; Minister of Communications, 1991–93; Minister for External Affairs, 1993. Hon. Vis. Prof., Univ. of Western Ontario, 1994–95. *Address:* Canadian Broadcasting Corporation, 250 Lanark Avenue, PO Box 3220, Station C, Ottawa, Ontario K1Y 1E4, Canada.

BEAUCHAMP, Sir Christopher Radstock Proctor-, 9th Bt *cr* 1744; solicitor with Gilbert Stephens, Exeter, retired; *b* 30 Jan. 1935; *s* of Rev. Sir Ivor Cuthbert Proctor-Beauchamp, 8th Bt, and Caroline Muriel (*d* 1987), *d* of late Frank Densham; *S* father, 1971; *m* 1965, Rosalind Emily Margot, 3rd *d* of G. P. Wainwright, St Leonards-on-Sea; two *s* one *d*. *Educ:* Rugby; Trinity College, Cambridge (MA). *Heir: s* Charles Barclay Proctor-Beauchamp [*b* 7 July 1969; *m* 1996, Harriet, *e d* of Anthony Meacock; one *s*]. *Address:* The Coach House, Balfour Mews, Sidmouth, Devon EX10 8XL.

BEAUCLERK, family name of **Duke of St Albans**.

BEAUFORT, 11th Duke of, *cr* 1682; **David Robert Somerset;** Earl of Worcester, 1514; Marquess of Worcester, 1642; Chairman, Marlborough Fine Art Ltd, since 1977; *b* 23 Feb. 1928; *s* of late Captain Henry Robert Somers Fitzroy de Vere Somerset, DSO (*d* 1965) (*g g s* of 8th Duke) and late Bettine Violet Somerset (*née* Malcolm) (*d* 1973); *S* cousin, 1984; *m* 1st, 1950, Lady Caroline Jane Thynne (*d* 1995), *d* of 6th Marquess of Bath and of Hon. Daphne Vivian; three *s* one *d*; 2nd, 2000, Miranda Morley. *Educ:* Eton. Formerly Lieutenant, Coldstream Guards. Pres., British Horse Soc., 1988–90. *Heir: s* Marquess of Worcester, *qv*. *Address:* Badminton, Glos GL9 1DB.

BEAUMONT, family name of **Viscount Allendale** and **Baron Beaumont of Whitley**.

BEAUMONT OF WHITLEY, Baron *cr* 1967 (Life Peer), of Child's Hill; **Rev. Timothy Wentworth Beaumont,** MA (Oxon); politician, priest and writer; *b* 22 Nov. 1928; *o s* of Major and Hon. Mrs M. W. Beaumont; *m* 1955, Mary Rose Wauchope; one *s* two *d* (and one *s* decd). *Educ:* Gordonstoun; Christ Church, Oxford; Westcott House, Cambridge. Asst Chaplain, St John's Cathedral, Hong Kong, 1955–57; Vicar, Christ Church Kowloon Tong, Hong Kong, 1957–59; Hon. Curate, St Stephen's Rochester Row, London, 1960–63; resigned orders, 1973; resumed orders, 1984; Vicar, St Philip and All Saints, with St Luke, Kew, 1986–91. Editor: Prism, 1960–63 and 1964; New Outlook, 1964, 1972–74; Chm., Studio Vista Books Ltd, 1963–68; Proprietor of New Christian, 1965–70. Food Columnist, Illustrated London News, 1976–80. Asst Dir (Public Affairs), Make Children Happy, 1977–78; Co-ordinator, The Green Alliance, 1978–80. Liberal Party Organisation: Jt Hon. Treas., 1962–63; Chm., Liberal Publications Dept, 1963–64; Head of Org., 1965–66; Chm., Liberal Party's Org. Cttee, 1966; Chm., Liberal Party, 1967–68; Pres., Liberal Party, 1969–70; Vice-Chm., Liberal Party Exec. and Dir, Policy Promotion, 1980–83; Mem., Lib Dem Policy Cttee, 1992–95. Liberal spokesman on education and the arts, H of L, 1968–86; Lib Dem spokesman on conservation and the countryside, H of L, 1993–98; Treas., All-Party Gp on St Helena and Dependencies,

1995–; Sec., All-Party Gp on Family Farms, 1998–; Vice-Chm., All-Party Gp on UK Overseas Territories, 1998–. Alternate Mem., Assemblies of Council of Europe and WEU, 1973–77, Leader of Liberal Delegn, 1977–78, Vice-Chm., Liberal Gp, 1977–78. Joined Green Party, 1999; spokesman on agriculture, 1999–. Pres., British Fedn of Film Socs, 1973–79. Chairman: Albany Trust, 1969–71; Inst. of Res. into Mental and Multiple Handicap, 1971–73; Exit, 1980–81. Mem., Exec. Cttee, British Council, 1974–78. Mem. Exec., Church Action on Poverty, 1983–86, 1991–94. *Publications:* (ed) Modern Religious Verse, 1965; ed and contrib., The Liberal Cookbook, 1972; (ed) New Christian Reader, 1974; (ed) The Selective Ego: the diaries of James Agate, 1976; Where shall I place my cross?, 1987; The End of the Yellowbrick Road, 1997. *Address:* 40 Elms Road, SW4 9EX. *T:* (020) 7498 8664.

BEAUMONT, Bill; *see* Beaumont, W. B.

BEAUMONT, Christopher; *see* Beaumont, H. C.

BEAUMONT, Christopher Hubert; a Recorder of the Crown Court, 1981–98; *b* 10 Feb. 1926; *s* of Hubert and Beatrix Beaumont; *m* 1st, 1959, Catherine Sanders Clark (*d* 1971); two *s*; 2nd, 1972, Sara Patricia Magee; one *d*. *Educ:* West Monmouth Sch., Pontypool; Balliol Coll., Oxford (MA). Served RN, 1944–47 (Sub-Lieut RNVR). Called to Bar, Middle Temple, 1950. Asst Dep. Coroner, Inner West London, 1963–81. Chm., Agricultural Land Tribunal, Eastern Area, 1985–98 (Dep. Chm., 1979–85). *Publications:* Law Relating to Sheriffs, 1968; Town and Country Planning Act 1968, 1969; Housing Act 1969, 1969; Town and Country Planning Acts 1971 and 1972, 1973; (with W. G. Nutley) Land Compensation Act 1973, 1973; (with W. G. Nutley) Community Land Act 1975, 1976; (ed) Planning Appeal Decisions, 1986– (with W. G. Nutley, 1986–98). *Address:* White Lodge, Crescent Road, Alverstoke, Gosport, Hants PO12 2DJ. *T:* (023) 9258 3184.

BEAUMONT, David Colin Baskcomb; HM Diplomatic Service, retired; High Commissioner, Botswana, 1995–98; *b* 16 Aug. 1942; *s* of Colin Baskcomb Beaumont and Denise Heather Smith; *m* 1965, Barbara Enid Morris; two *s* one *d*. *Educ:* St Benedict's Sch., Ealing. Joined CRO, 1961; Private Sec. to Special Rep. in Africa, Nairobi, 1965; Third Sec., Bahrain, 1967; Second Sec., FCO, 1970; Second Sec. (Commercial), Accra, 1974; First Sec., FCO, 1977; First Sec. (Develt), Kathmandu, 1981; First Sec. and Dep. Head of Mission, Addis Ababa, 1983; First Sec., later Counsellor, FCO, 1986; Head of Protocol Dept, 1989–94, and First Asst Marshal of the Diplomatic Corps, 1993–94, FCO. *Recreations:* tennis, walking, cooking. *Address:* 42 Harvey Road, Guildford, Surrey GU1 3SE. *T:* (01483) 539577. *Clubs:* MCC; Pirbright Tennis Association.

BEAUMONT, Captain Hon. Sir (Edward) Nicholas (Canning), KCVO 1994 (CVO 1986; LVO 1976); DL; Vice Lord-Lieutenant of Berkshire, 1989–94; *b* 14 Dec. 1929; 3rd *s* of 2nd Viscount Allendale, KG, CB, CBE, MC and Violet (*d* 1979), *d* of Sir Charles Seely, 2nd Bt; *m* 1953, Jane Caroline, *d* of Alexander Lewis Paget Falconer Wallace, of Candacraig, Strathdon, Aberdeenshire; two *s*. *Educ:* Eton. Joined Life Guards, 1948; Captain 1956; retired 1960. Assistant to Clerk of the Course, Ascot, 1964; Clerk of the Course and Sec. to Ascot Authy, 1969–94. Pres., Berks SJAB, 1988–94. DL Berks 1982; DL Northumberland, 1996. *Address:* Low Shield House, Sparty Lea, Allendale, Northumberland NE47 9UW. *T:* (01434) 685037.

BEAUMONT, Sir George Howland Francis, 12th Bt, *cr* 1661; late Lieutenant 60th Rifles; *b* 24 Sept. 1924; *s* of 11th Bt and Renée Muriel (*d* 1987), 2nd *d* of late Maj.-Gen. Sir Edward Northey, GCMG, CB; *S* father, 1933; *m* 1949, Barbara Singleton (marr. annulled, 1951); *m* 1963, Henrietta Anne (marr. diss. 1986), *d* of late Dr A. Waymouth and Mrs J. Rodwell, Riverside Cottage, Donnington, Berks; twin *d*. *Educ:* Stowe Sch. *Address:* Stretton House, Stretton-on-Fosse, near Moreton-in-Marsh, Glos GL56 9SB. *T:* (01608) 662845. *Club:* Lansdowne.

BEAUMONT, Rt Rev. Gerald Edward; an Assistant Bishop, Diocese of Perth, Western Australia (Bishop of Goldfields-Country Region), since 1998; *b* 18 Feb. 1940; *s* of John Beaumont and Marjorie Beaumont; *m* 1967, Elsa Lynette Sampson; two *d*. *Educ:* Australian Coll. of Theology (LTh); Royal Melbourne Inst. of Technology (BA Fine Arts). Deacon 1968, priest 1969, Melbourne; Curate: St Andrew's, Brighton, Vic., 1968–70; Geelong W, 1970–71; Vicar of Mooroolbark, 1971–74; Priest/Pilot, Carpentaria Aerial Mission, Dio. Carpentaria, Qld, 1974–75; Vicar, Armadale-Hawksburn, Vic., 1975–81; Priest-in-Charge, Kooyong, Vic., 1982–86; Vicar, E Melbourne, 1986–92; Canon Pastor, St George's Cathedral, Perth, WA, 1992–94; Rector, Ascension, Alice Springs, NT, 1995–98; Hon. Canon, Christ Church Cathedral, Darwin, NT, 1995–98. *Recreations:* painting (exhibiting professional artist), motorcycling. *Address:* PO Box 439, Kalgoorlie, WA 6430, Australia. *T:* (8) 90227382; *e-mail:* kalang@ludin.com.au. *Clubs:* Royal Automobile of Victoria (Melbourne); Ulysses (Perth).

BEAUMONT, His Honour (Herbert) Christopher, MBE 1948; a Circuit Judge, 1972–85; *b* 3 June 1912; *s* of late Gerald Beaumont, MC and bar, and Gwendolene Beaumont (*née* Haworth); *m* 1940, Helen Margaret Gordon Smail (*d* 2000), *d* of William Mitchell Smail; one *s* two *d*. *Educ:* Uppingham Sch.; Worcester Coll., Oxford. Indian Civil and Political Services, 1936–47; Private Sec. to Lord Radcliffe, Chm. of Indo-Pakistan Boundary Commn, 1947; Foreign Office, 1948–52. Called to the Bar, Inner Temple, 1951; Metropolitan Magistrate, 1962–72. Chm. of the London Juvenile Courts, 1964; Dep. Chm., North Riding QS, 1966–71; temp. Resident Judge, Cyprus, 1986. Mem., Parole Bd, 1974–76; a Chm., Police (Disciplinary) Appeal Tribunal, 1988–96. *Recreations:* travel in Europe, growing vegetables. *Address:* Mead House Cottage, Mariners Lane, Southend, Bradfield, Berks RG7 6HU. *T:* (0118) 974 4064. *Club:* Brooks's.
See also G. M. Waller.

BEAUMONT, (John) Michael, OBE 2001; Seigneur of Sark since 1974; *b* 20 Dec. 1927; *s* of late Lionel (Buster) Beaumont and Enid Beaumont (*née* Ripley), and *g s* of Dame Sibyl Hathaway, Dame of Sark; *m* 1956, Diana (*née* La Trobe-Bateman); two *s*. *Educ:* Loughborough Coll. (DLC). Aircraft Design Engr, 1952–70; Chief Techn. Engr, Beagle Aircraft, 1969–70; Design Engr, BAC GW Div., 1970–75. *Recreations:* theatre, music, gardening. *Heir:* *s* Christopher Beaumont, Major RE, *b* 4 Feb. 1957. *Address:* La Seigneurie, Sark, Channel Islands. *T:* (01481) 832017.

BEAUMONT, John Richard; Managing Director, Planet Online Ltd, since 1998; *b* 24 June 1957; *s* of Jim Beaumont and Betty Marie (*née* Jarratt); *m*; two *d*. *Educ:* Univ. of Durham (BA Geog.). Res. Asst, Univ. of Leeds, 1978–80; Lectr, Univ. of Keele, 1980–83; Consultant, Coopers & Lybrand (London and NY), 1983–85; Jt Man. Dir, Pinpoint Analysis Ltd, London, 1985–87; ICL Prof. of Applied Management Information Systems and Dir, European Centre for Inf. Resource Management, Univ. of Stirling, 1987–90; Prof. and Hd of Sch. of Management, Bath Univ., 1990–92. Man. Dir, Stratatech, 1986–93; Energis Communications Ltd: Strategy Planning Manager, 1993–94; Head of Corporate Strategy and Affairs, 1994–95; Dir of Marketing, 1995–96; Dir of Strategy and Business Develt, 1996–99. Dep. Chm. Supervisory Bd, Business Online AG, 1999–; Dir, Metro Hldgs Ltd, 1998–; non-executive Director: World Pay Ltd, 1999–; European Telecommunications and Technology Ltd, 1999–. Non-exec. Dir, Office of Nat. Statistics, 1996–99. Hon. Professor: QUB, 1990–93; City Univ., 1994–98. Mem. Council, ESRC, 1989–93. *Publications:* (with P. Keys) Future Cities, 1982; (with S. Williams) Projects in Geography, 1983; (with E. Sutherland) Information Resources Management, 1992; (jtly) Managing our Environment, 1993. *Recreations:* good wine, travel, golf, watching Rugby, reading and writing fiction. *Address:* 2 Holly Place, NW3 6QU. *Club:* Athenæum.

BEAUMONT, John Richard; Regional Chairman of Employment Tribunals (North West Region), since 1999; *b* 22 June 1947; *s* late Stanley and Winifred Beaumont; *m* 1986, Susan Margaret (*née* Blowers); one *s* two *d*, and one step *s*. *Educ:* Wolverhampton Grammar Sch.; Merton Coll., Oxford (BA 1969; MA 1973). Schoolmaster, Buckingham Coll., Harrow, 1969–71; Regl Organiser, W Midlands, 1971–73, Nat. Dir of Projects, 1973–74, Shelter; Senior Legal Officer: Alnwick DC, 1974; Thurrock BC, 1974–75; called to the Bar, Inner Temple, 1976; in practice at the Bar, Northern Circuit, 1976–94; Chm. of Industrial, then Employment, Tribunals, 1994–99 (pt-time, 1992–94). *Recreations:* walking, reading (especially Victorian history and literature), family picnics. *Address:* Regional Office of Employment Tribunals, Alexandra House, 14-22 The Parsonage, Manchester M3 2JA. *T:* (0161) 833 0581.

BEAUMONT, Hon. Sir Nicholas; *see* Beaumont, Hon. Sir E. N. C.

BEAUMONT, Peter John Luther, QC 1986; **His Honour Judge Beaumont;** a Circuit Judge, since 1989; Common Serjeant in the City of London, since 2001; *b* 10 Jan. 1944; *s* of S. P. L. Beaumont, OBE, and D. V. Beaumont; *m* 1970, Ann Jarratt; one *s* one *d*. *Educ:* Peterhouse, Zimbabwe; Univ. of Zimbabwe (BScEcon Hons). Called to the Bar, Lincoln's Inn, 1967 (Bencher, 2001); practised South Eastern Circuit; a Recorder, 1986. Member: Parole Bd, 1992–97; Criminal Cttee, Judicial Studies Bd, 2000–. Governor, Felsted Sch., 1990– (Chm., 1993–98). *Recreations:* golf, tennis, gardening. *Address:* Central Criminal Court, Old Bailey, EC4M 7EH. *T:* (020) 7248 3277. *Club:* Travellers.

BEAUMONT, Sir Richard Ashton, KCMG 1965 (CMG 1955); OBE 1949; HM Diplomatic Service, retired; *b* 29 Dec. 1912; *s* of A. R. Beaumont, FRCS, Uppingham, and Evelyn Frances (*née* Rendle); *m* 1st, 1942, Alou (*d* 1985), *d* of M. Camran, Istanbul; one *d*; 2nd, 1989, Melanie Anns, *d* of H. Brummell. *Educ:* Repton; Oriel Coll., Oxford. Joined HM Consular Service, 1936; posted Lebanon and Syria, 1936–41. Served War, 1941–44. Returned to Foreign Office, 1944; served in London, Iraq, Venezuela; Imperial Defence Coll., 1958; Head of Arabian Department, Foreign Office, 1959; Ambassador: to Morocco, 1961–65; to Iraq, 1965–67; Dep. Under-Sec. of State, FO, 1967–69; Ambassador to the Arab Republic of Egypt, 1969–72. Dir-Gen., Middle East Assoc., 1973–77; Chairman: Arab British Centre, 1976–77; Anglo-Arab Assoc., 1979–99; Arab–British Chamber of Commerce, 1980–96. Governor, SOAS, 1973–78. Trustee, Thomson Foundn, 1974–2000. *Address:* 82 Peterborough Road, SW6 3EB.

BEAUMONT, William Anderson, CB 1986; OBE (mil.) 1961; AE 1953; Speaker's Secretary, House of Commons, 1982–86; *b* 30 Oct. 1924; *s* of late William Lionel Beaumont and Mrs E. Taverner; *m* 1st, 1946, Kythé (*d* 1988), *d* of late Major K. G. Mackenzie, Victoria, BC; one *d*; 2nd, 1989, Rosalie, *widow* of Judge Michael Underhill, QC. *Educ:* Terrington Hall, York; Cranleigh Sch. (Entrance Exhibnr); Christ Church, Oxford (MA, DipEd). Served RAF, Navigator, 1942–47, 355 Sqdn, 232 Sqdn, SEAC (Flt Lt). Asst Master, Bristol Grammar Sch., 1951–54; Beaumont and Smith Ltd, Pudsey, 1954–66 (Man. Dir, 1958–66); Henry Mason (Shipley) Ltd (Man. Dir, 1966–76); Principal, Welsh Office, 1976–79; Asst Sec., Welsh Office, 1979–82. A Chm. of Assessors, CSSB, 1988–92. Dir, St David's Forum, 1986–92; Sec., Prince of Wales Award Gp, 1987–90; Mem., Awards Cttee, RAF Benevolent Fund, 1990–; Vice-Chm., Franco-British Soc., 1991–98. RAuxAF 3507 (Co. of Somerset) FCU, 1948–54; 3609 (W Riding) FCU, 1954–61 (Wing Comdr CO, 1958–61); Observer Comdr, No 18 (Leeds) Gp, Royal Observer Corps, 1962–75 (ROC Medal 1975). *Recreations:* pontificating, reluctant gardening. *Address:* 28 Halford Road, Richmond, Surrey TW10 6AP. *T:* (020) 8940 2390. *Clubs:* Royal Air Force, Civil Service; United Services Mess (Cardiff); Nothing (Richmond).

BEAUMONT, William Blackledge, (Bill), OBE 1982; Rugby Union footballer, retired; sports broadcaster and writer; Director, J. Blackledge & Son Ltd, since 1981; *b* 9 March 1952; *s* of Ronald Walton Beaumont and Joyce Beaumont; *m* 1977, Hilary Jane Seed; two *s*. *Educ:* Ellesmere Coll., Shropshire. Joined family textile business, 1971. First played Rugby Union for England, 1975; 34 caps (20 caps as Captain); Mem., British Lions, NZ tour, 1977; Captain, British Lions, S Africa tour, 1980; played for Lancashire Barbarians, retd 1982. Television includes A Question of Sport (BBC TV), 1982–96. *Publications:* Thanks to Rugby, 1982; Bill Beaumont's Tackle Rugby, 1983; Bill Beaumont's Sporting Year Book, 1984. *Recreations:* tennis, golf, water-skiing. *Clubs:* East India, MCC; Fylde Rugby Union Football; Royal Lytham St Anne's Golf.

BEAUMONT-DARK, Sir Anthony (Michael), Kt 1992; investment adviser; *b* Birmingham, 11 Oct. 1932; *s* of Leonard Cecil Dark; *m* 1959, Sheelagh Irene, *d* of R. Cassey; one *s* one *d*. *Educ:* Birmingham Coll. of Arts and Crafts; Birmingham Univ. Mem., Birmingham Stock Exchange, 1958–; Consultant: Smith, Keen, Cutler, subseq. Smith Keen Murray, 1985–95 (Sen. Partner, 1959–85); Brewin Dolphin, 1995–; Dep. Chm., J. Saville Gordon plc, 1994–99 (Dir, 1989–99); Director: Wigham Poland (Midlands) Ltd, 1960–75; Nat. Exhibition Centre Ltd, 1971–73; Cope Allman Internat. Ltd, 1972–83; Birmid Qualcast PLC, 1983–89; Henderson (formerly TR) High Income Trust PLC, 1990– (Chm., 1994–); Birmingham Executive Airways, 1983– (Chm., 1983–86); ADR Net, 1993–94. Mem., Central Housing Adv. Cttee, DoE, 1970–76. Member: Birmingham City Council, 1956–67 (Alderman, 1967–74, Hon. Alderman, 1976); W Midlands CC, 1973–87 (Chm., Finance Cttee, 1977–83). Contested (C): Birmingham, Aston, 1959, 1964; Birmingham, Selly Oak, 1992. MP (C) Birmingham, Selly Oak, 1979–92. Mem., Treasury and Civil Service Select Cttee, 1979–92. Governor: Aston Univ., 1980–94; Birmingham Univ., 1984–92. Trustee, Birmingham Copec Housing Trust, 1975–80. FRSA 1993. *Address:* 124 Lady Byron Lane, Knowle, Solihull, West Midlands B93 9BA.

BEAUREPAIRE, Dame Beryl (Edith), AC 1991; DBE 1981 (OBE 1975); *b* 24 Sept. 1923; *d* of late E. L. Bedggood; *m* 1946, Ian Francis Beaurepaire, CMG (*d* 1996); two *s*. *Educ:* Fintona Girls' Sch., Balwyn, Victoria; Univ. of Melbourne. ASO, WAAAF, 1942–45. Mem. Nat. Exec., YWCA Australia, 1969–77. Liberal Party of Australia: Chm., Victorian Women's Sect., 1973–76; Chm., Federal Women's Sect., 1974–76; Vice-Pres., Victorian Div., 1976–86. Mem., Federal Women's Adv. Cttee Working Party, 1977. Pres., Victorian Assoc. of Order of British Empire, 1988–90. Vice Pres., Citizen's Welfare Service, Vic, 1970–86; Convenor, Nat. Women's Adv. Council, Australia, 1978–82. Member: Council, Australian War Memorial, 1982–93 (Chm., 1985–93; Chm., Fund Raising Cttee, 1993–96); Australian Children's Television Foundation Bd, 1982–88; Bd, Victoria's 150th Authy, 1982–87; Australian Bi-centennial Multicultural Foundn,

1989–92. Chm., Bd of Management, Fintona Girls' Sch., 1973–87; Patron: Portsea Children's Camp, 1996–; Peninsula Health Care Network Foundn, 1996–; Epilepsy Foundn of Victoria Inc., 1999–; Australians Against Child Abuse, 1999–; Victorian Coll. of the Arts, 1999– (Patron, 25th Anniv. Cttee, 1996); Palliative Care Victoria, 1999–; Peninsula Hospice Service, 1999–; Children First Foundn, 2000–. Silver Jubilee Medal, 1977. *Recreations:* golf, swimming. *Address:* 18 Barton Drive, Mount Eliza, Vic 3930, Australia. *T:* (3) 97871129, *Fax:* (3) 97879389. *Clubs:* Alexandra (Melbourne); Peninsula Country Golf (Frankston).

BEAVEN, John Lewis, CMG 1986; CVO 1983 (MVO 1974); HM Diplomatic Service, retired; Ambassador to Sudan, 1986–90; *b* 30 July 1930; *s* of Charles and Margaret Beaven; *m* 1960, Jane Beeson (marr. diss.); one *s* one *d*; *m* 1975, Jean McComb Campbell. *Educ:* Newport (Gwent) High Sch. BoT, 1946; RAF, 1948–50; Asst Trade Comr, British High Commn, Karachi, 1956–60; Second Secretary (Commercial), British High Commn, Freetown, 1961–64; First Secretary (Commercial): British High Commn, Nicosia, 1964–66; Nairobi, 1966–68; FCO, 1969–72; Head of Chancery, British Embassy, Jakarta, 1972–74; Counsellor (Economic and Commercial), British High Commn, Lagos, 1975–77; Dep. Consul General and Dir, British Trade Develt Office, NY, 1978–82; Consul-General, San Francisco, 1982–86. *Recreations:* music, needlepoint, walking. *Address:* Scannell Road, Ghent, NY 12075–0354, USA. *T:* (518) 3922152, *Fax:* (518) 3927355; *e-mail:* beaven@att.net.

BEAVER, Rev. Dr William Carpenter, II; Director of Communications of the Church of England, since 1997; *b* 17 Sept. 1945; *s* of late William Carpenter Beaver, MD and Margaret Edith Beaver, MD (*née* Nelson); *m* 1979, Sarah Ann Wilks; two *s*. *Educ:* Colorado Coll., USA (BA 1967; Benezet Distinguished Alumnus, 2000); US Army Comd and Staff Coll. (psc 1980); Wolfson Coll., Oxford (Beit Sen. Schol., Rhodes House; DPhil 1976); St Stephen's House, Oxford (CertTh 1982). Served US Army, 1967–71 (Bronze Star (valour, thrice); Meritorious Service Medal; Air Medal; Combat Infantry Badge), Reserves, 1971–96. Exec. Dir, Univ. of Oxford Develt Records Project, and Jun. Res. Fellow, Wolfson Coll., Oxford, 1977–80; Dep. Hd, Corporate and Community Communications, J. Walter Thompson, 1980–83; Dir, Publicity, Barnardo's, 1983–89; Group Director: Public Affairs, Pergamon AGB Internat. Res., 1989–90; Corporate Affairs, Nat. Westminster Bank, 1990–92; Dir, Marketing, The Industrial Soc., 1992–97. Ordained deacon, 1982, priest, 1983; Assistant Curate: St John the Divine, Kennington, 1982–95; St Mary Redcliffe, Bristol, 1995–; St Andrew's, Holborn, 2001–; Hon. Priest-in-charge, St Andrew's, Avonmouth, 1995–98. *Recreation:* bicycling. *Address:* Church House, Great Smith Street, SW1P 3NZ. *T:* (020) 7898 1000. *Club:* Nikaean.

BEAVERBROOK, 3rd Baron *cr* 1917, of Beaverbrook, New Brunswick, and of Cherkley, Surrey; **Maxwell William Humphrey Aitken;** Bt 1916; Chairman, Beaverbrook Foundation, since 1985; Treasurer, European Democratic Union, 1990–92; *b* 29 Dec. 1951; *s* of Sir (John William) Max Aitken, 2nd Bt, DSO, DFC, and of Violet, *d* of Sir Humphrey de Trafford, 4th Bt, MC; *S* to disclaimed barony of father, 1985; *m* 1974, Susan Angela More O'Ferrall; two *s* two *d*. *Educ:* Charterhouse; Pembroke Coll., Cambridge. Beaverbrook Newspapers Ltd, 1973–77; Dir, Ventech, 1983–86; Chm., Ventech Healthcare Corp. Inc., 1986, 1988–92. Govt spokesman for Home Office and DTI, H of L, 1986; a Lord in Waiting (Government Whip), 1986–88; Dep. Treas., 1988–90, Treas., 1990–92, Cons. Party. Chm., Nat. Assoc. of Boys' Clubs, 1989–92. Mem. Council, Homeopathic Trust, 1986–92. *Recreation:* motor sport (Eur. GT Champion, 1998). *Heir: s* Hon. Maxwell Francis Aitken, *b* 17 March 1977. *Address:* 11 Old Queen Street, SW1H 9JA. *Clubs:* White's, Carlton; Royal Yacht Squadron; British Racing Drivers'.

BEAVIS, Air Chief Marshal Sir Michael (Gordon), KCB 1981; CBE 1977 (OBE 1969); AFC 1962; Director: Skye Pharma PLC (formerly Tubular Edgington Group, then Black & Edgington Group), since 1989; Alliance Aircraft Co., USA, since 2000; *b* 13 Aug. 1929; *s* of Walter Erle Beavis and Mary Ann (*née* Sarjantson); *m* 1950, Joy Marion (*née* Jones); one *s* one *d*. *Educ:* Kilburn Grammar School. Joined RAF 1947; commnd 1949; served Fighter Comd Squadrons 1950–54, RNZAF 1954–56; flew Vulcan aircraft, Bomber Comd, 1958–62; Staff Coll., 1963; MoD, 1964–66; OC No 10 Squadron (VC10s), 1966–68; Group Captain Flying, Akrotiri, Cyprus, 1968–71; Asst Dir, Defence Policy, MoD, 1971–73; RCDS, 1974; RAF Germany, 1975–77 (SASO 1976–77); Dir Gen. RAF Training, 1977–80; Comdt, RAF Staff Coll, 1980–81; AOC-in-C, RAF Support Comd, 1981–84; Dep. C-in-C, AFCENT, 1984–86. CIMgt. Freeman, City of London, 1980; Liveryman, GAPAN, 1983. *Recreations:* golf, ski-ing, travel. *Address:* c/o Lloyds TSB, 202 High Street, Lincoln LN5 7AP. *Club:* Royal Air Force.

BEAZER, Brian Cyril; Chairman and Chief Executive, Beazer (formerly C. H. Beazer (Holdings)) PLC, 1983–91; Chairman, Beazer Homes USA Inc., since 1992; *b* 22 Feb. 1935; *s* of late Cyril Henry George Beazer and of Ada Vera Beazer; *m* 1958, Patricia (*née* White); one *d*. *Educ:* Wells Cathedral School. Joined C.H. Beazer, 1958; Man. Dir, 1968; apptd Chm. and Chief Exec. on death of his father in 1983. *Recreations:* walking, reading. *Address:* The Weavers House, Castle Combe, Wiltshire SN14 7HX.

BEAZLEY, Christopher John Pridham; Member (C) Eastern Region, England, European Parliament, since 1999; *b* 5 Sept. 1952; *s* of Peter George Beazley, *qv*; *m* 1978, Christiane Marie Elyane (*née* Dillemann); two *s* one *d*. *Educ:* Shrewsbury; Bristol Univ. Formerly Nuffield Research Fellow, School of European Studies, Sussex Univ. Vice Chm., Lewes and Eastbourne branch, European Movement, 1980; Wealden DC, 1979–83. MEP (C) Cornwall and Plymouth, 1984–94; contested (C) Cornwall and W Plymouth, Eur. Parly elecns, 1994; European Parliament: spokesman on regl policy, 1984–89, on justice and home affairs, 1992–94; Vice-Chairman: Transport Cttee, 1989–91; Baltic States Delegn, 1991–94. *Club:* Oriental.

BEAZLEY, Hon. Kim Christian; MP (ALP) Brand, Perth, Australia, since 1996 (Swan, Perth, 1980–96); Leader of the Opposition, Australia, since 1996; Leader of the House of Representatives, Australia, 1988–96 (Vice-President, Executive Council, 1988–91); *b* 14 Dec. 1948; *s* of Hon. Kim Edward Beazley and Betty Beazley; *m* 1st, 1974, Mary Paltridge (marr. diss. 1989); two *d*; 2nd, 1990, Susanna Annus; one *d*. *Educ:* Univ. of Western Australia (MA); Oxford Univ. (Rhodes Scholar; MPhil). Tutor in Social and Political Theory, Murdoch Univ., WA, 1976–79, Lectr 1980. Minister of State for Aviation, and Minister Assisting the Minister for Defence, 1983–84; Special Minister of State, 1983–84; Minister of State for Defence, 1984–90; Minister for Transport and Communications, 1990–91, for Finance, 1991, for Employment, Educn and Training, 1991–93, for Finance, 1993–96; Dep. Prime Minister, 1995–96. Mem. Nat. Exec., ALP, 1991–94, 1996–. *Publication:* (with I. Clark) The Politics of Intrusion: the Super-Powers in the Indian Ocean, 1979. *Recreations:* swimming, reading. *Address:* Parliament House, Canberra, ACT 2600, Australia. *T:* (2) 62774022.

BEAZLEY, Peter George, CBE 1993; *b* 9 June 1922; *s* of Thomas Alfred and Agnes Alice Mary Beazley; *m* 1945, Joyce Marion Sulman; one *s* two *d*. *Educ:* Highgate Sch.; St John Baptist Coll., Oxford. Final Hons PPE, MA Oxon. Captain, Rifle Brigade, served in N Africa, Italy, Austria, 1942–47. Joined ICI, 1947; served in UK, Portugal, Germany, Belgium and S Africa as Manager, Gen. Manager, Divl Bd Dir, Vice Chm. and Man. Dir of associated cos, 1948–77; retd from ICI 1978. MEP (C) Bedfordshire, 1979–84, Bedfordshire South, 1984–94. Member: European Democratic Gp Bureau, 1982–83; Economic and Monetary Affairs and Industrial Policy Cttee, European Parlt, 1984–94 (Vice Chm., 1984–89); European Parlt Portuguese Parlt Jt delegn, 1979–84; European Parlt Japanese delegn, 1985–89; Vice Chm., SE Asia delegn, 1989–94. MRI; Mem., RIIA (Res. Fellow, 1977–78). *Publication:* The Role of Western Technology Transfer in the Development of the Soviet Union's Chemical Industry (with V. Sobeslavsky), 1979. *Recreations:* golf, gardening. *Address:* Rest Harrow, 14 The Combe, Ratton, Eastbourne, East Sussex BN20 9DB. *Club:* Oriental.

See also C. J. P. Beazley.

BEAZLEY, Thomas Alan George; QC 2001; *b* 2 March 1951; *s* of Derek Edwin George Beazley and Rosemary Janet Beazley; *m* 1980, Ingrid Ann Marrable; two *d*. *Educ:* Emmanuel Coll., Cambridge (BA; LLB). Called to the Bar, Middle Temple, 1979. *Recreations:* reading, travelling, cooking. *Address:* Blackstone Chambers, Blackstone House, Temple, EC4Y 9BW.

BECHER, Sir John (William Michael) Wrixon-, 6th Bt *cr* 1831, of Ballygiblin, co. Cork; Partner, Ford Reynolds and Associates Ltd, since 2000; Director, Old Street Productions Ltd; *b* 29 Sept. 1950; *s* of Sir William Fane Wrixon-Becher, 5th Bt, MC and Hon. Vanda (who later *m* 9th Earl of Glasgow), *d* of 4th Baron Vivian; *S* father, 2000. *Educ:* Ludgrove; Harrow; Neuchâtel Univ. FPC. Lloyds Non-Marine Underwriter, 1971–74; Lloyds Broker, Eckersley Hicks Ltd, 1974–82; Hutchison Craft Financial Services Ltd, 1982–87; Dir, Wise Speke Financial Services Ltd, 1987–93; Financial Consultant, HSBC Actuaries and Consultants Ltd, 1993–2000. *Recreations:* golf, shooting, fishing, all field sports. *Address:* 28 Atherton Street, SW11 2JE. *Clubs:* White's, Annabel's, MCC; I Zingari; Royal St George's; Swinley Forest.

BECHTEL, Stephen Davison, Jr; Chairman Emeritus: Bechtel Group, Inc., since 1990; Fremont Group, since 1995; *b* 1925; *s* of Stephen Davison Bechtel and Laura Peart. Joined Bechtel Group, Inc. (Engineers and Constructors), 1941; Pres., 1960; Chm., 1973–90. Mem., Bd of Trustees, CIT, 1967–96 (Life Trustee, 1997). Chairman: Business Council, 1987–88; Nat. Acad. of Engrg, 1982–86. Mem., President's Council, Purdue Univ., 1984–; Mem. Adv. Council, 1991–, Vice Chm. and Mem. Bd of Visitors, 1992–, Inst. for Internat. Studies, Stanford Univ. Numerous awards including: Herbert Hoover Medal, 1981; Chairman's Award, 1982, Nat. Engrg Award, 1997, Amer. Assoc. of Engrg Socs; President's Award, 1985, OPAL Award for Lifetime Achievement in Construction, 2000, ASCE; Nat. Medal of Technology, 1991; Founders Award, NAE, 1999; Engr of Distinction Award, Univ. of Colorado, 2000. Officer, Legion of Honour (France), 1979. *Address:* c/o Bechtel Group, Inc., PO Box 193965, San Francisco, CA 94119–3965, USA.

BECK, Rev. Brian Edgar, MA; President of the Methodist Conference, 1993–94; Secretary of the Conference, 1984–98; *b* 27 Sept. 1933; *o s* of late A. G. and C. A. Beck; *m* 1958, Margaret Ludlow; three *d*. *Educ:* City of London School; Corpus Christi College, Cambridge (1st Cl. Classical Tripos pts 1 and 2); Wesley House, Cambridge (1st Cl. Theol. Tripos pt 2). BA 1955, MA 1959. Ordained Methodist Minister, 1960; Asst Tutor, Handsworth Coll., 1957–59; E Suffolk Circuit Minister, 1959–62; St Paul's United Theological Coll., Limuru, Kenya, 1962–68; Tutor, Wesley House, Cambridge, 1968–80, Principal 1980–84. Sec., E African Church Union Consultation Worship and Liturgy Cttee, 1963–68; Mem., World Methodist Council, 1966–71, 1981–98; Co-Chm., Oxford Inst. of Methodist Theol. Studies, 1976–. Hon. Chaplain, Guild of St Bride, Fleet Street, 1994–. Fernley-Hartley Lectr, 1978; Vis. Prof., Wesley Theol Seminary, Washington, 1999. DD Lambeth, 1998. *Publications:* Reading the New Testament Today, 1977; Christian Character in the Gospel of St Luke, 1989; Gospel Insights, 1998; contributor to: Christian Belief, a Catholic-Methodist statement, 1970; Unity the Next Step?, 1972; Suffering and Martyrdom in the New Testament, 1981; Rethinking Wesley's Theology, 1998; Community-Unity-Communion, 1998; Managing the Church?, 2000; articles in NT Studies, Epworth Review. *Recreations:* walking, DIY, cross-stitch. *Address:* 26 Hurrell Road, Cambridge CB4 3RH. *T:* and *Fax:* (01223) 312260.

BECK, Clive; *b* 12 April 1937; *s* of Sir Edgar Charles Beck, CBE, and Mary Agnes Beck; *m* 1960, Philippa Flood; three *s* three *d*. *Educ:* Ampleforth College. 2nd Lieut, The Life Guards, 1956–57; John Mowlem & Co., 1957–67; SGB Group, 1967–86; Dep. Chm., John Mowlem & Co., 1986–92. Director: London Management Ltd, 1990–; Pioneer Concrete Holdings plc, 1990–. *Recreations:* golf, fishing. *Address:* 2 Parkside Gardens, Wimbledon, SW19 5EY. *Clubs:* Royal Wimbledon Golf, Swinley Forest Golf.

See also Sir E. P. Beck.

BECK, Sir (Edgar) Philip, Kt 1988; Chairman: John Mowlem & Co., 1979–95; Railtrack, 1999–2001; *b* 9 Aug. 1934; *s* of Sir Edgar Charles Beck, CBE, and Mary Agnes Beck; *m* 1st, 1957, Thomasina Joanna Jeal (marr. diss.); two *s*; 2nd, 1991, Bridget Cockerell (*née* Heathcoat-Amory). *Educ:* Ampleforth College; Jesus College, Cambridge (MA). Dir, John Mowlem, 1964, Dep. Chm., 1978–79. Chairman: FCEC, 1982–83; Export Group for Constructional Industries, 1986–88. Non-executive Director: Invensys; Delta; Kitagawa Europe. *Address:* Pylle Manor, Shepton Mallet, Somerset BA4 6TD. *Club:* Royal Yacht Squadron.

See also C. Beck.

BECK, (James Henry) John; Director of Industries and Farms, Prison Department, Home Office, 1976–80; *b* 5 April 1920; *s* of James Henry and Elizabeth Kate Beck; *m* 1942, Doris Peacock (*d* 1995); one *d* (and one *d* decd). *Educ:* Polytechnic Secondary Sch., Regent Street, W1. Entered Home Office as Clerical Officer, 1937; HM Forces, 1939; returned to Home Office as Executive Officer, 1946; Higher Exec. Officer, 1950; Sen. Exec. Officer, 1958; Principal, 1963; Asst Sec., 1968. *Address:* Scarlet Oaks, Ridgway, Pyrford, Woking, Surrey GU22 8PN. *T:* (01932) 346064.

BECK, Prof. (John) Swanson, FRSE 1984; Foundation Dean, International Medical College, Kuala Lumpur, 1993–97; Professor of Pathology, University of Dundee, 1971–93, now Professor Emeritus; *b* 22 Aug. 1928; *s* of late Dr John Beck and Mary (*née* Barbour); *m* 1960, Marion Tudhope Paterson; one *s* one *d*. *Educ:* Glasgow Acad.; Univ. of Glasgow. BSc, DSc, MB, ChB, MD, FRCPG, FRCPE, FRCPI, FRACP, FRCPath, FIBiol, CBiol, EurBiol. Lectr in Pathology, Univ. of Glasgow, 1958–63; Sen. Lectr in Pathology, Univ. of Aberdeen, 1963–71. Consultant Pathologist: N Eastern Regional Hosp. Bd, 1963–71; Eastern Regional Hosp. Bd, 1971–74; Tayside Health Bd, 1974–93. Chairman: Breast Tumour Panel, MRC, 1979–90; Biomedical Res. Cttee, SHHD, 1983–93 (Mem. 1975–79). Member: Cell Biology and Disorders Bd, MRC, 1978–82; Health Services Res. Panel, MRC, 1981–82; Chief Scientist's Cttee, SHHD, 1983–93; Tayside Health Bd, 1983–91; Nat. Biol Standards Bd, 1988–93 (Chm., 1991–93, Mem., 1993–, Scientific Policy Adv. Cttee); Med. Adv. Bd, LEPRA, 1988–. Mem. Council, RSE, 1987–90, 1997– (Convenor, Grants Cttee, 1991–94; Meetings Sec., 1997–98; Prog. Convenor, 1998–). Vis. Prof. of Pharmacy, Univ. of Strathclyde, 1996–. Distinguished Fellow, Internat. Med. Coll., 1998. DUniv Strathclyde, 1999. *Publications:* various papers in Jl of Pathology and other medical and scientific jls. *Recreations:* walking, gardening. *Address:* East Balloch Cottage, near Kirriemuir, Angus DD8 5EY. *T:* (01575) 574731, *Fax:* (01575) 575752; *e-mail:* jsbeck@clara.net. *Club:* New (Edinburgh).

BECK, Lydia Helena; *see* Lopes Cardozo, L. H.

BECK, Sir Philip; see Beck, Sir E. P.

BECK, Swanson; *see* Beck, J. S.

BECKE, Mrs Shirley Cameron, OBE 1974; QPM 1972; Vice-Chairman, 1976–83 and Regional Administrator, London Region, 1974–79, Women's Royal Voluntary Service, retired; *b* 29 April 1917; *er d* of late George L. Jennings, AMIGasE and Marion Jennings; *m* 1954, Rev. Justice Becke, MBE, TD, FCA (*d* 1990); no *c. Educ:* privately; Ealing Co. Gram. Sch. Trained in Gas Engineering, 1935–40. Joined Metropolitan Police as Constable, 1941; served in various ranks; Woman Commander, 1969–74. OStJ 1975. *Recreations:* reading, bridge. *Address:* 4 North Close, St Martin's Square, Chichester PO19 1NU. *T:* (01243) 784295.

BECKE, Lt-Col William Hugh Adamson, CMG 1964; DSO 1945; *b* 24 Sept. 1916; *er s* of late Brig.-Gen. J. H. W. Becke, CMG, DSO, AFC, and late Mrs A. P. Becke (*née* Adamson); *m* 1945, Mary Catherine, 3rd *d* of late Major G. M. Richmond, Kincairney, Murthly, Perthshire. *Educ:* Charterhouse; RMC Sandhurst. Commissioned in The Sherwood Foresters, 1937. British Military Mission to Greece, 1949–52; Asst Military Adviser to the High Commissioner for the UK in Pakistan, 1957–59; Military Attaché, Djakarta, 1962–64; retd 1966. Private Sec. and Comptroller to Governor of Victoria, 1969–74; Personnel Officer, Gas and Fuel Corp. of Vic, 1974–82. *Address:* 3 Chambers Street, South Yarra, Vic 3141, Australia. *Clubs:* Army and Navy; Melbourne, Victoria Racing (Melbourne).

BECKER, Boris; tennis administrator; *b* 22 Nov. 1967; *s* of late Karl-Heinz and Elvira Becker; *m* Barbara Feltus (marr. diss. 2001); two *s*; one *d*. West German Junior Champion, 1983; wins include: Young Masters' Junior Tournament, 1985; Wimbledon, 1985 (youngest winner), 1986, 1989; US Open, 1989; Australian Open, 1991, 1996; ATP World Champion, 1992, 1995; Davis Cup winner, 1988, 1989; retired as professional tennis player, 1999. *Address:* Nusslocher Strasse 51, 69181 Leimen, Baden, Germany.

BECKER, Prof. Gary Stanley, PhD; University Professor, Departments of Economics and Sociology, University of Chicago, since 1983; *b* 2 Dec. 1930; *s* of Louis William Becker and Anna (*née* Siskind); *m* 1st, 1954, Doria Slote (decd); two *d*; 2nd, 1979, Guity Nashat; two *s*. *Educ:* Princeton Univ. (AB *summa cum laude* 1951); Univ. of Chicago (AM 1953; PhD 1955). Asst Prof., Univ. of Chicago, 1954–57; Columbia University: Asst and Associate Prof of Econs, 1957–60; Prof. of Econs, 1960–68; Arthur Lehman Prof. of Econs, 1968–69; University of Chicago: Ford Foundn Vis. Prof. of Econs, 1969–70; Prof., 1970–83, Chm., 1984–85, Dept of Econs. Member: Domestic Adv. Bd, Hoover Instn, 1973–91 (Sen. Fellow, 1990–); Acad. Adv. Bd, Amer. Enterprise Inst. for Public Policy Res., 1987–91; Associate Mem., Inst. Fiscal and Monetary Policy, Min. of Finance, Japan, 1988–; Res. Associate, Econs Res. Center, Nat. Opinion Res. Center, 1980–. Columnist, Business Week, 1985–. Member: American Economic Association: Vice-Pres., 1974; Pres., 1987; Distinguished Fellow, 1988; Mont Pelerin Society, 1971–: Exec. Bd, 1985–96; Vice-Pres., 1989–90; Pres., 1990–92; Editl Bd, Amer. Econ. Rev., 1968–71; Amer. Statistical Assoc. (Fellow 1965); Econometric Soc. Member: Nat. Acad. Scis, 1975–; Internat. Union for Scientific Study of Population, 1982–; Amer. Philosophical Soc., 1986–; Founding Mem., Nat. Acad. Educn (Vice-Pres., 1965–67). Fellow: Amer. Acad. Arts and Scis, 1972; Nat. Assoc. of Business Economists, 1993; Pontifical Acad. of Sci., 1997. Hon. degrees: PhD: Hebrew Univ., Jerusalem, 1985; Palermo, 1993; LLD Knox Coll., Ill, 1985; Dr of Arts, Illinois, 1988; DSc: SUNY, 1990; Rochester, 1995; DHL: Princeton, 1991; Columbia, 1993; Hofstra, 1997; DBA Miami, 1995; DEconSc Warsaw Sch. of Econs, 1995; Dr Prague Univ. of Econs, 1995. John Bates Clark Medal, Amer. Econ. Assoc., 1967; Frank E. Seidman Dist. Award in Pol Econ., 1985; Merit Award, NIH, 1986; John R. Commons Award, Omicron Delta Epsilon, 1987; Nobel Prize for Economics, 1992. *Publications:* The Economics of Discrimination, 1957, 2nd edn 1971; Human Capital, 1964, 3rd edn 1993 (trans. Japanese 1975, Spanish 1984, Chinese 1987, Romanian 1997); Human Capital and the Personal Distribution of Income: an analytical approach, 1967; Economic Theory, 1971 (trans. Japanese, 1976); (ed jtly) Essays in the Economics of Crime and Punishment, 1974; (with G. Ghez) The Allocation of Time and Goods Over the Life Cycle, 1975; The Economic Approach to Human Behaviour, 1976 (trans. German 1982, Polish 1990, Chinese 1993, Romanian 1994); A Treatise on the Family, 1981, expanded edn 1991 (trans. Spanish 1987, Chinese 1988); Accounting for Tastes, 1996; The Economics of Life, 1996 (trans. Chinese 1997, Czech 1997, German 1998, Japanese 1998); Social Markets, 1999; contrib. chaps in numerous books and articles in jls incl. Jl Pol Econ., Qly Jl Econs, Amer. Econ. Rev., Jl Law and Econs, Jl Labor Econs, Business Econs, etc. *Address:* Department of Economics, University of Chicago, 1126 East 59th Street, Chicago, IL 60637, USA. *T:* (312) 7028168; 1308 East 58th Street, Chicago, IL 60637, USA.

BECKER, Judith Myfanwy Sarah; *see* Hall, J. M. S.

BECKERLEG, John; Director of Social Services, Buckinghamshire County Council, since 1999; *b* 12 Aug. 1956; *s* of Lewis Beckerleg and Doris (*née* Bundy); *m* 1983, April Cornelia Saunders; two *s* one *d*. *Educ:* Emmanuel Coll., Cambridge (MA 1981); MBA Henley Mgt Coll. 1998. CIPFA 1981. Chief Accountant, Cambs CC, 1985–87; Sen. Asst Co. Treas., Herts CC, 1987–91; Dep. Co. Treas., 1991–93, Dir of Finance, 1993–96, Dir of Corporate Services, 1996–99, Bucks CC. *Recreations:* theatre, genealogy. *Address:* Daffodil Cottage, Main Street, Grendon Underwood, Bucks HP18 0ST. *T:* (01296) 770595.

BECKERMAN, Wilfred, PhD; Fellow of Balliol College, Oxford, 1975–92, now Emeritus; Reader in Economics, Oxford University, 1978–92; *b* 19 May 1925; *s* of Morris and Mathilda Beckerman; *m* 1st, 1952, Nicole Geneviève Ritter (*d* 1979); one *s* two *d*; 2nd, 1991, Joanna Pasek; one *d*. *Educ:* Ealing County Sch.; Trinity Coll., Cambridge (MA, PhD). RNVR, 1943–46. Trinity Coll., Cambridge, 1946–50; Lecturer in Economics, Univ. of Nottingham, 1950–52; OEEC and OECD, Paris, 1952–61; National Inst. of Economic and Social Research, 1962–63; Fellow of Balliol Coll., Oxford, 1964–69; Economic Advr to Pres. of BoT (leave of absence from Balliol), 1967–69; Prof. of Political Economy, Univ. of London, and Head of Dept of Political Economy, UCL, 1969–75. Mem., Royal Commn on Environmental Pollution, 1970–73. Member: Exec. Cttee, NIESR, 1973–96; Council, Royal Economic Soc., 1990–93. Elie Halévy Vis. Prof. Institut d'Etudes Politiques, Paris, 1977; Resident Scholar, Woodrow Wilson Internat. Center for Scholars, Washington, DC, 1982. Consultant: World Bank; OECD; ILO. Pres., Section F (Economics), BAAS, 1978. *Publications:* The British Economy in 1975 (with associates), 1965; International Comparisons of Real Incomes, 1966; An Introduction to National Income Analysis, 1968; (ed and contrib.) The Labour Government's Economic Record, 1972; In Defence of Economic Growth, 1974; Measures of Leisure, Equality and Welfare, 1978; (ed and contrib.) Slow Growth in Britain: Causes and Consequences, 1979; Poverty and the Impact of Income Maintenance Programmes, 1979; (with S. Clark) Poverty and the Impact of Social Security in Britain since 1961, 1982; (ed and contrib.) Wage Rigidity and Unemployment, 1986; Small is Stupid, 1995; Growth, the Environment and the Distribution of Incomes, 1995; (with J. Pasek) Justice, Posterity and the Environment, 2001; articles in Economic Jl, Economica, Econometrica, Review of Economic Studies, Review of Economics and Statistics, etc. *Recreations:* various. *Address:* 1c Norham Gardens, Oxford OX2 6PS.

BECKETT, family name of **Baron Grimthorpe**.

BECKETT, Prof. Arnold Heyworth, OBE 1983; Professor of Pharmacy, Chelsea College (University of London), 1959–85, now Emeritus; *b* 12 Feb. 1920; *m* 1991, Prof. Bozena W. Hadzija. *Educ:* Baines Grammar Sch., Poulton-le-Fylde; Sch. of Pharmacy and Birkbeck Coll., University of London. FRPharmS (FPS 1942); BSc 1947; PhD 1950; DSc London, 1959. Head, Dept of Pharmacy, Chelsea Coll. of Sci. and Technology, 1959–79. Chm., Med. Commn, Internat. Tennis Fedn, 1985–93; Mem., Med. Commn, Internat. Olympic Cttee, 1968–93; Mem., British Olympic Assoc. Med. Commn, until 1986; Chm., Bd of Pharmaceutical Sciences, Fédération Internat. Pharmaceutique, 1960–80; Mem. Council, Pharmaceutical, later Royal Pharmaceutical, Soc. of GB, 1965–90 (Pres., 1981–82). Vis. Prof. to Univs, USA and Canada. Examr in Pharmaceut. Chem., Univs in UK, Nigeria, Ghana, Singapore. Internat. pharmaceutical consultant. Pereira Medal, 1942; STAS Medal, Belg. Chem. Soc., 1962; Hanbury Meml Medal, 1974; Charter Gold Medal, 1977; Mem. of Olympic Order, Silver Medal, 1980. Hon. DSc: Heriot-Watt, 1976; Uppsala, 1977; Leuven, 1982. *Publications:* (co-author) Practical Pharmaceutical Chemistry, 1962; Part 1, 3rd edn, 1975, Part 2, 3rd edn, 1976; founder Co-editor, Jl of Medicinal Chemistry; research contribs to 450 jls. *Recreations:* travel, sport, photography. *Address:* 20 Braybrooke Gardens, Upper Norwood, SE19 2UN.

BECKETT, Bruce Probart, FRIBA, FRIAS, FRTPI, FCIOB; Chartered Architect, Town and Country Planner and Building Consultant in private practice, 1984–97; *b* 7 June 1924; *s* of J. D. L. Beckett and Florence Theresa (*née* Probart); *m* 1957, Jean McDonald; two *s* three *d* (incl. twin *s* and *d*). *Educ:* Rondebosch Boys' High Sch., Cape Town; Univ. of Cape Town (BArch with distinction, 1950); University Coll. London (Diploma in Town Planning, 1963). Active Service SA Navy, 1943; Midshipman, 1943; Sub-Lieut, 1944; seconded RN, 1944; Lieut, 1946. ARIBA 1950, FRIBA 1968; FRIAS 1968. Mem. Inst. S African Architects, 1950; FRTPI (AMTPI 1966); FCIOB 1979. Private practice in S Africa, 1952–59, London, 1960. Sen. Architect, War Office, 1961; Superintending Grade Arch., Directorate-Gen. of Res. and Development, 1963–67; Chief Architect, 1967–84 and Dir of Bldg, 1978–84, Scottish Office, retd. Partner, Hutchison Locke & Monk, 1984–87. Dep. Leader, Timber Trade Mission to Canada, 1964. A Vice-Pres., RIBA, 1972–73, 1975–76, 1976–77; Hon. Librarian, 1976–78. Sec. of State for Scotland's nominee on ARCUK, 1970–85, RIBA nominee, 1985–97; Member Council: EAA, 1970–78; RIAS, 1971–78, 1984–87; RIBA, 1972–78; Member: Sec. of State for Environment's Construction and Housing Res. Adv. Council, 1968–79; Building Res. Estabt Adv. Cttees in England and Scotland, 1970–84; York Adv. Cttee for continuing educn for building professions, 1975–80. Assessor, to Scottish Cttee of Design Council, 1974–84; Civic Trust Adjudicator, 1985–87. *Publications:* papers on industrialised building, contract procedure, etc, in various jls; HMSO publications on Scottish housing, educational and health buildings. *Recreations:* sailing, walking. *Address:* Summerfield, Vines Cross Road, Horam, near Heathfield, East Sussex TN21 0HE. *T:* (01435) 812042; 15 Mayville Gardens, Edinburgh EH5 3DB. *T:* (0131) 556 2867. *Clubs:* Arts; New (Edinburgh); Kelvin (Kelvin Grove, Cape Town).

BECKETT, Maj.-Gen. Denis Arthur, CB 1971; DSO 1944; OBE 1960; *b* 19 May 1917; *o s* of late Archibald Beckett, Woodford Green, Essex; *m* 1946, Elizabeth (marr. diss. 1974), *er d* of late Col Guy Edwards, Upper Slaughter, Glos; one *s*; *m* 1978, Nancy Ann Hitt. *Educ:* Forest Sch.; Chard Sch. Joined Hon. Artillery Co., 1939; commnd into Essex Regt, 1940; served in W Africa, Middle East, Italy and Greece, 1940–45; DAA & QMG and Bde Major, Parachute Bdes, 1948–50; Instructor, RMA Sandhurst, 1951–53; Directing Staff, Staff Coll., Camberley, 1953–56; Second in Comd 3rd Bn Para. Regt, 1956–58; comd 2nd Bn Para. Regt, 1958–60; Directing Staff, JSSC, 1960–61; comd 19 Bde, 1961–63; idc 1964; DAG, BAOR, 1965–66; Chief of Staff, Far East Land Forces, 1966–68; Dir of Personal Services (Army), 1968–71, retired 1971. Trustee: Nehru Meml Centre Trust, 1975–; Airborne Forces Mus., 1985–94; Governor, Forest Sch., 1986–95. Liveryman, Coopers' Co., 1962–. *Address:* 12 Wellington House, Eton Road, NW3 4SY. *Clubs:* Army and Navy, Lansdowne.

BECKETT, Maj.-Gen. Edwin Horace Alexander, CB 1988; MBE 1974; Head of British Defence Staff, Washington, 1988–91, retired; *b* 16 May 1937; *s* of William Alexander Beckett and Doris Beckett; *m* 1963, Micaela Elizabeth Benedicta, *d* of Col Sir Edward Malet, Bt, OBE; three *s* one *d*. *Educ:* Henry Fanshawe School; RMA Sandhurst; ndc, psc, sq. Commissioned 1957 West Yorks Regt; regtl service in Aden (despatches 1968), Gibraltar, Germany and N Ireland; DAA&QMG 11 Armd Brigade, 1972–74; CO 1 PWO, 1976–78 (despatches 1977); GSO1 (DS) Staff Coll., 1979; Comdt Junior Div., Staff Coll., 1980; Comdr UKMF and 6 Field Force, 1981; Comdr UKMF, 1 Inf. Brigade and Tidworth Garrison, 1982; Director: Concepts, MoD, 1983–84; Army Plans and Programmes, MoD, 1984–85; C of S, HQ BAOR, 1985–88. Col Comdt, The King's Div., 1988–94; Col, PWO, 1996–2001. Dir, Corporate Affairs, IDV Ltd, 1991–96; Founder and Chm., British Brands Gp, 1992–96 (Pres., 1997–99); Chairman: Calvert Trust Exmoor, 1994–2000 (Trustee, 1994–); Exmoor Trust, 1999–. *Recreations:* fishing, picture framing, farming for fun. *Clubs:* Army and Navy, Pilgrims.

BECKETT, Frances Mary; Chief Executive, Shaftesbury Society, since 1995; *b* 20 Nov. 1951. *Educ:* Nottingham Poly. (CQSW); LSE (MSc Vol. Sector Orgn). Social Worker, Somerset CC, 1972–76; Student Advr, UCCF, 1976–80; Community Worker, 1981–86; Shaftesbury Society, 1986–: Social Work Advr, Community Care Co-ordinator, Urban Action Dir. *Publication:* Called to Action, 1989. *Recreations:* Church involvement, theatre, cinema, reading. *Address:* Shaftesbury Society, 16 Kingston Road, SW19 1JZ. *T:* (020) 8239 5555.

BECKETT, Rt Hon. Margaret (Mary), (Mrs L. A. Beckett); PC 1993; MP (Lab) Derby South, since 1983; Secretary of State for Environment, Food and Rural Affairs, since 2001; *b* 15 Jan. 1943; *d* of late Cyril and Winifred Jackson; *m* 1979, Lionel A. Beckett; two step *s*. *Educ:* Notre Dame High Sch., Norwich; Manchester Coll. of Sci. and Technol. Formerly: engrg apprentice (metallurgy), AEI, Manchester; exptl officer, Manchester Univ.; Labour Party res. asst; political adviser, Minister for Overseas Devel, 1974; Principal Researcher, Granada TV, 1979–83. Contested (Lab) Lincoln, Feb. 1974; MP (Lab) Lincoln, Oct. 1974–1979; PPS to Minister for Overseas Devel, 1974–75; Asst Govt Whip, 1975–76; Parly Under-Sec. of State, DES, 1976–79; Opposition front bench spokesman on health and social security, 1984–89; Mem., Shadow Cabinet, 1989–97; Shadow Chief Sec. to the Treasury, 1989–92; Shadow Leader, H of C, 1992–94;

Campaigns Co-ordinator and Dep. Leader, Lab Party, 1992–94; Actg Leader, Lab Party, May–July 1994; opposition front bench spokesman on health, 1994–95, on trade and industry, 1995–97; Pres., BoT, and Sec. of State for Trade and Industry, 1997–98; Pres. of the Council and Leader, H of C, 1998–2001. Mem. NEC, Labour Party, 1980–81, 1985–86, 1988–97. *Recreations:* cooking, reading, caravanning. *Address:* c/o House of Commons, SW1A 0AA.

BECKETT, Nikaila Susan; Chief Executive, NSB Retail Systems Plc, since 1995; *b* 16 June 1961; two *s*. IBM, UK, USA and Europe, 1979–95. *Recreations:* sailing, scuba diving, tennis, eating out. *Address:* Pembroke House, 7-9 Chesham Street, SW1X 8ND.

BECKETT, Sir Richard Gervase, 3rd Bt *cr* 1921; QC 1988; barrister; *b* 27 March 1944; *s* of Sir Martyn Gervase Beckett, 2nd Bt, MC, RIBA and Hon. Priscilla, *d* of 3rd Viscount Esher, GBE; *S* father, 2001; *m* 1976, Elizabeth Ann, *d* of Major Hugo Waterhouse; one *s* three *d*. *Educ:* Eton. Diploma in Economics (Oxford). Called to the Bar, Middle Temple, 1965; practice at the Bar, 1966–. *Recreation:* landscape. *Heir:* *s* Walter Gervase Beckett, *b* 16 Jan. 1987. *Address:* 33 Groveway, SW9 0AH. *T:* (020) 7735 3350. *Clubs:* White's, Pratt's, Portland.

BECKETT, Sir Terence (Norman), KBE 1987 (CBE 1974); Kt 1978; DL; Managing Director and Chief Executive, 1974–80 and Chairman, 1976–80, Ford Motor Co. Ltd; Director General, Confederation of British Industry, 1980–87 (Member, Council, 1976–80); *b* 13 Dec. 1923; *s* of late Horace Norman Beckett, MBE and late Clarice Lillian (*née* Allsop); *m* 1950, Sylvia Gladys Asprey; one *d*. *Educ:* Wolverhampton and S Staffs Tech. Coll. (Engrg Cadetship Diploma); London Sch. of Econs (BScEcon, Hon. Fellow, 1994). GIMechE, FIMechE, CEng, FIMI, FREng. Captain REME, British Army (UK, India, Malaya), 1945–48; RARO, 1949–62. Company Trainee, Ford Motor Co. Ltd, 1950; Asst in office of Dep. Chm. and Man. Dir, 1951; Man., Styling, Briggs Motor Bodies Ltd (Ford subsid.), 1954; Admin Man., Engrg, Briggs, 1955; Manager, Product Staff, 1955; Gen. Man., Product Planning Staff, 1961 (responsible for Cortina, Transit Van, 'D' series truck); Manager, Marketing Staff, 1963; Dir, Car Div., 1964; Exec. Dir, Ford Motor Co. Ltd, 1966 and Dir of Sales, 1968; Vice-Pres., European and Overseas Sales Ops, Ford of Europe Inc., 1969–74; Chm., Ford Motor Credit Co. Ltd, 1976–80; Director: ICI, 1976–80; Automotive Finance Ltd, 1974–77. Dep. Chm., CEGB, 1990 (Dir, 1987–90). Advr to Jt Cttee of MMB and Dairy Trade Fedn, 1987–94. Member: NEDC, 1980–87; Engineering Industries Council, 1975–80; BIM Council, 1976–77; Top Salaries Review Body, 1987–92; Grand Council, Motor and Cycle Trades Benevolent Fund (BEN), 1976–80; SMMT Council and Exec. Cttee, 1974–80; Council, Automobile Div., IMechE, 1979–80; Vice Pres. and Hon. Fellow, Inst. of the Motor Industry, 1974–80; Vice-Pres., Conference on Schs, Sci. and Technol., 1979–80; Chm., Governing Body, London Business Sch., 1979–86; Mem. Court, Cranfield Inst. of Technology, 1977–82; Governor, NIESR, 1978–; Governor and Mem. Court, LSE, 1978–99; Pro-Chancellor, Univ. of Essex, 1989–98 (Mem. Court, 1985–; Chm. Council, 1989–95). Mem. Court of Assts, Worshipful Co. of Engineers, 1983–85. DL Essex, 1991. Pres., IVCA, 1987–91. Patron: MSC Award Scheme for Disabled People, 1979–80; AIESEC, 1985. Lectures: Stamp, London Univ., 1982; Pfizer, Kent at Canterbury Univ., 1983. Hon. Fellow: Sidney Sussex Coll., Cambridge, 1981; London Business Sch., 1988; Hon. DSc: Cranfield, 1977; Heriot-Watt, 1981; Hon. DSc (Econ.) London, 1982; Hon. DTech: Brunel, 1991; Wolverhampton, 1995; DU Essex, 1995; Hon. DLitt Anglia Poly., 1998. CIMgt; FRSA 1984. Hambro Businessman of the Year, 1978; BIM Gold Medal, 1980. *Recreations:* travel, music. *Address:* c/o Barclays Bank plc, 74 High Street, Ingatestone, Essex CM4 9BW. *Club:* Athenæum.

BECKETT, William Cartwright, CB 1978; LLM; Solicitor to the Corporation of Lloyd's, 1985–93; *b* 21 Sept. 1929; *s* of late William Beckett and Emily (*née* Cartwright); *m* 1st, 1956, Marjorie Jean Hoskin; two *s*; 2nd, 1974, Lesley Margaret Furlonger. *Educ:* Salford Grammar Sch.; Manchester Univ. (LLB 1950, LLM 1952). Called to Bar, Middle Temple, 1952. Joined Treasury Solicitor's Dept, 1956; Board of Trade, 1965; Asst Solicitor, DEP, 1969; Under-Sec., DTI, 1972; Dep.-Sec. 1977; Legal Secretary, Law Officers' Dept, 1975–80; Solicitor, DTI, 1980–84. *Recreations:* music, golf. *Address:* Stocks Farm, New Road, Rayne, Essex CM7 8SY. *Club:* Reform.

BECKINGHAM, Peter; HM Diplomatic Service; Consul General and Director, Trade and Investment, Sydney, since 1999; *b* 16 March 1949; *s* of Rev. Leslie Beckingham and late Eileen Beckingham (*née* Grimsey); *m* 1975, Jill Mary Trotman; two *d*. *Educ:* Chigwell Sch.; Selwyn Coll., Cambridge (MA). MIEx 1998. Argo Record Co., 1970–1974; BOTB, 1974–79; Dir, British Inf. Services, NY, 1979–84; News Dept, FCO, 1984 (Hd, Press Centre, G7 Summit); Energy, Sci. and Space Dept, FCO, 1984–86; Hd, Horn of Africa Section, E Africa Dept, FCO, 1986–88; First Sec. (Commercial), Stockholm, 1988–92; Hd, Political Section, Canberra, 1992–96; Dir, Jt Export Promotion Directorate, FCO/DTI, 1996–99. *Publication:* (ed) Australia and Britain: the evolving relationship, 1993. *Recreations:* music, golf, tennis. *Address:* c/o Foreign and Commonwealth Office, King Charles Street, SW1A 2AH. *Clubs:* Union (Sydney); Royal Sydney Golf.

BECKLAKE, (Ernest) John (Stephen), PhD; CEng; Senior Research Fellow, Science Museum, since 1994; *b* 24 June 1943; *s* of Ernest and Evelyn Becklake; *m* 1965, Susan Elizabeth (*née* Buckle), BSc; two *s*. *Educ:* Bideford Grammar Sch.; Exeter Univ. (BSc, PhD). CEng 1988; MIEE 1988; FRAeS 1996. Engr, EMI Electronics, Wells, 1967–69; Post-Doctoral Fellow, Victoria Univ., BC, Canada, 1969–70; Sen. Scientist, Marconi Space and Def. Systems, Frimley, 1970–72; Science Museum: Asst Keeper, Dept of Earth and Space Sciences, 1972–80; Keeper, Dept of Elect. Engrg, Communications and Circulation, 1980–85; Keeper, Dept of Engrg, subseq. Head of Technology Gp, 1985–94. Mem., Internat. Acad. of Astronautics, 1988– (Chm., Hist. Cttee, 1996–). Man. Ed., DERA Hist. Project, DERA Farnborough, 1995–. Consultant, German Rocketry, Aerospace Mus., Cosford, 1997–. *Publications:* Man and the Moon, 1980; The Climate Crisis, 1989; The Population Explosion, 1990; Pollution, 1990; (ed) History of Rocketry and Astronautics, vol. XVI, 1995; (series editor) Exploration and Discovery, 1980–; technical pubns in Electronics Letters, Jl of Physics D, Jl of British Interplanetary Soc., and Spaceflight. *Recreations:* gardening, golf, rugby. *Address:* Tree Wood, Robin Hood Lane, Sutton Green, Guildford, Surrey GU7 4QY. *T:* (01483) 766931. *Club:* Puttenham Golf.

BECKMAN, Michael David; QC 1976; *b* 6 April 1932; *s* of Nathan and Esther Beckman; *m*; two *d*. *Educ:* King's Coll., London (LLB (Hons)). Called to the Bar, Lincoln's Inn, 1954. *Recreations:* various. *Address:* Bullards, Widford, Herts SG12 8SG. *T:* (0127984) 2669; (chambers) 11 Stone Buildings, Lincoln's Inn, WC2A 3TG. 12 North Pallant, Chichester PO19 1TQ.

BECKWITH, Prof. Athelstan Laurence Johnson, FRS 1988; FAA; FRACI; Professor of Organic Chemistry, Research School of Chemistry, Australian National University, 1981–96, now Emeritus (Dean, 1989–91); *b* 20 Feb. 1930; *s* of Laurence Alfred Beckwith and Doris Grace Beckwith; *m* 1953, Phyllis Kaye Marshall, Perth, WA; one *s* two *d*. *Educ:* Perth Modern Sch.; Univ. of WA (BSc Hons); Oxford Univ. (DPhil 1956). FAA 1973; FRACI 1973. Lectr in Chemistry, Adelaide Univ., 1953; CSIRO Overseas Student, 1954; Res. Officer, CSIRO Melbourne, 1957; Adelaide University: Lectr in Organic Chemistry, 1958; Prof., 1965–81; Dean of Science, 1972–73. Temp. Lectr, Imperial Coll., London, 1962–63; Vis. Lectr, Univ. of York, 1968; Carnegie Fellow, 1968. Federal Pres., RACI, 1965 (Rennie Medal, 1960; H. G. Smith Meml Medal, 1981; Organic Chemistry Medal, 1992; Leighton Medal, 1997); Treas., Aust. Acad. of Sci., 1997–. *Publications:* numerous articles in Jl of Chem. Soc., Jl of Amer. Chem. Soc., etc. *Recreations:* golf, music, walking. *Address:* 3/9 Crisp Circuit, Bruce, ACT 2617, Australia. *T:* (2) 62493234; (2) 62530696.

BECKWITH, John Lionel, CBE 1996; FCA; Chairman, Pacific Investments, since 1993; Founder Chairman, London & Edinburgh Trust PLC, 1971–92; *b* 19 March 1947; *s* of Col Harold Beckwith and Agnes Camilla McMichael (*née* Duncan); *m* 1975, Heather Marie Robbins; two *s* one *d*. *Educ:* Harrow Sch. FCA 1970; ATII 1970. Arthur Andersen & Co., 1969–71; with London & Edinburgh Trust PLC, 1971–92. Founder Chm., Rutland Trust plc, 1986–91; Chairman: Riverside PLC, 1993–97; Barbican Healthcare PLC, 1996–98. Director: Sporting Frontiers, 1996–; Harlequin FC, 1996–97. Member: Develt Bd, Cancer Relief Macmillan Fund; NCH Action for Children's 125th Anniversary Appeal Cttee. Vice-President: RNIB; Youth Clubs UK; Founder, and Chm. Bd of Trustees, Youth Sport Trust; Patron, Teenage Cancer Trust. Hon. DLitt Loughborough, 2000. Duke of Edinburgh Arthur Bell Trophy, 1999. *Recreations:* sport, music, ballet. *Address:* (office) 124 Sloane Street, SW1X 9BW. *Clubs:* MCC, Annabel's, Queen's; Old Harrovian Football; Royal Berkshire Golf, Royal Mid-Surrey Golf, St George's Hill Golf; Riverside Racquet Centre; Travellers (Paris).

See also P. M. Beckwith.

BECKWITH, Peter Michael; Chairman, PMB Holdings Ltd, since 1992; Deputy Chairman, Ambassador Theatre Group Ltd, since 1992; *b* 20 Jan. 1945; *s* of Col Harold Andrew Beckwith and Agnes Camilla McMichael Beckwith; *m* 1968, Paula Gay Bateman; two *d*. *Educ:* Harrow School; Emmanuel College, Cambridge (MA Hons; Hon. Fellow, 1999). Qualified Solicitor, 1970; Asst Solicitor, Norton Rose Botterell & Roche; London & Edinburgh Trust: Joint Founder and shareholder, 1972; Managing Director, 1983–86; Dep. Chm., 1987; Chm., 1992. Pres., Harbour Club, Milan, 1999–. Vice Patron, Cambridge Univ., 1992–; Trustee, Cambridge Foundn, 1997–. Gov., Harrow Sch., 1992. Hon. LLD Cantab, 2000. *Recreations:* tennis, ski-ing, opera, theatre, dogs, cycling. *Address:* PMB Holdings Ltd, Hill Place House, 55A High Street, SW19 5BA. *Clubs:* Riverside Racquets, Harbour; Downhill Only (Wengen); Harbour (Milan); Austria Haus (Vail).

See also J. L. Beckwith.

BECTIVE, Earl of; Thomas Michael Ronald Christopher Taylour; property consultancy with Bective Davidson, London, since 1995; *b* 10 Feb. 1959; *s* and *heir* of 6th Marquis of Headfort, *qv*; *m* 1987, Susan Jane, *er d* of late C. A. Vandervell and of Mrs Vandervell; two *s* two *d*. *Educ:* Harrow; RAC Cirencester. Formerly estate agent with Egerton, London. *Heir:* *s* Lord Kenlis, *qv*. *Address:* Shipton Manor, Shipton on Cherwell, Oxon OX5 1JL; (office) 1 Cadogan Street, SW3 2PP. *T:* (020) 7589 6677. *Clubs:* Lansdowne; Royal Dublin Society (Dublin).

BEDBROOK, Jack Harry, CEng, FRINA; FIMgt; RCNC; Managing Director, HM Dockyard, Devonport, 1979–84; *b* 8 Aug. 1924; *s* of Harry Bedbrook and Emma Bedbrook; *m* (marr. diss. 1989); three *d*; *m* 1996, Sylvia. *Educ:* Technical Coll., Portsmouth; RNC, Greenwich. Dir Gen. Ships Dept, Admiralty, 1946–51; Asst Constructor, Devonport, 1951–54; Dockyard Dept, Bath, 1954–56; Constructor, Gibraltar Dockyard, 1956–58; Admiralty Exptl Works, Haslar, 1958–62; Dir Gen. Ships Dept, 1962–65; Chief Constructor, Portsmouth, 1965–71; Project Manager, Rosyth, 1971–74; Prodn Dir, Devonport, 1974–77; Man. Dir, HM Dockyard, Rosyth, 1977–79. Registered Mem., Assoc. of Natural Medicines, 1994. *Recreations:* badminton, sailing, gardening, music, therapeutic massage. *Address:* Laxtons, Cargreen, Saltash, Cornwall PL12 6PA. *T:* (01752) 844519.

BEDDARD, Nicholas Elliot; His Honour Judge Beddard; a Circuit Judge, since 1986; *b* 26 April 1934; *s* of Terence Elliot Beddard and Ursula Mary Hamilton Howard; *m* 1964, Gillian Elisabeth Vaughan Bevan, 2nd *d* of Llewellyn and Molly Bevan; two *s* one *d*. *Educ:* Eton. National Service, 1952–54; commissioned, Royal Sussex Regt, 1953; TA (Royal Sussex Regt), 1955–64. United Africa Co., 1955–58; Asst Public Policy Executive, RAC, 1958–68; called to the Bar, Inner Temple, 1967; A Recorder, 1986. *Recreations:* choral singing, ski-ing, golf. *Address:* Ipswich Crown Court, Civic Drive, Ipswich IP1 2DX. *T:* (01473) 213841. *Clubs:* Lansdowne; Orford Sailing.

BEDDINGTON, Charles Richard; Metropolitan Magistrate, 1963–80; *b* 22 Aug. 1911; *s* of late Charles Beddington, Inner Temple, and Stella (*née* de Goldschmidt); *m* 1939, Debbie, *d* of late Frederick Appleby Holt and Rae Vera Franz, *d* of Sir George Hutchinson; two *s* one *d*. *Educ:* Eton (scholar); Balliol Coll., Oxford. Barrister, Inner Temple, 1934. Joined TA, 1939; served RA, 1939–45, Major. Practised at the Bar in London and on SE Circuit. Mem. Mental Health Review Tribunal (SE Metropolitan Area), 1960–63. *Address:* 21 Mytten Close, Cuckfield, West Sussex RH17 5LN. *T:* (01444) 454063.

BEDDINGTON, Prof. John Rex, PhD; FRS 2001; Professor of Applied Population Biology, since 1991, and Director, T. H. Huxley School of Environment, Earth Sciences and Engineering, since 1998, Imperial College, London; *b* 13 Oct. 1945; *s* of Harry Beddington and Mildred (*née* Weale); *m* 1st, 1968, Sarah West (marr. diss. 1972); one *s*; 2nd, 1973, Prof. Sally Baldwin (marr. diss. 1979); one *d*; 3rd, 1990, Caroline Hiller. *Educ:* Monmouth Sch.; London Sch. of Econs (BSc Econ, MSc); Edinburgh Univ. (PhD). Res. Asst, Edinburgh Univ., 1968–71; Lectr on Population Biol., York Univ., 1971–84; Imperial College, London: Reader in Applied Population Biol., 1984–91; Dir, Centre for Envmtl Technol., 1994–97. Sen. Fellow, Internat. Inst. for Envmt and Develt, 1980–83; Hd, UK Scientific Delegn, Commn for Conservation of Antarctic Living Marine Resources, 1983–; Dir, Fisheries Mgt Sci. Prog., DFID (formerly ODA), 1989–; Chm., Scientific Cttee, Indian Ocean Tuna Commn, 1998; Mem., NERC, 2000–. Chairman Trustees: People's Trust for Endangered Species, 1984–; Marine Educn and Conservation Trust, 1987–. Pres., Resource Modelling Assoc., 1992–94. Heidelberg Award for Envmtl Excellence, 1997. *Publications:* articles on ecology, population biol. and fisheries mgt. *Recreations:* hill-walking, art, birdwatching. *Address:* T. H. Huxley School of Environment, Earth Sciences and Engineering, RSM Building, Prince Consort Road, SW7 2BP. *T:* (020) 7594 9270. *Club:* Travellers.

BEDDOE, Sir David Sydney R.; *see* Rowe-Beddoe.

BEDDOW, Prof. Michael; Professor of German, University of Leeds, 1986–98; *b* 3 Sept. 1947; *s* of Austin Beddow and Ivy Beddow; *m* 1976, Helena Hajzyk; one *s*. *Educ:* West Park Grammar Sch., St Helens; St John's Coll., Cambridge. Trinity Hall, Cambridge: Res. Fellow, 1973–75; Staff Fellow, 1975–79; Lectr in German, KCL, 1979–86. Vice Chm. Governors, Silcoates Sch., Wakefield, 1993–2001. *Publications:* The Fiction of Humanity,

1982; Goethe's Faust I: a critical guide, 1986; Thomas Mann: Dr Faustus, 1994; articles and reviews in Jl European Studies, London German Studies, TLS, Publications of English Goethe Soc. *Recreations:* walking, choral singing, computer construction and programming. *Address:* 3 Oakwood Park, Leeds LS8 2PJ. *T:* (0113) 240 1561.

BEDFORD, 13th Duke of, *cr* 1694; **John Robert Russell;** Marquess of Tavistock, 1694; Earl of Bedford, 1550; Baron Russell of Chenies, 1540; Baron Russell of Thornhaugh, 1603; Baron Howland of Streatham, 1695; *b* 24 May 1917; *er s* of 12th Duke and Louisa Crommelin Roberta (*d* 1960), *y d* of Robert Jowitt Whitwell; *S* father 1953; *m* 1st, 1939, Clare Gwendolen Hollway, *née* Bridgman (*d* 1945); two *s*; 2nd, 1947, Lydia (marr. diss., 1960), *widow* of Capt. Ian de Hoghton Lyle, 3rd *d* of 3rd Baron Churston and late Duchess of Leinster; one *s*; 3rd, 1960, Mme Nicole Milinaire, *d* of Paul Schneider. Coldstream Guards, 1939; invalided out, 1940. *Publications:* A Silver-Plated Spoon, 1959; (with G. Mikes) Book of Snobs, 1965; The Flying Duchess, 1968; (with G. Mikes) How to Run a Stately Home, 1971. *Heir: s* Marquess of Tavistock, *qv*. *Address:* Château des Ligures, 2 rue Honoré Labande, Monte Carlo, MC 98000, Monaco. *Clubs:* Brooks's, Pratt's.

BEDFORD, Bishop Suffragan of, 1994–July 2002; **Rt Rev. John Henry Richardson;** *b* 11 July 1937; *s* of John Farquhar Richardson and Elizabeth Mary Richardson; *m* 1963, Felicity-Anne Lowes; three *d*. *Educ:* Winchester; Trinity Hall, Cambridge (BA 1961; MA 1965); Cuddesdon Coll., Oxford. Nat. Service, 1956–58 (despatches, Malaya, 1958). Ordained deacon, 1963, priest, 1964; Asst Curate, St George's, Stevenage, 1963–66; Curate, St Mary's, Eastbourne, 1966–68; Vicar: St Paul's, Chipperfield, 1968–75; St Mary's, Rickmansworth, 1975–86; RD, Rickmansworth, 1977–86; Vicar, St Michael's, Bishops Stortford, 1986–93; Hon. Canon, St Albans Cathedral, 1986–. *Recreations:* walking, bird-watching, windsurfing, fishing, energetic gardening. *Address:* (until July 2002) 168 Kimbolton Road, Bedford MK41 8DN. *T:* (01234) 357551, *Fax:* (01234) 218134; (from July 2002) The Old Rectory, Bewcastle, Cumbria CA6 6PS. *T:* (01697) 748338. *Clubs:* Royal Automobile; Leander.

BEDFORD, Archdeacon of; *see* Lesiter, Ven. M. L.

BEDFORD, David, FRAM, FTCL; Composer in Association, English Sinfonia, since 1993 (Youth Music Director, 1986–93); *b* 4 Aug. 1937; *s* of late Leslie Herbert Bedford and Lesley Florence Keitley Duff; *m* 1st, 1958, Maureen Parsonage; two *d*; 2nd, 1969, Susan Pilgrim; two *d*; 3rd, 1994, Allison Powell; one *s* one *d*. *Educ:* Lancing College; Royal Acad. of Music (ARAM; FRAM 1997); Trinity Coll. London (LTCL; FTCL 1998). Guy's Hosp. porter, 1956; teacher, Whitefield Sch., Hendon, 1965; teacher, 1968–80, and composer-in-residence, 1969–81, Queen's Coll., London; Assoc. Vis. Composer, Gordonstoun, 1983–88; Imogen Holst Composer in Residence, Dartington Coll. of Arts, 1996–97. Mem. Exec. Cttee, SPNM, 1982–88; Pres., British Music Information Centre, 1988–89; Chm., Assoc. of Professional Composers, 1991–93; Dep. Chm. (writer), PRS, 1999–; Chm., PRS Foundn, 2000–. Patron, Barnet Schs Music Assoc., 1987. Numerous compositions, many commissioned by major London orchestras and BBC; numerous recordings. *Recreations:* tennis, table tennis, cricket, astronomy, ancient history, philosophy, horror films. *Address:* 12 Oakwood Road, Bristol BS9 4NR. *T:* (0117) 962 4202; *e-mail:* dvbmus@aol.com. *Club:* Groucho.
See also S. J. R. Bedford.

BEDFORD, Steuart John Rudolf; freelance conductor; Artistic Director, English Sinfonia, since 1981; *b* 31 July 1939; *s* of late L. H. Bedford and Lesley Florence Keitley Duff; *m* 1st, 1969, Norma Burrowes, *qv*; 2nd, 1980, Celia, *er d* of Mr and Mrs G. R. Harding; two *d*. *Educ:* Lancing Coll., Sussex; Royal Acad. of Music. Fellow, RCO; FRAM; BA. Artistic Dir, 1974–98, and Exec. Artistic Dir, 1987–98, Aldeburgh Festival; Co-Artistic Dir, English Music Theatre Co., 1976–79. Royal Acad. of Music, 1965; English Opera Gp, now English Music Theatre, 1967–. Debut at Metropolitan, NY, 1974 (Death in Venice); new prodn of The Marriage of Figaro, 1975. Has conducted with English Opera Gp, Welsh National Opera, Florentine Opera, Luxembourg Philharmonic, Royal Scottish Nat. Orch., Bordeaux Opera, Opera Theatre of St Louis, NY City Opera; also at Royal Opera House, Covent Garden (operas incl. Owen Wingrave and Death in Venice, by Benjamin Britten, and Cosi Fan Tutte); also in Santa Fe, Buenos Aires, France, Belgium, Holland, Canada, Vienna, Denmark, etc. Recordings include a series of works by Benjamin Britten. *Recreations:* golf, gardening. *Address:* c/o Harrison Parrott Ltd, 12 Penzance Place, W11 4PA.
See also D. Bedford.

BEDFORD, Sybille, OBE 1981; CLit 1994; author; *b* 16 March 1911; *d* of Maximilian von Schoenebeck and Elizabeth Bernard; *m* 1935, Walter Bedford. *Educ:* privately, in Italy, England and France. Career in writing and literary journalism. Vice-Pres., PEN, 1979. FRSL. *Publications:* The Sudden View, A Visit to Don Otavio, 1953, 3rd edn 1982; A Legacy, 1956, repr. 1992, televised 1975; The Best We Can Do (The Trial of Dr Adams), 1958, 2nd edn 1989; The Faces of Justice, 1961; A Favourite of the Gods, 1962, 2nd edn 1993; A Compass Error, 1968, 2nd edn 1984; Aldous Huxley, a Biography: Vol I, The Apparent Stability, 1894–1939, 1973, 2nd edn 1987; Vol. II, The Turning Points, 1939–63, 1974, 3rd edn 1993; Jigsaw, 1989; As It Was (essays), 1990. *Recreations:* wine, reading, travel. *Address:* c/o Lutyens & Rubinstein, 231 Westbourne Park Road, W11 1EB. *Club:* PEN.

BEDFORD-JONES, Rt Rev. Michael Hugh Harold; a Suffragan Bishop of Toronto (Area Bishop of York–Scarborough), since 1994; *b* 29 Sept. 1942; *s* of Rev. Canon Hugh Bedford-Jones and Gretchen Flagler Bedford-Jones (*née* Gray); *m* 1967, Jeanne Yvonne Soules. *Educ:* Toronto Univ. (BA 1965; MA 1979); Univ. of Trinity Coll., Toronto (STB 1968). Ordained deacon, 1967, priest, 1968; St James' Cathedral, Toronto: Asst Curate, 1968–70; Dir of Christian Educn, 1970–74; Sen. Asst, 1974–75; Rector, Ch. of the Epiphany, Scarborough, 1976–83; Regl Dean, Scarborough, 1980–83; Rector, St Aidan, Toronto, 1983–88; Regl Dean, Toronto East, 1985–88; Exec. Asst to Bishop of Toronto, 1988–91; Canon, St James' Cathedral, 1990; Dean of Dio. of Ontario and Rector of St George's Cathedral, Kingston, Ont, 1991–94. Hon. DD Univ. of Trinity Coll., Toronto, 1997. *Recreations:* sailing, music, cottage life. *Address:* Bishop's Room, St Paul's Church, L'Amoreaux, 3333 Finch Avenue East, Scarborough, ON M1W 2R9, Canada. *T:* (416) 4977550, *Fax:* (416) 4974103; *e-mail:* mbj@total.net.

BEDI, Prof. Raman, DDS; FDSRCS; Professor and Head of Department of Transcultural Oral Health, Eastman Dental Institute, University College London, since 1996; *b* 20 May 1953; *s* of Satya-Paul Bedi and Raj Bedi (*née* Kaur); *m* 1986, Kathryn Jane Walter; three *s*. *Educ:* Headlands Sch.; Univ. of Bristol (BDS 1976, DDS 1993); Trinity Coll., Bristol (DipHE Theol. 1979); Univ. of Manchester (MSc 1986). FDSRCS 1982. Lecturer in Paediatric Dentistry: Univ. of Manchester, 1979–82; Univ. of Hong Kong, 1983–86; Univ. of Edinburgh, 1988–91; Sen. Lectr in Paediatric Dentistry, Univ. of Birmingham, 1991–96. Dir, WHO Collaborating Centre for Disability, Cultural and Oral Health, 1998–. Mem., Gen. Synod of C of E, 1995–. *Publications:* (ed with P. Jones) Betel-quid and Tobacco Chewing Among the Bangladeshi Community in the United Kingdom: usage and health issues, 1995; (with P. Jones) Embracing Goodwill: establishing healthy alliances with black organisations, 1996; (ed jtly) Dentists, Patients and Ethnic Minorities: towards the new millennium, 1996; (with P. A. Lowe) Best Practice in Primary Healthcare: oral healthcare delivery in a multi-ethnic society, 1997; (with J. Sardo Infirri) The Root Cause: oral health care in disadvantaged communities, 1999; contribs to scientific jls. *Recreations:* chess, tennis, travelling. *Address:* Oak Cottage, 12 Manor Way, Potters Bar, Herts EN6 1EL. *Club:* Royal Society of Medicine.

BEDINGFELD; *see* Paston-Bedingfeld.

BEDINGFIELD, Julian Peter; HM Diplomatic Service; First Secretary and Deputy Head of Mission, Ljubljana, since 1999; *b* 23 July 1945; *s* of Thomas William Bedingfield and Eileen Bedingfield (*née* Neves); *m* 1975, Margery Mary Jones Davies; one *s* two *d*. *Educ:* Sir Joseph Williamson's Mathematical Sch., Rochester. Joined Foreign Office, 1964: lang. trng, 1968; Scientific Attaché, Moscow, 1969–70; FCO, 1970–71; Düsseldorf, 1971–73; Bonn, 1973–75; Second Secretary: (Commercial), Dhaka, 1975–76; Dep. Hd of Mission, Ulan Bator, 1976–78; FCO, 1978–82; (Admin) and Consul, Berne, 1982–86; (Chancery/Inf.), Rabat, 1986–91; First Secretary: FCO, 1991–94; UK Delegn, NATO, Brussels, 1994–99. *Recreations:* travel, photography. *Address:* c/o Foreign and Commonwealth Office, King Charles Street, SW1A 2AH.

BEDNORZ, Johannes-Georg, PhD; Physicist at IBM Research Laboratory, Zürich, since 1982; *b* 16 May 1950. *Educ:* Swiss Federal Institute of Technology, Zürich. (Jtly) Nobel Prize for Physics, 1987. *Publications:* papers in learned jls on new super-conducting materials. *Address:* IBM Zürich Research Laboratory, Säumerstrasse 4, 8803 Rüschlikon, Switzerland.

BEDSER, Sir Alec (Victor), Kt 1997; CBE 1982 (OBE 1964); Chairman, England Cricket Selection Committee, 1968–81 (Member, 1961–85); *b* 4 July 1918; twin *s* of late Arthur and Florence Beatrice Bedser. *Educ:* Monument Hill Secondary Sch., Woking. Served with RAF in UK, France (BEF), N Africa, Sicily, Italy, Austria, 1939–46. Joined Surrey County Cricket Club, as Professional, 1938; awarded Surrey CCC and England caps, 1946, 1st Test Match v India, created record by taking 22 wickets in first two Tests; toured Australia as Member of MCC team, 1946–47, 1950–51, 1954–55; toured S Africa with MCC, 1948–49; held record of most number of Test wickets (236), since beaten, 1953; took 100th wicket against Australia (first English bowler since 1914 to do this), 1953; Asst Man. to Duke of Norfolk on MCC tour to Australia, 1962–63; Manager: MCC team to Australia, 1974–75; England team tour of Australia and India, 1979–80; Mem., MCC Cttee, 1982–85. Pres., Surrey CCC, 1987–88. Founded own company (office equipment and supplies) with Eric Bedser, 1955. Freeman, City of London, 1968; Liveryman, Worshipful Co. of Environmental Cleaners, 1988. *Publications:* (with E. A. Bedser) Our Cricket Story, 1951; Bowling, 1952; (with E. A. Bedser) Following On, 1954; Cricket Choice, 1981; (with Alex Bannister) Twin Ambitions (autobiog.), 1986. *Recreations:* cricket, golf. *Clubs:* MCC (Hon. Life Mem.; Life Vice Pres., 1999), East India, Devonshire, Sports and Public Schools; Surrey County Cricket (Hon. Life Mem.); West Hill Golf.

BEECHAM, Sir Jeremy (Hugh), Kt 1994; DL; Member, Newcastle upon Tyne City Council, since 1967 (Leader, 1977–94); Partner, Beecham Peacock (formerly Allan Henderson Beecham & Peacock), since 1968; *b* 17 Nov. 1944; *s* of Laurence and Florence Beecham; *m* 1968, Brenda Elizabeth (*née* Woolf); one *s* one *d*. *Educ:* Royal Grammar Sch., Newcastle upon Tyne; University Coll., Oxford (First Cl. Hons Jurisprudence; MA). Chm., OU Labour Club, 1964. Admitted Solicitor, 1968. Dir, Northern Develt Co., 1986–91. Newcastle upon Tyne City Council: Chairman: Social Services Cttee, 1973–77; Policy and Resources Cttee, 1977–94; Finance Cttee, 1979–85; Develt Cttee, 1995–97; Newcastle City Challenge, 1992–97. Chairman: AMA, 1991–97 (Dep. Chm., 1984–86; Vice Chm., 1986–91); Local Govt Assoc., 1995–; Vice Chm., Northern Regl Councils Assoc., 1986–91. Labour Party: Member: Local and Regl Govt Sub-Cttee, NEC, 1971–83, 1991–; NEC/Shadow Cabinet Wkg Pty on Future of Local Govt, 1984–87; Domestic and Internat. Policy Cttee, 1992–; Jt Policy Cttee, 1992–; NEC, 1998–. Member: RTPI Working Party on Public Participation in Planning, 1980–82; Historic Bldgs and Monuments Commn for England, 1983–87; Local and Central Govt Relns Res. Cttee, Joseph Rowntree Meml Trust, 1987–96; President's Cttee, Business in the Community, 1988–; Bd of Trustees, NE Civic Trust, 1989–92; NHS Modernisation Bd, 2000–. Pres., BURA, 1996–. Participant, Königswinter Conf., 1986. Member: Council of Management, Neighbourhood Energy Action, 1987–89; Council, Common Purpose, 1989–; President: Age Concern Newcastle, 1995–; Newcastle Choral Soc., 1997–. Contested (Lab) Tynemouth, 1970. DL Tyne and Wear, 1995. Hon. Freeman Newcastle upon Tyne, 1995. Hon. Fellow, Univ. of Northumbria (formerly Newcastle upon Tyne Poly.), 1989. Hon. DCL Newcastle, 1992. *Recreations:* reading, history, music, very amateur photography, the Northumbrian countryside. *Address:* (office) 7 Collingwood Street, Newcastle upon Tyne NE1 1JE; 39 The Drive, Gosforth, Newcastle upon Tyne NE3 4AJ. *T:* (0191) 285 1888. *Club:* Manors Social (Newcastle upon Tyne).

BEECHAM, Sir John Stratford Roland, 4th Bt *cr* 1914; *S* father, 1982. *Heir: b* Robert Adrian Beecham [*b* 6 Jan. 1942; *m* 1969, Daphne Mattinson; one *s* one *d*].

BEEDHAM, Brian James, CBE 1989; Associate Editor, The Economist, since 1989; *b* 12 Jan. 1928; *s* of James Victor Beedham and Nina Beedham (*née* Zambra); *m* 1960, Barbara Zollikofer. *Educ:* Leeds Grammar Sch.; The Queen's Coll., Oxford. RA, 1950–52. Asst Editor, Yorkshire Post, 1952–55; The Economist, 1955–: Washington correspondent, 1958–61; Foreign Editor, 1964–89. Commonwealth Fellowship, 1956–57. Fellow, Royal Geographical Society. *Recreations:* hillwalking, music, Kipling and Wodehouse. *Address:* 9 Hillside, SW19 4NH. *T:* (020) 8946 4454. *Club:* Travellers.

BEELS, Jonathan Sidney Spencer, CMG 1998; HM Diplomatic Service, retired; Consultant, Ministry of Defence, 1998–99; *b* 19 Jan. 1943; *s* of Sidney Beels and Joan Constance Beels (*née* Groves); *m* 1st, 1966, Patricia Joan Mills (marr. diss. 1982); one *s* one *d*; 2nd, 1983, Penelope Jane Aedy (marr. diss. 1998). *Educ:* Ardingly Coll.; St John's Coll., Cambridge (MA 1969). Entered Diplomatic Service, 1965; Prague, 1970–73; FCO, 1973–77; on loan to Northern Ireland Office, 1977–78; resigned from Diplomatic Service, 1979; Govt Service, Sultanate of Oman, 1979–83; Man. Dir, Control Risks (GS) Ltd, 1983–88; rejoined Diplomatic Service, 1988; Counsellor, Nicosia, 1992–93; FCO, 1994–98. *Recreations:* golf, shooting, tennis, motorcycling.

BEENSTOCK, Prof. Michael, PhD; Pinhas Sapir Professor of Economics, Hebrew University, Jerusalem, since 1996; *b* 18 June 1946; *s* of Sidney and Taubie Beenstock; *m* 1968, Ruchi Hager; one *s* four *d*. *Educ:* London Sch. of Econs and Political Science (BSc, MSc; PhD 1976). Econ. Advisor, HM Treasury, 1970–76; Economist, World Bank, Washington, DC, 1976–78; Sen. Res. Fellow, London Business Sch., 1978–81; Esmée Fairbairn Prof. of Finance and Investment, City Univ. Business Sch., 1981–87; Prof. of Econs, Hebrew Univ., Jerusalem, 1987–96 (Lady Davis Prof., 1987–89). *Publications:* The Foreign Exchange Market, 1978; A Neoclassical Analysis of Macroeconomic Policy, 1980; Health, Migration and Development, 1980; The World Economy in Transition, 1983,

2nd edn 1984; Insurance for Unemployment, 1986; Work, Welfare and Taxation, 1986; Modelling the Labour Market, 1988. *Recreation:* music. *Address:* Kefar Etzion 35/4, Jerusalem, Israel. *T:* (2) 6723184.

BEER, Prof. (Anthony) Stafford; international consultant cybernetics in management; Partner, Cwarel Isaf Institute, since 1999; Visiting Professor of Cybernetics: University of Sunderland, since 1997; Business School, University of Northumbria, since 1998; University of Stockholm, since 1999; *b* London, 25 Sept. 1926; *er s* of late William John and Doris Ethel Beer; *m* 1st, 1947, Cynthia Margaret Hannaway (marr. diss. 1968); four *s* one *d*; 2nd, 1968, Sallie Steadman (*née* Child) (marr. diss. 1995); one *s* two *d*; partner, Allenna Leonard, PhD. *Educ:* Whitgift Sch.; University Coll., London; MBA Manchester, 1970; DSc Sunderland, 2000. Lieut, 9th Gurkha Rifles 1945; Captain, Royal Fusiliers 1947. Man. of Operational Res. and Prodn Controller, S. Fox & Co., 1949–56; Head of Op. Res. and Cybernetics, United Steel, 1956–61; Man. Dir, SIGMA Science in General Management Ltd and Dir, Metra International, 1961–66; Develt Dir, International Publishing Corp.; Dir, International Data Highways Ltd; Chm., Computaprint Ltd, 1966–69; Advisor in Cybernetics to Ernst and Whinney (Canada), 1970–87; Dir, Metapraxis Ltd (UK), 1984–87; Chairman: Syncho Ltd (UK), 1986–99; Viable Systems Internat. (USA), 1987–88; Team Syntegrity Inc. (Canada), 1992–99. Visiting Professor: of Gen. Systems, Open Univ., 1970–71; of Cybernetics: Manchester Univ. Business Sch., 1969–94; Durham Univ. Business Sch., 1990–93; Res. Prof. of Managerial Cybernetics, European Business Sch., UC of Swansea, 1990–97. Scientific Dir, Project Cybersyn, Chile, 1971–73; Adjunct Prof. of Stats and Operations Res., Pennsylvania Univ. (Wharton Sch.), 1972–81, and of Social Systems Scis, 1981–87; Co-Dir, Project Urucib, Uruguay, 1986–87. Ex-Pres., Operational Res. Soc.; Ex-Pres., Soc. for Gen. Systems Res. (USA); Pres., World Orgn of Systems and Cybernetics (formerly of Gen. Systems and Cybernetics), 1981–; Mem. UK Automation Council, 1957–69; Mem. Gen. Adv. Council of BBC, 1961–69. Governor, Internat. Council for Computer Communication, 1973–93. Hon. Chm., The Stafford Beer Foundn, 1986–. Hon. Prof., Orgnl Transformation, Business Sch. (formerly Sch. of Inf. Sci. and Technol.), Liverpool John Moores Univ. (formerly Liverpool Poly.), 1990– (Hon. Fellow, 1996). Installation of Requiem (ten interactive paintings), Liverpool Metropolitan Cathedral, 1992–93. FWA 1986; FRSA 1991. Freeman, City of London, 1970. Hon. Fellow, St David's UC, Wales, 1989. Hon. LLD Concordia, Montreal, 1988; Dr Econ. Scis *hc* St Gallen, Switzerland, 2000. Silver Medal, Royal Swedish Acad. for Engrg Scis, 1958; Lanchester Prize (USA) for Ops Res., 1966; McCulloch Award (USA) for Cybernetics, 1970; Wiener Meml Gold Medal for Cybernetics, World Orgn of Gen. Systems and Cybernetics, 1984. *Publications:* Cybernetics and Management, 1959; Decision and Control, 1966; Management Science, 1967; Brain of the Firm, 1972 (new edn, 1981); Designing Freedom, 1974; Platform for Change, 1975; Transit (poems), 1977, extended edn 1983; The Heart of Enterprise, 1979; Diagnosing the System, for organizations, 1985; Pebbles to Computers: the thread, 1986; To Someone or Other (paintings), 1988; How Many Grapes Went into the Wine: Stafford Beer on the art and science of holistic management, ed Harnden and Leonard, 1994; Beyond Dispute: the invention of team syntegrity, 1994; chapters in numerous other books. *Recreations:* spinning, yoga, classics, staying put. *Address:* Cwarel Isaf, Pont Creuddyn, Llanbedr Pont Steffan, Ceredigion, Wales SA48 8PG; 34 Palmerston Square, Toronto, Ontario M6G 2S7, Canada. *Club:* Athenæum.

See also I. D. S. Beer.

BEER, Dame Gillian (Patricia Kempster), DBE 1998; FBA 1991; King Edward VII Professor of English Literature, University of Cambridge, 1994–Sept 2002; President, Clare Hall, Cambridge, 1994–2001; *b* 27 Jan. 1935; *d* of Owen Kempster Thomas and Ruth Winifred Bell; *m* 1962, John Bernard Beer, *qv*; three *s*. *Educ:* St Anne's Coll., Oxford (MA, BLitt; Hon. Fellow, 1990); LittD Cambridge. Asst Lectr, Bedford Coll., London, 1959–62; part-time Lectr, Liverpool Univ., 1962–64; Cambridge University: Asst Lectr 1966–71, Lectr, subseq. Reader in Literature and Narrative, 1971–89; Prof. of English, 1989–94; Fellow, Girton Coll., 1965–94. Vice-Pres., British Acad., 1994–96; Pres., Hist. of Science Sect., BAAS, 1998. Trustee, BM, 1992–. Chm., Poetry Book Soc., 1992–96. Chm. Judges, Booker Prize, 1997. Hon. Fellow, Univ. of Wales, Cardiff, 1996. Hon. LittD: Liverpool, 1995; Anglia Poly., 1997; Leicester, 1999. *Publications:* Meredith: a change of masks, 1970; The Romance, 1970; Darwin's Plots, 1983, 2nd edn 2000; George Eliot, 1986; Arguing with the Past, 1989; Open Fields, 1996; Virginia Woolf: the Common Ground, 1996. *Recreations:* singing, travel, conversation. *Address:* Clare Hall, Herschel Road, Cambridge CB3 9AL. *T:* (01223) 356384 and 332360.

BEER, Ian David Stafford, CBE 1992; MA; JP; Head Master of Harrow, 1981–91; Chairman, Winston Churchill Memorial Trust Council, since 1997 (Member, since 1990; Trustee, since 1998); *b* 28 April 1931; *s* of late William Beer and Doris Ethel Beer; *m* 1960, Angela Felce, *d* of Col E. S. G. Howard, MC, RA and Mrs E. S. G. Howard; two *s* one *d*. *Educ:* Whitgift Sch.; St Catharine's Coll., Cambridge (Exhibitioner). E-SU Walter Page Scholar, 1968. Second Lieut in 1st Bn Royal Fusiliers, 1950. Bursar, Ottershaw Sch., 1955; Guinness Ltd, 1956–57; House Master, Marlborough Coll., Wilts, 1957–61; Head Master: Ellesmere Coll., Salop, 1961–69; Lancing Coll., Sussex, 1969–81. Chairman: HMC Academic Cttee, 1977–79; HMC, 1980; Physical Educn Working Gp for Nat. Curriculum, 1990–91; ISJC, then ISC, 1997–2001 (Vice-Chm., 1994–97; Chm., Adv. Cttee, 1988–91); Vice-Chm., GBA, 1994–2001. Mem., Sports Council, 1992–94. Trustee, RMC Group plc Welfare Trust, 1983–. Evelyn Wrench Lectr, ESU, 1988, 1990. Governor: Whitgift Sch., 1986–91; Charterhouse Sch., 1991–93; Malvern Coll., 1991–2001; Mem. Council, Univ. of Buckingham, 1992–96. Chm. Editorial Bd, Rugby World and Post (formerly Rugby World, then Rugby Post), 1977–93. JP Shropshire, 1963–69, W Sussex, 1970–81, Mddx, 1981–91, Glos, 1992. Hon. FCP 1990. *Recreations:* Rugby Football Union (Mem. Exec. Cttee, 1984–95; Vice Pres., 1991–93; Pres., 1993–94) (formerly: played Rugby for England; CURFC (Capt.), Harlequins, Old Whitgiftians), swimming, reading, zoology, meeting people. *Address:* Winston Churchill Memorial Trust, 15 Queen's Gate Terrace, SW7 5PR. *Clubs:* East India, Devonshire, Sports and Public Schools; Hawks (Cambridge).

See also A. S. Beer.

BEER, James Edmund; Consultant: Nelson Hirst Group, 1978–88; Co-operative Bank Ltd, 1982–85; *b* 17 March 1931; *s* of Edmund Huxtable Beer and Gwendoline Kate Beer; *m* 1953, Barbara Mollie (*née* Tunley); two *s* one *d*. *Educ:* Torquay Grammar School. IPFA, FRVA, MBCS, MIMgt. Torquay Borough Council, 1951–54; Chatham, 1954–56; Wolverhampton, 1956–58; Doncaster, 1958–60; Chief Accountant, Bedford, 1960–62; Asst Borough Treas., Croydon, 1963–65; Dep. Treas., Leeds, 1965; Chief Financial Officer, Leeds, 1968; Dir of Finance, Leeds City Council, 1973–78. Director: Short Loan and Mortgage Co. Ltd, 1978–88; Short Loan (Leasing) Ltd, 1979–88; London Financial Futures Co. Ltd, 1982–88. Mem. Local Govt Financial Exec., CIPFA, 1974–78; Financial Adviser to AMA, 1974–78; Treas., Soc. of Metropolitan Treasurers, 1974–78; Member: LAMSAC Computer Panel, 1972–78; Yorks and Humberside Develt Assoc. London Section, 1970–; Past Examr, CIPFA; Adviser on Rate Support Grant, AMA, 1974–78; Treas., Leeds Grand Theatre & Opera House Ltd, 1974–78; Governor, Leeds Musical Festival, 1979–84. Freeman, City of London, 1972; Liveryman, Basketmakers' Co., 1982–92. *Publications:* contrib. professional jls. *Recreations:* theatre, swimming, Rugby (past playing mem., Torquay Athletic RUFC). *Address:* 48 High Ash Avenue, Alwoodley, Leeds LS17 8RG. *T:* (0113) 268 3907.

BEÉR, Prof. János Miklós, DSc, PhD; FREng; Professor of Chemical and Fuel Engineering, Massachusetts Institute of Technology (MIT), 1976–93, now Emeritus; Scientific Director, MIT Combustion Research Facilities, since 1980; *b* Budapest, 27 Feb. 1923; *s* of Sándor Beér and Gizella Trismai; *m* 1944, Marta Gabriella Csató. *Educ:* Berzsenyi Dániel Gymnasium, Budapest; Univ. of Budapest (Dipl-Ing 1950); PhD Sheffield, 1960, DSc(Tech) Sheffield, 1967. Heat Research Inst., Budapest: Research Officer, 1949–52; Head, Combustion Dept, 1952–56; Princ. Lectr (part-time), University of Budapest, 1953–56; Research Engr, Babcock & Wilcox Ltd, Renfrew, 1957; Research Bursar, University of Sheffield, 1957–60; Head, Research Stn, Internat. Flame Research Foundn, Ijmuiden, Holland, 1960–63; Prof., Dept of Fuel Science, Pa State Univ., 1963–65; Newton Drew Prof. of Chemical Engrg and Fuel Technology and Head of Dept, Univ. of Sheffield, 1965–76; Dean, Faculty of Engineering, Univ. of Sheffield, 1973–75; Programme Dir for Combustion, MIT Energy Lab., 1976–86. Hon. Supt of Res., Internat. Flame Res. Foundn, 1991. Member: Adv. Council on R&D for Fuel and Power, DTI, later Dept of Energy, 1973–76; Adv. Bd, Safety in Mines Research, Dept of Energy, 1974–76; Clean Air Council, DoE, 1974–76; Bd of Directors, The Combustion Inst., Pittsburgh, USA, 1974–86; Mem., Adv. Cttee, Italian Nat. Res. Council, 1974–; Chm., Clean Coal Utilization Project, US Nat. Acad. of Scis, 1987–88; Mem., US Nat. Coal Council (Adv. Council to Energy Sec.), 1993–. Gen. Superintendent of Research, Internat. Flame Research Foundn, 1972–89 (Hon. Supt of Res., 1990–). Australian Commonwealth Vis. Fellow, 1972; Fellow ASME, 1978 (Moody Award, 1964; Percy Nicholls Award, 1988); FREng (FEng 1979). Hon. Member: Hungarian Acad. of Scis, 1986; Hungarian Acad. of Engrng, 1991. Foreign Mem., Finnish Acad. of Technology, 1989. Dr *hc* Miskolc, Hungary, 1987; Budapest Tech. Sci., Hungary, 1997. Melchett Medal, Inst. Energy, London, 1985; Coal Science Gold Medal, BCURA, 1986; Alfred Edgerton Gold Medal, Combustion Inst., 1986; Axel Axelson Johnson Medal, Swedish Acad. of Engrg Scis, 1995; Energy System Award, AIAA, 1998. Editor, Fuel and Energy Science Monograph Series, 1966–. *Publications:* (with N. Chigier) Combustion Aerodynamics, 1972; (ed with M. W. Thring) Industrial Flames, 1972; (ed with H. B. Palmer) Developments in Combustion Science and Technology, 1974; (ed with N. Afgan) Heat Transfer in Flames, 1975; contribs to Nature, Combustion and Flame, Basic Engrg Jl, Amer. Soc. Mech. Engrg, Jl Inst. F, ZVDI, Internat. Gas Wärme, Proc. Internat. Symposia on Combustion, etc. *Recreations:* swimming, rowing, reading, music. *Address:* Department of Chemical Engineering, Massachusetts Institute of Technology, Cambridge, MA 02139, USA. *T:* (617) 2536661.

BEER, Prof. John Bernard, LittD; FBA 1994; Professor of English Literature, University of Cambridge, 1987–93, Professor Emeritus, since 1993; Fellow of Peterhouse, Cambridge, 1964–93, Emeritus Fellow, since 1993; *b* 31 March 1926; *s* of John Bateman Beer and Eva Chilton; *m* 1962, Gillian Patricia Kempster Thomas (*see* Dame G. P. K. Beer); three *s*. *Educ:* Watford Grammar Sch.; St John's Coll., Cambridge (MA, PhD); LittD Cantab 1995. Research Fellow, St John's Coll., Cambridge, 1955–58; Lectr, Manchester Univ., 1958–64; Univ. Lectr, Cambridge, 1964–78; Reader in English Literature, Cambridge, 1978–87. British Acad. Chatterton Lectr, 1964; Vis. Prof., Univ. of Virginia, 1975; Leverhulme Emeritus Fellowship, 1995–96; numerous lecture tours abroad. Pres., Charles Lamb Soc., 1989 . Gen. Ed., Coleridge's Writings, 1990–. *Publications:* Coleridge the Visionary, 1959; The Achievement of E. M. Forster, 1962; (ed) Coleridge's Poems, 1963, new edn 1999; Blake's Humanism, 1968; Blake's Visionary Universe, 1969; (ed) Coleridge's Variety: bicentenary studies, 1974; Coleridge's Poetic Intelligence, 1977; Wordsworth and the Human Heart, 1978; Wordsworth in Time, 1979; (ed with G. K. Das) E. M. Forster: a human exploration, 1979; (ed) A Passage to India: essays in interpretation, 1985; (ed) Aids to Reflection, 1993; Romantic Influences: contemporary, Victorian, modern, 1993; Against Finality, 1993; (ed) Questioning Romanticism, 1995; (ed) Selected Poems of Arthur Hugh Clough, 1998; Providence and Love: studies in Wordsworth, Channing, Myers, George Eliot and Ruskin, 1998; articles and reviews. *Recreations:* music, travel, walking in town and country. *Address:* 6 Belvoir Terrace, Cambridge CB2 2AA. *T:* (01223) 356384; *e-mail:* jbb1000@cam.ac.uk. *Club:* Royal Over-Seas League.

BEER, Ven. John Stuart; Archdeacon of Huntingdon, since 1997; Director of Ordinands, since 1987, Co-Director, since 1993, diocese of Ely; *b* 15 March 1944; *s* of John Gilbert Beer and late May (*née* Scott); *m* 1970, Susan, *d* of late Gordon and Jessie Spencer; two *s* one *d*. *Educ:* Roundhay Sch.; Pembroke Coll., Oxford (MA (Theol.) 1968); Westcott House, Cambridge (MA 1976). Advertising and Finance, Rowntree & Co. Ltd, York, 1965–69; ordained deacon, 1971, priest, 1972; Asst Curate, St John the Baptist, Knaresborough, 1971–74; Fellow and Chaplain, Fitzwilliam Coll., Cambridge, and Chaplain, New Hall, 1974–80; Rector of Toft with Hardwick, Caldecote and Childerley, 1980–87; Dir of Post Ordination Training and Dir of Studies for Readers, dio. of Ely, and Vicar of Grantchester, 1987–97. Mem., Ethics Cttee, Dunn Res. Inst., 1987–. Chm., Cathedral Pilgrims Assoc. Conf., 1987–97. *Publications:* Who is Jesus?, 1982; contribs to theol jls. *Recreations:* tennis, golf, music, wine. *Address:* The Rectory, Hemingford Abbots, Huntingdon PE28 9AN. *T:* (01480) 469856, *Fax:* (01480) 496073; *e-mail:* archdeacon.huntingdon@ely.anglican.org.

BEER, Air Vice-Marshal Peter George, CB 1995; CBE 1987 (OBE 1979); LVO 1974; Home Bursar, Jesus College, Oxford, since 1996; *b* 16 July 1941; *s* of Herbert George Beer and Kathleen Mary Beer; *m* 1975, Fiona Georgina Hamilton Davidson; two *s*. *Educ:* Hugh Sexey's Sch., Bruton. MA. Equerry to HM the Queen, 1971–74; Officer Commanding: No 55 Sqdn, 1977–79; RAF Brize Norton, 1984–86; Dir, RAF Plans and Programmes, 1989–91; Comdr British Forces, Falkland Is, 1991–92; Dir-Gen. Training and Personnel, RAF, 1992–94; COS, Personnel and Training Comd, RAF, 1994–95, retd. Non-exec. Dir, Oxford Radcliffe Hosps NHS Trust, 1999–. Vice-Pres., RAF Hockey Assoc. *Recreations:* cricket, opera. *Address:* Southfield, Stonehill Lane, Southmoor, Oxon OX13 5HU. *Club:* Royal Air Force.

BEER, Prof. Stafford; *see* Beer, Prof. A. S.

BEERLING, John William; freelance media consultant, film director, and writer, since 1994; Partner, The Great Outdoor Picture Co., since 1998; Managing Director, Classic Gold Digital Radio, since 2000; *b* 12 April 1937; *s* of Raymond Starr and May Elizabeth Julia Beerling; *m* 1st, 1959, Carol Ann Reynolds (marr. diss. 1991); one *s* one *d*; 2nd, 1993, Celia Margaret Potter (marr. diss. 1998); 3rd, 1999, Susan Patricia Guy. *Educ:* Sir Roger Manwood's Grammar Sch., Sandwich, Kent. National Service, RAF, wireless fitter, 1955–57. Joined BBC, 1957; Studio Manager, 1958; Producer, 1962; Head of Radio 1 Programmes, 1983; Controller, Radio 1, 1985–93. Chm., Radio Data Systems Forum, Geneva, 1993–; Dir, Stereo Pair, 1997–98. Gov., Brits Sch. for Performing Arts and Technology, 1995–. Pres., TRIC, 1992–93. *Publication:* Emperor Rosko's D. J.

Handbook, 1976. *Recreations:* photography, fishing, ski-ing. *Address:* Classic Gold Digital Ltd, Unique Broadcasting, 50 Lisson Street, NW1 5DF.

BEESLEY, Ian Blake; Partner, PricewaterhouseCoopers (formerly Price Waterhouse), since 1986; *b* 11 July 1942; *s* of Frank and Catherine Beesley; *m* 1st, 1964, Birgitte (*née* Smith) (marr. diss. 1982); 2nd, 1983, Elizabeth (*née* Wigley) (marr. diss. 1998); one *s* two *d*; 3rd, 2000, Edna (*née* Chivers); one step *s*. *Educ:* Manchester Grammar School; St Edmund Hall, Oxford (PPE). MA; Cert. in Statistics. Central Statistical Office, 1964–76; Chief Statistician, HM Treasury, 1976–78; Dep. Head, Unit supporting Lord Rayner, PM's adviser on efficiency, 1981–83; Under Sec. and Official Head of PM's Efficiency Unit, 1983–86. Alternate Mem., Jarratt Cttee on efficiency in universities, 1984–85; Mem., Croham Cttee to review function and operation of UGC, 1985–87. Member: Employment Service Adv. Gp, 1992–98; Expert Gp advising Govt on Nat. Experience Corps, 2000–. Mem., Council, Surrey Univ., 1986–92. FRSA 1990. Mem., Guild of Mgt Consultants, 1997–. *Publications:* Policy analysis and evaluation in British Government (RIPA seminar papers), 1983; (contrib.) Straight from the CEO, 1998; contribs to Jl Royal Statistical Soc.; articles on value for money in the arts. *Address:* c/o PricewaterhouseCoopers, 1 Embankment Place, Villiers Street, WC2N 6NN.

BEESLEY, Peter Frederick Barton; Registrar: Faculty Office of the Archbishop of Canterbury, since 1981; Diocese of Guildford, since 1981; (Joint) Diocese of Ely, since 1978; (Joint) Diocese of Hereford, since 1983; Senior Partner, Lee Bolton & Lee, since 2000 (Partner, since 1969); *b* 30 April 1943; *s* of Ronald Fitzgerald Barton Beesley and Mary Kurczyn (*née* Parker); *m* 1974, Elizabeth Jane Grahame; one *s* two *d*. *Educ:* King's School, Worcester; Exeter Univ. (LLB); Coll. of Law, Guildford. Articled Clerk and Asst Solicitor, Windeatt & Windeatt, 1965–68; Asst Solicitor, Lee Bolton & Lee, 1968–69. Jt Registrar, Dio. St Albans, 1969–78; Registrar, Woodard Corp., 1987–; Legal Advr, Nat. Soc. (C of E) for Promoting Religious Educn, 1975–; Secretary: Ecclesiastical Law Assoc., 1978–98 (Vice-Chm., 1998–2000; Chm., 2000–); Ecclesiastical Law Soc., 1987–; Mem. Legal Adv. Commn, General Synod of C of E, 1992–; Pres., City of Westminster Law Soc., 1991–92. Mem., Glaziers' Trust, 1996– (Vice-Chm., 1998–2000; Chm., 2000–). Liveryman, Glaziers' and Painters' of Glass Co., 1981 (Mem. Ct Assts, 1995–). Trustee, Arbory Trust, 2000–. Governor: Hampstead Parochial Sch., 1983– (Chm., 1986–95); Sarum Hall Sch., 1997–. *Publications:* (contrib. jtly) Encyclopaedia of Forms and Precedents, Vol. 13, Ecclesiastical Law, 1987; Anglican Marriage in England and Wales, a Guide to the Law for Clergy, 1992. *Address:* (office) 1 The Sanctuary, Westminster, SW1P 3JT. *T:* (020) 7222 5381. *Clubs:* Athenæum, St Stephen's Constitutional.

BEESON, Andrew Nigel Wendover; Executive Chairman, Beeson Gregory Group plc, since 2001; *b* 30 March 1944; *s* of Nigel Wendover Beeson (killed in action 1944) and Anne Beeson (*née* Sutherland, now Hodges); *m* 1st, 1971, Susan Gerard (marr. diss. 1983); one *s* one *d*; 2nd, 1986, Carrie Martin; one *d*. *Educ:* Eton Coll. Partner, Capel Cure Myers, 1972–85; Director: ANZ Merchant Bank, 1985–87; ANZ McCaughan, 1987–89; Founder, Beeson Gregory Holdings Ltd, 1989; CEO, 1989–2001, Dep. Chm., 2001, Beeson Gregory Gp. Founding Chm., City Gp for Small Cos, 1992–95; Director: European Assoc. Securities Dealers, 1995–; European Assoc. Securities Dealers Automatic Quotations, 1996–. Trustee, Tennis and Rackets Assoc., 1996. Achievement Award, Coopers & Lybrand, 1995. *Recreations:* Real tennis, shooting, collecting. *Address:* 21 Warwick Square, SW1V 2AB. *T:* (020) 7834 2903. *Clubs:* MCC, Pratt's, White's; Swinley Golf (Ascot).

BEESON, Prof. Paul Bruce, Hon. KBE 1973; FRCP; Professor of Medicine, University of Washington, 1974–82, now Emeritus; *b* 18 Oct. 1908; *s* of John Bradley Beeson, Livingston, Mont; *m* 1942, Barbara Neal, *d* of Ray C. Neal, Buffalo, NY; two *s* one *d*. *Educ:* Univ. of Washington, McGill Univ. Med. Sch. MD, CM, 1933. Intern, Hosp. of Univ. of Pa, 1933–35; Gen. practice of medicine, Wooster, Ohio, 1935–37; Asst Rockefeller Inst., 1937–39; Chief Med. Resident, Peter Bent Brigham Hosp., 1939–40; Instructor in Med., Havard Med. Sch., and Chief Phys., American Red Cross-Harvard Field Hosp. Unit, Salisbury, 1940–42; Asst and Assoc. Prof. of Med., Emory Med. Sch., 1942–46; Prof. of Med. Emory Med. Sch., 1946–52; Prof. of Med. and Chm. Dept of Med., Yale Univ., 1952–65; Nuffield Prof. of Clinical Med., Oxford Univ., and Fellow of Magdalen Coll., 1965–74, Hon. Fellow, 1975; Hon. Fellow RSM, 1976. Vis. Investigator, Wright-Fleming Inst., St Mary's Hosp., 1958–59. Pres., Assoc. Amer. Physicians, 1967; Master, Amer. Coll. of Physicians, 1970. Phillips Award, Amer. Coll. Physicians, 1975; Flexner Award, Assoc. Amer. Med. Colls, 1977. *Alumnus Summa Laude Dignatus*, Univ. of Washington, 1968; Hon. DSc: Emory Univ., 1968; McGill Univ., 1971; Yale Univ., 1975; Albany Med. Coll., 1975; Ohio Med. Coll., 1979. *Publications:* (ed jtly) The Oxford Companion to Medicine, 1986; edited: Cecil-Loeb Textbook of Medicine, 1959–82; Yale Journal Biology and Medicine, 1959–65; Journal Amer. Geriatric Soc., 1981–84; numerous scientific publications relating to infectious disease, pathogenesis of fever, pyelonephritis and mechanism of eosinophilia. *Address:* 21013 NE 122nd Street, Redmond, WA 98053, USA.

BEESON, Very Rev. Trevor Randall, OBE 1997; writer; Dean of Winchester, 1987–96, now Dean Emeritus; *b* 2 March 1926; *s* of late Arthur William and Matilda Beeson; *m* 1950, Josephine Grace Cope (*d* 1997); two *d*. *Educ:* King's Coll., London (AKC 1950; FKC 1987); St Boniface Coll., Warminster. RAF Met Office, 1944–47. Deacon, 1951; Priest, 1952; Curate, Leadgate, Co. Durham, 1951–54; Priest-in-charge and subseq. Vicar of St Chad, Stockton-on-Tees, 1954–65; Curate of St Martin-in-the-Fields, London, 1965–71; Vicar of Ware, Herts, 1971–76; Canon of Westminster, 1976–87; Treasurer, Westminster, 1978–82; Rector of St Margaret's, Westminster, 1982–87; Chaplain to Speaker of House of Commons, 1982–87. Chaplain of St Bride's, Fleet Street, 1967–84. Religious Programmes Advr, LWT, 1970–86. Chm., Christian Action, 1988–96. Gen. Sec., Parish and People, 1962–64; Editor, New Christian, and Man. Dir, Prism Publications Ltd, 1965–70; European Corresp. of The Christian Century (Chicago), 1970–83; Chm., SCM Press Ltd, 1978–87. Select Preacher, Oxford, 1980, 1991. Chm., KCL Theol Trust, 1990–. Mem. Council, WWF, 1987–94. MA (Lambeth) 1976; Hon. DLitt Southampton, 1999. *Publications:* New Area Mission, 1963; (jtly) Worship in a United Church, 1964; An Eye for an Ear, 1972; The Church of England in Crisis, 1973; Discretion and Valour: religious conditions in Russia and Eastern Europe, 1974; Britain Today and Tomorrow, 1978; Westminster Abbey, 1981; A Vision of Hope: the churches and change in Latin America, 1984; (contrib.) God's Truth, 1988; A Dean's Diary: Winchester 1987–1996, 1997; Window on Westminster, 1998; Rebels and Reformers, 1999; contrib. to DNB, Oxford Dictionary of the Church. *Recreations:* cricket, gardening. *Address:* 69 Greatbridge Road, Romsey, Hants SO51 8FE. *T:* (01794) 514627.

BEESTON, James; Chief Executive, Millennium Point Trust Co., since 1997; *b* 2 April 1947; *s* of Richard and Mary Beeston; *m* 1971, Christine, *d* of Barry and Enid Thomas; two *s*. *Educ:* King Edward's, Camp Hill; Birmingham Sch. of Planning. DipTP; MRTPI. Birmingham City Council: Public Works Dept, 1965–74; Central Area Planning Officer, 1974–80; Divl Planning Officer, 1980–85; Asst Dir of Develt, 1985–87; Project Controller, National Indoor Arena; Co-ordinator, first phase, Birmingham Olympics bid; Develt Manager and Dep. Chief Exec., Birmingham Heartlands Ltd, 1987–92; Chief Exec., Birmingham Heartlands Develt Corp., 1992–98. Member: Lunar Soc., Birmingham; Midlands Cttee, British Council for Offices, 1998–. *Publication:* (jtly) Negotiating with Planning Authorities. *Recreations:* family, cricket, sport, gardening. *Address:* Millennium Point Trust Co., Curzon Street Station, 1 Curzon Street, Digbeth, Birmingham B4 7XG. *T:* (0121) 303 4271, *Fax:* (0121) 303 4317.

BEETHAM, Geoffrey Howard, CB 1992; Legal Adviser to Department of Transport, 1983–93; Principal Assistant Solicitor, Treasury Solicitor's Department, 1983–93; *b* 9 Jan. 1933; *s* of Reginald Percy Beetham and Hetty Lilian Beetham (*née* Redman); *m* 1st, 1956, Valerie Douglass (marr. diss. 1975); three *d*; 2nd, 1977, Carol Ann Dorrell; two step *s*. *Educ:* City of London Sch.; St John's Coll., Oxford (BA Jurisp.). Nat. Service, RAF, 1951–53. Solicitor, 1960; Assistant Solicitor: Metropolitan Borough of Battersea, 1960–65; London Borough of Wandsworth, 1965–70; Sen. Legal Assistant and Asst Solicitor, DoE, 1970–77; Asst Solicitor, Dept of Transport, 1977–83. Legal Mem., Mental Health Review Tribunal, 1994–. *Recreations:* throwing pots, music, countryside.

BEETHAM, Marshal of the Royal Air Force Sir Michael (James), GCB 1978 (KCB 1976); CBE 1967; DFC 1944; AFC 1960; DL; FRAeS; Chief of the Air Staff, 1977–82; Air ADC to the Queen, 1977–82; *b* 17 May 1923; *s* of Major G. C. Beetham, MC; *m* 1956, Patricia Elizabeth Lane; one *s* one *d*. *Educ:* St Marylebone Grammar School. Joined RAF, 1941; pilot trng, 1941–42; commnd 1942; Bomber Comd: 50, 57 and 35 Sqdns, 1943–46; HQ Staff, 1947–49; 82 (Recce) Sqdn, E Africa, 1949–51; psa 1952; Air Min. (Directorate Operational Requirements), 1953–56; CO 214 (Valiant) Sqdn Marham, 1958–60; Gp Captain Ops, HQ Bomber Comd, 1962–64; CO RAF Khormaksar, Aden, 1964–66; idc 1967; Dir Ops (RAF), MoD, 1968–70; Comdt, RAF Staff Coll., 1970–72; ACOS (Plans and Policy), SHAPE, 1972–75; Dep. C-in-C, Strike Command, 1975–76; C-in-C RAF Germany, and Comdr, 2nd Tactical Allied Air Force, 1976–77. Hon. Air Cdre, 2620 (Co. of Norfolk) Sqdn, RAuxAF Regt, 1983–; Pres., Bomber Comd Assoc., 1986–. Chm., GEC Avionics Ltd, 1986–90 (Dir, 1984–91); Dir, Brixton Estate PLC, 1983–93. Chm. Trustees, 1983–99, Pres. Soc. of Friends, 1999–, RAF Museum; Pres., RAF Historical Soc., 1993–. Governor: Cheltenham Coll., 1983–89; Wymondham Coll., 1990–98. FRSA 1979; FRAeS 1982. DL Norfolk, 1989. Hon. Liveryman, GAPAN, 1983. Polish Order of Merit, 1998. *Recreations:* golf, tennis. *Clubs:* Royal Air Force (Pres., 1994–); Royal West Norfolk Golf.

See also Maj.-Gen. G. Risius.

BEETHAM, Roger Campbell, CMG 1993; LVO 1976; HM Diplomatic Service, retired; *b* 22 Nov. 1937; *s* of Henry Campbell and Mary Beetham; *m* 1st, 1965, Judith Rees (marr. diss. 1986); 2nd, 1986, Christine Marguerite Malerme. *Educ:* Peter Symonds Sch., Winchester; Brasenose Coll., Oxford (MA). Entered HM Diplomatic Service, 1960; FO, 1960–62; UK Delegation to Disarmament Conference, Geneva, 1962–65; Washington, 1965–68; News Dept, FCO, 1969–72; Head of Chancery, Helsinki, 1972–76; FCO, 1976; seconded to European Commission, Brussels, as Spokesman of the President, Rt Hon. Roy Jenkins, 1977–80; Counsellor (Econ. and Commercial), New Delhi, 1981–85; Head of Maritime, Aviation and Envmt Dept, FCO, 1985–90; Ambassador to Senegal and (non-resident) to Cape Verde, Guinea, Guinea-Bissau and Mali, 1990–93; UK Perm. Rep. (with personal rank of Ambassador) to Council of Europe, Strasbourg, 1993–97. European Manager, Surrey CC, 1998–2000. Order of the White Rose of Finland, 1976. *Publication:* (ed) The Euro Debate: persuading the people, 2001. *Recreations:* oenology, cooking, travel. *Address:* 32 Hillcroft Crescent, W5 2SQ. *Club:* Royal Over-Seas League.

BEETON, David Christopher, CBE 1998; Director General, British Casino Association, since 2000; *b* 25 Aug. 1939; *s* of Ernest Beeton and Ethel Beeton; *m* 1968, Brenda Lomax; two *s*. *Educ:* Ipswich Sch.; King's Coll., London Univ. (LLB). Solicitor. Chief Exec., Bath CC, 1973–85; Sec., National Trust, 1985–89; Chief Exec., Historic Royal Palaces, 1989–99. *Recreations:* swimming, historic buildings, cooking, music. *Address:* 5 Moreton Terrace Mews South, SW1V 2NU. *T:* and *Fax:* (020) 7834 2531.

BEEVOR, Antony James, FRSL; author; *b* 14 Dec. 1946; *s* of John Grosvenor Beevor and Carinthia Jane Beevor (*née* Waterfield); *m* 1986, Hon. Artemis Cooper, *d* of Viscount Norwich, *qv*; one *s* one *d*. *Educ:* Winchester Coll.; RMA Sandhurst. Served 11th Hussars (PAO), 1967–70; posts in mktg and advertising, London and Paris, 1971–75; occasional journalism and literary criticism. Member: Armed Forces into the 21st Century seminars, KCL, 1993–95; Exec. Council, French Theatre Season, 1996–97; Judge, Shiva Naipaul Meml Prize, 2000. Mem. Council, Soc. for Army Historical Res. Patron, Nat. Acad. of Writing. FRGS; FRSL 1999. Chevalier de l'Ordre des Arts et des Lettres (France), 1997. *Publications:* four novels; The Spanish Civil War, 1982; Inside the British Army, 1990; Crete: the battle and the resistance, 1991 (Runciman Prize); (with Artemis Cooper) Paris After the Liberation, 1994; Stalingrad, 1998 (Samuel Johnson Prize, Wolfson Prize for History, Hawthornden Prize, 1999). *Recreations:* reading, gardening. *Address:* 54 St Maur Road, SW6 4DP.

BEEVOR, Antony Romer; Senior Advisor, SG Hambros, since 2000 (Managing Director, 1998–2000); *b* 18 May 1940; *s* of late Miles Beevor and Sybil (*née* Gilliat); *m* 1970, Cecilia Hopton; one *s* one *d*. *Educ:* Winchester; New Coll., Oxford (BA). Admitted Solicitor, 1965. Ashurst Morris Crisp & Co., 1962–72 (on secondment as Sec., Panel on Takeovers and Mergers, 1969–71); joined Hambros Bank, 1972; Dir, 1974–98; Exec. Dir, 1985–98; on secondment, as Dir-Gen., Panel on Takeovers and Mergers, 1987–89 (Dep. Chm., 1999–); Director: Hambros plc, 1990–98; (non-exec.), Rugby Gp, 1993–2000; Gerrard Group, 1995–2000; Croda International, 1996– (Chm., 2001–); Helical Bar, 2000–; Nestor Healthcare Gp, 2000– (Chm., 2001–). Mem. Council, 1970–, Chm., 1999–, Fairbridge. *Recreations:* shooting, low level golf, the countryside. *Address:* SG House, 41 Tower Hill, EC3N 4HA. *T:* (020) 7676 6605. *Clubs:* Hurlingham, Brooks's.

BEEVOR, Sir Thomas Agnew, 7th Bt *cr* 1784; *b* 6 Jan. 1929; *s* of Comdr Sir Thomas Beevor, 6th Bt, and Edith Margaret Agnew (who *m* 2nd, 1944, Rear-Adm. R. A. Currie, CB, DSC; she *d* 1985); *S* father, 1943; *m* 1st, 1957, Barbara Clare (marr. diss., 1965), *y d* of Capt. R. L. B. Cunliffe, RN (retd); one *s* two *d*; 2nd, 1966, Carola (marr. diss. 1975), *d* of His Honour J. B. Herbert, MC; 3rd, 1976, Mrs Sally Bouwens, White Hall, Saham Toney, Norfolk. *Heir:* *s* Thomas Hugh Cunliffe Beevor [*b* 1 Oct. 1962; *m* 1988, Charlotte Louise, *e d* of Keith E. Harvey; two *s* one *d*]. *Address:* Hargham Hall, Norwich NR16 2JW.

BEEZLEY, His Honour Frederick Ernest; a Circuit Judge, 1976–93; *b* 30 Jan. 1921; *s* of Frederick William Beezley and Lilian Isabel (*née* Markham); *m* 1969, Sylvia Ruth (*née* Locke). *Educ:* Acton County Sch. Served War, Royal Signals, Combined Operations, 1940–46. Called to Bar, Gray's Inn, 1947; Res. Judge, Cambridge Crown Court, 1987–93. *Recreations:* fly-fishing, horse racing, musician with Ely Mil. Band. *Address:* White Lodge, 25 Northwold, Ely, Cambridge CB6 1BG.

BEFFA, Jean-Louis Guy Henri; Chevalier de la Légion d'Honneur; Officier de l'Ordre National du Mérite; Chairman and Chief Executive Officer, Compagnie de Saint-Gobain, since 1986; *b* 11 Aug. 1941; *m* 1967, Marie-Madeleine Brunel; two *s* one *d*. *Educ:* Ecole Polytechnique (Ing. au Corps des Mines); Dip. de l'Inst. d'Etudes Politiques de Paris. Compagnie de Saint-Gobain: Vice-Pres., Corporate Planning, 1974–77; Pres., Pipe Div., 1978–82; Chief Operating Officer, 1982–86. Order of Merit (Germany); Order of Rio Branco (Brazil). *Recreations:* golf, classical music. *Address:* c/o Compagnie de Saint-Gobain, Les Miroirs, 18 avenue d'Alsace, 92096 Paris la Défense cedex, France. *T:* 247623310.

BEGG, Prof. David; Director, Centre for Transport Policy, Robert Gordon University, since 1997; Chairman, UK Commission for Integrated Transport, since 1999; *b* 12 June 1956. *Educ:* Portobello Secondary Sch.; Heriot-Watt Univ. Mgt trainee, British Rail, 1979–81; Lectr in Econs, Napier Poly., then Napier Univ., 1981–97. Non-executive Director: BRB, 1997–99; Shadow SRA, 1999–2001; SRA, 2001–; Mem. Bd, Transport for London, 2000–. Member (Lab): Lothian Regl Council (Chm., Finance Cttee, 1990–94); Edinburgh City Council (Chm., Transport Cttee, 1994–99). *Recreations:* golf, watching football (Hibs). *Address:* Centre for Transport Policy, Robert Gordon University, Dolphin House, 4 Hunter Square, Edinburgh EH1 1QW.

BEGG, (Margaret) Anne; MP (Lab) Aberdeen South, since 1997; *b* 6 Dec. 1955; *d* of David Begg, MBE and Margaret Catherine Begg (*née* Ross). *Educ:* Brechin High Sch.; Univ. of Aberdeen (MA); Aberdeen Coll. of Education. English and History Teacher, Webster's High Sch., Kirriemuir, 1978–88; Asst Principal English Teacher, 1988–91, Principal English Teacher, 1991–97, Arbroath Acad. Member: Scottish Affairs Select Cttee, 1998–2001; Work and Pensions Select Cttee, 2001–. Mem., NEC, Lab Party, 1998–99. *Recreations:* reading, theatre, cinema, public speaking, meeting people. *Address:* House of Commons, SW1A 0AA. *T:* (020) 7219 2140.

BEGGS, Prof. Jean Duthie, PhD; FRS 1998; FRSE; SHEFC Professor of Molecular Biology, Wellcome Trust Centre for Cell Biology, Institute of Cell and Molecular Biology, University of Edinburgh, since 1999; *b* 16 April 1950; *d* of William Renfrew Lancaster and Jean Crawford Lancaster (*née* Duthie); *m* 1972, Dr Ian Beggs; two *s*. *Educ:* Glasgow High Sch. for Girls; Univ. of Glasgow (BSc Hons 1971; PhD 1974). FRSE 1995. Postdoctoral Fellow: Dept of Molecular Biol., Univ. of Edinburgh, 1974–77; Plant Breeding Inst., Cambridge, 1977–79; Beit Meml Fellow for Med. Res., 1976–79; Lectr, Dept of Biochem., ICSTM, 1979–85; University of Edinburgh: Royal Soc. Univ. Res. Fellow, Dept of Molecular Biol., 1985–89; Royal Soc. EPA Cephalosporin Fund Sen. Res. Fellow, 1989–99, Professorial Res. Fellow, 1994–99, Inst. Cell and Molecular Biol. Mem., EMBO, 1991; MAE 2000. *Publications:* research papers and reviews on gene cloning in yeast and molecular biology of RNA splicing. *Recreations:* walking, ski-ing, scuba diving, classical music. *Address:* Wellcome Trust Centre for Cell Biology, Institute of Cell and Molecular Biology, University of Edinburgh, King's Buildings, Mayfield Road, Edinburgh EH9 3JR. *T:* (0131) 650 5351.

BEGGS, John Robert, (Roy); MP (UU) East Antrim, since 1983 (resigned seat Dec. 1985 in protest against Anglo-Irish Agreement; re-elected Jan. 1986); *b* 20 Feb. 1936; *s* of John Beggs; *m* 1959, Wilma Lorimer; two *s* two *d*. *Educ:* Ballyclare High Sch.; Stranmillis Trng Coll. (Certificate/Diploma in Educn). Teacher, 1957–78, Vice-Principal, 1978–83, Larne High Sch. Mem., 1973–, Vice-Chm., 1981–, NE Educn and Library Bd; Pres., Assoc. of Educn and Liby Bds, NI, 1984–85 (Vice-Pres., 1983–84). Mem., Larne Borough Council, 1973–; Mayor of Larne, 1978–83; Mem. for N Antrim, NI Assembly, 1982–86. Mem., H of C Public Accounts Commn, 1984–. *Address:* House of Commons, SW1A 0AA; 9 Carnduff Road, Ballyvernstown, Larne, Co. Antrim BT40 3NJ. *T:* (028) 2827 3258.

See also R. Beggs.

BEGGS, Roy; Member (UU) Antrim East, Northern Ireland Assembly, since 1998; *b* 3 July 1962; *s* of John Robert Beggs, *qv* and Elizabeth Wilamina Beggs (*née* Lorimer); *m* 1989, Sandra Maureen Gillespie; two *s* one *d*. *Educ:* QUB (BEng Hons Industrial Engrg). Hon. Secretary: Ulster Young Unionist Council, 1986 and 1987; E Antrim UU Assoc., 1992–. Northern Ireland Assembly: Member: Higher and Further Educn, Trng & Employment Deptl Cttee; Public Accounts Cttee; Cttee of the Centre; Vice Chm., Cttee on Standards and Privileges. Mem. Cttee, Raloo Presbyterian Church. Gov., Glynn Primary Sch. *Recreations:* walking, cycling; Officer, 1st Raloo Boys' Brigade. *Address:* (office) 32c North Street, Carrickfergus, Northern Ireland BT38 7AQ. *T:* (028) 9336 2995, *Fax:* (028) 9336 8048; *e-mail:* roy.beggs@niassembly.gov.uk. *Club:* Larne Rugby Football.

BEGLEY, Kim Sean Robert; tenor; *b* 23 June 1952; *s* of late William Begley and of Elizabeth Begley (*née* Cooke); *m* 1986, Elizabeth Mary, *d* of Charles Collier; two *s*. Educ: Rock Ferry High Sch., Birkenhead; Wimbledon Sch. of Art (costume course); Guildhall Sch. of Music and Drama (theory, piano and voice); Nat. Opera Studio. Early career in theatre: Wardrobe Dept, Gateway Th., Chester; acted in Liverpool, Newbury, London and tours; with RSC, 1977–78; many rôles as principal tenor, Royal Opera House, 1983–89: operas included A Midsummer Night's Dream, King Priam, Florentine Tragedy, Otello, Das Rheingold, Tannhäuser, and Katya Kabanová; début: with Glyndebourne Touring Opera as Don Ottavio in Don Giovanni, 1986; with Glyndebourne Festival Opera as Gastone in La Traviata, 1988; subseq. rôles at Glyndebourne include: Graf Elemer in Arabella, 1989; Boris in Katya Kabanová, 1990; High Priest in Idomeneo, and Pellegrin in New Year, 1991; Laca in Jenůfa, 1992; Albert Gregor in The Makropulos Case, 1995 (also WNO, 1994, and Chicago Lyric Opera (US début), 1995); Florestan in Fidelio, 2001; other rôles include: Male Chorus in The Rape of Lucretia, ENO, 1993; Novagerio in Palestrina, Royal Opera House, 1997; also appearances at the Proms, at opera houses in Frankfurt, Geneva, Salzburg, Cologne, and at La Scala, Milan. *Address:* c/o IMG, 616 Chiswick High Road, W4 5RX.

BEHAR, Richard Victor Montague Edward; His Honour Judge Behar; a Circuit Judge, since 2000; *b* 14 Feb. 1941; *s* of Edward Behar and Eilleen Behar, *d* of Montague Evans; *m* 1982, Iwona Krystyna (*née* Grabowska); two *s* one *d*. *Educ:* Stowe Sch. (Schol.); St John's Coll., Oxford (MA). Called to the Bar, Middle Temple, 1965; in practice at the Bar, 1967–2000; SE Circuit; Asst Recorder, 1991–95; a Recorder, 1995–2000; part-time immigration and asylum adjudicator, 1998–2000. Chairman: Bar European Gp, 1988–90; British-Ukrainian Law Assoc., 1993–2000; Co-opted Mem., Internat. Relns Cttee, Gen. Council of Bar, 1988–2000. *Recreations:* foreign languages and travel, cinema, theatre, reading. *Address:* Kingston upon Thames Crown Court, 6–8 Penrhyn Road, Kingston upon Thames, Surrey KT1 2BB. *T:* (020) 8240 2500. *Club:* Oxford and Cambridge.

BEHRENS, Clive Owen John; His Honour Judge Behrens; a Circuit Judge, since 1996; *b* 14 Sept. 1948; *s* of Col William Edward Behrens and Dulcie Bella Behrens; *m* 1974, Clemency Anne Susan Butler; one *s* one *d*. *Educ:* Eton Coll.; Trinity Coll., Cambridge (BA Hons). Called to the Bar, Gray's Inn, 1972; in practice at the Bar, 1974–96; specialised in Chancery and commercial work; a Recorder, 1992–96. *Recreations:* golf, bridge, tennis, walking. *Address:* Birstwith House, Harrogate HG3 2NG. *Club:* Alwoodley (Leeds).

BEIGHTON, Leonard John Hobhouse, CB 1992; Deputy Chairman, Board of Inland Revenue, 1992–94 (Director General, 1988–92); *b* 20 May 1934; *s* of John Durant Kennedy Beighton, OBE and Leonora Hobhouse; *m* 1962, Judith Valerie Bridge (decd); one *s* one *d*. *Educ:* Tonbridge Sch.; Corpus Christi College, Oxford (MA PPE). Inland Revenue, 1957; seconded HM Treasury, 1968–69 (Private Sec. to Chief Sec.), and 1977–79. Director: Shared Interest Soc. Ltd, 1994– (Moderator, 1998–); World Vision UK, 1997–. Member: Council, Shaftesbury Soc., 1995– (Treas., 1998–99); Bd, New Era Housing Assoc., 1999– (Treas., 2000–). *Address:* 160 Tilt Road, Cobham, Surrey KT11 3HR.

BEILL, Air Vice-Marshal Alfred, CB 1986; Appeals Secretary, King Edward VII's Hospital for Officers, 1987–96; *b* 14 Feb. 1931; *s* of late Group Captain Robert Beill, CBE, DFC and Sophie Beill; *m* 1953, Vyvian Mary Crowhurst Archer; four *d*. *Educ:* Rossall Sch.; RAF Coll., Cranwell. Commnd RAF, 1952; served, 1952–64: RAF Marham, Stafford and Fauld; HQ Air Forces ME, Aden; RAF Supply Control Centre, Hendon; student, RAF Staff Coll., Andover, 1964; HQ FEAF, Singapore, 1965–67; student, JSSC, Latimer, 1968; OC Supply and Movements Sqdn, RAF Scampton, 1968–69; HQ Maintenance Comd, 1969–70; DS JSSC (later NDC), 1970–73; Comd Supply Officer, HQ NEAF, Cyprus, 1973–75; Dir of Engrg and Supply Policy (RAF), 1976–78; student, RCDS, 1978; Dir of Movements (RAF), 1979–82; Dir of Supply Policy and Logistics Plans (RAF), 1982–84; Dir Gen. of Supply (RAF), 1984–87, retired. ADC to the Queen, 1974–75. Life Vice Pres., RAF Swimming Assoc., 1987– (Pres., 1982–87). *Address:* c/o Lloyds TSB, Cox's & King's Branch, 7 Pall Mall, SW1Y 5NA. *Club:* Royal Air Force.

BEITH, Rt Hon. Alan (James), PC 1992; MP, Berwick-upon-Tweed since Nov. 1973 (L 1973–88, Lib Dem since 1988); Deputy Leader, Liberal Democrats, since 1992; *b* 20 April 1943; *o s* of James and Joan Beith, Poynton, Ches; *m* 1965, Barbara Jean Ward (*d* 1998); one *d* (one *s* decd); *m* 2001, Baroness Maddock, *qv*. *Educ:* King's Sch., Macclesfield; Balliol and Nuffield Colls, Oxford. BLitt, MA Oxon. Lectr, Dept of Politics, Univ. of Newcastle upon Tyne, 1966–73. Vice-Chm., Northumberland Assoc. of Parish Councils, 1970–71 and 1972–73; Jt Chm., Assoc. of Councillors, 1974–79; Member: Gen. Adv. Council of BBC, 1974–84; Hexham RDC, 1969–74; Corbridge Parish Council, 1970–74; Tynedale District Council, 1973–74; BBC NE Regional Adv. Council, 1971–74; NE Transport Users' Consultative Cttee, 1970–74. Mem., House of Commons Commn, 1979–97; UK Rep. to Council of Europe and WEU, 1976–84. Liberal Chief Whip, 1976–85; Dep. Leader, Liberal Party, 1985–88; spokesman on Educn, 1977–83; spokesman on parly and constitutional affairs, 1983–87; Lib. spokesman on foreign affairs, 1985–87 (Alliance spokesman on foreign affairs, 1987); Lib Dem spokesman on Treasury affairs, 1987–94, on Home affairs, 1994–99. Member: Select Cttee on Treasury affairs, 1987–94; Intelligence and Security Cttee, 1994–; Dep. Chm., Speaker's Cttee on Electoral Commn. Trustee, Historic Chapels Trust, 1993–. Hon. DCL Newcastle upon Tyne, 1998. Methodist Local Preacher. *Publications:* The Case for the Liberal Party and the Alliance, 1983; (jtly) Faith and Politics, 1987; chapter in The British General Election of 1964, ed Butler and King, 1965. *Recreations:* walking, music, boating, looking at old buildings. *Address:* House of Commons, SW1A 0AA. *T:* (020) 7219 3540. *Club:* National Liberal.

BÉJART, Maurice (Jean); choreographer; Director, Béjart Ballet Lausanne, since 1987; *b* 1 Jan. 1927; *s* of Gaston and Germaine Berger. *Educ:* Lycée de Marseilles. Début as ballet dancer with Marseilles Opéra, 1945; International Ballet, 1949–50; Royal Opera, Stockholm, 1951–52; co-founded Les Ballets de l'Etoile, later Ballet-Théâtre de Paris, 1954 (Dir, 1954–59); Director: Twentieth Century Ballet Co., 1959–87; Mudra Sch., 1972. Grand Prix National de la Musique, 1970; Prix Erasme de la danse, 1974. Chevalier des Arts et des Lettres; Commandeur de l'Ordre de Léopold (Belgium), 1982; Ordre du Soleil Levant (Japan), 1986; Grand Officier de l'Ordre de la Couronne (Belgium), 1988. Principal works include: La Belle au Boa, Symphonie pour un homme seul, 1955; Orphée, 1958; Le sacre du printemps, 1959; Boléro, 1961; The Tales of Hoffman, 1962; The Merry Widow, The Damnation of Faust, l'Oiseau de Feu, 1964; Romeo and Juliet, 1966; Messe pour le temps présent, 1967; Firebird, 1970; Song of a Wayfarer, Nijinsky: clown de Dieu, 1971; Le Marteau sans Maître, La Traviata, 1973; Ce que l'amour me dit, 1974; Notre Faust, 1975; Heliogabale, Pli selon Pli, 1976; Petrouchka, 1977; Gaîté Parisienne, Ce que la Mort me dit, 1978; Mephisto Waltzer, 1979; Casta Diva, Eros Thanatos, 1980; The Magic Flute, Les Chaises, Light, Les Uns et les Autres (film), Adagietto, 1981; Wien Wien nur du Allein, Thalassa Mare Nostrum, 1982; Salome, Messe pour le Temps Futur, Vie et mort d'une marionnette humaine, 1983; Dionysos, 1984; Le Concours, la Chauve Souris, 1985; Arepo, Malraux ou la Métamorphose des Dieux, 1986; Trois Etudes pour Alexandre, Souvenir de Léningrad, Après-midi d'un Faune, Fiche Signalétique, 1987; Patrice Chéreau …, Dibouk, Et Valse, Piaf, Paris-Tokyo, A force de partir …, 1988; 1789 et nous, Elégie pour elle, L …, aile, 1989; Ring um den Ring, Nijinsky Clown de dieu (theatrical version), Pyramides, Mozart Tangos, 1990; La Mort subite, La Tour, Paradoxe sur le comédien (film), Tod in Wien, Nijinski, 1991; Mr C, Episodes, A6-Roc, Le Mandarin merveilleux, La Crucifixion, Sissi, 1992; L'Art du pas de deux, AmoRoma, M(Mishima), Ballade de la rue Athina, 1993; King Lear–Prospero, Journal I, 1994; Ich stehe im Regen und warte, A propos de Shéhérazade, 1995; Le Presbytère n'a rien perdu de son charme ni le jardin de son éclat (Ballet for Life), IXe Symphonie, Juan Y Teresa, Barocco Bel Canto, 1997; Elton-Berg, 2000. *Publications:* Mathilde, ou le temps perdu (novel), 1963; La Reine Verte (play), 1963; L'autre chant de la danse, 1974; Un instant dans la vie d'autrui, 1979; La Mort Subite, 1991. *Address:* Béjart Ballet Lausanne, Case Postale 25, 1000 Lausanne 22, Switzerland.

BEKER, Prof. Henry Joseph, PhD; FREng; Chairman, e-Learning Foundation, since 2000; Visiting Professor of Information Technology, Royal Holloway (formerly Royal Holloway College, then Royal Holloway and Bedford New College), University of London, since 1984; *b* 22 Dec. 1951; *s* of Jozef and Mary Beker; *m* 1976, Mary Louise (*née* Keilthy); two *d*. *Educ:* Kilburn Grammar Sch.; Univ. of London (BSc Maths 1973, PhD 1976); Open Univ. (BA 1982). CEng, FIEE 1997 (MIEE 1984); FIS (MIS 1977); CStat 1993; CMath, FIMA 1994 (AFIMA 1978). Sen. Res. Asst, Dept of Statistics, University Coll. of Swansea, 1976–77; Principal Mathematician, Racal-Comsec Ltd, 1977–80, Chief Mathematician, 1980–83; Dir of Research, Racal Research Ltd, 1983–85; Dir of Systems, Racal-Chubb Security Systems Ltd, 1985–86; Man. Dir, Racal-Guardata Ltd, 1986–88; Chm., Zergo Hldgs, then Baltimore Technologies plc, 1989–2000 (Chief Exec., 1988–99). Chairman: Overnet Data Ltd, 2000–; BenefitsU Ltd, 2000–; Protx Ltd, 2000–; Shopcreator plc, 2000–; Bladerunner Ltd, 2001–; Director: Business HR Ltd, 2000–; KeyFree Ltd, 2000–; i-NET VCT plc, 2000–; Close Finsbury Eurotech Trust plc, 2000–. Mem. Council, British Mycological Soc. Vis. Prof. of IT, Westfield Coll., Univ. of London, 1983–84. Pres., IMA, 1998–99 (Vice Pres., 1988–89). Hon. Fellow, RHBNC, 2000. FREng 2000; MInstD 1995. Freeman, Co. of Information Technologies, 1995. *Publications:* Cipher Systems, 1982; Secure Speech Communications, 1985; Cryptography and Coding, 1989. *Recreations:* music, mycology, natural history, reading, travel. *Address:* 1 Cornhill, EC3V 3ND. *T:* (020) 7743 6386, *Fax:* (020) 7743 6388; *e-mail:* henry@hjbeker.com.

BEKOE, Dr Daniel Adzei; Regional Director, International Development Research Centre, Nairobi, 1986–92; *b* 7 Dec. 1928; *s* of Aristocles Silvanus Adzete Bekoe and Jessie Nadu (*née* Awuletey); *m* 1958, Theresa Victoria Anyisaa Annan (marr. diss. 1983); three *s* (and one *s* decd); *m* 1988, Bertha Augustina Ashia Randolph. *Educ:* Achimota Sch.; University Coll. of Gold Coast (BSc London); Univ. of Oxford (DPhil). Jun. Res. Asst, Univ. of Calif, LA, 1957–58; Univ. of Ghana (formerly University Coll. of Ghana): Lectr, 1958–63; Sen. Lectr, 1963–65; Associate Prof., 1965–74; Prof. of Chemistry, 1974–83; Vice-Chancellor, 1976–83; Dir, UNESCO Regl Office for Sci. and Technol. for Africa, 1983–85. Sabbatical year, Univ. of Calif, LA, 1962–63; Vis. Associate Prof., Univ. of Ibadan, 1966–67. Member: UN Univ. Council, 1980–83; UN Adv. Cttee on Science and Technology for Develt, 1980–82. President: ICSU, 1980–83; Ghana Acad. of Arts and Scis, 1993–96; African Assoc. of Pure and Applied Chem., 1995–98. *Publications:* articles on molecular structures in crystallographic and chemical jls; gen. articles in Proc. Ghana Acad. of Arts and Sciences. *Recreation:* music. *Address:* PO Box 3383, Accra, Ghana. *T:* (21) 774020.

BELCHER, John Rashleigh, FRCS; Consultant Thoracic Surgeon, NE Metropolitan Regional Hospital Board, 1950–82; Surgeon, London Chest Hospital, 1951–82; Thoracic Surgeon, Middlesex Hospital, 1955–82; *b* 11 Jan. 1917; *s* of late Dr Ormonde Rashleigh Belcher, Liverpool; *m* 1940, Jacqueline Mary, *d* of late C. P. Phillips; two *s* one *d*. *Educ:* Epsom Coll.; St Thomas' Hosp. MB BS 1939; FRCS 1942; MS 1945; Resident appointments at St Thomas' Hospital, 1939–46. RAF, 1940–46: Medical Service; general duties and surgical specialist; Squadron Leader. Resident and Asst posts at St Thomas', Brompton, London Chest, and Middlesex Hosps; followed by consultant appointments; co-editor, Brit. Jl of Diseases of the Chest. Pres., Assoc. of Thoracic Surgeons, 1980; Member: Thoracic Soc.; Cardiac Soc.; Amer. Coll. of Chest Physicians. Mem. Bd of Governors: Hosps for Diseases of Chest and Heart, 1961–80. Toured: for British Council, Far East 1969, Cyprus and Greece 1973, Yugoslavia 1977; for FCO, Indonesia 1971, Bolivia 1975; personal lecture tours, Nepal and India 1969, Jamaica 1973, Mexico 1975. Hunterian Prof., RCS, 1979. *Publications:* Thoracic Surgical Management, 1953; chapters in standard text-books; papers in British and foreign medical journals. *Recreations:* photography, picture framing, opera. *Address:* 23 Hornton Court, Kensington High Street, W8 7RT. *T:* (020) 7937 7006.

BELCHER, Ronald Harry, CMG 1958; Under-Secretary, Ministry of Overseas Development, 1965–75; *b* 5 Jan 1916; *s* of Harry Albert Belcher; *m* 1948, Hildegarde (*née* Hellyer-Jones) (*d* 2000); one *s*. *Educ:* Christ's Hosp., Horsham; Jesus Coll., Cambridge; Brasenose Coll., Oxford. BA (Hons Classics) Cantab 1937; Dipl. Class. Arch. Cantab 1938; BA Oxon 1938. Indian Civil Service, Punjab, 1939–48; Commonwealth Relations Office, 1948–65; seconded to Foreign Office for service in British Embassy, Washington, 1951–53; Private Sec., 1953–54; Asst Sec., 1954; Deputy High Commissioner for the UK in S Africa, 1956–59; Asst Under Sec. of State, CRO, 1960–61; British Dep. High Comr, Delhi, 1961–65. *Address:* Fieldview, Lower Road, Fetcham, Surrey KT22 9EJ.

BELCOURT, Norma Elizabeth, (Mrs Emile Belcourt); *see* Burrowes, N. E.

BELDAM, Rt Hon. Sir (Alexander) Roy (Asplan), Kt 1981; PC 1989; a Lord Justice of Appeal, 1989–2000; *b* 29 March 1925; *s* of George William Beldam and Margaret Frew Shettle (formerly Beldam, *née* Underwood); *m* 1953, Elisabeth Bryant Farr; two *s* one *d*. *Educ:* Oundle Sch.; Brasenose Coll., Oxford. Sub-Lt, RNVR Air Branch, 1943–46. Called to Bar, Inner Temple, 1950; Bencher, 1977; QC 1969; a Recorder of the Crown Court, 1972–81; Presiding Judge, Wales and Chester Circuit, Jan.–Oct. 1985; a Judge of the High Court of Justice, QBD, 1981–89. Chm., Law Commn, 1985–89. *Recreations:* sailing, cricket, naval history. *Address:* c/o Royal Courts of Justice, Strand, WC2A 2LL.

BELFALL, David John; Head of Housing and Area Regeneration Group, Scottish Executive (formerly Scottish Office) Development Department, since 1995; *b* 26 April 1947; *s* of Frederick Belfall and Ada Belfall (*née* Jacobs); *m* 1972, Lorna McLaughlan; one *s* one *d*. *Educ:* Colchester Royal Grammar Sch.; St John's Coll., Cambridge (BA Hons). Home Office, 1969–88; Under-Secretary, Scottish Office: Emergency Services, Home and Health Dept, 1988–91; Health Policy and Public Health Directorate, 1991–95. *Address:* (office) Victoria Quay, Edinburgh EH6 6QQ.

BELFAST, Earl of; Arthur Patrick Chichester; farmer; *b* 9 May 1952; *s* and *heir* of 7th Marquess of Donegall, *qv*; *m* 1989, Caroline, *er d* of Major Christopher Philipson; one *s* one *d*. *Educ:* Harrow; Royal Agricl Coll., Cirencester. Coldstream Guards. *Recreations:* hunting, shooting, fishing. *Heir:* *s* Viscount Chichester, *qv*. *Address:* Dunbrody Park, Arthurstown, Co. Wexford, Eire.

BELFAST, Dean of; *see* McKelvey, Very Rev. R. S. J. H.

BELHAM, David Ernest, CB 1975; Principal Assistant Solicitor (Under Secretary), Department of Employment, 1970–77, retired; *b* 9 Aug. 1914; *s* of Ernest George Belham and Grace Belham (*née* Firth); *m* 1938, Eunice Monica (*née* Vine); two *s* two *d*. *Educ:* Whitgift Sch.; Law Society's Sch. of Law. Solicitor (Hons), 1937. Private practice, 1937–39. Served War, RAFVR, 1940–46. Entered Solicitor's Department, Min. of Labour, 1946; Asst Solicitor, 1962. *Address:* 26 The Chase, Findon, Worthing, W Sussex BN14 0TT. *T:* (01903) 873771.

BELHAVEN and STENTON, 13th Lord *cr* 1647; **Robert Anthony Carmichael Hamilton;** *b* 27 Feb. 1927; *o s* of 12th Lord Belhaven and Stenton; *S* father, 1961; *m* 1st, 1952, Elizabeth Ann, *d* of late Col A. H. Moseley, Warrawee, NSW; one *s* one *d*; 2nd, 1973, Rosemary Lady Mactaggart (marr. diss. 1986), *o d* of Sir Herbert Williams, 1st Bt, MP; one *d* (adopted); 3rd, 1986, Malgorzata Maria, *d* of Tadeusz Hruzik-Mazurkiewicz, advocate, Krakow, Poland; one *d*. *Educ:* Eton. Commissioned, The Cameronians, 1947. Commander Cross, Order of Merit (Poland), 1995. *Recreation:* cooking. *Heir:* *s* Master of Belhaven, *qv*. *Address:* 710 Howard House, Dolphin Square, SW1V 3PQ. *Club:* Carlton.

BELHAVEN, Master of; Hon. Frederick Carmichael Arthur Hamilton; *b* 27 Sept. 1953; *s* of 13th Lord Belhaven and Stenton, *qv*; *m* 1st, 1981, Elizabeth Anne (marr. diss. 1988), *d* of S. V. Tredinnick, Wisborough Green, Sussex; two *s*; 2nd, 1991, Philippa Martha Gausel Whitehead, *d* of Sir Rowland Whitehead, Bt, *qv*; one *d*. *Educ:* Eton.

BELICH, Sir James, Kt 1990; Mayor of Wellington, New Zealand, 1986–92, retired; *b* 25 July 1927; *s* of Yakov Belich and Maria (*née* Batistich); *m* 1951, Valerie Frances Anzulovich; one *s* two *d*. *Educ:* Otahuhu Coll.; Auckland Univ.; Victoria Univ. of Wellington (BA Hons Econs); IBM Teaching Fellow, Massey Univ. Consular/Internat. Trade, Auckland, Sydney, Wellington, 1948–56; Economist, Market Res. Manager, Dir, Chief Exec. and Chm., Research, Marketing, Public Relns, Advertising, 1956–86. Member: Wellington Harbour Bd; Wellington Regional Council. Director: Air NZ, 1987–89; Lambton Harbour Overview Ltd (Chm.); Wellington Internat. Airport. Pres. and Exec., various orgns incl.: Pres., UNA, Wellington and NZ; Founder Pres., UNICEF, NZ. FInstD; Fellow, Inst. of Advertising. *Recreations:* reading, walking, bowls. *Address:* 4 Indus Street, Khandallah, Wellington 4, New Zealand. *T:* (4) 4793339. *Clubs:* Wellington, Wellington Central Rotary (Wellington).

BELISLE, Denton; management consultant; Manager, Social Security Board, Belize, since 1993; *b* 18 March 1948; *s* of George Nathaniel and Laura Ianthe Belisle; *m* 1974, Barrette Johnissa (*née* Sanz); three *s*. *Educ:* Univ. of West Indies (BSc Hons); Univ. of Newcastle upon Tyne. Agricl Officer, 1970–78; Projects Officer (Agric.), 1978–81; Investment Promotion Officer, 1981–83; Dep. Perm. Rep. to UN, 1983–84; Hd, Econs Div., Develt Finance Corp., 1984–85; Chargé d'Affaires *ai*, Washington, 1985; Actg High Comr, 1985–86, High Comr, 1986–87, London. *Recreations:* tennis, reading. *Address:* 10 Mango Street, Belmopan, Belize, Central America. *T:* (8) 23568. *Club:* Belmopan Tennis.

BELL, family name of **Baron Bell**.

BELL, Baron *cr* 1998 (Life Peer), of Belgravia in the City of Westminster; **Timothy John Leigh Bell,** Kt 1990; Chairman: Bell Pottinger (formerly Lowe Bell) Communications, since 1987; Chime Communications plc, since 1994; *b* 18 Oct. 1941; *s* of Arthur Leigh Bell and Greta Mary Bell (*née* Findlay); *m* 1988, Virginia Wallis Hornbrook; one *s* one *d*. *Educ:* Queen Elizabeth's Grammar Sch., Barnet, Herts. FIPA. ABC Television, 1959–61; Colman Prentis & Varley, 1961–63; Hobson Bates, 1963–66; Geers Gross, 1966–70; Man. Dir, Saatchi & Saatchi, 1970–75; Chm. and Man. Dir, Saatchi & Saatchi Compton, 1975–85; Gp Chief Exec., Lowe Howard-Spink Campbell Ewald, 1985–87; Dep. Chm., Lowe Howard-Spink & Bell, 1987–89. Dir, Centre for Policy Studies, 1989–92. Special Adviser to: Chm., NCB, 1984–86; South Bank Bd, 1985–86. Chm., Charity Projects, 1984–93 (Pres., 1993–). Member: Industry Cttee, SCF; Public Affairs Cttee, WWF, 1985–88; Public Relations Cttee, Greater London Fund for the Blind, 1979–86; Council, Royal Opera House, 1982–85; Steering Cttee, Percent Club. Governor, BFI, 1983–86. Council Mem., Sch. of Communication Arts, 1985–87. *Address:* (office) 7 Hertford Street, W1Y 7DY.

BELL, Alan Scott; Librarian, The London Library, 1993–2002; *b* 8 May 1942; *s* of late Stanley Bell and Iris Bell (*née* Scott), Sunderland; *m* 1966, Olivia Butt; one *s* one *d*. *Educ:* Ashville Coll., Selwyn Coll., Cambridge (BA 1963, MA 1967); MA Oxon 1981. FSA 1996. Asst Registrar, Royal Commn on Historical MSS, 1963–66; Asst Keeper, Nat. Library of Scotland, 1966–81; Librarian, Rhodes House Library, Univ. of Oxford, 1981–93. Vis. Fellow, All Souls Coll., Oxford, 1980. Adv. Editor, New DNB, 1993–. Chm., Marc Fitch Fund, 2001–. *Publications:* (ed) Scott Bicentenary Essays, 1973; (ed) Sir Leslie Stephen's Mausoleum Book, 1978; (ed) Henry Cockburn, 1979; Sydney Smith, 1980; (contrib.) Illustrated History of Oxford University, 1993. *Address:* 23 Upland Park Road, Oxford OX2 7RU. *T:* (01865) 515390. *Club:* Brooks's.

BELL, Alexander Gilmour, CB 1991; Chief Reporter for Public Inquiries, Scottish Office, 1979–93, Inquiry Reporter (Consultant), since 1993; *b* 11 March 1933; *s* of Edward and Daisy Bell; *m* 1966, Mary Chisholm; four *s*. *Educ:* Hutchesons' Grammar Sch.; Glasgow Univ. (BL). Admitted Solicitor, 1954. After commercial experience in Far East and in private practice, entered Scottish Office, as Legal Officer, 1967; Dep. Chief Reporter, 1973. *Recreations:* casual outdoor pursuits, choral music.

BELL, (Alexander) Scott, CBE 2000; Group Managing Director, Standard Life Assurance Co., 1988–2001; *b* 4 Dec. 1941; *s* of William Scott Bell and Irene Bell; *m* 1965, Veronica Jane (*née* Simpson); two *s* one *d*. *Educ:* Daniel Stewart's College, Edinburgh. FFA. Standard Life Assurance Co.: Asst Actuary for Canada, 1967; Dep. Actuary, 1972; South Region Manager, 1974; Asst Gen. Manager (Finance), 1979; Gen. Manager (Finance), 1985–88. Director: Bank of Scotland, 1988–96; Hammerson plc (formerly Hammerson Property and Develt Corp.), 1988–98; Prosperity SA, 1993–; Standard Life Healthcare, 1994–2001; Universities Superannuation Scheme Ltd, 1996–; Standard Life Bank, 1997–2001; Standard Life Investments, 1998–2001; Chm., Associated Scottish Life Offices, 1994–96. Dir, ABI, 1999–. Hon. Canadian Consul in Scotland, 1994–. Hon. DLitt Heriot-Watt, 1997. *Recreations:* travel, golf, reading. *Clubs:* New (Edinburgh); Hon. Co. of Edinburgh Golfers, Royal & Ancient Golf, Golf House (Elie), Bruntsfield Links Golfing Society.

BELL, His Honour Alistair Watson; a Circuit Judge, 1978–97; *b* Edinburgh, 31 March 1930; *s* of Albert William Bell and Alice Elizabeth Watson; *m* 1957, Patricia Margaret Seed; one *s* two *d*. *Educ:* Lanark Grammar Sch.; George Watson's Coll.; Univs of Edinburgh (MA) and Oxford (MA, BCL). 2nd Lieut RASC, 1955. Called to Bar, Middle Temple, 1955; Harmsworth Scholar, 1956; entered practice, Northern Circuit, 1957; a Recorder of the Crown Court, 1972–78. Hon. Recorder, Carlisle, 1990–98. Contested (L) Chorley, 1964 and Westmorland, 1966. *Recreations:* hill walking, with or without golf clubs, Edinburgh life and letters 1760–1840. *Address:* c/o Courts of Justice, Carlisle.

BELL, Andrew Montgomery; Sheriff of Lothian and Borders, since 1990; *b* 21 Feb. 1940; *s* of James Montgomery Bell and Mary Bell (*née* Cavaye), Edinburgh; *m* 1969, Ann Margaret Robinson; one *s* one *d*. *Educ:* Royal High Sch., Edinburgh; Univ. of Edinburgh (BL). Solicitor, 1961–74; called to Bar, 1975; Sheriff of S Strathclyde, Dumfries and Galloway at Hamilton, 1979–84; Sheriff of Glasgow and Strathkelvin, 1984–90. *Publication:* (contrib.) Stair Memorial Encyclopaedia of Scots Law, 1995. *Recreations:* reading, listening to music. *Address:* 5 York Road, Trinity, Edinburgh EH5 3EJ. *T:* (0131) 552 3859. *Club:* New (Edinburgh).

BELL, Arthur; *see* Bell, E. A.

BELL, Sir Brian (Ernest), KBE 1994 (OBE 1977); Chairman and Managing Director, Brian Bell & Co. Ltd, since 1956; *b* 3 July 1928; *s* of Ernest James Bell and Evelyn Ivy Alice Bell (*née* Zeller); *m* 1962, Jean Ann Clough (*d* 1992); one *s* one *d*. *Educ:* Chinchilla State Sch., Qld, Australia; Toowoomba Grammar Sch., Qld; Queensland Univ. (pharmaceutical chemist, 1949). Went to Papua New Guinea, 1954; Bulk Med. Store, Dept of Health, 1954–56; estabd first Appliance and Service Orgn, 1956. Mem., first Port Moresby CC, 1971–88 (Dep. Lord Mayor, 1973). Citizen of PNG, 1976. Hon. Consul for: Sweden, 1974–88 (Consul Gen., 1988–); Norway, 1984–88 (Consul Gen., 1988–). Mem., Salvation Army Adv. Bd, PNG, 1987–. Chm., Univ. of PNG Foundn, 1985–. Independence Medal (PNG), 1975; Silver Jubilee Medal, 1977; Tenth Anniversary Medal (PNG), 1985; Comdr, Royal Order of Polar Star (Sweden), 1990; Kt 1st Cl., Royal Order of Merit (Norway), 1992. *Recreation:* interest in community affairs. *Address:* Brian Bell and Co. Ltd, PO Box 1228, Boroko, Papua New Guinea. *T:* 3255411; *e-mail:* bbadmin@brianbell.com.pg. *Club:* Papua (Port Moresby).

BELL, Catherine Elisabeth Dorcas, (Mrs R. J. Weber), PhD; Director General, Competition and Markets Group (formerly Corporate and Consumer Affairs), Department of Trade and Industry, since 1999; *b* 26 April 1951; *d* of late Frank Douglas Howe and of Phyllis (*née* Walsh); *m* 1993, Richard John Weber; one *s*. *Educ:* Balshaw's Grammar Sch., Leyland, Lancs; Girton Coll., Cambridge (MA); Univ. of Kent (PhD). Joined Department of Trade and Industry, 1975; Pvte Sec. to Sec. of State for Trade and Industry, 1980–81; Principal, 1981; Asst Sec., 1986; Under Sec., 1991; Head of

Competition Policy Div., 1991–93; maternity leave, 1993–94; Resident Chm., CSSB, 1994–95; Hd of Central Policy Unit, 1995–97; Dir, Utilities Review Team, 1997–99, and Competition Policy, 1998–99. *Recreations:* opera, ski-ing, gardening. *Address:* Department of Trade and Industry, 1 Victoria Street, SW1H 0ET. *T:* (020) 7215 5589.

BELL, (Charles) Trevor; General Secretary, Colliery Officials and Staffs Area of the National Union of Mineworkers, 1979–89; Member, National Executive Committee of the National Union of Mineworkers, 1979–89; *b* 22 Sept. 1927; *s* of Charles and Annie Bell; *m* 1974, Patricia Ann Tappin. *Educ:* state schools; Technical Coll. (City and Guilds Engrg); Coleg Harlech, N Wales (Trades Union scholarship, 1955). Craftsman in coal mining industry, 1941. Mem., Labour Party, 1946–. *Recreations:* gardening, reading, bowls. *Address:* Wakefield, West Yorks WF2 6SH.

BELL, Prof. Colin Roy, FRSE; Principal and Vice Chancellor, University of Stirling, since 2001; *b* 1 March 1942; *s* of late Ernest Arthur Bell and Annie Bell (*née* Chaplin); *m* 1st, 1964, Jocelyn Mumford (marr. diss. 1986); one *s* one *d;* 2nd, 1987, Janette Webb; two *d. Educ:* Judd Sch., Tonbridge; Univ. of Keele (BA 1964); Univ. of Wales (MSc Econs 1966). Lectr, 1968–71, Sen. Lectr, 1971–73, Reader, 1973–75, Univ. of Essex; Prof. of Sociology, Univ. of NSW, 1975–79; Prof. of Sociology, Univ. of Aston, 1980–84; Social Scientist, Univ. of Leicester Med. Sch., 1985–86; Res. Fellow, Centre for Educnl Sociology, Univ. of Edinburgh, 1986–88; Prof. of Sociology, 1988–98, Vice Principal, 1993–98, Univ. of Edinburgh; Vice Chancellor and Principal, Univ. of Bradford, 1998–2001. Mem., SHEFC, 1999–. FRSE 1992. Founding Academician, Acad. of Social Scis, 1999. *Publications:* Middle Class Families, 1968; Community Studies, 1971; Power, Persistence and Change, 1975; Doing Sociological Research, 1977; Property, Paternalism and Power, 1977; Social Researching, 1984; articles in sociology and policy jls. *Recreations:* jazz, blues, domestic pursuits. *Address:* University of Stirling, Stirling FK9 4LA. *T:* (01786) 467018.

BELL, Cressida Iras; Director, Cressida Bell Ltd, since 1984; *b* 13 April 1959; *d* of late Prof. Quentin Bell, FRSL and of (Anne) Olivier Bell (*née* Popham). *Educ:* St Martin's Sch. of Art (BA Hons Fashion); Royal Coll. of Art (MA). Teacher (part-time), Central Sch. of Art, Duncan of Jordanstone Coll. of Art, St Martin's Sch. of Art, and RCA, 1984–90. Group exhibitions include: Duncan Grant & Cressida Bell, Sally Hunter Fine Art, 1984; Scarf Show, Liberty's, 1987; Arts & Crafts to Avant-Garde, RFH, 1992; Colour into Cloth, Crafts Council, 1994; Bloomsbury: 3 Generations, NY, 1996. Commissions include: scarf for BM, 1988; scarf for V&A, 1992; book jacket, Song of Love, 1991; interior, Zoo Studios, 1994; carpet for British Consulate, Hong Kong, 1996. *Publication:* The Decorative Painter, 1996. *Recreations:* travel, cookery, dress-making.

BELL, David Charles Maurice; Chairman, Financial Times, since 1996; Director for People, Pearson plc, since 1998; *b* 30 Sept. 1946; *s* of Roderick Martin Bell and Mary Frances Bell (*née* Wade); *m* 1972, Primrose Frances Moran; two *s* one *d. Educ:* Worth Sch.; Trinity Hall, Cambridge (BA 2nd Cl. Hons Hist.); Univ. of Pennsylvania (MA Econs and Pol Sci.). Oxford Mail and Times, 1970–72; Financial Times, 1972–: Washington Corresp., 1975–78; News Editor, Internat. Edn, 1978–80; Features Editor, 1980–85; Man. Editor, 1985–89; Advertisement Dir, 1989–93; Marketing Dir, 1992–93; Chief Exec., 1993–96. Dir, Pearson plc, 1996–. Member: UK Council, INSEAD, 1994–; Develt Bd, RNT, 2001–. Trustee, Common Purpose, 1994–; Patron, Ambache Chamber Orch., 1995–; Chairman: Millennium Bridge Trust, 1997–; Internat. Youth Foundn, 1998–. *Recreations:* cycling, theatre, Victorian social history. *Address:* 35 Belitha Villas, N1 1PE. *T:* (020) 7609 4000.

BELL, David John, CB 1998; FRICS; Commissioner of Valuation for Northern Ireland, 1988–98; Chief Executive, Valuation and Lands Agency, 1993–98; *b* 17 March 1938; *s* of James Bell and Elizabeth Bell; *m* 1962, Agnes Mona Eileen; two *d. Educ:* Regent House GS. FRICS 1981. Sen. Valuation Asst, Valuer I, Valuation Office, 1963–70; Department of the Environment, Northern Ireland: Divl Estates Surveyor (Belfast), 1975–80; Superintending Estates Surveyor, 1980–82; Chief Lands Officer, Lands Service, 1982–84; Asst Comr, 1984–87, Dep. Comr, 1987–88, Valuation and Lands Office, Dept of Finance and Personnel, NI. Hon. Fellow, Irish Auctioneers and Valuers Inst., 1996. *Recreations:* reading, gardening, church work, golf. *Address:* 1 Rockmount, Dundonald, Belfast BT16 2BY. *T:* (028) 9048 4241.

BELL, David Mackintosh; HM Diplomatic Service, retired; Lecturer in International Business Studies, Institut Supérieur Européen de Gestion, Lille; *b* 2 Aug. 1939; *s* of late David Little Bell and Kathleen Bell (*née* McBurnie); *m* 1st, 1963, Ann Adair Wilson (marr. diss.); one *s* one *d;* 2nd, 1996, Dominique Van Hille; two *s. Educ:* Ayr Acad.; Glasgow Univ. (MA 1959). Commonwealth Relations Office, 1960; served Karachi, Enugu, Havana and Mexico City; FCO, 1968–71; Budapest, 1971–74; 2nd, later 1st Sec., FCO, 1974–77; Commercial Consul, NY, 1977–81; FCO, 1981–86; Press Sec., Bonn, 1986–90; Consul-General, Lille, 1990–95; Consul-Gen., Zürich, and Dir, British Export Promotion in Switzerland and Liechtenstein, 1995–97. *Recreations:* reading, crosswords, cooking. *Address:* 6 rue de Wattignies, 59139 Noyelles-lez-Seclin, France. *T:* (3) 20327910; *e-mail:* dbell@nordnet.fr.

BELL, David Robert; Chief Executive, Bedfordshire County Council, since 2000; *b* 31 March 1959; *s* of Robert Bell and Marie Blackie Slater Bell; *m* 1981, Louise Caroline Poole; two *d. Educ:* Univ. of Glasgow (MA, MEd); Jordanhill Coll. of Educn (PGCE Primary). Teacher, Cuthbertson Primary Sch., Glasgow, 1982–85; Dep. Headteacher, Powers Hall Jun. Sch., Essex, 1985–88; Headteacher, Kingston Primary Sch., Essex, 1988–90; Asst Dir of Educn, Newcastle CC, 1990–93 and 1994–95; Harkness Fellow, Atlanta, Georgia, 1993–94; Chief Educn Officer, 1995–98, Dir of Educn and Libraries, 1998–2000, Newcastle CC. *Publications:* Parents' Guide to the National Curriculum (Primary), 1991; Parents' Guide to the National Curriculum (Secondary), 1991; Inspirations for History, 1992; Bright Ideas: maths projects, 1992. *Recreations:* Scottish country dancing, football, reading. *Address:* Bedfordshire County Council, County Hall, Cauldwell Street, Bedford MK42 9AP. *T:* (01234) 228013.

BELL, Dr Donald Atkinson, CEng; Technical Director, Marchland Consulting Ltd, since 1991; *b* 28 May 1941; *s* of late Robert Hamilton Bell and Gladys Mildred Bell; *m* 1967, Joyce Louisa Godber; two *s. Educ:* Royal Belfast Academical Instn; Queen's Univ., Belfast (BSc); Southampton Univ. (PhD); Glasgow Univ. (MSc). FIMechE; MIEE; FBCS. National Physical Lab., 1966–77; Dept of Industry, 1978–82; Dir, Nat. Engrg Lab., 1983–90; Hd of R&D, Strathclyde Inst., 1990–91. *Address:* Marchland Consulting Ltd, 108 East Kilbride Road, Glasgow G76 8JF. *T:* (0141) 644 2000; *e-mail:* donald@marchland.com.

BELL, Donald L.; *see* Lynden-Bell.

BELL, Prof. Donald Munro; international concert and opera artist; freelance; Professor of Music, Calgary University, since 1983; *b* 19 June 1934; one *s. Educ:* South Burnaby High Sch., BC, Canada. Made Wigmore Hall Debut, 1958; since then has sung at Bayreuth Wagner Festival, 1958, 1959, 1960; Lucerne and Berlin Festivals, 1959; Philadelphia and New York debuts with Eugene Ormandy, 1959; Israel, 1962; Russia Recital Tour, 1963; Glyndebourne Festival, 1963, 1973, 1974, 1982; with Deutsche Oper am Rhein, Düsseldorf, 1964–66; Scottish National Opera, 1974; Scottish Opera, 1978; Basler Kammer Orchestre, 1978; Australian Tour (Musica Viva), 1980. Prof. and Head of Vocal Dept, Ottawa Univ., 1979–82. Directed Opera Workshop at Univ. of Calgary. Member: Nat. Assoc. of Teachers of Singing, 1985–; Nat. Opera Assoc., 1985– (Dir, Alberta Br., 1986–90, for Canada, 1988–90). Has made recordings. Arnold Bax Medal, 1955. *Address:* University of Calgary, Faculty of Fine Arts, Department of Music, 2500 University Drive NW, Calgary, Alberta T2N 1N4, Canada; *e-mail:* dmbell@acs.ucalgary.ca.

BELL, Edith Alice, OBE 1981; Chief Nursing Officer, Welsh Office, 1972–81; *b* 14 Sept. 1919; *d* of George and Alice Bell. *Educ:* Girls' Grammar Sch., Lancaster. SRN University Hosp., Leeds; SCM St Luke's Hosp., Bradford; Cert. Royal Medico Psychological Assoc., Westwood Hosp., Bradford; Registered Nurse, Mentally Subnormal, Aston Hall, Derby. Ward Sister, Aston Hall Hosp., Derby, 1941–43; Sen. Asst Matron, Royal Albert Hosp., Lancaster, 1943–46; Dep. Matron, Darenth Park Hosp., Dartford, 1946–48; Gp Matron, Fountain Gp HMC, London, 1948–60; Management Services Officer, SE RHB, Scotland, 1960–63; Chief Regional Nursing Officer, E Anglian RHB, 1963–72. WHO Fellowship, 1951. Past Member: Gen. Nursing Council, England and Wales; Nat. Council of Nurses; Standing Nursing Adv. Cttee; Services Cttee, Internat. Council of Nurses; Jt Bd, Clinical Nursing Studies; Council, Queen's Inst. of Dist Nursing Service; SW Metrop. RHB: Nursing, Research and Trng Cttees. Chairman: Mental Nurses Cttee; Jt Organizations; Reg. Nursing Officers Gp; Royal Coll. of Nursing Br. Mem., NHS Reorganization Steering Cttee. Hon. Sec., Mental Hosp. Matrons Assoc.; Pres., Inst. of Religion and Medicine. Chm., CS Retirement Fellowship Gp, 1987– (Chm., N Lancs Br., 1989–; Mem., Cttee of Management, 1988–93, Welfare Cttee, 1988–93, Standing Orders Cttee, 1993–99). Chm., Old Girls' Assoc., Girls' Grammar Sch., Lancaster, 1987–95 (Mem. Cttee, 1995–). Mem. Cttees, local Abbeyfield Soc., 1983–. *Publications:* contribs to professional jls. *Recreations:* reading, travel, gardening, supporting ecumenical activities. *Address:* Tyla Teg, 51 Farmdale Road, Newlands, Lancaster LA1 4JB. *Club:* Civil Service.

BELL, Edward; Publisher, 1990–2000, and Chairman, 1992–2000, HarperCollins UK; Chairman, The Knowledge Source Ltd, since 2000; *b* 2 Aug. 1949; *s* of Eddie and Jean Bell; *m* 1969, Junette Bannatyne; one *s* two *d. Educ:* Airdrie High Sch. Cert. of Business Studies. With Hodder & Stoughton, 1970–85; Man. Dir, Collins General Div., 1985–89; launched Harper Paperbacks in USA, 1989; Dep. Chief Exec., 1990–91, Chief Exec., 1991–92, HarperCollins UK; Chm., HarperCollins India, 1994–2000. Non-executive Director: beCogent Ltd, 2000–; Haynes Publishing Gp plc; Management Diagnostics Ltd. *Recreations:* reading, golf, supporting Arsenal, opera, collecting old books. *Clubs:* Royal Automobile, Naval and Military; AutoWink (Epsom); Ferndown Golf.

BELL, Prof. (Ernest) Arthur, CB 1988; PhD; FLS, CChem, FRSC; CBiol, FIBiol; Director, Royal Botanic Gardens, Kew, 1981–88; Visiting Professor, King's College London, since 1982; Adjunct Professor, University of Texas at Austin, since 1990; *b* 20 June 1926; *s* of Albert Bell and Rachel Enid (*née* Williams), Gosforth, Northumberland; *m* 1952, Jean Swinton Ogilvie; two *s* one *d. Educ:* Dame Allan's Sch., Newcastle upon Tyne; Univ. of Durham (King's Coll., Newcastle upon Tyne) BSc; Trinity Coll., Univ. of Dublin (MA, PhD; Hon. Fellow, 1990). CChem, FRIC (now FRSC) 1961; FIBiol 1987. Res. Chemist, ICI, Billingham, 1946; Demonstr and holder of Sarah Purser Med. Res. Award, TCD, 1947; Asst to Prof. of Biochem., TCD, 1949; Lectr in Biochem., KCL, 1953; Reader in Biochem., Univ. of London, 1964–68; Prof. of Botany, Univ. of Texas, 1968–72; Prof. of Biology, London Univ., and Hd of Dept of Plant Scis, KCL, 1972–81; FKC 1982. Sen. Foreign Scientist Fellow, Nat. Sci. Foundn, USA, and Vis. Prof. of Biol., Univ. of Kansas, 1966; Visiting Professor: Univ. of Sierra Leone, 1977; Univ. of Reading, 1982–88; Cecil H. and Ida Green Vis. Prof., Univ. of British Columbia, 1987; Vis. Commonwealth Fellow, Australia, 1980; Emeritus Leverhulme Fellow, 1991–93. Scientific Dir, Texas Botanical Gardens Soc., 1988–. Consultant Dir, CAB-Internat. Mycological Inst. (formerly Commonwealth Mycol. Inst.), 1982–88; Member: Working Party on Naturally Occurring Toxicants in Food, 1983–94; Royal Mint Adv. Cttee, 1992–98. Hon. Botanical Adviser, Commonwealth War Graves Commn, 1983–89. President: Section K (Plant Biol.), BAAS, 1985–86; KCL Assoc., 1986–88; Vice Pres., Linnean Soc., 1983–85 (Mem. Council, 1980–85); Mem. Council, RHS, 1985–89; Hon. Mem., Phytochemical Soc. of Europe, 1985. *Publications:* contribs on plant biochem., chemotaxonomy, and chem. ecology to Phytochemistry, and Biochem. Jl. *Recreations:* walking, travel. *Address:* 3 Hillview, Wimbledon, SW20 0TA. *Club:* Athenæum.

BELL, Geoffrey Lakin; President, Geoffrey Bell and Co., New York, since 1982; Chairman, Guinness Mahon Holdings, 1987–93; *b* 8 Nov. 1939; *s* of Walter Lakin Bell and Ann (*née* Barnes); *m* 1973, Joan Abel; one *d. Educ:* Grimsby Technical Sch.; London School of Economics and Political Science. Economic Asst, HM Treasury, 1961–63; Vis. Scholar, Fed. Reserve System, principally with Federal Reserve Bank of St Louis, 1963–64; HM Treasury, also Special Lectr at LSE, 1964–66; Economic Advr, British Embassy, Washington, 1966–69; 1969–82: Asst to Chm., J. Henry Schroder Wagg; Dir, Schroder Wagg; Exec. Vice Pres., Schroder Internat. and Sen. Advr, Schroder Bank and Trust Co., NY; Special Columnist on Econs and Finance, The Times, 1969–74; Exec. Sec. and Mem., Gp of Thirty, 1978–. Mem., Court of Govs, LSE, 1994–. Cons. Editor, International Reports, 1983–93. *Publications:* The Euro-Dollar Market and the International Financial System, 1973; numerous articles on internat. econs and finance in UK and USA. *Address:* 17 Abbotsbury House, Abbotsbury Road, W14 8EN. *T:* (020) 7603 9408; 455 East 57th Street, New York, NY, USA. *T:* (212) 8381193. *Club:* Reform.

BELL, Sir (George) Raymond, KCMG 1973; CB 1967; Vice-President, European Investment Bank, 1973–78, retired; Hon. Vice-President, European Investment Bank, 1978; *b* 13 March 1916; *e s* of late William Bell and Christabel Bell (*née* Appleton); *m* 1944, Joan Elizabeth, *o d* of late W. G. Coltham and Christina Coltham; two *s* two *d. Educ:* Bradford Grammar Sch.; St John's Coll., Cambridge (Scholar). Entered Civil Service, Assistant Principal, 1938; Min. of Health, 1938; transf. Treasury, 1939; served War 1941–44, Royal Navy (Lieut RNVR). Principal, Civil Service, 1945; Asst Sec., 1951; Under-Sec., 1960; Dep. Sec., 1966; Dep. Sec. HM Treasury, 1966–72. Sec. (Finance), Office of HM High Commissioner for the UK in Canada, 1945–48; Counsellor, UK Permanent Delegn to OEEC/NATO, Paris, 1953–56; Principal Private Sec. to Chancellor of Exchequer, 1958–60. Mem. UK Delegation to Brussels Conference, 1961–62 and 1970–72. *Recreations:* music, reading, travel. *Address:* Quartier des Bories, Aouste-sur-Sye, 26400 Crest, Drôme, France. *T:* 475252694.

BELL, Griffin B.; Attorney-General, USA, 1977–79; *b* Americus, Georgia, 31 Oct. 1918; *s* of A. C. Bell and Thelma Pilcher; *m* 1943, Mary Foy Powell; one *s. Educ:* Southwestern Coll., Ga; Mercer Univ. (LLB *cum laude* 1948, LLD 1967). Served AUS, 1941–46, reaching rank of Major. Admitted to Georgia Bar, 1947; practice in Savannah and Rome, 1947–53. Partner in King and Spalding, Atlanta, 1953–59, 1976–77, 1979–, Managing Partner, 1959–61; United States Judge, 5th Circuit, 1961–76. Chairman: Atlanta Commn on Crime and Delinquency, 1965–66; CSCE, 1980. Mem., Vis. Cttee, Law Sch., Vanderbilt Univ.; Trustee, Mercer Univ.; Member: Amer. Law Inst.; Amer. Coll. of Trial Lawyers (Pres., 1985–86). *Address:* 206 Townsend Place NW, Atlanta, GA 30327, USA.

BELL, Guy Davies; Director, BAA plc, 1988–89; Managing Director, Gatwick Airport Ltd, 1985–89; *b* 19 May 1933; *s* of Percival and Margaret Bell; *m* 1958, Angela Mary Joan Bickersteth; two *s* one *d* (and one *s* decd). *Educ:* Sedbergh Sch. British Transport Docks Bd, 1963–68; British Airports Authority, 1968–86, Engrg Dir, 1977–85; BAA, 1986–89. *Recreations:* gardening, open air, music. *Club:* Royal Automobile.

BELL, Howard James; Chief Executive, Provident Financial plc, 1997–2001; *b* 28 March 1944; *m* 1969, Susan Vivienne Fell; one *s* (one *d* decd). *Educ:* Bradford Univ. (MBA). Yorkshire Imperial Metals Ltd, 1963–67; Provident Financial plc, 1967–2001: computer systems analyst, 1967–72; personnel and trng, 1972–80; Line Manager, 1980–89; Dir, 1989–2001. *Recreations:* sport, travel.

BELL, Prof. Ian Frederick Andrew, PhD; Professor of American Literature, University of Keele, since 1992; *b* 31 Oct. 1947; *s* of Frederick George Bell and Cecilia Bell; *m* 1983, Elizabeth Mary Tagart (marr. diss. 1989); two *s*; one *s*. *Educ:* West Bridgford Grammar Sch.; Univ. of Reading (BA 1970; PhD 1978). Lectr, Sen. Lectr and Reader in Amer. Lit., Univ. of Keele, 1973–92. *Publications:* Critic as Scientist: the modernist poetics of Ezra Pound, 1981; (ed) Ezra Pound: tactics for reading, 1982; (ed) Henry James: fiction as history, 1984; (ed jtly) American Literary Landscapes: the fiction and the fact, 1988; Henry James and the Past: readings into time, 1991; (ed) The Best of O. Henry, 1993; Washington Square: styles of money, 1993. *Recreations:* visual arts, cinema, music. *Address:* Department of American Studies, University of Keele, Staffs ST5 5BG. *T:* (01782) 583012.

BELL, James Steven, CMG 1989; CBE 1964; DFC 1946; QPM 1956; CPM 1950; Director General, Ministry of the Interior, Bahrain, retired; *b* 30 Sept. 1914; *s* of Lachlan Steven Bell and Mary (*née* Bertram). *Educ:* Whitehaven School. Grenadier Guards A Cadet, 1933–35; Kent County Constabulary, 1935–41; RAF, 1941–46; Nigeria Police, 1946–64; Bahrain Public Security, Ministry of the Interior, 1966–93. Nigerian Police Medal, 1960; Order of Bahrain 1st Cl., 1983; Bahrain Public Security Medal for Distinguished Service, 1988. *Recreations:* walking, reading, travel. *Address:* c/o Barclays Bank, Strand Street, Whitehaven, Cumbria CA28 7DL.

BELL, Jocelyn; *see* Bell Burnell, S. J.

BELL, Rear-Adm. John Anthony, CB 1977; Research Fellow, Exeter University, 1986–89, retired; Director, Naval Education Service, 1975–78; Chief Naval Instructor Officer, 1978–79; *b* 25 Nov. 1924; *s* of Mathew Bell, Dundee, and Mary Ann Ellen Bell (*née* Goss), London; *m* 1946, Eileen Joan Woodman; two *d* (and one *d* decd). *Educ:* St Ignatius Coll., Stamford Hill; London Univ. BA, BSc, LLB. Barrister, Gray's Inn, 1970. RM 1943–45; Schoolmaster, RN, Instr Lt, Courses, Reserve Fleet, service with RAN, 1945–52; HMS Implacable, Theseus, Admiralty, HMS Excellent, 1952–59; HMS Centaur, RN Staff Course, Staff of SACLANT, USA, Directing Staff, RN Staff Course, Western Fleet, 1959–69; Naval Educn Service, Dir, Dept of Naval Oceanography and Meteorology, 1969–75; Instr Captain 1969, Rear-Adm. 1975. Educn Sec. of the BBC, 1979–83; Dep. Chairman: Police Complaints Bd, 1983–85; (Discipline), Police Complaints Authority, 1985–86; Vice Chm., Educn Foundn for Visual Aids, 1986–88; Member: BEC Educn Cttee, 1975–79; C&G Policy Cttee, 1975–79; TEC, 1976–79; Cert. of Extended Educn Cttee, DES, 1978–79; FEFCE SW Cttee, 1993–99. Pres., Sea Cadet Corps, Gravesend, 1982–84; Vice-Pres., United Services Catholic Assoc., 1979–; Nat. Vice-Pres., RN Assoc., 1983–96 (Dep. Pres., 1996–). Chairman: Kent EC Cttee, 1982–84; RNLI, Wellington, 1988–98 (Pres., 1998–). Vice-Chm., Bd (formerly Court) of Govs, London Guildhall Univ. (formerly City of London Poly.), 1984–95; Governor: SOAS, London Univ., 1975–79; Somerset Coll. of Art and Technology, 1987–95 (Vice-Chm. of Govs, 1989–95); London Coll. of Furniture, 1988–90. Editor-in-Chief, Education Media International, 1988–2000. Hon. LLD London Guildhall, 1996. KSG 1983. *Recreations:* swimming, wines, travelling, France.

BELL, Prof. John Irving, DM; FRCP; Nuffield Professor of Clinical Medicine, University of Oxford, since 1992; Fellow of Magdalen College, Oxford, since 1990; *b* 1 July 1952; *s* of Robert Edward Bell and Mary Agnes (*née* Wholey). *Educ:* Univ. of Alberta, Canada (BSc Medicine); Oxford Univ. (BA Hons Physiol Sci.; BM, BCh; DM 1990). FRCP 1992. Rhodes Scholar, Univ. of Alberta and Magdalen Coll., Oxford, 1975. Postgraduate training in medicine, 1979–82 (John Radcliffe Hosp., Hammersmith Hosp., Guy's Hosp., Nat. Hosp. for Neurol Disease); Clinical Fellow in Immunology, Stanford Univ., USA, 1982–87; Wellcome Sen. Clin. Fellow, 1987–89, University Lectr, 1989–92, Oxford Univ. Mem., MRC, 1996–. Founder FMedSci 1998. Sen. Mem., OUBC, 1996–. *Publications:* scientific papers in immunology and genetics. *Recreations:* rowing, swimming, sailing. *Address:* Magdalen College, Oxford OX1 4AU. *T:* (01865) 221339. *Clubs:* Leander (Henley-on-Thames); Vincent's (Oxford).

BELL, Sir John Lowthian, 5th Bt *cr* 1885; *b* 14 June 1960; *s* of Sir Hugh Francis Bell, 4th Bt and Lady Bell (Mary Howson, MB, ChB, *d* of late George Howson, The Hyde, Hambledon); *S* father, 1970; *m* 1985, Venetia, *d* of J. A. Perry, Taunton; one *s* one *d*. *Recreations:* shooting, fishing. *Heir:* *s* John Hugh Bell, *b* 29 July 1988. *Address:* Arncliffe Hall, Ingleby Cross, Northallerton, N Yorks DL6 3PA.

BELL, Prof. (John) Nigel (Berridge), PhD; Professor of Environmental Pollution, Imperial College, University of London, since 1989; *b* 26 April 1943; *s* of John Edward Donald Bell and Dorothy Elise Bell (*née* White); *m* 1st, 1970, Jennifer Margaret Pollard (marr. diss. 1977); 2nd, 1978, Carolyn Mary Davies (marr. diss. 1992); three *s*. *Educ:* County Grammar Sch. of King Edward VII, Melton Mowbray; Univ. of Manchester (BSc Botany 1964; PhD Plant Ecol. 1969); Univ. of Waterloo, Ont. (MSc Biol. 1965). Teaching Fellow, Univ. of Waterloo, 1964–65; Res. Asst, Bedford Coll., Univ. of London, 1968–70; Imperial College, University of London: Res. Asst, 1970–72; Lectr, 1972–83; Sen. Lectr, 1983–87; Reader in Envmtl Pollution, 1987–89; Dir, Centre for Envmtl Technology, 1986–94; Dir, MSc Studies, 1994–; Head, Agricl and Envmtl Mgt Sect., Dept of Biology, 1986–. Hon. DES Waterloo, 1998. *Publications:* (ed) Ecological Aspects of Radionuclide Releases, 1983; Air Pollution Injury to Vegetation, 1986; (ed) Acid Rain and Britain's Natural Ecosystems, 1988; Air Pollution and Forest Health in the European Community, 1990; numerous papers in jls on air pollution and radioactive pollution. *Recreations:* classical music, travel, walking, railways. *Address:* T. H. Huxley School of Environment, Earth Sciences and Engineering, Royal School of Mines, Imperial College of Science, Technology and Medicine, Prince Consort Road, SW7 2BP. *T:* (020) 7594 9288; 48 Western Elms Avenue, Reading, Berks RG30 2AN. *T:* (0118) 958 0653.

BELL, Prof. John Stephen, DPhil; FBA 1999; Professor of Law, University of Cambridge, since 2001; *b* 5 May 1953; *s* of Harry Bell and Elsie Bell (*née* Walmsley); *m* 1983, Sheila Brookes; two *s*. *Educ:* Trinity Coll., Cambridge (BA 1974; MA 1977); Gregorian Univ., Rome (Baccalaureus in Philosophy 1976); Wadham Coll., Oxford (DPhil 1980). Asst, Inst de droit comparé, Paris II, 1974–75; Fellow and Tutor in Law, Wadham Coll., Oxford, 1979–89; Leeds University: Prof. of Public and Comparative Law, 1989–2001; Pro-Vice Chancellor for Teaching, 1992–94. Professeur associé: Univs of Paris I and Paris II, 1985–86; Univ. du Maine, 1995–96; Vis. Prof., Katholieke Univ., Brussels, 1993–. Mem., Res. Council, Eur. Univ. Inst., Florence, 1997–. Pres., SPTL, 1998–99. FRSA 1995. *Publications:* Policy Arguments in Judicial Decisions, 1983; French Constitutional Law, 1992; (with L. N. Brown) French Administrative Law, 4th edn 1993, 5th edn 1998; (with G. Engle) Cross on Statutory Interpretation, 3rd edn 1995; (jtly) Principles of French Law, 1998; (contrib.) New Directions in European Public Law, 1998; contribs to learned jls. *Recreation:* learning and speaking foreign languages. *Address:* Faculty of Law, University of Cambridge, 10 West Road, Cambridge CB3 9DZ.

BELL, Prof. Kathleen Myra, CBE 1978; Professor of Social Studies in the University of Newcastle upon Tyne, 1971–83, now Professor Emeritus; *b* 6 March 1920; *d* of late Walter Petty and late Myra Petty; *m* 1945, Rev. Jack Martin Bell (*d* 1993); one *s* one *d*. *Educ:* St Joseph's Coll., Bradford; Univ. of Manchester (Prize in Public Admin. 1940). Asst Personnel Officer, later Trng Officer, Min. of Supply ROF, 1942–45; Tutor and Lectr in Univ. Depts of Extra-Mural Studies, 1945–63; University of Newcastle upon Tyne: Lectr in Social Studies, 1963–67; Sen. Tutor, 1967–69; Sen. Lectr, 1969–71. Member: Lord Chancellor's Council on Tribunals, 1963–81 (Ch. person, Cttee on Functions of the Council, 1977–81); Social Admin. Cttee of Jt Univ. Council for Public and Social Admin., 1965–83; BBC Programmes Complaints Commn, 1978–81; Academic Adviser (apptd by Govt Chief Scientist) to DHSS Social Security Res. Policy Cttee, 1976–83; Expert Adviser to OECD Directorate for Social Affairs and Educn, for their project, Role of Women in the Economy, 1976–77; Mem., AHA for N Tyneside, 1974–77; Mem., Davies Cttee on Hosp. Complaints Procedure, 1971–73; Member Editorial Board: Jl of Social Policy, 1971–78; Jl of Social Welfare Law, 1977–. *Publications:* Tribunals in the Social Services, 1969; Disequilibrium in Welfare, 1973; Research Study on Supplementary Benefit Appeal Tribunals—Review of Main Findings, Conclusions and Recommendations, 1975; The Functions of the Council on Tribunals, 1980; various papers in Jl of Social Policy, Econ. and Social Admin, and other jls. *Address:* Silverton, 86 Trinity Road, Edinburgh EH5 3JU. *Club:* Scottish Arts (Edinburgh).

BELL, Leslie Gladstone, CEng, FRINA; RCNC; Director of Naval Ship Production, Ministry of Defence, 1977–79, retired; *b* 20 Oct. 1919; *s* of late John Gladstone Bell and Jessie Gray Bell (*née* Quigley); *m* 1963, Adriana Agatha Jacoba van den Berg; one *s* one *d*. *Educ:* Portsmouth Dockyard Tech. Coll.; Royal Naval Engineering Coll., Keyham; Royal Naval Coll., Greenwich. Staff Constructor Cdr, Home Fleet, 1953–56; Aircraft Carrier Design, 1956–59; Chief Constructor, Weapon Development, 1959–67; IDC, 1968; Asst Dir, Submarine Design, 1969–72; Director, Submarine Project Team, 1972–77. *Recreations:* gardening, golf, music. *Address:* Haytor, Old Midford Road, Bath, Avon BA2 7DH. *T:* (01225) 833357. *Club:* Bath Golf.

BELL, Lindsay Frances; Deputy Head, Domestic Affairs, Cabinet Office (on secondment), since 2000; *b* 29 April 1950; one *s* one *d*. *Educ:* University Coll. London (BA 1971); St Anne's Coll., Oxford (BPhil 1973). Department of the Environment, later Department of the Environment, Transport and the Regions, 1975–: Head: Finance Deptl Services, 1987–89; Water Regulation Div., 1989–90; Local Govt Reorgn Div., 1990–94; Local Authy Grants, 1994–97; Dir, Regl Policy, 1997–2000. *Address:* Cabinet Office, 70 Whitehall, SW1A 2AS.

BELL, Martin, OBE 1992; *b* 31 Aug. 1938; *s* of late Adrian Hanbury Bell and Marjorie H. Bell; *m* 1st, 1971, Nelly Lucienne Gourdon (marr. diss.); two *d*; 2nd, 1985, Rebecca D. Sobel (marr. diss.); 3rd, 1998, Fiona Goddard. *Educ:* The Leys Sch., Cambridge; King's Coll., Cambridge (MA). BBC TV News: Reporter, 1965–77; Diplomatic Correspondent, 1977–78; Chief Washington Correspondent, 1978–89; Berlin Correspondent, 1989–93; E European Correspondent, 1993–94; Foreign Affairs Correspondent, 1994–96; Special Correspondent, BBC Nine O'Clock News, 1997. Pool TV Reporter, 7th Armoured Bde, Gulf War, 1991. MP (Ind.) Tatton, 1997–2001. Contested (Ind. Bell) Brentwood and Ongar, 2001. DUniv Derby, 1996; Hon. MA: East Anglia, 1997; N London, 1997. RTS Reporter of the Year, 1977, TV Journalist of the Year, 1992. *Publications:* In Harm's Way, 1995; An Accidental MP, 2000. *Address:* 71 Denman Drive, NW11 6RA.

BELL, Martin George Henry; Senior Partner, Ashurst Morris Crisp, 1986–92; Director, Laird Group, since 1994; *b* 16 Jan. 1935; *s* of Leonard George Bell and Phyllis Bell (*née* Green); *m* 1965, Shirley Wrightson; two *s*. *Educ:* Charterhouse. Nat. Service, 1953–55. Articles, 1956–61, admitted Solicitor, 1961, Assistant, 1961, Partner, 1963, Ashurst Morris Crisp. *Recreation:* walking. *Address:* Mulberry, Woodbury Hill, Loughton, Essex IG10 1JB. *T:* (020) 8508 1188.

BELL, Michael John Vincent, CB 1992; Group Head of Strategic Analysis, BAE SYSTEMS (formerly British Aerospace), since 1999; *b* 9 Sept. 1941; *e s* of C. R. V. Bell, OBE and late Jane Bell, MBE; *m* 1983, Mary Shippen, *o d* of late J. W. Shippen and Mrs Margaret Shippen; one *s* two *d*. *Educ:* Winchester Coll.; Magdalen Coll., Oxford (BA Lit. Hum.). Res. Associate, Inst. for Strategic Studies, 1964; Ministry of Defence: Asst Principal, 1965; Principal, 1969; Asst Sec., 1975; on loan to HM Treasury, 1977–79; Asst Under Sec. of State (Resources and Programmes), 1982–84; Dir Gen. of Management Audit, 1984–86; Asst Sec. Gen. for Defence Plannning and Policy, NATO, 1986–88; Dep. Under-Sec. of State (Finance), 1988–92, (Defence Procurement), 1992–95; Dep. Chief of Defence Procurement (Support), 1995–96; Project Dir, European Consolidation, BAe (on secondment), 1996–99. *Recreations:* motorcycling, military history. *Address:* BAE SYSTEMS plc, Farnborough Aerospace Centre, Farnborough, Hants GU14 6YU.

BELL, Nigel; *see* Bell, J. N. B.

BELL, Nigel Christopher; CEng; Chief Executive, NHS Information Authority, since 1999; *b* 29 July 1959; *s* of Leonard Norman Bell and Marlene Bell (*née* Gould). *m* 1985, Colette Julia Stein; one *s* one *d*. *Recreations:* Kendal Grammar Sch.; Loughborough Univ. (BSc Hons Computer Studies); Sheffield Hallam Univ. (MSc Managing Change). MBCS 1987; CEng 1990. Analyst Programmer, Comshare, 1981–85; Project Co-ordinator, Honeywell Bull, 1985–87; Project Manager, Boots, 1987–88; Mgt Consultant, Price Waterhouse, 1988–93; Div. Dir, Eur. Inf. Systems, Low & Bonar, 1993–96; Vice-Pres., Inf. Systems and Services, Astra Charnwood, 1996–98; Inf. Systems and Technol. Dir for Drug Devlt, Astra AB, 1998–99. *Recreations:* Tae Kwon Do, fell-walking, motor cycling, chess. *Address:* NHS Information Authority, Aqueous II, Aston Cross, Rocky Lane, Birmingham B6 5RQ. *T:* (0121) 333 0102.

BELL, Prof. Peter Robert; Emeritus Professor of Botany, University of London; *b* 18 Feb. 1920; *s* of Andrew and Mabel Bell; *m* 1952, Elizabeth Harrison; two *s*. *Educ:* Simon

Langton School, Canterbury; Christ's Coll., Cambridge (MA 1949). University College London: Asst Lecturer in Botany, 1946; Lectr in Botany, 1949; Reader in Botany, 1967; Prof. of Botany, 1967; Quain Prof. of Botany and Head of Dept of Botany and Microbiol., 1978–85; Dean of Science, 1979–82; Mem. Council, 1979–85. Visiting Professor: Univ. of California, Berkeley, 1966–67; Univ. of Delhi, India, 1970. British Council Distinguished Visitor, NZ, 1976; many other visits overseas, including exploration of Ecuadorian Andes. Vice-Pres., Linnean Soc., 1962–65; Mem. Biological Sciences Cttee, 1974–79 (Chm. Panel 1, 1977–79), SRC. *Publications:* Darwin's Biological Work, Some Aspects Reconsidered, 1959; (with C. F. Woodcock) The Diversity of Green Plants, 1968, 3rd edn 1983; (trans., with D. E. Coombe) Strasburger's Textbook of Botany, 8th English edn, 1976; Green Plants: their origin and diversity, 1993, 2nd edn 2000; scientific papers on botanical topics, particularly reproductive cells of land plants, and on history of botany. *Recreation:* mountains. *Address:* 13 Granville Road, Barnet, Herts EN5 4DU. *T:* (020) 8449 9331.

BELL, Prof. Peter Robert Frank, MD; FRCS, FRCSGlas; Professor of Surgery, University of Leicester, since 1974; *b* 12 June 1938; *s* of Frank and Ruby Bell; *m* 1961, Anne Jennings; one *s* two *d*. *Educ:* Univ. of Sheffield (MB, ChB Hons 1961; MD 1969). FRCS 1965; FRCSGlas 1968. Postgrad. surg. career in Sheffield hosps, 1961–65; Lectr in Surgery, Univ. of Glasgow, 1965–68; Sir Henry Wellcome Travelling Fellow, Univ. of Colorado, 1968–69; Consultant Surgeon and Sen. Lectr, Western Infirm., Glasgow, 1969–74. President: Surgical Res. Soc., 1986–88; European Soc. of Vascular Surgery, 1994; Vascular Soc. of GB and Ireland, 1998–99; Mem. Council, RCS, 1992– (Vice Pres., 2001–). Founder FMedSci 1998. *Publications:* Surgical Aspects of Haemodialysis, 1974, 2nd edn 1983; Operative Arterial Surgery, 1982; Arterial Surgery of the Lower Limb, 1991; Surgical Management of Vascular Disease, 1992; pubns on vascular disease, transplantation and cancer in med. and surg. jls. *Recreations:* horticulture, oil painting, tennis. *Address:* Department of Surgery, Robert Kilpatrick Building, PO Box 65, Leicester Royal Infirmary, Leicester LE2 7LX.

BELL, Sir Raymond; *see* Bell, Sir G. R.

BELL, Robert Donald Murray, CB 1966; *b* 8 Oct. 1916; *s* of Robert William and Mary Caroline Bell; *m* 1941, Karin Anna Smith; one *s* one *d*. *Educ:* Christ's Hosp.; Clare Coll., Cambridge. First Class Honours, Natural Sciences Tripos (Physics), 1938. Joined Scottish Office, 1938. War of 1939–45: Royal Artillery, 1940–45 (Mil. Coll. of Science, Bury, 1943). Principal, Scottish Home Dept, 1946; Private Sec. to Sec. of State for Scotland, 1947–50; Under-Secretary in Scottish Depts, 1959–76.

BELL, Hon. Sir Rodger, Kt 1993; **Hon. Mr Justice Bell;** a Judge of the High Court of Justice, Queen's Bench Division, since 1993; a Judge of Employment Appeal Tribunal, since 1994; *b* 13 Sept. 1939; *s* of John Thornton Bell and Edith Bell; *m* 1969, (Sylvia) Claire Tatton Brown; one *s* three *d*. *Educ:* Brentwood Sch.; Brasenose Coll., Oxford (BA). Called to the Bar, Middle Temple, 1963, Bencher, 1989; QC 1982; a Recorder, 1980–93; Chm., NHS Tribunal, 1991–93; Legal Mem., Mental Health Review Tribunals, 1983–93; Mem., Parole Board, 1990–93. *Address:* Royal Courts of Justice, Strand, WC2A 2LL.

BELL, Prof. Ronald Leslie, CB 1988; FREng; FInstP; Director-General, Agricultural Development and Advisory Service and the Regional Organisation, and Chief Scientific Adviser, Ministry of Agriculture, Fisheries and Food, 1984–89; *b* 12 Sept. 1929; *s* of Thomas William Alexander Bell and Annie (*née* Mapleston); *m* 1954, Eleanor Joy (*née* Lancaster); one *s* two *d*. *Educ:* The City School, Lincoln; Univ. of Birmingham (BSc, PhD). Research Fellow, Royal Radar Estabt, Malvern, 1954–57; Imperial College, Univ. of London: Lectr in Metallurgy, 1957–62; Reader in Metallurgy, 1962–65; University of Southampton: Prof. of Engrg Materials, 1965–77; Head of Dept of Mech. Engrg, 1968; Dean of Faculty of Engrg and Applied Scis, 1970–72; Dep. Vice Chancellor, 1972–76; Dir, NIAE, 1977–84. Vis. Prof., Cranfield Inst. of Technology, 1979–89. Pres., British Crop Protection Council, 1985–89; Member: AFRC, 1984–89; Council, RASE, 1984–89. Sen. Treas., Methodist Church Div. of Ministries, 1992–96. FREng (FEng 1991). Hon. DSc Southampton, 1985. *Publications:* papers in learned jls dealing with twinning and brittle fracture of metals, grain boundary sliding and creep in metals, dislocations in semi-conductors, agricultural engineering. *Recreations:* the bassoon, musical acoustics, painting, Association football, gardening. *Address:* 3 Old Garden Court, Mount Pleasant, St Albans AL3 4RQ.

BELL, Scott; *see* Bell, Alexander Scott.

BELL, Stuart; MP (Lab) Middlesbrough, since 1983; Second Church Estates Commissioner, since 1997; barrister; *b* High Spen, Co. Durham, 16 May 1938; *s* of Ernest and Margaret Rose Bell; *m* 1st, 1960, Margaret, *d* of Mary Bruce; one *s* one *d*; 2nd, 1980, Margaret, *d* of Edward and Mary Allan; one *s*. *Educ:* Hookergate Grammar Sch. Formerly colliery clerk, newspaper reporter, typist and novelist. Called to the Bar, Gray's Inn, 1970. Conseil Juridique and Internat. Lawyer, Paris, 1970–77. Member: Newcastle City Council, 1980–83 (Mem., Finance, Health and Environment, Arts and Recreation Cttees; Chm., Youth and Community Cttee; Vice-Chm., Educn Cttee); Educn Cttee, AMA; Council of Local Educn Authorities; Newcastle AHA (T), 1980–83. Contested (Lab) Hexham, 1979. PPS to Dep. Leader of Opposition, Rt Hon. Roy Hattersley, 1983–84; Opposition front bench spokesman: on NI, 1984–87; on trade and industry, 1992–97. Chm., Finance and Services Cttee, 2000–; Mem., H of C Commn, 2000–. Founder Mem. and Vice Chm., British–Irish Inter Parly Body, 1990–93. Member: Fabian Soc.; Soc. of Lab. Lawyers; GMB. *Publications:* Paris 69 (novel), 1973; Days That Used To Be (novel), 1975; How to Abolish the Lords (Fabian Tract), 1981; Valuation for United States Customs Purposes, 1981; When Salem Came to the Boro: the true story of the Cleveland child abuse crisis, 1989; Annotation of The Children Act, 1989; Raising the Standard: the case for first past the post, 1998; Where Jenkins Went Wrong, 1999; Tony Really Loves Me (autobiog.), 2000. *Recreation:* writing. *Address:* House of Commons, SW1A 0AA.

BELL, Trevor; *see* Bell, C. T.

BELL, Walter (Fancourt), CMG 1967; *b* 7 Nov. 1909; *s* of Canon George Fancourt Bell; *m* 1948, Katharine Spaatz, Washington, DC, USA; no *c*. *Educ:* Tonbridge Sch. Barrister, Inner Temple. Vice-Consul (Acting): New York, 1935–40; Mexico City, 1940–41; New York, 1941–42; Foreign Office, London, 1942–45; 1st Sec., Brit. Embassy, Washington, DC, 1946–48; attached E Africa High Commn, Nairobi, Kenya, 1949–52; 1st Sec., Brit. High Commn, New Delhi, 1952–55; attached War Office, London, 1956–57; Adviser, Federal Govt, W Indies, 1957–60; attached Govt of Kenya, 1961–63; Counsellor, British High Commn, Nairobi, Kenya, 1963–67. US Medal of Freedom with Bronze Palm, 1946. *Recreation:* walking. *Address:* 6 Onslow Square, SW7 3NP. *Club:* Travellers.

BELL, William Archibald Ottley Juxon; Founder, 1980, Chairman, 1980–96, and President, since 1996, Heritage of London Trust; *b* 7 July 1919; *s* of Maj. William Archibald Juxon Bell and Mary Isabel Maude Bell (*née* Ottley); *m* 1947, Belinda Mary (*née* Dawson) (*d* 2001); three *s* three *d*. *Educ:* Eton; Trinity College, Oxford (MA(Hist.)). Temp. Captain, Welsh Guards, 1940–45. Entered HM Foreign Service, 1945; Political Private Sec. to Sir Terence Shone, UK High Comr in India, 1946–47; Sec. to Exec. Dirs, British S Africa Co., 1947–50; Partner and Dir, King & Shaxson Ltd (Bill-brokers), 1950–90. Mem. of Lloyd's, 1970. Mem., for Chelsea, GLC and ILEA, 1970–86. Chairman: Diocesan Bd of Finance for Oxon, 1973–76; GLC Historic Bldgs Cttee, 1977–81; Oxfordshire Buildings Trust, 1987–93; English Heritage Commemorative Plaques Working Gp, 1990–95; Member: Cttee, Oxfordshire Historic Churches Trust, 1970– (Pres., 1995–99); UK Cttee for European Architectural Heritage Year, 1973–75; London Adv. Cttee, English Heritage, 1986–90. High Sheriff, Oxon, 1978–79. *Recreations:* painting, shooting, golf, music. *Address:* 165 Cranmer Court, SW3 3HF. *T:* (020) 7589 1033; Jasmine House, The Green, Kingham OX7 6YD. *T:* (01608) 658030. *Clubs:* White's, Pratt's, Beefsteak.

BELL, William Bradshaw; JP; Member (UU) Lagan Valley, Northern Ireland Assembly, since 1998; *b* 9 Oct. 1935; *s* of Robert Bell and Mary Ann Bell; *m* 1969, Leona Maxwell; one *s* three *d*. *Educ:* Fane Street Primary School, Belfast; Grosvenor High School, Belfast. Member: for N Belfast, NI Constitutional Convention, 1975–76; Belfast City Council, 1976–85 (Unionist spokesman on housing, 1976–79; Lord Mayor of Belfast, 1979–80); for S Antrim, NI Assembly, 1982–86 (Dep. Chm., Finance and Personnel Cttee, 1984–86); Lisburn BC, 1989– (Chairman: Police Liaison Cttee, 1991; Finance Cttee, 1993–95; Economic Develt Cttee, 1996–98). Chm., NI Public Accounts Cttee, 1999–. Chm., NI Gas Employers' Bd, 1984–87. JP Belfast, 1985. *Recreations:* music, motoring, writing. *Address:* Parliament Buildings, Belfast BT4 3XX.

BELL, William Edwin, CBE 1980; Deputy Chairman, Enterprise Oil plc, 1991–97 (Chairman, 1984–91); *b* 4 Aug. 1926; *s* of late Cuthbert Edwin Bell and Winifred Mary Bell (*née* Simpson); *m* 1952, Angela Josephine Vaughan; two *s* two *d*. *Educ:* Birmingham University (BSc Civil Eng.); Royal School of Mines, Imperial College. Joined Royal Dutch Shell Group, 1948; tech. and managerial appts, Venezuela, USA, Kuwait, Indonesia; Shell International Petroleum Co. (Middle East Coordination), 1965–73; Gen. Man., Shell UK Exploration and Production and Dir, Shell UK, 1973; Man. Dir, Shell UK, 1976–79; Middle East Regional Coordinator and Dir, Shell International Petroleum Co., 1980–84, retired; non-exec. Dir, Costain Group, 1982–92. Pres., UK Offshore Operators Assoc., 1975–76. *Publications:* contribs to internat. tech. jls, papers on offshore oil industry develts. *Recreations:* golf, sailing. *Address:* Fordcombe Manor, near Tunbridge Wells, Kent TN3 0SE. *Club:* Nevill Golf.

BELL, Sir William Hollin Dayrell M.; *see* Morrison-Bell.

BELL, William Lewis, CMG 1970; MBE (mil.) 1945; retired; Information Officer, University of Oxford, 1977–84; *b* 31 Dec. 1919; *s* of Frederick Robinson Bell and Kate Harper Bell (*née* Lewis); *m* 1943, Margaret Giles; one *s* one *d*. *Educ:* Hymers Coll., Hull; Oriel Coll., Oxford. Served The Gloucestershire Regt (Major), 1940–46. Colonial Administrative Service, Uganda, 1946–63: Dep. Sec. to the Treasury, 1956–58; Perm. Sec., Min. of Social Services, 1958–63; Fellow, Economic Develt Inst., World Bank, 1958. Chm., Uganda National Parks, 1962; Pres., Uganda Sports Union, 1961–62. Director, Cox & Danks Ltd (Metal Industries Group), 1963–64. Sec. to the Governors, Westfield Coll., Univ. of London, 1964–65; Founding Head of British Develt Div. in the Caribbean, ODA, 1966–72; UK Dir, Caribbean Develt Bank, 1970–72; Founding Dir-Gen., Technical Educn and Training Org. for Overseas Countries, 1972–77. *Recreations:* cricket, Caribbeana. *Address:* Hungry Hatch, Fletching, E Sussex TN22 3SH. *Clubs:* MCC; Vincent's (Oxford).

BELL BURNELL, Prof. (Susan) Jocelyn, CBE 1999; PhD; FRAS, FInstP; astronomer; Professor of Physics, Open University, since 1991; *b* 15 July 1943; *d* of G. Philip and M. Allison Bell; *m* 1968, Martin Burnell (separated 1989); one *s*. *Educ:* The Mount Sch., York; Glasgow Univ. (BSc); New Hall, Cambridge (PhD; Hon. Fellow, 1996). FRAS 1969. Res. Fellowships, Univ. of Southampton, 1968–73; Res. Asst, Mullard Space Science Lab., UCL, 1974–82; Sen. Res. Fellow, 1982–86, SSO, 1986–89, Grade 7, 1989–91, Royal Observatory, Edinburgh. An Editor, The Observatory, 1973–76. Vis. Fellow, 1999, Vis. Prof. for Distinguished Teaching, 1999–2000, Princeton Univ.; Sackler Vis. Prof., Univ. of Calif, Berkeley, 2000; Philips Visitor, Haverford Coll., Pa, 1999; Tuve Fellow, Carnegie Instn of Washington, 2000. Lectures: Marie Curie, Inst. of Physics, 1994; Appleton, Univ., Edinburgh, 1994; Jansky, Nat. Radio Astronomy Observatory, USA, 1995; Royal Instn, 1996; Maddison, Keele Univ., 1997; Flamsteed, Derby Univ., 1997; Royal Soc., 1997; Hamilton, Princeton Univ., 1997; Women in Physics, Aust. Inst. of Physics, 1999; Bishop, Columbia Univ., NY, 1999. Mem., IAU, 1979–; Chm., Physics Trng and Mobility of Researchers Fellowships Panel, EC, 1996–98 (Vice Chm., 1995); Vice-Pres., RAS, 1995–97. Mem. Council, Open Univ., 1997–99. Trustee, Nat. Maritime Mus., 2000–. Foreign Mem., Onsala Telescope Bd, Sweden, 1996–. Hon. Mem., Sigma-Pi-Sigma, 2000. FRSA 1999. Hon. DSc: Heriot-Watt, 1993; Newcastle, 1995; Warwick, 1995; Cambridge, 1996; Glasgow, 1997; Sussex, 1997; St Andrews, 1999; London, 1999; Leeds, 2000; Haverford Coll., Penn, 2000; Williams Coll., Mass, 2000; DUniv York, 1994. Michelson Medal, Franklin Inst., Philadelphia (jtly with Prof. A. Hewish), 1973; J. Robert Oppenheimer Meml Prize, Univ. of Miami, 1978; Rennie Taylor Award, Amer. Tentative Soc., NY, 1978; (first) Beatrice M. Tinsley Prize, Amer. Astronomical Soc., 1987; Herschel Medal, RAS, 1989; Edinburgh Medal, City of Edinburgh, 1999; Targa Giuseppe Piazzi Award, Palermo, Sicily, 1999; Magellanic Premium, Amer. Philos. Soc., 2000. Discovered the first four pulsars (neutron stars), 1967–68. *Publications:* Broken for Life, 1989; (ed jtly) Next Generation Infrared Space Observatory, 1992; papers in Nature, Astronomy and Astrophysics, Jl of Geophys. Res., Monthly Notices of RAS. *Recreations:* Quaker interests, walking. *Address:* Department of Physics and Astronomy, The Open University, Walton Hall, Milton Keynes MK7 6AA.

BELL DAVIES, Vice-Adm. Sir Lancelot (Richard), KBE 1977; *b* 18 Feb. 1926; *s* of late Vice-Adm. R. Bell Davies, VC, CB, DSO, AFC, and Mrs Bell Davies, Lee on Solent, Hants; *m* 1949, Emmeline Joan (*née* Molengraaff), Wassenaar, Holland; one *s* two *d*. *Educ:* Boxgrove Preparatory Sch., Guildford; RN Coll., Dartmouth. War of 1939–45: Midshipman, HMS Norfolk, 1943 (Scharnhorst sunk); joined Submarines, 1944. First Command, HMS Subtle, 1953; subseq. commands: HMS Explorer, 1955; Comdr, HMS Leander, 1962; Captain: HMS Forth, also SM7, 1967, and HMS Bulwark, 1972; Rear-Adm., 1973. Ministry of Defence Posts: (Comdr) Naval Staff, 1960; (Captain) Naval Asst to Controller, 1964; Director of Naval Warfare, 1969; Comdr, British Naval Staff, Washington, and UK Rep. to Saclant, 1973–75; Supreme Allied Commander Atlantic's Rep. in Europe, 1975–78; Comdt, Nato Defence Coll., Rome, 1978–81. Chm., Sea Cadet Council, 1983–92; President: Square Rigger Club; HMS Norfolk Assoc.; Portsmouth Sea Cadets. Vice Pres., Trincomalee Trust. Pres., Southampton MND Assoc., 1998–. CIMgt (FBIM 1977). *Recreations:* sailing, gardening. *Address:* Wessex Bungalow, Satchell Lane, Hamble, Hampshire SO31 4HS. *T:* (023) 8045 7415. *Clubs:* Naval and Military; Royal Yacht Squadron, Royal Naval Sailing Association.

BELLAK, John George; Chairman, Severn Trent plc (formerly Severn-Trent Water Authority), 1983–94; *b* 19 Nov. 1930; *m* 1960, Mary Prudence Marshall; three *s* one *d*.

Educ: Uppingham; Clare College, Cambridge. MA (Economics). Sales and Marketing Dir, Royal Doulton, 1968–80, Man. Dir, 1980–83; Chairman: Royal Crown Derby, 1972–83; Lawleys Ltd, 1972–83. President: British Ceramic Manufacturers' Fedn, 1982–83; Fedn of European Porcelain and Earthenware Manufacturers, 1982–83; European Waste Water Group, 1991–93; Dep. Chm., Water Services Assoc., 1992 (Vice-Chm., 1990–91; Chm., 1991). Chm., Aberdeen High Income Trust (formerly Abtrust High Income Investment Trust), 1994–; Dir, Ascot Holdings, 1993–96. Mem., Grand Council, CBI, 1984–94. Mem. Court, Keele Univ., 1984–96. *Recreations:* ornithology, field sports, reading. *Address:* 1 Council House Court, Shrewsbury SY1 2AU. *Clubs:* Carlton, Beefsteak.

BELLAMY, Rear-Adm. Albert John, CB 1968; OBE 1956; CMath, FIMA; first Deputy Director, Polytechnic of the South Bank, 1970–80; *b* Upton-on-Severn, 26 Feb. 1915; *s* of late A. E. Bellamy and late Mrs A. E. Bellamy; *m* 1942, Dorothy Joan Lawson; one *s* one *d*. *Educ:* Hanley Castle Grammar Sch.; Downing Coll., Cambridge (Buchanan Exhibitioner; 1st cl. hons Pts I and II, Math. tripos, MA 1939). FIMA 1960; CMath 1992. Asst master, Berkhamsted Sch., 1936–39. Joined RN, 1939, as Instructor Lieut; Fleet Instr and Meteorological Officer, America and WI, 1948–50 (HMS Glasgow); Instr Comdr, 1950; Headmaster, RN Schs, Malta, 1951–54; HMS Ark Royal, 1955–56; Dean of the College, RN Engineering Coll., Manadon, Plymouth, 1956–60; Instr Capt., 1958; staff of Dir, Naval Educn Service, 1960–63; Dir of Studies, RN Electrical, Weapons and Radio Engineering Sch., HMS Collingwood, 1963–65; Instr Rear-Adm., 1965; Dir, Naval Educn Service and Hd of Instructor Branch, MoD, 1965–70. Mem., Home Office Extended Interview non-Service Mems Panel, 1980–87. *Recreations:* gardening, show jumping (BSJA representative for Dorset), crosswords, parish council work, finance work with two charities, keeping old age at bay by being involved. *Address:* The Cottage, Kington Magna, Gillingham, Dorset SP8 5EG. *T:* (01747) 838668.

BELLAMY, Sir Christopher (William), Kt 2000; President of the Appeal Tribunals, Competition Commission, since 1999; a Recorder, since 2000; *b* 25 April 1946; *s* of late William Albert Bellamy, TD, MRCS, LRCP and of Vyvienne Hilda, *d* of Albert Meyrick, OBE; *m* 1989, Deirdre Patricia (*née* Turner); one *s* two *d*. *Educ:* Tonbridge Sch.; Brasenose Coll., Oxford (MA). Called to the Bar, Middle Temple, 1968; Bencher, 1994. Taught in Africa, 1968–69; in practice at Bar, 1970–92; QC 1986; Asst Recorder, 1989–92; Judge: Court of First Instance, EC, 1992–99; Employment Appeal Tribunal, 2000–. Mem. Council, British Inst. of Internat. and Comparative Law, 2000–. Gov., Ravensbourne Coll. of Design and Communication, 1988–92. *Publications:* (with G. Child) Common Market Law of Competition, 1973, 5th edn (ed P. Roth), 2001; public lectures, papers and articles on legal matters. *Recreations:* history, walking, family life. *Address:* Competition Commission Appeal Tribunals, New Court, Carey Street, WC2A 2JT. *Club:* Athenæum.

BELLAMY, David James, OBE 1994; PhD; FLS; FIBiol; botanist; writer and broadcaster; *b* 18 Jan. 1933; *s* of Thomas Bellamy and Winifred (*née* Green); *m* 1959, Rosemary Froy; two *s* three *d*. *Educ:* London University: Chelsea Coll. of Science and Technology (BSc); Bedford Coll. (PhD). Lectr, then Sen. Lectr, Dept of Botany, Univ. of Durham, 1960–80; Hon. Prof. of Adult and Continuing Educn, 1980–82; Special Prof., then Special Prof. of Geog., Nottingham Univ., 1987–; Vis. Prof. of Natural Heritage Studies, Massey Univ., NZ, 1988–89; Hon. Prof., Univ. of Central Qld, 1999–. Dir, David Bellamy Associates, envmtl consultants, 1988–; Associate Dir, P-E Internat., 1993–. Founder Dir, Conservation Foundn; Trustee: WWF, 1985–89; Living Landscape Trust, 1985–; President: WATCH, 1982; YHA, 1983–; Population Concern, 1988–; Nat. Assoc. Envmtl Educn, 1989–; Assoc. of Master Thatchers, 1991–97; Council, Zool Soc. of London, 1991–94; Plantlife, 1994–; Wildflower Soc., 1995–98; Conservation Foundn, 1996–; Wildlife Trust Partnership, 1996–. Chair, Welsh Fest. of Countryside, 1999–. Governor, Repton Sch., 1983–89. Chief I Spy, 1983. Contested (Referendum) Huntingdon, 1997. Presenter and script writer for television and radio programmes, BBC and ITV; programmes include Longest Running Show on Earth, 1985; main series: Life in our Sea, 1970; Bellamy on Botany, 1973; Bellamy's Britain, 1975; Bellamy's Europe, 1977; Botanic Man, 1979; Up a Gum Tree, 1980; Backyard Safari, 1981; The Great Seasons, 1982; Bellamy's New World, 1983; You Can't See The Wood, 1984; Discovery, 1985; Seaside Safari, 1985; End of the Rainbow Show, 1985; Bellamy's Bugle, 1986; Turning the Tide, 1986; The End of the Rainbow Show, 1986; Bellamy's Bird's Eye View, 1988; Moa's Ark, 1990; Bellamy Rides Again, 1991, 1992; Wetlands, 1991; England's Last Wilderness, 1992; Blooming Bellamy, 1993; Routes of Wisdom, 1993; Bellamy's Border Raids: the Peak District, 1994; Westwatch, 1996; A Welsh Herbal, 1998; Making Tracks, 1998 and 1999; A Celtic Herbal, 1999; Kite Country, Bellamy and the Argonauts, 2000; The Challenge, 2000. FCIWEM 1996. Hon. Fellow, BICSc 1997; Hon. FLS 1997. Hon. Fellow, Univ. of Lancaster, 1997. DUniv Open, 1984; Hon. DSc: CNAA, 1990; Nottingham, 1993; Dunelm, 1995; Bournemouth, 1999; Kingston, 2000. Frances Ritchie Meml Prize, Rambler's Assoc., 1989; UNEP Global 500 Award, 1990; Environmental Communicator of the Year, British Assoc. of Communicators in Business, 1996; Guild of Travel Writers Award, 1996. Order of the Golden Ark (Netherlands), 1989. *Publications:* Peatlands, 1974; Bellamy on Botany, 1974; Bellamy's Britain, 1975; Bellamy's Europe, 1977; Life Giving Sea, 1977; Botanic Man, 1978; Half of Paradise, 1979; The Great Seasons, 1981; Backyard Safari, 1981; Discovering the Countryside with David Bellamy: vols I and II, 1982, vols III and IV, 1983; The Mouse Book, 1983; Bellamy's New World, 1983; The Queen's Hidden Garden, 1984; Turning the Tide, 1986; The Vanishing Bogs of Ireland, 1986; Bellamy's Changing Countryside, 4 vols, 1989; (with Brendan Quayle) England's Last Wilderness, 1989; England's Lost Wilderness, 1990; (with Jane Gifford) Wilderness in Britain, 1991; How Green Are You?, 1991; Tomorrow's Earth, 1991; (with Andrea Pfister) World Medicine, 1992; Blooming Bellamy, 1993; Poo, You and the Potoroo's Loo, 1997; (contrib.) The Blue UNESCO, 1999; The English Landscape, 2000; (consultant) The Countryside Detective, 2000. *Recreations:* children, ballet. *Address:* Mill House, Bedburn, Bishop Auckland, Co. Durham DL13 3NW.

BELLAMY, Prof. Edmund Henry, MA, PhD; Professor of Physics in the University of London, Westfield College, 1960–84, now Emeritus; *b* 8 April 1923; *s* of Herbert Bellamy and Nellie (*née* Ablett); *m* 1946, Joan Roberts; three *s*. *Educ:* Quarry Bank Sch., Liverpool; King's Coll., Cambridge. Lectr in Natural Philosophy, Univ. of Glasgow, 1951–59, Sen. Lectr, 1959–60; Vis. Physicist, Univ. of Pisa, 1960. Mem., Nuclear Physics Board of Science Research Council, 1965–66. Visiting Professor: Univ. of Stanford, 1966–67; Univ. of Pisa, 1985–86; Emeritus Fellow, Leverhulme Trust, 1987–89; Consultant, Univ. of Florida, 1990. *Publications:* numerous scientific papers in Proc. Phys. Soc. and other journals. *Recreations:* ski-ing, squash, travel, football, golf. *Address:* 134 Main Road, Long Hanborough, Witney, Oxon OX29 8JY. *T:* (01993) 882227.

BELLAMY, (Kenneth) Rex; Tennis Correspondent, The Times, 1967–89; *b* 15 Sept. 1928; *s* of Sampson Bellamy and Kathleen May Bellamy; *m* 1951, Hilda O'Shea; one step *d*. *Educ:* Yeovil; Woodhouse Grammar Sch., Sheffield. National Service, RA and RASC, 1946–49. Sports and Feature Writer, Sheffield Telegraph, 1944–46 and 1949–53; Sports Writer: Birmingham Gazette, 1953–56; The Times, 1956–89. World Championship Tennis award for service to tennis, 1988; International Tennis-writing Awards: 5 from Assoc. of Tennis Professionals, 1975–79 (award discontinued); 2 from Women's Tennis Assoc., 1977–78. *Publications:* Teach Yourself Squash (jtly), 1968; The Tennis Set, 1972; The Story of Squash, 1978 rev. edn as Squash—A History, 1988; The Peak District Companion, 1981; Walking the Tops, 1984; Game, Set and Deadline, 1986; Love Thirty, 1990; The Four Peaks, 1992. *Recreations:* hill-walking, golf. *Address:* 8 Guillards Oak, Midhurst, W Sussex GU29 9JZ. *Club:* Jesters (Hon. Mem.).

BELLAMY, Stephen Howard George Thompson; QC 1996; a Recorder, since 2000; *b* 27 Sept. 1950; *s* of George and Clarice Bellamy; *m* 1988, Rita James; one *d*. *Educ:* The Grammar Sch., Heckmondwike; Trinity Hall, Cambridge (MA Hons Law). ACIArb. Called to the Bar, Lincoln's Inn, 1974; Asst Recorder, 1997–2000; Dep. High Court Judge, 2000–. Asst Parly Boundary Comr, 2000–. Member: Cttee, Family Bar Assoc., 1989–96; General Council of the Bar, 1993–96. Mem., British Inst. of Internat. and Comparative Law, 1991–97. Fellow, Inst. of Advanced Legal Studies, 2000. *Recreations:* music, opera, ski-ing, gardening. *Address:* 1 King's Bench Walk, Temple, EC4Y 7DB. *T:* (020) 7936 1500, *Fax:* (020) 7936 1590.

BELLANY, Prof. Ian; Professor of Politics, University of Lancaster, since 1979; *b* 21 Feb. 1941; *s* of James Bellany and Jemima Bellany (*née* Emlay); *m* 1965, Wendy Ivey, *d* of Glyndwr and Bronwen Thomas; one *s* one *d*. *Educ:* Preston Lodge, Prestonpans; Firth Park Grammar Sch., Sheffield; Balliol Coll., Oxford (State Scholar, MA, DPhil). Foreign and Commonwealth Office, 1965–68; Res. Fellow in Internat. Relations, ANU, 1968–70; University of Lancaster: Lectr. later Sen. Lectr in Politics, 1970–79; Dir, Centre for Study of Arms Control and Internat. Security, 1979–90; Head, Dept of Politics, 1985–86. Leverhulme Res. Fellow, 1982; NATO Instl Fellow, 1989–90. Mem., Govt Adv. Panel on Disarmament, 1981–. Examr in Internat. Relations, LSE, 1985–88 and 1999–, in Internat. Studies, Birmingham Univ., 1990–93, in Internat. Relations, Aberdeen Univ., 1995–99. Founding Editor, Arms Control: Journal of Arms Control and Disarmament, 1980–91. *Publications:* Australia in the Nuclear Age, 1972; A Basis for Arms Control, 1991; Reviewing Britain's Defence, 1994; The Environment in World Politics, 1997; edited jointly: Antiballistic Missile Defences in the 1980s, 1983; The Verification of Arms Control Agreements, 1983; The Nuclear Non-Proliferation Treaty, 1985; New Conventional Weapons and Western Defence, 1987; contribs to jls. *Recreations:* broadcasting, coarse carpentry, computing. *Address:* 11 Spruce Avenue, Lancaster LA1 5LB. *T:* (01524) 68157.

BELLANY, John, CBE 1994; RA 1991 (ARA 1986); artist (painter); *b* Scotland, 18 June 1942; *s* of Richard Weatherhead Bellany and Agnes Craig Bellany; *m* 1st, 1964, Helen Margaret Percy (marr. diss. 1974); two *s* one *d*; 2nd, 1980, Juliet Gray (*née* Lister) (*d* 1985); 3rd, 1986 (for 2nd time), Helen Margaret Bellany. *Educ:* Cockenzie Public Sch., Scotland; Preston Lodge Sch., Scotland; Edinburgh Coll. of Art (DA); Royal Coll. of Art (MA Fine Art; ARCA). Lectr in Fine Art in various art colls and univs in Gt Britain, incl. Winchester Coll. of Art, Goldsmiths' Coll., London Univ., RCA; Artist in Residence, Victorian Coll. of the Arts, Melb., 1982. *One man exhibitions:* Nat. Portrait Gall., 1986; Fischer Fine Art, London, 1988–89, 1991; Scottish Nat. Gall. of Modern Art, 1989; Raab Gall., Berlin and Ruth Siegel Gall., NY, 1990; Fitzwilliam Mus., Cambridge, 1991; Kelvingrove Art Gall. and Mus., Glasgow, 1992; Beaux Arts Gall., London, 1997, 1998, 2000, 2001; Galeria K, Mexico City, 1997; Elaine Baker Gall., Florida, 1999; Soloman Gall., London, 2000; many others in Britain, USA, Australia, Europe; *retrospective exhibitions:* Scottish Nat. Gall. of Modern Art, Edin., and Serpentine Gall., London, 1986; Kunsthalle, Hamburg, 1988. Works represented in major museums and private collections throughout the world, incl. Tate Gall., V&A Mus., Mus. of Modern Art, NY, Metropolitan Mus., NY, Nat. Gall. of NSW, Melbourne. Sen. Fellow, RCA, 1999. Hon. Fellow Commoner, Trinity Hall, Cambridge, 1988. Hon. RSA 1987. Dr (*hc*) Edinburgh, 1996; Hon. DLitt Heriot-Watt, 1998. *Relevant publications:* John Bellany, by Victor Musgrave and Philip Rawson, 1982; John Bellany, a Retrospective, by Douglas Hall, 1986; John Bellany (Portraits) (The Maxi Hudson Collection), by Robin Gibson, 1986; John Bellany, by Richard Cork, 1986; John Bellany, Retrospective, by Prof. D. Werner Hofmann and Keith Hartley, 1988; John Bellany, by John McEwen, 1994. *Recreation:* climbing to and fro across Hadrian's Wall. *Address:* 2 Windmill Drive, SW4 9DE. *T:* (020) 8675 7909, *Fax:* (01799) 542062; 19 Great Stuart Street, Edinburgh EH2 7TP, *T:* (0131) 226 5183; Beaux Arts Gallery, 22 Cork Street, W1X 1HB. *T:* (020) 7437 5799; Berkeley Square Gallery, 23A Bruton Street, W1X 7DA. *T:* (020) 7493 7939. *Clubs:* Chelsea Arts; Scottish Arts (Edinburgh).

BELLENGER, Rev. Dr Dominic Terence Joseph, (Rev. Dom Aidan Bellenger), FSA; FRHistS; Director of Historical Research, Downside Abbey, since 1995; Parish Priest, St Benedict's, Stratton-on-the-Fosse, since 1999; *b* 21 July 1950; *s* of Gerald Bellenger and Kathleen Bellenger (*née* O'Donnell). *Educ:* Finchley Grammar Sch.; Jesus Coll., Cambridge (Scholar, MA, PhD); Angelicum Univ., Rome. Res. Student in History, 1972–78 and Lightfoot Schol. in Eccl. Hist., Cambridge, 1975–78; Assistant Master: St Mary's Sch., Cambridge, 1975–78; Downside Sch., 1978–82; Benedictine Monk, Downside Abbey, 1982; Priest, 1988; Housemaster, 1989–91, Head Master, 1991–95, Downside Sch.; Parish Priest, Little Malvern, 1995–99. Member: Cttee, Eccl. Hist. Soc., 1982–85; Cttee, English Benedictine Hist. Commn, 1987–; Council, Catholic Record Soc., 1990–99; Clifton Diocesan Educn Commn, 1995–; Trustee: Catholic Family Hist. Soc., 1990–99; Andrew C. Duncan Catholic History Trust, 1993–; Friends of Somerset Churches, 1996–; Somerset Record Soc., 1998–; Pres., English Catholic Hist. Assoc., 1991–. Governor: Moor Park Sch., Ludlow, 1991–99; St Antony's, Leweston, Sherborne, 1991–93; St Mary's Sch., Shaftesbury, 1992–96; Moreton Hall, Suffolk, 1995–; St Joseph's, Malvern, 1997–99; Downside Sch., 1999– (Vice Chm.). York Minster Lecture, 2001. Leverhulme Res. Award, 1986. FRSA. Editor, South Western Catholic History, 1982–; English correspondent, Rev. d'Hist. de l'Eglise de France, 1982–85. *Publications:* English and Welsh Priests 1558–1800, 1984; The French Exiled Clergy, 1986; (ed) Opening the Scrolls, 1987; (ed jtly) Les Archives du Nord, Calendar of 20 H, 1987; St Cuthbert, 1987; (ed jtly) Letters of Bede Jarrett, 1989; (ed) Fathers in Faith, 1991; (ed) The Great Return, 1994; (ed) Downside: a pictorial history, 1998; (jtly) Princes of the Church, 2001; (jtly) Medieval Worlds, 2002; contributor to many other books; articles in learned jls and periodicals. *Recreations:* books, church architecture, travel, visual arts, writing. *Address:* Downside Abbey, Stratton-on-the-Fosse, Bath BA3 4RJ. *T:* (01761) 235119.

BELLEW, family name of **Baron Bellew**.

BELLEW; *see* Grattan-Bellew.

BELLEW, 7th Baron *cr* 1848; **James Bryan Bellew;** Bt 1688; *b* 5 Jan. 1920; *s* of 6th Baron Bellew, MC, and Jeanie Ellen Agnes (*d* 1973), *d* of late James Ormsby Jameson; *S* father, 1981; *m* 1st, 1942, Mary Elizabeth (*d* 1978), *d* of Rev. Edward Eustace Hill; two *s* one *d*; 2nd, 1978, Gwendoline, formerly wife of Major P. Hall and *d* of late Charles Redmond Clayton-Daubeny. Served War of 1939–45, Irish Guards (Captain). *Heir:* *s* Hon. Bryan Edward Bellew [*b* 19 March 1943; *m* 1968, Rosemary Sarah, *d* of Major Reginald Kilner Brasier Hitchcock; one *s* (and one *s* decd)]. *Address:* c/o Royal Bank of Scotland, 45 The Promenade, Cheltenham, Glos GL50 1PY.

BELLINGER, Sir Robert (Ian), GBE 1967; Kt 1964; Chairman: Kinloch (PM) Ltd, 1946–75; National Savings Committee, 1970–75, and President, 1972–75; Director, Rank Organisation, 1971–83; *b* Tetbury, Glos, 10 March 1910; *s* of David Morgan Bellinger, Cardiganshire, and Jane Ballantine Deans, Edinburgh; *m* 1962, Christiane Marie Louise Janssens, Brussels; one *s* one *d*. *Educ:* Church of England sch. Elected Court of Common Council, 1953; Chm. City of London Freemen's Sch., 1957; Alderman for Ward of Cheap, 1958; Sheriff, City of London, 1962–63; Lord Mayor of London, 1966–67; one of HM Lieutenants, City of London, 1976–. Chairman: Panel for Civil Service Manpower Review, 1968–71; Adv. Cttee on Magistracy, City of London, 1968–76; Licensing Cttee, City of London; Finance Cttee, BBC; Governor, BBC, 1968–71; Trustee, St Paul's Cathedral Trust, 1977–96; Dir, Arsenal Football Club (Pres., 1997). Chairman: Anglo-Danish Soc., 1976–83; Danish Trade Adv. Bd, 1979–82. Past Master, Broderers' Company; Liveryman, Fletchers' Company. Hon. DSc City Univ., 1966. Gentleman Usher of the Purple Rod, Order of the British Empire, 1969–85. KStJ 1966; Commandeur, Ordre de Léopold, cl. III (Belgium), 1963; Comdr, Royal Order of the Phoenix (Greece), 1963; Officier, Ordre de la Valeur Camerounaise (Cameroons), 1963; Knight Comdr of the Order of Dannebrog (Denmark), 1977. *Recreations:* tennis, football, music, motoring. *Address:* Penn Wood, Fulmer, Bucks SL3 6JL. *T:* (01753) 662029. *Club:* City Livery.

BELLINGHAM, Prof. Alastair John, CBE 1997; FRCP, FRCPE, FRCPGlas, FRCPath; Chairman, NHS Information Authority, since 1999; Professor of Haematology, King's College London, 1984–97; *b* 27 March 1938; *s* of Stanley Herbert Bellingham and Sybil Mary Milne; *m* 1963, Valerie Jill Morford (*d* 1997); three *s*. *Educ:* Tiffin Boys' Sch., Kingston upon Thames; University Coll. Hosp. (MB BS). Research Fellow, Univ. of Washington, 1969–71; Sen. Lectr, UCH, 1971–74; Prof. of Haematology, Univ. of Liverpool, 1974–84; Hon. Consultant Haematologist, KCH, 1984–97. Transition Dir, Liverpool, Nat. Blood Service, 1997–99; Chm., Confidentiality Adv. Gp, DoH, 1997–. Mem. Bd, Inst. of Cancer Res., 1997–. Chm. Govs, St Dunstan's Coll., Catford, 1999–. Vice-Pres., 1990–93, Pres., 1993–96, RCPath; Past Pres., British Soc. for Haematology; Vice-Pres., Eur. Div., Internat Soc. Haematology, 1992–98. FFPath, RCPI, 1996. Hon. Fellow, Hong Kong Coll. of Path., 1995. *Publications:* contribs to books and jls on haematol., esp. red cell physiol. and inherited red cell disorders, incl. enzyme deficiencies, sickle cell disorders and thalassaemia. *Recreations:* oenology, viticulture, cricket, photography. *Address:* Broadstones, The Street, Teffont Magna, Salisbury SP3 5QP. *T:* (01722) 716267. *Club:* Savage.

BELLINGHAM, Sir Anthony Edward Norman, 8th Bt (2nd creation) *cr* 1796, of Castle Bellingham, co. Louth; Managing Director, City Financial Executive Recruitment, since 1980; *b* 24 March 1947; *yr s* of Sir Roger Carroll Patrick Stephen Bellingham, 6th Bt and of Mary, *d* of William Norman; *S* brother, 1999; *m* 1991, Denise Marie Moity (marr. diss. 1998); one *s*; *m* 1998, Namfon Bellingham. *Educ:* Rossall. *Heir: s* William Alexander Noel Henry Bellingham, *b* 19 Aug. 1991.

BELLINGHAM, Henry Campbell; MP (C) Norfolk North West, 1983–97 and since 2001; director of and consultant to companies, since 1998; *b* 29 March 1955; *s* of late Henry Bellingham; *m* 1993, Emma, *o d* of P. J. H. Whiteley and Lady Angela Whiteley. *Educ:* Eton; Magdalene Coll., Cambridge (BA 1977). Called to the Bar, Middle Temple, 1978. Underwriting Mem. of Lloyd's. Contested (C) Norfolk North West, 1997. PPS to Sec. of State for Transport, 1990–92, for Defence, 1992–95, for Foreign and Commonwealth Affairs, 1995–97. Chm., Cons. Council on Eastern Europe, 1989–94; Mem., Select Cttee on the Environment, 1987–90; officer, Cons. back bench cttees, 1983–90. *Clubs:* White's, Pratt's.

BELLIS, Bertram Thomas; Headmaster, The Leys School, Cambridge, 1975–86; *b* 4 May 1927; *s* of Rev. Thomas J. Bellis and Mary A. Bellis; *m* 1952, Joan Healey; two *s*. *Educ:* Kingswood Sch., Bath; St John's Coll., Cambridge (Exhibr in Maths, MA). Rossall Sch., 1951–55; Highgate Sch., 1955–65; Headmaster, Daniel Stewart's Coll., 1965–72; Principal, Daniel Stewart's and Melville Coll., 1972–75. Founding Dir, Mathematics in Educn and Industry Schools Project, 1963–65. Chm., Scottish Educn Dept Cttee on Computers and the Schools (reports, 1969 and 1972); Member: Council, Inst. of Math., 1975–79; Educational Research Bd, SSRC, 1975–80. Governor: Queenswood Sch., 1980–92; St John's Coll. Sch., 1981–86. Pres., Mathematical Assoc., 1971–72. Schoolmaster Fellow, Balliol Coll., Oxford, 1963; FIMA 1964; FRSE 1972. *Address:* 13 Marlborough Court, Grange Road, Cambridge CB3 9BQ.

BELLO, Mohammed, CON 1965; Chief Justice of Nigeria, 1987–95; *b* 1930; *s* of Mallam Muhammadu Gidado; *m* 1962; many *c*. *Educ:* Harvard Law School. Called to the Bar, Lincoln's Inn. Northern Nigeria appointments: Crown Counsel, 1956; Magistrate, 1961; Dir of Public Prosecutions, 1964; Judge of the High Court, 1966; Senior Puisne Judge, North-Central and Kwara States, 1968; occasional Acting Chief Justice, Northern State, 1969–75; Justice of Supreme Court of Nigeria, 1975. Fellow, Nigerian Inst. of Advanced Legal Studies, 1984. Hon. LLD: Ibadan, 1987; Ahmadu Bello, 1990; Lagos, 1992. *Recreation:* rambling. *Address:* 4 Umaru Dallaje Road, PO Box 365, Katsina, Nigeria. *T:* (65) 34964.

BELLOTTI, David Frank; agent, Bath Liberal Democrats, since 2000; *b* 13 Aug. 1943; *s* of Patrick Frank Bellotti and Elsie (*née* Venner); *m* 1st, 1965, Sheila (*née* Jones); one *s* one *d*; 2nd, 1973, Jennifer (*née* Compson) (marr. diss.); one *s*; 3rd, 1996, Josephine (*née* Brown). *Educ:* Exeter Sch.; YMCA National Coll. (Diploma in Youth Service); Brighton Polytechnic (Diploma in Counselling); Univ. of Sussex (MA). Civil Service, 1961–64; Young Men's Christian Association: student, Nat. Coll., 1964–65; Sec., St Helens, Llanelli, Norwich and Lewes, 1965–76; Regional Sec., South-East, 1977–81; Dir, Hove, 1981–90. Dep. Chm. and Chief Exec., Brighton and Hove Albion FC, 1993–97. Mem. (L, then Lib Dem), E Sussex CC, 1981–97 (Chm., 1993–94). Chm., Sussex Police Authy, 1993–95. Mem., Cttee of the Regions, EU, 1994–98. MP (Lib Dem) Eastbourne, Oct. 1990–1992; contested same seat, 1992. Contested (Lib Dem), European Parliamentary elections: E Sussex and Kent S, 1994; SE Reg., 1999. *Recreations:* Association Football, politics, snooker. *Address:* 8 Blenheim Close, Peasedown St John, Bath BA2 8TD. *Club:* National Liberal.

BELLOW, Saul; American writer; *b* 10 June 1915; *s* of Abraham and Liza Gordon Bellow; three *s*; *m* 1989, Janis Freedman; one *d*. *Educ:* Univ. of Chicago; Northwestern Univ. Hon. DLitt Northwestern Univ., 1962. Nobel Prize for Literature, 1976; Malaparté Prize for Literature, Italy, 1984. Commander, Legion of Honour (France), 1983; Commander, Order of Arts and Letters (France), 1985 (Croix de Chevalier, 1968). *Publications:* Dangling Man, 1944 (reissued 1972); The Victim, 1947; The Adventures of Augie March, 1953 (National Book Award, 1954); Seize the Day, 1956; Henderson the Rain King, 1959; Herzog, 1964 (National Book Award, Internat. Literary Prize, 1965); Mosby's Memoirs and Other Stories, 1969; Mr Sammler's Planet, 1970 (National Book Award, 1970); Humboldt's Gift, 1975 (Pulitzer Prize 1976); To Jerusalem and Back, 1976; The Dean's December, 1982; (short stories) Him with His Foot in His Mouth, 1984; More Die of Heartbreak, 1987; A Theft, 1989; The Bellarosa Connection, 1989; Something to Remember Me By: three tales, 1991; It All Adds Up (essays), 1994; The Actual, 1997; Ravelstein, 2000. *Address:* University Professors, Boston University, 745 Commonwealth Avenue, Boston, MA 02215, USA.

BELLOWS, James Gilbert; TV, newspaper, on-line executive; *b* 12 Nov. 1922; *s* of Lyman Hubbard Bellows and Dorothy Gilbert Bellows; *m* 1950, Marian Raines (decd); three *d*; *m* 1964, Maggie Savoy (decd); *m* 1971, Keven Ryan; one *d*. *Educ:* Kenyon Coll. (BA, LLB). Columbus (Ga) Ledger, 1947; News Editor Atlanta (Ga) Jl, 1950–57; Asst Editor, Detroit (Mich.) Free Press, 1957–58; Managing Editor Miami (Fla) News, 1958–61; Exec. Editor (News Ops), NY Herald Tribune, 1961–62; Editor, 1962–66; associate Editor, Los Angeles Times, 1966–75; Editor: Washington Star, 1975–78; Los Angeles Herald Examiner, 1979–82; Managing Editor, Entertainment Tonight (TV show), 1982–83; Exec. Editor, ABC-TV News, 1983–86; Dir of Editorial Develt, Prodigy, 1986–88; Managing Editor, USA Today on TV, 1988–89; Vice Pres. Editorial, MediaNews Gp, 1990–91; Los Angeles Bureau Chief, TV Guide, 1992–94; Exec. Editor, Excite Inc. Software, 1995–96; Chm., Editl Adv. Bd, Excite, 1997; Consultant, LA Daily News, 1998–99. Member: Kenyon Review Adv. Bd; Amer. Soc. of Newspaper Editors. *Address:* 2337 Canyonback Road, Los Angeles, CA 90049–6812, USA. *Club:* Bel-Air Country (Los Angeles).

BELMAHI, Mohammed; Ambassador of Morocco to the Court of St James's, since 1999; *b* 18 Aug. 1948; *s* of Redouane Belmahi and Aziza Filal Belmahi; *m* 1973, Åse Ask; one *d*. *Educ:* Ecole Nationale d'Architecture, Toulouse (Architect DPLG 1973); New York Univ. (Master of Urban Planning 1975; PhD Prog. in Public Admin 1976; MPhil 1985); Harvard Inst. for Internat. Develt, 1981. London Business Sch. (Sen. Exec. Prog.), 1991. UN Center for Housing, Building and Planning, NY, 1975–76; Min. of Housing and Land Use Planning, and Dir, Land Use Planning, Rabat, 1977–79; Prime Minister's Office, Rabat (Mem., State Owned Enterprise Reform Task Force), 1979–82; Dir of Tourism, Min. of Tourism, 1982–86; Dir Gen., Moroccan Nat. Tourist Bd, 1987–88; Mem., Exec. Cttee, ONA Hldg Gp, Casablanca, 1988–96; Dir Gen. for Real Estate and Tourism, and Dir Gen., Casablanca World Trade Center; Ambassador to India and Nepal, 1996–99. Officer, National Order of Merit (Portugal), 1991. *Recreations:* golf, swimming, collecting miniature elephants, drawing portraits, calligraphy (Arabic). *Address:* Embassy of Morocco, 49 Queen's Gate Gardens, SW7 5NE. *T:* (020) 7581 5001. *Clubs:* Travellers; Dar Es Salam Golf (Rabat).

BELMORE, 8th Earl of, *cr* 1797; **John Armar Lowry-Corry;** Baron Belmore, 1781; Viscount Belmore, 1789; *b* 4 Sept. 1951; *s* of 7th Earl of Belmore and Gloria Anthea, *d* of late Herbert Bryant Harker, Melbourne, Australia; *S* father, 1960; *m* 1984, Lady Mary Meade, *d* of 6th Earl of Clanwilliam; two *s* one *d*. *Educ:* Lancing; Royal Agricultural Coll., Cirencester. *Heir: s* Viscount Corry, *qv*. *Recreation:* fishing. *Address:* The Garden House, Castle Coole, Enniskillen, N Ireland BT74 6JY. *T:* (028) 6632 2463. *Club:* Kildare Street and University (Dublin).

BELOFF, Hon. Michael Jacob, MA; QC 1981; barrister and writer; President, Trinity College, University of Oxford, since 1996; *b* 18 April 1942; *s* of Baron Beloff, FBA and of Helen Dobrin; *m* 1969, Judith Mary Arkinstall; one *s* one *d*. *Educ:* Dragon Sch., Oxford; Eton Coll. (King's Schol.; Captain of Sch. 1960); Magdalen Coll., Oxford (Demy; H. W. C. Davis Prizeman, 1962; BA Hist. (1st cl.) 1963, Law 1965; MA 1967). Pres., Oxford Union Soc., 1962 (Sen. Trustee, 1997–); Oxford Union tour of USA, 1964. Called to the Bar, Gray's Inn, 1967 (Gerald Moody Schol., 1963; Atkin Schol., 1967), Bencher, 1988; Jt Head of Chambers, 4–5 Gray's Inn Sq., 1993–2000; a Recorder, 1985–95; a Dep. High Court Judge, 1989–99; a Judge of the Courts of Appeal, Jersey and Guernsey, 1995–. Vice-Pres., Interception of Communications (Bailiwick of Guernsey) Tribunal, 1998–; a Dep. Chm., Data Protection Tribunal, 2000–. Lectr in Law, Trinity Coll., Oxford, 1965–66. Legal Correspondent: New Society, 1969–79; The Observer, 1979–81; Columnist, San Diego Law Jl, 1999–. Vice-Pres., Administrative Law Bar Assoc., 1990 (first Chm., 1986–90, now Chm. Emeritus). Member: Bingham Law Reform Cttee on Discovery of Documents and Disclosure, 1982–; Sen. Salary Review Bd, 1995– (Chm., Judicial Sub-Cttee, 1998–); Court of Arbitration for Sport, 1996– (Mem., *ad hoc* Panel, Olympic Games, Atlanta, 1996, Sydney, 2000, Commonwealth Games, Kuala Lumpur, 1998). Chm., Oxford Univ. Tribunal into Alleged Plagiarism, 1990. Gov., Dragon Sch., Oxford, 1995–; Mem. Council, Cheltenham Ladies' Coll., 1996–. Chm., Jardine Scholarship Foundn, 2000–. For. Consultant, Law Counsel (Dacca), 1990–. Lectures: Statute Law Soc., 1994; Admin. Law Bar Assoc., 1995; John Kelly Meml, UC Dublin, 1997; Lasok, Univ. of Exeter, 1998; Atkin, Reform Club, 1999; K. Ramamani, Madras, 1999; Margaret Howard, Trinity Coll., Oxford, 2000. Consultant Editor: Judicial Review Bulletin, 1996; Commercial Law, 1994–96; Environmental Law, 1994–96; Gen. Ed., Internat. Sports Law Review, 2000–; an Associate Ed., DNB. Hon. Mem., Internat. Athletes' Club. FRSA 1996. Hon. Fellow, Soc. for Advanced Legal Studies, 1997. Fellow, Inst. of Continuing Professional Develt, 1998. Women's Legal Defence Award (first winner), 1991. *Publications:* A Short Walk on the Campus (ed with J. Aitken), 1966; The Plateglass Universities, 1968; The Sex Discrimination Act, 1976; (jtly) Sports Law, 1999; contributor to: Halsbury's Laws of England (contribution on Time), 1983, 2nd edn 1999; Judicial Safeguards in Administrative Proceedings, 1989; Judicial Review, 1991, 2nd edn 1998; Essays for Lord Cooke of Thorndon, 1997; Essays in Public Law in honour of Sir William Wade, 1998; Practitioner's Handbook of EC Law, 1998; Israel Among the Nations, 1998; Essays in Honour of Sir Louis Blom-Cooper, 1999; The Human Rights Act, 1999; contrib. several Festschriften, Encounter, Minerva, Irish Jurist, Political Qly, Current Legal Problems, Public Law, Statute Law Review, Modern Law Review, British Jl of Sport and Law, Denning Law Jl, Singapore Law Jl, NZ Law Jl, TLS, etc. *Recreation:* running. *Address:* President's Lodgings, Trinity College, Oxford OX1 3BH; 41 Campden Hill Square, W8 7JR; Blackstone Chambers, Blackstone House, Temple, EC4Y 7BW. *T:* (020) 7583 1770. *Clubs:* Reform, Royal Automobile (Steward, 1999–); Vincent's (Oxford); Achilles.

BELPER, 5th Baron *cr* 1856, of Belper, co. Derby; **Richard Henry Strutt;** *b* 24 Oct. 1941; *o s* of 4th Baron Belper and of Zara Sophie Kathleen Mary, *y d* of Sir Harry Mainwaring, 5th Bt; *S* father, 1999; *m* 1st, 1966, Jennifer Vivian (marr. diss. 1979), *d* of late Capt. Peter Winser; one *s* one *d*; 2nd, 1980, Judith Mary de Jonge (*née* Twynam). *Educ:* Harrow; RAC Cirencester. *Heir: s* Hon. Michael Henry Strutt, *b* 5 Jan. 1969. *Address:* The Park, Kingston on Soar, Nottingham NG11 0DH.

BELSTEAD, 2nd Baron *cr* 1938; **John Julian Ganzoni;** PC 1983; JP; Baron Ganzoni (Life Peer), 1999; Bt 1929; Lord-Lieutenant of Suffolk, since 1994; *b* 30 Sept. 1932; *o s* of 1st Baron Belstead and Gwendolen Gertrude Turner (*d* 1962); *S* father, 1958. *Educ:* Eton; Christ Church, Oxford. MA 1961. Parliamentary Under-Secretary of State: DES, 1970–73; NI Office, 1973–74; Home Office, 1979–82; Minister of State: FCO, 1982–83; MAFF, 1983–87; DoE, 1987–88; Dep. Leader, H of L, 1983–87; Leader, H of L and Lord Privy Seal, 1988–90; HM Paymaster General and Minister, NI Office, 1990–92. Chm., Parole Board, 1992–97. Chm., Assoc. of Governing Bodies of Public Schools, 1974–79. JP Borough of Ipswich, 1962; DL Suffolk, 1979. *Heir:* none. *Address:* House of Lords,

SW1A 0PW. *T:* (020) 7219 3000. *Clubs:* Boodle's; All England Lawn Tennis (Wimbledon); MCC.

BELTON, Prof. Peter Stanley, PhD; Head, Food Materials Division, Institute of Food Research, Biotechnology and Biological Sciences Research Council, since 1999; *b* 19 June 1947; *s* of Stanley Belton and Bertha (*née* Lawrence); *m* 1976, Teresa Stutz; three *s*. *Educ:* Cooper's Sch., Bow; Chelsea Coll., Univ. of London (BSc 1st Cl. Hons Chem. 1968; PhD 1972). University of East Anglia: Open Univ. Fellowship, 1971–72; ICI Fellowship, 1972–74; Res. Leader, Unilever Res., Port Sunlight, 1974–79; AFRC, later BBSRC, Institute of Food Research Norwich Laboratory: Hd, Molecular Spectroscopy Gp, 1979–87; Hd, Chem. Physics Dept, 1987–90; Hd, Food Structure & Biopolymer Technol. Dept, 1990–91; Hd, Food Colloid & Biopolymer Sci. Dept, 1991–92; Hd, Norwich Lab., 1992–99; Dep. Dir, Inst. of Food Res., AFRC, later BBSRC, 1994–99. Visiting Professor: Univ. of São Paulo, 1976; Centre D'Etudes Nucléaire, 1989; Hon. Prof., UEA, 1992. Member: SERC Instrumentation Panel, 1989–91; AFRC Food Res. Grants Bd, 1991–94; BBSRC Food Directorate, 1994–97; Internat. Scientific Cttee, Sciences des Aliments; Scientific Cttee, Ecole Européenne de Chimie Analytique. FIFST 1994. Member, Editorial Board: Jl Sci. Food & Agric., 1991–97; Jl of Magnetic Resonance Analysis, 1994–; Seminars in Food Analysis, 1997–99; Series Editor, Monographs in Food Analysis, 1994–. *Publications:* (jtly) From Arms Race to World Peace, 1991; contrib. books and jls. *Recreations:* coarse fishing, listening to music, making wine. *Address:* Institute of Food Research Norwich Laboratory, Norwich Research Park, Colney, Norwich NR4 7UA; 79 The Avenues, Norwich, Norfolk NR2 3QB. *T:* (01603) 465851.

BELTRAM, Geoffrey; Under-Secretary, Department of Health and Social Security, 1973–81; *b* 7 April 1921; *s* of George and Beatrice Dorothy Beltram; *m* 1945, Audrey Mary (*née* Harkett); one *s* one *d*. *Educ:* Dame Alice Owen's School. Tax Officer, Inland Revenue, 1938; served in RAF, 1941–46; Exec. Officer and Higher Exec. Officer, Min. of Town and Country Planning, 1947–51; Asst Principal, Nat. Assistance Bd, 1951–55; Principal 1955–63; Asst Sec. 1963–73 (NAB 1963–66, Min. of Social Security 1966–68, DHSS 1968–73). Vis. Res. Associate, LSE, 1981–84. Vis. social worker, Ind. Living Fund, 1988–93. *Publication:* Testing the Safety Net: a study of the Supplementary Benefit scheme, 1984. *Recreations:* literature, listening to music, opera, ballet, walking, swimming.

BEMIS, Michael Bruce; Chief Executive, London Electricity plc, 1997–99; *b* 24 March 1947; *m* 1981, Ann Elizabeth; one *d*. *Educ:* Univ. of Southern Mississippi (BS Accounting 1970); Harvard Business Sch. (Exec. Prog. 1989). Deloitte Haskins and Sells, 1970–82, Electricity Utility Specialist, and Partner; Sen. Vice Pres. and Chief Financial Officer, Entergy Arkansas Inc, 1982–89; President and Chief Operating Officer: Entergy Mississippi Inc, 1989–91; Entergy Louisiana, 1991–92; Exec. Vice Pres., Retail Services, Entergy Corp., 1992–97. FInstD 1997. *Recreation:* golf. *Clubs:* New Orleans Country (New Orleans); Wentworth Golf, Annandale Golf.

BEN AHMED, Mohamed, PhD; Minister of State for Scientific Research and Technology, Tunisia, since 1998; *b* Tunis, 28 March 1941; *m* Prof. Zeinib Benoshan; one *d*. *Educ:* Faculté des Sciences de Paris (PhD 1966); Institut de Recherche en Informatique, Paris (Doctorat d'Etat 1978). Lectr, Faculté des Sciences, Tunis, 1967–72; Researcher, Institut de Recherche en Informatique, Paris, 1972–77; Faculté des Sciences, Tunis: Sen. Lectr, 1977–78; Asst Prof., 1978–82; Dir, Computer Dept, 1981–84; Univ. Full Prof., 1983; Ecole Nationale des Sciences de l'Informatique, Univ. of Tunis: Founder and Dir, 1984–90; Prof., 1991–93, 1996–97; Chm., Nat. Computer Centre, 1993–95; Minister of State for Computer Scis at Prime Ministry, 1995–96; Ambassador of Tunisia to UK, 1997–98.

BEN-TOVIM, Atarah, (Mrs Douglas Boyd), MBE 1980 (for services to children's music); Artistic Director, Children's Music Foundation in Scotland, since 1995; Artistic Director, Children's Classic Concerts, since 1995; *b* 1 Oct. 1940; *d* of Tsvi Ben-Tovim and Gladys Ben-Tovim; *m*; one *d*; *m* 1976, Douglas Boyd. *Educ:* Royal Acad. of Music, London. ARAM 1967. Principal Flautist, Royal Liverpool Philharmonic Orchestra, 1962–75; children's concerts with Atarah's Band, 1973–88; Founder and Artistic Dir, Children's Concert Centre, 1975–95. Hon. DMus CNAA, 1991. *Publications:* Atarah's Book (autobiog.), 1976, 2nd edn 1979; Atarah's Band Kits (14 published), 1978–; Children and Music, 1979; (jtly) The Right Instrument For Your Child, 1985; You Can Make Music!, 1986; The Young Orchestral Flautist, Books 1–3, 1990; Queen Eleanor's Legacy, 1994; The Flute Book, 1997. *Recreations:* music, writing, France and the Mediterranean. *Address:* c/o Watson Little Ltd, Capo Di Monte, Windmill Hill, NW3 6RJ. *T:* (020) 7431 0770.

BENACERRAF, Prof. Baruj; Fabyan Professor of Comparative Pathology, Harvard Medical School, 1970–91, Professor Emeritus, since 1991; President: Dana-Farber, Inc., 1991–96; Dana-Farber Cancer Institute, Boston, 1980–91; *b* 29 Oct. 1920; *m* 1943, Annette Dreyfus; one *d*. *Educ:* Lycée Janson, Paris (BèsL 1940); Columbia Univ. (BS 1942); Medical Coll. of Virginia (MD 1945). Served US Army, 1946–48. Intern, Queens Gen. Hosp., NY, 1945–46; Res. Fellow, Dept of Micro-biol., Coll. of Physicians and Surgeons, Columbia Univ., 1948–49; Chargé de Recherches, CNRS, Hôpital Broussais, Paris, 1950–56; New York University School of Medicine: Asst Prof. of Pathol., 1956–58; Assoc. Prof. of Pathol., 1958–60; Prof. of Pathol., 1960–68; Chief, Lab. of Immunol., Nat. Inst. of Allergy and Infectious Diseases, NIH, Bethesda, 1968–70. Scientific Advr, WHO; Chm., Scientific Adv. Cttee, Centre d'Immunologie de Marseille, CNRS-INSERM; Member: Immunology A Study Sect., NIH, 1965–69; Adv. Council, National Inst. of Allergy and Infectious Disease, 1985–88; Scientific Adv. Cttee, Basel Inst. of Immunology, 1985–89; Member Scientific Advisory Board: Trudeau Foundn, 1970–76; Mass Gen. Hosp., 1971–74. President: Amer. Assoc. of Immunologists, 1973–74; Fedn of Amer. Socs for Exptl Biol., 1974–75; Internat. Union of Immunol Socs, 1980–83. Fellow, Amer. Acad. of Arts and Scis, 1972. Correspondent Emérite, Institut National de la Santé et de la Recherche Scientifique, 1988. Member: Nat. Acad. of Scis, 1973; Nat. Inst. of Med., 1981; Amer. Assoc. of Pathologists and Bacteriologists; Amer. Soc. for Exptl Pathol.; British Assoc. for Immunol.; French Soc. of Biol Chem.; Harvey Soc. Lectures: R. E. Dyer, NIH, 1969; Harvey, 1971, 1972; J. S. Blumenthal, Univ. of Minnesota, 1980. Hon. MD Geneva, 1980; Hon. DSc: Virginia Commonwealth Univ., 1981; NY Univ., 1981; Yeshiva Univ., 1982; Univ. Aix-Marseille, 1982; Columbia Univ., 1985; Adelphi Univ., 1988; Weizmann Inst., 1989; Harvard Univ., 1992; Univ. Bordeaux, 1993; Univ. Vienna, 1995. Rabbi Shai Shacknai Lectr and Prize, Hebrew Univ. of Jerusalem, 1974; T. Duckett Jones Meml Award, Helen Hay Whitney Foundn, 1976; Waterford Biomedical Science Award, 1980; (jtly) Nobel Prize for Physiology or Medicine, 1980; Rous-Whipple Award, Amer. Assoc. of Pathologists, 1985; Nat. Medal of Science, US, 1990. *Publications:* (with D. Katz) Immunological Tolerance, 1974; Immunogenetics and Immunodeficiency, 1975; (with D. Katz) The Role of Products of the Histocompatibility Gene Complex in Immune Responses, 1976; Textbook of Immunology, 1979; 650 articles in professional journals. *Recreations:* music, art collecting. *Address:* Dana-Farber Cancer Institute, 44 Binney Street, Boston, MA 02115, USA.

BÉNARD, André Pierre Jacques, Hon. KBE 1991; French business executive; Hon. Chairman, Eurotunnel, since 1996 (Co-Chairman, 1986–90, Chairman, 1990–94; non-executive Director, 1994–96); *b* 19 Aug. 1922; *s* of Marcel Bénard and Lucie Thalmann; *m* 1946, Jacqueline Preiss; one *s*. *Educ:* Lycée Janson-de-Sailly; Lycée Georges Clémenceau, Nantes; Lycée Thiers, Marseilles; Ecole Polytechnique, Paris. Joined Royal Dutch Shell Group, 1946; with Société Anonyme des Pétroles Jupiter, 1946–49; Société des Pétroles Shell Berre, 1950–59; Shell Française: Pres. Man. Dir, 1967–70; Regional Co-ordinator Europe, 1970; Man. Dir, 1971–83, Mem. Supervisory Bd, 1983–93, Royal Dutch Shell Group. Director: La Radiotechnique SA, Paris, 1980–95; Barclays Bank SA, Paris, 1989–96. Senior Adviser, Lazard Frères, NY, 1983–90. Mem. Bd, INSEAD, Fontainebleau, 1983–99. Hon. Pres., French Chamber of Commerce and Industry, Netherlands, 1980–; Chm., Autumn Fest., Paris, 1995–. Médaille des Evadés; Médaille de la Résistance; Chevalier du Mérite Agricole; Chevalier de l'Ordre National du Mérite; Comdr, Légion d'Honneur; Comdr, Order of Orange Nassau. *Recreations:* music, golf. *Address:* 45 Paulton's Square, SW3 5DT.

BENARROCH, Heather Mary, (Mrs E. J. Benarroch); *see* Harper, Heather.

BENAUD, Richard, OBE 1961; international sports consultant, journalist and media representative; television commentator: Nine Network, Australia, since 1977; Channel 4, since 1999; *b* 6 Oct. 1930; *s* of Louis Richard Benaud and Irene Benaud; *m* 1967, Daphne Elizabeth Surfleet; two *s* by previous marr. *Educ:* Parramatta High Sch. Captain, Australian Cricket Team, 28 Tests, played for Australia 63 Tests, Tours to England, 1953, 1956, 1961; first cricketer to achieve Test double, 2000 runs, 200 wickets, 1963. TV commentator, BBC, 1960–99. *Publications:* Way of Cricket, 1960; Tale of Two Tests, 1962; Spin Me a Spinner, 1963; The New Champions, 1965; Willow Patterns, 1972; Benaud on Reflection, 1984; The Appeal of Cricket, 1995; Anything but . . . An Autobiography, 1998. *Recreation:* golf. *Address:* (office) 19/178 Beach Street, Coogee, NSW 2034, Australia. *T:* (2) 96641124.

BENDALL, David Vere, CMG 1967; MBE 1945; HM Diplomatic Service, retired; *b* 27 Feb. 1920; *s* of John Manley Bendall; *m* 1941, Eve Stephanie Merrilees Galpin; one *d*. *Educ:* Winchester; King's Coll., Cambridge (BA). Served Grenadier Guards, 1940–46. Third Sec., Allied Force HQ, Caserta, 1946; Rome, 1947; FO, 1949; First Sec., Santiago, 1952; FO, 1955; seconded to NATO Secretariat, Paris 1957; FO, 1960; NATO Secretariat, Paris as Dep. Head, Economic and Finance Div. and Special Advisor on Defence Policy, 1962; Counsellor, 1962; Counsellor, Washington, 1965–69; Asst Under-Sec. of State for Western Europe, 1969–71. Chairman: Banque Morgan Grenfell en Suisse (formerly Morgan Grenfell Switzerland), 1974–90; Morgan Grenfell Internat. Ltd, 1979–85; Morgan Grenfell Italia, 1982–93; Banca Nazionale del Lavoro Investment Bank, 1986–94. Director: Morgan Grenfell (Holdings) Ltd, 1971–85; Morgan Grenfell France, 1986–90; Dep. Chm., Avon Cosmetics, 1979–90; Member: Morgan Grenfell Internat. Adv. Council, 1986–87; Internat. and London Adv. Bds, Banque de l'Indochine et de Suez, 1974–87. Chm., BRCS, 1980–85 (Vice-Chm., 1979–80); Vice-Chm., Finance Cttee, League of Red Cross Socs, 1981–85. OStJ 1985. *Recreations:* golf, tennis, shooting, languages. *Address:* 3 Eaton Terrace Mews, SW1W 8EU. *T:* (020) 7730 4229; Ashbocking Hall, near Ipswich, Suffolk IP6 9LG. *T:* (01473) 890262. *Club:* Boodle's.

BENDALL, Dr Eve Rosemarie Duffield; Chief Executive Officer, English National Board for Nursing, Midwifery and Health Visiting, 1981–86; *b* 7 Aug. 1927; *d* of Col F. W. D. Bendall, CMG, MA, and Mrs M. L. Bendall, LRAM, ARCM. *Educ:* Malvern Girls' Coll.; London Univ. (MA, PhD); Royal Free Hosp. (SRN). Ward Sister, Dorset County Hosp., 1953–55; Night Supt, Manchester Babies' Hosp., 1955–56; Nurse Tutor: United Sheffield Hosps Sch. of Nursing, 1958–61; St George's Hosp., London, 1961–63; Principal, Sch. of Nursing, Hosp. for Sick Children, Gt Ormond Street, 1963–69. Registrar, GNC, 1973–77. *Publications:* (jtly) Basic Nursing, 1963, 3rd edn 1970; (jtly) A Guide to Medical and Surgical Nursing, 1965, 2nd edn 1970; (jtly) A History of the General Nursing Council, 1969; So You Passed, Nurse (research), 1975. *Recreation:* auspicious ageing.

BENDALL, Vivian Walter Hough; surveyor and valuer in private practice, since 1956; *b* 14 Dec. 1938; *s* of late Cecil Aubrey Bendall and Olive Alvina Bendall (*née* Hough); *m* 1969, Ann Rosalind Jarvis (marr. diss. 1992). *Educ:* Coombe Hill House, Croydon; Broad Green Coll., Croydon. TechIRRV; AMRSH 1991. Mem. Croydon Council, 1964–78; Mem. GLC, 1970–73; Chm., Greater London Young Conservatives, 1967–68. Contested (C): Hertford and Stevenage, Feb. and Oct. 1974; Ilford North, 1997 and 2001. MP (C) Ilford North, March 1978–1997. Backbench Committees: Vice-Chm., Transport Cttee, 1982–83; Sec., Foreign and Commonwealth Affairs Cttee, 1981–84; Vice-Chm., Employment Cttee, 1984–87 (Jt Sec. 1981–84). Former Member: Central Council for Care of the Elderly; South Eastern Area Reg. Assoc. for the Blind; Dr Barnardo's New Mossford Home Fund Raising Cttee. FNAEA 1984. Hon. FASI. *Recreations:* cricket, motor sport. *Address:* (office) 25A Brighton Road, South Croydon, Surrey CR2 6EA. *T:* (020) 8688 0341. *Club:* St Stephen's Constitutional.

BENDER, Dr Brian Geoffrey, CB 1998; Permanent Secretary, Department for the Environment, Food and Rural Affairs (formerly Ministry of Agriculture, Fisheries and Food), since 2000; *b* 25 Feb. 1949; *s* of late Prof. Arnold Eric Bender; *m* 1974, Penelope Clark; one *s* one *d*. *Educ:* Greenford Grammar Sch.; Imperial Coll., London Univ. (BSc, PhD). Joined DTI, 1973; Private Sec. to Sec. of State for Trade, 1976–77; First Sec. (Trade Policy), Office of UK Permanent Rep. to EC, 1977–82; Principal (responsible for internat. steel issues), DTI, 1982–84; Counsellor (Industry), Office of UK Permanent Rep. to EC, 1985–89; Under Sec. and Dep. Head of European Secretariat, Cabinet Office, 1990–93; Hd of Regl Develt Div., DTI, 1993–94; Dep. Sec. and Head of European Secretariat, Cabinet Office, 1994–98; Head of Public Service Delivery, Cabinet Office, 1998–99; Permanent Sec., Cabinet Office, 1999–2000. *Address:* Department for the Environment, Food and Rural Affairs, Nobel House, 17 Smith Square, SW1P 3JR.

BENDERSKY, Pamela May H.; *see* Hudson-Bendersky.

BENDIGO, Bishop of, since 1995; **Rt Rev. Raymond David Bowden;** *b* 31 July 1937; *s* of Raymond Bowden and Mona Lillian Bowden (*née* Blaxell); *m* 1962, Linda Elizabeth Kleinschafer; two *s* one *d*. *Educ:* Newcastle Boys' High Sch., NSW; St John's Coll., Morpeth, ACT (ThL 1960; ThSchol 1970). Assistant Curate: St Peter's Cathedral, Armidale, 1960–64; St Paul, W Tamworth, 1964–65; Vicar: Warialda, 1965–69; Good Shepherd, Savona, NY, USA, 1969–71; Assoc. Rector, St Clement, Berkeley, Calif, 1971–72; Chaplain, Armidale Sch., 1973–74; Vicar, Glen Innes, 1974–82; Rector, Terrigal, 1982–92 and Archdeacon, Central Coast, 1985–92; Canon, Christ Church Cathedral, Newcastle, 1992–95; Archdeacon of Newcastle, 1992–95. *Publication:* Heroes of the Faith, 1998. *Recreations:* watching cricket, classical music, escape literature. *Address:* PO Box 2, Bendigo, Vic 3552, Australia. *T:* (3) 54434668.

BENDJAMA, Amar; Secretary General, Ministry of Foreign Affairs, Algeria, since 1996; *b* Constantine, Algeria, 1 Jan. 1951; *m*; two *c*. *Educ:* Nat. Sch. of Admin., Algiers. Ministry of Foreign Affairs, Algeria: Hd of Official Visits Desk, Protocol Dept, 1975–79; Counsellor, Moscow, 1980–84; Dep. Dir, European Dept, 1984–89; First Counsellor, Perm. Mission to UN in NY, and Dep. Rep. to Security Council, 1989–90; Chargé d'Affaires, Perm. Mission to UN in NY, 1990–91; Ambassador to Ethiopia, Djibouti and Eritrea, 1992–94; Ambassador to UK, 1994–96. Permanent Representative to OAU and UNECA, 1992–94; Chairman: Conf. Cttee, OAU, 1992–93; Adv. Cttee for Admin. and Budgetary Issues, OAU, 1993–94. *Address:* Ministry of Foreign Affairs, Place Med. Seddik Benyahia, El-Mouradia, Algiers, Algeria. *T:* (2) 692333, *Fax:* (2) 609333.

BENEDETTI, Renato Giovanni, RIBA; architect; Partner, McDowell+Benedetti, since 1996; Director, McDowell+Benedetti Ltd, since 1998; *b* 30 Nov. 1962; *s* of Giovanni Benedetti and Giulia (*née* Fugaccia). *Educ:* Cobourg Dist Collegiate Inst. East (Ontario Schol. 1981); Univ. of Waterloo Sch. of Architecture, Ontario (BES 1985; BArch 1988). RIBA 1996. Stonemason and bricklayer, 1976–81; Associate, David Chipperfield Architects, 1989–96; with Jonathan McDowell formed McDowell+Benedetti, 1996; main projects include: Smithfield Regeneration, Dublin, 1992; Oliver's Wharf Penthouse, Wapping, 1996; HQ Building, Options, London, 1997; (with YRM Architects) New Univ. of Commonwealth, Malaysia, 1998; Assoc. of Photographers, New Gall. and HQ, London, 1998; Nursing Home for Merchant Taylors' Co., Lewisham, 2000. Mem. Panel, Art for Architecture Award, RSA. FRSA 1999. *Recreations:* travel, arts, sport. *Address:* (office) 62 Rosebery Avenue, EC1R 4RR. *T:* (020) 7278 8810. *Clubs:* Architecture, Soho House.

BENEDICTUS, David Henry; writer and director for stage, television and radio; *b* 16 Sept. 1938; *s* of late Henry Jules Benedictus and Kathleen Constance (*née* Ricardo); *m* 1971, Yvonne Daphne Antrobus; one *s* one *d*. *Educ:* Stone House, Broadstairs; Eton College; Balliol College, Oxford (BA English); State Univ. of Iowa. News and current affairs, BBC Radio, 1961; Drama Director, BBC TV, 1962; Story Editor, Wednesday Play and Festival Series, BBC, 1965; Thames TV Trainee Director, at Bristol Old Vic, 1968; Asst Dir, RSC, Aldwych, 1970; Judith E. Wilson Vis. Fellow, Cambridge, and Fellow Commoner, Churchill Coll., Cambridge, 1981–82; Commissioning Editor, Drama Series, Channel 4 TV, 1984–86 (commissions included: The Manageress, 1987; Porterhouse Blue (Internat. Emmy), 1987); BBC Radio: Readings Editor, 1989–91; Editor, Readings, 1991; Editor, Radio 3 Drama, 1992; Sen. Producer, Serial Readings, 1993 (incl. The Bible, 1992; Arcadia, 1993; Jack, 1994; Macbeth, 1995). Writer in Residence: Sutton Library, Surrey, 1975; Kibbutz Gezer, Israel, 1978; Bitterne Library, Southampton, 1983–84. Antiques corresp., Standard, 1977–80; reviewer for books, stage, films, records, for major newspapers and magazines, principally The Economist. Dir, Kingston Books, 1988–90. Member: Amnesty International; Writers' Guild. Plays include: Betjemania, 1976, 1996; The Golden Key, 1982; What A Way To Run A Revolution!, 1985; You Say Potato, 1992. *Publications:* The Fourth of June, 1962; You're a Big Boy Now, 1963; This Animal is Mischievous, 1965; Hump, or Bone by Bone Alive, 1967; The Guru and the Golf Club, 1969; A World of Windows, 1971; The Rabbi's Wife, 1976; Junk, how and where to buy beautiful things at next to nothing prices, 1976; A Twentieth Century Man, 1978; The Antique Collector's Guide, 1980; Lloyd George (from Elaine Morgan's screenplay), 1981; Whose Life is it Anyway? (from Brian Clarke's screenplay), 1981; Who Killed the Prince Consort?, 1982; Local Hero (from Bill Forsyth's screenplay), 1983; The Essential London Guide, 1984; Floating Down to Camelot, 1985; The Streets of London, 1986; The Absolutely Essential London Guide, 1986; Uncle Ernie's System, 1988–; Little Sir Nicholas, 1990; (with Prof. Hans Kalmus) Odyssey of a Scientist, 1991; Sunny Intervals and Showers, 1992; The Stamp Collector, 1994; How to Cope When the Money Runs Out, 1998; numerous short stories for Radio 4 etc. *Recreations:* chess, tennis, cricket, auctions, table tennis, piano playing, horse racing, eating. *Address:* 95D Talfourd Road, SE15 5NN. *T:* (020) 7701 0989; *e-mail:* davidbenedictus@hotmail.com.

BENEDIKTSSON, Einar, MA; Knight Commander, Order of the Falcon, Iceland; Ambassador, Ministry of Foreign Affairs, Reykjavík, since 1997; Executive Director, Leifur Eiriksson Millennium Commission of Iceland, since 1997; *b* Reykjavík, 30 April 1931; *s* of Stefan M. Benediktsson and Sigridur Oddsdóttir; *m* 1956, Elsa Petursdóttir; three *s* two *d*. *Educ:* Colgate Univ., NY; Fletcher Sch. of Law and Diplomacy, Mass; London Sch. of Econs and Pol. Science; Inst. des Etudes Européennes, Turin. With OEEC, 1956–60; Head of Section, Mins of Econ. Affairs and Commerce, 1961–64, and Min. of For. Affairs, 1964; Counsellor, Paris, 1964–68; Head of Section, Min. of For. Affairs, 1968–70; Perm. Rep. to Internat. Orgns, Geneva, 1970–76; Chm., EFTA Council, 1975; Ambassador to France (also accredited to Spain and Portugal, and Perm. Rep. to OECD and UNESCO, 1976–82); Ambassador to UK and concurrently to The Netherlands, Nigeria and Ireland, 1982–86; Perm. Rep. to N Atlantic Council, 1986–90, and Ambassador to Belgium and Luxembourg, 1986–91; Ambassador to Norway, also to Poland and Czechoslovakia, 1991–93; Ambassador to USA, also accredited to Canada, Mexico, Chile, Argentina and Uruguay, 1993–97. Holds foreign decorations. *Address:* Landafundanefnd, Adalstraeti 6, 101 Reykjavík, Iceland. *T:* 5752000; (home) Hvassaleiti 28, 103 Reykjavík, Iceland. *T:* 5681943.

BENETTON, Luciano; industrialist; *b* 13 May 1935. Established Fratelli Benetton (with brothers), 1965; founder and Pres., Benetton, 1978; Benetton Holdings, 1981; Vice-Pres. and Man. Dir, Benetton Group SpA; Mem. Board, Edizione Holding SpA; Pres., Benetton Foundn. Mem., Italian Senate, 1992–94. Awards: Civiltà Veneta, 1986; Premio Creatività, 1992. *Publications:* contribs to La Biblioteca di Harvard, economic and business strategies, 1988. *Address:* Benetton Group SpA, via Villa Minelli 1, 31050 Ponzano Veneto (TV), Italy. *T:* (422) 4491.

BENGOUGH, Sir Piers (Henry George), KCVO 1986; OBE 1973; DL; Her Majesty's Representative, Ascot, 1982–97; *b* 24 May 1929; *s* of Nigel and Alice Bengough; *m* 1952, Bridget Shirley Adams; two *s*. *Educ:* Eton. Commnd 10th Royal Hussars (PWO), 1948; commanded Royal Hussars (PWO), 1971–73, retired. Formerly amateur rider; wins incl. Grand Military Gold Cup (4 times). Member: Jockey Club, 1965– (Steward, 1974–77, 1990–92); Horserace Betting Levy Board, 1978–81; Director: Cheltenham Steeplechase Co., 1977–90; Hereford Racecourse Co., 1974–2001; Ludlow Race Club, 1979–; Chm., Compensation Fund for Jockeys, 1981–89. Mem., HM Bodyguard, Hon. Corps of Gentlemen-at-Arms, 1981– (Standard Bearer, 1997–99). Hon. Col The Royal Hussars (PWO), 1983–90. DL Hereford and Worcester, 1987. *Recreations:* shooting, fishing. *Address:* Great House, Canon Pyon, Hereford HR4 8PD. *Clubs:* Cavalry and Guards, Pratt's.

BENHAM, George Frederick; Headmaster, Cardinal Hinsley RC High School, since 1999; *b* 26 Oct. 1946; *m* 1996, Elizabeth Maria; two *s*. *Educ:* Queen Mary Coll., London (BA 1969; MPhil 1972); Inst. of Educn, London Univ. (DipEd 1978; MA 1980). Lectr, Univ. of Aberdeen, 1971–75; teacher at various schs in London, 1975–85; Educn Advr, 1985–87; London Borough of Brent: Dep. Dir of Educn, 1987–88, Dir, 1989–95; Chief Exec., 1995–98. FRSA 1978; FIMgt (FBIM 1978). *Publications:* contribs on education to learned jls in USA, Holland, UK and Switzerland. *Address:* Cardinal Hinsley RC High School, Harlesden Road, NW10 3RN. *T:* (020) 8965 3947.

BENJAMIN, Prof. Bernard; Professor of Actuarial Science, The City University, London, 1973–75, now Emeritus; *b* 8 March 1910; *s* of Joseph and Lucy Benjamin, London; *m* 1937, May Pate (*d* 1977), Horham, Suffolk; two *d*. *Educ:* Colfe Grammar Sch.; Sir John Cass Coll. (London University). BSc (Hons); PhD London. LCC, 1928; statistician Public Health Dept, 1940; served War, 1943–46, RAF; statistician, General Register Office, 1952; Chief Statistician, 1954; Dir of Statistics, Ministry of Health, 1963–65; Dir of Research and Intelligence, GLC, 1965–70; Dir of Statistical Studies, CS College, 1970–73; Hon. Cons. in Med. Stats to Army, 1966. Chm., Statistics Users Council (formerly Standing Cttee of Statistics Users), 1971–90. Fellow: Inst. of Actuaries (a Vice-Pres. 1963; Pres., 1966–68; Gold Medal, 1975); Royal Statistical Soc. (Pres. 1970–71; Guy Medal in Gold, 1986); Galton Inst. (formerly Eugenics Soc.) (Pres., 1982–87; Galton Lectr, 1981). Hon. DSc: City Univ., London, 1981; Kent Univ. 1987. Internat. Insurance Prize of Italy, 1985. *Publications:* Social and Economic Factors in Mortality, 1965; Health and Vital Statistics, 1968; Demographic Analysis, 1969; The Population Census, 1970; (with H. W. Haycocks) The Analysis of Mortality and Other Actuarial Statistics, 1971; Statistics in Urban Administration, 1976; (ed) Medical Records, 1977; General Insurance, 1977; (jtly) The Analysis of Mortality and Other Actuarial Statistics, 1980, 3rd edn 1993; (jtly) Pensions: the problems of today and tomorrow, 1987; Population Statistics, 1989; (with Amal Soliman) Mortality on the Move, 1993; numerous medical and population statistical papers and contribs to Jl of Royal Statistical Society and Jl of Inst. of Actuaries. *Recreations:* gardening, painting (both kinds), music. *Address:* c/o Institute of Actuaries, Staple Inn Hall, High Holborn, WC1V 7QJ. *Club:* Athenæum.

BENJAMIN, Floella, OBE 2001; actress, independent producer and writer, Crystalrowe Ltd, since 1987; Chief Executive, Floella Benjamin Productions Ltd, since 1998; *b* 23 Sept. 1949; *d* of Roy Benjamin and Veronica Benjamin (*née* Dryce); *m* 1980, Keith Taylor; one *s* one *d*. *Educ:* Penge Girls' Sch. Chief Accountants Office, Barclays Bank, 1967–69; Actress: *stage:* Hair, Shaftesbury Th., 1970–72; Jesus Christ Superstar, Palace, 1972–74; Black Mikado, Cambridge Th., 1974–75; The Husband-in-Law, Comedy, 1976; *television:* Playschool, 1976–88; Playaway, 1976–82; Fast Forward, 1983–85; numerous dramas; also produced: Treehouse, 1987; Playabout, 1990–92; Hullaballoo, 1994; Caribbean Light, 1998; Jamboree, 1998–; Caribbean Kitchen, 1999; Taste of Barbados, 2000–; *film:* Black Joy, 1977. Dir, Knowledge Through Entertainment, 1997–. Member: Royal Mail Stamp Adv. Cttee, 1994–; British Bd of Film Classification Video Consultative Council, 1996–2000; Creative Cons. Gp, Millennium Dome, 1997–99; Foreign and Commonwealth Caribbean Adv. Gp, 1998–; British Bd of Film Classification Children's Viewing Adv. Gp, 2000–; Chm., Women of Year Lunch, 1996–2000; Chm., BAFTA, 1999– (Mem., 1990–; Vice-Chm., 1998–99); Governor: Nat. Film and Television Sch., 1995–; Commonwealth Inst., 1998–. *Publications:* Caribbean Cookery, 1986; *for children:* Floella's Fun Book, 1984; Why the Agouti Has No Tail, 1984; Floella's Funniest Jokes, 1985; Floella's Favourite Folk Tales, 1986; Fall About with Flo, 1986; Floella's Fabulous Bright Ideas, 1986; Floella's Floorboard Book, 1987; Flo and Aston's Books (series of six books), 1987; Snotty and the Rod of Power, 1987; Floella's Cardboard Box Book, 1987; Exploring Caribbean Food in Britain, 1988; For Goodness Sake, 1994; Skip Across the Ocean, 1995; Coming to England, 1995. *Recreations:* golf, cooking, running. *Address:* BAFTA, 195 Piccadilly, W1V 0LN. *T:* (020) 7734 0022. *Club:* Royal Commonwealth Society (Mem., Central Council).

BENJAMIN, George William John; composer, occasional conductor and pianist; *b* 31 Jan. 1960; *s* of William Benjamin and Susan Benjamin (*née* Bendon). *Educ:* Westminster School (private tuition with Peter Gellhorn); Paris Conservatoire (Olivier Messiaen); King's College, Cambridge (Alexander Goehr). MA, MusB. First London orchestral performance, BBC Proms, 1980; research at Institut de Recherche et Coordination Acoustique/Musique, Paris, 1984–87; Prince Consort Prof. of Composition, RCM, 1994– (Vis. Prof., 1987–94); Principal Guest Artist, Hallé Orch., 1993–96; operatic conducting début, Pelléas et Mélisande, La Monnaie, Brussels, 1999; performs, conducts and lectures on own and other contemp. music, GB, Europe, USA, Far East. Artistic Dir, contemp. music festivals, USA (San Francisco Symphony Orch.), France (Opéra Bastille), 1992, and London (South Bank), 1993. Artistic consultant, Sounding the Century, BBC R3, 1996–99. Featured composer: Salzburg Fest., 1995; Tanglewood Fest., 1999–2000. Hon. FRCM 1993. Mem., Bavarian Acad. of Arts, 2000. Lili Boulanger Award, USA, 1985; Koussevitzky Internat. Record Award, 1987; Gramophone Contemp. Music Award, 1990; Edison Award, Holland, 1998. Chevalier, Ordre des Arts et des Lettres (France), 1996. *Publications include: orchestral:* Altitude, 1977; Ringed by the Flat Horizon, 1980; A Mind of Winter, 1981; At First Light, 1982; Jubilation, 1985; Antara, 1987; Sudden Time, 1993; Three Inventions for Chamber Orchestra, 1995; Sometime Voices, 1996; Palimpsest, 2000; *chamber music:* Violin Sonata, 1977; Piano Sonata, 1978; Octet, 1978; Flight, 1979; Sortilèges, 1981; Three Studies for Solo Piano, 1985; Upon Silence, 1990, 1991; Viola, Viola, 1997. *Address:* c/o Faber Music Ltd, 3 Queen Square, WC1N 3AU.

BENJAMIN, Leanne; Principal, Royal Ballet Company, since 1993; *b* Australia, 1964. *Educ:* Royal Ballet Sch. (Adeline Genée Gold Medal). Joined Sadler's Wells Royal Ballet, 1983: Soloist, 1985–87; Principal, 1987–88; Principal: English Nat. Ballet, 1988–90; Deutsche Oper Ballet, Berlin, 1990–92; joined Royal Ballet Co., 1992. Numerous leading rôles; created: Greta in Metamorphosis; Gerda in The Snow Queen. Prix de Lausanne, 1981. *Address:* c/o Royal Ballet, Royal Opera House, Covent Garden, WC2E 9DB.

BENJAMIN, Dr Ralph, CB 1980; DSc, PhD, BSc, FCGI, FREng, FIEE; Visiting Professor: University College and Imperial College of Science, Technology and Medicine, University of London, since 1988; University of Bristol, since 1993; *b* 17 Nov. 1922; *s* of Charles Benjamin and Claire Benjamin (*née* Stern); *m* 1951, Kathleen Ruth Bull, BA; one *s* (and one *s* decd). *Educ:* in Germany and Switzerland; St Oswald's Coll., Ellesmere; Imperial Coll. of Science and Technology, London. DSc(Eng) London, 1970; FREng (FEng 1983); FCGI 1982. Joined Royal Naval Scientific Service, 1944; Senior Scientific Officer, 1949; Principal Scientific Officer, 1952; Senior Principal Scientific Officer (Special Merit), 1955; Deputy Chief Scientific Officer (Special Merit), 1960; Head of Research and Deputy Chief Scientist, Admiralty Surface Weapons Establishment, 1961; Dir and Chief Scientist, Admiralty Underwater Weapons Estab., 1964–71, and Dir, Underwater Weapons R&D (Navy), 1965–71; Chief Scientist, GCHQ, 1971–82; Head of Communications Techniques and Networks, SHAPE Technical Centre, The Hague, 1982–87. Hon. consultant: Univ. of Illinois; US Office of Naval Research, 1956. Mem. Council, IEE, 1994–97 (Chm., Bristol Area, 1992–93; Chm., Western Centre, 1995–96). IEE Marconi Premium, 1964; IERE Heinrich Hertz Premium, 1980, 1983. Council Mem., Brit. Acoustical Soc., 1971. Vis. Prof., Dept of Electrical and Electronic Engineering, Univ. of Surrey, 1973–80. Mem. Court, Brunel Univ., 1997–. FRSA 1984. Hon. DEng Bristol, 2000. *Publications:* Modulation, Resolution and Signal Processing for Radar Sonar and Related Systems, 1966; Five Lives in One (autobiog.), 1996; contribs to various advisory cttees, working parties, symposia, etc; articles in various professional jls. *Recreations:* work, hill-walking, ski-ing, swimming. *Address:* 13 Bellhouse Walk, Rockwell Park, Bristol BS11 0UE. *Club:* Athenæum.

BENN, Anthony, OBE 1945; *b* 7 Oct. 1912; *s* of late Francis Hamilton Benn and Arta Clara Benn (*née* Boal); *m* 1943, Maureen Lillian Kathleen Benn (*née* Denbigh) (*d* 1992); two *s* four *d*. *Educ:* Harrow; Christ Church, Oxford (Scholar). Oxford Univ. Cricket XI, 1935. Price & Pierce Ltd, 1935 (Director, 1947, Chm., 1956–72). Joined Surrey and Sussex Yeomanry, 1936. Served War of 1939–45 (OBE): Staff Coll., 1942; Instructor, Middle East Staff Coll., 1943. Comdr, Order of the Lion of Finland, 1958. *Recreation:* travel.

BENN, Edward, CMG 1981; Minister (Defence Equipment), British Embassy, Washington, 1978–82, retired; *b* 8 May 1922; *s* of John Henry Benn and Alice (*née* Taylor); *m* 1947, Joan Taylor; one *d*. *Educ:* High Storrs Grammar Sch., Sheffield; Sheffield Univ. (BEng; 1st Cl. Hons Civil Engrg; Mappin Medal, 1943). Operational Research with Army, 1943–48; India and Burma, 1944–46 (Major); entered War Office, 1948; tank research, Supt Special Studies, and later Dep. Dir, Army Op. Res. Estabt, 1961; Asst Sci. Adviser to SACEUR, Paris, 1962–65; Dep. Chief Sci. Adviser, Home Office, 1966–68; Dir, Defence Policy, MoD, 1968–75; Under Sec. and Dep. Chief Scientist (RAF), MoD, 1975–78. *Recreation:* golf. *Address:* 7 Hiatt Road, Minchinhampton, Glos GL6 9DB. *T:* (01453) 883005. *Clubs:* MCC; Minchinhampton Golf.

BENN, Hilary James Wedgwood; MP (Lab) Leeds Central, since June 1999; Parliamentary Under-Secretary of State, Department for International Development, since 2001; *b* 26 Nov. 1953; *s* of Rt Hon. Tony Benn, *qv*; *m* 1st, 1973, Rosalind Caroline Retey (*d* 1979); 2nd, 1982, Sally Christina Clark; three *s* one *d*. *Educ:* Holland Park Comprehensive Sch.; Sussex Univ. (BA Hons Russian and East European Studies). Res. Asst, Nat. Referendum Campaign, 1975; Res. Officer, 1975–93, Head of Res., 1993–96, Head of Policy and Communications, 1996–97, ASTMS, then MSF; Jt Sec., Finance Panel, Labour Party Commn of Inquiry, on secondment, 1980; Special Advr to Sec. of State for Educn and Employment, 1997–99. MSF Rep., Labour Party Nat. Policy Forum, 1994–97; Chair: Educn Cttee, ALA, 1988–90; Unions 21, 1995–99; Member: Educn Cttee, AMA, 1986–90; Envmt Policy Commn, Labour Party, 1994–97; Party into Power Task Force on Labour Party's Democracy, 1996–97. Mem., Envmt, Transport and the Regions Select Cttee, 1999–2001. Vice-Chair, PLP Educn and Employment Cttee, 2000; Pres., Acton CLP, 1979–82. Mem. (Lab) Ealing LBC, 1979–99 (Dep. Leader, 1986–90; Chair, Educn Cttee, 1986–90; Dep. Leader, Labour Gp, 1984–94). Contested (Lab) Ealing N, 1983, 1987. *Publication:* (contrib.) Beyond 2002: long-term policies for Labour, 1999. *Recreations:* watching sport, gardening. *Address:* House of Commons, SW1A 0AA.

BENN, Sir (James) Jonathan, 4th Bt *cr* 1914; Chairman, SCA Pension Trusts Ltd, 1988–98; *b* 27 July 1933; *s* of Sir John Andrews Benn, 3rd Bt, and of Hon. Ursula Lady Benn, *o d* of 1st Baron Hankey, PC, GCB, GCMG, GCVO, FRS; *S* father, 1984; *m* 1960, Jennifer Mary, *e d* of late Dr Wilfred Howells, OBE; one *s* one *d*. *Educ:* Harrow; Clare College, Cambridge (MA). Various positions with Reed International PLC (formerly A. E. Reed & Co.), 1957–88; Dir, Reed Paper & Board (UK) Ltd, 1971, Man. Dir 1976; Dir, Reed Group Ltd, 1976; Chm. and Chief Exec., Reed Paper & Board (UK) Ltd, 1977–90; Chm., Reedpack Paper Gp, 1988–90; Dir, Reedpack Ltd, 1988–90. Pres., British Paper and Board Industries Fedn, 1985–87. Dir, Broomhill Trust, 1991–96. *Recreations:* golf, skiing, music. *Heir:* *s* Robert Ernest Benn [*b* 17 Oct. 1963; *m* 1985, Sheila Margaret, 2nd *d* of Dr Alastair Blain]. *Address:* Fielden Lodge, Ightham, Kent TN15 9AN.
See also T. J. Benn.

BENN, Sir Jonathan; *see* Benn, Sir (James) J.

BENN, Timothy John; Chairman, Timothy Benn Publishing Ltd, 1983–97, and other companies; *b* 27 Oct. 1936; *yr s* of Sir John Andrews Benn, 3rd Bt, and of Hon. Ursula Helen Alers Hankey; *m* 1982, Christina Grace Townsend. *Educ:* Harrow; Clare Coll., Cambridge (MA); Princeton Univ., USA; Harvard Business Sch., USA (National Marketing Council Course; Scholarship Award). FInstM. 2nd Lieut Scots Guards, 1956–57. Benn Brothers Ltd: Board Member, 1961–82; Managing Director, 1972–82; Dep. Chm., 1976–81; Chm., Benn Brothers plc, 1981–82; Ernest Benn: Board Member, 1967–82; Managing Director, 1973–82; Chairman and Managing Director, 1974–82. Chairman: Bouverie Publishing Co., 1983–; Buckley Press (Publr, Post Magazine and Insurance Monitor, Re-insurance, Insurance Directory), 1984–97; Henry Greenwood and Co., 1987–98; Dalesman Publishing Co. (Publr, The Dalesman, Cumbria, Peak District magazine), 1989–; The Countryman Publishing Co., 2000–. Pres., Tonbridge Civic Soc., 1982–87. *Publication:* The (Almost) Compleat Angler, 1985. *Recreations:* writing, gardening, toymaking. *Address:* Brookfield, Fulbrook Lane, Elstead, Surrey GU6 8LG. *Club:* Flyfishers'.
See also Sir J. J. Benn.

BENN, Rt Hon. Tony; PC 1964; *b* 3 April 1925; *er* surv. *s* of 1st Viscount Stansgate, DSO, DFC, PC, former Labour MP and Cabinet Minister (*d* 1960); having unsuccessfully attempted to renounce his right of succession, 1955 and 1960, won a bye-election in May 1961 only to be prevented from taking seat; instigated Act to make disclaimer possible, and disclaimed title for life, 1963; *m* 1949, Caroline Middleton De Camp, MA (*d* 2000); three *s* one *d*. Served: RAFVR, 1943–45; RNVR, 1945–46. Joined Labour Party, 1943; Mem., NEC, 1959–60, 1962–93 (Chm., 1971–72); candidate for leadership of Labour Party, 1976, 1988, and for dep. leadership, 1971, 1981. MP (Lab): Bristol SE, Nov. 1950–1960 and Aug. 1963–1983; Chesterfield, 1984–2001; Postmaster-Gen., 1964–66, recommended establishment of GPO as public corp. and founded Giro; Minister of Technology, 1966–70, assumed responsibility for Min. of Aviation, 1967 and Min. of Power, 1969; opposition spokesman on Trade and Industry, 1970–74; Sec. of State for Industry and Minister for Posts and Telecommunications, 1974–75; Sec. of State for Energy, 1975–79. Pres., EEC Council of Energy Ministers, 1977. Pres., Campaign Gp, subseq. Socialist Campaign Gp of Lab. MPs, 1987–2001. Contested (Lab) Bristol East, 1983. Vis. Prof. of Pol Sci., LSE, 2001–. Pres., Labour Action for Peace. *Publications:* The Privy Council as a Second Chamber, 1957; The Regeneration of Britain, 1964; The New Politics, 1970; Speeches, 1974; Arguments for Socialism, 1979; Arguments for Democracy, 1981; (ed) Writings on the Wall: a radical and socialist anthology 1215–1984, 1984; Out of the Wilderness, Diaries 1963–1967, 1987; Fighting Back: speaking out for Socialism in the Eighties, 1988; Office Without Power, Diaries 1968–72, 1988; Against the Tide, Diaries 1973–76, 1989; Conflicts of Interest, Diaries 1977–80, 1990; A Future for Socialism, 1991; The End of an Era, Diaries 1980–1990, 1992; (jtly) Common Sense, 1993; Years of Hope: Diaries, Letters and Papers 1940–1962, 1994; The Benn Diaries 1940–1990, 1995; numerous pamphlets, videos and audio tapes. *Address:* 12 Holland Park Avenue, W11 3QU.
See also H. J. W. Benn.

BENN, Rt Rev. Wallace Parke; *see* Lewes, Suffragan Bishop of.

BENNER, Patrick, CB 1975; Deputy Secretary, Department of Health and Social Security, 1976–84; *b* 26 May 1923; *s* of Henry Grey and Gwendolen Benner; *m* 1952, Joan Christabel Draper; two *d*. *Educ:* Ipswich Sch.; University Coll., Oxford. Entered Min. of Health as Asst Princ., 1949; Princ., 1951; Princ. Private Sec. to Minister, 1955; Asst Sec., 1958; Under-Sec., Min. of Health, 1967–68, DHSS 1968–72; Dep. Sec., Cabinet Office, 1972–76. Chm., Rural Dispensing Cttee, 1987–91; Member: Exec. Council, Hosp. Saving Assoc., 1984–99; Exec. Cttee, Musicians Benevolent Fund, 1985–99 (Dep. Chm., 1996–99). *Address:* 12 Manor Gardens, Hampton, Middx TW12 2TU. *T:* (020) 8783 0848. *Club:* National Liberal.

BENNET, family name of **Earl of Tankerville**.

BENNETT, Alan; dramatist and actor; *b* 9 May 1934; *s* of Walter Bennett and Lilian Mary Peel; unmarried. *Educ:* Leeds Modern Sch.; Exeter Coll., Oxford (BA Modern History, 1957; Hon. Fellow, 1987). Jun. Lectr, Modern History, Magdalen Coll., Oxford, 1960–62. Trustee, National Gall., 1993–98. Hon. FRA 2000. Hon. DLitt Leeds, 1990. Co-author and actor, Beyond the Fringe, Royal Lyceum, Edinburgh, 1960, Fortune, London, 1961 and Golden, NY, 1962; author and actor, On the Margin (TV series), 1966; *stage plays:* Forty Years On, Apollo, 1968; Getting On, Queen's, 1971; Habeas Corpus, Lyric, 1973; The Old Country, Queen's, 1977; Enjoy, Vaudeville, 1980; Kafka's Dick, Royal Court, 1986; Single Spies (double bill: A Question of Attribution; An Englishman Abroad (also dir)), NT, 1988; The Wind in the Willows (adapted), NT, 1990; The Madness of George III, NT, 1991; Talking Heads, Comedy, 1992 and 1996; The Lady in the Van, Queen's, 1999; *BBC TV films:* A Day Out, 1972; Sunset Across the Bay, 1975; *TV Plays for LWT*, 1978–79: Doris and Doreen; The Old Crowd; Me! I'm Afraid of Virginia Woolf; All Day on the Sands; Afternoon Off; One Fine Day; *BBC TV plays:* A Little Outing, A Visit from Miss Prothero, 1977; Intensive Care, Say Something Happened, Our Winnie, Marks, A Woman of No Importance, Rolling Home; An Englishman Abroad, 1983; The Insurance Man, 1986; Talking Heads (series), 1988 (adapted for stage comedy, 1992); 102 Boulevard Haussmann, 1991; A Question of Attribution, 1991; Talking Heads 2 (series), 1998; Telling Tales (series), 2000; *BBC TV documentary:* Dinner at Noon, 1988; Portrait or Bust, 1994; The Abbey, 1995; *Channel 4:* Poetry in Motion, 1990; Poetry in Motion 2, 1992; *feature films:* A Private Function, 1984; Prick Up Your Ears, 1987; The Madness of King George, 1995. *Publications:* (with Cook, Miller and Moore) Beyond the Fringe, 1962; Forty Years On, 1969; Getting On, 1972; Habeas Corpus, 1973; The Old Country, 1978; Enjoy, 1980; Office Suite, 1981; Objects of Affection, 1982; A Private Function, 1984; The Writer in Disguise, 1985; Prick Up Your Ears (screenplay), 1987; Two Kafka Plays, 1987; Talking Heads, 1988 (Hawthornden Prize, 1989); Single Spies, 1989; The Lady in the Van, 1990; Poetry in Motion, 1990; The Wind in the Willows (adaptation), 1991; The Madness of George III, 1992; (jtly) Poetry in Motion 2, 1992; Writing Home, 1994 (collected articles); The Madness of King George (screenplay), 1995; The Clothes They Stood Up In, 1998; The Complete Talking Heads, 1998; The Lady in the Van, 2000; Father! Father! Burning Bright, 2000. *Address:* c/o Peters Fraser & Dunlop, Drury House, 34–43 Russell Street, WC2B 5HA. *T:* (020) 7344 1000.

BENNETT, (Albert) Edward; Director, G24 Nuclear Safety Assistance Co-ordination Centre, 1992–95, and Directorate of Nuclear Safety, Industry and the Environment, and Civil Protection (formerly of Nuclear Safety and Control of Chemical Pollution), 1987–95, European Commission; *b* 11 Sept. 1931; *s* of Albert Edward and Frances Ann Bennett; *m* 1957, Jean Louise Paston-Cooper; two *s*. *Educ:* University Coll. Sch., Hampstead; London Hosp. Med. Coll. MB BS London; FFCM 1972, FFOM 1984. Surgeon Lieut, RN, 1957–60; Senior Lectr, Dept of Clinical Epidemiology and Social Medicine, St. Thomas's Hosp. Med. Sch., 1964–70; Dir, Health Services Evaluation Gp, Univ. of Oxford, 1970–77; Prof. and Head of Dept of Clinical Epidemiology and Social Medicine, St George's Hosp. Med. Sch., Univ. of London, 1974–81; Director: Health and Safety Directorate, EEC, 1981–87. Hon. Editor, Internat. Jl of Epidemiology, 1977–81. *Publications:* Questionnaires in Medicine, 1975; (ed) Communications between Doctors and Patients, 1976; (ed) Recent Advances in Community Medicine, 1978; numerous sci. reports and contribs on epidemiology of chronic disease and evaluation of health services. *Recreations:* opera, gardening, browsing. *Address:* The Walled Garden, Liston, Sudbury, Suffolk CO10 7HT. *T:* (01787) 374746.
See also N. E. F. Bennett.

BENNETT, Andrew Francis; MP (Lab) Denton and Reddish, since 1983 (Stockport North, Feb. 1974–1983); teacher; *b* Manchester, 9 March 1939; *m*; two *s* one *d*. *Educ:* Birmingham Univ. (BSocSc). Joined Labour Party, 1957; Member, Oldham Borough Council, 1964–74. Member, National Union of Teachers. Contested (Lab) Knutsford, 1970; an Opposition spokesperson on educn, 1983–88. Jt Chm., Select Cttee on Envmt, Transport and Regl Affairs, 1997– (Chm., Envmt Sub-Cttee, 1997–). Interested especially in environment and education. *Recreations:* photography, walking, climbing. *Address:* 28 Brownsville Road, Stockport SK4 4PF; House of Commons, SW1A 0AA.

BENNETT, Andrew John, CMG 1998; Chief Natural Resources Adviser, Department for International Development (formerly Overseas Development Administration, Foreign and Commonwealth Office), since 1987; *b* 25 April 1942; *s* of Leonard Charles Bennett and Edna Mary Bennett (*née* Harding); *m* 1996, Yin Yin Jackson. *Educ:* St Edward's Sch., Oxford; University Coll. of N Wales (BSc Agr Scis 1965); Univ. of West Indies, Trinidad (DipTropAg 1967); Univ. of Reading (MSc Crop Protection 1970). VSO Kenya, 1965–66; Agricl Officer (Research), Govt of St Vincent, 1967–69; Maize Agronomist, Govt of Malawi, 1971–74; Crop Develt Manager, 1976–78, Chief Research Officer. 1978–79, S Region, Sudan; Asst Agricl Adviser, ODA, 1980–83; Natural Resources Adviser (ODA), SE Asia Develt Div., Bangkok, 1983–85; Head, British Develt Div. in Pacific (ODA), Fiji, 1985–87. FRSA 2000. Hon. DSc Cranfield, 1999. *Recreations:* walking, gardening. *Address:* Department for International Development, 1 Palace Street, SW1E 5HE.

BENNETT, Clive Ronald Reath, CEng; Chief Executive, Driver and Vehicle Licensing Authority, since 2000; *b* 20 Dec. 1947; *s* of Ron and Betty Bennett; *m* 1970, Pauline Weeks; two *d*. *Educ:* Hatfield Poly. (BSc). CEng 1971. Design Engr, Norton Abrasives Ltd, 1970–71; Industrial Engr, Radiomobile (Smiths Industries), 1971–73; Rank Xerox (UK) Ltd: Technical Service and Supply Dir, 1973–83; Gen. Manager, Supplies Distribn, 1983–84; Gen. Manager, Distribn, Polycell Products, 1984–87; Business Excellence Dir, Sara Lee Household and Personal Care, 1987–94; Gp Ops Dir, Norton Health Care, 1994–99. *Recreations:* music, swimming. *Address:* Driver and Vehicle Licensing Authority, Longview Road, Morriston, Swansea SA6 7JL. *T:* (01792) 782363.

BENNETT, Corinne Gillian, MBE 1988; FSA; historic buildings consultant, 1996–98; Cathedrals Architect at English Heritage, 1992–96; *b* 3 March 1935; *d* of Gilbert Wilson and Lucile (*née* Terroux); *m* 1979, Keith Charles Hugh Bennett. *Educ:* University Coll. London (BA Hons Arch. 1957; Inst. of Archaeology, London Univ. (Dip. Conservation of Historic Monuments 1964). ARIBA 1959. FSA 1996. Assistant Architect: Powell & Moya, 1958–61; Manning & Clamp, 1961–62; Architect, Ancient Monuments Br., MPBW, 1963–68; joined Purcell Miller Tritton, Associate, 1968, Partner, 1972–92. Consulting Surveyor, Archdeacons of Rochester Dio., 1969–84; Architect, Dean and Chapter of Winchester, 1974–89; Consultant Architect, Brighton BC (for Royal

Pavilion), 1981–91. Mem., Cathedrals Fabric Commn for England, 1996–. DHS 1979, DCHS 1988, DGCHS 2000. *Recreations:* opera, walking, gardening. *Club:* Arts.

BENNETT, Douglas Simon; Chief Executive, National Society for Epilepsy, 1997–2000; *b* 18 Aug. 1958. *Educ:* Bristol Univ. (LLB); Brunel Univ. (MA Public Sector Mgt 1989). Trainee Solicitor, Slaughter & May, 1980–82; admitted Solicitor, 1982; Society of Voluntary Associations: Inner London Co-ordinator, 1982–84; Asst Dir, 1984–86; Dep. Dir, 1986–88; Dir, Age Concern, Brent, 1989; Head of Planning, British Red Cross, 1989–97. *Recreations:* meals with friends, walking, swimming, reading, going to cinema and theatre.

BENNETT, Dudley Paul; His Honour Judge Dudley Bennett; a Circuit Judge, since 1993; *b* 4 Aug. 1948; *s* of late Patrick James Bennett and of Mary Bennett (*née* Edmondson); *m* 1986, Patricia Ann Martin; two *d*. *Educ:* Bradfield Coll.; LSE (LLB). Called to the Bar, Inner Temple, 1972; Recorder of the Crown Court, 1988–93. *Recreations:* travel, gardening, Afghan Hounds. *Address:* The Crown Court, Canal Street, Nottingham NG1 7EJ. *Club:* United Services (Nottingham).

BENNETT, Edward; *see* Bennett, A. E.

BENNETT, Air Vice Marshal Sir Erik Peter, KBE 1990; CB 1984; retired from RAF, 1991; Commander, Sultan of Oman's Air Force (in the rank of Air Marshal), 1974–90; *s* of Robert Francis and Anne Myra Bennett. *Educ:* The King's Hospital, Dublin. Air Adviser to King Hussein, 1958–62; RAF Staff College, 1963; Jt Services Staff Coll., 1968; RAF Coll. of Air Warfare, 1971. Order of Istiqlal (Jordan), 1960; Order of Oman, 1980; Order of Merit (Oman), 1989; Order of Sultan Qaboos (Oman), 1985; Medal of Honour (Oman), 1989. *Recreations:* riding, sailing, big game fishing. *Address:* Al Hail Farm, Seeb-Hail Al Awahir, PO Box 1751, Postal Code 111, Sultanate of Oman. *Clubs:* Royal Air Force, Beefsteak, Pratt's.

BENNETT, Rt Hon. Sir Frederic (Mackarness), Kt 1964; PC 1985; DL; *b* 2 Dec. 1918; 2nd *s* of late Sir Ernest Bennett and of Lady (Marguerite) Bennett; *m* 1945, Marion Patricia, *e d* of Cecil Burnham, OBE, FRCSE. *Educ:* Westminster. Served War of 1939–45, enlisted Middx Yeo., 1939; commissioned RA, 1940; commended for gallantry, 1941; Military Experimental Officer in Petroleum Warfare Dept, 1943–46, when released with rank of Major. TA&VRA, 1973–83. Called to English Bar, Lincoln's Inn, 1946, Southern Rhodesian Bar, 1947. Observer, Greek Communist War, 1947–49; Diplomatic correspondent, Birmingham Post, 1950–52. Contested (C) Burslem, 1945, Ladywood Div. of Birmingham, 1950. MP (C): Reading N, 1951–55; Torquay, Dec. 1955–1974; Torbay, 1974–87. PPS: to Under-Sec. of State, Home Office, 1953–55, to Minister of Supply, 1956–57, to Paymaster-Gen., 1957–59, and to Pres. of Bd of Trade, 1959–61. Chm. Exec. Cttee, CPA Gen. Council, 1971–73; Vice Pres., Council of Europe and WEU Assembly, 1979–87; Chairman, 1979–87: Pol Affairs Cttee, Council of Europe; Gen. Affairs Cttee, WEU; Federated Gp, Eur. Democrats and Christian Democrats. Lord of the Manor of Mawddwy. Co-Pres., ESU of Pakistan, 1988–. DL Greater London, 1990. Freeman, City of London, 1984. Hon. Dr of Law Istanbul, 1984. Comdr, Order of Phœnix, Greece, 1963; (Sithari) Star of Pakistan, 1st cl., 1964; Order of Al-Istiqlal, 1st cl., Jordan, 1980; Comdr, Order of Isabel la Católica, Spain, 1982; Order of Hilal-i-Quaid-i-Azam, Pakistan, 1983; Commander's Cross, Order of Merit, FRG, 1989; Order (first class) of Polonia Restituta, Poland, 1990 (Comdr, 1977; Grand Comdr's Cross, 1984); Knight of Vitezi, Hungary, 1990; Order of Cross of Terra Mariana (first class), Estonia, 1996; Knight's Cross, Order of Merit, Hungary, 2001. *Publications:* Speaking Frankly, 1960; Detente and Security in Europe, 1976; China and European Security, 1978; The Near and Middle East and Western European Security, 1979, 2nd edn 1980; Impact of Individual and Corporate Incentives on Productivity and Standard of Living, 1980; Fear is the Key: Ulster; Reds under the Bed, or the Enemy at the Gate—and Within, 1979, 3rd edn 1982. *Recreations:* shooting, fishing, yachting. *Address:* Cwmllecoediog, Aberangell, near Machynlleth, Powys SY20 9QP. *T:* (01650) 511430, *Fax:* (01650) 511469. *Clubs:* Carlton, Anglo-Belgian; Royal Torbay Yacht (Torquay).

BENNETT, His Honour Harry Graham; QC 1968; a Circuit Judge, 1972–91; Designated Circuit Judge, Leeds, 1988–91; *b* 19 Sept. 1921; *s* of Ernest and Alice Mary Bennett, Cleckheaton, Yorks; *m* 1987, Elizabeth, *widow* of Judge Allister Lonsdale. *Educ:* Whitcliffe Mount Grammar Sch., Cleckheaton; King's Coll., London. Royal Artillery, 1943–47. Called to Bar, Gray's Inn, 1948. Recorder: Doncaster, 1966–68; York, 1968–71 (Hon. Recorder, 1972–93); Crown Court, 1972; Dep. Chm., ER of Yorks QS, 1964–71. Chm., Agricl Land Tribunal (N Area), 1967–72; Chm., Cttee of Inquiry into Police Interrogation Procedures in NI, 1978–79.

BENNETT, Hon. Sir Hugh (Peter Derwyn), Kt 1995; **Hon. Mr Justice Bennett;** a Judge of the High Court of Justice, Family Division, since 1995; *b* 8 Sept. 1943; *s* of late Peter Ward Bennett, OBE, and Priscilla Ann Bennett; *m* 1969, Elizabeth (*née* Landon); one *s* three *d*. *Educ:* Haileybury and ISC; Churchill College, Cambridge (MA). Called to the Bar, Inner Temple, 1966, Bencher, 1993; an Assistant Recorder, 1987; QC 1988; a Recorder, 1990–95. Presiding Judge, NE Circuit, 1999–. Mem., Supreme Court Rule Cttee, 1988–92; Chm. (part-time), Betting Levy Appeal Tribunal, 1989–95. Hon. Legal Advr, Sussex County Playing Fields Assoc., 1988–95. Chm., Sussex Assoc. for Rehabilitation of Offenders, 1998–. Fellow of Woodard Corp., 1987–99; Mem. Council, Lancing Coll., 1981–95. *Recreations:* cricket, tennis, shooting, fishing. *Address:* Royal Courts of Justice, Strand, WC2A 2LL. *Clubs:* Pilgrims, MCC; Sussex.

See also Sir H. J. F. S. Cholmeley, Bt.

BENNETT, Hywel Thomas; actor; director; *b* Wales, 8 April 1944; *s* of Gordon Bennett and Sarah Gwen Bennett (*née* Lewis); *m* 1st, 1967, Cathy McGowan (marr. diss. 1988); one *d*; 2nd, 1996, Sandra Elayne Fulford. *Educ:* Henry Thornton Grammar School, Clapham; RADA (scholarship). *Stage:* Nat. Youth Theatre for 5 years; repertory, Salisbury and Leatherhead; first major roles in The Screwtape Letters and A Smashing Day, Arts Th., 1966; Shakespeare at Mermaid, Young Vic, Shaw Theatres; repertory, 1972–77 (roles included Jimmy Porter, in Look Back in Anger, Belgrade, and Hamlet, S Africa); Otherwise Engaged, Comedy, 1977; Night Must Fall, Shaw Th., 1977; Levantine, Her Majesty's, 1979; Terra Nova, Chichester, 1980; Fly Away Home, Lyric, Hammersmith, 1983; She Stoops to Conquer, Nat. Theatre, 1985; Toad of Toad Hall; Three Sisters, Albery, 1987; Edinburgh Festival, 1967 and 1990 (Long John Silver, in Treasure Island); *directed:* plays at provincial theatres incl. Lincoln, Leatherhead, Birmingham, Coventry, Sheffield and Cardiff; *films:* The Family Way, 1966; Twisted Nerve, 1968; The Virgin Soldiers, 1969; Loot, 1970; The Buttercup Chain, 1971; Endless Night, 1971; Alice in Wonderland, 1972; Twilight Zone, 1987; Murder Elite, 1990; War Zone, 1990; Age Unknown, 1992; Deadly Advice, 1994; Married to Malcolm, 1997; Misery Harbour, 1998; Nasty Neighbours, 1998; Vatel, 1999; Mary of Nazareth, 1999; *TV plays and films* include: Romeo and Juliet; The Idiot; A Month in the Country; Trust Me; Artemis 81; Frankie and Johnnie; The Other Side of Paradise; Murder Most Horrid; Frontiers; Karaoke; *TV series:* Malice Aforethought; Pennies from Heaven; Tinker, Tailor, Soldier, Spy; Shelley (10 series); Where the Buffalo Roam; Death of a Teddy Bear; The Consultant; Absent Friends; Myself a Mandarin; The Secret Agent; A Mind to Kill; Casualty; Virtual Murder; Neverwhere; Lock Stock; many radio plays, commercial voiceovers and film narrations. Hon. Fellow, Cardiff Univ., 1996. *Recreations:* fishing, golf, reading, walking. *Address:* c/o Gavin Barker Associates, 2D Wimpole Street, W1G 0EB. *T:* (020) 7499 4777. *Clubs:* Savile, Wig and Pen (Hon. Mem.).

BENNETT, Dr James Arthur; Director, Museum of the History of Science, and Fellow of Linacre College, University of Oxford, since 1994; *b* 2 April 1947; *s* of James Hutchinson Bennett and Margaret Anna Bennett (*née* McCune); *m* 1971, France Annie Ramette; two *d*. *Educ:* Grosvenor High Sch., Belfast; Clare Coll., Univ. of Cambridge (BA 1969; PhD 1974). Lectr, Univ. of Aberdeen, 1973–74; Archivist, Royal Astronomical Soc., 1974–1976; Curator of Astronomy, Nat. Maritime Mus. 1977–79; Curator, Whipple Mus. of Hist. of Sci., Cambridge, 1979–94; Sen. Res. Fellow, 1984–94, Sen. Tutor, 1992–94, Churchill Coll., Cambridge. Paul Bunge Prize, German Chemical Soc., 2001. *Publications:* The Mathematical Science of Christopher Wren, 1982; The Divided Circle, 1987; Church, State and Astronomy in Ireland, 1990; contrib. British Jl for Hist. of Sci., etc. *Recreation:* music. *Address:* Museum of the History of Science, Broad Street, Oxford OX1 3AZ. *T:* (01865) 277280.

BENNETT, Jana Eve, OBE 2000; Executive Vice President, Learning Channel, US Discovery Communications, Inc., since 1999; *b* 6 Nov. 1956; *d* of Gordon Willard Bennett and Elizabeth (*née* Cushing); *m* 1996, Richard Clemmow; one *s* one *d*. *Educ:* Bognor Regis Comprehensive Sch.; St Anne's Coll., Oxford (BA PPE); London Sch. of Econs (MSc with dist. Internat. Relns). Co-editor, Millennium, jl internat. relns; British Broadcasting Corporation: news trainee, 1978; news daily editor; series producer, then Ed., Antenna, 1987; Ed., Horizon, 1990; Head, BBC Science, 1994–97; Dir of BBC Prodn, and Dep. Chief Exec., BBC, 1997–99. FRTS 1999. *Publication:* The Disappeared: Argentina's dirty war, 1986. *Recreations:* mountaineering, travel, world music. *Address:* 7700 Wisconsin Avenue, Bethesda, MD 20814, USA. *T:* (301) 7715280, *Fax:* (301) 7713864.

BENNETT, Jeremy; *see* Bennett, John J. N.

BENNETT, John, MBE 1945; HM Senior Chief Inspector of Schools for Scotland, 1969–73; *b* 14 Nov. 1912; *m* 1940, Johanne R. McAlpine, MA; two *s* one *d*. *Educ:* Edinburgh Univ. MA (first class hons) 1934. Schoolmaster until 1951. Served War of 1939–45: Capt. REME, 79 Armd Div., 1940–46. HM Inspector of Schools, 1951. *Recreations:* mathematics, golf, bridge. *Address:* 35 Cadzow Drive, Cambuslang, Glasgow G72 8NF. *T:* (0141) 641 1058.

BENNETT, John Jerome Nelson, (Jeremy); independent producer; Director and Executive Producer, 3BM Television, since 1995; *b* 1 Dec. 1939; *s* of Denis Pengelley Bennett and Jill (*née* Nelson); *m* 1963, Tine Langkilde; three *s*. *Educ:* Haileybury; Clare Coll., Cambridge (Open Schol. in Hist.; MA); Copenhagen Univ. (Churchill Fellow). With British Council, 1963–65; BBC European Service, 1966–68; Producer/Dir, BBC TV documentaries, 1968–89; Producer, Richard Dimbleby Lecture, 1983–87; Exec. Producer, Contemporary Hist. Unit, 1989–92; freelance, 1993–95. *Productions* include: Cry Hungary, 1986 and 1996 (Blue Ribbon Award, American Film Fest.); Juan Carlos, King of All the Spaniards, 1980 and 1986; Alphabet: the Story of Writing (Silver Award, NY Film and TV Fest., 1980; Times Newcomer Award); Monty: in Love and War, 1987 (Blue Ribbon Award, American Film Fest.); Churchill, 1992; The Cuban Missile Crisis, 1992 (US Nat. Emmy Award); Chairman Mao: The Last Emperor, 1993; Hiroshima, 1995; The Suez Crisis, 1996; The Berlin Airlift, 1998; *TV histories of the BBC:* What Did You Do in the War, Auntie?, 1995; Auntie: The Inside Story, 1997. Chairman: Camberwell Soc., 1979–85; Southwark Envmt Trust, 1983–95; Groundwork Southwark, 1995–; Member: Bd, Cross River Partnership, 1995–; Bd, Groundwork Nat. Fedn, 1999–. Cross of Merit, Order of Vitez (Hungary), 1987. *Publication:* British Broadcasting and the Danish Resistance Movement 1940–45, 1966. *Recreations:* fishing, walking in Powys, the urban environment. *Address:* 30 Grove Lane, Camberwell, SE5 8ST. *T:* (020) 7703 9971.

BENNETT, Rt Rev. Manu Augustus, ONZ 1989; CMG 1981; DD; *b* 10 Feb. 1916; *s* of Rt Rev. F. A. Bennett, Bishop of Aotearoa, 1928–50, and Alice Rangioue Bennett; *m* 1944, Kathleen Clark; one *d*. *Educ:* Victoria Univ. Coll.; Univ. of Hawaii. BSc 1954. Deacon, 1939; Priest, 1940; Vicar of Tauranga, Te Puke Maori District, Dio. Waiapu, 1940–44; Chaplain to 2 NZEF, 1944–46; Pastor of Rangitikei South-Manawatu Pastorate, Dio. Wellington, 1946–52; Asst Vicar of Church of Holy Nativity, Honolulu, 1953–54; Pastor of Wellington Pastorate, 1952–57; Vicar of Ohinemutu Pastorate, Waikato, 1964–68; Bishop of Aotearoa, 1968–81. Nat. Council of Churches Chaplain, Dept of Justice. Mem., Waitangi Tribunal on Treaty Matters. Faculty Mem., Native Ministries Consortium, Vancouver Sch. of Theology, Univ. of BC; Kaumatua, Te Rau Kahikatea Unit, St John's Coll., Auckland. Hon. DD: Jackson Coll., 1964; Waikato, 1997. *Address:* 25c Eason Street, Rotorua, New Zealand.

BENNETT, Margaret Joan; Chief Executive, National Library for the Blind, since 1996; *b* 22 Dec. 1960; *d* of Rev. Canon Ian Frederick Bennett and Dr Rachel Bennett; *m* 1987, David Hill (marr. diss. 1994); one *s*. *Educ:* St Anne's Coll., Oxford (BA Hons PPE 1983). Chartered Accountant, KPMG, 1983–87; Finance Officer, West Midlands Arts, 1987–89; Asst Dir, North West Arts, 1989–91; Central Services Dir, Nottingham Community Housing Assoc., 1992–96. *Recreations:* the arts, reading, walking, music, cooking. *Address:* (home) 23 Endcliffe Rise Road, Sheffield S11 8RU. *T:* (0114) 268 3053; (office) National Library for the Blind, Cromwell Road, Stockport SK6 2SG. *T:* (0161) 355 2000.

BENNETT, Prof. Martin Arthur, FRS 1995; Professor, Research School of Chemistry, Australian National University, 1991–2000, Emeritus Professor, since 2001; *b* 11 Aug. 1935; *s* of late Arthur Edward Charles Bennett and Dorothy Ivy Bennett; *m* 1964, Rae Elizabeth Mathews; two *s*. *Educ:* Haberdashers' Aske's Hampstead Sch.; Imperial Coll. of Science and Technology, London (BSc 1957; PhD 1960; DSc 1974). FAA 1980. Postdoctoral Fellow, Univ. of S California, 1960–61; Turner and Newall Fellow, 1961–63, Lectr, 1963–67, UCL; Fellow, 1967–70, Sen. Fellow, 1970–79, Professorial Fellow, 1979–91, Res. Sch. of Chem., ANU. Adjunct Prof., RMIT, 2000–. Vis. Prof. and Vis. Fellow, univs in Canada, Germany, USA, Japan, China and NZ. Numerous awards, Aust. learned instns; Nyholm Medal, RSC, 1991; Max Planck Soc. Res. Award, 1994. *Publications:* chapters on Ruthenium in Comprehensive Organometallic Chemistry; contribs to learned jls. *Recreations:* golf, reading, foreign languages, esp. German and Japanese. *Address:* Research School of Chemistry, Australian National University, Canberra, ACT 0200, Australia. *T:* (2) 62493639; 21 Black Street, Yarralumla, ACT 2600, Australia. *T:* (2) 62824154.

BENNETT, Mrs Mary Letitia Somerville, MA; Principal, St Hilda's College, Oxford, 1965–80, Hon. Fellow 1980; Pro-Vice-Chancellor, Oxford University, 1979–80; *b* 9 Jan. 1913; *o c* of Rt Hon. H. A. L. Fisher, OM, and Lettice Ilbert; *m* 1955, John Sloman Bennett, CMG (*d* 1990). *Educ:* Oxford High Sch.; Somerville Coll. (Schol.); 2nd Cl.

Mods, 1st Cl. Lit. Hum.; Hon. Fellow, 1977. Jt Broadcasting Cttee, 1940–41; Transcription Service of BBC, 1941–45; Colonial Office, 1945–56. Mem., Hebdomodal Council, Oxford Univ., 1973–79. Hon. Sec., Society for the Promotion of Roman Studies, 1960–85. *Publication:* The Ilberts in India, 1995. *Address:* Rock Cottage, Thursley, Surrey GU8 6QJ; 25A Alma Place, Oxford OX4 1JW. *Club:* University Women's.

BENNETT, Neil Edward Francis; City Editor, Sunday Telegraph, since 1995; *b* 15 May 1965; *s* of Albert Edward Bennett, *qv*; *m* 1992, Carole Kenyon; two *d*. *Educ:* Westminster Sch.; University Coll. London (BA Medieval Archaeol.); City Univ. (Dip. Journalism). Staff writer, Investors Chronicle, 1987–89; The Times: Banking Corresp., 1989–92; Ed., Tempus column, 1992–94; Dep. Business Editor, 1994–95. Principal financial columnist, jagnotes-euro.com, 1999–2000. Jun. Wincott Foundn Award, 1992; Business Journalist of the Year, British Press Awards, 1998, 1999. *Recreations:* running, antiquarian book collecting, Irish Terriers. *Address:* Salters Hall, 4 Fore Street, EC2Y 5DT. *T:* (020) 7538 7901. *Club:* Capital.

BENNETT, Nicholas Jerome; JP; Chief Executive, Association of Consulting Engineers, since 1998; *b* 7 May 1949; *s* of Peter Ramsden Bennett and late Antonia Mary Flanagan; *m* 1995, Ruth, *er d* of Andrew and Alma Whitelaw, Barnham Broom, Norfolk. *Educ:* Sedgehill Sch.; Polytechnic of North London (BA Hons Philosophy); Univ. of London Inst. of Educn (PGCE Distinction); Univ. of Sussex (MA). Educnl publishing, 1974; schoolmaster, 1976–85; educn officer, 1985–87; Advr on public affairs, Price Waterhouse, 1993–98. Councillor (C), London Borough of Lewisham, 1974–82 (Leader of the Opposition, 1979–81); co-opted Mem., ILEA Educn Cttee, 1978–81. Mem., FEFCE, 1992–97. Contested (C): St Pancras N, 1973 and Greenwich, by-elec. 1974, GLC elections; Hackney Central, 1979. MP (C) Pembroke, 1987–92; contested (C): Pembroke, 1992; Reading W, 1997. PPS to Minister of State, Department of Transport, 1990; Parly Under-Sec. of State, Welsh Office, 1990–92. Member: Select Cttee on Welsh Affairs, 1987–90; Select Cttee on Procedure, 1988–90; Vice-Chm. (Wales), Cons. backbench Party Organisation Cttee, 1990. Chm., Nat. Council for Civil Protection, 1990. Mem., Western Front Assoc. FRSA 1998. JP, SW Div., Inner London, 1998. *Publication:* (contrib.) Primary Headship in the 1990s, 1989. *Recreations:* swimming, history, transport, browsing in second-hand bookshops, cinema, small scale gardening, visiting battlefields of First and Second World War. *Address:* 18 Upper Park Road, Bromley, Kent BR1 3MT. *T:* and *Fax:* (020) 8466 1363; *e-mail:* 106100.1253@compuserve.com.

BENNETT, Nicholas John, CEng, FIEE; Director General, Scrutiny and Analysis, Ministry of Defence, since 2001; *b* 30 Sept. 1948; *s* of John Douglas Bennett and Betty Yvonne Bennett (*née* Harker); *m* 1st, 1971, Susan Mary Worthington (*d* 1997); one *s* one *d*; 2nd, 2000, Lesley Ann Davie (*née* Thorpe). *Educ:* Bishop Wordsworth Sch., Salisbury; Brunel Univ. (BTech Hons Electronic Engrg 1971). CEng 1973 ; FIEE 1986 . Ministry of Defence: HQ No 90 (S) Gp, 1971–77; A&AEE, 1977–80; Hd, Engrg Design, RAF Signals Engrg Estabt, 1980–83; Principal D Air Radio, 1983–84; Asst Chief Design Engr, RAF Signals Engrg Estabt, 1984–86; Asst Dir, European Fighter Aircraft, 1986–89; rcds 1990; Hd, Civilian Mgt (Specialists) 2, 1991–92; Dir, Ops and Engrg, NATO European Fighter Aircraft Agency, 1992–96; Chief Exec., Specialist Procurement Services, 1996–99; Dir Gen., Human Resources, Defence Logistics Orgn, 1999–2001. *Recreations:* cricket, ski-ing, practical study of wine. *Address:* Ministry of Defence, Northumberland House, Northumberland Avenue, WC2N 5BP.

BENNETT, Patrick; QC 1969; a Recorder of the Crown Court, 1972–97; *b* 12 Jan. 1924; *s* of Michael Bennett; *m* 1951, Lyle Reta Pope; two *d*. *Educ:* Bablake Sch., Coventry; Magdalen Coll., Oxford. State Scholar, 1941, MA, BCL 1949. Served RNVR, 1943–46, Sub Lt. Called to Bar, Gray's Inn, 1949, Bencher 1976, Master of Students, 1980; Asst Recorder, Coventry, 1969–71; Dep. Chm., Lindsey QS, 1970–71. Mem., Mental Health Act Commn, 1984–86. Fellow: Internat. Soc. of Barristers, 1984; Nat. Inst. of Advocacy, 1980. Pres., Thomas More Soc., 1990–93. *Publications:* Assessment of Damages in Personal Injury and Fatal Accidents, 1980; The Common Jury, 1986; Trial Techniques, 1986. *Recreations:* food, flying. *Address:* (home) 22 Wynnstay Gardens, W8 6UR. *T:* (020) 7937 2110; 233 rue Nationale, Boulogne sur Mer, France. *T:* 321913339. *Club:* Spartan Flying (Denham).

BENNETT, Philip Hugh Penberthy, CBE 1972; FRIBA; FCIArb; Consultant, T. P. Bennett Partnership, architects, since 1980 (Partner, 1948–80, Senior Partner, 1967–80); *b* 14 April 1919; *o s* of late Sir Thomas Penberthy Bennett, KBE, FRIBA, and late Mary Langdon Edis; *m* 1943, Jeanne Heal; one *s* one *d*. *Educ:* Highgate Sch.; Emmanuel Coll., Cambridge (MA). Lieut (G) RNVR, 1940–46. Principal works: town centres at Bootle and Stratford (London); head offices for Norwich Union Insce Socs, Ford Motor Co. and other commercial cos; dept stores for United Africa Co. in Ghana and Nigeria, Bentalls (Kingston) and Fenwicks (Newcastle); extensions to Middlesex Hosp.; hostel for Internat. Students Trust; Cunard Internat. Hotel; flats for local authorities and private developers; buildings for airfield and dock develt. Chm., Building Regulations Adv. Cttee (DoE), 1965–77; former RIBA rep. on Jt Contracts Tribunal (Chm. 1973–78) and Nat. Jt Consultative Cttee (Chm. 1970); Mem. other cttees of RIBA and NEDO; Governor: Sch. of Building, 1952–72; Vauxhall Coll. of Further Educn, 1972–77; Member: Home Office Deptl Cttee enquiring into Fire Service, 1967–70; Adv. Council for Energy Conservation, 1974–76. Dir, BEC Building Trust Ltd, 1984–91. *Publications:* Architectural Practice and Procedure, 1981; chapter on building, in Britain 1984, 1963; articles in Building, Financial Times, etc. *Recreations:* travel, drawing, theatre. *Address:* Grey Walls, Park Lane, Aldeburgh, Suffolk IP15 5PH. *T:* (01728) 452766.

BENNETT, Gen. Sir Phillip (Harvey), AC 1985 (AO 1981); KBE 1983; DSO 1969; Chairman, Australian War Memorial Foundation, since 1996; National President, Order of Australia Association, 1997–2000; *b* 27 Dec. 1928; *m* 1955, Margaret Heywood; two *s* one *d*. *Educ:* Perth Modern Sch.; Royal Mil. Coll.; jssc, rcds, psc (Aust.). Served, 1950–57: 3rd Bn RAR, Korea (despatches 1951), Sch. of Infantry (Instr), 25 Cdn Bde, Korea, 1952–53, Pacific Is Regt, PNG, and 16th Bn Cameron Highlanders of WA; Commando training, Royal Marines, England, Malta and Cyprus, 1957–58; OC 2 Commando Co., Melb., 1958–61; Aust. Staff Coll., 1961–62; Sen. Instr, then Chief Instr, Officer Cadet Sch., Portsea, 1962–65; AAG Directorate of Personal Services, AHQ, 1965–67; Co. 1 RAR, 1967–69 (served Vietnam; DSO); Exchange Instr, Jt Services Staff Coll., England, 1969–71; COL Directorate of Co-ordination and Organization, AHQ, 1971–73; COS HQ Fd Force Comd, 1974–75; RCDS, England, 1976; Comdr 1st Div., 1977–79; Asst Chief of Def. Force Staff, 1979–82; Chief of General Staff, 1982–84; Chief of Defence Force, Australia, 1984–87; Governor, Tasmania, 1987–95. Hon. Col, Royal Tasmania Regt, 1987–95. KStJ 1988. Hon. LLD: New South Wales, 1987; Tasmania, 1992. *Recreations:* reading, golf. *Address:* c/o Commonwealth Club, ACT 2600, Australia. *Clubs:* Commonwealth, University House (Canberra).

BENNETT, Ralph Featherstone; *b* 3 Dec. 1923; *o s* of late Mr and Mrs Ralph J. P. Bennett, Plymouth, Devon; *m* 1948, Delia Marie, *o d* of late Mr and Mrs J. E. Baxter, Franklyns, Plymouth; two *s* two *d*. *Educ:* Plympton Grammar Sch.; Plymouth Technical Coll. Articled pupil to City of Plymouth Transport Manager, 1940–43; Techn. Asst, Plymouth City Transp., 1943–54; Michelin Tyre Co., 1954–55; Dep. Gen. Man., City of Plymouth Transp. Dept, 1955–58; Gen. Manager: Gt Yarmouth Transp. Dept, 1958–60; Bolton Transp. Dept, 1960–65; Manchester City Transp., 1965–68; London Transport Executive (formerly London Transport Board): Mem., 1968–71; Dep. Chm., 1971–78; Chief Exec., 1975–78; Chairman: London Transport Executive, 1978–80; London Transport International, 1976–80. Pres., Confedn of Road Passenger Transport, 1977–78; Vice-President: Internat. Union of Public Transport, 1978–81; CIT, 1979–82. CEng; FIMechE; FCIT; FRSA. *Address:* 3 Old Kennels Close, Winchester, Hants SO22 4LB. *T:* (01962) 867362.

BENNETT, Raymond Clayton Watson; His Honour Judge Raymond Bennett; a Circuit Judge, since 1989; *b* 20 June 1939; *s* of Harold Watson and Doris Helena Bennett (previously Watson); *m* 1965, Elaine Margaret Haworth; one *s* one *d*. *Educ:* Bury Grammar Sch.; Manchester Univ. (LLB). Solicitor, 1964–72; called to the Bar, Middle Temple, 1972; practising barrister, 1972–89; an Asst Recorder, 1984; a Recorder, 1988. Hon. Recorder, Burnley, 1998. *Recreations:* cycling, tennis, reading, painting, gardening, golf. *Address:* c/o The Crown Court, Hammerton Street, Burnley BB11 1XD.

BENNETT, Richard Clement W.; *see* Wheeler-Bennett.

BENNETT, Sir Richard Rodney, Kt 1998; CBE 1977; composer; Visiting Professor of Composition, Royal Academy of Music, since 1995; *b* 29 March 1936; *s* of H. Rodney and Joan Esther Bennett. *Educ:* Leighton Park Sch., Reading; Royal Academy of Music. Works performed, 1953–, at many Festivals in Europe, S Africa, USA, Canada, Australia, etc. Has written music for numerous films including: Indiscreet; The Devil's Disciple; Only Two Can Play; The Wrong Arm of the Law; Heavens Above; Billy Liar; One Way Pendulum; The Nanny; Far from the Madding Crowd; Billion Dollar Brain; Secret Ceremony; The Buttercup Chain; Figures in a Landscape; Nicholas and Alexandra; Lady Caroline Lamb; Voices; Murder on the Orient Express (SFTA award; Academy Award Nomination; Ivor Novello award, PRS); Permission to Kill; Equus (BAFTA Nomination); The Brinks Job; Yanks (BAFTA Nomination); Return of the Soldier; Four Weddings and a Funeral; Swann; also the music for television series: The Christians; L. P. Hartley trilogy; The Ebony Tower; Tender is the Night; The Charmer; Poor Little Rich Girl; The Hiding Place; The Story of Anne Frank; Gormenghast. Commissioned to write 2 full-length operas for Sadler's Wells: The Mines of Sulphur, 1965, A Penny for a Song, 1968; commnd to write opera for Covent Garden: Victory, 1970; other compositions include: Symphony No 1, 1965; Symphony No 2, 1967; (children's opera) All the King's Men, 1969; Guitar Concerto, 1970; Spells (choral work), 1975; Sonnets to Orpheus, 1979; Symphony No 3, 1987; Concerto for Stan Getz, 1990; Concerto for Trumpet, 1993; Partita, 1995; Reflections on a 16th Century Tune, 1999; Rondel (for large jazz ensemble), 1999; On Christmas Day (choral work), 1999; Seven Country Dances (for oboe and strings), 2000. *Publications include:* chamber music, orchestral music, educational music, song cycles, etc; articles for periodicals, about music. *Recreations:* cinema, modern jazz, painting. *Address:* c/o Novello & Co., 8–9 Frith Street, W1D 3JB.

BENNETT, Prof. Robert John, PhD; FBA 1991; Professor of Geography, and Fellow of St Catharine's College, University of Cambridge, since 1996; *b* 23 March 1948; *s* of Thomas Edward Bennett and Kathleen Elizabeth Robson; *m* 1971, Elizabeth Anne Allen; two *s*. *Educ:* Taunton's Sch., Southampton; St Catharine's Coll., Cambridge (BA 1970; PhD 1974). Lecturer: University Coll. London, 1973–78; Univ. of Cambridge, 1978–85; Fellow and Dir of Studies, 1978–85, Tutor, 1981–85, Fitzwilliam Coll., Cambridge; Prof. of Geography, LSE, 1985–96. Leverhulme Personal Res. Prof., 1996–2000. Vis. Prof., Univ. California at Berkeley, 1978; Guest Schol., Brookings Instn, Washington DC, 1978, 1979, 1981; Hubert Humphrey Inst. Fellow, Univ. Minnesota, 1985; Univ. Fellow, Macquarie, 1987; Snyder Lectr, Toronto, 1988. Treas., IBG, 1990–93; Vice Pres., RGS, 1993–95 and 1998–2001 (Mem. Council, 1990–2001); Chm., Council of British Geography, 1995–97. MInstD. Murchison Award, 1982, Founder's Medal, 1998, RGS. Gen. Editor, Government and Policy, 1982–; European Co-Editor, Geographical Analysis, 1985–88. *Publications:* Environmental Systems (with R. J. Chorley), 1978; Spatial Time Series, 1979; Geography of Public Finance, 1980; (ed) European Progress in Spatial Analysis, 1981; (ed with N. Wrigley) Quantitative Geography, 1981; Central Grants to Local Government, 1982; (with K. C. Tan) Optimal Control of Spatial Systems, 1984; Intergovernmental Financial Relations in Austria, 1985; (with A. G. Wilson) Mathematical Methods in Human Geography and Planning, 1985; (ed with H. Zimmerman) Local Business Taxes in Britain and Germany, 1986; (with G. Krebs) Die Wirkung Kommunaler Steuern auf die Steuerliche Belastung der Kapitalbildung, 1987; (with G. Krebs) Local Business Taxes in Britain and Germany, 1988; (ed) Territory and Administration in Europe, 1989; (ed) Decentralisation, Local Governments and Markets, 1990; (with G. Krebs) Local Economic Development Initiatives in Britain and Germany, 1991; (ed with R. C. Estall) Global Change and Challenge, 1991; (with A. McCoshan) Enterprise and Human Resource Development, 1993; (jtly) Local Empowerment and Business Services, 1994; (with G. Krebs and H. Zimmermann) Chambers of Commerce in Britain and Germany, 1994; (ed) Trade Associations in Britain and Germany, 1997. *Recreations:* the family, craftwork. *Address:* Department of Geography, University of Cambridge, Downing Place, Cambridge CB2 3EN.

BENNETT, Robin; adult educator; *b* 6 Nov. 1934; *s* of James Arthur Bennett, Major RA, and Alice Edith Bennett, Ipswich; *m* 1st, 1962, Patricia Ann Lloyd (marr. diss. 1991); one *s* one *d*; 2nd, 1992, Margaret Jane Allen. *Educ:* Northgate Grammar School, Ipswich; St. John's Coll., Univ. of Durham (BA); Queen's Coll., and Univ. of Birmingham (Dip Th); MEd Birmingham. Ordained deacon, 1960, priest, 1961; curacies and incumbencies in Essex and E London, 1960–75; appts in C of E educn, incl. Principal, Aston Training Scheme, 1977–82; Archdeacon of Dudley, 1985–86; left C of E and joined Soc. of Friends, 1988; Vice-Principal, Clapham Battersea Adult Educn Inst., 1986–89; Dep. Principal, Wandsworth Adult Coll., 1989–95. Mem. (Lab), Ludlow Town Council, 1999–. Gov., Fircroft Coll., 1983–99; Trustee, Woodbrooke Coll., 1998–2000. *Recreations:* travel, music, football. *Address:* 31 Poyner Road, Ludlow, Shropshire SY8 1QT. *T:* and *Fax:* (01584) 874752.

BENNETT, Sir Ronald (Wilfred Murdoch), 3rd Bt, *cr* 1929; *b* 25 March 1930; *o s* of Sir Wilfred Bennett, 2nd Bt, and Marion Agnes, OBE (*d* 1985), *d* of late James Somervell, Sorn Castle, Ayrshire, and step *d* of late Edwin Sandys Dawes; *S* father 1952; *m* 1st, 1953, Rose-Marie Audrey Patricia, *o d* of Major A. L. J. H. Aubépin, France and Co. Mayo, Ireland; two *d*; 2nd, 1968, Anne, *d* of late Leslie George Tooker; *m* 3rd. *Educ:* Wellington Coll.; Trinity Coll., Oxford. *Heir: cousin* Mark Edward Francis Bennett, *b* 5 April 1960. *Clubs:* Kampala, Uganda (Kampala).

BENNETT, Hon. William Richards; PC (Can.) 1982; Premier of British Columbia, 1975–86; *b* 14 April 1932; *y s* of late Hon. William Andrew Cecil Bennett, PC (Can.) and of Annie Elizabeth May Richards; *m* 1955, Audrey Lyne, *d* of late Jack James; four *s*. Began a business career. Elected MP for Okanagan South (succeeding to a constituency which had been held by his father), 1973; Leader of Social Credit Group in Provincial House, 1973; formed Social Credit Govt after election of Dec. 1975.

BENNETT-JONES, Peter; Chairman: Tiger Television, since 1988; PBJ Management, since 1988; Tiger Aspect Productions, since 1993; Tiger Aspect Pictures, since 1999; Comic Relief, since 1998; Director, Oxford Playhouse, since 2000; *b* 11 March 1955; *s* of Dr Nicholas and Ruth Bennett-Jones; *m* 1990, Alison E. Watts; two *s* one *d*. *Educ:* Winchester Coll.; Magdalene Coll., Cambridge (MA Law). Director: Oxford and Cambridge Shakespeare Co. Ltd, 1977–82; Pola Jones Assocs, 1977–82; Managing Director: Talkback, 1982–86; Corporate Communications Consultants Ltd, 1986–88. Hon. Golden Rose of Montreux, 1999. *Recreation:* simply messing about in boats. *Address:* (office) 7 Soho Street, W1D 3DQ; 8 Rawlinson Road, Oxford OX2 6UE. *T:* (01865) 515414. *Clubs:* Oxford and Cambridge, Groucho, Soho House.

BENNETTS, Rt Rev. Colin James; *see* Coventry, Bishop of.

BENNEY, (Adrian) Gerald (Sallis), CBE 1995; RDI 1971; goldsmith and silversmith; Professor of Silversmithing and Jewellery, Royal College of Art, 1974–83; *b* 21 April 1930; *s* of late Ernest Alfred Benney and Aileen Mary Benney; *m* 1957, Janet Edwards; three *s* one *d*. *Educ:* Brighton Grammar Sch.; Brighton Coll. of Art (Nat. Dip. in Art); RCA (DesRCA). FSIAD 1975. Estabd 1st workshop, Whitfield Place, London, 1955; Consultant Designer, Viners Ltd, 1957–69; began designing and making Reading civic plate, 1963; discovered technique of texturing on silver, 1964; moved workshop to Bankside, London, 1969; began prodn of Beenham Enamels, 1970; retired as goldsmith, 1999. Holds Royal Warrants of Appt to the Queen (designer and maker of 40th Anniversary Mace, for use at Commonwealth Ceremonies, 1992), the Duke of Edinburgh, Queen Elizabeth the Queen Mother and the Prince of Wales. Member: Govt's Craft Adv. Cttee, 1972–77; UK Atomic Energy Ceramics Centre Adv. Cttee, 1979–83; British Hallmarking Council, 1983–88. Metalwork Design Advisor to Indian Govt (UP State), 1977–78; Chm., Govt of India Hallmarking Survey, 1981; Export Advisor and Designer to Royal Selangor Pewter Co., Kuala Lumpur, 1986–. Consultant to Silver Trust, 1977– (commission of silver for loaning to No 10 Downing St and other govt estabs). Major Exhibns, Worshipful Co. of Goldsmiths, 1973, NY, 1994, Tel Aviv, 1995; major one man exhibn of oil paintings, Solomon Gall., 1988. Liveryman, Goldsmiths' Co., 1964. Hon. MA Leicester, 1963. Freeman, Borough of Reading, 1984. *Recreations:* walking, oil painting, landscape gardening. *Address:* The Old Rectory, Cholderton, Salisbury, Wilts SP4 0DW. *T:* (01980) 629614, *Fax:* (01980) 629461; (show rooms) 73 Walton Street, Knightsbridge, SW3 2HT, *T:* (020) 7589 7002. *Club:* Arts.

BENNION, Francis Alan Roscoe; writer; *b* 2 Jan. 1923; *o s* of Thomas Roscoe Bennion, Liverpool; *m* 1st, 1951, Barbara Elisabeth Braendle (separated 1971, marr. diss. 1975); three *d*; 2nd, 1977, Mary Field. *Educ:* John Lyon's, Harrow; Balliol Coll., Oxford. Pilot, RAFVR, 1941–46. Gibbs Law Scholar, Oxford, 1948. Called to Bar, Middle Temple, 1951 (Harmsworth Scholar); practised at Bar, 1951–53, 1985–94. Lectr and Tutor in Law, St Edmund Hall, Oxford, 1951–53; Office of Parly Counsel, 1953–65, and 1973–75; Dep. Parly Counsel, 1964; Parly Counsel, 1973–75; seconded to Govt of Pakistan to advise on drafting of new Constitution, 1956; seconded to Govt of Ghana to advise on legislation and drafting Constitution converting the country into a Republic, 1959–61. Sec., RICS, 1965–68; Governor, College of Estate Management, 1965–68. Co-founder and first Chm., Professional Assoc. of Teachers, 1968–72; Founder: Statute Law Soc., 1968 (Chm., 1978–79); Freedom Under Law, 1971; Dicey Trust, 1973; Towards One World, 1979; Statute Law Trust, 1991; founder and first Chm., World of Property Housing Trust (later Sanctuary Housing Assoc.), 1968–72 (Vice-Pres., 1986–); Co-founder, Areopagitica Educnl Trust, 1979. *Publications:* Constitutional Law of Ghana, 1962; Professional Ethics: The Consultant Professions and their Code, 1969; Tangling with the Law, 1970; Consumer Credit Control, 1976–2001; Consumer Credit Act Manual, 1978, 3rd edn 1986; Statute Law, 1980, 3rd edn 1990; Statutory Interpretation, 1984, 4th edn 2001; Victorian Railway Days, 1989; The Sex Code: Morals for Moderns, 1991; Statutes, in Halsbury's Laws of England, 1996; Understanding Common Law Legislation, 2001; articles and contribs to books on legal and other subjects. *Recreations:* studying Oxford origins, admiring the British Empire. *Address:* 29 Pegasus Road, Oxford OX4 6DS. *T:* (01865) 775164, *Fax:* (01395) 445822; *e-mail:* fbennion@aol.com. *Clubs:* Royal Commonwealth Soc., MCC.

BENSON, Sir Christopher (John), Kt 1988; FRICS; Chairman: Symphony Plastic Technologies plc, since 2000; Legacy plc, since 2000; Cross London Rail Links Ltd, since 2001; Principal, Inns of Court School of Law, since 2000; *b* 20 July 1933; *s* of Charles Woodburn Benson and Catherine Clara (*née* Bishton); *m* 1960, Margaret Josephine, OBE, JP, DL, *d* of Ernest Jefferies Bundy; two *s*. *Educ:* Worcester Cathedral King's Sch.; Thames Nautical Trng Coll., HMS Worcester. FRICS. Chartered surveyor and agricl auctioneer, Worcs, Herefords, Wilts, Dorset, Hants, 1953–64; Dir, Arndale Develts Ltd, 1965–69; Chm., Dolphin Develts Ltd, 1969–71; Man. Dir, 1976–88, Chm., 1988–93, MEPC; Chairman: The Boots Company, 1990–94 (Dir, 1989–94); Sun Alliance Gp, 1993–96 (Dir, 1988; Dep Chm., 1992–93), Royal & Sun Alliance Gp, 1996–97; Costain plc, 1993–96; Albright & Wilson, 1995–99; Dep. Chm., Thorn Lighting Gp, 1994–98. Dir, House of Fraser plc, 1982–86; Chairman: LDDC, 1984–88; Reedpack Ltd, 1989–90; Housing Corp., 1990–94; Funding Agency for Schs, 1994–97. Pres., British Property Fedn, 1981–83; Chm., Property Adv. Gp to DoE, 1988–90; Pres., London Chamber of Commerce and Industry, 2000–01; Mem. Council, CBI, 1990–97. Dir, Royal Opera House, 1984–92. Chm., Civic Trust, 1985–90; Trustee, Metropolitan Police Museum, 1986–; Vice President: Macmillan Cancer Relief (formerly Cancer Relief Macmillan Fund), 1991–2001; RSA, 1992–97; Pres., Nat. Deaf Children's Soc., 1995–. Lay-Gov., London Hosp. Med. Coll., 1993–95; Mem. Council, Marlborough Coll., 1982–90; Gov., Inns of Court Sch. of Law, 1996–. Freeman: City of London, 1975; Co. of Watermen and Lightermen, 1985; Liveryman: Co. of Gold and Silver Wyre Drawers, 1975; Guild of Air Pilots and Air Navigators, 1981. High Sheriff of Wilts, 2001. Lay Canon, Salisbury Cathedral, 2000. Hon. FRCPath 1992; Hon. FCIOB 1992. Hon. Fellow, Wolfson Coll., Cambridge, 1990. Hon. Bencher, Middle Temple, 1984. Hon. DSc: City, 2000; Bradford, 2000. *Recreations:* farming, aviation, opera, ballet. *Address:* 2, 50 South Audley Street, W1K 2QE. *T:* (020) 7629 2398. *Clubs:* Garrick, Royal Automobile, MCC; Australian (Sydney).

BENSON, David Holford; Chairman, Charter European Trust (formerly Kleinwort Charter Investment Trust), since 1992; *b* 26 Feb. 1938; *s* of Sir Rex Benson, DSO, MVO, MC, and Lady Leslie Foster Benson; *m* 1964, Lady Elizabeth Mary Charteris, *d* of 12th Earl of Wemyss and March, *qv*; one *s* two *d*. *Educ:* Eton Coll.; Madrid. CIGasE 1989. Shell Transport & Trading, 1957–63; Kleinwort Benson Gp, subseq. Dresdner Kleinwort Benson Gp, 1963–: Vice-Chm., 1989–92; non-exec. Dir, 1992–98. Non-executive Director: Marshall Cavendish, 1984–; Rouse Co., 1986–; BG Group plc (formerly British Gas), 1988–; Dover Corp., 1995–; Daniel Thwaites plc, 1998–; Vice Chm., Leach Internat. (formerly Leach Relais), 1992–. Chm., COIF Charities Funds (formerly Charities Official Investment Fund), 1984–; Trustee: Edward James Foundn, 1996–; UK Historic Bldg Preservation Trust, 1996–. *Recreation:* painting. *Address:* (office) 20 Fenchurch Street, EC3P 3DB; 11 Brunswick Gardens, W8 4AS. *T:* (020) 7727 4949. *Clubs:* White's, English-Speaking Union.

BENSON, Prof. Frank Atkinson, OBE 1988; DL; BEng, MEng (Liverpool); PhD, DEng (Sheffield); FIEE, FIEEE; Professor and Head of Department of Electronic and Electrical Engineering, University of Sheffield, 1967–87; Pro-Vice Chancellor, 1972–76; *b* 21 Nov. 1921; *s* of late John and Selina Benson; *m* 1950, Kathleen May Paskell; two *s*. *Educ:* Ulverston Grammar Sch.; Univ. of Liverpool. Mem. research staff, Admty Signal Estab., Witley, 1943–46; Asst Lectr in Electrical Engrg, University of Liverpool, 1946–49; Lectr 1949–59, Sen. Lectr 1959–61, in Electrical Engrg, University of Sheffield; Reader in Electronics, University of Sheffield, 1961–67. DL South Yorks, 1979. *Publications:* Voltage Stabilizers, 1950; Electrical Engineering Problems with Solutions, 1954; Voltage Stabilized Supplies, 1957; Problems in Electronics with Solutions, 1958; Electric Circuit Theory, 1959; Voltage Stabilization, 1965; Electric Circuit Problems with Solutions, 1967; Millimetre and Submillimetre Waves, 1969; Fields, Waves and Transmission Lines, 1991; many papers on microwaves, gas discharges and voltage stabilization in learned jls. *Address:* 64 Grove Road, Sheffield S7 2GZ. *T:* (0114) 236 3493.

BENSON, Glenwyn; Joint Director, Factual and Learning, and Member, Executive Committee, BBC, since 2001; *b* 23 Nov. 1947; *d* of late Tudor David, OBE and Nancy David; *m* 1974, Dr Ian Anthony Benson; one *s* one *d*. *Educ:* Nonsuch County Grammar Sch. for Girls, Cheam; Girton Coll., Cambridge (MA); Harvard Univ. (Frank Knox Fellow). Dep. Editor, Weekend World, LWT, 1986–88; BBC: Editor: On the Record, 1990–92; Panorama, 1992–95; Head: of Commng, Adult Educn, 1995–97; of Science, 1997–2000; Controller, Specialist Factual, 2000–01. Mem., BAFTA, 2000–. *Recreations:* gardening, music. *Address:* BBC, 201 Wood Lane, W12 7TS. *T:* (020) 8752 6178.

BENSON, Gordon Mitchell, OBE 2000; RA 2000; FRIAS; Partner, Benson+Forsyth, architects, established 1978; Member, Royal Fine Art Commission for Scotland, since 1993; *b* 5 Oct. 1946; *s* of William Benson and Gavina Dewar (*née* Mitchell); one *s* one *d*. *Educ:* Univ. of Strathclyde; Architectural Assoc. Sch of Architecture (AA Dip). SADG; FRIAS; ARIBA. London housing projects, Camden Council, 1968–78. Part-time Prof. of Architecture, Strathclyde Univ., 1986–90; Vis. Prof., Edinburgh Univ., 1991–96. *Built work:* Branch Hill Housing, 1974; Mansfield Rd Housing, 1975; Lambie St Housing, 1975; Maiden Lane, 1976; Marico Furniture Workshop and Residence, 1979; Boarbank Oratory, 1985; Physio Room, Cumbria, 1986; Pavilion, Glasgow Garden Fest., 1989; Machi Nakao: The Divided House, Jyohanna Mus., Japan, 1994; Gall. 22 Admin Bldg, Mus. of Scotland, 1997; Mus. of Scotland, 1998; extension, Nat. Gall. of Ireland, 2000. Has won numerous awards and competitions. *Publications:* contribs to Scotsman, Daily Telegraph, Sunday Times and professional jls incl. Architectural Rev., Architects Jl, Bldg Design, RIBA Jl, RSA Jl and overseas architectural jls. *Address:* (office) 37D Mildmay Grove North, N1 4RH. *T:* (020) 7359 0288.

BENSON, (Harry) Peter (Neville), CBE 1982; MC 1945; FCA; Chairman, Davy Corporation PLC, 1982–85; *b* 10 Feb. 1917; *s* of Harry Leedham Benson and Iolanthe Benson; *m* 1948, Margaret Young Brackenridge; two *s* one *d*. *Educ:* Cheltenham Coll. FCA 1946. Served War, S Staffs Regt, 1939–45 (Major; MC). Moore Stephens, 1946–48; John Mowlem, 1948–51; Dir, 1951–54, Man. Dir, 1954–57, Waring & Gillow; Dir, APV Co., 1957–66; Man. Dir, 1966–77, Chm., 1977–82, APV Holdings. Director: Rolls Royce Motors, 1971–80; Vickers Ltd, 1980–82. *Recreation:* golf. *Address:* The Gate House, Little Chesters, Nursery Road, Walton-on-the-Hill, Tadworth, Surrey KT20 7TX. *T:* (01737) 813767. *Club:* Walton Heath Golf.

BENSON, James; President, James Benson Associates Inc., since 1987; *b* 17 July 1925; *s* of Henry Herbert Benson and Olive Benson (*née* Hutchinson); *m* 1950, Honoria Margaret Hurley; one *d*. *Educ:* Bromley Grammar Sch., Kent; Emmanuel Coll., Cambridge (MA). RN, 1943–46. Manager, Res. and Promotion, Kemsley Newspapers, 1948–58; Dir, Mather & Crowther, 1959–65; Man. Dir, 1966–69, Chm., 1970–71 and 1975–78, Ogilvy & Mather Ltd; Vice-Chm., The Ogilvy Group (formerly Ogilvy & Mather Internat.) Inc., 1971–87. Chm., American Associates of the Royal Acad. Trust, 1983–. *Publications:* Above Us The Waves, 1953; The Admiralty Regrets, 1956; Will Not We Fear, 1961; The Broken Column, 1966; Silent Unseen, 1995. *Recreations:* swimming, walking, painting, reading. *Address:* 64 Harley House, Marylebone Road, NW1 5HL.

BENSON, Jeremy Keith; QC 2001; a Recorder, since 1997; *b* 17 Jan. 1953; *s* of Jack Henry Benson and Renee Esther Benson.*m* 1985, Dr Karen Judith Silkoff; two *s* one *d*. *Educ:* City of London Sch.; Essex Univ. (BA Hons 1973); St Peter's Coll., Saltley, Birmingham (PGCE 1974). Hd of Econs Dept, King's Heath Boys' Sch., 1974–76; called to the Bar, Middle Temple, 1978; Asst Recorder, 1993–97. Mem. Cttee, Criminal Bar Assoc., 1997–. Mem., Political Cartoon Soc. 2001–. *Recreations:* cricket, collecting political cartoons. *Address:* 2 Hare Court, Temple, EC4Y 7BH. *T:* (020) 7353 5324.

BENSON, John Trevor; QC 2001; a Recorder, since 1998; *b* 22 Jan, 1995; s of Trevor Benson and Ruth (*neé* Oliver); *m* 1984, Sheila Patricia Riordan; one *s* two *d*. *Educ:* Liverpool Univ. (LLB Hons). Called to the Bar, Middle Temple, 1978; pt-time Chm., Employment Tribunals, 1995–. *Recreations:* cookery, Liverpool FC, music. *Address:* (chambers) 14 Castle Street, Liverpool L2 0NE. *T:* (0151) 236 4421.

BENSON, Neil Winston, FCA; Senior Partner, Lewis Golden & Co., Chartered Accountants, since 1980; *b* 17 Oct. 1937; *s* of late John William Benson and Rebecca (*née* Winston); *m* 1960, Ann Margery Licht; one *s* one *d*. *Educ:* Clifton Coll. FCA 1961. Articled clerk with Hartleys, Wilkins and Flew, 1955–60; qualified as chartered accountant, 1961; Lewis Golden & Co.: Sen. Clerk, 1961–63; Partner, 1963–. Director: Davis Service Gp Plc, 1981– (Chm., 1989–); Shaftesbury Plc, 1986–; Moss Bros Gp Plc, 1989– (Chm., 1990–); Business Post Gp Plc, 1993– (Chm., 1995–). Gov., RSC, 1997– (Corp. of London Assessor, 1995–97). Hon. Treasurer and Trustee: Cystic Fibrosis Res. Trust, 1990–99; Liver Res. Trust, 1991–. *Recreations:* Real tennis, golf, watching Rugby, theatre, my Alvis. *Address:* 40 Queen Anne Street, W1M 0EL. *T:* (020) 7580 7313. *Clubs:* Royal Automobile, MCC, Saints and Sinners (Hon. Sec.; Chm., 1979); Highgate Golf, Lake Nona Golf (Orlando, Fla).

BENSON, Peter; *see* Benson, H. P. N.

BENSON, Peter Charles; His Honour Judge Peter Benson; a Circuit Judge, since 2001; *b* 16 June 1949; *s* of Robert Benson and Dorothy Benson (*née* Cartman). *Educ:* Bradford Grammar Sch.; Birmingham Univ. (BSocSc). Called to the Bar, Middle Temple, 1975; in practice at the Bar, Leeds, 1975–2001; a Recorder of the Crown Court, 1995–2001. *Recreations:* golf, wine, travel. *Address:* c/o Leeds Crown Court, 1 Oxford Row, Leeds LS1 3BG. *T:* (0113) 283 0040. *Clubs:* Royal Over-Seas League; Bradford; Ilkley Golf, Ganton Golf, Ilkley Bowling.

BENSON, Maj.-Gen. Peter Herbert, CBE 1974 (MBE 1954); Member, Lord Chancellor's Panel of Independent Inspectors, Planning Inspectorate, Departments of Environment and Transport, 1981–88; *b* 27 Oct. 1923; *s* of Herbert Kamerer Benson and Edith Doris Benson; *m* 1949, Diana Betty Ashmore; one *s* one *d*. Joined Army, 1944; commnd into S Wales Borderers, 1945; transf. to RASC, 1948, and Royal Corps of

Transport, 1965; served, Palestine, Cyprus, Malaya and Singapore (three times), Borneo, Africa and Australia; Comdr, 15 Air Despatch Regt, 1966–68; GSO1 (DS) Staff Coll., Camberley, and Australian Staff Coll., 1968–70; Col Q (Movements), MoD (Army), 1971–72; Comdr, 2 Transport Gp RCT (Logistic Support Force), 1972–73; Comdr, ANZUK Support Gp Singapore, Sen. British Officer Singapore, and Leader, UK Jt Services Planning Team, 1973–74; Chief Transport and Movements Officer, BAOR, 1974–76; Dir Gen. of Transport and Movements (Army) (formerly Transport Officer in Chief (Army)), MoD, 1976–78. Chm., Grants Cttee, Army Benevolent Fund, 1980–92. Col Comdt, RCT, 1978–90. Chm., Abbeyfield Soc., Beaminster, 1982–92. Pres., Army Officers' Golfing Soc., 1993–96. Liveryman, Co. of Carmen, 1977. *Recreations:* golf, wood turning, photography. *Club:* Lyme Regis Golf (Captain, 1993).

BENSON, Richard Anthony; QC 1995; a Recorder, since 1995; *b* 20 Feb. 1946; *s* of Douglas Arthur Benson and Muriel Alice Benson (*née* Fairfield); *m* 1967, Katherine Anne Smith (marr. diss. 1997); one *s* two *d*; *m* 2000, Sarah Levina Gaunt; two *s* one *d*. *Educ:* Wrekin Coll.; Coll. of Law; Inns of Court Sch. of Law. Sailing and overland expedition to Africa, 1964–65; articled to Bircham & Co. (Solicitors), 1965–67; joined Inner Temple as student, 1968; adventuring in Sudan, 1969–70; called to the Bar, Inner Temple, 1974; in practice on Midland and Oxford Circuit, specialising in criminal law; Asst Recorder, 1991–95. *Recreations:* flying (flew Atlantic via Greenland 1983), off-shore cruising, drama, writing and performing in reviews, after-dinner speaking, the company of friends! *Address:* 36 Bedford Row, WC1R 4JH. *T:* (020) 7421 8000. *Clubs:* Northampton and County; Bar Yacht.

BENSON, Richard Stuart Alistair; His Honour Judge Benson; a Circuit Judge, since 1993; *b* 23 Nov. 1943; *s* of late Frank Benson and of Jean Benson; *m* 1980, Susan (marr. diss. 1998). *Educ:* Clapham Coll.; Univ. of Nottingham (BA Politics). Called to the Bar, Gray's Inn, 1968; in practice at the Bar, firstly Midland Circuit, later Midland and Oxford Circuit, Nottingham, 1968–92; a Recorder, 1991–93. Member, Court of Appeal: St Helena, 1997–; Falkland Is, 2000–; British Antarctic Territory, 2000–. Mem., Nottingham Malt Whisky Soc. *Recreations:* steeplechasing, horses (Joint Master, Trent Valley Draghounds), books, France. *Address:* 1 High Pavement, Nottingham NG1 1HF. *T:* (0115) 941 8218. *Clubs:* Nottingham and Notts United Services; Darley Dale Fly Fishing, Beeston Fields Golf.

BENT, Margaret (Hilda), PhD; FBA 1993; musicologist; Senior Research Fellow, All Souls College, Oxford, since 1992; *b* 23 Dec. 1940; *d* of Horace Bassington and Miriam (*née* Simpson); *m*; one *s* one *d*. *Educ:* Haberdashers' Aske's Acton Sch.; Girton Coll., Cambridge (organ schol.; BA 1962; MusB 1963; MA; PhD 1969). Lectr, then Sen. Lectr, Music Dept, Goldsmiths' Coll., London Univ., 1972–75; Vis. Prof., then full Prof. and Chm., Music Dept, Brandeis Univ., 1975–81; Prof., later Chm., Music Dept, Princeton Univ., 1981–92. Guggenheim Fellow, 1983–84. Pres., Amer. Musicological Soc., 1984–86. For. Hon. Mem., Amer. Acad. of Arts and Scis, 1994. FRHistS 1995. Hon. DMus Glasgow, 1997. *Publications:* (ed jtly) Old Hall Manuscript, vols I and II 1969, vol III 1973; (ed jtly) John Dunstable, Complete Works, 1970; (ed) Four Anonymous Masses, 1979; Dunstaple, 1981; (ed jtly) Ciconia, 1985; (ed) Rossini, Il Turco in Italia, 1988; Fauvel Studies, 1998; (contrib.) New Grove Dictionary of Music and Musicians, 1980; contrib. Musica Disciplina, Jl of Amer. Musicol Soc., Early Music Hist. etc. *Address:* All Souls College, Oxford OX1 4AL. *T:* (01865) 279379.

BENTALL, Edward; *see* Bentall, L. E.

BENTALL, Hugh Henry, MB; FRCS; Professor of Cardiac Surgery, Royal Postgraduate Medical School, University of London, 1965–85, now Professor Emeritus at Imperial College School of Medicine at Hammersmith Hospital; *b* 28 April 1920; *s* of late Henry Bentall and Lilian Alice Greeno; *m* 1944, Jean, *d* of late Hugh Cameron Wilson, MD, FRCS; three *s* one *d*. *Educ:* Seaford Coll., Sussex; Medical Sch. of St Bartholomew's Hospital, London. RNVR, Surg Lieut, 1945–47. Consultant Thoracic Surgeon, Hammersmith Hosp., 1955–85; Lecturer in Thoracic Surgery, Postgraduate Medical Sch., London, 1959; Reader, 1962–65. Order of Yugoslav Flag with Gold Leaves, 1984. *Publications:* books and papers on surgical subjects. *Recreations:* sailing, antique horology. *Address:* Imperial College School of Medicine at Department of Surgery, Hammersmith Hospital, Ducane Road, W12 0NN. *T:* (020) 8743 2030. *Club:* Royal Naval Sailing Association (Portsmouth).

BENTALL, (Leonard) Edward; DL; FCA; Chairman, Bentalls, 1982–2001; *b* 26 May 1939; *s* of late Leonard Edward Rowan Bentall and Adelia Elizabeth Bentall (*née* Hawes); *m* 1964, Wendy Ann Daniel; three *d*. *Educ:* Stowe School. Articled Clerk, Dixon Wilson Tubbs & Gillett, 1958–64. Bentalls, 1965–: Management Accountant, Merchandise Controller, Merchandise Dir, Man. Dir, Chm. and Man. Dir, Chm. and Chief Exec. Non-exec. Dir, Associated Independent Stores, 1979–82. Pres., Textile Benevolent Assoc., 1991–95. Non-exec. Director: Kingston Hosp. Trust, 1990–98 (Dep. Chm., 1998); Riverside Radio, 1996–98. Governor: Brooklands Tech. Coll., 1981–90; Kingston Coll., 1990–; Kingston Grammar Sch., 1992–; Patron, Bedelsford Sch. Assoc., 1997–. Trustee and Chm., Exec. Cttee, Kingston and Dist Sea Cadet Corps TS Steadfast, 1994–; Chm. Bd of Trustees, Shooting Star Trust Children's Hospice Appeal, 2000–; Trustee, Spirit of Normandy Trust, 2000–. Vice-Pres., Surrey PGA, 1995–. Steward, Nat. Greyhound Racing Club, 1998–. Hon. Life Mem., Tamesis Sailing Club, 1997. FInstD. DL Greater London, 1999. *Address:* Runnymede, Sandpit Hall Road, Chobham, Woking, Surrey GU24 8AN. *T:* (01276) 858256. *Clubs:* Naval, MCC, Surrey Cricket, Saints and Sinners.

BENTHALL, Jonathan Charles Mackenzie; Director, Royal Anthropological Institute, 1974–2000; Editor, Anthropology Today, 1985–2000; *b* Calcutta, 12 Sept. 1941; *s* of Sir Arthur Paul Benthall, KBE and Mollie Pringle; *m* 1975, Zamira, *d* of Baron Menuhin, OM, KBE; two *s* and one step *s*. *Educ:* Eton (KS); King's Coll., Cambridge (MA). Sec., Inst. of Contemporary Arts, 1971–73. Member: UK Adv. Cttee, 1981–87, Overseas Adv. Cttee, 1985–86, 1990–96, Council, 1987–90, Assembly, 1990–98, SCF; Assoc. of Social Anthropologists, 1983; Bd, Internat. Broadcasting Trust, 1991–95; Trustee: Internat. NGO Trng and Res. Centre, 1997– (Chm., 1998–); Alliance of Religions and Conservation, 1997–. Hon. Res. Fellow, Dept of Anthropology, UCL, 1994–. Anthropology in Media Award, Amer. Anthropol Assoc., 1993; Patron's Medal, RAI, 2001. Chevalier de l'Ordre des Arts et des Lettres (France), 1973. *Publications:* Science and Technology in Art Today, 1972; (ed) Ecology: the Shaping Enquiry, 1972; (ed) The Limits of Human Nature, 1973; (ed jtly) The Body as a Medium of Expression, 1975; The Body Electric: patterns of western industrial culture, 1976; Disasters, Relief and the Media, 1993. *Recreations:* listening to music, swimming, mountain walking, books. *Address:* 212 Hammersmith Grove, W6 7HG. *T:* (020) 8749 5339, *Fax:* (020) 8743 4116. *Club:* Athenæum.

BENTHAM, Howard Lownds; QC 1996; a Recorder, since 1988; *b* 26 Feb. 1948; *s* of William Foster Bentham and Elsie Bentham; *m* 1978, Elizabeth Anne Owen; one *s*. *Educ:* Malvern Coll.; Liverpool Univ. (LLB). Called to the Bar, Gray's Inn, 1970; Asst Recorder, 1985–88. *Recreations:* motor racing, scuba diving, watching wildlife. *Address:* Peel Court Chambers, 45 Hardman Street, Manchester M3 3PL. *T:* (0161) 832 3791.

BENTHAM, Prof. Richard Walker; Professor of Petroleum and Mineral Law, and Director of the Centre for Petroleum and Mineral Law Studies, University of Dundee, 1983–90; Professor Emeritus, since 1991; *b* 26 June 1930; *s* of Richard Hardy Bentham and Ellen Walker (*née* Fisher); *m* 1956, Stella Winifred Matthews; one *d*. *Educ:* Campbell Coll., Belfast; Trinity Coll., Dublin (BA, LLB). Called to the Bar, Middle Temple, 1955. Lecturer in Law: Univ. of Tasmania, 1955–57; Univ. of Sydney, 1957–61; Legal Dept, The British Petroleum Co. PLC, 1961–83 (Dep. Legal Advisor, 1979–83). Founder Mem., Scottish Council for Internat. Arbitration (formerly Scottish Council for Arbitration), 1988–99; Mem. Council, Inst. of Internat. Business Law and Practice, ICC, 1988–94; British nominated Mem., Panel of Arbitrators, Dispute Settlement Centre, IEA, 1989–. Mem. and consultant, Russian Petroleum Legislation Project (sponsored by Univ. of Houston, World Bank and ODAS), 1991–96. FRSA 1986. *Publications:* articles in learned jls in UK and overseas. *Recreations:* cricket, military history, military modelling. *Address:* Earlham, 41 Trumlands Road, St Marychurch, Torquay, Devon TQ1 4RN. *T:* (01803) 314315.

BENTINCK, family name of **Earl of Portland**.

BENTINCK van SCHOONHETEN, Baron Willem Oswald; Ambassador of the Netherlands to the Court of St James's, and concurrently to Iceland, since 1999; *b* 9 March 1940; *s* of late Baron Oswald François Bentinck van Schoonheten and Meta Hendrica Bentinck van Schoonheten (*née* van der Slooten); *m* 1974, Corinne C. Elink Schuurman; two *s* one *d*. *Educ:* Univ. of Utrecht (Master of Law). Entered Netherlands Foreign Service, 1968; Buenos Aires, 1968–71; Rome, 1971–73; Internat. Relns Dept, Min. of Foreign Affairs, 1973–76; Perm. Rep., NY, 1976–79; Economic Counsellor, Moscow, 1979–81; Counsellor and Dep. Hd of Mission, Ottawa, 1981–84; Hd of Political Affairs Section and Dep. Dir, Atlantic Co-operation and Security Affairs Dept, Min. of Foreign Affairs, 1984–87; Minister and Deputy Head of Mission: Moscow, 1987–90; Washington, 1990–94; Ambassador to Madrid, 1994–98. Officer, Order of Orange Nassau (Netherlands), 1992; Kt, Order of Merit (Italy), 1972; Grand Cross, Order of Isabella la Católica (Spain), 1999. *Recreations:* shooting, golf. *Address:* (residence) 8 Palace Green, W8 4QA; (office) 38 Hyde Park Gate, SW7 5DP. *T:* (020) 7590 3299. *Clubs:* White's; Haagsche (Plaats Royaal).

BENTLEY, (Anthony) Philip; QC 1991; Barrister, Stanbrook & Hooper, Brussels, since 1980; *b* 5 Dec. 1948; *s* of late Kenneth Bentley and of Frances Elizabeth (*née* Scott); *m* 1980, Christine Anne-Marie Odile Bausier; two *s* two *d*. *Educ:* St George's Coll., Weybridge; St Catharine's Coll., Cambridge (MA). Called to the Bar, Lincoln's Inn, 1970. With ICI, 1973–77; Dilley & Custer, 1977–80. *Address:* (office) 42 rue du Taciturne, 1000 Brussels, Belgium. *T:* (2) 2305059.

BENTLEY, Rt Rev. David Edward; *see* Gloucester, Bishop of.

BENTLEY, David Jeffrey, CB 1993; Legal Consultant to government departments; *b* 5 July 1935; *s* of late Harry Jeffrey Bentley and Katherine (*née* Barnett). *Educ:* Watford Grammar School; New College, Oxford (BCL, MA). Called to the Bar, Lincoln's Inn, 1963; University teaching, 1957–79; Asst Parly Counsel, 1965–67; Legal Adviser's Branch, Home Office, 1979–95, Principal Asst Legal Advr, 1988–95; Legal Counsellor, FCO, 1995–97; Legal Consultant: FCO, 1997–98; Home Office, 1998–2000. *Recreations:* reading, listening to music, walking. *Address:* 192 Randolph Avenue, W9 1PE. *Club:* Oxford and Cambridge.

BENTLEY, David Ronald, QC 1984; **His Honour Judge Bentley;** a Circuit Judge, since 1988; *b* 24 Feb. 1942; *s* of Edgar Norman and Hilda Bentley; *m* 1978, Christine Elizabeth Stewart; two *s*. *Educ:* King Edward VII Sch., Sheffield; University Coll. London. LLB (Hons) 1963; LLM and Brigid Cotter Prize, London Univ., 1979; PhD Sheffield, 1994. Called to the Bar, Gray's Inn, 1969 (Macaskie Scholar). In practice at the bar, 1969–88; a Recorder, 1985–88. *Publications:* Select Cases from The Twelve Judges' Notebooks, 1997; Criminal Justice in Nineteenth-Century England, 1998; Victorian Men of Law, 2000. *Recreations:* legal history, watching Sheffield United.

BENTLEY, Ven. Frank William Henry; Archdeacon of Worcester and Canon Residentiary of Worcester Cathedral, 1984–99, now Emeritus; Chaplain to the Queen, since 1994; *b* 4 March 1934; *s* of Nowell and May Bentley; *m* 1st, 1957, Muriel Bland (*d* 1958); one *s*; 2nd, 1960, Yvonne Wilson (*d* 2000); two *s* one *d*. *Educ:* Yeovil School; King's College London (AKC). Deacon 1958, priest 1959; Curate at Shepton Mallet, 1958–62; Rector of Kingsdon with Podymore Milton and Curate-in-charge, Yeovilton, 1962–66; Rector of Babcary, 1964–66; Vicar of Wiveliscombe, 1966–76; Rural Dean of Tone, 1973–76; Vicar of St John-in-Bedwardine, Worcester, 1976–84; Rural Dean of Martley and Worcester West, 1979–84. Hon. Canon of Worcester Cathedral, 1981. *Recreations:* gardening, countryside. *Address:* The Chaplain's House, St Oswald's Close, Worcester WR1 1HR. *T:* (01905) 616619.

BENTLEY, Prof. George, FRCS, FRCSE; Professor of Orthopaedic Surgery, since 1982, and Director, since 1992, Institute of Orthopaedics, University College and Middlesex School of Medicine, University of London; *b* 19 Jan. 1936; *s* of George and Doris Bentley; *m* 1960, Ann Gillian Hutchings; two *s* one *d*. *Educ:* Rotherham Grammar Sch.; Sheffield Univ. (MB, ChB, ChM). FRCS 1964; FRCSE 2000. House Surgeon, Sheffield Royal Infirmary, 1959–61; Lectr in Anatomy, Birmingham Univ., 1961–62; Surg. Registrar, Sheffield Royal Infirm., 1963–65; Sen. Registrar in Orthopaedics, Nuffield Orthopaedic Centre and Radcliffe Infirm., Oxford, 1967–69; Instructor in Orth., Univ. of Pittsburgh, USA, 1969–70; Lectr, 1970–71, Sen. Lectr and Reader in Orth., 1971–76, Univ. of Oxford; Prof. of Orth. and Accident Surgery, Univ. of Liverpool, 1976–82; Hon. Consultant Orthopaedic Surgeon: Royal Nat. Orthopaedic Hosp., Stanmore; Middlesex Hosp. Vice-Pres., RCS, 2001–. FMedSci 1999. *Publications:* (ed) 3rd edn vols I and II, Rob and Smith Operative Surgery—Orthopaedics, 1979, 4th edn 1991; (ed) Mercer's Orthopaedic Surgery, 8th edn, 1983, 9th edn 1996; papers on cell-engineered cartilage grafting of joints, arthritis, accident surgery and scoliosis in leading med. and surg. jls. *Recreations:* golf, tennis, music. *Address:* Institute of Orthopaedics, Royal National Orthopaedic Hospital, Stanmore, Middx HA7 4LP. *T:* (020) 8954 2300.

BENTLEY, John Ransome; Chief Executive Officer, Netmedia Consultants plc; *b* 19 Feb. 1940; *m* 1st, 1960 (marr. diss. 1969); one *s* one *d*; two *d*; 2nd, 1982, Katherine Susan (marr. diss. 1986), *d* of Gerald Percy and the Marchioness of Bute. *Educ:* Harrow Sch. Chairman: Barclay Securities plc, Mills & Allen, British Lion Films, 1969–73; Intervision Video (Holdings) PLC, 1980–83; Faxcast Broadcast Corp., 1990–92; Viewcall America Inc., 1995–97. Inventor of Internet on TV, 1994. *Recreations:* life, politics by Internet, libertarianism; *e-mail:* johnbentley@easynet.co.uk.

BENTLEY, Philip; *see* Bentley, A. P.

BENTON, Joseph Edward; JP; MP (Lab) Bootle, since Nov. 1990; *b* 28 Sept. 1933; *s* of Thomas and Agnes Benton; *m* 1959, Doris Wynne; four *d*. *Educ:* St Monica's Primary and Secondary Sch.; Bootle Technical Coll. Nat. Service, RAF, 1955. Apprentice fitter and turner, 1949; former Personnel Manager, Pacific Steam Navigation Co.; Girobank, 1982–90. Councillor, Sefton Borough Council, 1970–90 (Leader, Labour Gp, 1985–90). An Opposition Whip, 1994–97. Mem., Speaker's Panel of Chairmen, 1992–94, 1998–. Mem., Select Cttee on Educn, 1997–98; Sec., All Party Parly Pro-Life Gp, 1992–; Member: British/Spanish Parly Gp, 1997–; British/Irish Parly Gp, 1997–. Mem., Bd Visitors, Liverpool Prison (Walton), 1974–81. Chm. of Govs, Hugh Baird Coll. of Technology, 1972–93. Assoc. Mem., IPM, 1965; MIL 1963. JP South Sefton, 1969. *Address:* c/o House of Commons, SW1A 0AA.

BENTON, Margaret Carole; Director, Theatre Museum, Victoria and Albert Museum, since 1990; *b* 14 April 1943; *d* of late Lawrence Benton and Mary Benton; *m* Stephen Green. *Educ:* The Red Maids Sch., Bristol; Univ. of Wales (BA Hons French). British Broadcasting Corporation: Radio, 1966; News, Paris Office, 1967; Schools Television, 1969; Gen. Features Television, 1970; COI (Overseas Documentaries/Co-prodns), 1971; BBC Television, Bristol, 1975; Nat. Museum of Photography, Film and Television, 1985. Member: Theatres Adv. Council; Council of Management (British Centre), Internat. Theatre Inst.; Museums Assoc.; Pres., Société Internationale des Bibliothèques et des Musées des Arts du Spectacle, 1992–96. Trustee, Peter Brook Empty Space Awards. Prod and dir. numerous television documentaries and other progs for BBC. *Recreations:* rural "idylling", theatre, cinema, visual arts, gardens, historic buildings. *Address:* c/o Theatre Museum, 1E Tavistock Street, WC2E 7PA. *T:* (020) 7943 4710.

BENTON, Rev. Canon Michael John; Priest-in-charge, Kingsclere, since 1996; Chaplain to the Queen, since 1998; *b* 3 Nov. 1938; *s* of William James Benton and Violet May Benton (*née* Pearse); *m* 1960, Frances Elizabeth Margaret Joyce Harris; two *s* one *d*. *Educ:* Chichester High Sch. for Boys; University Coll. London (BSc Hons 1960); Fitzwilliam House, Cambridge (CertEd 1961). Asst Biology Master, Alleynes GS, Stevenage, 1961–63; Head of Biology, Perse Sch., Cambridge, 1963–69; Lectr and Sen. Lectr, Biol Scis, King Alfred's Coll., Winchester, 1969–76. Theol study, Salisbury Theol Coll. and St George's Coll., Jerusalem, 1972–74; ordained deacon and priest, 1974; Hon. Curate, Weeke, 1974–76; full time priest in C of E, 1976–; Curate, Bursledon, 1976–78; Rector, Over Wallop with Nether Wallop, 1978–83; Rector, St Lawrence and St Maurice with St Swithun, Winchester, 1983–90; Dir of Educn, Dio. of Winchester, 1979–95; Hon. Canon, Winchester Cathedral, 1989–. *Publications:* regular Christian comment column for Hampshire Chronicle, 1988–; occasional papers and articles. *Recreations:* reading, science and faith debate (Mem. SOSc), history, bird-watching, growing shrub roses, watching vintage aircraft (Mem. Spitfire Soc.), archaeology. *Address:* The Vicarage, Fox's Lane, Kingsclere, Newbury, Berks RG20 5SL.

BENTON, Peter Faulkner, MA, CIMgt; Adviser, Stern Stewart Inc., since 1995; *b* 6 Oct. 1934; *s* of late S. F. Benton and Mrs H. D. Benton; *m* 1959, Ruth, *d* of late R. S. Cobb, MC, FRIBA and Mrs J. P. Cobb; two *s* three *d*. *Educ:* Oundle; Queens' Coll., Cambridge (MA Nat. Sciences). 2nd Lieut RE, 1953–55. Unilever Ltd, 1958–60; Shell Chemicals Ltd, 1960–63; Berger Jenson and Nicholson Ltd, 1963–64; McKinsey & Co. Inc., London and Chicago, 1964–71 (led reorgn of British gas industry, 1967–71); Gallaher Ltd, 1971, Dir, 1973–77; Man. Dir, Post Office Telecommunications, 1978–81; Dep. Chm., British Telecom, 1981–83. Dir Gen., BIM, 1987–92. Chairman: Saunders Valve Ltd, 1972–77; Mono Pumps Group, 1976–77; European Practice, Nolan, Norton & Co., 1984–87; Identica Ltd, 1992–93; Director: Singer and Friedlander, 1983–89; Woodside Communications, 1995–96; Mem., Supervisory Bd, Hiross Holdings AG, Austria, 1992–94. Dir, Turing Inst., 1985–94. Chairman: Enfield Dist HA, 1986–92; Enterprise Support Gp, 1993–96. Chm., Heating, Ventilating, Air Conditioning and Refrigerating Equipment Sector Working Party, NEDO, 1976–79; Member: Electronics Industry EDC, 1980–83; Econ. and Financial Policy Cttee, CBI, 1979–83; Special Adviser to EEC, 1983–84; Nat. Curriculum Science Wkg Gp, 1987–88; Indust. Develt Adv. Bd, DTI, 1988–94; Ind. Mem., British Liby Adv. Council, 1988–93; Internat. Adv. Bd for Science and Technology to Govt of Portugal, 1996–. Adviser, Arthur Andersen Société Coopérative, 1993–98. Vice-President: British Mech. Engrg Confedn, 1974–77; European Council of Management, 1989–93. Chairman: Ditchley Conf. on Inf. Technol., 1982; Financial Times Conf., World Electronics, 1983; World Bank Conf. on Catastrophe Avoidance, Washington, 1988, Karlstad, 1989; Vis. Gp, Inst. for Systems Engrg and Informatics, Italy, 1993; Inst. for Systems, Informatics and Safety, 1996; Euromoney Conf., New Delhi, 1998. Royal Signals Instn Lectr, London, 1980; ASLIB Lectr, 1988; Adam Smith Lectr, 1991. Pres., Highgate Literary and Scientific Instn, 1981–88. Chm., N London Hospice Gp, 1985–89. Governor, Molecule Club Theatre, 1985–91. *Publications:* Riding the Whirlwind, 1990; articles on management, science and IT. *Recreations:* reading, golf, conversation, looking at buildings. *Address:* Northgate House, Highgate Hill, N6 5HD. *T:* (020) 8341 1122; Dolphins, Polruan, Cornwall PL23 1PP. *Clubs:* Athenæum, Oxford and Cambridge, The Pilgrims; Blythe Sappers; Highgate Golf; Royal Fowey Yacht.

BENTON JONES, Sir Simon Warley Frederick; *see* Jones.

BENTSEN, Lloyd Millard, Jr; Chairman, New Holland, 1996–98; *b* 11 Feb. 1921; *s* of late Lloyd and of Edna Ruth Bentsen; *m* 1943, Beryl Ann Longino; two *s* one *d*. *Educ:* Univ. of Texas (LLB 1942). Served USAAF, 1942–45 (DFC; Air Medal). Admitted to Texas Bar, 1942; in private practice, 1945–48; Judge, Hidalgo County, Texas, 1946–48. Mem. of Congress, 1948–54; Mem. for Texas, US Senate, 1972–93; Sec. to US Treasury, 1993–94. Pres., Lincoln Consolidated, Houston, 1955–70. Democratic running mate to Michael Dukakis, US Presidential election, 1988. *Address:* 1111 Bagby Street, Suite 4700, Houston, TX 77002, USA.

BENYON, Thomas Yates; Director of various companies; *b* 13 Aug. 1942; *s* of late Thomas Yates Benyon and Joan Ida Walters; *m* 1968, Olivia Jane (*née* Scott Plummer); two *s* two *d*. *Educ:* Wellington Sch., Somerset; RMA Sandhurst. Lieut, Scots Guards, 1963–67. Insurance Broker, 1967–71; commodity broking, banking, 1971–78. Chm., Milton Keynes HA, 1989–94; Dir, Bucks Purchasing Authy, 1993–; Mem. Council, NAHAT. Councillor, Aylesbury Vale DC, 1976–79. Contested (C): Huyton, Feb. 1974; Haringey (Wood Green), Oct. 1974; MP (C) Abingdon, 1979–83; Vice Chm., Health and Social Services Cttee, 1982–83; Mem., Social Services Select Cttee, 1980–83. Chairman: Assoc. of Lloyd's Members, 1983–85; Soc. of Names, 1991–; Guild of Shareholders Ltd, 1995–; London Insurance Insider Ltd, 1995–. *Recreation:* family. *Address:* Old Rectory, Adstock, Buckingham MK18 2HY. *Club:* Pratt's.

BENYON, Sir William (Richard), Kt 1994; DL; landowner, since 1964; Vice Lord-Lieutenant, Berkshire, since 1994; *b* 17 Jan. 1930; *e s* of late Vice-Adm. R. Benyon, CB, CBE, and of Mrs Benyon, The Lambdens, Beenham, Berkshire; *m* Elizabeth Ann Hallifax; two *s* three *d*. *Educ:* Royal Naval Coll., Dartmouth. Royal Navy, 1947–56; Courtaulds Ltd, 1956–64. Mem., Berks CC, 1964–74. MP (C) Buckingham, 1970–83, Milton Keynes, 1983–92. PPS to Minister of Housing and Construction, 1972–74; Conservative Whip, 1974–76. Chairman: Peabody Trust, 1993–98; Ernest Cook Charitable Trust, 1993–. JP 1962–78, DL 1970, High Sheriff 1995, Berks. *Address:* Englefield House, Englefield, near Reading, Berkshire RG7 5EN. *T:* (0118) 930 2221, *Fax:* (0118) 930 3226; *e-mail:* benyon@netcomuk.co.uk. *Clubs:* Boodle's, Pratt's, Beefsteak.

BERASATEGUI, Vicente Ernesto; Ambassador of the Argentine Republic to the Court of St James's, since 2000; *b* 13 May 1934; *s* of Miguel Bernardo Gabriel Berasategui and Maria Luisa Rivanera Carles; *m* 1960, Teresita Mazza. *Educ:* Univ. of Buenos Aires (degree in Law); American Univ., Washington (Master in Internat. Relns and Orgn). Joined Argentine Foreign Service, 1954: Attaché, 1954–59; Hd, OAS Div., Foreign Min., 1960–61; Third, later Second, Sec., USA, 1961–65; Sec., Policy Making Cttee, Minister for Foreign Affairs, 1967–69; Dep. to Dir Gen. for Political Affairs, Foreign Min., 1970–72; Dep. Perm. Rep. to UN, Geneva, 1972–76; Minister, 1973; Ambassador, 1985; Dir for Western Eur. Affairs, Foreign Min., 1994–96; Ambassador to Denmark, 1997–2000. Rep., and Hd of delegns, to internat. confs, 1959–76 (Hd, Delegn to Conf. of Cttee on Disarmament, 1974–76); Mem., and Hd for meeting of delegns with heads of state and political consultations, 1971–98. United Nations posts include: Consultant, Centre for Disarmament, 1977–78; Sec., First Cttee of Gen. Assembly and Dep. Sec., Cttee on Disarmament, 1980; Dir, Geneva Br., Dept for Disarmament Affairs, 1983; Dep. Sec.-Gen., 1984–92, Sec.-Gen., 1992–93, Conf. on Disarmament (also Personal Rep. of Sec.-Gen. of UN). Dir, Sch. of Internat. Relns and Prof. of Theory of Internat. Relns and Contemp. Internat. Politics, Univ. of Salvador, 1967–70; Visiting Professor: of Foreign Policy, Sch. of Law, Univ. of Buenos Aires, 1971; Prog. of Diplomatic Studies, Grad. Inst. of Internat. Studies, Geneva, 1987–93; lectures on subjects concerning internat. relns, mainly disarmament, in Argentina, France and USA. Grand Cross, Order of Dannebrog (Denmark), 2000; Grand Officer, Order of Dist. Services (Peru), 1968; Commander: Order Bernardo O'Higgins (Chile), 1971; Order of Condor of the Andes (Bolivia), 1971; Order of Civil Merit (Spain), 1995; Order of Merit (Italy), 1995; Order of Merit (France), 1999. *Address:* 49 Belgrave Square, SW1X 8QZ. *T:* (020) 7235 3777; Embassy of the Argentine Republic, 65 Brook Street, W1K 4AH.

BERCOW, John Simon; MP (C) Buckingham, since 1997; *b* 19 Jan. 1963; *s* of late Charles Bercow and of Brenda Bercow (*née* Bailey). *Educ:* Finchley Manorhill Sch.; Univ. of Essex (BA 1st Cl. Hons Govt 1985). Nat. Chm., Fedn of Cons. Students, 1986–87; Credit Analyst, Hambros Bank, 1987–88; Public Affairs Consultant, Sallingbury Casey, later Rowland Sallingbury Casey, 1988–95; Dir, Rowland Co., 1994–95; Special Adviser to: Chief Sec. to Treasury, 1995; Sec. of State for Nat. Heritage, 1995–96; free-lance consultant, 1996–97. Councillor (C), Lambeth BC, 1986–90 (Dep. Leader, Opposition Gp, 1987–89). Vice-Chm., Cons. Collegiate Forum, 1987. Contested (C): Motherwell S, 1987; Bristol S, 1992. Opposition spokesman: on educn and employment, 1999–2000; on home affairs, 2000–01; Shadow Chief Sec. to HM Treasury, 2001–; Mem., Trade and Industry Select Cttee, 1998–99. Co-Dir, Advanced Speaking and Campaigning Course, 1989–. *Recreations:* tennis, swimming, reading, cinema. *Address:* House of Commons, SW1A 0AA; 31 Marsham Court, Marsham Street, SW1P 4JY.

BERESFORD, family name of **Baron Decies** and **Marquess of Waterford**.

BERESFORD, Sir (Alexander) Paul, Kt 1990; dental surgeon; MP (C) Mole Valley, since 1997 (Croydon Central, 1992–97); *b* 6 April 1946; *s* of Raymond and Joan Beresford; *m* Julie Haynes; three *s* one *d*. *Educ:* Richmond Primary Sch., Richmond, Nelson, NZ; Waimea Coll., Richmond; Otago Univ., Dunedin. Mem. (C), Wandsworth BC, 1978–94 (Leader of Council, 1983–92). Mem., Audit Commn, 1991–92. Parly Under-Sec. of State, DoE, 1994–97. *Address:* c/o House of Commons, SW1A 0AA.

BERESFORD, Prof. Maurice Warwick, FBA 1985; Professor of Economic History, University of Leeds, 1959–85, now Emeritus; *b* 6 Feb. 1920; *s* of late H. B. Beresford and Mrs N. E. Beresford. *Educ:* Boldmere and Green Lane Elementary Schs; Bishop Vesey's Grammar Sch., Sutton Coldfield; Jesus Coll., Cambridge (exhibnr and schol.). Goldsmiths' Co. Open Exhibnr; Historical Tripos, Pt I class I, 1940, Pt II class I, 1941; MA 1945. On Staff of Birmingham Univ. Settlement, 1941–42; Sub-warden, Percival Guildhouse, Rugby, 1942–43; Warden, 1943–48; University of Leeds: Lecturer, 1948–55; Reader, 1955–59; Dean, 1958–60; Chm., Sch. of Economic Studies, 1965–68, 1971–72, 1981–83; Chm. of Faculty Bd, 1968–70. Harrison Vis. Prof. of History, Coll. of William and Mary, Virginia, 1975–76; Vis. Prof. of History, Strathclyde Univ., 1987–90. Voluntary teacher, Wakefield Prison, 1975–92. Chairman: Yorks Citizens' Advice Bureaux Cttee, 1963–69; Parole Review Cttee, Leeds Prison, 1970–92; Northern Area Inst. for Study and Treatment of Delinquency, 1973–78; Co-opted Mem., City of Leeds Probation Cttee, 1972–78; SSRC, Economic and Social History Cttee, 1972–75. Minister's nominee, Yorkshire Dales National Park Cttee, 1964–71; Member: Consumer Council, 1966–71; Hearing Aids Council, 1969–71; Royal Commn on Historical Monuments (England), 1979–90. Hon. Vice-Pres., Yorks Archaeol Soc., 1986 (Medallist, 1989); Hon. Patron, Thoresby Soc., 1985. Hon. DLitt: Loughborough, 1984; Hull, 1986. *Publications:* The Leeds Chambers of Commerce, 1951; The Lost Villages of England, 1954, rev. edn 1998; History on the Ground, 1957, rev. edn 1998; (with J. K. S. St Joseph) Medieval England: an Aerial Survey, 1958, rev. edn 1979; Time and Place, 1962; New Towns of the Middle Ages, 1967, rev. edn 1988; (ed with G. R. J. Jones) Leeds and Its Region, 1967; (with J. G. Hurst) Deserted Medieval Villages, 1971, rev. edn 1989; (with H. P. R. Finberg) English Medieval Boroughs, 1973; (with B. J. Barber) The West Riding County Council 1889–1974, 1979; Walks Round Red Brick, 1980; Time and Place: collected essays, 1985; East End, West End, 1988; (with J. G. Hurst) Wharram Percy — Deserted Medieval Village, 1990; contribs to New DNB, Economic History Review, Agricultural History Review, Medieval Archaeology, etc. *Recreations:* music, theatre, maps, delinquency. *Address:* 4 Claremont Avenue, Leeds LS3 1AT. *T:* (0113) 245 4563.

BERESFORD, Meg; Manager, YMCA Centre, Wiston Lodge, since 1997 (Assistant Director, 1994–97); *b* 5 Sept. 1937; *d* of late John Tristram Beresford and of Anne Stuart-Wortley; *m* 1959, William Tanner; two *s*. *Educ:* Sherborne School for Girls; Seale Hayne Agricultural Coll., Newton Abbot; Univ. of Warwick. Community worker, Leamington Spa; Organising Sec., European Nuclear Disarmament, 1981–83; Gen. Sec., CND, 1985–90; gardener, 1991–92, Staff Co-ordinator, 1992–94, Iona Community. *Publications:* Into the Twenty First Century, 1989; contributor to End Jl, Sanity. *Recreations:* walking, reading, camping, music. *Address:* Wiston Lodge, Wiston, Biggar ML12 6HT.

BERESFORD-PEIRSE, Sir Henry Grant de la Poer, 6th Bt *cr* 1814; *b* 7 Feb. 1933; *s* of Sir Henry Campbell de la Poer Beresford-Peirse, 5th Bt, CB, and Margaret (*d* 1995), *d* of Frank Morison Seafield Grant, Knockie, Inverness-shire; *S* father, 1972; *m* 1966, Jadranka, *d* of Ivan Njerš, Zagreb, Croatia; two *s*. *Heir:* *s* Henry Njerš de la Poer Beresford-Peirse; *b* 25 March 1969.

BERESFORD-WEST, Michael Charles; QC 1975; a Recorder of the Crown Court, 1974–80; *b* 3 June 1928; *s* of late Arthur Charles, OBE, KPM and Ida Dagmar West; *m* 1st, 1956, Patricia Eileen Beresford (marr. diss.); two *s* one *d*; 2nd, 1986, Sheilagh Elizabeth Davies. *Educ:* St Peter's, Southbourne; Portsmouth Grammar Sch.; Brasenose Coll.,

Oxford (MA). Nat. Service, Intell. Corps, Middle East, SIME. Called to Bar, Lincoln's Inn, 1952, Inner Temple, 1980; Western Circuit, 1953–65; SE Circuit, 1965; a Chm., Independent Schools Tribunal and Tribunal (Children's Act 1948), 1974–80. *Recreations:* swimming, opera, music, golf, cruising. *Address:* 8 Lambert Jones Mews, Barbican, EC2Y 8DP. *T:* and *Fax:* (020) 7638 8804; 4 Farnham Hall, Farnham, Saxmundham, Suffolk IP17 1LB. *T:* and *Fax:* (01728) 602758. *Clubs:* Hampshire Hogs; Nomads; Aldeburgh Yacht, Bar Yacht; Aldeburgh Golf.

BERG, Adrian, RA 1992; *b* 12 March 1929; *s* of Charles Berg, MD, DPM and Sarah (*née* Sorby). *Educ:* Charterhouse; Gonville and Caius Coll., Cambridge (MA); Trinity Coll., Dublin (HDipEd); St Martin's Sch. of Art (Intermediate Arts & Crafts); Chelsea Sch. of Art (NDD); Royal Coll. of Art (ARCA; Hon. FRCA 1994). Nat. Service, 1947–49. Taught at various art schools, esp. Central Sch. of Art and Design and Camberwell Sch. of Arts and Crafts, 1961–78; Sen. Tutor, RCA, 1987–88. One-man exhibitions include: Arthur Tooth & Sons Ltd, London, 1964, 1967, 1969, 1972 and 1975; Galleria Vaccarino, Florence, 1973; Galerie Burg Diesdonk, Düsseldorf, 1976; Waddington and Tooth Galls, London, 1978; Waddington Galls, Montreal and Toronto and Grace Hokin, Inc., Chicago, 1979; London: Waddington Galls, 1981 and 1983; Serpentine Gall., 1973, 1984 and 1986; Piccadilly Gall., 1985, 1988, 1989, 1991, 1993 and 1999; Concourse Gall., Barbican Centre, 1993; Friends' Room, RA, 1999; Walker Art Gall., Liverpool, 1986; Victoria Art Gall., Bath, 1993; Plymouth City Mus. and Art Gall., 1993; Newport Mus. and Art Gall., Gwent, 1993; Mappin Gall., Sheffield, 1993; Hatton Gall., Newcastle, 1994; Royal Botanic Gdn, Edinburgh, 1994; Rye Art Gall., 1994. Lorne Scholarship, 1979–80. Gold Medal, Florence Biennale, 1973; minor and major prizes, John Moores Nat. Exhibns, 1980 and 1982; Major Prize, 3rd Tolly Cobbold, Eastern Arts Nat. Exhibn, 1981; Foundn for Art Award, NT, 1987. *Recreations:* imaginative reading, criticism. *Address:* The Piccadilly Gallery, 43 Dover Street, W1X 3RE. *T:* (020) 7629 2875.

BERG, Alan; District Judge (Magistrates' Courts) (formerly Stipendiary Magistrate), Greater Manchester, since 1994; *b* 17 Feb. 1943; *s* of Simon and Esther Berg; *m* 1967, Lorna Lewis; two *s*. *Educ:* King George V Grammar Sch., Southport; Law Coll., Liverpool. Solicitor in private practice, Liverpool, 1967–94; Sen. Partner, Canter Levin & Berg, 1980–93; Asst Stipendiary Magistrate, 1991–94. *Recreations:* gardening, swimming, worrying. *Address:* Manchester City Magistrates' Court, Crown Square, Manchester M60 1PR. *T:* (0161) 832 7272.

BERG, Geoffrey, MVO 1976; HM Diplomatic Service; Deputy Consul-General and Director of Trade, New York, since 1997; *b* 5 July 1945; *s* of Bertram Lionel Berg and Irene Amelia Berg; *m* 1970, Sheila Maxine Brown; one *s*. *Educ:* Woking County Grammar Sch. for Boys. Joined CRO, 1963; Diplomatic Service Admin, 1965–68; Latin American floater duties, 1968–70; Third Sec. (Vice-Consul), Bucharest, 1970–72; FCO, 1972–75; Second, later First Sec. (Inf.), Helsinki, 1975–79; FCO, 1979–84; First Sec. (Commercial), Madrid, 1984–88; FCO, 1988–90; Counsellor on secondment to DTI, 1990–93; Dep. Head of Mission, Mexico City, 1993–96. Chevalier First Cl., Order of Lion (Finland), 1976; Official Cross, Order of Civil Merit (Spain), 1988. *Recreations:* travel, photography. *Address:* c/o Foreign and Commonwealth Office, King Charles Street, SW1A 2AH. *Club:* Royal Over-Seas League.

BERG, Rev. John J.; *see* Johansen-Berg.

BERG, Prof. Paul, PhD; Cahill Professor in Cancer Research (Biochemistry), since 1994, and Director, Beckman Center for Molecular and Genetic Medicine, since 1985, Stanford University School of Medicine; *b* New York, 30 June 1926; *m* Mildred Levy; one *s*. *Educ:* Pennsylvania State Univ. (BS); Western Reserve Univ. (PhD). Pre-doctoral and post-doctoral med. research, 1950–54; scholar in cancer research, American Cancer Soc., Washington Univ., 1954; Asst to Associate Prof. of Microbiology, Washington Univ., 1955–59; Stanford Univ. Sch. of Medicine: Associate Prof. of Biochem., 1959–60; Prof., Dept of Biochem., 1960, Chm. 1969–74; Willson Prof. of Biochem., 1970–93; Non-resident Fellow, Salk Inst., 1973–83. Editor, Biochemical and Biophysical Res. Communications, 1959–68; Member: NIH Study, Sect. on Physiol Chem.; Editorial Bd, Jl of Molecular Biology, 1966–69; Bd of Sci. Advisors, Jane Coffin Childs Foundn for Med. Res.; Adv. Bds to Nat. Insts of Health, Amer. Cancer Soc., Nat. Sci. Foundn, MIT and Harvard, 1970–80; Council, Nat. Acad. of Scis, 1979. Former Pres., Amer. Soc. of Biological Chemists; Foreign Member: Japan Biochem. Soc., 1978; French Acad. of Scis, 1981; Royal Soc., 1992; Pontifical Acad. of Scis, 1996. Lectures: Harvey, 1972; Lynen, 1977; Weizmann Inst., 1977; Univ. of Pittsburgh, 1978; Priestly, Pennsylvania State Univ., 1978; Shell, Univ. of California at Davis, 1978; Dreyfus, Northwestern Univ., 1979; Jesup, Columbia Univ., 1980; Karl-August-Förster, Univ. of Mainz, 1980; David Rivett Meml, CSIR, Melb., 1980. Hon. DSc: Rochester and Yale Univs, 1978; Washington Univ., St Louis, 1986; Pennsylvania State Univ., 1995; numerous awards include: Eli Lilly Award, 1959; Calif. Scientist of the Year, 1963; Nat. Acad. of Scis, 1966, 1974; Amer. Acad. of Arts and Scis, 1966; Henry J. Kaiser, Stanford Univ. Sch. of Med., 1969, 1972; V. D. Mattia Prize of Roche Inst. for Molec. Biol., 1972; Gairdner Foundn Award, Nobel Prize in Chemistry, New York Acad. of Scis and Albert Lasker Med. Res. awards, 1980; National Medal of Science, 1983. *Publications:* (jtly) Genes and Genomes: a changing perspective, 1990; (jtly) Dealing with Genes: the language of heredity, 1992; many scientific articles and reviews. *Address:* Beckman Center–BO62, Stanford University Medical Center, Stanford, CA 94305, USA.

BERGANZA, Teresa; singer (mezzo-soprano); *b* Madrid, Spain; *d* of Guillermo and Maria Ascension Berganza; *m*; three *c*. Début in Aix-en-Provence, 1957; début in England, Glyndebourne, 1958; appeared at Glyndebourne, 1959; Royal Opera House, Covent Garden, 1959, 1960, 1963, 1964, 1976, 1977, 1979, 1981, 1984, 1985; Royal Festival Hall, 1960, 1961, 1962, 1967, 1971; appears regularly in Vienna, Milan, Aix-en-Provence, Holland, Japan, Edinburgh, Paris, Israel, America; Carmen, opening ceremonies, Expo 92, Seville; participated opening ceremonies, Barcelona Olympics, 1992. Mem. (first elected woman), Spanish Royal Acad. of Arts, 1994. Prizes: Lucretia Arana; Nacional Lírica, Spain; Lily Pons, 1976; Acad. Nat. du Disque Lyrique; USA record award; Harriet Cohen Internat. Music Award, 1974; Grand Prix Rossini; Médaille d'or, Ville Aix-en-Provence; International Critic Award, 1988. Charles Cross (6 times); Grand Cross, Isabel la Católica, Spain; Gran Cruz al Mérito en las Bellas Artes, Spain; Commandeur, l'Ordre des Arts et des Lettres, France. *Publication:* Flor de Soledad y Silencio, 1984. *Recreations:* music, books, the arts. *Address:* La Rossiniana, Archanda 5, PO Box 137, 28200 San Lorenzo del Escorial, Madrid, Spain. *T:* (1) 8960941, *Fax:* (1) 8960816.

BERGER, John; author and art critic; *b* London, 5 Nov. 1926; *s* of late S. J. D. Berger, OBE, MC, and Mrs Miriam Berger (*née* Branson). *Educ:* Central Sch. of Art; Chelsea Sch. of Art. Began career as a painter and teacher of drawing; exhibited at Wildenstein, Redfern and Leicester Galls, London. Art Critic: Tribune; New Statesman. Vis. Fellow, BFI, 1990–. Numerous TV appearances, incl.: Monitor; two series for Granada TV. Scenario: (with Alain Tanner) La Salamandre; Le Milieu du Monde; Jonas (New York Critics Prize for Best Scenario of Year, 1976); Play me Something (also principal rôle) (Europa Prize, Barcelona Film Fest., 1989). George Orwell Meml Prize, 1977; Lannan Foundn Lit. Award for Fiction, USA, 1989; State Prize for Artistic Achievement, Austria, 1990; Petrarca Award, Germany, 1991. *Publications: fiction:* A Painter of Our Time, 1958; The Foot of Clive, 1962; Corker's Freedom, 1964; G (Booker Prize, James Tait Black Meml Prize), 1972; Into their Labours (trilogy), 1992: Pig Earth, 1979; Once in Europa, 1989; Lilac and Flag, 1991; To The Wedding, 1995; Photocopies, 1996; King: a street story, 1999; *theatre:* with Nella Bielski: Question of Geography, 1986 (staged Marseilles, 1984, Paris, 1986 and by RSC, Stratford, 1987); Francisco Goya's Last Portrait, 1989; *non-fiction:* Marcel Frishman, 1958; Permanent Red, 1960; The Success and Failure of Picasso, 1965; (with J. Mohr) A Fortunate Man: the story of a country doctor, 1967; Art and Revolution, Moments of Cubism and Other Essays, 1969; The Look of Things, Ways of Seeing, 1972; The Seventh Man, 1975 (Prize for Best Reportage, Union of Journalists and Writers, Paris, 1977); About Looking, 1980; (with J. Mohr) Another Way of Telling, 1982 (televised, 1989); And Our Faces, My Heart, Brief as Photos, 1984; The White Bird, 1985 (USA, as The Sense of Sight, 1985); Keeping a Rendezvous (essays and poems), 1992; The Shape of a Pocket (essays), 2001; *translations:* (with A. Bostock): Poems on the Theatre, by B. Brecht, 1960; Return to My Native Land, by Aime Cesaire, 1969; (with Lisa Appignanesi) Oranges for the Son of Alexander Levy, by Nella Bielski, 1982. *Address:* Quincy, Mieussy, 74440 Taninges, France.

BERGER, Vice-Adm. Sir Peter (Egerton Capel), KCB 1979; LVO 1960; DSC 1949; MA; Bursar, 1981–91, and Fellow, Selwyn College, Cambridge, since 1981; *b* 11 Feb. 1925; *s* of late Capel Colquhoun Berger and Winifred Violet Berger (*née* Levett-Scrivener); *m* 1956, June Kathleen Pigou; three *d*. *Educ:* Harrow Sch. MA Cantab 1984. Served War of 1939–45: entered RN as a Cadet, 1943; Normandy and South of France landings in HMS Ajax, 1944; Sub-Lt, 1945; Lieut, 1946; Yangtse Incident, HMS Amethyst, 1949; Lt-Comdr, 1953; Comdr, 1956; Fleet Navigating Officer, Home Fleet, 1956–58; Navigating Officer, HM Yacht Britannia, 1958–60; Commanded HMS Torquay, 1962–64; Captain, 1964; Defence, Naval and Military Attaché, The Hague, 1964–66; commanded HMS Phoebe, 1966–68; Commodore, Clyde, 1971–73; Rear-Adm., 1973; Asst Chief of Naval Staff (Policy), 1973–75; COS to C-in-C Fleet, 1976–78; Flag Officer Plymouth, Port Admiral Devonport, Comdr Central Sub Area Eastern Atlantic and Comdr Plymouth Sub Area Channel, 1979–81, retired 1981. *Recreations:* shooting, fishing, history. *Address:* Carl's Barn, Church Road, Carlton, near Newmarket, Suffolk CB8 9JZ. *T:* (01223) 290241.

BERGERSEN, Dr Fraser John, AM 2000; FRS 1981; FAA 1985; Visiting Fellow, Division of Biochemistry and Molecular Biology, School of Life Sciences, 1994–2001, and University Fellow, 1996–98, Australian National University; *b* 26 May 1929; *s* of Victor E. and Arabel H. Bergersen; *m* 1952, Gladys Irene Heather; two *s* one *d*. *Educ:* Univ. of Otago, New Zealand (BSc, MSc (Hons)); Univ. of New Zealand (DSc 1962). Bacteriology Dept, Univ. of Otago, 1952–54; Div. of Plant Industry, CSIRO, Canberra, Aust., 1954–94, Chief Res. Scientist, 1972–94; formerly engaged part-time in scientific research in microbiology, with special reference to symbiotic nitrogen fixation in legume root-nodules. Foreign Sec., Aust. Acad. of Science, 1989–93. David Rivett Medal, CSIRO Officers' Assoc., 1968. *Publications:* Methods for Evaluating Biological Nitrogen Fixation, 1980; Root Nodules of Legumes: structure and functions, 1982; over one hundred and sixty articles and chapters in scientific journals and books. *Recreations:* music, gardening. *Address:* 13 Ferdinand Street, Campbell, ACT 2612, Australia. *T:* (2) 62477413.

BERGHUSER, Sir Hugo (Erich), Kt 1989; MBE 1981; *b* Germany, 25 Oct. 1935; *m* Christa; one *s* one *d*. *Educ:* Volksschule, Stiepel; Trade School, Bochum. Cabinet-maker. Embarked on ship to emigrate to Australia, 1958; ship (Skaubryn) caught fire and sank in the Indian Ocean; arrived in Papua New Guinea in 1959; active in the building industries, meat trade and timber sawmilling trade, employing over 700. MP, PNG, 1987–92; Minister for Civil Aviation, Tourism and Culture, 1987. Independence Medal, PNG, 1975; Silver Jubilee Medal, 1977; Service Medal, PNG, 1980; Long Service Medal, PNG, 1985. Distinctive Cross, 1st Cl. (Germany), 1986; Grand Cross (Germany), 1991; Hon. Consulate Gen. (Turkey). *Address:* PO Box 1785, Boroko, NCD, Papua New Guinea. *Club:* Papua.

BERGIN, Prof. Joseph, FBA 1996; Professor of History, University of Manchester, since 1996; *b* Kilkenny, 11 Feb. 1948; *s* of Cornelius Bergin and Brigid (*née* Phelan); *m* 1978, Sylvia Papazian; one *s* one *d*. *Educ:* Rockwell Coll., Co. Tipperary; University Coll., Dublin; Peterhouse, Cambridge. Lectr in History, Maynooth Coll., 1976–78; Manchester University: Lectr in History, 1978–88; Sen. Lectr, 1988–92; Reader, 1992–96. Visiting Professor: Lyon Univ., 1991–92; Ecole des Chartes, Paris, 1995. Prix Richelieu, Rueil-Malmaison, France, 1995. *Publications:* Cardinal Richelieu: power and the pursuit of wealth, 1985; Cardinal La Rochefoucauld, 1987; The Rise of Richelieu, 1991; The Making of the French Episcopate 1589–1661, 1996. *Recreations:* sports, book hunting, music. *Address:* 9 Sibley Road, Heaton Moor, Stockport, Cheshire SK4 4HH. *T:* (0161) 432 4650.

BERGMAN, (Ernst) Ingmar; Swedish film and theatre producer; Director, Royal Dramatic Theatre, Stockholm; director of productions on television; *b* Uppsala, 14 July 1918; *s* of a Chaplain to the Royal Court at Stockholm; *m* 1971, Mrs Ingrid von Rosen (*d* 1995); seven *c* (and one *s* decd) by previous marriages. *Educ:* Stockholm Univ. Producer, Royal Theatre, Stockholm, 1940–42; Producer and script-writer, Swedish Film Co., 1940–44; Theatre Director: Helsingborg, 1944–46; Gothenburg, 1946–49; Malmo, 1952–59. Produced: Hedda Gabler, Cambridge, 1970; Show, 1971; King Lear, 1985; Hamlet, 1986, Nat. Theatre, 1987; Miss Julie, Nat. Th., 1987; Lady from the Sea, Oslo, A Doll's House, Theatre Royal Glasgow, 1990. Films (British titles) produced include: Torment, 1943; Crisis, 1945; Port of Call, 1948; Summer Interlude, 1950; Waiting Women, 1952; Summer with Monika, 1952; Sawdust and Tinsel, 1953; A Lesson in Love, 1953; Journey into Autumn, 1954; Smiles of a Summer Night, 1955; The Seventh Seal, 1956–57; Wild Strawberries, 1957; So Close to Life, 1957; The Face, 1958; The Virgin Spring, 1960 (shown Edinburgh Fest., 1960); The Devil's Eye, 1961 (shown Edinburgh Fest., 1961); Through a Glass Darkly, 1961; Winter Light, 1962; The Silence, 1963; Now About all these Women, 1964 (first film in colour); Persona, 1967; Hour of the Wolf, 1968; Shame, 1968; The Rite, 1969; The Passion, 1970; The Fåro Document, 1970 (first documentary, shown Vienna Fest., 1980); The Touch, 1971; Cries and Whispers, 1972 (NY Film Critics Best Film Award, 1972); Scenes from a Marriage, 1974 (BBC TV Series, 1975; published, 1975; British première as play, Chichester, 1990); Face to Face, 1976 (BBC TV Series, 1979); The Serpent's Egg, 1977; Autumn Sonata, 1978; From the Life of the Marionettes, 1981; Fanny and Alexander, 1983 (published, 1989); screenplays: The Best Intentions, 1991; Faithless, 2000. Has gained several international awards and prizes for films; Goethe Prize, 1976; Great Gold Medal, Swedish Acad. of Letters, 1977. *Publications:* Four Stories, 1977; The Magic Lantern (autobiog.), 1988; Images: my life in film, 1994; Private Confessions, 1996.

BERGNE, (Alexander) Paul (A'Court), OBE 1985; HM Diplomatic Service, retired; author, broadcaster and consultant; *b* 9 Jan. 1937; *s* of Villiers A'Court Bergne and Diana Daphne Cuthbert (*née* Holman-Hunt); *m* 1963, Suzanne Hedwig Judith Wittich; one *s* one *d*. *Educ:* Winchester Coll.; Trinity Coll., Cambridge (BA); SOAS, London Univ. (MA). Krasicki Iran Expedn film cameraman, 1958–59; joined FO, 1959; served Vienna, 1961–63; Tehran, 1965–68; MECAS, 1970–72; Abu Dhabi, 1972–75; Cairo, 1975–77; Athens, 1980–84; Counsellor, Hong Kong, 1985–87; Cabinet Office, 1988–92; Ambassador to Uzbekistan, 1993–95, and to Tajikistan, 1994–95; Prin. Res. Officer, Res. and Analysis Dept, FCO, 1995–96. Director: Camco Trading Ltd, 1997–; London Information Network on Conflicts over State Building, 1999–. Specialist Advr, H of C Foreign Affairs Cttee, 1999–. Writer/presenter, radio series: Reports from the Silk Road, 1997; Hidden London, 1999. Persian Studies in Britain, 2001. Mem. Editl Bd, Central Asian Survey, 1998–. *Publications:* articles on art, architecture and archaeology of the Middle East. *Recreations:* mountain walking, numismatics, archaeology. *Address:* PO Box 414, Bourton on the Water, Cheltenham GL54 2YY.

BERGONZI, Prof. Bernard, FRSL; Professor of English, University of Warwick, 1971–92, now Emeritus; *b* 13 April 1929; *s* of late Carlo and Louisa Bergonzi; *m* 1st, 1960, Gabriel Wall (*d* 1984); one *s* two *d*; 2nd, 1987, Anne Samson. *Educ:* Wadham Coll., Oxford (BLitt, MA). Asst Lectr in English, Manchester Univ., 1959–62, Lectr, 1962–66; Sen. Lectr, Univ. of Warwick, 1966–71, Pro-Vice-Chancellor, 1979–82. Vis. Lectr, Brandeis Univ., 1964–65; Visiting Professor: Stanford Univ., 1982; Univ. of Louisville, 1988; Nene Coll., 1994–2000; Vis. Fellow, New Coll., Oxford, 1987. FRSL 1984. *Publications:* Descartes and the Animals (verse), 1954; The Early H. G. Wells, 1961; Heroes' Twilight, 1965; The Situation of the Novel, 1970; Anthony Powell, 1971; T. S. Eliot, 1972; The Turn of a Century, 1973; Gerard Manley Hopkins, 1977; Reading the Thirties, 1978; Years (verse), 1979; The Roman Persuasion (novel), 1981; The Myth of Modernism and Twentieth Century Literature, 1986; Exploding English, 1990; Wartime and Aftermath, 1993; David Lodge, 1995; War Poets and Other Subjects, 1999. *Recreations:* conversation, retrospection. *Address:* 19 St Mary's Crescent, Leamington Spa CV31 1JL. *T:* (01926) 883115.

BERGQUIST, Mats Fingal Thorwald, Hon. CMG 1983; PhD; Ambassador of Sweden to the Court of St James's, since 1997; *b* 5 Sept. 1938; *s* of Thorwald and Ingrid Bergquist; *m* 1st, 1968, Mariann Lübeck (*d* 1979); two *s*; 2nd, 1991, Agneta Lorichs; two *s*. *Educ:* Univ. of Lund (MA 1960; PhL 1964; PhD 1970). Joined Swedish Diplomatic Service, 1964: served: London, 1964–66; Perm. Mission to UN, NY, 1966–68; First Sec., subseq. Counsellor, Foreign Ministry, 1970–76; Counsellor, Washington, 1976–81; Asst Dep. Under Sec., 1981–85; Dep. Under Sec. for Political Affairs, 1985–87; Ambassador to: Israel, 1987–92; Finland, 1992–97. Commander: Légion d'Honneur (France), 1983; Order of Orange-Nassau (Netherlands), 1987; Grand Cross, Finnish Lion (Finland), 1994. *Publications:* Sweden and the EEC, 1970; War and Surrogate War, 1976; Balance of Power and Deterrence, 1988; Conflict Without End?, 1993; From Cold War to Lukewarm Peace, 1998. *Recreations:* music, tennis. *Address:* Embassy of Sweden, 11 Montagu Place, W1H 2AL. *T:* (020) 7917 6450. *Club:* Travellers.

BERGQUIST, Prof. Dame Patricia (Rose), DBE 1994; DSc; FRSNZ; Professor of Zoology, University of Auckland, since 1981; *b* 10 March 1933; *d* of William Smyth and Bertha Ellen Smyth (*née* Penny); *m* 1958, Peter Leonard Bergquist; one *d*. *Educ:* Devonport Primary Sch.; Takapuna Grammar; Univ. of Auckland (BSc 1954; MSc Hons 1957; PhD 1961; DSc 1979). University of Auckland: Lectr, then Sen. Lectr in Zool., 1958–69; Associate Prof., 1970–80; Head of Zool., 1986–92; Asst Vice-Chancellor Academic, 1989–96; Dep. Vice-Chancellor, 1993; Special Asst to Vice-Chancellor, 1997–. Research Fellow: Yale 1962 and 1968; Marseille, 1973; Natural Hist. Mus., London, 1978; Amer. Mus. of Natural Hist., 1990; Sen. Queen's Fellow in Marine Sci., Australia, 1984. FRSNZ 1981 (Hector Medal and Prize, 1989). *Publications:* Sponges, 1978; numerous papers and monographs in learned jls. *Recreations:* music, stamp collecting, swimming, wind-surfing. *Address:* Department of Anatomy, School of Medicine, University of Auckland, Private Bag 92019, Auckland, New Zealand. *T:* (9) 373599; 3A Pukerangi Crescent, Ellerslie, Auckland 5, New Zealand.

BERGSTRÖM, Prof. Sune, MD; Swedish biochemist; *b* 10 Jan. 1916; *s* of Sverker Bergström and Wera (*née* Wistrand). *Educ:* Karolinska Inst (MD 1944, DMedSci 1944). Squibb Inst., USA, 1941–42; Med. Nobel Inst., Stockholm, 1942–46; Basle Univ., 1946–47; Prof. of Biochemistry, Lund Univ., 1947–58; Prof. at Karolinska Inst, 1958–80, Dean of Med. Faculty, 1963–66, Rector, 1969–77. Consultant to WHO. Chm., Board, Nobel Foundn, 1975–87 (and Chm., Adv. Council, Med. Research, 1977–82). Member: Swedish Acad. of Scis; Swedish Acad. of Engineering; Amer. Acad. of Arts and Scis; Nat. Acad. of Scis, USA; Acad. of Sci., USSR; Acad. of Med. Scis, USSR; Papal Acad. of Sci.; Hon. Mem., Amer. Soc. of Biol. Chemists. Albert Lasker Basic Med. Research Award, 1977; (jtly) Nobel Prize for Physiology or Medicine, 1982. *Publications:* papers on heparin, autoxidation, bile acids and chlorestrol, prostaglandins. *Address:* Karolinska Institutet, Nobel Forum, Box 270, 17177 Stockholm, Sweden.

BERINGER, Guy Gibson; Senior Partner, Allen & Overy, since 2000; *b* 12 Aug. 1955; *s* of Lt Col Frederick Richard Beringer and Hazel Margaret Beringer (*née* Orr); *m* 1979, Margaret Catherine Powell; three *d*. *Educ:* Campbell Coll., Belfast; St Catharine's Coll., Cambridge (MA). Admitted Solicitor, 1980; joined Allen & Overy, 1980: Asst Solicitor, 1980–85; Partner, 1985–; Managing Partner, Corporate Dept, 1994–99. Mem., Law Soc., 1980–. *Recreations:* choral singing, golf, boating. *Address:* Allen & Overy, One New Change, EC4M 9QQ; The River House, Wey Road, Weybridge, Surrey KT13 8HR. *T:* (01932) 844868. *Club:* Hawks (Cambridge).

BERINGER, Prof. Sir John (Evelyn), Kt 2000; CBE 1993; Professor, School of Biological Sciences, since 1993, and Dean of Science, since 1996, University of Bristol; *b* 14 Feb. 1944; *s* of late Group Captain William Beringer and of Evelyn Joan Beringer (*née* Buckley); *m* 1970, Sheila Murray (*née* Gillies); three *s*. *Educ:* Univ. of Edinburgh (Scottish Dip. in Agric. 1965; BSc 1970); Univ. of East Anglia (PhD 1973). FIBiol 1985. Microbial Geneticist, John Innes Inst., 1970–80; Head, Dept of Microbiology, Rothamsted Exptl Station, Harpenden, 1980–84; University of Bristol: Dir, Molecular Genetics Unit, 1984–88; Head, Dept of Microbiology, 1986–90; Head, Dept of Botany, 1990–93. Chairman, advisory committees: Genetic Manipulation Planned Release Sub-Cttee, 1987–90; Releases to Envmt, 1990–99; Mem., NERC, 1996–. Fleming Lectr, Soc. for Gen. Microbiology, 1979. *Publications:* sci. contribs to biological jls and proceedings. *Recreations:* gardening, reading, travel, classic cars. *Address:* 92 Church Lane, Backwell, Bristol BS48 3JW. *T:* (01275) 462880.

BERIO, Luciano; composer; *b* 24 Oct. 1925; *s* of Ernesto Berio and Ada dal Fiume; *m* 1st, 1950, Cathy Berberian (marr. diss. 1964; she *d* 1983); one *d*; 2nd, 1964, Susan Oyama (marr. diss. 1971); one *s* one *d*; 3rd, 1977, Talia Pecker; two *s*. *Educ:* Liceo Classico, Oneglia; Conservatorio G. Verdi, Milan. Hon. degree in Composition, City Univ., London, 1979. Works include: Differences, 1958; Epifanie, 1959–63, revised as Epiphanies, 1991; Circles, 1960; Passaggio, 1962; Laborintus II, 1965; Sinfonia, 1968; Concerto for 2 pianos, 1972; Opera, 1969–74; Sequenzas I–XI for solo instruments, and for female voice, 1958–88; A-Ronne for five actors, 1974–75; Coro for chorus and orchestra, 1975–76; La Ritirata Notturna di Madrid, 1975; Ritorno degli Snovidenia, 1977; La Vera Storia, 1981; Un Re in Ascolto, 1983; Voci, 1984; Requies, 1985; Formazioni, 1986; Ricorrenze, 1987; Concerto II (Echoing Curves), 1988; Ofanim, 1988; Canticum Novissimi Testamenti, 1989; Rendering (Schubert), 1990; Continuo, 1991. *Address:* Il Colombaio, Radicondoli (Siena), Italy.

BERKELEY, 18th Baron *cr* 1421; **Anthony Fitzhardinge Gueterbock,** OBE 1989; Baron Gueterbock (Life Peer) 2000; Chairman, Rail Freight Group, since 1996; *b* 20 Sept. 1939; *o s* of Brig. E. A. L. Gueterbock (*d* 1984) and Hon. Cynthia Ella Gueterbock (*d* 1991), *sister* of Baroness Berkeley, 17th in line; *S* aunt, 1992; *m* 1st, 1965, Diane Christine (marr. diss. 1998), *e d* of Eric William John Townsend; two *s* one *d*; 2nd, 1999, Julia Rosalind, *d* of Michael Clarke. *Educ:* Eton; Trinity Coll., Cambridge (MA). CEng, MICE. Engineering, construction and planning, Sir Alexander Gibb & Partners, 1961–65; multi-disciplinary engineering and construction, planning and business develt, George Wimpey PLC, 1965–81; The Channel Tunnel Group/Eurotunnel, 1981–96. Chm., Piggyback Consortium, 1992–98. Hon. DSc Brighton, 1996. *Recreations:* ski-ing, sailing. *Heir:* *s* Hon. Thomas Fitzhardinge Gueterbock [*b* 5 Jan. 1969; *m* 1995, Helen Ruth, *er d* of Lt-Comdr Brian Walsh, RN retd]. *Address:* c/o Rail Freight Group, 6 Buckingham Gate, SW1E 6JP.

BERKELEY, Michael Fitzhardinge; composer and broadcaster; *b* 29 May 1948; *s* of late Sir Lennox Randal Berkeley and of Elizabeth Freda (*née* Bernstein); *m* 1979, Deborah Jane Coltman-Rogers; one *d*. *Educ:* Westminster Cathedral Choir Sch.; The Oratory Sch.; Royal Acad. of Music (ARAM 1984; FRAM 1996). Studied privately with Richard Rodney Bennett; rock musician; phlebotomist, St Bartholomew's Hosp., 1969–71; Presentation Asst, LWT, 1973; Announcer, BBC Radio 3, 1974–79; regular presenter of arts programmes for BBC (Meridian, World Service, Private Passions, Radio 3); introduces proms, concerts and festivals for BBC2 and Radio 3, BBC television documentaries and Glyndebourne for C4. Associate Composer: to Scottish Chamber Orch., 1979; to BBC Nat. Orch. of Wales, 2000–. Jt Artistic Dir, Spitalfields Fest., 1994–97; Artistic Dir, Cheltenham Fest., 1995–. Member: Exec. Cttee, Assoc. of Professional Composers, 1982–84; Central Music Adv. Cttee, BBC, 1986–90; Gen. Adv. Council, BBC, 1990–95; New Music Sub-Cttee, Arts Council of GB, 1984–86; Music Panel Adviser to Arts Council, 1986–90; Mem., Bd of Dirs, Royal Opera House, Covent Gdn, 1996–2001 (Mem., 1994–98, Chm., 1998–99, Opera Bd). Vis. Prof., Huddersfield Univ. (formerly Poly.), 1991–94. Governor: NYO, 1994–96; Royal Ballet, 2001–; Dir, Britten-Pears Foundn, 1996–. *Compositions: orchestral music:* Fanfare and National Anthem, 1979; Primavera, 1979; Flames, 1981; Gregorian Variations, 1982; Daybreak and a Candle End, 1985; Gethsemane Fragment, 1990; Secret Garden, 1998; The Garden of Earthly Delights, 1998; *for chamber or small orchestra:* Meditations, 1977 (Guinness Prize for Composition); Fantasia Concertante, 1978; Uprising: Symphony in one movement, 1980; Suite: the Vision of Piers the Ploughman, 1981; The Romance of the Rose, 1982; Coronach, 1988; Entertaining Master Punch, 1991; *concertos:* Concerto for Oboe and String Orch., 1977; Concerto for Cello and Small Orch., 1983; Concerto for Horn and String Orch., 1984; Organ Concerto, 1987; Clarinet Concerto, 1991; Viola Concerto, 1994; *chamber music:* String Trio, 1978; American Suite, 1980; Chamber Symphony, 1980; String Quartet No 1, 1981; Nocturne, 1982; Piano Trio, 1982; Music from Chaucer, 1983; Quintet for Clarinet and Strings, 1983; String Quartet No 2, 1984; The Mayfly, 1984; Pas de deux, 1985; For the Savage Messiah, 1985; Quartet Study, 1987; Catch Me if You Can, 1993; Torque and Velocity, 1997; *strings:* Etude de Fleurs, 1979; Sonata for Violin and Piano, 1979; Iberian Notebook, 1980; Variations on Greek Folk-Songs, 1981; Funerals and Fandangos, 1984; A Mosaic for Father Popieluszko, 1985; *guitar:* Lament, 1980; Worry Beads, 1981; Sonata in One Movement, 1982; Impromptu, 1985; Magnetic Field, 1995; *keyboard:* Passacaglia, 1978; Strange Meeting, 1978; Organ Sonata, 1979; Dark Sleep, 1994; *woodwind:* Three Moods, 1979; American Suite, 1980; Fierce Tears, 1984; Flighting, 1985; Keening, 1987; *vocal music for solo voice:* The Wild Winds, 1978; Rain, 1979; Wessex Graves, 1981; Songs of Awakening Love, 1986; Speaking Silence, 1986; *vocal/orchestral:* Love Cries, 1999 (adaptation from the Second Mrs Kong by Harrison Birtwistle); *choral music:* At the Round Earth's Imagin'd Corners, 1980; The Crocodile and Father William, 1982; Easter, 1982; As the Wind Doth Blow, 1983; Hereford Communion Service, 1985; Pasce Oves Meas, 1985; Verbum Caro Factum Est, 1987; The Red Macula, 1989; Night Song in the Jungle, 1990; Winter Fragments, 1996; Farewell, 1999; *oratorio:* Or Shall We Die?, 1983 (text by Ian McEwan; filmed for Channel 4); *opera:* libretti by David Malouf: Baa Baa Black Sheep, 1993; Jane Eyre, 2000; *ballet:* Bastet, 1988; *film music:* Captive, 1986; Twenty-one, 1990. *Publications:* The Music Pack, 1994; musical compositions; articles in The Observer, The Guardian, The Listener, The Sunday Telegraph, and Vogue. *Recreations:* looking at paintings, reading, walking and hill farming in mid-Wales. *Address:* c/o Oxford University Press, 70 Baker Street, W1U 7DN. *T:* (020) 7616 5900, *Fax:* (020) 7616 5901.

BERKELEY MILNE, Alexander; *see* Milne, A. B.

BERKLEY, David Nahum, QC 1999; a Recorder, since 2001; Deputy District Judge, since 1998; *b* 3 Dec. 1955; *s* of Harold Berkley and Doreen Berkley (*née* Wacks); *m* 1978, Deborah Fay Haffner; one *s* four *d*. *Educ:* Manchester Jewish Grammar Sch.; Gateshead Yeshiva; Univ. of Manchester (LLB (Hons)). Litigation Asst, Halliwell Landau, 1978–79; pupil of F. M. S. Hudson, 1979–80; called to the Bar, Middle Temple, 1979; Founding Head, Merchant Chambers, Northern Circuit, 1996. Faculty Mem., Nat. Inst. for Trial Advocacy, 1996–. Sec., N Circuit Commercial Bar Assoc., 1997–. *Recreation:* books. *Address:* Merchant Chambers, 1 North Parade, Parsonage Gardens, Manchester M3 2NH. *T:* (0161) 839 7070.

BERKOFF, Steven; actor, director and writer; *b* 3 Aug. 1937; *s* of Polly and Al Berks (formerly Berkovitch); *m* (marr. diss). *Educ:* Raines Foundation Grammar School, Stepney; Grocers' Co Sch., Hackney. *Plays acted*, 1965–: Zoo Story; Arturo Ui; *plays directed/acted/wrote*, 1969–: Metamorphosis (also directed on Broadway, 1989, Japan, 1992); Macbeth (directed and acted); Agamemnon; The Trial; The Fall of the House of Usher; East; Kvetch (Evening Standard Comedy of the Year Award, 1991); season of 3 plays, NT; Hamlet (directed and acted); Decadence (filmed, 1993); Brighton Beach Scumbags; Greek; West; One Man; Shakespeare's Villains (one-man show), Haymarket, 1998; *wrote and directed:* Sink the Belgrano, Mermaid, 1986, Acapulco, 1992; *directed:* Coriolanus, NY, 1988, Munich, 1991; Salomé, Edinburgh Festival, NT (and acted), 1989, Phoenix (and acted), 1990; The Trial, NT, 1991; Coriolanus, Mermaid (and acted), 1996; Massage, LA (and acted), 1997; East, Vaudeville, 1999; *films acted:* The Clockwork Orange; Barry Lyndon; The Passenger; McVicar; Outlands; Octopussy; Beverly Hills Cop; Rambo; Underworld; Revolution; Sins; Under the Cherry Moon; Absolute Beginners; Prisoner of Rio; The Krays; War and Remembrance; Decadence; Fair Game; Another 9½ Weeks; Legionnaire; Rancid Aluminium. *Publications:* East, 1977; Gross Intrusion (short stories), 1979; Decadence, 1982; Greek, 1982; West, 1985; Lunch, 1985; Harry's Xmas, 1985; Kvetch, 1987; Acapulco, 1987; Sink the Belgrano, 1987; Massage, 1987; America, 1988; I Am Hamlet, 1989; A Prisoner in Rio, 1989; The Theatre of

Steven Berkoff (photographic), 1992; Coriolanus in Deutschland, 1992; Free Association (autobiog.), 1996; Graft: tales of an actor (short stories), 1998; *play adaptations:* The Fall of the House of Usher, 1977; Agamemnon, 1977; The Trial, 1981; Metamorphosis, 1981; In the Penal Colony, 1988. *Recreations:* ping-pong, photography, travelling. *Address:* c/o Joanna Marston, 1 Clareville Grove Mews, SW7 5AH. *T:* (020) 7370 1080.

BERKSHIRE, Archdeacon of; *see* Russell, Ven. N. A.

BERKSON, David Mayer; a Recorder of the Crown Court, 1978–99; an Assistant Judge Advocate General, 1988–99; Deputy Judge Advocate General, Germany, 1994–99; Magistrate of the Standing Civilian Courts, 1991–99; *b* 8 Sept. 1934; *s* of Louis Berkson and Regina Berkson (*née* Globe); *m* 1961, Pamela Anne (*née* Thwaite); one *d. Educ:* Birkenhead School. Called to the Bar, Gray's Inn, 1957. Dep. Judge Advocate, 1984–87. Legal Mem., Mental Health Review Tribunal for the Mersey Area, 1982–84. Part-time Special Adjudicator, Immigration Appeal Authority, 1998–. *Club:* Lansdowne.

BERLINS, Marcel Joseph; journalist and broadcaster; *b* 30 Oct. 1941; *s* of Jacques and Pearl Berlins. *Educ:* schools in France and South Africa; Univ. of Witwatersrand (BComm, LLB); LSE (LLM). Legal Asst, Lord Chancellor's Dept, 1969–71; Legal Corresp. and leader writer, The Times, 1971–82; freelance writer and TV presenter, 1982–86; Editor, Law Magazine, 1987–88; presenter, Radio 4 Law in Action, 1988–; columnist, The Guardian, 1988–. *Publications:* Barrister behind Bars, 1974; (with Geoffrey Wansell) Caught in the Act, 1974; (with Clare Dyer) Living Together, 1982; (with Clare Dyer) The Law Machine, 1982, 4th edn 1994; (ed) The Law and You, 1986; numerous articles for newspapers, magazines and legal jls. *Recreations:* cinema, jazz. *Address:* 13 Hadley Street, NW1 8SS. *T:* (020) 7485 3965.

BERMAN, Edward David, (ED Berman), MBE 1979; social entrepreneur, playwright, theatre director and producer; educationalist; Founder, Chief Executive and Artistic Director, Inter-Action, since 1968; *b* 8 March 1941; 2nd *s* of Jack Berman and Ida (*née* Webber); naturalized British citizen, 1976. *Educ:* Harvard (BA Hons); Exeter Coll., Oxford (Rhodes Schol.); Dept of Educnl Studies, Oxford (1978–). *Plays:* 8 produced since 1966; *director: theatre:* (premières) *inter alia* Dirty Linen (London and Broadway), 1976, and The Dogg's Troupe (15 minute) Hamlet, (ed) by Tom Stoppard, 1976 (also filmed, 1976); The Irish Hebrew Lesson, 1976 and Samson and Delilah, 1978, by Wolf Mankowitz; Dogg's Hamlet, Cahoot's Macbeth, 1979, by Tom Stoppard; *producer: theatre:* 125 stage premières for adults and 170 new plays for children, London, 1967–89; *maker of films:* (educational) The Head, 1971; Two Weeler, 1972; Farm in the City, 1977; Marx for Beginners Cartoon (co-prod., voice dir), 1978; *actor:* over 1200 performances as Prof. Dogg, Otto Première Check, Super Santa. Editor: 18 community arts, action and constructive leisure handbooks, 1972–; 2 anthologies of plays, 1976–78. Trustee and Founder, Inter-Action Trust, 1968; Director and Founder: Ambiance Lunch-Hour Th. Club, 1968; Prof. Dogg's Troupe for Children, 1968; Labrys Trust, 1969; Inter-Action Advisory Service, 1970; Infilms, 1970; The Almost Free Th., 1971; Inprint Publishing Unit, 1972; City Farm 1, 1972; Alternative Education Project, 1973–84; Inter-Action Trust Ltd, 1974; Town and Country Inter-Action (Milton Keynes) Ltd, 1975; Ambiance Inter-Action Inc., 1976; Talacre Centre Ltd, 1977; Co-Founder: Inter-Action Housing Trust Ltd, 1970; NUBS, Neighbourhood Use of Bldgs and Space; Community Design Centre, 1974; Beginners Books Ltd, 1978; Inter-Action Housing Co-operative, 1978. Founder, Artistic Dir, BARC, British Amer. Rep. Co., 1978. Devised: Inter-Action Creative Game Method, 1967; Super Santa, Father Xmas Union, 1967–82; Chairman: Save Piccadilly Campaign, 1971–80; Talacre Action Gp, 1972; Nat. Assoc. of Arts Centres, 1975–79; Dir, Islington Bus Co., 1974–76; Treas., Fair Play for Children Campaign, 1975–77; Founder: City Farm Movement, 1976; WAC—Weekend Arts Coll., 1979; co-founder: Sport-Space, 1976; FUSION—London and Commonwealth Youth Ensemble, 1981. Founder and Co-Director: Internat. Inst. for Social Enterprise, 1980; Country Wings, 1981; OPS, Occupation Preparation Systems, 1982; Options Training Ltd, 1983; Social Enterprise Projects Ltd, 1984; Founder and Trustee, Inter-Action Social Enterprise Trust Ltd, Social Enterprise Foundn of Inter-Action, 1984; Cdre, Ships-in-the-City, 1988; Founder and Director: Network Inter-Action; Youth-Tech; Star Dome, 1989; Marketing and Business Services International Ltd, 1992. Special Adviser: on inner city matters to Sec. of State for the Environment, 1982–83; Ministry of Labour, Russia, 1992–94, Min. of Economy, 1993–. As community artist: created 17 formats for participatory theatre, 1968–85; Community Media Van, 1983; Community Cameos, 1977–83; MIY—Make It Yourself, 1978; RIY—Raise It Yourself, 1981; IES—Instant Enterprise Systems, 1981; Learning Domes, 1993; Public Art Workshop, 1994. *Publications:* Prof. R. L. Dogg's Zoo's Who I and II, 1975; Selecting Business Software, 1984; Make a Real Job of It, Breaks for Young Bands, 1985; How to Set Up a Small Business, 1987; Healthy Learning Songs & Activities, 1989; New Game Songs & Activities, 1989; The Democracy Handbook, 1999. *Recreations:* solitude, conversation, work, music. *Address:* Inter-Action, 27 Raleigh Court, Lymer Avenue, SE19 1LS. *T:* (020) 8670 3871.

BERMAN, Sir Franklin (Delow), KCMG 1994 (CMG 1986); HM Diplomatic Service, retired; barrister; Visiting Professor of International Law: University of Oxford, since 2000; University of Cape Town; *b* 23 Dec. 1939; *s* of Joshua Zelic Berman and Gertrude (*née* Levin); *m* 1964, Christine Mary Lawler; two *s* three *d* (triplets). *Educ:* Rondebosch Boys' High Sch., Cape Town; Univ. of Cape Town; Wadham and Nuffield Colls, Oxford (Hon. Fellow, Wadham Coll., 1995). BA, BSc Cape Town; MA Oxford. Rhodes Scholar, 1961; Martin Wronker Prizeman, 1963; called to Bar, Middle Temple, 1966 (Hon. Bencher, 1997). HM Diplomatic Service, 1965–99: Asst Legal Adviser, FO, 1965; Legal Adviser: British Military Govt, Berlin, 1971; British Embassy, Bonn, 1972; Legal Counsellor, FCO, 1974; Counsellor and Legal Adviser, UK Mission to UN, NY, 1982; FCO, 1985, Dep. Legal Advr, 1988, Legal Advr, 1991–99. Mem., Appeals Bd, WEU, 1994–96. Chairman: Diplomatic Service Assoc., 1979–82; Staff Tribunal, Internat. Oil Pollution Compensation Fund, 1986–. Member: Council of Management, British Inst. of Internat. and Comparative Law, 1992–; Council, British Br., Internat. Law Assoc., 1993–; Adv. Council, Centre for Advanced Study of European and Comparative Law, Oxford, 1995–2000; Adv. Council, Oxford Univ. Law Foundn, 1998–; Gov., Inst. of Advanced Legal Studies, Univ. of London, 1992–. J. C. Smith Vis. Fellow, Nottingham Univ., 1993. Hon. Fellow, Soc. of Advanced Legal Studies, 1997. Trustee: Greenwich Foundn for RNC, 1997–; Univ. of Cape Town Trust. Hon. QC 1992. Mem. Editl Bd, British Yearbook of Internat. Law, 1994–. *Recreations:* walking, reading, music, choral singing. *Address:* Essex Court Chambers, 24 Lincoln's Inn Fields, WC2A 3ED. *Club:* Oxford and Cambridge.

BERMAN, Lawrence Sam, CB 1975; retired; *b* 15 May 1928; *yr s* of late Jack and Violet Berman; *m* 1954, Kathleen D. Lewis (*d* 1996); one *s* one *d. Educ:* St Clement Danes Grammar Sch.; London Sch. of Economics. BSc (Econ) 1st cl. hons 1947; MSc (Econ) 1950. Res. Asst, LSE, 1947; Nuffield Coll., Oxford, 1948; Econ. Commn for Europe, 1949; Central Statistical Office: Asst Statistician 1952; Statistician 1955; Chief Statistician 1964; Asst Dir 1968; Dir of Statistics, Depts of Industry and Trade, 1972–83. Statistical Advr, Caribbean Tourism R&D Centre, Barbados, 1984–85. Editor, National Income Blue Book, 1954–60; Member: Council, Royal Statistical Soc., 1970–74 (Vice-Pres., 1973–74); Council, Internat. Assoc. for Research in Income and Wealth, 1980–85; ISI. *Publications:* Caribbean Tourism Statistical Reports; articles and papers in Jl of Royal Statistical Soc., Economica, Economic Trends, Statistical News, etc. *Recreations:* bridge, travel, theatre, collecting sugar tongs and bow ties. *Address:* 10 Carlton Close, Edgware, Mddx HA8 7PY. *T:* (020) 8958 6938.

BERMINGHAM, Gerald Edward; barrister; *b* Dublin, 20 Aug. 1940; *s* of late Patrick Xavier Bermingham and Eva Terescena Bermingham; *m* 1st, 1964, Joan (marr. diss.); two *s*; 2nd, 1978, Judith (marr. diss.); 3rd, 1998, Jilly; one *s. Educ:* Cotton College, N Staffs; Wellingborough Grammar School; Sheffield University (LLB Hons). Admitted Solicitor, 1967; called to the Bar, Gray's Inn, 1985. Councillor, Sheffield City Council, 1975–79, 1980–82. Contested (Lab) SE Derbyshire, 1979. MP (Lab) St Helens South, 1983–2001. *Recreations:* sport, reading, TV.

BERNARD, Beverley; Joint Deputy Chair, Commission for Racial Equality, since 2000; *b* 9 Aug. 1949; *d* of Edmund Blaize and Jane John Baptist; *m* 1974, Leslie Bernard; one *d. Educ:* Univ. of Westminster (BA Hons); Centre for Counselling and Psychotherapy Educn (Dip. Psych). Founder Trustee and CEO, Windsor Fellowship, 1985–95; Advr to Kagiso Trust, 1995–96, Man. Trustee, Nations Trust, 1995–98, RSA; trainee psychotherapist, 1998–2001. *Recreations:* movie buff, rough cooking, dreaming. *Address:* 27 Ford Square, E1 2HS. *Club:* Bougainvillea (Barbados).

BERNARD, Sir Dallas (Edmund), 2nd Bt *cr* 1954; international financial consultant; Chairman: National & Foreign Securities Trust Ltd, 1981–86; Thames Trust Ltd, 1983–86; *b* 14 Dec. 1926; *o s* of Sir Dallas Gerald Mercer Bernard, 1st Bt, and Betty (*d* 1980), *e d* of late Sir Charles Addis, KCMG; *S* father, 1975; *m* 1st, 1959 (marr. diss. 1979); two *d* (and one *d* decd); 2nd, 1979, Mrs Monica Montford, *d* of late James Edward Hudson; one *d. Educ:* Eton Coll.; Corpus Christi Coll., Oxford (MA). FCIS. Director: Dreyfus Intercontinental Investment Fund NV, 1970–91; Morgan Grenfell (Holdings) Ltd, 1972–79; Morgan Grenfell & Co. Ltd, 1964–77; Dominion Securities Ltd, Toronto, 1968–79; Italian Internat. Bank Plc, 1978–89; Dreyfus Dollar Internat. Fund Inc., 1982–91. Mem. Monopolies and Mergers Commn, 1973–79. Mem. Council, GPDST, 1988–93 (Finance Cttee, 1975–92). *Heir:* none. *Address:* 106 Cheyne Walk, SW10 0DG. *T:* (020) 7235 2318. *Club:* Lansdowne.

BERNARD, Daniel, Hon. CMG 1995; Hon. CBE 1992; Ambassador of France to the Court of St James's, since 1998; *b* 13 Sept. 1941; *m* 1964, Monique Beaumet; two *s* one *d. Educ:* Université de Lyon (LèsL (English)); Institut d'Etudes Politiques, Lyon (Dip.); Ecole Nationale d'Administration. Second Sec., Dublin, 1967–71; UN Directorate, Min. of Foreign Affairs, 1975–77; First Sec., Perm. Repn to EEC, 1977–81; Advr to Private Office of External Relations Minister, 1981–83; Deleg., Internat. Affairs Directorate, Industry and Res. Min., 1984; Diplomatic Advr to Prime Minister, 1984–86; Inspr, Min. of Foreign Affairs, 1986; seconded to EEC, 1987–88; Special Advr to Pres. of Nat. Assembly, 1988–90; Dir, Press Information and Communications Dept, and Min. Spokesman, Min. of Foreign Affairs, 1990–92; Prin. Private Sec. to Foreign Minister, 1992–93; Ambassador to Netherlands, 1993–95; Perm. Rep. to UN, Geneva, 1995–98. Chevalier: de l'Ordre National du Mérite (France), 1981; de la Légion d'Honneur (France), 1997. *Recreations:* music, sport. *Address:* French Embassy, 58 Knightsbridge, SW1X 7JT. *T:* (020) 7201 1006, *Fax:* (020) 7201 1003. *Club:* Travellers.

BERNARD, Daniel Camille; Chairman, since 1998, and Chief Executive Officer, since 1992, Carrefour Group; *b* 18 Feb. 1946; *s* of Paul Bernard and Simone (*née* Doise); *m* 1968, Chantal Leduc; one *s* two *d. Educ:* Lycée Camille Desmoulins, Cateau; Lycée Faidherbe, Lille; HEC Business Sch.; Univ. of Paris. Divl Manager, Mammouth, 1976–81; Chief Exec. Officer, Metro France, 1981–89; Mem. Bd, Metro Internat., 1990–92. *Recreations:* mountains, ski-ing, opera. *Address:* Carrefour, 6 avenue Raymond Poincaré, 75769 Paris cedex 16, France. *T:* 153701900.

BERNARD, Joan Constance, MA, BD; FKC; Principal of Trevelyan College, University of Durham, and Honorary Lecturer in Theology, 1966–79; *b* 6 April 1918; *d* of late Adm. Vivian Henry Gerald Bernard, CB, and Eileen Mary Bernard. *Educ:* Ascham Sch., Sydney, NSW; St Anne's Coll., Oxford Univ. (BA Lit. Hum. 1940, MA 1943); King's Coll., London (BD 1961). War Service, ATS, 1940–46; AA Comd, 1940–44; SO Air Def. Div., SHAEF, 1944–45 (mentioned in despatches 1945); Special Projectile Ops Gp, July-Nov. 1945. Dep. Admin. Officer, NCB, 1946–50; Asst Sec., Educn, Music and Drama, NFWI, 1950–57; full-time student, 1957–61; Warden, Canterbury Hall, Univ. of London, and part-time Lectr, Dept of Theol., KCL, 1962–65; FKC 1976. Mem., Ordination Candidates' Cttee, ACCM, 1972–91; Examining Chaplain to Bishop of Southwark, 1984–94. Mem., Fabric Adv. Cttee, Southwark Cathedral, 1992–97. FRSA 1984. *Recreations:* music (assisted John Tobin in Handel research for many years); mountaineering, photography, travel. *Address:* 89 Rennie Court, Upper Ground, SE1 9NZ.

BERNARD, Ralph Mitchell; Chief Executive, Classic FM plc, since 1997 (Director, since 1991); Chairman, GWR Group plc, since 2001; *b* 11 Feb. 1953; *s* of Reginald and Irene Bernard; *m* 1977, Lisa Anne Susan Kiené; four *d. Educ:* Caterham High Sch., Ilford. Copy boy, London News Service, 1970–71; Reporter: Express and Independent, Leytonstone, 1971–72; Stratford Express, 1972–73; Cambridge Evening News, 1973–75; radio journalist, 1975–78, Documentaries Ed., 1978–80, Radio Hallam, Sheffield; News Ed., Hereward Radio, Peterborough, 1980–82; Prog. Controller, 1982–83, Man. Dir, 1983–85, Wiltshire Radio; Pre-launch Manager, Classic FM, 1991. Chairman: London News Radio (LBC and News Direct), 1996–; Digital One Ltd, 1998–; Dir, Ind. Radio News, 1994–. Chm., Campaign Bd, Great Western Hosp., Swindon, 2000. Fellow, Radio Acad., 1999. Sony Gold Award, 2000. *Recreations:* music (most), walking, newspaper originals, cricket. *Address:* Classic FM House, Swallow Place, W1B 2AG. *T:* (020) 7343 9000.

BERNAYS, Rosamund; *see* Horwood-Smart, R.

BERNBAUM, Prof. Gerald; Vice-Chancellor and Chief Executive, South Bank University, 1993–2001; *b* 25 March 1936; *s* of Benjamin Bernbaum and Betty (*née* Sack); *m* 1959, Pamela Valerie Cohen (marr. diss. 1987); two *s. Educ:* Hackney Downs Grammar Sch.; LSE (BSc Econ 1957); London Inst. of Educn (PGCE 1958). Mitcham Grammar School for Boys: Asst Master, 1958–59; Head of Dept, 1959–62; Head of Dept, Rutherford Comprehensive Sch., 1962–64; University of Leicester School of Education: Lectr, 1964–70; Sen. Lectr, 1970–74; Prof. of Educn, 1974–93; Dir, 1976–85; Pro-Vice-Chancellor, 1985–87; Exec. Pro-Vice-Chancellor and Registrar, 1987–93. Hon. LLD Leicester, 2000; Hon. DLitt Assumption Univ., Bangkok. *Publications:* Social Change and the Schools, 1967; Knowledge and Ideology in the Sociology of Education, 1977; (ed) Schooling in Decline, 1978; (with H. Patrick and M. Galton) Educational Provision in Small Primary Schools, 1990; articles in Sociol Rev., Brit. Jl Educnl Studies. *Recreations:*

public affairs, professional sport, music. *Address:* c/o South Bank University, 103 Borough Road, SE1 0AA. *T:* (020) 7815 6004.

BERNERD, Elliott; Chairman, Chelsfield plc, since 1987; *b* 23 May 1945; *s* of late Geoffrey Bernerd and of Trudie Malawer (*née* Melzack); *m* 1st, 1968, Susan Elizabeth Lynton (marr. diss. 1989); two *d*; 2nd, 1992, Sonia Ramsay (*née* Ramalho). Chm. Wentworth Group Holdings Ltd, 1990–. Chairman: London Philharmonic Trust, 1987–94; South Bank Foundn, 1996–; South Bank Bd Ltd, 1998–. *Recreations:* tennis, skiing. *Address:* Chelsfield plc, 67 Brook Street, W1K 4NJ. *T:* (020) 7493 3977. *Clubs:* Savile, Cavalry and Guards, Royal Automobile; Wentworth.

BERNERS, Baroness (16th in line), *cr* 1455; **Pamela Vivien Kirkham;** *b* 30 Sept. 1929; *er d* of Harold Williams and Baroness Berners, 15th in line (*d* 1992); *S* to Barony of mother (called out of abeyance, 1995); *m* 1952, Michael Joseph Sperry Kirkham; two *s* one *d*. *Educ:* Bredenbury Court, Hereford; Stonar Sch., Wilts. Radcliffe Infirmary, Oxford (SRN, 1951). *Recreations:* painting, drawing, gardening, reading. *Heir:* *s* Hon. Rupert William Tyrwhitt Kirkham [*b* 18 Feb. 1953; *m* 1994, Lisa Carol Judy Lipsey; one *s*].

BERNERS-LEE, Prof. Timothy John, OBE 1997; FRS 2001; FREng; 3Com Founders Professor, since 1999, and Director, World Wide Web Consortium, Massachusetts Institute of Technology; *b* London, 8 June 1955. *Educ:* Emanuel Sch., London; Queen's Coll., Oxford (BA 1976; Hon. Fellow, 1999). Plessey Telecommunications Ltd, 1976–78; software engr, D. G. Nash Ltd, 1978; ind. consultant, 1978–80, incl. software consultancy, CERN, Geneva (wrote unpublished prog., Enquire, forerunner of World Wide Web); Founding Dir, responsible for tech. design, Image Computer Systems Ltd, 1981–84; Fellowship, CERN, 1984–94: global hypertext project, 1989, became World Wide Web, 1990 (available on Internet, 1991); designed URL (universal resource locator) and HTML (hypertext markup lang.); joined Lab. for Computer Sci., MIT, 1994. MacArthur Fellow, John D. and Catherine T. MacArthur Foundn, 1998. Distinguished FBCS; FREng 2001. Hon. DSc Oxon, 2001. *Publication:* Weaving the Web, 2000. *Address:* Laboratory for Computer Science, 545 Technology Square, Cambridge, MA 02139, USA.

BERNEY, Sir Julian (Reedham Stuart), 11th Bt *cr* 1620; *b* 26 Sept. 1952; *s* of Lieut John Reedham Erskine Berney (killed on active service in Korea, 1952), Royal Norfolk Regt, and of Hon. Jean Davina, *d* of 1st Viscount Stuart of Findhorn, PC, CH, MVO, MC; *S* grandfather, 1975; *m* 1976, Sheena Mary, *yr d* of Ralph Day and Ann Gordon Day; two *s* one *d*. *Educ:* Wellington Coll.; North-East London Polytechnic. FRICS 1992. *Recreation:* sailing. *Heir:* *s* William Reedham John Berney, *b* 29 June 1980. *Address:* Reeds House, 40 London Road, Maldon, Essex CM9 6HE. *T:* (01621) 853420. *Clubs:* Royal Ocean Racing; Royal Cruising.

BERNSTEIN, family name of **Baron Bernstein of Craigweil**.

BERNSTEIN OF CRAIGWEIL, Baron *cr* 2000 (Life Peer), of Craigweil, in the co. of West Sussex; **Alexander Bernstein;** Chairman, Granada Group plc, 1979–96 (Director, 1964–96); Director, Waddington Galleries, since 1966; *b* 15 March 1936; *s* of late Cecil Bernstein and of Myra Ella, *d* of Lesser and Rachel Lesser; *m* 1st, 1962, Vanessa Anne Mills (marr. diss. 1993); one *s* one *d*; 2nd, 1995, Angela Mary Serota. *Educ:* Stowe Sch.; St John's Coll., Cambridge. Man. Dir, 1964–68, Chm., 1977–86, Granada TV Rental Ltd; Jt Man. Dir, Granada Television Ltd, 1971–75. Trustee: Civic Trust for the North-West, 1964–86; Granada Foundn, 1968–; Theatres Trust, 1996–2000; Trusthouse Charitable Foundn, 1996–; Chairman: Royal Exchange Theatre, 1983–94 (Dep. Chm., 1980–83); Old Vic Theatre Trust, 1998–. Mem., Nat. Theatre Develt Council, 1996–98. Member of Court: Univ. of Salford, 1976–87; Univ. of Manchester, 1983–98. Hon. DLitt Salford 1981; Hon. LLD Manchester, 1996. *Address:* c/o House of Lords, SW1A 0PW.

BERNSTEIN, Howard; Chief Executive, Manchester City Council, since 1998; *b* 9 April 1953; *s* of Maurice and Miriam Bernstein; *m* 1980, Yvonne Selwyn; one *s* one *d* (and one *s* decd). *Educ:* Ducie High Sch., Manchester; London Univ. (ext.). Manchester City Council: Head of Urban Policy, 1980–86; Asst Chief Exec., 1986–90; Dep. Chief Exec., 1990–98; Dep. Clerk, 1986–98, Clerk, 1998–, Gtr Manchester PTA; Chief Exec., Manchester City Centre Task Force, 1996–. Sec., Commonwealth Games Organising Cttee, 1996–. *Recreations:* sport, particularly football and cricket. *Address:* Manchester City Council, Town Hall, Manchester M60 2LA. *T:* (0161) 234 3006.

BERNSTEIN, Her Honour Ingeborg, (Inge); a Circuit Judge, 1991–2001; *b* 24 Feb. 1931; *d* of Sarah and Eli Bernstein; *m* 1967, Eric Geoffrey Goldrein; one *s* one *d*. *Educ:* Peterborough County School; St Edmund's College, Liverpool; Liverpool University. Called to the Bar, Inner Temple, 1952; practice on Northern Circuit; a Recorder, 1978–91. Chm., Mental Health Review Tribunal; Mem., Mental Health Act Commn, 1984–86. *Recreation:* the domestic arts. *Address:* 7 Hale Road, Hale Village, Liverpool L24 5RB. *T:* (0151) 425 2155.

BERNSTEIN, Ronald Harold, DFC 1944; QC 1969; FCIArb; a Recorder of the Crown Court, 1974–90; *b* 18 Aug. 1918; *s* of late Mark and Fanny Bernstein; *m* 1955, Judy, *d* of David Levi, MS, and Vera Levi; three *s* one *d*. *Educ:* Swansea Grammar Sch.; Balliol Coll., Oxford. BA (Jurisprudence) 1939; FCIArb 1982. Served in RA, 1939–46, and in 654 Air OP Sqdn, RAF, 1942–46. Commanded 661 Air OP Sqdn, RAuxAF, 1954–56. Called to the Bar, Middle Temple, 1948, Bencher, 1975–. Mem., Gen. Council of the Bar, 1965–69; Vice-Pres., 1988–91, Vice-Pres. Emeritus, 1991–, CIArb. Pres., Highgate Soc., 1983–93. Hon. ARICS 1986; Hon. FSVA 1987. *Publications:* (jointly) The Restrictive Trade Practices Act, 1956; Handbook of Rent Review, 1981, and subseq. edns to 1997; Handbook of Arbitration Practice, 1987, 3rd edn 1997; Joint Ventures in Property, 1993; Essentials of Rent Review, 1995. *Address:* (professional) Falcon Chambers, Falcon Court, EC4Y 1AA. *T:* (020) 7353 2484; (home) (020) 8340 9933, *Fax:* (020) 8348 7676. *Club:* Athenæum.

BERRAGAN, Maj.-Gen. Gerald Brian, CB 1988; Chief Executive, Institute of Packaging, 1988–98; *b* 2 May 1933; *s* of William James and Marion Beatrice Berragan; *m* 1956, Anne Helen Kelly; three *s*. Commissioned REME 1954; attached 7th Hussars, Hong Kong, 1954–55; transf. RAOC 1956; served UK, Belgium, Germany and with 44 Para Bde (TA); Staff College, 1966; Nat. Defence Coll., 1972–73; Comdr RAOC 3 Div., 1973–76; AQMG HQ N Ireland, 1976–78; HQ DGOS, 1978–80; Comdt Central Ordnance Depot, Chilwell, 1980–82; Sen. Management Course, Henley, 1982; Comdt COD Bicester, 1982–83; Dir, Supply Ops (Army), 1983–85; Sen. Internat. Defence Management Course, USA, 1985; Dir Gen. of Ordnance Services, 1985–88. Col Comdt, RAOC, 1988–93, RLC 1993–98. UK Dir, World Packaging Orgn, 1988–98. FInstPkg. *Recreation:* tennis. *Clubs:* Athenæum, Army and Navy.

BERRIDGE, (Donald) Roy, CBE 1981; FREng; Chairman, South of Scotland Electricity Board, 1977–82 (Deputy Chairman, 1974–77); *b* 24 March 1922; *s* of Alfred Leonard Berridge and Pattie Annie Elizabeth (*née* Holloway); *m* 1945, Marie (*née* Kinder); one *d*. *Educ:* King's Sch., Peterborough; Leicester Coll. of Art and Technology. FREng (FEng 1979); FIMechE 1962. Taylor, Taylor & Hobson Ltd, Leicester, 1940; James Gordon & Co., 1946; British Electricity Authority, 1948; seconded to AERE, Harwell, 1952; Reactor Design Engr, CEGB, 1962; Chief Generation Design Engr, 1964–70; Dir-Gen., Gen. Develt Constr. Div., CEGB, 1970–72; Dir of Engrg, SSEB, 1972–74. Dir, Howden Gp, 1982–88. Member: N of Scotland Hydro-Electric Bd, 1977–82; Scottish Economic Council, 1977–83; CBI (Scottish Council), 1977–83. *Address:* East Gate, Chapel Square, Deddington, Oxon OX15 0SG.

BERRIDGE, Sir Michael (John), Kt 1998; PhD; FRS 1984; Fellow of Trinity College, Cambridge, since 1972; Head of Signalling Programme, Babraham Institute Laboratory of Molecular Signalling, since 1996; *b* 22 Oct. 1938; *s* of George Kirton Berridge and Stella Elaine Hards; *m* 1965, Susan Graham Winter; one *s* one *d*. *Educ:* University Coll. of Rhodesia and Nyasaland (BSc); Univ. of Cambridge (PhD). Post-doctoral Fellow: Univ. of Virginia, 1965–66; Case Western Reserve Univ., Cleveland, Ohio, 1966–69; AFRC Lab. of Molecular Signalling (formerly Unit of Insect Neurophysiology and Pharmacology), Dept of Zoology, Univ. of Cambridge, 1969–90; Babraham Inst. Lab. of Molecular Signalling, 1990–. Founder FMedSci 1998. King Faisal Internat. Prize in Sci., 1986; Jeantet Prize in Medicine, 1986; Gairdner Foundn Internat. Award, 1988; Lasker Basic Med. Res. Award, 1989; Dr H. P. Heineken Prize for Biochemistry and Biophysics, 1994; Wolf Foundn Prize in Medicine, 1995. *Publications:* papers in Jl Exptl Biol., Biochem. Jl and Nature. *Recreations:* golf, gardening. *Address:* The Babraham Institute, Babraham Hall, Babraham, Cambridge CB2 4AT. *T:* (01223) 496621.

BERRIEDALE, Lord; Alexander James Richard Sinclair; *b* 26 March 1981; *s* and *heir* of Earl of Caithness, *qv*. *Educ:* St David's Coll., Llandudno. *Recreations:* outdoor pursuits.

BERRILL, Sir Kenneth, GBE 1988; KCB 1971; Chairman, Moneda Chile Fund, since 1995; *b* 28 Aug. 1920; *m* 1st, 1941, Brenda West (marr. diss.); one *s*; 2nd, 1950, June Phillips (marr. diss.); one *s* one *d*; 3rd, 1977, Jane Marris. *Educ:* London Sch. of Economics; Trinity Coll., Cambridge. BSc(Econ) London; MA Cantab, 1949. Served War, 1939–45, REME. Economic Adviser to Turkey, Guyana, Cameroons, OECD, and World Bank. Univ. Lectr in Economics, Cambridge, 1949–69; Rockefeller Fellowship Stanford and Harvard Univs, 1951–52; Fellow and Bursar, St Catharine's Coll., Cambridge, 1949–62, Hon. Fellow, 1974; Prof., MIT, 1962; Fellow and First Bursar, King's Coll., Cambridge, 1962–69, Hon. Fellow, 1973; HM Treasury Special Adviser (Public Expenditure), 1967–69; Chm., UGC, 1969–73; Head of Govt Econ. Service and Chief Economic Advr, HM Treasury, 1973–74; Head of Central Policy Review Staff, Cabinet Office, 1974–80; Chm., Vickers da Costa Ltd and Vickers da Costa & Co. Hong Kong Ltd, 1981–85; Chm., SIB, 1985–88; Dep. Chm., 1982–87, Chm., 1987–90, Robert Horne Gp; Chm., Commonwealth Equities Fund, 1990–95. Mem., Stock Exchange, London, 1981–85. Member: Council for Scientific Policy, 1969–72; Adv. Bd for Research Councils, 1972–77; Adv. Council for Applied R&D, 1977–80; Brit. Nat. Commn for UNESCO, 1967–70; UN Cttee for Develt Planning, 1984–87; Inter-Univ. Council, 1969–73; UGC, Univ. of S Pacific, 1972–85; Council, Royal Economic Soc., 1972– (Vice Pres., 1986–); Adv. Bd, RCDS, 1974–80; Review Bd for Govt Contracts, 1981–85; Chm. Exec. Cttee, NIESR, 1988–96; (Nominated), Governing Council, Lloyd's, 1983–88. Dir, UK-Japan 2000 Gp, 1986–90. Advr, Nippon Credit Internat. Ltd, 1989–99; Dep. Chm., General Funds Investment Trust, 1982–85; Member: Baring Private Equity Partners Adv. Council, 1996–2000; Baring Eur. Private Equity Fund Adv. Council, 1999–; Director: Investing in Success Investment Trust, 1965–67; Ionian Bank, 1969–73; Dep. Chm., Universities' Superannuation Scheme, 1981–85 (Chm., Jt Negotiating Cttee, 1990–). Trustee: London Philharmonic, 1987–; Newnham Coll. Develt Trust, 1989–95; Nat. Extension Coll., 1990– (Vice-Chm. Trustees, 1997–); Res. Inst. for Consumer Affairs, 1990–96. Pro-Chancellor, and Chm. Council, Open Univ., 1983–96; Governor: Admin. Staff Coll., Henley, 1969–84; ODI, 1969–73; Mem. Council, Salford Univ., 1981–84. McDonnell Scholar, World Inst. for Develt Economic Res., 1988, 1990. Mem., Cambridge City Council, 1963–67. CIMgt (CBIM 1987). FRSA 1988; Hon. Fellow: LSE, 1970; Chelsea Coll., London, 1973; Hon. FKC 1989; Fellow, Open Univ., 1997. Hon. LLD: Cambridge, 1974; Bath, 1974; East Anglia, 1975; Leicester, 1975; DUniv Open, 1974; Hon. DTech Loughborough, 1974; Hon DSc Aston, 1974. Jephcott Lectr and Medallist, 1978; Stamp Meml Lectr, 1980. *Recreations:* gardening, sailing. *Address:* Salt Hill, Bridle Way, Grantchester, Cambs CB3 9NY. *T:* (01223) 840335, *Fax:* (01223) 845939. *Clubs:* Climbers (Hon. Mem.); Himalayan; Cambridge Alpine.

BERRIMAN, Sir David, Kt 1990; FCIB; CIMgt; Chairman, Association of Lloyd's Members, 1994–98 (Committee Member, 1993–98); *b* 20 May 1928; *s* of late Algernon Edward Berriman, OBE and late Enid Kathleen Berriman (*née* Sutcliffe); *m* 1st, 1955, Margaret Lloyd (*née* Owen) (marr. diss. 1970; she *d* 1995); two *s*; 2nd, 1971, Shirley Elizabeth (*née* Wright) (*d* 1993); 3rd, 1995, Patricia Ann Salter (*née* Walker). *Educ:* Winchester; New Coll., Oxford (MA, Dip. Econ. and Pol. Sc.); Harvard Business Sch. PMD course, 1961. First National City Bank of New York, 1952–56; Ford Motor Co. Ltd, 1956–60; AEI Hotpoint, 1960–63; Gen. Manager, United Leasing Corporation Ltd, 1963–64; Morgan Grenfell & Co. Ltd: Manager, 1964; Exec. Dir, 1968–73; Dir, Guinness Mahon & Co. Ltd, 1973–87 (Exec. Dir, 1973–85). Chairman: Bunzl Textile Holdings Ltd, 1981–88 (Dep. Chm., 1980); Alban Communications Ltd, 1988–90 (Dir, 1983–; Dep. Chm., 1987–88); Privatised Public Service Pension Plan Trustees Ltd, 1994–97; Director (non-exec.): Cable and Wireless, 1975–88; Sky Television (formerly Satellite Television), 1981–89 (Chm., 1981–85); Bahrein Telecommunications Corp., 1982–88; Britannia Building Soc., 1983–93; Ashenden Enterprises Ltd, 1983–; Videotron Hldgs plc, 1989–97; KDB Bank (UK) Ltd, 1991–98. Chairman: Lewisham and N Southwark DHA, 1981–84; NE Thames RHA, 1984–90. Member: Govt review body on Harland and Wolff diversification, 1980; Corp. of Lloyd's Disciplinary Bd, 1996–; Bd of Trade's Interim Action Cttee for the Film Industry, 1977–85; British Screen Adv. Council, 1985–91. Director: British Screen Finance Ltd, 1985–91; Nat. Film Develt Fund, 1985–91. Dep. Chm., Nat. Film and Television School, 1988–92 (Gov., 1977–92). Chairman: MacIntyre Care, 1978–92 (Gov., 1977–92); MacIntyre Charitable Trust, 1986–92; MacIntyre Foundn, 1993–95; Member, Council: Internat. Hosp. Fedn, 1985–86; King Edward's Hosp. Fund for London, 1985–90. Trustee: New Coll., Oxford Development Fund, 1983–95; Kent Community Housing Trust, 1990– (Dep. Chm., 1998–). *Recreations:* golf, lawn tennis. *Address:* Winwick House, Red Hill, Wateringbury, Kent ME18 5NN. *Clubs:* Royal Automobile, International Lawn Tennis; Wildernesse Golf (Sevenoaks); Royal St George's Golf.

BERRY, family name of **Baron Hartwell, Viscounts Camrose** and **Kemsley**.

BERRY, Anthony Arthur; Chairman, Berry Bros & Rudd Ltd, 1965–85; *b* 16 March 1915; *s* of Francis L. Berry and Amy Marie (*née* Freeman); *m* 1953, Sonia Alice, *d* of Sir Harold Graham-Hodgson, KCVO; one *s* one *d*. *Educ:* Charterhouse; Trinity Hall, Cambridge. Served War, RNVR, 1939–45, incl. 2¼ yrs in the Mediterranean. Joined the wine trade on leaving Cambridge, 1936; rejoined family firm of Berry Bros & Rudd on completion of war service; Dir, 1946–. Worshipful Co. of Vintners: Liveryman, 1946; Mem. Court, 1972–; Master, 1980–81. *Recreations:* golf, walking. *Clubs:* Boodle's, MCC;

Saintsbury; Bath and County (Bath); Royal Wimbledon Golf; Royal St George's Golf (Sandwich).

BERRY, Anthony Charles; QC 1994; a Recorder, since 2000; *b* 4 Oct. 1950; *s* of Geoffrey Vernon Berry and Audrey Millicent Berry (*née* Farrar); *m* 1977, Susan Carmen Traversi; three *s* one *d*. *Educ:* Downside Sch.; Lincoln Coll., Oxford (BA Phil. and Psychol.). Called to the Bar, Gray's Inn, 1976. Sec., Criminal Bar Assoc., 1991–93; Mem., Bar Council, 1993–95. *Recreations:* tennis, golf. *Address:* 9 Bedford Row, WC1R 4AZ. *T:* (020) 7489 2727.

BERRY, (Anthony) Scyld (Ivens); cricket correspondent, The Sunday Telegraph, since 1993; *b* 28 April 1954; *s* of Prof. Francis Berry, *qv*; *m* 1984, Sunita Ghosh; two *s* one *d*. *Educ:* Westbourne School, Sheffield; Ampleforth College; Christ's College, Cambridge (MA Oriental Studies). Cricket correspondent: The Observer, 1978–89; The Sunday Correspondent, 1989–90; The Independent on Sunday, 1991–93. *Publications:* Cricket Wallah, 1982; Train to Julia Creek, 1984; (ed) The Observer on Cricket, 1987; Cricket Odyssey, 1988; (with Phil Edmonds) 100 Great Bowlers, 1989. *Recreations:* playing village cricket, being at home. *Address:* c/o The Sunday Telegraph, 1 Canada Square, Canary Wharf, E14 5DT. *Club:* Hinton Charterhouse Cricket.

BERRY, Cicely Frances, (Mrs H. D. Moore), OBE 1985; Voice Director, Royal Shakespeare Co., since 1969; *b* 17 May 1926; *d* of Cecil and Frances Berry; *m* 1951, Harry Dent Moore (*d* 1978); two *s* one *d*. *Educ:* Eothen Sch., Caterham, Surrey; Central Sch. of Speech and Drama, London. Teacher, Central Sch. of Speech and Drama, 1948–68; 4-week Voice Workshops: Nat. Repertory Co. of Delhi, 1980; Directors and Actors in Australia (org. by Aust. Council), 1983; Directors, Actors, Teachers in China, Chinese Min. of Culture, 1984; text-based workshops: Theatre Voice, Stratford, 1992; Actors in Croatia, Poland, Bulgaria and the Netherlands, 1993; workshops: Writers in Stratford, 1993; Eur. League of Insts of Arts, Berlin, 1994; Theatre For A New Audience, NY, 1997 and 1998 (Artistic Associate, 1997); has also taught and lectured in Brazil; taught in Colombia and Croatia, 1998. Hon. Prof., de Montfort Univ.; Vis. Fellow, Central Sch. of Speech and Drama, 1994–. Organised: Internat. Voice Conf., Stratford, 1995, 1998; debate, Theatre and Citizenship, Barbican, 1997. Plays directed: Hamlet, Educn Dept, NT, 1985; King Lear, The Other Place, Stratford and Almeida Theatre, 1989. Patron of Northumberland and Leicester Youth Theatres. FRSAMD 1987. Hon. Dr, Nat. Acad. of Theatre Studies, Bulgaria, 1997; Hon. DLitt Birmingham, 1999. Sam Wanamaker Award, Globe Theatre, 2000. *Publications:* Voice and the Actor, 1973, 7th edn 2000; Your Voice and How to Use it Successfully, 1975, 2nd edn as Your Voice and How to Use it, 1994, new edn 2000; The Actor and the Text, 1987, new edn 2000; Text in Action, 2001.

BERRY, Sir Colin (Leonard), Kt 1993; DSc; FRCPath; Professor of Morbid Anatomy, University of London, at The London Hospital Medical College, since 1976; Warden of Joint Medical and Dental School, St Bartholomew's and Royal London Hospitals, and Vice-Principal for Medicine and Dentistry, Queen Mary and Westfield College, London University, 1995–96; *b* 28 Sept. 1937; *s* of Ronald Leonard Berry and Peggy-Caroline (*née* Benson); *m* 1960, Yvonne Waters; two *s*. *Educ:* privately, and Beckenham Grammar Sch.; Charing Cross Hosp. Med. Sch. (MB, BS; Governors' Clinical Gold Medal, Llewellyn Schol., Pierera Prize in Clinical Subjects, Steadman Prize in Path.); trained in Histopath., Charing Cross Hosp., 1962–64. MD 1968, PhD 1970, DSc 1993 (London). FRCPath 1979; FFPM 1991; FRCP 1993; FFOM 1995; FRCPE 1997. Lectr and Sen. Lectr, Inst. of Child Health, London, 1964–70; Reader in Pathology, Guy's Hosp. Med. Sch., 1970–76; Dean, London Hosp. Med. Coll., 1994–95. Gillson Scholar, Worshipful Soc. of Apothecaries, 1967–68 and 1970–72; Arris and Gail Lectr, RCS, 1973; Lectures: Bawden, BCPC, 1990; John Hull Grundy, Royal Army Med. Coll., 1992; Simonides, European Soc. of Pathology, 1993; Lucas, RCP, 1994. Chairman: Cttee on Dental and Surgical Materials, 1982–92 (Vice-Chm., 1979–82); Scientific Sub-Cttee on Pesticides, MAFF, 1984–87; Adv. Cttee on Pesticides, MAFF/DHSS, 1988–99 (Mem., 1982–87); Bd in Histology and Cytology, Union Européenne des Médecins Spécialistes, 1993–99; Member: Toxicology Review Panel, WHO, 1976–84, 1987–; Scientific Adv. Cttee on Pesticides, EEC, 1981–88; Cttee on Toxicity of Chemicals in Food, Consumer Products and the Environment, 1982–88; Cttee on Safety of Medicines, Dept. of Health, 1990–92; Ownership Bd, Pesticides Safety Directorate, 1994–99; Steering Gp on Envmt and Health, ESF, 1995–; MRC, 1990–; GMC, 1993–96 and 1998–; Chm., Physiological Systems and Disorders Bd, MRC, 1990–92 (Mem., 1988–). President: Developmental Path. Soc., 1976–79; European Soc. of Pathology, 1989–91 (Pres. elect, 1987–89); Pres. elect, 2001–02, Pres., June 2002–, British Acad. of Forensic Scis. Sec., Fedn of Assocs of Clinical Profs, 1987–; Chm. Council, Res. Defence Soc., 1993–99; Hon. Sec., ACP, 1982–85 (Meetings Sec., 1979–82). Scientific Advr, BIBRA, 1987–90. Treasurer, RCPath, 1988–93 (Asst Registrar, 1981–84). Asst to Court, Apothecaries' Soc., 1990–. Mem. Council, Imp. Soc. of Knights Bachelor, 1997–. Founder FMedSci 1998. Corresp. Mem., Deutsche Akad. der Naturforscher Leopoldina, 1993. *Publications:* Teratology: trends and applications, 1975; Paediatric Pathology, 1981, 3rd edn 1995; Diseases of the Arterial Wall, 1988; contrib. to many texts; numerous publns in Ljl of Path., Circulation Res. and other path. jls. *Recreations:* fishing, pond building. *Clubs:* Reform, Farmers'; Le Touquet Golf.

BERRY, Prof. Francis; Emeritus Professor of English Language and Literature, Royal Holloway College, University of London, since 1980; *b* 23 March 1915; *s* of James Berry and Mary Augusta Jane Berry (*née* Ivens); *m* 1st, 1947, Nancy Melloney (*d* 1967), *d* of Cecil Newton Graham; one *s* one *d*; 2nd, 1970, Patricia (marr. diss. 1975), *d* of John Gordon Thomson; 3rd, 1979, Eileen, *d* of Eric Charles Lear. *Educ:* Hereford Cathedral Sch.; Dean Close Sch.; University Coll., Exeter. BA London (1st cl. hons); MA Exeter. Solicitor's articled clerk, 1931; University Coll., Exeter, 1937. War Service, 1939–46. University Coll., Exeter, 1946; successively Asst Lectr, Lectr, Sen. Lectr, Reader in English Literature, and Prof. of English Literature, Univ. of Sheffield, 1947–70; Prof. of English Lang. and Lit., Royal Holloway Coll., Univ. of London, 1970–80. Visiting Lecturer: Carleton Coll., Minn, USA, 1951–52; University Coll. of the West Indies, Jamaica, 1957; W. P. Ker Vis. Lectr, Glasgow, 1979; Lectr for British Council: in India, 1966–67; tour of univs in Japan, 1983, of univs of New Zealand, 1988; Vis. Fellow, ANU, Canberra, 1979; Vis. Prof. of English, Univ. of Malaŵi, 1980–81. Pres. SW of England Shakespeare Trust, 1985. FRSL 1968. Hon. Fellow, RHBNC, London Univ., 1987. *Publications:* Gospel of Fire, 1933; Snake in the Moon, 1936; The Iron Christ, 1938; Fall of a Tower, 1942; Murdock and Other Poems, 1947; The Galloping Centaur, 1952, 2nd edn 1970; Herbert Read, 1953, 2nd edn 1961; (ed) An Anthology of Medieval Poems, 1954; Poets' Grammar: time, tense and mood in poetry, 1958, 2nd edn, 1974; Morant Bay and other poems, 1961; Poetry and the Physical Voice, 1962; The Shakespeare Inset, 1965, 2nd edn 1971; Ghosts of Greenland, 1967; John Masefield: the Narrative Poet, 1968; (ed) Essays and Studies for the English Association, 1969; Thoughts on Poetic Time, 1972; I Tell of Greenland (novel), 1977; From the Red Fort: new and selected poems, 1984; Collected Poems, 1994; contributor: Review of English Studies; Essays in Criticism; Poetry Nat. Review; BBC Radio Three, ABC, etc. *Recreations:* following first-class cricket, chess, travel, gardening. *Address:* 4 Eastgate Street, Winchester, Hants SO23 8EB. *T:* (01962) 854439.

See also A. S. I. Berry.

BERRY, Rt Rev. Fraser; *see* Berry, Rt Rev. R. E. F.

BERRY, (Gwenda) Lynne; Chief Executive, General Social Care Council, since 2001; *b* 27 Jan. 1953. Social Worker, Wandsworth LBC, 1976–79; Community Worker, Camden Council of Social Service, 1979–81; Lecturer: PCL, 1981–84; NISW, 1984–88; Social Services Inspector, DoH, 1988–90; Chief Exec., Family Welfare Assoc., 1990–96; Exec. Dir, Charity Commn, 1996–99; Chief Exec., EOC, 1999–2001. Non-exec. Dir, Europe Div., DTI. Chm., CPAG, 2001–; Trustee, Tomorrow Project, 2001–. Member of Council: Inst. of Educn, London Univ.; Franco-British Council. FRSA. *Publications:* contrib. books on Europe and social policy, complaints procedures and consumer rights, and jls on social policy and women's issues. *Address:* General Social Care Council, Goldings House, Hay's Lane, SE1 2HB. *T:* (020) 7397 5142; *e-mail:* lynneberry@gscc.co.uk.

BERRY, Dr James William; Director General (formerly Director) of Scientific and Technical Intelligence, 1982–89; *b* 5 Oct. 1931; *s* of Arthur Harold Berry and Mary Margaret Berry; *m* 1960, Monica Joan Hill; three *d*. *Educ:* St Mary's Coll., Blackburn; Municipal Technical Coll., Blackburn; Manchester Univ. (BSc); Leeds Univ. (PhD). FIEE. Royal Signals and Radar Estab., Malvern, 1956–60; Admiralty Surface Weapons Estab., Portsdown, 1960–76 (Head of Computer Div., 1972–76); Dir of Long Range Surveillance and Comd and Control Projs, MoD (PE), 1976–79; Dir Gen. Strategic Electronic Systems, MoD (PE), 1979–82. Organist, St Michael's RC Church, Leigh Park, Havant; 'cellist mem. of Petersfield Orch. *Recreations:* music (organ, 'cello, piano), walking, watching wild life, geriatric sport. *Club:* Civil Service.

BERRY, John, CBE 1968; DL; MA (Cantab); PhD (St Andrews); FRSE 1936; consultant on water impoundment biology, 1968–90; Conservation and Fisheries Adviser to: North of Scotland Hydro-Electric Board, 1968–89; South of Scotland Electricity Board, 1973–89; *b* Edinburgh, 5 Aug. 1907; *o s* of late William Berry, OBE, DL, Tayfield, Newport, Fife; *m* 1936, Hon. Bride Fremantle, MA (Cantab), 3rd *d* of 3rd Baron Cottesloe, CB; two *s* one *d*. *Educ:* Eton; Trinity Coll., Cambridge (BA 1929 (Zoo. Chem. Phys. Pt I and Law Pt II); MA 1933; PhD 1935). Salmon research, Fishery Bd for Scotland, 1930–31; Biological Research Station, University Coll., Southampton, Research Officer, 1932–36 and Dir, 1937–39. Press Censor for Scotland, 1940–44; Biologist and Information Officer, North of Scotland Hydro-Electric Bd, 1944–49; Dir of Nature Conservation in Scotland, 1949–67. Consultant Ecologist, Scottish Landowners' Fedn, 1984–87. Chm., Interdepartmental Salmon Res. Gp (UK and Ireland), 1971–82; Dir, British Pavilion, Expo '71, Budapest. Mem., Scottish Marine Biology Assoc., 1947–71 (RSE rep., Exec. Cttee, 1947; Mem Council, 1948–54, 1957–66). Pres. 1954–56, Vice-Pres. 1956–60, and Mem., 1966–72, Commn on Ecology, Internat. Union for Conservation of Natural Resources; UK rep., Exec. Bd, Internat. Wildfowl Research Bureau, 1963–72; Vice-President: RZS Scotland, 1959–82 (Hon. Life Fellow and Hon. Vice-Pres., 1982); Scottish Wildlife Trust; Vice-Pres. and Mem. Council, Wildfowl Trust, 1969– (Hon. Life Fellow, 1983); Hon. Life Fellow, RSPB, 1984. Mem. Court, Dundee Univ., and Delegate to Commonwealth Univs Congress, 1970–78. Hon. LLD Dundee, 1970; Hon. DSc St Andrews, 1991. DL Fife, 1969. *Publications:* The Status and Distribution of Wild Geese and Wild Duck in Scotland, 1939; various papers and articles on fresh-water fisheries, hydro-electric development and ornithology. *Recreations:* natural history (esp. wild geese and insects), music. *Address:* The Garden House, Tayfield, Newport-on-Tay, Fife DD6 8HA. *T:* (01382) 543118. *Club:* New (Edinburgh).

See also P. F. Berry.

BERRY, Lynne; *see* Berry, G. L.

BERRY, Sir Michael (Victor), Kt 1996; FRS 1982; Royal Society Research Professor, Bristol University, since 1988; *b* 14 March 1941; *s* of Jack and Marie Berry; *m* 1st, 1961, Eveline Ethel Fitt (marr. diss. 1970); two *s*; 2nd, 1971, Lesley Jane Allen (marr. diss. 1984); two *d*; 3rd, 1984, Monica Suzi Saiovici; one *s* one *d*. *Educ:* Univ. of Exeter (BSc; Hon. PhD 1991); Univ. of St Andrews (PhD). Bristol University: Res. Fellow, 1965–67; Lectr, 1967–74; Reader, 1974–78; Prof. of Physics, 1978–88. Bakerian Lectr, Royal Soc., 1987. Mem., Royal Scientific Soc., Uppsala, 1988; Foreign Member: US Nat. Acad. of Sci., 1995; Royal Netherlands Acad. of Arts and Scis, 2000. Hon. FInstP 1999. Maxwell Medal and Prize, Inst. of Physics, 1978; Dirac Medal and Prize, Inst. of Physics, 1990; Lilienfeld Prize, Amer. Physical Soc., 1990; Royal Medal, Royal Soc., 1990; Naylor Prize and Lectureship in Applied Maths, London Math. Soc., 1992; Science for Art Prize, LVMH, Paris, 1994; Hewlett Packard Europhysics Prize, 1995; Dirac Medal, Internat. Centre for Theoretical Physics, 1996; Kapitsa Medal, Russian Acad. of Scis, 1997; Wolf Prize for Physics, Wolf Foundn, Israel, 1998; Ig Nobel Prize for Physics, 2000. *Publications:* Diffraction of Light by Ultrasound, 1966; Principles of Cosmology and Gravitation, 1976; about 300 research papers, book reviews, etc, on physics. *Recreation:* anything but sport. *Address:* H. H. Wills Physics Laboratory, Tyndall Avenue, Bristol BS8 1TL. *T:* (0117) 928 8735.

BERRY, Nicholas (William); Chairman: Stancroft Trust Ltd, since 1972; Yeoman Investment Trust plc; Mintel International Ltd; *b* 3 July 1942; *yr s* of Baron Hartwell, MBE, TD; *m* 1977, Evelyn Prouvost; two *s*. *Educ:* Eton; Christ Church, Oxford. Publisher and investor; Man. Dir, 1976–91, Chm., 1981–91, Harrap Publishing; Chm., Manchester Ship Canal, 1986–87. Director: Fleming Asian (formerly Robert Fleming Far Eastern) Investment Trust, 1981–; Arlen, 1993–; Atlantic Telecom (formerly Caledonian Media Communications), 1994–; Fleming Mercantile Investment Trust, 1995–; Blackwells, 1997–. *Address:* Stancroft Trust, 20 Bride Lane, EC4Y 8JP. *T:* (020) 7583 3808. *Club:* White's.

See also Viscount Camrose.

BERRY, Paul L.; Member (DUP) Newry and Armagh, Northern Ireland Assembly, since 1998; *b* 3 June 1976. *Educ:* Craigavon Coll. of Further Educn. Sales person, hardware warehouse, 1994–96; examr, shoe firm, 1996–98. *Recreation:* interest in football.

BERRY, Very Rev. Peter Austin; Provost of Birmingham, 1986–99, now Emeritus; *b* 27 April 1935; *s* of Austin James Berry and Phyllis Evelyn Berry. *Educ:* Solihull Sch.; Keble Coll., Oxford (BA English, BTh, MA); St Stephen's House, Oxford. Intelligence Corps, 1954–56. Ordained deacon, 1962, priest, 1963; Chaplain to Bishop of Coventry, 1963–70; Midlands Regl Officer, Community Relations Commn, 1970–73; Canon Residentiary, Coventry Cathedral, 1973–86, Canon Emeritus 1987; Vice-Provost of Coventry, 1977–85. Mem., Gen. Synod of C of E, 1990–99; Church Comr, 1994–99. Chairman: Standing Adv. Cttee for Religious Educn, Birmingham, 1987–93; Birmingham Internat. Council, 1987–99 (Vice Pres., 1999–); Birmingham/Pakistan Friendship Assoc., 1995–99 (Vice Pres., 1999–); Pre-Raphaelite Soc., 1986–. Vice-Chm., Iqbal Acad. Life Fellow, Coventry Univ. (Fellow, Lanchester Coll., Coventry, 1985).

Hon. DD Birmingham, 1997. *Recreations:* music, theatre, architecture. *Address:* Reed Lodge, D5 Kenilworth Court, Hagley Road, Birmingham B16 9NU. *T:* (0121) 454 0021.

BERRY, Peter Fremantle, CMG 1999; Managing Director and Crown Agent, since 1988, Chairman, since 1998, Crown Agents for Oversea Governments and Administrations; *b* St Andrews, Fife, 17 May 1944; *s* of John Berry, *qv*; *m* 1972, Paola Padovani; one *s* two *d.* *Educ:* Eton Coll.; Lincoln Coll., Oxford (MA Hons Mod. History). Harrisons & Crosfield, London, 1966–73: Manager: Kuala Belait, Brunei, 1968; Indonesia, 1970; Anglo Indonesian Corp., London: Gen. Man., 1973; Dir, 1974–82; Crown Agents for Oversea Governments and Administrations, 1982–: Director: Asia and Pacific, based Singapore, 1982–84; ME, Asia and Pacific, based London, 1984–88; Chm. or Dir of many Crown Agents' subsidiaries and associates. Director: Thomas Tapling Ltd, 1987–; Anglo-Eastern Plantations Plc, 1991–93; Henderson TR Pacific Investment Trust, 1994–; Scottish Eastern Investment Trust, 1995–98; Kier Group plc, 1997–; Martin Currie Portfolio Investment Trust plc, 1999– (Chm., 2000–); Martin Currie Capital Return Trust plc, 1999–2000. Member: Management Bd, Resource, 1989–92; Internat. Bd, Transparency Internat., 1993–. Member: Rubber Growers Assoc., 1978–82; UK Task Force on Kuwait, 1991; UK–Japan 21st Century (formerly UK–Japan 2000) Gp, 1992– (Dir, 2000–); Whitehall Export Promotion Cttee, 1992–98; Internat. Cttee, CBI, 1997–; British Trade Internat. Sectors and Projects Gp, 1998–; Council: Malaysia, Singapore and Brunei Assoc., 1982–87; Indonesia Assoc., 1974–93 (Chm., 1986–89). Trustee, CAF, 2000– (Chm., Internat. Cttee, 2000–). FRSA. *Recreations:* wildlife and country pursuits in Britain and Italy, travel and international development. *Address:* St Nicholas House, St Nicholas Road, Sutton, Surrey SM1 1EL. *T:* (020) 8643 3311. *Club:* Royal Automobile.

BERRY, Prof. Peter Jeremy, FRCP, FRCPath, FRCPCH; Professor of Paediatric Pathology, University of Bristol, since 1991; *b* 21 March 1950; *s* of Peter Berry and Marjorie Berry (*née* Lang). *Educ:* Epsom Coll.; Magdalene Coll., Cambridge (BA, MB, BChir). Kent and Canterbury Hosp., 1975–77; Sen. Registrar in Histopathology, Addenbrooke's Hosp., 1977–81; Research Fellow, Children's Hosp., Denver, 1981–83; Consultant Paediatric Pathologist, Bristol Royal Hosp. for Sick Children, 1983–. *Publications:* chapters and papers on cot death and children's tumours. *Recreations:* walking, ski-ing, fishing, music. *Address:* Bristol Royal Hospital for Sick Children, St Michael's Hill, Bristol BS2 8BJ. *T:* (0117) 928 5310, *Fax:* (0117) 928 5312. *Clubs:* Athenæum, Royal Society of Medicine.

BERRY, Rt Rev. (Robert Edward) Fraser; Bishop of Kootenay, 1971–89; *b* Ottawa, Ont, 21 Jan. 1926; *s* of Samuel Berry and Claire Hartley; *m* 1951, Margaret Joan Trevorrow Baillie; one *s* one *d.* *Educ:* Sir George Williams Coll., Montreal; McGill Univ., Montreal; Montreal Diocesan Theological Coll. Assistant, Christ Church Cathedral, Victoria, BC, 1953–55; Rector: St Margaret's, Hamilton, Ont, 1955–61; St Mark's, Orangeville, Ont, 1961–63; St Luke's, Winnipeg, Manitoba, 1963–67; St Michael and All Angels, Kelowna, BC, 1967–71. Chaplain: RCAF Assoc. 883 (Kelowna) Wing, 1988–; Royal Canadian Legion 23 (Kelowna) Br., 1994–; Royal Canadian Mounted Police Okanagan Div., 1995–; (on call), Kelowna Gen. Hosp., 1992–, Asst (on call), St Andrew's, Okanagan Mission, Kelowna, 1992–. Chm., Church Relations, 1997–, Vice-Chm. Bd, 1998–, Habitat for Humanity, Kelowna. Hon. DD Montreal Diocesan Theol Coll., 1973. *Recreations:* reading, boating, angling, swimming, walking, computer communications. *Address:* 1857 Maple Street, Kelowna, BC V1Y 1H4, Canada. *T:* (604) 7622923; *e-mail:* refb@okanagan.net. *Clubs:* Vancouver (Vancouver); Kelowna Yacht.

BERRY, Prof. Robert James, FRSE 1981; FIBiol; Professor of Genetics in the University of London, 1974–2000, then Emeritus; *b* 26 Oct. 1934; *o s* of Albert Edward James Berry and Nellie (*née* Hodgson); *m* 1958, Anne Caroline Elliott, *d* of Charles Elliott and Evelyn Le Cornu; one *s* two *d.* *Educ:* Shrewsbury Sch.; Caius Coll., Cambridge (MA); University Coll. London (PhD; DSc 1976). Lectr, subseq. Reader, then Prof., in Genetics, at Royal Free Hospital Sch. of Medicine, 1962–78; Prof. of Genetics at University Coll. London, 1978–2000. Leverhulme Emeritus Fellow, 2001–. Gifford Lectr, Glasgow Univ., 1997–98. Mem., Human Fertilization and Embryology Authy, 1990–96. Member: Gen. Synod, 1970–90; Board of Social Responsibility of the General Synod, 1976–91; Natural Environment Research Council, 1981–87; Council, Zoological Soc. of London, 1986–90 (Vice-Pres., 1988–90); President: Linnean Soc., 1982–85; British Ecological Soc., 1987–89; Christians in Science (formerly Research Scientists' Christian Fellowship), 1993–95 (Chm., 1968–88); Mammal Soc., 1995–97; Chm., Environmental Issues Network, 1992–. Trustee, Nat. Museums and Galleries, Merseyside, 1986–94. Governor: Monkton Combe Sch., 1979–91; Walthamstow Hall Sch., 2001–. Templeton UK Award, 1996. *Publications:* Teach Yourself Genetics, 1965, 3rd edn 1977; Adam and the Ape, 1975; Inheritance and Natural History, 1977; (jtly) Natural History of Shetland, 1980; (ed) Biology of the House Mouse, 1981; Neo-Darwinism, 1982; (ed) Evolution in the Galapagos, 1984; (jtly) Free to be Different, 1984; Natural History of Orkney, 1985; (ed jtly) The People of Orkney, 1986; (ed jtly) Nature, Natural History and Ecology, 1987; (ed jtly) Changing Attitudes to Nature Conservation, 1987; God and Evolution, 1988; (ed jtly) Evolution, Ecology and Environmental Stress, 1989; (ed) Real Science, Real Faith, 1991; (ed jtly) Genes in Ecology, 1992; (ed) Environmental Dilemmas, 1993; God and the Biologist, 1996; (jtly) Science, Life and Christian Belief, 1998; Orkney Nature, 2000; (ed) The Care of Creation, 2000. *Recreation:* remembering hill-walking (especially Munros) and then dreaming. *Address:* Quarfseter, Sackville Close, Sevenoaks, Kent TN13 3QD. *T:* (01732) 451907.

BERRY, Dr Robert Langley Page, CBE 1979; Chairman, 1968–78, Deputy Chairman, 1978–79, Alcoa of Great Britain Ltd; *b* 22 Nov. 1918; *s* of Wilfred Arthur and Mabel Grace Berry; *m* 1946, Eleanor Joyce (*née* Cramp); one *s* one *d.* *Educ:* Sir Thomas Rich's Sch., Gloucester; Birmingham Univ. (BSc (Hons), PhD). Served war, Royal Engrs, 1939–45. ICI Metals Div., 1951–66, Director, 1960–66; Man. Dir, Impalco, 1966–68. Non-Exec. Dir, Royal Mint, 1981–86. Dir, Nat. Anti-Waste Prog., 1976–80. President: Inst. of Metals, 1973; Aluminium Fedn, 1974. Chm., Friends of Fairford Church, 1985–97. *Publications:* several, in scientific jls. *Recreations:* fly-fishing, gardening. *Address:* Waterloo Cottage, Waterloo Lane, Fairford, Glos GL7 4BP. *T:* (01285) 712038. *Club:* Army and Navy.

BERRY, Prof. Roger Julian, RD 1987; FRCP; FRCR; FFOM; Director, Westlakes Research Institute, Cumbria, 1992–95; Chairman, British Committee on Radiation Units and Measurements, 1995–2000 (Member, 1978–2000; Vice-Chairman, 1984–95); *b* 6 April 1935; *s* of Sidney Norton Berry and Beatrice (*née* Mendelson); *m* 1960, Joseline Valerie Joan (*née* Butler). *Educ:* Stuyvesant High Sch., New York; New York Univ. (BA); Duke Univ. (BSc, MD); Magdalen Coll., Oxford (MA, DPhil). MRC External Staff and Hd, Radiobiol. Lab., Churchill Hosp., Oxford, also Hon. Cons. Med. Radiobiologist, Oxford AHA, and Clin. Lectr, Univ. of Oxford, 1969–74; Hd, Neutrons and therapy-related effects gp, MRC Radiobiol. Unit, Harwell, 1974–76; Sir Brian Windeyer Prof. of Oncology, Mddx Hosp. Med. Sch., 1976–87; Dir, Health, Safety and Environmental Protection, British Nuclear Fuels, 1987–92. Member: Internat. Commn on Radiological Protection, 1985–89; Nat. Radiological Protection Bd, 1982–87; MRC Cttee on Effects of Ionizing Radiation, and Chm., Radiobiol. Sub-Cttee, 1983–87; DoE Radioactive Waste Management Cttee, 1984–87; DHSS Cttee on Med. Aspects of Radiation in the Environment, 1985–87, Black Enquiry on Windscale; HSC Adv. Cttee on Safety of Nuclear Installations, 1992–96; CBI Health and Safety Policy Cttee, 1988–92; CIA Health, Safety and Envmt Council, 1990–92. President: BIR, 1986–87; Radiology Sect., RSM, 1985–86; Chm., Sci. Adv. Cttee, Thames Cancer Registry, 1985–87. Surg. Captain, RNR, 1986, and PMO (Reserves), 1987–89. QHP 1987–89. Hon. Fellow, Amer. Coll. of Radiology, 1983. OStJ 1990. Editor, Cell and Tissue Kinetics, 1976–80. *Publications:* Manual on Radiation Dosimetry (jtly), 1970; contributor to Oxford Textbook of Medicine, Florey's Textbook of Pathology; over 190 sci. papers in Brit. Jl of Radiology, etc. *Recreations:* sailing, music, naval history. *Address:* 109 Fairways Drive, Mount Murray, Santon, Douglas, Isle of Man IM4 2JE. *T:* and *Fax:* (01624) 617959. *Clubs:* Royal Over-Seas League, Royal Naval Sailing Association.

BERRY, Dr Roger Leslie; MP (Lab) Kingswood, since 1992; *b* 4 July 1948; *s* of Mary Joyce Berry and Sydney Berry; *m* 1996, Alison Delyth. *Educ:* Dalton County Jun. Sch.; Huddersfield New Coll.; Univ. of Bristol (BSc); Univ. of Sussex (DPhil). Lectr in Econs and Associate Fellow, IDS, Univ. of Sussex, 1973–74; Lecturer in Economics: Univ. of Papua New Guinea, 1974–78; Univ. of Bristol, 1978–92. Avon County Council: Mem., 1981–93; Chm., Finance and Admin. Cttee, 1981–84; Dep. Leader of Council, 1985–86; Leader, Labour Group, 1986–92. Contested (Lab): Weston-super-Mare, 1983; Kingswood, 1987. Mem., Trade and Industry Select Cttee, 1995–; Sec., All-Party Disablement Gp, 1994–. Chair, Full Employment Forum, 1994–99. Dir, Tribune Publications Ltd, 1997–. Vice Pres., Disabled Drivers Assoc., 1997–; Trustee: Disabled Law Service, 1997–99; Snowdon Award Scheme, 1997–; Patron, Circomedia, 1997–. *Publications:* contribs to learned jls; newspaper articles and pamphlets. *Recreations:* travel, cooking, reading, cinema, theatre. *Address:* 9 Manor Road, Bristol BS16 2JD. *T:* (0117) 965 4889. *Club:* Kingswood Labour.

BERRY, (Roger) Simon; QC 1990; a Recorder, since 2000; *b* 9 Sept. 1948; *e s* of Kingsland Jutsum Berry and Kathleen Margaret Parker; *m* 1974, Jennifer Jane, *d* of Jonas Birtwistle Hall and Edith Emilé Vester; three *s.* *Educ:* St Brendan's Coll., Bristol; Manchester Univ. (LLB). Admitted Solicitor, 1973; Partner, Stanley, Wasbrough & Co., Solicitors, Bristol (later Veale Wasbrough), 1975–77; removed from Roll, 1977, at own request, in order to seek call to the Bar; called to the Bar, Middle Temple, 1977; Mem., Middle Temple and Lincoln's Inn; Harmsworth Benefactor's Law Schol.; Mem., Western Circuit, 1978–; in practice at Chancery Bar, 1978–; Asst Recorder, 1996–2000; Ordinary Bencher, Lincoln's Inn, 1998. Member: Bar Council, 1996–99 (Mem., Professional Conduct Cttee, 1996–99, and Practice Mgt and Develt Cttee, 1998–99); Chancery Bar Assoc., 1978– (Mem. Cttee, 1984, 1985); Professional Negligence Bar Assoc., 1991–; Property Bar Assoc., 2001–. Mem., Theatre Panel of Judges, Olivier Awards, 2000. *Publication:* (contrib.) Professional Negligence and Liability, 2000. *Recreations:* family, the performing arts, cycling, ski-ing, keeping fit. *Address:* 9 Old Square, Lincoln's Inn, WC2A 3SR. *T:* (020) 7405 4682. *Clubs:* Ski of Great Britain, Riverside.

BERRY, Scyld; *see* Berry, A. S. I.

BERRY, Simon; *see* Berry, Roger S.

BERRY, Thomas Henry S.; *see* Seager Berry.

BERTHOIN, Georges Paul; Chevalier, Légion d'Honneur, 1990; Médaille militaire, Croix de Guerre, Médaille de la Résistance avec Rosette, France, 1945; Executive Member of the Trilateral Commission (Japan, N America, W Europe), 1973–75, and since 1993 (Chairman, 1975–92, Hon. European Chairman, since 1992); Honorary International Chairman, the European Movement, since 1981 (Chairman, 1978–81); *b* Nérac, France, 17 May 1925; *s* of Jean Berthoin and Germaine Mourgnot; *m* 1st, 1950, Ann White Whittlesey; four *d*; 2nd, 1965, Pamela Jenkins; two *s.* *Educ:* Grenoble Univ.; École Sciences Politiques, Paris; Harvard Univ. Licencié ès Lettres (Philosophie), Licencié en Droit, Laureate for Economics (Grenoble). Lectr, McGill Univ., Montreal, 1948; Private Sec. to French Minister of Finance, 1948–50; Head of Staff of Superprefect of Alsace-Lorraine-Champagne, 1950–52. Joined High Authority of European Coal and Steel Community, and then Principal Private Sec. to its Pres. (Jean Monnet), 1952–53–55. Dep. Chief Rep. of ECSC in UK, 1956–67; Chargé d'Affaires for Commission of the European Communities (ECSC Euratom-Common Market), 1968; Principal Adviser to the Commission, and its Dep. Chief Rep. in London, 1969–70, Chief Representative, 1971–73. Member: Nine Wise Men Gp on Africa, 1988–89; Bd, Aspen Inst., Berlin; Adv. Bd, Johns Hopkins Univ. Bologna Center Sch. of Advanced Studies. Hon. Chm., Jean Monnet Assoc. Regular Lectr, RCDS, London. *Recreations:* art, theatre, walking, collecting objects. *Address:* 67 Avenue Niel, 75017 Paris, France.

BERTHON, Vice-Adm. Sir Stephen (Ferrier), KCB 1980; *b* 24 Aug. 1922; *s* of late Rear-Adm. C. P. Berthon, CBE and Mrs C. P. Berthon (*née* Ferrier); *m* 1948, Elizabeth Leigh-Bennett; two *s* two *d.* *Educ:* Old Malthouse, Swanage; RNC Dartmouth. Served War of 1939–45 at sea, Mediterranean, Atlantic, Russia; spec. communications, 1945–46; Flag Lieut Singapore, 1946–48; submarines, 1949–51; East Indies Flagship, 1951–52; HMS Mercury, 1952–54; Staff of Flag Officer Aircraft Carriers, 1954–56; Fleet Communications Officer Mediterranean, 1957–59; jssc 1959; Comdr HMS Mercury, 1959–61; Jt Planning Staff, 1961–64; Naval Attaché, Australia, 1964–66; Dir of Defence Policy, MoD, 1968–71; Cdre HMS Drake, 1971–73; Flag Officer Medway and Port Adm. Chatham, 1974–76; Asst Chief of Naval Staff (Op. Req.), 1976–78; Dep. Chief of Defence Staff (Operational Requirements), 1978–81; retired 1981. Jt MFH, Avon Vale Hunt, 1981–84. *Recreations:* hunting, riding, gardening, walking, painting. *Club:* Army and Navy.

BERTHOUD, Prof. Jacques Alexandre; Professor of English, Department of English and Related Literature, University of York, since 1980 (Head of Department, 1980–97; Deputy Vice-Chancellor, 1987–90); *b* 1 March 1935; *s* of Alexandre L. Berthoud and Madeleine (*née* Bourquin); *m* 1958, Astrid Irene (*née* Titlestad); one *s* two *d.* *Educ:* Univ. of the Witwatersrand, Johannesburg (BA and BA Hons). Lectr, English Dept, Univ. of Natal, Pietermaritzburg, 1960–67; Lectr, subseq. Sen. Lectr, English Dept, Univ. of Southampton, 1967–79. Vis. Fellow Commoner, Trinity College, Cambridge, 1990–91. British Chm., Amnesty Internat., 1978–80. *Publications:* (with Dr C. van Heyningen) Uys Krige, 1966; Joseph Conrad, the Major Phase, 1978; Joseph Conrad: au cœur de l'œuvre, 1992; (ed) books for OUP and Penguin Books. *Recreation:* sleeping. *Address:* 30 New Walk Terrace, Fishergate, York YO10 4BG. *T:* (01904) 629212.

BERTHOUD, Sir Martin (Seymour), KCVO 1985; CMG 1985; HM Diplomatic Service, retired; *b* 20 Aug. 1931; *s* of Sir Eric Berthoud, KCMG and late Ruth Tilston, *d* of Sir Charles Bright, FRSE; *m* 1960, Marguerite Joan Richarda Phayre; three *s* one *d.* *Educ:* Rugby Sch.; Magdalen Coll., Oxford (MA). Served with British Embassies in: Tehran, 1956–58; Manila, 1961–64; Pretoria/Cape Town, 1967–71; Tehran, 1971–73; Counsellor, Helsinki, 1974–77; Inspector, HM Diplomatic Service, 1977–79; Head of N.

American Dept, FCO, 1979–81; Consul-General, Sydney, 1982–85; High Comr, Trinidad and Tobago, 1985–91. EC Monitor, Croatia, 1991. Dir, The Wates Foundn, 1993–2000. Advr, Prisoners Abroad, 2001. EC Monitoring Mission Service Medal, 1994. Commander, Order of the Lion (Finland), 1976; Keys of City of San Fernando (Trinidad), 1991. *Recreations:* golf, tennis, bird-watching, acting as under-gardener to wife, grandchildren. *Address:* Gillyflower, Stoke by Nayland, Suffolk CO6 4RD. *T:* (01206) 263237. *Clubs:* Oxford and Cambridge; Vincent's (Oxford).

BERTIE, family name of **Earl of Lindsey and Abingdon**.

BERTRAM, Dr Brian Colin Ricardo; Special Projects Co-ordinator, Bristol Zoo Gardens, since 1995; *b* 14 April 1944; *s* of late Dr Colin Bertram and Dr (Cicely) Kate Bertram; *m* 1975, Katharine Jean Gillie; one *s* two *d*. *Educ:* Perse School, Cambridge; St John's Coll., Cambridge (BA 1965; MA 1968); PhD Cambridge, 1969. FIBiol 1981. Research Fellow, Serengeti Res. Inst., Tanzania, 1969–73; Sen. Res. Fellow, King's Coll., Cambridge, 1976–79; Curator of Mammals, 1980–87, and Curator of Aquarium and Invertebrates, 1982–87, Zoological Society of London; Dir-Gen., Wildfowl and Wetlands Trust, 1987–92. Vice-Pres., World Pheasant Assoc., 1990–97; Mem. Council, Zool Soc. of London, 1993–97, 1999. *Publications:* Pride of Lions, 1978; The Ostrich Communal Nesting System, 1992; Lions, 1998. *Recreations:* family, friends, zoology, garden, travel. *Address:* Fieldhead, Amberley, Stroud, Glos GL5 5AG. *T:* (01453) 872796. *Club:* Zoological.

BERTRAM, Dr Christoph; Director, Foundation Science and Policy, since 1998; *b* 3 Sept. 1937; German national; *m* 1st, 1967, Renate Edith Bergemann (marr. diss. 1980); 2nd, 1980, Ragnhild Lindemann; two *s* two *d*. *Educ:* Free Univ. Berlin and Bonn Univ. (law); Institut d'Etudes Politiques, Paris (political science). Dr of Law 1967. Joined Internat. Inst. for Strategic Studies as Research Associate, 1967, Asst Dir, 1969–74, Dir, 1974–82; Mem. Planning Staff, West German Min. of Defence, 1969–70. Political and Foreign Editor, 1982–85, Diplomatic Correspondent, 1986–98, Die Zeit. *Publications:* (with Alastair Buchan *et al.*) Europe's Futures—Europe's Choices, 1969; Mutual Force Reductions in Europe: the political aspects, 1972; (ed, with Johan J. Holst) New Strategic Factors in the North Atlantic, 1977; Arms Control and Technological Change, 1979; Europe in the Balance, 1995. *Recreations:* clocks, sailing. *Address:* Länderallee 11, 14052 Berlin, Germany.

BERTRAM, George, CB 1999; Director, National Services, Board of Inland Revenue, 2000–01; *b* 19 Sept. 1944; *s* of late George Bertram and of Muriel Bertram; *m* 1969, Jean Swales. *Educ:* Houghton-le-Spring Grammar Sch. Nat. Assistance Bd, Sunderland, 1964–70; Department of Health and Social Security, then Department of Social Security: Staff Trng, Billingham, 1970–73; Sunderland, 1973–76; Regl Office, Newcastle upon Tyne, 1976–80; South Shields, 1980–83; Manager: Peterlee, 1983; Hartlepool, 1983–84; Middlesbrough, 1984–89; Sunderland, 1989; Contributions Agency: Head of Field Ops, 1989–92; Dep. Chief Exec., and Dir of Compliance and Educn, 1992–94; actg Chief Exec., 1994–95; Dep. Chief Exec., and Dir of Ops, 1995–97; Chief Exec., 1997–99; Dir., Nat. Insce Contribns, Bd of Inland Revenue, 1999–2000. Mem., CSAB, 2000–. *Recreations:* sport, especially golf, cricket, football, gardening. *Address:* 8 Holmewood Drive, Rowlands Gill, Tyne and Wear NE39 1EL. *Club:* Garesfield Golf.

BERTRAM, Robert David Darney; Partner, Shepherd & Wedderburn, WS, 1992–98; *b* 6 Oct. 1941; *s* of late D. N. S. Bertram; *m* 1967, Patricia Joan Laithwaite; two *s*. *Educ:* Edinburgh Academy; Oxford Univ. (MA); Edinburgh Univ. (LLB (Hons), Berriedale Keith Prize). An Assistant Solicitor, Linklaters & Paines, London, 1968–69; Partner, Dundas & Wilson, CS, 1969–92. Associate, Institute of Taxation, 1970 (Mem., Technical Cttee, 1986); Examiner, Law Society of Scotland, 1972–75; Member: Scottish Law Commn, 1978–86; (part-time), VAT Tribunal, Scotland, 1984–92; Competition (formerly Monopolies and Mergers) Commn, 1998–. Non-exec. Dir, The Weir Group plc, 1983–. *Publications:* contribs to professional jls. *Address:* c/o Competition Commission, New Court, 48 Carey Street, WC2A 2JT. *Club:* Scottish Arts (Edinburgh).

BESCH, Anthony John Elwyn, FGSM; opera and theatre director, since 1950; Head of Opera Studies, Guildhall School of Music and Drama, 1986–89; *b* 5 Feb. 1924; *s* of late Roy Cressy Frederick Besch and Anne Gwendolen Besch. *Educ:* Rossall Sch., Lancs; Worcester Coll., Oxford (MA). FGSM 1989. Dir, opera and theatre, 1950–: Royal Opera House, Covent Garden; Glyndebourne Opera; English Nat. Opera, London Coliseum; Scottish Opera; Opera North; New Opera Co., London; Handel Opera Soc.; Edinburgh Festival; Wexford Festival; Deutsche Oper, Berlin; Royal Netherlands Opera; Théâtre de la Monnaie, Brussels; Opéra de Lyon; Teatro Colon, Buenos Aires; New York City Opera; San Francisco Opera; Canadian Opera Co.; Nat. Arts Centre, Canada; Australian Opera; State Opera, S Australia; Victoria State Opera. *Recreation:* gardening. *Address:* 201 Hammersmith Grove, W6 0NP. *Club:* Garrick.

BESGROVE, Maj.-Gen. Peter Vincent Ronald, CBE 1992; CEng, FIEE; Assistant Chief of Staff, J1 Headquarters Allied Forces South, since 1999; *b* 23 Oct. 1948; *s* of Ronald Alfred Besgrove and Josephine Besgrove (*née* Buckley); *m* 1971, Eileen McEwan; two *d*. *Educ:* Magdalen Coll. Sch.; Welbeck Coll.; Royal Military Coll. of Sci. (BSc Eng Hons). CEng 1985; FIEE 1997. Commnd REME, 1968: served BAOR, NI and England, 1968–79; Staff Coll., 1980; Dep. COS, 6 Armd Bde, 1981–83; Comd, 5 Armd Workshop, BAOR, 1983–84; jsdc 1985; DS, Staff Coll., 1985–87; Comd Maintenance 3 Armd Div., BAOR, 1987–89; Asst COS, HQ NI, 1989–91; Comdt, Sch. of Electrical and Mechanical Engrg, 1991–92; Comd, REME Trng Gp, 1992–93; rcds 1994; Dir of Manning (Army), 1995–97; Dir Gen. Equipment Support (Army), 1997–99. FIMgt. *Recreations:* fishing, shooting, sailing, DIY. *Address:* c/o Regimental HQ REME, Isaac Newton Road, Arborfield, Reading, Berks RG2 9NJ. *T:* (0118) 976 3672. *Club:* Army and Navy.

BESLEY, Christopher; a Metropolitan Magistrate, 1964–88; *b* 18 April 1916; *s* of late C. A. Besley, Tiverton; *m* 1947, Pamela, *d* of Dr W. E. David, Sydney, Australia; four *s* two *d*. *Educ:* King's Coll., Wimbledon; King's Coll., London. Barrister, Gray's Inn, 1938; practised Western Circuit. Served War of 1939–45, Devon Regt (wounded, N Africa). *Address:* Queen Elizabeth Building, Temple, EC4; 15 Belvedere Avenue, SW19 7PP. *Club:* Lansdowne.

BESLEY, Morrish Alexander, (Tim), AO 1992; FTSE; FIEAust; Chairman: Leighton Holdings Ltd, since 1990; Commonwealth Bank of Australia, 1991–99; *b* New Plymouth, NZ, 14 March 1947; *s* of Hugh Morrish Besley and Isabel (*née* Alexander); *m* 1952, Nancy Cave; three *s*. *Educ:* Univ. of New Zealand (BE Civil); Macquarie Univ. (BLegS). FIEAust 1982; FTSE (FTS 1985). Called to the Bar, NSW, 1985. Engr, Ministry of Works, NZ, 1950; Snowy Mts Hydro-Electric Authy, Australia, 1950–67; First Assistant Secretary: Dept of External Territories, Australia, 1967–73; Dept of Treasury, Australia, 1973–76 (Exec. Mem., Foreign Investment Rev. Bd, 1975–76); Sec., Commonwealth Dept of Business and Consumer Affairs, and Comptroller General of Customs, Australia, 1976–81; Monier Ltd: Man. Dir, 1982–87; Chm. and Chief Exec., 1987; Chairman: Monier Redland Ltd, 1988; Redland Australia, 1988–95; CIG Gp, 1988–93; Commonwealth Banking Corp., 1988–91. Director: Amcor Ltd, 1985–97; Fujitsu Australia Ltd, 1988–97; O'Connell Street Associates Pty Ltd, 1990–; Clyde Industries Ltd, 1991–96. Mem., NSW Council and Nat. Exec., Metal Trades Industry Assoc. (Pres., 1991–92). Chancellor, Macquarie Univ., 1994–. Chm., Sydney Royal Botanic Gardens Trust, 1988–92; Trustee, Royal Botanic Gdns Sydney Foundn, 1992–99; Governor, Australian Nat. Gall. Foundn, 1992–; Chm., Centenary Inst. Med. Res. Foundn, 1992–96; Mem., Aust. Bd of Reference, World Vision, 1992–. Pres., AATSE, 1998–. Mem., Red Shield Appeal Cttee, 1988–, Sydney Adv. Bd, 1994–99, Salvation Army. *Recreations:* golf, fishing. *Address:* Leighton Holdings, PO Box 1002, Crows Nest, NSW 2065, Australia; PO Box 304, Cammeray, NSW 2062, Australia. *Clubs:* Australian, Union (Sydney); National Press (Canberra); Elanora Country; Royal Sydney Yacht Squadron.

BESLEY, Prof. Timothy John, DPhil; FBA 2001; Professor of Economics, London School of Economics, since 1995; *b* 14 Sept. 1960; *s* of John Besley and June Besley (*née* Turton); *m* 1993, Gillian Nicola Paull; two *s*. *Educ:* Keble Coll., Oxford (BA PPE 1983); All Souls Coll., Oxford (MPhil; DPhil 1988). Prize Fellow, All Souls Coll., Oxford, 1984–91 and 1995–2000; Asst Prof., Princeton Univ., 1988–95; Dir, Suntory Toyota Internat. Centres for Econs and Related Disciplines, LSE, 2001–. Res. Fellow, Inst. for Fiscal Studies, 1995–. Co-Ed., Amer. Econ. Rev., 1999–. Fellow, Econometric Soc., 2000. *Publications:* contribs to Amer. Econ. Rev., Jl Political Econ., Econometrica, Qly Jl Econs and other scholarly jls. *Recreations:* squash, playing violin. *Address:* London School of Economics, Houghton Street, WC2A 2AE. *T:* (020) 7955 6702.

BESSBOROUGH, 11th Earl of, *cr* 1739 (Ire.); **Arthur Mountifort Longfield Ponsonby;** Baron Bessborough (Ire.) 1721; Viscount Duncannon (Ire.) 1722; Baron Ponsonby (GB) 1749; Baron Duncannon (UK) 1834; *b* 11 Dec. 1912; *s* of Hon. Cyril Myles Ponsonby (*d* 1915), 2nd *s* of 8th Earl, and Rita Narcissa Longfield (*d* 1977); *S* cousin, 1993; *m* 1st, 1939, Patricia (*d* 1952), *d* of Col Fitzhugh Minnigerode, Va, USA; one *s* one *d*; 2nd, 1956, Anne Marie Galitzine (marr. diss. 1963); 3rd, 1963, Madeleine Lola Margaret, *d* of Maj.-Gen. Laurence Grand, CB, CIE, CBE; two *s*. *Educ:* Harrow; Trinity Coll., Cambridge. Captain, Welsh Guards, 1940–46. *Heir:* *s* Viscount Duncannon, *qv*. *Address:* Roche Court, Winterslow, Wilts SP5 1BG. *T:* (01980) 862204.

BESSER, Prof. (Gordon) Michael, MD, DSc; FRCP, FMedSci; Professor of Medicine and Head of Department of Endocrinology and the Medical Professorial Unit, St Bartholomew's and the Royal London School of Medicine and Dentistry, Queen Mary and Westfield College (formerly St Bartholomew's Hospital Medical College), London University, at St Bartholomew's Hospital, since 1992, and at Royal London Hospital, since 1994; Consultant and Lead Clinician, Department of Endocrinology, Bart's and the London (formerly Royal Hospitals) NHS Trust, since 1994; *b* 22 Jan. 1936; *s* of Hyman Besser and Leah Besser (*née* Geller); *m* 1972; one *s* one *d*. *Educ:* Hove County Grammar Sch.; Bart's Med. Coll., Univ. of London (BSc, MB BS, MD, DSc). FRCP 1973. St Bartholomew's Hospital: Lectr in Medicine, 1966–70; Sen. Lectr and Hon. Consultant Physician, 1970–74; Prof. of Endocrinology, Med. Coll., 1974–92; Consultant and Physician i/c Dept of Endocrinology, 1974–; Dir of Medicine, 1989–93; Chief Exec., 1992–94. Consultant Endocrinologist to RN, 1989–. Vis. Prof., univs and med. estabts in Australasia, Canada, China, Hong Kong, Italy, Malta, S Africa, USA, Yugoslavia. Cttee work for RCP, RSocMed, Soc. for Endocrinology, Jt Cttee on Higher Med. Training; Medical Research Council: former Mem., Physiol. Systems Bd and Grants Cttee (Chm., 1984–86); Chm., Working Party on Hormone Replacement Therapy, 1992–95. Royal College of Physicians: Lectr, 1974, 1993, 1999; Censor, 1990–92; Sen. Vice-Pres. and Sen. Censor, 1995–97. Founder FMedSci 1998. Hon. MD Turin, 1985. Mem. Editl Bd, Clinics in Endocrinology and Metabolism, 1977–; former Mem. Editl Bd, Jl of Endocrinol., Neuroendocrinol., and Clinical Endocrinol. *Publications:* Fundamentals of Clinical Endocrinology (with R. Hall and J. Anderson), 2nd edn 1978, 3rd edn 1980, (ed with R. Hall) 4th edn 1989; Clinical Neuroendocrinology, 1977; Recent Advances in Medicine, 3 edns, 1981–87; (ed jtly) Endocrinology, 2nd edn 1989, 3rd edn 1994; Clinical Endocrinology, 1986, 2nd edn 1994; Clinical Diabetes, 1988; contribs to learned jls. *Recreations:* early Chinese ceramics, opera, ballet, theatre, keeping fit. *Address:* St Bartholomew's Hospital, EC1A 7BE. *T:* (020) 7601 8342. *Club:* Garrick.

BEST, family name of **Barons Best** and **Wynford**.

BEST, Baron *cr* 2001 (Life Peer), of Godmanstone in the County of Dorset; **Richard Stuart Best,** OBE 1988; Director, Joseph Rowntree Foundation (formerly Joseph Rowntree Memorial Trust), since 1988; *b* 22 June 1945; *s* of Walter Stuart Best, DL, JP and Frances Mary Chignell; *m* 1st, 1970, Ima Akpan (marr. diss. 1976); one *s* one *d*; 2nd, 1978, Belinda Janie Tremayne Stemp; one *s* one *d*. *Educ:* Shrewsbury School; University of Nottingham (BA). British Churches Housing Trust, 1968–73 (Dir, 1971–73); Dir, Nat. Fedn of Housing Assocs, 1973–88. Trustee: Sutton Housing Trust, 1971–84 (Dep. Chm., 1983–84); Internat. Year of Shelter for the Homeless 1987 Trust; Sustainability First Trust, 1999–; Chm., Omnium Central Housing Assoc., 1978–80; Committee Member: UK Housing Trust, 1976–88; Sutton Hastoe Housing Assoc., 1982–; Member: Social Policy Cttee, C of E Bd for Social Responsibility, 1986–91; BBC/IBA Central Appeals Cttee, 1989–91; Cttee, Assoc. of Charitable Foundns, 1989–92; DTI Foresight Panel on Built Envmt, 1999–; Comr, Rural Devel Commn, 1989–97; Bd Mem., Anchor Housing Assoc., 1985–88. Sec., Duke of Edinburgh's Inquiry into British Housing, 1984–91. Chm., UK Nat. Council for UN City Summit, 1995–96. *Publications:* Rural Housing: problems and solutions, 1981; Housing Associations 1890–1990, 1991; Housing After 2000 AD, 1992; The Inclusive Homes of the Future, 1999. *Address:* (office) The Homestead, 40 Water End, York YO30 6WP. *Club:* Travellers.

BEST, David William; Chairman, MMI Group plc, since 1996 (Chief Executive, 1995–96); *b* 1 Dec. 1949; *s* of William Robertson Best and Frances Best; *m* 1972, Margaret Smart Mitchell; one *s* one *d*. *Educ:* North Manchester Grammar Sch.; Univ. of Edinburgh. Mgt posts in pharmaceutical industry, 1973–88; Co-Founder, and Man. Dir, Medical Marketing Internat. Ltd (first private sector technology mgt co. in Europe), 1988–96; Founder and CEO, Bioscience Innovation Centre plc, 1996–; Chm., Cellfactors plc, 1998–2000; Dir, Healthy Living Centres (UK) Ltd, 1999–. Chm., BioStarter Initiative, 2001–. Dep. Chm., Med. and Scientific Div., World Fellowship, Duke of Edinburgh's Award, 1998–. *Recreation:* mountain walking. *Address:* MMI Group plc, Bioscience Innovation Centre, Cowley Road, Cambridge CB4 0DS. *T:* (01223) 477677. *Club:* Carlton.

BEST, Prof. Ernest; Professor of Divinity and Biblical Criticism, University of Glasgow, 1974–82, now Professor Emeritus; Dean of the Faculty of Divinity, 1978–80; *b* 23 May 1917; *s* of John and Louisa Elizabeth Best; *m* 1949, Sarah Elizabeth Kingston; two *d*. *Educ:* Methodist Coll., Belfast; Queen's Univ., Belfast (BA, MA, BD, PhD); Presbyterian Coll., Belfast. Asst Minister, First Bangor Presbyterian Church, 1943–49; Minister, Caledon and Minterburn Presbyt. Churches, 1949–63; Lectr (temp.), Presbyt. Coll., Belfast, 1953–54; Guest Prof., Austin Presbyt. Theol Seminary, Texas, 1955–57; Lectr in Biblical Lit. and Theol., St Andrews Univ., 1963–74 (Sen. Lectr 1971–74). Lectures: Nils W. Lund, Chicago, 1978; Manson Meml, Manchester Univ., 1978; Sprunt, Richmond, Virginia,

1985; Ethel M. Wood, London Univ., 1986. Vis. Prof. of New Testament Studies, Knox Coll., Dunedin, NZ, 1983; Vis. Fellow, Univ. of Otago, 1983; Gunning Fellow, New Coll., Edinburgh Univ., 1993. Jt Editor, Biblical Theology, 1962–72; Associate Editor, Irish Biblical Studies, 1978–. Hon. DD Glasgow, 1997. *Publications:* One Body in Christ, 1955; The Temptation and the Passion, 1965, 2nd edn 1990; The Letter of Paul to the Romans, 1967; 1 Peter, 1971; 1 and 2 Thessalonians, 1972; From Text to Sermon, 1977, 2nd edn 1988; Text and Interpretation (ed jtly), 1979; Following Jesus, 1981; Mark: the Gospel as story, 1983; Disciples and Discipleship, 1986; 2 Corinthians, 1987; Paul and His Converts, 1988; Interpreting Christ, 1993; Ephesians: a guide, 1993; Essays on Ephesians, 1997; Ephesians, 1998; contrib. Biblica, Ecumenical Review, Expository Times, Interpretation, Jl Theol Studies, New Testament Studies, Novum Testamentum, Scottish Jl Theology, Catholic Biblical Qly, Zeit. neu. test. Wiss. *Recreations:* vegetable growing, golf. *Address:* 13 Newmill Gardens, St Andrews, Fife KY16 8RY.

BEST, Dr Geoffrey Francis Andrew; Senior Associate Member, St Antony's College, Oxford, since 1988; *b* 20 Nov. 1928; *s* of Frederick Ebenezer Best and Catherine Sarah Vanderbrook (*née* Bultz); *m* 1955, Gwenllyan Marigold Davies; two *s* one *d*. *Educ:* St Paul's Sch.; Trinity Coll., Cambridge (MA, PhD). Army (RAEC), 1946–47; Choate Fellow, Harvard Univ., 1954–55; Fellow of Trinity Hall and Asst Lectr, Cambridge Univ., 1955–61; Lectr, Edinburgh Univ., 1961–66; Sir Richard Lodge Prof. of History, Edinburgh Univ., 1966–74; Prof. of History, Sch. of European Studies, 1974–85 (Hon. Prof., 1982–85), Dean, 1980–82, Univ. of Sussex; Academic Visitor, Dept of Internat. Relations, LSE, 1985–88. Vis. Prof., Chicago Univ., 1964; Visiting Fellow: All Souls Coll., Oxford, 1969–70; LSE, 1983–85; ANU, 1984; Fellow, Woodrow Wilson Internat. Center, Washington, DC, 1978–79. Lees Knowles Lectr, Cambridge, 1970; Joanne Goodman Lectr, Univ. of Western Ontario, 1981; Cyril Foster Lectr, Univ. of Oxford, 1999. Mem. Council, British Red Cross Soc., 1981–84, Hon. Consultant, 1985–91. Editor, Cambridge Review, 1953–54; Jt Editor, Victorian Studies, 1958–68; Editor, War and Society Newsletter, 1973–82. (Jtly) Paul Reuter Prize, ICRC, 1997. *Publications:* Temporal Pillars, 1964; Shaftesbury, 1964; Bishop Westcott and the Miners, 1968; Mid-Victorian Britain, 1971; (ed) Church's Oxford Movement, 1971; (jt ed) War, Economy and the Military Mind, 1976; Humanity in Warfare, 1980; War and Society in Revolutionary Europe, 1982; Honour Among Men and Nations, 1982; Nuremberg and After: the continuing history of war crimes and crimes against humanity, 1984; (ed jtly) History, Society and the Churches, 1985; (ed) The Permanent Revolution, 1988; War and Law since 1945, 1994; Churchill: a study in greatness, 2001; contrib. various jls. *Address:* 19 Buckingham Street, Oxford OX1 4LH.

BEST, Harold; MP (Lab) Leeds North West, since 1997; *b* 18 Dec 1937; *s* of Fred and Marie Patricia Best; *m* 1960, Mary Glyn; two *s* two *d*. *Educ:* Meanwood County Sch.; Leeds Coll. of Technol. Electrical technician; worked for Co-op Movt, in electrical contracting industry, and in educn (technical support). *Address:* House of Commons, SW1A 0AA.

BEST, Keith (Lander); Chief Executive, Immigration Advisory Service, since 1993; *b* 10 June 1949; *s* of late Peter Edwin Wilson Best and Margaret Louisa Best; *m* 1990, Elizabeth Margaret Gibson; two *d*. *Educ:* Brighton Coll.; Keble Coll., Oxford (BA (Hons) Jurisprudence; MA). Assistant Master, Summerfields Sch., Oxford, 1967; called to the Bar, Inner Temple, 1971; Lectr in Law, 1973. Served: 289 Parachute Battery, RHA (V), 1970–76; with RM on HMS Bulwark, 1976; Naval Gunfire Liaison Officer with Commando Forces (Major). Councillor, Brighton Borough Council (Chm. Lands Cttee, Housing Cttee), 1976–80. Dir, Prisoners Abroad, 1989–93. MP (C): Anglesey, 1979–83; Ynys Môn, 1983–87. PPS to Sec. of State for Wales, 1981–84. Former Chm., All Party Alcohol Policy and Services Gp; former Mem., Select Cttee on Welsh Affairs. Chairman: Bow Gp Defence Cttee; British Cttee for Vietnamese Refugees; Internat. Council of Parliamentarians' Global Action; World Federalist Movement, 1987–; Conservative Action for Electoral Reform, 1992–; Vauxhall Conservative Assoc., 1997–99; Electronic Immigration Network, 1998–; Electoral Reform Soc., 1998– (Mem. Council, 1996–; Chm., Mgt Cttee, 1997–); Member: Conservative Gtr London Area Exec. Cttee, 1997–; UN Disarmament Cttee; Young Conservative Nat. Adv. Cttee, 1978. Mem. Cttee, Assoc. of Lloyd's Mems. Founder Member: Two Piers Housing Co-operative, 1977; Brighton Housing Trust, 1976; school manager, Downs County First Sch. and Downs Middle Sch., 1976. *Publications:* Write Your Own Will, 1978 (paperback); The Right Way to Prove a Will, 1980 (paperback); contrib. District Councils Rev. *Recreations:* parachuting, walking, photography, travel. *Address:* 15 St Stephen's Terrace, SW8 1DJ; 7 Alderley Terrace, Holyhead, Anglesey LL65 1NL. *Clubs:* New Cavendish; Royal Artillery Mess (Woolwich); Holyhead Conservative.

BEST, Matthew Robert; Founder/Musical Director, Corydon Singers, since 1973, Corydon Orchestra, since 1991, Artistic Director, since 1996; *b* 6 Feb. 1957; *s* of Peter Best and Isabel Mary Best; *m* 1983, Rosalind Sandra Mayes; one *s* one *d*. *Educ:* Sevenoaks Sch.; King's Coll., Cambridge (Choral Schol.; MA Hons Music). Singer: Nat. Opera Studio, 1979–80; Principal bass, Royal Opera, 1980–86; Guest Artist, Royal Opera, Opera North, WNO, ENO, Scottish Opera, Netherlands Opera and others, 1982–; principal operatic rôles incl. Flying Dutchman, Scarpia, Pizarro, Wotan, Amfortas, Kurwenal, Jochanaan; has performed in concerts throughout Europe and at major European and American fests. Conductor: concert appearances at fests throughout UK and Europe, at South Bank and BBC Promenade concerts; Prin. Conductor, The Hanover Band, 1998–99; Guest Conductor with English Chamber Orch., London Mozart Players, City of London Sinfonia, Royal Seville SO, English Northern Philharmonia, New Queen's Hall Orch., Manchester Camerata and RTE Concert Orch.; has made numerous recordings of choral/orchestral music and opera. *Recreations:* reading, hill-walking. *Address:* c/o IMG Artists (Europe), Media House, 3 Burlington Lane, Chiswick, W4 2TH. *T:* (020) 8233 5800.

BEST, Sir Richard (Radford), KCVO 1990; CBE 1989 (MBE 1977); HM Diplomatic Service, retired; *b* 28 July 1933; *s* of Charles and Frances Best (*née* Raymond); *m* 1st, 1957, Elizabeth Vera Wait (*d* 1968); two *d*; 2nd, 1969, Mary Hill (*née* Wait); one *s*. *Educ:* Worthing High Sch.; University Coll. London (BA Hons). Home Office, 1957–66; HM Diplomatic Service, 1966–91: CO (formerly CRO), 1966–68; Lusaka, 1969–72; Stockholm, 1972–76; FCO, 1976–79; New Delhi, 1979–83; FCO, 1983–84; Dep. High Comr, Kaduna, 1984–88; Ambassador to Iceland, 1989–91; FCO, 1991. Mem., Patching Parish Council, 1993– (Chm., 1997–). BBC 'Brain of Britain', 1966. Life Mem., Kaduna Br., Nigeria–Britain Assoc. Grand Cross, Order of Icelandic Falcon, 1990. *Recreations:* gardening, churchwardening. *Address:* Holly Howe, The Street, Patching, near Worthing, West Sussex BN13 3XF.

BEST-SHAW, Sir John (Michael Robert), 10th Bt *cr* 1665; retired; *b* 28 Sept. 1924; *s* of Sir John James Kenward Best-Shaw, 9th Bt, Commander RN, and Elizabeth Mary Theodora (*d* 1986), *e d* of Sir Robert Hughes, 12th Bt; *S* father, 1984; *m* 1960, Jane Gordon, *d* of A. G. Guthrie; two *s* one *d* (and one *s* decd). *Educ:* Lancing; Hertford Coll., Oxford (MA); Avery Hill Coll., London (Teachers' Cert.). Captain Royal West Kent Regt, 1943–47. Royal Fedn of Malaya Police, 1950–58; church work, 1958–71; teaching, 1972–82. *Recreations:* bridge, writing. *Heir: s* Thomas Joshua Best-Shaw [*b* 7 March 1965; *m* 1992, Emily Susan, *d* of Vivian Rubin; two *s*]. *Address:* Belmont, 104 High Street, West Malling, Kent ME19 6NE. *T:* (01732) 843823. *Club:* Commonwealth.

BESTERMAN, Edwin Melville Mack, MD, MA, Cantab; FRCP; FACC; Honorary Consultant Cardiologist: Department of Medicine, University of the West Indies (Mona Faculty, Jamaica), since 1985; St Mary's Hospital, London, since 1985; Paddington Green Children's Hospital, since 1985; Hon. Consultant Physician, Department of Medicine, Hammersmith Hospital, since 1981; *b* 4 May 1924; *s* of late Theodore Deodatus Nathaniel Besterman and Evelyn, *y d* of Arthur Mack, NY; *m* 1978, Perri Marjorie Burrowes, *d* of R. Burrowes, Kingston, Jamaica, WI; four *s* by previous marriage. *Educ:* Stowe Sch.; Trinity Coll., Cambridge; Guy's Hospital. BA (Cantab) 1943 (1st cl. hons Physiology), MA 1948; MB, BChir 1947; MRCP 1949; MD 1955 (Raymond Horton Smith Prize); FRCP 1967; FACC 1985. Out-patient Officer, Guy's Hosp., 1947; House Physician, Post-graduate Medical Sch., Hammersmith, 1948; Registrar, Special Unit for Juvenile Rheumatism, Canadian Red Cross Memorial Hosp., Taplow, Berks, 1949–52; First Asst (Lectr), Inst of Cardiology and Nat. Heart Hosp., 1953–56; Sen. Registrar, Middlesex Hosp., 1956–62; Consultant Cardiologist: St Mary's Hosp., London, 1962–85; Paddington Green Children's Hosp., 1972–85. Member: Brit. Cardiac Soc.; Caribbean Cardiac Soc. Fellow, Amer. Coll. of Cardiology. Mem., Colony Photographic Club of Jamaica. *Publications:* (contrib.) Paul Wood, Diseases of the Heart and Circulation, 3rd edn, 1968; (contrib.) British Cardiology in the 20th Century, 2000; articles on phonocardiography, pulmonary hypertension, atherosclerosis, blood platelet function, lipid fractions and drug trials in angina and hypertension in Brit. Heart Jl, Brit. Med. Jl, Lancet, Circulation, Atherosclerosis Research, etc. *Recreations:* photography, gardening, dogs (Pres., German Shepherd Club, Jamaica). *Address:* PO Box 340, Stony Hill, Kingston 9, Jamaica, West Indies.

See also T. P. Besterman.

BESTERMAN, Tristram Paul; Director, Manchester Museum at University of Manchester, since 1994; *b* 19 Sept. 1949; *s* of Dr Edwin Melville Mack Besterman, *qv* and Audrey (*née* Heald); *m* 1977, Perry Garceau; two *s* one *d*. *Educ:* Stowe Sch.; Trinity Coll., Cambridge (BA 1971, MA 1979). FGS 1978; AMA 1979, FMA 1986. Studio Manager, BBC, 1971–73; Preparator's Asst, Geological and Mining Mus., Sydney, NSW, 1974; jackaroo, cattle station, Qld, 1974; Educn Asst, Sheffield City Museums, 1974–78; Dep. Curator and Keeper of Geology, Warwickshire Museums, 1978–85; City Curator, Plymouth City Museums and Art Gall., 1985–93. Chm., Ethics Cttee, Museums Assoc., 1994–. *Publications:* contribs to museological literature. *Recreations:* music, sampling antipodean wines and culture. *Address:* Manchester Museum, University of Manchester, Oxford Road, Manchester M13 9PL. *T:* (0161) 275 2650.

BETHE, Prof. Hans Albrecht, PhD; Professor of Theoretical Physics, Cornell University, 1937–75, now Professor Emeritus; *b* Strassburg, Germany, 2 July 1906; *m* 1939, Rose Ewald; one *s* one *d*. *Educ:* Goethe Gymnasium, Frankfurt on Main; Univs of Frankfurt and Munich. PhD Munich, 1928. Instructor in Theoretical Physics, Univs of Frankfurt, Stuttgart, Munich and Tübingen, 1928–33; Lectr, Univs of Manchester and Bristol, England, 1933–35; Asst Prof., Cornell Univ., Ithaca, 1935–37. Dir, Theoretical Physics Div. of Los Alamos Atomic Scientific Laboratory, 1943–46. Sabbatic leave to Cambridge Univ., academic year, 1955–56. Mem., President's Science Adv. Cttee, 1956–59. Member: Nat. Acad. Sciences; Amer. Physical Soc.; Amer. Astron. Soc.; For. Mem., Royal Society. Holds hon. doctorates in Science. US Medal of Merit, 1946; Planck Medal, German Physical Soc., 1955; Eddington Medal, Royal Astronomical Soc., 1961; Enrico Fermi Award, US Atomic Energy Commn, 1961; Nobel Prize for Physics, 1967. *Publications:* (jt author) Elementary Nuclear Theory, 1947; Mesons and Fields, 1955; Quantum Mechanics of One- and Two-Electron Atoms, 1957; Intermediate Quantum Mechanics, 1964; contributions to: Handbuch der Physik, 1933, 1954; Reviews of Mod. Physics, 1936–37, 1990; Physical Review; Astrophysical Jl. *Address:* Newman Laboratory of Nuclear Studies, Cornell University, Ithaca, NY 14853, USA.

BETHEL, David Percival, CBE 1983; Director, Leicester Polytechnic, 1973–87; *b* Bath, 7 Dec. 1923; *s* of William George Bethell and Elsie (*née* Cossins); *m* 1943, Margaret Elizabeth (*d* 1998), *d* of late Alexander Wrigglesworth; one *s* one *d*. *Educ:* King Edward VI Sch., Bath; Crypt Grammar Sch., Glos; West of England Coll. of Art; Bristol Univ., 1946–51; NDD, ATD, FSAE, FCSD, RWA. Served with RN, Far East, 1943–45. Lectr, Stafford Coll. of Art, 1951–56; Deputy Principal, Coventry Coll. of Art, 1956–65; Principal, Coventry Coll. of Art, 1965–69; Dep. Dir, Leicester Polytechnic, 1969–73. Pres., Nat. Soc. for Art Educn, 1965–66; Member: Nat. Adv. Cttee for Art Educn, 1965–71; Jt Summerson Coldstream Cttee, 1968–70; The Design Council, 1980–88; Nat. Adv. Bd for Local Authority Higher Educn, 1983–87; OECD Directing Gp for Management of Higher Educn, 1984–87; Cttee for Internat. Co-operation in Higher Educn, British Council, 1981–88; Chairman: CNAA Cttee for Art and Design (and Research Degrees Sub-Cttee), 1975–81; Educn and Trng Bd, Chartered Soc. of Designers, 1987–91; Study Team on Delivery of Primary Health Care Services, 1987–88; Cttee of Dirs of Polytechnics, 1978–80; Vice-Chm., Inter-Univs and Polytechnics Council for Higher Educn Overseas. Sometime Design Consultant to Massey Ferguson, Van Heusen, Monotype Corp., etc. British Council Adviser to Hong Kong Govt, 1971; Chairman: UGC/NAB Town & Country Planning Courses Cttee, 1985–86; Hong Kong Planning Cttee for Academic Accreditation, 1986–89; Hong Kong Council for Acad. Accreditation, 1989–92; Member: Hong Kong UPGC, 1982–92; World Council, INSEA; Council of Europe; Assessor, Partnership Trust, 1991–93; Convenor, W Midlands Br., Conservative Acad. Liaison Forum, 1993–. Chairman: Cyril Wood Meml Trust; Leicester Haymarket Theatre, 1979–85; Frame-Work Knitters Educnl Bursary Awards Cttee, 1992–; Mem. Council, RWA, 1993– (Sen. Vice-Pres., 1997–). Paintings and prints in Glos Libraries, Stafford Art Gallery, Coventry, RWA, private collections. Liveryman, Co. of Frame-Work Knitters (Steward, 1994–97; Mem., Ct of Assts, 1997–). Aust. Commonwealth Travelling Fellowship, 1979. FRSA. Hon. LLD Leicester, 1982; Hon. DLitt Loughborough, 1987; Hon. DEd UWE, 1998. *Publications:* A Case of Sorts, 1991; An Industrious People, 1991; 120 Woodcuts & the Bard, 1994; Initial Influences, 1996. *Recreations:* travel; study of art, design, architecture; archæology, music. *Address:* 48 Holmfield Road, Stoneygate, Leicester LE2 1SA. *Clubs:* Athenæum, Royal Over-Seas League.

BETHEL, Dr Keva Marie, CMG 1995; President, College of the Bahamas, 1995–98; *b* 18 Aug. 1935; *d* of late Sidney Alexander Eldon and of Rowena Beatrice Eldon (*née* Hill); *m* 1962, E. Clement Bethel (*d* 1987); one *s* one *d*. *Educ:* Girton Coll., Cambridge (BA, MA); Univ. of Alberta (PhD 1981). Government High School, Nassau, Bahamas: Asst Mistress, Spanish and French, 1959–66; Head, Mod. Langs Dept, 1966–72; Dep. Headmistress, 1972–75; College of the Bahamas: Chm., Div. of Humanities, 1975–77; Dean, Acad. Affairs, 1977–78; Vice Principal, 1979–81; Actg Principal, Jan.–June 1992; Principal, 1982–95. Hon. LLD Univ. of W Indies, 1998. *Publications:* (contrib.) Handbook of World Education, ed Walter Wickremasinghe, 1991; (contrib.) Educational Reform in the Commonwealth Caribbean, ed Errol Miller, 1999. *Recreations:* reading, music. *Address:* PO Box N1232, Nassau, New Providence, Bahamas.

BETHEL, Martin; QC 1983; a Recorder of the Crown Court, since 1979; *b* 12 March 1943; *o s* of late Rev. Ralph Bethel and Enid Bethel; *m* 1974, Kathryn Denby; two *s* one *d.* *Educ:* Kingswood Sch.; Fitzwilliam Coll., Cambridge (MA, LLM). Called to the Bar, Inner Temple, 1965; North-Eastern Circuit (Circuit Junior, 1969); a Dep. High Court Judge, 1995–. Member: Criminal Injuries Compensation Bd, 1999–2000; Criminal Injuries Compensation Appeals Panel, 2000–. Governor, Ashville Coll., Harrogate, 1989–2001. Pres., Runswick Bay Rescue Boat, 2001–. *Recreations:* family, sailing, ski-ing. *Address:* (chambers) Park Lane Chambers, 19 Westgate, Leeds LS1 2RD. *T:* (0113) 228 5000.

BETHELL, family name of **Barons Bethell** and **Westbury**.

BETHELL, 4th Baron *cr* 1922, of Romford; **Nicholas William Bethell;** Bt 1911; Member (C) London Region, European Parliament, since 1999; free-lance writer; *b* 19 July 1938; *s* of Hon. William Gladstone Bethell (*d* 1964) (3rd *s* of 1st Baron), and Ann Margaret Bethell (*d* 1996); *S* kinsman, 1967; *m* 1st, 1964, Cecilia Mary (marr. diss. 1971, she *d* 1977), *er d* of Prof. A. M. Honeyman; two *s*; 2nd, 1992, Bryony Lea Morgan, *e d* of Brian Griffiths; one *s.* *Educ:* Harrow; Pembroke Coll., Cambridge (PhD 1987). On editorial staff of Times Literary Supplement, 1962–64; a Script Editor in BBC Radio Drama, 1964–67. A Lord in Waiting (Govt Whip, House of Lords), June 1970–Jan. 1971. MEP (C), 1975–94 (London NW, 1979–94); contested (C) London NW, Eur. Parly elecns, 1994. Chm., Friends of Cyprus, 1981–; Pres., Friends of Gibraltar's Heritage, 1992–. Pres., Uxbridge Conservative Assoc., 1995–99. Vice Pres., Brill CC, 1997–. Comdr, Order of Merit (Poland), 1991. *Publications:* Gomulka: his Poland and his Communism, 1969; The War Hitler Won, 1972; The Last Secret, 1974; Russia Besieged, 1977; The Palestine Triangle, 1979; The Great Betrayal, 1984; Spies and Other Secrets, 1994; *translations:* Six Plays, by Slawomir Mrozek, 1967; Elegy to John Donne, by Joseph Brodsky, 1967; Cancer Ward, by A. Solzhenitsyn, 1968; The Love Girl and the Innocent, by A. Solzhenitsyn, 1969; The Ascent of Mount Fuji, by Chingiz Aitmatov, 1975; dramatic works for radio and TV; occasional journalism. *Recreations:* poker, tennis. *Heir:* *s* Hon. James Nicholas Bethell [*b* 1 Oct. 1967. *Educ:* Harrow; Edinburgh Univ.]. *Address:* Manor Farm, Brill, Bucks HP18 9SL. *T:* (01844) 238446. *Clubs:* Garrick, Pratt's.

BETHELL, Prof. Leslie Michael; Director, Centre for Brazilian Studies, University of Oxford, since 1997; Fellow, St Antony's College, Oxford, since 1997; *b* 12 Feb. 1937; *s* of late Stanley Bethell and of Bessie Bethell (*née* Stoddart); *m* 1961 (marr. diss. 1983); two *s.* *Educ:* Cockburn High Sch., Leeds; University Coll. London (BA, PhD). Lectr in History, Univ. of Bristol, 1961–66; Lectr 1966–74, Reader 1974–86, in Hispanic Amer. and Brazilian History, UCL; Prof. of Latin Amer. Hist., 1986–92, now Emeritus, and Dir, Inst. of Latin Amer. Studies, 1987–92, London Univ.; Sen. Res. Fellow, St Antony's Coll., Oxford, 1993–97. Visiting Professor: Instituto Universitario de Pesquisas do Rio de Janeiro, 1979; Univ. of California at San Diego, 1985; Woodrow Wilson Internat. Center for Scholars, Washington, 1986, 1996–97; Univ. of Chicago, 1992–93. Grand Officer, Nat. Order of the Southern Cross (Brazil), 1999 (Comdr, 1994). *Publications:* The Abolition of the Brazilian Slave Trade, 1970; (ed) The Cambridge History of Latin America: vols I and II, Colonial Latin America, 1984; vol. III, From Independence to *c* 1870, 1985; vols IV and V, From *c* 1870 to 1930, 1986; vol. VII, Mexico, Central America and the Caribbean since 1930, 1990; vol. VIII, Spanish South America since 1930, 1991; vol. VI, Economy, Society and Politics since 1930, Part 1, Economy and Society, Part 2, Politics and Society, 1994; vol XI, Bibliographical Essays, 1995; vol. X, Ideas, Culture and Society since 1930, 1995; (jtly) Latin America between the Second World War and the Cold War 1944–48, 1992; (jtly) A Guerra do Paraguai, 1995; articles and chapters on Latin American history, Brazilian history and politics, Britain and Latin America, and United States and Latin America. *Address:* Centre for Brazilian Studies, 92 Woodstock Road, Oxford OX2 7ND. *T:* (01865) 284460, *Fax:* (01865) 284461.

BETHUNE, Hon. Sir (Walter) Angus, Kt 1979; pastoralist; *b* 10 Sept. 1908; *s* of Frank Pogson Bethune and Laura Eileen Bethune; *m* 1936, Alexandra P., *d* of P. A. Pritchard; one *s* one *d.* *Educ:* Hutchin's Sch., Hobart; Launceston Church of England Grammar Sch. Served War, RAAF Air Crew, Middle East, 1940–43. Member, Hamilton Municipal Council, 1936–56, resigned (Dep. Warden, 1955–56). MHA, Wilmot, Tasmania, 1946–75, resigned; Leader of Opposition, 1960–69; Premier and Treasurer, Tasmania, 1969–72. Leader of Liberal Party, 1960–72, resigned. President: Clarendon Children's Homes, 1977–83; St John's Ambulance Brigade (Tasmania), 1979–86. OStJ 1982. *Address:* 1 Quinn Court, Sandy Bay, Tas 7005, Australia. *Clubs:* Tasmanian; Naval, Military and Air Force; Royal Autocar of Tasmania.

BETT, Sir Michael, Kt 1995; CBE 1990; MA; Chairman: Pace Micro Technology Plc, since 2000; Pensions Protection and Investment Accreditation Board, since 2000; First Civil Service Commissioner, 1995–2000; *b* 18 Jan. 1935; *s* of Arthur Bett, OBE and Nina Daniells; *m* 1959, Christine Angela Reid; one *s* two *d.* *Educ:* Aldenham Sch.; Pembroke Coll., Cambridge. Dir, Industrial Relations, Engrg Employers' Fedn, 1970–72; Personnel Dir, General Electric Co. Ltd, 1972–77; Dir of Personnel, BBC, 1977–81; British Telecom: Bd Mem. for Personnel, 1981–84; Corporate Dir, Personnel and Corporate Services, 1984–85; Man. Dir Local (Inland) Communications Services, 1985–87; Man. Dir, UK Communications, 1987–88; Man. Dir, British Telecom UK, 1988–91; Vice-Chm., 1990–91; Dep. Chm., 1991–94; non-exec. Dir, 1994–96. Chairman: Cellnet, 1991–99; Workhouse Ltd, 1992–95; Director: Compel Gp plc, 1993– (Chm., 2000–); KMG Financial Services, 1994–99; Eyretel Ltd, 1996–. Chairman: Nurses Pay Rev. Body, 1990–95; Social Security Adv. Cttee, 1993–95; Armed Forces Indep. Review on Manpower, 1994–95; Nat. Council, TEC, 1994–95; Inspectorate of the Security Industry, 1994–2000; Nat. Security Inspectorate, 2000–; Indep. Review of Pay and Conditions of Service in Higher Educn; Co Chm., British N Amer. Cttee, 1997–99; Member: Pay Bd, 1973–74; Training Levy Exemption Referee, 1975–82; Civil Service Arbitration Tribunal, 1977–83; Cttee of Inquiry into UK Prison Services, 1978–79; Cttee of Inquiry into Water Service Dispute, 1983; NHS Management Inquiry, 1983; Armed Forces Pay Review Body, 1983–87; Civil Service Coll. Adv. Council, 1983–88; Trng Commn (formerly MSC), 1985–89. Member Council: St Christopher's Hospice, 1993–99; Royal Hosp. for Neurodisability, 1996– (Chm., 1998–); Cranfield Inst. of Technology, 1982–87; Pro-Chancellor, Aston Univ., 1993–. Chairman: Bromley CABx, 1985–93; SCF, 1992–98. Chm. of Govs, Cranbrook Sch., 1992–. Dir, English Shakespeare Co., 1988–95; Chairman: One World Broadcasting Trust, 1996–; English Shakespeare Internat., 1997–2000. CIPD (Pres., 1992–98); CIMgt; FRSA. Hon. Col, 81 Signal Sqn (Vols), RCS, 1990–96. DBA (*hc*): IMCB, 1986; CNAA/Liverpool Poly., 1991; Hon. DSc Aston, 1996. *Recreations:* television and radio, theatre, music, cooking, gardening. *Address:* (office) 48 London Road, Sevenoaks, Kent TN13 1AS.

BETTISON, Norman George, QPM 2000; Chief Constable, Merseyside Police, since 1998; *b* 3 Jan. 1956; *s* of George and Betty Bettison. *Educ:* Queen's Coll., Oxford (MA Psychol. and Philosophy); Sheffield Hallam Univ. (MBA). Police officer, 1972–: S Yorks Police, 1972–93; W Yorks Police, 1993–98. Independence Medal (Rhodesia), 1980. *Address:* PO Box 59, Liverpool, Merseyside L69 1JD. *T:* (0151) 777 8000. *Club:* Royal Over-Seas League.

BETTRIDGE, Brig. John Bryan, CBE 1983; Principal, Emergency Planning College (formerly Civil Defence College), 1984–93; *b* 16 Aug. 1932; *s* of Henry George Bettridge and Dorothy Bettridge; *m* 1959, one *s* one *d.* *Educ:* Eastbourne Grammar School. Commissioned RA, 1951; regimental duty, 3 RHA and 52 Locating Regt, 1952–59; Instructor, RMA Sandhurst, 1959–61; Student, Staff Coll., Camberley, 1962; War Office, 1964–66; Bty Comd, 1 RHA, 1968–70; Comd, 3 RHA, 1973–75, Hong Kong; Chief Instructor, Tactics, RSA, 1976; Comd RA 2 Div., 1977–78; RCDS 1979; Dep. Comdt, Staff Coll., 1980–82; Comdt, RSA Larkhill, 1983–84. *Recreations:* golf, carpentry. *Address:* Cherry Garth, Main Street, Bishopthorpe, York YO23 2RB. *T:* (01904) 704270.

BETTS, Prof. Alan Osborn, PhD, MA, BSc, MRCVS; Principal and Dean, The Royal Veterinary College, University of London, 1970–89, now Emeritus Professor; *b* 11 March 1927; *s* of late A. O. and D. S. A. Betts; *m* 1st, 1952, Joan M. Battersby; one *s* one *d*; 2nd, 1990, Jane M. Jones (*see* J. M. Betts). *Educ:* Royal Veterinary Coll.; Magdalene Coll., Cambridge. Asst in Gen. Practice, 1949; Animal Health Trust Research Scholar, 1950–52; Demonstrator, Univ. of Cambridge, 1952–56; Commonwealth Fund Fellow, Cornell Univ., USA, 1955–56; University Lectr, Cambridge, 1956–64; Prof. of Veterinary Microbiology and Parasitology, Univ. of London, 1964–70; Vice-Chm., 1976–88, Acting Chm., 1989, Governing Body of Wye Coll.; Dep. Vice-Chancellor, Univ. of London, 1984–88. Leverhulme Vis. Fellow, Graduate Sch. of Admin, Univ. of Calif, Davis, 1982. Treasurer: BVA, 1967–70; RCVS, 1978–81; Pres., Vet. Res. Club, 1984–85. Member: Brit. Pharmacopoeia Commn, 1978–93; EC Adv. Cttee on Veterinary Trng, 1980–90; Bucks FHSA, 1992–96; Complaints Convenor, Bucks HA, 1998–. Mem. Council, Imperial Cancer Research Fund, 1988–97. Trustee: Hunterian Mus., RCSE, 1990–; Eastman Dental Res. Foundn, subseq. Eastman Foundn for Oral Res. and Trng, 1994–. Dalrymple-Champneys Cup and Medal of BVA, 1978; Faculty Medal, Vet. Faculty, Univ. of Munich, 1985. *Publications:* Viral and Rickettsial Infections of Animals, 1967; papers in microbiological, veterinary and management jls. *Recreations:* travel, gliding. *Address:* Lower Boycott, Dadford Road, Stowe, Buckingham MK18 5JZ. *T:* and *Fax:* (01280) 813287. *Club:* Athenæum.

BETTS, Air Vice-Marshal (Charles) Stephen, CBE 1963; MA; Head of Control and Inspection Division, Agency for the Control of Armaments, WEU, Paris, 1974–84; *b* 8 April 1919; *s* of H. C. Betts, Nuneaton; *m* 1st, 1943, Pauline Mary (deceased), *d* of Lt-Col P. Heath; two *d*; 2nd, 1964, Margaret Doreen (*d* 1993), *d* of Col W. H. Young, DSO; 3rd, 1996, Denys Mary, *d* of William de Montigny Clarke. *Educ:* King Edward's Sch., Nuneaton; Sidney Sussex Coll., Cambridge. Joined RAF 1941; Air Cdre 1966; Asst Comdt (Eng.), RAF Coll., Cranwell, 1971–72; Air Vice-Marshal 1972; AOC No 24 Group, RAF, 1972–73, retired 1974. *Recreations:* travel, music. *Address:* Cranford, Weston Road, Bath BA1 2XX. *T:* and *Fax:* (01225) 310995. *Club:* Royal Air Force.

BETTS, Charles Valentine, CB 1998; FREng, FRINA; Director General Submarines, and Deputy Controller of the Navy, Ministry of Defence, 1994–98; Head, Royal Corps of Naval Constructors, 1992–98; *b* 10 Jan. 1942; *s* of Harold Blair Betts and late Mary Ellis Betts (*née* France); *m* 1965, Rev. Patricia Joyce Bennett; two *s.* *Educ:* St Catharine's Coll., Cambridge (BA Hons, MA Mech. Scis); Royal Naval Coll., Greenwich (Prof. Cert., Naval Arch.); Univ. of London (MPhil Naval Arch.). CEng; FREng (FEng 1991). Asst Constructor, MoD, 1966–71; Lectr in Naval Arch., UCL, 1971–74; Constructor, HM Dockyard, Portsmouth, 1974–77; Constructor and Chief Constructor, MoD, Bath, 1977–83; Chief Constructor, MoD, London, 1983–85; Prof. of Naval Arch., UCL, 1985–89; Dir, Surface Ships B, MoD, Bath, 1989–92; Dir Gen., Surface Ships, MoD, 1992–94. Director (non-executive): BMT Group Ltd, 1999–; BMT Reliability Consultants Ltd, 2000–. Mem. Council, RINA, 1985–. Trustee, Alpha Internat. Ministries, 1993–. FRSA. *Publications:* (jtly) The Marine Technology Reference Book, 1990; papers in professional jls. *Recreations:* supporting my wife in her rôle as Vicar of Widcombe, Bath; cruising under sail, listening to music. *Address:* Hunters Lodge, North Road, Bathwick, Bath BA2 6HP. *T:* (01225) 464918, *Fax:* (01225) 445732. *Club:* Royal Naval Sailing Association.

BETTS, Clive James Charles; MP (Lab) Sheffield Attercliffe, since 1992; *b* 13 Jan. 1950; *s* of late Harold and Nellie Betts. *Educ:* Longley Sch., Sheffield; King Edward VII Sch., Sheffield; Pembroke Coll., Cambridge (BA Econ). Sheffield City Council: Councillor (Lab), 1976–92; Chm., Housing Cttee, 1980–86; Chm., Finance Cttee, 1986–88; Dep. Leader, 1986–87; Leader, 1987–92. Chm., S Yorks Pension Authority, 1989–92; Dep. Chm., AMA, 1988–91 (Chm., Housing Cttee, 1985–89). An Asst Government Whip, 1997–98; a Lord Comr of HM Treasury (Govt Whip), 1998–2001. Member: Treasury Select Cttee, 1995–96. Transport, Local Govt and the Regions Select Cttee, 2001–. Chm., 1995–96, Sec., 1995–97, Labour's Treasury Deptl Cttee; Labour Ldr's Campaign Team, 1995–96. *Recreations:* Sheffield Wednesday FC, cricket, squash, walking, real ale. *Address:* House of Commons, SW1A 0AA.

BETTS, Jane Margaret; Secretary-General, Law Society, 1996–2000; *b* 8 June 1953; *d* of James Gibson Jones and late Margaret Jones (*née* Finlayson); *m* 1990, Prof. Alan Osborn Betts, *qv.* *Educ:* Univ. of Leeds (BA); Cornell Univ. (EDP). MHSM. PA to Man. Dir, Fairclough Ltd, Leeds, 1976–79; University of London: PA to Principal and Information Officer, RVC, 1979–85; Admin. Assistant to Vice-Chancellor and Dep. Public Relations Officer, 1985–88; Sec., BPMF, 1988–96. FRSA 1996. *Recreations:* travel, music, photography. *Address:* Lower Boycott, Dadford Road, Stowe, Buckingham MK18 5JZ. *T:* and *Fax:* (01280) 813287. *Club:* Institute of Directors.

BETTS, Lily Edna Minerva, (Mrs John Betts); *see* Mackie, L. E. M.

BETTS, Rt Rev. Stanley Woodley, CBE 1967; *b* 23 March 1912; *yr s* of Hubert Woodley and Lillian Esther Betts. *Educ:* Perse Sch.; Jesus Coll., Cambridge (MA 1937); Ridley Hall, Cambridge. Curate of St Paul's Cheltenham, 1935–38; Chaplain, RAF, 1938–47 (despatches); Sen. Chaplain of BAFO, Germany, 1946–47; Comdt, RAF Chaplains' Sch., Dowdeswell Court, 1947; Chaplain, Clare Coll., Cambridge, 1947–49; Chaplain, Cambridge Pastorate, 1947–56; Proctor in Convocation, 1952–59; Vicar of Holy Trinity Cambridge, 1949–56; Exam. Chaplain to Bishop of Southwell, 1947–56; Select Preacher to University of Cambridge, 1955; Suffragan Bishop of Maidstone, 1956–66; Archbishop of Canterbury's Episcopal Representative with the three Armed Forces, 1956–66; Dean of Rochester, 1966–77. Chm., Bd of the Church Army, 1970–80; Vice-President: Lee Abbey, 1977–; Wadhurst Coll., 1984–97 (Chm. Council 1976–84). *Address:* 2 King's Houses, Pevensey, Sussex BN24 5JR. *T:* (01323) 762421. *Club:* National.

BETTS, Stephen; *see* Betts, C. S.

BEVAN, Rear-Adm. Christopher Martin, CB 1978; Under Treasurer Gray's Inn, 1980–89; *b* London, 22 Jan. 1923; *s* of Humphrey C. Bevan and Mary F. Bevan (*née* Mackenzie); *m* 1948, Patricia C. Bedford; one *s* three *d*. *Educ:* Stowe Sch., Bucks; Victoria Univ., Wellington, NZ. Trooper in Canterbury Yeoman Cavalry (NZ Mounted Rifles), 1941; joined RN as Ord. Seaman, 1942; served remainder of 1939–45 war, Mediterranean and N Atlantic; commissioned 1943; Comdr 1958; Captain 1967; Supt Weapons and Radio, Dockyard Dept, MoD (Navy), 1967–70; Asst Dir, Weapons Equipment (Surface), later, Captain Surface Weapons Acceptance, Weapons Dept, MoD (Navy), 1970–73; Dir, Naval Officer Appts (Engrs), 1973–76; ADC to the Queen, 1976; Rear-Adm. 1976; Flag Officer Medway and Port Adm. Chatham, 1976–78. *Recreations:* photography, theatre, music, travel. *Address:* c/o Messrs C. Hoare and Co., 37 Fleet Street, EC4P 4DQ. *Club:* Boodle's.

BEVAN, (Edward) Julian; QC 1991; *b* 23 Oct. 1940; *m* 1966, Bronwen Mary Windsor Lewis; two *s* two *d*. *Educ:* Eton. Called to the Bar, Gray's Inn, 1962, Bencher, 1989; Standing Counsel for the Inland Revenue, 1974; Jun. Treasury Counsel, 1977, Sen. Treasury Counsel, 1985, First Sen. Treasury Counsel, 1989–91, Central Criminal Court. *Address:* Queen Elizabeth Building, Temple, EC4Y 9BS. *Club:* Garrick.

BEVAN, Prof. Hugh Keith; JP; Professor of Law, University of Hull, 1969–89; *b* 8 Oct. 1922; *s* of Thomas Edward Bevan and Marjorie Avril Bevan (*née* Trick); *m* 1950, Mary Harris; one *d* (one *s* decd). *Educ:* Neath Grammar Sch.; University Coll. of Wales, Aberystwyth. LLB 1949, LLM 1966. Called to the Bar, Middle Temple, 1959. Served RA, 1943–46. University of Hull: Lectr in Law, 1950–61; Sen. Lectr in Law, 1961–69; Pro Vice-Chancellor, 1979–82; Wolfson College, Cambridge: Vis. Fellow, 1986 and 1989–90; Fellow, 1990–92; Hon. Fellow, 1992. Chm., Rent Assessment Cttees, 1982–92. Pres., Soc. of Public Teachers of Law, 1987–88. JP Kingston-upon-Hull, 1972 (Chm. of Bench, 1984–89). Hon. LLD: Hull, 1990; Sheffield, 2000. *Publications:* Source Book of Family Law (with P. R. H. Webb), 1964; Law Relating to Children, 1973; (with M. L. Parry) The Children Act 1975, 1978; Child Law, 1988; numerous articles. *Recreations:* music, golf. *Address:* Wolfson College, Cambridge CB3 9BB. *T:* (01223) 335900.

BEVAN, James David; Head, European Union Department (Internal), Foreign and Commonwealth Office, since 2000; *b* 13 July 1959; *s* of late Douglas Bevan and of Diana Bevan; *m* 1984, Janet Purdie; three *d*. *Educ:* Univ. of Sussex (BA Hons Social Anthropology). Joined FCO, 1982; Kinshasa, 1984–86; UK Delegn to NATO, Brussels, 1986–90; FCO, 1990–92; Paris, 1993; Washington, 1994–98; Head, Africa Dept (Equatorial), FCO, 1998–2000. *Recreations:* drumming, web browsing, pontificating. *Address:* c/o Foreign and Commonwealth Office, King Charles Street, SW1A 2AH.

BEVAN, John Penry Vaughan; QC 1997; a Recorder, since 1988; *b* 7 Sept. 1947; *s* of late Llewellyn Vaughan Bevan and of Hilda Molly Bevan; *m* 1st, 1971, Dinah Nicholson; two *d*; 2nd, 1978, Veronica Aliaga-Kelly; one *s* one *d*. *Educ:* Radley Coll.; Magdalene Coll., Cambridge (BA). Called to the Bar, Middle Temple, 1970. Sen. Treasury Counsel, CCC, 1989–97. *Recreation:* sailing. *Clubs:* Leander (Henley-on-Thames); Aldeburgh Yacht; Orford Sailing.

BEVAN, John Stuart, OBE 1995; consultant; Further Education Funding Council for England Ombudsman, 1996–2001; *b* 19 Nov. 1935; *s* of Frank Oakland and Ruth Mary Bevan; *m* 1960, Patricia Vera Beatrice (*née* Joyce); two *s* two *d*. *Educ:* Eggar's Grammar Sch.; Jesus Coll., Oxford; S Bartholomew's Hosp. Med. Coll. MA, MSc; FInstP. Health Physicist, UK Atomic Energy Authority, 1960–62; Lectr, then Sen. Lectr in Physics, Polytechnic of the South Bank (previously Borough Polytechnic), 1962–73; Inner London Education Authority: Asst Educn Officer, then Sen. Asst Educn Officer, 1973–76; Dep. Educn Officer, 1977–79; Dir of Educn, 1979–82; Sec., NAB, 1982–88; Dir of Educn Services, London Residuary Body, 1989–92; Chief Exec., ACFHE, 1992–93; Sec., Assoc. for Colls, 1993–94. Former Member, National Executive Committees: Nat. Union of Teachers; Assoc. of Teachers in Technical Instns (Pres., 1972–73). Chm., Nat. Youth Agency, 1996–. Scout Association: Asst, later Dep. Comr, Kent, 1982–99; Chm., Nat. Activities Bd, 1988–93; Nat. Comr for Activities, 1994–95; Chm., Programme and Trng, 1995–96; Chm., Cttee of Council, 1996–. Hon. Fellow: S Bank Univ. (formerly Poly of the S Bank), 1987; Westminster Coll., Oxford, 1990. DUniv Surrey, 1990; Hon. LLD CNAA, 1992. *Publications:* occasional papers in the educnl press. *Recreations:* scouting, mountaineering. *Address:* The Hollies, Great Asby, Appleby, Cumbria CA16 6HD. *T:* (01768) 353433.

BEVAN, Julian; *see* Bevan, E. J.

BEVAN, Sir Martyn Evan E.; *see* Evans-Bevan.

BEVAN, Prof. Michael John, PhD; FRS 1991; Investigator, Howard Hughes Medical Institute, and Professor, Department of Immunology, University of Washington, Seattle, since 1990; *b* 20 Sept. 1945; *s* of Thomas John Bevan and Doris Mary (*née* Prior); *m* 1985, Pamela Jean Fink; two *s*. *Educ:* Pontypridd Boys' Grammar Sch.; University Coll. London (BSc Zool. 1967; MSc Biochem. 1968); Nat. Inst. for Med. Research, London (PhD 1972). Postdoctoral Fellow, Salk Inst. for Biol Studies, La Jolla, Calif, 1973–76, Asst Res. Prof., 1976–77; Asst, then Associate, Prof., Dept of Biology, MIT, 1977–82; Associate, then Member, Dept of Immunology, Scripps Res. Inst., La Jolla, Calif, 1982–90. *Publications:* numerous original res. pubns in scientific jls incl. Nature, Science, Cell, Jl Exptl Medicine. *Recreation:* hiking. *Address:* Howard Hughes Medical Institute, Department of Immunology, University of Washington, 357370, Seattle, WA 98195, USA. *T:* (206) 6853610.

BEVAN, Dr Michael Webster; Head, Department of Molecular Genetics, John Innes Centre, Biotechnology and Biological Sciences Research Council; *b* 5 June 1952; *s* of John Vernon Bevan and Sue (*née* Webster); *m* 1982, Jane Foster; two *s*. *Educ:* Univ. of Auckland (BSc 1973; MSc Hons 1974); Univ. of Cambridge (PhD 1979). Res. Fellow, Washington Univ., St Louis, Mo, 1980; Higher Scientific Officer, 1982–84, SSO, 1984–86, PSO, 1986–88, Plant Breeding Inst., Cambridge; Hd, Dept of Molecular Genetics, Inst. of Plant Sci. Res., AFRC, subseq. John Innes Centre, BBSRC, 1988–. Rank Prize, Rank Foundn, 1986. *Publications:* contrib. numerous chapters in books and articles to learned jls. *Recreations:* reading modern literature, riding, ski-ing, walking. *Address:* 329 Unthank Road, Norwich NR4 7QA. *T:* (01603) 504181.

BEVAN, Sir Nicolas, Kt 2001; CB 1991; Speaker's Secretary, House of Commons, since 1993; *b* 8 March 1942; *s* of late Roger Bevan, BM, and Diana Mary Bevan (*née* Freeman); *m* 1982, Christine, *d* of N. A. Berry. *Educ:* Westminster Sch.; Corpus Christi Coll., Oxford (MA LitHum). Ministry of Defence: Asst Principal, 1964; Principal, 1969; Private Sec. to Chief of Air Staff, 1970–73; Cabinet Office, 1973–75; Asst Sec., 1976; RCDS 1981; Asst Under Sec. of State, 1985; Under Sec., Cabinet Office, 1992–93. *Recreation:* gardening. *Address:* House of Commons, SW1A 0AA.

BEVAN, Prof. Peter Gilroy, CBE 1983; MB, ChB; FRCS; Consultant Surgeon, Dudley Road Hospital, Birmingham, 1958–87; Professor of Surgery and Postgraduate Medical Education, University of Birmingham, 1981–87, now Emeritus Professor; *b* 13 Dec. 1922; *s* of Rev. Thomas John Bevan and Norah (*née* Gilroy); *m* 1st, 1949, Patricia Joan (*née* Laurie) (*d* 1985); one *s* one *d*; 2nd, 1990, Beryl Margaret (*née* Perry). *Educ:* King Edward VI High Sch., Birmingham; Univ. of Birmingham Medical Sch. (MB, ChB 1946; ChM 1958). LRCP MRCS 1946, FRCS 1952; Hon. FRCSI 1984. Served RAMC, BAOR, 1947–49 (Captain). Demonstrator in Anatomy, Univ. of Birmingham, 1949–51; Resident Surgical Officer, Birmingham Children's Hosp., 1954–55; Lectr in Surgery and Sen. Surgical Registrar, Queen Elizabeth Hosp., Birmingham, 1954–58; WHO Vis. Prof. of Surgery to Burma, 1969; Director, Board of Graduate Clinical Studies, Univ. of Birmingham, 1978–87; Pres., Birmingham Medical Inst., 1994– (Postgrad. Tutor, 1987–94). Royal College of Surgeons: Vice-Pres., 1980–82; Member: Council, 1971–83; Court of Patrons, 1988–; Bd of Hunterian Trustees, 1990–; Dir, Overseas Doctors Training Scheme Cttee, 1986–90. Founder Chm., W Midlands Oncology Assoc., 1974–79; Vice-Pres., Brit. Assoc. of Surgical Oncology, 1975–78; President: Pancreatic Soc. of GB, 1977; British Inst. of Surgical Technologists, 1980–95 (Hon. Fellow, British Inst. of Surgical and Dental Technologists, 1999); Assoc. of Surgeons of GB and Ireland, 1984–85 (Fellow, 1960–; Mem. Council, 1975–85); W Midlands Surgical Soc., 1986; Nat. Assoc. of Theatre Nurses, 1992–94. EEC: UK representative: on Monospecialist Section of Surgery, 1975–84; on Adv. Cttee on Medical Trng, 1980–85. Civil Consultant Advr in Gen. Surgery to RN, 1973–84; Med. Adviser, Midlands Div., Ileostomy Assoc., 1976–87. Chm., Adv. Cttee of Deans, 1986–88. Chairman: Steering Gp on Operating Theatres, Dept of Health, 1988–89; Jt Planning Adv. Cttee, Dept of Health, 1990–95; Medical Mem., Pensions Appeal Tribunals, 1987–89; Mem., Medical Appeals Tribunal, 1989–95. Former Member: Jt Planning Adv. Cttee; Central Manpower Cttee; Jt Consultants Cttee; Council for Postgraduate Med. Educn. Mem. Editl Bd, Health Trends, 1990–97. *Publications:* Reconstructive Procedures in Surgery, 1982; Handbook of General Surgery, 1992; various surgical papers in BMJ, Brit. Jl Surgery, Lancet, Annals of RCS; papers on illnesses of classical composers. *Recreations:* inland waterways, golf, photography, music, gardening. *Address:* 10 Russell Road, Moseley, Birmingham B13 8RD. *T:* (0121) 449 3055. *Clubs:* Royal Navy Medical; Edgbaston Golf (Birmingham).

BEVAN, Rev. Canon Richard Justin William, PhD; ThD; Chaplain to The Queen, 1986–92; Canon Emeritus, Carlisle Cathedral, since 1989 (Canon Residentiary, Carlisle Cathedral, 1982–89, Treasurer and Librarian, 1982–89, Vice-Dean, 1987–89); *b* 21 April 1922; *s* of Rev. Richard Bevan, Vicar of St Harmon, Radnorshire and Margaret Bevan; *m* 1948, Sheila Rosemary Barrow, Fazakerley, Liverpool; three *s* one *d* (and one *s* decd). *Educ:* St Edmund's Sch., Canterbury; St Augustine's Coll., Canterbury; Lichfield Theol Coll.; St Chad's Coll., Univ. of Durham (Theol. Prizeman; BA, LTh). ThD: Geneva Theol. Coll., 1972; Greenwich Univ., USA, 1990; PhD Columbia Pacific Univ., 1980. Ordained deacon, Lichfield Cathedral, 1945, priest, 1946; Asst Curate, Stoke-on-Trent, 1945–49; Chaplain, Aberlour Orphanage and licence to officiate, dio. of Moray, Ross and Caithness, 1949–51; Asst Master, Burnley Tech. High Sch., 1951–60; Asst Curate, Church Kirk, 1951–56, Whalley, 1956–60; Rector, St Mary-le-Bow, Durham and Chaplain to Durham Univ., 1960; Vicar, St Oswald's United Benefice, 1964–74; Convener of Chaplains, Univ. of Durham, 1964–74; Rector of Grasmere, 1974–82. Examg Chaplain to Bishop of Carlisle, 1970–; Chaplain, Durham Girls' High Sch., 1966–74; Vice-President: Friends of St Chad's Coll., 1990– (Governor, St Chad's Coll., 1969–89); Greenwich Sch. of Theology, 1997–. First Pres., and Founder Mem., Grasmere Village Soc., 1976–78; Dove Cottage Local Cttee, 1974–82. *Publications:* (ed) Steps to Christian Understanding, 1959; (ed) The Churches and Christian Unity, 1964; (ed) Durham Sermons, 1964; Unfurl the Flame (poetry), 1980; A Twig of Evidence: does belief in God make sense?, 1986; (contrib.) John Cosin: from priest to prince bishop, 1997; articles on ethics and culture. *Recreations:* poetry reading, musical appreciation, train spotting. *Address:* Beck Cottage, West End, Burgh-by-Sands, Carlisle CA5 6BT. *T:* (01228) 576781. *Club:* Victory Services.

BEVAN, Tim; film producer; Co-Founder and Co-Chairman, Working Title Films, since 1984; *m* 1992, Joely Richardson, *qv* (marr. diss.); one *d*. Formerly runner, Video Arts; co-founder, Aldabra, 1984. Film producer (jointly): A World Apart, 1988; Fools of Fortune, 1990; Drop Dead Fred, 1991; Bob Roberts, 1992; with Sarah Radclyffe: My Beautiful Laundrette, 1986; Sammy and Rosie Get Laid, 1987; Personal Services, 1987; Paperhouse, 1989; For Queen and Country, 1989; Dark Obsession, 1990; The Tall Guy, 1990; Chicago Joe and the Showgirl, 1990; London Kills Me, 1992; Rubin and Ed, 1992; with Eric Fellner: Posse, 1993; Romeo is Bleeding, 1993; Four Weddings and a Funeral, 1994; The Hudsucker Proxy, 1994; Loch Ness, 1995; Panther, 1995; French Kiss, 1995; Moonlight & Valentino, 1995; Dead Man Walking, 1995; Fargo, 1996; Bean, 1997; The Matchmaker, 1997; The Borrowers, 1997; The Hi-Lo Country, 1997; Elizabeth, 1998; The Big Lebowski, 1998; What Rats Won't Do, 1998; Notting Hill, 1999; Plunkett & Macleane, 1999; O Brother, Where Art Thou?, 2000; Billy Elliot, 2000; Bridget Jones's Diary, 2001; Captain Corelli's Mandolin, 2001; sole producer, High Fidelity, 2000. Television includes: Tales of the City, 1993; The Borrowers, 1993; More Tales of the City, 1998. *Address:* Working Title Films, Oxford House, 76 Oxford Street, W1D 1BS.

BEVAN, Sir Timothy (Hugh), Kt 1984; Deputy Chairman, Foreign & Colonial Investment Trust plc, 1993–98 (Director, 1988–98); *b* 24 May 1927; *y s* of late Hugh Bevan and Pleasance (*née* Scrutton); *m* 1952, Pamela, *e d* of late Norman and Margaret Smith; two *s* two *d*. *Educ:* Eton. Lieut Welsh Guards. Called to Bar, 1950. Joined Barclays Bank Ltd, 1950; Dir, 1966–93; Vice-Chm., 1968–73; Dep. Chm., 1973–81; Chm., 1981–87. Dir, BET, 1987–92 (Chm., 1988–91). Chm., Cttee of London Clearing Bankers, 1983–85. Mem., NEDC, 1986–87. *Recreations:* sailing, gardening. *Address:* c/o Barclays Bank, 54 Lombard Street, EC3V 9EX. *Clubs:* Cavalry and Guards, Royal Ocean Racing; Royal Yacht Squadron.

BEVAN, Rear-Adm. Timothy Michael, CB 1986; *b* 7 April 1931; *s* of Thomas Richard and Margaret Richmond Bevan; *m* 1970, Sarah Knight; three *s*. *Educ:* Eton College. psc(n), jssc. Entered RN, 1949; commanded: HMS Decoy, 1966; HMS Caprice, 1967–68; HMS Minerva, 1971–72; HMS Ariadne, 1976–78; HMS Ariadne, and Captain of 8th Frigate Sqdn, 1980–82; Britannia Royal Naval Coll., 1982–84; ACDS (Intelligence), 1984–87, retd. Dep. Dir, ACRE, The Rural Communities Charity, 1990–95; Chm., SSAFA Glos, 1996–2000.

BEVAN, Walter Harold, CBE 1977; FCIS; Chairman, Gateshead District Health Authority (formerly of Gateshead Area Health Authority), 1977–84; *b* 22 May 1916; *s* of late Walter Bevan and Sarah (*née* Grainger); *m* 1958, Patricia Edna Sadler, *d* of late Sir Sadler Forster, CBE, DCL; twin *s* and *d*. *Educ:* Gateshead Sch. FCIS 1961. 5th Bn Royal Northumberland Fusiliers, TA, 1938–42; served War: commissioned RA; Arakan campaign, Burma, with 81st W African Div., 1942–46; 4/5 Bn Royal Northumberland Fusiliers, TA, 1947–52. Asst to Sec., North Eastern Trading Estates Ltd, 1937, Chief Accountant 1956; English Industrial Estates Corporation: Chief Accountant, 1960; Sec., 1966; Finance Dir and Sec., 1973; Chief Exec. and Chm., Management Bd, 1974–79. Governor, Gateshead Technical Coll., 1971–81. *Publications:* articles on industrial estates and distribution of industry. *Recreations:* public and voluntary services, bowling, reading. *Address:* 26 Dryden Court, Gateshead NE9 5BY.

BEVERIDGE, Crawford William, CBE 1995; Executive Vice President, Sun Microsystems Inc., since 2000; *b* 3 Nov. 1945; *s* of William Wilson Beveridge and Catherine Crawford Beveridge; *m* 1977, Marguerite DeVoe; one *s* one *d*. *Educ:* Edinburgh Univ. (BSc); Bradford Univ. (MSc). Appts with Hewlett Packard in Scotland, Switzerland, USA, 1968–77; European Personnel Manager, Digital Equipment Corp., 1977–81; Vice-Pres., Human Resources, Analog Devices, 1982–85; Vice-Pres., Corporate Resources, Sun Microsystems, 1985–90; Chief Exec., Scottish Enterprise, 1991–2000. *Recreations:* music, cooking, paperweights. *Address:* Sun Microsystems Inc., 901 San Antonio Road, Palo Alto, CA 94303–4900, USA.

BEVERIDGE, John Caldwell; QC 1979; Recorder, Western Circuit, 1975–96; *b* 26 Sept. 1937; *s* of William Ian Beardmore Beveridge, *qv*; *m* 1st, 1972, Frances Ann Clunes Grant Martineau (marr. diss. 1988); 2nd, 1989, Lilian Moira Weston Adamson. *Educ:* Jesus Coll., Cambridge (MA, LLB). Called to the Bar, Inner Temple, 1963, Bencher, 1985; Western Circuit; called to the Bar, NSW, 1975, QC (NSW), 1980. Partner, Beveridge & Forwood, Zurich. Conservative Mem., Westminster City Council, 1968–72. Freeman, City of London. Jt Master, Westmeath Foxhounds, 1976–79. Comdr, Star of Honour (Ethiopia). *Recreations:* shooting, travelling. *Address:* 9 St James's Chambers, Ryder Street, SW1Y 6QA. *T:* (020) 7930 1118, *Fax:* (020) 7930 1119; Yeo Farm, Waterrow, Taunton TA4 2PT. *Clubs:* Beefsteak, Brooks's, Pratt's, Turf; Brook (New York).

BEVERIDGE, William Ian Beardmore, MA, ScD Cantab; DVSc Sydney; Professor of Animal Pathology, Cambridge, 1947–75; Emeritus Fellow of Jesus College; *b* 23 April 1908; *s* of J. W. C. and Ada Beveridge; *m* 1935, Patricia, *d* of Rev. E. C. Thomson; one *s*. *Educ:* Cranbrook Sch., Sydney; St Paul's Coll., University of Sydney; ScD Cantab 1974. Research bacteriologist, McMaster Animal Health Laboratory, Sydney, 1931–37; Commonwealth Fund Service Fellow at Rockefeller Inst. and at Washington, 1938–39; Walter and Eliza Hall Inst. for Medical Research, Melbourne, 1941–46; Visiting Worker, Pasteur Inst., Paris, 1946–47; Vis. Prof., Ohio State Univ., 1953; Guest Lectr, Norwegian Veterinary Sch., 1955; first Wesley W. Spink Lectr on Comparative Medicine, Minnesota, 1971. Consultant: WHO, Geneva, 1964–79; Bureau of Animal Health, Canberra, 1979–84; Vis. Fellow, John Curtin Sch. of Med. Res., ANU, Canberra, 1979–84, Fellow, University House, 1980–85. Chm. Permanent Cttee of the World Veterinary Assoc., 1957–75. DVM (*hc*) Hanover, 1963; Hon. Associate RCVS, 1963; Life Fellow, Aust. Vet. Assoc., 1963; Hon. Member: British Veterinary Assoc., 1970; Amer. Vet. Med. Assoc., 1973; World Veterinary Congresses, 1975; Univ. House, Canberra, 1986; Hon. Foreign Mem., Académie Royale de Médicine de Belgique, 1970; Foundation Fellow, Aust. Coll. Vet. Scientists, 1971; Mem., German Acad. for Scientific Research, Leopoldina, 1974; Hon. Dip., Hungarian Microbiological Assoc., Budapest, 1976. Karl F. Meyer Goldheaded Cane Award, 1971; Gamgee Gold Medal, World Vet. Assoc., 1975; Medal of Honour, French Nat. Cttee of World Vet. Assoc., 1976. *Publications:* The Art of Scientific Investigation, 1950; Frontiers in Comparative Medicine, 1972; Influenza: the last great plague, 1977; Seeds of Discovery, 1980; Viral Diseases of Farm Livestock, 1981; Bacterial Diseases of Cattle, Sheep and Goats, 1983; Fighting Diseases: my varied scientific career, 1997; articles on infectious diseases of man and domestic animals and comparative medicine, in scientific jls. *Recreation:* bush-walking. *Address:* 5 Bellevue Road, Wentworth Falls, Blue Mountains, NSW 2782, Australia. *T:* (2) 47571606.

See also J. C. Beveridge.

BEVERLEY, Bishop Suffragan of, since 2000; **Rt Rev. Martyn William Jarrett;** Episcopal Visitor for the Northern Province, since 2000; *b* 25 Oct. 1944; *s* of Frederick and Ivy Jarrett, Bristol; *m* 1968, Betty, *d* of Frank and Mabel Wallis, Bristol; two *d*. *Educ:* Cotham GS, Bristol; King's Coll., London (BD 1967); Hull Univ. (MPhil 1991); St Boniface, Warminster. Ordained deacon, 1968, priest, 1969; Curate: St George, Bristol, 1968–70; Swindon New Town, 1970–74; St Mary, Northolt, 1974–76; Vicar: St Joseph the Worker, Northolt West End, 1976–81; St Andrew, Hillingdon, 1981–83; Priest-in-charge, Uxbridge Moor, 1982–83; Vicar, St Andrew with St John, Uxbridge, 1983–85; Selection Sec., 1985–88, Sen. Selection Sec., 1989–91, ACCM; Vicar, Our Lady and All Saints, Chesterfield, 1991–94; Suffragan Bp of Burnley, 1994–2000. *Recreations:* psephology, vegetable gardening, reading. *Address:* 3 North Lane, Roundhay, Leeds LS8 2QJ. *T:* (0113) 265 4280, *Fax:* (0113) 265 4281.

BEVERLEY, Lt-Gen. Sir Henry (York La Roche), KCB 1991; OBE 1979; Commandant General Royal Marines, 1990–93; Director-General, Winston Churchill Memorial Trust, since 1993; *b* 25 Oct. 1935; *s* of Vice-Adm. Sir York Beverley, KBE, CB, and Lady Beverley; *m* 1963, Sally Anne Maclean; two *d*. *Educ:* Wellington College. DS Staff Coll., 1976–78; CO 42 Cdo RM, 1978–80; Comdt CTC RM, 1980–82; Director RM Personnel, MoD, 1983–84; Comd 3 Cdo Bde RM, 1984–86; Maj.-Gen. Trng and Reserve Forces RM, 1986–88; COS to CGRM, 1988–90. *Recreations:* golf, skiing. *Club:* Royal Thames Yacht.

BEVERLEY, Prof. Peter Charles Leonard, DSc; Professor of Tumour Immunology, University College London, since 1988; Scientific Head, Edward Jenner Institute for Vaccine Research, since 1995; *b* 7 March 1943; *s* of Samuel and Elinor Beverley; *m* 1967, Elisabeth A. Copleston; two *s* one *d*. *Educ:* University Coll. London (BSc, MB BS; DSc 1987). Research Fellow: NIMR, London, 1969–72; Sloan-Kettering Inst., NY, 1972–73; ICRF Tumour Immunology Unit, UCL, 1973–78; permanent staff mem., ICRF, 1978–95; Dep. Dir, 1988–92, Dir, 1992–95, Tumour Immunology Unit, UCL. *Publications:* contribs to immunological, biological and med. jls. *Recreations:* music, reading. *Address:* Edward Jenner Institute for Vaccine Research, Compton, Newbury, Berks RG20 7NN. *T:* (01635) 577900.

BEVINGTON, Christian Veronica; Her Honour Judge Bevington; a Circuit Judge, since 1998; *b* 1 Nov. 1939; *d* of late Michael Falkner Bevington and Dulcie Marian Bevington (*née* Gratton); *m* 1961, David Levitt, OBE (marr. diss. 1973); one *s* two *d*. *Educ:* St James's, W Malvern; London Sch. of Econs (LLB Hons). Called to the Bar: Inner Temple, 1961 (Bencher, 1994); Lincoln's Inn, *ad eundem* 1971. Co-Founder, Charitable Housing Trust, 1966: Company Sec. and Housing Manager, Circle 33 Housing Trust, 1966–76; joined Peat Marwick & Co., 1976; returned to full-time practice at the Bar, 1980; Head of Chambers, 1981–98; Recorder, 1994–98. Chm., Independent Inquiry for City and County of Cardiff, 1997. *Publication:* The Bevington Report, 1997. *Recreations:* music, travel.

BEVINGTON, Eric Raymond, CMG 1961; *b* 23 Jan. 1914; *s* of late R. Bevington and N. E. Bevington (*née* Sutton); *m* 1939, Enid Mary Selina (*née* Homer); one *s* one *d*. *Educ:* Monkton Combe Sch.; Loughborough Coll.; Queens' Coll., Cambridge. CEng, MIMechE. Cadet, HM Overseas Service, Gilbert and Ellice Islands, 1937; District Officer, Fiji, 1942; Sec., Commn of Enquiry into Cost of Living Allowances, Nigeria, 1945–46; Admin. Officer Cl I, Fiji, 1950; Asst Col Sec. (Develt), Fiji, 1951; Develt Comr, Brunei, 1954; Financial Sec., Fiji, 1958–61, Development Commissioner, 1962–63; Mem., Executive Council, Fiji, 1958–63; Senior Project Engineer, Wrigh Rain Ltd, 1964–67; Appeals Inspector, Min. of Housing and Local Govt, 1967–70; Sen. Housing and Planning Inspector, DoE, 1970–78. Mem., New Forest DC, 1979–83. *Publication:* The Things We Do For England, 1990. *Address:* The Old Parsonage Court, Flat 7, Otterbourne, Winchester, Hants SO21 2EP. *T:* (01962) 712560.

BEW, Prof. Paul Anthony Elliott, PhD; Professor of Irish Politics, Queen's University of Belfast, since 1991; *b* 22 Jan. 1950; *s* of Dr Kenneth Bew and Dr Mary Bew (*née* Leahy); *m* 1977, Prof. Greta Joyce Jones; one *s*. *Educ:* Brackenber House Sch.; Campbell Coll., Belfast; Pembroke Coll., Cambridge (MA; PhD 1974). Lectr, Sch. of Humanities, Ulster Coll., 1975–79; Queen's University, Belfast: Lectr in Eur. and American Hist., 1979–84; Lectr, 1984–87, Reader,1987–91, Dept of Politics. Vis. Lectr, Univ. of Pennsylvania, 1982–83; Parnell Fellow, Magdalene Coll., Cambridge, 1996–97; Vis. Prof., Surrey Univ., 1997–; Burns Vis. Schol., Boston Coll., 1999–2000. Historical Advr to Bloody Sunday Tribunal. Pres., Irish Assoc. for Econs and Cultural Relns, 1990–92; Exec. Mem., British Irish Assoc., 1995–. *Publications:* Land and the National Question in Ireland 1858–82, 1978; (jtly) The State in Northern Ireland, 1979, 2nd edn 1996; C. S. Parnell, 1980, 2nd edn 1991; (jtly) Séan Lemass and the Making of Modern Ireland, 1983; (jtly) The British State and the Ulster Crisis, 1985; Conflict and Conciliation in Ireland 1890–1910, 1987; (jtly) The Dynamics of Irish Politics, 1989; (ed jtly) Passion and Prejudice, 1993; (jtly) Northern Ireland: a chronology of the Troubles, 1993, rev. edn 1999; Ideology and the Irish Question, 1994; John Redmond, 1996; (jtly) The Northern Ireland Peace Process 1993–96, 1996; (jtly) Between War and Peace, 1997; contrib. numerous articles and reviews. *Recreations:* soccer, cinema, theatre. *Address:* Department of Politics, Queen's University of Belfast, 21 University Square, Belfast BT7 1NN. *T:* (028) 9024 5133.

BEWES, Rev. Preb. Richard Thomas; Rector, All Souls Church, Langham Place, since 1983; Prebendary of St Paul's Cathedral, since 1988; *b* 1 Dec. 1934; *s* of late Rev. Canon Cecil and Sylvia Bewes; *m* 1964, Elisabeth Ingrid Jaques; two *s* one *d*. *Educ:* Marlborough Sch.; Emmanuel Coll., Cambridge (MA); Ridley Hall, Cambridge. Deacon, 1959; priest, 1960; Curate of Christ Church, Beckenham, 1959–65; Vicar: St Peter's, Harold Wood, 1965–74; Emmanuel, Northwood, 1974–83. *Publications:* God in Ward 12, 1973; Advantage Mr Christian, 1975; Talking about Prayer, 1979; The Pocket Handbook of Christian Truth, 1981; John Wesley's England, 1981; The Church Reaches Out, 1981; The Church Overcomes, 1983; On The Way, 1984; Quest for Truth, 1985; Quest for Life, 1985; The Church Marches On, 1986; When God Surprises, 1986; The Resurrection, 1989; A New Beginning, 1989; Does God Reign?, 1995; Speaking in Public—Effectively, 1998; Great Quotations of the 20th Century, 1999; The Lord's Prayer, 2000; The Lamb Wins, 2000. *Recreations:* tennis, photography, audio-visual production. *Address:* 2 All Souls Place, W1N 3DB. *T:* (020) 7580 6029.

BEWICKE-COPLEY, family name of **Baron Cromwell**.

BEWLEY, Dame Beulah (Rosemary), DBE 2000; MD; FRCP, FFPHM, FRCPCH; Reader in Public Health Sciences, St George's Hospital Medical School, University of London, 1992–93, now Emeritus; *b* 2 Sept. 1929; *d* of John B. Knox and Ina E. (*née* Charles); *m* 1955, Thomas Henry Bewley, *qv*; one *s* four *d*. *Educ:* Alexandra Sch. and Coll., Dublin; Trinity Coll., Dublin (MA); LSHTM, Univ. of London (MSc Social Medicine 1971); MD 1977. FRCP 1992; FFPHM 1980. Qualified TCD, 1953; trained at Queen Elizabeth Hosp. for Children, London, Maudsley Hosp., London and Children's Hosp., Cincinatti; postgrad. trng at LSHTM and St Thomas's Hosp. Med. Sch.; Consultant, St Thomas' Hosp., 1974–79; Senior Lecturer and Hon. Consultant: KCH Med. Sch., 1979–83; LSHTM, 1979–86; St George's Hosp. Med. Sch., 1987–93; Undergrad. and postgrad. teacher/examr, Univ. of London, 1973–93; Chm., Bd of Studies in Public Health Medicine, London Univ., 1987–89; Postgrad. Acad. Tutor, SW Thames Reg., 1987–93. Mem., GMC, 1979–99 (Treas., 1992–99). Pres., Med. Women's Fedn, 1986. Mem. and Mem. Exec. Cttee, Women's Nat. Commn, 1992–99. FRSocMed 1969 (Vice Pres. and Past Pres., Section of Epidemiology and Public Health); FRCPCH (Mem., BPA 1985). Mem., London Chapter, Irish Georgian Soc. *Publications:* Choice not Chance, 1975; contrib. numerous articles and papers on research on children's smoking, adolescence, med. educn, women doctors and women's health. *Recreations:* piano, opera, travel. *Address:* 4 Grosvenor Garden Mews North, SW1W 0JP. *T:* (020) 7730 9592. *Club:* Reform.

BEWLEY, Edward de Beauvoir; Judge of the High Court of Hong Kong, 1980–96; Commissioner, Supreme Court of Brunei, since 1996 (with desig. Hon. Mr Justice Bewley); *b* 12 March 1931; *s* of Harold de Beauvoir Bewley and Phyllis Frances Cowdy; *m* 1st, 1956, Sheelagh Alice Brown; one *s*; 2nd, 1968, Mary Gwenefer Jones; three *d*. *Educ:* Shrewsbury School; Trinity College, Dublin. BA, LLB; Barrister at Law. Administrative Officer, Northern Rhodesia, 1956–59; English Bar, 1960–61; Resident Magistrate, Nyasaland, 1961–64; Magistrate, Hong Kong, 1964–76, District Judge, 1976–80. *Recreations:* golf, ski-ing, reading, music. *Address:* Ysgubor Fawr, Llanedwen, Llanfairpwll, Ynys Môn LL61 6PX. *T:* and *Fax:* (01248) 430162; Alpe des Chaux, 1882 Gryon sur Bex, Switzerland. *T:* and *Fax:* 244983325. *Clubs:* Hong Kong; Royal Irish Yacht (Dun Laoghaire), Holyhead Golf, Hong Kong Golf.

BEWLEY, Thomas Henry, Hon. CBE 1988; MA; MD; FRCP, FRCPI, FRCPsych; Consultant Psychiatrist, Tooting Bec and St Thomas' Hospitals, 1961–88, now Emeritus Consultant, St Thomas' Hospital; *b* 8 July 1926; *s* of Geoffrey Bewley and Victoria Jane Wilson; *m* 1955, Beulah Rosemary Knox (*see* Dame B. R. Bewley); one *s* four *d*. *Educ:* St Columba's College, Dublin; Trinity College, Dublin University (MA; MD 1958). FRCPsych 1972, Hon. FRCPsych 1989. Hon. MD Dublin, 1987. Qualified TCD, 1950; trained St Patrick's Hosp., Dublin, Maudsley Hosp., Univ. of Cincinnati. Hon. Sen. Lectr, St George's Hosp. Med. Sch., 1968–96. Member: Standing Adv. Cttee on Drug Dependence, 1966–71; Adv. Council on Misuse of Drugs, 1972–84; Consultant Adviser on Drug Dependence to DHSS, 1972–81; Consultant, WHO, 1969–78. Pres., RCPsych, 1984–87 (Dean, 1977–82); Jt Co-founder and Mem. Council, Inst. for Study of Drug Dependence, 1967–96. *Publications:* Handbook for Inceptors and Trainees in Psychiatry, 1976, 2nd edn 1980; papers on drug dependence, medical manpower and side effects of drugs. *Address:* 4 Grosvenor Gardens Mews North, SW1W 0JP. *T:* (020) 7730 9592. *Clubs:* Reform, London Chapter of Irish Georgian Society.

BEXON, Roger, CBE 1985; Chairman: Laporte plc, 1986–95; Goal Petroleum, 1990–96; Managing Director, British Petroleum Co., 1981–86, and Deputy Chairman, 1983–86; *b* 11 April 1926; *s* of late MacAlister Bexon, CBE, and Nora Hope Bexon (*née* Jenner); *m* 1951, Lois Loughran Walling; one *s* one *d*. *Educ:* Denstone Coll. (schol.); St John's Coll., Oxford (MA); Tulsa Univ. (MS). Geologist and petroleum engineer with Trinidad Petroleum Development Co. Ltd, 1946–57; management positions with British Petroleum Co., E Africa, 1958–59; Libya, 1959–60; Trinidad, 1961–64; London, 1964–66; Manager, North Sea Operations, 1966–68; General Manager, Libya, 1968–70; Regional Coordinator, Middle East, London, 1971–73; Gen. Manager, Exploration and Production, London, 1973–76; Managing Director, BP Exploration Co. Ltd, London,

1976–77; Dir and Sen. Vice Pres., 1977–80, and Dir, 1982–86, Standard Oil Co. of Ohio; Director: BP Canada Inc., 1983–87; BICC, 1985–92; Lazard Bros, 1986–91; Fenner plc, 1986–89; Cameron Iron Works, 1987–89; Astec (BSR) PLC, 1989–95. Mem. Council, British–N American Res. Assoc., 1986–95. *Publications:* general and technical contribs to internat. jls on oil and energy matters. *Recreations:* swimming, reading, crossword puzzles. *Address:* c/o 22 Hill Street, W1X 7FB. *T:* (020) 7496 4423.

BEYER, John Charles; HM Diplomatic Service; Head of Mediterranean Section, European Union Department, Foreign and Commonwealth Office, since 1999; *b* 29 April 1950; *s* of William Herbert Beyer and Doris Irene Beyer (*née* Tomline); *m* 1971, Letty Marindin Minns; one *s* one *d.* *Educ:* Abingdon Sch.; Queens' Coll., Cambridge (MA). Vis. Schol., Université de Paris VII, 1973–74; British Council Schol., Beijing Langs Inst., 1974–75; Lectr, Dept of Oriental Langs, Univ. of Calif, Berkeley, 1979–80; Researcher, Dept of Chinese Studies, Leeds Univ., 1980–82; Missions Exec., Sino-British Trade Council, 1983–85; Editor, China-Britain Trade Rev., 1985–90; Dir, Sino-British Trade Council, 1990–91; Dir, China-Britain Trade Gp, 1991–98. *Recreation:* family. *Address:* 44 South Hill Park, NW3 2SJ. *T:* (020) 7435 4795.

BEYFUS, Drusilla Norman; writer, editor, broadcaster; Tutor, Central St Martin's College of Art, since 1989; *d* of Norman Beyfus and Florence Noel Barker; *m* 1956, Milton Shulman, *qv*; one *s* two *d.* *Educ:* Royal Naval Sch.; Channing Sch. Woman's Editor, Sunday Express, 1950; columnist, Daily Express, 1952–55; Associate Editor, Queen magazine, 1956; Home Editor, The Observer, 1963; Associate Editor, Daily Telegraph magazine, 1966; Editor, Brides and Setting Up Home magazine, 1972–79; Associate Editor, 1979–87, Contributing Editor, 1987–88, Vogue magazine; Editor, Harrods Magazine, 1987–88; columnist, Sunday Telegraph, 1990–91; Contributing Editor, Telegraph Magazine, 1991–; columnist, You magazine (Mail on Sunday), 1994–. TV and radio appearances, incl. Call My Bluff and talks programmes. *Publications:* (with Anne Edwards) Lady Behave, 1956 (rev. edn 1969); The English Marriage, 1968; The Brides Book, 1981; The Art of Giving, 1987; Modern Manners, 1992; The Done Thing (series): Courtship, 1992; Parties, 1992; Business, 1993; Sex, 1993; The You Guide to Modern Dilemmas, 1997; contrib. to Sunday Times, Punch, New Statesman, Daily Telegraph, Daily Mail. *Recreations:* walking, modern art, cooking. *Address:* 51G Eaton Square, SW1W 9BE. *T:* (020) 7235 7162.

See also Marquis of Normanby, A. Shulman.

BEYNON, Ann; National Manager Wales, BT, since 1998; *b* 14 April 1953; *d* of Roger Talfryn Jones and Margaret Rose Beynon Jones; *m* 1st, 1976, John Trefor (marr. diss. 1983); 2nd, 1986, William Gwenlyn Parry (*d* 1991); one *s* one *d*; 3rd, 1996, Leighton Russell Andrews. *Educ:* UCNW, Bangor (BA Hons). Pres., Students' Union, UCNW, 1974–75. Administrator, Yr Academi Gymreig (Welsh Acad.), 1977–81; S4C, 1981–95: Press Officer, 1981–83; Head of Press and PR, 1983–91; Head, Political and Internat. Affairs, 1991–95; Dir of Business Develt, Cardiff Bay Develt Corp., 1995–98. Member: Royal Commn on H of L Reform, 1999; Welsh Lang. Bd, 1995–2000; Wales Cttee, EOC, 2000–. Gov., Nat. Film and TV Sch., 1995–. *Recreations:* reading, languages, tapestry, managing my late husband's literary estate. *Address:* 11 Waungron Road, Llandaff, Cardiff CF5 2JJ. *T:* (029) 2055 5425.

BEYNON, Ernest Geoffrey; Joint General Secretary, Assistant Masters and Mistresses Association, 1979–87; *b* 4 Oct. 1926; *s* of late Frank William George and Frances Alice Pretoria Beynon; *m* 1956, Denise Gwendoline Rees; two *s* one *d.* *Educ:* Borden Grammar Sch., Kent; Univ. of Bristol, 1944–47, 1949–50 (BSc (Hons Maths) 1947, CertEd 1950). National Service, Royal Artillery, 1947–49. Mathematics Master, Thornbury Grammar Sch., Glos, 1950–56; Mathematics Master and Sixth Form Master, St George Grammar Sch., Bristol, 1956–64; Asst Sec., Assistant Masters Assoc., 1964–78. Last Chm., Teachers' Panel, Burnham Primary and Secondary Cttee, 1985–87. Mem., Univ. of Bristol Court, 1986–; Trustee and Manager, Muntham House Sch., 1979–97. Treasurer: Welwyn Garden City Soc., 1988–; Welwyn Garden Decorative and Fine Arts Soc., 1992–99. Tower Captain, St John's, Lemsford. Hon. FCP, 1985. *Publications:* many reports/pamphlets for AMA, incl. The Middle School System, Mixed Ability Teaching, Selection for Admission to a University. *Recreations:* family, campanology, puzzles, special interest tours abroad, books. *Address:* 3 Templewood, Welwyn Garden City, Herts AL8 7HT. *T:* (01707) 321380.

BEYNON, Dr John David Emrys, FREng, FIEE; Principal, King's College London, 1990–92; *b* 11 March 1939; *s* of John Emrys and Elvira Beynon; *m* 1964, Hazel Janet Hurley; two *s* one *d.* *Educ:* Univ. of Wales (BSc); Univ. of Southampton (MSc, PhD). FIERE 1977; FIEE 1978; FREng (FEng 1988). Scientific Officer, Radio Res. Station, Slough, 1962–64; Univ. of Southampton: Lectr, Sen. Lectr and Reader, 1964–77; Prof. of Electronics, UWIST, Cardiff, 1977–79; University of Surrey: Prof. of Elec. Engrg, 1979–90; Head of Dept of Electronic and Elec. Engrg, 1979–83; Pro-Vice-Chancellor, 1983–87; Sen. Pro-Vice-Chancellor, 1987–90. Vis. Prof., Carleton Univ., Ottawa, 1975; Cons. to various cos, Govt estabts and Adviser to British Council, 1964–. Member: Accreditation Cttee, IEE, 1983–89; Adv. Cttee on Engrg and Technology, British Council, 1983–92; Technology Sub-Cttee, UGC, 1984–89; Nat. Electronics Council, 1985–91; Cttee 1, 1990–92, Main Cttee, 1991–94, CICHE; Adv. Cttee, Erasmus, 1990–92; Standing Cttee on Educn and Trng, Royal Acad. of Engrg, 1992–95; Adv. Council, British Liby, 1994–99; ITC, 1995–2000. Engrg Professors' Conference: Hon. Sec., 1982–84; Vice-Chm., 1984–85 and 1987–88; Chm., 1985–87. Chm., Westminster Christian Council, 1998–2000. FRSA 1982; FKC 1990. Hon. Fellow, UC Swansea, 1990. *Publications:* Charge-Coupled Devices and Their Applications (with D. R. Lamb), 1980; papers on plasma physics, semiconductor devices and integrated circuits, and engrg educn. *Recreations:* music, photography, travel. *Address:* 13 Great Quarry, Guildford, Surrey GU1 3XN.

BEYNON, Prof. John Herbert, DSc; FRS 1971; Professor Emeritus, University of Wales, since 1991; *b* 29 Dec. 1923; British; *m* 1947, Yvonne Lilian (*née* Fryer); no *c.* *Educ:* UC Swansea, Univ. of Wales (BSc (1st cl. hons Physics); DSc 1960). CPhys; FInstP; CChem; FRSC. Experimental Officer, Min. of Supply, Tank Armament Research, 1943–47; ICI Ltd (Organics Div.), 1947–74: Associate Research Man. i/c Physical Chemistry, 1962–70; Sen. Res. Associate, 1965–74; University College of Swansea, University of Wales (now University of Wales Swansea): first Hon. Professorial Fellow, and Lectr in Chemistry, 1967–74; Royal Soc. Res. Prof., 1974–86; Res. Prof., Depts of Physics and Chemistry, 1987–. Boomer Meml Fellow, Univ. of Minnesota, 1955; Prof. of Chemistry, Purdue Univ., Indiana, 1969–75; Associate Prof. of Molecular Sciences, Univ. of Warwick, 1972–74; Vis. Prof., Univ. of Essex, 1973–74, 1982–; Hon. Prof., Univ. of Warwick, 1977–; Associate, Institut Jožef Stefan, Ljubljana, 1980–. Chm., Science Curriculum Develt Cttee, Cttee for Wales, 1983–88; Pres., Assoc. for Sci. Educn, Wales, 1985–86. Founder Chm., British Mass Spectrometry Soc., 1960 (Hon. Mem. 1988); Founder Pres., Europ. Mass Spectrometry Soc., 1993–97. Hon. Member, Mass Spectrometry Societies: Japan, 1967; Yugoslavia, 1977; China, 1986; Italy, 1990. Editor, Internat. Jl of Mass Spectrom. Ion Processes, 1983–85; Founder Editor-in-Chief, Rapid Communications in Mass Spectrom., 1987–97. Hon. DSc: Purdue, USA, 1995; Babeş-Bolyai, Romania, 1997. Sigma-Xi Res. Award, Purdue Univ., USA, 1973; Hasler Award of Applied Spectroscopy, USA, 1979; Medal, Serbian Chemical Soc., 1981; Techmart Trophy, British Technol. Gp, 1984; Jan Marc Marci Medal, Czechoslovak Spectometry Soc., 1984; Field and Franklin Medal, Amer. Chem. Soc., 1987; Gold Medal: Internat. Mass Spectrometry Soc., 1985; British Mass Spectrometry Soc., 1987; Italian Mass Spectrometry Soc., 1992. *Publications:* Mass Spectrometry and its Applications in Organic Chemistry, 1960; Mass and Abundance Tables for use in Mass Spectrometry, 1963; The Mass Spectra of Organic Molecules, 1968; Table of Ion Energies for Metastable Transitions in Mass Spectrometry, 1970; Metastable Ions, 1973; An Introduction to Mass Spectrometry, 1981; Current Topics in Mass Spectrometry and Chemical Kinetics, 1982; Application of Transition State Theory to Unimolecular Reactions, 1983; papers in Proc. Royal Soc., Nature, Jl Sci. Inst., Jl Applied Physics, Chem. Soc., JACS, Trans Faraday Soc., Int. Jl Mass Spectrom. and Ion Physics, Org. Mass Spectrom., Anal. Chem., etc. *Recreations:* photography, golf. *Address:* 17 Coltshill Drive, Mumbles, Swansea SA3 4SN. *T:* and *Fax:* (01792) 368718. *Clubs:* Swansea Cricket and Football (Bd Mem., 1990–92), Swansea Sports (Chm., 1988–93); Bristol Channel Yacht; Buxton and High Peak Golf (Captain, 1965).

BEYNON, Timothy George, MA; FRGS 1983; President, British Dragonfly Society, since 2000; *b* 13 Jan. 1939; *s* of George Beynon and Fona I. Beynon; *m* 1973, Sally Jane Wilson; two *d.* *Educ:* Swansea Grammar Sch.; King's Coll., Cambridge (MA). City of London Sch., 1962–63; Merchant Taylors' Sch., 1963–78; Headmaster: Denstone Coll., 1978–86; The Leys Sch., Cambridge, 1986–90. Sen. Warden, Saltwells Local Nature Reserve, Dudley, 1992–99. *Recreations:* ornithology, fishing, sport, music, expeditions. *Address:* 34 Church Lane, Checkley, Stoke-on-Trent ST10 4NJ.

BEZOS, Jeffrey P.; Founder, and Chief Executive Officer, Amazon.com Inc., internet bookseller, since 1994; *b* 1963; *m* MacKenzie. *Educ:* Princeton Univ. (degree in elec. engrg and computer sci., *summa cum laude*, 1986). Formerly Mem. staff, FITEL; Bankers Trust Co., 1988–90 (Vice-Pres., 1990); D. E. Shaw & Co., 1990–94 (Sen. Vice-Pres., 1992–94). *Address:* Amazon.com Inc., 1200 12th Avenue South, Seattle, WA 98144, USA.

BHADESHIA, Prof. Harshad Kumar Dharamshi Hansraj, PhD; FRS 1998; CEng; Professor of Physical Metallurgy, since 1999, and Fellow of Darwin College, since 1993, University of Cambridge; *b* 27 Nov. 1953; *s* of Dharamshi Hansraj Bhadeshia and Narmda Dharamshi Bhadeshia; *m* 1978 (marr. diss. 1992); two *d.* *Educ:* City of London Poly. (BSc 1976); Univ. of Cambridge (PhD 1979). CEng. Technician: British Oxygen Co., 1970–72; Murex Welding Processes, 1972–73; University of Cambridge: engaged in res., 1976–79; SERC Res. Fellow, 1979–81; Demonstrator, 1981–85; Lectr in Physical Metallurgy, 1985–93; Reader in Physical Metallurgy, 1993–99. *Publications:* Geometry of Crystals, 1987; Bainite in Steels, 1992; (with R. W. K. Honeycombe) Steels, 1995; more than 260 res. papers. *Recreation:* squash.

BHASKAR, Prof. Krishan Nath; Founder, 1983, Director, 1988–94, Motor Industry Research Unit Ltd, Norwich; *b* 9 Oct. 1945; *s* of late Dr Ragu Nath Bhaskar and Mrs Kamla Bhaskar (*née* Dora Skill); *m* 1977, Fenella Mary (*née* McCann); one *s* one *d.* *Educ:* St Paul's Sch., London; London Sch. of Econs and Pol. Science (BSc Econ 1st Cl. Hons, MSc Econ). Lectr, LSE, 1968–70; Lectr in Accounting, Univ. of Bristol, 1970–78; Prof. of Accountancy and Finance, UEA, 1978–88. Founder, Computer Industry Res. Unit, 1985. *Publications:* (with D. Murray) Macroeconomic Systems, 1976; Building Financial Models: a simulation approach, 1978; Manual to Building Financial Models, 1978; The Future of the UK Motor Industry, 1979; The Future of the World Motor Industry, 1980; (with M. J. R. Shave) Computer Science Applied to Business Systems, 1982; The UK and European Motor Industry: analysis and future prospects, 1983; (jtly) Financial Modelling with a Microcomputer, 1984; (with R. J. Housden) Management Information Systems and Data Processing for the Management Accountant, 1985, new edn, as Information Technology Management, 1990; (with B. C. Williams) The Impact of Microprocessors on the Small Practice, 1985; A Fireside Chat on Databases for Accountants, 1985; Computer Security—Threats and Countermeasures, 1993; *reports:* A Research Report on the Future of the UK and European Motor Industry, 1984; Jaguar: an investor's guide, 1984; Car Pricing in Europe, 1984; (with G. R. Kaye) Financial Planning with Personal Computers, Vol. 1, 1985, Vol. 2, 1986; State Aid to the European Motor Industry, 1985, updated edn 1987; Demand Growth: a boost for employment?, 1985; Japanese Automotive Strategies: a European and US perspective, 1986; Quality and the Japanese Motor Industry: lessons for the West?, 1986; The Future of Car Retailing in the UK, 1987; A Single European Market? an automotive perspective, 1988; Rover: profile, progress and prospects, 1988; Automotive Trade Restrictions in Western Europe, 1989; The Greek Vehicle Market: future opportunities, 1989; Into the 1990s: future strategies of the vehicle producers of South Korea and Malaysia, 1990; UK Local Content of UK and European Cars, 1993; 1993 European Production Forecast, 1993. *Recreations:* gardening, vegetarian cooking, travel, wine.

BHATIA, Baron *cr* 2001 (Life Peer), of Hampton in the London Borough of Richmond-upon-Thames; **Amirali Alibhai Bhatia,** OBE 1997; Director, Casley Finance Ltd and Forbes Campbell (International) Ltd, since 1973; Chairman, Forbes Trust, since 1985; *b* 18 March 1932; *s* of Alibhai Bhatia and Fatma Alibhai Bhatia; *m* 1954, Nurbanu Amersi Kanji; three *d.* Career in manufacturing, Tanzania, 1960–72. Chm., SITPRO, 1998–; Board Member: E London TEC, 1991–; Nat. Lottery Charities Bd, 1995–2000; Local Investment Fund, 1997–; Project Fullemploy, 1997– (Chm., 1994–97); Mem., Prime Minister's Adv. Cttee for Queen's Award, 1999–. Chairman: Council of Ethnic Minority Vol. Sector Orgns, 1999–; Ethnic Minority Foundn, 1999–; Hon. Treas., Mem. Bd and Exec. Cttee, Internat. Alert, 1994–2000; Trustee: Oxfam, 1985–99 (Chm., Trading Bd, 1986–92); Community Develt Foundn, 1988–97 (Mem., Budget and Finance Cttee); Charities Evaluation Services, 1989–90; Water Aid, 2000–; St Christopher's Hospice, 1997– (Mem., Audit Cttee); Bd, Diana, Princess of Wales Meml Fund, 2001–. Trustee, High/Scope Educn Res. Foundn, Mich, 1985–97; Bd Mem., Tower Hamlets Coll., 1991–98. MInstD. Personality of the Year, UK Charity Awards, 2001. *Recreations:* reading, cricket, voluntary work. *Address:* The Forbes Trust, 9 Artillery Lane, E1 7LP. *T:* (020) 7377 8484. *Club:* Royal Commonwealth Society.

BHATNAGAR, Sir Rajeshwar Sarup, (Sir Roger), KNZM 1998; Chief Executive, R. B. Investments; *b* 26 Oct. 1942; separated; one *s* one *d.* Man. Dir, Sound Plus, 1980–93; Chm., Noel Leeming/Pacific Retail Gp, 1990–98. *Recreation:* fishing. *Address:* PO Box 99766, Newmarket, Auckland, New Zealand. *Club:* Auckland.

BHATTACHARYYA, Prof. Sushantha Kumar, CBE 1997; FREng; Professor of Manufacturing (formerly of Manufacturing Systems Engineering), University of Warwick, since 1980; *b* 6 June 1940; *s* of Sudhir Bhattacharyya and Hemanalini (*née* Chakraborty); *m* 1981, Bridie Rabbitt; three *d.* *Educ:* IIT, Kharagpur (BTech); Univ. of Birmingham (MSc, PhD). MIMechE, FIEE; FREng (FEng 1991). CAV Ltd, 1960–63; Prodn Engr, Joseph Lucas Ltd, 1964–68; University of Birmingham: Lectr, Dept of Engrg Prodn, 1970; Hd of Warwick Manufacturing Gp, 1980–. Advr, nat. and multinat. cos, UK and abroad.

Non-exec. Dir, Technology Rover Gp, 1986–92. Member: Nat. Consumer Council, 1990–93; Council for Sci. and Technology, 1993–; UK Technol. Foresight Panel on Manufg, 1994–97; W Midlands Regl Develt Agency, 1999–; Competitiveness Council, 1999–; Rover Task Force, 2000. Trustee, IPPR, 1998–. Hon. Professor: Hong Kong Poly. Univ., 1992; Univ. of Technol., Malaysia, 1993; Min. of Machinery, Beijing, 1994. Fellow, World Acad. of Prodn, 1999. CIMgt 1996. FIMgt. Hon. FILog 1996. DUniv Surrey, 1992; Hon. DEng Univ. of Technol., Malaysia. Mensforth Internat. Gold Medal, IEE, 1998; Sir Robert Lawrence Award, Inst. of Logistics and Transport, 2000. *Publications:* numerous, on operational and technological change in manufacturing industry. *Recreations:* family, flying, cricket. *Address:* Engineering Department, University of Warwick, Coventry CV4 7AL. *T:* (024) 7652 3155. *Club:* Athenæum.

BHOGAL, Rev. Inderjit; Minister, Sheffield Inner City Ecumenical Mission, since 1994; Director, Urban Theology Unit, Sheffield, since 1997; President, Methodist Conference, 2000–01; *b* Nairobi, 17 Jan. 1953; *m* 1986, Kathryn Anne; one *s* one *d.* *Educ:* Khalsa Sikh Sch., Nairobi; Blue Coat C of E Sch., Dudley; Dudley Tech. Coll.; Hartley Victoria Coll., Manchester (BA Manchester Univ. 1979); Westminster Coll., Oxford (MA 1991). Minister: Darlington Street Circuit, 1979–87; Carver Street Circuit, Sheffield, 1987–94. Co-ordinator, Wolverhampton Inter-Faith Gp, 1984–87; Mem., Sheffield Chaplaincy to Higher Educn, 1987–94 (Chm., 1990–94); Dir of Studies, Urban Theol. Unit, Sheffield, 1994–97. *Publication:* A Table for All, 2000. *Recreations:* walking, cooking, sport. *Address:* c/o Urban Theology Unit, 210 Abbeyfield Road, Sheffield S4 7AZ.

BHOWMICK, Dr Bimal Kanti, OBE 2001; FRCP; Consultant physician, since 1976, and Clinical Director, since 1993, Care of the Elderly, Glan Clwyd Hospital, Rhyl; *b* 13 Feb. 1940; *s* of late Jamini Mohan Bhowmick and of Ashalata Bhowmick; *m* 1969, Dr Aparna Banerjee; two *s* one *d.* *Educ:* Calcutta Univ. (MB BS; MD 1968). FRCP 1987. SHO, Victoria Hosp., Blackpool, 1969–71; SHO, 1971–72, Registrar, 1972–74, Burton Rd Hosp., Dudley; Sen. Registrar, H. M. Stanley Hosp., St Asaph, 1974–76. Associate Dean for Overseas Doctors in Wales, Sch. of Postgrad. Med. and Dental Educn, Univ. of Wales Coll. of Med., 1997–. Hon. Sen. Lectr, Inst. of Res., Univ. of Wales, Bangor, 1998–. Mem. Council, 1998–2001, Censor, 2001–, RCP. *Publications:* (contrib.) Parkinson's Disease and Parkinsonism in the Elderly, 2000; numerous contribs to learned jls. *Recreations:* reading, gardening, cinema. *Address:* Glan Clwd Hospital, Rhyl, Denbighshire, LL18 5UJ. *T:* (01745) 583910; Jamini Allt Goch, St Asaph, Denbighshire LL17 0BP.

BHUTTO, Benazir; Prime Minister of Pakistan, 1988–90, and, 1993–96; *b* 21 June 1953; *d* of late Zulfikar Ali Bhutto and of Begum Nusrat Bhutto; *m* 1987, Asif Ali Zardari; one *s* two *d.* *Educ:* Harvard Univ.; Lady Margaret Hall, Oxford (Dip. in Internat. Law and Diplomacy, 1977; Pres., Oxford Union Soc.; Hon. Fellow, 1989). Under house arrest, 1977–84; leader in exile, Pakistan People's Party, with Begum Nusrat Bhutto; returned to Pakistan, 1986. *Publications:* Perspective on Pakistan Foreign Policy, 1978; Daughter of the East, 1988. *Address:* Pakistan People's Party, 70 Clifton, Karachi 75600, Pakistan.

BIANCHERI, Boris, Hon. GCVO 1990; Chairman, Agenzia Nazionale Stampa Associata, since 1997; President, Institute for International Political Studies, Milan, since 1998; *b* 3 Nov. 1930; *s* of Augusto and Olga Wolff von Stomersee; *m* 1979, Flavia Arzeni; one *s* one *d.* *Educ:* Univ. of Rome (Law Degree). Joined Min. of Foreign Affairs, 1956; served Athens, 1959; Economic Dept, Min. of Foreign Affairs, 1964–67; Sec.-Gen., Commn for 1970 Osaka Exhibn, 1968; First Counsellor, Cultural Relations, Min. of Foreign Affairs, 1971; Political Counsellor, London, 1972–75; Chef de Cabinet, Sec. of State for Foreign Affairs, 1978; Minister, 1979; Ambassador, Tokyo, 1980–84; Dir Gen., Political Affairs, Min. of Foreign Affairs, 1985; Ambassador: UK, 1987–91; USA, 1991–95; Sec.-Gen., Min. of Foreign Affairs, 1995–97. Gran Croce, Ordine al Merito della Repubblica Italiana; numerous foreign orders. *Recreations:* gardening, boating, swimming, horse-riding. *Address:* Agenzia Nazionale Stampa Associata, Via delle Dataria 94, 00187 Rome, Italy. *Club:* Circolo Della Caccia (Rome).

BIBBY, Benjamin; *see* Bibby, J. B.

BIBBY, Sir Derek (James), 2nd Bt *cr* 1959, of Tarporley, Co. Palatine of Chester; MC 1945; DL; President, Bibby Line Group Ltd (formerly Bibby Line Ltd), since 1992 (Chairman, 1969–92); *b* 29 June 1922; *s* of Major Sir (Arthur) Harold Bibby, 1st Bt, DSO, DL, LLD, and of Marjorie, *d* of Charles J. Williamson; *S* father, 1986; *m* 1961, Christine Maud, *d* of late Rt Rev. F. J. Okell, MA, DD, Bishop of Stockport; four *s* one *d.* *Educ:* Rugby; Trinity Coll., Oxford (MA). Served War, Army, 1942–46. DL Cheshire, 1987. *Recreations:* shooting, gardening. *Heir:* *s* Michael James Bibby [*b* 2 Aug. 1963; *m* 1994, Beverley, *o d* of Donald Graham]. *Address:* Willaston Grange, Willaston, Neston, Cheshire CH64 2UN. *T:* (0151) 327 4913.

BIBBY, (John) Benjamin; Director, 1961–94, Chairman, 1970–78, J. Bibby & Sons PLC; *b* 19 April 1929; *s* of late J. P. and D. D. Bibby; *m* 1956, Susan Lindsay Paterson; two *s* one *d.* *Educ:* Oundle Sch.; St Catharine's Coll., Cambridge (MA). Called to the Bar, Gray's Inn, 1981. Held various positions in J. Bibby & Sons PLC, 1953–94. Mem. Council, Univ. of Liverpool, 1978–81; Mem. Exec. Cttee, West Kirby Residential Sch., 1978–87. Mem. Cttee, 1982–, Hon. Treas., 1987–, Nat. Squib Owners' Assoc. (Chm., 1983–87); Pres., Merseyside and Deeside Br., STA (formerly STA Schooners), 1992–. Fellow Commoner, St Catharine's Coll., Cambridge, 1996–. JP Liverpool 1975–81. *Publications:* (with C. L. Bibby) A Miller's Tale, 1978; A Birthday Ode and Other Verse, 1994; A Letter to a Grandson and Other Verse, 1994. *Recreations:* sailing, gardening. *Address:* Kirby Mount House, 1 Kirby Mount, West Kirby, Wirral, CH48 2HU. *T:* (0151) 625 8071. *Clubs:* Royal Thames Yacht; West Kirby Sailing; Royal Mersey Yacht; Royal Anglesey Yacht.

BIĆANIĆ, Prof. Nenad Josip Nikola, PhD; FICE, FIACM; Regius Professor of Civil Engineering, since 1994, and Head of Department of Civil Engineering, since 1997, University of Glasgow; *b* Zagreb, Croatia, 6 Sept. 1945; *s* of Vladimir Bićanić and Elizabeta (*née* Kostial-Zivanović); *m* 1969, Jasna Babić; one *s* one *d.* *Educ:* Zagreb Univ., Croatia (Dip. Ing 1968); Univ. of Wales, Swansea (PhD 1978). Structural Engr, Zagreb, 1968–69; Consulting Engr, Arnhem, Netherlands, 1969–72; Zagreb University: Lectr and Researcher, 1972–76; Docent, Prof., 1978–83; Prof., 1984–85; Lectr, Sen. Lectr, then Reader, Univ. of Wales, Swansea, 1985–94. Vis. Prof., Univ. of Colo, Boulder, 1983–84. FICE 1998; FIACM 1998. *Publications:* Computer Aided Analysis and Design of Concrete Structures, 1990; Computational Modelling of Concrete Structures, 1994, revd edn 1998; papers in learned and professional jls. *Recreations:* international folk-dancing, ski-ing, tennis. *Address:* 20 Ledcameroch Road, Bearsden, Glasgow G61 4AE. *T:* (0141) 942 0711. *Club:* College (Glasgow).

BICESTER, 3rd Baron *cr* 1938, of Tusmore; **Angus Edward Vivian Smith;** *b* 20 Feb. 1932; *s* of Lt-Col Hon. Stephen Edward Vivian Smith (*d* 1952) (2nd *s* of 1st Baron) and Elenor Anderson, *d* of Edward S. Hewitt, New York City; *S* uncle, 1968. *Educ:* Eton. *Heir:* *b* Hugh Charles Vivian Smith, *b* 8 Nov. 1934.

BICHARD, Sir Michael (George), KCB 1999; Rector, The London Institute, since 2001; *b* 31 Jan. 1947. *Educ:* Manchester Univ. (LLB); Birmingham Univ. (MSocSci). Chief Executive: Brent BC, 1980–86; Gloucestershire CC, 1986–90; Social Security Benefits Agency, 1990–95; Perm. Sec., Employment Dept Gp, April–July 1995; Jt Perm. Sec., July–Dec. 1995, Perm. Sec., 1996–2001, DfEE. Mem., ESRC, 1989–92. Hon. Fellow, Inst. of Local Govt Studies, Birmingham Univ. FIPD; CIMgt; FRSA. DUniv: Leeds Metropolitan, 1992; Middlesex, 2001; Hon. LLD Birmingham, 1999. *Address:* The London Institute, 65 Davies Street, W1K 5DA.

BICK; *see* Moore-Bick.

BICKERSTETH, Rt Rev. John Monier, KCVO 1989; Clerk of the Closet to The Queen, 1979–89; *b* 6 Sept. 1921; *yr s* of late Rev. Canon Edward Monier, OBE and Inez Katharine Bickersteth; *m* 1955, Rosemary, *yr d* of late Edward and Muriel Cleveland-Stevens, Gaines, Oxted; three *s* one *d.* *Educ:* Rugby; Christ Church, Oxford (MA 1953); Wells Theol College; Open Univ. Captain, Buffs and Royal Artillery, 1941–46. Priest, 1951; Curate, St Matthew, Moorfields, Bristol, 1950–54; Vicar, St John's, Hurst Green, Oxted, 1954–62; St Stephen's, Chatham, 1962–70; Hon. Canon of Rochester, 1968–70; Bishop Suffragan of Warrington, 1970–75; Bishop of Bath and Wells, 1975–87. A C of E delegate to 4th Assembly, WCC, 1968. Chaplain and Sub-Prelate, OStJ, 1977–96. Chairman: Royal Sch. of Church Music, 1977–88; Bible Reading Fellowship, 1978–90; Vice Chm., Central Bd of Finance of Church of England, 1981–84. Member: Marlborough Coll. Council, 1980–91; Wilts Wildlife Trust Council, 1989–95. Freeman of the City of London, 1979. *Publications:* (jtly) Clerks of the Closet in the Royal Household, 1991; (ed) The Bickersteth Diaries 1914–1918, 1995. *Address:* Beckfords, Newtown, Tisbury, Wilts SP3 6NY. *T:* (01747) 870479. *Club:* Royal Commonwealth Society.

BICKERTON, Frank Donald, CBE 1966; Director General, Central Office of Information, and Head of Government Information Service, 1971–74; *b* 22 June 1917; *s* of F. M. Bickerton and A. A. Hibbert; *m* 1945, Linda Russell; two *s.* *Educ:* Liverpool Collegiate Sch. Min. of Health, in Public Relations Div., 1935–40. Served War, RNVR, 1940–45. Min. of National Insurance (later Min. of Pensions and Nat. Insurance), 1946–61: initially Asst Press Officer and in charge of Information Div., 1952–61; Chief Information Officer, Min. of Transport, 1961–68; Controller (Home), COI, 1968–71. *Recreations:* walking, gardening. *Address:* 6 Diana Close, Granville Rise, Totland, Isle of Wight PO39 0EE.

BICKFORD, James David Prydeaux, CB 1995; Chairman, Bickford Associates; *b* 28 July 1940; *s* of William A. J. P. Bickford and late Muriel Bickford (*née* Smythe); *m* 1965, Carolyn Jane, *d* of late Major W. A. R. Sumner, RHA; three *s.* *Educ:* Downside; Law Society's College of Law, London. Admitted to Roll of Solicitors, 1963; Solicitor of the Supreme Court. In practice, J. J. Newcombe, Solicitors, Okehampton, 1963–69; Crown Counsel and Legal Advr to Govt of Turks and Caicos Islands, BWI, 1969–71; Asst Legal Advr, FCO, 1971–79 and 1982–84; Legal Advr, British Mil. Govt, Berlin, 1979–82; Legal Counsellor, FCO, 1984–87; Under Sec., MoD, and Legal Advr to Security and Intelligence Services, 1987–95. Judge Ben C. Green Lectr in Law, Case Western Reserve Univ., USA; Vis. Prof. of Law, Cleveland State Univ., USA. Mem., Panel of Legal Experts, Internat. Telecommunications Satellite Orgn, 1985–; Chm., Assembly of Internat. Maritime Satellite Orgn, 1985–87. Mem., Law Soc. Hon. Mem., Nat. Security Cttee, Amer. Bar Assoc. *Publications:* Land Dealings Simplified in the Turks and Caicos Islands, 1971; contribs on intelligence, organised crime and money-laundering issues to symposia, jls, media and internet. *Recreations:* the family, sailing, fishing. *Address:* c/o National Westminster Bank, Torrington, Devon EX38 8HP.

BICKNELL, Claud, OBE 1946; a Law Commissioner, 1970–75; a part-time Chairman of Industrial Tribunals, 1975–83; *b* Rowlands Gill, near Newcastle upon Tyne, 15 June 1910; 2nd *s* of Raymond Bicknell and Phillis Bicknell (*née* Lovibond); *m* 1st, 1934, Esther Irene (*d* 1958), *e d* of Kenneth Bell; one *s* two *d* (one *d* decd); 2nd, 1960, Christine Betty Reynolds, CBE (*d* 1999). *Educ:* Oundle Sch.; Queens' Coll., Cambridge. MA 1935. Pres., Cambridge Univ. Mountaineering Club, 1930–31. Admitted as a solicitor, 1934; Asst Solicitor, 1934–39, and partner, 1939–70, in firm of Stanton, Atkinson & Bird, Newcastle upon Tyne. Dir, Northern Corporation Ltd, 1939–53. Auxiliary Fire Service, Newcastle upon Tyne, 1939–41; Nat. Fire Service, 1941–45; Sen. Fire Staff Officer, Home Office, 1943–45. Mem. Planning Bd, Lake District Nat. Park, 1951–70 (Chm., Development Control Cttee, 1957–70). Chm., Newcastle upon Tyne Housing Improvement Trust Ltd, 1966–70. Pres., Newcastle upon Tyne Incorp. Law Soc., 1969. *Recreation:* mountains. *Address:* Aikrigg End Cottage, Burneside Road, Kendal LA9 6DZ. *Clubs:* Garrick, Alpine.
See also Sir J. R. Shelley, Bt.

BIDDER, Neil; QC 1998; a Recorder, since 1994; *b* 22 July 1953; *s* of Glyn Turner Bidder and Constance Mabel Bidder; *m* 1978, Madeleine Thomas; two *s.* *Educ:* Ogmore Grammar Sch.; Queens' Coll., Cambridge (BA 1974; MA 1977); Dalhousie Univ., Canada (LLM 1977). Called to the Bar, Lincoln's Inn, 1976; in practice at the Bar, 1976–. *Recreations:* choral singing, gardening, sport. *Address:* 33 Park Place, Cardiff CF1 3BA. *T:* (029) 2023 3313.

BIDDLE, Prof. Martin, OBE 1997; FBA 1985; FSA, FRHistS; Professor of Medieval Archaeology, University of Oxford, since 1997; Astor Senior Research Fellow in Medieval Archaeology, Hertford College, Oxford, since 1989; Director, Winchester Research Unit, since 1968; *b* 4 June 1937; *s* of Reginald Samuel Biddle and Gwladys Florence Biddle (*née* Baker); *m* 1966, Birthe, *d* of Landsretssagfører Axel Th. and Anni Kjølbye of Sønderborg, Denmark; two *d* (and two *d* by previous marr.). *Educ:* Merchant Taylors' Sch., Northwood; Pembroke Coll., Cambridge (MA 1965); MA Oxon 1967; MA Pennsylvania 1977. FSA 1964; FRHistS 1970; MIFA 1984. Second Lieut, 4 RTR, 1956; 1 Indep. Sqn, RTR, Berlin, 1956–57. Asst Inspector of Ancient Monuments, MPBW, 1961–63; Lectr in Medieval Archaeology, Univ. of Exeter, 1963–67; Vis. Fellow, All Souls Coll., Oxford, 1967–68; Dir, University Museum, and Prof. of Anthropology and of History of Art, Univ. of Pennsylvania, 1977–81; Lectr of The House, Christ Church, Oxford, 1983–86. Directed excavations and investigations: Nonsuch Palace, 1959–60; Winchester, 1961–71; (with Birthe Biddle): Repton, 1974–88, 1993; St Alban's Abbey, 1978, 1982–84, 1991, 1994–95; Holy Sepulchre, Jerusalem, 1989–90, 1992, 1993, 1998; Qasr Ibrim, Egypt, 1990, 1992, 1995, 2000. Archaeological Consultant: Canterbury Cathedral; St Alban's Abbey and Cathedral Church; Eurotunnel, etc. Chm., Rescue, Trust for British Archaeology, 1971–75. Mem., Royal Commn on Historical Monuments of England, 1984–95. Pres., Soc. for Medieval Archaeology, 1995–98. General Editor, Winchester Studies, 1976–. (With Birthe Biddle) Frend Medal, Soc. of Antiquaries, 1986. *Publications:* (with C. Heighway) The Future of London's Past, 1973; (with F. Barlow and others) Winchester in the Early Middle Ages, 1976; (with H.M. Colvin, J. Summerson and others) The History of the King's Works, vol. iv, pt 2, 1982; Object and Economy in Medieval Winchester, 1990; Approaches in Urban Archaeology, 1998; Nonsuch Palace: the domestic materials, 1998; The Tomb of Christ, 1999 (German edn, 1998); King Arthur's Round Table, 2000; papers on archaeological, historical and art-historical subjects in learned jls. *Recreations:* travel, esp. Hellenic travel, reading. *Address:* 19 Hamilton Road, Oxford OX2 7PY. *T:* and *Fax:* (01865) 559017. *Club:* Athenæum.

BIDDLESTONE, Prof. Anthony Joseph, PhD; CEng, FIChemE; Professor of Chemical Engineering, since 1993, Dean of Engineering, since 1998, University of Birmingham; *b* 8 Aug. 1937; *s* of William Albert and Ivy Evelyn Biddlestone; *m* 1973, Marion Summers; two *s*. *Educ:* George Dixon Grammar Sch., Birmingham; Univ. of Birmingham (BSc 1958; PhD 1961). CEng 1964; FIChemE 1973. University of Birmingham: Lectr, 1965–85; Sen Lectr, 1985–93; Hd, Sch. of Chem. Engrg, 1993–98. Chm., Accreditation Bd, IChemE, 1992–99. FRSA 1999. *Publications:* numerous contribs to refereed learned jls on aerobic biodegradation of organic wastes. *Recreations:* church music, organist, conductor. *Address:* Deans' Office, University of Birmingham, Edgbaston, Birmingham B15 2TT. *T:* (0121) 414 7452.

BIDDULPH, family name of **Baron Biddulph**.

BIDDULPH, 5th Baron *cr* 1903; **Anthony Nicholas Colin Maitland Biddulph;** interior designer; sporting manager; *b* 8 April 1959; *s* of 4th Baron Biddulph and of Lady Mary, *d* of Viscount Maitland (killed in action, 1943) and *g d* of 15th Earl of Lauderdale; *S* father, 1988; *m* 1993, Hon. Sian Diana, *y d* of Baron Gibson-Watt, *qv*; two *s*. *Educ:* Cheltenham; RAC, Cirencester. *Heir: s* Hon. Robert Julian Maitland Biddulph, *b* 8 July 1994. *Recreations:* shooting, fishing, painting. *Address:* 8 Orbel Street, SW11 3NZ; Makerstoun House, Kelso TD5 7PA. *Clubs:* Cavalry and Guards, Raffles, White's.

BIDDULPH, Constance; *see* Holt, C.

BIDDULPH, Sir Ian D'Olier, (Jack), 11th Bt *cr* 1664, of Westcombe, Kent; *b* 28 Feb. 1940; *s* of Sir Stuart Royden Biddulph, 10th Bt and Muriel Margaret (*d* 1995), *d* of Angus Harkness, Hamley Bridge, S Australia; *S* father, 1986; *m* 1967, Margaret Eleanor, *o d* of late John Gablonski, Oxley, Brisbane; one *s* two *d*. *Heir: s* Paul William Biddulph, *b* 30 Oct. 1967. *Address:* 17 Kendall Street, Oxley, Qld 4075, Australia.

BIDE, Sir Austin (Ernest), Kt 1980; Hon. President, Glaxo Holdings plc, 1985–95 (Chief Executive, 1973–80; Chairman, 1973–85); non-executive Chairman, BL plc, 1982–86 (Deputy Chairman, 1980–82; Director, 1977–86); *b* 11 Sept. 1915; *o s* of late Ernest Arthur Bide and Eliza Bide (*née* Young); *m* 1941, Irene (*née* Ward); three *d*. *Educ:* County Sch., Acton; Univ. of London. 1st cl. hons BSc Chemistry; FRSC, CChem. Govt Chemist's Dept, 1932–40; Research Chemist, Glaxo, 1940: i/c Chemical Develt and Intellectual Property, 1944–54; Dep. Sec., 1954–59; Sec., 1959–65; Dir, 1963–71; Dep. Chm., 1971–73; Dir, J. Lyons & Co. Ltd, 1977–78. Member: Review Body, UGC, 1985–87; Working Party on Biotechnology (under auspices of ACARD/ABRD and Royal Soc.) (Report 1980); Adv. Cttee on Industry to the Vice-Chancellors and Principals of UK Univs, 1984–87; Chm., Information Technology 1986 Cttee, 1986. Member: Adv. Council, Inst. of Biotechnological Studies, 1985–89; Council, Inst. of Manpower Studies, 1985–91; Chairman: Visiting Cttee, Open Univ., 1982–89; Adam Smith Inst., 1986– (Mem., 1985–). Chairman: QCA Ltd, 1985–89; Micro-test Res. Ltd, 1987–90; United Environmental Systems, 1988–90; CGEA (UK) Ltd, 1991–99; Comatech (UK) Ltd, 1992–99; Tyseley Waste Disposal, 1994–99; Onyx Environmental Group plc, 1998–99; Director: Oxford Consultancy Ltd, 1988–98 (Chm., 1994–98); Cie des Transports et Services Publiques, 1992–. Confederation of British Industry: Member: Council, 1974–85; President's Cttee, 1983–86; Chm., Res. and Technol. Cttee, 1977–86; Institute of Management (formerly British Institute of Management): CIMgt (FBIM 1972); Mem. Council, 1976–88; Chm., Finance Cttee, 1976–79; Vice-Pres., 1992–; Dir, BIM Foundn, 1977–79. Medical Research Council: Mem., 1986–90; Chm., Investment Cttee, 1988–90; Chm., Pensions Trust, 1988–90; Mem., AIDS Cttee, 1987–90; Trustee, Nat. AIDS Trust (Chm., until 1991); Co-founder, and Chm., World Humanity Action Trust, 1992–98. Member: Editl Adv. Bd, Science in Parlt, 1994–98; Foundn for Sci. and Technol., 1994–. Chm. Court, Freight Transport Assoc., 1992–; Mem. Court, British Shippers Council, 1984–92 (Chm., 1989–92); Trustee, British Motor Industry Heritage Trust, 1983–86. Chm., Salisbury Cathedral Spire Appeal Cttee, 1987–92; Trustee, Salisbury Cathedral Spire Trust, 1987–; Mem., Confraternity of Benefactors, Salisbury Cathedral, 1992–. Chm. of Appeal, RCS, 1992– (Patron, 1996–). Mem. Council, Imperial Soc. of Knights Bachelor, 1980–97. FIEx 1987; FInstD 1989; Hon. FIChemE 1983; Hon. FIIM 1983 (Vice-Pres., 1983); Hon. Fellow: Inst. Biotechnological Studies 1985; St Catherine's Coll., Oxford, 1987. Hon. DSc: QUB, 1986; CNAA, 1990; DUniv OU, 1991. Gold Medal, BIM, 1983; Duncan Davies Medal, R&D Soc., 1990. *Publications:* papers in learned jls on organic chemical subjects. *Recreation:* fishing. *Clubs:* Carlton, Hurlingham.

BIDGOOD, John Claude, MIEx; Director, Bidgood Holdings Ltd, 1947–97; *b* 12 May 1914; *s* of late Edward Charles Bidgood, Leeds; *m* 1945, Sheila Nancy Walker-Wood; one *s* two *d*. *Educ:* London Choir Sch.; Woodhouse Technical Sch. Served early part of War of 1939–45 as Pilot RAF. Mem. Leeds City Council, 1947–55 (late Chm. Works Cttee and City Architects Cttee); contested (C) N E Leeds, 1950, 1951; MP (C) Bury and Radcliffe, 1955–64; PPS to Joint Parly Secs, Min. of Pensions and Nat. Insurance, 1957–58; Mem. Parly Select Cttee on Estimates, 1958–64. Chm., Yorks Assoc. for the Disabled, 1950–58; Member: Inst. of Export; Leeds and Bradford Joint Aerodrome Cttee, 1951–55. Mayor, Chapeltown Corporation, 1987–88. Hon. Citizen, City of Atlanta, Georgia, 1960; Freeman, City of London, 1961; Liveryman and Mem., Worshipful Co. of Horners. *Recreations:* music, travel. *Address:* The Old Joinery, Walton, near Wetherby, W Yorks LS23 7DQ. *T:* (01937) 844028. *Club:* City Livery.

BIDSTRUP, (Patricia) Lesley, MD, FRCP, FRACP; Member, Medical Appeals Tribunal, 1970–88; private consulting concerned mainly with industrial medicine, since 1958; *b* 24 Oct. 1916; *d* of Clarence Leslie Bidstrup, Chemical Works Manager, South Australia, and Kathleen Helena Bidstrup (*née* O'Brien); *m* 1952, Ronald Frank Guymer, TD, MD, FRCP, FRCS, DPH, DIH; one step *s* one step *d*. *Educ:* Kadina High Sch. and Walford House, Adelaide, SA. MB, BS (Adel.) 1939; MD (Adel.) 1958; FRACP 1954; FRCP (Lond.) 1964. Resident Ho. Phys. and Registrar, Royal Adelaide Hosp., SA, 1939–41. Hon. Capt., AAMC, 1942–45. MO, UNRRA, Glyn-Hughes Hosp., Belsen, 1945–46. General practice: Acting Hon. Asst Phys., Royal Adelaide Hosp.; Tutor in Med., St Mark's Coll., Adelaide, and in Univ. of Adelaide Med. Sch.; Lectr in Med., Univ. of Adelaide Dental Faculty, 1942–45; Asst, Dept for Research in Industrial Medicine, MRC, 1947–58; Clinical Asst (Hon.), Chest Dept, St Thomas' Hosp., 1958–78. Member: Scientific Sub-Cttee on Poisonous Substances used in Agriculture and Food Storage, 1956–58; Industrial Injuries Adv. Council, 1970–83. Visiting Lectr, TUC Centenary Inst. of Occupational Health; Examiner for Diploma in Industrial Health: Conjoint Bd, 1965–71, 1980–82; Society of Apothecaries, 1970–76; External Examiner for Diploma in Industrial Health, Dundee, 1980–82. Fellow, Amer. Coll. of Occupational Medicine. William P. Yant Award, Amer. Industrial Hygiene Assoc., 1989. Mayoress, Royal Borough of Kingston-upon-Thames, 1959, 1960. *Publications:* The Toxicity of Mercury and its Compounds, 1964; chapters in: Cancer Progress, 1960; The Prevention of Cancer, 1967; Clinical Aspects of Inhaled Particles, 1972; contribs to Brit. Jl Indust. Med., Lancet, BMJ, Proc. Royal Soc. Med., ILO Encyclopaedia on Industrial Diseases. *Recreations:* people, theatre, music. *Address:* 11 Sloane Terrace Mansions, Sloane Terrace, SW1X 9DG. *T:* (020) 7730 8720.

BIDWELL, Sir Hugh (Charles Philip), GBE 1989; Deputy Chairman, ITE Group plc (formerly International Trade & Exhibitions J/V Ltd), since 1996; Lord Mayor of London, 1989–90; *b* 1 Nov. 1934; *s* of late Edward and Elisabeth Bidwell; *m* 1962, Jenifer Celia Webb; two *s* one *d*. *Educ:* Stonyhurst College. Nat. Service, 1953–55; commissioned E Surrey Regt, seconded to 1st Bn KAR, based Nyasaland. Viota Foods, 1956–70 (Dir, 1962–70); Dir, Robertson Foods, 1969–70; Chairman: Pearce Duff & Co. Ltd, 1970–84; Gill & Duffus Foods Ltd, 1984–85; British Invisibles, 1991–94; Non-executive Chairman: Riggs AP Bank Ltd, 1989–92; Julius Gp Ltd (formerly Octavian Gp Ltd), 1993–97; non-exec. Dep. Chm., London Forum, 1992–93; non-executive Director: Argyll Group plc, 1990–95; Rothschild Asset Mgt Ltd, 1992–98; Fleming Geared Income and Assets Investment Trust plc, 1993–97; Alpha Airports Gp plc, 1994–. Chm., London Tourist Bd, 1992–93; Member: Exec. Cttee, London Chamber of Commerce and Industry, 1976–85; Food from Britain Council, 1983–89 (Chm., Export Bd, 1983–86); European Trade Cttee, 1989–91; British-Soviet Chamber of Commerce, 1989–92; China-Britain (formerly Sino-British) Trade Gp, 1989–94; E. European Trade Gp, 1991–92; BOTB, 1992–94. Pres., British Food Export Council, 1980–87; Dep. Pres., Food and Drink Fedn, 1985–86. Alderman, Billingsgate Ward, 1979–96; Sheriff of the City of London, 1986–87. Master, Grocers' Co., 1984–85. President: Billingsgate Ward Club; Fishmongers' & Poulterers' Instn, 1980–98. *Recreations:* golf, fishing, tennis, cricket, shooting. *Address:* (office) 105 Salusbury Road, NW6 6RG. *T:* (020) 7596 5000. *Clubs:* Boodle's, White's, City of London, MCC; Royal & Ancient; Denham Golf, Royal St George's.

BIDWELL, Robin O'Neill, CBE 1999; PhD; Chairman and Chief Executive Officer, ERM, since 1993; *b* 15 Sept. 1944; *s* of late Philip John Bidwell and Ellen O'Neill Bidwell; *m* 1st, 1970, Caroline Margaret Budd (marr. diss. 1993); one *s* one *d*; 2nd, 1995, Veronica Rosemary Lucia Verey. *Educ:* Charterhouse; Christ Church, Oxford (BA 1966; MA 1970); Bradford Mgt Centre (PhD 1974). Joined ERL, now ERM, 1973: Dir, 1974–; Man. Dir, 1977–93. Non-exec. Dir, CU Envmtl Trust plc, now CGU Morley Qly High Income Trust plc, 1992–. Advr, Prince of Wales Business Leaders Forum, 1993–; Trustee, Heritage Trust, 1987–96; Member: Task Force on envmtl implications of 1992, EC, 1989–90; Bd, Sustainability Challenge Foundn, Netherlands, 1993–; NERC, 1996–; Adv. Cttee on Business and the Envmt, 1999–; Member Council: World Business Council for Sustainable Develt, 1997–; UK Roundtable on Sustainable Develt, 1998–2000. Mem. Exec. Cttee, Green Alliance, 1995–. *Recreations:* reshaping landscapes, ski-ing, reading. *Address:* Woodchester Park House, Nympsfield, Glos GL10 3UN. *T:* (office) (020) 7465 7331.

BIFFEN, Baron *cr* 1997 (Life Peer), of Tanat, in the co. of Shropshire; **William John Biffen;** PC 1979; DL; *b* 3 Nov. 1930; *s* of Victor W. Biffen; *m* 1979, Mrs Sarah Wood (*née* Drew); one step *s* one step *d*. *Educ:* Dr Morgan's Sch., Bridgwater; Jesus Coll., Cambridge (BA). Worked in Tube Investments Ltd, 1953–60; Economist Intelligence Unit, 1960–61. MP (C): Salop, Oswestry, Nov. 1961–1983; Shropshire N, 1983–97; Chief Sec. to the Treasury, 1979–81; Sec. of State for Trade, 1981–82; Lord Pres. of the Council, 1982–83; Leader of House of Commons, 1982–87 and Lord Privy Seal, 1983–87. Director: Glynwed International, 1987–2000; J. Bibby & Sons, 1988–97; Rockware Gp, 1988–91; Barlow International, 1998–2000. Trustee, The London Clinic, 1994–. DL Shropshire, 1993. *Publications:* Inside the House of Commons, 1989; Inside Westminster, 1996. *Address:* Tanat House, Llanyblodwel, Oswestry, Shropshire SY10 8NQ.

BIGG, Sally; *see* Gunnell, S.

BIGGAM, Sir Robin (Adair), Kt 1993; Chairman: Spectris (formerly Fairey Group plc), since 1996; Independent Television Commission, since 1997; *b* 8 July 1938; *s* of Thomas and Eileen Biggam; *m* 1962, Elizabeth McArthur McDougall; one *s* two *d*. *Educ:* Lanark Grammar Sch. Chartered accountant. Peat Marwick Mitchell, 1960–63; ICI, 1964–81; Director: ICL, 1981–84; Dunlop Holdings plc, 1984–85; Man. Dir, 1986–87, Chief Exec., 1987–91, Chm., 1992–96, BICC plc. Non Executive Director: Chloride Group plc, 1985–87; Lloyds Abbey Life plc (formerly Abbey Life Gp), 1985–90; Redland Gp plc, 1991–97; British Aerospace plc, 1994–; Foreign & Colonial German Investment Trust plc, 1995–98; British Energy plc, 1996–. Pres., German–British Chamber of Commerce, 1995–97. *Recreations:* golf, fishing, gardening, watching television. *Address:* Independent Television Commission, 33 Foley Street, W1P 7LB.

BIGGAR, (Walter) Andrew, CBE 1980 (OBE 1967); MC 1945; TD 1995; FRAgS; farming since 1956; *b* 6 March 1915; *s* of Walter Biggar and Margaret Sproat; *m* 1945, Patricia Mary Irving Elliot; one *s* one *d*. *Educ:* Sedbergh Sch., Cumbria; Edinburgh Univ. (BScAgric). FRAgS 1969. Commnd Royal Signals, 1938; War Service, 51st Highland Div., 1939–46; POW, Germany, 1940–45. Rowett Res. Inst., 1935–54. Director and Trustee: Scottish Soc. for Research in Plant Breeding, 1958–88; Animal Diseases Res. Assoc., 1966–96. Member: Farm Animals Welfare Adv. Cttee, 1967–77; ARC, 1969–80; Scottish Agricultural Develt Council, 1971–82; JCO Consultative Bd, 1980–84; Chm., Animals Bd, JCO, 1973–80. Chm., Moredun Animal Health Trust, 1988–94; Dir, Moredun Foundn, 1996–98. Governor: St Margaret's Sch., Edinburgh, 1960–81; Grassland Res. Inst., 1962–81 (Hon. Fellow, 1981); Scottish Crop Res. Inst., 1980–83. *Recreation:* photography. *Address:* Magdalenehall, St Boswells, Roxburghshire TD6 0EB. *T:* (01835) 823741.

BIGGART, (Thomas) Norman, CBE 1984; WS; Partner, Biggart Baillie & Gifford, WS, Solicitors, Glasgow and Edinburgh, 1959–95; *b* 24 Jan. 1930; *o s* of Andrew Stevenson Biggart, JP and Marjorie Scott Biggart; *m* 1956, Eileen Jean Anne Gemmell; one *s* one *d*. *Educ:* Morrisons Acad., Crieff; Glasgow Univ. (MA 1951, LLB 1954). Served RN, 1954–56 (Sub-Lt RNVR). Law Society of Scotland: Mem. Council, 1977–86; Vice-Pres., 1981–82; Pres., 1982–83. Mem., Council on Tribunals, and Chm., Scottish Cttee, 1990–98. Pres., Business Archives Council, Scotland, 1977–86. Member: Exec. Cttee, Scottish Council (Development and Industry), 1984–93; Scottish Tertiary Educn Adv. Council, 1984–87; Scottish Records Adv. Council, 1985–91. Director: Clydesdale Bank, 1985–97; Independent (formerly New Scotland) Insurance Gp, 1986–2000 (Chm., 1989–93); Beechwood Glasgow, 1989–97 (Chm., 1989–97). Trustee, Scottish Civic Trust, 1989–97. Hon. Mem., American Bar Assoc., 1982. OStJ 1968. *Recreations:* golf, hill walking. *Address:* Gailes, Kilmacolm, Renfrewshire PA13 4LZ. *T:* (01505) 872645. *Club:* The Western (Glasgow).

BIGGS, Vice-Adm. Sir Geoffrey (William Roger), KCB 1993; Military Adviser to ICL, since 1995; *b* 23 Nov. 1938; *s* of Vice-Adm. Sir Hilary Biggs, KBE, CB, DSO and Lady Biggs; *m* 1st, 1968, Marcia (*née* Leask) (marr. diss. 1978); three *s*; 2nd, 1981, Caroline Ann (*née* Daly); one *d*, and two step *s*. *Educ:* St Andrews, Eastbourne; Charterhouse. Joined RN 1956, Submarine Service, 1960; commanded HM Ships: Otus, 1969–70; Superb, 1978–79; Brilliant, 1984–85; Broadsword, 1985–86; Capt. 2nd Frigate Sqn, 1985–86; Dir of Naval Ops, 1986–89; Flag Officer Gibraltar, 1990; Comdr British Forces Gibraltar, 1990–92; Dep. Comdr and C of S to C-in-C Fleet, 1992–94; retd, 1995. Comdr, 1975; Capt., 1980; Rear-Adm., 1990; Vice-Adm., 1992. *Recreations:* lawnmowing, crosswords, family and friends. *Address:* c/o Naval Secretary, Victory Building, HM Naval Base, Portsmouth PO1 3LS.

BIGGS, Dr John, FRSC; Chairman, Free Church Federal Council, 1993–97 (Moderator, 1992–93); *b* 3 Jan. 1933; *s* of Horace James Biggs and Elsie Alice Biggs, Leicester; *m* 1965, Brenda Muriel Hicklenton. *Educ:* Wyggeston Grammar Sch. for Boys, Leicester; Downing Coll., Cambridge (Graystone Scholar). MA, PhD (Cantab). CChem; FRSC (FCS 1958). DSIR Res. Fellow, Cambridge, 1958–60; Lectr in Chemistry, Univ. of Hull, 1960–87. President: Baptist Students' Fedn, 1955–56; Yorkshire Baptist Assoc., 1973–74; Vice-Pres., Baptist Men's Movement, 1995–97, Pres., 1997–98; Baptist Union of GB: Chm., Home Mission Working Gp, 1981–88; Mem. Council, 1978–, Chm., 1990–94; Pres., 1989–90; Mem., Scholarships and Ministerial Trng Bursary Cttee, 1978–2001 (Chm., 1995–2001). Governor, Northern Baptist Coll., Manchester, 1989–2000; Chm., Relocation Steering Cttee, Baptist Theol Seminary, Prague, 1994–96 (Mem. Bd of Trustees, Rüschlikon, Zürich, 1989–94, Vice-Chm., 1992–94). Member: Envmtl Issues Network, CTBI (formerly CCBI), 1990–; Envmt Gp, Churches Together in Cumbria, 1997–; Steering Cttee, 1999–, and Adv. Panel, 1999–, Going for Green Eco-Congregation Scheme. *Recreations:* fell-walking, opera, photography. *Address:* Fellcroft, Easedale Road, Grasmere, Ambleside, Cumbria LA22 9QR. *Club:* Penn.

BIGGS, John; Member (Lab) City and East, London Assembly, Greater London Authority, since 2000; *b* 19 Nov. 1957; *s* of late Robert Edmund Biggs and of Mary Jeanette Biggs (*née* Phillips); *m* 1993, Christine Sibley; one *d. Educ:* Queen Elizabeth's Boys' Sch., Barnet; Bristol Univ. (BSc Hons Chem. 1979); Birkbeck Coll., London Univ. (Postgrad. Dip. Computer Sci. 1984); Westminster Univ. (Postgrad. Dip. Law 1996, Legal Practice Course 1998). Operating theatre orderly, 1979–80; lab. technician, 1980–83; systems analyst, 1984–91; self-employed computer consultant, 1991–92. Mem. (Lab), Tower Hamlets BC, 1988– (Leader of Opposition, 1991–94; Leader, 1994–95). Non-exec. Dir, Tower Hamlets HAT, 1996– (Vice-Chm., 1999–). Dir, Socialist Health Assoc., 1997–2000. *Recreations:* reading, walking, travel, psephology. *Address:* Greater London Authority, Romney House, 43 Marsham Street, SW1P 3PY. *T:* (020) 7983 4373; 7 Louisa Gardens, Stepney Green, E1 4NG. *T:* (020) 7790 9710.

BIGGS, John Sydney Grainge, MD; FRACOG; Postgraduate Medical Dean, University of Cambridge, and Eastern Region, NHS Executive, 1991–2001; *b* 16 Dec. 1935; *s* of Charles V. G. Biggs and Leah M. Biggs (*née* Price); *m* 1960 T. Glyndon Daley; three *s* two *d. Educ:* Carey Grammar Sch., Melbourne; Univ. of Melbourne (MB BS 1960); MD Aberdeen 1973; MA Cantab 1994. MRCOG 1966; FRACOG 1979; DHMSA 1993. House Officer, Royal Melbourne Hosp., 1961; RMO, Royal Children's Hosp., Melbourne, 1962; RMO and Registrar, Royal Women's Hosp., Melbourne, 1963–64; Lecturer in Obstetrics and Gynaecology: Univ. of Qld, 1965; Univ. of Aberdeen, 1966–69; University of Queensland: Sen. Lectr, 1969–72; Reader, 1973–82; Dean of Medicine and Prof., 1983–91. Hon. Prof., UEA, 1997– Pres., ASME, 1999– (Chm., 1996–99). *Publications:* contrib. to learned jls on ovarian structure and function, 1996–82, and medical educn, 1983–2001. *Recreations:* gardening, walking, reading. *Address:* 5 Wootton Way, Cambridge CB3 9LX. *T:* (01223) 323377. *Club:* Royal Society of Medicine.

BIGGS, Lewis; Director/Chief Executive, Liverpool Biennial of Contemporary Art, since 2000; *b* 22 April 1952; *s* of Lewis Ian Biggs and Penelope Torre Biggs (*née* Torr); *m* 1983, Ann Margaret Compton; one *s* one *d. Educ:* New Coll., Oxford (MA Mod. Hist. 1974); Courtauld Inst., Univ. of London (MA Hist. of Art 1979). Gallery Co-ordinator, Arnolfini Gall., Bristol, 1979–84; Exhibns Officer, British Council, 1984–87; Curator of Exhibns, Tate Gall., Liverpool, 1987–90; Curator, then Dir, Tate Gall., Liverpool, 1990–2000. Dir, Art Transpennine Ltd, 1996–. Member: Visual Arts Adv. Cttee, British Council, 1991–; Visual Arts Panel, Arts Council of England, 1996–99; NW Arts Bd, 1997–; Liverpool Cath. Fabric Adv. Cttee, 1995–98. Trustee, Liverpool Architecture and Design Trust, 1997–99; Dir, Liverpool Biennial Trust, 1998–2000. Associate Fellow, Univ. of Liverpool, 1992; Hon. Fellow, Liverpool John Moores Univ., 1998. *Address:* PO Box 55, Liverpool, L69 1BX. *T:* (0151) 709 7444, *Fax:* (0151) 709 7377; *e-mail:* lewis.biggs@biennial.org.uk.

BIGGS, Brig. Michael Worthington, CBE 1962 (OBE 1944); MA; CEng, MICE; *b* 16 Sept. 1911; *s* of late Lt-Col Charles William Biggs, OBE, Cheltenham and late Winifred Jesse Bell Biggs (*née* Dickinson); *m* 1940, Katharine Mary, *d* of late Sir Walter Harragin, CMG, QC, Colonial Legal Service, and Lady Harragin; two *d. Educ:* Cheltenham Coll.; RMA Woolwich; Pembroke Coll., Cambridge. MA (Cantab) 1966; MICE 1967. 2nd Lieut RE, 1931; served War of 1939–45, E Africa, Abyssinia (Bde Major), and Burma (GSO1 and CRE); Lt-Col 1942; Col 1954; Mil. Adviser to High Comr, Australia, 1954–57; Col GS, SME Chatham, 1957–60; Brig. 1960; Chief of Staff, E Africa Comd, 1960–62; Dir of Quartering (Army), MoD, 1963–66; retd, 1966. Group Building Exec., Forte's (Holdings) Ltd, 1966–67; Manager, Hatfield and Welwyn Garden City, Commn for New Towns, 1967–78. Member: Council, TCPA, 1978–86; Exec. Cttee, Hertfordshire Soc.; Chm., Herts Bldg Preservation Trust, 1978–86. Pres., KAR and EAF Officers' Dinner Club, 1972–97. Freeman, City of London, 1985. *Recreations:* golf, gardening. *Address:* 1 Mildmay Court, Odiham, Hampshire RG29 1AX. *T:* (01256) 702715. *Club:* Army and Navy.

BIGGS, Sir Norman (Parris), Kt 1977; Director, Banco de Bilbao, 1981–87; *b* 23 Dec. 1907; *s* of John Gordon Biggs and Mary Sharpe Dickson; *m* 1936, Peggy Helena Stammwitz (*d* 1990); two *s* one *d. Educ:* John Watson's Sch., Edinburgh. Bank of England, 1927–46; Dir, Kleinwort Sons & Co. Ltd, 1946–52; Esso Petroleum Company, Ltd: Dir, 1952–66, Chm., 1968–72; Chairman: Williams & Glyn's Bank Ltd, 1972–76; United International Bank Ltd, 1970–79; Deputy Chairman: National and Commercial Banking Gp Ltd, 1974–76; Privatbanken Ltd, 1980–83; Director: Royal Bank of Scotland, 1974–76; Gillett Bros Discount Co. Ltd, 1963–77. Mem., Bullock Cttee on Industrial Democracy, 1976. *Address:* Northbrooks, Danworth Lane, Hurstpierpoint, Sussex BN6 9LW. *T:* (01273) 832022.

BIGGS, Prof. Peter Martin, CBE 1987; PhD, DSc; FRS 1976; Director of Animal Health (formerly Animal Disease Research), Agricultural and Food Research Council, 1986–88, retired; Visiting Professor of Veterinary Microbiology, Royal Veterinary College, University of London, since 1982; *b* 13 Aug. 1926; *s* of Ronald Biggs and Cécile Biggs (*née* Player); *m* 1950, Alison Janet Molteno; two *s* one *d. Educ:* Bedales Sch.; Cambridge Sch., USA; Queen's Univ., Belfast; Royal Veterinary Coll., Univ. of London (BSc 1953, DSc 1975); Univ. of Bristol (PhD 1958). FRCVS, FRCPath, FIBiol, CBiol. Served RAF, 1944–48; Research Asst, Univ. of Bristol, 1953–55, Lectr, 1955–59; Houghton Poultry Research Station: Head of Leukosis Experimental Unit, 1959–74; Dep. Dir, 1971–74; Dir, 1974–86. Andrew D. White Prof.-at-Large, Cornell Univ., 1988–94. Sir William Dick Meml Lectr, Univ. of Edinburgh, 1974 and 1987; E.H.W. Wilmott Guest Lectr, Univ. of Bristol, 1977; Leeuwenhoek Prize Lectr, Royal Soc., 1997. Member: Veterinary Products Cttee, 1973–98; Management Bd, AFRC, 1986–88. Hon. Life Pres., World Vet. Poultry Assoc., 1985; President: Inst. of Biol., 1990–92; Internat. Assoc. for Comparative Res. on Leukemia and Related Diseases, 1981–83. Vice Pres., BVA, 1996–98. Founder FMedSci 1998. Hon. FRASE 1986. Hon. DVM Ludwig-Maximilians Univ., 1976; Dr *hc* Liège, 1991. Tom Newman Meml Award, 1964; Poultry Science Award, British Oil and Cake Mills, 1968; J. T. Edwards Meml Medal, 1969; Dalrymple-Champneys Cup and Medal, 1973; Bledisloe Veterinary Award, 1977; Wooldridge Meml Medal, 1978; Joszef Marek Meml Medal, Vet. Univ. of Budapest, 1979; Victory Medal, Central Vet. Soc., 1980; Gordon Meml Medal, Robert Fraser Gordon Meml Trust, 1989; Wolf Foundn Prize in Agric., 1989; Chiron Award, BVA, 1999. *Publications:* scientific papers on viruses and infectious disease. *Recreations:* music making, natural history, boating. *Address:* Willows, London Road, St Ives, PE27 5ES. *T:* and *Fax:* (01480) 463471. *Clubs:* Athenæum, Farmers'.

BIGHAM, family name of **Viscount Mersey**.

BIGNELL, (Francis) Geoffrey; Principal, Just Employment, Solicitors, since 1998; *b* 7 March 1949; *s* of Ernest Francis John Bignell and Olive Ethel Bignell (*née* Peatson); *m* 1978, Susan Rachel Harrison; two *s* one *d. Educ:* Isleworth Grammar Sch.; Trinity Hall, Cambridge (MA); Coll. of Law. Social work in Basildon and Worksop, 1971–74; articled to Notts CC, 1975–78; admitted Solicitor, 1977; Prosecuting Solicitor, Notts Police Authy, 1978–80; Asst and Sen. Asst Solicitor, Leics CC, 1980–83; Prin. Solicitor, Warwicks CC, 1983–87; Asst Sec.-Gen. (Management), Law Soc., 1987–95; Chief Executive: Law Soc. Services Ltd, 1995–97; Solicitors Property Centres Ltd, 1997–98. Non-executive Director: Cheviot Financial Services (formerly Cheviot Personal Pensions) Ltd, 1992–; Ambersham Holdings Ltd, 1998–; Lawyers Defence Union Ltd, 1999–; Peter Honey Publications Ltd, 2000–. Mem., Rail Passengers' (formerly Rail Users') Consultative Cttee for Southern England, 1997–. Gov., George Abbot Sch., 1995– (Vice-Chm., 1998–); Mem., Corp. of Guildford Coll., 1997– (Vice-Chm., 1998–). *Publications:* contribs to learned jls. *Recreations:* photography, shares, railways. *Address:* (office) Castle House, Castle Street, Guildford, Surrey GU1 3UW. *T:* (01483) 303636.

BIJUR, Peter Isaac; Chairman of the Board and Chief Executive Officer, Texaco Inc., 1996–2001; *b* 14 Oct. 1942; *m* 2000, Kjestine M. Anderson; two *s* one *d* from former marriage. *Educ:* Univ. of Pittsburgh (BA Pol. Sci. 1964); Columbia Univ. (MBA 1966). Texaco, 1966–2001: Manager, Buffalo sales dist, 1971–73; Asst Manager to Vice-Pres. for public affairs, 1973–75; Staff Co-ordinator, dept of strategic planning, 1975–77; Asst to Exec. Vice-Pres., 1977–80; Manager, Rocky Mountain Refining and Marketing, 1980–81; Asst to Chm. of Bd, 1981–83; Pres., Texaco Oil Trading & Supply Co., 1984; Vice-Pres., special projects, 1984–86; Pres. and Chief Exec., Don Mills, Texaco Canada, 1987–89; Chm., Pres. and Chief Exec., Texaco Canada Resources, Calgary, 1988–89; Chm., Texaco Ltd, 1989–91; Pres., Texaco Europe, 1990–92; Sen. Vice Pres., 1992–96, Vice Chm. Bd, 1996, Texaco Inc. *Address:* 1055 Washington Boulevard, Stamford, CT 06901, USA.

BILBY, Prof. Bruce Alexander, BA, PhD; FRS 1977; consultant; Professor of the Theory of Materials, University of Sheffield, 1966–84, now Emeritus; *b* 3 Sept. 1922; *e s* of late George Alexander Bilby and Dorothy Jean (*née* Telfer); *m* 1st, 1946, Hazel Joyce (*née* Casken); two *s* one *d*; 2nd, 1966, Lorette Wendela (*née* Thomas); two *s. Educ:* Dover Grammar Sch.; Peterhouse, Cambridge (BA); Univ. of Birmingham (PhD). Admiralty, 1943–46. Research, Birmingham, 1946–51; Univ. of Sheffield: Royal Soc. Sorby Res. Fellow, 1951–57; J. H. Andrew Res. Fellow, 1957–58; Reader in Theoretical Metallurgy, 1958–62, Prof., 1962–66. Has made contributions to theory of dislocations and its application to the deformation, transformation and fracture of metallic crystals. Rosenhain Medal, Inst. of Metals, 1963; Griffith Medal, European Structural Integrity Soc., 1994. *Publications:* contribs to learned jls. *Recreation:* sailing. *Address:* 32 Devonshire Road, Totley, Sheffield S17 3NT. *T:* (0114) 236 1086; Department of Mechanical Engineering, The University, Mappin Street, Sheffield S1 3JD. *T:* (0114) 222 7713.

BILDT, Carl; MP (Moderate Party), Sweden, since 1979; Special Envoy of UN Secretary General of Balkans, since 1999; *b* Halmstad, 15 July 1949; *s* of Daniel B. Bildt and Kerstin Bildt (*née* Andersson); *m* 1984, Mia Bohman; one *s* one *d*; *m* 1998, Anna Maria Corazza. *Educ:* Stockholm Univ. Mem., Stockholm CC, 1974–77; Under-Sec. of State for Co-ordination and Planning, Cabinet Office, 1979–81; Member: Parly Standing Cttee in Foreign Affairs, 1982–86; Adv. Council on Foreign Affairs, 1982–99; Submarine Defence Commn, 1982–83; 1984 Defence Cttee, 1984–87; Prime Minister of Sweden, 1991–94; EU Special Rep. to Conflict in Former Yugoslavia, and Co-Chm., Internat. Conf. on Former Yugoslavia, 1995; EU High Rep. for Civilian Peace Implementation in Bosnia and Herzegovinia, 1996–97. Moderate Party: Mem., Exec. Cttee, 1981–; Mem., Parly Gp Council, 1982–91; Chm., 1986–99. Mem., IISS, 1981–. Mem., Nordic Council, 1986– (Chm., Conservative Gp, 1988–91). Chm., Internat. Democratic Union, 1992–99. *Publications:* Landet Som Steg ut i Kylan, 1972; Framtid i Frihet, 1976; Hallänning, Svensk, Europé, 1991; Peace Journey, 1998. *Address:* Sveriges Riksdag, 10012 Stockholm, Sweden. *T:* (8) 7865390.

BILGER, Pierre; Chairman and Chief Executive Officer, ALSTOM, since 1998; *b* Colmar, 27 May 1940; *s* of Joseph Bilger and Suzanne Gillet; *m* 1966, Eliane Oyon; two *s* three *d. Educ:* Institut d'Etudes Politiques; Ecole Nationale d'Admin, Paris. Sen. posts at French Min. of Econ. and Finance (Inspection Générale des Finances and Budget Dept), 1967–82; sen. posts with Cie Générale d'Electricité, subseq. Alcatel Alsthom, then Alcatel, 1982–87 (Dep. Man. Dir, 1987); joined Alsthom, 1987; Pres. and CEO, GEC ALSTHOM, 1991–98. Non-exec. Dir, Société Générale, 1999. Mem. Adv. Bd, Renault-Nissan Internat., 2000. *Address:* ALSTOM, 25 avenue Kléber, 75795 Paris Cedex 16, France. *T:* (1) 47552000; 7 rue de l'Assomption, 75016 Paris, France.

BILL, (Edward) Geoffrey (Watson), OBE 1991; FSA, FRHistS; Lambeth Librarian, 1958–91; Lecturer and Archivist, Christ Church, Oxford, 1950–91; *b* 19 Feb. 1924; *s* of Edward Richard Bill and Anne (*née* Greenwood); *m* Margaret Nancy Finch; one *s* one *d. Educ:* Kingston Grammar Sch.; Balliol Coll., Oxford (MA). FRHistS 1983; FSA 1984. Served Army, 1943–46 (Lieut). Dept of Western MSS, Bodleian Library, Oxford, 1954–58. DLitt Lambeth, 1983. *Publications:* Christ Church Meadow, 1965; (with Dr J. F. A. Mason) Christ Church and Reform 1850–1867, 1970; University Reform in Nineteenth Century Oxford, 1973; Education at Christ Church Oxford 1660–1800, 1988; Catalogue of MSS in Lambeth Palace Library, 1972–83. *Recreation:* avoiding gardening. *Address:* 22 Helme Lodge, Kendal, Cumbria LA9 7QA.

BILLETT, Paul Rodney, CB 1981; *b* 19 Feb. 1921; *s* of late Arthur William and Grace Hilda Billett; *m* 1st, 1945, Muriel Gwendoline Marsh (*d* 1977); one *s*; 2nd, 1985, Eileen May Nourse. *Educ:* Commonweal and College Grammar Schools, Swindon. Entered Exchequer and Audit Dept, 1939. Served RASC, 1941–46. Deputy Secretary, Exchequer and Audit Dept, 1975–81 (retired). *Address:* Wynthorpe, Cornsland, Brentwood, Essex CM14 4JL. *T:* (01277) 224830.

BILLINGHAM, family name of **Baroness Billingham.**

BILLINGHAM, Baroness *cr* 2000 (Life Peer), of Banbury in the co. of Oxfordshire; **Angela Theodora Billingham;** JP; *b* 31 July 1939; widow; two *d. Educ:* Aylesbury GS; London Univ. Teacher, 1960–90; Examiner, 1990–95. Mayor of Banbury, 1976; Member (Lab): Banbury BC, 1970–74; Cherwell DC, 1974–84; Oxfordshire CC, 1993–94. Contested (Lab) Banbury, 1992. MEP (Lab) Northants and Blaby, 1994–99; contested (Lab) E Midlands Reg., 1999. Chief Whip, Party of European Socialists, EP, 1995–99. JP N Oxfordshire and Bicester, 1976. *Recreations:* tennis, gardening, bridge, cinema, grandchildren. *Address:* 6 Crediton Hill, NW6 1HP; c/o House of Lords, SW1A 0PW. *Club:* Cumberland Lawn Tennis (W Hampstead).

BILLINGHAM, Prof. Rupert Everett, MA, DPhil, DSc Oxon; FRS 1961; Professor and Chairman, Department of Cell Biology and Anatomy, Southwestern Medical School, University of Texas Health Science Center at Dallas, 1971–86; Professor Emeritus, 1990; *b* 15 Oct. 1921; *o s* of Albert Everett and Helen Louise Billingham, Oxford; *m* 1951, Jean Mary Morpeth; two *s* one *d. Educ:* City of Oxford High Sch.; Oriel Coll., Oxford. Served 1942–46, as Lieut RNVR. Asst Lectr, later Lectr in Zoology, University of Birmingham, 1947; Junior Research Fellow, British Empire Cancer Campaign, 1950; Intermediate Research Fellow, Brit. Emp. Cancer Campaign, 1953; Hon. Res. Asst, later Res. Associate, Dept of Zoology, University Coll., London, 1951; Wistar Prof. of Zoology, Univ. of Pennsylvania, USA, and Mem. of Wistar Institute of Anatomy and Biology, Philadelphia, 1957; Prof. and Chm., Dept of Medical Genetics, Univ. of Pennsylvania Med. Sch., Pa, 1965–71. Member: Allergy and Immunology Study Section, Nat. Insts of Health, US Public Health Service, 1958–62; Transplantation and Immunology Cttee, Nat. Insts of Health, 1968–70, 1971–73; Scientific Adv. Cttee, Massachusetts General Hospital, 1976–79; Nat. Allergy and Infectious Diseases Council, Nat. Insts of Health, 1980–83; Sigma Xi College of Nat. Lecturers, 1981–83; President: Transplantation Soc., 1974; Internat. Soc. for Immunology of Reproduction, 1983–86. Hon. Mem., British Transplantation Soc., 1988. Fellow, New York Acad. of Sciences, 1962; Fellow, Amer. Acad. of Arts and Sciences, 1965. Lectures: Herman Beerman, Soc. for Investigative Dermatology, 1963; I. S. Ravdin, Amer. College of Surgeons, 1964; *Sigma Xi*, Yale, 1965; Nat. Insts of Health, 1965; J. W. Jenkinson Meml, Oxford, 1965–66; Harvey, NY, 1966; Kinyoun, Nat. Inst. of Allergy and Infectious Diseases, 1979; Dist. Guest, Soc. for Gyn. Investigation, 1982. Hon. DSc: Trinity Coll., Hartford, Conn, 1965; Univ. of Pennsylvania, 1992. Alvarenga Prize, Coll. Physicians, Philadelphia, 1963; Hon. Award Medal, Amer. Assoc. of Plastic Surgeons, 1964; Adair Award, Amer. Gynecological Soc., 1971; AOA Honor Med. Soc., 1974. *Publications:* The Immunobiology of Transplantation (with W. K. Silvers), 1971; The Immunobiology of Mammalian Reproduction (with A. E. Beer), 1976; contribs to scien. jls on biology of skin, immunology of tissue transplantation and immunology of mammalian reproduction. *Recreations:* woodwork, gardening. *Address:* RR3, Box 86P, Vineyard Haven, MA 02568, USA. *T:* (508) 6937939.

BILLINGTON, Brian John, (Bill); consultant on roads and transport, since 1998; *b* 25 Feb. 1939; *s* of late Kenneth Jack Billington and Doris Violet Billington; *m* 1965, Gillian Elizabeth Annis; two *d. Educ:* Slough Grammar Sch.; The Polytechnic, Regent Street (BSc(Econ)); LSE (MSc). Lectr, The Polytechnic, Regent Street, 1966–68; Min. of Power, later Dept of Energy, 1969–74; Dept of Transport, later Dept of Envmt, Transport and the Regions, 1974–98; Highways Agency, 1994–98; Under Sec., 1991–98. *Address:* 100 Fox Lane, N13 4AX. *T:* (020) 8886 0898.

BILLINGTON, Dr James Hadley; Librarian of Congress, USA, since 1987; *b* 1 June 1929; *s* of Nelson Billington and Jane Coolbaugh; *m* 1957, Marjorie Anne Brennan; two *s* two *d. Educ:* Princeton Univ.; Balliol College, Oxford (Rhodes Scholar; DPhil 1953). Served US Army, 1953–56. Harvard University: Instructor in History, 1957–58; Asst Prof. of History and Res. Fellow, Russian Res. Center, 1958–59; Asst Prof. of History, 1958–61; Associate Prof. of History, 1962–64, Prof., 1964–73, Princeton; Dir, Woodrow Wilson Internat. Center for Scholars, Washington, 1973–87. Chm., Bd of Foreign Scholarships, 1971–73. Visiting Research Professor: Inst. of History, Acad. of Scis, USSR, 1966–67; Univ. of Helsinki, 1960–61; Ecole des Hautes Etudes en Scis Sociales, Paris, 1985, 1988; Vis. Lectr, USA, Europe, Asia; Guggenheim Fellow, 1960–61. Writer and host, The Face of Russia, TV series, 1998. Member: Amer. Acad. of Arts and Scis; Amer. Philosophical Soc.; numerous hon. degrees. Chevalier and Comdr, Ordre des Arts et des Lettres. *Publications:* Mikhailovsky and Russian Populism, 1958; The Icon and the Axe: an interpretive history of Russian culture, 1966; The Arts of Russia, 1970; Fire in the Minds of Men: origins of the Revolutionary Faith, 1980; Russia Transformed: breakthrough to hope, Moscow, August 1991, 1992; The Face of Russia, 1998; contribs to learned jls. *Address:* Office of the Librarian, Library of Congress, 101 Independence Avenue, Washington, DC 20540–1000, USA. *T:* (202) 7075205.

BILLINGTON, Kevin; film, theatre and television director; *b* 12 June 1934; *s* of Richard and Margaret Billington; *m* 1967, Lady Rachel Mary Pakenham (*see* Lady Rachel Billington); two *s* two *d. Educ:* Bryanston Sch.; Queens' Coll., Cambridge (BA); MusDip Open 1999. Film dir, BBC prog., Tonight, 1960–63; documentary film dir, BBC, 1963–67; films include: A Sort of Paradise; Many Mexicos; The Mexican Attitude; Twilight of Empire; Mary McCarthy's Paris; These Humble Shores; Matador; A Few Castles in Spain; The English Cardinal; A Socialist Childhood; Madison Avenue, USA; ATV documentary, All The Queen's Men. *Feature Film Director:* Interlude, 1967; The Rise and Rise of Michael Rimmer, 1969; The Light at the Edge of the World, 1970; Voices, 1974; Reflections, 1984. *Television Director:* And No One Can Save Her, 1973; Once Upon a Time is Now (documentary), 1978; The Music Will Never Stop (documentary), 1979; Henry VIII, 1979; The Jail Diary of Albie Sachs, 1980; The Good Soldier, 1981; Outside Edge, 1982; The Sonnets of William Shakespeare, 1984; Heartland, 1989; Small Doses, 1990; A Time to Dance, 1992. *Theatre Director:* Find Your Way Home, 1970; Me, 1973; The Birthday Party, 1974; The Caretaker, 1975; Bloody Neighbours, 1975; Emigrés, 1976; The Homecoming, 1978; Quartermaine's Terms, 1982; The Deliberate Death of a Polish Priest, 1985 (Channel Four, 1986); The Philanthropist, 1986; The Lover, and A Slight Ache (double bill), 1987; The Breadwinner, 1989; Veterans Day, 1989; Quartermaine's Terms, 1993; Old Times, 1994; Six Characters in Search of an Author, 1999; Our Country's Good, 1999. *Screenplay:* Bodily Harm, 2000. Chm., BAFTA, 1989–90 and 1990–91. Screenwriters' Guild Award, 1966 and 1967; Guild of TV Producers and Directors Award, 1966 and 1967. *Recreations:* swimming, Queen's Park Rangers. *Address:* The Court House, Poyntington, Sherborne, Dorset DT9 4LF. *Club:* Garrick.

BILLINGTON, Michael; Drama Critic of The Guardian, since 1971; *b* 16 Nov. 1939; *s* of Alfred Billington and Patricia (*née* Bradshaw); *m* 1978, Jeanine Bradlaugh. *Educ:* Warwick Sch.; St Catherine's Coll., Oxford (BA). Trained as journalist with Liverpool Daily Post and Echo, 1961–62; Public Liaison Officer and Director for Lincoln Theatre Co., 1962–64; reviewed plays, films and television for The Times, 1965–71. Film Critic: Birmingham Post, 1968–78; Illustrated London News, 1968–81; London Arts Correspondent, New York Times, 1978–; Drama Critic, Country Life, 1987–. Contributor to numerous radio and television Arts programmes, incl. Kaleidoscope, Critics' Forum, The Book Programme, Arena. Presenter, The Billington Interview and Theatre Call, BBC World Service. Writer and Presenter, television profiles of Peggy Ashcroft, Peter Hall and Alan Ayckbourn. Prof. of Drama, Colorado Coll., 1981. IPC Critic of the Year, 1974. *Publications:* The Modern Actor, 1974; How Tickled I Am, 1977; (ed) The Performing Arts, 1980; The Guinness Book of Theatre Facts and Feats, 1982; Alan Ayckbourn, 1983; Tom Stoppard, 1987; Peggy Ashcroft, 1988; (ed) Twelfth Night, 1990; One Night Stands, 1993; The Life and Work of Harold Pinter, 1996. *Recreations:* work, travel, cricket. *Address:* 15 Hearne Road, W4 3NJ. *T:* (020) 8995 0455.

BILLINGTON, Lady Rachel (Mary); writer; *b* 11 May 1942; *d* of 7th Earl of Longford, KG, PC, and of Countess of Longford, *qv*; *m* 1967, Kevin Billington, *qv*; two *s* two *d. Educ:* London Univ. (BA English). Work includes: short stories; four BBC radio plays; two BBC TV plays, Don't be Silly, 1979, Life After Death, 1981. Reviewer and feature writer. *Publications:* All Things Nice, 1969; The Big Dipper, 1970; Lilacs out of the Dead Land, 1971; Cock Robin, 1973; Beautiful, 1974; A Painted Devil, 1975; A Woman's Age, 1979; Occasion of Sin, 1982; The Garish Day, 1985; Loving Attitudes, 1988; Theo and Matilda, 1990; Bodily Harm, 1992; The Family Year, 1992; The Great Umbilical: mother, daughter, mother, 1994; Magic and Fate, 1996; Perfect Happiness: the sequel to Emma, 1996; Tiger Sky, 1998; *for children:* Rosanna and the Wizard-Robot, 1981; The First Christmas, 1983; Star-Time, 1984; The First Easter, 1987; The First Miracles, 1990; Life of Jesus, 1996; Life of St Francis, 1999. *Recreation:* nature. *Address:* The Court House, Poyntington, near Sherborne, Dorset DT9 4LF. *Clubs:* Society of Authors, PEN (Pres., 1997–2000).

BILLOT, Barbara Kathleen; Deputy Director (Under-Secretary), Department for National Savings, 1974–80; *b* 26 May 1920; *d* of Alfred Billot and Agnes Billot (*née* Hiner). *Educ:* Petersfield County High Sch. for Girls. Post Office Savings Bank: Clerical Officer 1938; Exec. Off. 1939; Higher Exec. Off. 1946; Sen. Exec. Off. 1953; Chief Exec. Off. 1957; Principal, Post Office Headquarters, 1960; Sen. Chief Exec. Off., PO Savings Dept, 1961; Principal Exec. Off. (Estabt Off.), 1969; Asst Sec., Dept for Nat. Savings, 1971. *Recreations:* reading, theatre-going. *Address:* 6 Springbank, Chichester, W Sussex PO19 4BX. *T:* (01243) 776295.

BILLS, David James, CBE 2001; Director General, Forestry Commission, since 1995; *b* 9 Feb. 1948; *s* of Nigel Bills and Sue Bills; *m* 1970, Michele Clutha Ellis; one *s* two *d. Educ:* Australian Nat. Univ. (BSc Forestry); MIT (SMP 1991). MICFor. Research Scientist, Australian Forest Res. Inst., 1970–74; Officer, Dept of Primary Industry, Australian Govt, 1974–77; various posts with Associated Pulp & Paper Mills and North Broken Hill Ltd, 1977–95 (Gen. Manager, Forest Products and Dir, 1986–95). Vice Pres., Australian Forest Develt Inst., 1982–86; Pres., Nat. Assoc. Forest Industries, 1992–95. Warden, Hobart Marine Bd, 1992–95. *Publications:* contribs to various scientific jls and to Australian Forestry Conf. Proc. *Recreations:* sailing, classic cars, ski-ing. *Address:* 17 Lansdowne Crescent, Edinburgh EH12 5EN. *T:* (0131) 538 4926. *Club:* Edinburgh Sports (Edinburgh).

bin YEOP, Tan Sri Abdul Aziz, Al-Haj; PSM (Malaysia); Hon. GCVO 1972; Member, Malaysian Parliament; Partner in legal firm, Aziz and Mazlan, Advocates and Solicitors, Kuala Lumpur, 1966–71, and since 1973; *b* 5 Oct. 1916; *m* 1942, Puan Sri Hamidah Aziz; seven *s* three *d. Educ:* King Edward VII Sch., Perak, Malaysia. Malay Administrative Service, 1937, called to Bar, Lincoln's Inn, 1950; Malayan Civil Service, 1951; First Asst State Sec., Perak 1954; London Univ. (course in Community Development), 1955. Permanent Sec., Min. of Agriculture, 1958–62; Dep. Sec., Malaysian Affairs Div., Prime Minister's Dept, 1962–64; Permanent Sec., Min. of Education, 1964–66. Chm. and Dir of firms in Malaysia, 1966–71. High Comr for Malaysia in London, 1971–73. First Chm., Bd of Governors of BERNAMA (Malaysia's National News Agency), 1967–71; Chairman: Council, Universiti Teknologi, Malaysia, 1974– (Pro-chancellor, 1977–80); Majlis Amanah Raayat, Malaysia, 1975–. *Recreations:* walking, reading, fishing. *Address:* c/o Aziz and Mazlan, Advocates and Solicitors, B-3-3 & B-3-4, 3rd Floor, Megan Phileo Promenade 189, Jalan Tun Razak, 50400 Kuala Lumpur, Malaysia. *T:* (3) 21617967, *Fax:* (3) 21633525; *e-mail:* azizmazlan@hotmail.com.

BINCHY, Maeve, (Mrs Gordon Snell); writer; *b* Dublin, 28 May 1940; *d* of William Binchy and Maureen Blackmore; *m* 1977, Gordon Snell, writer and broadcaster. *Educ:* Holy Child Convent, Killiney, Dublin; University College, Dublin. History teacher in girls' schs, 1960–68; columnist, Irish Times, 1968–. *Publications: novels:* Light a Penny Candle, 1982; Echoes, 1985; Firefly Summer, 1987; Circle of Friends, 1990 (filmed, 1995); Copper Beech, 1992; The Glass Lake, 1994; Evening Class, 1996; Tara Road, 1998; Scarlet Feather, 2000; *short stories:* Central Line, 1978; Victoria Line, 1980; Dublin 4, 1982; The Lilac Bus, 1984; Silver Wedding, 1988. *Recreations:* reading, theatre, very bad bridge, gardening. *Address:* Dalkey, Co. Dublin, Ireland.

BINDMAN, Geoffrey Lionel; Senior Partner, Bindman & Partners, Solicitors, since 1974; *b* 3 Jan. 1933; *s* of Dr Gerald and Lena Bindman; *m* 1961, Lynn Janice Winton; two *s* one *d. Educ:* Newcastle upon Tyne Royal Grammar Sch.; Oriel Coll., Oxford (BCL 1956; MA 1959). Admitted Solicitor, 1959; Teaching Fellow, Northwestern Univ., Ill, 1959–60; Partner, Lawford & Co., 1965–74. Legal adviser: Race Relations Bd, 1966–76; CRE, 1976–83. Visiting Professor of Law: UCLA, 1982; UCL, 1990–. Hon. Pres., Discrimination Law Assoc., 1999–; Chm., Soc. of Labour Lawyers, 1999–. Hon. LLD De Montfort, 2000. Liberty Award for Lifetime Human Rights Achievement, 1999. *Publications:* (jtly) Race and Law, 1972; (ed) South Africa: human rights and the rule of law, 1988. *Recreations:* walking, music, book collecting. *Address:* (office) 275 Gray's Inn Road, WC1X 8QB. *T:* (020) 7833 4433.

BING, Inigo Geoffrey; His Honour Judge Bing; a Circuit Judge, since 2000; *b* 1 April 1944; *s* of late Geoffrey Henry Cecil Bing, QC and Crystal Frances Bing; *m* 1980, Shirley-Anne Holmes (*née* Benka); three step *c. Educ:* St Olave's Grammar Sch., Southwark; Birmingham Univ. (LLB). Called to the Bar, Inner Temple, 1967; practised London and SE Circuit; a District Judge (Magistrates' Courts) (formerly a Metropolitan Stipendiary Magistrate), 1989–2000; a Recorder, 1996–2000. Mem. (Lab) London Borough of Lambeth, 1971–78 (Chm., F and GP Cttee, 1974–78); Co-founder, Lambeth Community Law Centre. Contested Braintree: (SDP) 1983; (SDP/Alliance) 1987. *Publication:* Criminal Procedure and Sentencing in the Magistrates' Court, 1990, 5th edn 1999. *Recreations:* reading, writing, music, travel. *Address:* Snaresbrook Crown Court, Hollybush Hill, E11 1QW; *e-mail:* ibing@lix.compulink.co.uk. *Club:* Reform.

BINGHAM, family name of **Barons Bingham of Cornhill** and **Clanmorris** and of **Earl of Lucan.**

BINGHAM OF CORNHILL, Baron *cr* 1996 (Life Peer); **Thomas Henry Bingham,** Kt 1980; PC 1986; Senior Lord of Appeal in Ordinary, since 2000; *b* 13 Oct. 1933; *o s* of late Dr T. H. Bingham and Dr C. Bingham, Reigate; *m* 1963, Elizabeth, *o d* of late Peter Loxley; two *s* one *d. Educ:* Sedbergh; Balliol Coll., Oxford (MA; Hon. Fellow, 1989).

Royal Ulster Rifles, 1952–54 (2nd Lt); London Irish Rifles (TA) 1954–59. Univ. of Oxford: Gibbs Schol. in Mod. Hist., 1956; 1st cl. Hons, Mod. Hist., 1957. Eldon Law Schol., 1957; Arden Schol., Gray's Inn, 1959; Cert. of Honour, Bar Finals, 1959; called to Bar, Gray's Inn, 1959; Bencher, 1979. Standing Jun. Counsel to Dept of Employment, 1968–72; QC 1972; a Recorder of the Crown Court, 1975–80; Judge of the High Court of Justice, Queen's Bench Div., and Judge of the Commercial Court, 1980–86; a Lord Justice of Appeal, 1986–92; Master of the Rolls, 1992–96; Lord Chief Justice, 1996–2000. Leader, Investigation into the supply of petroleum and petroleum products to Rhodesia, 1977–78; Chm., King's Fund Working Parties into Statutory Registration of Osteopaths and Chiropractors, 1989–93; Inquiry into the Supervision of BCCI, 1991–92; Comr, Interception of Communications Act 1985, 1992–94. Mem., Lord Chancellor's Law Reform Cttee; Chairman: Council of Legal Educn, 1982–86; Adv. Council, Centre for Commercial Law Studies, Queen Mary and Westfield Coll., London Univ., 1989–92; Adv. Council on Public Records, 1992–96; Magna Carta Trust, 1992–96; Royal Commn on Historical Manuscripts, 1994–. President: CIArb, 1991–95; British Records Assoc., 1992–96. Visitor: Balliol Coll., Oxford, 1986–; RPMS, 1989–; UCL, 1992–96; Nuffield Coll., Oxford, 1992–96; London Business Sch., 1992–; Templeton Coll., Oxford, 1996; Darwin Coll., Cambridge, 1996. Governor: Sedbergh, 1978–88; Atlantic Coll., 1984–89. Special Trustee, St Mary's Hosp., 1985–92 (Chm., 1988–92); Member: St Mary's Med. Sch. Delegacy, 1988–92; Council, KCL, 1989–93. Trustee, Pilgrim Trust, 1991–. Pres., Seckford Foundn, 1994–. Fellow, Winchester, 1983–93; Presentation Fellow, KCL, 1992; Fellow, QMW, 1993; Hon. Fellow: Amer. Coll. of Trial Lawyers, 1994; Coll. of Estate Mgt, 1996; UCL, 1997; Hon. Bencher: Inn of Court of NI, 1993; Inner Temple, 1999. Hon. LLD: Birmingham, 1993; Wales, London, 1998; Glamorgan, 1999; Dickinson Sch. of Law (Pennsylvania State Univ.), 2000; Hon. DCL Oxford, 1994; DU Essex, 1997. *Publications:* Chitty on Contracts, (Asst Editor) 22nd edn, 1961; The Business of Judging, 2000. *Address:* House of Lords, SW1A 0PW.

BINGHAM, Lord; George Charles Bingham; *b* 21 Sept. 1967; *s* and *heir* of 7th Earl of Lucan, *qv.* *Educ:* Eton; Trinity Hall, Cambridge.

[In 1999 Lord Bingham applied for a writ of summons to take his seat in the House of Lords as 8th Earl of Lucan but his application was not authorised by the Lord Chancellor.]

BINGHAM, Hon. Charlotte Mary Thérèse; playwright and novelist; *b* 29 June 1942; *d* of 7th Baron Clanmorris (John Bingham) and of Madeleine Mary, *d* of late Clement Ebel; *m* 1964, Terence Brady, *qv*; one *s* one *d.* *Educ:* The Priory, Haywards Heath; Sorbonne. *TV series* with Terence Brady: Boy Meets Girl; Take Three Girls; Upstairs Downstairs; Away From It All; Play for Today; No—Honestly; Yes—Honestly; Pig in the Middle; Thomas and Sarah; The Complete Lack of Charm of the Bourgeoisie; Nanny; Oh Madeline! (USA TV); Father Matthew's Daughter; Forever Green; The Upper Hand; *TV films:* Love With a Perfect Stranger, 1986; Losing Control, 1987; The Seventh Raven, 1987; This Magic Moment, 1988; Riders, 1990; Polo, 1993; *stage:* (contrib.) The Sloane Ranger Revue, 1985; I Wish, I Wish, 1989; (adaptation) The Shell Seekers, 1999. *Publications:* Coronet among the Weeds, 1963; Lucinda, 1965; Coronet among the Grass, 1972; Belgravia, 1983; Country Life, 1984; At Home, 1986; To Hear A Nightingale, 1988; The Business, 1989; In Sunshine or In Shadow, 1991; Stardust, 1992; By Invitation Only, 1993; Nanny, 1993; Change of Heart, 1994 (Romantic Novel of the Year Award, 1995, Romantic Novelists' Assoc.); Debutantes, 1995; The Nightingale Sings, 1996; Grand Affair, 1997; Love Song, 1998; The Kissing Garden, 1999; The Love Knot, 2000; The Blue Note, 2000; The Season, 2001; Summertime, 2001; with Terence Brady: Victoria, 1972; Rose's Story, 1973; Victoria and Company, 1974; Yes—Honestly, 1977. *Recreations:* horses, watching others garden. *Address:* c/o United Authors, Garden Studios, 11–15 Betterton Street, WC2H 9BP. *Club:* Society of Authors.

BINGHAM, Sir (Eardley) Max, Kt 1988; QC (Tas.) 1974; Chairman, Queensland Criminal Justice Commission, 1989–92; *b* 18 March 1927; *s* of Thomas Eardley and Olive Bingham; *m* 1952, Margaret Garrett Jesson; three *s* one *d.* *Educ:* Univ. of Tasmania (LLB (Hons)); Lincoln Coll., Oxford (BCL; Rhodes Schol., 1950); Univ. of California at Berkley (Harkness Commonwealth Fund Fellow, 1963). RANR, 1945–46. Legal practice, and teaching, Univ. of Tasmania, 1953–69. MHA Tasmania, 1969–84; Attorney-General, 1969–72; Leader of the Opposition, 1972–79, Dep. Leader of the Opposition, 1982; Dep. Premier of Tas., 1982–84. Mem., Nat. Crime Authority, 1984–87. Hon. LLD Tasmania, 1998. *Publications:* contribs to jls. *Recreations:* reading, sailing. *Address:* 14 Musgrove Road, Geilston Bay, Tas 7015, Australia. *Clubs:* Tasmanian, Royal Yacht of Tasmania (Hobart).

BINGHAM, Col Jeremy David S.; *see* Smith-Bingham.

BINGHAM, John, CBE 1991; FRS 1977; Plant Breeding International, Cambridge, 1981–91; *b* 19 June 1930; *s* of Thomas Frederick Bingham and Emma Maud Lusher; *m* 1983, Jadwiga Anna Siedlecka; one *s.* Mem. of staff, Plant Breeding Inst. of Cambridge, subseq. Plant Breeding Internat. Cambridge Ltd, 1954–91. Has researched in plant breeding, culminating in production of improved winter wheat varieties for British agriculture. Pres., Royal Norfolk Agricl Assoc., 1991. Hon. FRASE, 1983. Hon. ScD UEA, 1992. Res. Medal, RASE, 1975; Mullard Medal of Royal Society, 1975; Massey Ferguson Nat. Award for Services to UK Agric., 1984. *Recreations:* farming, conservation of wild life. *Address:* Hereward Barn, Church Lane, Mattishall Burgh, Dereham, Norfolk NR20 3QZ. *T:* (01362) 858354.

BINGHAM, Judith Caroline; composer; *b* 21 June 1952; *d* of Jack Bingham and Peggy (*née* MacGowan); *m* 1985, Andrew Petrow. *Educ:* High Storrs Grammar Sch., Sheffield; Royal Acad. of Music (Principal's Prize for Music, 1972; ARAM 1997). Mem., BBC Singers, 1983–95. *Major works:* The Divine Image, 1976; Cocaine Lil, 1977; Flynn, 1979; Chamouni, 1982; Cradle Song of the Blessed Virgin, Scenes From Nature, 1983; Just Before Dawn, 1985; A Cold Spell, 1987; Christmas Past, Christmas Present, 1988; Chartres, 1988; Dove Cottage by Moonlight, 1989; Four Minute Mile, 1991; The Stars Above, The Earth Below, 1991; Unpredictable But Providential, 1991; Irish Tenebrae, The Uttermost, 1992; O Magnum Mysterium, Santa Casa, Beyond Redemption, 1994; Evening Canticles, Epiphany, Salt in the Blood, The Red Hot Nail, 1995; The Mysteries of Adad, The Temple at Karnak, No Discord, 1996; Gleams of a Remoter World, The Waning Moon, Below the Surface Stream, Chapman's Pool, 1997; Missa Brevis, The Clouded Heaven, Bassoon Concerto, Unheimlich, Vorarlberg, Shelley Dreams, 1998; The Shooting Star, Walzerspiele, The Cathedral of Trees, Water Lilies, Otherworld, 1999; Necklace of Light, Annunciation, The Shepherd's Gift, St Bride, Assisted by Angels, These are Our Footsteps, 2000; 50 Shades of Green; The Shadow Side of Joy Finzi, 2001. BBC Young Composer, 1977. *Recreations:* art, books, friends. *Address:* c/o Maecenas Music, 5 Bushey Close, Old Barn Lane, Kenley, Surrey CR8 5AU. *T:* (020) 8660 4766.

BINGHAM, Sir Max; *see* Bingham, Sir E. M.

BINGHAM, Dr Sheila Anne, (Mrs S. H. Rodwell); Deputy Director, Dunn Human Nutrition Unit, MRC, since 1998; *b* 7 March 1947; *d* of Bernard Walter Harrison and Audrey Jean Harrison (*née* Wootton); *m* 1st, 1970, Roger Bingham (marr. diss. 1979); 2nd, 2000, Simon Hunter Rodwell. *Educ:* Loughborough High Sch.; King's Coll., London (BSc 1968; PhD 1983); MA Cantab 1996. Dietitian, University Coll. and St Phillip's Hosps, London, 1969–74; Dunn Human Nutrition Unit, 1976–: MRC Res Officer, 1976–88; MRC Scientific Staff, 1988–95; MRC Special Appt, 1995. Associate Lectr, Faculty of Clinical Medicine, Univ. of Cambridge, 1992–. Vis. Prof., Univ. of Ulster, 1994–. Mem., Cttee on Med. Aspects of Food Policy, 1991–2000. FRSoc Med 1993. *Publications:* Dictionary of Nutrition, 1977; Everyman Companion to Food and Nutrition, 1987; numerous articles in learned jls. *Recreations:* (in descending order of competence) sailing, dog training, tennis, cello. *Address:* 6 Pearces Yard, Grantchester, Cambridge CB3 9NZ. *T:* (01223) 845351.

BINGLEY, Juliet Martin, (Lady Bingley), MBE 1991; Research Social Worker, City Corporation Social Services, based at St Mark's Hospital, EC1, 1990–96 (Senior Social Worker, 1973–90); *b* 18 July 1925; *d* of Mary Kate Vick and Reginald Vick, OBE, MCh, FRCS; *m* 1948, Adm. Sir Alexander Noel Campbell Bingley, GCB, OBE (*d* 1972); one *s* two *d.* *Educ:* King Alfred School, Hampstead; London Sch. of Economics. Associated Mem., Inst. of Medical Social Workers. Social Worker, St Bartholomew's Hosp., 1945–48. Chairman: Nat. Assoc. of Mental Health, 1979–84; Good Practices in Mental Health, 1989–93; Vice-Chm., Nat. Assoc. for Colitis and Crohn's Disease, 1989–97; Vice Pres., Mind, 1996–. Counsellor, Dr Aubrey and Partners, Welwyn, Herts, 1990–. CStJ 1962. Companion of Honour, Republic of Malta, 1976. *Recreations:* music, gardening, reading, theatre, moving furniture, collecting Staffordshire figures, lawn mowing. *Address:* Hoddesdonbury Farm, Hoddesdon, Herts EN11 8LS. *T:* (01992) 463238.

BINMORE, Prof. Kenneth George, CBE 2001; PhD; FBA 1995; Professor of Economics, University College London, since 1991; *b* 27 Sept. 1940; *s* of Ernest George Binmore and Maud Alice (*née* Holland); *m* 1968, Josephine Ann Lee; two *s* two *d.* *Educ:* Imperial Coll., London (BSc; PhD 1964). Lectr, Reader and Prof. of Maths, LSE, 1969–88; Prof. of Econs, LSE and Univ. of Michigan, 1988–93; Dir, ESRC Centre for Econ. Learning and Social Evolution, 1994–. *Publications:* Mathematical Analysis, 1977, 2nd edn 1982; Logic, Sets and Numbers, 1980; Topological Ideas, 1981; Calculus, 1982; Economic Organizations as Games, 1986; Economics of Bargaining, 1986; Essays on the Foundations of Game Theory, 1991; Fun and Games, 1992; Frontiers of Game Theory, 1993; Game Theory and the Social Contract: vol. I, Playing Fair, 1994; vol. II, Just Playing, 1998; papers. *Recreation:* philosophy. *Address:* Newmills, Whitebrook, Monmouth, NP25 4TY. *T:* (01600) 860691; (office) (020) 7504 5864; (home) (020) 7700 5133.

BINNEY, Prof. James Jeffrey, DPhil; FRS 2000; FRAS, FInstP; Professor of Physics, University of Oxford, since 1996; Fellow and Tutor in Physics, Merton College, Oxford, since 1981; *b* 12 April 1950; *s* of Harry Augustus Roy Binney and Barbara Binney (*née* Poole); *m* 1993, Lucy Elliot Buckingham; one *s* one *d.* *Educ:* King's Coll. Sch., Wimbledon; Churchill Coll., Cambridge (BA 1971, MA 1975); Albert Ludwigs Univ., Freiburg im Breisgau; Christ Church and Magdalen Coll., Oxford (DPhil 1976). Fellow, Magdalen Coll., Oxford, 1975–79; Vis. Asst Prof., Princeton Univ., 1979–81; Lectr in Theoretical Physics, 1981–90, Reader, 1990–96, Oxford Univ. Lindemann Fellow, Princeton Univ., 1975–76; Fairchild Dist. Schol., CIT, 1983–84; Visiting Fellow: Univ. of Arizona, 1989; Princeton Univ., 1992; ANU, 1995. FRAS 1973. Maxwell Medal and Prize, Inst. Physics, 1986. *Publications:* jointly: Galactic Astronomy: structure and kinematics, 1981; Galactic Dynamics, 1987; PICK for Humans, 1990; The Theory of Critical Phenomena, 1992; Galactic Astronomy, 1998. *Recreations:* carpentry, stone and metalwork, walking. *Address:* Department of Theoretical Physics, University of Oxford, Keble Road, Oxford OX1 3NP. *T:* (01865) 273979.

BINNEY, Marcus Hugh Crofton, OBE 1983; FSA; writer, journalist, conservationist; Founder, 1975, and President, since 1984, Save Britain's Heritage (Chairman, 1975–84); *b* 21 Sept. 1944; *s* of late Lt-Col Francis Crofton Simms, MC and of Sonia, *d* of Rear-Adm. Sir William Marcus Charles Beresford-Whyte, KCB, CMG (she *m* 2nd, Sir George Binney, DSO); *m* 1st, 1966, Hon. Sara Anne Vanneck (marr. diss. 1976), *e d* of 6th Baron Huntingfield; 2nd, 1981, Anne Carolyn, *d* of Dr T. H. Hills, Merstham, Surrey; two *s.* *Educ:* Magdalene Coll., Cambridge (BA 1966). Architectural writer, 1968–77, Architectural Editor, 1977–84, Editor, 1984–86, Country Life; Ed., Landscape, 1987–88; envmt correspondent, Harpers & Queen, 1989–90; architecture correspondent, The Times, 1991–. Sec., UK Cttee, Internat. Council on Monuments and Sites, 1972–81; Director: Rly Heritage Trust, 1985–; HMS Warrior; Chm., Save Europe's Heritage, 1995–; President: Friends of City Churches, 1998– (Chm., 1995–98); Save Jersey's Heritage, 1990–. Television series: Co-Presenter, Great Houses of Europe, 1993, 1996, 1997. Exhibitions: (joint organizer) The Destruction of the Country House, V&A Mus., 1974; Change and Decay: the future of our churches, V&A Mus., 1977. FSA 1989. London Conservation Medal, 1985. *Publications:* (with Peter Burman): Change and Decay: the future of our churches, 1977; Chapels and Churches: who cares?, 1977; (with Max Hanna) Preservation Pays, 1978; (ed jtly) Railway Architecture, 1979; (ed jtly) Satanic Mills, 1979; (ed jtly) Our Past Before Us, 1981; (with Kit Martin) The Country House: to be or not to be, 1982; (with Max Hanna) Preserve and Prosper, 1983; The Architecture of Sir Robert Taylor, 1984; Our Vanishing Heritage, 1984; Country Manors of Portugal, 1987; (jtly) Bright Futures: the reuse of industrial buildings, 1990; Palace on the River, 1991; (with M. Watson-Smyth) The Save Action Guide, 1991; Châteaux of the Loire, 1992; (with R. Runciman) Glyndebourne: building a vision, 1994; The Châteaux of France: photographs by Frederick Evans 1906–7, 1994; Railway Architecture: the way ahead, 1995; (with Patrick Bowe) Houses and Gardens of Portugal, 1998; Town Houses: 800 years of evolution and innovation in urban design, 1998; Airport Builders, 1999; The Ritz Hotel, London, 1999; (with Graham Byfield) London Sketchbook: a city observed, 2001. *Address:* Domaine des Vaux, St Lawrence, Jersey JE3 1JG. *T:* (01534) 864424, *Fax:* (01534) 862612; *e-mail:* marcusbinney@psilink.co.uk.

BINNIE, David Stark, OBE 1979; General Manager, British Rail, London Midland Region, 1977–80; *b* 2 June 1922; *s* of Walter Archibald Binnie and Helen (*née* Baxter), Bonkle, Lanarkshire; *m* 1947, Leslie Archibald; one *s* one *d.* *Educ:* Wishaw High School. British Railways: Gen. and Signalling Asst to Gen. Manager Scottish Region, 1955; Asst District Operating Supt 1961, District Operating Supt 1963, Glasgow North; Divisional Movements Manager, Glasgow Div., 1965; Movements Manager, Scottish Region, 1967; Divisional Manager, SE Div., Southern Region, 1969; Asst Gen. Manager, Southern Region, 1970, Gen. Manager, 1972; Exec. Dir, Freight, BR Board, 1974–76. Lt-Col Engineer and Railway Staff Corps, RE (T&AVR). OStJ. *Recreation:* Dartmoor and Highland life. *Address:* Above Ways, Lower Knowle Road, Lustleigh, Devon TQ13 9TR. *T:* (01647) 277386.

BINNIE, Frank Hugh, FCSD; Chairman and Chief Executive, Binnie International, since 1998; *b* 1 March 1950; *s* of Dr Hugh Lawson Binnie and Isobel May Van Dijk (*née* Nairn); *m* 1996, Fiona Margaret Maclean Nicolson (*née* Hart); one *s* one *d*; and three *s* by previous marriage. *Educ:* Loughborough GS. FCSD 1992. Mgt trainee, Corah Textiles, Leicester, 1970–73; Ops Manager, Floreal Knitwear, Mauritius, 1973–76; Sales Manager,

Kemptons Knitwear, Leicester, 1976–79; Gen. Manager, Texport Unilever, 1979–82; Manager, Kilspindie Knitwear, Haddington, 1982–85; Dir and Co. Sec., Midlothian Enterprise, 1985–88; Man. Dir, Perkins, Hodgkinson & Gillibrand, 1988–90; Chief Exec., Design Council, Scotland, then Scottish Design, 1990–96. Chief Exec., Caledonian Foundn, 1996–97; Chief Executive Officer: Internet Soc. Scotland, 1998–; Scotland IS, 2000–; Executive Chairman: Scottish Internet Exchange, 1999–; Scotnom Ltd, 2000–; Internat. Soc. Foundn, 2001–; Broadband Scotland Ltd, 2001–; Chm., EBusiness Scotland Ltd, 1999–; Co-Founder, Ecommerce Exchange (Scotland) Ltd, 1999–; Sen. Consultant, Career Associates, 1998–. Vis. Prof., Strathclyde Univ., 1990–96; External Assessor: MBA, Westminster Univ., 1995–97; Design Mgt, De Montfort Univ., 1996–99. Chm., Sector Gp for Design, Scotvec, 1995–96. Mem. Exec. Council, Scottish Council of Develt and Industry. Formerly Mem. Bd, 1996 UK City of Architecture and Design. FRSA 1992; MInstD. *Recreations:* sailing, running, chess, classic cars. *Address:* (office) 150 St Vincent Street, Glasgow G2 5NE. *T:* (0141) 943 0859; *e-mail:* frankbinnie@msn.com.

BINNIG, Prof. Dr Gerd Karl; IBM Fellow, since 1986; Honorary Professor of Physics, University of Munich, since 1987; *b* 20 July 1947; *m* 1969, Lore; one *s* one *d.* *Educ:* J. W. Goethe Univ., Frankfurt/M (DipPhys; PhD). Research staff mem., IBM Zurich Res. Lab., in fields of superconductivity of semiconductors and scanning tunneling microscopy, 1978–, Gp Leader 1984–; IBM Almaden Res. Center, San José, and collab. with Stanford Univ., 1985–86; Vis. Prof., Stanford Univ., 1985–86. Member: Technology Council, IBM Acad., 1989–92; Supervisory Bd, Mercedes Automobil Holding AG, 1989–95. For. Associate Mem., Acad. of Scis, Washington, 1987. Hon. FRMS 1988. Scanning Tunneling Microscopy awards: Physics Prize, German Phys. Soc., 1982; Otto Klung Prize, 1983; (jtly) King Faisal Internat. Prize for Science and Hewlett Packard Europhysics Prize, 1984; (jtly) Nobel Prize in Physics, 1986; Elliot Cresson Medal, Franklin Inst., Philadelphia, 1987; Minnie Rosen Award, Ross Univ., NY, 1988. Grosses Verdienstkreuz mit Stern und Schulterband des Verdienstordens (FRG), 1987; Bayenischer Verdienstorden, 1992. *Recreations:* music, tennis, soccer, golf. *Address:* IBM Research Laboratory, Saeumerstrasse 4, 8803 Rueschlikon, Switzerland. *T:* (1) 7248111.

BINNING, Lord; George Edmund Baldred Baillie-Hamilton; *b* 27 Dec. 1985; *s* and *heir* of Earl of Haddington, *qv.*

BINNING, Kenneth George Henry, CMG 1976; consultant, public policy and international regulation, since 1992; *b* 5 Jan. 1928; *o s* of late Henry and Hilda Binning; *m* 1953, Pamela Dorothy, *o d* of A. E. and D. G. Pronger; three *s* one *d.* *Educ:* Bristol Grammar Sch.; Balliol Coll., Oxford. Joined Home Civil Service, 1950; Nat. Service, 1950–52; HM Treasury, 1952–58; Private Sec. to Financial Sec., 1956–57; AEA, 1958–65; seconded to Min. of Technology, 1965; rejoined Civil Service, 1968; Dir-Gen. Concorde, 1972–76 and Under-Sec., DTI later Dept of Industry, 1972–83. Mem., BSC, 1980–83; Director of Government Relations. NEI Internat. subseq. NEI plc, 1983–90; Rolls Royce plc, 1991–93; Dir, 1993–97, Consultant, 1992–99, Public Policy Unit Ltd. *Recreations:* music, gardening. *Address:* 12 Kemerton Road, Beckenham, Kent BR3 6NJ. *T:* (020) 8650 0273.

BINNS, David John, CBE 1989; Trust Board Secretary, Halton General Hospital NHS Trust, 1995–99 (non-executive Director, 1992–94); *b* 12 April 1929; *s* of Henry Norman Binns, OBE and Ivy Mary Binns; *m* 1957, Jean Margaret Evans; one *s* (one *d* decd). *Educ:* Fleetwood Grammar Sch.; Rossall Sch.; Sheffield Univ. LLB 1951. Solicitor 1954. Articled Clerk, Sheffield City Council, 1949; Asst Solicitor, Warrington County Borough Council, 1954; Dep. Town Clerk, Warrington County Borough Council, 1958; General Manager: Warrington Develt Corp., 1969–81; Warrington and Runcorn Develt Corp., 1981–89. Mem., Warrington DHA, 1990–92. *Recreations:* walking, gardening, music. *Address:* 4 Cedarways, Appleton, Warrington, Cheshire WA4 5EW. *T:* (01925) 262169. *Club:* Warrington (Warrington).

BINNS, Jacqueline Sukie, (Mrs W. A. T. Hills); artist/embroiderer, since 1986; *b* 24 May 1963; *d* of Dennis Binns and Eileen (*née* Andrews); *m* 1986, Warwick Alan Theodore Hills. *Educ:* Goldsmiths' Coll., London (BA Textiles 1986). Exhibitions include: Southwark Cathedral, Leicester Mus., Salisbury Cathedral, 1978; Gawthorpe Hall, Peterborough Cathedral, 1988; St Alban's Abbey, 1989, 1992; St Paul's Cathedral, 1990; Royal Sch. of Needlework, 1993; Sheffield Cath., Goldsmiths' Coll., 1997; Shrewsbury Abbey, 1998; Wimpole Hall, Cambridge, Winchester Cath., 1999; Guildford Cath., Portsmouth Cath., Alexandra Palace, 2000; works of art in private collections and cathedrals and churches in America, Australia, Europe and UK. *Recreations:* walking, the arts, costume. *Address:* 1 Cargill Road, Earlsfield, SW18 3EF. *T:* (020) 8874 0895; *e-mail:* jb@jacquiebinns.com.

BINNS, Rev. John Richard, PhD; Vicar, St Mary the Great with St Michael, Cambridge, since 1994; *b* 10 Jan. 1951. *Educ:* St John's Coll., Cambridge (MA 1976); King's Coll., London (PhD 1989); Coll. of the Resurrection, Mirfield. Ordained deacon, 1976, priest, 1977; Assistant Curate: Holy Trinity, Clapham, 1976–78; Clapham Old Town, 1978–80; Team Vicar, Mortlake with E Sheen, 1980–87; Vicar, Holy Trinity, Upper Tooting, 1987–94. *Publications:* Cyril of Scythopolis: lives of the Monks of Palestine, 1991; Ascetics and Ambassadors of Christ, 1994; Great St Mary's, Cambridge's University Church, 2000. *Address:* Great St Mary's Vicarage, 39 Madingley Road, Cambridge CB3 0EL. *T:* (01223) 355285.

BINNS, Malcolm; concert pianist; *b* 29 Jan. 1936; *s* of Douglas and May Binns. *Educ:* Bradford Grammar Sch.; Royal Coll. of Music (ARCM, Chappell Gold Medal, Medal of Worshipful Co. of Musicians). London début, 1957; Henry Wood Proms début, 1960; Royal Festival Hall début, 1961; Festival Hall appearances in London Philharmonic Orchestra International series, 1969–; toured with Scottish Nat. Orch., 1989; concerts at Aldeburgh, Leeds, Three Choirs (1975), Bath and Canterbury Festivals; regular appearances at Promenade concerts and broadcasts for BBC Radio; celebrated 60th birthday with series of concerts, 1996; series of recitals for BBC linking Clementi and Beethoven, 1997. First complete recording of Beethoven piano sonatas on original instruments, 1980; première recordings of Sir William Sterndale Bennett's piano concertos with London Philharmonic and Philharmonia Orchs, 1990; première recording of Stanford's re-discovered Third Piano Concerto, with RPO, 1996. *Recreation:* collecting antique gramophone records. *Address:* 233 Court Road, Orpington, Kent BR6 9BY. *T:* (01689) 831056.

BINNS, Hon. Patrick George; Premier and President of Executive Council, Prince Edward Island, Canada, since 1996; MLA (PC) District 5, Murray River-Gaspereaux, since 1996; *b* Saskatchewan, 8 Oct. 1948; *s* of Stan and Phillis Binns; *m* 1971, Carol MacMillan; three *s* one *d.* *Educ:* Univ. of Alberta (BA, MA 1971). Rural Develt Council, PEI, 1974–78; MLA (PC) 4th Kings, PEI, 1978–84; Minister: of Municipal Affairs, Labour, and Envmt, 1979–80; of Community Affairs, 1980–82; of Fisheries and of Industry, 1982–84; MP (PC) Cardigan, 1984–88; Parly Sec. to Minister of Fisheries and Oceans, 1984–88; Leader, PC Party, PEI, 1996–; Minister responsible for Intergovtl Affairs, 1996–. President: Island Bean Ltd, 1988–96; Pat Binns & Associates, 1988–96. Silver Jubilee Medal, 1977. *Recreations:* hockey, ski-ing. *Address:* (office) PO Box 2000, 95 Rochford Street, 5th Floor, Charlottetown, PE C1A 7N8, Canada. *T:* (902) 3684400; (home) Hopefield, Murray River RR#4, PE C0A 1W0, Canada. *T:* (902) 9622196.

BINNS, Susan May; Director, Internal Market and Financial Services, European Commission, since 1995; *b* 22 April 1948; *d* of Jack and Mollie Binns. *Educ:* Harrogate Coll.; LSE (BSc Econ Internat. Relations). HM Diplomatic Service, 1968; served FCO and Brussels; New Delhi, 1978–80; Cabinet of Ivor Richard, EC Member, Brussels, 1981–84; Counsellor, EC Delegations: Washington, 1985–88; Belgrade, 1988; Dep. Chef de Cabinet of Bruce Millan, EC Mem. resp. for regl policies, 1989–91, Chef de Cabinet, 1991–95. *Recreation:* tennis. *Address:* European Commission, 200 rue de la Loi, 1049 Brussels, Belgium. *T:* (2) 2963285.

BINTLEY, David Julian, CBE, 2001; choreographer; Director, Birmingham Royal Ballet, since 1995; *b* 17 Sept. 1957; *s* of David Bintley and Glenys Bintley (*née* Ellinthorpe); *m* 1981, Jennifer Catherine Ursula Mills; two *s.* *Educ:* Holme Valley Grammar School. Royal Ballet School, 1974; Sadler's Wells Royal Ballet, 1976; first professional choreography, The Outsider, 1978; first three act ballet, The Swan of Tuonela, 1982; Company Choreographer, 1983–85, Resident Choreographer, 1985–86, Sadler's Wells Royal Ballet; Resident Choreographer and Principal Dancer, Royal Ballet, 1986–93. Ballets created include: Carmina Burana, 1995; Far From the Madding Crowd, 1996; The Nutcracker Sweeties; The Protecting Veil, 1998; The Shakespeare Suite; Arthur, Part One, 2000; Arthur, Part Two, 2001; The Seasons, 2001. Evening Standard Award for Ballet, for Choros and Consort Lessons, both 1983; Laurence Olivier Award for Petrushka, 1984; Manchester Evening News Award for Dance, for Still Life at the Penguin Café, 1987, for Edward II, 1998. *Address:* Birmingham Royal Ballet, Birmingham Hippodrome, Thorp Street, Birmingham B5 4AU.

BIOBAKU, Dr Saburi Oladeni, CMG 1961; MA, PhD; Research historian and management consultant; Research Professor and Director, Institute of African Studies, University of Ibadan, 1976–83; *b* 16 June 1918; *s* of late Chief S. O. Biobaku, Aré of Iddo, Abeokuta; *m* 1949, Muhabat Folasade, *d* of Alhaji L. B. Agusto, barrister-at-law, Lagos; one *s.* *Educ:* Govt Coll., Ibadan; Higher Coll., Yaba; University Coll., Exeter; Trinity Coll., Cambridge. BA London, 1945; BA Cantab, 1947, MA 1951; PhD London, 1951. Education Officer, Nigeria, 1947–53; Registrar, University Coll., Ibadan, 1953–57; Dir, Yoruba Historical Research Scheme, 1956–; Sec. to Premier and Executive Council, Western Nigeria, 1957–61; Pro-Vice-Chancellor, Univ. of Ife, Nigeria, 1961–65; Vice-Chancellor, Univ. of Lagos, 1965–72; Chairman, Management Consultant Services Ltd, Lagos, 1972–76, 1983–. Hon. DLitt. Created: Aré of Iddo, Abeokuta, 1958; Agbakin of Igbore, 1972; Maye of Ife, 1980; Baapitan of Egbaland, 1980. *Publications:* The Origin of the Yoruba, 1955; The Egba and Their Neighbours, 1842–1872, 1957; Living Cultures of Nigeria, 1977; When We Were Young, 1993; A Window on Nigeria, 1996; When We Were No Longer Young, 1999; contribs to Africa, jl of Nigerian Historical Soc., Odu (Joint Ed.), etc. *Recreations:* soccer, tennis, badminton, swimming, walking. *Address:* PO Box 7741, Lagos, Nigeria. *T:* (home) (1) 4961430. *Clubs:* Metropolitan (Lagos); Dining (Ibadan).

BIRAN, Yoav; Ambassador; Senior Deputy Director General, with special responsibility for the Middle East and peace process, Ministry of Foreign Affairs, Jerusalem, since 1998 (Deputy Director General, 1993–98); *b* 17 July 1939; *s* of Michael and Rachel Barsky; *m* (marr. diss.); one *s* two *d;* *m* 1991, Mrs Jane Moonman. *Educ:* Hebrew University of Jerusalem (post grad. studies, history, internat. relns). Joined Min. of For. Affairs, Jerusalem, 1963; ME and Afr. Depts, 1963–65; Second Sec., Ethiopia, 1965–67; First Sec., Uganda, 1967–70; Prin. Asst to Asst Dir-Gen. in charge of World Jewry and Inf., 1970–72, Dep. Dir of Dir-Gen.'s Cabinet, 1972–74, Min. of For. Affairs; Mem., Israel Delegn to Geneva Peace Conf., Dec. 1973; Dir of Dept, Center for Res. and Policy Planning, Min. of For. Affairs, 1975–77; Minister Plenipotentiary, 1977–82, Chargé d'Affaires, 1982–83, London; elected Distinguished Mem., Israel For. Service and of Israel Civil Service, 1983; Asst Dir Gen., Admin, 1984–87, N Amer. and Disarmament Affairs, 1987–88, FO, Jerusalem; Ambassador to UK, 1988–93. *Recreations:* theatre, collecting antiquarian maps and books. *Address:* Ministry of Foreign Affairs, Hakirya, Romema, Jerusalem 91950, Israel.

BIRCH, Prof. Anthony Harold, PhD; FRSC 1988; Professor of Political Science, University of Victoria, British Columbia, 1977–89, now Emeritus; *b* 17 Feb. 1924; *o s* of late Frederick Harold Birch and Rosalind Dorothy Birch; *m* 1953, Dorothy Madeleine Overton, Bayport, New York; one *s* one *d.* *Educ:* The William Ellis Sch.; University Coll., Nottingham; London Sch. of Economics. BSc (Econ) London, with 1st cl. hons, 1945; PhD London, 1951. Asst Principal, Board of Trade, 1945–47; University of Manchester: Asst Lectr in Govt, 1947–51; Lectr, 1951–58; Senior Lectr in Government, 1958–61; Prof. of Political Studies, Univ. of Hull, 1961–70; Prof. of Political Sci., Exeter Univ., 1970–77. Commonwealth Fund Fellow at Harvard Univ. and University of Chicago, 1951–52. Consultant to Government of Western Region of Nigeria, 1956–58. Vis. Prof. Tufts Univ., 1968; Vis. Fellow, ANU, 1987. Vice-Pres., Internat. Political Sci. Assoc., 1976–79. *Publications:* Federalism, Finance and Social Legislation, 1955; Small-Town Politics, 1959; Representative and Responsible Government, 1964; The British System of Government, 1967, 10th edn 1998; Representation, 1971; Political Integration and Disintegration in the British Isles, 1977; Nationalism and National Integration, 1989; The Concepts and Theories of Modern Democracy, 1993, 2nd edn 2001; articles in various journals. *Recreations:* reading, music, bridge, camping. *Address:* 1901 Fairfield Road, Victoria, BC V8S 1H2, Canada.

BIRCH, Prof. Bryan John, FRS 1972; Professor of Arithmetic, University of Oxford, 1985–98; Fellow of Brasenose College, Oxford, 1966–98; *b* 25 Sept. 1931; *s* of Arthur Jack and Mary Edith Birch; *m* 1961, Gina Margaret Christ; two *s* one *d.* *Educ:* Shrewsbury Sch.; Trinity Coll., Cambridge (MA, PhD). Harkness Fellow, Princeton, 1957–58; Fellow: Trinity Coll., Cambridge, 1956–60; Churchill Coll., Cambridge, 1960–62; Sen. Lectr, later Reader, Univ. of Manchester, 1962–65; Reader in Mathematics, Univ. of Oxford, 1966–85. Deleg., OUP, 1988–98. Ed., Proc. London Math. Soc., 2001–. *Publications:* articles in learned jls, mainly on number theory; various editorships. *Recreations:* gardening (theoretical), opera, watching marmots. *Address:* Green Cottage, Boars Hill, Oxford OX1 5DQ. *T:* (01865) 735367; Mathematical Institute, 25–29 St Giles, Oxford. *T:* (01865) 273525; *e-mail:* birch@maths.ox.ac.uk.

BIRCH, Dennis Arthur, CBE 1977; DL; Councillor, West Midlands County Council, 1974–77; *b* 11 Feb. 1925; *s* of George Howard and Leah Birch; *m* 1948, Mary Therese Lyons; one *d.* *Educ:* Wolverhampton Municipal Grammar Sch. Wolverhampton County Borough Council: elected, 1952; served, 1952–74; Alderman, 1970–73; Mayor, 1973–74; Leader, 1967–73. Elected (following Local Govt reorganisation) Chm. West Midlands CC, 1974–76. DL West Midlands, 1979. *Address:* 3 Tern Close, Wolverhampton Road East, Wolverhampton WV4 6AU. *T:* (01902) 883837.

BIRCH, Frank Stanley Heath; public sector consultant; Commander, London District, St John Ambulance, since 1992 (Deputy Commander, 1990–92); *b* 8 Feb. 1939; *s* of late John Stanley Birch, CEng and Phyllis Edna Birch (*née* Heath), BA; *m* 1963, Diana Jacqueline Davies, BA; one *d*. *Educ:* Weston-super-Mare Grammar Sch. for Boys; Univ. of Wales (BA); Univ. of Birmingham (Inst. of Local Govt Studies). IPFA; MBIM. Entered local govt service, 1962; various appts, City Treasurer and Controller's Dept, Cardiff, 1962–69; Chief Internal Auditor, Dudley, 1969–73; Asst County Treasurer, 1973–74, Asst Chief Exec., 1974–76, W Midlands CC; Chief Exec., Lewisham, 1976–82; Town Clerk and Chief Exec., Croydon, 1982–90. Hon. Clerk, Gen. Purposes Cttee, 1982–90, Principal Grants Advr, 1983–86, London Boroughs Assoc.; Sec., London Co-ordinating Cttee, 1985–86. Dir, Croydon Business Venture Ltd, 1983–92. Chm., Lifecare NHS Trust, 1994–98. Freeman, City of London, 1980. FRSA 1980. KStJ 1997 (OStJ 1988; CStJ 1992; Mem. Council, London, 1986–); Vice-Pres., London SJAB, 1988–90. *Publications:* various articles on public admin and local govt management. *Recreations:* music, walking, caravanning, the countryside. *Address:* St John Ambulance, London (Prince of Wales's) District, Edwina Mountbatten House, 63 York Street, W1H 1PS.

BIRCH, Sir John (Allan), KCVO 1993; CMG 1987; HM Diplomatic Service, retired; Director, British Association for Central and Eastern Europe, since 1995; *b* 24 May 1935; *s* of late C. Allan Birch, MD, FRCP; *m* 1960, Primula Haselden; three *s* one *d*. *Educ:* Leighton Park Sch.; Corpus Christi Coll., Cambridge (MA). Served HM Forces, Middlesex Regt, 1954–56. Joined HM Foreign Service, 1959; served: Paris, 1960–63; Singapore, 1963–64; Bucharest, 1965–68; Geneva, 1968–70; Kabul, 1973–76; Royal Coll. of Defence Studies, 1977; Comprehensive Test Ban Treaty Negotiations, Geneva, 1977–80; Counsellor, Budapest, 1980–83; Hd of East European Dept, FCO, 1983–86; Ambassador and Dep. Perm. Rep. to UN, NY, 1986–89; Ambassador to Hungary, 1989–95. Dir, Schroder Emerging Countries Fund plc, 1996–. Mem. Council: SSEES, 1995–99; RIIA, 1997–; UCL, 1999–. Trustee, Wytham Hall, 1999–. *Recreations:* tennis, ski-ing, shooting, carpentry. *Address:* 185 Emery Hill Street, SW1P 1PD. *Club:* Athenæum.

BIRCH, John Anthony, MA, DMus; FRCM, FRCO(CHM), LRAM; Curator-Organist, Royal Albert Hall, since 1984; Professor, Royal College of Music, 1959–97, now Consultant; Organist: to the Royal Choral Society, since 1966; of the Royal Philharmonic Orchestra, since 1983; *b* 9 July 1929; *s* of late Charles Aylmer Birch and Mabel (*née* Greenwood), Leek, Staffs; unmarried. *Educ:* Trent Coll.; Royal Coll. of Music (ARCM; Pitcher Schol. of RCO). Nat. Service, Royal Corps of Signals, 1949–50. Organist and Choirmaster, St Thomas's Church, Regent Street, London, 1950–53; Accompanist to St Michael's Singers, 1952–58; Organist and Choirmaster, All Saints Church, Margaret Street, London, 1953–58; Sub-Organist, HM Chapels Royal, 1957–58; Organist and Master of the Choristers, Chichester Cathedral, 1958–80; Organist and Dir of Choir, Temple Church, 1982–97. With the Cathedral Organists of Salisbury and Winchester re-established the Southern Cathedrals Festival, 1960; Musical Advr, Chichester Festival Theatre, 1962–80; Choirmaster, Bishop Otter Coll., Chichester, 1963–69. Rep., 1950–66, and Man. Dir, 1966–73, C. A. Birch Ltd, Staffs. Accompanist, Royal Choral Soc., 1965–70; Examr to Associated Bd, Royal Schs of Music, 1958–77; a Gen. Ed., Novello & Co., 1967–77. Univ. Organist, 1967–94 and Vis. Lectr in Music, 1971–83, Univ. of Sussex. Special Comr, Royal Sch. of Church Music; Royal College of Organists: Mem. Council, 1964–; Pres., 1984–86; Hon. Treas., 1997–. Fellow, Corp. of SS Mary and Nicolas (Woodard Schs), 1973–; Governor: Hurstpierpoint Coll., 1974–93; St Catherine's, Bramley, 1981–89; Mem. Council, Corp. of Cranleigh and Bramley Schs, 1990. Trustee, Ouseley Trust. Has made concert appearances in France, Belgium, Italy, Germany, Switzerland, Netherlands, Spain, Portugal, Scandinavia and Far East; recital tours: Canada and US, 1966 and 1967, Australia and NZ, 1969, S Africa, 1978. FRSA. Hon. Bencher, Middle Temple, 1998. Freeman, City of London, 1991. DMus Lambeth, 1989; Hon. MA Sussex, 1971. *Address:* Fielding House, The Close, Salisbury, Wilts SP1 2EB. *T:* (01722) 412458, *Fax:* (01722) 412368. *Clubs:* Garrick; New (Edinburgh).

BIRCH, Lola; *see* Young, L.

BIRCH, Peter Gibbs, CBE 1992; Chairman: Land Securities PLC, since 1998; Kensington Group plc, since 2000; UCTX Ltd, since 2001; Chairman, Legal Services Commission, since 2000; *b* 4 Dec. 1937; *m* 1962, Gillian (*née* Benge); three *s* one *d*. *Educ:* Allhallows Sch., Devon. Royal West Kent Regt, seconded to Jamaica Regt, 1957–58 (2nd Lieut). Nestlé Co., UK, Singapore and Malaysia, 1958–65; Sales and Mkting Manager, Gillette, 1965; Gen. Sales Manager, Gillette Australia, 1969; Man. Dir, Gillette, NZ, 1971; Gen. Manager, Gillette, SE Asia (based Singapore), 1973; Gp Gen. Manager, Gillette, Africa, ME, Eastern Europe, 1975; Man. Dir, Gillette UK, 1981; Dir and Chief Exec., Abbey Nat. Building Soc., then Abbey Nat. plc, 1984–98. Chm., Trinity plc, 1998–99; Sen. non-exec. Dir, Trinity Mirror plc, 1999–; non-executive Director: Hoskyns Gp, 1988–93; Argos, 1990–98; Scottish Mutual Assurance, 1992–98; N. M. Rothschild & Sons, 1998–; Dalgety, 1993–98; PIC, 1998–2000; Coca-Cola Beverages, 1998–2000; Travellers Exchange Corp. Ltd, 1999–. Chm., Council of Mortgage Lenders, 1991–92. FCBSI. Pres., Middlesex Young People's (formerly Middlesex Assoc. of Boys') Clubs, 1988–. *Recreations:* active holidays, swimming. *Address:* N. M. Rothschild & Sons, New Court, St Swithin's Lane, EC4P 4DU. *T:* (020) 7280 5000.

BIRCH, Robert Edward Thomas, CBE 1979; Director General, Federation Against Copyright Theft, 1982–85; *b* 9 May 1917; *s* of late Robert Birch and Edith Birch; *m* 1946, Laura Pia Busini; two *d*. *Educ:* Dulwich Coll. Served RA, 1940–46; Africa, Italy, NW Europe; Major. Admitted solicitor, 1942; joined Solicitors' Dept, New Scotland Yard, 1946; Dep. Solicitor, 1968; Solicitor, 1976–82. *Recreations:* swimming, travel.

BIRCH, Robin Arthur, CB 1995; DL; voluntary worker; civil servant, retired; *b* 12 Oct. 1939; *s* of late Arthur and Olive Birch; *m* 1962, Jane Marion Irvine Sturdy; two *s*. *Educ:* King Henry VIII Sch., Coventry; Christ Church, Oxford (Marjoribanks Scholar, 1957; Craven Scholar, 1959; MA). Entered Min. of Health as Asst Principal, 1961; Private Sec. to Charles Loughlin, MP (Parly Sec.), 1965–66; Principal, 1966; seconded to: Interdeptl Social Work Gp, 1969–70; Home Office (Community Develt Project), 1970–72; Asst Sec., DHSS, 1973; Chm., Working Party on Manpower and Trng for Social Services, 1974–76 (Report, 1976); Principal Private Sec. to Rt Hon. Norman St John-Stevas, MP (Leader of the House of Commons), 1980–81; Under Sec., DHSS, 1982; Asst Auditor Gen., Nat. Audit Office, 1984–86, on secondment; Dir, Regl Orgn, 1988–90; Dep. Sec. (Policy), 1990–95, DSS. Hon. Sec., Friends of Christ Church Cathedral, Oxford, 1978–. Vice-Pres., Age Concern England, 1998– (Chm., 1995–98). Chairman: Oxfordshire Gp Homes, 1995–; Oxford CAB, 1997–; Low Vision Services Working Gp, 1998–99 (Report, 1999). Trustee: Oxfordshire Community Foundn, 1996–; Country Houses Assoc., 1998–. DL Oxfordshire, 1996. *Recreations:* family and friends; travel; music, mainly (but not exclusively) before 1827; byways of classical antiquity; model railway. *Address:* The Cathedral, Christ Church, Oxford OX1 1DP.

BIRCH, Sir Roger, Kt 1992; CBE 1987; QPM 1980; Chief Constable, Sussex Police, 1983–93; *b* 27 Sept. 1930; *s* of John Edward Lawrence Birch and Ruby Birch; *m* 1954, Jeanne Margaret Head; one *s*. *Educ:* King's Coll., Taunton. Cadet, Royal Naval Coll., Dartmouth, 1949–50; Pilot Officer, RAF, 1950–52. Devon Constabulary, 1954–72: Constable, uniform and CID; then through ranks to Chief Supt; Asst Chief Constable, Mid-Anglia Constab., 1972–74; Dep. Chief Constable, Kent Constab., 1974–78; Chief Constable, Warwickshire Constab., 1978–83. Dir, Police Extended Interviews, 1983–91; Pres., Assoc. of Chief Police Officers, 1987–88 (Vice-Pres., 1986–87; Chm., Traffic Cttee, 1983–86; Chm., Internat. Affairs Adv. Cttee, 1988–92); Vice Chm., Internat. Cttee, Internat. Assoc. of Chiefs of Police, 1989–93; Trustee: Police Dependants' Trust, 1981–93; Police Gurney Fund, 1983–91. Mem., St John Ambulance Council, Sussex, 1986–93. UK Vice-Pres., Royal Life Saving Soc., 1985–93 (Chm., SE Region, 1983–93). Mem. Council, IAM, 1984–93. Hon. Fellow, Centre for Legal Studies, 1993. Hon. LLD Sussex, 1991. *Publications:* articles on criminal intelligence, breath measuring instruments and on the urban environment, in learned jls. *Recreations:* swimming, music. *Club:* Royal Air Force.

BIRCH, Prof. William; *b* 24 Nov. 1925; *s* of Frederick Arthur and Maude Olive Birch; *m* 1950, Mary Vine Stammers; one *s* one *d*. *Educ:* Ranelagh Sch.; Univ. of Reading. BA 1949, PhD 1957. Royal Navy, 1943–46, Sub-Lt RNVR. Lectr, Univ. of Bristol, 1950–60; Prof. of Geography, Grad. Sch. of Geog., Clark Univ., Worcester, Mass, USA, 1960–63; Prof., and Chm. of Dept of Geog., Univ. of Toronto, Canada, 1963–67; Prof., and Head of Dept of Geog., Univ. of Leeds, 1967–75; Dir, Bristol Polytechnic, 1975–86. Visiting Professor: Inst. of Educn, London Univ., 1986–88; Univ. of Bristol, 1990–94. Pres., Inst. of British Geographers, 1976–77; Chm., Cttee of Directors of Polytechnics, 1982–84. Mem., ESRC, 1985–88. Hon. DLitt CNAA, 1989. *Publications:* The Isle of Man: a study in economic geography, 1964; The Challenge to Higher Education: reconciling responsibilities to scholarship and society, 1988; contribs on higher educn policy and on geography and planning, Trans Inst. Brit. Geographers, Geog. Jl, Economic Geog., Annals Assoc. Amer. Geographers, Jl Environmental Management, Studies in Higher Educn, etc. *Recreations:* yachting, travel, gardening, pottery. *Address:* 3 Rodney Place, Clifton, Bristol BS8 4HY. *T:* (0117) 973 9719.

BIRCH, Rt Hon. Sir William (Francis), GNZM 1999; PC 1992; consultant in public policy and affairs; company director; Minister of Finance, 1993–99, Treasurer, 1998–99, New Zealand; *b* 9 April 1934; *s* of Charles William Birch and Elizabeth Alicia (*née* Wells); *m* 1953, Rosa Mitchell; three *s* one *d*. Surveyor. Borough Councillor 1965–74, Dep. Mayor 1968–74, Pukekohe. MP (Nat.) Pukekohe, NZ, 1972–99; Jun. Opposition Whip, 1973–75; Sen. Govt Whip, 1975–78; Minister of: Energy, Science and Technol. and Nat. Develt, 1978–81; Energy, Regl Develt and Nat. Develt, 1981–84; Labour, Immigration and State Services, 1990–93; Employment, 1991–93; Health, 1993; Minister for Pacific Island Affairs, 1990–91. Chm., Internat. Energy Agency, 1983. *Recreation:* fishing. *Address:* Oira Road, RD2, Drury, New Zealand. *Clubs:* Rotary; Jaycee International.

BIRCHENOUGH, (John) Michael, BSc, PhD; Visiting Professor, School of Education, Open University, 1986–89; *b* 17 Jan. 1923; *s* of John Buckley Birchenough and Elsie Birchenough; *m* 1945, Enid Humphries; two *s*. *Educ:* Ashford Grammar Sch., Kent; Chiswick County Sch.; London Univ. Chemist, May & Baker Ltd, 1943–45; teaching posts, 1946–60; HM Inspector of Schools, 1960; Staff Inspector, 1966; Chief Inspector, 1968–72; Chief Inspector, ILEA, 1973–83; Res. Fellow, Sch. of Educn, Univ. of Bristol, 1983–86. Pres., Educn Section, BAAS Annual Meeting, Stirling, 1974. *Publications:* contribs to Jl of Chem. Soc. and other scientific jls. *Address:* 42 Hollies Drive, Edwalton, Nottingham NG12 4BZ.

BIRD, Prof. Adrian Peter, PhD; FRS 1989; Buchanan Professor of Genetics, Edinburgh University, since 1990; Director, Wellcome Trust Centre for Cell Biology, since 1999; *b* 3 July 1947; *s* of Kenneth George Bird and Aileen Mary Bird; *m* 1st, 1976; one *s* one *d*; 2nd, 1993, Dr Catherine Mary Abbott; one *s* one *d*. *Educ:* Queen Elizabeth's Grammar School, Hartlebury; Univ. of Sussex (BSc(Hons)); Univ. of Edinburgh (PhD 1971). Damon Runyan Fellow, Yale, 1972–73; postdoctoral fellowship, Univ. of Zurich, 1974–75; Medical Research Council, Edinburgh: scientific staff, Mammalian Genome Unit, 1975–87; Hd of Structural Studies Sect., Clin. and Population Cytogenetics Unit, 1987; Sen. Scientist, Inst. for Molecular Pathol., Vienna, 1988–90. Mem. Bd of Govs, Wellcome Trust, 2000–. Louis Jeantet Prize for Med. Res., 1999; Gabor Medal, Royal Soc., 1999. *Publications:* articles in Nature, Cell and other jls. *Recreations:* running, music, food. *Address:* Wellcome Trust Centre for Cell Biology, University of Edinburgh, King's Buildings, Mayfield Road, Edinburgh EH9 3JR. *T:* (0131) 650 5670.

BIRD, Rev. Dr Anthony Peter; General Medical Practitioner, since 1979; Principal of The Queen's College, Edgbaston, Birmingham, 1974–79; *b* 2 March 1931; *s* of late Albert Harry Bird and Noel Whitehouse Bird; *m* 1962, Sabine Boehmig; two *s* one *d*. *Educ:* St John's Coll., Oxford (BA LitHum, BA Theol, MA); Birmingham Univ. (MB, ChB, 1970). Deacon, 1957; Priest, 1958; Curate of St Mary's, Stafford, 1957–60; Chaplain, then Vice-Principal of Cuddesdon Theological Coll., 1960–64. General Medical Practitioner, 1972–73. Member: Home Office Policy Adv. Cttee on Sexual Offences, 1976–80; Parole Board, 1977–80. Freedom of Information Campaign Award, 1986. *Publication:* The Search for Health: a response from the inner city, 1981. *Recreations:* sailing, walking, music—J. S. Bach, innovation in primary health care, Wolverhampton Wanderers FC. *Address:* 93 Bournbrook Road, Birmingham B29 7BX.

BIRD, Prof. Colin Carmichael, CBE 2000; PhD; FRCPath, FRCPE, FRCSE, FMedSci; FRSE; Dean, Faculty of Medicine and Provost, Faculty Group of Medicine and Veterinary Medicine, University of Edinburgh, since 1995; *b* 5 March 1938; *s* of John and Sarah Bird; *m* 1964, Ailsa M. Ross; two *s* one *d*. *Educ:* Lenzie Acad.; Glasgow Univ. (MB ChB 1961; PhD 1967). FRCPath 1978 (MRCPath 1968); FRCPE 1989; FRCSE 1995; FRSE 1992. Research Fellow and Lectr in Pathology, Univ. of Glasgow, 1962–67; Lectr in Pathology, Univ. of Aberdeen, 1967–72; Sen. Lectr in Pathology, Univ. of Edinburgh, 1972–75; Professor of Pathology: Univ. of Leeds, 1975–86; Univ. of Edinburgh, 1986–95. Founder FMedSci 1998. *Publications:* contribs to various scientific jls on cancer and cancer genetics. *Recreations:* golf, walking, music, reading. *Address:* Faculty of Medicine, University of Edinburgh Medical School, Teviot Place, Edinburgh EH8 9AG. *T:* (0131) 650 3181. *Club:* New (Edinburgh).

BIRD, Ven. (Colin) Richard (Bateman); Archdeacon of Lambeth, 1988–99; *b* 31 March 1933; *s* of Paul James Bird and Marjorie Bird (*née* Bateman); *m* 1963, Valerie Wroughton van der Bijl; two *d* one *s*. *Educ:* privately; County Technical Coll., Guildford; Selwyn Coll., Cambridge (MA); Cuddesdon Theol Coll. Curate: St Mark's Cathedral, George, S Africa, 1958–61; St Saviour's Claremont, Cape Town, 1961–64; Rector, Parish of Northern Suburbs, Pretoria, 1964–66; Rector, Tzaneen with Duiwelskloof and Phalaborwa, N Transvaal, 1966–70; Curate, Limpsfield, Surrey, 1970–75; Vicar of St Catherine, Hatcham, 1975–88; RD, Deptford, 1980–85; Hon. Canon of Southwark, 1982–88; Priest-in-Charge, St Saviour's, Brixton Hill, 1989–94. *Recreations:* theatre and concert going, walking, bird-watching. *Address:* 32 Bristol Road, Bury St Edmunds, Suffolk IP33 2DL. *T:* (01284) 723810.

BIRD, Drayton Charles Colston; Founder, 1991, Chairman, since 1992, Drayton Bird Partnership; *b* 22 Aug. 1936; *s* of George Freeman Bird and Marjorie Louise Bird; *m* 1st, 1957, Pamela Bland (marr. diss.); two *s* one *d*; 2nd, 1971, Anna Te Paora (marr. diss.); 3rd, 1982, Cece Topley. *Educ:* Trent Coll.; Manchester Univ. Asst. Sec., Manchester Cotton Assoc., 1955–57; with sundry advertising agencies, 1957–68; Founder, Small Business Inst., 1968; publisher, Business Ideas newsletter, 1968–70; Co-Founder, then Man. Dir, Trenear-Harvey, Bird & Watson, 1977–85; Vice Chm., Ogilvy & Mather Direct Worldwide, 1985–91. Inaugural Fellow, Inst. Direct Mktng, 1996. *Publications:* Some Rats Run Faster, 1964; Commonsense Direct Marketing: the printed shop, 1982, 4th edn 2000; How To Write Sales Letters That Sell, 1994; Marketing Insights and Outrages, 1999. *Recreations:* music, reading, wine, writing. *Address:* Drayton Bird Partnership, MCB House, 133–137 Westbourne Grove, W11 2RS. *T:* (020) 7243 0196. *Club:* Wig and Pen.

BIRD, Harold Dennis, (Dickie), MBE 1986; umpire of first-class cricket, 1970–98, and of Test cricket, 1970–96; foundation Member, Independent International Panel of Umpires, 1993; *b* 19 April 1933; *s* of James Harold Bird and Ethel Bird; unmarried. *Educ:* Burton Road Primary Sch.; Raley Sch., Barnsley. Played county cricket for Yorkshire, 1956–60 (highest first-class score, 181 not out *v* Glamorgan, 1959), and Leicestershire, 1960–66; qualified MCC Advanced Cricket Coach, 1966; umpired 159 international matches (world record in 1996): 67 Tests (world record in 1994), incl. Queen's Silver Jubilee Test, Lord's, 1977, Centenary Test, Lord's, 1980, Bi-Centenary Test, Lord's, 1987, 3 in Zimbabwe, and WI *v* Pakistan series, 1993, in NZ, Pakistan and India, 1994, and Australia *v* Pakistan series, 1995; 92 one-day internationals, 1973–96 (world record in 1994); 4 World Cup tournaments, 1975–87, and Final at Lord's, 1975, 1979, 1983; Women's World Cup, and Final, NZ, 1982; finals of Gillette, NatWest, and Benson & Hedges competitions, Lord's, 1974–98; Rothmans Cup, 1983, 1985, Asia Cup, 1984, 1985, Champion's Cup, 1986, and Sharjah Tournament, 1993, UAE. Has travelled worldwide. Guest appearances on TV and radio progs include This is Your Life and Desert Island Discs. Freeman of Barnsley, 2000. DUniv Sheffield Hallam, 1996; Hon. LLD Leeds, 1997. Yorkshire Personality of the Year, 1977; Yorkshire Man of the Year, 1996; People of the Year Award, RADAR/Abbey Nat., 1996; Special Sporting Award, Variety Club of GB, 1997; English Sports Council (Yorks Reg.) Award, 1998; Barnsley Millennium of Merit Award, 2000. *Publications:* Not Out, 1978; That's Out, 1985; From the Pavilion End, 1988; Dickie Bird, My Autobiography, 1997; White Cap and Bails, 1999. *Recreations:* watching football, listening to Barbra Streisand, Nat King Cole, Diana Ross and Shirley Bassey records. *Address:* White Rose Cottage, 40 Paddock Road, Staincross, Barnsley, Yorks S75 6LE. *T:* (01226) 384491. *Clubs:* MCC (Hon. Life Mem., 1996), Lord's Taverners; Yorkshire CC (Hon. Life Mem., 1994); Leicestershire CC (Hon. Life Mem., 1996).

BIRD, John Anthony, MBE 1995; Chairman and Editor-in-Chief, The Big Issue, since 1996 (Managing Director, 1991–96); *b* 30 Jan. 1946; *s* of Alfred Ernest Bird and Eileen Mary (*née* Dunne); *m* 1st, 1965, Linda Stuart Haston (marr. diss.); one *d*; 2nd, 1973, Isobel Theresa, *d* of Sir Robert Ricketts, Bt, *qv*; one *s* one *d*. *Educ:* St Thomas Moores Secondary Mod. Sch.; Ealing Coll. (BA Hons Hum.). Gardening asst, Royal Borough of Kensington and Chelsea, 1963–64; printer, Acrow Engrg, 1964–73; bean canner, H. J. Heinz, 1973–74; printer: Pictorial Charts Educnl Trust, 1974–75; Broadoak Press, 1978–83; print and publishing consultant, 1983–91. *Recreations:* swimming, cycling, running, drinking, talking. *Address:* c/o The Big Issue, 236–240 Pentonville Road, N1 9JY. *T:* (020) 7526 3263.

BIRD, John Michael; actor and writer; *b* 22 Nov. 1936; *s* of Horace George Bird and Dorothy May Bird (*née* Haubitz); partner, Libby Crandon, musician. *Educ:* High Pavement Grammar Sch., Nottingham; King's Coll., Cambridge (BA 1958). Asst Artistic Dir, 1959–61, Associate Artistic Dir, 1961–63, Royal Court Theatre; writer and performer, The Establishment, 1961–64; Joint Founder: New York Establishment, 1963; New Theatre, NY, 1963. *Stage* includes: Luv, tour, 1971; Who's Who?, Arnaud, Guildford, 1972; Habeas Corpus, Lyric, 1973; The Ball Game, Open Space, 1978; *films:* Take a Girl Like You; The Seven Per Cent Solution; Yellow Pages; A Dandy in Aspic; *television* includes: Not so much a Programme, 1965–66; The Late Show, 1966; BBC3; A Series of Birds; With Bird Will Travel; John Bird/John Wells; Blue Remembered Hills; A Very Peculiar Practice; Travelling Man; El C.I.D., 1990, 1991, 1992; Rory Bremner—Who Else?, 1992–99 ((jtly) BAFTA Award for best light entertainment performance, 1997); The Long Johns, 1996–99; In the Red, 1998; Bremner, Bird and Fortune, 1999–; Chambers, 2000, 2001. *Publication:* (with John Fortune) The Long Johns, 1996. *Address:* c/o Chatto & Linnit Ltd, 123A King's Road, SW3 4PL. *T:* (020) 7352 7722.

BIRD, Judith Pamela; *see* Kelly, J. P.

BIRD, Michael James; Regional Chairman of Employment (formerly Industrial) Tribunals for Wales, since 1992; *b* 11 Nov. 1935; *s* of Walter Garfield and Ireen Bird; *m* 1963, Susan Harris; three *d*. *Educ:* Lewis Sch., Pengam; King's Coll., Univ. of London (LLB Hons). Solicitor (Hons) 1961. Assistant solicitor, 1961–62; Partner, T. S. Edwards & Son, 1962–67, Sen. Partner, 1967–84. Deputy Registrar of County and High Court, 1976–77; Chairman of Industrial Tribunal, Cardiff (part-time), 1977–83; Chm. of Industrial Tribunal, Bristol, 1984–87, Cardiff, 1987–92. Chm., Gwent Italian Soc., 1978–86 (Sec., 1976–78); Member: Royal Life Saving Soc., 1976– (President's Commendation, 1984); Amateur Swimming Assoc. (Advanced Teacher, 1981–); Newport and Maindee ASC; Crawshays Welsh RFC. *Recreations:* water sports, opera. *Address:* 17 Allt-yr-yn Avenue, Newport, Gwent NP9 5DA. *T:* (01633) 252000.

BIRD, Ven. Richard; *see* Bird, Ven. C. R. B.

BIRD, Richard; Director of Energy, Environment and Waste, Department for Environment, Food and Rural Affairs, since 2001; *b* 12 Feb. 1950; *s* of Desmond and late Betty Bird; *m* 1973, Penelope Anne Frudd; one *s* one *d*. *Educ:* King's Sch., Canterbury; Magdalen Coll., Oxford. Admin Trainee, DoE, 1971–73; Asst Private Sec. to Minister for Planning and Local Govt, 1974–75; Principal, Dept of Transport, 1975–78; First Sec., UK Rep. to EC, Brussels, 1978–82; Principal Private Sec. to Sec. of State for Transport, 1982–83; Asst Sec., 1983, Under Sec., 1990, Dept of Transport; Cabinet Office, 1992–94; Dir of Personnel, Dept of Transport, 1994–97; Dir, Urban, then Integrated, and Local Transport, DETR, 1997–2001. Mem., Oxford Univ. Fencing Club, 1969–71 (represented Britain at World Youth Fencing Championship, 1970). *Recreations:* choral singing, summer sports. *Address:* Department for Environment, Food and Rural Affairs, Ashdown House, 123 Victoria Street, SW1E 6DE. *T:* (020) 7944 6660.

BIRD, Sir Richard (Geoffrey Chapman), 4th Bt *cr* 1922; *b* 3 Nov. 1935; *er surv. s* of Sir Donald Bird, 3rd Bt, and of Anne Rowena (*d* 1969), *d* of late Charles Chapman; *S* father, 1963; *m* 1st, 1957, Gillian Frances (*d* 1966), *d* of Bernard Haggett, Solihull; two *s* four *d*; 2nd, 1968, Helen Patricia, *d* of Frank Beaumont, Pontefract; two *d*. *Educ:* Beaumont. *Heir: s* John Andrew Bird, *b* 19 Jan. 1964. *Address:* 39 Ashleigh Road, Solihull, W Midlands B91 1AF.

BIRD, Richard Herries, CB 1983; Deputy Secretary, Department of Education and Science, 1980–90; *b* 8 June 1932; *s* of late Edgar Bird and Armorel (*née* Dudley-Scott); *m* 1963, Valerie, *d* of Edward and Mary Sanderson; two *d*. *Educ:* Winchester Coll.; Clare Coll., Cambridge. Min. of Transport and Civil Aviation, 1955; Principal Private Sec. to Minister of Transport, 1966–67; CSD 1969; DoE 1971; DES 1973. *Address:* 53 Kippington Road, Sevenoaks, Kent TN13 2LL.

BIRD, Prof. Richard Simpson, PhD; Professor of Computation, since 1996 and Director, Computing Laboratory, since 1998, University of Oxford; Fellow, Lincoln College, Oxford, since 1988; *b* 13 Feb. 1943; *s* of John William Bird and Martha (*née* Solar); *m* 1967, Norma Christine Lapworth. *Educ:* St Olave's Grammar Sch.; Gonville and Caius Coll., Cambridge (MA); Inst. of Computer Sci., Univ. of London (MSc; PhD 1973). Lecturer: in Computer Sci., Reading Univ., 1972–83; Oxford Univ., 1983–88. *Publications:* Programs and Machines, 1977; Introduction to Functional Programming, 1988, 2nd edn 1998; Algebra of Programming, 1996. *Recreations:* jogging, bridge. *Address:* Stocks, Chapel Lane, Blewbury, Oxon OX11 9PQ. *T:* (01235) 850258; Lincoln College, Oxford OX1 3DR.

BIRD, Roger Charles; District Judge, Bristol County Court and District Registry of High Court, since 1987; *b* 28 April 1939; *s* of late Bertram Charles Bird and Olive Mary Bird; *m* 1964, Marie-Christine Snow; two *s*. *Educ:* Millfield Sch.; Univ. of Bristol (LLB Hons). Admitted solicitor, 1965; asst solicitor with various firms, 1965–69; Partner, Wilmot Thompson and Bird, Bristol, 1969–79; Registrar, Yeovil County Court, 1979–86. Member: Matrimonial Causes Rule Cttee, 1986–90; President's Adoption Cttee, Family Div.,1990–; Children Act Adv. Cttee, 1993–97; Lord Chancellor's Adv. Gp on Ancillary Relief, 1993–; Judicial Adv. Gp, Children and Family Court Adv. Support Service, 2000–01. Pres., Assoc. of Dist Judges, 1995–96. *Publications:* (with C. F. Turner) Bird and Turner's Forms and Precedents, 1985, 3rd edn 1992; (editor-in-chief) Sweet and Maxwell's Family Law Manual, 1985–96; Child Maintenance: the new law, 1992, 4th edn 2000; Domestic Violence, 1996, 3rd edn 2001; (with S. M. Cretney) Divorce: the new law, 1996; Ancillary Relief Handbook, 1998, 2nd edn 2000; Pension Sharing: the new law, 2000; (editor-in-chief) Emergency Remedies in the Family Courts, 2000; numerous articles in legal jls. *Recreations:* reading, listening to music, rural walks. *Address:* c/o Bristol County Court, Greyfriars, Lewins Mead, Bristol BS1 2NR. *T:* (0117) 929 4414. *Club:* National Liberal.

BIRDS, Prof. John Richard; Professor of Commercial Law, University of Sheffield, since 1989; *b* 20 June 1948; *s* of John Sidney Birds and Katharine Charlotte Birds; *m* 1973, Margaret Rhona Richardson; two *s* one *d*. *Educ:* Chesterfield Grammar Sch.; University College London (LLB, LLM). Lectr in Law: Newcastle Polytechnic, 1970; QMC, Univ. of London, 1972; University of Sheffield: Lectr in Law, 1978–82; Sen. Lectr, 1982–85; Reader, 1985–89; Head of Dept of Law, 1987–99. FRSA. *Publications:* Modern Insurance Law, 1982, 5th edn 2001; (with A. J. Boyle) Company Law, 1983, 4th edn 2000; (jtly) Secretarial Administration, 1984; (ed jtly) MacGillivray and Parkington on Insurance Law, 8th edn 1988, 9th edn (as MacGillivray on Insurance Law) 1997; articles in learned jls. *Recreations:* music, gardening, walking. *Address:* 93 Millhouses Lane, Sheffield S7 2HD. *T:* (0114) 236 0137; *e-mail:* j.birds@shef.ac.uk.

BIRDSALL, Derek Walter, RDI; freelance graphic designer; *b* 1 Aug. 1934; *s* of Frederick Birdsall and Hilda Birdsall (*née* Smith); *m* 1954, Shirley Thompson; three *s* one *d*. *Educ:* King's Sch., Pontefract, Yorks; Wakefield Coll. of Art, Yorks; Central Sch. of Arts and Crafts, London (NDD). National Service, RAOC Printing Unit, Cyprus, 1955–57. Lectr in Typographical Design, London Coll. of Printing, 1959–61; freelance graphic designer, working from his studio in Covent Garden, later Islington, 1961–; Founding Partner, Omnific Studios Partnership, 1983. Vis. Prof. of Graphic Art and Design, RCA, 1987–88. Consultant designer, The Independent Magazine, 1989–93; Tutor and designer of house-style for Prince of Wales's Inst. of Arch., 1991; Design Consultant, NACF, 1992–97; Consultant Designer to C of E, 1999–. Has broadcast on TV and radio on design subjects and his work; catalogue designs for major museums throughout the world have won many awards, incl. Gold Medal, New York Art Directors' Club, 1987. Mem., AGI, 1968–96; FCSD (FSIAD 1964); RDI 1982; FRSA; Hon. FRCA 1988. *Publications:* (with C. H. O'D. Alexander) Fischer *v* Spassky, 1972; (with C. H. O'D. Alexander) A Book of Chess, 1974; (with Carlo M. Cippola) The Technology of Man—a visual history, 1978; (with Bruce Bernard) Lucian Freud, 1996. *Recreations:* chess, poker. *Address:* 8 Compton Avenue, Islington, N1 2UN. *T:* (020) 7359 1201. *Club:* Chelsea Arts.

BIRDSALL, Mrs Doris, CBE 1985; Lord Mayor of Bradford Metropolitan District, 1975–76; *b* 20 July 1915; *d* of Fred and Violet Ratcliffe; *m* 1940, James Birdsall; one *s* one *d*. *Educ:* Hanson Girls' Grammar School. Mem. Bradford City Council, 1958, Chm. of Educn Cttee, 1972–74; former Mem. Bradford Univ. Council. Hon. MA Bradford, 1975; DUniv Bradford, 1993; Hon. LHD Lesley Coll., Mass, 1976. *Address:* 4 Flower Mount, Station Road, Baildon, Bradford, West Yorks BD17 6SB.

BIRDWOOD, family name of **Baron Birdwood**.

BIRDWOOD, 3rd Baron *cr* 1938, of Anzac and of Totnes; **Mark William Ogilvie Birdwood;** Bt 1919; Chairman: Martlet Ltd, since 1986; Fiortho plc, since 1995; *b* 23 Nov. 1938; *s* of 2nd Baron Birdwood, MVO, and Vere Lady Birdwood, CVO (*d* 1997); *S* father, 1962; *m* 1963, Judith Helen, *e d* of late R. G. Seymour Roberts; one *d*. *Educ:* Radley Coll.; Trinity Coll., Cambridge. Commnd RHG. Director: Wrightson Wood Ltd, 1979–86; Du Pont Pixel Systems (formerly Benchmark Technology); Comac plc, 1988–92; Scientific Generics, 1989–97; The Character Gp (formerly Toy Options) plc, 1995–; IMS plc, 1997–2000; Jasmin plc, 1998–2000. Mem., Select Cttee on Science and Technol., H of L, 1998–99. Res. Associate, LSE Centre for Philosophy of Nat. and Social Sci. Trustee of charities. Liveryman, Glaziers' Co. *Address:* 5 Holbein Mews, SW1W 8NW; Russell House, Broadway, Worcs WR12 7BU. *Clubs:* Brooks's, Carlton.

See also D. J. Montgomery, Earl of Woolton.

BIREEDO, Omer Yousif; Ambassador of Sudan to the Court of St James's, 1995–99; *b* 1 Jan. 1939; *s* of Yousif Bireedo and Fatima Hasan; *m* 1978, Kalthoum M. E. Barakat; one *s* two *d*. *Educ:* Univ. of Khartoum (BA); Delhi Univ. (MA). Sudanese Diplomatic Service: Third Sec., New Delhi, 1963–66; London, 1966–69; Dep. Dir, Consular Dept, Min. of Foreign Affairs, Khartoum, 1969–71; Uganda, 1971–73; Mission to UN, NY, 1973–76; Dir, Dept of Internat. Orgns, Min. of Foreign Affairs, Khartoum, 1976–78 and 1986–89; Ambassador and Perm. Rep. to UN and Internat. Orgns, Geneva and Vienna, 1978–83, NY, 1983–86; Ambassador to Saudi Arabia, 1989–92; 1st Undersec., Min. of Foreign Affairs, Khartoum, 1992–95. Republican Order (Sudan), 1972. *Recreations:* walking, reading. *Address:* c/o Ministry of Foreign Affairs, Khartoum, Sudan.

BIRGENEAU, Dr Robert Joseph, FRS 2001; President and Professor of Physics, University of Toronto, since 2000; *b* Toronto, 25 March 1942; *m* 1964, Mary Catherine Ware; one *s* three *d*. *Educ:* Univ. of Toronto (BSc 1963); Yale Univ. (PhD 1966). Grad. Student, 1963–66, Instructor, 1966–67, Dept of Engrg and Applied Sci., Yale Univ.; Nat.

Res. Council of Canada Postdoctoral Fellow, Oxford Univ., 1967–68; Bell Laboratories, Murray Hill, NJ: Mem., Tech. Staff, Physical Res. Lab., 1968–74; Res. Hd, Scattering and Low Energy Physics Dept, 1975; Consultant, 1977–80; Massachusetts Institute of Technology: Prof. of Physics, 1975–2000; Cecil and Ida Green Prof. of Physics, 1982–2000; Associate Dir, Res. Lab. of Electronics, 1983–86; Head: Solid State, Atomic and Plasma Physics, 1987–88; Dept of Physics, 1988–91; Dean, Sch. of Sci., 1991–2000. Consultant: IBM Res. Labs, NY, 1980–83; Sandia Nat. Labs, Albuquerque, 1985–90. Guest Sen. Physicist, Brookhaven Nat. Lab., NY, 1968–; Vis. Scientist, Riso Nat. Lab., Roskilde, Denmark, 1971, 1979. Numerous lectures at univs in USA, Canada, UK and Israel, incl. A. W. Scott Lecture, Cambridge Univ., 2000. Co-Chm., Polaroid Sci. and Technol. Bd, 1998–. Mem., Ext. Adv. Cttee, Physics Dept, Oxford Univ., 2000–. FAAAS 1982; Fellow: APS, 1980; Amer. Acad. Arts and Scis, 1987. Trustee, Boston Mus. of Sci., 1992–2001; Gov., Argonne Nat. Lab., 1992–2001; Mem., Adv. Council, Nippon Electric Co. Res. Inst., 1995–. Holds numerous awards and prizes. *Publications:* numerous contribs to learned jls on phases and phase transition behaviour of novel states of matter. *Address:* 93 Highland Avenue, Toronto, ON M4W 2A4, Canada.

BIRKENHEAD, Bishop Suffragan of, since 2000; **Rt Rev. David Andrew Urquhart;** *b* 14 April 1952; *s* of Hector Maconochie Urquhart, FRCSE and Elizabeth Mary Florence Urquhart (*née* Jones). *Educ:* Croftinloan; Rugby Sch.; Ealing Business Sch. (BA Hons); Wycliffe Hall, Oxford. Volunteer in Uganda, 1971; BP plc, 1972–82; ordained deacon, 1984, priest, 1985; Curate, St Nicholas, Kingston upon Hull, 1984–87; Team Vicar, Drypool, 1987–92; Vicar, Holy Trinity, Coventry, 1992–2000. Hon. Canon, Coventry Cathedral, 1999–2000. Chairman: Hull and E Yorks Faith in the City Gp, 1985–90; Chester Dio. Bd of Educn, 2001–; CMS, 1994–. Dir, Coventry City Centre Co., 1997–2000. Chm. Governors, Craven (LEA) Primary Sch., 1988–92; Gov., Rugby Sch., 1999–. Trustee, Triangle (1949) Trust, 1995–. Tallow Chandlers Medal, BP, 1977. *Recreations:* squash, fives (half blue, Rugby fives, 1984), watching films, collecting books on red deer. *Address:* Bishop's Lodge, 67 Bidston Road, Prenton, Wirral CH43 6TR. *T:* (0151) 652 2741; *e-mail:* bpbirkenhead@clara.net.

BIRKETT, family name of **Baron Birkett.**

BIRKETT, 2nd Baron *cr* 1958, of Ulverston; **Michael Birkett;** Chairman of Governors, BRIT School for Performing Arts and Technology; *b* 22 Oct. 1929; *s* of 1st Baron Birkett, PC and Ruth Birkett (*née* Nilsson, she *d* 1969); *S* father, 1962; *m* 1st, 1960, Junia Crawford (*d* 1973); 2nd, 1978, Gloria Taylor (*d* 2001); one *s*. *Educ:* Stowe; Trinity Coll., Cambridge. Asst Dir at Ealing Studios and Ealing Films, 1953–59; Asst Dir, 1959–61, on films including: The Mark; The Innocents; Billy Budd; Associate Producer: Some People, 1961–62; Modesty Blaise, 1965; Producer: The Caretaker, 1962; Marat/Sade, 1966; A Midsummer Night's Dream, 1967; King Lear, 1968–69; Director: The Launching and The Soldier's Tale, 1963; Overture and Beginners, the More Man Understands, 1964; Outward Bound, 1971. Vice Pres., British Bd of Film Classification, 1985–97. Dep. Dir, National Theatre, 1975–77; Consultant to Nat. Theatre on films, TV and sponsorship, 1977–79; Dir for Recreation and Arts, GLC, 1979–86; Adviser to South Bank Bd, 1986–89; Exec. Dir, Royal Philharmonic Soc., 1989–90; Dir, Olympic Festival 1990, Manchester, 1990. Chairman: Children's Film & TV Foundn, 1981–99; Theatres Adv. Council, 1986–; Adv. Cttee, Nat. Sound Archive, 1993–; Music Adv. Cttee, British Council, 1994–. Chm., Management Cttee, Park Lane Gp, 1991–. Master, Curriers' Co., 1975–76. *Recreations:* music, printing, horticulture. *Heir: s* Hon. Thomas Birkett, *b* 25 July 1982. *Address:* Great Allfields, Balls Cross, Petworth GU28 9JR.

BIRKETT, Peter Vidler; QC 1989; a Recorder, since 1989; *b* 13 July 1948; *s* of Neville Lawn Birkett, MA, MB BCh, FRES and Marjorie Joy Birkett; *m* 1976, Jane Elizabeth Fell; two *s*. *Educ:* Sedbergh School; Univ. of Leicester. Called to the Bar, Inner Temple, 1972, Bencher, 1996; practice on SE Circuit, 1973–77, on N Circuit, 1977– (Leader, 1999–). Asst Recorder, 1986–89. Mem., General Council of the Bar, 1999–. *Recreations:* golf, ski-ing, conversation, playing the piano. *Address:* 18 St John Street, Manchester M3 4EA. *T:* (0161) 834 9843. *Club:* Wilmslow Golf.

BIRKIN, Sir Derek; *see* Birkin, Sir J. D.

BIRKIN, Sir John (Christian William), 6th Bt *cr* 1905, of Ruddington Grange, Notts; Director, Compound Eye Productions, since 1987; *b* 2 July 1953; *s* of Sir Charles Lloyd Birkin, 5th Bt and Janet (*d* 1983), *d* of Peter Johnson; *S* father, 1985; *m* 1994, Emma Gage; one *s* one *d*. *Educ:* Eton; Trinity Coll., Dublin; London Film School. *Heir: s* Benjamin Charles Birkin, *b* 4 Nov. 1995. *Address:* Place Barton, Ashton, Exeter, Devon EX6 7QP.

BIRKIN, Sir (John) Derek, Kt 1990; TD 1965; Chairman, The RTZ Corporation PLC (formerly Rio Tinto-Zinc Corporation), 1991–96 (Chief Executive and Deputy Chairman, 1985–91); *b* 30 Sept 1929; *s* of Noah and Rebecca Birkin; *m* 1952, Sadie Smith; one *s* one *d*. *Educ:* Hemsworth Grammar Sch. Managing Director: Velmar Ltd, 1966–67; Nairn Williamson Ltd, 1967–70; Dep. Chm. and Man. Dir, Tunnel Holdings Ltd, 1970–75; Chm. and Man. Dir, Tunnel Holdings, 1975–82; Dir, Rio Tinto-Zinc, then RTZ, Corp., 1982–96, Dep. Chief Exec., 1983–85. Director: Smiths Industries, 1977–84; British Gas Corp., 1982–85; George Wimpey, 1984–92; CRA Ltd (Australia), 1985–94; Rio Algom Ltd (Canada), 1985–92; The Merchants Trust PLC, 1986–; British Steel plc (formerly BSC), 1986–92; Barclays PLC, 1990–95; Merck & Co. Inc. (USA), 1992–; Carlton Communications Plc, 1992–; Unilever PLC, 1993–2000; Watmoughs (Holdings) PLC, 1996–98. Member: Review Body on Top Salaries, 1986–89; Council, Industrial Soc., 1985–97. Dir, Royal Opera House, 1993–97 (Trustee, 1990–93). CIMgt (CBIM 1980); FRSA 1988. Hon. LLD Bath, 1998. *Recreations:* opera, Rugby, cricket.

BIRKMYRE, Sir James, 4th Bt *cr* 1921, of Dalmunzie, County of Perth; Director of Tournament Development, PGA European Tour, since 1994; *b* 29 Feb. 1956; *s* of Sir Archibald Birkmyre, 3rd Bt and of Gillian Mary (*née* Downes); *S* father, 2001; *m* 1990, Leslie Amanda, *d* of Dr Richard Lyon, Seal Beach, Calif; one *s*. *Educ:* Radley Coll.; Ecole Supérieure de Commerce, Neuchâtel; Ealing Tech. Coll. (BA Hons). Account Mgr, Collet Dickenson & Pearce Advertising, 1978–82; Account Dir, TBWA Advertising, 1982–87; Sponsorship Dir, The Wight Co., 1987–93; Man. Dir, Birchgrey, 1993–94. *Recreations:* tennis, fly-fishing, golf, ski-ing. *Heir: s* Alexander Birkmyre, *b* 24 May 1991. *Address:* Ashmore Green Cottage, Ashmore Green, near Newbury, Berks RG18 9EY. *T:* (01635) 862756. *Clubs:* MCC; Sunningdale Golf.

BIRKS, Lt-Gen. Anthony Leonard, CB 1993; OBE 1985 (MBE 1977); Chief of Defence Force, New Zealand Defence Force, 1995–99; *b* 30 Dec. 1941; *s* of Clifford Birks and Maisie Lola Gapes (*née* Brown); *m* 1964, Georgina May Ball, Bedfordshire; two *s* one *d*. *Educ:* St Andrew Coll., Christchurch; Nelson Coll.; RMA Sandhurst. Commissioned 1961; Platoon Comdr, 1 RNZIR, Mayala and Borneo, 1963–65; 1 Australian Task Force, Vietnam, 1968; 11 Field Force, Vietnam, 1970; Chief Instructor, Tactical Sch., 1977–78; Staff Coll., Australia, 1974; CO 2/1 RNZIR, 1979–81; Dir of Plans, Army, 1981–82; JSSC 1983; Comdr 3TF, 1985–87; Asst Chief Ops HQ, NZ Defence Force, 1988–89; RCDS 1990; Dep. Chief of Defence Staff HQ NZ Defence Force, 1991; CGS NZ Army, 1992–95. NZ Trustee, Prince's (formerly Prince of Wales') Trust, 2000–. *Recreations:* golf, motor-cycling. *Address:* 208 Pohutukawa Avenue, Ohope Beach, Whakatane, Bay of Plenty, New Zealand. *Club:* Wellington (Wellington).

BIRKS, His Honour Michael; a Circuit Judge, 1983–93; *b* 21 May 1920; *s* of late Falconer Moffat Birks, CBE, and Monica Katherine Lushington (*née* Mellor); *m* 1st, 1947, Ann Ethne (*d* 1999), *d* of Captain Henry Stafford Morgan; one *d*; 2nd, 1999, Anne Mary, *widow* of Lt-Col Richard Martin Power, RE. *Educ:* Oundle; Trinity Coll., Cambridge. Commissioned 22nd Dragoons, 1941; attached Indian Army, 1942, invalided out, 1943. Admitted Solicitor, 1946; Assistant Registrar: Chancery Div., High Court, 1953–60; Newcastle upon Tyne group of County Courts, 1960–61; Registrar: Birkenhead gp of County Courts, 1961–66; W London County Court, 1966–83; a Recorder of the Crown Court, 1979–83. Adv. Editor, Atkins Court Forms, 1966–91; Jt Editor, County Court Practice, 1976–83. Mem. County Court Rule Cttee, 1980–83. *Publications:* Gentlemen of the Law, 1960; Small Claims in the County Court, 1973; Enforcing Money Judgments in the County Court, 1980; contributed titles: County Courts and Interpleader (part), 4th edn Halsbury's Laws of England; Judgments and Orders (part), References and Inquiries (part), Service (part), and Transfer (part), County Courts Atkins Court Forms; contribs to legal jls. *Recreation:* painting. *Address:* Dreva, Rhinefield Road, Brockenhurst, Hants SO42 7SQ. *T:* (01590) 623353.

BIRKS, Prof. Peter Brian Herrenden, FBA 1989; Regius Professor of Civil Law, University of Oxford, and Fellow of All Souls College, Oxford, since 1989; *b* 3 Oct. 1941; *e s* of Dr Peter Herrenden Birks and Mary (*née* Morgan); *m* 1984, Jacqueline S. Berrington (*née* Stimpson). *Educ:* Trinity Coll., Oxford (MA; Hon. Fellow, 1994); University Coll., London (LLM; Fellow, 1993). DCL Oxon, 1991; LLD Edin., 1991. Lectr in Laws, UCL, 1966–71; Law Fellow, Brasenose Coll., Oxford, 1971–81; Prof. of Civil Law, and Head of Dept of Civil Law, Edinburgh Univ., 1981–87; Prof. of Law, Southampton Univ., 1988–89. Wisselleerstoelhouder, Faculty of Law, Univ. of Nijmegen, 1994–96; Vis. Prof., Univ. of Texas at Austin, 2001. Hon. Sec., SPTL, 1989–96 (Mem. Council, 1988–96); Member: Lord Chancellor's Adv. Cttee on Legal Educn, 1989–91; Social Sciences Cttee, Schs Exams and Assessment Council, 1989–91 (Chm., Law Cttee, 1988–89); Humanities Res. Bd, 1996–; Sec., Standing Conf. on Legal Educn, 1991–94. Consultant Editor, Restitution Law Review, 1993–. Mem., Eur. Acad. of Private Lawyers, 1994–. Hon. QC 1995. FRSA 1992. Hon. DJur Regensburg, 1996; Hon. LLD De Montfort, 1999. *Publications:* Introduction to the Law of Restitution, 1985; (ed with D. N. MacCormick) The Legal Mind, 1986; (with G. McLeod) The Institutes of Justinian, 1987; (ed) New Perspectives on the Roman Law of Property, 1989; Restitution: the future, 1992; (ed) Frontiers of Liability, vols 1 and 2, 1994; (ed) Reviewing Legal Education, 1994; (ed) Laundering and Tracing, 1995; (ed) Wrongs and Remedies in 21st Century, 1996; (ed) What are Law Schools For?, 1996; (ed) Privacy and Loyalty, 1997; (ed) The Classification of Obligations, 1997; English Private Law, 2000; articles on Roman law, legal history, legal educn, and restitution. *Address:* Oak Trees, Sandy Lane, Boars Hill, Oxford OX1 5HN. *T:* (01865) 735625; All Souls College, Oxford OX1 4AL. *T:* (01865) 279338, *Fax:* (01865) 279299. *Club:* Athenæum.

BIRLEY, Anthony Addison, CB 1979; Clerk of Public Bills, House of Commons, 1973–82, retired; *b* 28 Nov. 1920; *s* of Charles Fair Birley and Eileen Mia Rouse; *m* 1951, Jane Mary Ruggles-Brise; two *d*. *Educ:* Winchester (exhibnr); Christ Church, Oxford (MA). Served War in RA (Ayrshire Yeomanry), 1940–45, in North Africa and Italian campaigns (wounded). Asst Clerk, House of Commons, 1948; Clerk of Standing Cttees, 1970. *Recreations:* gardening, walking, racing. *Address:* Holtom House, Paxford, Chipping Campden, Glos GL55 6XH. *T:* (01386) 593318. *Club:* Army and Navy.

BIRLEY, Sir Derek, Kt 1989; Vice-Chancellor, University of Ulster, 1984–91; *b* 31 May 1926; *s* of late Sydney John and late Margaret Birley; *m* 1990, Prof. Norma Reid. *Educ:* Hemsworth Grammar Sch.; Queens' Coll., Cambridge (BA 1950, MA 1954). Royal Artillery, 1944–48; Schoolmaster, Queen Elizabeth Grammar Sch., Wakefield, 1952–55; Admin. Asst, Leeds Educn Cttee, 1955–59; Asst Educn Officer: Dorset, 1959–61; Lancs, 1961–64; Dep. Dir of Educn, Liverpool, 1964–70; Rector, Ulster Polytechnic, 1970–84. Hon. Fellow, Sheffield Poly., 1991. Hon. LLD QUB, 1991. *Publications:* The Education Officer and his World, 1970; (with Anne Dufton) An Equal Chance, 1971; Planning and Education, 1972; The Willow Wand, 1979; Sport and the Making of Britain, 1993; Land of Sport and Glory, 1994; Playing the Game, 1996; A Social History of English Cricket (William Hill Sports Book of the Year, Cricket Soc. Literary Award), 1999. *Recreations:* books, cricket, jazz. *Address:* Min Dowr, Hodder's Way, Cargreen, Saltash, Cornwall PL12 6NY.

BIRLEY, James Leatham Tennant, CBE 1990; FRCP, FRCPsych, DPM; Consultant Psychiatrist, Bethlem Royal and Maudsley Hospitals, 1969–90, Emeritus Psychiatrist, 1990; President, British Medical Association, 1993–94; *b* 31 May 1928; *s* of late Dr James Leatham Birley and Margaret Edith (*née* Tennant); *m* 1954, Julia Davies; one *s* three *d*. *Educ:* Winchester Coll.; University Coll., Oxford; St Thomas' Hosp., London. Maudsley Hospital: Registrar, 1960; Sen. Registrar, 1963; Mem. Scientific Staff, MRC Social Psychiatry Research Unit, 1965; Dean, Inst. of Psychiatry, 1971–82. Dean, 1982–87, Pres., 1987–90, RCPsych. *Publications:* contribs to scientific jls. *Recreations:* music, gardening. *Address:* Upper Bryn, Longtown, Hereford HR2 0NA.

BIRLEY, Michael Pellew, MA (Oxon); Housemaster, 1970–80, Assistant Master, 1980–84, Marlborough College; *b* 7 Nov. 1920; *s* of late Norman Pellew Birley, DSO, MC, and Eileen Alice Morgan; *m* 1949, Ann Grover (*née* Street); two *s* two *d*. *Educ:* Marlborough Coll.; Wadham Coll., Oxford. 1st class Classical Honour Moderations, 1940; 1st class *Litterae Humaniores*, 1947; MA 1946; Served War of 1939–45 with the Royal Fusiliers; joined up, Sept. 1940; commissioned, April 1941; abroad, 1942–45 (despatches); demobilised, Jan. 1946. Taught Classics: Shrewsbury Sch., 1948–50; Eton Coll., 1950–56; Headmaster, Eastbourne College, 1956–70. Member Council: Ardingly Coll., 1981–90; Marlborough Coll., 1985–90. Fellow, Woodard Corp., 1983–90. *Recreations:* gardening, wine-making. *Address:* Long Summers, Cross Lane, Marlborough, Wilts SN8 1LA. *T:* (01672) 512830.

BIRLEY, Prof. Susan Joyce, (Mrs David Norburn); Professor of Management, The Management School, Imperial College, since 1990; Director, Entrepreneurship Centre, since 2000; *m* 1st, 1964, Arwyn Hopkins (marr. diss. 1970); 2nd, 1975, Prof. David Norburn, *qv*. *Educ:* Nelson Grammar Sch.; University College London (BSc 1964); PhD London 1974. FSS. Teacher, Dunsmore Sch., 1964–66; Lectr, Lanchester Polytechnic, 1966–68; Lectr and Sen. Lectr, Poly. of Central London, 1968–72; Sen. Res. Fellow, City Univ., 1972–74; London Business School: Sen. Res. Fellow, 1974–79; Lectr in Small Business, 1979–82; University of Notre Dame, USA: Adjunct Associate Prof., 1978–82; Associate Prof. of Strategy and Entrepreneurship, 1982–85; Philip and Pauline Harris Prof. of Entrepreneurship, Cranfield Inst. of Technol., 1985–90. Academic Dir, European Foundn for Entrepreneurship Res., 1988–91. Member: CNAA, 1987–90; NI Economic Council, 1988–94; PCFC, 1988–92; Adv. Panel on Deregulation, DTI, 1989–91; Bd, LEDU, NI, 1992–93. Founder Director and Shareholder: Guidehouse Group, 1980–85;

Greyfriars Ltd, 1982–85; Newchurch & Co., 1986–97 (Chm.); Director: NatWest Bank, 1996–2000; Process Systems Enterprise Ltd, 1997–; IC Innovations Ltd, 1997–; BAE Systems, 2000–. Mem. Panel, Foresight Steering Gp, 1997–. Governor, Harris City Technol. Coll., 1990–92. Freeman, City of London, 1964. Mem. Editl Bds, various business jls. *Publications:* From Private to Public (jtly), 1977; The Small Business Casebook, 1979; The Small Business Casebook: teaching manual, 1980; New Enterprises, 1982; (contrib.) Small Business and Entrepreneurship, ed Burns and Dewhurst, 1989; (jtly) Exit Routes, 1989; (jtly) The British Entrepreneur, 1989; (ed) European Entrepreneurship: emerging growth companies, 1989; (ed jtly) International Perspectives on Entrepreneurship, 1992; Entrepreneurship Research: global perspectives, 1993; Mastering Enterprise, 1997; Mastering Entrepreneurship, 2000; numerous contribs to learned jls. *Recreation:* gardening. *Address:* The Management School, Imperial College of Science, Technology and Medicine, 53 Princes Gate, Exhibition Road, SW7 2PG.

BIRMINGHAM, Archbishop of, (RC), since 2000; **Most Rev. Vincent Gerard Nichols;** Titular Bishop of Othona; *b* 8 Nov. 1945; *s* of Henry Joseph Nichols and Mary Nichols (*née* Russell). *Educ:* St Mary's College, Crosby; Gregorian Univ., Rome (STL PhL); Manchester Univ. (MA Theol); Loyola Univ., Chicago (MEd). Chaplain, St John Rigby VI Form College, Wigan, 1972–77; Priest, inner city of Liverpool, 1978–81; Director, Upholland Northern Inst., with responsibility for in service training of clergy and for adult Christian educn, 1981–84; Gen. Sec., RC Bishops' Conf. of England and Wales, 1984–91; Auxiliary Bp of Westminster (Bp in N London), 1992–2000. Chairman: Catholic Educn Service, 1998–; Dept of Catholic Educn and Formation, RC Bishops' Conf. of Eng. and Wales, 1998–. Advr to Cardinal Hume and Archbishop Worlock, Internat. Synods of Bishops, 1980, 1983, 1985, 1987. Deleg. of Bishops' Conf. to Synod of Bishops, 1994; Mem., Synod of Bishops for Oceania, 1998, for Europe, 1999. *Publications:* Promise of Future Glory, 1997; articles in Priests and People, Business Economist. *Address:* Archbishop's House, 8 Shadwell Street, Birmingham B4 6EY. *T:* (0121) 236 9090.

BIRMINGHAM, Bishop of, 1987–May 2002; **Rt Rev. Mark Santer,** MA; *b* 29 Dec. 1936; *s* of late Rev. Canon Eric Arthur Robert Santer and Phyllis Clare Barlow; *m* 1st, 1964, Henriette Cornelia Weststrate (*d* 1994); one *s* two *d*; 2nd, 1997, Sabine Böhmig Bird. *Educ:* Marlborough Coll.; Queens' Coll., Cambridge (Hon. Fellow, 1991); Westcott House, Cambridge. Deacon, 1963; priest 1964; Asst Curate, Cuddesdon, 1963–67; Tutor, Cuddesdon Theological Coll., 1963–67; Fellow and Dean of Clare Coll., Cambridge, 1967–72 (and Tutor, 1968–72; Hon. Fellow, 1987); Univ. Asst Lectr in Divinity, 1968–72; Principal of Westcott House, Cambridge, 1973–81; Hon. Canon of Winchester Cathedral, 1978–81; Area Bishop of Kensington, 1981–87. Co-Chm., Anglican Roman Catholic Internat. Commn, 1983–98. Hon. DD Birmingham, 1998; DD Lambeth, 1999. *Publications:* (contrib.) The Phenomenon of Christian Belief, 1970; (with M. F. Wiles) Documents in Early Christian Thought, 1975; Their Lord and Ours, 1982; (contrib.) The Church and the State, 1984; (contrib.) Dropping the Bomb, 1985; articles in: Jl of Theological Studies; Theology. *Address:* Bishop's Croft, Old Church Road, Harborne, Birmingham B17 0BG. *T:* (0121) 427 1163, *Fax:* (0121) 426 1322.

BIRMINGHAM, Auxiliary Bishop of, (RC); *see* Pargeter, Rt Rev. P.

BIRMINGHAM, Dean of; *see* Mursell, Very Rev. A. G.

BIRMINGHAM, Archdeacon of; *see* Osborne, Ven. H. J.

BIRNBAUM, Michael Ian; QC 1992; a Recorder, since 1995; *b* 26 Feb. 1947; *s* of Samuel Birnbaum and Anne (*née* Zucker); *m* 1984, Aimee Dara Schachter. *Educ:* Southgate County Grammar Sch.; Christ Church, Oxford (BA Jurisp.). Called to the Bar, Middle Temple, 1969; practice mainly in criminal law, extradition and human rights; Asst Recorder, 1990–95; Chm., Africa Sub-Cttee, Bar Internat. Relns Cttee. *Publications:* two reports on the case in Nigeria of Ken Saro-Wiwa and others. *Recreations:* singing, opera, reading. *Address:* 9–12 Bell Yard, WC2A 2LF. *T:* (020) 7400 1800.

BIRNIE, Dr Esmond; Member (UU) Belfast South, Northern Ireland Assembly, since 1998; *b* 6 Jan. 1965; *s* of Dr James Whyte Birnie and Ruth Alexandra Birnie (*née* Bell). *Educ:* Gonville and Caius Coll., Cambridge (BA 1st Cl. Hons Econs 1986); Queen's Univ., Belfast (PhD Econs 1994). Res. Asst, NI Econ. Res. Centre, 1986–89; Lectr in Econs, 1989–2000, Sen. Lectr, 2000– (on leave of absence), QUB. UU Party spokesman on North–South affairs and British–Irish Council, 1999–. Chm., Cttee for Higher and Further Educn, Trng and Employment, NI Assembly, 1999–. *Publications:* Without Profit or Prophets, 1997; *jointly:* Closing the Productivity Gap, 1990; East German Productivity, 1993; The Competitiveness of Industry in Ireland, 1994; Competitiveness of Industry in the Czech Republic and Hungary, 1995; An Economics Lesson for Irish Nationalists and Republicans, 1995; Environmental Regulation, the Firm and Competitiveness, 1998; The Northern Ireland Economy, 1999. *Recreations:* cycling, jogging, art, architecture, music, church choir, active church member and Elder. *Address:* Northern Ireland Assembly, Parliament Buildings, Stormont, Belfast BT4 3SW. *T:* (028) 9029 1149; 32 Finaghy Road South, Finaghy, Belfast BT10 0DR.

BIRO, Bálint Stephen, (Val); illustrator, painter, and author of children's books; *b* Budapest, 6 Oct. 1921; *s* of late Dr Bálint Biro and Margaret Biro (*née* Gyulaházi); *m* 1st, 1945, Vivien Woolley (marr. diss. 1970; she *d* 1991); one *d*; 2nd, 1970, Marie-Louise Ellaway; one step *s* one step *d*. *Educ:* Cistercian Sch., Budapest; Central Sch. of Art, London. Nat. Fire Service, London, 1942–45; Studio Manager, Sylvan Press, 1944–46; Production Manager, C. & J. Temple, 1946–48; Art Dir, John Lehmann, 1948–53; weekly illustrations for Radio Times, 1951–72; freelance illustrator and designer of book covers, 1953–. Mem., Chesham UDC, 1966–70. Vice Chm., Bosham Assoc., 1989–91; Member: Soc. of Authors, 1970; Vintage Austin Register, 1961. Chm. of Govs, Amersham Coll. of Art and Design, 1974–84. *Publications:* author and illustrator of eighty-three books, including: Bumpy's Holiday, 1943; 36 Gumdrop titles, incl. Gumdrop: the adventures of a vintage car, 1965, Gumdrop's School Adventure, 2001; Hungarian Folk Tales, 1981 (trans. Spanish 1991); The Magic Doctor, 1982; The Hobyahs, 1985; Tobias and the Dragon, 1989; Look and Find ABC, 1990; Miranda's Umbrella, 1990; Rub-a-Dub-Dub Nursery Rhymes, 1991; Three Billy Goats Gruff, 1993; Lazy Jack, 1995; Jasper's Jungle Journey, 1995; Bears Can't Fly, 1996; Hansel and Gretel, 1996; Goldilocks and the Three Bears, 1998; Little Red Riding Hood, 2000; The Joking Wolf, 2001; illustrator of numerous books, including: Denys Val Baker, Worlds Without End, 1945; H. E. Todd, children's picture books, 1954–88; Jean Plaidy, historical novels, 1960–74; Anthony Hope, The Prisoner of Zenda, 1961; L. Frank Baum, Wizard of Oz books, 1965, 1967; Lord Tweedsmuir, One Man's Happiness, 1968; Eric Shipton, That Untravelled World, 1969; J. H. B. Peel, Country Talk books, 1970–81; The Good Food Guide, 1971; The Robert Carrier Cookery Course, 1974; Kenneth Grahame, Wind in the Willows, 1983; Margaret Mahy, The King's Jokes, 1987; My Oxford Picture Word Book, 1994; Ted Wragg, The Flying Boot reading scheme, 1994–95; Christina Butler, The Dinosaur's Egg, 1994; Anthony Trollope: The Landleagers, 1995; Golden Lion of Grandpere, 1997; G. K. Chesterton, Father Brown Stories, 1996; Michael Hardcastle, Carole's Camel, 1997; Anthony Buckeridge: Jennings Sounds the Alarm, 1999; Jennings Breaks the Record, 2000; Jennings Joins the Search Party, 2001. *Recreations:* vintage car rallies, painting, photography. *Address:* Bridge Cottage, Brook Avenue, Bosham, West Sussex PO18 8LQ. *T:* (01243) 574195. *Clubs:* Bosham Sailing; Vintage Sports-Car (Chipping Norton).

BIRRELL, Sir James (Drake), Kt 1993; FCA; FCBSI; Chief Executive, Halifax Building Society, 1988–93; *b* 18 Aug. 1933; *s* of James Russell Birrell, MA and Edith Marion Birrell, BSc (*née* Drake); *m* 1958, Margaret Anne Pattison; two *d*. *Educ:* Belle Vue Grammar School, Bradford. FCA 1955; FCBSI 1989. Boyce Welch & Co. (articled clerk), 1949–55; Pilot Officer, RAF, 1955–57; chartered accountant, Price Waterhouse, 1957–60; Accountant, ADA Halifax, 1960–61; Management Accountant, Empire Stores, 1961–64; Dir and Co. Sec., John Gladstone & Co., 1964–68; Halifax Building Society, 1968–93. Non-executive Director: Securicor, 1993–; Wesleyan Gen. Assce Soc., 1993–. Mem., Building Societies Commn, 1994–. *Recreations:* golf, gardening, archaeology, local history. *Address:* 4 Marlin End, Berkhamsted, Herts HP4 3GB.

BIRSE, Peter Malcolm; Chairman, Birse Group, 1999–2001 (Chairman and Chief Executive, 1970–99); *b* 24 Nov. 1942; *s* of Peter A. M. Birse and Margaret C. Birse; *m* 1969, Helen Searle; two *s* one *d*. *Educ:* Arbroath High Sch.; St Andrews Univ. (BScEng). MICE. Engineer, John Mowlem, 1963–66; Site Manager: Cammon (Ghana), 1966–68; Cammon (UK), 1968–69; Engineer, Foster Wheeler, 1969–70; founded Birse Group, 1970. *Recreations:* sailing, ski-ing. *Address:* c/o Birse Group, Humber Road, Barton-on-Humber, N Lincs DN18 5BW. *Club:* Royal Ocean Racing.

BIRT, family name of **Baron Birt**.

BIRT, Baron *cr* 2000 (Life Peer), of Liverpool in the County of Merseyside; **John Birt,** Kt 1998; Chairman, Lynx New Media, since 2000; Adviser, McKinsey & Co., New York, since 2000; Strategy Adviser to the Prime Minister, since 2001; *b* 10 Dec. 1944; *s* of Leo Vincent Birt and Ida Birt; *m* 1965, Jane Frances (*née* Lake); one *s* one *d*. *Educ:* St Mary's Coll., Liverpool; St Catherine's Coll., Oxford (MA; Hon. Fellow 1992). Producer, Nice Time, 1968–69; Joint Editor, World in Action, 1969–70; Producer, The Frost Programme, 1971–72; Executive Producer, Weekend World, 1972–74; Head of Current Affairs, LWT, 1974–77; Co-Producer, The Nixon Interviews, 1977; Controller of Features and Current Affairs, LWT, 1977–81; Dir of Programmes, LWT, 1982–87; Dep. Dir-Gen., 1987–92, Dir-Gen., 1992–2000, BBC. Advr to Prime Minister on Criminal Justice, 2000–01. Vis. Fellow, Nuffield Coll., Oxford, 1991–99. Member: Wilton Park Academic Council, 1980–83; Media Law Gp, 1983–94; Opportunity 2000 (formerly Women's Economic) Target Team, BITC, 1991–98; Internat. Council, Mus. of TV and Radio, NY, 1994–2000; Broadcasting Research Unit: Mem., Working Party on the new Technologies, 1981–83; Mem., Exec. Cttee, 1983–87. Vice-Pres., RTS, 1994–2000 (Fellow, 1989). CompIEE 1998. Hon. Fellow, Univ. of Wales Cardiff, 1997. Hon. DLitt: Liverpool John Moores, 1992; City, 1998; Hon. DLitt Bradford, 1999. Emmy Award, US Nat. Acad. of Television, Arts and Scis, 1995. *Publications:* various articles in newspapers and journals. *Recreation:* walking. *Address:* c/o House of Lords, SW1A 0PW.

BIRT, Prof. (Lindsay) Michael, AO 1986; CBE 1980; FTS; Vice-Chancellor, University of New South Wales, 1981–92; Chairman, Australian Science and Technology Council, 1992–93; *b* 18 Jan. 1932; *s* of Robert Birt and Florence Elizabeth Chapman; *m* 1959, Jenny Tapfield; two *s*. *Educ:* Melbourne Boys' High Sch.; Univ. of Melbourne; Univ. of Oxford. BAgrSc, BSc and PhD (Melb), DPhil (Oxon). FTS 1992. Univ. of Melbourne: Lectr in Biochemistry, 1960–63, Sen. Lectr in Biochem., 1964; Sen. Lectr in Biochem., Univ. of Sheffield, 1964–67; Foundn Prof. of Biochemistry, ANU, 1967–73; Vice-Chancellor designate, Wollongong Univ. Coll., Nov. 1973; Vice-Chancellor, Univ. of Wollongong, 1975–81; Emer. Prof., ANU, 1974. Hon. DLitt Wollongong, 1981; Hon. LLD Sheffield, 1988; Hon. DSc: New South Wales, 1992; Queensland, 1992; Dr (*hc*) Charles Sturt. *Publications:* Biochemistry of the Tissues (with W. Bartley and P. Banks), 1968 (London), 1970 (Germany, as Biochemie), 1972 (Japan); Not an Ivory Tower: the making of an Australian Vice-Chancellor, 1997. *Recreations:* music, reading. *Address:* 85 Florida Road, Palm Beach, NSW 2108, Australia. *T:* (2) 99744651. *Clubs:* Union, University and Schools (Sydney); Melbourne Cricket, Sydney Cricket.

BIRT, Michael Cameron St John; QC 1995; Deputy Bailiff, Jersey, since 2000; *b* 25 Aug. 1948; *s* of St John Michael Clive Birt and Mairi Araminta Birt (*née* Cameron); *m* 1973, Joan Frances Miller; two *s* one *d*. *Educ:* Marlborough Coll.; Magdalene Coll., Cambridge (MA Law). Called to the Bar, Middle Temple, 1970, to Jersey Bar, 1977; in practice: London, 1971–75; as Jersey advocate, with Ogier & Le Cornu, St Helier, 1976–93; Crown Advocate of Jersey, 1987–93; HM Attorney General, Jersey, 1994–2000. *Recreations:* ski-ing, yachting, golf. *Address:* Bailiff's Chambers, Royal Court House, St Helier, Jersey JE1 1BA. *T:* (01534) 502100, *Fax:* (01534) 502199. *Clubs:* Royal Channel Islands Yacht; Royal Jersey Golf.

BIRT, Ven. Canon William Raymond; Archdeacon of Berkshire, 1973–77; Archdeacon Emeritus, since 1985; Hon. Canon of Christ Church Cathedral, Oxford, 1980; *b* 25 Aug. 1911; *s* of Rev. Douglas Birt, Rector of Leconfield with Scorborough, and Dorothy Birt; *m* 1st, 1936, Marie Louise Jeaffreson (*d* 1990); one *s* two *d*; 2nd, 1994, Diana Bronwen Warren (*née* Montgomery). *Educ:* Christ's Hospital; Ely Theological Coll. Schoolmaster, Trent Coll., 1929–31; sub-editor, Daily Sketch, 1933–34; asst editor, Play Rights Publications, 1934–39. Major, 22nd Dragoons (RAC), 1941–46 (despatches). Editor: Winchester Publications, 1946–49; Country Life Books, 1949–56. Deacon, 1956; priest, 1957; Curate, Caversham, 1956–59; Vicar, St George, Newbury, 1959–71; Rector of West Woodhay, 1971–81, Asst Rector, 1981–91; Rural Dean of Newbury, 1969–73. *Recreations:* gardens and gardening. *Address:* 1 The Old Bakery, George Street, Kingsclere, Newbury, Berkshire RG20 5NQ. *T:* (01635) 297426.

BIRTS, Peter William; QC 1990; QC (NI) 1996; a Recorder, since 1989; *b* 9 Feb. 1946; *s* of John Claude Birts and Audrey Lavinia Birts; *m* 1st, 1971, Penelope Ann Eyre (marr. diss. 1997); two *d* one *s*; 2nd, 1997, Mrs Angela Forcer-Evans. *Educ:* Lancing College; St John's College, Cambridge (choral scholarship; MA). Called to the Bar, Gray's Inn, 1968, Bencher 1998; Mem., Gen. Council of the Bar, 1989–95 (Chm., Legal Aid and Fees Cttee, 1994–95). Member: Judicial Studies Bd (Main Bd and Civil and Family Cttee), 1991–96; County Court Rules Cttee, 1991–99; Legal Mem., Mental Health Review Tribunals, 1994–. Asst Parly Boundary Comr, 1992–. Gov., Benenden Sch., 1990–93. Freeman, City of London, 1967; Liveryman, Carpenters' Co., 1967–. *Publications:* Trespass: summary procedure for possession of land (with Alan Willis), 1987; Remedies for Trespass, 1990; (ed and contrib.) Butterworths Costs Service, 1999–. *Recreations:* music, shooting, fishing, walking. *Address:* 3 Pump Court, Temple, EC4Y 7AJ. *T:* (020) 7353 0711. *Club:* Hurlingham.

BIRTWISTLE, Maj.-Gen. Archibald Cull, CB 1983; CBE 1976 (OBE 1971); DL; Signal Officer in Chief (Army), 1980–83, retired; Master of Signals, 1990–97; *b* 19 Aug. 1927; *s* of Walter Edwin Birtwistle and Eila Louise Cull; *m* 1956, Sylvia Elleray; two *s* one *d*. *Educ:* Sir John Deane's Grammar School, Northwich; St John's Coll., Cambridge (MA

Mech. Sciences). CEng, MIEE. Commissioned, Royal Signals, 1949; served: Korea (despatches, 1952); UK; BAOR; CCR Sigs 1 (Br) Corps, 1973–75; Dep. Comdt, RMCS, 1975–79; Chief Signal Officer, BAOR, 1979–80. Col Comdt, Royal Corps of Signals, 1983–89, and 1990–97; Hon. Colonel: Durham and South Tyne ACF, 1983–88; 34 (Northern) Signal Regt (Vol.), TA, 1988–90. Pres., British Korean Veterans Assoc., 1997–. DL N Yorks, 1991. *Recreations:* all sports, especially Rugby (former Chairman, Army Rugby Union), soccer and cricket; gardening. *Address:* c/o National Westminster Bank PLC, 97 High Street, Northallerton, North Yorks DL7 8PS.

BIRTWISTLE, Sir Harrison, CH 2001; Kt 1988; composer; Henry Purcell Professor of Composition, King's College London, since 1994; *b* 1934; *m* Sheila; three *s*. *Educ:* Royal Manchester Coll. of Music; RAM (Hon. FRAM). Dir of Music, Cranborne Chase Sch., 1962–65. Composer-in-residence, London Philharmonic Orch., 1993–. Vis. Fellow, Princeton Univ., 1966–68; Cornell Vis. Prof. of Music, Swarthmore Coll., 1973; Vis. Slee Prof., State Univ. of NY at Buffalo, 1974–75. An Associate Dir, NT, 1975–88. Mem., Akademie der Kunst, Berlin. FKC 1998. Hon. DMus Sussex; Hon. DLitt Salford. Evening Standard Award for Opera, 1987, 1991; Ernst von Siemens Foundn Prize, 1995. Chevalier des Arts et des Lettres (France), 1986. *Publications:* Refrains and Choruses, 1957; Monody for Corpus Christi, 1959; Précis, 1959; The World is Discovered, 1960; Chorales, 1962, 1963; Entre'actes and Sappho Fragments, 1964; Three Movements with Fanfares, 1964; Tragoedia, 1965; Ring a Dumb Carillon, 1965; Carmen Paschale, 1965; The Mark of the Goat, 1965, 1966; The Visions of Francesco Petrarca, 1966; Verses, 1966; Punch and Judy, 1966–67 (opera); Three Lessons in a Frame, 1967; Linoii, 1968; Nomos, 1968; Verses for Ensembles, 1969; Down by the Greenwood Side, 1969; Hoquetus David (arr. of Machaut), 1969; Cantata, 1969; Ut Hermita Solvs, 1969; Medusa, 1969–70; Prologue, 1970; Nenia on the Death of Orpheus, 1970; An Imaginary Landscape, 1971; Meridian, 1971; The Fields of Sorrow, 1971; Chronometer, 1971; Epilogue—Full Fathom Five, 1972; Tombeau, 1972; The Triumph of Time, 1972; La Plage: eight arias of remembrance, 1972; Dinah and Nick's Love Song, 1972; Chanson de Geste, 1973; The World is Discovered, 1973; Grimethorpe Aria, 1973; 5 Chorale Preludes from Bach, 1973; Chorales from a Toyshop, 1973; Interludes from a Tragedy, 1973; The Mask of Orpheus, 1973–84 (opera) (Grawemeyer Award, Univ. of Louisville, 1987); Melencolia I, 1975; Pulse Field, Bow Down, Silbury Air, 1977; For O, for O, the Hobby-horse is forgot, 1977; Carmen Arcardiae Mechanicae Perpetuum, 1978; agm, 1979; On the Sheer Threshold of the Night, 1980; Quintet, 1981; Pulse Sampler, 1981; Deowa, 1983; Yan Tan Tethera, 1984; Still Movement, 1984; Secret Theatre, 1984; Songs by Myself, 1984; Earth Dances, 1986; Fanfare for Will, 1987; Endless Parade, 1987; Gawain, 1990 (opera); Four Poems by Jaan Kaplinski, 1991; Gawain's Journey, 1991; Antiphonies, 1992; The Second Mrs Kong, 1994 (opera); Cry of Anubis, 1995; Panic, 1995; Pulse Shadows, 1996; Slow Frieze, 1997; Exody, 1997; Harrison's Clocks, 1998; The Silk House Antiphonies, 1999; The Woman and the Hare, 1999; The Last Supper (opera), 2000; The Axe Manual, 2001. *Address:* c/o Allied Artists Agency, 42 Montpelier Square, SW7 1JZ.

BIRTWISTLE, Susan Elizabeth, (Lady Eyre); film and television producer; *d* of late Frank Edgar Birtwistle and Brenda Mary Birtwistle (*née* Higham); *m* 1973, Richard Charles Hastings Eyre (*see* Sir Richard Eyre); one *d*. Theatre director: Royal Lyceum Th. in Educn Co., 1970-72; Nottingham Playhouse Roundabout Co., 1973-78; freelance TV producer, 1980-: work includes: Hotel du Lac, 1986; Scoop; 'v'; Or Shall We Die?; Dutch Girls; Ball Trap on the Côte Sauvage; Anna Lee, 1993; Pride and Prejudice, 1995; Emma, 1996; King Lear, 1998; Wives and Daughters, 1999. Member: Arts Council Drama Panel, 1975-77; ACTT, 1979. *Publications:* The Making of Pride and Prejudice, 1995; The Making of Jane Austen's Emma, 1996. *Recreations:* gardening, theatre, music, books, croquet. *Address:* c/o Peter Murphy, Curtis Brown, 4th Floor, Haymarket House, 28-29 Haymarket, SW1Y 4SP. *T:* (020) 7396 6600.

BISCHOFF, Dr Manfred; Chairman, European Aeronautic Defence and Space Co., since 2000; *b* Calw, Germany, 22 April 1942. *Educ:* Univ. of Tubingen; Univ. of Heidelberg (MEc; Dr rer. pol. 1973). Asst Prof. for Econ. Politics and Internat. Trade, Alfred Weber Inst., Univ. of Heidelberg, 1968–76; joined Daimler-Benz AG, 1976; Project Co-ordinator for Mercedes Benz Cross Country Cars, Corporate Subsids, M & A Dept, 1976–81; Internat. Projects, M & A, Finance Dept, 1981–88 (Vice-Pres., Finance Cos and Corporate Subsids); Member, Board of Management: and Chief Financial Officer, Mercedes do Brasil, 1988–89; Deutsche Aerospace AG, later Daimler-Benz Aerospace AG, 1989–95; Daimler-Benz AG, later Daimler Chrysler AG, 1995–2000; Chairman: Bd of Mgt, 1995–2000, Supervisory Bd, 2000–, Dasa; Supervisory Bd, Airbus Industrie, 1998–; non-exec. Dir, Mitsubishi Motors Corp., 2000–. President: Eur. Assoc. Aerospace Industries, 1995–96; Fedn of German Aerospace Industries, 1996–2000. *Address:* European Aeronautic Defence and Space Co. EADS NV, Drentastraat 24, 1083 HK Amsterdam, Netherlands.

BISCHOFF, Sir Winfried Franz Wilhelm, (Sir Win), Kt 2000; Chairman, Citigroup, since 2000; Director: Schroders plc, since 1983 (Group Chief Executive, 1984–95; Chairman, 1995–2000); J. Henry Schroder & Co. Ltd, since 1978 (Chairman, 1983–94); *b* 10 May 1941; *s* of late Paul Helmut Bischoff and Hildegard (*née* Kühne); *m* 1972, Rosemary Elizabeth, *d* of Hon. Leslie Leathers; two *s*. *Educ:* Marist Brothers, Inanda, Johannesburg, S Africa; Univ. of the Witwatersrand, Johannesburg (BCom). Man. Dir, Schroders Asia Ltd, Hong Kong, 1971–82. Dep. Chm., Cable and Wireless, 1995– (non–exec. Dir, 1991–); non-executive Director: Land Securities, 1999–; McGraw-Hill Cos, Inc., 1999–; IFIL, Finanziaria di Partecipazioni SpA, 2000–; Eli Lilly & Co., 2000–. *Recreations:* opera, music, golf. *Address:* Citigroup Centre, 33 Canada Square, E14 5LB. *T:* (020) 7658 6565. *Clubs:* Woking Golf, Swinley Forest Golf, Frilford Heath Golf; 300 (Japan).

BISCOE, Prof. Timothy John; Pro-Provost, China, University College London, 1996–99; *b* 28 April 1932; *s* of late Rev. W. H. Biscoe and Mrs M. G. Biscoe; *m* 1955, Daphne Miriam (*née* Gurton); one *s* two *d*. *Educ:* Latymer Upper School; The London Hospital Medical College. BSc (Hons) Physiology, 1953; MB, BS 1957; DSc London, 1993; FRCP 1983. London Hospital, 1957–58; RAMC Short Service Commission, 1958–62; Physiologist, CDEE, Porton Down, 1959–62; ARC Inst. of Animal Physiology, Babraham, 1962–65; Res. Fellow in Physiology, John Curtin Sch. of Med. Res., Canberra, 1965–66; Associate Res. Physiologist, Cardiovascular Res. Inst., UC Medical Center, San Francisco, 1966–68; University of Bristol: Res. Associate, Dept of Physiology, 1968–70; 2nd Chair of Physiology, 1970–79; Head of Dept of Physiology, 1975–79. University College London: Jodrell Prof. of Physiology, 1979–92; Vice Provost, 1990–92; Hon. Fellow, 1996; Dep. Vice-Chancellor, Univ. of Hong Kong, 1992–95. McLaughlin Vis. Prof., McMaster Univ., Ont, 1986; Hooker Distinguished Vis. Prof., McMaster Univ., 1990. Hon. Sec., Physiological Soc., 1977–82; Member Council: Harveian Soc., 1983–86; Research Defence Soc., 1983–90 (Hon. Sec., 1983–86). Mem., Academia Europaea, 1991. *Publications:* papers on neurophysiology in Journal of Physiology, etc. *Recreations:* looking, listening, reading. *Address:* University College London, Gower Street, WC1E 6BT. *Club:* Garrick.

BISHKO, Roy Colin; Founder, and Co-Chairman, Tie Rack Ltd, since 1999 (Chairman, 1981–99); *b* 2 March 1944; *s* of Isidore Bishko and Rae Bishko; *m* 1969, Barbara Eileen (*née* Hirsch); one *s* one *d*. *Educ:* Grey Coll., Bloemfontein, SA; Univ. of S Africa (Attorney's Admission 1967). With Schlesinger Orgn, 1969–74; Dir, Dorrington Investment Co. Ltd, 1974–76; Man. Dir, Chaddesley Investments, London, 1976–78. FRSA 1992. *Recreation:* golf.

BISHOP, family name of **Baroness O'Cathain**.

BISHOP, Alan Henry, CB 1989; HM Chief Inspector of Prisons for Scotland, 1989–94; *b* 12 Sept. 1929; *s* of Robert Bishop and May Watson; *m* 1959, Marjorie Anne Conlan; one *s* one *d*. *Educ:* George Heriot's Sch., Edinburgh; Edinburgh Univ. (MA 1st Cl. Hons Econ. Science, 1951, 2nd Cl. Hons History, 1952). Served RAF Educn Br., 1952–54. Asst Principal, Dept of Agric. for Scotland, 1954; Private Sec. to Parly Under-Secs of State, 1958–59; Principal, 1959; First Sec., Agric. and Food, Copenhagen and The Hague, 1963–66; Asst Sec., Scottish Develt Dept, 1968; Asst Sec., Commn on the Constitution, 1969–73; Asst Under-Sec. of State, 1980–84, Principal Establishment Officer, 1984–89, Scottish Office. *Recreations:* contract bridge (Pres., Scottish Bridge Union, 1979–80), theatre, golf. *Address:* Beaumont Court, 19/8 Wester Coates Gardens, Edinburgh EH12 5LT. *T:* (0131) 346 4641. *Clubs:* New (Edinburgh); Melville Bridge, Murrayfield Golf.

BISHOP, Ven. (Anthony) Peter, CB 2001; Associate Priest, Tewkesbury with Walton Cardiff and Twyning, since 2001; *b* 24 May 1946; *s* of Geoffrey Richard Bishop and Dora Annie Bishop; *m* 1970, Ruth Isabel Jordan; two *s*. *Educ:* London Coll. of Divinity; St John's Coll., Nottingham (LTh 1971; MPhil 1983). Civil Servant, MoT, 1963–67; ordained deacon 1971, priest 1972; Curate, Beckenham, 1971–75; RAF Chaplain, 1975–2001: Asst Chaplain-in-Chief, 1991–98; Chaplain-in-Chief, and Archdeacon, RAF, 1998–2001. QHC 1996–2001. Canon of Lincoln, 1998–2001. Mem., Gen. Synod of C of E, 1998–2001. Mem. Council, RAF Benevolent Fund, 1998–2001; Vice-Pres., RAFA, 1998–2001. FRSA 1983; FRAeS 1999. *Recreations:* walking, history, biography, cookery, travelling in France. *Address:* The Vicarage, Church End, Twyning, Tewkesbury, Glos GL20 6DA. *Club:* Royal Air Force.

BISHOP, Dr Arthur Clive; Deputy Director, British Museum (Natural History), 1982–89, and Keeper of Mineralogy, 1975–89; *b* 9 July 1930; *s* of late Charles Henry Bishop and Hilda (*née* Clowes); *m* 1962, Helen (*née* Bennison); one *d*. *Educ:* Wolstanton County Grammar Sch., Newcastle, Staffs; King's Coll., Univ. of London (FKC 1985). BSc 1951, PhD 1954. Geologist, HM Geological Survey, 1954; served RAF Educn Br., 1955–57; Lectr in Geology, Queen Mary Coll., Univ. of London, 1958; Principal Sci. Officer, British Museum (Natural History), 1969, Deputy Keeper 1972. Geological Society: Daniel Pidgeon Fund, 1958; Murchison Fund, 1970; Vice-Pres., 1977–78; Mineralogical Society: Gen. Sec., 1965–72; Vice-Pres., 1973–74; Pres., 1986–87; Pres., Geologists' Assoc., 1978–80 (Halstead Medallist, 1999); Vice-Pres., Inst. of Science Technology, 1973–82. Mem. d'honneur, La Société Jersiaise, 1983. *Publications:* An Outline of Crystal Morphology, 1967; (with W. R. Hamilton and A. R. Woolley) Hamlyn Guide to Minerals, Rocks and Fossils, 1974, rev. edn as Philip's Minerals, Rocks and Fossils, 1999; papers in various jls, mainly on geology of Channel Is and Brittany, and on dioritic rocks. *Recreations:* drawing and painting. *Address:* 4 Viewfield Road, Bexley, Kent DA5 3EE. *T:* (020) 8302 9602.

BISHOP, Prof. David Hugh Langler, PhD, DSc; FIBiol; Fellow, St Cross College, Oxford, 1984–98, now Emeritus; Director, Natural Environment Research Council Institute of Virology and Environmental Microbiology (formerly Institute of Virology), 1984–95; *b* 31 Dec. 1937; *s* of late Reginald Samuel Harold Bishop and of Violet Rosina May Langler; *m* 1st, 1963, Margaret Duthie (marr. diss.); one *s* one *d*; 2nd, 1971, Polly Roy (marr. diss.); one *s*; 3rd, 1999, Margreta Buijs; one *s* one *d*. *Educ:* Liverpool Univ. (BSc 1959, PhD 1962); MA 1984, DSc 1988, Oxon. FIBiol 1989. Postdoctoral Fellow, CNRS, Gif-sur-Yvette, 1962–63; Research Associate, Univ. of Edinburgh, 1963–66, Univ. of Illinois, 1966–69; Asst Prof., 1969–70, Associate Prof., 1970–71, Columbia Univ.; Associate Prof., 1971–75, Prof., 1975, Rutgers Univ.; University of Alabama at Birmingham: Prof., 1975–84; Sen. Scientist, Comprehensive Cancer Center, 1975–84; Chm., Dept of Microbiology, 1983–84; Adjunct Prof., Dept of Internat. Health, 1996–99. Vis. Fellow, Lincoln Coll., Oxford, 1981–82; Vis. Prof. of Virology, Oxford Univ., 1984–97; Hon. Prof., Dept of Microbiol., Univ. of Qld, 1997–2000. Nathaniel A. Young Award in Virology, 1981. *Publications:* Rhabdoviruses, 1979; numerous contribs to books and jls. *Recreation:* hill walking. *Address:* 12 Chemin du Haut Morier, 41000 Blois Les Grouets, Loir et Cher, France.

BISHOP, Prof. Dorothy Vera Margaret, DPhil; Professor of Developmental Neuropsychology, since 1999, and Wellcome Principal Research Fellow, since 1998, University of Oxford; *b* 14 Feb. 1952; *d* of Aubrey Francis Bishop and Annemarie Sofia Bishop (*née* Eucken); *m* 1976, Patrick Michael Anthony Rabbitt, *qv*. *Educ:* St Hugh's Coll., Oxford (BA Hons 1973; MA; DPhil 1978); Inst. of Psychiatry, Univ. of London (MPhil 1975). Res. Officer, Neuropsychology Unit, Dept of Clinical Neurology, Univ. of Oxford, 1975–82; Sen. Res. Fellow, MRC, at Univs of Newcastle upon Tyne and Manchester, 1982–91; Sen. Res. Scientist, MRC Applied Psychology Unit, Cambridge, 1991–98. Adjunct Prof., Univ. of Western Australia, 1998. Mem., ESRC, 1996–2000. *Publications:* (ed with K. Mogford) Language Development in Exceptional Circumstances, 1988; Handedness and Developmental Disorders, 1990; Uncommon Understanding: development and disorders of language comprehension in children, 1997; (ed with L. B. Leonard) Speech and Language Impairments in Children, 2000. *Recreations:* Victorian novels, pre-1945 films. *Address:* Department of Experimental Psychology, South Parks Road, Oxford OX1 3UD. *T:* (01865) 271386.

BISHOP, Sir Frederick (Arthur), Kt 1975; CB 1960; CVO 1957; Director-General of the National Trust, 1971–75; *b* 4 Dec. 1915; *o s* of A. J. Bishop, Bristol; *m* 1940, Elizabeth Finlay Stevenson (*d* 1999); two *s* one *d*. *Educ:* Colston's Hospital, Bristol. LLB (London). Inland Revenue, 1934. Served in RAF and Air Transport Auxiliary, 1942–46. Ministry of Food, 1947, where Principal Private Secretary to Ministers, 1949–52; Asst Secretary, Cabinet Office, 1953–55; Principal Private Secretary to the Prime Minister, 1956–59; Deputy Secretary: of the Cabinet, 1959–61; Min. of Agriculture, Fisheries and Food, 1961–64; Perm. Sec., Min. of Land and Natural Resources, 1964–65, resigned. Chm., Home Grown Timber Advisory Cttee, 1966–73; Member: BBC Gen. Adv. Council, 1971–75; Crafts Adv. Council, 1973–75. Director: S. Pearson & Son Ltd, 1965–70; Pearson Longman, 1970–77; English China Clays Ltd, 1975–86; Devon and Cornwall Bd, Lloyds Bank, 1976–86. *Address:* Manor Barn, Church Road, Bramshott, Liphook GU30 7SQ.

BISHOP, George Robert, CBE 1993; DPhil; FRSE; CPhys, FInstP; Director General, Ispra Establishment, Joint Research Centre, European Commission, Ispra, Italy, 1983–92, retired (Director, 1982–83); *b* 16 Jan. 1927; *s* of George William Bishop and Lilian Elizabeth Garrod; *m* 1952, Adriana Giuseppina, *d* of Luigi Caberlotto and Giselda Mazzariol; two *s* one *d*. *Educ:* Christ Church, Oxford (MA, DPhil). ICI Research Fellow,

Univ. of Oxford, 1951; Research Fellow, St Antony's Coll., Oxford, 1952; Chercheur, Ecole Normale Supérieure, Paris, 1954; Ingénieur-Physicien, Laboratoire de l'Accelerateur Linéaire, ENS, Orsay, 1958; Prof., Faculté des Sciences, Univ. de Paris, 1962; Kelvin Prof. of Natural Philosophy, Univ. of Glasgow, 1964–76; Dir, Dept of Natural and Physical Sciences, JRC, Ispra, 1974–82. Hon. DSc, Strathclyde, 1979. *Publications:* Handbuch der Physik, Band XLII, 1957; β and X-Ray Spectroscopy, 1960; Nuclear Structure and Electromagnetic Interactions, 1965; numerous papers in learned jls on nuclear and high energy physics. *Recreations:* literature, music, swimming, tennis, gardening, travel. *Address:* via Favretti 23/A, Mogliano Veneto, 31021 (TV), Italy. *T:* (41) 455813.

BISHOP, James Drew; writer and editor; Chairman, National Heritage, since 1998 (Trustee, since 1995); *b* 18 June 1929; *s* of late Sir Patrick Bishop, MBE, MP, and Vera Drew; *m* 1959, Brenda Pearson; two *s*. *Educ:* Haileybury; Corpus Christi Coll., Cambridge. Reporter, Northampton Chronicle & Echo, 1953; joined editorial staff of The Times, 1954; Foreign Correspondent, 1957–64; Foreign News Editor, 1964–66; Features Editor, 1966–70; Editor, Illustrated London News, 1971–87; Editor-in-Chief, Illustrated London News Publications, 1987–94. Director: Illustrated London News & Sketch Ltd, 1973–94; International Thomson Publishing Ltd, 1980–85. Chm., Assoc. of British Editors, 1987–96. Mem. Adv. Bd, 1970–, Chm., 2000–, Annual Register (contributor, Amer. sect., 1960–88); Chm. Editl Bd, Natural World, 1981–97. *Publications:* A Social History of Edwardian Britain, 1977; Social History of the First World War, 1982; (with Oliver Woods) The Story of The Times, 1983; (ed) The Illustrated Counties of England, 1985; The Sedgwick Story, 1998. *Recreations:* reading, walking, looking and listening. *Address:* 67 Parliament Hill, NW3 2TB. *T:* (020) 7435 4403, *Fax:* (020) 7435 0778; Black Fen, Scotland Street, Stoke by Nayland, Suffolk CO6 4QF., *T:* and *Fax:* (01206) 262315. *Clubs:* Oxford and Cambridge, MCC.

BISHOP, John Edward; His Honour Judge Bishop; a Circuit Judge, since 1993; *b* 9 Feb. 1943; *s* of Albert George Bishop and Frances Marion Bishop; *m* 1968, Elizabeth Ann Grover; two *d*. *Educ:* St Edward's Sch., Oxford. Articled to P. F. Carter-Ruck at Messrs Oswald Hickson Collier & Co., WC2, 1962–66; admitted solicitor, 1966; Partner: Messrs Copley Clark & Co., Sutton, 1969–81; Messrs Tuck & Mann, Epsom, 1981–85; Registrar: Woolwich County Court, 1985–88; Croydon County Court, 1988–93 (District Judge, 1992–93); an Asst Recorder, 1987–90; a Recorder, 1990–93. Pres., Mid-Surrey Law Soc., 1980–81. *Recreations:* golf, walking, music, reading, garden, family. *Address:* Kingston-upon-Thames County Court, St James' Road, Kingston-upon-Thames, Surrey KT1 2AD. *Club:* Walton Heath Golf.

BISHOP, Dr John Edward Lucas; freelance musician; *b* 23 Feb. 1935; *s* of late Reginald John Bishop and of Eva Bishop (*née* Lucas). *Educ:* Cotham Sch., Bristol; St John's Coll., Cambridge (Exhibr); Reading and Edinburgh Univs. MA, MusB Cantab; DMus Edin.; FRCO (CHM); ADCM; Hon. FBSM. John Stewart of Rannoch Schol. (Univ. prize) 1954. Organist and Asst Dir of Music, Worksop Coll., Notts, 1958–69; Dir of Music, Worksop Coll., 1969–73; Birmingham School of Music: Dir of Studies, 1973–74; Sen. Lectr, 1974–79; Principal Lectr, Head of Organ Studies and Head of Admissions, 1979–87. Dir of Music, Cotham Parish Church, Bristol, 1976–90; Hon. Dir of Music, St Paul's Church, Birmingham, 1986; Dir, Bristol Highbury Singers, 1978–90; Consultant, Wells Cathedral Sch., 1986–93. Organ recitalist (incl. many broadcasts) and choral conductor (Conductor, 1997–2000, Pres., 2000–, Portishead Choral Soc.), pianist, coach and adjudicator, 1960–. Former Pres., Sheffield, Birmingham and Bristol Organists' Assocs; Member: Council, ISM, 1991–97; Music Adv. Panel, Henleaze Concert Soc., 1995–; Bd of Mgt, Emerald Chamber Players, 1997–. *Publications:* various articles on history and practice of church music and 19th century organ design. *Recreations:* walking, ecclesiology, savouring the countryside, cities and towns, railways, architecture. *Address:* 98 High Kingsdown, Bristol BS2 8ER. *T:* (0117) 942 3373.

BISHOP, Prof. (John) Michael, MD; Professor of Microbiology and Immunology, since 1972, and of Biochemistry and Biophysics, since 1982, University Professor, since 1994, Director, G. W. Hooper Research Foundation, since 1981, and Chancellor, since 1998, University of California, San Francisco; *b* 22 Feb. 1936; *s* of John and Carrie Bishop; *m* 1959, Kathryn Putman; two *s*. *Educ:* Gettysburg Coll., Gettysburg (AB); Harvard Univ., Boston (MD). Intern/Asst Resident in Internal Med., Mass. Gen. Hosp., 1962–64; Res. Associate, NIAID, NIH, 1964–67; Vis. Scientist, Heinrich-Pette Inst., Hamburg, 1967–68; Asst Prof., Microbiology, 1968–70, Associate Prof., Microbiology, 1970–72, Univ. of California. Member: Nat. Acad. of Scis, 1980–; Amer. Acad. of Arts and Scis, 1984–. Hon. DSc Gettysburg, 1983. Albert Lasker Award for Basic Med. Res., 1982; Passano Foundn Award, 1983; Warren Triennial Prize, 1983; Armand Hammer Cancer Res. Award, 1984; Gen. Motors Cancer Res. Award, 1984; Gairdner Foundn Internat. Award, 1984; ACS Medal of Honor, 1985; (jtly) Nobel Prize in Physiology or Medicine, 1989. *Publications:* The Rise of the Genetic Paradigm, 1995; Proto-oncogenes and Plasticity in Cell Signaling, 1995; over 400 pubns in refereed sci. jls. *Recreations:* music, reading, theatre. *Address:* 1542 HSW, University of California, San Francisco, CA 94143–0552, USA. *T:* (415) 4763211.

BISHOP, Kenneth Anthony, CMG 1998; OBE 1973; HM Diplomatic Service, retired; *b* 22 Jan. 1938; *s* of Charles William Bishop and Mary Ann Bishop (*née* Bell); *m* 1962, Christine Mary Pennell; one *s* one *d*. *Educ:* Wade Deacon GS, Widnes; Emmanuel Coll., Cambridge (BA Hons Mod. Langs 1961). Nat. Service, RAF, 1956–58. Joined Foreign Office, 1961; Principal Conf. Interpreter, 1968–98, Res. Counsellor, 1981–98, FCO Research Department: Moscow, 1963–65; Berlin Four-Power Negotiations, 1970–71; Bonn, 1971–72; Geneva Comprehensive Test Ban Talks, 1978–81; Royal Visit to Russia, 1994; Anglo-Soviet/Russian summits, 1961–98. Medal for Outstanding Contribution to the UK/USA Intelligence Relationship, CIA, 1997. *Recreations:* church-based charity work in Russia, hill walking, choral singing. *Address:* 33 Lansdowne Road, Sevenoaks, Kent TN13 3XU. *T:* (01732) 452718. *Club:* Royal Commonwealth Society.

BISHOP, Malcolm Leslie; QC 1993; a Recorder, since 2000; *b* 9 Oct. 1944; *s* of late John Bishop and Irene Bishop (*née* Dunn). *Educ:* Ruabon Grammar Sch.; Regent's Park Coll., Oxford Univ. (Samuel Davies Prizeman; Hon. Mods in Theology, BA Jurisprudence, MA). Chm., OU Dem. Lab. Club, 1966. Called to the Bar, Inner Temple, 1968; in practice on Wales and Chester Circuit. A Dep. High Court Judge, Family Div., 1997; an Asst Recorder, 1998–2000. Circuit Rep., Bar Council, 1987–92; Mem., Exec. Cttee, Family Law Bar Assoc., 1985–. Contested (Lab), Bath, Feb. and Oct. 1974. *Recreations:* politics, wine. *Address:* 30 Park Place, Cardiff CF1 3BA. *T:* (029) 2039 8421; 2 Paper Buildings, Temple, EC4Y 7ET. *T:* (020) 7556 5500. *Clubs:* Oxford and Cambridge; Cardiff and County (Cardiff).

BISHOP, Michael; *see* Bishop, J. M.

BISHOP, Sir Michael (David), Kt 1991; CBE 1986; Chairman: British Midland Plc (formerly Airlines of Britain Holdings Plc), since 1978; British Regional Air Lines Group, and Manx Airlines, since 1982; *b* 10 Feb. 1942; *s* of Clive Leonard Bishop. *Educ:* Mill Hill School. Joined: Mercury Airlines, Manchester, 1963; British Midland Airways, 1964; Director: Airtours plc, 1987– (Dep. Chm., 1996–2001); Williams Plc, 1993–. Member: E Midlands Electricity Bd, 1980–83; E Midlands Reg. Bd, Central Television, 1981–89; Dep. Chm., 1991–93, Chm., 1993–97, Channel 4 Television Corp. Chm., D'Oyly Carte Opera Trust Ltd, 1989–. Hon. Mem., Royal Soc. of Musicians of GB, 1989. *Address:* Donington Hall, Castle Donington, near Derby DE74 2SB. *T:* (01332) 854000. *Clubs:* Brooks's; St James's (Manchester).

BISHOP, Michael William; JP; Director: Manchester Care Ltd, since 1995; Heritage Care Ltd, since 1999; *b* 22 Oct. 1941; *s* of Ronald Lewis William and Gwendoline Mary Bishop; *m* Loraine Helen Jones; two *s* one *d*. *Educ:* Manchester Univ. (BA (Econs) IIi Hons); Leicester Univ. (CertAppSocStudies). Director of Social Services: Cleveland CC, 1981–89; Manchester City Council, 1989–95. Member: Registered Homes Tribunal, 1995; Mancunian Community Health NHS Trust, 1996– (Vice-Chm., 1998–; Chair, Audit Cttee, 1998–). Trustee, RNID, 1996–. JP Manchester City, 1996. *Recreations:* horse riding and competing. *Address:* 12 Higher Chisworth, Chisworth, Glossop SK13 5SA. *T:* (01457) 867837.

BISHOP, Ven. Peter; *see* Bishop, A. P.

BISHOP, Prof. Peter Orlebar, AO 1986; DSc; FRS 1977; FAA; Professor Emeritus, Australian National University, since 1983; Hon. Research Associate, Department of Anatomy and Histology, University of Sydney, since 1987; *b* 14 June 1917; *s* of Ernest John Hunter Bishop and Mildred Alice Havelock Bishop (*née* Vidal); *m* 1942, Hilare Louise Holmes; one *s* two *d*. *Educ:* Barker Coll., Hornsby; Univ. of Sydney (MB, BS, DSc). Neurol Registrar, Royal Prince Alfred Hosp., Sydney, 1941–42; Surgeon Lieut, RANR, 1942–46; Fellow, Postgrad. Cttee in Medicine (Sydney Univ.) at Nat. Hosp., Queen Square, London, 1946–47 and Dept Anatomy, UCL, 1947–50; Sydney University: Res. Fellow, Dept Surgery, 1950–51; Sen. Lectr, 1951–54, Reader, 1954–55, Prof. and Head, Dept Physiology, 1955–67; Prof. and Head of Dept of Physiology, John Curtin School of Medical Res., ANU, 1967–82; Vis. Fellow, ANU, 1983–87. Visiting Professor: Japan Soc. for Promotion of Science, 1974, 1982; Katholieke Universiteit Leuven, Belgium, 1984–85; Guest Prof., Zürich Univ., 1985; Vis. Fellow, St John's Coll., Cambridge, Jan.–Oct. 1986. FAA 1967; Fellow: Aust. Postgrad. Fedn in Medicine, 1969; Nat. Vision Res. Inst. of Australia, 1983. Hon. Member: Neurosurgical Soc. of Aust., 1970; Ophthalmol Soc. of NZ, 1973; Aust. Assoc. of Neurologists, 1977; Australian Neuroscience Soc., 1986; Aust. Physiol and Pharmacol Soc., 1987. Hon. MD Sydney, 1983. (Jtly) Australia Prize, 1993. *Publications:* contribs on physiological optics and visual neurophysiology. *Recreation:* bushwalking. *Address:* Department of Anatomy and Histology, University of Sydney, NSW 2006, Australia; Villa 41, Lutanda Manor, 14 Victoria Road, Pennant Hills, NSW 2120, Australia.

BISHOP, Stanley Victor, MC 1944; management consultant; *b* 11 May 1916; *s* of George Stanley Bishop, MA; *m* 1946, Dorothy Primrose Dodds, Berwick-upon-Tweed; two *s* one *d*. *Educ:* Leeds. Articled to Beevers & Adgie, Leeds; CA 1937. Served War of 1939–45: enlisted London Scottish (TA), 1938; commissioned, West Yorkshire Regt, 1940; served overseas, 1940–45, Middle East, India and Burma (MC) (Hon. Major). Joined Albert E. Reed and Co. Ltd, 1946; Brush Group, 1951; Massey Ferguson Ltd, 1959–79; Perkins Diesel Engine Group, 1963. Man. Dir, British Printing Corp., 1966–70; Chm. and Dir various cos, 1970–73 and 1979–92; Dir, Massey-Ferguson Europe Ltd, 1973–79. Has lectured to British Institute of Management, Institute of Chartered Accountants, Oxford Business Summer School, etc. *Publication:* Business Planning and Control, 1966. *Recreation:* pottering.

BISHOP, Stephen; *see* Kovacevich, S.

BISHOP-KOVACEVICH, Stephen; *see* Kovacevich, S.

BISS, Adele, (Mrs R. O. Davies); Chairman, A. S. Biss & Co., since 1996; *b* 18 Oct. 1944; *d* of Robert and Bronia Biss; *m* 1973, Roger Oliver Davies, *qv*; one *s*. *Educ:* Cheltenham Ladies' Coll.; University Coll. London (BSc Econ). Unilever, 1968; Thomson Holidays, 1970; Chief Exec., Biss Lancaster, 1978–88; Chm., BTA and English Tourist Bd, 1993–96. Director: Aegis plc, 1985–90; BR, 1987–92; European Passenger Services, 1990–; Harry Ramsden's, 1995–. Gov., Middx Univ., 1995–; Member Council: GDST (formerly GPDST), 1996–; UCL, 1997–. FRSA. *Recreations:* piano, hiking, ski-ing. *Address:* A. S. Biss & Co., 100 Rochester Row, SW1P 1JP. *T:* (020) 7828 3030, *Fax:* (020) 7828 5505.

BISSELL, Claude Thomas, CC 1969; MA, PhD; FRSC 1957; Professor, University of Toronto, 1971–83, now Emeritus (President of the University, 1958–71); *b* 10 Feb. 1916; *m* 1945, Christina Flora Gray; one *d*. *Educ:* University of Toronto; Cornell Univ. BA 1936, MA 1937, Toronto; PhD Cornell, 1940. Instructor in English, Cornell, 1938–41; Lecturer in English, Toronto, 1941–42. Canadian Army, 1942–46; demobilised as Capt. University of Toronto: Asst Prof. of English, 1947–51; Assoc. Prof. of English, 1951–56; Prof. of English, 1962; Asst to Pres., 1948–52; Vice-Pres., 1952–56; Dean in Residence, University Coll., 1946–56; Pres., Carleton Univ., Ottawa, 1956–58; Chm., The Canada Council, 1960–62. President, Nat. Conference of Canadian Universities and Colleges, 1962–; Chairman, Canadian Universities Foundation, 1962–; President, World University Service of Canada, 1962–63. Visiting Prof. of Canadian Studies, Harvard, 1967–68. Aggrey-Fraser-Guggisberg Meml Lectr, Ghana Univ., 1976. Hon. DLitt: Manitoba, 1958; W Ontario, 1971; Lethbridge, 1972; Leeds, 1976; Toronto, 1977; Hon. LLD: McGill, 1958; Queen's, 1959; New Brunswick, 1959; Carleton, 1960; Montreal, 1960; St Lawrence, 1962; British Columbia, 1962; Michigan, 1963; Columbia, 1965; Laval, 1966; Prince of Wales Coll., 1967; Windsor, 1968; St Andrews, 1972. *Publications:* (ed) University College, A Portrait, 1853–1953, 1953; (ed) Canada's Crisis in Higher Education, 1957; (ed) Our Living Tradition, 1957; (ed) Great Canadian Writing, 1966; The Strength of the University, 1968; Halfway up Parnassus, 1974; The Humanities in the University, 1977; The Young Vincent Massey, 1981; The Imperial Canadian, 1986; Ernest Buckler Remembered, 1989; number of articles on literary subjects in Canadian and American jls. *Address:* 229 Erskine Avenue, Toronto, ON M4P 1Z5, Canada. *Clubs:* Arts and Letters, York (Toronto); Cercle Universitaire (Ottawa).

BISSELL, Frances Mary; freelance writer; *b* 19 Aug. 1946; *d* of Robert Maloney and Mary Maloney (*née* Kelly); *m* 1970, Thomas Emery Bissell; one step *d*. *Educ:* Univ. of Leeds (BA Hons French). VSO Nigeria, 1965–66; Assistante, Ecole Normale, Albi, 1968–69; British Council, 1970–87; The Times Cook, 1987-2000; food and cookery writer, cook and consultant, 1983–, TV presenter, 1995–. Guest cook: Mandarin Oriental, Hong Kong, 1987, 1990, 1995; London Intercontinental, 1987, 1988 and 1996; Manila Peninsula, 1989; Colombo Hilton, Sri Lanka, 1991; The Dusit Thani, Bangkok, 1992; George V, Paris, 1994; The Mark, NY, 1997, 1999 and 2000; Rio Suites Hotel, Las Vegas, 1997; guest teacher: Bogotá Hilton, Colombia, 1988; Ballymaloe Cooking Sch., Ireland, 1990; The Times cookery evenings at Leith's Sch. of Food and Wine, 1991; Learning for Pleasure, Spain, 1995 and 1996. Member judging panel: THF Hotels Chef of the Year

1988 and 1990; Annual Catey Award Function Menu, 1989–94; A Fresh Taste of Britain, Women's Farming Union, 1989; UK Finals, Prix Taittinger, 1993, 1994; Roux Diners Club Scholarship, 1995–98; Roux Scholarship, 2000–; Shackleton Fund Fellowship, 2001. Founder Mem., Guild of Food Writers, 1985. Chef Mem., Acad. of Culinary Arts (formerly Académie Culinaire de France), 1997. Columnist, Caterer & Hotelkeeper, 1988–94. Glenfiddich Cookery Writer of the Year, 1994; James Beard Foundn Award, USA, 1995. *Television:* Frances Bissell's Westcountry Kitchen, 1995; Frances Bissell's Christmas Cooking, 1996. *Publications:* A Cook's Calendar, 1985; The Pleasures of Cookery, 1986; Ten Dinner Parties for Two, 1988; Sainsbury's Book of Food, 1989 (US edn, as The Book of Food, 1994); Oriental Flavours, 1990; The Real Meat Cookbook, 1992; The Times Cookbook, 1993; Frances Bissell's West Country Kitchen, 1996; (with Tom Bissell) An A–Z of Food and Wine in Plain English, 1999; The Organic Meat Cookbook, 1999; Modern Classics, 2000; contrib. to Caterer and Hotelkeeper, Sunday Times Mag., Homes and Gardens, House & Garden, Country Living, Decanter, Country Life. *Recreations:* travelling and reading. *Address:* c/o Macmillan, 25 Eccleston Place, SW1W 9NF.

BISSON, Hon. Claude, OC 1999; Counsel, McCarthy Tétrault, Montreal, since 1996; a Judge of the Court of Appeal, Quebec, 1980–96; Chief Justice of Quebec, 1988–94; *b* 9 May 1931; *m* 1957, Louisette Lanneville; two *s* one *d*. *Educ:* Univ. de Laval, Quebec (BA 1950; LLL 1953). Called to Bar, Quebec, 1954. Superior Court Judge, Montreal, 1969–80. *Address:* (office) 1170 Peel Street, 5th Floor, Montreal, QC H3B 4S8, Canada.

BISSON, Rt Hon. Sir Gordon (Ellis), Kt 1991; PC 1987; Judge of the Court of Appeal: New Zealand, 1986–91; Samoa, 1994–2000; Kiribati, 1999; Chairman, New Zealand Banking Ombudsman Commission, 1992–97; *b* 23 Nov. 1918; *s* of Clarence Henry Bisson and Ada Ellis; *m* 1948, Myra Patricia Kemp; three *d*. *Educ:* Napier Boys High Sch.; Victoria Coll., Wellington; Univ. of NZ. LLB. Served War of 1939–45, RN and RNZN, 1940–45 (mentioned in despatches); Lt Comdr RNZNVR. Partner, Bisson Moss Robertshawe & Co., Barristers and Solicitors, Napier, NZ, 1946–78; Crown Solicitor, Napier, 1961; Judge, Courts Martial Appeal Ct, 1976; Judge of Supreme Ct, 1978. Vice-President: NZ Law Soc., 1974–77; NZ Sect., Internat. Commn of Jurists, 1979–92. Chairman: Indep. Tribunal for Allocation of Meat Export Quotas, 1995–97; New Entrants Allocation Cttee, NZ Meat Bd. *Publication:* (jtly) Criminal Law and Practice in New Zealand, 1961. *Recreations:* tennis, fly-fishing, golf. *Address:* 341/4 Fergusson Drive, Heretaunga, Wellington 6007, New Zealand. *Clubs:* Wellington, Wellington Golf (Wellington, NZ).

BISZTYGA, Jan; Officer's Cross of the Order of Polonia Restituta 1970; Order of Merit 1973; Political Adviser to Minister of Interior and Administration, Poland, since 1997; *b* 19 Jan. 1933; *s* of Kazimierz Biszytyga; *m* 1956, Otylia; one *s*. *Educ:* Jagiellonian Univ. (MSc Biochemistry). Asst Professor, Jagiellonian Univ., Cracow, 1954–57; political youth movement, 1956–59; Min. for Foreign Affairs, 1959–63; Attaché, New Delhi, 1963–64; Min. for Foreign Affairs, 1964–69; Head of Planning Dept, Min. for Foreign Affairs, 1969–71; Dep. Foreign Minister, 1972–75; Ambassador in Athens, 1975–78, to UK, 1978–81; Ideology Dept, Polish United Workers' Party; expert in Office of Pres. of Polish Republic, 1990–91; Advr on Foreign Trade Enterprise, Euroamer, 1991–94; Advr to PM's Office, 1994–97. *Recreations:* game shooting, fishing, history. *Address:* (home) Jaworzyńska 11–18, Warsaw, Poland; (office) Al. Jerozolimskie 87, Warsaw 02–001, Poland. *T:* (22) 251922, *Fax:* (22) 218676.

BJELKE-PETERSEN, Hon. Sir Johannes, KCMG 1984; Premier of Queensland, 1968–87; *b* Dannevirke, NZ, 13 Jan. 1911; *s* of late C. G. Bjelke-Petersen, Denmark; *m* 1952, Florence Isabel (Senator for Queensland in Commonwealth Parliament, 1981–93), *d* of J. P. Gilmour; one *s* three *d*. *Educ:* Taabinga Valley Sch.; corresp. courses, and privately. MLA National Party (formerly Country Party): for Nanango, 1947–50; for Barambah, 1950–87; Minister for Works and Housing, Qld, 1963–68. *Address:* Bethany, Kingaroy, Queensland 4610, Australia.

BJERREGAARD, Ritt Jytte; MP (Social Dem.) Lejre, Denmark, since 1999; Minister for Food, Agriculture and Fisheries, Denmark, since 2000; *b* Copenhagen, 19 May 1941; *d* of Gudmund Bjerregaard and Rita (*née* Hærslev); *m* 1966, Prof. Søren Mørch. Qualified as teacher, 1964. MP (Social Dem.), Otterup (Fyn), Denmark, 1971–95; Minister for: Educn, 1973 and 1975–78; Social Affairs, 1979–81; Mem., EC, 1995–99. Chm., Social Dem. Parly Gp, 1981–82 and 1987–92 (Dep. Chm., 1982–87). Pres., Danish European Movt, 1992–94. Mem., Trilateral Commn, 1982–. Vice-Pres., Danish delgn, CSCE, 1992–94. Vice-Pres., Socialist Internat. Women, 1992–94. *Publications:* books on educn and politics in Denmark, including: Strid, 1979; Til venner og fjender, 1982; I opposition, 1987; (with S. Mørch) Fyn med omliggende oor, 1989; Verden er saa stor, saa stor, 1990, etc; articles in Danish jls. *Recreation:* growing apples. *Address:* Ministry of Food, Agriculture and Fisheries, Holbergsgade 2, 1057 Copenhagen K, Denmark; Stestrup Old 17, 4360 Kirke Eskilstrup, Denmark.

BJØRNSON, Maria Elena; theatre designer, since 1969; *b* Paris, 16 Feb. 1949; *d* of Bjørn Bjørnson and Maria Prodan. *Educ:* Byam Shaw Sch. of Art (Pre-Dip); Central Sch. of Art and Design (MA). Ext. Examr, Central St Martin's Theatre Dept, 1993–. Designs include: *stage:* Scapino (costumes), NT, 1969; 13 productions for Citizens' Th., Glasgow; Antony and Cleopatra, Bankside Globe, 1973; Hedda Gabler, Duke of York's, 1977; Vieux Carre (costumes), Piccadilly, 1978; The Cherry Orchard, Chichester, 1981; The Lonely Road, Old Vic, 1985; Phantom of the Opera, Her Majesty's, 1986, NY and worldwide 1987 (numerous awards, UK and overseas, incl. Drama mag., 1987; Tony Award for Best Set and Best Costumes, 1987; Drama Critics' Award, LA, 1988); Follies, Shaftesbury, 1987 (Best Design award, Drama mag., 1988); Aspects of Love, Prince of Wales', 1989, NY, 1990; Phèdre, Aldwych, 1998; Britannicus, 1998, Plenty, 1999, Albery; The Cherry Orchard, RNT, 2000; Cat on a Hot Tin Roof, Lyric, 2001; *Royal Shakespeare Co.:* The Way of the World, 1978; Hamlet, 1984; Measure for Measure, 1974, 1991; A Midsummer Night's Dream, 1981; The Tempest, 1982; Camille, 1984; The Blue Angel, 1991; *Royal Ballet:* Sleeping Beauty, 1994; *opera:* Katya Kabanova, 1971, The Gambler, 1974, Wexford Fest.; Macbeth, La Scala, Milan, 1997; *Scottish Opera:* Rake's Progress (costumes), 1971; Tristan and Isolde (costumes), 1973; The Magic Flute (costumes), 1974; The Golden Cockerel (costumes), 1975; Die Meistersinger, 1976; Jenufa, Il Seraglio (costumes), The Bartered Bride (costumes), Hansel and Gretel (costumes), 1978; Don Giovanni, Katya Kabanova, 1979; The Cunning Little Vixen, 1980; House of the Dead, 1987; *Welsh National Opera:* Jenufa, 1975; Il Trovatore, 1976; The Makropulos Case, 1978; Ernani, 1979; Cunning Little Vixen, 1980; House of the Dead, 1982; *English National Opera:* Toussaint, 1977; Die Walkyrie, 1983; Carmen, 1986; Queen of Spades, 1987; Cunning Little Vixen, 1988; *Opera North:* Rigoletto, 1979; Don Giovanni, 1981; Werther, 1982; *Royal Opera:* Tales of Hoffman, 1980; Der Rosenkavalier (costumes), 1984; Donnerstag aus Licht, 1985; Katya Kabanova, 1994; *Glydebourne:* Così fan tutte, 1991; also for productions in Sydney, Kassel, Houston, Geneva, Florence, Paris, the Netherlands, Canada, and the provinces. *Recreations:* travel, running away. *Address:* c/o Judy Daish Associates, 2 St Charles Place, W10 6EG. *Club:* Peg's.

BLACH, Rolf Karl, MD; FRCS, FRCOphth; Ophthalmologist, St Dunstan's, since 1967; Consultant Surgeon, Moorfields Eye Hospital, 1970–95; Dean, Institute of Ophthalmology, London University, 1985–91; *b* 21 Jan. 1930; *s* of Paul Samuel Blach and Hedwig Jeanette Blach; *m* 1960, Lynette Cecilia Sceales; two *s* one *d*. *Educ:* Berkhamsted Sch.; Trinity Coll., Cambridge (MA); St Thomas' Hosp. MD 1965; FRCS 1962; FRCOphth (FCOphth 1989). Capt. RAMC, 1957–58. Jun. medical appts, St Thomas' Hosp. and Moorfields Eye Hosp., 1955–62; Sen. Registrar, Middlesex Hosp., 1962–63; Consultant Ophthalmic Surgeon, St Mary's Hosp., 1963–70; Hon. Consultant Ophthalmologist, RPMS, Hammersmith, 1967–70. Dep. Master, Oxford Ophthal. Congress, 1985. Vice Chm., British Council for Prevention of Blindness, 1996–. Liveryman, Soc. of Apothecaries, 1970. *Publications:* articles on ophthalmology, esp. medical and surgical retina. *Recreations:* my family, aspects of history and economics, a little sport. *Address:* Summers, Northfield Avenue, Lower Shiplake, Henley-on-Thames, Oxon RG9 3PB. *T:* (0118) 940 4549, *Fax:* (0118) 940 2848. *Clubs:* Royal Society of Medicine; Phyllis Court (Henley-on-Thames).

BLACK OF CROSSHARBOUR, Baron *cr* 2001 (Life Peer), of Crossharbour in the London Borough of Tower Hamlets; **Conrad Moffat Black,** OC 1990; PC (Can.) 1992; Chairman and Chief Executive Officer, Hollinger Inc., since 1985; *b* 25 Aug. 1944; *m* 1st, 1978, Joanna Catherine Louise Hishon (name changed by deed poll in 1990 from Shirley Gail Hishon) (marr. diss., 1992); two *s* one *d*; 2nd, 1992, Barbara Amiel. *Educ:* Carleton Univ. (BA); Laval Univ. (LLL); MA History McGill, 1973. Chm. and Chief Exec., Ravelston Corp., 1979–; Chm., 1979–, Chief Exec., 1985–, Argus Corp.; Chm. and CEO, Southam Inc., 1996–; Chairman: Saturday Night Magazine Inc., 1987–; The Telegraph plc, 1987–95 (Dir, 1985–95); Director: Canadian Imperial Bank of Commerce, 1977–; Brascan, 1986–; The Spectator (1828) Ltd, 1990–; Sotheby's, 1997–. Chm., Adv. Bd, The National Interest, Washington, 1992–; Member: Steering Cttee, Bilderberg Meetings, 1986; Adv. Bd, Council on Foreign Relns, 1995–; Board: Hudson Inst., USA; Centre for Policy Studies, 2000–. Hon LLD: St Francis Xavier, 1979; McMaster, 1979; Carleton, 1989; Hon. LittD Univ. of Windsor, 1979. KLJ. *Publications:* Duplessis, 1977, rev. edn as Render Unto Caesar, 1998; A Life in Progress (autobiog.), 1993. *Address:* c/o 10 Toronto Street, Toronto, ON M5C 2B7, Canada. *T:* (416) 3638721; The Telegraph plc, 1 Canada Square, Canary Wharf, E14 5DT. *Clubs:* Athenæum, Beefsteak, Garrick, White's; Everglades, Beach (Palm Beach); Toronto, York, Granite Toronto Golf (Toronto); University, Mount Royal (Montreal).

BLACK, Alastair Kenneth Lamond, CBE 1989; DL; Under Sheriff of Greater London, 1974–94; Clerk, Bowyers' Company, 1985–94; *b* 14 Dec. 1929; *s* of Kenneth Black and Althea Joan Black; *m* 1st, 1955, Elizabeth Jane (*d* 1995), *d* of Sir Henry Darlington, KCB, CMG, TD; one *s* two *d*; 2nd, 1997, Mrs Susan Mary Miller. *Educ:* Sherborne Sch.; Law Soc. Coll. of Law. Admitted solicitor, 1953. Nat. Service, Intelligence Corps, 1953–55, Lieut. Partner in Messrs Burchell & Ruston, Solicitors, 1953–94. Dep. Sheriff, Co. of London, then Greater London, 1953–74; DL Greater London, 1978. Mem. Council, Shrievalty Assoc., 1985–91; Vice-Pres., Under Sheriffs Assoc., 1985–87, Pres., 1987–93. Member: House of Laity, Gen. Synod, 1982–97; (a Chm., Gen. Synod, 1991); Dioceses Commn, 1986–91; Ecclesiastical Fees Adv. Commn, 1986–96; Bd of Social Responsibility, 1992–96. Lay Reader, 1983–97. Governor, St Matthew's C of E Infant Sch., Cobham, 1995–97. *Publications:* contributions to: Halsbury's Laws of England, 4th edn, vols 25, 1978 (rev. edn 1994), and 42, 1983 (rev. edn 1999); Atkin's Court Forms, 3rd edn, vols 19, 1972 (rev. edn 1985), 22, 1968, and 36, 1977 (rev. edn 1988); Enforcement of a Judgement, 8th edn, 1993. *Recreations:* horseracing, gardening, travel. *Address:* Ashdene Farm, Priors Dean, Petersfield, Hants GU32 1BP. *T:* (01730) 827535.

BLACK, Dr Aline Mary; Headteacher, Colchester County High School for Girls, 1987–98; *b* 2 July 1936; *d* of Maurice and Harriet Rose; *m* 1972, David Black. *Educ:* Manchester Univ.; Birkbeck and King's Colls, London (BSc Hons Physics 1957; PGCE 1959; BSc Hons Chemistry 1970; PhD 1973). Res. Physicist, Richard, Thomas & Baldwins, 1957–58; Physics Teacher, Sir William Perkins' Sch., 1959–61; Head of Physics, City of London Sch. for Girls, 1961–71; Science Advr, Waltham Forest LBC, 1973–75; Science and Maths Advr, Bexley LBC, 1975–77; Headteacher: Leyton Sen. High Sch. for Girls, 1977–82; Gravesend Grammar Sch. for Girls, 1982–87. *Recreations:* fruit farming, flying, sailing. *Address:* Oxley House, Abberton, Colchester CO5 7NR. *T:* (01206) 735239.

BLACK, Col Anthony Edward Norman, OBE 1981; Chief Executive Commissioner, Scout Association, 1987–95; *b* 20 Jan. 1938; *s* of late Arthur Norman Black and Phyllis Margaret Ranicar; *m* 1963, Susan Frances Copeland; two *s*. *Educ:* Brighton College; RMA Sandhurst. Commissioned RE, 1957; served Kenya, Aden, Germany, Cyprus; Army Staff Course, Camberley, 1970; GSO1 Ghana Armed Forces Staff Coll., 1976–78; CO 36 Engr Regt, 1978–80; Col GS MGO Secretariat, 1980–82; Comd Engrs Falkland Islands, 1983; Comdt, Army Apprentices Coll., Chepstow, 1983–86; retired 1987. *Recreations:* gardening, bird watching, driving Ferraris. *Address:* National Westminster Bank, 50 High Street, Egham, Surrey TW20 9EU.

BLACK, Barrington (Malcolm); His Honour Judge Barrington Black; a Circuit Judge, since 1993; *b* 16 Aug. 1932; *s* of Louis and Millicent Black; *m* 1962, Diana Heller, JP; two *s* two *d*. *Educ:* Roundhay Sch.; Leeds Univ. (Pres. of Union, 1952; Vice-Pres., NUS, 1953–54; LLB). Admitted Solicitor, 1956. Served Army, 1956–58, commnd RASC. Partner, Walker, Morris & Coles, 1958–69; Sen. Partner, Barrington Black, Austin & Co., 1969–84. An Asst Recorder, 1987–91, a Recorder, 1991–93; a Metropolitan Stipendiary Magistrate, 1984–93. Chairman: Inner London Juvenile Court, 1985–93; Family Court, 1991–93. Mem. Court and Council, Leeds Univ., 1979–84. Councillor, Harrogate Bor. Council, 1964–67; contested (L) Harrogate, 1964. *Recreations:* ski-bobbing, opera, music. *Address:* Harrow Crown Court, Harrow, HA1 4TU.

BLACK, Prof. Carol Mary, MD; FRCP, FMedSci; Professor of Rheumatology, University College London, since 1994; Medical Director, Royal Free NHS Trust, since 2000; Vice-President, Royal College of Physicians, London, 1998–March 2002; *b* 26 Dec. 1939; *d* of Edgar and Annie Herbert; *m* 1973, James Black (marr. diss. 1983). *Educ:* Univ. of Bristol (BA Hist. 1962; Dip. Med. Social Studies 1963; MB ChB 1970; MD 1974). FRCP 1988. Res. Fellow, Univ. of Bristol Sch. of Medicine, 1971–73; Consultant Rheumatologist: W Middx Univ. Hosp., 1981–89; Royal Free NHS Trust, 1989–91. Member: Nat. Specialist Adv. Gp, 1999–; Appraisal Cttee, NICE, 2000–. Vice-Chm., Clin. Interest Gp, Wellcome Trust, 1997–; Mem., Scientific Co-ordinating Cttee, Arthritis Res. Campaign, 1999–; Founder Member and Chairman: UK Scleroderma Gp, 1985–; Eur. Scleroderma Club, 1997. Mem. Council, Section of Clin. Immunol. and Allergy, RSocMed, 1997– (Pres., 1997–99). FMedSci 1999; Mem., Assoc. Physicians, 1997. Hon. Member: Italian Soc. Rheumatol., 1995; Turkish Soc. Rheumatol., 1995–. Mem., editl bds, various scientific jls. *Publications:* (with A. R. Myers) Systemic Sclerosis, 1985; (with J. Jayson) Scleroderma, 1988; contrib. scientific and med. papers in learned jls. *Recreations:* music, walking, travel, theatre. *Address:* 2 Ferncroft Avenue, Hampstead, NW3 7PG. *T:* (020) 7794 0560.

BLACK, Charles Stewart Forbes; a District Judge (Magistrates' Courts) (formerly a Metropolitan Stipendiary Magistrate), since 1993 (Chairman, Youth Courts, since 1994); *b* 6 Feb. 1947; *s* of Roger Bernard Black and Mary Agnes (*née* Murray); *m* 1976, Mhairi Shuna Elspeth McNab; one *d*. *Educ:* Kent Coll., Canterbury; Council of Legal Educn. Called to the Bar, Inner Temple, 1970; *ad eundem* Gray's Inn, 1973; Head of Chambers, 1981–93. *Recreations:* ski-ing, reading, playing with computers. *Address:* c/o Tower Bridge Magistrates' Court, 211 Tooley Street, SE1 2JY.

BLACK, Cilla, OBE 1997; entertainer; *b* 27 May 1943; *née* Priscilla Maria Veronica White; *m* 1969, Bobby Willis (*d* 1999); three *s*. *Television series include:* Cilla (8 series), 1968–76; Cilla's World of Comedy, 1976; Surprise, Surprise, 1984–; Blind Date, 1985–; The Moment of Truth, 1998–; *films:* Ferry Cross the Mersey, 1964; Work is a Four-Letter Word, 1968; *recordings include:* (singles): Anyone Who Had a Heart, 1964; You're My World, 1964; It's For You, 1964; You've Lost that Lovin' Feeling, 1965; Love's Just a Broken Heart, 1966; Alfie, 1966; Don't Answer Me, 1966; Step Inside Love, 1968; Surround Yourself With Sorrow, 1969; Conversations, 1969; Something Tells Me, 1971; (albums): Cilla, 1965; Cilla Sings a Rainbow, 1966; Sher-oo!, 1968. Top TV Female Personality, Sun Awards, 1970, 1971, 1972, 1973 and 1974 (including a Gold Award); Favourite Female Personality on TV Awards, TV Times, 1986, 1988, 1989 and 1990; Top Female Comedy Star, Writers' Guild of GB, 1975; Variety Club Showbusiness Personality, 1991; Lew Grade Award, BAFTA, 1995. *Publications:* Step Inside, 1985; Through the Years: my Life in Pictures, 1993.

BLACK, Colin Hyndmarsh; Chairman: Kleinwort Benson Investment Management Ltd, 1988–95; Merchants Trust, 1993–2000 (Director, 1992–2000); *b* 4 Feb. 1930; *s* of Daisy Louise (*née* Morris) and Robert Black; *m* 1955, Christine Fleurette Browne; one *s* one *d*. *Educ:* Ayr Acad.; Fettes Coll.; St Andrews Univ. (MA); Edinburgh Univ. (LLB). Brander and Cruickshank, Aberdeen, 1957–71 (Partner in charge of investment management); Globe Investment Trust, 1971–90, Dep Chm., 1983–90. Chairman: Scottish Widows' Fund and Life Assurance Soc., 1987–95; Assoc. of Investment Trust Cos, 1987–89; Non-executive Director: Temple Bar Investment Trust, 1963–2000; Clyde Petroleum, 1976–96; Electra Investment Trust, 1975–94; Kleinwort Benson Gp plc, 1988–95; Scottish Power plc, 1990–95; East German Investment Trust, 1990–96; Govett Asian Smaller Cos Investment Trust, 1994–2000 (Chm., 1994–2000); Postern Fund Management Ltd, 1996–99; PFM Carried Interest Ltd, 1996–2000. *Recreations:* golf, gardening, reading, watching cricket, walking Labradors. *Address:* 15 Tudor Close, Fairmile Park Road, Cobham, Surrey KT11 2PH. *T:* (01932) 865656. *Club:* Wisley Golf (Mem. Bd, 1994–96).

BLACK, Sir David; *see* Black, Sir R. D.

BLACK, Don, OBE 1999; lyric writer; *b* 21 June 1938; *s* of Betsy and Morris Blackstone; *m* 1958, Shirley Berg; two *s*. *Educ:* Hackney Central Sch. Professional lyric writer, 1960–; collaborates with Andrew Lloyd Webber, John Barry, Jule Styne, Elmer Bernstein and other leading composers; musicals include: Billy, 1974; Song and Dance, 1982; Aspects of Love, 1989; Sunset Boulevard, 1993; The Goodbye Girl, 1997. Numerous awards, UK and USA, including: Academy Award, 1966, for song Born Free; Tony Award, 1995, for Sunset Boulevard (Best Book for a musical, and Best Score, lyrics). *Recreations:* snooker, swimming. *Address:* c/o John Cohen, Clintons, 55 Drury Lane, WC2B 5SQ. *T:* (020) 7379 6080. *Clubs:* Royal Automobile, Groucho, Tramp.

BLACK, Sir Douglas (Andrew Kilgour), Kt 1973; MD, FRCP; Professor of Medicine, Manchester University and Physician, Manchester Royal Infirmary, 1959–77, now Emeritus; Chief Scientist, Department of Health and Social Security, 1973–77; *b* 29 May 1913; *s* of late Rev. Walter Kilgour Black and Mary Jane Crichton; *m* 1948, Mollie Thorn; one *s* two *d*. *Educ:* Forfar Academy; St Andrews Univ. BSc 1933; MB, ChB 1936; MD 1940; MRCP 1939; FRCP 1952; FACP, FRACP, FRCPGlas, 1978; FRCPath, FRCPI, FRCPE, 1979; FRCPsych, 1982; FRCGP, FRCOG, FFPHM (FFCM 1983); FFOM 1984. MRC Research Fellow, 1938–40; Beit Memorial Research Fellow, 1940–42. Major RAMC, 1942–46. Lecturer, then Reader, in Medicine, Manchester Univ., 1946–58. Horder Travelling Fellow, 1967; Sir Arthur Sims Commonwealth Travelling Prof., 1971; Rock Carling Fellow, 1984. Lectures: Goulstonian, RCP, 1953; Bradshaw, RCP, 1965; Lumleian, RCP, 1970; Harben, RIPH&H, 1973; Crookshank, RCR, 1976; Harveian Orator, RCP, 1977; Maurice Bloch, Glasgow, 1979; Linacre, St John's Coll., Cambridge, 1980; Lloyd Roberts, RSM, 1980; John Locke, Soc. of Apothecaries, 1990; Thomas Young, St George's Hosp. Med. Sch., 1990; Annual, Office of Health Econs, 1994. Secretary, Manchester Medical Soc., 1957–59. Member: Medical Research Council, 1966–70 and 1971–77 (Chm., Clinical Res. Bd, 1971–73); Assoc. of Physicians; Medical Research Soc.; Renal Assoc., etc. President: RCP, 1977–83; Section X, British Assoc., 1977; Medical Protection Soc., 1982–85; BMA, 1984–85; Hon. Mem., Manchester Lit. and Phil. Soc., 1991. Trustee, 1968–77, Chm., 1977–83, Smith Kline & French Foundn. Chm., Research Working Group on Inequalities in Health, 1977–80. Hon. FMedSci 2000. Hon. DSc: St Andrews, 1972; Manchester, 1978; Leicester, 1980; Cambridge, 1994; Hon. LLD Birmingham, 1984; Hon. MD Sheffield, 1984. KStJ 1989. *Publications:* Sodium Metabolism in Health and Disease, 1952; Essentials of Fluid Balance, 4th edn, 1967; The Logic of Medicine, 1968; (ed) Renal Disease, 4th edn, 1979; An Anthology of False Antitheses (Rock Carling Lecture), 1984; Invitation to Medicine, 1987; Recollections and Reflections, 1987; contributions to various medical journals. *Recreations:* reading and writing. *Address:* The Old Forge, Duchess Close, Whitchurch-on-Thames, near Reading, RG8 7EN. *T:* (0118) 984 4693. *Club:* Athenæum.

BLACK, Air Vice-Marshal George Philip, CB 1987; OBE 1967; AFC 1962 (Bar 1971); FRAeS; Royal Air Force, retired 1987; Defence Consultant, BAE SYSTEMS; *b* 10 July 1932; *s* of William and Elizabeth Black; *m* 1954, Ella Ruddiman (*née* Walker); two *s*. *Educ:* Hilton Acad., Aberdeen. Joined RAF, 1950; flying trng in Canada, 1951; served, 1952–64: fighter pilot; carrier pilot (on exchange to FAA); Flying Instr; HQ Fighter Comd; commanded No 111 (Fighter) Sqdn, 1964–66; Mem., Lightning Aerobatic Team, 1965; commanded Lightning Operational Conversion Unit, 1967–69; commanded No 5 (Fighter) Sqdn, 1969–70 (Huddleston Trophy); JSSC, 1970; Air Plans, MoD, 1971–72; Stn Comdr, RAF Wildenwrath, and Harrier Field Force Comdr, RAF Germany, 1972–74; Gp Captain Ops HQ 38 Gp, 1974–76; RCDS, 1977; Gp Captain Ops HQ 11 (Fighter) Gp, 1978–80; Comdr Allied Air Defence Sector One, 1980–83; Comdt ROC, 1983–84; DCS (Ops), HQ AAFCE, 1984–87. Air ADC to the Queen, 1981–83. Sen. Defence Advr, subseq. Dir, Mil. Marketing, GEC–Ferranti, 1987–93; Dir, Mil. Business Develt, Marconi Electronic Systems, subseq. BAE SYSTEMS, 1993–2000. FIMgt (FBIM 1977). FRAeS 2001. *Recreations:* military aviation history, railways. *Address:* BAE SYSTEMS, The Grove, Warren Lane, Stanmore, Middx HA7 4LY. *Club:* Royal Air Force.

BLACK, Guy Vaughan; Director, Press Complaints Commission, since 1996; *b* 6 Aug. 1964; *s* of Thomas Black and Monica Black (*née* Drew). *Educ:* Brentwood Sch., Essex; Peterhouse, Cambridge (John Cosin Schol.; Sir Herbert Butterfield Prize for History, 1985; MA). Graduate Trainee, Corporate Banking Div., BZW, 1985–86; Desk Officer, Conservative Res. Dept, 1986–89; Special Advr to Sec. of State for Energy, 1989–92; Account Dir, Westminster Strategy, 1992–94; Associate Dir, Lowe Bell Good Relns, 1994–96. Mem. (C), Brentwood DC, 1988–92. FRSA 1997. *Recreations:* music, cats, reading. *Address:* (office) 1 Salisbury Square, EC4Y 8JB. *T:* (020) 7353 1248. *Clubs:* Athenæum, London Press (Hon. Mem.).

BLACK, James Walter; QC 1979; *b* 8 Feb. 1941; *s* of Dr James Black and Mrs Clementine M. Black (*née* Robb); *m* 1st, 1964, Jane Marie Keyden; two *s* one *d*; 2nd, 1985, Diana Marjorie Day (*née* Harris); one *d*. *Educ:* Harecroft Hall, Gosforth, Cumbria; Trinity Coll., Glenalmond, Perthshire; St Catharine's Coll., Cambridge (MA). Called to the Bar, Middle Temple, 1964, NSW Bar, 1986; a Recorder, 1976–87. *Recreations:* fishing, sailing, golf. *Address:* Edmund Barton Chambers, Level 44 MLC Centre, Martin Place, Sydney, NSW 2000, Australia.

BLACK, Sir James (Whyte), Kt 1981; OM 2000; FRCP; FRS 1976; Professor of Analytical Pharmacology, King's College Hospital Medical School, University of London, 1984–93, now Emeritus; Chancellor, Dundee University, since 1992; *b* 14 June 1924; *m* 1994, Rona McLeod Mackie, *qv*. *Educ:* Beath High Sch., Cowdenbeath; Univ. of St Andrews (MB, ChB). Asst Lectr in Physiology, Univ. of St Andrews, 1946; Lectr in Physiology, Univ. of Malaya, 1947–50; Sen. Lectr, Univ. of Glasgow Vet. Sch., 1950–58; ICI Pharmaceuticals Ltd, 1958–64; Head of Biological Res. and Dep. Res. Dir, Smith, Kline & French, Welwyn Garden City, 1964–73; Prof. and Head of Dept of Pharmacology, University College, London, 1973–77; Dir of Therapeutic Research, Wellcome Res. Labs, 1978–84. Mem., British Pharmacological Soc., 1961–. Hon. FRSE 1986. Hon. Fellow, London Univ., 1990. Mullard Award, Royal Soc., 1978; (jtly) Nobel Prize for Physiology or Medicine, 1988. *Address:* James Black Foundation, 68 Half Moon Lane, SE24 9JE.

BLACK, Hon. Dame Jill (Margaret), DBE 1999; **Hon. Mrs Justice Black;** a Judge of the High Court of Justice, Family Division, since 1999; *b* 1 June 1954; *d* of Dr James Irvine Currie and Margaret Yvonne Currie; *m* 1978, David Charles Black; one *s* one *d*. *Educ:* Penrhos Coll., Colwyn Bay; Durham Univ. (BA Hons Law). Called to the Bar, Inner Temple, 1976; QC 1994; a Recorder, 1999. *Publications:* Divorce: the things you thought you'd never need to know, 1982, 5th edn 1997; A Practical Approach to Family Law, 1986, 5th edn 1998; (with J. Bridge and T. Bond) The Working Mother's Survival Guide, 1988; (jtly) The Family Court Practice, annually, 1993–. *Address:* Royal Courts of Justice, Strand, WC2A 2LL.

BLACK, John Alexander; QC 1998; *b* 23 April 1951; *s* of John Alexander Black and late Grace Gardiner Black (*née* Cornock); *m* 1977, Penelope Anne Willdig; one *s* two *d*. *Educ:* St James' Choir Sch., Grimsby; Hull Univ. (LLB 1974). Called to the Bar, Inner Temple, 1975. *Recreations:* classical music, motor cars, political history. *Address:* 18 Red Lion Court, EC4 3EB.

BLACK, Adm. Sir (John) Jeremy, GBE 1991 (MBE 1963); KCB 1987; DSO 1982; Stia Negara Brunei 1963; Vice Admiral of the United Kingdom and Lieutenant of the Admiralty, since 2001 (Rear Admiral of the United Kingdom, 1997–2001); *b* 17 Nov. 1932; *s* of Alan H. Black and G. Black; *m* 1958, Alison Pamela Barber; two *s* one *d*. *Educ:* Royal Naval College, Dartmouth (entered 1946). Korean War and Malayan Emergency, 1951–52; qualified in gunnery, 1958; commanded HM Ships: Fiskerton, 1960–62 (Brunei Rebellion, 1962), Decoy, 1969 (Comdr 1969, Captain 1974); Fife, 1977; RCDS 1979; Director of Naval Operational Requirements, Naval Staff, 1980–81; commanded HMS Invincible (Falklands), 1982–83; Flag Officer, First Flotilla, 1983–84; ACNS (Policy), Oct.-Dec. 1984; ACNS, 1985–86; Dep. CDS (Systems), 1986–89; C-in-C Naval Home Comd, 1989–91; Flag ADC, 1989–91. Chairman: Remy and Associates (UK) Ltd, 1992–96; Applied Visuals Ltd, 1998–2000; Berry Birch & Noble, 1999–; Director: Devonport Management Ltd, 1992–97; Macallan-Glenlivet plc, 1993–96; Global Emerging Markets Europe Ltd, 1993–96; St Davids Investment Trust, 1996–98; Gosport Seaport Ltd, 1993–; Consultant: Shorts, 1992–98; British Aerospace, 1993–97; Krug Champagne, 1996–99. Trustee, Imperial War Mus., 1991–98; Chm., Britain at War Mus., 1999–. Mem. Council, RUSI, 1987–89. Gov., Wellington Coll., 1992–; Chm. Govs, Eagle House, 1998–. Chairman: Whitbread Round the World Race Cttee, 1990–94; Royal Navy Club of 1765 and 1785, 1992–95; Governor, Ocean Youth Club, 1991–95 (Chm., World Voyage, 1994–97). Life Vice Cdre, RNSA, 1991 (Cdre, 1989–91). *Recreations:* sailing, history. *Clubs:* Boodle's; Royal Yacht Squadron.

BLACK, John Newman, CEng, FICE, FIMarE; FRGS; Partner, Robert West and Partners, Chartered Consulting Engineers, 1988–90; *b* 29 Sept. 1925; *s* of late John Black and late Janet Black (*née* Hamilton); *m* 1952, Euphemia Isabella Elizabeth Thomson; two *d*. *Educ:* Cumberland and Medway Technical Colls. Civil and marine engrg naval stations and dockyards, UK and abroad, incl. Singapore, Hong Kong, Colombo, Gibraltar and Orkney Isles, 1941–64; joined PLA as Civil Engr, 1964; Planning and Construction, Tilbury Docks, 1964–66; Planning Manager, 1967; seconded to Thames Estuary Develt Co. Ltd, for work on Maplin Airport/Seaport Scheme, 1969; Asst Dir Planning, PLA, 1970; Director: Maplin, 1972; Tilbury Docks, 1974; all London Docks, 1977; Man. Dir, 1978–81; Bd Mem., 1978–86, Chief Exec., 1982–86, and Dep. Chm., 1985–86, PLA. Dep. Chm., PLA (Met. Terminals) Ltd, 1974; Director: PLACON Ltd (PLA's cons. subsid. co.), 1972; Orsett Depot Ltd, 1974; Port Documentation Services Ltd (Chm.), 1978; Chairman: Thames Riparian Housing Assoc., 1974; PLA Group Property Holdings, 1984. Member: Exec. Council, British Ports Assoc., 1982–86; Exec. Cttee, Nat. Assoc. of Port Employers, 1982–86 (Vice-Chm., 1984–86); British Nat. Cttee, Permt Internat. Assoc. of Navigation Congresses, 1981–; London Maritime Assoc., 1975; Council, ICHCA Internat., 1985–86; Nat. Exec. Cttee, ICHCA (UK), 1985–88. Co-Adviser to Indian Govt on port ops and potential, 1968; lectures: for UN, Alexandria, 1975; for ESCAP (UN), Bangkok, 1983. FInstPet. Freeman: City of London, 1977; Watermen and Lightermen of River Thames, 1977. *Publications:* numerous articles and papers in Geographical Jl, Civil Engr and other learned jls. *Recreations:* shooting, fishing. *Address:* Westdene Cottage, Tanyard Hill, Shorne, near Gravesend, Kent DA12 3EN.

BLACK, John Nicholson, MA, DPhil, DSc; FRSE; Principal, Bedford College, University of London, 1971–81; *b* 28 June 1922; *e s* of Harold Black, MD, FRCP, and Margaret Frances Black (*née* Nicholson); *m* 1st, 1952, Mary Denise Webb (*d* 1966); one *s* one *d*; 2nd, 1967, Wendy Marjorie Waterston; two *s*. *Educ:* Rugby Sch.; Exeter Coll., Oxford. MA 1952, DPhil 1952, Oxford; DSc 1965, Adelaide; FRSE 1965. Served War, RAF, 1942–46. Oxford Univ., 1946–49; BA Hons Cl. 1 (Agri.) 1949; Agricl Research Council Studentship, 1949–52; Lectr, Sen. Lectr, Reader, Univ. of Adelaide (Waite Agricl Research Inst.), 1952–63; André Mayer Fellowship (FAO), 1958; Prof. of Forestry and Natural Resources, Univ. of Edinburgh, 1963–71. Dir and Sec., The Wolfson Foundn, 1981–87; Dir, The Wolfson Family Charitable Trust, 1987–89. Tutor in Ceramic Restoration, Missenden Abbey, 1993–98. Mem., NERC, 1968–74; Mem. Council and Finance Cttee, RAF Benevolent Fund, 1989–97. Conductor, City of Burnside Symphony Orch., SA, 1956–63; Chm., Donizetti Soc., 1984–87. *Publications:* The Dominion of Man, 1970; Donizetti's Operas in Naples, 1983; The Italian Romantic Libretto, 1984; (contrib.

entries (26) on Italian librettists) The New Grove Dictionary of Opera, 1992; British Tinglazed Earthenware, 2001; papers on: ecological subjects in scientific jls (70); Italian opera libretti (30); history of ceramics (3). *Recreations:* music, repair and restoration of porcelain and pottery, lecturing on English delftware. *Address:* Paddock House, Pyrton, near Watlington, Oxford OX49 5AP. *T:* (01491) 612600.

BLACK, Hon. Michael Eric John, AC 1998; **Hon. Chief Justice Black;** Chief Justice, Federal Court of Australia, since 1991; *b* 22 March 1940; *s* of Col E. R. E. Black, OBE; *m* 1963, Margaret Dungan; one *s* one *d. Educ:* St John's on the Hill, Chepstow; Wesley Coll., Melbourne; Univ. of Melbourne (LLB). Practice, Victorian Bar, 1964–90, ACT Bar, 1974–90; QC Victoria 1980, QC Tasmania 1984. Mem. Board, Royal Melbourne Hosp., 1986–90 (Chm., Ethics Cttee); The Defence Force Advocate, 1987–90. *Address:* Chief Justice's Chambers, Federal Court of Australia, 305 William Street, Melbourne, Vic 3000, Australia.

BLACK, Michael Jonathan; QC 1995; a Recorder, since 1999; *b* 31 March 1954; *s* of Samuel and Lillian Black; *m* 1984, Ann, *e d* of Keith and Rosa Pentol; two *s. Educ:* Stand Grammar Sch.; University College London (LLB). FCIArb 1991. Called to the Bar, Middle Temple, 1978; an Asst Recorder, 1995–99; a Dep. Judge, Technology and Construction Court, 1999–. Asst Comr, Parly Boundary Commn for England, 2000–. Mem., Civil Procedure Cttee, 2000–. Vis. Res. Fellow, UMIST, 1996–. FInstCES 2001. Freeman, Arbitrators' Co., 2000. *Address:* 2 Temple Gardens, Temple, EC4Y 9AY. *T:* (020) 7822 1200, *Fax:* (020) 7822 1300; Byrom Street Chambers, 12 Byrom Street, Manchester M3 4PP. *T:* (0161) 829 2100, *Fax:* (0161) 829 2101; *e-mail:* mblack@2templegardens.co.uk.

BLACK, Neil Cathcart, OBE 1989; Principal Oboist, English Chamber Orchestra, 1970–98; *b* 28 May 1932; *s* of Harold Black and Margaret Frances Black; *m* 1st, 1960, Jill (*née* Hemingsley); one *s* two *d*; 2nd, 1984, Janice Mary (*née* Knight). *Educ:* Rugby; Exeter College, Oxford (BA History). Entered musical profession, 1956; Principal Oboist: London Philharmonic Orch., 1959–61; in various chamber orchs, incl. London Mozart Players, Acad. of St Martin-in-the-Fields, 1965–72; oboe soloist internationally. Hon. RAM 1969. *Recreations:* wine, travel.

BLACK, Prof. Paul Joseph, OBE 1983; PhD; FInstP; Professor of Science Education, University of London, 1976–95 (in School of Education, King's College, 1985–95), now Emeritus Professor; Visiting Professor, Stanford University, California, since 1999; *b* 10 Sept. 1930; *s* of Walter and Susie Black; *m* 1957, Mary Elaine Weston; four *s* one *d. Educ:* Rhyl Grammar Sch.; Univ. of Manchester (BSc); Univ. of Cambridge (PhD). FInstP 1986. Royal Society John Jaffé Studentship, 1953–56. Univ. of Birmingham: Lectr in Physics, 1956–66; Reader in Crystal Physics, 1966–74; Prof. of Physics (Science Education), 1974–76; Dir, Centre for Science and Maths Educn, Chelsea Coll., Univ. of London, 1976–85; subseq., following merger of colls, Head, Centre for Educnl Studies, KCL, 1985–89 (FKC 1990); Dean, Faculty of Educn, Univ. of London, 1978–82. Educnl Consultant: to Nuffield Chelsea Curriculum Trust, 1978–93 (Chm., 1996–98); to OECD, 1988–96; Consultant to: World Bank, 1991; US Nat. Sci. Foundn, 1992. Vice-Pres., Royal Instn of Great Britain, 1983–85; Chairman: National Curriculum Task Gp on Assessment and Testing, DES, 1987–88; Internat. Commn on Physics Educn, 1993–99 (Mem., 1987–93); S London Cttee, RC Archdio. of Southwark Schs' Commn, 1996–; Dep. Chm., Grubb Inst. for Behavioural Studies, 1990– (Mem. Council, 1983–; Chm., 1985–90; Hon. Vice-Pres., 1997); Member: School Curriculum Develt Cttee, 1984–88; Nat. Curriculum Council, 1988–91 (Dep. Chm., 1989–91); Exec., Univs Council for Educn of Teachers, 1982–86; Res. Grants Bd, ESRC, 1987–90; Exec., Editl Cttee for Nat. Sci. Educn Standards, Nat. Res. Council, USA, 1994–95; US Nat. Acad. of Scis Bd on Testing and Assessment, 1995–99. President: Groupe Internat. de la Recherche sur l'Enseignement de la Physique, 1984–91; Educn Section, British Assoc., 1992–93; Vice Pres. and Mem. Council, IUPAP, 1997–99; Hon. Pres., Assoc. for Science Educn, 1986 (Hon. Life Mem., 1986); Hon. Mem., Standing Conf. on Sch. Science and Technol., 1989. Trustee: Nat. Energy Foundn, 1992–2000; One Plus One Marriage and Partnership Research, 1996– (Chair of Trustees, 1997–). Hon. Mem., CGLI, 1989. FRSA 1990; Osher Fellow, San Francisco Exploratorium, 1993. DUniv Surrey, 1991. Bragg Medal, Inst. of Physics, 1973; Medal, Internat. Commn on Physics Educn, 2000. Kt of St Gregory, 1973. *Publications:* (jtly) Nuffield Advanced Physics Project, 1972; (contrib.) Higher Education Learning Project Books, 1977; (jtly) Open Work in Science, 1992; Nuffield Primary Science books (for Key Stages 1 and 2), 1993; (ed jtly) Children's Informal Ideas in Science, 1993; (ed jtly) Teachers Assessing Pupils: lessons from science classrooms, 1995; (jtly) Primary SPACE Project Research Reports: Light, 1990, Electricity, 1991, Processes of Life, 1992, The Earth in Space, 1994; (ed jtly) Changing the Subject, 1996; Testing: friend or foe, 1998; papers on crystallography, physics and science, technology education, and assessment in education. *Address:* 16 Wilton Crescent, SW19 3QZ. *T:* (020) 8542 4178.

BLACK, Peter Malcolm; Member (Lib Dem) South Wales West, National Assembly for Wales, since 1999; *b* 30 Jan. 1960; *s* of John Malcolm and Joan Arlene Black; *m* 1st, 1984, Patricia Mary Hopkin (marr. diss. 1995); 2nd, 2000, Angela Lynette Jones. *Educ:* Wirral Grammar Sch. for Boys; University Coll. of Swansea (BA Hons English and History). Exec. Officer, Land Registry for Wales, 1983–99. Member: (L) Swansea City DC, 1984–96; (Lib Dem) City and County of Swansea Unitary Council, 1996–. Chm., Lib Dem Wales, 1995–97 (Sec., Finance and Admin. Cttee, 1996–99). *Recreations:* theatre, poetry, films. *Address:* 115 Cecil Street, Manselton, Swansea SA5 8QL.

BLACK, Prof. Robert; QC (Scot.) 1987; FRSE; Professor of Scots Law, University of Edinburgh, since 1981; *b* 12 June 1947; *s* of James Little Black and Jeannie Findlay Lyon. *Educ:* Lockerbie Acad.; Dumfries Acad.; Edinburgh Univ. (LLB); McGill Univ., Montreal (LLM); Lord Pres. Cooper Meml Prize, Univ. of Edinburgh, 1968; Vans Dunlop Scholarship, Univ. of Edinburgh, 1968; Commonwealth Scholarship, Commonwealth Scholarship Commn, 1968. Advocate, 1972; Lectr in Scots Law, Univ. of Edinburgh, 1972–75; Sen. Legal Officer, Scottish Law Commn, 1975–78; in practice at Scottish Bar, 1978–81; Temp. Sheriff, 1981–95. Chm., Inquiry into operations of Monklands DC, 1994–95. Gen. Editor, The Laws of Scotland: Stair Memorial Encyclopaedia, 1988–96 (Dep., then Jt, Gen. Editor, 1981–88). FRSA 1991; FRSE 1992; Founding Fellow, Inst. of Contemporary Scotland, 2000. *Publications:* An Introduction to Written Pleading, 1982; Civil Jurisdiction: the new rules, 1983; articles in UK and S African legal jls. *Recreation:* seeking a solution to the Lockerbie impasse. *Address:* 6/4 Glenogle Road, Edinburgh EH3 5HW. *T:* (0131) 557 3571; *e-mail:* Robert.Black@ed.ac.uk. *Club:* Royal Over-Seas League.

BLACK, Sir (Robert) David, 3rd Bt *cr* 1922; DL; *b* 29 March 1929; *s* of Sir Robert Andrew Stransham Black, 2nd Bt, ED, and Ivy (*d* 1980), *d* of late Brig.-Gen. Sir Samuel Wilson, GCMG, KCB, KBE; *S* father, 1979; *m* 1st, 1953, Rosemary Diana (marr. diss. 1972), *d* of Sir Rupert John Hardy, 4th Bt; two *d* (and one *d* decd); 2nd, 1973, Dorothy Maureen, *d* of Major Charles R. Eustace Radclyffe and *widow* of A. R. D. Pilkington. *Educ:* Eton. Lieut, Royal Horse Guards, 1949; Captain 1953; Major 1960; retired, 1961. Served with Berkshire and Westminster Dragoons, TA, 1964–67, and Berkshire Territorials, TAVR III, 1967–69; Vice-Chm., Berkshire, Eastern Wessex TAVRA, 1985–92. Joint Master, Garth and South Berks Foxhounds, 1965–73. Hon. Col, 94 (Berks Yeo.) Signal Sqn (TA), 1988–98. DL Caithness, 1991; High Sheriff, Oxfordshire, 1993. *Recreations:* shooting, stalking, fishing. *Heir:* none. *Address:* Beech Farm House, Woodcote, near Reading, Berks RG8 0PX. *T:* (01491) 682234; Shurrery Lodge, Shebster, Thurso, Caithness KW14 7RB. *T:* (01847) 811252. *Club:* Cavalry and Guards.

BLACK, Prof. Robert Denis Collison, FBA 1974; Professor of Economics, and Head of Department of Economics, Queen's University Belfast, 1962–85, now Emeritus; *b* 11 June 1922; *s* of William Robert Black and Rose Anna Mary (*née* Reid), Dublin; *m* 1953, Frances Mary, *o d* of William F. and Mary Weatherup, Belfast; one *s* one *d. Educ:* Sandford Park Sch.; Trinity Coll., Dublin (Hon. Fellow, 1982). BA 1941, BComm 1941, PhD 1943, MA 1945. Dep. for Prof. of Polit. Economy, Trinity Coll., Dublin, 1943–45; Asst Lectr in Economics, Queen's Univ., Belfast, 1945–46, Lectr, 1946–58, Sen. Lectr, 1958–61, Reader, 1961–62. Rockefeller Post-doctoral Fellow, Princeton Univ., 1950–51; Visiting Prof. of Economics, Yale Univ., 1964–65; Dean of Faculty of Economics and Social Sciences, QUB, 1967–70; Pro-Vice-Chancellor, 1971–75. President: Statistical & Social Inquiry Soc. of Ireland, 1983–86; Section F, BAAS, 1984–85. Distinguished Fellow, History of Economics Soc., USA, 1987. MRIA 1974. Hon. DSc(Econ) QUB, 1988. *Publications:* Centenary History of the Statistical Society of Ireland, 1947; Economic Thought and the Irish Question 1817–1870, 1960; Catalogue of Economic Pamphlets 1750–1900, 1969; Papers and Correspondence of William Stanley Jevons, Vol. I, 1972, Vol. II, 1973, Vols III-VI, 1977, Vol. VII, 1981; Ideas in Economics, 1986; Economic Theory and Policy in Context, 1995; articles in Economic Jl, Economica, Oxford Econ. Papers, Econ. History Review, etc. *Recreations:* travel, music. *Address:* Queen's University, Belfast, Northern Ireland BT7 1NN. *T:* (028) 9024 5133.

BLACK, Rona McLeod, (Lady Black); *see* MacKie, R. M.

BLACK, Sheila (Psyche), OBE 1986; feature writer; Director, MAI plc (formerly Mills and Allen International), 1976–92; *b* 6 May 1920; *d* of Clement Johnston Black, CA, and Mildred Beryl Black; *m* 1st, 1939, Geoffrey Davien, Sculptor (marr. diss. 1951); one *d* (one *s* decd); 2nd, 1951, L. A. Lee Howard (marr. diss. 1973). *Educ:* Dorset; Switzerland; RADA. Actress, until outbreak of War of 1939–45; Asst to production manager of an electrical engineering factory. Post-war, in advertising; then in journalism, from the mid-fifties; Woman's Editor, Financial Times, 1959–72; specialist feature writer, The Times, 1972–79; Chm., Interflex Data Systems (UK) Ltd, 1975–83. Features writer for The Director, Financial Weekly, Punch, Mediaworld, and many newspapers and magazines. Chairman: Nat. Gas Consumers' Council, 1981–86; Gas Consumers Council, 1986–88; Dir, Money Management Council, 1985–90; Member: Furniture Develt Council, 1967–70; Liquor Licensing Laws Special Cttee, 1971–72; (part-time) Price Commn, 1973–77; Nat. Consumer Council, 1981–91; Calcutt Cttee on Privacy and Related Matters, 1989–90. Dir, Countrywide Workshops Charitable Trust, 1982–88 and 1989–93. Mem. Council, Inst. of Directors, 1975–90. Freeman, City of London, 1985. *Publications:* The Black Book, 1976; Mirabelle: cuisine de qualité et tradition, 1979; The Reluctant Money Minder, 1980; various others. *Recreations:* gardening, grandchildren, football. *Address:* 12A Earls Court Gardens, SW5 0TD.

BLACK, Stewart; *see* Black, C. S. F.

BLACK, Timothy Reuben Ladbroke, CBE 1994; Founder and Chief Executive, Marie Stopes International, since 1975; *b* 7 Jan. 1937; *s* of Stephen Joscelyn Ladbroke Black and Dorothy Joyce (*née* Bedford, now Mrs Paul Fletcher); *m* 1962, Jean Carter; two *d. Educ:* Dartington Hall Sch., Devon; Brighton Tech. Coll.; St George's Hosp., London Univ. (MB BS); Univ. of Northern Carolina (MPH 1970). MRCS 1962; LRCP 1962, MRCP 1966; DTM&H 1968; CDipAF 1989. Jun. House Officer, Harare Hosp., Salisbury, Rhodesia, 1962–63; Sen. House Officer, Croydon General and Mayday Hosps, 1963–64; Medical Registrar, Harefield Hosp., 1964–65; Consultant Physician, Rabaul and E Sepik Reg., New Guinea Med. Service, 1967; GP, NZ, 1968; Population Studies Fellow, Population Council and Ford Foundn, Univ. of N Carolina, 1969–70; Population Services International: Co-founder, 1970; Vice-Pres., 1970–75; Africa Regl Dir, Nairobi, Kenya, 1972–74. Chm., Options Consultancy Services Ltd; Vice Pres., DKT Internat. FRSTM&H 1970; FIMgt 1985; FCIM 1989. *Publications:* numerous articles in population/family planning jls covering service delivery and mgt issues. *Recreations:* gardening, geese, hill-walking, trees, reading. *Address:* Gorsedene, Lower Beeding, Sussex RH13 6PX. *Club:* Royal Society of Medicine.

BLACKADDER, Elizabeth Violet, OBE 1982; RA 1976; RSA 1972; artist; Her Majesty's Painter and Limner in Scotland, since 2000; *b* 24 Sept. 1931; *m* 1956, John Houston. *Educ:* Falkirk High Sch.; Univ. of Edinburgh; Edinburgh Coll. of Art. Lectr, Sch. of Drawing and Painting, Edinburgh Coll. of Art, 1962–86. Exhibns, Mercury Gall., London, 1965–; retrospective exhibitions: Scottish Arts Council, 1981; Aberystwyth Arts Centre, 1989; Talbot Rice Gall., Edinburgh, 2000. Work in collections including: Scottish Nat. Gall. of Modern Art; Scottish Nat. Portrait Gall.; Nat. Portrait Gall.; Government Art Collection; Kettle's Yard, Cambridge; Hunterian Art Gall., Glasgow. Hon. FRIAS 1986; Hon. FRSE 1994. Hon. DLitt: Heriot-Watt, 1989; Strathclyde, 1998; Dr (*hc*) Edinburgh, 1990; Hon. LLD Aberdeen, 1997. *Address:* c/o Royal Scottish Academy, The Mound, Edinburgh EH2 2EL.

BLACKBEARD, Roy Warren; High Commissioner for Botswana in the United Kingdom, since 1998; *b* 16 April 1953. *Educ:* Kimberley Boys' High Sch. Official Learner, Metallurgy, De Beers, 1972–79; Audit Clerk, Price Waterhouse, 1973–74; CEO, Blackbeard & Co. (Pty) Ltd, 1974–89; ranch manager, 1974–96. MP, Serowe N, 1989–98; Asst Minister, 1992–94, Minister, 1994–97, of Agriculture, Botswana. Mem., Central DC, 1979–89 (Member: Gen. Purposes and Finance Cttee, 1979–89; Livestock Industry Adv. Cttee, 1979–89). Treas., Youth Wing, Botswana Democratic Party, 1980–96. Dir, Air Botswana, 1979–89. *Recreations:* sporting, skeet shooting, theatre, cinema, tennis. *Address:* Botswana High Commission, 6 Stratford Place, W1N 9AE. *T:* (020) 7499 0031, *Fax:* (020) 7495 8595; 34 Winnington Road, Hampstead, N2 0UB.

BLACKBOURN, Prof. David Gordon, PhD; FRHistS; Professor of History, since 1992, Coolidge Professor of History, since 1997, Harvard University; *b* 1 Nov. 1949; *s* of Harry Blackbourn and Pamela Jean (*née* Youngman); *m* 1985, Deborah Frances Langton; one *s* one *d. Educ:* Leeds Modern Grammar Sch.; Christ's Coll., Cambridge (BA Hons Hist. 1970); MA 1974, PhD 1976, Cambridge. Res. Fellow, Jesus Coll., Cambridge, 1973–76; Lectr in History, QMC, Univ. of London, 1976–79; Birkbeck College, University of London: Lectr, 1979–85; Reader, 1985–89; Prof. of Mod. European History, 1989–92. Research Fellow: Inst. of European Hist., Mainz, 1974–75; Alexander von Humboldt Foundn, Bonn-Bad Godesberg, 1984–85; John Simon Guggenheim Meml Foundn, NY, 1994–95; Vis. Kratter Prof. of European Hist., Stanford Univ., 1989–90. Annual Lect., German Histl Inst., London, 1998. Mem., Editl Bd, Past and Present, 1988–. Sec. 1979–81, Mem. Cttee 1981–86, German Hist. Soc.; Member, Academic

Advisory Board: German Hist. Inst., London, 1983–92; Inst. for European Hist., Mainz, 1995–. FRHistS 1987. *Publications:* Class, Religion and Local Politics in Wilhelmine Germany, 1980; (with Geoff Eley) Mythen Deutscher Geschichtsschreibung, 1980 (Japanese edn 1983); (with Geoff Eley) The Peculiarities of German History, 1984; Populists and Patricians, 1987; (ed with Richard J. Evans) The German Bourgeoisie, 1991; Marpingen: apparitions of the Virgin Mary in Bismarckian Germany, 1993 (Amer. Historical Assoc. prize for best book in German history); The Fontana History of Germany: the long nineteenth century 1780–1918, 1997. *Recreations:* reading, jazz and classical music, sport, family. *Address:* Minda de Gunzburg Center for European Studies, Harvard University, 27 Kirkland Street, Cambridge, MA 02138, USA. *T:* (617) 4954303, *Fax:* (617) 4958509.

BLACKBURN, Bishop of, since 1989; **Rt Rev. Alan David Chesters;** *b* 26 Aug. 1937; *s* of Herbert and Catherine Rebecca Chesters; *m* 1975, Jennie Garrett; one *s*. *Educ:* Elland Grammar Sch., W Yorks; St Chad's Coll., Univ. of Durham (BA Mod. History); St Catherine's Coll., Oxford (BA Theol., MA); St Stephen's House, Oxford. Curate of St Anne, Wandsworth, 1962–66; Chaplain and Head of Religious Education, Tiffin School, Kingston-upon-Thames, 1966–72; Director of Education and Rector of Brancepeth, Diocese of Durham, 1972–84; Hon. Canon of Durham Cathedral, 1975–84; Archdeacon of Halifax, 1985–89. A Church Comr, 1982–98 (Mem., Bd of Governors, 1984–89, 1992–98). Mem., General Synod, 1975– (Mem., Standing Cttee, 1985–89, 1990–95); Chm., C of E Bd of Educn, and Council, Nat. Soc., 1999–. Member: Countryside Commn, 1995–99; Countryside Agency, 1999–2001. Entered House of Lords, 1995. *Recreations:* railways, walking, reading. *Address:* Bishop's House, Ribchester Road, Blackburn BB1 9EF.

BLACKBURN, Archdeacon of; *no new appointment at time of going to press.*

BLACKBURN, Dean of; *see* Armstrong, Very Rev. C. J.

BLACKBURN, Vice Adm. David Anthony James, (Tom), CB 1999; LVO 1978; Master of HM's Household, since 2000; an Extra Equerry to the Queen, since 2000; *b* 18 Jan. 1945; *s* of late Lieut J. Blackburn, DSC, RN, and late Mrs M. J. G. Pickering-Pick; *m* 1973, Elizabeth Barstow; three *d*. *Educ:* Taunton Sch. RNC Dartmouth, 1963; HMS Kirkliston (in comd), 1972–73; Equerry-in-Waiting to the Duke of Edinburgh, 1976–78; Exec. Officer, HMS Antrim, 1978–81; MoD (Navy), 1981–83; Comdr, HMS Birmingham, 1983–84; MoD (Navy), 1984–86; HMS York (in comd) and Captain Third Destroyer Sqn, 1987–88; Dir, Naval Manpower and Trng (Seamen), MoD, 1988–90; Cdre, Clyde, and Naval Base Comdr, Clyde, 1990–92; HMS Cornwall (in comd) and Captain, Second Frigate Sqn, 1992–93; Defence Attaché and Hd of British Defence Staff, Washington, 1994–97; COS to Comdr Allied Naval Forces Southern Europe, 1997–99. *Clubs:* Army and Navy; Royal Cruising.

BLACKBURN, Elizabeth; QC 1998; *b* 5 Oct. 1954; *d* of Robert Arnold Parker and Edna Parker (*née* Baines); *m* 1979, John Blackburn, *qv*; two *s*. *Educ:* City of London Sch. for Girls; Manchester Univ. (BA Hons English 1976). Called to the Bar, Middle Temple, 1978 (Harmsworth Schol.); in practice at the Bar, 1978–, specialising in commercial and admiralty law, 1980–; Examr, High Court, 1987–90. *Recreations:* family life, gardening, France. *Address:* 4 Field Court, Gray's Inn, WC1R 5EA. *T:* (020) 7440 6900.

See also R. S. Parker.

BLACKBURN, Prof. Elizabeth Helen, (Mrs J. W. Sedat), PhD; FRS 1992; Professor of Microbiology and Immunology and of Biochemistry and Biophysics, University of California, San Francisco, since 1990 (Chair, Department of Microbiology and Immunology, 1993–99); *b* 26 Nov. 1948; *d* of Harold Stewart Blackburn and Marcia Constance (*née* Jack); *m* 1975, John William Sedat; one *s*. *Educ:* Univ. of Melbourne (BSc Hons 1970; MSc 1972); Cambridge Univ. (PhD 1975). University of California, Berkeley: Asst Prof., Dept of Molecular Biol., 1978–83; Associate Prof., 1983–86; Prof. of Molecular Biology, 1986–90. Pres., Amer. Soc. for Cell Biol., 1998. Mem., Amer. Acad. Arts and Scis; For. Associate, Nat. Acad. of Scis, USA, 1993. Hon. DSc Yale, 1991. Award for Molecular Biol., Nat. Acad. Scis, USA, 1990. *Publications:* research and review articles in Nature, Science, Cell. *Recreations:* music, playing the piano. *Address:* Department of Biochemistry and Biophysics, University of California, Box 0448, San Francisco, CA 94143–0448, USA. *T:* (415) 4764912.

BLACKBURN, (Jeffrey) Michael; DL; Deputy Chairman, Town Centre Securities plc, since 1999; *b* 16 Dec. 1941; *s* of Jeffrey and Renee Blackburn; *m* 1987, Louise Clair Jouny; two *s*; and one *s* one *d* from a previous marriage. *Educ:* Northgate Grammar Sch., Ipswich. FCIB. Chief Manager, Lloyds Bank Business Adv. Service, 1979–83; Dir and Chief Exec., Joint Credit Card Co. Ltd, 1983–87; Dir and Chief Exec., Leeds Permanent Building Soc., 1987–93; Chief Exec., Halifax Building Soc., subseq. Halifax plc, 1993–98. Chairman: Watson Wyatt Systems, 2000–; ID Data, 2000–; Director: DFS Furniture plc; George Wimpey PLC; Jacobs Hldgs plc. Pres., CIB, 1998–99. Mem. Court, Leeds Univ., 1989–2000. Gov., NYO, 1999–; Trustee, Duke of Edinburgh's Award, 1998–. CIMgt; FRSA. DL W Yorkshire, 1998. DUniv Leeds Metropolitan, 1998; Hon. DLitt Huddersfield, 1998. *Recreations:* music, theatre. *Address:* Town Centre Securities, Town Centre House, Merrion Centre, Leeds LS2 8LY. *Club:* Oriental.

BLACKBURN, John; QC 1984; barrister; *b* 13 Nov. 1945; *s* of Harry and Violet Blackburn; *m* 1st, 1970, Alison Nield (marr. diss. 1978); 2nd, 1979, Elizabeth Parker (*see* E. Blackburn); two *s*. *Educ:* Rugby Sch.; Worcester Coll., Oxford (Scholar, 1967; Gibbs Prize in Law, 1967). Called to the Bar, Middle Temple, 1969 (Astbury Law Scholar), Bencher, 1993. Practising barrister, 1970–. *Recreations:* cricket, golf, paintings, wine. *Address:* 1 Atkin Building, Gray's Inn, WC1R 5BQ.

BLACKBURN, Ven. John; QHC 1999; Archdeacon of HM Land Forces, since 1999 and Chaplain-General, since 2000; *b* 3 Dec. 1947; *m* 1970, Anne Elisabeth Woodcock; two *d*. *Educ:* University Coll., Cardiff (DipTh); St Michael's Coll., Llandaff (DPS 1971); Open Univ. (BA Hons 1988; AdvDipEd). Deacon 1971, priest 1972; Curate, Risca, 1971–76; Chaplain, HM Forces, 1976–, Dep. Chaplain-Gen., 1999–2000. FRSA 1999. *Recreations:* travelling, game shooting, reading, English watercolours. *Address:* North Manor, Tilshead, Wilts SP3 4RZ. *T:* (01980) 620436. *Club:* Army and Navy.

BLACKBURN, Michael; *see* Blackburn, J. M.

BLACKBURN, Michael John, FCA; Chairman, Touche Ross & Co., 1990–92 (Managing Partner, 1984–90); *b* 25 Oct. 1930; *s* of Francis and Ann Blackburn; *m* 1955, Maureen (*née* Dale); one *s* two *d*. *Educ:* Kingston Grammar Sch. Joined Touche Ross, 1954; Partner, 1960. Chm., GEI International, 1990–95; Deputy Chairman: Aerostructures Hamble Hldgs, 1992–95; Blue Arrow Hldgs, 1992–96; Director: Chubb Security, 1992–97; William Hill Gp, 1992–99; Steel, Burrill Jones, 1992–99; Wolverhampton Wanderers FC, 1995–97. Chm., Voices for Hospices, 1990–. *Recreations:* horse racing, the garden.

BLACKBURN, Peter Hugh, FCA; Chairman and Chief Executive, Nestlé UK, 1991–96, and 1997–2001; *b* 17 Dec. 1940; *s* of Hugh Edward Blackburn and Sarah Blackburn (*née* Moffatt); *m* 1967, Gillian Mary Popple; three *d*. *Educ:* Douai Sch., Reading; Leeds Univ. (BA Hons Philosophy and French); Poitiers Univ. (Dipl. French); Inst. of Chartered Accts; AMP, Harvard Business Sch., 1976. R. S. Dawson & Co., Bradford (articles), 1962–66; various positions within John Mackintosh and Rowntree Mackintosh, 1966–91; Chm., Rowntree UK, 1985–91; Head, Nestlé Chocolate, Confectionery and Biscuit Strategy Group, 1989–90; Pres. and Dir Gen., Nestlé France, 1996–97. President: ISBA, 1998–2000; FDF, 2000–01. Nat. Pres., Modern Languages Assoc., 1987–89; Chm., Council, Festival of Languages Young Linguist Competition, 1985–89. Mem., Council of Industry and Higher Educn, 1990–92. Mem. Council, York Univ., 1989–92, 2001–. York Merchant Adventurers, 1989. FIGD 1991. Hon. FIL 1989. Hon. DLitt Bradford, 1991. Chevalier du Tastevin, 1984. *Recreations:* fell walking, swimming, photography. *Address:* c/o Nestlé Rowntree Division, York YO91 1XY.

BLACKBURN, Ven. Richard Finn; Archdeacon of Sheffield and Residentiary Canon, Sheffield Cathedral, since 1999; *b* 22 Jan. 1952; *s* of William Brow Blackburn and Ingeborg Lerche-Thomsen; *m* 1980, Helen Claire Davies; one *s* three *d*. *Educ:* Aysgarth Sch.; Eastbourne Coll.; St John's Coll., Durham Univ. (BA); Hull Univ. (MA); Westcott House, Cambridge. National Westminster Bank, 1976–81; deacon 1983, priest 1984; Curate, St Dunstan and All Saints, Stepney, 1983–87; Priest-in-charge, St John the Baptist, Isleworth, 1987–92; Vicar of Mosborough, 1992–99; RD of Attercliffe, 1996–99; Hon. Canon, Sheffield Cathedral, 1998–99. Dignitary in Convocation, 2000–. Governor: Worksop Coll., 2000–; Ranby House Sch., 2000–. *Recreations:* rowing, walking, gardening, music. *Address:* Sheffield Diocesan Church House, 95–99 Effingham Street, Rotherham, South Yorks S65 1BL. *T:* (01709) 512449; 34 Wilson Road, Sheffield S11 8RN.

BLACKBURN, Prof. Simon Walter, PhD; Professor of Philosophy, University of Cambridge, since 2001; Edna J. Koury Distinguished Professor of Philosophy, University of North Carolina, USA, since 1990; *b* 12 July 1944; *s* of Cuthbert and Edna Blackburn; *m* 1968, Angela Bowles; one *s* one *d*. *Educ:* Trinity Coll., Cambridge (BA 1965; PhD 1970). Research Fellow, Churchill Coll., Cambridge, 1967–70; Fellow and Tutor in Philosophy, Pembroke Coll., Oxford, 1970–90. Visiting Professor: Princeton Univ., 1987; Ohio State Univ., 1988; Adjunct Prof., ANU, 1993–. Editor, Mind, 1984–90. *Publications:* Reason and Prediction, 1973; Spreading the Word, 1984; Essays in Quasi Realism, 1993; Oxford Dictionary of Philosophy, 1994; Ruling Passions, 1998; Think, 1999; Being Good, 2001. *Recreations:* hill-walking, sailing, photography. *Address:* 141 Thornton Road, Cambridge CB3 0NE. *T:* (01223) 528278.

BLACKBURN, Vice Adm. Tom; *see* Blackburn, Vice Adm. D. A. J.

BLACKBURNE, Hon. Sir William (Anthony), Kt 1993; **Hon. Mr Justice Blackburne;** Judge of the High Court of Justice, Chancery Division, since 1993; Vice-Chancellor of the County Palatine of Lancaster, since 1998; *b* 24 Feb. 1944; *m* 1996, Vivien, *d* of A. C. Webber. *Address:* Royal Courts of Justice, Strand, WC2A 2LL.

BLACKER, Gen. Sir (Anthony Stephen) Jeremy, KCB 1992; CBE 1987 (OBE 1979); FIMechE; Master-General of the Ordnance, Ministry of Defence, 1991–95; *b* 6 May 1939; *s* of Kenneth Anthony Blacker, CBE and late Louise Margaret Blacker (*née* Band); *m* 1973, Julia Mary (*née* Trew); two *d*. *Educ:* Sherborne School; RMA Sandhurst; Corpus Christi Coll., Cambridge (BA Hons). FIMechE 1990. Commissioned Royal Tank Regt, 1959; Staff Coll., 1971; MA to VCGS, 1976–79; Comd 1 RTR, 1979–81; Mil. Dir of Studies, RMCS, 1981–82; Comd 11 Armd Brigade, 1982–84; Principal Staff Officer to Chief of Defence Staff, 1985–87; Comdt, RMCS, 1987–89; ACDS (Operational Requirements), Land Systems, MoD, 1989–91. Col Comdt, REME, 1987–92, RTR, 1988–95, RAC, 1993–95; Hon. Col, Royal Yeo. and Westminster Dragoons, 1997–. *Recreations:* ski-ing, tennis, golf, investment trusts.

BLACKER, Dr Carmen Elizabeth, FBA 1989; Lecturer in Japanese, 1958–91, and Fellow of Clare Hall, 1965–91, now Fellow Emeritus, Cambridge University; Professor, Ueno Gakuen University, Tokyo, since 1996; *b* 13 July 1924; *d* of Carlos Paton Blacker, MC, GM, MA, MD, FRCP and Helen Maud Blacker (*née* Pilkington). *Educ:* Benenden School; School of Oriental Studies, London University; Somerville Coll., Oxford (Hon. Fellow, 1991). PhD London Univ., 1957. Visiting Professor: Columbia Univ., 1965; Princeton Univ., 1979; Ueno Gakuen Univ., Tokyo, 1991; Toronto Univ., 1992; Vis. Fellow, Kyoto Univ., 1986. Pres., Folklore Soc., 1982–84 (Hon. Mem., 1988). Minakata Kumagusu Prize, 1997. Order of the Precious Crown (Japan), 1988. *Publications:* The Japanese Enlightenment: a study of the writing of Fukuzawa Yukichi, 1964; The Catalpa Bow: a study of Shamanistic practices in Japan, 1975, rev. edn 1986; Collected Papers, 2000; articles in Monumenta Nipponica, Folklore, Trans of Asiatic Soc. of Japan, Asian Folklore Studies, etc. *Recreations:* walking, comparative mythology. *Address:* Willow House, Grantchester, Cambridge CB3 9NF. *T:* (01223) 840196. *Club:* University Women's.

BLACKER, Gen. Sir Cecil (Hugh), GCB 1975 (KCB 1969; CB 1967); OBE 1960; MC 1944; Adjutant-General, Ministry of Defence (Army), 1973–76, retired; ADC (General) to the Queen, 1974–76; *b* 4 June 1916; *s* of Col Norman Valentine Blacker and Olive Georgina (*née* Hope); *m* 1947, Felicity Mary, *widow* of Major J. Rew and *d* of Major I. Buxton, DSO; two *s*. *Educ:* Wellington Coll. Joined 5th Royal Inniskilling Dragoon Guards, 1936; Commanded 23rd Hussars, 1945; Instructor, Staff Coll., Camberley, 1951–54; Commanded 5th Royal Inniskilling Dragoon Guards, 1955–57; Military Asst to CIGS, 1958–60; Asst Commandant, RMA, Sandhurst, 1960–62; Commander, 39 Infantry Brigade Group, 1962–64; GOC 3rd Div., 1964–66; Dir, Army Staff Duties, MoD, 1966–69; GOC-in-C Northern Command, 1969–70; Vice-Chief of the General Staff, 1970–73. Colonel Commandant: RMP, 1971–76; APTC, 1971–76; Col, 5th Royal Inniskilling Dragoon Guards, 1972–81. Member: Jockey Club, 1954– (Dep. Sen. Steward, 1984–86); Horserace Betting Levy Bd, 1981–84; President: BSJA, 1976–80; BEF, 1980–84. *Publications:* The Story of Workboy, 1960; Soldier in the Saddle, 1963; Monkey Business, 1993. *Recreations:* painting; amateur steeplechase rider, 1947–54; represented GB in World Modern Pentathlon Championships, 1951; represented GB in Showjumping, 1959–61. *Address:* Cowpasture Farm, Hook Norton, Banbury, Oxon OX15 5BY.

BLACKER, Captain Derek Charles, RN; Director of Personnel, Orion Royal Bank Ltd, 1984–88; *b* 19 May 1929; *s* of Charles Edward Blacker and Alexandra May Farrant; *m* 1952, Brenda Mary Getgood (*d* 2001); one *s* one *d*. *Educ:* County Sch., Isleworth; King's Coll., Univ. of London (BSc Hons 1950). Entered RN, 1950; specialisations: navigation, meteorology, oceanography; HMS Birmingham, HMS Albion, BRNC Dartmouth, HMS Hermes, 1956–69; Comdr 1965; NATO Commands: SACLANT, 1969; CINCHAN, 1972; SACEUR, 1974; Captain 1975; Dir of Public Relations (RN), 1977–79; Bd Pres., Admiralty Interview Bd, 1980; staff of C-in-C, Naval Home Comd, 1980–81; Dir of Naval Oceanography and Meteorology, MoD, 1981–84. Naval ADC to the Queen,

1983–84. *Recreations:* music, golf, country pursuits. *Address:* Frenchacre, 16 Coach Road, Newton Abbot, Devon TQ12 1EW. *Club:* Army and Navy.

BLACKER, Lt-Gen. Sir Jeremy; *see* Blacker, Lt-Gen. Sir A. S. J.

BLACKER, Norman; Executive Director, British Gas, 1989–95; *b* 22 May 1938; *m* 1st, 1961, Jennifer Mary Anderson (*d* 1992); 2nd, 1994, Carol Anderson. *Educ:* Wolverton Grammar School. IPFA; CIGasE; CIMgt. British Gas: Dir of Finance, Northern Reg., 1976–80; Dir of Finance, 1980–84; Chm., N Eastern Region, then British Gas N Eastern, 1985–89; Managing Director: Eastern Regions, 1989–91; Regl Services, 1991–92; Gas Business, 1992–94. Chm., Nat. Council for Hospice and Specialist Palliative Care Services, 1994–2000. *Address:* 4 White Heather Court, Hythe Marina Village, Hythe SO45 6DT.

BLACKETT, Sir Hugh Francis, 12th Bt *cr* 1673, of Newcastle, Northumberland; *b* 11 Feb. 1955; *e s* of Major Sir Francis Hugh Blackett, 11th Bt and his 1st wife, Elizabeth Eily Barrie (*née* Dennison) (*d* 1982); *S* father, 1995; *m* 1982, Anna, *yr d* of J. St G. Coldwell; one *s* three *d*. *Educ:* Eton. *Heir: s* Henry Douglas Blackett, *b* 2 Feb. 1992.

BLACKETT-ORD, His Honour Andrew James, CVO 1988; a Circuit Judge, 1972–87; Vice-Chancellor, County Palatine of Lancaster, 1973–87; *b* 21 Aug. 1921; 2nd *s* of late John Reginald Blackett-Ord, Whitfield, Northumberland; *m* 1945, Rosemary Bovill; three *s* one *d*. *Educ:* Eton; New Coll., Oxford (MA). Scots Guards, 1943–46; called to Bar, 1947, Bencher, Lincoln's Inn, 1985; County Court Judge, 1971. Mem. Council, Duchy of Lancaster, 1973–87. Chancellor, dio. of Newcastle-upon-Tyne, 1971–98. *Recreations:* reading, art, shooting, country life, travel. *Address:* Helbeck Hall, Brough, Kirkby Stephen, Cumbria CA17 4DD. *T:* (017683) 41323. *Clubs:* Garrick, Lansdowne.

BLACKHAM, Vice-Adm. Sir Jeremy (Joe), KCB 1999; Deputy Chief of Defence Staff (Equipment Capability), Ministry of Defence, since 1999; *b* 10 Sept. 1943; *s* of Rear-Adm. Joseph Leslie Blackham, *qv*; *m* 1971, Candy Carter. *Educ:* Bradfield Coll., Berks; Open Univ. (BA 1st Cl. Hons 1979); RN Staff Course, 1974. Joined RN, 1961; Spanish Interpreter, 1966; commanded HM Ships Beachampton, 1969–70, Ashanti, 1977–79, Nottingham, 1984–85; RCDS 1986; Commandant, RN Staff Coll., Greenwich, 1987–89; Dir of Naval Plans, 1989–92; Captain, HMS Ark Royal, 1992–93 (Comdr RN Task Group, Adriatic); DG, Naval Personnel Strategy and Plans, 1993–95; ACNS and Adm. Pres., RNC, Greenwich, 1995–97; Dep. Comdr, Fleet, 1997–99; DCDS (Progs and Personnel), 1999. Lectr, RUSI and defence organs. Member: Council, RUSI; RIIA; Chm., Blackheath Conservatoire of Music and Arts, 2000–. Liveryman, Shipwrights' Co., 1999–. *Publications:* articles on defence, strategic affairs and walking. *Recreations:* cricket, music, theatre, language, travel, walking. *Address:* c/o Lloyds TSB, 15 The Village, Blackheath, SE3 9LH. *Clubs:* Royal Commonwealth Society, MCC.

BLACKHAM, Rear-Adm. Joseph Leslie, CB 1965; DL; *b* 29 Feb. 1912; *s* of Dr Walter Charles Blackham, Birmingham, and Margaret Eva Blackham (*née* Bavin); *m* 1938, Coreen Shelford Skinner, *er d* of Paym. Captain W. S. Skinner, CBE, RN; one *s* one *d*. *Educ:* West House Sch., Edgbaston; RNC Dartmouth. Specialised in Navigation; served war of 1939–45; JSSC 1950; Comdr, RNC Greenwich, 1953–54; Captain 1954; Admty, 1955–57; Sen. Officer, Reserve Fleet at Plymouth, 1957–59; Admty Naval Staff, 1959–61; Cdre. Supt, HM Dockyard, Singapore, 1962–63; Rear-Adm. 1963; Admiral Supt, HM Dockyard, Portsmouth, 1964–66; retired. Mem., IoW Hosp. Management Cttee, 1968–74; Vice-Chm., IoW AHA 1974–82; Chm., Family Practitioners Cttee, IoW, 1974–85; Mem., Bd of Visitors, HM Prison, Parkhurst, 1967–82 (Chm., 1974–77). CC Isle of Wight, 1967–77 (Chm., 1975–77); DL Hants and IoW, 1970–87; High Sheriff, IoW, 1975. Mentioned in despatches for service in Korea, 1951. SBStJ 1991. *Address:* Trinity Cottage, Love Lane, Bembridge, Isle of Wight PO35 5NH. *T:* (01983) 874386.

See also Vice-Adm. Sir J. J. Blackham, Rear-Adm. R. O. Irwin.

BLACKLEY, Air Vice-Marshal Allan Baillie, CBE 1983; AFC; BSc; Principal, Emergency Planning College, 1993–97; *b* 28 Sept. 1937. Flight Lieut, 1961; Sqn Leader, 1968; Wing Comdr, 1974; Directorate of Air Staff Plans, Dept of CAS, Air Force Dept, 1977; Gp Capt., 1980; OC RAF Valley and ADC to the Queen, 1980–82; Gp Capt (Air Defence) RAF Strike Comd, 1982–83; Dir (Air Defence), MoD, 1984–85; Air Cdre, 1985; Comdt, RAF CFS, Scampton, 1985–87; SASO, No 11 Gp, 1987–89; Dep. COS (Ops), HQ AFCENT, 1989–91; AO Scotland and NI, 1991–93. Chm., Lincs and Notts Air Ambulance Charitable Trust, 1998–2001. *Address:* Robin Lodge, 40 Horncastle Road, Woodhall Spa, Lincs LN10 6UZ.

BLACKLEY, Ian Lorimer; HM Diplomatic Service, retired; *b* 14 Dec. 1946; *s* of late John Lorimer Blackley and Christina Ferrier (*née* Aitken); *m* 1981, Pamela Ann Helena Belt; one *s*. *Educ:* Sedbergh Sch.; St Catharine's Coll., Cambridge (MA). Joined Diplomatic Service, 1969; MECAS, Lebanon, 1971–72; Third Sec., Tripoli, 1972–73; Second Sec., Berlin, 1973–74; First Sec., Damascus, 1974–77; FCO, 1977–80; Head of Chancery and HM Consul, Beirut, 1980–82; First Sec. (Agric.), The Hague, 1982–86; Asst Head, ME Dept, FCO, 1986–88; Counsellor, Kuwait, 1988–90; British Rep. to Govt of Occupied Kuwait in Exile, Aug. 1990–March 1991; Counsellor, Damascus, 1991–93; Spokesman, EU Electoral Mission, Palestinian Elections, 1995–96; Sen. Observer, British Mission to Yemeni Elections, 1997. *Recreations:* fly fishing, Islamic art. *Address:* Berscar, Closeburn, Thornhill, Dumfriesshire DG3 5JJ.

BLACKLOCK, Sir Norman (James), KCVO 1993 (CVO 1989); OBE 1974; FRCS; Professor and Head of Department of Urological Surgery, Victoria University of Manchester, at Withington Hospital, 1978–91, now Professor Emeritus; an Extra Gentleman Usher to the Queen, since 1993; *b* 5 Feb. 1928; 2nd *s* of Prof. John and Ella Blacklock; *m* 1956, Marjorie Reid; one *s* one *d*. *Educ:* McLaren High Sch., Perthshire; Glasgow Univ. (MB ChB 1950). FRCS 1957. Jun. appts, Royal Inf. and Western Inf., Glasgow, 1950–51; Nat. Service, RN, 1951–54, Surg. Lieut, HMSs Theseus and Warrior; Surg. Registrar and Lectr, Glasgow Royal Inf., 1954–56; Surg. Registrar, Ipswich and St Bart's Hosps, 1956–58; Royal Navy: Surg. Specialist, then Cons. in Gen. Surg., serving in naval hosps at Chatham, Devonport, Malta and Portsmouth, 1958–70; Cons. in Surg. and Urol., and Dir of Surg. Res., 1970–78; retd in rank of Surg. Capt., 1978; Dir, Lithotripter Centre, Withington Hosp., 1987–91. Med. Advr to HM Queen on overseas visits, 1976–93; Hon. Cons. in Urol., RN, 1978–93. Former Ext. Examnr in Surgery, univs of Edinburgh, Newcastle upon Tyne and King Saud, Riyadh; Chm., Mil. Educn Cttee, Manchester Univ., 1986–91. Chm., Health Care Cttee, BSI, 1970–91 (mem. cttees concerned with safety of med. equipment etc). Member: Council, British Assoc. of Urolog. Surgs, 1975–78, 1987–91; Adv. Cttee in Urol., RCS, 1987–91. Gilbert Blane Medal, RCS and RCP, 1970; Errol Eldridge Prize, RN Med. Service, 1972. *Publications:* contributor to: Scientific Foundations of Urology, 1976, 3rd edn 1990; Urinary Infection, 1983; Textbook of Geriatric Medicine and Gerontology, 1985, 2nd edn 1991; Urinary Calculous Disease, 1979; Prostate Cancer, 1981; Western Diseases: their emergence and prevention, 1981; Recent Advances in Urology, 3rd edn 1981; Urolithiasis: clinical and basic research, 1982; Textbook of Genito-Urinary Surgery, 2 vols, 1985; Therapy of Prostatitis, 1986; Diagnostic Techniques in Urology, 1990; Tropical Urology and Renal Disease, 1992; many contribs to learned jls. *Recreations:* gardening, cookery, bread-making, pottering. *Address:* c/o Registrar, University of Manchester, Oxford Road, Manchester M13 9PT.

BLACKMAN, Elizabeth Marion; MP (Lab) Erewash, since 1997; *b* 26 Sept. 1949; *m* Derek Blackman; one *s* one *d*. *Educ:* Carlisle County Sch. for Girls; Prince Henry's Grammar Sch., Otley; Clifton Coll., Nottingham (BEd Hons). Hd, Upper Sch., Bramcote Park Comp., Nottingham. PPS to Sec. of State for Defence, 2000–. Mem., Treasury Select Cttee, 1997–2000. *Address:* House of Commons, SW1A 0AA.

BLACKMAN, Sir Frank (Milton), KA 1985; KCVO 1985 (CVO 1975); OBE 1969 (MBE 1964); Ombudsman for Barbados, 1987–93; *b* 31 July 1926; *s* of late A. Milton Blackman and Winnifred Blackman (*née* Pile); *m* 1st, 1958, Edith Mary Knight (*d* 1994); one *s*; 2nd, 1995, Norma Cox Astwood. *Educ:* Wesley Hall Boys' Sch., Barbados; Harrison Coll., Barbados. Clerical Officer, Colonial Secretary's Office, 1944–56; Sec., Public Service Commn, 1956–57; Asst. Sec., Colonial Sec.'s Office, 1957; Cabinet Office/Premier's Office, 1958–66; Clerk of the Legislative Council, 1958–64; Perm. Sec./Cabinet Sec., 1966–86; Head of CS, 1981–86. *Address:* Lausanne, Rendezvous Hill, Christ Church, Barbados. *T:* 4273463.

BLACKMAN, Gilbert Albert Waller, CBE 1978 (OBE 1973); FREng, FIMechE; Chairman, Central Electricity Generating Board, Jan.–March 1990, retired; *b* 28 July 1925; *s* of Ernest Albert Cecil Blackman and Amy Blackman; *m* 1948, Lilian Rosay. *Educ:* Wanstead County High Sch.; Wandsworth Tech. Coll. (CEng, FIMechE 1967). Hon. FInstE (FInstF 1964). Commnd RE, 1945–48. Trainee Engr, London Div., Brit. Electricity Authority, 1948–50; various appts in power stns, 1950–63; Central Electricity Generating Board: Stn Supt, Belvedere, 1963–64; Asst Reg. Dir, E Midlands Div., 1964–67; Asst Reg. Dir, Midlands Reg., 1967–70; Dir of Generation, Midlands Reg., 1970–75; Dir Gen., N Eastern Reg., 1975–77; Mem., 1977–90; Dep. Chm. and Prodn Man. Dir, 1986–89; Chm., British Electricity Internat. Ltd, 1988–90; Dir, Nat. Power, 1990–94. *Recreations:* music, photography, walking. *Address:* Gryphon Lodge, 15 Norton Park, Sunninghill, Berks SL5 9BW. *T:* (01344) 624374.

See also L. C. F. Blackman.

BLACKMAN, Dr Lionel Cyril Francis; Director, British American Tobacco Co. Ltd, 1980–84 (General Manager, Group Research and Development, 1978–80); *b* 12 Sept. 1930; *s* of Ernest Albert Cecil Blackman and Amy McBane; *m* 1955, Susan Hazel Peachey (marr. diss. 1983); one *s* one *d*. *Educ:* Wanstead High Sch.; Queen Mary Coll., London. BSc 1952; PhD 1955. Scientific Officer, then Senior Research Fellow, RN Scientific Service, 1954–57; ICI Research Fellow, then Lectr in Chemical Physics of Solids, Imperial Coll., London, 1957–60; Asst Dir (London), then Dir, Chemical Research Div., BR, 1961–64; Dir of Basic Research, then Dir Gen., British Coal Utilisation Research Assoc., 1964–71; Director: Fibreglass Ltd (subsid. of Pilkington Bros Ltd), 1971–78; Compocem Ltd, 1975–78; Cemfil Corp. (US), 1975–78; Vice-Pres., Cementos y Fibras SA (Spain), 1976–78. Chm., Hockering Residents Assoc., 1995–. CEng; CChem; FRSC; DIC; SFInstE. *Publications:* (ed) Modern Aspects of Graphite Technology, 1970; Athletics World Records in the 20th Century, 1988; papers in various scientific and technical jls on dropwise condensation of steam, ferrites, sintering of oxides, graphite and its crystal compounds, glass surface coatings, glass reinforced cement. *Recreations:* gardening, music, wine. *Address:* Griffin House, Knowl Hill, The Hockering, Woking, Surrey GU22 7HL. *T:* (01483) 766328.

See also G. A. W. Blackman.

BLACKMORE, Prof. Stephen; Regius Keeper, Royal Botanic Garden Edinburgh, since 1999; *b* 30 July 1952; *s* of Edwin Arthur and Josephine Blackmore; *m* 1973, Patricia Jane Melrose Hawley; one *s* one *d*. *Educ:* Univ. of Reading (BSc 1973; PhD 1976). Botanist and Administrator, Royal Society Aldabra Research Station, Indian Ocean, 1976–77; Head of Nat. Herbarium and Lectr in Botany, Univ. of Malaŵi, 1977–80; Head of Palynology Section, Dept of Botany, BM (Natural Hist.), 1980–90; Keeper of Botany, 1990–99, Associate Dir, 1992–95, Natural Hist. Mus. Visiting Professor: Reading Univ., 1995–; Glasgow Univ., 1999–. Pres., Systematics Assoc., 1994–97; Chm., UK Systematics Forum, 1993–99. Trustee, Little Sparta Trust, 2001–. *Publications:* Bee Orchids, 1985; Buttercups, 1985; (ed jtly) Pollen and Spores: form and function, 1986; (ed jtly) Evolution, Systematics and Fossil History of the Hamamelidae, 2 vols, 1989; (ed jtly) Microspores: evolution and ontogeny, 1990; (ed jtly) Pollen and Spores: patterns of diversification, 1991; (ed jtly) An Atlas of Plant Sexual Reproduction, 1992; (ed jtly) Systematics Agenda 2000: The Challenge For Europe, 1996; Pollen and Spores: morphology and biology, 2000; contribs to professional jls. *Recreations:* hill walking, photography, blues guitar music. *Address:* (office) 20A Inverleith Row, Edinburgh EH3 5LR. *T:* (0131) 248 2930.

BLACKSELL, Henry Oliver; QC 1994; **His Honour Judge Blacksell;** a Circuit Judge, since 1996; *b* 28 Nov. 1948; *s* of James Edward Blacksell, MBE and Joan Simmons Yates Blacksell (*née* Yates); *m* 1st, 1971, Diana Frances Mary Burton (marr. diss. 1985); 2nd, 1986, Miranda Jane, *d* of His Honour W. A. L. Allardice, *qv*; one *s* one *d*. *Educ:* Barnstaple Grammar Sch.; Exeter Univ. (LLB). Called to the Bar, Inner Temple, 1972; a Recorder, 1993–96. *Recreations:* family, theatre, ancient humour. *Address:* Crown Court, Middlesex Guildhall, SW1P 3BB. *Club:* Harlequin Rugby Football.

BLACKSHAW, Alan, OBE 1992; VRD 1970; business consultant and author; *b* 7 April 1933; *s* of late Frederick William Blackshaw and Elsie (*née* MacDougall); *m* 1st, 1956, Jane Elizabeth Turner (marr. diss. 1983); one *d*; 2nd, 1984, Dr Elspeth Paterson Martin, *d* of late Rev. Gavin C. Martin and Agnes Martin; one *s* two *d*. *Educ:* Merchant Taylors' Sch., Crosby; Wadham Coll., Oxford (MA). Royal Marines (commnd), 1954–56, and RM Reserve, 1956–76. Entered Home Civil Service, Min. of Power, 1956; 1st Sec., UK Delegn to OECD, Paris, 1965–66; Principal Private Sec. to Minister of Power, 1967–69; with Charterhouse Gp on loan, 1972–73; Dept of Energy: Under Sec., 1974; Offshore Supplies Office, 1974–78 (Dir-Gen., 1977–78); Coal Div., 1978–79; Consultant, NCB, 1979–86. Consultant Dir, Strategy Internat., 1980–91; Director: Paths for All Partnership, 1996–97; Badenoch, Moray and Strathspey Enterprise, 1998–2000. Member: Scottish Council for Develt and Industry, 1974–78; Offshore Energy Technol. Bd, 1977–78; Ship and Marine Technol. Requirements Bd, 1977–78; Scottish Sports Council, 1990–95; Scottish Natural Heritage, 1992–97 (Chairman: Task Force on Access, 1992–94; Audit Cttee, 1994–97); Adventure Activities Licensing Authy, 1996–; UN Inter-Agency Gp on Mountains, 1996–; Bd, Cairngorms Partnership, 1998– (Chm., Recreational Forum, 1998–); Rights of Way Survey Steering Gp, Countryside Agency, 2000–. University of Highlands and Islands Project: Academic Advr, 1997–; Chm., Working Gp on Tourism and Leisure, 1998–99; Mem., Scis and Envmt Faculty Bd, 1999–. Libel damages against Daily Telegraph (upheld in Ct of Appeal, 1983) and Daily Mail, 1981. Pres., Oxford Univ. Mountaineering Club, 1953–54; Climbers' Club: Sec., 1956–61; Vice-Pres., 1973–75; Hon. Mem., 1998; Alpine Club: Editor, Alpine Jl, 1968–70; Vice-Pres., 1979–81; Trustee, 1980–90; Hon. Mem., 1998; British Mountaineering Council: Pres., 1973–76; Patron, 1979–; Chairman: Standing Adv. Cttee on Mountain Trng Policy, 1980–86 and

1990–93; Ski Touring and Mountaineering Cttee, 1981–91. Chairman: Sports Council's Nat. Mountain Centre (formerly Nat. Centre for Mountain Activities), Plas y Brenin, 1986–95; Mountaineering Cttee, UIAA, 1990–2000 (Mem., 1985–; Dep. Chm., 1989–90); UIAA Gp on competitions in mountain areas, 1993–, on mountain access, 1995–99; UK Mountain Trng Bd, 1991–94; Scottish Adventure Activities Forum, 1999–; Interim Wkg Gp on Leadership in Outdoor Activities, Sports Council, 1990–91; Leader, British Alpine Ski Traverse, 1972; UIAA Special Rep., UN Year of the Mountains 2002, 2000–; Adviser on public access to land: Scottish Envmt Link, 1994–; CCPR, 1997–; Hon. Advr, Mountaineering Council of Scotland, 1994–. Pres., Snowsport Scotland (formerly Scottish Nat. Ski Council), 1994– (Chm., 1991–94); Ski Club of Great Britain: Vice-Pres., 1977–80, 1983–85; Pres., 1997–; Pery Medal, 1977; Hon. Mem., 1992; Pres., Eagle Ski Club, 1979–81 (Hon. Mem., 1982); British Ski Federation: Vice-Pres., 1983–84; Chm., 1984–86. Sec., Edinburgh Br., Oxford Soc., 1989–98. Hon. Advr, Venture Scotland, 1995–. Freeman, City of London. FRGS; FInstPet. *Publication:* Mountaineering, 1965, 3rd revision 1975. *Recreations:* mountaineering, ski-ing, sailing. *Address:* Rhu Grianach, Kingussie Road, Newtonmore, Inverness-shire PH20 1AY. *T:* (01540) 673239; Les Autannes, Le Tour, Argentière, 74440, France. *T:* 450541220. *Club:* Royal Scottish Automobile (Glasgow).

BLACKSHAW, William Simon; Headmaster of Brighton College, 1971–87; *b* 28 Oct. 1930; *s* of late C. B. Blackshaw, sometime Housemaster, Cranleigh School and Kathleen Mary (who *m* 1965, Sir Thomas McAlpine, 4th Bt); *m* 1956, Elizabeth Anne Evans; one *s* one *d* (and one *s* decd). *Educ:* Sherborne Sch.; Hertford Coll., Oxford. 2nd cl. hons Mod. Langs. Repton School: Asst Master, 1955–71; Head of Modern Languages Dept, 1961–66; Housemaster, 1966–71. Chm., Bankside Gall., 1994–2000. Chm., Sussex Schs Cricket Assoc., 1994–96. Hon. RWS. *Publications:* Regardez! Racontez!, 1971; A History of Bilton Grange School, 1997. *Recreations:* philately, painting, cricket, golf. *Address:* Squash Court, The Green, Rottingdean, East Sussex BN2 7HA.

BLACKSTONE, Baroness *cr* 1987 (Life Peer), of Stoke Newington in Greater London; **Tessa Ann Vosper Blackstone,** PC 2001; PhD; Minister of State (Minister for Arts), Department for Culture, Media and Sport, since 2001; *b* 27 Sept. 1942; *d* of late Geoffrey Vaughan Blackstone, CBE, GM, QFSM and of Joanna Blackstone; *m* 1963, Tom Evans (marr. diss.; he *d* 1985); one *s* one *d*. *Educ:* Ware Grammar Sch.; London School of Economics (BScSoc, PhD). Associate Lectr, Enfield Coll., 1965–66; Asst Lectr, then Lectr, Dept of Social Administration, LSE, 1966–75; Adviser, Central Policy Review Staff, Cabinet Office, 1975–78; Prof. of Educnl Admin, Univ. of London Inst. of Educn, 1978–83; Dep. Educn Officer (Resources), then Clerk and Dir of Education, ILEA, 1983–87; Master, Birkbeck Coll., London Univ., 1987–97. Fellow, Centre for Studies in Social Policy, 1972–74; Special Rowntree Visiting Fellow, Policy Studies Inst., 1987. Chm., Gen. Adv. Council of BBC, 1987–91; First Chm., Inst. for Public Policy Research, 1988–97. Director: Project Fullemploy, 1984–91; Thames Television, 1991–92; Royal Opera House, 1987–97. Chm. Ballet Bd, 1991–97; Member: Planning Bd, Arts Council of GB, 1986–90; Management Cttee, King Edward's Hosp. Fund for London, 1990–95; Gov. and Mem. of Council, Ditchley Foundn, 1990–97; Gov., Royal Ballet, 1991–. Vice Pres., VSO, 1992–. Opposition spokesman, House of Lords: on educn and science, 1988–92; on foreign affairs, 1992–97; Minister of State, DfEE, 1997–2001. Trustee: Architecture Foundn, 1991–97; Nat. Hist. Mus., 1992–97. *Publications:* Students in Conflict (jtly), 1970; A Fair Start, 1971; Education and Day Care for Young Children in Need, 1973; The Academic Labour Market (jtly), 1974; Social Policy and Administration in Britain, 1975; Disadvantage and Education (jtly), 1982; Educational Policy and Educational Inequality (jtly), 1982; Response to Adversity (jtly), 1983; Testing Children (jtly), 1983; Inside the Think Tank (jtly), 1988; Prisons and Penal Reform, 1990; Race Relations in Britain, 1997. *Address:* Department for Culture, Media and Sport, 2–4 Cockspur Street, SW1Y 5DH.

BLACKWELL, family name of **Baron Blackwell.**

BLACKWELL, Baron *cr* 1997 (Life Peer), of Woodcote in the co. of Surrey; **Norman Roy Blackwell;** Director, Dixons Group, since 2000; Chairman: Centre for Policy Studies, since 2000; Smart Stream Technologies Ltd, since 2001; *b* 29 July 1952; *s* of Albert Blackwell and Frances Blackwell (*née* Lutman); *m* 1974, Brenda Clucas; three *s* two *d*. *Educ:* RAM (Jun. Exhibnr); Trinity Coll., Cambridge (MA); Wharton Business Sch., Univ. of Pennsylvania (AM, MBA; PhD 1976). With Plessey Co., 1976–78; Partner, McKinsey & Co., 1978–95, elected Partner, 1984; Special Advr, Prime Minister's Policy Unit, 1986–87 (on leave of absence); Head, Prime Minister's Policy Unit, 1995–97; Dir, Gp Develt, NatWest Gp, 1997–2000; Special Advr, KPMG Corp. Finance, 2000–. Director: Corporate Services Gp, 2000–; Slough Estates, 2001–. *Recreations:* classical music, walking. *Address:* c/o House of Lords, SW1A 0PW. *Clubs:* Carlton, Royal Automobile.

BLACKWELL, Sir Basil (Davenport), Kt 1983; FREng; Chief Executive, 1974–85, and Chairman, 1985, Westland PLC (formerly Westland Aircraft Ltd) (Vice-Chairman, 1974–84, Deputy Chairman, 1984); retired; *b* Whitkirk, Yorks, 8 Feb. 1922; *s* of late Alfred Blackwell and late Mrs H. Lloyd; *m* 1948, Betty Meggs, *d* of late Engr Captain Meggs, RN; one *d*. *Educ:* Leeds Grammar Sch.; St John's Coll., Cambridge (MA; Hughes Prize); London Univ. (BScEng). FIMechE; FRAeS (Gold Medal, 1982); CIMgt. Sci. Officer, Admiralty, 1942; Rolls-Royce Ltd, 1945; Engine Div., Bristol Aeroplane Co. Ltd, 1949; Bristol Siddeley Engines Ltd: Dep. Chief Engr, 1959; Sales Dir, 1963; Man. Dir, Small Engine Div., 1965 (subseq. Small Engines Div. of Rolls-Royce Ltd). Commercial Dir, Westland Aircraft Ltd, 1970–72; Westland Helicopters Ltd: Man. Dir, 1972; Chm., 1976–85; Chairman: British Hovercraft Corp., 1979–85; Normalair-Garrett Ltd, 1979–85. Member Council: BIM; CBI; NDIC; SBAC (Vice-Pres., 1978; Pres., 1979 and 1980; Dep. Pres., 1980); EEF (Vice-Pres., 1983–85); Bath Univ., 1986–95. Pres., AECMA, 1984–85 (Président d'honneur 1985); Chm., Astrid Trust, 1986–93. Hon. DSc, 1984, Chancellor's Medal, 1997, Bath Univ. *Publications:* (jtly) The Global Challenge of Innovation, 1991; contrib. professional jls. *Recreations:* gardens and gardening. *Address:* High Newland, Newland Garden, Sherborne, Dorset DT9 3AF. *T:* (01935) 813516. *Club:* Oxford and Cambridge.

BLACKWELL, Prof. Donald Eustace, MA, PhD; Savilian Professor of Astronomy, University of Oxford, 1960–88, now Emeritus; Fellow of New College, Oxford, 1960–88, now Emeritus; *b* 27 May 1921; *s* of John Blackwell and Ethel Bowe; *m* 1951, Nora Louise Carlton; two *s* two *d*. *Educ:* Merchant Taylors' Sch.; Sandy Lodge; Sidney Sussex Coll., Cambridge. Isaac Newton Student, University of Cambridge, 1947; Stokes Student, Pembroke Coll., Cambridge, 1948; Asst Director, Solar Physics Observatory, Cambridge, 1950–60. Various Astronomical Expeditions: Sudan, 1952; Fiji, 1955; Bolivia, 1958 and 1961; Canada, 1963; Manuae Island, 1965. Pres., RAS, 1973–75. *Publications:* papers in astronomical journals. *Address:* 4 Pullens Field, Headington, Oxford OX3 0BU.

BLACKWELL, Rt Rev. Douglas Charles; a Suffragan Bishop of Toronto (Area Bishop of Trent-Durham), since 1988; *b* 3 June 1938; *s* of late William John Blackwell and Ethel N. Blackwell (*née* Keates); *m* 1963, Sandra Dianne Griffiths; one *s* two *d*. *Educ:* Wycliffe Coll., Univ. of Toronto (DipTh, LTh). Deacon 1963, priest 1964; Asst Curate, St Stephen's, Calgary, 1964; Vicar, Cochrane Mission, Diocese of Calgary, 1966; Rector, St Paul's, North Battleford, Diocese of Saskatoon, 1969; Regional Dean of Battleford, 1970; Archdeacon of Battlefords–Lloydminster, 1973; Asst Director, Aurora Conf. Centre, Diocese of Toronto, 1974; Executive Asst to Archbishop of Toronto, 1977; Canon of St James's Cathedral, Toronto, 1978; Archdeacon of York, 1986. Hon. DD Wycliffe Coll., Toronto, 1990. *Address:* 135 Adelaide Street East, Toronto, ON M5C 1L8, Canada. *T:* (416) 3636021.

BLACKWELL, Prof. Jenefer Mary; Glaxo Professor of Molecular Parasitology, Cambridge, since 1991; Professorial Fellow, Newnham College, Cambridge, since 1993; Director, Cambridge Institute for Medical Research, since 1998; *b* 8 Dec. 1948; *d* of Frank Blackwell and Elsie Winifred Broadhurst; *m* 1973, Simon John Miles; one *s* one *d*. *Educ:* Univ. of Western Australia (BSc 1969 (1st Cl. Hons Zoology); PhD 1974 (Population Genetics)). Cons. Biologist and Res. Officer, WA Govt Depts, 1973–74; Lectr in Biol., Avery Hill Coll. of Educn, London, 1975–76; London School of Hygiene and Tropical Medicine: Res. Fellow, Ross Inst. of Tropical Hygiene, 1976–82; Wellcome Trust Sen. Lectr, Dept of Trop. Hygiene, 1982–88, Dept of Med. Parasitology, 1988–91 (and Head, Immunobiol. of Parasitic Diseases Unit); Reader, Univ. of London, 1989–91. Faculty Mem., Molecular Biol. of Parasitism Course, Marine Biol. Labs, Wood's Hole, Mass, 1988. *Publication:* (with D. Wakelin) Genetics of Resistance to Bacterial and Parasitic Infection, 1988. *Recreations:* music, walking. *Address:* Cambridge Institute for Medical Research, Wellcome Trust/MRC Building, Addenbrooke's Hospital, Hills Road, Cambridge CB2 2XY. *T:* (01223) 336947.

BLACKWELL, John Charles, CBE 1988; education consultant, since 1995; farmer; *b* 4 Nov. 1935; *s* of Charles Arthur Blackwell and Louisa Amy Blackwell (*née* Sellers); *m* 1st, 1961, Julia Rose; one *s*; 2nd, 1978, Inger Beatrice Lewin; one step *s*. *Educ:* Glynn Grammar Sch., Ewell; Dudley Coll. of Educn (Cert. in Educn); Bristol Univ. (BA, MEd, PhD). Metropolitan Police Cadet, 1952–53; RAF, 1954–56; teacher, Dempsey Secondary Sch., London, 1958–60; British Council, 1966–95: Asst Rep., Tanzania, 1966–70; Educn Officer, Calcutta, 1971–72; Asst Educn Adviser, New Delhi, 1973–75; Head, Schools and Teacher Educn Unit, 1976–78; attached British Embassy, Washington, 1979; Dir, Educn Contracts Dept, 1980–83; Rep., Indonesia, 1983–89; Controller, later Dir, Sci. and Educn Div., 1989–92; Develt Advr, 1993–95. *Recreations:* boating, fishing, reading. *Address:* Agriomata, Paralia Vergas, Kalamata, Messinia 24100, Greece. *T:* and *Fax:* 72197524.

BLACKWELL, Julian, (Toby); DL; President, since 1995, and Chairman, 1996–99, Blackwell Ltd; Chairman, The Blackwell Group Ltd, 1980–94; *b* 10 Jan. 1929; *s* of Sir Basil Henry Blackwell and late Marion Christine, *d* of John Soans; *m* 1953, Jennifer Jocelyn Darley Wykeham; two *s* one *d*. *Educ:* Winchester; Trinity Coll., Oxford. Served 5th RTR, 1947–49; 21st SAS (TA), 1950–59. Dir and Chm., various Blackwell companies, 1956–. Chm. Council, ASLIB, 1966–68 (Vice-Pres., 1982); Co-founder and Chm., Mail Users' Assoc., 1975–78 and 1987–90; Pres., Booksellers' Assoc., 1980–82; Chairman: Thames Business Advice Centre, 1986–97; Heart of England TEC, 1989–94; Fox FM, 1989–98. Chm., Son White Meml Trust, 1991–. DL Oxon 1987, High Sheriff, 1991–92. Hon. DLitt Robert Gordon, 1997; DUniv Sheffield Hallam, 1998; Hon. Dr Oxford Brookes, 1999. *Recreations:* sailing, saving firewood. *Address:* c/o 50 Broad Street, Oxford OX1 3BQ. *T:* (01865) 792111. *Clubs:* Special Forces; Royal Yacht Squadron; Leander (Henley); Royal Southern Yacht (Southampton).

BLACKWOOD, family name of **Baron Dufferin and Clandeboye.**

BLAHNIK, Manolo; designer of shoes and furniture, since 1973; Director, Manolo Blahnik International Ltd, since 1973; *b* Canary Is, 28 Nov. 1942; *s* of late E. Blahnik and of Manuela Blahnik. *Educ:* Univ. of Geneva; Louvre Art Sch., Paris. Fashion Council of America Award, 1987, 1990, 1997; Balenciaga Award, 1989; Antonio Lopez Award, Hispanic Inst., Washington, 1990; British Fashion Council Award, 1990, 1999; American Leather New York Award, 1991; Silver Slipper Award, Houston Mus. of Fine Art, 1999 (first awarded to a shoe designer). *Recreations:* travel, painting. *Address:* 49–51 Old Church Street, SW3 5BS. *T:* (020) 7352 8622.

BLAIKLEY, Robert Marcel; HM Diplomatic Service, retired; *b* 1 Oct. 1916; *s* of late Alexander John Blaikley and late Adelaide Blaikley (*née* Miller); *m* 1942, Alice Mary Duncan; one *s* one *d*. *Educ:* Christ's Coll., Finchley; St John's Coll., Cambridge. Served HM Forces, 1940–46. Inland Revenue, 1946–48; General Register Office, 1948–65, Asst Secretary, 1958; transferred to Diplomatic Service as Counsellor, 1965; on loan to Colonial Office, 1965–66; Head of Aviation and Telecommunications Dept, CO, 1966–68; Counsellor, Jamaica, 1968–71, Ghana, 1971–73. *Recreations:* reading, growing shrubs. *Address:* 23 Deanery Walk, Avonpark, Winsley Road, Limpley Stoke, Bath BA2 7JQ.

BLAIN, Prof. Peter George, PhD; FRCP, FRCPE, FFOM; CBiol, FIBiol; Professor of Environmental Medicine, University of Newcastle Upon Tyne, since 1986; *b* 15 March 1951; *s* of Reginald Blain and Margaret (*née* Graham); *m* 1977, Patricia Anne Crawford; two *s* one *d*. *Educ:* Univ. of Newcastle upon Tyne (BMed.Sci.; MB, BS; PhD 1988). MFOM 1990, FFOM 1997; FRCP 1990; FRCPE 1991; CBiol 1986; FIBiol 1989. Jun. hosp. doctor, Royal Victoria Infirmary, Newcastle upon Tyne, 1975–79; University of Newcastle upon Tyne: Lectr in Clinical Pharmacol., 1979–80; Wellcome Res. Fellow in Clinical Pharmacol. and Neurology, 1980–81; First Asst in Clinical Pharmacol., 1981–85; Hd, Biomed. Scis and Human Toxicol. Res., ICI plc, 1985–86. Consultant Physician: Freeman Gp of Hosps NHS Trust (formerly Freeman Hosp.), 1988–; Royal Victoria Infirmary NHS Trust (formerly Royal Victoria Inf.), 1988–; Newcastle Hosps NHS Trust, 1998–; Consultant in Envmtl Medicine and Toxicol., Northern and Yorks RHA, 1992–. *Publications:* contrib. to textbooks in toxicol. and medicine; res. papers in acad. jls in toxicol. *Recreation:* hill walking. *Address:* Department of Environmental Medicine, Medical School, Newcastle upon Tyne NE2 4HH. *T:* (0191) 222 7195, *Fax:* (0191) 222 6442; *e-mail:* p.g.blain@ncl.ac.uk.

BLAIN, Sophie Clodagh Mary; *see* Andreae, S. C. M.

BLAIR, Rt Hon. Anthony Charles Lynton, (Tony); PC 1994; MP (Lab) Sedgefield, since 1983; Prime Minister and First Lord of the Treasury, since 1997; Leader of the Labour Party, since 1994; *b* 6 May 1953; *s* of Leo Charles Lynton Blair and late Hazel Blair; *m* 1980, Cherie Booth, *qv*; three *s* one *d*. *Educ:* Durham Choristers School; Fettes College, Edinburgh; St John's College, Oxford. Called to the Bar, Lincoln's Inn, 1976; Hon. Bencher, 1994. Leader of the Opposition, 1994–97. *Publications:* New Britain: my vision of a young country, 1996; The Third Way, 1998. *Address:* 10 Downing Street, SW1A 2AA. *T:* (020) 7270 3000. *Clubs:* Trimdon Colliery and Deaf Hill Working Men's, Constituency Labour (Trimdon); Fishburn Working Men's.

See also W. J. L. Blair.

BLAIR, Bruce Graeme Donald; QC 1989; a Recorder, since 1995; *b* 12 April 1946; *s* of late Dr Donald Alexander Sangster Blair, MA, MD, DPM and Eleanor Violet Blair (*née* Van Ryneveld); *m* 1970, Susanne Blair (*née* Hartung); three *d* (and one *s* decd). *Educ:* Harrow School; Magdalene College, Cambridge. Called to the Bar, Middle Temple, 1969, Bencher, 1997. *Publication:* Practical Matrimonial Precedents (jtly), 1989. *Recreations:* bridge, tennis, turf. *Address:* 1 Mitre Court Buildings, Temple, EC4Y 7BS. *T:* (020) 7797 7070. *Clubs:* Reform, MCC.

BLAIR, Lt-Gen. Sir Chandos, KCVO 1972; OBE 1962; MC 1941 and bar, 1944; GOC Scotland and Governor of Edinburgh Castle, 1972–76; *b* 25 Feb. 1919; *s* of Brig.-Gen. Arthur Blair and Elizabeth Mary (*née* Hoskyns); *m* 1947, Audrey Mary Travers (*d* 1997); one *s* one *d*. *Educ:* Harrow; Sandhurst. Commnd into Seaforth Highlanders, 1939; comd 4 KAR, Uganda, 1959–61; comd 39 Bde, Radfan and N. Ireland. GOC 2nd Division, BAOR, 1968–70; Defence Services Secretary, MoD, 1970–72. Col Comdt, Scottish Div., 1972–76; Col, Queen's Own Highlanders, 1975–83. *Recreations:* golf, fishing, shooting. *Club:* Naval and Military.

BLAIR, Cherie; *see* Booth, C.

BLAIR, Claude, OBE 1994; FSA 1956; Keeper, Department of Metalwork, Victoria and Albert Museum, 1972–82; *b* 30 Nov. 1922; *s* of William Henry Murray Blair and Lilian Wearing; *m* 1952, Joan Mary Greville Drinkwater (*d* 1996); one *s*. *Educ:* William Hulme's Grammar Sch., Manchester; Manchester Univ. (MA). Served War, Army (Captain RA), 1942–46. Manchester Univ., 1946–51; Asst, Tower of London Armouries, 1951–56; Asst Keeper of Metalwork, V&A, 1956–66; Dep. Keeper, 1966–72. Hon. Editor, Jl of the Arms and Armour Soc., 1953–77. Consultant to Christie's, 1983–; Member: Arch. Adv. Panel, Westminster Abbey, 1979–98; Council for the Care of Churches, 1991–96 (Mem. Exec. Cttee, 1983–91); Trustee, Churches Conservation Trust (formerly Redundant Churches Fund), 1982–97. Vice-Pres., Soc. of Antiquaries, 1990–93; Hon. Pres., Meyrick Soc., 1979–94; Hon. Vice-President: Soc. for Study of Church Monuments, 1984– (Hon. Pres., 1978–84); Monumental Brass Soc. Hon. Liveryman, Cutlers' Co. Liveryman: Goldsmiths' Co.; Armourers and Brasiers' Co. Medal of Museo Militar, Barcelona, 1969; Medal of Arms and Armour Soc., 1986; Gold Medal, Soc. of Antiquaries, 1998. *Publications:* European Armour, 1958 (2nd edn, 1972); European and American Arms, 1962; The Silvered Armour of Henry VIII, 1965; Pistols of the World, 1968; Three Presentation Swords in the Victoria and Albert Museum, 1972; The James A. de Rothschild Collection: Arms, Armour and Miscellaneous Metalwork, 1974; (gen. editor and contrib.) Pollard's History of Firearms, 1983; (ed) The History of Silver, 1987; (gen. editor and contrib.) The Crown Jewels, 1998; numerous articles and reviews in Archaeological Jl, Jl of Arms and Armour Soc., Connoisseur, Waffen und Kostümkunde, etc. *Recreations:* travel, looking at churches, listening to music. *Address:* 90 Links Road, Ashtead, Surrey KT21 2HW. *T:* (01372) 275532. *Clubs:* Civil Service, Royal Over-Seas League.

BLAIR, Sir Edward Thomas H.; *see* Hunter-Blair.

BLAIR, Prof. Gordon Purves, CBE 1995; PhD, DSc; FREng, FIMechE, FSAE; Professor of Mechanical Engineering, Queen's University of Belfast, 1976–96, now Emeritus; *b* 29 April 1937; *s* of Gordon Blair and Mary Helen Jones Blair; *m* 1964, Norma Margaret Millar; two *d*. *Educ:* Queen's Univ. of Belfast (BSc; PhD 1962; DSc 1978). CEng, FIMechE 1977; FSAE 1979; FREng (FEng 1982). Asst Prof., New Mexico State Univ., 1962–64; Queen's University of Belfast: Lectr, 1964–71; Sen. Lectr, 1971–73; Reader, 1973–76; Head of Dept of Mechl and Industrial Engrg, 1982–89, and of Dept of Mechl and Manufacturing, Aeronautical and Chemical Engrg, 1987–89; Dean, Faculty of Engrg, 1985–88; Pro-Vice-Chancellor, 1989–94. Chm., Automobile Div., IMechE, 1991. *Publications:* The Basic Design of Two-Stroke Engines, USA, 1990; Design and Simulation of Two-Stroke Engines, 1996; Design and Simulation of Four-Stroke Engines, 1999; wide pubn in IMechE and SAE Jls on design and develt of internal combustion engines. *Recreations:* golf, fishing, motorcycles. *Address:* 9 Ben Madigan Park South, Newtownabbey, N Ireland BT36 7PX. *T:* (028) 9077 3280. *Clubs:* Royal Automobile; Cairndhu Golf; Royal Portrush Golf.

BLAIR, Ian Charles; City Treasurer, Nottingham City Council, since 1991; *b* 31 Aug. 1947; *s* of John Blair and Robina Poppy Blair (*née* Carr); *m* 1974, Jennifer Mary Hodgson; one *s* one *d*. *Educ:* Liberton Sch., Edinburgh; Open Univ. (BA 1995). CPFA (IPFA 1969). Trainee Accountant, then Accountant, Midlothian CC, 1964–72; Sen. Accountant, Scottish Special Housing Assoc., 1972–75; Sen. Asst Treas., Lothian Health Bd, 1975–81; City Treas., Bath CC, 1981–91. Advr, ADC, 1992–97. Chm., S Wales and West, CIPFA, 1991; Pres., Audit Cttee, Eurocities, 1999–; Mem., Exec., Soc. Municipal Treasurers, 1999–. *Publications:* contribs to prof. jls. *Recreations:* family, sports (Hearts FC and Bath RFC), theatre. *Address:* c/o Nottingham County Council, The Guildhall, Burton Street, Nottingham NG1 2DE. *T:* (0115) 915 4000.

BLAIR, Ian Warwick, QPM 1999; Deputy Commissioner, Metropolitan Police, since 2000; *b* 19 March 1953; *yr s* of late Francis James Blair and Sheila Kathleen Blair; *m* 1980, Felicity Jane White; one *s* one *d*. *Educ:* Wrekin Coll.; Harvard High Sch., LA; Christ Church, Oxford (MA). Joined Metropolitan Police, 1974; uniform and CID posts, 1974–91; Chief Supt, SO to HM Chief Inspector of Constabulary, 1991–93; Asst Chief Constable, 1994–97, des. Dep. to Chief Constable, 1997, Thames Valley Police; Chief Constable, Surrey Police, 1998–2000. Vis. Fellow, Internat. Centre for Advanced Studies, NY Univ., 1998. *Publication:* Investigating Rape: a new approach for police, 1985. *Recreations:* ski-ing, tennis, golf, theatre. *Address:* New Scotland Yard, Broadway, SW1H 0BG. *T:* (020) 7230 2636.

BLAIR, Michael Campbell; barrister in private practice; Chairman Personal Investment Authority, since 2000; Investment Management Regulatory Organisation, since 2000; Securities and Futures Authority, since 2001; *b* 26 Aug. 1941; *s* of Sir Alastair Campbell Blair, KCVO and late Catriona Hatchard Blair (*née* Orr); *m* 1966, Halldóra Isabel (*née* Tunnard); one *s*. *Educ:* Rugby Sch.; Clare Coll., Cambridge (MA, LLM); Yale Univ., USA (Mellon Fellow; MA). Called to the Bar, Middle Temple, 1965 (Harmsworth Law Scholar); Bencher, 1995. Lord Chancellor's Dept, 1966–87: Private Sec. to the Lord Chancellor, 1968–71; Sec., Law Reform Cttee, 1977–79; Under Sec., 1982–87; Circuit Administrator, Midland and Oxford Circuit, 1982–86; Hd, Courts and Legal Services Gp, 1986–87. Attended Cabinet Office Top Management Programme, 1986. Securities and Investments Board: Dir of Legal Services, 1987–91; General Counsel, 1991–93; Head of Policy and Legal Affairs, 1993–95; Dep. Chief Exec. and Gen. Counsel, 1996–98; Gen. Counsel to Bd, FSA, 1998–2000. Director: Financial Services Compensation Scheme Ltd, 2000–; Investors Compensation Scheme Ltd, 2001. Mem., Appeals Tribunal, Competition Commn, 2000–. Chairman: Bar Assoc. for Commerce, Finance and Industry, 1990–91; Bar Conf., 1993; Member: Gen. Council of the Bar, 1989–98 (Chm., Professional Standards Cttee, 1994; Treas., 1995–98); Council of Legal Educn, 1992–97. Vis. Prof., Univ. of Reading, 1998–. Hon. QC 1996. FRSA 1992. *Publications:* Sale of Goods Act 1979, 1980; Financial Services: the new core rules, 1991; (ed) Blackstone's Guide to the Bank of England Act 1998, 1998; (ed) Blackstone's Guide to the Financial Services and Markets Act 2000, 2001; legal articles in Modern Law Rev., New Law Jl, Civil Justice Qly, Jl of Internat. Banking and Financial Law, etc. *Address:* 3 Burbage Road, SE24 9HJ. *T:* (020) 7274 7614. *Club:* Athenæum.

BLAIR, Capt. (Robert) Neil, RN; CVO 2001 (LVO 1997); Private Secretary, Treasurer and Extra Equerry to the Duke of York, 1990–2001; Private Secretary to Princess Alexandra, the Hon. Lady Ogilvy, 1995–2001; *b* 14 July 1936; *s* of Harley Blair and Jane Blair (*née* Tarr); *m* 1960, Barbara Jane, *d* of Ian and Monica Rankin; two *s* one *d*. *Educ:* St John's Coll., Johannesburg; BRNC, Dartmouth. Joined RN, 1954: served HMY Britannia, 1958–59 and 1970–71; FAA, 1961–70; in command: HMS Shavington, 1965–67; HMS Ashanti, 1972–74; HMS Royal Arthur, 1978; Comdr, RNC, Dartmouth, 1979–80; Naval and Air Attaché, Athens, 1982–85; Defence and Naval Attaché, The Hague, 1986–89. Younger Brother, Trinity House, 1991. *Recreations:* photography, cricket, hill-walking, music. *Address:* c/o Naval Secretary, Ministry of Defence, Victory Building, HM Naval Base, Portsmouth PO1 3LS. *Clubs:* Army and Navy, MCC.

BLAIR, Robin Orr, LVO 1999; Lord Lyon King of Arms and Secretary of the Order of the Thistle, since 2000; *b* 1 Jan. 1940; *s* of Sir Alastair Campbell Blair, KCVO and late Catriona Hatchard Blair (*née* Orr); *m* 1972, Elizabeth Caroline McCallum Webster (d 2000); two *s* one *d*. *Educ:* Cargilfield; Rugby; St Andrews Univ. (MA); Edinburgh Univ. (LLB). WS 1965. Partner: Davidson & Syme WS, 1967–72; Dundas & Wilson CS, 1972–97 (Managing Partner, 1976–83, 1988–91); Turcan Connell WS, 1997–2000. Chm., Top Flight Leisure Gp, 1987–98 (non-exec. Dir, 1977–98); non-exec. Dir, Tullis Russell & Co. Ltd, 1977–98. Chm., Scottish Solicitors' Staff Pension Scheme, 1985–91. Hon. Sec., Assoc. of Edinburgh Royal Tradesmen, 1966–91. Purse Bearer to Lord High Comr to Gen. Assembly, C of S, 1988–. Mem., Royal Co. of Archers. *Address:* 2 Greenhill Park, Edinburgh EH10 4DW. *T:* (0131) 447 4847; Court of the Lord Lyon, HM New Register House, Edinburgh EH1 3YT. *T:* (0131) 556 7255. *Clubs:* New (Edinburgh); Hon. Company of Edinburgh Golfers.

See also M. C. Blair.

BLAIR, Thomas Alexander; QC (NI) 1958; Chief Social Security (formerly National Insurance) Commissioner (Northern Ireland), 1969–83; *b* 12 Dec. 1916; *s* of late John Blair and Wilhelmina Whitla Blair (*née* Downey); *m* 1947, Ida Irvine Moore; two *s* one *d*. *Educ:* Royal Belfast Academical Instn; Queen's Univ. Belfast (BA, LLB). Served War, in Royal Navy, 1940–46 (commissioned, 1941). Called to Bar of N Ireland, 1946. Chairman: Wages Councils; War Pensions Appeal Tribunal. Sen. Crown Counsel for Co. Tyrone; Mem. Departmental Cttee on Legal Aid. Apptd Dep. Nat. Insurance Umpire, 1959; Pres., Industrial Tribunals (NI), 1967–69; Chief Nat. Insurance Commissioner (NI), 1969. *Recreations:* sport, reading. *Address:* 3/2 Perdrixknowe, 82 Colinton Road, Edinburgh EH14 1AF. *T:* (0131) 443 1242.

BLAIR, Tony; *see* Blair, A. C. L.

BLAIR, William James Lynton; QC 1994; a Recorder, since 1998; *b* 31 March 1950; *s* of Leo Charles Lynton Blair and late Hazel Elizabeth (*née* Corscadden); *m* 1982, Katy Tse. *Educ:* Fettes Coll., Edinburgh; Balliol Coll., Oxford (BA 1971). Called to the Bar, Lincoln's Inn, 1972; Asst Recorder, 1996–98. Visiting Professor of Law: LSE, 1994–; Centre for Commercial Law Studies, QMW, 1999–. Consultant, IMF, 1991–. Member: Banking Law Sub-Cttee, Law Soc., 1988–; Internat. Monetary Law Cttee, Internat. Law Assoc., 1996–. Hon. Fellow, Soc. for Advanced Legal Studies, 1997. *Publications:* (ed) Encyclopaedia of Banking Law, 1982; (jtly) Banking and the Financial Services Act, 1993, 2nd edn, as Banking and Financial Services Regulation, 1998; (ed) Bullen, Leake and Jacob's Precedents of Pleading, 14th edn, 2001; contrib. other legal books and jls. *Recreations:* travel, walking.

See also A. C. L. Blair.

BLAIR-OLIPHANT, Air Vice-Marshal David Nigel Kington, CB 1966; OBE 1945; *b* 22 Dec. 1911; *y s* of Col P. L. K. Blair-Oliphant, DSO, Ardblair Castle, Blairgowrie, Perthshire, and Laura Geraldine Bodenham; *m* 1942, Helen Nathalie Donald (*d* 1983), *yr d* of Sir John Donald, KCIE; one *s* (and one *s* and one *d* decd). *Educ:* Harrow; Trinity Hall, Cambridge (BA). Joined RAF, 1934; Middle East and European Campaigns, 1939–45; RAF Staff Coll., 1945–48; Group Capt. 1949; Air Cdre 1958; Director, Weapons Engineering, Air Ministry, 1958–60; British Defence Staffs, Washington, 1960–63; Acting Air Vice-Marshal, 1963; Pres., Ordnance Board, 1965–66; Air Vice-Marshal, 1966. *Address:* 9 Northfield Road, Sherfield-on-Lodon, Hook, Hants RG27 0DR. *T:* (01256) 882724. *Club:* Royal Air Force.

BLAIS, Hon. Jean Jacques; PC (Can.) 1976; QC (Can.) 1978; Counsel, Marusyk, Miller & Swain, Ottawa, since 1999; *b* 27 June 1940; *m* 1968, Maureen Ahearn; two *s* one *d*. *Educ:* Secondary Sch., Sturgeon Falls; Univ. of Ottawa (BA, LLB). Professional lawyer. MP (L) Nipissing, Ontario, 1972, re-elected 1974, 1979, 1980; defeated Sept. 1984; Parliamentary Sec. to Pres. of Privy Council, 1975; Post Master General, 1976; Solicitor General, 1978; Minister of Supply and Services, and Receiver General, 1980; Minister of Nat. Defence, 1983–84. Lectr in Private Internat. Law, Ottawa Univ., 1986–88. Dir, Canada Israel Industrial R & D Foundn, 1994–. Mem., Security and Intelligence Review Cttee, 1984–91; Dep. Chm., Provisional Election Commn, Bosnia and Herzegovina, 1998–. Chairman: Canadian Inst. of Strategic Studies, 1993–; Bd, Pearson Internat. Peacekeeping Center, 1994–. Pres. Exec. Cttee, Bd of Govs, Univ. of Ottawa. *Recreations:* squash, skiing, swimming. *Address:* (office) 270 Albert Street, 14th Floor, Ottawa, ON K1P 5G8, Canada. *T:* (613) 5679348, *Fax:* (613) 5637671; *e-mail:* jjblais@mbm-law.com.

BLAKE, family name of **Baron Blake.**

BLAKE, Baron *cr* 1971 (Life Peer), of Braydeston, Norfolk; **Robert Norman William Blake,** FBA 1967; JP; Provost of The Queen's College, Oxford, 1968–87, Hon. Fellow, 1987; a Pro-Vice-Chancellor, Oxford University, 1971–87; Joint Editor, Dictionary of National Biography, 1980–90; *b* 23 Dec. 1916; *er s* of William Joseph Blake and Norah Lindley Daynes, Brundall, Norfolk; *m* 1953, Patricia Mary (*d* 1995), *e d* of Thomas Richard Waters, Great Plumstead, Norfolk; three *d*. *Educ:* King Edward VI Grammar Sch., Norwich; Magdalen Coll., Oxford (MA), 1st Cl. Final Honour Sch. of Modern Greats, 1938; Eldon Law Scholar, 1938. Served War of 1939–45; Royal Artillery; North African campaign, 1942; POW in Italy, 1942–44; escaped, 1944; despatches, 1944. Student and Tutor in Politics, Christ Church, Oxford, 1947–68; Censor, 1950–55; Senior Proctor, 1959–60; Ford's Lectr in English History for 1967–68; Mem., Hebdomadal Council, 1959–81. Member: Royal Commn on Historical Manuscripts, 1975–97 (Chm., 1982–89); Bd of Trustees, BM, 1978–88; Bd, Channel 4, 1983–86. Chm., Hansard Soc. Commn on Electoral Reform, 1975–76; Pres., Electoral Reform Soc., 1986–93. Mem. (Conservative) Oxford City Council, 1957–64. Rhodes Trustee, 1971–87 (Chm., 1983–87). Prime Warden, Dyers' Co., 1976–77. High Bailiff of Westminster Abbey and Searcher of the Sanctuary, 1988–89; High Steward of Westminster Abbey, 1989–99. Hon. Student, Christ Church, Oxford, 1977; Hon. Fellow, Pembroke Coll., Cambridge, 1992.

Hon. DLitt: Glasgow, 1972; East Anglia, 1983; Westminster Coll., Fulton, Mo, 1987; Buckingham, 1988. *Publications:* The Private Papers of Douglas Haig, 1952; The Unknown Prime Minister (Life of Andrew Bonar Law), 1955; A History of the Norwich Union Life Insurance Society, 1958; Disraeli, 1966, repr. 1998; The Conservative Party from Peel to Churchill, 1970, 2nd edn, The Conservative Party from Peel to Thatcher, 1985, 3rd edn, The Conservative Party from Peel to Major, 1997; The Office of Prime Minister, 1975; (ed with John Patten) The Conservative Opportunity, 1976; A History of Rhodesia, 1977; Disraeli's Grand Tour, 1982; (ed) The English World, 1982; The Decline of Power 1915–1964, 1985; (ed jtly) Salisbury: the man and his policies, 1987; (ed) Oxford Illustrated Encyclopaedia, Vol. 4, World History from 1800, 1989; (ed with Roger Louis) Churchill, 1993; Winston Churchill: a pocket biography, 1998; Jardine Matheson, Traders of the Far East, 1999. *Address:* Riverview House, Brundall, Norfolk NR13 5LA. *T:* (01603) 712133. *Clubs:* Beefsteak, Pratt's, Oxford and Cambridge; Vincent's (Oxford); Norfolk County.

BLAKE, Sir Alfred (Lapthorn), KCVO 1979 (CVO 1975); MC 1945; DL; Director, The Duke of Edinburgh's Award Scheme, 1967–78; Consultant with Blake Lapthorn, Solicitors, Portsmouth and area, 1985–2000 (Partner, 1949–85, Senior Partner, 1983–85); *b* 6 Oct. 1915; *s* of late Leonard Nicholson Blake and Nora Woodfall Blake (*née* Lapthorn); *m* 1st, 1940, Beatrice Grace Nellthorp (*d* 1967); two *s*; 2nd, 1969, Alison Kelsey Dick, Boston, Mass, USA. *Educ:* Dauntsey's Sch. LLB (London), 1938. Qual. Solicitor and Notary Public, 1938. Royal Marines Officer, 1939–45: Bde Major 2 Commando Bde, 1944; Lieut-Col comdg 45 (RM) Commando and Holding Operational Commando, 1945 (despatches). Mem., Portsmouth CC, 1950–67 (Past Chm., Portsmouth Educn Cttee); Lord Mayor of Portsmouth, 1958–59. Mem., Youth Service Development Coun., 1960–66; Pres., Portsmouth Youth Activities Cttee, 1976–; Patron: Elizabeth Foundn, 1984–; Portsmouth Family Welfare, 1987–. Lay Canon, Portsmouth Cathedral, 1962–72. Hon. Fellow, Portsmouth Univ. (formerly Poly.), 1981. DL Hants, 1991. *Recreation:* golf. *Address:* Flat 32, Jupiter Court, Gunwharf Quays, Portsmouth PO1 3TS. *T:* (023) 9234 3936.

BLAKE, Prof. Andrew, PhD; FREng, FIEE; Senior Research Scientist, Microsoft Research Ltd, since 1999; Fellow Clare Hall, Cambridge, since 2000; *b* 12 March 1956; *s* of Alan Geoffrey Blake and Judith Anne Blake (*née* Hart); *m* 1982, Fiona Anne-Marie Hewitt; one *s* one *d*. *Educ:* Rugby Sch.; Trinity Coll., Cambridge (MA); Univ. of Edinburgh (PhD 1983). FIEE 1994; FREng (FEng 1998). Kennedy Meml Fellow, MIT, 1977–78; Research Scientist, Ferranti Edinburgh, 1978–80; University of Edinburgh: Res. Associate, 1980–83; Lectr in Computer Sci., 1983–87; Fellow, Exeter Coll., 1987–99; Prof. of Engrg Sci., 1996–99; Royal Soc. Res. Fellow, 1984–87; University of Oxford: Lectr in Image Processing, 1987–96; Fellow, Exeter Coll., 1987–99; Prof. of Engrg Sci., 1996–99; Royal Soc. Sen. Res. Fellow, 1998–99; Vis. Prof of Information Engrg, 1999–. *Publications:* (with A. Zisserman) Visual Reconstruction, 1987; (with T. Troscianko) AI and the Eye, 1990; (with A. Yuille) Active Vision, 1992; (with M. Isard) Active Contours, 1998; articles on machine vision, robotics, visual psychology. *Address:* Microsoft Research Ltd, St George House, 1 Guildhall Street, Cambridge CB2 3NH.

BLAKE, Andrew Nicholas Hubert; His Honour Judge Blake; a Circuit Judge, since 1999; *b* 18 Aug. 1946; *s* of late John Berchmans Blake and of Beryl Mary Blake; *m* 1978, Joy Ruth Shevloff; one *s*. *Educ:* Ampleforth Coll.; Hertford Coll., Oxford (MA Hist.). Called to the Bar, Inner Temple, 1971; in practice in Manchester, 1972–99. *Recreations:* ski-ing, fishing, cycling, the Turf. *Address:* Preston Crown Court, Ringway, Preston PR1 2LL. *Club:* Norbury Fishing.

BLAKE, Carole Rae; Joint Managing Director, Blake Friedmann Literary Agency Ltd, since 1983; *b* 29 Sept. 1946; *née* Blake; *d* of Maisie Lock and step *d* of Gilbert Lock; *m* 1st, 1970, David Urbani (marr. diss. 1982); 2nd, 1983, Julian Friedmann (marr. diss. 1996). *Educ:* Pollards Hill Co. Secondary Sch. Rights Manager, George Rainbird Ltd, 1963–70; Rights and Contracts Manager: Michael Joseph Ltd, 1970–74; W. H. Allen Ltd, 1974–75; Marketing Dir, Sphere Books Ltd, 1975–76; founded Carole Blake Literary Agency Ltd, subseq. Blake Friedmann Literary Agency Ltd, 1976. Pres., Assoc. of Authors' Agents, 1991–93. Mem., Soc. of Bookmen, 1991– (Chm., 1997–98); Dir, Book Trade Benevolent Soc., 1999–. Mem. Adv. Bd, Publishing Studies, City Univ. *Publication:* From Pitch to Publication, 1999. *Recreations:* reading, classical music, gardening, wildlife, Medieval and Ancient Egyptian history. *Address:* (office) 122 Arlington Road, NW1 7HP. *T:* (020) 7284 0408, *Fax:* (020) 7284 0442; *e-mail:* carole@blakefriedmann.co.uk.

BLAKE, Prof. Christopher, CBE 1991; FRSE; Chairman, Glenrothes Development Corporation, 1987–96; *b* 28 April 1926; *s* of George Blake and Eliza Blake; *m* 1951, Elizabeth McIntyre; two *s* two *d*. *Educ:* Dollar Academy; St Andrews Univ. MA St Andrews 1950, PhD St Andrews 1965. Served in Royal Navy, 1944–47. Teaching posts, Bowdoin Coll., Maine, and Princeton Univ., 1951–53; Asst, Edinburgh Univ., 1953–55; Stewarts & Lloyds Ltd, 1955–60; Lectr and Sen. Lectr, Univ. of St Andrews, 1960–67; Sen. Lectr and Prof. of Economics, 1967–74, Bonar Prof. of Applied Econs, 1974–88, Univ. of Dundee. Dir, Alliance Trust plc, 1974–94; Chm., William Low & Co. plc, 1985–90 (Dir, 1980–90). Member: Council for Applied Science in Scotland, 1978–86; Royal Commn on Envtl Pollution, 1980–86. Treasurer, RSE, 1986–89. *Publications:* articles in economic and other jls. *Recreation:* golf. *Address:* Westlea, 14 Wardlaw Gardens, St Andrews, Fife KY16 9DW. *T:* (01334) 473840. *Clubs:* New (Edinburgh); Royal and Ancient (St Andrews).

BLAKE, Clifford Douglas, AM 1988; PhD; Vice-Chancellor, Charles Sturt University, 1990–2001; *b* 27 Aug. 1937; *s* of William Oscar Blake and Isobel Florence Blake (*née* Keown). *Educ:* Muswellbrook High Sch.; Univ. of Sydney (BScAgr); Univ. of London (PhD). FAIAS. Lectr and Sen. Lectr in Plant Pathology, Univ. of Sydney, 1963–70; foundation Principal, Riverina College of Advanced Educn, subseq. renamed Riverina-Murray Inst. of Higher Educn, 1971–90. Pres., Aust. Higher Educn Industrial Assoc., 1992–99; Member, Board of Directors: Open Learning Agency of Australia Pty, 1993–96; Australian Vice Chancellors' Cttee, 1994–99; Convenor, NSW Vice Chancellors' Cttee, 1996–98. Gov., Commonwealth of Learning, 1992–2000; Chm., Nat. Cttee on Distance Educn, 1994–95. Freeman, City of Wagga Wagga, 1996; Hon. Citizen, City of Bathurst, 1998. *Publication:* (ed) Fundamentals of Modern Agriculture, 1967, 3rd edn 1971. *Recreation:* travel. *Address:* 55 Waratah Road, Wentworth Falls, NSW 2782, Australia. *Clubs:* University and Schools, Union (Sydney).

BLAKE, David Charles, Eur Ing, CEng, FIMechE; Partner, Bee Services, since 1997; *b* 23 Sept. 1936; *s* of Walter David John Blake and Ellen Charlotte Blake; *m* 1st, 1959, Della Victoria Stevenson (marr. diss. 1996); two *s*; 2nd, 1996, Christine Emmett; one *d*. *Educ:* South East Essex Technical Sch.; South East Essex Technical Coll. British Transport Commn, later British Railways Board, 1953–96: Engrg apprentice, Stratford Locomotive Works, 1953–57; Technical Management, BR Eastern Reg., 1957–69; Construction Engr, W Coast Main Line Electrification, 1969–74; Area Maintenance Engineer: Motherwell Scottish Reg., 1974–75; Shields Scottish Reg., 1975–76; Rolling Stock Engr, Scottish Reg., 1976–78; Electrical Engr, E Reg., 1978–80; Chief Mechanical and Electrical Engr, Southern Reg., 1980–82; Director: Manufacturing and Maintenance Policy, BRB, 1983–87; Mech. and Elec. Engrg, BRB, 1987–90; Man. Dir, King's Cross Projects Gp, BRB, 1990–93; Man. Dir, Vendor Unit, BRB, 1993–96. Non-exec. dir, Engineering Link Ltd, 1999–. *Recreations:* gardening, hill walking. *Address:* The Windmill, Morcott, Rutland LE15 9DQ. *T:* (01572) 747000, *Fax:* (01572) 747373.

BLAKE, Prof. David Leonard; Professor of Music, University of York, since 1976; *b* 2 Sept. 1936; *s* of Leonard Blake and Dorothy Blake; *m* 1960, Rita Muir; two *s* one *d*. *Educ:* Latymer Upper School; Gonville and Caius College, Cambridge (BA 1960, MA 1963); Deutsche Akademie der Künste, Berlin, GDR. School teacher: Ealing Grammar Sch., 1961–62; Northwood Secondary Sch., 1962–63; University of York: Granada Arts Fellow, 1963–64; Lectr in Music, 1964; Sen. Lectr, 1971–76. *Recordings* (own compositions): Violin concerto: In Praise of Krishna; Variations for Piano; The Almanack. *Compositions* include: String Quartet No 1, 1962; It's a Small War (musical for schools), 1962; Chamber Symphony, 1966; Lumina (text from Ezra Pound's Cantos) (cantata for soprano, baritone, chorus and orch.), 1969; Metamorphoses, for large orch., 1971; Nonet, for wind, 1971; The Bones of Chuang Tzu (cantata for baritone and piano), 1972; In Praise of Krishna: Bengali lyrics, 1973; String Quartet No 2, 1973; Violin Concerto, 1976; Toussaint (opera), 1974–77; From the Mattress Grave (song cycle), 1978; Nine Songs of Heine, 1978; Clarinet Quintet, 1980; String Quartet No 3, 1982; Rise Dove, for bass and orch., 1983; The Plumber's Gift (opera), 1985–88; Cello Concerto, 1992; Three Ritsos Choruses, 1992; The Griffin's Tale, for baritone and orch., 1994; Diversions on Themes of Hanns Eisler, for alto sax. and piano, 1995; The Fabulous Adventures of Alexander the Great, for chorus and orch. of young people, 1996; Scoring a Century (entertainment), 1999; The Shades of Love, for bass and small orch., 2000. *Publication:* (ed) Hanns Eisler: a miscellany, 1995. *Recreation:* political debate. *Address:* Mill Gill, Askrigg, Leyburn, North Yorks DL8 3HR. *T:* (01969) 650364.

BLAKE, Sir Francis Michael, 3rd Bt *cr* 1907; *b* 11 July 1943; *o s* of Sir F. Edward C. Blake, 2nd Bt and Olive Mary (*d* 1946) *d* of Charles Liddell Simpson; *S* father, 1950; *m* 1968, Joan Ashbridge, *d* of F. C. A. Miller; two *s*. *Educ:* Rugby. *Heir:* *s* Francis Julian Blake [*b* 17 Feb. 1971; *m* 2000, Dr Jennifer Armstrong, *o d* of Peter Armstrong]. *Address:* The Dower House, Tillmouth Park, Cornhill-on-Tweed, Northumberland TD12 4UR. *T:* (01890) 882443.

BLAKE, Howard David, OBE 1994; FRAM; composer; *b* 28 Oct. 1938; *s* of Horace C. Blake and Grace B. Blake (*née* Benson). FRAM 1989. Dir, PRS, 1978–87; Co-founder, Assoc. of Professional Composers, 1980. *Compositions: concert works:* The Song of Francis, 1976; Benedictus, 1979; Sinfonietta for brass ensemble, 1981; Clarinet Concerto, 1984; Shakespeare Songs, 1987; Festival Mass, 1987; Diversions for Cello and Orchestra, 1989; Four Songs of the Nativity, 1990; Piano Concerto for Princess of Wales, 1990; Violin Concerto for City of Leeds, 1993; The Land of Counterpane, 1995; Charter for Peace (commissioned by FCO for 50th anniv. of UN), 1995; All God's Creatures, 1995; Lifecycle for solo piano, 1996; Flute Concerto, 1996; Still Falls the Rain, 1998; *stage works:* Henry V, 1984, As You Like It, 1985, RSC; The Snowman (ballet), 1993; Eva (ballet), Gothenburg Opera House, 1996; *film and television scores include:* The Duellists, 1977; The Snowman (TV), 1982; A Month in the Country, 1986 (BFI Anthony Asquith Award); Granpa (TV), 1987; A Midsummer Night's Dream (RSC and Channel 4), 1996; The Bear (TV), 1998; My Life So Far, 1999. *Recreations:* reading, walking, swimming. *Address:* Studio Flat 6, 18 Kensington Court Place, W8 5BJ. *T:* (020) 7937 1966, *Fax:* (020) 7938 1969. *Clubs:* Garrick, Groucho, Chelsea Arts.

BLAKE, John Michael; Managing Director, Blake Publishing, since 1991; *b* 6 Nov. 1948; *s* of late Major Edwin Blake, MBE, and of Joyce Blake; *m* 1968, Diane Sutherland Campbell; one *s* two *d*. *Educ:* Westminster City Grammar Sch.; North-West London Polytechnic. Reporter: Hackney Gazette, 1966; Evening Post, Luton, 1969; Fleet Street News Agency, 1970; Columnist: London Evening News, 1971; London Evening Standard, 1980; The Sun, 1982; Asst Editor, Daily Mirror, 1985; Editor, The People, 1988–89; Pres., Mirror Group Newspapers (USA), 1989; Exec. Producer, Sky Television, 1990. *Publications:* Up and Down with The Rolling Stones, 1978; All You Needed Was Love, 1981. *Recreations:* messing about in boats, distance running, travel. *Address:* Blake Publishing Ltd, 3 Bramber Court, 2 Bramber Road, W14 9PB.

BLAKE, Mary Netterville, MA; Headmistress, Manchester High School for Girls, 1975–83; *b* 12 Sept. 1922; *d* of John Netterville Blake and Agnes Barr Blake. *Educ:* Howell's Sch., Denbigh; St Anne's Coll., Oxford (MA). Asst Mistress, The Mount Sch., York, 1945–48; Head of Geography Dept, King's High Sch., Warwick, 1948–56; Associate Gen. Sec., Student Christian Movement in Schools, 1956–60; Head Mistress, Selby Grammar Sch., 1960–75. Pres., Assoc. of Headmistresses, 1976–77; first Pres., Secondary Heads Assoc., 1978. *Address:* 29 Crown Lea Court, Borrowdale Road, Malvern, Worcs WR14 3NG. *T:* (01684) 564359.

BLAKE, Nicholas John Gorrod; QC 1994; barrister; a Recorder, since 2000; *b* 21 June 1949; *s* of Leslie Gorrod Blake and Jean Margaret (*née* Ballinger); *m* 1986, Clio Whittaker; one *s* two *d* (and one *s* decd). *Educ:* Cranleigh Sch.; Magdalene Coll., Cambridge (BA Hons Hist.); Inns of Court Sch. of Law. Called to the Bar, Middle Temple, 1974; Asst Recorder, 1999–2000. Human rights lawyer specialising in asylum, immigration and miscarriage of justice cases. Chm., Immigration Lawyers Practitioners Assoc., 1994–97. Member: Cttee, Haldane Soc. of Socialist Lawyers, 1979–87; Council, Justice, 1995–. *Publications:* Police Law and the People, 1974; (jtly) Wigs and Workers, 1980; (jtly) New Nationality Law, 1983; (ed jtly) Immigration Law and Practice, 3rd edn 1991, 4th edn 1995. *Recreation:* the visual arts. *Address:* Matrix Chambers, Griffin Building, Gray's Inn, WC1R 5LN. *T:* (020) 7404 3447; *e-mail:* nickblake@matrixlaw.co.uk.

BLAKE, Sir Peter (James), KBE 1995 (OBE 1991 MBE 1983); Chief Executive Officer, Team New Zealand Ltd, America's Cup Defence 2000, 1994–2000; Captain, Seamaster, blakexpeditions, since 2000; *b* 1 Oct. 1948; *m* 1979, Pippa Glanville; one *s* one *d*. *Educ:* Takapuna GS, Auckland; Auckland Tech. Inst. (NZCE (Mech.)). Began sailing at age of 5; first long ocean race, NZ to Pacific Islands (1200 miles), at age of 16; built own Van de Stadt 23 foot keelboat, Bandit, at age of 18; won NZ Jun. Offshore Gp Champ., Bandit, 1967–68; Watch Leader, Cape Town/Rio de Janeiro race, Ocean Spirit, 1971; Whitbread Round the World Yacht Race: Watch Leader: Burton Cutter, 1973–74; Heath's Condor, 1977–78; Skipper/Navigator: Ceramco NZ, 1981–82 (Southern Ocean Trophy); Lion NZ, 1985–86; Skipper/Project Manager, Steinlager 2, 1989–90 (Southern Ocean Trophy, Overall Race hons); Skipper, Miama/Montego Bay race, Condor, 1979 (race record); Manager, NZ Admirals Cup Team in UK, 1982; winner: Around Australia 2-handed race, Steinlager 1, 1988; America's Cup, Black Magic, 1995 (with NZ team won NZ Supreme Sports Award); has taken part in most major ocean races around the world. With Sir Robin Knox-Johnson, set non-stop around the world sailing record, 74 days 22 hours 17 minutes 22 secs, Enza NZ, 1994. Captain, Antarctic Explorer, Cousteau Soc., 1997–2000. Life Mem., Royal NZ Yacht Squadron, 1995. Trustee, NZ Internat. Yachting Trust, 1985–; Mem., Assoc. of Cape Horners, 1978–; Pres., Jules Verne Assoc., 1995–. NZ Yachtsman of the Year, 1982, (jtly) 1989–90; NZ Sportsman of the Year, 1990; Hobson Medal, NZ

Maritime Assoc., 1994; British Yachtsman of the Year, 1995; Sir Francis Chichester Trophy, RYS, 1995; Prix de l'Aventure Sportive, Académie des Sports, 1996. *Publications:* Blake's Odyssey, 1982; Peter Blake's Yachting Book, 1984; Lion New Zealand, 1986; Peter Blake: adventurer, 1996. *Recreations:* flying, scuba diving, piano, yachting. *Address:* Longshore, 3 Western Parade, Emsworth, Hants PO10 7HS. *T:* (01243) 377027. *Clubs:* West Mersea Yacht (Life Mem.), Ocean Cruising, Emsworth Sailing, Royal Southern Yacht (Hon. Mem.), Royal Southampton Yacht (Hon. Mem.), Royal Yacht Squadron (Hon. Mem.); Royal Port Nicholson Yacht (Wellington).

BLAKE, Peter Thomas, CBE 1983; RA 1980 (ARA 1974); RDI 1987; ARCA; painter; *b* 25 June 1932; *s* of Kenneth William Blake; *m* 1963, Jann Haworth (marr. diss. 1982); two *d*; *m* 1987, Chrissy Wilson; one *d*. *Educ:* Gravesend Tech. Coll.; Gravesend Sch. of Art; RCA. Works exhibited: ICA, 1958, 1960; Guggenheim Competition, 1958; Cambridge, 1959; RA, 1960; Musée d'Art Moderne, Paris, 1968; Waddington Galls, 1970, 1972, 1977 and 1990; Stedlijk Mus., Amsterdam, 1973; Kunstverein, Hamburg, 1973; Gemeentemuseum, Arnhem, 1974; Palais des Beaux-Arts, Brussels, 1974; Galleria Documenta, Turin, 1982; retrospective exhibns, Tate Gall., 1983, Gal. Claude Bernard, Paris, 1984, Nishimura Gall., Tokyo, 1988, Nat. Gall., 1996; works in public collections: Trinity Coll., Cambridge; Carlisle City Gall.; Tate Gall.; Arts Council of GB; Mus. of Modern Art, NY; V & A Mus.; Mus. Boymans-van Beuningen, Rotterdam; Calouste Gulbenkian Foundn, London; RCA; Whitworth Art Gall., Univ. of Manchester; Baltimore Mus. of Art, Md. Third Associate Artist, Nat. Gall., 1994. *Publications:* illustrations for: Oxford Illustrated Old Testament, 1968; Roger McGough, Summer with Monica, 1978; cover illustration, Arden Shakespeare: Othello, 1980; Anthony and Cleopatra, 1980; Timon of Athens, 1980; contribs to: Times Educnl Supp.; Ark; Graphis 70; World of Art; Architectural Rev.; House and Garden; Painter and Sculptor. *Recreations:* sculpture, wining and dining, going to rock and roll concerts, boxing and wrestling matches; living well is the best revenge. *Address:* c/o Waddington Galleries Ltd, 11 Cork Street, W1X 2LT.

BLAKE, Quentin Saxby, OBE 1988; RDI 1981; freelance artist and illustrator, since 1957; Visiting Professor, Royal College of Art, since 1989; first Children's Laureate, 1999–2001; *b* 16 Dec. 1932; *s* of William Blake and Evelyn Blake. *Educ:* Downing Coll., Cambridge (MA; Hon. Fellow, 2000). Royal College of Art: Tutor, 1965–77; Head, Dept of Illustration, 1978–86; Vis. Tutor, 1986–89; Sen. Fellow, 1988. Exhibitions of watercolour drawings, Workshop Gallery: Invitation to the Dance, 1972; Runners and Riders, 1973; Creature Comforts, 1974; Water Music, 1976; exhibitions of illustration work: Chris Beetles Gall., 1993, 1996; retrospective: Nat. Theatre, 1984; Paris, 1995, 1999. Curator: Tell Me A Picture, Nat. Gall., 2001; A Baker's Dozen, Bury St Edmunds, 2001; The Magic Pencil, British Council, 2001. Hon. Fellow, Brighton Univ. Hon. Dr: London Inst., 2000; RCA, Northumbria, 2001. *Publications:* (author and illustrator) for children: Patrick, 1968; Jack and Nancy, 1969; Angelo, 1970; Snuff, 1973; The Adventures of Lester, 1977; Mr Magnolia, 1980 (Fedn of Children's Bk Gps Award; Kate Greenaway Medal, 1981); Quentin Blake's Nursery Rhyme Book, 1983; The Story of the Dancing Frog, 1984; Mrs Armitage on Wheels, 1987; Quentin Blake's ABC, 1989; All Join In, 1990; Cockatoos, 1991; Simpkin, 1993; Clown, 1995 (Bologna Ragazzi Prize, 1996); Mrs Armitage and the Big Wave, 1997; Dix Grenouilles, 1997; The Green Ship, 1998; Zagazoo, 1998; Fantastic Daisy Artichoke, 1999; (editor and illustrator) for children: Custard and Company, by Ogden Nash, 1979; The Quentin Blake Book of Nonsense Verse, 1994; The Quentin Blake Book of Nonsense Stories, 1996; The Laureate's Party, 2000; (illustrator) for children: Russell Hoban: How Tom Beat Captain Najork and his Hired Sportsmen, 1974 (Whitbread Lit. Award, 1975; Hans Andersen Honour Book, 1975); A Near Thing for Captain Najork, 1976; The Rain Door, 1986; Hilaire Belloc: Algernon and Other Cautionary Tales, 1991; Roald Dahl: The Enormous Crocodile, 1978; The Twits, 1980; George's Marvellous Medicine, 1981; Revolting Rhymes, 1982; The BFG, 1982; The Witches, 1983; Dirty Beasts, 1984; The Giraffe and the Pelly and Me, 1985; Matilda, 1988; Rhyme Stew, 1989; Esio Trot, 1990; Dahl Diary, 1991; My Year, 1993; Danny Champion of the World, 1994; Roald Dahl's Revolting Recipes, 1994; Charlie and the Chocolate Factory, 1995; Charlie and the Great Glass Elevator, 1995; James and the Giant Peach, 1995; The Magic Finger, 1995; Fantastic Mr Fox, 1996; John Yeoman: Featherbrains, 1993; The Singing Tortoise, 1993; The Family Album, 1993; The Do-It-Yourself House that Jack Built, 1994; Mr Nodd's Ark, 1995; Up with Birds!, 1997; The Princes' Gifts, 1997; The Heron and the Crane, 1999; Joan Aiken, The Winter Sleepwalker, 1994; books by Clement Freud, Sid Fleischman, Michael Rosen, Sylvia Plath, Margaret Mahy and Dr Seuss; (illustrator) for adults: Aristophanes, The Birds, 1971; Lewis Caroll, The Hunting of the Snark, 1976; Stella Gibbons, Cold Comfort Farm, 1977; Evelyn Waugh, Black Mischief, 1980, Scoop, 1981; George Orwell, Animal Farm, 1984; Cyrano de Bergerac, Voyages to the Sun and Moon, 1991; Cervantes, Don Quixote, 1995; Charles Dickens, A Christmas Carol, 1995; Victor Hugo, The Hunchback of Notre Dame, 1998; *non-fiction:* (author) La Vie de la Page, 1995; (jtly) Drawing for the Artistically Undiscovered, 2000; Words and Pictures, 2000; Woman with a Book (drawings), 2000; Tell me a Picture, 2001. *Address:* 30 Bramham Gardens, SW5 0HF. *T:* (020) 7373 7464.

BLAKE, Sir Richard; *see* Blake, Sir T. R. V.

BLAKE, Richard Frederick William; Editor, Whitaker's Almanack, 1981–86; *b* 9 April 1948; *s* of late Frederick William Blake and Doris Margaret Blake; *m* 1973, Christine Vaughan; one *d*. *Educ:* Archbishop Tenison's Grammar School. Joined J. Whitaker & Sons, Ltd (Whitaker's Almanack Dept), 1966; apptd Asst Editor of Whitaker's Almanack, 1974. *Recreation:* listening to music. *Address:* 118 Warren Drive, Elm Park, Hornchurch, Essex RM12 4QX.

BLAKE, Sir (Thomas) Richard (Valentine), 17th Bt *cr* 1622, of Menlough; *b* 7 Jan. 1942; *s* of Sir Ulick Temple Blake, 16th Bt, and late Elizabeth Gordon (she *m* 1965, Vice-Adm. E. Longley-Cook, CB, CBE, DSO); *S* father, 1963; *m* 1st, 1976, Mrs Jacqueline Hankey; 2nd, 1982, Bertice Reading (marr. diss. 1986; she *d* 1991); 3rd, 1991, Wendy, *widow* of Anthony Ronald Roberts. *Educ:* Bradfield Coll., Berks. Member, Standing Council of Baronets. *Recreations:* classic cars, horses, gardening. *Heir: kinsman* Anthony Telio Bruce Blake [*b* 5 May 1951; *m* 1988, Geraldine, *d* of Cecil Shnaps]. *Address:* Old Janes, River, near Petworth, West Sussex GU28 9AY; 46 chemin du Peylong Sud, route des Arcs, 83510 Lorgues, Var, France. *Clubs:* Cowdray Park Polo, Gordon-Keeble Owners, Rolls-Royce Enthusiasts, Goodwood Road Racing.

BLAKE-JAMES, Linda Elizabeth; *see* Sullivan, L. E.

BLAKELEY, Trevor, CEng; FRINA; FIMarE; FIMechE; Chief Executive, Royal Institution of Naval Architects, since 1997; *b* 22 Nov. 1943; *m* 1965, Patricia Challenger; one *s* one *d*. *Educ:* Goole Grammar Sch.; BRNC Dartmouth; RNEC Manadon (BSc 1968); BA Open Univ. 1995. CEng 1973; FIMarE 1996; FIMechE 1996; FRINA 1997. Joined RN, 1963; served as engineering specialist; retired 1996. Mem. Ct, Cranfield Univ., 1999–. Mem., Shipwrights' Co., 1999–. *Recreations:* theatre, music, horse riding. *Address:* Royal Institution of Naval Architects, 10 Upper Belgrave Street, SW1X 8BQ. *T:* (020) 7235 4622.

BLAKEMORE, Prof. Colin (Brian), FRS 1992; Waynflete Professor of Physiology, Oxford University, since 1979; Fellow of Magdalen College, since 1979; *b* 1 June 1944; *s* of Cedric Norman Blakemore and Beryl Ann Smith; *m* 1965, Andrée Elizabeth Washbourne; three *d*. *Educ:* King Henry VIII Sch., Coventry; Corpus Christi Coll., Cambridge (Smyth Scholar; BA 1965; MA 1969; ScD 1988; Hon. Fellow, 1994); Univ. of Calif, Berkeley (PhD 1968); Magdalen Coll., Oxford (MA 1979; DSc 1989). FIBiol, CBiol 1996. Harkness Fellow, Neurosensory Lab., Univ. of Calif, Berkeley, 1965–68; Cambridge University: Fellow and Dir of Medical Studies, Downing Coll., 1971–79; Univ. Demonstr in Physiol., 1968–72; Univ. Lectr in Physiol., 1972–79; Leverhulme Fellow, 1974–75; Royal Soc. Locke Res. Fellow, 1976–79; Dir, McDonnell-Pew Centre for Cognitive Neuroscience, Oxford, 1989–; Dir, MRC IRC for Cognitive Neurosci., 1996–. Chm., Neurobiology and Mental Health Bd Grants Cttee, MRC, 1977–79. Vis. Professor: NY Univ., 1970; MIT, 1971; Royal Soc. Study Visit, Keio Univ., Tokyo, 1974; Lethaby Prof., RCA, 1978; Storer Vis. Lectr, Univ. of Calif, Davis, 1980; Vis. Scientist, Salk Inst., 1982, 1983, 1992; Macallum Vis. Lectr, Univ. of Toronto, 1984; McLaughlin Vis. Prof., McMaster Univ., Ont, 1992; Regents' Prof., Univ. of Calif, Davis, 1995–96; Spinoza Prof., Univ. of Amsterdam, 1996. Chm. Council, BAAS, 2001–(Pres., Gen. Section, 1989; Pres., 1997–98, Vice-Pres., 1990–97, 1998–); Pres., British Neuroscience Assoc., 1998–2000; Hon. Pres., World Cultural Council, 1983–. Founder and Mem., Bd of Govs, Internat. Brain Injury Assoc. (Nat. Head Injury Foundn Inc., Washington), 1993–; Mem. Professional Adv. Panel, and Patron, Headway (Nat. Head Injuries Assoc.), 1997–; Member: Council, Internat. Brain Res. Org., 1973–; BBC Science Consultative Group, 1975–79; British Nat. Cttee for Physiol. Scis, 1988–90; Professional Adv. Cttee, Schizophrenia: A National Emergency, 1989–; Adv. Gp on Non-Ionising Radiation, NRPB, 1992–; Council, Fedn of European Neuroscience Socs, 1998–; Nat. Cttee for 2000 Forum for European Neurosci., Brighton, 1998–2000; Ind. Expert Gp on Mobile Phones, DoH, 1999–2000; Prog. Mgt Cttee, UK Telecoms Health Res. Prog., 2000–. Mem. Exec. Cttee, Dana Alliance for Brain Initiatives, NY, 1996–; Chief Exec., European Dana Alliance for the Brain, 1996–. Royal Society: Chairman: Wkg Gp, Public Prog., 2001–; Sci. Educn Grants Cttee, 2001; Member: Sci. in Soc. Cttee, 2001–; Jt Acad. Med. Scis Wkg Gp on Sci. of Transmissible Spongiform Encephalopothies, 2000–. Hon. Associate: Rationalist Press Assoc., 1986–; Rationalist Internat., 2000–; Founder Mem. Cttee, Harkness Fellowships Assoc., 1997–; Patron: Assoc. for Art, Sci., Engrg and Technol., 1997–; Clifton Scientific Trust, Bristol, 1999–; Patron, 1996–, and Scientific Advr, Bristol 2000. BBC Reith Lectr, 1976; Presenter: The Mind Machine, BBC2 series, 1988; The Next Big Thing, BBC TV series, 2000; Lectures: Aubrey Lewis, Inst. of Psych., 1979; Lord Charnwood, Amer. Acad. of Optometry, 1980; Vickers, Neonatal Soc., 1981; Harveian, Harveian Soc. of London, 1982; Christmas, Royal Instn, 1982; Earl Grey Meml, Newcastle Univ., 1982; George Frederic Still, BPA, 1983; Edridge-Green, RCS, 1984; Plenary, European Neuroscience Assoc., 1984; Mac Keith Meml, Brit. Paediatric Neurology Assoc., 1985; Halliburton, KCL, 1986; Cairns Meml, Cambridge Univ., 1986; Bertram Louis Abrahams, RCP, 1986; Norman McAlister Gregg (also Medal), RACO, 1988; Dietrich Bodenstein, Univ. of Va, 1989; Charnock Bradley, Univ. of Edinburgh, 1989; Doyne, Oxford Ophthalmol Congress, 1989 (also Medal); G. L. Brown, Physiol Soc., 1990; Sir Douglas Robb, Univ. of Auckland, 1991; Schs' Christmas, RSE, 1992; James Law, Cornell, 1994; Royal Soc., ASE, 1995; Newton, Cos of Spectacle Makers, and Clockmakers and Scientific Instrument Makers, 1997; Cockcroft, UMIST, 1997; Conway, South Place Ethical Soc., 1998; David Oppenheimer Meml, Oxford, 2000. Founder FMedSci 1998. Foreign Mem., Royal Netherlands Acad. of Arts and Scis, 1993. Hon. Mem., Physiol Soc., 1998. Freeman, City of London, 1998; Mem., Co. of Spectacle Makers, 1997, Liveryman, 1998. Hon. Fellow: Cardiff Univ., 1998; Downing Coll., Cambridge, 1999. Hon. DSc: Aston, 1992; Salford, 1994. Robert Bing Prize, Swiss Acad. of Med. Sciences, 1975; Richardson Cross Medal, S Western Ophthalmol Soc., 1978; Copeman Medal, Corpus Christi Coll., Cambridge, 1976; Man of the Year, Royal Assoc. for Disability and Rehabilitation, 1978; Phi Beta Kappa Award in Sci., 1978; John Locke Medal, Apothecaries' Soc., 1983; Prix du Docteur Robert Netter, Acad. Nat. de Médecine, Paris, 1984; Cairns Medal, Cairns Meml Fund, 1986; Michael Faraday Award, Royal Soc., 1989; John P. McGovern Science and Soc. Medal, Sigma XI, USA, 1990; Montgomery Medal, RCSI and Irish Ophthalmol Soc., 1991; Osler Medal, RCP, 1993; Ellison-Cliffe Medal, RSM, 1993; Annual Review Prize, Physiol Soc., 1994; Charles F. Prentice Award, Amer. Acad. of Optometry, 1994; Alcon Prize, Alcon Res. Inst., 1996; Meml Medal, Charles Univ., Prague, 1998; Charter Award, IBiol, 2001; Alfred Meyer Award, British Neuropathol Soc., 2001. *Publications:* Handbook of Psychobiology (with M. S. Gazzaniga), 1975; Mechanics of the Mind, 1977; (with S. A. Greenfield) Mindwaves, 1987; The Mind Machine, 1988, 2nd edn 1994; (with H. B. Barlow and M. Weston-Smith) Images and Understanding, 1990; Vision: coding and efficiency, 1990; (with S. D. Iversen) Gender and Society, 2000; (with S. Jennett) Oxford Companion to the Body, 2001; res. reports in Jl of Physiol., Jl of Neuroscience, Nature, etc. *Recreation:* wasting time. *Address:* University Laboratory of Physiology, Parks Road, Oxford OX1 3PT. *Club:* Chelsea Arts (Hon. Mem., 1992).

BLAKEMORE, Michael Howell; freelance director; *b* Sydney, NSW, 18 June 1928; *s* of late Conrad Blakemore and Una Mary Blakemore (*née* Litchfield); *m* 1st, 1960, Shirley (*née* Bush); one *s*; 2nd, 1986, Tanya McCallin; two *d*. *Educ:* The King's Sch., NSW; Sydney Univ.; Royal Academy of Dramatic Art. Actor with Birmingham Rep. Theatre, Shakespeare Memorial Theatre, etc, 1952–66; Co-dir, Glasgow Citizens Theatre (1st prod., The Investigation), 1966–68; Associate Artistic Dir, Nat. Theatre, 1971–76. Dir, Players, NY, 1978. Resident Dir, Lyric Theatre, Hammersmith, 1980. Best Dir, London Critics, 1972. *Productions include:* A Day in the Death of Joe Egg, Comedy, 1967, Broadway 1968; Arturo Ui, Saville, 1969, Israel, 1969; Forget-me-not Lane, Apollo, 1971; Design for Living, Phoenix, 1973; Knuckle, Comedy, 1974; Separate Tables, Apollo, 1976; Privates on Parade, Aldwych (RSC), transf. Piccadilly, 1977; Candida, Albery, 1977; All My Sons, Wyndam's, 1981; Benefactors, Vaudeville, 1984, NY, 1986; Made in Bangkok, Aldwych, 1986; Lettice and Lovage, Globe, 1987, NY, 1990 (Outer Critics Circle Award, NY, 1990); Uncle Vanya, Vaudeville, 1988; City of Angels, Broadway, 1989 (Outer Critics Circle Award, NY, 1990), Prince of Wales Th., 1993; Tosca, WNO, 1992; Here, Donmar Warehouse, 1993; The Sisters Rosensweig, Old Vic, 1994; Now You Know, Hampstead, 1995; Sylvia, Apollo, 1996; Alarms and Excursions, Gielgud, 1998; Mr Peter's Connections, Almeida, 2000; *National Theatre:* The National Health, 1969; Long Day's Journey Into Night, 1971; The Front Page, Macbeth, 1972; The Cherry Orchard, 1973; Plunder, 1976; After the Fall, 1990; Copenhagen, 1998, transf. Duchess, then Montparnasse, Paris, 1999 (Mohère Award, Tony Award, Drama Desk Award, 2000); *Royal Court Theatre:* Widowers' Houses, 1970; Don's Party, 1975; *Lyric Theatre, Hammersmith:* Make and Break, 1980; Travelling North, 1980; The Wild Duck, 1980; Noises Off, 1982 (transf. to Savoy, 1982, NY, 1983 (Drama Desk Award, NY, 1983–84; Outer Critics Circle Award, NY, 1983; Hollywood Drama-League Award, LA, 1984); *foreign productions include:* The White Devil, Minneapolis, 1976; Hay Fever, 1976, The Seagull, 1979, Aarhus; Mourning Becomes Electra, Melbourne, 1980; Death

Defying Acts, NY, 1995; The Life (musical), Broadway, NY, 1997; Kiss Me Kate, Broadway, NY, 1999 (Tony Award, Drama Desk Award, 2000). *Films:* A Personal History of the Australian Surf, 1981 (Standard film award, 1982); Privates on Parade, 1983; Country Life, 1995 (Film Critics Circle of Australia Award, 1994). *Publication:* Next Season, 1969 (novel). *Recreation:* surfing. *Address:* 18 Upper Park Road, NW3 2UP. *T:* (020) 7483 2575, *Fax:* (020) 7483 2476.

BLAKENEY, Hon. Allan Emrys, OC 1992; PC (Canada) 1982; Visiting Scholar, University of Saskatchewan, Saskatoon, since 1990; *b* Bridgewater, NS, 7 Sept. 1925; *m* 1st, 1950, Mary Elizabeth (Molly) Schwartz (*d* 1957), Halifax, NS; one *s* one *d*; 2nd, 1959, Anne Gorham, Halifax; one *s* one *d. Educ:* Dalhousie Univ. (BA, LLB); Queen's Coll., Oxford (MA). Univ. Medal for Achievement in Coll. of Law, Dalhousie; Rhodes Schol. Sec. and Legal Adviser, Saskatchewan Crown Corps, 1950; Chm., Saskatchewan Securities Commn, 1955–58; private law practice, 1958–60 and 1964–70. MLA, Saskatchewan, 1960–88; formerly Minister of Educn, Provincial Treas. and Health Minister; Chm., Wascana Centre Authority, 1962–64; Opposition Financial Critic, 1964–70; Dep. Leader, 1967–70; Federal New Democratic Party President, 1969–71; Saskatchewan NDP Leader and Leader of Opposition, 1970; Premier, 1971–82; Leader of Opposition, Sask, 1982–87. Prof. of Public Law, Osgoode Hall Law Sch., York Univ., Toronto, 1988–90. Hon. DCL Mount Allison; Hon. LLD: Dalhousie; York; Western Ontario; Regina; Saskatchewan. *Recreations:* reading, swimming, formerly ice hockey and badminton. *Address:* 1752 Prince of Wales Avenue, Saskatoon, SK S7K 3E5, Canada; College of Law, 15 Campus Drive, University of Saskatchewan, Saskatoon, SK S7N 5A6, Canada.

BLAKENHAM, 2nd Viscount *cr* 1963, of Little Blakenham; **Michael John Hare;** Chairman, Board of Trustees, Royal Botanic Gardens, Kew, since 1997 (Trustee, since 1991); *b* 25 Jan. 1938; *s* of 1st Viscount Blakenham, PC, OBE, VMH, and Hon. Beryl Nancy Pearson (*d* 1994), *d* of 2nd Viscount Cowdray; *S* father, 1982; *m* 1965, Marcia Persephone, *d* of late Hon. Alan Hare, MC; one *s* two *d. Educ:* Eton College; Harvard Univ. (AB Econ.). National Service, 1956–57. English Electric, 1958; Harvard, 1959–61; Lazard Brothers, 1961–63; Standard Industrial Group, 1963–71; Royal Doulton, 1972–77; Pearson, 1977–97 (Chief Exec., 1978–90; Chm., 1983–97). Chairman: The Financial Times, 1983–93; MEPC plc, 1993–98 (Dir, 1990–98); UK Chm., Japan 2001, 1999–; Partner, Lazard Partners, 1984–97; Director: Lazard Bros, 1975–97; Sotheby's Holdings Inc., 1987–; UK-Japan 21st Century (formerly UK-Japan 2000) Group, 1990–; Lafarge, 1997–; Mem., Internat. Adv. Gp, Toshiba, 1997–. Member, House of Lords Select Committee: on Science and Technol., 1985–88; on Sustainable Develt, 1994–95. Chm., RSPB, 1981–86; Mem., Nature Conservancy Council, 1986–90; Pres., Sussex Wildlife Trust, 1983–. *Address:* 1 St Leonard's Studios, SW3 4EN.

BLAKER, family name of **Baron Blaker**.

BLAKER, Baron *cr* 1994 (Life Peer), of Blackpool in the County of Lancashire, and of Lindfield in the County of West Sussex; **Peter Allan Renshaw Blaker,** KCMG 1983; PC 1983; MA; *b* Hong Kong, 4 Oct. 1922; *s* of late Cedric Blaker, CBE, MC and Louisa Douglas Blaker (*née* Chapple); *m* 1953, Jennifer, *d* of late Sir Pierson Dixon, GCMG, CB; one *s* two *d. Educ:* Shrewsbury; Trinity Coll., Toronto (BA, 1st class, Classics); New Coll., Oxford (MA). Served 1942–46: Argyll and Sutherland Highlanders of Canada (Capt., wounded). Admitted a Solicitor, 1948. New Coll., Oxford, 1949–52; 1st Class, Jurisprudence, Pass degree in PPE. Pres. Oxford Union. Called to Bar, Lincoln's Inn, 1952. Admitted to HM Foreign Service, 1953; HM Embassy, Phnom Penh, 1955–57; UK High Commn, Ottawa, 1957–60; FO, 1960–62; Private Sec. to Minister of State for Foreign Affairs, 1962–64. Attended Disarmament Conf., Geneva; UN Gen. Assembly, 1962 and 1963; signing of Nuclear Test Ban Treaty, Moscow, 1963. MP (C) Blackpool South, 1964–92; an Opposition Whip, 1966–67; PPS to Chancellor of Exchequer, 1970–72; Parliamentary Under-Secretary of State: (Army), MoD, 1972–74; FCO, 1974; Minister of State: FCO, 1979–81; for the Armed Forces, MoD, 1981–83. Joint Secretary: Conservative Parly Foreign Affairs Cttee, 1965–66; Trade Cttee, 1967–70; Exec. Cttee of 1922 Cttee, 1967–70; Vice-Chm., All-Party Tourism Cttee, 1974–79; Member: Select Cttee on Conduct of Members, 1976–77; Public Accounts Commn, 1987–92; Intelligence and Security Cttee, 1996–97; Chairman: Hong Kong Parly Gp, 1970–72, 1983–92; Cons. For. and Commonwealth Affairs Cttee, 1983–92 (Vice-Chm., 1974–79); Mem. Exec. Cttee, British-American Parly Gp, 1975–79; Hon. Sec., Franco-British Parly Relations Cttee, 1975–79. Chm., Bd, Royal Ordnance Factories, 1972–74; Chm. Governors, Welbeck Coll., 1972–74; Mem. Council: Chatham House, 1977–79, 1986–90; Council for Arms Control, 1983–99; Freedom Assoc., 1984–97; Vice-Chm., Peace Through NATO, 1983–93; Vice-Pres., 1983–92, Patron, 1993–, Cons. Foreign and Commonwealth Council; Mem. Council, Britain-Russia Centre (formerly GB-USSR Assoc.), 1974–79, and 1992–2000 (Vice-Chm., 1983–92); Governor, Atlantic Inst., 1978–79; Trustee, Inst. for Negotiation and Conciliation, 1984–92. Chm., Maclean Hunter Cablevision Ltd, 1989–94; company director; farmer. *Publications:* Coping with the Soviet Union, 1977; Small is Dangerous: micro states in a macro world, 1984. *Recreations:* sailing, opera, shooting. *Address:* House of Lords, SW1A 0PW.

BLAKER, George Blaker, CMG 1963; Under-Secretary, HM Treasury, 1955–63, and Department of Education and Science, 1963–71 retired; *b* Simla, India, 30 Sept. 1912; *m* 1938, Richenda Dorothy Buxton (*d* 1987); one *d. Educ:* Eton; Trinity Coll., Cambridge. Private Sec. to Ministers of State in the Middle East, 1941–43; Cabinet Office, 1943; Private Sec. to Sec. of War Cabinet, 1944; Principal Private Sec. to Minister of Production and Presidents of the Board of Trade, 1945–47; accompanied Cabinet Mission to India, 1946; Sec. of UK Trade Mission to China, 1946; HM Treasury, 1947; UK Treasury Representative in India, Ceylon and Burma, 1957–63. President: Surrey Trust for Nature Conservation, 1969–80; Scientific and Medical Network, 1986– (Hon. Sec., 1973–86). Gold Medal, Royal Soc. for the Protection of Birds, 1934. *Address:* Lake House, Vann Lake Road, Ockley, Surrey RH5 5NS.

BLAKER, Sir John, 3rd Bt *cr* 1919; *b* 22 March 1935; *s* of Sir Reginald Blaker, 2nd Bt, TD, and Sheila Kellas, *d* of Dr Alexander Cran; *S* father, 1975; *m* 1st, 1960, Catherine Ann (marr. diss. 1965), *d* of late F. J. Thorold; 2nd, 1968, Elizabeth Katherine, *d* of late Col John Tinsley Russell, DSO. *Address:* Stantons Farm, East Chiltington, near Lewes, East Sussex BN7 3BB.

BLAKEY, David Cecil, CBE 1998; QPM 1993; DL; HM Inspector of Constabulary, since 1999; *b* 1943; *s* of Cecil and Elsie Jane Blakey; *m* 1966, Wendy Margaret Cartwright; one *s* one *d. Educ:* Jarrow Grammar Sch.; Univ. of Newcastle upon Tyne (MBA). VSO, Sarawak, 1962; Constable, Durham Constabulary, 1963; Police National Computer, 1972–76; Supt, Durham, 1979; Chief Supt, Northumbria, 1984; Asst Chief Constable, West Mercia, 1986; RCDS, 1989; Deputy Chief Constable: Leics, 1989–90; West Mercia, 1990–91; Chief Constable, W Mercia, 1991–99. Pres., ACPO, 1997–98. DL Worcs, 1999. *Recreations:* books, history. *Address:* (office) Bridge House, Sion Place, Clifton Down, Bristol BS8 4XA.

BLAKEY, (Diana) Kristin; *see* Henry, D. K.

BLAKISTON, Sir Ferguson Arthur James, 9th Bt *cr* 1763; entrepreneur and writer; *b* 19 Feb. 1963; *er s* of Sir Arthur Norman Hunter Blakiston, 8th Bt, and Mary Ferguson (*d* 1982), *d* of late Alfred Ernest Gillingham, Cave, S Canterbury, NZ; *S* father, 1977; *m* 1993, Linda Jane, *d* of late Robert John Key, Queenstown, NZ; one *d. Educ:* Lincoln Coll., NZ (Diploma in Agriculture 1983); Auckland Inst. of Technology (Cert. in Marketing, 1993); NZ Inst. of Business Studies (Diploma in Travel Writing). *Heir: b* Norman John Balfour Blakiston, Executive Officer; *b* 7 April 1964. *Address:* Cortington, 8 Waimi Terrace, Geraldine, New Zealand.

BLAKSTAD, Michael Björn; Chief Executive, since 1984, Chairman, since 1994, Workhouse Ltd; Director, Zenith Entertainment (formerly TEAM) plc, since 1991; *b* 18 April 1940; *s* of late Clifford and Alice Blakstad; *m* 1965, Patricia Marilyn Wotherspoon; one *s* twin *d. Educ:* Ampleforth Coll.; Oriel Coll., Oxford (MA Lit. Hum.). General trainee, BBC, 1962–68; Producer, Yorkshire Television, 1968–71; freelance TV producer, 1971–74; Programme Editor, BBC, 1974–80; Dir of Programmes, TV South, 1980–84. Founder and Managing Director, Blackrod, 1980 (Chm., 1981–84); Chairman and Chief Executive: Workhouse Productions, 1984–88; Chrysalis Television Ltd, 1988–90; Chairman: Filmscreen Internat. Ltd, 1984–86; Friday Productions, 1984–88; Blackrod Interactive Services, 1988–90; Winchester Independent Radio Ltd, 1995–; Jt Chief Exec., Videodisc Co., 1984–88; Dir, Chrysalis Gp. Director: IPPA, 1986–90; Internat. Video Communications Assoc., 1988–90; Winchester Theatre Royal, 1988–95 (Chm., 1990–95). Awards include: Radio Industries Club, 1975, 1977, 1979; RTS, 1976; BAFTA/Shell Prize, 1976; BIM/John Player, 1976; Nyon, 1978. Hon. MSc Salford, 1983; FRSA; MRI. *Publications:* The Risk Business, 1979; Tomorrow's World looks to the Eighties, 1979; (with Aldwyn Cooper) The Communicating Organisation, 1995. *Recreations:* golf, writing. *Address:* The Tudor House, Workhouse Lane, East Meon, Hants GU32 1PD. *Club:* Reform.

BLAMEY, Marjorie; botanical illustrator and wildlife artist, since 1970; *b* 13 March 1918; *d* of Dr Arthur Percival Day and Janetta Day; *m* 1941, Philip Bernard Blamey; two *s* two *d. Educ:* private schools; Italia Conti Stage Sch.; RADA. Actress and part-time photographer, prior to 1939; farmer, Cornwall, 1948–70. *Publications* include: wrote and illustrated: Learn to Paint Flowers in Watercolour, 1986; Painting Flowers, 1997; illustrated: R. Mabey, Food for Free, 1972; R. Fitter: Wild Flowers of Britain and Northern Europe, 1974, 5th edn 1996 (trans. 8 langs); Handguide to Wild Flowers, 1979; Collins Gem Guide to Wild Flowers, 1980; Wild Flowers of Britain and Ireland, 2001; C. Grey-Wilson: Alpine Flowers of Europe, 1979, 2nd edn 1995; The Illustrated Flora of Britain and Northern Europe, 1989; Mediterranean Wild Flowers, 1993; P. Blamey: Collins Gem Guide to Fruits, Nuts and Berries, 1984; Wild Flowers by Colour, 1997. *Recreations:* bird watching, gardening, travel, walking, cooking, my family, painting!

BLAMIRE, Roger Victor; veterinary consultant; Director of Veterinary Field Services, Ministry of Agriculture, Fisheries and Food, 1979–83; *b* 9 July 1923; *s* of Thomas Victor Blamire and Anetta Elizabeth (*née* Lawson); *m* 1947, Catherine Maisie Ellis Davidson; two *d. Educ:* Kendal Sch.; Royal (Dick) Veterinary Coll., Edinburgh. MRCVS, DVSM. RAVC, 1945–48 (Captain); served India, Burma and Malaya. MAF, 1949; Asst Vet. Officer, City of London, 1949; Dep. Chief Advr on Meat Inspection, MOF, 1952; Dep. Dir, Vet. Field Services, MAFF, 1968. Hon. FRSH, 1979. *Recreations:* walking, gardening, listening to music. *Address:* 5 Atbara Road, Teddington, Middx TW11 9PA. *T:* (020) 8943 4225.

BLAMIRE-BROWN, John; DL; County Clerk and Chief Executive, Staffordshire County Council, 1973–78; *b* 16 April 1915; *s* of Rev. F. J. Blamire Brown, MA; *m* 1945, Joyce Olivia Pearson; two *s. Educ:* Cheam Sch.; St Edmund's Sch., Canterbury. Solicitor 1937. Served War of 1939–45, Royal Marines (Captain). Asst Solicitor, Wednesbury, 1937; West Bromwich, 1946; Staffs CC, 1948; Deputy Clerk of County Council and of Peace, 1962; Clerk, Staffs CC, 1972; Clerk to Lieutenancy, 1972–78; Sec., Staffs Probation and After Care Cttee; Hon. Sec., W Mids Planning Authorities Conf., 1972–78. Dep. Chm., Manpower Services Commn Area Board, Staffs, Salop, W Midlands (North), 1978–83. Mem. Council, Beth Johnson Foundn, 1978–83; Governor, Newcastle-under-Lyme Endowed Schools, 1978–83; Chm., St Giles Hospice Ltd, 1979–84. Pres., Codsall Civic Soc., 1991–. DL Staffs, 1974. *Recreations:* local history, gardening, painting. *Address:* The Mount, Codsall Wood, Wolverhampton, West Midlands WV8 1QS. *T:* (01902) 842044.

BLANC, Christian; Chairman, Merrill Lynch France SA and Vice-Chairman, Merrill Lynch Europe, since 2000; *b* Talence, Gironde, 17 May 1943; *s* of Marcel Blanc and Encarna (*née* Miranda); *m* 1973, Asa Birgitta Hagglund; two *d. Educ:* Institut d'Etudes Politiques, Bordeaux (Dip.). Asst Dir, Sopexa Scandinave, 1969; Dep. to Controller, Mission for Territorial Equipment, 1970–74; Hd of Bureau, Sec. of State for Youth and Sports, 1974–76; Asst Gen. Delegate, Tech. Interministerial Agency for Leisure and Fresh Air, 1976–80; Dir of Cabinet, Commn of EC, Brussels, 1981–83; Prefect: Commune of Haute-Pyrénées, 1983–84; Govt of New Caledonia, 1985; Seine and Marne, 1985–89; without portfolio, 1989. Pres. and Dir-Gen., Régie Autonome des Transports Parisiens, 1989–92; Pres., Air France, 1993–97. Director: Middle East Airlines, 1998–99; Carrefour; Cap Gemini. Dir, Chancery, Univ. of Paris. Pres. External Selection Cttee for Recruitment of Sen. Treasury Officials, 2000–. Officer, Légion d'Honneur (France), 1988; Officier, Ordre National du Merite (France), 1994. *Publication:* Le Lièvre et la Tortue, 1994. *Address:* Merrill Lynch France SA, 112 Avenue Kleber, 75116 Paris, France.

BLANC, Raymond René; chef; Patron and Chairman, Blanc Restaurants Ltd, since 1984; *b* 19 Nov. 1949; *m*; two *s. Educ:* CEG de Valdahon; Lycée technique de horlogerie, Besançon. Chef de rang, 1971; Manager and chef de cuisine, 1976; proprietor and chef, Les Quat' Saisons, Summertown, 1977; Dir and Chm., Maison Blanc, 1978–88; proprietor, Le Petit Blanc, 1984–88; Chef/patron and Chairman, Le Manoir aux Quat' Saisons, 1984–; co-owner: Le Petit Blanc Brasserie/Rôtisserie, Oxford, 1996–; Le Petit Blanc, Cheltenham, 1998–; Le Petit Blanc, Birmingham, 1999–; Le Petit Blanc, Manchester, 2000–. TV series, Blanc Mange, 1994. Academicien Mentor, Academie Culinaire de France. Master Chef Great Britain. Hon. DBA Oxford Brookes Univ., 1999. Personalité de l'année, 1990. Commandeur de l'Assoc. Internat. des Maîtres Conseils en Gastronomie Française. *Publications:* Recipes from Le Manoir aux Quat' Saisons, 1988; Cooking for Friends, 1991; Blanc Mange, 1994; A Blanc Christmas, 1996; Blanc Vite, 1998. *Recreations:* reading, tennis, riding, classical and rock music. *Address:* Le Manoir aux Quat' Saisons, Church Road, Great Milton, Oxford OX44 7PD.

BLANCH, Mrs Lesley, MBE 2001; FRSL; author; *b* 1907; *m* 2nd, 1945, Romain Kacew (Romain Gary) (marr. diss. 1962; he *d* 1980). *Educ:* by reading, and listening to conversation of elders and betters. FRSL 1969. *Publications:* The Wilder Shores of Love (biog.), 1954; Round the World in Eighty Dishes (cookery), 1956; The Game of Hearts (biog.), 1956; The Sabres of Paradise (biog.), 1960; Under a Lilac Bleeding Star (travels), 1963; The Nine Tiger Man (fict.), 1965; Journey into the Mind's Eye (autobiog.), 1968;

Pavilions of the Heart (biog.), 1974; Pierre Loti: portrait of an escapist (biog.), 1983; From Wilder Shores: the tables of my travels (travel/autobiog.), 1989. *Recreations:* travel, opera, acquiring useless objects, animal welfare, gardening. *Address:* 9 Chemin Vallaya, Garavan-Menton 06500, France. *Club:* Taharir (formerly Mahommed Ali) (Cairo).

BLANCH, Sir Malcolm, KCVO 1998 (CVO 1992; LVO 1981; MVO 1968); Clerk Comptroller to Queen Elizabeth the Queen Mother, 1967–98; *b* 27 May 1932; *s* of late John and Louie Blanch; *m* 1957, Jean Harding Richardson; two *s*. *Educ:* Dinnington Sch., Yorks. Served RN, 1949–56. Asst Keeper and Steward in Royal Yachts, Victoria & Albert, 1953, Britannia, 1954–56; Queen Elizabeth the Queen Mother's Household, 1957–98: Clerk Accountant, 1960–67. Freeman, City of London, 1989. *Recreations:* gardening, music. *Address:* 12 Bishop's Drive, East Harnham, Salisbury, Wilts SP2 8NZ. *T:* (01722) 329862.

BLANCH, Dr Michael Dennis, TD and bar 1990; Chief Executive, Falkland Islands Government, since 2000; *b* 22 Oct. 1946; *s* of Harold Clement Blanch and Jane Emily Blanch; *m* 1973, Penelope Ann Worthington; two *s*. *Educ:* William Ellis Sch.; Univ. of Birmingham (BScSoc 1969; DipEd 1970; PhD 1975). AMA 1979. Keeper of Education, Nat. Army Mus., 1973–77; Sen. Museums Keeper, Rotherham MBC, 1977–79; Asst Dir, Libraries, Oldham MBC, 1979–81; Dir of Museums, 1981–84, Dir of Leisure Services, 1984–88, Calderdale MBC; County Leisure Services Officer, Shropshire CC, 1988–91; Chief Executive: Eastbourne BC, 1991–95; London Borough of Bromley, 1995–2000. FIMgt 1985. *Publications:* War and Weapons, 1976; Soldiers, 1980. *Recreations:* mountain biking, hill walking, sailing, previously Territorial Army. *Address:* Sulivan House, Stanley, Falkland Islands. *T:* 21036.

BLANCHARD, Francis; Commandeur de la Légion d'Honneur; Member, French Economic and Social Council, since 1989; *b* Paris, 21 July 1916; *m* 1940, Marie-Claire Boué; two *s*. *Educ:* Univ. of Paris. French Home Office; Internat. Organisation for Refugees, Geneva, 1947–51; Internat. Labour Office, Geneva, 1951–89: Asst Dir-Gen., 1956–68; Dep. Dir-Gen., 1968–74; Dir-Gen., 1974–89. Dr *hc* Brussels, Cairo and Manila. *Recreations:* ski-ing, hunting, riding. *Address:* Prébailly, 01170 Gex, France. *T:* 450415170.

BLANCHARD, Rt Hon. Peter; PC 1998; Rt Hon. Justice Blanchard; a Judge of the Court of Appeal, New Zealand, since 1996; *b* 2 Aug. 1942; *s* of Cyril Francis Blanchard and Zora Louis Blanchard (now Parkinson); *m* 1968, Judith Isabel Watts; one *s* one *d*. *Educ:* King's Coll., Auckland; Univ. of Auckland (LLM 1968); Harvard Univ. (Frank Knox Fellow, 1968; Fulbright Fellow, 1968; LLM 1969). Admitted barrister and solicitor, Supreme Court of NZ, 1966; Partner: Grierson Jackson & Partners, 1968–83; Simpson Grierson, 1983–92; Judge, High Court of NZ, 1992–96. Comr, Law Commn, 1990–94. *Publications:* Company Receiverships in Australia and New Zealand, 1982, 2nd edn (jtly) 1994; Handbook on Agreements for Sale and Purchase of Land, 1988, 4th edn 1987. *Recreations:* reading, music, theatre, walking. *Address:* Court of Appeal of New Zealand, PO Box 1606, Wellington, New Zealand. *T:* (4) 9143540.

BLANCO WHITE, Thomas Anthony; QC 1969; *b* 19 Jan. 1915; *s* of late G. R. Blanco White, QC, and Amber Blanco White, OBE; *m* 1950, Anne Katherine Ironside-Smith; two *s* one *d*. *Educ:* Gresham's Sch.; Trinity Coll., Cambridge. Called to Bar, Lincoln's Inn, 1937, Bencher 1977, retired 1993. Served RAFVR, 1940–46. *Publications:* Patents for Inventions, 1950, 1955, 1962, 1974, 1983, etc. *Recreations:* gardening, photography. *Address:* 72 South Hill Park, NW3 2SN.

BLAND, Christopher Donald Jack; Lord–Lieutenant of the Isle of Wight, since 1995; Chairman, Hovertravel Ltd, since 1965; *b* 8 Oct. 1936; *s* of Christopher Donald James Bland and Iris Raynor Bland; *m* 1962, Judith Anne Louise Maynard; one *s* three *d*. *Educ:* Sandroyd Prep. Sch.; Clayesmore Public Sch. Nat. Service, Gordon Highlanders, later Lieut RE, 1955–57. Rolls Royce Ltd, 1957–61; Britten Norman Aircraft Co., 1961–65; Hovertravel Ltd (world's first hovercraft operator), 1965; Sen. Partner, Norwood, 1981–; Dir, Red Funnel Gp PLC, 1986; Chm., Vectis Transport PLC, 1988–. Mem., Albany Prison Bd, 1978–88; Chm., IoW HA, 1988–90. High Sheriff, IoW, 1989–90. *Recreations:* flying vintage aircraft, vintage sports cars, tinkering with water mills. *Address:* Yafford House, Shorwell, Isle of Wight PO30 3LH. *T:* (home) (01983) 740428; (office) (01983) 565181. *Club:* Royal Yacht Squadron.

BLAND, Sir (Francis) Christopher (Buchan), Kt 1993; Chairman, British Telecommunications plc, since 2001; *b* 29 May 1938; *e s* of James Franklin MacMahon Bland and Jess Buchan Bland (*née* Brodie); *m* 1981, Jennifer Mary, Viscountess Enfield, *er d* of late Rt Hon. W. M. May, PC, FCA, MP, and of Mrs May, Mertoun Hall, Holywood, Co. Down; one *s* and two step *s* two step *d*. *Educ:* Sedbergh; The Queen's Coll., Oxford (Hastings Exhibnr). 2nd Lieut, 5th Royal Inniskilling Dragoon Guards, 1956–58; Lieut, North Irish Horse (TA), 1958–69. Dir, NI Finance Corp., 1972–76; Dep. Chm., IBA, 1972–80; Chairman: Sir Joseph Causton & Sons, 1977–85; LWT (Hldgs), 1984–94; Century Hutchinson Group, 1984–89; Phicom, subseq. Life Sciences Internat., 1987–97; NFC, 1994–2000; Director: Nat. Provident Instn, 1978–88; Storehouse plc, 1988–93. Chm. Bd of Govs, BBC, 1996–2001. Mem. GLC, for Lewisham, 1967–70; Chm., ILEA Schs Sub-Cttee, 1970; Mem. Burnham Cttee, 1970; Chm., Bow Group, 1969–70; Editor, Crossbow, 1971–72; Mem., Prime Minister's Adv. Panel on Citizen's Charter, 1991–94; Chm., Chancellor's Private Finance Panel, 1995–96 (Mem., 1994–96). Chairman: NHS Rev. Gp on Nat. Trng Council and Nat. Staff Cttees, 1982; Hammersmith and Queen Charlotte's Hosps (formerly Hammersmith) SHA, 1982–94; Hammersmith Hosps NHS Trust, 1994–96. Governor, Prendergast Girls Grammar Sch. and Woolwich Polytechnic, 1968–70; Mem. Council: RPMS, 1982–96 (Hon. Fellow, 1997); St Mary's Med Sch., 1984–88. Hon. LLD South Bank, 1994. *Publications:* Bow Group pamphlet on Commonwealth Immigration; (with Linda Kelly) Feasts, 1987. *Recreations:* fishing, skiing; formerly: Captain, OU Fencing Team, 1961; Captain, OU Modern Pentathlon Team, 1959–60; Mem. Irish Olympic Fencing Team, 1960. *Address:* Blissamore Hall, Clanville, Andover, Hants SP11 9HL. *T:* (01264) 772274; 10 Catherine Place, SW1E 6HF. *T:* (020) 7834 0021. *Club:* Beefsteak.

BLAND, Louise Sarah, (Mrs S. Bland); *see* Godfrey, L. S.

BLAND, Lt-Col Sir Simon (Claud Michael), KCVO 1982 (CVO 1973; MVO 1967); Extra Equerry to Princess Alice Duchess of Gloucester and the Duke and Duchess of Gloucester, since 1989 (Comptroller, Private Secretary and Equerry, 1972–89); *b* 4 Dec. 1923; *s* of late Sir Nevile Bland, KCMG, KCVO, and Portia (*née* Ottley); *m* 1954, Olivia, *d* of late Major William Blackett, Arbigland, Dumfries; one *s* three *d*. *Educ:* Eton College. Served War of 1939–45, Scots Guards, in Italy; BJSM, Washington, 1948–49; 2nd Bn, Scots Guards, Malaya, 1949–51; Asst Mil. Adviser at UK High Commn, Karachi, 1959–60; Comptroller and Asst Private Sec. to late Duke of Gloucester, 1961–74 and Private Sec. to late Prince William, 1968–72. Dir, West End Bd, Commercial Union, 1964–; Vice-Pres., Raleigh Internat. (formerly Operation Raleigh), 1989–96. Chm., Coll. of St Barnabas, 1993–97; Member Council: Pestalozzi Children's Village Trust, 1989–; Elizabeth Finn Trust (formerly DGAA Homelife), 1990–; Order of St John for Kent, 1990–; President: Friends of Edenbridge Hosp., 1990–; Lingfield Br., Riding for the Disabled, 1990–. Freeman, City of London, 1988. KStJ 1988. *Address:* Totties, Mill Hill, Edenbridge, Kent TN8 5DB. *T:* and *Fax:* (01732) 862340. *Club:* Buck's.

BLANDFORD, Marquess of; Charles James Spencer-Churchill; *b* 24 Nov. 1955; *e s* and *heir* of 11th Duke of Marlborough, *qv*; *m* 1990, Rebecca Mary, *d* of Peter Few Brown; one *s*. *Educ:* Pinewood; Harrow; RAC, Cirencester; Royal Berks Coll. of Agric. *Heir:* *s* Earl of Sunderland, *qv*. *Address:* Blenheim Palace, Woodstock, Oxon; 16 Lawrence Street, SW3 5NE. *Clubs:* Turf, Tramp's, Annabel's; Racquet and Tennis (New York).

BLANDFORD, Eric George, CBE 1967; formerly a Judge of the Supreme Court of Aden; *b* 10 March 1916; *s* of George and Eva Blanche Blandford; *m* 1940, Marjorie Georgina Crane; one *s*. *Educ:* Bristol Grammar Sch. Admitted Solicitor Supreme Court, England, 1939; LLB (London) 1939. War Service, 1939–46 (despatches): India, Burma, Malaya; rank on release Temp. Major RA. Solicitor in London, 1946–51; Asst Comr of Lands, Gold Coast, 1951; Dist Magistrate, Gold Coast, 1952; called to the Bar, Inner Temple, 1955; Chief Registrar, Supreme Court, Gold Coast, 1956; Registrar of High Court of Northern Rhodesia, 1958; Judge, Supreme Court of Aden, 1961–68; Dep. Asst Registrar of Criminal Appeals, 1968–78; Asst Registrar of Criminal Appeals, Royal Courts of Justice, 1978–81. Chm. Aden Municipality Inquiry Commn, 1962. *Publication:* Civil Procedure Rules of Court, Aden, 1967. *Recreation:* local history research. *Address:* Hays Park, Sedgehill, Shaftesbury, Dorset SP7 9JR.

BLANDFORD, Prof. Roger David, FRS 1989; Richard Chace Tolman Professor of Theoretical Astrophysics, California Institute of Technology, since 1989; *b* 28 Aug. 1949; *s* of Jack George and Janet Margaret Blandford; *m* 1972, Elizabeth Denise Kellett; two *s*. *Educ:* King Edward's Sch., Birmingham; Magdalene Coll., Cambridge Univ. (BA, MA, PhD; Bye Fellow 1973). Res. Fellow, St John's Coll., Cambridge, 1973–76; Inst. for Advanced Study, Princeton, 1974–75; CIT, 1976–. Fellow, Amer. Acad. of Arts and Scis, 1993. *Address:* 130–33 Caltech, Pasadena, CA 91125, USA. *T:* (626) 3954200.

BLANDY, Prof. John Peter, CBE 1995; MA, DM, MCh, FRCS, FACS; Consultant Surgeon: The Royal London (formerly London) Hospital, 1964–92; St Peter's Hospital for the Stone, 1969–92; Professor of Urology, University of London, 1969–92, now Emeritus; *b* 11 Sept. 1927; *s* of late Sir E. Nicolas Blandy, KCIE, CSI, ICS and Dorothy Kathleen (*née* Marshall); *m* 1953, Anne, *d* of Hugh Mathias, FRCS, Tenby; four *d*. *Educ:* Clifton Coll.; Balliol Coll., Oxford (Hon. Fellow, 1992); London Hosp. Med. Coll. BM, BCh 1951; MA 1953; FRCS 1956; DM 1963; MCh 1963; FACS 1980. House Phys. and House Surg., London Hosp., 1952; RAMC, 1953–55; Surgical Registrar and Lectr in Surgery, London Hosp., 1956–60; exchange Fellow, Presbyterian St Luke's Hosp., Chicago, 1960–61; Sen. Lectr, London Hosp., 1961; Resident Surgical Officer, St Paul's Hosp., 1963–64. McLaughlin-Gallie Vis. Prof., Royal Coll. of Physicians and Surgeons of Canada, 1988. Member: BMA; RSM (Hon. FRSocMed 1995); Council, RCS, 1982–94 (Hunterian Prof., 1964; Hunterian Orator, 1991; a Vice-Pres., 1992–94); GMC, 1992–96; Internat. Soc. Pædiatric Urol. Surg.; Internat. Soc. of Urological Surgeons; British Assoc. Urological Surgeons (Pres., 1984); President: European Assoc. of Urology, 1986–88; European Bd of Urology, 1991–92. Chm., Nat. Confidential Enquiry into Perioperative Deaths, 1992–97. Fellow, Assoc. of Surgeons; Hon. FRCSI 1992; Hon. Fellow, Urological Society: of Australasia, 1973; of Canada, 1986; of Denmark, 1986; of Germany, 1987; of The Netherlands, 1990; of Romania, 1991; of Japan, 1991; Hon. Fellow: Mexican Coll. of Urology, 1974; Amer. Urol Assoc., 1989. Maurice Davidson Award, Fellowship of Postgrad. Med., 1980; St Peter's Medal, British Assoc. of Urol Surgs, 1982; Francisco Diaz Medal, Spanish Urol Assoc., 1988; Grégoir Medal, Eur. Assoc. of Urology, 2001. *Publications:* (with A. D. Dayan and H. F. Hope-Stone) Tumours of the Testicle, 1970; Transurethral Resection, 1971, 4th edn (with R. G. Notley) 1998; (ed) Urology, 1976, 2nd edn (with C. G. Fowler) 1995; Lecture Notes on Urology, 1976, 5th edn 1998; Operative Urology, 1978; (ed with B. Lytton) The Prostate, 1986; (with J. Moors) Urology for Nurses, 1989; (ed with R. T. D. Oliver and H. F. Hope-Stone) Urological and Genital Cancer, 1989; (ed with J. S. P. Lumley) History of the Royal College of Surgeons, 2000; papers in surgical and urological jls. *Recreation:* painting. *Address:* 362 Shakespeare Tower, Barbican, EC2Y 8NJ. *T:* (020) 7638 4095.

BLANK, Sir (Maurice) Victor, Kt 1999; Chairman: The Great Universal Stores plc, since 2000 (Director, since 1993; Deputy Chairman, 1996–2000); Trinity Mirror PLC, since 1999; *b* 9 Nov. 1942; *s* of Joseph Blank and Ruth Blank (*née* Levey); *m* 1977, Sylvia Helen (*née* Richford); two *s* one *d*. *Educ:* Stockport Grammar Sch.; St Catherine's Coll., Oxford (MA; Domus Fellow, 1998). Solicitor of the Supreme Court. Joined Clifford-Turner as articled clerk, 1964: Solicitor, 1966; Partner, 1969; Charterhouse Bank: Dir, and Head of Corporate Finance, 1981; Chief Exec., 1985–96; Chm., 1985–97; Chief Exec., 1985–96, Chm., 1991–97, Charterhouse plc; Dir, Charterhouse Eur. Hldg, 1993– (Chm., 1993–97); Chm., Mirror Group plc, 1998–99. Non-executive Director: Coats Viyella, 1989– (Dep. Chm., 1999–); Williams (formerly Williams Hldgs) plc, 1995–2000; Sen. Ind. Dir, Chubb plc, 2000–. Mem., 1998–, Chm., 1999–, Industrial Develt Adv. Bd. Chm., Wellbeing, 1989–. Oxford University: Chm., Adv. Bd, Develt Prog., 1999–; Mem., Council, 2000–. Mem., RSA. CIMgt 2000. Hon. FRCOG 1998. *Publication:* (jtly) Weinberg and Blank on Take-Overs and Mergers, 3rd edn 1971 to 5th edn 1989. *Recreations:* family, cricket, tennis, theatre. *Address:* The Great Universal Stores plc, Nightingale House, 65 Curzon Street, W1J 8PE. *T:* (020) 7318 6209, *Fax:* (020) 7318 6233.

BLANNING, Prof. Timothy Charles William, LittD; FBA 1990; Professor of Modern European History, University of Cambridge, since 1992; Fellow, Sidney Sussex College, Cambridge, since 1968; *b* 21 April 1942; *s* of Thomas Walter Blanning and Gwendolyn Marchant (*née* Jones); *m* 1988, Nicky Susan Jones. *Educ:* King's Sch., Bruton, Somerset; Sidney Sussex Coll., Cambridge (BA, MA; PhD 1967; LittD 1998). University of Cambridge: Res. Fellow, Sidney Sussex Coll., 1965–68; Asst Lectr in History, 1972–76; Lectr in History, 1976–87; Reader in Modern European History, 1987–92. *Publications:* Joseph II and Enlightened Despotism, 1970; Reform and Revolution in Mainz 1740–1803, 1974; The French Revolution in Germany, 1983; The Origins of the French Revolutionary Wars, 1986; The French Revolution: aristocrats versus bourgeois?, 1987; Joseph II, 1994; The French Revolutionary Wars 1787–1802, 1996; (ed) The Oxford Illustrated History of Modern Europe, 1996; (ed) The Rise and Fall of the French Revolution, 1996; (ed) History and Biography: essays in honour of Derek Beales, 1996; The French Revolution: class war or culture clash?, 1998; (ed) Reform in Great Britain and Germany 1750–1850, 1999; (ed) The Short Oxford History of Europe: the eighteenth century, 2000; (ed) The Short Oxford History of Europe: the nineteenth century, 2000. *Recreations:* music, gardening, dog-walking. *Address:* Sidney Sussex College, Cambridge CB2 3HU. *T:* (01223) 338800. *Club:* Athenæum.

BLANTYRE, Archbishop of, (RC), since 1968; **Most Rev. James Chiona;** *b* 1924. *Educ:*; Nankhunda Minor Seminary, Malaŵi; Kachebere Major Seminary, Malaŵi. Priest, 1954; Asst Parish Priest, 1954–57; Prof., Nankhunda Minor Seminary, 1957–60; study of Pastoral Sociology, Rome, 1961–62; Asst Parish Priest, 1962–65; Auxiliary Bishop of

Blantyre and Titular Bishop of Bacanaria, 1965; Vicar Capitular of Archdiocese of Blantyre, 1967. *Recreation:* music. *Address:* Archbishop's House, PO Box 385, Blantyre, Malawi. *T:* (10) 633516.

BLASHFORD-SNELL, Col John Nicholas, OBE 1996 (MBE 1969); Ministry of Defence consultant (on staff, 1983–91); Director, The Starting Point Appeal, Merseyside Youth Association, since 1993; *b* 22 Oct. 1936; *s* of late Rev. Prebendary Leland John Blashford Snell and Gwendolen Ives Sadler; *m* 1960, Judith Frances (*née* Sherman); two *d.* *Educ:* Victoria Coll., Jersey, CI; RMA, Sandhurst. Commissioned Royal Engineers, 1957; 33 Indep. Fd Sqdn RE Cyprus, 1958–61; comd Operation Aphrodite (Expedition) Cyprus, 1959–61; Instructor: Junior Leaders Regt RE, 1962–63; RMA Sandhurst, 1963–66; Adjt 3rd Div. Engineers, 1966–67; comd Great Abbai Expedn (Blue Nile), 1968; sc RMCS Shrivenham and Camberley, 1968–69; comd Dahlak Quest Expedn, 1969–70; GSO2 MoD, 1970–72; comd British Trans-Americas Expedn, 1971–72; OC 48 Fd Sqdn RE, service in Belize, Oman, Ulster, 1972–74; comd Zaire River Expedn, 1974–75; CO Junior Leaders Regt RE, 1976–78; Dir of Operations, Operation Drake, 1977–81; on staff (GSO1), MoD, 1978–82; in command, The Fort George Volunteers, 1982–83. Operation Raleigh: Operations Dir, 1982–88; Dir Gen., 1989–91; Leader, Kota Mama expedn, 1995–. Hon. Chairman: Scientific Exploration Soc., 1969–; Operation New World, 1995–99. Freeman, City of Hereford, 1984. Hon. DSc Durham, 1986; Hon. DEng Bournemouth, 1997. Darien Medal (Colombia), 1972; Livingstone Medal, RSGS, 1975; Patron's Medal, RGS, 1993; Gold Medal, Instn of RE, 1994. La Paz Medal (Bolivia), 2000. *Publications:* Weapons and Tactics (with Tom Wintringham), 1970; (with Richard Snailham) The Expedition Organiser's Guide, 1970, 2nd edn 1976; Where the Trails Run Out, 1974; In the Steps of Stanley, 1975, 2nd edn 1975; (with A. Ballantine) Expeditions the Experts' Way, 1977, 2nd edn 1978; A Taste for Adventure, 1978; (with Michael Cable) Operation Drake, 1981; Mysteries: encounters with the unexplained, 1983; Operation Raleigh, the Start of an Adventure, 1987; (with Ann Tweedy) Operation Raleigh, Adventure Challenge, 1988; (with Ann Tweedy) Operation Raleigh, Adventure Unlimited, 1990; Something lost behind the Ranges, 1994; (with Rula Lenska) Mammoth Hunt, 1996; (with Richard Snailham) Kota Mama, 2000. *Recreations:* motoring, shooting, underwater diving, food, wine. *Address:* c/o Scientific Exploration Society, Expedition Base, Motcombe, Dorset SP7 9PB. *Fax:* (01747) 851351. *Clubs:* Wig and Pen, Buck's; Artists' (Liverpool); Galley Hill Shooting (Hon. Pres.); Explorers' (New York).

BLATCH, family name of **Baroness Blatch**.

BLATCH, Baroness *cr* 1987 (Life Peer), of Hinchingbrooke in the county of Cambridgeshire; **Emily May Blatch,** CBE 1983; PC 1993; *b* 24 July 1937; *d* of Stephen Joseph and Sarah Triggs; *m* 1963, John Richard Blatch, AFC; two *s* one *d* (of whom one *s* one *d* are twins) (and one *s* decd). *Educ:* Prenton, Birkenhead; Huntingdonshire College. WRAF, 1955–59; Ministry of Aviation, 1959–63. Member: Bd, Peterborough Develt Corp., 1984–89; Cambs CC, 1977–89 (Leader, 1981–85); ACC, 1981–85; European Econ. and Social Cttee, 1986–87; Cons. Nat. Local Govt Adv. Cttee, 1988–92. Baroness in Waiting (Govt Whip), H of L, 1990; Parly Under-Sec. of State for the Envmt, 1990–91; Minister of State: DoE, 1991–92; DFE, 1992–94; Home Office, 1994–97; Opposition front bench spokesman on educn and employment, 1997–2000; Dep. Leader of Opposition, H of L, 2000–. Chm., Anglo-American Community Relations Cttee, RAF Alconbury, 1985–91. Pres., Nat. Benevolent Inst., 1989–. Member: Air League Council, 1998–; Air Cadet Council, 1998–; Trustee, RAF Mus., 1998–. Paul Harris Fellow, Rotary Club, 1992. FRSA 1985. Hon. LLD Teesside, 1997. *Recreations:* music, theatre. *Address:* House of Lords, SW1A 0PW. *Club:* Royal Air Force.

BLATCHLEY, Geraldine; *see* James, G.

BLATCHLY, John Marcus, MA, PhD; FSA 1975; Headmaster, Ipswich School, 1972–93; *b* 7 Oct. 1932; *s* of late Alfred Ernest Blatchly and Edith Selina Blatchly (*née* Giddings); *m* 1955, Pamela Winifred, JP, *d* of late Major and Mrs L. J. Smith; one *s* one *d.* *Educ:* Sutton Grammar Sch., Surrey; Christ's Coll., Cambridge (Natural Scis Triposes; BA, MA, PhD). Instr Lieut RN, 1954–57. Asst Master and Head of Science Dept: King's Sch., Bruton, 1957–62; Eastbourne Coll., 1962–66; Charterhouse, 1966–72 (PhD awarded 1967 publication of work carried out with Royal Society grants at these three schools). Pres., Suffolk Inst. of Archaeology and History, 1975–2001; Chm., Suffolk Records Soc., 1988–. Editor, Conference and Common Room (Journal of HMC Schools), 1987–92; Hon. Treas., 1990–92, Hon. Associate Mem., 1993, HMC; lead inspector to HMC schs, 1994–2000. Co-ed., Bookplate Jl, 1994–98. Gov., Norwich Sch., 1993–; Trustee, Oakham Sch., 1993–. Hon. LittD UEA, 1993. *Publications:* Organic Reactions, vol. 19, 1972 (jtly, with J. F. W. McOmie); The Topographers of Suffolk, 1976, 5th edn 1988; (with Peter Eden) Isaac Johnson of Woodbridge, 1979; Eighty Ipswich Portraits, 1980; (ed) Davy's Suffolk Journal, 1983; The Town Library of Ipswich: a history and catalogue, 1989; The Bookplates of Edward Gordon Craig, 1997; Some Suffolk and Norfolk Ex-Libris, 2000; (jtly) The Journal of Wilham Dowsing, 2001; many papers in chemical, educnl, archaeological and antiquarian jls. *Recreations:* East Anglian history, music, books. *Address:* 11 Burlington Road, Ipswich, Suffolk IP1 2HS.

BLATHERWICK, Sir David (Elliott Spiby), KCMG 1997 (CMG 1990); OBE 1973; HM Diplomatic Service, retired; Chairman, British Egyptian Chamber of Commerce, since 1999; *b* 13 July 1941; *s* of Edward S. Blatherwick; *m* 1964, (Margaret) Clare Crompton; one *s* one *d.* *Educ:* Lincoln Sch.; Wadham Coll., Oxford. Entered FO, 1964; Second Sec., Kuwait, 1968; First Sec., Dublin, 1970; FCO, 1973; Head of Chancery, Cairo, 1977; Head, Pol Affairs Dept, NI Office (Belfast), 1981; Hd, Energy, Science and Space Dept, FCO, 1983; sabbatical leave at Stanford Univ., Calif, 1985–86; Counsellor and Hd of Chancery, UK Mission to UN, NY, 1986–89; Prin. Finance Officer and Chief Inspector, FCO, 1989–91; Ambassador to: Republic of Ireland, 1991–95; Egypt, 1995–99. *Publication:* The International Politics of Telecommunications, 1987. *Recreations:* music, sailing, walking. *Club:* Athenæum.

BLATTER, Joseph Sepp; President, Fédération Internationale de Football Association, since 1998; *b* 10 March 1936; *s* of Joseph and Berta Blatter-Nellen; *m* (marr. diss.); one *d.* *Educ:* Univ. of Lausanne (BA Business Admin and Econs). Gen. Sec., Swiss Ice-Hockey Fedn, 1964–66; Press Officer, Swiss Sports Orgn, 1966–68; Dir, Sports Timing and PR, Longines SA, 1968–75; Technical Dir, 1975–81, Gen. Sec. and CEO, 1981–98, FIFA. Mem., IOC, 1999–. Hon. Mem., Swiss FA. Olympic Order, 1994. Kt, Sultanate of Pahang, 1990; Order of Good Hope (S Africa), 1998. *Recreations:* crosswords, tennis, books (detective stories). *Address:* FIFA, Hitzigweg 11, PO Box 85, 8030 Zurich, Switzerland. *T:* (1) 3849595.

BLAUG, Prof. Mark, PhD; FBA 1989; Professor of the Economics of Education, University of London Institute of Education, 1967–84, now Professor Emeritus; *b* 3 April 1927; *s* of Bernard Blaug and Sarah (*née* Toeman); *m* 1st, 1946, Rose Lapone (marr. diss.); 2nd, 1954, Brenda Ellis (marr. diss.); one *s*; 3rd, 1969, Ruth M. Towse; one *s.* *Educ:* Queen's Coll., NY (BA); Columbia Univ. (MA, PhD). Asst Prof., Yale Univ., 1954–62; Sen. Lectr, then Reader, Univ. of London Inst. of Educn, 1963–67; Lectr, LSE, 1963–78. Consultant Prof., Univ. of Buckingham, 1984–92, now Prof. Emeritus; Visiting Professor: Exeter Univ., 1989–; Univ. of Amsterdam, 1999–; Erasmus Univ., Rotterdam, 2000–. Guggenheim Foundn Fellow, 1958–59. Dist. Fellow, Hist. of Econs Soc., 1988. Editl Consultant, Edward Elgar Publishing, 1986–. Foreign Hon. Mem., Royal Netherlands Acad. of Arts and Scis, 1984. Hon. DSc Buckingham, 1993. *Publications:* Ricardian Economics, 1958; Economic Theory in Retrospect, 1962, 5th edn 1996; (jtly) The Causes of Graduate Unemployment in India, 1969; Introduction to the Economics of Education, 1970; Education and the Employment Problem in Developing Countries, 1973; (jtly) The Practice of Manpower Forecasting, 1973; The Cambridge Revolution?, 1974; The Methodology of Economics, 1980, 2nd edn 1992; Who's Who in Economics, 1983, 3rd edn 1999; Great Economists Since Keynes, 1984, 2nd edn 1998; Great Economists Before Keynes, 1986; Economic History and the History of Economics, 1986; The Economics of Education and the Education of an Economist, 1987; Economic Theories: True or False?, 1990; Keynes: Life, Ideas and Legacy, 1990; (jtly) Appraising Economic Theories, 1991; (jtly) Quantity Theory of Money, 1995; Not Only an Economist, 1997. *Recreations:* talking, walking, sailing. *Address:* Vliet 30, 2311 RE Leiden, Netherlands. *T:* (71) 5663222; Langsford Barn, Peter Tavy, Tavistock, Devon PL9 9LY. *T:* (01822) 810562.

BLAYNEY, Elizabeth Carmel, (Eily); Head of Library and Records Department and Departmental Record Officer (Assistant Secretary), Foreign and Commonwealth Office, 1977–85, retired; *b* 19 July 1925; *d* of William Blayney, MRCS, LRCP, Medical Practitioner (previously County Inspector, RIC) of Harrold, Beds, and Mary Henrietta *d* of John Beveridge, sometime Town Clerk of Dublin. *Educ:* St Mary's Convent, Shaftesbury; The Triangle, S Molton Street. Chartered Librarian. Served War, WTS(FANY) in UK, India and Ceylon (Force 136), 1944–46. Library Asst, Hampstead Borough Libraries, 1947–50; Assistant Librarian: RSA, 1950–52; CO/CRO Jt Library, CRO, 1953; Head of Printed Library, FO, 1959–68; Librarian i/c, ODM, 1968–69; Librarian, FCO, 1969–77. *Address:* 6 Bamville Wood, East Common, Harpenden, Herts AL5 1AP. *T:* (01582) 715067.

BLAZWICK, Iwona Maria Anna; Director, Whitechapel Art Gallery, since 2001; *b* 14 Oct. 1955; *d* of Wojciech Blaszczyk and Danuta Mondry-Blaszczyk. *Educ:* Exeter Univ. (BA 1977). Curator, 1980–85, Dir of Exhibns, 1987–93, Inst. of Contemporary Arts, London; Dir, A.I.R. Gall., 1985–87; Commng Editor, Phaidon Press, 1993–97; Curator, then Hd of Exhibns, Tate Gall. of Modern Art, 1997–2001. Art critic, lectr and broadcaster on contemporary art, 1985–; Vis. Lectr, RCA, 1993–97. Curator: Ha-Ha: Contemporary British Artists in an 18th Century Park, Univ. of Plymouth and Nat. Trust, 1993; (jtly) On Taking a Normal Situation, Mus. of Contemporary Art, Antwerp, 1993; Now Here, Louisiana Mus., Denmark, 1996; New Tendencies in British and Japanese Art, Toyama Mus. of Modern Art, Japan, 1996. *Publications:* An Endless Feast: on British situationism, 1988; Lawrence Weiner, 1993; Ilya Kabakov, 1998; exhibn catalogues; contribs to jls. *Recreations:* cinema, dancing, travel, photography. *Address:* 80–82 Whitechapel High Street, E1 7QX. *Club:* Blacks.

BLEACKLEY, David, CMG 1979; DPhil; Head, Overseas Division, and Assistant Director, Institute of Geological Sciences, 1975–80; *b* 1 Feb. 1919; *s* of Alfred Mason and Hilda Gertrude Bleackley; *m* 1st, 1945, Peggy Florence Chill (*d* 1966); one *s* one *d*; 2nd, 1973, Patricia Clavell Strakosch (*née* Hore); two step *s* one step *d.* *Educ:* City of Oxford Sch.; The Queen's Coll., Oxford (BA 1939, MA 1942, DPhil 1960). Served War, Royal Engineers, 1939–45. Geologist: Shell Oil Co., 1946–50; Geological Survey, British Guiana, 1954–57, Dep. Dir, 1957–60; Overseas Geological Surveys, 1960–65; Dep. Head, Overseas Div., Inst. of Geological Sciences, 1965–75. FIMM 1969; FGS 1943. *Publications:* papers in various jls. *Recreation:* country pursuits. *Address:* Well Farm, Dagnall, near Berkhamsted, Herts HP4 1QU. *T:* (01442) 843232.

BLEAKLEY, Rt Hon. David Wylie, CBE 1984; PC (NI) 1971; President, Church Mission (formerly Church Missionary) Society, 1983–97; *b* 11 Jan. 1925; *s* of John Wesley Bleakley and Sarah Bleakley (*née* Wylie); *m* 1949, Winifred Wason; three *s.* *Educ:* Ruskin Coll., Oxford; Queen's Univ., Belfast. MA, DipEconPolSci (Oxon). Belfast Shipyard, 1940–46; Oxford and Queen's Univ., 1946–51; Tutor in Social Studies, 1951–55; Principal, Belfast Further Educn Centre, 1955–58; Lectr in Industrial Relations, Kivukoni Coll., Dar-es-Salaam, 1967–69; Head of Dept of Economics and Political Studies, Methodist Coll., Belfast, 1969–79; Chief Exec., Irish Council of Churches, 1980–92. MP (Lab) Victoria, Belfast, Parliament of N Ireland, 1958–65; contested: (Lab) East Belfast, General Elections, 1970, Feb. and Oct. 1974. Minister of Community Relations, Govt of NI, March-Sept. 1971; Member (NILP), E Belfast: NI Assembly, 1973–75; NI Constitutional Convention, 1975–76. Contested (Lab) Belfast E, NI Assembly, 1998. Mem., Cttee of Inquiry on Police, 1978. Chm., NI Standing Adv. Commn on Human Rights, 1980–84. Mem., Labour Delegn, NI Peace Talks, 1996–. Irish Deleg. to ACC, 1976; Delegate to WCC, to Conf. of European Churches. WEA and Open Univ. tutor; Vis. Sen. Lectr in Peace Studies, Univ. of Bradford, 1974–. Mem., Press Council, 1987–90. Hon. MA Open, 1975. *Publications:* Ulster since 1800: regional history symposium, 1958; Young Ulster and Religion in the Sixties, 1964; Peace in Ulster, 1972; Faulkner: a biography, 1974; Saidie Patterson, Irish Peacemaker, 1980; In Place of Work, 1981; The Shadow and Substance, 1983; Beyond Work—Free to Be, 1985; Will the Future Work, 1986; Europe: a Christian vision, 1992; Ageing and Ageism in a Technological Society, 1994; Peace in Ireland: two states, one people, 1995; Europe: obligations and opportunities for Christians, 1997; C. S. Lewis: at home in Ireland, 1998; regular contribs to BBC and to press on community relations and industrial studies. *Address:* 8 Thornhill, Bangor, Co. Down, Northern Ireland BT19 1RD. *T:* (028) 9145 4898, *Fax:* (028) 9127 4274.

BLEANEY, Prof. Brebis, CBE 1965; FRS 1950; MA, DPhil; Warren Research Fellow, Royal Society, 1977–80, Leverhulme Emeritus Fellow, 1980–82; Fellow, 1957–77, Senior Research Fellow, 1977–82, Wadham College, Oxford, now Emeritus Fellow; Dr Lee's Professor of Experimental Philosophy, University of Oxford, 1957–77, now Emeritus Professor; *b* 6 June 1915; *m* 1949, Betty Isabelle Plumpton; one *s* one *d.* *Educ:* Westminster City Sch.; St John's Coll., Oxford. Lecturer in Physics at Balliol Coll., Oxford, 1947–50. Research Fellow, Harvard Univ. and Mass Institute of Technology, 1949. University Demonstrator and Lectr in Physics, Univ. of Oxford, 1945–57; Fellow and Lectr in Physics, St John's Coll., Oxford, 1947–57; Tutor, 1950–57; Hon. Fellow, 1968. Visiting Prof. in Physics in Columbia Univ., 1956–57; Harkins Lectr, Chicago Univ., 1957; Kelvin Lectr, Instn Electrical Engineers, 1962; Morris Loeb Lectr, Harvard Univ., 1981; Cherwell Simon Meml Lectr, Oxford Univ., 1981–82; John and Abigail Van Vleck Lectr, Univ. of Minnesota, 1985; Visiting Professor: Univ. of California, Berkeley, 1961; Univ. of Pittsburgh, 1962–63; Manitoba, 1968; La Plata, Argentina, 1971; Amer. Univ. in Cairo, 1978; Univ. of NSW, 1981. Mem. Council for Scientific and Industrial Res., 1960–62; Chm., British Radiofrequency Spectroscopy Gp, 1983–85. Fellow, Internat. Electron Paramagnetic Resonance Soc., 1995 (Gold Medallist, 1999); FRSSAf 1995. FRSA 1971. Corr. Mem. Acad. of Sciences, Inst. of France, 1974, Associé Etranger, 1978; For. Hon. Mem., Amer. Acad. of Arts and Scis, 1978; Hon. Prof., Kazan Univ., 1994. DSc *hc* Porto, Portugal, 1987. Charles Vernon Boys Prize, Physical Soc., 1952;

Hughes Medal, Royal Society, 1962; ISMAR Prize, Internat. Soc. for Magnetic Resonance, 1983; Holweck Medal and Prize, Inst. of Physics and Société Française de Physique, 1984; Zavoisky Prize, Kazan, Physical-Technical Inst., 1992. *Publications:* (with B. I. Bleaney) Electricity and Magnetism, 1957, 3rd edn, 1976, revd edn in 2 vols, 1989; (with A. Abragam) Electron Paramagnetic Resonance, 1970, revd edn 1986; over 300 papers in Proceedings of the Royal Society and Proceedings of the Physical Society, etc. *Recreations:* music, travel. *Address:* Clarendon Laboratory, Parks Road, Oxford OX1 3PU.

BLEARS, Hazel Anne; MP (Lab) Salford, since 1997; Parliamentary Under-Secretary of State, Department of Health, since 2001; *b* 14 May 1956; *d* of Arthur and Dorothy Blears; *m* 1989, Michael Halsall. *Educ:* Wardley Grammar Sch.; Trent Poly. (BA Hons Law). Trainee Solicitor, Salford Council, 1978–80; in private practice, 1980–81; Solicitor: Rossendale Council, 1981–83; Wigan Council, 1983–85; Principal Solicitor, Manchester City Council, 1985–97. Mem. (Lab) Salford City Council, 1984–92. Contested (Lab): Tatton, 1987; Bury S, 1992. *Recreations:* dance, motorcycling. *Address:* House of Commons, SW1A 0AA. *T:* (020) 7219 6595.

BLEASDALE, Alan; writer and producer; *b* 23 March 1946; *s* of George and Margaret Bleasdale; *m* 1970, Julia Moses; two *s* one *d*. *Educ:* St Aloysius RC Jun. Sch., Huyton; Wade Deacon Grammar Sch., Widnes; Padgate Teachers Trng Coll. (Teacher's Cert.). Schoolteacher, 1967–75. *TV series: writer:* Boys from the Blackstuff, 1982 (BPG TV Award for Best Series, 1982; Best British TV Drama of the Decade, ITV Achievement of the Decade Awards, 1989); Scully, 1984; The Monocled Mutineer, 1986; (also prod) GBH, 1991 (BPG TV Award for Best Drama Series, 1992); (also prod) Jake's Progress, 1995 (Best Writer Award, Monte Carlo Internat. TV Fest., 1996); (also prod) Melissa, 1997; (adapt.) Oliver Twist, 1999 (Best TV Drama Series, TRIC Award, 2000); *producer:* Alan Bleasdale Presents, 1994; Soft Sand, Blue Sea, 1997. Hon. DLitt Liverpool Poly., 1991. BAFTA Writers Award, 1982; RTS Writer of the Year, 1982. *Publications: novels:* Scully, 1975; Who's been sleeping in my bed, 1977; *play scripts:* No more sitting on the Old School Bench, 1979; Boys from the Blackstuff, 1982; Are you lonesome tonight?, 1985 (Best Musical, London Standard Drama Awards, 1985); Having a Ball, 1986; It's a Madhouse, 1986; The Monocled Mutineer, 1986; On the Ledge, 1993; *film script:* No Surrender, 1986. *Recreation:* rowing. *Address:* c/o The Agency, 24 Pottery Lane, Holland Park, W11 4LZ. *T:* (020) 7727 1346.

BLEASDALE, Cyril, OBE 1988; FCIT; FIMgt; transport consultant; Managing Director, Railnews Ltd, since 1996; Deputy Chairman, Transaid Worldwide, since 1998; *b* 8 July 1934; *s* of Frederick and Alice Bleasdale; *m* 1970, Catherine; two *d*. *Educ:* Evered High Sch., Liverpool; Stanford Univ., Calif (Sen. Exec. Program). Man. Dir, Freightliner Ltd, 1975–82; Dir, Inter City British Rail, 1982–86; Gen. Manager, BR London Midland Region, 1986–90; Dir, Scotrail, 1990–94. Chm., Stevenage Business Initiative Ltd, 1997–. *Recreations:* music, fitness. *Address:* 8 Long Ridge, Aston, Stevenage SG2 7EW. *Club:* Royal Automobile.

BLEASDALE, Paul Edward; QC 2001; a Recorder of the Crown Court, since 1996; *b* 18 Dec. 1955; *s* of William Arthur Bleasedale and Dorothy Elizabeth Bleasedale; *m* 1991, Dr Sarah Alexandra Nicholson; one *s* one *d*. *Educ:* Langley Park Sch. for Boys, Beckenham; Queen Mary Coll., London (LLB 1977). Called to the Bar, Inner Temple, 1978; Asst Recorder, 1992–96. Dep. Chm., Agricl Lands Tribunal, 1994–. *Recreations:* family holidays, outdoor sports. *Address:* 5 Fountain Court, Steelhouse Lane, Birmingham B4 6DR.

BLEASE, family name of **Baron Blease**.

BLEASE, Baron *cr* 1978 (Life Peer), of Cromac in the City of Belfast; **William John Blease;** JP; *b* 28 May 1914; *e s* of late William and Sarah Blease; *m* 1939, Sarah Evelyn Caldwell (*d* 1995); three *s* one *d*. *Educ:* elementary and technical schs; Nat. Council of Labour Colls; WEA. Retail Provision Trade (apprentice), 1929; Retail Grocery Asst (Branch Manager), 1938–40; Clerk, Belfast Shipyard, 1940–45; Branch Manager, Co-operative Soc., Belfast, 1945–59; Divl Councillor, Union of Shop Distributive Workers, 1948–59; NI Officer, 1959–75, Exec. Consultant, 1975–76, Irish Congress of Trade Unions; Divl Chm. and Nat. Exec. Mem., Nat. Council of Labour Colls, 1948–61; Exec. Mem., NI Labour Party, 1949–59 (Dep. Chm., 1957–58); Trustee, LPNI, 1986–90. Labour Party Spokesman in House of Lords, on N Ireland, 1979–82; Mem., British-Irish Inter-Parly Body, 1997–; Trade Union Side Sec., NI CS Industrial Jt Council, 1975–77. Member: NI Co-operative Develt Agency, 1987–92 (Patron, 1993–); NI Economic Council, 1964–75; Review Body on Local Govt, NI, 1970–71; Review Body on Ind. Relations, NI, 1970–73; Working Party on Discrimination in Employment, NI, 1972–73; NI Trng Res. Cttee, 1966–80; NI Regional Adv. Bd, BIM, 1971–80; NUU Vocational Guidance Council, 1974–83; Ind. Appeals Tribunals, 1974–76; Local Govt Appeals Tribunal, 1974–83; Irish Council of Churches Working Party, 1974–93; IBA, 1974–79; Standing Adv. Commn on Human Rights, NI, 1977–79; Police Complaints Bd, 1977–80; Conciliation Panel, Ind. Relations Agency, 1978–89; Security Appeal Bd, NI SC Commn, 1979–88; Chm., Community Service Order Cttee, 1979–80; Rapporteur, EEC Cross Border Communications Study on Londonderry/Donegal, 1978–80. President: NI Assoc., NACRO, 1982–85; NI Hospice, 1981–85 (Patron, 1986–); E Belfast Access Council for Disabled, 1982–88; NI Widows Assoc., 1985–89; Mem., Belfast Housing Aid, 1989–95. Trustee: Belfast Charitable Trust for Integrated Educn, 1984–88; TSB Foundn, NI, 1986–96. Hon. Mem., NI Cttee, Duke of Edinburgh's Award Scheme (Chm., NI Anniversary Appeal, 1981–82). Member: Bd of Govs, St Mae Nissis Coll., 1981–90; Mgt Bd, Rathgael Young People's Centre, 1989–93. Ford Foundn Travel Award, USA, 1959. Duke of Edinburgh's Sword, 1981. Hon. Res. Fellow, Univ. of Ulster, 1976–83; Jt Hon. Res. Fellow, TCD, 1976–79. Hon. FBIM 1981 (MBIM 1970). JP Belfast, 1976–. Hon. DLitt New Univ. of Ulster, 1972; Hon. LLD QUB, 1982. *Publication:* Encyclopaedia of Labour Law, vol. 1: The Trade Union Movement in Northern Ireland, 1983. *Recreations:* gardening, reading.

BLEDISLOE, 3rd Viscount *cr* 1935; **Christopher Hiley Ludlow Bathurst;** QC 1978; *b* 24 June 1934; *s* of 2nd Viscount Bledisloe, QC, and Joan Isobel Krishaber (*d* 1999); *S* father, 1979; *m* (marr. diss. 1986); two *s* one *d*. *Educ:* Eton; Trinity Coll., Oxford. Called to the Bar, Gray's Inn, 1959; Bencher, 1986. Elected Mem., H of L, 1999. *Heir: s* Hon. Rupert Edward Ludlow Bathurst, *b* 13 March 1964. *Address:* Lydney Park, Glos GL15 6BT. *T:* (01594) 842566; Fountain Court, Temple, EC4Y 9DH. *T:* (020) 7583 3335.

BLEEHEN, Prof. Norman Montague, CBE 1994; Cancer Research Campaign Professor of Clinical Oncology, 1975–95, and Hon. Director of MRC Unit of Clinical Oncology and Radiotherapeutics, 1975–95, University of Cambridge (Director, Radiotherapeutics, and Oncology Centre, 1984–92); Fellow of St John's College, Cambridge, since 1976; *b* 24 Feb. 1930; *s* of Solomon and Lena Bleehen; *m* 1969, Tirza, *d* of Alex and Jenny Loeb. *Educ:* Manchester Grammar Sch.; Haberdashers' Aske's Sch.; Exeter Coll., Oxford (Francis Gotch medal, 1953); Middlesex Hosp. Med. School. BA 1951, BSc 1953, MA 1954, BM, BCh 1955, Oxon; MRCP 1957, FRCP 1973; FRCR 1964; DMRT 1962. MRC Res. Student, Biochem. Dept, Oxford, 1951; house appts: Middlesex Hosp., 1955–56; Hammersmith Hosp., 1957; Asst Med. Specialist Army, Hanover, 1957; Med. Specialist Army, Berlin, 1959 (Captain); Jun. Lectr in Medicine, Dept of Regius Prof. of Medicine, Oxford, 1959–60; Registrar and Sen. Registrar in Radiotherapy, Middlesex Hosp. Med. Sch., 1961–66; Lilly Res. Fellow, Stanford Univ., 1966–67; Locum Consultant, Middlesex Hosp., 1967–69; Prof. of Radiotherapy, Middlesex Hosp. Med. Sch., 1969–75. Consultant advr to CMO, DHSS, for radiation oncology, 1986–92. Cantor Lectr, RSA, 1979; Simon Lectr, RCR, 1986. Member: Jt MRC/CRC Cttee for jtly supported insts, 1971–74; Coordinating Cttee for Cancer Res., 1973–79, 1987–; Council, Imperial Cancer Res. Fund, 1973–76; Council, Brit. Inst. of Radiology, 1974–77; Sci. Cttee, Cancer Res. Campaign, 1976–90; MRC Cell Bd, 1980–84; UICC Fellowships Cttee, 1983–87; Council, European Organisation for Treatment of Cancer, 1983–88; Council, RCR, 1987–90; Vice-President: Bd of Dirs, Internat. Assoc. for Study of Lung Cancer, 1980–82, 1985–94; EEC Cancer Experts Cttee, 1987–96; Pres., Internat. Soc. of Radiation Oncology, 1985–89; Chairman: MRC Lung Cancer Wkg Party, 1973–89; MRC Brain Tumour Wkg Party, 1978–89; MRC Cancer Therapy Cttee, 1972–88; British Assoc. for Cancer Res., 1976–79; Soc. for Comparative Oncology, 1983–86. Hon. FACR 1984. Hon. Dr, Faculty of Pharmacy, Bologna, 1990. Roentgen Prize, British Inst. of Radiology, 1986. *Publications:* (ed jtly) Radiation Therapy Planning, 1983; (Scientific Editor) British Medical Bulletin 24/1, The Scientific Basis of Radiotherapy, 1973; various on medicine, biochemistry, cancer and radiotherapy. *Recreations:* gardening, television. *Address:* 21 Bentley Road, Cambridge CB2 2AW. *T:* (01223) 354320.

BLELLOCH, Sir John (Niall Henderson), KCB 1987 (CB 1983); Permanent Under-Secretary of State, Northern Ireland Office, 1988–90; *b* 24 Oct. 1930; *s* of late Ian William Blelloch, CMG and Leila Mary Henderson; *m* 1958, Pamela, *d* of late James B. and E. M. Blair; one *s* (and one *s* decd). *Educ:* Fettes Coll.; Gonville and Caius Coll., Cambridge (BA). Nat. Service, RA, 1949–51 (commnd 1950). Asst Principal, War Office, 1954; Private Sec. to successive Parly Under Secs of State, 1956–58; Principal, 1958; MoD, 1964–80; London Business Sch. (EDP 3), 1967; Asst Sec., 1968; RCDS, 1974; Asst Under-Sec. of State, 1976; Dep. Sec., NI Office, 1980–82; Dep. Under-Sec of State (Policy and Programmes), MoD, 1982–84; Second Permanent Under-Sec. of State, MoD, 1984–88. Mem., Security Commn, 1991–; Jt Chm., Sentence Review Commn, NI, 1998–. Comr, Royal Hosp. Chelsea, 1988–94. Mem. Cttee, 1993–, Vice-Chm., 1995–99, Automobile Assoc.; Pres., Emergency Planning Soc., 1993–. Trustee: RAF Mus., 1993–; Cheshire Foundn, 1996–; Gov., Fettes Coll., 1992–. *Recreations:* golf, ski-ing, learning the piano. *Address:* c/o Bank of Scotland, St James's Gate, 14–16 Cockspur Street, SW1 5BL. *Clubs:* Royal Mid-Surrey Golf, Sherborne Golf.

BLENKINSOP, Dorothy, CBE 1990; Regional Nursing Officer, Northern Regional Health Authority, 1973–89, retired; *b* 15 Nov. 1931; *d* of late Joseph Henry Blenkinsop, BEM, and Thelma Irene (*née* Bishop). *Educ:* South Shields Grammar Sch. for Girls. MA (Dunelm) 1978. SRN 1953; SCM 1954; Health Visitors Cert. 1962. Ward Sister, Royal Victoria Infirmary, Newcastle upon Tyne, 1955–61; Health Visitor, S Shields, 1962–64; Dep. Matron, Gen. Hosp., S Shields, 1964–67; Durham Hospital Management Committee: Prin. Nurse, Durham City Hosps, 1967–69; Prin. Nursing Officer (Top), 1969–71; Chief Nursing Officer, 1971–73. Chm., S Tyneside Health Care Trust, 1992–96. Local Preacher, Methodist Church. Hon. MSc CNAA, 1990. *Publications:* (with E. G. Nelson): Changing the System, 1972; Managing the System, 1976; articles in nursing press. *Recreation:* gardening. *Address:* 143 Temple Park Road, South Shields, Tyne and Wear NE34 0EN. *T:* (0191) 456 1429.

BLENNERHASSETT, Sir (Marmaduke) Adrian (Francis William), 7th Bt, *cr* 1809; *b* 25 May 1940; *s* of Lieut Sir Marmaduke Blennerhassett, 6th Bt, RNVR (killed in action, 1940), and Gwenfra (*d* 1956), *d* of Judge Harrington-Morgan, Churchtown, Co. Kerry, and of Mrs Douglas Campbell; *S* father 1940; *m* 1972, Carolyn Margaret, *yr d* of late Gilbert Brown; one *s* one *d*. *Educ:* Michael Hall, Forest Row; McGill Univ.; Imperial Coll., Univ. of London (MSc); Cranfield Business Sch. (MBA). FRGS. *Recreations:* sailing, ski-ing, adventure travelling. *Heir: s* Charles Henry Marmaduke Blennerhassett, *b* 18 July 1975. *Address:* 54 Staveley Road, Chiswick, W4 3ES. *Club:* Travellers.

BLESSED, Brian; actor, author and climber; *b* 9 Oct. 1936; *s* of William Blessed and Hilda Blessed (*née* Wall); *m* 1st, Anne Bomann (marr. diss.); one *d*; 2nd, 1978, Hildegard Neil (*née* Zimmermann); one *d*. *Educ:* Bolton-on-Dearne Sch.; Bristol Old Vic Theatre Sch. *Stage:* worked in rep., Nottingham, Birmingham, etc; Incident at Vichy, Phoenix, 1966; The Exorcism, Comedy, 1967; State of Revolution, NT, 1977; The Devil's Disciple, 1979 and The Eagle has Two Heads, Chichester; Hamlet, Richard III, and Henry V, RSC, 1984–85; dir., The Glass Menagerie, tour 1998; one-man show, An Evening with Brian Blessed, tours 1992–93, 1995–96; musicals: Old Deuteronomy, in Cats, New London, 1981; Metropolis, Piccadilly, 1989; Hard Times, Haymarket, 2000; narrator, Morning Heroes (Arthur Bliss), with LSO, 1991, and other works; *films include:* The Trojan Women, 1971; Man of La Mancha, 1972; Flash Gordon, 1980; Henry V, 1989; Robin Hood, Prince of Thieves, 1991; Much Ado About Nothing, 1993; Hamlet, 1997; Star Wars—The Phantom Menace, 1998; Walt Disney's Tarzan, 1999; Mumbo Jumbo, 2000; *television includes:* series: Fancy Smith, in Z Cars, 1962–78; The Little World of Don Camillo, 1980; The Black Adder, 1983; My Family and Other Animals, 1987; serials: The Three Musketeers, 1966; I, Claudius, 1976; Return to Treasure Island, 1986; War and Remembrance, 1988; Catherine the Great, 1995; Tom Jones, 1997. Has made expeditions to Mt Everest, 1991 (film, Gallahad of Everest, won Canadian Grand Prix, Banff Fest., 1992), 1993, 1996, N Pole, and Venezuela. *Publications:* The Turquoise Mountain, 1991; The Dynamite Kid, 1992; Nothing's Impossible, 1994; Quest for the Lost World, 1999. *Address:* c/o AIM, Nederlander House, 7 Great Russell Street, WC1B 3NH.

BLESSLEY, Kenneth Harry, CBE 1974 (MBE 1945); ED; Valuer and Estates Surveyor, Greater London Council, 1964–77; *b* 28 Feb. 1914; *s* of Victor Henry le Blond Blessley and Ellen Mary Blessley; *m* 1946, Gwendeline MacRae; two *s*. *Educ:* Haberdashers' Aske's Hampstead Sch.; St Catharine's Coll., Cambridge (MA); Coll. of Estate Management. FRICS. Private practice, West End and London suburbs. Served War of 1939–45, TA Royal Engrs, Persia, Middle East, Sicily, Italy (despatches 1942 and 1944). Sen. Property Adviser, Public Trustee, 1946–50; Dep. County Valuer, Mddx CC, 1950–53; County Valuer, Mddx CC, 1953–65. Mem. Urban Motorways Cttee, 1970–72; Chm., Covent Garden Officers' Steering Gp, 1970–77; Chm., Thamesmead Officers' Steering Gp, 1971–76; Pres., Assoc. of Local Authority Valuers and Estate Surveyors, 1962 and 1972; Mem. Gen. Council, RICS, 1972–78, Pres., Gen. Practice Div., 1976–77. Pres., Old Haberdashers' Assoc., 1963 (Pres. RFC, 1966–68); Vice-Pres., Cambridge Univ. Land Soc., 1985–86. *Publications:* numerous articles and papers on compensation, property valuation and development. *Recreations:* music, drama, sport, motoring. *Address:* 99 Maplehurst Road, Summersdale, Chichester, West Sussex PO19 4RP. *T:* (01243) 528188.

BLETHYN, Brenda Anne; actress; *b* 20 Feb. 1946; *d* of William Charles Bottle and Louisa Kathleen Bottle; partner, 1977, Michael Mayhew. *Educ:* St Augustine's RC Sch.,

Ramsgate; Thanet Tech. Coll., Ramsgate; Guildford Sch. of Acting. *Theatre* includes: work with NT, 1975–90, incl. Mysteries, 1979, Double Dealer, 1982, Dalliance, 1987, Beaux' Stratagem, 1989, Bedroom Farce; A Doll's House, 1987, Born Yesterday, 1988, An Ideal Husband, 1992, Royal Exchange, Manchester; Steaming, Comedy, 1981; Benefactors, Vaudeville, 1984; Wildest Dreams, RSC, 1993; The Bed Before Yesterday, Almeida, 1994; Habeas Corpus, Donmar Warehouse, 1996; Absent Friends, NY; *films:* The Witches; A River Runs Through It, 1992; Secrets and Lies, 1996; Remember Me, 1996; Music From Another Room, 1997; Girls' Night, In the Winter Dark, 1998; Little Voice, Daddy and Them, 1999; Night Train, Saving Grace, 2000; Pumpkin, Yellow Bird, Anne Frank–The Whole Story, 2001; *television* includes: Henry VI Part I, 1981; King Lear, 1983; Chance in a Million (3 series), 1983–85; The Labours of Erica, 1987; The Bullion Boys, 1993; The Buddah of Suburbia, 1993; Sleeping with Mickey, 1993; Outside Edge (3 series), 1994–96; First Signs of Madness (Mona), 1996. Mem., Poetry Soc., 1976–. Hon. DLitt Kent. Numerous awards incl. Best Actress Awards for Secrets and Lies: Cannes Film Fest., 1996; Boston Film Critics, 1997; LA Film Critics, 1997; Golden Globe, 1997; London Film Critics, 1997; BAFTA, 1997. *Recreations:* reading, swimming, cryptic crosswords. *Address:* c/o ICM, 76 Oxford Street, W1N 0AX. *T:* (020) 7636 6565.

BLEWETT, Hon. Neal, AC 1995; DPhil; FRHistS; FASSA; High Commissioner for Australia in the United Kingdom, 1994–98; *b* 24 Oct. 1933; *s* of James and Phyllis Blewett; *m* 1962, Jill Myford (*d* 1988); one *s* one *d*. *Educ:* Launceston High Sch.; Univ. of Tasmania (Dip Ed, MA); Jesus Coll., Oxford (MA; Hon. Fellow, 1998); St Antony's Coll., Oxford (DPhil). FRHistS 1975. Oxford University: Sen. Schol., St Antony's Coll., 1959–61; Lectr, St Edmund Hall, 1961–63; Lectr in Politics, Univ. of Adelaide, 1964–69; Flinders University, S Australia: Reader, 1970–74; Prof., Dept of Pol Theory and Instns, 1974–77. MP (Lab) Bonython, SA, 1977–94; Mem., Jt Hse Cttee on Foreign Affairs and Defence, 1977–80; Deleg. to Australian Constitutional Convention, 1978; Opposition Spokesman on health and Tasmanian affairs, 1980–83; Minister for: Health, 1983–87; Community Services and Health, 1987–90; Trade and Overseas Develt, 1990–91; Social Security, 1991–93. Vis. Prof., Faculty of Medicine, Univ. of Sydney, 1998–. Member Council: Univ. of Adelaide, 1972–74; Torrens Coll. of Advanced Educn, 1972–78. Exec. Bd Mem., WHO, 1995–98. Nat. Pres., Australian Inst. of Internat. Affairs, 1998–. Hon. LLD Tasmania; Hon. DLitt Hull. *Publications:* The Peers, the Parties and the People, 1972; (jtly) Playford to Dunstan: the politics of transition, 1971; A Cabinet Diary, 1999. *Recreations:* bush-walking, reading, cinema. *Address:* 32 Fitzroy Street, Leura, NSW 2780, Australia.

BLEWITT, Major Sir Shane (Gabriel Basil), GCVO 1996 (KCVO 1989; CVO 1987; LVO 1981); Keeper of the Privy Purse and Treasurer to the Queen, 1988–96; an Extra Equerry to the Queen, since 1996; *b* 25 March 1935; *s* of late Col Basil Blewitt; *m* 1969, Julia Morrogh-Bernard, *widow* of Major John Morrogh-Bernard, Irish Guards, and *d* of late Mr Robert Calvert; one *s* one *d* (and one step *s* one step *d*). *Educ:* Ampleforth Coll.; Christ Church, Oxford (MA Hons Mod. Languages). Served Irish Guards, 1956–74; Antony Gibbs and Sons, 1974; Asst Keeper, 1975–85, Dep. Keeper, 1985–88, of the Privy Purse; Receiver-General, Duchy of Lancaster, 1988–96. Member: Council, King Edward VII Hosp. for Officers, 1988–; Instn, King Edward VII Hosp., Midhurst, 1996–; Gen. Council, King's Hosp. Fund, 1988–. *Recreations:* gardening, shooting. *Club:* White's.

BLIGH, family name of **Earl of Darnley**.

BLIN-STOYLE, Prof. Roger John, FRS 1976; Professor of Theoretical Physics, University of Sussex, 1962–90, now Emeritus; *b* 24 Dec. 1924; *s* of Cuthbert Basil St John Blin-Stoyle and Ada Mary (*née* Nash); *m* 1949, Audrey Elizabeth Balmford; one *s* one *d*. *Educ:* Alderman Newton's Boys' Sch., Leicester; Wadham Coll., Oxford (Scholar). MA, DPhil Oxon; FInstP; ARCM. Served Royal Signals, 1943–46 (Lieut). Pressed Steel Co. Res. Fellow, Oxford Univ., 1951–53; Lectr in Math. Physics, Birmingham Univ., 1953–54; Sen. Res. Officer in Theoret. Physics, Oxford Univ., 1952–62; Fellow and Lectr in Physics, Wadham Coll., Oxford, 1956–62, Hon. Fellow, 1987; Vis. Associate Prof. of Physics, MIT, 1959–60; Vis. Prof. of Physics, Univ. of Calif, La Jolla, 1960; Sussex University: Dean, Sch. of Math. and Phys. Sciences, 1962–68; Pro-Vice-Chancellor, 1965–67; Dep. Vice-Chancellor, 1970–72; Pro-Vice-Chancellor (Science), 1977–79. Chm., School Curriculum Develt Cttee, 1983–88. Member: Royal Greenwich Observatory Cttee, 1966–70; Nuclear Physics Bd, SRC, later SERC, 1967–70, 1982–84; Mem. Council, 1982–83, Chm. Educn Cttee, 1992–94, Royal Soc.; President: Inst. of Physics, 1990–92; Assoc. for Sci. Educn, 1993–94. Editor: Reports on Progress in Physics, 1977–82; Student Physics Series, 1983–87. Hon. DSc Sussex, 1990. Rutherford Medal and Prize, IPPS, 1976. Silver Jubilee Medal, 1977. *Publications:* Theories of Nuclear Moments, 1957; Fundamental Interactions and the Nucleus, 1973; Nuclear and Particle Physics, 1991; Eureka!, 1997; papers on nuclear and elementary particle physics in scientific jls. *Recreation:* making music. *Address:* 14 Hill Road, Lewes, E Sussex BN7 1DB. *T:* (01273) 473640.

BLISHEN, Anthony Owen, OBE 1968; HM Diplomatic Service, retired; Counsellor, Foreign and Commonwealth Office, 1981–92; *b* 16 April 1932; *s* of Henry Charles Adolphus Blishen, MBE and Joan Cecile Blishen (*née* Blakeney); *m* 1st, 1963, Sarah Anne Joscelyne (marr. diss. 1994); three *s* one *d*; 2nd, 1994, Elizabeth Appleyard (*née* West). *Educ:* Clayesmore Sch., Dorset; SOAS, London Univ. Commnd Royal Hampshire Regt, 1951; Lt 1st Bn: BAOR, 1953; Malaya, 1953–55; Captain, GSO3 HQ 18 Inf. Bde, Malaya, 1955–56; attached HQ Land Forces, Hong Kong (language trng), 1957–59; GSO3 HQ Far East Land Forces, Singapore, 1960–62; FO, 1963–65; First Sec. and Consul, Peking, 1965–67; First Sec., FCO, 1968–70; Chargé d'Affaires (ad interim), Ulan Bator, 1970; Trade Comr (China trade), Hong Kong, 1971–73; First Sec., FCO, 1973–77; First Sec., 1977–78, Counsellor, 1978–81, Tokyo. *Recreations:* Renaissance music (founded Aragon Consort, 1990), oriental languages. *Address:* 331 Petersham Road, Ham, Richmond, Surrey TW10 7DB.

BLISS, Prof. Christopher John Emile, PhD; FBA 1988; Nuffield Professor of International Economics, Oxford University, since 1992, and Fellow of Nuffield College, Oxford, since 1977; *b* 17 Feb. 1940; *s* of John Llewlyn Bliss and Patricia Paula (*née* Dubern); *m* 1983, Ghada (*née* Saqf El Hait); one *s*, and one *s* two *d* by previous marr. *Educ:* Finchley Catholic Grammar Sch.; King's Coll., Cambridge (BA 1962, MA 1964, PhD 1966). Fellow of Christ's Coll., Cambridge, 1965–71; Asst Lectr, 1965–67, and Lectr, 1967–71, Cambridge Univ.; Prof. of Econs, Univ. of Essex, 1971–77; Nuffield Reader in Internat. Econs, Oxford Univ., 1977–92. Dir, General Funds Investment Trust Ltd, 1980–87. Fellow, Econometric Soc., 1978–96. Editor or Asst Editor, Rev. of Econ. Studies, 1967–71; Managing Editor: Oxford Economic Papers, 1989–96; Economic Jl, 1996–. *Publications:* Capital Theory and the Distribution of Income, 1975; (with N. H. Stern) Palanpur: the economy of an Indian village, 1982; Economic Theory and Policy for Trading Blocks, 1994; papers and reviews in learned jls. *Recreation:* music. *Address:* Nuffield College, Oxford OX1 1NF. *T:* (01865) 278573.

BLISS, Dr Timothy Vivian Pelham, FRS 1994; Head, Division of Neurophysiology, National Institute for Medical Research, since 1988; *b* 27 July 1940; *s* of Pelham Marryat Bliss and Elizabeth Cotton Bliss (*née* Sproule); *m* 1st, 1975, Virginia Catherine Morton-Evans (*née* O'Rorke); one step *s* two step *d*; one *d* by Katherine Sarah Clough; 2nd, 1994, Isabel Frances Vasseur (*née* Wardrop); two step *s*. *Educ:* Dean Close Sch.; McGill Univ. (BSc 1963; PhD 1967). Mem., scientific staff, MRC, 1967–. Vis. Prof., Dept of Physiology, UCL, 1993–. Founder FMedSci 1998. Bristol Myers Squibb Award for Neuroscience, 1991; Feldberg Prize, 1994. *Publications:* numerous papers on the neural basis of memory and other aspects of the neurophysiology of the brain. *Recreations:* naval history, wine. *Address:* 15 Highgate West Hill, N6 6NP. *T:* (020) 8341 1215; *e-mail:* tbhss@nimr.mrc.ac.uk. *Club:* Academy.

BLIX, Hans, PhD, LLD; Executive Chairman, UN Monitoring, Verification and Inspection Commission for Iraq, since 2000; *b* 28 June 1928; *s* of Gunnar Blix and Hertha Blix (*née* Wiberg); *m* 1962, Eva Margareta Kettis; two *s*. *Educ:* Univ. of Uppsala; Columbia Univ.; Univ. of Cambridge (PhD); Stockholm Univ. (LLD). Associate Prof. in International Law, 1960; Ministry of Foreign Affairs, Stockholm: Legal Adviser, 1963–76; Under-Secretary of State, in charge of internat. development co-operation, 1976; Minister for Foreign Affairs, 1978; Under-Secretary of State, in charge of internat. development co-operation, 1979. Dir Gen., IAEA, 1981–97, now Dir Gen. Emeritus. Member: Sweden's delegn to UN General Assembly, 1961–81; Swedish delegn to Conference on Disarmament in Geneva, 1962–78. Hon. doctorates: Moscow State Univ., 1987; Bucharest Univ., 1994; Univ. of Managua, 1996. Foratom Award, 1994. *Publications:* Treaty Making Power, 1959; Statsmyndigheternas Internationella Förbindelser, 1964; Sovereignty, Aggression and Neutrality, 1970; The Treaty-Maker's Handbook, 1974. *Recreations:* ski-ing, hiking. *Address:* UNMOVIC, Room S-3120H, United Nations, New York, NY 10017, USA.

BLIZZARD, Robert John; MP (Lab) Waveney, since 1997; *b* 31 May 1950; *s* of late Arthur Blizzard and Joan Blizzard; *m* 1978, Lyn Chance; one *s* one *d*. *Educ:* Univ. of Birmingham (BA Hons 1971). Head of English: Crayford Sch., Bexley, 1976–86; Lynn Grove High Sch., Gorleston, 1986–97. Mem. (Lab), Waveney DC, 1987–97 (Leader, 1991–97). PPS to Minister of State, MAFF, 1999–2001, to Minister of State for Work, DWP, 2001–. Mem., Envmtl Audit Select Cttee, 1997–99; Chairman: British–Brazilian All Pty Gp, 1997–; British Offshore Oil and Gas Industry All Pty Gp, 1999–; Vice Chm., Envmt, Transport and the Regions PLP Cttee, 1997–. *Recreations:* walking, ski-ing, travel, listening to jazz. *Address:* House of Commons, SW1A 0AA. *T:* (020) 7219 3000. *Clubs:* Waveney Labour (Lowestoft); Royal Norfolk and Suffolk Yacht (Lowestoft).

BLOBEL, Prof. Günter, MD, PhD; John D. Rockefeller Jr Professor, since 1992, and Head of Laboratory of Cell Biology, Rockefeller University, New York; *b* Waltersdorf, Germany (now Poland), 21 May 1936; US citizen; *m* Laura Maioglio. *Educ:* Univ. of Tübingen (MD 1960); Univ. of Wisconsin (PhD 1967). Intern, German hosps, 1960–62; Laboratory of Cell Biology, Rockefeller University, New York: Fellow, 1967–69; Asst Prof., 1969–73; Associate Prof., 1973–76; Prof., 1976–92. Investigator, Howard Hughes Medical Inst., 1986–. Member: US Nat. Acad. of Scis, 1983; Amer. Acad. of Arts and Scis. Founder and Pres. Bd of Dirs, Friends of Dresden Inc. Nobel Prize for Physiology or Medicine, 1999. *Publications:* contribs to books and jls. *Address:* Laboratory of Cell Biology, Rockefeller University, 1230 York Avenue, New York, NY 10021, USA; Apt 10D, 1100 Park Avenue, New York, NY 10128, USA.

BLOCH, Prof. Maurice Emile Félix, PhD; FBA 1990, Professor of Anthropology, University of London at London School of Economics, since 1984; *b* 21 Oct. 1939; *s* of late Pierre Bloch and of Claude Kennedy; step *s* of John Stodart Kennedy, FRS; *m* 1963, Jean Helen Medlicott; one *s* one *d*. *Educ:* Lycée Carnot, Paris; Perse Sch., Cambridge; LSE (BA 1962); Fitzwilliam Coll., Cambridge (PhD 1968). Asst Lectr, Univ. of Wales, Swansea, 1968; Lectr, LSE, 1969; Reader, London Univ., 1977. Corresp. Mem., Académie Malgache, Madagascar, 1965. *Publications:* Placing the Dead, 1971; Marxism and Anthropology, 1983; From Blessing to Violence, 1986; Ritual, History and Power, 1989; Prey into Hunter, 1992; How We Think They Think, 1998. *Recreation:* book binding. *Address:* Department of Anthropology, London School of Economics, Houghton Street, WC2A 2AE. *T:* (020) 7405 7686.

BLOCH, Dame Merle Florence; *see* Park, Dame Merle F.

BLOCH, Michael Gordon; QC 1998; *b* 18 Oct. 1951; *s* of John and Thelma Bloch; *m* Caroline Williams (marr. diss.); two *d*; *m* 1998, Lady Camilla Bingham, *yr d* of 7th Earl of Lucan and of Veronica Mary (*née* Duncan). *Educ:* Bedales Sch.; Corpus Christi Coll., Cambridge (MA); UEA (MPhil). Called to the Bar, Lincoln's Inn, 1979; in practice as a barrister, 1979–. Trustee, Childline. Gov., Bedales Sch. *Recreations:* squash, cinema. *Address:* Wilberforce Chambers, 8 New Square, Lincoln's Inn, WC2A 3QP. *Club:* Royal Automobile.

BLOCH, Selwyn Irving; QC 2000; *b* 23 Feb. 1952; *s* of Rev. Cecil Maurice Bloch and Esther Bloch; *m* 1983, Brenda Igra; three *d*. *Educ:* Potchefstroom Boys' High Sch.; Witwatersrand Univ. (BA); Stellenbosch Univ. (LLB). Attorney, S Africa, 1977–; called to the Bar, Middle Temple, 1982; in practice at the Bar, 1983–. *Publication:* (jtly) Employment Covenants and Confidential Information, 1993, 2nd edn 1999. *Recreations:* listening to music, walking, reading, theatre. *Address:* Littleton Chambers, 3 King's Bench Walk North, EC4Y 7HR. *T:* (020) 7797 8699.

BLOCK, David Greenberg, AC 1988 (AO 1983); *b* 21 March 1936; *s* of Emanuel Block and Hannah Greenberg; *m* 1959, Naomi Denfield; one *s* three *d*. *Educ:* King Edward VII Sch., Johannesburg; Univ. of Witwatersrand (BJuris cum laude). Joined Schroder-Darling & Co., 1964, Dir, 1967–72; Chairman: David Block & Associates, 1972–81; Trinity Properties, 1984–90; George Ward Group, 1986–89; Dep. Chm., Concrete Constructions, 1990; Director: CSR, 1977–88; Kalamazoo Holdings, 1986–94; Dep. Chm., Pacific Magazines & Publishing, 1991–95; Dir, Lloyds Bank NZA, Chm., Lloyds Internat., Dir, Lloyds Merchant Bank (UK) and Adviser, Lloyds Merchant Bank Holdings, 1981–86; Consultant, Coudert Brothers, 1986–91; Adviser: Coopers & Lybrand, 1986–93; S. G. Warburg Group, 1987–95. Consultant: to Prime Minister and Cabinet, 1986–89; to govts, cos and instns, 1986–96; to Premier's Dept, NSW, 1987–88; Mem., Cttee of Enquiry into inflation and taxation, 1975; Chm., Efficiency Scrutiny Unit and Admin. Reform Unit, 1986–88. Comr, Aust. Film Commn, 1978–81; Chm., Sydney Opera House Trust, 1981–89; Trustee, Japanese Friends of Sydney Opera House Foundn, 1992–96; Councillor: Asia-Australian Inst., 1991–96; Nat. Heart Foundn, 1994–96; Gov., Aust. Nat. Gall. Foundn, 1992–96. Dir, Univ. of NSW Foundn, 1989–96. Fellow, Senate of Univ. of Sydney, 1983–87. FAICD; FAIM; FSIA. Hon. LLD New South Wales, 1992. *Recreations:* swimming, squash, music, theatre. *Address:* 30 Clarke Street, Vaucluse, NSW 2030, Australia. *T:* (2) 93376211. *Club:* University (Sydney).

BLOEMBERGEN, Prof. Nicolaas; Gerhard Gade University Professor, Harvard University, 1980–90, now Emeritus; *b* 11 March 1920; *m* 1950, Huberta Deliana Brink; one *s* two *d*. *Educ:* Univ. of Utrecht (BA, MA); Univ. of Leiden (PhD). Research Associate, Leiden, 1947–48; Harvard University: Associate Prof., 1951; Gordon McKay Prof. of Applied Physics, 1957; Rumford Prof. of Physics, 1974. Hon. DSc: Laval Univ.,

1987; Connecticut Univ., 1988; Univ. of Hartford, 1990; Univ. of Massachusetts at Lowell, 1994; Moscow State Univ., 1997; N Carolina State Univ., 1998. Stuart Ballantine Medal, Franklin Inst., 1961; Nat. Medal of Science, 1974; Lorentz Medal, Royal Dutch Acad. of Science, 1978; Alexander von Humboldt Senior US Scientist Award, Munich, 1980; (jtly) Nobel Prize in Physics, 1981; IEEE Medal of Honor, 1983; Dirac Medal, Univ. of NSW, 1983. Commander, Order of Orange Nassau (Netherlands), 1983. *Publications:* Nuclear Magnetic Relaxation, 1948 (New York 1961); Nonlinear Optics, 1965, reprinted 1996; Encounters in Magnetic Resonance, 1996; Encounters in Nonlinear Optics, 1996; over 300 papers in scientific jls. *Address:* Optical Sciences Center, University of Arizona, Tuscon, AZ 85721, USA. *T:* (520) 6263479.

BLOEMFONTEIN, Bishop of, since 1997; **Rt Rev. (Elistan) Patrick Glover;** *b* 1 Feb. 1944; *s* of Rev. Chirho Glover and Sylvia Glover; *m* 1971, Kirsteen Marjorie Bain; two *s* two *d*. *Educ:* King Edward VII High Sch., Johannesburg; Rhodes Univ. (BA); Keble Coll., Oxford (BA Theol 1968; MA 1978); St Paul's Theol Coll., Grahamstown. Deacon 1969, priest 1970; Curate: St Peter's Church, Krugersdorp, 1969–71; St Martin's-in-Veld, Johannesburg, 1971–74; Rector: St Catherine's, Johannesburg, 1975–83; St George's, Johannesburg, 1983–86; Dean of Bloemfontein, 1987–94; Suffragan Bishop of Bloemfontein, 1994–97. *Recreations:* squash, scuba diving, jogging. *Address:* Bishop's House, 16 York Road, Waverley, Bloemfontein 9300, OFS, S Africa. *T:* (office) (51) 4476053, (home) (51) 4364351. *Club:* Bloemfontein.

BLOFELD, Sir John (Christopher Calthorpe), Kt 1991; DL; a Judge of the High Court of Justice, Queen's Bench Division, 1990–2001; *b* 11 July 1932; *s* of late T. R. C. Blofeld, CBE; *m* 1961, Judith Anne, *er d* of Alan Mohun and Mrs James Mitchell; two *s* one *d*. *Educ:* Eton; King's Coll., Cambridge. Called to Bar, Lincoln's Inn, 1956, Bencher, 1990; QC 1975; a Recorder of the Crown Court, 1975–82; a Circuit Judge, 1982–90; Presiding Judge, SE Circuit, 1993–96. Inspector, Dept of Trade, 1979–81. Chancellor: Dio. St Edmundsbury and Ipswich, 1973; Dio. of Norwich, 1998–. DL Norfolk, 1991. *Recreations:* cricket, gardening. *Club:* Boodle's.

BLOIS, Sir Charles (Nicholas Gervase), 11th Bt, *cr* 1686; farming since 1965; *b* 25 Dec. 1939; *s* of Sir Gervase Ralph Edmund Blois, 10th Bt and Mrs Audrey Winifred Blois (*née* Johnson) (*d* 1997); *S* father, 1968; *m* 1967, Celia Helen Mary Pritchett; one *s* one *d*. *Educ:* Harrow; Trinity Coll., Dublin; Royal Agricultural Coll., Cirencester. Australia, 1963–65. FRGS 1992. *Recreations:* yachting, shooting, travel. *Heir: s* Andrew Charles David Blois, *b* 7 Feb. 1971. *Address:* Red House, Westleton, Saxmundham, Suffolk IP17 3EQ. *T:* (01728) 648200. *Clubs:* Cruising Association; Ocean Cruising.

BLOKH, Alexandre, PhD, (pen-name **Jean Blot**); writer, since 1956; Vice President, PEN Club, since 1998 (International Secretary, 1982–98); *b* Moscow, 31 March 1923; *s* of Arnold Blokh, man of letters, and Anne (*née* Berlinrote); *m* 1956, Nadia Ermolaiev. *Educ:* Bromsgrove Public Sch., Worcester; Univ. of Paris (PhD Law, PhD Letters). International Civil Servant, United Nations, 1947–62: New York, until 1956; Geneva, 1958–62; Director, Arts and Letters, UNESCO, Paris, 1962–81. Critic, arts and letters, in reviews: Arche, Preuves, NRF. Prix des Critiques, 1972; Prix Valéry Larbaud, 1977; Prix Cazes, 1982; Grand Prix de la Critique, 1986; Prix International de la Paix, 1990. Officier, Ordre des Arts et des Lettres, 1997. *Publications: novels:* Le Soleil de Cavouri, 1956; Les Enfants de New York, 1959; Obscur Ennemi, 1961; Les Illusions Nocturnes, 1964; La Jeune Géante, 1969; La Difficulté d'aimer, 1971; Les Cosmopolites, 1976; Gris du Ciel, 1981; Tout l'été, 1985; Sainte Imposture, 1988; Le Juif Margolin, 1998; *essays:* Marguerite Yourcenar; Ossip Mandelstam; Là où tu iras; Sporade; Ivan Gontcharov; La Montagne Sainte; Albert Cohen; Si loin de Dieu et autres voyages; Bloomsbury; Retour en Asie; Vladimir Nabokov; Moïse, notre contemporain. *Address:* 34 Square Montsouris, 75014 Paris. *T:* (1) 45893416.

BLOM-COOPER, Sir Louis (Jacques), Kt 1992; QC 1970; Independent Commissioner for the Holding Centres, Northern Ireland, 1993–2000; a Judge of the Courts of Appeal, Jersey and Guernsey, 1989–96; *b* 27 March 1926; *s* of Alfred Blom-Cooper and Ella Flesseman, Rotterdam; *m* 1952 (marr. diss. 1970); two *s* one *d*; *m* 1970, Jane Elizabeth, *e d* of Maurice and Helen Smither, Woodbridge, Suffolk; one *s* two *d*. *Educ:* Port Regis Prep. Sch.; Seaford Coll.; King's Coll., London (FKC 1994); Municipal Univ. of Amsterdam; Fitzwilliam Coll., Cambridge. LLB London, 1952; Dr Juris Amsterdam, 1954. HM Army, 1944–47: Capt., E Yorks Regt. Called to Bar, Middle Temple, 1952; Bencher, 1978. Mem., Home Secretary's Adv. Council on the Penal System, 1966–78. Chairman: Panel of Inquiry into circumstances surrounding the death of Jasmine Beckford, 1985; Cttee of Inquiry into complaints about Ashworth Hosp., 1991–92; Commissioner of Inquiry: into allegations of arson and political corruption in the Turks and Caicos Is, 1986 (report published, 1986); into the N Creek Develt Project, Turks and Caicos Is, 1986–87. Chairman: Indep. Cttee for the Supervision of Standards of Telephone Information Services, 1986–93; Mental Health Act Commn, 1987–94; Commn on the future of Occupational Therapy, 1988–89; Press Council, 1989–90; Review of Mental Health Services in S Devon, 1994; Georgina Robinson Inquiry Cttee, 1994; Jason Mitchell Inquiry Panel, 1996. Vice-Pres., Howard League for Penal Reform, 1984– (Chm., 1973–84). Chm., BBC London Local Radio Adv. Council, 1970–73. Jt Dir, Legal Res. Unit, Bedford Coll., Univ. of London, 1967–82; Vis. Prof., QMC, London Univ., 1983–88. Trustee, Scott Trust (The Guardian Newspaper), 1982–88. Joint Editor, Common Market Law Reports. JP Inner London, 1966–79 (transf. City of London, 1969). FRSA 1984. Hon. DLitt: Loughborough, 1991; Ulster, 1994; UEA, 1998. *Publications:* Bankruptcy in Private International Law, 1954; The Law as Literature, 1962; The A6 Murder (A Semblance of Truth), 1963; (with T. P. Morris) A Calendar of Murder, 1964; Language of the Law, 1965; (with O. R. McGregor and Colin Gibson) Separated Spouses, 1970; (with G. Drewry) Final Appeal: a study of the House of Lords in its judicial capacity, 1972; (ed) Progress in Penal Reform, 1975; (ed with G. Drewry) Law and Morality, 1976; The Birmingham Six and Other Cases, 1997; contrib. to Modern Law Review, Criminal Law Review, Public Law, Brit. Jl of Criminology, Brit. Jl of Sociology. *Recreations:* watching and reporting on Association football, reading, music, writing, broadcasting. *Address:* 1 Southgate Road, N1 3JP. *T:* (020) 7704 1514; Glebe House, Montgomery, Powys SY15 6QA. *T:* (01686) 668458, 668079. *Clubs:* Athenæum, MCC.

BLOMEFIELD, Sir (Thomas) Charles (Peregrine), 6th Bt *cr* 1807; Fine Art Consultant; *b* 24 July 1948; *s* of Sir Thomas Edward Peregrine Blomefield, 5th Bt, and of Ginette, Lady Blomefield; *S* father, 1984; *m* 1975, Georgina Geraldine, *d* of late Commander C. E. Over, Lugger End, Portscatho, Cornwall; one *s* two *d*. *Educ:* Wellington Coll., Berks; Mansfield Coll., Oxford. Christie's, 1970–75; Wildenstein and Co., 1975–76; Director, Lidchi Art Gallery, Johannesburg, 1976–78; Man. Director, Charles Blomefield and Co., 1980–. *Recreations:* travel, listening to music. *Heir: s* Thomas William Peregrine Blomefield, *b* 16 July 1983. *Address:* Attlepin Farm, Chipping Campden, Glos GL55 6PP.

BLOMQVIST, Leif; Hon. GCVO 1995; Knight Commander, Order of the Lion of Finland, 1995; Knight, 1st Class, Order of White Rose of Finland, 1975; Ambassador of Finland: to Belgium, since 1996; to NATO, since 1997; *b* 20 March 1937; *s* of Viktor Hardy Blomqvist and Harriet Ellinor Knowles; *m* 1965, Marianne Sand, PhD. *Educ:* Univ. of Helsinki (LLM). Entered Finnish diplomatic service, 1965; Attaché, Addis Ababa, 1967–70; 2nd Sec., Tel Aviv, 1970–71; Dept of External Econ. Relns, Foreign Ministry, 1971–73; 1st Sec., Finnish Mission to CSCE, Geneva, 1973–75; Counsellor, Finnish Permanent Mission, Geneva, 1975–77; Vice-Chm., Finnish Delegn to CSCE follow-up meeting, Belgrade, 1977–78; Counsellor, Min. for Foreign Affairs, 1978–80; Dir and Dep. Dir Gen., External Econ. Relations, 1980–85; Ambassador to European Communities, Brussels, 1985–90; Ambassador, Min. for Foreign Affairs, 1990–91; Ambassador to UK, 1991–96. Comdr, Order of North Star (Sweden); Grosses Verdienstkreutz (Germany); Kt Comdr, Order of White Falcon (Iceland). *Recreations:* oriental rugs, English furniture. *Address:* Embassy of Finland, avenue des Arts 58, 1000 Brussels, Belgium.

BLONDEL, Prof. Jean Fernand Pierre; Professor of Political Science, European University Institute, Florence, 1985–94; *b* Toulon, France, 26 Oct. 1929; *s* of Fernand Blondel and Marie Blondel (*née* Santelli); *m* 1st, 1954, Michèle (*née* Hadet) (marr. diss. 1979); two *d*; 2nd, 1982, Mrs Theresa Martineau. *Educ:* Collège Saint Louis de Gonzague and Lycée Henri IV, Paris; Institut d'Etudes Politiques and Faculté de Droit, Paris; St Antony's Coll., Oxford. Asst Lectr, then Lectr in Govt, Univ. of Keele, 1958–63; Vis. ACLS Fellow, Yale Univ., 1963–64; Prof. of Government, 1964–84, and Dean, Sch. of Comparative Studies, 1967–69, Univ. of Essex. Visiting Professor: Carleton Univ., Canada, 1969–70; Univ. of Siena, 1996–; Vis. Schol., Russell Sage Foundn, NY, 1984–85. Exec. Dir, European Consortium for Political Res., 1970–79. Member: Royal Swedish Acad. of Scis, 1990; Academia Europaea, 1993. Hon. DLitt Salford, 1990; Dr *hc*: Essex, 1992; Univ. Catholique de Louvain, 1992; Univ. of Turku, 1995. *Publications:* Voters, Parties and Leaders, 1963; (jtly) Constituency Politics, 1964; (jtly) Public Administration in France, 1965; An Introduction to Comparative Government, 1969; (jtly) Workbook for Comparative Government, 1972; Comparing Political Systems, 1972; Comparative Legislatures, 1973; The Government of France, 1974; Thinking Politically, 1976; Political Parties, 1978; World Leaders, 1980; The Discipline of Politics, 1981; The Organisation of Governments, 1982; (jtly) Comparative Politics, 1984; Government Ministers in the Contemporary World, 1985; Political Leadership, 1987; (ed jtly) Western European Cabinets, 1988; Comparative Government, 1990; (ed jtly) The Profession of Cabinet Minister in Western Europe, 1991; (ed jtly) Governing Together, 1993; (ed jtly) Party and Government, 1996; (jtly) People and Parliament in the European Union, 1998; (ed jtly) Democracy, Governance and Economic Performance, 1999; (ed jtly) The Nature of Party Government, 2000; articles in: Political Studies, Parliamentary Affairs, Public Administration, Revue Française de Science Politique, European Jl of Political Research, etc. *Recreation:* holidays in Provence. *Address:* 15 Marloes Road, W8 6LQ. *T:* (020) 7370 6008; 17 Via Santo Spirito, 50125 Florence, Italy.

BLOOD, Baroness *cr* 1999 (Life Peer), of Blackwatertown in the county of Armagh; **May Blood,** MBE 1995; Information Officer, Great Shankhill Partnership Co. Ltd, since 1994; Founding Member, Northern Ireland Women's Coalition, since 1996; *b* 26 May 1938; *d* of William and Mary Blood. *Educ:* Donegall Road Primary Sch.; Linfield Secondary Sch. Cutter/Supervisor, Blackstaff Linen Mill Co. Ltd, 1952–90; Manager, Cairn Martin Wood Products, 1991–94. DUniv Ulster, 1998; Hon. Dr QUB, 2000. *Recreations:* home decorating, reading, gardening. *Address:* 7 Black Mountain Place, Belfast BT13 3TT. *T:* (028) 9032 6514.

BLOOD, Bindon, (Peter); Director, Western Marketing Consultants Ltd, since 1987; Senior Industrialist and Enterprise Counsellor for Department of Trade and Industry, 1986–94; *b* 24 Sept. 1920; *o s* of Brig. William Edmunds Robarts Blood, CBE, MC, Croix de Guerre, and Eva Gwendoline (*née* Harrison); *m* 1953, Elizabeth Ann, *d* of Harold Drummond Hillier, MC; one *s* one *d*. *Educ:* Imperial Service Coll., Windsor. Family public works and civil engineering business, 1938–41; served Royal Engineers, 1941–46 (despatches 1944); Engineering Div., Forestry Commn, 1946–48; regular commn, RE, 1948; Second i/c, RE Officer Training Unit, 1948–51; Staff Coll., Camberley, 1951; Sec., Army Bd, NATO Mil. Agency for Standardisation, 1952–53; invalided from service, 1953; Intelligence Co-ordination Staff, FO, 1953–58; Founder and formerly Managing Director: Isora Integrated Ceilings Ltd; Clean Room Construction Ltd; Mitchel and King (Sales) Ltd; Dep. Chm. and Group Marketing Dir, King Group. Institute of Marketing: Dir of Marketing Services, 1971; Dir-Gen., 1972–84. Chm., Industrial Market Research Ltd, 1984–87. Gov., Berks Coll. of Art and Design, 1975–89 (Chm. of Govs, 1981–86). FRSA, FInstM. *Recreations:* photography, furniture restoration, travel, music, local community activities. *Address:* 8 Woodhurst South, Ray Mead Road, Maidenhead, Berks SL6 8NZ. *T:* and *Fax:* (01628) 626600.

BLOOM, André Borisovich; *see* Anthony, Metropolitan.

BLOOM, Anthony Herbert; Director, RIT Capital Partners plc, since 1988; *b* 15 Feb. 1939; *s* of Joseph Bloom and Margaret Roslyn Bloom; *m* 1973, Gisela von Mellenthin; two *s* two *d*. *Educ:* Univ. of Witwatersrand (BCom, LLB); Harvard Law Sch. (LLM); Stanford Graduate Sch. of Business (Sloan Fellow, 1970). Hayman Godfrey and Sanderson, S Africa, 1960–64; joined Premier Gp Ltd, S Africa, 1966, Dir, 1969; Dep. Chm., 1975–79, Chm., 1979–88; Director: Barclays Nat. Bank, later First Nat. Bank of Southern Africa Ltd, 1980–88; Liberty Life Assoc., 1982–88; South African Breweries Ltd, 1983–89; CNA Gallo Ltd, 1983–88; Dir and Dep. Chm., Sketchley, 1990–; Chm., CINE-UK Ltd, 1995–. Dir, Ballet Rambert, 1995–; Mem., British Library Bd, 1995–. *Recreations:* opera, ballet, theatre, music. *Address:* 8 Hanover Terrace, NW1 4RJ. *T:* (020) 7723 3422.

BLOOM, Charles; QC 1987; **His Honour Judge Bloom;** a Circuit Judge, since 1997; *b* 6 Nov. 1940; *s* of Abraham Barnett Bloom and Freda Bloom (*née* Craft); *m* 1967, Janice Rachelle Goldberg; one *s* one *d*. *Educ:* Manchester Central Grammar School; Manchester University. LLB Hons 1962. Called to the Bar, Gray's Inn, 1963; practised on Northern Circuit, 1963–97; a Recorder, 1983–97. Chm., Medical Appeal Tribunals, 1979–97. Mem., Larner Vinifloral Soc., 1996–. *Recreations:* tennis, horticulture. *Address:* c/o Circuit Administrator's Office, Northern Circuit, 15 Quay Street, Manchester M60 9FD. *Club:* Friedland Postmusaf Tennis (Cheadle).

BLOOM, Claire; *b* London, 15 Feb. 1931; *d* of late Edward Bloom and of Elizabeth Bloom; *m* 1st, 1959, Rod Steiger (marr. diss. 1969); one *d*; 2nd, 1969; 3rd, 1990, Philip Roth (marr. diss. 1995). *Educ:* Badminton, Bristol; America and privately. First work in England, BBC, 1946. Stratford: Ophelia, Lady Blanche (King John), Perdita, 1948; The Damask Cheek, Lyric, Hammersmith, 1949; The Lady's Not For Burning, Globe, 1949; Ring Round the Moon, Globe, 1949–50. Old Vic: 1952–53: Romeo and Juliet; 1953: Merchant of Venice; 1954: Hamlet, All's Well, Coriolanus, Twelfth Night, Tempest; 1956: Romeo and Juliet (London, and N American tour). Cordelia, in Stratford Festival Company, 1955 (London, provinces and continental tour); Duel of Angels, Apollo, 1958; Rashomon, NY, 1959; Altona, Royal Court, 1961; The Trojan Women, Spoleto Festival, 1963; Ivanov, Phoenix, 1965; A Doll's House, NY, 1971; Hedda Gabler, 1971; Vivat! Vivat Regina!, NY, 1971; A Doll's House, Criterion, 1973 (filmed 1973); A Streetcar

Named Desire, Piccadilly, 1974; Rosmersholm, Haymarket, 1977; The Cherry Orchard, Chichester Fest., 1981, Cambridge, Mass, 1994; When We Dead Waken, Almeida, 1990; A Long Day's Journey into Night, ART, Cambridge, Mass, 1996; Electra, McCarter Th., Princeton, NJ, 1998, transf. NY, 1999; Conversations After a Burial, Almeida, 2000. One-woman performances: These Are Women, 1981– (US tour, 1981–82); Enter the Actress, 1998–. First film, Blind Goddess, 1947; *films include:* Limelight; The Man Between; Richard III; Alexander the Great; The Brothers Karamazov; The Buccaneers; Look Back in Anger; Three Moves to Freedom; The Brothers Grimm; The Chapman Report; The Haunting; 80,000 Suspects; Alta Infedelta; Il Maestro di Vigevano; The Outrage; The Spy Who Came in From The Cold; Charly; Three into Two won't go; A Severed Head; Red Sky at Morning; Islands In The Stream; The Clash of the Titans, 1979; Always, 1984; Sammy and Rosie Get Laid, 1987; Crimes and Misdemeanors, 1989; Daylight, 1997. *Television:* first appearance on television programmes, 1952, since when she has had frequent successes on TV in the US: In Praise of Love, 1975; Anastasia, 1986; Queenie, 1986; BBC: A Legacy, 1975; The Ghost Writer, 1983; Shadowlands, 1985 (BAFTA award Best TV Actress); Time and the Conways, 1985; Oedipus the King, 1986; What the Deaf Man Heard, 1997; BBC Shakespeare: Katharine in Henry VIII, 1979; Gertrude in Hamlet, 1980; the Queen in Cymbeline, Lady Constance in King John, 1983; ITV: series: Brideshead Revisited, 1981; Intimate Contact, 1987; Shadow on the Sun, 1988; play, The Belle of Amherst, 1986; Channel Four: series, The Camomile Lawn, 1992; The Mirror Crack'd, 1992; Remember, 1993; A Village Affair, 1994; Family Money, 1996; series, Imogen's Face, 1998; The Lady in Question, 1999. Many appearances as narrator in both contemporary and classic repertoire. Distinguished Vis. Prof., Hunter Coll., NY, 1989. *Publications:* Limelight and After (autobiog.), 1982; Leaving a Doll's House (autobiog.), 1996. *Recreations:* opera, music. *Address:* c/o Jeremy Conway, 18–21 Jermyn Street, SW1Y 6HB.

BLOOM, Louise Anne; Member (Lib Dem), London Assembly, Greater London Authority, since 2000; *b* 7 April 1964; *d* of Christopher George Harris and Patricia Rose Harris (*née* Fray, now Lindsley); *m* 1987, Charles Neil Bloom (separated); two *d*. *Educ:* Kingston Poly. (BA Hons Applied Soc. Sci. 1985). Worked for various advertising agencies, 1985–90; freelance orgn mgt of press and publicity events, 1991–97; res. and admin assistant to Lib Dem councillors, Royal Bor. of Kingston upon Thames, 1991–93; Asst to Co-ordinator of Ind. Living Scheme, Kingston Assoc. of Disabled People, 1997; Inf. and Volunteer Develt Officer, Richmond Advice and Inf. on Disability, 1998–2000. *Recreations:* theatre, music, reading, history, thinking up ways to keep my children entertained and away from the television. *Address:* Greater London Authority, Romney House, 43 Marsham Street, SW1P 3PY. *T:* (020) 7983 4383.

BLOOM, Margaret Janet; Director of Competition Policy, Office of Fair Trading, since 1997; *b* 28 July 1943; *d* of John Sturrock and Jean Elizabeth Sturrock (*née* Ranken); *m* 1965, Prof. Stephen Robert Bloom, *qv*; two *s* two *d*. *Educ:* Sherborne Sch. for Girls; Girton Coll., Cambridge (MA). Economist, then Dep. Gp Economist, John Laing and Son, 1965–69; Gp Economist, Tarmac, 1969–70; Sen. Project Manager, NEDO, 1970–86; Sci. and Technol. Secretariat, Cabinet Office, 1986–89; Res. and Technol. Policy Div., 1989–91, Competition Policy Div., 1991–93, Finance and Resource Mgt Div., 1993–95, DTI; Head, Agencies Privatisation Team, 1995–96, Dir, Agencies Gp B, 1996, Cabinet Office. Pt-time Lectr, 1977–80, Ext. Examr, 1985–88, for MSc in Architecture, UCL. *Recreations:* family, foreign travel, eating out, rambling. *Address:* Office of Fair Trading, Fleetbank House, 2–6 Salisbury Square, EC4Y 8JX. *T:* (020) 7211 8843, *Fax:* (020) 7211 8545; *e-mail:* margaret.bloom@oft.gov.uk.

BLOOM, Prof. Stephen Robert, MD, DSc; FRCP, FRCPath, FMedSci; Professor of Medicine, since 1982, Director of Metabolic Medicine, and Chief of Service for Chemical Pathology, since 1994, Imperial College School of Medicine (formerly Royal Postgraduate Medical School), London University, since 1994; Consultant Physician, Hammersmith Hospital, since 1982; *b* 24 Oct. 1942; *s* of Arnold and Edith Bloom; *m* 1965, Margaret Janet Sturrock (*see* M. J. Bloom); two *s* two *d*. *Educ:* Queens' Coll., Cambridge (MA 1968; MD 1979); Middlesex Hosp. Med. Sch.; DSc London 1982. FRCP 1978; FRCPath 1993. Middlesex Hospital: Gastro House Physician, 1967–68; Cardiology House Physician, 1968; Casualty Med. Officer, 1969; Leverhulme Res. Schol., Inst. of Clin. Res., 1970; Med. Unit Registrar, 1970–72; MRC Clin. Res. Fellow, 1972–74; House Surgeon, Mount Vernon Hosp., 1968–69; Endocrinology House Physician, Hammersmith Hosp., 1969–70; Sen. Lectr, 1974–78, Reader in Medicine, 1978–82, RPMS, Hammersmith Hosp.; Dir, Endocrinol. Clin. Service, 1982–, and Chm., Div. of Investigative Sci., 1997–, ICSM (formerly RPMS). Copp Lectr, Amer. Diabetes Assoc.; Goulstonian Lectr, RCP; Amer. Endocrine Soc. Transatlantic Lectr; Lawrence Lectr, British Diabetic Assoc. Sen. Censor, RCP, 1999–; Sec., Endocrine Soc., 1999–. Founder FMedSci, 1998. *Publications:* Toohey's Medicine, 15th edn, 1994; (with J. Lynn) Surgical Endocrinology, 1993. *Recreations:* walking, jogging, travelling, opera. *Address:* Department of Metabolic Medicine, Imperial College School of Medicine, 6th Floor Commonwealth Building, Hammersmith Campus, Du Cane Road, W12 0NN. *T:* (020) 8383 3242.

BLOOMER, Jonathan William, FCA; Chief Executive Prudential plc, since 2000 (Deputy Group Chief Executive, 1999–2000); *b* 23 March 1954; *s* of Derick William Bloomer and Audrey Alexandra Bloomer; *m* 1977, Anne Elizabeth Judith May; one *s* two *d*. *Educ:* Halesowen Grammar Sch.; Imperial Coll., London (BSc, ARCS 1974). FCA 1982. Partner, Arthur Andersen, 1987–94; Gp Finance Dir, Prudential Corp. plc, 1995–99. CIMgt 1996. *Recreations:* sailing, flying. *Address:* Prudential plc, Laurence Pountney Hill, EC4R 0HH. *T:* (020) 7548 3100.

BLOOMFIELD, Barry Cambray, MA, FLA; Director, Collection Development, Humanities and Social Sciences, British Library, 1985–90; *b* 1 June 1931; *s* of Clifford Wilson Bloomfield and Eileen Elizabeth (*née* Cambray); *m* 1958, Valerie Jean Philpot. *Educ:* East Ham Grammar Sch.; University College of the South-West, Exeter; University Coll. London; Birkbeck Coll., London. Served in Intelligence Corps, Malaya, 1952–54. Assistant, National Central Library, 1955; Librarian, College of S Mark and S John, Chelsea, 1956–61; Asst Librarian, London Sch. of Economics, 1961–63; Dep. Librarian, 1963–72, Librarian, 1972–78, School of Oriental and African Studies; Dir, India Office Library and Records, British Library (formerly FCO), 1978–85 and concurrently Keeper, Dept of Oriental MSS and Printed Bks, British Library, 1983–85. Chm., SCONUL Group of Orientalist Libraries, 1975–80; President: Bibliographical Soc., 1990–92 (Vice-Pres., 1979–90); Private Libraries Assoc., 1998–2001; Assoc. of Independent Libraries, 2000–; Vice-Pres., Philip Larkin Soc., 1995–; Member: Council, Royal Asiatic Soc., 1980–84, 1996–2000; British Assoc. for Cemeteries in S Asia, 1980–90; Britain-Burma Soc., 1980–90; Exec. Cttee, Friends of the Nat. Libraries, 1981–96; Chm., Rare Books Gp, LA, 1991–95; International Federation of Library Associations: Chairman: Sect. on Bibliography, 1985–89; Div. of Bibliographic Control, 1985–89; Mem., Professional Bd, 1987–89. Trustee, Shakespeare Birthplace Trust, 1987–91. Vis. Professor, Univ. of Florida, 1963; Vis. Fellow, Univ. of Hawaii, 1977. FLA 1959 (Hon. FLA 1998). Hon. Mem., ABA, 1999. Walford Award, LA, 1998. *Publications:* New Verse in the '30s, 1960; W. H. Auden: a bibliography, 1964, 2nd edn 1972; (ed) Autobiography of Sir J. P. Kay Shuttleworth, 1964; (ed with V. J. Bloomfield, J. D. Pearson) Theses on Africa, 1964; (ed) Theses on Asia, 1967; (ed) The Acquisition and Provision of Foreign Books by National and University Libraries in the UK, 1972; An Author Index to Selected British 'Little' Magazines, 1976; Philip Larkin: a bibliography 1933–1976, 1979, 2nd edn 2001; (ed) Middle East Studies and Libraries, 1980; Brought to Book, 1995; (ed) A Directory of Rare Books and Special Collections in the United Kingdom and Ireland, 2nd edn, 1997; numerous articles in library and bibliog. jls. *Recreations:* reading, music. *Address:* Brambling, 24 Oxenturn Road, Wye, Kent TN25 5BE. *T:* (01233) 813038. *Club:* Civil Service.

BLOOMFIELD, Keith George; HM Diplomatic Service; Head, Counter Terrorism Policy Department, Foreign and Commonwealth Office, since 1998; *b* 2 June 1947; *s* of George William Bloomfield and Edith Joan Bloomfield; *m* 1976, Genevieve Charbonneau; three *d*. *Educ:* Kilburn Grammar Sch.; Lincoln Coll., Oxford (MA). Home Civil Service, 1969–80; Office of UK Rep. to EC, Brussels, 1980–85; FCO, 1985–87; Head of Chancery, Cairo, 1987–90; Dep. Head of Mission, Algiers, 1990–94; Counsellor (Political and Mgt), Rome, 1994–96; Minister and Dep. Head of Mission, Rome, 1997–98. *Recreations:* music, tennis, reading. *Address:* c/o Foreign and Commonwealth Office, SW1A 2AH. *T:* (home) (020) 7610 4036; Les Hommeaux, Combrée, 49520, France.

BLOOMFIELD, Sir Kenneth Percy, KCB 1987 (CB 1982); Chairman, Northern Ireland Higher Education Council, since 1993; *b* 15 April 1931; *o c* of late Harry Percy Bloomfield and Doris Bloomfield, Belfast; *m* 1960, Mary Elizabeth Ramsey; one *s* one *d*. *Educ:* Royal Belfast Academical Instn; St Peter's Coll., Oxford (MA; Hon. Fellow, 1991). Min. of Finance, N Ireland, 1952–56; Private Sec. to Ministers of Finance, 1956–60; Dep. Dir, British Industrial Develt Office, NY, 1960–63; Asst and later Dep. Sec. to Cabinet, NI, 1963–72; Under-Sec., Northern Ireland Office, 1972–73; Sec. to Northern Ireland Executive, Jan.–May 1974; Permanent Secretary: Office of the Executive, NI, 1974–75; Dept of Housing, Local Govt and Planning, NI, 1975–76; Dept of the Environment, NI, 1976–81; Dept of Commerce, NI, 1981–82; Dept of Economic Develt, 1982–84; Head, NICS, and Second Perm. Under Sec. of State, NI Office, 1984–91. Nat. Gov. and Chm. of Broadcasting Council for NI, BBC, 1991–99. Review of Dental Remuneration, 1992; Consultant, Crown Appts Review Gp, 1999–2001. Comr, NI Victims Commn, 1997–98 (report published 1998); Jt Internat. Comr, Commn for Location of Victims Remains, 1999–2001. Chairman: Chief Executives' Forum for NI Public Services, 1991–97; Review of Criminal Injuries Compensation in NI, 1998–99; Pres., NI Council, Stationery Office, 1998–2000. Mem., NI Adv. Bd, Bank of Ireland, 1991–; Member of Board: Co-operation North, 1991–93; Opera, NI, 1992–97; Member: Statute Law Adv. Cttee, 1993–97; Nat. Steering Cttee, Give as You Earn, 1992–93; Adv. Cttee, Constitution Unit, 1997; Jersey Review of Machinery of Govt, 1999–2000. Chm., Children in Need Trust, 1992–98; Mem. Bd, Green Park Hosp. Trust, 1993–2001; Patron: Belfast Improved Houses, 1992–; NI Council for Integrated Educn, 1998–. Senator (Crown nominee), QUB, 1991–93; Pres., Ulster People's Coll., 1996–. Governor, Royal Belfast Academical Instn, 1984–. Bass Ireland Lectr, Univ. of Ulster, 1991. Hon. LLD QUB, 1991; DUniv Open, 2000. Dr Ben Wilson Trophy for Individual or Corporate Excellence, NI Chamber of Commerce and Industry, 1990. *Publications:* Stormont in Crisis (a memoir), 1994; *contributions to:* Hope and History, 1996; Broadcasting in a Divided Community, 1996; People and Government: questions for Northern Ireland, 1997; Cool Britannia, 1998; various jls and periodicals. *Recreations:* history, travel, swimming. *Address:* 16 Larch Hill, Holywood, Co. Down BT18 0JN. *T:* (028) 9042 8340.

BLOOR, Prof. David; Professor of Applied Physics, University of Durham, since 1989 (Chairman, Department of Physics, 1993–96); *b* 25 July 1937; *s* of Alfred Edwin Bloor and Gladys Ellen Bloor (*née* Collins); *m* 1960, Margaret E. A. Avery; four *s* (and one *s* decd). *Educ:* Queen Mary College London (BSc, PhD). CPhys, FInstP. Lectr, Dept of Physics, Univ. of Canterbury, NZ, 1961–64; Queen Mary College London: Lectr, Dept of Physics, 1964; Reader, 1980–84; Prof. of Polymer Physics, 1984–89. Humboldt Fellow: Univ. of Stuttgart, 1975–76; Univ. of Bayreuth, 1997–98; Erskine Fellow, Univ. of Canterbury, NZ, 1983; Royal Society SERC Indust. Fellow, GEC Marconi Res. Centre, 1985–86; Sir Derman Christopherson Foundn Fellow, Univ. of Durham, 1996–97. Mem., Exec. Cttee, Canon Foundn in Europe, 2000–. *Publications:* contribs to professional jls. *Recreations:* cycling, gardening. *Address:* Applied Physics Group, Department of Physics, University of Durham, South Road, Durham DH1 3LE. *T:* (0191) 374 2391.

BLOSSE, Sir Richard Hely L.; *see* Lynch-Blosse.

BLOT, Jean; *see* Blokh, A.

BLOUNT, Sir Walter (Edward Alpin), 12th Bt *cr* 1642; DSC 1943 and two Bars 1945; farmer; *b* 31 Oct. 1917; *s* of Sir Edward Robert Blount, 11th Bt, and Violet Ellen (*d* 1969), *d* of Alpin Grant Fowler; *S* father, 1978; *m* 1954, Eileen Audrey, *d* of late Hugh B. Carritt; one *d*. *Educ:* Beaumont College; Sidney Sussex Coll., Cambridge (MA). Served RNVSR, 1939–47 (MTBs). Qualified as Solicitor, 1950; practised Gold Coast, West Africa, 1950–52; London and Cambridge, 1952–76. Farmer, Tilkhurst, East Grinstead, Sussex, 1978–. *Recreation:* sailing. *Heir:* none. *Address:* Tilkhurst, Imberhorne Lane, East Grinstead, Sussex RH19 1TY. *T:* (01342) 323018; Regent House, Seaview, IoW PO34 5ET. *Clubs:* Bembridge Sailing, Seaview Yacht, Cambridge Cruising, RNVR Sailing, Island Sailing.

BLOW, Bridget Penelope; Chief Executive, ITNET, since 1994; *b* 2 June 1949; *m* Rod Blow (marr. diss.); one *d*. *Educ:* Caistor Grammar Sch. Systems Develt, Grimsby BC, 1968–79; Human Resources Dir, Divl Dir, Dir of Technol., then Exec. Dir, FI Gp, 1979–92; Systems Dir, ITNET, 1992–94. Dir, Bank of England, 2000–. Mem. Council, Industrial Soc., 2000–. CIMgt. NatWest Midlands Business Woman of the Year, 1996. *Recreations:* golf, gym, tennis. *Address:* ITNET Ltd, Laburnum House, Laburnum Road, Bournville, Birmingham B30 2BD.

BLOW, Prof. David Mervyn, FRS 1972; Professor of Biophysics, 1977–94, now Emeritus, and Senior Research Fellow, since 1994, Imperial College, University of London; *b* 27 June 1931; *s* of Rev. Edward Mervyn and Dorothy Laura Blow; *m* 1955, Mavis Sears; one *s* one *d*. *Educ:* Kingswood Sch.; Corpus Christi Coll., Cambridge (MA, PhD). FInstP. Fulbright Scholar, Nat. Inst. of Health, Bethesda, Md, and MIT, 1957–59; MRC Unit for Study of Molecular Biological Systems, Cambridge, 1959–62; MRC Lab. of Molecular Biology, Cambridge, 1962–77; College Lectr and Fellow, Trinity Coll., Cambridge, 1968–77; Imperial College, London: Dean, Royal Coll. of Sci., 1981–84; Head, Dept of Physics, 1991–94. Pres., British Crystallographic Assoc., 1984–87. For. Associate Mem., Acad. des Scis, Paris, 1992. Mem. Governing Body, Imperial Coll., London, 1987–94. Social Colours, Imperial Coll. Students' Union, 1986, 1989. Biochem. Soc. CIBA Medal, 1967; (jtly) Charles Léopold Meyer Prize, 1979; (jtly) Wolf Foundn Prize for Chemistry, 1987. *Publications:* papers and reviews in scientific jls. *Recreations:* walking, sailing. *Address:* Blackett Laboratory, Imperial College of Science, Technology and Medicine, University of London, SW7 2BZ.

BLOW, Joyce, (Mrs Anthony Darlington), OBE 1994; Chairman, Child Accident Prevention Trust, since 1996; *b* 4 May 1929; *d* of late Walter Blow and Phyllis (*née* Grainger); *m* 1974, Lt-Col J. A. B. Darlington, RE retd. *Educ:* Bell Baxter Sch., Cupar, Fife; Edinburgh Univ. (MA Hons). FIPR 1964. John Lewis Partnership, 1951–52; FBI, 1952–53; Press Officer, Council of Indust. Design, 1953–63; Publicity and Advertising Manager, Heal & Son Ltd, 1963–65; entered Civil Service on first regular recruitment of direct entry Principals from business and industry: BoT, 1965–67; Monopolies Commn (gen. enquiry into restrictive practices in supply of prof. services), 1967–70; DTI, 1970, Asst Sec. 1972; Dept of Prices and Consumer Protection, 1974–77; Under-Secretary: OFT, 1977–80; DTI, 1980–84; Chairman: Mail Order Publishers' Authy, 1985–92; Direct Marketing Assoc. Authy, 1992–97. Chm., E Sussex FHSA, 1990–96. Pres., Assoc. for Quality in Healthcare, 1991–94; Vice-Pres., Trading Standards Inst. 1985–; Bd Mem., BSI, 1987–97 (Chm., Consumer Policy Cttee, 1987–93). Founder Mem. and Past Pres., Women in Public Relations. Trustee, Univ. of Edinburgh Develt Trust, 1990–94; Chm., PR Educn Trust, 1992–97. Freeman, City of London. Hon. FIPR; FIMgt; FRSA. *Publication:* Consumers and International Trade: a handbook, 1987. *Recreations:* music, particularly opera; travel, France. *Address:* 17 Fentiman Road, SW8 1LD. *T:* (020) 7735 4023; 9 Crouchfield Close, Seaford, E Sussex. *Clubs:* Arts, Reform.

BLOW, Sandra, RA 1978 (ARA 1971); *b* 14 Sept. 1925; *d* of Jack and Lily Blow. *Educ:* St Martin's School of Art; Royal Academy Sch.; Accademia di Belle Arti, Rome. Tutor, Painting School, Royal Coll. of Art, 1960–75. *Individual Exhibitions:* Gimpel Fils, 1952, 1954, 1960, 1962; Saidenburg Gallery, NY, 1957; New Art Centre, London, 1966, 1968, 1971, 1973; Francis Graham-Dixon, 1991; Newlyn, 1995; New Millennium Gall., St Ives, 1997; *retrospective:* Royal Acad's Sackler Galls, 1994. Represented in group exhibitions in Britain (including British Painting 74, Hayward Gall.; Tate, St Ives, 1995, 1997), USA, Italy, Denmark, France, Ireland, UAE; first etching exhibited RA, 1996. Won British Section of Internat. Guggenheim Award, 1960; 2nd prize, John Moore's Liverpool Exhibition, 1961; Arts Council Purchase Award, 1965–66; Korn/Ferry Picture of the Year Award, 1998. *Official Purchases:* Peter Stuyvesant Foundation; Nuffield Foundation; Arts Council of Great Britain; Arts Council of N Ireland; Walker Art Gallery, Liverpool; Allbright Knox Art Gallery, Buffalo, NY; Museum of Modern Art, NY; Tate Gallery; Chantry Bequest; Gulbenkian Foundation; Min. of Public Building and Works; Contemp. Art Society; Victoria and Albert Museum; Fitzwilliam Museum, Cambridge; City of Leeds Art Gall.; Graves Art Gall., Sheffield; Heathrow Airport (glass screen). *Address:* c/o Royal Academy of Arts, Piccadilly, W1V 0DS.

BLOWERS, Dr Anthony John, CBE 1985; JP, DL; CBiol; FIBMS; Commissioner, Mental Health Act Commission, 1987–95; Director, Ogilvy Public Relations Worldwide, since 1999; *b* 11 Aug. 1926; *e s* of late Geoffrey Hathaway and Louise Blowers; *m* 1948, Yvonne Boiteux-Buchanan; two *s* one *d. Educ:* Sloane Sch., Chelsea; Sir John Cass Coll.; Univ. of London; Univ. of Surrey (PhD 1982). FIMLS 1983; CBiol 1984. Served War, RCS, 1944–45; served: RAMC, 1945–46; RWAFF, 1946–48. Min. of Agriculture, 1948–59, Exptl Officer, 1953–59; Sandoz Pharmaceuticals, 1959–91; Sen. Res. Officer, 1973–87; Psychopharmacology Consultant, 1987–91; Consultant in Bacteriology, Mansi Labs, 1973–90. Dir, Corporate Affairs, Magellan Medical Communications, 1990–99. Vis. Res. Fellow, Roehampton Inst., 1998–; Vis. Lectr, Dept of Psychiatry of Addictive Behaviour, St George's Hosp. Med. Sch., 1999–. Chairman: W Surrey and NE Hants HA, 1981–86; Mental Health and Learning Disabilities Monitoring Gp, SW Surrey HA, 1991–95; Member: Surrey AHA, 1973–80 (Vice Chm., 1976–77); SW Thames RHA, 1980–81; Mental Health Review Tribunal, 1975–99; Nat. Standing Cttees on Consent to Treatment and Community Care, 1992–95. Admin. Sec., All-Party Parly Gp on R & D in Fertility and Contraception, 1994–. Member: Chertsey UDC, 1964–74 (Chm., 1969–70, 1973–74); Runnymede BC, 1973–84 (Chm., 1973–74); Surrey CC, 1970–85 (Vice Chm., Social Services Cttee, 1973–77); Surrey Police Authority, 1973–90 (Chm., 1981–85); Chairman: Runnymede and Elmbridge Police Community Liaison Cttee, 1983–94; Surrey Drug Action Team, 1995–. Chm. SE Region, and Mem. Nat. Adv. Council, Duke of Edinburgh's Award, 1990–98; Chm., Surrey Magistrates' Soc., 1988–94; Member: Council, Magistrates' Assoc., 1986–91; Bd of Visitors, Coldingley Prison, 1978–93; Court, Surrey Univ., 1986–; Surrey Scout Council, 1991–; Pres., Runnymede Scout Council, 1970–84. Vice-President: Hosp. Saving Assoc., 1994–; Parkinson's Disease Soc., 1995– (Actg Chief Exec., 1995); Mem. Council, 1986–, Trustee, 1995–, Psychiatry Res. Trust; Chm., Knight Foundn for Cystic Fibrosis Appeal, 1997–. Governor: Fullbrook Sch., 1967–85 (Chm., 1981–85); Ottershaw Sch., 1975–81 (Chm., 1979–81). Liveryman, Worshipful Soc. of Apothecaries, 1988– (Yeoman, 1983–88); Freeman, City of London, 1983; Hon. Freeman, Bor. of Runnymede, 1985. JP 1970, DL 1986, High Sheriff, 1990–91, Surrey. St John Ambulance: Asst Dir Gen., 1985–91; Dir Gen., 1991–94; Actg Chief Comdr, 1991–92; Comdr, Surrey, 1987–91; Chm., St John Fellowship, 1995–. KStJ 1991 (Mem., Chapter-Gen., 1991–99; Mem. Priory, England and the Islands, 1999–). *Publications:* The Isolation of Salmonellae, 1978; Tardive Dyskinesia, 1982; contribs to med. and scientific books and jls. *Recreations:* tackling drug misuse; fund-raising, gardening. *Address:* Westward, 12 Birch Close, Boundstone, Farnham, Surrey GU10 4TJ. *T:* (01252) 792769.

BLUCK, Duncan Robert Yorke, CBE 1990 (OBE 1984); Chairman: British Tourist Authority, 1984–90; English Tourist Board, 1984–90; Director, John Swire & Sons, 1984–99; *b* 19 March 1927; *s* of Thomas Edward Bluck and Ida Bluck; *m* 1952, Stella Wardlaw Murdoch; one *s* three *d. Educ:* Taunton Sch. RNVR, 1944–47. Joined John Swire & Sons, 1948; Dir, 1964–99, Chief Exec., 1971–84, Chm., 1980–84, Cathay Pacific Airways; Chairman: John Swire & Sons (HK) Ltd, 1980–84; Swire Pacific Ltd, 1980–84; Swire Properties Ltd, 1980–84. Dir, Hongkong and Shanghai Banking Corp., 1981–84. Chairman: English Schools Foundn (Hongkong), 1978–84; Hongkong Tourist Assoc., 1981–84; Kent Economic Develt Bd, 1986–91; Cystic Fibrosis Trust, 1996–. Governor, Marlborough House Sch., 1986–; Mem. Ct, Univ. of Kent, 1991–. JP Hong Kong, 1981–84. *Recreations:* sailing, swimming. *Address:* Elfords, Hawkhurst, Kent TN18 4RP. *T:* (01580) 752153. *Clubs:* Hongkong, Sheko (Hongkong); Rye Golf.

BLUE, Rabbi Lionel, OBE 1994; Lecturer, Leo Baeck College, since 1967; Convener of the Beth Din (Ecclesiastical Court) of the Reform Synagogues of Great Britain, 1971–88; *b* 6 Feb. 1930; *s* of late Harry and Hetty Blue. *Educ:* Balliol Coll., Oxford (MA History); University Coll. London (BA Semitics); Leo Baeck Coll., London (Rabbinical Dip). Ordained Rabbi, 1960; Minister to Settlement Synagogue and Middlesex New Synagogue, 1960–63; European Dir, World Union for Progressive Judaism, 1963–66; Co-Editor, Forms of Prayer, 1967–; broadcaster, 1967–; Feature Writer: The Universe, 1979–; The Standard, 1985–86; The Tablet, 1994–. Scriptwriter and presenter, TV series, In Search of Holy England, 1989. Templeton (UK) Prize, 1993. *Publications:* To Heaven with Scribes and Pharisees, 1975; (jtly) A Taste of Heaven, 1977; (ed jtly) Forms of Prayer (Sabbath and Daily), 1977; A Backdoor to Heaven, 1979, revd edn 1985; (ed jtly) Forms of Prayer (Days of Awe), 1985; Bright Blue, 1985; (jtly) Simply Divine, 1985; Kitchen Blues, 1985; Bolts from the Blue, 1986; Blue Heaven, 1987; (jtly) Daytrips to Eternity, 1987; (jtly) The Guide to the Here and Hereafter, 1988; Blue Horizons, 1989; Bedside Manna, 1991; (jtly) How to Get Up When Life Gets You Down, 1992; (jtly) The Little Blue Book of Prayer, 1993; Tales of Body and Soul, 1994; (jtly) Kindred Spirits: a year of readings, 1995; My Affair with Christianity (autobiog.), 1998; (jtly) Sun, Sand and Soul, 1999. *Recreations:* window shopping, package holidays, monasteries, cooking. *Address:* Leo Baeck College, 80 East End Road, N3 2SY. *T:* (020) 8349 4525.

BLUGLASS, Prof. Robert Saul, CBE 1995; MD; FRCP, FRCPsych; Professor of Forensic Psychiatry, University of Birmingham, 1979–96, now Emeritus; Hon. Consultant, Reaside Clinic, Birmingham, since 1995; *b* 22 Sept. 1930; *s* of Henry Bluglass and Fay (*née* Griew); *m* 1962, Jean Margaret Kerry (*née* Montgomery); one *s* one *d. Educ:* Warwick Sch., Warwick; Univ. of St Andrews (MB, ChB 1957, MD 1967). DPM 1962; MRCPsych 1971, FRCPsych 1976; MRCP 1994, FRCP 1997. Formerly, Sen. Registrar in Psych., Royal Dundee Liff Hosp. and Maryfield Hosp., Dundee; Consultant in Forensic Psychiatry: W Midlands RHA and the Home Office, 1967–94; S Birmingham Mental Health NHS Trust, 1994–95 (Med. Dir, 1995–96); Consultant i/c Midland Centre for For. Psych., All Saints Hosp., Birmingham, 1967–93; Clinical Dir, Reaside Clinic, Birmingham, 1986–95. Birmingham University: Hon. Lectr, 1968–75, Sen. Clin. Lectr in For. Psych., 1975–79; Regl Postgrad. Tutor in Forensic Psych., 1967–95; Jt Dir, Midland Inst. of For. Medicine, 1975–87. Dep. Regional Advr in Psychiatry, W Midlands RHA, 1985–87, Regional Advr, 1987–92; Specialist Advr, H of C Select Cttee on Social Services, 1985–87, on Health, 2000–01; Consultant Advr in Psych., RAF, 1992–; Advr in For. Psych., Bd of Corrections, Health Service, NSW, 1996–97. Member: Adv. Cttee on Alcoholism, DHSS, 1975–80; Adv. Council on Probation, Home Office, 1974–77; Mental Health Review Tribunal, 1979–; Mental Health Act Commn, 1983–85; Forensic Psych. Res. Liaison Gp, DHSS; Rev. of Services for Mentally Disordered Offenders (Reed Cttee), DoH, 1991–94; Inquiry into care and mgt of Christopher Edwards and Richard Linford, 1996–98; Judicial Inquiry into Personality Disorder Unit at Ashworth Special Hosp., 1997–99. Royal College of Psychiatrists: Mem., Ct of Electors, 1976–79; Mem. Council, Exec. and Finance Cttees, 1973–76, 1976–78, 1980–86, 1986–91; Vice-Pres., 1983–85; Chm., For. Psych. Specialist Section, 1978–82; Chm., Midlands Div., 1986–91; Chm., Midlands Soc. of Criminology, 1981–95 (Sec., 1970–81); Past Pres., Sect. of Psych., Birmingham Med. Inst.; Vice-Pres., RAF Psych. Soc.; Mem., Brit. Acad. of For. Sciences. FRSocMed 1975. Baron ver Heyden de Lancey Law Prize, RSocMed, 1983. *Publications:* Psychiatry, The Law and The Offender, 1980; A Guide to the Mental Health Act 1983, 1983; (ed with Prof. Sir Martin Roth) Psychiatry, Human Rights and the Law, 1985; (ed with Dr Paul Bowden) The Principles and Practice of Forensic Psychiatry, 1990; articles in Brit. Jl of Hosp. Med., BMJ, Brit. Jl of Psych., and Med., Science and the Law. *Recreations:* water-colour painting, cooking, gardening, swimming. *Address:* c/o Reaside Clinic, Birmingham Great Park, Bristol Road South, Rubery, Rednal, Birmingham B45 9BE.

BLUMBERG, Prof. Baruch Samuel, MD, PhD; Director, Astrobiology Institute, NASA, Ames Research Center, California, since 1999; Senior Advisor to the Administrator, NASA, Washington, since 2000; Fox Chase Distinguished Scientist, Senior Advisor to the President, Fox Chase Cancer Center, since 1989; University Professor of Medicine and Anthropology, University of Pennsylvania, since 1977; *b* 28 July 1925; *s* of Meyer Blumberg and Ida Blumberg; *m* 1954, Jean Liebesman Blumberg; two *s* two *d. Educ:* Union Coll. (BS Physics, 1946); Columbia University Coll. of Physicians and Surgeons (MD 1951); Balliol Coll., Oxford (PhD Biochemistry, 1957; Hon. Fellow, 1977). FRCP 1984. US Navy, 1943–46 (Lieut JG). US Public Health Service (rank of med. dir, col), and Chief, Geographic Medicine and Genetics Sect., Nat. Insts. of Health, Bethesda, Md, 1957–64; Associate Dir for Clinical Res., then Vice-Pres. for Population Oncology, Fox Chase Cancer Center, 1964–89; Clin. Prof., Dept of Epidemiology, Univ. of Washington Sch. of Public Health, 1983–89; Master of Balliol Coll., Oxford, 1989–94. George Eastman Vis. Prof., Oxford Univ., 1983–84; Lokey Vis. Prof., Program in Human Biology, Stanford Univ., 1997–98; Fellow, Center for Advanced Study in Behavioural Scis, Stanford Univ. Mem. Nat. Acad. of Sciences, Washington. Hon. DSc: Univ. of Pittsburgh, 1977; Union Coll., Schenectady, NY, 1977; Med. Coll. of Pa, 1977; Dickinson Coll., Carlisle, Pa, 1977; Hahnemann Med. Coll., Philadelphia, Pa, 1977; Indian Acad. of Scis, 1977; Elizabethtown Coll., Pa, 1988; Ball State Univ., Muncie, 1989; Dr *hc* Univ. of Paris VII, 1978. (Jt) Nobel Prize in Physiology or Medicine, 1976. *Publications:* (ed) Genetic Polymorphisms and Geographic Variations in Disease, 1961; (ed jtly) Medical Clinics of North America: new developments in medicine, 1970; (ed jtly) Hepatitis B: the virus, the disease and the vaccine, 1984; *chapters in:* McGraw-Hill Encyclopedia of Science and Technology Yearbook, 1962; The Genetics of Migrant and Isolate Populations, ed E. Goldschmidt, 1963; Hemoglobin: its precursors and metabolites, ed F. W. Sunderman and F. W. Sunderman, Jr, 1964; McGraw-Hill Yearbook of Science and Technology, 1970; (also co-author chapter) Viral Hepatitis and Blood Transfusion, ed G. N. Vyas and others, 1972; Hematology, ed W. J. Williams and others, 1972; Progress in Liver Disease, Vol. IV, ed H. Popper and F. Schaffner, 1972; Australia Antigen, ed J. E. Prier and H. Friedman, 1973; Drugs and the Liver, ed. W. Gerok and K. Sickinger, 1975 (Germany); (*jtly*) *chapters in:* Progress in Medical Genetics, ed A. G. Steinberg and A. G. Bearn, 1965 (also London); Viruses Affecting Man and Animals, ed M. Sanders and M. Schaeffer, 1971; Perspectives in Virology, 1971; Transmissable Disease and Blood Transfusion, ed T. J. Greenwalt and G. A. Jamieson, 1975; Physiological Anthropology, ed A. Damon, 1975; Hepatite a Virus B et Hemodialyse, 1975 (Paris); Onco-Developmental Gene Expression, 1976; contrib. symposia; over 460 articles in scientific jls. *Recreations:* rock climbing, cycling, canoeing, cattle raising. *Address:* Fox Chase Cancer Center, 7701 Burholme Avenue, Philadelphia, PA 19111, USA. *T:* (215) 7283164. *Clubs:* Athenæum; Explorers (NY).

BLUME, Hilary Sharon Braverman, (Mrs M. A. Norton); Founder and Director, Charities Advisory Trust (formerly Charity Trading Advisory Group), since 1979; *b* 9 Jan. 1945; *d* of Henry and Muriel Braverman; *m* 1st, 1965, Prof. Stuart Blume (marr. diss. 1977); two *s*; 2nd, 1977, Michael Aslan Norton, OBE; one *d. Educ:* London Sch. of Econs (BSc Econ.); Univ. of Sussex (MPhil). Fund raiser: War on Want, 1971–74; SHAC, 1975–79. Comr, Nat. Lottery Commn, 1999–2000. Vice Chm., Finnat House Trust. Patron, Trees for London. *Publications:* Fund-raising: a comprehensive handbook, 1977; (jtly) Accounting and Financial Management for Charities, 1979, 2nd edn 1985; Charity Trading Handbook, 1981; Charity Christmas Cards, 1984; Museum Trading Handbook, 1987; Charity Shops Handbook, 1995. *Address:* Charities Advisory Trust, Radius Works, Back Lane, Hampstead, NW3 1HL.

BLUMENTHAL, W(erner) Michael, PhD; US Secretary of the Treasury, 1977–79; *b* Germany, 3 Jan. 1926. *Educ:* Univ. of California at Berkeley; Princeton Univ. Research Associate, Princeton Univ., 1954–57; Vice-Pres., Dir, Crown Cork Internat. Corp., 1957–61; Dep. Asst Sec. of State for Econ. Affairs, Dept of State, 1961–63; Dep. Special Rep. of the President (with rank Ambassador) for Trade Negotiations, 1963–67; Pres., Bendix Internat., 1967–70; Bendix Corp.: Dir, 1967–77; Vice-Chm., 1970–71; Pres. and Chief Operating Officer, 1971–72; Chm. and Chief Exec. Officer, 1972–77; Burroughs Corp. subseq. Unisys: Chief Exec. Officer, 1980–90; Vice-Chm., 1980; Chm., 1981–90; Lazard Frères & Co. LLC, 1990–96. Director: Tenneco, Inc.; Daimler-Benz InterServices;

Internat. Adv. Bd, Chemical Bank; Mem., Business Council. *Address:* 227 Ridgeview Road, Princeton, NJ 08540, USA.

BLUMER, Rodney Milnes, (Rodney Milnes); Chief Opera Critic, The Times, since 1992; *b* 26 July 1936; *s* of Charles Eric Milnes Blumer and Kathleen Bertha Croft. *Educ:* Rugby School; Christ Church, Oxford (BA Hons Hist.). Editorial Dir, Rupert Hart-Davis Ltd, 1966–68; Music Critic, Queen magazine, later Harpers and Queen, 1968–87; Opera Critic: The Spectator, 1970–90; Evening Standard, 1990–92; Opera magazine: contribs, 1971–; Editl Bd, 1973; Associate Editor, 1976; Editor, 1986–99. Pres., Critics' Circle, 1988–90. Kt, Order of White Rose (Finland). *Publications:* numerous opera translations. *Recreation:* travel. *Address:* 3/23 Northwood Hall, N6 5PH.

BLUMGART, Prof. Leslie Harold, MD; FRCS, FRCSE, FRCSGlas, FACS; Enid A. Haupt Professor of Surgery, Memorial Sloane-Kettering Cancer Center, New York, since 1991 (Chief, Section of Hepato-Biliary Surgery, since 1995; Director, Programme on Hepato-Biliary Diseases, since 1995); Professor of Surgery, Cornell University Medical Center, since 1992; *b* 7 Dec. 1931, of S African parentage; *m* 1955, Pearl Marie Navias (decd); *m* 1968, Sarah Raybould Bowen; two *s* two *d*. *Educ:* Jeppe High Sch., Johannesburg, SA; Univ. of Witwatersrand (BDS); Univ. of Sheffield (MB, ChB Hons; MD 1969). Prize Medal, Clin. Med. and Surg.; Ashby-de-la-Zouche Prize, Surg., Med., Obst. and Gynaecol. FRCS 1966, FRCSGlas 1973, FRCSE 1976. General dental practice, Durban, SA, 1954–59; Sen. Surgical Registrar, Nottingham Gen. Hosp. and Sheffield Royal Infirmary, 1966–70; Sen. Lectr and Dep. Dir, Dept of Surgery, Welsh Nat. Sch. of Med., also Hon. Cons. Surg., Cardiff Royal Inf., 1970–72; St Mungo Prof. of Surgery, Univ. of Glasgow, and Hon. Cons. Surg., Glasgow Royal Inf., 1972–79; Prof. of Surgery, Royal Postgrad. Sch. of London and Dir of Surgery, Hammersmith Hosp., 1979–86; Prof. of Surgery, Univ. of Bern, 1986–91. Moynihan Fellow, Assoc. of Surgs of Gt Brit. and Ire., 1972; Mayne Vis. Prof., Univ. of Queensland, Brisbane, 1976; Vis. Prof., Univ. of Lund, Sweden, 1977; Nimmo Vis. Prof., Adelaide Univ., 1982; Purvis Oration, 1974; President's Oration, Soc. for Surgery of Aliment. Tract, Toronto, 1977; Lectures: Honyman Gillespie, Univ. of Edinburgh, 1978; Walton, RCPGlas, 1984; Monsarrat, Univ. of Liverpool, 1985; Legg Meml, KCH, 1985; Philip Sandblom, Lund Univ., Sweden, 1986; T. E. Jones Meml, Cleveland Clinic, USA, 1986; L. W. Edwards, Vanderbilt Univ., USA, 1987; Ernest Miles, British Assoc. Surg. Oncology, 1995. Member: BMA, 1963–; Assoc. of Surgs of GB and Ire., 1971–; Surgical Research Soc., 1971–; Brit. Soc. of Gastroenterology, 1972–; Swiss Surg. Soc., 1987–; Internat. Hepato-Biliar Pancreatic Assoc., 1992–; Amer. Surgical Assoc., 1993–; Soc. Surgical Oncology, 1994–. Hon. Member: Soc. for Surgery of Aliment. Tract, USA, 1977; Soc. Amer. Endoscopic Surgs, 1986–; Danish Surg. Soc., 1988; Yugoslavian Surg. Soc., 1988; French Surg. Soc., 1990; Pres., Internat. Biliary Assoc., 1987. Hon. DSc Sheffield, 1998. Acral Medal, Swedish Soc. Surgery, 1990. Order of Prasidda, Prabala-Gorkha-Dakshin Bahu, Nepal, 1984. *Publications:* (ed with A. C. Kennedy), Essentials of Medicine and Surgery for Dental Students, 3rd edn 1977, 4th edn 1982; (ed) The Biliary Tract, 1982; (ed) Surgery of the Liver and Biliary Tract, vols 1 and 2, 1988, 2nd edn 1994; chapters in books; numerous publications concerned with medical educn, gastrointestinal surgery and aspects of oncology with particular interests in surgery of the liver, pancreas and biliary tract and hepatic pathophysiology in med. and surgical jls. *Recreations:* water colour painting, wood carving. *Address:* Memorial Sloane-Kettering Cancer Center, 1275 York Avenue, New York, NY 10021, USA. *T:* (212) 6395526; 447 E 57th Street #3E, New York, NY 10022, USA.

BLUNDELL, Commandant Daphne Mary, CB 1972; Director, WRNS, 1970–73; *b* 19 Aug. 1916. *Educ:* St Helen's Sch., Northwood; Bedford Coll., London. Worked for LCC as Child Care Organiser. Joined WRNS, Nov. 1942; commnd 1943; served in Orkneys, Ceylon, E Africa; Malta, 1954–56; Staff of Flag Officer Naval Air Comd, 1964–67; Staff of C-in-C Portsmouth, 1967–69; Supt WRNS Training and Drafting, 1969–70. Supt 1967; Comdt 1970, retd 1973; Hon. ADC to the Queen, 1970–73. *Address:* 15 Northbrook Drive, Northwood, Mddx HA6 2YU.

BLUNDELL, Prof. Derek John; Professor of Environmental Geology, University of London, 1975–98, now Emeritus Professor of Geophysics; Dean of Research and Enterprise, Royal Holloway, University of London, 1995–98; *b* 30 June 1933; *s* of Frank and Mollie Blundell; *m* 1960, Mary Patricia, *d* of Archibald and Mildred Leonard. *Educ:* Univ. of Birmingham (BSc); Imperial Coll., London (DIC, PhD). Res. Fellow 1957, Lectr 1959, in Geology, Univ. of Birmingham; Sen. Lectr 1970, Reader 1972, in Geophysics, Univ. of Lancaster; Royal Soc. Vis. Prof., Univ. of Ghana, 1974; Prof. of Environmental Geol., Univ. of London, first at Chelsea Coll. (Hd of Geol. Dept), 1975, then at Royal Holloway and Bedford New Coll., 1985–98; Hd of Geol. Dept, 1992–97; Hon. Associate, Royal Holloway, 2001. Leverhulme Emeritus Fellow, 1998–2000. Pres., Geological Soc., 1988–90. Mem., Academia Europaea, 1990. Coke Medal, Geological Soc., 1993. *Publications:* (jtly) A Continent Revealed: the European geotraverse, 1992; Lyell: the past is the key to the present, 1998; contribs to learned jls mainly relating to seismic exploration of the earth's crust, to earthquake hazards and, early on, to palæomagnetism. *Recreations:* travel, golf. *Address:* Springwood, Tite Hill, Englefield Green, Surrey TW20 0NF. *T:* (01784) 433170. *Club:* Athenæum.

BLUNDELL, John; General Director, Institute of Economic Affairs, since 1993; *b* 9 Oct. 1952; *s* of James Blundell and Alice Margaret Blundell (*née* Taylor); *m* 1977, Christine Violet Lowry; two *s*. *Educ:* King's Sch., Macclesfield; London Sch. of Econs, Univ. of London. Head of Press, Parly Liaison and Res. Office, Fedn of Small Businesses, 1976–82; Councillor (C), Lambeth BC, 1978–82; Institute for Humane Studies, George Mason University: Dir, Public Affairs, 1982–85; Exec. Vice-Pres., 1985–88; Pres., 1988–91; Trustee, 1991–; Atlas Economic Research Foundation, Fairfax, Virginia: Pres., 1987–91; Chm., Exec. Cttee, 1991–; Director: Inst. for Economic Studies, Europe (formerly Inst. for Humane Studies Europe), Paris, 1988–; Fraser Inst., Vancouver, 1987–92; Humane Studies Foundn, 1988–91; Atlas Economic Res. Foundn (UK), 1993–; Centre for the New Europe, Brussels, 1998–; Founder Director: Inst. for Justice, Washington, 1991–93; Athens Inst., Alexandria, Va, 1992–2000; Founder Trustee, Buckeye Inst. for Public Policy Solutions, Dayton, Ohio, 1989–; Pres., Charles G. Koch and Claude R. Lambe Charitable Foundns, Washington DC, 1991–93. Co-founder and Chm., Inst. for Children, Cambridge, Mass, 1993–98. Advr, Business Wise, 1993–98; Mem. Adv. Bd, Inst. de Libre Empresa, Peru, 2000–. Mem. Council, Fairbridge, 1998–. Member: Mont Pelerin Soc., 1990– (Mem. Bd, 1998–); Philadelphia Soc., 1994–. Pres., Bd of Regents, Congressional Schs of Virginia, 1988–92. Associate Ed. for Internat. Business, Mid-Atlantic Jl of Business, 1996–. *Publications:* (with Brian Gosschalk) Beyond Left and Right, the New Politics of Britain, 1998; (with Colin Robertson) Regulation Without the State, 1999; (jtly) Regulation Without the State...The Debate Continues, 2000; papers, contribs to jls, forewords, introductions, newspaper columns and magazine articles. *Recreations:* cricket, golf, genealogy, Morgan sports cars, minimising the role of the state and maximising individual liberty. *Address:* 43 Ponsonby Place, SW1P 4PS; (office) 2 Lord North Street, SW1P 3LB. *T:* (020) 7799 3745, *Fax:* (020) 7799 2137; *e-mail:* jblundell@iea.org.uk; Alpine Lake, Terra Alta, WV 26764, USA. *T:* (304) 789 2115. *Club:* Marin Cricket (Calif, USA).

BLUNDELL, Prof. Richard William, FBA 1997; Professor of Economics, University College London, since 1984; Leverhulme Personal Research Professor, since 1999; Director of Research, Institute for Fiscal Studies, since 1987; *b* 1 May 1952; *s* of Horace Leon and Marjorie Blundell; *m* 1984, Anne Gaynor Aberdeen; one *s* one *d*. *Educ:* Univ. of Bristol (BSc 1st cl. Hons Econs with Stats); LSE (MSc Econometrics). Lectr in Econometrics, Univ. of Manchester, 1975–85; Head, Dept of Economics, UCL, 1988–92; Dir, ESRC Centre for Microecon. Analysis of Fiscal Policy, Inst. Fiscal Studies, 1991–. Visiting Professor: Univ. of BC, 1980–81; MIT, 1993; Univ. of Calif at Berkeley, 1994, 1999. Member, Council: Royal Econ. Soc., 1990–94; European Econs Assoc., 1997– (Yrjo Johnsson Prize, 1995); Eur. Econ. Assoc., 1997–; Econometric Soc., 1998– (Fellow, 1991; Frisch Prize, 2000); Programme Chm., European Econometric Soc. Meetings, 1992. Member, Editorial Board: Rev. Econ. Studies, 1983–93 (Asst Ed, 1984–88); Jl Applied Econometrics, 1986–89; Fiscal Studies, 1986–; Jl of Human Resources, 1995–97. Editor: Jl of Econometrics, 1991–96; Econometrica, 1997–. *Publications:* Unemployment, Search and Labour Supply, 1986; The Measurement of Household Welfare, 1994; contrib. Econometrica, Rev. Econ. Studies, Econ. Jl, Jl Econometrics. *Recreations:* saxophone, guitar, jazz music, African music, travel. *Address:* Department of Economics, University College London, Gower Street, WC1E 6BT. *T:* (020) 7679 5863; *e-mail:* r.blundell@ucl.ac.uk.

See also Sir T. L. Blundell.

BLUNDELL, Sir Thomas Leon, (Sir Tom), Kt 1997; FRS 1984; Sir William Dunn Professor of Biochemistry, since 1995, and Head of Department of Biochemistry, since 1996, Cambridge University; Fellow of Sidney Sussex College, Cambridge, since 1995; *b* 7 July 1942; *s* of Horace Leon Blundell and Marjorie Blundell; one *s*; *m* 1987, Bancinyane Lynn Sibanda; two *d*. *Educ:* Steyning Grammar Sch.; Brasenose Coll., Oxford (BA, DPhil; Hon. Fellow, 1989). Postdoctoral Res. Fellow, Laboratory of Molecular Biophysics, Oxford Univ., 1967–72; Jun. Res. Fellow, Linacre Coll., Oxford, 1968–70; Lectr, Biological Scis, Sussex Univ., 1973–76; Prof. of Crystallography, Birkbeck Coll., Univ. of London, 1976–90; Dep. Chm. and Dir Gen., AFRC, 1991–94; Chief Exec. and Dep. Chm., BBSRC, 1994–96 (on secondment). Director: International Sch. of Crystallography, 1981–; Babraham Inst., Cambridge, 1997–. Founder and non-exec. Dir, Astex Technology, 1999–. Chm., Royal Commn on Envmtl Pollution, 1998–. Member: Council, AFRC, 1985–90; MRC AIDS Res. Steering Cttee, 1987–90; ACOST, 1988–90; Council, SERC, 1989–90 (Mem., 1979–82, Chm., 1983–87, Biological Scis Cttee; Mem., Science Bd, 1983–87); ABRC, 1991–94; Council, Royal Soc., 1997–99; R&D Bd, SmithKline Beecham, 1997–2000; Bd, Parly OST, 1998–. Hon. Dir, ICRF Unit of Structural Molecular Biology, 1989–96. Lectures: Plenary, Internat. Congress of Crystallography, 1969, 1978 and 1993; Gerhardt Schmidt, Weizman Inst., Israel, 1983; Plenary, Europ. Cryst. Meeting, 1983; Ferdinand Springer, Fedn of Europ. Biochemical Socs, 1984; Plenary, Asian and Ocean Biochemical Soc., 1986; Plenary, Fedn of European Biochemical Socs, 1987; Plenary, Internat. Juvenile Diabetes Congress, 1988; Plenary, Internat. Congress of Biochem., 1991. Councillor, Oxford CBC, 1970–73 (Chm. Planning Cttee, 1972–73). Scientific Consultant, Oxford Molecular Ltd, 1996–99; Chm., Scientific Adv. Bd, Bioprocessing Ltd, 1997–; Industrial Consultant: Celltech, 1981–86 (non-exec. Dir, 1997–; Chm., Scientific Adv. Bd, 1998–); Pfizer Central Res., Groton, USA and Sandwich, UK, 1984–90; Abingworth Management Ltd, 1988–90. Dir, Lawes Agricl Trust, 1998–; Trustee, Daphne Jackson Trust, 1996–. Governor, Birkbeck Coll., 1985–89. Founder FMedSci 1998. Hon. Fellow, Linacre Coll., Oxford, 1991. Hon. FRASE 1993; Hon. FIChemE 1995. Hon. DSc: Edinburgh, East Anglia, 1993; Sheffield, Strathclyde, 1994; Warwick, Antwerp, 1995; Nottingham, 1996; UWE, 1997; Sussex, Pavia, 2001; DUniv Stirling, 2000. Alcon Award for Dist. Work in Vision Research, 1985; Gold Medal, Inst. of Biotechnological Studies, 1987; Sir Hans Krebs Medal, Fedn of European Biochemical Socs, 1987; Ciba Medal, UK Biochemical Soc., 1988; Feldberg Prize for Biology and Medicine, 1988; Gold Medal, SCI, 1995; Pfizer Eur. Award for Innovation, 1998. Joint Editor: Progress in Biophysics and Molecular Biology, 1979–; Current Opinion in Structural Biology, 1996–; Member Editorial Advisory Board: Biochemistry, 1986–89; Protein Engineering, 1986–; Protein Science, 1992–98; Structure, 1993–. *Publications:* Protein Crystallography, 1976; papers in Jl of Molecular Biology, Nature, European Jl of Biochemistry, etc. *Recreations:* playing jazz, listening to opera, walking, international travel. *Address:* Department of Biochemistry, Tennis Court Road, Cambridge CB2 1GA.

See also R. W. Blundell.

BLUNDEN, Sir George, Kt 1987; Deputy Governor, Bank of England, 1986–90 (Executive Director, 1976–84, Non-Executive Director, 1984–85); Joint Deputy Chairman, Leopold Joseph Holdings, 1984–85 and 1990–94; *b* 31 Dec. 1922; *s* of late George Blunden and Florence Holder; *m* 1949, Anne, *d* of late G. J. E. and Phyllis Bulford; two *s* one *d*. *Educ:* City of London Sch.; University Coll., Oxford (MA). Royal Sussex Regt, 1941–45. Bank of England, 1947–55; IMF, 1955–58; Bank of England: rejoined 1958; Dep. Chief Cashier, 1968–73; Chief of Management Services, 1973–74; Head of Banking Supervision, 1974–76. Director: Eagle Star Hldgs, 1984–85; Portals Hldgs, 1984–86; Grindlays Hldgs, 1984–85. Advr, Union Bank of Switzerland in London, 1990–94. Chairman: Group of Ten Cttees, BIS, Basle, on Banking Regulations and Supervisory Practices, 1974–77, on Payments Systems, 1981–83; cttee to oversee estabt and operation of Code of Banking Practice, 1990–94; London Pensions Fund Authy, 1989–92. Chm. Governors, St Peter's Gp of Hosps, 1978–82; Chm., St Peter's Hosps Special Trustees, 1982–96; Chm., Inst. of Urology, 1982–88 (Hon. Treasurer, 1975–78); Mem. Council, Imperial Cancer Res. Fund, 1981–94 (Treas., 1988–91; Chm., 1991–94). Chairman: Samuel Lewis Housing Trust, 1985 (Trustee, 1980–85); Centre for Study of Financial Innovation, 1995–98. President: Inst. of Business Ethics, 1994–96; British-Malaysia Soc., 1989–94. Member: Court, Mermaid Theatre Trust, 1979–84; Council, RCM, 1983–89 (Dep. Chm., 1990–97; Hon. FRCM 1987). Mem., Livery, Goldsmiths' Co., 1987. Hon. Fellow, UEA, 1997. *Address:* Ashdale, Gunthorpe, Melton Constable, Norfolk NR24 2NS. *T:* (01263) 860359. *Clubs:* Reform, MCC; Norfolk (Norwich).

BLUNDEN, Sir Philip (Overington), 7th Bt *cr* 1766, of Castle Blunden, Kilkenny; artist and art restorer; *b* 27 Jan. 1922; *s* of Sir John Blunden, 5th Bt and Phyllis Dorothy (*d* 1967), *d* of Philip Crampton Creaghe; *S* brother, 1985; *m* 1945, Jeannette Francesca Alexandra, *e d* of Captain D. Macdonald, RNR; two *s* one *d*. *Educ:* Repton. Served RN, 1941–46 (1939–45 Star, Atlantic Star, Defence Medal). Estate Manager, Castle Blunden, 1947–60; engaged in marketing of industrial protective coatings, 1962–83; in art and art restoration, 1976–. *Recreations:* fishing, field sports, swimming, tennis, reading. *Heir:* *s* Hubert Chisholm Blunden [*b* 9 Aug. 1948; *m* 1975, Ellish O'Brien; one *s* one *d*]. *Club:* Royal Dublin Society (Life Mem.).

BLUNKETT, Rt Hon. David; PC 1997; MP (Lab) Sheffield, Brightside, since 1987; Secretary of State for the Home Department, since 2001; *b* 6 June 1947; *m* (marr. diss.); three *s*. *Educ:* night sch. and day release, Shrewsbury Coll. of Technol. and Richmond

Coll. of Further Educn, Sheffield; Nat. Cert. in Business Studies, E Midlands Gas Bd; Sheffield Univ. (BA Hons Pol Theory and Instns); Huddersfield Holly Bank Coll. of Educn (Tech.) (PGCFE). Tutor in Industrial Relns, Barnsley Coll. of Technol., 1974–87. Elected to Sheffield City Council (at age of 22), 1970; Chm., Family and Community Services Cttee, 1976–80; Leader, 1980–87; Dep. Chm., AMA, 1984–87. Joined Labour Party at age of 16; Chm., Labour Party NEC, 1993–94 (Dep. Chm., 1992–93; Mem., 1983–98); Chm., Labour Party Cttee on Local govt, 1984–92. Front bench spokesman on the environment, with special responsibility for local govt and poll tax, 1988–92, on health, 1992–94, on educn, 1994–95, on educn and employment, 1995–97 (Mem., Shadow Cabinet, 1992–97); Sec. of State for Educn and Employment, 1997–2001. *Publications:* (jtly) Local Enterprise and Workers' Plans, 1981; (jtly) Building from the Bottom: the Sheffield Experience, 1983; (jtly) Democracy in Crisis: the town halls respond, 1987; On a Clear Day, 1995. *Address:* House of Commons, SW1A 0AA.

BLUNT, Charles William; Chief Executive Officer, American Chamber of Commerce in Australia, since 1990; *b* Sydney, 19 Jan. 1951; *s* of R. S. G. Blunt; *m* Gail; two *s*. *Educ:* Sydney Univ. (BEcon). AASA; CPA. Exec. appts in mining, finance and agricultural industries. MP (Nat. Party) Richmond, NSW, 1984–90; Leader, Parly Nat. Party, 1989–90; opposition Minister, 1984–90, variously for: Sport, Recreation and Tourism; Social Security; Transport and Communications; Community Services and Aged Care; Trade and Resources. Former Mem., parly cttees and official delegns. *Recreations:* tennis, reading. *Address:* PO Box 66, Wahroonga, NSW 2076, Australia; American Chamber of Commerce in Australia, Suite 4, Gloucester Walk, 88 Cumberland Street, Sydney, NSW 2000, Australia. *Clubs:* Union, American (Sydney).

BLUNT, Crispin Jeremy Rupert; MP (C) Reigate, since 1997; *b* 15 July 1960; *s* of Maj. Gen. Peter Blunt, *qv*; *m* 1990, Victoria Ainsley Jenkins; one *s* one *d*. *Educ:* Wellington Coll.; RMA, Sandhurst; Durham Univ. (BA 1984); Cranfield Inst. of Technology (MBA 1991). Commnd, 13th/18th Royal Hussars (QMO), 1980; Troop Leader: UK and Cyprus, 1980–81; BAOR, 1984–85; Regtl Signals Officer/Ops Officer, BAOR/UK, 1985–87; Sqn Leader, 2IC UK, 1987–89; resigned commn, 1990; Rep., Forum of Private Business, 1991–92; Consultant, Politics Internat., 1993; Special Advr to Sec. of State for Defence, 1993–95, to Foreign Sec., 1995–97. Member: Select Cttee on Defence, 1997–2000; Select Cttee on Envmt, Transport and the Regions, 2000–01. Sec., Cons. Foreign and Commonwealth Affairs Cttee, 1997–2001. *Recreations:* cricket, sport, travel, bridge, food and wine. *Address:* House of Commons, SW1A 0AA. *T:* (020) 7219 3000. *Clubs:* Royal Automobile; Redhill Constitutional (Redhill); Fantasians Cricket.

BLUNT, David John; QC 1991; a Recorder of the Crown Court, since 1990; writer; *b* 25 Oct. 1944; *s* of late Vernon Egerton Rowland Blunt and of Catherine Vera Blunt; *m* 1976, Zaibonessa Ebrahim; one *s* one *d*. *Educ:* Farnham Grammar Sch.; Trinity Hall, Cambridge (MA Hons). Called to the Bar, Middle Temple, 1967, Bencher, 2000. Asst Recorder, 1985–90. Contested (L): Lambeth Central, 1978, 1979; Cornwall SE, 1983. First TV play broadcast, 1976. *Recreations:* walking, running, cycling, reading, writing, old cars. *Address:* 4 Pump Court, Temple, EC4Y 7AN. *T:* (020) 7353 2656.

BLUNT, Sir David Richard Reginald Harvey, 12th Bt *cr* 1720; *b* 8 Nov. 1938; *s* of Sir Richard David Harvey Blunt, 11th Bt and Elisabeth Malvine Ernestine, *d* of Comdr F. M. Fransen Van de Putte, Royal Netherlands Navy (retd); *S* father, 1975; *m* 1969, Sonia Tudor Rosemary (*née* Day); one *d*. *Heir: kinsman:* Robin Anthony Blunt, CEng, MIMechE [*b* 23 Nov. 1926; *m* 1st, 1949, Sheila Stuart (marr. diss. 1962), *d* of C. Stuart Brindley; one *s*; 2nd, 1962, June Elizabeth, *d* of Charles Wigginton; one *s*].

BLUNT, Oliver Simon Peter; QC 1994; a Recorder, since 1995; *b* 8 March 1951; *s* of Maj.-Gen. Peter Blunt, *qv* and Adrienne (*née* Richardson); *m* 1979, Joanna Margaret Dixon; one *s* three *d*. *Educ:* Bedford Sch.; Southampton Univ. (LLB 1973). Called to the Bar, Middle Temple, 1974; Asst Recorder, SE Circuit, 1991–95. *Recreations:* cricket, golf, ski-ing, swimming, mini-rugby coach. *Address:* Furnival Chambers, 32 Furnival Street, EC4A 1JQ. *T:* (020) 7405 3232. *Clubs:* Roehampton; Barnes Cricket; Rosslyn Park Rugby.

BLUNT, Maj.-Gen. Peter, CB 1978; MBE 1955; GM 1959; *b* 18 Aug. 1923; *s* of A. G. Blunt and C. M. Blunt; *m* 1949, Adrienne, *o d* of Gen. T. W. Richardson; three *s*. Joined Army aged 14 yrs, 1937; commnd Royal Fusiliers; served Duke of Cornwall's LI and Royal Scots Fusiliers, until 1946; foreign service, 1946–49; Staff Coll., 1957; Jt Services Staff Coll., 1963; RCDS, 1972; comd 26 Regt, Bridging, 1965; GSO 1 Def. Plans, FARELF, 1968; Comdr RCT 1 Corps, 1970; Dep. Transport Officer-in-Chief (Army), later Transp. Off.-in-Chief, 1973; Asst Chief of Personnel and Logistics (Army), MoD, 1977–78; Asst Chief of Defence Staff (Personnel and Logistics), MoD, 1978–79. Man. Dir, Earls Court Ltd, 1979–80; Exec. Vice-Chm., Brompton and Kensington Special Catering Co. Ltd, 1979–80; Jt Man. Dir, Angex-Watson, 1980–83; Dir, Associated Newspapers, 1984–90; Chm. and Man. Dir, Market Sensors, 1986–88; Man. Dir, 1980–88, non-exec. Chm., 1988–90, Angex Ltd; Chm., Argus Shield Ltd, 1988–89. Rep. Col Comdt, RCT, 1987–89 (Col Comdt, 1974–89). Specially apptd Comr, Royal Hosp., Chelsea, 1979–85. Exec. Mem., Caravan Club, 1989–. Liveryman, Co. of Carmen, 1973. *Recreations:* fishing, caravanning. *Address:* Harefield House, Crowood Lane, Ramsbury, Marlborough, Wilts SN8 2PT. *T:* (01672) 520296. *Club:* RCT Luncheon (Patron).

See also C. J. R. Blunt, O. S. P. Blunt.

BLYE, Douglas William Alfred, CMG 1979; OBE 1973; Secretary for Monetary Affairs, Hong Kong Government, 1977–85; *b* 15 Dec. 1924; *s* of William Blye and Ethel Attwood; *m* 1955, Juanita, (June), Buckley. *Educ:* King's Road Sch., Herne Bay; Maidstone Polytechnic. ACMA. Served War, RAF, 1941–46. Various commercial and industrial appts in UK, 1947–55; Govt of Fedn of Malaya, 1955–58; Hong Kong Govt, 1958–85; Econ. and Financial Advr, Govt of Dubai, 1986–87. *Recreations:* squash, tennis. *Address:* Middlefield, The Street, Goodnestone, Canterbury, Kent CT3 1PG. *T:* (01304) 842196. *Club:* Royal Automobile.

BLYTH, family name of **Barons Blyth** and **Blyth of Rowington**.

BLYTH, 4th Baron *cr* 1907; **Anthony Audley Rupert Blyth;** Bt 1895; *b* 3 June 1931; *er s* of 3rd Baron Blyth and Edna Myrtle (*d* 1952), *d* of Ernest Lewis, Wellington, NZ; *S* father, 1977; *m* 1st, 1954, Elizabeth Dorothea (marr. diss., 1962), *d* of R. T. Sparrow, Vancouver, BC; two *d* (one *s* decd); 2nd, 1963, Oonagh Elizabeth Ann, *yr d* of late William Henry Conway, Dublin; one *s* one *d*. *Educ:* St Columba's College, Dublin. *Heir: s* Hon. James Audley Ian Blyth, *b* 1970. *Address:* Blythwood Estate, Athenry, Co. Galway.

BLYTH OF ROWINGTON, Baron *cr* 1995 (Life Peer), of Rowington in the County of Warwickshire; **James Blyth,** Kt 1985; Chairman, Diageo plc, since 2000 (Director, since 1998); Senior Advisor, Greenhill & Co., since 2000; *b* 8 May 1940; *s* of Daniel Blyth and Jane Power Carlton; *m* 1967, Pamela Anne Campbell Dixon; one *d* (one *s* decd). *Educ:* Spiers Sch.; Glasgow Univ. Mobil Oil Co., 1963–69; General Foods Ltd, 1969–71; Mars Ltd, 1971–74; General Manager: Lucas Batteries Ltd, 1974–77; Lucas Aerospace Ltd, 1977–81; Head of Defence Sales, MoD, 1981–85; Managing Director: Plessey Electronic Systems, 1985–86; The Plessey Co plc, 1986–87; The Boots Co.: Chief Exec., 1987–98; Dep. Chm., 1994–98; Chm., 1998–2000. Non-executive Director: Imperial Gp PLC, 1984–86; Cadbury-Schweppes PLC, 1986–90; British Aerospace, 1990–94; Anixter Internat. Inc., 1995–; NatWest Gp, 1998–2000. Chm., Adv. Panel on Citizen's Charter, 1991–97. Pres., ME Assoc., 1988–93; Patron, Combined Services Winter Sports Assoc., 1997–. Gov., London Business Sch., 1987–96 (Hon. Fellow, 1997). Liveryman, Coachmakers' and Coach Harness Makers' Co. Hon. LLD Nottingham, 1992. *Recreations:* ski-ing, tennis, paintings, theatre. *Address:* Diageo plc, 8 Henrietta Place, W1G 0NB. *Clubs:* East India, Queen's.

BLYTH, Sir Charles, (Sir Chay), Kt 1997; CBE 1972; BEM 1967; Managing Director, The Challenge Business Ltd (formerly Crownfields Ltd), since 1989; Organiser, BT Global Challenge Round the World Yacht Race 1996–97, since 1994; *b* 14 May 1940; *s* of Robert and Jessie Blyth; *m* 1st, 1962, Maureen Margaret Morris (marr. diss. 1992); one *d*; 2nd, 1995, Felicity Rayson. *Educ:* Hawick High School. HM Forces, Para. Regt, 1958–67. Cadbury Schweppes, 1968–69; Dir, Sailing Ventures (Hampshire) Ltd, 1969–73. Organiser, British Steel Challenge Round World Yacht Race 1992–93, 1989–93. Rowed North Atlantic with Captain John Ridgway, June-Sept. 1966; circumnavigated the world westwards solo in yacht British Steel, 1970–71; circumnavigated the world eastwards with crew of paratroopers in yacht Great Britain II, and Winner, Elapsed Time Prize Whitbread Round the World Yacht Race, 1973–74; Atlantic sailing record, Cape Verde to Antigua, 1977; won Round Britain Race in yacht Great Britain IV, 1978 (crew Robert James); won The Observer/Europe 1 doublehanded transatlantic race in record time, 1981 (crew Robert James); Number One to Virgin Atlantic Challenge II successful attempt on the Blue Riband, 1986. Pres., Inst. of Professional Sales, 1998. Yachtsman of the Year, 1971, Special Award for outstanding services to yachting, Yachting Journalists Assoc., 1994; Chichester Trophy, RYS, 1971. Freeman of Hawick, 1972. *Publications:* A Fighting Chance, 1966; Innocent Aboard, 1968; The Impossible Voyage, 1971; Theirs is the Glory, 1974; The Challenge, 1993. *Recreations:* sailing, horse-riding, hunting. *Address:* Trepen House, Menheniot, Liskeard, Cornwall PL14 3PN. *Clubs:* Special Forces, Royal Ocean Racing; Royal Southern Yacht, Royal Western Yacht.

BLYTH, John Douglas Morrison, CMG 1981; HM Diplomatic Service, retired; *b* 23 July 1924; *s* of late William Naismith Blyth and Jean (*née* Morrison); *m* 1st, 1949, Gabrielle Elodie (*née* Belloc) (*d* 1971); three *s* two *d*; 2nd, 1973, Lucy Anne (*née* Alcock); one *s* one *d*. *Educ:* Christ's Coll.; Lincoln Coll., Oxford (MA); Downing Coll., Cambridge (MA). Served War, RNVR, 1942–46. Editor, The Polar Record (publd by Scott Polar Res. Inst., Cambridge), 1949–54; joined FO, 1954; served: Geneva, 1955; Athens, 1959; Leopoldville, 1963; Accra, 1964; FO, 1966; Athens, 1968; FCO, 1972; Vienna, 1974; FCO, 1977. Pres., Hélène Heroys Literary Foundn, 1975–. Hon. Sec., Suffolk Preservation Soc., 1985–94. *Publications:* articles in The Polar Record. *Recreations:* gardening, military history, enjoying wine. *Address:* Crownland Hall, Walsham-le-Willows, Suffolk IP31 3BU. *T:* (01359) 259369. *Club:* Naval and Military.

BLYTHE, His Honour James Forbes, TD 1946; a Circuit Judge, 1978–92; Solicitor; *b* Coventry, 11 July 1917; *s* of J. F. Blythe and Dorothy Alice (*née* Hazlewood); *m* 1949, Margaret, *d* of P. D. Kinsey; two *d*. *Educ:* Wrekin Coll.; Birmingham Univ. (LLB). Commissioned TA, Royal Warwickshire Regt, 1936–53 (Major); served War of 1939–45 with BEF in France (Dunkirk), 1939–40; Central Mediterranean Force (Tunisia, Sicily, Italy, Corsica, S France and Austria), 1942–45; Air Liaison Officer GSO II (Ops) with RAF (despatches); GSO II (Ops) 10 Corps, 1945. Admitted solicitor, 1947; private practitioner in partnership in Coventry and Leamington Spa, 1948. HM Deputy Coroner for City of Coventry and Northern Dist of Warwickshire, 1954–64; HM Coroner for City of Coventry, 1964–78; a Recorder of the Crown Court, 1972–78. Pres., Warwicks Law Soc., 1978–79. *Recreations:* shooting, sailing; past player and Sec. Coventry Football Club (RU). *Address:* Hazlewood, Upper Ladyes' Hill, Kenilworth, Warwickshire CV8 2FB. *Clubs:* Army and Navy; Drapers (Coventry); Leamington Tennis Court.

BLYTHE, Mark Andrew, CB 1999; Principal Assistant Solicitor, Treasury Solicitor's Department, since 1989, and Legal Adviser, HM Treasury, since 1993; *b* 4 Sept. 1943; *s* of John Jarratt Blythe and Dorothy Kathleen Blythe; *m* 1972, Brigid Helen Frazer (*née* Skemp); two *s* one *d*. *Educ:* King Edward VII Grammar Sch., Sheffield; University Coll., Oxford (BCL, MA; Open Schol. in Classics, 1961; Gibbs Prize in Law, 1963). Called to the Bar, Inner Temple, 1966; Attorney, NY Bar, 1980. Teaching Associate, Univ. of Pennsylvania Law Sch., 1965–66; Chancery Bar, 1967–77; Legal Consultant, NY, 1978–80; Treasury Solicitor's Dept, 1981–; Assistant Solicitor, European Div., 1986–89; Hd, Central Adv. Div., 1989–93. *Address:* Treasury Chambers, Parliament Street, SW1P 3AG.

BLYTHE, Rex Arnold; Under-Secretary, Board of Inland Revenue, 1981–86, retired; *b* 11 Nov. 1928; *s* of late Sydney Arnold Blythe and Florence Blythe (*née* Jones); *m* 1953, Rachel Ann Best; one *s* two *d*. *Educ:* Bradford Grammar Sch.; Trinity Coll., Cambridge (MA Classics). Entered Inland Revenue as Inspector of Taxes, 1953; Sen. Inspector, 1962; Principal Inspector, 1968; Asst Sec., 1974. *Recreations:* golf, photography, walking, travel. *Address:* 18A Kirkwick Avenue, Harpenden, Herts AL5 2QX. *T:* (01582) 715833. *Club:* MCC.

BLYTHE, Ronald George; writer, since 1953; *b* 6 Nov. 1922; *s* of Albert George Blythe and Matilda Elizabeth (*née* Elkins). *Educ:* St Peter's and St Gregory's Sch., Sudbury, Suffolk. Librarian, 1943–53. Soc. of Authors' Travel Scholarship, 1969. Editor, Penguin Classics, 1966–87. Assistant, Aldeburgh Fest., 1955–57; Member: Eastern Arts Lit. Panel, 1975–85; Cttee, Centre of E Anglian Studies, UEA, 1975–80; Soc. of Authors' Management Cttee, 1980–85; Chm., Essex Fest., 1981–84. Pres., John Clare Soc., 1981–. FRSL 1969. Hon. MA UEA, 1990. *Publications:* A Treasonable Growth, 1960; Immediate Possession, 1961; The Age of Illusion, 1963; William Hazlitt: selected writings, 1970; Akenfield (Heinemann Award), 1969; Aldeburgh Anthology, 1972; (ed jtly) Works of Thomas Hardy, 1978; The View in Winter, 1979; (ed) Writing in a War: stories, essays and poems of 1939–45, 1982; Places, 1982; From the Headlands, 1982; The Stories of Ronald Blythe (Angel Prize for Literature), 1985; Divine Landscapes, 1986; Each Returning Day: the pleasure of diaries, 1989; Private Words: letters and diaries of the Second World War, 1991; Word from Wormingford, 1997; First Friends, 1998; Going to See George and other outings, 1999; Talking About John Clare, 1999; The Papers of the Late Lieutenant, 2000; Out of the Valley, 2000; The Circling Year, 2001. *Recreations:* walking, looking, listening. *Address:* Bottengoms Farm, Wormingford, Colchester, Essex CO6 3AP. *T:* (01206) 271308.

BOADEN, Helen; Controller, BBC Radio 4, since 2000; *b* 1 March 1956; *d* of William John Boaden and Barbara Mary Boaden; *m* 1994, Stephen Burley. *Educ:* Univ. of Sussex (BA Hons English 1978). Care Asst, Hackney Social Services, 1978; Reporter: Radio WBAI, NY, 1979; Radio Tees and Radio Aire, 1980–83; Producer, BBC Radio Leeds, 1983–85; Reporter: File on 4, Radio 4, 1985–91; Brass Tacks, BBC 2, 1985–91;

Presenter: Woman's Hour, Radio 4, 1985–91; Verdict, Channel 4, 1991–; Editor, File on 4, Radio 4, 1991–94; Head: Network Current Affairs, BBC Manchester, 1994–97; Business Progs, BBC News, 1997; Current Affairs and Business Progs, 1998–2000. *Recreations:* walking, food, travel. *Address:* c/o BBC, Broadcasting House, Portland Place, W1A 1AA. *T:* (020) 7580 4468.

BOAG, Prof. John Wilson; Professor of Physics as Applied to Medicine, University of London, Institute of Cancer Research, 1965–76, now Emeritus; *b* Elgin, Scotland, 20 June 1911; *s* of John and Margaret A. Boag; *m* 1938, Isabel Petrie; no *c. Educ:* Universities of Glasgow, Cambridge and Braunschweig. Engineer, British Thomson Houston Co., Rugby, 1936–41; Physicist, Medical Research Council, 1941–52; Visiting Scientist, National Bureau of Standards, Washington, DC, 1953–54; Physicist, British Empire Cancer Campaign, Mount Vernon Hospital, 1954–64; Royal Society (Leverhulme) Visiting Prof. to Poland, 1964. President: Hosp. Physicists' Assoc., 1959; Assoc. for Radiation Res. (UK), 1972–74; Internat. Assoc. for Radiation Res., 1970–74; British Inst. of Radiology, 1975–76. L. H. Gray Medal, ICRU, 1973; Barclay Medal, BIR, 1975. *Publications:* (jtly) Kapitza in Cambridge and Moscow, 1990; papers on radiation dosimetry, statistics, radiation chemistry, radiodiagnosis. *Address:* 88 Craiglockhart Road, Edinburgh EH14 1EP.

BOAL, (John) Graham; QC 1993; **His Honour Judge Boal;** a Senior Circuit Judge, and Permanent Judge at Central Criminal Court, since 1996; *b* 24 Oct. 1943; *s* of late Surg. Captain Jackson Graham Boal, RN, and late Dorothy Kenley Boal; *m* 1978, Elizabeth Mary East; one *s. Educ:* Eastbourne Coll.; King's Coll. London (LLB). Called to the Bar, Gray's Inn, 1966, Bencher, 1991; Junior Treasury Counsel, 1977–85; Sen. Prosecuting Counsel to the Crown, 1985–91; First Sen. Counsel to the Crown at CCC, 1991–93; a Recorder, 1985–96. Vice Chm., Criminal Bar Assoc., 1991–93. *Recreations:* theatre, golf, watching cricket. *Address:* Central Criminal Court, Old Bailey, EC4M 7EH. *Clubs:* Garrick, MCC; Royal Wimbledon Golf, Royal West Norfolk Golf.

BOAM, Maj.-Gen. Thomas Anthony, CB 1987; CBE 1978 (OBE 1973); Trustee, Leonard Cheshire, and Chairman, Leonard Cheshire South Region, since 1997; *b* 14 Feb. 1932; *s* of late Lt-Col T. S. Boam, OBE, and of Mrs Boam; *m* 1961, Penelope Christine Mary Roberts; one *s* two *d. Educ:* Bradfield Coll.; RMA Sandhurst. Commissioned Scots Guards, 1952; Canal Zone, Egypt (with 1SG), 1952–54; GSO3, MO4 War Office, 1959–61; psc 1962; Kenya (with 2 Scots Guards), 1963–64; DAA&QMG 4 Guards Bde, 1964–65; Malaysia (with 1SG), 1966–67; BM 4 Guards Bde, 1967–69; GSO1 (DS) Staff Coll., Camberley, 1970–71; CO 2SG, 1972–74; RCDS 1974–75; Comd BAAT Nigeria, 1976–78; BGS (Trg) HQ UKLF, 1978; Dep. Comdr and COS Hong Kong, 1979–81; Hd of British Defence Staff Washington, and Defence Attaché, 1981–84, Mil. Attaché, 1981–83; Comdr, British Forces Hong Kong, and Maj.-Gen., Brigade of Gurkhas, 1985–87. MEC, Hong Kong, 1985–87. Dir, British Consultants Bureau, 1988–95. Governor: Hayes Dashwood Foundn, 1992–; Queen Alexandra Hosp. Home, 1996–. *Recreations:* shooting, fishing, gardening, sport. *Address:* Bury Gate House, Pulborough, W Sussex RH20 1HA. *Clubs:* Army and Navy, MCC.

BOARDMAN, family name of **Baron Boardman**.

BOARDMAN, Baron *cr* 1980 (Life Peer), of Welford in the County of Northamptonshire; **Thomas Gray Boardman,** MC 1944; TD 1952; DL; Chairman, National Westminster Bank, 1983–89 (Director, 1979–89; Chairman, Eastern Region, 1979–83); *b* 12 Jan. 1919; *s* of John Clayton Boardman, late of Daventry, and Janet Boardman, formerly Houston; *m* 1948, (Norah Mary) Deirdre, *widow* of John Henry Chaworth-Musters, Annesley Park, Nottingham, and *d* of late Hubert Vincent Gough; two *s* one *d. Educ:* Bromsgrove. Served Northants Yeomanry, 1939–45 and subsequently; Commanding Northants Yeomanry, 1956. Qualified as a Solicitor, 1947. MP (C) Leicester SW, Nov. 1967–74, Leicester South Feb.-Sept. 1974; Minister for Industry, DTI, 1972–74; Chief Sec. to Treasury, 1974. Hon. Treas., Cons. Party, 1981–82. Chairman: Chamberlain Phipps Ltd, 1958–72; The Steetley Co. Ltd, 1978–83 (Dir, 1975–83); Heron Internat. NV, 1993–95; Director: Allied Breweries Ltd, 1968–72 and 1974–77 (Vice-Chm., 1975–76); MEPC, 1980–89; Mem. Adv. Bd, LEK Partnership, 1990–97. Pres., Assoc. of British Chambers of Commerce, 1977–80. Chm., Cttee of London and Scottish Bankers, 1987–89. Mem., Exec. Assoc. of Cons. Peers, 1981–84, 1991–95. Freeman, City of London, 1984; HM Lieut, City of London, 1989–; DL Northants, 1977–, High Sheriff, Northants, 1979. *Recreation:* riding. *Address:* 29 Tufton Court, Tufton Street, SW1P 3QH. *T:* (020) 7222 6793; The Manor House, Welford, Northampton NN6 6HX. *T:* (01858) 575235. *Club:* Cavalry and Guards.

See also Baron Ellenborough.

BOARDMAN, Christopher Miles, MBE 1993; professional cyclist, retired 2000; *b* 26 Aug. 1968; *s* of Keith and Carole Boardman; *m* 1988, Sally-Ann Edwards; three *s* one *d.* Gold Medal, Individual Pursuit, Olympic Games, Barcelona, 1992; World Champion: Pursuit, 1994; Time Trial, 1994; Yellow Jersey Holder, Tour de France, 1994, 1997, 1998; Silver Medal, Time Trial, World Championship, 1996; Bronze Medal, Time Trial, Olympic Games, Atlanta, 1996; World Champion, 4,000 Pursuit, 1996; World One Hour Record Holder: 52.270 km, 1993; 56.375 km, 1996; (under new regulations) 49.441 km, 2000. Mem., Sports Council for England, 1995–96, English Sports Council, 1996–. Hon. DSc Brighton, 1997; Hon. MSc Liverpool, 1995. Man of Year Award, Cheshire Life mag., 1997. *Publication:* (with Andrew Longmore) The Complete Book of Cycling, 2000. *Address:* Beyond Level Four, Lindfield House, Station Approach, Meols, Wirral L47 8XA. *T:* (0151) 632 3383.

BOARDMAN, Faith; Chief Executive, London Borough of Lambeth, since 2000; *b* 21 Aug. 1950; *d* of Kenneth Mills and Vera Mills (*née* Waterson); *m* 1974, David Boardman; one *s* one *d. Educ:* Lady Margaret Hall, Oxford (MA Modern Hist.). Fast-stream grad. trainee, 1972–77, Grade 7, VAT Policy, 1977–79, HM Customs and Excise; Fiscal Policy, HM Treasury, 1979–83; HM Customs and Excise: Tobacco Taxation, 1983–86; Personnel Policy, 1986–89, Grade 5, 1988; Chief Exec. (Collector), London Central, 1989–95; Chief Exec., (Grade 3) Contributions Agency, DSS, 1995–97; Grade 2, 1997; Chief Exec., CSA, 1997–2000. Financial Services Woman of Year Award, 1990. *Recreations:* family, friends, music, hill-walking. *Address:* Lambeth Town Hall, Brixton Hill, Brixton, SW2 1RW.

BOARDMAN, Sir John, Kt 1989; FSA 1957; FBA 1969; Lincoln Professor of Classical Archaeology and Art, and Fellow of Lincoln College, University of Oxford, 1978–94 (Hon. Fellow, 1995); *b* 20 Aug. 1927; *s* of Frederick Archibald Boardman; *m* 1952, Sheila Joan Lyndon Stanford; one *s* one *d. Educ:* Chigwell Sch.; Magdalene Coll., Cambridge (BA 1948, MA 1951, Walston Student, 1948–50; Hon. Fellow 1984). 2nd Lt, Intell. Corps, 1950–52. Asst Dir, British Sch. at Athens, 1952–55; Asst Keeper, Ashmolean Museum, Oxford, 1955–59; Reader in Classical Archaeology, Univ. of Oxford, 1959–78; Fellow of Merton Coll., Oxford, 1963–78, Hon. Fellow, 1978. Geddes-Harrower Prof., Aberdeen Univ., 1974; Vis. Prof., Australian Inst. of Archaeology, 1987; Prof. of Ancient History, Royal Acad., 1989–; Lectures: Andrew W. Mellon, Washington, 1993; Myres Meml, Oxford, 1993. Editor: Journal of Hellenic Studies, 1958–65; Lexicon Iconographicum, 1972–99; Cambridge Ancient History, 1978–94. Conducted excavations on Chios, 1953–55, and at Tocra in Libya, 1964–65. Delegate, OUP, 1979–89. Pres. Fédn Internat. des Assocs d'Etudes Classiques, 1994–97. Corresponding Fellow: Bavarian Acad. of Scis, 1969; Athens Acad., 1997; Fellow, Inst. of Etruscan Studies, Florence, 1983; Hon. Fellow, Archaeol Soc. of Athens, 1989 (Vice Pres., 1998–); Member: Amer. Philosophical Soc., 1999; Accad. dei Lincei, Rome, 1999; Foreign Mem., Royal Danish Acad., 1979; Mem. associé, Acad. des Inscriptions et Belles Lettres, Institut de France, 1991 (Correspondant, 1985); Hon. Mem., Archaeol Inst. of America, 1993. Hon. MRIA, 1986. Hon. Dr: Dept of Archaeology and History, Univ. of Athens, 1991; Sorbonne, 1994. Cromer Greek Prize, 1959, Kenyon Medal, 1995, British Acad. *Publications:* Cretan Collection in Oxford, 1961; Date of the Knossos Tablets, 1963; Island Gems, 1963; Greeks Overseas, 1964, rev. edn 1999; Greek Art, 1964, rev. edns 1973, 1984, 1996; Excavations at Tocra, vol. I 1966, vol. II 1973; Pre-Classical, 1967, repr. 1978; Greek Emporio, 1967; Engraved Gems, 1968; Archaic Greek Gems, 1968; Greek Gems and Finger Rings, 1970, repr. 2001; (with D. Kurtz) Greek Burial Customs, 1971; Athenian Black Figure Vases, 1974; Athenian Red Figure Vases, Archaic Period, 1975; Intaglios and Rings, 1975; Corpus Vasorum, Oxford, vol. 3, 1975; Greek Sculpture, Archaic Period, 1978; (with M. Robertson) Corpus Vasorum, Castle Ashby, 1978; (with M. L. Vollenweider) Catalogue of Engraved Gems, Ashmolean Museum, 1978; (with D. Scarisbrick) Harari Collection of Finger Rings, 1978; (with E. La Rocca) Eros in Greece, 1978; Escarabeos de Piedra de Ibiza, 1984; La Ceramica Antica, 1984; Greek Sculpture, Classical Period, 1985; (with D. Finn) The Parthenon and its Sculptures, 1985; (jtly) The Oxford History of the Classical World, 1986; Athenian Red Figure Vases, Classical Period, 1989; (jtly) The Oxford History of Classical Art, 1993; The Diffusion of Classical Art in Antiquity, 1994; Greek Sculpture, Later Classical, 1995; Early Greek Vase Painting, 1998; Persia and the West, 2000; Greek Vases, 2001; articles in jls. *Address:* 11 Park Street, Woodstock, Oxford OX20 1SJ. *T:* (01993) 811259. *Club:* Athenæum.

BOARDMAN, Norman Keith, AO 1993; PhD, ScD; FRS 1978; FAA; FTSE; Chief Executive, Commonwealth Scientific and Industrial Research Organization, 1986–90 (post-retirement Fellow, 1990–99); *b* 16 Aug. 1926; *s* of William Robert Boardman and Margaret Boardman; *m* 1952, Mary Clayton Shepherd; two *s* five *d. Educ:* Melbourne Univ. (BSc 1946, MSc 1949); St John's Coll., Cambridge (PhD 1954, ScD 1974). FAA 1972; FTSE (FTS 1986). ICI Fellow, Cambridge, 1953–55; Fulbright Scholar, Univ. of Calif, LA, 1964–66. Res. Officer, Wool Res. Section, CSIRO, 1949–51; CSIRO Div. of Plant Industry: Sen. Res. Scientist, 1956; Principal Res. Scientist, 1961; Sen. Prin. Res. Scientist, 1966; Chief Res. Scientist, 1968; Mem. Exec., 1977–85, Chm. and Chief Exec., 1985–86, CSIRO. Member: Aust. Res. Grants Cttee, 1971–75; Council, ANU, 1979–89 and 1990–91; Bd, Aust. Centre for Internat. Agricl Research, 1982–88; Nat. Water Research Council, 1982–85; Prime Minister's Science Council, 1989–90. Director: Sirotech Ltd, 1986–90; Landcare Aust. Ltd, 1990–98. Pres., Aust. Biochem. Soc., 1976–78; Sec. of Sci. Policy, Aust. Acad. of Sci., 1993–97 (Treas., 1978–81). Corresp. Mem., Amer. Soc. of Plant Physiologists. Hon. DSc Newcastle, NSW, 1988. David Syme Res. Prize, Melbourne Univ., 1967; Lemberg Medal, Aust. Biochem. Soc., 1969. *Publications:* scientific papers on plant biochemistry, partic. photosynthesis and structure, function and biogenesis of chloroplasts; papers on science and technology policy. *Recreations:* reading, tennis, listening to music. *Address:* 6 Somers Crescent, Forrest, ACT 2603, Australia. *T:* (2) 62951746. *Club:* Commonwealth (Canberra).

BOAS, John Robert Sotheby, (Bob); Trustee, National Heritage Memorial Fund and Heritage Lottery Fund, since 1998; *b* 28 Feb. 1937; *s* of Edgar Henry Boas and Mary Katherine Boas; *m* 1965, Elisabeth Gersted; one *s* one *d* (and one *s* decd). *Educ:* Corpus Christi Coll., Cambridge (BA Maths (Sen. Optimes)). FCA 1964. Price Waterhouse, 1960–65; ICI, 1965–66; S. G. Warburg, 1966–95; Dir, 1971–95; Vice Chm., 1990–95; Man. Dir, SBC Warburg, 1995–97; Advr, UBS Warburg (formerly Warburg Dillon Read), 1998–. Non-executive Director: Chesterfield Properties, 1978–99; ENO, 1990–99; Norwich Union, 1998–2000; Invesco Continental Smaller Cos Trust, 1998–; Trident Safeguards Ltd, 1998–; Land Command Mgt Bd, 1998–. Dir, SFA, 1988–96. *Recreations:* opera, music, art, theatre, reading, golf, travelling. *Address:* 22 Mansfield Street, W1G 9NR. *Club:* Arts.

BOASE, Martin; Chairman, Omnicom UK plc, 1989–95; *b* 14 July 1932; *s* of Prof. Alan Martin Boase and Elizabeth Grizelle Boase; *m* 1st, 1960, Terry Ann Moir (marr. diss. 1971); one *s* one *d*; 2nd, 1974, Pauline Valerie Brownrigg; one *s* one *d. Educ:* Bedales Sch.; Rendcomb Coll.; New Coll., Oxford. MA; FIPA 1976. Executive, The London Press Exchange, Ltd, 1958–60; Pritchard Wood and Partners, Ltd: Manager, 1961–65; Dir, then Dep. Man. Dir, 1965–68; Founding Partner, The Boase Massimi Pollitt Partnership, Ltd, 1968; Chm., Boase Massimi Pollitt plc, 1977–89 (Jt Chm., 1977–79). Chairman: Maiden Outdoor, 1993–; Kiss 100 FM, 1993–2000; Herald Investment Trust, 1994–; Investment Trust of Investment Trusts, 1995–; Heal's, 1997–; Global Professional Media plc, 1999–; Jupiter Dividend & Growth Investments Trust, 1999–; Director: Omnicom Gp Inc., 1989–93; EMAP plc, 1991–2000; Matthew Clark plc, 1995–98; New Star Investment Trust, 2000–. Chairman: Advertising Assoc., 1987–92; British Television Advertising Awards Ltd, 1993–2000. Dir, Oxford Playhouse Trust, 1991–97. *Recreation:* the Turf. *Address:* (office) 12 Bishop's Bridge Road, W2 6AA.

BOATENG, Rt Hon. Paul (Yaw); PC 1999; MP (Lab) Brent South, since 1987; Financial Secretary, HM Treasury, since 2001; barrister-at-law; *b* 14 June 1951; *s* of Eleanor and Kwaku Boateng; *m* 1980, Janet Alleyne; two *s* three *d. Educ:* Ghana Internat. Sch.; Accra Acad.; Apsley Grammar Sch.; Bristol Univ. (LLB Hons); Coll. of Law. Admitted Solicitor, 1976; Solicitor, Paddington Law Centre, 1976–79; Solicitor and Partner, B. M. Birnberg and Co., 1979–87; called to the Bar, Gray's Inn, 1989. Legal Advr, Scrap Sus Campaign, 1977–81. Greater London Council: Mem. (Lab) for Walthamstow, 1981–86; Chm., Police Cttee, 1981–86; Vice-Chm., Ethnic Minorities Cttee, GLC, 1981–86. Contested (Lab) Hertfordshire W, 1983. Chairman: Afro-Caribbean Educn Resource Project, 1978–86; Westminster CRC, 1979–81. Opposition frontbench spokesman: on treasury and economic affairs, 1989–92; on legal affairs, LCD, 1992–97; Parly Under-Sec. of State, DoH, 1997–98; Minister of State, 1998–2001, and Dep. Home Sec., 1999–2001, Home Office. Mem., H of C Environment Cttee, 1987–89. Member: Home Sec.'s Adv. Council on Race Relations, 1981–86; WCC Commn on prog. to combat racism, 1984–91; Police Training Council, 1981–85; Exec., NCCL, 1980–86. Chm. Governors, Priory Park Sch., 1978–84; Governor, Police Staff Coll., Bramshill, 1981–84; Mem. Ct, Bristol Univ., 1994–. Mem. Bd, ENO, 1984–97. Broadcaster. *Publication:* (contrib.) Reclaiming the Ground, 1993. *Recreations:* escapist. *Address:* House of Commons, SW1A 0AA. *Clubs:* Mangrove; Black and White Café (Bristol).

BOBROW, Prof. Martin, CBE 1995; FRCP, FRCPath, FMedSci; Professor of Medical Genetics, Cambridge University, since 1995; *b* 6 Feb. 1938; *s* of Joe and Bessie Bobrow; *m* 1963, Lynda Geraldine Strauss; three *d. Educ:* Univ. of the Witwatersrand (BSc Hons 1958; MB BCh 1963; DSc Med 1979). MRCPath 1978, FRCPath 1990; FRCP 1986.

Clin. Sci. Officer, MRC Population Genetics Res. Unit, 1965–72; Consultant in Clin. Genetics, Oxford, and Mem., MRC Ext. Sci. Staff, Genetics Lab., Oxford Univ., 1974–81; Prof. of Human Genetics, Univ. of Amsterdam, 1981–82; Prince Philip Prof. of Paediatric Res., UMDS of Guy's and St Thomas' Hosps, London Univ., 1982–95. Mem. Council, 1988–92, 1993–94, Chm., Molecular and Cellular Medicine Bd, 1992–95, MRC; Chairman: Cttee on Med. Aspects of Radiation in the Envt, 1985–92; Unrelated Live Donor Transplant Regulatory Authy, 1990–99; Nat. Council, Muscular Dystrophy Gp, 1995– (Mem., 1980–, Chm., 1993–95, Res. Cttee); Member: Black Adv. Gp on Possible Increased Incidence of Cancer in West Cumbria, 1983–84; Cttee to examine the ethical implications of gene therapy, 1989–93; NHS Central R&D Cttee, DoH, 1991–97; Gene Therapy Adv. Cttee, 1993–94; Lewisham NHS Trust Bd, 1994–95; Nuffield Council on Bioethics, 1996–; Human Genetics Adv. Commn, 1997–99. Governor, Wellcome Trust, 1996–. FRCPCH 1997; Founder FMedSci 1998. *Publications:* papers in sci. books and jls. *Address:* Department of Medical Genetics, Wellcome/MRC Building, Addenbrooke's Hospital, Cambridge CB2 2XY.

BOCK, Prof. Claus Victor, MA, DrPhil; Professor of German Language and Literature, Westfield College, University of London, 1969–84, now Emeritus; Hon. Research Fellow, Queen Mary and Westfield College (formerly Westfield College), since 1984, Fellow, 1993; *b* Hamburg, 7 May 1926; *o s* of Frederick Bock, merchant and manufacturer, and Margot (*née* Meyerhof). *Educ:* Quaker Sch., Eerde, Holland; Univs of Amsterdam, Manchester, Basle. DrPhil (insigni cum laude) Basle 1955. Asst Lectr in German, Univ. of Manchester, 1956–58; University of London: Lectr, Queen Mary Coll., 1958–69; Reader in German Lang. and Lit., 1964; Chm., Bd of Studies in Germanic Langs and Lit., 1970–73; Hon. Dir, Inst. of Germanic Studies, 1973–81 (Hon. Fellow, 1989); Dean, Fac. of Arts, 1980–84; Mem., Senate, 1981–83; Mem., Acad. Council, 1981–83; Mem., Central Research Fund (A), 1981–84. Mem. Council, English Goethe Soc., 1965–; Chm., Stichting Castrum Peregrini, 1984–98 (Mem., 1971–). Hon. Pres., Assoc. of Teachers of German, 1973–75. Mem., Maatschappij der Nederlandse Letteren, 1977. Mem. Editl Bd, Bithell Series of Dissertations, 1978–84. Officer, Order of Merit (FRG), 1984. *Publications:* Deutsche erfahren Holland 1725–1925, 1956; Q. Kuhlmann als Dichter, 1957; ed (with Margot Ruben) K. Wolfskehl Ges. Werke, 1960; ed (with G. F. Senior) Goethe the Critic, 1960; Pente Pigadia und die Tagebücher des Clement Harris, 1962; ed (with L. Helbing) Fr. Gundolf Briefwechsel mit H. Steiner und E. R. Curtius, 1963; Wort-Konkordanz zur Dichtung Stefan Georges, 1964; ed (with L. Helbing) Fr. Gundolf Briefe Neue Folge, 1965; A Tower of Ivory?, 1970; (with L. Helbing and K. Kluncker) Stefan George: Dokumente seiner Wirkung, 1974; (ed) London German Studies, 1980; (with K. Kluncker) Wolfgang Cordan: Jahre der Freundschaft, 1982; Untergetaucht unter Freunden, 1985,4th edn 1998; Besuch im Elfenbeinturm (selected essays), 1990; (ed) W. Frommel Templer und Rosenkreuz, 1991; (ed) W. Frommel Meditationen, 1994; (ed) W. Frommel Briefe an die Eltern 1920–1959, 1997; articles in English and foreign jls and collections. *Recreation:* foreign travel. *Address:* c/o Castrum Peregrini Presse, PB 645, 1000 AP Amsterdam, Netherlands. *T:* (20) 6230043.

BOCK, Dieter; Chairman, Advanta AG, Frankfurt, since 1986; *b* 3 March 1939; *s* of Rudolf Bock and Helene (*née* Dannert); *m* 1985, Olga Giro; four *s*. *Educ:* Marburg; Munich Univ. Chief Exec., and Man. Dir, Lonrho plc, 1993–96; Vice-Chm., TrizecHahn Corp., 1997–98. Senator, Univ. of Cottbus, Germany, 1999–. Hon. Citizen, Houston, Texas. *Recreation:* sailing. *Address:* 18a St James's Place, SW1A 1NH. *Clubs:* Athenæum; Royal Cape Yacht (Cape Town).

BODDINGTON, Ewart Agnew; JP; DL; Chairman, The Boddington Group PLC (formerly Boddingtons' Breweries), 1970–88 (President, 1989–95); *b* 7 April 1927; *m* 1954, Vine Anne Clayton (*d* 1989); two *s* one *d*. *Educ:* Stowe Sch., Buckingham; Trinity Coll., Cambridge (MA). Jt Man. Dir, Boddingtons', 1957, Man. Dir, 1980. Dir, Northern Bd, National Westminster Bank, 1977–92. Pres., Inst. of Brewing, 1972–74; Chm., Brewers' Soc., 1984–85; Mem., Brewers' Co., 1980–. JP Macclesfield, 1959; High Sheriff of Cheshire, 1978–79; DL Cheshire 1993. Chethams' School of Music: Feoffee, 1953– (Chm., 1969–92); Gov., 1953–99 (Chm., 1969–83). Trustee, NSPCC, 1993–. Hon. MA Manchester, 1977. *Recreations:* shooting, fishing, music. *Address:* Fanshawe Brook Farm, Henbury, Macclesfield SK11 9PP. *T:* (01260) 224387.

BODDY, Jack Richard, MBE 1973; JP; Group Secretary, Agricultural and Allied Workers Trade Group, Transport and General Workers Union, 1982–87 (General Secretary, National Union of Agricultural and Allied Workers, 1978–82); *b* 23 Aug. 1922; *s* of Percy James Boddy and Lucy May Boddy, JP; *m* 1943, Muriel Lilian (*née* Webb) (*d* 1987); three *s* one *d*; *m* 1990, (Margaret) Joan Laws. *Educ:* City of Norwich Sch. Agricultural worker, 1939; farm foreman, 1943. District Organiser: Lincolnshire NUAAW, 1953; Norfolk NUAAW, 1960. Mem., TUC Gen. Council, 1978–83. Leader, Workers' side, Agricl Wages Bd, 1978–87. Member: Agricl Cttee, EDC, 1978–88; Economic and Social Cttee, EEC, 1980–90; Food and Drink Cttee, EDC, 1984–87; Industrial Injuries Adv. Cttee, DHSS, 1983–87. Mem., Swaffham Town Council, 1987– (Dep. Mayor, 1990–91; Mayor, 1991–92); Breckland District Council: Mem., 1987–99; Chm., Housing Cttee, 1995–98; Vice Chm., Planning Cttee, 1995–98; Chm., Eco-tech Cttee, 1995–98; Vice Chm., 1997–98; Chm., 1998–99. Pres., Mid Norfolk Mencap, 1988–91. Freeman, City of Norwich. JP Swaffham, 1947. *Recreations:* caravanning, gardening. *Address:* The Brambles, 2b Spinners Lane, Swaffham, Norfolk PE37 7ND. *T:* (01760) 722916.

BODDY, Prof. Keith, CBE 1998 (OBE 1989); PhD, DSc; FRSE; Professor of Medical Physics, University of Newcastle upon Tyne, and Head of Regional Medical Physics Department, Northern Regional Health Authority, 1978–98; *b* 1 Nov. 1937; *s* of late Ernest Boddy and Edith Mary Boddy; *m* 1960, Sylvia Mary (*née* Goodier); two *s*. *Educ:* Liverpool Univ. (BSc 1959); St Bartholomew's Hosp. Med. Coll. (MSc 1961); Glasgow Univ. (PhD 1971); Strathclyde Univ. (DSc 1976). FRSE 1980; FInstP 1969; FIPEM (FIPSM 1988; Hon. FIPEM 1998). Head of Health Physics, AEI Res. Lab., Aldermaston Court, 1959–63; Lectr, 1963–67, Sen. Lectr, 1967–78, and Head of Health Physics and Nuclear Medicine Unit, Scottish Univs Res. and Reactor Centre. Numerous eponymous lectures. Member: Radioactive Waste Mgt Adv. Cttee, 1989–; Cttee on Med. Aspects of Radiation in the Envmt, 1991–; Ionising Radiations Adv. Cttee, 1995–. President: Hosp. Physicists Assoc., 1986–88; Inst. of Physical Scis in Medicine, 1986–88; Internat. Orgn for Med. Physics, 1994–97; Internat. Union for Physical and Engrg Scis in Medicine, 1997–2000; Hon. Member: British Nuclear Medicine Soc., 1980; RCR, 1981; BIR, 1997. Hon. FSRP 1999. Hon. DSc De Montfort, 1997. Glazebrook Medal and Prize, Inst. of Physics, 1991; Skinner Medal, RCR, 1999. *Publications:* numerous papers, lectures, contribs to books; contribs to reports of nat. cttees. *Recreations:* walking, gardening, crosswords, logic puzzles, music, family activities, stray animals. *Address:* 2 Eppleton Hall, Colliery Lane, Hetton-le-Hole, Tyne and Wear DH5 0QZ. *T:* and *Fax:* (0191) 526 4315.

BODEN, Prof. Margaret Ann, ScD, PhD; FBA 1983; Professor of Philosophy and Psychology, University of Sussex, since 1980; *b* 26 Nov. 1936; *d* of late Leonard Forbes Boden, OBE, LLB and Violet Dorothy Dawson; *m* 1967, John Raymond Spiers, *qv* (marr. diss. 1981); one *s* one *d*. *Educ:* City of London Sch. for Girls; Newnham Coll., Cambridge (Major schol. in Med. Scis; Sarah Smithson Scholar in Moral Scis; MA; Associate, 1981–93; ScD 1990); Harvard Grad. Sch. (Harkness Fellow; AM; PhD in Cognitive and Social Psychology). Asst Lectr, then Lectr, in Philosophy, Birmingham Univ., 1959–65; Sussex University: Lectr, 1965–72; Reader, 1972–80; Founding Dean, Sch. of Cognitive Sciences, later Cognitive and Computing Sciences, 1987. Vis. Scientist, Yale Univ., 1979. Co-founder, Dir, 1968–85, Sec., 1968–79, Harvester Press. Founding Chm., Hist. and Philosophy of Psychology Sect., BPsS, 1983; Pres., Sect. X, BAAS, 1993; Vice-Pres., and Chm. of Council, Royal Instn of GB, 1993–95 (Mem. Council, 1992–95). Member: Council for Science and Society, 1986–91 (Trustee, 1990–91); ABRC, 1989–90 (Chm., Working Gp on Peer-Review, 1989–90); Animal Procedures Cttee, Home Office, 1994–98; Council, Royal Inst. of Philosophy, 1987–; Council, British Acad., 1988–91 (Vice-Pres., 1989–91). Mem., Bd of Curators, Sch. of Advanced Study, Univ. of London, 1995–. Mem., Soc. of Authors, 1982–98. Trustee, Eric Gill Trust, 1993–. Mem., Academia Europaea, 1993; Fellow, Amer. Assoc. for Artificial Intelligence, 1993; FRSA 1992. Hon. DSc Sussex, 2001. Leslie McMichael Premium, IERE, 1977. *Publications:* Purposive Explanation in Psychology, 1972; Artificial Intelligence and Natural Man, 1977; Piaget, 1979; Minds and Mechanisms, 1981; Computer Models of Mind, 1988; Artificial Intelligence in Psychology, 1989; (ed) The Philosophy of Artificial Intelligence, 1990; The Creative Mind: myths and mechanisms, 1990; (ed) Dimensions of Creativity, 1994; (ed) The Philosophy of Artificial Life, 1996; (ed) Artificial Intelligence, 1996; General Editor: Explorations in Cognitive Science; Harvester Studies in Cognitive Science; Harvester Studies in Philosophy; contribs to philosophical and psychological jls. *Recreations:* dress-making, dreaming about the South Pacific. *Address:* School of Cognitive and Computing Sciences, University of Sussex, Brighton BN1 9QH. *T:* (01273) 678386. *Club:* Reform.

BODEY, Hon. Sir David (Roderick Lessiter), Kt 1999; **Hon. Mr Justice Bodey;** a Judge of the High Court of Justice, Family Division, since 1999; Family Division Liaison Judge for North Eastern Circuit, since 2001; *b* 14 Oct. 1947; *s* of late Reginald Augustus Bodey, FIA and Betty Francis Bodey; *m* 1976, Ruth (*née* MacAdorey); one *s* one *d*. *Educ:* King's Sch., Canterbury; Univ. of Bristol (LLB Hons 1969). Called to the Bar, Middle Temple, 1970 (Harmsworth Scholar, 1970), Bencher, 1998; QC 1991; an Asst Recorder, 1989; a Recorder, 1993–98; a Dep. High Court Judge, 1994–98; Family Div. Liaison Judge for London, 1999–2001. Legal Assessor, 1983–94, Sen. Legal Assessor, 1994–98, UKCC. Mem., Supreme Court Procedure Cttee, 1995–97. Chm., Family Law Bar Assoc., 1997–98 (Sec., 1995–97); Mem., Family Cttee, Justice, 1995–98. Fellow, Internat. Acad. of Matrimonial Lawyers, 1995. *Recreations:* music, marathon running. *Address:* Royal Courts of Justice, Strand, WC2A 2LL. *Club:* Lansdowne.

BODGER; *see* Steele-Bodger.

BODINHAM, Susan; *see* Sowden, S.

BODMER, Sir Walter (Fred), Kt 1986; FRCPath; FRS 1974; FIBiol; Principal, Hertford College, Oxford, since 1996; *b* 10 Jan. 1936; *s* of late Dr Ernest Julius and Sylvia Emily Bodmer; *m* 1956, Julia Gwynaeth Pilkington, FMedSci (*d* 2001); two *s* one *d*. *Educ:* Manchester Grammar Sch.; Clare Coll., Cambridge (BA 1956; MA, PhD 1959). FRCPath 1984; FIBiol 1990. Research Fellow 1958–61, Official Fellow 1961, Hon. Fellow 1989, Clare Coll., Cambridge; Demonstrator in Genetics, Univ. of Cambridge, 1960–61; Asst Prof. 1962–66, Associate Prof. 1966–68, Prof. 1968–70, Dept of Genetics, Stanford Univ.; Prof. of Genetics, Univ. of Oxford, 1970–79; Dir of Res., 1979–91, Dir Gen., 1991–96, ICRF. Non-exec. Dir, Fisons plc, 1990–96. Chm., BBC Sci. Consultative Gp, 1981–87; Member: BBC Gen. Adv. Council, 1981–91 (Chm., 1987); Council, Internat. Union Against Cancer, 1982–90; Adv. Bd for Res. Councils, 1983–88; Council, Found for Sci. and Technol., 1995–; Chairman: COPUS, 1990–93; Orgn of European Cancer Insts, 1990–93; NRPB, 1998–; President: Royal Statistical Soc., 1984–85 (Vice-Pres., 1983–84; Hon. Fellow, 1997); BAAS, 1987–88 (Vice-Pres., 1989–; Chm., Council, 1996); ASE, 1989–90; Human Genome Orgn, 1990–92; British Soc. for Histocompatibility and Immunogenetics, 1990–91 (Hon. Mem. 1992); EACR, 1994–96; British Assoc. for Cancer Res., 1998–; first Pres., Internat. Fedn of Assocs for Advancement of Sci. and Technol., 1992–94; Vice-President: Royal Instn, 1981–82; Parly and Scientific Cttee, 1990–93; Hon. Vice-Pres., Res. Defence Soc., 1990–. Trustee: BM (Natural History), 1983–93 (Chm., Bd of Trustees, 1989–93); Sir John Soane's Mus., 1982–. Chancellor, Salford Univ., 1995–. Chm. Bd of Dirs, Laban Centre for Movement and Dance, 1998–; Mem. Bd of Patrons, St Mark's Hosp. and Academic Inst., 1996. Founder FMedSci 1998. Hon. Member: British Soc. of Gastroenterology, 1989; Amer. Assoc. of Immunologists, 1985; St Mark's Assoc., 1995; For. Associate, US Nat. Acad. of Scis, 1981; For. Mem., Amer. Philosophical Soc., 1989; For. Hon. Mem., Amer. Acad. Arts and Scis, 1972; Fellow, Internat. Inst. of Biotechnology, 1989; Hon. Fellow: Keble Coll., Oxford, 1982; Green Coll., Oxford, 1993; Hon. FRCP 1985; Hon. FRCS 1986; Hon. FRSocMed 1994. Hon. DSc: Bath, Oxford, 1988; Hull, Edinburgh, 1990; Bristol, 1991; Loughborough, 1993; Lancaster, Aberdeen, 1994; Plymouth, 1995; London, Salford, 1996; UMIST, 1997; DUniv Surrey, 1990; Laurea *hc* in Medicine and Surgery, Univ. of Bologna, 1987; Dr *hc*: Leuven, 1992; Masaryk, 1994; Hon. MD Birmingham, 1992; Hon. LLD Dundee, 1993. William Allan Meml Award, Amer. Soc. Human Genetics, 1980; Conway Evans Prize, RCP/Royal Soc., 1982; Rabbi Shai Shacknai Meml Prize Lectr, 1983; John Alexander Meml Prize and Lectureship, Univ. of Pennsylvania Med. Sch., 1984; Rose Payne Dist. Scientists Lectureship, Amer. Soc. for Histocompatibility and Immunogenetics, 1985; Bernal Lectr, Royal Soc., 1986; Neil Hamilton-Fairley Medal, RCP, 1990; Faraday Award, Royal Soc., 1994; Harveian Orator, RCP, 1996. *Publications:* The Genetics of Human Populations (with L. L. Cavalli-Sforza), 1971; (with A. Jones) Our Future Inheritance: choice or chance?, 1974; (with L. L. Cavalli-Sforza) Genetics, Evolution and Man, 1976; (with Robin McKie) The Book of Man, 1994; research papers in genetical, statistical and mathematical jls, etc. *Recreations:* playing the piano, riding, swimming, scuba diving. *Address:* Hertford College, Oxford OX1 3BW. *T:* (01865) 279407. *Club:* Athenæum.

BODMIN, Archdeacon of; *see* Cohen, Ven. C. R. F.

BODY, Sir Richard (Bernard Frank Stewart), Kt 1986; *b* 18 May 1927; *s* of Lieut-Col Bernard Richard Body, formerly of Hyde End, Shinfield, Berks; *m* 1959, Marion, *d* of late Major H. Graham, OBE; one *s* one *d*. *Educ:* Reading Sch.; Inns of Court Sch. of Law. RAF (India Comd), 1945–48. Called to the Bar, Middle Temple, 1949; Chm., E London Poor Man's Lawyer Assoc., 1952–59. Contested (C) Rotherham, 1950; Abertillery bye-election, 1950; Leek, 1951; MP (C): Billericay Div., Essex, 1955–Sept. 1959: Holland with Boston, 1966–97, Boston and Skegness, 1997–2001. Member: Jt Select Cttee on Consolidation of Law, 1975–91; Commons Select Cttee on Agric., 1979–87 (Chm., 1986–87). Jt Chm., Council, Get Britain Out referendum campaign, 1975. Chm. Trustees, Centre for European Studies, 1991–. Pres., William Cobbett Soc., 1996–; Chm., Ruskin Soc., 1997–. Chm., Internat. Assoc. of Masters of Bloodhounds, 1997–. Dir, New European Publications Ltd, 1986–; Editor, World Review, 1996–. *Publications:* The Architect and the Law, 1954; (contrib.) Destiny or Delusion, 1971; (ed jtly) Freedom and

Stability in the World Economy, 1976; Agriculture: The Triumph and the Shame, 1982; Farming in the Clouds, 1984; Red or Green for Farmers, 1987; Europe of Many Circles, 1990; Our Food, Our Land, 1991; The Breakdown of Europe, 1998; England for the English, 2001. *Recreation:* trying to catch trout. *Address:* Jewell's Farm, Stanford Dingley, near Reading, Berks RG7 6LX. *T:* (0118) 9744295. *Clubs:* Athenæum, Carlton, Reform, Savage.

BOE, Norman Wallace; Deputy Solicitor to Secretary of State for Scotland, 1987–96; *b* 30 Aug. 1943; *s* of late Alexander Thomson Boe and Margaret Wallace Revans; *m* 1968, Margaret Irene McKenzie; one *s* one *d*. *Educ:* George Heriot's Sch., Edinburgh; Edinburgh Univ. LLB Hons 1965. Admitted Solicitor, 1967. Legal apprentice, Lindsays, WS, 1965–67; Legal Asst, Menzies & White, WS, 1967–70; Office of Solicitor to Sec. of State for Scotland, 1970–96. Volunteer with Volunteer Stroke Service, Chest, Heart and Stroke, Scotland, 1996–. *Recreations:* golf, gardening, travelling.

BOEGNER, Jean-Marc; Grand Officier, Légion d'Honneur; Commandeur, Ordre National du Mérite; Ambassadeur de France, 1973; *b* 3 July 1913; *s* of Marc and Jeanne Boegner; *m* 1945, Odilie de Moustier; three *d*. *Educ:* Lycée Janson-de-Sailly; Ecole Libre des Sciences Politiques; Paris University (LèsL). Joined French diplomatic service, 1939; Attaché: Berlin, 1939; Ankara, 1940; Beirut, 1941; Counsellor: Stockholm, 1945; The Hague, 1947; Ministry of Foreign Affairs, Paris, 1952–58; Counsellor to Charles de Gaulle, 1958–59; Ambassador to Tunisia, 1959–60; Permanent Representative of France: to EEC, 1961–72; to OECD, 1975–78. *Publication:* Le Marché commun de Six à Neuf, 1974. *Address:* 19 rue de Lille, 75007 Paris, France.

BOEVEY, Sir Thomas (Michael Blake) C.; *see* Crawley-Boevey.

BOGDANOR, Prof. Vernon Bernard, CBE 1998; FBA 1997; Professor of Government, since 1996, and Fellow of Brasenose College, since 1966, Oxford University; *b* 16 July 1943; *s* of Harry Bogdanor and Rosa (*née* Weinger); *m* 1972, Judith Evelyn Beckett (marr. diss. 2000); two *s*. *Educ:* Bishopshalt Sch.; The Queen's College, Oxford (BA 1st Cl. PPE 1964; MA 1968). Sen. Tutor, Brasenose Coll., Oxford, 1979–85, 1996–97; Reader in Government, Oxford Univ., 1990–96. Special Advr, H of L Select Cttee on European Communities, 1982–83; Advr on Constitutional and Electoral Matters to Czechoslovak, Hungarian, and Israeli Govts, 1988–; Special Advr, H of C Public Service Cttee, 1996; Mem., UK Delegn to CSCE Conf., Oslo, 1991. Mem. Council, Hansard Soc. for Parly Govt, 1981–97. Hon. Fellow, Soc. for Advanced Legal Studies, 1997. FRSA 1992. *Publications:* (ed) Disraeli: Lothair, 1975; Devolution, 1979; The People and the Party System, 1981; Multi-Party Politics and the Constitution, 1983; (ed) Democracy and Elections, 1983; (ed) Coalition Government in Western Europe, 1983; What is Proportional Representation?, 1984; (ed) Parties and Democracy in Britain and America, 1984; (ed) Constitutions in Democratic Politics, 1988; (ed) The Blackwell Encyclopaedia of Political Science, 1992; (jtly) Comparing Constitutions, 1995; The Monarchy and the Constitution, 1995; Politics and the Constitution: essays on British Government, 1996; Power and the People: a guide to constitutional reform, 1997; Devolution in the United Kingdom, 1999; contribs to learned jls. *Recreations:* music, walking, talking. *Address:* Brasenose College, Oxford OX1 4AJ. *T:* (01865) 277830.

BOGDANOV, Michael; Artistic Director, English Shakespeare Company, since 1986; *b* 15 Dec. 1938; *s* of Francis Benzion Bogdin and Rhoda Rees Bogdin; *m* 1966, Patsy Ann Warwick (marr. diss. 2000); two *s* one *d*; *m* 2000, Ulrike Engel Brecht; one *s* one *d*. *Educ:* Lower School of John Lyon, Harrow; Univ. of Dublin Trinity Coll. (MA); Univs of the Sorbonne, and Munich. Writer, with Terence Brady, ATV series, Broad and Narrow, 1965; Producer/Director with Telefis Eireann, 1966–68; opening production of Theatre Upstairs, Royal Court, A Comedy of the Changing Years, 1969; The Bourgeois Gentilhomme, Oxford Playhouse, 1969; Asst Dir, Royal Shakespeare Theatre Co., 1970–71; Associate Dir, Peter Brook's A Midsummer Night's Dream, Stratford 1970, New York 1971, World Tour 1972; Dir, Two Gentlemen of Verona, São Paulo, Brazil, 1971; Associate to Jean Louis Barrault, Rabelais, 1971; Associate Director: Tyneside Th. Co., 1971–73; Haymarket Th., Leicester; Director: Phoenix Th., Leicester, 1973–77; Young Vic Th., London, 1978–80; an Associate Dir, Nat. Theatre, 1980–88; Intendant (Chief Exec.), Deutsche Schauspielhaus, Hamburg, 1989–92. Directed: The Taming of the Shrew, RSC, Stratford 1978, London 1979 (SWET Dir of the Year award, 1979); The Seagull, Toho Th. Co., Tokyo, 1980; Shadow of a Gunman, RSC, 1980; The Knight of the Burning Pestle, RSC, 1981; Hamlet, Dublin, 1983; Romeo and Juliet, Tokyo, 1983, RSC, 1986, Lyric, Hammersmith, 1993; The Mayor of Zalamea, Washington, 1984; Measure for Measure, Stratford, Ont, 1985; Mutiny (musical), 1985; Donnerstag aus Licht, Royal Opera House, 1985; Julius Caesar, Schauspielhaus, Hamburg, 1986 (also filmed by ZDF TV); Reineke Fuchs, Schauspielhaus, Hamburg, 1987; The Canterbury Tales, Prince of Wales, 1987; Montag, Stockhausen Opera, La Scala, Milan, 1988 (world première); Hamlet, Hamburg, 1989; The Venetian Twins, Swan, 1993; Hair, Old Vic, 1993; The Hostage, Barbican, 1994; Faust, Swan, 1995; Peer Gynt, Munich, 1995; Timon of Athens, Chicago, 1997; Troilus and Cressida, Olympic Arts Fest., Sydney Opera House, 2000; National Theatre productions: Sir Gawain and the Green Knight, The Hunchback of Notre Dame, 1977–78; The Romans in Britain, Hiawatha, 1980; One Woman Plays, The Mayor of Zalamea, The Hypochondriac, 1981; Uncle Vanya, The Spanish Tragedy, 1982; Lorenzaccio, 1983; You Can't Take it With You, 1983; Strider, 1984; English Shakespeare Co. productions: Henry IV (Parts I and II), Henry V, UK tour, European tour, Old Vic, and Canada, 1986–87; The Wars of the Roses (7 play history cycle), UK, Europe and world tour, 1987–89 (Laurence Olivier Award, Dir of the Year, 1989); Coriolanus, The Winter's Tale, UK and world tour, 1990–91; Macbeth, UK tour, 1992; The Tempest, 1992; Beowulf, 1997; As You Like It, 1998; Antony and Cleopatra, 1998. *Television:* deviser and presenter, Shakespeare Lives, series, 1983; director: Shakespeare on the Estate (documentary), Bard on the Box series, 1995 (BAFTA, RTS, and Banff Film Fest. Awards); films: The Tempest in Butetown, 1996; Macbeth, 1997; Light in the Valley, 1998; Light on the Hill, 1999; A Light in the City, 2001. Co-author, plays, adaptations and children's theatre pieces. Hon. Prof., Univ. of Wales, 1993; Sen. Fellow, De Montfort Univ., 1992; Fellow, Sunderland Univ., 1997; Hon. FWCMD 1994; Hon. Fellow in Drama, TCD, 1997. *Publication:* (jtly) The English Shakespeare Company, 1990. *Recreations:* cricket, wine, music, sheep. *Address:* c/o Peter Murphy, Curtis Brown, Haymarket House, 28–29 Haymarket, SW1Y 4SP.

BOGDANOVICH, Peter; American film director, writer, producer, actor; *b* Kingston, NY, 30 July 1939; *s* of Borislav Bogdanovich and Herma (*née* Robinson); *m* 1962, Polly Platt (marr. diss. 1970); two *d*; *m* 1988, L. B. Straten. Owner: Crescent Moon Productions, Inc., LA, 1986; Holly Moon Co. Inc., LA, 1992. Member: Dirs Guild of America; Writers' Guild of America; Acad. of Motion Picture Arts and Sciences. *Theatre:* Actor, Amer. Shakespeare Fest., Stratford, Conn, 1956, NY Shakespeare Fest., 1958; Dir and producer, off-Broadway: The Big Knife, 1959; Camino Real, Ten Little Indians, Rocket to the Moon, 1961; Once in a Lifetime, 1964. *Films include:* The Wild Angels (2nd-Unit Dir, co-writer, actor), 1966; Targets (dir, co-writer, prod., actor), 1968; The Last Picture Show (dir, co-writer), 1971 (NY Film Critics' Award for Best Screenplay, British Acad. Award for Best Screenplay); Directed by John Ford (dir, writer, interviewer), 1971; What's Up, Doc? (dir, co-writer, prod.), 1972 (Writers' Guild of America Award for Best Screenplay); Paper Moon (dir, prod.), 1973 (Silver Shell Award, Spain); Daisy Miller (dir, prod.), 1974 (Brussels Festival Award for Best Director); At Long Last Love (dir, writer, prod.), 1975; Nickelodeon (dir, co-writer), 1976; Saint Jack (dir, co-writer, actor), 1979 (Pasinetti Award, Critics' Prize, Venice Festival); They All Laughed (dir, writer), 1981; Mask (dir), 1985; Illegally Yours (dir, prod.), 1988; Texasville (dir, prod., writer), 1990; Noises Off (dir, exec. prod.), 1992; The Thing Called Love (dir), 1993. *Television:* The Great Professional: Howard Hawks, BBC, 1967; CBS This Morning (weekly commentary), 1987–89; Prowler, CBS, 1995; Blessed Assurance, To Sir With Love II, CBS-MOW, 1996. *Publications:* The Cinema of Orson Welles, 1961; The Cinema of Howard Hawks, 1962; The Cinema of Alfred Hitchcock, 1963; John Ford, 1968; Fritz Lang in America, 1969; Allan Dwan: the last pioneer, 1971; Pieces of Time: Peter Bogdanovich on the Movies 1961–85, 1973, enlarged 1985; The Killing of the Unicorn: Dorothy Stratten, 1960–1980, a Memoir, 1984; (ed with introd.) A Year and a Day Engagement Calendar, annually, 1991–; This is Orson Welles, 1992; Who The Devil Made It, 1997; features on films in Esquire, New York Times, Village Voice, Cahiers du Cinema, Los Angeles Times, New York Magazine, Vogue, Variety etc, 1961–. *Address:* c/o William Peiffer, 30 Lane of Acres, Haddonfield, NJ 08033, USA.

BOGGIS, Andrew Gurdon, MA; Warden of Forest School, since 1992; *b* 1 April 1954; *s* of Lt-Col (Edmund) Allan (Theodore) Boggis and Myrtle (Eirene) Boggis (*née* Donald); *m* 1983, Fiona Mary Cocke; two *d* one *s*. *Educ:* Marlborough Coll.; New Coll., Oxford (MA); King's Coll., Cambridge (PGCE). Asst Master, Hitchin Boys' Sch., 1978–79; Eton College: Asst Master, 1979–92; Master-in-College, 1984–92. Mem., Ind. Schs Exam. Bd, 1992– (Chm., Langs Cttee, 1997–). Liveryman, Skinners' Co., 1990–. Governor: King's Coll. Sch., Cambridge, 1994–99; Skinners' Co.'s Sch. for Girls, 1997–. *Publications:* articles and reviews. *Recreations:* music, cookery, reading. *Address:* Forest School, College Place, Snaresbrook, E17 3PY. *T:* (020) 8520 1744. *Club:* East India.

BOGGIS, John Graham; QC 1993; **His Honour Judge Boggis;** a Circuit Judge, since 1996; a Chancery Circuit Judge, since 1997; *b* 2 April 1949; *s* of Robert Boggis and Joyce Meek; *m* 1976, Jennifer Coultas; three *s*. *Educ:* Whitgift Sch.; Univ. of London (LLB); Univ. of Keele (MA). Called to the Bar, Lincoln's Inn, 1972; a Recorder, 1994–96. Asst Boundary Comr, 1993–95. Member: Chancery Bar Assoc., 1982–84; Senate of the Inns of Court and Bar, 1984–85. Staff Rep. Gov., Sherborne Sch., 1993–98. *Recreation:* boating. *Address:* Priory Law Courts, 33 Bull Street, Birmingham B4 6DS.

BOGGIS-ROLFE, Hume, CB 1971; CBE 1962; farmer; *b* 20 Oct. 1911; *s* of Douglass Horace Boggis-Rolfe and Maria Maud (*née* Bailey); *m* 1941, Anne Dorothea, *e d* of Capt. Eric Noble, Henley-on-Thames; one *s* one *d* (and one *s* decd). *Educ:* Westminster Sch.; Freiburg Univ.; Trinity Coll., Cambridge. Called to Bar, Middle Temple, 1935. Army, Intelligence Corps, 1939–46 (Lieut-Col). Private Sec. to Lord Chancellor, 1949–50; Asst Solicitor in Lord Chancellor's Office, 1951–65; Sec. to Law Commn, 1965–68; Deputy Clerk of the Crown in Chancery, and Asst Perm. Sec. to Lord Chancellor, 1968–75, and Deputy Secretary, Lord Chancellor's Office, 1970–75. Master, Merchant Taylors' Co., 1971–72. Chm., Friends of the Elderly and Gentlefolks' Help, 1977–84. *Recreations:* gardening, travelling. *Address:* The Grange, Wormingford, Colchester, Essex, CO6 3AU. *T:* (01787) 227303. *Club:* Athenæum.

BOGLE, Ellen Gray, CD 1987; Special Envoy of Jamaica to Association of Caribbean States and CARICOM, since 1997; *d* of late Victor Gray Williams and Eileen Avril Williams; *m* (marr. diss.); one *s* one *d*. *Educ:* St Andrew High Sch., Jamaica; Univ. of the West Indies, Jamaica (BA). Dir of For. Trade, Min. of For. Affairs, Jamaica, 1978–81; Dir, Jamaica Nat. Export Corp., 1978–81; High Comr to Trinidad and Tobago, Barbados, E Caribbean and Guyana, and Ambassador to Suriname, 1982–89; High Comr, UK, 1989–93, and Ambassador to Denmark, Norway, Sweden, Spain and Portugal, 1990–93; Perm. Sec., Min. of Industry, Tourism and Commerce, subseq. Industry, Investment and Commerce, Jamaica, 1993–96; Min. of Foreign Affairs and Foreign Trade, 1996–. *Recreations:* gardening, reading, cooking, table tennis. *Address:* Ministry of Foreign Affairs and Foreign Trade, 21 Dominica Drive, Kingston 5, Jamaica.

BOGLE, Dr Ian Gibb, FRCGP; Chairman of Council, British Medical Association, since 1998; general practitioner, Priory Medical Centre, Liverpool, since 1962; *b* 11 Dec. 1938; *s* of Dr John G. Bogle and Muriel Bogle (*née* Stoll); *m* 1962, Dorothy Edwards; two *d*. *Educ:* Liverpool Coll.; Liverpool Univ. (MB ChB 1961). FRCGP 1997. Member: Liverpool Exec. Health Council, 1972–74; Liverpool FPC, 1974–90 (Vice Chm., 1987–88); Liverpool AHA, 1978–90; Section 63 Wkg Party, DHSS, 1985; Standing Med. Adv. Cttee, DoH, 1991–. Secretary: Liverpool Div., BMA, 1978–82 (Pres., 1977); Jt Cttee on Post Graduate Trng for Gen. Practice, 1985–90; Chairman: Anfield CAB, 1970–74; Gen. Med. Services Cttee, 1990–97. Hon. MD Liverpool, 1999. *Recreations:* golf, photography, travel, music. *Address:* Priory Medical Centre, Belmont Grove, Liverpool L6 4EW. *T:* (0151) 260 9119; (home) 111 Alder Road, W Derby, Liverpool L12 2BA. *T:* (0151) 228 2653; BMA House, Tavistock Square, WC1H 9JP. *T:* (020) 7383 6100. *Club:* Athenæum.

BOGSCH, Arpad, Dr jur; Director General, World Intellectual Property Organization, 1973–97 (Deputy Director General, 1963–73); *b* 24 Feb. 1919; *s* of Arpad Bogsch and Emilia Taborsky; *m* 1994, Adèle Fankhauser; one *s* one *d* by former marriage. *Educ:* Univ. of Budapest (Dr jur); Univ. of Paris (Dr jur); George Washington Univ. (LLM). Called to the Budapest Bar, 1940, to the Washington DC Bar, 1952. Private law practice, Budapest, 1940–48; Legal Officer, Unesco, Paris, 1948–54; Legal Adviser, Library of Congress, Washington DC, 1954–63. Hon. Prof. of Law, Peking Univ., 1991. LLD *hc*: Jabalpur, 1978; George Washington, 1985; Colombo, 1987; Kyung Hee, Korea, 1991; Eötvös Lóránd, Budapest, 1991; Bucharest, 1991; Delhi, 1992; Moscow, 1993; Charles Univ., Prague, 1994; Kiev, 1995; Mathias Bel, Slovakia, 1996; Tbilisi, 1996. Decorations from: Sweden, 1967; Austria, 1977; Spain, 1980; Senegal and Republic of Korea, 1981; Bulgaria, 1985; France, Japan and Thailand, 1986; Hungary, 1991; Colombia, France and Senegal, 1992; Germany, 1993; Tanzania, 1995; Hungary and Cuba, 1996; Sweden, 1997. *Address:* 12 chemin du Vieux-Bois, 1292 Chambesy, Switzerland. *T:* (22) 7582267.

BOHAN, William Joseph, CB 1988; Assistant Under Secretary of State, Home Office, 1979–89, retired; *b* 10 April 1929; *s* of John and Josephine Bohan; *m* 1955, Brenda Skevington (*d* 1995); one *s* (one *d* decd). *Educ:* Finchley Catholic Grammar Sch.; Cardinal Vaughan Sch., Kensington; King's Coll., Cambridge (Chancellor's Classical Medallist, 1952). Home Office: Asst Principal, 1952; Principal, 1958; Sec., Cttee on Immigration Appeals, 1966–67; Asst Sec., 1967. Chm., European Cttee on Crime Problems, 1987–89. *Recreations:* languages and literature, walking. *Address:* 16 Mostyn Road, SW19 3LJ. *T:* (020) 8542 1127.

BOHR, Prof. Aage Niels, DSc, DrPhil; physicist, Denmark; Professor of Physics, University of Copenhagen, 1956–92; *b* Copenhagen, 19 June 1922; *s* of late Prof. Niels Bohr and Margrethe Nørlund; *m* 1st, Marietta Bettina (*née* Soffer) (*d* 1978); two *s* one *d*;

2nd, 1981, Bente, *d* of late Chief Physician Johannes Meyer and Lone (*née* Rubow) and *widow* of Morten Scharff. *Educ:* Univ. of Copenhagen. Jun. Scientific Officer, Dept of Scientific and Industrial Research, London, 1943–45; Research Asst, Inst. for Theoretical Physics, Univ. of Copenhagen, 1946; Dir, Niels Bohr Inst. (formerly Inst. for Theoretical Physics), 1963–70. Bd Mem., Nordita, 1958–74, Dir, 1975–81. Member: Royal Danish Acad. of Science, 1955–; Royal Physiolog. Soc., Sweden, 1959–; Royal Norwegian Acad. of Sciences, 1962–; Acad. of Tech. Sciences, Copenhagen, 1963–; Amer. Phil. Soc., 1965–; Amer. Acad. of Arts and Sciences, 1965–; Nat. Acad. of Sciences, USA, 1971–; Royal Swedish Acad. of Sciences, 1974–; Yugoslavia Acad. of Sciences, 1976–; Pontificia Academia Scientiarum, 1978–; Norwegian Acad. of Sciences, 1979–; Polish Acad. of Sciences, 1980–; Finska Vetenskaps-Societeten, 1980–; Deutsche Akademie der Naturforscher Leopoldina, 1981–. Awards: Dannie Heineman Prize, 1960; Pius XI Medal, 1963; Atoms for Peace Award, 1969; H. C. Ørsted Medal, 1970; Rutherford Medal, 1972; John Price Wetherill Medal, 1974; (jointly) Nobel Prize for Physics, 1975; Ole Rømer Medal, 1976. Dr *hc*: Manchester, 1961; Oslo, 1969; Heidelberg, 1971; Trondheim, 1972; Uppsala, 1975. *Publications:* Rotational States of Atomic Nuclei, 1954; (with Ben R. Mottelson) Nuclear Structure, vol. I, 1969, vol. II 1975; contrib. learned jls. *Address:* Strandgade 34, 1st Floor, 1401 Copenhagen K, Denmark.

BOHUSZ-SZYSZKO, Dame Cicely (Mary Strode); *see* Saunders, Dame C. M. S.

BOILEAU, Sir Guy (Francis), 8th Bt *cr* 1838; antique dealer; *b* 23 Feb. 1935; *s* of Sir Edmond Charles Boileau, 7th Bt, and of Marjorie Lyle, *d* of Claude Monteath D'Arcy; *S* father, 1980; *m* 1962, Judith Frances, *d* of George Conrad Hannan; two *s* three *d*. *Educ:* Xavier College, Melbourne; Royal Military Coll., Duntroon, Australia. Lieut, Aust. Staff Corps, 1956; Platoon Comdr, 3rd Bn, Royal Aust. Regt, Malaysia, 1957–58; Observer, UN Mil. Observer Gp in India and Pakistan, 1959–60; Instructor, Aust. Army Training Team, Vietnam, 1963–64; attached US Dept of Defence, Washington, DC, 1966–68; Security Adviser, Dept of the Administrator, Territory of Papua-New Guinea, 1970–71; CO, Army Intelligence Centre, 1972–74; Directing Staff (Instructor), Aust. Staff Coll., 1975–76; SO1 Personnel, HQ Third Mil. Dist, 1979. *Recreations:* boating, fishing. *Heir: s* Nicolas Edmond George Boileau, *b* 17 Nov. 1964. *Address:* 14 Faircroft Avenue, Glen Iris, Victoria 3146, Australia. *T:* (3) 98228273. *Club:* The Heroes (Toorak, Victoria).

BOISSIER, Martin Scobell; Vice Lord-Lieutenant of Derbyshire, 1992–2001; *b* 14 May 1926; *s* of Ernest Gabriel Boissier, DSC and Doris Mary Boissier (*née* Bingham); *m* 1955, Margaret Jean Blair, JP; one *s* one *d*. *Educ:* Bramcote Prep. Sch., Scarborough; RN Naval Coll., Dartmouth. Service in RN, 1943–58; qualified as Pilot, 1947; Lt-Comdr, retired 1958. Aiton & Co., Derby, 1958, Dir, 1976, retired 1988; Gp Personnel Controller and local Dir, Whessoe, 1980–88; former Director: Silkolene; ATV (Midlands). Mem., East Reg. Bd, Central ITV, 1982–92. Chm., Derbys FHSA, 1990–97. Vice-Pres., Arkwright Soc., Cromford; Pres., Royal Sch. for the Deaf, Derby; Vice-Pres., Derby Sea Cadet Corps. Freeman, City of London, 1978; Liveryman, Tinplate Workers alias Wire-workers' Co., 1978 (Mem., Ct of Assts, 1994–). DL 1977, High Sheriff, 1978–79, Derbys. *Recreations:* gardening; appreciation of art, music and wine; needlework, charity work. *Address:* Ithersay Cottage, Idridgehay, Belper, Derbyshire DE56 2SB. *T:* (01773) 550210. *Clubs:* Army and Navy, MCC; County (Derby); Royal Naval Sailing Assoc. (Portsmouth); Carsington Sailing (Derbys).

See also R. H. Boissier.

BOISSIER, Roger Humphrey, CBE 1992; Chairman: Pressac plc (formerly Pressac Holdings PLC), since 1990 (non-executive Director, since 1984); Royal Crown Derby Porcelain Co. Ltd, since 2000; Kalon Pension Trustees Ltd, 1992–2002; *b* 30 June 1930; *y s* of late Ernest Boissier, DSC, CEng, FIEE and Doris Boissier (*née* Bingham), of Bingham's Melcombe; *m* 1965, (Elizabeth) Bridget (Rhoda), *e d* of Sir Gerald Ley, Bt, TD and Rosemary, Lady Ley; one *s* one *d*. *Educ:* Harrow. International Combustion, 1950–52; Cooper-Parry, Hall, Doughty & Co. 1952–53; Merz & McLellan, 1953–55; Aiton & Co, 1955–83, Man. Dir, 1975–83; Exec Dir, Whessoe plc, 1975–83. Non-executive Director: Edward Lumley Hldgs, 1988–; Kalon Gp plc, 1992–99 (Chm., 1992–95); Allott & Lomax (Holdings) Ltd, 1996–2000 (Advr, 1984–96); Derbyshire BS, 1972–81; Simmonds Precision NV, 1976–82; Ley's Foundries & Engineering, 1977–82; Severn Trent Water Authy, then Severn Trent plc, 1986–98; British Gas plc, 1986–96 (pt-time Mem., British Gas Corp., 1981–86); T & N plc, 1987–98; AMEC Power, 1992–94; AMEC Mechanical and Electrical Services, 1994–96. Mem. Exec., British Energy Assoc. (formerly Brit. Nat. Cttee, World Energy Council), 1975– (Chm., 1977–80); Member: E Midlands Econ. Planning Council, 1972–75; CBI Central Council (selected Mem. from E Midlands regn), 1973–82. Pro-Chancellor and Dep. Chm. Council, Loughborough Univ., 2000–; Mem. Council, Univ. of Derby, 1998–; Gov., Harrow Sch., 1976–96 (Dep. Chm., 1988–96). High Sheriff of Derbyshire, 1987–88. Freeman, City of London, 1971; Master, Co. of Tin Plate Workers alias Wire Workers, 1988–89. CIGasE 1983; Companion, Inst. of Energy, 1991; FInstD 1984; FRSA 1987. Hon. DTech Loughborough, 2001. *Recreations:* cars, foreign travel, reading, meeting people. *Address:* Easton House, The Pastures, Repton, Derby DE65 6GG. *T:* (01283) 702274, *Fax:* (01283) 701489; *e-mail:* boissier@pressac.com. *Clubs:* Brooks's, MCC; Surrey County Cricket; County (Derby).

See also M. S. Boissier.

BOIZOT, Peter James, MBE 1986; DL; founded PizzaExpress Ltd, 1965; President, PizzaExpress Plc, since 1996 (Chairman, 1993–96); *b* 16 Nov. 1929; *s* of late Gaston Charles and Susannah Boizot. *Educ:* King's Sch., Peterborough (chorister, Peterborough Cathedral); St Catharine's Coll., Cambridge. MA (BA (Hons) History). Captain, MV Yarvic, 1951. Various jobs, predominantly in sales field, 1953–64; Chm. and Man. Dir, PizzaExpress Ltd, 1965–93; Dir, Connoisseur Casino, 1970–82. Publisher, monthly magazines: BOZ (formerly Jazz Express), 1983–; Hockey Sport (formerly Hockey Digest), 1995–; World Hockey, 1995. Proprietor: Pizza on the Park, 1976–; Kettners Restaurant, Soho, 1980–; Great Northern Hotel, Peterborough, 1993–. Founder and Chm., Soho Restaurateurs Assoc., 1980–. Founder and Dir, Soho Jazz Fest., 1986–. Dir, CENTEC, 1990–93. Chm., Westminster Chamber of Commerce, 1992–95. Mem., Royal Acad. Adv. Bd, 1988–91. Fellow Commoner, St Catharine's Coll., Cambridge, 1996. Contested (L) Peterborough, Feb. and Oct. 1974. Founder Mem., Soho Soc., 1972. Pres., Hampstead and Westminster Hockey Club, 1986–; a Vice-Pres., Hockey Assoc., 1990–; Chm., Peterborough United FC, 1997–. DL Cambs, 1998. FHCIMA 1989. Hon. LLD Westminster, 1995. Bolla Award, 1983; Hotel and Caterer Food Service Award, 1989. Commendatore, Al Merito della Repubblica Italiana, 1996 (Cavaliere Ufficiale, 1983). *Publication:* PizzaExpress Cook Book, 1976, rev. edn 1991. *Recreations:* hockey, presenting jazz, cabaret, dining out. *Address:* 10 Lowndes Square, SW1X 9HA. *T:* (020) 7235 9100. *Clubs:* National Liberal, Royal Automobile; Hawks (Cambridge); Vincent's (Oxford).

BOK, Derek; Professor of Law, since 1961, 300th Anniversary University Professor, since 1991, and President, 1971–91, Harvard University; *b* Bryn Mawr, Pa, 22 March 1930; *s* of late Curtis and Margaret Plummer Bok (later Mrs William S. Kiskadden); *m* 1955, Sissela Ann Myrdal, *d* of late Prof. Karl Gunnar Myrdal and Alva Myrdal; one *s* two *d*. *Educ:* Stanford Univ., BA; Harvard Univ., JD; Inst. of Political Science, Univ. of Paris (Fulbright Scholar); George Washington Univ., MA in Economics. Served AUS, 1956–58. Asst Prof. of Law, Harvard Univ., 1958–61, Dean of Law Sch., 1968–71. *Publications:* The First Three Years of the Schuman Plan, 1955; (ed with Archibald Cox) Cases and Materials on Labor Law, 5th edn 1962, 6th edn 1965, 7th edn 1969, 8th edn 1977; (with John Dunlop) Labor and the American Community, 1970; Beyond the Ivory Tower, 1982; Higher Learning, 1986; Universities and the future of America, 1990; The Cost of Talent, 1993; The State of the Nation, 1996; The Shape of the River, 1998. *Recreations:* gardening, tennis, skiing. *Address:* c/o John F. Kennedy School of Government, Harvard University, Cambridge, MA 02138, USA.

BOKHARY, Syed Kemal Shah; Hon. Mr Justice Bokhary; a Permanent Judge, Hong Kong Court of Final Appeal, since 1997; *b* 25 Oct. 1947; *s* of Syed Daud Shah Bokhary and Halima Bokhary (*née* Arculli); *m* 1977, Verina Saeeda Chung (*see* V. S. Bokhary); three *d*. *Educ:* King George V Sch., Hong Kong. Called to the Bar, Middle Temple, 1970; QC (Hong Kong) 1983; practised in Hong Kong and before the Judicial Cttee of the Privy Council, London, 1971–89; Judge of High Court, Hong Kong, 1989–93; Justice of Appeal, Supreme Court of Hong Kong, 1993–97. Mem., Law Reform Commn, 2000–. Mem. Bd, Law Faculty, 1994–, and Chm., Law and Professional Legal Educn Depts Adv. Cttee, 1997–, City Univ., Hong Kong; Chm., Adv. Bd, Centre for Criminology, Dept. of Sociology, Univ. of Hong Kong, 1999–. Hon. Lectr, Dept of Professional Legal Educn, Univ. of Hong Kong, 2000–. Mem., RSAA, 1988–. FRAI 1998. Mem., Welsh and W of England Bullmastiff Soc.; Life Mem., Southern Bullmastiff Soc. Mem. Editl Adv. Bd, Halsbury's Laws of Hong Kong, 1993–. *Publications:* articles in Hong Kong Law Jl and other learned jls. *Recreations:* dogs, opera, anthropology, reading, walking, travel, shooting. *Address:* Court of Final Appeal, 1 Battery Path, Hong Kong. *Clubs:* Hong Kong Jockey, Hong Kong Country, Aberdeen Marina, Hong Kong Clay Target Shooting Association, Hong Kong Rifle Association, Hong Kong Kennel (President).

BOKHARY, Verina Saeeda; Hon. Mrs Justice Bokhary; a Judge of the Court of First Instance of the High Court (formerly Judge of the High Court), Hong Kong, since 1996; *b* 5 Feb. 1950; *d* of Chung Hon-Wing and Hung Shui-Chan; *m* 1977, Syed Kemal Shah Bokhary, *qv*; three *d*. Called to the Bar, Lincoln's Inn, 1971; Temp. Asst Registrar, Royal Courts of Justice, Chancery Div., 1972; Legal Asst, HM Customs & Excise, 1972–76; Legal Officer, Unofficial Mems of the Exec. and Legislative Council Office, Hong Kong, 1976–78; in private practice, Hong Kong, 1978–85; Hong Kong Judiciary: Magistrate, 1985–87; Adjudicator, 1987–89; Dist Court Judge, 1989–95. Chm., Release under Supervision Bd, 1998–; Dep. Pres., Long-term Prison Sentences Rev. Bd, 1997–. *Recreations:* homelife, antiques, reading. *Address:* High Court, 38 Queensway, Hong Kong. *T:* 28254312.

BOKSENBERG, Prof. Alexander, CBE 1996; PhD; FRS 1978; FInstP; FRAS; Research Professor, University of Cambridge and PPARC Senior Research Fellow, Universities of Cambridge and London, since 1996; Extraordinary Fellow, Churchill College, Cambridge, since 1996; Director, Royal Observatories, 1993–96: Royal Greenwich Observatory, Cambridge; Royal Observatory, Edinburgh; Isaac Newton Group of optical telescopes, Canary Islands; Joint Astronomy Centre, Hawaii; *b* 18 March 1936; *s* of Julius Boksenberg and Ernestina Steinberg; *m* 1960, Adella Coren; one *s* one *d*. *Educ:* Stationers' Co.'s Sch.; Univ. of London (BSc, PhD). Dept of Physics and Astronomy, University Coll. London: SRC Res. Asst, 1960–65; Lectr in Physics, 1965–75; Head of Optical and Ultraviolet Astronomy Res. Group, 1969–81; Reader in Physics, 1975–78; SRC Sen. Fellow, 1976–81; Prof. of Physics and Astronomy, 1978–81; Dir, Royal Greenwich Observatory, 1981–93. Sherman Fairchild Dist. Schol., CIT, 1981–82; Visiting Professor: Dept of Physics and Astronomy, UCL, 1981–; Astronomy Centre, Univ. of Sussex, 1981–89; Hon. Prof. of Experimental Astronomy, Univ. of Cambridge, 1991–. Chm., New Industrial Concepts Ltd, 1969–81. Chairman: SRC Astronomy II Cttee, 1980–81; Gemini Telescopes Project Expert Cttee, 1992 (Chm., UK Steering Cttee, 1992–93; Mem., USA Oversight Cttee, 1993–94); Mem. and Pres., Internat. Scientific Cttee, Canary Is Observatories, 1981–95; Member: ESA Hubble Space Telescope Instrument Definition Team, 1973–; S African Astronomical Observatory Adv. Cttee, 1978–85; British Council Science Adv. Cttee, 1987–91; Anglo-Australian Telescope Bd, 1989–91 (Dep. Chm., 1991–92); Hubble Space Telescope Users Cttee, 1990–91; Fachbeirat, Max Planck Inst. für Astronomie, 1991–95; European Southern Observatory Vis. Cttee, 1993–; formerly mem. or chm. of more than 40 other councils, boards, cttees, panels or courts, 1970–. Exec. Ed., Experimental Astronomy, 1995–. Mem. Council and Trustee, Royal Soc., 1995–97. Pres., W London Astronomical Soc., 1978–; Hon. Pres., Astronomical Soc. of Glasgow, 1995–. Founding Member: Academia Europaea, 1989; European Astronomical Soc., 1990. Mem. Council, Churchill Coll., Cambridge, 1998–. Fellow, UCL, 1991. FRAS 1965 (Hannah Jackson Medal, 1998); FInstP 1998; FRSA 1984. Clockmakers' Co.: Freeman, 1984; Liveryman, 1989; Mem., Court of Assts, 1994–; Master, 2000. Asteroid (3205) Boksenberg, named 1988. Dr *hc* l'Observatoire de Paris, 1982; DSc *hc* Sussex, 1991. *Publications:* (ed jtly) Modern Technology and its Influence on Astronomy, 1990; over 240 contribs to learned jls. *Recreation:* ski-ing. *Address:* University of Cambridge, Institute of Astronomy, The Observatories, Madingley Road, Cambridge CB3 0HA. *T:* (01223) 339909. *Club:* Athenæum.

BOLAM, James; actor; *b* Sunderland, 16 June 1938; *s* of Robert Alfred Bolam and Marion Alice Bolam (*née* Drury). *Educ:* Bede Grammar Sch., Sunderland; Bemrose Sch., Derby. First stage appearance, The Kitchen, Royal Court, 1959; later plays include: Events While Guarding the Bofors Gun, Hampstead, 1966; In Celebration, Royal Court, 1969; Veterans, Royal Court, 1972; Treats, Royal Court, 1976; Who Killed 'Agatha' Christie?, Ambassadors, 1978; King Lear (title rôle), Young Vic, 1981; Run for Your Wife!, Criterion, 1983; Arms and the Man, Cambridge; Who's Afraid of Virginia Woolf?, Birmingham, 1989; Victory, Chichester, 1989; Jeffrey Bernard is Unwell, Apollo, 1990; Glengarry Glen Ross, Donmar Warehouse, 1994; Wild Oats, National, 1995; Endgame, Nottingham Playhouse, 1999; Semi-Detached, Chichester, 1999. *Films:* A Kind of Loving, 1962; Half a Sixpence, 1967; Otley, 1969; Crucible of Terror, 1971; Straight on till Morning, 1972; In Celebration, 1974; Murder Most Foul; The Likely Lads, 1976; The Great Question; Seaview Knights; Clockwork Mice; Stella Does Tricks; Island on Bird Street; End of the Affair, 1999; It Was an Accident, 2000. *Television series:* The Likely Lads, 1965–69; Whatever Happened to the Likely Lads?, 1973; When the Boat Comes In, 1975–77; The Limbo Connection (Armchair Thriller Series); Only When I Laugh; The Beiderbecke Affair; Room at the Bottom; Andy Capp; The Beiderbecke Tapes; The Beiderbecke Connection; Second Thoughts; Eleven Men Against Eleven; Have your Cake, The Missing Postman, 1997; Pay and Display, Dirty Tricks, Close and True, 2000; Dr Shipman, 2001; also As You Like It, Macbeth, in BBC Shakespeare. *Address:* c/o Jane Brand, ICM, 76 Oxford Street, W1N 0AX.

BOLAND, John Anthony; Public Trustee and Accountant General, 1987–91 (Public Trustee, 1980–87); *b* 23 Jan. 1931; *s* of late Daniel Boland, MBE, and Hannah Boland (*née* Barton), Dublin; *m* 1972, Ann, *d* of late James C. Doyle and Maureen Doyle. *Educ:* Castleknock Coll.; Xavier Sch.; Christian Brothers, Synge Street; Trinity Coll., Dublin

(MA, LLB). Called to the Bar, Middle Temple, 1956; called to Irish Bar, 1967. Joined Public Trustee Office, 1956; Chief Administrative Officer, 1974–79; Asst Public Trustee, 1979–80. Hon. Member, College Historical Soc., TCD, 1954. Trustee, London Trust for TCD (formerly TCD (Univ. of Dublin) Trust), 1980–. Asst Editor, The Supreme Court Practice, 1984–91. *Recreations:* walking, foreign travel, theology. *Address:* 22 Waltham Terrace, Blackrock, Co. Dublin, Ireland. *T:* and *Fax:* (1) 278 0120. *Club:* Kildare Street and University (Dublin).

BOLEAT, Mark John; company director and business consultant; *b* 21 Jan. 1949; *s* of Paul Boleat and Peggy Boleat (*née* Still); *m* 1991, Elizabeth Ann Baker (*née* Barker). *Educ:* Victoria College, Jersey; Lanchester Polytechnic and Univ. of Reading (BA Econ, MA Contemp. European Studies). FCIB. Asst Master, Dulwich College, 1972; Economist, Indust. Policy Group, 1973; The Building Societies Association: Asst Sec., 1974; Under Sec., 1976; Dep. Sec., 1979; Dep. Sec.-Gen., 1981; Sec.-Gen., 1986; Dir-Gen., 1987. Sec.-Gen., Internat. Union of Housing Finance Instns (formerly Internat. Union of Building Socs and Savings Assocs), 1986–89; Mem. Bd, Housing Corp., 1988–93; Chm., Circle 33 Housing Trust, 1990–93; Dir-Gen., ABI, 1993–99; Chm., Open Door Finance, 2000–; Director: Abbey National Life plc, 1999–; Scottish Mutual plc, 1999–; Camino Gp, 2000–; Countryside Properties, 2001–. Member: NCC, 2000–; Gibraltar Services Commn, 2000–. *Publications:* The Building Society Industry, 1982; National Housing Finance Systems: a comparative study, 1985; Housing in Britain, 1986; (with Adrian Coles) The Mortgage Market, 1987; Building Societies: the regulatory framework, 1988, 3rd edn 1992; Trade Association Strategy and Management, 1996; Models of Trade Association Co-operation, 2000; Best Practice in Trade Association Commerce, 2001; articles on housing, insurance and finance. *Recreations:* reading, writing, squash, golf. *Address:* 26 Westbury Road, Northwood, Middx HA6 3BU. *Clubs:* East India; Moor Park Golf.

BOLES, Sir Jeremy John Fortescue, 3rd Bt *cr* 1922; *b* 9 Jan. 1932; *s* of Sir Gerald Fortescue Boles, 2nd Bt, and Violet Blanche (*d* 1974), *er d* of late Major Hall Parlby, Manadon, Crown Hill, S Devon, *S* father, 1945; *m* 1st, 1955, Dorothy Jane (marr. diss. 1970), *yr d* of James Alexander Worswick; two *s* one *d*; 2nd, 1970, Elisabeth Gildroy Willis Fleming (marr. diss. 1981), *yr d* of Edward Phillip Shaw; one *d*; 3rd, 1982, Marigold Aspey, *e d* of Donald Frank Seckington. *Heir: s* Richard Fortescue Boles [*b* 12 Dec. 1958; *m* 1990, Allison Beverley, *d* of Brian MacDonald; one *s* one *d*]. *Address:* Buttys, Stogumber, Taunton TA4 3TD.

BOLES, Sir John Dennis, (Sir Jack), Kt 1983; MBE 1960; DL; Director General of the National Trust, 1975–83; *b* 25 June 1925; *s* of late Comdr Geoffrey Coleridge Boles and Hilda Frances (*née* Crofton); *m* 1st, 1953, Benita (*née* Wormald) (*d* 1969); two *s* three *d*; 2nd, 1971, Lady Anne Hermione, *d* of 12th Earl Waldegrave, KG, GCVO. *Educ:* Winchester Coll. Rifle Brigade, 1943–46. Colonial Administrative Service (later Overseas Civil Service), North Borneo (now Sabah), 1948–64; Asst Sec., National Trust, 1965, Sec., 1968; Mem., Devon and Cornwall Regl Cttee, Nat. Trust, 1985–95. Dir, SW Region Bd, Lloyds Bank plc, 1984–91. Trustee, Ernest Cook Trust. Devon: DL 1991; High Sheriff 1993–94. *Address:* Rydon House, Talaton, near Exeter, Devon EX5 2RP. *Club:* Army and Navy.

See also J. D. Fishburn.

BOLGER, Rt Hon. James Brendan, (Jim), ONZ 1997; PC 1991; Ambassador for New Zealand to the United States, since 1998; *b* 31 May 1935; *s* of Daniel Bolger and Cecilia (*née* Doyle); *m* 1963, Joan Maureen Riddell; six *s* three *d*. *Educ:* Opunake High Sch. Sheep and cattle farmer, Te Kuiti, 1965–. Federated Farmers: Br. Chm., 1967–72; sub-provincial Chm., 1970–72; Vice-Pres., Waikato, 1971–72; Mem., Dominion Exec., 1971–72. MP (Nat. Party) King Country, 1972–98; Parly Under-Sec., Min. of Agric. and Fisheries, Min. of Maori Affairs, then Minister i/c of Rural Banking Finance Corp., 1975–77; Minister of Fisheries and Associate Minister of Agric., 1977–78; Minister of Labour, 1978–84; Minister of Immigration, 1978–81; Leader of Nat. Party, 1986–97; Leader of the Opposition, 1986–90; Prime Minister of NZ, 1990–97. Pres., ILO, 1983. Silver Jubilee Medal, 1977; NZ Commemoration Medal, 1990; NZ Suffrage Centennial Medal, 1993. *Recreations:* tramping, fishing, reading, Rugby, cricket. *Address:* New Zealand Embassy, 37 Observatory Circle NW, Washington, DC 20008, USA; Mangarino Road, Te Kuiti, New Zealand.

BOLGER, Margaret Anne; *see* Ford, M. A.

BOLINGBROKE, 7th Viscount *cr* 1712, **AND ST JOHN,** 8th Viscount *cr* 1716; **Kenneth Oliver Musgrave St John;** Bt 1611; Baron St John of Lydiard Tregoze, 1712; Baron St John of Battersea, 1716; Director, Italian importing companies; *b* 22 March 1927; *s* of Geoffrey Robert St John, MC (*d* 1972) and Katherine Mary (*d* 1958), *d* of late A. S. J. Musgrave; *S* cousin, 1974; *m* 1st, 1953, Patricia Mary McKenna (marr. diss. 1972); one *s*; 2nd, 1972, Jainey Anne McRae (marr. diss. 1987); two *s*. *Educ:* Eton; Geneva Univ. Chairman, A&P Gp of Cos, 1958–75; Director: Shaw Savill Holidays Pty Ltd; Bolingbroke and Partners Ltd; Wata Investment Inc., Panama. Pres., Travel Agents Assoc. of NZ, 1966–68; Dir, World Assoc. of Travel Agencies, 1966–75; Chm., Aust. Council of Tour Wholesalers, 1972–75. Fellow, Aust. Inst. of Travel; Mem., NZ Inst. of Travel. *Recreations:* golf, cricket, tennis, history. *Heir: s* Hon. Henry Fitzroy St John, *b* 18 May 1957. *Address:* PO Box 25.069, Christchurch, New Zealand; 5110 Conference Street, Christchurch, New Zealand. *Club:* Christchurch (Christchurch, NZ).

BOLKESTEIN, Frederik, (Frits); Member, European Commission, since 1999; *b* 4 April 1933; *m* 1988, Femke Boersma; two *s* one *d*. *Educ:* Oregon State Coll., USA; Gemeentelijke Univ., Amsterdam; Univ. of Leiden (Master of Law). Shell Group, 1960–76: posts in E Africa, Honduras, El Salvador, UK, Indonesia and France; Dir, Shell Chimie, Paris, 1973–76. Mem. Parliament (VVD), Netherlands, 1978–82, 1986–88 and 1989–99; Minister for Foreign Trade, 1982–86; Minister of Defence, 1988–89; Chm., VVD Parly Gp, 1990–98. Pres., Liberal Internat., 1996–99. MRIIA. Chm., Amsterdam Bach Soloists. *Address:* European Commission, Rue de la Loi 200, 1049 Brussels, Belgium.

BOLLAND, Alexander; QC (Scot.) 1992; *b* 21 Nov. 1950; *s* of James Bolland and Elizabeth Agnes (*née* Anderson); *m* 1973, Agnes Hunter, *d* of Dr George Pate Moffat, Crookedholm; one *s* two *d*. *Educ:* Kilmarnock Acad.; Univ. of St Andrews (BD 1973); Glasgow Univ. (LLB 1976). Admitted to Faculty of Advocates, 1978; Capt., Directorate of Army Legal Services, later Army Legal Corps, 1978–80; Standing Jun. Counsel to Dept of Employment in Scotland, 1988–92; Temp. Sheriff, 1988–99; part-time Chm., Employment (formerly Industrial) Tribunals, 1993–. *Recreations:* Hellenistics, walking, reading. *Address:* The Old Dairy, 60 North Street, St Andrews, Fife KY16 9AH. *T:* (01334) 474599. *Clubs:* Naval and Military; New (Edinburgh).

BOLLAND, (David) Michael; Head of Comedy and Entertainment, BBC Scotland, since 2001 (Head of Arts and Entertainment, 1996–2001); *b* 27 Feb. 1947; *s* of Allan Bolland and Eileen Lindsay; *m* 1987, Katie Lander; one *s*, one *d*, and one *s* two *d* by former marrs. *Educ:* Hillhead High School, Glasgow. Film editor, BBC Scotland, 1965–73; TV Producer, BBC TV, 1973–81; Channel Four Television: Commissioning Editor, Youth, 1981–83; Senior Commissioning Editor, Entertainment, 1983–87; Asst Dir of Programmes, and Head of Art and Entertainment Gp, 1987–88; Controller Arts and Entertainment, and Dep. Dir of Progs, 1988–90; Man. Dir, Initial Films and Television, 1990; Man. Dir, Channel X Ltd, 1990–96; Project Dir, Channel X Broadcasting (Scotland) Ltd, 1991–95. Chairman: Edinburgh Internat. TV Fest., 1990; Producers' Alliance for Film and Television, 1995. Member: RTS; BAFTA. *Recreation:* catching up with the world. *Address:* BBC Scotland, Queen Margaret Drive, Glasgow G12 8DG.

BOLLAND, Sir Edwin, KCMG 1981 (CMG 1971); HM Diplomatic Service, retired; Ambassador to Yugoslavia, 1980–82; *b* 20 Oct. 1922; *m* 1948, Winifred Mellor; one *s* three *d* (and one *s* decd). *Educ:* Morley Grammar Sch.; University Coll., Oxford. Served in Armed Forces, 1942–45. Foreign Office, 1947; Head of Far Eastern Dept, FO, 1965–67; Counsellor, Washington, 1967–71; St Antony's Coll., Oxford, 1971–72; Ambassador to Bulgaria, 1973–76; Head of British delegn to Negotiations on MBFR, 1976–80. *Recreations:* walking, gardening. *Address:* 2A Dukes Meadow, Stapleford, Cambridge CB2 5BH. *T:* (01223) 847139.

BOLLAND, Hugh Westrope; Vice Chairman, Schroder Investment Management Ltd, 1999–2000; *b* 14 May 1946; *s* of late Gp Capt. Guy Alfred Bolland, CBE; *m* 1972, Marian Wendy Elton; two *s* one *d*. *Educ:* St Edward's Sch., Oxford; Univ. of Exeter (BA (Hons) Econs). Joined Schroders, 1970; Man. Dir, Schroders Asia Ltd, Hong Kong, 1984–87; Chief Exec., Schroders Australia Ltd, 1987–90; Chm., Schroder Unit Trusts Ltd, 1990–92; Jt Chief Exec., 1995–96, Chief Exec., 1997–99, Schroder Investment Management Ltd (Dir, 1990–2000); Dir, Schroder Split Fund plc, 1993–. Gov., St Edward's Sch., Oxford. *Recreations:* sailing, golf, music. *Clubs:* Hong Kong, Hong Kong Jockey (Hong Kong); Woking Golf, Royal Motor Yacht.

BOLLAND, Mark William; Deputy Private Secretary to HRH the Prince of Wales, since 1997 (Assistant Private Secretary, 1996–97); *b* 10 April 1966; *s* of late Robert Arthur Bolland and of Joan Bolland (*née* Barker). *Educ:* Kings Manor Sch., Middlesbrough; Univ. of York (BSc Hons). Public Affairs Exec., Public Affairs Internat. Ltd, Toronto, 1987; Mkting Exec., IBM (UK) Ltd, 1987–88; Res. Manager, and Advr to Dir Gen., Advertising Standards Authy, 1988–91; Exec. Asst to Chm., 1991–92, Dir, 1992–96, Press Complaints Commn. *Address:* (office) St James's Palace, SW1A 1BS. *T:* (020) 7930 4832.

BOLLAND, Michael; *see* Bolland, D. M.

BOLLERS, Hon. Sir Harold (Brodie Smith), Kt 1969; CCH 1982; Chairman, Elections Commission, 1982; Chief Justice of Guyana, 1966–80; *b* 5 Feb. 1915; *s* of late John Bollers; *m* 1st, 1951, Irene Mahadeo (*d* 1965); two *s* one *d*; 2nd, 1968, Eileen Hanoman; one *s*. *Educ:* Queen's Coll., Guyana; King's Coll., London; Middle Temple. Called to the Bar, Feb. 1938; Magistrate, Guyana, 1946, Senior Magistrate, 1959; Puisne Judge, Guyana, 1960. *Recreations:* reading, walking. *Address:* 252 South Road, Bourda, Georgetown, Guyana.

BOLLOBÁS, Dr Béla; Fellow of Trinity College, Cambridge, since 1972; Distinguished Professor of Excellence in Combinatorics, University of Memphis, Tennessee, since 1995; *b* 3 Aug. 1943; *s* of Béla Bollobás and Emma Varga; *m* 1969, Gabriella Farkas; one *s*. *Educ:* Univ. of Budapest (BA 1966; Dr rer nat 1967); Univ. of Cambridge (PhD 1972; DSc 1984). Res. Scientist, Hungarian Acad. of Scis, 1966–69; Vis. Scientist, Soviet Acad. of Scis, 1967–68; Vis. Fellow, Oxford, 1969; Cambridge University: Res. Fellow, 1970–72, Dir of Studies in Maths, 1972–96, Trinity Coll.; Asst Lectr, 1971–74, Lectr in Maths, 1974–85; Reader in Pure Maths, 1985–96. Foreign Mem., Hungarian Acad. of Scis, 1990. *Publications:* Extremal Graph Theory, 1978; Graph Theory, 1979; Random Graphs, 1985; Combinatorics, 1986; Linear Analysis, 1990; Modern Graph Theory, 1998; Polynomials of Graphs and Knots, 2000; over 250 papers in learned jls. *Recreations:* books, opera, theatre, tennis, swimming, jogging, windsurfing, riding, ski-ing. *Address:* Trinity College, Cambridge CB2 1TQ; 5 Selwyn Gardens, Cambridge CB3 9AX. *T:* (01223) 354872; 1644 Neshoba Trace Cove, Germantown, TN 38138, USA. *T:* (901) 7514162.

BOLSOVER, John Derrick; Chairman and Chief Executive, Baring Asset Management Holdings Ltd, since 1995; *b* 21 June 1947; *m* 1st, 1971, Susan Elizabeth Peacock; two *s* one *d*; 2nd, 1994, Kate Woollett. *Educ:* Repton Sch.; McGill Univ., Canada (BA). Director: Baring Internat. Investment Mgt Ltd (Hong Kong), 1973–85; Baring Asset Mgt (Japan) Ltd, 1986–; Baring Asset Mgt Ltd, 1994–; Dep. Chm., Baring Hldgs Ltd, 1995–97; Dir, Baring Asset Mgt Hldgs Inc., 1996–98. *Recreation:* sport. *Address:* (office) 155 Bishopsgate, EC2M 3XY. *T:* (020) 7628 6000, *Fax:* (020) 7638 7928. *Clubs:* Boodle's, City; Sunningdale Golf, Valderrama Golf.

BOLT, David Ernest, CBE 1984; FRCS; President, British Medical Association, 1987–88; *b* 21 Sept. 1921; *s* of Rev. E. A. J. Bolt and Hilda I. Bolt; *m* 1955, Phyllis Margaret, (Peggy), Fudge; two *d*. *Educ:* Queen Elizabeth's Hosp., Bristol; Univ. of Bristol. MB ChB 1945; FRCS 1950. Senior Surgical Registrar, W Middx Hosp. and St Mary's Hosp., Paddington, 1955–60; Consultant Surgeon, W Middx Hosp., 1960–82; Hon. Lectr, Charing Cross Hosp., 1972–82. British Medical Association: Mem., Central Cttee for Hosp. Med. Service (Dep. Chm., 1975–79; Chm., 1979–83); Dep. Chm., Jt Consultants' Cttee, 1979–83; Mem. Council, 1975–83. Mem., GMC, 1979–89 (Chm., Professional Conduct Cttee). *Publications:* articles on surgical subjects in professional jls. *Recreations:* motor boat cruising, tree planting, reading, walking. *Address:* Feniton House, Feniton, Honiton, Devon EX14 0BE. *T:* (01404) 850921. *Club:* Royal Society of Medicine.

BOLT, (Mohan) Paul; Director of Strategy and Communications, Department for Culture, Media and Sport, 1998–2001; *b* 8 Feb. 1954; *s* of Sydney Bolt and Jaya Bolt (*née* Chandran); *m* 1991, Carol Spekes. *Educ:* Trinity Coll., Cambridge (BA 1975); Open Univ. (MBA 1995). Joined Home Office as admin trainee, 1975: Principal, 1980–89; Hd, Mgt Div., 1989–92; Department of National Heritage, then Department for Culture, Media and Sport: Head: Libraries Div., 1992–94; Fundamental Expenditure Rev., 1994–95; Broadcasting Bill Team, 1995–96; Broadcasting Policy Div., 1996–98. *Recreations:* cricket, theatre, reading, bridge. *Address:* Department for Culture, Media and Sport, 2/4 Cockspur Street, SW1Y 5DH. *Clubs:* Reform; Lancashire County Cricket.

BOLT, Air Marshal Sir Richard (Bruce), KBE 1979 (CBE 1973); CB 1977; DFC 1945; AFC 1959; Chairman, Pacific Aerospace Corp. of New Zealand, 1982–95; *b* 16 July 1923; *s* of George Bruce Bolt and Mary (*née* Best); *m* 1st, 1946, June Catherine South (*d* 1984); one *s* one *d*; 2nd, 1987, Janice Caroline Tucker. *Educ:* Nelson Coll., NZ. Began service with RNZAF in mid 1942; served during 2nd World War in RAF Bomber Command (Pathfinder Force); Chief of Air Staff, NZ, 1974–76; Chief of Defence Staff, NZ, 1976–80. *Recreations:* fly fishing, golf, horse racing. *Club:* Wellington (Wellington, NZ).

BOLTON, 8th Baron *cr* 1797, of Bolton Castle, co. York; **Harry Algar Nigel Orde-Powlett;** *b* 14 Feb. 1954; *s* of 7th Baron Bolton and of Hon. Christine, *e d* of 7th Baron Forester; *S* father, 2001; *m* 1977, Philippa, *d* of Major Peter Tapply; three *s*. *Educ:* Eton.

Heir: s Hon. Thomas Orde-Powlett, *b* 16 July 1979. *Address:* Wensley Hall, Wensley, Leyburn, N Yorks DL8 4HN. *T:* (01969) 623674.

BOLTON, Bishop Suffragan of, since 1999; **Rt Rev. David Keith Gillett;** *b* 25 Jan. 1945; *s* of Norman and Kathleen Gillett; *m* 1988, Valerie Shannon. *Educ:* Leeds Univ. (BA Theol. 1st cl. 1965; MPhil 1968). Curate, St Luke's, Watford, 1968–71; Northern Sec., Pathfinders and Church Youth Fellowship's Assoc., 1971–74; Lectr, St John's Coll., Nottingham, 1974–79; Co-Leader, Christian Renewal Centre for Reconciliation, NI, 1979–82; Vicar of St Hugh's, Luton, 1982–88; Principal, Trinity Theol Coll., Bristol, 1988–99. Mem., Gen. Synod of C of E, 1985–88, 1990–99. Hon. Canon of Bristol Cathedral, 1991–99. *Publications:* Learning in the Local Congregation, 1979; The Darkness where God is, 1983; Trust and Obey, 1993; (ed jtly) Treasure in the Field: the Archbishops' Companion to the Decade of Evangelism, 1993; co-author and contributor to various books and reference works. *Recreations:* photography, gardening. *Address:* Bishop's Lodge, Bolton Road, Hawkshaw, Bury, Lancs BL8 4JN. *T:* (01204) 882955, *Fax:* (01204) 882988.

BOLTON, Archdeacon of; *no new appointment at time of going to press.*

BOLTON, Beatrice Maud; Her Honour Judge Bolton; a Circuit Judge, since 2001; *b* 26 July 1953; *d* of late Arthur Henry Bolton and of Freda Bolton; divorced; one *s. Educ:* Newcastle upon Tyne Church High Sch.; Sheffield Univ. (LLB Hons). Called to the Bar, Gray's Inn, 1975; Asst Recorder, 1994–98; a Recorder, 1998–2001. *Recreations:* playing tennis, gardening, football, in particular Newcastle United FC. *Address:* Newcastle upon Tyne Combined Court Centre, Quayside, Newcastle upon Tyne NE1 3LA.

BOLTON, Group Captain David; Director, Royal United Services Institute, 1981–94 (Deputy Director, 1980–81); *b* 15 April 1932; *o s* of late George Edward and Florence May Bolton; *m* 1955, Betty Patricia Simmonds; three *d. Educ:* Bede Sch., Co. Durham. Commnd RAF Regt, 1953; subsequent service in Egypt, Jordan, Singapore, Aden, Cyprus, Malta and Germany; RAF Staff Coll., 1969; National Def. Coll., 1972; Central Planning Staff, MoD, 1973–75; OC 33 Wing RAF Regt, 1975–77; Comdt RAF Regt Depot, Catterick, 1977–80; retd 1980. Chm., Macbeth Associates, 1994–2000; Vice-Chm., TASC Eur., 1994–97. Member: RUSI Council, 1973–79; IISS, 1964–90; RIIA, 1975; Council, British Atlantic Cttee, 1981–91; Bd of War Studies, Univ. of London, 1984–92; a founding Mem., Adv. Bd, British-American Project, 1985–99. Hon. Steward, Westminster Abbey, 1981–. Trench Gascoigne Essay Prize, RUSI, 1972. Editor: Brassey's Defence Year Bk, 1982–92; MacMillan-RUSI Defence Studies, 1982–94; RUSI Internat. Security Review, 1992–94. *Publications:* contrib. learned jls. *Recreations:* choral music, international affairs, gardening. *Address:* Churchfield House, Churchfield Lane, Benson, Oxon OX10 6SH. *Club:* Royal Air Force.

BOLTON, David Michael William; education consultant; Head Master, Dame Alice Owen's School, 1982–94; *b* 29 Feb. 1936; *s* of William Benedict Bolton and Edith Phyllis Bolton; *m* 1961, Janet Christine Fleming; two *s* one *d. Educ:* St Francis Xavier's Coll., Liverpool; St Edmund Hall, Oxford (BA 1960; MA 1964); DipEd London 1971. Nat. Service, RAF (Coastal Command), 1955–57. Reckitt & Colman Ltd, 1960–62; Alleyn's Sch., Dulwich, 1962–63; Housemaster, Highgate Sch., 1963–72; Dep. Head, Chancellor's Sch., Herts, 1972–74; Headmaster, Davenant Foundn Grammar Sch., 1974–82. OFSTED Inspector, 1995–. Mem. Council, Secondary Heads Assoc., 1991–94 (Chm., Area Five). Governor, St Albans High School for Girls, 1997–. FRSA 1993. Freeman, City of London, 1994. *Publications:* articles and reviews in TES. *Recreations:* reading, music, jazz especially, travel, walking, sport. *Address:* 29 Normandy Avenue, Barnet, Herts EN5 2HU.

BOLTON, Prof. Eric James, CB 1987; Professor of Teacher Education, Institute of Education, University of London, 1991–96; *b* 11 Jan. 1935; *s* of late James and Lilian Bolton; *m* 1960, Ann Gregory; one *s* twin *d. Educ:* Wigan Grammar Sch.; Chester Coll.; Lancaster Univ. MA. English teacher at secondary schs, 1957–68; Lectr, Chorley Teacher Training Coll., 1968–70; Inspector of Schs, Croydon, 1970–73; HM Inspector of Schs, 1973–79; Staff Inspector (Educnl Disadvantage), 1979–81; Chief Inspector of Schools, DES, 1981–83, Sen. Chief Inspector of Schools, 1983–91. Chairman: Book Trust, 1997–2000 (Vice Chm., 1996–97); ITC Schs Adv. Cttee, 1997–2000; Member: Educn Adv. Cttee, LSO, 1997–; Bd, New Opportunities Fund, 1998–; Educn Cttee, NESTA, 1999–; Trustee, Foundn of Young Musicians, 1992–. *Publications:* Verse Writing in Schools, 1964; various articles in educnl jls. *Recreations:* reading, music and opera, fly fishing. *Address:* 50 Addington Road, Sanderstead, South Croydon, Surrey CR2 8RB.

BOLTON, Sir Frederic (Bernard), Kt 1976; MC; FIMarE; Chairman: The Bolton Group, 1953–91; Dover Harbour Board, 1982–88 (Member, 1957–62 and 1980–88); *b* 9 March 1921; *s* of late Louis Hamilton Bolton and late Beryl Dyer; *m* 1st, 1950, Valerie Margaret Barwick (*d* 1970); two *s*; 2nd, 1971, Vanessa Mary Anne Robarts; two *s* two *d. Educ:* Rugby. Served War, with Welsh Guards, 1940–46 (MC 1945, Italy); Northants Yeomanry, 1952–56. Member: Lloyd's, 1945–; Baltic Exchange, 1946–. Chm., Atlantic Steam Nav. Co. & Subs, 1960–71; Dir, B.P. Tanker Co., 1968–82; Mem., Brit. Rail Shipping & Int. Services Bd, 1970–82 (later Sealink UK Ltd). Pres., Chamber of Shipping of UK, 1966; Mem., Lloyd's Register of Shipping Gen. Cttee, 1961–86; Chairman: Ship & Marine Technol. Requirements Bd, 1977–81; British Ports Assoc., 1985–88; Pilots' Nat. Pension Fund, 1991–94; Member: PLA, 1964–71; Nat. Ports Council, 1967–74; President: Inst. of Marine Engineers, 1968–69 and 1969–70; British Shipping Fedn, 1972–75; Internat. Shipping Fedn, 1973–82; Gen. Council of British Shipping, 1975–76; British Maritime League, 1985–91. Hon. Treas., W Oxfordshire Cons. Assoc., 1991–95. Hon. FNI. Grafton Hunt: Jt Master, 1956–67, Chm., 1967–72. *Recreations:* country sports. *Address:* Pudlicote, near Charlbury, Oxon OX7 3HX. *Club:* City of London.

BOLTON, Prof. Geoffrey Curgenven, AO 1984; DPhil; Pro-Chancellor, Murdoch University, since 2000; Professor of History, Edith Cowan University, 1993–96, now Emeritus; *b* 5 Nov. 1931; *s* of Frank and Winifred Bolton, Perth, W Australia; *m* 1958, (Ann) Carol Grattan; two *s. Educ:* North Perth State Sch.; Wesley Coll., Perth; Univ. of Western Australia; Balliol Coll., Oxford, (DPhil). FRHistS 1967; FAHA 1974; FASSA 1976. Res. Fellow, ANU, 1957–62; Sen. Lectr, Monash Univ., 1962–65; Prof. of Modern Hist., Univ. of Western Australia, 1966–73; Prof. of History, 1973–82 and 1985–89, and Pro-Vice-Chancellor, 1973–76, Murdoch Univ.; Prof. of Australian Studies, Univ. of London, 1982–85; Prof. of Australian Hist., Univ, of Queensland, 1989–93. Vis. Fellow, All Souls Coll., Oxford, 1995. Mem. Council, Australian Nat. Maritime Museum, Sydney, 1985–91. Boyer Lectr, Australian Broadcasting Corp., 1992. FRSA. General Editor, Oxford History of Australia, 1987–91. DUniv Murdoch, 1995. *Publications:* Alexander Forrest, 1958; A Thousand Miles Away, 1963; The Passing of the Irish Act of Union, 1966; Dick Boyer, 1967; A Fine Country to Starve In, 1972; Spoils and Spoilers: Australians Make Their Environment, 1981; Oxford History of Australia, vol. 5, 1990; Daphne Street, 1997; Claremont: a history, 1999; Edmund Barton, 2000; articles in learned jls. *Recreation:* sleep. *Address:* 6 Melvista Avenue, Claremont, WA 6010, Australia. *Club:* Athenæum.

BOLTON, Ivor; conductor; Music Director, Glyndebourne Touring Opera, since 1992; *b* 17 May 1958; *s* of Cyril John Bolton and Elsie Bolton (*née* Worthington); *m* 1984, Tessa Wendy Knighton, *qv*; one *s. Educ:* Queen Elizabeth's GS, Blackburn; Clare Coll., Cambridge (MusB, MA); Royal Coll. of Music (schol.); Nat. Opera Studio. FRCO (CHM) 1976; LRAM 1976. Conductor, Schola Cantorum of Oxford, 1981–82; Music Dir, St James's, Piccadilly, 1982–90; Chorus Master, Glyndebourne, 1985–88; Music Dir, English Touring Opera, 1990–93; Chief Conductor, Scottish Chamber Orchestra, 1993–96. Founder Dir, St James's Baroque Players, 1984–; Founder and Music Dir, Lufthansa Fest. of Baroque Music, 1985–. Bayerische Staatsoper début, 1994; Royal Opera début, world première of Goehr's Arianna, 1995. Has made several recordings. *Recreation:* football (keen follower of Blackburn Rovers). *Address:* 171 Goldhurst Terrace, NW6.

BOLTON, John Eveleigh, CBE 1972; DSC 1945; DL; Chairman and Managing Director, Growth Capital Ltd, since 1968; Chairman: Hall Bolton Estates Ltd; Riverview Investments Ltd; *b* 17 Oct. 1920; *s* of late Ernest and Edith Mary Bolton; *m* 1948, Gabrielle Healey Hall (*d* 1989), *d* of late Joseph and Minnie Hall; one *s* one *d. Educ:* Ilkley Sch.; Wolverhampton Sch.; Trinity Coll., Cambridge (Cassel Travelling Schol., 1948; BA Hons Econs 1948, MA 1953); Harvard Business School (Baker Schol., 1949; MBA with dist., 1950). Articled pupil to Chartered Acct, 1937–40; intermed. exam. of Inst. of Chartered Accts, 1940. Served War of 1939–45 (DSC): Destroyers, Lt RNVR, 1940–46. Research for Harvard in British Industry, 1950–51; Finance Dir, Solartron Laboratory Instruments Ltd, Kingston-upon-Thames, 1951–53 (Chm., 1953); Chm. and Man. Dir: Solartron Engineering Ltd, 1952; The Solartron Electronic Group Ltd, Thames Ditton and subseq. Farnborough, Hants, 1954–63 (Dep. Chm., 1963–65). Director or former Director: NCR Co. Ltd; Alphameric PLC; Black & Decker Group Inc.; Black & Decker Holdings Inc.; Black & Decker Investment Co.; Black & Decker Corp.; Plasmec PLC; Dawson International plc; Johnson Wax Ltd; Redland plc; Hoskyns plc; Business Advisers Ltd; Camperdowne Investment Holdings Ltd; Pres., Develt Capital Gp Ltd, 1984–88. A Gen. Comr of Income Tax, 1964–. British Institute of Management: Chm. Council, 1964–66; Bowie Medal 1969; CIMgt; Life Vice-Pres.; Pres., Engrg Industries Assoc., 1981–84; Chm. and Founder Subscriber: Advanced Management Programmes Internat. Trust; Foundn for Management Educn; Business Grads Assoc.; Dir, Management Publications Ltd, 1966–73 (Chm., 1969); Mem. Exec. Cttee, AA; Hon. Treasurer, Surrey Univ., 1975–82 (Past Chm.); Member: Sub-Cttee on Business Management Studies, UGC; Council of Industry for Management Educn; Harvard Business Sch. Vis. Cttee, 1962–75; Adv. Cttee on Industry, Cttee of Vice-Chancellors, 1984; Business Educn Forum, 1969–74. Mem. Org. Cttee, World Research Hospital. Member: UK Automation Council, 1964–65; Adv. Cttee for Management Efficiency in NHS, 1964–65; Cttee for Exports to New Zealand, 1965–68; Adv. Cttee, Queen's Award to Industry, 1972–; Council, Inst. of Dirs; Chm., Economic Develt Cttee for the Rubber Industry, 1965–68; Vice-Chm., Royal Commn on Local Govt in England, 1966–69; Chm., Committee of Inquiry on Small Firms, 1969–71. Trustee, Small Business Research Trust. Life FRSA. DL Surrey, 1974; High Sheriff of Surrey, 1980–81. DUniv Surrey, 1982; Hon. DSc Bath, 1986. *Publications:* articles in newspapers and journals; various radio and TV broadcasts on industrial topics. *Recreations:* shooting, swimming, gardening, opera, antiques. *Address:* Sunnymead, Tite Hill, Englefield Green, Surrey TW20 0NH. *T:* (01784) 435172. *Clubs:* Harvard Club of London, Institute of Directors.

BOLTON, Roger William; General Secretary, Broadcasting, Entertainment, Cinematograph and Theatre Union, since 1993; *b* 7 Sept. 1947; *s* of William and Honara Bolton; *m* 1974, Elaine Lewis; one *d. Educ:* St Thomas More's Sch., London. Photographic Asst, Boots The Chemists, 1960–64; photographer: Belgrave Press Bureau, 1964–69; BBC TV News, 1969–79; Trade Union Official: Assoc. of Broadcasting Staff, 1979–84; Broadcasting Entertainment Trades Alliance, 1984–93. Mem., British Screen Adv. Council, 1994–. Gov., Nat. Film and TV Sch., 1994–. *Address:* (office) 111 Wardour Street, W1V 4AY. *T:* (020) 7437 8506.

BOLTON, Tessa Wendy; *see* Knighton, T. W.

BOMBAY, Archbishop of, (RC), since 1997; **His Eminence Cardinal Ivan Cornelius Dias,** DCnL; *b* 14 April 1936; *s* of late Carlos Nazario Dias and Maria Martins Dias. *Educ:* Pontifical Ecclesiastical Academy, Rome. DCnL Lateran Univ., Rome, 1964. Ordained priest, Bombay, 1958. Trained for Diplomatic Service, 1961–64; Foreign Service of Holy See, 1964–97; served Vatican Secretariat of State, preparing visit of HH the Pope to Bombay, Internat. Eucharistic Congress, 1964; Sec., Apostolic Nunciatures in Scandinavian countries, Indonesia and Madagascar, 1965–73; Chief of Desk at Vatican Secretariat of State for USSR, Baltic States, Byelorussia, Ukraine, Poland, Bulgaria, China, Vietnam, Laos, Cambodia, S Africa, Namibia, Lesotho, Swaziland, Zimbabwe, Ethiopia, Rwanda, Burundi, Uganda, Zambia, Kenya, Tanzania, 1973–82; Titular Archbishop of Rusubisir and Apostolic Pro-Nuncio to Ghana, Togo and Benin, 1982–87; Apostolic Pro-Nuncio: S Korea, 1987–91; Albania, 1991–97. Cardinal, 2001. Member: Pontifical Council for Culture, Vatican, 1998–; Congregation for Divine Worship and Discipline of the Sacraments, 1999–; Congregation for the Doctrine of Faith, 2000–; Consultor, Congregation for the Evangelization of Peoples, 1998–. *Address:* Archbishop's House, 21 Nathalal Parekh Marg, Fort, Mumbai 400 001 (Maharashtra), India. *T:* (22) 2021093/2021193/2021293, *Fax:* (22) 2853872.

BOMFORD, David Robert Lee; Senior Restorer of Paintings, National Gallery, since 1974; Secretary-General, International Institute for Conservation, since 1994; *b* 31 March 1946; *s* of Donald James Bomford and Margaret Vanstone Bomford (*née* Spalding); *m* 1st, 1969, Helen Graham (marr. diss. 1989); one *s* two *d*; 2nd, 1990, Zahira Véliz; one *s* one *d. Educ:* Merchant Taylors' Sch.; Univ. of Sussex (BSc 1967; MSc 1968). Asst Restorer, National Gall., 1968–74. Editor, Studies in Conservation, 1981–91. Vis. Prof., Churubusco Nat. Inst. of Conservation, Mexico City, 1987; Slade Prof. of Fine Art, Univ. of Oxford, 1996–97. FIIC 1979. *Publications:* Art in the Making: Rembrandt, 1988; Art in the Making: Italian painting before 1400, 1989; Art in the Making: Impressionism, 1990; Conservation of Paintings, 1997; Venice through Canaletto's Eyes, 1998; Colour, 2000. *Recreations:* walking, travel, theatre. *Address:* National Gallery, Trafalgar Square, WC2N 5DN; 80 Stamford Brook Road, W6 0XN. *T:* (020) 8749 8685.

BOMFORD, Nicholas Raymond, MA; Head Master of Harrow, 1991–99; *b* 27 Jan. 1939; *s* of late Ernest Raymond Bomford and of Patricia Clive Bomford (*née* Brooke), JP; *m* 1966, Gillian Mary Reynolds; two *d. Educ:* Kelly Coll.; Trinity Coll., Oxford (MA, Mod. History). Teaching appts, 1960–64; Lectr in History and Contemp. Affairs, BRNC, Dartmouth, 1964–66, Sen. Lectr, 1966–68; Wellington Coll., 1968–76 (Housemaster, 1973–76); Headmaster: Monmouth Sch., 1977–82; Uppingham Sch., 1982–91. Chm., Jt Standing Cttee, HMC/IAPS, 1986–89; Nat. Rep., HMC Cttee, 1990–91. Mem. Navy Records Soc. (Councillor, 1967–70, 1973–76, 1984–88). Governor: Sherborne Sch. for Girls, 1994– (Chm., 2000–); Elstree Prep. Sch., 1996– (Chm., 2001–); Lord Wandsworth Coll., 1999–; Kelly Coll., 1999–; Malvern Coll., 2000–. Freeman, Haberdashers' Co., 1992. *Publications:* Documents in World History, 1914–70, 1973; (contrib.) Dictionary of World History, 1973. *Recreations:* shooting (Captain OURC, 1959–60; England VIII

(Elcho match), 1960), fishing, gardening, music, enjoying Welsh border country and Southern France. *Address:* Long Meadow House, Millend, Newland, Glos GL16 8NF.

BOMPAS, Anthony George; QC 1994; *b* 6 Nov. 1951; *s* of Donald George Bompas, *qv*; *m* 1981, Donna Linda, *d* of J. O. Schmidt; two *s* one *d*. *Educ:* Merchant Taylors' Sch., Northwood; Oriel Coll., Oxford (Schol., MA). Called to the Bar, Middle Temple, 1975; Junior Counsel (Chancery), DTI, 1989–94. Liveryman, Merchant Taylors' Co., 1982–. *Address:* 4 Stone Buildings, Lincoln's Inn, WC2A 3XT. *T:* (020) 7242 5524.

BOMPAS, Donald George, CMG 1966; Managing Executive, Philip and Pauline Harris Charitable Trust, since 1986; *b* 20 Nov. 1920; *yr s* of Rev. E. Anstie Bompas; *m* 1946, Freda Vice, *y d* of F. M. Smithyman, Malawi; one *s* one *d*. *Educ:* Merchant Taylors' Sch., Northwood; Oriel Coll., Oxford (MA Oxon 1947). Overseas Audit Service, 1942–66, retired; Nyasaland, 1942–47; Singapore, 1947–48; Malaya, then Malaysia, 1948–66; Deputy Auditor-General, 1957–60; Auditor-General, Malaya, then Malaysia, 1960–66. Dep. Sec., Guy's Hosp. Med. and Dental Schools, 1966–69, Sec., 1969–82; Dep. Sec., 1982–83, Sec., 1984–86, UMDS of Guy's and St Thomas's Hosps (Hon. Fellow, 1996). Chm., Univ. of London Purchasing Gp, 1976–82. Mem. Exec., Federated Pension Schemes, 1979–86. Mem. Council and Exec. Cttee, Technology (formerly City Technology) Colls Trust, 1990–2000; Trustee, Bacon's Coll., 1991–; Gov., St Olave's and St Saviour's Grammar Sch. Foundn, 1992–2001. FKC 1998. Liveryman, Merchant Taylors' Co., 1951. JMN (Hon.) Malaya, 1961. *Address:* 8 Birchwood Road, Petts Wood, Kent BR5 1NY. *T:* and *Fax:* (01689) 821661. *Club:* Royal Commonwealth Society.

See also A. G. Bompas.

BON, Michel Marie; Chairman, France Telecom, since 1995; *b* 5 July 1943; *s* of Emmanuel Bon and Mathilde (*née* Aussedat); *m* 1971, Catherine de Sairigné; one *s* three *d*. *Educ:* Lycée Champollion, Grenoble; Ecole supérieure des scis économiques et commerciales, Paris; Inst. d'Etudes Politiques, Paris; Ecole Nat. d'Administration, Paris. Insp. of Finance, Min. of Finance, 1971–75; Crédit National, 1975–78; Caisse Nat. de Crédit Agricole, 1978–85; Carrefour, 1985–93 (Chm. and Chief Exec. Officer, 1990–93); Dir, Agence Nationale pour l'Emploi, France, 1993–95. *Address:* 4 avenue de Camoëns, 75116 Paris, France.

BONA, Sir Kina, KBE 1993; High Commissioner for Papua New Guinea in the United Kingdom, since 1996; *b* 14 Feb. 1954; *m* 1990, Judith Lilian Sharples; one *d*. *Educ:* Univ. of Papua New Guinea (LLB 1976); Legal Officer, PNG, 1976–78; Teaching Fellow, Univ. of PNG, 1979; Sen. Legal Officer, 1980–82; Asst. Sec., Dept of Justice, 1985–87; Public Prosecutor, PNG, 1988–94. *Address:* (office) 14 Waterloo Place, SW1Y 4AR.

BONALLACK, Sir Michael (Francis), Kt 1998; OBE 1971; Captain, Royal and Ancient Golf Club of St Andrews, since 1999 (Secretary, 1983–99); *b* 31 Dec. 1934; *s* of Sir Richard (Frank) Bonallack, CBE; *m* 1958, Angela Ward; one *s* three *d*. *Educ:* Chigwell; Haileybury. National Service, 1953–55 (1st Lieut, RASC). Joined family business, Bonallack and Sons Ltd, later Freight Bonallack Ltd, 1955; Director, 1962–74; Dir, Buckley Investments, 1976–84. Chairman: Golf Foundn, 1977–83; Professional Golfers' Assoc., 1976–82; Pres., English Golf Union, 1982. DUniv Stirling, 1994. *Recreation:* golf (British Amateur Champion, 1961, 1965, 1968, 1969, 1970; English Amateur Champion, 1962–63, 1965–67 and 1968; Captain, British Walker Cup Team, 1971; Bobby Jones Award for distinguished sportsmanship in golf, 1972). *Address:* Clatto Lodge, Blebo Craigs, Cupar, Fife KY15 5UF. *T:* (01334) 850600. *Clubs:* Golf House (Elie); Pine Valley (USA).

BOND, Alan; *b* 22 April 1938; *s* of Frank and Kathleen Bond; *m* 1st, 1956, Eileen Teresa Hughes (marr. diss. 1992); two *s* one *d* (and one *d* decd); 2nd, 1995, Diana Bliss. *Educ:* Perivale Sch., Ealing, UK; Fremantle Boys' Sch., W Australia. Chairman, Bond Corporation Holdings Ltd, 1969–90 (interests in property, brewing, electronic media, oil and gas, minerals, airships); Chairman: North Kalgurli Mines Ltd, 1985–89; Gold Mines of Kalgoorlie Ltd, 1987–89; Dallhold Investments Pty, 1987. Founder, Bond Univ., Qld, 1991. Syndicate Head, America's Cup Challenge 1983 Ltd; Australia II Winners of 1983 America's Cup Challenge, following three previous attempts: 1974 Southern Cross, 1977 Australia, 1980 Australia. Australian of the Year, 1977. AO 1984. *Recreation:* yachting. *Address:* GPO Box H555, Perth, WA 6001, Australia. *Clubs:* Royal Ocean Racing; Young Presidents Organisation, Royal Perth Yacht, Cruising Yacht, Western Australian Turf (WA).

BOND, Prof. Brian James, FRHistS; Professor of Military History, King's College, University of London, 1986–2001, now Emeritus; *b* 17 April 1936; *s* of Edward Herbert Bond and Olive Bessie Bond (*née* Sartin); *m* 1962, Madeleine Joyce Carr. *Educ:* Sir William Borlase's Sch., Marlow; Worcester Coll., Oxford (BA Hist. 1959); King's Coll. London (MA Hist. 1962; FKC 1996). FRHistS 1978. Nat. Service, 1954–56, commnd RA. Tutor in Mod. Hist., Univ. of Exeter, 1961–62; Lectr, Univ. of Liverpool, 1962–66; King's College London: Lectr in War Studies, 1966–78; Reader, 1978–86. Vis. Prof., Univ. of Western Ontario, 1972–73; Visiting Fellow: Brasenose Coll., Oxford, 1992–93; All Souls Coll., Oxford, 2000. Liddell Hart Lectr, KCL, 1997; Lees Knowles Lectr, Cambridge Univ., 2000; War Studies Lectr, KCL, 2001. Mem. Council, RUSI, 1972–84. Pres., British Commn for Mil. Hist., 1986–. Member Editorial Board: Jl Contemp. Hist., 1988–; Jl Strategic Studies, 1978–; Jl Mil. Hist. (USA), 1992–96; War in Hist., 1994–; an Associate Editor, New DNB, 1996–. *Publications:* (ed) Victorian Military Campaigns, 1967, 2nd edn 1994; The Victorian Army and the Staff College, 1972; (ed) Chief of Staff: the diaries of Lt-Gen. Sir Henry Pownall 1933–1944, vol. 1, 1972, vol. 2, 1974; Britain, France and Belgium, 1939–1940, 1975, 2nd edn 1990; Liddell Hart: a study of his military thought, 1977, 2nd edn 1991; British Military Policy between the Two World Wars, 1980; War and Society in Europe 1870–1970, 1984; (ed with S. Robbins) Staff Officer: the diaries of Lord Moyne 1914–1918, 1987; (ed) The First World War and British Military History, 1991; (ed) Fallen Stars: eleven studies of twentieth century military disasters, 1991; The Pursuit of Victory: from Napoleon to Saddam Hussein, 1996; (ed with N. Cave) Haig: a reappraisal 70 years on, 1999. *Recreations:* gardening, visiting country houses, observing and protecting wild animals (especially foxes). *Address:* Olmeda, Ferry Lane, Medmenham, Marlow, Bucks SL7 2EZ. *T:* (01491) 571293.

BOND, Rt Rev. (Charles) Derek; appointed Bishop Suffragan of Bradwell, 1976, Area Bishop, 1984–92; Hon. Assistant Bishop, dioceses of Gloucester and Worcester, since 1992; *b* 4 July 1927; *s* of Charles Norman Bond and Doris Bond; *m* 1951, Joan Valerie Meikle; two *s* two *d*. *Educ:* Bournemouth Sch.; King's Coll., London. AKC (2nd hons). Curate of Friern Barnet, 1952; Midlands Area Sec. of SCM in Schools and Public Preacher, dio. Birmingham, 1956; Vicar: of Harringay, 1958; of Harrow Weald, 1962; Archdeacon of Colchester, 1972–76. Nat. Chm., CEMS, 1983–86; Chm., Retired Clergy Assoc., 1998–. *Recreation:* travel. *Address:* Ambleside, 14 Worcester Road, Evesham, Worcs WR11 4JU. *T:* (01386) 446156; *e-mail:* dbondbp@tinyonline.co.uk.

BOND, Edward; playwright and director; *b* 18 July 1934; *m* 1971, Elisabeth Pablé. Northern Arts Literary Fellow, 1977–79. Hon. DLitt Yale, 1977. George Devine Award, 1968; John Whiting Award, 1968. *Opera Libretti:* We Come to the River (music by Hans Werner Henze), 1976; The English Cat (music by Hans Werner Henze), 1983; *ballet libretto:* Orpheus, 1982; *translations:* Chekhov, The Three Sisters, 1967; Wedekind, Spring Awakening, 1974; Wedekind, Lulu—a monster tragedy, 1992. *Publications:* Collected Poems 1978–1985, 1987; Notes on Post-Modernism, 1990; Selected Letters (5 vols), 1994–2000; Selected Notebooks, vol. 1, 2000, vol. 2, 2001; The Hidden Plot: notes on theatre and the state, 2000; *plays:* The Pope's Wedding, 1962; Saved, 1965; Narrow Road to the Deep North, 1968; Early Morning, 1968; Passion, 1971; Black Mass, 1971; Lear, 1972; The Sea, 1973; Bingo, 1974; The Fool, 1976; A-A-America! (Grandma Faust, and The Swing), 1976; Stone, 1976; The Woman, 1978; The Bundle, 1978; Theatre Poems and Songs, 1978; The Worlds and The Activist Papers, 1980; Restoration, 1981; Summer: a play for Europe, 1982; Derek, 1983; Human Cannon, 1984; The War Plays (part 1, Red Black and Ignorant; part 2, The Tin Can People; part 3, Great Peace), 1985; Jackets, 1989; In The Company of Men, 1990; September, 1990; Olly's Prison (TV), 1993; Tuesday (TV), 1993; Coffee: a tragedy, with notes on imagination, 1995; At the Inland Sea: a play for young people, 1996; Eleven Vests, 1997; The Crime of the Twenty-first Century, 1998; The Children: a play for two adults and sixteen children, 2000; Chair: a play for radio, 2000; Have I None, 2000. *Recreation:* the study of physics, because in physics the problems of human motives do not have to be considered (for the benefit of newspaper reporters, especially those with no sense of humour: this is a joke, as anyone who had attended a rehearsal with actors would know). *Address:* c/o Casarotto Ramsay, 60–66 Wardour Street, W1V 3HP.

BOND, Maj.-Gen. Henry Mark Garneys, OBE 1993; JP; Vice Lord-Lieutenant of Dorset, 1984–99; *b* 1 June 1922; *s* of W. R. G. Bond, Tyneham, Dorset; unmarried. *Educ:* Eton. Enlisted as Rifleman, 1940; commnd in Rifle Bde, 1941; served Middle East and Italy; seconded to Parachute Regt, 1947–50; ADC to Field Marshal Viscount Montgomery of Alamein, 1950–52; psc 1953; served in Kenya, Malaya, Cyprus and Borneo; Comd Rifle Bde in Cyprus and Borneo, 1964–66; Comd 12th Inf. Bde, 1967–68; idc 1969; Dir of Defence Operational Plans and Asst Chief of Defence Staff (Ops), 1970–72; retd 1972. President: Dorset Natural History and Archaeological Soc., 1972–75; Dorset Br., CPRE, 1990–95; Dorset Community Council, 1988–97; Dorset Assoc. of Parish Councils, 1990–97; Chm., Dorset Police Authy, 1980–92. Mem., Dorset CC, 1973–85 (Vice-Chm., 1981–85). JP Dorset, 1972 (Chm., Wareham Bench, 1984–89). High Sheriff of Dorset, 1977, DL Dorset, 1977. Chm., Governors of Milton Abbey Sch., 1982–94 (Visitor, 1994–98). *Recreations:* forestry, reading. *Address:* Moigne Combe, Dorchester, Dorset DT2 8JA. *T:* (01305) 852265. *Club:* Boodle's.

BOND, Jennie, (Mrs James Keltz); Court Correspondent, BBC News, since 1989; *b* 19 Aug. 1950; *d* of Kenneth and Pamela Bond; *m* 1982, James Keltz; one *d*, and one step *s* one step *d*. *Educ:* St Francis Coll., Letchworth; Univ. of Warwick. Reporter: Richmond Herald, 1972–75; Evening Mail, Uxbridge, 1975–77; News Producer, BBC, 1977–86; News Correspondent, BBC, 1986–89. *Publication:* Reporting Royalty (autobiog.), 2001. *Recreations:* family, walking by the sea. *Address:* BBC Television Centre, Wood Lane, W12 7RJ.

BOND, Sir John (Reginald Hartnell), Kt 1999; Group Chairman, HSBC Holdings plc, since 1998 (Group Chief Executive, 1993–98); Chairman: HSBC Bank (formerly Midland Bank) Plc, since 1998; HSBC Bank Middle East (formerly British Bank of the Middle East), since 1998; *b* 24 July 1941; *s* of late Capt. R. H. A. Bond, OBE and of E. C. A. Bond; *m* 1968, Elizabeth Caroline Parker; one *s* two *d*. *Educ:* Tonbridge Sch., Kent; Cate Sch., Calif, USA (E-SU Scholar). Joined Hongkong & Shanghai Banking Corp., 1961; worked in Hong Kong, Thailand, Singapore, Indonesia and USA; Chief Exec., Wardley Ltd (Merchant Banking), 1984–87; Hongkong & Shanghai Banking Corporation: Exec. Dir, 1988–91; responsible for: Americas, 1988–89; commercial banking, based in Hong Kong, 1990–91; Pres. and Chief Exec., Marine Midland Banks Inc., Buffalo, USA, 1991–92. Chairman: Hongkong Bank of Canada, 1987–98; HSBC Americas Inc., 1997–; HSBC Bank USA (formerly Marine Midland Bank), 1997–; Director: Hang Seng Bank Ltd, 1990–96; HSBC Hldgs, 1990–; Midland Bank, 1993– (Dep. Chm., 1996–98); Bank of England, 2001–; non-executive Director: London Stock Exchange, 1994–99; British Steel, 1994–98; Orange plc, 1996–99; Ford Motor Co., 2000–. Chm., Inst. of Internat. Finance, Washington. FCIB (FIB 1982). Hon. DEc Richmond, American Univ. in London, 1998; Hon. DLitt Loughborough, 2000. *Recreations:* golf, ski-ing, reading biography. *Address:* HSBC Holdings plc, 10th Floor, 10 Lower Thames Street, EC3R 6AE. *T:* (020) 7260 9158. *Clubs:* MCC; Royal Ashdown Forest Golf; Hong Kong (Hong Kong); John's Island (Florida).

BOND, Prof. (John) Richard, PhD; FRS 2001; FRSC; Professor, since 1987, University Professor, since 1999, and Director, since 1996, Canadian Institute for Theoretical Astrophysics; *b* 15 May 1950; *s* of Jack Parry Bond and Margaret (*née* Sandham). *Educ:* Univ. of Toronto (BSc); Calif Inst. of Technol. (MS, PhD 1979). FRSC 1996. Res. Asst, Kellogg Lab., CIT, 1973–78; Postdoctoral Fellow, Univ. of Calif, Berkeley, 1978–81; Res. Fellow, Inst. of Astronomy, Cambridge, 1982–83; Asst Prof., 1981–85, Associate Prof., 1985–87, Stanford Univ.; Associate Prof., 1985–87, Actg Dir, 1990–91, Canadian Inst. for Theoretical Astrophysics. Fellow, APS, 1998. *Address:* Canadian Institute for Theoretical Astrophysics, University of Toronto, 60 St George Street, Toronto, ON M5S 3H8, Canada. *T:* (416) 9786874.

BOND, Sir Kenneth (Raymond Boyden), Kt 1977; Vice-Chairman, The General Electric Company plc, 1985–90 (Financial Director, 1962–66; Deputy Managing Director, 1966–85), retired; *b* 1 Feb. 1920; *s* of late James Edwin and Gertrude Deplidge Bond; *m* 1958, Jennifer Margaret, *d* of late Sir Cecil and Lady Crabbe; two *s* three *d* (and one *s* decd). *Educ:* Selhurst Grammar School. Served TA, Europe and Middle East, 1939–46. FCA 1960 (Mem. 1949). Partner, Cooper & Cooper, Chartered Accountants, 1954–57; Dir, Radio & Allied Industries Ltd, 1957–62. Member: Industrial Develt Adv. Bd, 1972–77; Cttee to Review the Functioning of Financial Instns, 1977–80; Audit Commn, 1983–86; Civil Justice Rev. Adv. Cttee, 1985–88. *Recreation:* bowls. *Address:* Woodstock, Wayside Gardens, Gerrards Cross, Bucks SL9 7NG. *T:* (01753) 883513. *Club:* The Addington Golf.

BOND, Dr Martyn Arthur; Director, Federal Trust, since 1999; *b* 10 Oct. 1942; *s* of Jack Bond and Muriel Caroline Janet (*née* Webb); *m* 1965, Dinah Macfarlane; two *s* one *d*. *Educ:* Portsmouth Grammar Sch.; Peter Symonds Sch.; Winchester Coll.; Queens' Coll., Cambridge (MA); Univ. of Sussex (DPhil 1971); Univ. of Hamburg. Producer, BBC, 1966–70; Lectr in W European Studies, NUU, 1970–73; Press Officer, Gen. Secretariat, Council of Ministers of EC, 1974–81; BBC Rep., Berlin, 1981–83; Principal Adminr, Gen. Secretariat, Council of Ministers of EC, 1983–88; Dir, UK Office of EP, 1989–99. Mem. Bd, Europe-China Assoc., 1976–82; Founder Mem., Quaker Council for European Affairs, 1979–. Chm., Internat. Adv. Council, 1987–94, Sen. Fellow, 1995–, Salzburg Seminar in American Studies. Vis. Prof. of European Politics, RHBNC, 1999–. Dir, London Press Club, 2000–. Dir, English Coll. Foundn, 1993–; Gov., English Coll. in Prague, 1995–. FRSA 1992. *Publications:* A Tale of Two Germanies, 1991; (ed) Eminent Europeans, 1996; (ed) The Treaty of Nice Explained, 2001; contrib. to Jl Legislative

Studies, German Life and Letters, Parliament Mag. *Recreation:* Europe. *Club:* National Liberal.

BOND, Michael, OBE 1997; author; *b* 13 Jan. 1926; *s* of Norman Robert and Frances Mary Bond; *m* 1950, Brenda Mary Johnson (marr. diss. 1981); one *s* one *d*; *m* 1981, Susan Marfrey Rogers. *Educ:* Presentation College, Reading. RAF and Army, 1943–47; BBC Cameraman, 1947–66; full-time author from 1966. Paddington TV series, 1976. *Publications: for children:* A Bear Called Paddington, 1958; More About Paddington, 1959; Paddington Helps Out, 1960; Paddington Abroad, 1961; Paddington at Large, 1962; Paddington Marches On, 1964; Paddington at Work, 1966; Here Comes Thursday, 1966; Thursday Rides Again, 1968; Paddington Goes to Town, 1968; Thursday Ahoy, 1969; Parsley's Tail, 1969; Parsley's Good Deed, 1969; Parsley's Problem Present, 1970; Parsley's Last Stand, 1970; Paddington Takes the Air, 1970; Thursday in Paris, 1970; Michael Bond's Book of Bears, 1971, 1992; Michael Bond's Book of Mice, 1972; The Day the Animals Went on Strike, 1972; Paddington Bear, 1972; Paddington's Garden, 1972; Parsley the Lion, 1972; Parsley Parade, 1972; The Tales of Olga da Polga, 1972; Olga Meets her Match, 1973; Paddington's Blue Peter Story Book, 1973; Paddington at the Circus, 1973; Paddington Goes Shopping, 1973; Paddington at the Sea-side, 1974; Paddington at the Tower, 1974; Paddington on Top, 1974; Windmill, 1975; How to make Flying Things, 1975; Eight Olga Readers, 1975; Paddington's Loose End Book, 1976; Paddington's Party Book, 1976; Olga Carries On, 1976; Paddington's Pop-up Book, 1977; Paddington Takes the Test, 1979; Paddington's Cartoon Book, 1979; J. D. Polson and the Liberty-Head Dime, 1980; J. D. Polson and the Dillogate Affair, 1981; Paddington on Screen, 1981; Olga Takes Charge, 1982; The Caravan Puppets, 1983; Paddington at the Zoo, 1984; Paddington and the Knickerbocker Rainbow, 1984; Paddington's Painting Exhibition, 1985; Paddington at the Fair, 1985; Oliver the Greedy Elephant, 1985; Paddington at the Palace, 1986; Paddington Minds the House, 1986; Paddington's Busy Day, 1987; Paddington and the Marmalade Maze, 1987; Paddington's Magical Christmas, 1988; Paddington and the Christmas Surprise, 1997; Paddington at the Carnival, 1998; Paddington's Scrap Book, 1999; Paddington in Hot Water, 2000; Paddington's Party Tricks, 2000; Paddington Goes to Hospital, 2001; Olga Moves House, 2001; with Karen Bond: Paddington Posts a Letter, 1986; Paddington at the Airport, 1986; Paddington's London, 1986; *for adults:* Monsieur Pamplemousse, 1983; Monsieur Pamplemousse and the Secret Mission, 1984; Monsieur Pamplemousse on the Spot, 1986; Monsieur Pamplemousse Takes the Cure, 1987; The Pleasures of Paris, 1987; Monsieur Pamplemousse Aloft, 1989; Monsieur Pamplemousse Investigates, 1990; Monsieur Pamplemousse Rests His Case, 1991; Monsieur Pamplemousse Stands Firm, 1992; Monsieur Pamplemousse on Location, 1992; Monsieur Pamplemousse takes the Train, 1993; Monsieur Pamplemousse Afloat, 1998; Monsieur Pamplemousse on Probation, 2000; *autobiography:* Bears and Forebears: a life so far, 1996. *Recreations:* photography, travel, cars, wine. *Address:* The Agency, 24 Pottery Lane, W11 4LZ. *T:* (020) 7727 1346.

BOND, Sir Michael (Richard), Kt 1995; FRCPsych, FRCPGlas, FRCSE; Professor of Psychological Medicine, University of Glasgow, 1973–98 (Vice Principal, 1986–97; Administrative Dean, Faculty of Medicine, 1991–97); *b* 15 April 1936; *s* of Frederick Richard Bond and Dorothy Bond (*née* Gardner); *m* 1961, Jane Issitt; one *s* one *d*. *Educ:* Magnus Grammar Sch., Newark, Notts; Univ. of Sheffield (MD, PhD). FRSE 1998. Ho. Surg./Ho. Phys., Royal Inf., Sheffield, 1961–62; Asst Lectr/Res. Registrar, Univ. Dept of Surgery, Sheffield, 1962–64; Res. Registrar/Lectr, Univ. Dept of Psychiatry, Sheffield, 1964–67; Sen. Ho. Officer/Res. Registrar, Registrar/Sen. Registrar, Inst. of Neurological Scis, Glasgow, 1968–71; Lectr in Neurosurgery, Univ. Dept of Neurosurgery, Glasgow, 1971–73. Locum Cons. Neurosurgeon, Oxford, 1972; Hon. Cons. Psychiatrist, Greater Glasgow Health Bd, 1973–98. Member: UGC, 1982–91; UFC, 1991–93; SHEFC, 1992–96; Chm., Jt Med. Adv. Cttee, 1992–95. Pres., Pain Soc., 1999–2001; Councillor, Internat. Assoc. for Study of Pain, 1981–83, 1996– (Pres. elect, 1999–); Mem. Council, St Andrews Ambulance Assoc., 1995–2000. Dir, Prince and Princess of Wales Hospice, Glasgow, 1997–. Chm., Head Injuries Trust for Scotland, 1989–99; Trustee, Lloyds TSB Foundn, 1999–. Gov., High Sch., Glasgow, 1990– (Dep. Chm., 1999–). FRSA 1992. Hon. DSc Leicester, 1996. *Publications:* Pain, its nature, analysis and treatment, 1979, 2nd edn 1984; (co-ed) Rehabilitation of the Head Injured Adult, 1983, 2nd edn 1989; papers on psychological and social consequences of severe brain injury, psychological aspects of chronic pain and cancer pain, 1963–, and others on similar topics. *Recreations:* painting, collecting antique books, forest walking, ornithology, gardening. *Address:* 33 Ralston Road, Bearsden, Glasgow G61 3BA. *T:* (home) (0141) 942 4391; (work) (0141) 330 3692. *Club:* Athenæum.

BOND, Richard; *see* Bond, J. R.

BOND, Richard Douglas; Senior Partner, Herbert Smith, since 2000; *b* 23 July 1946; *s* of Douglas Charles Bond and Vera Eileen Bond; *m* 1973, Anthea Mary Charrington (*d* 1996); two *d*. *Educ:* Berkhamsted Sch. Articled Clerk, Halsey, Lightly & Hemsley, 1964–69; joined Herbert Smith, 1969; seconded to BNOC, 1976–78; Partner, 1977; Head of Corporate, 1993–2000. Member: Law Soc.; Internat Bar Assoc. Mem., Solicitors' Co. *Recreations:* golf, cricket, theatre. *Address:* (office) Exchange House, Primrose Street, EC2A 2HS. *T:* (020) 7374 8000. *Clubs:* MCC, Lansdowne.

BOND, Richard Henry; His Honour Judge Bond; a Circuit Judge, since 1997; *b* 15 April 1947; *s* of Ashley Raymond Bond and Hester Mary Bond (*née* Bowles); *m* 1987, Annabel Susan Curtis; one *s* one *d*. *Educ:* Sherborne Sch. Called to the Bar, Inner Temple, 1970. *Recreations:* architecture, walking, gardening. *Address:* Combined Court Centre, Deansleigh Road, Bournemouth BH7 7DS. *Clubs:* Travellers, Royal Automobile.

BOND-WILLIAMS, Noel Ignace, CBE 1979; Director, National Exhibition Centre Ltd, 1970–89; *b* 7 Nov. 1914; *s* of late W. H. Williams, Birmingham; *m* 1939, Mary Gwendoline Tomey (*d* 1989); one *s* two *d*. *Educ:* Oundle Sch.; Birmingham Univ. (BSc). FIM, FIMgt. Pres. Guild of Undergrads 1936–37, Pres. Guild of Grads 1947, Birmingham Univ. Various appts in metal industry; Director: Enfield Rolling Mills Ltd, 1957–65; Delta Metal Co. Ltd, 1967–77; Vice-Chm., 1978–79, Chm., 1979–83, Remploy Ltd; Dir, 1972–85, and Vice-Chm., 1979–85, Lucas (Industries) Ltd. Industrial Adviser, DEA, 1965–67. Pres., Birmingham Chamber of Commerce, 1969. Member: Commn on Industrial Relations, 1971–74; Price Commn, 1977–79. Mem. Council, Industrial Soc., 1947–78; Pres., Brit. Non-ferrous Metals Fedn, 1974–75. Pro-Chancellor, Univ. of Aston in Birmingham, 1970–81. Hon. DSc Aston, 1975. *Publications:* papers and articles on relationships between people in industry. *Recreation:* sailing. *Address:* Courtyard House, High Street, Lymington, Hants SO41 9AH. *T:* (01590) 672593. *Clubs:* Metallics; Royal Cruising, Royal Lymington Yacht.

BONDEVIK, Rev. Kjell Magne; MP (KrF) Norway, since 1973; Prime Minister of Norway, 1997–2000; *b* Molde, Norway, 3 Sept. 1947; *s* of Johannes and Margit Bondevik; *m* 1970, Bjørg Rasmussen; two *s* one *d*. *Educ:* Free Faculty of Theology, Oslo (*Candidatus Theologiae* 1975). Ordained priest, Lutheran Church of Norway, 1979. State Sec., Prime Minister's Office, 1972–73; Minister of Church and Educn, 1983–86; Minister of Foreign Affairs, 1989–90. *Address:* Stortinget, 0026 Oslo, Norway.

BONDI, Prof. Sir Hermann, KCB 1973; FRS 1959; FRAS; Master of Churchill College, Cambridge, 1983–90, Fellow, since 1990; Professor of Mathematics, King's College, London, since 1954 (titular since 1971, emeritus since 1985); *b* Vienna, 1 Nov. 1919; *s* of late Samuel and Helene Bondi, New York; *m* 1947, Christine M. Stockman, *d* of late H. W. Stockman, CBE; two *s* three *d*. *Educ:* Realgymnasium, Vienna; Trinity Coll., Cambridge (MA). Temporary Experimental Officer, Admiralty, 1942–45; Fellow Trinity Coll., Cambridge, 1943–49, and 1952–54; Asst Lecturer, Mathematics, Cambridge, 1945–48; University Lecturer, Mathematics, Cambridge, 1948–54. Dir-Gen., ESRO, 1967–71; Chief Scientific Advr, MoD, 1971–77; Chief Scientist, Dept of Energy, 1977–80; Chm. and Chief Exec., NERC, 1980–84. Research Associate, Cornell Univ., 1951; Visiting Prof. Cornell Univ., 1960; Raman Prof., Indian Acad. of Scis, 1996. Lectures: Harvard Coll. Observatory, 1953; Lowell, Boston, Mass, 1953; Halley, Oxford, 1962; Tarner, Cambridge, 1965; Lees-Knowles, Cambridge, 1974; Conway Meml, London, 1992. Chairman: Space Cttee, MoD, 1964–65; Nat. Cttee for Astronomy, 1963–67; Adv. Council on Energy Conservation, 1980–82; IFIAS 1984–97. Secretary, Royal Astronomical Soc., 1956–64; Mem., SRC, 1973–80. President: Inst. of Mathematics and its Applications, 1974–75; British Humanist Assoc., 1982–99; Assoc. of British Science Writers, 1981–85; Soc. for Res. into Higher Educn, 1981–97; Assoc. for Science Educn, 1982; Hydrographic Soc., 1985–87; Rationalist Press Assoc., 1982–. Member: Science Policy Foundn; Mem., Ct, London Univ., 1963–67. Hon. Fellow, Indian Acad. of Scis, 1996. FKC 1968. Hon. DSc: Sussex 1974; Bath 1974; Surrey 1974; York 1980; Southampton 1981; Salford, 1982; Birmingham, 1984; St Andrews, 1985; Hon. DTech Plymouth, 1995; Dr *hc* Vienna, 1993. Hon. FIEE 1979; Hon. FInstP 1992; Hon. FIMA 1993. Einstein Soc. gold medal, 1983; Gold Medal, Inst. of Mathematics and its Applications, 1988; G. D. Birla Internat. Award for Humanism, 1990; Decoration of Honour for Sci. and Art, Austria, 1997. *Publications:* Cosmology, 1952 (2nd edn, 1960); The Universe at Large, 1961; Relativity and Commonsense, 1964; Assumption and Myth in Physical Theory, 1968; (with Dame Kathleen Ollerenshaw) Magic Squares of Order Four, 1982; Science, Churchill and me (autobiog.), 1990; papers on astrophysics, etc, in Proc. Royal Society, Monthly Notices, Royal Astronomical Society, Proc. Cam. Phil. Society, etc. *Recreations:* walking, travelling. *Address:* Churchill College, Cambridge CB3 0DS; 60 Mill Lane, Impington, Cambridge CB4 9XN.

BONE, Charles, PPRI, ARCA; President, Royal Institute of Painters in Water Colours, 1979–89; Governor, Federation of British Artists, 1976–81 and since 1983 (Member, Executive Council, 1983–84 and 1986–88); *b* 15 Sept. 1926; *s* of William Stanley and Elizabeth Bone; *m* Sheila Mitchell, FRBS, ARCA, sculptor; two *s*. *Educ:* Farnham Coll. of Art; Royal Coll. of Art (ARCA). FBI Award for Design. Consultant, COSIRA, 1952–70; Craft Adviser, Malta Inds Assoc., Malta, 1952–78; Lecturer, Brighton Coll. of Art, 1950–86; Director, RI Galleries, Piccadilly, 1965–70. Many mural paintings completed, including those in Eaton Square and Meretea, Italy; oils and water colours in exhibns of RA, London Group, NEAC and RBA, 1950–; 42 one-man shows, 1950–; works in private collections in France, Italy, Malta, America, Canada, Japan, Australia, Norway, Sweden, Germany. Designer of Stourhead Ball, 1959–69; produced Ceramic Mural on the History of Aerial Photography. Critic for Arts Review. Mem. Council, RI, 1964– (Vice-Pres. 1974). Hon. Member: Medical Art Soc.; Soc. Botanical Artists. Hon. FCA (Can.). Hunting Gp Prize for a British Watercolour, 1984. *Film:* Watercolour Painting: a practical guide, 1990. *Publications:* author and illustrator: Waverley, 1991; Authors Circle, 1998; Cathedrals, 2000. *Address:* Winters Farm, Puttenham, Guildford, Surrey GU3 1AR. *T:* (01483) 810226.

BONE, Prof. (James) Drummond; Principal, Royal Holloway and Bedford New College, University of London, since 2000; *b* 11 July 1947; *s* of William Drummond Bone, ARSA, RSW and Helen Bone (*née* Yuill); *m* 1970, Vivian Clare Kindon. *Educ:* Ayr Acad.; Univ. of Glasgow (MA); Balliol Coll., Oxford (Snell Exhibnr, 1968–72). Lectr, English and Comparative Literature, Univ. of Warwick, 1972–80; University of Glasgow: Lectr, 1980–89, Sen. Lectr, 1989–95, in English Literature; Dean, Faculty of Arts, 1991–95; Vice-Principal, 1995–99; Prof. of English Literature, 1995–2000. Jt Editor, Romanticism jl, 1993–. FRSA 1995. *Publications:* Writers and their Work: Byron, 2000; Cambridge Companion to Byron, 2002. *Recreations:* music, ski-ing, Maseratis. *Address:* Royal Holloway and Bedford New College, Egham, Surrey TW20 0EX. *T:* (01784) 443033. *Clubs:* Athenæum; Glasgow Arts (Glasgow).

BONE, Rt Rev. John Frank Ewan; Area Bishop of Reading, 1989–96; *b* 28 Aug. 1930; *s* of Jack and Herberta Blanche Bone; *m* 1954, Ruth Margaret Crudgington; two *s* two *d* and one adopted *s*. *Educ:* Monkton Combe School, Bath; St Peter's Coll., Oxford (MA); Ely Theological Coll.; Whitelands Coll. of Education (Grad. Cert. in Education). Ordained, 1956; Assistant Curate: St Gabriel's, Warwick Square, 1956–60; St Mary's, Henley on Thames, 1960–63; Vicar of Datchet, 1963–76; Rector of Slough, 1976–78; Rural Dean of Burnham, 1974–77; Archdeacon of Buckingham, 1978–89. Mem. of General Synod, 1980–85. *Recreations:* collecting antique maps and prints, classical music, walking. *Address:* 4 Grove Road, Henley-on-Thames, Oxon RG9 1DH.

BONE, Quentin; JP; MA, DPhil; FRS 1984; zoologist; Hon. Research Fellow, Marine Biological Association UK; *b* 17 Aug. 1931; *s* of late Stephen Bone (landscape painter) and Mary Adshead (mural painter); *m* 1958, Susan Elizabeth Smith; four *s*. *Educ:* Warwick Sch.; St John's Coll., Oxon. Naples Scholarship, 1954; Fellow by examination, Magdalen Coll., Oxford, 1956. Zoologist at Plymouth Laboratory, 1959–91 (Marine Biol Assoc., DCSO). *Publications:* Biology of Fishes (with N. B. Marshall), 1983, 2nd edn (with J. S. Blaxter also), 1994; (ed) Biology of Pelagic Tunicates, 1998; papers on fish and invertebrates, mainly in Jl of Mar. Biol Assoc. UK. *Address:* Marchant House, 98 Church Road, Plymstock, Plymouth PL9 9BG.

BONE, Roger Bridgland, CMG 1996; HM Diplomatic Service; Ambassador to Brazil, since 1999; *b* 29 July 1944; *s* of late Horace Bridgland Bone and Dora R. Bone (*née* Tring); *m* 1970, Lena M. Bergman; one *s* one *d*. *Educ:* William Palmer's Sch., Grays; St Peter's Coll., Oxford (MA). Entered HM Diplomatic Service, 1966; UK Mission to UN, 1966; FCO, 1967; 3rd Sec., Stockholm, 1968–70; 2nd Sec., FCO, 1970–73; 1st Secretary: Moscow, 1973–75; FCO, 1975–78; 1st Sec., UK Perm. Representation to European Communities, Brussels, 1978–82; Asst Private Sec. to Sec. of State for Foreign and Commonwealth Affairs, 1982–84; Vis. Fellow, Harvard Univ. Center for Internat. Affairs, 1984–85; Counsellor, 1985–89, and Head of Chancery, 1987–89, Washington; Counsellor, FCO, 1989–91; Asst Under Sec. of State, FCO, 1991–95; Ambassador to Sweden, 1995–99. *Recreations:* music, wine. *Address:* c/o Foreign and Commonwealth Office, SW1A 2AH.

BONE, Prof. Thomas Renfrew, CBE 1987; Deputy Principal, University of Strathclyde, 1992–96; *b* 2 Jan. 1935; *s* of James Renfrew Bone and Mary Williams; *m* 1959, Elizabeth Stewart; one *s* one *d*. *Educ:* Greenock High Sch.; Glasgow Univ. MA 1st cl. English 1956, MEd 1st cl. 1962, PhD 1967. Teacher, Paisley Grammar Sch., 1957–62; Lecturer: Jordanhill Coll. of Educn, 1962–63; Glasgow Univ., 1963–67; Jordanhill College of Education: Hd of Educn Dept, 1967–71; Principal, 1972–92. FCCEA 1984; FRSGS

1997. *Publications:* Studies in History of Scottish Education, 1967; School Inspection in Scotland, 1968; *chapters in:* Whither Scotland, 1971; Education Administration in Australia and Abroad, 1975; Administering Education: international challenge, 1975; European Perspectives in Teacher Education, 1976; Education for Development, 1977; Practice of Teaching, 1978; World Yearbook of Education, 1980; The Management of Educational Institutions, 1982; The Effective Teacher, 1983; Strathclyde: changing horizons, 1985; The Changing Role of the Teacher, 1987; Teacher Education in Europe, 1990; Educational Leadership: challenge and change, 1992. *Recreation:* golf. *Address:* 7 Marchbank Gardens, Paisley PA1 3JD. *Clubs:* Western Gailes Golf; Paisley Burns.

BONELL, Carlos Antonio; guitarist; concert artist since 1969; *b* London, 23 July 1949; *s* of Carlos Bonell and Ana Bravo; *m* 1975, Pinuccia Rossetti; two *s*. *Educ:* William Ellis Sch., Highgate; Royal Coll. of Music (Hon. RCM 1973). Lectr, City Lit, 1970; Prof., RCM 1972. Début as solo guitarist, Purcell Room, 1971; GLAA Young Musician, 1973; resident guitarist, London Contemp. Dance Theatre, 1974; concert tours and recording with John Williams & Friends, 1975; first solo album, 1975; concerto début, RFH, 1977; NY début, 1978; Carlos Bonell Ensemble début, QEH, 1983, and tours in Europe and Far East; soloist with all major UK orchestras; commissioned and first performed Sonata by Stephen Oliver, 1981; first performance of: guitar concertos by Bryan Kelly, 1979, Barrington Pheloung, 1994, Armand Coeck, 1997; recorded Rodrigo's Concierto de Aranjuez, 1981; first recording of Carlos Bonell Ensemble, The Sea in Spring, 1997; numerous other solo records and awards. *Publications:* Spanish folk songs and dances, 1975; Gaspar Sanz airs and dances, 1977; A Tarrega collection, 1980; First Pieces for solo guitar, 1980; The romantic collection, 1983; The classical collection, 1983; Spanish folk songs for 3 guitars, 1984; Purcell: 3 pieces, 1984; Tarrega Fantasia, 1984; Technique Builder, 1998; Carlos Bonell Guitar Series, 1998. *Recreations:* cinema, reading, history, playing the guitar, listening to music. *Address:* Bravo Music International, PO Box 19060, N7 0ZD. *Fax:* (020) 7689 9964; *e-mail:* carlos@carlosbonell.com; 5A Dalmeny Mansions, 77 Anson Road, N7 0AX.

BONELLI, Pierre Sauveur Ernest; Chief Executive Officer, Sema Group plc, 1988–2001; *b* 28 May 1939; *s* of Pierre Bonelli and Victoria Bonelli (*née* Seren); *m* 1962, Harriet Becker; three *s*. *Educ:* Ecole Polytechnique, Paris; Harvard Business Sch. (MBA 1965). Joined Texas Instruments, Dallas, 1966: engr, 1966–68; Financial Manager, 1968–75; Vice-Pres. i/c US Digital Circuits Div., 1975; Gen. Manager, 1971, then Pres.-Gen. Manager, 1971–76, Texas Instruments France; Sema-Metra, Paris: Dir Gen., 1976–82; CEO, 1982–88; Sema-Metra merged with CAP Gp, UK, 1988 to form Sema Gp. Mem., Adv. Bd and Technol. Regulatory Bd, Bank of France. Mem. Adv. Council, LSO. Légion d'Honneur (France), 1993.

BONELLO DU PUIS, Dr George, KOM 1995; High Commissioner for Malta in London, since 1999; *b* 24 Jan. 1928; *s* of Joseph Bonello and Josephine (*née* Du Puis); *m* 1957, Mary Iris sive Iris Gauci Maistre'; two *s* one *d*. *Educ:* St Catherine's High Sch., Malta; The Lyceum, Malta; Royal Univ. of Malta (LLD 1952). Law Practice, 1953–87 and 1995–98. MP, Malta, 1971–96; Minister of Finance, 1987–92; Minister for Econ. Services, 1992–95. Chm., Sliema Wanderers FC, 1961–87. *Recreations:* billiards and sports in general, football in particular. *Address:* Malta High Commission, 36–38 Piccadilly, W1V 0PQ; 16 Kensington Square, W8 5HH. *T:* (020) 7937 5535; The Park, Antonio Nani Street, Ta'Xbiex, Malta. *T:* 335415. *Clubs:* Royal Over-Seas League; Casino Maltese (Valletta, Malta).

BONEY, Guy Thomas Knowles; QC 1990; a Recorder, since 1985; a Deputy High Court Judge, since 1994; *b* 28 Dec. 1944; *o c* of Thomas Knowles Boney, MD and Muriel Hilary Eileen Long, FRCS; *m* 1976, Jean Harris Ritchie, *qv*; two *s*. *Educ:* Winchester College; New College, Oxford (BA 1966; MA 1987). Called to the Bar, Middle Temple, 1968 (Harmsworth Scholar), Bencher, 1997; in practice on Western Circuit, 1969–; Head of Pump Court Chambers, 1992–. *Publications:* The Road Safety Act 1967, 1971; contribs to: Halsbury's Laws of England, 4th edn (Road Traffic); horological jls. *Recreations:* horology, music (Organist, King's Somborne Parish Church, 1980–), amateur theatre. *Address:* 3 Pump Court, Temple, EC4Y 7AJ. *Club:* Reform.

BONEY, Jean Harris, (Mrs G. T. K. Boney); *see* Ritchie, J. H.

BONFIELD, Sir Peter (Leahy), Kt 1996; CBE 1989; FREng; Chief Executive, British Telecommunications plc, 1996–2002; *b* 3 June 1944; *s* of George and Patricia Bonfield; *m* 1968, Josephine Houghton. *Educ:* Hitchin Boys' Grammar School; Loughborough Univ. (BTech Hons; Hon. DTech, 1988). FIEE 1990, FBCS 1990, FCIM 1990; FREng (FEng 1993). Texas Instruments Inc., Dallas, USA, 1966–81; Group Exec. Dir, ICL, 1981–84; Chm. and Man. Dir, STC Internat. Computers Ltd, 1984–90; Chm. and Chief Exec., 1985–96, Dep. Chm., 1997–2000, ICL plc; Dep. Chief Exec., STC plc, 1987–90. Director: BICC PLC, 1992–96; AstraZeneca plc (formerly Zeneca Gp), 1995–; MCI Inc., 1996–98; Mem., Internat. Adv. Bd, Salomon Smith Barney, 1999–. Member: European Round Table; EU-Japan Business Dialogue Round Table; Ambassador for British Business. Mem., British Quality Foundn, 1993– (Vice-Pres.). Mem., CS Coll. Adv. Council, 1993–97. FRSA 1992. Freeman, City of London, 1990; Liveryman, Information Technologists' Co., 1992. Hon. Citizen, Dallas, Texas. Hon. doctorates from univs of Loughborough, Surrey, Mid Glamorgan, Nottingham, Nottingham Trent, Brunel, Open, Northumbria at Newcastle, Kingston, Cranfield, Essex and London. Mountbatten Medal, Nat. Electronics Council, 1995; Gold Medal, Inst. of Mgt, 1996. Comdr, Order of the Lion (Finland), 1995. *Recreations:* music, sailing, ski-ing. *Address:* c/o BT Centre, 81 Newgate Street, EC1A 7AJ. *Club:* Royal Automobile.

BONFIELD, Prof. William, CBE 1998; PhD; FREng; Professor of Medical Materials, University of Cambridge, since 2000; *b* 6 March 1937; *s* of Cecil William Bonfield and Ellen Gertrude Bonfield; *m* 1960, Gillian Winifred Edith Cross; one *s* two *d*. *Educ:* Letchworth GS; Imperial College, London (Perry Meml and Bessemer Medals; BScEng, PhD, DIC, ARSM). CEng, FIM; FREng (FEng 1993). Honeywell Res. Center, Hopkins, Minn, USA, 1961–68; Queen Mary, later Queen Mary and Westfield College, London: Reader in Materials Science, 1968; Prof. of Materials, 1974–99; Head, Dept of Materials, 1980–90; Chm., Sch. of Engineering, 1981–88; Dean of Engineering, 1985–89; Dir, Univ. of London IRC in Biomedical Materials, 1991–99. Vis. Prof., Chulalongkorn Univ., Bangkok, 1988; OCMR Dist. Vis. Prof., Univ. of Toronto, 1990; Vis. Prof., Henry Ford Hosp., Detroit, 1992; Hon. Prof., Univ. of Sichuan, 1992. Lectures: Royal Microscopical Soc., 1992; Mellor Meml, Inst. of Materials, 1993; Prof. Moore Meml, Univ. of Bradford, 1994; Dist. Scholar, QUB, 1994; C. W. Hall Meml, SW Res. Inst., San Antonio, Texas, 1996; Hatfield Meml, Univ. of Sheffield, 1996; CSE Internat., Royal Acad. of Engrg, 1998; Hawksley Meml, IMechE, 1999. Project Leader, EEC Concerted Action in Skeletal Implants, 1989–96. Chm., Med Engrg Cttee, 1989, Mem., Materials Cttee, later Materials Commn, 1983–88, SERC; Institute of Materials: Chairman: Biomaterials Cttee, 1989–96; Biomedical Applications Div., 1996–; Vice-Pres., 1998–; Member: Materials Sci. Bd, 1989–95; Council, 1996–; Member: Jt Dental Cttee, 1984–89; DoH Cttee on Dental and Surgical Materials, 1986–90; Directive Council, Internat. Soc. for Bio-analoging Skeletal Implants, 1988–95; Jl Cttee, Internat. Fedn for Med. and Biol Engrg, 1989–; Techl Cttee, BSI, 1992–; Metallurgy and Materials Res. Assessment Panel, HEFC, 1995–96; Materials Foresight Panel, OST, 1995–; Chm., UK Focus on Med. Engrg, Royal Acad. of Engrg, 1998–. Chm., London Metallurgical Soc., 1991; Sec. Gen., Internat. Soc. for Ceramics in Medicine, 1998–. Director: Abonetics Ltd, 1996–; Biocompatibles plc, 2000–. Hon. Member: Canadian Ortho. Res. Soc., 1983; Materials Res. Soc. of India, 1993. Griffith Medal, Inst. of Metals, 1991; Royal Soc. Armourers' and Brasiers' Co. Medal, 1991; George Winter Award, Eur. Soc. for Biomaterials, 1994; Kelvin Medal, ICE, 1995; Acta Metallurgica J. Herbert Holloman Award, 2000. Freeman: Armourers' and Brasiers' Co., 1994 (Liveryman, 1999; Mem., Ct of Assts, 2001–); City of London, 1998. Chm., Editl Bd, Materials in Electronics, 1990–; Mem., Editl Bd, Jl of Applied Polymer Sci., 1992–; Editor, Jl of Materials Science, 1973–; Founding Editor: Jl of Materials Science Letters, 1981–; Materials in Medicine, 1990–. *Publications:* Bioceramics, 1991; over 300 research papers on biomaterials, biomechanics and physical metallurgy in sci. jls. *Recreations:* cycling, British Cycling Coaching Scheme coach. *Address:* Department of Materials Science and Metallurgy, University of Cambridge, New Museums Site, Pembroke Street, Cambridge CB2 3QZ. *Clubs:* Athenæum; North Road Cycling.

BONGERS de RATH, Paul Nicholas; international relations consultant in urban affairs, Bongers de Rath, since 1996; *b* 25 Oct. 1943; *s* of Henry Bongers and late Marjorie Bongers (*née* Luxton); *m* 1968, Margaret Collins; two *s* two *d*. *Educ:* Bradfield Coll.; New Coll., Oxford (MA); DPA Univ. of London (external), 1968. Administrative Trainee, City of Southampton, 1965–68; Personal Asst to Chief Exec., City of Nottingham, 1968–69; Administrator, Council of Europe, 1969–71; Assistant Secretary: AMC, 1971–74; AMA, 1974–78; Exec. Sec., British Sections, IULA/CEMR, 1978–88; Dir, Local Govt Internat. Bureau, 1988–95. Special Advr, CEMR, 1996–; Consultant, World Assocs of Cities and Local Authorities Co-ordination, 1996–99; Special Rep., Bremen Initiative, 1999–. Hon. Sec., Local Govt Gp for Europe, 1999–. Mem., Rotary Club, 1996–. *Publications:* Local Government and 1992, 1990, 2nd edn as Local Government and the European Single Market, 1992; articles in local govt jls. *Recreations:* family, music, countryside, travel, the arts. *Address:* The Old Gordon House, 215 High Street, Aldeburgh, Suffolk IP15 5DN. *Club:* Reform.

BONHAM, Major Sir Antony Lionel Thomas, 4th Bt *cr* 1852; DL; late Royal Scots Greys; *b* 21 Oct. 1916; *o s* of Maj. Sir Eric H. Bonham, 3rd Bt, and Ethel (*d* 1962), *y d* of Col Leopold Seymour; *S* father, 1937; *m* 1944, Felicity, *o d* of late Col. Frank L. Pardoe, DSO, Bartonbury, Cirencester; three *s*. *Educ:* Eton; RMC. Served Royal Scots Greys, 1937–49; retired with rank of Major, 1949. DL Glos 1983. *Heir: s* (George) Martin (Antony) Bonham [*b* 18 Feb. 1945; *m* 1979, Nenon Baillieu (marr. diss. 1992), *e d* of R. R. Wilson and Hon. Mrs Wilson, Durford Knoll, Upper Durford Wood, Petersfield, Hants; one *s* three *d*]. *Address:* Greystones, The Croft, Fairford, Glos GL7 4BB. *T:* (01285) 712258.

BONHAM, Derek Charles, FCA, FCT; Chairman: Imperial Tobacco Group plc, since 1996; Cadbury Schweppes plc, since 2000; Marconi, since 2001; *b* 12 July 1943. *Educ:* Bedford Sch. Chartered Accountant, Whinney Murray; Management Accountant, Staflex Internat.; Hanson plc: Dep. Financial Controller, 1971; Finance Dir, 1981; Chief Exec., 1992–97; Dep. Chm., 1993–97; Chm., Energy Gp, 1997–98. Non-executive Director: USI, 1995–96; Glaxo-Wellcome, 1995–2001. Member: Accounting Standards Cttee, 1987–90; Financial Accounting Standards Adv. Council, USA, 1990–93. *Address:* 150 Brompton Road, SW3 1HX. *T:* (020) 7584 6798, *Fax:* (020) 7584 6485.

BONHAM, Nicholas; Deputy Chairman, Bonhams & Brooks (formerly W. & F. C. Bonham & Sons Ltd), since 1987; *b* 7 Sept. 1948; *s* of late Leonard Charles Bonham and Diana Maureen (*née* Magwood); *m* 1977, Kaye Eleanor (*née* Ivett) (marr. diss. 1999); two *d*. *Educ:* Trent College. Joined W. & F. C. Bonham & Sons Ltd, Fine Art Auctioneers, 1966; Dir, 1970; Man. Dir, 1975–87. Director: Montpelier Properties, 1970–95; Bonhams Gp, 1995–. *Recreations:* sailing, tobogganing, ski-ing, golf, swimming. *Address:* Montpelier Galleries, Montpelier Street, SW7 1HH. *T:* (020) 7393 3900, *Fax:* (020) 7393 3980. *Clubs:* Kennel; Royal Thames Yacht, South West Shingles Yacht, Seaview Yacht; Berkshire Golf; St Moritz Tobogganing, St Moritz Sporting.

BONHAM CARTER, Helena; actress; *b* 26 May 1966; *d* of Hon. Raymond Bonham Carter, *qv* and Elena Bonham Carter (*née* Propper de Callejón). *Educ:* Hampstead High Sch. for Girls; Westminster Sch. *Films include:* Lady Jane, 1985; A Room with a View, 1986; A Hazard of Hearts, 1988; The Mask, 1988; St Francis of Assisi, 1989; Getting it Right, 1989; Hamlet, 1990; Where Angels Fear to Tread, 1990; Howard's End, 1992; Fatal Deception, 1993; Mary Shelley's Frankenstein, 1994; Mighty Aphrodite, 1996; Twelfth Night, 1996; Margaret's Museum, 1997; Portraits Chinois, 1997; Keep the Aspidistra Flying, 1997; The Wings of the Dove, 1998; The Theory of Flight, 1998; The Revengers' Comedies, 1999; Fight Club, 1999; Planet of the Apes, 2001; *television includes:* Miami Vice, 1987; The Vision, 1988; Arms and the Man, 1988; Dancing Queen, 1993; A Dark Adapted Eye, 1994; *theatre includes:* Woman in White, Greenwich, 1988; The Chalk Garden, Windsor, 1989; House of Bernarda Alba, Nottingham Playhouse, 1991; The Barber of Seville, Palace, Watford, 1992; Trelawney of the Wells, Comedy, 1992; *radio:* The Reluctant Debutante; Marie Antoinette; The Seagull. *Recreation:* reading. *Address:* c/o Conway van Gelder Ltd, 18/21 Jermyn Street, SW1Y 6HP. *T:* (020) 7287 0077.

BONHAM CARTER, Hon. Raymond Henry; Executive Director, S. G. Warburg & Co. Ltd, 1967–77; retired in 1979 following disability; *b* 19 June 1929; *s* of Sir Maurice Bonham Carter, KCB, KCVO, and Lady Violet Bonham Carter, DBE (later Baroness Asquith of Yarnbury); *m* 1958, Elena Propper de Callejon; two *s* one *d*. *Educ:* Winchester Coll.; Magdalen Coll., Oxford (BA 1952); Harvard Business Sch. (MBA 1954). Irish Guards, 1947–49. With J. Henry Schröder & Co., 1954–58; acting Advr, Bank of England, 1958–63; Alternate Exec. Dir for UK, IMF, and Mem., UK Treasury and Supply Delegn, Washington, 1961–63; S. G. Warburg & Co. Ltd, 1964; Director: Transport Development Group Ltd, 1969–77; Banque de Paris et des Pays Bas NV, 1973–77; Mercury Securities Ltd, 1974–77; seconded as Dir, Industrial Develt Unit, DoI, 1977–79. Mem. Council, Internat. Inst. for Strategic Studies (Hon. Treasurer, 1974–84). *Address:* 7 West Heath Avenue, NW11 7QS.

See also H. Bonham Carter.

BONHAM-CARTER, Victor; Joint Secretary, Society of Authors, 1971–78, Consultant, 1978–82; Secretary, Royal Literary Fund, 1966–82; *b* 13 Dec. 1913; *s* of Gen. Sir Charles Bonham-Carter, GCB, CMG, DSO, and Gabrielle Madge Jeanette (*née* Fisher); *m* 1st, 1938, Audrey Edith Stogdon (marr. diss. 1979); two *s*; 2nd, 1979, Cynthia Claire Sanford. *Educ:* Winchester Coll.; Magdalene Coll., Cambridge (MA); Hamburg and Paris. Worked on The Countryman, 1936–37; Dir, School Prints Ltd, 1937–39, 1945–60; Army, R Berks Regt and Intell. Corps, 1939–45; farmed in W Somerset, 1947–59; historian of Dartington Hall Estate, Devon, 1951–66; on staff of Soc. of Authors, 1963–82. Active in Exmoor National Park affairs, 1955–; Pres., Exmoor Soc., 1975–; Partner, Exmoor Press, 1969–89. *Publications:* The English Village, 1952; (with W. B. Curry) Dartington Hall,

1958; Exploring Parish Churches, 1959; Farming the Land, 1959; In a Liberal Tradition, 1960; Soldier True, 1965; Surgeon in the Crimea, 1969; The Survival of the English Countryside, 1971; Authors by Profession, vol. 1 1978, vol. 2 1984; Exmoor Writers, 1987; The Essence of Exmoor, 1991; What Countryman, Sir?, 1996; many contribs to jls, radio, etc on country life and work; also on authorship matters, esp. Public Lending Right. *Recreations:* music, conversation. *Address:* The Mount, Milverton, Taunton TA4 1QZ.

BONINGTON, Sir Christian (John Storey), Kt 1996; CBE 1976; mountaineer, writer and photographer; *b* 6 Aug. 1934; *s* of Charles Bonington, journalist, and Helen Anne Bonington (*née* Storey); *m* 1962, Muriel Wendy Marchant; two *s* (and one *s* decd). *Educ:* University Coll. Sch., London. RMA Sandhurst, 1955–56; commnd Royal Tank Regt, 1956–61. Unilever Management Trainee, 1961–62; writer and photographer, 1962–. Climbs: Annapurna II, 26,041 ft (1st ascent) 1960; Central Pillar Freney, Mont Blanc (1st ascent), 1961; Nuptse, 25,850 ft (1st ascent), 1961; North Wall of Eiger (1st British ascent), 1962; Central Tower of Paine, Patagonia (1st ascent), 1963; Mem. of team, first descent of Blue Nile, 1968; Leader: successful Annapurna South Face Expedition, 1970; British Everest Expedition, 1972; Brammah, Himalayas (1st ascent), 1973; co-leader, Changabang, Himalayas (1st ascent), 1974; British Everest Expedition (1st ascent SW face), 1975; Ogre (1st ascent), 1977; jt leader, Kongur, NW China (1st ascent), 1981; Shivling West (1st ascent), 1983; Mt Vinson, highest point of Antarctica (1st British ascent), 1983; reached Everest summit, 1985; Panch Chuli II (W Ridge), Kumaon, Himalayas (1st ascent), 1992; Mejslen, Greenland (1st ascent), 1993; Rang Rik Rank, Kinnaur, Himalayas (1st ascent), 1994; Drangnag Ri (1st ascent), 1995; Danga (1st ascent), 2000. President: British Mountaineering Council, 1988–91 (Vice-Pres., 1976–79, 1985–88; Chm., Mountain Heritage Trust, 2000–); British Orienteering Fedn, 1985–; NT Lake Dist Appeal, 1989–; Council for National Parks, 1992–2000 (Life Vice-Pres., 2000); Vice-President: Army Mountaineering Assoc., 1980–; YHA, 1990–. Non-exec. Chm., Berghaus Ltd, 1998–. Trustee, Outward Bound, 1998– (Chm., Risk Mgt Cttee, 1998–). Pres., LEPRA, 1983. MInstD 1992. FRGS (Founders' Medal, 1974); FRPS 1991; FRSA 1996. Hon. Fellow: UMIST, 1976; Lancashire Polytechnic, 1991. Hon. MA Salford, 1973; Hon. DSc: Sheffield, 1976; Lancaster, 1983; Hon. DCL Northumbria, 1996; Hon. Dr Sheffield Hallam, 1998. Lawrence of Arabia Medal, RSAA, 1986; Livingstone Medal, RSGS, 1991. *Publications:* I Chose to Climb (autobiog.), 1966; Annapurna South Face, 1971; The Next Horizon (autobiog.), 1973; Everest, South West Face, 1973; Everest the Hard Way, 1976; Quest for Adventure, 1981; Kongur: China's elusive summit, 1982; (jtly) Everest: the unclimbed ridge, 1983; The Everest Years, 1986; Mountaineer (autobiog.), 1989; The Climbers, 1992; (with Robin Knox-Johnston) Sea, Ice and Rock, 1992; Chris Bonington's Lake District, 1997; (with Charles Clarke) Tibet's Secret Mountain, 1999; Boundless Horizons (autobiog.), 2000; Quest for Adventure, 2000. *Recreations:* mountaineering, ski-ing, orienteering. *Address:* Badger Hill, Nether Row, Hesket Newmarket, Wigton, Cumbria CA7 8LA. *T:* (01697) 478286; *e-mail:* chris@bonington.com. *Clubs:* Alpine (Pres., 1996–99), Alpine Ski, Army and Navy, Climbers, Fell and Rock Climbing, Border Liners, Carlisle Mountaineering; American Alpine.

BONINO, Emma; Member, European Parliament, 1979–94 and since 1999; *b* 9 March 1948. *Educ:* Bocconi Univ., Milan (BA 1972). Mem., Italian Chamber of Deputies, 1976–94; posts include: Chm., Radical Party Gp, 1979–81; Mem., Bureau of Parlt, 1992–94; Mem., European Commn, 1994–99. Transnational Radical Party: Pres., 1991–93; Sec., 1993–95. *Recreations:* snorkling, scuba-diving. *Address:* European Parliament, Rue Wiertz, 1047 Brussels, Belgium.

BONNER, Paul Max, OBE 1999; Director, Secretariat, ITV Network Centre, 1993–94; *b* 30 Nov. 1934; *s* of Jill and late Frank Bonner; *m* 1956, Jenifer Hubbard; two *s* one *d*. *Educ:* Felsted Sch., Essex. National Service commission, 1953–55. Local journalism, 1955; Radio production, BBC Bristol, 1955–57; Television production, BBC Bristol, 1957–59, BBC Lime Grove, 1959–62; Television Documentary prodn and direction, BBC Lime Grove and Kensington House, 1962–74; Editor, Community Programmes for BBC, 1974–77; Head of Science and Features Programmes for BBC, 1977–80; Channel Controller, Channel Four TV, 1980–83; Exec. Dir and Programme Controller, Channel Four TV, 1983–87; Dir, Programme Planning Secretariat, ITVA, 1987–93. A Manager, Royal Instn, 1982–85; Governor, Nat. Film and TV School, 1983–88; Director: Broadcasting Support Services, 1982–93; House of Commons Broadcasting Unit Ltd, 1989–91; Parly Broadcasting Unit, 1991–94; Chm., Sponsorship and Advertising Cttee, EBU, 1991–94; Member: Bd, Children's Film Unit, 1989–97; COPUS, 1986–92 (Chm., Broadcast Trust, 1995–98). FRTS 1989. *Publications:* Independent Television in Britain: Vol. 5, ITV and the IBA 1981–1992, 1998; *documentaries include:* Strange Excellency, 1964; Climb up to Hell, 1967; Lost: Four H Bombs, 1967; Search for the Real Che Guevara, 1971; Who Sank the Lusitania?, 1972. *Recreations:* photography, the theatre, sailing, walking, listening to good conversation. *Address:* North View, Wimbledon Common, SW19 4UJ. *Clubs:* Reform, Chelsea Arts.

BONNET, Maj.-Gen. Peter Robert Frank, CB 1991; MBE 1975; Colonel Commandant, Royal Regiment of Artillery, 1990–2000; *b* 12 Dec. 1936; *s* of James Robert and Phyllis Elsie Bonnet; *m* 1961, Sylvia Mary Coy; two *s*. *Educ:* Royal Military Coll. of Science, Shrivenham. BSc (Engrg). Commnd from RMA Sandhurst, 1958; RMCS Shrivenham, 1959–62; apptd to RHA, 1962; Staff trng, RMCS and Staff Coll., Camberley, 1969–70; Comd (Lt-Col), 26 Field Regt, RA, 1978–81; Comd RA (Brig.) 2nd Div., 1982–84; attendance at Indian Nat. Defence Coll., New Delhi, 1985; Dir RA, 1986–89 (Maj.-Gen. 1986); GOC Western Dist, 1989–91, retd 1992. Gen. Sec., Officers' Pensions Soc., 1995–2000; Dir, OPS Investment Co. Ltd, 1995–2000; Man. Trustee, OPS Widows' Fund, 1995–2000; Mem., Council Officers' Assoc., 1995–. Hon. Col, 26 Field Regt RA, 1992–99. Vice-Pres., Nat. Artillery Assoc., 1989–99. Trustee: Kelly Holdsworth Meml Trust, 1996–; Council, Age Concern, 1998–99. *Publications:* International Terrorism, 1985; A Short History of the Royal Regiment of Artillery, 1994. *Recreations:* tennis, sculpture, painting. *T:* (01398) 341324. *Club:* Army and Navy.

BONNETT, Prof. Raymond, CChem, FRSC; Scotia Research Professor, Queen Mary and Westfield College, London, since 1994; *b* 13 July 1931; *s* of Harry and Maud Bonnett; *m* 1956, Shirley Rowe; two *s* one *d*. *Educ:* County Grammar Sch., Bury St Edmunds; Imperial Coll. (BSc, ARCS); Cambridge Univ. (PhD); DSc London 1972. Salters' Fellow, Cambridge, 1957–58; Res. Fellow, Harvard, 1958–59; Asst Prof., Dept of Chemistry, Univ. of British Columbia, 1959–61; Lectr in Organic Chem., 1961–66, Reader in Organic Chem., 1966–74, Prof. 1974–94, Hd of Dept of Chemistry, 1982–87, QMC, then QMW London Univ. *Publications:* sci. papers, esp. in Jls of Royal Soc. of Chemistry and Biochemical Soc. *Recreations:* theatre, bookbinding, gardening. *Address:* Elmbank, 19 Station Road, Epping, Essex CM16 4HG. *T:* (01992) 573203.

BONNEY, George Louis William, MS, FRCS; Consulting Orthopædic Surgeon, St Mary's Hospital, London, since 1984; *b* 10 Jan. 1920; *s* of late Dr Ernest Bonney and Gertrude Mary Williams; *m* 1950, Margaret Morgan; two *d*. *Educ:* Eton (Scholar); St Mary's Hospital Medical Sch. MB, BS, MRCS, LRCP 1943; FRCS 1945; MS (London) 1947. Formerly: Surg.-Lieut RNVR; Research Assistant and Senior Registrar, Royal National Orthopædic Hospital; Consultant Orthopædic Surgeon: Southend Group of Hospitals; St Mary's Hosp., London, 1954–84 (Sen. Consultant, 1979–84). Travelling Fellowship of British Postgraduate Med. Fedn, Univ. of London, 1950. Watson-Jones Lectr, RCS, 1976. Sen. FBOA; Hon. Fellow, Medical Defence Union; Mem., SICOT. *Publications:* (jtly) Surgical Disorders of the Peripheral Nerves, 1998; chapters in: Operative Surgery, 1957; Clinical Surgery, 1966; Clinical Orthopædics, 1983, 2nd edn 1995; Micro-reconstruction of Nerve Injuries, 1987; Current Therapy in Neurologic Disease, 1987; Medical Negligence, 1990, 3rd edn 2000; Clinical Neurology, 1991; Medical Negligence: cranium, spine and nervous system, 1999; papers in medical journals on visceral pain, circulatory mechanisms, nerve injuries and on various aspects of orthopædic surgery. *Recreations:* fishing, shooting, photography, music. *Address:* 6 Wooburn Grange, Grange Drive, Wooburn Green, Bucks HP10 0QU. *T:* (01628) 525598. *Club:* Leander.

BONNEY, James William; QC 1995; *b* 5 Sept. 1948; *s* of late James Henry Bonney, inshore fisherman, and of Alice Bonney (*née* Butler); *m* 1975, Judith Anne, *d* of Montague William Lacey; one *s* one *d*. *Educ:* St John the Divine C of E Sch.; King Edward VII Sch., Lytham; Keble Coll., Oxford (BA 1974; BCL 1975; MA 1983). Admitted Solicitor, 1970; Asst Solicitor, 1970–75; called to the Bar, Lincoln's Inn, 1975 (Jenkin's Schol.); Vis. Tutor in Jurisprudence, Keble Coll., Oxford, 1975–76; Mem., Northern Circuit, 1976–; a Dep. High Court Judge, Chancery Div., 1996–. Member: Chancery Bar Assoc., 1977–; Ecclesiastical Law Soc., 1988–; Assoc. of Contentious Trust and Probate Specialists, 1998–; Property Bar Assoc., 2000–; Professional Negligence Bar Assoc., 2001–; Bar European Gp, 2001–. Reader, St Cuthbert's Parish Church, Lytham, 1983–. *Recreation:* choral singing. *Address:* 10 Old Square, Lincoln's Inn, WC2A 3SU. *T:* (020) 7405 0758; 24 Norfolk Road, Lytham, Lancs FY8 4JG. *T:* (01253) 794259; Flat 5, 24 Old Buildings, Lincoln's Inn, WC2A 3UP. *T:* (020) 7404 8663. *Club:* Lytham Yacht.

BONNICI, Carmelo M.; *see* Mifsud Bonnici.

BONOMY, Hon. Lord; Iain Bonomy; a Senator of the College of Justice in Scotland, since 1997; *b* 15 Jan. 1946; *s* of late John Bonomy and of Mary Gray Bonomy (*née* Richardson); *m* 1969, Janet (*née* Gray); two *d*. *Educ:* Dalziel High Sch., Motherwell; Univ. of Glasgow (LLB Hons). Apprentice solicitor, East Kilbride Town Council, 1968–70; Asst solicitor, then Partner, Ballantyne & Copland, solicitors, Motherwell, 1970–83; admitted Faculty of Advocates, 1984; Advocate Depute, then Home Advocate Depute, 1990–96; QC (Scot.) 1993. *Recreations:* golf, gardening, travel, football terraces (now stands). *Address:* Parliament House, Parliament Square, Edinburgh EH1 1RQ. *Clubs:* Torrance House Golf, East Kilbride Golf, Motherwell Football and Athletic.

BONOMY, Iain; *see* Bonomy, Hon. Lord.

BONSALL, Sir Arthur (Wilfred), KCMG 1977; CBE 1957; *b* 25 June 1917; *s* of late Wilfred Bonsall and Sarah Bonsall; *m* 1941, Joan Isabel Wingfield (*d* 1990); four *s* three *d*. *Educ:* Bishop's Stortford Coll.; St Catharine's Coll., Cambridge. 2nd Cl. Hons Mod. Langs. Joined Air Ministry, 1940; transf. to FO 1942; IDC, 1962; Dir, Govt Communications HQ, 1975–78. *Recreation:* coarse gardening. *Address:* 1 Coxwell Court, Coxwell Street, Cirencester, Glos GL7 2BQ.

See also See also F. F. Bonsall.

BONSALL, Prof. Frank Featherstone, FRS 1970; Professor of Mathematics, University of Edinburgh, 1965–84, now Emeritus; *b* 1920; *s* of late Wilfred Bonsall and Sarah Bonsall; *m* 1947, Gillian Patrick. *Educ:* Bishop's Stortford Coll.; Merton Coll., Oxford. *Publications* (all with J. Duncan): Numerical Ranges of Operators on Normed Spaces and of Elements of Normed Algebras, 1971; Numerical Ranges II, 1973; Complete Normed Algebras, 1973. *Recreation:* walking.

See also Sir A. W. Bonsall.

BONSER, Rt Rev. David; Bishop Suffragan of Bolton, 1991–99; *b* 1 Feb. 1934; *s* of George Frederick and Alice Bonser; *m* 1960, Shirley Wilkinson; one *s* two *d*. *Educ:* Hillhouse Secondary Sch., Huddersfield; King's Coll., London Univ. (AKC); Manchester Univ. (MA). Curate: St James's, Heckmondwike, 1962–65; St George's, Sheffield, 1965–68; Rector of St Clement's, Chorlton-cum-Hardy, 1968–82; Hon. Canon of Manchester Cathedral, 1980–82; Area Dean of Hulme, 1981–82; Archdeacon of Rochdale, 1982–91; Team Rector, Rochdale Team Ministry, 1982–91 (Vicar of St Chad's, 1982–86). *Recreations:* theatre, reading, walking, ski-ing, music, soup-making. *Address:* 82 Birchfield Drive, Marland, Rochdale OL11 4NY. *T:* (01706) 352522.

BONSEY, Martin Charles Brian, LVO 2000; Official Secretary to the Governor-General of Australia, since 1998; *b* 2 May 1948; *s* of Thory Richmond and Frances Mary Bonsey; *m* 1971, Joan Hair. *Educ:* Univ. of Melbourne (BA Hons Hist. and Pol Sci.); Australian Nat. Univ. (LLB). Public servant, Australia, 1974–. Secretary: Order of Australia, 1998–; Australian Bravery Decorations Council, 1998–. CStJ 1999. *Address:* Government House, Canberra, ACT 2600, Australia. *T:* (2) 62833507.

BONSOR, Sir Nicholas (Cosmo), 4th Bt *cr* 1925; *b* 9 Dec. 1942; *s* of Sir Bryan Cosmo Bonsor, 3rd Bt, MC, TD, and of Elizabeth, *d* of late Captain Angus Valdimar Hambro; *S* father, 1977; *m* 1969, Hon. Nadine Marisa Lampson, *d* of 2nd Baron Killearn; two *s* three *d* (including twin *d*). *Educ:* Eton; Keble College, Oxford (MA). Served Royal Buckinghamshire Yeomanry, 1964–69. Called to the Bar, Inner Temple, 1967; practised at the Bar, 1967–75. Mem., CLA Legal and Parly Sub-Cttee, 1978–82. MP (C) Nantwich, 1979–83, Upminster, 1983–97; contested (C) Upminster, 1997. Minister of State, FCO, 1995–97. Chm., Select Cttee on Defence, 1992–95; Sec., Cons. Tourism Sub-Cttee, 1979–80; Vice-Chairman: Cons. Foreign Affairs Cttee, 1981–83; Cons. Defence Cttee, 1987–90. Mem. Council, RUSI, 1992–95, 1997–98. Chairman: Food Hygiene Bureau, later Checkmate Plc, 1986–95; Leadership (UK) Ltd, 2000–; Pres. and non-exec. Dir, Liscombe Hldgs, 1997–2000. Chairman: Cyclotron Trust for Cancer Treatment, 1984–92 (Pres., 1992–); British Field Sports Soc., 1987–93; Standing Council of the Baronetage, 1990–93 (Vice-Chm., 1987–90); Baronets' Trust, 1993–95 (Trustee, 1986–95); Verdin Home for Mentally Handicapped, 1981–85. Mem., Council of Lloyd's, 1987–92. Hon. Col, 60 Signals Sqdn (V), 2000–. FRSA 1970. *Publications:* political pamphlets on law and trades unions and defence. *Recreations:* sailing, shooting, military history. *Heir:* *s* Alexander Cosmo Walrond Bonsor, *b* 8 Sept. 1976. *Clubs:* White's, Pratt's; Royal Yacht Squadron.

BONVIN, Jane Anne Marie, (Mrs S. M. Poulter); Her Honour Judge Bonvin; a Circuit Judge, since 1995; *b* 15 Dec. 1946; *d* of Jean Albert Bonvin and Phyllis Margaret (*née* Boyd); *m* 1972, Sebastian Murray Poulter (*d* 1998). *Educ:* Putney High Sch.; Bristol Univ. (LLB Hons). Law Lectr, IVS, Lesotho, 1969–71; called to the Bar, Gray's Inn, 1971; barrister, Western Circuit, 1972–77 and 1979–95. Editor, Lesotho Law Reports, 1977–79. *Recreations:* gardening, tennis, travel. *Address:* c/o Third Floor, Southside Offices, The Law Courts, Winchester, Hants SO23 9EL. *T:* (01962) 876004, 876005.

BONYNGE, Dame Joan; *see* Sutherland, Dame Joan.

BONYNGE, Richard, AO 1983; CBE 1977; opera conductor; *b* Sydney, 29 Sept. 1930; *s* of C. A. Bonynge, Epping, NSW; *m* 1954, Dame Joan Sutherland, *qv*; one *s*. *Educ:* Sydney Conservatorium (pianist). Official debut, as Conductor, with Santa Cecilia Orch. in Rome, 1962; conducted first opera, Faust, Vancouver, 1963. Has conducted in most leading opera houses in world, and in Edinburgh, Vienna and Florence Fests. Has been Princ. Conductor and Artistic/Musical Dir of cos, incl. Sutherland/Williamson Internat. Grand Opera Co., Aust., 1965; Vancouver Opera, 1974–77; Australian Opera, 1976–85. Many opera and ballet recordings; also recital discs with Sutherland, Tebaldi, Tourangeau and Pavarotti, and many orchestral and ballet anthologies. *Publication:* (with Dame Joan Sutherland) The Joan Sutherland Album, 1986. *Address:* c/o Ingpen and Williams, 26 Wadham Road, SW15 2LR.

BOOKER, Christopher John Penrice; journalist and author; *b* 7 Oct. 1937; *s* of late John Booker and Margaret Booker; *m* 1979, Valerie, *d* of late Dr M. S. Patrick, OBE; two *s*. *Educ:* Dragon Sch., Oxford; Shrewsbury Sch.; Corpus Christi Coll., Cambridge (History scholar). Liberal News, 1960; jazz critic, Sunday Telegraph, 1961; Editor, Private Eye, 1961–63, and regular contributor, 1965–; resident scriptwriter, That Was The Week That Was, 1962–63, and Not So Much A Programme, 1963–64; contributor to Spectator, 1962–, Daily Telegraph, 1972– (Way of the World column, as Peter Simple II, 1987–90), and to many other newspapers and jls; columnist, Sunday Telegraph, 1990–. Wrote extensively on property develt, planning and housing, 1972–77 (with Bennie Gray, Campaigning Journalist of the Year, 1973); City of Towers—the Rise and Fall of a Twentieth Century Dream (TV prog.), 1979. Mem., Cowgill enquiry into post-war repatriations from Austria, 1986–90. *Publications:* The Neophiliacs: a study of the revolution in English life in the 50s and 60s, 1969; (with Candida Lycett-Green) Goodbye London, 1973; The Booker Quiz, 1976; The Seventies, 1980; The Games War: a Moscow journal, 1981; (with Lord Brimelow and Brig. A. Cowgill) The Repatriations from Austria in 1945, 1990; (with Richard North) The Mad Officials: how the bureaucrats are strangling Britain, 1993; The Castle of Lies: why Britain must leave the European Union, 1996; A Looking Glass Tragedy: the controversy over the repatriations from Austria in 1945, 1997; Scared To Death: an anatomy of the food scare phenomenon, 1999; contrib. Private Eye anthologies, 1962–, incl. The Secret Diary of John Major, 1992–95, St Albion Parish News, 1998. *Recreations:* the psychology of storytelling, nature, music, following Somerset cricket team. *Address:* The Old Rectory, Litton, Bath BA3 4PW. *T:* (01761) 241263.

BOOKER, Gordon Alan, FIWEM; utility adviser; Deputy Director General of Water Services, 1990–98; *b* 17 Feb. 1938; *s* of Frederick William Booker and Beryl Booker; *m* 1957, Anne Christine Pike; two *s* one *d*. *Educ:* Dronfield Grammar Sch.; Sheffield Univ. (BEng (Hons) 1960). MICE 1963; FIWEM 1966. Sheffield Water, 1960–65; Birmingham Water, 1965–70; W Glam Water, 1970–74; Welsh Water, 1974–80; Chief Exec., E Worcester Water, 1980–89; Managing Director: Biwater Supply, 1987–90; Bournemouth and W Hants Water Cos, 1989–90. Mem., Council, Water Res. Centre, 1985–90; mem. and chm. of several water industry cttees on automation and leakage control. *Publications:* Water Distribution Systems, 1984; Telemetry and Control, 1986; contrib. Procs of ICE and of IWSA, reports for DoE and NWC, and Jls of IWEM and IAWPRC. *Recreations:* walking, painting. *Address:* 106 The Holloway, Droitwich, Worcs WR9 7AH. *T:* (01905) 772432; Sheplegh Court, Blackawton, Devon TQ9 7AH.

BOOKER, Pamela Elizabeth; *see* Alexander, P. E.

BOOKER-MILBURN, Donald; Sheriff of Grampian, Highland and Islands, since 1983; *b* Dornoch, 20 May 1940; *s* of late Captain Booker Milburn, DSO, MC, Coldstream Guards, and late Betty Calthrop Calthrop; *m* 1963, Marjorie Lilian Elizabeth Burns; one *s* one *d*. *Educ:* Trinity College, Glenalmond; Grenoble Univ.; Jesus Coll., Cambridge (BA); Edinburgh Univ. (LLB). Admitted to Faculty of Advocates, 1968; Standing Junior Counsel to RAF, 1977–80; Sheriff of Lothian and Borders, 1980–83. *Recreations:* golf, skiing. *Address:* Clashmore House, Clashmore, Dornoch, Sutherland IV25 3RG. *Clubs:* Royal & Ancient Golf (St Andrews); Royal Dornoch Golf.

BOOLELL, Sir Satcam, GOSK 1999; Kt 1977; High Commissioner for Mauritius in London, since 1996; *b* New Grove, Mauritius, 11 Sept. 1920; *s* of Sahadewoo Boolell and Cossilah Choony; *m* 1st, 1948, Inderjeet Kissoodaye (*d* 1986); two *s* one *d*; 2nd, 1987, Myrtha Poblete. *Educ:* primary and secondary schs in New Grove, Mare d'Albert, Rose Belle, and Port-Louis; LSE (LLB Hons 1951). Called to the Bar, Lincoln's Inn, 1952. Civil servant, Mauritius, 1944–48. Minister of Agric. and Natural Resources, 1959–82; Minister of Economic Planning, 1983–84; Dep. Prime Minister, Attorney General, Minister of Justice and Minister of External Affairs and Emigration, 1986–90. Mem. Central Exec., 1955–, Leader, 1985–90, Advr, 1990–, Mauritius Labour Party. Rep. Mauritius, internat. confs. Founder, English and French daily newspaper, The Nation. Hon. DCL Mauritius, 1986. GCSG 1999. Comdr, Légion d'Honneur (France), 1990. *Publications:* The Untold Stories, 1997; Reminiscences of Travels Abroad, 1998. *Recreations:* travel books, walking in the countryside. *Address:* Mauritius High Commission, 32–33 Elvaston Place, SW7 5NW; 4bis Bancilhon Street, Port Louis, Mauritius. *T:* 2080079, *Fax:* 2089207.

BOON, (George) Peter (Richard); HM Diplomatic Service; High Commissioner to Cameroon and non-resident Ambassador to Chad, Central African Republic, Gabon and Equatorial Guinea, since 1998; *b* 2 Nov. 1942; *s* of George Alan James Boon and Enid Monica Boon (*née* Smith); *m* 1971, Marie Paule Calicis; one *s*. *Educ:* Repton Sch., Derbys. Joined CRO, later FCO, 1963; Bombay, 1966–69; Brussels, 1969–71; Vienna, 1971–74; on secondment to DTI, 1974–75; FCO, 1975–78; The Hague, 1978–81; Spokesman, BMG, Berlin, 1981–86; FCO, 1986–90; First Sec. (Political), Dhaka, 1990–93; FCO, 1994–97. *Address:* c/o Foreign and Commonwealth Office, King Charles Street, SW1A 2AH.

BOORD, Sir Nicolas (John Charles), 4th Bt *cr* 1896; scientific translator; English training specialist; *b* 10 June 1936; *s* of Sir Richard William Boord, 3rd Bt, and of Yvonne, Lady Boord, *d* of late J. A. Hubert Bird; *S* father, 1975; *m* 1965, Françoise Renée Louise Mouret. *Educ:* Eton (Harmsworth Lit. Prize, 1952); Sorbonne, France; Societa Dante Alighieri, Italy; Univ. of Santander, Spain. *Publications:* (trans. jtly) The History of Physics and the Philosophy of Science—Selected Essays (Armin Teske), 1972; numerous translations of scientific papers for English and American scientific and technical jls. *Recreations:* English and French literature and linguistics. *Heir:* *b* Antony Andrew Boord [*b* 21 May 1938; *m* 1960, Anna Christina von Krogh; one *s* one *d*]. *Address:* 61 Traverse Le Mée, 13009 Marseille, France. *T:* 4731395.

BOORMAN, Anthony John; Principal Ombudsman (Insurance), Financial Ombudsman Service, since 2000; *b* 14 Nov. 1958; *s* of William Harry and Margaret Boorman; *m* 1984, Alison Drury; two *s*. *Educ:* Kent Coll., Canterbury; New Coll., Oxford (BA). Various posts, Electricity Consumers' Council, 1985–90, Dir, 1989–90; Dir, Office of Electricity Regulation, 1990–98; Dep. Dir Gen., Office of Gas and Electricity Mkts, 1998–2000. *Address:* Financial Ombudsman Service, South Quay Plaza, 183 Marsh Wall, E14 9SR.

BOORMAN, Lt-Gen. Sir Derek, KCB 1986 (CB 1982); Lieutenant of the Tower of London, 1989–92; *b* 13 Sept. 1930; *s* of late N. R. Boorman, MBE, and of Mrs A. L. Boorman (*née* Patman); *m* 1st, 1956, Jennifer Jane Skinner (*d* 1991); two *d* (one *s* decd); 2nd, 1992, Mrs Nicola Cox. *Educ:* Wolstanton Grammar Sch.; RMA Sandhurst. Commnd N Staffords, 1950; Adjt 1 Staffords, 1958–59; Staff Coll., 1961; HQ 48 Gurkha Inf. Bde, 1962–64; Jt Services Staff Coll., 1968; CO 1 Staffords, 1969–71; Instr, Staff Coll., 1972–73; Comdr 51 Inf. Bde, 1975–76; RCDS, 1977; Dir, Public Relations (Army), 1978–79; Director of Military Operations, 1980–82; Comdr, British Forces Hong Kong, and Maj.-Gen. Bde of Gurkhas, 1982–85; Chief of Defence Intelligence, 1985–88. Colonel: 6th Queen Elizabeth's Own Gurkha Rifles, 1983–88; Staffordshire Regt (Prince of Wales's), 1985–90. Director: Tarmac Construction, 1988–95. Chairman: KCH Trust, 1992–93; Royal Hosps NHS Trust, 1994–97; Health Care Projects Ltd, 1998–. Mem., Security Commn, 1991–96. Dep. Pro-Chancellor, Univ. of Kent, 2000–. *Recreations:* gardening, music, taking wife out to dinner.

BOORMAN, Edwin Roy Pratt; DL; Chairman and Chief Executive, Kent Messenger Group, since 1986 (Managing Director, 1965–86); Chairman, Messenger Print Ltd, 1970–98; *b* 7 Nov. 1935; *s* of late H. R. P. Boorman, CBE and Enid (*née* Starke); *m* 1st, Merrilyn Ruth Pettit (marr. diss. 1982); four *d*; 2nd, 1983, Janine Craske; one *s*. *Educ:* Rydal; Queens' Coll., Cambridge (MA Econ. History). National Service, 1954–56. Cambridge Univ., 1956–59; Kent Messenger, 1959; Editor: South Eastern Gazette, 1960–62; Kent Messenger, 1962–65. Councillor, Newspaper Soc., 1990– (Vice-Pres., 2000–01). Pres., Dickens Area Newsagents' Benevolent Assoc., 1975–. Vice Chm., Royal British Legion Industries, 1995– (Pres., RBL, Kent, 1998–). Chairman: KABC–Kent Youth Trust (formerly Kent Assoc. of Boys' Clubs), 1988–; N Kent Success, 1993–96; Kent River Walk, 1998–. Trustee: Chatham Historic Dockyard, 1992–97; Kent Air Ambulance; County Dir, St John Ambulance; Chm., Kent Council, Order of St John, 1997. Pres., Loose Amenities Assoc. Patron, Kent Child Witness Service, 1999–. Governor: Sutton Valence Sch.; Canterbury Christ Church Coll., 1996–. Tax Comr, Maidstone District 2. Formerly Liveryman, Stationers' and Newspapermakers' Co. (Mem., Ct of Assts, 1987–2000). High Sheriff, Kent, 1997; DL Kent, 2001. *Recreation:* sailing. *Address:* Redhill Farm, 339 Redhill, Wateringbury, Kent ME18 5LB. *Clubs:* Carlton; Maidstone, Kent CC; Veteran Car (Ashwell, Herts); Royal Yachting Association, Medway Yacht, Ocean Cruising.

BOORMAN, John, CBE 1994; film director; *b* 18 Jan. 1933; *m* 1956, Christel Kruse; one *s* three *d*. *Educ:* Salesian Coll., Chertsey. Film Editor, ITN, 1955–58; Dir and Producer, Southern TV, 1958–60; Head of Documentaries, BBC Bristol. *Films include:* Catch us if you Can, 1965; Point Blank, 1967; Hell in the Pacific, 1968; Leo the Last, 1969; Deliverance, 1970; Zardoz, 1973; The Heretic, 1976; Excalibur, 1981; The Emerald Forest, 1985; Hope and Glory, 1987; Where the Heart Is, 1989; I Dreamt I Woke Up, 1991; Beyond Rangoon, 1995; Two Nudes Bathing, 1995; The General, 1998; The Tailor of Panama, 2001. Gov., BFI, 1983–94. *Publications:* The Legend of Zardoz, 1973; Money into Light, 1985; Hope and Glory, 1987; Projections: (ed) no 1, 1992; (joint editor): no 2, 1993; no 3, 1994; nos 4 and 4½, 1995; nos 5 and 6, 1996; no 7, 1997; no 8, 1998. *Address:* Merlin Films International, 16 Pembroke Street, Dublin 2, Ireland.

BOORSTIN, Dr Daniel J., FRHistS; (12th) Librarian of Congress, 1975–87, now Emeritus; *b* 1 Oct. 1914; *s* of Samuel Boorstin and Dora (*née* Olsan); *m* 1941, Ruth Carolyn Frankel; three *s*. *Educ:* schs in Tulsa, Okla; Harvard Univ. (AB, summa cum Laude); Balliol Coll., Oxford (Rhodes Schol., BA Juris. 1st Cl. Hons, BCL 1st Cl. Hons); Yale Univ. Law Sch. (Sterling Fellow, JSD). Called to Bar, Inner Temple, 1937; admitted Mass Bar, 1942. Instr, tutor in history and lit., Harvard Univ. and Radcliffe Coll., 1938–42; Lectr, legal history, Law Sch., Harvard, 1939–42; Sen. Attorney, Office of Lend Lease Admin, Washington, DC, 1942–43; Office of Asst SG, USA, 1942–43; Asst Prof. of History, Swarthmore Coll., 1942–44; Univ. of Chicago, 1944–69: Asst Prof., 1944–49; Associate Prof., Preston and Sterling Morton Distinguished Prof. of Amer. History, 1956–69. During his 25 years tenure at Chicago, Visiting Lectr at Rome and Kyoto Univs, Sorbonne and Cambridge (Fellow, Trinity Coll., and Pitt Prof. of Amer. History and Instns; LittD 1968). Smithsonian Institution: Dir, Nat. Museum History and Techn., 1969–73; Sen. Historian, 1973–75. Many public service membership assignments, trusteeships, and active concern with a number of Amer. Assocs, esp. those relating to Amer. history, educn and cultural affairs. Past Pres., American Studies Assoc. Hon. FAGS. Hon. LittD Sheffield, 1979; Hon. DLitt: Cambridge, 1968; East Anglia, 1980; Sussex, 1983; numerous other hon. degrees. Watson-Davis Prize of the History of Science, Soc. for Discoverers, 1986; Charles Frankel Prize, Nat. Endowment for the Humanities, 1989; Nat. Book Award Medal for Distinguished Contribution to American Letters, 1989; Jefferson Medal, Amer. Phil Soc., 1999. Officier de L'Ordre de la Couronne, Belgium, 1980; Chevalier, Légion d'Honneur, France, 1984; Grand Officer, Order of Prince Henry the Navigator, Portugal, 1985; First Class Order of the Sacred Treasure, Japan, 1986. *Publications: include:* The Mysterious Science of the Law, 1941; The Lost World of Thomas Jefferson, 1948; The Genius of American Politics, 1953; The Americans: The Colonial Experience, 1958 (Bancroft Prize); America and the Image of Europe, 1960; The Image, 1962; The Americans: The National Experience, 1965 (Parkman Prize); The Decline of Radicalism, 1969; The Sociology of the Absurd, 1970; The Americans: The Democratic Experience, 1973 (Pulitzer Prize for History and Dexter Prize, 1974); Democracy and Its Discontents, 1974; The Exploring Spirit (BBC 1975 Reith Lectures), 1976; The Republic of Technology, 1978; (with Brooks M. Kelley) A History of the United States, 1980; The Discoverers, 1984 (Watson-Davis Prize), illustrated edn 1991; Hidden History, 1987; The Creators, 1992; Cleopatra's Nose, 1994; The Daniel J. Boorstin Reader, 1996; The Seekers, 1998; *for young readers:* Landmark History of the American People, vol. I, From Plymouth to Appomattox, 1968; vol. II, From Appomattox to the Moon, 1970; New Landmark History of the American People, 1987; *edited:* Delaware Cases 1792–1830, 1943; An American Primer, 1966; American Civilization, 1971; The Chicago History of American Civilization (30 vols). *Address:* (home) 3541 Ordway Street, NW, Washington, DC 20016, USA. *T:* (202) 9661853; (office) Library of Congress, Washington, DC 20540, USA. *Clubs:* Cosmos (Washington); Elizabethan (Yale); International House (Japan).

BOOTE, Robert Edward, CVO 1971; first Director General, Nature Conservancy Council, 1973–80; *b* 6 Feb. 1920; *s* of Ernest Haydn Boote and Helen Rose Boote; *m* 1948, Vera (*née* Badian); one *s* one *d*. *Educ:* London Univ. (BSc Econ Hons). DPA; FREconS 1953–61; AIPR 1957–61; FCIS 1960–81. War service, 1939–46, Actg Lt-Col, Hon. Major. Admin. Officer, City of Stoke-on-Trent, 1946–48; Chief Admin. Officer, Staffs County Planning and Develt Dept, 1948–54; Principal, 1954–64, Dep. Dir, 1964–73, Nature Conservancy. Sec. 1965–71, formerly Dep. Sec., Countryside in 1970 Confs, 1963, 1965, 1970 and numerous study groups; Mem., Pesticides Cttee, 1958–73; Chm., Broadland Report, 1963–65; UK Deleg. to Council of Europe Cttee for Conservation of Nature and Natural Resources, 1963–71; Mem., Countryside Review Cttee, 1977–79; a Chief Marshal to the Queen, 1970; various posts in meetings of UN, UNESCO, EEC and OECD, 1968–81; Chm. Preparatory Gp for Eur. Conservation Year 1970; Chm. Organising Cttee for European Conservation Conf. 1970 (Conf. Vice-Pres.); Chm. European Cttee, 1969–71; Consultant for European Architectural Heritage Year

1975; Advr, H of L Select Cttee on Europ. Communities, 1980–81. A Vice-Pres. and Chm., Euro Fedn of Nature and Nat. Parks, 1980–81; International Union for Conservation of Nature and Natural Resources: Treas., 1975–78; Mem., Governing Council and Bureau, 1975–81; a Vice-Pres., 1978–81; Rep., Internat. Conf. on Antarctic Marine Living Resources, 1980; Chm., Antarctica Resolution, 1981; Election Officer, 1984; Founder and Chm., 1974–80, Mem., 1980–85, UK Cttee. Council Member: FFPS, 1979–83; RGS, 1983–86; BTCV (Vice-Pres.) 1980–; RSNC (Vice-Pres.) 1980–99; RSNC Wildlife Appeal, 1983–87; WWF, 1980–86; Ecological Parks Trust, 1980–85; YPTES (Chm.), 1982–87; Friends of ENO, 1980–87; Common Ground Internat., 1981–85; Cttees for UK Conservation and Develt Prog., 1980–83; HGTAC, Forestry Commn, 1981–87; Conservator, Wimbledon and Putney Commons, 1981–97; Patron, CSV, 1978–85; Chairman: Instn of Environmental Sciences, 1981–84; Seychelles Appeal Cttee, Royal Soc., 1980–87; Chm., Gp A, Ditchley Foundn Anglo/Amer. Conf. on Environment, 1970; Lead Speaker, Eurogespracht, Vienna, 1970; Mem., Entretiens Ecologiques de Dijon, 1981; UK Officer Rep., Eur. Environment Ministers Conf., 1976; Judge, Berlin world agro/environ films and TV competitions, 1970, 1972, 1974 and 1980. Initiator and Chm., Age Resource, 1988–98, now Chm. Emeritus; a Vice-Pres., Age Concern, 1990–. Trustee and Hon. Treas., New Renaissance Gp, 1995–. FRSA 1971. Hon. Associate, Landscape Inst., 1971; Hon. MRTPI, 1978. Greek Distinguished Service Medal, 1946; van Tienhoven European Prize, 1980; Merit Award, IUCN, 1984; Alfred Toepfer Prize for European nature protection, Goethe Foundn, 1995. Adviser: Macmillan Guide to Britain's Nature Reserves, 1980–94; Shell Better Britain Campaign, 1980–91. Member Editorial Boards: Internat. Jl of Environmental Studies, 1975–; Town Planning Review, 1979–85; Internat. Jl Environmental Educn and Information, 1981–83. Helped to prepare: Pacemaker (film), 1970 (also appeared in); Man of Action, BBC Radio, 1977. *Publications:* (as Robert Arvill) Man and Environment, 1967 (5th edn 1984); numerous papers, articles, addresses, TV and radio broadcasts, over 4 decades in UK and internat. professional confs in 50 countries. *Recreations:* travel, theatre, music, dancing. *Address:* 3 Leeward Gardens, SW19 7QR. *T:* (020) 8946 1551.

BOOTH; *see* Gore-Booth.

BOOTH; *see* Sclater-Booth, family name of Baron Basing.

BOOTH, His Honour Alan Shore; QC 1975; a Circuit Judge, 1976–93; *b* Aug. 1922; 4th *s* of Parkin Stanley Booth and Ethel Mary Shore; *m* 1954, Mary Gwendoline Hilton; one *s* one *d*. *Educ:* Shrewsbury Sch.; Liverpool Univ. (LLB). Served War of 1939–45, RNVR, Fleet Air Arm, 1833 Sqdn (despatches 1944): Sub-Lt 1942; HMS Illustrious, Eastern and Pacific Fleets, 1943–45; Lieut 1944. Called to Bar, Gray's Inn, 1949. A Recorder of the Crown Court, 1972–76. Mem. Mgt Cttee, Hoylake Cottage Hosp., 1996–. Governor, Shrewsbury Sch., 1969. Guide, Chester Cathedral, 1996–. Pres., Liverpool Ramblers AFC, 1992–94. *Recreations:* golf, grandchildren, gardening. *Address:* 18 Abbey Road, West Kirby, Wirral CH48 7EW. *T:* (0151) 625 5796. *Clubs:* Royal Liverpool Golf; Royal and Ancient (St Andrews).

BOOTH, Rt Hon. Albert Edward; PC 1976; CIMechE 1985; *b* 28 May 1928; *e s* of Albert Henry Booth and Janet Mathieson; *m* 1957, Joan Amis; three *s*. *Educ:* St Thomas's Sch., Winchester; S Shields Marine Sch.; Rutherford Coll. of Technology. Engineering Draughtsman. Election Agent, 1951 and 1955. County Borough Councillor, 1962–65. Exec. Dir, S Yorks Passenger Transport Exec., 1983–87. MP (Lab) Barrow-in-Furness, 1966–83; Minister of State, Dept of Employment, 1974–76; Sec. of State for Employment, 1976–79; Opposition spokesman on transport, 1979–83. Chm., Select Cttee on Statutory Instruments, 1970–74. Treasurer, Labour Party, 1984. Contested (Lab): Tynemouth, 1964; Barrow and Furness, 1983; Warrington South, 1987. *Address:* 30b Albemarle Road, Beckenham, Kent BR3 5HJ. *T:* (020) 8650 5982.

BOOTH, Anthony John, CBE 1993; CEng, FIEE; Chairman, Ericsson Ltd, since 1994; *b* 18 March 1939; *s* of Benjamin and Una Lavinia Booth; *m* 1965, Elspeth Marjorie (*née* Fraser); one *s* one *d*. *Educ:* Bungay Grammar Sch.; London Univ. (BScEng, DMS). Joined Post Office Res. Dept, 1957; Exec. Engr and Sen. Exec. Engr, Telecom HQ, 1965–71; Asst Staff Engr, Central HQ Appointments, 1971–74; Head of Section and Div., External Telecom Exec., 1974–78; Head of Div., THQ, 1978–79; Dir, Internat. Networks, 1979–80; Regional Dir, London Region, 1980–83; Corporate Dir, British Telecommunications PLC, 1984–94; Managing Director: BT International, 1983–91; Business Communications, 1991–92; Special Businesses and Internat. Affairs Div., 1992–94. Director: Echo Plastics Ltd, 1998–; Protek Network Mgt Ltd; RB Phusion Ltd, 2001–. Mem., HEFCE, 1996–. Gov., and Chm. Finance Cttee, Polytechnic of W London, 1991–92; Chm. of Govs, Thames Valley Univ., 1993–96; Mem. Council, Univ. of Surrey, 1998–. Member, Guild of Freemen of City of London, 1982–. Chm., SE Reg., RLSS, 1997–2001. FInstD 1997 (Chm., W Surrey, 1999–); CIMgt (CBIM 1986; Mem. Bd of Companions, 1999–); FRSA 1991. Hon. DPhil Thames Valley, 1998. *Recreations:* opera, golf. *Address:* 63 Hillsborough Park, Camberley, Surrey GU15 1HG.

BOOTH, Brian George; JP; Chairman, Preston Acute Hospitals NHS Trust, since 1997; Vice-Chancellor, University of Central Lancashire (formerly Rector and Chief Executive, Lancashire Polytechnic), 1989–98; *b* 6 Sept. 1942; *s* of George and Ada Booth; *m* 1965, Barbara Ann (*née* Wright); two *d*. *Educ:* Univ. of Manchester (BA Econ 1964); Brunel Univ. (MTech 1972). FSS 1968–2000. Asst Lectr in Statistics, High Wycombe Coll. of Technology, 1965–68; Lectr, Sen. Lectr, and Principal Lectr, Kingston Polytechnic, 1968–73; Head, Dept of Business and Admin, 1974–78, Dean, Faculty of Business and Management, 1978–82, Preston Polytechnic; Dep. Dir, Preston Polytechnic, later Lancashire Polytechnic, 1982–89. Chair of Bd, Preston Business Venture, 1983–92; Chair of Trustees, Preston Postgrad. Med. Centre, 1990–96; Director: Lancs Partnership Against Crime, 1997–; Central Lancs Develt Agency, 1998–2000; (non-exec.), Student Loans Co. Ltd, 1998–. Trustee, Nat. Football Museum, 1996–. JP Preston, 1987. CIMgt 1992. DUniv Central Lancashire, 1998. *Recreations:* golf, watching Preston North End. *Address:* 9 Moorfield Close, Fulwood, Preston, Lancs PR2 9SW. *T:* (01772) 864243, *Fax:* (01772) 865636.

BOOTH, Cherie, (Mrs A. C. L. Blair); QC 1995; a Recorder, since 1999; *b* 23 Sept. 1954; *d* of Anthony and Gale Booth; *m* 1980, Rt Hon. Anthony Charles Lynton Blair, *qv*; three *s* one *d*. *Educ:* St Edmund's RC Primary Sch., Liverpool; Seafield Grammar Sch., Crosby; London Sch. of Economics (LLB; Hon. Fellow, 1999). Called to the Bar, Lincoln's Inn, 1976, Bencher, 1999; an Asst Recorder, 1996–99; barrister specialising in public law and employment law. Contested (Lab) Thanet North, 1983. Vice Pres., Kids Club Network, 1998–; Patron: Home Start, Islington, 1997–; Sargent Cancer Care for Children, 1998–; Breast Cancer Care, 1997–; SHADO, 1998–; Islington Music Centre, 1999–; Victim Support, London, 1999–. Trustee: Refuge, 1995–; Citizenship Foundn, 1995–. Fellow: Inst. of Advanced Legal Studies, 1998; Internat. Soc. of Lawyers for Public Service, 1999; FRSA. Chancellor, Liverpool John Moores Univ., 1999– (Fellow, 1997). DUniv Open, 1999; Hon. LLD Westminster, 1999. *Recreations:* theatre, the arts, keeping fit, enjoying my children. *Address:* Matrix Chambers, Gray's Inn, WC1R 5LN. *T:* (020) 7404 3447.

BOOTH, Sir Christopher (Charles), Kt 1983; Harveian Librarian, Royal College of Physicians, 1989–97; *b* 22 June 1924; *s* of Lionel Barton Booth and Phyllis Petley Duncan; *m* 1st, 1959, Lavinia Loughridge, Belfast; one *s* one *d*; 2nd, 1970, Soad Tabaqchali; one *d*; *m* 2001, Joyce Singleton. *Educ:* Sedbergh Sch., Yorks; University of St Andrews; MB 1951, MD 1958 (Rutherford Gold Medal). Junior appointments at Dundee Royal Infirmary, Hammersmith Hosp. and Addenbrooke's Hosp., Cambridge; successively Medical Tutor, Lecturer in Medicine and Senior Lecturer, Postgraduate Medical School of London; Prof. and Dir of Dept of Medicine, RPMS, London Univ., 1966–77; Dir, Clin. Res. Centre, MRC, 1978–88. Member: Adv. Bd to Res. Councils, 1976–78; MRC, 1981–84; Chm., Medical Adv. Cttee, British Council, 1979–85; President: British Soc. of Gastroenterology, 1978–79; BMA, 1986–87; RSocMed, 1988; Johnson Soc., 1987–88; Soc. Social History of Medicine, 1990. Hon. Prof., UCL, 2001. Chm., Royal Naval Personnel Cttee, 1985–91. Trustee, Coeliac Soc., 1968–93 (Chm., 1968–83). FRCP 1964; FRCPEd 1967; Hon. FACP 1973; Hon. FRSocMed 1991. For. Mem., Amer. Philosophical Soc., 1981. Docteur (*hc*): Paris, 1975; Poitiers, 1981; Hon. LLD Dundee, 1982; Laurea (*hc*) Bologna, 1991. Dicke Gold Medal, Dutch Soc. of Gastroenterology, 1973; Ludwig Heilmeyer Gold Medal, German Soc. for Advances in Internal Medicine, 1982; Gold Medal, BMA, 1992. Chevalier de l'Ordre National du Mérite (France), 1977. *Publications:* (with Betsy C. Corner) Chain of Friendship: Letters of Dr John Fothergill of London, 1735–1780, 1971; (with G. Neale) Disorders of the Small Intestine, 1985; Doctors in Science and Society, 1987; papers in med. jls on relationship of nutritional disorders to disease of the alimentary tract, and on medical history. *Recreations:* fishing, history. *Address:* 1 Kings Lodge, Pembroke Road, Ruislip, Middx HA4 8NH. *T:* (01895) 677811.

BOOTH, Prof. Clive, PhD; Chairman, Teacher Training Agency, since 1997; Deputy Chairman, South East England Development Agency, since 1999; *b* 18 April 1943; *s* of Henry Booth and Freda Frankland; *m* 1969, Margaret Sardeson. *Educ:* King's Sch., Macclesfield; Trinity Coll., Cambridge (1st cl. Hons Nat Scis Tripos; MA 1969); Univ. of California, Berkeley (Harkness Fellow, 1973; MA 1974; PhD 1976). Joined DES, 1965; Prin. Pvte Sec. to Sec. of State for Educn and Science, 1975–77; Asst Sec., 1977–81; Dep. Dir, Plymouth Polytechnic, 1981–84; Mem., HM Inspectorate, DES, 1984–86; Dir, Oxford Poly., 1986–92; Vice-Chancellor, 1992–97, Prof. Emeritus, 1997, Oxford Brookes Univ. Asst Comr, Nat. Commn on Educn, 1992–94. Member: Governing Council, SRHE, 1981–90; Adv. Cttee, Brunel Univ. Educn Policy Centre, 1986–91; Computer Bd for Univs and Res. Councils, 1987–92; CNAA Cttee for Information and Develt Services, 1987–92; Fulbright Academic Administrators Selection Cttee, 1988–97; British Council Cttee for Internat. Co-operation in Higher Educn, 1988–96 (Chm., 1994–); Council for Industry and Higher Educn, 1990–97; Fulbright Commn, 1992–97; Royal Soc. Study Gp on Higher Educn, 1991–97; UFC Inf. Systems Cttee, 1991–93; Oxford Science Park Adv. Cttee, 1990–; Oxford Inst. of Nursing Bd, 1991–95; Commonwealth Scholarships Commn, 1992–96; UK ERASMUS Council, 1992–97 (Chm., 1993–97); Oxford Trust Adv. Council, 1992–; Bd, British Inst., Paris, 1997–; Know How Fund Mgt Cttee, DFID, 1998–2000. Chairman: PCFC Steering Gp on Statistical Information, 1989–93; Heart of England Educn Forum, 1997–; Review Body for Nurses, Midwives and Professions Allied to Medicine, 1998–; Vice-Chm., CVCP, 1992–97. Chairman: Oxfordshire Learning Partnership, 1999–; Mgt Cttee, Oxfordshire Connexions, 2000–; Director: Thames Action Resource Gp for Educn and Trng, 1986–2000; Thames Valley Technology Centre, 1989–; British Council, 1995–97 (Sen. Advr, 1997–). Leverhulme Res. Fellow, 1983. Governor: Headington and Wheatley Park Schs; Westminster Coll., Oxford, 1997–2000. Jt Ed., Higher Educn Qly, 1986–; Mem., Editorial Bd, Oxford Review of Educn, 1990–. DUniv Oxford Brookes, 2000. *Recreations:* cycling, walking, bridge, opera. *Address:* 43 St John Street, Oxford OX1 2LH. *T:* (01865) 557762, *Fax:* (01865) 558886; *e-mail:* cbooth@brookes.ac.uk.

BOOTH, Sir Douglas Allen, 3rd Bt *cr* 1916; writer and producer for television, writer for films; *b* 2 Dec. 1949; *s* of Sir Philip Booth, 2nd Bt, and Ethel, *d* of Joseph Greenfield, NY, USA; *S* father 1960; *m* 1991, Yolanda Marcela (*née* Scantlebury); one *d*. *Educ:* Beverly Hills High Sch.; Harvard Univ. (Harvard Nat. Scholarship, Nat. Merit Scholarship, 1967); BA (*magna cum laude*) 1975. *Recreations:* music, back-packing. *Heir:* *b* Derek Blake Booth [*b* 7 April 1953; *m* 1981, Elizabeth Dreisbach; one *s* one *d*]. *Address:* 22933 Portage Circle Drive, Topanga, CA 90290, USA.

BOOTH, Eric Stuart, CBE 1971; FRS 1967; FREng; Chairman, Yorkshire Electricity Board, 1972–79; *b* 14 Oct. 1914; *s* of Henry and Annie Booth; *m* 1945, Mary Elizabeth Melton (*d* 1987); two *d*; *m* 1988, Pauline Margaret Ford. *Educ:* Batley Grammar Sch.; Liverpool Univ. Apprentice, Metropolitan Vickers Electrical Co. Ltd, 1936–38; Technical Engineer, Yorks Electric Power Co., 1938–46; Dep., later City Electrical Engineer and Manager, Salford Corporation, 1946–48; various posts associated with construction of Power Stations with British, later Central Electricity Authority, 1948–57, Dep. Chief Engineer (Generation Design and Construction), 1957; Chief Design and Construction Engineer, 1958–59, Bd Mem. for Engrg, 1959–71, CEGB. Part-time Mem., UKAEA, 1965–72; Pres., IEE, 1976–77. Dir, British Electricity Internat., 1979–84; Consultant to Electricity Council, 1979–84. FREng (FEng 1976). Hon. FIEE 1986. Hon. DTech Bradford, 1980. *Address:* Pinecroft, Upper Dunsforth, York YO26 9RU. *T:* (01423) 322821.

BOOTH, Sir Gordon, KCMG 1980 (CMG 1969); CVO 1976; HM Diplomatic Service, retired; Chairman, The Ritz Hotel Casino Ltd, since 1998; *b* 22 Nov. 1921; *s* of Walter and Grace Booth, Bolton, Lancs; *m* 1944, Jeanne Mary Kirkham; one *s* one *d*. *Educ:* Canon Slade Sch.; London Univ. (BCom). Served War of 1939–45: Capt. RAC and 13/18th Royal Hussars, 1941–46. Min. of Labour and Bd of Trade, 1946–55; Trade Comr, Canada and West Indies, 1955–65; Mem. HM Diplomatic Service, 1965–80; Counsellor (Commercial), British Embassy in Copenhagen, 1966–69; Dir, Coordination of Export Services, DTI, 1969–71; Consul-General, Sydney, 1971–74; HBM Consul-Gen., NY, and Dir-Gen. of Trade Develt in USA, 1975–80; Chm., SITPRO Bd, 1980–86. Chm., London Clubs Internat. plc, 1992–95; Director: Hanson PLC (formerly Hanson Trust), 1981–89; Bechtel Ltd, 1983–92; Allders Internat. Ltd, 1992–96. *Recreations:* golf, bridge. *Address:* Penthouse B, Forsyte Shades, Canford Cliffs, Dorset BH14 8LA. *T:* (01202) 706682. *Club:* Walton Heath Golf.

BOOTH, Hartley; Chairman, UBTIC, British Trade International, since 1999; *b* 17 July 1946; *s* of late V. W. H. Booth and Eilish (*née* Morrow); *m* 1977, Adrianne Claire Cranefield; two *s* one *d*. *Educ:* Queen's Coll., Taunton; Bristol Univ. (LLB); Downing Coll., Cambridge (LLM, PhD). Called to the Bar, Inner Temple, 1970 (Scholar); in practice, 1970–84; Special Advr to Prime Minister and Mem., 10 Downing Street Policy Unit, 1984–88; Chief Exec., British Urban Develt, 1988–90; Consultant, Berwin Leighton (Solicitors), 1997–99; Director: Edexcel, 1999–; Canford Gp plc. MP (C) Finchley, 1992–97. PPS to Minister of State, FCO, 1992–94. Mem. Select Committees: Home Affairs, 1992; European Legislation, 1992; Public Service, 1995–97; Chm., Urban Affairs Select Cttee, 1994–97. Vice President: Royal Life Saving Soc., 1990–; British Urban Regeneration Assoc., 1991–94 (Chm., 1990–91); AMA, 1992. Chm., Resources for Autism. European Editor, Current Law Year Books, 1974–84. *Publications:* British Extradition Law and Procedure, vol. I 1979, vol. II 1980; Return Ticket, 1994. *Recreations:* writing, swimming, delving into history, poetry. *Address:* c/o Berwin Leighton, Adelaide House, London Bridge, EC4R 9HA.

BOOTH, Prof. Ian Westerby, MD; FRCP, FRCPCH; Head, Academic Department of Paediatrics and Child Health, and Director, Institute of Child Health, since 1993, Sir Leonard Parsons Professor of Paediatrics and Child Health, since 1996, and Associate Dean, Medical School, since 2000, University of Birmingham; *b* 15 Aug. 1948; *s* of William Westerby Booth and Audrey Iris (*née* Corless). *Educ:* Sir George Monoux Grammar Sch., London; King's Coll. Hosp. Med. Sch., Univ. of London (BSc Hons Physiol. 1969; MB BS 1972; MSc with Dist. Biochem. 1982; MD 1987). DRCOG 1974; DCH 1975; MRCP 1977, FRCP 1991; Founder FRCPCH 1997. Eden Res. Fellow, RCP, 1980–83; Lectr, Inst. Child Health, London, 1983–85; University of Birmingham: Sen. Lectr in Paediatrics and Child Health, 1985–92; Prof. of Paediatric Gastroenterology and Nutrition, 1992–96; Hon. Consultant Paediatric Gastroenterologist, 1985–, Dir of Educn, 1998–, Mem. Exec. Bd, 1995–, Children's Hosp., Birmingham. Department of Health: Vice-Chm., Adv. Cttee on Borderline Substances, 1990–97; Member: Panel on Novel Foods, 1992–98; Wkg Gp on Nutritional Adequacy of Infant Formulas, 1994–96; Mem., Med. and Res. Adv. Gp, HEA, 1994–99. Pres., British Soc. Paediatric Gastroenterology and Nutrition, 1995–98 (Sec., 1985–89); Royal College of Paediatrics and Child Health: Chairman: Standing Cttee on Nutrition, 1996–; Academic Bd, 1998–; Wkg Gp on Intestinal Failure, 1998–; Mem., Safety and Efficiency Register of New Interventional Procedures, Acad. of Med. Royal Colls, 1996–. Associate Ed., Archives of Diseases of Childhood, 1993–96. *Publications:* (with E. Wozniak) Pocket Picture Guides in Clinical Medicine: Paediatrics, 1984; (with D. A. Kelly) An Atlas of Paediatric Gastroenterology and Hepatology, 1996; contribs to learned jls on paediatric gastroenterology and nutrition. *Recreation:* walking to restaurants. *Address:* University of Birmingham, Institute of Child Health, Whittall Street, Birmingham B4 6NH. *T:* (0121) 333 8717, *Fax:* (0121) 333 8701; *e-mail:* i.w.booth@bham.ac.uk.

BOOTH, John Antony W.; *see* Ward-Booth.

BOOTH, John Barton, FRCS; Physician, St Bridget's Hospice, Douglas, since 2000; Consultant Otolaryngologist, London (later Royal London) Hospital, 1972–98, and Royal Hospital of St Bartholomew, 1995–98, now Hon. Consulting Otolaryngologist, Barts and the London (formerly Royal Hospitals) NHS Trust; *b* 19 Nov. 1937; *s* of (Percy) Leonard Booth and Mildred Amy (*née* Wilson); *m* 1966, Carroll Griffiths; one *s*. *Educ:* Canford Sch., Dorset; King's Coll., London (AKC 1963); King's Coll. Hosp. Med. Sch. (MB, BS 1963). FRCS 1968. House Surgeon: Birmingham Accident Hosp., 1964; Hosp. for Sick Children, Gt Ormond St, 1965; House Surgeon, Registrar, Sen. Registrar, RNTNEH, 1966–70; Sen. Registrar, Royal Free Hosp., 1970–72; Clin. Asst, Neuro-Otology, Nat. Hosp. for Nervous Diseases, 1968, 1971; Consultant Surgeon, RNTNEH, 1973–78; Civil Consultant (Otology), RAF, 1983–2000, now Hon. Consultant; Hon. Consultant, St Luke's Hosp. for the Clergy, 1983–2000; Hon. Consultant Laryngologist: Musicians Benevolent Fund, 1974–2000; Royal Coll. of Music, 1974–2000; Newspaper Press Fund, 1982–2000; Royal Opera House, Covent Gdn, 1983–2000; Royal Soc. of Musicians of GB, 1987–2000; Concert Artists Assoc., 1987–2000; Webber-Douglas Acad. of Dramatic Art, 1987–2000. Hunterian Prof., RCS, 1980–81. Hon. Chm., IXth British Acad. Conf. in Otolaryngol., 1995. Vice-Chm., 1960–61, Chm., 1961–62, Vice-Pres., 1962–63, Fedn of Univ. Conservatives; Mem., Gen. Purposes and Exec. Cttees, Cons. Party, 1961–62. FRSocMed 1967 (Mem. Council, 1980–88 and 1993–96; Hon. Sec., 1996–98; Pres., Otology Sect., 1996–97; Pres., United Services Section, 1999–2001; Vice-Pres., History of Medicine Section, 2000–). MRAeS (Medical Aviation Gp) 1990; Mem., Amer. Neurotology Soc., 1994; Corresp. Mem., Amer. Acad. of Otolaryngology, 1998; Hon. Mem., Amer. Otological Soc., 1995. FZS 1996. Howell Meml Prize (jtly), Univ. of London, 1988. Editor, Jl of Laryngology and Otology, 1987–92 (Asst Editor, 1979–87; Abstract Editor, 1987–94). *Publications:* (ed) Vol. 3, The Ear, of 5th edn of Scott-Brown's Otolaryngology, 1987, 6th edn 1997; chapters in: Rob and Smith, Operative Surgery, 3rd edn 1976; Audiology and Audiological Medicine, vol. I, 1981; Otologic Medicine and Surgery, 1988. *Recreations:* golf, music, the arts. *Address:* 44 The Crofts, Castletown, Isle of Man IM9 1LZ. *T:* (01624) 823837. *Clubs:* Royal Automobile, MCC; Royal & Ancient Golf (St Andrews).

BOOTH, Dame Margaret (Myfanwy Wood), DBE 1979; Chairman, National Family and Parenting Institute, since 1999; a Judge of the High Court, Family Division, 1979–94; *b* 11 Sept. 1933; *d* of late Alec Wood Booth and Lilian May Booth; *m* 1st, 1982, Joseph Jackson, QC (*d* 1987); 2nd, 1993, Peter Glucksmann. *Educ:* Northwood Coll.; University Coll., London (LLM; Fellow, 1982). Called to the Bar, Middle Temple, 1956; Bencher, 1979. QC 1976. Chairman: Family Law Bar Assoc., 1976–78; Matrimonial Causes Procedure Cttee, 1982–85; Inner London Adv. Cttee on Justices of the Peace, 1990–93; Children Act Procedure Adv. Cttee, 1990; Children Act 1989 Adv. Cttee, 1991–93 (report published, 1996); Bar Central Selection Bd, 1993–96; Family Law Cttee, Justice, 1993–98. Pres., Family Mediators Assoc., 1994–95; Chm. Govs, UK Coll. of Family Mediators, 1996–99. Vis. Prof. of Law, Liverpool Univ., 1994–99. Trustee: Rowntree Foundn, 1996–; Apex Charitable Trust Ltd, 1996– (Chm., 1997–); Pres., Alone in London, 1998–; Patron, The Place to Be, 1999–; Governor, Northwood Coll., 1975–96; Member, Council: UCL, 1980–84; Liverpool Univ., 1994–99 (Vice-Pres., 1996–99). Hon. LLD Liverpool, 1992. *Publications:* (co-ed) Rayden on Divorce, 10th edn 1967, (cons. ed.) 17th edn 1997; (co-ed) Clarke Hall and Morrison on Children, 9th edn 1977, (cons. ed.) 10th edn 1985. *Address:* 15 Wellington House, Eton Road, NW3 4SY. *Club:* Reform.

BOOTH, Martin, FRSL; writer; *b* 7 Sept. 1944; *s* of William John Kenneth Booth and Alice Joyce Booth (*née* Pankhurst); *m* 1968, Helen Barber; one *s* one *d*. *Educ:* Hong Kong and Kenya. Started writing at the age of 17, encouraged by Edmund Blunden; addicted to the habit ever since. Fellow Commoner: St Peter's Coll., Oxford, 1972; Corpus Christi Coll., Cambridge, 1980. FRSL 1980. *Publications include: fiction:* Hiroshima Joe, 1985; A Very Private Gentleman, 1991; Adrift in the Oceans of Mercy, 1996; The Industry of Souls, 1998; *children's fiction:* Music on the Bamboo Radio, 1997; War Dog, 1998; Panther, 1999; PoW, 2000; *non-fiction:* Carpet Sahib: a life of Jim Corbett, 1986; Rhino Road, 1992; The Dragon and the Pearl: a Hong Kong notebook, 1994; Opium: a history, 1996; The Doctor, The Detective and Arthur Conan Doyle, 1997; The Dragon Syndicates, 1999; A Magick Life: a biography of Aleister Crowley, 2000; also film scripts, wildlife documentaries, feature films, verse, literary criticism and journalism. *Recreations:* torpedoing pretension, hounding hypocrisy. *Address:* c/o Gillon Aitken Associates, 29 Fernshaw Road, SW10 0TG. *T:* (020) 7351 7561.

BOOTH, Sir Michael Addison John W.; *see* Wheeler-Booth.

BOOTH, Michael John; QC 1999; *b* Salford, 24 May 1958; *s* of Eric Charles Booth and Iris Booth (*née* Race); *m* 1987, Sarah Jane Marchington; two *s* one *d*. *Educ:* Manchester Grammar Sch. (Schol.); Trinity Coll., Cambridge (Open Schol.; MA Hons Law). Pres., Cambridge Union Soc., Michaelmas, 1979. Called to the Bar, Lincoln's Inn, 1981. Mem., Manchester GS's winning team, ESU Nat. Schools Public Speaking Comp., 1975. *Recreations:* walking, swimming, reading, watching football, wine. *Address:* 40 King Street, Manchester M2 6BA. *T:* (0161) 832 9082.

BOOTH, Peter John Richard; Textile National Trade Group Secretary, Transport and General Workers' Union, since 1986; *b* 27 March 1949; *s* of Eric Albert and Edith Booth; *m* 1970, Edwina Ivy; three *s*. *Educ:* Little London Infant Sch.; Rawdon Littlemore Junior Sch., Rawdon; Benton Park Secondary Modern School. Dyers' Operative, 1964; National Union of Dyers, Bleachers and Textile Workers: District Officer, 1973; Nat. Research Officer, 1975; Nat. Organiser, 1980; transf. to TGWU, 1982; Nat. Trade Group Organiser, 1982. Mem., Yorks and Humberside Regional Innovation Strategy, 1998–. Director: Man-Made Fibres Industry Trng Adv. Bd, 1986–; Apparel, Knitting & Textiles Alliance, 1989–; Nat. Textile Trading Orgn, 1998; Member: Internat. Textile, Garment and Leather Workers Fedn, 1986– (Pres., 1996–); Confedn of British Wool Textiles Trng Bd, 1986–; Carpet Industry Trng Council, 1986– (Chm.); Nat. Textile Trng Gp, 1989– (Vice Pres.); Presidium, European TU Cttee, 1990–; Textiles Industry Adv. Cttee, 1994–; Cotton & Allied Textiles Industry Adv. Cttee, 1986–; Chm., Wool Textile and Clothing Industry Action Cttee, 1996–. FRSA. *Publication:* The Old Dog Strike, 1985. *Recreations:* walking, gardening, dominoes, chess. *Address:* 8 Gladding Road, Hammond Street, Cheshunt EN7 6XB.

BOOTH, Richard George William Pitt; Chairman, Richard Booth (Bookshops) Ltd, Bookseller, since 1961; Chairman, Welsh Booksellers Association, since 1987; *b* 12 Sept. 1938; *m* 1987, Hope Estcourt Stuart (*née* Barrie). *Educ:* Rugby; Univ. of Oxford. Founding father of following towns as centres of bookselling: Hay-on-Wye, 1961; Redu, 1984; Becherel, 1988; Montolieu, 1989; Bredevoort, 1992; Fjaerland, 1996; Dalmellington, 1997. Life Pres., Internat. Book Town Movt, 2000. *Publications:* Country Life Book of Book Collecting, 1976; Independence for Hay, 1977. *Recreations:* creating a monarchy in Hay (began home rule movement, 1 April 1977), gardening. *Address:* Hay Castle, Hay-on-Wye, via Hereford HR3.

BOOTH, Prof. Roger Hignett, CEng; Royal Academy of Engineering Visiting Professor, Department of Engineering, University of Oxford, since 1998; *b* 3 May 1940; *s* of David and Elsie Booth; *m* 1st, 1968, Maureen (*née* Howell) (marr. diss. 1996); two *s*; 2nd, 1997, Thelly (*née* Price). *Educ:* Bentham Grammar Sch.; Birmingham Univ. (BSc Chem. Engrg). MIChemE 1966; CEng 1973. Royal Dutch/Shell Gp (posts in UK, Indonesia, USA, Netherlands, Pakistan), 1961–96; Dir, Solar Century Hldgs Ltd, 1999–. Mem., Renewable Energy Adv. Cttee, DTI, 1995–. Clerk, Newnham Parish Council, 1998–. *Publications:* articles on renewable energy and sustainable develt. *Recreations:* golf, walking, dining with friends, listening to music. *Address:* Firtree Cottage, Newnham Road, Newnham, Hook RG27 9AE. *T:* (01256) 762456. *Club:* Tylney Park Golf.

BOOTH, Sarah Ann; *see* Hinkley, S. A.

BOOTH, Vernon Edward Hartley; *see* Booth, H.

BOOTH, Rev. Preb. William James, LVO 1999; Sub-Dean of Her Majesty's Chapels Royal, Deputy Clerk of the Closet, Sub-Almoner and Domestic Chaplain to The Queen, since 1991; Prebendary, St Paul's Cathedral, since 2000; *b* 3 Feb. 1939; *s* of William James Booth and Elizabeth Ethel Booth. *Educ:* Ballymena Acad., Co. Antrim; TCD (MA). Curate, St Luke's Parish, Belfast, 1962–64; Chaplain, Cranleigh Sch., Surrey, 1965–74. Priest-in-Ordinary to The Queen, 1976–91; Priest-Vicar of Westminster Abbey, 1987–91. Chaplain, Westminster School, London, 1974–91. Organiser, PHAB annual residential courses at Westminster (and formerly at Cranleigh). *Recreations:* music, hi-fi, cooking. *Address:* Marlborough Gate, St James's Palace, SW1A 1BG. *T:* (020) 7930 6609.

BOOTHBY, Sir Brooke (Charles), 16th Bt *cr* 1660, of Broadlow Ash, Derbyshire; Chairman, Adventure Activity Licensing Authority, since 1996; *b* 6 April 1949; *s* of Sir Hugo Robert Brooke Boothby, 15th Bt and (Evelyn) Ann (*d* 1993), *d* of late H. C. R. Homfray; *S* father, 1986; *m* 1976, Georgiana Alexandra, *o d* of late Sir John Wriothesley Russell, GCVO, CMG; two *d*. *Educ:* Eton; Trinity Coll., Cambridge (BA Econs). Chm., Associated Quality Services, 1994–; Man. Dir, 1979–95, Vice Chm., 1995–, Fontygary Parks Ltd (formerly Fontygary Leisure). Chairman: Historic Houses Assoc. Inheritance Cttee, 1984–86; Nat. Caravan Council Parks Div., 1987–90. President: Glamorgan Br., CLA, 1992–94; Vale of Glamorgan Nat. Trust, 1998–. High Sheriff, South Glamorgan, 1986–87. *Recreation:* gardening. *Heir: kinsman* George William Boothby [*b* 18 June 1948; *m* 1977, Sally Louisa Thomas; three *d*]. *Address:* Fonmon Castle, Barry, South Glamorgan CF62 3ZN. *T:* (01446) 710206, *Fax:* (01446) 711687.

BOOTHMAN, Campbell Lester; His Honour Judge Boothman; a Circuit Judge, since 1988; *b* 3 Sept. 1942; *s* of Gerald and Ann Boothman; *m* 1966, Penelope Evelyn Pepe; three *s*. *Educ:* Oundle; King's College, London. Called to the Bar, Inner Temple, 1965. A Recorder, 1985–88. *Recreations:* skiing, squash. *Address:* The Glen, Tower House Lane, Wraxall, Bristol BS19 1JX.

BOOTHMAN, Derek Arnold, FCA; Chairman, Ian Anthony (Holdings) Ltd, since 1997; Deputy Chairman, Teather & Greenwood Holdings plc (formerly Northumbrian Residential Properties, then NRP plc), since 2000 (non-executive Director, since 1994; Chairman, 1998–2000); *b* 5 June 1932; *s* of Eric Randolph Boothman and Doris Mary Boothman; *m* 1958, Brenda Margaret; one *s* one *d*. *Educ:* William Hulme's Grammar Sch., Manchester. Articled to J. Needham & Co., 1948; Mem., ICA, 1954; National Service, RAF, 1954–56; Partner: J. Needham & Co. (now part of Binder Hamlyn), 1957; Binder Hamlyn, Chartered Accts, 1974–88. Dep. Chm., Central Manchester Develt Corp., 1988–96. Non-executive Director: Remploy Ltd, 1987–; L. Gardner Gp, 1995–. President: Manchester Chartered Accountants Students Soc., 1967–68; Manchester Soc. of Chartered Accountants, 1968–69; Institute of Chartered Accountants in England and Wales: Council Member, 1969–91; Treasurer, 1981–83; Vice-Pres., 1983–85; Dep. Pres., 1985–86; Pres., 1986–87. Member, Accounting Standards Cttee, 1974–82. Gov., William Hulme's Grammar Sch., 1982– (Chm., 1988–99); Mem. Ct, Univ. of Manchester, 1990–99. Liveryman, Worshipful Company of Chartered Accountants, 1976–. *Publications:* contribs to professional press and lectures on professional topics, internationally. *Recreations:* cricket, gardening, travel. *Address:* Ashworth Dene, Wilmslow Road, Mottram St Andrew, Cheshire SK10 4QH. *T:* (01625) 829101. *Clubs:* St James's (Manchester); Withington Golf (Manchester) (past Captain).

BOOTHMAN, Nicholas, CEng; Director of Technology, Metropolitan Police Service, 1992–2000; *b* 16 Dec. 1941; *s* of late Frederick Boothman and Sarah Ellen (*née* Kirk); *m* 1964, Ernestine Carole Jane Billings; one *d*. *Educ:* Threshfield Sch.; Ermysteds Grammar Sch., Skipton; Univ. of Birmingham (BSc Physics). CEng, MIEE 1972. Research at GEC Hirst Res. Centre, Wembley, 1963–72; project management of communication systems for RAF, MoD (PE), 1972–77; Project Manager, Metropolitan Police Office, 1977–88; Chief Engr, Metropolitan Police, 1988–92. *Recreations:* amateur musician, watching cricket, railways, unavoidable gardening. *Address:* 35 Clarence Road, Teddington, Middx TW11 0BN.

BOOTHROYD, Baroness *cr* 2000 (Life Peer), of Sandwell in the co. of West Midlands; **Betty Boothroyd;** PC 1992; Speaker of the House of Commons, 1992–2000; *b* Yorkshire, 8 Oct. 1929; *d* of Archibald and Mary Boothroyd. *Educ:* Dewsbury Coll. of Commerce and Art. Personal/Political Asst to Labour Ministers. Delegate to N Atlantic Assembly, 1974. MP (Lab) West Bromwich, May 1973–1974, West Bromwich West, 1974–92 (when elected Speaker); MP West Bromwich West, 1992–2000. An Asst Govt Whip, Oct. 1974–Nov. 1975; Dep. Chm. of Ways and Means, and Dep. Speaker, 1987–92. Member: Select Cttee on Foreign Affairs, 1979–81; Speaker's Panel of Chairmen, 1979–87; House of Commons Commn, 1983–87. Mem., European Parlt, 1975–77. Mem., Labour Party NEC, 1981–87. Contested (Lab): SE Leicester (by-elec.), 1957; Peterborough (gen. elec.), 1959; Nelson and Colne (by-elec.), 1968; Rossendale (gen. elec.), 1970. Chancellor, Open Univ., 1994–. Freeman: Borough of Sandwell, 1992; Borough of Kirklees, 1992; City of London, 1993. Hon. LLD: Birmingham, 1992; South Bank, 1992; Leicester, 1993; Cambridge, 1994; Hon. DLitt Bradford, 1993; DUniv: Leeds Metropolitan, 1993; North London, 1993; Hon. DCL Oxford, 1995. *Publication:* Betty Boothroyd: the autobiography, 2001. *Address:* House of Lords, SW1A 0PW.

BOOTLE, Roger Paul; Managing Director, Capital Economics Ltd, since 1999; *b* 22 June 1952; *s* of David Bootle and Florence (*née* Denman); *m* 1993, Sally Broomfield; one *s* two *d*. *Educ:* Merton Coll., Oxford (BA PPE 1973); Nuffield Coll., Oxford (MPhil Econs 1975). Chief Economist: Capel-Cure Myers, 1982–86; Lloyds Merchant Bank, 1986–89; Greenwell Montagu, 1989–92; HSBC Markets, 1992–96; Gp Chief Economist, HSBC, 1996–98. Vis. Prof., Manchester Business Sch., 1995–. Mem., Chancellor of the Exchequer's Panel of Indep. Econ. Advrs, 1997; Specialist Advr, H of C Treasury Cttee, 1998–. Econ. Advr, Deloitte & Touche, 1999–. Columnist: The Times, 1997–99; Sunday Telegraph, 1999–. *Publications:* (with W. T. Newlyn) Theory of Money, 1978; Index-Linked Gilts, 1985; The Death of Inflation, 1996. *Recreations:* squash, horse-racing, classical music, bridge. *Address:* 150 Buckingham Palace Road, SW1W 9TR. *T:* (020) 7823 5000.

BOOTLE-WILBRAHAM, family name of **Baron Skelmersdale**.

BORBIDGE, Hon. Robert Edward; Senior Associate, Strategic Communications Australia, since 2001; *b* Ararat, Vic, 12 Aug. 1954; *s* of Edward A. Borbidge and Jean Borbidge; *m* 1984, Jennifer Gooding; one *s* one *d*. *Educ:* Ararat High Sch., Vic; Overberg High Sch., S Africa. Dist Governor, Rotary Internat., 1974–75; Mem. Bd, Gold Coast Visitors' Bureau, 1980. MLA (Nat.) Surfers Paradise, Qld, 1980–2001; formerly Mem., Qld Parly Delegn, Qld Govt Cttees on Transport, Tourism, Nat. Parks, Sport and Arts, Ind. and Commerce, Local Govt, Main Roads and Police; Minister: for Industry, Small Business, Communications and Technol., 1987–89; for Ind., Small Business, Technol. and Tourism, then for Police, Emergency Services and Corrective Services, and subseq. for Tourism and for Envmt, Conservation and Forestry, 1989; Opposition spokesman on Small Business, Manufg and Regl Develt and Assisting Leader on Econ. and Trade Develt, 1990–91; Dep. Leader of Opposition, 1989–91, Leader, 1991–96 and 1998–2001; Premier of Qld and Minister responsible for Ethnic Affairs, 1996–98; Leader, Qld Nat. Party-Lib. Party Coalition, 1992–2001. *Recreations:* travel, reading, tourism, swimming. *Address:* (office) PO Box 1500, Milton, Qld 4064, Australia.

BORCHERDS, Prof. Richard Ewen, FRS 1994; Professor of Mathematics, University of California at Berkeley, 1993–96 and since 1999; *b* 29 Nov. 1959; *s* of Dr Peter Howard Borcherds and Margaret Elizabeth Borcherds; *m* Ursula Gritsch. *Educ:* Trinity Coll., Cambridge (BA, MA; PhD 1985). Research Fellow, Trinity Coll., Cambridge, 1983–87; Morrey Asst Prof., Univ. of California, Berkeley, 1987–88; Cambridge University: Royal Society Univ Res. Fellow, 1988–92; Lectr, 1992–93; Royal Soc. Prof., Dept of Maths, 1996–99. Fields Medal, Internat. Mathematical Union, 1998. *Publications:* papers in math. jls. *Address:* Department of Mathematics, University of California, 970 Evans Hall # 3840, Berkeley, CA 94720-3840, USA.

BORDER, Allan Robert, AO 1989; with Castlemaine Perkins, 1984–98; professional cricketer, 1977–96; Captain, Australian cricket team, 1984–94; *b* 27 July 1955; *s* of John and Sheila Border; *m* 1980, Jane, *d* of John and Eve Hiscox; two *s* two *d*. *Educ:* N Sydney Tech. Sch.; N Sydney High Sch. First class cricket début, for NSW, 1976; professional cricketer, Queensland State, 1977–96 (Captain, 1983–84); Test début, 1978; played 156 Test matches for Australia, with record of 93 as Captain, scored 27 centuries and 2 double centuries, record total of 11,174 Test runs, also took 39 wickets and record 156 catches; in all first-class cricket matches to 1994, had scored 25,551 runs incl. 68 centuries, and taken 102 wickets and 345 catches. Mem., Nat. Cricket Selection Panel, Aust., 1998–. With Ronald McConnell Hldgs, 1980–84. *Address:* c/o Australian Cricket Board, 90 Jolimont Street, Jolimont, Vic 3002, Australia.

BOREEL, Sir Francis (David), 13th Bt, *cr* 1645; Counsellor, Netherlands Foreign Service, 1966–87 (Attaché, 1956), retired; *b* 14 June 1926; *s* of Sir Alfred Boreel, 12th Bt and Countess Reiniera Adriana (*d* 1957), *d* of Count Francis David Schimmelpenninck; *S* father 1964; *m* 1964, Suzanne Campagne; three *d*. *Educ:* Utrecht Univ. *Recreations:* tennis, sailing. *Heir: kinsman* Stephen Gerard Boreel [*b* 9 Feb. 1945; *m* Francien P. Kooyman; one *s*]. *Address:* Kapellestraat 25, 4351 A. L. Veere, Netherlands.

BOREHAM, Sir Leslie Kenneth Edward, Kt 1972; a Judge of the High Court, Queen's Bench Division, 1972–92; Presiding Judge, North Eastern Circuit, 1974–80; Deputy Chairman, Agricultural Lands Tribunal; *b* 19 Oct. 1918; *o s* of Harry Edward and Mary Amelia Boreham; *m* 1941, Rachel (*d* 1998), *o c* of Trevor Morgan and Elizabeth Harding; one *s* one *d*. *Educ:* Bungay Grammar Sch. Served War of 1939–45, RAF. Called to the Bar at Lincoln's Inn, Nov. 1947, Bencher 1972; admitted to Bar of St Helena, 1962. Joined South-Eastern Circuit. Dep. Chm. 1962–65, Chm. 1965–71, East Suffolk QS; QC 1965; Recorder of Margate, 1968–71. Chm., Lord Chancellor's Cttee on Trng of Magistrates, 1974–82; Pres., Central Council of Probation Cttees, 1976–82; Parole Bd, 1979–81 (Vice Chm., 1981). *Recreations:* gardening, golf. *Address:* c/o Royal Courts of Justice, Strand, WC2A 2LL.

BORELAND-KELLY, Dame Lorna (May), DBE 1998; JP; Team Manager, Children and Families Mayday Hospital, Croydon, since 2000; *b* 9 Aug. 1952; *d* of James Boreland and Hortence Boreland (*née* Boyd); *m* Anthony Owen Kelly; three *s* three *d*. *Educ:* North London Univ. (CQSW 1991). Sen. Practitioner, Social Work Children and Families, St Thomas' Hosp., 1997–2000. Chair of Govs, Lambeth Coll. Mem., Union of Catholic Mothers. FRSA. JP S Westminster, 1991. *Recreations:* reading, writing short stories (never to be published), watching my sons swim. *Address:* c/o Lambeth College, 45 Clapham Common, Southside, SW4 9BL. *T:* (020) 7501 5602.

BORG, Alan Charles Nelson, CBE 1991; PhD; FSA; Director, Victoria and Albert Museum, 1995–2001; *b* 21 Jan. 1942; *s* of late Charles John Nelson Borg and Frances Mary Olive Hughes; *m* 1st, 1964, Anne (marr. diss.), *d* of late Dr William Blackmore; one *s* one *d*; 2nd, 1976, Lady Caroline, *d* of late Captain Lord Francis Hill, *yr s* of 6th Marquess of Downshire; two *d*. *Educ:* Westminster Sch.; Brasenose Coll., Oxford (MA); Courtauld Inst. of Art (PhD). Lecteur d'anglais, Université d'Aix-Marseille, 1964–65; Lectr, History of Art, Indiana Univ., 1967–69; Asst Prof. of History of Art, Princeton Univ., 1969–70; Asst Keeper of the Royal Armouries, HM Tower of London, 1970–78; Keeper, Sainsbury Centre for Visual Arts, Univ. of E Anglia, 1978–82; Dir Gen., Imperial War Mus., 1982–95. Member: British Nat. Cttee for Hist. of Second World War, 1982–95; Bd of War Studies, KCL, 1982–95; COPUS, 1992–95; Council, Museums Assoc., 1992–95; Adv. Cttee on Public Records, 1993–; Court of Advisers, St Paul's Cathedral, 1996–; Bd of Mgt, Courtauld Inst. of Art, 1998–; Chm., Nat. Inventory of War Memls, 1988–95; Admin. Council, Louvre Mus., 1999–. Chm., Nat. Mus. Dirs' Conf., 1998–2000. President: Elizabethan Club, 1994–2000; Meyrick Soc., 1994–. Governor: Thomas Coram Foundn for Children, 1995–; Westminster Sch., 1998–. Freeman, City of London, 1997; Liveryman, Painter Stainers' Co., 1997. Hon. FRCA 1991. *Publications:* Architectural Sculpture in Romanesque Provence, 1972; European Swords and Daggers in the Tower of London, 1974; Torture and Punishment, 1975; Heads and Horses, 1976; Arms and Armour in Britain, 1979; (ed with A. R. Martindale) The Vanishing Past: studies presented to Christopher Hohler, 1981; War Memorials, 1991; articles in learned jls. *Recreations:* fencing (Oxford blue, 1962, 1963), music, travel. *Address:* Telegraph House, 36 West Square, SE11 4SP. *Clubs:* Beefsteak, Special Forces.

BORG, Björn Rune; professional tennis player, 1972–2000; *b* 6 June 1956; *s* of Rune and Margaretha Borg; *m* 1980, Mariana Simionescu (marr. diss. 1984); one *s* by Jannike Bjorling; *m* 1989, Loredana Berte (marr. diss. 1992). *Educ:* Blombacka Sch., Södertälje. Started to play tennis at age of 9; won Wimbledon junior title, 1972; became professional player in 1972. Mem., Swedish Davis Cup team, annually 1972–80 (youngest player ever in a winning Davis Cup team, 1975). Championship titles: Italian, 1974, 1978; French, 1974, 1975, 1978, 1979, 1980, 1981; Wimbledon, record of 5 consecutive singles titles, 1976–80; World Champion, 1978, 1979, 1980; Masters, 1980, 1981. *Publication:* (with Eugene Scott) Björn Borg: my life and game, 1980. *Address:* c/o International Management Group, The Pier House, Strand on the Green, Chiswick, W4 3NN.

BORG COSTANZI, Prof. Edwin J., MOM 1999; Rector, University of Malta, 1964–80 and 1988–91; *b* 8 Sept. 1925; 2nd *s* of late Michael Borg Costanzi and M. Stella (*née* Camilleri); *m* 1948, Lucy Valentino; two *s* one *d*. *Educ:* Lyceum, Malta; Royal University of Malta (BSc, BE&A); Balliol College, Oxford (BA 1946, MA 1952); Malta Rhodes Scholar, 1945. Professor of Mathematics, Royal University of Malta, 1950–64; Vis. Fellow, Univ. of Southampton, 1980–82; Professorial Res. Fellow, 1982–85, Hd of Dept of Computer Sci., 1985–87, Brunel Univ. Chm., 1976–77, Mem., 1965–66, 1968–69, 1972–74, 1977–78, Council of ACU. Chairman: Public Service Reform Commn, 1988–89; Public Service Commn, Malta, 1991–95. Hon. DLitt Malta, 1993. *Address:* 35 Don M. Rua Street, Sliema, SLM 10, Malta. *Clubs:* Casino, Maltese (Valletta, Malta).

BORINGDON, Viscount; Mark Lionel Parker; *b* 22 Aug. 1956; *s* and *heir* of 6th Earl of Morley, *qv*; *m* 1983, Carolyn Jill, *d* of Donald McVicar, Meols, Wirral, Cheshire; three *d*. *Educ:* Eton. Commissioned, Royal Green Jackets, 1976. *Address:* Pound House, Yelverton, Devon PL20 7LJ.

BÖRJESSON, Rolf Libert; Chief Executive, Rexam PLC, since 1996; *b* 27 Sept. 1942; *s* of Stig Allan Börjesson and Brita Ahlström; *m* 1969, Kristina Ivarsson; two *d*. *Educ:* Chalmers Univ., Gothenburg (MSc Chem. Engrg). With Steenberg & Flygt, 1968–71; ITT Europe, Brussels, 1971–74; President: Sund Akesson/Sundpacma, 1974–77; AB Securitas Industrier, 1977–81; Wayne Europe, 1981–87; PLM AB: Exec. Vice Pres., 1987–88; Chief Operating Officer, 1988–90; Pres. and CEO, 1990–96. *Recreations:* shooting, ski-ing, riding. *Address:* Rexam PLC, 4 Millbank, SW1P 3XR. *T:* (020) 7227 4100. *Club:* Naval and Military.

BORLAUG, Norman Ernest, PhD; Consultant, International Center for Maize and Wheat Improvement, since 1979; *b* 25 March 1914; *s* of Henry O. and Clara Vaala Borlaug; *m* 1937, Margaret Gibson; one *s* one *d*. *Educ:* Univ. of Minnesota (BS 1937; MS 1940; PhD 1942). US Forest Service (USDA), 1935–1937–1938; Biologist, Dupont de Nemours & Co, 1942–44; Rockefeller Foundation: Plant Pathologist and Genetist, Wheat Improvement, 1944–60; Associate Dir, Inter-American Food Crop Program, 1960–63; Dir of Wheat Res. and Production Program, International Center for Maize and Wheat Improvement (CIMMYT), 1964–79. Dir, Population Crisis Cttee, 1971; Asesor Especial, Fundación para Estudios de la Población (Mexico), 1971–; Member: Adv. Council, Renewable Natural Resources Foundn, 1973–; Citizens' Commn on Science, Law and Food Supply, 1973–; Council for Agricl Science and Tech., 1973–; Commn on Critical Choices for Americans 1973–. Mem., Nat. Acad. of Scis (USA), 1968; Foreign Mem., Royal Soc., 1987. Outstanding Achievement Award, Univ. of Minnesota, 1959; Sitara-Imtiaz (Star of Distinction) (Pakistan), 1968, Hilal-I-Imtiaz 1978. Nobel Peace Prize, 1970. Holds numerous hon. doctorates in Science, both from USA and abroad; and more than 30 Service Awards by govts and organizations, including US Medal of Freedom, 1977. *Publications:* more than 70 scientific and semi-popular articles. *Recreations:* hunting, fishing, baseball, wrestling, football, golf. *Address:* c/o International Center for Maize and Wheat Improvement (CIMMYT), Apartado Postal 6–641, Lisboa 27, 06600 Mexico DF, Mexico.

BORLEY, Lester, CBE 1993; Secretary General, 1993–96, Member Council, since 1990, Europa Nostra, The Hague; *b* 7 April 1931; *er s* of Edwin Richard Borley and Mary Dorena Davies; *m* Mary Alison, *e d* of Edward John Pearce and Kathleen Florence Barratt; three *d*. *Educ:* Dover Grammar Sch.; Queen Mary Coll. and Birkbeck Coll., London Univ. Pres. of Union, QMC, 1953; Dep. Pres., Univ. of London Union, 1954; ESU debating team tour of USA, 1955. Joined British Travel Assoc., 1955; Asst to Gen. Manager, USA, 1957–61; Manager: Chicago Office, 1961–64; Australia, 1964–67; West Germany, 1967–69; Chief Executive: Scottish Tourist Bd, 1970–75; English Tourist Bd, 1975–83; Dir, Nat. Trust for Scotland, 1983–93. Member: Exec. Cttee, Scotland's Garden Scheme, 1970–75, 1983–93; Council, Nat. Gardens Scheme, 1975–83; Park and Gardens Cttee, Zool Soc. of London, 1979–83; Internat. Cultural Tourism Cttee, ICOMOS, 1990–; Chm., Cultural Tourism Cttee, ICOMOS (UK), 1993–. Advr, World Monuments Fund, NY, 1995–. Governor, Edinburgh Film House, 1987–96 (Hon. Vice Pres., 1996–); Trustee: Cromarty Arts Trust, 1995–; Hopetoun House Preservation Trust, 1998–. Visiting Lecturer: Acad. Istropolitana Nova, Bratislava, 1993–; Coll. of New Europe, Krakow, 1998–; Faculty Mem., Salzburg Seminar, 1996. Founder Fellow, Tourism Soc., 1978. FRSA 1982. Hon. FRSGS 1989. Hon. DLitt Robert Gordon Inst. of Technology, Aberdeen, 1991. Honorable Kentucky Col, 1963. *Publications:* English Cathedrals and Tourism, 1979; Historic Cities and Sustainable Tourism, 1995; Sustaining the Cultural Heritage of Europe, 1998; (ed) Dear Maurice: Culture and Identity in late 20th Century Scotland, 1998; contributor to: Patronage of the Arts by Foundations and NGOs in Europe, 1991; Universal Tourism, 1992; Cultural Tourism, 1994; Manual of Heritage

Management, 1994; Tourism and Culture, 1996; Il Paesaggio Culturale nelle strategia europea, 1996; Preserving the Built Heritage, 1997. *Recreations:* listening to music, looking at pictures, gardening. *Address:* 4 Belford Place, Edinburgh EH4 3DH. *T:* and *Fax:* (0131) 332 2364; The Old Schoolhouse, Wester Elchies, Morayshire AB3 9SD. *Club:* New (Edinburgh).

BORN, Prof. Gustav Victor Rudolf, FRCP 1976; FRS 1972; FKC; Professor of Pharmacology, King's College, University of London, 1978–86, now Emeritus; Research Director, The William Harvey Research Institute, St Bartholomew's Hospital Medical College, since 1989; *b* 29 July 1921; *s* of late Prof. Max Born, FRS; *m* 1st, 1950, Wilfrida Ann Plowden-Wardlaw (marr. diss., 1961); two *s* one *d*; 2nd, 1962, Dr Faith Elizabeth Maurice-Williams; one *s* one *d*. *Educ:* Oberrealschule, Göttingen; Perse Sch., Cambridge; Edinburgh Academy; University of Edinburgh. Vans Dunlop Scholar; MB, ChB, 1943; DPhil (Oxford), 1951, MA 1956. Med. Officer, RAMC, 1943–47; Mem. Scientific Staff, MRC, 1952–53; Research Officer, Nuffield Inst. for Med. Research, 1953–60 and Deptl Demonstrator in Pharmacology, 1956–60, University of Oxford; Vandervell Prof. of Pharmacology, RCS and Univ. of London, 1960–73; Sheild Prof. of Pharmacology, Univ. of Cambridge, and Fellow, Gonville and Caius Coll., Cambridge, 1973–78. Vis. Prof. in Chem., NW Univ., Illinois, 1970; William S. Creasy Vis. Prof. in Clin. Pharmacol., Brown Univ., 1977; Prof. of Fondation de France, Paris, 1982–84. Hon. Dir, MRC Thrombosis Res. Gp, 1964–73. Scientific Advr, Vandervell Foundn, 1967–; Pres., Internat. Soc. on Thrombosis and Haemostasis, 1977–79; Adviser (formerly Trustee), Heineman Med. Res. Center, Charlotte, NC, 1981–; Vice-Pres., Alzheimer Res. Trust, 1997–. Member: Editl Board, Handbook of Experimental Pharmacology; Cttee of Enquiry into Relationship of Pharmaceut. Industry with Nat. Health Service (Sainsbury Cttee), 1965–67; Kuratorium, Lipid Liga, Munich; Kuratorium, Ernst Jung Foundn, Hamburg, 1983–91; Kuratorium, Shakespeare Prize, Hamburg, 1991–98; Forensic Science Adv. Gp, Home Office. Hon. Life Mem., New York Acad. of Scis. Lectures: Beyer, Wisconsin Univ., 1969; Sharpey-Schäfer, Edinburgh Univ., 1973; Cross, RCS, 1974; Wander, Bern Univ., 1974; Johnson Meml, Paris, 1975; Lo Yuk Tong Foundn, Hong Kong Univ., and Heineman Meml, Charlotte, NC, 1978; Carlo Erba Foundn, Milan, 1979; Sir Henry Dale, RCS, 1981; Rokitansky, Vienna, and Oration to Med. Soc., London, 1983. Mem., Akad. Leopoldina; Hon. Mem., German Physiological Soc.; Corresp. Member: German Pharmacological Soc.; Royal Belgian Acad. of Medicine; Rheinisch-Westfälische Akad. der Wissenschaften, Düsseldorf. Hon. Fellow, St Peter's Coll., Oxford, 1972; FKC 1988. Hon. D de l'Univ.: Bordeaux, 1978; Paris, 1987; Hon. MD: Münster, 1980; Leuven, 1981; Edinburgh, 1982; Munich, 1989; Hon. DSc: Brown Univ., 1987; Loyola Univ., 1995. Albrecht von Haller Medal, Göttingen Univ., 1979; Ratschow Medal, Internat. Kur. of Angiology, 1980; Auenbrugger Medal, Graz Univ., 1984; Royal Medal, Royal Soc., 1987; Morawitz Prize, German Soc. for Cardiovascular Res., 1990; Pfleger Prize, Robert Pfleger Foundn, Bamberg, 1990; Alexander von Humboldt Award, 1995; Internat. Sen. Aspirin Prize, 1995; Gold Medal for Medicine, Ernst Jung Foundn, Hamburg, 2001. Chevalier de l'Ordre National de Mérite, France, 1980. *Publications:* articles in scientific jls and books. *Recreations:* music, history, being in the country. *Address:* William Harvey Research Institute, Charterhouse Square, EC1M 6BQ. *T:* (020) 7982 6070; 5 Walden Lodge, 48 Wood Lane, N6 5UU. *Club:* Garrick.

BORODALE, Viscount; Sean David Beatty; *b* 12 June 1973; *s* and *heir* of 3rd Earl Beatty, *qv*.

BORRETT, Louis Albert Frank; a Chairman, Police Disciplinary Appeals, 1987–89; *b* 8 Aug. 1924; *e s* of late Albert B. Borrett and Louise Alfreda Eudoxie Forrestier; *m* 1946, Barbara Betty, *er d* of late Frederick Charles Bamsey and of Lily Gertrude Thompson. *Educ:* France and England; Folkestone Teachers' Trng Coll.; King's Coll., Univ. of London (LLB 1954). Called to the Bar, Gray's Inn, 1955. Served War, Army: volunteered, 1940; RASC, London Dist and South Eastern Comd; commnd Royal Sussex Regt, 1944; served India and Burma Border; Intell. Officer, 9th Royal Sussex, during invasion of Malaya, 1945; GSO III (Ops), ALFSEA, 1946 (Burma Star, Defence Medal, Victory Medal); demob., 1946 (Captain). Schoolmaster, 1947–53; barrister, in practice on South-Eastern circuit, 1955–86; a Recorder, 1980–89. Assist Comr, Boundary Commn, 1964–67. *Recreations:* music, the French language. *Address:* 54 Farm Close, East Grinstead, West Sussex RH19 3QG.

BORRETT, Neil Edgar; non-executive Chairman, Matek Business Media, since 1994; *b* 10 March 1940; *m* 1965; two *d*. *Educ:* Coll. of Estate Management. FRICS 1969. Dir of property cos, 1963–90; Dir, Property Hldgs, DoE, 1990–96; Chief Exec., Property Advisers to the Civil Estate, 1996–97; Dir Urban Estate, Crown Estate, 1997–2000. Gov., South Bank Univ., 1996–. *Address:* Matek Business Media, Genisis House, Field Place Estate, Byfleets Lane, Broadbridge Heath, W Sussex RH12 3PB. *T:* (01403) 276300.

BORRIE, Baron *cr* 1995 (Life Peer), of Abbots Morton in the County of Hereford and Worcester; **Gordon Johnson Borrie,** Kt 1982; QC 1986; Chairman, Advertising Standards Authority, since 2001; *b* 13 March 1931; *s* of Stanley Borrie, Solicitor; *m* 1960, Dorene, *d* of Herbert Toland, Toronto, Canada; no *c*. *Educ:* John Bright Grammar Sch., Llandudno; Univ. of Manchester (LLB, LLM). Barrister-at-Law and Harmsworth Scholar of the Middle Temple; called to Bar, Middle Temple, 1952; Bencher, 1980. Nat. Service: Army Legal Services, HQ Brit. Commonwealth Forces in Korea, 1952–54. Practice as a barrister, London, 1954–57; Lectr and later Sen. Lectr, Coll. of Law, 1957–64; University of Birmingham: Sen. Lectr in Law, 1965–68; Prof. of English Law and Dir, Inst. of Judicial Admin, 1969–76; Dean of Faculty of Law, 1974–76; Hon. Prof. of Law, 1989–; Dir Gen. of Fair Trading, 1976–92. Member: Parole Bd for England and Wales, 1971–74; CNAA Legal Studies Bd, 1971–76; Circuit Adv. Cttee, Birmingham Gp of Courts, 1972–74; Council, Consumers' Assoc., 1972–75; Consumer Protection Adv. Cttee, 1973–76; Equal Opportunities Commn, 1975–76; Chm., Commn on Social Justice, 1992–94. Director: Woolwich plc (formerly Woolwich Building Soc.), 1992–2000; Three Valleys Water, 1992–; Mirror Group, 1993–99; UAPT/Infolink, 1993–94; TeleWest Communications Group, 1994–2001; General Utilities, 1998–. Chm., Accountancy Foundn, 2000–. Mem., H of L Select Cttee on the EC, 1996–2000. Pres., Inst. of Trading Standards Admin, 1992–96 (Vice-Pres., 1985–92, and 1996–). Sen. Treasurer, Nat. Union of Students, 1955–58. Hon. Mem., SPTL, 1989. Contested (Lab): Croydon, NE, 1955; Ilford, S, 1959. Gov., Birmingham Coll. of Commerce, 1966–70. FRSA 1982. Hon. LLD: City of London Polytechnic, 1989; Manchester Univ., 1990; Hull Univ., 1991; Dundee Univ., 1993; W of England Univ., 1997; DUniv Nottingham Trent, 1996. *Publications:* Commercial Law, 1962, 6th edn 1988; The Consumer, Society and the Law (with Prof. A. L. Diamond), 1963, 4th edn 1981; Law of Contempt (with N. V. Lowe), 1973, 3rd edn 1995; The Development of Consumer Law and Policy (Hamlyn Lectures), 1984. *Recreations:* gastronomy, piano playing, travel. *Address:* Manor Farm, Abbots Morton, Worcestershire WR7 4NA. *T:* (01386) 792330; 4 Brick Court, Temple, EC4Y 9AD. *T:* (020) 7353 4434. *Clubs:* Garrick, Reform (Chm., 1990–91).

BORRIELLO, Prof. (Saverio) Peter, PhD; Director, Central Public Health Laboratory, since 1995; *b* 29 Oct. 1953; *s* of Pasquale Borriello and Margaret Rose (*née* Taylor); partner, Helen Georgina Archer; one *s* one *d*. *Educ:* Oldbury Grammar Sch., W Midlands; University Coll. London (BSc; Fellow 1998); Central Public Health Lab. and St Thomas's Hosp. Med. Sch. (PhD 1981). MRCPath 1987, FRCPath 1998. MRC Clinical Research Centre: Upjohn Res. Fellow, 1979–82; Res. Scientist, 1982–86; Head of Gp, 1986–92; University of Nottingham: Head of Gp, Dept of Microbiol., 1992–93; personal chair, 1993; Founding Dir, Inst. of Infections and Immunity, 1993–95; Special Prof., 1996–2001. Vis. Prof., LSHTM, 1997–March 2002. Oakley Lectr, Pathol Soc. of GB and Ireland, 1990. *Publications:* Antibiotic Associated Diarrhoea and Colitis, 1984; Clostridia in Gastro-intestinal Disease, 1985; Clinical and Molecular Aspects of Anaerobes, 1990; papers in scientific jls. *Recreations:* antiques and bric a brac, interesting facts, questioning. *Address:* Central Public Health Laboratory, 61 Colindale Avenue, Colindale, NW9 5HT. *T:* (020) 8358 3223.

BORROW, David Stanley; MP (Lab) South Ribble, since 1997; *b* 2 Aug. 1952; *s* of James Borrow and Nancy (*née* Crawshaw). *Educ:* Mirfield Grammar Sch., W Yorks; Lanchester Poly. (BA Hons Econs). Trainee, Yorkshire Bank, 1973–75; Lancashire Valuation Tribunal: Asst Clerk, 1975–78; Dep. Clerk, 1978–81; Dep. Clerk, Manchester S Valuation Tribunal, 1981–83; Clerk to Tribunal, Merseyside Valuation Tribunal, 1983–97. Pres., Soc. of Clerks of Valuation Tribunals, 1990–92 and 1996–97. Mem. (Lab) Preston BC, 1987– (Leader, 1992–94, 1995–97). *Address:* House of Commons, SW1A 0AA; 117 Garstang Road, Preston PR2 3EB. *T:* (01772) 787792. *Club:* Lostock Hall Labour (Lostock Hall).

BORTHWICK, family name of **Baron Borthwick**.

BORTHWICK, 24th Lord *cr* 1450 (Scot.); **John Hugh Borthwick of That Ilk;** Baron of Heriotmuir and Laird of Crookston, Midlothian; Hereditary Falconer of Scotland to the Queen; DL; landowner; *b* 14 Nov. 1940; *er twin s* of 23rd Lord Borthwick and Margaret Frances (*d* 1976), *d* of Alexander Campbell Cormack; *S* father, 1996; *m* 1974, Adelaide, *d* of A. Birkmyre; two *d*. *Educ:* Gordonstoun; Edinburgh School of Agriculture (SDA, NDA). DL Midlothian, 2001. *Recreations:* wild trout fishing, stalking, stamp and cigarette card collecting. *Heir: twin b* Hon. James Henry Alexander Borthwick, Master of Borthwick [*b* 14 Nov. 1940; *m* 1972, Elspeth, *d* of Lt-Col A. D. MacConachie; one *s*]. *Address:* Crookston, Heriot, Midlothian EH38 5YS. *T:* (01875) 835236. *Club:* New (Edinburgh).

BORTHWICK, Sir John Thomas, 3rd Bt *cr* 1908; MBE 1945; *b* 5 Dec. 1917; *S* to Btcy of uncle (1st and last Baron Whitburgh), 1967; *m* 1st, 1939; three *s*; 2nd, 1962; two *s*. *Heir:* *s* Antony Thomas Borthwick, *b* 12 Feb. 1941.

BORTHWICK, Kenneth W., CBE 1980; JP; DL; Rt Hon. Lord Provost of the City of Edinburgh, 1977–80; Lord Lieutenant of the City and County of Edinburgh, 1977–80; *b* 4 Nov. 1915; *s* of Andrew Graham Borthwick; *m* 1942, Irene Margaret Wilson, *d* of John Graham Wilson, Aberdeen; two *s* one *d*. *Educ:* George Heriot Sch., Edinburgh. Served War of 1939–45: Flying Officer, RAF. Elected Edinburgh Town Council, 1963; Lothian Regional Council, 1974–77; Edinburgh District Council, 1976. Judge of Police, 1972–75. Member: Lothians River Bd, 1969–73; Organising Cttee, Commonwealth Games, Edinburgh, 1970; Edinburgh and Lothian Theatre Trust, 1975–76; Lothian and Borders Police Bd, 1975–77; British Airports Authorities Consultative Cttee, 1977–80; Convention of Scottish Local Authorities, 1977; Scottish Council Develt and Industry, 1977; Chairman: Edinburgh Dist. Licensing Court, 1975–77; Edinburgh Internat. Festival Soc., 1977–80; Edinburgh Military Tattoo Policy Cttee, 1977–80; Queen's Silver Jubilee Edinburgh Appeal Fund, 1977; Organising Cttee, XIII Commonwealth Games, Scotland 1986, 1983–86. Dean, Consular Corps, Edinburgh and Leith, 1991–92. Curator of Patronage, Univ. of Edinburgh, 1977–80. Governor, George Heriot Sch., 1965–73. Vice-President (ex officio): RZS of Scotland, 1977–80; Lowland TA&VRA, 1977–80. DL City of Edinburgh, 1980. Hon. Consul for Malaŵi, 1982, Hon. Consul Gen., 1993–94. OStJ. Commander, Order of the Lion (Malaŵi), 1993. *Recreations:* golf, gardening. *Address:* 17 York Road, Edinburgh EH5 3EJ. *Club:* Caledonian (Hon. Mem.).

BORWICK, family name of **Baron Borwick**.

BORWICK, 4th Baron, *cr* 1922; **James Hugh Myles Borwick;** Bt *cr* 1916; MC 1944; Major HLI retired; *b* 12 Dec. 1917; *s* of 3rd Baron and Irene Phyllis, *d* of late Thomas Main Paterson, Littlebourne, Canterbury; *S* father 1961; *m* 1954, Hyllarie Adalia Mary, *y d* of late Lieut-Col William Hamilton Hall Johnston, DSO, MC, DL, Bryn-y-Groes, Bala, N Wales; four *d*. *Educ:* Eton; RMC, Sandhurst. Commissioned as 2nd Lieut HLI, 1937; Capt. 1939; Major 1941; retired, 1947. *Recreations:* field sports, sailing. *Heir: half b* Hon. Robin Sandbach Borwick [*b* 22 March 1927; *m* 1950, Hon. Patricia Garnett, *o d* of Baron McAlpine of Moffat; two *s* one *d*]. *Address:* Leys Farm, Bircher, Leominster, Hereford HR6 0AZ. *T:* (01568) 780367. *Club:* Royal Ocean Racing.

BORYSIEWICZ, Prof. Sir Leszek (Krzysztof), Kt 2001; PhD; FRCP; Principal, Imperial College School of Medicine, since 2001; *b* 13 April 1951; *s* of Jan Borysiewicz and Zofia Helena Woloszyn; *m* 1976, Gwenllian Sian Jones; two *d*. *Educ:* Cardiff High Sch.; Welsh Nat. Sch. of Medicine (BSc, MB BCh 1975); Univ. of London (PhD 1986). MRCP 1979, FRCP 1989. Hosp. appts at University Hosp. of Wales, Hammersmith Hosp., Nat. Hosp. for Nervous Diseases and Ealing Hosp., 1975–79; Registrar, Dept of Medicine, Hammersmith Hosp., 1979–80; Royal Postgraduate Medical School: MRC Clinical Trng Fellow, 1980–82; Lister Res. Fellow and Sen. Lectr, 1982–86; Wellcome Trust Sen. Lectr in Infectious Diseases, Addenbrooke's Hosp., Cambridge, 1987–88; Lectr in Medicine, Univ. of Cambridge, 1988–91; Prof. of Medicine, Univ. of Wales Coll. of Medicine, 1991–2001. Mem., MRC, 1995–2000 (Chm., Molecular and Cell Bd, 1996–2000). Founder FMedSci 1998. Mem., Polish Acad. Arts and Scis, 1996. *Publications:* papers on immunology and pathogenesis of virus infection and viral induced cancer. *Recreations:* Rugby football, cricket. *Address:* Imperial College School of Medicine, South Kensington Campus, SW7 2AZ. *T:* (020) 7594 8800, *Fax:* (020) 7594 9833; *e-mail:* l.borysiewicz@ic.ac.uk.

BOSANQUET, Prof. Nicholas; Professor of Health Policy, Imperial College, University of London, since 1993; *b* 17 Jan. 1942; *s* of Lt Col Neville Richard Gustavus Bosanquet and Nancy Bosanquet; *m* 1st, 1974, Anne Connolly (marr. diss. 1993); two *d*; 2nd, 1996, Anna Zarzecka. *Educ:* Winchester Coll.; Clare Coll., Cambridge (BA Hist.); Yale Univ. (Mellon Fellow); London Sch. of Econs (MSc Econs). Econ. Advr, NBPI, 1967–69; Lecturer in Economics: LSE, 1969–72; King's Fund Coll., 1973–86; City Univ., 1977–84; Sen. Research Fellow, Centre for Health Econs, Univ. of York, 1984–88; Prof. of Health Policy, RHBNC, Univ. of London, 1988–93. Special Advr, Health Cttee, H of C, 1988–90, 2000–. Consultant: WHO, 1989; World Bank, 1993. Arbitrator, ACAS, 1983–90. Non-executive Director: Abbey Health, 1998–2000; TTH Primary Care Trust, 2001–. Health Policy Advr, Care UK plc, 1995–. MInstD. *Publications:* Industrial Relations in the NHS: the search for a system, 1980; After the New Right, 1983; Family Doctors and Economic Incentives, 1989; contrib. to econ. and med. jls. *Recreations:* visiting battlefields, brainstorming with Americans and others about military history. *Address:* 231 High Street, Hampton Hill, Middx TW12 1NP.

BOSCAWEN, family name of **Viscount Falmouth**.

BOSCAWEN, Rt Hon. Robert Thomas, MC 1944; PC 1992; *b* 17 March 1923; 4th *s* of 8th Viscount Falmouth and Dowager Viscountess Falmouth, CBE; *m* 1949, Mary Alice, JP London 1961, *e d* of Col Sir Geoffrey Ronald Codrington, KCVO, CB, CMG, DSO, OBE, TD; one *s* two *d*. *Educ:* Eton; Trinity College, Cambridge. Served Coldstream Guards, 1941–50 (with 1st (armoured) Bn Coldstream Guards, Normandy to N Germany, wounded 1945); NW Europe, 1944–45; attached to British Red Cross Civilian Relief Orgn in occupied Europe, 1946–47. Mem., London Exec. Council, Nat. Health Service, 1954–65; Underwriting Mem. of Lloyd's, 1952–. Contested Falmouth and Camborne (C), 1964, 1966; MP (C) Wells, 1970–83, Somerton and Frome, 1983–92. An Asst Govt Whip, 1979–81; a Lord Comr of HM Treasury, 1981–83; Vice-Chamberlain of HM Household, 1983–86, Comptroller, 1986–88. Mem., Select Cttee on Expenditure, 1974; Vice-Chm., Conservative Parly Health and Social Security Cttee, 1974–79. Mem. Parly Delegns, USSR 1977, Nepal 1981; led Parly Delegn to UN Assembly, 1987, to Canada, 1991. *Recreations:* sailing, shooting. *Address:* Ivythorn Manor, Street, Somerset BA16 0TZ. *Clubs:* Pratt's; Royal Yacht Squadron.

BOSE, Mihir, FICA; freelance author and journalist, since 1987; *b* 12 Jan. 1947; *s* of Kiran Chandra Bose and Sova Rani Bose; *m* 1986, Kalpana (marr. diss. 1999); one *d*. *Educ:* St Xavier's High Sch.; St Xavier's Coll., Bombay (BSc Physics and Maths). Cricket Corresp., LBC, 1974–75; For. Corresp., Sunday Times, Spectator, New Society, 1975–78; freelance writer, 1979; Editor: Property Guide, 1980–81; International Fund Guide, 1980–81; Pensions, 1981–83; Financial Planning Ed. 1983–84, City Ed. 1984–86, Dep. Ed. 1985–86, Financial Weekly; City Features Ed., London Daily News, 1986–87; freelance writer, mainly on regular contract basis, specialising in finance, sports and feature writing for Sunday Times, Spectator, Mail on Sunday, Daily Telegraph, Independent, The Times, Guardian, 1987–. Mem., Gambling Review Body, Home Office, 2000–01. *Publications:* Keith Miller, 1979, 2nd edn 1980; The Lost Hero, 1982; All in a Day's Work, 1983; The Aga Khan, 1984; A Maidan View, 1986; The Crash, 1988, 3rd edn 1989, incl. Jap. edn; Insurance: are you covered?, 1988, 2nd edn 1991; Crash – a new money crisis, 1989; (jtly) Fraud, 1989; Cricket Voices, 1990; How to Invest in a Bear Market, 1990; History of Indian Cricket, 1990; Michael Grade: screening the image, 1992; (jtly) Behind Closed Doors, 1992; Sporting Colours, 1994; False Messiah: the life and times of Terry Venables, 1996; Sporting Alien, 1996; Sporting Babylon, 1999; Manchester Unlimited: the rise and rise of the world's premier football club, 1999. *Recreations:* running his own cricket team, reading, films, travelling. *Clubs:* Reform, MCC; Saturday (Calcutta).

BOSNICH, Prof. Brice, PhD; FRS 2000; Professor of Chemistry, University of Chicago, since 1987; *b* 3 June 1936; *s* of Frank Bosnich and Zorka (*née* Setimo); *m* 1992, Jayne Seberling. *Educ:* St Gregory's Coll., Australia; Univ. of Sydney (BSc); ANU (PhD 1962). DSIR Fellow, 1962–63, ICI Fellow, 1963–66, Lectr, 1966–69, UCL; University of Toronto: Associate Prof., 1969–75; Prof., 1975–87; Killam Fellow, 1979–81. Noranda Award in Inorganic Chem., CIC, 1978; Organometallic Award, 1994, Nyholm Award Medal, 1995, RSC; Award in Inorganic Chem., ACS, 1998. *Publications:* Asymmetric Catalysis, 1993; contrib. numerous papers to learned scientific jls. *Recreations:* art, Asian collection. *Address:* Department of Chemistry, University of Chicago, 5735 South Ellis Avenue, Chicago, IL 60637, USA. *T:* (773) 7020287.

BOSONNET, Paul Graham, CBE 1995; Chairman, G. A. Day, since 1996; *b* 12 Sept. 1932; *s* of Edgar Raymond Bosonnet and Sylvia Gladys Cradock; *m* 1958, Joan Colet Cunningham; one *s* two *d*. *Educ:* St John's College, Southsea. FCA. Accountant, British Oxygen Co., 1957; Dir, BOC International, 1976; Dep. Chm., BOC Gp, 1985–92; Dep. Chm., British Telecommunications plc, 1991–95. Chm., Logica, 1990–95; Director: MAM Gp, 1991–98; Lucas Varity (formerly Lucas Industries), 1993–97. Vice Chm., Council, Royal Holloway (formerly RHBNC), Univ. of London, 1986–95. *Recreations:* genealogy, walking. *Address:* The Old House Cottage, Pyrford Road, Pyrford, Surrey GU22 8UE. *T:* (01932) 342991.

BOSSANO, Hon. Joseph John; MP (Gibraltar Socialist Labour Party); Chief Minister, Gibraltar, 1988–96; *b* 10 June 1939; *s* of Maria Teresa and Oscar Bossano; *m* (marr. diss.); three *s* one *d*; *m* 1988, Rose Torrilla. *Educ:* Gibraltar Grammar School; Univ. of London (BScEcon); Univ. of Birmingham (BA). Factory worker, 1958–60; Seaman, 1960–64; Health Inspector, 1964–68; student, 1968–72; building worker, 1972–74; Union leader, 1974–88; MP 1972–; Leader of Opposition, 1984–88. *Recreations:* thinking, cooking, gardening. *Address:* 2 Gowlands Ramp, Gibraltar.

BOSSOM, Hon. Sir Clive, 2nd Bt *cr* 1953; *b* 4 Feb. 1918; *s* of late Baron Bossom (Life Peer); *S* to father's Baronetcy, 1965; *m* 1951, Lady Barbara North, *sister* of 9th Earl of Guilford; three *s* one *d*. *Educ:* Eton. Regular Army, The Buffs, 1939–48; served Europe and Far East. Kent County Council, 1949–52; Chm. Council Order of St John for Kent, 1951–56; Mem. Chapter General, Order of St John (Mem., Jt Cttee, 1961–93; Chm., Ex-Services War Disabled Help and Homes Dept, 1973–87; Almoner, 1987–93). Contested (C) Faversham Div., 1951 and 1955. MP (C) Leominster Div., Herefordshire, 1959–Feb. 1974; Parliamentary Private Secretary: to Jt Parly Secs, Min. of Pensions and Nat. Insce, 1960–62; to Sec. of State for Air, 1962–64; to Minister of Defence for RAF, 1964; to Home Secretary, 1970–72. Chm., Europ Assistance Ltd, 1973–88. President: Anglo-Belgian Union, 1970–73, 1983–85 (Vice-Pres., 1974–82, 1985–); Anglo-Netherlands Soc., 1978–89 (Vice Pres., 1989–); BARC, 1985–91; Vice-President: Industrial Fire Protection Assoc., 1981–88; Fédération Internationale de L'Automobile, 1975–81 (Vice-Pres. d'Honneur, 1982–); Internat. Social Service, 1989– (Internat. Pres., 1984–89); Chairman: RAC, 1975–78 (Vice Pres., 1998–); RAC Motor Sports Council, 1975–81; RAC Motor Sports Assoc. Ltd, 1979–82; Iran Soc. 1973–76; Mem. Council, RGS, 1982–86. Trustee, Brooklands Museum Trust, 1987–95; Vice-Pres., First Gear Foundn, 1996–. Liveryman of Worshipful Company of Grocers (Master, 1979). FRSA (Mem. Council, 1971–77). KStJ 1961. Badge of Honour, British Red Cross, 1993. Comdr, Order of Leopold II; Order of Homayoun III (Iran), 1977; Comdr, Order of the Crown (Belgium), 1977; Kt Comdr, Order of Orange Nassau (Netherlands), 1980. *Recreation:* travel. *Heir:* *s* Bruce Charles Bossom [*b* 22 Aug. 1952; *m* 1985, Penelope Jane, *d* of late Edward Holland-Martin and of Mrs Holland-Martin, Overbury Court, Glos; one *s* two *d*]. *Address:* 97 Cadogan Lane, SW1X 9DU. *T:* (020) 7245 6531; Rotherdown, Grove Lane, Petworth, Sussex GU28 0BT. *T:* (01798) 342329. *Clubs:* Royal Automobile, Carlton.

BOSSY, Prof. John Antony, PhD; FRHistS; FBA 1993; Professor of History, University of York, 1979–2000, now Emeritus; *b* 30 April 1933; *s* of Frederick James Bossy and Kate Louise Fanny Bossy (*née* White). *Educ:* St Ignatius' Coll., London; Queens' Coll., Cambridge (BA 1954; PhD 1961). FRHistS 1975. Res. Fellow, Queens' Coll., Cambridge, 1959–62; Lectr in Hist., Goldsmiths' Coll., London, 1962–66; Lectr, then Reader, in Mod. Hist., QUB, 1966–78. Mem., Editl Bd, Past and Present, 1972–. *Publications:* The English Catholic Community 1570–1850, 1976; Christianity in the West 1400–1700, 1984; Giordano Bruno and the Embassy Affair, 1991; Peace in the Post-Reformation, 1998. *Recreations:* chess, piano, smoking. *Address:* 80 Stockton Lane, York YO31 1BS. *T:* (01904) 424801.

See also Rev. M. J. F. Bossy.

BOSSY, Rev. Michael Joseph Frederick, SJ; Assistant Priest, Corpus Christi Church, Brixton, since 1998; Rector, Stonyhurst College, 1993–97 (Headmaster, 1972–85); *b* 22 Nov. 1929; *s* of F. J. Bossy and K. Bossy (*née* White). *Educ:* St Ignatius Coll., Stamford Hill; Heythrop Coll., Oxon (STL); Oxford Univ. (MA). Taught at: St Ignatius Coll., Stamford Hill, 1956–59; St Francis Xavier's Coll., Liverpool, 1963–64; Stonyhurst Coll., 1965–85; Asst Priest, 1986–88, Rector and Parish Priest, 1988–92, Parish of St Aloysius, Glasgow; Actg Parish Priest, St Mary of the Angels, Liverpool, 1998. *Recreation:* watching games. *Address:* Corpus Christi, 11 Trent Road, Brixton Hill, SW2 5BJ.

See also J. A. Bossy.

BOSTOCK, Prof. Christopher John, PhD; Director, BBSRC Institute for Animal Health, since 1997; *b* 29 May 1942; *s* of John Major Leslie Bostock and Mildred Lilian Bostock; *m* 1st, 1963, Yvonne Pauline Kendrick (marr. diss. 1990); one *s* two *d*; 2nd, 1992, Patricia Roberts. *Educ:* Univ. of Edinburgh (BSc Hons; Sir Ramsay Wright Post-Grad. Schol., 1965; PhD 1968). Univ. Demonstr., Univ. of Edinburgh, 1965–69; Vis. Fellow, Univ. of Colorado, 1969–71; Res. Fellow, Univ. of St Andrews, 1971–72; Res. Scientist, MRC Clin. and Population Cytogenetics Unit, Edinburgh, 1972–77; Res. Scientist, 1977–83, Asst Dir, 1983–85, MRC Mammalian Genome Unit; Head of Molecular Biology: Animal Virus Res. Inst., AFRC, 1985–89; Inst. for Animal Health, AFRC, then BBSRC, 1989–97. Visiting Professor: Univ. of Wisconsin, 1985; Dept of Clin. Veterinary Sci., Univ. of Bristol, 1998–; Sch. of Animal and Microbial Scis, Univ. of Reading, 2000–. *Publications:* (with Adrian Sumner) The Eukaryotic Chromosome, 1978; scientific res. papers on chromosomes, tumour cell drug resistance, infectious disease agents. *Recreations:* French country life, walking, building. *Address:* Institute for Animal Health, Compton, Newbury, Berks RG20 7NN.

BOSTOCK, David John, CMG 1998; Head of European Secretariat, Cabinet Office, 1999–2000; *b* 11 April 1948; *s* of John C. Bostock and Gwendoline G. (*née* Lee); *m* 1975, Beth Ann O'Byrne; one *s* one *d*. *Educ:* Cheltenham Grammar Sch.; Balliol Coll., Oxford (BA Mod. Hist. 1969); University Coll. London (MSc Econs of Public Policy 1978). VSO, Indonesia, 1970. Joined HM Treasury, 1971; Second Sec., Office of UK Permanent Rep. to EC, 1973–75; Principal: HM Treasury, 1975–81; Cabinet Office (Economic Secretariat), 1981–83; Asst Sec., HM Treasury, 1983–85; Financial and Econ. Counsellor, Office of UK Permanent Rep. to EC, 1985–89; Under Sec. and Head of EC Gp, HM Treasury, 1990–94; UK Dep. Perm. Rep. to EU, 1995–98. *Recreations:* choral singing, walking, looking at old buildings, drinking beer. *Address:* Cabinet Office, 70 Whitehall, SW1A 2AS.

BOSTOCK, Prof. Hugh, PhD; FRS 2001; Professor of Neurophysiology, Institute of Neurology, University College London, since 1996; *b* 25 Aug. 1944; *s* of Edward and Alice Bostock; *m* 1975, Kate Shaw; two *s* one *d*. *Educ:* Merton Coll., Oxford (BA); University Coll. London (MSc, PhD 1974). Institute of Neurology, London University, 1974–: Lectr, 1976–87; Sen. Lectr, 1987–92; Reader, 1992–96. *Publications:* contrib. papers to Jl Physiol., Brain and similar jls. *Address:* Newton House, Bridge Street, Olney, Bucks MK46 4AB.

BOSTOCK, James Edward, RE 1961 (ARE 1947); ARCA London; painter and engraver; *b* Hanley, Staffs, 11 June 1917; *s* of William George Bostock, pottery and glass-worker, and Amy (*née* Titley); *m* 1939, Gwladys Irene (*née* Griffiths); three *s*. *Educ:* Borden Grammar Sch., Sittingbourne; Medway Sch. of Art, Rochester; Royal College of Art. War Service as Sgt in Durham LI and Royal Corps of Signals. Full-time Teacher, 1946–78; Vice-Principal, West of England Coll. of Art, 1965–70; Academic Develt Officer, Bristol Polytechnic, 1970–78. Elected Mem. of Soc. of Wood Engravers, 1950. Mem. Council. Soc. of Staffs Artists, 1963. Mem., E Kent Art Soc., 1980. Exhibited water-colours, etchings, wood engravings and drawings at RA, NEAC, RBA, RE, RI and other group exhibitions and in travelling exhibitions to Poland, Czechoslovakia, South Africa, Far East, New Zealand, USA, Sweden, Russia and Baltic States, and the provinces. One-man shows: Mignon Gall., Bath; Univ. of Bristol; Bristol Polytechnic; Margate Liby Gall.; Deal Liby Gall.; Broadstairs Liby Gall.; Folkestone Liby Gall.; Phillip Maslen Gall., Canterbury; Exeter Mus.; Hereford Mus.; Oxford Univ.; 20th Century Gall., SW6. Works bought by V & A Museum, British Museum, British Council, Hull, Swindon, Stoke-on-Trent and Bristol Education Cttees, Hunt Botanical Library, Pittsburgh, Hereford Mus., Medici Soc., and private collectors. Commissioned work for: ICI Ltd, British Museum (Nat. Hist.), Odhams Press, and other firms and public authorities. *Publications:* Roman Lettering for Students, 1959; wood engraved illustrations to Poems of Edward Thomas, 1988; articles in: Times, Guardian, Staffordshire Sentinel, Studio, Artist; reproductions in: Garrett, History of British Wood Engraving, 1978; Garrett, British Wood Engraving of the Twentieth Century, 1980. *Address:* White Lodge, 80 Lindenthorpe Road, Broadstairs, Kent CT10 1DB. *T:* (01843) 869782.

BOSTON, family name of **Baron Boston of Faversham**.

BOSTON, 10th Baron *cr* 1761; **Timothy George Frank Boteler Irby;** Bt 1704; *b* 27 March 1939; *s* of 9th Baron Boston, MBE, and Erica N. (*d* 1990), *d* of T. H. Hill; *S* father, 1978; *m* 1967, Rhonda Anne, *d* of R. A. Bate; two *s* one *d*. *Educ:* Clayesmore School, Dorset; Southampton Univ. (BSc Econ.). *Heir:* *s* Hon. George William Eustace Boteler Irby, BSc [*b* 1 Aug. 1971; *m* 1998, Nicola Sydney Mary, *d* of William Reid; one *s* one *d*]. *Address:* Cae'r Borth, Moelfre, Anglesey LL72 8NN. *T:* (01248) 410249.

BOSTON OF FAVERSHAM, Baron *cr* 1976 (Life Peer), of Faversham, Kent; **Terence George Boston;** QC 1981; barrister; a Deputy Speaker, House of Lords, since 1991; *b* 21 March 1930; *yr surv. s* of late George T. Boston and Kate (*née* Bellati); *m* 1962, Margaret Joyce (Member: SE Metropolitan Regional Hospital Board, 1970–74; Mental Health Review Appeals Tribunal (SE Metropolitan area), 1970–74; market research consultant), *er d* of late R. H. J. Head and Mrs E. M. Winters, and step *d* of late H. F. Winters, Melbourne, Australia. *Educ:* Woolwich Polytechnic Sch.; King's Coll., University of London. Dep. President, University of London Union, 1955–56. Commnd in RAF during Nat. Service, 1950–52; later trained as pilot with University of London Air Sqdn. Called to the Bar, Inner Temple, 1960. BBC News Sub-Editor, External Services, 1957–60; Senior BBC Producer (Current Affairs), 1960–64; also Producer of Law in Action series (Third Programme), 1962–64. Chm., TVS Entertainment, 1980–90. Joined Labour Party, 1946; contested (Lab) Wokingham, 1955 and 1959; MP (Lab) Faversham, Kent, June 1964–70; PPS to: Minister of Public Building and Works, 1964–66; Minister of Power, 1966–68; Minister of Transport, 1968–69; Asst Govt Whip, 1969–70; Minister of State, Home Office, 1979; opp. front bench spokesman on home affairs, 1979–84, on defence, 1984–86; Prin. Dep. Chm. of Cttees, 1992–94, Chm. of Cttees, 1994–2000, H of L. UK Deleg. to UN Gen. Assembly, XXXIst, XXXIInd and XXXIIIrd Sessions, 1976–78. Member: Executive Cttee, International Union of Socialist Youth, 1950; Select Cttee on Broadcasting Proceedings of Parliament, 1966; Speaker's Conference on Electoral Law, 1965–68. Trustee, Parly Lab. Party Benevolent Fund, 1967–70. Founder

Vice-Chm., Great Britain—East Europe Centre, 1967–69; Chm., The Sheppey Gp, 1967–. *Recreations:* opera (going, not singing), fell-walking. *Address:* House of Lords, SW1A 0PW.

BOSTON, David Merrick, OBE 1976; MA; Director (formerly Curator), Horniman Public Museum and Public Park Trust (formerly Horniman Museum and Library), London, 1965–93; Hon. Curator, and tenant of National Trust, Quebec House; *b* 15 May 1931; *s* of late Dr H. M. Boston, Salisbury, Wilts; *m* 1961, Catharine, *d* of Rev. Prof. E. G. S. Parrinder, *qv*; one *s* two *d*. *Educ:* Rondebosch, Cape Town; Bishop Wordsworth's, Salisbury; Selwyn Coll., Cambridge; Univ. of Cape Town. BA History Cantab 1954; MA 1958. RAF, 1950–51; Adjt, Marine Craft Trng School. Field survey, S African Inst. of Race Relations, 1955; Keeper of Ethnology, Liverpool Museums, 1956–62; Asst Keeper, British Museum, New World archaeology and ethnography, 1962–65. Chm., British Nat. Cttee of Internat. Council of Museums, 1976–80; Vice-Chm., Internat. Cttee for Museums of Ethnography, 1989–95; Member, Council: Museums Assoc., 1969–70; Royal Anthropological Inst., 1969 and 1998– (Vice-Pres., 1972–75, 1977–80, 1995–98, Hon. Sec., 1985–88, Hon. Librarian, 1992–). Visiting Scientist: National Museum of Man, Ottawa, 1970; Japan Foundation, Tokyo, 1986. Consultant, Prog. for Belize, 1994–. Gov., Dolmetsch Foundn, 1983–. Vice President: Dulwich Decorative & Fine Arts Soc., 1987–; Friends of the Horniman, 1995–99; Mem. Cttee, Wolfe Soc., 1999–. Trustee, Haslemere Museum, 1996–. FMA; FRAS; FRGS; FRSA. Ordenom Jugoslavenske Zastave sa zlatnom zvezdom na ogrlici (Yugoslavia), 1981. *Publications:* Pre-Columbian Pottery of the Americas, 1980; contribs to learned jls and encyclopaedias and on Pre-European America, in World Ceramics (ed R. J. Charleston). *Address:* Quebec House, Westerham, Kent TN16 1TD. *T:* (01959) 562206.

BOSTON, Richard; writer; *b* 29 Dec. 1938. *Educ:* Stowe; Regent Street Polytechnic School of Art; King's Coll., Cambridge (MA). Taught English in Sicily, Sweden and Paris; acted in Jacques Tati's Playtime. Glenfiddich Special Award, 1976. Editorial staff of Peace News, TLS, New Society; columnist and feature writer, The Guardian, at intervals, 1972–2001. Editor: The Vole, 1977–80; Quarto, 1979–82. *Publications:* The Press We Deserve (ed), 1969; An Anatomy of Laughter, 1974; The Admirable Urquhart, 1975; Beer and Skittles, 1976; Baldness Be My Friend, 1977; The Little Green Book, 1979; C. O. Jones's Compendium of Practical Jokes, 1982; Osbert: a portrait of Osbert Lancaster, 1989; Boudu Saved from Drowning, 1994; Starkness at Noon, 1997. *Recreation:* procrastination. *Address:* The Old School, Aldworth, Reading, Berks RG8 9TJ. *T:* (01635) 578587.

BOSTRIDGE, Dr Ian Charles; concert and operatic tenor; *b* 25 Dec. 1964; *s* of late Leslie John Bostridge and of Lilian Winifred (*née* Clark); *m* 1992, Lucasta Miller; one *s*. *Educ:* Dulwich Coll. Prep. Sch.; Westminster Sch. (Queen's Schol.); St John's Coll., Oxford (MA, DPhil Hist. 1990); St John's Coll., Cambridge (MPhil Hist. and Philosophy of Sci.). North Sen. Schol., St John's Coll., Oxford, 1988–90; Jun. Res. Fellow, and British Acad. Postdoctoral Res. Fellow, Corpus Christi Coll., Oxford, 1992–95. Professional début as Young Sailor in Tristan, RFH/LPO, 1993; operatic stage début as Lysander, Midsummer Night's Dream, Australian Opera at Edinburgh Fest., 1994; Royal Opera House début, Salome, 1995; Wigmore Hall recital début, 1995; début with ENO, Tamino, 1996; Carnegie Hall début, 1999; other rôles include: Nerone, L'Incoronazione di Poppaea; Belmonte, Die Entführung aus dem Serail; Vasek, The Bartered Bride; Quint, The Turn of the Screw; recitals include: Munich, Salzburg and Berlin Fests, Châtelet; Concertgebouw; Lincoln Center; Schubert's Winterreise (film and documentary), Channel 4, 1997 (Prague TV Award). Maggio Musicale. Has made numerous recordings. NFMS award, 1990; Young Concert Artists' Trust award, 1992; Début Award, Royal Philharmonic Soc., 1995; Solo Vocal Award, Gramophone, 1996, 1998; Classical Music Award, South Bank Show, 1996; Munich Fest. Prize, 1998; Choc de l'Année Award, 1998; Edison Award, 1999. *Publications:* Witchcraft and its Transformations c1650–c1750, 1997; reviews and articles in The Times, TLS, Wall St Jl, etc. *Recreations:* reading, cooking, looking at pictures. *Address:* c/o Askonas Holt Ltd, Lonsdale Chambers, 27 Chancery Lane, WC2A 1PF. *T:* (020) 7400 1700, *Fax:* (020) 7400 1799.

BOSVILLE MACDONALD OF SLEAT, Sir Ian Godfrey, 17th Bt, *cr* 1625; DL; FRICS, MRSH; 25th Chief of Sleat; *b* 18 July 1947; *er s* of Sir (Alexander) Somerled Angus Bosville Macdonald of Sleat, 16th Bt, MC, 24th Chief of Sleat and of Mary, Lady Bosville Macdonald of Sleat; *S* father 1958; *m* 1970, Juliet Fleury, *o d* of late Maj.-Gen. J. M. D. Ward-Harrison, OBE, MC; one *s* two *d*. *Educ:* Pinewood Sch.; Eton Coll.; Royal Agricultural Coll. ARICS 1972; FRICS 1986. Member (for Bridlington South), Humberside CC, 1981–84. MRSH 1972; Mem., Econ. Res. Council, 1979–. Chairman: Rural Develt Commn, Humberside, 1988–95; Rural Partnership ER of Yorks Council, 2000–; President: Humber and Wolds Rural Community Council, 1996–; British Food and Farming in Humberside, 1989; Humberside Young Farmers, 1989–96; British Red Cross: Mem. Council and Trustee, 1995–97; Nat. Trustee, 2001–; Chm., N of England Reg., 2000–; President: Humberside Br., 1988–96; Hull and ER Br., 1996–. High Sheriff, Humberside, 1988–89; DL ER of Yorks, 1997. *Heir: s* Somerled Alexander Bosville Macdonald, younger of Sleat, *b* 30 Jan. 1976. *Recreation:* ornithology. *Address:* Thorpe Hall, Rudston, Driffield, East Yorkshire YO25 4JE. *T:* (01262) 420239. *Clubs:* Lansdowne, White's; New, Puffin's (Edinburgh).

BOSWALL, Sir (Thomas) Alford H.; *see* Houstoun-Boswall.

BOSWELL, Lt-Gen. Sir Alexander (Crawford Simpson), KCB 1982; CBE 1974 (OBE 1971; MBE 1962); DL; Lieutenant-Governor and Commander-in-Chief, Guernsey, 1985–90; *b* 3 Aug. 1928; *s* of Alexander Boswell Simpson Boswell and Elizabeth Burns Simpson Boswell (*née* Park); *m* 1956, Jocelyn Leslie Blundstone Pomfret, *d* of Surg. Rear-Adm. A. A. Pomfret, CB, OBE; five *s*. *Educ:* Merchiston Castle Sch.; RMA, Sandhurst. Enlisted in Army, 1947; Commnd, Argyll and Sutherland Highlanders, Dec. 1948; regimental appts, Hong Kong, Korea, UK, Suez, Guyana, 1949–58; sc Camberley, 1959; Mil. Asst (GS02) to GOC Berlin, 1960–62; Co. Comdr, then Second in Comd, 1 A and SH, Malaya and Borneo, 1963–65 (despatches 1965); Directing Staff, Staff Coll., Camberley, 1965–68; CO, 1 A and SH, 1968–71; Col GS Trng Army Strategic Comd, 1971; Brig. Comdg 39 Inf. Bde, 1972–74; COS, 1st British Corps, 1974–76; NDC (Canada), 1976–77; GOC 2nd Armd Div., 1978–80; Dir, TA and Cadets, 1980–82; GOC Scotland and Governor of Edinburgh Castle, 1982–85. Chairman: Scottish Veterans' Residences, 1991–; Officers Assoc. (Scottish Br.), 1991–98. Col, Argyll and Sutherland Highlanders, 1972–82; Hon. Col, Tayforth Univs OTC, 1982–86; Col Comdt, Scottish Div., 1982–86; Hon. Col, Scottish Transport Regt RLC(V), 1993–96. Captain of Tarbet, 1974–82. KStJ 1985. DL East Lothian, 1993. *Address:* c/o Bank of Scotland, 52 Shandwick Place, Edinburgh EH2 4SB.

BOSWELL, Lindsay Alice; QC 1997; *b* Nairobi, 22 Nov. 1958; *d* of Graham Leonard William Boswell and Erica Boswell (*née* Mayers); *m* 1987, Jonathan James Acton Davis, *qv*; one *s*. *Educ:* St Mary's, Ascot; Brooke House; University Coll. London (BSc Econ Hons); City Univ. (Dip. Law). Called to the Bar, Gray's Inn, 1982. *Recreation:* gardens. *Address:* 4 Pump Court, Temple, EC4Y 7AN. *T:* (020) 7842 5555.

BOSWELL, Timothy Eric; MP (C) Daventry, since 1987; *b* 2 Dec. 1942; *s* of late Eric New Boswell and of Joan Winifred Caroline Boswell; *m* 1969, Helen Delahay, *d* of Rev. Arthur Rees; three *d*. *Educ:* Marlborough Coll.; New Coll., Oxford (MA; Dip. Agricl Econs). Conservative Res. Dept, 1966–73 (Head of Econ. Section, 1970–73); managed family farming business, 1974–87; part-time Special Adviser to Minister of Agriculture, Fisheries and Food, 1984–86. Chm., Leics, Northants and Rutland Counties Br., NFU, 1983; Mem. Council, 1966–90, Pres., 1984–90, Perry Foundn (for Agricl Res.); Mem., AFRC, 1988–90. PPS to Financial Sec. to the Treasury, 1989–90; an Asst Govt Whip, 1990–92; a Lord Comr of HM Treasury (a Govt Whip), 1992; Parly Under-Sec. of State, DFE, 1992–95; Parly Sec., MAFF, 1995–97; Opposition frontbench spokesman on Treasury matters, 1997, on trade and industry, 1997–99, on further and higher educn and disabilities, 1999–2001. Mem., Select Cttee for Agriculture, 1987–89; Sec., Cons. Backbench Cttee on Agriculture, 1987–89; Chm., All-Party Charity Law Review Panel, 1988–90. Treas., 1976–79, Chm., 1979–83, Daventry Constituency Cons. Assoc. Contested (C) Rugby, Feb. 1974. *Recreations:* the countryside, shooting, snooker, poetry. *Address:* House of Commons, SW1A 0AA. *T:* (020) 7219 3520. *Club:* Farmers'.

BOSWOOD, Anthony Richard; QC 1986; *b* 1 Oct. 1947; *s* of late Noel Gordon Paul Boswood and of Cicily Ann Watson; *m* 1973, Sarah Bridget Alexander; three *d*. *Educ:* St Paul's Sch.; New Coll., Oxford (BCL, MA). Called to Bar, Middle Temple, 1970, Bencher, 1995. *Recreations:* opera, riding, gardening, olive farming. *Address:* Fountain Court, Temple, EC4Y 9DH. *T:* (020) 7583 3335; Podere Casanuova, Pieveasciata, Castelnuovo Berardenga (SI), Italy; South Hay House, Binsted, Alton, Hants GU35 9NR; *e-mail:* a.boswood@dial.pipex.com.

BOSWORTH, Prof. Clifford Edmund, FBA 1992; Professor of Arabic Studies, Manchester University, 1967–90, now Emeritus; Hon. Fellow, Manchester University, since 1990; *b* 29 Dec. 1928; *s* of Clifford Bosworth and Gladys Constance Gregory; *m* 1957, Annette Ellen Todd; three *d*. *Educ:* St John's College, Oxford (MA Mod. Hist.); Edinburgh Univ. (MA Arabic, Persian, Turkish; PhD). Dept of Agriculture for Scotland, 1952–54; Lectr in Arabic, St Andrews Univ., 1956–67. Vis. Associate Prof., Univ. of Toronto, 1965–66; Vis. Prof., UCLA, 1969; Center for Humanities Fellow, Princeton, 1984. Hon. Prof., Univ. of Wales, 1997–. Pres., British Soc. for Middle Eastern Studies, 1983–85. Avicenna Silver Medal, UNESCO, 1998. *Publications:* The Ghaznavids, 1963; The Islamic Dynasties, 1967, 2nd edn as The New Islamic Dynasties, 1996; Sistan under the Arabs, 1968; The Book of Curious and Entertaining Information, 1968; The Medieval Islamic Underworld, 1976; The Later Ghaznavids, 1977; Al-Maqrizi's Book of contention and strife, 1981; Medieval Arabic Culture and Administration, 1982; The History of al-Tabari (annotated trans.), vols 5, 30, 32–3, 1987–99; The History of the Saffarids of Sistan and the Maliks of Nimruz, 1994; The Arabs, Byzantium and Iran, 1996. *Recreations:* walking, listening to music, collecting detective fiction. *Address:* 11 Prince's Road, Heaton Moor, Stockport, Cheshire SK4 3NQ. *T.* (0161) 432 6464.

BOSWORTH, (John) Michael (Worthington), CBE 1972; FCA; Deputy Chairman, British Railways Board, 1972–83 (Vice-Chairman, 1968–72); *b* 22 June 1921; *s* of Humphrey Worthington Bosworth and Vera Hope Bosworth; *m* 1955, Patricia Mary Edith Wheelock; one *s* one *d*. *Educ:* Bishop's Stortford Coll. Served Royal Artillery, 1939–46. Peat, Marwick, Mitchell & Co., 1949–68, Partner, 1960. Chairman: British Rail Engineering Ltd, 1969–71; British Rail Property Bd, 1971–72, British Rail Shipping and International Services Ltd, later Sealink UK Ltd, 1976–84; BR Hovercraft Ltd, 1976–81; British Transport Hotels, 1978–83; British Rail Investments Ltd, 1981–84; British Rail Trustee Co., 1984–86; Director: Hoverspeed (UK) Ltd, 1981–89; British Ferries, 1984–90. Vice Pres., Société Belgo-Anglaise des Ferry-Boats, 1979–87. Dir, Compass Hotels Ltd, 1988–99. *Recreations:* ski-ing, vintage cars. *Address:* Cross Farm, Yetminster, Sherborne, Dorset DT9 6LG.

BOSWORTH, Sir Neville (Bruce Alfred), Kt 1987; CBE 1982; Consultant, Grove Tompkins Bosworth, Solicitors, Birmingham, since 1989; *b* 18 April 1918; *s* of W. C. N. Bosworth; *m* 1945, Charlotte Marian Davis; one *s* two *d*. *Educ:* King Edward's Sch., Birmingham; Birmingham Univ. LLB. Admitted Solicitor, 1941; Sen. Partner, Bosworth, Bailey Cox & Co., Birmingham, 1941–89. Birmingham City Council, 1950–96; County Bor. Councillor (Erdington Ward), 1950–61; Alderman, 1961–74; Dist Councillor (Edgbaston Ward), 1973–96; Hon. Alderman, 1996; Lord Mayor of Birmingham, 1969–70; Dep. Mayor, 1970–71; Leader of Birmingham City Council, 1976–80, 1982–84; Leader of Opposition, 1972–76, 1980–82 and 1984–87; Cons. Gp Leader, 1972–87 (Dep. Gp Leader, 1971–72); Chairman: Gen. Purposes Cttee, 1966–69; Finance Cttee, 1976–80, 1982–84; National Exhibn Centre Cttee, 1976–80. Chm., W Midlands Police Bd, 1985–86. County Councillor (Edgbaston Ward), W Midlands CC, 1973–86; Chm., Legal and Property Cttee, 1977–79; Vice-Chm., Finance Cttee, 1980–81. Chm., Sutton Coldfield Cons. Assoc., 1963–66; Vice-Chm., Birmingham Cons. Assoc., 1972–87; Mem., Local Govt Adv. Cttee, National Union of Cons. and Unionist Assocs, 1973–87; Pres., Edgbaston Constituency Cons. Assoc., 1992–. Vice Chm., Assoc. of Metropolitan Authorities, 1978–80, and Mem. Policy Cttee, 1976–80; Vice-Pres., Birmingham and Dist Property Owners Assoc.; Dir, Nat. Exhibn Centre Ltd, 1970–72, 1974–96; Mem., W Midlands Econ. Council, 1978–79. Trustee, several charitable trusts; Mem. Council, Birmingham Univ., 1962–91; Governor, King Edward VI Schs, Birmingham, 1970–87 (Dep. Bailiff, 1979–80). Hon. Freeman, City of Birmingham, 1982. *Recreations:* politics, football, bridge. *Address:* Hollington, Luttrell Road, Four Oaks, Sutton Coldfield, Birmingham B74 2SR. *T:* (0121) 308 0647; 54 Newhall Street, Birmingham B3 3QG. *T:* (0121) 236 9341.

BOTHA, Pieter Willem, DMS 1976; Star of South Africa, 1979; State President, Republic of South Africa, 1984–89 (Prime Minister, and Minister of National Intelligence Service, 1978–84); *b* 12 Jan. 1916; *s* of Pieter Willem and Hendriena Christina Botha; *m* 1st, 1943, Anna Elizabeth Rossouw (*d* 1997); two *s* three *d*; 2nd, 1998, Barbara Nola Robertson. *Educ:* Paul Roux; Bethlehem, Orange Free State; Univ. of Orange Free State, Bloemfontein. MP for George, 1948–84; Deputy Minister of the Interior, 1958; Minister of Community Development and of Coloured Affairs, 1961; Minister of Public Works, 1964; Minister of Defence, 1966–80. Leader of the National Party in the Cape Province, 1966–86; Chief Leader of Nat. Party, 1978–89. Hon. Doctorate in: Military Science, Stellenbosch Univ., 1976; Philosophy, Orange Free State Univ., 1981; DAdmin *hc* Pretoria Univ., 1985. Grand Cross of Military Order of Christ, Portugal, 1967; Order of Propitious Clouds with Special Grand Cordon, Taiwan, 1980; Grand Collar, Order of Good Hope, Republic of S Africa, 1985. *Relevant publication:* Voice from the Wilderness, by Dr Daan Prinsloo, 1997. *Recreations:* horseriding, walking, reading, small game hunting. *Address:* Die Anker, Wilderness 6560, South Africa.

BOTHA, Roelof Frederik, (Pik), DMS 1981; MP (National Party), 1977–96; Minister of Energy, South Africa, 1994–96; Leader, Transvaal National Party, 1992–96; *b* 27 April 1932; *m* 1953, Helena Susanna Bosman; two *s* two *d*; *m* 1998, Ina Joubert. *Educ:* Volkskool, Potchefstroom; Univ. of Pretoria (BA, LLB). Dept of Foreign Affairs, 1953; diplomatic missions, Europe, 1956–62; Mem. team from S Africa, in SW Africa case,

Internat. Court of Justice, The Hague, 1963–66, 1970–71; Agent for S African Govt, Internat. Court of Justice, 1965–66; Legal Adviser, Dept of Foreign Affairs, 1966–68; Under-Sec. and Head of SW Africa and UN Sections, 1968–70. National Party, MP for Wonderboom, 1970–74. Mem., SA Delegn to UN Gen. Assembly, 1967–69, 1971, 1973–74. Served on select Parly Cttees, 1970–74. South African Permanent Representative to the UN, NY, 1974–77; South African Ambassador to the USA, 1975–77. Minister of Foreign Affairs, 1977–94; Minister of Information, 1978–86. Grand Cross, Order of Good Hope, 1980; Order of the Brilliant Star with Grand Cordon, 1980. *Address:* PO Box 16176, Pretoria North 0116, South Africa.

BOTHAM, Ian Terence, OBE 1992; cricketer, retired 1993; Chairman, Mission Logistics Ltd, since 2000; *b* 24 Nov. 1955; *s* of Leslie and Marie Botham; *m* 1976, Kathryn Waller; one *s* two *d. Educ:* Milford Junior Sch.; Buckler's Mead Secondary Sch., Yeovil. Bowler and batsman; County Cricket Clubs: Somerset, 1974–87 (Captain, 1983–85; Hon. Life Mem., 1993); Worcestershire, 1987–91; Durham, 1992–93 (Hon. Life Mem.). England Test cricketer, 1977–92 (Captain, 1980–81); scored 1,000 runs and took 100 wickets in 21 Tests at age 23, 1979; scored 3,000 runs and took 300 wickets in Tests to 1982; first player to score a century and take 10 wickets in a Test match, Bombay, 1979; made 100 runs and took 8 wickets in 3 Tests, 1978, 1980, 1984; made 5,200 runs, took 383 wickets and 120 catches in 102 Tests; played cricket for Queensland, football for Scunthorpe and Yeovil. Technical Dir of bowling, England Cricket Team, 1996–. Marathon walks for leukaemia research incl. Land's End to John o'Groats and Alps; takes part in pantomimes; columnist, Daily Mirror. Team captain, A Question of Sport, BBC, 1989–96. Mem., Sky cricket commentary team, 1995–. *Publications:* Ian Botham on Cricket, 1980; (with Ian Jarrett) Botham Down Under, 1983; (with Kenneth Gregory) Botham's Bedside Cricket Book, 1983; (with Peter Roebuck) It Sort of Clicks, 1986, rev. edn 1987; (with Jack Bannister) Cricket My Way, 1989; Botham: my autobiography, 1994; (with Peter Hayter) The Botham Report, 1997. *Address:* North Yorkshire. *Club:* MCC (Hon. Mem. 1994).

BOTHROYD, Shirley Ann, (Mrs Ian Mayes); barrister; First Prosecuting Counsel to the Inland Revenue at the Central Criminal Court and Inner London Crown Court, since 1991; *b* 23 July 1958; *d* of Reginald Bothroyd and Audrey (*née* Bryant); *m* 1986, Ian Mayes, *qv*; two *s*. Called to the Bar, Middle Temple, 1982; Second Prosecuting Counsel to Inland Revenue, 1989–91. *Recreations:* ski-ing, scuba diving, family activities, organizing others. *Address:* Littleton Chambers, 3 King's Bench Walk North, Temple, EC4Y 7HR. *T:* (020) 7797 8600.

BOTHWELL, Rt Rev. John Charles, DD; Archbishop of Niagara and Metropolitan of Ontario, 1985–91; *b* 29 June 1926; *s* of William Alexander Bothwell and Anne Bothwell (*née* Campbell); *m* 1951, Joan Cowan; three *s* two *d. Educ:* Runnymede Public School; Humberside Coll. Inst., Toronto; Trinity Coll., Univ. of Toronto (BA 1948, LTh 1951, BD 1952; DD 1972). Asst Priest, St James' Cathedral, Toronto, 1951–53; Sen. Assistant at Christ Church Cathedral, Vancouver, 1953–56; Rector: St Aidan's, Oakville, Ont, 1956–60; St James' Church, Dundas, Ont, 1960–65; Canon of Christ Church Cathedral, Hamilton, Ont, 1963; Dir of Programs for Niagara Diocese, 1965–69; Exec. Dir of Program, Nat. HQ of Anglican Church of Canada, Toronto, 1969–71; Bishop Coadjutor of Niagara, 1971–73; Bishop of Niagara, 1973–85. Chancellor, Trinity Coll., Univ. of Toronto, 1991–. Hon. Sen. Fellow, Renison Coll., Univ. of Waterloo, 1988. Hon. DD: Huron Coll., Univ. of Western Ont, 1989; Wycliffe Coll., Univ. of Toronto, 1989. *Publications:* Taking Risks and Keeping Faith, 1985; An Open View: keeping faith day by day, 1990; Old Time Religion or Risky Faith: the challenge and the vision, 1993. *Recreations:* golf, cross-country ski-ing, swimming. *Address:* #406-1237 Northshore Boulevard E, Burlington, ON L7S 2H8, Canada. *T:* (905) 6348649, *Fax:* (905) 6341049.

BOTT, Catherine Jane; soprano; *b* 11 Sept. 1952; *d* of Maurice Bott and Patricia Bott (*née* Sherlock). *Educ:* King's High Sch. for Girls, Warwick; Guildhall Sch. of Music and Drama (GGSM). Concert singer specialising in baroque vocal music; worldwide concert engagements, incl. world première of Francis Grier's Five Joyful Mysteries, 2000; radio broadcasts; numerous recordings with leading ensembles and orchestras, recital recordings and recordings of operatic roles, incl. Purcell's Dido, Messaggiera (l'Orfeo), Drusilla (l'Incoronazione di Poppea), and Mandane (Artaxerxes). Occasional presenter, BBC Radio 3. *Recreations:* exploring London, going to the ballet, learning Spanish. *Address:* c/o MAS, Masters Yard, 180A South Street, Dorking, Surrey RH4 2ES.

BOTT, Ian Bernard, FREng; Director, Admiralty Research Establishment, Ministry of Defence, 1984–88, retired; consultant engineer, since 1989; *b* 1 April 1932; *s* of late Edwin Bernard and Agnes Bott; *m* 1955, Kathleen Mary (*née* Broadbent); one *s* one *d. Educ:* Nottingham High Sch.; Southwell Minster Grammar Sch.; Stafford Technical Coll.; Manchester Univ. BSc Hons Physics; FIEE, FInstP; FREng (FEng 1985). Nottingham Lace Industry, 1949–53. Royal Air Force, 1953–55. English Electric, Stafford, 1955–57; Royal Radar Estabt, 1960–75 (Head of Electronics Group, 1973–75); Counsellor, Defence Research and Development, British Embassy, Washington DC, 1975–77; Ministry of Defence: Dep. Dir Underwater Weapons Projects (S/M), 1977–79; Asst Chief Scientific Advr (Projects), 1979–81; Dir Gen., Guided Weapons and Electronics, 1981–82; Principal Dep. Dir, AWRE, MoD, 1982–84. Mem. Council, Fellowship of Engrg, 1987–90. Hon. Chm., Portsmouth Area Hospice, 1989–94 (Hon. Life Vice Pres., 1998). Trustee, Panasonic Trust, 1993–96. Freeman, City of London, 1985; Liveryman, Co. of Engineers, 1985. *Publications:* papers on physics and electronics subjects in jls of learned socs. *Recreations:* golf, horology, music. *Address:* The Lodge, Brand Lane, Ludlow, Shropshire SY8 1NN; *e-mail:* bottfreng@lodge.enta.net. *Club:* Royal Automobile.

BOTT, Prof. Martin Harold Phillips, FRS 1977; Professor, 1966–88, Research Professor, 1988–91, in Geophysics, University of Durham, now Professor Emeritus; *b* 12 July 1926; *s* of Harold Bott and Dorothy (*née* Phillips); *m* 1961, Joyce Cynthia Hughes; two *s* one *d. Educ:* Clayesmore Sch. Dorset; Magdalene Coll., Cambridge (Scholar). MA, PhD. Nat. Service, 1945–48 (Lieut, Royal Signals). Durham University: Turner and Newall Fellow, 1954–56; Lectr, 1956–63; Reader, 1963–66. Anglican Lay Reader. Mem. Council, Royal Soc., 1982–84. Murchison Medallist, Geological Soc. of London, 1977; Clough Medal, Geol Soc. of Edinburgh, 1979; Sorby Medal, Yorkshire Geol Soc., 1981; Wollaston Medal, Geol Soc. of London, 1992. *Publications:* The Interior of the Earth, 1971, 2nd edn 1982; papers in learned jls. *Recreations:* walking, mountains, garden slavery. *Address:* 11 St Mary's Close, Shincliffe, Durham DH1 2ND. *T:* (0191) 3864021.

BOTTAI, Bruno; President: Società Dante Alighieri, since 1996; Fondazione Premio Balzan, since 1999; *b* 10 July 1930; *s* of Giuseppe Bottai and Cornelia Ciocca. *Educ:* Univ. of Rome (law degree). Joined Min. for For. Affairs, 1954; Vice Consul, Tunis, 1956; Second Sec., Perm. Representation to EC, Brussels, 1958; Gen. Secretariat, Co-ord. Service, Min. for For. Affairs, 1961; Counsellor, London, 1966; Dep. Chef de Cabinet, Min. for For. Affairs, 1968; Minister-Counsellor, Holy See, 1969; Diplomatic Advr to Pres., Council of Ministers, 1970; Hd of Press and Inf. Dept 1972, Dep. Dir-Gen. of Political Affairs 1976, Min. for For. Affairs; Ambassador to Holy See and Sovereign Mil. Order of Malta, 1979; Dir-Gen. Pol. Affairs, Min. for For. Affairs, 1981; Ambassador to UK, 1985–87; Sec. Gen., Min. of Foreign Affairs, Italy, 1987–94; Ambassador of Italy to the Holy See, 1994–97. Numerous decorations from Europe, Africa, Latin Amer. countries, Holy See, Malta. *Publications:* political essays and articles. *Recreations:* modern paintings and modern sculpture, theatre, reading, walking. *Address:* Piazza Firenze 27, 00186 Rome, Italy.

BOTTING, Maj.-Gen. David Francis Edmund, CB 1992; CBE 1986; Director General of Ordnance Services, Ministry of Defence, 1990–93; *b* 15 Dec. 1937; *s* of Leonard Edmund Botting and Elizabeth Mildred Botting (*née* Stacey); *m* 1962, Anne Outhwaite; two *s. Educ:* St Paul's School, London. National Service, RAOC, 1956; commissioned Eaton Hall, 1957; Regular Commission, 1958; regtl appts, Kineton, Deepcut, Borneo, Singapore and Malaya, 1957–67; sc 1968; BAOR, 1972–74; 1 Div., 1974–75; 3rd Div., 1981–82; Col AQ 1 Div., 1982–85; Comd Sup. 1 (BR) Corps, 1987; ACOS HQ UKLF, 1987–90. Rep. Col Comdt, RAOC, 1993; Col Comdt, RLC, 1993–. Trustee, Army Benevolent Fund, 1997–. FILDM 1991; MInstPS 1991. Freeman, City of London, 1990; Liveryman, Co. of Gold and Silver Wyre Drawers, 1991. *Recreations:* sport, esp. golf, philately, furniture restoration. *Clubs:* Army and Navy; Tidworth Golf.

BOTTING, (Elizabeth) Louise, CBE 1993; Chairman, Douglas Deakin Young, since 1988 (Managing Director, 1982–88); *b* 19 Sept. 1939; *d* of Robert and Edith Young; marr. diss.; two *d*; *m* 1989, L. A. Carpenter, *qv. Educ:* Sutton Coldfield High School; London Sch. of Economics (BSc Econ.). Kleinwort Benson, 1961–65; Daily Mail, 1970–75; British Forces Broadcasting, 1971–83; Douglas Deakin Young, financial consultancy, 1975–. Director: Trinity International, 1991–99; CGU (formerly General Accident), 1992–2000; London Weekend Television, 1992–94; 102, Stratford-upon-Avon Radio Station, 1996–; Camelot plc, 1999–. Presenter, BBC Moneybox, 1977–92. Mem. Top Salaries Review Body, 1987–94. *Address:* Douglas Deakin Young Ltd, 22–25a Sackville Street, W1X 2DH. *T:* (020) 7439 3344.

See also J. R. C. Young.

BOTTO DE BARROS, Adwaldo Cardoso; Director-General, International Bureau of Universal Postal Union, 1985–94; *b* 19 Jan. 1925; *s* of Julio Botto de Barros and Maria Cardoso Botto de Barros; *m* 1951, Neida de Moura; one *s* two *d. Educ:* Military Coll., Military Engineering Inst. and Higher Military Engineering Inst., Brazil. Railway construction, 1952–54; Dir, industries in São Paulo and Curitiba, 1955–64; Dir, Handling Sector, São Paulo Prefecture, Financial Adviser to São Paulo Engrg Faculty and Adviser to Suzano Prefecture, 1965–71; Regional Dir, São Paulo, 1972–74; Pres., Brazilian Telegraph and Post Office, Brasília-DF, 1974–84. Mem. and Head, numerous delegns to UPU and other postal assocs overseas, 1976–84. Numerous Brazilian and foreign hons and decorations. *Recreations:* philately, sports.

BOTTOMLEY, Sir James (Reginald Alfred), KCMG 1973 (CMG 1965); HM Diplomatic Service, retired; *b* 12 Jan. 1920; *s* of Sir (William) Cecil Bottomley, KCMG, and Alice Thistle Bottomley (*née* Robinson), JP; *m* 1941, Barbara Evelyn Vardon (*d* 1994); two *s* two *d* (and one *s* decd). *Educ:* King's College Sch., Wimbledon; Trinity Coll., Cambridge. Served with Inns of Court Regt, RAC, 1940–46. Dominions Office, 1946; Pretoria, 1948–50; Karachi, 1953–55; Washington, 1955–59; UK Mission to United Nations, 1959; Dep. High Commissioner, Kuala Lumpur 1963–67; Assst Under-Sec. of State, Commonwealth Office (later FCO), 1967–70; Dep. Under-Sec. of State, FCO, 1970–72; Ambassador to South Africa, 1973–76; Perm. UK Rep. to UN and other Internat. Organisations at Geneva, 1976–78; Dir, Johnson Matthey plc, 1979–85. Mem., British Overseas Trade Bd, 1972. *Recreation:* golf. *Address:* 22 Beaufort Place, Thompson's Lane, Cambridge CB5 8AG. *T:* (01223) 328760.

See also P. J. Bottomley.

BOTTOMLEY, Peter James; MP (C) Worthing West, since 1997 (Greenwich, Woolwich West, June 1975–1983, Eltham, 1983–97); *b* 30 July 1944; *er s* of Sir James Bottomley, *qv*; *m* 1967, Virginia Garnett (*see* Rt Hon. Virginia Bottomley); one *s* two *d. Educ:* comprehensive sch.; Westminster Sch.; Trinity Coll., Cambridge (MA). Driving, industrial sales, industrial relations, industrial economics. Contested (C) GLC elect., Vauxhall, 1973; (C) Woolwich West, gen. elecs, 1974. PPS to Minister of State, FCO, 1982–83, to Sec. of State for Social Services, 1983–84, to Sec. of State for NI, 1990; Parly Under Sec. of State, Dept of Employment, 1984–86, Dept of Transport, 1986–89, NI Office, 1989–90. Secretary: Cons. Parly Social Services Cttee, 1977–79; Cons. Parly For. and Commonwealth Cttee, 1979–81. Mem., Transport House Br., T&GWU, 1971–; Mem., Commonwealth Trade Unionists Appeal, 1999; Pres., Cons. Trade Unionists, 1978–80; Vice-Pres., Fedn of Cons. Students, 1980–82. Chairman: British Union of Family Orgns, 1973–80; Family Forum, 1980–82; Church of England Children's Soc., 1983–84. Member Council: MIND, 1981–82; NACRO, 1997–; Trustee, Christian Aid, 1978–84. Parly Swimming Champion, 1980–81, 1984–86; Captain, Parly Football Team; occasional Parly Dinghy Sailing Champion. Mem., Ct of Assts, Drapers' Co. Castrol/Inst. of Motor Industry Road Safety Gold Medal, 1988. *Recreations:* children, book reviewing. *Address:* House of Commons, SW1A 0AA.

BOTTOMLEY, Rt Hon. Virginia (Hilda Brunette Maxwell); PC 1992; JP; MP (C) Surrey South West, since May 1984; *b* 12 March 1948; *d* of late W. John Garnett, CBE and of Barbara (*née* Rutherford-Smith); *m* Peter Bottomley, *qv*; one *s* two *d. Educ:* Putney High Sch.; Univ. of Essex (BA); London Sch. of Econs and Pol Science (MSc). Research for Child Poverty Action Gp, 1971–73; behavioural scientist, 1973–84. Vice Chm., National Council of Carers and their Elderly Dependants, 1982–88. Director: Mid Southern Water Co., 1987–88; Odgers International, 2000–. Mem., MRC, 1987–88. Contested (C) IoW, 1983. PPS: to Minister of State for Educn and Science, 1985–86; to Minister for Overseas Develt, 1986–87; to Sec. of State for Foreign and Commonwealth Affairs, 1987–88; Parly Under-Sec. of State, DoE, 1988–89; Minister for Health, 1989–92; Secretary of State: for Health, 1992–95; for Nat. Heritage, 1995–97. Mem., Select Cttee on Foreign Affairs, 1997–99. Sec., Cons. Backbench Employment Cttee, 1985; Fellow, Industry Parlt Trust, 1987. Vice-Chm., British Council, 1998–. Co-Chm., Women's Nat. Commn, 1991–92. Patron, Cruse Bereavement Care. Mem., Court of Govs, LSE, 1985–; Gov., Ditchley Foundn, 1991–. JP Inner London, 1975 (Chm., Lambeth Juvenile Court, 1981–84). Freeman, City of London, 1988. *Recreation:* family. *Address:* House of Commons, SW1A 0AA. *T:* (020) 7219 6499. *Club:* Seaview Yacht.

BOTTOMS, Sir Anthony Edward, Kt 2001; FBA 1997; Wolfson Professor of Criminology, since 1984 and Director of the Institute of Criminology, 1984–98, University of Cambridge; Fellow of Fitzwilliam College, Cambridge, since 1984 (President, 1994–98); *b* 29 Aug. 1939; *yr s* of James William Bottoms, medical missionary, and Dorothy Ethel Bottoms (*née* Barnes); *m* 1962, Janet Freda Wenger; one *s* two *d. Educ:* Eltham Coll.; Corpus Christi Coll., Oxford (MA); Corpus Christi Coll., Cambridge (MA); Univ. of Sheffield (PhD). Probation Officer, 1962–64; Research Officer, Inst. of Criminology, Univ. of Cambridge, 1964–68; Univ. of Sheffield: Lecturer, 1968–72; Sen. Lectr, 1972–76; Prof. of Criminology, 1976–84; Dean of Faculty of Law, 1981–84. Canadian Commonwealth Vis. Fellow, Simon Fraser Univ., BC, 1982; Visiting Professor: QUB, 1999–2000; Univ. of Sheffield, 2000–. Member: Parole Bd for England and Wales,

1974–76; Home Office Res. and Adv. Gp on Long-Term Prison System, 1984–90. Editor, Howard Journal of Penology and Crime Prevention, 1975–81. Sellin–Glueck Award, Amer. Soc. of Criminology, 1996. *Publications:* (jtly) Criminals Coming of Age, 1973; (jtly) The Urban Criminal, 1976; (jtly) Defendants in the Criminal Process, 1976; The Suspended Sentence after Ten Years (Frank Dawtry Lecture), 1980; (ed jtly) The Coming Penal Crisis, 1980; (ed jtly) Problems of Long-Term Imprisonment, 1987; (jtly) Social Inquiry Reports, 1988; (jtly) Intermediate Treatment and Juvenile Justice, 1990; Crime Prevention facing the 1990s (James Smart Lecture), 1990; Intensive Community Supervision for Young Offenders, 1995; (jtly) Prisons and the Problem of Order, 1996; (jtly) Criminal Deterrence and Sentence Severity, 1999; (ed jtly) Community Penalties, 2001; various articles and reviews. *Address:* Institute of Criminology, 7 West Road, Cambridge CB3 9DT. *T:* (01223) 335360.

BOTTONE, Bonaventura; tenor; *b* 19 Sept. 1950; *s* of Bonaventura Bottone and Kathleen (*née* Barnes); *m* 1973, Jennifer Dakin; two *s* two *d*. *Educ:* Lascelles Secondary Mod. Sch., Harrow; Royal Acad. Music (ARAM 1984; FRAM 1998). Has appeared at numerous international venues, including: Nice Opera, 1982; Houston Opera, 1987; Royal Opera House, Covent Garden (début 1987); London Coliseum; Glyndebourne Fest. (début 1990); Bavarian State Opera, Munich (début 1991); Fundação de São Carlos, Lisbon (début 1994); Chicago Lyric Opera (début 1994); New Israeli Opera, Tel Aviv (début 1995); Metropolitan Opera, NY (début 1998); Opera del Teatro Municipal, Santiago (début 1998); Paris Opéra Bastille (début 2000); Atlanta Opera (début 2001). Has performed with ENO, Royal Opera Co., Scottish Opera, Opera North and Welsh Opera; rôles include: Alfredo in La Traviata, Italian Tenor in Der Rosenkavalier, Governor General in Candide, Nanki-Poo in Mikado, Lenski in Eugene Onegin, Alfred in Die Fledermaus, Narraboth in Salome, Duke of Mantua in Rigoletto, Pinkerton in Madam Butterfly, Turridù in Cavalleria Rusticana, title rôle, Damnation of Faust, title rôle, Doctor Ox's Experiment (world première), Rodolfo in La Bohème. Riccardo in Un Ballo in Maschera. Has made numerous recordings. *Recreations:* gardening, boating. *Address:* c/o Stafford Law Associates, 6 Barham Close, Weybridge, Surrey KT13 9PR.

BOTWOOD, Richard Price; Director-General, Chartered Institute of Transport, 1989–98; *b* 1 June 1932; *s* of Allan Bertram and Hilda Amelia Botwood; *m* 1964, Victoria Sanderson; one *s* one *d*. *Educ:* Oundle School. Sec., Tozer Kemsley & Millbourn, 1952–56; Dir, International Factors, 1956–61; Asst Man. Dir, Melbray Group, 1961–73; Chm. and Man. Dir, W. S. Sanderson (Morpeth), wine and spirit merchants, 1973–85; Dir-Gen., Air Transport Users' Cttee, 1986–89. *Recreations:* opera, gardening, embroidery, golf. *Address:* 34 Brook Green, W6 7BL. *T:* (020) 7603 5277.

BOUCHARD, Hon. Lucien; PC (Can.) 1988; Prime Minister of Quebec, 1996–2001; Member for Jonquière, Quebec National Assembly, 1996–2001; *b* 22 Dec. 1938; *m* Audrey Best; two *s*. *Educ:* Collège de Jonquière; Université Laval (BA, BSocSc, LLB 1964). Called to the Bar, Quebec, 1964; in private practice, Chicoutimi, 1964–85. Pres., Saguenay Bar, 1978; Mem., Admin. Cttee and Chm., Specialisation Cttee, Quebec Bar. Ambassador to France, 1985–88; Secretary of State, 1988–89; Minister of the Envmt, 1989–90. MP (C), 1988–90, (Ind), 1990–91, (Bloc Québécois), 1991–96, Lac-St-Jean; Chm. and Leader, Bloc Québécois, 1991–96; Leader of Opposition, Quebec, 1993–96; Leader, Parti Québécois, 1996–2001. *Publications:* (jtly) Martin-Bouchard Report, 1978; A visage découvert, 1992 (trans. English 1994); specialised articles in legal and labour relns jls. *Address:* c/o Office of the Prime Minister, 885 Grande Allée Est, Quebec G1A 1A2, Canada.

BOUCHER, Prof. Robert Francis, CBE 2000; PhD; FREng, FIMechE; Vice-Chancellor, University of Sheffield, since 2001; *b* 25 April 1940; *s* of Robert Boucher and Johanna (*née* Fox); *m* 1965, Rosemary Ellen Maskell; two *s* one *d* (and one *s* decd). *Educ:* St Ignatius Coll.; Borough Poly.; Nottingham Univ. (PhD 1966). FIMechE 1992; FREng (FEng 1994); FASME 1997; MIEE. ICI Post-doctoral Fellow, Nottingham Univ., 1966; Queen's University, Belfast: Res. Fellow, 1966–68; Lectr, 1968–70; University of Sheffield: Lectr, 1970–76; Sen. Lectr, 1976–85; Prof. of Mech. Engrg, 1985–95; Pro-Vice-Chancellor, 1992–95; Principal and Vice-Chancellor, UMIST, 1995–2000. Chm., Engrg Profs' Council, 1993–95; Senator, Engrg Council, 1995–99; Member: Council, Royal Acad. of Engrg, 1996–99; Bd, British Council, 1996– (Mem., 1996–, Chm., 1997–, CICHE); User Panel, EPSRC, 1997–. Internat. Sector Gp, CVCP, 1995– (Chm., 1997–). Chairman: CSU Ltd, 1998–; Marketing Manchester, 1999–2000; Mem. Bd of Patrons, Alliance Française de Manchester, 1997–2000. FRSA 1987. Hon. DHL SUNY, 1998. *Publications:* in engrg jls and confs incl. Proc. IMechE, Trans ASME, Trans IEEE, Inst. of Physics jls. *Recreations:* hill-walking, music, exercise. *Address:* University of Sheffield, Firth Court, Western Bank, Sheffield S10 2TN. *Club:* Athenæum.

BOUCHIER, Prof. Ian Arthur Dennis, CBE 1990; Professor of Medicine, University of Edinburgh, 1986–97; Chief Scientist, Scottish Office Department of Health (formerly Home and Health Department), 1992–97; *b* 7 Sept. 1932; *s* of E. A. and M. Bouchier; *m* 1959, Patricia Norma Henshilwood; two *s*. *Educ:* Rondebosch Boys' High Sch., Cape Town; Univ. of Cape Town. MB, ChB, MD, FRCP, FRCPE, FFPHM; FRSE, FIBiol. Groote Schuur Hospital: House Officer, 1955–58; Registrar, 1958–61; Asst Lectr, Royal Free Hosp., 1962–63; Instructor in Medicine, Boston Univ. Sch. of Medicine, 1964–65; Sen. Lectr 1965–70, Reader in Medicine 1970–73, Univ. of London; Prof. of Medicine, 1973–86, and Dean, Faculty of Medicine and Dentistry, 1982–86, Univ. of Dundee. Pres., World Organisation of Gastroenterology, 1990–98 (Sec. Gen., 1982–90); British Society of Gastroenterology: Mem. Council, 1987–90; Chm. Educn Cttee, 1987–90; Pres., 1994–95; Trustee, 1999–. Member: Chief Scientist Cttee, Scotland, 1980–97; MRC, 1982–86; Council, RCPE, 1984–90. Goulstonian Lectr, RCP, 1971; Sydney Watson Smith Lectr, RCPE, 1991. Visiting Professor of Medicine: Michigan Univ., 1979; McGill Univ., 1983; RPMS, 1984; Shenyang Univ., Hong Kong Univ., 1988. FRSA. Founder FMedSci 1998. Hon. FCP (SoAf); Founder FMedSci 1998. Hon. Mem., Japanese Soc. Gastroenterology; Corresp. Member: Soc. Italiana di Gastroenterologia; Royal Catalonian Acad. of Medicine. Chm., Editl Bd, Current Opinion in Gastroenterology, 1987–91; Member, Editorial Board: Baillière's Clinical Gastroenterology, 1987–98; Hellenic Jl of Gastroenterology, 1988–; Internat. Gastroenterology, 1988–98. *Publications:* (ed jtly) Bilirubin Metabolism, 1967; (ed) Clinical Investigation of Gastrointestinal Function, 1969, 2nd edn 1981; (ed) Seventh Symposium on Advanced Medicine, 1971; (ed) Diseases of the Biliary Tract, vol. 2, 1973; Gastroenterology, 1973, 3rd edn 1982; (jtly) Aspects of Clinical Gastroenterology, 1975; (ed jtly) Clinical Skills, 1976, 2nd edn 1982; (ed) Recent Advances in Gastroenterology 3, 1976, 4, 1980, 5, 1983; (ed jtly) Textbook of Gastroenterology, 1984; (ed jtly) Inflammatory Bowel Disease, 1986, 2nd edn 1993; (ed jtly) Davidson's Principles and Practice of Medicine, 15th edn 1987 to 17th edn 1995; (ed jtly) Clinical Investigations in Gastroenterology, 1988; (ed) Jaundice, 1989; (ed jtly) Infectious Diarrhoea, 1993; (ed jtly) Gastroenterology Clinical Science and Practice, vols 1 and 2, 2nd edn 1993; (ed jtly) Quality Assurance in Medical Care, 1993; (ed jtly) French's Index of Differential Diagnosis, 13th edn 1996; 600 scientific papers and communications. *Recreations:* history of whaling, music of Berlioz, cooking.

BOUGH, Francis Joseph; broadcaster; Presenter, London News Radio, 1994–97; *b* 15 Jan. 1933; *m*; three *s*. *Educ:* Oswestry; Merton College, Oxford (MA). With ICI, 1957–62; BBC, 1962–89; presenter of Sportsview, 1964–67, of Grandstand, 1967–82, of Nationwide, 1972–83, of breakfast television, 1983–87, of Holiday, 1987–88; presenter: 6 o'clock Live, LWT, 1989–92; Sky TV, 1989–90; LBC Radio, 1992–96; Travel Live, on Travel TV (cable and satellite), 1996–. Former Oxford soccer blue, Shropshire sprint champion. *Publications:* Cue Frank! (autobiog.), 1980; Frank Bough's Breakfast Book, 1984. *Address:* c/o The Roseman Organisation, Suite 9, The Power House, 70 Chiswick High Road, W4 1SY.

BOUGHEY, Sir John (George Fletcher), 11th Bt *cr* 1798; medical practitioner; *b* 12 Aug. 1959; *s* of Sir Richard James Boughey, 10th Bt, and of Davina Julia (now the Lady Loch), *d* of FitzHerbert Wright; *S* father, 1978. *Educ:* Eton; Univ. of Zimbabwe (MB ChB 1984); LRCPE; LRCSE; LRCPSGlas 1990; MRCPI 1994. *Heir:* *b* James Richard Boughey [*b* 29 Aug. 1960; *m* 1989, Katy Fenwicke-Clennell; two *s* two *d*]. *Address:* The Cobbles, Shillingstone, Blandford Forum, Dorset DT11 0SF.

BOULDING, Hilary; Director of Music, Arts Council of England, since 1999; *b* 25 Jan. 1957; *d* of James Frederick Boulding and Dorothy Boulding (*née* Watson). *Educ:* St Hilda's Coll., Oxford (BA Hons Music). TV Dir, 1981–85, TV Producer, 1985–92, BBC Scotland; Head of Arts and Music, BBC Wales, 1992–97; Commissioning Editor, Music (Policy), BBC Radio 3, 1997–99. *Recreations:* music, gardening. *Address:* Arts Council of England, 14 Great Peter Street, SW1P 3NQ. *T:* (020) 7973 6495.

BOULDING, Philip Vincent; QC 1996; *b* 1 Feb. 1954; *s* of Vincent Fergusson Boulding and Sylvia Boulding; *m* 1988, Helen Elizabeth Richardson; one *s* one *d*. *Educ:* Downing Coll., Cambridge (Scholar; BA Law 1st Cl. Hons 1976; LLM 1977; MA 1979; Rugby Blue). Called to the Bar, Gray's Inn, 1979; practice in London and South East, internat. arbitration practice in FE (esp. Hong Kong), regular arbitrator and adjudicator in commercial contract disputes, esp. in engrg and construction law; admitted to Hong Kong Bar, 1997. Pres., Cambridge Univ. Amateur Boxing Club, 1990–94 (Vice-Pres., 1994–2000). Gov., Hills Road VI Form Coll., Cambridge, 1997–2000. *Recreations:* Rugby, tennis, swimming, shooting. *Address:* Keating Chambers, 10 Essex Street, WC2R 3AA. *Clubs:* Royal Automobile; Hawks (Cambridge).

BOULEZ, Pierre; Hon. CBE 1979; composer, conductor; Director, Institut de Recherche et de Coordination Acoustique/Musique, 1976–91; *b* Montbrison, Loire, France, 26 March 1925. *Educ:* Saint-Etienne and Lyon (music and higher mathematics); Paris Conservatoire. Studied with Messiaen and René Leibowitz. Theatre conductor, Jean-Louis Barrault Company, Paris, 1948; visited USA with French Ballet Company, 1952. Has conducted major orchestras in his own and standard classical works in Great Britain, Europe, USA, S America and Asia, also conducted Wozzeck in Paris and Frankfurt; Parsifal at Bayreuth, 1966–70; The Ring, at Bayreuth, 1976–80; Chief Conductor, BBC Symphony Orchestra, 1971–75; Music Dir, NY Philharmonic, 1971–77. Hon. DMus: Cantab, 1980; Oxon, 1987, etc. Charles Heidsieck Award for Outstanding Contribution to Franco-British Music, 1989. Interested in poetry and aesthetics of Baudelaire, Mallarmé and René Char. *Compositions include:* Sonata No 1 (piano), 1946; Sonatine for flute and piano, 1946; Sonata No 2 (piano), 1948; Polyphonie X for 18 solo instruments, 1951; Visage nuptial (2nd version), 1951, rev. version, 1989; Structures for 2 pianos, 1952; Le Marteau sans Maître (voice and 6 instruments), 1954; Sonata No 3 (piano), 1956; Deux Improvisations sur Mallarmé for voice and 9 instruments, 1957; Doubles for orchestra, 1958; Poésie pour Pouvoir for voices and orchestra, 1958; Soleil des Eaux (text by René Char) for chorus and orchestra, 1958; Pli selon Pli: Hommage à Mallarmé, for voice and orchestra, 1960; Eclat, 1965; Domaines for solo clarinet, 1968; Cummings ist der Dichter (16 solo voices and instruments), 1970; Eclat/Multiples, 1970; Explosante Fixe (8 solo instruments), 1972; Rituel, for orchestra, 1975; Messagesquisses (7 celli), 1977; Notations, for orch., 1980; Répons, for orch. and live electronics, 1981–86; Mémoriale, 1984; Dérive, 1985; Dialogue de l'Ombre Double, 1986; Anthèmes, for violin solo, 1991; … explosante/fixe . . . , for 3 flutes, large ensemble and electronics, 1993; Sur Incises, 1998. *Publications:* Penser la musique d'aujourd'hui, 1966 (Boulez on Music Today, 1971); Relevés d'apprenti, 1967; Par volonté et par hasard, 1976; Points de Repère, 1981; Orientations, 1986; Jalons, 1989; Le pays fertile—Paul Klee, 1989. *Address:* IRCAM, 1 place Igor Stravinsky, 75004 Paris, France. *Fax:* (1) 44781540.

BOULIND, Mrs (Olive) Joan, CBE 1975; Fellow, 1973–79, and Tutor, 1974–79, Hughes Hall, Cambridge; *b* 24 Sept. 1912; *e d* of Douglas Siddall and Olive Raby; *m* 1936, Henry F. Boulind (decd), MA, PhD; one *s* (and one *s* one *d* decd). *Educ:* Wallasey High Sch., Cheshire; Univ. of Liverpool (BA 1st class Hons History, Medieval and Modern; DipEd); MA Cantab 1974. Teacher: Wirral Co. Sch. for Girls, 1934–36; Cambridgeshire High Sch. for Girls, 1963. Nat. Pres., Nat. Council of Women, 1966–68 (Sen. Vice-Pres., 1964–66); Co-Chm., Women's Consultative Council, 1966–68; Leader, British delegn to conf. of Internat. Council of Women, Bangkok, 1970; Co-Chm., Women's Nat. Commn, 1973–75; Co-Chm., UK Co-ordinating Cttee for Internat. Women's Year, 1975; Chm., Westminster College Management Cttee, 1980–88. Member: Commn on the Church in the Seventies, Congregational Church in England and Wales, 1970–72 (Vice-Chm., 1971–72); Ministerial Trng Cttee, United Reformed Church, 1972–79 and 1982–86 (Chm., 1982–86); East Adv. Council, BBC, 1976–84 (Chm. 1981–84). Deacon, Emmanuel Congregational Ch., Cambridge, 1958–66. Trustee, Homerton Coll. of Educn, 1955–94. *Recreations:* reading, travel, music. *Address:* 28 Rathmore Road, Cambridge CB1 7AD.

BOULTER, Prof. Donald, CBE 1991; FIBiol; Head of Department of Biological Sciences, University of Durham, 1988–91 (Professor of Botany and Head of Department of Botany, 1966–88); Director of Durham University Botanic Garden, 1966–91; *b* 25 Aug. 1926; *s* of late George Boulter and Vera Boulter; *m* 1956, Margaret Eileen Kennedy; four *d*. *Educ:* Portsmouth Grammar Sch.; Christ Church, Oxford (BA, MA, DPhil). FIBiol 1970. Served RAF, 1945–48. Sessel Fellow, Yale Univ., 1953–54; Asst Lectr in Botany, King's Coll., London, 1955–57; Lectr 1957–64, Sen. Lectr 1964–66, Liverpool Univ. Vis. Prof., Univ. of Texas, Austin, 1967. Chm., Plant Science Res. Ltd, 1992–96. Member: AFRC, 1985–89; Biological Scis Sub-Cttee, UFC (formerly UGC), 1988–89; Chm., Plants & Soils Res. Grant Bd, 1986–89; Pres., Sect. K, BAAS, 1981. Dep. Chm. Governing Body, AFRC Inst. of Horticultural Res., 1987–90; Member, Governing Body: Scottish Crop Res. Inst., 1986–92; AFRC Inst. of Plant Sci. Res., 1989–92; Dep. Chm., John Innes Centre, 1993–97; Trustee, John Innes Foundn, 1994–97. Mem., Exec. Cttee, Horticultural Res. Internat., 1990–97. FRSA 1972. Tate & Lyle Award for Phytochem., 1975. *Publications:* (ed) Chemotaxonomy of the Leguminosae, 1971; (ed) Encyclopedia of Plant Physiology, vol. 14B: Nucleic Acids and Proteins, 1982; papers in sci. jls on molecular evolution, genetic engrg of crops, biochem. and molecular biol of seed develt. *Recreation:* travel. *Address:* 5 Crossgate, Durham DH1 4PS. *T:* (0191) 3861199.

BOULTER, Patrick Stewart, FRCSE, FRCS, FRCP; Consultant Surgeon Emeritus, Royal Surrey County Hospital and Regional Radiotherapy Centre, since 1991; President,

Royal College of Surgeons of Edinburgh, 1991–94; *b* 28 May 1927; *s* of Frederick Charles Boulter, MC and Flora Victoria Boulter of Annan, Dumfriesshire; *m* 1946, Patricia Mary Eckersley Barlow, *d* of S. G. Barlow of Lowton, Lancs; two *d*. *Educ:* King's Coll. Sch.; Carlisle GS; Guy's Hosp. Med. Sch., Univ. of London (Sands Cox Schol. in Physiology, 1952; MB BS Hons and Gold Medal, 1955). FRCS 1958; FRCSE 1958; FRCPE 1993; FRCPSGlas 1993; FRCP 1997. Guy's Hospital and Medical School, University of London: House Surgeon, 1955–56; Res. Fellow, Dept of Surgery, 1956–57; Lectr in Anatomy, 1956–57; Sen. Surgical Registrar, 1959–62; Hon. Consultant Surgeon, 1963; Surgical Registrar, Middlesex Hosp., 1957–59; Consultant Surgeon, Royal Surrey County and St Luke's Hosps, Guildford, 1962–91; Vis. Surgeon, Cranleigh and Cobham Hosps, 1962–91; Surgical Dir, Jarvis Breast Screening Centre, DHSS, 1978–91. Sen. Mem., British Breast Gp (Mem., 1962–). Visiting Professor: Surrey Univ., 1986– (Hon. Reader, 1968–80); univs in USA, Australia, NZ, Pakistan and India; Wilson Wang Prof. in Surgery, Chinese Univ. of HK, 1993. Examnr, RCSGlas, and Univs of Edinburgh, London, Nottingham, Newcastle, Singapore and Malaya; Overseas Advr for sen. acad. appts in surgical specialities, Univ. of Malaya, 1993–; Ext. Advr for sen. surg. posts, King Saud Univ., Riyadh, 1993–; Advr, Anti-Cancer Council of Vic, Aust., 1992–. Mem. Clin. Adv. Gp, Health Risk Resources Internat., 1995–; Trustee and Mem., Health and Welfare Cttee, Thalidomide Trust, 1995–; Overseas Mem., Australian and NZ Breast Cancer Study Gp, 1989–. Chm., Conf. of Colls and Faculties (Scotland), 1992–94; Mem., Senate of Surgery of UK and Ire., 1992–95; Fellow, Assoc. of Surgeons of GB and Ire., 1962 (Mem. Council, and Chm., Educn Adv. Cttee, 1986–90); Royal College of Surgeons: Handcock Prize, 1955; Surgical Tutor, 1964; Regl Advr, 1975; Penrose May teacher, 1985–; Royal College of Surgeons of Edinburgh: Examnr, 1979; Mem. Council, 1984–; Vice-Pres., 1989–91; Regent, 1995. Hon. FRACS 1985; Hon. FCS(SA) 1992; Hon. FCSSL 1992; Hon. FRCSI 1993; Hon. FCSHK 1993; Hon. FFAEM 1997; Mem., Acad. of Medicine of Malaysia, 1993; Hon. Member: N Pacific Surgical Assoc., USA, 1991; Assoc. of Surgeons of India, 1993; Soc. of Surgeons of Nepal, 1994; Surgical Res. Soc., 1995; Fellow, Acad. of Medicine of Singapore, 1994. Internat. Master Surgeon, Internat. Coll. of Surgeons, 1994. DUniv Surrey, 1996. Hon. Citizen, State of Nebraska, USA, 1967. *Publications:* articles and book chapters on surgical subjects, esp. breast disease, surgical oncology and endocrine surgery. *Recreations:* mountaineering, ski-ing, fly-fishing. *Address:* Quarry Cottage, Salkeld Dykes, Penrith, Cumbria CA11 9LL. *T:* (01768) 898822. *Clubs:* Alpine, Caledonian; New (Edinburgh); Yorkshire Fly Fishers; Swiss Alpine (Pres., Assoc. of British Members, 1978–80).

BOULTING, Roy; Producer and Joint Managing Director, Charter Film Productions Ltd, since 1973; *b* 21 Nov. 1913; *s* of Arthur Boulting and Rose Bennett. *Educ:* HMS Worcester; Reading Sch. Formed independent film production company with twin brother John, 1937. Served War of 1939–45, RAC, finishing as Capt.; films directed for Army included Desert Victory (Oscar), Tunisian Victory and Burma Victory. Producer: Brighton Rock, 1947; Seven Days to Noon, 1950; Private's Progress, 1955; Lucky Jim (Edinburgh Festival), 1957; I'm All Right Jack, 1959; Heavens Above!, 1962. Director: Pastor Hall, 1939; Thunder Rock, 1942; Fame is the Spur, 1947; The Guinea Pig, 1948; High Treason, 1951; Singlehanded, 1952; Seagulls over Sorrento, Crest of the Wave, 1953; Josephine and Men, 1955; Run for the Sun, 1955; Brothers in Law, 1956; Happy is the Bride, 1958; Carlton-Browne of the FO, 1958–59; I'm All Right Jack, 1959; The Risk, 1960; The French Mistress, 1960; Suspect, 1960; The Family Way, 1966; Twisted Nerve, 1968; There's a Girl in My Soup, 1970; Soft Beds, Hard Battles, 1974; Danny Travis, 1978; The Last Word, 1979; The Moving Finger, 1984. *Play:* (with Leo Marks) Favourites, 1977. Dir, British Lion Films Ltd, 1958–72. Mem. Adv. Council, Dirs' and Producers' Rights Soc., 1988–. Hon. Dr RCA, 1990. Evening Standard Award for outstanding contribn to British films, 1997. *Address:* Charter Film Productions Ltd, Twickenham Film Studios, St Margarets, Twickenham, Middlesex TW1 2AW. *Club:* Lord's Taverners.

BOULTON, Sir Clifford (John), GCB 1994 (KCB 1990; CB 1985); DL; Clerk of the House of Commons, 1987–94; *b* 25 July 1930; *s* of Stanley Boulton and Evelyn (*née* Hey), Cocknage, Staffs; *m* 1955, Anne, *d* of Rev. E. E. Raven, Cambridge; one adopted *s* one adopted *d*. *Educ:* Newcastle-under-Lyme High School; St John's Coll., Oxford (exhibnr). MA (Modern History). National Service, RAC, 1949–50; Lt Staffs Yeomanry (TA). A Clerk in the House of Commons, 1953–94: Clerk of Select Cttees on Procedure, 1964–68 and 1976–77; Public Accounts, 1968–70; Parliamentary Questions, 1971–72; Privileges, 1972–77; Clerk of the Overseas Office, 1977–79; Principal Clerk, Table Office, 1979–83; Clerk Asst, 1983–87. A school Governor and subsequently board mem., Church Schools Company, 1965–79; Trustee, Oakham Sch., 1998–. Trustee, Industry and Parliament Trust, 1991–95. Mem., Standing Cttee on Standards in Public Life, 1994–2000. Chm., Standards Cttee, Rutland CC, 2000–. DL Rutland, 1997. Hon. LLD Keele, 1993. *Publications:* (ed) Erskine May's Parliamentary Practice, 21st edn, 1989; contribs to Halsbury's Laws of England, 4th edn, and Parliamentary journals. *Recreations:* visual arts, the countryside. *Address:* 2 Main Street, Lyddington, Oakham LE15 9LT. *T:* (01572) 823487.

BOULTON, David John; His Honour Judge Boulton; a Circuit Judge, since 2001; *b* 2 July 1945; *s* of late John Ellis and Hilda May Boulton; *m* 1971, Suzanne Proudlove. *Educ:* Quarry Bank High Sch., Liverpool; Liverpool Univ. (LLB). Called to the Bar, Middle Temple, 1970; specialised in crime; Standing Counsel for Inland Revenue, Customs and Excise, and DTI; a Recorder, 1989–2001. *Recreations:* wine, gardens, travel. *Address:* c/o The Crown Court, Ringway, Preston PR1 2LL. *Clubs:* Racquet (Liverpool); Lancashire CC.

BOULTON, Prof. Geoffrey Stewart, OBE 2000; FRS 1992; FRSE; Regius Professor of Geology and Mineralogy, since 1986, Vice-Principal, since 1999, University of Edinburgh; *b* 28 Nov. 1940; *s* of George Stewart and Rose Boulton; *m* 1964, Denise Bryers Lawns; two *d*. *Educ:* Longton High Sch.; Birmingham Univ. BSc, PhD, DSc. FGS 1961; FRSE 1989. British Geol Survey, 1962–64; Demonstrator, Univ. of Keele, 1964–65; Fellow, Univ. of Birmingham, 1965–68; Hydrogeologist, Kenya, 1968; Lectr, then Reader, Univ. of E Anglia, 1968–86; Provost and Dean, Faculty of Sci. and Engrg, Univ. of Edinburgh, 1994–99. Prof., Amsterdam Univ., 1980–86. Mem., Royal Commn on Envmtl Pollution, 1994–2000. NERC: Chairman: Polar Sci. Bd, 1992–95; Earth Sci. and Technol. Bd, 1994–98; Mem. Council, 1993–98; Royal Society: Chm., Sect. Cttee 5 for Earth Sci. and Astronomy, 1993–95; Mem., Council, 1997–99. Member: NCC Scotland, 1991–92; SHEFC, 1997– (Chm., Res. Policy Cttee, 2000–); Council, Scottish Assoc. for Marine Sci., 1997–. UK Deleg. to IUGS, 1996–99. President: Geol Soc. of Edinburgh, 1991–93; Quaternary Res. Assoc., 1991–94. Seligman Crystal, Internat. Glaciol. Soc., 2001. *Publications:* numerous articles in learned jls on glaciology, quaternary, marine and polar geology. *Recreations:* violin, mountaineering, sailing. *Address:* 19 Lygon Road, Edinburgh EH16 5QD.

BOULTON, Prof. James Thompson, FBA 1994; Deputy Director, Institute for Advanced Research in Arts and Social Sciences (formerly Institute for Advanced Research in the Humanities), University of Birmingham, since 1999 (Fellow, 1984; Director, 1987–99); *b* 17 Feb. 1924; *e s* of Harry and Annie M. P. Boulton; *m* 1949, Margaret Helen Leary; one *s* one *d*. *Educ:* University College, Univ. of Durham; Lincoln Coll., Oxford. BA Dunelm 1948; BLitt Oxon 1952; PhD Nottingham 1960. FRSL 1968. Served as pilot in RAF, 1943–46 (Flt-Lt). Lectr, subseq. Sen. Lectr and Reader in English, Univ. of Nottingham, 1951–64; John Cranford Adams Prof. of English, Hofstra Univ., NY, 1967; Prof. of English Lit., Univ. of Nottingham, 1964–75, Dean, Faculty of Arts, 1970–73; University of Birmingham: Prof. of English Studies and Head of Dept of English Lang. and Lit., 1975–88, Prof. Emeritus, 1989; Dean of Faculty of Arts, 1981–84; Public Orator, 1984–88. Chm. of Govs, Fircroft Coll., Selly Oak, 1985–92. Editor, Renaissance and Modern Studies, 1969–75, 1985. General Editor: The Letters of D. H. Lawrence, 1973–; The Works of D. H. Lawrence, 1975–. Hon. DLitt: Dunelm, 1991; Nottingham, 1993. *Publications:* (ed) Edmund Burke: A Philosophical Enquiry into…the Sublime and Beautiful, 1958, rev. edn 1987; (ed) C. F. G. Masterman: The Condition of England, 1960; The Language of Politics in the Age of Wilkes and Burke, 1963, 2nd edn 1975; (ed) Dryden: Of Dramatick Poesy etc, 1964; (ed) Defoe: Prose and Verse, 1965, 2nd edn 1975; (with James Kinsley) English Satiric Poetry: Dryden to Byron, 1966; (ed and contrib.) Renaissance and Modern Essays, 1966; (ed) Lawrence in Love: Letters from D. H. Lawrence to Louie Burrows, 1968; (ed) Samuel Johnson: The Critical Heritage, 1971; (with S. T. Bindoff) Research in Progress in English and Historical Studies in the Universities of the British Isles, vol. 1, 1971, vol. 2, 1976; (ed) Defoe: Memoirs of a Cavalier, 1972, rev. edn 1991; (ed) The Letters of D. H. Lawrence, vol. 1, 1979, vol. 2 (jtly), 1982, vol. 3 (jtly), 1984, vol. 4 (jtly), 1987, vol. 5 (jtly), 1989, vol. 6 (jtly), 1991, vol. 7 (jtly), 1993, vol. 8, 2000, Selected Letters, 1997; (ed jtly) The Writings and Speeches of Edmund Burke, vol. 1, The Early Writings, 1997; D. H. Lawrence: man of learning, 2000; *contributed to:* The Familiar Letter in the 18th Century, 1966; D. H. Lawrence, 1980; Renaissance and Modern Studies, 1985; D. H. Lawrence in Italy and England, 1999; papers in Durham Univ. Jl, Essays in Criticism, Renaissance and Modern Studies, Modern Drama, etc. *Recreation:* gardening. *Address:* Institute for Advanced Research in Arts and Social Sciences, University of Birmingham, Edgbaston, Birmingham B15 2TT.

BOULTON, Sir William (Whytehead), 3rd Bt *cr* 1944; Kt 1975; CBE 1958; TD 1949; Secretary, Senate of the Inns of Court and the Bar, 1974–75; *b* 21 June 1912; *s* of Sir William Boulton, 1st Bt, and Rosalind Mary (*d* 1969), *d* of Sir John Davison Milburn, 1st Bt, of Guyzance, Northumberland; *S* brother, 1982; *m* 1944, Margaret Elizabeth, *o d* of late Brig. H. N. A. Hunter, DSO; one *s* two *d*. *Educ:* Eton (Captain of Oppidans, 1931); Trinity Coll., Cambridge. Called to Bar, Inner Temple, 1936; practised at the Bar, 1937–39. Secretary, General Council of the Bar, 1950–74. Gazetted 2nd Lieut TA (Essex Yeo.), 1934; retired with rank of Hon. Lieut-Col, 1949; served War of 1939–45: with 104th Regt RHA (Essex Yeo.) and 14th Regt RHA, in the Middle East, 1940–44; Staff Coll., Camberley, 1944. Control Commission for Germany (Legal Div.), 1945–50. *Publications:* A Guide to Conduct and Etiquette at the Bar of England and Wales, 1st edn 1953, 6th edn, 1975. *Heir:* *s* John Gibson Boulton, *b* 18 Dec. 1946. *Address:* The Quarters House, Alresford, near Colchester, Essex CO7 8AY. *T:* (01206) 822450.

BOUNDS, (Kenneth) Peter; Chief Executive, Liverpool City Council, 1991–99; a Civil Service Commissioner, since 2001; *b* 7 Nov. 1943; *s* of Rev. Kenneth Bounds and Doris Bounds; *m* 1965, Geraldine Amy Slee; two *s*. *Educ:* Ashville College, Harrogate. Admitted Solicitor, 1971. Dir of Admin, Stockport MBC, 1973–82; Chief Exec., Bolton MBC, 1982–91. Pres., Assoc. of Dist Secs, 1980–81; Chm., Soc. of Metropolitan Chief Execs, 1997; Company Secretary: Greater Manchester Econ. Develt Ltd, 1986–91; NW Tourist Bd, 1986–91; Royal Liverpool Philharmonic Soc., 2000– (Dir, 1993–2000; Dep. Chm., 1997–2000). Chairman: Liverpool City Challenge, 1991–95; Liverpool City of Learning, 1994–97; Liverpool Partnership Gp, 1994–99. Member: President's Council, Methodist Church, 1981–84; Bd of Trustees for Methodist Church Purposes, 1983–. Patron, Centre for Tomorrow's Company, 1997–. Hon. Fellow, Bolton Inst. of Higher Educn, 1991. FRSA 1994. *Recreations:* music, theatre. *Address:* The Coach House, 42 Church Road, Woolton, Liverpool L25 6DD.

BOURDEAUX, Rev. Canon Michael Alan; Director, Keston Institute, Oxford (formerly Keston College, Kent), 1969–99; *b* 19 March 1934; *s* of Richard Edward and Lillian Myra Bourdeaux; *m* 1st, 1960, Gillian Mary Davies (*d* 1978); one *s* one *d*; 2nd, 1979, Lorna Elizabeth Waterton; one *s* one *d*. *Educ:* Truro Sch.; St Edmund Hall, Oxford (MA Hons Mod. Langs); Wycliffe Hall, Oxford (Hons Theology); BD Oxon 1969. Moscow State Univ., 1959–60; Deacon, 1960; Asst Curate, Enfield Parish Church, Mddx, 1960–64; researching at Chislehurst, Kent, on the Church in the Soviet Union, with grant from Centre de Recherches, Geneva, 1965–68. Vis. Prof., St Bernard's Seminary, Rochester, NY, 1969; Vis. Fellow, LSE, 1969–71; Research Fellow, RIIA, Chatham House, 1971–73; Dawson Lectr on Church and State, Baylor Univ., Waco, Texas, 1972; Chavasse Meml Lectr, Oxford Univ., 1976; Kathryn W. Davis Prof. in Slavic Studies, Wellesley Coll., Wellesley, Mass, 1981; Moorhouse Lectr, Melbourne, 1987; Vis. Fellow, St Edmund Hall, Oxford, 1989–90; Vis. Prof., Inst. for Econ., Political and Cultural Develt, Notre Dame Univ., Ind., 1993; Croall Lectr, Univ. of Edinburgh, 2002. Mem., High-Level Experts' Gp on For. Policy and Common Security, EC, 1993–94. Hon. Canon, Rochester Cathedral, 1990–99, now Canon Emeritus; Hon. Dir, Iffley Fest., 1996. Founded Keston College, a research centre on religion in the Communist countries, 1969. Founder of journal, Religion in Communist Lands, 1973, retitled Religion, State and Society: the Keston Jl, 1992. Mem. Council, Britain–Russia Centre, 1991–2000. DD Lambeth, 1996. Templeton Prize for Progress in Religion, 1984. Order of Grand Duke Gediminas (Lithuania), 1999. *Publications:* Opium of the People, 1965, 2nd edn 1977; Religious Ferment in Russia, 1968; Patriarch and Prophets, 1970, 2nd edn 1975; Faith on Trial in Russia, 1971; Land of Crosses, 1979; Risen Indeed, 1983; (with Lorna Bourdeaux) Ten Growing Soviet Churches, 1987; Gorbachev, Glasnost and the Gospel, 1990, rev. US edn, The Gospel's Triumph over Communism, 1991; (ed) The Politics of Religion in Russia and the New States of Eurasia, 1995; (ed jtly) Proselytism and Orthodoxy in Russia, 1999. *Recreations:* choral singing, officiating, as Member British Tennis Umpires Assoc., at Wimbledon and abroad. *Address:* Keston Institute, 4 Park Town, Oxford OX2 6SH. *T:* (01865) 311022; 101 Church Way, Iffley, Oxford OX4 4EG. *T:* (01865) 777276. *Club:* Athenæum.

BOURDILLON, Mervyn Leigh; JP; Lord-Lieutenant of Powys, 1986–98; *b* 9 Aug. 1924; *s* of late Prebendary G. L. Bourdillon; *m* 1961, Penelope, *d* of late P. W. Kemp-Welch, OBE; one *s* three *d*. *Educ:* Haileybury. Served RNVR, 1943–46. Forestry Comr, 1973–76. Mem. Brecon County Council, 1962–73; DL 1962, JP 1970, High Sheriff 1970, Brecon; Vice Lord-Lieutenant, Powys, 1978–86. KStJ 1994. *Address:* Llwyn Madoc, Beulah, Llanwrtyd Wells, Powys LD5 4TU.

BOURDILLON, Peter John, FRCP; Consultant in Cardiovascular Disease (formerly in Clinical Physiology (Cardiology)), Hammersmith Hospital, since 1975; on secondment to Academy of Medical Royal Colleges, from Department of Health, 1997–2001; *b* 10 July 1941; *s* of John Francis Bourdillon and Pamela Maud Bourdillon (*née* Chetham); *m* 1964, Catriona Glencairn-Campbell, FGA, *d* of Brig. W. Glencairn-Campbell, OBE and Lady Muir-Mackenzie; one *s* two *d*. *Educ:* Rugby Sch.; Middlesex Hosp. Med. Sch. (MB BS

1965). MRCP 1968, FRCP 1983. House physician and surgeon posts in London, 1965–68; Medical Registrar: Middlesex Hosp., 1969–70; Hammersmith Hosp., 1970–72; Sen. Registrar in Cardiol., Hammersmith Hosp., 1972–74; part-time MO, 1975–81, part-time SMO, 1981–91, Hd of Med. Manpower and Educn Div., 1991–93, DHSS, then DoH; Head (Grade 3), Health Care (Med.), then Specialist Clin. Services, Div., DoH, 1993–97. Hon. Sen. Lectr, RPMS, later ICSM, London Univ., 1979–. QHP 1996–99. *Publications:* contrib. to med. jls. *Recreations:* writing software, golf, ski-ing. *Address:* 13 Grove Terrace, NW5 1PH. *T:* (020) 7485 6839. *Clubs:* Royal Society of Medicine; Highgate Golf.

BOURDON, Derek Conway, FIA; Director, 1981–84, and General Manager, 1979–84, Prudential Assurance Co. Ltd; Director, London and Manchester Group PLC, 1986–94; *b* 3 Nov. 1932; *s* of late Walter Alphonse Bourdon and Winifred Gladys Vera Bourdon; *m* 1st, Camilla Rose Bourdon (marr. diss.); one *s* one *d*; 2nd, Jean Elizabeth Bourdon. *Educ:* Bancroft's School. FIA 1957. RAF Operations Research (Pilot Officer), 1956–58. Joined Prudential, 1950; South Africa, 1962–65; Dep. General Manager, 1976–79. Chairman, Vanbrugh Life, 1974–79. Member, Policyholders Protection Board, 1980–84; Chm., Industrial Life Offices Assoc., 1982–84 (Vice-Chm., 1980–82). *Recreations:* golf, bridge. *Clubs:* Sloane; Barton-on-Sea Golf.

BOURKE, family name of **Earl of Mayo**.

BOURKE, Christopher John; Metropolitan Stipendiary Magistrate, 1974–96; *b* 31 March 1926; *e s* of late John Francis Bourke of the Oxford Circuit and late Eileen Winifred Bourke (*née* Beddoes); *m* 1956, Maureen, *y d* of late G. A. Barron-Boshell; two *s* one *d*. *Educ:* Stonyhurst; Oriel Coll., Oxford. Served Army, 1944–48: commnd Glos Regt; served BAOR and Jamaica (ADC to Governor). Called to Bar, Gray's Inn, 1953; Oxford Circuit, 1954–55; Dir of Public Prosecutions Dept, 1955–74. *Recreations:* landscape painting, ballet. *Address:* 61 Kingsmead Road, SW2 3HY. *T:* (020) 8671 3977.

See also Baron Derwent.

BOURKE, (Elizabeth) Shân (Josephine) L.; *see* Legge-Bourke.

BOURKE, Martin; HM Diplomatic Service; Deputy High Commissioner, New Zealand, since 2000; *b* 12 March 1947; *s* of Robert Martin Bourke and Enid Millicent Bourke (*née* Love); *m* 1973, Anne Marie Marguerite Hottelet; four *s*. *Educ:* Stockport Grammar Sch.; University Coll. London (BA Hons 1969); King's Coll. London (MA 1970). Joined FCO, 1970; Brussels, 1971–73; Singapore, 1974–76; Lagos, 1978–80; on loan to DTI, 1980–84; Consul (Commercial), Johannesburg, 1984–88; Asst Head, Envmt, Sci. and Energy Dept, FCO, 1990–93; Gov., Turks and Caicos Islands, 1993–96; Area Manager, Prince's Trust (on secondment), 1996–99. *Recreations:* walking, tennis, reading, theatre, amateur dramatics. *Address:* c/o Foreign and Commonwealth Office, SW1A 2AH. *Club:* Royal Over-Seas League.

BOURKE, Rt Rev. Michael; *see* Wolverhampton, Bishop Suffragan of.

BOURN, James; HM Diplomatic Service, retired; *b* 30 Aug. 1917; *s* of James and Sarah Gertrude Bourn; *m* 1st, 1944, Isobel Mackenzie (*d* 1977); one *s*; 2nd, 1981, Moya Livesey (*d* 1993). *Educ:* Queen Elizabeth's Grammar Sch., Darlington; Univ. of Edinburgh (MA Hons 1979). Executive Officer, Ministry of Health, 1936. War of 1939–45; served (Royal Signals), in India, North Africa and Italy; POW; Captain. Higher Exec. Officer, Ministry of National Insurance, 1947; Asst Principal, Colonial Office, 1947; Principal, 1949; Secretary to the Salaries Commission, Bahamas, 1948–49; Private Sec. to Perm. Under-Sec., 1949; seconded to Tanganyika, 1953–55; UK Liaison Officer to Commn for Technical Co-operation in Africa (CCTA), 1955–57; Commonwealth Relations Office, 1961; seconded to Central African Office, 1962; Dar es Salaam, 1963; Deputy High Commissioner in Zanzibar, Tanzania, 1964–65; Counsellor and Dep. High Comr, Malawi, 1966–70; Ambassador to Somalia, 1970–73; Consul-General, Istanbul, 1973–75. *Address:* c/o National Westminster Bank, 20 Market Place, Richmond, North Yorks DL10 4QF. *Club:* Royal Commonwealth Society.

BOURN, Sir John (Bryant), KCB 1991 (CB 1986); Comptroller and Auditor General, since 1988; Auditor General for Wales, since 1999; *b* 21 Feb. 1934; *s* of late Henry Thomas Bryant Bourn and Beatrice Grace Bourn; *m* 1959, Ardita Ann Fleming; one *s* one *d*. *Educ:* Southgate County Grammar Sch.; LSE. 1st cl. hons BScEcon 1954, PhD 1958. Air Min. 1956–63; HM Treasury, 1963–64; Private Sec. to Perm. Under-Sec., MoD, 1964–69; Asst Sec. and Dir of Programmes, Civil Service Coll., 1969–72; Asst Sec., MoD, 1972–74; Under-Sec., Northern Ireland Office, 1974–77; Asst Under-Sec. of State, MoD, 1977–82; Dep. Sec., Northern Ireland Office, 1982–84; Dep. Under Sec. of State (Defence Procurement), MoD, 1985–88. Vis. Prof., LSE, 1983–. Chm., Multi-Lateral Audit Adv. Gp, World Bank, 1999–; Member: Financial Reporting Council, 1990–; Financial Reporting Review Panel, 1991–. FCIPS 1995; CIMgt 1994. Hon. Fellow: Brighton Univ., 1989; LSE, 1995. Hon. LLD Brunel, 1995; DUniv Open, 1998. *Publications:* articles and reviews in professional jls. *Recreations:* swimming, tennis. *Address:* National Audit Office, 157–197 Buckingham Palace Road, SW1W 9SP.

BOURNE, Prof. Frederick John, CBE 1995; Professor of Animal Health, University of Bristol, since 1988; *b* 3 Jan. 1937; *s* of Sidney John Bourne and Florence Beatrice Bourne; *m* 1959, Mary Angela Minter; two *s*. *Educ:* Univ. of London (BVetMed); Univ. of Bristol (PhD). MRCVS 1961. Gen. vet. practice, 1961–67; University of Bristol: Lectr in Animal Husbandry, 1967–76; Reader in Animal Husbandry, 1976–80; Prof. and Hd of Dept of Veterinary Medicine, 1980–88; Dir, AFRC, subseq. BBSRC, Inst. for Animal Health, 1988–97. Vis. Prof., Univ. of Reading, 1990–97. Chm., Govt Ind. Scientific Gp for Control of Cattle TB, 1998–. For. Mem., Polish Acad. of Sci., 1994. *Publications:* over 200 contribs to variety of jls, incl. Immunology, Vet. Immunology and Immunopath., Res. in Vet. Sci., Infection and Immunity. *Recreations:* gardening, fishing, golf, cricket, music. *Address:* Westlands, Jubilee Lane, Langford, Bristol BS40 5EJ. *T:* (01934) 852 464.

BOURNE, Gordon Lionel, FRCS, FRCOG; Hon. Consultant, Department of Obstetrics and Gynæcology, St Bartholomew's Hospital, London; Hon. Consultant Gynæcologist to Royal Masonic Hospital, since 1986 (Consultant, 1972–86); *b* 3 June 1921; *s* of Thomas Holland Bourne and Lily Anne (*née* Clewlow); *m* 1948, Barbara Eileen Anderson; three *s* one *d*. *Educ:* Queen Elizabeth Grammar Sch., Ashbourne; St Bartholomew's Hosp.; Harvard Univ. MRCS, LRCP 1945, FRCS 1954; MRCOG 1956, FRCOG 1962; FRSocMed. Highlands Hosp., 1948; Derbs Royal Infirm., 1949; City of London Mat. Hosp., 1952; Hosp. for Women, Soho, 1954; Gynæcol Registrar, Middlesex Hosp., 1956; Sen. Registrar, Obsts and Gynae., St Bartholomew's Hosp., 1958; Nuffield Trav. Fellow, 1959; Res. Fellow, Harvard, 1959; Cons. Gynæcol., St Luke's Hosp., 1963. Arris and Gale Lectr, RCS, 1964; Mem. Bd of Professions Suppl. to Medicine, 1964; Regional Assessor in Maternal Deaths, 1974; Examr in Obsts and Gynae., Univs of London, Oxford and Riyadh, Jt Conjt Bd and RCOG, Central Midwives Bd; Mem. Ct of Assts, Haberdashers' Co., 1968, Master, 1984; Mem. Bd of Governors, 1971–83, Chm., 1980–83, Haberdashers' Aske's Schs, Hatcham; Mem., 1983–95, Chm., 1987–95, Bd of Governors, Haberdashers' Aske's Schs, Elstree. *Publications:* The Human Amnion and Chorion, 1962; Shaw's Textbook of Gynæcology, 9th edn, 1970; Recent Advances in Obstetrics and Gynæcology, 11th edn, 1966—13th edn, 1979; Modern Gynæcology with Obstetrics for Nurses, 4th edn, 1969 and 5th edn, 1973; Pregnancy, 1972, 6th edn 1994; numerous articles in sci. and professional jls. *Recreations:* ski-ing, water-ski-ing, shooting, swimming, writing, golf. *Address:* Oldways, Bishop's Avenue, N2 0BN. *T:* (020) 8458 4788. *Club:* Carlton.

BOURNE, Margaret Janet, OBE 1982; Chairman, CORDA Ltd, since 1992; *b* 18 Aug. 1931; *d* of Thomas William Southcott and Nora Annie Southcott (*née* Pelling); *m* 1960, George Brian Bourne. *Educ:* Twickenham Grammar Sch.; Royal Holloway Coll. (BSc). MRAeS 1962; CEng, FIEE 1997. Fairey Engineering, 1953–62; Army Operational Res. Estabt, 1962–65; Defence Operational Analysis Estabt, 1965–76; Asst Dir, Scientific Adv. Gp Army, 1976–80; Hd of Assessments Div., ASWE, 1980–82; Hd of Weapon Dept, ASWE, 1982–84; Dep. Dir, Admiralty Res. Estabt, 1984–87; Asst Chief Scientific Advr (Capabilities), MoD, 1987–91. *Recreations:* playing early music, gardening, natural history. *Address:* c/o CORDA Ltd, Apex Tower, 7 High Street, New Malden, Surrey KT3 4LH.

BOURNE, Matthew Christopher, OBE 2001; director and choreographer; Artistic Director and Joint Founder Member, Adventures in Motion Pictures, since 1987; *b* 13 Jan. 1960; *s* of Harold Jeffrey, (Jim), Bourne and June Lillian Bourne (*née* Handley). *Educ:* Laban Centre for Movement and Dance (BA Hons Dance and Theatre 1986; Hon. Fellow 1997). Dir, Spitfire Trust, 1996–; Mem. Bd, Laban Centre for Movt and Dance, 1999–; Mem., Hon. Cttee, Dance Cares, 1995–. *Works* include: *for Adventures in Motion Pictures,* created and directed: Overlap Lovers, 1987; Spitfire, 1988; The Infernal Galop, 1989; Green Fingers, 1990; Town and Country, 1991; Deadly Serious, 1992; Nutcracker, 1992; The Percys of Fitzrovia, 1992; Highland Fling, 1994; Swan Lake, 1995 (Olivier Award, 1996; LA Drama Critics Award, 1997; 2 Tony Awards, 1999; 3 Drama Desk Awards, 1999; 2 Outer Critics' Circle Awards, 1999; Astaire Award, 1999); Cinderella, 1997; The Car Man (Evening Standard Award), 2000; *for other companies,* choreographed: As You Like It, RSC, 1989; Leonce and Lena, Crucible, Sheffield, 1989; Children of Eden, Prince Edward Theatre, 1991; A Midsummer Night's Dream, Aix-en-Provence Fest., 1991; The Tempest, NYT, 1991; Show Boat, Malmö Stadsteater, 1991; Peer Gynt, Ninagawa Co., Oslo, Barbican, 1994; Watch with Mother, Nat. Youth Dance Co., 1994; Oliver!, London Palladium, 1994; My Fair Lady, RNT, 2001; as performer, created numerous rôles in AMP prodns on stage and in films; *films choreographed* include: Late Flowering Lust, 1993; Drip: a narcissistic love story, 1993. *Recreations:* old movies, theatre and music, reading obituaries. *Address:* c/o Adventures in Motion Pictures, Suite 3, 140A Gloucester Mansions, Cambridge Circus, WC2H 8HD. *T:* (020) 7836 8716; c/o Duncan Heath, ICM, Oxford House, 76 Oxford Street, W1N 0AX. *T:* (020) 7636 6565. *Club:* Soho House.

BOURNE, Nicholas; Member (C) Mid & West Wales, and Leader of Conservatives, National Assembly for Wales, since 1999; *b* 1 Jan. 1952; *s* of late John Morgan Bourne and of Joan Edith Mary Bourne. *Educ:* King Edward VI Sch., Chelmsford; UCW, Aberystwyth (LLB 1st Cl. Hons; LLM 1976); Trinity Coll., Cambridge (LLM). Called to the Bar, Gray's Inn, 1976. Supervisor in Law: Corpus Christi Coll., Cambridge, 1974–80; St Catharine's Coll., Cambridge, 1974–82; LSE, 1975–77; Principal, Chart Univ. Tutors Ltd, 1979–88; Co. Sec. and Dir, Chart Foulks Lynch plc, 1984–88; Dir, Holborn Gp Ltd, 1988–91; Swansea Institute: Prof. of Law, 1991–96, Dean, 1992–96, Swansea Law Sch.; Asst Principal, 1996–98. Lectr in Co. Law, Univ. of London Ext. Degree Prog. at UCL, 1991–96; Sen. Lectr in Law, South Bank Univ., 1991–92; Vis. Lectr, Hong Kong Univ., 1996–. Member: Editl Bd, Malaysian Law News, 1991–; Editl Adv. Bd, Business Law Rev., 1991–. Member: NE Thames RHA, 1990–92; W Glamorgan HA, 1994–97. MInstD 1984. *Publications:* Duties and Responsibilities of British Company Directors, 1982; British Company Law and Practice, 1983; Business Law for Accountants, 1987; Lecture Notes for Company Law, 1993, 3rd edn 1998; Essential Company Law, 1994, 2nd edn 1997; Business Law and Practice, 1994; (with B. Pillans) Scottish Company Law, 1996, 2nd edn 1999; contrib. to business and co. law jls. *Recreations:* walking, tennis, badminton, squash, theatre, cricket, travel, cinema. *Address:* National Assembly for Wales, Cardiff Bay, Cardiff CF99 1NA. *T:* (029) 2089 8351. *Club:* Oxford and Cambridge.

BOURNE, (Rowland) Richard; Head, Commonwealth Policy Studies Unit, Institute of Commonwealth Studies, London University, since 1999; *b* 27 July 1940; *s* of late Arthur Brittan and Edith Mary Bourne; *m* 1966, Juliet Mary, *d* of John Attenborough, CBE; two *s* one *d*. *Educ:* Uppingham Sch., Rutland; Brasenose Coll., Oxford (BA Mod. Hist.). Journalist, The Guardian, 1962–72 (Education correspondent, 1968–72); Asst Editor, New Society, 1972–77; Evening Standard: Dep. Editor, 1977–78; London Columnist, 1978–79; Founder Editor, Learn Magazine, 1979; Dep. Dir, Commonwealth Inst., 1983–89; Dir, Commonwealth Human Rights Initiative, 1990–92 (Chm., Trustee Cttee, 1994–); consultant, 1993–94; Co-Dir, Commonwealth Values in Educn Project, Inst. of Educn, London Univ., 1995–98; Dir, Commonwealth Non-Govtl Office for S Africa and Mozambique, 1995–97. Consultant: Internat. Broadcasting Trust, 1980–81; Adv. Council for Adult and Continuing Educn, 1982. Chm., Survival Internat., 1983–98. Chm., Brazilian Contemporary Arts, 1995–98. Treas., Anglo-Portuguese Foundn, 1985–87. *Publications:* Political Leaders of Latin America, 1969; (with Brian MacArthur) The Struggle for Education, 1970; Getulio Vargas of Brazil, 1974; Assault on the Amazon, 1978; Londoners, 1981; (with Jessica Gould) Self-Sufficiency, 16–25, 1983; Lords of Fleet Street, 1990; News on a Knife-Edge, 1995; Britain in the Commonwealth, 1997; (ed) Universities and Development, 2000. *Recreations:* theatre, fishing, supporting Charlton Athletic. *Address:* 36 Burney Street, SE10 8EX. *T:* (020) 8853 0642. *Clubs:* Royal Automobile, Royal Commonwealth Society.

BOURNE-ARTON, Simon Nicholas; QC 1994; a Recorder, since 1993; *b* 5 Sept. 1949; *s* of late Major Anthony Temple Bourne-Arton, MBE; *m* 1974, Diana Carr-Walker; two *s* one *d*. *Educ:* Aysgarth Prep. Sch.; Harrow; Teesside Poly. (HND Bus. Studies); Leeds Univ. (LLB Hons). Called to the Bar, Inner Temple, 1975. *Recreations:* living in the country, golf, tennis, being with family and friends, drinking wine. *Address:* Park Court Chambers, 16 Park Place, Leeds LS1 1SJ.

BOURNEMOUTH, Archdeacon of; *see* Harbidge, Ven. A. G.

BOURNS, Prof. Arthur Newcombe, OC 1982; FRSC 1964; President and Vice-Chancellor, 1972–80, Professor of Chemistry 1953–81, now Emeritus, McMaster University; *b* 8 Dec. 1919; *s* of Evans Clement Bourns and Kathleen Jones; *m* 1943, Marion Harriet Blakney; two *s* two *d*. *Educ:* schs in Petitcodiac, NB; Acadia Univ. (BSc); McGill Univ. (PhD). Research Chemist, Dominion Rubber Co., 1944–45; Lectr, Acadia Univ., 1945–46; Asst Prof. of Chemistry, Saskatchewan Univ., 1946–47; McMaster University: Asst Prof., 1947–49; Associate Prof., 1949–53; Dean, Faculty of Grad. Studies, 1957–61; Chm., Chemistry Dept, 1965–67; Vice-Pres., Science and Engrg Div., 1967–72; Actg Pres., 1970. Nuffield Trav. Fellow in Science, University Coll., London, 1955–56. Chm., Gordon Res. Conf. on Chem. and Physics of Isotopes (Vice-Chm. 1959–60; Chm., 1961–62); Nat. Res. Council of Canada: Mem. Grant Selection Cttee in

Chem., 1966–69 (Chm. 1968–69); Mem. Council, 1969–75; Mem. Exec. Cttee, 1969–75; Mem. or Chm. various other cttees; Natural Scis and Engrg Res. Council: Member: Council, 1978–85; Exec. Cttee, 1978–85; Allocations Cttee, 1978–86; Cttee on Strategic Grants, 1978–83; Chm., Grants and Scholarships Cttee, 1978–83; Mem., Adv. Cttee on University/Industry Interface, 1979–83; Vis. Res. Officer, 1983–84. Member: Ancaster Public Sch. Bd, 1963–64; Bd, Royal Botanic Gdns, 1972–80 (Vice-Chm.); Cttee on Univ. Affairs, Prov. Ontario; Canadian Cttee for Financing Univ. Res., 1978–80; Council of Ontario Univs, 1972–80; Bd of Dirs and Exec. Cttee, Assoc. of Univs and Colleges of Canada, 1974–77; Mohawk Coll. Bd of Dirs, 1975–82; Council, Canadian Inst. for Advanced Research, 1983–89; Chm., Internat. Adv. Cttee, Chinese Univ. Develt Project, 1985–92; Pres. and Chm. Exec. Cttee, Canadian Bureau for Internat. Educn, 1973–76. McMaster Univ. Med. Centre: Member: Bd of Trustees, 1972–80; Exec. Cttee, 1972–80. Director: Nuclear Activation Services, 1978–80; Slater Steel Industries Ltd, 1975–79. British Council Lectr, 1963. Assoc. Editor, Canadian Jl Chemistry, 1966–69; Mem. Editorial Bd, Science Forum, 1967–73. FCIC 1954 (Chm. Hamilton Section, 1952–53; Mem. Educn Cttee, 1953–59; Mem. Council, 1966–69; Montreal Medal, 1976). Hon. Prof., Jiangxi Univ., China, 1989. Hon. DSc: Acadia, 1968; McGill, 1977; New Brunswick, McMaster, 1981; Hon. LLD Brock, 1980. *Address:* No 2411, 100 Burloak Drive, Burlington, ON L7L 6P6, Canada. *T:* (905) 6396964.

BOUSHER, Stephen; Principal Assistant Solicitor, Board of Inland Revenue, since 2000; *b* 13 Feb. 1952; *s* of Leslie Arthur and Clare Bousher; *m* 1974, Jan Townsend; one *s* one *d*. *Educ:* Bec Grammar Sch., Tooting; Southampton Univ. (LLB). Called to the Bar, Gray's Inn, 1975; Board of Inland Revenue, 1976–: Asst Solicitor, 1988-2000; Team Leader, Tax Simplification, then Tax Law Rewrite, Project, 1996–2000. *Recreations:* cinema, watching sport, arguing with Holden, listening to The Grateful Dead, travelling. *Address:* c/o Solicitor's Office, Board of Inland Revenue, East Wing, Somerset House, Strand, WC2R 1LB.

BOUTROS-GHALI, Boutros, PhD; Secretary-General: La Francophonie, since 1997; United Nations, 1992–96; *b* Cairo, 14 Nov. 1922; *m* Maria Leia Nadler. *Educ:* Cairo Univ. (LLB 1946); Paris Univ. (PhD 1949). Prof. of Internat. Law and Internat. Relns, and Head, Dept of Political Scis, Cairo Univ., 1949–77; Minister of State for Foreign Affairs, Egypt, 1977–91; Dep. Prime Minister for Foreign Affairs, 1991–92. Mem., Secretariat, Nat. Democratic Party, 1980–92; MP 1987–92. Mem., UN Commn of Internat. Law, 1979–92. Founder and Editor: Al Ahram Iktisadi, 1960–75; Al-Siyassa Dawlya. *Publications:* Contribution à l'étude des ententes régionales, 1949; Cours de diplomatie et de droit diplomatique et consulaire, 1951; (jtly) Le problème du Canal de Suez, 1957; (jtly) Egypt and the United Nations, 1957; Le principe d'égalité des états et les organisations internationales, 1961; Contribution à une théorie générale des Alliances, 1963; Foreign Policies in a World of Change, 1963; L'Organisation de l'unité africaine, 1969; Le mouvement Afro-Asiatique, 1969; Les difficultés institutionelles du panafricanisme, 1971; La ligue des états arabes, 1972; Les Conflits de frontières en Afrique, 1973; Unvanquished: a US–UN saga, 1999; also many books in Arabic and numerous contribs to periodicals and learned jls. *Address:* 2 Avenue Epnipgiza, Cairo, Egypt.

BOUVERIE; *see* Pleydell-Bouverie, family name of Earl of Radnor.

BOVENIZER, Vernon Gordon Fitzell, CMG 1948; Assistant Under-Secretary of State, Ministry of Defence, 1964–68, retired; *b* 22 July 1908; *s* of Rev. Michael Fitzell Bovenizer and Mary Gordon; *m* 1937, Lillian Cherry (*d* 1970), *d* of John Henry Rowe, Cork; two *s* two *d*. *Educ:* Liverpool Coll.; Sidney Sussex Coll., Cambridge (Scholar). War Office, 1931–45; Control Commission for Germany, 1945, until return to War Office, 1948; Asst Private Sec. to Secretaries of State for War, 1936, and 1940–42; Resident Clerk, 1934–37; Asst Sec., 1942, civilian liaison with US Armies in the UK; Establishment Officer and Dir of Organisation, CCG, 1945–47; Asst Sec. and Dep. Comptroller of Claims, War Office, 1948–58; Counsellor, UK Delegation to NATO, 1958–60; Asst Under-Sec. of State, War Office, 1960–68. US Medal of Freedom, 1945. *Address:* Walhampton Lodge, Lymington, Hants SO41 5SB. *Club:* Reform.

BOVEY, Kathleen Margaret; *see* Wales, K. M.

BOVEY, Dr Leonard; Editor, Materials & Design, since 1985; Head of Technological Requirements Branch, Department of Industry, 1977–84; *b* 9 May 1924; *s* of late Alfred and Gladys Bovey; *m* 1943, Constance Hudson (*d* 1987); one *s* one *d*. *Educ:* Heles Sch., Exeter; Emmanuel Coll., Cambridge (BA, PhD). FInstP; CPhys. Dunlop Rubber, 1943–46; Post-doctoral Fellow, Nat. Res. Council, Ottawa, 1950–52; AERE Harwell, 1952–65; Head W Mids Regional Office, Birmingham, Min. of Technology, 1966–70; Regional Dir, Yorks and Humberside, DTI, 1970–73; Counsellor (Scientific and Technological Affairs), High Commn, Ottawa, 1974–77. Foreign correspondent, Soc. for Advancement of Materials and Processes Engineering (USA) Jl, 1987–. Mem., London Diplomatic Sci. Club. *Publications:* Spectroscopy in the Metallurgical Industry, 1963; papers on spectroscopy in Jl Optical Soc. Amer., Spectrochimica Acta, Jl Phys. Soc. London. *Recreations:* repairing neglected household equipment, work, reading (particularly crime novels), walking, theatre, music. *Address:* 32 Radnor Walk, Chelsea SW3 4BN. *T:* (020) 7352 4142. *Club:* Civil Service.

BOVEY, Philip Henry; Director Legal Services, Department of Trade and Industry, since 1996; Legal Adviser to Regulatory Impact (formerly Deregulation, then Better Regulation) Unit, Cabinet Office, since 1995; *b* 11 July 1948; *s* of Norman Henry Bovey and Dorothy Yvonne Kent Bovey; *m* 1974, Jenet Alison, *d* of late Rev. Canon J. M. McTear and Margaret McTear; one *s* one *d*. *Educ:* Rugby; Peterhouse, Cambridge (schol.; MA). Solicitor. 3rd Sec., FCO, 1970–71; with Slaughter and May, 1972–75; Legal Assistant, 1976; Sen. Legal Assistant, 1976; Depts of Trade and Industry, 1976–77; Cabinet Office, 1977–78; Depts of Trade, Industry, Prices and Consumer Protection, then DTI, 1978–; Asst Solicitor, 1982; Under-Sec., 1985. Companies Act Inspector, 1984–88 (report published 1988). *Recreation:* photography. *Address:* 102 Cleveland Gardens, Barnes, SW13 0AH. *T:* (020) 8876 3710.

BOWATER, Sir Euan David Vansittart, 3rd Bt *cr* 1939, of Friston, Suffolk; *b* 9 Sept. 1935; *s* of Sir Noël Vansittart Bowater, 2nd Bt, GBE, MC, and Constance Heiton (*d* 1993), *d* of David Gordon Bett; *S* father, 1984; *m* 1964, Susan Mary Humphrey, *d* of late A. R. O. Slater, FCA; two *s* two *d*. *Educ:* Eton; Trinity Coll., Cambridge (BA). *Recreations:* travel, golf, music. *Heir:* *s* Moray David Vansittart Bowater, *b* 24 April 1967.

BOWATER, Sir J(ohn) Vansittart, 4th Bt *cr* 1914; *b* 6 April 1918; *s* of Captain Victor Spencer Bowater (*d* 1967) (3rd *s* of 1st Bt) and Hilda Mary (*d* 1918), *d* of W. Henry Potter; *S* uncle, Sir Thomas Dudley Blennerhassett Bowater, 3rd Bt, 1972; *m* 1943, Joan Kathleen, (*d* 1982), *d* of late Wilfrid Scullard; one *s* one *d*. *Educ:* Branksome School, Godalming, Surrey. Served Royal Artillery, 1939–46. *Heir:* *s* Michael Patrick Bowater [*b* 18 July 1949; *m* 1968, Alison, *d* of Edward Wall; four *d*]. *Address:* 214 Runnymede Avenue, Bournemouth, Dorset BH11 9SP. *T:* (01202) 571782.

BOWCOCK, John Brown, FICE; consulting engineer; Senior Consultant, Sir Alexander Gibb & Partners Ltd, 1996–99 (Director, 1989–96; Chairman, 1993–95); *b* 25 Oct. 1931; *s* of John Brown Bowcock and Mabel Bowcock; *m* 1955, Pauline Mary Elizabeth Dalton; three *d*. *Educ:* Hastings Grammar Sch.; St Catherine's Coll., Oxford (MA). FICE 1971; FIMechE 1986. Nat. service, RAF, 1954–56. Joined Sir Alexander Gibb & Partners, 1957: worked on water resource projects overseas incl. Kariba (Zimbabwe), Roseires (Sudan) and Latiyan (Iran), 1957–70; responsible for major dam projects and Drakensberg pumped storage project, SA, 1970–78; Partner, 1978–89; Chief Exec., 1989–93. Chairman: British Dam Soc., 1992–93; British Consultants Bureau, 1991–92; ACE, 1995–96. *Recreations:* golf, music, reading. *Address:* Lothlorien, Crowsley Road, Shiplake, Oxon RG9 3JU. *T:* (0118) 940 4443. *Clubs:* Royal Air Force; Huntercombe Golf (Henley).

BOWDEN, Rev. Andrew; *see* Bowden, Rev. R. A.

BOWDEN, Sir Andrew, Kt 1994; MBE 1961; *b* 8 April 1930; *s* of William Victor Bowden, Solicitor, and Francesca Wilson; *m* 1970, Benita Napier; one *s* one *d*. *Educ:* Ardingly College. Paint industry, 1955–68; Man. Dir, Personnel Assessments Ltd, 1969–71; Man. Dir, Haymarket Personnel Selection Ltd, 1970–71; Director: Sales Education & Leadership Ltd, 1970–71; Jenkin and Purser (Holdings) Ltd, 1973–77. Mem., Wandsworth Borough Council, 1956–62. Contested (C): N Hammersmith, 1955; N Kensington, 1964; Kemp Town, Brighton, 1966. MP (C) Brighton, Kemptown, 1970–97; contested (C) same seat, 1997. Jt Chm., All Party Old Age Pensioners Parly Gp, 1972–97; Chm., All Party BLESMA Gp, 1975–97; Mem. Select Cttee on Expenditure, 1973–74, on Abortion, 1975, on Employment, 1979–83. Mem., Council of Europe, 1987–97. Nat. Chm., Young Conservatives, 1960–61. Internat. Chm., People to People, 1981–83. Nat. Pres., Captive Animals Protection Soc., 1978–98. Mem., Chichester Dio. Synod. Mem. School Council, Ardingly Coll., 1982–97. *Recreations:* birdwatching, chess, golf. *Address:* 4 Carden Avenue, Brighton BN1 8NA. *Club:* Carlton.

BOWDEN, Sir Frank Houston, 3rd Bt *cr* 1915; MA Oxon; retired industrialist and landowner; *b* 10 Aug. 1909; *o s* of Sir Harold Bowden, 2nd Bt, GBE, and of Vera, *d* of Joseph Whitaker, JP, FZS; *S* father 1960; *m* 1st, 1934, Marie-José, *d* of Charles Stiénon and Comtesse Laure de Messey; one *s*; 2nd, 1937, Lydia Eveline (*d* 1981), *d* of Jean Manolovici, Bucharest; three *s*; 3rd, 1989, Oriol Annette Mary, *d* of Charles Hooper Bath. *Educ:* Rugby; Merton Coll., Oxford. Served with RNVR, 1939–44. President: University Hall, Buckland, 1967–71; British Kendo Association, 1969; Thame Br., RN Assoc. Hon. Vice-Pres., 3rd World Kendo Championships, 1976. Vice-Pres., Oxfordshire County Scout Council, 1970–. Pres., Merton Soc., 1976–80. Order of the Rising Sun, Gold Rays with Rosette (Japan), 2000. *Recreation:* collecting weapons and armour, particularly Japanese (Vice-Chm., Japan Soc. of London, 1970–75, 1979–82, 1984–87, Vice-Pres., 1987–), photography, entomology. *Heir:* *s* Nicholas Richard Bowden, *b* 13 Aug. 1935. *Clubs:* White's, Royal Thames Yacht.

BOWDEN, Gerald Francis, TD 1971; barrister, chartered surveyor and university lecturer; *b* 26 Aug. 1935; *s* of Frank Albert Bowden and Elsie Bowden (*née* Burrill); *m* 1967, Heather Elizabeth Hill (*née* Hall) (*d* 1984); two *d*, and one step *s* one step *d*. *Educ:* Battersea Grammar School; Magdalen College, Oxford. MA; FRICS 1984. Called to the Bar, Gray's Inn, 1963. Worked in advertising industry, 1964–68; property marketing and investment, 1968–72; Principal Lecturer in Law, Dept of Estate Management, Polytechnic of the South Bank, 1972–83; Vis. Lectr, Kingston Univ., 1993–. Chm. Panel, Examination in Public of Suffolk Co. Structure Plan, 1993. Mem. GLC for Dulwich, 1977–81; a co-opted Mem., ILEA, 1981–84. MP (C) Dulwich, 1983–92; contested (C) Dulwich, 1992. PPS to Minister for Arts, 1990–92. Mem., Select Cttee on Educn, Sci. and Arts, 1990–92. Vice-Chairman: Cons. Backbench Educn Cttee, 1987–89; Cons. Backbench Arts and Heritage Cttee, 1987–92. Pres., Greater London Conservative Trade Unionists, 1985–88. Pres., Southwark Chamber of Commerce, 1986–89. Chairman: Walcot Educn Foundn (formerly Soc.), 1978–; Lambeth and Southwark Housing Soc., 1973–84; London Rent Assessment Panel, 1994–; Leasehold Valuation Tribunal, 1994–; Pres., Appeal Tribunal on Building Regulation, 1995–. Chm., Magdalen Soc., 1991–; Trustee, Magdalen Develt Trust, 1991–. Mem. Council, Royal Albert Hall, 1994–. Estates Gov., Alleyn's Coll. of God's Gift, Dulwich, 1992–. After Nat. Service, continued to serve in TA until 1984 (Lt-Col). *Publications:* An Introduction to the Law of Contract and Tort, 1977; The Housing Act, 1988. *Recreations:* gardening, books, pictures, renovating old houses. *Address:* 130 Kennington Park Road, SE11 4DJ. *T:* (020) 7582 7361. *Clubs:* Oxford and Cambridge, Chelsea Arts, Garrick.

BOWDEN, Logan S.; *see* Scott Bowden.

BOWDEN, Rt Rev. Raymond David; *see* Bendigo, Bishop of.

BOWDEN, Rev. Canon (Robert) Andrew; Rector of Coates, Rodmarton and Sapperton with Frampton Mansell, since 1979; Chaplain to the Queen, since 1992; Local Ministry Officer, Diocese of Gloucester, since 1993; *b* 13 Nov. 1938; *s* of Charles Bowden and Miriam (*née* Howard-Tripp); *m* 1966, Susan (*née* Humpidge); three *d*. *Educ:* Clifton Coll., Bristol; Worcester Coll., Oxford (Scholar; BA 1962; DipTh 1963; MA 1967; BDQ 1968); Cuddesdon Coll., Oxford. Ordained deacon, 1965, priest, 1966. Curate: St George, Wolverhampton, 1965–69; St Luke's, Duston, 1969–72; Rector, Byfield, 1972–79. Chaplain, Royal Agricl Coll., Cirencester, 1979–93; Rural Advr to dio. of Gloucester, 1981–93; Mem., Archbp's Commn on Rural Areas, 1988–90. Hon. Canon, Gloucester Cathedral, 1990–. Hon. Res. Fellow, Centre for Theology and Educn, Trinity Coll., Carmarthen, 1995–. *Publications:* Ministry in the Countryside, 1994; (with M. West) Dynamic Local Ministry, 2000. *Recreations:* breeding old breeds of poultry, Riding for the Disabled. *Address:* Coates Rectory, Cirencester, Glos GL7 6NR. *T:* and *Fax:* (01285) 770235.

BOWDEN, Prof. Ruth Elizabeth Mary, OBE 1980; DSc London, MB, BS, FRCS; Professor of Anatomy, Royal Free Hospital School of Medicine, University of London, 1951–80, now Emeritus; Sir William Collins Professor of Human and Comparative Anatomy, Royal College of Surgeons of England, 1984–89; Hon. Research Fellow, Institute of Neurology, 1980–96; *b* 21 Feb. 1915; *o c* of late Frank Harold and Louise Ellen Bowden. *Educ:* Westlands Sch.; St Paul's Girls' Sch.; London (Royal Free Hospital) Sch. of Medicine for Women, University of London. House Surg. and later House Physician, Elizabeth Garrett Anderson Hosp. (Oster House branch), 1940–42; House Surg., Royal Cancer Hosp., 1942; Grad. Asst in Nuffield Dept of Orthopaedic Surgery, Peripheral Nerve Injury Unit, Oxford, 1942–45; Asst Lecturer in Anatomy, Royal Free Hospital Sch. of Medicine, 1945; later Lecturer, then University Reader in Human Anatomy, 1949; Rockefeller Travelling Fellowship, 1949–50; Hunterian Prof., RCS, 1950; part-time Lectr, Dept of Anatomy, St Thomas's Hosp. Med. Sch., 1980–83. WHO Consultant in anatomy, Khartoum Univ., 1972, 1974, 1977. President: Anat. Soc. of Gt Brit. and Ireland, 1970; Medical Women's Fedn, 1981. Member: Exec. Cttee, Women's Nat. Commn, 1984–89; Exec. Cttee, N London Hospice Gp, 1986–97 (Mem. Council, 1986–98; Chm., Professional Sub-Cttee, 1986–90); Exec. Cttee, 1988–97, and Med. Adv. Bd, 1992, LEPRA. Member, later Convenor: Acad. Awards Cttee, British Fedn of

University Women, 1956–94; Cttee for Awards and Fellowships, Internat. Fedn of University Women, 1986–92. FRSocMed; Fellow: Brit. Orthopaedic Assoc.; Linnean Soc. Life Vice-President: Chartered Soc. of Physiotherapy (Chm., 1960–70); Inst. of Science Technology (Pres., 1960–65); Riding for the Disabled Assoc. DCLJ 1988, DMLJ 1984. Jubilee Medal, 1977; Wood Jones Medal, RCS, 1988. *Publications:* Peripheral Nerve Injuries, 1958; (contrib.) Surgery of the Spine, ed G. Findlay and R. Owen, 1992; contribs to Peripheral Nerve Injuries Report of Medical Research Council; contrib. to Oxford Companion to Medicine; contribs to medical and scientific jls. *Recreations:* reading, music, painting, walking, gardening, carpentry. *Address:* 6 Hartham Close, Hartham Road, N7 9JH. *T:* (020) 7607 3464.

BOWDERY, Martin Howard; QC 2000; *b* 2 July 1956; *s* of Ray Bowdery and Beryl Bowdery (*née* Porter); *m* 1982, Corinne Taylor (marr. diss. 1999); two *s* four *d*. *Educ:* Trinity Sch. of John Whitgift; Pembroke Coll., Oxford (BA PPE 1978). Called to the Bar, Inner Temple, 1980; practising Barrister, 1982–. Ed., Internat. Construction Law Rev., 1983–87. *Publications:* contributor to: Construction Contract Reform: a plea for sanity, 1999; Construction Law Handbook, 2000. *Address:* 1 Atkin Building, Gray's Inn, WC1R 5AT. *T:* (020) 7404 0102.

BOWDON, Humphrey Anthony Erdeswick B.; *see* Butler-Bowdon.

BOWE, Colette, PhD; *b* 27 Nov. 1946; *d* of Philip Bowe and Norah (*née* Hughes). *Educ:* Notre Dame High Sch., Liverpool; Queen Mary Coll., Univ. of London (BSc Econs, PhD); LSE (MSc Econs). Research Officer, LSE, 1969–70; Econ. Advr, Nat. Ports Council, 1971–73; Department of Industry: Econ. Advr, 1975–78; Principal, 1979–81; Department of Trade and Industry: Asst Sec., 1981–84; Dir of Information, 1984–87; Controller of Public Affairs, IBA, 1987–89; Dir, SIB, 1989–93; Chief Exec., PIA, 1994–97; Exec. Chm., Save & Prosper and Fleming Fund Mgt (Luxembourg), 1998–2001. Non-exec. Dir, Thames Water Utilities Ltd, 2001–. Mem., Statistics Commn, 2000–. Mem., Council, QMW, 1993–. Hon. Fellow: Liverpool John Moores Univ., 1995; Soc. for Advanced Legal Studies, 1998–. *Recreations:* walking, music, films. *Address:* 18 Elia Street, N1 8DE. *T:* (020) 7713 8040.

BOWE, David Robert; Member (Lab) Yorkshire and the Humber Region, European Parliament, since 1999 (Cleveland and Yorkshire North, 1989–94; Cleveland and Richmond, 1994–99); *b* Gateshead, 19 July 1955; *m* 1978, Helena Scattergood; one *s* one *d*. *Educ:* Sunderland Polytechnic; Bath Univ. BSc; PGCE. Former science teacher. Mem., Middlesbrough Borough Council, 1983–89 (Chm., Monitoring and Review Cttee). European Parliament: Mem., Cttee on Envmt, Public Health and Consumer Protection, 1989–; substitute Member: Cttee on Econ. and Monetary Affairs, 1994–99; Industry Cttee, 1999–. Mem., UNISON. *Address:* (constituency office) 2 Blenheim Terrace, Leeds LS2 9JG. *T:* (0113) 245 8993, *Fax:* (0113) 244 2782.

BOWEN, Anthony John; Lector, Faculty of Classics, since 1990, and Orator, since 1993, University of Cambridge; Fellow of Jesus College, Cambridge, since 1995; *b* 17 May 1940; *s* of Dr Reginald Bowen and Dorothy Bowen (*née* Jinks). *Educ:* Bradfield Coll., Berks; St John's Coll., Cambridge. Teacher: Bradfield Coll., 1963–67 (producer of Greek play, 1961, 1964, 1967); Shrewsbury Sch., 1967–90. Contested (L/Alliance) Shrewsbury and Atcham, 1983. Member: (L, then Lib Dem) Shropshire CC, 1981 89, (Lib Dem) Cambridgeshire CC, 1997–. *Publications:* Aeschylus, Cheophori, 1986; The Story of Lucretia, 1987; Plutarch, the Malice of Herodotus, 1992; Xenophon, Symposium, 1998. *Recreations:* travel, politics, music, golf, godchildren. *Address:* Jesus College, Cambridge CB5 8BL. *T:* (01223) 339309. *Clubs:* National Liberal; Royal St David's Golf.

BOWEN, Maj.-Gen. Bryan Morris, CB 1988; Paymaster-in-Chief and Inspector of Army Pay Services, 1986–89, retired; *b* 8 March 1932; *s* of Frederick Bowen and Gwendoline Bowen (*née* Morris); *m* 1955, Suzanne Rowena (*née* Howell); two *d*. *Educ:* Newport High Sch.; Exeter Univ. FCMA; ndc, psc†, sq, pfc. Joined RE, 1953, served UK and BAOR; transf. RAPC, 1958; Paymaster 1/6 QEO Gurkha Rifles, Malaya and UK, 1960–63; Army Cost and Management Accounting Services, 1963–68; DAAG, MoD, 1968–70; Exchange Officer, US Army, Washington, DC, 1970–72; Nat. Defence Coll., 1972–73; DS, RMCS Shrivenham, 1973–76; AAG, MOD, 1976–79; Col (Principal), MoD F4(AD), 1979–81; Chief Paymaster, Army Pay Office (Officers Accounts), 1981–82; Dep. Paymaster-in-Chief, 1982–85. Col Comdt, RAPC, 1990–92; Dep. Col Comdt, AGC, 1992–93. Mem. Council, CIMA, 1990–94; Chm., Oxfordshire Cttee, Army Benevolent Fund, 1990–92; Special Comr, Duke of York's Royal Mil. Sch., Dover, 1990–2000 (Chm., 1992–2000); Dir, United Services Trustee, 1990–2000. Freeman, City of London, 1987. *Recreations:* golf, church affairs. *Address:* Foxlea, Yew Tree Farm, Goodworth Clatford, Andover, Hants SP11 7QY.

BOWEN, Carolyn Elizabeth Cunningham, (Mrs S. J. Bowen); *see* Sinclair, C. E. C.

BOWEN, Charles John; Chief Executive, Booker, 1993–98; *b* 11 Dec. 1941; *s* of John and late Millicent Bowen; *m* 1965, Naomi Stevens; one *s* one *d*. *Educ:* Exeter Univ. (BA Econs and Stats). Fellow, Royal Statistical Soc. Market Research Manager, ICI Paints Div., 1965–67; Product Manager, Unilever, 1967–73; Marketing Manager and Dir, General Foods UK, 1973–78; Gen. Manager, General Foods, Puerto Rico, 1978–82; Vice-Pres., General Foods Corp., USA, 1982–88; Exec. Dir, Hillsdown Holdings, 1988–93. Non-exec. Dir, Legal & General Gp, 1996–99. *Club:* Travellers.

BOWEN, Prof. David Aubrey Llewellyn, FRCP, FRCPE, FRCPath; Professor of Forensic Medicine, University of London, 1977–89, now Emeritus; Head of Department of Forensic Medicine and Toxicology, Charing Cross Hospital Medical School, 1973–89 (Charing Cross and Westminster Medical School, 1985–89); Hon. Consultant Pathologist, Charing Cross Hospital, 1973–89; *b* 31 Jan. 1924; *s* of late Dr Thomas Rufus Bowen and Catherine (*née* Llewellyn); *m* 1st, 1950, Joan Rosemary Davis (*d* 1973); two *s* one *d*; 2nd, 1975, Helen Rosamund Landcastle. *Educ:* Caterham Sch.; Garw Secondary Sch., Pontycymmer; University College of Wales, Cardiff; Corpus Christi Coll., Cambridge (MA); Middlesex Hosp. Med. Sch. (MB BChir 1947); DipPath 1955; DMJ Soc. of Apoth. of London 1962. FRCPE 1971; FRCPath 1975; FRCP 1982. Ho. posts at W Middlesex Hosp. and London Chest Hosp., 1947 and 1950; RAMC, 1947–49; Jun. Resident Pathologist, Bristol Royal Inf., 1950–51; Registrar in Path., London Chest Hosp., 1951–52; Registrar and Sen. Registrar in Clin. Path., National Hosp. for Nervous Diseases, 1952–56; Asst Pathologist and Sen. Registrar, Royal Marsden Hosp., 1956–57; Demonstr 1957–63, Lectr 1963–66, in Forensic Medicine, St George's Hosp. Med. Sch.; Sen. Lectr 1966–73, Reader 1973–77, in Forensic Medicine, Vice-Dean 1974–78, Charing Cross Hosp. Med. Sch.; Lectr in Forensic Medicine, Oxford Univ., 1974–89. Chairman: Div. of Pathology, Charing Cross Hosp., 1976–78; Apptd and Recog. Teachers in Path., Charing Cross Hosp. Med. Sch., 1980–82; Examiner: Univ. of Riyadh, Saudi Arabia, 1978–81; on Forensic Med., RCPath, 1976–90; for Diploma of Med. Jurisprudence, Soc. of Apothecaries of London, 1970–93; for MD (Forensic Medicine) and Diploma in Legal Medicine, Univ. of Sri Lanka, 1985. Lectr, Metropolitan Police Trng Coll., Hendon, 1976–84; W. D. L. Fernando Oration to Medical Legal Soc. of Sri Lanka, 1985. Chm., Quality Assce and Scientific Standards Cttee, Adv. Bd for Forensic Pathol., Home Office, 1990–96. Vice-President: Medico-Legal Soc., 1977–90; Medical Defence Union, 1979–91; President: British Assoc. in Forensic Med., 1977–79; W London Medico-Chirurgical Soc., 1987–88; Member: British Academy in Forensic Sci. and Forensic Sci. Soc., 1960–91 (Mem. Council, 1965–67); British Div. of Internat. Acad. of Path., 1974–93; Acad. Internat. de Médicine Légale et de Méd. Sociale, 1976–90; RCPath Adv. Cttee on Forensic Path., 1973–76 and 1980–82. Liveryman, Apothecaries' Soc., 1972–. Vice-Pres., Old Caterhamians Assoc., 1987–88. *Publications:* sci. papers in numerous med., forensic med. and path. jls. *Recreations:* horses, golf, jogging. *Address:* 19 Letchmore Road, Radlett, Herts WD7 8HU. *T:* (01923) 856936.

BOWEN, Prof. (David) Keith, DPhil; FRS 1998; FREng; President, Bede Scientific Inc., since 1996; Professor of Engineering, University of Warwick, 1989–97, now Emeritus; *b* 10 May 1940; *s* of Harold Lane Bowen and Muriel Bowen; *m* 1968, Beryl Lodge; one *s*. *Educ:* Christ's Hosp.; St Edmund Hall, Oxford (MA 1966; DPhil Metallurgy 1967). FREng (FEng 1997); FIM 1983; CPhys 1998, FInstP 1998. SRC Res. Fellow, Oxford Univ., 1966–68; Department of Engineering, University of Warwick: Lectr, 1968–78; Sen. Lectr, 1978–85; Reader, 1985–89. Vis. Prof., MIT, 1987. *Publications:* (with C. R. Hall) Microscopy of Materials, 1975; (with B. K. Tanner) High Resolution X-Ray Diffractometry and Topography, 1998; more than 100 articles in learned jls. *Recreations:* music (orchestral and chamber clarinet player), woodwork. *Address:* Bede Scientific Inc., 14 Inverness Drive East, Suite G-104, Englewood, CO 80112, USA. *T:* (303) 7908647; *e-mail:* keith@bede.com.

BOWEN, Desmond John; Director, Private Office of the Secretary General, NATO, since 1999; *b* 11 Jan. 1949; *s* of John and Deborah Bowen; *m* 1979, Susan Brandt; one *s* one *d*. *Educ:* Charterhouse; University Coll., Oxford (MA). Parachute Regt, 1970–73; joined MoD, 1973; seconded to FCO, 1978–81, 1987–91; Private Sec. to Permanent Under Sec. of State, 1982–85; Dir Gen. of Mktg, Defence Export Services Orgn, 1995–97; Fellow, Center for Internat. Affairs, Harvard Univ., 1997–98; Asst Under Sec. of State (Service Personnel Policy), 1998–99. *Recreations:* mountains, squash. *Address:* c/o Ministry of Defence, Whitehall, SW1A 2HB.

BOWEN, Edward Farquharson, TD 1976; QC (Scot.) 1992; Sheriff-Principal of Glasgow and Strathkelvin, since 1997; Temporary Judge, Court of Session, since 2000; *b* 1 May 1945; *s* of late Stanley Bowen, CBE; *m* 1975, Patricia Margaret Brown, *y d* of Rev. R. Russell Brown, Perth; two *s* two *d*. *Educ:* Melville Coll., Edinburgh; Edinburgh Univ. (LLB 1966). Enrolled as Solicitor in Scotland, 1968; admitted to Faculty of Advocates, 1970. Standing Jun. Counsel: to Scottish Educn Dept, 1977–79; to Home Office in Scotland, 1979; Advocate-Depute, 1979–83; Sheriff of Tayside Central and Fife, 1983–90; Partner, Thorntons, WS, 1990–91. Chm. (part-time), Industrial Tribunals, 1995–97; Mem. Criminal Injuries Compensation Bd, 1996–97. Comr of Northern Lights, 1997–. Served RAOC (TA and T&AVR), 1964–80. *Recreations:* golf, curling. *Address:* The Old Manse, Lundie, Angus DD2 5NW. *Clubs:* New (Edinburgh); Royal & Ancient Golf (St Andrews); Hon. Company of Edinburgh Golfers; Panmure Golf; Lundie and Auchterhouse Curling.

BOWEN, Maj.-Gen. Esmond John, CB 1982; Director, Army Dental Service, 1978–82; *b* 6 Dec. 1922; *s* of Major Leslie Arthur George Bowen, MC, and Edna Grace Bowen; *m* 1948, Elsie (*née* Midgley) (*d* 1996); two *s* two *d* (and one *d* decd). *Educ:* Clayesmore Sch.; Univ. of Birmingham. LDS Birmingham 1946. Commd Lieut, RADC, 1947; Captain 1948; Major 1955; Lt-Col 1962; Chief Instructor, Depot and Training Establishment RADC, 1966–69; CO Nos 2 and 3 Dental Groups, 1969–74; Asst Dir, Army Dental Service, 1974–76; Comdt, HQ and Training Centre, RADC, 1976–77; Brig. 1977; Dep. Dir, Dental Service, HQ BAOR, 1977–78. QHDS, 1977–82. Col Comdt, RADC, 1982–87. OStJ 1975. *Recreations:* target rifle and muzzle loading shooting. *Address:* 72 Winchester Road, Andover, Hants SP10 2ER. *T:* (01264) 323252. *Club:* Lansdowne.

BOWEN, Sir Geoffrey (Fraser), Kt 1977; Managing Director, Commercial Banking Company of Sydney Ltd, Australia, 1973–76, retired (General Manager, 1970–73); *m* 1st, Ruth (decd), *d* of H. E. Horsburgh; two *s* one *d*; 2nd, Isabel, *d* of H. T. Underwood. *Address:* Unit 56 The Cotswolds, 28 Curagul Road, North Turramurra, NSW 2074, Australia.

BOWEN, Geraint Robert Lewis, FRCO; Organist and Director of Music, Hereford Cathedral, since 2001; *b* 11 Jan. 1963; *s* of Kenneth John Bowen and Angela Mary Bowen (*née* Evenden); *m* 1987, Catherine Lucy Dennis; two *s*. *Educ:* Haverstock Sch.; William Ellis Sch.; Jesus Coll., Cambridge (organ schol.; BA 1986, MA 1989); Trinity Coll., Dublin (MusB 1987). FRCO 1987. Assistant Organist: Hampstead Parish Ch and St Clement Danes Ch, 1985–86; St Patrick's Cathedral, Dublin, 1986–89; Hereford Cathedral, 1989–94; Organist and Master of the Choristers, St Davids Cathedral, and Artistic Dir, St Davids Cathedral Fest., 1995–2001. *Recreations:* growing vegetables, railways, travel, typography, walking. *Address:* 7 College Cloisters, The Close, Hereford HR1 2NG. *T:* (01432) 374238, *Fax:* (01432) 374213.

BOWEN, Jeremy Francis John; Presenter, BBC Breakfast, since 2000; *b* 6 Feb. 1960; *s* of Gareth Bowen and Jennifer Bowen (*née* Delany); partner, Julia Williams; one *d*. *Educ:* Cardiff High Sch.; University Coll. London (BA Hons Hist.); Johns Hopkins Univ. Sch. of Advanced Internat. Studies, Washington and Bologna, Italy (MA Internat. Affairs). Joined BBC, 1984: news trainee, 1984–85; financial news reporter, 1986–87; Foreign Correspondent, 1987–2000: Radio Corresp., Geneva, 1987; Foreign Affairs Corresp., TV, 1988–95; Middle East Corresp., 1995–2000; has covered major stories in more than 60 countries, incl. ten wars. Journalism award: NY TV Fest., 1993; Monte Carlo TV Fest., 1994. *Recreations:* sport, cooking, not travelling. *Address:* c/o BBC News, Television Centre, W12 7RJ.

BOWEN, John Griffith; playwright and novelist; freelance drama producer for television; *b* 5 Nov. 1924; *s* of Hugh Griffith Bowen and Ethel May Cook; unmarried. *Educ:* Queen Elizabeth's Grammar Sch., Crediton; Pembroke Coll., Oxford; St Antony's Coll., Oxford. Frere Exhibition for Indian Studies, Oxford, 1951 52 and 1952–53. Asst Editor, The Sketch, 1954–57; Advertising Copywriter and Copy Chief, 1957–60; Consultant on TV Drama, Associated TV, 1960–67; productions for Thames TV, LWT, BBC. *Publications:* The Truth Will Not Help Us, 1956; After the Rain, 1958; The Centre of the Green, 1959; Storyboard, 1960; The Birdcage, 1962; A World Elsewhere, 1965; The Essay Prize, 1965; Squeak, 1983; The McGuffin, 1984 (filmed for TV, 1986); The Girls, 1986; Fighting Back, 1989; The Precious Gift, 1992; No Retreat, 1994; *plays:* I Love You, Mrs Patterson, 1964; After the Rain, 1967; Fall and Redemption, 1967; Little Boxes, 1968; The Disorderly Women, 1968; The Corsican Brothers, 1970; The Waiting Room, 1970; Robin Redbreast, 1972; Heil Caesar, 1973; Florence Nightingale, 1975; Which Way Are You Facing?, 1976; Singles, 1977; Bondage, 1978; The Inconstant Couple (adaptation of Marivaux, L'Heureux Stratagème), 1978; Uncle Jeremy, 1981; The Geordie Gentleman (adaptation of Molière's Le Bourgeois Gentilhomme), 1987; Cold Salmon, 1998. *Address:* Old Lodge Farm, Sugarswell Lane, Edgehill, Banbury, Oxon OX15 6HP.

BOWEN, Keith; *see* Bowen, D. K.

BOWEN, Hon. Lionel Frost, AC 1991; MHR (Lab) Kingsford-Smith, NSW, 1969–90; Attorney-General of Australia, 1984–90; Chairman, National Gallery, Canberra, 1990–95; *b* 28 Dec. 1922; *m* 1953, Claire Clement; five *s* three *d. Educ:* Sydney Univ. (LLB). Alderman, 1948, Mayor, 1949–50, Randwick Council; MLA, NSW, 1962–69; Postmaster Gen., 1972–74; Special Minister of State, 1974–75; Minister for Manufg Industry, 1975; Dep. Leader, Opposition, 1977–83; Minister for Trade, 1983–84; Dep. Prime Minister, 1983–90. *Recreations:* surfing, reading. *Address:* 24 Mooramie Avenue, Kensington, NSW 2033, Australia.

BOWEN, Sir Mark Edward Mortimer, 5th Bt *cr* 1921, of Colworth, Co. Bedford; *b* 17 Oct. 1958; *s* of Sir Thomas Frederic Charles Bowen, 4th Bt and of Jill, *d* of Lloyd Evans; *S* father, 1989; *m* 1983, Kerry Tessa, *d* of Michael Moriarty; one *s* one *d. Heir: s* George Edward Michael Bowen, *b* 27 Dec. 1987. *Address:* Bowood, 31 Ashley Road, Thames Ditton, Surrey KT7 0NH.

BOWEN, Most Rev. Michael George; *see* Southwark, Archbishop and Metropolitan of, (RC).

BOWEN, Thomas Edward Ifor L.; *see* Lewis-Bowen.

BOWEN, William G(ordon), PhD; President, The Andrew W. Mellon Foundation, since 1988; President, Princeton University, 1972–88, now Emeritus; *b* 6 Oct. 1933; *s* of Albert A. and Bernice C. Bowen; *m* 1956, Mary Ellen Maxwell; one *s* one *d. Educ:* Denison Univ. (AB); Princeton Univ. (PhD). Princeton University: Asst Prof. of Economics, Associate Prof. of Economics; Prof. of Econs, 1958–88; Provost, 1967–72; Sen. Fellow, Woodrow Wilson Sch. of Public and Internat. Affairs, 1988. Director: NCR, 1975–91; Reader's Digest, 1985–97; Merck, 1986–; DeWitt and Lila Wallace-Reader's Digest Funds, 1986–97; American Express, 1988–; Teachers' Insce and Annuity Assoc., 1995–; Coll. Retirement Equities Fund, 1995–; (first) Chm., JSTOR, 1995–. Trustee, Center for Advanced Study in the Behavioral Sciences, 1986–92; Regent, Smithsonian Instn, 1980–92; Mem. Bd of Dirs, Denison Univ., 1992–. Hon. LLD: Denison, Rutgers, Pennsylvania and Yale, 1972; Harvard, 1973; Jewish Theol Seminary, 1974; Seton Hall Univ., 1975; Dartmouth and Princeton, 1987; Brown, 1988; Michigan, 1995; Hon. DHL: Morehouse Coll., 1992; Hartwick Coll., 1992; Hon. DSc Lafayette Coll., 1992; Hon. DEconSc Cape Town, 1996. *Publications:* Economic Aspects of Education, 1964; (with W. J. Baumol) Performing Arts: the Economic Dilemma, 1966; (with T. A. Finegan) Economics of Labor Force Participation, 1969; Ever the Teacher, 1987; (with Julie Ann Sosa) Prospects for Faculty in the Arts & Sciences, 1989; (with N. L. Rudenstine) In Pursuit of the PhD, 1992; Inside the Boardroom: governance by directors and trustees, 1994; (jtly) The Charitable Nonprofits, 1994; (with Derek Bok) The Shape of the River: long-term consequences of considering race in college and university admissions, 1998; contribs to Amer. Econ. Review, Economica, Quarterly Jl of Economics, etc. *Address:* 140 E 62 Street, New York, NY 10021, USA. *T:* (212) 8388400.

BOWER, Michael Douglas; Leader, Sheffield Metropolitan District Council, 1992–98; *b* 25 Aug. 1942; *s* of Stanley Arthur Bower and Rachael Farmer; *m;* two *d. Educ:* Colwyn Bay Grammar Sch.; Royal Coll. of Advanced Technol., Salford. Civil engr, 1961–64; journalist, 1965–77; with The Star, Sheffield, 1968–77; Regional Organiser, NUJ, 1977–81; Organiser, Sheffield Co-operative Develt Gp, 1981–94. Mem., Press Council, 1976–77. Mem., Sheffield Metropolitan DC, 1976–98 (Chm., Educn Cttee, 1983). Contested (Lab) Hallam Div. of Sheffield, 1979. *Recreations:* walking, golf. *Address:* 366 Walkley Bank Road, Sheffield S6 5AR. *T:* (0114) 233 5753. *Club:* Carlton Working Men's (Gleadless, Sheffield).

BOWER, Thomas Michael; writer and journalist; *b* 28 Sept. 1946; *s* of George Bower and Sylvia Bower; *m* 1st, 1971, Juliet Ann Oddie (marr. diss. 1981); two *s;* 2nd, 1985, Veronica Judith Colleton Wadley; one *s* one *d. Educ:* William Ellis Sch.; London Sch. of Econs (LLB). Called to the Bar, Gray's Inn, 1969; with BBC TV, 1970-95: researcher, 24 Hours, 1970-72; producer, Midweek, 1972-76; Dep. Ed. and Producer, Panorama, 1976-86; Producer, Documentaries, 1986-95; contributor, Daily Mail, 1996-2001. Best TV Documentary, Fest. dei Popoli, 1987; Fipa d'Or, Cannes, for best TV documentary, The Confession, 1991; Chairman's Award, BPA, 1991. *Publications:* Blind Eye to Murder, a Pledge Betrayed, 1981; Klaus Barbie, Butcher of Lyons, 1984; The Paperclip Conspiracy, 1987; Maxwell the Outsider, 1988; The Red Web, 1989; Tiny Rowland, a Rebel Tycoon, 1993; The Perfect English Spy, Sir Dick White, 1995; Heroes of World War 2, 1995; Maxwell: the Final Verdict, 1995; Blood Money: the Swiss, the Nazis and the looted billions, 1997; Fayed: the unauthorised biography, 1998; Branson, 2000; The Paymaster: Geoffrey Robinson, Maxwell and New Labour, 2001. *Recreations:* walking, ski-ing, shooting. *Address:* 10 Thurlow Road, NW3 5PL. *T:* (020) 7435 9776. *Clubs:* Garrick, Beefsteak.

BOWERING, Christine, DL; MA; Chairman, Nottingham City Hospital NHS Trust, since 1998; Headmistress, Nottingham High School for Girls (GPDST), 1984–96; *b* 30 June 1936; *d* of Kenneth Soper and Florence E. W. Soper; *m* 1960, Rev. John Anthony Bowering; one *s* one *d. Educ:* St Bernard's Convent, Westcliff-on-Sea; Newnham Coll., Cambridge (MA). Assistant Teacher: St Bernard's Convent; Ursuline Convent, Brentwood; Sheffield High Sch. (GPDST). Mem., Engineering Council, 1988–91. Dir, Queen's Med. Centre, Nottingham, 1993–98. Chairman: Educn Cttee, GSA, 1989–93; Indep. Schs Curriculum Cttee, 1992–94; Mem., Educn Cttee, Goldsmiths' Co., 1992–. Gov., Nottingham Trent Univ. (formerly Nottingham Poly.), 1989–96 (Mem., 1990–, Chm., 1990–96, Employment Cttee). Assoc. Mem., Newnham Coll., Cambridge, 1991–. Trustee, Southwell Dio. Council for Family Care, 1998–. FRSA 1994. DL Notts, 2000. Hon. DLitt Nottingham, 1996. *Address:* Linthwaite Cottage, Main Street, Kirklington, Newark NG22 8ND. *T:* (01636) 816995, *Fax:* (01636) 813743.

BOWERING, Ven. Michael Ernest; Archdeacon of Lindisfarne, 1987–2000; *b* 25 June 1935; *s* of Hubert James and Mary Elizabeth Bowering; *m* 1962, Aileen (*née* Fox); one *s* two *d. Educ:* Barnstaple Grammar School; Kelham Theological Coll. Curate: St Oswald, Middlesbrough, 1959–62; Huntington with New Earswick, York, 1962–64; Vicar, Brayton with Barlow, 1964–72; RD of Selby, 1971–72; Vicar, Saltburn by the Sea, 1972–81; Canon Residentiary of York Minster and Secretary for Mission and Evangelism, 1981–87. *Recreation:* crosswords. *Address:* Old Timbers, Westway, Crayke, York YO61 4TE. *T:* (01347) 823682.

BOWERS, John Simon; QC 1998; *b* 2 Jan. 1956; *s* of Alfred and Irene Bowers; *m* 1982, Suzanne Franks; one *s* two *d. Educ:* Lincoln Coll., Oxford (MA, BCL). Called to the Bar, Middle Temple, 1979; in practice at the Bar, 1979–. Chairman: Employment Appeal Tribunal Users' Gp, 1995–99; (part-time), Employment Tribunals, 2001–; Hon. Legal Advr, Public Concern at Work, 1997–; Mediator, Centre for Dispute Resolution, 1998–. Vice-Chm., Employment Law, Bar Assoc., 1999–; Member: Liaison Cttee, Govt Human Rights Task Force, 1999–; Bar Council Race Relations Cttee, 1999–; Bar Disciplinary Tribunal, 2001–. *Publications:* Bowers on Employment Law, 1980, 5th edn 2000; (jtly) Atkins Court Forms, vol. 38, 1986, 1999; (jtly) Modern Law of Strikes, 1987; Industrial Tribunal Procedure, 1987, 2nd edn, as Employment Tribunal Procedure, 1998; (jtly) The Employment Act 1988, 1988; Termination of Employment, 1988, 3rd edn 1995; (jtly) Transfer of Undertakings: the legal pitfalls, 1989, 6th edn 1996; (jtly) Basic Procedure in Courts and Tribunals, 1990; (jtly) Textbook on Employment Law, 1990, 5th edn 1998; (jtly) Employment Law Update, 1991; Transfer of Undertakings Encyclopaedia, 1998; Whistleblowing: the new law, 2000; Employment Law and Human Rights, 2000; (contrib.) Bullen & Leake on Pleadings; many articles in legal jls. *Recreations:* football, walking, cycling. *Address:* Littleton Chambers, 3 King's Bench Walk, Temple, EC4Y 7HR.

BOWERS, Michael John; Managing Director, Tamoil Shipping Ltd, 1995; *b* 1 Oct. 1933; *s* of Arthur Patrick and Lena Frances Bowers; *m* 1959, Caroline (*née* Clifford); two *d. Educ:* Cardinal Vaughan Sch., Kensington. BP Group: various appts in Supply, Distribution Planning and Trading, 1951–73; Vice-Pres. and Dir, BP North America Inc. (NY), 1973–76; Man. Dir and Chief Exec. Officer, BP Gas, 1976–81; Dir, BP Shipping/BP Exploration, 1980–81; Regional Co-ordinator, Western Hemisphere, 1981–83; Chief Exec., International Petroleum Exchange of London Ltd, 1983–85; Man. Dir, TW Oil (UK), 1985–88. *Recreations:* gardening, tennis, bridge, chess.

BOWERS, Peter Hammond; His Honour Judge Bowers; a Circuit Judge, since 1995; *b* 22 June 1945; *s* of Edward Hammond Bowers and Elsie Bowers; *m* 1970, Brenda Janet Burgess; two *s* one *d. Educ:* Acklam Hall, Middlesbrough. Admitted solicitor, 1966; in private practice, 1966–70; Prosecuting Solicitor, 1970–72; called to the Bar, Inner Temple, 1972; barrister, N Eastern Circuit, 1972–95. *Recreations:* cricket, aspiring artist, antiques, paintings, armchair sportsman. *Address:* Irving House, Appleton Wiske, Northallerton DL6 2AU.

BOWERS, Roger George, CMG 1997; OBE 1984; PhD; Director, R. G. Bowers & Associates, since 1996; *b* 23 May 1942; *s* of George Albert Bowers and Hilda Mary Bowers (*née* Wells); *m* 1963, Gweneth Iris Pither (marr. diss.); one *s* one *d. Educ:* Royal Grammar Sch., Guildford; Wadham Coll., Oxford (BA); Reading Univ. (MPhil; PhD). Joined British Council, 1964; Tutor to Overseas Students, Univ. of Birmingham, 1965; Asst Regl Dir, Cape Coast, Ghana, 1965–69; seconded to Eng. Lang. Trng Inst., Allahabad, 1971–73; Asst Regl Educ. Advr, Calcutta, 1973–76; Eng. Lang. Consultancies Dept, 1978–80; seconded to Ain Shams Univ., Cairo, 1980–84; Dir, Eng. Lang. Services Dept, 1984–85; Dep. Controller, 1985–89, Controller, then Dir, 1989–93, Eng. Lang. and Lit. Div.; Asst Dir-Gen. (Manchester), and Dir of Professional Services, 1993–96. Dir, World of Language Ltd, 1997–. Jt Editor, Cambridge Handbooks for Language Teachers, 1985–92; Member: Editorial Cttee, ELT Documents, 1984–93; Bd of Management, ELT Jl, 1985–96. Chief Exec., Trinity Coll., London, 1998– (Mem. Council, 1997–98); Mem. Corp., Trinity Coll. of Music, 1999–. Trustee, A. S. Hornby Educnl Trust, 1997–. FRSA 1993. *Publications:* In Passing, 1976; Talking About Grammar, 1987; Word Play, 1990. *Recreations:* fishing, cooking, eating. *Address:* 25 Hillbrow, Richmond Hill, Surrey TW10 6BH. *T:* (020) 8948 6342.

BOWERS-BROADBENT, Christopher Joseph St George; organist and composer; *b* 13 Jan. 1945; *s* of Henry W. Bowers-Broadbent and Doris E. Bowers-Broadbent (*née* Mizen); *m* 1970, Deirdre Ann Cape; one *s* one *d. Educ:* King's Coll., Cambridge (Chorister); Berkhamsted Sch.; Royal Acad. of Music (Rec.Dip.; FRAM 1983). Organist and Choirmaster, St Pancras Parish Church, 1965–88; début recital, 1966; Organist, W London Synagogue, 1973–; Organist and Choirmaster, Gray's Inn, 1983–. Prof., RAM, 1975–92. Numerous recordings. *Publications include:* sacred and secular compositions; Collected Church Pieces, 1972; chamber operas: The Pied Piper, 1972; The Seacock Bane, 1979; The Last Man, 1983. *Recreations:* sketching, silence. *Address:* 94 Colney Hatch Lane, N10 1EA. *T:* (020) 8883 1933.

BOWERY, Prof. Norman George, PhD; DSc; Professor of Pharmacology, since 1995, and Head of Neuroscience, since 1999, Medical School, University of Birmingham; *b* 23 June 1944; *s* of George Bowery and Olga (*née* Beevers); *m* 1970, Barbara Joyce (*née* Westcott); one *s* two *d. Educ:* Christ's Coll., Finchley; NE Surrey Coll. of Technology; St Bartholomew's Med. Coll., Univ. of London (PhD 1974; DSc 1987). MIBiol 1970. Res. Asst, CIBA Labs, 1963–70; Res. Student, St Bart's Med. Coll., London, 1970–73; Postdoctoral Res. Fellow, Sch. of Pharmacy, London Univ., 1973–75; Lectr in Pharmacology, 1975–82, Sen. Lectr in Pharm., 1982–84, St Thomas's Hosp. Med. Sch.; Section Leader, Neuroscience Res. Centre, Merck, Sharp & Dohme, Harlow, 1984–87; Wellcome Prof. of Pharmacol., Sch. of Pharmacy, London Univ., 1987–95. Pres., British Pharmacol Soc., 1999–2000. Laurea in pharmacy *hc* Florence, 1992. Biological Council Medal, 1991. *Publications:* Actions and Interactions of GABA and Benzodiazepines, 1984; GABAergic Mechanisms in the Mammalian Periphery, 1986; GABA: basic mechanisms to clinical applications, 1989; $GABA_B$ Receptors in Mammalian Function, 1990; GABA: transport, receptors and metabolism, 1996; The GABA Receptors, 1996. *Recreations:* gardening, socializing, walking, family life. *Address:* The Medical School, University of Birmingham, Edgbaston, Birmingham B15 2TT. *T:* (0121) 414 4506.

BOWES, Michael Anthony; QC 2001; a Recorder, since 2000; *b* 12 Dec. 1956; *s* of late Michael Philip Bowes and of Patricia Bowes; *m* 1987, Amanda Wissler; two *d. Educ:* St George's Coll., Weybridge; Manchester Univ. (LLB). Called to the Bar, Middle Temple, 1980; in practice, Western Circuit, 1996 –; specialising in criminal law, fraud and financial regulatory work. *Publication:* (ed and contrib.) Archbold, Criminal Pleading: evidence and practice, 1999–. *Recreations:* ski-ing, riding, tennis. *Address:* 2 King's Bench Walk, Temple, EC4Y 7DE. *T:* (020) 7353 1746.

BOWES, Richard Noel; Deputy Chairman, Willis Faber plc and Chairman, Willis Faber and Dumas, 1985–88, retired; *b* 17 Dec. 1928; *m* 1961, Elizabeth Lyle; one *s* two *d. Educ:* Epsom College; Worcester Coll., Oxford (MA). Called to the Bar, Gray's Inn, 1950. RN, 1950–53. Willis Faber and Dumas, 1953–88. *Address:* Fairacre, Enton, Godalming, Surrey GU8 5AQ. *T:* (01483) 416544.

BOWES, Roger Norman; Chief Executive, Association for Information Management (Aslib), since 1989; *b* 28 Jan. 1943; *s* of late Russell Ernest Bowes and Sybil Caroline Rose Bowes (*née* Bell); *m* 1st, 1961, Denise Hume Windsor (marr. diss. 1974); one *d;* 2nd, 1977, Ann Rosemary O'Connor (*née* Hamstead) (marr. diss. 1988). *Educ:* Chiswick and Dorking Grammar Schools. Advertisement Executive: Associated Newspapers, 1962–67; IPC/Mirror Gp Newspapers, 1967–70; Marketing Exec./Sales Manager, Mirror Gp, 1970–75; Media Dir, McCann Erickson Advertising, 1976–78; Mirror Gp Newspapers: Adv. Dir, 1978–81; Dep. Chief Exec., 1982–83; Chief Exec., 1984; Man. Dir, Guinness Enterprises, 1985; Chief Exec., Express Gp Newspapers, 1985–86; Chm., Citybridge, 1987–97. Member: Europ. Council of Information Assocs; British Council Libraries Adv. Cttee; Treas., Internat. Fedn for Information and Documentation. FRSA 1994. *Recreations:*

political and military history, cookery, architectural restoration, classic cars. *Address:* Aslib, Staple Hall, Stone House Court, EC3A 7PB. *T:* (020) 7903 0000, *Fax:* (020) 7903 0011; *e-mail:* aslib@aslib.com.

BOWES LYON, family name of **Earl of Strathmore**.

BOWES LYON, Simon Alexander, FCA; director of investment companies; Lord-Lieutenant of Hertfordshire, since 1986; *b* 17 June 1932; *s* of Hon. Sir David Bowes Lyon, KCVO, and Rachel Bowes Lyon (*née* Spender Clay) (*d* 1996); *m* 1966, Caroline, *d* of Rt Rev. Victor Pike, CB, CBE, DD, and of Dorothea Pike; three *s* one *d*. *Educ:* Eton; Magdalen Coll., Oxford (BA). KStJ 1997. *Recreations:* botany, gardening, shooting, music. *Address:* St Paul's Walden Bury, Hitchin, Herts SG4 8BP. *T:* (01438) 871218; *e-mail:* boweslyon@aol.com.

BOWETT, Sir Derek (William), Kt 1998; CBE 1983; QC 1978; LLD; FBA 1983; Whewell Professor of International Law, Cambridge University, 1981–91; Professorial Fellow of Queens' College, Cambridge, 1982–91 (Hon. Fellow, 1991); *b* 20 April 1927; *s* of Arnold William Bowett and Marion Wood; *m* 1953, Betty Northall; two *s* one *d*. *Educ:* William Hulme's Sch., Manchester; Downing Coll., Cambridge. MA, LLB, LLD (Cantab), PhD (Manchester). Called to the Bar, Middle Temple, 1953, Hon. Bencher, 1975. Lectr, Law Faculty, Manchester Univ. 1951–59; Legal Officer, United Nations, New York, 1957–59; Cambridge University: Lectr, Law Faculty, 1960–76, Reader, 1976–81; Fellow of Queens' Coll., 1960–69, President 1969–82. Gen. Counsel, UNRWA, Beirut, 1966–68. Member: Royal Commn on Environmental Pollution, 1973–77; Internat. Law Commn, 1991–96. Commander, Order of Dannebrog (Denmark), 1993; Grand Cross, Civil Order, Jose Cecilio del Valle (Honduras), 1993. *Publications:* Self-defence in International Law, 1958; Law of International Institutions, 1964; United Nations Forces, 1964; Law of the Sea, 1967; Search for Peace, 1972; Legal Régime of Islands in International Law, 1978; The International Court of Justice: process, practice and procedure, 1997. *Recreation:* music. *Address:* 228 Hills Road, Cambridge CB2 2QE. *T:* (01223) 210688.

BOWEY, Prof. Angela Marilyn, PhD; Director, Pay Advice and Research Centre, Gibraltar, since 1987 (Glasgow, 1986); Professor of Business Administration, Strathclyde Business School, University of Strathclyde, Glasgow, 1976–87; *b* 20 Oct. 1940; *d* of Jack Nicholas Peterson and Kathleen (*née* Griffin); *m* 1st, 1960, Miklos Papp; two *s* one *d*; 2nd, 1965, Gregory Bowey (marr. diss. 1980); one *s* one *d*. *Educ:* Withington Girls Sch., Manchester; Univ. of Manchester (BA Econ, PhD). Technical Asst, Nuclear Power Gp, 1961–62; Asst Lectr, Elizabeth Gaskell Coll. of Educn, 1967–68; Manchester Business School: Res. Associate, 1968–69; Res. Fellow, 1969–72; Lectr, 1972–76. Vis. Professor: Admin. Staff Coll. of India, 1975; Western Australian Inst. of Technology, 1976; Univ. of WA, 1977; Prahran Coll. of Advanced Educn, Australia, 1978; Massey Univ., NZ, 1978. ACAS Arbitrator, 1977–92; Dir, Pay and Rewards Res. Centre, 1978–85; Comr, Equal Opportunities Commn, 1980–86; Member: Scottish Econ. Council, 1980–83; Police Adv. Bd (Scotland) (formerly Adv. Panel on Police), 1983–88. Gov., Scottish Police Coll., 1985–88. Chm., Glass Mus. Trust, Paihia, NZ, 1994–. Editor, Management Decision, 1979–82. *Publications:* Job and Pay Comparisons (with Tom Lupton), 1973, 2nd edn 1974; A Guide to Manpower Planning, 1974, 2nd edn 1977; (with Tom Lupton) Wages and Salaries, 1974, 2nd edn 1982; Handbook of Salary and Wage Systems, 1975, 2nd edn 1982; The Sociology of Organisations, 1976; (with Richard Thorpe and Phil Hellier) Payment Systems and Productivity, 1986; Managing Salary and Wage Systems, 1987; articles in Brit. Jl of Indust. Relations, Jl of Management Studies, and Management Decision; *e-mail:* dr.bowey@gainshare.co.nz.

BOWEY, Olwyn, RA 1975 (ARA 1970); practising artist (painter); *b* 10 Feb. 1936; *o d* of James and Olive Bowey. *Educ:* West Hartlepool Sch. of Art; Royal Coll. of Art. One-man shows: Zwemmer Gall., 1961; New Grafton Gall., 1969; also exhibited at Leicester Gall., Royal Academy; work purchased through Chantrey Bequest for Tate Gall., Royal Academy, Min. of Works, etc.

BOWIE, Rev. (Alexander) Glen, CBE 1984; Principal Chaplain (Church of Scotland and Free Churches), Royal Air Force, 1980–84, retired; *b* 10 May 1928; *s* of Alexander Bowie and Annie (*née* McGhie); *m* 1952, Mary McKillop (*d* 1991); two *d*. *Educ:* Stevenston High Sch.; Irvine Royal Acad.; Glasgow Univ. (BSc 1951; Dip Theol 1954); BA Open Univ., 1977. Nat. Service, RAF, 1947–49. Assistant, Beith High Church, 1952–54; ordained, 1954; entered RAF Chaplains' Br., 1955; served: RAF Padgate, 1955–56; Akrotiri, 1956–59; Stafford, 1959–61; Butzweilerhof, 1961–64; Halton, 1964–67; Akrotiri, 1967–70; RAF Coll., Cranwell, 1970–75; Asst Principal Chaplain, 1975; HQ Germany, 1975–76; HQ Support Comd, 1976–80. Acting Chaplain to Moderator of Church of Scotland, in London, 1985–; Moderator, Ch of Scotland Presbytery of England, 1988–89. QHC 1980–84; Hon. Chaplain, Royal Scottish Corp., 1981–2001. Editor, Scottish Forces Bulletin, 1985–95. *Recreations:* oil painting, travel, leading Holy Land tours. *Address:* 16 Weir Road, Hemingford Grey, Huntingdon, Cambs PE18 9EH. *T:* (01480) 381425. *Club:* Royal Air Force.

BOWIE, David; international recording artist and performer; film and stage actor; video and film producer; graphic designer; *b* 8 Jan. 1947; *s* of Hayward Stenton Jones and late Margaret Mary Burns; *m* (marr. diss.); one *s*; *m* 1992, Iman Abdul Majid; one *d*. *Educ:* Stansfield Road Sch., Brixton. Artiste from age of 16; many major recordings, 1970–, and video productions, 1979–; numerous live musical stage performances; guest appearances on television shows. Actor: *films:* The Man who Fell to Earth, 1976; Just a Gigolo, 1978; The Hunger, 1982; Merry Christmas, Mr Lawrence, 1983; Ziggy Stardust and the Spiders from Mars, 1983; Absolute Beginners, 1986; Labyrinth, 1986; Into the Night; The Last Temptation of Christ, 1988; The Linguini Incident, 1990; Basquiat, 1997; *stage:* The Elephant Man, New York 1980; *television:* Baal, 1982. Recipient of internat. music and entertainment awards. *Recreations:* painting, ski-ing. *Address:* c/o Isolar, Suite 220, 641 5th Avenue, New York, NY 10022, USA.

BOWIE, Rev. Glen; *see* Bowie, Rev. A. G.

BOWIE, Graham Maitland, CBE 1992; Chief Executive, Lothian Regional Council, 1986–94; *b* 11 Nov. 1931; *s* of John Graham Bowie and Agnes Bowie; *m* 1962, Maureen Jennifer O'Sullivan; one *s* two *d*. *Educ:* Alloa Academy; Univ. of St Andrews (MA); Univ. of Glasgow (LLB). National Service, 1956–58. Asst Sec., Glasgow Chamber of Commerce, 1958–60; Product Planner, Ford Motor Co., 1960–64; Edinburgh Corp. Educn Dept, 1964–69; ILEA, 1969–75; Dir of Policy Planning, Lothian Regional Council, 1975–86. Mem., Nat. Lotteries Charities Bd, 1994–97. *Recreations:* walking, travel, the arts. *Address:* 8 Keith Crescent, Edinburgh EH4 3NH.

BOWIE, Prof. Malcolm McNaughtan, DPhil; FBA 1993; FRSL; Marshal Foch Professor of French Literature, since 1992, and Director, European Humanities Research Centre, since 1998, University of Oxford; Fellow of All Souls College, Oxford, since 1992; *b* 5 May 1943; *s* of George Alexander Bowie and Beatrice Georgina Betty (*née* Strowger); *m* 1979, Alison Mary Finch; one *s* one *d*. *Educ:* Woodbridge Sch.; Univ. of Edinburgh (MA 1965); Univ. of Sussex (DPhil 1970); MA Cantab 1969; MA Oxon 1992. FRSL 1999. Asst Lectr in French, UEA, 1967–69; University of Cambridge: Asst Lectr, 1969–72; Lectr, 1972–76; Fellow and Dir of Studies, Clare Coll., 1969–76, Tutor, 1971–76; University of London: Prof. of French Lang. and Lit., 1976–92; Hd, Dept of French, QMC, 1976–89; Founding Dir, Inst. of Romance Studies, 1989–92 (Hon. Sen. Res. Fellow, 1993). Vis. Prof., Univ. of California, Berkeley, 1983; Vis. Dist. Prof., Grad. Center, CUNY, 1989; Vis. Fellow, Centre for Res. in Philosophy and Lit., Univ. of Warwick, 1991; Vis. Prof., Collège de France, Paris, 2001– Sept. 2002. Lectures: Andrew W. Mellon, Bucknell Univ., 1990; Cassal, London Univ., 1999. President: Assoc. of Univ. Profs of French, 1982–84; Soc. for French Studies, 1994–96; British Comparative Lit. Assoc., 1998–. Member: Exec. Cttee, Univs Council for Modern Langs, 1994–96; Council, British Academy, 1999–. Mem., Academia Europaea, 1989. Gen. Editor, French Studies, 1980–87; Founding Gen. Editor, Cambridge Studies in French, 1980–95; Editor, Jl Inst. Romance Studies, 1992. Hon. DLit QMW, 1997. Truman Capote Award for Literary Criticism, 2001. Chevalier, 1987, Officier, 1996, de l'Ordre des Palmes Académiques (France). *Publications:* Henri Michaux: a study of his literary works, 1973; Mallarmé and the Art of Being Difficult, 1978; Freud, Proust and Lacan: theory as fiction, 1987; Lacan, 1991; Psychoanalysis and the Future of Theory, 1993; Proust Among the Stars, 1998; (jtly) A Short History of French Literature, 2002; contribs to learned jls and collective works. *Address:* All Souls College, Oxford OX1 4AL. *T:* (01865) 279379.

BOWIE, Stanley Hay Umphray, DSc; FRS 1975; FREng; FRSE, FIMM, FMSA; FSAScot; Consultant Geologist; Assistant Director, Chief Geochemist, Institute of Geological Sciences, 1968–77; *b* 24 March 1917; *s* of Dr James Cameron and Mary Bowie; *m* 1948, Helen Elizabeth, *d* of Dr Roy Woodhouse and Florence Elizabeth Pocock; two *s*. *Educ:* Grammar Sch. and Univ. of Aberdeen (BSc, DSc). Meteorological Office, 1942; commissioned RAF, 1943; HM Geological Survey of Gt Britain: Geologist, Sen. Geologist and Principal Geologist, 1946–55; Chief Geologist, Atomic Energy Div., 1955–67; Chief Consultant Geologist to UKAEA, 1955–77. Visiting Prof. of Applied Geology, Univ. of Strathclyde, 1968–85; Vis. Prof., Imperial Coll., London, 1985–92. Principal Investigator, Apollo 11 and 12 lunar samples, 1969–71; Chairman: Internat. Mineralogical Assoc., Commn on Ore Microscopy, 1970–78; Royal Soc. Sectl Cttee 5, 1977–79; Royal Soc. Working Party on Envtl Geochem. and Health, 1979–81; DoE Res. Adv. Gp, Radioactive Waste Management, 1984–85; Mem., Radioactive Waste Management Adv. Cttee, 1978–82. Vice-Pres., Shetland Sheep Breeders Gp, 1992– (Chm., 1989–91). Vice-Pres., Geological Soc., 1972–74; Mem. Council, Mineralogical Soc., 1954–57, 1962–65 (Chairman: Applied Mineralogy Gp, 1969–72; Geochem. Gp, 1972–75). FGS 1959; FMSA 1963; FRSE 1970; FIMM 1972 (Pres. 1976–77), Hon. FIMM 1987; FREng (FEng 1976); FSAScot 1992. Silver Medal, RSA, 1959; Team Mem., Queen's Award for Technol Achievement, 1990 (for develt of Inductively Coupled Plasma Mass Spectrometer). *Publications:* (ed jtly) Uranium Prospecting Handbook, 1972; (ed jtly) Mineral Deposits of Europe, Vol. 1: North-West Europe, 1978; (with P. R. Simpson) The Bowie-Simpson System for the Microscopic Determination of Ore Minerals, 1980; (ed jtly) Environmental Geochemistry and Health, 1985; (with C. Bowie) Radon and Health—The Facts, 1991; contributions to: Nuclear Geology, 1954; Physical Methods in Determinative Mineralogy, 1967, 2nd edn 1977; Uranium Exploration Geology, 1970; Proceedings of the Apollo Lunar Science Conference, 1970; Proceedings of the Second Lunar Science Conference, 1971; Uranium Exploration Methods, 1973; Recognition and Evaluation of Uraniferous Areas, 1977; Theoretical and Practical Aspects of Uranium Geology, 1979; Nuclear Power Technology, 1983; Applied Environmental Geochemistry, 1983; numerous papers in scientific and technical jls on uranium geology and economics, mineralogy, geophysics and geochemistry, and articles on rare breeds of domesticated animals. *Recreations:* preservation of rare breeds, gardening, photography. *Address:* Tanyard Farm, Clapton, Crewkerne, Somerset TA18 8PS. *T:* (01460) 72093.

BOWIS, John Crocket, OBE 1981; Member (C) London Region, European Parliament, since 1999; *b* 2 Aug. 1945; *s* of Thomas Palin Bowis and Georgiana Joyce (*née* Crocket); *m* 1968, Caroline May (*née* Taylor); two *s* one *d*. *Educ:* Tonbridge Sch.; Brasenose Coll., Oxford (MA). Tutor, Cumberland Lodge, Windsor Great Park Student Conference Centre, 1966–67; Cons. Party Agent, Peterborough, Derby, Harborough and Blaby, 1968–72; Conservative Central Office: National Organiser, Fedn of Cons. Students, 1972–75; Nat. Organiser, Cons. Trade Unionists, 1975–79; Dir of Community Affairs, 1979–81; Campaign Dir, 1981–82, Public Affairs Dir, 1983–87, British Insurance Brokers Assoc.; Press and Parly Consultant, Nat. Fedn of Self-employed and Small Firms, 1982–83. Councillor (C) Royal Bor. of Kingston upon Thames, 1982–86 (Chm. of Educn, 1985–86). MP (C) Battersea, 1987–97; contested (C) same seat, 1997. PPS to Minister for Local Govt and Inner Cities, DoE, 1989–90, to Sec. of State for Wales, 1990–93; Parly Under-Sec. of State, DoH, 1993–96, Dept of Transport, 1996–97. Mem., Select Cttee on Members' Interests, 1987–90; Vice-Chm., All Party Gp on Social Sci., 1988–93; Chm., All Party Somali Gp, 1991–97. Secretary: Cons. Inner Cities Cttee, 1987–89; Cons. Educn Cttee, 1988–89; Cons. Arts and Heritage Cttee, 1988–89; Parliamentary Adviser to: ACFHE, 1987–93; Assoc. for Coll. Management, 1990–93; ATL (formerly AMMA), 1992–93. European Parliament: Party spokesman on envmt, health and consumer affairs, 1999–; Rapporteur: on food safety, 2000–01; on health and enlargement, 2000–. Internat. Policy Advr to WHO at Inst. of Psychiatry, 1997–; Consultant, SANE, 1999–. Vice-Pres., Internat. Soc. for Human Rights, 1988–; Chm., Nat. Council for Civil Protection, 1992–93. Hon. Jt Pres., British Youth Council, 1987–93; Member: Council, Internat. Social Service (UK), 1997–; Bd, Churches Educn and Develt Partnership for Southern Africa, 1998–; Bd, Internat. Inst. for Special Needs Offenders, 1998–; Adv. Bd, Geneva Initiative on Psychiatry, 1999–. Trustee: Nat. Aids Trust, 1997–; Epilepsy Res. Foundn, 1997–; Share Community, 1997–. Director: London Actors' Theatre Co., 1990–95; Battersea Arts Centre, 1991–; Royal Nat. Theatre, 1992–95; South Bank Centre, 1992–95; Mem. Bd, Mosaic Clubhouse, 1998–. *Recreations:* theatre, music, art, sport. *Address:* PO Box 262, New Malden KT3 4WJ. *Fax:* (020) 8395 7463.

BOWKER, Prof. John Westerdale; Hon. Canon of Canterbury Cathedral, since 1985; Adjunct Professor of Religion, North Carolina State University, since 1986; Adjunct Professor of Religious Studies, University of Pennsylvania, since 1986; *b* 30 July 1935; *s* of Gordon Westerdale Bowker and Marguerite (*née* Burdick); *m* 1963, Margaret Roper; one *s*. *Educ:* St John's Sch., Leatherhead; Worcester Coll., Oxford (MA); Ripon Hall, Oxford. National Service, RWAFF, N Nigeria, 1953–55. Henry Stephenson Fellow, Sheffield Univ., 1961; Deacon, St Augustine's, Brocco Bank, Sheffield, 1961; Priest and Dean of Chapel, Corpus Christi Coll., Cambridge, 1962; Asst Lectr, 1965, Lectr, 1970, Univ. of Cambridge; Prof. of Religious Studies, Univ. of Lancaster, 1974–85; Dean, 1984–91 and Fellow, 1984–93, Trinity Coll., Cambridge. Gresham Prof. of Divinity, 1992–97; Fellow, Gresham Coll., London, 1997. Lectures: Wilde, Univ. of Oxford, 1972–75; Staley, Rollins Coll., Florida, 1978–79; Public, Univ. of Cardiff, 1984; Riddell, Newcastle Univ., 1985; Boutwood, Univ. of Cambridge, 1985; Harris Meml, Toronto, 1986; Boardman, Univ. of Pa, 1988; Montefiore, Univ. of Southampton, 1989; Scott

Holland, London Univ., 1989; Bicentary, Univ. of Georgetown, Washington, 1989; Heslington, York, 1997; Member: Durham Commn on Religious Educn, 1967–70; Root Commn on Marriage and Divorce, 1967–71; Archbps' Commn on Doctrine, 1977–86; Patron, Marriage Research Inst.; Hon. Pres., Stauros; Vice-President: Inst. on Religion in an Age of Science, 1980; Culture and Animals Foundn, 1984–92; Pres., Christian Action on AIDS, 1987–91. *Publications:* The Targums and Rabbinic Literature, 1969, 2nd edn 1979; Problems of Suffering in Religions of the World, 1970, 3rd edn 1987; Jesus and the Pharisees, 1973; The Sense of God, 1973, 2nd edn 1995; The Religious Imagination and the Sense of God, 1978; Uncle Bolpenny Tries Things Out, 1973; Worlds of Faith, 1983; (ed) Violence and Aggression, 1983; Licensed Insanities: religions and belief in God in the contemporary world, 1987; The Meanings of Death, 1991 (HarperCollins Religious Book Award, 1993); A Year to Live, 1991; Hallowed Ground: the religious poetry of place, 1993; (ed jtly) Themes in Religious Studies, 1994; Voices of Islam, 1995; Is God a Virus? Genes, Culture and Religion, 1995; World Religions, 1997; The Oxford Dictionary of World Religions, 1997; The Complete Bible Handbook: an illustrated companion, 1998 (Benjamin Franklin Award, 1999). *Recreations:* books, painting, poetry. *Address:* 14 Bowers Croft, Cambridge CB1 8RP.

BOWKETT, Alan John; venture capitalist and organic farmer; Chairman: Acordis BV, since 2000; Metzeler APS SA, since 2000; *b* 6 Jan. 1951; *er s* of John and Margaret Bowkett; *m* 1975, Joy Dianne Neale; three *s* two *d*. *Educ:* King Charles I Grammar Sch., Kidderminster; University College London (BSc Econ); London Business Sch. (MSc Econ). Corporate Planning Manager, Lex Service, 1977–83; Corporate Develt Manager, BET, 1983–85; Man. Dir, Boulton & Paul, 1985–87; Chief Executive: United Precision Industries, 1987–91; Berisford Internat., then Berisford plc, 1992–99. Director: Anglian Group, 1992–94; Pallasinvest SA (Luxembourg), 1992–98; Greene King, 1993–; Chm., Calder Gp Ltd, 1994–96. Councillor (C) London Borough of Ealing, 1978–82 (Chm., Social Services); Dep. Chm., Ealing Acton Cons. Assoc., 1982–84. Council Mem., UEA, 1988–94 (Treasurer, 1990–94; Hon. Fellow, 1997). FRSA 1993. *Recreations:* growing vegetables, shooting, opera, Italy, listening to Archers. *Address:* Allée du Croître 3, Brussels 1000, Belgium. *Club:* Carlton.

BOWLBY, Prof. Rachel Helena, PhD; Professor of English and Related Literature, University of York, since 1999; *b* 29 Jan. 1957; *d* of Ronald and Elizabeth Bowlby; one *d*. *Educ:* St Anne's Coll., Oxford (1st Cl. Hon. Mods Latin and Greek Lit. 1977; BA 1st Cl. Hons English 1979); Yale Univ. (PhD Comparative Lit. 1983). University of Sussex: Lectr in English, 1984–90; Sen. Lectr, 1990–92; Reader, 1992–94; Prof., 1994–97; Oxford University: Fellow, St Hilda's Coll., 1997–99; Prof. of English, 1998–99. *Publications:* Just Looking, 1985; Virginia Woolf, 1988; Still Crazy after all these Years: women, writing and psychoanalysis, 1992; Shopping with Freud, 1993; Feminist Destinations and Further Essays on Virginia Woolf, 1997; Carried Away: the invention of modern shopping, 2000. *Address:* Department of English, University of York, Heslington, York YO10 5DD. *T:* (01904) 434717.

BOWLBY, Sir Richard Peregrine Longstaff, 3rd Bt *cr* 1923, of Manchester Square, St Marylebone; *b* 11 Aug. 1941; *s* of Edward John Mostyn Bowlby, CBE, MD (*d* 1990), 2nd *s* of Sir Anthony Alfred Bowlby, 1st Bt, KCB, KCMG, KCVO, and Ursula, *d* of Dr T. G. Longstaff; *S* uncle, 1993; *m* 1963, Xenia, *o d* of R. P. A. Garrett; one *s* one *d*. *Heir: s* Benjamin Bowlby [*b* 2 Nov. 1966; *m* 1992, Mylanna Sophia, *er d* of M. C. Colyer; two *s* one *d*]. *Address:* Boundary House, Wyldes Close, NW11 7JB.

BOWLBY, Rt Rev. Ronald Oliver; Assistant Bishop, Diocese of Lichfield, since 1991; *b* 16 August 1926; *s* of Oliver and Helena Bowlby; *m* 1956, Elizabeth Trevelyan Monro; three *s* two *d*. *Educ:* Eton Coll.; Trinity College, Oxford (MA; Hon. Fellow, 1991); Westcott House, Cambridge. Curate of St Luke's, Pallion, Sunderland, 1952–56; Priest-in-charge and Vicar of St Aidan, Billingham, 1956–66; Vicar of Croydon, 1966–72; Bishop of: Newcastle, 1973–80; Southwark, 1980–91. Chairman: Hospital Chaplaincies Council, 1975–82; Social Policy Cttee, Bd for Social Responsibility, 1986–90; Mem., Anglican Consultative Council, 1977–85. President: Nat. Fedn of Housing Assocs, 1988–94; Churches' Nat. Housing Coalition, 1991–94. Hon. Fellow, Newcastle upon Tyne Polytechnic, 1980. *Publications:* contrib. Church without Walls, ed Lindars, 1969; contrib. Church and Politics Today, ed Moyser, 1985. *Recreations:* walking, gardening, music. *Address:* 4 Uppington Avenue, Shrewsbury SY3 7JL.
See also R. H. Bowlby.

BOWLER, Geoffrey, FCIS; Chief General Manager, Sun Alliance & London Insurance Group, 1977–87; *b* 11 July 1924; *s* of James Henry Bowler and Hilda May Bowler. *Educ:* Sloane Sch., Chelsea. FCIS 1952. Dir, British Aviation Insurance Co., 1976–87 (Chm., 1977–83). Dep. Chm., British Insurance Assoc., 1977, Chm. 1979–80. *Address:* 13 Green Lane, Purley, Surrey CR8 3PP. *T:* (020) 8660 0756.

BOWLER, Ian John, CBE 1971 (OBE 1957); Chairman, International Management & Engineering Group Ltd, since 1973 (Managing Director, 1964–68); *b* 1920; *s* of Major John Arthur Bowler; *m* 1963, Hamideh, *d* of Prince Yadollah Azodi, GCMG; two *d*; and one step *s* one step *d*. *Educ:* King's Sch., Worcester; privately; Oxford Univ. Director of Constructors, John Brown, 1961–64; Pres., Iranian Management & Engrg Gp, 1965. Director: IMEG (Offshore) Ltd, 1974–; MMC Gas, Kuala Lumpur. Mem., RNLI, 1983–. Sec., Azerbaijan Foundn, 1992. MInstPet. *Publication:* Predator Birds of Iran, 1973. *Recreations:* ornithology, yachting. *Address:* IMEG, King's House, 10 Haymarket, SW1Y 4BP. *T:* (020) 7321 2611. *Clubs:* Royal Thames Yacht, Ocean Cruising; S.R.R. (La Rochelle, France).

BOWLES, Prof. Dianna Joy, PhD; Professor of Biochemistry, and Co-Founder, Plant Laboratory, University of York, since 1994; *b* 1 May 1948; *d* of Bertie James Bowles and Cicely (*née* Mee). *Educ:* Univ. of Newcastle upon Tyne (BSc Hons 1970); New Hall, Cambridge (PhD 1973). Research Fellow: Univ. of Kaiserslautern, 1973–75; Univ. of Regensburg, 1975; Weizmann Inst., 1976; Univ. of Cambridge, 1976–77; EMBL, 1978; University of Leeds, 1979–93, Prof., 1991–93. Scientific Advr, Ownership Bd, MAFF Central Science Lab., 1995–. Member: ODA Scientific Adv. Gp, Plant Scis Prog., 1993–97; BBSRC Cttees, 1995–2000; EU Framework 5 External Adv. Gp, 1998–. Founder, York Centre for Novel Agricl Products, 1999. Founding Ed., and Ed.-in-Chief, Plant Jl, 1991–. *Publications:* articles in jls. *Recreations:* Upper Nidderdale, Wasdale Head, Herdwick sheep. *Address:* Plant Laboratory, Department of Biology, University of York, York YO10 5YW. *T:* (01904) 434334.

BOWLES, Godfrey Edward; Managing Director, Pearl Group, 1989–94; *b* 21 Dec. 1935; *s* of Llewellyn Crowley Bowles and Florence Jane Edwards; *m* 1958, Elizabeth Madge Dunning; two *s* two *d*. *Educ:* Commonweal Grammar Sch., Swindon; Exeter Coll., Oxford (MA). Emigrated to Australia, 1959; joined Australian Mutual Provident Society: Dep. Manager, Wellington, NZ, 1976; Manager, WA Br., Perth, 1980; Manager, Victoria Br., Melbourne, 1983; Chief Manager, Corporate Services, Sydney, 1986; Gen. Manager, AMP Corporate, Sydney, 1988; returned to UK after acquisition of Pearl Gp by AMP Soc., 1989. Dir, Royal Liver Assce Ltd. Chairman: Gtr Peterborough Partnership; ASBAH. *Recreations:* running, cycling, reading, music, theatre, cinema.

BOWLES, Peter; actor; *b* 16 Oct. 1936; *s* of Herbert Reginald Bowles and Sarah Jane (*née* Harrison); *m* 1961, Susan Alexandra Bennett; two *s* one *d*. *Educ:* High Pavement Grammar Sch., Nottingham; RADA (schol.; Kendal Prize 1955). London début in Romeo and Juliet, Old Vic, 1956; *theatre* includes: Happy Haven, Platonov, Royal Court, 1960; Bonne Soupe, Wyndham's, 1961; Afternoon Men, Arts, 1962; Absent Friends, Garrick, 1975; Dirty Linen, Arts, 1976; Born in the Gardens, Globe, 1980; Some of My Best Friends Are Husbands, nat. tour, 1985; The Entertainer, Shaftesbury, 1986; Canaries Sometimes Sing, Albery, 1987; Man of the Moment, Globe, 1990; Otherwise Engaged (also dir), nat. tour, 1992; Separate Tables, Albery, 1993; Pygmalion, Chichester, 1994; Present Laughter, nat. tour, 1994, Aldwych, 1996; In Praise of Love, Apollo, 1995; Gangster No 1, Almeida, 1995; The School for Wives, Piccadilly, 1997; Major Barbara, The Misanthrope, Piccadilly, 1998; Sleuth, tour, 1999; Hedda Gabler, tour, 1999; The Beau, Th. Royal, Haymarket, 2001; *films* include: Blow Up, 1966; The Charge of the Light Brigade, 1967; Laughter in the Dark, 1968; A Day in the Death of Joe Egg, 1970; The Steal, 1994; The Hollywood Ten, 2000; *TV films:* Shadow on the Sun, 1988; Running Late (also co-prod), 1992; Little White Lies, 1998; Love and War in the Apennines; *television series* include: Rumpole of the Bailey, 1976–92; To the Manor Born, 1979–82; Only when I Laugh, 1979–82; The Bounder, 1982–83; The Irish RM, 1983–85; Lytton's Diary, 1984–86 (also co-created series); Executive Stress, 1987–88; Perfect Scoundrels, 1990–92 (also co-created series). Comedy Actor of the Year, Pye Awards, 1984; ITV Personality of the Year, Variety Club of GB, 1984. *Recreations:* motoring, physical jerks. *Address:* c/o Conway Van Gelder, 18–21 Jermyn Street, SW1Y 6HP.

BOWLES, Timothy John; Master of the Supreme Court (Chancery Division), since 1999; *b* 20 March 1951; *s* of late Arthur Ernest Bowles and of Elizabeth Mary Bowles; *m* 1987, Michelle Martine Riley; two *s*. *Educ:* Downside Sch.; Durham Univ. FCIArb 1994. Called to the Bar, Gray's Inn, 1973 (Mould Schol.); in practice at the Bar, 1973–99; Dep. Chancery Master, 1996–99. Legal Chairman: South and South Eastern Rent Assessment Panel, 1994–2001; London Rent Assessment Panel, 1997–2001; Dep. Chm., Agricl Land Tribunal, 1995–. Gov., King Edward VI Grammar Sch. (The Royal Grammar Sch.), Guildford, 2001–. Ed., Civil Court Practice, 2001–. *Recreations:* sailing, cricket. *Address:* Hillbrow, 44 Harvey Road, Guildford, Surrey GU1 3SE; Dolphins, 3 Church Hill, St Mawes, Cornwall TR2 5DP. *Clubs:* Cruising Association, Bar Yacht; St Mawes Sailing; Merrow Cricket.

BOWLEY, Martin Richard; QC 1981; a Recorder of the Crown Court, 1979–88; *b* 29 Dec. 1936; *s* of late Charles Colin Stuart Bowley and Mary Evelyn Bowley; partner, 1976, Julian Marquez Bedoya (*d* 1990). *Educ:* Magdalen Coll. Sch., Oxford; Queen's Coll., Oxford (Styring Exhibnr, 1955; MA; BCL 1961). National Service, 1955–57: commnd Pilot Officer as a Fighter Controller; served 2nd Tactical Air Force, 1956–57. Called to the Bar, Inner Temple, 1962, Bencher, 1994; Midland and Oxford Circuit; Member: Senate and Bar Council, 1985–86; Gen. Council of Bar, 1987–88, 1989–94 (Treas., 1992–94); Chm., Bar Cttee, 1987. Member: Lord Chancellor's Standing Commn on Efficiency, 1986–87; Marre Cttee on Future of Legal Profession, 1987–88; Home Office Steering Gp on Sexual Offences Law Reform, 1999–2000. Trustee, Bar Free Repn Unit, 1997–. Pres., Bar Lesbian and Gay Gp, 1994–. Stonewall Lectr, 1994. Chm., Questors Theatre, 1972–84 and 1988–93 (Sec., 1963–72); Mem. Standing Cttee, Little Theatre Guild of GB, 1974–84 (Vice-Chm., 1979–81, Chm., 1981–84; Hon. Associate, 1997). Mem., Stonewall Gp, 1999–. *Publications:* (contrib.) Advising Gay and Lesbian Clients, 1999; contrib. to nat. and legal periodicals. *Recreations:* playing at theatre, watching cricket, island hopping, supporting Stonewall. *Address:* Flat E, 23/24 Great James Street, WC1N 3ES. *T:* (020) 7831 1674; 36 Bedford Row, WC1R 4JH. *T:* (020) 7421 8000. *Clubs:* MCC, Surrey CC; Questors.

BOWMAN; *see* Kellett-Bowman.

BOWMAN, Alan Keir, PhD; FBA 1994; Official Student of Christ Church, and Lecturer in Ancient History, University of Oxford, since 1977; *b* Manchester, 23 May 1944; *s* of late Cyril Bowman and of Freda (*née* Bowman); *m* 1966, Jacqueline Frayman; one *s* one *d*. *Educ:* Manchester Grammar Sch.; Queen's Coll., Oxford (MA); Univ. of Toronto (MA, PhD 1969). Canada Council Postdoctoral Fellow, 1969–70; Asst Prof. of Classics, Rutgers Univ., 1970–72; Lectr in Ancient Hist., Manchester Univ., 1972–77; Sen. Censor, Christ Church, Oxford, 1988–90; Dir, Centre for Study of Ancient Documents, Oxford Univ., 1995–. Vis. Mem., Inst. for Advanced Study, Princeton, 1976, 1981; British Acad. Res. Reader, 1991–93. Chm., Roman Res. Trust, 1990–. FSA 1999. *Publications:* The Town Councils of Roman Egypt, 1971; Egypt after the Pharaohs, 1986, 3rd edn 1996; (jtly) The Vindolanda Writing-Tablets, 1994; Life and Letters on the Roman Frontier: Vindolanda and its people, 1994, 2nd edn 1998 (British Archaeological Book Award, 1998); (jtly) Literacy and Power in the Ancient World, 1994; (ed jtly) The Cambridge Ancient History, 2nd edn, Vol. X, 1996, Vol. XI, 2000; (ed jtly) Agriculture in Egypt from Pharaonic to modern times, 1998; contrib. learned jls. *Recreations:* photography, music, cricket, tennis, walking. *Address:* Christ Church, Oxford OX1 1DP. *T:* (01865) 276202. *Club:* Emeriti (Oxford).

BOWMAN, Claire Margaret; *see* Makin, C. M.

BOWMAN, (Edwin) Geoffrey, CB 1991; Parliamentary Counsel, since 1984; *b* Blackpool, Lancs, 27 Jan. 1946; *er s* of late John Edwin Bowman and Lillian Joan Bowman (*née* Nield); *m* 1969, Carol Margaret, *er d* of late Alexander Ogilvie and Ethel Ogilvie; two *s* one *d*. *Educ:* Roundhay Sch., Leeds; Trinity Coll., Cambridge (Senior Scholar; BA 1st cl., LLB 1st cl., MA, LLM). Called to Bar, Lincoln's Inn (Cassel Scholar), 1968; in practice, Chancery Bar, 1969–71; joined Parliamentary Counsel Office, 1971 (seconded to Law Commission, 1977–79, 1996–98); Dep. Parly Counsel, 1981–84. *Publication:* The Elements of Conveyancing (with E. L. G. Tyler), 1972. *Recreation:* music (bassoon), history. *Address:* Parliamentary Counsel Office, 36 Whitehall, SW1A 2AY. *T:* (020) 7210 6629. *Club:* Les Amis du Basson Français (Paris).

BOWMAN, Eric Joseph; consultant, since 1986; *b* 1 June 1929; *s* of late Joseph John Bowman and Lilley Bowman; *m* 1951, Esther Kay; one *d*. *Educ:* Stationers' Company's School; College of Estate Management. FRICS. Private practice, 1945–51; Royal Engineers, 1951–53; private practice, 1953–54; Min. of Works, 1954–63; Min. of Housing and Local Govt, 1963–73; Directorate of Diplomatic and Post Office Services, MPBW, later DoE, 1973–80; Directorate of Quantity Surveying Services, DoE, 1980–83; Dir of Building and Quantity Surveying Services, PSA, DoE, 1983–86. *Recreations:* fly fishing, walking, swimming, gardening, reading. *Address:* Mearsons Farm, Hubbersty Head, Crosthwaite, near Kendal, Cumbria LA8 8JB. *T:* (01539) 568400.

BOWMAN, Geoffrey; *see* Bowman, E. G.

BOWMAN, James Thomas, CBE 1997; counter-tenor; Teacher of Voice, Guildhall School of Music, since 1983; *b* Oxford, 6 Nov. 1941; *s* of Benjamin and Cecilia Bowman. *Educ:* Ely Cathedral Choir Sch.; King's Sch., Ely; New Coll., Oxford (MA (History) 1967; DipEd 1964; Hon. Fellow, 1998). Lay Vicar, Westminster Abbey, 1969; Gentleman in Ordinary, HM Chapel Royal, St James's Palace, 2000. Many concert performances with Early Music Consort, 1967–76; operatic performances with: English Opera Gp, 1967; Sadler's Wells Opera, 1970–; Glyndebourne Festival Opera, 1970–; Royal Opera, Covent Gdn, 1972; Sydney Opera, Australia, 1978; Opéra Comique, Paris, 1979; Le Châtelet, Paris, 1982; Geneva, 1983; Scottish Opera, 1985; La Scala, Milan, 1988, 1991; La Fenice, Venice, 1991; Paris Opera, 1991; Badisches Staatsteater, Karlsruhe, 1984; in USA at Santa Fe and Wolf Trap Festivals, Dallas and San Francisco Operas; at Aix-en-Provence Fest., 1979; operatic roles include: Oberon, in A Midsummer Night's Dream; Endymion, in La Calisto; the Priest, in Taverner; Polinesso, in Ariodante; Apollo, in Death in Venice; Astron, in The Ice Break; Ruggiero in Alcina; title rôles: Giulio Cesare; Tamerlano; Xerxes; Scipione; Giustino; Orlando; Ottone. Extensive discography of opera, oratorio and contemporary music. Hon. DMus Newcastle, 1996. Medal, City of Paris, 1992. Officier, Ordre des Arts et des Lettres (France), 1995. *Recreations:* ecclesiastical architecture, collecting records. *Address:* 4 Brownlow Road, Redhill RH1 6AW.

BOWMAN, Sir Jeffery (Haverstock), Kt 1991; FCA; Chairman: Mid Essex Hospital Services NHS Trust, 1993–99; Masthead Insurance Underwriting PLC, 1993–99; *b* 3 April 1935; *s* of Alfred Haverstock Bowman and Doris Gertrude Bowman; *m* 1963, Susan Claudia Bostock; one *s* two *d*. *Educ:* Winchester Coll. (schol.); Trinity Hall, Cambridge (major schol.; BA Hons 1st cl. in Law). Served RHG, 1953–55 (commnd, 1954). Price Waterhouse: articled in London, 1958; NY, 1963–64; admitted to partnership, 1966; Mem., Policy Cttee, 1972–91; Dir of Tech. Services, 1973–76; Dir, London Office, 1979–81; Sen. Partner, 1982–91; Chm., Price Waterhouse Europe, 1988–93; Jt Chm., Price Waterhouse World Firm, 1992–93. Dir, Gibbs Mew, 1995–97. Auditor, Duchy of Cornwall, 1971–93. Vice-Pres., Union of Indep. Cos, 1983–93; Member: Council, ICAEW, 1986–90 (Mem., Accounting Standards Cttee, 1982–87); Council, Industrial Soc., 1985–93; Economic and Financial Policy Cttee, CBI, 1987–93; City Capital Markets Cttee, 1989–93; Council, Business in the Community, 1985–91. Chairman: Court of Appeal (Civil Div.) Review, 1996–97; Crown Office Review, 1999–2000. Trustee, Royal Botanic Gdns, Kew, 1995–. Gov., Brentwood Sch., 1985–97. FRSA 1989. *Recreations:* golf, opera, gardening, sailing. *Address:* The Old Rectory, Boreham, Chelmsford, Essex CM3 3EP. *T:* (01245) 467233. *Club:* Garrick.

BOWMAN, Dr John Christopher, CBE 1986; PhD; FIBiol; independent environmental consultant, since 1993; Managing Director (Europe and Africa), Brown & Root Environmental, 1991–93; *b* 13 Aug. 1933; *s* of M. C. Bowman and C. V. Simister; *m* 1961, S. J. Lorimer; three *d*. *Educ:* Manchester Grammar Sch.; Univ. of Reading (BSc); Univ. of Edinburgh (PhD). Geneticist, later Chief Geneticist, Thornbers, Mytholmroyd, Yorks, 1958–66. Post-doctoral Fellow, North Carolina State Univ., Raleigh, NC, USA, 1964–65; University of Reading: Prof. of Animal Production, 1966–81; Head of Dept of Agric., 1967–71; Dir, Univ. Farms, 1967–78; Dir, Centre for Agricl Strategy, 1975–81; Sec., NERC, 1981–89; Chief Exec., NRA, 1989–91. Dir, Certa Foundn, 1998–. Chm., Sonning Parish Council, 1994–98. Hon. DSc Cranfield, 1990. *Publications:* An Introduction to Animal Breeding, 1974; Animals for Man, 1977; (with P. Susmel) The Future of Beef Production in the European Community, 1979; (jtly) Hammond's Farm Animals, 1983. *Recreations:* golf, tennis, gardening. *Address:* Court Mill, Lower Street, Merriott, Som TA16 5NL.

BOWMAN, Sir Paul Humphrey Armytage, 5th Bt *cr* 1884, of Holmbury St Mary, Surrey; *b* 10 Aug. 1921; *s* of Major Humphrey Ernest Bowman, CMG, CBE (*d* 1965), and Frances Guinevere Armytage (*d* 1923), and *great nephew* of Sir William Paget Bowman, 2nd Bt; *S* cousin, 1994; *m* 1st, 1943, Felicité Anne Araminta MacMichael (marr. diss. 1947); 2nd, 1947, Gabrielle May Currie (marr. diss. 1974); one *d*; 3rd, 1974, Elizabeth Deirdre Churchill (*d* 1993). *Educ:* Eton. Served War, 1940–46, Coldstream Guards (Major); twice wounded. Dir, Hill Samuel Co. Ltd, 1962–78. *Heir: cousin* Martin Ramsay Bowman, *b* 10 Nov. 1928. *Address:* 3/414 Edgecliff Road, Woollahra, Sydney, NSW 2025, Australia.

BOWMAN, Penelope Jill; *see* Watkins, P. J.

BOWMAN, Philip, FCA; Chief Executive, Allied Domecq plc, since 1999; *b* 14 Dec. 1952; *s* of Thomas Patrick Bowman and Norma Elizabeth (*née* Deravin). *Educ:* Westminster Sch.; Pembroke Coll., Cambridge (MA). FCA 1983. Price Waterhouse, London, 1974–78; Gibbs Bright & Co. Pty Ltd, Melbourne, 1978–83; Granite Industries Inc., Atlanta, 1983–85; Bass plc, London, 1985–95: Finance Dir, 1991–94; Chief Exec., Retail Div., 1994–95; Finance Dir, Coles Myer Ltd, Melbourne, 1995–96; Chm., Liberty plc, 1998–2000. Non-exec. Dir, BSkyB Gp plc, 1994–. *Recreations:* scuba diving, entomology, opera, computers and electronics. *Address:* Allied Domecq plc, The Pavilions, Bridgwater Road, Bedminster Down, Bristol BS13 8AR. *Clubs:* Victoria Racing, Royal Automobile of Victoria (Melbourne).

BOWMAN, Richard Alan; Master of the Supreme Court, Chancery Division, since 1996; *b* 3 Oct. 1943; *s* of Harry Bowman and Gladys Bowman (*née* Croft); *m* 1970, Joanna Mary Lodder; two *s* one *d*. *Educ:* Clifton; St George's Sch., Newport, RI; Keble Coll., Oxford (MA). FCIArb 1995. Admitted solicitor, 1970; Dep. Chancery Master, 1988–96. Chm., Legal Aid Commn, General Synod of C of E, 1996. *Address:* Royal Courts of Justice, Strand, WC2A 2LL.

BOWMAN, Sarah Meredith; District Judge, Principal Registry (Family Division), since 1993; *b* 24 May 1949; *d* of Alexander Dennis Bowman and Jean Bowman; *m* 1984, Jake Downey; three *s*. *Educ:* Notting Hill and Ealing High Sch.; Leeds Univ. (BA). Called to the Bar, Middle Temple, 1976; Barrister, 1976–93. *Recreation:* my family. *Address:* (Principal Registry Family Division), First Avenue House, 42–49 High Holborn, WC1V 6NP.

BOWMAN, Dr Sheridan Gail Esther, FSA; Keeper, Department of Scientific Research, British Museum, since 1989; *b* Westlock, Alta, Canada, 11 March 1950; *o d* of late Otto Michael Bowman and of Eva (*née* McKnight). *Educ:* Whitehaven County Grammar Sch., Cumbria; St Anne's Coll., Oxford (Open Scholar; MA; DPhil Physics, 1976); Chelsea Coll., London (MSc Maths, 1981); (extramural) London Univ. (Dip. in Archaeol., 1985). FSA 1987 (a Vice Pres., 1993). Scientific Officer, BM, 1976. *Publications:* Radiocarbon Dating, 1990; (ed) Science and the Past, 1991; papers on scientific techniques, particularly dating, applied to archaeology. *Recreations:* heath and fell walking, gardening, theatre. *Address:* Department of Scientific Research, British Museum, WC1B 3DG. *T:* (020) 7323 8669.

BOWMAN-SHAW, Sir (George) Neville, Kt 1984; Chairman: Bowmans Mechanical Handling Ltd, since 1995; Samuk Ltd, since 1995; Bowman Lift Trucks Ltd, since 1997; *b* 4 Oct. 1930; *s* of George Bowman-Shaw and Hazel Bowman-Shaw (*née* Smyth); *m* 1962, Georgina Mary Blundell; two *s* one *d* (and one *s* decd). *Educ:* Caldicott Preparatory Sch.; then private tutor. Farming Trainee, 1947; Management Trainee in Engineering Co., 1948. Commissioned in 5th Royal Inniskilling Dragoon Guards, 1950. Sales Manager: Matling Ltd, Wolverhampton, 1953; Materials Handling Equipment (GB) Ltd, London, and Matbro Ltd, London, 1955; Chairman: Boss Trucks Ltd, 1959–95; Lancer Boss Gp Ltd, 1966–94; Lancer Boss Ireland Ltd, 1966–94; Lancer Boss Fördergeräte Vertriebsges. (Austria), 1966–94; Boss France SA, 1967–94; Steinbock GmbH, 1983–94; Boss Trucks España SA, 1987–94; FOREXIA (UK) Ltd, 1994–97. Member: Development Commn, 1970–77; Design Council, 1979–84; BOTB, 1982–85. High Sheriff, Bedfordshire, 1987–88. *Recreations:* shooting, vintage tractors. *Address:* Toddington Manor, Toddington, Bedfordshire LU5 6HJ. *T:* (01525) 872576. *Clubs:* Cavalry and Guards, Buck's, MCC.

BOWMONT AND CESSFORD, Marquis of; Charles Robert George Innes-Ker; *b* 18 Feb. 1981; *s* and *heir* of Duke of Roxburghe, *qv* and of Lady Jane Dawnay, *qv*. *Educ:* Eton Coll.; Newcastle Univ. *Recreations:* motor racing, golf, tennis, fishing. *Address:* Floors Castle, Kelso TD5 7RW.

BOWN, Jane Hope, (Mrs M. G. Moss), CBE 1995 (MBE 1985); Photographer for The Observer, since 1950; *b* 13 March 1925; *d* of Charles Wentworth Bell and Daisy Bown; *m* 1954, Martin Grenville Moss, *qv*; two *s* one *d*. *Educ:* William Gibbs Sch., Faversham. Chart corrector, WRNS, 1944–46; student photographer, Guildford School of Art, 1946–50. Hon. DLitt Bradford, 1986. Barry Award, What the Papers Say, 1995. *Publications:* The Gentle Eye: a book of photographs, 1980; Women of Consequence, 1986; Men of Consequence, 1987; The Singular Cat, 1988; Pillars of the Church, 1991; Jane Bown: Observer, 1996; Faces, 2000. *Recreations:* restoring old houses, chickens. *Address:* Old Mill House, 50 Broad Street, Alresford, Hampshire SO24 9AN. *T:* (01962) 732419.

BOWN, Prof. Lalage Jean, OBE 1977; FRSE; FEIS; CCIPD; Director, Department of Adult and Continuing Education, University of Glasgow, 1981–92, now Professor Emeritus; *b* 1 April 1927; *d* of Arthur Mervyn Bown, MC and Dorothy Ethel (*née* Watson); two foster *d*. *Educ:* Wycombe Abbey Sch.; Cheltenham Ladies' Coll.; Somerville Coll., Oxford (MA); Oxford Post-grad. Internship in Adult Education. FEIS 1990; FRSE 1991; CCIPD (FIPD 1993). Resident Tutor: University Coll. of Gold Coast, 1949–55; Makerere University Coll., Uganda, 1955–59; Asst Dir, then Dep. Dir, Extramural Studies, Univ. of Ibadan, Nigeria, 1960–66; Dir, Extramural Studies and Prof. (*ad personam*), Univ., of Zambia, 1966–70; Prof. of Adult Educn, Ahmadu Bello Univ., Nigeria, 1971–76, Univ. of Lagos, Nigeria, 1977–79; Dean of Educn, Univ. of Lagos, 1979–80; Vis. Fellow, Inst. of Development Studies, 1980–81. Hon. Professor: Internat. Centre for Educn in Develt, Warwick Univ., 1992–97; Inst. of Educn, Univ. of London, 1998–99. Member: Bd, British Council, 1981–89; Scottish Community Educn Council, 1982–88; Exec. Cttee, Scottish Inst. of Adult and Continuing Educn, 1982–88; Bd, Network Scotland, 1983–88; Bd of Trustees, Nat. Museums of Scotland, 1987–97; Council, Insite Trust, 1987–95; Bd of Trustees, Womankind, 1988–96; Interim Trustee, Books for Develt, 1987–90; British Mem., Commonwealth Standing Cttee on Student Mobility and Higher Educn Co-operation, 1989–94; Trustee, World Univ. Service, UK, 1997–; Mem. Exec., Council for Educn in the Commonwealth, 2000– (Chm., Wkg Gp on Student Mobility, 1998–2000). Governor, Inst. of Develt Studies, 1982–91, President: Develt Studies Assoc., 1984–86; British Comparative and Internat. Educn Soc., 1985–86; Vice-President: WEA, 1989–95 (Hon. Vice-Pres., 1984–88); Commonwealth Assoc. for Educn and Trng of Adults, 1990–93; Hon. Pres., British Assoc. for Literacy in Develt, 1993–98. Hon. Vice-Pres., Townswomen's Guilds, 1984–. Hon. Life Member: People's Educnl Assoc., Ghana, 1973; African Adult Educn Assoc., 1976. DUniv: Open, 1975; Paisley, 1993; Stirling, 1994; Dr (*hc*) Edinburgh, 1993. William Pearson Tolley Medal, Syracuse Univ., USA, 1975; Meritorious Service Award, Nigerian Nat. Council for Adult Educn, 1979. *Publications:* (ed with Michael Crowder) Proceedings of First International Congress of Africanists, 1964; Two Centuries of African English, 1973; (ed) Adult Education in Nigeria: the next 10 years, 1975; A Rusty Person is Worse than Rusty Iron, 1976; Lifelong Learning: prescription for progress, 1979; (ed with S. H. O. Tomori) A Handbook of Adult Education for West Africa, 1980; (ed with J. T. Okedara) An Introduction to Adult Education: a multi-disciplinary and cross-cultural approach for developing countries, 1980; Preparing the Future: women, literacy and development, 1991; (ed) Towards a Commonwealth of Scholars: a new vision for the Nineties, 1994; numerous articles in learned jls. *Recreations:* travel, reading, entertaining friends. *Address:* 1 Dogpole Court, Dogpole, Shrewsbury SY1 1ES. *T:* (01743) 356155, *Fax:* (01743) 233626. *Club:* Royal Over-Seas League.

BOWNESS, family name of **Baron Bowness.**

BOWNESS, Baron *cr* 1995 (Life Peer), of Warlingham in the County of Surrey and of Croydon in the London Borough of Croydon; **Peter Spencer Bowness,** Kt 1987; CBE 1981; DL; Partner, Weightman, Sadler (formerly Horsley, Weightman, Richardson and Sadler), Solicitors, Purley, since 1970; *b* 19 May 1943; *s* of Hubert Spencer Bowness and Doreen (Peggy) Bowness; *m* 1969, Marianne Hall (marr. diss.); one *d*; *m* 1984, Mrs Patricia Jane Cook; one step *s*. *Educ:* Whitgift Sch., Croydon. Admitted Solicitor, 1966. Croydon Council: Mem. (C), 1968–98: Leader, 1976–94; Leader of the Opposition, 1994–96; Mayor of Croydon, 1979–80; Chm., London Boroughs Assoc., 1978–94; Dep. Chm., Assoc. of Metropolitan Authorities, 1978–80. Opposition spokesman on the envmt, transport and the regions, H of L, 1997–98. Member: Audit Commn, 1983–95; London Residuary Body, 1985–93; Nat. Training Task Force, 1989–92; UK Delegn, CLRAE (Council of Europe), 1990–98; UK Mem., Mem. Bureau, and Mem. Transportation and Telecommunications Commn, EC Cttee of the Regions, 1994–98; Mem., UK Delegn to EU Charter of Fundamental Rights Drafting Convention, 1999–2000. Gov., Whitgift Foundn, 1982–94. Hon. Col, 151 (Greater London) Transport Regt RCT (V), 1988–93. DL Greater London, 1981; Freeman, City of London, 1984. *Recreations:* travel, gardening, our two dachshunds. *Address:* Three Gables, 10 Westview Road, Warlingham, Surrey CR6 9JD. *T:* (office) (020) 8660 6455.

BOWNESS, Sir Alan, Kt 1988; CBE 1976; Director of the Tate Gallery, 1980–88; Director, Henry Moore Foundation, 1988–94 (Member, Committee of Management, 1984–88 and since 1994); *b* 11 Jan. 1928; *er s* of George Bowness and Kathleen (*née* Benton); *m* 1957, Sarah Hepworth-Nicholson, *d* of Ben Nicholson, OM, and Dame Barbara Hepworth, DBE; one *s* one *d*. *Educ:* University Coll. Sch.; Downing Coll., Cambridge (Hon. Fellow 1980); Courtauld Inst. of Art, Univ. of London (Hon. Fellow 1986). Worked with Friends' Ambulance Unit and Friends' Service Council, 1946–50; Reg. Art Officer, Arts Council of GB, 1955–57; Courtauld Inst., 1957–79, Dep. Dir, 1978–79; Reader, 1967–78, Prof. of Hist. of Art, 1978–79, Univ. of London. Vis. Prof., Humanities Seminar, Johns Hopkins Univ., Baltimore, 1969. Mem. Internat. Juries: Premio Di Tella, Buenos Aires, 1965; São Paulo Bienal, 1967; Venice Biennale, 1986; Lehmbruck Prize, Duisburg, 1970; Rembrandt Prize, 1979–88; Heiliger Prize, 1998. Arts Council: Mem., 1973–75 and 1978–80; Mem., Art Panel, 1960–80 (Vice-Chm., 1973–75, Chm., 1978–80); Mem., Arts Film Cttee, 1968–77 (Chm., 1972–75). Member:

Fine Arts Cttee, Brit. Council, 1960–69 and 1970–92 (Chm., 1981–92); Exec. Cttee, Contemp. Art Soc., 1961–69 and 1970–86; Kettle's Yard Cttee, Univ. of Cambridge, 1970–99; Cultural Adv. Cttee, UK National Commn for UNESCO, 1973–82. Governor, Chelsea Sch. of Art, 1965–93; Hon. Sec., Assoc. of Art Historians, 1973–76; Dir, Barbara Hepworth Museum, St Ives, Cornwall, 1976–88. Mem. Council, RCA, 1978–99 (Hon. Fellow 1984). Trustee: Yorkshire Sculpture Park, 1979–; Handel House, 1994– (Chm., 1997–). Hon. Fellow, Bristol Polytechnic, 1980. Hon. FRIBA 1994. Hon. DLit Liverpool, 1988; Hon. DLitt: Leeds, 1995; Exeter, 1996. Exhibitions arranged and catalogued include: 54:64 Painting and Sculpture of a Decade (with L. Gowing), 1964; Dubuffet, 1966; Sculpture in Battersea Park, 1966; Van Gogh, 1968; Rodin, 1970; William Scott, 1972; French Symbolist Painters (with G. Lacambre), 1972; Ceri Richards, 1975; Courbet (with M. Laclotte), 1977. Chevalier, l'Ordre des Arts et des Lettres, France, 1973. *Publications:* William Scott Paintings, 1964; Impressionists and Post Impressionists, 1965; (ed) Henry Moore: complete sculpture 1955–64 (vol. 3) 1965, 1964–73 (vol. 4) 1977, 1974–80 (vol. 5) 1983, 1949–54 (vol. 2) 1987, 1980–86 (vol. 6) 1988; Modern Sculpture, 1965; Barbara Hepworth Drawings, 1966; Alan Davie, 1967; Recent British Painting, 1968; Gauguin, 1971; Barbara Hepworth: complete sculpture 1960–70, 1971; Modern European Art, 1972; Ivon Hitchens, 1973; (contrib.) Picasso 1881–1973, ed R. Penrose, 1973; (contrib.) The Genius of British Painting, ed D. Piper, 1975; The Conditions of Success, 1989; Bernard Meadows, 1994; articles in Burlington Magazine, TLS, Observer, and Annual Register. *Recreations:* going to concerts, theatre, opera. *Address:* 91 Castelnau, SW13 9EL. *T:* (020) 8846 8520; 16 Piazza, St Ives, Cornwall TR26 1NQ. *T:* (01736) 795444. *Club:* Athenæum.

BOWRING, Air Vice-Marshal John Ivan Roy, CB 1977; CBE 1971; CEng, FRAeS; FIMgt; management consultant, aircraft maintenance, retired; Head of Technical Training and Maintenance, British Aerospace (formerly British Aircraft Corporation), Riyadh, Saudi Arabia, 1978–88, retired; *b* 28 March 1923; *s* of Hugh Passmore Bowring and Ethel Grace Bowring; *m* 1945, Irene Mary Rance; two *d. Educ:* Great Yarmouth Grammar Sch., Norfolk; Aircraft Apprentice, RAF Halton-Cosford, 1938–40; Leicester Tech. Coll.; commissioned, RAF, 1944; NW Europe, 1944–47; RAF, Horsham St Faith's, Engrg duties, 1947–48; RAF South Cerney, Pilot trng, 1949; Engr Officer: RAF Finningly, 1950–51; RAF Kai-Tak, 1951–53; Staff Officer, AHQ Hong Kong, ADC to Governor, Hong Kong, 1953–54; Sen. Engr Officer, RAF Coltishall, 1954–56; exchange duties with US Air Force, Research and Develt, Wright Patterson Air Force Base, Ohio, 1956–60; RAF Staff Coll., Bracknell, 1960; Air Min. Opl Requirements, 1961–64; OC Engrg Wing, RAF St Mawgan, 1964–67; Head of F111 Procurement Team, USA, 1967–68; OC RAF Aldergrove, NI, 1968–70; RCDS, 1971; Dir of Engrg Policy, MoD, 1972–73; AO Engrg, RAF Germany, 1973–74; SASO, RAF Support Comd, 1974–77; AO Maintenance, 1977. *Recreations:* sailing, golf. *Club:* Royal Air Force.

BOWRING, Peter, CBE 1993; Chairman, C. T. Bowring & Co. Ltd, 1978–82; Director, Marsh & McLennan Cos Inc., New York, 1980–85 (Vice-Chairman, 1982–84); *b* 22 April 1923; *e s* of Frederick Clive Bowring and Agnes Walker (*née* Cairns); *m* 1946, Barbara Ekaterina Brewis (marr. diss.); one *s* one *d*; *m* 1986, Mrs Carole Dear. *Educ:* Shrewsbury Sch. Served War, 1939–45: commnd Rifle Bde, 1942; served in Egypt, N Africa, Italy, Austria (mentioned in despatches, 1945); demobilised 1946. Joined Bowring Group of Cos, 1947: Dir, C. T. Bowring & Co. Ltd, 1956–84, Dep. Chm. 1973–78; Chairman: C. T. Bowring Trading (Holdings) Ltd, 1967–84; Bowmaker (Plant) Ltd, 1972–83; Bowring Steamship Co. Ltd, 1974–82; Bowmaker Ltd, 1978–82; C. T. Bowring (UK) Ltd, 1980–84. Director: City Arts Trust Ltd, 1984–94 (Chm., 1987–94); Independent Primary and Secondary Educn Trust, 1986–. Mem. of Lloyd's, 1968–98. Chm., Help the Aged Ltd, 1977–87, Pres., 1988–2000. Dir, Centre for Policy Studies, 1983–88. Vice Pres., Aldeburgh Foundn, 1989– (Chm., 1982–89). Chairman: Inter-Action Social Enterprise Trust, 1989–91; Bd of Governors, St Dunstan's Educnl Foundn, 1977–91; Dulwich Picture Gall. Consultative Cttee, 1989–96; Mem. Bd of Governors, Shrewsbury Sch., 1969–97. Trustee: Ironbridge Gorge Mus. Develt Trust, 1989–93; Spry Trust (formerly Upper Severn Navigation Trust), 1989–; Third Age Challenge (formerly ReAction) Trust, 1991–96; Wakefield (Tower Hill, Trinity Square) Trust, 1986–. Member: Guild of Freemen of City of London; Co. of World Traders (Master, 1989–90); Liveryman, Insurers' Co.; Freeman, Co. of Watermen and Lightermen. FRSA; FZS; FInstD. *Publication:* The Last Minute, 2000. *Recreations:* sailing, motoring, listening to music, photography, cooking, travel. *Address:* Flat 79, New Concordia Wharf, Mill Street, SE1 2BB. *T:* (020) 7237 0818. *Clubs:* Royal Thames Yacht, Little Ship, Royal Green Jackets, City Livery.

BOWRING, Prof. Richard John; Master, Selwyn College, Cambridge, since 2000; Professor of Japanese Studies, University of Cambridge, since 1985; *b* 6 Feb. 1947; *s* of late Richard Arthur Bowring and of Mabel Bowring (*née* Eddy); *m* 1970, Susan (*née* Povey); one *d. Educ:* Blundell's Sch.; Downing Coll., Cambridge (PhD 1973; LittD 1997). Lectr in Japanese, Monash Univ., 1973–75; Asst Prof. of Japanese, Columbia Univ., NY, 1978–79; Associate Prof. of Japanese, Princeton Univ., NJ, 1979–84; Cambridge University: Lectr in Japanese, 1984; Chm, Faculty Bd of Oriental Studies, 1987–89, 1998–2000; Fellow, Downing Coll., 1985–2000; Hon. Fellow, 2000. British Acad. Reader, 1995–97. Trustee, Cambridge Foundn, 1989–98. Advr, UFC, subseq. HEFCE, 1992–94. Gov., SOAS, 1994–99. *Publications:* Mori Ogai and the Modernization of Japanese Culture, 1979; trans., Murasaki Shikibu: her diary and poetic memoirs, 1982; Murasaki Shikibu: The Tale of Genji, 1988; An Introduction to Modern Japanese, 1992; (ed) Cambridge Encyclopedia of Japan, 1993; The Diary of Lady Murasaki, 1996. *Address:* The Master's Lodge, Selwyn College, Cambridge CB3 9DQ.

BOWRON, John Lewis, CBE 1986; solicitor; Secretary-General, The Law Society, 1974–87; *b* 1 Feb. 1924; *e s* of John Henry and Lavinia Bowron; *m* 1950, Patricia, *d* of Arthur Cobby; two *d. Educ:* Grangefield Grammar Sch., Stockton-on-Tees; King's Coll., London (LLB, FKC 1976). Principal in Malcolm Wilson & Cobby, Solicitors, Worthing, 1952–74. Member of the Council of the Law Society, 1969–74. Chm. (part-time), Social Security Appeal Tribunals, 1988–96; Agent (part-time) Crown Prosecution Service, 1988–93. *Recreations:* golf, music. *Address:* Hurworth, Sanctuary Lane, Storrington, Pulborough, West Sussex RH20 3JD. *T:* (01903) 746949.

See also M. R. Bowron.

BOWRON, Margaret Ruth, (Mrs A. T. Davy); QC 2001; *b* 8 July 1956; *d* of John Lewis Bowron, *qv*; *m* 1988, Anthony Tallents Davy; two *d. Educ:* Convent of Our Lady of Sion, Worthing; Brighton and Hove High Sch., Brighton; King's Coll., London (LLB 1977). Called to the Bar, Inner Temple, 1978; in practice as barrister, specialising in clinical negligence and related work, 1978–. *Recreations:* walking, theatre, travel. *Address:* (chambers) 1 Crown Office Row, Temple, EC4Y 7HH. *T:* (020) 7797 7500.

BOWSER of Argaty and the King's Lundies, David Stewart, JP; a Forestry Commissioner, 1974–82; *b* 11 March 1926; *s* of late David Charles Bowser, CBE and Maysie Murray Bowser (*née* Henderson); *m* 1951, Judith Crabbe; one *s* four *d. Educ:* Harrow; Trinity Coll., Cambridge (BA Agric). Captain, Scots Guards, 1944–47. Member: Nat. Bd of Timber Growers Scotland Ltd (formerly Scottish Woodland Owners' Assoc.), 1960–82 (Chm. 1972–74); Regional Adv. Cttee, West Scotland Conservancy, Forestry Commn, 1964–74 (Chm. 1970–74). Chm., Scottish Council, British Deer Soc., 1989–94; Mem., Blackface Sheep Breeders' Assoc. (Vice-Pres., 1981–83; Pres., 1983–84); Pres., Highland Cattle Soc., 1970–72. Trustee, Scottish Forestry Trust, 1983–89. Mem. Perth CC, 1954–61; JP Co. Perth, 1956. *Recreation:* fishing. *Address:* Auchlyne, Killin, Perthshire FK21 8RG.

BOWSHER, Peter Charles, QC 1978; FCIArb; **His Honour Judge Bowsher;** a Judge of the Technology and Construction Court of the High Court, since 1998 (an Official Referee, 1987–98); *b* 9 Feb. 1935; *s* of Charles and Ellen Bowsher; *m* 1960, Deborah, *d* of Frederick Wilkins and Isobel Wilkins (*née* Copp), Vancouver; two *s. Educ:* Ardingly; Oriel Coll., Oxford (MA). FCIArb 1990. Commnd Royal Artillery, 1954; Territorial Army XX Rifle Team, 1957. Called to the Bar, Middle Temple, 1959, Bencher, 1985. A Recorder, 1983–87. Harmsworth Scholar; Blackstone Entrance Scholar. A Legal Assessor to GMC and GDC, 1979–87. Indep. Review Body, Modified Colliery Review Procedure, 1986–87; Adjudicator, Crown Prosecution Service (Transfer of Staff) Regulations, 1985, 1986–87. Mem. Council, Soc. for Computers and Law, 1990–95. Member: IT and the Courts Cttee, 1991–; Judicial Cttee, British Acad. of Experts, 1992–. *Recreations:* photography, music. *Address:* Royal Courts of Justice, Strand, WC2A 2LL. *Clubs:* Brooks's, Royal Automobile.

BOWTELL, Dame Ann (Elizabeth), DCB 1997 (CB 1989); Permanent Secretary, Department of Social Security, 1995–99; *b* 25 April 1938; *d* of John Albert and Olive Rose Kewell; *m* 1961, Michael John Bowtell; two *s* two *d. Educ:* Kendrick Girls' Sch., Reading; Girton Coll., Cambridge (MA). Asst Principal, Nat. Assistance Board, 1960; Principal: Nat. Assistance Board, 1964; Min. of Social Security, 1966; DHSS, 1968; Asst Sec., 1973, Under Sec., 1980, DHSS; Dep. Sec., DHSS, later DSS, 1986; Principal Establishment and Finance Officer, DoH (on secondment), 1990–93; First Civil Service Comr and Dep. Sec., Cabinet Office, 1993–95; Dep. Sec., DSS, 1995. Chm., CS Healthcare, 2000–. Trustee: St Christopher's Hospice, Sydenham, 2000–; Joseph Rowntree Foundn, 2001–. *Recreations:* bird watching, music, walking. *Address:* 26 Sidney Road, Walton-on-Thames, Surrey KT12 2NA.

BOWYER, family name of **Baron Denham.**

BOWYER, Gordon Arthur, OBE 1970; RIBA; FCSD; Partner, BLB Architects (formerly Gordon Bowyer & Partners, then Bowyer Langlands Batchelor), Chartered Architects, 1948–92; *b* 21 March 1923; *s* of Arthur Bowyer and Kathleen Mary Bowyer; *m* 1950, Ursula Meyer; one *s* one *d. Educ:* Dauntsey's Sch.; Polytechnic of Central London. Architect and designer in private practice, in partnership with Ursula Bowyer, Iain Langlands and Stephen Batchelor, 1948–92. Practice started with design of Sports Section, South Bank Exhibn, Fest. of Britain, 1951; schs and hostel for handicapped children in Peckham, Bermondsey and Dulwich, 1966–75; housing for Southwark, GLC, Family Housing Assoc., London & Quadrant Housing Assoc. and Greenwich Housing Soc., 1969–83; numerous office conversions for IBM (UK), 1969–89; Peckham Methodist Church, 1975; new offices and shops for Rank City Wall at Brighton, 1975 and Folkestone, 1976; Treasury at Gloucester Cathedral, 1976; conservation at Vanbrugh Castle, Greenwich, 1973, Charlton Assembly Rooms, 1980, Hill Hall, Essex, 1982; lecture theatre, library and accommodation, Jt Services Defence Coll., RNC, Greenwich, 1983; Cabinet War Rooms Museum, Whitehall (with Alan Irvine), 1984; refurbishment of Barry Rooms at Nat. Gall., Stuart & Georgian Galls at Nat. Portrait Gall. and East Hall of Science Museum; new Prints & Drawings and Japanese Gall. at BM; gall. for Japanese prints, Fitzwilliam Mus. Advisory architect: Science Mus., 1992–96; Trustees' Buildings Cttee, Nat. Maritime Mus., 1993–96. Hon. Sec., SIAD, 1957–58. Mem. Council, Friends of the Nat. Maritime Mus., 1985–; Trustee, Nat. Maritime Museum, 1977–93. *Address:* 111 Maze Hill, SE10 8XQ. *Club:* Arts.

BOWYER, William, RA 1981 (ARA 1974); RP, RBA, RWS; Head of Fine Art, Maidstone College of Art, 1971–82; *b* 25 May 1926; *m* 1951, Vera Mary Small; two *s* one *d. Educ:* Burslem School of Art; Royal College of Art (ARCA). Former Hon. Sec., New English Art Club. *Recreations:* cricket (Chiswick and Old Meadonians Cricket Clubs), snooker. *Address:* 12 Cleveland Avenue, Chiswick, W4 1SN. *T:* (020) 8994 0346. *Club:* Arts.

BOWYER-SMYTH, Sir Thomas Weyland; *see* Smyth.

BOX, Prof. George Edward Pelham, BEM 1946; FRS 1985; Emeritus Professor of Statistics and Engineering, since 1992, and Director of Research, Center for Quality and Productivity, since 1990, University of Wisconsin-Madison; *b* 18 Oct. 1919; *s* of Harry and Helen (Martin) Box; *m* 1st, 1945, Jessie Ward; 2nd, 1959, Joan G. Fisher; one *s* one *d*; 3rd, 1985, Claire Louise Quist. *Educ:* London University (BSc Maths and Statistics 1947, PhD 1952, DSc 1961). Served War of 1939–45 in Army; res. at Chemical Defence Exptl Station, Porton. Statistician and Head Statn, Statistical Res. Section, ICI, Blackley, 1948–56; Dir, Stats Tech. Res. Group, Princeton Univ., 1956–60; Prof. of Stats, 1960–92, and Vilas Res. Prof., Dept of Stats, 1980–92, Univ. of Wisconsin-Madison. Res. Prof., Univ. of N Carolina, 1952–53; Ford Foundn Vis. Prof., Harvard Business Sch., 1965–66; Vis. Prof., Univ. of Essex, 1970–71. President: Amer. Statistical Assoc., 1978; Inst. of Mathematical Statistics, 1979. Fellow, Amer. Acad. of Arts and Scis, 1974. Hon. DSc: Rochester, NY, 1975; Carnegie Mellon, 1989; Don Carlos III, Madrid, 1995; Waterloo, Canada, 1999; Conservatoire nat. des arts et métiers, Paris, 2000. Numerous medals and awards. *Publications:* Statistical Methods in Research and Production, 1957; Design and Analysis of Industrial Experiments, 1959; Evolutionary Operation: a statistical method for process improvement, 1969; Time Series Analysis Forecasting and Control, 1970; Bayesian Inference in Statistical Analysis, 1973; Statistics for Experimenters, 1977; Empirical Model Building and Response Surfaces, 1986; Statistical Control by Monitoring and Feedback Adjustment, 1997; Box on Quality and Discovery, 2000. *Address:* Center for Quality and Productivity Improvement, University of Wisconsin-Madison, 610 Walnut Street, Madison, WI 53705, USA. *T:* (608) 2632520.

BOX, John Allan Hyatt, OBE 1998; RDI 1992; free-lance production designer of films; *b* 27 Jan. 1920; *s* of late Allan Cyril Box and Bertha (*née* Storey); *m* 1st, 1944, Barbara Courtenay Linton (marr. diss. 1951); 2nd, 1953, Doris Lee (decd); two *d. Educ:* Ceylon; Highgate Sch.; Sch. of Architecture, London Poly. ARIBA 1948. Served RAC and RTR, 1940–46 (mentioned in despatches, Normandy, 1944). Entered film industry, 1948: films designed include: The Million Pound Note, 1954; The Inn of the Sixth Happiness, 1958; Our Man in Havana, 1959; The World of Suzie Wong, 1960; Lawrence of Arabia, 1961 (Academy Award 1962); Doctor Zhivago, 1965 (Academy Award 1966); A Man for All Seasons, 1966 (BAFTA Award 1967); Oliver!, 1967 (Academy Award 1968); Nicholas and Alexandra, 1970 (Academy Award 1970); Travels with My Aunt, 1972; The Great Gatsby, 1973 (BAFTA Award 1974); Rollerball, 1974 (BAFTA Award 1975); A Passage to India, 1984; Black Beauty, 1994; First Knight, 1995; produced: The Looking Glass War, 1969. FRSA 1993. Award for special contribution to films, BAFTA, 1991; Critics' Circle Award for Lifetime Achievement, 1999. *Recreations:* painting, visiting art galleries and exhibitions, interest in cricket and Rugby. *Address:* 5 Elm Bank Mansions, The Terrace, Barnes, SW13 0NS. *T:* (020) 8876 9125.

BOXALL, Barbara Ann, (Mrs Lewis Boxall); *see* Buss, B. A.

BOXER, Anna; *see* Ford, A.

BOXER, Charles Ian; *b* 11 Feb. 1926; *s* of Rev. William Neville Gordon Boxer and Margaret Boxer; *m* 1968, Hilary Fabienne Boxer. *Educ:* Glasgow High Sch.; Edinburgh Univ. (BL). Church of England ministry, 1950–54; apprentice to solicitors, 1954–58; Mem., Dominican Order (RC), 1958–67; Sen. Community Relations Officer for Wandsworth, 1967–77; Dir, Community Affairs and Liaison Div., Commn for Racial Equality, 1977–81. Communicator of the Year, BAIE Awards, 1976. *Recreation:* music. *Address:* Parish Farmhouse, Hassell Street, Hastingleigh, near Ashford, Kent TN25 5JE. *T:* (01233) 750219.

BOXER, Air Cdre Henry Everard Crichton, CB 1965; OBE 1948; idc, ndc, psc; *b* 28 July 1914; *s* of late Rear-Adm. Henry P. Boxer; *m* 1st, 1938, Enid Anne Louise (*d* 1994), *d* of late Dr John Moore Collyns; two *s* two *d*; 2nd, 1996, Hope Poland (*d* 1998). *Educ:* Shrewsbury Sch.; RAF Coll., Cranwell. Commissioned RAF, 1935; No 1 Fighter Squadron, 1935–37; No 1 Flying Training Sch., 1937–39; Specialist Navigator, 1939. Served War of 1939–45, in UK, S Africa and Europe. BJSM, Washington, DC, 1945–48; directing Staff, RAF Staff Coll., 1949–50; Coastal Command, 1951–52; Nat. Defence Coll., Canada, 1952–53; Air Ministry, 1953–56; OC, RAF Thorney Island, 1956–58. ADC to the Queen, 1957–59; IDC, 1959; Sen. Air Liaison Officer and Air Adviser to British High Comr in Canada, 1960–62; AO i/c Admin, HQ Coastal Comd, 1962–65; Dir of Personnel (Air), MoD (RAF), 1965–67; retd, 1967. Counsellor (Defence Equipment), British High Commn, Ottawa, 1967–74; retd, 1975. *Address:* 42 Courtenay Place, Lymington, Hants SO41 3NQ. *T:* (01590) 672584. *Club:* Royal Air Force.

BOXSHALL, Dr Geoffrey Allan, FRS 1994; Deputy Chief Scientific Officer, Natural History Museum, since 1997; *b* 13 June 1950; *s* of John Edward Boxshall and Sybil Irene Boxshall (*née* Baker); *m* 1972, Roberta Gabriel Smith; one *s* three *d*. *Educ:* Churcher's Coll., Petersfield; Leeds Univ. (BSc, PhD). British Museum (Natural History), subseq. Natural History Museum: Higher SO, 1974–76; SSO, 1976–80; PSO, 1980–91; SPSO, 1991–97. *Publications:* (jtly) Dictionary of Ecology, Evolution and Systematics, 1982, 2nd edn 1998; (jtly) Cambridge Illustrated Dictionary of Natural History, 1987; (ed jtly) Biology of Copepods, 1988; (jtly) Copepod Evolution, 1991; (ed jtly) Pathogens of Wild and Farmed Fish: sea lice, 1993; numerous papers in scientific jls. *Recreations:* tennis, reading, lexicography, travel. *Address:* Department of Zoology, Natural History Museum, Cromwell Road, SW7 5BD. *T:* (020) 7942 5749. *Club:* Zoological.

BOYACK, Sarah; Member (Lab) Edinburgh Central, Scottish Parliament, since 1999; Minister for Transport and Planning, since 2001 (for Transport and the Environment, 1999–2000, for Transport, 2000–01); *d* of late Jim Boyack. MRTPI. Former Sen. Planning Officer, Central Regl Council; Lectr in Planning, Edinburgh Coll. of Art. *Address:* Scottish Parliament, Edinburgh EH99 1SP.

BOYCE, Sir Graham Hugh, KCMG 2001 (CMG 1991); HM Diplomatic Service; *b* 6 Oct. 1945; *s* of Comdr Hugh Boyce, DSC, RN and Madeleine Boyce (*née* Manley); *m* 1970, Janet Elizabeth Spencer; one *s* three *d*. *Educ:* Hurstpierpoint Coll.; Jesus Coll., Cambridge (MA). VSO, Antigua, 1967; HM Diplomatic Service, 1968; Ottawa, 1971; MECAS, 1972–74; 1st Sec., Tripoli, Libya, 1974–77; FCO, 1977–81; Kuwait, 1981–85; Asst Hd of ME Dept, FCO, 1985–86; Counsellor and Consul-Gen., Stockholm, 1987–90; Ambassador and Consul-Gen., Doha, 1990–93; Counsellor, FCO, 1993–96; Ambassador to Kuwait, 1996–99; Ambassador to Egypt, 1999–2001. *Recreations:* tennis, golf, reading. *Address:* c/o Foreign and Commonwealth Office, King Charles Street, SW1A 2AH.
See also Adm. Sir M. C. Boyce.

BOYCE, Joseph Frederick, JP; FRICS; General Manager, Telford Development Corporation, 1980–86; *b* 10 Aug. 1926; *s* of Frederick Arthur and Rosalie Mary Boyce; *m* 1953, Nina Margaret, *o d* of A. F. Tebb, Leeds; two *s*. *Educ:* Roundhay Sch., Leeds; Leeds Coll. of Technology. Articled Pupil and Sen. Assistant, Rex Procter & Miller, Chartered Quantity Surveyors, 1942–53; Sen. Quantity Surveyor, Bedford Corp., 1953–55; Group Quantity Surveyor, Somerset CC, 1955–60; Principal Quantity Surveyor, Salop CC, 1960–64; Telford Development Corporation: Chief Quantity Surveyor, 1964–71; Technical Dir, 1971–76; Dep. Gen. Manager, 1976–80. JP Shrewsbury, 1975. *Publications:* technical articles and publications on new towns, in learned journals. *Recreations:* gardening, hill walking, music, fine wine. *Address:* Grasse, Alpes-Maritimes, France.

BOYCE, Adm. Sir Michael (Cecil), GCB 1999 (KCB 1995); OBE 1982; Chief of the Defence Staff, since 2001; Aide-de-Camp to the Queen, since 2001; *b* 2 April 1943; *s* of Comdr Hugh Boyce, DSC, RN and late Madeleine Boyce (*née* Manley); *m* 1971, Harriette Gail Fletcher (separated 1994); one *s* one *d*. *Educ:* Hurstpierpoint Coll.; BRNC, Dartmouth. Joined RN, 1961; qualified Submarines, 1965 and TAS, 1970; served in HM Submarines Anchorite, Valiant, and Conqueror, 1965–72; commanded: HM Submarines: Oberon, 1973–74; Opossum, 1974–75; Superb, 1979–81; HMS Brilliant, 1983–84; Captain (SM), Submarine Sea Training, 1984–86; RCDS, 1988; Sen. Naval Officer, ME, 1989; Dir Naval Staff Duties, 1989–91; Flag Officer: Sea Training, 1991–92; Surface Flotilla, 1992–95; Comdr, Anti-Submarine Warfare Striking Force, 1992–94; Second Sea Lord, and C-in-C Naval Home Comd, 1995–97; C-in-C Fleet, C-in-C Eastern Atlantic Area and Comdr Naval Forces N Western Europe, 1997–98; First Sea Lord and Chief of Naval Staff, and First and Principal Naval ADC to the Queen, 1998–2001. Gov., Alleyn's Sch., 1995–. Freeman, City of London, 1999. Younger Brother, Trinity House, 1999. Comdr, Legion of Merit (US), 1999. *Recreations:* squash, tennis, windsurfing. *Address:* c/o Naval Secretary, Victory Building, HM Naval Base, Portsmouth PO1 3LS.
See also Sir G. H. Boyce.

BOYCE, Michael David; DL; Chief Executive, Cardiff Bay Development Corporation, 1992–2000; *b* 27 May 1937; *s* of Clifford and Vera Boyce; *m* 1962, Audrey May Gregory; one *s* one *d*. *Educ:* Queen Elizabeth's Sch., Crediton. DMA 1962; Dip. in French, UC Cardiff, 1984. Admitted Solicitor, 1968. Asst Solicitor, 1968–69, Sen. Asst Solicitor, and Asst Clerk of the Peace, 1969–71, Exeter CC; Dep. Town Clerk, 1971–73, Dep. Chief Exec., 1973–74, Newport, Gwent; County Solicitor, S Glam, 1974–87; Chief Exec., S Glam CC, and Clerk to Lieutenancy, 1987–92. Sec., Lord Chancellor's Adv. Cttee, 1987–92. Director: Cardiff Marketing Ltd, 1990–94; Cardiff Business Technology Centre Ltd, 1979–87; S Glam Youth Opportunities Ltd, 1979–87; New Openings Ltd, 1979–87; S Glam Investments Ltd, 1979–87. Member: Bd, S Glam TEC, 1987–95; Cardiff Chamber of Commerce & Trade, 1987–2000; S and Mid Glam Area Manpower Bd, 1976–79; Council, Cardiff Common Purpose, 1995–. Advr, ACC, 1976–87; Legal Adviser: Assembly of Welsh Counties, 1976–87; Council of Museums in Wales, 1979–85; Hon. Solicitor, S Glam Probation and After-care Cttee, 1974–85. Member: Sports Council for Wales, 1980–82; BBC Wales Indep. Assessment Panel on Sport, 1997. Trustee: Glam County History Trust Ltd, 1974–85; S Wales Community Foundn, 1996–99. Mem. Council, Univ. of Wales Coll. of Cardiff, 1987–93; Gov., Welsh Coll. of Music and Drama, 1992–98. Chm., Cardiff City AFC, 1993–95. FWCMD 1999. DL S Glam, 1993. *Recreations:* France and French, Association Football, music, railways, travel. *Address:* 1 White Oaks Drive, Old St Mellons, Cardiff CF3 5EX. *T:* (029) 2079 1927.

BOYCE, Peter John, AO 1995; PhD; Vice-Chancellor, Murdoch University, Western Australia, 1985–96; Hon. Professor of Political Science, University of Tasmania, since 2000 (Visiting Professor, 1996); *b* 20 Feb. 1935; *s* of Oswald and Marjorie Boyce; *m* 1962, Lorinne Peet; one *s* two *d*. *Educ:* Wesley Coll., Perth, WA; Univ. of Western Australia (MA); Duke Univ., USA (PhD). Res. Fellow, then Fellow, Dept of Internat. Relns, ANU, 1964–66; Nuffield Fellow, St Antony's Coll., Oxford, 1966–67; Sen. Lectr, then Reader, in Political Science, Tasmania Univ., 1967–75; Prof. of Pol. Science and Hd, Dept of Govt, Queensland Univ., 1976–79; Prof. of Politics and Hd of Dept, Univ. of W Australia, 1980–84. Visiting Fellow: Corpus Christi Coll., Cambridge, 1989; Merton Coll., Oxford, 1996; Christ Church, Oxford, 1997. Exec. Mem., Aust.-NZ Foundn, 1979–83; Member: Aust. Human Rights Commn, 1981–86; Consultative Cttee on Relns with Japan, 1983–85; Asia Business Council of WA, 1993–96. Lay Canon of St George's Cath., Perth, 1986–96. Editor, Australian Outlook, 1973–77. *Publications:* Malaysia and Singapore in International Diplomacy, 1968; Foreign Affairs for New States, 1977; (co-ord. ed.) Dictionary of Australian Politics, 1980; (co-ord. ed.) Politics in Queensland, 1980; (co-ord. ed.) The Torres Strait Treaty, 1981; (ed) Independence and Alliance, 1983; Diplomacy in the Market Place, 1991. *Recreations:* gardening, walking, church music. *Address:* Windrush, 20 Fisher Avenue, Lower Sandy Bay, Tas 7005, Australia. *T:* (03) 62252009.

BOYCE, Most Rev. Philip; *see* Raphoe, Bishop of, (RC).

BOYCE, Sir Robert (Leslie), 3rd Bt *cr* 1952; FRCSE; Specialist Registrar in Ophthalmology, Royal Victoria Infirmary, Newcastle upon Tyne, since 1998; *b* 2 May 1962; *s* of Sir Richard (Leslie) Boyce, 2nd Bt, and of Jacqueline Anne (who *m* 2nd, 1974, Christopher Boyce-Dennis), *o d* of Roland A. Hill; *S* father, 1968; *m* 1985, Fiona, second *d* of John Savage, Whitmore Park, Coventry; one *s* one *d*. *Educ:* Cheltenham Coll; Salford Univ. (BSc 1984, 1st cl. hons); Nottingham Univ. (BMedSci 1991, 1st cl. hons; BM BS 1993). FRCSE 1998. Sen. House Officer in Ophthalmology, Manchester Royal Eye Hosp., 1995–98. *Heir: s* Thomas Leslie Boyce, *b* 3 Sept. 1993.

BOYCE, Walter Edwin, OBE 1970; Director of Social Services, Essex County Council, 1970–78; *b* 30 July 1918; *s* of Rev. Joseph Edwin Boyce and Alice Elizabeth Boyce; *m* 1942, Edna Lane (*née* Gargett); two *d*. *Educ:* High Sch. for Boys, Trowbridge, Wilts. Admin. Officer, Warwickshire CC, 1938–49. Served war, commnd RA; Gunnery sc, 1943; demob. rank Major, 1946. Dep. County Welfare Officer: Shropshire, 1949–52; Cheshire, 1952–57; Co. Welfare Officer, Essex, 1957–70. Adviser to Assoc. of County Councils, 1965–78; Mem., Sec. of State's Adv. Personal Social Services Council, 1973 until disbanded, 1980 (Chm., People with handicaps Gp); Mem., nat. working parties on: Health Service collaboration, 1972–74; residential accommodation for elderly and mentally handicapped, 1974–78; boarding houses, 1981. Pres., County Welfare Officers Soc., 1967–68. Governor, Queen Elizabeth's Foundn for the Disabled, 1980–. *Recreations:* sailing, golf, in sports, particularly Rugby and athletics, voluntary services, travel. *Address:* Highlanders Barn, Newmans Green, Long Melford, Suffolk CO10 0AD.

BOYCE, William, QC 2001; a Recorder, since 1997; *b* 29 July 1951. *Educ:* St Joseph's Acad. Grammar Sch., Blackheath; Univ. of Kent (BA). Called to the Bar, Gray's Inn, 1976; Jun. Treasury Counsel, 1991–97, Sen. Treasury Counsel, 1997–2001, CCC. *Address:* Queen Elizabeth Building, Temple, EC4Y 9BS. *T:* (020) 7583 5766.

BOYCOTT, Geoffrey; cricket commentator; *b* 21 Oct. 1940; *s* of late Thomas Wilfred Boycott and Jane Boycott. *Educ:* Kinsley Modern Sch.; Hemsworth Grammar Sch. Played cricket for Yorkshire, 1962–86, received County Cap, 1963, Captain of Yorkshire, 1970–78. Played for England, 1964–74, 1977–82; scored 100th first-class hundred, England v Australia, 1977, 150th hundred, 1986; passed former world record no of runs scored in Test Matches, Delhi, Dec. 1981. Mem., General Cttee, Yorks CCC, 1984–93. Commentator: BBC TV; Trans World Internat.; Channel 9; SABC; Talk Radio. *Publications:* Geoff Boycott's Book for Young Cricketers, 1976; Put to the Test: England in Australia 1978–79, 1979; Geoff Boycott's Cricket Quiz, 1979; On Batting, 1980; Opening Up, 1980; In the Fast Lane, 1981; Master Class, 1982; Boycott, The Autobiography, 1987; Boycott on Cricket, 1990; Geoffrey Boycott on Cricket, 1999. *Recreations:* golf, tennis. *Address:* c/o Yorkshire County Cricket Club, Headingley Cricket Ground, Leeds, Yorks LS6 3BY.

BOYCOTT, Rosie; Editor, The Express, 1998–2001; *b* 13 May 1951; *d* of Charles Boycott and Betty Boycott; *m* 1983, David Leitch (marr. diss. 1998); one *d*; *m* 1999, Charles Anthony Frederick Howard, *qv*. *Educ:* Cheltenham Ladies' Coll.; Kent Univ. (pure maths). Has worked on: Frendz mag., 1971; Spare Rib (Founder and Editor), 1971–72; Luka (Buddhist Jl of America), 1973–75; Osrati (Kuwait), 1976–79; Honey mag., 1979–81 (Dep. Ed.); Daily Mail, 1984–85; Sunday Telegraph, Harpers & Queen, 1989–92; Editor: Esquire, 1992–96; Independent on Sunday, 1996–98; The Independent, 1998. Trustee, Warchild. Editor of Year (Magazines), 1994, 1995. *Publications:* Batty, Bloomers & Boycott; A Nice Girl Like Me; All for Love. *Recreations:* riding, ski-ing, tennis, reading, arts. *Club:* Groucho.

BOYD, family name of **Baron Kilmarnock**.

BOYD OF MERTON, 2nd Viscount *cr* 1960, of Merton-in-Penninghame, Co. Wigtown; **Simon Donald Rupert Neville Lennox-Boyd;** Chairman, Iveagh Trustees Ltd, since 1992; *b* 7 Dec. 1939; *e s* of 1st Viscount Boyd of Merton, CH, PC, and Lady Patricia Guinness, *d* of 2nd Earl of Iveagh, KG, CB, CMG, FRS; *S* father, 1983; *m* 1962, Alice Mary (JP, DL, High Sheriff of Cornwall, 1987–88), *d* of late Major M. G. D. Clive and of Lady Mary Clive; two *s* two *d*. *Educ:* Eton; Christ Church, Oxford. Dep. Chm., Arthur Guinness & Sons, 1981–86. Chairman: SCF, 1987–92 (Vice-Chm., 1979–82); Stonham Housing Assoc., 1992–99. Trustee, Guinness Trust, 1974–. *Heir: s* Hon. Benjamin Alan Lennox-Boyd [*b* 21 Oct. 1964; *m* 1993, Sheila Carroll; two *s* one *d*. *Address:* Ince Castle, Saltash, Cornwall PL12 4QZ. *T:* (01752) 842672; 9 Warwick Square, SW1V 2AA. *T:* (020) 7821 1618. *Club:* Royal Yacht Squadron.

BOYD, Alan Robb; SSC; NP; Director, Public Sector Unit, McGrigor Donald, solicitors, since 1997; *b* 30 July 1953; *er s* of Alexander Boyd and Mary Herd Boyd; *m* 1973, Frances Helen Donaldson; two *d*. *Educ:* Irvine Royal Acad.; Univ. of Dundee (LLB 1974); Open Univ. (BA 1985). Admitted solicitor, 1976; Principal Legal Asst, Shetland Is Council, 1979–81; Principal Solicitor, Glenrothes Develt Corp., 1981–84; Legal Advr, Irvine Develt Corp., 1984–97. Mem. Council, Law Soc. of Scotland, 1985–97 (Vice-Pres.,

1994–95; Pres., 1995–96). *Recreations:* golf, music, gardening. *Address:* 45 Craigholm Road, Ayr KA7 3LJ. *T:* (01292) 262542. *Club:* Turnberry Golf.

BOYD, Sir Alexander Walter, 3rd Bt *cr* 1916; *b* 16 June 1934; *s* of late Cecil Anderson Boyd, MC, MD, and Marjorie Catharine, *e d* of late Francis Kinloch, JP, Shipka Lodge, North Berwick; *S* uncle, 1948; *m* 1958, Molly Madeline, *d* of late Ernest Arthur Rendell; two *s* three *d*. *Heir: s* Ian Walter Rendell Boyd [*b* 14 March 1964; *m* 1986, LeeAnn Dillon; three *s*].

BOYD, Atarah, (Mrs Douglas Boyd); *see* Ben-Tovim, A.

BOYD, Christopher; *see* Boyd, T. C.

BOYD, Rt Hon. Colin David; PC 2000; Lord Advocate, Scottish Executive, since 2000; *b* 7 June 1953; *s* of Dr David Hugh Aird Boyd and Betty Meldrum Boyd; *m* 1979, Fiona Margaret MacLeod; two *s* one *d*. *Educ:* Wick High Sch.; George Watson's Coll., Edinburgh; Manchester Univ. (BA Econ); Edinburgh Univ. (LLB). Solicitor, 1978–82; called to the Bar, Scotland, 1983; Legal Associate, Royal Town Planning Inst., 1990; Advocate Depute, 1993–95; QC (Scot.) 1995; Solicitor General: for Scotland, 1997–99; Scottish Exec., 1999–2000. FRSA 2000. *Publication:* (contrib.) The Legal Aspects of Devolution, 1997. *Recreations:* walking, reading. *Address:* Crown Office, 25 Chambers Street, Edinburgh EH1 1LA.

BOYD, (David) John; QC 1982; arbitrator; Chairman: Axxia Systems Ltd, since 1995; Alpha Consulting Group Ltd, since 1999; *b* 11 Feb. 1935; *s* of David Boyd and Ellen Jane Boyd (*née* Gruer); *m* 1960, Raija Sinikka Lindholm, Finland; one *s* one *d*. *Educ:* Eastbourne Coll.; St George's Sch., Newport, USA (British-Amer. schoolboy schol.); Gonville and Caius Coll., Cambridge (MA). FCIArb 1979. Various secretarial posts, ICI, 1957–62; Legal Asst, Pfizer, 1962–66; called to the Bar, Gray's Inn, 1963, Bencher 1988; Sec. and Legal Officer, Henry Wiggin & Co., 1966; Asst Sec. and Sen. Legal Officer (UK), Internat. Nickel, 1968; Dir, Impala Platinum, 1972–78; Sec. and Chief Legal Officer, 1972–86, and Dir, 1984–86, Inco Europe; practising barrister, 1986; Director: Legal Services, 1986–93, Public Affairs and Communications, 1993–95, Digital Equipment Co.; Digital Equipment Scotland, 1987–95. Gen. Comr of Income Tax, 1978–83; Immigration Adjudicator, 1995–; Vice-Pres., Council of Immigration Judges, 1998–2000. Chm., Bar Assoc. for Commerce, Finance and Industry, 1980–81; Mem., Senate of Inns of Court and Bar, 1978–81. Sec. Gen., Assoc. des Juristes d'Entreprise Européens (European Company Lawyers Assoc.), 1983–84. Dir, Centre for European Dispute Resolution, 1991–94. Legal Advisor to Review Bd for Govt Contracts, 1984–91. Chm., CBI Competition Panel, 1988–93; Mem., Electricity Panel, Monopolies and Mergers Commn, 1991–98. Mem., Exec. Cttee, Royal Acad. of Dancing, 1991–98; Chm., The Place Th. and Contemp. Dance Trust, 1995–98; Dir, Oxford Orch. da Camera, 1996–2001. *Recreations:* theatre-going, holidaying in France, viticulture. *Address:* Beeches, Upton Bishop, Ross-on-Wye, Herefordshire HR9 7UD. *T:* (01989) 780214, *Fax:* (01989) 780538. *Club:* Leander.

BOYD, Dennis Galt, CBE 1988; Chief Conciliation Officer, Advisory, Conciliation and Arbitration Service, 1980–92; *b* 3 Feb. 1931; *s* of late Thomas Ayre Boyd and Minnie (*née* Galt); *m* 1953, Pamela Mary McLean; one *s* one *d*. *Educ:* South Shields High School for Boys. National Service, 1949–51; Executive Officer, Civil Service: Min. of Supply/Min. of Defence, 1951–66; Board of Trade, 1966–69; Personnel Officer, Forestry Commission, 1969–75; Director of Corporate Services Health and Safety Executive, Dept of Employment, 1975–79; Director of Conciliation (ACAS), 1979–80. Hon. FIPM 1985. *Recreations:* golf, compulsory gardening. *Address:* Dunelm, Silchester Road, Little London, Tadley RG26 5EW.

BOYD, Ian Robertson; HM Stipendiary Magistrate, West Yorkshire, 1982–89; a Recorder of the Crown Court, 1983–88; *b* 18 Oct. 1922; *s* of Arthur Robertson Boyd, Edinburgh, and Florence May Boyd (*née* Kinghorn), Leeds; *m* 1952, Joyce Mary Boyd (*née* Crabtree); one *s* one *d*. *Educ:* Roundhay Sch.; Leeds Univ. (LLB (Hons)). Served Army, 1942–47: Captain Green Howards; Royal Lincolnshire Regt in India, Burma, Malaya, Dutch East Indies. Leeds Univ., 1947; called to Bar, Middle Temple, 1952; practised North Eastern Circuit, 1952–72; HM Stipendiary Magistrate, sitting at Hull, 1972–82. Sometime Asst/Dep. Recorder of Doncaster, Newcastle, Hull and York. *Recreation:* gardener manqué.

BOYD, James Edward, CA; Director and Financial Adviser, Denholm group of companies, 1968–96; *b* 14 Sept. 1928; *s* of Robert Edward Boyd and Elizabeth Reid Sinclair; *m* 1956, Judy Ann Christey Scott; two *s* two *d*. *Educ:* Kelvinside Academy; The Leys Sch., Cambridge. CA Scot. (dist.) 1951. Director: Lithgows (Hldgs), 1962–87; Ayrshire Metal Products plc, 1965–93 (Chm., 1991–93); Invergordon Distillers (Holdings) plc, 1966–88; GB Papers plc, 1977–87; Jebsens Drilling plc, 1978–85; Scottish Widows' Fund & Life Assurance Soc., 1981–93 (Dep. Chm., 1988–93); Shanks & McEwan Gp Ltd, 1983–94; Scottish Exhibn Centre Ltd, 1983–89; British Linen Bank Ltd, 1983–94 (Gov., 1986–94); Bank of Scotland, 1984–94; Yarrow PLC, 1984–86 (Chm., 1985–86); Bank of Wales, 1986–88; Save and Prosper Gp Ltd, 1987–89; James River UK Hldgs Ltd, 1987–90; Chairman: London & Gartmore Investment Trust plc, 1978–91; English & Caledonian Investment plc, 1981–91. Partner, McClelland Ker & Co. CA (subseq. McClelland Moores & Co.), 1953–61; Finance Director: Lithgows Ltd, 1962–69; Scott Lithgow Ltd, 1970–78; Chm., Fairfield Shipbuilding & Engrg Co. Ltd, 1964–65; Man. Dir, Invergordon Distillers (Holdings) Ltd, 1966–67; Director: Nairn & Williamson (Holdings) Ltd, 1968–75; Carlton Industries plc, 1978–84. Dep. Chm., BAA plc (formerly British Airports Authority), 1985–94; Member: CAA (part-time), 1984–85; Clyde Port Authority, 1974–80; Working Party on Scope and Aims of Financial Accounts (the Corporate Report), 1974–75; Exec. Cttee, Accountants Jt Disciplinary Scheme, 1979–81; Mem. Council, Inst. of Chartered Accountants of Scotland, 1977–83 (Vice-Pres., 1980–82, Pres., 1982–83). Mem. Council, Glenalmond Coll., 1983–92. *Recreations:* tennis, golf, gardening, painting. *Address:* Dunard, Station Road, Rhu, Dunbartonshire, Scotland G84 8LW. *T:* (01436) 820441.

BOYD, John; *see* Boyd, D. J.

BOYD, Sir John (Dixon Iklé), KCMG 1992 (CMG 1985); HM Diplomatic Service, retired; Master, Churchill College, Cambridge, since 1996; *b* 17 Jan. 1936; *s* of Prof. James Dixon Boyd and late Amélie Lowenthal; *m* 1st, 1968, Gunilla Kristina Ingegerd Rönngren; one *s* one *d*; 2nd, 1977, Julia Daphne Raynsford; three *d*. *Educ:* Westminster Sch.; Clare Coll., Cambridge (BA; Hon. Fellow, 1994); Yale Univ. (MA). Joined HM Foreign Service, 1962; Hong Kong, 1962–64; Peking, 1965–67; Foreign Office, 1967–69; Washington, 1969–73; 1st Sec., Peking, 1973–75; secondment to HM Treasury, 1976; Counsellor: (Economic), Bonn, 1977–81; (Economic and Soc. Affairs), UK Mission to UN, 1981–84; Asst Under-Sec. of State, FCO, 1984; Political Advr, Hong Kong, 1985–87; Dep. Under-Sec. of State, FCO, 1987–89; Chief Clerk, FCO, 1989–92; Ambassador to Japan, 1992–96. Non-exec. Dir, BNFL, 1997–2000. UK Rep., ASEM Vision Gp, 1998–2000. Trustee: BM, 1996– (Chm., July 2002–); Wordsworth Trust, 1997–; GB Sasakawa Foundn, 2001–; RAND Europe (UK), 2001–; Syndic, Fitzwilliam Mus., 1997–. Gov., RSC, 1996–. Chairman: Bd of Govs, Bedales Sch., 1996–; David Davies Meml Inst., 1997–; Trustees, Cambridge Union Soc., 1997–. Vice-Chm., Menuhin Prize, 1996–. *Recreations:* music, fly fishing. *Address:* Churchill College, Cambridge CB3 0DS.

See also R. D. H. Boyd.

BOYD, John MacInnes, CBE 1990; QPM 1984; HM Chief Inspector of Constabulary for Scotland, 1993–96; *b* 14 Oct. 1933; *s* of late F. Duncan Boyd and M. Catherine MacInnes; *m* 1957, Sheila MacSporran; two *s*. *Educ:* Oban High School. Paisley Burgh Police, 1956–67; Renfrew and Bute Constabulary, 1967–75; Strathclyde Police, 1975–84 (Asst Chief Constable, 1979–84); Chief Constable, Dumfries and Galloway Constabulary, 1984–89; HM Inspector of Constabulary for Scotland, 1989–93. Pres., Scotland, ACPO, 1988–89. *Recreations:* golf, gardening, reading, photography. *Address:* Beechwood, Lochwinnoch Road, Kilmacolm PA13 4DZ.

BOYD, Hon. Sir Mark Alexander L.; *see* Lennox-Boyd.

BOYD, Michael; Associate Director, Royal Shakespeare Theatre, since 1996; *b* 6 July 1955; *s* of John Truesdale Boyd and Sheila Boyd; one *s* one *d* by Marcella Evaristi; one *d* by Caroline Hall. *Educ:* Latymer Upper Sch.; Daniel Stewart's Coll.; Univ. of Edinburgh (MA English Lit.). Trainee Dir, Malaya Bronnaya Th., Moscow, 1979; Asst Dir, Belgrade Th., Coventry, 1980–82; Associate Dir, Crucible Th., Sheffield, 1982–84; Founding Artistic Dir, Tron Th., Glasgow, 1985–96. Hon. Prof., Univ. of Michigan, 2001. *Productions:* for Tron Theatre: The Guid Sisters, 1989, Tremblay's The Real World, 1991 (also Toronto, NY and Montreal); (with I. Glen) Macbeth, 1993; The Trick is to Keep Breathing (also Royal Court and World Stage Fest., Toronto), 1995; for Royal Shakespeare Co.: The Broken Heart, 1994; The Spanish Tragedy, 1996; Measure for Measure, 1997; Troilus and Cressida (also Tel Aviv and USA), 1999; A Midsummer Night's Dream (also NY), 1999; Romeo and Juliet, 2000; Henry VI, Parts 1, 2 and 3, and Richard III (also USA), 2001; West End: Miss Julie, Haymarket, 2000. *Recreations:* cooking, football, walking, swimming, reading, music. *Address:* c/o Royal Shakespeare Theatre, Waterside, Stratford upon Avon, Warks CV37 6BB. *Address:* T: (01789) 296655.

BOYD, Morgan Alistair, CMG 1990; Adviser, Commonwealth Development Corporation, 1994–2000; *b* 1 May 1934; *s* of Norman Robert Boyd and Kathleen Muriel Boyd; *m* 1959, Judith Mary Martin. *Educ:* Marlborough College; Wadham College, Oxford (BA, MA 1955). FRGS 1957. Commonwealth Development Corporation: Management trainee, 1957; Exec., Malaysia, 1958–66; Manager, East Caribbean Housing, Barbados, 1967–70; Gen. Manager, Tanganyika Develt Finance Co., 1970–74; Advr, Industrial Develt Bank, Kenya, 1975; Regl Controller, Central Africa, 1976–80, East Africa, 1981–82; Dep. Gen. Manager, Investigations, London, 1983–84; Dir of Ops, 1985–89; Dep. Gen. Manager, 1989–91; Dep. Chief Exec., 1991–94. Director: EDESA Management, Switzerland, 1995–97; Tea Plantations Investment Trust PLC, 1998–; AMREF UK, 1999– (Chm., 2001). Chm., Southern Africa Business Assoc., 1995–. Member: RSA 1990–; Council, Royal African Soc., 1992– (Vice-Chm., 1996–); Management Council, Africa Centre, 1995–. *Publication:* Royal Challenge Accepted, 1962. *Recreations:* music, sailing, travel. *Address:* 7 South Hill Mansions, South Hill Park, NW3 2SL. *T:* (020) 7435 1082. *Clubs:* Naval, English-Speaking Union.

BOYD, Norman Jonathan; Member, Antrim South, Northern Ireland Assembly (UKU, 1998–99, NIU, since 1999); *b* 16 Oct. 1961; *s* of William and Jean Boyd; *m* 1984, Sylvia Christine (*née* Brindley); one *s* one *d*. *Educ:* Belfast High Sch.; Newtownabbey Technical Coll. (BEC Nat. Cert. in Business Studies with Distinction, 1982). Joined Halifax Bldg Soc., later Halifax plc, 1980: posts included Deptl Manager, Asst Branch Manager, and Manager. Member: Apprentice Boys of Derry, Carrickfergus, 1988– (Chm., Ballymena and Dist Amalgamated Cttee, 1996–97); Kilroot True Blues Loyal Orange Lodge, 1988–; Kilroot Royal Arch Purple Chapter, 1989–; Royal Black Instn, Carrickfergus, 1993–. Formerly Mem., Boys' Bde (President's Badge, 1979; Queen's Badge, 1980). *Recreations:* sport—soccer, caravanning, theatre, cinema, programme collecting. *Address:* 18 Woodford Park, Newtownabbey, Co. Antrim BT36 6TJ. *T:* (028) 9084 4297, *Fax:* (028) 9083 6644; (office) 38 Main Street, Ballyclare, Co. Antrim BT39 9AA, *T:* (028) 9334 9132, *Fax:* (028) 9334 9128.

BOYD, Prof. Robert David Hugh, FRCP, FFPHM, FRCPCH, FMedSci; Principal, St George's Hospital Medical School, University of London, since 1996; Professor of Paediatrics, since 1996 and Pro-Vice Chancellor (Medicine), since 2000, University of London; *b* 14 May 1938; *s* of James Dixon Boyd and Amélie Boyd; *m* 1966, Meriel Cornelia Talbot; one *s* two *d*. *Educ:* Ley's Sch.; Clare Coll., Cambridge (MA; MB, BChir); University Coll. Hosp., London. FRCP 1977; FFPHM 1997; FRCPCH 1997. Jun. med. posts, Hosp. for Sick Children, Gt Ormond St, Brompton Hosp., UCH, 1962–65; Sir Stuart Halley Res. Fellow and Sen. Registrar, UC Hosp. and Med. Sch., 1966–71; Goldsmith's MRC Travelling Fellow, Univ. of Colo Med. Center, 1971–72; Sen. Lectr and Hon. Consultant, UCH Med. Sch., 1972–80; Asst Registrar, RCP, 1980–81; University of Manchester Medical School: Prof. of Paediatrics, 1981–96; Dean, 1989–93; Hon. Consultant: St Mary's Hosp., Manchester and Booth Hall Children's Hosp., Manchester, 1981–96; St George's Healthcare NHS Trust, 1996–. Chm., Nat. Primary Care R&D Centre, Manchester, Salford and York Univs, 1994–96. Vis. Prof., Oregon Health Scis Univ., 1988. Ed., Placenta, 1989–95. Chm., Manchester HA, 1994–96. Member: Standing Med. Adv. Cttee, 1988–92; Standing Cttee on Postgrad. Med. and Dental Educn, 1995–99; Jt Med. Adv. Cttee, HEFCs, 1994–99; Univs UK (formerly CVCP), 1997– (Mem. Health Cttee, 1997–); Scientific Adv. Cttee, AMRC, 1996–; Council, RVC, 1999–; Chm., Council of Heads of UK Med. Schs, 2001–. Mem., Taskforce supporting R & D in NHS, 1994. Sec., 1977–80, Chm., 1987–90, Acad. Bd, BPA. Co-opted Gov., Kingston Univ., 1998–. Pres., 1942 Club, 1998–99. Founder FMedSci 1998. *Publications:* (jtly) Paediatric Problems in General Practice, 1982, 3rd edn 1996; contribs to Placental and Fetal Physiol. and Paediatrics. *Recreations:* cooking, reading, holidays. *Address:* St George's Hospital Medical School, Cranmer Terrace, SW17 0RE. *T:* (020) 8725 5008; The Stone House, Adlington, Macclesfield, Cheshire SK10 4NU. *T:* (01625) 872400.

See also Sir J. D. I. Boyd.

BOYD, Sir Robert (Lewis Fullarton), Kt 1983; CBE 1972; FRS 1969; Professor of Physics in the University of London, 1962–83, now Emeritus; Director, Mullard Space Science Laboratory of Department of Physics and Astronomy of University College, London, 1965–83; *b* 1922; *s* of late William John Boyd, PhD, BSc; *m* 1st, 1949, Mary (*d* 1996), *d* of late John Higgins; two *s* one *d*; 2nd, 1998, Betty, *d* of late Herbert Frank Chelmsford, *widow* of Stanley Robinson. *Educ:* Whitgift Sch.; Imperial Coll., London (BSc (Eng) 1943); University Coll., London (PhD 1949; Fellow 1988). FIEE 1967; FInstP 1972. Exp. Officer at Admty Mining Estabt, 1943–46; DSIR Res. Asst, 1946–49; ICI Res. Fellow, 1949–50, Maths Dept, UCL; ICI Res. Fellow, Physics Dept, UCL, 1950–52; Lectr in Physics, UCL, 1952–58, Reader in Physics, UCL, 1959–62. Prof. of Astronomy (part-time), Royal Institution, 1961–67; IEE Appleton Lectr, 1976; Bakerian Lectr, Royal

Soc., 1978; Halley Lectr, Univ. of Oxford, 1981. Chairman: Meteorol Res. Cttee, MoD, 1972–75; Astronautics Cttee, MoD, 1972–77; Member: BBC Science Cons. Gp, 1970–79; SRC, 1977–81 (Chm., Astronomy, Space and Radio Bd, 1977–80); Council, Physical Soc., 1958–60; Council, RAS, 1962–66 (Vice-Pres., 1964–66); British Nat. Cttee on Space Res., 1976–87. Pres., Victoria Inst., 1965–76. Trustee, Nat. Maritime Museum, 1980–89. Governor: St Lawrence Coll., 1965–76; Croydon Coll., 1966–80; Southlands Coll., 1976–94; Chm., London Bible Coll., 1983–90. Hon. DSc Heriot-Watt, 1979. *Publications:* The Upper Atmosphere (with H. S. W. Massey), 1958; Space Research by Rocket and Satellite, 1960; Space Physics, 1975; papers in sci. jls on space sci. and other topics. *Recreations:* elderly Rolls Royce motors, model engineering. *Address:* 9 Cherwell Gardens, Chandlers Ford, Eastleigh SO53 2NH.

BOYD, Robert Stanley, CB 1982; Solicitor of Inland Revenue, 1979–86; *b* 6 March 1927; *s* of Robert Reginald Boyd (formerly Indian Police) and Agnes Maria Dorothea, *d* of Lt-Col Charles H. Harrison; *m* 1965, Ann, *d* of Daniel Hopkin. *Educ:* Wellington; Trinity Coll., Dublin (BA, LLB). Served RN, 1945–48. Called to Bar, Inner Temple, 1954. Joined Inland Revenue, 1959; Prin. Asst Solicitor, 1971–79. *Address:* Great Beere, North Tawton, Devon EX20 2BR.

BOYD, Stewart Craufurd; QC 1981; a Recorder, since 1994; *b* 25 Oct. 1943; *s* of late Leslie Balfour Boyd, CBE, and Wendy Marie Boyd; *m* 1970, Catherine Jay; one *s* three *d. Educ:* Winchester Coll.; Trinity Coll., Cambridge (MA). Called to the Bar, Middle Temple, 1967, Bencher, 1989. Dep. Chm., FSA, 1999–. *Publications:* (ed) Scrutton, Charterparties, 18th edn 1972, 19th edn 1984; (with Sir Michael Mustill) The Law and Practice of Commercial Arbitration, 1982, 1989; contrib. Civil Justice Rev., Arbitration Internat., Lloyd's Commercial and Maritime Law Qly. *Recreations:* boats, pianos, gardens. *Address:* 1 Gayton Crescent, NW3 1TT. *T:* (020) 7431 1581.

BOYD, (Thomas) Christopher; farmer, 1963–96; *b* 14 Aug. 1916; *m*; one *s* two *d*. Army, 1940–44; civil servant, 1939 and 1944–48; MP (Lab) Bristol NW, 1955–59; Chelsea Borough Councillor, 1953–59. *Address:* The Quillet, Appledore, Kent TN26 2DD.

BOYD, Dame Vivienne (Myra), DBE 1986 (CBE 1983); Vice Chairperson, Hutt Diabetic Foundation, since 1992; *b* 11 April 1926; *d* of Hugh France Lowe and Winifred May Lowe (*née* Shearer); *m* 1948, Robert Macdonald Boyd; three *d* (one *s* decd). *Educ:* Eastern Hutt Sch.; Hutt Valley High Sch.; Victoria Coll., Univ. of New Zealand (MSc (Hons)). President: Dunedin Free Kindergarten Assoc., 1965; NZ Baptist Women's League, 1966; Nat. Council of Women of NZ, 1978–82; NZ Baptist Union of Churches and Missionary Soc., 1984–85; Wellington Br., NZ Epilepsy Assoc., 1994–96. Member: Royal Commn on Nuclear Power Generation, 1976–78; Equal Opportunities Tribunal, 1979–89; Advertising Standards Council, subseq. Advertising Standards Complaints Bd, 1988–97; Envmtl Choice Mgt Adv. Cttee, 1990–98; chaired: Abortion Supervisory Cttee, 1979–80; Women and Recreation Conf., 1981; Review of Preparation and Initial Employment of Nurses, 1986–92; Consumer Council, NZ, 1983–88 (Mem., 1975–88); Consumers' Inst. of NZ Inc., 1988–89 (Mem. Bd, 1989–90); Convener, Internat. Council of Women Standing Cttee on Social Welfare, 1982–88. Mem., NZ Medic Alert Trust Bd, 1995–. Chm., Taita Home and Hosp. for the Elderly, 1989–92. Trustee, Celebrating Women Trust, 1998–. Silver Jubilee Medal, 1977. *Recreations:* reading, gardening. *Address:* 1/38 Kings Cresent, Lower Hutt, New Zealand. *T:* (4) 5695028.

BOYD, William Andrew Murray, FRSL; author; *b* 7 March 1952; *s* of Dr Alexander Murray Boyd and Evelyn Boyd; *m* 1975, Susan Anne (*née* Wilson). *Educ:* Gordonstoun Sch.; Glasgow Univ. (MA Hons English and Philosophy); Jesus Coll., Oxford. Lecturer in English, St Hilda's Coll., Oxford, 1980–83; Television Critic, New Statesman, 1981–83. FRSL 1983. Hon. DLitt: St Andrews, 1997; Stirling, 1997; Glasgow, 2000. Chevalier de l'Ordre des Arts et des Lettres (France), 1991. *Publications:* A Good Man in Africa, 1981 (Whitbread Prize 1981, Somerset Maugham Award 1982); On the Yankee Station (short stories), 1981; An Ice-Cream War, 1982 (John Llewellyn Rhys Prize, 1982); Stars and Bars, 1984; School Ties (screenplays), 1985; The New Confessions, 1987; Brazzaville Beach, 1990 (James Tait Black Meml Prize, 1990; McVitie's Prize, 1991); The Blue Afternoon, 1993 (Sunday Express Book of the Year Award, 1993; LA Times Book Award for Fiction, 1995); The Destiny of Nathalie X (short stories), 1995; Armadillo, 1998; Nat Tate: an American artist, 1998. *Screenplays:* Good and Bad at Games (TV), 1983; Dutch Girls (TV), 1985; Scoop (TV), 1987; Stars and Bars, 1988; Aunt Julia and the Scriptwriter, 1990; Mr Johnson, 1990; Chaplin, 1992; A Good Man in Africa, 1994; The Trench, 1999 (also Dir); Sword of Honour (TV), 2001; Armadillo (TV), 2001. *Recreations:* tennis, strolling. *Address:* c/o The Agency, 24 Pottery Lane, Holland Park, W11 4LZ.

BOYD-CARPENTER, (Marsom) Henry, CVO 1994; Senior Partner, Farrer & Co., Solicitors, since 2000 (Partner, since 1968); Private Solicitor to the Queen, since 1995; *b* 11 Oct. 1939; *s* of Francis Henry Boyd-Carpenter and Nina Boyd-Carpenter (*née* Townshend); *m* 1971, Lesley Ann Davies; one *s* one *d. Educ:* Charterhouse; Balliol Coll., Oxford (BA 1962; MA 1967). Admitted solicitor, 1966; Solicitor to Duchy of Cornwall, 1976–94. Law Society: Mem., 1966–; Hon. Auditor, 1979–81. Member: Council, Prince of Wales's Inst. of Architecture, 1995–99; Bd, British Library, 1999–. Hon. Steward, Westminster Abbey, 1980–; Hon. Legal Advr, Canterbury Cathedral Trust Fund, 1994–. Mem. Governing Body, Charterhouse, 1981– (Chm., 2000–); Governor: Sutton's Hosp. in Charterhouse, 1994–; St Mary's Sch., Gerrards Cross, 1967–70. Member: RHS Governance Wkg Party, 2000–01; Council, Chelsea Physic Garden, 1983–; Trustee: Nat. Gardens Scheme, 1998–; Merlin Trust, 1998–; Mem., Bd of Trustees, Inst. of Cancer Res., 2001–. *Recreations:* reading, listening to music, hill-walking, gardening. *Address:* 66 Lincoln's Inn Fields, WC2A 3LH; Guardswell House, Brockenhurst Road, South Ascot, Berks SL5 9HA. *Club:* Brooks's.

BOYD-CARPENTER, Hon. Sir Thomas (Patrick John), KBE 1993 (MBE 1973); Chairman: Social Security Advisory Committee, since 1995; Moorfields Eye Hospital NHS Trust, since 2001; senior consultant, since 1996 and Director, since 1997, People in Business; *b* 16 June 1938; *s* of Baron Boyd-Carpenter, PC; *m* 1972, Mary-Jean (*née* Duffield); one *s* two *d. Educ:* Stowe. Commnd 1957; served UK, Oman, Malaya, Borneo and Germany; Instr, Staff Coll., 1975–77; Defence Fellowship, Aberdeen Univ., 1977–78; CO 1st Bn Scots Guards, 1979–81; Comdr 24 Inf. Brigade, 1983–84; Dir, Defence Policy, 1985–87; COS, HQ BAOR, 1988–89; ACDS (Programmes), 1989–92; DCDS (Progs and Personnel), 1992–96; retd in rank of Lt-Gen. Chairman: Kensington & Chelsea and Westminster HA, 1996–2001; Adv. Bd on Family Law, 1997–2001. *Publication:* Conventional Deterrence: into the 1990s, 1989. *Recreations:* reading, gardening. *Address:* c/o Barclays Bank, 6 Market Place, Newbury, Berks RG14 5AY.
See also Baroness Hogg.

BOYDE, Prof. Patrick, PhD; FBA 1987; Serena Professor of Italian, 1981–Sept. 2002, and Fellow of St John's College, since 1965, University of Cambridge; *b* 30 Nov. 1934; *s* of late Harry Caine Boyde and Florence Colonna Boyde; *m* 1956, Catherine Mavis Taylor; four *s. Educ:* Braintree County High Sch.; Wanstead County High Sch.; St John's Coll., Cambridge. BA 1956, MA 1960, PhD 1963. Nat. service, commnd RA, 1956–58. Research, St John's Coll., Cambridge, 1958–61; Asst Lectr in Italian, Univ. of Leeds, 1961–62; Asst Lectr, later Lectr, Univ. of Cambridge, 1962–81. Corresp. Fellow, Accademia Nazionale dei Lincei, 1986. *Publications:* Dante's Lyric Poetry (with K. Foster), 1967; Dante's Style in his Lyric Poetry, 1971; Dante Philomythes and Philosopher: Man in the Cosmos, 1981; Perception and Passion in Dante's Comedy, 1993; Human Vices and Human Worth in Dante's Comedy, 2000. *Recreations:* walking, music.

BOYER, John Leslie, OBE 1982; Chief Executive, Zoological Society of London, 1984–88; *b* 13 Nov. 1926; *s* of Albert and Gladys Boyer; *m* 1953, Joyce Enid Thomasson; one *s* two *d. Educ:* Nantwich; Acton Grammar Sch. Served Army, 1944–48: commnd into South Lancashire Regt, 1946, and attached to Baluch Regt, then Indian Army. Joined Hongkong and Shanghai Banking Corp., 1948: served Hong Kong, Burma, Japan, India, Malaysia, Singapore; General Manager, Hong Kong, 1973; Director, March 1977; Dep. Chm., Sept. 1977–81; Chm., Antony Gibbs Hldgs Ltd, 1981–83. *Recreations:* walking, swimming, bridge, reading. *Address:* Friars Lawn, Norwood Green Road, Norwood Green, Mddx UB2 4LA. *T:* (020) 8574 8489. *Clubs:* Oriental; Shek O (Hong Kong); Tanglin (Singapore).

BOYER, Prof. Paul Delos, PhD; Professor of Biochemistry, University of California at Los Angeles, since 1963; *b* 31 July 1918; *s* of Dell Delos Boyer and Grace Guymon; *m* 1939, Lyda Wicker; one *s* two *d. Educ:* Brigham Young Univ.; Univ. of Wisconsin (PhD 1943). Res. Asst, Univ. of Wisconsin, 1939–43; Instructor, Stanford Univ., 1943–45; University of Minnesota: Associate Prof., 1946–53; Prof., 1953–56; Hill Prof. of Biochemistry, 1956–63; Dir, Molecular Biology Inst., 1965–83, Biotechnology Prog., 1985–89, UCLA. Editor, Annual Biochemistry Review, 1964–89. ACS Award, 1955; Tolman Medal, ACS, 1981; Rose Award, Amer. Soc. of Biochemistry and Molecular Biology, 1989; (jtly) Nobel Prize for Chemistry, 1997. *Publications:* (ed jtly) The Enzymes, vol. 2, 1970 to vol. 20, 1992; papers on biochem. and molecular biology. *Address:* University of California, Los Angeles, Molecular Biology Institute, 408 Milgard Avenue, Los Angeles, CA 90024, USA; 1033 Somera Road, Los Angeles, CA 90077, USA.

BOYERS, (Raphael) Howard, DFC 1945; Regional Chairman of Industrial Tribunals, Sheffield, 1984–87, retired 1988; *b* 20 Oct. 1915; *yr s* of late Bernard Boyers and Jennie Boyers; *m* 1st, 1949, Anna Moyra Cowan (*d* 1984); three *d*; 2nd, 1985, Estelle Wolman (*née* Davidson), JP; two step *s* one step *d. Educ:* King Edward VI Grammar School, Retford. Admitted Solicitor, 1939. Served War, RAF, 1940–45; 130 Sqdn, 10 Gp Fighter Comd, 1941; 51 Sqdn, 4 Gp Bomber Comd, 1944–45. Sen. Partner, Boyers Howson & Co., 1946–72. Clerk of the Peace, City of Sheffield, 1964–71; Chairman: VAT Tribunals, 1972–75; Industrial Tribunals, 1975–80; acting Regional Chm., 1980–84. Pres., Rep. Council of Sheffield and Dist Jews, 1963–67 and 1973–74. *Recreations:* theatre, music, watching football. *Address:* 49 Cortworth Road, Sheffield S11 9LN. *T:* (0114) 235 3534. *Club:* Royal Air Force.

BOYES, Sir Brian Gerald B.; *see* Barratt-Boyes.

BOYES, James Ashley; Headmaster of City of London School, 1965–84; *b* 27 Aug. 1924; *s* of late Alfred Simeon Boyes and of Edith May Boyes; *m* 1st, 1949, Diana Fay (*née* Rothera), MA Cantab; two *d*; 2nd, 1973, April Tanner (*née* Rothery). *Educ:* Rugby Sch., Clare Coll., Cambridge. Lieut RNVR; N Russian convoys and Brit. Pacific Fleet, 1942–46. Cambridge Univ., 1942, 1946–48; 1st class Hons Mod. Hist., 1948; Mellon Fellowship, Yale Univ., 1948–50; MA Yale, 1950. Asst Master, Rugby Sch., 1950–55; Headmaster, Kendal Grammar Sch., Westmorland, 1955–60; Dir of Studies, Royal Air Force Coll., Cranwell, 1960–65. Since retirement engaged in work for the mentally ill; Vice-Chair, Nat. Schizophrenia Fellowship, 1989–. *Recreations:* squash racquets, sailing. *Address:* 12 Linver Road, SW6 3RB. *Clubs:* Royal Automobile, Hurlingham; Harlequins RUFC (Hon. Mem.); Hawks (Cambridge); Royal Windermere Yacht.

BOYES, Kate Emily Tyrrell, (Mrs C. W. Sanders); Chairman, Civil Service Selection Boards, since 1978; *b* 22 April 1918; *e d* of S. F. Boyes, Sandiacre, Derbyshire; *m* 1944, Cyril Woods Sanders, *qv*; one *s* three *d. Educ:* Long Eaton Grammar Sch.; (Scholar) Newnham Coll., Cambridge. Economics Tripos, 1939; MA (Cantab). Administrative Class, BoT, Home Civil Service, 1939; Private Sec. to Parly Sec., 1942–45; Principal, 1945; Sec. to Council on Prices, Productivity and Incomes, 1958–60; Asst Sec., 1961; Speechwriter to President of BoT, 1963–64; Under-Sec., Europe, Industry and Technology Div., DTI, later Dept of Trade, 1972–78. Member: Council, National Trust, 1967–79; Exec., Keep Britain Tidy Gp, 1980–. *Recreations:* climbing, sailing, ski-ing, archæology. *Address:* 41 Smith Street, SW3 4EP. *T:* (020) 7352 8053; Giles Point, Winchelsea, Sussex TN36 4AA. *T:* (01797) 226431; Canower, Cashel, Connemara, Ireland. *Clubs:* Ski Club of Gt Britain; Island Cruising (Salcombe).

BOYES, Roland; *b* 12 Feb. 1937; *m* 1962, Patricia James; two *s. Educ:* London Univ. (BSc Econ 1968); Bradford Univ. (MSc). Teacher, 1961–74; Asst Dir, Social Services Dept, Durham CC, 1975–79. Member (Lab) Durham, European Parliament, 1979–84. MP (Lab) Houghton and Washington, 1983–97; an opposition frontbench spokesman on: Parly environment team, 1985–88; Parly defence team, 1988–92; Member, Select Committee: on Envmt, 1992–94; on Nat. Heritage, 1994–97; Mem., Speaker's Panel of Chairmen, 1994–97. Founder Chm., All Party Photography Gp, 1987–97. Member GMB. Chm., Tribune Gp, 1985–86. Dir, Hartlepool United AFC, 1987–. Hon. degree, Sunderland, 1997. *Publication:* People in Parliament, 1990. *Address:* 12 Spire Hollin, Peterlee, Co. Durham SR8 1DA. *T:* (0191) 586 3917.

BOYLAN, Prof. Patrick John, PhD; FMA; FGS; Professor of Arts Policy and Management, City University, since 1990; *b* 17 Aug. 1939; *s* of Francis Boylan and Mary Doreen (*née* Haxby), Hull, Yorks; *m* Pamela Mary Inder. *Educ:* Marist Coll., Hull; Univ. of Hull (BSc 1960; PGCE 1961); Univ. of Leicester (PhD 1985). Museums Diploma (with Distinction), Museums Assoc., 1966. FMA 1972; FGS 1973. Asst Master, Marist Coll., Hull, 1961–63; Keeper of Geology and Natural History, Kingston upon Hull Museums, 1964–68; Dir of Museums and Art Gallery, Exeter City Council, 1968–72; Dir of Museums and Art Gall., Leicester City Council, 1972–74; Dir of Museums and Arts, Leics County Council, 1974–90. International Council of Museums: Chm., Internat. Cttee for Training of Personnel, 1983–89; Chm., UK Nat. Cttee, 1987–93; Mem., Adv. Cttee, 1983–93; Mem., Exec. Council, 1989–; Vice-Pres., 1992–. Councillor, Museums Assoc., 1970–71 and 1986– (Centenary Pres., 1988–90); Chm., Library Cttee, Geol Soc., 1984–87. Consultant: UNESCO; Jt UN/UNESCO World Commn on Culture and Devel; Council of Europe, etc. Freeman, City of London, 1991; Liveryman, Framework Knitters' Co., 1991–. FIMgt (FBIM 1990; MBIM 1975); FRSA 1990. *Publications:* Ice Age in Yorkshire and Humberside, 1983; The Changing World of Museums and Art Galleries, 1986; Museums 2000: politics, people, professionals and profit, 1991; Review of Convention on Protection of Cultural Property in the Event of Armed Conflict, 1993; over 180 papers in learned jls and chapters in books on museums, cultural policy, mgt, prof. training, geology, natural history and history of science. *Recreations:* the arts (especially opera and contemporary arts and crafts), history of science research, avoiding gardening. *Address:* Department of Arts Policy and Management, City University,

Frobisher Crescent, Barbican, EC2Y 8HB. *T:* (020) 7477 8750, *Fax:* (020) 7477 8887; *e-mail:* p.boylan@city.ac.uk; The Deepings, Gun Lane, Knebworth, Herts SG3 6BJ. *T:* (01438) 812658.

BOYLAND, Prof. Eric, (Dick), PhD London; DSc Manchester; Professor of Biochemistry, University of London, at Chester Beatty Research Institute, Institute of Cancer Research, Royal Marsden Hospital, 1948–70, now Emeritus Professor; Visiting Professor in Environmental Toxicology, London School of Hygiene and Tropical Medicine, 1970–76; *b* Manchester, 24 Feb. 1905; *s* of Alfred E. and Helen Boyland; *m* 1931, Margaret Esther (*d* 1985), *d* of late Maj.-Gen. Sir Frederick Maurice, KCMG, CB; two *s* one *d*. *Educ:* Manchester Central High Sch.; Manchester Univ. BSc Tech. 1926; MSc 1928; DSc 1936. Research Asst in Physiology, Manchester Univ., 1926–28; Grocers' Company Scholar and Beit Memorial Fellow for Med. Research at Lister Institute for Preventive Medicine, 1928–30, and Kaiser Wilhelm Institut für Medizinische Forschung, Heidelberg, 1930–31; Physiological Chemist to Royal Cancer Hosp., London, 1931; Reader in Biochemistry, University of London, 1935–47. Research Officer in Ministry of Supply, 1941–44; Ministry of Agriculture, 1944–45. Consultant to Internat. Agency for Research on Cancer, Lyon, 1970–72; Member WHO Panel on Food Additives. Hon. FFOM, RCP, 1982. Hon. PhD Frankfurt, 1982; Hon. MD Malta, 1985. Judd Award for Cancer Research, New York, 1948. *Publications:* The Biochemistry of Bladder Cancer, 1963; Modern Trends in Toxicology, vol. I, 1962, vol. II, 1974; scientific papers in biochemistry and pharmacology. *Recreation:* looking at paintings. *Clubs:* Athenæum; Rucksack (Manchester).

BOYLE, family name of **Earls of Cork, Glasgow,** and **Shannon**.

BOYLE, Viscount; Richard Henry John Boyle; *b* 19 Jan. 1960; *s* and *heir* of 9th Earl of Shannon, *qv*. *Address:* Edington House, Edington, Bridgwater, Somerset TA7 9JS.

BOYLE, Alan Gordon; QC 1991; *b* 31 March 1949; *s* of late Dr Michael Morris Boyle and of Hazel Irene Boyle; *m* 1981, Claudine-Aimée Minne-Vercruysse; two *d*. *Educ:* Royal Shrewsbury Sch.; St Catherine's Coll., Oxford (MA). Called to the Bar, Lincoln's Inn, 1972. *Recreations:* walking, music. *Address:* Serle Court Chambers, 6 New Square, Lincoln's Inn, WC2A 3QS. *T:* (020) 7242 6105.

BOYLE, Leonard Butler, CBE 1977; Director and General Manager, Principality Building Society, Cardiff, 1956–78; *b* 13 Jan. 1913; *s* of Harold and Edith Boyle; *m* 1938, Alice Baldwin Yarborough (*d* 1989); two *s*. *Educ:* Roundhay Sch., Leeds. FCIB. Chief of Investment Dept, Leeds Permanent Building Soc., 1937; Asst Man., Isle of Thanet Bldg Soc., 1949; Jt Asst Gen. Man., Hastings and Thanet Bldg Soc., 1951, Sec. 1954. Building Socs Assoc.: Mem. Council, 1956–78 (Chm. Gen. Purposes Cttee, 1958–60; Chm. Develt Cttee, 1967–71); Chm. of Council, 1973–75 (Dep. Chm. 1971–73; Vice-Pres., 1978); Vice-Pres., CIB (formerly CBSI), 1982–. *Recreations:* gardening, walking, golf. *Address:* Northwick Cottage, Marlpit Lane, Seaton, Devon EX12 2HH. *T:* (01297) 22194.

BOYLE, Prof. Nicholas, PhD; FBA 2001; Professor of German Literary and Intellectual History, University of Cambridge, since 2000; Fellow, Magdalene College, Cambridge, since 1968; *b* 18 June 1946; *e s* of late Hugh Boyle and of Margaret Mary Faith (*née* Hopkins, now Mrs R. G. Boothroyd); *m* 1983, Rosemary Angela Devlin; one *s* three *d*. *Educ:* King's Sch., Worcester; Magdalene Coll., Cambridge (schol.; BA 1967; MA; PhD 1976). University of Cambridge: Res. Fellow in German, Magdalene Coll., 1968–72; Lectr in German, Magdalene and Girton Colls, 1972–74; Univ. Asst Lectr in German, 1974–79, Lectr, 1979–93, Reader, 1993–2000, Hd of Dept, 1996–2001; Sec., Faculty Bd of Mod. and Medieval Langs, 1982–85; Tutor, Magdalene Coll., 1984–93. Scholar, Alexander von Humboldt Foundn, 1978, 1980–81; British Acad. Res. Reader in Humanities, 1990–92; Res. Fellow, John Rylands Res. Inst., Univ. of Manchester, 1993; Fellow, Wissenschaftskolleg, Berlin, 1994–95. W. Heinemann Prize, RSL, 1992; J. G. Robertson Meml Prize, Univ. of London, 1994; Goethe Medal, 2000. *Publications:* (ed with M. Swales) Realism in European Literature: essays in honour of J. P. Stern, 1986; Goethe: Faust, Part One, 1987; Goethe: the poet and the age, Vol. 1, 1991 (trans. German 1995), Vol. 2, 2000 (trans. German, 1999); Who Are We Now?: Christian humanism and the global market from Hegel to Heaney, 1998; articles in New Blackfriars, German Life and Letters, French Studies, etc. *Recreation:* enjoying other people's gardens. *Address:* Magdalene College, Cambridge CB3 0AG. *T:* (01223) 332137; 20 Alpha Road, Cambridge CB4 3DG. *T:* (01223) 364310.

BOYLE, Roger Michael, FRCP; Consultant Cardiologist, York District Hospital, since 1983; National Director for Heart Disease, since 2000; *b* 27 Jan. 1948; *s* of late Dr Michael Morris Boyle and of Hazel Irene Boyle; *m* 1975, Susan Scutt (separated); three *s*. *Educ:* Shrewsbury Sch.; London Hosp. Med. Sch., London Univ. (MB BS 1972). House physician and surgeon, then SHO, London Hosp., 1972–75; Registrar, Chelmsford Hosp., 1975–78; Res. Fellow, Wythenshawe Hosp., Manchester, 1978–80; Lectr in Cardiovascular Studies, Univ. of Leeds, 1980–83. FESC. *Publications:* contribs to cardiovascular jls on coronary heart disease and trng in cardiology. *Recreations:* sailing, playing the piano, walking. *Address:* The Paddocks House, 42 Main Street, Copmanthorpe, York YO2 3SU. *Club:* Percuil Sailing.
See also A. G. Boyle.

BOYLE, Sir Stephen Gurney, 5th Bt *cr* 1904; *b* 15 Jan. 1962; *s* of Sir Richard Gurney Boyle, 4th Bt, and of Elizabeth Ann, *yr d* of Norman Dennes; *S* father, 1983. Chm., Co-operative property services. *Heir: b* Michael Desmond Boyle, *b* 16 Sept. 1963. *Recreations:* music, watching cricket, bridge. *Address:* 19 Gibb Croft, Harlow, Essex CM18 7JL.

BOYNE, 11th Viscount *cr* 1717 (Ire.); **Gustavus Michael Stucley Hamilton-Russell;** Baron Hamilton 1715; Baron Brancepeth (UK) 1866; *b* 27 May 1965; *o s* of 10th Viscount Boyne and of Rosemary Anne, *d* of Sir Dennis Stucley, 5th Bt; *S* father, 1995; *m* 1991, Lucy, *d* of George Potter; three *s* one *d* (incl. twin *s*). *Educ:* Harrow; RAC Cirencester. Dip. Rural Estate Management; ARICS 1991. Chartered Surveyor with Carter Jonas. *Recreations:* country sports, tennis, ski-ing. *Heir: s* Hon. Gustavus Archie Edward Hamilton-Russell, *b* 30 June 1999. *Address:* Burwarton House, Bridgnorth, Shropshire WV16 6QH. *T:* (01746) 787221. *Club:* Turf.

BOYNE, Donald Arthur Colin Aydon, CBE 1977; Director, 1974–85, Consultant, 1984–86, The Architectural Press; *b* 15 Feb. 1921; 2nd *s* of late Lytton Leonard Boyne and Millicent (*née* Nisbet); *m* 1947, Rosemary Pater; two *s* one *d*. *Educ:* Tonbridge Sch.; Architectural Assoc. School of Architecture, 1943–47. Indian Army, 8/13 FF Rifles, 1940–43. Editor, Architects' Jl, 1953–70; Chm., Editorial Bd, Architectural Review and Architects' Jl, 1971–84. Hon. FRIBA 1969. *Address:* Pound House, Southover, Wells, Somerset BA5 1UH. *T:* (01749) 674704.

BOYNE, Maj.-Gen. John, CB 1987; MBE 1965; CEng, FIMechE; FIMgt; company director, since 1988; *b* 7 Nov. 1932; *s* of John Grant Boyne and Agnes Crawford (*née* Forrester); *m* 1956, Norma Beech; two *s*. *Educ:* King's Sch., Chester; Royal Military Coll. of Science, Shrivenham (BScEng 1st Cl. Hons). CEng, FIMechE 1975. Served in Egypt, Cyprus, Libya and UK, 1951–62; Staff Coll., Camberley, 1963; DAQMG(Ops) HQ MEC, Aden, 1964–66; OC 11 Infantry Workshop, REME, BAOR, 1966–67; Jt Services Staff Coll., 1968; GSO2 MoD, 1968–70; GSO1 (DS), Staff Coll., 1970–72; Comdr REME, 2nd Div., BAOR, 1972–73; AAG MoD, 1973–75; CSO (Personnel) to CPL, MoD, 1975–76; Dep. Dir Elec. and Mech. Engrg, 1st British Corps, 1976–78; RCDS, 1979; Dep. Dir Personal Services (Army), MoD, 1980–82; Vice Adjutant Gen. and Dir of Manning (Army), MoD, 1982–85; Dir Gen., Electrical and Mechanical Engrg, Logistic Executive (Army), MoD, 1985–88. Col Comdt, REME, 1988–93 (Rep. Col Comdt, 1989–90). Trustee, Army Benevolent Fund, 1986–. Vice Pres., Army Football Assoc., 1988–. FIMgt (FBIM 1975). *Recreations:* music, philately, football. *Address:* c/o HSBC, 48 High Street, Runcorn, Cheshire WA7 1AN.

BOYNTON, Sir John (Keyworth), Kt 1979; MC 1944; LLB; MRTPI; DL; Chief Executive, Cheshire County Council, 1974–79; Solicitor; *b* 14 Feb. 1918; *s* of late Ernest Boynton, Hull; *m* 1st, 1947, Gabrielle Stanglmaier, Munich (*d* 1978); two *d*; 2nd, 1979, Edith Laane, The Hague. *Educ:* Dulwich Coll. Served War, 15th Scottish Reconnaissance Regt, 1940–46 (despatches, MC). Dep. Clerk, Berks CC, 1951–64; Clerk, Cheshire CC, 1964–74. Member: Planning Law Cttee of Law Soc., 1964–88; Economic Planning Council for NW, 1965; Exec. Council of Royal Inst. of Public Admin., 1970; Council of Industrial Soc., 1974–93; Council, PSI, 1978–83. Pres., RTPI, 1976. Election Commissioner, Southern Rhodesia, 1979–80. DL Cheshire 1975. *Publications:* Compulsory Purchase and Compensation, 1964, 7th edn 1994; Job at the Top, 1986. *Recreation:* golf. *Address:* 40 High Sheldon, Sheldon Avenue, N6 4NJ. *T:* (020) 8348 5234. *Club:* Army and Navy.

BOYS, Rt Hon. Sir Michael H.; *see* Hardie Boys.

BOYS, Penelope Ann, (Mrs D. C. H. Wright); Deputy Director General, Office of Fair Trading, since 2000; *b* 11 June 1947; *d* of late Hubert John Boys and of Mollie Blackman Boys; *m* 1977, David Charles Henshaw Wright. *Educ:* Guildford County Sch. for Girls. Exec. Officer, DES, 1966–69; Asst Principal, Min. of Power, 1969–72; Private Sec., Minister without Portfolio, 1972–73; Principal, Dept of Energy, 1973–78; seconded to BNOC, 1978–80; Head of Internat. Unit, Dept of Energy, 1981–85; seconded to HM Treasury as Head, ST2 Div., 1985–87; Dir of Personnel, Dept of Energy, 1987–89; Dep. Dir Gen., Office of Electricity Regulation, 1989–93; Head of Personnel, DTI, 1993–96; Sec., Monopolies and Mergers, later Competition, Commn, 1996–2000. *Recreations:* entertaining, racing, music. *Address:* Office of Fair Trading, Fleetbank House, 2–6 Salisbury Square, EC4Y 8JX.

BOYS-GREENE, Jenny; *see* Greene, J.

BOYS SMITH, Stephen Wynn, CB 2001; Director-General, Immigration and Nationality Directorate, Home Office, since 1998; *b* 4 May 1946; *s* of late Rev. Dr John Sandwith Boys Smith and Gwendolen Sara Boys Smith (*née* Wynn); *m* 1971, Linda Elaine Price; one *s* one *d*. *Educ:* Sherborne Sch.; St John's Coll., Cambridge (MA); Univ. of British Columbia (MA). Home Office, 1968; Asst Private Sec. to Home Sec., 1971–73; Central Policy Review Staff, Cabinet Office, 1977; Home Office, 1979; Private Sec. to Home Sec., 1980–81; NI Office, 1981; Principal Private Sec. to Sec. of State for NI, 1981–82; Home Office, 1984; Principal Private Sec. to Home Sec., 1985–87; Asst Under Sec. of State, Home Office, 1989–92; Under Sec., HM Treasury, 1992–95; Dep. Sec. and Head of Police Dept, Home Office, 1995–96; Dir, Police Policy, Home Office, 1996–98. *Recreations:* gardening, reading. *Address:* (office) Apollo House, 36 Wellesley Road, Croydon CR9 3RR.

BOYSE, Prof. Edward Arthur, MD; FRS 1977; Distinguished Professor, University of Arizona, Tucson, 1989–94, now Emeritus Professor; Member, Sloan-Kettering Institute for Cancer Research, New York, 1967–89; Professor of Biology, Cornell University, 1969–89; *b* 11 Aug. 1923; *s* of late Arthur Boyse, FRCO, and Dorothy Vera Boyse (*née* Mellersh); *m* 1951, Jeanette (*née* Grimwood) (marr. diss. 1987); two *s* one *d*; *m* 1987, Judith Bard. *Educ:* St Bartholomew's Hosp. Med. Sch., Univ. of London. MB BS 1952; MD 1957. Aircrew, RAF, 1941–46, commnd 1943. Various hospital appts, 1952–57; research at Guy's Hosp., 1957–60; research appts at NY Univ. and Sloan-Kettering Inst., 1960–89. Amer. Cancer Soc. Res. Prof., 1977. Member: Amer. Acad. of Arts and Scis, 1977; Nat. Acad. of Scis, USA, 1979. Cancer Research Institute Award in Tumor Immunology, 1975; Isaac Adler Award, Rockefeller and Harvard Univs, 1976. *Publications:* papers relating genetics and immunology to development and cancer. *Address:* Department of Microbiology and Immunology, University of Arizona Health Sciences Center, 1501 N Campbell Avenue, Tucson, AZ 85724, USA.

BOYSON, Rt Hon. Sir Rhodes, Kt 1987; PC 1987; *b* 11 May 1925; *s* of Alderman William Boyson, MBE, JP and Mrs Bertha Boyson, Haslingden, Rossendale, Lancs; *m* 1st, 1946, Violet Burletson (marr. diss.); two *d*; 2nd, 1971, Florette MacFarlane. *Educ:* Haslingden Grammar Sch.; UC Cardiff; Manchester Univ. (BA, MA); LSE (PhD); Corpus Christi Coll., Cambridge. Served with Royal Navy. Headmaster: Lea Bank Secondary Modern Sch., Rossendale, 1955–61; Robert Montefiore Secondary Sch., Stepney, 1961–66; Highbury Grammar Sch., 1966–67; Highbury Grove Sch., 1967–74. Chm., Nat. Council for Educnl Standards, 1974–79. Chm., Churchill Press and Constitutional Book Club, 1969–79. Councillor: Haslingden, 1957–61; Waltham Forest, 1968–74 (Chm. Establishment Cttee, 1968–71); Chm., London Boroughs Management Services Unit, 1968–70. Formerly Youth Warden, Lancs Youth Clubs. Contested (C) Eccles, 1970. MP (C) Brent North, Feb. 1974–1997; contested (C) same seat, 1997. Vice-Chm., Cons Parly Educn Cttee, 1975–76; Hon. Sec. Cons. Adv. Cttee on Educn, 1975–78; Opposition spokesman on educn, 1976–79; Parly Under-Sec. of State, DES, 1979–83; Minister of State: for Social Security, DHSS, 1983–84; NI Office, 1984–86; for Local Govt, DoE, 1986–87. Non-executive Dir. Black's Leisure, 1998–. *Publications:* The North-East Lancashire Poor Law 1838–1871, 1965; The Ashworth Cotton Enterprise, 1970; (ed) Right Turn, 1970; (ed) Down with the Poor, 1971; (ed) Goodbye to Nationalisation, 1972; (ed) Education: Threatened Standards, 1972; (ed) The Accountability of Schools, 1973; Oversubscribed: the story of Highbury Grove, 1974; Crisis in Education, 1975; (jt ed) Black Papers on Education, 1969–77; (ed) 1985: An Escape from Orwell's 1984, 1975; Centre Forward, 1978; Speaking My Mind (autobiog.), 1995; Boyson on Education, 1996. *Recreations:* reading, writing, talk, hard work, meeting friends, inciting the millenialistic Left in education and politics. *Address:* 71 Paines Lane, Pinner, Middx HA5 3BX. *T:* (020) 8866 2071. *Clubs:* Carlton; Churchill (N Wembley), Wembley Conservative.

BRABAZON, family name of **Earl of Meath**.

BRABAZON OF TARA, 3rd Baron *cr* 1942; **Ivon Anthony Moore-Brabazon;** DL; *b* 20 Dec. 1946; *s* of 2nd Baron Brabazon of Tara, CBE, and Henriette Mary (*d* 1985), *d* of late Sir Rowland Clegg; *S* father, 1974; *m* 1979, Harriet Frances, *o d* of Mervyn P. de Courcy Hamilton, Salisbury, Zimbabwe; one *s* one *d*. *Educ:* Harrow. Mem., Stock Exchange, 1972–84. A Lord in Waiting (Govt Whip), 1984–86; Parly Under-Sec. of

State, Dept of Transport, 1986–89; Minister of State: FCO, 1989–90; Dept of Transport, 1990–92; Opposition spokesman on Transport, H of L, 1998–; elected Mem., H of L, 1999. Mem., RAC Public Policy Cttee, 1992–99. Dep. Chm., Foundn for Sport and the Arts, 1992–. President: UK Warehousing Assoc., 1992–; British Internat. Freight Assoc., 1997–99; Inst. of the Motor Industry, 1998–. DL Isle of Wight, 1993. *Recreations:* sailing, Cresta Run. *Heir: s* Hon. Benjamin Ralph Moore-Brabazon, *b* 15 March 1983. *Address:* House of Lords, SW1A 0PW. *Clubs:* Royal Yacht Squadron; Bembridge Sailing, St Moritz Tobogganing, New Zealand Golf.

BRABBINS, Martyn Charles; Associate Principal Conductor, BBC Scottish Symphony Orchestra, since 1994; Principal Conductor: Sinfonia 21, since 1994; Huddersfield Choral Society, since 1998; *b* 13 Aug. 1959; *s* of Herbert Henry Brabbins and Enid Caroline Brabbins; *m* 1985, Karen Maria Evans; two *s* one *d. Educ:* Goldsmiths' Coll., Univ. of London (BMus, MMus); Leningrad State Conservatoire. Professional début with Scottish Chamber Orch., 1988; Associate Conductor, BBC Scottish SO, 1992–94; Conducting Consultant, RSAMD, 1996–; has conducted most major British orchestras, and orchestras abroad, incl. NDR Hanover, Orch. Philharmonic Gran Canaria, Lahti SO, Tapiola Sinfonietta, St Petersburg Philharmonic, Bergen Philharmonic, Ensemble Intercontemporain; also conducted: Don Giovanni, Kirov Opera, 1988; Magic Flute, ENO, 1995; Montpellier Opera, 1999. Has made recordings. Winner, Leeds Conductors Competition, 1988. *Recreation:* family. *Address:* c/o Allied Artists, 42 Montpelier Square, SW7 1JZ. *T:* (020) 7589 6243.

BRABHAM, Sir John Arthur, (Sir Jack), Kt 1979; OBE 1966; retired, 1970, as Professional Racing Driver; Managing Director: Jack Brabham (Motors) Ltd; Engine Developments Ltd; *b* Sydney, Australia, 2 April 1926; *m* 1st, Betty Evelyn Beresford (marr. diss.); three *s*; 2nd, Margaret Taylor. *Educ:* Hurstville Technical Coll., Sydney. Served in RAAF, 1944–46. Started own engineering business, 1946; Midget Speedway racing, 1946–52; several championships (Australian, NSW, South Australian); numerous wins driving a Cooper-Bristol, Australia, 1953–54; to Europe, 1955; Australian Grand Prix, 1955 and 1963 (debut of Repco Brabham); World Champion Formula II, 1958, also many firsts including Casablanca, Goodwood, Brands Hatch, NZ Grand Prix, Belgian Grand Prix; Formula II Champion of France, 1964–66. World Champion Driver: (after first full Formula I Season with 2·5-litre car), 1959–60, 1960–61, 1966. First in Monaco and British Grandes Epreuves, 1959; won Grand Prix of: Holland, Belgium, France, Britain, Portugal, Denmark, 1960; Belgium, 1961. Elected Driver of the Year by Guild of Motoring Writers, 1959, 1966 and 1970, Sportsman of the Year by Australian Broadcasting Co., 1959; left Cooper to take up building own Grand Prix cars, 1961; debut, 1962; first ever constructor/driver to score world championship points, 1963; cars finished first: French GP; Mexican GP, 1964; Formula II and Formula III cars world-wide success, 1963; awarded Ferodo Trophy, 1964 and again, 1966; British Saloon Car Championship, 1965; won French Grand Prix and British Grand Prix, 1966; won French Grand Prix, 1967. RAC Gold Medal, 1966; BARC Gold Star, 1959, 1960 and 1966; Formula I Manufacturers' Championship, 1966, 1967. *Publications:* Jack Brabham's Book of Motor Racing, 1960; When the Flag Drops, 1971; contribs to British journals. *Recreations:* photography, water ski-ing, under-water swimming, flying. *Address:* 5 Ruxley Lane, Ewell, Surrey KT19 0JB. *Clubs:* Royal Automobile, British Racing and Sports Car, British Racing Drivers'; Australian Racing Drivers'.

BRABOURNE, 7th Baron, *cr* 1880; **John Ulick Knatchbull,** CBE 1993; Bt 1641; film and television producer; Director, Thames Television, 1975–93 (Chairman, 1990–93); *b* 9 Nov. 1924; *s* of 5th Baron and Lady Doreen Geraldine Browne (Order of the Crown of India; DStJ) (*d* 1979), *y d* of 6th Marquess of Sligo; *S* brother, 1943; *m* 1946, Lady Patricia Edwina Victoria Mountbatten (*see* Countess Mountbatten of Burma); four *s* two *d* (and one *s* decd). *Educ:* Eton; Oxford. *Films produced:* Harry Black, 1958; Sink the Bismarck!, 1959; HMS Defiant, 1961; Othello, 1965; The Mikado, 1966; Romeo and Juliet; Up the Junction, 1967; Dance of Death, 1968; Tales of Beatrix Potter, 1971; Murder on the Orient Express, 1974; Death on the Nile, 1978; Stories from a Flying Trunk, 1979; The Mirror Crack'd, 1980; Evil Under the Sun, 1982; A Passage to India, 1984; Little Dorrit, 1987. TV Series: National Gallery, 1974; A Much-Maligned Monarch, 1976; Leontyne, 1987. Director: Copyright Promotions Gp, 1974– (Vice Chm., 1995–); Thorn EMI, 1981–86. Governor: BFI, 1979–94 (Fellow, 1985); National Film Sch., 1980–95; Mem., British Screen Adv. Council, 1985–97; Trustee: BAFTA, 1975–; Science Museum, 1984–94; Nat. Mus. of Photography, Film and Television, 1984–94. Pres., Kent Trust for Nature Conservation, 1958–97. Governor: Gordonstoun Sch., 1964–94; United World Colls, 1965–96; Norton Knatchbull Sch., 1969–95; Wye Coll., later Imperial Coll. at Wye, 1955–99 (Provost, 1994–99). University of Kent: Pro-Chancellor, 1992–98; Mem. Council, 1968–98. *Heir: s* Lord Romsey, *qv. Address:* Newhouse, Mersham, Ashford, Kent TN25 6NQ. *T:* (01233) 503636, *Fax:* (01233) 502244.

BRACEGIRDLE, Dr Brian; FSA, FRPS, FIBiol; Research Consultant in microscopy, and Fellow, Science Museum, since 1990; *b* 31 May 1933; *o c* of Alfred Bracegirdle; *m* 1st, 1958, Margaret Lucy Merrett (marr. diss. 1974); one *d*; 2nd, 1975, Patricia Helen Miles; no *c. Educ:* King's Sch., Macclesfield; Univ. of London (BSc); PhD 1975 (UCL). DipRMS 1975. FRPS 1969; FBIPP (FIIP 1970); FIBiol 1976; FSA 1981. Technician in industry, 1950–57; Biology Master, Erith Grammar Sch., 1958–61; Sen. Lectr in Biol., S Katharine's Coll., London, 1961–64; Head, Depts of Nat. Science and Learning Resources, Coll. of All Saints, London, 1964–77; Science Museum: Keeper, Wellcome Mus. of Hist. of Medicine, 1977; Head of Dept of Med. Scis, and Head of Collections Management Div., 1987–89; Asst Dir, 1987–89. Hon. Lectr in History of Medicine, UCL, 1978–90; Hon. Res. Fellow in Hist. of Sci., Imperial Coll., 1990–93. Hon. Treasurer, ICOM (UK), 1978–89. Chm., Inst. of Medical and Biological Illustration, 1983–84; President: Assoc. Européenne de Musées de l'Histoire des Sciences Medicales, 1983–90; Quekett Microscopical Club, 1985–88; Vice-Pres., Royal Microscopical Soc., 1988–90. Ed., Quekett Jl of Microscopy, 1998–. *Publications:* Photography for Books and Reports, 1970; The Archaeology of the Industrial Revolution, 1973; The Evolution of Microtechnique, 1978, 1987; (ed) Beads of Glass: Leeuwenhoek and the early microscope, 1984; Scientific Photomacrography, 1995; Notes on Modern Microscope Manufacturers, 1996; Microscopical Mounts and Mounters, 1998; (with W. H. Freeman): An Atlas of Embryology, 1963, 1978; An Atlas of Histology, 1966; An Atlas of Invertebrate Structure, 1971; An Advanced Atlas of Histology, 1976; (with P. H. Miles): An Atlas of Plant Structure, vol. I, 1971; An Atlas of Plant Structure, Vol. II, 1973; Thomas Telford, 1973; The Darbys and the Ironbridge Gorge, 1974; An Atlas of Chordate Structure, 1977; (with J. B. McCormick) The Microscopic Photographs of J. B. Dancer, 1993; (with S. Bradbury) Modern Photomicrography, 1995; (with S. Bradbury) Introduction to Light Microscopy, 1998; papers on photography for life sciences, on scientific topics, and on history of science/medicine. *Recreations:* walking, music, travel, garden railways. *Address:* Cold Aston Lodge, Cold Aston, Cheltenham, Glos GL54 3BN. *T:* (01451) 820181.

BRACEWELL, Hon. Dame Joyanne (Winifred), (Dame Joyanne Copeland), DBE 1990; **Hon. Mrs Justice Bracewell;** a Judge of the High Court of Justice, Family Division, since 1990; *b* 5 July 1934; *d* of Jack and Lilian Bracewell; *m* 1963, Roy Copeland; one *s* one *d. Educ:* Manchester Univ. (LLB, LLM). Called to Bar, Gray's Inn, 1955; pupillage at the Bar, 1955–56; Mem., Northern Circuit, 1956–; a Recorder of the Crown Court, 1975–83; QC 1978; a Circuit Judge, 1983–90. Family Div. Liaison Judge for London, 1990–97. Chm., Children Act Adv. Cttee, 1993–97. Consulting Editor: Butterworth's Family Law Service, 1989–; Family Practice, 1993–. FRSA 1994. Hon. LLD Manchester, 1991. *Recreations:* antiques, cooking, reading, walking, wildlife conservation. *Address:* Royal Courts of Justice, Strand, WC2A 2LL.

BRACEWELL-SMITH, Sir Charles, 4th Bt *cr* 1947, of Keighley; *b* 13 Oct. 1955; *s* of Sir George Bracewell Smith, 2nd Bt, MBE, and Helene Marie (*d* 1975), *d* of late John Frederick Hydock, Philadelphia, USA; *S* brother, 1983; *m* 1977, Carol Vivien Hough (*d* 1994); *m* 1996, Nina Kakkar. Founder, Homestead Charitable Trust, 1990. *Recreations:* mysticism, theology, philosophy, psychology. *Heir:* none. *Address:* The Hermitage, 7 Clarence Gate Gardens, Glentworth Street, NW1 6AY. *Clubs:* Royal Automobile, Arsenal Football.

BRACK, Rodney Lee; Chief Executive, Horserace Betting Levy Board, since 1993; *b* 16 Aug. 1945; *s* of Sydney William Brack and Mary Alice Brack (*née* Quested); *m* 1973, Marilyn Carol Martin; two *s* one *d. Educ:* Whitgift Sch. FCA 1979. Chartered Accountant, 1963–68; Finance Manager, Daily Mirror Gp, 1969–75; Man. Dir, Leisure Div., EMI, 1976–80; Dir, Leisure Div., Lonrho, 1981–84; Financial Controller and Dep. Chief Exec., Horserace Betting Levy Bd, 1985–92. *Recreations:* music, theatre, cricket, golf. *Address:* Horserace Betting Levy Board, 52 Grosvenor Gardens, SW1W 0AU. *T:* (020) 7333 0043. *Clubs:* MCC, Royal Automobile.

BRACK, Terence John, CB 1994; Assistant Under-Secretary of State (General Finance), Ministry of Defence, 1989–94; *b* 17 April 1938; *s* of late Noël D. J. Brack and Tertia Brack; *m* 1983, Christine Mary, *d* of late Douglas and Evelyn Cashin. *Educ:* Bradfield Coll., Berkshire; Caius Coll., Cambridge Univ. (BA Hist. (1st cl. Hons), MA). Pilot Officer, Secretarial Br., RAF, 1956–58. Entered Air Ministry, subseq. MoD, 1961; Private Sec. to Parly Under-Sec. of State for Defence (RAF), 1964–66; Principal, 1966; seconded to HM Treasury, 1968–72; Asst Sec., 1973; Head, Finance and Sec. Div. for Controller of the Navy, 1975–78; Head, Defence Secretariat Div. for Equipment Requirements, 1978–81; RCDS, 1982; Head, Finance and Sec. Div. (Air Launched Guided Weapons and Electronics), 1983–84; Asst Under-Sec. of State (Naval Personnel), 1985–89. Vice-Chm., Management Bd, Royal Hosp. Sch., Holbrook, 1985–89. Pres., London Manx Soc., 2001. *Recreations:* walking, travel, family history projects.

BRACKENBURY, (Frederick Edwin) John (Gedge), CBE 2000; Chairman: Pubmaster Group Ltd, since 1991; Active Media Capital Ltd, since 2000; *b* 9 Feb. 1936; *s* of Claude Russell Brackenbury and Florence Edna Brackenbury; *m* 1st, 1958, Pauline Hinchliffe (marr. diss. 1977); one *s* two *d*; 2nd, 1978, Desiree Sally Taylor; one *s. Educ:* Mercers Sch., London. Justerini & Brooks Ltd, 1954–62 (Dir, 1958–62); Man. Dir, City Cellars, 1962–65; Chm., Morgan Furze, 1965–67; Dir, IDV Ltd, 1967–72; Founder, Brackenbury consultancy co., 1972–75; Exec. Dir, G. & W. Walker, 1975–83 (Gp Operational Dir, Brent Walker, 1976–83); Man. Dir, All Weather Sports Activities Ltd, 1983–88; Exec. Dir, Brent Walker Gp Plc, 1988–96. Non-executive Director: Western Wines Ltd, 1997–; Aspen Gp Plc, 1997–99; Hotel and Catering Trng Co., 1998–; SFI Gp Plc, 1998–; Holsten (UK) Ltd, 2000–. Chairman: Business in Sport & Leisure, 1985–; Hospitality Trng Foundn, 1997–; Dir, Tourism & Hospitality Educn Trust, 1999–. *Recreations:* golf, tennis, viticulture. *Address:* 8 Moore Street, SW3 2QN. *Clubs:* Carlton, Hurlingham; Walton Heath Golf (Surrey).

BRACKENBURY, Air Vice-Marshal Ian, CB 2000; OBE 1987; CEng, FIMechE; Director, Rolls-Royce Defence (Europe), since 2001; *b* 28 Aug. 1945; *s* of Capt. D. E. Brackenbury and R. Brackenbury (*née* Grant). Directorate of Aircraft Engrg, 1975; Engrg Staff, Strike Comd, 1981; joined Dept for Supply and Orgn, 1986, Dir of Support Mgt, 1993; Dir of Support Mgt, HQ Logistics Comd, 1994; Dir, Helicopter Support, Chief of Fleet Support, 1995–97; Air Officer Engrg and Supply, Strike Comd, 1997–98; Dir Gen. Defence Logistics (Ops and Policy), MoD, 1998–2000. *Address:* PO Box 3, Felton, Bristol BS34 7QE. *Club:* Royal Air Force.

BRACKENBURY, John; *see* Brackenbury, F. E. J. G.

BRACKENBURY, Ven. Michael Palmer; Archdeacon of Lincoln, 1988–95, now Emeritus; *b* 6 July 1930; *s* of Frank Brackenbury and Constance Mary (*née* Palmer); *m* 1953, Jean Margaret, *d* of Oscar Arnold Harrison and May (*née* Norton). *Educ:* Norwich School; Lincoln Theological Coll. ACII 1956. RAF, 1948–50. Asst Curate, South Ormsby Group, 1966–69; Rector of Sudbrooke with Scothern, 1969–77; RD of Lawres, 1973–78; Diocesan Dir of Ordinands, Lincoln, 1977–87; Personal Assistant to Bishop of Lincoln, 1977–88; Canon and Prebendary of Lincoln, 1979–95; Diocesan Lay Ministry Adviser, Lincoln, 1986–87. Mem., Gen. Synod of C of E, 1989–95. Mem., Ecclesiastical Law Soc., 1988–. Chm. Lincs Award Bd, Prince's Trust, 1996–. *Recreations:* music, reading, travel. *Address:* 18 Lea View, Ryhall, Stamford, Lincs PE9 4HZ. *T:* (01780) 752415.

BRACKLEY, Rt Rev. Ian James; *see* Dorking, Suffragan Bishop of.

BRACKS, Hon. Stephen (Phillip); MLA (ALP) Williamstown, Victoria, since 1994; Premier of Victoria, and Minister for Multicultural Affairs, since 1999; *b* 15 Oct. 1954; *m* 1983, Terry Horsfall; two *s* one *d. Educ:* St Patrick's Coll., Ballarat; Ballarat Univ. (Dip. Business Studies, Grad. DipEd). Secondary commerce teacher, 1976–81; employment project worker and municipal recreation officer, 1981–85; Exec. Dir, Ballarat Educn Centre, 1985–89; Statewide Manager, Victoria's Employment Progs, 1989–93 (on secondment as Ministerial Advr to Premiers of Victoria, 1990); Principal Advr to Fed. Parly Sec. for Transport and Communications, 1993; Exec. Dir, Victorian Printing Industry Trng Bd, 1993–94. Government of Victoria: Shadow Minister for Employment, Industrial Relns and Tourism, 1994–96; Shadow Treas. and Shadow Minister for Finance and Industrial Relns, 1996–99; Dep. Chm., Public Accounts and Estimates Cttee, 1996–99; Shadow Treas. and Shadow Minister for Multicultural Affairs, March–Oct. 1999; Treas., 1999–2000. Leader, State Parly Labor Party, March–Oct. 1999. *Recreations:* camping, distance swimming, tennis, football supporter. *Address:* 1 Treasury Place, Melbourne, Vic 3002, Australia.

BRADBEER, Sir (John) Derek (Richardson), Kt 1988; OBE 1973; TD 1965; DL; Partner, Wilkinson Maughan (formerly Wilkinson Marshall Clayton & Gibson), 1961–97; President of the Law Society, 1987–88; *b* 29 Oct. 1931; *s* of late William Bertram Bradbeer and Winifred (*née* Richardson); *m* 1962, Margaret Elizabeth Chantler (DL Northumberland); one *s* one *d. Educ:* Canford Sch.; Sidney Sussex Coll., Cambridge (MA). Nat. Service, 2nd Lieut RA, 1951–52; TA, 1952–77: Lt-Col Comdg 101 (N) Med. Regt RA(V), 1970–73; Col, Dep. Comdr 21 and 23 Artillery Bdes, 1973–76; Hon. Col, 101 (N) Field Regt, RA(V), 1986–91. Admitted Solicitor, 1959. Member: Criminal

Injuries Compensation Bd, 1988–2000; Criminal Injuries Compensation Appeals Panel, 1996–. Member: Disciplinary Cttee, Inst. of Actuaries, 1989–96; Insurance Brokers Registration Council, 1992–96. Mem. Council, 1973–94, Vice-Pres., 1986–87, Law Soc.; Pres., Newcastle upon Tyne Incorp. Law Soc., 1982–83; Gov., Coll. of Law, 1983– (Chm., 1990–99). Director: Newcastle and Gateshead Water plc, 1978–; Sunderland and South Shields Water plc, 1990–; Dir and Chm., R. B. Bolton (Mining Engrs), 1990–; Chm., North East Water, 1992–; Dep. Chm., Northumbrian Water Gp, 1996–. UK Vice-Pres., Union Internationale des Avocats, 1988–92. Chm., N of England TA&VRA, 1990–96 (Vice-Chm., 1988–90). DL Tyne and Wear, 1988. *Recreations:* reading, gardening, sport. *Address:* Forge Cottage, Shilvington, Newcastle upon Tyne NE20 0AP. *T:* (01670) 775214. *Clubs:* Army and Navy; Northern Counties (Newcastle upon Tyne).

BRADBOURN, Philip Charles, OBE 1994; Member (C) West Midlands Region, European Parliament, since 1999; *b* 9 Aug. 1951; *s* of Horace and Elizabeth Bradbourn. *Educ:* Tipton Grammar Sch.; Worcester Coll. of Higher Educn; Wulfrun Coll. of Further Educn, Wolverhampton (DMA 1972). Local govt officer, 1967–87; Advr to Leader of Opposition, Wolverhampton BC, 1987–99. *Recreation:* gardening. *Address:* (office) Radclyffe House, 66–68 Hagley Road, Edgbaston, Birmingham B16 8PF. *T:* (0845) 606 0239.

BRADBURN, John; Chief Registrar of the High Court of Justice in Bankruptcy, 1984–88; Registrar of the Companies Court and Clerk of the Restrictive Practices Court, 1980–88; *b* 4 April 1915; *s* of Harold and Fanny Louise Bradburn; *m* 1948, Irène Elizabeth Norman, JP, *yr d* of Denham Grindley and Bertha Norman; two *s*. *Educ:* Repton; Trinity Coll., Oxford (MA). Served War, 1939–46; Oxfordshire and Bucks LI; Major. Called to the Bar, Inner Temple, 1939; practised at Chancery Bar, Lincoln's Inn, 1946–79 (Bencher, 1972–); a Conveyancing Counsel of the Supreme Court, 1977–80; Lord Chancellor's Legal Visitor, Ct of Protection, 1980–83. Mem., Gen. Council of the Bar, 1962–66. *Recreation:* freemasonry. *Address:* West Mews, 11 Calcot Court, Calcot Park, Reading, Berks RG31 7RW. *T:* (0118) 942 5418. *Club:* MCC.

BRADBURY, family name of **Baron Bradbury**.

BRADBURY, 3rd Baron *cr* 1925, of Winsford, Co. Chester; **John Bradbury;** *b* 17 March 1940; *s* of 2nd Baron Bradbury and of his 1st wife, Joan, *o d* of W. D. Knight; *S* father, 1994; *m* 1968, Susan, *d* of late W. Liddiard; two *s*. *Educ:* Gresham's Sch.; Univ. of Bristol. *Heir: s* Hon. John Timothy Bradbury, *b* 16 Jan. 1973. *Address:* 10 Clifton Hill, NW8 0QG.

BRADBURY, Anita Jean, (Mrs Philip Bradbury); *see* Pollack, A. J.

BRADBURY, Anthony Vincent; His Honour Judge Bradbury; a Circuit Judge, since 1992; *b* 29 Sept. 1941; *s* of late Alfred Charles Bradbury, OBE and Noreen Vincent Bradbury; *m* 1966, Rosalie Anne Buttrey; one *d*. *Educ:* Kent College, Canterbury; Univ. of Birmingham (Sir Henry Barber Law Scholar; LLB). Solicitor 1965; Principal, Bradbury & Co., 1970–81; Registrar, then Dist Judge, Ilford County Court, 1981–91; a Recorder of the Crown Court, 1990. Wandsworth Mem., GLC and ILEA, 1967–70. Contested (C): N Battersea, 1970; S Battersea, Feb. 1974. *Publications:* contribs to Wisden Cricketers' Almanack and to cricketing periodicals. *Recreations:* walking, watching cricket, writing for pleasure. *Address:* Bow County Court, 96 Romford Road, E15 4EG. *Clubs:* MCC; Yorkshire CC; Cricket Writers'.

BRADBURY, Edgar; Managing Director, Skelmersdale Development Corporation, 1976–85; *b* 5 June 1927; *s* of Edgar Furniss Bradbury and Mary Bradbury; *m* 1954, Janet Mary Bouchier Lisle; two *s* one *d*. *Educ:* Grove Park Sch., Wrexham; The High Sch., Newcastle, Staffs; King's Coll., Durham Univ. LLB (Hons). Solicitor. Asst Solicitor: Scarborough BC, 1952–54; St Helens CBC, 1954–57; Dep. Town Clerk, Loughborough, 1957–59; Town Clerk and Clerk of the Peace, Deal, 1960–63; Legal Dir, Skelmersdale Develt Corp., 1963–76. Vice-Chm., W Lancs Health Authority, 1984–94 (Mem., 1982–94). *Recreations:* tennis, bridge.

BRADBURY, Surgeon Vice-Adm. Sir Eric (Blackburn), KBE 1971; CB 1968; FRCS 1972; Medical Director-General of the Navy, 1969–72; Chairman, Tunbridge Wells District Health Authority, 1981–84; *b* 2 March 1911; *s* of late A. B. Bradbury, Maze, Co. Antrim; *m* 1939, Elizabeth Constance Austin (*d* 1991); three *d*. *Educ:* Royal Belfast Academical Instn; Queen's Univ., Belfast; MB, BCh 1934; DMRD (London) 1949; Hon. LLD 1973. Joined RN (Medical Service), 1934; served at sea in HMS Barham, HMS Endeavour, HMS Cumberland, 1935–38 and in HMS Charybdis and HMHS Oxfordshire, 1941–45; served in RN Hospitals: Haslar, Chatham, Plymouth and Malta; Med. Officer-in-Charge, RN Hosp., Haslar, and Comd MO, Portsmouth, 1966–69. QHP 1966–72.

BRADBURY, Ray Douglas; author; *b* Waukegan, Ill, USA, 22 Aug. 1920; *s* of Leonard S. Bradbury and Esther Moberg; *m* 1947, Marguerite Susan McClure; four *d*. *Educ:* Los Angeles High Sch. First Science-Fiction stories, 1941–44; stories sold to Harpers', Mademoiselle, The New Yorker, etc., 1945–56. Stories selected for: Best American Short Stories, 1946, 1948, 1952, 1958; O. Henry Prize Stories, 1947, 1948; and for inclusion in numerous anthologies. *Screenplays:* Moby Dick, 1954; Icarus Montgolfier Wright, 1961; The Martian Chronicles, 1964; The Picasso Summer, 1968; The Halloween Tree, 1968; The Dreamers; And The Rock Cried Out. Benjamin Franklin Award for Best Story Published in an Amer. Magazine of General Circulation, 1954; 1000 dollar Grant from Inst. of Arts and Letters, 1954. *Publications: novels:* Dark Carnival, 1947; Fahrenheit 451, 1953 (filmed); (for children) Switch on the Night, 1955; Dandelion Wine, 1957; Something Wicked This Way Comes, 1962 (filmed 1983; adapted for stage, 1986); The Small Assassin, 1973; Mars and the Minds of Man, 1973; The Mummies of Guanajuato, 1978; The Ghosts of Forever, 1981; Death is a Lonely Business, 1986; The Toynbee Convector, 1989; A Graveyard for Lunatics, 1990; *short stories:* The Martian Chronicles, 1950 (English edn, The Silver Locusts, 1957); The Illustrated Man, 1951 (filmed with The Day It Rained Forever); The Golden Apples of the Sun, 1953; The October Country, 1955; A Medicine for Melancholy (English edn, The Day It Rained Forever), 1959; (for children) R Is For Rocket, 1962; (for children) S Is For Space, 1962; The Machineries of Joy, 1964; The Autumn People, 1965; The Vintage Bradbury, 1965; Tomorrow Midnight, 1966; Twice Twenty-Two, 1966; I Sing the Body Electric!, 1969; Long After Midnight, 1976; Quicker than the Eye, 1998; Driving Blind, 1998; *general:* Zen and the Art of Writing, 1973; *poems:* When Elephants Last in the Dooryard Bloomed, 1973; Where Robot Mice and Robot Men Run Round in Robot Towns, 1977; This Attic where the Meadow Greens, 1980; The Haunted Computer and the Android Pope, 1981; *plays:* The Meadow, 1947; The Anthem Sprinters (one-act), 1963; The World of Ray Bradbury (one-act), 1964; The Wonderful Ice Cream Suit and Other Plays (one-act), 1965; Any Friend of Nicholas Nickleby's is a Friend of Mine, 1968; Pillar of Fire, 1975. *Recreations:* oil painting, ceramics, collecting native masks. *Address:* 10265 Cheviot Drive, Los Angeles, CA 90064, USA.

BRADBURY, Rear-Adm. Thomas Henry, CB 1979; *b* 4 Dec. 1922; *s* of Thomas Henry Bradbury and Violet Buckingham; *m* 1st, 1945, Beryl Doreen Evans (marr. diss. 1979; she *d* 1985); one *s* one *d*; 2nd, 1979, Sarah Catherine, *d* of Harley Hillier and Mrs Susan Hillier. *Educ:* Christ's Hosp. CO HMS Jufair, 1960–62; Supply Officer, HMS Hermes, 1965–67; Sec. to Controller of Navy, MoD, 1967–70; CO HMS Terror, 1970–71; RCDS, 1972; Dir, Naval Admin. Planning, MoD, 1974–76; Flag Officer, Admiralty Interview Bd, 1977–79. Gp Personnel Dir, Inchcape Gp of Cos, 1979–86; Gp Personnel Exec., Davy Corp., 1987–91. Non-exec. Dir, Eastbourne HA, 1990–93. *Recreation:* gardening in Sussex and Andalucia. *Address:* Padgham Down, Dallington, Heathfield, E Sussex TN21 9NS. *T:* (01435) 830208.

BRADBY, Prof. David Henry, PhD; Professor of Drama and Theatre Studies, University of London, at Royal Holloway (formerly Royal Holloway and Bedford New College), since 1988; *b* 27 Feb. 1942; *s* of late Edward Lawrence Bradby; *m* 1965, Rachel Anderson, writer; three *s* one *d*. *Educ:* Rugby Sch.; Trinity College, Oxford (MA); PhD Glasgow; CertEd Bristol. Lectr, Glasgow Univ., 1966–70; University of Kent at Canterbury: Lectr, 1971; Sen. Lectr, 1979–85; Reader in French Theatre Studies, 1985–88; Prof. of Theatre Studies, Univ. of Caen, 1983–84. Dir, Orange Tree Theatre, Richmond, 1990–. FRSA. Chevalier des Arts et des Lettres (France), 1997. *Publications:* People's Theatre (with John McCormick), 1978; The Theatre of Roger Planchon, 1984; Modern French Drama 1940–1980, 1984, 2nd edn, as Modern French Drama 1940–1990, 1991; (with David Williams) Directors' Theatre, 1988; Le Théâtre Français Contemporain, 1990; The Theatre of Michael Vinaver, 1993; (with Annie Sparks) Mise en Scène: French theatre now, 1997. *Recreation:* forestry. *Address:* Department of Drama and Theatre Studies, Royal Holloway, University of London, Egham, Surrey TW20 0EX.

BRADDICK, Prof. Oliver John, PhD; Professor of Psychology and Head, Department of Experimental Psychology, Oxford University, since 2001; Fellow, Magdalen College, Oxford, since 2001; *b* 16 Nov. 1944; *s* of Henry John James Braddick and Edith Muriel Braddick; *m* 1979, Prof. Janette Atkinson; two *s* two *d*. *Educ:* Trinity Coll., Cambridge (MA; PhD 1968). Cambridge University: Lectr, 1969–86; Reader in Vision, 1986–93; Fellow, Trinity Coll., 1968–72; Prof. of Psychol., 1993–2001, Hd of Dept, 1998–2001, UCL. Associate, Brown Univ., USA, 1968–69. FMedSci 2001. Trustee, Assoc. for Res. in Vision and Ophthalmol., 1999–. *Publications:* numerous articles on vision and its develt in scientific jls and books. *Recreations:* family life, the arts. *Address:* Department of Experimental Psychology, University of Oxford, South Parks Road, Oxford OX1 3UD. *T:* (01865) 271444.

BRADEN, Hugh Reginald, CMG 1980; DL; Mayor of Worthing, 1991–92; *b* 30 Jan. 1923; *s* of late Reginald Henry Braden and Mabel Braden (*née* Selby); *m* 1946, Phyllis Grace Barnes; one *d*. *Educ:* Worthing High School for Boys; Brighton College of Technology. Joined War Office, 1939; served War, Royal Navy, 1942–45; Far East Land Forces, 1946–50; British Army of the Rhine, 1953–56; War Office and Min. of Defence, 1956–66; jssc 1967; British Embassy, Washington, 1968–70; Min. of Defence, 1971–80 (Asst Under Sec. of State, 1978–80). Dir, A. B. Jay, 1981–90. Borough Councillor, Worthing, 1983–95; Chm., Worthing Cons. Assoc., 1992–95. DL W Sussex, 1993. *Address:* Field House, Honeysuckle Lane, High Salvington, Worthing, West Sussex BN13 3BT. *T:* (01903) 260203.

BRADES, Susan Deborah F.; *see* Ferleger Brades.

BRADFIELD, John Richard Grenfell, CBE 1986; PhD; Senior Bursar, Trinity College, Cambridge, 1956–92; Founder, and Manager, Cambridge Science Park, 1970–92; *b* 20 May 1925; *s* of Horace and Ada Bradfield; *m* 1951, Jane Wood; one *s*. *Educ:* Trinity Coll., Cambridge (schol. 1942; MA, PhD). Research Fellow in Cell Biology, Trinity Coll., Cambridge, 1947; Commonwealth (Harkness) Fellow, Chicago, 1948; Jun. Bursar, Trinity Coll., Cambridge, 1951. Director: Cambridge Water Co., 1965–95; Cambridge Building Soc., 1968–95; Biotechnology Investments, 1989–; Anglian Water, 1989–93 (Bd Mem., 1975–89); 3i Bioscience Investment Trust, 2000–; Chm., Abbotstone Agricl Property Unit Trust, 1975–. Chairman: Addenbrooke's NHS Trust, 1993–96; Commn for the New Towns, 1995–98. Darwin College, Cambridge: proposed foundn, 1963; Hon. Fellow, 1973. Hon. LLD Cambridge, 1992. FRSA 1990. *Publications:* scientific papers on cell biology. *Recreations:* walking, arboretum-visiting. *Address:* Trinity College, Cambridge CB2 1TQ. *T:* (01223) 338400.

BRADFORD, 7th Earl of, *cr* 1815; **Richard Thomas Orlando Bridgeman;** Bt 1660; Baron Bradford, 1794; Viscount Newport, 1815; *b* 3 Oct. 1947; *s* of 6th Earl of Bradford, TD, and Mary Willoughby (*d* 1986), *er d* of Lt-Col T. H. Montgomery, DSO; *S* father, 1981; *m* 1979, Joanne Elizabeth, *d* of B. Miller; three *s* one *d*. *Educ:* Harrow; Trinity College, Cambridge. Owner of Porters English Restaurant of Covent Garden. *Publications:* (compiled) My Private Parts and the Stuffed Parrot, 1984; The Eccentric Cookbook, 1985; Stately Secrets, 1994. *Heir: s* Viscount Newport, *qv*. *Address:* Woodlands House, Weston-under-Lizard, Shifnal, Salop TF11 8PX. *T:* (office) (01952) 850566, *Fax:* (01952) 850697; *e-mail:* bradfordr@porters.uk.com.

BRADFORD, Bishop of, since 1992; **Rt Rev. David James Smith;** *b* 14 July 1935; *s* of Stanley James and Gwendolen Emie Smith; *m* 1961, Mary Hunter Moult; one *s* one *d*. *Educ:* Hertford Grammar School; King's College, London (AKC; FKC 1999). Assistant Curate: All Saints, Gosforth, 1959–62; St Francis, High Heaton, 1962–64; Long Benton, 1964–68; Vicar: Longhirst with Hebron, 1968–75; St Mary, Monkseaton, 1975–81; Felton, 1982–83; Archdeacon of Lindisfarne, 1981–87; Bishop Suffragan of Maidstone, 1987–92; Bishop to the Forces, 1990–92. DUniv Bradford, 2001. *Recreations:* fell walking, reading novels. *Address:* Bishopscroft, Ashwell Road, Bradford, West Yorkshire BD9 4AU. *T:* (01274) 545414, *Fax:* (01274) 544831; *e-mail:* bishbrad@nildram.co.uk.

BRADFORD, Dean of; *no new appointment at time of going to press.*

BRADFORD, Archdeacon of; *see* Wilkinson, Ven. G. A.

BRADFORD, Barbara Taylor; author; *b* Leeds, 10 May 1933; *d* of late Winston and Freda Taylor; *m* 1963, Robert Bradford. Jun. Reporter, 1949–51, Women's Editor, 1951–53, Yorkshire Evening Post; Fashion Editor, Woman's Own, 1953–54; columnist, London Evening News, 1955–57; Exec. Editor, London American, 1959–62; moved to USA, 1964; Editor, National Design Center Magazine, 1965–69; syndicated columnist, 1968–81. Hon. DLitt: Leeds, 1989; Bradford, 1995; Hon. DHL Teikyo Post, Conn, 1996. *Publications:* Complete Encyclopedia of Homemaking Ideas, 1968; A Garland of Children's Verse, 1968; How to be the Perfect Wife, 1969; Easy Steps to Successful Decorating, 1971; How to Solve Your Decorating Problems, 1976; Decorating Ideas for Casual Living, 1977; Making Space Grow, 1979; Luxury Designs for Apartment Living, 1981; *novels:* A Woman of Substance, 1979 (televised, 1985); Voice of the Heart, 1983; Hold the Dream, 1985 (televised, 1986); Act of Will, 1986; To Be the Best, 1988; The Women in His Life, 1990; Remember, 1991; Angel, 1993; Everything to Gain, 1994; Dangerous to Know, 1995; Love in Another Town, 1995; Her Own Rules, 1996; A

Secret Affair, 1996; Power of a Woman, 1997; A Sudden Change of Heart, 1999; Where You Belong, 2000; The Triumph of Katie Byrne, 2001. *Address:* Bradford Enterprises, 450 Park Avenue, New York, NY 10022–2605, USA. *T:* (212) 308 7390, *Fax:* (212) 935 1636.

BRADFORD, (Sir) Edward Alexander Slade, 5th Bt, *cr* 1902 (but does not use the title); *b* 18 June 1952; *s* of Major Sir Edward Montagu Andrew Bradford, 3rd Bt (*d* 1952) and of his 2nd wife, Marjorie Edith (*née* Bere); *S* half-brother, Sir John Ridley Evelyn Bradford, 4th Bt, 1954. *Heir: uncle* Donald Clifton Bradford [*b* 22 May 1914; *m* 1949, Constance Mary Morgan; two *d*].

BRADFORD, Prof. Eric Watts, MDS (Sheffield); DDSc (St Andrews); Professor of Dental Surgery, 1959–85, now Emeritus, and Pro-Vice-Chancellor, 1983–85, University of Bristol; *b* 4 Nov. 1919; *e s* of E. J. G. and C. M. Bradford; *m* 1946, Norah Mary Longmuir; two *s* three *d. Educ:* King Edward VII Sch., Sheffield; High Storrs Grammar Sch., Sheffield; Univ. of Sheffield (Robert Styring Scholar). LDS, Sheffield, 1943; BDS, Sheffield, 1944; MDS, Sheffield, 1950; DDSc St Andrews, 1954. Lieut, Army Dental Corps, Nov. 1944; Capt., Nov. 1945. Lectr, Univ. of Sheffield, 1947–52; Senior Lectr, Univ. of St Andrews, 1952–59; Dean, Faculty of Medicine, Bristol University, 1975–79. Mem., Gen. Dental Council, 1979–85. *Publications:* many papers on dental anatomy in British and other journals. *Address:* 9 Cedar Court, Glenavon Park, Sneyd Park, Bristol BS9 1RL. *T:* (0117) 968 1849.

BRADFORD, Hon. Max(well Robert); MP (Nat. Party), Rotorua, since 1996 (Tarawera, 1990–96); *b* 19 Jan. 1942; *s* of Robert and Ella Bradford; *m* 1st, 1967, Dr Janet Grieve (marr. diss. 1988); 2nd, 1991, Rosemary Young; two step *d. Educ:* Christchurch Boys' High Sch.; Univ. of Canterbury, NZ (MCom Hons). NZ Treasury, 1966–69, 1973–78; Economist, IMF, Washington, 1969–73; Dir of Advocacy, Employers' Fedn, 1978–85; Chief Exec., Bankers Assoc., 1985–87; Sec.-Gen., Nat. Party, 1987–89; Minister: for Enterprise and Commerce, 1996–99; of Defence, 1997–99; for Tertiary Educn, 1999. *Recreations:* sailing, music, reading, fishing, ski-ing. *Address:* Parliament House, Wellington, New Zealand; Lake Okareka, Rotorua, New Zealand. *T:* (4) 4719577; *e-mail:* max.bradford@parliament.govt.nz. *Club:* Wellington.

BRADING, Prof. David Anthony, PhD, LittD; FBA 1995; Professor of Mexican History, University of Cambridge, since 1999; Fellow of Clare Hall, Cambridge, since 1995; *b* 26 Aug. 1936; *s* of Ernest Arthur Brading and Amy Mary (*née* Driscoll); *m* 1966, Celia Wu; one *s. Educ:* Pembroke Coll., Cambridge (BA; LittD 1991); UCL (PhD 1965). Asst. Prof., Univ. of Calif, Berkeley, 1965–71; Associate Prof., Yale Univ., 1971–73; Cambridge University: Lectr, 1973–92; Reader in Latin American Hist., 1992–99. Hon. Prof., Univ. of Lima, 1993. *Publications:* Miners and Merchants in Bourbon Mexico, 1971; Haciendas and Ranchos in the Mexican Bajío, 1979; The Origins of Mexican Nationalism, 1985; The First America, 1991; Church and State in Bourbon Mexico, 1994; Mexican Phoenix, 2001. *Recreations:* music, walking. *Address:* 28 Storey's Way, Cambridge CB3 0DT. *T:* (01223) 352098. *Club:* Oxford and Cambridge.

BRADLEY, Andrew; *see* Bradley, J. A.

BRADLEY, Anna Louise; Director, National Consumer Council, since 1999; *b* 29 July 1957; *d* of Donald Bradley and Angela Lucy Bradley (*née* Bradley, now Ratcliffe); *m* 1995, Norman Howard Jones; one *s* one *d. Educ:* Camden Sch. for Girls; Warwick Univ. (BA Phil, 1978; MBA 1994). Sen. Sub-Editor, Marshall Cavendish Partworks Ltd, 1978–82; Consumers' Association: Sen. Project Leader, 1982–87; Project Manager, Food and Health, 1987–88; Head, Food and Health, 1988–91; Dep. Research Dir, 1991–93; Exec. Dir and Co. Sec., Inst. for the Study of Drug Dependence Ltd, 1993–98. Jt Asst Sec., All Party Drugs Misuse Gp, 1994–98; Member: Adv. Council on the Misuse of Drugs, 1996–98; Agriculture, Envmt and Biotechnol. Commn, 2000–. Mem., Mgt Cttee, Patients' Assoc., 1985–88. *Publications:* Healthy Eating, 1989; (ed) Understanding Additives, 1988; acad. and research papers in Lancet, Jl Human Nutrition, Dietetics, etc. *Address:* 17 Beverley Road, Colchester CO3 3NG. *T:* (01206) 512741.

BRADLEY, Anne; *see* Smith, A.

BRADLEY, Anthony Wilfred; barrister and legal author; *b* 6 Feb. 1934; *s* of David and Olive Bradley (*née* Bonsey); *m* 1959, Kathleen Bryce; one *s* three *d. Educ:* Dover Grammar Sch.; Emmanuel Coll., Cambridge (BA 1957, LLB 1958, MA 1961). Solicitor of the Supreme Court, 1960 (Clifford's Inn Prize); called to the Bar, Inner Temple, 1989. Asst Lectr, 1960–64, Lectr, 1964–68, Cambridge, and Fellow of Trinity Hall, 1960–68; Prof. of Constitutional Law, 1968–89, Dean, Faculty of Law, 1979–82, Prof. Emeritus, 1990, Univ. of Edinburgh. Vis. Reader in Law, UC, Dar es Salaam, 1966–67; Vis. Prof. of Public Law, Univ. of Florence, 1984. Chairman: Edinburgh Council for Single Homeless, 1984–88; Social Security Appeal Tribunal, 1984–89; Member: Wolfenden Cttee on Voluntary Orgns, 1974–78; Social Scis and Law Cttee, SSRC, 1975–79; Social Studies Sub-Cttee, UGC, 1985–89; Cttee of Inquiry into Local Govt in Scotland, 1980; Cttee to review local govt in Islands of Scotland, 1983–84. Ed., Public Law, 1986–92. Hon. LLD: Staffordshire, 1993; Edinburgh, 1998. *Publications:* (with M. Adler) Justice, Discretion and Poverty, 1976; (with D. J. Christie) The Scotland Act 1978, 1979; (ed) Wade and Bradley, Constitutional and Administrative Law, 9th edn 1978 – 11th edn 1993, subseq. Bradley and Ewing, Constitutional and Administrative Law, 12th edn 1997; Administrative Law (in Stair Meml Encyc. of the Laws of Scotland), 1987, 2nd edn 2000; (with J. S. Bell) Governmental Liability, 1991; (jtly) European Human Rights Law: text and materials, 1995, 2nd edn 2000; articles in legal jls. *Recreation:* music. *Address:* Cloisters, 1 Pump Court, Temple, EC4Y 7AA. *T:* (020) 7827 4000; Morland, Sheepstead, near Marcham, Abingdon, Oxon OX13 6QG. *T:* (01865) 390774.

BRADLEY, Averil Olive, (Mrs J. W. P. Bradley); *see* Mansfield, A. O.

BRADLEY, Prof. Benjamin Arthur de Burgh, PhD; FRCP, FRCPath; Director, University of Bristol Department of Transplantation Sciences, since 1992; *b* 17 Sept. 1942; *s* of Reuben Stephen Bradley and Elsie Marjorie Bradley (*née* Burke); *m* 1968, Anne White; four *d. Educ:* Silcoates Sch., Wakefield; Bilston Grammar Sch.; Birmingham Univ. Med. Sch. (MB ChB 1965); Birmingham Univ. (MSc 1967; PhD 1970). FRCPath 1986 (MRCPath 1974); FRCP 1999. House surgeon and house physician, United Birmingham Hosps, 1965–66; MRC Res. Fellow, Dept of Surgery and Exptl Pathology, Univ. of Birmingham, 1967–70; Asst Dir of Res., Dept of Surgery, Univ. of Cambridge, 1970–75; Asst Prof., Dept of Immunhaematology, Univ. of Leiden, 1975–79; Dir, UK Transplant Service, 1979–92. Member: Scientific Policy Adv. Cttee, Nat. Inst. for Biol Standards, 1991–96; Bd, Jenner Educnl Trust, 1992–; Scientific Cttee, Foundn for Nephrology, 1992–. President: Eur. Foundn for Immunogenetics, 1988–89; British Soc. for Histocompatibility and Immunogenetics, 1996–98. Chm., Editl Bd, European Jl Immunogenetics, 1989–. Hon. MA Cantab, 1974. *Publications:* (with S. M. Gore) Renal Transplantation: sense and sensitization, 1986; Editor and contributor to annual reports of: UK Transplant Service, 1979–90; Transplantation Services and Statistics in UK and Eire, 1991; contrib. textbooks and med. jls on clinical organ and tissue transplantation and immunology and genetics of transplantation. *Recreation:* competitive sailing. *Address:* East Barn, The Pound, Lower Almondsbury, Bristol BS12 4EF; University of Bristol Department of Transplantation Sciences, Southmead Health Services, Westbury-on-Trym, Bristol BS10 5NB. *T:* (0117) 959 5340, *Fax:* (0117) 950 6277. *Club:* Royal Society of Medicine.

BRADLEY, Dr (Charles) Clive; Consultant, Sharp Laboratories of Europe Ltd, since 1999 (Managing Director, 1990–99); *b* 11 April 1937; *s* of late Charles William Bradley and Winifred Smith; *m* 1965, Vivien Audrey Godley; one *s* one *d. Educ:* Longton High Sch.; Birmingham Univ. (BSc Hons in Physics, 1958); Emmanuel Coll., Cambridge (PhD 1962). FInstP 1997. Nat. Phys. Lab., 1961–67; MIT, USA, 1967, 1969; Nat. Bureau of Standards, USA, 1968; Nat. Phys. Lab., 1969–75; DoI, 1975–82, SPSO and Head of Energy Unit, 1978–82; Counsellor (Science and Technology), British Embassy, Tokyo, 1982–88; DCSO and Head of Secretariat, ACOST, Cabinet Office, 1988–90. Vis. Prof., Univ. of Oxford, 1999–. Dep. Comr Gen. for Britain, Sci. Expo Tokyo, 1985. Mem., Oxford Univ. Adv. Council on Continuing Educn, 1993–. A. F. Bulgin Prize, IERE, 1972. *Publications:* High Pressure Methods in Solid State Research, 1969; contribs to jls on lasers, metals and semiconductors. *Recreations:* tennis, gardening. *Address:* 8 Montrose Gardens, Oxshott, Surrey KT22 0UU. *Club:* Athenæum.

BRADLEY, (Charles) Stuart, CBE 1990; Managing Director, Associated British Ports, 1988–95; Director, Associated British Ports Holdings, since 1988; *b* 11 Jan. 1936; *s* of Captain Charles Bradley, OBE and Amelia Jane Bradley; *m* 1959, Kathleen Marina (*née* Loraine); one *s* one *d* (and one *s* decd). *Educ:* Penarth County Sch.; University Coll. Southampton (Warsash). Master Mariner, 1961; FCIT 1978. Deck Officer, P&OSN Co., 1952–64; joined British Transport Docks Bd, subseq. Associated British Ports, 1964; Dock and Harbour Master, Silloth, 1968–70; Dock Master, 1970–74, Dock and Marine Superintendent, 1974–76, Plymouth; Docks Manager, Lowestoft, 1976–78; Port Manager, Barry, 1978–80; Dep. Port Manager, 1980–85, Port Manager, 1985–87, Hull; Asst Man. Dir (Resources), 1987–88; Chm., Red Funnel Gp, 1989–2000. Younger Brother, Trinity House, 1994–. *Recreations:* Welsh Rugby football, cycling, walking, theatre. *Address:* c/o 150 Holborn, EC1N 2LR. *T:* (020) 7430 1177. *Clubs:* Oriental, Honourable Company of Master Mariners; Cardiff Athletic.

BRADLEY, Clive; *see* Bradley, Charles C.

BRADLEY, Clive, CBE 1996; Chief Executive, The Publishers Association, 1976–97; Convenor, Confederation of Information Communication Industries, since 1984; *b* 25 July 1934; *s* of late Alfred and Kathleen Bradley. *Educ:* Felsted Sch., Essex; Clare Coll., Cambridge (Scholar; MA); Yale Univ. (Mellon Fellow). Called to the Bar, Middle Temple. Current Affairs Producer, BBC, 1961–63; Broadcasting Officer, Labour Party, 1963–64; Political Editor, The Statist, 1965–67; Gp Labour Adviser, IPC, 1967–69; Dep. Gen. Man., Daily and Sunday Mirror, 1969–71; Controller of Admin, IPC Newspapers, 1971–72; i/c IPC local radio applications, 1972–73; Dir i/c new prodn arrangements, The Observer, 1973–75. Dep. Chairman: Central London Valuation Tribunal; Member: Gen. Assembly, Organising Cttee, World Congress on Books, London, 1982; PA delegns to USSR, China, Australia/NZ, Southern Africa and Canada; IPA Congresses, Stockholm, 1980, Mexico City, 1984, London (also organiser), 1988, New Delhi, 1992, Barcelona, 1996; DTI Inf. Age Partnership, 1997–; DCMS Creative Industries Export Promotion Adv. Gp, 1998–. Trustee: Age Concern, Richmond, 1998– (Chm., 2001–); Cambrian Centre, Richmond, 2000–. Governor, Felsted Sch. Contested (Lab) S Kensington, by-election, March 1968. *Publications:* Which Way?, 1970; (ed) The Future of the Book, 1982; articles on politics, economics, the press, television, industrial relations. *Recreations:* reading, travel. *Address:* 8 Northumberland Place, Richmond, Surrey TW10 6TS. *T:* (020) 8940 7172; *e-mail:* Clive_Bradley@cici.demon.co.uk. *Clubs:* Reform, Groucho; Elizabethan (Yale).

BRADLEY, Prof. Daniel Joseph, PhD; FRS 1976; FInstP; Professor of Optical Electronics, Trinity College Dublin, since 1980; Emeritus Professor of Optics, London University, 1980; *b* 18 Jan. 1928; *s* of late John Columba Bradley and Margaret Mary Bradley; *m* 1958, Winefride Marie Therese O'Connor; four *s* one *d. Educ:* St Columb's Coll., Derry; St Mary's Trng Coll., Belfast; Birkbeck and Royal Holloway Colls, London (BSc Maths, BSc Physics, PhD). Primary Sch. Teacher, Derry, 1947–53; Secondary Sch. Teacher, London area, 1953–57; Asst Lectr, Royal Holloway Coll., 1957–60; Lectr, Imperial Coll. of Science and Technol., 1960–64; Reader, Royal Holloway Coll., 1964–66; Prof. and Head of Dept of Pure and Applied Physics, QUB, 1966–73; Prof. of Optics, 1973–80, and Head of Physics Dept, 1976–80, Imperial Coll., London. Vis. Scientist, MIT, 1965; Consultant, Harvard Observatory, 1966. Lectures: Scott, Cambridge, 1977; Tolansky Meml, RSA, 1977. Chairman: Laser Facility Cttee, SRC, 1976–79; British Nat. Cttee for Physics, 1979–80; Quantum Electronics Commn, IUPAP, 1982–85; Member: Rutherford Lab. Estab. Cttee, SRC, 1977–79; Science Bd, SRC, 1977–80; Council, Royal Soc., 1979–80. Gov., Sch. of Cosmic Physics, DIAS, 1981–95. MRIA 1969; Fellow, Optical Soc. of America, 1975. Hon. DSc: NUU, 1983; QUB, 1986. Thomas Young Medal, Inst. of Physics, 1975; Royal Medal, Royal Soc., 1983; C. H. Townes Award, Optical Soc. of America, 1989. *Publications:* papers on optics, lasers, spectroscopy, chronoscopy and astronomy in Proc. Roy. Soc., Phil. Mag., Phys. Rev., J. Opt. Soc. Amer., Proc. IEEE, Chem. Phys. Letts, Optics Communications. *Recreations:* television, walking, DIY. *Address:* Trinity College, Dublin 2, Ireland. *T:* (1) 6772941.

See also D. D. C. Bradley.

BRADLEY, Prof. David John, DM; FRCP; FRCPath; FFPHM; FIBiol; Director, Ross Institute, London School of Hygiene and Tropical Medicine, since 1974; Professor of Tropical Hygiene, University of London, 1974–2000, now Ross Professor Emeritus of Tropical Public Health; *b* 12 Jan. 1937; *s* of late Harold Robert and of Mona Bradley; *m* 1961, Lorne Marie, *d* of late Major L. G. Farquhar and Marie Farquhar; two *s* two *d. Educ:* Wyggeston Sch., Leicester; Selwyn Coll., Cambridge (Scholar); University Coll. Hosp. Med. Sch. (Atchison Schol., Magrath Schol., Trotter Medal in Surgery, Liston Gold Medal in Surgery, BA Nat. Scis Tripos, Med. Scis and Zoology, 1st cl. Hons, Frank Smart Prize Zool.; MB, BChir, MA 1960); DM Oxon 1972. FIBiol 1974, FFPHM (FFCM 1979); FRCPath 1981; FRCP 1985. Med. Res. Officer, Ross Inst. Bilharzia Res. Unit, Tanzania, 1961–64; Lectr, 1964–66, Sen. Lectr, 1966–69, Makerere Univ. of East Africa, Uganda; Trop. Res. Fellow of Royal Soc., Sir William Dunn Sch. of Pathology, Oxford, 1969–73; Sen. Res. Fellow, Staines Med. Fellow, Exeter Coll., Oxford, 1971–74; Clinical Reader in Path., Oxford Clinical Med. Sch., 1973–74; Chm., Div. of Communicable and Tropical Diseases, LSHTM, 1982–88. Vis. Prof., Univ. of Wales Coll. of Medicine, 1994–. Co-Director, Malaria Ref. Lab., PHLS, 1974–; Hon. Consultant in Public Health Medicine, PHLS and Kensington, Chelsea and Westminster, 1974–; Hon. Consultant in Trop. and Communicable Diseases, Bloomsbury DHA, 1983–; Dir, WHO Collaborating Centre Envtl Control of Vectors, 1983–; Mem., Bd of Trustees, Internat. Centre for Diarrhoeal Disease Res., Bangladesh, 1979–85 (Chm., 1982–83); Consultant Advisor to

Dir, Royal Tropical Inst., Amsterdam, 1980–90; Advr, Indep. Internat. Commn on Health Res.; Res. Advr to Dean, LSHTM, 1989–; Member: WHO Expert Adv. Panel on Parasitic Diseases, 1972–; Tech. Adv. Gp, Diarrhoea Programme, 1979–85; Panel of Experts on Envtl Management, 1981–; External Review Gp on Trop. Diseases Programme, 1987; Task Force on Health Res. for Develt, 1991–93; Chm., Rev. Cttee, Swiss Tropical Inst., 1994–. Pres., RSTM&H, 1999–2001. FMedSci 1999; For. Corresp. Mem., Royal Belgian Acad. of Medicine, 1984; Corresp. Mem., German Tropenmediziningesellschaft, 1980; Hon. FIWEM (Hon. FIPHE, 1981). Editor, Jl of Trop. Med. and Hygiene, 1981–; Founding Ed., Tropical Medicine and Internat. Health. Chalmers Medal, 1980, Macdonald Medal, 1996, RSTM&H. *Publications:* (with G. F. and A. U. White) Drawers of Water, 1972; (with E. E. Sabben-Clare and B. Kirkwood) Health in Tropical Africa during the Colonial Period, 1980; (with R. G. Feachem, D. D. Mara and H. Garelick) Sanitation and Disease, 1983; (jtly) Travel Medicine, 1989; (jtly) The Impact of Development Policies on Health, 1990; (jtly) The Malaria Challenge, 1999; papers in learned jls. *Recreations:* natural history, landscape gardens, travel. *Address:* Ross Institute, London School of Hygiene and Tropical Medicine, Keppel Street, WC1E 7HT. *T:* (020) 7927 2216; Flat 3, 1 Taviton Street, WC1H 0BT. *T:* (020) 7383 0228.

BRADLEY, David Rice; Director of Development, King's College School, Wimbledon, since 2000; *b* 9 Jan. 1938; *s* of George Leonard Bradley and Evelyn Annie Bradley; *m* 1962, Josephine Elizabeth Turnbull Fricker (*née* Harries); two *s*. *Educ:* Christ Coll., Brecon; St Catharine's Coll., Cambridge (Exhibnr; MA English); Edinburgh Univ. (Dip. in Applied Linguistics). Nat. service commn, S Wales Borderers. British Council: served: Dacca, 1962–65; Allahabad, 1966–69; New Delhi, 1969–70; Dir of Studies, British Inst., Madrid, 1970–73; Department of the Environment: Principal, Res. Admin, 1973–76; Planning, Develt Control, 1976–78; Inner Cities, 1978–79; Rayner Study (develt of Management Inf. System for Ministers), 1979–80; Central Policy Planning Unit, 1980–81; Study of Local Govt Finance (Grade 5), 1981–82; on special leave, Gwilym Gibbon Res. Fellow, Nuffield Coll., Oxford, 1982–83; Finance, Envmtl Servs, 1983–86; London Urban Develt, sponsorship of LDDC, 1986–88; Dir (G3), Merseyside Task Force, DoE, 1988–90; Chief Exec., London Borough of Havering, 1990–95; Man. Consultant, CSC Computer Scis Ltd, 1995–96; Head, Corporate Funding, Univ. of Oxford, 1997–2000. Vis. Fellow, Nuffield Coll., Oxford, 1993–2001. Mem., DoE Adv. Panel on appointments to Sponsored Bodies, 1996–98; non-exec. Dir, E Thames Housing Gp, 1997–98. Mem. Council, Sch. of Mgt Studies, Oxford Univ., 1995–98. Hon. Sec., London Planning and Develt Forum, 1990–. *Recreation:* gardening. *Address:* 7 Paget Place, Warren Road, Kingston upon Thames, Surrey KT2 7HZ. *T:* (020) 8549 4929.

BRADLEY, Prof. Denise Irene, AO 1995; Vice Chancellor and President, University of South Australia, since 1997; *b* 23 March 1942; *d* of Richard Francis Haren and Lillian Irene (*née* Ward); *m* 1st, 1962, Michael James Bradley (marr. diss. 1985); four *s*; 2nd, 1987, Bruce Simpson King. *Educ:* Sydney Univ. (BA); Adelaide Univ. (DipEd 1964); Univ. of NSW (DipLib 1973); Flinders Univ. (MSocAdmin 1986). Women's Advr, Dept of Educn, S Australia, 1977–80; South Australia College of Advanced Education: Dean, Faculty of Educn and Humanities, 1983–86; Dir (Academic), 1986–88; Dep. Principal, 1988–90; Principal, 1990; University of South Australia: Dep. Vice Chancellor, 1991–92; Dep. Vice Chancellor (Academic), 1992–95; Dep. Vice Chancellor and Vice Pres., 1995–96. *Recreation:* reading. *Address:* University of South Australia, GPO Box 2471, Adelaide, SA 5001, Australia.

BRADLEY, Prof. Donal Donat Conor, PhD; CPhys; Professor of Experimental Solid State Physics, since 2000 and Deputy Director, Centre for Electronic Materials and Devices, since 2001, Imperial College, University of London; *b* 3 Jan. 1962; *s* of Daniel Joseph Bradley, *qv*; *m* 1989, Beverley Diane Hirst; one *s* two *d*. *Educ:* Wimbledon Coll., London; Imperial Coll., Univ of London (BSc 1st Cl. Hons 1983; ARCS); Cavendish Lab., Univ. of Cambridge (PhD 1987). Unilever Res. Fellow in Chem. Physics, Corpus Christi Coll., Cambridge, 1987–89; Toshiba Res. Fellow, Toshiba R&D Center, Kawasaki, Japan, 1987–88; Asst Lectr in Physics, Univ. of Cambridge, 1989–93; Churchill College, Cambridge: Lectr and Fellow, 1989–93; Dir of Studies, 1992–93; Tutor, 1992–93; University of Sheffield: Reader in Physics, 1993–95; Warden, Tapton Hall, 1994–99; Prof. of Physics, 1995–2000; Dir, Centre for Molecular Materials, 1995–2000; Royal Soc. Amersham Internat. Sen. Res. Fellow, 1996–97; Leverhulme Trust Res. Fellow, 1997–98. Member: SERC/EPSRC Laser Facility Cttee Panel, 1991–95; EPSRC Functional Materials Coll., 1995–. MInstP 1990; Member: European Physical Soc., 1993; European Optical Soc., 1994; Optical Soc. Amer., 1994; APS, 1995; European Materials Res. Soc., 1995. Ed., Organic Electronics, 2000–. Co-inventor, conjugated polymer electroluminescence; co-founder, Cambridge Display Technol. Ltd. FRSA 1983. RSA Silver Medal, Outstanding Grad., RCS, 1983; Daiwa Award for Anglo-Japanese Collaboration, 1994. *Publications:* numerous papers in learned jls and 15 patents on polymer optoelectronics. *Recreations:* DIY, cinema, music, military history. *Address:* Blackett Laboratory, Imperial College, Prince Consort Road, SW7 2BZ; *e-mail:* don@bradleyhome.net.

BRADLEY, Prof. Donald Charlton, CChem, FRSC; FRS 1980; Professor of Inorganic Chemistry, 1965–87, and Head of Chemistry Department, 1978–82, Fellow, 1988, Queen Mary College, University of London; Emeritus Professor, University of London, since 1988; *b* 7 Nov. 1924; *m* 1st, 1948, Constance Joy Hazeldean (*d* 1985); one *s*; 2nd, 1990, Ann Levy (*née* MacDonald). *Educ:* Hove County School for Boys; Birkbeck Coll., Univ. of London (BSc 1st Cl. Hons Chemistry, PhD, DSc). Research Asst, British Electrical and Allied Industries Research Assoc., 1941–47; Asst Lectr in Chemistry, 1949–52, Lectr in Chemistry, 1952–59, Birkbeck Coll.; Prof. of Chemistry, Univ. of Western Ontario, Canada, 1959–64. Univ. of London: Chm., Bd of Studies in Chemistry and Chemical Industries, 1977–79; Mem. Senate, 1981–87. MRI 1979 (Mem. Council, 1987–93; Hon. Sec., 1988–93); Royal Society of Chemistry: Pres. Dalton Div., 1983–85; Ludwig Mond Medal and Lectr, 1987. Exec. Editor, Polyhedron, 1982–97. Gov., Haberdashers' Aske's Schs, Elstree, 1973–95. Freeman: Haberdashers' Co., 1995; City of London, 1996. Member: Samuel Pepys Club, 1995–; Aldersgate Ward Club, 1996–. FRSA 1982. Royal Medal, Royal Soc., 1998. *Publications:* (jtly) Metal Alkoxides, 1978; Alkoxo and Anyloxo Derivatives of Metals, 2001; numerous pubns on synthesis and structure of metallo-organic compounds, co-ordination chemistry and inorganic polymers, mainly in Jl of Chemical Soc. *Recreations:* travelling, listening to music, amateur interest in archaeology. *Address:* Department of Chemistry, Queen Mary, University of London, Mile End Road, E1 4NS. *T:* (020) 7975 5025.

BRADLEY, Edgar Leonard, OBE 1979; Metropolitan Stipendiary Magistrate, 1967–83; *b* 17 Nov. 1917; 2nd *s* of Ernest Henry and Letitia Bradley, W Felton, Oswestry; *m* 1942, Elsa, *o d* of Colin and Elizabeth Matheson, Edinburgh; two *s* three *d*. *Educ:* Malvern Coll.; Trinity Hall, Cambridge. BA 1939; MA 1944. Called to Bar, Middle Temple, 1940. Served 1940–46, RA; Capt. and Adjt, 1943–45; Major, GSO2, Mil. Govt of Germany, 1946. Practised at Bar, 1946–51, SE Circuit, Central Criminal Ct, S London and Surrey Sessions. Legal Dept of Home Office, 1951–54. Sec., Departmental Cttee on Magistrates' Courts Bill, 1952; Sec. of Magistrates' Courts Rule Cttee, 1952–54; Clerk to Justices: Wrexham and Bromfield, 1954–57; Poole, 1957–67. Justices' Clerks Society: Mem. Council, 1957–67; Hon. Sec., 1963–67. Mem., Nat. Adv. Council on Trng of Magistrates, 1965–67; Magistrates' Association: Vice Pres., 1984–; Mem. Council, 1968–84; Chm. Legal Cttee, 1973–82. Adv. tour of Magistrates' Courts in Ghana, 1970. *Publications:* (with J. J. Senior) Bail in Magistrates' Courts, 1977; articles in legal jls. *Recreations:* golf, music. *Address:* 55 St Germains, Bearsden, Glasgow G61 2RS. *T:* (0141) 942 5831. *Clubs:* Army and Navy; Buchanan Castle Golf (Glasgow).

BRADLEY, Prof. (John) Andrew, PhD; FRCSGlas; Professor of Surgery, University of Cambridge, since 1997; Hon. Consultant Surgeon, Addenbrooke's Hospital, Cambridge, since 1997; *b* 24 Oct. 1950; *s* of Colin Bradley and Christine Bradley (*née* Johnstone Miller); *m* 1987, Eleanor Mary Bolton; two *s*. *Educ:* Salendine Nook Secondary Sch., Huddersfield; Huddersfield Coll. of Tech.; Univ. of Leeds (MB ChB 1975); Univ. of Glasgow (PhD 1982). FRCSGlas 1979. Lectr in Surgery, Glasgow Univ., 1978–84; Cons. Surgeon, Western Infirmary, Glasgow, 1984–94; Prof. of Surgery, Univ. of Glasgow, 1994–97; Hon. Cons. Surgeon, Western Infirmary, Glasgow, 1994–97. Pres., British Transplantation Soc., 1999–2002. Founder FMedSci 1998; FRCS *ad eundem* 1999. *Publications:* articles in sci. jls, mainly in the field of organ transplantation and immunology. *Recreations:* ski-ing, mountaineering. *Address:* University Department of Surgery, Box 202, Level 9, Addenbrooke's Hospital, Cambridge CB2 2QQ.

BRADLEY, Rt Hon. Keith (John Charles); PC 2001; MP (Lab) Manchester, Withington, since 1987; Minister of State, Home Office, since 2001; *b* 17 May 1950; *m*; two *s* one *d*. *Educ:* Manchester Polytechnic (BA Hons); York Univ. (MPhil). Former health service administrator, North West RHA. Mem., Manchester City Council, 1983–88. Opposition spokesman on social security, 1991–96, on transport, 1996–97; Parly Under-Sec. of State, DSS, 1997–98; Treasr of HM Household (Dep. Chief Whip), 1998–2001. Joined Labour Party, 1973; Mem., Manchester Withington Co-op Party. Member: MSF; UNISON. *Address:* House of Commons, SW1A 0AA. *T:* (020) 7219 5124; 56 Kingston Road, Didsbury, Manchester M20 2SB. *T:* (constituency office) (0161) 446 2047.

BRADLEY, Michael John, CMG 1990; QC (Cayman Islands) 1983; Constitutional Adviser, Overseas Territories Department, Foreign and Commonwealth Office, since 2001; Law Revision Commissioner for the Cayman Islands, since 1994; *b* 11 June 1933; *s* of late Joseph Bradley and Catherine Bradley (*née* Cleary); *m* 1965, Patricia Elizabeth Macauley, MBE; one *s*. *Educ:* St Malachy's Coll., Belfast; Queen's Univ., Belfast (LLB Hons). Solicitor, Law Soc. of NI, 1964; Attorney, Supreme Ct, Turks and Caicos Is, 1980; Barrister-at-law, Eastern Caribbean Supreme Ct, 1982. Solicitor, NI, 1964–67; State Counsel, Malawi, 1967–69; Volume Editor, Halsbury's Laws, 1970; Sen., later Chief, Parly Draftsman, Botswana, 1970–72; UN Legal Advr to Govt of Antigua, 1973–76; Reg. Legal Draftsman to Govts of E Caribbean, British Develt Div. in the Caribbean, FCO, 1976–82; Attorney General: British Virgin Is, 1977–78; Turks and Caicos Is, 1980; Montserrat, 1981; Cayman Is, 1982–87; Gov., Turks and Caicos Is, 1987–93. British Dependent Territories Law Reform and Law Revision Consultant, 1993. Pres., Cayman Gaelic FC, 2000–. *Recreations:* reading, philately, travel, good wine. *Address:* 11 The Lays, Goose Street, Beckington, Somerset BA3 6SS. *T:* and *Fax:* (01373) 831059; c/o Law Revision Commission, PO Box 907, George Town, Grand Cayman, Cayman Islands, West Indies. *T:* 9454731, *Fax:* 9455925. *Clubs:* Civil Service, Royal Over-Seas League.

BRADLEY, Peadar John; Member (SDLP) Down South, Northern Ireland Assembly, since 1998; *b* 28 April 1940; *s* of William T. Bradley and Annie E. Barry; *m* 1962, Leontia Martin; three *s* five *d*. *Educ:* St Colman's Coll., Newry, Co. Down. Mem., Irish Auctioneers and Valuers Inst., 1986. Salesman, 1958–65; Agricl Rep., 1965–78; Property Negotiator, 1978–81; self-employed Estate Agent, 1981–99. Mem., Newry and Mourne DC, 1981–. *Recreations:* Gaelic games, part-time farming, travel. *Address:* 10 Corrags Road, Newry, Co. Down BT34 2NJ. *T:* (028) 3026 2062; (office) (028) 4177 2228. *Club:* Naomh Mhuire, Cumann Luth Chleas Gael (Boireann).

BRADLEY, Peter Charles Stephen; MP (Lab) The Wrekin, since 1997; *b* 12 April 1953; *s* of Fred and Trudie Bradley; *m* Annie Hart; one *s* one *d* (twins). *Educ:* Abingdon Sch.; Univ. of Sussex (BA Hons 1975); Occidental Coll., LA. Res. Dir, Centre for Contemporary Studies, 1979–85; Dir, Good Relations Ltd, 1985–93; Man. Dir, Millbank Consultants Ltd, 1993–97. Mem. (Lab), Westminster CC, 1986–96 (Dep. Leader, Labour Gp, 1990–96). PPS to Minister of State for Rural Affairs, 2001–. Mem., Select Cttee on Public Admin, 1997–99; Chm., Rural Gp of Labour MPs, 1997–2001. *Recreations:* playing/watching cricket, supporting Aston Villa, walking and reading (both slowly), the pub. *Address:* House of Commons, SW1A 0AA; Wrekin Labour Party, 9A Queen Street, Wellington, Telford TF1 1EH. *Club:* Warwickshire County Cricket.

BRADLEY, Ven. Peter David Douglas; Archdeacon of Warrington, since 2001; Team Rector, Upholland, since 1994; *b* 4 June 1949; *m* 1970, Pat Dutton; three *s*. *Educ:* Brookfield Comp. Sch., Kirkby; Lincoln Theol Coll.; Ian Ramsey Coll., Brasted; Nottingham Univ. (BTh 1979). Ordained deacon, 1979, priest, 1980; Curate, Upholland Team, 1979–83; Vicar, Holy Spirit, Dovecot, Liverpool, 1983–94; Dir, Continuing Ministerial Educn, dio. Liverpool, 1989–2001. Mem., Gen. Synod of C of E, 1990–. Hon. Canon, Liverpool Cathedral, 2000. *Recreations:* walking, reading. *Address:* The Rectory, 1a College Road, Upholland, Skelmersdale WN8 0PY. *T:* (01695) 622936.

BRADLEY, Maj.-Gen. Peter Edward Moore, CB 1968; CBE 1964 (OBE 1955); DSO 1946; Trustee, Vindolanda Trust, 1982–85 (Secretary, 1975–82); *b* 12 Dec. 1914; *s* of late Col Edward de Winton Herbert Bradley, CBE, DSO, MC, DL; *m* Margaret, *d* of late Norman Wardhaugh of Haydon Bridge, Northumberland; three *s*. *Educ:* Marlborough; Royal Military Academy, Woolwich. 2nd Lieut, Royal Signals, 1934. Served War of 1939–45; India, Middle East, Italy and North West Europe (DSO 6th Airborne Div.). Lieut-Col 1954; Col 1957; Brig. 1962; Maj.-Gen. 1965; Signal Officer in Chief (Army), Ministry of Defence, 1965–67; Chief of Staff to C-in-C Allied Forces Northern Europe, Oslo, 1968–70, retired. Dunlop Ltd, 1970–75. Col Comdt, Royal Signals, 1967–82, Master of Signals, 1970–82; Col Gurkha Signals, 1967–74. CEng, FIEE, 1966; FIMgt (FBIM 1970). *Address:* c/o RHQ Royal Signals, Blandford Camp, Blandford Forum, DT11 8RH.

BRADLEY, Peter Richard; Chief Executive, London Ambulance Service NHS Trust, since 2000; *b* 28 Dec. 1957; *s* of John and Mary Bradley; *m* 1978, Mary Elisabeth Verhoeff; one *s* two *d*. *Educ:* Temple Moor Grammar Sch., Leeds; Otago Univ., NZ (MBA). With Commercial Bank of Australia, Auckland, 1973–76; St John Ambulance Service, Auckland, 1976–95; qualified paramedic, 1986; Chief Ambulance Officer, 1993–95; joined London Ambulance Service NHS Trust, 1996; Dir of Ops, 1998–2000. OStJ 1994 (SBStJ 1992). *Recreations:* reading, sport, music. *Address:* Edgware House, 63 High Street, Knaphill, Surrey GU21 2PX. *T:* (01483) 481179.

BRADLEY, Richard Alan; Headmaster, Rivers Country Day School, Massachusetts, USA, 1981–91, retired; *b* 6 Oct. 1925; *s* of late Reginald Livingstone Bradley, CBE, MC, and of Phyllis Mary Richardson; *m* 1971, Mary Ann Vicary; one *s* two *d* by previous marriage. *Educ:* Marlborough Coll.; Trinity Coll., Oxford (Scholar). 2nd cl. hons Mod. History. Royal Marines, 1944–46; Oxford, 1946–48; Club Manager, Oxford and Bermondsey Club, 1949. Asst Master: Dulwich Coll., 1949–50; Tonbridge Sch., 1950–66 (Head of History Dept, 1957–66; Housemaster of Ferox Hall, 1961–66); Warden of St Edward's Sch., Oxford, 1966–71; Headmaster, Ridley Coll., Canada, 1971–81. *Recreations:* games, dramatics, mountains. *Address:* 10 Carver Hill, South Natick, MA 01760, USA. *Club:* Vincent's (Oxford).

BRADLEY, Prof. Richard John, FSA, FSAScot; FBA 1995; Professor of Archaeology, Reading University, since 1987; *b* 18 Nov. 1946; *s* of John Newsum Bradley and Margaret Bradley (*née* Saul); *m* 1976, Katherine Bowden. *Educ:* Portsmouth Grammar Sch.; Magdalen Coll., Oxford (MA). MIFA. Lectr in Archaeology, 1971–84, Reader, 1984–87, Reading Univ. Mem., Royal Commn on Historical Monuments of England, 1987–99. *Publications:* (with A. Ellison) Rams Hill: a Bronze Age Defended Enclosure and its Landscape, 1975; The Prehistoric Settlement of Britain, 1978; (ed with J. Barrett) Settlement and Society in the British Later Bronze Age, 1980; The Social Foundations of Prehistoric Britain, 1984; (ed with J. Gardiner) Neolithic Studies, 1984; The Passage of Arms: an archæological analysis of prehistoric hoards and votive deposits, 1990, rev. edn 1998; (with J. Barrett and M. Green) Landscape, Monuments and Society, 1991; (ed with J. Barrett and M. Hall) Papers on the Prehistoric Archaeology of Cranborne Chase, 1991; Altering the Earth: the origins of monuments in Britain and Continental Europe, 1993; (with M. Edmonds) Interpreting the Axe Trade: production and exchange in Neolithic Britain, 1993; (jtly) Prehistoric Land Divisions on Salisbury Plain: the work of the Wessex Linear Ditches Project, 1994; Rock Art and the Prehistory of Atlantic Europe, 1997; The Significance of Monuments, 1998; An Archaeology of Natural Places, 2000; The Good Stones: a new investigation of the Clava Cairns, 2000; contribs to learned jls. *Recreations:* literature, twentieth century music, watercolours, secondhand bookshops. *Address:* Department of Archaeology, The University, Whiteknights, Reading RG6 6AA. *T:* (0118) 931 8130.

BRADLEY, Robin Alistair, CBE 2000; CEng; Chief Executive, Atomic Weapons Establishment, Aldermaston, 1997–2000; *b* 3 Aug. 1938; *s* of Cyril Robert Bradley and Phyllis Mary (*née* Stalham); *m* 1964, Marguerite Loftus; one *s* two *d*. MIMechE 1972; CEng 1972. MoD, 1962–65; Hunting Engrg, Ampthill, 1965–72; Manager, Defence Progs (Australia), Hunting Systems, S Australia, 1972–75; Chief Project Engr, Project Manager, then Divl Manager Engrg, Hunting Engrg, Ampthill, 1975–90; Ops Director, AWE/Hunting Brown Root/AEA, Aldermaston (originally on secondment), 1990–96. *Recreations:* athletics, climbing, gardening. *Address:* c/o Hunting plc, 3 Cockspur Street, SW1 5BQ.

BRADLEY, Roger Thubron, FICFor; FIWSc; Chairman: UK Forestry Accord, since 1996; Forth District Salmon Fishery Board, since 1998; *b* 5 July 1936; *s* of Ivor Lewis Bradley and Elizabeth Thubron; *m* 1959, Ailsa Mary Walkden; one *s* one *d*. *Educ:* Lancaster Royal Grammar Sch.; St Peter's Coll., Oxford (MA). FICFor 1980; FIWSc 1985. Asst District Officer, Kendal, 1960; Mensuration Officer, Alice Holt, 1961; Working Plans Officer, 1967; District Officer, North Argyll, 1970; Asst Conservator, South Wales, 1974; Conservator, North Wales, 1977; Forestry Commission: Dir, and Sen. Officer for Wales, 1982–83; Dir, Harvesting and Marketing, Edinburgh, 1983–85; Forestry Comr, 1985–95; Hd of Forestry Authy, 1992–95. Chm., Edinburgh Centre for Tropical Forestry, 1996–99. Chm., Commonwealth Forestry Assoc., 1988–90; Pres., Inst. of Chartered Foresters, 1996–98. *Publications:* Forest Management Tables, 1966, 2nd edn 1971; Forest Planning, 1967; Thinning Control in British Forestry, 1967, 2nd edn 1971; various articles in Forestry, etc. *Recreation:* sailing. *Club:* Royal Commonwealth Society.

BRADLEY, Stanley Walter; business consultant, since 1988; Director, W. Hart & Son (Saffron Walden) Ltd, since 1991; Director General, British Printing Industries Federation, 1983–88; *b* 9 Sept. 1927; *s* of Walter Bradley; *m* 1955, Jean Brewster; three *s* one *d*. *Educ:* Boys' British Sch., Saffron Walden. Joined Spicers Ltd, 1948: held posts in prodn, marketing and gen. management; Personnel Dir, 1973–83; Dir, Capital Spicers Ltd, Eire, 1971–83. Dir, Harman Gp, 1988–91. Chm., BPIF Manufg Stationery Industry Gp, 1977–81; Pres., E Anglian Printing Industries Alliance, 1978–79; Mem., Printing Industries Sector Working Party, 1979–87, Chm., Communications Action Team, 1980–85, NEDC. *Recreations:* painting, golf, fishing. *Address:* Dale House, Hogs Lane, Chrishall, Royston, Herts SG8 8RB. *T:* (01763) 838820.

BRADLEY, Stuart; *see* Bradley, C. S.

BRADLEY, Thomas George; Director, British Section, European League for Economic Co-operation, 1979–91; *b* 13 April 1926; *s* of George Henry Bradley, Kettering; *m* 1953, Joy, *d* of George Starmer, Kettering; two *s*. *Educ:* Kettering Central Sch., Northants. Elected to Northants County Council, 1952, County Alderman, 1961; Mem., Kettering Borough Council, 1957–61. Transport Salaried Staffs' Association: Branch Officer, 1946–58; Mem. Exec. Cttee, 1958–77; Treasurer, 1961–64; Pres., 1964–77; Acting Gen. Sec., 1976–77. MP Leicester NE, July 1962–1974, Leicester E, 1974–83 (Lab, 1962–81, SDP, 1981–83); PPS: to Minister of Aviation, 1964–65; to Home Secretary, 1966–67; to Chancellor of the Exchequer, 1967–70; Chm., Select Cttee on Transport, 1979–83. Vice-Chm., Labour Party, 1974–75, Chm., 1975–76; Mem., Labour Party NEC, 1966–81. Contested: (Lab) Rutland and Stamford, 1950, 1951 and 1955; (Lab) Preston S, 1959; (SDP) Leicester E, 1983. *Address:* The Orchard, 111 London Road, Kettering, Northants NN15 7PH. *T:* (01536) 513019.

BRADLEY, William Ewart; Special Commissioner of Income Tax, 1950–75; *b* 5 Sept. 1910; *s* of W. E. Bradley, Durham City; *m* 1949, Mary Campbell Tyre; two *s*. *Educ:* Johnston Sch., Durham; LSE, London Univ. Inland Revenue, 1929–50. *Address:* Abbeyfield House, 3 Kinburn Terrace, St Andrews, Fife KY16 9DU.

BRADLEY GOODMAN, Michael; *see* Goodman, M. B.

BRADMAN, Godfrey Michael, FCA; Chairman: European Land & Property Corporation plc, since 1992; European Land & Property Investments Co., since 1993; Pondbridge Europe Ltd, since 1994; *b* 9 Sept. 1936; *s* of William Bradman and Anne Bradman (*née* Goldsweig); *m* 1975, Susan Bennett; two *s* three *d*. FCA 1961. Sen. Partner, Godfrey Bradman and Co. (Chartered Accountants), 1961–69; Chm. and Chief Exec., London Mercantile Corp. (Bankers), 1969; Chm., Rosehaugh plc, 1979–91; Jt Chm., Victoria Quay Ltd, 1993–. Founder and Mem., CLEAR (Campaign for Lead-Free Air) Ltd, 1981–91; Jt Founder, 1983, and Hon. Pres., Campaign for Freedom of Information, 1983–; Founder and Chm., Citizen Action and European Citizen Action, 1983–91 (Dir, AIDS Policy Unit, 1987–90); Chm., Friends of the Earth Trust, 1983–91; Council Mem., UN Internat. Year of Shelter for the Homeless, 1987; Pres., Soc. for the Protection of Unborn Children Educnl Res. Trust, 1987–; Founder and Jt Chm., Parents Against Tobacco Campaign; Founder, Opren Victims Campaign. Mem. governing body, LSHTM, 1988–91. Hon. Fellow, Downing Coll., Cambridge, 1997 (Wilkins Fellow, 1999). *Recreations:* his children, reading, riding. *Address:* 15 Hanover Terrace, NW1 4RJ. *T:* (020) 7706 0189.

BRADNEY, John Robert; HM Diplomatic Service, retired; *b* 24 July 1931; *s* of Rev. Samuel Bradney, Canon Emeritus of St Alban's Abbey, and Constance Bradney (*née* Partington); *m* 1st, Jean Marion Halls (marr. diss. 1971); one *s* two *d*; 2nd, 1974, Sandra Cherry Smith, JP, *d* of Richard Arthur Amyus Smith, MC. *Educ:* Christ's Hospital. HM Forces, 1949–51, Herts Regt and RWAFF; Colonial Police, Nigeria, 1953–65; HM Diplomatic Service, 1965–86: First Sec., Lagos, 1974; FCO, 1977–86 (Counsellor, 1985); Advr, Govt of Oman, 1986–89. DSM Oman, 1989. *Recreations:* salmon and trout fishing, gardening, ornithology. *Address:* Barclays Bank PLC, Penrith, Cumbria CA11 7YB. *Club:* Royal Over-Seas League.

BRADSHAW, family name of **Baron Bradshaw**.

BRADSHAW, Baron *cr* 1999 (Life Peer), of Wallingford in the county of Oxfordshire; **William Peter Bradshaw;** Senior Visiting Research Fellow, Centre for Socio-Legal Studies, Wolfson College, Oxford, 1985–2000; Supernumerary Fellow, Wolfson College, Oxford, since 1988; *b* 9 Sept. 1936; *s* of Leonard Charles Bradshaw and Ivy Doris Bradshaw; *m* 1957, Jill Hayward; one *s* one *d*. *Educ:* Univ. of Reading (BA Pol. Economy, 1957; MA 1960). FCIT 1987 (MCIT 1966). Joined Western Region of British Railways as Management Trainee, 1959; various appts, London and W of England Divs; Divl Manager, Liverpool, 1973; Chief Operating Man., LMR, 1976, Dep. Gen. Man. 1977; Chief Ops Man., BR HQ, 1978; Dir, Policy Unit, 1980; Gen. Man., Western Region, BR, 1983–85; Prof. of Transport Mgt, Univ. of Salford, 1986–92; Chm., Ulsterbus and Citybus Ltd, 1987–93. Member: Thames Valley Police Authority, 1997– (Vice Chm., 1999–); BRB, later Strategic Rail Authy, 1999–2001; Commn for Integrated Transport, 1999–2001; Chm., Bus Appeals Body, 1998–2000. Mem. (Lib Dem) Oxfordshire CC, 1993–. Special Advr to Transport Select Cttee, H of C, 1992–97. *Recreations:* growing hardy plants; playing member of a brass band. *Address:* House of Lords, SW1A 0PW. *Club:* National Liberal.

BRADSHAW, Prof. Anthony David, PhD; FRS 1982; Holbrook Gaskell Professor of Botany, University of Liverpool, 1968–88, now Emeritus; *b* 17 Jan. 1926; *m* Betty Margaret Bradshaw; three *d*. *Educ:* St Paul's Sch., Hammersmith; Jesus Coll., Cambridge (BA 1947; MA 1951); PhD Wales 1959. FIBiol 1971. Lectr, 1952–63, Sen. Lectr, 1963–64, Reader in Agricl Botany, 1964–68, UCNW, Bangor. Member: Nature Conservancy Council, 1969–78; Natural Environment Res. Council, 1969–74; Bd of Management, Sports Turf Res. Inst., 1976– (Vice Pres., 1982–). President: British Ecological Soc., 1981–83; Inst. Ecology and Envmtl Management, 1991–94. Trustee, Nat. Museums and Galls on Merseyside, 1986–96 (Vice Chm., 1995–). Hon. Fellow, Indian Nat. Acad. Sci., 1990. FLS 1982; FIEEM 1994 (MIEEM 1991). Hon. DSc: Lancaster, 1998, Hong Kong Baptist Univ., 2000. *Publications:* (ed jtly) Teaching Genetics, 1963; (with M. J. Chadwick) The Restoration of Land, 1980; (with others) Quarry Reclamation, 1982; (with others) Mine Wastes Reclamation, 1982; (with R. A. Dutton) Land Reclamation in Cities, 1982; (with Alison Burt) Transforming our Waste Land: the way forward, 1986; (ed jtly) Ecology and Design in Landscape, 1986; (ed jtly) The Treatment and Handling of Wastes, 1992; (with B. Hunt and T. J. Walmsley) Trees in the Urban Landscape, 1995; contribs to symposia and learned jls. *Recreations:* sailing, gardening, appreciating land. *Address:* 58 Knowsley Road, Liverpool L19 0PG.

BRADSHAW, Benjamin Peter James; MP (Lab) Exeter, since 1997; Parliamentary Under-Secretary of State, Foreign and Commonwealth Office, since 2001; *b* 30 Aug. 1960; *s* of Peter Bradshaw and Daphne Bradshaw (*née* Murphy); partner, Neal Thomas Dalgleish. *Educ:* Thorpe St Andrew Sch., Norwich; Univ. of Sussex (BA Hons). Reporter: Express and Echo, Exeter, 1984–85; Eastern Daily Press, Norwich, 1985–86; BBC Radio Devon, Exeter, 1986–89; BBC Radio Corresp., Berlin, 1989–91; reporter, World At One and World This Weekend, BBC Radio 4, 1991–97. Member: European Legislation Select Cttee, 1997–2001; Ecclesiastical Cttee, 1997–2001. Member: Christian Socialist Movement, 1997–; Lab. Campaign for Electoral Reform, 1997–. Mem., Inst. of Internat. and Foreign Affairs. Consumer Journalist of Year, Argos, 1988; Journalist of Year, Anglo-German Foundn, 1990; Sony News Reporter Award, 1993. *Recreations:* cycling, walking in Devon, classical music, cooking, gardening. *Address:* House of Commons, SW1A 1AA. *T:* (020) 7219 6597, (Constituency office) (01392) 424464. *Club:* Whipton Labour (Exeter).

BRADSHAW, Ian Cameron; Chief Executive, NHS Logistics Authority, since 2000; *b* 12 Sept. 1941; *s* of Kenneth Bradshaw and Margaret Bradshaw (*née* Pirie); *m* 1962, Margaret Gilmour Milligan. *Educ:* Coatbridge High Sch.; Burnbank Coll. of Engrg. MCIPS 1990; FILog 1997; FCIT 1999. Engrg Apprentice, NCB, 1956–62; Traffic Div., Strathclyde Police, 1962–69; gen. mgt trainee, subseq. Gen. Manager, 1969–76, Distribution Dir, 1976–79, Man. Dir, 1979–83, Glasgow Hiring Co. (Transport Develt Gp plc); Trent Regional Health Authority: Project Manager, 1984–88; Regl Supplies Officer, 1988–89; Chief Exec., Trent Purchasing Agency, 1989–92; NHS Supplies Authority: Chief Exec., Central Div., 1992–94; Nat. Dir of Logistics, 1994–96; Man. Dir, Wholesaling Div., 1996–2000. FIMgt 1980. *Recreations:* fly fishing, gardening, all forms of woodworking, dining out, listening to classical music. *Address:* The Gables, 178 Derby Road, Cromford, Matlock, Derbys DE4 3RN. *T:* (01629) 822782.

BRADSHAW, Sir Kenneth (Anthony), KCB 1986 (CB 1982); Member, Advisory Board, Compton Verney Opera Project, since 1997 (Administrator, 1988–97); *b* 1 Sept. 1922; *s* of late Herbert and Gladys Bradshaw. *Educ:* Ampleforth Coll.; St Catharine's Coll., Cambridge (1st Cl. Hons History); MA 1947. War Service, 1942–45; served with Royal Ulster Rifles (2nd Bn), NW Europe. Temp. Asst Principal, Min. of Supply, Oct.-Dec. 1946; a Clerk in the House of Commons, 1947–87; seconded as Clerk of the Saskatchewan Legislature, 1966 session; Clerk of Overseas Office, 1972–76; Clerk of the House of Commons, 1983–87. Pres., Assoc. of Secs Gen. of Parlts, IPU, 1986–87 (Jt Sec., 1955–71; Vice-Pres., 1984–86). *Publication:* (with David Pring) Parliament and Congress, 1972, new edn 1982. *Address:* 6 Melton Court, Old Brompton Road, SW7 3JQ. *Club:* Garrick.

BRADSHAW, Martin Clark; planning consultant, MB Consultants, since 1995; Director, Civic Trust, 1987–95; *b* 25 Aug. 1935; *s* of late Cyril Bradshaw and Nina Isabel Bradshaw; *m* 1st, 1959, Patricia Anne Leggatt (*d* 1981); two *s* one *d*; 2nd, 1986, Gillian Rosemary Payne; three step *s* one step *d*. *Educ:* King's Sch., Macclesfield; St John's Coll., Cambridge (MA); Univ. of Manchester (DipTP); MRTPI. Staff Surveyor, Lands and Surveys Dept, Uganda Protectorate, 1958–63; Asst Planning Officer, Planning Dept, City of Manchester, 1963–67; Asst Dir, City of Toronto Planning Bd, 1967–70; Asst Chief Planner, Cheshire CC, 1970–72; Asst County Planning Officer, Leics CC, 1972–73; Exec. Dir, Planning and Transport, 1973–81, Dir of Planning, 1981–86, W Yorks MCC; DoE Local Plans Inspectorate, 1986–87. Mem. Council, 1989–2001, Pres., 1993, RTPI. Gen. Comr for Income Tax, Oxford, 2000–. FRSA 1985. Hon. FRIBA 1995. *Recreations:* theatre, art, golf.

BRADSHAW, Prof. Peter, FRS 1981; Thomas V. Jones Professor of Engineering, Department of Mechanical Engineering, Stanford University, 1988–95, now Emeritus; *b* 26 Dec. 1935; *s* of Joseph W. N. Bradshaw and Frances W. G. Bradshaw; *m* 1968, Sheila Dorothy (*née* Brown). *Educ:* Torquay Grammar Sch.; St John's Coll., Cambridge (BA). Scientific Officer, Aerodynamics Div., National Physical Lab., 1957–69; Imperial College, London: Sen. Lectr, Dept of Aeronautics, 1969–71; Reader, 1971–78; Prof. of Experimental Aerodynamics, 1978–88. *Publications:* Experimental Fluid Mechanics, 1964, 2nd edn 1971; An Introduction to Turbulence and its Measurement, 1971, 2nd edn 1975; (with T. Cebeci) Momentum Transfer in Boundary Layers, 1977; (ed) Topics in Applied Physics: Turbulence, 1978; (with T. Cebeci and J. H. Whitelaw) Engineering Calculation Methods for Turbulent Flow, 1981; (with T. Cebeci) Convective Heat Transfer, 1984; author or co-author of over 100 papers in Jl of Fluid Mechanics, AIAA Jl, etc. *Recreations:* ancient history, walking. *Address:* c/o Department of Mechanical Engineering, Stanford University, Stanford, CA 94305–3030, USA.

BRADSHAW, Peter Nicholas, PhD; film critic, The Guardian, since 1999; *b* 19 June 1962; *s* of Albert Desmond Bradshaw and Mollie Bradshaw (*née* Fine); partner, Dr Caroline Hill. *Educ:* Haberdashers' Aske's Sch., Elstree; Pembroke Coll., Cambridge (BA 1st Cl. Hons 1984; PhD 1989). Evening Standard: reporter, Londoner's Diary, 1989–92; leader writer and columnist, 1992–99. Writer/performer: radio: The Skivers, 1995; For One Horrible Moment, 1999; television: Baddiel's Syndrome, 2000. *Publications:* Not Alan Clark's Diaries, 1998; Lucky Baby Jesus (novel), 1999. *Recreations:* swimming, dozing. *Address:* The Guardian, 119 Farringdon Road, EC1R 3ER. *T:* (020) 7278 2332.

BRADTKE, Hon. Robert Anthony; Executive Secretary, National Security Council, since 1999; *b* 11 Oct. 1949; *s* of Albert Bradtke and Lucille Bradtke (*née* Gale); *m* 1983, Marsha Barnes. *Educ:* Univ. of Notre Dame; Bologna Center; Johns Hopkins Univ.; Univ. of Virginia. Joined Foreign Service, US Dept of State, 1973; served in: Georgetown, 1973–75; Zagreb, 1976–78; Office of Eastern European Affairs, Dept of State, 1978–81; Moscow, 1983–86; Bonn, 1986–90; Office of Congressional Affairs, Dept of State, 1990–94 (Dep. Asst Sec. of State, 1992–94); Exec. Asst to Sec. of State, 1994–96; Minister and Dep. Chief of Mission, London, 1996–99. Superior Honor Award, Dept of State, 1988, 1996. *Recreations:* hiking, reading, baseball. *Address:* National Security Council, The White House, Washington, DC 20504, USA.

BRADWELL, Area Bishop of, since 1993; **Rt Rev. Dr Laurence Alexander Green, (Laurie);** *b* 26 Dec. 1945; *s* of Leonard Alexander and Laura Elizabeth Green; *m* 1969, J. Victoria Bussell; two *d*. *Educ:* King's Coll. London (BD Hons, AKC); New York Theological Seminary, NY State Univ. (STM, DMin); St Augustine's Coll., Canterbury. Curate, St Mark, Kingstanding, Birmingham, 1970–73; Vicar, St Chad, Erdington, Birmingham, 1973–83; Industrial Chaplain, British Steel Corp., 1975–83; Lectr in Urban Studies, Urban Theol. Unit, Sheffield, 1976–82; Principal, Aston Training Scheme, 1983–89; Hon. Curate, Holy Trinity, Birchfield, Handsworth, 1983–89; Team Rector, All Saints, Poplar, 1989–93; Tutor in Urban Theology, Sheffield Univ., 1989–93. *Publications:* Power to the Powerless, 1987; (jtly) A Thing Called Aston (ed Todd), 1987; Let's Do Theology, 1989; God in the Inner City, 1993; (jtly) God in the City, 1995; (contrib.) Urban Christ, 1997; (contrib.) Gospel from the City, 1997; (jtly) A Reader in Urban Theology, 1998; The Impact of the Global: an urban theology, 2001; contrib. St George's Windsor Review. *Recreations:* folk and jazz music, running. *Address:* Bishop's House, Orsett Road, Horndon-on-the-Hill, Essex SS17 8NS. *T:* (01375) 673806, *Fax:* (01375) 674222; *e-mail:* lauriegr@globalnet.co.uk, bishoplaurie@chelmsford.anglican.org.

BRADY, Very Rev. Ernest William; Dean of Edinburgh, 1976–82 and 1985–86; *b* 10 Nov. 1917; *s* of Ernest and Malinda Elizabeth Brady; *m* 1948, Violet Jeanne Louise Aldworth (*d* 1993); one *s* one *d*. *Educ:* Harris Academy, Dundee (Dux and Classics Medallist, 1936); Univ. of St Andrews; Edinburgh Theological Coll. (Luscombe Schol. 1942). LTh (Dunelm) 1942. Deacon 1942, Priest 1943; Asst Curate, Christ Church, Glasgow, 1942; Asst Curate, St Alphage, Hendon, 1946; Rector, All Saints, Buckie, 1949; Rector, All Saints, Edinburgh, 1957; Chaplain, Royal Infirmary of Edinburgh, 1959–74; Priest-in-Charge, Priory Church of St Mary of Mount Carmel, South Queensferry, 1974–82; Canon of St Mary's Cathedral, Edinburgh, 1967, Hon. Canon, 1983; Synod Clerk, Diocese of Edinburgh, 1969. Sub-dean, Collegiate Church of St Vincent, Edinburgh (Order of St Lazarus of Jerusalem), 1982–89. Kt of Holy Sepulchre of Jerusalem (Golden Cross with Crown), 1984. *Recreations:* Holy Land pilgrimage, choral music, ecclesiastical vestments and embroidery. *Address:* 44 Glendevon Place, Edinburgh EH12 5UJ. *T:* (0131) 337 9528.

BRADY, Graham Stuart; MP (C) Altrincham and Sale West, since 1997; *b* 20 May 1967; *s* of John Brady and Maureen Brady (*née* Birch); *m* 1992, Victoria Anne Lowther; one *s* one *d*. *Educ:* Altrincham Grammar Sch.; Univ. of Durham (BA Hons Law 1989); Chm., Durham Univ. Cons. Assoc., 1987; Chm., Northern Area Cons. Collegiate Forum, 1987–89. Shandwick plc, 1989–90; Centre for Policy Studies, 1990–92; Public Affairs Dir, Waterfront Partnership, 1992–97. PPS to Chm. Cons. Party, 1999–2000; an Opposition Whip, 2000–; opposition frontbench spokesman on educn and employment, 2000–01, on educn, 2001–. Mem., Educn and Employment Select Cttee, 1997–2001; Jt Chm., All Party Railfreight Gp, 1998–99; Vice-Chm., All Party Gp on Advertising, 1999–. Sec., Cons. backbench Educn and Employment Cttee, 1997–; Mem. Exec., 1922 Cttee, 1998–2000. Vice-Chm., E Berks Cons. Assoc., 1992–95. *Recreations:* family, friends. *Address:* House of Commons, SW1A 0AA.

BRADY, Prof. (John) Michael, FRS 1997; FREng; BP Professor of Information Engineering, Oxford University, since 1985; Fellow of Keble College, Oxford, since 1985; *b* 30 April 1945; *s* of late John and of Priscilla Mansfield; *m* 1967, Naomi Friedlander; two *d*. *Educ:* Manchester Univ. (BSc (1st Cl. Hons Mathematics) 1966; Renold Prize 1967; MSc 1968); Australian National Univ. (PhD 1970). FREng (FEng 1992); FIEE 1992; FInstP 1997. Lectr, Computer Science, 1970, Sen. Lectr 1979, Essex Univ.; Sen. Res. Scientist, MIT, 1980; EPSRC Sen. Fellow, 1994–99. Member: ACOST, 1990–93; Bd, UKAEA, 1994–; Nat. Technology Foresight Steering Gp, 1994–97; Chm., IT Adv. Bd, 1989–94. Member Board: Guidance and Control Systems, 1991–; Oxford Instruments, 1995–; AEA Technology, 1995–; OMIA, 1997; Surgister, 1997–; OXIVA, 1999. DU Essex, 1996; Hon. DSc: Manchester, 1998; Southampton, 1999; Hon. DEng Liverpool, 1999; Dr (*hc*) Univ. Paul Sabatier, Toulouse, 2000. Faraday Medal, IEE, 2000; Millennium Medal, IEEE, 2000. *Publications:* Theory of Computer Science, 1975; Computer Vision, 1981; Robot Motion, 1982; Computational Theory of Discourse, 1982; Robotics Research, 1984; Artificial Intelligence and Robotics, 1984; Robotics Science, 1989; Mammographic Image Analysis, 1999; contribs to jls on computer vision, medical image analysis, robotics, artificial intelligence, computer science. *Recreations:* squash, music, winetasting.

BRADY, Nicholas Frederick; Secretary of the US Treasury, 1988–93; Chairman: Darby Overseas Investments Ltd, since 1994; Darby Emerging Markets Investments, LDC, since 1994; *b* 11 April 1930; *s* of James Brady and Eliot Brady; *m* 1952, Katherine Douglas; three *s* one *d*. *Educ:* Yale Univ. (BA 1952); Harvard Univ. (MBA 1954). Joined Dillon Read & Co. Inc., 1954; Vice-Pres., 1961; Pres. and Chief Exec. Officer, 1971; Chm. and Chief Exec. Officer, 1982–88. Mem., US Senate, Apr.–Dec. 1982. Posts on federal commns include: Chairman: Commn on Executive, Legislative and Judicial Salaries, 1984; Task Force on Market Mechanisms, 1987–88; Member: Commn on Strategic Forces, 1983; Bipartisan Commn on Central America, 1984; Commn on Defense Mgt, 1986. Chairman: Templeton Latin American Investment Trust, 1994–; Templeton Emerging Markets Investment Trust, 1994–; Templeton Central and E European Investment Co., 1996–; Director: Christiana Cos Inc., 1993–; H. J. Heinz Co., 1993–; Amerada Hess Corp., 1994–; Merchant Bankers Asociados SA, 1995–. *Address:* c/o Darby Overseas Investments Ltd, 1133 Connecticut Avenue NW, Suite 200, Washington, DC 20036, USA.

BRADY, Scott; QC (Scot.) 2000; *b* 31 Oct. 1962; *s* of John Brady and Miriam Cameron Brown. *Educ:* Ardrossan Acad., Ayrshire; Edinburgh Univ. (LLB); Glasgow Univ. (DipLP). Admitted Advocate, Scottish Bar, 1987; Advocate Depute, 1993–97; called to the Bar, Middle Temple, 1998. *Address:* c/o Advocates' Library, Parliament House, Edinburgh EH1 1RF. *T:* (0131) 226 5071. *Clubs:* Caledonian, Scottish Arts (Edinburgh).

BRADY, Most Rev. Sean; *see* Armagh, Archbishop of, (RC).

BRADY, Terence Joseph; playwright, novelist and actor, since 1962; *b* 13 March 1939; *s* of late Frederick Arthur Noel and Elizabeth Mary Brady; *m* Charlotte Mary Thérèse Bingham, *qv*; one *s* one *d*. *Educ:* Merchant Taylors', Northwood; TCD (BA Moderatorship, History and Polit. Science). Actor: Would Anyone who saw the Accident?, The Dumb Waiter, Room at the Top, 1962; Beyond the Fringe, 1962–64; Present from the Corporation, In the Picture, 1967; Quick One 'Ere, 1968; films include: Baby Love; Foreign Exchange; TV appearances include plays, comedy series and shows, incl. Nanny, 1981, and Pig in the Middle, 1981, 1982, 1983. Writer for *radio:* Lines from my Grandfather's Forehead (BBC Radio Writers' Guild Award, Best Radio Entertainment, 1972); *television:* Broad and Narrow; TWTWTW; with Charlotte Bingham: TV series: Boy Meets Girl; Take Three Girls; Upstairs Downstairs; Away From It All; Play for Today; Plays of Marriage; No—Honestly; Yes—Honestly; Thomas and Sarah; Pig in the Middle; The Complete Lack of Charm of the Bourgeoisie; Nanny; Oh Madeline! (USA TV); Father Matthew's Daughter; Forever Green; adapted for television: Love with a Perfect Stranger; Losing Control, 1987; The Seventh Raven, 1987; This Magic Moment, 1988; Riders, 1990; Polo, 1993; Lorna Doone, 1997; The Lost Domain (film), 1999; *stage:* (contrib.) The Sloane Ranger Revue, 1985; I wish I wish, 1989; The Shell Seekers (adapted 1999); Downstairs Upstairs, 1999. Member: Soc. of Authors, 1988–; Point to Point Owners Assoc., 1988–. Dir, Wincanton Racecourse. *Publications:* Rehearsal, 1972; The Fight Against Slavery, 1976; Blueprint, 1998; with Charlotte Bingham: Victoria, 1972; Rose's Story, 1973; Victoria and Company, 1974; Yes—Honestly, 1977; (with Michael Felton) Point-to-Point, 1990; regular contribs to Daily Mail, Living, Country Homes and Interiors, Punch, Sunday Express, Mail on Sunday. *Recreations:* painting, music, horse racing and breeding, avoiding dinner parties, tilting at windmills. *Address:* c/o Hurley Lowe Management, 3a Imperial Studios, Imperial Road, SW6 2AG. *Club:* PEN.

BRAGG, family name of **Baron Bragg**.

BRAGG, Baron *cr* 1998 (Life Peer), of Wigton in the co. of Cumbria; **Melvyn Bragg;** writer; Presenter and Editor, The South Bank Show, for ITV, since 1978; Controller of Arts, London Weekend Television, since 1990 (Head of Arts, 1982–90); *b* 6 Oct. 1939; *s* of Stanley Bragg and Mary Ethel (*née* Parks); *m* 1st, 1961, Marie-Elisabeth Roche (*d* 1971); one *d*; 2nd, 1973, Catherine Mary Haste; one *s* one *d*. *Educ:* Nelson-Thomlinson Grammar Sch., Wigton; Wadham Coll., Oxford (MA; Hon. Fellow, 1995). BBC Radio and TV Producer, 1961–67; writer and broadcaster, 1967–. Novelist, 1964–. Presenter: 2nd House, 1973–77, Read all About It (also editor), 1976–77, BBC TV series; Two Thousand Years, 1999, Who's Afraid of the Ten Commandments?, 2000, The Apostles, 2001, ITV series;BBC Radio 4: Start the Week, 1988–98; On Giants' Shoulders, 1998; In Our Time, 1998–; Routes of English, 1999–. Dep. Chm., 1985–90, Chm., 1990–95, Border Television. Mem. Arts Council, and Chm. Literature Panel of Arts Council, 1977–80. President: Cumbrians for Peace, 1982–; Northern Arts, 1983–87; Nat. Campaign for the Arts, 1986–; Nat. Acad. of Writing; MIND; Appeal Chm., RNIB Talking Books Appeal. Chancellor, Leeds University, 1999–. Governor, LSE, 1997–. Domus Fellow, St Catherine's Coll., Oxford, 1990. FRSL; FRTS. Hon. FLA 1994. Hon. Fellow: Lancashire Polytechnic, 1987; Univ. of Wales, Cardiff, 1996. Hon. DLitt: Liverpool, 1986; Lancaster, 1990; CNAA, 1990; South Bank, 1997; DUniv Open, 1987; Hon. LLD St Andrews, 1993; Hon. DCL Northumbria, 1994. *Plays:* Mardi Gras, 1976 (musical); Orion (TV), 1977; The Hired Man, 1984 (musical); King Lear in New York, 1992; *screenplays:* Isadora; Jesus Christ Superstar; (with Ken Russell) Clouds of Glory. *Publications:* Speak for England, 1976; Land of the Lakes, 1983 (televised); Laurence Olivier, 1984; Rich: the life of Richard Burton, 1988; The Seventh Seal: a study on Ingmar Bergman, 1993; On Giants' Shoulders, 1998; *novels:* For Want of a Nail, 1965; The Second Inheritance, 1966; Without a City Wall, 1968; The Hired Man, 1969; A Place in England, 1970; The Nerve, 1971; Josh Lawton, 1972; The Silken Net, 1974; A Christmas Child, 1976; Autumn Manoeuvres, 1978; Kingdom Come, 1980; Love and Glory, 1983; The Maid of Buttermere, 1987; A Time to Dance, 1990 (televised 1992); Crystal Rooms, 1992; Credo, 1996; The Soldier's Return, 1999 (W. H. Smith Lit. Award, 2000); A Son of War, 2001; articles for various English jls. *Recreations:* walking, books. *Address:* 12 Hampstead Hill Gardens, NW3 2PL. *Clubs:* Garrick, Groucho, PEN.

BRAGG, Stephen Lawrence, MA, SM; FREng; FIMechE; FRAeS; Administrator, Cambridge Office, American Friends of Cambridge University, 1988–93; Fellow, Wolfson College, Cambridge, 1982–91, now Emeritus Fellow; *b* 17 Nov. 1923; *e s* of Sir Lawrence Bragg, CH, OBE, MC, FRS and Lady Bragg, CBE; *m* 1951, Maureen Ann (*née* Roberts); three *s*. *Educ:* Rugby Sch.; Cambridge Univ.; Massachusetts Inst. of Technology. BA 1945, MA 1949 (Cambridge); SM 1949 (MIT). FREng (FEng 1981). Rolls-Royce Ltd, 1944–48; Commonwealth Fund Fellow, 1948–49; Wm Jessop Ltd, Steelmakers, 1949–51; Rolls-Royce Ltd, 1951–71: Chief Scientist, 1960–63; Chief Research Engineer, 1964–68; Dir, Aero Div., 1969–71. Vice-Chancellor, Brunel Univ., 1971–81. Eastern Region Broker, SERC, 1981–83. Dir in Industrial Co-operation, Cambridge Univ., 1984–87. Chm., Cambridge DHA, 1982–86. Member: Univ. Grants Cttee, 1966–71; Aeronautical Research Council, 1970–73; Court of ASC, Henley, 1972–81; SRC Engineering Bd, 1976–79; Airworthiness Requirements Bd, 1979–81; Chm., Adv. Cttee on Falsework, 1973–75. Pres., Railway and Canal Histl Soc., 1998–2000. Corresp. Mem., Venezuelan Acad. Sci., 1975. Hon. DEng Sheffield, 1969; Hon. DTech Brunel, 1982. *Publications:* Rocket Engines, 1962; articles on Jet Engines, Research Management, University/Industry Collaboration, etc. *Recreation:* railway history. *Address:* 22 Brookside, Cambridge CB2 1JQ. *T:* (01223) 362208. *Club:* Athenæum.

See also Sir Mark Heath, D. P. Thomson.

BRAGGE, Nicolas William; Master of the Supreme Court, Chancery Division, since 1997; *b* 13 Dec. 1948; *o s* of late Norman Bragge and Nicolette Hilda Bragge (*née* Simms);

m 1973, Pamela Elizabeth Brett; three *s*. *Educ:* S Kent Coll. of Technol., Ashford; Holborn Coll. of Law and Inns of Court Sch. of Law (LLB Hons London). Called to the Bar, Inner Temple, 1972; in practice, Intellectual Property and Chancery Bars, 1974–97; Dep. Chancery Master, 1993–97. Chm. (part-time), Social Security and Disability Appeal Tribunals, 1990–97; Dep. Social Security Comr, 1996–98. Jt Ed., Civil Procedure, 2001–. *Address:* Royal Courts of Justice, Strand, WC2A 2LL.

BRAHAM, Allan John Witney, PhD; Keeper and Deputy Director, the National Gallery, 1978–92; *b* 19 Aug. 1937; *s* of Dudley Braham and Florence Mears; *m* 1963, Helen Clare Butterworth; two *d*. *Educ:* Dulwich Coll.; Courtauld Inst. of Art, Univ. of London (BA 1960, PhD 1967). Asst Keeper, National Gall., 1962, Dep. Keeper, 1973. Arts Council Exhibn (with Peter Smith), François Mansart, 1970–71; National Gall. Exhibitions: (co-ordinator and editor) The Working of the National Gallery, 1974; Velázquez, The Rokeby Venus, 1976; Giovanni Battista Moroni, 1978; Italian Renaissance Portraits, 1979; El Greco to Goya, 1981; Wright of Derby "Mr and Mrs Coltman", 1986. *Publications:* Dürer, 1965; Murillo (The Masters), 1966; The National Gallery in London: Italian Painting of the High Renaissance, 1971; (with Peter Smith) François Mansart, 1973; Funeral Decorations in Early Eighteenth Century Rome, 1975; (with Hellmut Hager) Carlo Fontana: The Drawings at Windsor Castle, 1977; The Architecture of the French Enlightenment, 1980 (Hitchcock Medal, Banister Fletcher Prize; French edn 1982); National Gall. catalogues: The Spanish School (revised edn), 1970, and booklets: Velázquez, 1972; Rubens, 1972; Architecture, 1976; Italian Paintings of the Sixteenth Century, 1985; contrib. prof. jls, etc. *Recreation:* history of architecture. *Address:* 1/55 Buckley Road, NW6 7LX.

BRAIDEN, Prof. Paul Mayo, PhD; FREng, FIMechE, FIEE; CPhys; Sir James Woodeson Professor of Manufacturing Engineering, since 1983 and Head, Department of Mechanical, Materials and Manufacturing Engineering, 1992–97, University of Newcastle upon Tyne; *b* 7 Feb. 1941; *s* of late Isaac Braiden and of Lilian Braiden (*née* Mayo); *m* 1st, 1967, Elizabeth Marjorie Spensley (marr. diss. 1993); 2nd, 1993, Lesley Howard. *Educ:* Univ. of Sheffield (BEng, MEng, PhD). CEng, FIMechE 1978; FIEE 1983; FREng (FEng 1994); CPhys, MInstP 1973. Asst Prof., Carnegie Mellon Univ., Pittsburgh, 1968–70; Atomic Energy Research Establishment, Harwell: SSO, 1970–73; PSO, 1973–76; Lectr, then Sen. Lectr, Dept of Engrg, Univ. of Durham, 1976–83. Science and Engineering Research Council: Chm., Engrg Design Cttee, 1990–94; Member: Engrg Bd, 1990–91; Engrg Res. Commn, 1991–94; Cttee on Electro-Mechanical Engrg, 1989–91; Automotive Design Prog., 1989–91; Panel on the Innovative Manufg Initiative, 1993–94. Chm., DTI Working Party on Advanced Mfg Technol., 1987–89. Chm., Northern Reg. and Council Mem., IProdE, 1988–90; Hon. Sec. for Mechanical Subjects, Royal Acad. Engrg, 1997–2000. Mem. Bd, Entrust, 1984–91. Mem., Nat. Cttee for Revision of Methodist Hymn Book, 1979–82. *Publications:* articles on materials behaviour, stress analysis, manufacturing technol. and systems in various jls. *Recreations:* music, especially opera/oratorio (trained singer, tenor voice), cycling, ski-ing. *Address:* Department of Mechanical, Materials and Manufacturing Engineering, University of Newcastle upon Tyne, Stephenson Building, Claremont Road, Newcastle upon Tyne NE1 7RU. *T:* (0191) 222 6210.

BRAILSFORD, (Sidney) Neil; QC (Scot.) 1994; *b* 15 Aug. 1954; *s* of Sidney James Brailsford and Jean Thelma Moar Leighton or Brailsford; *m* 1984, Elaine Nicola Robbie; three *s*. *Educ:* Daniel Stewart's Coll., Edinburgh; Stirling Univ. (BA); Edinburgh Univ. (LLB). Admitted Faculty of Advocates, 1981, Treasurer, 2000–; called to the Bar, Lincoln's Inn, 1990. *Recreations:* travel, horse riding, food and wine, American history. *Address:* 29 Warriston Crescent, Edinburgh EH3 5LB. *T:* (0131) 556 8320; Pleasant Street, Grafton, VT 05146, USA. *T:* (802) 8432120. *Club:* New (Edinburgh),

BRAIN, family name of **Baron Brain**.

BRAIN, 2nd Baron *cr* 1962, of Eynsham; **Christopher Langdon Brain;** Bt 1954; *b* 30 Aug. 1926; *s* of 1st Baron Brain, MA, DM, FRS, FRCP and Stella, *er d* of late Reginald L. Langdon-Down; *S* father 1966; *m* 1953, Susan Mary, *d* of George P. and Ethelbertha Morris; three *d*. *Educ:* Leighton Park Sch., Reading; New College, Oxford. MA 1956. Royal Navy, 1946–48. Liveryman, 1955, Upper Warden, 1974–75, Asst, 1980–2000, Renter Bailiff, 1983–84, Upper Bailiff, 1984–85, Worshipful Co. of Weavers. Chm., Rhone-Alps Regional Council, British Chamber of Commerce, France, 1967. ARPS 1970. *Recreations:* bird watching, fly-fishing. *Heir:* *b* Hon. Michael Cottrell Brain, MA, DM, FRCP, FRCP Canada, Prof. of Medicine, McMaster Univ. [*b* 6 Aug. 1928; *m* 1960, Dr the Hon. Elizabeth Ann Herbert, *e d* of Baron Tangley, KBE; one *s* two *d*]. *Address:* Alexandra House, 8 Cross Street, Moretonhampstead, Devon TQ13 8NL. *Club:* Oxford and Cambridge Sailing Society.

BRAIN, Albert Edward Arnold; Regional Director (East Midlands), Department of the Environment, and Chairman of Regional Economic Planning Board, 1972–77; *b* 31 Dec. 1917; *s* of Walter Henry and Henrietta Mabel Brain; *m* 1947, Patricia Grace Gallop; two *s* one *d*. *Educ:* Rendcomb Coll., Cirencester; Loughborough College. BSc (Eng) London, external; DLC hons Loughborough; CEng, MICE, MIMunE. Royal Engineers, 1940–46; Bristol City Corp., 1946–48; Min. of Transport: Asst Engr, London, 1948–54; Civil Engr, Wales, 1954–63; Sen. Engr, HQ, 1963–67; Asst Chief Engr, HQ, 1967–69; Divl Road Engr, W Mids, then Regional Controller (Roads and Transportation), 1969–72. Pres., Old Rendcombian Soc., 1986–91. *Recreation:* gardening. *Address:* Withyholt Lodge, Moorend Road, Charlton Kings, Cheltenham GL53 9BW. *T:* (01242) 576264.

BRAIN, Charlotte; *see* Atkins, C.

BRAIN, Sir (Henry) Norman, KBE 1963 (OBE 1947); CMG 1953; *b* 19 July 1907; *s* of late B. Brain, Rushall, Staffs; *m* 1939, Nuala Mary, *d* of late Capt. A. W. Butterworth; one *s* (and one *s* decd). *Educ:* King Edward's Sch., Birmingham; The Queen's Coll., Oxford (MA). Entered the Consular Service, 1930, and served at Tokyo, Kobe, Osaka, Tamsui, Manila, Mukden, Shanghai and Dairen; interned by Japanese, 1941–42; repatriated and served in Foreign Office, 1943; appointed to Staff of Supreme Allied Comdr, South-East Asia, 1944–46; Political Adviser to Saigon Control Commission, 1945; served with Special Commissioner in South-East Asia, at Singapore, 1946–48; Counsellor in Foreign Office, 1949; Inspector of HM Foreign Service Estabts, 1950–53; Minister, Tokyo, 1953–55; Ambassador to Cambodia, 1956–58; Asst Under-Sec. of State, FO, 1958–61; Ambassador to Uruguay, 1961–66, retired, 1966. Chairman: Royal Central Asian Soc., 1970–74; Japan Soc. of London, 1970–73; Pres., British Uruguayan Soc., 1974–. *Recreations:* music, golf.

BRAIN, Dame Margaret Anne, DBE 1994 (OBE 1989); FRCOG; President, Royal College of Midwives, 1987–94 (Member Council, 1970–96); *b* 23 April 1932; *d* of late Charles and Leonora Brain; *m* 1985, Peter Wheeler (*d* 1988), MBE, FRCS, FRCOG. *Educ:* Northampton High Sch.; Westminster Hosp. (SRN 1953); Northampton and Epsom Hosps (SCM 1956); Sheffield Hosp. (MTD 1966). FRCOG *ad eund* 1991. Med. Missionary, USPG St Columba's Hosp., Hazaribagh, Bihar, India, 1959–65; Dep. Matron, Barratt Maternity Home, Northampton, 1966–68; Prin. Midwifery Officer, Reading HMC, 1968–73; Dist Nursing Officer, W Berks DHA, 1974–77; Chief Admin. Nursing Officer, S Glamorgan HA, 1977–88, retd. Member: Nat. Staff Cttee for Nurses and Midwives, 1978–86; Maternity Services Adv. Cttee, 1981–85; Standing Midwifery Cttee, Welsh Nat. Bd, 1982–87; Perinatal Mortality Initiative Steering Gp for Wales, 1983–85; Standing Nursing and Midwifery Adv. Cttee, 1987–93; Women's Nat. Commn, 1990–92; Alternate Treas., 1972–78, Treas., 1978–90, Internat. Confedn of Midwives. Hon. DSc City, 1995. *Address:* Squirrels, Castle Farm, Lower Broad Oak Road, West Hill, Ottery St Mary, Devon EX11 1UF. *T:* (01404) 812958.

BRAIN, Rt Rev. Peter Robert; *see* Armidale, Bishop of.

BRAIN, Rt Rev. Terence John; *see* Salford, Bishop of, (RC).

BRAININ, Norbert, OBE 1960; concert violinist; formed Amadeus Ensemble, incorporating Amadeus Trio, 1988; Professor of Chamber Music: Hochschule für Musik, Cologne, since 1976; Royal Academy of Music, since 1986; *b* Vienna, 12 March 1923; *s* of Adolph and Sophie Brainin; *m* 1948, Kathe Kottow; one *d*. *Educ:* High Sch., Vienna. Commenced musical training in Vienna at age of seven and continued studies there until 1938; emigrated to London in 1938 and studied with Carl Flesch and Max Rostal; won Carl Flesch prize for solo violinists at the Guildhall Sch. of Music, London, 1946. Formed Amadeus String Quartet, 1947, Leader until disbanded in 1987. Professor: (annual) Amadeus Quartet Course, RAM; of Violin, Scuola di Musica di Fiesole, 1974; of Violin, Hochschule für Musik Franz Liszt Weimar, 1995. DUniv York, 1968; Hon. DMus London, 1983; Dr *hc* Venezuela, 1996. Grosse Verdienstzeichen, Vienna, 1999. Grand Cross of Merit, 1st cl. Fed. Republic of Germany, 1972; Cross of Honour for Arts and Science (Austria), 1972. *Address:* 19 Prowse Avenue, Bushey Heath, Herts WD2 1JS. *T:* (020) 8950 7379, *Fax:* (020) 8209 1907.

BRAITHWAITE, (Arthur) Bevan (Midgley), OBE 1993; FREng; Chief Executive, TWI, since 1988; *b* 27 July 1939; *s* of Frederick Arthur Bevan Braithwaite and Magnhild Katrina Braithwaite (*née* Dahl); *m* 1961, Rosemary Kerry Conrad Cooke; one *s* two *d*. *Educ:* Leighton Park Sch.; Jesus Coll., Cambridge (MA). FREng 1999. Joined British Welding Res. Assoc., subseq. The Welding Inst., then TWI, 1961; Dir of Develt, 1966–84; Man. Dir, 1984–88. Mem., Eastern Reg. IDB, 1994–98; Dir, Granta Park, 1997–. Mem., EPSRC, 1996–2001 (Chm., User Panel, 1996–2000). Pres., Internat. Inst. Welding, 1999–. *Publications:* contribs to various jls; several patents. *Recreations:* steam engines, house restoration. *Address:* TWI, Granta Park, Great Abington, Cambridge CB1 6AL. *T:* (01223) 891162.

BRAITHWAITE, His Honour Bernard Richard; a Circuit Judge (formerly County Court Judge), 1971–88; *b* 20 Aug. 1917; *s* of Bernard Leigh Braithwaite and Emily Dora Ballard Braithwaite (*née* Thomas); unmarried. *Educ:* Clifton; Peterhouse, Cambridge. BA (Hons), Law. Served War: 7th Bn Somerset LI, 1939–43; Parachute Regt, 1943–46; Captain, Temp. Major. Called to Bar, Inner Temple, 1946. *Recreations:* hunting, sailing. *Address:* Summerfield House, Uley, Gloucestershire GL11 5BZ. *Club:* Boodle's.

BRAITHWAITE, Bevan; *see* Braithwaite, A. B. M.

BRAITHWAITE, Eustace Ricardo; writer and lecturer; *b* Georgetown, British Guyana (now Guyana). *Educ:* Cambridge Univ. Served War of 1939–45, Fighter Pilot, RAF. Schoolteacher, London, 1950–57; Welfare Officer, LCC, 1958–60; Human Rights Officer, World Veterans Fedn, Paris, 1960–63; Education Consultant, UNESCO, Paris, 1963–66; Permanent Rep. of Guyana to UN, 1966–68; Ambassador of Guyana to Venezuela, 1968–70. Ainsfield-Wolff Prize, 1967; Franklin Peace Prize, 1968. *Publications:* To Sir With Love, 1959; Paid Servant, 1962; A Kind of Homecoming, 1962; Choice of Straws, 1965; Reluctant Neighbours, 1972; Honorary White, 1976. *Recreations:* tennis, birdwatching.

BRAITHWAITE, Sir (Joseph) Franklin (Madders), Kt 1980; DL; CIMgt; Chairman: Baker Perkins Holdings plc, 1980–84; Peterborough Independent Hospital plc, 1981–87; *b* 6 April 1917; *s* of late Sir John Braithwaite and Martha Janette (*née* Baker); *m* 1939, Charlotte Isabel, *d* of late Robert Elmer Baker, New York; one *s* one *d*. *Educ:* Bootham Sch.; King's Coll., Cambridge, 1936–39 (BA 1939, MA 1955). Served Army, 1940–46 (Captain). Joined Baker Perkins Ltd, 1946, Director 1950, Vice-Chm. 1956; Chairman, Baker Perkins Exports Ltd, 1966; Man. Dir, Baker Perkins Holdings Ltd, 1971. Director, Lloyds Bank Ltd, Eastern Counties Regional Board, 1979–87. Member: Mech. Engrg Industry Economic Development Cttee, 1974–79; Management Board, 1978–82, Commercial and Econ. Cttee, 1977–84, Engrg Employers' Fedn; Board of Fellows, 1974–79, Economic and Social Affairs Cttee, 1979–84, BIM. Mem., Peterborough Develt Corp., 1981–88, Dep. Chm. 1982–88. President, Process Plant Assoc., 1977–79, Hon. life Vice-Pres., 1981. DL Cambs, 1983. *Recreations:* music, golf. *Address:* 7 Rutland Terrace, Stamford, Lincs PE9 2QD. *T:* (01780) 751244. *Club:* Army and Navy.

BRAITHWAITE, Sir Rodric (Quentin), GCMG 1994 (KCMG 1988 CMG 1981); HM Diplomatic Service, retired; Senior Advisor, since 1994, and Managing Director, Deutsche Bank (formerly Deutsche Morgan Grenfell); *b* 17 May 1932; *s* of Henry Warwick Braithwaite and Lorna Constance Davies; *m* 1961, Gillian Mary Robinson; three *s* one *d* (and one *s* decd). *Educ:* Bedales Sch.; Christ's Coll., Cambridge (1st cl. Mod. Langs, Pts I and II; Hon. Fellow, 1989). Mil. Service, 1950–52. Joined Foreign (subseq. Diplomatic) Service, 1955; served Djakarta, Warsaw and FO, 1957–63; Moscow, 1963–66; Rome, 1966–69; FCO, 1969–72; Vis. Fellow, All Souls Coll., Oxford, 1972–73; Head of European Integration Dept (External), FCO, 1973–75; Head of Chancery, Office of Permanent Rep. to EEC, Brussels, 1975–78; Head of Planning Staff, FCO, 1979–80; Asst Under Sec. of State, FCO, 1981; Minister Commercial, Washington, 1982–84; Dep. Under-Sec. of State, FCO, 1984–88; Ambassador to Russia, 1988–92; Prime Minister's foreign policy advr, 1992–93. Member: European Strategy Bd, ICL plc, 1994–99; Supervisory Bd, Deutsche Bank, Moscow, 1998–99; Adv. Bd, Sirocco Aerospace, 1999–; Chm., Morgan Grenfell Securities, 1995–97. Chm. Council, Britain–Russia Centre, 1995–99; Mem. Council, VSO, 1994–99. Dir, ENO, 1992–99. Chm., Moscow Sch. of Political Studies, 1998–. Gov., RAM, 1993– (Chm. of Govs, 1998–; Hon. FRAM 1996). Trustee, BBC Marshall Plan for the Mind, 1995–98. Hon. LLD, 1997, Hon. Prof., 1999, Birmingham. *Publications:* (jtly) Engaging Russia, 1995; Russia in Europe, 1999. *Recreations:* chamber music (viola), sailing, Russia. *Address:* Deutsche Bank, 23 Great Winchester Street, EC2P 2AX.

BRAITHWAITE, William Thomas Scatchard; QC 1992; a Recorder, 1993–99; *b* 20 Jan. 1948; *s* of late John Vernon Braithwaite and Nancy Phyllis Braithwaite; *m* 1972, Sheila Edgecombe; one *s* one *d*. *Educ:* Gordonstoun Sch.; Liverpool Univ. (LLB Hons). Called to the Bar, Gray's Inn, 1970; joined chambers in Liverpool, 1970; Asst Recorder of the Crown Court, 1990. Consultant Editor, Kemp and Kemp, The Quantum of Damages, 1995–. *Publication:* (ed jtly) Medical Aspects of Personal Injury Litigation, 1997. *Recreations:* cars, wine. *Address:* Exchange Chambers, Pearl Assurance House, Derby Square, Liverpool L2 9XX; 2 Crown Office Row, Temple, EC4Y 7HJ.

BRAKE, Thomas Anthony; MP (Lib Dem) Carshalton and Wallington, since 1997; *b* 6 May 1962; *s* of Michael and Judy Brake; *m* 1998, Candida Goulden; one *s* one *d*. *Educ:* Imperial Coll., London (BSc Hons Physics); Lycée International, France (Internat. Baccalauréat). Formerly Principal Consultant, Cap Gemini, (IT services). Lib Dem spokesman: on envmt, 1997; on transport, local govt and the regions, 2001–; a Lib Dem Whip, 2000–. Mem., Accommodation and Works Cttee, H of C, 2001–. *Publication:* (jtly) Costing the Earth, 1991. *Recreations:* running, travel, eating, cinema. *Address:* House of Commons, SW1A 0AA.

BRAMALL, family name of **Baron Bramall**.

BRAMALL, Baron *cr* 1987 (Life Peer), of Bushfield in the County of Hampshire; **Field Marshal Edwin Noel Westby Bramall,** KG 1990; GCB 1979 (KCB 1974); OBE 1965; MC 1945; JP; HM Lord-Lieutenant of Greater London, 1986–98; Chief of the Defence Staff, 1982–85; *b* 18 Dec. 1923; *s* of late Major Edmund Haselden Bramall and Mrs Katherine Bridget Bramall (*née* Westby); *m* 1949, Dorothy Avril Wentworth Vernon; one *s* one *d*. *Educ:* Eton College. Commnd into KRRC, 1943; served in NW Europe, 1944–45; occupation of Japan, 1946–47; Instructor, Sch. of Infantry, 1949–51; psc 1952; Middle East, 1953–58; Instructor, Army Staff Coll., 1958–61; on staff of Lord Mountbatten at MoD, 1963–64; CO, 2 Green Jackets, KRRC, Malaysia during Indonesian confrontation, 1965–66; comd 5th Airportable Bde, 1967–69; idc 1970; GOC 1st Div. BAOR, 1971–73; Lt-Gen., 1973; Comdr, British Forces, Hong Kong, 1973–76; Gen., 1976; C-in-C, UK Land Forces, 1976–78; Vice-Chief of Defence Staff (Personnel and Logistics), 1978–79; Chief of the General Staff, 1979–82; Field Marshal, 1982. ADC (Gen.), 1979–82. Col Comdt, 3rd Bn Royal Green Jackets, 1973–84; Col, 2nd Goorkhas, 1976–86; President: Greater London TAVRA, 1986–98; Gurkha Bde Assoc., 1987–97. Hon. Life Vice Pres., MCC, 1997 (Mem. Cttee, 1985–94; Pres., 1988–89; Trustee, 1994–97). A Trustee, Imperial War Museum, 1983–98 (Chm., 1989–98). JP London 1986. KStJ 1986. *Publication:* (jtly) The Chiefs, 1993. *Recreations:* cricket, painting, travel. *Address:* House of Lords, SW1A 0PW. *Clubs:* Travellers, Army and Navy, Pratt's, MCC, I Zingari, Free Foresters.

BRAMALL, Margaret Elaine, OBE 1969; MA; JP; Vice-President, National Council for One Parent Families (formerly National Council for the Unmarried Mother and her Child) (Director, 1962–79); *b* 1 Oct. 1916; *d* of Raymond Taylor, MA and Nettie Kate Taylor, BA; *m* 1939, E. A. Bramall, later Sir Ashley Bramall (marr. diss.; he *d* 1999); two *s*. *Educ:* St Paul's Girls' Sch., Hammersmith; Somerville Coll., Oxford (BA 1939, MA 1942); LSE (Social Science Hon. Certif. 1950); Inst. of Almoners (Certif. 1951). Lectr, Applied Social Studies Course, Surrey Univ., 1979–89. Member: Probation Case Cttee; Management Cttee, Humming Bird Housing Assoc. Chm., Richmond on Thames Action for Southern Africa. JP Richmond 1965. *Publications:* contrib., One Parent Families, ed Dulan Barber, 1975; contrib. social work jls. *Recreations:* gardening, family. *Address:* 74 Fifth Cross Road, Twickenham, Mddx TW2 5LE. *T:* (020) 8894 3998.

BRAMLEY, Prof. Sir Paul (Anthony), Kt 1984; FRCS, FDSRCS; Professor of Dental Surgery, University of Sheffield, 1969–88, now Emeritus; *b* 24 May 1923; *s* of Charles and Constance Bramley; *m* 1952, Hazel Morag Boyd, MA, MB ChB; one *s* three *d*. *Educ:* Wyggeston Grammar Sch., Leicester; Univ. of Birmingham. MB ChB, BDS. HS, Queen Elizabeth Hosp., Birmingham, 1945; Capt., RADC, 224 Para Fd Amb., 1946–48; MO, Church of Scotland, Kenya, 1952; Registrar, Rooksdown House, 1953–54; Consultant Oral Surgeon, SW Region Hosp. Bd, 1954–69; Dir, Dept of Oral Surgery and Orthodontics, Plymouth Gen. Hosp. and Truro Royal Infirmary, 1954–69; Civilian Consultant, RN, 1959–88, now Emeritus; Dean, Sch. of Clinical Dentistry, Univ. of Sheffield, 1972–75. Consultant Oral Surgeon, Trent Region, 1969–88. Chm., Dental Protection Ltd, 1989–95. Member: General Dental Council, 1973–89; Council, Medical Protection Soc., 1975–95; Council, RCS, 1975–83 (Tomes Lectr, 1980; Dean of Faculty of Dental Surgery, 1980–83; Colyer Gold Medal, 1988); Royal Commission on NHS; Dental Strategy Review Group; Chm., Standing Dental Adv. Cttee; Consultant Adviser, DHSS; Hon. Sec., British Assoc. of Oral Surgeons, 1968–72, Pres., 1975; President: S Yorks Br., British Dental Assoc., 1975; Oral Surgery Club of GB, 1985–86; Inst. of Maxillofacial Technol., 1987–89; BDA, 1988–89. Adviser, Prince of Songkla Univ., Thailand, 1982–; External Examiner to RCS, RCSI, RCSG, RACDS, Univs of Birmingham, Baghdad, Hong Kong, London, Singapore, Trinity College Dublin, Cardiff, NUI. Pres., Norman Rowe Educnl Trust, 1993–95; Chm., Cavendish Br., NADFAS, 1996–99. Lay Reader, dios of Winchester and Exeter, 1953–68. Hon. FRACDS. Hon. DDS: Birmingham, 1987; Prince of Songkla Univ., 1989; Hon. MD Sheffield, 1994. Fellow, Internat. Assoc. of Oral and Maxillofacial Surgeons. Bronze Medal, Helsinki Univ., 1990. *Publications:* (with J. Norman) The Temporomandibular Joint: disease, disorders, surgery, 1989; scientific articles in British and foreign medical and dental jls. *Address:* Greenhills, Back Lane, Hathersage S32 1AR.

BRAMMA, Harry Wakefield, FRCO; Organist and Director of Music, All Saints', Margaret Street, since 1989; Director, Royal School of Church Music, 1989–98; *b* 11 Nov. 1936; *s* of late Fred and Christine Bramma. *Educ:* Bradford Grammar Sch.; Pembroke Coll., Oxford (MA). FRCO 1958 (Harding Prize). Dir of Music, King Edward VI Grammar Sch., Retford, Notts, 1961; Asst Organist, Worcester Cathedral, 1963; Dir of Music, The King's Sch., Worcester, 1965; Organist, Southwark Cathedral, 1976. Vis. Music Supervisor, King's Coll., Cambridge, 1998–2000; Music Tutor, Christ Church, Oxford, 2000–. Conductor, Kidderminster Choral Soc., 1972–79. Examnr, Associated Bd of Royal Schs of Music, 1978–89. Mem. Council, RCO, 1979–96, Hon. Treas., 1987–96; Mem., Archbishops' Commn on Church Music, 1989–92; Organ Advr, Dio. of Southwark, 1976–93 and 1999–; Mem., Ct of Advrs, St Paul's Cathedral, 1993–99. Hon. Sec., Cathedral Organists' Assoc., 1989–98; Pres., Southwark and S London Soc. of Organists, 1976–; Vice Pres., Church Music Soc. Patron, Herbert Howells Soc. FGCM 1988; FRSCM 1994. Hon. Mem., Assoc. of Anglican Musicians, USA. Hon. DLitt Bradford, 1995. *Recreations:* travel, walking. *Address:* 8 Margaret Street, W1N 7LG. *Club:* Athenæum.

BRAMPTON, Sally Jane, (Mrs Jonathan Powell); novelist; *b* 15 July 1955; *d* of Roy and Pamela Brampton; *m* 1981, Nigel Cole (marr. diss. 1990); *m* 1990, Jonathan Leslie Powell, *qv*; one *d*. *Educ:* Ashford Sch., Ashford, Kent; St Clare's Hall, Oxford; St Martin's School of Art, London. Fashion Writer, Vogue, 1978; Fashion Editor, Observer, 1981; Editor, Elle (UK), 1985–89; Associate Editor, Mirabella, 1990–91; Editor, Red, 2000. Vis. Prof., Central St Martin's Coll. of Art and Design, 1997–. TV documentary: Undressed: the history of 20th century fashion, C4, 1998. *Publications:* Good Grief, 1992; Lovesick, 1995; Concerning Lily, 1998; Love, Always, 2000. *Address:* 139 Randolph Avenue, Maida Vale, W9 1DN. *Club:* Groucho.

BRAMSON, David; Senior Partner, Nabarro Nathanson, since 1995; *b* 8 Feb. 1942; *s* of late Israel Bramson and of Deborah Bramson (*née* Warshinsky); *m* 1966, Lilian de Wilde; one *s* one *d*. *Educ:* Willesden Co. Grammar Sch.; University Coll. London (LLB). Solicitor: Mobil Oil Co. Ltd, 1966–68; Nabarro Nathanson, 1968– (Partner, 1969–). Member, Policy Cttee, British Property Fedn, 1995–; Trustee, Investment Property Forum Educnl Trust, 1997–. Lectr on commercial property, 1996–. *Publications:* contrib. to jls on commercial property topics. *Recreations:* opera, theatre, visual arts, herding cats. *Address:* Nabarro Nathanson, Lacon House, Theobalds Road, WC1X 8RW. *T:* (020) 7524 6000. *Club:* Royal Automobile.

BRAMWELL, Richard Mervyn; QC 1989; *b* 29 Sept. 1944; *s* of Clifford and Dorothy Bramwell; *m* 1968, Susan Green; one *d*. *Educ:* Stretford Grammar Sch.; LSE (LLB, LLM). Called to the Bar, Middle Temple, 1967. *Publications:* Taxation of Companies and Company Reconstructions, 1973, 7th edn 1999; Inheritance Tax on Lifetime Gifts, 1987. *Recreations:* hunting, tennis. *Address:* 3 Temple Gardens, Temple, EC4Y 9AU. *T:* (020) 7353 7884.

BRANAGH, Kenneth Charles; actor and director; *b* 10 Dec. 1960; *s* of William and Frances Branagh; *m* 1989, Emma Thompson, *qv* (marr. diss. 1997). *Educ:* Meadway Comprehensive Sch., Reading; Royal Academy of Dramatic Art (Bancroft Gold Medalist). *Theatre:* Another Country, Queen's, 1982 (SWET Award, Most Promising Newcomer; Plays and Players Award); The Madness; Francis; Henry V, Golden Girls, Hamlet, Love's Labours Lost, 1984–85; Tell Me Honestly (also author); Across the Roaring Hill; The Glass Maze; Hamlet, RSC, 1992; formed Renaissance Theatre Company, 1987: Romeo and Juliet (also dir); Public Enemy (also author); Much Ado About Nothing; As You Like It; Hamlet; Look Back in Anger (also televised); A Midsummer Night's Dream (also dir); King Lear (also dir); Coriolanus; *directed:* Twelfth Night (also televised); The Life of Napoleon; (with Peter Egan) Uncle Vanya; *films include:* A Month in the Country, 1987; High Season, 1987; Henry V (also dir), 1989 (Evening Standard Best Film of the Year, 1989; Oscar, Best Costume Design, 1990; BFI Award, Best Film and Technical Achievement, 1990; Young European Film of the Year, 1990; NY Critics Circle Award, Best New Dir; European Actor of the Year, 1990); Dead Again (also dir), 1991; Peter's Friends (also dir), Swan Song (dir), 1992; Swing Kids, Much Ado About Nothing (also dir), 1993; Mary Shelley's Frankenstein (also dir), 1994; (writer and dir) In the Bleak Midwinter, 1995; Othello, 1995; Hamlet (also dir), 1997; The Proposition, 1997; The Gingerbread Man, 1998; The Theory of Flight, 1998; Celebrity, 1999; Wild Wild West, 1999; Love's Labour's Lost (also dir), 2000; *television includes:* Billy Trilogy, 1982; Fortunes of War, 1987; Boy in the Bush; To the Lighthouse; Strange Interlude; Ghosts, 1987; The Lady's Not for Burning; Shadow of a Gunman, 1995; *radio includes:* Hamlet, and Romeo and Juliet (both also co-dir); King Lear; Anthem for the Doomed Youth; Diaries of Samuel Pepys; Mary Shelley's Frankenstein. *Publications:* Public Enemy (play), 1988; Beginning (autobiog.), 1989; *screenplays:* Henry V; Much Ado About Nothing; Hamlet; In the Bleak Midwinter. *Recreations:* reading, playing guitar. *Address:* Shepperton Studios, Shepperton, Mddx TW17 0QD.

BRANCH, Prof. Michael Arthur, CMG 2000; PhD; Director, School of Slavonic and East European Studies, since 1980, and Professor of Finnish, since 1986, London University, at University College London, since 1999; *b* 24 March 1940; *s* of Arthur Frederick Branch and Mahala Parker; *m* 1963, Ritva-Riitta Hannele, *d* of Erkki Kari, Heinola, Finland; three *d*. *Educ:* Shene Grammar Sch.; Sch. of Slavonic and East European Studies, Univ. of London (BA 1963; PhD 1967). School of Slavonic and East European Studies: Asst Lectr and Lectr in Finno–Ugrian Studies, 1967–72; Lectr, 1972–77, and Reader in Finnish, 1977; Chm., Dept of East European Language and Literature, 1979–80. Fellow, UCL, 2001. Corresponding Member: Finno–Ugrian Soc., 1977; Finnish Literature Soc. (Helsinki), 1980. Hon. PhD Oulu (Finland), 1983. Comdr, Lion of Finland, 1980; Comdr, Polish Order of Merit, 1992; Comdr, Estonian Terra Mariana Cross, 2000. *Publications:* A. J. Sjögren, 1973; (jtly) Finnish Folk Poetry: Epic, 1977; (jtly) A Student's Glossary of Finnish, 1980; (ed) Kalevala, 1985; (jtly) Edith Södergran, 1992; (jtly) The Great Bear, 1993; (jtly) Uses of Tradition, 1994; (jtly) Finland and Poland in the Russian Empire, 1995; (ed) The Writing of National History and Identity, 1999. *Recreations:* gardening, walking. *Address:* 33 St Donatt's Road, SE14 6NU. *Club:* Athenæum.

BRAND, family name of **Viscount Hampden**.

BRAND, Alexander George, MBE 1945; *b* 23 March 1918; *s* of David Wilson Brand and Janet Ramsay Brand (*née* Paton); *m* 1947, Helen Constance Campbell; one *s* one *d*. *Educ:* Ayr Academy; Univ. of Glasgow. MA 1940, LLB 1948. Admitted Solicitor, 1948. Served in Royal Air Force, 1940–46 (Flt Lt). Legal Asst: Dumbarton CC, 1948; in Office of Solicitor to the Secretary of State for Scotland, 1949; Sen. Legal Asst, 1955; Asst Solicitor, 1964; Dep. Solicitor, 1972–79. Sec. of Scottish Law Commn, 1965–72. Traffic Comr and Dep. Licensing Authty, Scotland, 1979–88. *Recreations:* golf, theatre, music, reading.

BRAND, Prof. Charles Peter, FBA 1990; Professor of Italian, 1966–88, and Vice-Principal, 1984–88, University of Edinburgh; *b* 7 Feb. 1923; *er s* of Charles Frank Brand and Dorothy (*née* Tapping); *m* 1948, Gunvor, *yr d* of Col I. Hellgren, Stockholm; one *s* three *d*. *Educ:* Cambridge High Sch.; Trinity Hall, Cambridge. War Service, Intelligence Corps, 1943–46. Open Maj. Scholar, Trinity Hall, 1940; 1st Class Hons Mod. Languages, Cantab, 1948; PhD Cantab, 1951. Asst Lecturer, Edinburgh Univ., 1952; Cambridge University: Asst Lecturer, subsequently Lecturer, 1952–66; Fellow and Tutor, Trinity Hall, 1958–66. Pres., MHRA, 1995. Cavaliere Ufficiale, 1975, Commendatore, 1988, al Merito della Repubblica Italiana. General Editor, Modern Language Review, 1971–77; Editor, Italian Studies, 1977–. *Publications:* Italy and the English Romantics, 1957; Torquato Tasso, 1965; Ariosto: a preface to the Orlando Furioso, 1974; (ed) Cambridge History of Italian Literature, 1996; contributions to learned journals. *Recreations:* sport, travel, gardening. *Address:* 21 Succoth Park, Edinburgh EH12 6BX.

BRAND, Geoffrey Arthur; Under-Secretary, Department of Employment, 1972–85; *b* 13 June 1930; *s* of late Arthur William Charles Brand and Muriel Ada Brand; *m* 1954, Joy Trotman; two *d*. *Educ:* Andover Grammar Sch.; University Coll., London. Entered Min. of Labour, 1953; Private Sec. to Parly Sec., 1956–57; Colonial Office, 1957–58; Private Sec. to Minister of Labour, 1965–66; Asst. Sec., Industrial Relations and Research and Planning Divisions, 1966–72. Mem., Archbishop of Canterbury's (later Bishops') Adv. Gp on Urban Priority Areas, 1986–98. FRSA 1985. *Address:* Cedarwood, Seer Green, Beaconsfield, Bucks HP9 2UH. *T:* (01494) 676637.

BRAND, Jo; writer and comedian; *m*. Formerly psychiatric nurse. Comedy includes stand-up. Television series: Jo Brand Through the Cakehole, 1995; A Big Slice of Jo Brand, 1996; Jo Brand's Commercial Breakdown, 1999–; Head on Comedy with Jo Brand, 2000. Radio series: Windbags (with Donna McPhail); Seven Ages of Man, 2000. Former columnist, The Independent; columnist, Nursing Times, 2000. British Comedy Award, 1992. *Publications:* Load of Old Balls: ranking of men in history, 1995; Load of Old Ball Crunchers: women in history, 1996; (with Helen Griffin) Mental (play), 1996. *Address:* c/o Richard Stone Partnership, 2 Henrietta Street, WC2E 8PS.

BRAND, Dr Paul Anthony, FBA 1998; Senior Research Fellow of All Souls College, Oxford, since 1999; *b* 25 Dec. 1946; *s* of Thomas Joseph Brand and Marjorie Jean Brand (*née* Smith); *m* 1970, Vanessa Carolyn Alexandra Rodrigues. *Educ:* Hampton Grammar Sch.; Magdalen Coll., Oxford (BA 1967; DPhil 1974). Asst Keeper, Public Record Office, 1970–76; Lectr in Law, UCD, 1976–83; research, 1983–93; Res. Fellow, Inst. of Historical Res., Univ. of London, 1993–99; Fellow, All Souls Coll., Oxford, 1997–99. Vis. Fellow, All Souls Coll., Oxford, 1995; Vis. Prof., Columbia Univ. Law Sch., 1995; Dist. Vis. Prof., Arizona Center for Medieval and Renaissance Studies and Merriam Vis. Prof. of Law, Arizona State Univ., 2000. *Publications:* The Origins of the English Legal Profession, 1992; The Making of the Common Law, 1992; The Earliest English Law Reports, vol. I, vol. II, 1996. *Recreations:* theatre, looking at buildings. *Address:* All Souls College, Oxford OX1 4AL. *T:* (01865) 279286; 155 Kennington Road, SE11 6SF. *T:* (020) 7582 4051.

BRAND, Dr Peter; General Practitioner, Brading, Isle of Wight, since 1977; *b* 16 May 1947; *s* of L. H. Brand and J. Brand (*née* Fredricks); *m* 1972, Jane Vivienne Attlee; two *s*. *Educ:* Thornbury Grammar Sch., Glos; Birmingham Univ. Med. Sch. MRCS; LRCP; DObstRCOG; MRCGP. Chm., IoW Div., BMA, 1980–84. Contested (Lib Dem) Isle of Wight, 1992, 2001; MP (Lib Dem) Isle of Wight, 1997-2001. *Recreations:* boating, preservation of 17th century domestic architecture. *Address:* Beechgrove, Brading, Isle of Wight PO36 0DE. *Clubs:* National Liberal; Island Sailing, Brading Haven Yacht.

BRANDES, Lawrence Henry, CB 1982; Under Secretary and Head of Office of Arts and Libraries, 1978–82; *b* 16 Dec. 1924; *m* 1950, Dorothea Stanyon; one *s* one *d*. *Educ:* Beltane Sch.; London Sch. of Economics. Min. of Health, 1950; Principal Private Sec. to Minister, 1959; Nat. Bd for Prices and Incomes, 1966; Dept of Employment and Productivity, 1969; Under-Sec., DHSS, 1970; HM Treasury, 1975. Director: Dance Umbrella, 1984–94; London Internat. Festival of Theatre, 1985–92. Member: Dulwich Picture Gall. Man. Cttee, 1984–94 (acting Chm., 1992; Chm., 1994); Museums and Galls Commn (Chm., Conservation Cttee), 1988–92. Chm., Textile Conservation Centre, 1993–98. Mem. Delegacy, Goldsmiths' Coll., 1983–88. Trustee, SS Great Britain, 1987–98. *Address:* 4 Hogarth Hill, NW11 6AX.

BRANDO, Marlon; American actor, stage and screen; *b* Omaha, Nebraska, 3 April 1924; *s* of Marlon Brando; *m* 1957, Anna Kashfi (marr. diss., 1959); one *s*. *Educ:* Libertyville High Sch., Illinois; Shattuck Military Academy, Minnesota. Entered Dramatic Workshop of New School for Social Research, New York, 1943; has studied with Elia Kazan and Stella Adler. *Plays include:* I Remember Mama, Broadway, 1944; Truckline Café, 1946; Candida, 1946; A Flag is Born, 1946; The Eagle Has Two Heads, 1946; A Streetcar Named Desire, 1947. *Films include:* The Men, 1950; A Streetcar Named Desire, 1951; Viva Zapata!, 1952; Julius Cæsar, 1953; The Wild Ones, 1953; Désirée, 1954; On the Waterfront, 1954; Guys and Dolls, 1955; Tea House of the August Moon, 1956; Sayonara, 1957; The Young Lions, 1958; The Fugitive Kind, 1960; Mutiny on the Bounty, 1962; The Ugly American, 1963; Bedtime Story, 1964; The Saboteur, Code Name-Morituri, 1965; The Chase, 1966; Appaloosa, 1966, Southwest to Sonora, 1966; A Countess from Hong Kong, 1967; Reflections in a Golden Eye, 1967; Candy, 1968; The Night of the Following Day, 1969; Quiemad!, 1970; The Nightcomers, 1971; The Godfather, 1972; Last Tango in Paris, 1972; The Missouri Breaks, 1975; Apocalypse Now, 1977; Superman, 1978; The Formula, 1981; A Dry White Season, 1990; The Freshman, 1990; Christopher Columbus, 1992; Don Juan DeMarco, 1994; The Island of Doctor Moreau, 1996; The Score, 2001. Directed, produced and appeared in One-Eyed Jacks, 1959. Academy Award, best actor of year, 1954, 1972. *Publication:* Songs My Mother Taught Me (autobiog.), 1994.

BRANDON, (David) Stephen; QC 1996; *b* 18 Dec. 1950; *s* of late James Osbaldeston Brandon and Dorothy Brandon (*née* Wright); *m* 1982, (Helen) Beatrice Lee; one *d*. *Educ:* Univ. of Nottingham (BA); Univ. of Keele (LLM). Lectr in Law, Univ. of Keele, 1975–85; called to the Bar, Gray's Inn, 1978; in practice at Revenue Bar, 1981–. *Publications:* Taxation of Non-Resident and Migrant Companies, 1989; Foreign Companies and the Problem of UK Residence, 1991; Taxation of Non-UK Resident Companies and Their Shareholders, 2001; various articles. *Recreations:* art (esp. collecting early woodcuts), opera, nurturing woodlands. *Address:* 24 Old Buildings, Lincoln's Inn, WC2A 3UP. *T:* (020) 7242 2744; Clopton Manor, Clopton, Northants NN14 3DZ.

BRANDON, Prof. Peter Samuel, FRICS; Professor of Quantity and Building Surveying, since 1985, and Director of Strategic Development, since 2001, University of Salford; *b* 4 June 1943; *s* of Samuel Brandon and Doris Eileen Florence Brandon (*née* Downing); *m* 1968, Mary Ann Elizabeth Canham; one *s* two *d*. *Educ:* Bournemouth Grammar Sch.; Bristol Univ. (MSc Architecture); DSc Salford. Private practice and local govt, 1963–69; Lectr, Portsmouth Poly., 1969–73; Prin. Lectr, Bristol Poly., 1973–81; Head of Dept, Portsmouth Poly., 1981–85; Salford University: Chm., Surveying Dept, 1985–93; Pro-Vice-Chancellor, 1993–2001; Dir, Res. and Grad. Coll., 1993–2001. Royal Institution of Chartered Surveyors: Chm., Res. Cttee, 1987–91; Mem. Gen. Council representing Gtr Manchester, 1989–93; Mem., Exec. Bd, QS Div., 1991–; Science and Engineering Research Council: Chm., Construction Cttee, 1991–94; Chm., Building Design Technology and Management Sub-Cttee, 1990–91; Member: Engrg Res. Commn, 1991–94; DTI Technology Foresight Panel for Construction, 1994; Chm., Built Envmt Panel for HEFC RAE, 1996 and 2001. Hon. Mem., ASAQS. *Publications:* Cost Planning of Buildings, 1980, 7th edn 1999; (ed) Building Cost Techniques, 1982; Microcomputers in Building Appraisal, 1983; (ed) Quality and Profit in Building Design, 1984; Computer programs for Building Cost Appraisal, 1985; Building, Cost Modelling and Computers, 1987; Expert Systems: the strategic planning of construction projects, 1988; (ed) Investment, Procurement & Performance in Construction, 1991; (ed) Management, Quality and Economics in Building, 1991; (ed) Integration of Construction Information, 1995; (ed) Client Centered Approach to Knowledge Based Systems, 1995; Evaluation of the Built Environment Sustainability, 1997; (ed) Cities and Sustainability, 2000. *Recreations:* mountain biking alongside canals, walking, travel, modern art. *Address:* Research and Graduate College, University of Salford, Salford M5 4WT. *T:* (0161) 295 5164, *Fax:* (0161) 745 5553. *Club:* Royal Over-Seas League.

BRANDON, Stephen; *see* Brandon, D. S.

BRANDON-BRAVO, Martin Maurice, FIMgt; *b* 25 March 1932; *s* of late Issac, (Alfred), and Phoebe Brandon-Bravo; *m* 1964, Sally Anne Wallwin; two *s*. *Educ:* Latymer Sch. FIMgt (FBIM 1980). Joined Richard Stump Ltd, later Richard Stump (1979), 1952; successively Floor Manager, Factory Manager, Production Dir and Asst Man. Dir; Man. Dir., 1979–83; non-exec. Dir, 1983–; Dir, Hall & Earl Ltd, 1970–83. Mem., Nottingham City Council, 1968–70 and 1976–87; Chm., 1970–73, Pres., 1975–83, Nottingham West Cons. Party Orgn; Dep. Chm., City of Nottingham Cons. Fedn. Contested (C): Nottingham East, 1979; Nottingham South, 1992. MP (C) Nottingham South, 1983–92; PPS to Minister of State for Housing and Urban Affairs, 1985–87, to Minister of State, Home Office, 1987–89, to Home Sec., 1989–90, to Lord Privy Seal and Leader of the House of Lords, 1990–92. Mem., Notts CC, 1993–. Contested (C) Nottingham and Leicestershire NW, Eur. Parly elecns, 1994. Mem., Nat. Water Sport Centre Management Cttee, 1972–83; President: Amateur Rowing Assoc., 1993–; Nottingham and Union Rowing Club; Trustee, Henley River and Rowing Mus, 1993–. *Recreation:* rowing (holder of Internat. Licence). *Address:* The Old Farmhouse, 27 Rectory Place, Barton-in-Fabis, Nottingham NG11 0AL. *T:* (0115) 983 0459, *Fax:* (0115) 983 0457. *Club:* Leander.

BRANDRETH, Gyles Daubeney; author, broadcaster; *b* 8 March 1948; *s* of late Charles Brandreth and of Alice Addison; *m* 1973, Michèle Brown; one *s* two *d*. *Educ:* Lycée Français de Londres; Betteshanger Sch., Kent; Bedales Sch., Hants; New Coll., Oxford (Scholar). Pres. Oxford Union, Editor of Isis. Chairman: Archway Productions Ltd, 1971–74; Victorama Ltd, 1974–93; Complete Editions Ltd, 1988–93; Director: Colin Smythe Ltd, 1971–73; Newarke Wools Ltd, 1988–92; J. W. Spear & Sons, 1992–95. Dep. Chm., Unicorn Heritage, 1987–90; children's publisher, André Deutsch Ltd, 1997–2000; consultant ed., Whitaker's Almanack, 1997–. Freelance journalist, 1968–: contrib. Observer, Guardian, Express, Daily Mail, Daily Mirror, Daily Telegraph, Evening Standard, Spectator, Punch, Homes & Gardens, She, Woman's Own; Columnist: Honey, 1968–69; Manchester Evening News, 1971–72; Woman, 1972–73, 1986–88; TV Times, 1989–92; Press Assoc. weekly syndicated column in USA, 1981–85; Ed., Puzzle World, 1989–92; Ed.-at-Large, Sunday Telegraph Review, 1999–. MP (C) City of Chester, 1992–97; contested (C) same seat, 1997. PPS to Financial Sec. to Treasury, 1993–94, to Sec. of State for Nat. Heritage, 1994–95, to Sec. of State for Health, 1995; an Asst Govt Whip, 1995–96; a Lord Comr, HM Treasury, 1996–97. Sponsor, 1994 Marriage Act. Broadcaster, 1969–: TV series incl.: Child of the Sixties, 1969; Puzzle Party, 1977; Chatterbox, 1977–78; Memories, 1982; Countdown, 1983–90 and 1997–; TV-am, 1983–90; Railway Carriage Game, 1985; Catchword, 1986; Discovering Gardens, 1990–91; CBS News, 1992–; (with Hinge and Bracket) Dear Ladies (TV scripts); (with Julian Slade) Now We Are Sixty (play); Theatrical producer, 1971–86: Through the Looking-Glass, 1972; Oxford Theatre Fest., 1974, 1976; The Dame of Sark, Wyndham's, 1974; The Little Hut, Duke of York's, 1974; Dear Daddy, Ambassador's, 1976; Cambridge Fest., 1986; also Son et Lumière; appeared as Baron Hardup in Cinderella, Guildford, 1989, Wimbledon, 1990. Founder: National Scrabble Championships, 1971; British Pantomime Assoc., 1971; Teddy Bear Mus., Stratford-upon-Avon, 1988. Dir, Europ. Movement's People for Europe campaign, 1975; Mem., Better English Campaign, 1995–97. Appeals Chm., 1983–89, Chm., 1989–93, Vice-Pres., 1993–, NPFA. Three times holder, world record for longest-ever after-dinner speech (4 hrs 19 mins, 1976; 11 hrs, 1978; 12 hrs 30 mins, 1982). *Publications:* over fifty books since Created in Captivity, 1972; most recent: Under the Jumper (autobiog.), 1993; Who is Nick Saint? (novel), 1996; Venice Midnight (novel), 1998; Breaking the Code (diaries), 1999; John Gielgud, 2000; Brief Encounters: meetings with remarkable people, 2001; over seventy books for children. *Address:* c/o International Artistes, 235 Regent Street, W1R 8AX.

BRANDRICK, David Guy, CBE 1981; Secretary, British Coal Corporation (formerly National Coal Board), 1972–89, retired; Director: Coal Staff Superannuation Scheme Trustees Ltd (formerly British Coal Staff Scheme Superannuation Trustees Ltd), since 1989; CMT Pension Trustee Services Ltd, since 1993; *b* 17 April 1932; *s* of Harry and Minnie Brandrick; *m* 1956, Eunice Fisher (*d* 1999); one *s* one *d*. *Educ:* Newcastle-under-Lyme High Sch.; St John's Coll., Oxford (MA). Joined National Coal Board, 1955; Chairman's Office, 1957; Principal Private Secretary to Chairman, 1961; Departmental Sec., Production Dept, 1963; Dep. Sec. to the Bd, 1967. *Recreation:* walking.

BRANDT, Paul Nicholas; His Honour Judge Brandt; a Circuit Judge, since 1987; *b* 21 Nov. 1937; *s* of late Paul Francis and of Barbara Brandt. *Educ:* St Andrew's Sch., Eastbourne; Marlborough Coll.; New Coll., Oxford (BA 2nd Cl. Hons Sch. of Jurisprudence). Called to the Bar, Gray's Inn, 1963; a Recorder, 1983–87. *Recreations:* sailing, shooting, Rugby football. *Address:* Colchester County Court, Falkland House, 25 Southway, Colchester, Essex CO3 3EG. *Clubs:* Royal Harwich Yacht (Woolverstone, Suffolk), Bar Yacht.

BRANDT, Peter Augustus; Chairman, Atkins Fulford Ltd, since 1977; *b* 2 July 1931; *s* of late Walter Augustus Brandt and late Dorothy Gray Brandt (*née* Crane); *m* 1962, Elisabeth Margaret (*née* ten Bos); two *s* one *d*. *Educ:* Eton Coll.; Trinity Coll., Cambridge (MA). Joined Wm Brandt's Sons & Co. Ltd, Merchant Bankers, 1954; Mem. Bd, 1960; Chief Executive, 1966; resigned, 1972. Director: London Life Assoc., 1962–89; Corp. of Argentine Meat Producers (CAP) Ltd and affiliates, 1970; Edward Bates (Holdings) Ltd, 1972–77; Edward Bates & Sons Ltd, 1972–77 (Chm., 1974–77). Mem., Nat. Rivers Authy (formerly Nat. Rivers Adv. Cttee), 1988–95. *Recreations:* sailing, rowing, steam engines, wild fowl. *Address:* Spout Farm, Boxford, Suffolk CO10 5HA. *Clubs:* Boodle's; Leander (Henley-on-Thames).

BRANKIN, Rhona; Member (Lab) Midlothian, Scottish Parliament, since 1999; *d* of Edward and Joyce Lloyd; *m* Peter Jones; two *d* by former marriage. *Educ:* Aberdeen Univ. (BEd 1975); Moray House Coll. (Dip. Special Educnl Needs 1989). Teacher, 1975–94; Lectr in Special Educnl Needs, Northern Coll., Dundee, 1994–99. Dep. Minister for Culture and Sport, 1999–2001, for Rural Develt, 2001–, Scottish Exec. Former Chair, Scottish Labour Party. *Recreations:* sport, the arts. *Address:* Scottish Parliament, Edinburgh EH99 1SP.

BRANN, Col William Norman, OBE 1967; ERD; Lord Lieutenant for County Down, 1979–90, retired; *b* 16 Aug. 1915; *s* of Rev. William Brann, BA, LLB, and Francesca Brann; *m* 1950, Anne Elizabeth Hughes; one *s* two *d*. *Educ:* Campbell Coll., Belfast. With Beck & Scott Ltd, Food Importers, Belfast, 1934–80, Chm., 1984–98. Served War of 1939–45, Army, France and Far East; TA, 1947–53. Hon. ADC to HE the Governor of N Ireland, 1952–72. Belfast Harbour Comr, 1960–79. Chm., Somme Hosp. for Ex Service Men and Women, retd; Pres., Burma Star Assoc., NI. County Down: DL 1974–79; JP 1980; High Sheriff, 1982. KStJ 1991. *Recreations:* gardening, hunting. *Address:* 23 Ballymoney Road, Craigantlet, Newtownards, Co. Down BT23 4TG. *T:* (028) 9042 2224. *Club:* Ulster Reform (Belfast).

BRANNEN, Peter; Director, International Labour Office, London, since 1992; *b* 1 Dec. 1941; *s* of Joseph Brannen and Monica Brannen (*née* Cairns); *m* 1966, Julia Mary Morgan; two *s*. *Educ:* Ushaw Coll., Durham; Univ. of Manchester (BA Hons Econs 1964). Account Exec., McCann Erickson Advertising, 1964; Sen. Res. Asst, Univ. of Durham, 1966–69; Senior Research Fellow: Univ. of Bradford, 1969–72; Univ. of Southampton Med. Sch., 1973; Department of Employment: Special Advr, 1974; Chief Res. Officer, 1975–86; Head of Internat. Relns, 1989–91. Visiting Fellow: ANU, 1987; Nuffield Coll., Oxford, 1988; Sen. Vis. Fellow, PSI, 1988; Vis. Prof. in Management, Southampton Univ., 2000–. Mem., Mgt, Indust. Relns and other cttees, SSRC, 1975–81; Chm., British Workplace Indust. Relns Surveys, 1980–89; Member: Admin Bd, European Foundn, 1986–92 (Dep. Chm., 1991); Employment Labour and Social Affairs Cttee, OECD, 1990–92; Employment Cttee, Council of Europe, 1990–92. FRSA 2000. Editl Bd, Work, Employment and Society, 1986–90. *Publications:* Entering the World of Work, 1975; The Worker Directors, 1976; Authority and Participation in Industry, 1983; various contribs to anthologies and learned jls on economic sociology. *Recreations:* sailing, gardening, drinking wine, music. *Address:* Hillside Cottage, Hyde Lane, Hyde, Fordingbridge, Hants SP6 2QP. *T:* (01425) 653333. *Clubs:* National Liberal; Royal Southampton Yacht.

BRANSON, Rear Adm. Cecil Robert Peter Charles, CBE 1975; *b* 30 March 1924; *s* of Cecil Branson and Marcelle Branson; *m* 1946, Sonia Moss; one *d. Educ:* RNC, Dartmouth. Served, HMS Dragon, W Africa, S Atlantic, Indian Ocean and Far East (present during time of fall of Singapore and Java), 1941–42; Sub-Lieut's Courses, 1942–43; qual. as submarine specialist, served in HM S/M Sea Rover, Far East, 1944–45; various appts in S/Ms, 1945–53; First Lieut, HMS Defender, 1953–55; jssc; CO, HMS Roebuck, Dartmouth Trng Sqdn, 1957; Staff, Flag Officer Flotillas Mediterranean, 1959–60; Jt Planning Staff, MoD, 1960–62; Exec. Officer, HMS Victorious, Far East, 1962–64; CO, HMS Rooke, Gibraltar, 1965; NATO Def. Coll., 1965; Defence Planning Staff, MoD, 1966–68; CO, HMS Phoebe, and Captain (D) Londonderry Sqdn, 1968–70; Naval Attaché, Paris, 1970–73; CO, HMS Hermes, 1973–74 (Hermes headed RN task force evacuating Brit. and foreign subjects from Cyprus beaches after Turkish invasion, 1973); Asst Chief of Naval Staff (Ops), MoD, 1975–77; retired. Man. Dir, UK Trawlers Mutual Insurance Assoc., 1977–85. *Club:* Army and Navy.

BRANSON, Edward James, MA; public relations and publicity services; a Metropolitan Stipendiary Magistrate, 1971–87; barrister-at-law; *b* 10 March 1918; *s* of late Rt Hon. Sir George Branson, PC, sometime Judge of High Court, and late Lady (Mona) Branson; *m* 1949, Evette Huntley, *e d* of late Rupert Huntley Flindt; one *s* two *d. Educ:* Bootham Sch., York; Trinity Coll., Cambridge. Served War, 1939–46, Staffordshire Yeomanry: Palestine, Egypt, and Western Desert, 1941–42; GSO 3 (Ops) attd 2 NZ Div. for Alamein, 1942; GS02 (Ops), attd 6 (US) Corps for Salerno and Anzio landings, 1943–44; subseq. GSO2 (Ops) 53 (W) Div. in Germany. Called to the Bar, Inner Temple, 1950; practised London and SE Circuit. *Recreations:* shooting, fishing, archaeology. *Address:* Cakeham Manor, West Wittering, W Sussex PO20 8LG.
See also Sir R. Branson.

BRANSON, Sir Richard (Charles Nicholas), Kt 2000; Founder and Chairman, Virgin Retail Group, Virgin Communications, Virgin Travel Group, Virgin Hotels Group, Virgin Direct Ltd, Virgin Bride Ltd, Virgin Net Ltd and Virgin Express Holdings Plc; Life President, Virgin Music Group (sold to Thorn-EMI, 1992); *b* 18 July 1950; *s* of Edward James Branson, *qv*; *m* 1st, 1969 (marr. diss.); 2nd, 1989, Joan Templeman; one *s* one *d. Educ:* Stowe. Editor, Student magazine, 1968–69; set up Student Advisory Centre (now Help), 1970. Founded Virgin Mail-Order Co., 1969, followed by Virgin Retail, Virgin Record Label, Virgin Music Publishing, Virgin Recording Studios; estabd Virgin Record subsids in 25 countries, 1980–86; founded Virgin Atlantic Airways, 1984; Voyager Gp Ltd formed 1986, encompassing interests in travel, clubs and hotels; Virgin Records launched in US, 1987; founded: Virgin Radio, 1993; Virgin Rail Gp Ltd, 1996. Pres., UK 2000, 1988– (Chm., 1986–88); Dir, Intourist Moscow Ltd, 1988–90. Launched charity, The Healthcare Foundn, 1987. Captain, Atlantic Challenger II, winner Blue Riband for fastest crossing of Atlantic by a ship, 1986; with Per Lindstrand, first to cross Atlantic in hot air balloon, 1987, and Pacific, 1991 (longest flight in hot air balloon, 6700 miles, and fastest speed, 200 mph, 1991). *Publication:* Losing My Virginity: the autobiography, 1998. *Address:* c/o Virgin Group Ltd, 120 Campden Hill Road, W8 7AR. *T:* (020) 7229 1282.

BRANT, Colin Trevor, CMG 1981; CVO 1979; HM Diplomatic Service, retired; *b* 2 June 1929; *m* 1954, Jean Faith Walker; one *s* two *d. Educ:* Christ's Hospital, Horsham; Sidney Sussex Coll., Cambridge (MA). Served Army, 4th Queen's Own Hussars, active service, Malaya, 1948–49; Pilot, Cambridge Univ. Air Squadron, 1951–52. Joined Sen. Br., Foreign Office, 1952; MECAS, Lebanon, 1953–54; Bahrain, 1954; Amman, 1954–56; FO, 1956–59; Stockholm, 1959–61; Cairo, 1961–64; Joint Services Staff Coll., Latimer, Bucks, 1964–65 (jssc); FO, 1965–67; Head of Chancery and Consul, Tunis, 1967–68; Asst Head, Oil Dept, FCO, 1969–71; Counsellor (Commercial), Caracas, 1971–73; Counsellor (Energy), Washington, 1973–78; Ambassador to Qatar, 1978–81; FCO Fellow, St Antony's Coll., Oxford, 1981–82; Consul Gen., and Dir Trade Promotion for S Africa, Johannesburg, 1982–87. Consultant, Carmichael & Sweet, Portsmouth, 1990–93; Dir, Internat. Energy Management Ltd, 1994–96. Donation Governor, Christ's Hosp., 1980–97, Almoner 1989–95. *Recreations:* music, painting, history. *Address:* 67 Merton Court, Rutherway, Oxford OX2 6QZ. *Club:* Royal Over-Seas League.

BRASH, Rev. Alan Anderson, OBE 1962; Moderator, Presbyterian Church of New Zealand, 1978–79; *b* 5 June 1913; *s* of Thomas C. Brash, CBE, New Zealand, and Margaret Brash (*née* Allan); *m* 1938, Eljean Ivory Hill; one *s* one *d. Educ:* Dunedin Univ., NZ (MA); Edinburgh Univ. (BD). Parish Minister in NZ, 1938–46 and 1952–56; Gen. Sec., NZ Nat. Council of Churches, 1947–52 and 1957–64, East Asia Christian Conf., 1958–68; Dir, Christian Aid, London, 1968–70; Dir, Commn on Inter-Church Aid, Refuge and World Service, WCC, 1970–73; Dep. Gen. Sec., WCC, 1974–78. Hon. DD Toronto, 1971. *Address:* 8 Gatonby Place, Avonhead, Christchurch, New Zealand.
See also D. T. Brash.

BRASH, Dr Donald Thomas; Governor, Reserve Bank of New Zealand, since 1988; *b* 24 Sept. 1940; *s* of Rev. Alan Anderson Brash, *qv*; *m* 1st, 1964, Erica Beatty; one *s* one *d*; 2nd, 1989, Je Lan Lee; one *s. Educ:* Christchurch Boys' High Sch.; Canterbury Univ., NZ (BA Hist. and Econs 1961; MA 1st Cl. Hons Econs 1962); Australian Nat. Univ. (PhD 1966). IBRD, Washington, 1966–71; Gen. Manager, Broadbank Corp. Ltd, 1971–81; Managing Director: NZ Kiwifruit Authy, 1982–86; Trust Bank Gp, 1986–88. *Publications:* New Zealand's Debt Servicing Capacity, 1964; American Investment in Australian Industry, 1966. *Recreation:* growing kiwifruit. *Address:* Reserve Bank of New Zealand, 2 The Terrace, PO Box 2498, Wellington, New Zealand. *T:* (4) 4722029.

BRASH, Robert, CMG 1980; HM Diplomatic Service, retired; Ambassador to Indonesia, 1981–84; *b* 30 May 1924; *s* of Frank and Ida Brash; *m* 1954, Barbara Enid Clarke; three *s* one *d. Educ:* Trinity Coll., Cambridge (Exhbnr). War Service, 1943–46. Entered Foreign Service, 1949; Djakarta, 1951–55; FO, 1955–58; First Sec., 1956; Jerusalem, 1958–61; Bonn, 1961–64; Bucharest, 1964–66; FCO, 1966–70; Counsellor, 1968; Canadian Nat. Defence Coll., 1970–71; Counsellor and Consul-Gen., Saigon, 1971–73; Counsellor, Vienna, 1974–78; Consul-Gen., Düsseldorf, 1978–81. Chm., Guildford Rambling Club, 1986–91. *Recreations:* walking, gardening, stained glass, golf. *Address:* Woodbrow, 495 Woodham Lane, Woking, Surrey GU21 5SR.

BRASHER, Christopher William, CBE 1996; President, London Marathon Ltd, since 1995 (Founder and Chairman, 1981–95); Chairman: Brasher Leisure Ltd, since 1977; The Brasher Boot Co., since 1992; *b* 21 Aug. 1928; *s* of William Kenneth Brasher, CBE and Katie Howe Brasher; *m* 1959, Shirley Bloomer; one *s* two *d. Educ:* Rugby Sch.; St John's Coll., Cambridge (MA). Pres., Mountaineering Club and Athletic Club, Cambridge Univ. Management Trainee and Jun. Executive, Mobil Oil Co., 1951–57; Sports Editor, 1957–61, columnist and Olympic Corresp., 1961–91, The Observer; BBC Television: Reporter, Tonight, 1961–65; Editor, Time Out, and Man Alive, 1964–65; Head of Gen. Features, 1969–72; reporter/producer, 1972–81. Man. Dir, Fleetfoot Ltd, 1979–95; Chairman: Reebok UK Ltd, 1990–92; Berghaus, 1993–98. Co-Founder and Chm., British Orienteering Fedn (formerly English Orienteering Assoc.), 1966–69 (Vice-Pres., 1984–). Trustee, London Marathon Charitable Trust, 1981–; Founder, 1983, and Trustee, 1983–92, 1996–, John Muir Trust; Chairman: Chris Brasher Trust, 1988–; Petersham Trust, 1999–. Rep. GB, Olympic Games, 1952 and 1956; Gold Medal for 3,000 metres Steeplechase, 1956. DUniv Stirling, 1989; Hon. DSc Kingston, 1996. OStJ 1995. National Medal of Honour, Finland, 1975; Sports Writer of the Year (British Press Awards), 1968, 1976. *Publications:* The Red Snows (with Sir John Hunt), 1960; Sportsmen of our Time, 1962; Tokyo 1964: a diary of the XVIIIth Olympiad, 1964; Mexico 1968: a diary of the XIXth Olympics, 1968; Munich 72, 1972; (ed) The London Marathon: the first ten years, 1991. *Recreations:* mountains, fishing, horse racing, orienteering, social running. *Address:* The White House, Chaddleworth, Berks RG20 7DY. *T:* (01488) 638498. *Clubs:* Travellers, Alpine, Hurlingham; Ranelagh Harriers (Petersham); Thames Hare and Hounds (Kingston Vale).

BRASLAVSKY, Dr Nicholas Justin; QC 1999; a Recorder, since 2001; *b* 9 Feb. 1959; *s* of late Rev. Cyril and of Stella Braslavsky; *m* 1990, Jane Margolis; two *s* one *d. Educ:* Blackpool Grammar Sch.; High Pavement Grammar Sch., Nottingham; Univ. of Birmingham (LLB Hons 1979; PhD 1982). Called to the Bar, Inner Temple, 1983; in practice at the Bar, 1983–. *Address:* 40 King Street, Manchester M2 6BA; 5 Park Place, Leeds LS1 2RU; 3 Paper Buildings, EC4Y 7EU.

BRASNETT, John, CMG 1987; HM Diplomatic Service, retired; Deputy High Commissioner, Bombay, 1985–89; *b* 30 Oct. 1929; *s* of late Norman Vincent Brasnett and of Frances May Brasnett (*née* Hewlett); *m* 1956, Jennifer Ann Reid; one *s* one *d. Educ:* Blundells Sch.; Selwyn Coll., Cambridge (BA). Served Royal Artillery, 1948–49. Colonial Administrative Service, Uganda, 1953–65; retired from HM Overseas CS as Dep. Administrator, Karamoja District, 1965; entered HM Diplomatic Service, 1965; 1st Sec., OECD Delegn, 1968; Dep. High Comr, Freetown, 1970; FCO, 1973; Olympic Attaché, Montreal, 1975–76; Dep. High Comr, Accra, 1977–80; Counsellor (Econ. and Commercial), Ottawa, 1980–85. *Recreations:* reading, photography. *Address:* 8 Croft Way, Sevenoaks, Kent TN13 2JX.

BRASSEY, family name of **Baron Brassey of Apethorpe**.

BRASSEY OF APETHORPE, 3rd Baron *cr* 1938, of Apethorpe; **David Henry Brassey;** Bt 1922; OBE 1994; JP; Vice Lord-Lieutenant of Northamptonshire, since 2000; *b* 16 Sept. 1932; *er s* of 2nd Baron Brassey of Apethorpe, MC, TD, and late Lady Brassey of Apethorpe; *S* father, 1967; *m* 1st, 1958, Myrna Elizabeth (*d* 1974), *o d* of late Lt-Col John Baskervyle-Glegg; one *s*; 2nd, 1978, Caroline, *y d* of late Lt-Col G. A. Evill; two *d.* Commissioned, Grenadier Guards, 1951; Major, 1966, retired, 1967. JP 1970, DL 1972, Northants. *Heir: s* Hon. Edward Brassey, *b* 9 March 1964. *Address:* The Manor House, Apethorpe, Peterborough PE8 5DL. *T:* (01780) 470231. *Club:* White's.

BRATBY, Jean Esme Oregon; *see* Cooke, J. E. O.

BRATHWAITE, Rt Hon. Nicholas (Alexander), Kt 1995; OBE; PC 1994; Prime Minister of Grenada, 1990–95; *b* Carriacou, 8 July 1925; *s* of Charles and Sophia Brathwaite; *m*; three *s* one *d. Educ:* Univ. of W Indies (BEd 1967). Formerly: teacher; Sen. Tutor, then Principal, Teachers' Coll.; Chief Educn Officer, Min. of Social Affairs, Grenada; Regl Dir, Commonwealth Youth Prog., Caribbean Centre, 1974–83; Chm., Interim Council, Grenada, 1983–84; Leader, Nat. Democratic Congress, 1989–95; formerly Minister of: Finance; Home Affairs; Nat. Security; Foreign Affairs; Personnel and Mgt; Carriacou and Petit Martinique Affairs. *Address:* Villa A, St George's, Grenada.

BRATT, Guy Maurice, CMG 1977; MBE 1945; HM Diplomatic Service, retired; Counsellor, Foreign and Commonwealth Office, 1977–80; *b* 4 April 1920; *s* of late Ernst Lars Gustaf Bratt and late Alice Maud Mary Bratt (*née* Raper); *m* 1945, Françoise Nelly Roberte Girardet; two *s* one *d. Educ:* Merchant Taylors' Sch.; London Univ. (BA). Served Army, 1939–46 (MBE): Major, Royal Signals. Solicitor 1947. Asst Sec., Colonial Develt Corp.; joined HM Foreign (subseq. Diplomatic) Service, 1952; served FO, 1952–54; Berlin, 1954–56; Brussels, 1956–58; FO, 1958–62; Vienna, 1962–66; FCO, 1966–70; Geneva, 1970–72; FCO, 1972–74; Washington, 1974–77. Mem. various gps of Chiltern Soc. *Publications:* The Bisses of Valais: man-made watercourses in Switzerland, 1995; articles in railway and model railway jls. *Recreations:* music, railways, mountaineering. *Address:* 2 Orchehill Rise, Gerrards Cross, Bucks SL9 8PR. *T:* (01753) 883106. *Club:* Travellers.

BRATTON, Prof. Jacqueline Susan, DPhil; Professor of Theatre and Cultural History, Royal Holloway, University of London, since 1992 (Head of Drama and Theatre, 1994–2001); *b* 23 April 1945; *d* of Jack Stanley Bratton and Doris Nellie Bratton (*née* Reynolds); partner, Jane Elizabeth Traies. *Educ:* St Anne's Coll., Oxford (BA 1966; DPhil 1969). Lectr, 1969–83, Reader in English Literature, 1983–84, Bedford Coll., Univ. of London; Reader in Theatre and Cultural History, RHBNC, 1984–92. Series Editor, Shakespeare in Production, 1994–; Editor, Nineteenth Century Theatre, 1996–2001. *Publications:* The Victorian Popular Ballad, 1975; The Impact of Victorian Children's Fiction, 1981; (ed) Music Hall: Performance and Style, 1986; King Lear: a stage history edition, 1987; Acts of Supremacy, 1991; (ed) Melodrama: stage picture screen, 1994. *Recreations:* hill walking, writing fiction. *Address:* Department of Drama, Royal Holloway, University of London, Egham TW20 0EX.

BRATZA, Hon. Sir Nicolas (Dušan), Kt 1998; **Hon. Mr Justice Bratza;** a Judge of the High Court, Queen's Bench Division, since 1998; Judge of the European Court of Human Rights, since 1998 (Section President, 1998–2000); *b* 3 March 1945; *s* of late Milan Bratza, concert violinist, and Hon. Margaret Bratza (*née* Russell). *Educ:* Wimbledon Coll.; Brasenose Coll., Oxford (BA 1st Cl. Hons, MA). Instructor, Univ. of Pennsylvania Law Sch., 1967–68; called to Bar, Lincoln's Inn, 1969 (Hardwicke and Droop Schol.), Bencher, 1993; Jun. Counsel to the Crown, Common Law, 1979–88; QC 1988; a Recorder, 1993–98; UK Mem., European Commn of Human Rights, 1993–98. Vice-Chm., British Inst. of Human Rights, 1990–98 (Gov., 1983–); Mem., Bd of Mgt, British Inst. of Internat. and Comparative Law, 1999–. Mem., Editl Bd, European Human Rights Law Review, 1996–. *Publications:* (jtly) Contempt of Court, and Crown Proceedings, in Halsbury's Laws of England, 4th edn. *Recreations:* music, cricket. *Address:* European Court of Human Rights, Council of Europe, 67075 Strasbourg, France. *T:* 388412018, *Fax:* 388412730. *Clubs:* Garrick, MCC.

BRAUDE, Prof. Peter Riven, PhD; FRCOG; Professor and Head of Division of Women's and Children's Health, Guy's, King's and St Thomas' School of Medicine, King's College, London (formerly Head of Department of Obstetrics and Gynaecology, United Medical and Dental Schools of Guy's and St Thomas' Hospitals), since 1991; Director, Centre for Pre-implantation Genetic Diagnosis, Guy's and St Thomas' Hospital NHS Trust, since 1999; *b* Johannesburg, 29 May 1948; *s* of Dr Barnett Braude and Sylvia (*née* Grunberg); *m* 1973, Beatrice Louise Roselaar; two *s. Educ:* Univ. of Witwatersrand (BSc 1968; MB BCh 1972); Jesus Coll., Cambridge (MA 1975; PhD 1981). DPMSA 1983; MRCOG 1982, FRCOG 1993. Lectr in Physiology and Pharmacology, Univ. of Witwatersrand Med. Sch., 1973; Demonstrator, Dept of Anatomy, Univ. of Cambridge,

1974–79; sen. house officer appts, St Mary's Hosp., London and Addenbrooke's Hosp., Cambridge, 1979–81; Sen. Res. Associate, Dept of Obstetrics and Gynaecol., Univ. of Cambridge, 1981–83; Registrar in Obstetrics and Gynaecol., Rosie Maternity Hosp., Cambridge, 1983–85; University of Cambridge: Clinical Lectr in Obstetrics and Gynaecol., 1985–88; MRC Clinical Res. Consultant, Clinical Sch., 1988–89; Consultant and Sen. Lectr, Dept of Obstetrics and Gynaecol., 1989–90; Clinical Dir for Women's Services, 1993–94, Dir, Assisted Conception Unit and Fertility Service, 1993–99, Guy's and St Thomas' Hosp. NHS Trust. Mem., HFEA, 1999–. Exec. Sec., Assoc. Profs of Obstetrics and Gynaecol., 1993–95. Mem., Med. Adv. Bd, Tommy's Campaign, 1993–99. Mem. Editl Bd, Molecular Human Reproduction, 1992–. *Publications:* contribs to scientific jls on develt of the human embryo *in vitro*, assisted conception techniques, treatment of infertility, ethics and politics of new reproductive technologies and laparoscopic surgery. *Recreations:* hooked on, but not necessarily very good at, ski-ing, narrow boating, music, wine-tasting, gardening, Apple Macs. *Address:* GKT Division of Women's and Children's Health, St Thomas' Hospital, Lambeth Palace Road, SE1 7EH. *T:* (020) 7922 8105; *e-mail:* peter.braude@kcl.ac.uk.

BRAUTASET, Tarald Osnes; Ambassador of Norway to the Court of St James's, since 2000; *b* 28 Sept. 1946; *s* of Alv Brautaset and Birgit Osnes Brautaset; *m* 1975, Elisabeth Mohr; two *d*. *Educ:* Univ. of Oslo (MA Pol Sci.). Joined Norwegian Diplomatic Service, 1975: 2nd Sec., Abidjan, 1975–77; 1st Sec., Paris, 1977–80; Hd of Div., Min. of Foreign Affairs, Oslo, 1980–88; Counsellor, Mission to EU, Brussels, 1988–94; Dep. Dir Gen., 1994–96, Dir Gen., 1996–98, Dep. Sec. Gen., 1998–2000, Min. of Foreign Affairs, Oslo. Comdr, Order of St Olav (Norway), 2000. *Recreation:* gardening. *Address:* Royal Norwegian Embassy, 25 Belgrave Square, SW1X 8QD.

BRAVO, Martin Maurice B.; *see* Brandon-Bravo.

BRAY, Angela Lavinia; Member (C) West Central, London Assembly, Greater London Authority, since 2000; *b* 13 Oct. 1953; *d* of Benedict and Patricia Bray. *Educ:* Downe House, Newbury; St Andrews Univ. (MA Hons Medieval Hist.). Presenter, British Forces Broadcasting, Gibraltar, 1979–80; presenter, producer and reporter, LBC Radio, 1980–88; Hd, Broadcasting Unit, Cons. Central Office, 1989–91; Press Officer, Rt Hon. John Major's Leadership Campaign, Nov. 1990; Press Sec. to Chm., Conservative Party, 1991–92; Public Affairs Consultant, 1992–2000. Contested (C) E Ham, 1997. Pres., Kensington and Chelsea Cons. Pol Forum, 2000–; Vice Pres., Hammersmith and Fulham Cons. Assoc., 2000–. *Recreations:* tennis, music, history, walking my dogs. *Address:* Greater London Authority, Romney House, 43 Marsham Street, SW1P 3PY. *T:* (020) 7983 4360.

BRAY, Denis Campbell, CMG 1977; CVO 1975; JP; Chairman, Denis Bray Consultants Ltd, Hong Kong, since 1985; *b* 24 Jan. 1926; *s* of Rev. Arthur Henry Bray and Edith Muriel Bray; *m* 1952, Marjorie Elizabeth Bottomley; four *d* (one *s* decd). *Educ:* Kingswood Sch.; Jesus Coll., Cambridge (MA). BScEcon London. RN, 1947–49. Colonial Service Devonshire Course, 1949–50; Admin. Officer, Hong Kong, 1950; Dist Comr, New Territories, 1971; Hong Kong Comr in London, 1977–80; Sec. for Home Affairs, Hong Kong, 1973–77 and 1980–84, retd. Chairman: English Schools Foundn, Hong Kong, 1985–91; Jubilee Sports Centre, Hong Kong, 1985–89; Dir, Hong Kong Philharmonic, 1985–. Director: First Pacific Davies Ltd, 1986–99; Herald Holdings Ltd, 1987–; Leighton Asia Ltd, 1990–2000; Exec. Dir, Community Chest of Hong Kong, 1985–92. Pres., Hong Kong Yachting Assoc., 1989–91. JP 1960–85, and 1987. *Address:* 8A-7 Borrett Mansions, 8–9 Bowen Road, Hong Kong. *T:* 25263630. *Clubs:* Travellers, London Rowing; Leander (Henley-on-Thames); Hong Kong, Hong Kong Jockey, Royal Hong Kong Yacht; Tai Po Boat.
See also J. W. Bray.

BRAY, Jeremy William, PhD; *b* 29 June 1930; *s* of Rev. Arthur Henry Bray and Mrs Edith Muriel Bray; *m* 1953, Elizabeth (*née* Trowell); four *d*. *Educ:* Aberystwyth Grammar Sch.; Kingswood Sch.; Jesus Coll., Cambridge (PhD 1956). Researched in pure mathematics at Cambridge, 1953–55; Choate Fellow, Harvard Univ., USA, 1955–56; Technical Officer, Wilton Works of ICI, 1956–62. Contested (Lab) Thirsk and Malton, 1959. MP (Lab): Middlesbrough West, 1962–70; Motherwell and Wishaw, Oct. 1974–1983; Motherwell South, 1983–97. Parly Sec., Min. of Power, 1966–67; Jt Parly Sec., Min. of Technology, 1967–69; Opposition spokesman on science and technology, 1983–92. Member: Select Cttee on Nationalised Industries, 1962–64; Estimates Cttee, 1964–66 (Chm., Sub-cttee, 1964–66); Expenditure Cttee, 1978–79; Select Cttee on Treasury and Civil Service, 1979–83 (Chm., Sub-cttee, 1981–82); Select Cttee on Sci. and Technol., 1992–97; Bd, Parly Office of Sci. and Technol., 1993–97; Chairman: Labour, Science and Technol. Group, 1964–66; All-Party Parly Mental Health Gp, 1994–97; Vice Pres., Parlt and Sci. Cttee, 1993–97; Vice Chairman: Parly Engrg Gp, 1993–97; British-Chinese Parly Gp, 1987–95. Dir, Mullard Ltd, 1970–73; Consultant, Battelle Res. Centre, Geneva, 1973; Sen. Res. Fellow, 1974, Vis. Prof., 1975–79, Univ. of Strathclyde; Vis. Res. Fellow, Imperial Coll., 1989–93. Mem. Adv. Council, Save British Science, 1993–. Dep. Chm., Christian Aid, 1972–84; Co-Dir, Programme of Res. into Econometric Methods, QMC and Imperial Coll., 1971–74. Chm., Fabian Soc., 1971–72. Hon. DSc Leicester, 1995. *Publications:* Decision in Government, 1970; Production Purpose and Structure, 1982; Fabian pamphlets and articles in jls. *Recreation:* sailing. *Address:* 21 Horn Lane, Linton, Cambs CB1 6HT. *T:* (01223) 890434.
See also D. C. Bray.

BRAY, Prof. Kenneth Noel Corbett, PhD; FRS 1991; CEng; Hopkinson and Imperial Chemical Industries Professor of Applied Thermodynamics, 1985–97, now Emeritus, and Fellow of Girton College, 1985–97, Cambridge University; *b* 19 Nov. 1929; *s* of Harold H. Bray and Effie E. Bray; *m* 1958, Shirley Maureen Culver; two *s* one *d*. *Educ:* Univ. of Cambridge (BA); Univ. of Southampton (PhD); MSE Princeton; CEng; MRAeS; MAIAA. Engr in Research Dept, Handley Page Aircraft, 1955–56; University of Southampton, 1956–85: Dean, Faculty of Engrg and Applied Science, 1975–78; Head, Dept of Aeronautics and Astronautics, 1982–85. Vis. appt, Avco-Everett Res. Lab., Mass, USA, 1961–62; Vis. Prof., MIT, 1966–67; Vis. Res. Engr, Univ. of California, San Diego, 1975, 1983. *Publications:* on topics in gas dynamics, chemically reacting flows, molecular energy transfer processes and combustion. *Recreations:* walking, wood carving, gardening. *Address:* 23 De Freville Avenue, Cambridge CB4 1HW.

BRAY, Maj.-Gen. Paul Sheldon, CB 1991; Paymaster-in-Chief and Inspector of Army Pay Services, 1989–92, now retired; *b* 31 Jan. 1936; *s* of Gerald Bray and Doris (*née* Holt); *m* 1958, Marion Diana Naden; one *s* two *d*. *Educ:* Purbrook Park County High Sch.; RMA Sandhurst; Southampton Univ. (BA 1995; MA 1998). ndc, psc†, sq, pfc. Commissioned RA 1956; served BAOR, Cyprus, UK; transf. RAPC 1965; served Malaya, N Wales, MoD, HQ UKLF, HQ Scotland, HQ NE District; OC RAPC Training Centre, 1976–77; NDC 1978; DS RMCS Shrivenham, 1979–82; MoD 1982; Chief Paymaster, Army Pay Office (Officers' Accounts), 1982–83; Comdt, Defence ADP Training Centre, 1983–85; Chief Paymaster ADP, RAPC Computer Centre, 1985–89. Chm. Trustees, Friends of Winchester Cathedral, 1996–. Governor, King's Sch., Winchester, 1992–. *Recreations:* music, theatre, travel, oenology, rearranging the garden. *Address:* c/o Corps HQ, RAPC Worthy Down, Winchester, Hants SO21 2RG.

BRAY, Richard Winston Atterton; His Honour Judge Bray; a Circuit Judge, since 1993; *b* 10 April 1945; *s* of Winston Bray, *qv* and Betty Atterton (*née* Miller); *m* 1978, Judith Elizabeth Margaret Ferguson; one *s* three *d*. *Educ:* Rugby Sch.; Corpus Christi Coll., Oxford (BA). Called to the Bar, Middle Temple, 1970; practiced on Midland and Oxford Circuit; Asst Recorder, 1983–87; Recorder, 1987–93. *Recreations:* cricket, Real tennis, astronomy. *Address:* 36 Bedford Row, WC1R 4JH. *Clubs:* MCC, I Zingari, Frogs.

BRAY, William John, CBE 1975; FREng; Director of Research, Post Office, 1966–75 (Dep. Director, 1965); *b* 10 Sept. 1911; British; *m* 1936, Margaret Earp (*d* 1998); one *d* (and one *d* decd). *Educ:* Imperial Coll., London Univ. Electrical engineering apprenticeship, Portsmouth Naval Dockyard, 1928–32; Royal and Kitchener Scholarships, Imperial Coll., 1932–34; entered PO Engineering Dept as Asst Engineer, 1934; Commonwealth Fund Fellowship (Harkness Foundation) for study in USA, 1956–57; Staff Engineer, Inland Radio Br., PO Engineering Dept, 1958. Vis. Prof., UCL, 1974–78. External Examr, MSc (Communications), Imperial Coll., London, 1976–80. Participation in work of International Radio Consultative Cttee of International Telecommunication Union and European Postal and Telecommunication Conferences; Consultant to UK Council for Educnl Technology, 1976–78. Associate Mem., World Innovation Foundn, 1999. MSc(Eng), FCGI, DIC, FIEE; FREng (FEng 1978). DUniv Essex, 1976. J. J. Thomson Medal, IEE, 1978. *Publications:* Memoirs of a Telecommunications Engineer, 1983; The Communications Miracle: telecommunication pioneers from Morse to the Information Superhighway, 1995; Then, Now and Tomorrow: the autobiography of a communications engineer, 1999; papers in Proc. IEE (IEE Ambrose Fleming Radio Sect. and Electronics Div. Premium Awards), IEE Review. *Recreation:* writing. *Address:* The Pump House, Bredfield, Woodbridge, Suffolk IP13 6AH. *T:* (01394) 385838; *e-mail:* bray@btinternet.com.

BRAY, Winston, CBE 1970; Deputy Chairman and Deputy Chief Executive, BOAC, 1972–74; Member Board, BOAC, 1971–74; Member Board, BAAC Ltd (formerly BOAC (AC Ltd), 1969–74; *b* 29 April 1910; *s* of late Edward Bray and Alice Walker; *m* 1937, Betty Atterton Miller (*d* 1999); one *s* one *d* (and one *d* decd). *Educ:* Highgate Sch.; London Univ. (BCom). Missouri Pacific Railroad, USA, 1932; Asst to Traffic Manager, British Airways, 1938; Traffic Dept, BOAC, 1940; Sales Promotion Supt, 1946; Sales Manager, 1950; Sales Planning Manager, 1954; Dir of Planning, 1964; Planning Dir, 1969; Dep. Managing Dir, 1972. FCIT. *Recreations:* sailing, gardening. *Address:* Altenburg, Trafford Road, Great Missenden, Bucks HP16 0BT.
See also R. W. A. Bray.

BRAYBROOKE, 10th Baron *cr* 1788; **Robin Henry Charles Neville;** Lord-Lieutenant of Essex, since 1992; Hereditary Visitor of Magdalene College, Cambridge; Patron of three livings; farmer and landowner; *b* 29 Jan. 1932; *s* of 9th Baron Braybrooke and Muriel Evelyn (*d* 1962), *d* of William C. Manning; *S* father, 1990; *m* 1st, 1955, Robin Helen Brockhoff (marr. diss. 1974); four *d* (inc. twins) (and one *d* decd); 2nd, 1974, Linda Norman (marr. diss. 1998); three *d*; 3rd, 1998, Mrs Perina Fordham. *Educ:* Eton; Magdalene Coll., Cambridge (MA); RAC Cirencester. Commnd Rifle Bde, 1951; served 3rd Bn King's African Rifles in Kenya and Malaya, 1951–52. Dir of Essex and Suffolk Insurance Co. until amalgamation with Guardian Royal Exchange. Member: Saffron Walden RDC, 1959–69; for Stansted, Essex CC, 1969–72; Council of CLA, 1965–83; Agricl Land Tribunal, Eastern Area, 1975–. Chairman: Price Trust, 1983–95; Rural Develt Commn for Essex, 1984–90. Pres., Essex Show, 1990. DL Essex, 1980. DU Essex, 2000. *Recreations:* railway and airfield operating, photography, motorcycling. *Heir: kinsman* George Neville, *b* 23 March 1943. *Address:* Abbey House, Audley End, Saffron Walden, Essex CB11 4JB. *T:* (01799) 522484, *Fax:* (01799) 513270. *Clubs:* Boodle's, Farmers'.
See also Earl of Derby.

BRAYBROOKE, Rev. Marcus Christopher Rossi; non-stipendiary priest, Marsh and Toot Baldon, Dorchester Team Ministry, Oxford, since 1993; *b* 16 Nov. 1938; *s* of late Lt-Col Arthur Rossi Braybrooke and of Marcia Nona Braybrooke; *m* 1964, Mary Elizabeth Walker, JP, BSc, CQSW; one *s* one *d*. *Educ:* Cranleigh School; Magdalene College, Cambridge (BA, MA); Madras Christian College; Wells Theological College; King's College, London (MPhil). Curate, St Michael's, Highgate, 1964–67; Team Vicar, Strood Clergy Team, 1967–73; Rector, Swainswick, Langridge, Woolley, 1973–79; Dir of Training, Dio. of Bath and Wells, 1979–84; Hon. priest-in-charge, Christ Church, Bath, 1984–91; Exec. Director, Council of Christians and Jews, 1984–87; Preb., Wells Cathedral, 1990–93; Chaplain, Chapel of St Mary Magdalene, Bath, 1992–93. World Congress of Faiths: Chm., 1978–83 and 1992–99; a Vice-Pres., 1986–97; Co-Pres., 1997–; Chm., Internat. Cttee, 1988–93; Chm., Internat. Interfaith Orgns Co-ordinating Cttee, 1990–93; Trustee: Internat. Interfaith Centre, 1993–2000; Internat. Peace Council, 1995–; Council for Parlt of World Religions, 1995–. Examng Chaplain to Bishop of Bath and Wells, 1984–88. Sir Sigmund Sternberg Award for contributions to Christian-Jewish relations, 1992. Editor: World Faiths Insight, 1976–91; Common Ground, 1987–93. *Publications:* Together to the Truth, 1971; The Undiscovered Christ of Hinduism, 1973; Interfaith Worship, 1974; Interfaith Organizations: a historical directory, 1980; Time to Meet, 1990; Wide Embracing Love, 1990; Pilgrimage of Hope, 1992; Stepping Stones to a Global Ethic, 1992; Be Reconciled, 1992; (ed with Tony Bayfield) Dialogue with a Difference, 1992; Love Without Limit, 1995; Faith in a Global Age, 1995; How to Understand Judaism, 1995; A Wider Vision: a history of the World Congress of Faiths, 1996; The Wisdom of Jesus, 1997; (contrib.) The Miracles of Jesus, 1997; (ed with Jean Potter) All in Good Faith, 1997; (contrib.) The Journeys of St Paul, 1997; The Explorers' Guide to Christianity, 1998; (ed with Peggy Morgan) Testing the Global Ethic, 1999; Christian–Jewish Dialogue: the next steps, 2000; contrib. to various theol books and jls incl. Theology, Modern Believing (formerly The Modern Churchman), The Tablet, The Expository Times. *Recreations:* gardening, swimming, travel, photography. *Address:* The Rectory, Marsh Baldon, Oxford OX44 9LS. *T:* (01865) 343215, *Fax:* (01865) 343575; *e-mail:* MarcusBray@aol.com.

BRAYE, Baroness (8th in line) *cr* 1529, of Eaton Braye, Co. Bedford; **Mary Penelope Aubrey-Fletcher;** DL; *b* 28 Sept. 1941; *d* of 7th Baron Braye and Dorothea (*d* 1994), *yr d* of late Daniel C. Donoghue, Philadelphia; *S* father, 1985; *m* 1981, Lt-Col Edward Henry Lancelot Aubrey-Fletcher, Grenadier Guards. *Educ:* Assumption Convent, Hengrave Hall; Univ. of Warwick. Pres., Blaby Cons. Assoc., 1986–; Dep. Pres., Northants Red Cross, 1983–92; Chm. School Cttee, St Andrew's Occupational Therapy School, 1988–93. Governor: St Andrew's Hosp., Northampton, 1978–; Three Shires Hosp., Northampton, 1983–. High Sheriff of Northants, 1983; JP South Northants, 1981–86; DL Northants 1998. *Co-heiresses: cousins* Linda Kathleen Fothergill [*b* 2 May 1930, *née* Browne; *m* 1965, Comdr Christopher Henry Fothergill, RN; two *s*; Theresa Beatrice Browne *b* 9 Aug. 1934]. *Address:* Stanford Hall, Lutterworth, Leics LE17 6DH.

BRAYFIELD, Celia Frances; author; *b* 21 Aug. 1945; *d* of Felix Francis Brayfield and Helen (Ada Ellen) Brayfield; one *d*. *Educ:* St Paul's Girls' Sch.; Univ. of Grenoble. Sec.,

1964–67; trainee, Nova mag., 1968; sec., The Observer, 1969; feature writer, Daily Mail, 1969–71; TV columnist, Evening Standard, 1974–82; TV critic, The Times, 1984–88; columnist, Sunday Telegraph, 1988–90; feature writer, The Times, 1998–; contrib. to other pubns. Mem., Cttee of Mgt, NCOPF, 1989–. Mem., Cttee of Mgt, Soc. of Authors, 1995–98; Dir, Nat. Acad. Writing, 1999–. *Publications:* Glitter: the truth about fame, 1985; Bestseller, 1996; *fiction:* Pearls, 1986; The Prince, 1990; White Ice, 1993; Harvest, 1993; Getting Home, 1998; Sunset, 1999; Heartswap, 2000. *Recreations:* family life, the arts. *Address:* c/o Curtis Brown Ltd, Haymarket House, 28/29 Haymarket, SW1Y 4SP. *T:* (020) 7396 6600. *Clubs:* Groucho, Chelsea Arts.

BRAYNE, Richard Bolding, MBE 1957; Clerk of the Worshipful Company of Ironmongers, 1973–90 (Asst Clerk, 1971; Master, 1993–94); *b* 28 Oct. 1924; 3rd *s* of late Brig. Frank Lugard Brayne, MC, CSI, CIE, ICS, and late Iris Goodeve Brayne, K-i-H; *m* 1947, Anne Stoddart Forrest; one *s* two *d*. *Educ:* Sherborne Sch.; Pembroke Coll., Cambridge. Indian Army, 3rd (Peshawar) Indian Mountain Battery, FF, India, Burma and Far East, 1942–46. Entered Colonial Service as DO, Tanganyika, 1948; Staff Officer to HRH The Princess Margaret's tour of Tanganyika, 1956; Dist Comr, 1957; Principal, Admin. Trng Centre and Local Govt Trng Centre, 1960. Prin. Asst Sec., Min. of Educn, 1963; Mem., E African UGC and Makerere Univ. College Council, 1963; retd from Colonial Service, 1964. Sec., Brit. Paper and Board Makers' Assoc., 1964; Trng Adviser and Develt Manager, Construction Industry Trng Bd, 1966. Member: Exec. Cttee, Nat. Assoc. of Almshouses, 1972–2000 (Chm., 1981–87); Council, Royal Surgical Aid Soc., 1972–95 (Chm., 1982–87). *Recreations:* golf, bridge, gardening.

BRAZAUSKAS, Dr Algirdas Mykolas; President, Republic of Lithuania, 1993–98; *b* Rokishkis, Lithuania, 22 Sept. 1932; *s* of Kazimieras Brazauskas and Zofija Brazauskiene; *m* 1958, Julija Styraite–Brazauskiene; two *d*. *Educ:* Polytech. of Kaunas; Dr 1974. Construction work, Hydro-electric Power Stn, River Nemunas and other constructive orgns, 1956–65; Minister, Lithuanian SSR Bldg Materials Industry, 1965–67; Vice-Chm., Lithuanian SSR Planning Cttee, 1967–77; Dep., Supreme Council of Lithuanian SSR, 1969–90; Sec., 1977–88, First Sec., 1988–90, Central Cttee, Communist Party of Lithuania; Republic of Lithuania: Chm., Democratic Labour Party, 1990–93; Dep., Supreme Council and Parliament, 1990–93; Chm. Presidium, Supreme Council, 1990; Dep. Prime Minister, 1990–91. Hon. Dr: Vilnius Tech., Lithuania, 1994; Kiev, Ukraine, 1994. Royal Order of Seraphim (Sweden), 1995; Grand-Croix, Ordre de la Rose Blanche (Finland), 1995; Order of White Eagle (Poland), 1995; Order of Gen. San Martin (Argentina), 1996; Collar, Order of the Libertador (Venezuela), 1996; Gran Cordon de la Medallia de la Republica Oriental de Uruguay, 1996. *Publication:* Lithuanian Divorce, 1992. *Recreations:* yachting, hunting. *Address:* Turniškus 30, 2016 Vilnius, Lithuania. *T:* (2) 778787.

BRAZIER, Julian William Hendy, TD; MP (C) Canterbury, since 1987; *b* 24 July 1953; *s* of Lt-Col P. H. Brazier; *m* 1984, Katharine Elizabeth, *d* of Brig. P. M. Blagden; three *s* (inc. twins). *Educ:* Wellington Coll.; Brasenose Coll., Oxford (schol. in maths; MA); London Business Sch. Chm., Oxford Univ. Cons. Assoc., 1974. Charter Consolidated, 1975–84, Sec., Exec. Cttee of Bd, 1981–84; management consultant to industry, H. B. Maynard, internat. management consultants, 1984–87. Contested (C) Berwick-upon-Tweed, 1983. PPS to Minister of State, HM Treasury, 1990–92, to Sec. of State for Employment, 1992–93. Mem., Defence Select Cttee, 1997–; Vice Chm., Cons. Backbench Defence Cttee, 1993–; Sec., Cons. Backbench Finance Cttee, 1990. Served 13 yrs in TA, principally with airborne forces. *Publications:* pamphlets on defence, economic policy, social security and family issues. *Recreations:* science, philosophy, cross-country running. *Address:* House of Commons, SW1A 0AA.

BRAZIER, Prof. Margaret Rosetta, OBE 1997; Professor of Law, University of Manchester, since 1990; *b* 2 Nov. 1950; *d* of Leslie Jacobs and Mary Jacobs (*née* Pickering); *m* 1974, Rodney John Brazier, *qv*; one *d*. *Educ:* Univ. of Manchester (LLB 1971). Called to the Bar, Middle Temple, 1973. University of Manchester: Lectr, 1971–83, Sen. Lectr, 1983–89, Reader, 1989–90, in Law; Dir of Legal Studies, Centre for Social Ethics and Policy, 1987–; Dir, Inst. of Medicine Law and Bioethics, 1996–. Chairman: Animal Procedures Cttee, 1993–98; Review of Surrogacy, DoH, 1997–98; Mem., Nuffield Council on Bioethics, 1995–. *Publications:* Medicine, Patients and the Law, 1987, 2nd edn 1993; (jtly) Protecting the Vulnerable: autonomy and health care, 1991; (Gen. Ed.) Clerk & Lindsell on Torts, 17th edn 1995; (ed) Street on Torts, 8th edn to 10th edn 1998. *Recreations:* literature, theatre, cooking. *Address:* Faculty of Law, University of Manchester, Manchester M13 9PL. *T:* (0161) 275 3593.

BRAZIER, Rev. Canon Raymond Venner; Vicar, St Matthew and St Nathanael, Kingsdown, Bristol, since 1984; Chaplain to the Queen, since 1998; *b* 12 Oct. 1940; *s* of Harold and Doris Brazier; *m* 1964, Elizabeth Dawn Radford; three *d*. *Educ:* Brockley County Sch., London; Bishop Otter Coll., Chichester; Wells Theol Coll. Assistant teacher: St Martin's County Secondary Boys' Sch., Shenfield, Essex, 1963–66; Kingswood Secondary Boys' Sch., Kingswood, Bristol, 1966–68; ordained deacon 1971, priest 1972; Curate, St Gregory the Great, Horfield, Bristol, 1971–75; Priest-in-charge, 1975–79, Vicar, 1979–84, St Nathanael with St Katharine, Bristol; also Priest-in-charge, St Matthew, Kingsdown, Bristol, 1980–84; Rural Dean of Horfield, 1985–91; Priest-in-charge, Bishopston, Bristol, 1993–97. Hon. Canon, Bristol Cathedral, 1994–. Hon. Chaplain, Colston's Girls Sch., Bristol, 1976–. *Recreations:* reading, listening to music, watching sport, cooking, walking. *Address:* 11 Glentworth Road, Redland, Bristol BS6 7EG. *T:* (0117) 942 4186.

BRAZIER, Prof. Rodney John, FRHistS; Professor of Constitutional Law, University of Manchester, since 1992; *b* 13 May 1946; *s* of late Eric Brazier and Mildred Brazier (*née* Davies); *m* 1974, Margaret Rosetta Jacobs (*see* M. R. Brazier); one *d*. *Educ:* Buckhurst Hill County High Sch.; Univ. of Southampton (LLB 1968). Called to the Bar, Lincoln's Inn, 1970; Additional Bencher, 2000. University of Manchester: Asst Lectr, 1968–70; Lectr, 1970–78; Sen. Lectr in Law, 1978–89; Reader in Constitutional Law, 1989–92; Dean, Faculty of Law, 1992–94. Chm., Consumer Credit Appeal Tribunals, 1992–. JP Manchester, 1982–89. FRHistS 1994. *Publications:* Constitutional Practice, 1988, 3rd edn 1999; Constitutional Texts, 1990; Constitutional Reform: reshaping the British political system, 1991, 2nd edn 1998; Ministers of the Crown, 1997; (jtly) Constitutional & Administrative Law, 8th edn 1998; articles in legal jls. *Recreations:* family, reading, television, walking the dog. *Address:* School of Law, University of Manchester, Oxford Road, Manchester M13 9PL. *T:* (0161) 275 3575.

BRAZIER-CREAGH, Maj.-Gen. Sir (Kilner) Rupert, KBE 1962 (CBE 1947); CB 1954; DSO 1944; Secretary of the Horse Race Betting Levy Board, 1961–65; Director of Staff Duties, War Office, 1959–61, retired; *b* 12 Dec. 1909; 2nd *s* of late Lt-Col K. C. Brazier-Creagh; *m* 1st, 1938, Elizabeth Mary (*d* 1967), *d* of late E. M. Magor; one *s* two *d*; 2nd, 1968, Mrs Marie Nelson. *Educ:* Rugby; RMA, Woolwich. 2nd Lieut, 1929; served War of 1939–45 (despatches, DSO); Bde Major, 9th Armoured Div., 1941; GSO1 12th Corps, 1943; Commanded 25th Field Regt, 1944; BGS 21st Army Group and BAOR, 1945–48 (CBE); idc 1949; DDRA, War Office, 1950; CRA 11th Armoured Div., 1951–52; Chief of Staff Malaya Command, 1952–55 (despatches, CB); Asst Comdt, Staff Coll., 1955–57; Chief of Staff, Eastern Command, 1957–59. Officer, American Legion of Merit, 1945. *Recreation:* racing. *Address:* Travis Corners Road, Garrison, NY 10524, USA.

BREACH, Gerald Ernest John; Director, Project Group, Export Credits Guarantee Department, 1988–90; *b* 14 March 1932; *s* of Ernest Albert Breach and Jane Breach; *m* 1st, 1958, Joan Elizabeth Eckford; one *s* one *d*; 2nd, 1988, Sylvia Eileen Harding. *Educ:* Roan Sch., Greenwich. Nat. Service, Royal Signals, 1950–52. Joined: ECGD, 1952; ECGD Management Bd, 1988. *Recreations:* boating, rambling, bellringing. *Address:* Clunbury, Shropshire.

BREADALBANE AND HOLLAND, Earldom of, *cr* 1677; dormant since 1995;

BREADEN, Very Rev. Robert William; Dean of Brechin since 1984; Rector of St Mary's, Broughty Ferry, since 1972; *b* 7 Nov. 1937; *s* of Moses and Martha Breaden; *m* 1970, Glenice Sutton Martin; one *s* four *d*. *Educ:* The King's Hospital, Dublin; Edinburgh Theological Coll. Deacon 1961, priest 1962; Asst Curate, St Mary's, Broughty Ferry, 1961–65; Rector, Church of the Holy Rood, Carnoustie, 1965–72; Canon of St Paul's Cathedral, Dundee, 1977. *Recreations:* gardening, horse riding; Rugby enthusiast. *Address:* St Mary's Rectory, 46 Seafield Road, Broughty Ferry, Dundee DD5 3AN. *T:* (01382) 477477, *Fax:* (01382) 477434; *e-mail:* Ateallach@aol.com.

BREALEY, Prof. Richard Arthur, FBA 1999; Special Adviser to the Governor, Bank of England, since 1998; Visiting Professor of Finance, London Business School, since 1998; *b* 9 June 1936; *s* of late Albert Brealey and of Irene Brealey; *m* 1967, Diana Cecily Brown Kelly; two *s*. *Educ:* Queen Elizabeth's, Barnet; Exeter Coll., Oxford (MA, 1st Cl. Hons PPE). Sun Life Assce Co. of Canada, 1959–66; Keystone Custodian Funds of Boston, 1966–68; London Business School: Prudential Res. Fellow, 1968–74; Sen. Lectr, 1972–74; Prof. of Finance, 1974–97; Barclaytrust Prof. of Investment, 1974–82; Midland Bank Prof. of Corporate Finance, 1982–91; Tokai Bank Prof. of Finance, 1993–97; Dep. Prin., 1984–88; Governor, 1984–88. Director: Swiss Helvetia Fund Inc., 1987–96; Sun Life Assurance Co. of Canada UK Hldgs plc, 1994–97; Tokai Derivative Products, 1995–97. Pres., European Finance Assoc., 1975; Dir, Amer. Finance Assoc., 1979–81. *Publications:* An Introduction to Risk and Return from Common Stocks, 1969, 2nd edn 1983; Security Prices in a Competitive Market, 1971; (with J. Lorie) Modern Developments in Investment Management, 1972, 2nd edn 1978; (with S. C. Myers) Principles of Corporate Finance, 1981, 6th edn 2000; (with S. C. Myers and A. J. Marcus) Fundamentals of Corporate Finance, 1995, 3rd edn 2000; articles in professional jls. *Recreations:* ski-ing, rock climbing, horse riding. *Address:* Haydens Cottage, The Pound, Cookham, Berks SL6 9QE. *T:* (01628) 520143.

BREAM, Julian, CBE 1985 (OBE 1964); guitarist and lutenist; *b* 15 July 1933; *e s* of Henry G. Bream; *m* 1st, Margaret Williamson; one adopted *s*; 2nd, 1980, Isobel Sanchez. *Educ:* Royal College of Music (Junior Exhibition Award, 1945 and Scholarship, 1948). Began professional career at Cheltenham, 1947; London début, Wigmore Hall, 1950; subsequently has appeared in leading world festivals in Europe, USA, Australia and Far East. A leader in revival of interest in Elizabethan Lute music, on which he has done much research; has encouraged contemporary English compositions for the guitar. Formed Julian Bream Consort, 1960; inaugurated Semley Festival of Music and Poetry, 1971. DUniv Surrey, 1968. Villa-Lobos Gold Medal, 1976. *Recreations:* playing the guitar; cricket, table tennis, gardening, backgammon. *Address:* c/o Hazard Chase, Norman House, Cambridge Place, Cambridge CB2 1NS.

BREARLEY, Christopher John Scott, CB 1994; consultant; *b* 25 May 1943; *s* of Geoffrey Brearley and Winifred (*née* Scott); *m* 1971, Rosemary Stockbridge; two *s*. *Educ:* King Edward VII Sch., Sheffield; Trinity Coll., Oxford. MA 1964, BPhil 1966. Entered Ministry of Transport, 1966; Private Sec. to Perm. Sec., 1969–70; Principal, DoE, 1970; Sec. to Review of Develt Control Procedures (Dobry), DoE, 1973–74; Private Sec. to the Secretary of the Cabinet, Cabinet Office, 1974–76; Asst Sec., 1977; Under Sec., 1981; Dir of Scottish Services, PSA, 1981–83; Cabinet Office, 1983–85; Department of the Environment, 1985–97: Deputy Secretary: Local Govt, 1990–94; Local Govt and Planning, 1994–95; Local and Regl Develt, 1996–97; Dep. Sec., later Dir Gen., Planning, Roads and Local Transport, DETR, 1997–2000. Non-exec. Dir, Housing Div., Tarmac plc, 1986–88. Sec., Review of Child Protection in the Catholic Ch, 2000–01. Mem., Policy Cttee, CPRE, 2001–. Member: Bd, Public Finance Foundn, 1990–98; Public Policy Adv. Bd, QMW, 1995–. Governor, Watford Grammar Sch. for Boys, 1988– (Chm. of Govs, 1998–); Trustee, Watford Grammar Schs, 1992–. Trustee: Motability Tenth Anniv. Trust, 2001–; Motorway Archive Trust, 2001–. FRSA 1991. Freeman, City of London. *Recreations:* crosswords, walking. *Address:* 35 South Road, Chorleywood, Herts WD3 5AS. *T:* (01923) 283848. *Clubs:* Oxford and Cambridge; New (Edinburgh).

BREARLEY, (John) Michael, OBE 1978; psychoanalyst; *b* 28 April 1942; *s* of Horace and late Midge Brearley; lives with Mana Sarabhai; two *c*. *Educ:* City of London Sch.; St John's Coll., Cambridge (MA; Hon. Fellow, 1998). Lectr in Philosophy, Univ. of Newcastle upon Tyne, 1968–71. Middlesex County Cricketer, intermittently, 1961–82, capped 1964, Captain, 1971–82; played first Test Match, 1976; Captain of England XI, 1977–80, 1981. Mem., British Psycho-Analytical Soc., 1991 (Associate Mem., 1985). Hon. LLD Lancaster, 1999. *Publications:* (with Dudley Doust) The Return of the Ashes, 1978; (with Dudley Doust) The Ashes Retained, 1979; Phoenix: the series that rose from the ashes, 1982; The Art of Captaincy, 1985; (with John Arlott) Arlott in Conversation with Mike Brearley, 1986; articles for The Observer. *Club:* MCC (Hon. Life Mem.).

BREARLEY-SMITH, Anne Margaret; *see* Luther, A. M.

BREARS, Peter Charles David, FMA, FSA; writer and museums consultant, since 1994; *b* 30 Aug. 1944; *s* of Charles Brears and Mary (*née* Fett). *Educ:* Castleford Technical High Sch.; Leeds Coll. of Art (DipAD 1967). FMA 1980; FSA 1980. Hon. Asst, Wakefield City Museum, 1957–66; Keeper of Folk Life, Hampshire CC, 1967–69; Curator: Shibden Hall, Halifax, 1969–72; Clarke Hall, Wakefield, 1972–75; Castle Museum, York, 1975–79; Dir, Leeds City Museums, 1979–94. Chm., Leeds Symposium for Food History, 1986–; Founder, 1975, and Mem., 1975–, Group for Regional Studies in Museums, subseq. Social Hist. Curators Gp, 1975; Mem., Social History and Industrial Classification Wkg Party, 1978–; Pres., Soc. for Folk Life Studies, 1995–96. Sophie Coe Prize for food writing, Oxford Symposium for Food History, 1997. *Publications:* The English Country Pottery, 1971; Yorkshire Probate Inventories, 1972; The Collectors' Book of English Country Pottery, 1974; Horse Brasses, 1981; The Gentlewoman's Kitchen, 1984; Traditional Food in Yorkshire, 1987; North Country Folk Art, 1989; Of Curiosities and Rare Things, 1989; Treasures for the People, 1989; Images of Leeds, 1992; Leeds Describ'd, 1993; Leeds Waterfront, 1994; The Country House Kitchen, 1996; Ryedale Recipes, 1998; A Taste of Leeds, 1998; The Old Devon Farmhouse, 1998; All the King's Cooks, 1999; The Compleat Housekeeper, 2000; articles in Folk Life, Post-Medieval Archaeology, etc; museum guides and catalogues. *Recreations:* hill walking, drawing, history re-enactment, cookery. *Address:* 4 Woodbine Terrace, Headingley, Leeds LS6 4AF. *T:* (0113) 275 6537.

BRECHIN, Bishop of, since 1997; **Rt Rev. Neville Chamberlain;** *b* 24 Oct. 1939; *s* of Albert Victor Chamberlain and Miriam Chamberlain; *m* 1964, Diana Hammill; three *s* one *d*. *Educ:* Salford Grammar Sch.; Nottingham Univ. (BA Theol.; MA Applied Social Studies; CQSW); Ripon Hall, Oxford (DPSA 1962). Ordained deacon, 1963, priest, 1964; Asst Curate, St Paul's, Birmingham, 1963–64; Priest-in-charge, St Michael's, Birmingham, 1964–69; Rector, Deer Creek Parish, USA, 1967–68; Vicar, St Michael's Anglican/Methodist Church, Birmingham, 1969–72; Probation Officer, Grimsby, 1972–74; Exec. Sec., Lincoln Diocesan Social Responsibility Cttee, 1974–82; Rector, St John the Evangelist, Edinburgh, 1982–97. Prebend and Canon, Lincoln Cathedral, 1979–. *Recreations:* golf, cycling, cinema. *Address:* Diocesan Centre, Pine Grove, 334 Perth Road, Dundee DD2 1EQ. *T:* (01382) 640007, *Fax:* (01382) 630083; *e-mail:* office@brechin.anglican.org.

BRECHIN, Dean of; *see* Breaden, Very Rev. R. W.

BRECKENRIDGE, Prof. Alasdair Muir, CBE 1995; MD; FRCP; FRCPE; FRSE; Professor of Clinical Pharmacology, University of Liverpool, since 1974; *b* 7 May 1937; *s* of Thomas and Jane Breckenridge; *m* 1967, Jean Margaret Boyle; two *s*. *Educ:* Bell Baxter Sch., Cupar, Fife; Univ. of St Andrews (MB, ChB Hons 1961); Univ. of London (MSc 1968); Univ. of Dundee (MD Hons 1974). FRCP 1974; FRCPE 1988; FRSE 1991. House Phys. and Surg., Dundee Royal Infirm., 1961–62; Asst, Dept of Medicine, Univ. of St Andrews, 1962–63; successively House Phys., Registrar, Sen. Registrar, Tutor, Lectr and Sen. Lectr, Hammersmith Hosp. and RPMS, 1964–74. Non-exec. Dir, 1990–94, Vice Chm., 1993–94, Mersey RHA (Chm., Jan.–July 1993; Chm., Res. Cttee, 1987–91); Vice Chm., NW RHA, 1994–96 (Dir of R & D, 1994–96); Chm., NW Reg., NHS Exec., 1996–99. NHS Advr in Clin. Pharm. to CMO, 1982–94; Mem., NHS Adv. Cttee on Drugs, 1985–98 (Vice Chm., 1986–98). Committee on Safety of Medicines: Mem., 1982– (Vice Chm., 1996–98; Chm., 1999–); Chm., Adverse Reactions Subgroup, 1987–92; Chm., Adverse Reactions to Vaccination and Immunisation Sub Cttee, 1989–92; Chm., Sub Cttee on Safety and Efficacy, 1993–95. Medical Research Council: Mem., 1992–96; Member: Clin. Trials Cttee, 1983–; Physiol Systems and Disorders Bd, 1987–91 (Vice Chm., 1990–91); AIDS Therapeutic Cttee, 1989– (Chm., 1993–). Royal College of Physicians: Mem. Council, 1983–86; Mem., Res. Cttee, 1983–88; Mem., Clin. Pharm. Cttee, 1990–95; Mem. Adv. Res. Cttee, 1993–98; Goulstonian Lectr, 1975. British Pharmacological Society: Mem., 1972–; Foreign Sec., 1984–91; Chm., Clin. Section, 1988–93; Lilly Medal, 1994; Chm. Edtl Bd, British Jl of Clin. Pharmacol., 1983–87. Member: Panel on Tropical and Infectious Disease, Wellcome Trust, 1984–87; Res. Cttee, British Heart Foundn, 1977–82; Steering Cttee for Chemotherapy of Malaria, WHO, 1987–91; Exec. Cttee, Internat. Union of Pharm., 1981–87; Central R&D Cttee, NHS, 1991–94; Jt Med. Adv. Cttee, HEFCE, 1995– (Chm., 1998–); Cttee on Proprietary Medicinal Products of EU, 2001–. Mem., Assoc. of Physicians, 1975–. Founder FMedSci 1998. Paul Martini Prize in Clin. Pharm., Paul Martini Foundn, 1974; Poulson Medal, Norwegian Pharmacol Soc., 1988. Exec. Editor, Pharmacology and Therapeutics, 1982–98. *Publications:* papers on clinical pharmacology in various jls. *Recreations:* hill-walking, golf, music. *Address:* Cree Cottage, Feather Lane, Heswall, Wirral L60 4RL. *T:* (0151) 342 1096.

BRECKNOCK, Earl of; James William John Pratt; *b* 11 Dec. 1965; *s* and *heir* of Marquess Camden, *qv*. *Educ:* Eton.

BRECON, Dean of; *see* Davies, Very Rev. J. D. E.

BREDIN, Maj.-Gen. Humphrey Edgar Nicholson, CB 1969; DSO 1944 (and bars, 1945 and 1957); MC 1938 (and bar, 1939); DL; Appeals Secretary, Cancer Research Campaign, Essex and Suffolk, 1971–83; *b* 28 March 1916; *s* of Lieut-Colonel A. Bredin, late Indian Army, and Ethel Bredin (*née* Homan); *m* 1st, 1947, Jacqueline Geare (marr. diss. 1961; she *d* 1997); one *d*; 2nd, 1965, Anne Hardie (*d* 1995); two *d*. *Educ:* King's School, Canterbury; RMC, Sandhurst. Commissioned Royal Ulster Rifles, 1936; Commanded: 6th Royal Inniskilling Fusiliers, 1944; 2nd London Irish Rifles, 1945; Eastern Arab Corps, Sudan Defence Force, 1949–53; 2nd Parachute Regt, 1956–57; 99th Gurkha Infty Bde Group, 1959–62. Campaigns: Dunkirk, 1940; N Africa, 1943; Italy, 1943–45; Palestine, 1937–39 and 1946–47; Suez, 1956; Cyprus, 1956–57; Singapore-Malaya Internal Security, 1959–62; Chief of British Commander-in-Chief's Mission to Soviet Forces in Germany, 1963–65; Commanded 42nd Div. (TA), 1965–68. Brig. 1964; Maj.-Gen. 1965; Dir, Volunteers, Territorials and Cadets, 1968–71; retired 1971. Col Comdt, The King's Division, 1968–71; Col of the Regt, Royal Irish Rangers, 1979–85; Hon. Col D (London Irish Rifles) Co., 4th (V) Bn, The Royal Irish Rangers, 1980–86. Chm. Essex Co. Cttee, Army Benevolent Fund, 1983–92; President: Dunkirk Veterans Clacton and Colchester Assoc., 1983–99; 78th Div. Battleaxe Club, 1991–95. DL Essex, 1984. *Recreations:* shooting, fishing, gardening. *Address:* c/o Rodmead Farm, Maiden Bradley, Warminster, Wilts BA12 7HP. *T:* (01985) 844689.

BREED, Colin Edward; MP (Lib Dem) Cornwall South East, since 1997; *b* 4 May 1947; *s* of Alfred Breed and Edith Violet Breed; *m* 1968, Janet Courtiour; one *s* one *d*. *Educ:* Torquay GS. ACIB. Junior, to Area Manager, Midland Bank plc, 1964–81; Manager, Venture Capital Fund, later Man. Dir, Dartington & Co. Ltd, 1981–91; Consultant, Corporate Finance, Allied Provincial Stockbrokers, 1991–92; Dir, Gemini Abrasives Ltd, 1992–97. Mem., GMC, 1999–. *Recreations:* golf, watching live sport. *Address:* 10 Dunheved Road, Saltash, Cornwall PL12 4BW.

BREEN, Geoffrey Brian; His Honour Judge Breen; a Circuit Judge, since 2000; *b* 3 June 1944; *s* of Ivor James Breen and late Doreen Odessa Breen; *m* 1978, Lucy Bolaños (marr. diss. 1999); one *s* one *d*. *Educ:* Harrow High School. Articled to Stiles Wood & Co., Harrow, 1962–67; admitted Solicitor, 1967; Partner, Stiles, Wood, Head & Co, 1970–75; Sen. Partner, Stiles, Breen & Partners, 1976–86; Partner, Blaser Mills & Newman, Bucks and Herts, 1976–86; a Metropolitan Stipendiary Magistrate, subseq. Dist Judge (Magistrates' Courts), 1986–2000; Asst Recorder, 1989–93; Recorder, 1993–2000. Chairman: Youth Courts, 1989–93; Family Proceedings Courts, 1991–2000. Mem., British Acad. of Forensic Scis, 1989–. *Recreations:* classical guitar, reading, do-it-yourself. *Address:* Luton Crown Court, 7 George Street, Luton, Beds LU1 2AA.

BREEN, Richard James, PhD; FBA 1999; Official Fellow, Nuffield College, Oxford, since 2000; *b* 25 Aug. 1954; *s* of Edward Francis Breen and Emily Breen (*née* Wolstenholme); *m* 1st, 1981, Eleanor Burgess (marr. diss. 1993); 2nd, 1997, Mary Christine O'Sullivan. *Educ:* St Thomas Aquinas Grammar Sch., Leeds; Fitzwilliam Coll., Cambridge (BA 1976; MA 1979; PhD 1981). Research Officer, then Sen. Research Officer, Economic and Social Research Inst., Dublin, 1980–91; Professor of Sociology: QUB, 1991; European Univ. Inst., Florence, 1997. MRIA 1998. *Publications:* Understanding Contemporary Ireland, 1990; Social Class and Social Mobility in the Republic of Ireland, 1996; numerous contribs to learned jls. *Recreations:* music, chess, reading, hill walking. *Address:* Nuffield College, Oxford, OX1 1NF. *T:* (01865) 278500.

BREEZE, Alastair Jon, CMG 1990; HM Diplomatic Service; Counsellor, Foreign and Commonwealth Office, 1987–94; *b* 1 June 1934; *s* of Samuel Wilfred Breeze and Gladys Elizabeth Breeze; *m* 1960, Helen Burns Shaw; two *s* one *d*. *Educ:* Mill Hill School; Christ's College, Cambridge (Scholar; MA 1959). Served Royal Marines, 1953–55. Foreign Office, 1958; 3rd Sec., Jakarta, 1960–62; FO, 1962–64; 2nd Sec., seconded to Colonial Office for service in Georgetown, 1964–66; 1st Sec., Tehran, 1967–71; FCO, 1971–72; 1st Sec., Islamabad, 1972–75, Lagos, 1976–79; FCO, 1979–83; Counsellor, UK Mission to UN, NY, 1983–87. *Recreations:* sailing, ornithology. *Address:* Dryhill Cottage, Sundridge, Kent TN14 6AA.

BREEZE, Dr David John, FSA, FSAScot, FRSE; Chief Inspector of Ancient Monuments, Historic Scotland, since 1989; *b* Blackpool, 25 July 1944; *s* of Reginald C. Breeze and Marian (*née* Lawson); *m* 1972, Pamela Diane Silvester; two *s*. *Educ:* Blackpool Grammar Sch.; University Coll., Durham Univ. (BA; PhD 1970). FSAScot 1970; FSA 1975; FRSE 1991; MIFA 1990. Inspector of Ancient Monuments, Scotland, 1969–88, Principal Inspector, 1988–89. Vis. Prof., Durham Univ., 1994–; Hon. Prof., Edinburgh Univ., 1996. Chm., Hadrian's Wall Pilgrimage, 1989 and 1999; Member: Hadrian's Wall Adv. Cttee, English Heritage, 1977–97; Internat. Cttee, Congress of Roman Frontier Studies, 1983–; President: South Shields Archaeol and Historical Soc., 1983–85; Soc. of Antiquaries of Scotland, 1987–90. Trustee, Senhouse Museum Trust, 1985–. FRSA. Corresp. Mem., German Archaeol Inst., 1979. *Publications:* (with Brian Dobson) Hadrian's Wall, 1976, 4th edn 2000; (with D. V. Clarke and G. Mackay) The Romans in Scotland, 1980; The Northern Frontiers of Roman Britain, 1982; Roman Forts in Britain, 1983, 2nd edn 1987; (ed) Studies in Scottish Antiquity, 1984; Hadrian's Wall, a Souvenir Guide, 1987, 3rd edn 1996; A Queen's Progress, 1987; The Second Augustan Legion in North Britain, 1989; (ed) Service in the Roman Army, 1989; (with Anna Ritchie) Invaders of Scotland, 1991; (with Brian Dobson) Roman Officers and Frontiers, 1993; Roman Scotland: frontier country, 1996; (with G. Munro) The Stone of Destiny, 1997; Historic Scotland, 1998; contribs to British and foreign jls. *Recreations:* reading, walking, travel. *Address:* Historic Scotland, Longmore House, Salisbury Place, Edinburgh EH9 1SH. *T:* (0131) 668 8724.

BREHONY, Dr John Albert Noel, CMG 1991; Adviser to Board on Middle East Affairs, Rolls-Royce PLC, since 1999; *b* 11 Dec. 1936; *s* of Patrick Paul Brehony and Agnes Maher; *m* 1961, Jennifer Ann (*née* Cox); one *s* one *d*. *Educ:* London Oratory Sch.; Univ. of Durham (BA, PhD). Tutor, Durham Univ., 1960; Economist Intell. Unit, 1961; Res. Fellow, Jerusalem (Jordan), 1962; Lectr, Univ. of Libya, 1965–66; FO, 1966; Kuwait, 1967–69; Aden, 1970–71; Amman, 1973–77; Cairo, 1981–84; Counsellor, FCO, 1984–92; Dir of Middle East Affairs, Rolls-Royce PLC, 1992–99. Chm., Menas Associates, 2001–. Chm., Middle East Assoc., 1996–97; Pres., British Soc. of ME Studies, 2000–. Chm., British Inst. at Amman for Archaeol. and Hist., 1992–99. Special Advr, SOAS, 1999–. *Recreations:* Middle Eastern history, tennis, golf, opera. *Address:* (office) c/o 65 Buckingham Gate, SW1E 6AT. *Club:* Athenæum.

BREITMEYER, Brig. Alan Norman; DL; Lieutenant, HM Body Guard, Honourable Corps of Gentlemen at Arms, 1993–94 (Member, 1976–94; Harbinger, 1992–93); *b* 14 March 1924; *s* of Cecil Breitmeyer and Clare Herbert-Smith; *m* 1st, 1952, Hon. June Jane Barrie (marr. diss. 1977); one *s* one *d*; 2nd, 1978, Susan Irwin (*née* Lipscomb). *Educ:* Winchester Coll.; RMA Sandhurst. Commissioned Grenadier Guards, 1943; served NW Europe, 1944–45 (despatches 1945); ADC to Field Marshal Montgomery, 1948–50 (despatches, Palestine, 1948); Staff College, 1954; commanded 2nd Bn Grenadier Guards, 1964–66; commanding Grenadier Guards, 1966–69; Brig., 1971; Dep. Comdr, NE Dist, 1972–74, retired 1974. County Councillor, Cambs, 1977–85. DL Cambs, 1978; High Sheriff Cambs, 1984. *Recreation:* shooting. *Address:* Bartlow Park, Cambs CB1 6PP. *T:* (01223) 891609. *Clubs:* Boodle's, Pratt's.

BREMNER, Rory Keith Ogilvy; satirical impressionist and writer (content provider); *b* 6 April 1961; *s* of late Major Donald Stuart Ogilvy Bremner and Anne Ulithorne Bremner (*née* Simpson); *m* 1986, Susan Shackleton (marr. diss. 1994); *m* 1999, Tessa Campbell Fraser; one *d*. *Educ:* Wellington Coll.; King's Coll. London (BA Hons French and German 1983). Television series: Now–Something Else, 1986–87; Rory Bremner, 1988–92; Rory Bremner–Who Else?, 1993–99; Bremner, Bird and Fortune, 1999–. Opera translations: Silver Lake (Weill), 1999; Carmen (Bizet), 2001. British Comedy Award, 1993; BAFTA Award for Best Light Entertainment Performance, 1995, 1996; RTS Awards, 1995, 1999, 2000; Channel 4 political humorist of the year, 1998, 2000. *Recreations:* cricket, tennis, riding, opera, travel. *Address:* c/o Richard Stone Partnership, 2 Henrietta Street, WC2E 8PS. *T:* (020) 7497 0849. *Clubs:* Queen's, Lord's Taverners.

BRENCHLEY, Thomas Frank, CMG 1964; HM Diplomatic Service, retired; *b* 9 April 1918; *m* 1946, Edith Helen Helfand (*d* 1980); three *d*. *Educ:* privately and at Sir William Turner's Sch., Coatham; Merton Coll., Oxford (Modern History postmastership; Classical Hon. Mods, 1938; MA Philos. and Ancient Hist., 1946; Mem., Sen. Common Room, 1987; Hon. Fellow 1991; DPhil 2001); Open Univ. (BA 1986; BSc 1996). CS quals in Arabic, Norwegian and Polish. Served with Royal Corps of Signals, 1939–46; Major on Staff of Military Attaché, Ankara, 1943–45; Director, Telecommunications Liaison Directorate, Syria and Lebanon, 1945–46. Civil Servant, GCHQ, 1947; transferred to Foreign Office, 1949; First Secretary: Singapore, 1950–53; Cairo, 1953–56; FO, 1956–58; MECAS, 1958–60; Counsellor, Khartoum, 1960–63; Chargé d'Affaires, Jedda, 1963; Head of Arabian Department, Foreign Office, 1963–67; Assistant Under-Secretary of State, Foreign Office, 1967–68; Ambassador to: Norway, 1968–72; Poland, 1972–74; Vis. Fellow, Inst. for Study of Conflict, 1974–75; Dep. Sec., Cabinet Office, 1975–76. Dep. Sec. Gen. and Chief Exec., Arab-British Chamber of Commerce, 1976–83; Chairman: Institute for Study of Conflict, 1983–89; Res. Inst. for Study of Conflict and Terrorism, 1989–94; Pres., Internat. Inst. for Study of Conflict, Geneva, 1989–91. Dir, Center for Security Studies, Washington DC, 1988–90. *Publications:* New Dimensions of European Security (ed), 1975; Norway and her Soviet Neighbour: NATO's Arctic Frontier, 1982; Diplomatic Immunities and State-sponsored Terrorism, 1984; Living With Terrorism: the problem of air piracy, 1986; Britain and the Middle East: an economic history 1945–87, 1989; Aegean Conflict and the Law of the Sea, 1990. *Recreation:* collecting (and sometimes reading) books. *Address:* 19 Ennismore Gardens, SW7 1AA. *Club:* Travellers (Chm., 1991–94).

BRENDEL, Alfred, Hon. KBE 1989; concert pianist since 1948; *b* 5 Jan. 1931; *s* of Albert Brendel and Ida Brendel (*née* Wieltschnig); *m* 1960, Iris Heymann-Gonzala (marr. diss. 1972); one *d*; *m* 1975, Irene Semler; one *s* two *d*. Studied piano with: S. Deželić, 1937–43; L. V. Kaan, 1943–47; also under Edwin Fischer, P. Baumgartner and E. Steuermann; composition with Artur Michl, harmony with Franjo Dugan, Zagreb. Vienna State Diploma, 1947; Premio Bolzano Concorso Busoni, 1949. Hon. RAM; FRNCM 1990; Hon. RCM 1999; Hon. Mem., Amer. Acad. of Arts and Sciences, 1984; Korrespondierendes Mitglied, Bayer. Akad. der Wissenschaften; Hon. Fellow, Exeter

Coll., Oxford, 1987; Hon. DMus: London, 1978; Sussex, 1980; Oxford, 1983; Warwick, 1991; Yale, 1992; Cologne, 1995; Exeter, 1998. Busoni Foundn Award, 1990; Gold Medal, Royal Philharmonic Soc., 1993. Commandeur des Arts et des Lettres, 1985; Orden pour le Mérite für Wissenschaften und Künste, 1991. Concerts: most European countries, North and Latin America, Australia and New Zealand, also N and S Africa and Near and Far East. Many appearances Vienna and Salzburg Festivals, 1960–. Other Festivals: Athens, Granada, Bregenz, Würzburg, Aldeburgh, York, Cheltenham, Edinburgh, Bath, Puerto Rico, Barcelona, Prague, Lucerne, Dubrovnik, etc. Many long playing records (Bach to Schoenberg) incl. first complete recording of Beethoven's piano works (Grand Prix du Disque, 1965). Cycle of Beethoven Sonatas: London, 1962, 1977, 1982–83, 1992–95; Copenhagen, 1964; Vienna, 1965, 1982–83; Puerto Rico, 1968; BBC and Rome, 1970; Munich and Stuttgart, 1977; Amsterdam, Paris and Berlin, 1982–83; New York, 1983; 14 Eur. and 4 N Amer. cities, 1992–96; Cycle of Schubert piano works 1822–28 in 19 cities, incl. London, Paris, Amsterdam, Berlin, Vienna, New York, Los Angeles, 1987–88. *Television (series):* Schubert Piano Music (13 films), Bremen, 1978; Alfred Brendel Masterclass, BBC, 1983; Liszt Années de Pèlerinage, BBC, 1986; Schubert Last Three Sonatas, BBC, 1988. *Publications:* Musical Thoughts and Afterthoughts (Essays), 1976; Music Sounded Out, 1990; Fingerzeig, 1996; Störendes Lachen während des Jaworts, 1997; One Finger Too Many, 1998; Kleine Teufel, 1999; Ausgerechnet Ich, 2000; Alfred Brendel on Music: collected essays, 2001; essays on music, in: HiFi Stereophonie, Music and Musicians, Phono, Fono Forum, Osterreichische Musikzeitschrift, Gramophone, Die Zeit, New York Rev. of Books, Frankfurter Allgemeine, Neue Zürcher Zeitung, etc. *Recreations:* literature, art galleries, architecture, unintentional humour, "kitsch". *Address:* Ingpen & Williams, 26 Wadham Road, SW15 2LR. *T:* (020) 8874 3222.

BRENIKOV, Prof. Paul, FRTPI; Professor and Head of Department of Town and Country Planning, University of Newcastle upon Tyne, 1964–86, now Professor Emeritus; *b* 13 July 1921; *o s* of Pavel Brenikov and Joyce Mildred Jackson, Liverpool; *m* 1943, Margaret (*d* 1994), *e d* of Albert McLevy, Burnley, Lancs; two *s* one *d*. *Educ:* St Peter's Sch., York; Liverpool Coll.; Univ. of Liverpool (BA (Hons Geog.), MA, DipCD). War service with RNAS, 1941–46. Sen. Planning Officer, Lancs CC, 1950–55; Lectr, Dept of Civic Design, Univ. of Liverpool, 1955–64; Planning Corresp., Architect's Jl, 1957–63; Environmental Planning Consultant: in UK, for former Bootle CB, 1957–64; Govt of Ireland, 1963–67; overseas, for UN; Chile, 1960–61; E Africa, 1964; OECD; Turkey, 1968. Royal Town Planning Institute: Mem. Council, 1967–78; Chm., Northern Br., 1973–74. Member: Subject Cttee of UGC, 1975–86; DoE Local Plans Inspector's Panel, 1985–. FRSA 1979 (Chm., NE Region, RSA, and Council Mem., 1997–2000). *Publications:* contrib. Social Aspects of a Town Development Plan, 1951; contrib. Land Use in an Urban Environment, 1961; (jtly) The Dublin Region: preliminary and final reports, 1965 and 1967; other technical pubns in architectural, geographical, planning and sociological jls. *Recreations:* drawing, painting, listening to music, walking, reading. *Address:* 46 Mitchell Avenue, Jesmond, Newcastle upon Tyne NE2 3LA. *T:* (0191) 281 2773.

BRENNAN, family name of **Baron Brennan**.

BRENNAN, Baron *cr* 2000 (Life Peer), of Bibury in the co. of Gloucestershire; **Daniel Joseph Brennan;** QC 1985; a Recorder of the Crown Court, since 1982; *b* 19 March 1942; *s* of late Daniel Brennan and Mary Brennan; *m* 1968, Pilar, *d* of late Luis Sanchez Hernandez; four *s*. *Educ:* St Bede's Grammar Sch., Bradford; Victoria University of Manchester (LLB Hons). President, University Union, 1964–65. Called to the Bar: Gray's Inn, 1967 (Bencher, 1993); King's Inns, Dublin, 1990. Mem., Criminal Injuries Compensation Bd, 1989–97; Chm., Gen. Council of the Bar, 1999 (Vice Chm., 1998). FRSA 2000. Hon. LLD: Nottingham Trent, 1999; Manchester, 2000. Cross of St Raimond de Penafort (Spain), 2000. *Publications:* Provisional Damages, 1986; (contrib.) Bullen and Leake, Precedents of Pleading, 13th edn 1990, 14th edn 2001; (gen. ed.) Personal Injury Manual, 1997. *Address:* Matrix Chambers, Gray's Inn, WC1R 5LN. *T:* (020) 7404 3447, *Fax:* (020) 7404 3448.

BRENNAN, Anthony John Edward, CB 1981; Deputy Secretary, Northern Ireland Office, 1982–87; *b* 24 Jan. 1927; 2nd *s* of late Edward Joseph Brennan and Mabel Brennan (*née* West); *m* 1958, Pauline Margery, *d* of late Percy Clegg Lees; two *s* one *d*. *Educ:* St Joseph's; London Sch. of Economics (Leverhulme Schol.). BSc Econ 1946. Served Army, RA, RAEC, 1946–49; Asst Principal, Home Office, 1949; Private Sec. to Parly Under-Sec. of State, 1953–54; Principal, 1954; Principal Private Sec. to Home Sec., 1963; Asst Sec., 1963; Asst Under Sec. of State, Criminal Dept, 1971–75, Immigration Dept, 1975–77; Dep. Under-Sec. of State, Home Office, 1977–82. Sec., Royal Commn on Penal System, 1964–66; Mem., UN Cttee on Crime Prevention and Control, 1979–84. *Recreations:* theatre, athletics. *Club:* Athenæum.

BRENNAN, Archibald Orr, (Archie), OBE 1981; studio artist and lecturer, since 1984; *s* of James and Jessie Brennan; *m* 1956, Elizabeth Hewitt Carmichael (marr. diss.); three *d*. *Educ:* Boroughmuir Sch., Edinburgh; Edinburgh College of Art (DA). Training as tapestry weaver/student, 1947–62; Lectr, Edinburgh College of Art, 1962–78; Dir, Edin. Tapestry Co., 1962; co-ordinator/designer of all embellishment, new Nat. Parlt Bldg, PNG, 1978–84. Pres., Society of Scottish Artists, 1977–78; Chm., British Craft Centre, 1977–78; travelling lectr, UK, USA, Canada, Australia, PNG, 1962–78; Vis. Artist, PNG, 1978. Fellow, ANU, 1974–75. *Publications:* articles in various jls.

BRENNAN, Edward A.; Chairman and Chief Executive Officer, 1986–95, and President, 1989, Sears, Roebuck & Co.; *b* 16 Jan. 1934; *s* of Edward Brennan and Margaret (*née* Bourget); *m* 1955, Lois Lyon; three *s* three *d*. *Educ:* Marquette Univ., Wisconsin (BA). Joined Sears as salesman in Madison, Wisconsin, 1956; asst store manager, 1958, asst buyer, 1960, store manager, 1967 and other positions in diff. locations, to 1969; Asst Manager, NY group, 1969–72; Gen. Manager, Sears Western NY group, 1972–75; Admin. Asst to Vice-Pres., Sears Eastern Territory, 1975; Gen. Manager, Boston group, 1976; Exec. Vice Pres., Southern Territory, 1978; Pres., Sears, Roebuck, 1980; Chm. and Chief Exec., Sears Merchandise Group, 1981; Pres. and chief operating officer, Sears, Roebuck & Co., 1984; dir of other cos. Member: President's Export Council; Business Roundtable; Conference Bd; business adv. council, Chicago Urban League; Civic Cttee, Commercial Club; Chm., Board of Governors, United Way of America; Member, Boards of Trustees: Savings and Profit Sharing Fund of Sears Employees; Univs of DePaul and Marquette; Chicago Museum of Science and Industry. *Address:* c/o Sears, Roebuck and Co., 3333 Beverly Road, Hoffman Estates, IL 60179, USA.

BRENNAN, Hon. Sir (Francis) Gerard, AC 1988; KBE 1981; Non-Permanent Judge, Court of Final Appeal of Hong Kong, since 2000; Chancellor, University of Technology, Sydney, since 1998; *b* 22 May 1928; *s* of Hon. Mr Justice (Frank Tenison) Brennan and Mrs Gertrude Brennan; *m* 1953, Dr Patricia (*née* O'Hara); three *s* four *d*. *Educ:* Christian Brothers Coll., Rockhampton, Qld; Downlands Coll., Toowoomba, Qld; Univ. of Qld (BA, LLB). Called to the Queensland Bar, 1951; QC (Australia) 1965. Judge, Aust. Indust. Court, and Additional Judge of Supreme Court of ACT, 1976–81; Judge, Fed. Court of Australia, 1977–81; Justice of the High Court, 1981–95; Chief Justice of Australia, 1995–98; Foundn Scientia Prof. of Law, Univ. of NSW, 1998–99; external Judge, Supreme Court, Republic of Fiji, 1999–2000. President: Admin. Appeals Tribunal, 1976–79; Admin. Review Council, 1976–79; Bar Assoc. of Qld, 1974–76; Aust. Bar Assoc., 1975–76; National Union of Aust. Univ. Students, 1949. Member: Exec. Law Council of Australia, 1974–76; Aust. Law Reform Commn, 1975–77. Hon. LLD: TCD, 1988; Queensland, 1996; ANU, 1996; Melbourne, 1998; UTS, 1998; Hon. DLitt Central Queensland, 1996; DUniv Griffith, 1996. *Address:* (office) Suite 2604, Piccadilly Tower, 133 Castlereagh Street, Sydney, NSW 2000, Australia. *T:* (2) 92618704, *Fax:* (2) 92618113. *Club:* Australian (Sydney).

BRENNAN, Kevin Denis; MP (Lab) Cardiff West, since 2001; *b* 16 Oct. 1959; *s* of Michael John Brennan and Beryl Marie Brennan (*née* Evans); *m* 1988, Amy Lynn Wack; one *d*. *Educ:* St Alban's RC Comprehensive Sch., Pontypool; Pembroke Coll., Oxford (BA); UC, Cardiff (PGCE); Univ. of Glamorgan (MSc). Volunteer organiser/news ed., Cwmbran Community Press, 1982–84; Hd, Econs and Business Studies, Radyr Comprehensive Sch., 1985–94; Res. Officer for Rhodri Morgan, MP, 1995–2000; Special Advr to First Minister, Nat. Assembly for Wales, 2000. *Recreations:* Rugby (watching now), music, golf, cricket. *Address:* House of Commons, SW1A 0AA; Transport House, 1 Cathedral Road, Cardiff CF11 9SD. *Club:* Canton Labour (Cardiff).

BRENNAN, Timothy Roger; QC 2001; a Recorder, since 2000; *b* 11 April 1958; *s* of John Gerald Brennan, MSc and Edna Brennan (*née* Rees), MB BCh.*m* 1988, Heulwen Rees; three *s*. *Educ:* Olchfa Sch., Swansea; Balliol Coll., Oxford (BCL, MA). Called to the Bar, Gray's Inn, 1981 (Atkin Schol. 1981); Addnl Jun. Counsel to Inland Revenue (Common Law), 1991–97, Jun. Counsel, 1997–2001; Asst Recorder, 1997–2000. Mem., Gen. Council of the Bar, 1987, 1988 (Mem., Professional Conduct and Complaints Cttee, 1989 and 1995–98). *Publications:* contribs to various tech. legal pubns. *Recreations:* cycling, swimming, music. *Address:* Devereux Chambers, Devereux Court, WC2R 3JH. *T:* (020) 7353 7534.

BRENNAN, Ursula Mary; Group Director, Working Age and Children's Services, Department for Work and Pensions, since 2001; *b* 28 Oct. 1952; *d* of Philip and Mary Burns; *m* 1975, Denis Brennan. *Educ:* Univ. of Kent at Canterbury (BA Hons English and Amer. Lit). ILEA, 1973–75; Department of Health and Social Security, later of Social Security, 1975–2001; Head, Disability Benefits Policy, 1990–93; Dir, IT Services Agency, 1993–95; Dir, Change Management, Benefits Agency, 1995–97; Gp Dir, Working Age Services, 1997–2001. *Address:* Department for Work and Pensions, The Adelphi, 1/11 John Adam Street, WC2N 6HT.

BRENNER, Sydney, CH 1987; DPhil; FRCP; FRS 1965; Distinguished Research Professor, Salk Institute, La Jolla, California, since 2001; Member of Scientific Staff, MRC, 1957–92; Fellow of King's College, Cambridge, since 1959; *b* Germiston, South Africa, 13 Jan. 1927; *s* of Morris Brenner and Lena (*née* Blacher); *m* 1952, May Woolf Balkind; one *s* two *d* (and one step *s*). *Educ:* Germiston High School; University of the Witwatersrand, S Africa; Oxford University (Hon. Fellow, Exeter Coll., 1985). MSc 1947, MB, BCh 1951, Univ. of the Witwatersrand; DPhil Oxon, 1954; FRCP 1979; Hon. FRCPath 1990. Director: MRC Lab. of Molecular Biol., Cambridge, 1979–86; MRC Molecular Genetics Unit, Cambridge, 1986–92; Mem., Scripps Res. Inst., La Jolla, 1992–94. Pres. and Dir of Res., Molecular Scis Inst., Berkeley, Calif, 1996–2001. Mem., MRC, 1978–82, 1986–90. Hon. Prof. of Genetic Medicine, Cambridge Univ., 1989–97. Carter-Wallace Lectr, Princeton, 1966, 1971; Gifford Lectr, Glasgow, 1978–79; Dunham Lectr, Harvard, 1984; Croonian Lectr, Royal Soc., 1986. External Scientific Mem., Max-Planck Soc., 1988; Mem., Academia Europaea, 1989; Foreign Hon. Member, American Academy of Arts and Sciences, 1965; Foreign Associate: Nat. Acad. of Sciences, USA, 1977; Royal Soc. of S Africa, 1983; Académie des Sciences, Paris, 1992; Mem., Deutsche Akademie der Naturforscher, Leopoldina, 1975 (Gregor Mendel Medal, 1970); Foreign Member: Amer. Philosophical Soc., 1979; Real Academia de Ciencias, Spain, 1985; Correspondant Scientifique Emerite, Institut National de la Santé et de la Recherche Médicale, Paris, 1991; Hon. Member: Chinese Soc. of Genetics, 1989; Assoc. of Physicians of GB and Ireland, 1991; Alpha Omega Alpha Honor Med. Soc., 1994; German Soc. Cell Biol., 1999. Fellow, Amer. Acad. of Microbiol., 1996. Hon. FRSE 1979. Hon. FIASc 1989. Hon. DSc: Dublin, 1967; Witwatersrand, 1972; Chicago, 1976; London, 1982; Leicester, 1983; Oxford, 1985; Rockefeller, 1996; Columbia, 1997; La Trobe, 1999; Hon. LLD: Glasgow, 1981; Cambridge, 2001; Hon. DLitt Nat. Univ. of Singapore, 1995; Dr rer. nat. *hc* Jena, 1998. Warren Triennial Prize, 1968; William Bate Hardy Prize, Cambridge Philosophical Soc., 1969; (jtly) Lasker Award for Basic Medical Research, 1971; Royal Medal, Royal Soc., 1974; (jtly) Prix Charles Leopold Mayer, French Acad. of Science, 1975; Gairdner Foundn Annual Award, 1978; Krebs Medal, FEBS, 1980; CIBA Medal, Biochem. Soc., 1981; Feldberg Foundn Prize, 1983; Neil Hamilton Fairley Medal, RCP, 1985; Rosenstiel Award, Brandeis Univ., 1986; Prix Louis Jeantet de Médecine, Switzerland, 1987; Genetics Soc. of America Medal, 1987; Harvey Prize, Technion-Israel Inst. of Technol., 1987; Hughlings Jackson Medal, RSocMed, 1987; Waterford Bio-Medical Sci. Award, Res. Inst. of Scripps Clinic, USA, 1988; Kyoto Prize, Inamori Foundn, 1990; Gairdner Foundn Internat. Award, Canada, 1991; Copley Medal, Royal Soc., 1991; King Faisal Internat. Prize for Science, King Faisal Foundn, Saudi Arabia, 1992; Bristol-Myers Squibb Award for Dist. Achievement in Neurosci. Res., NY, 1992; Albert Lasker Award for Special Achievement, 2000. *Publications:* papers in scientific journals. *Recreation:* rumination. *Address:* King's College, Cambridge CB2 1ST.

BRENT, Prof. Leslie Baruch, FIBiol; Professor Emeritus, University of London, since 1990; *b* 5 July 1925; *s* of Charlotte and Arthur Baruch; *m* 1st, 1954, Joanne Elisabeth Manley (marr. diss. 1991); one *s* two *d*; 2nd, 1991, Carol Pamela Martin. *Educ:* Bunce Court Sch., Kent; Birmingham Central Technical Coll.; Univ. of Birmingham; UCL. BSc Birmingham, PhD London; FIBiol 1964. Laboratory technician, 1941–43; Army service, 1943–47, Captain; Lectr, Dept of Zoology, UCL, 1954–62; Rockefeller Res. Fellow, Calif Inst. of Technology, 1956–57; Res. scientist, Nat. Inst. for Med. Res., 1962–65; Prof. of Zoology, Univ. of Southampton, 1965–69; Prof. of Immunology, St Mary's Hosp. Med. Sch., London, 1969–90. European Editor, Transplantation, 1963–68; Gen. Sec., British Transplantation Soc., 1971–75 (Hon. Mem., 1988); Pres., The Transplantation Society, 1976–78 (Medawar Prize, 1994); Chairman: Wessex Br., Inst. of Biol., 1966–68; Organising Cttee, 9th Internat. Congress of The Transplantation Soc., 1978–82; Fellowships Cttee, Inst. of Biol., 1982–85; Art Cttee, St Mary's Hosp. Med. Sch., 1988–92. Pres., Guild of Undergrads, Birmingham Univ., 1950–51. Chairman: Haringey Community Relations Council, 1979–80; Haringey SDP, 1981–83. Governor, Yerbury Sch., 1999–. Hon. MRCP 1986. Hon. Mem., British Transplantation Soc., 1988; hon. mem. of several foreign scientific socs. Vice-Chancellor's Prize, Birmingham Univ., 1951; Scientific Medal, Zool Soc., 1963; Peter Medawar Medal, Internat. Transplantation Soc., 1994. Played hockey for UAU and Staffs, 1949–51. Co-editor, Immunology Letters, 1983–90. *Publications:* (ed jtly) Organ Transplantation: current clinical and immunological concepts, 1989; History of Transplantation Immunology,

1997; articles in scientific and med. jls on transplantation immunology. *Recreations:* music, singing (Crouch End Festival Chorus), fell-walking, novels. *Address:* 30 Hugo Road, N19 5EU.

BRENT, Michael Leon; QC 1983; a Recorder, 1990–2000; a Deputy High Court Judge, 1994–2000; *b* 8 June 1936; *m* 1965, Rosalind Keller; two *d. Educ:* Manchester Grammar Sch.; Manchester Univ. (LLB Hons). Called to the Bar, Gray's Inn, 1961; practised on: Northern Circuit, 1961–67 (Circuit Junior, 1964); Midland and Oxford Circuit, 1967–2000. Mem. Bd, Criminal Injuries Compensation Appeals Panel, 1999-. *Address:* 9 Gough Square, EC4A 3DG.

BRENT, Prof. Richard Peirce, PhD; DSc; Professor of Computing Science, and Fellow of St Hugh's College, University of Oxford, since 1998; *b* 20 April 1946; *s* of Oscar and Nancy Brent; *m* 1969, Erin O'Connor; two *s. Educ:* Melbourne Grammar Sch.; Monash Univ. (BSc 1968; DSc 1981); Stanford Univ. (PhD 1971). FAA 1982; FIEEE 1991. IBM Res., Yorktown Heights, NY, 1971–72; Australian National University: Res. Fellow, 1972–73; Fellow, 1973–76; Sen. Fellow, 1976–78; Foundation Prof. of Computer Science, 1978–98. Visiting Professor: Stanford Univ., 1974–75; Univ. of Calif at Berkeley, 1977–78; Harvard Univ., 1997. Fellow, ACM, 1994. Aust. Math. Soc. Medal, 1984. *Publications:* Algorithms for Minimization without Derivatives, 1973; Computational Complexity and the Analysis of Algorithms, 1980. *Recreations:* music, chess, factoring Fermat numbers. *Address:* Oxford University Computing Laboratory, Wolfson Building, Parks Road, Oxford OX1 3QD. *T:* (01865) 283505.

BRENTFORD, 4th Viscount *cr* 1929, of Newick; **Crispin William Joynson-Hicks;** Bt of Holmbury, 1919; Bt of Newick, 1956; Partner, Taylor Joynson Garrett (formerly Joynson-Hicks), 1961–95; *b* 7 April 1933; *s* of 3rd Viscount Brentford and Phyllis (*d* 1979), *o d* of late Major Herbert Allfrey, Tetbury, Glos; *S* father, 1983; *m* 1964, Gillian Evelyn Schluter (*see* Viscountess Brentford); one *s* three *d. Educ:* Eton; New College, Oxford. Admitted solicitor, 1960. Master, Girdlers' Co., 1983–84. *Heir: s* Hon. Paul William Joynson-Hicks, *b* 18 April 1971. *Address:* Cousley Place, Wadhurst, East Sussex TN5 6HF. *T:* (01892) 783737.

BRENTFORD, Viscountess; Gillian Evelyn Joynson-Hicks, OBE 1996; FCA; Third Church Estates Commissioner, since 1999; *b* 22 Nov. 1942; *d* of Gerald Edward Schluter, OBE; *m* 1964, Crispin William Joynson-Hicks (*see* Viscount Brentford); one *s* three *d. Educ:* West Heath Sch. FCA 1965. Director: Edward Schluter & Co. (London) Ltd, 1971–88; M. A. F. Europe, 1990–97. Mem., General Synod of C of E, 1990–; a Church Comr, 1991–98 (Mem., Bd of Govs, 1993–98); Chm., House of Laity, Chichester dio., 1991–99; Mem., Crown Appts Commn, 1995–. Pres., CMS, 1998–. High Sheriff, E Sussex, 1998–99. *Recreations:* family, gardens, travel. *Address:* Cousley Place, Wadhurst, East Sussex TN5 6HF.

BRENTON, Anthony Russell, CMG 2001; HM Diplomatic Service; Director, Foreign and Commonwealth Office, since 1998; *b* 1 Jan. 1950; *s* of Ivan Bernard Brenton and Jean Sylvia (*née* Rostgard); *m* 1981, Susan Mary Penrose; one *s* two *d. Educ:* Queens' Coll. Cambridge (BA); Open Univ. (MPhil). Joined HM Diplomatic Service, 1975; Cairo, 1978–81; European Communities Dept, FCO, 1981–85; with UK Perm. Repn to EC, 1985–86; Dep. Chef de Cabinet, EC, 1986–89; Counsellor, 1989; Head, UN Dept, FCO, 1989–90; Envmt, Sci. and Energy Dept, FCO, 1990–92; Fellow, Centre for Internat. Affairs, Harvard Univ., 1992–93; Counsellor, Moscow, 1994–98. *Publication:* The Greening of Machiavelli, 1994. *Recreation:* history. *Address:* c/o Foreign and Commonwealth Office, King Charles Street, SW1A 2AH.

BRENTON, Howard; playwright; *b* 13 Dec. 1942; *s* of Donald Henry Brenton and Rose Lilian (*née* Lewis); *m* 1970, Jane Fry; two *s. Educ:* Chichester High Sch. for Boys; St Catharine's Coll., Cambridge (BA Hons English). Hon. Dr North London. *Full-length stage plays:* Revenge, 1969; Hitler Dances, and Measure for Measure (after Shakespeare), 1972; Magnificence, 1973; The Churchill Play, 1974; Government Property, 1975; Weapons of Happiness, 1976 (Evening Standard Award); Epsom Downs, 1977; Sore Throats, 1979; The Romans in Britain, 1980; Thirteenth Night, 1981; The Genius, 1983; Bloody Poetry, 1984; Greenland, 1988; H. I. D. (Hess is Dead), 1989; Berlin Bertie, 1992; In Extremis, 1997; Kit's Play, 2000; *one-act stage plays:* Gum and Goo, Heads, The Education of Skinny Spew, and Christie in Love, 1969; Wesley, 1970; Scott of the Antartic, and A Sky-blue Life, 1971; How Beautiful with Badges, 1972; Mug, 1973; The Thing (for children), 1982; *collaborations:* (with six others) Lay-By, 1970; (with six others) England's Ireland, 1971; (with David Hare) Brassneck, 1973; (with Trevor Griffiths, David Hare and Ken Campbell), Deeds, 1978; (with Tony Howard) A Short Sharp Shock, 1980; (with Tunde Ikoli) Sleeping Policemen, 1983; (with David Hare) Pravda, 1985 (London Standard Award); (with Tariq Ali) Iranian Nights, 1989; (with Tariq Ali) Moscow Gold, 1990; Playing Away (opera), 1994 (score by Benedict Mason); (with Tariq Ali) Ugly Rumours, 1998; (with Tariq Ali and Andy de la Tour) Collateral Damage, 1999; (with Tariq Ali and Andy de la Tour) Snogging Ken, 2000; *television plays:* Lushly, 1971; Brassneck (adaptation of stage play), 1974; The Saliva Milkshake, 1975 (also perf. theatre); The Paradise Run, 1976; Desert of Lies, 1984; *television series:* Dead Head, 1986; *radio play:* Nasser's Eden, 1998; *translations:* Bertolt Brecht, The Life of Galileo, 1980; Georg Buchner, Danton's Death, 1982; Bertolt Brecht, Conversations in Exile, 1982; Goethe, Faust, 1995. *Publications:* Diving for Pearls (novel), 1989; Hot Irons: diaries, essays, journalism, 1995; many plays published. *Recreation:* painting. *Address:* c/o Casarotto Ramsay Ltd, 60–66 Wardour Street, W1V 3HP. *T:* (020) 7287 4450.

BRENTON, Timothy Deane; QC 1998; *b* 4 Nov. 1957; *s* of late Comdr R. W. Brenton, RN and of P. C. D. Brenton; *m* 1981, Annabel Louisa Robson; one *s* one *d. Educ:* King's Sch., Rochester; BRNC, Dartmouth; Bristol Univ. (LLB 1st cl. Hons 1979). RN, 1975–79; Lectr in Law, King's Coll. London, 1980; called to the Bar, Middle Temple, 1981; in practice at the Bar, 1981–. Mem., Editl Bd, International Maritime Law, 1994–. *Recreations:* golf, country pursuits, music. *Address:* 7 King's Bench Walk, Inner Temple, EC4Y 7DS. *T:* (020) 7910 8300.

BRENTWOOD, Bishop of, (RC), since 1980; **Rt Rev. Thomas McMahon;** *b* 17 June 1936. *Educ:* St Bede's GS, Manchester; St Sulpice, Paris; Wonersh. Ordained priest, 1959; Asst Priest, Colchester, 1959–64; Priest, Westcliff-on-Sea, 1964–69; Parish Priest, Stock, 1969–; Chaplain, Univ. of Essex, 1972–80. Former Member: Nat. Ecumenical Commn, Liturgical Commn; Chairman: Brentwood Ecumenical Commn, 1979; Cttee for Pastoral Liturgy, 1983–96; Essex Churches Consultative Council, 1984–; Cttee for Church Music, 1985–; Mem., London Church Leaders Gp, 1980–. Pres., Essex Show, 1992. DU Essex, 1991. *Address:* Bishop's House, Stock, Ingatestone, Essex CM4 9BU. *T:* (01277) 840268.

BRERETON, Donald, CB 2001; Director, Disability and Carers, Department for Work and Pensions (formerly Director, Disability, Department of Social Security), since 2000; *b* 18 July 1945; *s* of Clarence Vivian and Alice Gwendolin Brereton; *m* 1969, Mary Frances Turley; one *s* two *d. Educ:* Plymouth Coll.; Univ. of Newcastle upon Tyne (BA Hons Pol. and Soc. Admin). VSO, Malaysia, 1963–64. Asst Principal, Min. of Health, 1968; Asst Private Sec. to Sec. of State for Social Services, 1971; Private Sec. to Perm. Sec., DHSS, 1972; Prin., Health Services Planning, 1973; Private Sec. to Sec. of State for Social Services, 1979–82; Asst Sec., DHSS Policy Strategy Unit, 1982–83; Sec. to Housing Benefit Rev. Team, 1984; Asst Sec., Housing Benefit, 1985–89; Under Sec., Head of Prime Minister's Efficiency Unit, 1989–93; Under Sec., Social Security Policy Gp, DSS, 1993–2000. *Recreations:* squash, holidays, books, gardening, bridge. *Address:* Department for Work and Pensions, The Adelphi, 1–11 John Adam Street, WC2N 6HT.

BRETHERTON, James Russell; Secretary, since 1990, and Director of Corporate Services, since 1998, United Kingdom Atomic Energy Authority; *b* 28 March 1943; *y s* of Russell Frederick Bretherton, CB and Jocelyn Nina Mathews; *m* 1968, Harriet Grace Drew, *d* of Sir Arthur Charles Walter Drew, KCB; two *s. Educ:* King's Sch., Canterbury; Wadham Coll., Oxford (MA History). Voluntary Service as Asst Dist Officer, Nigeria, 1965–66; Asst Principal, Min. of Fuel and Power, 1966–70; Principal, Min. of Technol., 1970–76; Principal Private Sec. to Sec. of State for Energy, 1976–78; Head of Oil Industry Div., Internat. Energy Agency, Paris, 1980–82; Asst Sec., Dept of Energy, 1983–86; Principal Finance and Programmes Officer, UKAEA, 1986–89; Commercial and Planning Dir, AEA Technology, 1990–94; Dir, Property Mgt and Services, UKAEA, 1994–98. *Recreations:* gardening, walking, bassoon playing. *Address:* Highview, 15 Hid's Copse Road, Cumnor Hill, Oxford OX2 9JJ. *T:* (01865) 863388; Authers Cottage, Cotleigh, Honiton, Devon EX14 9HD. *T:* (01404) 831243.

See also P. C. Drew.

BRETSCHER, Barbara Mary Frances, (Mrs M. S. Bretscher); *see* Pearse, B. M. F.

BRETSCHER, Mark Steven, PhD; FRS 1985; Senior Member of Scientific Staff, Division of Cell Biology, Medical Research Council Laboratory of Molecular Biology, Cambridge, since 1972 (Head of Division, 1984–95); *b* 8 Jan. 1940; *s* of late Egon Bretscher, CBE and Hanni (*née* Greminger); *m* 1978, Barbara Mary Frances Pearse, *qv*; one *s* one *d. Educ:* Abingdon Sch., Berks; Gonville and Caius Coll., Cambridge (MA, PhD). Res. Fellow, Gonville and Caius Coll., Cambridge, 1964–70; Mem., Scientific Staff, MRC Lab. of Molecular Biology, Cambridge, 1965–. Vis. Professor: Harvard Univ., 1975; Stanford Univ., 1984. Friedrich Miescher Prize, Swiss Biochemical Soc., 1979. *Publications:* papers in scientific jls on protein biosynthesis, membrane structure and cell locomotion. *Recreation:* gardening. *Address:* Ram Cottage, Commercial End, Swaffham Bulbeck, Cambridge CB5 0ND. *T:* (01223) 811276; *e-mail:* msb@mrc-lmb.cam.ac.uk.

BRETT, family name of **Viscount Esher** and **Baron Brett**.

BRETT, Baron *cr* 1999 (Life Peer), of Lydd in the county of Kent; **William Henry Brett;** General Secretary, Institution of Professionals, Managers and Specialists, 1989–99; *b* 6 March 1942; *s* of William Joseph Brett and Mary Brett (*née* Murphy); *m* 1st, 1961, Jean Valerie (marr. diss. 1986); one *s* one *d*; 2nd, 1994, Janet Winters; two *d. Educ:* Radcliffe Secondary Technical College, Manchester. British Railways, 1958–64; TSSA, 1964–66; NW Organiser, NUBE (now BIFU), 1966–68; E Midlands Divl Officer, ASTMS, 1968–74; Asst Sec., IPCS later IPMS, Asst Gen. Sec., 1980, elected Gen. Sec., 1988. Mem., Gen. Council, TUC, 1989–99. Exec. Sec., Internat. Fedn of Air Traffic Electronic Assocs, 1984–92; Mem. Public Services Internat. Exec. Cttee, 1989–99. International Labour Organisation: Mem. Governing Body, Geneva, 1991– (Vice Pres., 1993–); Pres., Worker Group, 1993–. FRSA. *Publication:* International Labour in the 21st Century, 1994. *Recreations:* travelling, reading. *Address:* Sycamore House, 2 Mill Road, Lydd, Romney Marsh, Kent TN29 9EP. *T:* (01797) 321597, *Fax:* (01797) 322148; *e-mail:* BBRETT4571@aol.com. *Club:* Lydd War Memorial.

BRETT, Sir Charles (Edward Bainbridge), Kt 1990; CBE 1981; Consultant, L'Estrange & Brett, Solicitors, Belfast, 1994–98 (Partner, 1954–94); *b* 30 Oct. 1928; *s* of Charles Anthony Brett and Elizabeth Joyce (*née* Carter); *m* 1953, Joyce Patricia Worley; three *s. Educ:* Rugby Sch.; New Coll., Oxford (Schol.; MA History). Solicitor, 1953. Journalist, Radiodiffusion Française and Continental Daily Mail, 1949–50. Member: Child Welfare Council of Northern Ireland, 1958–61; Northern Ireland Cttee, National Trust, 1956–83 and 1985–93 (Mem. Council, 1975–89); Board, Arts Council of N Ireland, 1970–76, and 1994–98 (Vice-Chm., 1994–98); Chairman: N Ireland Labour Party, 1962; Ulster Architectural Heritage Soc., 1968–78 (Pres., 1979–); HEARTH Housing Assoc., 1978 and 1985–2000 (Vice-Pres., 2000–); NI Housing Exec., 1979–84 (Mem. Bd, 1971–77, Vice-Chm., 1977–78); Internat. Fund for Ireland, 1986–89. Mem. Bd, Irish Architectural Archive, Dublin, 1985–88. Hon. Mem., Royal Society of Ulster Architects, 1973; Hon. MRIAI 1988; Hon. FRIBA 1987. Hon. LLD QUB, 1989. *Publications:* Buildings of Belfast 1700–1914, 1967, rev. edn 1985; Court Houses and Market Houses of Ulster, 1973; Long Shadows Cast Before, 1978; Housing a Divided Community, 1986; Buildings of County Antrim, 1996; Five Big Houses of Cushendun, 1997; Buildings of County Armagh, 1999; lists and surveys for Ulster Architectural Heritage Soc., National Trusts of Guernsey and Jersey, and Alderney Soc; (as Albert Rechts) Handbook to a Hypothetical City, 1986. *Club:* Oxford and Cambridge.

BRETT, Lionel; *see* Esher, 4th Viscount.

BRETT, Michael John Lee; freelance financial journalist, part-time lecturer and writer, since 1982; *b* 23 May 1939; *s* of late John Brett and Margaret Brett (*née* Lee). *Educ:* King's Coll. Sch., Wimbledon; Wadham Coll., Oxford (BA Modern Langs). Investors Review, 1962–64; Fire Protection Assoc., 1964–68; Investors Chronicle, 1968–82: Dep. Editor, 1973–77; Editor, 1977–82. Past Director: Throgmorton Publications; Financial Times Business Publishing Div. *Publications:* Finance for Business: private sector finance; (contrib.) Valuation and Investment Appraisal; How to Read the Financial Pages; Property and Money, 1990. *Recreations:* travelling, reading.

See also S. A. L. Brett.

BRETT, Richard John; Managing Director, Solution Partners Ltd, since 1996; *b* 23 October 1947; *s* of Henry William Brett and Dorothy Ada Brett; *m* 1st, 1972, Alison Elizabeth Lambert (marr. diss. 1991); one *d*; 2nd, 1991, Maria Antoinette Brown. *Educ:* Univ. of Bradford (MSc). FCA; Associate, Inst. of Taxation. Leonard C. Bye, Chartered Accountants, Middlesbrough, 1964; ICI Petro-chemicals, 1971; Finance Director: Chloride Shires, 1976; Chloride Automotive Batteries, 1979; Westpark, 1981; Thorn EMI Datatech, 1985–88; Gp Dir, Finance and Mgt Services, CAA, 1988–96. *Recreation:* music. *Address:* Solution Partners Ltd, Garrick House, 27–32 King Street, WC2E 8JD.

BRETT, Simon Anthony Lee; writer; *b* 28 Oct. 1945; *s* of late Alan John Brett and Margaret Agnes Brett (*née* Lee); *m* 1971, Lucy Victoria McLaren; two *s* one *d. Educ:* Dulwich College; Wadham College, Oxford (BA Hons). Department store Father Christmas, 1967; BBC Radio Producer, 1968–77; LWT Producer, 1977–79. Chm., Soc. of Authors, 1995–97. Radio and television scripts, incl. After Henry, No Commitments. *Publications: Charles Paris crime novels:* Cast, In Order of Disappearance, 1975; So Much Blood, 1976; Star Trap, 1977; An Amateur Corpse, 1978; A Comedian Dies, 1979; The

Dead Side of the Mike, 1980; Situation Tragedy, 1981; Murder Unprompted, 1982; Murder in the Title, 1983; Not Dead, Only Resting, 1984; Dead Giveaway, 1985; What Bloody Man Is That?, 1987; A Series of Murders, 1989; Corporate Bodies, 1991; A Reconstructed Corpse, 1993; Sicken And So Die, 1995; Dead Room Farce, 1997; *Mrs Pargeter crime novels:* A Nice Class of Corpse, 1986; Mrs, Presumed Dead, 1988; Mrs Pargeter's Package, 1990; Mrs Pargeter's Pound of Flesh, 1992; Mrs Pargeter's Plot, 1996; Mrs Pargeter's Point of Honour, 1998; *other crime novels:* A Shock to the System, 1984; Dead Romantic, 1985; The Three Detectives and the Missing Superstar, 1986; The Three Detectives and the Knight-in-Armour, 1987; The Christmas Crimes at Puzzel Manor, 1991; Singled Out, 1995; The Body on the Beach, 2000; Death on the Downs, 2001; *crime short stories:* A Box of Tricks, 1985; Crime Writers and Other Animals, 1998; *humorous books:* The Child-Owner's Handbook, 1983; Molesworth Rites Again, 1983; Bad Form, 1984; People-Spotting, 1985; The Wastepaper Basket Archive, 1986; How to Stay Topp, 1987; After Henry, 1987; The Booker Book, 1989; How to be a Little Sod, 1992; Look Who's Walking, 1994; Not Another Little Sod!, 1997; *anthologies:* The Faber Book of Useful Verse, 1981; (with Frank Muir) The Book of Comedy Sketches, 1982; Take a Spare Truss, 1983; The Faber Book of Parodies, 1984; The Faber Book of Diaries, 1987; *stage play:* Silhouette, 1998. *Recreations:* writing, reading, Real tennis, unreal fantasies. *Address:* Frith House, Burpham, Arundel, West Sussex BN18 9RR. *T:* (01903) 882257. *Clubs:* Groucho, Detection.

See also M. J. L. Brett.

BRETT, Timothy Edward William; Chief Executive, Tayside Health Board, 1998–2001; *b* 28 March 1949; *s* of Reuben Brett and Edna Brett (*née* Waterman); *m* 1972, Barbara Jane Turnbull; two *s* one *d* (and one *s* decd). *Educ:* Gravesend GS for Boys; Bristol Univ. (BSc Hons). FHSM, DipHSM, GradIPD. VSO Teacher, Min. of Educn, Sierra Leone, 1971–73; Nat. Admin. Trainee, Leeds RBH, later Yorks RHA, 1973–75; Sen. Admin. Asst (Planning & Personnel), Leeds AHA, 1975–76; Business Manager, Nixon Meml Hosp., Methodist Church–Overseas Div., Segbwema, Sierra Leone, 1976–78; Community Services Adminr, Humberside AHA, 1978; Dep. Adminr, Derbyshire Royal Infirmary, 1979–80; Unit Adminr, Plymouth Gen. Hosp., 1981–85; Unit Adminr, 1985–87, Unit Gen. Manager, 1987–93, Dundee Gen. Hosps Unit; Chief Exec., Dundee Teaching Hosps NHS Trust, 1993–98. *Recreations:* hill-walking, swimming, theatre, church activities, Rotarian. *Address:* Woodend Cottage, Hazelton Walls, Cupar, Fife KY15 4QL. *T:* (01382) 632598.

BRETT-HOLT, Alexis Fayrer; Director, Legal Services B, Department of Trade and Industry, since 2001; *b* 7 March 1950; *d* of Raymond Arthur Brett-Holt and late Jacqueline Fayrer Brett-Holt (*née* Fayrer Hosken); *m* 1980, (John) Gareth Roscoe, *qv*; one *s* one *d*. *Educ:* Wimbledon High Sch.; St Anne's Coll., Oxford (BA). Called to the Bar, Lincoln's Inn, 1973; Department of the Environment: Legal Asst, 1974–78; Sen. Legal Asst, 1978–85; Asst Solicitor, 1985–89; Assistant Solicitor: DoH, 1989–93; DoE, 1993–97; Dir, Legal Services C, 1997–2001. *Address:* Solicitor's Office, Department of Trade and Industry, 10 Victoria Street, SW1H 0NN. *T:* (020) 7215 3247. *Club:* CWIL.

BRETTEN, George Rex; QC 1980; barrister-at-law; *b* 21 Feb. 1942; *s* of Horace Victor Bretten and Kathleen Edna Betty Bretten; *m* 1965, Maureen Gillian Crowhurst; one *d*. *Educ:* King Edward VII Sch., King's Lynn; Sidney Sussex Coll., Cambridge (MA, LLM). Lectr, Nottingham Univ., 1964–68; Asst Director, Inst. of Law Research and Reform, Alberta, Canada, 1968–70; called to the Bar, Lincoln's Inn, 1965, a Bencher 1989; in practice, 1971–. *Publication:* Special Reasons, 1977. *Recreations:* gardening, walking, tennis. *Address:* Stonehill House, Horam, Heathfield, East Sussex TN21 0JN. *T:* (01825) 872820. *Club:* Athenæum.

BREW, David Allan; Chief Executive, Institute of Chartered Accountants of Scotland, since 2000; *b* 19 Feb. 1953; *s* of Kenneth Frederick Cecil Brew and Iris May (*née* Sharpe). *Educ:* Kettering Grammar Sch.; Heriot-Watt Univ. (BA 1st Cl. Hons 1974; Pres., Students' Assoc., 1974–75); Univ. of Strathclyde (MSc 1976); European Univ. Inst., Florence. Scottish Office, 1979–81; Adminr, Directorate-Gen. V, EC, Brussels, 1981–84; Scottish Office: Principal, Glasgow, 1984–88, Edinburgh, 1988–90; Head: Electricity Privatisation Div., 1990–91; Eur. Funds and Co-ordination Div., 1991–95; Sea Fisheries Div., 1995–98; Devolution Team, Constitution Secretariat, Cabinet Office, 1998–2000. Mem. Court, Heriot-Watt Univ., 1985–91, 2000–. *Publications:* (contrib.) Changing Patterns of Relations between the National Parliaments and the European Parliament, 1979; (contrib.) European Electoral Systems Handbook, 1979; (contrib.) The European Parliament: towards a uniform procedure for direct elections, 1981. *Recreations:* languages, music, film, gastronomy. *Address:* 1 Dundas Street, Edinburgh EH3 6QG. *T:* (0131) 556 4692.

BREW, Richard Maddock, CBE 1982; DL; Chairman, Budget Boilers Ltd, since 1984; *b* 13 Dec. 1930; *s* of late Leslie Maddock Brew and Phyllis Evelyn Huntsman; *m* 1953, Judith Anne Thompson Hancock; two *s* two *d*. *Educ:* Rugby Sch.; Magdalene Coll., Cambridge (BA). Called to the Bar, Inner Temple, 1955. After practising for short time at the Bar, joined family business, Brew Brothers Ltd, SW7, 1955, and remained until takeover, 1972. Chm., Monks Dormitory Ltd, 1979–93; Regl Dir, Lloyds Bank, 1988–91. Mem., NE Thames RHA, 1982–90 (Vice-Chm., 1982–86); Chm., Tower Hamlets DHA, 1990–93. Farms in Essex. Member: Royal Borough of Kensington Council, 1959–65; Royal Borough of Kensington and Chelsea Council, 1964–70; Greater London Council: Mem., 1968–86; Alderman, 1968–73; Vice-Chm., Strategic Planning Cttee, 1969–71; Chm., Covent Garden Jt Development Cttee, 1970–71 and Environmental Planning Cttee, 1971–73; Mem. for Chingford, 1973–86; Dep. Leader of Council and Leader, Policy and Resources Cttee, 1977–81; Dep. Leader, Cons. Party and Opposition Spokesman on Finance, 1981–82; Leader of the Opposition, 1982–83. Mem., Nat. Theatre Bd, 1982–86. Mem., Pony Club Council, 1975–93. High Sheriff, Greater London, 1988–89. DL Greater London, 1989. *Recreations:* hunting, gardening. *Address:* Holm Close, Kilton, Somerset TA5 1ST. *T:* (01278) 741293. *Clubs:* Carlton, MCC.

BREWER, David William, CMG 1999; JP; FCII; Chairman, GB-China Centre, since 1997; Senior Consultant, International Financial Services, London, since 2001; Consultant, Asia Pacific Region, Marsh Inc., since 1999; *b* 28 May 1940; *s* of Dr H. F. Brewer and Elizabeth Brewer (*née* Nickell-Lean); *m* 1985, Tessa Suzanne Mary Jordá; two *d*. *Educ:* St Paul's Sch.; Univ. of Grenoble. FCII 1966. Joined Sedgwick Group, 1959: Rep., Japan, 1976–78; Director: Sedgwick Far East Ltd, 1982–99 (Chm., 1993–97); Develt Cos, 1982–98; Sedgwick Internat. Risk Mgt Inc., 1990–99; Chairman: Sedgwick Insce and Risk Mgt Consultants (China) Ltd, 1993–97; Sedgwick Japan Ltd, 1994–97. Dir, Sumitomo Marine & Fire Insce Co. (Europe) Ltd, 1985–98; Dir and Sen. Consultant, British Invisibles, 1998-2001; Mem., Eur. Adv. Bd, Credit Lyonnais, 2000–. Mem., Action Japan Cttee, DTI, 1996–2000. Mem. Council, and Hon. Treas., China-Britain Business Council, 1991– (Chm., International Financial Services, London/China-Britain Business Council Financial Services Cttee, 1993–); Exec. Chm., UK-China Forum, 2000–; Mem., UK-Korea Forum for the Future, 2000–. Dir, City of London Sinfonia, 1988–; Mem., Adv. Council, LSO, 1999–; Mem. Council, Spitalfields Fest., 1989–. Chm., City of London Br., RNLI, 1997– (Mem., 1989–); Vice-Pres., City of London Sector, BRCS, 1986–. Governor: City of London Poly., 1979–90; Corp. of Sons of the Clergy, 1993–; Almoner, Christ's Hosp., 1998–. Trustee: Lord Mayor's 800th Anniversary Awards Trust, 1997–; Guildhall Sch. Trust Foundn, 1999–. Alderman, City of London, Ward of Bassishaw, 1996– (Mem. Ct of Common Council, 1992–96); Liveryman, Merchant Taylors' Co., 1968– (Mem., Ct of Assts, 1985–; Master, 2001–July 2002). Churchwarden, St Lawrence Jewry, 1996–. JP City of London, 1979. *Recreations:* music (especially opera and choral music), golf, mechanical gardening, chocolate, paronomasia. *Address:* 16 Cowley Street, SW1P 3LZ. *T:* (020) 7222 5481; Orchard Cottage, Hellandbridge, Bodmin, Cornwall PL30 4QR. *T:* (01208) 841268. *Clubs:* Garrick, City of London, MCC; St Enodoc Golf.

BREWER, Prof. Derek Stanley, LittD; Master of Emmanuel College, Cambridge, 1977–90; Professor of English, University of Cambridge, 1983–90, now Professor Emeritus; *b* 13 July 1923; *s* of Stanley Leonard Brewer and Winifred Helen Forbes; *m* 1951, Lucie Elisabeth Hoole; three *s* two *d*. *Educ:* elementary school; The Crypt Grammar Sch.; Magdalen Coll., Oxford (Matthew Arnold Essay Prize, 1948; BA, MA 1948); Birmingham Univ. (PhD 1956). LittD Cantab 1980. Commnd 2nd Lieut, Worcestershire Regt, 1942; Captain and Adjt, 1st Bn Royal Fusiliers, 1944–45. Asst Lectr and Lectr in English, Univ. of Birmingham, 1949–56; Prof. of English, Internat. Christian Univ., Tokyo, 1956–58; Lectr and Sen. Lectr, Univ. of Birmingham, 1958–64; Lectr in English, Univ. of Cambridge, 1965–76, Reader in Medieval English, 1976–83; Fellow of Emmanuel Coll., Cambridge, 1965–77, Life Fellow 1990. Founder, D. S. Brewer Ltd, for the publication of academic books, 1972; now part of Boydell and Brewer Ltd (Dir, 1979–96). Mem., Council of the Senate, Cambridge, 1978–83; Chairman: Fitzwilliam Museum Enterprises Ltd, 1978–90; Univ. Library Synd., 1980–93; English Faculty Bd, Cambridge, 1984–86, 1989. Lectures: Sir Israel Gollancz Meml, British Academy, 1974; first William Matthews, Univ. of London, 1982; first Geoffrey Shepherd Meml, Univ. of Birmingham, 1983; Ballard Mathews, Univ. of Wales, Bangor, 1996. Sandars Reader, Univ. of Cambridge, 1991. First British Council Vis. Prof. of English to Japan, 1987; Vis. Prof., Japan Soc. for Promotion of Science, 1988; Cline Distinguished Vis. Prof., Univ. of Texas at Austin, 1992; Francqui Internat. Chair in Human Sciences, univs in Belgium, 1998. President: The English Assoc., 1982–83, 1987–90; Internat. Chaucer Soc., 1982–84; Chairman Trustees: Chaucer Heritage Trust, 1992–; British Taiwan Cultural Inst., 1990–; Trustee (Treas.), SOS Villages (UK), 1990–; Hon. Trustee, Osaka Univ. of Arts, 1987–. Hon. Mem., Japan Acad., 1981 (Commemorative Medal, 1997); Corresp. Fellow, Medieval Soc. of America, 1987. Hon. LLD: Keio Univ., Tokyo, 1982; Harvard Univ., 1984; Hon. DLitt: Birmingham, 1985; Williams Coll., USA, 1990; DUniv: York, 1985; Sorbonne, 1988; Univ. of Liège, 1990. Seatonian Prize, Univ. of Cambridge, 1969, 1972, 1983, 1986, 1988, 1993, 1999, (jtly) 1979, 1980, 1992, (*prox. acc.*) 1985, 1990. Editor, The Cambridge Review, 1981–86. *Publications:* Chaucer, 1953, 3rd edn 1973; Proteus, 1958 (Tokyo); (ed) The Parlement of Foulys, 1960; Chaucer in his Time, 1963; (ed and contrib.) Chaucer and Chaucerians, 1966; (ed) Malory's Morte Darthur: Parts Seven and Eight, 1968; (ed and contrib.) Writers and their Backgrounds: Chaucer, 1974; (ed) Chaucer: the Critical Heritage, 1978; Chaucer and his World, 1978; Symbolic Stories, 1980, 2nd edn 1988; (ed jtly) Aspects of Malory, 1981; English Gothic Literature, 1983; Tradition and Innovation in Chaucer, 1983; Chaucer: the Poet as Storyteller, 1984; Chaucer: an introduction, 1984; (ed) Beardsley's Le Morte Darthur, 1985; (with E. Frankl) Arthur's Britain: the land and the legend, 1985; (ed) Studies in Medieval English Romances, 1988; (ed) Medieval Comic Tales, 1996; (ed) A Critical Companion to the Gawain-poet, 1997; (ed) The Middle Ages after the Middle Ages, 1997; A New Introduction to Chaucer, 1998; Seatonian Exercises and Other Verses, 2000; Chaucer's World, 2000; numerous articles in learned jls, reviews, etc. *Recreations:* reading, walking, looking at paintings and antiquities, travelling, publishing other people's books. *Address:* 240 Hills Road, Cambridge CB2 2QE; Emmanuel College, Cambridge CB2 3AP. *T:* (01223) 334200.

BREWSTER, (Elsie) Yvonne, OBE 1993; Artistic Director, Talawa Theatre Co., since 1986; *b* 7 Oct. 1938; *d* of Claude Noel Clarke and Kathleen Vanessa Clarke; *m* 1st, 1961, John Roger Francis Jones (marr. diss. 1965); 2nd, 1971, Starr Edmund Francis Home Brewster; one *s*. *Educ:* Rose Bruford Coll. of Speech and Drama (Dip.). LRAM. Stage, TV and radio actress, 1960–; theatre, film, TV and radio director, 1965–; Drama Officer, Arts Council of GB, 1982–84. Mem., London Arts Bd, 1993–99; Trustee, Theatres Trust, 1992–; Patron, Rose Bruford Coll., 1994–. Non-executive Director: Riverside Mental Health NHS Trust, 1994–99; Kensington, Chelsea, Westminster and Brent NHS Trust, 1999–. FRSA 1992. *Publications:* Black Plays, Vol. 1, 1987, Vol. 2, 1989, Vol. 3, 1995. *Recreations:* reading, London. *Address:* 32 Buckley Road, NW6 7LU. *Fax:* (020) 7372 6307.

BREWSTER, Richard Philip; Chief Executive, Scope, since 1995; *b* 25 May 1952; *s* of Peter and Patricia Brewster; *m* 1975, Lindy Udale; three *s* one *d*. *Educ:* Leeds Grammar Sch.; Trinity Coll., Oxford (BA Hons). ICI, 1976–86: Sales Rep., 1976–79; Product Man., 1979–81; Purchasing Man., 1981–83; Marketing Man., 1983–86; Nat. Appeals Manager, Oxfam, 1986–89; Dir of Mkting, Spastics Soc., then Scope, 1989–95. *Recreations:* arts, watching sport. *Address:* Scope, 6–10 Market Road, N7 9PW.

BREYER, Stephen Gerald; Associate Justice, Supreme Court of the United States, since 1994; *b* 15 Aug. 1938; *s* of Irving Breyer and Anne (*née* Roberts); *m* 1967, Joanna Hare; one *s* two *d*. *Educ:* Stanford Univ. (AM 1959); Magdalen Coll., Oxford (Marshall Schol.; BA 1st Cl. Hons PPE 1961; Hon Fellow 1995); Harvard Law Sch. (LLB 1964). Law Clerk, US Supreme Court, 1964–65; Special Asst to Asst Attorney Gen., US Dept of Justice, 1965–67; Harvard University: Asst Prof. of Law, 1967–70; Prof. of Law, Harvard Law Sch., 1970–80, Lectr, 1981–; Prof., Kennedy Sch. of Govt, 1977–80; Asst Special Prosecutor, Watergate Special Prosecution Force, 1973; US Court of Appeals for First Circuit: Circuit Judge, 1980–94; Chief Judge, 1990–94. US Senate Judiciary Committee: Special Counsel, Admin. Practices Subcttee, 1974–75; Chief Counsel, 1979–80; Mem., US Sentencing Commn, 1985–89. Vis. Lectr, Coll. of Law, Sydney, Aust., 1975; Vis. Prof., Univ. of Rome, 1993. Fellow: Amer. Acad. of Arts and Scis; Amer Bar Foundn. *Publications:* (with P. MacAvoy) The Federal Power Commission and the Regulation of Energy, 1974; (with R. Stewart) Administrative Law and Regulatory Policy, 1979, 3rd edn 1992; Regulation and its Reform, 1982; Breaking the Vicious Circle: toward effective risk regulation, 1993; contrib. chapters in books; numerous articles in law jls and reviews. *Address:* Supreme Court Building, One First Street NE, Washington, DC 20543-0001, USA. *T:* (202) 4793000.

BRICE, (Ann) Nuala, PhD; Special Commissioner of Taxes, since 1999 (Deputy Special Commissioner, 1992–99); Chairman, VAT and Duties Tribunals (formerly VAT Tribunals), since 1992 (part-time Chairman, 1992–99); *b* 22 Dec. 1937; *d* of William Connor and Rosaleen Gertrude Connor (*née* Gilmartin); *m* 1963, Geoffrey James Barrington Groves Brice, QC (*d* 1999); one *s*. *Educ:* Loreto Convent, Manchester; University Coll. London. LLB (Hons), LLM 1976, PhD 1982, London. Admitted Solicitor of the Supreme Court, 1963 (Stephen Heelis Gold Medal and John Peacock

Conveyancing Prize, 1963). The Law Society: Asst Solicitor, 1963; Asst Sec., 1964; Sen. Asst Sec., 1973; Deptl Sec., 1982; Asst Sec.-Gen., 1987–92. Sec., Revenue Law Cttee, 1972–82. Vis. Associate Prof. of Law, Tulane Univ., 1990–99; Vis. Prof. of Law, Univ. of Natal, 1996–99. *Recreations:* reading, music, gardening. *Address:* (office) 15/19 Bedford Avenue, WC1B 3AS. *T:* (020) 7631 4242. *Club:* University Women's.

BRICE, Air Cdre Eric John, CBE 1971 (OBE 1957); CEng; AFRAeS; RAF retd; stockbroker; *b* 12 Feb. 1917; *s* of Courtenay Percy Please Brice and Lilie Alice Louise Brice (*née* Grey); *m* 1942, Janet Parks, Roundhay, Leeds, Yorks; two *s* one *d. Educ:* Loughborough Coll. (DLC). Joined RAF, 1939; served War, MEAF, 1943–46 (Sqdn Ldr). Air Ministry, 1946–50; Parachute Trg Sch., 1950–52; Wing Comdr, 1952; RAE, Farnborough, 1952–58; Comd, Parachute Trg Sch., 1958–60; RAF Coll., Cranwell, 1960–61; Gp Capt., 1961; RAF Halton, 1961–64; Comd, RAF Innsworth, Glos, 1964–66; Dir, Physical Educn, RAF, MoD, 1966–68; Air Cdre, 1968; Dep. AOA, RAF Headqrs, Maintenance Comd, 1968–71; April 1971, retd prematurely. MIMgt. *Recreations:* athletics (Combined Services and RAF athletic blues); Rugby football (RAF trialist and Blackheath Rugby Club); captained Loughborough Coll. in three sports. *Address:* Durns, Boldre, Lymington, Hampshire SO41 8NE. *T:* (01590) 672196. *Clubs:* Royal Air Force; Royal Lymington Yacht.

BRICE, Nuala; *see* Brice, A. N.

BRICHTO, Rabbi Dr Sidney; Senior Vice-President, Union of Liberal and Progressive Synagogues, since 1992; Lecturer, Oxford Centre for Postgraduate Hebrew Studies, since 1991; *b* 21 July 1936; *s* of Solomon and Rivka Brichto; *m* 1st, 1959, Frances Goldstein (decd); one *s* one *d*; 2nd, 1971, Cathryn Goldhill; two *s. Educ:* New York Univ. (BA); Hebrew Union Coll., NY (MA, MHL, DD); University College London (Study Fellowship). Associate Minister, Liberal Jewish Synagogue, 1961–64; Founder and Principal, Evening Inst. for Study of Judaism, 1962–65; Exec. Vice-Pres. and Dir, ULPS, 1964–89; Dir, Joseph Levy Charitable Foundn, 1989–99. Chairman: Conf. of Rabbis, ULPS, 1969–70, 1974–75; Council of Reform and Liberal Rabbis, 1974–76; Chief Rabbi's Consultative Cttee on Jewish-non-Jewish Relations, 1976–78. Vice-Pres., Nat. Assoc. of Bereavement Services, 1992–98. Founder and Chm., Adv. Cttee, Israel Diaspora Trust, 1982–; Mem. Exec. Council, Leo Baeck Coll., 1964–74; Dir, Inst. for Jewish Policy Res., 1996–99; Gov., Oxford Centre for Hebrew and Jewish Studies, 1994–. *Publications:* Funny…you don't look Jewish, 1995; (ed jtly) Two Cheers for Secularism, 1998; (ed and trans.) The People's Bible: Genesis, 2000; Samuel, 2000; Song of Songs, 2000; St Luke and the Apostles, 2000; The Conquest of Canaan, 2001; The Genius of Paul, 2001; The Exodus and the Laws of Moses, 2001; contribs to Service of the Heart (Liberal Jewish Prayer Book) and to national and Jewish jls. *Recreations:* pleasant lunches, reading, writing. *Address:* 3 Amberley Close, Pinner, Middx HA5 3BH. *T:* (020) 8933 6216; *e-mail:* sidney@brichto.com. *Club:* Athenæum.

BRICKELL, Christopher David, CBE 1991; VMH 1976; Director General, Royal Horticultural Society, 1985–93; *b* 29 June 1932; *s* of Bertram Tom Brickell and Kathleen Alice Brickell; *m* 1963, Jeanette Scargill Flecknoe; two *d. Educ:* Queen's College, Taunton; Reading Univ. (BSc Horticulture). Joined Royal Horticultural Society Garden, Wisley, 1958: Asst Botanist, 1958; Botanist, 1960; Sen. Scientific Officer, 1964; Dep. Dir, 1968; Dir, 1969–85. Pres., Internat. Soc. for Hortl Sci., 1999–Aug. 2002. George Robert White Medal of Honor, Mass Hort. Soc., 1988; Inst. of Horticulture Award, 1997. *Publications:* Daphne: the genus in cultivation, 1976; Pruning, 1979; The Vanishing Garden, 1986; An English Florilegium, 1987; (ed and contrib.) The Gardener's Encyclopaedia of Plants and Flowers, 1989; (ed and contrib.) The RHS Encyclopaedia of Gardening, 1992; Garden Plants, 1995; (ed and contrib.) The RHS A–Z of Garden Plants, 1996; botanical papers in Flora Europaea, European Garden Flora, and Flora of Turkey; horticultural and botanical papers in RHS Jl, The New Plantsman and Alpine Garden Soc. Bulletin. *Recreations:* gardening, sailing, squash, tennis. *Address:* The Camber, Nutbourne, Pulborough, West Sussex RH20 2HE.

BRICKWOOD, Sir Basil (Greame), 3rd Bt *cr* 1927; *b* 21 May 1923; *s* of Sir John Brickwood, 1st Bt and Isabella Janet Gibson (*d* 1967), *d* of James Gordon; *S* half-brother, 1974; *m* 1956, Shirley Anne Brown; two *d. Educ:* King Edward's Grammar Sch., Stratford-upon-Avon; Clifton. Served War, RAF, 1940–46. *Club:* Royal Air Force.

BRIDEN, Prof. James Christopher, PhD, DSc; CGeol; FGS; Professor of Environmental Studies and Director of the Environmental Change Institute, University of Oxford, since 1997; Fellow, Linacre College, Oxford, since 1997; Hon. Professor, University of Leeds, since 1986; *b* 30 Dec. 1938; *s* of late Henry Charles Briden and of Gladys Elizabeth (*née* Jefkins); *m* 1968, Caroline Mary (*née* Gillmore); one *s* one *d. Educ:* Royal Grammar Sch., High Wycombe; St Catherine's Coll., Oxford (MA); ANU (PhD 1965; DSc 1994). FGS 1962; CGeol 1990. Research Fellow: Univ. of Rhodesia, 1965–66; Univ. of Oxford, 1966–67; Univ. of Birmingham, 1967–68; University of Leeds: Lectr, 1968–73; Reader, 1973–75; Prof. of Geophysics, 1975–86; Head, Dept of Earth Sciences, 1976–79 and 1982–85; Dir of Earth Scis, NERC, 1986–94; Vis. Prof. (NERC Res. Prof.), Univ. of Oxford, 1994–96. Canadian Commonwealth Fellow and Vis. Prof., Univ. of Western Ontario, 1979–80. Mem., NERC, 1981–86; Chairman: Jt Assoc. for Geophysics, 1981–84 (Chm., Founding Cttee, 1978–79); Exec. Cttee, Ocean Drilling Prog., 1994–96; Member: Science and Engrg (formerly Science) Cttee, British Council, 1990–96; Governing Council, Internat. Seismol Centre, 1978–83; Council: Eur. Geophysical Soc., 1976–84; RAS, 1978–79 (FRAS 1962); Geol Soc., 1992–95. Fellow, Amer. Geophysical Union, 1994. Murchison Medal, Geol Soc., 1984. Editor, Earth and Planetary Science Letters, 1971–97; Ed.-in-chief, Envmtl Sci. and Policy, 2001–. *Publications:* (with A. G. Smith) Mesozoic and Cenozoic Palaeocontinental World Maps, 1977; (with A. G. Smith and A. M. Hurley) Phanerozoic Palaeocontinental World Maps, 1981; over 80 papers on palaeomagnetism, palaeoclimates, tectonics and aspects of geophysics. *Recreations:* opera-, music-, theatre-going, various sports. *Address:* Environmental Change Institute, 5 South Parks Road, Oxford OX1 3UB. *T:* (01865) 281203.

BRIDGE, family name of **Baron Bridge of Harwich**.

BRIDGE OF HARWICH, Baron *cr* 1980 (Life Peer), of Harwich in the County of Essex; **Nigel Cyprian Bridge;** Kt 1968; PC 1975; a Lord of Appeal in Ordinary, 1980–92; *b* 26 Feb. 1917; *s* of late Comdr C. D. C. Bridge, RN; *m* 1944, Margaret Swinbank; one *s* two *d. Educ:* Marlborough College. Army Service, 1940–46; commnd into KRRC, 1941. Called to the Bar, Inner Temple, 1947; Bencher, 1964, Reader, 1985, Treasurer, 1986; Junior Counsel to Treasury (Common Law), 1964–68; a Judge of High Court, Queen's Bench Div., 1968–75; Presiding Judge, Western Circuit, 1972–74; a Lord Justice of Appeal, 1975–80. Mem., Security Commn, 1977–85 (Chm. 1982–85); Chm., C of E Synodical Govt Review, 1993–97. Hon. Fellow, Amer. Coll. of Trial Lawyers, 1984. Hon. Fellow, Wolfson Coll., Cambridge, 1989. *Address:* House of Lords, SW1A 0PW.
See also Very Rev. A. C. Bridge.

BRIDGE, Very Rev. Antony Cyprian; Dean of Guildford, 1968–86; *b* 5 Sept. 1914; *s* of late Comdr C. D. C. Bridge, RN; *m* 1st, 1937, Brenda Lois Streatfeild (*d* 1995); one *s* two *d*; 2nd, 1996, Diana Joyce Readhead. *Educ:* Marlborough College. Scholarship to Royal Academy School of Art, 1932. Professional painter thereafter. War of 1939–45: joined Army, Sept. 1939; commissioned Buffs, 1940; demobilised as Major, 1945. Ordained, 1955; Curate, Hythe Parish Church till 1958; Vicar of Christ Church, Lancaster Gate, London, 1958–68. Mem., Adv. Council V&A Museum, 1976–79. FSA 1987. *Publications:* Images of God, 1960; Theodora: portrait in a Byzantine landscape, 1978; The Crusades, 1980; Suleiman The Magnificent, 1983; One Man's Advent, 1985; Richard the Lionheart, 1989. *Recreations:* bird-watching, reading. *Address:* 34 London Road, Deal, Kent CT14 9TE.
See also Baron Bridge of Harwich.

BRIDGE, Dame Jill; *see* Macleod Clark, Dame J.

BRIDGE, John, GC 1944; GM 1940 and Bar 1941; Director of Education for Sunderland Borough Council (formerly Sunderland County Borough Council), 1963–76, retired; *b* 5 Feb. 1915; *s* of late Joseph Edward Bridge, Culcheth, Warrington; *m* 1945, F. J. Patterson; three *d. Educ:* London Univ. BSc Gen. Hons, 1936 and BSc Special Hons (Physics), 1937; Teacher's Dip., 1938. Schoolmaster: Lancs CC, Sept.–Dec. 1938; Leighton Park, Reading, Jan.–Aug. 1939; Firth Park Grammar Sch., Sheffield, Sept. 1939–Aug. 1946 (interrupted by war service). Served War: RNVR June 1940–Feb. 1946, engaged on bomb and mine disposal; demobilised as Lt Comdr RNVR. *Recreations:* gardening, travel, fell walking, photography. *Address:* 37 Park Avenue, Roker, Sunderland SR6 9NJ. *T:* (0191) 548 6356.

BRIDGE, Keith James, CBE 1997; consultant; *b* 21 Aug. 1929; *s* of late James Henry Bridge and Lilian Elizabeth (*née* Nichols); *m* 1960, Thelma Ruby (*née* Hubble); three *d* (and one *s* decd). *Educ:* Sir George Monoux Grammar Sch., Walthamstow; Corpus Christi Coll., Oxford (MA). CIPFA 1959; CIMgt (CBIM 1978). Local govt service, 1953; Dep. City Treasurer, York, 1965; Borough Treas., Bolton, 1967; City Treas., Manchester, 1971; County Treasurer, Greater Manchester Council, 1973; Chief Exec., Humberside CC, 1978–83. Mem., W Yorks Residuary Body, 1985–91. Financial Adviser to Assoc. of Metrop. Authorities, 1971–78; Mem. Council, 1972–84, Pres., 1982–83, Chartered Inst. of Public Finance and Accountancy; Pres., Soc. of Metropolitan Treasurers, 1977–78. Member: Audit Commn for Local Authorities in Eng. and Wales, 1983–86; Exec. Council, Business in the Community, 1982–84; Bd, Public Finance Foundn, 1984–90; Educn Transfer Council (formerly Educn Assets Bd), 1988–2000 (Chm., 1996–2000); Football Licensing Authy, 1990–96. Dir, Phillips & Drew, 1987–89. Chm., York Diocesan Pastoral Cttee, 1989–94. Governor: Univ. of Lincolnshire and Humberside (formerly Humberside Poly.), 1989–98; E Yorks Coll., 2000–. Hon. LLD Lincs and Humberside, 1999. Freeman, City of London, 1986. *Publications:* papers in professional jls. *Recreations:* gardening, literature, music. *Address:* 1 Fairlawn, Molescroft, Beverley, N Humberside HU17 7DD. *T:* (01482) 887652.

BRIDGEMAN, family name of **Earl of Bradford** and **Viscount Bridgeman**.

BRIDGEMAN, 3rd Viscount *cr* 1929, of Leigh, **Robin John Orlando Bridgeman,** CA; *b* 5 Dec. 1930; *s* of Hon. Geoffrey John Orlando Bridgeman, MC, FRCS (*d* 1974) (2nd *s* of 1st Viscount) and Mary Meriel Gertrude Bridgeman (*d* 1974), *d* of Rt Hon. Sir George John Talbot; *S* uncle, 1982; *m* 1966, (Victoria) Harriet Lucy, *d* of Ralph Meredyth Turton; three *s* (and one *s* decd). *Educ:* Eton. CA 1958. 2nd Lieut, Rifle Bde, 1950–51. Partner: Fenn & Crosthwaite, 1973; Henderson Crosthwaite & Co., 1975–86; Director: Nestor-BNA, 1988–94; Guinness Mahon & Co. Ltd, 1988–90; Chm., Asset Management Investment Co. plc, 1994–2001. Opposition Whip, H of L, 1999–; elected Mem., H of L, 1999. Dir., Bridgeman Art Library Ltd, 1972–; Chm., Friends of Lambeth Palace Liby, 1992–. Chm., Hosp. of St John and St Elizabeth, 1999–; Special Trustee, Hammersmith Hosp., 1986–99; Treasurer, Florence Nightingale Aid in Sickness Trust, 1995–; Gov., Reed's Sch., 1994– (Chm.). Mem. Court, New England Co., 1986– (Treas., 1996–). *Recreations:* shooting, ski-ing, gardening, music. *Heir: s* Hon. Luke Robinson Orlando Bridgeman [*b* 1 May 1971; *m* 1996, Victoria Rose, *y d* of late Henry Frost]. *Address:* 19 Chepstow Road, W2 5BP. *T:* (020) 7727 5400; Watley House, Sparsholt, Winchester SO21 2LU. *T:* (01962) 776297. *Clubs:* Beefsteak, MCC; Pitt.

BRIDGEMAN, (John) Michael, CB 1988; Chief Registrar of Friendly Societies and Industrial Assurance Commissioner, 1982–91; First Commissioner (Chairman), Building Societies Commission, 1986–91; *b* 26 April 1931; *s* of late John Wilfred Bridgeman, CBE and Mary Bridgeman (*née* Wallace); *m* 1958, June Bridgeman, *qv*; one *s* four *d. Educ:* Marlborough Coll.; Trinity Coll., Cambridge. Asst Principal, BoT, 1954; HM Treasury, 1956–81, Under Sec., 1975–81. *Address:* Bridge House, Culverden Park Road, Tunbridge Wells, Kent TN4 9QX.

BRIDGEMAN, John Stuart, CBE 2001; TD 1995; DL; Director: Regulatory Impact Unit, Cardew & Co., since 2001; Oxford Psychologists Press, since 2001; Chairman: Direct Marketing Authority; howtocomplain.com Ltd; competition consultant, Norton Rose; *b* 5 Oct. 1944; *s* of late James Alfred George Bridgeman and Edith Celia (*née* Watkins); *m* 1967, Lindy Jane Fillmore; three *d. Educ:* Whitchurch Sch., Cardiff; University Coll., Swansea (BSc) (Hon. Fellow, Univ. of Wales, Swansea, 1997); McGill Univ., Montreal. Alcan Inds, 1966–69; Aluminium Co. of Canada, 1969–70; Alcan Australia, 1970; Commercial Dir, Alcan UK, 1977–80; Vice-Pres. (Europe), Alcan Basic Raw Materials, 1978–82; Dir, Saguenay Shipping, 1979–82; Divl Man. Dir, Alcan Aluminium (UK) Ltd, 1981–82; Managing Director: Extrusion Div., Brit. Alcan Aluminium plc, 1983–87; Brit. Alcan Enterprises, 1987–91; Dir, Corporate Planning, Alcan Aluminium Ltd, Montreal, 1992–93; Man. Dir, British Alcan Aluminium plc, 1993–95; Dir-Gen. of Fair Trading, 1995–2000; Chm., GPC Europe, 2000–01. Chm., Luxfer Hldgs, 1988–91. Member: British Airways NE Consumer Council, 1978–86; Monopolies and Mergers Commn, 1990–95; Adv. Council, Consumer Policy Inst., 2000–. Vis. Prof. of Mgt, Keele Univ., 1992–; Vis. Prof. in Mgt, Imperial Coll., London, 2001–. Vice-President: Aluminium Fedn, 1995; Trading Standards Inst., 2001–. Chairman: N Oxon Business Gp, 1984–92; Enterprise Cherwell Ltd, 1985–91; Oxfordshire Economic Partnership, 2000–; Dir, Heart of England TEC, 1989– (Chm., 2000–). Commnd TA and Reserve Forces, 1978; QOY, 1981–84; Maj. REME (V), 1985–94; Staff Coll., 1986; SO2 Employer Support SE Dist, 1994–95. Hon. Col, 5 (QOOH) Sqdn, 39 (Skinners) Signal Regt (V), 1996–. Mem., TAVRA Oxon and E Wessex, 1985–2000. Member: Defence Science Adv. Council, 1991–94; Nat. Employer Liaison Cttee for Reserve Forces, 1992– (Chm., 1998–); SE RFCA, 2001–. Member: UK-Canada Colloquium, 1993–; UK-Canada Chamber of Commerce, 1993– (Vice-Pres., 1995–96; Pres., 1997–98); Canada Club, 1994–. Gov., N Oxon Coll., 1985– (Chm., 1989; Vice Chm., 1997–). Trustee: Oxfordshire Community Foundn, 1995–; Oxford Orch. da Camera, 1996–2001; Oxfordshire Yeomanry Trust, 1997–. Pres., Oxfordshire Gliding Club, 1998–. CIMgt, FInstD, FRGS, FRSA. Liveryman, Turners' Co. DL Oxon, 1989; High Sheriff, Oxon, 1995–96. Hon. Dr Sheffield Hallam, 1996. US Aluminium Assoc. Prize, 1988. *Recreations:* education, gardening, public affairs, shooting, ski-ing. *Address:* Cardew & Co., 12 Suffolk Street, SW1Y 4HQ. *T:* (020) 7930 0777, *Fax:* (020) 7925 0647. *Clubs:* Reform; Glamorgan County Cricket.

BRIDGEMAN, Mrs June, CB 1990; Deputy Chair, Equal Opportunities Commission, 1991–94; *b* 26 June 1932; *d* of Gordon and Elsie Forbes; *m* 1958, John Michael Bridgeman, *qv*; one *s* four *d*. *Educ:* variously, England and Scotland; Westfield Coll., London Univ. (BA; Fellow, QMW, 1993). Asst Principal, BoT, 1954; subseq. served in DEA, NBPI, Min. of Housing and Local Govt, DoE; Under Secretary: DoE 1974–76; Central Policy Review Staff, Cabinet Office, 1976–79; Dept of Transport, 1979–90. Mem., BSE Inquiry, 1998–. Mem., Central Bd of Finance, C of E, 1979–83; Bishops Selector for ACCM, 1974–89. Member of Council: PSI, 1984–90; NCOPF, 1994–; GDST (formerly GPDST), 1995–. Vice-Pres., Fawcett Soc., 1994–. Trustee, Rees Jeffreys Road Fund, 1992–. Governor: Bromley High Sch.; Kent Coll. FRSA 1991. *Recreations:* feminism, learning the piano accordion. *Address:* Bridge House, Culverden Park Road, Tunbridge Wells TN4 9QX. *T:* (01892) 525578.

BRIDGEMAN, Michael; *see* Bridgeman, J. M.

BRIDGER, Rev. Dr Francis William; Principal, Trinity Theological College, Bristol, since 1999; *b* 27 May 1951; *s* of Harry Edward George Bridger and Harriet Rose Bridger; *m* 1975, Renee Winifred; one *s* two *d*. *Educ:* Pembroke Coll., Oxford (BA 1973; MA 1978); Trinity Coll., Bristol; Bristol Univ. (PhD 1981). Ordained deacon, 1978, priest, 1979; Asst Curate, St Jude, Mildmay Park and St Paul, Canonbury, 1978–82; Lectr and Tutor, St John's Coll., Nottingham, 1982–90; Vicar, St Mark, Woodthorpe, 1990–99. Adjunct Prof. of Pastoral Care and Counselling, Fuller Theol Seminary, Calif., 1999–. *Publications:* The Cross and the Bomb, 1983; Videos, Permissiveness and the Law, 1984; Children Finding Faith, 1988, 2nd edn 2000 (trans. French and German, 1995); Counselling in Context, 1995, 2nd edn 1998; Celebrating the Family, 1995; Why Can't I have Faith?, 1998; The Diana Phenomenon, 1998; contrib. to Tyndale Bull., Anvil, Theology. *Recreations:* politics, current affairs, media, Star Trek. *Address:* Trinity College, Stoke Hill, Bristol BS9 1JP. *T:* (0117) 968 2803, *Fax:* (0117) 968 7470.

BRIDGER, Rev. Canon Gordon Frederick; Principal, Oak Hill Theological College, 1987–96; *b* 5 Feb. 1932; *s* of late Dr John Dell Bridger and Hilda Bridger; *m* 1962, Elizabeth Doris Bewes; three *d*. *Educ:* Christ's Hospital, Horsham; Selwyn Coll., Cambridge (MA Hons Theology); Ridley Hall, Cambridge. Curate, Islington Parish Church, 1956–59; Curate, Holy Sepulchre Church, Cambridge, 1959–62; Vicar, St Mary, North End, Fulham, 1962–69; Chaplain, St Thomas's Episcopal Church, Edinburgh, 1969–76; Rector, Holy Trinity Church, Heigham, Norwich, 1976–87; RD Norwich (South), 1981–86; Exam. Chaplain to Bishop of Norwich, 1981–86; Hon. Canon, Norwich Cathedral, 1984–87, now Hon. Canon Emeritus. Dir, Open Theol Coll., 1993–97; Mem. Court, Middlesex Univ., 1996–. Hon. MA Middlesex, 1996. *Publications:* The Man from Outside, 1969, rev. edn 1978; A Day that Changed the World, 1975; A Bible Study Commentary (I Corinthians—Galatians), 1985; reviews in The Churchman, Anvil and other Christian papers and magazines. *Recreations:* music, sport, reading. *Address:* 4 Common Lane, Sheringham, Norfolk NR26 8PL.

BRIDGES, family name of **Baron Bridges**.

BRIDGES, 2nd Baron *cr* 1957; **Thomas Edward Bridges,** GCMG 1988 (KCMG 1983 CMG 1975); HM Diplomatic Service, retired; *b* 27 Nov. 1927; *s* of 1st Baron Bridges, KG, PC, GCB, GCVO, MC, FRS, and late Hon. Katharine Dianthe, *d* of 2nd Baron Farrer; *S* father, 1969; *m* 1953, Rachel Mary, *y d* of late Sir Henry Bunbury, KCB; two *s* one *d*. *Educ:* Eton; New Coll., Oxford. Entered Foreign Service, 1951; served in Bonn, Berlin, Rio de Janeiro and at FO (Asst Private Sec. to Foreign Secretary, 1963–66); Head of Chancery, Athens, 1966–68; Counsellor, Moscow, 1969–71; Private Sec. (Overseas Affairs) to Prime Minister, 1972–74; RCDS 1975; Minister (Commercial), Washington, 1976–79; Dep. Under Sec. of State, FCO, 1979–82; Ambassador to Italy, 1983–87. Mem., Select Cttee on Eur. Communities, H of L, 1988–92 and 1994–98; elected Mem., H of L, 1999. Dir, Consolidated Gold Fields, 1988–89. Indep. Bd Mem., Securities and Futures Authority (formerly Securities Assoc.), 1989–97. Chairman: UK Nat. Cttee for UNICEF, 1989–97; British–Italian Soc., 1991–97. Mem., E Anglian Regl Cttee, NT, 1988–97. Pres., Dolmetsch Foundn. Trustee, Rayne Foundn. *Heir: s* Hon. Mark Thomas Bridges [*b* 25 July 1954; *m* 1978, Angela Margaret, *er d* of J. L. Collinson, Mansfield, Notts; one *s* three *d*]. *Address:* 56 Church Street, Orford, Woodbridge, Suffolk IP12 2NT.
See also M. E. Aston.

BRIDGES, Brian; public affairs consultant; *b* 30 June 1937; 4th *s* of late William Ernest Bridges; *m* 1970, Jennifer Mary Rogers. *Educ:* Harrow Weald County Grammar Sch.; Univ. of Keele (BA 1961). Sec., Univ. of Keele Union, 1959–60. Joined Civil Service, 1961; Principal, 1967; Asst Sec. 1975; Under Sec., DHSS, 1985; Dir of Estabts and Personnel, DHSS, 1985–88; Under Sec. i/c of NHS dental, pharmaceutical and optical services and pharmaceutical industry, DoH, 1988–92; Under Sec. i/c Environmental and Food Safety, DoH, 1992–95. *Recreations:* long walks in the tow of dogs, a range of practical and intellectual pursuits including carpentry and local history. *Address:* Townsend House, Ullingswick, Herefordshire HR1 3JQ. *T:* and *Fax:* (01432) 841312.

BRIDGES, Rt Rev. Dewi Morris; Bishop of Swansea and Brecon, 1988–98; *b* 18 Nov. 1933; *s* of Harold Davies Bridges and Elsie Margaret Bridges; *m* 1959, Rhiannon Williams; one *s* one *d*. *Educ:* St David's University College, Lampeter (BA 1954, 1st cl. Hons History); Corpus Christi Coll., Cambridge (BA 1956 II 1, Pt 2 Theol. Tripos, MA 1960); Westcott House, Cambridge. Assistant Curate: Rhymney, Gwent, 1957–60; Chepstow, 1960–63; Vicar of St James', Tredegar, 1963–65; Lecturer and Senior Lectr, Summerfield Coll. of Education, Kidderminster, 1965–69; Vicar of Kempsey, Worcester, 1969–79; RD of Upton-upon-Severn, 1974–79; Rector of Tenby, Pembs, 1979–88; RD of Narberth, 1980–82; Archdeacon of St Davids, 1982–88. Member: Court, 1989–98, and Council, 1989–95, UCW, Swansea; Council, Univ. of Wales, Lampeter (formerly St David's UC, Lampeter), 1992–98. *Recreations:* walking, gardening, photography. *Address:* Llys Dewi, 1 Greystones Crescent, Mardy, Abergavenny, Monmouthshire NP7 6JY.

BRIDGES, Prof. James Wilfrid; Professor of Toxicology, since 1979 and Dean for International Strategy, since 2000, University of Surrey; *b* 9 Aug. 1938; *s* of Wilfrid Edward Seymour Bridges and Mary Winifred Cameron. *Educ:* Bromley Grammar Sch.; Queen Elizabeth Coll., London Univ.; St Mary's Hosp. Med. Sch., London Univ. BSc, DSc, PhD; MRCPath; FRSC, CChem; FIBiol; FIOSH; MInstEnvSci. Lectr, St Mary's Hosp. Med. Sch., 1962–68; University of Surrey: Senior Lectr then Reader, Dept of Biochemistry, 1968–78; Res. Dir, Robens Inst. of Industrial and Envmtl Health and Safety, 1978–95; Dean, Faculty of Science, 1988–92; Hd, European Inst. of Health and Med. Scis, 1995–2000. Visiting Professor: Univ. of Texas at Dallas, 1973, 1979; Univ. of Rochester, NY, 1974; Mexico City, 1991; Sen. Scientist, Nat. Inst. of Envtl Health Scis, N Carolina, 1976. Chm., British Toxicology Soc., 1980–81; First Pres., Fedn of European Toxicology Socs, 1985–88. Member: Vet. Products Cttee, 1982–96; EC Scientific Cttee on Animal Nutrition, 1991–97; EU Scientific Steering Cttee (Public Health), 1997–; Chm., EU Harmonisation of Risk Assessment Working Party; Pres., EU Scientific Adv. Cttee on Toxicology, Ecotoxicology and the Envmt, 1997–; Mem., HSE WATCH Cttee; Chm., Vet. Residues Cttee, 2001–. *Publications:* (ed jtly) Progress in Drug Metabolism, 10 vols, 1976–88; over 300 research papers and reviews in scientific jls. *Recreations:* theatre going, various sports. *Address:* Senate House, Surrey University, Guildford GU2 5XH; Liddington Lodge, Liddington Hall Drive, Guildford GU3 3AE.

BRIDGES, Dame Mary (Patricia), DBE 1981; *b* 6 June 1930; *d* of Austin Edward and Lena Mabel Fawkes; *m* 1951, Bertram Marsdin Bridges; one step *s*. Chm., Honiton Div. Cons. Assoc., 1968–71; Pres., Western Provincial Area, Nat. Union of Cons. and Unionist Assocs, 1987–. Women's Section of Royal British Legion: Pres., Exmouth Br., 1965–; Chm., Devon County Women's Section, 1979–91; County Vice Pres., 1991; County Pres., 1997–; SW Area Rep. to Central Cttee, 1985–89; Nat. Vice-Chm., 1989–92; Nat. Chm., 1992–95; Nat. Life Vice-Pres., 1999; Mem. House Cttee, Dunkirk Meml House, 1994–99. Former Mem., Exe Vale HMC; Pres., Exmouth Council of Voluntary Service (Founder Chm., 1975). Member: Exec., Resthaven, Exmouth, 1970–2001 (Chm., League of Friends, 1971–90); Devon FPC, 1985–91; President: Exmouth and Budleigh Salterton Br., CRUSE, 1980–88; Exmouth Campaign Cttee, Cancer Research, 1981– (Chm., 1975–81); Founder Pres., Exmouth Br., British Heart Foundn, 1984. Mem., SW Electricity Consultative Council, 1982–90 (Chm., Devon Cttee, 1986–90); Mem., Exmouth Cttee, LEPRA, 1962–87 (Hon. Sec., 1964–87); Dir, Home Care Trust, 1988–; Co-optative Trustee, Exmouth Welfare Trust, 1979–; Co-founder, and Trustee, Exmouth and Lympstone Hospiscare, 1986– (Pres., 1994–); founder Trustee, Exmouth Adventure Trust for Girls, 1987–90 (Patron, 1990–); Exec. Mem., St Loye's Coll. Foundn for Trng the Disabled for Commerce and Industry, 1988–; Governor, Rolle Coll., Exmouth, 1982–88. Hon. Life Member: Retford Cricket Club, 1951; Exmouth Cricket Club, 1997 (Hon. Vice-Pres., 1981; Pres., 1992–2001). *Recreations:* cricket, reading. *Address:* Walton House, Fairfield Close, Exmouth, Devon EX8 2BN. *T:* (01395) 265317.

BRIDGES, Ven. Peter Sydney Godfrey; Archdeacon of Warwick, 1983–90, now Emeritus; Canon-Theologian of Coventry Cathedral, 1977–90, now Emeritus; *b* 30 Jan. 1925; *s* of Sidney Clifford Bridges and Winifred (*née* Livette); *m* 1952, Joan Penlerick (*née* Madge); two *s*. *Educ:* Raynes Park Grammar Sch.; Kingston upon Thames Sch. of Architecture; Lincoln Theol College. ARIBA 1950, Dip. Liturgy and Architecture 1967. Gen. and ecclesiastical practice, 1950–54; Lectr, Nottingham Sch. of Architecture, 1954–56. Deacon, 1958; Priest, 1959. Asst Curate, Hemel Hempstead, 1958–64; Res. Fellow, Inst. for Study of Worship and Religious Architecture, Univ. of Birmingham, 1964–67 (Hon. Fellow, 1967–72 and 1978); Warden, Anglican Chaplaincy and Chaplain to Univ. of Birmingham, 1965–68; Lectr, Birmingham Sch. of Arch., 1967–72; eccles. architect and planning consultant, 1968–75; Chm., New Town Ministers Assoc., 1968–72; Co-Dir, Midlands Socio-Religious Res. Gp, 1968–75; Dir, Chelmsford Diocesan R&D Unit, 1972–77; Archdeacon of Southend, 1972–77; Archdeacon of Coventry, 1977–83. Advr for Christian Spirituality, Dio. of Coventry, 1990–93. Mem., Cathedrals Advisory Commn for England, 1981–86. Chm., Painting and Prayer, 1989–94. *Publications:* Socio-Religious Institutes, Lay Academies, etc, 1967; contrib. Church Building, res. bulletins (Inst. for Study of Worship and Relig. Arch.), Clergy Review, Prism, Christian Ministry in New Towns, Cathedral and Mission, Church Architecture and Social Responsibility. *Recreations:* architecture, singing, painting. *Address:* Saint Clare, 25 Rivermead Close, Romsey, Hants SO51 8HQ. *T:* (01794) 512889.

BRIDGES, Sir Phillip (Rodney), Kt 1973; CMG 1967; *b* 9 July 1922; *e s* of late Captain Sir Ernest Bridges and Lady Bridges; *m* 1st, 1951, Rosemary Ann Streeten (marr. diss. 1961); two *s* one *d*; 2nd, 1962, Angela Mary (*née* Dearden), *widow* of James Huyton. *Educ:* Bedford School. Military Service (Capt., RA) with Royal W African Frontier Force in W Africa, India and Burma, 1941–47; Beds Yeo., 1947–54. Admitted Solicitor (England), 1951; Colonial Legal Service, 1954; Barrister and Solicitor, Supreme Court of The Gambia, 1954; Solicitor-General of The Gambia, 1963; QC (Gambia) 1964; Attorney-General of The Gambia, 1964–68; Chief Justice of The Gambia, 1968–83. *Address:* Weavers, Coney Weston, Bury St Edmunds, Suffolk IP31 1HG. *T:* (01359) 221316. *Club:* Travellers.

BRIDGEWATER, Allan, CBE 1998; Chairman, Swiss Re Group UK, since 1998; *b* 26 Aug. 1936; *m* 1960, Janet Bridgewater; three *d*. *Educ:* Wyggeston Grammar Sch., Leicester. ACII, Chartered Insurer, FCIPD, CIMgt. Norwich Union Insurance Group: Dir, 1985–97; Group Chief Exec., 1989–97. Director: Riggs Bank Europe, 1991–; Fox Pitt Kelton, 2000–; NCM Hldgs NV, 2000–. Pres., Chartered Insurance Inst., 1989–90; Chm., Assoc. of British Insurers, 1993–95. Pres., Endeavour Training, 1997– (Chm., 1987–97); Chm., C of E Pensions Bd, 1998–. Special Prof., Business Sch., Univ. of Nottingham, 1995–. Trustee: (and Treas.) Duke of Edinburgh's Commonwealth Study Conf., 1993–; Industry in Educn, 1993–97; Soc. for the Protection of Life from Fire, 1991–. Gov., Chartered Insurance Inst. College, 1985–. FRSA 1989. Freeman, City of London, 1991; Liveryman, Insurers' Co., 1991–.

BRIDGLAND, Milton Deane, AO 1987; FTS, FRACI, FAIM; Chairman, ICI Australia Ltd, 1980–93; *b* 8 July 1922; *s* of late Frederick H. and Muriel E. Bridgland, Adelaide; *m* 1945, Christine L. Cowell; three *d*. *Educ:* St Peter's Coll., Adelaide; Adelaide Univ. (BSc). Joined ICI Australia Ltd, 1945; Technical Manager, Plastics Gp, 1955–62; Ops Dir, 1962–67, Man. Dir, 1967–71, Dulux Australia Ltd; Exec. Dir 1971, Man. Dir, 1978–84, ICI Australia Ltd. Chairman: Jennings Properties, later Centro Properties Ltd, 1985–92; ANZ Banking Group Ltd, 1989–92 (Dir, 1982–92; Dep Chm., 1987–89); Director: Jennings Group (formerly Industries) Ltd, 1984–92; Freeport–McMoRan Australia Ltd, 1987–89. President: Aust. Chemical Industry Council, 1977; Aust. Industry Develt Assoc., 1982–83. Vice President: Aust. Business Roundtable, 1983; Business Council of Australia, 1983–84; Dir, Aust. Inst. of Petroleum, 1980–84; Mem., National Energy Adv. Cttee, 1977–80. Member, Board of Management: Univ. of Melbourne Grad. Sch. of Management, 1983–86; Crawford Fund for Internat. Agricl Res., 1989–94. Chm. Adv. Bd, Salvation Army, Southern Territory, 1986–90. Mem., Cook Soc. *Recreations:* the arts, gardening. *Address:* 1/42 Glen Street, Hawthorn, Vic 3122, Australia. *T:* (3) 98193939.

BRIDGWATER, Prof. John, FREng, FIChemE; Shell Professor of Chemical Engineering, and Professorial Fellow of St Catharine's College, Cambridge University, since 1993; *b* 10 Jan. 1938; *s* of Eric and Mary Bridgwater; *m* 1962, Diane Louise Tucker; one *s* one *d*. *Educ:* Solihull Sch.; St Catharine's Coll., Cambridge (Major Scholar; MA, PhD, ScD); Princeton Univ. (MSE). FREng (FEng 1987). Chemical Engineer, Courtaulds, 1961–64; University of Cambridge: Demonstrator in Chem. Engrg, 1964–69; Univ. Lectr in Chem. Engrg and Fellow, St Catharine's Coll., 1969–71; Esso Res. Fellow in Chem. Engrg, Hertford Coll., Oxford, 1971–73; Univ. Lectr in Engrg Sci., Univ. of Oxford and Lubbock Fellow in Engrg, Balliol Coll., 1973–80; University of Birmingham: Prof., 1980–93; Head, Sch. of Chem. Engrg, 1983–89; Dean, Faculty of Engrg, 1989–92; Gp Leader in Inter-Disciplinary Res. Centre in Materials for High Performance Applications, 1989–93; Hd, Dept of Chemical Engrg, Cambridge Univ., 1993–98. Vis. Associate Prof., Univ. of British Columbia, 1970–71; Vis. Prof., Univ. of Calif at

Berkeley, 1992–93. Mem., Engrg Bd, SERC, 1986–89; Chm., Process Engrg Cttee, SERC, 1986–89. Pres., IChemE, 1997–98 (Vice-Pres., 1995–97). Chm., Editl Bd, Chem. Engrg Science, 1996– (Exec. Editor, 1983–96). *Publications:* (with J. J. Benbow) Paste Flow and Extrusion, 1993; papers on chem. and process engineering in professional jls. *Address:* Department of Chemical Engineering, University of Cambridge, Pembroke Street, Cambridge CB2 3RA. *T:* (01223) 334798.

BRIDLE, Rear-Adm. Gordon Walter, CB 1977; MBE 1952; *b* 14 May 1923; *s* of Percy Gordon Bridle and Dorothy Agnes Bridle; *m* 1944, Phyllis Audrey Page; three *s*. *Educ:* King Edward's Grammar Sch., Aston, Birmingham; Northern Grammar Sch., Portsmouth; Royal Dockyard Sch., Portsmouth (Whitworth Scholar); Imperial Coll., London (ACGI). CEng, FIEE. jssc. Loan Service, Pakistan, 1950–52; served HM Ships: Implacable, St James, Gambia, Newfoundland, Devonshire; Proj. Manager, Sea Slug and Sea Dart, Mins of Aviation/Technol.; comd HMS Collingwood, 1969–71; Dir, Surface Weapons Projects, ASWE; Asst Controller of the Navy, 1974–77. *Address:* 25 Heatherwood, Midhurst, Sussex GU29 9LH. *T:* (01730) 812838.

BRIDLE, Ronald Jarman, FREng; private consultant and inventor, Cardiff University Industry Centre, since 1989, and Hon. Professor, Cardiff University, since 1991; *b* 27 Jan. 1930; *s* of Raymond Bridle and Dorothy (*née* Jarman); *m* Beryl Eunice (*née* Doe); two *d*. *Educ:* West Monmouth Grammar Sch.; Bristol Univ. (BSc). FREng (FEng 1979); FICE, FIHE. Graduate Asst, Monmouthshire CC, 1953–55; Exec. Engr, Gold Coast Govt, 1955–57; Sen. Engr, Cwmbran Develt Corp., 1957–60; Principal Designer, Cardiff City, 1960–62; Project Engr, Sheffield-Leeds Motorway, West Riding CC, 1962–65; Dep. County Surveyor II, Cheshire CC, 1965–67; Dir, Midland RCU, DoE, 1967–71; Dep. Chief Highway Engr, 1971–73, Under-Sec., Highways 1, 1973–75, Chief Highway Engr, 1975–76, DoE; Chief Highway Engr, Dept of Transport, 1976–80; Controller of R&D, Dept of Transport, and Dir, Transport and Road Res. Lab., 1980–84; Dir, Key Resources Internat., 1984–87. Dir (Technology and Develt), Mitchell Cotts PLC, 1984–86; Chm., Permanent Formwork Ltd, 1987–89. FRSA. Former Member: Council, ICE; EDC for Civil Engrg; Past Pres., IHE; Mem. Bd., BSI, 1979–85; Chm., Building and Civil Engineering Council, BSI, 1979–85. *Publications:* papers in jls of ICE, IHE and internat. confs. *Recreations:* golf, painting. *Address:* Parsonage Farm, Kemeys Commander, Usk, Gwent NP5 1SU. *T:* (01873) 880929. *Club:* Royal Automobile.

BRIDPORT, 4th Viscount, *cr* 1868; **Alexander Nelson Hood;** Baron Bridport, 1794; 7th Duke of Bronte in Sicily (*cr* 1799); Managing Partner, Bridport & Cie SA, since 1991; *b* 17 March 1948; *s* of 3rd Viscount Bridport and Sheila Jeanne Agatha (*d* 1996), *d* of Johann van Meurs; *S* father, 1969; *m* 1st, 1972, Linda Jacqueline Paravicini (marr. diss.), *d* of Lt-Col and Mrs V. R. Paravicini; one *s*; 2nd, 1979, Mrs Nina Rindt-Martyn (marr. diss. 1999); one *s*. *Educ:* Eton; Sorbonne. *Heir: s* Hon. Peregrine Alexander Nelson Hood, *b* 30 Aug. 1974. *Address:* 1 Place Longemalle, 1204 Geneva, Switzerland. *T:* (22) 8177000, *Fax:* (22) 8177050. *Club:* Brooks's.

BRIEGEL, Geoffrey Michael Olver; Deputy Master of the Court of Protection, 1977–83; *b* 13 July 1923; *s* of late Roy C. Briegel, TD, and Veria Lindsey Briegel; *m* 1947, Barbara Mary Richardson; three *s* one *d*. *Educ:* Highgate Sch. Served War, RAF, 1942–46 (514 Sqdn Bomber Command). Called to Bar, Lincoln's Inn, 1950; Public Trustee Office, 1954; Clerk of the Lists, Queen's Bench Div., and Legal Sec. to Lord Chief Justice of England, 1963; Dep. Circuit Administrator, South Eastern Circuit, 1971. Legacy Officer, Inst. of Cancer Res., Royal Cancer Hosp., 1983–97. *Recreations:* theatre, cinema, music, boating, all sports. *Club:* Royal Air Force.

BRIEN, Alan; novelist and journalist; *b* 12 March 1925; *s* of Ernest Brien and Isabella Brien (*née* Patterson); *m* 1st, 1947, Pamela Mary Jones (*d* 1998); three *d*; 2nd, 1961, Nancy Newbold Ryan (*d* 1980); one *s* one *d*; 3rd, 1973, Jill Sheila Tweedie (*d* 1993); 4th, 1996, Jane Hill. *Educ:* Bede Grammar Sch., Sunderland; Jesus Coll., Oxford. BA (Eng Lit). Served war RAF (air-gunner), 1943–46. Associate Editor: Mini-Cinema, 1950–52; Courier, 1952–53; Film Critic and Columnist, Truth, 1953–54; TV Critic, Observer, 1954–55; Film Critic, 1954–56, columnist, 1956–58, Evening Standard; Drama Critic and Features Editor, Spectator, 1958–61; Columnist, Daily Mail, 1958–62; Columnist, Sunday Dispatch, 1962–63; Political Columnist, Sunday Pictorial, 1963–64; Drama Critic, Sunday Telegraph, 1961–67; Columnist: Spectator, 1963–65; New Statesman, 1966–72; Punch, 1972–84; Diarist, 1967–75, Film Critic, 1976–84, Sunday Times. Foreign correspondent: New York (for Evening Standard), 1956–58; Moscow (for Sunday Times), 1974; Saigon (for Sunday Times, Punch), 1972. Regular broadcaster on radio, 1952–, and television, 1955–. Hannen Swaffer (now IPC) Critic of Year, 1966, 1967. *Publications:* Domes of Fortune (essays), 1979; Lenin: the novel (novel), 1987; All Right For Some (autobiog.), 2000. *Recreations:* procrastination, empyromancy. *Address:* The Cottage at 36A, Highgate High Street, N6 5JG.

BRIERLEY, Christopher Wadsworth, CBE 1987; Senior Adviser, Natural Gas Development Unit, World Bank, Washington, USA, 1990–94; Managing Director, Resources and New Business, 1987–89, and Member of the Board, 1985–89, British Gas plc (formerly British Gas Corporation); *b* 1 June 1929; *s* of Eric Brierley and Edna Mary Lister; *m* 1st, Dorothy Scott (marr. diss. 1980); two *d*; 2nd, 1984, Dilwen Marie Srobat (*née* Morgan). *Educ:* Whitgift Middle School, Croydon. FCMA, ACIS. Branch Accountant, Hubert Davies & Co., Rhodesia, 1953–56; private business, N Rhodesia, 1956–59; Accountant, EMI, 1960; Chief Accountant, EMI Records, 1965; Dir of Finance, Long & Hambly, 1968; Chief Accountant, E Midlands Gas Bd, 1970; Director of Finance: Eastern Gas Bd, 1974; British Gas, 1977; Dir, 1980, Man. Dir, 1982, Economic Planning, British Gas. *Recreation:* music. *Address:* 6 Stobarts Close, Knebworth, Herts SG3 6ND. *T:* (01438) 814988.

BRIERLEY, David, CBE 1986; Advisory Director, Royal Shakespeare Company, since 1996; *b* 26 July 1936; *s* of Ernest William Brierley and Jessie Brierley; *m* 1962, Ann Fosbrooke Potter; two *s*. *Educ:* Romiley County Primary Sch.; Stockport GS; Clare Coll., Cambridge (Exhibnr; Cert Ed 1959; MA; Pres., 1958–59, Trustee, 1969–, CU Amateur Dramatic Club). Teacher: Perse Sch., Cambridge, 1958–59; King Edward VI Sch., Macclesfield, 1959–61; Royal Shakespeare Company: Asst Stage Manager, and Stage Manager, Royal Shakespeare Theatre, 1961–63; Gen. Stage Manager, 1963–66; Asst to Dir, 1966–68; Gen. Manager, Sec. to Govs and Dir, various associated cos, 1968–96. Member: Council of Mgt, Royal Shakespeare Theatre Trust, 1982–; Trustees and Guardians, Shakespeare's Birthplace, 1984–96. Director: West End Theatre Managers Ltd, 1975–96; Theatre Royal, Plymouth, 1997–; Clwyd Theatr Cymru, 1997–; Hall for Cornwall Trust, 1999–. Chairman: Grant Aided Theatres Standing Cttee, Soc. of London Theatre, 1975–96; Theatres Nat. Cttee, 1986–96; Mem., Theatres Trust, 1996–; Adv. Bd Actors Centre, 1996–. Mem. and chm. of panels and cttees, Arts Council of GB, 1975–94; Arts Council of England: Member: Drama Adv. Panel, 1994–96; Nat. Lottery Adv. Panel, 1996–; Council, 1997–; Chairman: Stabilisation Cttee, 1996–; Audit Cttee, 1998–; Chairman: Drama and Dance Adv. Cttee, British Council, 1997–; South West Arts, 1997–98. Member: Cambridge Univ. Careers Service Syndicate, 1980–88; Council, Warwick Univ., 1984–91; Gov., Stratford-upon-Avon Coll., 1971–96. Hon. DLitt Warwick, 1996. Special Award, 10th Internat. Congress, Internat. Soc. for the Performing Arts, 1996. *Recreation:* reading. *Address:* Tredenham Cottage, Tredenham Road, St Mawes, Truro, Cornwall TR2 5AN. *T:* (01326) 270478.

BRIERLEY, John David, CB 1978; retired Civil Servant; *b* 16 March 1918; *s* of late Walter George Brierley and late Doris Brierley (*née* Paterson); *m* 1956, Frances Elizabeth Davis; one (adopted) *s* one (adopted) *d*. *Educ:* elementary schools, London and Croydon; Whitgift Sch., Croydon; Lincoln Coll., Oxford. *Lit Hum.* BA Hons, 1940. Served War: Army, RASC, 1940–46. Ministry of Education, later DES, 1946–77: Under-Sec., 1969; Principal Finance Officer, 1969–75; Under Sec., 1969–77. Dean of Studies, Working Mens' Coll., NW1, 1978–81 (Mem. Corp., 1980–94); Governor, Croydon High Sch. (GPDST), 1980–91. *Recreations:* fell-walking, cycling, photography, music. *Address:* Little Trees, Winterbourne, near Newbury, Berks RG20 8AS. *T:* (01635) 248870.

BRIERLEY, Sir Ronald (Alfred), Kt 1988; Chairman, Guinness Peat Group plc (formerly GPG plc), since 1990; *b* Wellington, 2 Aug. 1937; *s* of J. R. Brierley. *Educ:* Wellington Coll. Editor, New Zealand Stocks and Shares, 1957–63; Chairman: Brierley Investments Ltd, 1961–89 (Founder, 1961; Founder Pres. 1989–); Industrial Equity Ltd, 1966–89; Chm., Bank of New Zealand, 1987–88 (Dir, 1985–88; Dep. Chm., 1986). *Address:* Guinness Peat Group plc, 2nd Floor, 21–26 Garlick Hill, EC4V 2AU. *Clubs:* American National, City Tattersall's (NSW).

BRIERS, Richard David, OBE 1989; actor since 1955; *b* 14 Jan. 1934; *s* of Joseph Briers and Morna Richardson; *m* 1957, Ann Davies; two *d*. *Educ:* Rokeby Prep. Sch., Wimbledon; Ridgeway Sch., Wimbledon. RADA, 1954–56 (silver medal). First appearance in London in Gilt and Gingerbread, Duke of York's, 1959. *Plays:* (major parts in): Arsenic and Old Lace, Vaudeville, 1965; Relatively Speaking, Duke of York's, 1966; The Real Inspector Hound, Criterion, 1968; Cat Among the Pigeons, Prince of Wales, 1969; The Two of Us, Garrick, 1970; Butley, Criterion, 1972; Absurd Person Singular, Criterion, 1973; Absent Friends, Garrick, 1975; Middle Age Spread, Lyric, 1979; The Wild Duck, Lyric, Hammersmith, 1980; Arms and the Man, Lyric, 1981; Run for Your Wife, Shaftesbury, 1983; Why Me?, Strand, 1985; The Relapse, Chichester, 1986; Twelfth Night, Riverside Studios, 1987 (televised 1988); Midsummer Night's Dream, and King Lear, Renaissance Theatre world tour, 1990; Wind in the Willows, Nat. Theatre, 1991; Uncle Vanya, Lyric, Hammersmith, 1991; Coriolanus, Chichester, 1992; Home, Wyndham's, 1994; A Christmas Carol, Lyric, Hammersmith, 1996; The Chairs, Royal Court Downstairs, 1997; Spike, Nuffield Th., Southampton, 2001. *Television series:* Brothers-in-Law; Marriage Lines; The Good Life; OneUpManShip; The Other One; Norman Conquests; Ever-Decreasing Circles; All In Good Faith; Monarch of the Glen, 2000. *Films:* Henry V, 1989; Much Ado About Nothing, and Swan Song, 1993; Mary Shelley's Frankenstein, 1994; In the Bleak Midwinter, 1995; Hamlet, 1997; Love's Labours Lost, 1999; Unconditional Love, 2000. *Publications:* Natter Natter, 1981; Coward and Company, 1987; A Little Light Weeding, 1993; A Taste of the Good Life, 1995. *Recreations:* reading, gardening. *Address:* c/o Hamilton Asper Management, Ground Floor, 24 Hanway Street, W1P 9DD.

BRIGDEN, Wallace, MA, MD, FRCP; Consulting Physician: London Hospital, and Cardiac Department, London Hospital; National Heart Hospital; Consulting Cardiologist to the Royal Navy, now Emeritus; *b* 8 June 1916; *s* of Wallis Brigden and Louise Brigden (*née* Clarke); *m* 1st, 1942, Joan Mack (marr. diss. 1966); two *s* one *d*; 2nd, 1966, Everel Sankey; one *s*, and one step *s*. *Educ:* Latymer School; University of Cambridge; King's College Hospital; Yale University. Senior Scholar, King's College, Cambridge; First Class Natural Sciences Tripos, Parts I and II, 1936, 1937; Henry Fund Fellowship, Yale University, USA, 1937–38; Burney Yeo Schol., King's College Hospital, 1938. RAMC, 1943–47, Med. Specialist and O/C Medical Division. Lecturer in Medicine, Post-Grad. Med. School of London; Physician, Hammersmith Hospital, 1948–49; Asst Physician, later Consultant Physician, London Hospital and Cardiac Dept of London Hosp., 1949–81; Asst Physician, later Consultant Physician, National Heart Hospital, 1949–81; Cons. Cardiologist, Special Unit for Juvenile Rheumatism, Taplow, 1955–59; Director Inst. of Cardiology, 1962–66. Cons. Physician to Munich Re-Insurance Co., 1974–. Pres., Assurance Medical Society, 1987–89. St Cyres Lectr, 1956; R. T. Hall Lectr, Australia and New Zealand, 1961; Hugh Morgan Vis. Prof., Vanderbilt Univ., 1963. Late Assistant Editor, British Heart Journal. Mem. British Cardiac Society and Assoc. of Physicians. *Publications:* Section on Cardio-vascular disease in Price's Textbook of Medicine; Myocardial Disease, Cecil-Loeb Textbook of Medicine; contributor to the Lancet, British Heart Jl, British Medical Jl. *Recreation:* painting. *Address:* Willow House, 38 Totteridge Common, N20 8NE. *T:* (020) 8959 6616.

BRIGGS, family name of **Baron Briggs**.

BRIGGS, Baron *cr* 1976 (Life Peer), of Lewes, E Sussex; **Asa Briggs,** MA, BSc (Econ); FBA 1980; Provost, Worcester College, Oxford, 1976–91; Chancellor, Open University, 1978–94; *b* 7 May 1921; *o s* of William Walker Briggs and Jane Briggs, Keighley, Yorks; *m* 1955, Susan Anne Banwell, *o d* of late Donald I. Banwell, Keevil, Wiltshire; two *s* two *d*. *Educ:* Keighley Grammar School; Sidney Sussex College, Cambridge (1st cl. History Tripos, Pts I and II, 1940, 1941; 1st cl. BSc (Econ.), Lond., 1941). Gerstenberg studentship in Economics, London, 1941. Served in Intelligence Corps, 1942–45. Fellow of Worcester College, Oxford, 1945–55; Reader in Recent Social and Economic History, Oxford, 1950–55; Member, Institute for Advanced Study, Princeton, USA, 1953–54; Faculty Fellow of Nuffield College, Oxford, 1953–55; Professor of Modern History, Leeds Univ., 1955–61; University of Sussex: Professor of History, 1961–76; Dean, School of Social Studies, 1961–65; Pro Vice-Chancellor, 1961–67; Vice-Chancellor, 1967–76. Chm. Bd of Governors, Inst. of Develt Studies, 1967–76. Visiting Professor: ANU, 1960; Chicago Univ., 1966, 1972; Sen. Gannett Fellow, Columbia Univ., 1988, 1996. Lectures: Gregynog, Univ. of Wales, 1981; Ford, Oxford Univ., 1991; Ellen McArthur, Cambridge Univ., 1992. Dep. Pres., WEA, 1954–58, Pres., 1958–67. Mem., UGC, 1959–67; Chm., Cttee on Nursing, 1970–72 (Cmnd 5115, 1972). Trustee: Glyndebourne Arts Trust, 1966–91; Internat. Broadcasting Inst., 1968–87 (Hon. Trustee, 1991–); (Chm.) Heritage Educn Gp, 1976–86; Civic Trust, 1976–86; Chairman: Standing Conf. for Study of Local History, 1969–76; Council, European Inst. of Education, 1975–90; Commonwealth of Learning, 1988–93; Govs and Trustees, Brighton Pavilion, 1975–; Adv. Bd for Redundant Churches, 1983–89; Eurydice Consultative Gp, 1996–2000; Vice-Chm. of Council, UN Univ., 1974–80; Governor, British Film Institute, 1970–77; President: Social History Soc., 1976–; Victorian Soc., 1983–; The Ephemera Soc., 1984–; Brontë Soc., 1989–96; British Assoc. for Local History, 1984–86; Assoc. of Research Associations, 1986–88; Vice-Pres., Historical Assoc., 1986–. Mem., Ct of Governors, Administrative Staff Coll., 1971–91. Mem., Amer. Acad. of Arts and Sciences, 1970. Hon. Fellow: Sidney Sussex Coll., Cambridge, 1968; Worcester Coll., Oxford, 1969; St Catharine's Coll., Cambridge, 1977. Hon. DLitt: East Anglia, 1966; Strathclyde, 1973; Leeds, 1974; Cincinnati, 1977; Liverpool, 1977; Open Univ., 1979; Birmingham, 1989; Missouri, Teesside, 1993; Hon. DSc Florida Presbyterian, 1966; Hon. LLD: York, Canada, 1968; New England, 1972; Sussex, 1976; Bradford, 1978; Rochester, NY, 1980; Ball State, 1985; E Asia, 1987;

George Washington, 1988; Southampton, 1995; Tulane, 1996. Marconi Medal for Communications History, 1975; Médaille de Vermeil de la Formation, Fondation de l'Académie d'Architecture, 1979; Snow Medal, Royal Coll. of Anaesthetists, 1991. *Publications:* Patterns of Peace-making (with D. Thomson and E. Meyer), 1945; History of Birmingham (1865–1938), 1952; Victorian People, 1954; Friends of the People, 1956; The Age of Improvement, 1959, rev. edn 2000; (ed) Chartist Studies, 1959; (ed with John Saville) Essays in Labour History, Vol. I, 1960, Vol. II, 1971, Vol. III, 1977; (ed) They Saw it Happen, 1897–1940, 1961; A Study of the Work of Seebohm Rowntree, 1871–1954, 1961; History of Broadcasting in the United Kingdom: vol. I, The Birth of Broadcasting, 1961; vol. II, The Golden Age of Wireless, 1965; vol. III, The War of Words, 1970; vol. IV, Sound and Vision, 1979; vol. V, Competition 1955–1974, 1995; Victorian Cities, 1963, 2nd edn 1996; William Cobbett, 1967; How They Lived, 1700–1815, 1969; (ed) The Nineteenth Century, 1970; (ed with Susan Briggs) Cap and Bell, 1973; (ed) Essays in the History of Publishing, 1974; Iron Bridge to Crystal Palace: impact and images of the Industrial Revolution, 1979; Governing the BBC, 1979; The Power of Steam, 1982; Marx in London, 1982; A Social History of England, 1983, 3rd edn 1999; Toynbee Hall, 1984; Collected Essays, 2 vols, 1985, vol. III 1991; The BBC: the first fifty years, 1985; (with Joanna Spicer) The Franchise Affair, 1986; Victorian Things, 1988, 2nd edn 1996; Haut Brion, 1994; The Channel Islands, Occupation and Liberation 1940–1945, 1995; (ed jtly) Fins de Siècle: how centuries end 1400–2000, 1996; (with Patricia Clavin) Modern Europe 1789–1989, 1997; Chartism, 1998; Go To It!: working for victory on the Home Front 1939–1945, 2000. *Recreation:* travelling. *Address:* The Caprons, Keere Street, Lewes, Sussex BN7 1TY. *Clubs:* Beefsteak, Oxford and Cambridge.

BRIGGS, David John, FRCO; Organist, Gloucester Cathedral, 1994–Easter 2002; composer and concert organist; *b* 1 Nov. 1962; *s* of late J. R. Briggs and of J. A. Briggs (*née* Jones); *m* 1986, Elisabeth Anne Baker; one *d. Educ:* Solihull Sch. (Music Schol.); King's Coll., Cambridge (Organ Schol.; MA 1987). FRCO 1980; ARCM 1986. Asst Organist, Hereford Cathedral, 1985–88; Organist, Truro Cathedral, 1989–94. Vis. Tutor in Improvisation, RNCM, 1995–; Vis. Prof. of Improvisation, RAM, 2001–. Festival Conductor, Gloucester Three Choirs Fest., 1995. Recital tours, Australia, NZ and USA, 1997. Has made numerous recordings. FRSA 1993. *Publications:* compositions: Truro Eucharist, 1990; The Music Mountain, 1991; Te Deum Laudamus, 1998; Creation, 2000; *transcriptions:* Cochereau, Improvisations on Alouette, gentille Alouette, 1993; Cantem toto la Gloria, 1997; Suite de Danses improvisées, 1998; Improvisations sur Venez, Divin Messie, 1998; Triptique Symphonique, 1998; (for organ) Mahler, Symphony No 5. *Recreation:* training for private pilot's licence. *Address:* (until Easter 2002) 7 Miller's Green, Gloucester GL1 2BN. *T:* (01452) 524764; c/o Philip Truckenbrod Concert Artists, 97 South Street, West Hartford, CT 06110–1960, USA. *Fax:* (860) 5107788.

BRIGGS, Prof. Derek Ernest Gilmor, PhD; FRS 1999; Professor of Palaeontology, since 1994, and Head, Department of Earth Sciences, since 1997, University of Bristol; *b* 10 Jan. 1950; *s* of John Gilmor Briggs and Olive Evelyn Briggs (*née* Scanlon); *m* 1972, Jennifer Olive Kershaw; three *s. Educ:* Sandford Park Sch., Dublin; Trinity Coll., Dublin (Foundn Scholar; BA Geology); Sidney Sussex Coll., Cambridge (MA, PhD). Res. Fellow, Cambridge, 1974–77; Goldsmiths' College, London University: Department of Geology: Lectr, 1977; Sen. Lectr, 1980; Principal Lectr and Dep. Dean of Sci. and Maths, 1982–85; Bristol University: Lectr, 1985, Reader, 1988, Dept of Geol.; Asst Dir, Biogeochemistry Res. Centre, 1990–97. Res. Associate, Royal Ontario Mus., Toronto, 1983–; Vis. Scientist, Field Mus. of Nat. History, Chicago, 1983; Dist. Vis. Scholar, Univ. of Adelaide, 1994; Benedum Lectr, Univ. of W Virginia, 1994. Editor, Palaeontology and Special Papers in Palaeontology, 1982–86. Lyell Medal, Geol Soc., 2000. Premio Capo d'Orlando, Italy, 2000. *Publications:* (ed with K. C. Allen) Evolution and the Fossil Record, 1989; (ed with P. R. Crowther) Palaeobiology: a synthesis, 1990; (ed with P. A. Allison) Taphonomy: releasing the data locked in the fossil record, 1991; (jtly) The Fossils of the Burgess Shale, 1994; The Fossils of the Hunsrück Slate, 1998; (ed with P. R. Crowther) Palaeobiology II, 2001; contribs to learned jls. *Recreations:* the outdoors, natural history, golf. *Address:* Department of Earth Sciences, University of Bristol, Wills Memorial Building, Queen's Road, Bristol BS8 1RJ. *T:* (0117) 954 5423; Longroof, All Saints' Lane, Clevedon, North Som BS21 6AU.

BRIGGS, Rt Rev. George Cardell, CMG 1980; Bishop of Seychelles, 1973–79; *b* Latchford, Warrington, Cheshire, 6 Sept. 1910; *s* of George Cecil and Mary Theodora Briggs; unmarried. *Educ:* Worksop Coll., Notts; Sidney Sussex Coll., Cambridge (MA); Cuddesdon Theological Coll. Deacon 1934; priest 1935; Curate of St Alban's, Stockport, 1934–37; Missionary priest, Diocese of Masasi, Tanzania, 1937; Archdeacon of Newala and Canon of Masasi, 1955–64; Rector of St Alban's, Dar-es-Salaam, 1964–69; Warden of St Cyprian's Theological Coll., Masasi, 1969–73; Asst Bishop, Diocese of Derby, and Assistant Priest, parish of St Giles, Matlock, 1979–80. *Recreations:* walking, reading, music. *Address:* College of St Barnabas, Blackberry Lane, Lingfield, Surrey RH7 6NJ. *T:* (01342) 870747. *Club:* Royal Commonwealth Society.

BRIGGS, Very Rev. George Peter N.; *see* Nairn-Briggs.

BRIGGS, Isabel Diana, (Mrs Michael Briggs); *see* Colegate, I. D.

BRIGGS, John; *see* Briggs, P. J.

BRIGGS, Dr (Michael) Peter; Chief Executive (formerly Executive Secretary), British Association for the Advancement of Science, since 1990; *b* 3 Dec. 1944; *s* of late Hewieson Briggs and of Doris (*née* Habberley); *m* 1969, Jennifer Elizabeth Watts; one *s* one *d. Educ:* Abbeydale Boys' Grammar Sch., Sheffield; Univ. of Sussex (BSc, DPhil). Jun. Res. Fellow in Theoretical Chem., Univ. of Sheffield, 1969–71; Res. Assistant, Dept of Architecture, Univ. of Bristol, 1971–73; Deputation Sec., Methodist Church Overseas Div., 1973–77; Area Sec. (Herts and Essex), Christian Aid, BCC, 1977–80; British Association for the Advancement of Science: Educn Manager, 1980–86; Public Affairs Man., 1986–88; Dep. Sec., 1988–90. Mem. Council, Internat. Council for Advancement of Scientific Literacy, 1992–. Sec., Assoc. of British Science Writers, 1986–. Chairman: Management Cttee, Methodist Church Div. of Social Responsibility, 1983–86; Methodist Youth World Affairs Management Cttee, 1984–92. FRSA 1990. *Recreation:* walking. *Address:* British Association for the Advancement of Science, 23 Savile Row, W1S 2EZ. *T:* (020) 7973 3500.

BRIGGS, Michael Townley Featherstone; QC 1994; Attorney General, Duchy of Lancaster, since 2001; *b* 23 Dec. 1954; *s* of Capt. James William Featherstone Briggs, RN and Barbara Nadine Briggs (*née* Pelham Groom); *m* 1981, Beverly Ann Rogers; three *s* one *d. Educ:* Charterhouse; Magdalen Coll., Oxford (BA History). Called to the Bar, Lincoln's Inn, 1978; Jun. Counsel to Crown Chancery, 1990–94. *Recreations:* sailing, singing (solo and choral), cooking, garden railways. *Address:* Serle Court, 6 New Square, Lincoln's Inn, WC2A 3QS. *T:* (020) 7242 6105. *Clubs:* Bar Yacht; Emsworth Sailing.

BRIGGS, Patrick David, MA; Principal, Kolej Tuanku Ja'afar, Malaysia, since 1997; *b* 24 Aug. 1940; *s* of late Denis Patrick Briggs and of Nancy Sylvester (*née* Jackson); *m* 1968, Alicia Dorothy O'Donnell; two *s* one *d. Educ:* Pocklington Sch.; Christ's Coll., Cambridge (MA). Bedford Sch., 1965–87 (Sen. Housemaster, 1983–87); Head Master, William Hulme's GS, 1987–97. Rugby Blue, Cambridge, 1962; England Rugby trialist, 1968 and 1969; Mem. Barbarians, 1968–69; RFU staff coach, 1973–95; England Under-23 Rugby coach, 1975–80; Team Manager, England Students Rugby, 1988–95. *Publication:* The Parents' Guide to Independent Schools, 1979. *Recreations:* cricket, Rugby, golf, fell walking, poetry, theatre. *Address:* Kolej Tuanku Ja'afar, 71700 Mantin, Negeri Sembilan, Malaysia. *T:* (6) 7582561. *Clubs:* East India, Devonshire, Sports and Public Schools, XL; Hawks (Cambridge); Quidnuncs, Cheshire County Cricket, Lancashire County Cricket; Royal Selangor (Kuala Lumpur).

BRIGGS, Peter; *see* Briggs, M. P.

BRIGGS, (Peter) John; a Recorder of the Crown Court, 1978–97; *b* 15 May 1928; *s* of late Percy Briggs and Annie M. Folker; *m* 1956, Sheila Phyllis Walton; one *s* three *d. Educ:* King's Sch., Peterborough; Balliol Coll., Oxford. MA, BCL. Called to the Bar, Inner Temple, 1953. Legal Member: Mersey Mental Health Review Tribunal, 1969 (Dep. Chm., 1971, Chm., 1981–94); North-West Mental Health Review Tribunal, 1994–98; NW and W Midlands Mental Health Review Tribunal, 1998–2000. Pres., Merseyside Medico-Legal Soc., 1982–84. Chm., Merseyside Opera, 1996–99. *Recreation:* music, particularly amateur operatics. *Address:* 15 Dean's Lawn, Berkhamsted, Herts HP4 3AZ. *T:* (01442) 871488.

BRIGGS, Raymond Redvers, DFA; FCSD; freelance illustrator, since 1957; author, since 1961; *b* 18 Jan. 1934; *s* of Ernest Redvers Briggs and Ethel Bowyer; *m* 1963, Jean Taprell Clark (*d* 1973). *Educ:* Rutlish Sch., Merton; Wimbledon School of Art; Slade School of Fine Art. NDD; DFA London. Part-time Lecturer in Illustration, Faculty of Art, Brighton Polytechnic, 1961–87. *Publications:* The Strange House, 1961; Midnight Adventure, 1961; Ring-A-Ring O'Roses, 1962; Sledges to the Rescue, 1963; The White Land, 1963; Fee Fi Fo Fum, 1964; The Mother Goose Treasury, 1966 (Kate Greenaway Medal, 1966); Jim and the Beanstalk, 1970; The Fairy Tale Treasury, 1972; Father Christmas, 1973 (Kate Greenaway Medal, 1973); Father Christmas Goes On Holiday, 1975; Fungus The Bogeyman, 1977; The Snowman, 1978 (animated film, 1982); Gentleman Jim, 1980 (play, Nottingham Playhouse, 1985); When the Wind Blows, 1982 (play, BBC Radio and Whitehall Th., 1983; text publd 1983; cassette 1984; animated film, 1987); Fungus the Bogeyman Plop-Up Book, 1982; The Tin-Pot Foreign General and the Old Iron Woman, 1984; The Snowman Pop-Up, 1986; Unlucky Wally, 1987; Unlucky Wally Twenty Years On, 1989; The Man, 1992; The Bear, 1994; Ethel & Ernest, 1998; UG, Boy Genius of the Stone Age, 2001. *Recreations:* gardening, reading, walking, second-hand bookshops. *Address:* Weston, Underhill Lane, Westmeston, Hassocks, Sussex BN6 8XG. *Clubs:* Groucho, Royal Over-Seas League.

BRIGHOUSE, Prof. Timothy Robert Peter; Chief Education Officer, Birmingham City Council, since 1993; Visiting Professor, Keele University, since 1993; *b* 15 Jan. 1940; *s* of Denison Brighouse and Mary Howard Brighouse; *m* 1st, 1962, Mary Elizabeth Demers (marr. diss. 1988); one *s* one *d*; 2nd, 1989, Elizabeth Ann (formerly Kearney). *Educ:* St Catherine's College, Oxford (MA Modern History); DipEd. Head of History Dept, Cavendish Grammar Sch., Buxton, 1962–64; Dep. Head and Warden, Chepstow Comm. Coll., 1964–66; Asst Educn Officer, Monmouthshire Educn Dept, 1966–69; Sen. Asst Educn Officer, Bucks Educn Dept, 1969–74; Under-Sec., Educn, ACC, 1974–76; Dep. Educn Officer, ILEA, 1976–78; Chief Educn Officer, Oxon, 1978–89; Prof. of Educn and Hd of Dept, Keele Univ., 1989–93. Jt Vice-Chm., Standards Task Force, 1997–99. Hon. Prof., Birmingham Univ., 1996–. Hon. DEd (CNAA) Oxford Poly., 1989; Hon. DLitt Exeter, 1996; Hon. PhD UCE, 1996. *Publications:* Revolution in Education and Training (jt editor and author), 1986; Managing the National Curriculum (jt editor and author), 1990; What Makes a Good School, 1991; Successful Schooling, 1991. *Recreations:* gardening, politics. *Address:* Willowbank, Old Road, Headington, Oxford OX3 8ZA. *T:* (01865) 766995.

BRIGHT, Andrew John; QC 2000; a Recorder, since 2000; *b* 12 April 1951; *e s* of late J. H. Bright and of Freda Bright (*née* Cotton); *m* 1976, Sally Elizabeth Carter; three *s* one *d. Educ:* Wells Cathedral Sch.; University Coll. London (LLB Hons). Called to the Bar, Middle Temple, 1973; in practice at the Bar in field of criminal law, S Eastern Circuit, 1975–. Co-opted Mem. Cttee, Criminal Bar Assoc., 1993–95. *Recreations:* river and canal boating, fishing, music. *Address:* 9 Bedford Row, WC1R 4AZ.

BRIGHT, Colin Charles; HM Diplomatic Service; Head of Commonwealth Co-ordination Department, Foreign and Commonwealth Office, since 1998; *b* 2 Jan. 1948; *s* of William Charles John Bright and Doris (*née* Sutton); *m* 1st, 1978, Helen-Anne Michie; 2nd, 1990, Jane Elizabeth Gurney Pease; one *s* one *d* (and one *d* decd). *Educ:* Christ's Hospital; St Andrews Univ. (MA Hons 1971). FCO, 1975–77; Bonn, 1977–79; FCO, 1979–83; seconded to Cabinet Office, 1983–85; British Trade Develt Office, NY, 1985–88; Dep. Head of Mission, Berne, 1989–93; Consul Gen., Frankfurt, 1993–97. *Address:* c/o Foreign and Commonwealth Office, SW1A 2AH.

BRIGHT, Sir Graham (Frank James), Kt 1994; Chairman, since 1977, Managing Director, since 1970, Dietary Foods Ltd; Chairman, International Sweeteners Association, since 1997; *b* 2 April 1942; *s* of late Robert Frank Bright and Agnes Mary (*née* Graham); *m* 1972, Valerie, *d* of late E. H. Woolliams; one *s. Educ:* Hassenbrook County Sch.; Thurrock Technical Coll. Marketing Exec., Pauls & White Ltd, 1958–70. Contested (C): Thurrock, 1970 and Feb. 1974; Dartford, Oct. 1974. MP (C) Luton East, 1979–83, Luton South, 1983–97; contested (C) Luton South, 1997; contested (C) Eastern Region, EP elecns, 1999. PPS to Ministers of State, Home Office, 1984–87, DoE, 1988–89, to Paymaster Gen., 1989–90, to Prime Minister, 1990–94. Mem. Select Cttee on House of Commons Services, 1982–84. Jt Sec. to Party Aviation Gp, 1984–90; Chm., Cons. Backbench Smaller Businesses Cttee, 1983–84, 1987–88 (Vice-Chm., 1980–83; Sec., 1979–80); Vice-Chairman: Cons. Backbench Food and Drink Sub-Cttee, 1983 (Sec., 1983–85); Backbench Aviation Cttee, 1987–88; former Sec., Space Sub-Cttee; Introduced Private Member's Bills: Video Recordings Act, 1984; Entertainment (Increased Penalties) Act, 1990. Member: Thurrock Bor. Council, 1966–79; Essex CC, 1967–70. Chm., Eastern Area CPC, 1977–79; Mem., Nat. CPC, 1980–97; Vice Chm., YC Org., 1970–72; Pres., Eastern Area YCs, 1981–98; a Vice Chm., Cons. Party, 1994–97. Vice-Chm., Small Business Bureau, 1980–89, and 1991–97 (Dir, 1989–91). *Publications:* pamphlets on airports, small businesses, education. *Recreations:* golf, gardening. *Address:* 54 Vestry Court, Monck Street, Westminster, SW1P 2BQ. *Club:* Carlton.

BRIGHTLING, Peter Henry Miller; Assistant Under Secretary of State, Ministry of Defence, 1973–81; *b* 12 Sept. 1921; *o s* of late Henry Miller Brightling and Eva Emily Brightling (*née* Fry); *m* 1951, Pamela Cheeseright; two *s* two *d. Educ:* City of London Sch.; BSc(Econ), London. War of 1939–45: Air Ministry, 1939–40; MAP, 1940–41; served in RAF, 1941–46. Ministry of: Supply, 1946–59; Aviation, 1959–67; Technology, 1967–70;

Aviation Supply, 1970–71; MoD (Procurement Executive), 1971. *Address:* 5 Selwyn Road, New Malden, Surrey KT3 5AU. *T:* (020) 8942 8014.

BRIGHTMAN, family name of **Baron Brightman**.

BRIGHTMAN, Baron *cr* 1982 (Life Peer), of Ibthorpe in the County of Hampshire; **John Anson Brightman,** Kt 1970; PC 1979; a Lord of Appeal in Ordinary, 1982–86; *b* 20 June 1911; 2nd *s* of William Henry Brightman, St Albans, Herts; *m* 1945, Roxane Ambatielo; one *s*. *Educ:* Marlborough College; St John's College, Cambridge (Hon. Fellow, 1982). Called to the Bar, Lincoln's Inn, 1932; Bencher 1966. QC 1961. Able Seaman, Merchant Navy, 1939–40; RNVR (Lieut-Commander), 1940–46; anti-sub. warfare base, Tobermory; N Atlantic and Mediterranean convoys; staff, SEAC; RNSC, 1944; Assistant Naval Attaché, Ankara, 1944. Attorney-General of the Duchy of Lancaster, 1969–70; Judge of the High Court of Justice, Chancery Div., 1970–79; a Lord Justice of Appeal, 1979–82; Judge, Nat. Industrial Relns Court, 1971–74. Chairman, House of Lords Select Committee: on Charities, 1983–84; on Abortion Law, 1987–88; on City of Bristol Develt, 1988; on Spitalfields Market, 1989; on British Waterways, 1991; on Property Law, 1994; on Private Internat. Law, 1994–95; on Family Homes and Domestic Violence, 1995; Member: Cttee on Parly procedures for tax simplification, 1996; Ecclesiastical Cttee, 1997–; H of L Working Gp on procedure, 1998; Jt Cttee on Tax Simplification Bills, 2001–. Mem., General Council of the Bar, 1956–60, 1966–70. Mem. Adv. Cttee, Inst. of Advanced Legal Studies, 2000–. Chm., Tancred's Charities, 1982–96. FRGS. *Recreations:* Arctic travel, cross-country ski-ing, mountain walking, sailing. *Address:* House of Lords, SW1A 0PW. *T:* (020) 7219 2034.

BRIGHTON, Wing Comdr Peter, BSc; CEng, FIEE, FRAeS; independent consultant; *b* 26 March 1933; *s* of late Henry Charles Brighton and Ivy Irene Brighton (*née* Crane); *m* 1959, Anne Maureen Lewis Jones; one *d* (one *s* decd). *Educ:* Wisbech Grammar Sch.; Reading Univ. (BSc); RAF Technical Coll. and Staff Coll. CEng 1966; FIEE 1980; FRAeS 1981. Pilot, Engr and Attaché, RAF, 1955–71. Man. Dir, Rockwell-Collins UK, 1974–77; Regional Man. Dir, Plessey Co., 1977–78; Man. Dir, Cossor Electronics Ltd, 1978–85; British Aerospace PLC: Divl Man. Dir, 1985–87; Co. Dir of Operations, 1988; Dir Gen., EEF, 1989–91. Chm., Princess Alexandra Hosp. NHS Trust, 1996–97. Pres., Electronic Engineering Assoc., 1984–85. Mem. Ct, Cranfield Inst. of Technology, 1989–92. CIMgt (CBIM 1984). Liveryman, Coachmakers and Coach Harness Makers Co., 1989; Freeman of City of London, 1989. *Publications:* articles on aviation topics in learned jls. *Recreations:* flying (current pilot's licence), bridge, golf. *Address:* St Andrew's Cottage, Church Lane, Much Hadham, Herts SG10 6DH. *T:* (01279) 842309. *Club:* Royal Air Force.

BRIGHTY, (Anthony) David, CMG 1984; CVO 1985; HM Diplomatic Service, retired; Ambassador to Spain, and concurrently (non resident) to Andorra, 1994–98; *b* 7 Feb. 1939; *s* of C. P. J. Brighty and Winifred (*née* Turner); *m* 1963, Diana Porteous (marr. diss. 1979; she *d* 1993); two *s* two *d*; *m*, 1997, Susan Olivier. *Educ:* Northgate Grammar Sch., Ipswich; Clare Coll., Cambridge (BA). Entered FO, 1961; Brussels, 1962–63; Havana, 1964–66; FO, 1967–69, resigned; joined S. G. Warburg & Co., 1969; reinstated in FCO, 1971; Saigon, 1973–74; UK Mission to UN, NY, 1975–78; RCDS, 1979; Head of Personnel Operations Dept, FCO, 1980–83; Counsellor, Lisbon, 1983–86; Dir, Cabinet of Sec.-Gen. of NATO, 1986–87; Resident Chm., CSSB, 1988; Ambassador to Cuba, 1989–91; Ambassador to Czech and Slovak Fed. Republic, later to Czech Republic and (non-resident) to Slovakia, 1991–94. Non-exec. Dir, EFG Private Bank Ltd, 1999–. Chm., Consultative Cttee on Remuneration (NATO, OECD, etc), 1999–. Dep. Chm., Anglo-Spanish Soc. *Address:* 15 Provost Road, NW3 4ST.

BRIGSTOCKE, family name of **Baroness Brigstocke**.

BRIGSTOCKE, Baroness *cr* 1990 (Life Peer), of Kensington in the Royal Borough of Kensington and Chelsea; **Heather Renwick Brigstocke,** CBE 2000; Chairman, English-Speaking Union of the Commonwealth, 1993–99; High Mistress of St Paul's Girls' School, 1974–89; *b* 2 Sept. 1929; *d* of late Sqdn-Ldr J. R. Brown, DFC and Mrs M. J. C. Brown, MA; *m* 1st, 1952, Geoffrey Brigstocke (*d* 1974); three *s* one *d*; 2nd, 2000, Baron Griffiths, *qv*. *Educ:* Abbey Sch., Reading; Girton Coll., Cambridge (MA, Pt I Classics, Pt II Archaeolog. and Anthropol.); Univ. Winchester Reading Prize, 1950. Classics Mistress, Francis Holland Sch., London, SW1, 1951–53; part-time Classics Mistress, Godolphin and Latymer Sch., 1954–60; part-time Latin Teacher, National Cathedral Sch., Washington, DC, 1962–64; Headmistress, Francis Holland Sch., London, NW1, 1965–74. Comr, Museums and Galls Commn, 1992–2000. Member: Council, London House for Overseas Graduates, 1965–91 (Vice-Chm., 1975–80); Council, Middlesex Hosp. Med. Sch., 1971–80; Cttee, AA, 1975–90; Council, RHC, 1977–85; Council, The City Univ., 1978–83; Pres., Girls' Schools Assoc., 1980–81; Vice Pres., C & G, 1993–. Member: Health Educn Authority, 1989–98; Modern Foreign Langs Wkg Gp, 1989–90. Non-exec. Dir, 1982–90, Mem., Programme Adv. Bd, 1990–93, LWT; Ind. Dir, The Times, 1990–; Associate Dir, Great Universal Stores, 1993–96; non-exec. Dir, Burberrys, 1993–96. Member Council: RSA, 1983–87; St George's House, Windsor, 1984–90; Pres., Bishop Creighton House Settlement, Fulham, 1977–; Chairman: Thames LWT Telethon Trust, 1990; Menerva Educnl Trust, 1991–93; Mem. Council, Nat. Literacy Trust, 1993–; Chm. of Trustees, Geffrye Mus., 1990–2000; Trustee: Nat. Gall., 1975–82; Kennedy Meml Trust, 1980–85; Technology Colls Trust (formerly City Technology Colls Trust), 1987–; GB Sasakawa Foundn, 1994–. Governor: Mus. of London, 1986–92; Wellington Coll., 1975–87; Royal Ballet Sch., 1977–92; United World College of the Atlantic, 1980–85; Forest Sch., 1982–90; Imperial Coll., 1991–98; Gordonstoun Sch., 1991–93; Chm. of Govs, Landau Forte Coll., Derby, 1993– (Gov., 1992–). Hon. Bencher, Inner Temple, 1992. *Address:* House of Lords, SW1A 0PW. *T:* (020) 7219 3000.

BRIGSTOCKE, Adm. Sir John (Richard), KCB 1997; Chief Executive Officer, St Andrew's Group of Hospitals, since 2000; *b* 30 July 1945; *s* of late Rev. Canon George Edward Brigstocke and Mollie (*née* Sandford); *m* 1979, Heather Day; two *s*. *Educ:* Marlborough Coll.; BRNC, Dartmouth; RNC Greenwich; RCDS. Joined RN, 1962; commands: HMS Upton; HMS Bacchante; HMS York (Capt. (D) 3rd Destroyer Squadron); Naval Plans, MoD, 1980–81 and 1982–84; BRNC Dartmouth, 1987–88; HMS Ark Royal; FO, 2nd Flotilla, subseq. Comdr, UK Task Gp, 1991–93; ACNS, 1993–95; Adm. Pres., RNC, Greenwich, 1994–95; Flag Officer, Surface Flotilla, 1995–97; Second Sea Lord, and C-in-C Naval Home Comd, and Flag ADC to the Queen, 1997–2000. Director: Ind. Healthcare Assoc., 2000–; Three Shires Hosp., 2000–. Younger Brother, Trinity House, 1981. Freeman, City of London, 1995. *Recreations:* family, ski-ing, riding. *Address:* c/o Naval Secretary, Victory Building, HM Naval Base, Portsmouth PO1 3LS.

BRIMACOMBE, Prof. John Stuart, FRSE, FRSC; Roscoe Professor of Chemistry, University of Dundee, since 1969; *b* Falmouth, Cornwall, 18 Aug. 1935; *s* of Stanley Poole Brimacombe and Lillian May Kathleen Brimacombe (*née* Candy); *m* 1959, Eileen (*née* Gibson); four *d*. *Educ:* Falmouth Grammar Sch.; Birmingham Univ. (DSc). DSc Dundee Univ. Lectr in Chemistry, Birmingham Univ., 1961–69. Meldola Medallist, 1964. *Publications:* (co-author) Mucopolysaccharides, 1964; numerous papers, reviews, etc, in: Jl Chem. Soc., Carbohydrate Research, etc. *Recreations:* sport, swimming. *Address:* 29 Dalhousie Road, Barnhill, Dundee DD5 2SP. *T:* (01382) 779214.

BRIMELOW, Alison Jane; Comptroller General and Chief Executive, Patent Office, since 1999; *b* 6 June 1949. HM Diplomatic Service, 1973–76; DTI, 1976–. *Address:* Patent Office, Concept House, Cardiff Road, Newport NP10 8QQ.

BRIMS, Maj. Gen. Robin Vaughan, CBE 1999 (OBE 1991; MBE 1986); General Officer Commanding 1 (UK) Armoured Division, since 2000; *b* 27 June 1951; *s* of late David Vaughan Brims and of Eve Georgina Mary Brims. *Educ:* Winchester Coll. Commissioned LI, 1970; sc 1982–83; CO 3rd Bn LI, 1989–91; Comdr, 24 Airmobile Bde, 1995–96; COS, NI, 1997–98; Dir, Army Resources and Plans, 1999; Comdr, Multinat. Div. (South West), 2000. *Recreation:* sport. *Address:* RHQ The Light Infantry, Peninsula Barracks, Romsey Road, Winchester, Hants SO23 8TS.

BRINCKMAN, Sir Theodore (George Roderick), 6th Bt *cr* 1831; publisher; *b* 20 March 1932; *s* of Sir Roderick Napoleon Brinckman, 5th Bt, DSO, MC, and Margaret Wilson Southam; *S* father, 1985; *m* 1st, 1958, Helen Mary Anne Cook (marr. diss. 1983); two *s* one *d*; 2nd, 1983, Hon. Greta Sheira Bernadette Murray, formerly wife of Christopher Murray, and *d* of Baron Harvington, AE, PC. *Educ:* Trinity College School, Port Hope, Ontario; Millfield; Christ Church, Oxford; Trinity Coll., Toronto (BA). *Heir: s* Theodore Jonathan Brinckman, *b* 19 Feb. 1960. *Address:* Monk Bretton, Barnsley, Cirencester, Glos GL7 5EJ. *T:* (01285) 740564. *Clubs:* White's; University (Toronto).

BRIND, (Arthur) Henry, CMG 1973; HM Diplomatic Service, retired; *b* 4 July 1927; *o s* of late T. H. Brind and late N. W. B. Brind; *m* 1954, Barbara Harrison; one *s* one *d*. *Educ:* Barry; St John's Coll., Cambridge. HM Forces, 1947–49. Colonial Administrative Service: Gold Coast/Ghana, 1950–60; Regional Sec., Trans-Volta Togoland, 1959. HM Diplomatic Service, 1960–87: Acting High Comr, Uganda, 1972–73; High Comr, Mauritius, 1974–77; Ambassador to Somali Democratic Republic, 1977–80; Vis. Research Fellow, RIIA, 1981–82; High Comr, Malaŵi, 1983–87. Grand Comdr, Order of Lion of Malaŵi, 1985. *Publication:* Lying Abroad (memoirs), 1999. *Recreations:* walking, swimming, books. *Address:* 20 Grove Terrace, NW5 1PH. *T:* (020) 7267 1190. *Club:* Reform.

BRINDED, Malcolm Arthur; Country Chairman, Shell UK Ltd, since 1999; Managing Director, Shell Exploration and Production, since 1998; *b* 18 March 1953; *s* of Cliff and Gwen Brinded; *m* 1975, Carola Telford; three *s*. *Educ:* Churchill Coll., Cambridge (BSc 1st Cl. Hons Engrg 1974). Shell Internat., The Hague, 1974–75; Project Engr, Brunei Shell Petroleum, 1975–80, Facilities Engr, Shell UK Exploration and Prodn, 1980–82; on secondment to Dept of Energy as Policy Advr, 1982–84; Nederlands Aardolie MIJ, 1984–86; Shell Gp, 1987–88; Engrg Dir, Shell Oman, 1988–92; Shell UK Exploration and Prodn, 1993–. *Recreations:* music, mountain biking, Rugby. *Address:* Shell UK Ltd, Shell Mex House, The Strand, WC2R 0DX.

BRINDLE, Ian; Deputy Chairman, Financial Reporting Review Panel, since 2001; *b* 17 Aug. 1943; *s* of John Brindle and Mabel Brindle (*née* Walsh); *m* 1967, Frances Elisabeth Moseby; two *s* one *d*. *Educ:* Blundells School; Manchester Univ. (BA Econ). FCA 1969. Price Waterhouse: articled in London, 1965; Toronto, 1971; admitted to partnership, 1976; Mem., Supervisory Cttee, 1988–98; Dir, Audit and Business Advisory Services, 1990–91; Mem., UK Exec., 1990–98; Sen. Partner, 1991–98; company merged with Coopers & Lybrand, 1998; UK Chm., PricewaterhouseCoopers, 1998–2001. Member: Auditing Practices Cttee, CCAB, 1986–90 (Chm., 1990); Accounting Standards Bd, 1993–2001 (Mem. Urgent Issues Task Force, 1991–93); Council, ICAEW, 1994–97; Financial Reporting Council, 1995–. Auditor, Duchy of Cornwall, 1993–. *Recreations:* tennis, golf. *Address:* Milestones, Packhorse Road, Bessels Green, Sevenoaks, Kent TN13 2QP.

BRINDLE, Jane; *see* Cox, Josephine.

BRINDLE, Michael John; QC 1992; a Recorder, since 2000; *b* 23 June 1952; *s* of John Arthur Brindle and Muriel Jones; *m* 1988, Heather Mary (*née* Pearce); one *s* two *d*. *Educ:* Westminster Sch.; New Coll., Oxford (Ella Stephens Schol. in Classics; 1st Cl. Hons Mods, 1972; 1st Cl. Jurisprudence, 1974; MA). Called to the Bar, Lincoln's Inn, 1975 (Hardwicke Scholar). Chm., Commercial Bar Assoc., 2001– (former Treas.). Chm. Trustees, Public Concern at Work. *Recreations:* classical music, travel, bridge. *Address:* Fountain Court, Temple, EC4Y 9DH.

BRINDLE, Dr Michael John, CBE 1998; FRCP, FRCR, FRCPC, FRCPE, FRCSE; Consultant Radiologist, The Queen Elizabeth Hospital, King's Lynn, 1972–98; President, Royal College of Radiologists, 1995–98; *b* 18 Nov. 1934; *s* of Dr W. S. Brindle and P. M. Brindle; *m* 1960, Muriel Eileen Hayward; two *s* two *d*. *Educ:* Liverpool Univ. (MB ChB 1958; MD 1967; MRad 1971). FRCPC 1972; FRCR 1989; FRCP 1998; FRCPE 1999; FRCSE 1999. Surgeon Lieut, RN, 1959–62. Consultant, Royal Alexandra Hosp., Edmonton, Alberta, 1966–72. Treas., RCR, 1990–95. Hon. FRCGP 1998. *Recreations:* bird-watching, golf. *Address:* The Orchard, Hall Lane, South Wootton, King's Lynn, Norfolk PE30 3LQ. *T:* (01553) 672825.

BRINDLEY, Prof. Giles Skey, MA, MD; FRS 1965; FRCP; Professor of Physiology in the University of London at the Institute of Psychiatry, 1968–91, now Emeritus; *b* 30 April 1926; *s* of late Arthur James Benet Skey and Dr Margaret Beatrice Marion Skey (*née* Dewhurst), later Brindley; *m* 1st, 1959, Lucy Dunk Bennell (marr. diss.); 2nd, 1964, Dr Hilary Richards; one *s* one *d*. *Educ:* Leyton County High School; Downing College, Cambridge (Hon. Fellow, 1969); London Hospital Medical College. Various jun. clin. and res. posts, 1950–54; Russian lang. abstractor, British Abstracts of Medical Sciences, 1953–56; successively Demonstrator, Lectr and Reader in Physiology, Univ. of Cambridge, 1954–68; Fellow: King's Coll., Cambridge, 1959–62; Trinity Coll., Cambridge, 1963–68. Hon. Dir, MRC Neurological Prostheses Unit, 1968–92; Hon. Consultant Physician, Maudsley Hosp., 1971–92. Chm. of Editorial Board, Journal of Physiology, 1964–66 (Member 1959–64). Visiting Prof., Univ. of California, Berkeley, 1968. Hon. FRCS 1988; Hon. FRCSE 2000. Liebrecht-Franceschetti Prize, German Ophthalmological Soc., 1971; Feldberg Prize, Feldberg Foundn, 1974; St Peter's Medal, British Assoc. of Urological Surgeons, 1987. *Publications:* Physiology of the Retina and Visual Pathway, 1960, 2nd edn 1970; papers in scientific, musicological and medical journals. *Recreations:* ski-ing, cross-country and track running (UK over-65 record holder, 2000m and 3000m steeplechase, silver medallist, 2000m steeplechase and 800m (men over 65), World Veterans' Track and Field Championships, Finland, 1991), designing, making and playing various musical instruments (inventor of the logical bassoon). *Address:* 102 Ferndene Road, SE24 0AA. *T:* (020) 7274 2598.

BRINDLEY, John Frederick, CB 1996; Circuit Administrator, South Eastern Circuit, 1995–97; *b* 25 Sept. 1937; *s* of Harold and Eva Brindley; *m* 1960, Judith Ann Sherratt; one *d. Educ:* Leek Grammar Sch. Lord Chancellor's Department: Court Business Officer, Midland and Oxford Circuit, 1971; HQ Personnel Officer, 1976; Courts Administrator, Exeter Group, 1981; Head, Civil Business Div. HQ, 1987; Court Service Management Gp, 1988; Court Service Business Gp, 1991. Chm., CSSB, 1998–. *Recreations:* hockey, cricket, amateur theatricals. *Address:* Sidmouth, Devon. *Club:* Athenæum.

BRINDLEY, Lynne Janie; Chief Executive, British Library, since 2000; *b* 2 July 1950; *d* of Ivan Blowers and Janie Blowers (*née* Williams); adopted *d* of Ronald Williams and Elaine Williams (*née* Chapman), 1958; *m* 1972, Timothy Stuart Brindley. *Educ:* Truro High Sch.; Univ. of Reading (BA 1971); UCL (MA 1975). FIInfSc 1990; FLA 1990. Head of Mktg and of Chief Exec.'s Office, British Library, 1979–85; Dir of Library and Information Services, and Pro-Vice Chancellor, Aston Univ., 1985–90; Principal Consultant, KPMG, 1990–92; Librarian and Dir of Information Services, LSE, 1992–97; Librarian and Pro-Vice Chancellor, Univ. of Leeds, 1997–2000. Visiting Professor: Knowledge Mgt, Univ. of Leeds, 2000–; Information Mgt, Leeds Metropolitan Univ., 2000–. Member: Lord Chancellor's Adv. Cttee on Public Records, 1992–98; Jt Inf. Systems Cttee, HEFCs, 1992–98 (Chair, Electronic Libraries Prog., 1993–98); Review of Higher Educn Libraries, HEFCs, 1992–93; Internat. Cttee on Social Sci. Inf., UNESCO, 1992–97; Res. Resources Bd, ESRC, 1997–; Liby and Inf. Commn, DCMS, 1999–2000; Stanford Univ. Adv. Council for Libraries and Inf. Resources, 1999–. Trustee, Thackray Med. Mus., Leeds, 1999–. FRSA 1993. Freeman, City of London, 1989; Liveryman, Goldsmiths' Co., 1993–. Hon. DLitt Nottingham Trent, 2001. *Publications:* numerous articles on electronic libraries and information mgt. *Recreations:* classical music, theatre, modern art, hill walking. *Address:* British Library, 96 Euston Road, NW1 2DB. *Club:* Reform.

BRINDLEY, Stephen, FCIH; therapeutic counsellor/psychotherapist; Chief Executive, North Hull Housing Action Trust, 1991–99; *b* 18 April 1947; *s* of Bernard Patrick and Marjorie Yvonne Brindley; *m* 1969, Elaine Gillian Hill (*d* 1998); two *d. Educ:* Wolverhampton Grammar Tech. Sch.; Univ. of Essex. FCIH 1981. Various local govt housing positions, 1969–81; Dir of Housing, Hull CC, 1981–91. *Recreation:* music. *Address:* The Old Farmhouse, 47 Main Street, Brandesburton, Driffield, E Yorks YO25 8RL.

BRINK, Prof. André Philippus, DLitt; Professor of English, University of Cape Town, since 1991; *b* 29 May 1935; *s* of Daniel Brink and Aletta Wilhelmina Wolmarans; *m*; three *s* one *d. Educ:* Potchefstroom Univ. (MA Eng. Lit. 1958, MA Afr. Lit. 1959); Rhodes Univ. (DLitt 1975). Rhodes University: Lectr, 1961; Sen. Lectr, 1975; Associate Prof., 1977; Prof. of Afrikaans and Dutch Literature, 1980–90. Hon. DLitt Witwatersrand, 1985. Prix Médicis étranger, 1981; Martin Luther King Meml Prize, 1981. Chevalier de la Légion d'honneur, 1982; Commandeur, l'Ordre des Arts et des Lettres, 1992. *Publications:* in Afrikaans: Die meul teen die hang, 1958; over 40 titles (novels, plays, travel books, literary criticism, humour); in English: Looking on Darkness, 1974; An Instant in the Wind, 1976; Rumours of Rain, 1978; A Dry White Season, 1979; A Chain of Voices, 1982; Mapmakers (essays), 1983; The Wall of the Plague, 1984; The Ambassador, 1985; (ed with J. M. Coetzee) A Land Apart, 1986; States of Emergency, 1988; An Act of Terror, 1991; The First Life of Adamastor, 1993; On the Contrary, 1993; Imaginings of Sand, 1996; Reinventing a Continent (essays), 1996; Devil's Valley, 1998; The Rights of Desire, 2000. *Address:* Department of English, University of Cape Town, Rondebosch, 7701, South Africa.

BRINK, Prof. David Maurice, DPhil; FRS 1981; Professor of History of Physics, University of Trento, Italy, 1993–98; *b* 20 July 1930; *s* of Maurice Ossian Brink and Victoria May Finlayson; *m* 1958, Verena Wehrli; one *s* two *d. Educ:* Friends' Sch., Hobart; Univ. of Tasmania (BSc); Univ. of Oxford (DPhil). Rhodes Scholar, 1951–54; Rutherford Scholar, 1954–58; Lectr, 1954–58, Fellow and Tutor, 1958–93, Balliol Coll., Oxford; Univ. Lectr, 1958–89, H. J. G. Moseley Reader in Physics, 1989–93, Oxford Univ., retd. Instructor, MIT, 1956–57. Rutherford Medal and Prize, Inst. of Physics, 1982. *Publications:* Angular Momentum, 1962, 3rd edn 1993; Nuclear Forces, 1965; Semi-classical Methods in Nucleus–Nucleus Scattering, 1985. *Recreations:* birdwatching, mountaineering. *Address:* 34 Minster Road, Oxford OX4 1LY. *T:* (01865) 246127.

BRINKLEY, Robert Edward; HM Diplomatic Service; Head, Foreign and Commonwealth Office/Home Office Joint Entry Clearance Unit, since 2000; *b* 21 Jan. 1954; *s* of Thomas Edward Brinkley and Sheila Doris Brinkley (*née* Gearing); *m* 1982, (Frances) Mary Webster (*née* Edwards); three *s. Educ:* Stonyhurst Coll.; Corpus Christi Coll., Oxford (MA). Entered HM Diplomatic Service, 1977: FCO, 1977–78; Mem., UK Delegn to Comprehensive Test Ban Negotiations, Geneva, 1978; Second Sec., Moscow, 1979–82; First Secretary: FCO, 1982–88; Bonn, 1988–92; FCO, 1992–95; Counsellor and Head, Fundamental Expenditure Rev. Unit, FCO, 1995–96; Political Counsellor, Moscow, 1996–99. *Recreations:* walking, reading, music (violin). *Address:* c/o Foreign and Commonwealth Office, King Charles Street, SW1A 2AH.

BRINLEY JONES, Robert; *see* Jones.

BRINSDEN, Peter Robert, FRCOG; Consultant and Medical Director, Bourn Hall Clinic, Cambridge, since 1989; *b* 2 Sept. 1940; *s* of Dudley and Geraldine Brinsden; *m* 1967, Gillian Susan Heather; two *s. Educ:* Rugby Sch.; King's Coll. London; St George's Hosp., London (MB BS 1966). MRCS 1966; LRCP 1966; FRCOG 1989. House officer appts, 1967; Medical Officer, Royal Navy, 1966–82: appointments: HMS Glamorgan, 1967–68; RN Hosps, Haslar, Plymouth, Malta and Gibraltar, 1968–78; civilian hosps, Southampton and Portsmouth, 1972–74; Surgeon Comdr, 1976; Consultant Obstetrician and Gynaecologist, RN Hosps, Portsmouth and Plymouth, 1978–82; retd 1982; Consultant: King Fahd Hosp., Riyadh, 1982–84; Bourn Hall and Wellington Hosp., 1985–89. Affiliated Lectr, Univ. of Cambridge Clinical Sch., Addenbrooke's Hosp., 1992–. Inspector, HFEA, 1997–. Gov., Newton Primary Sch., Cambs, 1998–. *Publications:* (ed) A Textbook of In-Vitro Fertilization and Assisted Reproduction, 1992, 2nd edn 1999; contrib. numerous medical articles and book chapters on infertility and assisted reproduction. *Recreations:* sailing, sub-aqua diving, computing, photography. *Address:* Manor Farm, Yelling, Cambs PE19 6SD. *T:* (01480) 880272; *e-mail:* BrinsdenP@aol.com. *Club:* Royal Society of Medicine.

BRINTON, Helen Rosemary; MP (Lab) Peterborough, since 1997; *b* 23 Dec. 1954; *d* of George Henry Dyche and Phyllis May Dyche (*née* James); *m* (marr. diss.); two *c. Educ:* Spondon Pank Grammar Sch.; Bristol Univ. (BA Hons Eng Lit. 1976; MA Medieval Lit. 1978; PGCE 1979). English Teacher, 1979–97. Examr, English Lit. and Lang., London, Cambridge and Northern Exam. Bds, 1985–97. *Publications:* contrib. to various political jls. *Recreations:* reading novels and political biography, modern films and theatre. *Address:* House of Commons, SW1A 0AA. *T:* (020) 7219 3000.

BRINTON, Timothy Denis; self-employed broadcasting consultant, presentation tutor and communications adviser, retired 1999; *b* 24 Dec. 1929; *s* of late Dr Denis Hubert Brinton; *m* 1st, 1954, Jane-Mari Coningham; one *s* three *d*; 2nd, 1965, Jeanne Frances Wedge; two *d. Educ:* Summer Fields, Oxford; Eton Coll., Windsor; Geneva Univ.; Central Sch. of Speech and Drama. BBC staff, 1951–59; ITN, 1959–62; freelance, 1962–99. Mem., Kent CC, 1974–81. Chm., Dartford Gravesham HA, 1988–90. MP (C): Gravesend, 1979–83; Gravesham, 1983–87. Member: Court, 1979–95, Council, 1995–98, Univ. of London; Med. Sch. Council, St Mary's Hosp., Paddington, 1983–88; Gov., Wye Coll., London Univ., 1989–97. Mem., RTS. *Address:* 4/21 Grimston Gardens, Folkestone, Kent CT20 2PU. *T:* (01303) 226558, *Fax:* (01303) 227019.

BRISBANE, Archbishop of; *no new appointment at time of going to press.*

BRISBANE, Archbishop of, (RC), since 1992; **Most Rev. John Alexius Bathersby,** STD; *b* 26 July 1936; *s* of John Thomas Bathersby and Grace Maud Bathersby (*née* Conquest). *Educ:* Pius XII Seminary, Banyo, Qld, Australia; Gregorian Univ., Rome (STL, STD). Priest, 1961; Asst Priest, Goondiwindi, 1962–68; Spiritual Dir, Banyo Seminary, 1973–86; Bishop of Cairns, 1986–92. *Recreation:* bush walking. *Address:* Wynberg, 790 Brunswick Street, Brisbane, Qld 4005, Australia. *T:* (7) 32243364.

BRISBANE, Assistant Bishops of; *see* Appleby, Rt Rev. R. F.; Noble, Rt Rev. J. A.; Williams, Rt Rev. R. J. C.

BRISBY, John Constant Shannon McBurney; QC 1996; *b* 8 May 1956; *s* of late Michael Douglas James McBurney Brisby and Liliana Daneva-Hadjikaltcheva Drenska; *m* 1985, Claire Alexandra Anne, *d* of Sir Donald Logan, *qv. Educ:* Westminster Sch.; Christ Church, Oxford (Schol.; MA). 2nd Lieut, 5th Royal Inniskilling Dragoon Guards, 1974. Called to the Bar, Lincoln's Inn, 1978 (Mansfield Schol.); in practice as barrister, 1980–. Member, Executive Council: Friends of Bulgaria, 1991–; British-Bulgarian Legal Assoc., 1991–. *Publication:* (contrib.) Butterworth's Company Law Precedents, 4th edn. *Recreations:* hunting, ski-ing, tennis, music, reading, art and architecture. *Address:* 4 Stone Buildings, Lincoln's Inn, WC2A 3XT. *T:* (020) 7242 5524.

BRISCO, Sir Campbell Howard, 9th Bt *cr* 1982, of Crofton Place, Cumberland; livestock farmer and manager; *b* 11 Dec. 1944; *s* of Gilfred Rimington Brisco (*d* 1981) and Constance Freda Brisco (*d* 1980), 2nd *d* of Charles John Polson, Masterton, NZ; *S* cousin, 1995; *m* 1969, Kaye Janette, *d* of Ewan William McFadzien; two *s* one *d. Educ:* Southland Boys' High Sch. *Recreation:* sport. *Heir: s* Kent Rimington Brisco, *b* 24 Sept. 1972. *Address:* 134 Park Street, Winton, Southland, New Zealand. *T:* (3) 2369068.

BRISCOE, Brian Anthony; Chief Executive, Local Government Association, since 1996; *b* 29 July 1945; *s* of Anthony Brown Briscoe and Lily Briscoe; *m* 1969, Sheila Mary Cheyne; three *s. Educ:* Newcastle Royal Grammar Sch.; St Catharine's Coll., Cambridge (MA, DipTP). MRTPI, ARICS. Asst Planner, Derbyshire CC, 1967–71; Section Head, Herefordshire CC, 1971–74; Asst Chief Planner, W Yorks CC, 1974–79; Dep. County Planning Officer, Herts CC, 1979–88; County Planning Officer, Kent CC, 1988–90; Chief Exec., Herts CC, 1990–96. FRSA; CIMgt. *Publications:* contribs to planning and property jls; chapter in English Structure Planning, 1982. *Recreations:* family, golf, Newcastle United FC. *Address:* Local Government Association, Local Government House, Smith Square, SW1P 3HZ.

BRISCOE, Sir John Geoffrey James, 6th Bt *cr* 1910, of Bourn Hall, Bourn, Cambridge; *b* (posthumously) 4 Nov. 1994; *o s* of Sir (John) James Briscoe, 5th Bt and of Felicity Mary (now Mrs Whitley), *e d* of David Melville Watkinson; *S* father, 1994. *Heir: uncle:* Edward Home Briscoe [*b* 27 March 1955; *m* 1st, 1979, Anne Lister (marr. diss. 1989); one *s* one *d*; 2nd, 1994, Sandy Elizabeth King (*née* Lloyd)].

BRISCOE, John Hubert Daly, LVO 1997; Apothecary to HM Household, Windsor, and to HM the Queen Mother's Household at Royal Lodge, 1986–97; Master, Worshipful Society of Apothecaries of London, 2000–01; *b* 19 March 1933; only *s* of Dr Arnold Daly Briscoe and Doris Winifred Briscoe (*née* Nicholson); *m* 1958, Janet Anne Earlam; one *s* four *d. Educ:* St Andrew's Sch., Eastbourne; Winchester Coll.; St John's Coll., Cambridge (MA); St Thomas's Hosp. (MB BChir); DObstRCOG 1959; MRCGP 1968. MO, Overseas CS, Basutoland, 1959–62; Asst in gen. practice, Aldeburgh, 1963–65; Principal in gen. practice, Eton, 1965–97; Medical Officer: Eton Coll., 1965–97; St George's Sch., Windsor Castle, 1976–97. Pres., MOs of Schs Assoc., 1989–91. FRSocMed 1995. Hon. MO, Guards' Polo Club, 1966–83. Hon. Mem., Windsor and Dist Med. Soc., 1999. Hon. Auditor, Eur. Union of Sch. and Univ. Health and Medicine, 1981–89. Lay Steward, St George's Chapel, Windsor Castle, 1999. Hon. Licentiate, Apothecaries' Hall, Dublin, 2001. *Publications:* contrib. papers on influenza vaccination and adolescent medicine. *Recreations:* growing vegetables, pictures. *Address:* Wistaria House, 54/56 Kings Road, Windsor, Berks SL4 2AH. *T:* (01753) 855321.

BRISE, Sir John Archibald R.; *see* Ruggles-Brise.

BRISON, Ven. William Stanley; Team Rector, Pendleton, Manchester, 1994–98; *b* 20 Nov. 1929; *s* of William P. Brison and Marion A. Wilber; *m* 1951, Marguerite Adelia Nettleton; two *s* two *d. Educ:* Alfred Univ., New York (BS Eng); Berkeley Divinity School, New Haven, Conn (STM, MDiv). United States Marine Corps, Captain (Reserve), 1951–53. Engineer, Norton Co., Worcester, Mass, 1953–54. Vicar, then Rector, Christ Church, Bethany, Conn, 1957–69; Archdeacon of New Haven, Conn, 1967–69; Rector, Emmanuel Episcopal Church, Stamford, Conn, 1969–72; Vicar, Christ Church, Davyhulme, Manchester, 1972–81; Rector, All Saints', Newton Heath, Manchester, 1981–85; Area Dean of North Manchester, 1981–85; Archdeacon of Bolton, 1985–92, then Archdeacon Emeritus; CMS Missionary, Nigeria, 1992–94; Lectr, St Francis of Assisi Theol Coll., Zaria, 1992–94. *Recreations:* squash, grandchildren. *Address:* 2 Scott Avenue, Bury, Lancs BL9 9RS.

BRISTER, William Arthur Francis, CB 1984; Deputy Director General of Prison Service, 1982–85; *b* 10 Feb. 1925; *s* of Arthur John Brister and Velda Mirandoli; *m* 1949, Mary Speakman; one *s* one *d* (and one *s* decd). *Educ:* Douai Sch.; Brasenose Coll., Oxford (MA 1949). Asst Governor Cl. II, HM Borstal, Lowdham Grange, 1949–52; Asst Principal, Imperial Trng Sch., Wakefield, 1952–55; Asst Governor II, HM Prison, Parkhurst, 1955–57; Dep. Governor, HM Prison: Camp Hill, 1957–60; Manchester, 1960–62; Governor, HM Borstal: Morton Hall, 1962–67; Dover, 1967–69; Governor II, Prison Dept HQ, 1969–71; Governor, HM Remand Centre, Ashford, 1971–73; Governor I, Prison Dept HQ, 1973–75, Asst Controller, 1975–79; Chief Inspector of the Prison Service, 1979–81; HM Dep. Chief Inspector of Prisons, 1981–82. Mem., Parole Board, 1986–89. Nuffield Travelling Fellow, Canada and Mexico, 1966–67. *Recreations:* shooting, music, Venetian history. *Clubs:* Oxford and Cambridge, English-Speaking Union.

BRISTOL, 8th Marquess of, *cr* 1826; **Frederick William Augustus Hervey;** Baron Hervey of Ickworth, 1703; Earl of Bristol, 1714; Earl Jermyn, 1826; Hereditary High Steward of the Liberty of St Edmund; student at Edinburgh University; *b* 19 Oct. 1979; *s* of 6th Marquess of Bristol and of his 3rd wife, Yvonne Marie, *d* of Anthony Sutton; *S* half-brother, 1999. *Educ:* Eton Coll. *Recreations:* ski-ing, water sports, shooting, stalking, travel.

Heir: kinsman Timothy Hugh Hervey [*b* 5 Feb. 1960; *m* 1992, Susan Mary Peacham; one *s* two *d*]. *Address:* Rosa-Maris, 29 Avenue des Papalins, Fontvieille, Monaco 98000.

BRISTOL, Bishop of, since 1985; **Rt Rev. Barry Rogerson;** *b* 25 July 1936; *s* of Eric and Olive Rogerson; *m* 1961, Olga May Gibson; two *d*. *Educ:* Magnus Grammar School; Leeds Univ. (BA Theology). Midland Bank Ltd, 1952–57; Leeds Univ. and Wells Theol Coll., 1957–62; Curate: St Hilda's, South Shields, 1962–65; St Nicholas', Bishopwearmouth, Sunderland, 1965–67; Lecturer, Lichfield Theological Coll., 1967–71, Vice-Principal, 1971–72; Lectr, Salisbury and Wells Theol Coll., 1972–75; Vicar, St Thomas', Wednesfield, 1975–79; Team Rector, Wednesfield Team Ministry, 1979; Bishop Suffragan of Wolverhampton, 1979–85. Chm., ABM (formerly ACCM), 1987–93; Mem. Central Cttee, WCC, 1991– (Mem., Faith and Order Commn, 1987–98); Pres., CTBI, 1999–2002. Chm., Melanesian Mission, 1979–. Hon. LLD Bristol, 1993. *Recreations:* cinema, stained glass windows. *Address:* Bishop's House, Clifton Hill, Bristol BS8 1BW.

BRISTOL, Dean of; *see* Grimley, Very Rev. R. W.

BRISTOL, Archdeacon of; *see* McClure, Ven. T. E.

BRISTOW, Alan Edgar, OBE 1966; FRAeS; Managing Director, then Chairman, Bristow Helicopters Ltd, 1954–85; *b* 3 Sept. 1923; *m* 1945; one *s* one *d*. *Educ:* Portsmouth Grammar School. Cadet, British India Steam Navigation Co., 1939–43; Pilot, Fleet Air Arm, 1943–46; Test Pilot, Westland Aircraft Ltd, 1946–49; Helicopair, Paris/Indo-China, 1949–51; Man. Dir, Air Whaling Ltd (Antarctic Whaling Expedns), 1951–54; Dir, British United Airways Ltd, 1960–70, Man. Dir 1967–70; Chairman: Briway Transit Systems Ltd, 1987–94; Alanta Ltd, 1996–. Invented water beds for cows and horses, 1995, patented 1997. Cierva Memorial Lectr, RAeS, 1967. FRAeS 1967. Croix de Guerre (France), 1950. *Publications:* papers to RAeS. *Recreations:* flying, shooting, sailing, farming, four-in-hand driving. *Address:* Baynards Park Estate, Cranleigh, Surrey GU6 8EE. *T:* (01483) 277170.

BRISTOW, Hon. Sir Peter (Henry Rowley), Kt 1970; a Judge of the High Court, Queen's Bench Division, 1970–85; *b* 1 June 1913; *s* of Walter Rowley Bristow, FRCS and Florence (*née* White); *m* 1st, 1940, Josephine Noel Leney (*d* 1969); one *s* (one *d* decd); 2nd, 1975, Elsa, *widow* of H. B. Leney. *Educ:* Eton; Trinity College, Cambridge. Pilot, RAFVR, 1935–45; tutor, Empire Central Flying Sch., 1942–43. Called to the Bar, Middle Temple, 1936, Bencher 1961, Treasurer 1977; QC 1964; Mem., Inns of Court Senate, 1966–70 (Hon. Treas., 1967–70); Judge, Court of Appeal, Guernsey, and Court of Appeal, Jersey, 1965–70; Dep. Chm., Hants QS, 1964–71; Judge of the Commercial Court and Employment Appeals Tribunal, 1976–78; Vice-Chm., Parole Bd, 1977–78 (Mem. 1976); Presiding Judge, Western Circuit, 1979–82. *Publication:* Judge for Yourself, 1986. *Recreations:* fishing, gardening. *Address:* The Folly, Membury, Axminster, Devon EX13 7AG.

BRITISH COLUMBIA, Metropolitan of; *see* Kootenay, Archbishop of.

BRITTAIN, Clive Edward; racehorse trainer, since 1972; *b* 15 Dec. 1933; *s* of Edward John Brittain and Priscilla Rosalind (*née* Winzer); *m* 1957, Maureen Helen Robinson. *Educ:* Calne Secondary Mod. Sch. Winning horses trained include: Julio Mariner, St Leger, 1978; Pebbles, 1000 Guineas, 1984; Eclipse, Dubai Champion and Breeders Cup Turf, 1985; Jupiter Island, Japan Cup, Tokyo, 1986; Mystiko, 2000 Guineas, 1991; Terimon, Juddmont Internat., 1991; User Friendly, Oaks, Irish Oaks, Yorkshire Oaks, St Leger, 1992; Sayyedati, 1000 Guineas, and Jacque le Marois, 1993, Sussex Stakes, 1995; Luso, Hong Kong Vase, 1996 and 1997; Crimplene, Irish 1000 Guineas, 2000. *Recreation:* shooting. *Address:* Carlburg, 49 Bury Road, Newmarket, Suffolk CB8 7BY. *T:* (01638) 664347. *Club:* Jockey Club Rooms (Newmarket).

BRITTAN OF SPENNITHORNE, Baron *cr* 2000 (Life Peer), of Spennithorne in the County of North Yorkshire; **Leon Brittan,** Kt 1989; PC 1981; QC 1978; DL; Vice-Chairman, UBS Warburg, since 2000; Member, 1989–99, a Vice-President, 1989–93 and 1995–99, European Commission (formerly Commission of the European Communities); *b* 25 Sept. 1939; *s* of late Dr Joseph Brittan and Mrs Rebecca Brittan; *m* 1980, Diana Peterson (*see* Diana Brittan); two step *d*. *Educ:* Haberdashers' Aske's Sch.; Trinity Coll., Cambridge (MA); Yale Univ. (Henry Fellow). Chm., Cambridge Univ. Conservative Assoc., 1960; Pres., Cambridge Union, 1960; debating tour of USA for Cambridge Union, 1961. Called to Bar, Inner Temple, 1962; Bencher, 1983. Chm., Bow Group, 1964–65; contested (C) North Kensington, 1966 and 1970. MP (C): Cleveland and Whitby, Feb. 1974–1983; Richmond, Yorks, 1983–88. Editor, Crossbow, 1966–68; formerly Mem. Political Cttee, Carlton Club; Vice-Chm. of Governors, Isaac Newton Sch., 1968–71; Mem. European North American Cttee, 1970–78; Vice-Chm., Nat. Assoc. of School Governors and Managers, 1970–78; Vice-Chm., Parly Cons. Party Employment Cttee, 1974–76; opposition front bench spokesman on Devolution, 1976–79, on employment, 1978–79; Minister of State, Home Office, 1979–81; Chief Sec. to the Treasury, 1981–83; Sec. of State for Home Dept, 1983–85; Sec. of State for Trade and Industry, 1985–86. Consultant, Herbert Smith, 2000–; Adv. Dir, Unilever, 2000–. Distinguished Vis. Scholar, Yale Univ., 2000–. Chancellor, Univ. of Teesside, 1993–. Chm., Soc. of Cons. Lawyers, 1986–88. DL N Yorks, 2001. Hon. DCL: Newcastle, 1990; Durham, 1992; Hon. LLD: Hull, 1990; Bath, 1995; Dr *hc* Edinburgh, 1991; Hon. DLitt Bradford, 1992; Hon. DEc Korea, 1997. *Publications:* Defence and Arms Control in a Changing Era, 1988; Hersch Lauterpacht Memorial Lectures, 1990; European Competition Policy, 1992; The Europe We Need, 1994; Globalisation *vs* Sovereignty (Rede Lect., 1997); A Diet of Brussels, 2000; (contrib.) The Conservative Opportunity; pamphlets: Millstones for the Sixties (jtly), Rough Justice, Infancy and the Law, How to Save Your Schools, To spur, not to mould, A New Deal for Health Care, Discussions on Policy, Monetary Union. *Recreations:* opera, art, cricket, walking. *Address:* c/o House of Lords, SW1A 0PW. *Clubs:* Carlton, White's, Pratts, MCC.

See also Sir Samuel Brittan.

BRITTAN OF SPENNITHORNE, Lady; Diana Brittan, CBE 1995; JP; Chairman, Community Fund (formerly National Lottery Charities Board), since 1999; *b* 14 Oct. 1940; *d* of Leslie Howell Clemetson and Elizabeth Agnes Clemetson (*née* Leonard); *m* 1st, 1965, Dr Richard Peterson (marr. diss. 1979); two *d*; 2nd, 1980, Leon Brittan (*see* Baron Brittan of Spennithorne). *Educ:* Westonbirt Sch., Tetbury. Man. Editor, Eibis Internat., London, 1977–88. Deputy Chairman: HFEA, 1990–97; EOC, 1994–96 (Comr, 1989–94); Mem., Lord Chancellor's Adv. Cttee on Legal Educn and Conduct, 1997–99. Chm., Rathbone Community Industry, 1991–; Trustee: Action on Addiction, 1993–98; Runnymede Trust, 1995– (Chm., 1998–99); Open Univ. Foundn, 1996–2000; Multiple Birth Foundn, 1998–; Pres., Townswomen's Guild, 1996–. Mem., Bd of Mgt, British Sch. of Brussels, 1989–99. JP City of London, 1984. Distinguished Associate, Darwin Coll., Cambridge, 1998. *Recreations:* gardening, travel, cinema, cards, walking. *Address:* Lower Garden House, Spennithorne, Leyburn, N Yorks DL8 5PR.

BRITTAN, Sir Samuel, Kt 1993; Principal Economic Commentator, Financial Times, since 1966 (Assistant Editor, 1978–95); *b* 29 Dec. 1933; *s* of late Joseph Brittan, MD, and of Rebecca Brittan (*née* Lipetz). *Educ:* Kilburn Grammar Sch.; Jesus Coll., Cambridge (Hon. Fellow, 1988). 1st Class in Economics, 1955; MA Cantab. Various posts in Financial Times, 1955–61; Economics Editor, Observer, 1961–64; Adviser, DEA, 1965. Fellow, Nuffield Coll., Oxford, 1973–74, Vis. Fellow, 1974–82; Vis. Prof. of Economics, Chicago Law Sch., 1978; Hon. Prof. of Politics, Warwick Univ., 1987–92. Mem., Peacock Cttee on Financing the BBC, 1985–86. Pres., David Hume Soc., 1996–99. Hon. DLitt Heriot-Watt, 1985; DU Essex, 1994. Financial Journalist of the Year Award 1971; George Orwell Prize (for political journalism), 1980; Ludwig Erhard Prize (for economic writing), 1988. Chevalier de la Légion d'Honneur, 1993. *Publications:* The Treasury under the Tories, 1964, rev. edn, Steering the Economy, 1969, 1971; Left or Right: The Bogus Dilemma, 1968; The Price of Economic Freedom, 1970; Capitalism and the Permissive Society, 1973, rev. edn as A Restatement of Economic Liberalism, 1988; Is There an Economic Consensus?, 1973; (with P. Lilley) The Delusion of Incomes Policy, 1977; The Economic Consequences of Democracy, 1977; How to End the Monetarist Controversy, 1981; The Role and Limits of Government, 1983; Capitalism with a Human Face, 1995; Essays: moral, political and economic, 1998; articles in various jls. *Address:* c/o Financial Times, Number One Southwark Bridge, SE1 9HL.

See also Baron Brittan of Spennithorne.

BRITTEN, Alan Edward Marsh; Chairman, English Tourism Council, since 1999; Board Member, British Tourist Authority, since 1997; *b* 26 Feb. 1938; *s* of Robert Harry Marsh Britten and Helen Marjorie (*née* Goldson); *m* 1967, Judith Clare Akerman; two *d*. *Educ:* Radley; Emmanuel Coll., Cambridge (MA English); Williams Coll., Mass (American Studies). Mobil Oil Co.: joined 1961; marketing and planning, UK, USA, Italy; Chief Exec., Mobil Cos in E Africa, 1975–77, Denmark, 1980–81, Portugal, 1982–84, Benelux, 1984–86; Managing Dir, Mobil Oil Co., 1987–89; Manager, Internat. Planning, Mobil Oil Corp., 1989–90; Vice-President: Mobil Europe, 1991–97; Country Management, 1993–97; non-exec. Dir, Mobil Oil Co. Ltd, 1997–. Dir, Europia, 1994–97. Mem., Council for Aldeburgh Foundn, 1989–99; Pres., Friends of Aldeburgh Prodns, 2000–. Member: Council, Royal Warrant Holders' Assoc. (Pres., 1997–98); Adv. Board, Ten Days at Princeton; Council, UEA, 1996–. Trustee, Queen Elizabeth Scholarship Trust, 1997– (Chm., 1999–). *Recreations:* music, travel, gardening, letter writing. *Address:* c/o English Tourism Council, Black's Road, W6 9EL. *T:* (020) 8846 9000. *Clubs:* Garrick, Noblemen & Gentlemen's Catch; Aldeburgh Golf.

BRITTENDEN, (Charles) Arthur; Senior Consultant, Bell Pottinger (formerly Lowe Bell) Communications Ltd, since 1988; Director of Corporate Relations, News International, 1981–87; General Manager (Editorial), Times Newspapers, 1982–87; Director, Times Newspapers Ltd, 1982–87; *b* 23 Oct. 1924; *o s* of late Tom Edwin Brittenden and Caroline (*née* Scrivener); *m* 1st, 1953, Sylvia Penelope Cadman (marr. diss. 1960); 2nd, 1966, Ann Patricia Kenny (marr. diss. 1972); 3rd, 1975, Valerie Arnison. *Educ:* Leeds Grammar School. Served in Reconnaissance Corps, 1943–46. Yorkshire Post, 1940–43, 1946–49; News Chronicle, 1949–55; joined Sunday Express, 1955: Foreign Editor, 1959–62; Northern Editor, Daily Express, 1962–63; Dep. Editor, Sunday Express, 1963–64; Exec. Editor, 1964–66, Editor, 1966–71, Daily Mail; Dep. Editor, The Sun, 1972–81. Dir, Harmsworth Publications Ltd, 1967–71; Man. Dir, Wigmore Cassettes, 1971–72. Dir, Dowson-Shurman Associates Ltd, 1990–. Mem., 1982–86, Jt Vice-Chm., 1983–86, Press Council. *Address:* 22 Park Street, Woodstock, Oxon OX20 1SP.

BRITTLE, (Benjamin) Cliff; Chairman, Management Board, Rugby Football Union, 1996–98; *b* 11 Jan. 1942; *s* of Benjamin James Brittle and Amy Brittle; *m* (marr. diss.). *Educ:* Longton High Sch., Stoke-on-Trent. With NCR, 1960–62; started business, 1962, retd 1987. FIMgt. *Recreations:* golf, Rugby. *Address:* The Hollies, Main Road, Baldrine, Isle of Man IM4 6DQ. *T:* (01624) 861011.

BRITTON, Andrew James Christie; Director, National Institute of Economics and Social Research, 1982–95; *b* 1 Dec. 1940; *s* of late Prof. Karl William Britton and Sheila Margaret Christie; *m* 1963, Pamela Anne, *d* of His Honour Edward Sutcliffe, QC; three *d*. *Educ:* Royal Grammar Sch., Newcastle upon Tyne; Oriel Coll., Oxford (BA); LSE (MSc). Joined HM Treasury as Cadet Economist, 1966; Econ. Asst, 1968; Econ. Adviser, 1970; Sen. Econ. Adviser: DHSS, 1973; HM Treasury, 1975; London Business Sch., 1978–79; Under Sec., HM Treasury, 1980–82. Mem., Treasury Panel of Indep. Forecasters, 1993–95. Vis. Prof., Univ. of Bath, 1998–. Licensed Reader, Dio. of Southwark, 1986–. Member: Industry and Econ. Affairs Cttee, Bd for Social Responsibility, Gen. Synod, 1989– (Mem. of Bd, 1992–96); Bd of Finance, Dio. of Southwark, 1998– (Vice Chm., 1999–2000; Chm., 2000–). Exec. Sec., Churches' Enquiry into Unemployment and the Future of Work, 1995–97. *Publications:* (ed) Employment, Output and Inflation, 1983; The Trade Cycle in Britain, 1986; (ed) Policymaking with Macroeconomic Models, 1989; Macroeconomic Policy in Britain 1974–87, 1991; Monetary Regimes of the Twentieth Century, 2001. *Address:* 2 Shabden Park, High Road, Chipstead, Surrey CR5 3SF.

BRITTON, Prof. Celia Margaret, PhD; FBA 2000; Carnegie Professor of French, University of Aberdeen, since 1991; *b* 20 March 1946; *d* of Prof. James Nimmo Britton and Jessie Muriel Britton. *Educ:* New Hall, Cambridge (MA Mod. and Medieval Langs 1969; Postgrad. Dip. Linguistics 1970); Univ. of Essex (PhD Literary Stylistics 1973). Temp. Lectr in French, KCL, 1972–74; Lectr in French Studies, Univ. of Reading, 1974–91. Pres., Soc. for French Studies, 1996–98. *Publications:* Claude Simon: writing the visible, 1987; The Nouveau Roman: fiction, theory and politics, 1992; Edouard Glissant and Postcolonial Theory, 1999; numerous articles on French and Francophone literature and film. *Recreations:* travel, cinema, cookery. *Address:* Department of French, University of Aberdeen, Taylor Building, Aberdeen AB9 2UB. *T:* (01224) 272163.

BRITTON, Prof. Denis King, CBE 1978; Professor of Agricultural Economics at Wye College, University of London, 1970–83, now Emeritus Professor; Hon. Fellow, Wye College, 1986; *b* 25 March 1920; *s* of Rev. George Charles Britton and Harriet Rosa (*née* Swinstead); *m* 1942, Margaret Alice Smith; one *s* two *d*. *Educ:* Caterham School; London School of Economics, London University (BSc (Econ.)). Asst Statistician, Ministry of Agriculture and Fisheries, 1943–47; Lecturing and Research at University of Oxford, Agricultural Economics Res. Inst., 1947–52; MA Oxon 1948 (by decree); Economist, United Nations Food and Agriculture Organisation, Geneva, 1952–59; Gen. Manager, Marketing and Economic Res., Massey-Ferguson (UK) Ltd, 1959–61; Prof. of Agricultural Economics, Univ. of Nottingham, 1961–70; Dean, Faculty of Agriculture and Horticulture, Univ. of Nottingham, 1967–70. Member: EDC for Agriculture, 1966–83; Home Grown Cereals Authority, 1969–87; Adv. Council for Agriculture and Horticulture, 1973–80; Adv. Cttee, Nuffield Centre for Agric. Strategy, 1975–80; MAFF Gp to review Eggs Authority, 1985; Chairman: Council, Centre for European Agricl Studies, Wye Coll., 1974–79; Forestry Commn Rev. Gp on Integration of Farming and Forestry, 1983–84; President: Internat. Assoc. of Agric. Economists, 1976–79; British Agric. Economics Soc., 1977–78; Special Adviser, House of Commons Select Cttee on

Agric., 1980–83. Vis. Prof., Uppsala, 1973; Winegarten Lecture, NFU, 1981. Farmers' Club Cup, 1966. FSS 1943; FRAgS 1970; FRASE 1980. Hon. DAgric, Univ. of Bonn, 1975; Hon. DEcon, Univ. of Padua, 1982. *Publications:* Cereals in the United Kingdom, 1969; (with Berkeley Hill) Size and Efficiency in Farming, 1975; (with H. F. Marks) A Hundred Years of British Food and Farming: a statistical survey, 1989; (ed) Agriculture in Britain: changing pressures and policies, 1990; articles in Jl of Royal Statistical Society, Jl of Agricultural Economics, Jl of RSA, etc. *Recreations:* music, golf. *Address:* 29 Chequers Park, Wye, Ashford, Kent TN25 5BB.

BRITTON, Sir Edward (Louis), Kt 1975; CBE 1967; General Secretary, National Union of Teachers, 1970–75; retired; *b* 4 Dec. 1909; *s* of George Edwin and Ellen Alice Britton; *m* 1936, Nora Arnald; no *c.* *Educ:* Bromley Grammar School, Kent; Trinity College, Cambridge. Teacher in various Surrey schools until 1951; Headmaster, Warlingham County Secondary School, Surrey, 1951–60; General Secretary, Association of Teachers in Technical Institutions, 1960–68. Pres., National Union of Teachers, 1956–57. Sen. Res. Fellow, Educn Div., Sheffield Univ., 1975–79; Mem. of staff, Christ Church Coll., Canterbury, 1979–86. Vice-Pres., NFER, 1979–; Member: TUC General Council, 1970–74; Beloe Cttee on Secondary Schs Exams, 1960; Schools Council, 1964–75; Adv. Cttee for Supply and Trng of Teachers, 1973–75; Burnham Primary and Secondary Cttee, 1956–75 (Jt Sec. and Leader of Teachers' Panel, 1970–75); Burnham Further Educn Cttee, 1959–69 (Jt Sec. and Leader of Teachers' Panel, 1961–69); Officers' Panel, Soulbury Cttee (and Leader), 1970–75; Staff Panel, Jt Negotiating Cttee Youth Leaders (and Leader), 1970–75; Warnock Cttee on Special Educn, 1974–78; Council and Exec., CGLI, 1974–77; Central Arbitration Cttee, 1977–83. Chm., Nat. Centre for Cued Speech for the Deaf, 1986–88. FCP, 1967; Hon. FEIS, 1974. Hon. DEd CNAA, 1969. *Publications:* many articles in educational journals. *Address:* 40 Nightingale Road, Guildford, Surrey GU1 1ER.

BRITTON, John William; independent consultant, since 1993; *b* 13 Dec. 1936; *s* of John Ferguson and Dinah Britton; *m* 1961, Maisie Rubython; one *s* one *d.* *Educ:* Bedlington Grammar Sch.; Bristol Univ. (BScEng 1st Cl. Hons). Royal Aircraft Establishment, Bedford, 1959–83: Hd, Flight Res. Div., 1978–80; Chief Supt and Hd, Flight Systems Bedford Dept, 1981–83; RCDS 1984; Dir, Avionic Equipment and Systems, MoD PE, 1985–86; Science and Technology Assessment Office, Cabinet Office, 1987; Dir Gen. Aircraft 3, MoD PE, 1987–90; Asst Chief Scientific Advr (Projects), MoD, 1990–92, retd. *Recreations:* wine, painting, motor racing (watching), gardening (especially dahlias and fuchsias). *Address:* 6 The Drive, Sharnbrook, Bedford MK44 1HU.

BRITTON, Paul John James, CB 2001; Head, Economic and Domestic Affairs Secretariat, Cabinet Office, since 2001; *b* 17 April 1949; *s* of Leonard Britton and Maureen Britton (*née* Vowles); *m* 1972, Pauline Bruce; one *s* one *d.* *Educ:* Clifton Coll.; Magdalene Coll., Cambridge (BA 1971; MA 1974). Department of the Environment: Admin trainee, 1971–75; Private Sec. to Second Perm. Sec., 1975–77; Principal, 1977; Dept of Transport, 1979–81; DoE, 1981–97: Private Sec. to Minister for Housing and Construction, 1983–84; Asst Sec., 1984; Grade 4, 1991; Dir of Local Govt Finance Policy, 1991–96; Under Sec., 1992; Dir, Envmt Protection Strategy, 1996–97; Dep. Dir, Constitution Secretariat, 1997–98, Dep. Head, Econ. and Domestic Affairs Secretariat, 1998–2001, Cabinet Office; Dir, Town and Country Planning, DTLR, 2001. *Recreations:* architectural history, photography, topography. *Address:* Cabinet Office, 70 Whitehall, SW1A 2AS. *T:* (020) 7270 0140.

BRITZ, Jack; General Secretary, Clearing Bank Union, 1980–83; independent human resources consultant, since 1983; *b* 6 Nov. 1930; *s* of Alfred and Hetty Britz; *m* 1955, Thelma Salaver; one *s* two *d.* *Educ:* Luton Grammar School. Entered electrical contracting industry, 1944; various posts in industry; Director, Rolfe Electrical Ltd, 1964–65. National Recruitment Officer, EETPU, 1969–74; short period with Commission on Industrial Relations as sen. industrial relations officer, 1974; Personnel Manager, Courage Eastern Ltd, 1974–77; Gp Personnel Director, Bowthorpe Group Ltd, 1977–80. HR Interim Mgt, 1989–. Advr, Investors in People, 1998–. NVQ Assessor, mgt and trng, 1992–. *Recreations:* walking, history, wargaming, etc. *Address:* Holmwood, Church Place, Pulborough, W Sussex RH20 1AF.

See also L. Britz.

BRITZ, Lewis; Executive Councillor, Electrical, Electronic, Telecommunication & Plumbing Union, 1983–95; Member, Industrial Tribunals, 1990–2000; *b* 7 Jan. 1933; *s* of Alfred and Hetty Britz; *m* 1960, Hadassah Rosenberg; four *d.* *Educ:* Hackney Downs Grammar Sch.; Acton Technical Coll. (OND Elec. Engrg); Nottingham Univ. (BSc (Hons) Engrg). Head of Research, 1967–71, Nat. Officer, 1971–83, EETPU. Director: LEB, 1977–87; British Internat. Helicopters, 1987–92; Esca Services, 1990–; Chm., JIB Pension Scheme Trustee Co. Ltd, 1997–. Mem., Monopolies and Mergers Commn, 1986–92. Sat in Restrictive Practices Court, 1989. *Recreation:* philately. *Address:* 30 Braemar Gardens, West Wickham, Kent BR4 0JW. *T:* (020) 8777 5986.

See also J. Britz.

BRIXWORTH, Bishop Suffragan of; *no new appointment at time of going to press.*

BROAD, Rev. Hugh Duncan; Vicar of Gloucester St George and St Margaret, Whaddon, since 1997; Member, Crown Appointments Commission, since 1997; *b* 28 Oct. 1937; *s* of Horace Edward Broad and Lucy Broad; *m* 1988, Jacqueline Lissaman; two *d.* *Educ:* Shropshire Inst. of Agriculture; Bernard Gilpin Soc., Durham Univ.; Lichfield Theol Coll.; Hereford Coll. of Education. Curate, Holy Trinity, Hereford, 1967–72; Asst Master, Bishop of Hereford's Bluecoat Sch., 1972–74; Curate, St Peter and St Paul, Fareham, 1974–76; Vicar, All Saints with St Barnabas, Hereford, 1976–90; Rector, Matson, 1990–97. Chaplain: Victoria Eye Hosp., Hereford, 1976–90; Selwyn Sch., Gloucester, 1990–97. Mem., Gen. Synod, C of E, 1995–. *Recreations:* theatre, music, cricket. *Address:* St George's Vicarage, Grange Road, Tuffley, Gloucester GL4 0PE. *T:* (01452) 520851.

BROADBENT, Sir Andrew George, 5th Bt *cr* 1893, of Brook Street, co. London and Longwood, co. Yorkshire; *b* 26 Jan. 1963; *s* of Sqn Ldr Sir George Broadbent, AFC, RAF, 4th Bt and Valerie Anne, *o d* of Cecil Frank Ward; *S* father, 1992. *Educ:* Oakley Hall Prep. Sch., Cirencester; Monkton Combe Sch.; RMA, Sandhurst. Commnd, PWO Regt Yorks, 1984; retd 1994. *Recreations:* music, reading, walking, following sport. *Heir:* *uncle* Robert John Dendy Broadbent, *b* 4 Nov. 1938.

BROADBENT, Christopher Joseph St George B.; *see* Bowers-Broadbent.

BROADBENT, Dr Edward Granville, FRS 1977; FREng, FRAeS, FIMA; Visiting Professor, Imperial College of Science and Technology (Mathematics Department), London University, since 1983; *b* 27 June 1923; *s* of Joseph Charles Fletcher Broadbent and Lucetta (*née* Riley); *m* 1949, Elizabeth Barbara (*née* Puttick). *Educ:* Huddersfield Coll.; St Catharine's Coll., Cambridge (State Scholarship, 1941; Eng Scholar; MA, ScD). FRAeS 1959; FIMA 1965. Joined RAE (Structures Dept), 1943; worked on aero-elasticity (Wakefield Gold Medal, RAeS, 1960); transf. to Aerodynamics Dept, 1960; worked on various aspects of fluid mechanics and acoustics; DCSO (IM), RAE, 1969–83, retired. Gold Medal, RAeS, 1991. *Publication:* The Elementary Theory of Aero-elasticity, 1954. *Recreations:* bridge, chess, music, theatre. *Address:* 11 Three Stiles Road, Farnham, Surrey GU9 7DE. *T:* (01252) 714621.

BROADBENT, James, (Jim); actor, since 1972; *b* Lincoln, 24 May 1949; *s* of late Roy and Dee Broadbent; *m* 1987, Anastasia Lewis; two step *s.* *Educ:* Leighton Park Sch., Reading; Hammersmith Coll. of Art; LAMDA. Joined Nat. Theatre of Brent, 1983, appeared in: The Messiah, 1983; (jt writer) The Complete Guide to Sex, 1984; (jt writer) The Greatest Story Ever Told, 1987; Founder Member, Science Fiction Theatre of Liverpool: Illuminatus!, 1976; The Warp, 1978; *other theatre* includes: Hampstead Theatre: Ecstacy, 1979; Goose Pimples, 1980; Royal Shakespeare Co.: Our Friends in the North, Clay, 1981; National Theatre: The Government Inspector, 1984; A Place with the Pigs, 1988; Royal Court: Kafka's Dick, 1986; The Recruiting Officer, Our Country's Good, 1988; Old Vic: A Flea in Her Ear, 1989; Donmar: Habeas Corpus, 1996; *films* include: The Time Bandits, 1981; Brazil, 1985; The Good Father, 1986; Life is Sweet, Enchanted April, 1991; A Sense of History (also writer), The Crying Game, 1992; Widow's Peak, 1993; Princess Caraboo, Bullets over Broadway, Wide Eyed and Legless, 1994; Richard III, 1995; The Borrowers, 1997; The Avengers, Little Voice, 1998; Topsy-Turvy, 1999 (Best Actor, Venice Film Fest., Evening Standard British Film Awards, London Film Critics' Circle, 2001); Bridget Jones's Diary, Gangs of New York, Moulin Rouge, 2001; *television series* include: Victoria Wood as Seen on TV; Blackadder; Only Fools and Horses; Gone to the Dogs; Gone to Seed; The Peter Principle. *Recreations:* walking, cooking, golf, wood carving, cinema, reading. *Address:* c/o ICM, 76 Oxford Street, W1N 0AX. *T:* (020) 7636 6565. *Club:* Two Brydges.

BROADBENT, (John) Michael; international wine auctioneer and wine writer; non-executive Director, Christie's Fine Art Ltd, since 1998; Director, Christie Manson & Woods, 1967–99; *b* 2 May 1927; *s* of late John Fred Broadbent and Hilary Louise Broadbent; *m* 1954, Daphne Joste; one *s* one *d.* *Educ:* Rishworth Sch., Yorks; Bartlett Sch. of Architecture, UCL (Cert. in Architecture 1952). Commissioned RA, 1945–48 (Nat. Service). Trainee, Laytons Wine Merchants, 1952–53; Saccone & Speed, 1953–55; John Harvey & Sons, Bristol, 1955–66 (Dir, 1963); Head, Wine Dept, Christie's, 1966–92; Chm., Christie's South Kensington, 1978–79. Wine Trade Art Society: Founder Mem., 1955; Chm., 1972–; Institute of Masters of Wine: Mem. Council, 1966–78; Chm., 1971–72; Chm., Central Panel MW Examn Bd, 1982–85. Distillers' Company: Liveryman, 1964–80; Mem. Council, 1981–; Master, 1990–91; International Wine and Food Society: Life Mem.; Mem. Council, 1969–92; Internat. Pres., 1985–92; Gold Medal, 1989; Chm., Wine and Spirit Benevolent Soc., 1991–92. Numerous awards from wine socs and other instns. Chevalier, Ordre National du Mérite, 1979; La Médaille de la Ville de Paris, Echelon Vermeil, 1989; Wine Spectator Annual Lifetime Achievement Award, 1991; Man of the Year, Decanter magazine, 1993. *Publications:* Wine Tasting, 1st edn 1968 (numerous foreign edns); The Great Vintage Wine Book, 1980 (foreign edns); Pocket Guide to Wine Tasting, 1988; The Great Vintage Wine Book II, 1991; Pocket Guide to Wine Vintages, 1992; The Bordeaux Atlas, 1997; contribs to Decanter and other jls. *Recreations:* piano, painting. *Address:* Chippenham Lodge, Old Sodbury, Avon BS17 6RQ; (office) 87/88 Rosebank, SW6 6LJ. *Fax:* (020) 7386 9723. *Clubs:* Brooks's, Saintsbury.

BROADBENT, Miles Anthony Le Messurier; Chairman, The Miles Partnership, since 1996; *b* 1936; *m* 1980, Robin Anne Beveridge; two *s* two *d.* *Educ:* Shrewsbury Sch.; Magdalene Coll., Cambridge Univ. (MA); Harvard Bus. Sch. (MBA). *Recreations:* tennis, golf. *Address:* Bennet House, 54 St James's Street, SW1A 1JT. *T:* (020) 7495 7772. *Clubs:* Boodle's; St George's Hill Tennis; St George's Hill Golf, Burhill Golf, Wisley Golf.

BROADBENT, Rt Rev. Peter Alan; *see* Willesden, Area Bishop of.

BROADBENT, Richard John; Chairman, HM Customs and Excise, since 2000; *b* 22 April 1953; *s* of John Barclay Broadbent and Faith Joan Laurie Broadbent; *m* 1974, Rosalind Scarland; one *s* one *d.* *Educ:* Queen Mary Coll., Univ. of London (BSc); Univ. of Manchester (MA). Admin. Trainee, 1975, Principal, 1979, Private Sec. to Chief Sec., 1984–86, HM Treasury; Harkness Fellow, 1983–84; Schroders plc: Manager, 1986–88, Asst Dir, 1988–89, Dir, 1989–99, J. Henry Schroder & Co. Ltd; Head, European Corporate Finance, 1995–99; Gp Man. Dir, Corporate Finance, and Mem., Gp Exec. Cttee, 1998–99. MSI. *Recreations:* walking, reading, cooking. *Address:* HM Customs and Excise, New King's Beam House, 22 Upper Ground, SE1 9PJ. *T:* (020) 7865 5001. *Club:* Two Brydges.

BROADBENT, Simon Hope; Visiting Fellow, National Institute of Economic and Social Research, since 1994; *b* 4 June 1942; *s* of Edmund Urquhart Broadbent, CBE and late Doris Hope; *m* 1966, Margaret Ann Taylor; two *s* one *d.* *Educ:* University College School; Hatfield College, Durham (BA); Magdalen College, Oxford (BPhil). Malawi Civil Service, 1964; Economic Adviser, FCO, 1971; First Sec., UK Treasury and Supply delegn, Washington, 1974; seconded to Bank of England, 1977; Senior Economic Adviser and Joint Head, Economists Dept, FCO, 1978; Centre for Econ. Policy Res., and Graduate Inst. of Internat. Studies, Geneva, 1984. Hd of Econ. Advrs, later Chief Econ. Advr, FCO, 1984–93. Trustee, Anglo-German Foundn, 1994–. *Recreation:* boating. *Address:* 40 Parliament Hill, NW3 2TN. *T:* (020) 7435 4159, *Fax:* (020) 7435 0752.

BROADBRIDGE, family name of **Baron Broadbridge**.

BROADBRIDGE, 4th Baron *cr* 1945, of Brighton, co. Sussex; **Martin Hugh Broadbridge;** Bt 1937; *b* 29 Nov. 1929; *s* of Hon. Hugh Broadbridge and Marjorie Broadbridge; *S* cousin, 2000; *m* 1st, 1954, Norma Sheffield (marr. diss. 1967); one *s* one *d*; 2nd, 1968, Elizabeth Trotman. *Educ:* St George's Coll., Weybridge; Univ. of Birmingham (BSc 1954). Dist Officer, Northern Nigeria, HMOCS, 1954–63; Dir and Manager, specialist road surface treatments co., 1963–92; consultant, 1992–95. *Recreations:* game fishing, natural history. *Heir:* *s* Hon. Richard John Martin Broadbridge [*b* 20 Jan. 1959; *m* 1980, Jacqueline Roberts; one *s* one *d*]. *Address:* 23A Westfield Road, Barton-on-Humber, North Lincolnshire DN18 5AA. *T:* (01652) 632895.

BROADFOOT, Prof. Patricia Mary, DSc, PhD; Professor of Education, since 1992, and Dean of Social Sciences, since 1999, University of Bristol; *b* 13 July 1949; *d* of late Norman John Cole, VRD, sometime MP and Margaret Grace Cole (*née* Potter); *m* 1971, John Ledingham Broadfoot (marr. diss. 1977); *m* 1980, David Charles Rockey, *yr s* of Prof. Kenneth Rockey; two *s* one *d.* *Educ:* Queen Elizabeth's Girls' Grammar Sch., Barnet; Leeds Univ. (BA 1970); Edinburgh Univ. (MEd 1977); Open Univ. (PhD 1984); PGCE London 1971; DSc Univ. of Bristol 2000. Teacher, Wolmer's Boys' Sch., Jamaica, 1971–73; Researcher, Scottish Council for Res. in Educn, 1973–77; Lectr and Sen. Lectr, Westhill Coll., Birmingham, 1977–81; University of Bristol: Lectr, 1981–90; Reader, 1990–92; Hd, Sch. of Educn, 1993–97. Visiting Scholar: Macquarie Univ., Aust., 1987; Univ. of Western Sydney, 1992. Member: ESRC Res. Grants Bd, 1998–99; Conseil

Scientifique de l'Institut Nat. de Recherche Pedagogique, 1998–99. President: British Educnl Res. Assoc., 1987–88; British Assoc. for Internat. and Comparative Educn, 1997–98. Mem. Coll. of Fellows, Internat. Bureau of Educn, Geneva, 1999–. Founding AcSS, 1999 (Mem., Commn on Social Scis). Editor: Comparative Education, 1993–; Assessment in Education, 1994–. *Publications:* Assessment, Schools and Society, 1979; (with J. D. Nisbet) The Impact of Research on Education, 1981; (with H. D. Black) Keeping Track of Teaching, 1982; (ed) Selection, Certification and Control, 1984; (ed) Profiles and Records of Achievement, 1986; Introducing Profiling, 1987; (with M. Osborn) Perceptions of Teaching, 1993; (jtly) The Changing English Primary School, 1994; Education, Assessment and Society, 1996; (ed jtly) Learning from Comparing, 1999; (jtly) Promoting Quality in Education, 2000; (jtly) Policy, Practice and Teacher Experience, 2000. *Recreations:* gardening, travel, horse-riding. *Address:* Amercombe, Kingswood, Glos GL12 8RS. *T:* (01453) 844436.

BROADHURST, Rt Rev. John Charles; *see* Fulham, Suffragan Bishop of.

BROADLEY, Ian R.; *see* Rank-Broadley.

BROADLEY, John Kenneth Elliott, CMG 1988; HM Diplomatic Service, retired; Ambassador to the Holy See, 1988–91; *b* 10 June 1936; *s* of late Kenneth Broadley and late Rosamund Venn (*née* Elliott); *m* 1961, Jane Alice Rachel (*née* Gee); one *s* two *d*. *Educ:* Winchester Coll.; Balliol Coll., Oxford (Exhibnr, MA). Served Army, 1st RHA, 1954–56. Entered HM Diplomatic Service, 1960; Washington, 1963–65; La Paz, 1965–68; FCO, 1968–73; UK Mission to UN, Geneva, 1973–76; Counsellor, Amman, 1976–79; FCO, 1979–84; Dep. Governor, Gibraltar, 1984–88. Non-Service Mem., Home Office Extended Interview Panel, 1994–. Mem. Assembly, CTBI (formerly CCBI), 1992–; Chm. of Trustees, Overseas Bishopric Fund, 1999–; Trustee, Kainos Community, 1999–. Reader, St Saviour and St Nicholas, Brockenhurst, 1998–. Chm. of Govs, Ballard Sch., 1998–. *Recreations:* golf, tennis. *Address:* The Thatched Cottage, Tile Barn Lane, Brockenhurst, Hants SO42 7UE. *Club:* Royal Automobile.

BROCAS, Viscount; Patrick John Bernard Jellicoe; *b* 29 Aug. 1950; *s* and *heir* of 2nd Earl Jellicoe, *qv*; *m* 1971, separated 1971, marr. diss. 1981; two *s* (*b* 1970, 1977). *Educ:* Eton. Profession, engineer.

BROCK, Jonathan Simon; QC 1997; FCIArb; a Recorder, since 2000; *b* 13 July 1952; *s* of Rev. Preb. Patrick Laurence Brock, MBE and Patricia Addinsell Brock, RIBA; *m* 1st, 1977 (marr. diss. 1988); two *s* one *d*; 2nd, 1989, Lindsey Frances Oliver; two *s*. *Educ:* St Paul's Sch.; Corpus Christi Coll., Cambridge (MA 1975). FCIArb 1989. Called to the Bar, Lincoln's Inn, 1977. An Asst Recorder, 1994–2000. Member: Bar Council, 1992–98 (Chm., Commonwealth Internat. Relns Sub-cttee, 1993–98); Court of Appeal Users' Cttee, 1996–; Bar Standing Rep., UK Inter-Professional Gp, 1993–. Vice-Chm., London Common Law and Commercial Bar Assoc., 1999–. *Publication:* (ed) Woodfall on the Law of Landlord and Tenant. *Recreations:* cricket, football, ski-ing. *Address:* Falcon Chambers, Falcon Court, EC4Y 1AA. *Clubs:* Athenæum, MCC; Snakepit Strollers (Chm.).

BROCK, Katharine, (Kay); Assistant Private Secretary to the Queen, since 1999; *b* 23 May 1953; *d* of George Roland Stewart Sandeman and Helen Stewart Sandeman (*née* McLaren); *m* 1978, George Laurence Brock; two *s*. *Educ:* Sherborne Sch. for Girls; Somerville College, Oxford (BA Hons 1975); London Business Sch. (MBA 1988). MAFF, 1975–85 (Private Sec. to Perm. Sec., 1980–81); consultant in internat. trade, 1985–88; Spicers Consulting Gp, 1988–89; Dir, PDN Ltd, 1990–91; Ext. Relns Directorate, EC, 1992–95; Advr to UK Knowhow Fund and EBRD, 1995–99. *Recreations:* family, music, Italy. *Address:* Buckingham Palace, SW1A 1AA. *Club:* Farmers.

BROCK, Michael George, CBE 1981; Warden of St George's House, Windsor Castle, 1988–93; *b* 9 March 1920; *s* of late Sir Laurence George Brock and Ellen Margery Brock (*née* Williams); *m* 1949, Eleanor Hope Morrison; three *s*. *Educ:* Wellington Coll. (Schol.); Corpus Christi Coll., Oxford (Open Schol.; First Cl. Hons Mod. Hist. 1948; MA 1948). FRHistS 1965; FRSL 1983. War service (Middlesex Regt), 1940–45. Corpus Christi Coll., Oxford: Jun. Res. Fellow, 1948–50; Fellow and Tutor in Modern History and Politics, 1950–66, Fellow Emeritus, 1977; Hon. Fellow, 1982; Oxford University: Jun. Proctor, 1956–57; Univ. Lectr, 1951–70; Mem., Hebdomadal Council, 1965–76, 1978–86; Vice Pres. and Bursar, Wolfson Coll., Oxford, 1967–76; Prof. of Educn and Dir, Sch. of Educn, Exeter Univ., 1977–78; Warden of Nuffield Coll., Oxford, 1978–88; Pro-Vice-Chancellor, Oxford Univ., 1980–88. Church Comr, 1990–93. Hon. Fellow: Wolfson Coll., Oxford, 1977; Nuffield Coll., Oxford, 1988; Hon FSRHE 1986. Hon. DLitt Exeter, 1982. *Publications:* The Great Reform Act, 1973; (ed with Eleanor Brock) H. H. Asquith: Letters to Venetia Stanley, 1982; (ed with M. Curthoys) The History of the University of Oxford, vols vi and vii: Nineteenth-Century Oxford, Part 1, 1997, Part 2, 2000; many articles on historical topics and on higher education. *Address:* 11 Portland Road, Oxford OX2 7EZ. *Clubs:* Athenæum; Oxford Union.

BROCK, Dr Sebastian Paul, FBA 1977; Reader in Syriac Studies, University of Oxford, since 1991; Fellow of Wolfson College, Oxford, since 1974; *b* 24 Feb. 1938; *m* 1966, Helen M. C. (*née* Hughes). *Educ:* Eton College; Trinity Coll., Cambridge (BA 1962, MA 1965); MA and DPhil Oxon 1966. Asst Lectr, 1964–66, Lectr, 1966–67, Dept of Theology, Univ. of Birmingham; Fellow, Selwyn Coll., Cambridge, 1967–72; Lectr, Hebrew and Aramaic, Univ. of Cambridge, 1967–74; Lectr in Aramaic and Syriac, Univ. of Oxford, 1974–90. Corresp. Mem., Syriac Section, Iraqi Acad., 1979. Editor, JSS, 1987–90. Hon. Dr Pontificio Istituto Orientale, Rome, 1992; Hon. DLitt Birmingham, 1998. *Publications:* Pseudepigrapha Veteris Testamenti Graece II; Testamentum Iobi, 1967; The Syriac Version of the Pseudo-Nonnos Mythological Scholia, 1971; (with C. T. Fritsch and S. Jellicoe) A Classified Bibliography of the Septuagint, 1973; The Harp of the Spirit: Poems of St Ephrem, 1975, 2nd edn 1983; The Holy Spirit in Syrian Baptismal Tradition, 1979; Sughyotho Mgabyotho, 1982; Syriac Perspectives on Late Antiquity, 1984; Turgome d'Mor Ya'qub da-Srug, 1984; The Luminous Eye: the spiritual world vision of St Ephrem, 1985, 2nd edn 1992; (with S. A. Harvey) Holy Women of the Syrian Orient, 1987; Vetus Testamentum Syriace III. 1: Liber Isaiae, 1987; The Syriac Fathers on Prayer and the Spiritual Life, 1987; Malpanuto d-abohoto suryoye d-'al ṣluto, 1988; St Ephrem: Hymns on Paradise, 1990; Studies in Syriac Christianity, 1992; Luqoto d-Mimre, 1993; Bride of Light: hymns on Mary from the Syriac churches, 1994; Isaac of Nineveh: the second part, ch. IV–XLI, 1995; Catalogue of Syriac Fragments (New finds) in the Library of the Monastery of St Catherine, Mount Sinai, 1995; The Recensions of the Septuaginta Version of I Samuel, 1996; A Brief Outline of Syriac Literature, 1997; contrib. Jl of Semitic Studies, JTS, Le Muséon, Oriens Christianus, Orientalia Christiana Periodica, Parole de l'Orient, Revue des études arméniennes. *Address:* Wolfson College, Oxford OX2 6UD; Oriental Institute, Pusey Lane, Oxford OX1 2LE.

BROCK, Timothy Hugh C.; *see* Clutton-Brock.

BROCK, Prof. William Ranulf, FBA 1990; Fellow of Selwyn College, Cambridge, since 1947; Professor of Modern History, University of Glasgow, 1967–81, now Emeritus; *b* 16 May 1916; *s* of Stewart Ernst Brock and Katherine Helen (*née* Temple Roberts); *m* 1950, Constance Helen (*née* Brown) (*d* 2000); one *s* one *d*. *Educ:* Christ's Hosp.; Trinity Coll., Cambridge (MA, PhD). Prize Fellow 1940 (in absentia). Military service (Army), 1939–45; Asst Master, Eton Coll., 1946–47. Commonwealth Fund Fellow, Berkeley, Calif, Yale and Johns Hopkins, 1952–53, 1958; Vis. Professor: Michigan Univ., 1968; Washington Univ., 1970; Maryland Univ., 1980; Charles Warren Fellow, Harvard Univ., 1976; Leverhulme Emeritus Fellow, 1981. Hon. LittD Keele, 1998. *Publications:* Lord Liverpool and Liberal Toryism, 1941; The Character of American History, 1960; An American Crisis, 1963; The Evolution of American Democracy, 1970; Conflict and Transformation 1844–1877, 1973; The Sources of History: the United States 1790–1890, 1975; Parties and Political Conscience, 1979; Scotus Americanus, 1982; Investigation and Responsibility, 1985; Welfare, Democracy and the New Deal, 1988; (with P. H. M. Cooper) Selwyn College: a history, 1994; contrib. New Cambridge Mod. History, Vols VII and XI; articles and reviews in History, Jl Amer. Studies, Jl Amer. Hist., Amer. Nineteenth Cent. Hist., etc. *Recreation:* antiques. *Address:* 49 Barton Road, Cambridge CB3 9LG. *T:* (01223) 313606.

BROCKBANK, Maj.-Gen. John Myles, (Robin), CBE 1972; MC 1943; Vice Lord-Lieutenant of Wiltshire, 1990–96; *b* 19 Sept. 1921; *s* of Col J. G. Brockbank, CBE, DSO, and Eireine Marguerite Robinson; *m* 1953, Gillian Findlay, *yr d* of Sir Edmund Findlay, 2nd Bt of Aberlour; three *s* one *d*. *Educ:* Eton Coll.; Oxford Univ. Commissioned into 12 Royal Lancers, 1941. Served War, North Africa, Italy, 1941–45. Served Germany: 1955–58, 1964–68 and 1970–72; Cyprus, 1959; USA, 1961–64; Staff Coll., 1950; IDC 1969; CO, 9/12 Royal Lancers; Comdr, RAC, HQ 1 Corps; Chief of Staff, 1 Corps; Dir, RAC, 1972–74; Vice-Adjutant General, MoD, 1974–76, retd. Col, 9/12 Lancers, 1982–85. Dir, British Field Sports Soc., 1976–84. Chm., Wilts Trust for Nature Conservation, 1984–90. DL Wilts 1982. *Recreations:* field sports, gardening, bird watching. *Address:* Manor House, Steeple Langford, Salisbury, Wilts SP3 4NQ. *T:* (01722) 790353.

BROCKES, Prof. Jeremy Patrick, PhD; FRS 1994; MRC Research Professor, Department of Biochemistry and Molecular Biology, University College London, since 1997; Member, Ludwig Institute for Cancer Research, since 1991; *b* 29 Feb. 1948; *s* of Bernard A. Brockes and Edna (*née* Heaney). *Educ:* Winchester Coll.; St John's Coll., Cambridge (BA 1969); Edinburgh Univ. (PhD 1972). Muscular Dystrophy Assoc. of America Postdoctoral Fellow, Dept of Neurobiology, Harvard Med. Sch., 1972–75; Research Fellow, MRC Neuroimmunology Project, UCL, 1975–78; Asst, then Associate, Prof., Div. of Biology, CIT, 1978–83; Staff Mem., MRC Biophysics Unit, KCL, 1983–88; scientific staff, Ludwig Inst. for Cancer Res., UCL/Middlesex Hosp. Br., 1988–97; Prof. of Cell Biology, UCL, 1991–97. Mem. Scientific Adv. Bd, Cambridge Neuroscience Inc., 1987–2000. Brooks Lectr, Harvard Med. Sch., 1997. MAE 1989. Scientific Medal: Zool Soc. of London, 1986; Biol Council, 1990. *Publications:* Neuroimmunology, 1982; papers in scientific jls. *Recreation:* soprano saxophone. *Address:* Department of Biochemistry, University College London, Gower Street, WC1E 6BT. *T:* (020) 7504 4483.

BROCKET, 3rd Baron, *cr* 1933; **Charles Ronald George Nall-Cain;** Bt 1921; *b* 12 Feb. 1952; *s* of Hon. Ronald Charles Manus Nall-Cain (*d* 1961), and of Elizabeth Mary (who *m* 2nd, 1964, Colin John Richard Trotter), *d* of R. J. Stallard; *S* grandfather, 1967; *m* 1982, Isabell Maria Lorenzo (marr. diss. 1994), *o d* of Gustavo Lorenzo, New York; two *s* one *d*. *Educ:* Eton. 14/20 Hussars, 1970–75 (Lieut). Pres., Herts Chamber of Commerce and Industry, 1992; Chm., Business Link Hertfordshire, 1994. Chm., Trust for Information and Prevention (drug prevention initiatives), 1993. Chm., British Motor Centenary Trust; Dir, De Havilland Museum Trust; Patron, Guild of Guide Lectrs, 1992. *Heir: s* Hon. Alexander Christopher Charles Nall-Cain, *b* 30 Sept. 1984.

BROCKHOUSE, Dr Bertram Neville, CC 1995 (OC 1982); FRS 1965; Professor of Physics, McMaster University, Canada, 1962–84, now Emeritus; *b* 15 July 1918; *s* of Israel Bertram Brockhouse and Mable Emily Brockhouse (*née* Neville); *m* 1948, Doris Isobel Mary (*née* Miller); four *s* two *d*. *Educ:* University of British Columbia (BA); University of Toronto (PhD). Served War of 1939–45 with Royal Canadian Navy. Lectr, University of Toronto, 1949–50; Research Officer, Atomic Energy of Canada Ltd, 1950–59; Branch Head, Neutron Physics Br., 1960–62. Foreign Member: Royal Swedish Acad. of Sciences, 1984; Amer. Acad. of Arts and Sciences, 1990. Hon. DSc: Waterloo, 1969; McMaster, 1984; Toronto, 1995; UBC, and Dalhousie, 1996. Nobel Prize for Physics (jtly), 1994. *Publications:* some 75 papers in learned journals. *Address:* PO Box 7338, Ancaster, Ontario L9G 3N6, Canada. *T:* (905) 648 6329.

BROCKINGTON, Prof. Colin Fraser; Professor of Social and Preventive Medicine, Manchester University, 1951–64, Emeritus, 1964; *b* 8 Jan. 1903; *s* of late Sir William Brockington; *m* 1933, Dr Joyce Margaret Furze; three *s* one *d*. *Educ:* Oakham Sch.; Gonville and Caius Coll., Cambridge; Guy's Hosp., London. MD, MA, DPH, BChir Cantab, MSc Manchester, MRCS, MRCP; barrister-at-law, Middle Temple. Medical Superintendent, Brighton Infectious Diseases Hosp. and Sanatorium, 1929; Asst County Medical Officer, Worcs CC, 1930–33; general medical practice, Kingsbridge, Devon, 1933–36; Medical Officer of Health, Horsham and Petworth, 1936–38; Dep. County Medical Officer of Health, Warwickshire CC, 1938–42; County Medical Officer of Health: Warwickshire CC, 1942–46; West Riding CC, 1946–51. Member: Central Adv. Council for Educn (Eng.), 1945–56; Central Training Council in Child Care (Home Office), 1947–53; Adv. Council for Welfare of Handicapped (Min. of Health), 1949–54; Nursing Cttee of Central Health Services Council (Min. of Health), 1949–51; Council of Soc. of Med. Officers of Health, 1944–66; Public Health Cttee of County Councils Assoc., 1945–49. Chairman: WHO Expert Cttee on School Health, 1950; Symposium on "Mental Health-Public Health Partnership," 5th Internat. Congress on Mental Health, Toronto, 1954; WHO Research Study Group on Juvenile Epilepsy, 1955; UK Cttee of WHO, 1958–61. Took part as Expert in Technical Discussions on Rural Health at World Health Assembly, 1954; Far Eastern Lecture Tour for British Council, 1956–57; visited India, 1959, 1962, S America 1960, Jordan 1966–67, Spain 1967, Arabia 1968, Turkey 1955, 1969, 1970, 1972, Greece 1970, for WHO. Lecture Tour: S Africa and Middle East, 1964. *Publications:* Principles of Nutrition, 1952; The People's Health, 1955; A Short History of Public Health, 1956, 2nd edn 1966; World Health, 1958, 4th edn (electronic) 1996; The Health of the Community, 1955, 1960, 1965; Public Health in the Nineteenth Century, 1965; The Social Needs of the Over-Eighties, 1966; The Health of the Developing World, 1985; wide range of contribs to learned jls. *Recreations:* bookbinding, travel. *Address:* Werneth, Silverburn, Ballasalla, Isle of Man IM9 2DT. *T:* (01624) 3465.

BROCKLEBANK, Sir Aubrey (Thomas), 6th Bt *cr* 1885; ACA; Chairman, Tardis Transcommunications Plc, 1996–2001; director of companies; *b* 29 Jan. 1952; *s* of Sir John Montague Brocklebank, 5th Bt, TD, and of Pamela Sue, *d* of late William Harold Pierce, OBE; *S* father, 1974; *m* 1st, 1979, Dr Anna-Marie Dunnet (marr. diss. 1989); two *s*; 2nd, 1997, Hazel Catherine, *yr d* of Brian Roden; one *s*. *Educ:* Eton; University Coll., Durham (BSc Psychology). *Recreations:* deep sea tadpole wrestling, shooting, motor racing. *Heir: s*

Aubrey William Thomas Brocklebank, *b* 15 Dec. 1980. *Address:* Hunters Lodge, St Andrews Lane, Titchmarsh, Northants NN14 3DN. *Club:* Brooks's.

BROCKLEBANK-FOWLER, Christopher; certified management consultant; *b* 13 Jan. 1934; 2nd *s* of Sidney Straton Brocklebank Fowler, MA, LLB Cantab; *m* 1st, 1957, Joan Nowland (marr. diss. 1975); two *s*; 2nd, 1975, Mrs Mary Berry (marr. diss. 1986); 3rd, 1996, Mrs Dorothea Rycroft (marr. diss. 2000). *Educ:* Perse Sch., Cambridge; DipAgr Agricl Corresp. Coll., Oxford, 1952. Farm pupil on farms in Suffolk, Cambridgeshire and Norfolk, 1950–55. National service (submarines), Sub-Lt, RNVR, 1952–54. Farm Manager, Kenya, 1955–57; Lever Bros Ltd (Unilever Cos Management Trainee), 1957–59; advertising and marketing consultant, 1959–79; Chm., Overseas Trade and Develt Agency Ltd, 1979–83; Man. Dir, Cambridge Corporate Consultants Ltd, 1985–87. Mem. Bow Group, 1961–81 (Chm., 1968–69; Dir, Bow Publications, 1968–71). Mem. London Conciliation Cttee, 1966–67; Vice-Chm. Information Panel, Nat. Cttee for Commonwealth Immigrants, 1966–67; Mem. Exec. Cttee, Africa Bureau, 1970–74; Chm., SOS Childrens Villages, 1978–84. MP King's Lynn, 1970–74, Norfolk North West, 1974–83 (C, 1970–81, SDP, 1981–83); Chm., Conservative Parly Sub-Cttee on Horticulture, 1972–74; Vice-Chairman: Cons. Parly Cttee on Agriculture, 1974–75; Cons. Parly Foreign and Commonwealth Affairs Cttee, 1979 (Jt Sec., 1974–75, 1976–77); Cons. Parly Trade Cttee, 1979–80; SDP Agriculture Policy Cttee, 1982–83; Chairman: UN Parly Gp, 1979–83 (Jt Sec., 1971–78); Cons. Parly Overseas Develt Sub-Cttee, 1979–81; SDP Third World Policy Cttee, 1981–87; Member: Select Cttee for Overseas Develt, 1973–79; Select Cttee on Foreign Affairs, 1979–81; SDP Nat. Steering Cttee, 1981–82; SDP Nat. Cttee, 1982; SDP Parly spokesman on Agriculture, 1981–82, on Overseas Develt, 1981–83, on Foreign Affairs, 1982–83. Contested: (C) West Ham (North), 1964; (SDP) 1983, (SDP/Alliance) 1987, Norfolk North West; (Lib. Dem.) Norfolk South, 1992. Mem., Labour Party, 1996–. Vice Chm., Centre for World Devel Educn, 1980–83; Governor, Inst. of Develt Studies, 1978–81. Vice Pres., Inst. of Mgt Consultancy, 1999. Fellow, De Montfort Univ., 1992. MCIM; MCAM; FIMgt; FCMC; Hon. Fellow IDS. *Publications:* pamphlets and articles on race relations, African affairs, overseas development. *Recreations:* painting, fishing, shooting, swimming.

BROCKLEHURST, Prof. John Charles, CBE 1988; FRCP, FRCPE, FRCPGlas; Professor of Geriatric Medicine, University of Manchester, 1970–89, now Emeritus; Associate Director, Research Unit, Royal College of Physicians, 1989–98; *b* 31 May 1924; *s* of late Harold John Brocklehurst and Dorothy Brocklehurst; *m* 1956, Susan Engle; two *s* one *d*. *Educ:* Glasgow High Sch.; Ayr Academy; Univ. of Glasgow (MB ChB 1947; MD Hons 1950). Christine Hansen Research Fellow, Glasgow Univ., 1948–49; RAMC (to rank of Major), 1949–51; Medical Registrar, Stobhill Hosp., and Asst Lectr, Dept of Materia Medica and Therapeutics, Glasgow Univ., 1952–53 and 1958–59; MO, Grenfell Mission, Northern Newfoundland and Labrador, 1955–57; Cons. Geriatrician, Bromley Hosp. Gp and Cray Valley and Sevenoaks Hosp. Gp, 1960–69; Cons. in Geriatric and Gen. Med., Guy's Hosp., London, 1969–70. Dir, Univ. of Manchester Unit for Biological Aging Research (formerly Geigy Unit for Res. in Aging), 1974–89. Chm., Age Concern England, 1973–77, Hon. Vice-Pres., 1980–; Governor, Research into Ageing (formerly British Foundn for Age Research), 1980–97; President: Soc. of Chiropodists, 1977–83; British Geriatrics Soc., 1984–86; Trustee, Continence Foundn, 1992–97. Vis. Professor of Geriatric Med. and Chm., Div. of Geriatric Med., Univ. of Saskatchewan, Canada, 1978–79. Hon. MSc Manchester 1974. Bellahouston Gold Medal, Univ. of Glasgow, 1950; Willard Thomson Gold Medal, Amer. Geriatrics Soc., 1978; Sandoz Prize, Internat. Assoc. of Gerontology, 1989; Founder's Medal, British Geriatrics Soc., 1990. *Publications:* Incontinence in Old People, 1951; The Geriatric Day Hospital, 1971; ed and part author, Textbook of Geriatric Medicine and Gerontology, 1973, 5th edn 1998; Geriatric Care in Advanced Societies, 1975; (jtly) Geriatric Medicine for Students, 1976, 3rd edn, 1986; (jtly) Progress in Geriatric Day Care, 1980; (jtly) Colour Atlas of Geriatric Medicine, 1983, 2nd edn 1991; (ed and part author) Urology: the elderly, 1985; Geriatric Pharmacology and Therapeutics, 1985; (jtly) British Geriatric Medicine in the 1980s, 1987. *Recreations:* painting, the mandoline. *Address:* 59 Stanneylands Road, Wilmslow, Cheshire SK9 4EX. *Club:* East India and Devonshire.

BROCKLESBY, Prof. David William, CMG 1991; FRCVS; Professor of Tropical Animal Health and Director of Centre for Tropical Veterinary Medicine, Royal (Dick) School of Veterinary Studies, University of Edinburgh, 1978–90, now Emeritus; *b* 12 Feb. 1929; *s* of late David Layton Brocklesby, AFC, and Katherine Jessie (*née* Mudd); *m* 1957, Jennifer Mary Hubble, MB, BS; one *s* three *d*. *Educ:* Terrington Hall Sch.; Sedbergh Sch.; Royal Vet. Coll., Univ. of London; London Sch. of Hygiene and Tropical Med. MRCVS 1954; FRCVS (by election) 1984; MRCPath 1964, FRCPath 1982; DrMedVet Zürich 1965. Nat. Service, 4th Queen's Own Hussars (RAC), 1947–49. Vet. Res. Officer (Protozoologist), E Afr. Vet. Res. Org., Muguga, Kenya, 1955–66; Hd of Animal Health Res. Dept, Fisons Pest Control, 1966–67; joined ARC Inst. for Res. on Animal Diseases, Compton, as Parasitologist, 1967; Hd of Parasitology Dept, IRAD, 1969–78. Member: Senatus Academicus, Univ. of Edinburgh, 1978–90; Governing Body, Animal Virus Res. Inst., Pirbright, 1979–86; Bd, Edinburgh Centre of Rural Economy, 1981–88; Council, RCVS, 1985–89. Mem. Editorial Board: Research in Veterinary Science, 1970–88; Tropical Animal Health and Production, 1978–90; British Vet. Jl, 1982–90. *Publications:* papers in sci. jls and chapters in review books, mainly on tropical and veterinary protozoa. *Recreations:* formerly squash and golf, now TV and The Times. *Address:* Lynwood, Honeyfield Road, Jedburgh, Borders TD8 6JN. *T:* (01835) 863472.

BROCKMAN, Rev. John St Leger, CB 1988; Permanent Deacon, St Joseph's RC Church, Epsom, since 1988; Assistant Director for Permanent Diaconate, Diocese of Arundel and Brighton, since 1996; *b* 24 March 1928; *s* of late Prof. Ralph St Leger Brockman and Estelle Wilson; *m* 1954, Sheila Elizabeth Jordan; one *s* two *d* (and one *d* decd). *Educ:* Ampleforth; Gonville and Caius Coll., Cambridge. MA, LLB. Called to the Bar, Gray's Inn, 1952. Legal Asst, Min. of National Insurance, 1953; Sen. Legal Asst, Min. of Pensions and National Insurance, 1964; Asst Solicitor, DHSS, 1973; Under Sec. and Principal Asst Solicitor, DHSS, 1978; Solicitor to DHSS, to Registrar General and to OPCS, 1985–89. *Publications:* compiled and edited: The Law relating to Family Allowances and National Insurance, 1961; The Law relating to National Insurance (Industrial Injuries), 1961. *Address:* 304 The Greenway, Epsom, Surrey KT18 7JF. *T:* (01372) 812915.

BRÖDER, Ernst-Günther, DEcon; German economist and financial executive; international consultant; *b* Cologne, 6 Jan. 1927. *Educ:* Univs of Cologne, Mayence, Freiburg and Paris. Corporate staff, Bayer AG Leverkusen, 1956–61; Projects Dept, World Bank, 1961–64; Kreditanstalt für Wiederaufbau, 1964–84: Manager, 1969–75; Mem., Bd of Management, 1975–84; Bd of Management Spokesman, 1980–84; European Investment Bank: a Dir, 1980–84; Pres., and Chm. of Bd of Dirs, 1984–93; Hon. Pres., 1993–; Chm., 1994–96, 1998–99, Mem., 1997–98, 1999, Inspection Panel, World Bank. Member: Special Adv. Gp, Asian Develt Bank, 1981–82; Panel of Conciliators, Internat. Centre for Settlement of Investment Disputes, 1976–. *Address:* 15 Op den Aessen, 6231 Bech, Luxembourg.

BRODIE, Sir Benjamin David Ross, 5th Bt *cr* 1834; *b* 29 May 1925; *s* of Sir Benjamin Collins Brodie, 4th Bt, MC, and Mary Charlotte (*d* 1940), *e d* of R. E. Palmer, Ballyheigue, Co. Kerry; *S* father, 1971; *m*; one *s* one *d*. *Educ:* Eton. Formerly Royal Corps of Signals. *Heir:* *s* Alan Brodie.

BRODIE, Elizabeth, (Mrs S. E. Brodie); *see* Gloster, E.

BRODIE of Lethen, Ewen John; Lord Lieutenant of Nairnshire, since 1999; Director, John Gordon & Son, since 1992; *b* 16 Dec. 1942; *s* of Major David J. Brodie of Lethen, OBE and Diana, *d* of Maj. Gen. Sir John Davidson, KCMG, CB, DSO; *m* 1967, Mariota, *yr d* of Lt-Col Ronald Steuart-Menzies of Culdares; three *d*. *Educ:* Harrow. Lieut, Grenadier Guards, 1961–64; IBM (UK) Ltd, 1965–74; estate mgt, 1975–. DL Nairn, 1980. *Recreation:* countryside sports. *Address:* Lethen House, Nairn IV12 5PR. *T:* (01667) 452079. *Club:* New (Edinburgh).

BRODIE, Huw David; Director, Agriculture Department, National Assembly for Wales, since 1999; *b* 20 July 1958; *s* of John Handel James Brodie and June (*née* Mustow); *m* 1985, Benita Humphries; one *s*. *Educ:* Trinity Coll., Cambridge (MA Hist.). Joined Dept of Employment, 1980; MSC and Trng Agency, 1983–90; Head of Policy Analysis Br., Trng Agency, 1987; TEC Policy Team, 1988; Asst Dir, Trng Agency, Wales, 1990–92; joined Welsh Office, 1992: Trng, Educn and Enterprise Dept, 1992–94; Head of Industrial and Trng Policy Div., Industry and Trng Dept, 1994–97; Agriculture Dept, 1997–99. *Recreations:* history, archaeology, hill walking. *Address:* National Assembly for Wales, Cathays Park, Cardiff CF10 3NQ.

BRODIE OF BRODIE, (Montagu) Ninian (Alexander), DL; JP; Chief of Clan Brodie; landowner since 1953; *b* 12 June 1912; *s* of I. A. M. Brodie of Brodie (*d* 1943) and C. V. M. Brodie of Brodie (*née* Hope) (*d* 1958); *m* 1939, Helena Penelope Mills Budgen (*d* 1972); one *s* one *d*. *Educ:* Eton. Stage, films, TV, 1933–40 and 1945–49. Served Royal Artillery, 1940–45. JP Morayshire, 1958; Hon. Sheriff-Substitute, 1958; DL Nairn, 1970. *Recreations:* shooting, collecting pictures. *Heir:* *s* Alastair Ian Ninian Brodie, Younger of Brodie [*b* 7 Sept. 1943; *m* 1968, Mary Louise Johnson (marr. diss. 1986); two *s* one *d*]. *Address:* Brodie Castle, Forres, Moray IV36 2TE, Scotland. *T:* (01309) 641202.

BRODIE, Philip Hope; QC (Scot.) 1987; *b* 14 July 1950; *s* of Very Rev. Peter Philip Brodie and Constance Lindsay Hope; *m* 1983, Carol Dora McLeish; two *s* one *d*. *Educ:* Dollar Academy; Edinburgh Univ. (LLB Hons); Univ. of Virginia (LLM). Admitted Faculty of Advocates, 1976; called to the Bar, Lincoln's Inn, 1991; Standing Junior Counsel, MoD (Scotland) PE, and HSE, 1983–87; Advocate-Depute, 1997–99. Mem., Mental Welfare Commn for Scotland, 1985–96. Part-time Chairman: Industrial Tribunals, 1987–91; Medical Appeal Tribunals, 1991–96. *Recreations:* fencing, walking, reading. *Address:* 2 Cobden Crescent, Edinburgh EH9 2BG. *T:* (0131) 667 2651.

BRODIE, Robert, CB 1990; Solicitor to the Secretary of State for Scotland, 1987–98; *b* 9 April 1938; *s* of Robert Brodie, MBE and Helen Ford Bayne Grieve; *m* 1970, Jean Margaret McDonald; two *s* two *d*. *Educ:* Morgan Acad., Dundee; St Andrews Univ. (MA 1959, LLB 1962). Admitted Solicitor, 1962. Office of Solicitor to the Sec. of State for Scotland: Legal Asst, 1965; Sen. Legal Asst, 1970; Asst Solicitor, 1975; Dep. Dir, Scottish Courts Admin, 1975–82; Dep. Solicitor to Sec. of State for Scotland, 1984–87. Temporary Sheriff, 1999; part-time Sheriff, 2000–; part-time Chm., Employment Tribunals (Scotland), 2000–. Chm., Scottish Assoc. of CABx, 1999–. *Recreations:* music, hill-walking. *Address:* 8 York Road, Edinburgh EH5 3EH. *T:* (0131) 552 2028.

BRODIE, Stanley Eric; QC 1975; a Recorder of the Crown Court, 1975–89; *b* 2 July 1930; *s* of late Abraham Brodie, MB, BS and Cissie Rachel Brodie; *m* 1956, Gillian Rosemary Joseph; two *d*; *m* 1973, Elizabeth Gloster, *qv*; one *s* one *d*. *Educ:* Bradford Grammar Sch.; Balliol Coll., Oxford (MA). Pres., Oxford Univ. Law Soc., 1952. Called to Bar, Inner Temple, 1954 (Bencher, 1984, Reader, 1999, Treas., 2000); Mem. NE Circuit, 1954; Lectr in Law, Univ. of Southampton, 1954–55. Mem., Bar Council, 1987–89. *Recreations:* opera, boating, winter sports, fishing. *Address:* Skeldon House, Dalrymple, Ayrshire KA6 6ED. *T:* (01292) 560223; 39 Clarendon Street, SW1V 4RE. *T:* (020) 7821 0975. *Clubs:* Athenæum, Flyfishers'.

BRODIE-HALL, Sir Laurence (Charles), Kt 1982; AO 1993; CMG 1976; Director, 1962–82, Consultant, 1975–82, Western Mining Corporation; Chairman, West Australian Foundation for the Museum of Science and Technology; *b* 10 June 1910; *m* 1st, 1940, Dorothy Jolly (decd); three *s* two *d*; 2nd, 1978, Jean Verschuer (AM 2001). *Educ:* Sch. of Mines, Kalgoorlie (Dip. Metallurgy 1947, DipME 1948). Served War, RAE. Geologist, Central Norseman Gold Corp., 1948–49; Tech. Asst to Man. Dir, Western Mining Corp., 1950–51; Gen. Supt, Gt Western Consolidated, 1951–58; Gen. Supt, 1958–68, Exec. Dir, WA, 1967–75, Western Mining Corp.; Chairman: Gold Mines of Kalgoorlie (Aust.) Ltd, 1974–82; Central Norseman Gold Corp. NL, 1974–82; Westintech Innovation Corp. Ltd, 1984–88; Director: Ansett WA (formerly Airlines WA), 1983–93; Coolgardie Gold NL, 1985–93; former Chm. or Dir of many subsidiaries, and Dir, Alcoa of Australia Ltd, 1971–83. Pres., WA Chamber of Mines, 1970–75 (Life Mem.); Past Pres., Australasian Inst. of Mining and Metallurgy (Institute Medal, 1977, Hon. Life Mem., 1987); Chairman: WA State Cttee, CSIRO, 1971–81; Bd of Management, WA Sch. of Mines, to 1991. Hon. DTech, WA Inst. Technology, 1978. *Address:* (office) 2 Cliff Street, West Perth, WA 6005, Australia. *Club:* Weld (Perth).

BRODRICK, family name of **Viscount Midleton.**

BRODRICK, Michael John Lee; His Honour Judge Brodrick; a Circuit Judge, since 1987; Resident Judge, Winchester Combined Court, since 1999; *b* 12 Oct. 1941; *s* of His Honour Norman John Lee Brodrick, QC and late Ruth, *d* of Sir Stanley Unwin, KCMG; *m* 1969, Valerie Lois Stroud; one *s* one *d*. *Educ:* Charterhouse; Merton Coll., Oxford (2nd Jurisp.). Called to the Bar, Lincoln's Inn, 1965, Bencher, 2000; Western Circuit; a Recorder, 1981–87. Judicial Mem., Transport Tribunal, 1986. Member: Senate of Inns of Court and Bar, 1979, served 1979–82; Wine Cttee, Western Circuit, 1982–86; Cttee, Council of Circuit Judges, 1990–. Liaison Judge to SE Hants Magistrates, 1989–93, to IoW Magistrates, 1989–94, to NE and NW Hants Magistrates, 1999–. Mem., Lord Chancellor's Adv. Cttee for the Appointment of Magistrates, for Portsmouth, 1990–93, for SE Hants, 1993–2000. Counsellor to Dean and Chapter, Winchester Cathedral, 1993–. *Recreation:* gardening.

BRODY, William Ralph, PhD, MD; FIEEE; President, Johns Hopkins University, since 1996; *b* 4 Jan. 1944; *m* Wendyce H.; one *s* one *d*. *Educ:* Massachusetts Inst. of Technol. (BS Electrical Engrg 1965; MS 1966); Stanford Univ. Sch. of Medicine (MD 1970); Stanford Univ. (PhD Electrical Engrg 1972). Dip. Amer. Bd Radiol., 1977. Stanford University School of Medicine: Fellow, Dept of Cardiovascular Surgery, 1970–71; Intern, Dept of Surgery, 1971–72; Resident, Dept of Cardiovascular Surgery, 1972–73; Clin. Associate, Nat. Heart, Lung and Blood Inst., Bethesda, Md, 1973–75; Resident, Dept of Radiol., Univ. of Calif, San Francisco, 1975–77; Stanford University School of Medicine: Dir, Res. Labs, Div. of Diagnostic Radiol., 1977–84; Associate Prof. of Radiol., 1977–82;

Dir, Advance Imaging Techniques Lab., 1978–84; Prof. of Radiol., 1982–86 (on leave of absence, 1984–86); Radiologist-in-Chief, Johns Hopkins Hosp., 1987–94; Johns Hopkins University School of Medicine: Martin Donner Prof. and Dir, Dept of Radiol., 1987–94; secondary appt in biomed. engrg and jt appt in electrical and computer engrg, 1987–94; Prof. of Radiol., Univ. of Minn, 1994–96. Founder, Resonex Inc., 1983: Consultant, 1983–84; Pres., 1984–86; Pres. and CEO, 1986–87; Chm., 1987–89. Mem., Inst. of Medicine, NAS. Founding Fellow, Amer. Inst. Med. and Biol Engrg; Fellow: Amer. Coll. Cardiol.; Amer. Coll. Radiol.; Council on Cardiovascular Radiol., Amer. Heart Assoc.; Internat. Soc. Magnetic Resonance in Medicine. *Publications:* (ed) Digital Radiography: proceedings of the Stanford Conference on digital radiography, 1981; Digital Radiography, 1984; (ed with G. S. Johnston) Computer Applications to Assist Radiology, 1992; contrib. numerous book chapters and to conf. proceedings and tech. reports; contrib. numerous articles to jls, incl. Radiol., Jl Thoracic Cardiovascular Surgery, Med. Phys., IEEE Trans Biomed. Engrg, Investigative Radiol., Amer. Jl Radiol. *Address:* Johns Hopkins University, 242 Garland Hall, 3400 North Charles Street, Baltimore, MD 21218, USA.

BROERS, Sir Alec (Nigel), Kt 1998; DL; PhD, ScD; FRS 1986; FREng; FIEE; FInstP; Professor of Electrical Engineering, Cambridge University, 1984–96, now Emeritus; Vice-Chancellor, Cambridge University, since 1996; Fellow, Churchill College, Cambridge, since 1990 (Master, 1990–96); President, Royal Academy of Engineering, since 2001; *b* 17 Sept. 1938; *s* of late Alec William Broers and of Constance Amy (*née* Cox); *m* 1964, Mary Therese Phelan; two *s*. *Educ:* Geelong Grammar School; Melbourne Univ. (BSc Physics 1958, Electronics 1959); Gonville and Caius College, Cambridge (BA Mech Scis 1962; PhD Mech Scis 1966; ScD 1991; Hon. Fellow, 1996). FIEE 1984; FREng (FEng 1985); FInstP 1991. IBM Thomas Watson Research Center: Research Staff Mem., 1965–67; Manager, Electron Beam Technology, 1967–72; Manager, Photon and Electron Optics, 1972–80; IBM Fellow, 1977; IBM East Fishkill Laboratory: Manager, Lithography Systems and Technology Tools, 1981–82; Manager, Semiconductor Lithography and Process Develt, 1982–83; Manager, Advanced Develt, 1983–84; Mem., Corporate Tech. Cttee, IBM Corporate HQ, 1984; Cambridge University: Hd of Electrical Div., 1984–92, and of Dept of Engrg, 1992–96; Fellow, Trinity Coll., 1985–90 (Hon. Fellow, 1999). Non-executive Director: Vodafone Gp, 1998–2000; Vodafone AirTouch Plc, 2000–. Mem., EPSRC, 1994–2000. Mem. Council, Univ. of Melbourne. Mem. Council, Royal Acad. of Engineering, 1993–96. Foreign Associate, Nat. Acad of Engrg, USA, 1994. DL Cambs, 2000. Hon. Fellow, Univ. of Wales, Cardiff, 2001. Hon. FIEE, 1996. Hon. DEng Glasgow, 1996; Hon. DSc Warwick, 1997; Hon. LLD Melbourne, 2000; Hon. DTech Greenwich, 2000; DUniv Anglia Polytech. Univ., 2000. Prize for Industrial Applications of Physics, Amer. Inst. of Physics, 1982; Cledo Brunetti Award, IEEE, 1985. *Publications:* patents and papers on electron microscopy, electron beam lithography, integrated circuit fabrication. *Recreations:* music, small-boat sailing, skiing, tennis. *Address:* The Old Schools, Trinity Lane, Cambridge CB2 1TN.

BROGAN, Prof. (Denis) Hugh (Vercingetorix); R. A. Butler Professor of History, University of Essex, 1992–98, now Research Professor; *b* 20 March 1936; *s* of Prof. Sir Denis Brogan, FBA and late Olwen Brogan (*née* Kendall). *Educ:* St Faith's Sch., Cambridge; Repton Sch.; St John's Coll., Cambridge (BA Hist. 1959; MA 1964). Staff mem., The Economist, 1960–63; Harkness Fellow, 1962–64; Fellow, St John's Coll., Cambridge, 1963–74; Lectr, then Reader, Dept of Hist., Univ. of Essex, 1974–92. *Publications:* Tocqueville, 1973; The Times Reports The American Civil War, 1975; The Life of Arthur Ransome, 1984; The Longman History of the United States of America, 1985, repr. as The Penguin History of the United States of America, 1990; Mowgli's Sons: Kipling and Baden-Powell's Scouts, 1987; (with Anne P. Kerr) Correspondance et Conversations d'Alexis de Tocqueville et Nassau William Senior, 1991; Kennedy, 1996; (ed) Signalling from Mars: the letters of Arthur Ransome, 1997. *Recreation:* collecting English epitaphs. *Address:* Department of History, University of Essex, Colchester, Essex CO4 3SQ. *T:* (01206) 872232. *Club:* Reform.

BROINOWSKI, John Herbert, CMG 1969; FCA; finance and investment consultant; Senior Partner, J. H. Broinowski & Storey, Chartered Accountants, 1944–54; Founder/ Chairman and Managing Director, Consolidated Metal Products Ltd, 1954–70; Chairman, Vielun Poll Hereford Stud, since 1955; *b* 19 May 1911; *s* of late Dr G. H. Broinowski and late Mrs Ethel Broinowski (*née* Hungerford); *m* 1939, Jean Gaerloch Broinowski, *d* of Sir Norman and Lady Kater; one *s* one step *s*. *Educ:* Sydney Church of England Grammar Sch. Served Australian Imperial Forces (Captain), 1940–44, New Guinea. Chief Exec. and Dep. Chm., Schroder Darling and Co. Ltd, 1963–73; Exec. Chm., Sims Consolidated Ltd, 1970–83; Chairman: Zip Heaters Ltd, 1987–93; Utilux Ltd, 1977–93; Allied Lyons Australia, 1982–92; Director: Electrical Equipment Ltd, 1954–77; Readers Digest Aust., 1955–77; Mount Morgan Ltd, 1962–67 (Chm.); Peko-Wallsend Ltd, 1962–83; South British United Insurance Gp, 1965–73; Hoyts Theatres Ltd, 1968–79 (Chm.); Compunet Ltd, 1969–77 (Chm.); Orient Lloyd Gp, Singapore, 1970–87 (Chm.); Doulton Aust. Ltd, 1972–77; Robe River Ltd, 1972–73; Aquila Steel Co. Ltd, 1973–81 (Chm.); Formfit Ltd, 1974–79 (Chm.); John Sands Ltd, 1974–77; Clive Hall Ltd, 1974–84 (Chm.); Castlemaine Tooheys Ltd, 1977–83 (Dep. Chm.); Hin Kong Ltd, 1977–86 (Chm.); Judson Steel Corp., San Francisco, 1979–83 (Chm.). Chm., Photographic Index of Australian Wildlife, 1980–93. Hon. Life Member: Aust. Council for Rehabilitation of the Disabled (Pres., 1964–68); NSW Soc. for Crippled Children (Pres., 1970–77); Vice-Pres., Internat. Soc. for Rehabilitation of the Disabled, 1966–72. *Publication:* A Family Memoir, 1993. *Address:* 7 South Avenue, Double Bay, Sydney, NSW 2028, Australia. *T:* (2) 93287534. *Clubs:* Australian (Sydney); Royal Sydney Golf.

BROKE; *see* Willoughby de Broke.

BROKE, Col George Robin Straton, LVO 1977; Director, Association of Leading Visitor Attractions, since 1996; Equerry-in-Waiting to the Queen, 1974–77; *b* 31 March 1946; *s* of Maj.-Gen. R. S. Broke, *qv*; *m* 1978, Patricia Thornhill Shann, *d* of Thomas Thornhill Shann; one *s*. *Educ:* Eton. Commissioned into Royal Artillery, 1965; CO 3 RHA, 1987–89. Mem., HM Bodyguard, Hon. Corps of Gentlemen-at-Arms, 1997–. Mem. Bd of Management, King Edward VII's Hosp., London, 1994–96; Member: Exec. Council, BLESMA, 1994–96; Grants Cttee, Army Benevolent Fund, 1994–. Dir, Hedley Foundn, 1998–. Mem. Governing Council, Union Jack Club, 1994–96. *Recreation:* country pursuits. *Address:* St Mary's Lodge, Bircham, King's Lynn, Norfolk PE31 6QR. *T:* (01485) 578402. *Clubs:* Cavalry and Guards, Queen's.

BROKE, Maj.-Gen. Robert Straton, CB 1967; OBE 1946; MC 1940; *b* 15 March 1913; *s* of Rev. Horatio George Broke and Mary Campbell Broke (*née* Adlington); *m* 1939, Ernine Susan Margaret Bonsey (*d* 1997); two *s*. *Educ:* Eton College (KS); Magdalene College, Cambridge (BA). Commissioned Royal Artillery, 1933. Served War of 1939–45: France, 1940; Abyssinia, 1940–41 (despatches); Syria, 1941 (despatches); N Africa, 1942–43. Commander Royal Artillery: 5th Division, 1959; 1st Division, 1960; 1st (British) Corps 1961; Northern Army Group, 1964–66, retired. Col Comdt, RA, 1968–78; Representative Col Comdt, 1974–75. Dir, Wellman Engrg Corp., later Wellman plc, and Chm. of six cos within the Group, 1968–88. Chm., Iron and Steel Plant Contractors Assoc., 1972, 1977. Pres., Metallurgical Plantmakers' Fedn, 1977–79. Treas., London Appeals, Macmillan Cancer Relief (formerly Cancer Relief Macmillan Fund), 1989–97. *Recreations:* country sports. *Address:* Ivy Farm, Holme Hale, Thetford, Norfolk IP25 7DJ. *T:* (01760) 440225. *Club:* Army and Navy.

See also G. R. S. Broke.

BROME, Vincent; author; *s* of Nathaniel Gregory and Emily Brome. *Educ:* Streatham Grammar School; Elleston School; privately. Formerly: Feature Writer; Editor, Menu Magazines; Min. of Information; Asst Editor, Medical World. Since then author biographies, novels, plays and essays; broadcaster. Mem., British Library Adv. Cttee, 1975–82. *Plays:* The Sleepless One (prod. Edin), 1962; BBC plays. *Publications:* Anthology, 1936; Clement Attlee, 1947; H. G. Wells, 1951; Aneurin Bevan, 1953; The Last Surrender, 1954; The Way Back, 1956; Six Studies in Quarrelling, 1958; Sometimes at Night, 1959; Frank Harris, 1959; Acquaintance With Grief, 1961; We Have Come a Long Way, 1962; The Problem of Progress, 1963; Love in Our Time, 1964; Four Realist Novelists, 1964; The International Brigades, 1965; The World of Luke Jympson, 1966; Freud and His Early Circle, 1967; The Surgeon, 1967; Diary of A Revolution, 1968; The Revolution, 1969; The Imaginary Crime, 1969; Confessions of a Writer, 1970; The Brain Operators, 1970; Private Prosecutions, 1971; Reverse Your Verdict, 1971; London Consequences, 1972; The Embassy, 1972; The Day of Destruction, 1975; The Happy Hostage, 1976; Jung—Man and Myth, 1978; Havelock Ellis—philosopher of sex, 1981; Ernest Jones: Freud's alter ego, 1983; The Day of the Fifth Moon, 1984; J. B. Priestley, 1988; The Other Pepys, 1992; Love in the Plague, 2001; Retribution, 2001; contrib. The Times, Sunday Times, Observer, Guardian, New Statesman, New Society, Encounter, Spectator, TLS etc. *Recreations:* writing plays and talking. *Address:* 45 Great Ormond Street, WC1N 3HZ. *T:* (020) 7405 0550. *Club:* Savile.

BROMHEAD, (Sir) John Desmond Gonville, (6th Bt *cr* 1806); *S* father, 1981, but does not use title. *Heir:* *cousin* John Edmund de Gonville Bromhead [*b* 10 Oct. 1939; *m* 1965, Janet Frances, *e d* of Harry Vernon Brotherton, Moreton-in-Marsh, Glos; one *s* one *d*].

BROMLEY, Archdeacon of; *see* Norman, Ven. G.

BROMLEY, Lance Lee, MA; MChir; FRCS; Director of Medical and Health Services, Gibraltar, 1982–85; Honorary Consultant Cardiothoracic Surgeon, St Mary's Hospital, W2; *b* 16 Feb. 1920; *s* of late Lancelot Bromley, MChir, FRCS, of London and Seaford, Sussex, and Dora Ridgway Bromley, Dewsbury, Yorks; *m* 1952, Rosemary Anne Holbrook; three *d*. *Educ:* St Paul's School; Caius Coll., Cambridge. Late Capt. RAMC. Late Travelling Fell. Amer. Assoc. for Thoracic Surgery. Consultant Thoracic Surgeon, St Mary's Hosp., 1953–80; Consultant Gen. Surgeon, Teddington Hosp., 1953–80. *Publications:* various contributions to medical journals. *Recreations:* sailing, golf. *Address:* 26 Molyneux Street, W1H 5HW. *T:* (020) 7262 7175. *Club:* Royal Ocean Racing.

See also See also Sir Charles Knowles, Bt.

BROMLEY, Sir Michael (Roger), KBE 1998; Chairman, Air Nuigini; Chairman and Chief Executive Officer, Collins & Leahy Pty Ltd, 1998–2000; *b* 19 July 1948; *s* of Harry and Joan Margaret Bromley; *m* 1st, 1972, Thienne Brands (marr. diss. 1976); one *d*; 2nd, 1982, Peta Lynette Baynes (marr. diss. 1998); one *s* three *d*. *Educ:* Kikori Bush Sch., PNG, by corresp.; Mount Hagen Park Sch., PNG; Southport Sch., Qld, Australia. Collins & Leahy: Merchandise Operator, then Night Security, then truck driver, 1966–73; Man. Dir, 1982–98; Gen. Manager, Bromley & Manton, 1973–82. *Recreations:* polocrosse, flying (pilot), scuba diving, sailing. *Club:* Goroka Polocrosse.

BROMLEY, Prof. Peter Mann; Professor of English Law, University of Manchester, 1985–86 (Professor of Law, 1965–85), now Professor Emeritus; *b* 20 Nov. 1922; *s* of Frank Bromley and Marion Maud (*née* Moy); *m* 1963, Beatrice Mary, *d* of Eric Charles Cassels Hunter and Amy Madeleine (*née* Renold). *Educ:* Ealing Grammar Sch.; The Queen's College, Oxford (MA 1948). Called to the Bar, Middle Temple, 1951. Served War, Royal Artillery, 1942–45. University of Manchester: Asst Lectr 1947–50, Lectr 1950–61, Sen. Lectr 1961–65; Dean, Faculty of Law, 1966–68, 1972–74 and 1981–83; Pro-Vice-Chancellor, 1977–81; Principal, Dalton Hall, 1958–65. Vis. Prof. of Law, Univ. of Buckingham, 1987–88. Chm., Cttee on Professional Legal Educn in NI, 1983–85; Member: Adv. Cttee on Legal Educn, 1972–75; University Grants Cttee, 1978–85 (Chm., Social Studies Sub-cttee, 1979–85); Commonwealth Scholarship Commn, 1986–92. Editor, Butterworths Family Law Service, 1983–96. *Publications:* Family Law, 1957, 9th edn (with N. V. Lowe and G. Douglas), 1998; (contrib.) Parental Custody and Matrimonial Maintenance, 1966; (contrib.) Das Erbrecht von Familienangehörigen, 1971; (contrib.) The Child and the Courts, 1978; (contrib.) Adoption, 1984; (contrib.) Children and the Law, 1990; (contrib.) Droit Sans Frontières, 1991; articles in various legal jls. *Recreations:* walking, theatre, listening to music. *Address:* 7A Hawthorn Avenue, Wilmslow, Cheshire SK9 5BR. *T:* (01625) 526516. *Club:* Oxford and Cambridge.

BROMLEY, Sir Rupert Charles, 10th Bt *cr* 1757; *b* 2 April 1936; *s* of Major Sir Rupert Howe Bromley, MC, 9th Bt, and Dorothy Vera (*d* 1982), *d* of late Sir Walford Selby, KCMG, CB, CVO; *S* father, 1966; *m* 1962, Priscilla Hazel, *d* of late Maj. Howard Bourne, HAC; three *s*. *Educ:* Michaelhouse, Natal; Rhodes Univ.; Christ Church, Oxford. *Recreations:* equestrian. *Heir:* *s* Charles Howard Bromley [*b* 31 July 1963; *m* 1998, Marie, *d* of W. J. Taylor; one *s*]. *Address:* The Old Manse, Glencairn, Simon's Town, 7975, South Africa.

BROMLEY-DAVENPORT, William Arthur; landowner; chartered accountant; Lord-Lieutenant of Cheshire, since 1990; *b* 7 March 1935; *o s* of Lt-Col Sir Walter Bromley-Davenport, TD, DL and Lenette, *d* of Joseph Y. Jeanes, Philadelphia; *m* 1962, Elizabeth Watts, Oldwick, NJ; one *s* one *d*. *Educ:* Eton; Cornell Univ., NY. Mem. ICA, 1966. National Service, 2nd Batt. Grenadier Guards, 1953–54; Hon. Col 3rd (Vol.) Batt. 22nd (Cheshire) Regt, 1985. Owns land in UK and Norway. Mem. Cttee (past Chm.) Cheshire Br., CLA, 1962–. Pres., Cheshire Scout Council, 1990– (Chm., 1981–90). Chm. of Govs, King's Sch., Macclesfield, 1986–. JP 1975, DL 1982, High Sheriff 1983–84, Cheshire. *Address:* Capesthorne Hall, Macclesfield SK11 9JY; Fiva, Aandalsnes, Norway.

BROMWICH, Prof. Michael; CIMA Professor of Accounting and Financial Management, London School of Economics and Political Science, since 1985; *b* 29 Jan. 1941; *s* of William James Bromwich and Margery (*née* Townley); *m* 1972, Christine Margaret Elizabeth Whitehead (OBE 1991). *Educ:* Wentworth High Sch., Southend; London School of Economics (BScEcon 1965); FCMA. Ford Motor Co., 1958–62 and 1965–66; Lectr, LSE, 1966–70; Professor: UWIST, 1971–77; Univ. of Reading, 1977–85. Mem. Council, ICMA, 1980–85; Vice Pres., ICMA, later CIMA, 1985–87, Pres., CIMA, 1987–88. Mem., Accounting Standards Cttee, 1981–84; Additional Mem., Monopolies and Mergers Commn, 1992–; Research Grants Bd, ESRC, 1992–96. Hon. DEcon Lund Univ., Sweden, 1993. *Publications:* Economics of Capital Budgeting, 1976; Economics of Accounting Standard Setting, 1985; (jtly) Management Accounting: evolution not revolution, 1989; (jtly) Housing Association Accounting, 1990; Financial Reporting,

Information and Capital Markets, 1992; Management Accounting: pathways to progress, 1994; Accounting for Overheads: critique and reforms, 1997; co-ed others, incl. Essays in British Accounting Research; many articles. *Recreations:* working and eating in restaurants. *Address:* 14 Thornhill Road, N1 1HW. *T:* (020) 7607 9323.

BRON, Prof. Anthony John, FRCS, FCOphth; Head, Nuffield Laboratory of Ophthalmology, since 1973, and Clinical Professor of Ophthalmology, since 1989, University of Oxford; Fellow of Linacre College, Oxford, since 1975; *b* 3 Feb. 1936; *s* of late Sydney and Fagah Bron; *m* 1st, 1961, Sandra Ruth Shoot (*d* 1976); one *s* one *d* (and one *s* decd); 2nd, 1981, Diana S. Shortt; one step *s* three step *d*. *Educ:* London Univ. (BSc 1957; MB BS 1961); Guy's Hosp. (DO 1964). LRCP 1960; MRCS 1960, FRCS 1968; FCOphth 1989. Guy's Hosp., 1961–63; Clin. Fellow in Ophthalmol., Johns Hopkins Univ., 1964–65; Res. Assistant, Inst. of Ophthalmol., 1965; Moorfields Eye Hospital: Chief Clin. Assistant, 1965; Resident Surg. Officer, 1965–68; Lectr, 1968–70; Sen. Lectr and Hon. Consultant, 1970–73; Margaret Ogilvie's Reader in Ophthalmol., Oxford Univ., 1973–89; Hon. Consultant, Oxford Eye Hosp., 1989–. Pres., Ophthalmic Section, RSM, 1986; Vice Pres., Jt Eur. Res. Meetings in Ophthal. and Vision, 1994–95; Chm., Assoc. for Eye Res., 1993–95. Mem., Soc. of Scholars, Johns Hopkins Univ., 1991. Founder FMedSci 1998. Hon. MA Oxon, 1973. *Publications:* (contrib.) The Inborn Errors of Metabolism, 1974; The Unquiet Eye, 1983, 2nd edn 1987; (jtly) Lens Disorders, 1996; (ed and contrib.) Wolff's Anatomy of the Eye and Orbit, 1997; papers on the cornea, tears and crystalline lens. *Recreations:* drawing, photography, musing on Life. *Address:* Nuffield Laboratory of Ophthalmology, Walton Street, Oxford OX2 6AW. *T:* (01865) 248996. *Club:* Athenæum.
See also E. Bron.

BRON, Eleanor; actress and writer; *d* of late Sydney and Fagah Bron. *Educ:* North London Collegiate Sch., Canons, Edgware; Newnham Coll., Cambridge (BA Hons Mod. Langs). De La Rue Co., 1961. Director: Actors Centre, 1982–93; Soho Theatre Co., since 1993. Appearances include: revue, Establishment Nightclub, Soho, 1962, and New York, 1963; Not so much a Programme, More a Way of Life, BBC TV, 1964; several TV series written with John Fortune, and TV series: Making Faces, written by Michael Frayn, 1976; Pinkerton's Progress, 1983; *TV plays and films include:* Nina, 1978; My Dear Palestrina, 1980; A Month in the Country, 1985; Quartermaine's Terms, 1987; Changing Step, 1989; The Hour of the Lynx, 1990; The Blue Boy, 1994; Vanity Fair, 1998; Gypsy Girl, Randall & Hopkirk (Deceased), 2001. *Stage roles include:* Jennifer Dubedat, The Doctor's Dilemma, 1966; Jean Brodie, The Prime of Miss Jean Brodie, 1967, 1984; title role, Hedda Gabler, 1969; Portia, The Merchant of Venice, 1975; Amanda, Private Lives, 1976; Elena, Uncle Vanya, 1977; Charlotte, The Cherry Orchard, 1978; Margaret, A Family, 1978; On Her Own, 1980; Goody Biddy Bean; The Amusing Spectacle of Cinderella and her Naughty, Naughty Sisters, 1980; Betrayal, 1981; Heartbreak House, 1981; Duet for One, 1982; The Duchess of Malfi, 1985; The Real Inspector Hound, and The Critic (double bill), 1985; Jocasta and Ismene, Oedipus and Oedipus at Colonus, 1987; Infidelities, 1987; The Madwoman of Chaillot, 1988; The Chalk Garden, 1989; The Miser, and The White Devils, 1991; opera, Die Glückliche Hand, Nederlandse Oper, Amsterdam, 1991; Desdemona—if you had only spoken! (one-woman show), 1992; Gertrude, Hamlet, 1993; Agnes, A Delicate Balance, 1996; A Perfect Ganesh, 1996; Doña Rosita: the Spinster, 1997; Be My Baby, 1998; Making Noise Quietly, 1999. *Films include:* Help!; Alfie; Two for the Road; Bedazzled; Women in Love; The National Health; The Day that Christ Died, 1980; Turtle Diary, 1985; Little Dorrit, 1987; The Attic, 1988; Deadly Advice, 1994; Black Beauty, A Little Princess, 1995; The House of Mirth, 2000. Author: song-cycle with John Dankworth, 1973; verses for Saint-Saens' Carnival of the Animals, 1975 (recorded). *Publications:* Is Your Marriage Really Necessary (with John Fortune), 1972; (contrib.) My Cambridge, 1976; (contrib.) More Words, 1977; Life and Other Punctures, 1978; The Pillow Book of Eleanor Bron, 1985; (trans.) Desdemona – if you had only spoken!, by Christine Brückner, 1992; Double Take, 1996. *Address:* c/o Rebecca Blond Associates, 69A King's Road, SW3 4NX.
See also A. J. Bron.

BRONFMAN, Edgar Miles; Executive Vice Chairman, Vivendi Universal, since 2000; *b* 20 June 1929; *s* of late Samuel Bronfman and of Saidye Rosner. *Educ:* Trinity College Sch., Port Hope, Ont., Canada; Williams Coll., Williamstown, Mass, US; McGill Univ., Montreal (BA 1951). Chm., Joseph E. Seagram & Sons, Inc. (Pres., 1957); Pres., 1971, CEO, 1975–94, Chm., 1975–2000, The Seagram Company Ltd; Dir, E. I. duPont de Nemours & Co. Pres., World Jewish Congress, 1980–. Hon. LHD Pace Univ., NY, 1982; Hon. Dr Laws Williams Coll., Williamstown, 1986. *Address:* Vivendi Universal, 375 Park Avenue, New York, NY 10152, USA. *T:* (212) 5727000.

BROOK, Anthony Donald, FCA; Chairman, Ocean Radio Group (formerly Ocean Sound) Ltd, 1994–2000; *b* 24 Sept. 1936; *s* of Donald Charles Brook and Doris Ellen (*née* Emmett); *m* 1965, Ann Mary Reeves (*d* 2000); two *d*. *Educ:* Eastbourne Coll. FCA 1970 (ACA 1960). Joined Associated Television Ltd, 1966; Financial Controller, ATV Network Ltd, 1969; Dir of External Finance, IBA, 1974; Finance Dir/Gen. Man., ITC Entertainment Ltd, 1978; Dep. Man. Dir, Television South plc, 1981; Man. Dir (Television), TVS Entertainment, 1984–89, Man. Dir Broadcasting, 1989–91; Man. Dir, TVS Television Ltd, 1986–89; Dep. Chm. and Man. Dir, TVS Entertainment plc, 1991–93; Chairman: SelecTV, 1993–95; Advanced Media Gp plc, 1994–95; Southern Screen Commn, 1996–99. *Recreations:* sailing, travel, golf. *Address:* 18 Brookvale Road, Highfield, Southampton SO17 1QP. *Clubs:* Royal Southern Yacht (Hamble, Hants); Tamesis (Teddington, Mddx).

BROOK, Prof. Charles Groves Darville, MD; FRCP; Professor of Paediatric Endocrinology, University College London, 1989–2000, now Emeritus; Consultant Paediatrician, Middlesex Hospital, 1974–2000, and Gt Ormond Street Hospital, 1994–2000, now Hon. Consulting Paediatric Endocrinologist; Director, London Centre for Paediatric Endocrinology, 1994–2000; *b* 15 Jan. 1940; *s* of Air Vice-Marshal William Arthur Darville Brook, CB, CBE, and of Marjorie Jean Brook (*née* Grant, now Hamilton); *m* 1963, Hon. Catherine Mary Hawke, *d* of 9th Baron Hawke; two *d*. *Educ:* Rugby Sch.; Magdalene Coll., Cambridge (MA); St Thomas's Hosp. Med. Sch. (MD 1964). FRCP 1979; FRCPCH 1997. Resident posts at St Thomas' and Gt Ormond St Hosps, 1964–74; Res. Fellow, Kinderspital, Zurich, 1972; University College London: Sen. Lectr in Paediatric Endocrinology, 1983–89; Academic Dir of Endocrinology, 1997–2000. Fellow, UCL Hosps, 2000. Andrea Prader Prize, European Soc. for Paediatric Endocrinology, 2000. *Publications:* Practical Paediatric Endocrinology, 1978; Clinical Paediatric Endocrinology, 1981, 4th edn 2001; Essential Endocrinology, 1982, 4th edn 2001; Growth Assessment in Childhood and Adolescence, 1982; All About Adolescence, 1985; Current Concepts in Paediatric Endocrinology, 1987; The Practice of Medicine in Adolescence, 1993; A Guide to the Practice of Paediatric Endocrinology, 1993; Essential Endocrinology, 1996; numerous papers on endocrinology in med. jls. *Recreations:* fishing, walking, gardening, DIY. *Address:* Middlesex Hospital, Mortimer Street, W1T 3AA. *T:* (020) 8521 0553; *e-mail:* c.brook@ucl.ac.uk.
See also Air Vice-Marshal D. C. G. Brook.

BROOK, Air Vice-Marshal David Conway Grant, CB 1990; CBE 1983; Civil Emergencies Adviser, Home Office, 1989–93; *b* 23 Dec. 1935; *s* of late Air Vice-Marshal William Arthur Darville Brook, CB, CBE and of Jean Brook (now Jean Hamilton); *m* 1961, Jessica (*née* Lubbock); one *s* one *d*. *Educ:* Marlborough Coll.; RAF Coll. Pilot, Nos 263, 1 (Fighter) and 14 Sqdns, 1957–62 (Hunter aircraft; fighter combat leader); ADC to AOC-in-C Near East Air Force, 1962–64; CO No 1 (Fighter) Sqdn, 1964–66 (Hunter Mk 9); RN Staff Course, 1967 (psc); RAF Adviser to Dir Land/Air Warfare (MoD Army), 1968–69; Wing Comdr Offensive Support, Jt Warfare Estab., 1970–72; CO No 20 (Army Cooperation) Sqdn, 1974–76 (Harrier); Station Comdr, RAF Wittering, 1976–78 (Harrier); RCDS, 1979 (rcds); Principal Staff Officer to Chief of Defence Staff, 1980–82; SASO, HQ RAF Germany, 1982–85; Air Officer Scotland and NI, 1986–89. *Publications:* contrib. to Brasseys Annual. *Recreations:* golf, music, canal boating, walking. *Club:* Royal Air Force.
See also Prof. C. G. D. Brook.

BROOK, (Gerald) Robert, CBE 1981; Chief Executive, 1977–86, and Chairman, 1985–86, National Bus Company (Deputy Chairman, 1978–85); *b* 19 Dec. 1928; *s* of Charles Pollard Brook and Doris Brook (*née* Senior); *m* 1957, Joan Marjorie Oldfield; two *s* one *d*. *Educ:* King James Grammar Sch., Knaresborough. FCIS, FCIT. Served Duke of Wellington's Regt, 1947–49. Appointments in bus companies, from 1950; Company Secretary: Cumberland Motor Services Ltd, 1960; Thames Valley Traction Co. Ltd, 1963; General Manager: North Western Road Car Co. Ltd, 1968; Midland Red Omnibus Co. Ltd, 1972; Regional Director, National Bus Company, 1974; Chm., Fleetsoftware Ltd, 1998–. Pres., CIT, 1987–88. *Publications:* papers for professional instns and learned socs. *Recreation:* reading military history. *Address:* Pleinmont, 24 Hookstone Drive, Harrogate, N Yorks HG2 8PP. *Club:* Army and Navy.

BROOK, Air Vice-Marshal John Michael, CB 1993; FRCGP; Director General, Royal Air Force Medical Services, 1991–94, retired; *b* 26 May 1934; *s* of late Norman Brook and Nellie Brook (*née* Burns); *m* 1959, Edna Kilburn; one *s* three *d*. *Educ:* Mirfield Grammar Sch.; Leeds Univ. (MB ChB 1957). MRCGP 1972, FRCGP 1992; Dip AvMed RCP 1974; MFOM 1981. Commissioned 1959; served Laarbruch, Stafford, Muharraq, Watton, Linton-on-Ouse, MoD; SMO, RAF Finningley, 1974–76; MoD, 1976; SMO RAF Brize Norton, 1978–81; OC RAF Av. Med. Trng Centre, 1981–83; RAF Exchange Officer, USAF HQ Systems Command, 1983–86; OC Defence Services Med. Rehabilitation Unit, 1986–87; OC Central Med. Estabt, 1987–89; Dep. Principal MO, HQ Strike Comd, 1989–91; Dep. Surgeon Gen., Health Services, 1991–93. QHS 1991–94. OStJ 1980. *Recreations:* all music, travel, walking. *Address:* 2 Vicarage Fields, Hemingford Grey, Cambs PE28 9BY. *Club:* Royal Air Force.

BROOK, Leopold, BScEng, FICE, FIMechE; Director, Renishaw plc, since 1980; *b* 2 Jan. 1912; *s* of Albert and Kate Brook, Hampstead; *m* 1st, 1940, Susan (*d* 1970), *d* of David Rose, Hampstead; two *s*; 2nd, 1974, Mrs Elly Rhodes; two step *s* one step *d*. *Educ:* Central Foundation School, London; University College, London. L. G. Mouchel & Partners, Cons. Engineers, 1935–44; Simon Engineering Ltd, 1944–77 (Chief Exec., 1967–70; Chm., 1970–77); Chairman: Associated Nuclear Services Ltd, 1977–90; Brown & Sharpe Group (UK), 1979–88. Fellow, UCL, 1970–. CIMgt; FRSA 1973. *Recreations:* music, theatre, walking. *Address:* 55 Kingston House North, Prince's Gate, SW7 1LW. *T:* (020) 7584 2041. *Clubs:* Athenæum, Hurlingham.
See also R. E. Rhodes.

BROOK, Peter Stephen Paul, CH 1998; CBE 1965; Producer; Co-Director, The Royal Shakespeare Theatre; *b* 21 March 1925; 2nd *s* of Simon and Ida Brook; *m* 1951, Natasha Parry, stage and film star; one *s* one *d*. *Educ:* Westminster; Greshams; Magdalen College, Oxford (Hon. Fellow, 1991). Productions include: The Tragedy of Dr Faustus, 1942; The Infernal Machine, 1945; Birmingham Repertory Theatre: Man and Superman, King John, The Lady from the Sea, 1945–46; Stratford: Romeo and Juliet, Love's Labour's Lost, 1947; London: Vicious Circle, Men Without Shadows, Respectable Prostitute, The Brothers Karamazov, 1946; Director of Productions, Royal Opera House, Covent Garden, 1947–50: Boris Godunov, La Bohème, 1948; Marriage of Figaro, The Olympians, Salome, 1949. Dark of the Moon, 1949; Ring Round the Moon, 1950; Measure for Measure, Stratford, 1950, Paris, 1978; The Little Hut, 1950; The Winter's Tale, 1951; Venice Preserved, 1953; The Little Hut, New York, Faust, Metropolitan Opera House, 1953; The Dark is Light Enough; Both Ends Meet, 1954; House of Flowers, New York, 1954; The Lark, 1955; Titus Andronicus, Stratford, 1955; Hamlet, London, Moscow, 1955, Paris 2000, London, 2001; The Power and the Glory, 1956; Family Reunion, 1956; The Tempest, Stratford, 1957; Cat on a Hot Tin Roof, Paris, 1957; View from the Bridge, Paris, 1958; Irma la Douce, London, 1958; The Fighting Cock, New York, 1959; Le Balcon, Paris, 1960; The Visit, Royalty, 1960; King Lear, Stratford, Aldwych and Moscow, 1962; The Physicists, Aldwych, 1963; Sergeant Musgrave's Dance, Paris, 1963; The Persecution and Assassination of Marat..., Aldwych, 1964 (New York, 1966); The Investigation, Aldwych, 1965; US, Aldwych, 1966; Oedipus, National Theatre, 1968; A Midsummer Night's Dream, Stratford, 1970, NY, 1971; Timon of Athens, Paris, 1974 (Grand Prix Dominique, 1975; Brigadier Prize, 1975); The Ik, Paris, 1975, London, 1976; Ubu Roi, Paris, 1977; Antony and Cleopatra, Stratford, 1978, Aldwych, 1979; Ubu, Young Vic, 1978; Conference of the Birds, France, Australia, NY, 1980; The Cherry Orchard, Paris, 1981, NY, 1988; La tragédie Carmen, Paris, 1981, NY, 1983 (Emmy Award, and Prix Italia, 1984); The Mahabharata, Avignon and Paris, 1985, Glasgow, 1988, televised, 1989 (Internat. Emmy Award 1990); Woza Albert, Paris, 1988; Carmen, Glasgow, 1989; The Tempest, Glasgow and Paris, 1990; Impressions de Pelléas, Paris, 1992; L'Homme Qui, Paris, 1993, The Man Who, Nat. Theatre, 1994, New York, 1995; Qui Est Là, Paris, 1995; Oh les Beaux Jours, Lausanne, Paris, Moscow, Tbilisi, 1995, London, 1997; Don Giovanni, Aix, 1998; Je Suis un Phenomène, Paris, 1998; Le Costume, Paris, 1999, Young Vic, 2001; The Tragedy of Hamlet, Paris, 2000, Young Vic, 2001; work with Internat. Centre of Theatre Research, Paris, Iran, W Africa, and USA, 1971, Sahara, Niger and Nigeria, 1972–73. *Directed films:* The Beggar's Opera, 1952; Moderato Cantabile, 1960; Lord of the Flies, 1962; The Marat/Sade, 1967; Tell Me Lies, 1968; King Lear, 1969; Meetings with Remarkable Men, 1979; The Tragedy of Carmen, 1983. Hon. DLitt: Birmingham; Strathclyde, 1990; Oxford, 1994. SWET award, for outstanding contribn by UK theatre artist to US theatre season, 1983. Freiherr von Stein Foundn Shakespeare Award, 1973. Commandeur de l'Ordre des Arts et des Lettres; Officer of the Legion of Honour (France), 1995. *Publications:* The Empty Space, 1968; The Shifting Point (autobiog.), 1988; Le Diable c'est l'Ennui, 1991; There Are No Secrets, 1993; Threads of Time: a memoir, 1998; Evoking Shakespeare, 1999. *Recreations:* painting, piano playing and travelling by air. *Address:* c/o CICT, 37 bis Boulevard de la Chapelle, 75010 Paris, France.

BROOK, Prof. Richard John, OBE 1988; ScD; FREng; Director, Leverhulme Trust, since 2001; Professor of Materials Science, since 1995, and Professorial Fellow, St Cross College, since 1991, Oxford University (on leave of absence); *b* 12 March 1938; *s* of Frank Brook and Emily Sarah (*née* Lytle); *m* 1961, Elizabeth Christine Aldred; one *s* one *d*. *Educ:* Univ. of Leeds (BSc Ceramics); MIT (ScD Ceramics). FREng (FEng 1998). Res. Asst,

MIT, 1962–66; Asst Prof. of Materials Science, Univ. of S California, 1966–70; Gp Leader, AERE, 1970–74; Prof. and Head of Dept of Ceramics, Univ. of Leeds, 1974–88; Scientific Mem., Max Planck Soc. and Dir, Max Planck Inst. Metallforschung, Stuttgart, 1988–91; Cookson Prof. of Materials Sci., 1991–95, and Head, Dept of Materials, 1992–94, Oxford Univ.; Chief Exec., EPSRC, 1994–2001. Chairman, Materials Cttee, 1985–88, Materials Commn, 1992–94, SERC; Ext. Mem., Res. Cttee, British Gas, 1989–; Mem., ESTA, 1994–98; Chm., EU Res. Orgns Hds of Res. Councils, 1997–99. Mem., Curatorium Körber Award, 1995–. Pres., British Ceramic Soc., 1984–86; Vice-Pres., Inst. of Materials, 1993–; Fellow, Inst. of Ceramics, 1978 (Pres., 1984–86); Dist. Life Fellow, American Ceramic Soc., 1995; Mem. d'Honneur, Soc. Française Métallurgie Matériaux, 1995–. Mem. Senate, Max Planck Soc., 1999–. Hon. Prof., Univ. of Stuttgart, 1990–. Mellor Meml Lectr, Swansea, 1989; Stuijts Meml Lectr, Maastricht, 1989. Dr *hc* Aveiro, 1995; Hon. DSc: Bradford, 1996; Loughborough, 2000; Brunel, Nottingham Trent, 2001. Editor, Jl of European Ceramic Soc., 1989–. *Publications:* papers in publications of Inst. of Materials, Amer. Ceramic Soc., European Ceramic Soc. *Recreation:* Europe. *Address:* Leverhulme Trust, 1 Pemberton Row, EC4A 3BG.

BROOK, Robert; *see* Brook, G. R.

BROOK, Rowland Stuart; Director of Social Services, Nottinghamshire County Council, since 1995; *b* 17 Nov. 1949; *s* of Geoffrey Brook and Eileen Brook; *m* 1971, Susan Heward; three *s* one *d*. *Educ:* Warwick Univ.; Hull Univ.; Bradford Univ. (MA). Probation Officer, Humberside Probation Service, 1973–77; Humberside County Council: Sen. Social Worker, 1977–81; Area Manager, 1981–84; Principal Officer, Dyfed CC, 1984–87; Asst Dir (Ops), Rotherham MBC, 1987–89; Asst Dir, Bradford MBC, 1989–92; Dep. Dir, Notts CC Social Services Dept, 1992–94. *Recreations:* family, sport, music. *Address:* Plumtree House, Station Road, Plumtree, Notts NG12 5NA.

BROOK-PARTRIDGE, Bernard; Partner, Carsons, Brook-Partridge & Co. (Planning Consultants), since 1972; *b* Croydon, 1927; *o s* of late Leslie Brook-Partridge and late Gladys Vere Burchell (*née* Brooks), Sanderstead; *m* 1st, 1951, Enid Elizabeth Hatfield (marr. diss. 1965); one *d* (and one *d* decd); 2nd, 1967, Carol Devonald, *o d* of late Arnold Devonald Francis Lewis and late Patricia (*née* Thomas), Gower, S Wales; two *s*. *Educ:* Selsdon County Grammar Sch.; Cambridgeshire Tech. Coll.; Cambridge Univ.; London Univ.; Gray's Inn. Military Service, 1945–48. Studies, 1948–50. Cashier/Accountant, Dominion Rubber Co. Ltd, 1950–51; Asst Export Manager, British & General Tube Co. Ltd, 1951–52; Asst Sec., Assoc. of Internat. Accountants, 1952–59; Sec.-Gen., Institute of Linguists, 1959–62; various teaching posts, Federal Republic of Germany, 1962–66; Special Asst to Man. Dir, M. G. Scott Ltd, 1966–68. Business consultancy work on own account, incl. various dirships with several client cos, 1968–72; Chairman: Brompton Troika Ltd, 1985–; Daldorch Estates Ltd, 1995–98; Wilding Properties Ltd, 1995–; Deputy Chairman: World Trade Centre Ltd, 1997–; Central London Masonic Centre Ltd, 2000–; Director: Edmund Nuttall Ltd, 1986–92; Kyle Stewart, 1989–92; Ethical Developments Ltd, 1999–; Paramount Hills Ltd, 2001–. Local Govt and Pol Advisor to Transmanche-Link UK, 1988 and 1989. Contested (C) St Pancras North, LCC, 1958; Mem. (C) St Pancras Metropolitan Borough Council, 1959–62. Prospective Parly Cand. (C), Shoreditch and Finsbury, 1960–62; contested (C) Nottingham Central, 1970. Greater London Council: Mem. for Havering, 1967–73, for Havering (Romford), 1973–85; Chm., 1980–81; Chairman: Planning and Transportation (NE) Area Bd, 1967–71; Town Develt Cttee, 1971–73, Arts Cttee, 1977–78, Public Services and Safety Cttee, 1978–79; Opposition spokesman: for Arts and Recreation, 1973–77; for Police Matters, 1983–85; Member: Exec. Cttee, Greater London Arts Assoc., 1973–78; Council and Exec., Greater London and SE Council for Sport and Recreation, 1977–78; GLC Leaders' Cttee with special responsibility for Law and Order and Police Liaison matters, 1977–79; Dep. Leader, Recreation and Community Services Policy Cttee, 1977–79. Vice-Pres., SPCK, 1993– (Gov. and Trustee, 1976–93); Member: BBC Radio London Adv. Council, 1974–79; Gen. Council, Poetry Soc., 1977–86 (Treas., 1982–84); Board Member: Peterborough Develt Corp., 1972–88 (Chm., Queensgate Management Services); London Festival Ballet (and Trustee), 1977–79; Young Vic Theatre Ltd, 1977–88 (Chm., 1983–87); London Orchestral Concert Bd Ltd, 1977–78; ENO, 1977–78; London Contemp. Dance Trust, 1979–84; Governor and Trustee, Sadler's Wells Foundn, 1977–79; Chairman: London Music Hall Trust, 1983–96; London Symphony Chorus Develt Cttee, 1981–88; Samuel Lewis Housing Trust, 1985–92 (Trustee, 1976–94); Council, Royal Philharmonic Soc., 1991–99 (Chm., 1991–95); Exec. Cttee, Henley Soc., 1994–; Pres., British Sch. of Osteopathy Appeal Fund, 1980–84. President: City of London Rifle League, 1980–; Gtr London Horse Show, 1982–85; Gtr London (County Hall) Br., Royal British Legion, 1988–. An active Freemason, 1973–. FCIS (Mem. Council, 1981–97, Treas., 1984, Vice-Pres. 1985, Pres., 1986); MIMgt. Hon. FIIE. Hon. PhD Columbia Pacific, 1982. Order of Gorkha Dakshina Bahu (2nd cl.), Nepal, 1981. *Publications:* Europe—Power and Responsibility: Direct Elections to the European Parliament (with David Baker), 1972; numerous contribs to learned jls and periodicals on linguistics and translation, the use of language, political science and contemporary politics. *Recreations:* conversation, opera, classical music and being difficult. *Address:* 28 Elizabeth Road, Henley-on-Thames, Oxfordshire RG9 1RG. *T:* (01491) 412080, *Fax:* (01491) 412090; *e-mail:* bernard@brook-partridge.freeserve.co.uk. *Clubs:* Athenæum; Leander (Henley).

BROOKE, family name of **Viscounts Alanbrooke** and **Brookeborough** and **Baron Brooke of Sutton Mandeville**.

BROOKE, Lord; Charles Fulke Chester Greville; *b* 27 July 1982; *s* and *heir* of Earl of Warwick, *qv*.

BROOKE OF ALVERTHORPE, Baron *cr* 1997 (Life Peer), of Alverthorpe in the co. of West Yorkshire; **Clive Brooke;** Joint General Secretary, Public Services Tax and Commerce Union, 1996–98; *b* 21 June 1942; *s* of Mary Brooke (*née* Colbeck) and John Brooke; *m* 1967, Lorna Hopkin Roberts. *Educ:* Thornes House School, Wakefield. Asst Sec., 1964–82, Dep. Gen. Sec., 1982–88, Gen. Sec., 1988–95, Inland Revenue Staff Fedn. Trade Union Congress: Member: Gen. Council, 1989–96; Exec. Cttee, 1993–96. Member: Council of Civil Service Unions, 1982–97 (Chm., Major Policy Cttee, 1996–97); H of C Speaker's Commn on Citizenship, 1988; Exec. Cttee, Involvement and Participation Assoc., 1991–; Council, Inst. for Employment Studies, 1994–; Pensions Compensation Bd, 1996–. Trustee: Duke of Edinburgh Study Conf., 1993– (Mem., Canada Conf., 1980); Community Services Volunteers, 1989–; IPPR, 1997–. Mem., Labour Party. Mem., Churches Enquiry on Employment and Future of Work, 1995–96. Mem., H of L EU Select Cttee, 1999–, and Chm., Sub-Cttee B (Energy, Industry and Transport), 1998–. Jt Patron, Neighbourhood Initiatives Foundn, 1999–. *Recreations:* spiritual and community issues, politics, sailing, walking my cairn terrier. *Address:* House of Lords, SW1A 0PW. *T:* (020) 7219 5353.

BROOKE OF SUTTON MANDEVILLE, Baron *cr* 2001 (Life Peer), of Sutton Mandeville in the County of Wiltshire; **Peter Leonard Brooke,** CH 1992; PC 1988; *b* 3 March 1934; *s* of Lord Brooke of Cumnor, PC, CH and Lady Brooke of Ystradfellte, DBE; *m* 1st, 1964, Joan Margaret Smith (*d* 1985); three *s* (and one *s* decd); 2nd, 1991, Lindsay Allinson. *Educ:* Marlborough; Balliol College, Oxford (MA); Harvard Business School (MBA). Vice-Pres., Nat. Union of Students, 1955–56; Chm., Nat. Conf., Student Christian Movement, 1956; Pres., Oxford Union, 1957; Commonwealth Fund Fellow, 1957–59. Research Assistant, IMEDE, Lausanne, 1960–61; Spencer Stuart & Associates, Management Consultants, 1961–79 (Director of parent company, 1965–79, Chairman 1974–79); lived in NY and Brussels, 1969–73. Dir, Hambros plc, 1997–98. Mem., Camden Borough Council, 1968–69. Chm., St Pancras N Cons. Assoc., 1976–77. Contested (C) Bedwellty, Oct. 1974; MP (C) City of London and Westminster South, Feb. 1977–1997, Cities of London and Westminster, 1997–2001. An Asst Govt Whip, 1979–81; a Lord Comr of HM Treasury, 1981–83; Parly Under Sec. of State, DES, 1983–85; Minister of State, HM Treasury, 1985–87; Paymaster Gen., HM Treasury, 1987–89; Chm., Conservative Party, 1987–89; Secretary of State: for NI, 1989–92; for Nat. Heritage, 1992–94. Chm., H of C Select Cttee on NI, 1997–2001. Mem., British Irish Parly Body, 1997–. Chm., Building Socs Ombudsman Council, 1996–. President: British Antique Dealers Assoc., 1995–; British Art Market Fedn, 1996–; IAPS, 1980–83; Mem. Council, Marlborough Coll., 1977–83, 1992–95; Lay Mem., Univ. of London Council, 1994– (Dep. Chm., 2001–). Chm., Churches Conservation Trust, 1995–98. Trustee: Wordsworth Trust, 1975–2001; Cusichaca Project, 1978–98; Conf. on Trng in Archtl Conservation, 1994–97. FSA 1998. Sen. Fellow, RCA, 1987; Presentation Fellow, KCL, 1989; Hon. Fellow, QMW, 1996. Hon. DLitt Westminster, 1999; Hon. Dr London Guildhall, 2001. *Recreations:* churches, conservation, cricket, visual arts. *Address:* c/o House of Lords, SW1A 0PW. *Clubs:* Beefsteak, Brooks's, City Livery, Coningsby (Pres.), Grillions, MCC, I Zingari, St George's (Hanover Square) Conservative.

See also Rt Hon. Sir H. Brooke.

BROOKE, Sir Alistair Weston, 4th Bt *cr* 1919, of Almondbury; *b* 12 Sept. 1947; *s* of Major Sir John Weston Brooke, 3rd Bt, TD, and Rosemary (*d* 1979), *d* of late Percy Nevill, Birling House, West Malling, Kent; *S* father, 1983; *m* 1982, Susan Mary, *d* of Barry Charles Roger Griffiths, MRCVS, Church House, Norton, Powys; one *d*. *Educ:* Repton; Royal Agricultural Coll., Cirencester. *Recreations:* shooting, farming, racehorse training. *Heir: b* Charles Weston Brooke [*b* 27 Jan. 1951; *m* 1984, Tanya Elizabeth, *d* of Antony Thelwell Maurice; one *s* two *d*]. *Address:* Wootton Farm, Pencombe, Hereford. *T:* (01885) 400615.

BROOKE, Annette Lesley; MP (Lib Dem) Dorset Mid and Poole North, since 2001; *b* 7 June 1947; *m* Mike Brooke; two *d*. *Educ:* Romford Tech. Sch.; LSE (BSc Econ); Hughes Hall, Cambridge (Cert Ed). Teacher of econs and social scis in schs and colls in Reading, Aylesbury and Poole; Hd of Econs, Talbot Heath Sch., Bournemouth, 1984–94; Tutor, Open Univ., 1971–91. Partner, Broadstone Minerals. Mem. (Lib Dem), Poole BC, 1986– (Chairman: Planning Cttee, 1991–96; Educn Cttee, 1996–2000; Mayor, 1997–98; Gp Leader, 2000–). *Address:* (office) Liberal Hall, 14 York Road, Broadstone, Dorset BH18 8ET; c/o House of Commons, SW1A 0AA.

BROOKE, Arthur Caffin, CB 1972; Chairman, Arts Council of Northern Ireland, 1982–86 (Member, 1979–86); *b* 11 March 1919; *s* of late Rev. James M. Wilmot Brooke and Constance Brooke; *m* 1942, Margaret Florence Thompson; two *s*. *Educ:* Abbotsholme Sch.; Peterhouse, Cambridge (MA). Served War, Royal Corps of Signals, 1939–46. Northern Ireland Civil Service, 1946–79; Ministry of Commerce, 1946–73: Asst Sec., Head of Industrial Development Div., 1955; Sen. Asst Sec., Industrial Development, 1963; Second Sec., 1968; Permanent Sec., 1969; Permanent Sec., Dept of Educn, 1973–79. *Address:* 4 Camden Court, Brecon, Powys LD3 7RP. *T:* (01874) 625617.

BROOKE, Prof. Christopher Nugent Lawrence, CBE 1995; MA; LittD; FSA; FRHistS; FBA 1970; Dixie Professor of Ecclesiastical History, University of Cambridge, 1977–94, now Dixie Professor Emeritus; Fellow, Gonville and Caius College, Cambridge, 1949–56 and since 1977 (Life Fellow, 1994); *b* 23 June 1927; *y s* of late Professor Zachary Nugent Brooke and Rosa Grace Brooke; *m* 1951, Rosalind Beckford, *d* of Dr and Mrs L. H. S. Clark; two *s* (and one *s* decd). *Educ:* Winchester College (Scholar); Gonville and Caius College, Cambridge (Major Scholar). BA 1948; MA 1952; LittD 1973. Army service in RAEC, Temp. Captain 1949. Cambridge University: College Lecturer in History, 1953–56; Praelector Rhetoricus, 1955–56; Asst Lectr in History, 1953–54; Lectr, 1954–56; Prof. of Mediæval History, University of Liverpool, 1956–67; Prof. of History, Westfield Coll., Univ. of London, 1967–77. Member: Royal Commn on Historical Monuments (England), 1977–83; Reviewing Cttee on Export of Works of Art, 1979–82. Vice-Pres., Soc. of Antiquaries, 1975–79, Pres., 1981–84. Corresp. Fellow, Medieval Acad. of America, 1981; Corresponding Member: Monumenta Germaniae Historica, 1988; Bavarian Acad. of Scis, 1997. DUniv York, 1984. Lord Mayor's Midsummer Prize, City of London, 1981. *Publications:* The Dullness of the Past, 1957; From Alfred to Henry III, 1961; The Saxon and Norman Kings, 1963; Europe in the Central Middle Ages, 1964, 3rd edn 2000; Time the Archsatirist, 1968; The Twelfth Century Renaissance, 1970; Structure of Medieval Society, 1971; Medieval Church and Society (sel. papers), 1971; (with W. Swaan) The Monastic World, 1974; (with G. Keir) London, 800–1216, 1975; Marriage in Christian History, 1977; (with R. B. Brooke) Popular Religion in the Middle Ages, 1000–1300, 1984; A History of Gonville and Caius College, 1985; The Church and the Welsh Border, 1986; (with J. R. L. Highfield and W. Swaan) Oxford and Cambridge, 1988; The Medieval Idea of Marriage, 1989; (jtly) David Knowles Remembered, 1991; A History of the University of Cambridge, vol. IV, 1870–1990, 1993; Jane Austen: illusion and reality, 1999; (with R. B. Brooke) Churches and Churchmen in Medieval Europe (selected papers), 1999; (jtly) A History of Emmanuel College, Cambridge, 1999; part Editor: The Book of William Morton, 1954; The Letters of John of Salisbury, vol. I, 1955, vol. II, 1979; Carte Nativorum, 1960; (with A. Morey) Gilbert Foliot and his letters, 1965 and (ed jtly) The Letters and Charters of Gilbert Foliot, 1967; (with D. Knowles and V. London) Heads of Religious Houses, England and Wales 940–1216, 1972; (with D. Whitelock and M. Brett) Councils and Synods, vol. I, 1981; (with Sir Roger Mynors) Walter Map, De Nugis Curialium (revision of M. R. James edn), 1983; (with M. Brett and M. Winterbottom) Hugh the Chanter, History of the Church of York (revision of C. Johnson edn), 1990; contributed to: A History of St Paul's Cathedral, 1957; A History of York Minster, 1977; general editor: Oxford (formerly Nelson's) Medieval Texts, 1959–87; Nelson's History of England, etc; articles and reviews in English Historical Review, Cambridge Historical Journal, Studies in Church History, Bulletin of Inst. of Historical Research, Downside Review, Traditio, Bulletin of John Rylands Library, Jl of Soc. of Archivists, etc. *Address:* Gonville and Caius College, Cambridge CB2 1TA.

BROOKE, (Christopher) Roger (Ettrick); Chairman, Innisfree Management Ltd, since 1995; *b* 2 Feb. 1931; *s* of late Ralph Brooke and Marjorie (*née* Lee); *m* 1958, Nancy Belle Lowenthal; three *s* one *d*. *Educ:* Tonbridge; Trinity Coll., Oxford (MA). Served HM Diplomatic Service: Bonn, 1955–57; Southern Dept, FO, 1958–60; Washington, 1960–63; Tel Aviv, 1963–66. Dep. Man. Dir, IRC, 1966–69; Man. Dir, Scienta SA, 1969–71; Dir, Pearson Gp, 1971–79; Gp Man. Dir, EMI, 1979–80; Chief Exec., 1980–90, and Chm., 1991–99, Candover Investments plc. Chm., Audit Commn, 1995–98. Director: Slough Estates plc, 1980–; Lambert Fenchurch Gp (formerly Lowndes Lambert Gp Holdings) PLC, 1991–99; Tarmac plc, 1994–99; Wembley PLC, 1995–99; Pi Capital

Ltd, 1999–, and various other cos; Dep. Chm., Carillion plc, 1999–; Chairman: Accord plc, 1999–; Advent VCT2 plc, 1998–. *Publication:* Santa's Christmas Journey, 1985. *Recreations:* golf, tennis, theatre, reading, travel. *Address:* Water Meadow, Swarraton, near Alresford, Hants SO24 9TQ. *T:* (01962) 732259. *Club:* Woking Golf.

BROOKE, Sir Francis (George Windham), 4th Bt *cr* 1903; Director, European Equities, Merrill Lynch Investment Managers; *b* 15 Oct. 1963; *s* of Sir George Cecil Francis Brooke, 3rd Bt, MBE, and of Lady Melissa Brooke, *er d* of 6th Earl of Dunraven and Mount-Earl, CB, CBE, MC; *S* father, 1982; *m* 1989, Hon. Katharine Elizabeth, *o d* of Baron Hussey of North Bradley, *qv* and Lady Susan Hussey, *qv*; one *s* two *d*. *Educ:* Eton; Edinburgh University (MA Hons). AIIMR 1993. Dir, Foreign & Colonial Mgt Ltd, 1994–97. *Heir: s* George Francis Geoffrey Brooke, *b* 10 Sept. 1991. *Address:* 65 Sterndale Road, W14 0HU. *Clubs:* Turf, White's; Royal St George's (Sandwich).

BROOKE, Rt Hon. Sir Henry, Kt 1988; PC 1996; **Rt Hon. Lord Justice Brooke;** a Lord Justice of Appeal, since 1996; *b* 19 July 1936; *s* of Lord Brooke of Cumnor, PC, CH and Lady Brooke of Ystradfellte, DBE; *m* 1966, Bridget Mary Kalaugher; three *s* one *d*. *Educ:* Marlborough College; Balliol Coll., Oxford. MA (1st Cl. Classical Hon. Mods, 1st Cl. Lit. Hum.). Called to the Bar, Inner Temple, 1963, Bencher, 1987; Junior Counsel to the Crown, Common Law, 1978–81; QC 1981; a Recorder, 1983–88; a Judge of the High Court, QBD, 1988–96. Chm., Law Commn, 1993–95; Counsel to the Inquiry, Sizewell 'B' Nuclear Reactor Inquiry, 1983–85; DTI Inspector, House of Fraser Hldgs plc, 1987–88. Mem., Bar Council, 1987–88 (Chairman: Professional Standards Cttee, 1987–88; Race Relations Cttee, 1989–91); Chairman: Computer Cttee, Senate of the Inns of Court and the Bar, 1985–86; London Common Law and Commercial Bar Assoc., 1988 (Vice-Chm., 1986–87); Ethnic Minority Adv. Cttee, Judicial Studies Bd, 1991–94; Council, Centre for Crime and Justice Studies (formerly Inst. for Study and Treatment of Delinquency), 1997–. Member: Information Technology and the Courts Cttee, 1986–87, 1990–96; Judicial Studies Bd, 1992–94. Pres., Soc. for Computers and Law, 1992–. Trustee, Wordsworth Trust, 1995–. *Publications:* Institute Cargo Clauses (Air), 1986; (contrib.) Halsbury's Laws of England, 4th edn, and to legal jls. *Address:* Royal Courts of Justice, Strand, WC2A 2LL. *Club:* Brooks's.
See also Baron Brooke of Sutton Mandeville.

BROOKE, Prof. John Hedley, PhD; Andreas Idreos Professor of Science and Religion, Director, Ian Ramsey Centre, and Fellow of Harris Manchester College, Oxford University, since 1999; *b* 20 May 1944; *s* of Hedley Joseph Brooke and Margaret Brooke (*née* Brown); *m* 1972, Janice Marian Heffer. *Educ:* Fitzwilliam Coll., Cambridge (MA; PhD 1969). Res. Fellow, Fitzwilliam Coll., Cambridge, 1967–68; Tutorial Fellow, Univ. of Sussex, 1968–69; Lancaster University: Lectr, 1969–80; Sen. Lectr, 1980–91; Reader in History of Science, 1991–92; Prof. of History of Science, 1992–99. (Jtly) Gifford Lectr, Glasgow Univ., 1995–96. President: Historical Section, BAAS, 1996–97; British Soc. for History of Science, 1996–98; Corresp. Mem., Internat. Acad. of History of Science, 1993. Ed., British Jl for the History of Science, 1989–93. *Publications:* Science and Religion: some historical perspectives, 1991; Thinking about Matter: studies in the history of chemical philosophy, 1995; (jtly) Reconstructing Nature: the engagement of science and religion, 1998; many articles on history of chemistry and history of natural theology. *Recreations:* music (opera), foreign travel, chess, walking, rhododendrons. *Address:* Harris Manchester College, Oxford OX1 3TD. *T:* (01865) 271006.

BROOKE, John Stephen P.; *see* Pitt-Brooke.

BROOKE, Michael Eccles Macklin; QC 1994; a Recorder, since 2000; *b* 8 May 1942; *s* of late Reginald Eccles Joseph Brooke and Beryl Cicely Brooke (*née* Riggs); *m* 1st, 1972, Annie Sophie (marr. diss. 1985), *d* of André Vautier; three *s*; 2nd, 1996, Mireille, *d* of late Colin Colahan; two step *d*. *Educ:* Froebel Sch., Datchet; Lycée Français de Londres; Edinburgh Univ. (LLB). Called to the Bar, Gray's Inn, and in practice, 1968–; admitted Avocat, Cour d'Appel, Paris. *Recreations:* boating, comparing England and France. *Address:* 4 New Square, Lincoln's Inn, WC2A 3RJ. *T:* (020) 7822 2000.

BROOKE, Sir Richard (David Christopher), 11th Bt *cr* 1662, of Norton Priory, Cheshire; *b* 23 Oct. 1938; *s* of Sir Richard (Neville) Brooke, 10th Bt and Lady Mabel Kathleen Brooke (*d* 1985), *d* of 8th Earl of Roden; *S* father, 1997; *m* 1st, 1963, Carola Marion (marr. diss. 1978), *e d* of Sir Robert Erskine-Hill, 2nd Bt; two *s*; 2nd, 1979, Lucinda, *d* of John Frederick Voelcker. *Educ:* Eton College. MSI. Lt, Scots Guards, 1957–58. Partner, Rowe & Pitman, 1968–86; Dir, S. G. Warburg Gp and Dep. Chm., S. G. Warburg Securities, 1986–90; Pres. and Chm., S. G. Warburg (USA) Inc., 1988–90; Chm., J. O. Hambro & Partners, 1990–97. Director: Potter Partners, 1987–90; Govett Atlantic Investment Trust plc, 1990–92; Contracyclical Investment Trust, 1990–96; J. O. Hambro & Co., 1990–97; Exeter Preferred Capital Investment Trust plc, 1991–; Gartmore American Securities plc, 1991–95; Govett American Smaller Companies Investment Trust plc, 1992–98; HCG Lloyd's Investment Trust plc, 1994–96; Templeton Emerging Markets Investment Trust plc, 1994–; Templeton Latin America Investment Trust plc, 1994–; Templeton Central and Eastern European Investment Trust plc, 1995–98; Avocet Mining plc, 1995–; Fidelity Special Values plc, 1995–; Chairman: Armstrong International Ltd, 1990–; N Atlantic Smaller Cos Investment Trust plc, 1993–98; Govett Global Smaller Cos Investment Trust plc, 1994–97. Member: Internat. Capital Mkts Adv. Bd, NY Stock Exchange, 1987–89; Cttee, Soc. of Merchants Trading into Europe, 1988–; National Association of Securities Dealers Inc.: Mem., Internat. Markets Adv. Bd, 1991–98; Vice Chm. Bd of Governors, 1994–95. *Recreations:* travel, antiques and fine art, wines, boating. *Heir: er s* Richard Christopher Brooke, *b* 10 July 1966. *Address:* The Manor House, Cholderton, Wilts SP4 0DW. *T:* (01980) 629200; Château Rouzaud, St Victor-Rouzaud, 09100 Pamiers, France. *Clubs:* Boodle's, Pratt's; Tarporley Hunt (Cheshire); The Brook (NY).

BROOKE, Rodney George, CBE 1996; DL; Secretary, Association of Metropolitan Authorities, 1990–97; Visiting Fellow, Nuffield Institute for Health Service Studies, University of Leeds, since 1989; *b* 22 Oct. 1939; *s* of George Sidney Brooke and Amy Brooke; *m* 1967, Dr Clare Margaret Cox; one *s* one *d*. *Educ:* Queen Elizabeth's Grammar Sch., Wakefield. Admitted solicitor (hons), 1962. Rochdale County Bor. Council, 1962–63; Leicester CC, 1963–65; Stockport County Bor. Council, 1965–73; West Yorkshire Metropolitan County Council: Dir of Admin, 1973–81; Chief Exec. and Clerk, 1981–84; Clerk to W Yorks Lieutenancy, 1981–84; Chief Exec., Westminster City Council, 1984–89; Clerk to Gtr London Lieutenancy, 1987–89; Chm., Bradford HA, 1989–90; Dir, Riverside Health Trust, 2000–. Secretary: Yorks and Humberside Tourist Board, 1974–84; Yorks and Humberside Develt Assoc., 1974–84; Hon. Sec., London Boroughs Assoc., 1984–90; Dir, Foundn for IT in Local Govt, 1988–92; Chairman: Electricity Consumers' Cttee (Yorks), 1997–2000; National Electricity Consumers Council, 1999–2000. Associate: Local Govt Mgt Bd, 1997–; Politics Internat., 1998–. Member: Action London, 1988–90; Exec., SOLACE, 1981–84, 1987–89; CS Final Selection Bd, 1991–2000. Chm., Durham Univ. Centre for Public Management Res., 1994–97; Vis. Res. Fellow, RIPA, 1989–92; Sen. Vis. Res. Fellow, Sch. of Public Policy, Birmingham Univ., 1997–. Dir, Dolphin Square Trust, 1987–; Chm., London NE, Royal Jubilee and Prince's Trusts, 1984–91. Trustee, Community Develt Foundn, 1996–2000. Associate, Ernst & Young, 1989–90. Editl Advr, Longman Gp, 1989–90. Hon. Fellow, Inst. of Govt Studies, Birmingham Univ. FRSA. Freeman, City of London, 1993. DL Greater London, 1989. National Order of Merit (France), 1984; Nat. Order of Aztec Eagle (Mexico), 1985; Medal of Merit (Qatar), 1985; Order of Merit (Germany), 1986; Legion of Merit (Senegal), 1988. *Publications:* Managing the Enabling Authority, 1989; The Environmental Role of Local Government, 1990; (jtly) City Futures in Britain and Canada, 1990; (jtly) The Public Service Manager's Handbook, 1992; (jtly) Strengthening Local Government in the 1990s, 1997; (jtly) Ethics in Public Service for the New Millennium, 2000; The Consumer's-Eye View of Utilities, 2000; articles on local govt. *Recreations:* skiing, opera, Byzantium. *Address:* Stubham Lodge, Clifford Road, Middleton, Ilkley, West Yorks LS29 0AX. *T:* (01943) 601869; 706 Grenville House, Dolphin Square, SW1V 3LR. *T:* (020) 7798 8086. *Clubs:* Athenæum, Ski Club of Great Britain.

BROOKE, Roger; *see* Brooke, C. R. E.

BROOKE-LITTLE, John Philip Brooke, CVO 1984 (MVO 1969); Norroy and Ulster King of Arms, and King of Arms, Registrar and Knight Attendant on the Most Illustrious Order of St Patrick, 1980–95; Librarian, 1974–94, and Treasurer, 1978–95, College of Arms; Clarenceux King of Arms, 1995–97; *b* 6 April 1927; *s* of late Raymond Brooke-Little, Unicorns House, Swalcliffe; *m* 1960, Mary Lee, *o c* of late John Raymond Pierce; three *s* one *d*. *Educ:* Clayesmore Sch; New Coll., Oxford (MA). Earl Marshal's staff, 1952–53; Gold Staff Officer, Coronation, 1953; Bluemantle Pursuivant of Arms, 1956–67; Richmond Herald, 1967–80; Registrar, Coll. of Arms, 1974–82. Dir, Heralds' Museum, 1991–97; Adviser on heraldry: Nat. Trust, 1983–; Shrievalty Assoc., 1983–. Founder of Heraldry Soc., 1947 (Chm., 1947–97; Pres., 1997–); Hon. Editor, The Coat of Arms, 1950–; Fellow, Soc. of Genealogists, 1969; Hon. Fellow, 1979, and Trustee, Inst. of Heraldic and Genealogical Studies. Chm., Harleian Soc., 1984–; Pres., English Language Literary Trust, 1985–96. Governor Emeritus, Clayesmore Sch. (Chm., 1971–83). Trustee, RAF Heraldic Trust, 1996. Freeman and Liveryman, Scriveners' Co. of London (Master, 1985–86). FSA 1961. KStJ 1975; Knight of Malta, 1955, Knight Grand Cross of Grace and Devotion, Order of Malta, 1974 (Chancellor, British Assoc., 1973–77); Comdr Cross of Merit of Order of Malta, 1964; Cruz Distinguida (1st cl.) de San Raimundo de Peñafort, 1955; Grand Cross of Grace, Constantinian Order of St George, 1975. *Publications:* Royal London, 1953; Pictorial History of Oxford, 1954; Boutell's Heraldry, 1970, 1973, 1978 and 1983 (1963 and 1966 edns with C. W. Scott-Giles); Knights of the Middle Ages, 1966; Prince of Wales, 1969; Fox-Davies' Complete Guide to Heraldry, annotated edn, 1969; (with Don Pottinger and Anne Tauté) Kings and Queens of Great Britain, 1970; An Heraldic Alphabet, 1973, rev. edn 1997; (with Marie Angell) Beasts in Heraldry, 1974; The British Monarchy in Colour, 1976; Royal Arms, Beasts and Badges, 1977; Royal Ceremonies of State, 1979; genealogical and heraldic articles. *Recreations:* designing, humming. *Address:* Heyford House, Lower Heyford, Bicester, Oxon OX6 3NZ. *T:* and *Fax:* (01869) 340337. *Club:* Chelsea Arts (Hon. Member).

BROOKE-ROSE, Prof. Christine; novelist and critic; Professor of English Language and Literature, University of Paris, 1975–88 (Lecturer, 1969–75); *b* 16 Jan. 1923. *Educ:* Somerville Coll., Oxford (MA 1953; Hon. Fellow, 1997); PhD London 1954. Research and criticism, 1955–. Reviewer for: The Times Literary Supplement, The Times, The Observer, The Sunday Times, The Listener, The Spectator, and The London Magazine, 1956–68; took up post at Univ. of Paris VIII, Vincennes, 1969. Has broadcast in book programmes on BBC, and on 'The Critics', and ABC Television. Hon. LittD East Anglia, 1988. Travelling Prize of Society of Authors, 1964; James Tait Black Memorial Prize, 1966; Arts Council Translation Prize, 1969. *Publications: novels:* The Languages of Love, 1957; The Sycamore Tree, 1958; The Dear Deceit, 1960; The Middlemen, 1961; Out, 1964; Such, 1965; Between, 1968; Thru, 1975; Amalgamemnon, 1984; Xorandor, 1986; Verbivore, 1990; Textermination, 1991; Remake, 1996; Next, 1998; Subscript, 1999; *criticism:* A Grammar of Metaphor, 1958; A ZBC of Ezra Pound, 1971; A Rhetoric of the Unreal, 1981; Stories, Theories and Things, 1991; *short stories:* Go when you see the Green Man Walking, 1969; short stories and essays in various magazines, etc. *Recreations:* people, books. *Address:* c/o Cambridge University Press, PO Box 110, Cambridge CB2 3RL.

BROOKE TURNER, Alan, CMG 1980; HM Diplomatic Service, retired; Director, British Association for Central and Eastern Europe (formerly Great Britain/East Europe Centre), 1987–95; *b* 4 Jan. 1926; *s* of late Arthur Brooke Turner, MC; *m* 1954, Hazel Alexandra Rowan Henderson; two *s* two *d*. *Educ:* Marlborough; Balliol Coll., Oxford (Sen. Schol.). 1st cl Hon. Mods 1949; 1st cl. Lit. Hum. 1951. Served in RAF, 1944–48. Entered HM Foreign (subseq. Diplomatic) Service, 1951; FO, 1951; Warsaw, 1953; 3rd, later 2nd Sec. (Commercial), Jedda, 1954; Lisbon, 1957; 1st Sec., FO, 1959 (UK Delegn to Nuclear Tests Conf., Geneva, 1962); Cultural Attaché, Moscow, 1962; FO, 1965; Fellow, Center for Internat. Affairs, Harvard Univ., 1968; Counsellor, Rio de Janeiro, 1969–71; Head of Southern European Dept, FCO, 1972–73; Counsellor and Head of Chancery, British Embassy, Rome, 1973–76; Civil Dep. Comdt and Dir of Studies, NATO Defense Coll., Rome, 1976–78; Internat. Inst. for Strategic Studies, 1978–79; Minister, Moscow, 1979–82; Ambassador to Finland, 1983–85. Member: Council, Anglican Centre, Rome, 1976–77; Anglican Synod Wkg Gp on Peacemaking, 1986–88; Council, SSEES, 1987–95 (Chm., 1989–92). *Recreations:* music, reading. *Address:* Poultons, Moor Lane, Dormansland, Lingfield, Surrey RH7 6NX. *Club:* Travellers.

BROOKEBOROUGH, 3rd Viscount *cr* 1952, of Colebrooke; **Alan Henry Brooke,** Bt 1822; DL; farmer; a Personal Lord in Waiting to the Queen, since 1997; *b* 30 June 1952; *s* of 2nd Viscount Brookeborough, PC and of Rosemary Hilda (*née* Chichester); *S* father, 1987; *m* 1980, Janet Elizabeth, *d* of J. P. Cooke, Doagh, Ballyclare. *Educ:* Harrow; Millfield. Commissioned 17th/21st Lancers, 1971; transferred 4th (County Fermanagh) Bn, UDR, 1977; Company Commander, 1981–83; Royal Irish Regt (Co. Comdr, 1988–93); Lt-Col, 1993, transf. to RARO. Now farms and runs an estate with a shooting/fishing tourist enterprise. Member: EEC Agricl Sub-Cttee, House of Lords, 1988–92, 1993–97; EC Select Cttee and Sub-Cttee B (energy, industry and transport), H of L, 1998–; elected Mem., H of L, 1999. Non-exec. Dir, Green Park Unit Hosp. Trust, 1993–; Chm., Basel International (Jersey), 1996–. Hon. Col, 4th/5th Bn, Royal Irish Rangers, 1997–. DL 1987, High Sheriff 1995, Co. Fermanagh. *Recreations:* shooting, fishing. *Heir: b* Hon. Christopher Arthur Brooke [*b* 16 May 1954; *m* 1990, Amanda Hodges; three *s*]. *Address:* Colebrooke, Brookeborough, Co. Fermanagh, N Ireland BT94 4DW. *T:* (01365) 531402. *Club:* Cavalry and Guards.

BROOKER, Alan Bernard; JP, DL; FCA; Chairman: Kode International, 1988–98; E. T. Heron & Co., 1991–96; *b* 24 Aug. 1931; *s* of late Bernard John Brooker and of Gwendoline Ada (*née* Launchbury); *m* 1957, Diana (*née* Coles); one *s* two *d*. *Educ:* Chigwell School, Essex. FCA 1954. Served 2nd RHA (2nd Lieut), 1954–56. Articled, Cole, Dickin & Hills, Chartered Accountants, 1949–54, qualified 1954; Manager, Cole, Dickin & Hills, 1956–58; Accountant, Independent Dairies, 1958–59; Asst Accountant, Exchange Telegraph Co., 1959–64; Dir, 1964–87, Chm. and Chief Exec., 1980–87, Extel Group. Chm., Serif Cowells, then Serif, 1990–93; Vice-Chairman: Provident Financial,

1983–94; James Martin Associates, 1987–89; Non-executive Director: Pauls plc, 1984–85; Aukett Associates, 1988–; Plysu, 1988–99; PNA Holdings, 1988–89; Addison Worldwide, 1990–94; Eastern Counties Newspapers (formerly East Anglian Daily Times), 1990–96; ACAL plc, 1996–. Member: Council, CBI London Region, 1980–83; Companies Cttee, CBI, 1979–83; Council, CPU, 1975–88. Appeal Chm., Newspaper Press Fund, 1985–86. Governor: Chigwell School, 1968– (Chm., 1978–99); Felixstowe Coll., 1986–94. Freeman, City of London; Liveryman, Stationers and Newspapermakers' Co. (Court Asst, 1985–; Master, 1995–96). Churchwarden, St Bride's, Fleet Street, 1986–. JP Essex 1972 (Chm. of Bench, Epping and Ongar, 1995–99); DL Essex 1982. FRSA 1980. *Recreations:* cricket, golf. *Address:* Plowlands, Laundry Lane, Little Easton, Dunmow, Essex CM6 2JW. *Clubs:* East India, MCC; Royal Worlington and Newmarket Golf.

BROOKER, Mervyn Edward William; Headmaster, King Edward VI Camp Hill School for Boys, since 1995; *b* 24 March 1954; *s* of Derek and Hazel Brooker; *m* 1976, Brigid Mary O'Rorke; two *d. Educ:* Lancaster Royal Grammar Sch.; Burnley Grammar Sch.; Jesus Coll., Cambridge (BA Hons Geography 1975; PGCE 1976; cricket blue, 1976). Teacher (Geography and Games): County High Sch., Saffron Walden, 1976–80; Royal Grammar Sch., Worcester, 1980–88; Highfields Sch., Wolverhampton, 1988–91; King Edward VI Camp Hill Sch. for Boys, 1992– (Dep. Headmaster, 1992–95); Pres., Camp Hill Old Edwardians Assoc., 1999–. Vice Chair: Yardley Educnl Trust, 1995–; Birmingham Secondary Heads Assoc., 1998–. Played cricket for: Combined Univs CC, 1976; Cambs CCC, 1976–80 (county cap, 1978); Staffs CCC, 1982–86; Birmingham Cricket League XI, 1984; Midlands Clubs Cricket Conf., 1986–90; Hereford and Worcester Cricket Assoc., 1981–86; Staffs Club Cricket League XI, 1994. *Recreations:* cricket, sport in general, hill walking, foreign travel. *Address:* King Edward VI Camp Hill School for Boys, Vicarage Road, King's Heath, Birmingham B14 7QJ. *T:* (0121) 444 3188. *Clubs:* Old Wulfrunians (Wolverhampton); Tything Tramps (Worcester); Camp Hill Rugby (Pres.), Camp Hill Old Edwardians CC (Pres.).

BROOKES, family name of **Baron Brookes**.

BROOKES, Baron *cr* 1975 (Life Peer), of West Bromwich; **Raymond Percival Brookes,** Kt 1971; Life President, GKN plc (formerly Guest, Keen & Nettlefolds Ltd) (Group Chairman and Chief Executive, 1965–74); *b* 10 April 1909; *s* of William and Ursula Brookes; *m* 1937, Florence Edna Sharman; one *s*. Part-time Mem., BSC, 1967–68. First Pres., British Mechanical Engrg Confedn, 1968–70; a Vice-Pres., Engrg Employers' Fedn, 1967–75. Member: Council, UK S Africa Trade Assoc. Ltd, 1967–74; Council, CBI, 1968–75; BNEC, 1969–71; Wilberforce Ct of Inquiry into electricity supply industry dispute, Jan. 1971; Industrial Develt Adv. Bd, 1972–75. Member: Exec. Cttee, 1970–, Council, 1969–, Pres., 1974–75, Soc. of Motor Manufacturers & Traders Ltd; Court of Governors, Univ. of Birmingham, 1966–75; Council, Univ. of Birmingham, 1968–75. Pres., Motor Ind. Res. Assoc., 1973–75. Chm., Rea Bros (IoM) Ltd, 1976–89; Director: Plessey Co. Ltd, 1974–89; AMF Inc., 1975–78. *Recreations:* golf, fly-fishing. *Address:* GKN plc, PO Box 55, Redditch, Worcs B98 0TL; (private) Mallards, Santon, Isle of Man IM4 1EH.

BROOKES, Beata Ann, CBE 1996; *b* 21 Jan. 1931. *Educ:* Lowther College, Abergele; Univ. of Wales, Bangor; studied politics in USA (US State Dept Scholarship). Former social worker, Denbighshire CC; company secretary and farmer. Contested (C) Widnes, 1955, Warrington, 1963, Manchester Exchange, 1964. Contested (C) N Wales, European Parly Elecn, 1989. MEP (C) N Wales, 1979–89; Mem., Educn and Agricl Cttees. Member: Clwyd AHA, 1973–80 (Mem., Welsh Hosp. Bd, 1963–74); Clwyd Family Practitioner Cttee; Clwyd CC Social Services Cttee, 1973–81; Flintshire Soc. for Mentally Handicapped; N Wales Council for Mentally Handicapped; Council for Professions Supplementary to Medicine; Exec. Cttee, N Wales Cons. Group. Pres., N Wales Assoc. for the Disabled. *Address:* The Cottage, Wayside Acres, Bodelwyddan, near Rhyl, North Wales.

BROOKES, James Robert; Director (non-executive): The Knowledge Group, since 1998; Smart South West, since 1999; Consultant, SOCITM; *b* 2 Sept. 1941; *s* of James Brookes and Hettie Brookes (*née* Colley); *m* 1964, Patricia Gaskell; three *d. Educ:* Manchester Grammar Sch.; Corpus Christi Coll., Oxford (MA Maths). FBCS; CEng 1990; Eur Ing, 1991. Various posts as systems and applications programmer in develt, tech. support and sales; Northern Branch Manager, Univs and Nat. Research Region, Ferranti/Internat. Computers, 1962–67; Computer Services Manager, Queen's Univ. Belfast, 1967–69; Operations Manager, Univ. of Manchester Regional Computer Centre, 1969–75; Director: SW Univs Regional Computer Centre, 1975–87; Bath Univ. Computer Service, 1983–87; Inf. Services Orgn, Portsmouth Univ., 1992–95; Head of Information Systems, Avon and Somerset Constabulary, 1995–98. Co-founder and non-exec Chm., Praxis Systems, 1983; Chief Exec., 1986–91, Consultant, 1991–92, BCS. Vis. Prof., Business Sch., Strathclyde Univ., 1991–98. Mem. Council, PITCOM, 1989– (Prog. Exec., 1997–2000); Hon. Sec., Council of European Professional Information Socs, 1991–93. FRSA 1988. Freeman, City of London, 1989; Liveryman, Information Technologists' Co. (Mem., 1988). *Recreations:* sailing, fellwalking, cycling, bridge, squash, badminton. *Address:* 29 High Street, Marshfield, Chippenham, Wilts SN14 8LR. *T:* (home) (01225) 891294, (office) (0117) 900 7539; *e-mail:* jr.brookes@btinternet.com. *Club:* Oxford and Cambridge.

BROOKES, John; landscape designer; *b* 11 Oct. 1933; *s* of Edward Percy Brookes and Margaret Alexandra Brookes. *Educ:* Durham; Dip. Landscape, UCL. Asst to Brenda Colvin, 1957, to Dame Sylvia Crowe, 1958–61; private practice, 1964–; Director: Inchbald Sch. of Garden Design, 1970–78; Inchbald Sch. of Interior Design, Tehran, 1978–80; founded Clock House Sch. of Garden Design, Sussex, 1980; gardening corresp., Evening Standard, 1988–89; Principal Lectr, Kew Sch. of Garden Design, 1990–93. Chm., Soc. of Garden Designers, 1997–2000. Design workshops and lectures, UK and overseas; design and construction of gardens, and consultancies, UK, Europe, Japan, USA. *Publications:* Room Outside, 1969; Gardens for Small Spaces, 1970; Garden Design and Layout, 1970; Living in the Garden, 1971; Financial Times Book of Garden Design, 1975; Improve Your Lot, 1977; The Small Garden, 1977; The Garden Book, 1984; A Place in the Country, 1984; The Indoor Garden Book, 1986; Gardens of Paradise, 1987; The Country Garden, 1987; The New Small Garden Book, 1989; Garden Design Book, 1991; Planting the Country Way, 1994; Garden Design Workbook, 1994; Home and Garden Style, 1996; The New Garden, 1998. *Recreations:* reading, pottering, entertaining. *Address:* Clock House, Denmans, Fontwell, near Arundel, West Sussex BN18 0SU. *T:* (01243) 542808, *Fax:* (01243) 544064.

BROOKES, Nicholas Kelvin, FCA; Chief Executive, Spirent (formerlyBowthorpe) plc, since 1995; *b* 19 May 1947; *s* of Stanley Brookes and Jean (*née* Wigley); *m* 1968, Maria Rosa Crespo; two *s* one *d. Educ:* Harrow Sch. FCA 1971. Articles for ACA, Hart Bros Reddall & Co., London, 1965–69; joined Texas Instruments, 1975; Man. Dir, Canada, 1980–85; Man. Dir, Europe, 1985–92; Vice-Pres., Texas Instruments Inc. and Pres., Materials and Controls Gp, 1992–95. Non-executive Director: De La Rue plc, 1997–; Corp. Financiera ALBA SA, Spain, 1999–. FInstD. *Recreations:* tennis, badminton, opera. *Address:* Spirent plc, Spirent House, Crawley Business Quarter, Fleming Way, Crawley, W Sussex RH10 9QL. *Club:* Reform.

BROOKES, Peter C.; *see* Cannon-Brookes.

BROOKES, Peter Derek; Political Cartoonist, The Times, since 1993; *b* 28 Sept. 1943; *s* of George Henry Brookes and Joan Elizabeth Brookes; *m* 1971, Angela Harrison; two *s. Educ:* Heversham Grammar Sch., Westmorland; RAF Coll., Cranwell (BA London Ext.); Central School of Art and Design (BA). Freelance illustrator, 1969–; Cover Artist, The Spectator, 1986–98; stamp designs for Royal Mail, 1995 and 1999; contributor to: The Times, Sunday Times, Radio Times, New Statesman, The Listener, Spectator, TLS and Glyndebourne Fest. Opera Books. Illustration Tutor: Central Sch. of Art and Design, 1977–79; RCA, 1979–89. Mem., AGI, 1988–. FRSA 2000. Political Cartoonist of the Year, Cartoon Art Trust Awards, 1996 and 1998. *Publications:* Nature Notes, 1997; Nature Notes: the new collection, 1999; Nature Notes III, 2001. *Recreations:* music, QPR, arguing. *Address:* 30 Vanbrugh Hill, Blackheath, SE3 7UF. *T:* (020) 8858 9022.

BROOKING, Barry Alfred, MBE 1972; JP; Chief Executive, British Psychological Society, since 2000; *b* 2 Feb. 1944; *s* of Alfred Brooking and Winifred Joan Brooking; *m* 1978, Julia Irene McBride (marr. diss. 1993). *Educ:* Milford Haven GS; Sir Joseph Williamson's Math. Sch., Rochester; Birkbeck Coll., London Univ. (BA 1976, MA 1980). MInstM, MIPD, ACP. Royal Navy, 1965–81: BRNC Dartmouth, 1965; HMS Pembroke, 1966–67; HMS Diamond, 1968–69; CTC RM, Lympstone, 1969; 41 Cdo RM, 1969–70; 40 Cdo RM, 1970–72; HMS Raleigh, 1972–75; RN Sch. of Educnl and Trng Technol., 1976–78; ARE, 1978–81. Business Adminr, Med. Protection Soc., 1981–91; Regl Dir, St John Ambulance, 1992–95; Chief Exec., Parkinson's Disease Soc., 1995–99. Member: Surrey Magistrates' Soc., 1985–2000; Surrey Magistrates' Courts Cttee, 1993–95; Surrey Probation Cttee, 1993–95; Surrey Magistrates' Club, 1995–; Leics Magistrates' Soc., 2001–; Dep. Chm., North and East PSD, Surrey, 1995–97. Chm., Brooking Soc., 1993– (Mem., 1980–). MRTS. JP Surrey, 1985–2000, Leics, 2001. Business Develt Award, Surrey TEC, 1994. *Publications:* Naval Mathematics Self-Tuition Text, 1966; Naval English Self-Tuition Text, 1966; Naval Mathematics Programmed-Learning Text, 1967; Royal Navy CCTV Production Techniques Handbook, 1977; (contrib.) Educational Technology in a Changing World: aspects of educational technology Vol. XII, 1978; ARE reports, booklets, articles in jls. *Recreations:* travel, theatre, cinema, music, history, sport. *Address:* 9 Hawkmoor Parke, Bovey Tracey, Devon TQ13 9NL; (office) St Andrews House, 48 Princess Road East, Leicester LE1 7DR.

BROOKING, Maj.-Gen. Patrick Guy, CB 1988; CMG 1997; MBE 1975; DL; *b* 4 April 1937; *s* of late Captain C. A. H. Brooking, CBE, RN, and G. M. J. White (*née* Coleridge); *m* 1964, Pamela Mary Walford; one *s* one *d. Educ:* Charterhouse Sch.; Alliance Française, Paris, 1955. Commnd 5th Royal Inniskilling Dragoon Guards, 1956; early career served in England, W Germany, NI, Cyprus (UN); Staff Coll., Camberley, 1969; Mil. Asst to Comdr 1st British Corps, 1970–71; Bde Major 39 Bde, Belfast, 1974–75; comd his regt, 1975–77; Instr Army Staff Coll., 1978; COS, 4 Armd Div., 1979–80; RCDS 1981; Comdr 33 Armd Bde, Paderborn Garrison, 1982–83; Dep. COS, HQ UKLF, 1984–85; Commandant and GOC Berlin (British Sector), 1985–89; Dir Gen., Army Manning and Recruiting, 1990; retd 1991. Chief Exec. Officer, Worldwide Subsidiaries, KRONE AG, Berlin, 1991–97. Colonel: 5th Royal Inniskilling Dragoon Guards, 1991–92; Royal Dragoon Guards (on foundn), 1992–94. Chairman: Internat. Club, Berlin, 1994–; British-German Assoc., 2000–. Freeman, City of London, 1964; Mem., Broderers' Co., 1964. DL Wilts, 1997. Verdienstorden des Landes, Berlin, 1996. *Recreations:* tennis, golf, choral singing, painting. *Address:* c/o National Westminster Bank, PO Box 411, 34 Henrietta Street, WC2E 8NN. *Club:* Cavalry and Guards.

BROOKING, Trevor David, CBE 1999 (MBE 1981); football broadcaster, since 1984; Chairman, Sport England, since 1999; *b* 2 Oct. 1948; *s* of Henry and Margaret Brooking; *m* 1970, Hilkka Helina Helakorpi; one *s* one *d. Educ:* Ilford County High Sch. Professional footballer with West Ham United, 1965–84: played 642 games; scored 111 goals; FA Cup winner, 1975, *v* Fulham, 1980, *v* Arsenal (scoring only goal); won Football League Div. 2, 1980–81; 47 appearances for England, 1974–82. Chm., Eastern Council for Sport and Recreation, 1986–95; Mem., Sport England (formerly Sports Council, then English Sports Council), 1989– (Vice-Chm., 1994–96). *Publications:* Trevor Brooking (autobiog.), 1981; Trevor Brooking's 100 Great British Footballers, 1988. *Recreations:* golf, tennis.

BROOKMAN, family name of **Baron Brookman**.

BROOKMAN, Baron *cr* 1998 (Life Peer), of Ebbw Vale in the co. of Gwent; **David Keith Brookman;** General Secretary, Iron and Steel Trades Confederation, 1993–99; *b* 3 Jan. 1937; *s* of George Henry Brookman, MM and Blodwin Brookman (*née* Nash); *m* 1958, Patricia Worthington; three *d. Educ:* Nantyglo Grammar Sch., Gwent. Nat. Service, RAF, 1955–57. Steel worker, Richard Thomas & Baldwin, Ebbw Vale, 1953–55 and 1957–73; Iron & Steel Trades Confederation: Organiser, 1973–85; Asst Gen. Sec., 1985–93. Trades Union Congress: Member: Educn Adv. Cttee for Wales, 1976–82; Steel Cttee, 1985–90; Gen. Council, 1992–99. Member: Brit. Steel Jt Accident Prevention Adv. Cttee, 1985–93; Brit. Steel Adv. Cttee on Educn and Trng, 1986–93; Nat. Steel Co-ordinating Cttee, 1991–99 (Chm., 1993–99); Consultative Cttee, ECSC, 1993–; Operatives' Secretary: Jt Ind. Council for Slag Ind., 1985–93; Brit. Steel Long Products portfolio of cos Jt Standing Cttee, 1993–98; Brit. Steel Strip Trade Bd, 1993–98; Mem. Bd, UK Steel Enterprise (formerly Brit. Steel (Ind.) Ltd), 1993–; Jt Sec., European Works Council, British Steel, 1996–98. Member Executive Council: European Metalworkers' Fedn, 1985–95 (Mem., Steel Cttee, 1994–99); CSEU, 1989–93; International Metalworkers' Federation: Hon. Sec., Brit. Section, 1993–99; Pres., Iron and Steel and Non-Ferrous Metals Dept, 1993–99. Labour Party: Member: Exec. Cttee, Wales, 1982–85; Nat. Constitutional Cttee, 1987–91; NEC, 1991–92. Trustee, Julian Melchett Trust, 1985–95. Gov., Gwent Coll. of HE, 1980–84. *Recreations:* cricket, Rugby, reading, keep fit, golf. *Address:* 4 Bassett Close, Redbourn, Herts AL3 7JY. *T:* (01582) 792066.

BROOKNER, Dr Anita, CBE 1990; Reader, Courtauld Institute of Art, 1977–88; *b* 16 July 1928; *o c* of Newson and Maude Brookner. *Educ:* James Allen's Girls' Sch.; King's Coll., Univ. of London (FKC 1990); Courtauld Inst.; Paris. Vis. Lectr, Univ. of Reading, 1959–64; Slade Professor, Univ. of Cambridge, 1967–68; Lectr, Courtauld Inst. of Art, 1964. Fellow, New Hall, Cambridge. *Publications:* Watteau, 1968; The Genius of the Future, 1971; Greuze: the rise and fall of an Eighteenth Century Phenomenon, 1972; Jacques-Louis David, 1980; (ed) The Stories of Edith Wharton, Vol. 1, 1988, Vol. 2, 1989; Soundings, 1997; Romanticism and its Discontents, 2000; *novels:* A Start in Life, 1981; Providence, 1982; Look at Me, 1983; Hotel du Lac, 1984 (Booker McConnell Prize; filmed for TV, 1986); Family and Friends, 1985; A Misalliance, 1986; A Friend from England, 1987; Latecomers, 1988; Lewis Percy, 1989; Brief Lives, 1990; A Closed Eye, 1991; Fraud, 1992; A Family Romance, 1993; A Private View, 1994; Incidents in the Rue Laugier, 1995; Altered States, 1996; Visitors, 1997; Falling Slowly, 1998; Undue

Influence, 1999; The Bay of Angels, 2001; articles in Burlington Magazine, etc. *Address:* 68 Elm Park Gardens, SW10 9PB. *T:* (020) 7352 6894.

BROOKS, family name of **Barons Brooks of Tremorfa** and **Crawshaw**.

BROOKS OF TREMORFA, Baron *cr* 1979 (Life Peer), of Tremorfa in the County of South Glamorgan; **John Edward Brooks;** DL; *b* 12 April 1927; *s* of Edward George Brooks and Rachel Brooks (*née* White); *m* 1948 (marr. diss. 1956); one *s* one *d*; *m* 1958, Margaret Pringle; two *s*. *Educ:* elementary schools; Coleg Harlech. Secretary, Cardiff South East Labour Party, 1966–84; Member, South Glamorgan CC, 1973–93 (Leader, 1973–77, 1986–92; Chm., 1981–82). Contested (Lab) Barry, Feb. and Oct. 1974; Parliamentary Agent to Rt Hon. James Callaghan, MP, Gen. Elections, 1970, 1979. Chm., Labour Party, Wales, 1978–79. Opposition defence spokesman, 1980–81. Steward, 1986–, Vice Chm., 1999–2000, Chm., 2000–, British Boxing Bd of Control. Chairman: Welsh Sports Hall of Fame, 1988–; Sportsmatch Wales, 1992–. DL S Glam, 1994. *Recreations:* reading, most sports. *Address:* 46 Kennerleigh Road, Rumney, Cardiff, S Glam CF3 9BJ.

BROOKS, Alan; Director, Horace Clarkson plc, since 1993; *b* 30 Dec. 1935; *s* of Charles and Annie Brooks; *m* 1959, Marie Curtis; one *s* two *d*. *Educ:* Leeds Univ. (BSc 1st Cl. Mining Engineering; 1st Cl. Cert. of Competency, Mines and Quarries). Asst Mine Manager, Winsford Salt Mine, ICI, 1961–66; British Gypsum: Dep. Mines Agent, 1966–71; Dir, Midland Region, 1971–74; Production Dir, 1974–77; Dep. Man. Dir, 1977–85; Man. Dir, 1985–88; Chm., 1988; Gp Man. Dir, Gypsum Products, BPB Industries, subseq. BPB Gypsum Industries, 1988–93; Chm., Anglo United plc, 1993–98. Chairman: Westroc Industries, Canada, 1988; Inveryeso, Spain, 1991; Dir, Falkland Is Hldgs, 1998–2000. *Recreation:* fell walking. *Address:* The Chantry, Little Casterton, Stamford PE9 4BE.

BROOKS, Caroline St J.; *see* St John-Brooks.

BROOKS, Prof. Christopher Leonard, DPhil; FSA; Professor of Victorian Culture, Exeter University, since 2001; *b* 23 Jan. 1949; *s* of Donald and Lilian Brooks. *Educ:* Grammar Sch., Plympton; Manchester Univ. (BA 1971); Lincoln Coll., Oxford (DPhil 1979). Exeter University: Lectr in English, 1976–92; Senior Lectr in Victorian Studies, 1992–98; Reader in Victorian Culture, 1998–2001; Hd, Sch. of English and American Studies, 1990–93. Victorian Society: Mem., Main Cttee, 1980–; Vice-Chm., 1987–93; Chm., 1993–2001. Member: Exeter DAC for Care of Churches, 1982–96; Technical Adv. Cttee, Exeter Cathedral, 1982–88; Wallpaintings Cttee, Council for Care of Churches, 1988–91; Fabric Cttee, Exeter Cathedral, 1990–; Fabric Cttee, Truro Cathedral, 1990–97; English Heritage: Adv. Cttee on Cathedrals and Churches, 1993–2001; Places of Worship Panel, 2001–; Historic Settlements and Landscapes Adv. Cttee, 2001–. Sec., Devon Bldgs Gp, 1985–95; Mem., Kensal Green Cemetery Adv. Cttee, 1990–. Mem. Council, Royal Archaeol Inst., 1993–96. Mem., Steering Gp for Albert Meml, DNH, 1993–94; Trustee, Albert Meml Trust, 1994–99. Leverhulme Trust Res. Fellow, 1997–98. *Publications:* Signs for the Times: symbolic realism in the mid-Victorian world, 1984; (with D. Evans) The Great East Window of Exeter Cathedral, 1988; Mortal Remains: the history and present state of the Victorian and Edwardian cemetery, 1989; (ed with A. Saint) The Victorian Church: architecture and society, 1995; The Albert Memorial, 1995; (with P. Faulkner) The White Man's Burdens: an anthology of British Poetry of the Empire, 1996; The Gothic Revival, 1999; (ed) The Albert Memorial: The Prince Consort National Memorial, its history, contexts and conservation, 2000. *Recreations:* pubs, cricket. *Address:* 48 Park Street, Crediton, Devon EX17 3EH; Victorian Society, 1 Priory Gardens, Bedford Park, W4 1TT. *T:* (020) 8994 1019; School of English, Queen's Building, University of Exeter, Exeter, Devon EX4 4QH. *T:* (01392) 264265.

BROOKS, Diana D., (Dede); President and Chief Executive Officer: Sotheby's Holdings Inc., 1994–2000 (also Director); Sotheby's North and South America, 1990–2000; *m* Michael C. Brooks; one *s* one *d*. *Educ:* Miss Porter's Sch., Farmington; Yale Univ. (BA Amer. Studies, 1973). Lending officer, Nat. Banking Gp, Citibank, 1973–79; joined Sotheby's New York, 1979; Sotheby's North America: Sen. Vice Pres. and Chief Financial and Admin. Officer, 1982; Exec. Vice Pres., 1984; Chief Operating Officer, 1985; Pres., 1987; Chief Exec. Officer, 1990. Trustee: Yale Univ.; Deerfield Acad., Mass; Henry Francis du Pont Winterthur Mus.; Meml Sloan–Kettering Cancer Center; Discover & Co.; Central Park Conservatory. *Address:* c/o Sotheby's, 34–35 New Bond Street, W1A 2AA.

BROOKS, Douglas; Consultant, Douglas Brooks Associates, 1992–98; *b* 3 Sept. 1928; *s* of Oliver Brooks and Olive Brooks; *m* 1952, June Anne (*née* Branch); one *s* one *d*. *Educ:* Newbridge Grammar Sch.; University Coll., Cardiff (Dip. Soc. Sc.). CIPM. Girling Ltd: factory operative, 1951–53; Employment Officer, 1953–56; Hoover Ltd: Personnel Off., 1956–60; Sen. Personnel Off., 1960–63; Dep. Personnel Man., 1963–66; Indust. Relations Advr, 1966–69; Gp Personnel Man., 1969–73; Personnel Dir, 1973–78; Group Personnel Manager, Tarmac Ltd, 1979–80; Director: Walker Brooks and Partners Ltd, 1980–91; Flexello Castors & Wheels plc, 1987–91. Member: Council, SSRC, later ESRC, 1976–82; BBC Consultative Gp on social effects of television, 1978–80; Hon. Soc. Cymmrodorion, 1981– (Mem. Council, 1992–). Vis. Fellow, PSI, 1982–84. Vice-Pres., IPM, 1972–74. Chm., Wooburn Fest. Soc. Ltd, 1978–86; Trustee, Ledbury Poetry Fest., 2001–. *Publications:* (with M. Fogarty) Trade Unions and British Industrial Development, 1986; various articles in professional jls. *Recreations:* talking, music, reading, gardening, cooking. *Address:* Gloucester House, The Southend, Ledbury, Herefordshire HR8 2HD. *T:* (01531) 631546. *Club:* Reform.

BROOKS, Edwin, PhD; FAIM, FCIM; Deputy Principal, Charles Sturt University, 1988–89; *b* Barry, Glamorgan, 1 Dec. 1929; *s* of Edwin Brooks and Agnes Elizabeth (*née* Campbell); *m* 1956, Winifred Hazel Soundie; four *s* one *d*. *Educ:* Barry Grammar Sch.; St John's Coll., Cambridge. PhD (Camb) 1958. National Service, Singapore, 1948–49. MP (Lab) Bebington, 1966–70. Univ. of Liverpool: Lectr, Dept of Geography, 1954–66 and 1970–72; Sen. Lectr, 1972–77; Dean, College Studies, 1975–77; Riverina College of Advanced Education, later Riverina-Murray Institute of Higher Education, then Charles Sturt University: Dean of Business and Liberal Studies, 1977–82; Dean of Commerce, 1982–88; Dir, Albury-Wodonga Campus, 1982; Dean Emeritus, 1990. Wagga Wagga Base Hospital: Dir, 1989–96; Dep. Chm., 1989–93; Chm., 1995–96; Riverina Dist Health Service: Dir and Dep. Chm., 1994–96; Treas., 1995–96. Councillor, Birkenhead, 1958–67. Mem., Courses Cttee, Higher Educn Bd of NSW, 1978–82; Dir, Australian Business Educn Council, 1986–89. Pres., Wagga Wagga Chamber of Commerce, 1988–90. FAIM 1983; FCIM 1989; ACIS 1995. *Publications:* This Crowded Kingdom, 1973; (ed) Tribes of the Amazon Basin in Brazil, 1973. *Recreations:* gardening, listening to music, computing. *Address:* Inchnadamph, Gregadoo Road, Wagga Wagga, NSW 2650, Australia. *T:* (2) 69226798.

BROOKS, Most Rev. Francis Gerard, DD, DCL; Bishop of Dromore (RC), 1976–99, now Bishop Emeritus; *b* Jan. 1924. Priest, 1949. Formerly President, St Colman's Coll., Violet Hill, Newry. *Address:* Drumiller House, Jerrettspass, Newry, Co. Down BT34 1TS. *T:* (028) 3082 1508, (028) 3082 1367.

BROOKS, John Ashton, CBE 1989; FCIB; Director: Midland Bank plc, 1981–91; Hongkong and Shanghai Banking Corp., 1989–91; Thomas Cook Group Ltd, 1983–94 (Chairman, 1988–92); *b* 24 Oct. 1928; *s* of Victor Brooks and Annie (*née* Ashton); *m* 1959, Sheila (*née* Hulse); one *s* one *d*. *Educ:* Merchant Taylors' Sch., Northwood. Joined Midland Bank, 1949; Manager: 22 Victoria Street Br., 1970; Threadneedle Street Br., 1972; Gen. Man., Computer Operations, 1975; Dep. Gp Chief Exec., Midland Group, 1981–89. President: Chartered Inst. of Bankers, 1987–89; Assoc. of Banking Teachers, 1990–98. Trustee, Charities Aid Foundn, 1990–99; Dir and Chm., CafCash Ltd (formerly Charities Aid Foundn Money Management Ltd), 1993–99. *Recreations:* reading, walking. *Club:* Institute of Directors.

BROOKS, Prof. John Stuart, PhD, DSc; FInstP; Vice-Chancellor, University of Wolverhampton, since 1998; *b* 8 March 1949; *s* of Ernest and Maude Brooks; *m* 1971, Jill Everil (*née* Pusey); two *s*. *Educ:* Cheshunt Grammar Sch.; Sheffield Univ. (BSc; PhD 1973; DSc 1998). CPhys, FInstP 1985; CEng 1992. Lectr, Sheffield City Poly., 1973–84; Head of Applied Physics Dept, 1984–90; Dir, Materials Res. Inst., 1990–92; Asst Principal, Sheffield Hallam Univ., 1992–98. *Publications:* 75 papers on materials and spectroscopy in learned jls. *Recreations:* travel, walking, music, bridge. *Address:* University of Wolverhampton, Wulfrana Street, Wolverhampton WV1 1SB. *T:* (01902) 322102.

BROOKS, Leslie James, CEng, FRINA; RCNC; Deputy Director of Engineering (Constructive), Ship Department, Ministry of Defence (Procurement Executive), 1973–76, retired; *b* 3 Aug. 1916; *yr s* of late C. J. D. Brooks and Lucy A. Brooks, Milton Regis, Sittingbourne, Kent; *m* 1941, Ruth Elizabeth Olver, Saltash, Cornwall; two *s*. *Educ:* Borden Grammar Sch., Sittingbourne, Kent; HM Dockyard Schs, Sheerness and Chatham; Royal Naval Engrg Coll., Keyham; RNC, Greenwich. War of 1939–45: Asst Constructor, Naval Construction Dept, Admty, Bath, 1941–44; Constr Lt-Comdr on Staff of Allied Naval Comdr, Exped. Force, and Flag Officer, Brit. Assault Area, 1944. Constr in charge Welding, Naval Constrn Dept, Admty, Bath, 1945–47; Constr Comdr, Staff of Comdr-in-Chief, Brit. Pacific Fleet, 1947–49; Constr in charge, No 2 Ship Tank, Admty Experiment Works, Haslar, Gosport, 1949–54. Naval Constrn Dept, Admty, Bath: Constr, Merchant Shipping Liaison, 1954–56; Chief Constr in charge of Conversion of First Commando Ships, and of Operating Aircraft Carriers, 1956–62; Dep. Supt, Admty Exper. Works, Haslar, 1962–64; Senior Officers War Course, RNC Greenwich, 1964–65; Ship Dept, Bath: Asst Dir of Naval Constrn, Naval Constrn Div., MoD(N), 1965–68; Asst Dir of Engrg (Ships), MoD(PE), 1968–73; Dep. Dir of Engrg/Constr., MoD(PE), 1973. Mem., Royal Corps of Naval Constructors. *Recreations:* walking, photography, natural history. *Address:* Merrymeet, Perrymead, Bath BA2 5AY. *T:* (01225) 832856.

BROOKS, Mel; producer, writer, director, actor; *b* Brooklyn, 1926; *m* Florence Baum; two *s* one *d*; *m* 1964, Anne Bancroft; one *s*. TV script writer for series: Your Show of Shows, 1950–54; Caesar's Hour, 1954–57; (co-created) Get Smart, 1965. Films: (cartoon) The Critic (Academy Award), 1963; writer and director: The Producers (Academy Award), 1968 (adapted for stage, NY, 2001); Young Frankenstein, 1974; writer, director and actor: The Twelve Chairs, 1970; Blazing Saddles, 1974; Silent Movie, 1976; writer, director, actor and producer: High Anxiety, 1977; History of the World Part 1, 1981; Spaceballs, 1987; Life Stinks, 1991; Robin Hood: Men in Tights, 1993; Dracula: Dead and Loving It, 1995; actor, producer: To Be Or Not To Be, 1983. Film productions include: The Elephant Man, 1980; The Fly; Frances; My Favorite Year; 84 Charing Cross Road. Several album recordings. *Address:* c/o The Culver Studios, 9336 W Washington Boulevard, Culver City, CA 90232–2600, USA.

BROOKS, Prof. Nicholas Peter, DPhil; FSA, FRHistS; FBA 1989; Professor and Head of Department of Medieval History, University of Birmingham, since 1985; *b* 14 Jan. 1941; *s* of late W. D. W. Brooks, CBE; *m* 1967, Chloë Carolyn Willis; one *s* one *d*. *Educ:* Winchester Coll.; Magdalen Coll., Oxford (Demy; MA DPhil). FRHistS 1970; FSAScot 1970–85; FSA 1974. Lectr in Medieval Hist., 1964–78, Sen. Lectr, 1978–85, St Andrews Univ.; Birmingham University: Chm., Sch. of History, 1987–89; Chm., Jun. Year Abroad prog., 1988–95; Dean, Faculty of Arts, 1992–95. Chm., British Acad./RHistS Anglo-Saxon Charters Project, 1994–. General Editor: Studies in the Early Hist. of Britain, 1978–2000; Studies in Early Medieval Britain, 1999–. *Publications:* (ed) Latin and the Vernacular Languages in Early Medieval Britain, 1981; The Early History of the Church of Canterbury, 1984; (ed) St Oswald of Worcester, 1996; Anglo-Saxon Myths: State and Church 400–1066, 2000; Communities and Warfare 700–1400, 2000; numerous articles in festschriften, Medieval Archaeology, Anglo-Saxon England, Trans of RHistS, etc. *Recreations:* gardening, bridge, swimming, walking. *Address:* Department of Medieval History, University of Birmingham, Edgbaston, Birmingham B15 2TT. *T:* (0121) 414 5736.

BROOKS, Peter Malcolm; Chairman of European Corporate Coverage, Clifford Chance, since 1999; Chairman: Enodis plc, since 2000 (non-executive Director, since 1997); *b* 12 Feb. 1947; *s* of Roger Morrison Brooks and Phyllis Fuller Brooks (*née* Hopkinson); *m* 1987, Patricia Margaret Garrett; one *s*; and one *s* by a previous marriage. *Educ:* Marlborough Coll.; Southampton Univ. (LLB). Solicitor, MacFarlanes, 1970–84 (Partner, 1977–84); Clifford Chance: Partner, 1984–96; Hd of Corporate Practice, 1992–96; General Counsel, Deutsche Morgan Grenfell, 1997–99. Non-exec. Chm., Chesterton International plc, 2000; non-exec. Dir, NCL Holdings ASA, 2000–. *Recreations:* opera, theatre, travel, cricket, rackets. *Address:* c/o Clifford Chance, 200 Aldersgate Street, EC1A 4JJ. *T:* (020) 7006 1143. *Club:* MCC.

BROOKS, Richard John; Arts Editor, Sunday Times, since 1999; *b* 5 Feb. 1946; *s* of late Peter John Brooks and Joan Brooks; *m* 1978, Jane Mannion; two *d*. *Educ:* University College Sch.; Bristol Univ. (BA). Reporter, Bristol Evening Post, 1968–71; Journalist: BBC Radio, 1972–79; Economist, 1979–80; Sunday Times, 1980–85; Media and Culture Editor, Observer, 1986–99. *Recreations:* playing golf and tennis, supporting Arsenal, watching films. *Address:* Sunday Times, 1 Pennington Street, E1 9XW. *T:* (020) 7782 5735.

BROOKS, Robert; Chairman, Bonhams and Brooks Ltd, since 2000; *b* 1 Oct. 1956; *s* of William Frederick Brooks and Joan Patricia (*née* Marshall); *m* 1981, Evelyn Rachel Durnford; two *s* one *d*. *Educ:* St Benedict's Sch., Ealing. Joined Christie's South Kensington Ltd, 1975, Dir, 1984–87; Dir, Christie Manson and Woods Ltd, 1987–89; established Brooks (Auctioneers) Ltd, 1989; acquired and merged with W. & F. C. Bonham and Sons Ltd, 2000. FIA Gp N European Touring Car Champion, 1999. *Recreations:* motor racing, golf, cricket. *Address:* Montpelier Galleries, Montpelier Street, SW7 1HH. *T:* (020) 7393 3900. *Club:* British Racing Drivers'.

BROOKS, Stuart Armitage, CMG 2001; OBE 1991; HM Diplomatic Service; Counsellor, Foreign and Commonwealth Office, 1997–2001; *b* 15 May 1948; *s* of Frank and Audrey Brooks; *m* 1975, Mary-Margaret Elliott; two *d*. *Educ:* Churchill Coll.,

Cambridge (MA). Entered FCO, 1970: Vice-Consul, Rio de Janeiro, 1972–74; Second Sec., on secondment to Home CS, 1974–75; Second, later First, Sec., Lisbon, 1975–78; First Secretary: FCO, 1978; Moscow, 1979–82; FCO, 1982–87; Stockholm, 1987–91; FCO, 1991–93; Counsellor, Vienna, 1993–97. *Recreations:* music, horticulture. *Address:* c/o Foreign and Commonwealth Office, King Charles Street, SW1A 2AH.

BROOKS, Timothy Gerald Martin; JP; farmer; Lord-Lieutenant of Leicestershire, since 1989; *b* 20 March 1929; *s* of late Hon. Herbert William Brooks, *s* of 2nd Baron Crawshaw, and of Hilda Muriel (*née* Steel); *m* 1951, Hon. Ann Fremantle, *d* of 4th Baron Cottesloe, GBE, TD and late Lady Elizabeth Harris; three *s* two *d*. *Educ:* Eton; RAC, Cirencester (NDA). Set up farm and garden centre, Wistow, 1953; Dir, Thomas Tapling & Co. Ltd. Mem., Harborough DC, 1975–89 (Chm., 1983–84). Chm. Governors, Wyggeston's Hosp., Leicester, 1988–96. Churchwarden, St Wistan's, Wistow. JP 1960, High Sheriff, 1979–80, Leics. *Recreations:* arts, shooting. *Address:* Wistow Hall, near Great Glen, Leicester LE8 0QF.

BROOKSBANK, Sir (Edward) Nicholas, 3rd Bt *cr* 1919; with Christie's, 1974–97; *b* 4 Oct. 1944; *s* of Sir Edward William Brooksbank, 2nd Bt, TD, and of Ann, 2nd *d* of Col T. Clitherow; *S* father, 1983; *m* 1970, Emma, *d* of Baron Holderness, *qv*; one *s* one *d*. *Educ:* Eton. Royal Dragoons, 1963–69; Blues and Royals, 1969–73; Adjutant, 1971–73. *Heir: s* (Florian) Tom (Charles) Brooksbank, *b* 9 Aug. 1982. *Address:* Menethorpe Hall, Malton, North Yorks.

BROOKSBANK, Sir Nicholas; *see* Brooksbank, Sir E. N.

BROOM, Prof. Donald Maurice; Colleen Macleod Professor of Animal Welfare, University of Cambridge, since 1986; Fellow, since 1987, and President, since 2001, St Catharine's College, Cambridge; *b* 14 July 1942; *s* of late Donald Edward Broom and of Mavis Edith Rose Broom; *m* 1971, Sally Elizabeth Mary Riordan; three *s*. *Educ:* Whitgift Sch.; St Catharine's Coll., Cambridge (MA, PhD). Lectr, 1967, Sen. Lectr, 1979, Reader, 1982, Dept of Pure and Applied Zoology, Univ. of Reading. Vis. Asst Prof., Univ. of California, Berkeley, 1969; Vis. Lectr, Univ. of W Indies, Trinidad, 1972; Vis. Scientist, CSIRO Div. of Animal Prodn, Perth, WA, 1983. Member: EEC Farm Animal Welfare Expert Gp, 1981–89; EU Scientific Cttee on Animal Health and Animal Welfare, 1997–; Scientific Advr, Council of Europe Standing Cttee of Eur. Convention for Protection of Animals kept for Farming Purposes, 1987–2000; Chm., EU Scientific Veterinary Cttee on Animal Welfare, 1990–97; EU Rep., Quadripartite Wkg Gp on Humane Trapping Standard, 1995–96. Hon. Res. Associate, BBSRC Inst. of Grassland and Envmtl Res. (formerly AFRC Inst. for Grassland and Animal Production), 1985–. Member: Council, Assoc. for Study of Animal Behaviour, 1971–83 (Hon. Treas., 1971–80); Internat. Ethological Cttee, 1976–79; Council, Soc. for Vet. Ethology, 1981–89 (Vice-Pres., 1986–87, 1989–91; Pres., 1987–89); NERC Special Cttee on Seals, 1986–96; Farm Animal Welfare Council, MAFF, 1991–99; BSI Panel on ISO Animal (Mammal) Traps, 1993–98; Animal Procedures Cttee, Home Office, 1998–. Trustee, Farm Animal Care Trust, 1986– (Chm., 1999–). Hon. Coll. Fellow, Myerscough Coll., Univ. of Central Lancs, 1999. Hon. DSc De Montfort, 2000. George Fleming Prize, British Vet. Jl, 1990; British Soc. of Animal Sci./RSPCA Award for Innovative Develts in Animal Welfare, 2001. *Publications:* Birds and their Behaviour, 1977; Biology of Behaviour, 1981; (ed jtly) The Encyclopaedia of Domestic Animals, 1986; (ed) Farmed Animals, 1986; (with A. F. Fraser) Farm Animal Behaviour and Welfare, 1990; (with K. G. Johnson) Stress and Animal Welfare, 1993; numerous papers in behaviour, psychol, zool, ornithol, agricl and vet. jls. *Recreations:* squash, water-polo, modern pentathlon, ornithology. *Address:* Department of Clinical Veterinary Medicine, Madingley Road, Cambridge CB3 0ES. *T:* (01223) 337697; *e-mail:* dmb16@cam.ac.uk. *Club:* Hawks (Cambridge).

BROOM, Air Marshal Sir Ivor (Gordon), KCB 1975 (CB 1972); CBE 1969; DSO 1945; DFC 1942 (Bar to DFC 1944, 2nd Bar 1945); AFC 1956; international aerospace consultant, since 1977; Chairman: Gatwick Handling Ltd, 1982–93; Farnborough Aerospace Development Corporation, 1985–92; *b* Cardiff, 2 June 1920; *s* of Alfred Godfrey Broom and Janet Broom; *m* 1942, Jess Irene Broom (*née* Cooper); two *s* one *d*. *Educ:* West Monmouth Grammar Sch.; Pontypridd County Sch., Glam. Joined RAF, 1940; commissioned, 1941; 114 Sqdn, 107 Sqdn, 1941; CFS Course, 1942; Instructor on: 1655 Mosquito Trg Unit; 571 Sqdn, 128 Sqdn; commanded 163 Sqdn, 1943–45; HQ, ACSEA, 1945–46; commanded 28 (FR) Sqdn, 1946–48; RAF Staff Coll. Course, Bracknell, 1949; Sqdn Comdr, No 1 ITS, 1950–52; No 3 Flying Coll. Course, Manby, 1952–53; commanded 57 Sqdn, 1953–54; Syndicate Leader, Flying Coll., Manby, 1954–56; commanded Bomber Command Development Unit, Wittering, 1956–59; Air Secretary's Dept, 1959–62; commanded RAF Bruggen, 1962–64; IDC, 1965–66; Dir of Organisation (Establishments), 1966–68; Commandant, Central Flying School, 1968–70; AOC No 11 (Fighter) Gp, Strike Comd, 1970–72. Dep. Controller, 1972–74, Controller, 1974–77, Nat. Air Traffic Services; Mem., CAA Bd, 1974–77. Dir, Plessey Airports Ltd, 1982–86. Pres., Mosquito Aircrew Assoc., 1993–. Vice-Pres., RAFA, 1981–. President: Pathfinder Assoc., 1990–93; Blenheim Soc., 1990–. QCVSA 1955. *Recreations:* golf, skiing. *Address:* Cherry Lawn, Bridle Lane, Loudwater, Rickmansworth, Herts WD3 4JB. *Clubs:* Royal Air Force; Moor Park Golf (Pres., 1992–97).

BROOM, Peter David; HM Diplomatic Service; Consul General, Cape Town, since 2000; *b* 7 Aug. 1953; *s* of Albert Leslie Broom and Annie Myfannwy Broom; *m* 1976, Vivienne Louise Pyatt; five *d*. *Educ:* Hillside Sch., Finchley. Entered FCO, 1970; Attaché: Oslo, 1974–77; Jedda, 1977–79; Islamabad, 1979–81; FCO, 1981–84; Mbabane, 1984–87; New Delhi, 1987–89; Second Sec., FCO, 1989–91; Consul (Commercial), Brisbane, 1991–97; Consul and Dep. High Comr, Yaoundé, 1997–2000. *Recreations:* sport, history. *Address:* c/o Foreign and Commonwealth Office, King Charles Street, SW1A 2AH; 7 Sunny Hill, Waldringfield, Suffolk IP12 4QS.

BROOME, David McPherson, CBE 1995 (OBE 1970); farmer; British professional show jumper; *b* Cardiff, 1 March 1940; *s* of Fred and Amelia Broome, Chepstow, Gwent; *m* 1976, Elizabeth, *d* of K. W. Fletcher, Thirsk, N Yorkshire; three *s*. *Educ:* Monmouth Grammar Sch. for Boys. European Show Jumping Champion (3 times); World Show Jumping Champion, La Baule, 1970; Olympic Medallist (Bronze) twice, 1960, 1968; King George V Gold Cup 6 times (a record, in 1990). Mounts include: Sunsalve, Aachen, 1961; Mr Softee, Rotterdam, 1967, and Hickstead, 1969; Beethoven, La Baule, France, 1970, as (1st British) World Champion; Sportsman and Philco, Cardiff, 1974; Professional Champion of the World. *Publications:* Jump-Off, 1971; (with S. Hadley) Horsemanship, 1983. *Recreations:* hunting (MFH), shooting, golf. *Address:* Mount Ballan Manor, Port Skewett, Caldicot, Monmouthshire, Wales NP26 5UN.

BROOME, Prof. John, PhD; FBA 2000; FRSE; White's Professor of Moral Philosophy, University of Oxford, since 2000; Fellow, Corpus Christi College, Oxford, since 2000; *b* 17 May 1947; *s* of Richard and Tamsin Broome; *m* 1970, Ann Rowland; one *s* one *d*. *Educ:* Trinity Hall, Cambridge (BA); Bedford Coll., Univ. of London (MA); Massachusetts Inst. Technol. (PhD 1972). Lectr in Econs, Birkbeck Coll., London Univ., 1972–78; Reader in Econs, 1979–92, Prof. of Econs and Philosophy, 1992–95, Univ. of Bristol; Prof. of Philosophy, Univ. of St Andrews, 1995–2000. Visiting posts: Univ. of Va, 1975; All Souls Coll., Oxford, 1982–83; ANU, 1986, 1993; Princeton Univ., 1987–89; Univ. of Washington, 1988; Univ. of BC, 1993–94; Uppsala Univ., 1997–98. Ed., Economics and Philosophy, 1994–99. FRSE 1999. *Publications:* The Microeconomics of Capitalism, 1983; Weighing Goods, 1991; Counting the Cost of Global Warming, 1992; Ethics Out of Economics, 1999. *Recreation:* sailing. *Address:* Corpus Christi College, Oxford OX1 4JF; 4 Southgait Close, St Andrews, Fife KY16 9QH.

BROOME, John Lawson, CBE 1987; Founder and Chairman, Alton Towers Theme Park, since 1980 (Chief Executive, 1980–90); *b* 2 Aug. 1943; *s* of late Albert Henry and Mary Elizabeth Broome; *m* 1972, Jane Myott Bagshaw; one *s* two *d*. *Educ:* Rossall School. School master, 1960–65; Dir, JLB Investment Property Group, 1961–, and numerous other companies; Chm. and Chief Exec., Adventure World Theme Park, 1997–99. Member: ETB and BTA, 1982–92; Internat. Assoc. of Amusement Parks and Attractions, USA, 1986–89 (Chm., Internat. Cttee; Chm., Internat. Council, 1986–89). Vice-Pres., Ironbridge Gorge Museum Trust. Governor, Staffordshire Univ. (formerly N Staffs Poly.), 1984–95. Vis. Prof., Sunderland Univ., 1996–. *Recreations:* ski-ing, travelling, antiques, old paintings, objets d'art, fine gardens, restoration of historic properties. *Address:* Dallicote Hall, Bridgnorth, Shropshire WV15 5PL. *T:* (office) (01691) 610794. *Clubs:* Grosvenor (Chester); St James's (Manchester).

BROOMFIELD, Alexander Bryan; Chairman, Aberdeen Royal Hospitals NHS Trust, 1992–96; *b* 13 Jan. 1937; *s* of late William P. Broomfield, OBE and Eliza M. Broomfield; *m* 1960, Morag Carruthers. *Educ:* Aberdeen Grammar Sch. 26 years with Town & County Motor Garage Ltd; Man. Dir, retired 1992. Member: Grampian Health Bd, 1990–92; Bd, Scottish SHA, 1980–88; Council, Aberdeen Chamber of Commerce, to 1995 (Pres., 1978–79); Vice-Chm., Aberdeen Airport Consultative Cttee, 1990–. *Recreations:* walking, fishing, golf. *Address:* 5 Carnegie Gardens, Aberdeen AB15 4AW. *Clubs:* Royal Northern and University (Aberdeen); Royal Aberdeen Golf.

BROOMFIELD, Sir Nigel (Hugh Robert Allen), KCMG 1993 (CMG 1986); HM Diplomatic Service, retired; Director, Ditchley Foundation, since 1999; *b* 19 March 1937; *s* of Col Arthur Allen Broomfield and Ruth Sheilagh Broomfield; *m* 1963, Valerie Fenton; two *s*. *Educ:* Haileybury Coll.; Trinity Coll., Cambridge (BA (Hons) English Lit.). Commnd 17/21 Lancers, 1959, retired as Major, 1968. Joined FCO as First Sec., 1969; First Secretary: British Embassy, Bonn, 1970–72; British Embassy, Moscow, 1972–74; European Communities Dept, London, 1975–77; RCDS, 1978; Political Advr and Head of Chancery, British Mil. Govt, Berlin, 1979–81; Head of Eastern European and Soviet Dept, 1981–83, and Head of Soviet Dept, 1983–85, FCO; Dep. High Comr and Minister, New Delhi, 1985–88; Ambassador to GDR, 1988–90; Dep. Under Sec. of State (Defence), FCO, 1990–92, Ambassador to Germany, 1993–97. Non-exec. Dir, TI Gp Plc, 1998–; Advr, Arthur Anderson, 1997. Captain, Cambridge Squash Rackets and Real Tennis, 1957–58; British Amateur Squash Champion, 1958–59 (played for England, 1957–60). *Recreations:* tennis, golf, reading, music. *Address:* Ditchley Foundation, Ditchley Park, Enstone, Chipping Norton, Oxon OX7 4ER. *Clubs:* Royal Automobile, MCC, All England Lawn Tennis; Hawks (Cambridge).

BROPHY, Michael John Mary; Chief Executive, Charities Aid Foundation, since 1982; *b* 24 June 1937; *s* of Gerald and Mary Brophy; *m* 1962, Sarah Rowe; three *s* one *d*. *Educ:* Ampleforth Coll.; Royal Naval Coll., Dartmouth. Entered Royal Navy, 1955; retired as Lt-Comdr, 1966. Associate Dir, J. Walter Thompson, 1967–74; Appeals Dir, Spastics Soc., 1974–82. Dir, European Foundn Centre, 1989–98 (Chm., 1994–95); Chm., Euro Citizens Action Service, 1996–. *Recreation:* sailing. *Address:* 8 Oldlands Hall, Herons Ghyll, Uckfield, E Sussex TN22 3DA. *Club:* Athenæum.

BROSAN, Dr George Stephen, CBE 1982; TD 1960; Director, North East London Polytechnic, 1970–82; *b* 8 Aug. 1921; *o s* of Rudolph and Margaret Brosan; *m* 1952, Maureen Dorothy Foscoe; three *d*. *Educ:* Kilburn Grammar Sch.; Faraday House; The Polytechnic; Birkbeck Coll., London. Faraday Scholar, 1939. PhD 1951; DFH 1957; CEng 1976, Eur Ing 1989, Hon. FIEE 1991 (FIEE 1964); CMath 1982; MRIN 1983. Teaching staff, Regent Street Polytechnic, 1950–58; Head of Dept, Willesden Coll. of Technology, 1958–60; Further Educn Officer, Middlesex CC, 1960–62; Principal, Enfield Coll. of Technology, 1962–70. Pres., Tensor Club of GB, 1973–82; Pres., IProdE, 1975–77 (Hon. FIProdE 1980–91); Mem. Council, BIM, 1975–79; Chairman: CEI Educn Cttee, 1978–79; Accountancy Educn Consultative Bd, 1979–82. Life Mem., ASME, 1977. Hon. MIED 1967; Hon. Mem., Council for Educn in the Commonwealth, 1983. CIMgt (FBIM 1975). Chevalier du Tastevin, 1976; Yachtmaster Ocean, 1986. *Publications:* (jtly) Advanced Electrical Power and Machines, 1966; (jtly) Patterns and Policies in Higher Education, 1971; numerous articles and papers in academic and professional press. *Recreation:* computing. *Address:* Winton Dene, Ashen, Sudbury, Suffolk CO10 8JN; Tartagli Alti, Paciano 06060, Province of Perugia, Italy. *Club:* Reform.

See also Prof. N. J. Mackintosh.

BROSNAN, Pierce; actor; *b* Navan, Co. Meath, 16 May 1953; *s* of Tom Brosnan and May Smith; *m* 1977, Cassandra Harris (*d* 1991); one *s*, and one step *s* one step *d*; *m* 2001, Keely Shaye Smith; two *s*. *Educ:* Drama Centre, London. Asst stage manager, Theatre Royal, York; *stage* appearances include: Red Devil Battery Sign; Filumena; Wait Until Dark; *television* includes: The Manions of America series, 1981; Remington Steele series (title rôle), 1982–87; Nancy Astor, 1984; Noble House 1988; Around the World in 80 Days, 1989; Robinson Crusoe, 1996; *films* include: Nomads, 1986; The Fourth Protocol, 1987; The Deceivers, 1988; Mr Johnson, 1991; Lawnmower Man, 1992; Mrs Doubtfire, 1993; Love Affair, 1994; The Mirror has Two Faces, 1996; Mars Attacks!, 1996; Dante's Peak, 1997; The Nephew, 1998 (also prod); The Thomas Crown Affair, 1999 (also prod); Grey Owl, 2000; The Taylor of Panama, 2001; rôle of James Bond in: GoldenEye, 1995; Tomorrow Never Dies, 1997; The World is Not Enough, 1999. *Address:* c/o Guttman Associates, 118 South Beverly Drive, Suite 201, Beverly Hills, CA 90212, USA.

BROTHERHOOD, Air Cdre William Rowland, CBE 1952; retired as Director, Guided Weapons (Trials), Ministry of Aviation (formerly Supply), 1959–61; *b* 22 Jan. 1912; *s* of late James Brotherhood, Tintern, Mon.; *m* 1939, Margaret (*d* 1981), *d* of late Ernest Sutcliffe, Louth, Lincs; one *s* one *d*. *Educ:* Monmouth School; RAF College, Cranwell. Joined RAF, 1930; Group Captain, 1943; Air Commodore, 1955; Director, Operational Requirements, Air Ministry, 1955–58. *Address:* Fisherman's Cottage, 25 Dial Close, Seend, Melksham, Wilts SN12 6NP. *T:* (01380) 828189.

BROTHERS, Air Cdre Peter Malam, CBE 1964; DSO 1944; DFC 1940, and Bar, 1943; Managing Director, Peter Brothers Consultants Ltd, 1973–86; *b* 30 Sept. 1917; *s* of late John Malam Brothers; *m* 1939, Annette, *d* of late James Wilson; three *d*. *Educ:* N. Manchester Sch. (Br. of Manchester Grammar). Joined RAF, 1936; Flt-Lieut 1939; RAF Biggin Hill, Battle of Britain, 1940; Sqdn-Ldr 1941; Wing Comdr 1942; Tangmere Fighter Wing Ldr, 1942–43; Staff HQ No. 10 Gp, 1943; Exeter Wing Ldr, 1944; US Comd and Gen. Staff Sch., 1944–45; Central Fighter Estab., 1945–46; Colonial Service, Kenya, 1947–49; RAF Bomber Sqdn, 1949–52; HQ No. 3 Gp, 1952–54; RAF Staff Coll.,

1954; HQ Fighter Comd, 1955–57; Bomber Stn, 1957–59; Gp Capt., and Staff Officer, SHAPE, 1959–62; Dir of Ops (Overseas), 1962–65; Air Cdre, and AOC Mil. Air Traffic Ops, 1965–68; Dir of Public Relations (RAF), MoD (Air), 1968–73; retired 1973. Freeman, Guild Air Pilots and Air Navigators, 1966 (Liveryman, 1968; Warden, 1971; Master, 1974–75); Freeman, City of London, 1967. Editorial Adviser, Defence and Foreign Affairs publications, 1973–76. Patron, Spitfire Assoc., Australia, 1971–; Vice-President: Spitfire Soc., 1984–; Devon Emergency Volunteers, 1980–93 (Chm., 1981–93). *Recreations:* golf, sailing, fishing, swimming, flying. *Address:* c/o National Westminster Bank, Topsham, Devon EX3 0HB. *Clubs:* Royal Air Force; Deanwood Park Golf.

BROTHERSTON, Leslie William, (Lez); freelance production designer, since 1984; *b* 6 Oct. 1961; *s* of L. Brotherston and Irene Richardson. *Educ:* Prescot Grammar Sch., Prescot, Liverpool; Central Sch. of Art and Design (BA Hons Th. Design 1984). First design for Letter to Brezhnev (film); work with Northern Ballet Theatre includes: The Brontes, Strange Meeting, Romeo and Juliet; Giselle, 1997; Dracula, 1997; The Hunchback of Notre Dame, 1998; Carmen (Barclays Th. Award for Outstanding Achievement in Dance, TMA Award), 1999; designs for *dance* include: for Adventures in Motion Pictures: Highland Fling, 1994; Swan Lake, Piccadilly, 1996, transf. NY (Tony Award for Best Costume Design, Drama Desk Awards for Best Costume Design and Best Set Design, Outer Critics Award for Outstanding Costume Design, 1999); Cinderella, Piccadilly, 1997 (Olivier Award for Outstanding Achievement in Dance, 1998); Greymatter, Rambert; for Scottish Ballet: Just Scratchin' the Surface, Nightlife, 1999; Aladdin, 2000; *theatre* includes: Greenwich: Prisoner of Zenda; Handling Bach, 1995; The Last Romantics, Northanger Abbey, 1996; David Copperfield, Side by Side by Sondheim, 1997; Rosencrantz and Guildenstern are Dead, RNT, 1995; Alarms and Excursions, Gielgud, 1998; Spend, Spend, Spend, Piccadilly, 1999; A Woman of No Importance, Royal Exchange, 2000; *opera* includes prodns for Opera Zuid, Hong Kong Arts Fest., Opera North, Glyndebourne Touring Opera, Teatro Bellini, Royal Danish Opera, Opera NI; *musicals* include: Side by Side by Sondheim, Greenwich; Cabaret, Sheffield Crucible; Maria Friedman by Special Arrangement, Donmar Warehouse. *Address:* c/o Cassie Mayer Management, 34 Kingly Court, W1R 5LE. *T:* (020) 7434 1242; 26 Bow Brook, Mace Street, Bethnal Green, E2 0PW. *T:* (020) 8981 8764. *Club:* Soho House.

BROTHERTON, Ven. John Michael; Archdeacon of Chichester and Canon Residentiary of Chichester Cathedral, since 1991; *b* 7 Dec. 1935; *s* of late Clifford and Minnie Brotherton; *m* 1963, Daphne Margaret Yvonne, *d* of Sir Geoffrey Meade, KBE, CMG, CVO; three *s* one *d*. *Educ:* St John's Coll., Cambridge (MA); Cuddesdon Coll., Oxford; Univ. of London Inst. of Educn (PGCE). Ordained: deacon, 1961; priest, 1962; Asst Curate, St Nicolas, Chiswick, 1961–64; Chaplain, Trinity Coll., Port of Spain, Trinidad, 1965–69; Rector of St Michael's, Diego Martin, Trinidad, 1969–75; Vicar, St Mary and St John, Oxford, and Chaplain, St Hilda's Coll., Oxford, 1976–81; Rural Dean of Cowley, 1978–81; Vicar, St Mary, Portsea, 1981–91. Mem., Legal Adv. Commn, C of E, 1996–. Hon. Canon, St Michael's Cathedral, Kobe, Japan, 1986. Proctor in Convocation, 1995–. *Recreations:* travel, walking. *Address:* 4 Canon Lane, Chichester, West Sussex PO19 1PX. *T:* (01243) 779134, *Fax:* (01243) 536452.

BROTHERTON, Michael Lewis; formed Michael Brotherton Associates, Parliamentary Consultants, 1986; *b* 26 May 1931; *s* of late John Basil Brotherton and Maud Brotherton; *m* 1968, Julia, *d* of Austin Gerald Comyn King and Katherine Elizabeth King, Bath; three *s* one *d*. *Educ:* Prior Park; RNC Dartmouth. Served RN, 1949–64: qual. Observer 1955; Cyprus, 1957 (despatches); Lt-Comdr 1964, retd. Times Newspapers, 1967–74. Chm., Beckenham Conservative Political Cttee, 1967–68; contested (C) Deptford, 1970; MP (C) Louth, Oct. 1974–1983. Pres., Hyde Park Tories, 1975. Mem., Select Cttee on violence in the family, 1975–76. Chm., Friends, 1995–99, Chm., Library Cttee, 1997–99, Boston Parish Church. *Recreations:* cricket, cooking, gardening, talking. *Address:* The Old Vicarage, Wrangle, Boston, Lincs PE22 9EP. *T:* (01205) 870688. *Clubs:* Conservative Working Men's, Louth (Louth); Castaways; Cleethorpes Conservative; Immingham Conservative.

BROTHWOOD, Rev. John, MRCP, FRCPsych, FFOM; Hon. Curate, St Barnabas, Dulwich, 1991–99; *b* 23 Feb. 1931; *s* of late Wilfred Cyril Vernon Brothwood and Emma Bailey; *m* 1957, Dr Margaret Stirling Meyer; one *d* (one *s* decd). *Educ:* Marlborough Coll.; Peterhouse, Cambridge (Schol.); Middlesex Hosp. MB BChir (Cantab) 1955; MRCP 1960, DPM (London) 1964, FFCM 1972, FRCPsych 1976, FFOM 1988. Various posts in clinical medicine, 1955–64; joined DHSS (then Min. of Health) as MO, 1964; SPMO and Under Secretary, DHSS, 1975–78; CMO, Esso Petroleum (UK) and Esso, subseq. Exxon, Chemicals, 1979–90. Lay Reader, Parish of St Barnabas, Dulwich, 1982–91; Southwark Ordination Course, 1988–91; deacon, 1991; priest, 1992. Mem. Council, Missions to Seamen, 1994–2001. *Publications:* various. *Recreations:* diverse. *Address:* 98 Woodwarde Road, SE22 8UT. *T:* (020) 8693 8273.

BROUCHER, David Stuart; HM Diplomatic Service; UK Permanent Representative to Conference on Disarmament, Geneva (with personal rank of Ambassador), since 2001; *b* 5 Oct. 1944; *s* of Clifford Broucher and Betty Broucher (*née* Jordan); *m* 1971, Marion Monika Blackwell; one *s*. *Educ:* Manchester Grammar School; Trinity Hall, Cambridge (MA Modern Languages). Foreign Office, 1966; British Military Govt, Berlin, 1968; Cabinet Office, 1972; Prague, 1975; FCO, 1978; UK Perm. Rep. to EC, 1983; Counsellor, Jakarta, 1985–89; Economic Counsellor, Bonn, 1989–93; Counsellor, FCO, 1994; Asst Under Sec. of State, FCO, 1995–97; Ambassador to Czech Republic, 1997–2001. *Recreations:* music, golf, sailing. *Address:* c/o Foreign and Commonwealth Office, SW1A 2AH.

BROUGH, Dr Colin, FRCPE; FFCM; Chief Administrative Medical Officer, Lothian Health Board, 1980–88; *b* 4 Jan. 1932; *s* of Peter Brough and Elizabeth C. C. Chalmers; *m* 1957, Maureen Jennings; four *s* one *d*. *Educ:* Bell Baxter Sch., Cupar; Univ. of Edinburgh (MB ChB). DPH 1965; DIH 1965; FFCM 1978; MRCPE 1981; FRCPE 1982. House Officer, Leicester General Hosp. and Royal Infirmary of Edinburgh, 1956–57; Surg.-Lieut, Royal Navy, 1957–60; General Practitioner, Leith and Fife, 1960–64; Dep. Medical Supt, Royal Inf. of Edinburgh, 1965–67; ASMO, PASMO, Dep. SAMO, South-Eastern Regional Hosp. Board, Scotland, 1967–74; Community Medicine Specialist, Lothian Health Board, 1974–80. *Recreations:* golf, shooting, fishing, first aid. *Address:* The Saughs, Gullane, East Lothian EH31 2AL. *T:* (01620) 842179.

BROUGH, Edward; Chairman, Volker Stevin (UK) Ltd, 1980–82; *b* 28 May 1918; *s* of late Hugh and Jane Brough; *m* 1941, Peggy Jennings; two *s*. *Educ:* Berwick Grammar School; Edinburgh University (MA). Joined Unilever Ltd, 1938. War service, KOSB, 1939–46 (Captain). Rejoined Unilever, 1946; Commercial Dir, 1951, Man. Dir, 1954, Lever's Cattle Foods Ltd; Chairman, Crosfields (CWG) Ltd, 1957; Lever Bros & Associates Ltd: Development Dir, 1960; Marketing Dir, 1962; Chm., 1965; Hd of Unilever's Marketing Div., 1968–71; Dir of Unilever Ltd and Unilever NV, 1968–74, and Chm. of UK Cttee, 1971–74. Chm., Adriaan Volker (UK) Ltd, 1974–80. Mem., NBPI, 1967–70. FIMgt (FBIM 1967). *Recreations:* flyfishing, golf. *Address:* Flat 8, Ferndown Court, Frensham Road, Lower Bourne, Farnham, Surrey GU10 3PZ; St John's, Chagford, Devon TQ13 8HJ. *Club:* Farmers'.

BROUGH, Michael David, FRCS; Consultant Plastic Surgeon: University College London Hospitals, Royal Free and Whittington Hospitals, since 1982; St Luke's Hospital for the Clergy, since 1986; King Edward VII's Hospital for Officers, since 1992; *b* 4 July 1942; *s* of late Kenneth David Brough and Frances Elizabeth Brough (*née* Davies); *m* 1974, Dr Geraldine Moira Sleigh; two *s* two *d*. *Educ:* Westminster Sch.; Christ's Coll., Cambridge (MA); Middlesex Hosp. Med. Sch. (MB, BChir). Med. posts at Middlesex and Central Middlesex Hosps, 1968–71; Surgical trng posts, Birmingham Hosps, 1971–74; Plastic Surgery trng posts, Mount Vernon Hosp., London, Odstock Hosp., Salisbury, Whithington Hosp., Manchester, 1975–80; Cons. Plastic Surg., St Andrews Hosp., Billericay, Queen Elizabeth Hosp., Hackney, Whipps Cross Hosp., 1980–82. Hon. Sen. Lectr in Plastic Surgery, London Univ., 1985–. Hon. Sec., Phoenix Appeal, 1988–95. President: Plastic Surg. Sect., RSM, 1990–91; BAPS, 2002. *Publications:* chapters in books; contribs to med. jls on plastic and reconstructive surgery. *Recreations:* family, ski-ing, Modern Pentathlon Half-Blue, 1964. *Address:* The Consulting Suite, 82 Portland Place, W1N 3DH. *T:* (020) 7935 8910. *Club:* Hawks (Cambridge).

BROUGHAM, family name of **Baron Brougham and Vaux**.

BROUGHAM AND VAUX, 5th Baron *cr* 1860; **Michael John Brougham,** CBE 1995; *b* 2 Aug. 1938; *s* of 4th Baron and Jean (*d* 1992), *d* of late Brig.-Gen. G. B. S. Follett, DSO, MVO; *S* father, 1967; *m* 1st, 1963, Olivia Susan (marr. diss. 1968), *d* of Rear-Admiral Gordon Thomas Seccombe Gray, CB, DSC; one *d*; 2nd, 1969, Catherine Gulliver (marr. diss. 1981), *d* of late W. Gulliver; one *s*. *Educ:* Lycée Jaccard, Lausanne; Millfield School. Dep. Chm. of Cttees, H of L, 1992–; a Dep. Speaker, H of L, 1995–; elected Mem., H of L, 1999. President: RoSPA, 1986–89; Nat. Health and Safety Gps Council, 1994–. Chm., Tax Payers Soc., 1989–91. Chm., European Secure Vehicle Alliance, 1992–. *Heir: s* Hon. Charles William Brougham, *b* 9 Nov. 1971. *Address:* 11 Westminster Gardens, Marsham Street, SW1P 4JA.

BROUGHAM, Christopher John; QC 1988; *b* 11 Jan. 1947; *s* of late Lt-Comdr Patrick Brougham and of Elizabeth Anne (*née* Vestey); *m* 1974, Mary Olwen (*née* Corker); one *s* three *d*. *Educ:* Radley Coll.; Worcester Coll., Oxford (BA Hons). Called to the Bar, Inner Temple, 1969; Dep. High Court Bankruptcy Registrar, 1984. Dep. Churchwarden, Christ Church, Kensington, 1980–95. *Publications:* (contrib.) Encyclopedia of Financial Provision in Family Matters, 1998–; (jtly) Muir Hunter on Personal Insolvency, 2000–. *Recreations:* music, crossword puzzles. *Address:* 3/4 South Square, Gray's Inn, WC1R 5HP. *T:* (020) 7696 9900.

BROUGHER, Kerry; Chief Curator, Hirshhorn Museum and Sculpture Garden, since 2000; *b* 25 Sept. 1952; *s* of Russell Brougher and Margaret Brougher (*née* Smith); *m* 1987, Nora Halpern; two *d*. *Educ:* Univ. of Calif at Irvine (BA 1974); UCLA (MA 1978). Museum of Contemporary Art, Los Angeles: Asst Curator, 1982–87; Associate Curator, 1987–93; Curator, 1993–97; Dir, MOMA, Oxford, 1997–2000. Visitor, Ashmolean Mus., Univ. of Oxford, 1998–; Vis. Fellow, Nuffield Coll., Oxford, 1999–. Mem. Bd of Advrs, Filmforum, Los Angeles, 1994–. FRSA 2000. *Publications:* The Image of Abstraction, 1988; The Beatrice and Philip Gersh Collection, 1989; Wolfgang Laib, 1992; Robert Irwin, 1993; Hiroshi Sugimoto, 1993; Hall of Mirrors: art and film since 1945, 1996; Jeff Wall, 1997; Gustav Metzger, 1998; Notorious: Alfred Hitchcock and contemporary art, 1999; Ed Ruscha, 2000; Enclosed and Enchanted, 2000; Open City: street photographs since 1950, 2001. *Address:* Hirshhorn Museum and Sculpture Garden, Independence Avenue at Seventh Street SW, Washington, DC 20560–0350, USA.

BROUGHSHANE, 3rd Baron *cr* 1945; **William Kensington Davison,** DSO 1945; DFC 1942; *b* 25 Nov. 1914; *yr s* of 1st Baron Broughshane and Beatrice Mary (*d* 1971), *d* of Sir Owen Roberts; *S* brother, 1995. *Educ:* Shrewsbury Sch.; Magdalen Coll., Oxford. Called to the Bar, Inner Temple, 1939. Served War, 1939–45 (Wing Commander, RAF). *Recreations:* music, opera, ballet, reading. *Address:* 3 Godfrey Street, SW3 3TA. *T:* (020) 7352 7826. *Club:* Garrick.

BROUGHTON, family name of **Baron Fairhaven**.

BROUGHTON, Sir David (Delves), 13th Bt *cr* 1660, of Broughton, Staffordshire; *b* 7 May 1942; *s* of Lt-Comdr P. J. D. Broughton, RN, *g g g s* of Rev. Sir Henry Delves Broughton, 8th Bt, and of his 1st wife, Nancy Rosemary, *yr d* of J. E. Paterson; *S* kinsman, 1993; *m* 1969, Diane, *d* of R. L. Nicol. *Heir: half b* Geoffrey Delves Broughton, *b* 1962. *Address:* 31 Mayfield Court, Sandy, Beds SG19 1NF.

BROUGHTON, Martin Faulkner, FCA; Chairman, British American Tobacco plc, since 1998; *b* 15 April 1947; *m* 1974, Jocelyn Mary Rodgers; one *s* one *d*. *Educ:* Westminster City Grammar Sch. FCA 1969. Career in BAT Group: British-American Tobacco Co.: travelling auditor, 1971–74; Head Office, 1974–80; Souza Cruz, Brazil, 1980–85; Eagle Star, 1985–88 and (Chm.) 1992–93; Chm., Wiggins Teape Gp, 1989–90; Finance Dir, 1988–92; Man. Dir, Financial Services, 1992–98; Gp Chief Exec. and Dep. Chm., BAT Industries, 1993–98. Non-exec. Director: Whitbread, 1993–2000; British Airways, 2000–. Chm., CBI Cos Cttee, 1995–99; Member: Takeover Panel, 1996–99; Financial Reporting Council, 1998–. Ind. Dir, British Horseracing Bd, 1999–. *Recreations:* theatre, golf. *Address:* British American Tobacco plc, Globe House, 4 Temple Place, WC2R 2PG. *T:* (020) 7845 1000. *Club:* Hever Golf (Hever).

BROUGHTON, Dr Peter, FREng; Project Manager, Maureen Platform Re-Float and Decommissioning Project, Phillips Petroleum UK Ltd, since 1998; *b* 8 Sept. 1944; *s* of late Thomas Frederick Broughton and Mary Theodosia Broughton (*née* Bracewell); *m* 1968, Janet Mary, *d* of late Ronald George Silveston; two *s*. *Educ:* Rowlinson Technical Sch., Sheffield; Manchester Univ. (BSc 1966; PhD 1970). FICE; FIStructE; FIMarE; FRINA; FREng (FEng 1996). Engrg Surveyor, Lloyd's Register of Shipping, 1971–74; Partner, Campbell Reith and Partners, 1974–75; Sen. Structural Engr, Burmah Oil Development, 1975–76; Supervising Structural Engr, BNOC, 1977–79; Phillips Petroleum Co., 1979–: Sen Structl Engr, 1979–82, Civil Engrg Supervisor, 1982–86, UK; Project Engr and Co. Rep., Ekofisk Protective Barrier Project, Norway, 1986–90; Engrg and Procurement Manager, Judy/Joanne Develt Project, UK, 1990–94; Project Manager for Substructures, Ekofisk II Develt Project, Norway, 1994–98. Vis. Prof., Dept of Civil Engrg, ICSTM, 1991–. Stanley Grey Award, IMarE, 1992; George Stephenson Medal, 1993, Bill Curtin Medal, 1997, Overseas Premium, 1998, David Hislop Award, 1999, ICE. *Publications:* The Analysis of Cable and Catenary Structures, 1994; numerous technical papers on offshore structures. *Recreations:* walking, fishing, swimming. *Address:* Appletrees, 30 Portsmouth Road, Camberley, Surrey GU15 1JX. *T:* (01276) 23215.

BROUN, Sir William (Windsor), 13th Bt *cr* 1686 (NS), of Colstoun, Haddingtonshire; FCA; *b* 11 July 1917; *e s* of William Arthur Broun (*d* 1925) and Marie Victoria Broun (*d* 1964), *d* of William McIntyre; *S* cousin, 1995; *m* 1952, D'Hrie, *d* of late Frank R. King, Bingara, NSW; two *d*. *Educ:* North Sydney High Sch. FCA 1991. Vice Pres., Scottish

Australian Heritage Council. Member: Royal Agricl Soc. of NSW; Royal Armoured Corps Assoc. *Recreations:* golf, bowls. *Heir: b* Hulance Haddington Broun [*b* 10 March 1919; *m* 1947, Joy Maude (*d* 1995), *d* of late A. L. Stack, Mosman, NSW; one *s* two *d*]. *Address:* Tamarisk Gardens, 12/2–4 Reed Street, Cremorne, NSW 2090, Australia. *T:* (2) 99041020. *Clubs:* Royal Automobile of Australia (Sydney); Cromer Golf; Bombay Presidency Golf; Mosman Bowling.

BROWALDH, Tore; Grand Cross, Order of Star of the North, 1974; Kt Comdr's Cross, Order of Vasa, 1963; Hon. Chairman, Svenska Handelsbanken, since 1988; Deputy Chairman, Nobel Foundation, since 1966; *b* 23 Aug. 1917; *s* of Knut Ernfrid Browaldh and Ingrid Gezelius; *m* 1942, Gunnel Eva Ericson; three *s* one *d*. *Educ:* Stockholm Univ. (MA Politics, Economics and Law, 1941). Financial Attaché, Washington, 1943; Asst Sec., Royal Cttee of Post-War Econ. Planning, and Admin. Sec., Industrial Inst. for Econ. and Social Res., 1944–45; Sec. to Bd of Management, Svenska Handelsbanken, 1946–49; Dir of Econ., Social, Cultural and Refugee Dept, Secretariat Gen., Council of Europe, Strasbourg, 1949–51; Exec. Vice Pres., Confedn of Swedish Employers, 1951–54; Chief Gen. Man., Svenska Handelsbanken, 1955–66, Chm., 1966–78, Vice-Chm., 1978–88. Chairman: Svenska Cellulosa AB, 1965–88; Sandrew theater and movie AB, 1963–; Swedish IBM, 1978–; Swedish Unilever AB, 1977–; Industrivärden, 1976–88; Deputy Chairman: Beijerinvest AB, 1975–82; AB Volvo, 1977–88; Director: Volvo Internat. Adv. Bd, 1980–88; IBM World Trade Corp., Europe/ME/Africa, New York, 1979–88; Unilever Adv. Bd, Rotterdam and London, 1976–88. Member: Swedish Govt's Econ. Planning Commn, 1962–73 and Res. Adv. Bd, 1966–70; Consultative Cttee, Internat. Fedn of Insts for Advanced Study, 1972–; UN Gp of Eminent Persons on Multinational Corporations, 1973–74. Member: Royal Swedish Acad. of Sciences; Hudson Inst., USA; Soc. of Scientists and Members of Parlt, Sweden; Royal Swedish Acad. of Engrg Sciences; Royal Acad. of Arts and Sciences, Uppsala; World Acad. of Art and Scis. Dr of Technol. *hc* Royal Inst. of Technol., 1967; Dr of Econs *hc* Gothenburg, 1980. St Erik's Medal, Sweden, 1961; Gold Medal for public service, Sweden, 1981. *Publications:* Management and Society, 1961; (autobiography): vol. I, The Pilgrimage of a Journeyman, 1976; vol. II, The Long Road, 1980; vol. III, Against the Wind, 1984. *Recreations:* jazz, piano, golf, chess. *Address:* (office) Svenska Handelsbanken, Kungsträdgårdsgatan 2, 10670 Stockholm, Sweden. *T:* (8) 229220; (home) Sturegatan 14, 11436 Stockholm. *T:* (8) 6619643. *Club:* Sällskapet (Stockholm).

BROWN, Alan James; HM Diplomatic Service, retired; Deputy Commissioner-General, UN Relief and Works Agency for Palestine Refugees, 1977–84; *b* 28 Aug. 1921; *s* of W. Y. Brown and Mrs E. I. Brown; *m* 1966, Joy Aileen Key Stone (*née* McIntyre); one *s*, and two step *d*. *Educ:* Magdalene College, Cambridge (MA). Served with HM Forces, 1941–47; CRO 1948; 2nd Sec., Calcutta, 1948–50; CRO, 1951; Private Sec. to Parly Under-Secretary of State, 1951–52; 1st Secretary, Dacca, Karachi, 1952–55; CRO, 1955–57; Kuala Lumpur, 1957–62; CRO, 1962–63; Head of Information Policy Dept, 1963–64; Dep. High Comr, Nicosia, 1964; Head of Far East and Pacific Dept, CRO, 1964–66; Dep. High Comr, Malta, 1966–70; Dep High Comr, later Consul-Gen., Karachi, 1971–72; Ambassador to Togo and Benin, 1973–75; Head of Nationality and Treaty Dept, FCO, 1975–77. *Recreation:* sailing. *Address:* Oakwood, Treworthal Road, Perranarworthal, Truro TR3 7QB. *T:* (01872) 863027. *Club:* Oxford and Cambridge.

BROWN, Hon. Alan John; Agent-General for Victoria, 1997–2000; *b* Wonthaggi, Vic, 25 Jan. 1946; *m* 1972, Paula McBurnie; three *s* one *d*. Councillor, Wonthaggi BC, 1970–78, Mayor, 1974–77; MLA (L): Westernport, Vic, 1979–85; Gippsland W, Vic, 1985–96; Victorian Shadow Minister for: Youth, Sport and Recreation, 1982; Aboriginal Affairs and Housing, 1982–85; Correctional Services, 1984–85; Resources, 1985; Tspt, 1985–89; Dep. Leader of Opposition, 1987–89; Leader of Opposition, 1989–91; Shadow Minister for Tspt, 1991–92; Minister for Tspt, 1992–96. *Recreations:* motor cycle riding, vintage cars, farming. *Address:* Bridgewater Park, RMB 4580, Korumburra, Vic 3950, Australia.

BROWN, Alan Thomas, CBE 1978; DL; Chief Executive, Oxfordshire County Council, 1973–88; *b* 18 April 1928; *s* of Thomas Henry Brown and Lucy Lilian (*née* Betts); *m* 1962, Marie Christine East; two *d*. *Educ:* Wyggeston Grammar Sch., Leicester; Sidney Sussex Coll., Cambridge (Wrangler, Maths Tripos 1950, MA 1953). Fellow CIPFA, 1961. Asst, Bor. Treasurer's Dept, Wolverhampton, 1950–56; Asst Sec., IMTA, 1956–58; Dep. Co. Treas., Berks CC, 1958–61; Co. Treas., Cumberland CC, 1961–66; Town Clerk and Chief Exec., Oxford City Council, 1966–73. Member: SE Econ. Planning Council, 1975–79; Audit Commn, 1989–95. DL Oxon 1978. *Recreations:* chess, horticulture, music, reading. *Address:* 4 Malkin Drive, Beaconsfield, Bucks HP9 1JN. *T:* (01494) 677933.

BROWN, Alan Winthrop, CB 1992; Head of Health Policy Division, Health and Safety Executive, 1992–94; *b* 14 March 1934; *s* of James Brown and Evelyn V. Brown (*née* Winthrop); *m* 1959, Rut Berit (*née* Ohlson); two *s* one *d*. *Educ:* Bedford Sch.; Pembroke Coll., Cambridge (BA Hons); Cornell Univ., NY (MSc). Joined Min. of Labour, 1959; Private Sec. to Minister, 1961–62; Principal, 1963; Asst Sec., 1969. Dir of Planning, Employment Service Agency, 1973–74; Under-Sec. and Head of Incomes Div., DoE, 1975; Chief Exec., Employment Service Div., 1976–79, Trng Services Div., 1979–82, MSC; Hd Electricity Div., Dept of Energy, 1983–85; Dir, Personnel and Management Services, Dept of Employment, 1985–89; Dir, Resources and Planning, HSE, 1989–92. Chm., Godalming Trust, 1999. Lay Mem., Waverley Primary Care Gp, 2000–. *Publications:* papers on occupational psychology and industrial training. *Recreations:* history of art, poetry, gardening, croquet. *Address:* Groton, Ballfield Road, Godalming, Surrey GU7 2HE.

BROWN, Alexander Douglas G.; *see* Gordon-Brown.

BROWN, Prof. Alice, PhD; Professor of Politics, since 1997 and Vice-Principal, since 1999, University of Edinburgh; Co-Director, Governance of Scotland Forum, since 1998; *b* 30 Sept. 1946; *m* Alan James Brown; two *d*. *Educ:* Boroughmuir High Sch., Edinburgh; Stevenson Coll., Edinburgh; Univ. of Edinburgh (MA 1983; PhD 1990). Lectr in Econs, Univ. of Stirling, 1984–85; University of Edinburgh: Lectr, 1985–92; Sen. Lectr in Politics, 1992–97; Hd, Dept of Politics, 1995; Hd, Planning Unit, 1996; Chm., Mergers Cttee, 2001–. Chm., Community Planning Task Force (Scotland), 2001–; Member: SHEFC, 1998–; Cttee on Standards in Public Life, 1999–; Res. Grants Bd, ESRC; Adv. Gp, EOC, Scotland, 1995–. Founder Member: Engender (women's res. and campaigning gp), 1991–; Scottish Women's Co-ordination Gp, 1992–. Bd Mem., Centre for Scottish Public Policy (formerly John Wheatley Centre), 1992. Asst Ed., Scottish Affairs jl, 1992–. *Publications:* (co-ed) The Scottish Government Yearbook, 1989–91; The New Politics of Scotland, 2001; jointly: A Major Crisis?, 1996; Politics and Society in Scotland, 1996; Gender Equality in Scotland, 1997; The Scottish Electorate, 1999; New Scotland, New Politics?, 2001. *Address:* Governance of Scotland Forum, Chisholm House, High School Yards, Edinburgh EH1 1LZ.

BROWN, Dr Andrew Edward; Director, English Nature, since 1998; *b* 9 May 1954; *s* of James Andrew Brown and Gwyneth Brown (*née* Watkins); *m* 1980, Christina Joyce Binks; two *d*. *Educ:* University Coll., Cardiff (BSc Zool. and Envmtl Studies); Leicester Poly. (PhD Freshwater Ecol.). Res. Officer and Tutor, Sussex Univ., 1980–81; Lectr, Bayero Univ., Kano, Nigeria, 1981–83; Nature Conservancy Council: Asst Regl Officer, Cheshire, 1983–86; Develt Officer, Scotland, 1986–89; Sen. Officer, York, 1989–90; English Nature: Strategic Planner, 1990–94; Corporate Manager, 1994–96; Chief Officer, Jt Nature Conservation Cttee, 1996–98. Mem., Broads Authority, 1999–. *Publications:* contrib. to books on freshwater ecology; papers in scientific jls. *Recreations:* reading, DIY, walking, travel, ski-ing. *Address:* The Yews, 39 King Street, West Deeping, Peterborough PE6 9HP. *T:* (01778) 343229.

BROWN, Andrew William; Director General, Advertising Association, since 1993; *b* 3 March 1946; *s* of Harry Brown and Geraldine (*née* O'Leary); *m* 1977, Shelby Ann Hill. *Educ:* St Edmund's Coll., Ware, Herts. J. Walter Thompson Co. Ltd. 1965–93, Board Dir, 1982–93. Chm., CAM Foundn, 1994–96. Dir, Advertising Standards Bd of Finance, 1993–; Chm., Cttee of Advertising Practice, 1999–; Mem., ITC Advertising Adv. Cttee, 1999–. *Recreations:* cricket, theatre, London, Bodmin Moor. *Address:* Advertising Association, Abford House, 15 Wilton Road, SW1V 1NJ; 81 Westbourne Terrace, W2 6QS; Berrio Brook, North Hill, Launceston, Cornwall PL15 7NL. *Clubs:* Reform, MCC; XL.

BROWN, Prof. Archibald Haworth, FBA 1991; Professor of Politics, University of Oxford, since 1989; Fellow, St Antony's College, Oxford, since 1971 (Sub-Warden, 1995–97); Director, Russian and East European Centre, since 1999; *b* 10 May 1938; *s* of late Rev. Alexander Douglas Brown and of Mary Brown (*née* Yates); *m* 1963, Patricia Susan Cornwell; one *s* one *d*. *Educ:* Annan Acad.; Dumfries Acad.; City of Westminster Coll.; LSE (BSc Econ, 1st Cl. Hons 1962). MA Oxon 1972. Reporter, Annandale Herald and Annandale Observer, 1954–56. National Service, 1956–58. Lectr in Politics, Glasgow Univ., 1964–71; British Council exchange scholar, Moscow Univ., 1967–68; Lectr in Soviet Instns, Univ. of Oxford, 1971–89. Visiting Professor: of Political Science, Yale Univ. and Univ. of Connecticut, 1980; Columbia Univ., NY, 1985; Univ. of Texas, Austin, 1990–91; INSEAD, 1991; Distinguished Vis. Fellow, Kellogg Inst. for Internat. Studies, Univ. of Notre Dame, 1998; Henry L. Stimson Lectures, Yale Univ., 1980. Mem. Council, SSEES, Univ. of London, 1992–98. *Publications:* Soviet Politics and Political Science, 1974; (ed jtly and contrib.) The Soviet Union since the Fall of Khrushchev, 1975, 2nd edn 1978; (ed jtly and contrib.) Political Culture and Political Change in Communist States, 1977, 2nd edn 1979; (ed jtly and contrib.) Authority, Power and Policy in the USSR: essays dedicated to Leonard Schapiro, 1980; (ed jtly and contrib.) The Cambridge Encyclopedia of Russia and the Soviet Union, 1982; (ed jtly and contrib.) Soviet Policy for the 1980s, 1982; (ed and contrib.) Political Culture and Communist Studies, 1984; (ed and contrib.) Political Leadership in the Soviet Union, 1989; (ed and contrib.) The Soviet Union: a biographical dictionary, 1990; (ed and contrib.) New Thinking in Soviet Politics, 1992; (ed jtly and contrib.) The Cambridge Encyclopedia of Russia and the Former Soviet Union, 1994; The Gorbachev Factor, 1996 (W. J. M. Mackenzie Prize, Pol Studies Assoc., 1998; Alec Nove Prize, British Assoc. for Slavonic and E Eur. Studies, 1998); (ed jtly and contrib.) The British Study of Politics in the Twentieth Century, 1999; (ed and contrib.) Contemporary Russian Politics: a reader, 2001; (ed jtly and contrib.) Political Leadership in the Russian Transition, 2001; The Demise of Marxism–Leninism in Russia, 2002; papers in academic jls and symposia. *Recreations:* novels and political memoirs, opera, watching football and cricket. *Address:* St Antony's College, Oxford OX2 6JF. *T:* (01865) 284748.

BROWN, Gen. Arnold, OC 1982; International Leader, and General, Salvation Army, 1977–81; *b* 13 Dec. 1913; *s* of Arnold Rees Brown and Annie Brown; *m* 1939, Jean Catherine Barclay; two *d*. *Educ:* Belleville Collegiate, Canada. Commnd Salvation Army Officer, 1935; Editor, Canadian War Cry, 1937–47; Nat. Publicity Officer, Canada, 1947–62; Nat. Youth Officer, Canada, 1962–64; Head of Internat. Public Relations, Internat. HQ, London, 1964–69; Chief of Staff, 1969–74; Territorial Comdr, Canada and Bermuda, 1974–77. Freeman, City of London, 1978. Hon. LHD Asbury Coll., USA, 1972; Hon. DD Olivet Coll., USA, 1981. *Publications:* What Hath God Wrought?, 1952; The Gate and the Light, 1984; Fighting for His Glory, 1988; Yin: the mountain the wind blew here, 1988; With Christ at the Table, 1991; Occupied Manager—Unoccupied Tomb, 1994; Reading Between the Lines, 1997. *Recreations:* reading, writing, music. *Address:* 1200 Don Mills Road, Suite 416, North York, ON M3B 3N8, Canada. *Club:* Rotary of London and Toronto.

BROWN, Rt Rev. Arthur Durrant; a Suffragan Bishop of Toronto, 1981–93 (Bishop of York–Scarborough); *b* 7 March 1926; *s* of Edward S. Brown and Laura A. Durrant; *m* 1949, Norma Inez Rafuse; three *d*. *Educ:* Univ. of Western Ontario (BA 1949); Huron College (LTh 1949). Ordained deacon, 1949; priest, 1950, Huron. Rector: of Paisley with Cargill and Pinkerton, 1948–50; of Glenworth and St Stephen, London, Ont., 1950–53; of St John, Sandwich, Windsor, Ont., 1953–63; of St Michael and All Angels, Toronto, 1963–80; Canon of Toronto, 1972–74; Archdeacon of York, Toronto, 1974–80. Member: Nat. Exec. Council, Anglican Church of Canada, 1969–81; Judicial Council of Ontario, 1978–85; Multi-Cultural Council of Ontario, 1985–87; Press Council of Ontario, 1986. Hon. Chm. Adv. Bd, Cdn Foundn on Compulsive Gambling (Ontario), 1983–; Chairman: Canadian Friends to West Indian Christians, 1982–; Royal Visit Children's Fund, 1984–. Columnist, Toronto Sunday Sun, 1974–86. Mem., Corp. of Huron Coll., 1961–86; Chancellor, Renison Coll., 1994–2001, Chancellor Emeritus, 2001. City of Toronto Civic Award, 1981. Hon. DD: Huron Coll., 1976; Wycliffe Coll., 1981; Trinity Coll., 1999. Distinguished Service Award, 5th Caribbean Anglican Consultation, 1999. *Address:* 45 Livingston Road # 810, Scarborough, ON M1E 1K8, Canada.

BROWN, A(rthur) I(vor) Parry, FRCA; Anæsthetist: London Hospital, 1936–73; London Chest Hospital, 1946–73; Harefield Hospital, 1940–73; Royal Masonic Hospital, 1950–73; retired; *b* 23 July 1908; *s* of A. T. J. Brown; *m* Joyce Marion Bash. *Educ:* Tollington Sch., London; London Hospital. MRCS, LRCP, 1931; MB, BS London, 1933; DA, 1935; FFARCS, 1951. Member of the Board of the Faculty of Anæsthetists, RCS; Pres., Sect. of Anæsthetics, RSM, 1972–73; Fellow, Assoc. of Anæsthetists; Member, Thoracic Soc. *Publications:* chapter in Diseases of the Chest, 1952; contributions to: Thorax, Anæsthesia. *Address:* Long Thatch, Church Lane, Balsham, Cambridge CB1 6DS. *T:* (01223) 893012.

BROWN, Prof. Arthur Joseph, CBE 1974; FBA 1972; Professor of Economics, University of Leeds, 1947–79, now Emeritus; Pro-Vice-Chancellor, Leeds University, 1975–77; *b* 8 Aug. 1914; *s* of J. Brown, Alderley Edge, Cheshire; *m* 1938, Joan H. M., *d* of Rev. Canon B. E. Taylor, Holy Trinity, Walton Breck, Liverpool; two *s* (and one *s* decd). *Educ:* Bradford Grammar School; Queen's College, Oxford (Hon. Fellow, 1985). First Class Hons in Philosophy, Politics and Economics, 1936, MA, DPhil 1939. Fellow of All Souls College, Oxford, 1937–46; Lectr in Economics, Hertford College, Oxford,

1937–40; on staff of: Foreign Research and Press Service, 1940–43; Foreign Office Research Dept, 1943–45; Economic Section, Offices of the Cabinet, 1945–47. Head of Dept of Economics and Commerce, University of Leeds, 1947–65. Visiting Professor of Economics, Columbia University, City of New York, Jan.-June 1950. President Section F, British Assoc. for the Advancement of Science, 1958; Member: East African Economic and Fiscal Commn, 1960; UN Consultative Group on Economic and Social Consequences of Disarmament, 1961–62; First Secretary of State's Advisory Group on Central Africa, 1962; Hunt Cttee on Intermediate Areas, 1967–69; UGC, 1969–78 (Vice-Chm., 1977–78). Pres., Royal Economic Soc., 1976–78, Vice-Pres., 1978–. Chairman, Adv. Panel on Student Maintenance Grants, 1967–68. Vis. Prof. ANU, 1963; directing Regional Economics project, National Institute of Economic and Social Research, 1966–72. Hon. DLitt: Bradford, 1975; Kent, 1979; Hon. LLD Aberdeen, 1978; Hon. LittD Sheffield, 1979. *Publications:* Industrialisation and Trade, 1943; Applied Economics-Aspects of the World Economy in War and Peace, 1948; The Great Inflation, 1939–51, 1955; Introduction to the World Economy, 1959; The Framework of Regional Economics in the United Kingdom, 1972; (with E. M. Burrows) Regional Economic Problems, 1977; (with J. Darby) World Inflation since 1950: a comparative international study, 1985; articles in various journals. *Recreations:* gardening and walking. *Address:* 24 Moor Drive, Leeds LS6 4BY. *T:* (0113) 275 5799. *Club:* Athenæum.

See also W. A. Brown.

BROWN, Sir (Austen) Patrick, KCB 1995; Deputy Chairman, Kvaerner Corporate Development Ltd, 1998–99; *b* 14 April 1940; *m* 1966, Mary (*née* Bulger); one *d. Educ:* Royal Grammar School, Newcastle upon Tyne; School of Slavonic and East European Studies, Univ. of London. Carreras Ltd, 1961–69 (Cyprus, 1965–66, Belgium, 1967–68); Management Consultant, Urwick Orr & Partners, UK, France, Portugal, Sweden, 1969–72; DoE, 1972; Asst. Sec., Property Services Agency, 1976–80, Dept of Transport, 1980–83; Under Sec., Dept of Transport, 1983–88; Dep. Sec., DoE, 1988–90; Second Perm. Sec., and Chief Exec., PSA, DoE, 1990–91; Perm. Sec., Dept of Transport, 1991–97. Vis. Prof., Newcastle Univ., 1998–. Director: Hunting PLC, 1998–; Go-Ahead Group, 1999–; Arlington Securities plc, 1999–. Trustee, Charities Aid Foundn, 1998–; Chm. Trustees, Mobility Choice, 1998–. *Club:* Royal Automobile.

BROWN, Barry; *see* Brown, James B. C.

BROWN, Benjamin Robert; Special Correspondent, BBC Television News, since 1998; *b* 26 May 1960; *s* of late Antony Victor Brown and of Sheila Mary Brown; *m* 1991, Geraldine Anne Ryan; one *s* two *d. Educ:* Sutton Valence Sch., Kent; Keble Coll., Oxford (BA Hons PPE); Centre for Journalism Studies, UC, Cardiff. Reporter: Radio Clyde, 1982; Radio City, 1982–85; Independent Radio News, 1985–88; BBC Television News: Corresp., 1988–91; Moscow Corresp., 1991–94; Foreign Affairs Corresp., 1994–98. *Publication:* (with D. Shukman) All Necessary Means: inside the Gulf War, 1991. *Recreations:* reading, cinema, following Liverpool Football Club. *Address:* c/o BBC Television News, World Affairs Unit, Room 2505, Television Centre, Wood Lane, W12 7RJ.

BROWN, Adm. Sir Brian (Thomas), KCB 1989; CBE 1983; Chairman, P-E International plc, 1995–98; Director: Cray Electronics plc, 1991–96; Lorien plc, since 1996; *b* 31 Aug. 1934; *s* of late Walter Brown and Gladys (*née* Baddeley); *m* 1959, Veronica, *d* of late Wing Comdr and Mrs J. D. Bird; two *s. Educ:* Peter Symonds' School. Joined RN 1952; pilot in 898 and 848 Sqdns, 1959–62; Dep. Supply Officer, HMY Britannia, 1966–68; Supply Officer, HMS Tiger, 1973–75; Secretary to: VCNS, 1975–78; First Sea Lord, 1979–82; rcds 1983; CO HMS Raleigh, 1984–85; DGNPS, 1986; Dir Gen., Naval Manpower and Trng, 1986–88, and Chief Naval Supply and Secretariat Officer, 1987–88; Chief of Naval Personnel, Second Sea Lord and Admiral Pres., RNC, Greenwich, 1988–91, retired. Chairman: King George's Fund for Sailors, 1993–; Exec. Cttee, Nuffield Trust for Forces of the Crown, 1996–; Pres., Victory Services Assoc., 1993–. CIMgt (CBIM 1989); FIPD (FIPM 1990). Hon. DEd CNAA, 1990. Freeman, City of London, 1989; Liveryman, Gardeners' Co., 1991. *Recreations:* cricket, gardening, fishing. *Address:* The Old Dairy, Stoner Hill House, Froxfield, Petersfield, Hants GU32 1DX. *Club:* Army and Navy.

BROWN, Bruce; *see* Brown, John B.

BROWN, Bruce Macdonald; Director, 1993–97, and Chairman, Research Committee, since 1993, New Zealand Institute of International Affairs; *b* 24 Jan. 1930; *s* of John Albert Brown and Caroline Dorothea Brown (*née* Jorgensen); *m* 1st, 1953, Edith Irene (*née* Raynor) (*d* 1989); two *s* one *d*; 2nd, 1990, Françoise Rousseau (*d* 1995). *Educ:* Victoria University of Wellington (MA Hons). Private Secretary to Prime Minister, 1957–59; Second Sec., Kuala Lumpur, 1960–62; First Sec. (later Counsellor), New Zealand Mission to UN, New York, 1963–67; Head of Administration, Min. of Foreign Affairs, Wellington, 1967–68; Director, NZ Inst. of International Affairs, 1969–71; NZ Dep. High Commissioner, Canberra, 1972–75; Ambassador to Iran, 1975–78, and Pakistan, 1976–78; Asst Sec., Min. of Foreign Affairs, 1978–81; Dep. High Comr in London, 1981–85; Ambassador to Thailand, Vietnam and Laos, 1985–88, to Burma, 1986–88; High Comr to Canada, also accredited to Barbados, Guyana, Jamaica and Trinidad and Tobago, 1988–92. *Publications:* The Rise of New Zealand Labour, 1962; (ed) Asia and the Pacific in the 1970s, 1971; (ed) New Zealand in World Affairs, Vol. III, 1972–1990, 1999. *Recreations:* reading, golf. *Address:* New Zealand Institute of International Affairs, PO Box 600, Wellington, New Zealand.

BROWN, Carter; *see* Brown, John C.

BROWN, Cedric Harold, FREng, FIGasE, FICE; consultant; Chairman: CB Consultants, since 1996; Intellihome plc, since 1997; Atlantic Caspian Resources plc, since 1999; *b* 7 March 1935; *s* of late William Herbert Brown and Constance Dorothy Brown (*née* Frances); *m* 1956, Joan Hendry; one *s* three *d. Educ:* Sheffield, Rotherham and Derby Colleges of Technology. Pupil Gas Distribution Engineer, E Midlands Gas Bd, 1953–58, Tech. Asst, 1958–59; Engineering Asst, Tunbridge Wells Borough Council, 1959–60; engineering posts, E Midlands Gas Bd, 1960–75 (Chief Engineer, 1973–75); Dir of Engineering, E Midlands Gas, 1975–78; British Gas Corp., subseq. British Gas plc: Asst Dir (Ops) and Dir (Construction), 1978–79; Dir, Morecambe Bay Project, 1980–87; Regl Chm., British Gas W Midlands, 1987–89; Dir, Man. Dir, Exploration and Production, 1989; Man. Dir, Regl Services, 1989–91; Sen. Man. Dir, 1991–92; Chief Exec., 1992–96. Dir, Bow Valley Industries, 1988–92. Mem., Adv. Council on Business and the Envmt, 1993–95. Pres., IGasE, 1996–97. FREng (FEng 1990). Liveryman, Engineers' Co., 1988–. *Publications:* tech. papers to professional bodies. *Recreations:* sport, countryside, places of historic interest. *Address:* Atlantic Caspian Resources plc, Albemarle House, 1 Albemarle Street, W1X 3AF.

BROWN, (Cedric Wilfred) George E.; *see* Edmonds-Brown.

BROWN, Charles Dargie, FREng; consulting engineer, retired; Joint Chairman, Mott, Hay & Anderson, Consulting Engineers, 1981–89; *b* 13 April 1927; *s* of William Henry Brown and Jean Dargie; *m* 1952, Sylvia Margaret Vallis; one *s* one *d. Educ:* Harris Acad., Dundee; St Andrews Univ. (BScEng, 1st Cl. Hons.). FICE; FREng (FEng 1981). Joined staff of Mott, Hay & Anderson, 1947; engaged on highways, tunnels and bridge works, incl. Tamar Bridge, Forth Road Bridge, George Street Bridge, Newport, Kingsferry and Queensferry Bridges, 1947–65; Partner and Director, 1965. Principally concerned with planning, design and supervision of major works, 1965–89, incl. Mersey Queensway tunnels and new London Bridge, and projects in Hong Kong (Tsing Ma Bridge), Malaysia (Pahang River Bridges), highway and bridge works in Indonesia and USA; participated in develt of underground rly systems in Melbourne and Singapore. Member, Smeatonian Soc. of Civil Engrs, 1984–. Hon. LLD Dundee, 1982. *Publications:* papers to Instn of Civil Engrs, on Kingsferry Bridge, George St Bridge, London Bridge and Mersey tunnels; also various papers to engrg confs. *Recreations:* golf, gardening, bird watching, reading. *Address:* Mallards Mere, Russell Way, Petersfield, Hants GU31 4LD. *T:* (01730) 267820. *Club:* Royal Automobile.

BROWN, Christina Hambley; *see* Brown, Tina.

BROWN, Christopher; Director and Chief Executive, National Society for Prevention of Cruelty to Children, 1989–95; *b* 21 June 1938; *s* of Reginald Frank Greenwood Brown and Margaret Eleanor Brown; *m* 1968, Helen Margaret, *d* of George A. Woolsey and Hilda M. Woolsey; three *s* one *d. Educ:* Hertford Grammar Sch.; KCL. AKC; Home Office Cert. in Probation. Ordained deacon, 1963, priest, 1964; Assistant Curate, Diocese of Southwark: St Hilda's, Crofton Park, 1963; St Michael's, Wallington, 1964–67. Probation Officer, Nottingham, 1968–72; Sen. Probation Officer, W Midlands, 1972–74; Asst Dir, Social Services, Solihull, 1974–76; Asst Chief Probation Officer, Hereford and Worcester, 1976–79; Chief Probation Officer: Oxfordshire, 1979–86; Essex, 1986–89. Member: Parole Bd, 1985–87; Trng Cttee, Inst. for Study and Treatment of Delinquency, 1986–89; Professional Adv. Cttee, NSPCC, 1986–89; Chm., Social Issues Cttee, Assoc. of Chief Officers of Probation, 1985–87. Mem., Green Coll., Oxford, 1981–86. Licensed to officiate, Dio. Chelmsford, 1986–. *Publications:* contribs to various jls on social work practice and community issues, 1971–. *Recreations:* walking, reading, music, conversation, gardening.

BROWN, Christopher David, MA; Headmaster, Norwich School, 1984–Aug. 2002; *b* 8 July 1944; *s* of E. K. Brown; *m* 1972, Caroline Dunkerley; two *d. Educ:* Plymouth College; Fitzwilliam College, Cambridge. MA. Assistant Master: The Leys School, Cambridge, 1967–71; Pangbourne College, 1971–73; Radley College, 1973–84 (Head of English, 1975–84). Chairman: Choir Schs Assoc., 1997–99; HMC, 2001. *Address:* 16 The Close, Norwich NR1 4DZ.

BROWN, Dr Christopher Paul Hadley; Director, Ashmolean Museum, and Fellow, Worcester College, Oxford, since 1998; *b* 15 April 1948; *s* of late Arthur Edgar Brown and of Florence Marjorie Brown; *m* 1975, Sally Madeleine Stockton; one *s* one *d. Educ:* Merchant Taylors' Sch.; St Catherine's Coll., Oxford (BA Hons Modern History, Dip. History of Art); Courtauld Inst. of Art, Univ. of London (PhD). National Gallery: Asst Keeper, 1971, with responsibility for Dutch and Flemish 17th cent. paintings; Dep. Keeper, 1979; Keeper, then Chief Curator, 1989–98. Trustee, Dulwich Picture Gall., 1993–. Vis. Prof., Univ. of St Andrews, 1996–. Lectures: Ferens Fine Art, Univ. of Hull, 1980; Cargill, Univ. of Glasgow, 1987; Jasper Walls, Pierpont Morgan Library, NY, 1991; Visual Arts, QUB, 1999. Fellow, Netherlands Inst. for Advanced Study, Wassenaar, 1993–94. Member: Consultative Cttee, Burlington Mag.; Cttee of Mgt, Royal Mus. of Fine Arts, Antwerp. *Publications:* Carel Fabritius, 1981; Van Dyck, 1982; Scenes of Everyday Life: seventeenth-century Dutch genre painting, 1984; Dutch Landscape (catalogue), 1986; The Drawings of Anthony van Dyck, 1991; (jtly) Rembrandt: the master and his workshop (catalogue), 1991; Making and Meaning: Rubens's landscapes, 1996; (jtly) Van Dyck 1599–1641, 1999; National Gallery catalogues, incl. The Dutch School 1600–1900, 1990; contribs to art magazines, UK and overseas. *Address:* Ashmolean Museum, Oxford OX1 2PB. *T:* (01865) 278005, *Fax:* (01865) 278018; *e-mail:* christopher.brown@ashmus.ox.ac.uk.

BROWN, Craig; *see* Brown, J. C.

BROWN, Craig Edward Moncrieff; freelance writer since 1977; *b* 23 May 1957; *s* of Peter Brown and Jennifer (*née* Bethell); *m* 1987, Frances Welch; one *s* one *d. Educ:* Farleigh House; Eton Coll.; Bristol Univ. Drama Dept. Columnist on: Sunday Telegraph, Daily Telegraph, Private Eye, Independent on Sunday, Guardian (as Wallace Arnold, and Bel Littlejohn); specializing in parody and satire. What the Papers Say Gen. Pleasure Award, 1996. *Publications:* The Marsh-Marlow Letters, 1984; A Year Inside, 1989; The Agreeable World of Wallace Arnold, 1990; Rear Columns, 1992; Welcome to My Worlds!, 1993; Craig Brown's Greatest Hits, 1993; The Hounding of John Thomas, 1994; The Private Eye Book of Craig Brown Parodies, 1995; (ed jtly) Colin Welch, The Odd Thing About the Colonel and Other Pieces, 1997; Hug Me While I Weep (For I Weep For the World): the lonely struggles of Bel Littlejohn, 1998. *Recreations:* swimming in the sea, drinking, shopping. *Address:* c/o Private Eye, Carlisle Street, W1V 5RG.

BROWN, Sir (Cyril) Maxwell Palmer, (Sir Max), KCB 1969 (CB 1965); CMG 1957; Permanent Secretary, Department of Trade, March–June 1974; *b* 30 June 1914; *s* of late Cyril Palmer Brown; *m* 1940, Margaret May Gillhespy; three *s* one *d. Educ:* Wanganui College; Victoria University College, NZ; Clare College, Cambridge. Princ. Private Secretary to Pres. Board of Trade, 1946–49; Monopolies Commn, 1951–55; Counsellor (Commercial) Washington, 1955–57; returned to Board of Trade; Second Permanent Sec., 1968–70; Sec. (Trade), DTI, 1970–74; Mem., 1975–81, Dep. Chm., 1976–81, Monopolies and Mergers Commn. Director: John Brown & Co., 1975–82; ERA Technology Ltd, 1974–86; RHP Gp plc (formerly Ransome Hoffmann Pollard Ltd), 1975–88. *Address:* 20 Cottenham Park Road, Wimbledon, SW20 0RZ. *T:* (020) 8946 7237.

BROWN, Dr Daniel McGillivray, BSc, PhD, ScD; FRS 1982; FRSC; Emeritus Reader in Organic Chemistry, Cambridge University, since 1983; Fellow of King's College, Cambridge, since 1953; *b* 3 Feb. 1923; *s* of David Cunninghame Brown and Catherine Stewart (*née* McGillivray); *m* 1953, Margaret Joyce Herbert; three *d* (one *s* decd). *Educ:* Glasgow Acad.; Glasgow Univ. (BSc); London Univ. (PhD); Cambridge Univ. (PhD, ScD). FRSC 2001. Res. Chemist, Chester Beatty Res. Inst., 1945–53; Asst Dir of Res., 1953–58, Lectr, 1959–67, Reader in Org. Chem., 1967–83, Cambridge Univ.; Vice-Provost, King's Coll., Cambridge, 1974–81. Vis. Professor: Univ. of Calif, LA, 1959–60; Brandeis Univ., 1966–67. *Publications:* scientific papers, mainly in chemical and molecular biology jls. *Recreations:* modern art, gardening. *Address:* 60 Hartington Grove, Cambridge CB1 7UE. *T:* (01223) 245304.

BROWN, Prof. David Anthony, PhD; FRS 1990; FIBiol; Professor of Pharmacology, Middlesex Hospital Medical School and University College London, since 1987; *b* 10 Feb.

1936; *s* of Alfred William and Florence Brown; *m* Susan Hames; two *s* one *d.* *Educ:* Univ. of London (BSc, BSc, PhD). Asst Lectr 1961–65, Lectr 1965–73, Dept of Pharmacology, St Bart's Hosp. Med. Coll.; Dept of Pharmacology, School of Pharmacy, Univ. of London: Sen. Lectr, 1973–74; Reader, 1974–77; Professor, 1977–79; Wellcome Professor, 1979–87. Visiting Professor: Univ. of Chicago, 1970; Univ. of Iowa, 1971, 1973; Univ. of Texas, 1979, 1980, 1981; Vis. Scientist, Armed Forces Radiobiology Res. Inst., Bethesda, Md, 1976; Fogarty Schol.-in-Residence, NIH, Bethesda, 1985–86. Member: Physiological Soc., 1970; British Pharmacological Soc., 1965–; Biochemical Soc., 1969–; Academia Europaea, 1990. *Publications:* contribs to Jl of Physiology, British Jl of Pharmacology. *Recreation:* filling in forms. *Address:* Department of Pharmacology, University College London, Gower Street, WC1E 6BT.

BROWN, Prof. David Clifford; writer on music; Professor of Musicology, Southampton University, 1983–89, now Professor Emeritus; *b* 8 July 1929; *s* of Bertram and Constance Brown; *m* 1953, Elizabeth (*née* Valentine); two *d.* *Educ:* Sheffield Univ. (BA, MA, BMus); PhD Southampton Univ. LTCL. RAF 1952–54. Schoolmaster, 1954–59; Music Librarian, London Univ., 1959–62; Southampton University: Lectr in Music, 1962; Sen. Lectr, 1970; Reader, 1975. Many broadcast talks and scripts incl. series: Tchaikovsky and his World, 1980; Tchaikovsky: a fateful gift, 1984; A Sympathetic Person, 1989–90. Mem. Edtl Cttee, Musica Britannica, 1980–. *Publications:* (ed jtly) Thomas Weelkes: collected anthems, 1966; Thomas Weelkes, 1969; Mikhail Glinka, 1974; John Wilbye, 1974; Tchaikovsky, vol. 1, 1978, vol. 2, 1982 (Derek Allen Prize, British Acad.), vol. 3, 1986, vol. 4, 1991 (Yorkshire Post Music Book Award, 1991); Tchaikovsky Remembered, 1993; Musorgsky, 2001; contribs to jls and periodicals. *Recreation:* walking. *Address:* Braishfield Lodge West, Braishfield, Romsey, Hants SO51 0PS. *T:* (01794) 368163.

BROWN, David Colin, CMG 1995; HM Diplomatic Service, retired; Consultant, Home Estates Department, Foreign and Commonwealth Office, 1997 (Head, 1989–97); Project Director, Refurbishment of Foreign Office, Whitehall, 1989–97; *b* 10 Aug. 1939; *yr s* of Alan James Brown and Catherine Mary Brown; *m* 1960, Ann Jackson; two *s* one *d.* *Educ:* Lymm Grammar Sch. Joined CRO, 1960; Tech. Aid Administrator, Lagos, 1960–63; Admin Officer, Kingston, Jamaica, 1964–66; Diplomatic Service Admin Office, 1966–68; Second Sec., FCO, 1968; Vice-Consul (Commercial), Johannesburg, 1969–73; seconded to Commn on Rhodesian Opinion, Bulawayo, 1971; News Dept, FCO, 1974–77; Dep. High Comr, Port Louis, 1977–81; Overseas Inspectorate, 1981–83; Asst Hd, W Indian and Atlantic Dept, FCO, 1983–86; Dep. Consul Gen., Milan, 1986–89; Counsellor, 1989. *Recreations:* walking, gardening, building conservation.

BROWN, David John Bowes, CBE 1982; FCSD; Chairman, Multidrive Ltd, since 1996; *b* 2 Aug. 1925; *s* of Matthew and Helene Brown; *m* 1st, 1954, Patricia Robson (marr. diss. 1982); two *s* two *d*; 2nd, 1986, Eve Watkinson (marr. diss. 1998). *Educ:* King James Grammar Sch., Knaresborough; Leeds College of Technology. Logging Contractor, UK and W Africa, 1946–60; joined Hunslet Engine Co. as Designer/Draughtsman, 1960–62; designed and patented transmission and exhaust gas conditioning systems for underground mines tractors; joined Chaseside as Chief Designer, 1962–65; designed and patented 4 wheel drive loading shovels; became Director and Chief Executive; joined Muir-Hill Ltd as Man. Dir, 1965–73; designed and patented 4 wheel drive tractors, cranes, steering systems, transmissions, axles; started DJB Engineering Ltd, 1973 (which became Artix Ltd, 1985); designed, manufactured and sold a range of off highway articulated dump trucks in Peterlee, Co. Durham; the company gained 4 Queen's Awards and 1 Design Council Award; formed Brown Design Engineering Ltd, 1987 for design and building of Telescopic Handlers and the patented Multidrive system; both cos sold to Caterpillar Inc., 1996; founded Multidrive Ltd, 1996, for design and manuf. of tractors, construction trucks and military vehicles. FRSA. *Address:* Ravensthorpe Manor, Boltby, Thirsk, North Yorks YO7 2DX; Multidrive Ltd, Thirsk Industrial Park, York Road, Thirsk, North Yorks YO7 3BX. *T:* (01845) 521500.

BROWN, David K.; *see* Kennett Brown.

BROWN, Sir David (Martin), Kt 2001; FREng, FIEE; Chairman, Motorola Ltd, since 1997; *b* 14 May 1950; *s* of Alan Brown and Laura Marjorie Brown (*née* Richardson); *m* 1975, Denise Frances Bowers; two *s.* *Educ:* Portsmouth Poly. (BSc Electrical Engrg); CEng 1980; FIEE 1985; FREng 1999. With Standard Telephones and Cables, 1979–91; joined Motorola, 1991: Director: UK Ops, Cellular Infrastructure, 1991–93; GSM Product Mgt, 1993–95; Sen. Dir, Radio Access, 1995–97. President: ASE, 1998; Fedn of Electronics Industry, 1999–2000; Mem. Council, IEE, 1986–90, 1997–. MIMgt (MBIM 1976). *Recreations:* literature, art, theatre. *Address:* Bridleway Cottage, Stanmore, Newbury, Berks RG20 8SR.

BROWN, David Rodney H.; *see* Heath-Brown.

BROWN, Rev. Canon Prof. David William, PhD; Van Mildert Professor of Divinity, University of Durham and Canon of Durham Cathedral, since 1990; *b* 1 July 1948; *s* of David William Brown and Catherine Smith. *Educ:* Keil Sch., Dumbarton; Edinburgh Univ. (MA 1st cl. Classics 1970); Oriel Coll., Oxford (BA 1st cl. Phil. and Theol. 1972); Clare Coll., Cambridge (PhD 1976); Westcott House, Cambridge. Fellow, Chaplain and Tutor in Theol. and Phil., Oriel Coll., Oxford and Univ. Lectr in Theol., 1976–90. Vice-Chm., Doctrine Commn of C of E, 1990–95. *Publications:* Choices: ethics and the Christian, 1983; The Divine Trinity, 1985; Continental Philosophy and Modern Theology, 1987; Invitation to Theology, 1989; (ed) Newman: a man for our time, 1990; The Word To Set You Free, 1995; (ed jtly) The Sense of the Sacramental, 1995; (with D. Fuller) Signs of Grace, 1995; (ed jtly) Christ: the Sacramental Word, 1996; Tradition and Imagination: revelation and change, 1999; Discipleship and Imagination: Christian tradition and truth, 2000. *Recreations:* gardening, art, listening to music. *Address:* 14 The College, Durham DH1 3EQ. *T:* (0191) 386 4657; Theology Department, Abbey House, Palace Green, Durham DH1 3RS. *T:* (0191) 374 2064.

BROWN, Vice-Adm. Sir David (Worthington), KCB 1984; *b* 28 Nov. 1927; *s* of late Captain J. R. S. Brown, RN and of Mrs D. M. E. Brown; *m* 1958, Etienne Hester Boileau; three *d.* *Educ:* HMS Conway. Joined RN, 1945; commanded HM Ships MGB 5036, MTB 5020, Dalswinton, Chailey, Cavendish, Falmouth, Hermione, Bristol; Dir, Naval Ops and Trade, 1971–72; Dir of Officers Appointments (Exec.), 1976–78; Asst Chief of Defence Staff (Ops), 1980–82; Flag Officer Plymouth, Port Adm. Devonport, 1982–85. Younger Brother of Trinity House. FIPD. *Recreations:* sailing, fishing. *Club:* Army and Navy.

BROWN, Hon. Dean Craig; MP (L) Finniss, South Australia, since 1993; Minister for Human Services, South Australia, since 1997; *b* Adelaide, 5 Aug. 1943; *m* 1979, Rosslyn Judith Wadey; one *s* one *d.* *Educ:* Unley High Sch.; Univ. of New England, NSW (BRurSc, MRurSc); Australian Admin. Staff Coll.; S Australian Inst. of Technol. (Fellowship Dip. in Business Admin). MP (L) Davenport, 1973–85; Shadow Minister for Industrial Affairs, 1975–79; Minister for Industrial Affairs and for Public Works, 1979–82; Shadow Minister, 1982–85, for: Public Works; Transport; Technology; agricl consultant, 1986–92; MP (L) Alexandra, 1992–93; Leader of Opposition, 1992–93; Shadow Minister for Multicultural and Ethnic Affairs, 1992–93; Premier of SA, and Minister for Multicultural and Ethnic Affairs, 1993–96; Minister: for IT, 1995–96; for Industrial Affairs, Aboriginal Affairs, and Inf. and Contract Services, 1996–97. *Publications:* contribs to political, technical and scientific jls. *Recreations:* jogging, fishing, gardening. *Address:* GPO Box 2555, Adelaide, SA 5001, Australia.

BROWN, Sir Derrick H.; *see* Holden-Brown.

BROWN, Sir Douglas (Denison), Kt 1983; Chairman, 1981–87 and Managing Director, 1954–87, James Corson & Co. Ltd; *b* 8 July 1917; *s* of Robert and Alice Mary Brown; *m* 1941, Marion Cruickshanks Emmerson (*d* 1992); one *s* one *d.* *Educ:* Bablake Sch., Coventry. Served Army, 1940–46: RE, 1940–41; commnd RA, 1941; India, ME, N Africa, Italy; mentioned in despatches; retd in rank of Major. Member: Exec. Cttee, Clothing Manufrs of GB, 1967–82; Cttee, Wooltac, 1988– (Vice Chm., 1982–92); Exec., BCIA, 1988–90 (Hon. Mem., Yorks Humberside BCIA, 1990); Chairman: Leeds and Northern Clothing Assoc., 1975–77; Clothing Initiative, 1988–90; Leeds Clothing and Textile Centre, 1993–97. Chairman: NW Leeds Cons. Assoc., 1961–74 (Pres. 1974); Yorks Area Cons. Assoc., 1978–83 (Treasurer, 1971–78); Mem., Nat. Exec. Cttee, Cons. and Unionist Assoc., 1971–90; Mem., Cons. Bd of Finance, 1971–78. Director: Computer Internat., 1993–94; Castleton Computers, 1995–2000. Mem., Gas Consumer Council, NE Area, 1981–86; Bd Mem., Yorkshire Water Authority, 1983–86. President: Water Aid Yorkshire, 1988; Leeds Gardeners' Fedn, 1991–94 and 1998; Vice-Chm., St Edmund's PCC, Roundhay, 1981–96. Chm., Bd of Governors, Jacob Kramer Coll. of Further Educn, 1978–92 (Gov., 1975–93); Chm. Govs, Leeds Coll. of Art and Design, 1993–2000; Governor, Cross Green High Sch., 1989–96 (Chm., 1995–96). *Recreations:* gardening, Rugby, cricket, golf. *Address:* One Oak, 12 Elmete Grove, Leeds LS8 2JY. *T:* (0113) 273 5470.

BROWN, Hon. Sir Douglas (Dunlop), Kt 1989; **Hon. Mr Justice Douglas Brown;** a Judge of the High Court of Justice, Queen's Bench Division, since 1996 (Family Division, 1989–96); Presiding Judge, Northern Circuit, since 1998; *b* 22 Dec. 1931; *s* of late Robert Dunlop Brown, MICE, and Anne Cameron Brown; *m* 1960, June Margaret Elizabeth McNamara; one *s.* *Educ:* Ryleys Sch., Alderley Edge; Manchester Grammar Sch.; Manchester Univ. (LLB). Served in RN, 1953–55; Lieut, RNR. Called to Bar, Gray's Inn, 1953; Bencher, 1989; practised Northern Circuit from 1955; Mem. General Council of Bar, 1967–71; Asst Recorder, Salford City QS, 1971; a Recorder of the Crown Court, 1972–80; QC 1976; a Circuit Judge, 1980–88; Family Div. Liaison Judge, Northern Circuit, 1990–95. Mem., Parole Bd for England and Wales, 1985–87. *Recreations:* cricket, golf, music. *Address:* Royal Courts of Justice, Strand, WC2A 2LL. *Clubs:* St James's (Manchester); Wilmslow Golf; Royal Porthcawl Golf.

BROWN, Edmund Gerald, Jr, (Jerry Brown); lawyer, writer and politician; Mayor of Oakland, California, since 1999; *b* 7 April 1938; *s* of late Edmund Gerald Brown and of Bernice (*née* Layne). *Educ:* Univ. of California at Berkeley (BA 1961); Yale Law School (JD 1964). Admitted to California Bar, 1965; Research Attorney, Calif. Supreme Court, 1964–65; with Tuttle & Taylor, LA, 1966 69, Sec. of State, Calif., 1970–74; Gov. of California, 1975–83; Attorney with Fulbright Jaworski, 1986–91. Democratic Candidate for US Senator from California, 1982; Chm., California Democratic Party, 1989–91; Candidate for Democratic Presidential Nomination, 1992. Founder and Chm., We the People Legal Foundn, 1992. Trustee, Los Angeles Community Colls, 1969–70. *Address:* 1 City Hall Plaza, Oakland, CA 94612, USA; 200 Harrison Street, Oakland, CA 94610, USA.

BROWN, Prof. Edwin Thomas, AC 2001; PhD, DSc Eng; FREng; FTSE; FIEAust; FIMM; Senior Consultant, Golder Associates Pty Ltd, since 2001; Senior Deputy Vice-Chancellor, University of Queensland, Australia, 1996–2001 (Deputy Vice-Chancellor, 1990–96; Dean of Engineering, 1987–90); *b* 4 Dec. 1938; *s* of George O. and Bessie M. Brown. *Educ:* Castlemaine High Sch.; Univ. of Melbourne (BE 1960, MEngSc 1964); Univ. of Queensland (PhD 1969); Univ. of London (DSc Eng 1985). MICE 1976; MASCE 1965; FIMM 1980; FIEAust 1987 (MIEAust 1965); FTSE (FTS 1990). Engr, State Electricity Commn of Victoria, 1960–64; James Cook Univ. of North Queensland (formerly UC of Townsville): Lectr, 1965–69; Sen. Lectr, 1969–72; Associate Prof. of Civil Engrg, 1972–75; Imperial College, Univ. of London: Reader in Rock Mechanics, 1975–79; Prof. of Rock Mechanics, 1979–87; Dean, RSM, 1983–86; Hd, Dept of Mineral Resources Engrg, 1985–87. Res. Associate, Dept of Civil and Mineral Engrg, Univ. of Minnesota, 1970; Sen. Visitor, Dept of Engrg, Univ. of Cambridge, 1974; Vis. Prof., Dept of Mining and Fuels Engrg, Univ. of Utah, 1979. Chm., British Geotechnical Soc., 1982–83; Pres., Internat. Soc. for Rock Mechanics, 1983–87; Mem. Council, AATSE, 1997–98. Foreign Mem., Royal Acad. (formerly Fellowship) of Engrg, 1989. Instn of Mining and Metallurgy: Consolidated Gold Fields Gold Medal, 1984; Sir Julius Wernher Meml Lecture, 1985. Editor-in-Chief, Internat. Jl of Rock Mechanics and Mining Sciences, 1975–82. *Publications:* (with E. Hoek) Underground Excavations in Rock, 1980; (ed) Rock Characterization, Testing and Monitoring, 1981; (with B. H. G. Brady) Rock Mechanics for Underground Mining, 1985, 2nd edn 1993; (ed) Analytical and Computational Methods in Engineering Rock Mechanics, 1987; papers on rock mechanics in civil engrg and mining jls. *Recreations:* cricket, jazz. *Address:* 5121 Bridgewater Crest, 55 Baildon Street, Kangaroo Point, Qld 4169, Australia. *T:* (7) 38919833.

BROWN, Elizabeth, (Mrs Ray Brown); *see* Vaughan, E.

BROWN, Prof. Eric Herbert, PhD; Professor of Geography, University College London, 1966–88, Honorary Research Fellow, since 1988; *b* 8 Dec. 1922; *s* of Samuel Brown and Ada Brown, Melton Mowbray, Leics; *m* 1945, Eileen (*née* Reynolds) (*d* 1984), Llanhowell, Dyfed; two *d.* *Educ:* King Edward VII Grammar Sch., Melton Mowbray; King's Coll., London (BSc 1st Cl. Hons). MSc Wales, PhD London. Served War: RAF Pilot, Coastal Comd, 1941–45. Asst Lectr, then Lectr in Geography, University Coll. of Wales, Aberystwyth, 1947–49; University College London: Lectr, then Reader in Geog., 1950–66; Dean of Students, 1972–75; Alumnus Dir, 1989–91; Mem. Senate, Univ. of London, 1981–86. Vis. Lectr, Indiana Univ., USA, 1953–54; Vis. Prof., Monash Univ., Melbourne, 1971. Mem., NERC, 1981–84. Geographical Adviser, Govt of Argentina, 1965–66, 1992–94; Hon. Mem., Geograph. Soc. of Argentina, 1968. Chairman: British Geomorphol Res. Group, 1971–72; British Nat. Cttee for Geog., 1985–90. Royal Geographical Society: Back Grant, 1961; Hon. Sec., 1977–87; Vice-Pres., 1988–89, Hon. Vice-Pres., 1989; Hon. Fellow, 1989; Pres., Inst. of British Geographers, 1978. Foreign Mem., Polish Acad. of Scis and Letters, 1992. *Publications:* The Relief and Drainage of Wales, 1961; (with W. R. Mead) The USA and Canada, 1962; (ed) Geography Yesterday and Tomorrow, 1980; contrib. Geog. Jl, Phil. Trans Royal Soc., Proc. Geologists' Assoc., Trans Inst. of British Geographers, and Geography. *Recreations:* watching Rugby football, wine. *Address:* Monterey, Castle Hill, Berkhamsted, Herts HP4 1HE. *T:* (01442) 864077. *Clubs:* Athenæum, Geographical.

BROWN, Captain Eric Melrose, CBE 1970 (OBE 1945; MBE 1944); DSC 1942; AFC 1947; RN; Vice-President, European Helicopter Association, since 1992 (Chief Executive, 1980–92); *b* 21 Jan. 1919; *s* of Robert John Brown and Euphemia (*née* Melrose); *m* 1942, Evelyn Jean Margaret Macrory (*d* 1998); one *s*. *Educ:* Royal High Sch., Edinburgh; Edinburgh University. MA 1947. Joined Fleet Air Arm as Pilot, 1939; Chief Naval Test Pilot, 1944–49 (RN Boyd Trophy, 1948); Resident British Test Pilot at USN Air Test Center, Patuxent River, 1951–52; CO No 804 Sqdn, 1953–54; Comdr (Air), RN Air Stn, Brawdy, 1954–56; Head of British Naval Air Mission to Germany, 1958–60; Dep. Dir (Air), Gunnery Div., Admty, 1961; Dep. Dir, Naval Air Warfare and Adviser on Aircraft Accidents, Admty, 1962–64; Naval Attaché, Bonn, 1965–67; CO, RN Air Stn, Lossiemouth, 1967–70. Chief Exec., British Helicopter Adv. Bd, 1970–87, Vice-Pres., 1988–. Chm., British Aviation Bicentenary Exec. Cttee, 1984. FRAeS 1964 (Pres., 1982–83; Chm., RAeS Rotorcraft Sect., 1973–76). Hon. FEng (Pakistan) 1984; Hon. Fellow, Soc. of Experimental Test Pilots, 1984. Liveryman, GAPAN, 1978. British Silver Medal for Practical Achievement in Aeronautics, 1949; Anglo-French Breguet Trophy, 1983; Bronze Medal, Fédération Aéronautique Internationale, 1986; US Carrier Aviation Test Pilot Hall of Honor, 1995; Gold Medal, British Assoc. of Aviation Consultants, 1997. *Publications:* Wings on My Sleeve, 1961; (jtly) Aircraft Carriers, 1969; Wings of the Luftwaffe, 1977; Wings of the Navy, 1980; The Helicopter in Civil Operations, 1981; Wings of the Weird and the Wonderful, vol. 1, 1982, vol. 2, 1985; Duels in the Sky, 1989; Testing for Combat, 1994. *Recreations:* travel, philately, bridge. *Address:* Carousel, New Domewood, Copthorne, W Sussex RH10 3HF. *T:* (01342) 712610. *Clubs:* Naval and Military, City Livery; Explorers' (NY).

BROWN, Frank Henry, OBE 1975; HM Diplomatic Service, retired; *b* 6 Sept. 1923; *s* of late Thomas Henry Brown and Ada Katherine Brown (*née* Clifton); *m* 1943, Sheila Desiree (*d* 1997), *d* of late Rev. Canon John Rees and Elsie Rees; one *s* three *d*. *Educ:* LCC Bonneville Road, Clapham; Bec Sch., Tooting Bec. C. & E. Morton Ltd, 1940; Colonial Office, 1940–42; RN, 1942–46; Colonial Office, subseq. Commonwealth Office, then Foreign and Commonwealth Office, 1946–83: St Helena, 1948–50; Gold Coast/Ghana, 1954–57; Financial Sec., New Hebrides, 1971–75; Dep. High Comr, Guyana, 1978–80; Asst Head, Nationality and Treaty Dept, FCO, 1980–83. *Recreations:* Christian service, grandparenting to 10, appreciating nature. *Address:* 143 Mitchley Avenue, Sanderstead, Surrey CR2 9HP. *T:* (020) 8657 6824. *Club:* Civil Service.

BROWN, Prof. Fred, OBE 1999; FRS 1981; Adjunct Professor, School of Epidemiology and Public Health, Yale University, since 1990; Professorial Fellow, Queen's University, Belfast, since 1986; *b* 31 Jan. 1925; *m* 1948, Audrey Alice Doherty; two *s*. *Educ:* Burnley Grammar Sch.; Manchester Univ. BSc 1944, MSc 1946, PhD 1948. Asst Lectr, Manchester Univ., 1946–48; Lectr, Bristol Univ. Food Preservation Res. Station, 1948–50; Senior Scientific Officer: Hannah Dairy Res. Inst., Ayr, 1950–53; Christie Hosp. and Holt Radium Inst., Manchester, 1953–55; Head, Biochemistry Dept, 1955–83, and Dep. Dir, 1980–83, Animal Virus Res. Inst., Pirbright, Surrey; Hd of Virology Div., Wellcome Res. Labs, Beckenham, Kent, 1983–90; Prof. of Microbiology, Univ. of Surrey, 1989–90. Vis. Scientist, US Dept of Agric., Plum Is. Animal Disease Centre, NY, 1995–. Mem., Spongiform Encephalopathy Adv. Cttee, 1990–98. Hon. DSc QUB, 1992. *Publications:* papers on viruses causing animal diseases, in scientific journals. *Recreations:* watching cricket, Association football, listening to classical music, fell walking. *Address:* Syndal, Glaziers Lane, Normandy, Surrey GU3 2DF. *T:* (01483) 811107.

BROWN, Prof. Gavin, PhD; FAA; Vice-Chancellor and Principal, University of Sydney, since 1996; *b* Fife, Scotland, 27 Feb. 1942; *s* of F. B. D. and A. D. D. Brown; *m* 1966, Barbara Routh; one *s* one *d*. *Educ:* Univ. of St Andrews (MA); Univ. of Newcastle upon Tyne (PhD 1966). FAA 1981. Asst Lectr, then Lectr, and Sen. Lectr in Maths, Liverpool Univ., 1966–75; University of New South Wales: Prof. of Pure Maths, 1976–92, now Emeritus; Hd, Dept of Pure Maths, 1976–81, 1986–89; Hd, Sch. of Maths, 1981–85; Dean: Faculty of Sci., 1989–92; Bd of Studies in Sci. & Maths, 1990–92; Dep. Vice-Chancellor, 1992–93, Vice-Chancellor, 1994–96, Univ. of Adelaide. Visiting Professor: Univ. of Paris, 1975; Univ. of York, 1979; Univ. of Cambridge, 1986. Hon. LLD St Andrews, 1998. *Publications:* numerous contribs to various maths jls. *Recreation:* racing. *Address:* University of Sydney, NSW 2006, Australia. *T:* (2) 93513058.

BROWN, Rev. Canon Geoffrey Harold; Vicar of St Martin-in-the-Fields, 1985–95; *b* 1 April 1930; *s* of Harry and Ada Brown; *m* 1963, Elizabeth Jane Williams; two *d*. *Educ:* Monmouth Sch.; Trinity Hall, Cambridge. MA. Asst Curate, St Andrew's, Plaistow, 1954–60; Asst Curate, St Peter's, Birmingham and Sub-Warden of Pre-Ordination Training Scheme, 1960–63; Rector: St George's, Newtown, Birmingham, 1963–73; Grimsby, 1973–85. Hon. Canon Lincoln Cathedral, 1978; Canon Emeritus, 1985. FRSA 1991. *Recreations:* the countryside, photography, theatre. *Address:* 8 Worcester Close, Hagley, near Stourbridge, W Midlands DY9 0NP.

BROWN, Geoffrey Howard; journalist, The Times; *b* 1 March 1949; *s* of John Howard Brown and Nancy (*née* Fardoe); *m* 1985, Catherine Ann Surowiec. *Educ:* King Henry VIII Grammar Sch., Coventry; Pembroke Coll., Cambridge (BA); Royal Coll. of Art (Sch. of Film and TV, MA). Dep. Film Critic, Financial Times, 1977–81; Film Critic, Radio Times, 1981–89; Dep. Film Critic, 1981–90, Film Critic, 1990–98, The Times. *Publications:* Walter Forde, 1977; Launder and Gilliat, 1977; Der Produzent: Michael Balcon und der Englische Film, 1981; (contrib.) Michael Balcon: the pursuit of British cinema, 1984; The Common Touch: the films of John Baxter, 1989; (contrib.) The British Cinema Book, 1997; (contrib.) The Unknown 1930s, 1998; (contrib.) British Cinema of the 90s, 2000. *Recreation:* music. *Address:* The Times, 1 Pennington Street, E1 9XN. *T:* (020) 7782 5167.

BROWN, Geoffrey Robert C.; *see* Clifton-Brown.

BROWN, Sir George (Francis) Richmond, 5th Bt *cr* 1863, of Richmond Hill; *b* 3 Feb. 1938; *o s* of Sir Charles Frederick Richmond Brown, 4th Bt and of Audrey Baring; *S* father, 1995; *m* 1978, Philippa Willcox; three *s*. *Educ:* Eton. Served Welsh Guards, 1956–70; Extra Equerry to HRH The Duke of Edinburgh, 1961–63; ADC to Governor of Queensland, 1964–66; Adjt, 1st Bn Welsh Guards, 1967–69. *Heir: s* Sam George Richmond Brown, *b* 27 Dec. 1979. *Address:* Mas de Sudre, 81600 Gaillac, France. *T:* 563410132. *Club:* Pratt's.

BROWN, Sir George (Noel), Kt 1991; Law Revision Commissioner, Belize, 1998–99; Chief Justice, Belize, 1990–98; *b* 13 June 1942; *s* of late Noel Todd Brown and Elma Priscilla Brown; *m* 1974, Magdalene Elizabeth Bucknor; two *d*, and one *s* one *d* from previous marriage. *Educ:* St Michael's Coll., Belize City; Carlton Univ., Ottawa (Cert. in Public Admin); Univ. of WI (LLB Hons); Norman Manley Law Sch., Council of Legal Educn, Univ. of WI (Legal Educn Cert.); Nairobi Law Sch., Kenya (Commonwealth Cert. in Legislative Drafting). Customs Examiner, Customs and Excise Dept, 1960–67; Clerk of Courts, Magistracy Dept, 1967–69; Admin. Asst, and Actg Trade Adminr, Min. of Trade and Ind., 1970–72; Actg Magistrate, Belize Judicial Dist and Itinerant countrywide, 1972–73; Crown Counsel, Attorney General's Ministry, 1978–81; Solicitor General, 1981–84; Puisne Judge, Supreme Court Justice, 1984–85 and 1986–90; Actg Chief Justice, 1985–86; Dep. Governor-Gen., Belize, 1985–94. Mem., Belize Adv. Council, 1985–. Chm., Belize Maritime Trust. *Publications:* Consumer Society and the Law, 1976; contribs to Caribbean Law Rev. *Recreations:* yachting, football (soccer), especially coaching and managing primary and secondary schools teams. *Address:* 6203 Buttonwood Bay, Belize City, PO Box 236, Belize, Central America. *T:* (2) 33824. *Club:* Belize Yacht (Belize City).

BROWN, Prof. George William, OBE 1995; FBA 1986; Member, External Scientific Staff, Medical Research Council, since 1980; Hon. Professor of Sociology, Royal Holloway and Bedford New College, London University, since 1980; *b* 15 Nov. 1930; *s* of late William G. Brown and Lily Jane (*née* Hillier); *m* 1st, 1954, Gillian M. Hole (marr. diss. 1970); one *s* one *d*; 2nd, 1978, Seija T. Sandberg (marr. diss. 1987); one *d*; 3rd, 1990, Elizabeth A. Davies; one *s*. *Educ:* Kilburn Grammar Sch.; University Coll. London (BA Anthropol. 1954); LSE (PhD 1961). Scientific Staff, DSIR, 1955–56; MRC Social Psychiatry Res. Unit, Inst. of Psychiatry, 1956–67; joined Social Res. Unit, Bedford Coll., London Univ., 1967; Prof. of Sociology, London Univ. and Jt Dir, Social Res. Unit, Bedford Coll., 1973–80. Mem., Academia Europaea, 1990. Founder FMedSci 1998. Hon.FRCPsych, 1987. *Publications:* (jtly) Schizophrenia and Social Care, 1966; (with J. K. Wing) Institutionalism and Schizophrenia, 1970; (with T. O. Harris) Social Origins of Depression, 1978; Life Events and Illness, 1989; numerous contribs to jls. *Address:* 1 Redberry Grove, SE26 4DA. *T:* (020) 8699 0120.

BROWN, Prof. Gillian, CBE 1992; Professor of English as an International Language, University of Cambridge, since 1988; Fellow of Clare College, Cambridge, since 1988; *b* 23 Jan. 1937; *d* of Geoffrey Rencher Read and Elsie Olive Chapman; *m* 1959, Edward Keith Brown; three *d*. *Educ:* Perse Sch. for Girls; Girton Coll., Cambridge (MA); Univ. of Edinburgh (PhD 1971); LittD Cantab 1997. Lectr, University Coll. of Cape Coast, Ghana, 1962–64; Lectr, 1965–81, Reader, 1981–83, Univ. of Edinburgh; Prof., Univ. of Essex, 1983–88 (Dean of Social Scis, 1985–88); Dir, Res. Centre for English and Applied Linguistics, Univ. of Cambridge, 1988–. Mem., ESRC Educn and Human Devlt Cttee, 1983–87; Chm., Research Grants Board, ESRC, 1987–90; Member: Kingman Cttee, 1987–88; UGC, subseq. UFC, 1988–91; Council, Philological Soc., 1988–93; British Council English Teaching Adv. Cttee, 1989–94; Cttee of Mgt, British Inst. in Paris, 1990–. Curator, Sch. of Advanced Studies, Univ. of London, 1994–. Gov., Bell Educnl Trust, 1987–92. Dr *hc* Univ. of Lyon, 1987. Member, Editorial Boards: Jl of Semantics; Jl of Applied Linguistics; Second Language Acquisition Res. *Publications:* Phonological Rules and Dialect Variation, 1972; Listening to Spoken English, 1977; (with George Yule) Discourse Analysis, 1983; Speakers, Listeners and Communication, 1995; articles in learned jls. *Address:* Clare College, Cambridge CB2 1TL.

BROWN, Prof. Godfrey Norman; Professor of Education, University of Keele, 1967–80, now Emeritus; Director, Betley Court Gallery, 1980–94; *b* 13 July 1926; *s* of Percy Charles and Margaret Elizabeth Brown; *m* 1960, Dr Freda Bowyer; three *s*. *Educ:* Whitgift Sch.; School of Oriental and African Studies, London; Merton Coll., Oxford (MA, DPhil). Army service, RAC and Intelligence Corps, 1944–48. Social Affairs Officer, UN Headquarters, NY, 1953–54; Sen. History Master, Barking Abbey Sch., Essex, 1954–57; Lectr in Educn, University Coll. of Ghana, 1958–61; Sen. Lectr, 1961, Prof., 1963, Univ. of Ibadan, Nigeria; Dir, Univ. of Keele Inst. of Educn, 1967–80. Visiting Prof., Univ. of Rhodesia and Nyasaland, 1963; Chm., Assoc. for Recurrent Educn, 1976–77; Mem., Exec. Cttee and Bd of Dirs, World Council for Curriculum and Instruction, 1974–77. OECD Consultant on teacher education, Portugal, 1980. Vice-Pres., Community Council of Staffs, 1984–. Collector of the Year Award, Art and Antiques, 1981; Newcastle-under-Lyme Civic Award for Conservation, 1990. *Publications:* An Active History of Ghana, 2 vols, 1961 and 1964; Living History, 1967; Apartheid, a Teacher's Guide, 1981; Betley Through the Centuries, 1985; This Old House: a domestic biography, 1987; ed (with J. C. Anene) Africa in the Nineteenth and Twentieth Centuries, 1966; ed, Towards a Learning Community, 1971; ed (with M. Hiskett) Conflict and Harmony in Education in Tropical Africa, 1975; contrib. educnl and cultural jls. *Recreations:* family life, art history, conservation, writing. *Address:* Betley Court, Betley, near Crewe, Cheshire CW3 9BH. *T:* (01270) 820652.

BROWN, Rt Hon. Gordon; *see* Brown, Rt Hon. James G.

BROWN, Harold, PhD; Partner, Warburg Pincus & Co., since 1990; Counselor, Center for Strategic and International Studies, since 1992; *b* 19 Sept. 1927; *s* of A. H. Brown and Gertrude Cohen Brown; *m* 1953, Colene McDowell; two *d*. *Educ:* Columbia Univ. (AB 1945, AM 1946, PhD in Physics 1949). Res. Scientist, Columbia Univ., 1945–50, Lectr in Physics, 1947–48; Lectr in Physics, Stevens Inst. of Technol., 1949–50; Res. Scientist, Radiation Lab., Univ. of Calif, Berkeley, 1951–52; Gp Leader, Radiation Lab., Livermore, 1952–61; Dir, Def. Res. and Engrg, Dept of Def., 1961–65; Sec. of Air Force, 1965–69; Pres., Calif Inst. of Technol., Pasadena, 1969–77; Sec. of Defense, USA, 1977–81; Vis. Prof., 1981–84, Chm., 1984–92, Johns Hopkins Foreign Policy Inst., Sch. of Advanced Internat. Studies. Sen. Sci. Adviser, Conf. on Discontinuance of Nuclear Tests, 1958–59; Delegate, Strategic Arms Limitations Talks, Helsinki, Vienna and Geneva, 1969–77. Member: Polaris Steering Cttee, 1956–58; Air Force Sci. Adv. Bd, 1956–61; (also Consultant) President's Sci. Adv. Cttee, 1958–61. Chm., Commn on Roles and Capabilities, US Intelligence Cttee, 1995–96. Hon. DEng Stevens Inst. of Technol., 1964; Hon. LLD: Long Island Univ., 1966; Gettysburg Coll., 1967; Occidental Coll., 1969; Univ. of Calif, 1969; Hon. ScD: Univ. of Rochester, 1975; Brown Univ., 1977; Univ. of the Pacific, 1978; Univ. of S Carolina, 1979; Franklin and Marshall Coll., 1982; Chung Ang Univ. (Seoul, Korea), 1983. Member: Amer. Phys. Soc., 1946; Nat. Acad. of Engrg, 1967; Amer. Acad. of Arts and Scis, 1969; Nat. Acad. of Scis, 1977. One of Ten Outstanding Young Men of Year, US Jun. Chamber of Commerce, 1961; Columbia Univ. Medal of Excellence, 1963; Air Force Exceptl Civil. Service Award, 1969; Dept of Def. Award for Exceptionally Meritorious Service, 1969; Joseph C. Wilson Award, 1976; Presidential Medal of Freedom, 1981; Enrico Fermi Award, US Dept of Energy, 1993. *Publications:* Thinking About National Security: defense and foreign policy in a dangerous world, 1983; (ed) The Strategic Defense Initiative: shield or snare?, 1987. *Address:* Center for Strategic and International Studies, Suite 400, 1800 K Street, NW, Washington, DC 20006, USA. *Club:* City Tavern (Washington, DC).

BROWN, Harold Arthur Neville, CMG 1963; CVO 1961; HM Diplomatic Service, retired; *b* 13 Dec. 1914; *s* of Stanley Raymond and Gladys Maud Brown; *m* 1939, Mary McBeath Urquhart (*d* 1994); one *s* one *d*. *Educ:* Cardiff High School; University College, Cardiff. Entered Ministry of Labour as 3rd Class Officer, 1939; Asst Principal, 1943; Private Sec. to Permanent Sec. of Min. of Labour and Nat. Service, 1944–46; Principal, 1946; Labour Attaché, Mexico City (and other countries in Central America and the Caribbean), 1950–54; transferred to Foreign Office, 1955; Head of Chancery, Rangoon, 1958 and 1959; British Ambassador in Liberia, 1960–63; Corps of Inspectors, Foreign Office, 1963–66; Ambassador to Cambodia, 1966–70; Consul-General, Johannesburg, 1970–73; Minister, Pretoria, Cape Town, 1973–74. Knight Great Band of the Humane

Order of African Redemption, 1962. *Address:* 14 Embassy Court, King's Road, Brighton BN1 2PX.

BROWN, Harold James, AM 1980; BSc, ME; Hon. DSc; FIEAust; FIREE; retired; management consultant, Adelaide, South Australia, 1976–85; Technical Director, Philips Industries Holdings Ltd, Sydney, 1961–76; *b* 10 July 1911; *s* of Allison James and Hilda Emmy Brown; *m* 1936, Hazel Merlyn Dahl Helm; two *s* two *d. Educ:* Fort Street Boys' High Sch.; Univ. of Sydney, NSW, Australia. BSc 1933; BE (Univ. Medal) 1935; ME (Univ. Medal) 1945; Hon. DSc 1976. Research Engineer, Amalgamated Wireless Australasia Ltd, 1935–37; Electrical Engineer, Hydro-electric Commission of Tasmania, 1937–39; Research Officer and Principal Research Officer, Council for Scientific and Industrial Research, 1939–45; Chief Communications Engineer, Australian Nat. Airways Pty Ltd, 1945–47; Prof. of Electrical Engineering, Dean of Faculty of Engineering and Asst Director, NSW Univ. of Technology, 1947–52; Controller R&D, Dept of Supply, Melbourne, 1952–54; Controller, Weapons Research Establishment, Department of Supply, Commonwealth Government of Australia, 1955–58; Technical Director, Rola Co. Pty Ltd, Melbourne, 1958–61. Silver Jubilee Medal, 1977. *Publications:* numerous technical articles in scientific journals. *Recreations:* gardening, bowling. *Address:* 20 Woodbridge, 6 Island Drive, West Lakes, SA 5021, Australia.

BROWN, (Harold) Vivian (Bigley); Chief Executive, Export Credits Guarantee Department, since 1997; *b* 20 Aug. 1945; *s* of late Alec Sidney Brown and Joyce Brown (*née* Bigley); *m* 1970, Jean Josephine Bowyer, *yr d* of Sir Eric Bowyer, KCB, KBE and Lady Bowyer; two *s. Educ:* Leeds Grammar Sch.; St John's Coll., Oxford (BA); St Cross Coll., Oxford (BPhil Islamic Philosophy). Min. of Technology, 1970; DTI, 1972–74 (Private Sec. to Permanent Sec., 1972–73); FCO, 1975–79 (First Sec. Commercial Jeddah); DTI, 1979–86; Hd of Sci. and Technol. Assessment Office, Cabinet Office, 1986–89; Hd of Competition Policy Div., 1989–91; Hd of Investigations Div., 1991–92, of Deregulation Unit, 1992–94, of Small Firms and Business Link, 1994–96, DTI; Dep. Dir Gen. and Dir, Business Link, DTI, 1996–97. *Publication:* Islamic Philosophy and the Classical Tradition (with S. M. Stern and A. Hourani), 1972. *Recreations:* playing piano, cycling, cooking. *Address:* Export Credits Guarantee Department, 2 Exchange Tower, Harbour Exchange Square, E14 9GS.

BROWN, Hazel Christine P.; *see* Parker-Brown.

BROWN, Henry Thomas C.; *see* Cadbury-Brown.

BROWN, Prof. Herbert Charles, PhD; R. B. Wetherill Research Professor Emeritus, Purdue University, 1978 (Professor, 1947–60, R. B. Wetherill Research Professor, 1960–78); *b* 22 May 1912; *s* of Charles Brown and Pearl (*née* Gorinstein); *m* 1937, Sarah Baylen; one *s. Educ:* Wright Jun. Coll., Chicago (Assoc. Sci. 1935); Univ. of Chicago (BS 1936; PhD 1938). University of Chicago: Eli Lilly Postdoctoral Res. Fellow, 1938–39; Instr, 1939–43; Wayne University: Asst Prof., 1943–46; Associate Prof., 1946–47. Member: Nat. Acad. of Sciences, USA, 1957–; Amer. Acad. of Arts and Sciences, 1966–; Hon. Mem., Phi Lambda Upsilon, 1961–; Hon. Fellow, Chem. Soc., London, 1978– (Centenary Lectr, 1955; C. K. Ingold Medal, 1978); Foreign Fellow, Indian Nat. Science Acad., 1978–. Hon. Dr of Science: Univ. of Chicago, 1968; Wayne State Univ., 1980; Hebrew Univ. Jerusalem, 1980; Pontifica Univ. Catolica de Chile, 1980; Wales, 1982; Purdue, 1982, etc. (Jtly) Nobel Prize in Chemistry, 1979. American Chemical Society: Harrison Howe Award, Rochester Sect., 1953; Nichols Medal, NY Sect., 1959; Linus Pauling Medal, Oregon and Puget Sound Sects, 1968; Roger Adams Medal, Organic Div., 1971; Priestley Medal, 1981; Oesper Award, Cincinnati Sect., 1990; Herbert C. Brown Medal and Award, 1998. Award for Creative Res. in Org. Chem., Soc. of Organic Chem. Mfg Assoc., 1960; Herbert Newby McCoy Award, Purdue Univ., 1965 (1st co-recipient); Nat. Medal of Science, US Govt, 1969; Madison Marshall Award, 1975; Allied Chemical Award for Grad. Trng and Innovative Chem., 1978 (1st recipient); Perkins Medal, Amer. Sect., Soc. of Chemical Industry, 1982; Gold Medal, Amer. Inst. Chem., 1985; Chem. Sci. Award, Nat. Acad. of Scis, 1987; G. M. Kossolopoff Medal, Auburn Sect., Amer. Chem. Soc., 1987. Order of the Rising Sun, Gold and Silver Star (Japan), 1989. *Publications:* Hydroboration, 1962; Boranes in Organic Chemistry, 1972; Organic Syntheses via Boranes, 1975; The Non-classical Ion Problem, 1977; (with A. Pelter, K. Smith) Borane Reagents, 1988; over 1140 scientific articles in Jl Amer. Chem. Soc., Jl Org. Chem., Jl Organometal. Chem., and Synthesis. *Recreations:* travel, photography. *Address:* Department of Chemistry, Purdue University, West Lafayette, IN 47907, USA. *T:* (317) 4945316.

BROWN, Hugh Dunbar; *b* 18 May 1919; *s* of Neil Brown and Grace (*née* Hargrave); *m* 1947, Mary Glen Carmichael; one *d. Educ:* Allan Glen's School and Whitehill Secondary School, Glasgow. Formerly Civil Servant, Ministry of Pensions and National Insurance. Member of Glasgow Corporation, 1954; Magistrate, Glasgow, 1961. MP (Lab) Provan Div. of Glasgow, 1964–87. Parly Under-Sec. of State, Scottish Office, 1974–79. *Recreation:* golf. *Address:* 29 Blackwood Road, Milngavie, Glasgow G62 7LB.

BROWN, Col Hugh Goundry, TD 1968; FRCS; Vice Lord-Lieutenant, Tyne & Wear, since 1993; *b* 25 Feb. 1927; *s* of Charles Frank Brown and Edith Temple Brown (*née* Smithson); *m* 1961, Ann Mary Crump; one *s* two *d. Educ:* Durham Univ. (MB BS 1949). FRCS 1958. Nat. Service, RMO, 1 (Nyasaland) Bn, KAR, 1950–52. TA 1 (N) Gen. Hosp., 1952–73; OC, 201 (N) Gen. Hosp., 1970–73, Hon. Col, 1982–87. Consultant Plastic Surgeon, Royal Victoria Inf., Newcastle upon Tyne and Sen. Lectr in plastic surgery, Univ. of Newcastle upon Tyne, 1968–92. President: Brit. Soc. for Surgery of the Hand, 1985; Brit. Assoc. Plastic Surgeons, 1988; Brit. Assoc. Clinical Anatomists, 1989. QHS 1972. Tyne & Wear: DL 1986; High Sheriff, 1992. *Publications:* contrib. Brit. Jl Plastic Surgery, Hand, Brit. Jl Anaesthesia. *Recreations:* family, fell-walking. *Address:* 12 Lindisfarne Road, Jesmond, Newcastle upon Tyne NE22 2HE. *T:* (0191) 281 4141. *Club:* Northern Counties (Newcastle).

BROWN, Prof. Ian James Morris, PhD; playwright; Professor of Drama, since 1995, Dean of Arts, since 1999, and Director, Scottish Centre for Cultural Management and Policy, since 1996, Queen Margaret University College (formerly Queen Margaret College), Edinburgh; *b* 28 Feb. 1945; *s* of Bruce Beveridge Brown and Eileen Frances Scott Carnegie; *m* 1st, 1968, Judith Ellen Sidaway (marr. diss. 1997); one *s* one *d*; 2nd, 1997, Nicola Dawn Axford. *Educ:* Dollar Academy; Edinburgh Univ. MA Hons, MLitt, DipEd; Crewe and Alsager Coll. (PhD). Playwright, 1969–; Schoolmaster, 1967–69, 1970–71; Lectr in Drama, Dunfermline Coll., 1971–76; British Council: Asst Rep., Scotland, 1976–77; Asst Regional Dir, Istanbul, 1977–78; Crewe and Alsager College: Head of Drama, 1978–79; Head of Performance Arts, 1979–82; Programme Leader, BA Hons Drama Studies, 1982–86; Programme Dir, Alsager Arts Centre, 1980–86; Drama Dir, Arts Council of GB, 1986–94; Reader, 1994–95, Head, Dept of Drama, 1995–99, Queen Margaret Coll., Edinburgh. Chm., Scottish Soc. of Playwrights, 1973–75, 1984–87, 1997–99; convenor, NW Playwrights' Workshop, 1982–85; Member: NW Arts Assoc. Drama panel, 1980–83, General Arts panel, 1983–86; Arts Council of GB Drama panel, 1985–86; British Theatre Institute: Vice-Chm., 1983–85; Chm., 1985–87. Chm., Dionysia World Fest. of Contemp. Theatre, Chianti, Italy, 1991–94. Productions: Mother Earth, 1970; The Bacchae, 1972; Positively the Last Final Farewell Performance (ballet), 1972; Rune (choral work), 1973; Carnegie, 1973; The Knife, 1973; The Fork, 1976; New Reekie, 1977; Mary, 1977; Runners, 1978; Mary Queen and the Loch Tower, 1979; Joker in the Pack, 1983; Beatrice, 1989; (jtly) First Strike, 1990; The Scotch Play, 1991; Bacchai, 1991; Wasting Reality, 1992; Margaret, 2000; A Great Reckonin, 2000. FRSA 1991. *Publications:* articles on drama, theatre and arts policy. *Recreations:* theatre, sport, travel, cooking. *Address:* Queen Margaret University College, Clerwood Terrace, Edinburgh EH12 8TS.

BROWN, Col James, CVO 1985; RNZAC (retd); *b* 15 Aug. 1925; *y s* of late John Brown and Eveline Bertha (*née* Cooper), Russells Flat, North Canterbury, NZ; *m* 1952, Patricia Sutton; two *d. Educ:* Christchurch Boys' High Sch., NZ; Royal Military Coll., Duntroon, Australia (grad 1947). NZ Regular Army, 1947–71: active service, Korea, 1951–52; Comptroller of Household to Gov.-Gen. of NZ, 1961–62; Reg. Comr of Civil Defence, Dept of Internal Affairs, NZ, 1971–77; Official Sec. to Governor-Gen. of NZ, 1977–85; Gen. Sec., Duke of Edinburgh's Award Scheme in NZ, 1986–94. Col Comdt, RNZAC, 1982–86; Pres., NZ Army Assoc., 1986–94. *Recreations:* fishing, shooting. *Address:* 2 Te Maku Grove, Waikanae, New Zealand. *Club:* Wellington (Wellington).

BROWN, Dr (James) Barry (Conway), OBE 1978; Subject Assessor, Higher Education Funding Council for England, since 1995; *b* 3 July 1937; *s* of Frederick Clarence and Alys Brown; *m* 1963, Anne Rosemary Clough; two *s* one *d. Educ:* Cambridge Univ. (BA Nat. Sci 1959; MA 1963); Birmingham Univ. (MSc 1960; PhD 1963). Research Officer, CEGB, Berkeley Nuclear Labs, 1963–67; British Council: Sen. Sci. Officer, Sci. Dept, 1967–69; Sci. Officer, Madrid, 1969–72, Paris, 1972–78; Head, Sci. and Technology Group, 1978–81; Rep. and Cultural Counsellor, Mexico, 1981–85; Dep. Controller (Higher Educn Div.), 1985–89; Dir, EC Liaison Unit (Higher Education), Brussels, 1989–91; Dir, Poland, 1992–94. Treas., St Mary's Church, Purley-on-Thames, 1994–2000. *Recreations:* music, travel in (and study of) countries of posting, singing, reading. *Address:* 42 Hazel Road, Purley-on-Thames, Reading RG8 8BB. *T:* (0118) 941 7581.

BROWN, (James) Craig, CBE 1999; Director of Football Development, Scottish Football Association, since 1993 (International Team Manager, 1993–2001); *b* 1 July 1940; *s* of Hugh and Margaret Brown; *m* 1964 (separated 1981); two *s* one *d. Educ:* Scottish Sch. of Physical Educn (DipPE (Distinction)); BA Open Univ. 1976. Lectr in Primary Educn, Craigie Coll. of Educn, 1969–86. Professional footballer: Rangers FC, 1958–60; Dundee FC, 1960–65; Falkirk FC, 1965–67; Asst Manager, Motherwell FC, 1974–77; Manager, Clyde FC, 1977–86; Asst Nat. Coach, 1986–93, Nat. Coach, 1993–2001, Scottish Football Assoc. DUniv Paisley, 1998. *Publications:* (jtly) Activity Methods in the Middle Years, 1975; Craig Brown (autobiog.), 1998. *Recreations:* golf, reading, travel. *Address:* Scottish Football Association, National Stadium, Hampden Park, Glasgow G42 9BA; 53 Sycamore Crescent, Ayr KA7 3NS.

BROWN, Rt Hon. (James) Gordon; PC 1996; MP (Lab) Dunfermline East, since 1983; Chancellor of the Exchequer, since 1997; *b* 20 Feb. 1951; *s* of late Rev. Dr John Brown and of J. Elizabeth Brown; *m* 2000, Sarah Jane Macaulay. *Educ:* Kirkcaldy High Sch.; Edinburgh Univ. MA 1972; PhD 1982. Rector, Edinburgh Univ., 1972–75; Temp. Lectr, Edinburgh Univ., 1976; Lectr, Glasgow Coll. of Technology, 1976–80; Journalist and Current Affairs Editor, Scottish TV, 1980–83. Mem., TGWU. Chm., Labour Party Scottish Council, 1983–84; Opposition Chief Sec. to the Treasury, 1987–89; Opposition Trade and Industry Sec., 1989–92; Opposition Treasury Sec., 1992–97. Contested (Lab) S Edinburgh, 1979. *Publications:* (ed) The Red Paper on Scotland, 1975; (with H. M. Drucker) The Politics of Nationalism and Devolution, 1980; (ed) Scotland: the real divide, 1983; Maxton, 1986; Where There is Greed, 1989; (with J. Naughtie) John Smith: Life and Soul of the Party, 1994; (with T. Wright) Values, Visions and Voices, 1995. *Recreations:* reading and writing, football and tennis. *Address:* House of Commons, SW1A 0AA.

BROWN, Jerry; *see* Brown, E. G.

BROWN, Joe, MBE 1975; freelance guide and climber, and film maker for television and cinema; *b* 26 Sept. 1930; *s* of J. Brown, Longsight, Manchester; *m* 1957, Valerie Gray; two *d. Educ:* Stanley Grove, Manchester. Started climbing while working as plumber in Manchester; pioneered new climbs in Wales in early 1950's; gained internat. reputation after climbing West Face of Petit Dru, 1954; climbed Kanchenjunga, 1955; Mustagh Tower, 1956; Mt Communism, USSR, 1962; Trango Tower, 1976; Cotaphxi, 1979; Mt Kenya, 1984; Mt McInley, 1986; other expdns: El Torro, 1970; Bramah 2, 1978; Thalaysagar, 1982; Everest NE Ridge, 1986 and 1988. Climbing Instructor, Whitehall, Derbs, 1961–65; opened climbing equipment shops, Llanberis, 1965, Capel Curig, 1970; Leader of United Newspapers Andean Expedn, 1970; Roraima Expedn, 1973. Hon. Fellow, Manchester Polytechnic, 1970. *Publication:* (autobiog.) The Hard Years, 1967. *Recreations:* mountaineering, ski-ing, fishing. *Address:* Menai Hall, Llanberis, Gwynedd LL55 4HA. *T:* (01286) 870327. *Club:* Climbers' (Brynrefail, Caernarfon).

BROWN, John, CBE 1982; FREng, FIEE; Part-time Dean of Technology, Brunel University, 1988–91; *b* 17 July 1923; *s* of George Brown and Margaret Ditchburn Brown; *m* 1st, 1947, Maureen Dorothy Moore (*d* 1991); one *d*; 2nd, 1992, Dr Helen Crawford Gladstone. *Educ:* Edinburgh University. Radar Research and Development Estabt, 1944–51; Lectr, Imperial Coll., 1951–54; University Coll., London: Lectr, 1954–56; Reader, 1956–64; Prof., 1964–67; seconded to Indian Inst. of Technology as Prof. of Electrical Engrg, 1962–65; Prof. of Elect. Engineering, Imperial Coll. of Science and Technology, 1967–81 (Head of Dept, 1967–79); Tech. Dir, Marconi Electrical Devices Ltd, 1981–83; Dir, Univ. and Schs Liaison, GEC, 1983–88. Mem., SRC, 1977–81 (Chm., Engrg Bd, 1977–81); Chm., Joint ESRC-SERC Cttee, 1988–91; Member: Engrg Group, Nat. Advisory Bd, 1983–84; Engrg Cttee, CNAA, 1985–87; Accreditation Cttee, CNAA, 1987–89. Pres., IEE, 1979–80 (Vice-Pres., 1975–78; Dep. Pres., 1978–79); Pres., IEEIE, 1981–85 (Treasurer, 1989–99). Governor: S Bank Polytechnic, 1985–90; Willesden Coll. of Technology, 1985–86. FREng (FEng 1984). Hon. FIElecIE 1986. Hon. DLitt Nanyang Technol Univ., Singapore, 1996. *Publications:* Microwave Lenses, 1953; (with H. M. Barlow) Radio Surface Waves, 1962; Telecommunications, 1964; (with R. H. Clarke) Diffraction Theory and Antennas, 1980; papers in Proc. IEE, etc. *Recreation:* gardening. *Address:* 28 Dale Side, Gerrards Cross, Bucks SL9 7JE.

BROWN, John, CMG 1989; HM Diplomatic Service, retired; *b* 13 July 1931; *s* of John Coultas Scofield Brown and Sarah Ellen Brown (*née* Brown); *m* 1955, Christine Ann Batchelor; one *d.* Export Credits Guarantee Dept, 1949; Nat. service, Grenadier Guards, 1949–51; Board of Trade, 1967; seconded to HM Diplomatic Service, 1969; Diplomatic Service, 1975; First Secretary and Head of Chancery, Accra, 1977; FCO, 1979, Counsellor, 1981; Counsellor (Commercial) and Dir of Trade Promotion, British Trade Develt Office, NY, 1984; Consul-Gen., Toronto, and Dir, Trade Promotion and

Investment, 1989–91. *Recreations:* walking, public speaking. *Club:* Royal Over-Seas League.

BROWN, John B.; *see* Blamire-Brown.

BROWN, (John) Bruce, FRICS; Chairman, Lambert Smith Hampton, since 1988; *b* 15 June 1944; *s* of late Bruce Brown and of Margaret Mary (*née* Roberts); *m* 1967, Daphne Jane Walker; one *s* two *d. Educ:* Acton Park, Wrexham; Grove Park, Wrexham; Coll. of Estate Management, London Univ. (BSc). FRICS 1977. Surveyor, Samuel Walker & Son, 1967–68; Estates Surveyor, Bracknell Develt Corp., 1968–69; Sen. Develt Surveyor, Town & City Properties, 1969–71; Sen. Partner, Anthony Brown Stewart, 1971–88. *Recreations:* motor-racing, vintage and veteran cars. *Address:* Mimosa House, 12 Princes Street, W1R 7RD. *T:* (020) 7494 4000; Radmore Farm, Wappenham, Towcester, Northants NN12 8SX.

BROWN, Prof. John Campbell, PhD; DSc; Regius Professor of Astronomy, University of Glasgow, since 1996; Astronomer Royal for Scotland, since 1995; *b* 4 Feb. 1947; *s* of John Brown and Jane Livingston Stewart Brown (*née* Campbell); *m* 1972, Dr Margaret Isobel Logan; one *s* one *d. Educ:* Hartfield Primary; Dumbarton Acad.; Glasgow Univ. (BSc 1st Cl. Hons Physics and Astronomy 1968; PhD 1973; DSc 1984). University of Glasgow: Research Asst, 1968–70; Lectr, 1970–78; Sen. Lectr, 1978–80; Reader, 1980–84; Prof. of Astrophysics, 1984–96. Fellow: Univ. of Tubingen, 1971–72; Univ. of Utrecht, 1973–74; Vis. Fellow, Nat. Center for Atmospheric Res., Colorado, 1977; NASA Associate Prof., Univ. of Md, 1980; Nuffield/NSF Fellow, UCSD and Univ. of Amsterdam, 1984; Brittingham Prof., Univ. of Wisconsin-Madison, 1987; Visiting Fellow, 1999: Univ. of Amsterdam; ETH Zürich; Observatoire de Paris; NASA Goddard SFC; Univ. of Wisconsin-Madison. Hon. Professor: Univ. of Edinburgh, 1996–; Univ. of Aberdeen, 1998–. FRAS 1973 (Vice Pres., 1986–87); FRSE 1984 (Mem. Council, 1997–2000); FInstP 1996; Associate Mem., Brazilian Acad. of Scis, 1988. Kelvin Prize and Medal, Univ. of Glasgow, 1984; Kelvin Medal, Royal Philosophical Soc., Glasgow, 1996; Robinson Lectr and Medal, Armagh Observatory, 1998. *Publications:* (with I. J. D. Craig) Inverse Problems in Astronomy, 1986; (ed with J. T. Schmeltz) The Sun: a laboratory for astrophysics, 1992; numerous papers in Astrophysical Jl, Astronomy and Astrophysics, Solar Physic, Nature, etc. *Recreations:* oil-painting, lapidary and silvercraft, woodwork, photography, conjuring, reading, cycling, hiking. *Address:* Department of Physics and Astronomy, University of Glasgow, Glasgow G12 8QQ. *T:* (0141) 330 5182; 21 Bradfield Avenue, Glasgow G12 0QH. *T:* (0141) 339 1688.

BROWN, (John) Carter, Hon. CBE 1993; Director, National Gallery of Art, Washington, DC, 1969–92, now Director Emeritus; Chairman, US Commission of Fine Arts, since 1971; Chairman, Ovation Inc., the Arts Network, since 1993; *b* 8 Oct. 1934; *s* of John Nicholas Brown and Anne Kinsolving Brown; *m* 1976, Pamela Braga Drexel (marr. diss. 1991); one *s* one *d. Educ:* Harvard (AB *summa cum laude* 1956; MBA 1958); Inst. of Fine Arts, NY Univ. (Museum Trng Prog., Metropol. Museum of Art; MA 1961). Studied: with Bernard Berenson, Florence, 1958; Ecole du Louvre, Paris, 1958–59; Rijksbureau voor Kunsthistorische Documentatie, The Hague, 1960. National Gallery of Art: Asst to Dir, 1961–63; Asst Dir, 1964–68; Dep. Dir, 1968–69. Mem., Federal Council on Arts and Humanities, 1971–. Treas., White House Historical Assoc., 1969–; Mem., Cttee for Preservation of the White House. Mem. Bd of Govs, John Carter Brown Liby; Trustee: Brown Univ.; Doris Duke Charitable Foundn; John F. Kennedy Center for Performing Arts; Morris and Gwendolyn Cafritz Foundn; Nat. Geographic Soc.; Storm King Art Center; World Monuments Fund; Newport Restoration Foundn. Chm., Pritzker Prize Jury, 1979–. Mem., Amer. Philosophical Soc., 1992; Fellow, Amer. Acad. of Arts and Scis, 1993; Hon. Mem., Amer. Inst. of Architects, 1975; Hon. FRA 1991. Holds 17 hon. degrees. Gold Medal of Honor, National Arts Soc., 1972; Gold Medal of Honor, Nat. Inst. of Social Sciences, 1987; Nat. Medal of Arts, USA, 1991. Commandeur, l'Ordre des Arts et des Lettres, France, 1975; Chevalier de la Légion d'Honneur, France, 1976; Knight, Order of St Olav, Norway, 1979; Comdr, Order of the Republic, Egypt, 1979; Comdr, Order of Orange-Nassau, Netherlands, 1982; Commendatore, Order of Merit of Italian Republic, 1984; Kt Comdr, Order of Isabel la Católica, Spain, 1985; Austrian Cross of Honor for Arts and Letters, 1986; Comdr, Royal Order of the Polar Star, Sweden, 1988; Grande Oficial, Order of Prince Henry the Navigator, Portugal, 1992. Phi Beta Kappa, 1956. Author/Dir, (film), The American Vision, 1966; author and narrator, (TV), Rings of Passion: five emotions in world art. *Publications:* Rings: five passions in world art, 1996; contrib. professional jls and exhibn catalogues. *Recreations:* sailing, riding, photography. *Address:* (office) Suite 621, 1201 Pennsylvania Avenue NW, Washington, DC 20004, USA. *Clubs:* Knickerbocker, New York Yacht (New York).

BROWN, John Domenic Weare; Chairman, John Brown Publishing Ltd, since 1987 (Managing Director, 1987–99); *b* 29 May 1953; *s* of Sir John Gilbert Newton Brown, *qv*; *m* 1987, Claudia Zeff; one *s* one *d. Educ:* Westminster Sch.; London Coll. of Printing. Managing Director: Eel Pie Publishing, 1982; Virgin Books, 1983–87; Founder, John Brown Publishing Ltd (magazine publisher), 1987. Marcus Morris Award, PPA, 1997. *Recreations:* sport (mainly watching), music (mainly listening), cars (mostly dreaming). *Address:* c/o John Brown Publishing, The New Boathouse, 136-142 Bramley Road, W10 6SR. *T:* (020) 7565 3000. *Clubs:* Groucho, Soho House.

BROWN, Rt Rev. John Edward; Bishop in Cyprus and the Gulf, 1987–95; Episcopal Canon, St George's Cathedral, Jerusalem, 1987–95; an Assistant Bishop, Diocese of Lincoln, since 1995; *b* 13 July 1930; *s* of Edward and Muriel Brown; *m* 1956, Rosemary (*née* Wood); one *s. Educ:* Wintringham Grammar Sch., Grimsby; Kelham Theological Coll., Notts. BD London. Deacon 1955, priest 1956; Master, St George's School, Jerusalem; Curate, St George's Cathedral, Jerusalem; Chaplain of Amman, Jordan, 1954–57; Curate-in-Charge, All Saints, Reading, 1957–60; Missionary and Chaplain, All Saints Cathedral, Khartoum, Sudan, 1960–64; Vicar: Stewkley, Buckingham, 1964–69; St Luke's, Maidenhead, 1969–73; Bracknell, Berkshire, 1973–77; Rural Dean of Sonning, 1974–77; Archdeacon of Berkshire, 1978–86. *Recreations:* walking; Middle East and African studies. *Address:* 130 Oxford Street, Cleethorpes DN35 0BP. *T:* (01472) 698840.

BROWN, Sir John (Gilbert Newton), Kt 1974; CBE 1966; MA; Vice President, Blackwell Group Ltd, since 1987 (Director, 1980–87); *b* 7 July 1916; *s* of John and Molly Brown, Chilham, Kent; *m* 1946, Virginia, *d* of late Darcy Braddell and Dorothy Braddell; one *s* two *d. Educ:* Lancing Coll.; Hertford Coll., Oxford (MA Zoology). Bombay Branch Oxford University Press, 1937–40; commissioned Royal Artillery, 1941; served with 5th Field Regiment, 1941–46; captured by the Japanese at Fall of Singapore, 1942; prisoner of war, Malaya, Formosa and Japan, 1942–45; returned Oxford University Press, 1946; Sales Manager, 1949; Publisher, 1956–80; Chm., University Bookshops (Oxford) Ltd; Chm., 1980–83, Dep. Chm., 1983–87, Dir, 1980–87, B. H. Blackwell Ltd; Chm., 1983–85, Dir, 1983–87, Basil Blackwell Ltd (formerly Basil Blackwell Publisher Ltd); Director: Willshaw Booksellers Ltd, Manchester, 1966–89; Book Tokens Ltd, 1973–89; Archival Facsimiles Ltd, 1986–89; John Brown Publishing Ltd, 1989–. President, Publishers' Association, 1963–65. Member: Nat. Libraries Cttee; EDC for Newspapers, Printing and Publishing Industry, 1967–70; Adv. Cttee on Scientific and Technical Information, 1969–73; Communication Adv. Cttee for UK Nat. Cttee for UNESCO; Royal Literary Fund (Asst Treasurer); Bd of British Library, 1973–79; Royal Soc. Cttee on Scientific Information; Mem. Bd, British Council, 1968–81; Open Univ. Visiting Cttee. Professorial Fellow, Hertford Coll., Oxford, 1974–80. FRSA 1964. *Address:* Milton Lodge, Great Milton, Oxford OX44 7NJ. *T:* (01844) 279217. *Club:* Garrick.

BROWN, (John) Michael, CBE 1986; HM Diplomatic Service, retired; *b* 16 Nov. 1929; *m* 1955, Elizabeth Fitton; one *s* one *d.* Served at: Cairo, 1954–55; Doha, 1956–57; FO, 1957–60; Havana, 1960–62; FO, 1962–64; Jedda, 1965–66; Maseru, 1966–67; Bogotá, 1967–69; FCO, 1969–71; Ankara, 1971–73; Tripoli, 1973–75; FCO, 1976–79; Ambassador to Costa Rica and Nicaragua, 1979–82; Consul-Gen., Geneva, 1983–85. *Address:* Springfield House, Donhead St Andrew, Shaftesbury, SP7 9DZ.

BROWN, Dr John Michael, FRS 1996; Lecturer and Tutor in Chemistry, Dyson Perrins Laboratory, Oxford University and Fellow of Wadham College, since 1974; *b* 24 Dec. 1939; *s* of John Caulfield Brown and Winefride Brown; *m* 1963, Una Horner; one *s* one *d. Educ:* Manchester Univ. (BSc 1960; PhD 1963). Various postdoctoral appts, 1963–66; Lectr in Chemistry, Warwick Univ., 1966–74. Tilden Lectr, RSC, 1991. Organometallic Prize, RSC, 1993. *Publications:* (jtly) Mechanism in Organic Chemistry, 1971; articles and reviews in UK, US and European jls. *Recreations:* countryside (UK and France), good writing, grandchildren, Man Utd. *Address:* Dyson Perrins Laboratory, South Parks Road, Oxford OX1 3QY. *T:* (01865) 275642, *Fax:* (01865) 275674; *e-mail:* john.brown@chem.ox.ac.uk.

BROWN, John Russell; Visiting Professor of Theatre, Middlesex University, since 2000 (Research Consultant, 1994); *b* 15 Sept. 1923; *yr s* of Russell Alan and Olive Helen Brown, Coombe Wood, Somerset; *m* 1961, Hilary Sue Baker; one *s* two *d. Educ:* Monkton Combe Sch.; Keble Coll., Oxford. Sub-Lieut (AE) RNVR, 1944–46. Fellow, Shakespeare Inst., Stratford-upon-Avon, 1951–55; Lectr and Sen. Lectr, Dept of English, Birmingham Univ., 1955–63; Hd of Dept of Drama and Theatre Arts, Univ. of Birmingham, 1964–71; Prof. of English, Sussex Univ., 1971–82; Prof. of Theatre Arts, State Univ. of NY at Stony Brook, 1982–85; Prof. of Theatre, Univ. of Michigan, Ann Arbor, 1985–97; Artistic Dir, Project Theatre, Michigan Univ., 1985–89. Reynolds Lectr, Colorado Univ., 1957; Vis. Prof. Graduate Sch., New York Univ., 1959; Mellon Prof. of Drama, Carnegie Inst., Pittsburgh, 1964; Vis. Prof., Zürich Univ., 1969–70; Univ. Lectr in Drama, Univ. of Toronto, 1970; Vis. Prof., Columbia Univ., NY, 1998. Robb Lectr, Univ. of Auckland, 1976; Lansdowne Visitor, Univ. of Victoria, BC, 1990. Associate, NT, 1973–88. Member: Adv. Council of Victoria and Albert Museum, 1980–83; Adv. Council of Theatre Museum, 1974–83 (Chm., 1979–83); Arts Council of GB, 1980–83, and Chm. Drama Panel, 1980–83 (formerly Dep. Chm.). *Theatre productions include:* Twelfth Night, Playhouse, Pittsburgh, 1964; Macbeth, Everyman, Liverpool, 1965; The White Devil, Everyman, 1969; Crossing Niagara, Nat. Theatre at the ICA, 1975; They Are Dying Out, Young Vic, 1976; Old Times, British Council tour of Poland, 1976; Judgement, Nat. Theatre, 1977; Hamlet (tour), 1978; Macbeth, Nat. Theatre (co-director), 1978; The Vienna Notes and The Nest, Crucible, Sheffield, 1979; Company, Nat. Theatre, 1980; Faith Healer, Nat. Theatre and Santa Fe, 1982, and, with Candida, British Council tour of India, 1983; The Double Bass, Nat. Theatre, 1984; The Daughter-in-Law, Antique Pink, Oedipus, Waiting for Godot, Don Juan, Every Good Boy, Project Theater, Ann Arbor, Mich, USA, 1985–89; Richard II, Nat. Theatre, Educn Project Tour, 1987; Much Ado About Nothing, Playhouse, Cincinnati, 1989; Burn This, 1989, On the Verge, 1991, Dunedin, NZ; Arden of Faversham, Empty Space, Seattle, 1991; Life Sentences, Group Theater of Mich, 1994. General Editor: Stratford-upon-Avon Studies, 1960–67; Stratford-upon-Avon Library, 1964–69; Theatre Production Studies, 1981–2002; Theatre Concepts, 1992–95; Theatres of the World, 2001–. *Publications:* (ed) The Merchant of Venice, 1955; Shakespeare and his Comedies, 1957; (ed) The White Devil, 1960; Shakespeare: The Tragedy of Macbeth, 1963; (ed) The Duchess of Malfi, 1965; (ed) Henry V, 1965; Shakespeare's Plays in Performance, 1966; Effective Theatre, 1969; Shakespeare's The Tempest, 1969; Shakespeare's Dramatic Style, 1970; Theatre Language, 1972; Free Shakespeare, 1974; Discovering Shakespeare, 1981; Shakespeare and his Theatre, 1982; A Short Guide to Modern British Drama, 1983; Shakescenes, 1993; (ed) Oxford Illustrated History of Theatre, 1995; William Shakespeare: writing for performance, 1996; What is Theatre?, 1997; New Sites for Shakespeare: theatre, the audience and Asia, 1999; Shakespeare: the Tragedies, 2001; articles in Shakespeare Survey, Critical Quarterly, Tulane Drama Review, Studies in Bibliography, New Theatre Qly, Theatre Res. Internat., etc. *Recreations:* gardening, travel. *Address:* Court Lodge, Hooe; The Circle, SE1.

BROWN, Joseph Lawler, CBE 1978; TD 1953; FMIC; CIMgt; DL; Chairman and Managing Director, The Birmingham Post & Mail Ltd, 1973–77; *b* 22 March 1921; *s* of late Neil Brown; *m* 1950, Mabel Smith, SRN, SCM; one *s* one *d. Educ:* Peebles; Heriot-Watt Coll., Edinburgh. BA Hons Open Univ. FCIM (FInstM 1976); CIMgt (FBIM 1978). Served War, The Royal Scots, 1939–47 (Major). The Scotsman Publications Ltd, 1947–60; Coventry Newspapers Ltd: Gen. Man., 1960; Jt Man. Dir, 1961; Man. Dir, 1964–69; The Birmingham Post & Mail Ltd: Dep. Man. Dir, 1970; Man. Dir, 1971. Director: Cambridge Newspapers Ltd, 1965–69; Press Assoc., 1968–75 (Chm. 1972); Reuters Ltd, 1972–75; BPM (Holdings) Ltd, 1973–81. Pres., Birmingham Chamber of Industry and Commerce, 1979–80. Exec. Chm., Birmingham Venture, 1981–85. Mem., Bromsgrove and Redditch DHA, 1982–84; Mem., Hereford and Worcester Family Practitioner Cttee, 1982–83. Mem. Council, Regular Forces Employment Assoc., 1983–87; Warden, Neidpath Castle, Peebles, 1983–84. Mem., Peebles Guildry Corp., 1991–97. Life Mem., Court, Birmingham Univ., 1980; Bailiff, Schs of King Edward the Sixth in Birmingham, 1987–88. DL County of W Midlands, 1976. Kt, Mark Twain Soc., 1979. Commendatore, Order Al Merito Della Repubblica Italiana, 1973. *Publication:* (with J. C. Lawson) History of Peebles 1850–1990, 1990. *Address:* 1 Norbury Close, Church Hill North, Redditch, Worcs B98 8RP. *T:* (01527) 597887.

BROWN, Prof. Judith Margaret, (Mrs P. J. Diggle), FRHistS; Beit Professor of Commonwealth History, Oxford and Fellow of Balliol College, since 1990; *b* India, 9 July 1944; *d* of late Rev. Wilfred George Brown and Joan M. Brown; *m* 1984, Peter James Diggle; one *s. Educ:* Sherborne Sch. for Girls; Girton Coll., Cambridge (BA 1965; PhD 1968; MA 1969); MA, DPhil Oxon 1990. Research Fellow, Official Fellow and Dir of Studies in History, Girton Coll., Cambridge, 1968–71; Lectr, Sen. Lectr, Reader Elect in History, Univ. of Manchester, 1971–90. Trustee, Charles Wallace (India) Trust, 1996–; Chm. Trustees, Friends of Delhi Brotherhood Soc., 1997–99. Governor: Bath Spa UC, 1997–; SOAS, London Univ., 1999–. Hon. DSocSc Natal, 2001. *Publications:* Gandhi's Rise to Power: Indian politics 1915–1922, 1972; Gandhi and Civil Disobedience: the Mahatma in Indian politics 1928–1934, 1977; Men and Gods in a Changing World, 1980; Modern India: the origins of an Asian democracy, 1984, 2nd edn 1994; Gandhi: prisoner of hope, 1989, 2nd edn 1998 (trans. Italian, 1995); (ed with R. Foot) Migration: the Asian experience, 1994; (ed with M. Prozesky) Gandhi and South Africa: principles and politics, 1996; (ed with R. Foot) Hong Kong's Transitions 1842–1997, 1997; Nehru, 1999; (ed with W. R. Louis) The Oxford History of the British Empire, vol. IV: the twentieth

century, 1999. *Recreations:* classical music, gardening, walking. *Address:* Balliol College, Oxford OX1 3BJ. *T:* (01865) 277736.
See also P. W. H. Brown.

BROWN, Julia Elizabeth; *see* King, J. E.

BROWN, Julian Francis, RDI 1998; owner, StudioBrown, since 1990; *b* 8 Sept. 1955; *s* of Oliver and Barbara Brown; *m* 1986, Louise Mary Aron; two *s* one *d. Educ:* Leicester Poly. (BA Hons Industrial Design 1978); RCA (MDes 1983). Designer: David Carter Associates, 1979–80; Porsche Design, Austria, 1983–86; Partner, Lovegrove & Brown, 1986–90. Guest Prof., Hochschule der Kunste, Berlin, 1991–92. Ext. Examnr in Industrial Design, RCA, 1997–99. *Address:* StudioBrown, 6 Princes Building, George Street, Bath BA1 2ED. *T:* (01225) 481735.

BROWN, June P.; *see* Paterson-Brown.

BROWN, (Laurence Frederick) Mark; His Honour Judge Mark Brown; a Circuit Judge, since 2000; *b* 16 March 1953; *s* of Rt Rev. Ronald Brown, *qv*; *m* 1978, Jane Margaret Boardman; one *s. Educ:* Bolton Sch.; St John's Coll., Univ. of Durham (BA Jt Hons Law/Econs). Called to the Bar, Inner Temple, 1975; practised, Northern Circuit, 1976–2000; Asst Recorder, 1993–97, a Recorder, 1997–2000; Asst Boundary Comr, England and Wales, 2000. Pt-time tutor in Law, Univ. of Liverpool, 1977–82; Head of advocacy training, Northern Circuit, 1998–2001. Counsel to Chief Constable at Police Disciplinary Hearings, 1989–2000; Member: Panel, Disciplinary Tribunals of Council of Inns of Court, 1994–2000; Merseyside Area Criminal Justice Strategy Cttee, 1997–2000; Northern Circuit Exec. Cttee and Advocacy Studies Bd, Bar Council, 1998–2000. *Recreations:* golf, ballroom dancing, gardening. *Address:* Liverpool Combined Court Centre, Queen Elizabeth II Law Courts, Derby Square, Liverpool L2 1XA. *T:* (0151) 473 7373. *Club:* Royal Liverpool Golf.

BROWN, Prof. Lawrence Michael, ScD; FRS 1982; Professor of Physics, University of Cambridge, since 1990; Founding Fellow, Robinson College, Cambridge, since 1977; *b* 18 March 1936; *s* of Bertson Waterworth Brown and Edith Waghorne; *m* 1965, Susan Drucker; one *s* two *d. Educ:* Univ. of Toronto (BASc); Univ. of Birmingham (PhD); ScD Cantab 1992. Athlone Fellow, Univ. of Birmingham, 1957; W. M. Tapp Research Fellow, Gonville and Caius Coll., Cambridge, 1963; University Demonstrator, Cavendish Laboratory, 1965; Lectr, 1970–83, Reader, 1983–90, Cambridge Univ.; Lectr, Robinson Coll., Cambridge, 1977–90. *Publications:* many papers on structure and properties of materials and electron microscopy in Acta Metallurgica and Philosophical Magazine. *Address:* 74 Alpha Road, Cambridge CB4 3DG. *T:* (01223) 337291.

BROWN, Prof. L(ionel) Neville, OBE 1988; Professor of Comparative Law, University of Birmingham, 1966–90, Emeritus Professor, since 1990; Leverhulme Fellow, 1990– 92; *b* 29 July 1923; *s* of Reginald P. N. Brown and Fanny Brown (*née* Carver); *m* 1957, Mary Patricia Vowles; three *s* one *d. Educ:* Wolverhampton Grammar Sch.; Pembroke Coll., Cambridge (Scholar; 1st Cl. Class. Tripos Pt I and Law Tripos Pt II; MA, LLM); Lyons Univ. (Dr en Droit). RAF, 1942–45; Cambridge, 1945–48; articled to Wolverhampton solicitor, 1948–50; Rotary Foundn Fellow, Lyons Univ., 1951–52; Lectr in Law, Sheffield Univ., 1953–55; Lectr in Comparative Law, Birmingham Univ., 1956, Sen. Lectr, 1957; Sen. Res. Fellow, Univ. of Michigan, 1960. Mem., Council on Tribunals, 1982–88; Chm., Birmingham Social Security Appeal Tribunal, 1988–96. Visiting Professor: Univ. of Tulane, New Orleans, 1968; Univ. of Nairobi, 1974; Laval, 1975, 1979, 1983, 1990; Limoges, 1986; Mauritius, 1988, 1989; Aix-en-Provence, 1991. Commonwealth Foundn Lectr (Caribbean), 1975–76. Pres., SPTL, 1984–85. Reader, C of E, Lichfield Dio., 1971–. Dr *hc* Limoges, 1989; Hon. LLD Laval, 1992. Officier dans l'Ordre des Palmes Académiques, 1987. *Publications:* (with F. H. Lawson and A. E. Anton) Amos and Walton's Introduction to French Law, 2nd edn 1963 and 3rd edn 1967; (with J. F. Garner) French Administrative Law, 1967, 5th edn (with J. S. Bell) 1998; (with F. G. Jacobs) Court of Justice of the European Communities, 1977, 5th edn (with T. Kennedy), 2000. *Recreations:* landscape gardening, country walking, music. *Address:* Willow Rise, 14 Waterdale, Compton Road West, Wolverhampton, West Midlands WV3 9DY. *T:* (01902) 426666. *Club:* Oxford and Cambridge.

BROWN, Prof. Margaret Louise, PhD; Professor of Mathematics Education, King's College, London, since 1990; *b* 30 Sept. 1943; *d* of (Frederick) Harold Seed and Louisa Seed (*née* Shearer); *m* 1970, Hugh Palmer Brown; three *s. Educ:* Merchant Taylors' Sch. for Girls, Liverpool; Newnham Coll., Cambridge (BA Math. 1965; MA 1968); Inst. of Education, London Univ. (PGCE 1966); Chelsea Coll., Univ. of London (PhD 1981). Math. Teacher, Cavendish Sch., Hemel Hempstead, 1966–69; Lectr in Math. Educn, 1969–83, Sen. Lectr, 1983–86, Chelsea Coll., Univ. of London; Reader in Math. Educn, 1986–90, Head of Sch. of Educn, 1992–96, KCL; FKC 1996. Member: Nat. Curriculum Math. Wkg Gp, 1987–88; Numeracy Task Force, 1997–98; Chair: Jt Math. Council of UK, 1991–95; Trustees, School Math. Project, 1996–; President: Math. Assoc., 1990–91; British Educnl Res. Assoc., 1997–98. *Publications:* (jtly) Statistics and Probability, 1972, 2nd edn 1977; (jtly) Low Attainers in Mathematics 5–16, 1982; (jtly) Children Learning Mathematics, 1984; Graded Assessment in Mathematics, 1992; (jtly) Intuition or Evidence?, 1995; (jtly) Effective Teachers of Numeracy, 1997; papers in jls and contribs to books on math. educn. *Recreations:* walking, music. *Address:* School of Education, King's College London, Cornwall House, Waterloo Road, SE1 8WA. *T:* (020) 7848 3088; (home) 34 Girdwood Road, SW18 5QS. *T:* (020) 8789 4344.

BROWN, (Marion) Patricia; Under-Secretary (Economics), Treasury, 1972–85; *b* 2 Feb. 1927; *d* of late Henry Oswald Brown and Elsie Elizabeth (*née* Thompson). *Educ:* Norwich High Sch. for Girls; Newnham Coll., Cambridge. Central Economic Planning Staff, Cabinet Office, 1947; Treasury, 1948–54; United States Embassy, London, 1956–59; Treasury, 1959–85. Mem. Council, Royal Holloway and Bedford New Coll., London Univ., 1985–98 (Hon. Fellow, 1999). *Recreations:* bird watching, walking. *Address:* 28 The Plantation, SE3 0AB. *T:* (020) 8852 9011.

BROWN, Mark; *see* Brown, L. F. M.

BROWN, Martin; Commissioner, since 1993, and Director, Customs and Tax Practice, since 2001, HM Customs and Excise; *b* 26 Jan. 1949; *s* of late Clarence Brown and of Anne Brown; *m* 1971, Frances Leithead; two *s. Educ:* Bolton Sch.; New Coll., Oxford (MA). Joined Customs and Excise as Admin. Trainee, 1971; Private Sec. to Minister of State and to Financial Sec., HM Treasury, 1974–76; Principal, HM Customs and Excise, 1976; Customs adviser to Barbados Govt, 1984–86; HM Customs and Excise: Asst Sec., 1987; Director: Customs, 1993; Central Ops, 1994–96; VAT Policy, 1996–2000. *Recreations:* theatre, singing, walking, gardening, pottering. *Address:* HM Customs and Excise, New King's Beam House, 22 Upper Ground, SE1 9PJ. *T:* (020) 7865 5015. *Club:* Hale (Leigh Road) Tennis.

BROWN, Sir Max; *see* Brown, Sir C. M. P.

BROWN, Sir Mervyn, KCMG 1981 (CMG 1975); OBE 1963; HM Diplomatic Service, retired; *b* 24 Sept. 1923; *m* 1949, Elizabeth Gittings. *Educ:* Ryhope Gram. Sch., Sunderland; St John's Coll., Oxford. Served in RA, 1942–45. Entered HM Foreign Service, 1949; Third Secretary, Buenos Aires, 1950; Second Secretary, UK Mission to UN, New York, 1953; First Secretary, Foreign Office, 1956; Singapore, 1959; Vientiane, 1960; again in Foreign Office, 1963–67; Ambassador to Madagascar, 1967–70; Inspector, FCO, 1970–72; Head of Communications Operations Dept, FCO, 1973–74; Asst Under-Sec. of State (Dir of Communications), 1974; High Comr in Tanzania, 1975–78, and concurrently Ambassador to Madagascar; Minister and Dep. Perm. Representative to UN, 1978; High Comr in Nigeria, 1979–83, and concurrently Ambassador to Benin. Chairman: Visiting Arts Unit of GB, 1983–89; Council, King's Coll., Madrid, 1995–; Vice-Pres., Commonwealth Youth Exchange Council, 1984–87. Pres., Britain-Nigeria Assoc., 2000–; Chm., Anglo-Malagasy Soc., 1986–. *Publications:* Madagascar Rediscovered, 1978; A History of Madagascar, 1995; War in Shangri-La, 2001. *Recreations:* music, tennis, history, cooking. *Address:* 195 Queen's Gate, SW7 5EU. *Clubs:* Royal Commonwealth Society, Hurlingham, All England Lawn Tennis.

BROWN, Michael; *see* Brown, J. M.

BROWN, Air Vice-Marshal Michael John Douglas; non-executive Director, CSE International (formerly Centre for Software Engineering) Ltd, since 1993; consulting engineer; *b* 9 May 1936; *s* of late N. H. B. Brown, AMIERE; *m* 1st, 1961, Audrey (*d* 1994); one *s*; 2nd, 1997, Ruth, *d* of late H. G. Willey, Weobley, Herefordshire. *Educ:* Drayton Manor, W7; RAF Technical Coll., Henlow; Trinity Hall, Cambridge (MA). CEng 1968; CMath, FIMA 1991; FRIN 1998; FRAeS 2000. Commnd RAF Technical Br., 1954; Cambridge Univ. Air Sqdn, 1954–57; RAF pilot trng, 1958–59; served in Bomber Comd, 1959–61; signals duties in Kenya (also assisted with formation of Kenya Air Force), 1961–64; advanced weapons course, 1965–66; Defence Operational Analysis Estabt, 1966–69; RAF Staff Coll., 1970; MoD Operational Requirements Staff, 1971–73; RAF Boulmer, 1973–75; USAF Air War Coll., 1975–76; HQ RAF Strike Comd, 1976–78; Comdr, RAF N Luffenham, 1978–80; rcds 1981; Dir, Air Guided Weapons, MoD (PE), 1983–86; Dir Gen., Strategic Electronic Systems, MoD (PE), 1986–91. Vice-Chm., Herefordshire RBL, 1997–2000; Vice-President: SSAFA, Powys, 1993–; RAFA, Hereford, 1997–; Regl Rep. for S Wales, SSAFA Nat. Council, 1997–. Freeman, City of London, 2000; Freeman, 2000, Liveryman, 2001, Engineers' Co. *Club:* Royal Air Force.

BROWN, Ven. Michael René Warneford; Archdeacon of Nottingham, 1960–77, now Archdeacon Emeritus; *b* 7 June 1915; *s* of late George and Irene Brown; *m* 1978, Marie Joyce Chaloner, *d* of late Walter Dawson, and of Sarah Dawson, Burbage, Leics; three step *s. Educ:* King's School, Rochester; St Peter's College, Oxford; St Stephen's House, Oxford (MA). Deacon 1941; priest, 1942; Asst Master, Christ's Hospital, 1939–43; Curate of West Grinstead, 1941–43. Chap. RNVR, 1943–46; chaplain and Dean of St Peter's College and Curate of St Mary the Virgin, Oxford, 1946; Lecturer, RN College, Greenwich, 1946–47; Librarian, 1948–50 and Fellow, 1948–52, of St Augustine's Coll., Canterbury; Priest-in-charge of Bekesbourne, 1948–50; Asst Secretary, CACTM, 1950–60. Examining Chaplain: to Bishop of Southwell, 1954–77; to Archbishop of Canterbury, 1959–60; Commissary to Bishop of Waikato, 1958–70; Hon. Officiating Chaplain, RM, Deal, Kent, 1987–96. Member: Church of England Pensions Board, 1966–84; Church Commissioners' Redundant Churches Cttee, 1978–88; Chm., Redundant Churches' Uses Cttee in Canterbury Dio., 1980–89; Vice-Chm., Diocesan Adv. Cttee for the Care of Churches, 1980–93; Church Commissioner, 1968–78. *Recreations:* antiquarian and aesthetic, especially English paintings and silver. *Address:* Faygate, 72 Liverpool Road, Walmer, Deal, Kent CT14 7LR. *T:* (01304) 361326. *Club:* Athenæum.

BROWN, Michael Russell; journalist; *b* 3 July 1951; *s* of Frederick Alfred Brown and Greta Mary Brown, OBE (*née* Russell). *Educ:* Andrew Cairns Secondary Modern Sch., Sussex; Univ. of York (BA (Hons) Economics and Politics). Graduate Management Trainee, Barclays Bank Ltd, 1972–74; Lecturer and Tutor, Swinton Conservative Coll., 1974–75; part-time Asst to Michael Marshall, MP, 1975–76; Law Student, 1976–77, Member of Middle Temple; Personal Asst to Nicholas Winterton, MP, 1976–79. MP (C) Brigg and Scunthorpe, 1979–83, Brigg and Cleethorpes, 1983–97; contested (C) Cleethorpes, 1997. PPS to Hon. Douglas Hogg, Minister of State, DTI, 1989–90, FCO, 1990–92; PPS to Sir Patrick Mayhew, Sec. of State for NI, 1992–93; an Asst Govt Whip, 1993–94. Mem., Energy Select Cttee, 1986–89; Sec., 1981–87, Vice-Chm., 1987–89, Conservative Party N Ireland Cttee. Political columnist, The Independent, 1998–. *Recreations:* cricket, walking. *Address:* 78 Lupus Street, SW1V 3EL. *T:* (020) 7630 9045. *Club:* Reform.

BROWN, Prof. Michael Stuart, MD; Regental Professor, University of Texas; Professor of Internal Medicine and Genetics, University of Texas Southwestern Medical School at Dallas, since 1974; *b* 13 April 1941; *s* of Harvey and Evelyn Brown; *m* 1964, Alice Lapin; two *d. Educ:* Univ. of Pennsylvania (AB 1962, MD 1966). Resident in Internal Medicine, Mass. Gen. Hosp., Boston, 1966–68; Research Scientist, NIH, Bethesda, 1968–71; Asst Prof., Univ. of Texas Southwestern Med. Sch. at Dallas, 1971–74; Associate Prof., 1974–76. Mem. Bd Dirs, Pfizer Inc. For. Mem., Royal Soc., 1991. Lounsbery Award, 1979; Albert D. Lasker Award, 1985; (jtly) Nobel Prize in Medicine or Physiology for the discovery of receptors for Low Density Lipoproteins, a fundamental advance in the understanding of cholesterol metabolism, 1985; US Nat. Medal of Science, 1987. *Publications:* numerous papers to learned jls. *Address:* Department of Molecular Genetics, University of Texas Southwestern Medical School, 5323 Harry Hines Boulevard, Dallas, TX 75235, USA.

BROWN, Prof. Morris Jonathan, FRCP; Professor of Clinical Pharmacology, Cambridge University, and Hon. Consultant Physician, Addenbrooke's Hospital, since 1985; Fellow of Gonville and Caius College, and Director of Clinical Studies, Cambridge, since 1989; *b* 18 Jan. 1951; *s* of Arnold and Irene Brown; *m* 1977, Diana Phylactou; three *d. Educ:* Harrow; Trinity College, Cambridge (MA, MD); MSc London. FRCP 1987. Lectr, Royal Postgraduate Medical School, 1979–82; Senior Fellow, MRC, 1982–85. Oliver-Sharpey Lectr, RCP, 1992. Chm., Med. Res. Soc., 1991–. FMedSci 1999. *Publications:* Advanced Medicine 21, 1985; (jtly) Clinical Pharmacology, 1996; articles on adrenaline and cardiovascular disease, genetics and therapy of hypertension, prevention of myocardial infarction by vitamin E. *Recreations:* violin and oboe playing, tennis. *Address:* 104 Grange Road, Cambridge CB3 9AA.

BROWN, Rt Hon. Nicholas (Hugh); PC 1997; MP (Lab) Newcastle upon Tyne East and Wallsend, since 1997 (Newcastle upon Tyne East, 1983–97); Minister of State for Work, Department for Work and Pensions, since 2001; *b* 13 June 1950; *s* of late R. C. Brown and of G. K. Brown (*née* Tester). *Educ:* Swatenden Secondary Modern Sch.; Tunbridge Wells Tech. High Sch.; Manchester Univ. (BA 1971). Trade Union Officer, GMWU Northern Region, 1978–83. Mem., Newcastle upon Tyne City Council, 1980–84. Opposition front-bench spokesman: on legal affairs, 1984–87; on Treasury affairs, 1987–94; on health, 1994–95; Dep. Chief Opposition Whip, 1995–97; Parly Sec. to HM Treasury (Govt Chief Whip), 1997–98; Minister, Agriculture, Fisheries and Food,

1998–2001. *Address:* House of Commons, SW1A 0AA. *Clubs:* Shieldfield Workingmen's, West Walker Social, Newcastle Labour (Newcastle); Lindisfarne (Wallsend).

BROWN, Prof. Nigel Leslie, PhD; Professor of Molecular Genetics and Microbiology, University of Birmingham, since 1988; *b* 19 Dec. 1948; *s* of Leslie Charles Brown and Beryl (*née* Brown); *m* 1971, Gayle Lynnette Blackah; two *d. Educ:* Beverley Grammar Sch.; Univ. of Leeds (BSc 1971; F. C. Happold Prize; PhD 1974). CBiol, FIBiol 1989; CChem, FRSC 1990. ICI Fellow, MRC Lab. of Molecular Biology, Cambridge, 1974–76; Lectr in Biochemistry, 1976–81, Royal Soc. EPA Cephalosporin Fund Sen. Res. Fellow, 1981–88, Univ. of Bristol. Vis. Fellow in Genetics, Univ. of Melbourne, 1987–88; Leverhulme Trust Res. Fellow, 2000–01. Biotechnology and Biological Sciences Research Council: Chairman: Genes and Develtl Biology Cttee, 1997–2000; Studentships and Fellowships Cttee, 2000–; Mem., Strategy Bd, 1997–. Member: Res. Careers Initiative, 1997–98; Lunar Soc., 1998–. Hon. Pres., W Midlands Reg., ASE, 1997–98. Mem. Editl Bd, Molecular Microbiology, 1986–97; Chief Ed., Fedn of Eur. Microbiology Socs Microbiology Reviews, 2000–. *Publications:* contribs to scientific jls and books. *Recreations:* travel, house renovation. *Address:* School of Biosciences, University of Birmingham, Edgbaston, Birmingham B15 2TT. *T:* (0121) 414 5467, *Fax:* (0121) 414 5907; *e-mail:* n.l.brown@bham.ac.uk.

BROWN, Patricia; *see* Brown, M. P.

BROWN, Sir Patrick; *see* Brown, Sir A. P.

BROWN, Paul G.; Executive Director, UK Retail Banking, Lloyds Bank plc, 1991–97, retired; *b* 10 Sept. 1942; *s* of Col E. G. Brown and Alice Brown (*née* Van Weyenberghe); *m* 1969, Jessica Faunce; one *s* two *d. Educ:* Belgium, Germany and UK. Management appts with Lloyds Bank plc in Germany, Switzerland, USA and UK, 1960–97. *Recreations:* sailing, ski-ing.

BROWN, Sir Peter (Randolph), Kt 1997; Conservative Constituency Agent for Huntingdon, since 1985; *b* 30 Aug. 1945; *s* of Stanley Percival Brown and late Dorothy Ida Brown (*née* Bagge); *m* 1983, Antonia Brenda Taylor; one *s* one *d. Educ:* Bushey Sch., New Malden, Surrey. With Inland Revenue, 1961–67; Conservative Constituency Agent: London Bor. of Newham, 1967–70; Lambeth, Norwood, 1970–74; Kingston upon Thames, 1974–85; Cons. Eur. Constituency Agent, Cambridge and N Beds, 1987–90. Qualified Mem., Nat. Soc. of Cons. and Unionist Agents, 1968; Mem., Inst. of Supervisory Mgt, 1994. Freeman, City of London, 1992. *Recreations:* reading, following international tennis, gardening. *Address:* Huntingdon Constituency Conservative Association, Archers Court, 8 Stukeley Road, Huntingdon PE18 6XG. *Club:* St Neots Conservative.

BROWN, Prof. Peter Robert Lamont, FBA 1971; FRHistS; Rollins Professor of History, Princeton University since 1986 (Visiting Professor, 1983–86); *b* 26 July 1935; *s* of James Lamont and Sheila Brown, Dublin; *m* 1st, 1959, Friedl Esther (*née* Löw-Beer); two *d*; 2nd, 1980, Patricia Ann Fortini; 3rd, 1989, Elizabeth Gilliam. *Educ:* Aravon Sch., Bray, Co. Wicklow, Ireland; Shrewsbury Sch.; New Coll., Oxford (MA). Harmsworth Senior Scholar, Merton Coll., Oxford and Prize Fellow, All Souls Coll., Oxford, 1956; Junior Research Fellow, 1963, Sen. Res. Fellow, 1970–73, All Souls Coll.; Fellow, All Souls Coll., 1956–75; Lectr in Medieval History, Merton Coll. Oxford, 1970–75; Special Lectr in late Roman and early Byzantine History, 1970–73, Reader, 1973–75, Univ. of Oxford; Prof. of History, Royal Holloway Coll., London Univ., 1975–78; Prof. of History and Classics, Univ. of Calif. at Berkeley, 1978–86. Fellow, Amer. Acad. of Arts and Scis, 1978. Hon. DTheol Fribourg, 1975; Hon. DHL Chicago, 1978; Hon. DLitt: TCD, 1990; Wesleyan Univ., Conn, 1993. *Publications:* Augustine of Hippo: a biography, 1967; The World of Late Antiquity, 1971; Religion and Society in the Age of St Augustine, 1971; The Making of Late Antiquity, 1978; The Cult of the Saints: its rise and function in Latin Christianity, 1980; Society and the Holy in Late Antiquity, 1982; The Body and Society: men, women and sexual renunciation in Early Christianity, 1989; Power and Persuasion in Late Antiquity: towards a Christian Empire, 1992; Authority and the Sacred: aspects of the christianization of the Roman world, 1995; The Rise of Western Christendom: triumph and diversity, AD 200–1000, 1996. *Address:* Department of History, Princeton University, Princeton, NJ 08544, USA.

BROWN, Peter Wilfred Henry, CBE 1996; Secretary of the British Academy, since 1983; *b* 4 June 1941; *s* of late Rev. Wilfred George Brown and Joan Margaret (*née* Adams); *m* 1968, Kathleen Clarke (marr. diss.); one *d. Educ:* Marlborough Coll.; Jesus Coll., Cambridge (Rustat Schol.). Assistant Master in Classics, Birkenhead Sch., 1963–66; Lectr in Classics, Fourah Bay Coll., Univ. of Sierra Leone, 1966–68; Asst Sec., School of Oriental and African Studies, Univ. of London, 1968–75; Dep. Sec., British Academy, 1975–83 (Actg Sec., 1976–77). Member: British Library Adv. Council, 1983–88; CNAA Cttee for Arts and Humanities, 1985–87; Cttee for Research, 1987–89; Council, Soc. for Protection of Sci. and Learning, 1997–. Member: Governing Body, British Assoc. for Central and Eastern Europe (formerly GB/E Europe Centre), 1983–96; Conseil Internat. de la Maison Suger, Paris, 1988–; Council: Britain–Russia Centre (formerly GB/USSR Assoc.), 1983–94; SSEES, Univ. of London, 1984–99; Committee of Management: Inst. of Archaeol., Univ. of London, 1984–86; Inst. of Classical Studies, Univ. of London, 1984–99; Warburg Inst., Univ. of London, 1987–93; Bd, Inst. of Histl Res., London Univ., 1994–99. Fellow, National Humanities Center, N Carolina, 1978. Hon. DLitt Birmingham, 1995. Kt Grand Cross, Order of Merit (Poland), 1995. *Recreations:* travel on business, reading, listening to classical music, photography. *Address:* The British Academy, 10 Carlton House Terrace, SW1Y 5AH. *T:* (020) 7969 5200; 34 Victoria Road, NW6 6PX. *Club:* Athenæum.

See also J. M. Brown.

BROWN, Philip Anthony Russell, CB 1977; Director of Policy, Investment Management Regulatory Organisation, 1985–93; *b* 18 May 1924; *e s* of late Sir William Brown, KCB, KCMG, CBE, and of Elizabeth Mabel (*née* Scott); *m* 1954, Eileen (*d* 1976), *d* of late J. Brennan; *m* 1976, Sarah Elizabeth Dean (*see* S. E. Brown). *Educ:* Malvern; King's Coll., Cambridge. Entered Home Civil Service, Board of Trade, 1947; Private Sec. to Perm. Sec., 1949; Principal, 1952; Private Sec. to Minister of State, 1953; Observer, Civil Service Selection Board, 1957; returned to BoT, 1959; Asst Sec., 1963; Head of Overseas Information Co-ordination Office, 1963; BoT, 1964; Under-Sec., 1969; Head of Establishments Div. 1, BoT, later DTI, 1969; Head of Cos Div., DTI, 1971; Dep. Sec., Dept of Trade, 1974–83. Head of External Relations, Lloyd's of London, 1983–85; Dir, NPI, 1985–90. Mem., Disciplinary Cttee, ICA, 1985–96. Mem., London Adv. Bd, Salvation Army, 1982–92. *Publications:* (contrib.) Multinational Approaches: corporate insiders, 1976; Poems from Square Mile, 1992; articles in various jls. *Recreations:* reading, gardening, music. *Address:* 32 Cumberland Street, SW1V 4LX. *Club:* Oxford and Cambridge.

BROWN, Ralph, RA 1972 (ARA 1968); sculptor; *b* 24 April 1928; *m* 1st, 1952, M. E. Taylor (marr. diss. 1963); one *s* one *d*; 2nd, 1964, Caroline Ann Clifton-Trigg; one *s. Educ:* Leeds Grammar School. RAF, 1946–48. Studied Royal College of Art, 1948–56; in Paris with Zadkine, 1954; travel scholarships to Greece 1955, Italy 1957. Tutor, RCA, 1958–64. Sculpture Prof., Salzburg Festival, Summer 1972. Work exhibited: John Moores, Liverpool (prizewinner 1957), Tate Gallery, Religious Theme 1958, Arnhem Internat. Open Air Sculpture, 1958; Middelheim Open Air Sculpture, 1959; Battersea Park Open Air Sculpture, 1960, 1963, 1966, 1977; Tokyo Biennale, 1963; British Sculptors '72, RA, 1972; Holland Park Open Air, 1975; Sculpture of the Century, Salisbury Cathedral and Canary Wharf, London, 1999. One man Shows: Leicester Galls, 1961, 1963; Archer Gall., 1972; Salzburg 1972; Munich 1973; Montpellier 1974; Marseilles 1975; Oxford 1975; Taranman Gall., 1979; Browse & Darby Gall., 1979; Beaux Arts, Bath, 1983, 1987; Charles Foley Gall., Columbus, US, 1984; Lloyd Shine Gall., Chicago, 1984; Falle Gall., Jersey, 1995; Bruton Gall., Leeds, 1999; Retrospective, Leeds City Art Gall. and Warwick Arts Centre, 1988. Work in Collections: Tate Gallery, Arts Council, Contemp. Art Society, Kröller-Müller, Gallery of NSW, Stuyvesant Foundation, City of Salzburg, Nat. Gallery of Wales, Allbright-Knox Gall., and at Leeds, Bristol, Norwich, Aberdeen, etc; public sculpture in Harlow New Town Market Square and Jersey Zoo. *Address:* Southanger Farm, Chalford, Stroud, Glos GL6 8HP. *T:* (01285) 760243.

BROWN, Rt Rev. Mgr Ralph, JCD; Vicar General, Archdiocese of Westminster, 1976–99; *b* 30 June 1931; *s* of John William and Elizabeth Josephine Brown. *Educ:* Highgate Sch.; St Edmund's Coll., Old Hall Green, Herts; Pontifical Gregorian Univ., Rome. Licence in Canon Law, 1961, Doctorate, 1963. Commnd Middlesex Regt, 1949; Korea, 1950. Ordained priest, Westminster Cathedral, 1959; Vice-Chancellor, Vice Officialis, dio. of Westminster, 1964–69; Officialis, 1969–76, Officialis, subseq. Judicial Vicar, 1988–, Westminster; Canonical Advr to British Mil. Ordinariate, 1987–. Pres., Canon Law Soc. of GB and Ireland, 1980–86, Sec., 1986–89. Apptd Papal Chamberlain, 1972; National Co-ordinator for Papal Visit to England and Wales, 1982; Prelate of Honour to HH the Pope, 1987; Protonotary Apostolic, 1999. Elected to Old Brotherhood of English Secular Clergy, 1987. Hon. Member: Canon Law Soc. of Aust. and NZ, 1975; Canadian Canon Law Soc., 1979; Canon Law Soc. of Amer., 1979. KHS 1985; KCHS 1991 (Prior, Westminster sect., 1996). *Publications:* Marriage Annulment, 1969, rev. edn 1990; (ed) Matrimonial Decisions of Great Britain and Ireland, 1969–; co-translator, The Code of Canon Law in English Translation, 1983; (ed jtly) The Canon Law: Letter and Spirit: a practical guide to the Code of Canon Law, 1995; articles in Heythrop Jl, Studia Canonica, Theological Digest, The Jurist. *Address:* Flat 3, 8 Morpeth Terrace, SW1P 1EQ. *T:* (020) 7798 9035/9020. *Club:* Anglo-Belgian.

BROWN, Hon. Sir Ralph Kilner, Kt 1970; OBE (mil.) 1945; TD 1952; DL; a Judge of the High Court, Queen's Bench Division, 1970–84; a Judge of Employment Appeal Tribunal, 1976–84; *b* 28 Aug. 1909; *s* of Rev. A. E. Brown, CIE, MA, BSc; *m* 1943, Cynthia Rosemary Breffit; one *s* two *d. Educ:* Kingswood School; Trinity Hall, Cambridge (Squire Law Scholar; MA). Barrister, Middle Temple (Harmsworth Scholar; Bencher, 1964; Master Reader, 1982); Midland Circuit, 1934 and Northern Circuit, 1975. TA 1938; War Service, 1939–46; DAQMG NW Europe Plans; DAAG HQ53 (Welsh) Div.; AQMG (Planning), COSSAC; Col Q (Ops) and Brig. Q Staff HQ 21 Army Group (despatches, OBE); Hon. Col, TARO, 1952. QC 1958; Recorder of Lincoln, 1960–64; Recorder of Birmingham, 1964–65; Chairman, Warwicks QS, 1964–67 (Dep. Chm., 1954–64); a Judge of the Central Criminal Court, 1965–67; Recorder of Liverpool, and Judge of the Crown Court at Liverpool, 1967–69; Presiding Judge, N Circuit, 1970–75. Chairman, Mental Health Review Tribunal, Birmingham RHB Area, 1962–65. Contested (L) Oldbury and Halesowen, 1945 and 1950; South Bucks, 1959 and 1964; Pres., Birmingham Liberal Organisation, 1946–56; Pres., and Chm., W Midland Liberal Fedn, 1950–56; Mem., Liberal Party Exec., 1950–56. Pres., Birmingham Bn, Boys Bde, 1946–56; Mem., Exec., Boys Bde, 1950–55; Former Member: CCPR; Cttee of RNIB; Cttee of RNID. Former Mem., Governing Body, Kingswood Sch. DL Warwickshire, 1956. Guild of Freemen, City of London. *Publications:* The Office of Reader in the Middle Temple, 1982; Top Brass and No Brass, 1991. *Recreations:* watching athletics (represented Cambridge University and Great Britain; British AAA Champion 440 yds hurdles, 1934); cricket, Rugby football. *Address:* 174 Defoe House, Barbican, EC2Y 8ND. *Clubs:* Naval and Military; Hawks (Cambridge).

BROWN, Rev. Raymond; *see* Brown, Rev. Robert R.

BROWN, Rev. Raymond, PhD; Senior Minister, Victoria Baptist Church, Eastbourne, 1987–93, retired; *b* 3 March 1928; *s* of Frank Stevenson Brown and Florence Mansfield; *m* 1966, Christine Mary Smallman; one *s* one *d. Educ:* Spurgeon's Coll., London (BD, MTh); Fitzwilliam Coll., Cambridge (MA, BD, PhD). Minister: Zion Baptist Church, Cambridge, 1956–62; Upton Vale Baptist Church, Torquay, 1964–71; Tutor in Church History, Spurgeon's Coll., London, 1971–73, Principal 1973–86. Pres., Evangelical Alliance, 1975–76; Trustee, Dr Daniel Williams's Charity, 1980–; Nat. Chaplain, Girls' Brigade, 1986–90. *Publications:* Their Problems and Ours, 1969; Let's Read the Old Testament, 1971; Skilful Hands, 1972; Christ Above All: the message of Hebrews, 1982; Bible Study Commentary: 1 Timothy-James, 1983; The English Baptists of the Eighteenth Century, 1986; The Bible Book by Book, 1987; Be My Disciple, 1992; The Message of Deuteronomy: not by bread alone, 1993; Collins Gem Bible Guide, 1993; Four Spiritual Giants, 1997 (US edn as Giants of the Faith, 1997); The Message of Nehemiah: God's servant in a time of change, 1998; contribs to: What the Bible Says, 1974; Dictionary of Christian Spirituality, 1983; My Call to Preach, 1986; Encyclopedia of World Faiths, 1987; New Dictionary of Theology, 1988; The Empty Cross, 1989; Dictionary of Evangelical Biography, 1995; Oxford Dictionary of World Religions, 1997; Oxford Dictionary of the Christian Church, 1998. *Recreations:* music, walking. *Address:* 5 The Paddock, Eaton Ford, Cambs PE19 7SA. *T:* (01480) 475136.

BROWN, Richard George; His Honour Judge Richard Brown; a Circuit Judge, since 1992; *b* Durham, 10 April 1945; *m* 1969, Ann Patricia Bridget Wade; one *s* one *d* (and one *s* decd). *Educ:* Bournville Grammar Sch.; Technical Sch., Birmingham; London Sch. of Economics (LLB Hons); Inns of Court Sch. of Law. Insurance clerk, 1961–62; shop assistant, 1962–63; bus conductor, 1963–64; Trainee Radio Officer, Merchant Navy, 1964–65; taxi driver, 1965–66; assistant, school for maladjusted children, 1966–67; driver, public service vehicle, 1967–68. Called to the Bar, Middle Temple, 1972 (Blackstone Entrance Exhibnr). Asst Recorder, 1986–90; a Recorder of the Crown Court, 1990–92. Resident and Liaison Judge, Crown Courts in E Sussex, 1996–. Vice Pres., E Sussex Magistrates' Assoc., 1997–. Chm., Bd of Govs, Farney Close Sch., 1984–86. *Recreations:* watching sport, travel, being with the family. *Address:* Lewes Crown Court, High Street, Lewes, East Sussex BN7 1YB. *T:* (01273) 480400.

BROWN, Robert; His Honour Judge Robert Brown; a Circuit Judge, since 1988; *b* 21 June 1943; *s* of Robert and Mary Brown; *m* 1st, 1964, Susan (marr. diss. 1971); one *s* one *d*; 2nd, 1973, Carole; two step *s. Educ:* Arnold Sch., Blackpool; Downing Coll., Cambridge (Exhibnr; BA, LLB). Called to Bar, Inner Temple, 1968 (Major Schol.); a

Recorder, 1983–88. *Recreation:* golf. *Address:* c/o Courts of Justice, Earl Street, Carlisle CA1 1DJ. *Club:* Royal Lytham St Annes Golf.

BROWN, Robert; Member (Lib Dem) Glasgow, Scottish Parliament, since 1999; *b* 25 Dec. 1947; *s* of Albert Edward Brown and Joan Brown; *m* 1977, Gwen Morris; one *s* one *d*. *Educ:* Gordon Schools, Huntly; Univ. of Aberdeen (LLB 1st Cl. Hons). Legal Apprentice and Asst, Edmonds and Ledingham, Solicitors, Aberdeen, 1969–72; Procurator Fiscal, Dumbarton, 1972–74; Asst, 1974–75, Partner, 1975–99, Consultant, 1999–, Ross Harper and Murphy, Solicitors, Glasgow. Lib Dem spokesman on communities and housing, Scottish Parlt, 1999–. *Recreations:* history, science fiction. *Address:* 1 Douglas Avenue, Burnside, Rutherglen, Glasgow G73 4RA; (constituency) Olympic House, Suite 1, 2nd Floor, 142 Queen Street, Glasgow G1 1BU. *T:* (0141) 243 2421; *e-mail:* robert.brown.msp@scottish.parliament.uk.

BROWN, Robert Burnett; Associate, PE-International and Public Administration International, since 1996; *b* 10 Aug. 1942; *s* of late David Brown and of Isabella Dow; *m* 1972, Anne Boschetti. *Educ:* Kirkcaldy High Sch.; Edinburgh Univ. (1st cl. Hons BSc Chemistry). Min. of Social Security, 1967; DHSS, 1971–83; Cabinet Office and HM Treasury, 1983–87; DHSS and DSS, 1987–89; Under Sec., DSS, 1989–96. *Recreations:* jazz, rock and roll, football, Greece.

BROWN, Sir Robert C.; *see* Crichton-Brown.

BROWN, Robert Glencairn; Director (formerly Deputy Chief Officer), Housing Corporation, 1986–91; *b* 19 July 1930; *s* of William and Marion Brown (*née* Cockburn); *m* 1957, Florence May Stalker; two *s*. *Educ:* Hillhead High Sch., Glasgow. Commnd, RCS, 1949–51. Forestry Commn, 1947–68; seconded to CS Pay Res. Unit, 1963–64 and to Min. of Land and Natural Resources, 1964–68; Min. of Housing and Local Govt, later DoE, 1968–71; seconded to Nat. Whitley Council, Staff Side, 1969; Asst Dir, Countryside Commn, 1971–77; Department of the Environment: Asst Sec., 1977–83; Under Sec., 1983–86. Chm., W Middx Centre, Nat. Trust, 1989–93. *Recreations:* golfing, gardening, ski-ing, reading. *Address:* 2 The Squirrels, Pinner, Middx HA5 3BD. *T:* (020) 8866 8713. *Clubs:* Ski Club of Great Britain; Pinner Hill Golf.

BROWN, Prof. Robert Hanbury, AC 1986; FRS 1960; Professor of Physics (Astronomy), in the University of Sydney, 1964–81, now Emeritus Professor; *b* 31 Aug. 1916; *s* of Colonel Basil Hanbury Brown and Joyce Blaker; *m* 1952, Hilda Heather Chesterman; two *s* one *d*. *Educ:* Tonbridge School; Brighton Technical College; City and Guilds College, London. BSc (Eng), London (external), 1935; DIC, 1936; DSc Manchester, 1960. MIEE, 1938. Air Ministry, Bawdsey Research Station, working on radar, 1936–42; British Air Commission, Washington, DC, 1942–45; Principal Scientific Officer, Ministry of Supply, 1945–47; Consulting Engineer, Sir Robert Watson-Watt and partners, 1947–49; ICI Research Fellow of Manchester University, 1949; Professor of Radio-Astronomy in the University of Manchester, 1960–63. Pres., Internat. Astronomical Union, 1982–85. ARAS 1986; FAA 1967. Hon. Mem., Aust. Optical Soc., 1987; Hon. MRIN 1997; Hon. FNA 1975; Hon. FASc 1975; Hon. Fellow, Royal Astronomical Soc. of Canada, Astronomical Soc. of India, 1987. Hon. DSc: Sydney, 1984; Monash, 1984. Holweck Prize, 1959; Eddington Medal, 1968; Lyle Medal, 1971; Britannica Australia Award, 1971; Hughes Medal, 1971; Michelson Medal, Franklin Inst., 1982; ANZAAS Medal, 1987. *Publications:* The Exploration of Space by Radio, 1957; The Intensity Interferometer, 1974; Man and the Stars, 1978; Photons, Galaxies and Stars, 1985; Wisdom of Science, 1986; Boffin, 1991; publications in Physical and Astronomical Journals. *Address:* White Cottage, Penton Mewsey, Andover, Hants SP11 0RQ.

BROWN, Rev. (Robert) Raymond; Methodist Minister, responsible for lay training and development, Melton Mowbray, since 1994; *b* 24 March 1936; *s* of Robert Brown and Elsie (*née* Dudson); *m* 1959, Barbara (*née* Johnson); three *s* one *d*. *Educ:* Stockport Sch.; Univ. of Leeds (BA Hons Philosophy); Univ. of Manchester (BD Hons Theology). Ordained Methodist minister, 1959; Minister: Luton Industrial Coll. and Mission, 1959–64; Heald Green and Handforth, 1964–67; commnd RAF Chaplain, 1967; Vice Principal, RAF Chaplains' Sch., 1978–83; Comd Chaplain, RAF Germany, 1983–87; Asst Prin. Chaplain, 1987–90, Prin. Chaplain, 1990–94, Ch of Scotland and Free Churches, RAF. QHC 1990–94. *Recreations:* music and drama (amateur singer and actor), writing for pleasure. *Address:* Trinity Cottage, 6 Church Terrace, Melton Mowbray, Leics LE13 0PW. *T:* (01664) 61179. *Club:* Royal Air Force.

BROWN, Robert Ross Buchanan, CBE 1968; CEng, FIEE; Chairman, Southern Electricity Board, 1954–74; *b* 15 July 1909; 2nd *s* of Robert and Rhoda Brown, Sydney, Australia; *m* 1940, Ruth Sarah Aird; one *s* two *d*. *Educ:* The King's School, Sydney; Sydney University; Cambridge University. BA (Cantab.), BSc. Deputy Gen. Manager, Wessex Electricity Co., 1938. Captain 4th County of London Yeomanry, 1940–45. Gen. Manager, Wessex Electricity Co., 1945; Deputy Chairman, Southern Electricity Board, 1948. *Recreations:* gardening, golf. *Address:* Mumbery Lodge, School Hill, Wargrave, Reading, Berks RG10 8DY.

BROWN, Dr Roger John; Principal, Southampton Institute, since 1998; *b* 26 June 1947; *s* of John Richard Brown and Beatrice Anne (*née* Clamp); *m* 1st, 1971, Mary Elizabeth George (*see* M. E. Francis) (marr. diss. 1991); 2nd, 1992, Josephine Anne Titcomb. *Educ:* St Olave's Grammar Sch., Bermondsey; Queens' Coll., Cambridge (Haynes Exhibnr in History; MA); Inst. of Educn, Univ. of London (PhD). Admin. Officer, ILEA, 1969–75; Sec., William Tyndale Schs' Inquiry, 1975–76; Principal, Dept Industry, Dept Trade, Cabinet Office, OFT, DTI, 1976–84; Assistant Secretary: DoE, 1984–86; DTI, 1986–90; Sec., PCFC, 1990–91; Chief Exec., Cttee of Dirs of Polytechnics, 1991–93; Chief Exec., HEQC, 1993–97. Visiting Professor: Univ. of London Inst. of Educn, 1996–98; Middx Univ., 1997–99; Goldsmiths' Coll., 1997–99; Univ. of Surrey Roehampton (formerly Roehampton Inst.), 1997–; Univ. of East London, 2000–; City Univ., 2001–. Vice-Chm., Standing Conf. of Principals, 1999–. *Publications:* Educational Policy Making: an analysis, 1983; The Post-Dearing Quality Agenda, 1998; contribs to educnl jls. *Recreations:* opera, cinema, jazz, collecting books about music. *Address:* Southampton Institute, East Park Terrace, Southampton SO14 0YN. *T:* (023) 8031 9000.

BROWN, Roland George MacCormack; Legal Adviser, Technical Assistance Group, Commonwealth Secretariat, 1975–87; *b* 27 Dec. 1924; 2nd *s* of late Oliver and of Mona Brown; *m* 1964, Irene Constance (*d* 2000), *d* of Rev. Claude Coltman; two *s* one *d*. *Educ:* Ampleforth College; Trinity College, Cambridge. Called to the Bar, Gray's Inn, Nov. 1949. Practised at the Bar, Nov. 1949–May 1961; Attorney-Gen., Tanganyika, later Tanzania, 1961–65; Legal Consultant to Govt of Tanzania, 1965–72; Fellow, Inst. of Develt Studies, Sussex Univ., 1973–75; on secondment as Special Adviser to Sec. of State for Trade, 1974. *Publication:* (with Richard O'Sullivan, QC) The Law of Defamation. *Recreation:* swimming.

BROWN, Rt Rev. Ronald; Bishop Suffragan of Birkenhead, 1974–92; *b* 7 Aug. 1926; *s* of Fred and Ellen Brown; *m* 1951, Joyce Hymers (*d* 1987); one *s* one *d*. *Educ:* Kirkham Grammar Sch.; Durham Univ. (BA, DipTh). Vicar of Whittle-le-Woods, 1956; Vicar of St Thomas, Halliwell, Bolton, 1961; Rector and Rural Dean of Ashton-under-Lyne, 1970. *Publications:* Bishop's Brew, 1989; Good Lord, 1992; Bishop's Broth, 2000. *Recreations:* antiques and golf. *Address:* Hurst Cottage, Moss Lane, Lathom, near Burscough, Lancs L40 4BA. *T:* (01704) 897314.

See also L. F. M. Brown.

BROWN, Ronald, (Ron); *b* Edinburgh, 1940; *s* of James Brown and Margaret McLaren; *m* 1963, May Smart; two *s*. *Educ:* Pennywell Primary Sch., Edinburgh; Ainslie Park High Sch., Edinburgh; Bristo Technical Inst., Edinburgh. National Service, Royal Signals. Five yrs engrg apprenticeship with Bruce Peebles and Co. Ltd, East Pilton, Edinburgh. Chm., Pilton Br., AUEW; President: AEU, Pilton, 1992–98; AEEU, Edinburgh, 1998–2000; formerly: Chm. Works Cttee, Edinburgh Dist of SSEB; Convenor of Shop Stewards, Parsons Peebles Ltd, Edinburgh. Formerly Councillor for Central Leith, Edinburgh Town Council; Regional Councillor for Royston/Granton, Lothian Reg. Council, 1974–79. MP (Lab) Edinburgh Leith, 1979–92; contested (Ind. Lab) Edinburgh Leith, 1992. Member: Lothian and Borders Fire Bd, 1974–79; Central Scotland Water Develt Bd, 1974–79. EC Mem. and Vice Chair, Edinburgh Trade Union Council, 1998–2000. Mem. Mgt Cttee, Leith CAB, 1998–2000. Columnist, Edinburgh Echo, 1998–2000.

BROWN, Ronald William; JP; consultant, since 1991; Deputy Director General, Federation of Master Builders, 1987–91 (Director of Industrial Relations, 1984–87); *b* 7 Sept. 1921; *s* of George Brown; *m* 1944, Mary Munn; one *s* two *d*. *Educ:* Elementary School, South London; Borough Polytechnic. Sen. Lectr in Electrical Engineering, Principal of Industrial Training Sch. Leader of Opposition, Wanstead and Woodford BC, 1953–56; Leader, Camberwell Borough Council, 1956; Alderman and Leader, London Bor. of Southwark, 1964. MP Shoreditch and Finsbury, 1964–74, Hackney South and Shoreditch, 1974–83 (Lab, 1964–81, SDP, 1981–83); Asst Govt Whip, 1966–67; contested (SDP) Hackney South and Shoreditch, 1983. Member: Council of Europe Assembly and WEU, 1965–76; European Parlt, 1977–79. Chm., Energy Commn, Rapporteur on Science, Technology and Aerospace questions; Parly Advr to Furniture, Timber and Allied Trades Union, 1967–81. Member: Council of Europe, 1979–83; WEU, 1979–83. Member: Bldg Cttee, Construction ITB, 1985–90; NW Thames RHA, 1974–88; E London and City HA Local Res. and Ethics Cttee, 1994–. St Bartholomew's Hospital: Member: Bd of Govs, 1964–74; Jt Res. Bd, 1980–; Local Res. and Ethics Cttee, 1980–94 (Vice-Chm., 1992–94); St Bartholomew's Hospital Medical College: Gov., 1974–95; Mem. Exec. Cttee, 1978–95; Treas., 1978–86. Trustee: St Mark's Res. Foundn, 1974–2001; St Mark's Educnl Trust, 1995–2001. Estate Gov., Alleyn's Coll. of God's Gift, 1961–82 (Chm., Bd of Govs, 1976–78). FIMgt. JP Co. London, 1961. *Address:* 45 Innings Drive, Pevensey Bay, E Sussex BN24 6BH.

BROWN, Ronald William; Deputy Legal Adviser and Solicitor to Ministry of Agriculture, Fisheries and Food, to Forestry Commission and to (EEC) Intervention Board for Agricultural Produce, 1974–82; *b* 21 April 1917; *o s* of late William Nicol Brown and Eleanor Brown (*née* Dobson); *m* 1958, Elsie Joyce (*d* 1983), *er d* of late Sir Norman Guttery, KBE, CB and Lady Guttery (*née* Crankshaw); two *s*. *Educ:* Dover Coll.; Corpus Christi Coll., Cambridge (MA). War service, 1939–45, King's Own Royal Regt (Lancaster), France, W Desert, Burma (Chindits) (Major). Called to Bar, Gray's Inn, 1946. Entered Legal Dept, Min. of Agric. and Fisheries, 1948; Asst Solicitor, MAFF, 1970. *Address:* 18 Tracery, Park Road, Banstead, Surrey SM7 3DD. *T:* (01737) 358569. *Club:* Royal Automobile.

BROWN, Rosemary Jean; *see* Atkins, R. J.

BROWN, Rowland Percival, OBE 1993; MA; JP; legal consultant, Secondary Heads Association, since 1993; Headmaster, Royal Grammar School, High Wycombe, 1975–93; *b* 8 Jan. 1933; *s* of late Percy and Gladys Mabel Brown; *m* 1959, Jessie Doig Connell; three *d*. *Educ:* Queen Mary's Sch., Basingstoke; Worcester Coll., Oxford (MA French and Russian, 1956). Called to the Bar, Inner Temple, 1966; ESU Walter Page Scholar, 1976. Intelligence Corps, 1951–53, Second Lieut. Hampton Sch., 1957–62; Head of Modern Langs, Tudor Grange Grammar Sch., Solihull, 1962–67; Head Master, King Edward VI Sch., Nuneaton, 1967–75. Legal Sec., Headmasters' Assoc. and SHA, 1975–85; Pres., SHA, 1985–86. Oxford Univ. Delegacy of Local Exams, 1986–96; Mem., RAF OASC Selection Bd, 1970–96. Educnl Advr, World Challenge Expedns, 1993–. Liveryman, Feltmakers' Co., 1991–. JP Bucks, 1978. *Publications:* Heads Legal Guide, 1984; The School Management Handbook, 1993; The Education Acts, 1998. *Recreations:* golf, walking, theatre, following sport. *Address:* Wildwood, Manor Road, Penn, Bucks HP10 8JA. *Club:* Phyllis Court (Henley).

BROWN, Roy Dudley; Director, Association of West European Shipbuilders, 1977–83; *b* 5 Aug. 1916; *y s* of late Alexander and Jessie Brown; *m* 1941, Maria Margaret Barry McGhee (*d* 1996); one *s* one *d*. *Educ:* Robert Gordon's Coll., Aberdeen; Aberdeen Univ. (MA 1935, LLB 1937). In private law practice, Glasgow, 1937–38; joined Shipbldg Conf., London, 1938; War Service, RN; Jt Sec. on amalgamation of Shipbldg Conf., Shipbldg Employers Fedn, and Dry Dock Owners and Repairers Central Council into Shipbuilders and Repairers National Assoc., 1967; Dep. Dir, 1973, until dissolution of Assoc. on nationalization, 1977. Sec., Shipbldg Corp. Ltd, 1943–77. Freeman, Shipwrights' Co. *Recreations:* golf, wine, gardening. *Address:* 109 Upper Selsdon Road, Sanderstead, Surrey CR2 0DP. *T:* (020) 8657 7144.

BROWN, Russell; *see* Brown, J. R.

BROWN, Russell Leslie; MP (Lab) Dumfries, since 1997; *b* 17 Sept. 1951; *s* of Howard Russell Brown and Muriel Brown (*née* Anderson); *m* 1973, Christine Margaret Calvert; two *d*. *Educ:* Annan Acad. Various posts with ICI, 1974–97, Plant Operative, 1992–97. Member: Dumfries and Galloway Regl Council, 1986–96 (Chm., Public Protection Cttee, 1990–94); Annandale and Eskdale DC, 1988–96; Dumfries and Galloway UA, 1995–97. *Recreations:* walking, football. *Address:* 56 Wood Avenue, Annan DG12 6DE. *T:* (01461) 205365.

BROWN, Prof. Sally Ann, PhD; FRSE, AcSS; Professor of Education, since 1990, and Deputy Principal, since 1996, University of Stirling; *b* 15 Dec. 1935; *d* of Fred Compigné-Cook and Gwendoline Cook (*née* Barrett); *m* 1959, Charles Victor Brown (*d* 1991); two *s*. *Educ:* Bromley High Sch.; University College London (BSc Hons 1957); Smith Coll., Mass (MA 1958); Jordanhill Coll., Glasgow (Teaching Cert. 1966); Univ. of Stirling (PhD 1975). FRSE 1996. Lectr in Physics, Univ. of Ife and Nigerian Coll. of Tech., 1960–64; Principal Teacher of Science, Helensburgh, 1964–70; Sen. Res. Fellow, Univ. of Stirling, 1970–80; Consultant and Adviser, Scottish Educn Dept, 1980–84; Dir, Scottish Council for Res. in Educn, 1986–90 (Fellow, 1992). Chair: Univs' Assoc. for Continuing Educn (Scotland), 2000; Educn Panel, 2001 RAE. Chair Adv. Bd, Gaelic Res. Centre, Leirsinn, 2000. FRSA 1989; FEIS 1997; AcSS 2000. *Publications:* What Do They Know?, 1980; Making Sense of Teaching, 1993; Special Needs Policy in the 1990s, 1994; numerous academic works. *Recreations:* theatre, music, golf. *Address:* 30A Chalton Road, Bridge of

Allan, Stirling FK9 4EF. *T:* (01786) 833671; Department of Education, University of Stirling, Stirling FK9 4LA. *T:* (01786) 467600. *Club:* Royal Commonwealth Society.

BROWN, Sarah Elizabeth; Member, Competition (formerly Monopolies and Mergers) Commission, since 1998; *b* 30 Dec. 1943; *d* of Sir Maurice Dean, KCB, KCMG and Anne (*née* Gibson); *m* 1976, Philip A. R. Brown, *qv*. *Educ:* St Paul's Girls' Sch.; Newnham Coll., Cambridge (BA Nat. Sci.). Joined BoT as Asst Principal, 1965; Private Sec. to Second Perm. Sec., 1968; Principal, 1970; DTI, 1971–96: Asst. Sec., 1978; Sec. to Crown Agents Tribunal, 1978–82; Personnel Management Div., 1982–84; Head of Financial Services Bill team, 1984–86; Under Sec., 1986; Head of Companies Div., 1986–91; Head of Enterprise Initiative Div., 1991–93, and Small Firms Div., 1992–93; Head of Small Firms and Business Link Div., 1993–94; Head of Companies Div., 1994–96; Dir, Company Law, 1996. Comr, Friendly Socs Commn, 1997–2001. Dir, Remploy Ltd, 1997–2000; Mem. Bd, Look Ahead Housing Assoc., 1996–; Associate Mem., Kensington & Chelsea and Westminster HA, 1996–99; non-executive Director: Kent and Sussex Weald NHS Trust, 1999–2000; Financial Services Compensation Scheme, 2000–. Mem., Civil Service Appeals Bd, 1998–. *Recreations:* travel, theatre, gardening. *Address:* 32 Cumberland Street, SW1V 4LX.

BROWN, Rt Hon. Sir Simon Denis, Kt 1984; PC 1992; **Rt Hon. Lord Justice Simon Brown;** a Lord Justice of Appeal, since 1992; Vice-President, Court of Appeal (Civil Division), since 2001; *b* 9 April 1937; *s* of late Denis Baer Brown and Edna Elizabeth (*née* Abrahams); *m* 1963, Jennifer Buddicom; two *s* one *d*. *Educ:* Stowe Sch.; Worcester Coll., Oxford (Hon. Fellow, 1993). Commnd 2nd Lt RA, 1955–57. Called to the Bar, Middle Temple, 1961 (Harmsworth Schol.); Master of the Bench, Hon. Soc. of Middle Temple, 1980; a Recorder, 1979–84; First Jun. Treasury Counsel, Common Law, 1979–84; a Judge of the High Court of Justice, QBD, 1984–92. President: Security Service Tribunal, 1989–2000; Intelligence Services Tribunal, 1995–2000; Intelligence Services Comr, 2000–. *Recreations:* golf, skiing, theatre, reading. *Address:* Royal Courts of Justice, Strand, WC2A 2LL. *Clubs:* Garrick; Denham Golf.

BROWN, Simon Staley; QC 1995; a Recorder, since 2000; *b* 23 Aug. 1952; *s* of Peter Brown and Celia Rosamond Brown; *m* 1981, Kathleen Margaret Wain, (Kathy Brown-Garden, writer); one *s* one *d*. *Educ:* Harrow Sch.; Queens' Coll., Cambridge (MA). Called to the Bar, Inner Temple, 1976 (Governing Bencher, 1995; Chm., Estates Cttee, 2000); an Asst Recorder, 1997–2000. Asst to Boundary Commn. Member: Professional Negligence, and Technology and Construction Cttees, Bar Assoc.; London Common Law and Commercial Bar Assoc. Mem., RHS. *Publication:* (contrib.) Emden's Construction Law. *Recreations:* gardening, cricket, golf. *Address:* Crown Office Chambers, One Paper Buildings, Temple, EC4Y 7EP. *T:* (020) 7797 8100; *e-mail:* brown@crownofficechambers.com.

BROWN, Rt Hon. Sir Stephen, GBE 1999; Kt 1975; PC 1983; a Lord Justice of Appeal, 1983–88; President of the Family Division, 1988–99; *b* 3 Oct. 1924; *s* of Wilfrid Brown and Nora Elizabeth Brown, Longdon Green, Staffordshire; *m* 1951, Patricia Ann, *d* of Richard Good, Tenbury Wells, Worcs; two *s* (twins) three *d*. *Educ:* Malvern College; Queens' College, Cambridge (Hon. Fellow, 1984). Served RNVR (Lieut), 1943–46. Barrister, Inner Temple, 1949; Bencher, 1974; Treas., 1994. Dep. Chairman, Staffs QS, 1963–71; Recorder of West Bromwich, 1965–71; QC 1966; a Recorder, and Honorary Recorder of West Bromwich, 1972–75; a Judge of the High Court, Family Div., 1975–77, QBD, 1977–83; Presiding Judge, Midland and Oxford Circuit, 1977–81. Member: Parole Board, England and Wales, 1967–71; Butler Cttee on mentally abnormal offenders, 1972–75; Adv. Council on Penal System, 1977; Chairman: Adv. Cttee on Conscientious Objectors, 1971–75; Council of Malvern Coll., 1976–94; Pres., Edgbaston High Sch., 1989–. Hon. FRCPsych 2000. Hon. LLD: Birmingham, 1985; Leicester, 1997; UWE, 2000. *Recreation:* sailing. *Address:* 78 Hamilton Avenue, Harborne, Birmingham B17 8AR. *Club:* Garrick.

BROWN, Sir Stephen (David Reid), KCVO 1999; HM Diplomatic Service; High Commissioner, Singapore, since 2001; *b* 26 Dec. 1945; *s* of Albert Senior Brown and Edna Brown; *m* 1966, Pamela Denise Gaunt; one *s* one *d*. *Educ:* Leeds Grammar Sch.; RMA Sandhurst; Univ. of Sussex (BA Hons). Served HM Forces, RA, 1966–76; FCO, 1976–77; 1st Sec., Nicosia, 1977–80; 1st Sec. (Commercial), Paris, 1980–85; FCO, 1985–89; DTI, 1989; Consul-Gen., Melbourne, 1989–94; Commercial Counsellor and Dir of Trade Promotion, Peking, 1994–97; Ambassador, Republic of Korea, 1997–2000. *Recreations:* reading, ski-ing, motor sport. *Address:* c/o Foreign and Commonwealth Office, King Charles Street, SW1A 2AH.

BROWN, Stuart Christopher; QC 1991; a Recorder, since 1992; Visiting Teaching Fellow, Leeds Metropolitan University, since 1994; *b* 4 Sept. 1950; *s* of late Geoffrey Howard Brown and of Olive Baum; *m* 1973, Imogen Lucas; two *d*. *Educ:* Acklam High Sch., Middlesbrough; Worcester Coll., Oxford (BA, BCL). Called to the Bar, Inner Temple, 1974, Bencher, 1998. Practises on NE Circuit; an Asst Recorder, 1988–92. *Recreations:* family, theatre, walking. *Address:* Cherry Hill, Staircase Lane, Leeds LS16 9JD; Park Lane Chambers, 19 Westgate, Leeds LS1 2RD.

BROWN, Susan Mary; *see* Spindler, S. M.

BROWN, Sir Thomas, Kt 1974; Chairman, Eastern Health and Social Services Board, Northern Ireland (formerly NI Hospitals Authority), 1967–84, retired; *b* 11 Oct. 1915; *s* of Ephraim Hugh and Elizabeth Brown; *m* 1988, Dr Eleanor A. Thompson. *Educ:* Royal Belfast Academical Institution. Admitted Solicitor, 1938. Mem., Royal Commn on NHS, 1976–79. *Recreation:* boating. *Address:* Westgate, Portaferry, Co. Down, Northern Ireland BT22 1PF. *T:* (028) 4272 8309.

BROWN, Rt Rev. Thomas John; *see* Wellington (NZ), Bishop of.

BROWN, Timothy Charles; Fellow, and Director of Music, Clare College, Cambridge, since 1979; *b* 9 Dec. 1946; *s* of Roland Frederick John Brown and Ruth Margery Brown (*née* Dawe). *Educ:* Westminster Abbey Choir Sch.; Dean Close Sch., Cheltenham; King's Coll., Cambridge (alto choral schol.; MA); Westminster Coll., Oxford (DipEd). Music Master, Hinchingbrooke Sch., Huntingdon, 1969–72; Dir of Music, Oundle Sch., 1972–79. Mem., Scholars' Vocal Ensemble, 1969–72. Director: Choir of Clare Coll., Cambridge, 1979–; Cambridge Univ. Chamber Choir, 1986–2000; English Voices, 1995–. *Publication:* (ed) William Walton: shorter choral works, 1999. *Recreations:* travelling, gardening, walking. *Address:* Clare College, Cambridge CB2 1TL. *T:* (01223) 333264.

BROWN, Tina, (Christina Hambley Brown), CBE 2000; Partner and Chairman, Talk Media, since 1998; Chairman and Editor-in-Chief, Talk magazine, since 1998; *b* 21 Nov. 1953; *d* of late Bettina Iris Mary Kohr Brown and George Hambley Brown; *m* 1981, Harold Matthew Evans, *qv*; one *s* one *d*. *Educ:* Univ. of Oxford (MA). Columnist for Punch, 1978; Editor, Tatler, 1979–83; Editor in Chief, Vanity Fair Magazine, 1984–92; Editor, The New Yorker, 1992–98. Catherine Pakenham Prize, Most Promising Female Journalist (Sunday Times), 1973; Young Journalist of the Year, 1978. *Plays:* Under the Bamboo Tree (Sunday Times Drama Award), 1973; Happy Yellow, 1977. *Publications:* Loose Talk, 1979; Life as a Party, 1983. *Address:* Talk, 152 West 57th Street, 56th floor, New York, NY 10019, USA.

BROWN, Prof. Valerie Kathleen, PhD; Director, Centre for Agri-Environmental Research, and Research Professor in Agro-Ecology, University of Reading, since 2000; *b* 11 May 1944; *d* of Reginald Brown and Kathleen (*née* Southerton); *m* 1970, Dr Clive Wall. *Educ:* Imperial Coll., London Univ. (BSc Zoology 1966; PhD Entomology 1969; DIC 1969). ARCS 1966. Lectr, Royal Holloway Coll., London Univ., 1969–74; Imperial College of Science, Technology and Medicine: Lectr, 1975–84; Sen. Lectr, 1984–89; Reader, 1989–94; CAB International: Dir, Internat. Inst. of Entomology, 1994–98; Dir, CABI Bioscience: Environment, 1998–2000. *Publications:* Grasshoppers, 1983, 2nd edn 1992; (ed) Insect Life History Strategies, 1983; Multitrophic Interactions, 1997; (ed) Herbivores between Plants and Predators, 1999. *Recreations:* bird watching, cultivation of alpine plants, wine tasting. *Address:* Department of Agriculture, University of Reading, Earley Gate, PO Box 236, Reading RG6 6AT. *T:* (0118) 931 6535.

BROWN, Vivian; *see* Brown, H. V. B.

BROWN, Prof. William Arthur; Montague Burton Professor of Industrial Relations, University of Cambridge, since 1985; Master, Darwin College, Cambridge, since 2000; *b* 22 April 1945; *s* of Prof. Arthur Joseph Brown, *qv*; *m* 1993, Kim Hewitt; two step *d*. *Educ:* Leeds Grammar Sch.; Wadham Coll., Oxford (BA Hons). Economic Asst, NBPI, 1966–68; Res. Associate, Univ. of Warwick, 1968–70; SSRC's Industrial Relations Research Unit, University of Warwick: Res. Fellow, 1970–79; Dep. Dir, 1979–81; Dir, 1981–85; University of Cambridge: Fellow, Wolfson Coll., 1985–2000; Chairman: Faculty of Econs and Politics, 1992–96; Sch. of Humanities and Soc. Scis, 1993–96. Ind. Chm., Nat. Fire Brigades Disputes Cttee, 1998–. Member: Low Pay Commn, 1997–; Council, ACAS, 1998–. *Publications:* Piecework Bargaining, 1973; The Changing Contours of British Industrial Relations, 1981; The Individualisation of Employment Contracts in Britain, 1999; articles in industrial relations jls, etc. *Recreations:* walking, gardening. *Address:* Darwin College, Cambridge CB3 9EU.

BROWN, Sir William Brian P.; *see* Pigott-Brown.

BROWN, William Charles Langdon, CBE 1992 (OBE 1982); Deputy Group Chief Executive and Deputy Chairman, Standard Chartered PLC, 1988–91 (Director, 1987–94); Deputy Chairman, Standard Chartered Bank, 1989–91; *b* 9 Sept. 1931; *s* of Charles Leonard Brown and Kathleen May Tizzard; *m* 1959, Nachiko Sagawa; one *s* two *d*. *Educ:* John Ruskin Sch., Croydon; Ashbourne Grammar Sch., Derbyshire. Joined Westminster Bank, 1947; transf. to Standard Chartered Bank (formerly Chartered Bank of India, Australia and China, the predecessor of Chartered Bank), 1954; Standard Chartered Bank: Tokyo, 1954–59; Bangkok, 1959–62; Hong Kong, 1962–69; Man., Singapore, 1969–72; Country Man., Bangkok, 1972–75; Area Gen. Man., Hong Kong, 1975–87. Various additional positions in Hong Kong, 1975–87, include: MLC Hong Kong; Chm., Hong Kong Export Credit Insce Corp. Adv. Bd; Mem. Council, Hong Kong Trade Develt Council; Chm., Hong Kong Assoc. of Banks; Director: Mass Railway Corp.; Wing Lung Bank Ltd. Director: Hong Kong Investment Trust, 1991–96; Kexim Bank (UK) Ltd, 1992–; Arbuthnot Latham & Co. Ltd, 1993–99; Chm., Atlantis Japan Growth Fund Ltd, 1996–. Treas., Royal Commonwealth Soc. and Commonwealth Trust, 1991–96. FCIB 1984; FInstD 1988. Hon. DSSc Chinese Univ. of Hong Kong, 1987. *Recreations:* mountain walking, snow ski-ing, yoga, philately, photography, calligraphy, classical music. *Address:* Appleshaw, 11 Central Avenue, Findon Valley, Worthing, Sussex BN14 0DS. *T:* (01903) 873175; Penthouse B, 15 Portman Square, W1H 6LJ. *T:* (020) 7487 5741, *Fax:* (020) 7486 3005. *Clubs:* Oriental, Royal Automobile; Hong Kong, Shek-O, Ladies Recreation (Hong Kong); Tanglin (Singapore).

BROWN, Dr William Christopher, OBE 1966; RDI 1977; Founder, Brown Beech & Associates, 1987; *b* 16 Sept. 1928; *s* of William Edward Brown and Margaret Eliza Brown; *m* 1964, Celia Hermione Emmett. *Educ:* Monmouth Sch.; University Coll., Southampton (BScEng); Imperial Coll. of Science and Technol., London (DIC); FIC 1987. Partner, Freeman, Fox & Partners, 1970–85. Principal designer for major bridges, incl.: Volta River, 1956; Forth Road, 1964; Severn and Wye, 1966; Auckland Harbour, 1969; Erskine, 1971; Bosporus, 1973; Avonmouth, 1975; Humber, 1981; Bosporus 2, 1988. Holds patents on new concepts for long-span bridges, incl. Messina Straits. Designer for radio telescopes in Australia and Canada, and for other special structures. Master, Faculty of RDI, 1983–85. Hon. FRIBA 1978. Hon. Dr: Bosporus Univ., 1988; RCA, 1998. McRobert Award, 1970; Construction Industry Award, Engrg News Record, 1989; Gustave Trasenster Medal, Liège Univ., 1992; UK and European steel design awards, 1968, 1971, 1976. *Publications:* technical papers for engrg instns in UK and abroad. *Recreations:* archaeology, photography, motoring. *Address:* 1 Allen Mansions, Allen Street, W8 6UY. *T:* (020) 7937 6550. *Club:* Royal Over-Seas League.

BROWN, Rev. William Martyn; *b* 12 July 1914; *s* of Edward Brown, artist; *m* 1939, Elizabeth Lucy Hill; one adopted *s*. *Educ:* Bedford School; Pembroke College, Cambridge (Scholar). 1st Class Honours in Modern Languages, 1936, MA 1947. Assistant Master, Wellington College, 1936–47; Housemaster 1943–47; Headmaster: The King's School, Ely, 1947–55; Bedford School, 1955–75. Commissioner of the Peace, 1954. Ordained 1976; Priest-in-charge, Field Dalling and Saxlingham, 1977–84; RD of Holt, 1984–88. *Recreation:* watercolour painting. *Address:* Lodge Cottage, Field Dalling, Holt, Norfolk NR25 7AS. *T:* (01328) 830403.

BROWNE, family name of **Baron Kilmaine, Baron Oranmore, Marquess of Sligo**.

BROWNE OF MADINGLEY, Baron *cr* 2001 (Life Peer), of Cambridge in the County of Cambridgeshire; **Edmund John Phillip Browne,** Kt 1998; FREng, FIMM, FInstP, FInstPet; Chief Executive Officer, BP (formerly BP Amoco) plc, since 1998; *b* 20 Feb. 1948; *s* of late Edmund John Browne and Paula (*née* Wesz). *Educ:* King's Sch., Ely; St John's Coll., Cambridge (MA Hons; Hon. Fellow, 1997); Stanford Grad. Sch. of Business (MS Business). FIMM 1987; FREng (FEng 1993); FInstP 1993. Joined British Petroleum Co., 1966; Gp Treasurer and Chief Exec., BP Finance Internat., 1984–86; Executive Vice-President and Chief Financial Officer: Standard Oil Co., 1986–87; BP America, 1987–89; Chief Exec. Officer, Standard Oil Prodn Co., 1987–89; Man. Dir and CEO, BP Exploration Co., 1989–95; Man. Dir, 1991–98, and Gp Chief Exec., 1995–98, British Petroleum Co. plc. Non-executive Director: SmithKline Beecham, 1995–99; Intel Corp., 1997–; Mem. Supervisory Bd, DaimlerChrysler AG, 1998–2001. Trustee, BM, 1995–. Chm., Adv. Bd, Stanford Grad. Sch. of Business, 1995–97, now Chm. Emeritus; Mem. Governing Body, London Business Sch., 1996–. A Vice Pres. and Mem. Bd, Prince of Wales Business Leaders Forum. CIMgt 1993. Hon. FIChemE; Hon. FIMechE 2001. Prince Philip Medal, Royal Acad. of Engrg, 1999. *Recreations:* opera, photography, books, pre-Columbian art. *Address:* BP plc, Britannic House, 1 Finsbury Circus, EC2M 7BA. *T:* (020) 7496 4488. *Club:* Athenæum.

BROWNE, Andrew Harold; full-time Chairman of Industrial Tribunals, Nottingham Region, 1983–96 (part-time Chairman, 1975–83); *b* 2 Dec. 1923; *s* of late Harold and Ada Caroline Browne; *m* 1951, Jocelyn Mary Vade Ashmead; two *s* one *d*. *Educ:* Repton; Trinity Hall, Cambridge (MA). ACIArb 1983. Served Royal Navy, 1942–46; Lieut RNVR. Admitted Solicitor, 1950; Partner in firm of Wells & Hind, Nottingham, 1952–83. Dep. Clerk of the Peace, Nottingham QS, 1951–55. Chairman, National Insurance Local Tribunal, Nottingham, 1965–83; Member, E Midland Rent Assessment Panel, 1966–83 (Vice-Pres., 1972–83). Lay Chm., Bingham Deanery Synod, 1987–96. Chm., Reserve Forces Reinstatement Cttee, 1991–93. Hon. Mem., Notts Law Soc., 1996. *Recreations:* rural England, organ music. *Address:* The House in the Garden, Elton, near Nottingham NG13 9LA. *T:* (01949) 850419. *Club:* Aula.

BROWNE, Angelica Elizabeth; *see* Mitchell, A. E.

BROWNE, Sir Anthony Arthur Duncan M.; *see* Montague Browne.

BROWNE, Anthony Edward Tudor; author and illustrator of children's books, since 1976; *b* 11 Sept. 1946; *s* of Jack and Doris Browne; *m* 1980, Jane Franklin; one *s* one *d*. *Educ:* Whitcliffe Mount GS, Cleckheaton; Leeds Coll. of Art (BA 1967). Medical Artist, Manchester Royal Infirmary, 1969–71; designer of greetings cards, Gordon Fraser Gall., 1972–86. Silver Medal, US Soc. of Illustrators, 1994; Hans Christian Andersen Award, 2000. *Publications: author and illustrator:* Through the Magic Mirror, 1976; Walk in the Park, 1977; Bear Hunt, 1979; Bear Goes to Town, 1982; Gorilla, 1983 (Kurt Maschler Award, 1983; Kate Greenaway Medal, 1984; Boston Globe Horn Book Award, 1986; Netherlands Silver Pencil Award, 1989); Willy the Wimp, 1984; Piggybook, 1985; Willy the Champ, 1985; I Like Books, 1988; The Tunnel, 1989 (Netherlands Silver Pencil Award, 1990); Changes, 1990; Willy and Hugh, 1991; Zoo, 1992 (Kate Greenaway Medal, 1992); Big Baby, 1993; Willy the Wizard, 1995; Look What I've Got!, 1996; Things I Like, 1997; Willy the Dreamer, 1997; Voices in the Park, 1998 (Kurt Maschler Award); Willy's Pictures, 1999; My Dad, 2000; *illustrator:* Hansel and Gretel (adapted from trans. by Eleanor Quarrie), 1981; Annalena McAfee, The Visitors Who Came to Stay, 1984; Sally Grindley, Knock, Knock!, Who's There?, 1985; Annalena McAfee, Kirsty Knows Best, 1987; Lewis Carroll, Alice's Adventures in Wonderland, 1988 (Kurt Maschler Award, 1988); Gwen Strauss, Trail of Stones (poems), 1990; Gwen Strauss, The Night Shimmy, 1991; Janni Howker, The Topiary Garden, 1993; King Kong (from story by Edgar Wallace and Merian C. Cooper), 1994; Ian McEwan, The Daydreamer, 1994. *Recreations:* playing cricket, swimming, being with my children. *Address:* c/o Walker Books Ltd, 87 Vauxhall Walk, SE11 5HJ. *T:* (020) 7793 0909. *Club:* St Nicholas at Wade Cricket.

BROWNE, Benjamin James; QC 1996; a Recorder, since 2000; *b* 25 April 1954; *s* of Percy Basil Browne, *qv* and Jenefer Mary Browne; *m* 1987, Juliet Mary Heywood; one *s* one *d*. *Educ:* Eton Coll.; Christ Church, Oxford (MA). Called to the Bar, Inner Temple, 1976. An Asst Recorder, 1998–2000. *Recreations:* country pursuits, gardening. *Address:* 2 Temple Gardens, Temple, EC4Y 9AY. *T:* (020) 7583 6041. *Club:* Boodle's.

BROWNE, Bernard Peter Francis K.; *see* Kenworthy-Browne.

BROWNE, Air Cdre Charles Duncan Alfred, CB 1971, DFC 1944; RAF, retired; *b* 8 July 1922; *m* 1946, Una Felicite Leader (*d* 2001); (one *s* decd). War of 1939–45: served Western Desert, Italy, Corsica and S France in Hurricane and Spitfire Sqdns; post war service in Home, Flying Training, Bomber and Strike Commands; MoD; CO, RAF Brüggen, Germany, 1966–68; Comdt, Aeroplane and Armament Exp. Estab., 1968–71; Air Officer i/c Central Tactics and Trials Orgn, 1971–72. *Club:* Royal Air Force.

BROWNE, Colin; *see* Browne, J. C. C.

BROWNE, Rt Rev. Denis George; *see* Hamilton (NZ), Bishop of, (RC).

BROWNE, Desmond Henry; MP (Lab) Kilmarnock and Loudoun, since 1997; Parliamentary Under-Secretary of State, Northern Ireland Office, since 2001; *b* 22 March 1952; *s* of Peter and Maureen Browne. *Educ:* St Michael's Acad., Kilwinning; Univ. of Glasgow. Apprentice Solicitor, Jas Campbell & Co., 1974–76; Solicitor, 1976; Asst Solicitor, 1976–80, Partner, 1980–85, Ross Harper & Murphy; Partner, McCluskey Browne, 1985–92; admitted, Faculty of Advocates, 1993. Contested (Lab) Argyll and Bute, 1992. *Recreations:* football, reading. *Address:* House of Commons, SW1A 0AA.

BROWNE, Desmond John Michael; QC 1990; Recorder, since 1994; *b* 5 April 1947; *s* of Sir Denis John Browne, KCVO, FRCS and of Lady Moyra Browne, *qv*; *m* 1973, Jennifer Mary Wilmore; two *d*. *Educ:* Eton College; New College, Oxford (Scholar). Called to the Bar, Gray's Inn, 1969, Bencher, 1999. *Recreations:* Australiana, Venice, Sussex Downs. *Address:* 5 Raymond Buildings, Gray's Inn, WC1R 5BP. *T:* (020) 7242 2902. *Clubs:* Brooks's, Beefsteak.

BROWNE, Gillian Brenda B.; *see* Babington-Browne.

BROWNE, (James) Nicholas; QC 1995; a Recorder, since 1993; *b* 25 April 1947; *o s* of late James Christopher Browne, MC and Winifred Browne (*née* Pirie); *m* 1981, Angelica Elizabeth Mitchell, *qv*; two *d*. *Educ:* Cheltenham Coll.; Liverpool Univ. (LLB 1969). Called to the Bar, Inner Temple, 1971; Midland and Oxford Circuit, 1971–; Asst Recorder, 1990–93. Mem., Bar Council, 1992–94. Chairman, Code of Practice Appeal Board: Prescription Medicines Code of Practice Authy; Assoc. of British Pharmaceutical Industry, 2000–. *Recreations:* cricket, squash, theatre, spending time with family and friends. *Address:* 36 Bedford Row, WC1R 4JH. *T:* (020) 7421 8000. *Club:* Cumberland Lawn Tennis.

BROWNE, John Anthony; a District Judge (Magistrates' Courts) (formerly Stipendiary Magistrate), S Yorkshire, since 1992; *b* 25 Aug. 1948; *s* of George Henry Browne and Margaret Browne (now Wheeler); *m* 1971, Dr Jill Lesley Atfield; one *s* three *d*. *Educ:* St Peter's de la Salle, Bournemouth; Sheffield Univ. (LLB Hons). Admitted solicitor, 1975; in private practice with Elliot Mather Smith, Chesterfield and Mansfield, 1975–92. *Recreations:* tennis, hill-walking, ski-ing, running (slowly), reading, supporting Sheffield Wednesday. *Address:* The Magistrates' Court, Castle Street, Sheffield S3 8LU. *T.* (0114) 276 0760.

BROWNE, (John) Colin (Clarke); Partner, The Maitland Consultancy, since 2000; *b* 25 Oct. 1945; *s* of late Ernest Browne, JP and Isobel Sarah Browne (*née* McVitie); *m* 1984, Karen Lascelles Barr; one *s*. *Educ:* Wallace High Sch., Lisburn, Co. Antrim; Trinity Coll., Dublin (BA). Post Office, then British Telecommunications, 1969–94: Dir, Chairman's Office, 1980–85; Chief Exec., Broadband Services, 1985–86; Dir, Corporate Relations, 1986–94; Dir of Corporate Affairs, BBC, 1994–2000. Vice-Pres., Inst. of Trading Standards Admin, 1994–. Mem., HDA (formerly HEA), 1996–. Trustee: BBC Children in Need, 1994–2000; One World Broadcasting Trust, 1997–; Mem. Bd Trustees, Inst. of Internat. Communications, 1998–2000. *Recreations:* sport, music, reading. *Address:* The Maitland Consultancy, Orion House, 5 Upper St Martin's Lane, WC2H 9EA. *T:* (020) 7379 5151. *Club:* Tulse Hill Hockey.

BROWNE, John Ernest Douglas Delavalette; Vice President, Investments, Salomon Smith Barney Inc. (Citigroup), since 1995; *b* Hampshire, 17 Oct. 1938; *s* of late Col Ernest Coigny Delavalette Browne, OBE, and Victoria Mary Eugene (*née* Douglas); *m* 1st, 1965, Elizabeth Jeannette Marguerite Garthwaite (marr. diss.); 2nd, 1986, Elaine Margaret Schmid Boylen. *Educ:* Malvern; RMA Sandhurst; Cranfield Inst. of Technology (MSc); Harvard Business Sch. (MBA). Served Grenadier Guards, British Guiana (Battalion Pilot), Cyprus, BAOR, 1959–67; Captain 1963; TA, Grenadier Guards (Volunteers), 1981–91, Major 1985. Associate, Morgan Stanley & Co., New York, 1969–72; Pember & Boyle, 1972–74; Man. Dir, Falcon Finance Mgt Ltd, 1978–95; Director: Middle East Operations, European Banking Co., 1974–78; Worms Investments, 1981–83; Scansat (Broadcasting) Ltd, 1988–93; Internat. Bd, World Times (Boston), 1988–; Tijari Finance Ltd, 1989–92; Adviser: Barclays Bank Ltd, 1978–84; Trustees Household Div., 1979–83. Director: Churchill Private Clinic, 1980–91; Drug Free America, 1998–. Councillor (C), Westminster Council, 1974–78. MP (C) Winchester, 1979–92; introduced: Trades Description Act (Amendment) Bill, 1988; Protection of Animals (Amendment) Act, 1988; Protection of Privacy Bill, 1989; Armed Forces (Liability for Injury) Bill, 1991. Member: H of C Treasury Select Cttee, 1982–87; Social Services Select Cttee, 1991–92; Secretary: Conservative Finance Cttee, 1982–84; Conservative Defence Cttee, 1982–83; Chm., Conservative Smaller Business Cttee, 1984–87; Treas., Lords and Commons Anglo-Swiss Soc., 1979–92 (Treas., 1984–87; Sec., 1987–92); UK deleg. to N Atlantic Assembly, 1986–92 (rapporteur on human rights, 1989–92). Contested: (Ind. C) Winchester, 1992; (Ind. Against a Federal Europe) Hampshire South and Wight, EP election, 1994; (UK Ind.) Falmouth and Camborne, 2001. Mem., NFU. Mem., Winchester Preservation Trust, 1980–90; Patron, Winchester Cadets Assoc., 1980–90; Trustee, Winnall Community Assoc., 1981–94; President: Winchester Gp for Disabled People, 1982–92; Hursley Cricket Club, 1985–90. Mem. Court, Univ. of Southampton, 1979–90; Governor, Malvern Coll., 1982–. Liveryman, Goldsmiths' Co., 1982–. OStJ 1979 (Mem., Chapter Gen., 1985–90). Interests include: economics, gold and internat. monetary affairs, defence, broadcasting. *Publications:* various articles on finance, gold (A New European Currency—The Karl, K), defence, Middle East, Soviet leadership. *Recreations:* riding, sailing, shooting, ski-ing, golf. *Address:* 20 Sutton Place South, New York, NY 10022, USA; *e-mail:* johndbrowne@attglobal.net; john.d.browne@rrsmb.com. *Clubs:* Boodle's, Turf, Special Forces.

BROWNE, Air Vice-Marshal John Philip Ravenscroft, CBE 1985; engineering consultant; *b* 27 April 1937; *s* of late Charles Harold Browne and Lorna Browne (*née* Bailey); *m* 1962, Gillian Dorothy Smith; two *s*. *Educ:* Brockenhurst County High Sch.; Southampton Univ. (BSc(Eng)). CEng, FICE, FRAeS. Commissioned Airfield Construction Branch, RAF, 1958; appts in NEAF and UK, 1959–66; transf. to Engineer Branch, 1966; RAF Coll., Cranwell, 1966–67; aircraft engineering appts, RAF Valley and MoD, 1967–71; RAF Staff Coll., 1972; OC Engrg Wing, RAF Valley, 1973–75; staff appts, MoD and HQ RAF Germany, 1975–82; MoD (PE), 1982–89: Asst Dir, Harrier Projects, 1982–85, Dir, Electronics Radar Airborne, 1985–86, Dir, Airborne Early Warning, 1986–89; Dir Gen. Support Services (RAF), MoD, 1989–92; RAF retd, 1992; Dir Engrg, 1992–95, Dir Systems, 1995–96, NATS, CAA. Trustee, Bletchley Park Trust, 2000–. FIMgt. *Publication:* (with M. T. Thurbon) Electronic Warfare, 1998. *Recreations:* reading, writing, aviation, military history, photography, music. *Address:* c/o Lloyds TSB, New Milton, Hants BH25 6HU. *Club:* Royal Air Force.

BROWNE, Mervyn Ernest, CBE 1976; ERD 1954; HM Diplomatic Service, retired 1976; *b* 3 June 1916; *s* of late Ernest Edmond Browne and of Florence Mary Browne; *m* 1st, 1942, Constance (*née* Jarvis) (*d* 1988); three *s*; 2nd, 1991, Cecily (*née* Baker). *Educ:* Stockport Sec. Sch.; St Luke's Coll., Exeter; University Coll., Exeter. BScEcon London; BA Exeter. RA, 1940–46; TA, 1947–53; AER, RASC, 1953–60. Distribution of industry res., BoT, 1948–56; HM Trade Comr Service: Trade Comr, Wellington, NZ, 1957–61 and Adelaide, 1961–64; Principal Trade Comr, Kingston, Jamaica, 1964–68; HM Diplomatic Service: Counsellor (Commercial), Canberra, 1968–70; Dir, Brit. Trade in S Africa, Johannesburg, 1970–73; Consul-Gen., 1974–76 and Chargé d'Affaires, 1974 and 1976, Brit. Embassy, Manila. *Recreations:* militaria, lepidoptery, squash rackets. *Address:* 32 Cydonia Court, Earlsdon Way, Highcliffe, Dorset BH23 5TD. *T:* (01425) 278529.

BROWNE, Lady Moyra (Blanche Madeleine), DBE 1977 (OBE 1962); Governor, 1987–99, Vice President, since 1999, Research into Ageing (formerly British Foundation for Age Research) (National Chairman, Support Groups, 1987–93); *b* 2 March 1918; *d* of 9th Earl of Bessborough, PC, GCMG; *m* 1945, Sir Denis John Browne, KCVO, FRCS (*d* 1967); one *s* one *d*. *Educ:* privately. Enrolled Nurse (General) (State Enrolled Nurse, 1946). Dep. Supt-in-Chief, 1964, Supt-in-Chief, 1970–83, St John Amb. Bde. Vice-Chm. Central Council, Victoria League, 1961–65; Vice-Pres., Royal Coll. of Nursing, 1970–85. Hon. Mem., British Assoc. of Paediatric Surgeons, 1990. GCStJ 1984. *Recreations:* music, fishing, travel. *Address:* 16 Wilton Street, SW1X 7AX. *T:* (020) 7235 1419.

See also D. J. M. Browne.

BROWNE, Nicholas; *see* Browne, James N.

BROWNE, Nicholas Walker, CMG 1999; HM Diplomatic Service; Ambassador to Iran, since 1999 (Chargé d'Affaires, Tehran, 1997–99); *b* 17 Dec. 1947; *s* of Gordon Browne and Molly (*née* Gray); *m* 1969, Diana Aldwinckle; two *s* two *d*. *Educ:* Cheltenham Coll.; University Coll., Oxford (Open Scholar) (BA). Third Sec., FCO, 1969–71; Tehran, 1971–74; Second, later First Sec., FCO, 1974–76; on loan to Cabinet Office, 1976–80; First Sec. and Head of Chancery, Salisbury, 1980–81; First Sec., FCO, 1981–84; First Sec. (Envmt), Office of UK Rep., Brussels, 1984–89; Chargé d'Affaires, Tehran, 1989; Counsellor, FCO, 1989–90; Counsellor (Press and Public Affairs), Washington, and Hd of British Information Services, NY, 1990–94; Hd of Middle East Dept, FCO, 1994–97. *Recreations:* travel, theatre, BBC sport, family gatherings. *Address:* c/o Foreign and Commonwealth Office, King Charles Street, SW1A 2AH.

BROWNE, Percy Basil; DL; Chairman, Devon & Exeter Steeplechases Ltd, 1990–96; *b* 2 May 1923; *s* of late Captain W. P. Browne, MC; *m* 1st, 1947, Pamela Exham (*d* 1951); one *s*; 2nd, 1953, Jenefer Petherick (marr. diss. 1991); two *s* one *d*; 3rd, 1991, Susan, *widow* of Rupert Arkell. *Educ:* The Downs, Colwall; Eton College. Served War of 1939–45 with Royal Dragoons in Italy and NW Europe. Rode in Grand National, 1953. MP (C) Torrington Division of Devon, 1959–64. Dir, Appledore Shipbuilders Ltd, 1965–72 (former Chm.); Chairman: N Devon Meat Ltd, 1982–86; Western Counties Bldg Soc., 1983–85; West of England Bldg Soc., 1987–89 (Vice-Chm., 1985–87); Vice-Chm., Regency & West of England Bldg Soc., 1989–90. Mem., SW Reg. Hosp. Bd, 1967–70. Chm., Minister of Agriculture's SW Regl Panel, 1985–88. High Sheriff, Devon, 1978; DL Devon, 1984. *Address:* Newtown Farm, Semington, Trowbridge BA14 6JU. *T:* (01225) 708082.

See also B. J. Browne.

BROWNE, Peter K.; *see* Kenworthy-Browne.

BROWNE, Robert William M.; *see* Moxon Browne.

BROWNE, Sheila Jeanne, CB 1977; Principal, Newnham College, Cambridge, 1983–92; *b* 25 Dec. 1924; *d* of Edward Elliott Browne. *Educ:* Lady Margaret Hall, Oxford (MA; Hon. Fellow 1978); Ecole des Chartes, Paris. Asst Lectr, Royal Holloway Coll., Univ. of London, 1947–51; Tutor and Fellow of St Hilda's Coll., Oxford and Univ. Lectr in French, Oxford, 1951–61, Hon. Fellow, St Hilda's Coll., 1978; HM Inspector of Schools, 1961–70; Staff Inspector, Secondary Educn, 1970–72; Chief Inspector, Secondary Educn, 1972; Dep. Sen. Chief Inspector, DES, 1972–74, Senior Chief Inspector, 1974–83. Member: CNAA, 1985–93; Franco-British Council, 1987–95; Marshall Aid Commemoration Comr, 1987–92. Trustee, Gladstone Meml Trust, 1991–. Chm. Council, Selly Oak Colls, 1992–93. Hon. Fellow: Thames Valley Univ. (formerly Ealing Tech. Coll., then Poly. of W London), 1984; RHBNC, 1987; Lancashire Polytechnic, 1989; Univ. (formerly Poly.) of N London, 1989. Hon. DLitt Warwick, 1981; Hon. LLD: Exeter, 1984; Birmingham, 1987. *Recreations:* medieval France, enjoying Oxford. *Address:* 101 Walton Street, Oxford OX2 6EB. *T:* (01865) 511128.

BROWNE-CAVE, Sir Robert C.; *see* Cave-Browne-Cave.

BROWNE-EVANS, Hon. Dame Lois (Marie), DBE 1999; JP; MP (Progressive Lab) Devonshire North, Bermuda, since 1963; Minister of Legislative Affairs, since 1998; Attorney-General of Bermuda, since 1999; *b* 1 June 1927; *d* of James T. Browne and Emmeline Browne (*née* Charles); *m* 1958, John Evans; one *s* two *d*. *Educ:* King's Coll., London (LLB). Called to the Bar: Middle Temple, June 1953; Bermuda, Dec. 1953; Jamaica, 1966; in practice at the Bar, own chambers, 1954–99. Leader of the Opposition, Bermuda, 1968–85; Shadow Minister of Legislative Affairs, 1985. Mem., Internat. Fedn of Women Lawyers. Hon. Rep. of Govt of Jamaica, Bermuda. *Recreations:* reading, travel. *Address:* c/o Attorney General's Chambers, 4th Floor, Global House, 43 Church Street, Hamilton HM 12, Bermuda. *Clubs:* Devonshire Recreation, Bermuda Business and Professional Women's (Bermuda).

BROWNE-WILKINSON, family name of **Baron Browne-Wilkinson**.

BROWNE-WILKINSON, Baron *cr* 1991 (Life Peer), of Camden, in the London Borough of Camden; **Nicolas Christopher Henry Browne-Wilkinson,** Kt 1977; PC 1983; a Lord of Appeal in Ordinary, 1991–2000; Senior Law Lord, 1999–2000; *b* 30 March 1930; *s* of late Canon A. R. Browne-Wilkinson and Molly Browne-Wilkinson; *m* 1st, 1955, Ursula de Lacy Bacon (*d* 1987); three *s* two *d*; 2nd, 1990, Mrs Hilary Tuckwell. *Educ:* Lancing; Magdalen Coll., Oxford (BA; Hon. Fellow, 1993). Called to Bar, Lincoln's Inn, 1953 (Bencher, 1977); QC 1972. Junior Counsel: to Registrar of Restrictive Trading Agreements, 1964–66; to Attorney-General in Charity Matters, 1966–72; in bankruptcy, to Dept of Trade and Industry, 1966–72; a Judge of the Courts of Appeal of Jersey and Guernsey, 1976–77; a Judge of the High Court, Chancery Div., 1977–83; a Lord Justice of Appeal, 1983–85; Vice-Chancellor of the Supreme Court, 1985–91. Pres., Employment Appeal Tribunal, 1981–83. Pres., Senate of the Inns of Court and the Bar, 1984–86. Hon. Fellow, St Edmund Hall, Oxford, 1987. *Recreation:* gardening. *Address:* House of Lords, SW1A 0PW.
See also S. Browne-Wilkinson.

BROWNE-WILKINSON, Simon; QC 1998; barrister; *b* 18 Aug. 1957; *s* of Baron Browne-Wilkinson, *qv*; *m* 1988, Megan Tresidder (*d* 2001); one *s* one *d*. *Educ:* City of London Sch.; Magdalen Coll., Oxford (BA Jurisprudence 1979). Called to the Bar, Lincoln's Inn, 1981; in practice at the Bar, 1981–. *Recreation:* sailing. *Address:* Serle Court, 6 New Square, Lincoln's Inn, WC2A 3QS. *T:* (020) 7242 6105.

BROWNING, Angela Frances; MP (C) Tiverton and Honiton, since 1997 (Tiverton, 1992–97); *b* 4 Dec. 1946; *d* of late Thomas Pearson and of Linda Pearson; *m* 1968, David Browning; two *s*. *Educ:* Westwood Girls' Grammar Sch.; Reading Coll. of Technol.; Bournemouth Coll. of Technol. FInstSMM. Management Consultant. Parly Sec., MAFF, 1994–97; Opposition spokesman: on educn and disability, 1997–98; on trade and industry, 1999–2000; Shadow Leader, H of C, 2000–01. Vice Pres., InstSMM, 1997–. Mem. and Special Counsellor to Nat. Autistic Soc.; Nat. Vice Pres., Alzheimer's Disease Soc., 1997–. *Recreations:* supporting family of keen oarsmen, theatre, opera. *Address:* House of Commons, SW1A 0AA. *T:* (020) 7219 5067.

BROWNING, (David) Peter (James), CBE 1984; MA; Chief Education Officer: Southampton, 1969–73; Bedfordshire, 1973–89; *b* 29 May 1927; *s* of late Frank Browning and Lucie A. (*née* Hiscock); *m* 1953, Eleanor Berry, *d* of late J. H. Forshaw, CB, FRIBA; three *s*. *Educ:* Christ's Coll., Cambridge (Engl. and Mod. Langs Tripos); Sorbonne; Univs of Strasbourg and Perugia. Personal Asst to Vice-Chancellor, Liverpool Univ., 1952–56; Teacher, Willenhall Comprehensive Sch., 1956–59; Sen. Admin. Asst, Somerset LEA, 1959–62; Asst Dir of Educn, Cumberland LEA, 1962–66; Dep. Chief Educn Officer, Southampton LEA, 1966–69. Member: Schools Council Governing Council and 5–13 Steering Cttee, 1969–75; Council, Univ. of Southampton, 1970–73; C of E Bd of Educn Schools Cttee, 1970–75; Council, Nat. Youth Orch., 1972–77; Merchant Navy Trng Bd, 1973–77; British Educnl Administration Soc. (Chm., 1974–78; Founder Mem., Council of Management); UGC, 1974–79; Taylor Cttee of Enquiry into Management and Govt of Schs, 1975–77; Governing Body, Centre for Inf. on Language Teaching and Research, 1975–80; European Forum for Educational Admin (Founder Chm., 1977–84); Library Adv. Council (England), 1978–81; Bd of Governors, Camb. Inst. of Educn (Vice-Chm., 1980–89); Univ. of Cambridge Faculty Bd of Educn, 1983–92; Council of Management, British Sch. Tech., 1984–87, Trust Dir, 1987–92; Lancaster Univ. Council, 1988–97 (Treas., 1993–97); Dir, Nat. Educnl Resources Inf. Service, 1988–91; Member: Carlisle Diocesan Bd of Educn, 1989–97 (Chm., 1992–97); Council, Open Coll. of NW, 1991–94; Cumbria Arts in Educn Trust, 1992–95 (Chm., 1992–95); Carlisle DAC for Care of Churches, 1993–2000 (Chm., 1993–2000); Chairman: Armitt (Liby and Mus.) Trust, 1994–2000 (Mem., 1992–); Armitt Liby and Mus. Centre Co., 1996–2000 (Mem., 1996–); Armitt Centre Enterprises Co., 1997–. Governor: Gordonstoun Sch., 1985–92; Lakes Sch., Windermere, 1988–92; Charlotte Mason Coll. of Higher Educn, Ambleside, 1988–92; London Coll. of Dance, 1990–93. Consultant, Ministry of Education: Sudan, 1976; Cyprus, 1977; Italy, 1981. Sir James Matthews Meml Lecture, Univ. of Southampton, 1983. FRSA 1981–93. Cavaliere, Order of Merit (Republic of Italy), 1985; Médaille d'honneur de l'Oise, 1988; Commandeur, Ordre des Palmes Académiques (Republic of France), 1989 (Officier, 1985). *Publications:* Editor: Julius Caesar for German Students, 1957; Macbeth for German Students, 1959; contrib. London Educn Rev., Educnl Administration jl, and other educnl jls. *Recreations:* music, community affairs, travel. *Address:* Park Fell, Skelwith Bridge, near Ambleside LA22 9NP. *T:* (015394) 33978, *Fax:* (015394) 81552; 43/45 Chilkwell Street, Glastonbury BA6 8DE, *T:* (01458) 832514.

BROWNING, Most Rev. Edmond Lee; Presiding Bishop of the Episcopal Church in the United States, 1986–97; *b* 11 March 1929; *s* of Edmond Lucian Browning and Cora Mae Lee; *m* 1953, Patricia A. Sparks; four *s* one *d*. *Educ:* Univ. of the South (BA 1952); School of Theology, Sewanee, Tenn (BD 1954). Curate, Good Shepherd, Corpus Christi, Texas, 1954–56; Rector, Redeemer, Eagle Pass, Texas, 1956–59; Rector, All Souls, Okinawa, 1959–63; Japanese Lang. School, Kobe, Japan, 1963–65; Rector, St Matthews, Okinawa, 1965–67; Archdeacon of Episcopal Church, Okinawa, 1965–67; first Bishop of Okinawa, 1967–71; Bishop of American Convocation, 1971–73; Executive for National and World Mission, on Presiding Bishop's Staff, United States Episcopal Church, 1974–76; Bishop of Hawaii, 1976–85. Chm., Standing Commn on World Mission, 1979–82. Member: Exec. Council, Episcopal Church, 1982–85; Anglican Consultative Council, 1982–91. Hon. DD: Univ. of the South, Sewanee, Tenn, 1970; Gen. Theol Seminary, 1986; Church Divinity Sch. of the Pacific, 1987; Seabury Western Seminary, 1987; Hon. DHL: Chaminade Univ., Honolulu, 1985; St Paul's Coll., Lawrenceville, Va, 1987. *Publication:* Essay on World Mission, 1977. *Address:* 5164 Imai Road, Hood River, OR 97031, USA. *T:* (212) 9225322.

BROWNING, Rt Rev. George Victor; *see* Canberra and Goulburn, Bishop of.

BROWNING, Ian Andrew; DL; Chief Executive, Wiltshire County Council, 1984–96; Clerk to the Wiltshire Police Authority, since 1976; *b* 28 Aug. 1941; *m* 1967, Ann Carter; two *s*. *Educ:* Liverpool Univ. (BA Hons Pol Theory and Instns). Solicitor. Swindon BC, 1964–70; WR, Yorks, 1970–73; S Yorks CC, 1973–76; Wilts CC, 1976–96. DL Wilts, 1996. *Recreations:* golf, travel, ornithology. *Address:* 10 The Picquet, Bratton, Westbury, Wiltshire BA13 4RU.

BROWNING, Prof. Keith Anthony, PhD; FRS 1978; Director, Joint Centre for Mesoscale Meteorology, since 1992, and Professor in Department of Meteorology, since 1995, University of Reading; *b* 31 July 1938; *s* of late Sqdn Ldr James Anthony Browning and Amy Hilda (*née* Greenwood); *m* 1962, Ann Muriel (*née* Baish), BSc, MSc; one *s* two *d*. *Educ:* Commonweal Grammar Sch., Swindon, Wilts; Imperial Coll. of Science and Technology, Univ. of London. BSc, ARCS, PhD, DIC. Research atmospheric physicist, Air Force Cambridge Research Laboratories, Mass, USA, 1962–66; in charge of Meteorological Office Radar Research Lab., RSRE, Malvern, 1966–85; Dep. Dir (Phys. Res.), 1985–89, Dir of Res., 1989–91, Met. Office, Bracknell; Principal Research Fellow, 1966–69; Principal Scientific Officer, 1969–72; Sen. Principal Scientific Officer, 1972–79; Dep. Chief Scientific Officer, 1979–89; Chief Scientific Officer, 1989–91. Ch. Scientist, Nat. Hail Res. Experiment, USA, 1974–75; Vis. Prof., Dept of Meteorology, Univ. of Reading, 1988–94. World Climate Research Programme: Member: British Nat. Cttee, 1988–89; Scientific Steering Gp, Global Energy and Water Cycle Expmt, 1988–96; WMO/ICSU Scientific Cttee, 1990–94; Chm., Cloud System Sci. Panel, 1992–96; World Weather Research Programme: Mem., WMO Interim Sci. Steering Cttee, 1996–98; Mem., Sci. Steering Cttee, 1998–. Member: Council, Royal Met. Soc., 1971–74 (Vice-Pres., 1979–81, 1987–88 and 1990–91; Pres., 1988–90; Mem., Accreditation Bd, 1993–99; Chm., 1994–99); Editing Cttee, Qly Jl RMetS, 1975–78; Inter-Union Commn on Radio Meteorology, 1975–78; Internat. Commn on Cloud Physics, 1976–84; British Nat. Cttee for Physics, 1979–84; British Nat. Cttee for Geodesy and Geophysics, 1983–89 (Chm., Met. and Atmos. Phys. Sub-Cttee, 1985–89, Vice-Chm., 1979–84); NERC, 1984–87; British Nat. Cttee for Space Res., 1986–89 (Remote Sensing Sub-Cttee, 1986–89); Royal Soc. Interdisciplinary Sci. Cttee for Space Res., 1990–91. MAE, 1989; For. Associate, US Nat. Acad. of Engrg, 1992. UK Nat. Correspondent, Internat. Assoc. of Meteorology and Atmospheric Physics, 1991–94. L. F. Richardson Prize, 1968, Buchan Prize, 1972, William Gaskell Meml Medal, 1982, RMetS; L. G. Groves Meml Prize for Meteorology, Met. Office, 1969; Meisinger Award, 1974, Jule Charney Award, 1985, Amer. Met. Soc. (Fellow of the Society, 1975); Charles Chree Medal and Prize, Inst. of Physics, 1981. *Publications:* (ed) Nowcasting, 1982; (ed jtly) Global Energy and Water Cycles, 1999; meteorological papers in learned jls, mainly in Britain and USA. *Recreations:* home and garden.

BROWNING, Peter; *see* Browning, D. P. J.

BROWNING, Philip Harold Roger; a District Judge (Magistrates' Courts) (formerly Stipendiary Magistrate), Shropshire, since 1994; *b* 25 Aug. 1946; *s* of Harold and Barbara Browning; *m* 1972, Linda; two *s*. *Educ:* Hele's Sch., Exeter; Surbiton County Grammar Sch.; Windsor Grammar Sch.; Coll. of Law. Articled T. W. Stuchbery & Son, Windsor and Maidenhead, 1964–69; admitted solicitor, 1969; Asst Solicitor, Baily, Williams & Lucas, Saffron Walden, 1969–71; Prosecuting Solicitor, Devon, 1972–81; Clerk to Justices: Axminster, Exmouth, Honiton and Wonford, 1981–85; Norwich, 1985–94. *Recreations:* thinking, reading, writing, listening to music, choral singing, playing the piano, computing. *Address:* Telford Magistrates' Court, Telford Square, Malinsgate, Telford TF3 4HX. *T:* (01952) 204500.

BROWNING, Rex Alan, CB 1984; Deputy Secretary, Overseas Development Administration, 1981–86, retired; *b* 22 July 1930; *s* of Gilbert H. W. Browning and Gladys (*née* Smith); *m* 1961, Paula McKain; three *d*. *Educ:* Bristol Grammar Sch.; Merton Coll., Oxford (Postmaster) (MA). HM Inspector of Taxes, 1952; Asst Principal, Colonial Office, 1957; Private Sec. to Parly Under-Sec. for the Colonies, 1960; Principal, Dept of Techn. Co-operation, 1961; transf. ODM, 1964; seconded to Diplomatic Service as First Sec. (Aid), British High Commn, Singapore, 1969; Asst Sec., 1971; Counsellor, Overseas Develt, Washington, and Alternate UK Exec. Dir, IBRD, 1973–76; Under-Secretary: ODM, 1976–78; Dept of Trade, 1978–80; ODA, 1980–81. *Address:* Taranaki House, Trusham, near Newton Abbot, Devon TQ13 0NR.

BROWNING, Rev. Canon Wilfrid Robert Francis; Canon Residentiary of Christ Church Cathedral, Oxford, 1965–87, Hon. Canon since 1987; *b* 29 May 1918; *s* of Charles Robert and Mabel Elizabeth Browning; *m* 1948, Elizabeth Beeston; two *s* two *d*. *Educ:* Westminster School; Christ Church, Oxford; Cuddesdon Coll., Oxford. MA, BD Oxon. Deacon 1941, priest 1942, dio. of Peterborough; on staff of St Deiniol's Library, Hawarden, 1946–48; Vicar of St Richard's, Hove, 1948–51; Rector of Great Haseley, 1951–59; Lectr, Cuddesdon Coll., Oxford, 1951–59 and 1965–70; Canon Residentiary of Blackburn Cath. and Warden of Whalley Abbey, Lancs, 1959–65; Director of Ordinands and Post-Ordination Trng (Oxford dio.), 1965–85; Dir of Trng for Non-Stipendiary Ordinands and Clergy, 1972–88; Tutor, Westminster Coll., Oxford, 1993–2000. Examining Chaplain: Blackburn, 1960–70; Manchester, 1970–78; Oxford, 1965–89. Member of General Synod, 1973–85; Select Preacher, Oxford Univ., 1972, 1981. *Publications:* Commentary on St Luke's Gospel, 1960, 6th edn 1981; Meet the New Testament, 1964; ed, The Anglican Synthesis, 1965; Handbook of the Ministry, 1985; A Dictionary of the Bible, 1996. *Address:* 33 Dunstone Road, Plymstock, Plymouth PL9 8RJ. *T:* (01752) 403039; 42 Alexandra Road, Oxford OX2 0DB. *T:* (01865) 723464.

BROWNLEE, Prof. George; Professor of Pharmacology, King's College, University of London, 1958–78, retired; now Emeritus Professor; *b* 8 Sept. 1911; *s* of late George R. Brownlee and of Mary C. C. Gow, Edinburgh; *m* 1940, Margaret P. M. Cochrane (*d* 1970), 2nd *d* of Thomas W. P. Cochrane and Margaret P. M. S. Milne, Bo'ness, Scotland; three *s*; 2nd, 1977, Betty Jean Gaydon (marr. diss. 1981), *o d* of Stanley H. Clutterham and

Margaret M. Fox, Sidney, Australia. *Educ:* Tynecastle Sch.; Heriot Watt Coll., Edinburgh, BSc 1936, DSc 1950, Glasgow; PhD 1939, London. Rammell Schol., Biological Standardization Labs of Pharmaceutical Soc., London; subseq. Head of Chemotherapeutic Div., Wellcome Res. Labs, Beckenham; Reader in Pharmacology, King's Coll., Univ. of London, 1949. Editor, Jl of Pharmacy and Pharmacology, 1955–72. FKC, 1971. *Publications:* (with Prof. J. P. Quilliam) Experimental Pharmacology, 1952; papers on: chemotherapy of tuberculosis and leprosy; structure and pharmacology of the polymyxins; endocrinology; toxicity of drugs; neurohumoral transmitters in smooth muscle, etc., in: Brit. Jl Pharmacology; Jl Physiology; Biochem. Jl; Nature; Lancet; Annals NY Acad. of Science; Pharmacological Reviews, etc. *Recreations:* collecting books, making things. *Address:* 602 Gilbert House, Barbican, EC2Y 8BD. *T:* (020) 7638 9543. *Club:* Athenæum.
See also G. G. Brownlee.

BROWNLEE, Prof. George Gow, PhD; FMedSci; FRS 1987; E. P. Abraham Professor of Chemical Pathology, Sir William Dunn School of Pathology, University of Oxford, since 1980; Fellow of Lincoln College, Oxford, since 1980; *b* 13 Jan. 1942; *s* of Prof. George Brownlee, *qv*; *m* 1966, Margaret Susan Kemp; one *d* (one *s* decd). *Educ:* Dulwich College; Emmanuel Coll., Cambridge (MA, PhD). Scientific staff of MRC at Laboratory of Molecular Biology, Cambridge, 1966–80. Fellow, Emmanuel Coll., Cambridge, 1967–71. Founder FMedSci 1998. Colworth Medal, 1977, Wellcome Trust Award, 1985, Biochemical Soc.; Owren Medal (Norway), 1987; Haemophilia Medal (France), 1988. *Publications:* Determination of Sequences in RNA (Vol. 3, Part I of Laboratory Techniques in Biochemistry and Molecular Biology), 1972; scientific papers in Jl of Molecular Biology, Nature, Cell, Nucleic Acids Research, etc. *Recreations:* gardening, cricket. *Address:* Sir William Dunn School of Pathology, South Parks Road, Oxford OX1 3RE. *T:* (01865) 275559.

BROWNLIE, Albert Dempster; Vice-Chancellor, University of Canterbury, Christchurch, New Zealand, 1977–98; *b* 3 Sept. 1932; *s* of Albert Newman and Netia Brownlie; *m* 1955, Noelene Eunice (*née* Meyer); two *d*. *Educ:* Univ. of Auckland, NZ (MCom). Economist, NZ Treasury, 1954–55. Lecturer, Sen. Lectr, Associate Prof. in Economics, Univ. of Auckland, 1956–64; Prof. and Head of Dept of Economics, Univ. of Canterbury, Christchurch, 1965–77. Chairman: Monetary and Economic Council, 1972–78; Australia-NZ Foundn, 1979–83; UGC Cttee to Review NZ Univ. Educn, 1980–82; NZ Vice-Chancellors' Cttee, 1983–84, 1993; Member: Commonwealth Experts Group on New Internat. Economic Order, 1975–77; Commonwealth Experts Gp on Econ. Growth, 1980; Wage Hearing Tribunal, 1976. Associate Mem., World Innovation Foundn, 1999. Silver Jubilee Medal, 1977. *Publications:* articles in learned jls. *Address:* 66 Clyde Road, Christchurch 4, New Zealand. *T:* (3) 3487629.

BROWNLIE, Prof. Ian, CBE 1993; QC; DCL; FBA; International Law practitioner; Chichele Professor of Public International Law, and Fellow of All Souls College, University of Oxford, 1980–99; *b* 19 Sept. 1932; *s* of John Nason Brownlie and Amy Isabella (*née* Atherton); *m* 1st, 1957, Jocelyn Gale; one *s* two *d*; 2nd, 1978, C. J. Apperley, LLM. *Educ:* Alsop High Sch., Liverpool; Hertford Coll., Oxford (Gibbs Scholar, 1952; BA 1953); King's Coll., Cambridge (Humanitarian Trust Student, 1955). DPhil Oxford, 1961; DCL Oxford, 1976. Called to the Bar, Gray's Inn, 1958, Bencher, 1987; QC 1979. Lectr, Nottingham Univ., 1957–63; Fellow and Tutor in Law, Wadham Coll., Oxford, 1963–76 and Lectr, Oxford Univ., 1964–76; Prof. of Internat. Law, LSE, Univ. of London, 1976–80. Reader in Public Internat. Law, Inns of Ct Sch. of Law, 1973–76; Dir of Studies, Internat. Law Assoc., 1982–91. Member: Panel of Conciliators and Panel of Arbitrators, ICSID (World Bank), 1988–; Internat. Law Commn, UN, 1996–; Judge, 1995–, Pres., 1996–, Eur. Nuclear Energy Tribunal. Delegate, OUP, 1984–94. Lectr, Hague Acad. of Internat. Law, 1979, 1995. Editor, British Year Book of International Law, 1974–99. Mem., Inst. of Internat. Law, 1985 (Associate Mem., 1977). FBA 1979. Japan Foundn Award, 1978. Comdr, Royal Norwegian OM, 1993. *Publications:* International Law and the Use of Force by States, 1963; Principles of Public International Law, 1966, 5th edn 1998 (Russian edn, ed G. I. Tunkin, 1977; Japanese edn, 1989; Portuguese edn, 1998; Certif. of Merit, Amer. Soc. of Internat. Law, 1976); Basic Documents in International Law, 1967, 3rd edn 1983; The Law Relating to Public Order, 1968; Basic Documents on Human Rights, 1971, 3rd edn 1992; Basic Documents on African Affairs, 1971; African Boundaries, a legal and diplomatic encyclopaedia, 1979; State Responsibility, part 1, 1983; (ed jtly) Liber Amicorum for Lord Wilberforce, 1987. *Recreation:* travel. *Address:* Blackstone Chambers, Blackstone House, Temple, EC4Y 9BW. *T:* (020) 7583 1770.

BROWNLOW, 7th Baron *cr* 1776; **Edward John Peregrine Cust;** Bt 1677; Chairman and Managing Director of Harris & Dixon (Underwriting Agencies) Ltd, 1976–82; *b* 25 March 1936; *o s* of 6th Baron Brownlow and Katherine Hariot (*d* 1952), 2nd *d* of Sir David Alexander Kinloch, 11th Bt, CB, MVO; *S* father, 1978; *m* 1964, Shirlie Edith, 2nd *d* of late John Yeomans, The Manor Farm, Hill Croome, Upton-on-Severn, Worcs; one *s*. *Educ:* Eton. Member of Lloyd's, 1961–88, and 1993–; Director: Hand-in-Hand Fire and Life Insurance Soc. (branch office of Commercial Union Assurance Co. Ltd), 1962–82; Ermitage International Ltd, 1988–99. High Sheriff of Lincolnshire, 1978–79. CStJ 1999 (Chm. Council, Jersey, 1996–). *Heir: s* Hon. Peregrine Edward Quintin Cust, *b* 9 July 1974. *Address:* La Maison des Prés, St Peter, Jersey JE3 7EL. *Clubs:* White's, Pratt's; United (Jersey).

BROWNLOW, Air Vice-Marshal Bertrand, (John), CB 1982; OBE 1967; AFC 1962; FRAeS; aviation consultant, since 1997; *b* 13 Jan. 1929; *s* of Robert John Brownlow and Helen Louise Brownlow; *m* 1958, Kathleen Shannon; one *s* one *d* (and one *s* decd). *Educ:* Beaufort Lodge Sch. Joined RAF, 1947; 12 and 101 Sqdns, ADC to AOC 1 Gp, 103 Sqdn, 213 Sqdn, Empire Test Pilots' Sch., OC Structures and Mech. Eng Flt RAE Farnborough, RAF Staff Coll., Air Min. Op. Requirements, 1949–64; Wing Comdr Ops, RAF Lyneham, 1964–66; Jt Services Staff Coll., 1966–67; DS RAF Staff Coll., 1967–68; Def. and Air Attaché, Stockholm, 1969–71; CO Experimental Flying, RAE Farnborough, 1971–73; Asst Comdt, Office and Flying Trng, RAF Coll., Cranwell, 1973–74; Dir of Flying (R&D), MoD, 1974–77; Comdt, A&AEE, 1977–80; Comdt, RAF Coll., Cranwell, 1980–82; Dir Gen., Trng, RAF, 1982–83, retired 1984. Exec. Dir, Marshall of Cambridge (Engineering), subseq. Dir, Marshall Aerospace, 1987–94. Mem., CAA, 1994–96. FRAeS 1981. Silver Medal, Royal Aero Club, 1983, for servs to RAF gliding. *Recreations:* squash, tennis, golf, gliding (Gold C with two diamonds). *Address:* Woodside, Abbotsley Road, Croxton, St Neots PE19 6SZ. *T:* (01480) 880663. *Club:* Royal Air Force.

BROWNLOW, James Hilton, CBE 1984; QPM 1978; Adviser on Ground Control, Football Association, 1990–94; HM Inspector of Constabulary for North Eastern England, 1983–89; *b* 19 Oct. 1925; *s* of late Ernest Cuthbert Brownlow and Beatrice Annie Elizabeth Brownlow; *m* 1947, Joyce Key; two *d*. *Educ:* Worksop Central School. Solicitor's Clerk, 1941–43; served war, RAF, Flt/Sgt (Air Gunner), 1943–47. Police Constable, Leicester City Police, 1947; Police Constable to Det. Chief Supt, Kent County Constabulary, 1947–69; Asst Chief Constable, Hertfordshire Constabulary, 1969–75; Asst to HM Chief Inspector of Constabulary, Home Office, 1975–76; Dep. Chief Constable, Greater Manchester Police, 1976–79; Chief Constable, S Yorks Police, 1979–82. Mem., Parole Bd, 1991–94. Queen's Commendation for Brave Conduct, 1972. Officer Brother OStJ 1981. *Recreations:* golf, gardening.

BROWNLOW, Air Vice-Marshal John; *see* Brownlow, Air Vice-Marshal B.

BROWNLOW, Kevin; author; film director; *b* 2 June 1938; *s* of Thomas and Niña Brownlow; *m* 1969, Virginia Keane; one *d*. *Educ:* University College School. Entered documentaries, 1955; became film editor, 1958, and edited many documentaries; with Andrew Mollo dir. feature films: It Happened Here, 1964; Winstanley, 1975; dir. Charm of Dynamite, 1967, about Abel Gance, and restored his classic film Napoleon (first shown London, Nov. 1980, NY, Jan. 1981). With David Gill produced and directed TV series: Hollywood, 1980; Thames Silents, 1981–90 (incl. The Big Parade); Channel Four Silents, 1991– (incl. Sunrise); Unknown Chaplin, 1983; British Cinema—Personal View, 1986; Buster Keaton: a Hard Act to Follow, 1987; Harold Lloyd—The Third Genius, 1990; D. W. Griffith, Father of Film, 1993; Cinema Europe—The Other Hollywood, 1995; Universal Horror, 1998; Lon Chaney: a thousand faces, 2000. *Publications:* The Parade's Gone By . . ., 1968; How it Happened Here, 1968; The War, the West and the Wilderness, 1978; Hollywood: the Pioneers, 1979; Napoleon: Abel Gance's classic film, 1983; Behind The Mask of Innocence, 1991; David Lean: a biography, 1996; Mary Pickford Rediscovered, 1999; many articles on film history. *Recreation:* motion pictures. *Address:* Photoplay Productions, 21 Princess Road, NW1 8JR.

BROWNLOW, Peter; Managing Director and Financial Director, Border Television plc, since 1996; *b* 4 June 1945; *s* of Frederick and Margaret Brownlow; *m* 1972, Judith Margaret Alton; two *s*. *Educ:* Rothwell Grammar Sch.; Leeds Poly. ACMA 1970. Company Accountant: John Menzies plc, 1967–70; United Newspapers, 1970–82; Co. Sec., Border Television plc, 1982–84; Financial Dir, 1984–96, non-exec. Dep. Chm., 1995–, Cumberland Building Soc. Director: Century Radio Ltd, 1993–; Century Radio 106 Ltd, 1996–; Century Radio 105 Ltd, 1997–; Sun FM Ltd, 1997–; Border Radio Hldgs, 1997–. *Recreations:* sailing, fell walking, gardening. *Address:* Border Television plc, Television Centre, Carlisle CA1 3NT.

BROWNRIGG, Sir Nicholas (Gawen), 5th Bt *cr* 1816; *b* 22 Dec. 1932; *s* of late Gawen Egremont Brownrigg and Baroness Lucia von Borosini, *o d* of Baron Victor von Borosini, California; *S* grandfather, 1939; *m* 1959, Linda Louise Lovelace (marr. diss. 1965), Beverly Hills, California; one *s* one *d*; *m* 1971, Valerie Ann, *d* of Julian A. Arden, Livonia, Michigan, USA. *Educ:* Midland Sch., Stanford Univ. *Heir: s* Michael Gawen Brownrigg [*b* 11 Oct. 1961; *m* Margaret Dillon, *d* of Dr Clay Burchell; one *s*]. *Address:* PO Box 548, Ukiah, CA 95482, USA.

BROWNSWORD, Andrew; Chairman and Chief Executive, Andrew Brownsword Group, since 1993; Chairman, Bath Rugby plc, since 1998; *s* of Douglas and Eileen Brownsword; *m* 1983, Christina Brenchley; two *d*. *Educ:* Harvey Grammar Sch., Folkestone. Formed A. Brownsword and Co., wholesale distributors of greetings cards and stationery, 1971; formed the Andrew Brownsword Collection Ltd, 1975; acquired Gordon Fraser Gallery, 1989; greetings cards business acquired by Hallmark Cards, 1994. *Recreations:* sailing, ski-ing, hill-walking. *Address:* 4 Queen Square, Bath BA1 2HA. *Clubs:* Royal Thames Yacht; British Ski.

BROWSE, Lillian Gertrude, CBE 1998; author; private archivist; *d* of Michael Browse and Gladys Browse (*née* Meredith); *m* 1st, 1934, Ivan H. Joseph; 2nd, 1964, Sidney H. Lines. *Educ:* Barnato Park, Johannesburg. Studied with Margaret Craske at Cecchetti Ballet Sch., London, 1928–30; joined Dolin-Nemtchinova ballet co., 1930; gave up ballet and worked at Leger Galls, London, 1931–39; organised war-time exhibns at Nat. Gall. and travelling exhibns for CEMA, 1940–45, also exhibns for Inst. of Adult Educn; Organising Sec., Red Cross picture sale, Christie's, 1942; founder partner, Roland, Browse & Delbanco, 1945; Founder Dir, Browse & Darby, 1977–81. Ballet Critic, Spectator, 1950–54. Organised: Sickert exhibn, Edinburgh, 1953; Sickert centenary exhibn, Tate Gall., 1960; exhibited own private collection at Courtauld Inst. Galls, 1983. Hon. Fellow, Courtauld Inst., 1986. *Publications:* Augustus John Drawings, 1941; Sickert, 1943; (ed) Ariel Books on the Arts, 1946; Degas Dancers, 1949; William Nicholson: Catalogue Raisonné, 1955; Sickert, 1960; Forain, the Painter, 1978; Duchess of Cork Street: an autobiography of an art dealer, 1999; contribs to Apollo, Sunday Times, Country Life, Burlington Magazine and various articles. *Recreation:* gardening.

BROWSE, Sir Norman (Leslie), Kt 1994; MD; FRCS, FRCP; Professor of Surgery and Senior Consultant Surgeon, St Thomas's Hospital Medical School, 1981–96, now Professor Emeritus; Consulting Surgeon, St Thomas' Hospital, since 1996; President, Royal College of Surgeons, 1992–95; *b* 1 Dec. 1931; *s* of Reginald and Margaret Browse; *m* 1957, Dr Jeanne Menage; one *s* one *d*. *Educ:* St Bartholomew's Hosp. Med. Coll. (MB BS 1955); Bristol Univ. (MD 1961). FRCS 1959; FRCP 1993. Capt. RAMC, Cyprus, 1957–59. Lectr in Surgery, Westminster Hosp., 1962–64; Harkness Fellow, Res. Associate, Mayo Clinic, Rochester, Minn, 1964–65; St Thomas's Hospital Medical School: Reader in Surgery, 1965–72; Prof. of Vascular Surgery, 1972–81. Sims Travelling Prof., 1990; Arris & Gale Lectr, 1966, Vicary Lectr, 2000, RCS. Hon. Consultant (Vascular Surgery) to: Army, 1980–96; RAF, 1982–96. President: European Soc. for Cardiovascular Surgery, 1982–84; Assoc. of Profs of Surgery, 1985–87; Surgical Res. Soc., 1990–92; Venous Forum, RSM, 1989–91; Vascular Surgical Soc. of GB and Ireland, 1991–92; Mem. Council, RCS, 1986–95 (Mem., Ct of Patrons, 1996–); Co-Chm., Senate of Surgery, 1993–95; Chm., Jt Consultants Cttee, 1994–98. Chairman: British Atherosclerosis Soc., 1988–91; Lord Brock Meml Trust, 1994–2001; Vice-Chm., British Vascular Foundn, 1997–. Trustee, Restoration of Appearance and Function Trust, 1996–2001; Patron, INPUT Trust, 1999–. Gov., Amer. Coll. of Surgeons, 1997–. Mem. Council, Marlborough Coll., 1990–2001. FKC 2000. Hon. FRCP&SGlas 1993; Hon. FSACM 1993; Hon. FRACS 1994; Hon. FDS RCS 1994; Hon. FFAEM 1994; Hon. FRSCI 1995; Hon. FACS 1995; Hon. FRCSE 1996. Hon. Member: Amer. Surgical Vascular Soc., 1987; Australian Vascular Soc., 1987; Amer. Vascular Biol. Soc., 1988; Amer. Venous Forum, 1991; Soc. for Clin. Vascular Surg., USA, 1993. Distinguished Alumnus, Mayo Clinic, 1993; Hon. Academician, Acad. of Athens, 1995. Hon. Freeman, Barbers' Co., 1997. *Publications:* Physiology and Pathology of Bed Rest, 1964; Symptoms and Signs of Surgical Disease, 1978; Reducing Operations for Lymphoedema, 1986; Diseases of the Veins, 1988; Diseases of the Lymphatics, 2001; papers on all aspects of vascular disease. *Recreations:* marine art, mediaeval history, sailing. *Address:* Corbet House, Butes Lane, Alderney, Channel Islands GY9 3UW. *T:* (01481) 823716.

BRUBECK, David Warren; jazz musician, composer; *b* Concord, Calif, 6 Dec. 1920; *s* of Howard Brubeck and Elizabeth Ivey; *m* 1942, Iola Whitlock; five *s* one *d*. *Educ:* Univ. of the Pacific (BA); graduate study with Darius Milhaud, Mills Coll. Leader, Dave Brubeck Octet, and Trio, 1946–; formed Dave Brubeck Quartet, 1951; played colls, fests, clubs and symphony orchs; 3 month tour of Europe and Middle East (for US State Dept) and tours in Aust., Japan, USSR and S America. Numerous recordings. Has composed: *ballet:* Points on Jazz, 1962; Glances, 1976; *orchestral:* Elementals, 1963; They All Sang Yankee Doodle, 1976; *flute and guitar:* Tritonis, 1979; *piano:* Reminiscences of the Cattle Country, 1946; Four by Four, 1946; *oratorios:* The Light in the Wilderness, 1968; Beloved Son, 1978; The Voice of the Holy Spirit, 1985; *cantatas:* Gates of Justice, 1969; Truth is Fallen, 1971; La Fiesta de la Posada, 1975; In Praise of Mary, 1989; *chorus and orchestra:* Pange Lingua Variations, 1983; Upon This Rock Chorale and Fugue, 1987; Lenten Triptych, 1988; Joy in the Morning, 1991; *mass:* To Hope!, a celebration, 1980; *SATB Chorus:* I See Satie, 1987; Four New England Pieces, 1988; Earth is our mother (with chamber orch.), 1992; over 250 *jazz* compositions incl. Blue Rondo à la Turk; In Your Own Sweet Way; The Duke. Duke Ellington Fellow, Yale Univ., 1973. Hon. PhD: Univ. of Pacific; Fairfield Univ.; Bridgeport Univ., 1982; Mills Coll., 1982; Niagara Univ., 1989; Kalamazoo Coll., 1991. Hollywood Walk of Fame. Winner, jazz polls conducted by Downbeat, Melody Maker, Cashbox, Billboard and Playboy magazines, 1952–55; Broadcast Music Inc. Jazz Pioneer Award, 1985; Compostela Humanitarian award, 1986; Connecticut Arts award, 1987; American Eagle award, Nat. Music Council, 1988; Pantheon of the Arts, Univ. of the Pacific, 1989; Gerard Manley Hopkins Award, Fairfield Univ., 1990; Distinguished Achievement Award, Simon's Rock Coll., 1991; Connecticut Bar Assoc. Award, 1992; Nat. Medal of the Arts, USA, 1994; Lifetime Achievement Award, Nat. Acad. of Recording Arts and Scis, 1996. Officier de l'Ordre des Arts et des Lettres (France), 1990. *Address:* Derry Music, 601 Montgomery Street, Suite 800, San Francisco, CA 94111, USA; c/o Sutton Artists Corporation, 20 West Park Avenue, Suite 305, Long Beach, NY 11561, USA; Box 216, Wilton, CT 06897, USA.

BRUCE, family name of **Barons Aberdare,** and **Bruce of Donington,** of **Lord Balfour of Burleigh,** and of **Earl of Elgin.**

BRUCE; *see* Hovell-Thurlow-Cumming-Bruce.

BRUCE, Lord; Charles Edward Bruce; DL; Director: Scottish Lime Centre Trust; Environmental Trust for Scotland; Association for the Protection of Rural Scotland; *b* 19 Oct. 1961; *s* and *heir* of 11th Earl of Elgin, *qv*; *m* 1990, Amanda, *yr d* of James Movius; two *s* one *d*; *m* 2001, Dr Alice Enders. *Educ:* Eton College; Univ. of St Andrews (MA Hons). A Page of Honour to HM the Queen Mother, 1975–77. DL Fife, 1997. *Heir: s* Hon. James Andrew Charles Robert Bruce, Master of Bruce, *b* 16 Nov. 1991. *Address:* The Abbey House, Culross, Fife KY12 8JB. *T:* (01383) 880333, *Fax:* (01383) 881218.

BRUCE OF DONINGTON, Baron *cr* 1974 (Life Peer), of Rickmansworth; **Donald William Trevor Bruce;** economist; Chartered Accountant, Baker Tilly; writer; *b* 3 Oct. 1912; *s* of late W. T. Bruce, Norbury, Surrey; *m* 1st, 1939, Joan Letitia Butcher (marr. diss.); one *s* two *d* (and one *d* decd); 2nd, 1981, Cyrena Shaw Heard. *Educ:* Grammar School, Donington, Lincs; FCA 1947. Re-joined Territorial Army, March 1939; commissioned, Nov. 1939; Major, 1942; served at home and in France until May 1945 (despatches). MP (Lab) for North Portsmouth, 1945–50; Parliamentary Private Sec. to Minister of Health, 1945–50; Member Min. of Health delegn to Sweden and Denmark, 1946, and of House of Commons Select Cttee on Public Accounts, 1948–50. MEP, 1975–79. Opposition spokesman on Treasury, economic and industrial questions, House of Lords, 1979–83, on trade and industry, 1983–86, on Treasury and economic questions, 1986–90. *Publications:* (jtly) The State of the Nation, 1997; miscellaneous contributions on political science and economics to newspapers and periodicals. *Address:* Hobson House, 2 Bloomsbury Street, WC1B 3ST.

BRUCE, Christopher, CBE 1998; dancer, choreographer, opera producer; Artistic Director, Rambert Dance Company, since 1994; Resident Choreographer, Houston Ballet, since 1989; *b* Leicester, 3 Oct. 1945; *m* Marian Bruce; two *s* one *d*. *Educ:* Ballet Rambert Sch. Joined Ballet Rambert Company, 1963; leading dancer with co. when re-formed as modern dance co., 1966; Associate Dir, 1975–79; Associate Choreographer, 1979–87; Associate Choreographer, London Fest. Ballet, later English Nat. Ballet, 1986–91. Leading roles include: Pierrot Lunaire, The Tempest (Tetley); L'Apres-Midi d'un Faune (Nijinsky); Cruel Garden (also choreographed with Lindsay Kemp); choreographed: for Ballet Rambert: George Frideric (1st work), 1969; For These Who Die as Cattle, 1971; There Was a Time, 1972; Weekend, 1974; Ancient Voices of Children, 1975; Black Angels, 1976; Cruel Garden, 1977; Night with Waning Moon, 1979; Dancing Day, 1981; Ghost Dances, 1981; Berlin Requiem, 1982; Concertino, 1983; Intimate Pages, 1984; Sergeant Early's Dream, 1984; Ceremonies, 1986; Crossing, 1994; Meeting Point, 1995; Quicksilver, 1996; Stream, 1997; Four Scenes, 1998; God's Plenty, 1999; for London Festival Ballet, later English National Ballet: Land, 1985; The World Again, 1986; The Dream is Over, 1987; Swansong, 1987; Symphony in Three Movements, 1989; for Tanz Forum, Cologne: Wings, 1970; Cantata, 1981; for Nederlands Dans Theater: Village Songs, 1981; Curses and Blessings, 1983; Moonshine, 1993; for Houston Ballet: Gautama Buddha, 1989; Journey, 1990; Nature Dances, 1992; for Geneva: Rooster, 1991 (restaged for London Contemporary Dance Theatre, 1992); Kingdom, 1993; for London Contemporary Dance Theatre, Waiting, 1993; works for Royal Ballet, Batsheva Dance Co., Munich Opera Ballet, Gulbenkian Ballet Co., Australian Dance Theatre, Royal Danish Ballet, Royal Swedish Ballet. Kent Opera: choreographed and produced: Monteverdi's Il Ballo delle Ingrate, 1980; Combattimento di Tancredi e Clorinda, 1981; chor. John Blow's Venus and Adonis, 1980; co-prod Handel's Agrippina, 1982. Choreographed Mutiny (musical), Piccadilly, 1985. TV productions: Ancient Voices of Children, BBC, 1977; Cruel Garden, BBC, 1981–82; Ghost Dances, Channel 4, 1982, Danmark Radio, 1990; Requiem, Danish-German co-prodn, 1982; Silence is the end of our Song, Danish TV, 1984. Hon. DA De Montfort, 2000. Evening Standard's inaugural Dance Award, 1974; Internat. Theatre Inst. Award, 1993; Evening Standard Ballet Award for outstanding artistic achievement, 1996. *Address:* c/o Rambert Dance Co., 94 Chiswick High Road, W4 1SH; Houston Ballet, 1916 West Gray, PO 13150, Houston, TX 77219-3150, USA.

BRUCE, David, CA; Partner, Deloitte Haskins & Sells, 1974–87; *b* 21 Jan. 1927; *s* of David Bruce and Margaret (*née* Gregson); *m* 1955, Joy Robertson McAslan (*d* 1999); four *d*. *Educ:* High School of Glasgow. Commissioned, Royal Corps of Signals, 1947–49. Qualified as Chartered Accountant, 1955; Partner, Kerr McLeod & Co., Chartered Accountants, 1961 (merged with Deloitte Haskins & Sells, 1974); retired 1987. Vice-Pres., Inst. of Chartered Accountants of Scotland, 1978–79 and 1979–80, Pres. 1980–81. Mem., Council on Tribunals, 1984–90 (Mem., Scottish Cttee, 1984–90). *Address:* 8 Beechwood Court, Bearsden, Glasgow G61 2RY.

BRUCE, Fiona; Presenter: BBC Television News, since 1999; Crimewatch UK, since 2000; *b* 25 April 1964; *d* of John and Rosemary Bruce; *m* 1995, Nigel; one *s*. *Educ:* Hertford Coll., Oxford (MA French/Italian). Joined BBC, 1989: researcher, Panorama, 1989–91; reporter: Breakfast News, 1991–92; First Sight, 1992–93; Public Eye, 1993–95; Newsnight, 1995–98; Presenter: Antiques Show, 1998–; Six O'Clock News, 1999–. *Recreations:* playing with my son, playing the piano, eating out. *Address:* c/o BBC News, TV Centre, Wood Lane, W12 7RJ.

BRUCE, Sir (Francis) Michael Ian; *see* Bruce, Sir Michael Ian.

BRUCE, George John Done, RP 1959; painter of portraits, landscapes, still life, flowers; *b* 28 March 1930; *s* of 11th Lord Balfour of Burleigh, Brucefield, Clackmannan, Scotland and Violet Dorothy, *d* of Richard Henry Done, Tarporley, Cheshire.*b* of 12th Lord Balfour of Burleigh, *qv*. *Educ:* Byam Shaw Sch. of Drawing and Painting; by his portrait sitters. Pres., Royal Soc. of Portrait Painters, 1991–94 (Hon. Sec., 1970–84; Vice-Pres., 1984–89). *Recreations:* ski-ing, windsurfing, talking books. *Address:* 6 Pembroke Walk, W8 6PQ. *T:* (020) 7937 1493. *Club:* Athenæum.

BRUCE, George Robert, OBE 1984; poet and critic; *b* 10 March 1909; *s* of Henry George Bruce and Jeannie Roberta (*née* Gray); *m* 1935, Elizabeth Duncan (*d* 1994); one *s* one *d*. *Educ:* Fraserburgh Acad.; Aberdeen Univ. (MA 1st Cl. Hons English Lit. and Lang. 1932). Teacher of English and Hist., Dundee High Sch., 1933–46; gen. progs producer, Aberdeen, 1946–56, Features Producer, Edinburgh, 1956–70, BBC; Th. and Literary Critic, Sunday Times, 1964–76; (First) Fellow in Creative Writing, 1971–73, Extramural Lectr, 1973, Glasgow Univ. Visiting Professor: Union Theol Seminary, Richmond, Va, 1974; Coll. of Wooster, Ohio, 1976–77; St Andrews Presbyterian Coll., Laurinburg, N Carolina, 1985. Writer-in-Residence, Prescott Coll., Arizona, 1974; Scottish-Australian Writing Fellow, 1982. Hon. Member: Cockburn Assoc., 1975; Saltire Soc., 1986; Hon. Pres., Scottish Poetry Liby, 1991. Hon. DLitt: Coll. of Wooster, Ohio, 1977; Aberdeen, 2000. *Publications: poetry:* Sea Talk, 1944; Selected Poems, 1947; Landscapes and Figures, 1967; The Collected Poems of George Bruce, 1970; The Red Sky Poems, 1985; Perspective: poems 1970–1986, 1987; Pursuit: poems 1986–1998 (Scottish Book of Year, Saltire Soc.), 1999; Today Tomorrow: the collected poems of George Bruce 1933–2000, 2001; (with John Bellany) Woman of the North Sea (art/poetry), 2001; also ed anthologies of Scottish poetry; *non-fiction:* (with T. S. Halliday) Scottish Sculpture, 1946; Neil M. Gunn, 1971; Anne Redpath, 1974; The City of Edinburgh, 1974, rev. edn 1977; Festival in the North: the story of the Edinburgh Festival, 1975; William Soutar 1898–1943: the man and the poet, 1978; To Foster and Enrich: the first fifty years of the Saltire Society, 1986. *Recreation:* receiving and visiting friends. *Address:* 25 Warriston Crescent, Edinburgh EH3 5LB. *T:* (0131) 556 3848.

BRUCE, Sir Hervey (James Hugh); *see* Bruce-Clifton, Sir H. J. H.

BRUCE, Ian Cameron; freelance writer; Chairman, Ian Bruce Associates Ltd, since 1975; Consultant; Engineering Manufacturing Training Authority; TRG Ltd; *b* 14 March 1947; *s* of Henry Bruce and Ellen Flora Bruce (*née* Bingham); *m* 1969, Hazel Bruce (*née* Roberts); one *s* three *d*. *Educ:* Chelmsford Tech. High Sch.; Bradford Univ.; Mid-Essex Tech. Coll. Mem., Inst. of Management Services. Student apprentice, Marconi, 1965–67; Work Study Engineer: Marconi, 1967–69; Pye Unicam, 1969–70; Haverhill Meat Products, 1970–71; Factory Manager and Work Study Manager, BEPI (Pye), 1971–74; Factory Manager, Sinclair Electronics, 1974–75; Chm. and Founder, gp of Employment Agencies and Management Consultants, 1975–. MP (C) Dorset South, 1987–2001; contested (C) same seat, 2001. PPS to Social Security Ministers, 1992–94. Member, Select Committee: on Employment, 1990–92; on Science and Technol., 1995–97; on Information, 1997–2001; Vice-Chm., PITCOM, 1997–2001; Jt Chm., All Party Street Children Gp, 1992–2001; Vice Chairman: Cons. Employment Cttee, 1992; Cons. Social Security Cttee, 1995–97 (Sec., 1991–92); Cons. Educn and Employment Cttee, 1995–2001; Cons. Trade and Industry Cttee, 1999–2001; Pres., Cons. Technol. Forum, 1999–2001. Jt Chm., British Cayman Island Gp, 1995–2001; Vice Chm., British-Nepal Gp, 1993–2001; Secretary: British-Finnish Gp, 1995–2001; British-Romanian Gp, 1995–2001; Vice-Chm., European Informatics Market, 1993–. Parly Consultant to Telecommunication Managers Assoc., 1989–2001, to Trevor Gilbert Assoc., 1993–2001, to Fedn of Recruitment and Employment Services, 1996–97. *Publications:* numerous articles in press and magazines, both technical and political. *Recreations:* scouting, badminton, writing, wind surfing, sailing, camping, squash, ski-ing. *Address:* 14 Preston Road, Weymouth, Dorset DT3 6PZ. *T:* (01305) 833320; *e-mail:* ianbruce@supanet.com.

BRUCE, Ian Waugh; Director-General, Royal National Institute for the Blind, since 1983; Hon. Director, and Visiting Professor, Centre for Voluntary Sector and Not-for-Profit Management, City University Business School, since 1991; *b* 21 April 1945; *s* of Thomas Waugh Bruce and Una (*née* Eagle); *m* 1971, Anthea Christine, (Tina), *d* of Dr P. R. Rowland, FRSC; one *s* one *d*. *Educ:* King Edward VI Sch., Southampton; Central High Sch., Arizona; Univ. of Birmingham (BSocSc Hons 1968). CIMgt 1991. Apprentice Chem. Engr, Courtaulds, 1964–65; Marketing Trainee, then Manager, Unilever, 1968–70; Appeals and PR Officer, then Asst Dir, Age Concern England, 1970–74; Dir, The Volunteer Centre UK, 1975–81; Controller of Secretariat, then Asst Chief Exec., Bor. of Hammersmith and Fulham, 1981–83. Chm., Coventry Internat. Centre, 1964; spokesman, Artists Now, 1973–77. Consultant, UN Div. of Social Affairs, 1970–72; Mem., Prime Minister's Gp on Voluntary Action, 1978–79; Founding Sec., Volunteurope, Brussels, 1979–81; Adviser, BBC Community Progs Unit, 1979–81. Member: Art Panel, Art Film Cttee and New Activities Cttee, Arts Council of GB, 1967–71; National Good Neighbour Campaign, 1977–79; Exec. Cttee, NCVO, 1978–81, 1990–94; Council, Retired Executives Action Clearing House, 1978–83; Adv. Council, Centre for Policy on Ageing, 1979–83; Educn Adv. Council, IBA, 1981–83; Disability Alliance Steering Cttee, 1985–93; Exec. Cttee, Age Concern England, 1986–92; Nat. Adv. Council on Employment of People with Disabilities, 1987–98; DHSS Cttee on Inter-Agency Collaboration on Visual Handicap, 1987–88; Bd, Central London TEC, 1990–97 (Dep. Chm., 1996–97); Bd, Focus TEC, 1997–99; Co-Chair, Disability Benefits Consortium, 1988–; Chair: Nat. Adv. Cttee, Johns Hopkins Univ. Comparative Non Profit Study, 1996–99; Res. Cttee, Nat. Giving Campaign, 2001–. FRSA 1991. Hon. DSocSc Birmingham, 1995. Sir Raymond Priestley Expeditionary Award, Univ. of Birmingham, 1968. *Publications:* Public Relations and the Social Services, 1972; (jtly) Patronage of the Creative Artist, 1974; Blind and Partially Sighted Adults in Britain, 1992; Meeting Need: successful charity marketing, 1994, 2nd edn 1998; papers on visual handicap, voluntary and community work, old people, contemporary art, management and marketing. *Recreations:* the arts, the countryside. *Address:* 54 Mall Road, W6 9DG. *Club:* ICA.

BRUCE, Hon. James Michael Edward, CBE 1992; JP; Founder and Chairman, Scottish Woodlands Ltd, 1967–93; *b* 26 Aug. 1927; *s* of 10th Earl of Elgin, KT, CMG, TD and Hon. Katherine Elizabeth Cochrane, Countess of Elgin, DBE (*d* 1989); *m* 1st, 1950, Hon. (Margaret) Jean Dagbjørt Coats (marr. diss.), *d* of 2nd Baron Glentanar; two *s* one *d* (and one *s* decd); 2nd, 1975, Morven-Anne Macdonald (*d* 1994); two *s* two *d*; 3rd, 2000, Mrs Mary Elizabeth Hamilton. *Educ:* Eton; RAC, Cirencester (Goldstand Medal). FInstD. Served Scots Guards, 2nd Lieut. Mem., Home Grown Timber Adv. Cttee, 1969–93; Dir, Forest Industry Cttee, 1989–93. Vice-Pres., Scottish Opera, 1985–94. FRSA (Council Mem., 1988–95); Hon. Fellow: Game Conservancy, 1993; Scottish Council for Development and Industry, 1993. JP Perth, 1962. *Recreations:* gardens, boats, fishing, shooting. *Address:* Dron House, Balmanno, Perth PH2 9HG. *T:* (01738) 812786. *Clubs:* Pratt's; New (Edinburgh).

BRUCE, Malcolm Gray; MP Gordon, since 1983 (L 1983–88, Lib Dem since 1988); *b* 17 Nov. 1944; *s* of David Stewart Bruce and Kathleen Elmslie (*née* Delf); *m* 1st, 1969, Veronica Jane Wilson (marr. diss. 1992); one *s* one *d*; 2nd, 1998, Rosemary Vetterlein; one *d*. *Educ:* Wrekin Coll., Shropshire; St Andrews Univ. (MA 1966); Strathclyde Univ. (MSc 1970). Liverpool Daily Post, 1966–67; Buyer, Boots Pure Drug Co., 1967–68; A. Goldberg & Son, 1968–69; Res. Information Officer, NE Scotland Develt Authority, 1971–75; Marketing Dir, Noroil Publishing House (UK), 1975–81; Jt Editor/Publisher/Dir, Aberdeen Petroleum Publishing, 1981–84. Called to the Bar, Gray's Inn, 1995. Dep. Chm., Scottish Liberal Party, 1975–84 (Energy Spokesman, 1975–83); Liberal Parly Spokesman on Scottish Affairs, 1983–85, on Energy, 1985–87, on Trade and Industry, 1987–88; Alliance Parly Spokesman on Employment, 1987; Lib Dem Spokesman on Natural Resources (energy and conservation), 1988–90, on Trade and Industry, 1992–94, on Treasury affairs, 1994–99; Chm., Parly Lib Dems, 1999–2001. Member: Select Cttee on Trade and Industry, 1992–94, Treasury, 1994–98; Standards and Privileges Cttee, 1999–. Leader, Scottish Liberal Democrats, 1988–92. Rector of Dundee Univ., 1986–89. Vice-Pres., Nat. Deaf Children's Soc., 1990– (Pres., Grampian Br., 1985–). *Publications:* A New Life for the Country: a rural development programme for West Aberdeenshire, 1978; Putting Energy to Work, 1981; (with others) A New Deal for Rural Scotland, 1983; (with Paddy Ashdown) Growth from the Grassroots, 1985. *Recreations:* theatre, music, travel, fresh Scottish air. *Address:* Grove Cottage, Grove Lane, Torphins AB31 4HJ. *T:* (01339) 889120.

BRUCE, Sir Michael Ian, 12th Bt *cr* 1628; partner, Gossard-Bruce Co., from 1953; President, Newport Sailing Club Inc., since 1978; *b* 3 April 1926; *s* of Sir Michael William Selby Bruce, 11th Bt and Doreen Dalziel, *d* of late W. F. Greenwell; *S* father 1957; holds dual UK and US citizenship; has discontinued first forename, Francis; *m* 1st, 1947, Barbara Stevens (marr. diss., 1957), *d* of Frank J. Lynch; two *s*; 2nd, 1961, Frances Keegan (marr. diss., 1963); 3rd, 1966, Marilyn Ann (marr. diss., 1975), *d* of Carter Mulally; 4th, Patricia Gail (marr. diss. 1991), *d* of Frederich Root; 5th, 1994, Alessandro Conforto, MD. *Educ:* Forman School, Litchfield, Conn; Pomfret, Conn. Served United States Marine Corps, 1943–46 (Letter of Commendation); S Pacific area two years, Bismarck Archipelago, Bougainville, Philippines. Master Mariner's Ticket, 1968; Pres., Newport Academy of Sail, Inc., 1979–; Owner, American Maritime Co. Mem., US Naval Inst. *Recreations:* sailing, spear-fishing. *Heir:* *s* Michael Ian Richard Bruce, *b* 10 Dec. 1950. *Address:* 3424 Via Oporto #204, Newport Beach, CA 92663, USA. *T:* (714) 6757100. *Clubs:* Rockaway Hunt; Lawrence Beach; Balboa Bay (Newport Beach).

BRUCE, Michael Stewart Rae; *see* Marnoch, Rt Hon. Lord.

BRUCE, Prof. Victoria Geraldine, OBE 1997; PhD; CPsychol, FBPsS; FRSE; FBA 1999; Professor of Psychology, University of Stirling, since 1992 (Deputy Principal (Research), 1995–2001); *b* 4 Jan. 1953; *d* of Charles Frederick Bruce and Geraldine Cordelia Diane (*née* Giffard); *m* 1st, 1978, John Paul Fox (marr. diss.); 2nd, 1984, Anthony Michael Burton. *Educ:* Newcastle upon Tyne Church High Sch.; Newnham Coll., Cambridge (BA Nat. Scis 1974; MA, PhD Psychol. 1978). CPsychol, FBPsS 1989. University of Nottingham: Lectr, 1978–88; Reader, 1988–90; Prof. of Psychology, 1990–92. Member: Neuroscis Bd, MRC, 1989–92; ESRC, 1992–96 (Chm., Res. Progs Bd, 1992–); SHEFC, 1995– (Chm., Res. Policy Adv. Cttee, 1980–); Chm., Psychology Panel, RAE, HEFCE, 1996, 2001. President: Eur. Soc. for Cognitive Psychology, 1996–98; BPsS, 2001–March 2002. Editor, British Jl of Psychology, 1995–2000. FRSE 1996. *Publications:* (with P. R. Green) Visual Perception: physiology, psychology and ecology, 1985, 3rd edn (jtly) 1996; Recognising Faces, 1988; (with G. W. Humphreys) Visual Cognition: computational, experimental and neuropsychological perspectives, 1989; (ed) Face Recognition (special edn of European Jl of Cognitive Psychology), 1991; (ed jtly) Processing the Facial Image, 1992; (ed with A. M. Burton) Processing Images of Faces, 1992; (ed with G. W. Humphreys) Object and Face Recognition (special issue of Visual Cognition), 1994; (with I. Roth) Perception and Representation: current issues, 2nd edn 1995; (ed) Unsolved Mysteries of the Mind: tutorial essays in cognition, 1996; (with A. Young) In the Eye of the Beholder: the science of face perception, 1998; numerous articles in learned jls and edited books. *Recreations:* dogs, walking, games. *Address:* Department of Psychology, University of Stirling, Stirling FK9 4LA. *T:* (01786) 467640.

BRUCE-CLIFTON, Sir Hervey (James Hugh), 7th Bt *cr* 1804; hotelier, Oaklands Country Manor; *b* 3 Sept. 1952; *s* of Sir Hervey John William Bruce, 6th Bt, and Crista, (*d* 1984), *y d* of late Lt-Col Chandos De Paravicini, OBE; changed name to Bruce-Clifton on inheriting Clifton estate, 1996; *S* father, 1971; *m* 1st, 1979, Charlotte (marr. diss. 1991), *e d* of Jack Gore; one *s* one *d*; 2nd, 1992, Joanna, *y d* of Frank Pope; two *s*. *Educ:* Eton; Officer Cadet School, Mons. Major, the Grenadier Guards, 1984–96. *Recreations:* bungee jumping, body surfing, riding, tapestry. *Heir:* *s* Hervey Hamish Peter Bruce, *b* 20 Nov. 1986. *Address:* PO Box 19, Van Reenen 3372, Natal, South Africa. *Club:* Cavalry and Guards.

BRUCE-GARDNER, Sir Robert (Henry), 3rd Bt *cr* 1945, of Frilford, Berks; Director, Department of Conservation and Technology, Courtauld Institute, since 1990; *b* 10 June 1943; *s* of Sir Douglas Bruce-Gardner, 2nd Bt and of his 1st wife, Monica Flumerfelt (*née* Jefferson; decd); *S* father, 1997; *m* 1979, Veronica Ann Hand Oxborrow; two *s*. *Educ:* Uppingham; Reading Univ. (BA Fine Art); Courtauld Inst., Univ. of London (Dip.). Courtauld Institute: Asst Lectr, Dept of History of Art, 1968; Asst to Hd, 1970–76, Lectr, 1976–90, Dept of Technol. *Publications:* catalogue contrib., Metropolitan Mus., NY; contrib. The Conservator. *Recreation:* Himalayan travel. *Heir:* *s* Edmund Thomas Peter Bruce-Gardner, *b* 28 Jan. 1982. *Address:* Courtauld Institute of Art, Somerset House, Strand WC2R 0RN. *T:* (020) 7873 2197. *Club:* Travellers.

BRUCE-LOCKHART, Alexander John, (Sandy), OBE 1995; Leader, Kent County Council, since 1997; *b* 4 May 1942; *s* of John McGregor Bruce-Lockhart, CB, CMG, OBE and Margaret Evelyn Bruce-Lockhart (*née* Hone); *m* 1966, Tess Pressland; two *s* one *d*. *Educ:* Dragon Sch., Oxford; Sedbergh Sch., Yorks; Royal Agricultural Coll., Cirencester. Farmer, Zimbabwe, 1963–65, Kent, 1966–. Kent County Council: Mem., 1989–; Leader, Cons. Gp, 1993–; Pres., Transmanche Euroregion, 1998–99. Chm., Envmt and Regeneration Exec., LGA, 1999–. Pres., Maidstone Cons. Assoc., 1993–98 (Chm., 1989–92). *Recreations:* walking, shooting, tennis, family. *Address:* Upper Boy Court Farm, Headcorn, Kent TN27 9LA. *T:* (01622) 890651.

BRUCE LOCKHART, Logie, MA; Headmaster of Gresham's School, Holt, 1955–82; *b* 12 Oct. 1921; *s* of late John Harold Bruce Lockhart; *m* 1944, Josephine Agnew; two *s* two *d* (and one *d* decd). *Educ:* Sedbergh School; St John's College, Cambridge (Schol. and Choral Studentship). RMC Sandhurst, 1941; served War of 1939–45; 9th Sherwood Foresters, 1942; 2nd Household Cavalry (Life Guards), 1944–45. Larmor Award, 1947; Asst Master, Tonbridge School, 1947–55. Sponsor, Nat. Council for Educnl Standards. *Publications:* The Pleasures of Fishing, 1981; Stuff and Nonsense, 1996. *Recreations:* fishing, writing, music, natural history, games; Blue for Rugby football, 1945, 1946, Scottish International, 1948, 1950, 1953; squash for Cambridge, 1946. *Address:* Mead Barn, New Road, Blakeney, Norfolk NR25 7PA. *T:* (01263) 740588.

BRUDENELL-BRUCE, family name of **Marquess of Ailesbury**.

BRÜGGEN, Frans; conductor; formerly recorder player; Principal Guest Conductor, Orchestre de Paris, since 1998; *b* Amsterdam, 30 Oct. 1934. *Educ:* Conservatory and Univ. of Amsterdam. Prof., Royal Hague Conservatoire, 1955; formerly: Erasmus Prof., Harvard Univ.; Regents Prof., Univ. of Calif, Berkeley. Founder, Orch. of The Eighteenth Century, 1981; Artistic Dir, Stavanger Symphony Orch., 1990–94; guest conductor: Concertgebouw Orch., Amsterdam; Vienna Philharmonic Orch.; Rotterdam Philharmonic Orch.; Orch. of the Age of Enlightenment; Birmingham Philharmonic Orch.; Stockholm Philharmonic Orch. *Address:* c/o Askonas Holt Ltd, Lonsdale Chambers, 27 Chancery Lane, WC2A 1PF.

BRUINVELS, Peter Nigel Edward; Principal, Peter Bruinvels Associates, media management and public affairs consultants, founded 1986; Managing Director, Bruinvels News & Media, since 1992; news broadcaster, political commentator and freelance journalist; *b* 30 March 1950; *er s* of Stanley and Ninette Maud Bruinvels; *m* 1980, Alison Margaret, *o d* of Major David Gilmore Bacon, RA retd; two *d*. *Educ:* St John's Sch., Leatherhead; London Univ. (LLB Hons); Council of Legal Educn. Co. Sec., BPC Publishing, 1978–81; Sec./Lawyer, Amari PLC, 1981–82; Management Consultant and company director, 1982–. Chm., Dorking CPC, 1979–83; Mem., Cons. Nat. Union Exec., 1976–81. MP (C) Leicester E, 1983–87; contested (C): Leicester E, 1987; The Wrekin, 1997. Jt Chm., British Parly Lighting Gp; Vice-Chairman: Cons. Backbench Cttee on Urban Affairs and New Towns, 1984–87; Cons. Backbench Cttee on Education, 1985–87; Sec., Anglo-Netherlands Parly Gp, 1983–87; Chm., British-Malta Parly Gp, 1984–87; Member: Cons. Backbench Cttee on Home Affairs, 1983–87; Cons. Backbench Cttee on NI, 1983–87; Life Mem., British-Amer. Parly Gp, 1983. Promoter, Crossbows Act, 1987. Campaign Co-ordinator, Eastbourne, gen. election, 1992. Pres., Dorking Conservatives, 1995– (Chm., 1992–95). Director: Aalco Nottingham Ltd, 1983–88; Radio Mercury and Allied Radio, 1994–97. Special Advr, DTI Deregulation Task Force on Pharmaceuticals and Chemicals, 1993. Ind. Lay Chm., NHS Complaints Procedure, 1999–; Member: Social Security Appeals Tribunal, 1994–99; Child Support Appeals Tribunal, 1995–99. Mem., Surrey LEA, 1997– (Admissions Adjudicator, Schs Orgn Cttee, 1999–). Inspector, Denominational Ch Schs, OFSTED, 1994–. Church Comr, 1992– (Member: Pastoral and Houses Cttee, 1993–; Bd of Govs, 1998–; Mgt Adv. Cttee, 1999–); Member: Guildford Dio. Synod 1979–; Gen. Synod, 1985– (Mem. Legislative Cttee, 1991–96 and 2000–); Guildford Diocesan Bd of Educn, 1994–; Gen. Synod Bd of Educn, 1996–; Clergy Discipline (Doctrine) Gp, 1999–; Dir, Church Army, 1999– (Chm., Remuneration Cttee, 1999–). Mem., Jersey Wildlife Preservation Trust. Chm., Surrey Schs Orgn Cttee, 2000–. Gov., UC of Ripon and York St John, 1999–; Mem. Ct, Univ. of Sussex, 2001–. MIPR 1981; FRSA 1986; FCIM 1998 (Hon. MCIM 1987; Pres., Norwest Midlands, 1997–98); MCIJ (MJI 1988); Fellow, Industry and Parliament Trust. Granted Freedom, City of London, 1980. *Publications:* Zoning in on Enterprise, 1982; Light up the Roads, 1984; Sharing in Britain's Success—a Study in Widening Share Ownership, Through Privatisation, 1987; Investing in Enterprise—a Comprehensive Guide to Inner City Regeneration and Urban Renewal, 1989. *Recreations:* political campaigning, the media, Church of England. *Address:* 14 High Meadow Close, Dorking, Surrey RH4 2LG. *T:* (01306) 887082, (office) 887680, *Fax:* (0870) 133 1756. *Clubs:* Carlton, Inner Temple, Corporation of Church House.

BRUMFIT, Prof. Christopher John; Professor of Education, since 1984, Director, Centre for Language in Education, since 1986, University of Southampton; *b* 25 Oct. 1940; *s* of late John Raymond Brumfit and of Margaret May Brumfit (*née* Warner; she *m* 2nd, 1942, Frank Greenaway, *qv*); *m* 1st, 1965, Elizabeth Ann Sandars (marr. diss.); one *s*; 2nd, 1986, Rosamond Frances Mitchell; one *s*. *Educ:* Glyn Grammar Sch., Epsom; Brasenose Coll., Oxford (BA English Lang. and Lit.); Univ. of Essex (MA Applied Linguistics); PhD London 1983; Makerere Coll., Univ. of East Africa (DipEd). Head of English, Tabora Govt Sch., Tanzania, 1964–68; Lectr in Educn, Univ. of Dar es Salaam, 1968–71; Lectr in English and Linguistics, City of Birmingham Coll. of Educn, 1972–74; Lectr in Educn with ref. to English for Speakers of Other Languages, Univ. of London Inst. of Educn, 1974–80; Reader in Educn, Univ. of London, 1980–84; Southampton University: Head, Sch. of Educn, 1986–90; Dean, Faculty of Educnl Studies, 1990–93 and 1996–99; Head, Res. and Grad. Sch. of Educn, 1997–2000. Vis. Prof. of English, Univ. of Vienna, 2000–01. Chairman: BAAL, 1982–85; British Council English Teaching Adv. Cttee, 1991–98; British Assoc. of TESOL Qualifying Instns, 1991–94; Vice-Pres., Assoc. Internat. de Linguistique Appliquée, 1984–87; Member: Lang. Cttee, 1981–, Educn Cttee, 1992–, ESU; Lit. Adv. Cttee, British Council, 1989–97; Res. Cttee, Centre for Inf. on Lang. Teaching, 1991–; Bd, English 2000, 1996–98. Editor: ELT Documents, 1982–90; Review of English Language Teaching, 1990–96. Founding AcSS, 1999; Founding Fellow, British Inst. of English Lang. Teaching, 2000. *Publications:* (jtly) Teaching English as a Foreign Language, 1978; (with K. Johnson) The Communicative Approach to Language Teaching, 1979; Problems and Principles in English Teaching, 1980; English for International Communication, 1982; (with J. Roberts) An Introduction to Language and Language Teaching, 1983; (with M. Finocchiaro) The Functional-Notional Approach, 1983; Teaching Literature Overseas, 1983; Language Teaching Projects for the Third World, 1983; Communicative Methodology in Language Teaching, 1984; General English Syllabus Design, 1984; Language and Literature Teaching, 1985; (jtly) English as a Second Language in the UK, 1985; The Practice of Communicative Teaching, 1986; (with R. A. Carter) Literature and Language Teaching, 1986; Language in Teacher Education, 1988; (with R. Mitchell) Research in the Language Classroom, 1990; Literature on Language, 1991; Assessment in Literature Teaching, 1992; (with R. Bowers) Applied Linguistics and English Language Teaching, 1992; (with M. G. Benton) Teaching Literature, 1993; The Council of Europe and Language Teaching, 1995; (jtly) Language Education in the National Curriculum, 1995; Individual Freedom in Language Teaching, 2001; academic and professional papers. *Recreations:* Russian literature, academic cricket, opera, walking. *Address:* 4 The Finches, Southampton SO17 1UB. *T:* (023) 8055 7346. *Club:* Athenæum.

BRUMMELL, David; Legal Secretary to the Law Officers, since 2000; *b* 18 Dec. 1947; *s* of Ernest Brummell and Florence Elizabeth Brummell (*née* Martin). *Educ:* Nottingham High Sch.; Queens' Coll., Cambridge (MA Law 1973); Inst. of Linguistics (Dips in French, German and Spanish). Articled clerk, 1971–73, Asst Solicitor, 1973–75, Simmons & Simmons, Solicitors, London; Legal Adviser: Devon CC, 1975–77; W Sussex CC, 1977–79; Legal Asst, then Sen. Legal Asst, OFT, 1979–84; Treasury Solicitor's Department: Sen. Legal Asst, 1984–86, Grade 6, 1986, Central Adv. Div.; Grade 5, 1986–89; Litigation Div., 1989–2000, Head, 1995–2000. *Recreations:* tennis, swimming, music, languages. *Address:* 14A The Gateways, Park Lane, Richmond, Surrey TW9 2RB. *T:* (020) 8948 1247. *Clubs:* Athenæum; Thames Hare and Hounds.

BRUNA, Dick; graphic designer; writer and illustrator of children's books; *b* 23 Aug. 1927; *s* of A. W. Bruna and J. C. C. Erdbrink; *m* 1953, Irene de Jongh; two *s* one *d*. *Educ:* Primary Sch. and Gymnasium, Utrecht, Holland; autodidact. Designer of book jackets, 1945–, and of posters, 1947– (many prizes); writer and illustrator of children's books, 1953– (1st book, The Apple); also designer of postage stamps, murals, greeting cards and picture postcards. Exhibn based on Miffy (best-known character in children's books): Gemeentemuseum, Arnhem, 1977; Frans Halsmus. Haarlem, 1989; Centre Pompidou, Paris, 1991. Member: Netherlands Graphic Designers; Authors League of America Inc.; PEN Internat.; Alliance Graphique Internat. *Publications:* 100 titles published and 100 million copies printed by 2000; children's books translated into 41 languages. *Address:* (studio) 3 Jeruzalemstraat, 3512 KW, Utrecht. *T:* (30) 2316042. *Club:* Art Directors (Netherlands).

BRUNDIN, Clark Lannerdahl, PhD; Director, School of Management Studies, University of Oxford, 1992–96; President, Templeton College, Oxford, 1992–96; *b* 21 March 1931; *s* of late Ernest Walfrid Brundin and Elinor Brundin (*née* Clark); *m* 1959, Judith Anne (*née* Maloney); two *s* two *d*. *Educ:* Whittier High Sch., California; California Inst. of Technology; Univ. of California, Berkeley (BSc, PhD); MA Oxford. Electronics Petty Officer, US Navy, 1951–55. Associate in Mech. Engrg, UC Berkeley, 1956–57; Demonstr. Dept of Engrg Science, Univ. of Oxford, 1957–58; Res. Engr, Inst. of Engrg Res., UC Berkeley, 1959–63; Univ. Lectr, Dept of Engrg Sci., Univ. of Oxford, 1963–85, Vice-Chm., Gen. Bd of the Faculties, 1984–85; Jesus College, Oxford: Fellow and Tutor in Engrg, 1964–85; Sen. Tutor, 1974–77; Estates Bursar, 1978–84; Hon. Fellow, 1985; Vice Chancellor, Univ. of Warwick, 1985–92. Vis. Prof., Univ. of Calif Santa Barbara, 1978; Vis. Schol., Center for Studies in Higher Educn, UC Berkeley, 1997–. Mem., CICHE, 1987–96. Director: Cokethorpe Sch. Educnl Trust, 1983–96; Heritage Projects (Oxford) Ltd, 1985–97; Blackwell Science Ltd, 1990–98; Finsbury Growth Trust plc, 1995–2000; CAF America, 1997–2000 (Pres., 1998–2000); Chm., Anchor Housing Assoc., 1985–91 (Bd Mem., 1985–94). Governor: Magdalen College Sch., 1987–99; Coventry Sch. Foundn, 1991–99. CIMgt. *Publications:* articles on rarefied gas dynamics in sci. lit. *Recreations:* sailing, mending old machinery, music of all sorts. *Address:* 28 Observatory Street, Oxford OX2 6EW. *Club:* Fowey Gallants Sailing (Fowey, Cornwall).

BRUNDLE, Martin John; presenter and commentator, Formula One, ITV, since 1997; *b* 1 June 1959; *s* of late Alfred Edward John Brundle and of Alma Brundle (*née* Coe); *m* 1981, Elizabeth Mary Anthony; one *s* one *d*. *Educ:* King Edward VII Grammar Sch., King's Lynn; Norfolk Coll. of Arts and Technol. Formula One racing driver, 1984–96 (158 Grands Prix): World Sportscar Champion, 1988; winner: Daytona 24 hours, 1988; Le Mans 24 hours, 1990. *Recreations:* helicopter flying, motor biking. *Address:* Brundle House, Tottenhill, King's Lynn, Norfolk PE33 0SR. *Club:* British Racing Drivers' (Chm., 2000–) (Silverstone).

BRUNDTLAND, Gro Harlem, MD; Norwegian physician and politician; Director General, World Health Organisation, since 1998; *b* 20 April 1939; *d* of Gudmund and Inga Harlem; *m* 1960, Arne Olav Brundtland; two *s* one *d* (and one *s* decd). *Educ:* Oslo and Harvard Univs. MPH. MO, Directorate of Health, 1966–68; Asst Med. Dir, Oslo Bd of Health, 1968–74; Minister of Environment, 1974–79; MP (Lab) Oslo, 1977–96; Dep. Leader, Labour Party, 1975–81; Dep. Leader, Labour Parly Gp, 1979–81, Leader, 1981–90; Prime Minister of Norway, Feb.–Oct. 1981, 1986–89 and 1990–96. Mem., Indep. Commn on Disarmament and Security Issues; Vice-Pres., Socialist Internat.; Chm., UN World Commn on Envmt and Develt. Hon. DCL Oxon, 2001. *Publications:* articles on preventive medicine, school health and growth studies, internat. issues. *Recreation:* cross-country ski-ing. *Address:* World Health Organisation, 20 avenue Appia, 1211 Geneva 27, Switzerland.

BRUNEI, HM Sultan of; *see* Negara Brunei Darussalam.

BRUNER, Jerome Seymour, MA, PhD; Watts Professor of Psychology, University of Oxford, 1972–80; G. H. Mead University Professor, New School for Social Research, New York, 1980–88; Research Professor of Psychology, New York University, since 1987; Adjunct Professor of Law, New York University, since 1991; Fellow, New York Institute for the Humanities; *b* New York, 1 Oct. 1915; *s* of Herman and Rose Bruner; *m* 1st, 1940, Katherine Frost (marr. diss. 1956); one *s* one *d*; 2nd, 1960, Blanche Marshall McLane (marr. diss. 1984); 3rd, 1987, Carol Fleisher Feldman. *Educ:* Duke Univ. (AB 1937): Harvard Univ. (AM 1939, PhD 1941). US Intelligence, 1941; Assoc. Dir, Office Public Opinion Research, Princeton, 1942–44; govt public opinion surveys on war problems, 1942–43; political intelligence, France, 1943; Harvard University: research, 1945–72; Prof. of Psychology, 1952–72; Dir, Centre for Cognitive Studies, 1961–72. Lectr, Salzburg Seminar, 1952; Bacon Prof., Univ. of Aix-en-Provence, 1965. Editor, Public Opinion Quarterly, 1943–44; Syndic, Harvard Univ. Press, 1962–63. Member: Inst. Advanced Study, 1951; White House Panel on Educnl Research and Develt. Guggenheim Fellow, Cambridge Univ., 1955; Fellow: Amer. Psychol Assoc. (Pres., 1964–65; Distinguished Scientific Contrib. award, 1962); Amer. Acad. Arts and Sciences; Swiss Psychol Soc. (hon.); Soc. Psychol Study Social Issues (past Pres.); Amer. Assoc. Univ. Profs; Puerto Rican Acad. Arts and Sciences (hon.). Hon. DHL Lesley Coll., 1964; Hon. DSc: Northwestern Univ., 1965; Sheffield, 1970; Bristol, 1975; Hon. MA, Oxford, 1972; Hon. DSocSci, Yale, 1975; Hon. LLD: Temple Univ., 1965; Univ. of Cincinnati, 1966; Univ. of New Brunswick, 1969; Hon. DLitt: North Michigan Univ., 1969; Duke Univ., 1969; Dr *hc*: Sorbonne, 1974; Leuven, 1976; Ghent, 1977; Madrid, 1987; Free Univ., Berlin, 1988; Columbia, 1988; Stirling, 1990; Rome, 1992; Harvard, Bologna, Geneva, 1996. Internat. Balzan Prize, Fondazione Balzan, 1987. *Publications:* Mandate from the People, 1944; (with Krech) Perception and Personality: A Symposium, 1950; (with Goodnow and Austin) A Study of Thinking, 1956; (with Smith and White) Opinions and Personality, 1956; (with Bresson, Morf and Piaget) Logique et Perception, 1958; The Process of Education, 1960; On Knowing: Essays for the Left Hand, 1962; (ed) Learning about Learning: A conference report, 1966; (with Olver, Greenfield, and others) Studies in Cognitive Growth, 1966; Toward a Theory of Instruction, 1966; Processes of Cognitive Growth: Infancy, Vol III, 1968; The Relevance of Education, 1971; (ed Anglin) Beyond the Information Given: selected papers of Jerome S. Bruner, 1973; (with Connolly) The Growth of Competence, 1974; (with Jolly and Sylva) Play: its role in evolution and development, 1976; Under Five in Britain, 1980; Communication as Language, 1982; In Search of Mind: essays in autobiography, 1983; Child's Talk, 1983; Actual Minds, Possible Worlds, 1986; Acts of Meaning, 1990; The Culture of Education, 1996; (with A. G. Amsterdam) Minding the Law, 2000; contribs technical and professional jls. *Recreation:* sailing. *Address:* 200 Mercer Street, New York, NY 10012, USA. *Clubs:* Royal Cruising; Century (New York); Cruising Club of America.

BRUNNER, Adrian John Nelson; QC 1994; a Recorder, since 1990; *b* 18 June 1946; *s* of late Comdr Hugh Brunner, DSC, RN and of Elizabeth Brunner; *m* 1970, Christine Anne Hughes; one *s* four *d*. *Educ:* Ampleforth Coll.; BRNC; Coll. of Law. Served RN, 1963–66. Called to the Bar, Inner Temple, 1968 (Major Schol., 1967). *Recreations:* yachting, shooting. *Address:* Furneaux Pelham Hall, Buntingford, Herts SG9 0LB; Holborn Head Farm, Scrabster, Caithness KW14 7UW. *Clubs:* Royal Yacht Squadron, Bar Yacht.

BRUNNER, Hugo Laurence Joseph; JP; Lord-Lieutenant of Oxfordshire, since 1996; *b* 17 Aug. 1935; *s* of Sir Felix Brunner, 3rd Bt and Dorothea Elizabeth (*née* Irving); *m* 1967, Mary Rose Pollen; five *s* one *d*. *Educ:* Eton; Trinity Coll., Oxford (MA Hons; Hon. Fellow, 1994). With OUP, 1958–65 (First Rep., Hong Kong, 1960–62); Sales Dir, Chatto & Windus, publishers, 1966–76; Dep. Gen. Publisher, OUP, 1977–79; Man. Dir, then Chm., Chatto & Windus, 1979–85. Director: Caithness Glass Ltd, 1966–96 (Chm., 1984–91); Brunner Investment Trust PLC, 1987–99; SCM Press Ltd, 1991–97. Contested (L) Torquay, 1964 and 1966. Chm., Oxford DAC for Care of Churches, 1985–98. Governor: St Edward's Sch., Oxford, 1991–; Ripon Coll. Cuddesdon, 1992–. Dep. Steward, Univ. of Oxford, 2001. High Sheriff, 1988–89, DL 1993, JP 1996, Oxon. Hon. LLD Oxford Brookes, 1999. *Recreations:* hill-walking, church visiting, study of animal-powered engines. *Address:* 26 Norham Road, Oxford OX2 6SF. *T:* (01865) 316431. *Clubs:* Reform, Chelsea Arts.

BRUNNER, Sir John Henry Kilian, 4th Bt *cr* 1895; *b* 1 June 1927; *s* of Sir Felix John Morgan Brunner, 3rd Bt, and of Dorothea Elizabeth, OBE, *d* of late Henry Brodribb Irving; *S* father, 1982; *m* 1955, Jasmine Cecily, *d* of late John Wardrop Moore; two *s* one *d*. *Educ:* Eton; Trinity Coll., Oxford (BA 1950). Served as Lieut RA. On staff, PEP, 1950–53; Talks producer, 1953; Economic Adviser, Treasury, 1958–61; Asst Manager, Observer, 1961. *Heir:* *s* Nicholas Felix Minturn Brunner, *b* 16 Jan. 1960. *Address:* 138 Victoria Avenue, Dalkeith, WA 6009, Australia.

BRUNNING, David Wilfrid; His Honour Judge Brunning; a Circuit Judge, since 1988; Designated Civil Judge, Nottingham Group, since 1999; *b* 10 April 1943; *s* of Wilfred and Marion Brunning; *m* 1967, Deirdre Ann Shotton; three *s*. *Educ:* Burton upon Trent Grammar Sch.; Worcester Coll., Oxford (BA 1965, DPA 1966). Called to the Bar, Middle Temple, 1969; Midland and Oxford Circuit, 1970–88; Assigned Judge and Designated Care Judge, Nottingham County Court, 1995–98. *Recreations:* campanology, squash, walking, wine, music. *Address:* Nottingham County Court, Canal Street, Nottingham NG1 7EJ.

BRUNO, Franklin Roy, (Frank), MBE 1990; professional boxer, 1982–96; *b* 16 Nov. 1961; *s* of late Robert Bruno and of Lynette Bruno (*née* Campbell); *m* 1990, Laura Frances Mooney; one *s* two *d*. *Educ:* Oak Hall Sch., Sussex. Amateur boxer, Sir Philip Game Amateur Boxing Club, 1977–80: 21 contests, 20 victories; London ABA and Nat. ABA Heavyweight Champion, 1980; professional career, 1982–96: 45 contests, 40 victories; European Champion, 1985–86; WBC World Heavyweight Champion, 1995. Pantomime appearances: Aladdin, Dominion, 1989; Nottingham, 1990; Robin Hood, Bristol, 1991; Jack and the Beanstalk, Bradford, 1996; Goldilocks, Birmingham, 1997, Southampton, 1999. Sports Personality of Year, Stars Orgn for Spastics, 1989, 1990. *Publications:* Know What I Mean?, 1987; Eye of the Tiger, 1992; From Zero to Hero, 1996. *Recreations:* swimming, training, driving, eating, shopping for good clothes. *Address:* PO Box 2266, Brentwood, Essex CM15 0AQ. *Fax:* (01277) 822209.

BRUNSDEN, Prof. Denys, PhD; Professor of Geography, Department of Geography, King's College, University of London, 1983–96, now Emeritus; *b* 14 March 1936; *s* of Francis Stephen Brunsden and Mabel Florence (*née* Martin); *m* 1961, Elizabeth Mary Philippa (*née* Wright); one *s* one *d*. *Educ:* Torquay Grammar Sch. for Boys; King's Coll., Univ. of London (BSc Hons Geography; PhD 1963). King's College, London: Tutorial Student, 1959–60; Asst Lectr, 1960–63; Lectr, 1963–75; Reader, 1975–83; Fellow, 1998. Vis. Lectr, 1964–65, Erskine Fellow, 1988, Univ. of Canterbury, NZ; Vis. Associate Prof., Louisiana State Univ., 1971; Vis. Prof., Univ. of Durham, 1996–2002. Founder Consultant, Geomorphological Services Ltd, 1972. Chairman: British Geomorphol Res. Gp, 1985–86; Wkg Pty for Collaboration in Internat. Geomorphology, 1985–; President: Geographical Assoc., 1986–87 (Hon. Mem., 1996); Internat. Assoc. of Geomorphologists, 1989–93 (Sen. Past Pres., 1993–97; Hon. Fellow 1997); Vice-Pres., RGS, 1984–87; Hon. Mem., Polish Assoc. of Geomorphologists, 1993. Hon. DSc Plymouth, 2000. Gill Meml Award, RGS (for contribs to study of mass movement and fieldwork), 1977; Republic of China Award Lectr, 1988–89; Assoc. of American Geographers Honours, 1991; Linton Award, British Geomorphological Res. Gp, 1993; William Smith Medal, Geol Soc. of London, 2000. *Publications:* Dartmoor, 1968; Slopes, Forms and Process, 1970; (with J. C. Doornkamp) The Unquiet Landscape, 1971 (USA 1976, Australia 1976, Germany 1977); (with J. B. Thornes) Geomorphology and Time, 1977; (with C. Embleton and D. K. C. Jones) Geomorphology: present problems, future prospects, 1978; (with J. C. Doornkamp and D. K. C. Jones) The Geology, Geomorphology and Pedology of Bahrain, 1980; (with R. U. Cooke, J. C. Doornkamp and D. K. C. Jones) The Urban Geomorphology of Drylands, 1982; (with D. B. Prior) Slope Instability, 1984; (with R. Gardner, A. S. Goudie and D. K. C. Jones) Landshapes, 1989; Natural Disasters, 1990; (with A. S. Goudie) The Environment of the British Isles: an Atlas, 1995; (with R. Dikau) Landslide Recognition, 1996. *Recreations:* making walking sticks and shepherd's-crooks, painting, reading thrillers, watching TV, enjoying dinner parties and fine wine, talking, travelling to exotic places, eating, drinking and relaxing in the Drôme. *Address:* Department of Geography, King's College London, Strand, WC2R 2LS. *Club:* Geographical.

BRUNSDON, Norman Keith; Chairman, Anglican Foundation for Aged Care, 1993–2001; Director, Arthur Yates & Co. Ltd, 1993–2001; *b* 11 Jan. 1930; *s* of late G. A. Brunsdon; *m* 1953, Ruth, *d* of late W. Legg; one *s* one *d*. *Educ:* Wagga Wagga High Sch., NSW. FCA. Price Waterhouse, Australia: joined, 1951; Partner, 1963; Mem. Policy Cttee (Bd), 1970–86; Partner-in-Charge, Sydney, 1975–81; Chm. and Sen. Partner, Australia, 1982–86; World Firm Policy Cttee (Bd) and Council of Firms, 1979–86; Agent Gen. for NSW in London, 1989–91. Chm., Aust. Govt's Taxation Adv. Cttee, 1979–83; Trustee, Econ. Develt of Aust. Cttee, 1977–86. Vice-Pres., Thai-Aust. Chamber of Commerce & Industry, 1982–85; Member: Pacific Basin Econ. Council, 1982–86; Aust. Japan Business Co-op. Cttee, 1982–86. Member: Standing Cttee, C of E Dio. Sydney, 1969–74; C of E Children's Homes Cttee, 1974–84 (Treasurer, 1969–75; Acting Chm., 1972–73); Chm., Anglican Retirement Villages, dio. Sydney, 1991–98. Governor, King's Sch., Parramatta, 1977–86; Trustee, Bark Endeavour Foundn Pty Ltd, 1992–2001. Hon. Mem., Cook Soc. Freeman, City of London, 1989. FAICD. *Recreations:* music, opera, theatre, reading, sailing, golf. *Address:* 71 Coolawin Road, Northbridge, NSW 2063, Australia. *T:* (2) 99580641, *Fax:* (2) 99672835. *Clubs:* Australian (Sydney); Royal Sydney Yacht Squadron.

BRUNSKILL, Ronald William, OBE 1990; MA, PhD; FSA; lecturer and author; Professor, Centre for Conservation Studies, School of Architecture (formerly School of the Built Environment), De Montfort University, 1995–2001; *b* 3 Jan. 1929; *s* of William Brunskill and Elizabeth Hannah Brunskill; *m* 1960, Miriam Allsopp; two *d*. *Educ:* Bury High Sch.; Univ. of Manchester (BA Hons Arch. 1951, MA 1952, PhD 1963). Registered Architect and ARIBA, 1951; FSA 1975. National Service, 2nd Lieut RE, 1953–55. Studio Asst in Arch., Univ. of Manchester, 1951–53; Architectural Asst, LCC, 1955; Asst in Arch., Univ. of Manchester, 1955–56; Commonwealth Fund Fellow (arch. and town planning), MIT, 1956–57; Architect to Williams Deacon's Bank, 1957–60; Manchester

University: Lectr, 1960–73; Sen. Lectr, 1973–84; Reader in Architecture, 1984–89; Hon. Fellow, Sch. of Architecture, 1989–95; Architect in private practice, 1960–66; Partner, Carter, Brunskill & Associates, chartered architects, 1966–69, Consultant, 1969–73. Vis. Prof., Univ. of Florida, Gainesville, 1969–70; Hon. Vis. Prof., De Montfort Univ., 1994–95. President: Vernacular Arch. Gp, 1974–77; Cumberland and Westmorland Antiquarian and Archaeol Soc., 1990–93 (Vice-Pres., 1975–90); Friends of Friendless Churches, 1999– (Chm., 1990–98); Vice-President: Weald and Downland Museum Trust, 1980–; Ancient Monuments Soc., 2000– (Hon. Architect, 1983–88; Vice-Chm., 1988–90; Chm., 1990–2000); Urban Parks Adv. Panel, Heritage Lottery Fund, 1995–99; Member: Historic Bldgs Council for England, 1978–84; Royal Commn on Ancient and Historical Monuments of Wales, 1983–97 (Vice Chm., 1993–97); Historic Buildings and Monuments Commn (English Heritage), 1989–95 (Member: Historic Buildings Adv. Cttee, 1984–95 (Chm., 1989–95); Ancient Monuments Adv. Cttee, 1984–90; Chm., Cathedrals and Churches Adv. Cttee, 1989–95); Cathedrals Adv. Commn for England, 1981–91; Cathedrals Fabric Commn for England, 1991–96; Manchester DAC for Care of Churches, 1973–79 and 1987–93; Manchester Cathedral Fabric Cttee, 1987–96; Blackburn Cathedral Fabric Cttee, 1989–96 (Chm.); Chester Cathedral Fabric Cttee, 1989–94; Council, Soc. for Folk Life Studies, 1969–72 and 1980–83. Trustee, British Historic Buildings Trust, 1985–92. Hon. DA De Montfort, 2001. Neale Bursar, RIBA, 1962; President's Award, Manchester Soc. of Architects, 1977. *Publications:* Illustrated Handbook of Vernacular Architecture, 1971, 3rd edn (enlarged) 1987; Vernacular Architecture of the Lake Counties, 1974; (with Alec Clifton-Taylor) English Brickwork, 1977; Traditional Buildings of Britain, 1981, 2nd edn (enlarged) 1992; Houses (in series, Collins Archaeology), 1982; Traditional Farm Buildings of Britain, 1982, 2nd edn (enlarged) 1987; Timber Building in Britain, 1985, 2nd edn (enlarged) 1994; Brick Building in Britain, 1990; Houses and Cottages of Britain, 1997; Traditional Farm Buildings and their Conservation, 1999; Vernacular Architecture: an illustrated handbook, 2000; Traditional Buildings of Cumbria, 2002; articles and reviews in archaeol and architectural jls. *Recreation:* enjoying the countryside. *Address:* Three Trees, 8 Overhill Road, Wilmslow SK9 2BE. *T:* (01625) 522099; 159 Glan Gors, Harlech, Gwynedd LL46 2SA. *Club:* Athenæum.

BRUNSON, Michael John, OBE 2000; broadcaster and journalist; Political Editor, ITN, 1986–2000; *b* 12 Aug. 1940; *s* of Geoffrey Brunson and Ethel (*née* Mills); *m* 1965, Susan Margaret Brown; two *s*. *Educ:* Bedford Sch.; Queen's Coll., Oxford (BA Theol. 1963; MA). VSO, Sierra Leone, 1963–64; BBC General Trainee, 1964–65; Reporter, BBC SE Radio News, 1965–66; Asst Producer, BBC TV Current Affairs, 1966–68; Independent Television News: Reporter, 1968–72; Washington Corresp., 1972–77; Reporter, 1977–80; Diplomatic Editor, 1980–86; Campaign Reporter with Mrs Thatcher, 1979 and 1983 Gen. Elections. Chairman: Parly Lobby Journalists, 1994; Parly Press Gall., 1999. Member: Govt Adv. Gp on Citizenship Educn, 1997–98; Preparation for Adult Life Gp, QCA, 1998; Adult Learning Cttee, Learning and Skills Council, 2001–. Trustee, Citizenship Foundn, 2000–. Columnist, The House Mag. (H of C), 1989–90, 1997–99; Pol Ed., Saga Magazine, 2000–. RTS News Event Award, 1994; RTS Judges' Award for Lifetime Achievement, 2000. *Publication:* A Ringside Seat (autobiog.), 2000. *Recreations:* gardening, listening to music. *Address:* c/o Knight Ayton Management, 114 St Martin's Lane, WC2N 4AZ. *T:* (020) 7836 5333. *Club:* Oxford and Cambridge.

BRUNT, Peter Astbury, FBA 1969; Camden Professor of Ancient History, Oxford University, and Fellow of Brasenose College, 1970–82; *b* 23 June 1917; *s* of Rev. Samuel Brunt, Methodist Minister, and Gladys Eileen Brunt. *Educ:* Ipswich Sch.; Oriel Coll., Oxford. Open Schol. in History, Oriel Coll., Oxford, 1935; first classes in Class. Mods, 1937, and Lit. Hum., 1939; Craven Fellowship, 1939. Temp. Asst Principal and (later) Temp. Principal, Min. of Shipping (later War Transport), 1940–45. Sen. Demy, Magdalen Coll., Oxford, 1946; Lectr in Ancient History, St Andrews Univ., 1947–51; Fellow and Tutor of Oriel Coll., Oxford, 1951–67, Dean, 1959–64, Hon. Fellow, 1973; Fellow and Sen. Bursar, Gonville and Caius Coll., Cambridge, 1968–70. Editor of Oxford Magazine, 1963–64; Chm., Cttee on Ashmolean Museum, 1967; Deleg., Clarendon Press, 1971–79; Mem. Council, British Sch. at Rome, 1972–87; Pres., Soc. for Promotion of Roman Studies, 1980–83. *Publications:* Thucydides (selections in trans. with introd.), 1963; Res Gestae Divi Augusti (with Dr J. M. Moore), 1967; Social Conflicts in the Roman Republic, 1971; Italian Manpower 225 BC-AD 14, 1971, rev. edn 1987; (ed) Arrian's Anabasis (Loeb Classical Library), vol. I, 1976, vol. II, 1983; The Fall of the Roman Republic and related essays, 1988; Roman Imperial Themes, 1990; Studies in Ancient Greek History and Thought, 1992; articles in classical and historical jls. *Address:* 37 Woodstock Close, Woodstock Road, Oxford OX2 8DB. *T:* (01865) 553024.

BRUNT, Rev. Prof. Peter William, CVO 2001; OBE 1994; MD, FRCP, FRCPE; Physician to the Queen in Scotland, 1983–2001; Consultant Physician and Gastroenterologist, Grampian Health Board, Aberdeen, since 1970; Clinical Professor of Medicine, University of Aberdeen, since 1996; Non-Stipendiary Minister, Bieldside, since 1996; *b* 18 Jan. 1936; *s* of late Harry Brunt and Florence J. J. Airey; *m* 1961, Dr Anne Lewis, *d* of Rev. R. H. Lewis; three *d*. *Educ:* Manchester Grammar Sch.; Cheadle Hulme Sch.; King George V Sch.; Univ. of Liverpool (MB, ChB 1959; MD 1967). Gen. Med. training, Liverpool Royal Infirmary and Liverpool Hosps, 1959–64; Research Fellow, Johns Hopkins Univ. Sch. of Medicine, Baltimore, USA, 1965–67; Lectr in Medicine, Edinburgh Univ., 1967–68; Senior Registrar, Gastrointestinal Unit, Western Gen. Hosp., Edinburgh, 1968–69; Clin. Sen. Lectr in Medicine, Aberdeen Univ., 1970–96. Hon. Lectr in Medicine, Royal Free Hosp. Sch. of Medicine, Univ. of London, 1969–70. Mem., Assoc. of Physicians of GB and Ireland (Pres., 1995–96). Ordained deacon, 1996, priest, 1997, Scottish Episcopal Church. *Publications:* (with M. Losowsky and A. E. Read) Diseases of the Liver and Biliary System, 1984; (with P. F. Jones and N. A. G. Mowat) Gastroenterology, 1984. *Recreations:* mountaineering, music, operatics, Crusaders' Union. *Address:* 17 Kingshill Road, Aberdeen AB15 5JY. *T:* (01224) 314204.

BRUNTISFIELD, 2nd Baron *cr* 1942, of Boroughmuir; **John Robert Warrender,** OBE 1963; MC 1943; TD 1967; DL; Bt 1715; *b* 7 Feb. 1921; *s* of 1st Baron Bruntisfield, MC and Dorothy (*d* 1975), *y d* of Col R. H. Rawson, MP; *S* father, 1993; *m* 1st, 1948, (Anne) Moireen Campbell (*d* 1976), 2nd *d* of Sir Walter Campbell, KCIE; two *s* two *d*; 2nd, 1977, Mrs Shirley Crawley (*d* 1981), *o d* of E. J. L. Ross; 3rd, 1985, Mrs (Kathleen) Joanna Graham, JP, *o d* of David Chancellor. *Educ:* Eton; RMC, Sandhurst. Royal Scots Greys (2nd Dragoons), 1939–48; ADC to Governor of Madras, 1946–48; comd N Somerset Yeomanry/44th Royal Tank Regt, 1957–62; Dep. Brigadier RAC (TA), Southern and Eastern Commands, 1962–67. Mem., Queen's Body Guard for Scotland (Royal Co. of Archers) (Brigadier, 1973–85). DL Somerset 1965. *Recreations:* shooting, fishing. *Heir: s* Hon. Michael John Victor Warrender [*b* 9 Jan. 1949; *m* 1978, Baroness Walburga von Twickel; one *s*]. *Address:* 18 Warriston Crescent, Edinburgh EH3 5LB. *T:* (0131) 556 3701. *Clubs:* Puffin's, New (Edinburgh).

See also Hon. R. H. Warrender.

BRUNTON, Sir (Edward Francis) Lauder, 3rd Bt *cr* 1908; physician; *b* 10 Nov. 1916; *s* of Sir Stopford Brunton, 2nd Bt, and Elizabeth, *o d* of late Professor J. Bonsall Porter; *S* father, 1943; *m* 1946, Marjorie, *o d* of David Sclater Lewis, MSc, MD, CM, FRCP (C); one *s* one *d*. *Educ:* Trinity College School, Port Hope; Bryanston School; McGill Univ. BSc 1940; MD, CM 1942; served as Captain, RCAMC. Hon. attending Physician, Royal Victoria Hosp., Montreal. Fellow: American Coll. of Physicians; Internat. Soc. of Hematology; Life Mem., Montreal Mus. of Fine Arts; Life Governor, Art Gall. of Nova Scotia. *Heir: s* James Lauder Brunton, MD, FRCP(C) [*b* 24 Sept. 1947; *m* 1967, Susan, *o d* of Charles Hons; one *s* one *d*]. *Address:* PO Box 140, Guysborough, Nova Scotia B0H 1N0, Canada.

BRUNTON, Sir Gordon (Charles), Kt 1985; Chairman: Communications and General Consultants, since 1985; The Racing Post plc, 1985–97; Verity Group plc (formerly Wharfedale plc), 1991–97; Green Field Leisure Group Ltd, since 1992; Telme.com (formerly PhoneLink) plc, since 1993; *b* 27 Dec. 1921; *s* of late Charles Arthur Brunton and late Hylda Pritchard; *m* 1st, 1946, Nadine Lucile Paula Sohr (marr. diss. 1965); one *s* two *d* (and one *s* decd); 2nd, 1966, Gillian Agnes Kirk; one *s* one *d*. *Educ:* Cranleigh Sch.; London Sch. of Economics. Commnd into RA, 1942; served Indian Army, Far East; Mil. Govt, Germany, 1946. Joined Tothill Press, 1947; Exec. Dir, Tothill, 1956; Man. Dir, Tower Press Gp of Cos, 1958; Exec. Dir, Odhams Press, 1961; joined Thomson Organisation, 1961; Man. Dir, Thomson Publications, 1961; Dir, Thomson Organisation, 1963; Chm., Thomson Travel, 1965–68; Man. Dir and Chief Exec., Internat. Thomson Orgn plc (formerly Thomson British Hldgs) and The Thomson Orgn Ltd, 1968–84; Pres., Internat. Thomson Orgn Ltd, 1978–84. Director: Times Newspapers Ltd, 1967–81; Sotheby Parke Bernet Group, 1978–83 (Chm., 1982–83, Chm. Emeritus, Sotheby's Holding Inc., 1983); Cable and Wireless plc, 1981–91; Yattendon Investment Trust, 1985–; Chairman: Bemrose Corp., 1978–91; Martin Currie Pacific Trust, 1985–92; Community Industry, 1985–92; Euram Consulting, 1985–92; Cavendish Shops, 1985–93; Mercury Communications, 1986–90; Cavendish Retail, 1987–; Ingersoll Publications, 1988–91. President: Periodical Publishers Assoc., 1972–74, 1981–83; Nat. Advertising Benevolent Soc., 1973–75 (Trustee, 1980–); History of Advertising Trust, 1981–84; CPU, 1991–94; Chm., EDC for Civil Engrg, 1978–84; Member: Printing and Publishing Ind. Trng Bd, 1974–78; Supervisory Bd, CBI Special Programmes Unit, 1980–84; Business in the Community Council, 1981–84; Chm., Independent Adoption Service, 1986–. Mem., South Bank Bd, Arts Council, 1985–92. Governor: LSE, 1971–95 (Fellow, 1978); Ashridge Management Coll., 1983–86; Ct of Governors, Henley—The Management Coll., 1983–85; Mem. Council, Templeton College (formerly Oxford Centre for Management Studies), 1976–95; Mem., Finance Cttee, OUP, 1985–91. *Recreations:* books, breeding horses. *Address:* (office) North Munstead, North Munstead Lane, Godalming, Surrey GU8 4AX. *T:* (01483) 424181, *Fax:* (01483) 426043. *Club:* Garrick.

BRUNTON, Sir Lauder; *see* Brunton, Sir E. F. L.

BRUS, Prof. Wlodzimierz, PhD; Professor of Modern Russian and East European Studies, University of Oxford, 1985–88, now Emeritus Professor; Professorial Fellow, Wolfson College, 1985–88, now Emeritus Fellow; Senior Research Fellow, St Antony's College, Oxford, 1989–91; *b* 23 Aug. 1921; *s* of Abram Zylberberg and Helena (*née* Askanas); changed surname to Brus, 1944; *m* 1st, 1940, Helena Wolińska; 2nd, 1945, Irena Stergień; two *d*; 3rd, 1956, Helena Wolińska; one *s*. *Educ:* Saratov, USSR (MA Economic Planning); Warsaw, Poland (PhD Pol. Econ.). Polish Army, 1944–46. Junior Editor, Nowe Drogi (theoretical journal of Polish Workers' (later United Workers') Party), 1946–49; Asst (later Associate) Prof. of Political Economy, Central Sch. of Planning & Statistics, Warsaw, 1949–54; Hd of Dept of Political Economy, Inst. of Social Sciences attached to Central Cttee, Polish United Workers' Party, 1950–56; Prof. of Political Econ., Univ. of Warsaw, 1954–68; Dir, Research Bureau, Polish Planning Commn, 1956–68; Vice-Chm., Econ. Adv. Council of Poland, 1957–63; research worker, Inst. of Housing, Warsaw, 1968–72; Vis. Sen. Res. Fellow, Univ. of Glasgow, 1972–73; Sen. Res. Fellow, St Antony's Coll., Oxford, 1973–76; Univ. Lectr and Fellow, Wolfson Coll., Oxford, 1976–85. Visiting Professor (or Senior Fellow): Rome, 1971; Catholic Univ. of Louvain, 1973; Columbia, 1982; Johns Hopkins Bologna Centre, 1983; Siena, 1991. Consultant to World Bank, 1980–82, 1984. Officers' Cross, Order of Polonia Restituta, Poland, 1954; Polish and Soviet war medals, 1944, 1945. *Publications:* The Law of Value and Economic Incentives, 1956 (trans Hungarian, 1957); General Problems of Functioning of the Socialist Economy, 1961 (published in 10 langs); Economics and Politics of Socialism, 1973 (published in 6 langs); Socialist Ownership and Political Systems, 1975 (published in 8 langs); Economic History of Eastern Europe, 1983 (published in 6 langs); (with K. Laski) From Marx to the Market: socialism in search of an economic system, 1989; contribs to Soviet Studies, Jl of Comparative Economics, Cambridge Jl of Economics. *Recreations:* walking, swimming. *Address:* 21 Bardwell Court, Bardwell Road, Oxford OX2 6SX. *T:* (01865) 553790.

BRUTON, John (Gerard); TD (Fine Gael), Meath, Dáil Eireann (Parliament of Ireland), since 1969; *b* 18 May 1947; *s* of Matthew Joseph Bruton and Doris Bruton (*née* Delany); *m* 1981, Finola Gill; one *s* three *d*. *Educ:* St Dominic's Coll., Dublin; Clongowes Wood Coll., Co. Kildare; University Coll., Dublin (BA, BL); King's Inns, Dublin; called to the Bar, 1972. National Secretary, Fine Gael Youth Group, 1966–69. Mem., Dáil Committee of Procedure and Privileges, 1969–73, 1982–; Fine Gael Spokesman on Agriculture, 1972–73; Parliamentary Secretary: to Minister for Education, 1973–77; to Minister for Industry and Commerce, 1975–77; Fine Gael Spokesman: on Agriculture, 1977–81; on Finance, Jan.-June 1981; Minister: for Finance, 1981–82, for Industry and Energy, 1982–83, for Industry, Trade, Commerce and Tourism, 1983–86, for Finance, 1986–87; Fine Gael Spokesman on Industry and Commerce, 1987–89, on education, 1989; Leader of the House, 1982–86; Taoiseach (Prime Minister of Ireland), 1994–97; Leader of the Opposition, 1997–2001. Dep. Leader, 1987–90, Leader, 1990–2001, Fine Gael. Pres., EEC Industry, Research and Internal Market Councils, July–Dec. 1984. Member: Parly Assembly, Council of Europe, 1989–90; British-Irish Parly Body, 1993–94; Parly Assembly, WEU, 1997–98. Vice President: Christian Democrat Internat., 1998–; EPP, 1999–. Schumann Medal, 1998. *Recreations:* reading history, tennis. *Address:* Cornelstown, Dunboyne, Co. Meath. *T:* (1) 6183000.

BRYAN, Sir Arthur, Kt 1976, Lord-Lieutenant of Staffordshire, 1968–93; President, Waterford Wedgwood Holdings plc and a Director, Waterford Glass Group plc, 1986–88 (Managing Director, 1963–85, Chairman, 1968–86, Wedgwood); *b* 4 March 1923; *s* of William Woodall Bryan and Isobel Alan (*née* Tweedie); *m* 1947, Betty Ratford; one *s* one *d*. *Educ:* Longton High Sch., Stoke-on-Trent. Served with RAFVR, 1941–45. Joined Josiah Wedgwood & Sons Ltd, 1947; London Man., 1953–57; General Sales Man., 1959–60; Director and President, Josiah Wedgwood & Sons Inc. of America, 1960–62; Director: Josiah Wedgwood & Sons Ltd, Barlaston, 1962; Josiah Wedgwood & Sons (Canada) Ltd; Josiah Wedgwood & Sons (Australia) Pty Ltd; Phoenix Assurance Co., 1976–85; Friends' Provident Life Office, 1985–92; Rank Organisation, 1985–94; United Kingdom Fund Inc., 1987–. Member: BOTB, 1978–82 (Chm., N American Adv. Gp, 1973–82); British-American Associates, 1988–94; Marshall Aid Commem. Cttee, 1988–94. Pres., British Ceramic Manufacturers' Fedn, 1970–71; Mem., Design Council,

1977–82. Mem. Ct, Univ. of Keele. Fellow, Inst. of Marketing (grad. 1950); CIMgt (FBIM 1968); Comp. Inst. Ceramics. KStJ 1972. Hon. MUniv Keele, 1978; Hon. DLitt Staffordshire, 1993. *Recreations:* walking, reading. *Address:* Parkfields Cottage, Tittensor, Stoke-on-Trent, Staffs ST12 9HQ. *T:* (01782) 372686.

BRYAN, Dora May, (Mrs William Lawton), OBE 1996; actress; *b* 7 Feb. 1924; *d* of Albert Broadbent and Georgina (*née* Hill); *m* 1954, William Lawton; one *s* (and one *s* one *d* adopted). *Educ:* Hathershaw Council Sch., Lancs. Pantomimes: London Hippodrome, 1936; Manchester Palace, 1937; Alhambra, Glasgow, 1938; Oldham Repertory, 1939–44; followed by Peterborough, Colchester, Westcliff-on-Sea. ENSA, Italy, during War of 1939–45. Came to London, 1945, and appeared in West End Theatres: Peace in our Time; Travellers' Joy; Accolade; Lyric Revue; Globe Revue; Simon and Laura; The Water Gypsies; Gentlemen Prefer Blondes; Six of One; Too True to be Good; Hello, Dolly!; They Don't Grow on Trees; Rookery Nook, Her Majesty's, 1979; The Merry Wives of Windsor, Regent's Park, 1984; She Stoops to Conquer, Nat. Theatre, 1985; The Apple Cart, Haymarket, 1986; Charlie Girl, Victoria Palace, 1986, Birmingham, 1988; Pygmalion, Plymouth, New York, 1987; 70, Girls, 70, Vaudeville, 1991; The Birthday Party, NT, 1994; Hello Dora (one-woman show), tour, 1996; Miss Prism, in The Importance of Being Earnest, tour, 1999; Talking Heads, tour, 2000; Chichester Festival seasons, 1971–74 and 1995–97; London Palladium season, 1971; London Palladium Pantomime season, 1973–74. Has also taken parts in farces televised from Whitehall Theatre. *Films include:* The Fallen Idol, 1949; A Taste of Honey, 1961 (British Acad. Award); Two a Penny, 1968; Great St Trinian's Train Robbery, 1970; Apartment Zero, 1989. *TV series:* appearances on A to Z; Sunday Night at the London Palladium; According to Dora, 1968; Both Ends Meet, 1972; Mother's Ruin, 1994; Last of the Summer Wine, 2001. Cabaret in Canada, Hong Kong and Britain. Has made recordings. *Publication:* According to Dora (autobiog.), 1987, 2nd edn 1996. *Recreations:* reading, patchwork quilts. *Address:* 118 Marine Parade, Brighton BN2 1DD. *T:* (01273) 603235.

BRYAN, Gerald Jackson, CMG 1964; CVO 1966; OBE 1960; MC 1941; Member, Lord Chancellor's Panel of Independent Inquiry Inspectors, 1982–91; *b* 2 April 1921; *yr s* of late George Bryan, OBE, LLD, and Ruby Evelyn (*née* Jackson), Belfast; *m* 1947, Georgiana Wendy Cockburn, OStJ, Hon. Belonger, BVI, *d* of late William Barraud and Winnifred Hull; one *s* two *d*. *Educ:* Wrekin Coll.; RMA, Woolwich; New Coll., Oxford. Regular Commn, RE, 1940; served Middle East with No 11 (Scottish) Commando, 1941; retd 1944, Capt. (temp. Maj.). Apptd Colonial Service, 1944; Asst District Comr, Swaziland, 1944; Asst Colonial Sec., Barbados, 1950; Estabt Sec., Mauritius, 1954; Administrator, Brit. Virgin Is, 1959; Administrator of St Lucia, 1962–67, retired; Govt Sec. and Head of Isle of Man Civil Service, 1967–69; General Manager: Londonderry Develt Commn, NI, 1969–73; Bracknell Develt Corp., 1973–82. Director: Lovaux Engrg Co. Ltd, 1982–88; MDSL Estates Ltd, 1988–2001. Sec. Gen., Assoc. of Contact Lens Manufacturers, 1983–88. Mem. (C), Berks CC, 1983–85. Treasurer, 1979–99, Vice-Chm., 1999–2002, Gordon Foundn; Gov., Gordon's Sch. (formerly Gordon Boys' Home), Woking, 1979–2002. Chm., St John Council for Berks, 1981–88. KStJ 1985, Mem., Chapter Gen., 1987–96. FIMgt. Hon. Belonger, BVI. *Recreation:* swimming. *Address:* Whitehouse, Murrell Hill Lane, Binfield, Bracknell, Berks RG42 4BY. *T:* (01344) 425447. *Clubs:* Royal Commonwealth Society; Leander.

BRYAN, Kenneth John; Chairman, Southampton University Hospitals NHS Trust, since 1996; *b* 22 July 1939; *s* of late Patrick Joseph Bryan and Elsie May Bryan; *m* 1962 (marr. diss. 1999); one *d*. *Educ:* De La Salle Coll.; Farnborough GS. Insurance Broker, Lloyds, 1957–59; Major, British Army, 1959–78; Sen. Mgt Cons., KPMG, 1978–79; Hongkong and Shanghai Banking Corporation: Financial Controller, Hong Kong office, 1979–86; Sen. Manager, Banking Services, 1986–88; Hd of Gp Finances, 1988–93; Chief Financial Officer, Midland Bank, 1993–96. Chm., Hampshire Autistic Soc., 2001– (Trustee, 1996–). Gov., Barton Peverill Coll., 1998–. *Recreations:* golf, fly fishing. *Address:* 5 Bracken Hall, Bracken Place, Chilworth, Southampton SO16 3ET. *T:* (023) 8076 8991, *Fax:* (023) 8076 0773; *e-mail:* kjbryan@easicom.com. *Club:* Army and Navy.

BRYAN, Margaret, CMG 1988; HM Diplomatic Service, retired; Ambassador to Panama, 1986–89; *b* 26 Sept. 1929; *d* of late James Grant and Dorothy Rebecca Galloway; *m* 1952, Peter Bernard Bryan (marr. diss. 1981). *Educ:* Cathedral Sch., Shanghai; Croydon High Sch.; Girton Coll., Cambridge (MA Modern Languages). Second, later First, Secretary, FCO, 1962–80; Head of Chancery and Consul, Kinshasa, 1980–83; Counsellor, Havana, 1983–86. *Recreations:* theatre, travel, cookery, embroidery. *Address:* 10 Park Road, Blockley, Moreton-in-Marsh, Glos GL56 8BZ. *Club:* Royal Over-Seas League.

BRYAN, Sir Paul (Elmore Oliver), Kt 1972; DSO 1943; MC 1943; *b* 3 Aug. 1913; *s* of Rev. Dr J. I. Bryan, PhD; *m* 1st, 1939, Betty Mary (*née* Hoyle) (*d* 1968); two *d* (and one *d* decd); 2nd, 1971, Cynthia, *d* of Sir Patrick Ashley Cooper and of Lady Ashley Cooper, Hexton Manor, Herts, and *widow* of Patrick Duncan. *Educ:* St John's School, Leatherhead (Scholar); Caius College, Cambridge (MA). War of 1939–45; 6th Royal West Kent Regt; enlisted, 1939; commissioned, 1940; Lieut-Col, 1943; served in France, N Africa, Sicily, Italy; Comdt 164th Inf. OCTU (Eaton Hall), 1944. Sowerby Bridge UDC, 1947; contested Sowerby, March 1949, 1950 and 1951. MP (C): Howden Div. of ER Yorks, 1955–83; Boothferry, 1983–87. Assistant Government Whip, 1956–58; Parliamentary Private Secretary to Minister of Defence, 1956; a Lord Commissioner of the Treasury, 1958–61; Vice-Chairman, Conservative Party Organisation, 1961–65; Conservative Front Bench Spokesman on Post Office and broadcasting, 1965; Minister of State, Dept of Employment, 1970–72. Chm., All Party Hong Kong Parly Gp, 1974–84; Vice-Chm., Conservative 1922 Cttee, 1977–87. Chm., Croydon Cable Television, subseq. United Artists Cables Internat. (London South), 1985–; Director: Granada TV Rental Ltd, 1966–70; Granada Television, 1972–83; Granada Theatres, 1973–83; Greater Manchester Independent Radio Ltd, 1972–84; Scottish Lion Insurance Co. Ltd, 1981–95; Hewetson Holdings Ltd, 1983–91; (alternate) Port of Felixstowe, 1991–94; Dep. Chm., Furness Withy and Co. Ltd, 1984–89 (Dir, 1983–). *Publication:* Wool, War and Westminster, 1993. *Address:* Park Farm, Sawdon, near Scarborough, North Yorks YO13 9EB. *T:* (01723) 859370; 5 Westminster Gardens, Marsham Street, SW1P 4JA. *T:* (020) 7834 2050.

BRYAN, Robert Patrick, OBE 1980; security consultant; Police Adviser to Foreign and Commonwealth Office, and Inspector General of Dependent Territories Police, 1980–85, retired; *b* 29 June 1926; *s* of Maurice Bryan and Elizabeth (*née* Waite); *m* 1948, Hazel Audrey (*née* Braine) (*d* 1990); three *s*. *Educ:* Plaistow Secondary Sch.; Wanstead County High Sch. Indian Army (Mahratta LI), 1944–47. Bank of Nova Scotia, 1948–49; Metropolitan Police: Constable, 1950; Dep. Asst Commissioner, 1977, retired 1980. National Police College: Intermediate Comd Course, 1965; Sen. Comd Course, 1969; occasional lecturer. RCDS 1974. Chm., Los Zapateros (cobblers), 1998–99. Chm., Food Distribn Security Assoc., 1988–99. Gov., Corps of Commissionaires, 1993–97. Governor, Hampton Sch., 1978–97. *Publications:* contribs to police and related pubns, particularly on community relations and juvenile delinquency. *Address:* c/o National Westminster Bank, High Street, Teddington, Mddx TW11 8EP.

BRYANS, Dame Anne (Margaret), DBE 1957 (CBE 1945); DStJ; Chairman, Order of St John of Jerusalem and BRCS Service Hospitals Welfare and VAD Committee, 1960–89; Vice-Chairman, Joint Committee, Order of St John and BRCS, 1976–81; *b* 29 Oct. 1909; *e d* of late Col Rt Hon. Sir John Gilmour, 2nd Bt, GCVO, DSO, MP of Montrave and late Mary Louise Lambert; *m* 1932, Lieut-Comdr J. R. Bryans, RN, retired (*d* 1990); one *s*. *Educ:* privately. Joined HQ Staff British Red Cross Society, 1938; Deputy Commissioner British Red Cross and St John War Organisation, Middle East Commission, 1943; Commissioner Jan.-June 1945. Dep. Chm., 1953–64, Vice-Chm., 1964–76, Exec. Cttee, BRCS; Lay Mem., Council for Professions Supplementary to Med., 1973–79. Member: Bd of Governors, Eastman Dental Hosp., 1973–79; Camden and Islington AHA, 1974–79; Vice-Pres., Open Sect., RSocMed, 1975, Pres. 1980–82; former Member: ITA, later IBA; Govt Anglo-Egyptian Resettlement Bd; BBC/ITA Appeals Cttee; Med. Sch. St George's Hosp.; Special Trustee and former Chm., Royal Free Hosp. and Friends of Royal Free Hosp.; former Chairman: Bd of Governors, Royal Free Hosp.; Council, Florence Nightingale Hosp.; Vice-Pres., Royal Coll. of Nursing; former Governor, Westminster Hosp. FRSocMed 1976; Hon. FRSocMed 1994. *Address:* 25 Links Road, Lundin Links, Leven, Fife KY8 5QD. *Club:* Royal Lymington Yacht.

BRYANT, (Alan) Christopher, OBE 1995; Life President, Bryant Group plc (formerly Bryant Holdings Ltd), since 1992 (Managing Director, 1960–88; Chairman, 1962–92); *b* 28 July 1923; *s* of Ebenezer John Bryant and Ivy Maud Bryant (*née* Seymour); *m* 1951, Jean Mary Nock; four *d*. *Educ:* West House School, Birmingham; Malvern Coll.; Birmingham Univ. (BSc (Hons)). FCIOB 1958. Engineer Officer, Fleet Air Arm, 1944–47 (Sub-Lieut, RNVR); Project Manager, 1946–48, Director, 1948–86, C. Bryant & Son Ltd. Non-exec. Dir, BSG International plc, 1985–94. Chm., 1969–95, Pres., 1987–, Birmingham YMCA; Hon. Treas., Nat. Council of YMCAs, 1991–95. Hon. DEng Birmingham, 1992. *Recreations:* sailing, shooting, walking. *Clubs:* Naval; South Caernarvonshire Yacht.

BRYANT, Christopher; *see* Bryant, A. C.

BRYANT, Christopher John; MP (Lab) Rhondda, since 2001; *b* 11 Jan. 1962; *s* of Rees Bryant and Anne Gracie Bryant (*née* Goodwin). *Educ:* Cheltenham Coll.; Mansfield Coll., Oxford (MA); Ripon Coll., Cuddesdon (MA, DipTh). Ordained deacon, 1986, priest, 1987; Asst Curate, All Saints, High Wycombe, 1986–89; Youth Chaplain, Dio. Peterborough, 1989–91; Organiser, Holborn & St Pancras Lab. Party, 1991–93; Local Govt Devlt Officer, Lab. Party, 1993–94. London Manager, Common Purpose, 1994–96; freelance writer, 1996–98; Hd, Eur. Affairs, BBC, 1998–2000. *Publications:* (ed) Reclaiming the Ground, 1993; (ed) John Smith: an appreciation, 1995; Possible Dreams, 1996; Stafford Cripps: the first modern Chancellor, 1997; Glenda Jackson: the biography, 1998. *Recreations:* theatre, modern art, Spain. *Address:* House of Commons, SW1A 0AA. *T:* (020) 7219 8315; *e-mail:* bryantc@parliament.uk. *Club:* Ferndale Rugby Football (Vice-Pres.) (Rhondda).

BRYANT, David John, CBE 1980 (MBE 1969); international bowler, 1958–92; *b* 27 Oct. 1931; *s* of Reginald Samuel Harold Bryant and Evelyn Claire (*née* Weaver); *m* 1960, Ruth Georgina (*née* Roberts); two *d*. *Educ:* Weston Grammar Sch.; St Paul's Coll., Cheltenham; Redland Coll., Bristol (teacher training colls). National Service, RAF, 1950–52; teacher trng, 1953–55; schoolmaster, 1955–71; company director, sports business, 1971–78; Dir, Drakelite Ltd (Internat. Bowls Consultant), 1978–97. World Singles Champion, 1966, 1980 and 1988; World Indoor Singles Champion, 1979, 1980 and 1981; World Indoor Pairs Champion, 1986, 1987, 1989, 1990, 1991 and 1992; Kodak Masters International Singles Champion, 1978, 1979 and 1982; Gateway International Masters Singles Champion, 1984, 1985, 1986, 1987; Woolwich International Singles Champion, 1988, 1989; World Triples Champion, 1980; Commonwealth Games Gold Medallist: Singles: 1962, 1970, 1974 and 1978; Fours: 1962. Numerous national and British Isles titles, both indoor and outdoor. England Indoor Team Captain, 1993, 1994. *Publications:* Bryant on Bowls, 1966; Bowl with Bryant, 1984; Bryant on Bowls, 1985; The Game of Bowls, 1990; Bowl to Win, 1994. *Recreations:* angling, gardening. *Address:* 47 Esmond Grove, Clevedon, Somerset BS21 7HP. *Clubs:* Clevedon Bowling, Clevedon Conservative.

BRYANT, David Michael Arton; His Honour Judge Bryant; a Circuit Judge, since 1989; *b* 27 Jan. 1942; *s* of Lt-Col and Mrs A. D. Bryant; *m* 1969, Diana Caroline, *d* of Brig. and Mrs W. C. W. Sloan; two *s* one *d*. *Educ:* Wellington Coll.; Oriel Coll., Oxford (Open Scholar; MA). Called to the Bar, Inner Temple, 1964; practised North Eastern Circuit, 1965–89. A Recorder, 1985–89. *Recreations:* gardening, shooting, tennis, Byzantine history. *Address:* Teesside Combined Court Centre, Russell Street, Middlesbrough TS1 2AE. *Club:* Carlton.

BRYANT, Rt Rev. Denis William, DFC 1942; retired; *b* 31 Jan. 1918; *s* of Thomas and Beatrice Maud Bryant; *m* 1940, Dorothy Linda (*née* Lewis); one *d*. *Educ:* Clark's Coll., Ealing; Cardiff Techn. Coll. Joined RAF; Wireless Operator/Air Gunner, 1936; Navigator, 1939; France, 1940 (despatches); Pilot, 1943; commn in Secretarial Br., 1948; Adjt, RAF Hereford, 1950; Sqdn-Ldr i/c Overseas Postings Record Office, Gloucester, 1951; Sqdn-Ldr DP7, Air Min., 1953. Ordinand, Queen's Coll., Birmingham, 1956; Deacon, 1958; Priest, 1959; Rector of Esperance, 1961–67; Archdeacon of Goldfields, 1966–67; Bishop of Kalgoorlie, 1967 until 1973 when Kalgoorlie became part of Diocese of Perth; Asst Bishop of Perth, and Archdeacon and Rector of Northam, 1973–75; Rector of Dalkeith, WA, 1975–85. Hon. Chaplain, Anglican Homes, 1985–. *Recreations:* squash, tennis, oil painting. *Address:* U3 Dorothy Genders Village, 99 McCabe Street, Mosman Park, WA 6012, Australia. *T:* (8) 93854515.

BRYANT, Air Vice-Marshal Derek Thomas, CB 1987; OBE 1974; Air Officer Commanding, Headquarters Command and Staff Training and Commandant, Royal Air Force Staff College, 1987–89, retired; *b* 1 Nov. 1933; *s* of Thomas Bryant and Mary (*née* Thurley); *m* 1956, Patricia Dodge; one *s* one *d*. *Educ:* Latymer Upper Grammar Sch., Hammersmith. Fighter pilot, 1953; Qualified Flying Instructor, 1957; Sqdn Comdr, 1968–74; OC RAF Coningsby, 1976–78; SASO HQ 38 Gp, 1982–84; Dep. Comdr, RAF Germany, 1984–87; various courses and staff appts. *Recreations:* gardening, golf. *Address:* The Old Stables, Lower Swell, Fivehead, Taunton, Somerset TA3 6PH. *Club:* Royal Air Force.

BRYANT, Prof. Greyham Frank, PhD; FREng, FIEE; FIMA; Professor of Control, Imperial College, London University, since 1982; *b* 3 June 1931; *s* of Ernest Noel Bryant and Florence Ivy (*née* Russell); *m* 1955, Iris Sybil Jardine; two *s*. *Educ:* Reading Univ.; Imperial Coll. (PhD). FIMA 1973; FIEE 1987; FREng (FEng 1988). Sen. Scientific Officer, Iron and Steel Res., London, 1959–64; Imperial College: Res. Fellow, 1964–67; Reader in Industrial Control, 1975–82. Chm., Broner Consultants, 1979–88; Director: Greycon Consultants, 1985–2000; Circulation Research, 1989–. *Publications:* Automation of Tandem Mills (jtly), 1973; (with L. F. Yeung) Multivariable Control and System Design Techniques, 1996; papers on design of management control schemes, multivariable control and modelling, in learned jls. *Recreation:* music. *Address:* 18 Wimborne Avenue, Norwood Green, Middlesex UB2 4HB. *T:* (020) 8574 5648. *Club:* Athenæum.

BRYANT, John Martin, FREng, FIM; Joint Chief Executive, Corus Group plc, 1999–2000; *b* 28 Sept. 1943; *s* of William George Bryant and Doris Bryant; *m* 1965, Andrea Irene Emmons; two *s* one *d*. *Educ:* West Monmouth Sch.; St Catharine's Coll., Cambridge (BA Nat. Sci. 1965; MA). CEng, FIM 1993. Trainee, Steel Co. of Wales, 1965; British Steel, 1967–99: Production/Technical Mgt, Port Talbot works, 1967–78; Works Manager, Hot Rolled Products, Port Talbot, 1978–87; Project Manager, Hot Strip Mill Develt, 1982–87; Works Manager, Cold Rolled Products, Shotton, 1987–88; Dir, Coated Products, 1988–90; Dir, Tinplate, 1990–92; Man. Dir, Strip Products, 1992–96; Exec. Dir, 1996–99; Chief Exec., 1999. Dir, Bank of Wales plc, 1996–. FREng 2000. Hon. DSc Wales, 2000. *Recreations:* squash, watching Rugby and cricket.

BRYANT, Judith Marie, (Mrs H. M. Hodkinson), SRN; retired; Fellow, King's Fund College, 1990–94 (part-time Fellow, 1986–90); *b* 31 Dec. 1942; *d* of Frederic John Bryant and Joan Marion (*née* Summerfield); *m* 1986, Prof. Henry Malcolm Hodkinson, *qv*. *Educ:* City of London Sch. for Girls; The London Hosp. (SRN 1964); Brunel Univ. (MPhil 1983). Ward Sister, UCH, 1965–69; Nursing Officer, subseq. Sen. Nursing Officer, Northwick Park Hosp., Harrow, 1969–75; Divl Nursing Officer, Harrow, 1975–78; Dist Nursing Officer, Enfield, 1978–82, Victoria, 1982–85; Chief Nursing Officer and Dir of Quality Assurance, Riverside HA, 1985–86; Regl Nursing Officer, NE Thames RHA, 1986–90. Florence Nightingale Meml Scholar, USA and Canada, 1970. Adviser, DHSS Res. Liaison Cttee for the Elderly, 1977–83; Member: SW Herts DHA, 1981–86; NHS Training Authority, Nurses and Midwives Staff Training Cttee, 1986–89; 1930 Fund for Dist Nurses, 1985–; Cttee, Nurseline, 1996–2000. *Publication:* (with H. M. Hodkinson) Sherratt? A Natural Family of Staffordshire Figures, 1991. *Recreations:* opera, gardening. *Address:* 8 Chiswick Square, Burlington Lane, W4 2QG. *T:* (020) 8747 0239.

BRYANT, Julius John Victor, FSA; Director of Museums and Collections, English Heritage, since 1995; *b* 17 Dec. 1957; *s* of late Robert Bryant and of Dena Bryant (*née* Bond); *m* 1984, Barbara Ann Coffey; one *s*. *Educ:* St Alban's Sch.; University College London; Courtauld Inst. of Art. Paintings Cataloguer, Sotheby's, 1980–81; Mus. Asst, V&A Mus., 1982–83; Asst Curator, 1983–88, Acting Curator, 1989, Iveagh Bequest, Kenwood; Hd of Museums Div., 1990–93, Dir of London Historic Properties, 1993–95, English Heritage. Visiting Fellow: Yale Center for British Art, 1985; Huntington Liby and Art Gall., Calif, 1992. Member: London Museums Consultative Cttee, 1989–99; Exec. Council, Area Museums Service for SE England, 1992–95; Art Museum Directors' Conf. (formerly Conf. of Nat. and Regl Mus. Dirs), 1998–; Hampstead Heath Mgt Cttee, 1990–95; Council, Furniture History Soc., 1998–2000; Internat. Cttee, Historic House Museums, 1999–. Pres., Hampstead Heath Fine and Decorative Art Soc., 1989–. FSA 1999. Editor, Collections Review, 1997–. *Publications:* Marble Hill: the design and use of a Palladian estate, 1986; Finest Prospects, 1986; The Victoria and Albert Museum Guide, 1986; Marble Hill House, 1988; Mrs Howard: a woman of reason, 1988; (jtly) The Landscape of Kenwood, 1990; The Iveagh Bequest, Kenwood, 1990; Robert Adam, 1992; (ed) London Historic House Museums Review, 1993; London's Country House Collections, 1993; (jtly) The Trojan War: sculptures by Anthony Caro, 1994, 3rd edn 1998; Turner: painting the nation, 1996; contribs to New DNB, Grove Dictionary of Art; exhibn catalogues; articles in jls. *Recreations:* shopping for museums, running, family life. *Address:* English Heritage, 23 Savile Row, W1R 2HD. *T:* (020) 7973 3535.

BRYANT, Ven. Mark Watts; Archdeacon of Coventry, since 2001; *b* 8 Oct. 1949; *s* of Douglas William and Kathleen Joyce Bryant; m 1976, Elisabeth Eastaugh; two *s* one *d*. *Educ:* St John's Sch., Leatherhead; St John's Coll., Univ. of Durham (BA); Cuddesdon Theol Coll. Ordained deacon, 1975, priest, 1976; Curate, Addlestone, 1975–79; Asst Priest, 1979–83; Vicar, 1983–88, St John Studley, Trowbridge; Chaplain, Trowbridge FE Coll., 1979–83; Dir of Ordinands and Hd, Vocations and Trng Dept, Dio. Coventry, 1988–96; Team Rector, Caludon, Coventry, 1996–2001. *Recreations:* music, walking, popular television. *Address:* 9 Armorial Road, Coventry CV3 6GH. *T:* (024) 7641 7750.

BRYANT, Michael Dennis, CBE 1988; actor; Royal National Theatre player, since 1977, Associate Director, since 1996; *b* 5 April 1928; *s* of William and Ann Bryant; *m* 1st, 1958, Josephine Martin (marr. diss. 1980); two *s* two *d*; 2nd, 1990, Judith Mary Coke. *Educ:* Battersea Grammar Sch. Merchant Navy, 1945; Army, 1946–49; drama sch., 1949–51; theatre and television, 1957–77; RSC, 1964–65. Rôles with National, subseq. Royal National, Theatre include: Hieronimo, in Spanish Tragedy; Iago, in Othello; Lenin, in State of Revolution (Best Actor, SWET awards, 1977); title rôle, in Mayor of Zalamea (Best Actor, British Theatrical Assoc. awards, 1981); Enobarbus, in Antony and Cleopatra, and Gloucester, in King Lear (Best Supporting Actor: Olivier awards, 1987; (for Enobarbus) London Critics awards, 1987); Prospero, in The Tempest, 1988; Polonius, in Hamlet, 1989; Racing Demon, 1990; The Wind in the Willows, 1990; Murmuring Judges, 1991; Doolittle, in Pygmalion, 1992; Trelawny of the Wells, 1993; The Absence of War, 1993; Johnny on a Spot, 1994; York, in Richard II, 1995; John Gabriel Borkman, 1996; Fool, in King Lear, 1997; Peter Pan, 1998; Money, Summerfolk, 1999; The Cherry Orchard, 2000. *Recreation:* rambling. *Address:* 19 Deanhill Court, Upper Richmond Road West, SW14 7DJ.

BRYANT, Prof. Peter Elwood, FRS 1991; Watts Professor of Psychology, Oxford University, since 1980; Fellow of Wolfson College, Oxford, since 1980; *b* 24 June 1937; *s* of Michael Bryant; *m* (marr. diss.); one *s* two *d*; *m* 1995, T. Nunes. *Educ:* Blundell's Sch.; Clare College, Cambridge (BA 1963; MA 1967); London Univ. (PhD). University Lecturer in Human Experimental Psychology, Oxford, 1967–80; Fellow, St John's Coll., Oxford, 1967–80. Editor, British Jl of Developmental Psychol., 1982–88. President's award, BPsS, 1984. *Publications:* Perception and Understanding in Young Children, 1974; (with L. Bradley) Children's Reading Problems, 1985; (with U. Goswami) Phonological Skills and Learning to Read, 1990; (with T. Nunes) Children Doing Mathematics, 1996; (with T. Nunes) Learning & Teaching Mathematics: an international perspective, 1997. *Address:* Wolfson College, Oxford OX2 6UD.

BRYANT, Peter George Francis; Under Secretary, Department of Trade and Industry, 1989–92; *b* 10 May 1932; *s* of late George Bryant, CBE and Margaret Bryant; *m* 1961, Jean (*née* Morriss); one *s* one *d*. *Educ:* Sutton Valence Sch.; Birkbeck Coll., London Univ. (BA). Min. of Supply, 1953–55; BoT, 1955–69; 1st Sec. (Commercial), Vienna (on secondment), 1970–72; Dir of British Trade Drive in S Germany, 1973; Department of Trade (later Department of Trade and Industry), 1974–85; seconded to HM Diplomatic Service as Consul-Gen., Düsseldorf, 1985–88, and Dir-Gen. of Trade and Investment Promotion, FRG, 1988.

BRYANT, Richard Charles, CB 1960; Under-Secretary, Board of Trade, 1955–68; *b* 20 Aug. 1908; *s* of Charles James and Constance Byron Bryant, The Bounds, Hernhill, Faversham, Kent; *m* 1938, Elisabeth Ellington (*d* 1994), *d* of Dr. A. E. Stansfeld, FRCP; two *s* two *d*. *Educ:* Rugby; Oriel College, Oxford. Entered Board of Trade, 1932; Ministry of Supply, 1939–44. *Address:* Marsh Farm House, Brancaster, Norfolk PE31 8AE. *T:* (01485) 210206. *Club:* Travellers.

BRYANT, Thomas, CMG 1995; HM Diplomatic Service, retired; Consul General, Zürich, 1991–95; *b* 1 Nov. 1938; *s* of George Edward Bryant and Ethel May Bryant (*née* Rogers); *m* 1961, Vivien Mary Theresa Hill (separated 1998); twin *s* one *d*. *Educ:* William Ellis Sch., London; Polytechnic of Central London (DMS). Nat. service, Army, 1957–59. Entered FO, 1957; Hong Kong, 1963; Peking, 1963–65; Vice Consul, Frankfurt, 1966–68; Second Sec., Tel Aviv, 1968–72; First Sec., FCO, 1973–76; Vienna, 1976–80; FCO, 1980–82, Counsellor, 1982; Hd of Finance Dept, 1982–84; Consul-Gen., Munich, 1984–88; Dep. High Comr, Nairobi, 1988–91. Gov., William Ellis Sch., London, 1995. *Recreations:* cricket, soccer, tennis, classical music, laughter. *Address:* 36 Fulmar Drive, East Grinstead, W Sussex RH19 3NN. *Club:* Muthaiga (Nairobi).

BRYARS, Donald Leonard; Commissioner of Customs and Excise, 1978–84 and Director, Personnel, 1979–84, retired; *b* 31 March 1929; *s* of late Leonard and Marie Bryars; *m* 1953, Joan (*née* Yealand); one *d*. *Educ:* Goole Grammar Sch.; Leeds Univ. Joined Customs and Excise as Executive Officer, 1953, Principal, 1964, Asst Sec., 1971; on loan to Cabinet Office, 1976–78; Director, General Customs, 1978–79. Dir (non-exec.), The Customs Annuity Benevolent Fund Inc., 1986–. Trustee, Milton's Cottage Trust, 1993–. *Address:* 15 Cedars Walk, Chorleywood, Rickmansworth, Herts WD3 5GD. *T:* (01923) 446752. *Club:* Civil Service (Chm., 1981–85).

BRYARS, Gavin; *see* Bryars, R. G.

BRYARS, John Desmond, CB 1982; Deputy Under Secretary of State (Finance and Budget), Ministry of Defence, 1979–84, retired; *b* 31 Oct. 1928; *s* of William Bryars, MD and Sarah (*née* McMeekin); *m* 1964, Faith (*d* 2000), *d* of Frederick Momber, ARCM and Anne Momber. *Educ:* St Edward's Sch., Oxford; Trinity Coll., Oxford (schol.; MA). Army, 1946–48. Entered Civil Service, Air Ministry, 1952; HM Treasury, 1960–62; Private Sec. to Sec. of State for Air, 1963–64, to Minister of Defence, RAF, 1964–65; Asst Sec., MoD, 1965–73; RCDS 1973; Asst Under-Sec. of State, MoD, 1973–75 and 1977–79; Under Sec., Cabinet Office, 1975–77. *Address:* 42 Osterley Road, Osterley, Isleworth, Middlesex TW7 4PN. *Club:* Royal Commonwealth Society.

BRYARS, (Richard) Gavin; composer; *b* 16 Jan. 1943; *s* of Walter Joseph Bryars and Miriam Eleanor Bryars (*née* Hopley); *m* 1971, Angela Margaret Bigley (marr. diss. 1993); two *d*; *m* 1999, Anna Tchernakova; one *s*, and one step *d*. *Educ:* Goole Grammar Sch.; Sheffield Univ. (BA Hons Philosophy). Freelance bassist, 1963–66; Mem. trio, Joseph Holbrooke (improvising), 1964–66, 1998–; Lecturer: Northampton Tech. Coll. and Sch. of Art, 1966–67; Portsmouth Coll. of Art, 1969–70; Sen. Lectr, Leicester Poly., 1970–85; Prof. of Music, Leicester Poly., later De Montfort Univ., 1985–96 (part-time, 1994–96). Visiting Professor: Univ. of Victoria, BC; Univ. of Hertfordshire. Founder and Dir, Gavin Bryars Ensemble, 1979–. Mem., Collège de Pataphysique, France, 1974– (Pres., sous-commn des Cliques Claques, 1984–). *Compositions* include: The Sinking of the Titanic, 1969; Jesus' Blood Never Failed Me Yet, 1971; Out of Zaleski's Gazebo, 1977; My First Homage, 1978; The Cross Channel Ferry, 1979; The Vespertine Park, The English Mail-Coach, 1980; Les Fiançailles, Allegrasco, 1983; On Photography, Effarene, 1984; String quartet No 1, 1985; Pico's Flight, Sub Rosa, 1986; By the Vaar, The Old Tower of Löbenicht, 1987; Invention of Tradition, Glorious Hill, Doctor Ox's Experiment (Epilogue), 1988; Incipit Vita Nova, 1989; Cadman Requiem, 1989, revd 1996; Alaric I or II, 1989; After the Requiem, String Quartet No 2, 1990; The Black River, The Green Ray, 1991; The White Lodge, 1991; (with Juan Munoz) A Man in a Room Gambling, Die Letzen Tage, 1992; The War in Heaven, The North Shore, 1993; Three Elegies for Nine Clarinets, One Last Bar Then Joe Can Sing, The East Coast, 1994; The South Downs, In Nomine (after Purcell), After Handel's Vesper, Cello Concerto, 1995; The Adnan Songbook, 1996; The Island Chapel, And so ended Kant's travelling in this world, 1997; String Quartet no 3, 1998; First Book of Madrigals, 1998–99; The Porazzi Fragment, 1999; Violin Concerto, 2000; *opera:* Medea, for Opéra de Lyon, 1982, revd 1984, 1995; Doctor Ox's Experiment, for ENO, 1998; *ballet:* Four Elements, 1990; Wonderlawn, 1994; 2, 1995; BIPED, 2000. Has made recordings. *Recreations:* supporting, from a distance, Yorkshire CCC and Queen's Park Rangers FC; dalmatians. *Address:* c/o Schott & Co. Ltd, 48 Great Marlborough Street, W1V 2BN. *T:* (020) 7494 1487.

BRYCE, Gabe Robb, OBE 1959; Sales Manager (Operations) British Aircraft Corporation, 1965–75; occupied in breeding dogs and boarding cats, until retirement from animal world, 1987; *b* 27 April 1921; *m* 1943, Agnes Lindsay; one *s* one *d*. *Educ:* Glasgow High School. Served in RAF, 1939–46. Vickers-Armstrongs (Aircraft) Ltd, 1946–60 (Chief Test Pilot, 1951–60). Participated as First or Second Pilot, in Maiden Flights of following British Aircraft: Varsity; Nene Viking; Viscount 630, 700 and 800; Tay Viscount; Valiant; Pathfinder; Vanguard; VC-10; BAC 1–11; Chief Test Pilot, British Aircraft Corporation, 1960–64. Fellow Soc. of Experimental Test Pilots (USA), 1967. Sir Barnes Wallis Meml Medal, GAPAN, 1980. *Recreations:* squash, tennis. *Address:* 8 Rowan Green, Rosslyn Park, Weybridge, Surrey KT13 9NF. *T:* (01932) 858996.

BRYCE, Sir Gordon; *see* Bryce, Sir W. G.

BRYCE, Gordon, RSA 1993 (ARSA 1976); RSW 1976; painter; Head of Fine Art, Gray's School of Art, Aberdeen, since 1986; *b* 30 June 1943; *s* of George and Annie Bryce; *m* 1st, 1966, Margaret Lothian (marr. diss. 1976); two *s*; 2nd, 1984, Hilary Duthie; one *s* two *d*. *Educ:* Edinburgh Acad.; George Watson's Coll., Edinburgh; Edinburgh Coll. of Art. Dip. in Art. Exhibited widely in UK, Europe and USA, 1965–; 30 one-man exhbns of painting, UK and overseas; paintings in public and private collections, UK, Europe, USA, Canada. *Recreation:* fly fishing. *Address:* Sylva Cottage, 2 Culter House Road, Milltimber, Aberdeen AB1 0EN. *T:* (01224) 733274.

BRYCE, Ian James G.; *see* Graham-Bryce.

BRYCE, Rt Rev. Jabez Leslie; *see* Polynesia, Bishop in.

BRYCE, Sir (William) Gordon, Kt 1971; CBE 1963; Chief Justice of the Bahamas, 1970–73; *b* 2 Feb. 1913; *s* of James Chisholm Bryce and Emily Susan (*née* Lees); *m* 1940, Molly Mary, *d* of Arthur Cranch Drake; two *d*. *Educ:* Bromsgrove Sch.; Hertford Coll., Oxford (MA). Called to Bar, Middle Temple. War Service, 1940–46 (Major). Colonial Service: Crown Counsel, Fiji, 1949; Solicitor General, Fiji, 1953; Attorney General: Gibraltar, 1956; Aden, 1959; Legal Adviser, S Arabian High Commn, 1963; Attorney General, Bahamas, 1966. Comr, revised edn of Laws: of Gilbert and Ellice Islands, 1952; of Fiji, 1955; Comr, Bahamas Law Reform and Revision Commn, 1976. *Recreations:* riding, gardening. *Address:* Nevis, Broad Lane, Brancaster, Norfolk PE31 8AU.

BRYCE-SMITH, Prof. Derek, PhD, DSc; CChem, FRSC; Professor of Organic Chemistry, University of Reading, 1965–89, part-time, 1989–91, now Emeritus; *b* 29 April 1926; *s* of Charles Philip and Amelia Smith; *m* 1st, 1956, Marjorie Mary Anne Stewart (*d* 1966); two *s* two *d*; 2nd, 1969, Pamela Joyce Morgan; two step *d*. *Educ:*

Bancrofts Sch., Woodford Wells; SW Essex Tech. Coll.; West Ham Municipal Coll.; Bedford Coll., London. Research Chemist: Powell Duffryn Res. Ltd, 1945–46; Dufay-Chromex Ltd, 1946–48; Inst. of Petroleum Student, Bedford Coll., 1948–51; ICI Post-doctoral Fellow, KCL, 1951–55; Asst Lectr in Chem., KCL, 1955–56; Lectr in Chem., 1956–63, Reader, 1963–65, Reading Univ. Founding Chm., European Photochem. Assoc., 1970–72; Founding Vice-Chm., UK Br., Internat. Solar Energy Soc., 1973–74; Chm., RSC Photochemistry Gp, 1981–92. John Jeyes Endowed Lectureship and Silver Medal, RSC, 1984–85. *Publications:* (with R. Stephens) Lead or Health, 1980, 2nd edn 1981; (with E. Hodgkinson) The Zinc Solution, 1986; (RSC Senior Reporter and contrib.) Photochemistry: a review of chemical literature, vols 1–25, 1970–94; contribs to learned jls in the fields of photochem., organometallic chem., environmental chem. and philosophy of sci. *Recreations:* gardening, making music. *Address:* Highland Wood House, Mill Lane, Kidmore End, Reading, Berks RG4 9HB. *T:* (0118) 972 3132.

BRYDEN, David John, PhD; FSA; Property Manager, Felbrigg Hall and Sheringham Park, National Trust, 1997–2001; *b* 23 Nov. 1943; *s* of George Bryden and Marion (*née* Bellingham); *m* 1964, Helen Margaret Willison; two *s*. *Educ:* Univ. of Leicester (BSc(Engrg)); Linacre Coll., Oxford (Dip. in Hist. and Philos. of Sci.); Gonville and Caius Coll., Cambridge (MA 1973); St Edmund's Coll., Cambridge (PhD 1993). FSA 1993. Asst Keeper II, Royal Scottish Mus., 1966–70; Curator, Whipple Mus. of Hist. of Sci., Univ. of Cambridge, 1970–78; Fellow and Steward, St Edmund's House, 1977–78; Asst Keeper I, Science Mus. Library, 1979–87; Academic Administrator, Gresham Coll., 1987–88; Keeper, Dept of Sci., Technol. and Working Life, Nat. Museums of Scotland, 1988–96. *Publications:* Scottish Scientific Instrument Makers 1600–1990, 1972; Napier's Bones: a history and instruction manual, 1992; (jtly) A Classified Bibliography on the history of scientific instruments, 1997; articles on early scientific instruments, history of science and technology, printing history and bibliography, numismatics. *Address:* 11 Pensham Hill, Pershore, Worcs WR10 3HA.

BRYDEN, William Campbell Rough, (Bill Bryden), CBE 1993; director and writer; Head of Drama Television, BBC Scotland, 1984–93; *b* 12 April 1942; *s* of late George Bryden and of Catherine Bryden; *m* 1971, Hon. Deborah Morris, *d* of Baron Killanin, MBE, TD; one *s* one *d*. *Educ:* Hillend Public Sch.; Greenock High Sch. Documentary writer, Scottish Television, 1963–64; Assistant Director: Belgrade Theatre, Coventry, 1965–67; Royal Court Th., London, 1967–69; Associate Director: Royal Lyceum Th., Edinburgh, 1971–74; National Th., subseq. RNT, 1975–85; Dir, Cottesloe Theatre (Nat. Theatre), 1978–80. Director: *opera:* Parsifal, 1988, The Cunning Little Vixen, 1990, Royal Opera House, Covent Garden; The Silver Tassie, Coliseum, 2000; *stage:* Bernstein's Mass, GSMD, 1987; A Life in the Theatre, Haymarket, 1989; The Ship, Harland and Wolff Shipyard, Glasgow, 1990; Cops, Greenwich, 1991; A Month in the Country, Albery, 1994; The Big Picnic, Harland and Wolff Shipyard, Glasgow (also writer), 1994 (televised 1996); Son of Man, RSC, 1995; Uncle Vanya, Chichester, 1996; Three Sisters, Birmingham, 1998. *Television:* Exec. Producer: Tutti Frutti, by John Byrne, 1987 (Best Series, BAFTA awards); The Play on 1 (series), 1989; Dir, The Shawl, by David Mamet, 1989. Member Board, Scottish Television, 1979–85. Dir of the Year, Laurence Olivier Awards, 1985, Best Dir, Brit. Th. Assoc. and Drama Magazine Awards, 1986, and Evening Standard Best Dir Award, 1985 (for The Mysteries, NT, 1985). *Publications: plays:* Willie Rough, 1972; Benny Lynch, 1974; Old Movies, 1977; *screenplay:* The Long Riders, 1980; *films:* (writer and director) Ill Fares The Land, 1982; The Holy City (for TV), 1985; Aria, 1987. *Recreation:* music.

BRYDON, Donald Hood, OBE 1993; Chairman and Chief Executive, AXA Investment Managers SA, since 1997; *b* 25 May 1945; *s* of James Hood Brydon and Mary Duncanson (*née* Young); *m* 1st, 1971, Joan Victoria (marr. diss. 1995); one *s* one *d*; 2nd, 1996, Corrine Susan Jane Green. *Educ:* George Watson's Coll., Edinburgh; Univ. of Edinburgh (BSc). Econs Dept, Univ. of Edinburgh, 1967–70; British Airways Pension Fund, 1970–77; Barclays Investment Manager's Office, 1977–81; Dep. Man. Dir, Barclays Investment Mgt Ltd, 1981–86; BZW Investment Management Ltd: Dir, 1986–88; Man. Dir, 1988–91; BZW Asset Management Ltd: Chm. and Chief Exec., 1991–94; non-exec. Chm., 1994–95; Barclays de Zoete Wedd: Dep. Chief Exec., 1994–96; Acting Chief Exec., 1996. Director: London Stock Exchange, 1991–98; Edinburgh Inca Investment Trust, 1996–; Allied Domecq, 1997–; Nycomed Amersham, 1997–; Edinburgh UK Tracker Trust, 1997–; Sun Life and Provincial Hldgs, 1997–2000. Pres., Eur. Asset Mgt Assoc., 1999–. Chm., Eur. Children's Trust, 1999–. *Publications:* (jtly) Economics of Technical Information Services, 1972; (jtly) Pension Fund Investment, 1988. *Recreation:* golf. *Address:* (office) 7 Newgate Street, EC1A 7NX. *Club:* Caledonian.

BRYER, Prof. Anthony Applemore Mornington, FSA 1972; Professor of Byzantine Studies, University of Birmingham, 1980–99, now Emeritus; Senior Research Fellow, King's College London, since 1996; *b* 31 Oct. 1937; *e s* of late Group Captain Gerald Mornington Bryer, OBE and of Joan Evelyn (*née* Grigsby); *m* 1st, 1961, Elizabeth Lipscomb (*d* 1995); three *d*; 2nd, 1998, Jennifer Ann Banks, widow. *Educ:* Canford Sch.; Sorbonne Univ.; Balliol Coll., Oxford (Scholar; BA, MA; DPhil 1967); Athens Univ. Nat. Service, RAF (Adjutant), 1956–58. University of Birmingham: Research Fellow, 1964–65, Lectr, 1965–73, Sen. Lectr, 1973–76, in Medieval History; Reader in Byzantine Studies, 1976–79; Dir of Byzantine Studies, 1969–76; Dir, Centre for Byzantine, Ottoman and Modern Greek Studies, 1976–94; Public Orator, 1991–98. Fellow, Inst. for Advanced Res. in Humanities, Univ. of Birmingham, 1999–. Visiting Fellow: Dumbarton Oaks, Harvard, 1971–; Merton Coll., Oxford, 1985. Founder, annual British Byzantine Symposia, 1966 (Dir, 1966–); Chm., British Nat. Cttee, Internat. Byzantine Assoc., 1989–95 (Sec., 1976–89); former Vice-Pres., Nat. Trust for Greece; Mem., Managing Cttees, British Sch. at Athens and British Inst. of Archaeology, Ankara; Consultant to Cyprus Govt on res. in humanities, 1988–89; field trips to Trebizond and Pontos, 1959–; Hellenic Cruise lectr, 1967–; British Council specialist lectr, Greece, Turkey, Latvia, Albania and Australia; Loeb Lectr, Harvard, 1979; Vis. Byzantinist, Medieval Acad. of America, 1987; Wiles Lectr, QUB, 1990; Runciman Lectr, KCL, 1997. Chm., Runciman Award, 1999. Co-founder, Byzantine and Modern Greek Studies, 1975–. *Publications:* Byzantium and the Ancient East, 1970; Iconoclasm, 1977; The Empire of Trebizond and the Pontos, 1980; (with David Winfield) The Byzantine Monuments and Topography of the Pontos, 2 vols, 1985; (with Heath Lowry) Continuity and Change in late Byzantine and Early Ottoman Society, 1986; Peoples and Settlement in Anatolia and the Caucasus 800–1900, 1988; The Sweet Land of Cyprus, 1993; Mount Athos, 1996; articles in learned jls. *Recreations:* travel, Dodonium design. *Address:* 33 Crosbie Road, Harborne, Birmingham B17 9BG. *T:* (0121) 427 1207. *Clubs:* Buckland (Birmingham); Lochaline Social (Morvern); Black Sea (Trabzon).

BRYER, Dr David Ronald William, CMG 1996; Chief Executive, World Faiths Development Dialogue, since 2001; *b* 15 March 1944; *s* of late Ronald John William Bryer and Betty Gertrude Bryer (*née* Rawlinson); *m* 1980, Margaret Isabel, *e d* of Sir Eric Bowyer, KCB, KBE and Elizabeth (*née* Nicholls); one *s* one *d*. *Educ:* King's Sch., Worcester; Worcester Coll., Oxford (MA, DPhil); Manchester Univ. (Dip. Teaching English Overseas). Teaching and research, Lebanon and Britain, 1964–65, 1967–74 and 1979–81; Asst Keeper, Ashmolean Museum, 1972–74; Oxfam, 1975–2001: Field Dir, Middle East, 1975–79; Co-ordinator, Africa, 1981–84; Overseas Dir, 1984–91; Dir, 1992–2001. Vis. Fellow, British Acad., 1972. Chm., Steering Cttee for Humanitarian Response, Geneva, 1995–97. Chairman: Eurostep, 1993–94; British Overseas Aid Gp, 1998–2000. Member: Council, VSO; Wilton Park Academic Council, 1999–; Court, Oxford Brookes Univ., 1999–. *Publications:* The Origins of the Druze Religion, 1975; contrib. Der Islam; articles on humanitarian and development issues. *Recreations:* family and friends, travel, esp. Eastern Mediterranean, walking. *Address:* 5 First Turn, Upper Wolvercote, Oxford OX2 8AG.

BRYMER, Jack, OBE 1960; Hon. RAM; Principal Clarinettist, London Symphony Orchestra, 1972–87; *b* 27 Jan. 1915; *s* of J. and Mrs M. Brymer, South Shields, Co. Durham; *m* 1939, Joan Richardson, Lancaster; one *s*. *Educ:* Goldsmiths' College, London University (FGCL 1991). Schoolmaster, Croydon, general subjects, 1935–40. RAF, 1940–45. Principal Clarinettist: Royal Philharmonic Orchestra, 1946–63; BBC Symphony Orchestra, 1963–72; Prof., Royal Acad. of Music, 1950–58; Prof., Royal Military Sch. of Music, Kneller Hall, 1969–73; Prof., Guildhall Sch. of Music and Drama, 1981–; Member of Wigmore, Prometheus and London Baroque ensembles; Director of London Wind Soloists. Has directed recordings of the complete wind chamber music of Mozart, Beethoven, Haydn and J. C. Bach. Presenter of several BBC music series, inc. At Home (nightly). Has taken a life-long interest in mainstream jazz, and in later life has toured and performed as soloist with many of finest British and American players in that field. Pres., ISM, 1993. Hon. RAM 1955; FGSM 1986; FRNCM 1992. Hon. MA Newcastle upon Tyne, 1973; Hon. DMus: Kingston, 1993; de Montfort, 1995. Cobbett Medal, Worshipful Co. of Musicians, 1989. *Publications:* The Clarinet (Menuhin Guides), 1976; From Where I Sit (autobiog.), 1979; In the Orchestra, 1987. *Recreations:* golf, tennis, swimming, carpentry, gardening, music. *Address:* 31 Sycamore Court, Hoskins Road, Oxted, Surrey RH8 9JQ. *T:* (01883) 712843. *Club:* Croham Hurst Golf.

BRYSON, Col (James) Graeme, OBE (mil.) 1954; TD 1949; JP; Vice Lord-Lieutenant of Merseyside, 1979–89; *b* 4 Feb. 1913; 3rd *s* of John Conway Bryson and Oletta Bryson; *m* Jean (*d* 1981), *d* of Walter Glendinning; two *s* four *d* (and one *s* decd). *Educ:* St Edward's Coll.; Liverpool Univ. (LLM); Open Univ. (BSc 1994). Admitted solicitor, 1935. Commnd 89th Field Bde RA (TA), 1936; served War, RA, 1939–45 (Lt-Col 1944); comd 470 (3W/Lancs) HAA Regt, 1947–52, and 626 HAA Regt, 1952–55; Bt-Col 1955; Hon. Col 33 Signal Regt (V), 1975–81. Sen. Jt Dist Registrar and Liverpool Admiralty Registrar, High Court of Justice, Liverpool, and Registrar of Liverpool County Court, 1947–78; Dep. Circuit Judge, Northern Circuit, 1978–82. President: Assoc. of County Court Registrars, 1969; Liverpool Law Soc., 1969; W Lancs Co., 1959–79 (Hon. Life Pres., 1993), City of Liverpool, 1965–, NW Area, 1979–90, Royal British Legion; Merseyside Council of Ex-Service and Regtl Assocs, 1975–89 (Hon. Life Pres., 1989). Chm., Med. Appeal Tribunal, 1978–85; Member: Lord Chancellor's Cttee for enforcement of debts (Payne), 1965–69; IOM Commn to reform enforcement laws, 1972–74; Vice-Patron, Nat. Assoc. for Employment of Regular Sailors, Soldiers and Airmen, 1989– (Mem. Council, 1952–89); Vice President: RA Officers Assoc., 1996; RA Assoc., Liverpool, 1996. Kt, Hon. Soc. of Knights of the Round Table, 1987–. FRSA 1989. JP Liverpool, 1956; DL Lancs, 1965, later Merseyside. The Queen's Commendation for Brave Conduct, 1961. KHS 1974; KCHS 1990; KCSG 1996. *Publications:* (jtly) Execution, in Halsbury's Laws of England, 3rd edn 1976; Shakespeare in Lancashire, 1997; A Cathedral in My Time, 2000; (jtly) Liverpool Lawyers of the 20th Century, 2001. *Recreations:* local history, boating. *Address:* Sunwards, 2 Thirlmere Road, Hightown, Liverpool L38 3RQ. *T:* (0151) 929 2652. *Clubs:* Athenæum (Liverpool; Pres., 1969); Lancashire County Cricket.

BRYSON, Adm. Sir Lindsay (Sutherland), KCB 1981; FRSE 1984; FREng; Director, 1985–97, Chairman, 1990–97, ERA Technology; Lord Lieutenant of East Sussex, 1989–2000; *b* 22 Jan. 1925; *s* of James McAuslan Bryson and Margaret Bryson (*née* Whyte); *m* 1951, Averil Curtis-Willson; one *s* two *d*. *Educ:* Allan Glen's Sch., Glasgow; London Univ. (External) (BSc (Eng)); FIEE (Hon. FIEE 1991), FRAeS. Engrg Cadet, 1942; Electrical Mechanic, RN, 1944; Midshipman 1946; Lieut 1948; Comdr 1960; Captain 1967; comd HMS Daedalus, RNAS Lee-on-Solent, 1970–71; RCDS 1972; Dir, Naval Guided Weapons, 1973; Dir, Surface Weapons Project (Navy), 1974–76; Dir-Gen. Weapons (Naval), 1977–81; and Chief Naval Engr Officer, 1979–81; Controller of the Navy, 1981–84. Chm., Marine Technology Directorate, 1986–92; Dep. Chm., GEC-Marconi (formerly The Marconi Co. and GEC Avionics), 1987–90; Director (non-executive): Molins, 1988–99; Elswick, 1990–94. Pres., Sussex Sci. and Technol. Regl Orgn, 1990–94. Chairman: New Sussex Opera, 1990–99; Brighton Festival Trust, 1991–; Brighton West Pier Trust, 1995–. Institution of Electrical Engineers: Vice-Pres., 1982–84; Dep. Pres., 1984–85; Pres., 1985–86; Faraday Lectr, 1976–77. President: Soc. of Underwater Technol., 1989–91; Assoc. of Project Managers, 1991–95. Worshipful Co. of Cooks: Liveryman, 1964; Assistant, 1980; Warden, 1985; Second Master, 1986; Master, 1987; Liveryman, Worshipful Co. of Engrs, 1988. Chairman of Council: Sussex Univ., 1989–95 (Vice-Chm., 1988–89); Brighton Coll., 1990–98 (Governor, 1986–99). Chm., Old Market Trust (Hanover Band), 1996–. Hon. Fellow, Paisley Coll. of Technology, 1986; Hon. FIMechE, 1991; Hon. DSc Strathclyde, 1987; Hon DSc(Eng) Bristol, 1988; Hon LLD Sussex, 1995. KStJ 1990. *Publications:* contrib. Jl RAeS, Jl IEE, Trans RINA, Seaford Papers, Control Engineering. *Recreations:* opera, fair weather sailing, gardening. *Address:* 74 Dyke Road Avenue, Brighton BN1 5LE. *T:* (01273) 553638, *Fax:* (01273) 562478; *e-mail:* lbryson@aol.com.uk. *Clubs:* Army and Navy, MCC; Sussex; Sussex CC.

BUCCLEUCH, 9th Duke of, *cr* 1663, **AND QUEENSBERRY,** 11th Duke of, *cr* 1684; **Walter Francis John Montagu Douglas Scott,** KT 1978; VRD; JP; Baron Scott of Buccleuch, 1606; Earl of Buccleuch, Baron Scott of Whitchester and Eskdaill, 1619; Earl of Doncaster and Baron Tynedale (Eng.), 1662; Earl of Dalkeith, 1663; Marquis of Dumfriesshire, Earl of Drumlanrig and Sanquhar, Viscount of Nith, Torthorwold, and Ross, Baron Douglas, 1684; Hon. Captain RNR; President of the Council, the Queen's Body Guard for Scotland, Royal Company of Archers, 1996–2001; Lord-Lieutenant of Roxburgh, 1974–98, of Ettrick and Lauderdale, 1975–98; Chancellor, Order of the Thistle, since 1992; *b* 28 Sept. 1923; *o s* of 8th Duke of Buccleuch, KT, PC, GCVO, and Vreda Esther Mary (*d* 1993), *er d* of late Major W. F. Lascelles and Lady Sybil Lascelles, *d* of 10th Duke of St Albans; *S* father, 1973; *m* 1953, Jane, *d* of John McNeill, QC, Appin, Argyll; three *s* one *d*. *Educ:* Eton; Christ Church, Oxford. Served War of 1939–45, RNVR. MP (C) Edinburgh North, 1960–73; PPS to the Sec. of State for Scotland, 1962–64. Chairman: Buccleuch Heritage Trust, 1985–; Living Landscape Trust, 1986–; Assoc. of Lord Lieutenants, 1990–98; President: Royal Highland & Agricultural Soc. of Scotland, 1969; St Andrew's Ambulance Assoc.; Royal Scottish Agricultural Benevolent Inst.; Scottish Nat. Inst. for War Blinded; Royal Blind Asylum & School; RADAR; Galloway Cattle Soc.; East of England Agricultural Soc., 1976; Commonwealth Forestry Assoc., 1979–99; Royal Scottish Forestry Soc., 1994–96; Vice-Pres., Children First; Hon. President: Moredun Foundn for Animal Welfare; Scottish Agricultural Organisation Soc. FRAgS 1995. DL, Selkirk 1955, Roxburgh 1962, Dumfries 1974; JP Roxburgh 1975. Countryside Award, Countryside Commn and CLA, 1983; Bledisloe Gold Medal, RASE,

1992. *Recreations:* country pursuits, painting, classical music, tormenting a French horn, works of art study, overseas travel. *Heir: s* Earl of Dalkeith, *qv.*

BUCHAN, family name of **Baron Tweedsmuir**.

BUCHAN, 17th Earl of, *cr* 1469; **Malcolm Harry Erskine;** Lord Auchterhouse, 1469; Lord Cardross, 1610; Baron Erskine, 1806; *b* 4 July 1930; *s* of 16th Earl of Buchan and of Christina, Dowager Countess of Buchan (*d* 1994), *d* of late Hugh Woolner and adopted *d* of late Lloyd Baxendale; *S* father, 1984; *m* 1957, Hilary Diana Cecil, *d* of late Sir Ivan McLannahan Power, 2nd Bt; two *s* two *d. Educ:* Eton. *Heir: s* Lord Cardross, *qv. Address:* Newnham House, Newnham, Basingstoke, Hants RG27 9AS. *Club:* Carlton.

BUCHAN OF AUCHMACOY, Captain David William Sinclair; Chief of the Name of Buchan; *b* 18 Sept. 1929; *o s* of late Captain S. L. Trevor, late of Lathbury Park, Bucks, and late Lady Olivia Trevor, *e d* of 18th Earl of Caithness; changed name from Trevor through Court of Lord Lyon King of Arms, 1949, succeeding 18th Earl of Caithness as Chief of Buchan Clan; *m* 1961, Susan Blanche Fionodbhar Scott-Ellis, *d* of 9th Baron Howard de Walden and 5th Baron Seaford, TD; four *s* one *d. Educ:* Eton; RMA Sandhurst. Commissioned 1949 into Gordon Highlanders; served Berlin, BAOR and Malaya; ADC to GOC, Singapore, 1951–53; retired 1955. Member of London Stock Exchange. Sen. Partner, Messrs Gow and Parsons, 1963–72. Comr, Inland Revenue, 1974–76. Member: Queen's Body Guard for Scotland; The Pilgrims; Friends of Malta GC; Cook Soc., 1982–; Council, Royal Sch. of Needlework, 1987–96; Cons. Industrial Fund Cttee, 1988–97. Gov., London Clinic, 1988–. Mem., Worshipful Company of Broderers (Master, 1992). Vice-President: Aberdeenshire CCC, 1962–; Bucks CCC, 1984–. JP Aberdeenshire, 1959–96; JP London, 1972–95. KStJ 1987 (OStJ 1981). *Recreations:* bridge, reading. *Address:* 30 Chipstead Street, SW6 3SS; Auchmacoy House, Ellon, Aberdeenshire AB41 8RB. *T:* (01358) 720229. *Clubs:* White's, Turf, MCC, Pratt's, Pitt.

BUCHAN, Dennis Thorne, RSA 1991 (ARSA 1975); painter; *b* 25 April 1937; *s* of David S. Buchan and Mary Buchan (*née* Clark); *m* 1965, Elizabeth Watson (marr. diss. 1977); one *s* one *d. Educ:* Arbroath High Sch.; Dundee Coll. of Art; Patrick Allan Fraser Coll., Arbroath; Dundee Coll. of Art (DA 1958). Nat. Service, RAEC, 1960–62. Lectr in Drawing and Painting, Duncan of Jordanstone Coll. of Art, 1965–94. Mem., SSA, 1961–74. *Solo exhibitions:* Douglas and Foulis Gall., 1965; Saltire Soc., Edinburgh Fest., 1974; Compass Gall., 1975, A Span of Shores, 1994; *group exhibitions* include: Six Coastal Artists, Demarco Gall., Edinburgh, 1965; Seven Painters in Dundee, Scottish Nat. Gall. of Modern Art, and tour, 1972; Compass Contribution, Tramway, Glasgow, 1990; Scottish Contemporary Painting, Flowers East, London, 1993; Five Scottish Artists, Centre d'Art en l'Ille, Geneva, 1994; work in private and public collections throughout UK and USA. Keith Prize, 1962, Latimer, 1973, William McCauley Award, 1988, Gillies Bequest, 1991, Royal Scottish Acad. *Recreations:* non specific. *Address:* 8 Inchcape Road, Arbroath, Angus DD11 2DF. *T:* (01241) 873080.

BUCHAN, Janey, (Jane O'Neil Buchan); Member (Lab) Glasgow, European Parliament, 1979–94; *b* 30 April 1926; *d* of Joseph and Christina Kent; *m* 1945, Norman Findlay Buchan, MP (*d* 1990); one *s. Educ:* secondary sch.; commercial coll. Housewife, Socialist; occasional scriptwriting and journalism. Mem., Strathclyde Regl Council, 1974–79 (Vice-Chm., Educn Cttee); Chm., local consumer gp; formerly Chm., Scottish Gas Consumers' Council. *Recreations:* books, music, theatre, watching television whenever and wherever I can and defending the freedom of action of viewers and programme makers. *Address:* 72 Peel Street, Glasgow G11 5LR. *T:* (0141) 339 2583.

BUCHAN, Hon. Ursula Margaret Bridget, (Hon. Mrs Wide); gardening journalist and author; *b* 25 June 1953; twin *d* of Baron Tweedsmuir, *qv*; *m* 1979, Charles Thomas Wide, *qv*; one *s* one *d. Educ:* Littlemore Grammar Sch.; Oxford High Sch. for Girls; New Hall, Cambridge (MA); Royal Botanic Gardens, Kew (Dip. Hort.). Freelance journalist, 1980–; gardening columnist: Spectator, 1984–; Observer, 1987–93; Sunday Telegraph, 1993–97; Independent, 1998–. *Publications:* An Anthology of Garden Writing, 1986; The Pleasures of Gardening, 1987; (with Nigel Colborn) The Classic Horticulturist, 1987; Foliage Plants, 1988, 2nd edn 1993; The Village Show, 1990; Wall Plants and Climbers, 1992; (with David Stevens) The Garden Book, 1994; Gardening for Pleasure, 1996; Plants for All Seasons, 1999; Good in a Bed: garden writings from The Spectator, 2001. *Recreations:* gardening, fell walking, watching Rugby Union, reading. *Address:* c/o Curtis Brown, Haymarket House, 28–29 Haymarket, SW1Y 4SP.

BUCHAN-HEPBURN, Sir (John) Alastair (Trant Kidd), 7th Bt *cr* 1815, of Smeaton Hepburn, Haddingtonshire; Director, Broughton Ales Ltd, since 1995; *b* 27 June 1931; *s* of John Trant Buchan-Hepburn (*d* 1953), *g g s* of 2nd Bt, and Edith Margaret Mitchell (*née* Robb) (*d* 1980); *S* cousin, 1992; *m* 1957, Georgina Elizabeth, *d* of late Oswald Morris Turner, MC; one *s* three *d. Educ:* Charterhouse; St Andrews Univ.; RMA, Sandhurst. 1st King's Dragoon Guards, 1952–57; Captain, 1954; ADC to GOC-in-C, Malaya, 1954–57. Arthur Guinness & Son Co. Ltd, 1958–86; Dir, Broughton Brewery Ltd, 1987–95. Mem. Cttee, St Andrews Br., RBL. Life Mem., St Andrews Preservation Trust, 1984–; Mem., Baronets' Trust, 1992–. *Recreations:* golf, fishing, shooting, tennis, travel in Scottish Islands, antiquities. *Heir: s* (John) Christopher (Alastair) Buchan-Hepburn [*b* 9 March 1963; *m* 1990, Andrea Unwin]. *Address:* Chagford, 60 Argyle Street, St Andrews, Fife KY16 9BU. *T:* (01334) 472161. *Club:* Royal and Ancient Golf (St Andrews).

BUCHANAN, Sir Andrew George, 5th Bt *cr* 1878; farmer; Lord-Lieutenant and Keeper of the Rolls for Nottinghamshire, since 1991; *b* 21 July 1937; *s* of Major Sir Charles Buchanan, 4th Bt, and Barbara Helen (*d* 1986), *o d* of late Lt-Col Rt Hon. Sir George Stanley, PC, GCSI, GCIE; *S* father, 1984; *m* 1966, Belinda Jane Virginia (*née* Maclean), JP, DL, *widow* of Gresham Neilus Vaughan; one *s* one *d*, and one step *s* one step *d. Educ:* Eton; Trinity Coll., Cambridge; Wye Coll., Univ. of London. Nat. Service, 2nd Lieut, Coldstream Guards, 1956–58. Chartered Surveyor with Smith-Woolley & Co, 1965–70. Chm., Bd of Visitors, HM Prison Ranby, 1983 (Vice-Chm. 1982). Commanded A Squadron (SRY), 3rd Bn Worcs and Sherwood Foresters (TA), 1971–74; Hon. Col, B Sqn (SRY), Queen's Own Yeo., 1989–94. High Sheriff, Notts, 1976–77; DL Notts, 1985. KStJ 1991. *Recreations:* skiing, walking, forestry. *Heir: s* George Charles Mellish Buchanan, *b* 27 Jan. 1975. *Address:* Hodsock Priory, Blyth, Worksop, Notts S81 0TY. *T:* (01909) 591204, *Fax:* (01909) 591578; *e-mail:* andrew.buchanan@talk21.com. *Club:* Boodle's.

BUCHANAN, Sir Charles Alexander James L.; *see* Leith-Buchanan.

BUCHANAN, Prof. Sir Colin (Douglas), Kt 1972; CBE 1964; Lieut-Colonel; consultant with Colin Buchanan & Partners, 47 Princes Gate, London; *b* 22 Aug. 1907; *s* of William Ernest and Laura Kate Buchanan; *m* 1933, Elsie Alice Mitchell (*d* 1984); two *s* one *d. Educ:* Berkhamsted School; Imperial College, London. Sudan Govt Public Works Dept, 1930–32; Regional planning studies with F. Longstreth Thompson, 1932–35; Ministry of Transport, 1935–39. War Service in Royal Engineers, 1939–46 (despatches). Ministry of Town and Country Planning (later Ministry of Housing and Local Govt), 1946–61; Urban Planning Adviser, Ministry of Transport, 1961–63; Prof. of Transport, Imperial Coll., London, 1963–72; Prof. of Urban Studies and Dir, Sch. for Advanced Urban Studies, Bristol Univ., 1973–75. Vis. Prof., Imperial Coll., London, 1975–78. Member: Commn on Third London Airport, 1968–70; Royal Fine Art Commn, 1972–74. Pres., CPRE, 1980–85. Pres., Friends of the Vale of Aylesbury, 1985–94. Hon. DCL Oxon, 1972; Hon. DSc: Leeds, 1972; City, 1972. *Publications:* Mixed Blessing, The Motor in Britain, 1958; Traffic in Towns (Ministry of Transport report), 1963, (paperback edn), 1964; The State of Britain, 1972; No Way to the Airport, 1981; numerous papers on town planning and allied subjects. *Recreations:* photography, carpentry, caravan touring. *Address:* Appletree House, Lincombe Lane, Boars Hill, Oxford OX1 5DU. *T:* (01865) 739458.

BUCHANAN, Rt Rev. Colin Ogilvie; *see* Woolwich, Area Bishop of.

BUCHANAN, Prof. David Alan, PhD; Professor of Organizational Behaviour, School of Business, De Montfort University, since 1995; *b* 26 July 1949; *s* of David Stewart and Harriet Buchanan; *m* 1974, Lesley Fiddes Fulton; one *s* one *d. Educ:* Heriot-Watt Univ. (BA Hons); Univ. of Edinburgh (PhD). Personnel Asst, Lothian Regl Council, Edinburgh, 1976–77; Lecturer in Organizational Behaviour: Napier Poly., Edinburgh, 1977–79; Univ. of Glasgow, 1979–86, Sen. Lectr, 1986–89; Prof. of Human Resource Management, Loughborough Univ. of Technology, 1989–95; Dir, Loughborough Univ. Business Sch., 1992–95. FRSA. *Publications:* The Development of Job Design Theories and Techniques, 1979; (with A. A. Huczynski) Organizational Behaviour: an introductory text, 1985, 4th edn 2001, Student Workbook, 1994, Instructor's Manual, 2001; (ed jtly) The New Management Challenge: information systems for improved performance, 1988; (with J. McCalman) High Performance Work Systems: the digital experience, 1989; with D. Boddy: Organizations in the Computer Age: technological imperatives and strategic choice, 1983; Managing New Technology, 1986; The Technical Change Audit: action for results, 1987; Take the Lead: interpersonal skills for project managers, 1992; The Expertise of the Change Agent: public performance and backstage activity, 1992; (with R. Badham) Power, Politics, and Organizational Change, 1999; numerous contribs to learned jls. *Recreations:* music, reading, photography, fitness. *Address:* 18 Ascott Gardens, West Bridgford, Nottingham NG2 7TH.

BUCHANAN, Sir Dennis; *see* Buchanan, Sir R. D.

BUCHANAN, Rt Rev. Duncan; *see* Buchanan, Rt Rev. G. D.

BUCHANAN, Rev. Canon Eric; Vicar of St Mary's, Higham Ferrers, 1990–97; Chaplain to the Queen, since 1992; *b* 2 Feb. 1932; *s* of Oswald Stanley Buchanan and Dorothy Aletta Buchanan (*née* Parkinson); *m* 1st, 1961, Julie Anne Taylor (*d* 1977); one *s* two *d*; 2nd, 1977, Julie Annette Howard (*née* Chamberlain); one step *s* two step *d. Educ:* Rotherham Grammar Sch.; Leeds Univ. (BA Hons Phil.); Coll. of the Resurrection, Mirfield. Ordained deacon, 1956, priest, 1957; Asst Curate, St Mark's, Coventry, 1956–59; Asst Chaplain, Univ. of London, 1959–64; Vicar: St Luke's, Duston, Northants, 1964–79; All Hallows, Wellingborough, 1979–90. Rural Dean of Wootton, 1974–79; Non-residentiary Canon of Peterborough Cathedral, 1977–97, Canon Emeritus, 1997–. Chm., House of Clergy, Peterborough Diocesan Synod, 1978–91. *Recreations:* listening to classical music and jazz, gardening, theatre, detective fiction. *Address:* 8 College Street, Higham Ferrers, Northants NN10 8DZ. *T:* (01933) 411232.

BUCHANAN, Rt Rev. (George) Duncan; Bishop of Johannesburg, 1986–2000; *b* 23 April 1935; *s* of Wyndam Kelsey Fraser Buchanan and Phyllis Rhoda Dale Buchanan (*née* Nichols); *m* 1959, Diana Margaret Dacombe; two *d. Educ:* St John's Coll., Johannesburg; Rhodes Univ., Grahamstown (BA 1957); Gen. Theological Seminary (MDiv 1959). Curate, St Paul's Church, Durban, 1960; Rector, Parish of Kingsway, Natal, 1961–65; Diocesan Theol Tutor, Dio. Natal, 1963–65; Sub Warden, St Paul's Theol Coll., Grahamstown, 1966–76, Warden, 1976–86; Dean, St Mary's Cathedral, Johannesburg, May–Sept. 1986; Archdeacon of Albany, Diocese of Grahamstown, 1975–86. Chairman: Church Unity Commn, 1989–2000; Theol Educn by Extension Coll., 1993–2000; SA Anglican Theol Commn, 1995–2000. Hon. DD General Theological Seminary, 1987. *Publications:* The Counselling of Jesus, 1985; (ed) Meeting the Future: Christian leadership in South Africa, 1995. *Recreations:* carpentry, reading. *Address:* 35 East Street, East Town, Johannesburg 2195, South Africa. *T:* and *Fax:* (11) 7829201.

BUCHANAN, Isobel Wilson, (Mrs Jonathan King); soprano; *b* 15 March 1954; *d* of Stewart and Mary Buchanan; *m* 1980, Jonathan Stephen Geoffrey King (otherwise Jonathan Hyde, actor); two *d. Educ:* Cumbernauld High Sch.; Royal Scottish Academy of Music and Drama (DRSAMD 1974). Australian Opera principal singer, 1975–78; freelance singer, 1978–; British debut, Glyndebourne, 1978; Vienna Staatsoper debut, 1978; American debut: Santa Fé, 1979; Chicago, 1979; New York, 1979; German debut, Cologne, 1979; French debut, Aix-en-Provence, 1981; ENO debut, 1985; Paris Opera debut, 1986. Performances also with Scottish Opera, Covent Garden, Munich Radio, Belgium, Norway, etc. Various operatic recordings. *Recreations:* reading, gardening, cooking, yoga.

BUCHANAN, Prof. James McGill; Holbert L. Harris University Professor, since 1983 and Advisory General Director, Center for the Study of Public Choice, since 1988 (General Director, 1969–88), George Mason University; *b* 2 Oct. 1919; *s* of James Buchanan and Lila Scott; *m* 1945, Anne Bakke. *Educ:* Middle Tennessee State Coll. (BS 1940); Univ. of Tennessee (MA 1941); Univ. of Chicago (PhD 1948). Lieut, USNR, 1941–46. Professor of Economics: Univ. of Tennessee, 1950–51; Florida State Univ., 1951–56; Univ. of Virginia, 1956–62, 1962–68 (Paul G. McIntyre Prof.); UCLA, 1968–69; Virginia Polytechnic Inst., 1969–83 (Univ. Dist. Prof.). Fulbright Res. Scholar, Italy, 1955–56; Ford Faculty Res. Fellow, 1959–60; Fulbright Vis. Prof., Univ. of Cambridge, 1961–62. Fellow, Amer. Acad. of Arts and Scis; Dist. Fellow, Amer. Econ. Assoc. (Seidman Award, 1984). Hon. Dr, US and overseas Univs. Nobel Prize for Economics, 1986. *Publications:* Prices, Incomes and Public Policy (jtly), 1954; Public Principles of Public Debt, 1958; The Public Finances, 1960; Fiscal Theory and Political Economy, 1960; (with G. Tullock) The Calculus of Consent, 1962; Public Finance in Democratic Process, 1966; The Demand and Supply of Public Goods, 1968; Cost and Choice, 1969; (with N. Devletoglou) Academia in Anarchy, 1970; (ed jtly) Theory of Public Choice, 1972; (with G. F. Thirlby) LSE Essays on Cost, 1973; The Limits of Liberty, 1975; (with R. Wagner) Democracy in Deficit, 1977; Freedom in Constitutional Contract, 1978; What Should Economists Do?, 1979; (with G. Brennan) The Power to Tax, 1980; (ed jtly) Towards a Theory of the Rent-Seeking Society, 1980; (ed jtly) The Theory of Public Choice II, 1984; (with G. Brennan) The Reason of Rules, 1985; Liberty Market and State, 1985; (jtly) El Analisis Economico de lo Politico, 1985; (ed jtly) Deficits, 1987; Economics: between predictive science and moral philosophy, 1987; Economía y Política, 1987; Maktens Gränser, 1988; (ed) Explorations into Constitutional Economics, 1989; Essays on the Political Economy, 1989; Stato, mercato e libertà, 1989; The Economics and the Ethics of Constitutional Order, 1991; Constitutional Economics, 1991; Better than Plowing and Other Personal Essays, 1992; Ethics and Economic

Progress, 1994; (ed jtly) Return to Increasing Returns, 1994; Post-Socialist Political Economy, 1997; (with R. Congleton) Politics by Principle, not Interest, 1998. *Address:* Center for the Study of Public Choice, Buchanan House, George Mason University, Fairfax, VA 22030–4444, USA; PO Drawer G, Blacksburg, VA 24063–1021, USA.

BUCHANAN, John David, MBE 1944; ERD 1989; DL; Headmaster of Oakham School, Rutland, 1958–77; *b* 26 Oct. 1916; *e s* of late John Nevile Buchanan and Nancy Isabel (*née* Bevan); *m* 1st, 1946, Janet Marjorie (*d* 1990), *d* of late Brig. J. A. C. Pennycuick, DSO; three *s* four *d* (and one *s* decd); 2nd, 1992, Banoo Ramsamy. *Educ:* Stowe; Trinity College, Cambridge (MA). Served with Grenadier Guards, 1939–46; Adjutant, 3rd Bn Grenadier Guards, 1941–43 (despatches, 1943); Brigade Major, 1st Guards Bde, 1944–45; Private Secretary to Sir Alexander Cadogan, Security Council for the UN, 1946. Assistant Master, Westminster Under School, 1948; Assistant Master, Sherborne School, 1948–57. Administrator, Inchcape Educational Scholarship Scheme, 1978–94; Educnl Consultant to Jerwood Foundn, 1978–. FRSA 1991. DL Leics, 1980. *Publications:* Operation Oakham, 1984; Oakham Overture to Poetry, 1985; Oakham Orations, 1995. *Recreation:* gardening. *Address:* Rose Cottage, Owston, Leics LE15 8DN.

BUCHANAN, Dr John Gordon St Clair; Executive Director and Chief Financial Officer, BP (formerly BP Amoco) plc, since 1998; *b* Auckland, NZ, 9 June 1943; *s* of Russell Penman Buchanan and Marguerite, (Ginette), St Clair Stuart (*née* Cabouret); *m* 1967, Rosemary June Johnston; one *s* one *d*. *Educ:* Auckland Grammar Sch.; Univ. of Auckland (MSc Hons I, PhD Organic Chemistry); Harvard Business Sch. (PMD 1977). Post-Doctoral Res. Fellow, Wolfson Coll., Oxford, 1968–69; joined British Petroleum, 1970: various operational, commercial, and marketing posts for BP Oil, 1970–76; seconded to Central Policy Rev. Staff, Cabinet Office, 1976–77; BP Switzerland, 1978–80; Manager, Mkting and Ops, BP NZ, 1980–82; Asst Gen. Manager, Supply Dept, 1982–85; Gen. Manager, Gp Corporate Planning, 1985–88; Chief Operating Officer and Dep. Chief Exec., BP Chemicals, 1988–95; Gp Treas. and Chief Exec., BP Finance, 1995–96; Man. Dir and Chief Financial Officer, BP Co. plc, 1996–98. Non-exec. Dir, Boots Co., 1997–. Mem., Accounting Standards Bd, 1997–2001. Vice-Pres., SCI, 1991–93. Mem., Main Cttee, Hundred Gp of Finance Dirs, 1998–. Chm., Univ. of Auckland UK Trust, 2001–. *Recreations:* golf, ski-ing, Polynesian culture. *Address:* BP plc, Britannic House, 1 Finsbury Circus, EC2M 7BA. *T:* (020) 7496 4375. *Club:* Tandridge Golf (Surrey).

BUCHANAN, John M.; *see* Macdonald-Buchanan.

BUCHANAN, Vice-Adm. Sir Peter (William), KBE 1980; *b* 14 May 1925; *s* of Lt-Col Francis Henry Theodore Buchanan and Gwendolen May Isobel (*née* Hunt); *m* 1953, Audrey Rowena Mary (*née* Edmondson); three *s* one *d*. *Educ:* Malvern Coll. Joined RN, 1943; served in HM Ships King George V, Birmingham, destroyers and frigates; comd HMS Scarborough 1961–63; Far East, 1963–65 (despatches); HMS Victorious, 1965–67; British Antarctic Survey, 1967–68; comd HMS Endurance, 1968–70; MoD, 1970–72; comd HMS Devonshire, 1972–74; MoD, 1974–76; ADC to the Queen, 1975–76; Rear-Adm. 1976; Naval Sec., 1976–78; Vice-Adm., 1979; Chief of Staff, Allied Naval Forces Southern Europe, 1979–82. Mem., Lord Chancellor's Panel of Independent Inspectors, 1983–95. Younger Brother of Trinity House, 1963. Liveryman, Shipwrights' Co., 1984; Master, Guild of Freemen of City of London, 1996. MRIN; FNI. *Recreation:* sailing. *Clubs:* Caledonian; Royal Yacht Squadron.

BUCHANAN, Sir (Ranald) Dennis, Kt 1991; MBE 1976; Chairman and Managing Director, Flight West Airlines Pty Ltd, since 1987; *b* Sydney, 6 Nov. 1932; *s* of Stanley Brisbane Buchanan and Jessica (*née* Hall); *m* 1956, Della Agnes Brown; four *s* five *d* (and one *s* decd). *Educ:* All Saints Coll., Bathurst, NSW. Joined Gibbes Sepik Airways Ltd, Wewak, PNG, 1949; purchased Territory Airlines Ltd, 1957 (renamed Talair Pty Ltd, 1975), Chm. and Man. Dir, 1958–93. *Recreation:* farming. *Address:* PO Box 1580, Port Vila, Vanuata. *T:* 26481; Flight West Airlines, PO Box 1126, Eagle Farm, Qld 4009, Australia. *T:* (7) 32121201, *Fax:* (7) 32121522.

BUCHANAN, Richard; JP; *b* 3 May 1912; *s* of late Richard Buchanan and late Helen Henderson; *m* 1st, 1938, Margaret McManus (*d* 1963); six *s* two *d*; 2nd, 1971, Helen Duggan, MA, DipEd. *Educ:* St Mungo's Boys' School; St Mungo's Academy; Royal Technical Coll. Councillor, City of Glasgow, 1949–64 (Past Chm. Libraries, Schools and Standing Orders Cttees); Hon. City Treasurer, 1960–63. MP (Lab) Springburn, Glasgow, 1964–79; PPS to Treasury Ministers, 1967–70; Mem. Select Cttees: Public Accounts; Services. Chm., West Day School Management, 1958–64; Governor, Notre Dame College of Education, 1959–64, etc. Chm., Belvidere Hospital; Member Board of Managers, Glasgow Royal Infirmary; Hon. Pres., Scottish Library Assoc. (Pres., 1963); Life Mem., Scottish Secondary Teachers' Assoc., 1979; Chairman: Scottish Central Library; Adv. Cttee, Nat. Library of Scotland; Cttee on Burrell Collection; H of C Library Cttee; St Mungo's Old Folks' Day Centre, 1979–85; Director, Glasgow Citizens Theatre. Pres., Buchanan Soc., 1989–91. JP Glasgow, 1954. Hon. FLA, 1979. *Recreations:* theatre, walking, reading. *Address:* 18 Gargrave Avenue, Garrowhill, Glasgow G69 7LP. *T:* (0141) 771 7234. *Club:* St Mungo's Centenary (Glasgow).

BUCHANAN, Prof. Robert Angus, OBE 1993; PhD; FSA; FRHistS; Founder and Director, Centre for the History of Technology, Science and Society, 1964–95, Professor of the History of Technology, 1990–95, University of Bath, now Emeritus Professor; Director, National Cataloguing Unit for the Archives of Contemporary Scientists, 1987–95; *b* 5 June 1930; *s* of Roy Graham Buchanan and Bertha (*née* Davis); *m* 1955, Brenda June Wade; two *s*. *Educ:* High Storrs Grammar Sch. for Boys, Sheffield; St Catharine's Coll., Cambridge (MA, PhD). FRHistS 1978; FSA 1990. Educn Officer to Royal Foundn of St Katharine, Stepney, 1956–60 (Co-opted Mem., LCC Educn Cttee, 1958–60); Asst Lectr, Dept of Gen. Studies, Bristol Coll. of Science and Technol. (now Univ. of Bath), 1960; Lectr, 1961, Sen. Lectr, 1966, Head of Humanities Gp, Sch. of Humanities and Social Scis, 1970–95, Reader in Hist. of Technol., 1981–90, Univ. of Bath. Vis. Lectr, Univ. of Delaware, USA, 1969; Vis. Fellow, ANU, Canberra, 1981; Vis. Lectr, Huazhong (Central China) Univ. of Science and Tech., Wuhan, People's Repub. of China, 1983; Jubilee Chair in History of Technol., Chalmers Univ., Göteborg, Sweden, Autumn term, 1984. Royal Comr, Royal Commn on Historical Monuments (England), 1979–93; Sec., Res. Cttee on Indust. Archaeology, Council for British Archaeology, 1972–79; President: (Founding), Bristol Indust. Archaeology Soc., 1967–70; Assoc. for Indust. Archaeology, 1974–77; Newcomen Soc. for History of Engrg and Technol., 1981–83; Internat. Cttee for History of Technol., 1993–97 (Sec.-Gen., 1981–93); Vice Pres., Soc. of Antiquaries, 1995–99; Chm., Water Space Amenity Commn's Working Party on Indust. Archaeology, 1982–83; Member: Properties Cttee, National Trust, 1974–; Technol Preservation Awards Cttee, Science Museum, 1973–81. FRSA 1993–99. Hon. Fellow, Science Mus., 1992. Hon. DSc (Engrg) Chalmers Univ., Göteborg, Sweden, 1986. Leonardo da Vinci Medal, Soc. for Hist. of Technol., 1989. *Publications:* Technology and Social Progress, 1965; (with Neil Cossons) Industrial Archaeology of the Bristol Region, 1969; Industrial Archaeology in Britain, 1972, 2nd edn 1982; (with George Watkins) Industrial Archaeology of the Stationary Steam Engine, 1976; History and Industrial Civilization, 1979; (with C. A. Buchanan) Industrial Archaeology of Central Southern England, 1980; (with Michael Williams) Brunel's Bristol, 1982; The Engineers: a history of the engineering profession in Britain, 1989; The Power of the Machine, 1992. *Recreations:* Cambridge Judo half-blue, 1955; rambling, travelling, exploring. *Address:* 13 Hensley Road, Bath BA2 2DR. *T:* (01225) 311508.

BUCHANAN, Sir Robert Wilson, (Sir Robin), Kt 1991; DL; CA; Chairman, NHS Supplies Authority, 1991–95; *b* 28 Sept. 1930; *s* of Robert Downie and Mary Hobson Buchanan; *m* Naomi Pauline (*née* Lewis); three *d*. *Educ:* Dumbarton Acad.; Glasgow Acad. Mem., Inst. of Chartered Accts of Scotland, 1953. CA, Bath, 1965–. Chairman: Bath DHA, 1982–88; Wessex RHA, 1988–93; Vice-Chm., NHS Training Authy, 1983–88; Mem., Bath City Council, 1978–86. Mem. Council, Bath Internat. Fest., 1970–88 (Chm., 1982–86, 1988); Trustee, Robin Buchanan Charitable Trust, 1985–. Mem. Council, 1985–, Treasurer, 1995–, Bath Univ.; Mem. Council, Southampton Univ., 1990–93; Gov., Millfield Sch., 1992–2000 (Treas., 1963–92; Chm., 1997–2000). DL Avon, 1992, Somerset, 1996. *Recreations:* golf, beach walking. *Address:* Stonewalls, Beechwood Road, Combe Down, Bath BA2 5JS. *T:* (01225) 833768; Cassia Heights, Royal Westmoreland, Barbados.

BUCHANAN-DUNLOP, Richard; QC 1966; *b* 19 April 1919; *s* of late Canon W. R. Buchanan-Dunlop and Mrs R. E. Buchanan-Dunlop (*née* Mead); *m* 1948, Helen Murray Dunlop; three *d*. *Educ:* Marlborough College; Magdalene College, Cambridge. Served in Royal Corps of Signals, 1939–46 (Hon. Major). BA (Hons) Law, Cambridge, 1949; Harmsworth Scholar, 1950. Called to the Bar, 1951. *Publications:* Skiathos and other Poems, 1984; Old Olive Men, 1986; Hie Paeeon: songs from the Greek Isles, 1989. *Recreations:* painting, writing. *Address:* Skiathos, Greece.

BUCHANAN-DUNLOP, Col Robert Daubeny, (Robin), CBE 1987 (OBE 1982); Clerk, Goldsmiths' Company, since 1988; *b* 11 Aug. 1939; *o s* of late Col Robert Arthur Buchanan-Dunlop of Drumhead, OBE, The Cameronians (Scottish Rifles) and Patricia Buchanan-Dunlop (*née* Upton); *m* 1972, Nicola Jane Goodhart; two *s*. *Educ:* Loretto Sch. National Service, The Cameronians (Scottish Rifles), 1959–61; Regular Commission, 1961; transf. to Scots Guards; served Kenya, Aden, Sharjah, Germany, NI (despatches); Staff Coll., 1971; HQ 1 Div., 1973–75; Armed Forces Staff Coll., USA, 1978; Directing Staff, Canadian Land Forces Staff Coll., 1978–79; CO 8th (Co. Tyrone) Bn, UDR, 1979–81; COS 52 Lowland Bde, 1982–84; COS NI, 1984–86; Dep. Dir, UK C-in-C Cttees, 1987; retired. Mem., Queen's Body Guard for Scotland (Royal Company of Archers), 1987–. Chm., Lead Body, Jewellery and Allied Industries, 1994–98. Mem., British Hallmarking Council, 1988–. Member: Council, Goldsmiths' Coll., 1989; Governing Body: Imperial Coll., 1989–2001; London Guildhall Univ., 1997–. Hon. MA London Guildhall, 1994. *Recreations:* walking, gardening, visual arts. *Address:* Goldsmiths' Hall, Foster Lane, EC2V 6BN. *T:* (020) 7606 7010. *Club:* Army and Navy.

BUCHANAN-JARDINE, Sir Andrew Rupert John; *see* Jardine.

BUCHWALD, Art, (Arthur); American journalist, author, lecturer and columnist; *b* Mount Vernon, New York, 20 Oct. 1925; *s* of Joseph Buchwald and Helen (*née* Kleinberger); *m* 1952, Ann McGarry, Warren, Pa; one *s* two *d*. *Educ:* University of Southern California. Sergeant, US Marine Corps, 1942–45. Columnist, New York Herald Tribune: in Paris, 1949–62; in Washington, 1962–. Syndicated columnist whose articles appear in 550 newspapers throughout the world. Mem., AAAL, 1986–. Pulitzer Prize for outstanding commentary, 1982. *Publications:* (mostly published later in England) Paris After Dark, 1950; Art Buchwald's Paris, 1954; The Brave Coward, 1957; I Chose Caviar, 1957; More Caviar, 1958; A Gift from the Boys, 1958; Don't Forget to Write, 1960; Art Buchwald's Secret List to Paris, 1961; How Much is That in Dollars?, 1961; Is it Safe to Drink the Water?, 1962; I Chose Capitol Punishment, 1963; . . . and Then I told the President, 1965; Son of the Great Society, 1966; Have I Ever Lied to You?, 1968; The Establishment is Alive and Well in Washington, 1969; Sheep on the Runway (Play), 1970; Oh, to be a Swinger, 1970; Getting High in Government Circles, 1971; I Never Danced at the White House, 1973; I Am not a Crook, 1974; Bollo Caper, 1974; Irving's Delight, 1975; Washington is Leaking, 1976; Down the Seine and up the Potomac, 1977; The Buchwald Stops Here, 1978; Laid Back in Washington, 1981; While Reagan Slept, 1984; You Can Fool All of the People All the Time, 1985; I Think I Don't Remember, 1987; Whose Rose Garden is it Anyway?, 1989; Lighten Up, George, 1991; Leaving Home: a memoir, 1994; I'll Always Have Paris, 1996. *Recreations:* tennis, chess, marathon running.

BUCK, John Stephen; HM Diplomatic Service; Head, Public Diplomacy Department, Foreign and Commonwealth Office, since 2000; *b* 10 Oct. 1953; *s* of Frederick George Buck and Amelia Ellen Buck (*née* Stevens); *m* 1980, Jean Claire Webb; one *s* one *d*. *Educ:* East Ham GS; York Univ. (BA History 1975); Wolfson Coll., Oxford (MSc Applied Social Studies, 1979; CQSW 1979). Middlesex Probation Service, 1975–77; social worker, Oxfordshire Social Services, 1979; joined HM Diplomatic Service, 1980; Second Sec., Sofia, 1982; First Sec., FCO, 1984; Head of Chancery, Lisbon, 1988; FCO, 1992; Counsellor, on loan to Cabinet Office, Prin. Private Sec. to Chancellor of the Duchy of Lancaster, 1994; Counsellor and Dep. High Comr, Republic of Cyprus, 1996–2000. *Recreations:* music, reading, swimming. *Address:* c/o Foreign and Commonwealth Office, King Charles Street, SW1A 2AH.

BUCK, Karen Patricia; MP (Lab) Regent's Park and Kensington North, since 1997; *b* 30 Aug. 1958; partner, Barrie Taylor; one *s*. *Educ:* Chelmsford High Sch.; LSE (BSc, MSc, MA). R&D worker, Outset, 1979–83; London Borough of Hackney: Specialist Officer, Developing Services and Employment for Disabled People, 1983–86; Public Health Officer, 1986–87; Lab. Party Policy Directorate (Health), 1987–92; Co-ordinator, Lab. Party Campaign Strategy, 1992–96. Member: Social Security Select Cttee, 1997–2001; Work and Pensions Select Cttee, 2001–. Chm., London Gp of Labour MPs, 1998–. *Address:* House of Commons, SW1A 0AA.

BUCK, Prof. Kenneth William, PhD, DSc; Professor of Plant and Fungal Virology, Imperial College of Science, Technology and Medicine, University of London, since 1986 (Head, Microbiology and Plant Pathology Section, then Plant and Microbial Sciences Section, 1986–2001); *b* 16 Feb. 1938; *s* of William Buck and Nellie Sebra (*née* Turner); *m* 1961, Gwendoline Maureen Patterson; three *d*. *Educ:* Univ. of Birmingham (BSc 1st Cl. Hons 1959; PhD 1962; DSc 1983). Res. Fellow, Univ. of Birmingham, 1962–65; Imperial College, University of London: Lectr, Dept of Biochem., 1965–81; Reader, Dept of Biol., 1981–86; Chairman: Sub-Bd of Examrs in Microbiol., 1981–98; Bd of Examrs in Biol., 2000–; Panel of Vis. Examrs in Microbiol., London Univ., 1988–96. Sec., Cttee on Non-Specific Immunity, MRC, 1968–71; Member: Plants and Envmt Res. Grants Bd, AFRC, 1992–94; Plant and Microbial Scis Cttee, BBSRC, 1994–97. International Committee on Taxonomy of Viruses: Mem., Exec. Cttee, 1981–93; Mem., 1975–, Chm., 1981–87, Fungal Virus Sub-cttee; Sec., 1984–90; Vice-Pres., 1990–93; Mem., Plant Virus Sub-cttee, 1999–; Chm., Narnaviridae Study Gp, 2000–. Chm. of workshops on fungal virol. and plant virus replication, Internat. Congress of Virology, triennially, 1981–93, 1999; Mem., Internat. Adv. Cttee, XII Internat. Congress of Virology, Paris, 2002. Mem., Soc.

for Gen. Microbiol., 1975–. Editor, Jl of Gen. Virology, 1991–96 (Mem., Editl Bd, 1985–90, 1997–2001); Mem., Editl Bd, Virology, 1998–. *Publications:* (ed) Fungal Virology, 1986; numerous papers in scientific jls and books. *Recreations:* genealogy, mountain walking. *Address:* Department of Biological Sciences, Sir Alexander Fleming Building, Imperial College of Science, Technology and Medicine, Imperial College Road, SW7 2AZ. *T:* (020) 7594 5362.

BUCK, Prof. Margaret Ann; Head of College, Central Saint Martins College of Art & Design, since 1991, and Assistant Rector, since 1989, The London Institute; *b* 23 Nov. 1948; *d* of William Ewart Buck and Winifred Annie Buck; *m* 1985, David Martin Burrows; one *s* one *d* (twins). *Educ:* Gloucestershire Coll. of Art and Design (DipAD Fine Art); Royal Coll. of Art (MA Furniture Design). Head of Dept, then Dep. Head of Sch., Central Sch. of Art and Design, 1986; Dep. Head of Sch., Camberwell Sch. of Arts and Crafts, 1987–89; Head, Camberwell Coll. of Arts, London Inst., 1989–91. Mem. Cttee, Theatre Mus., 2000–; Trustee: Arts Foundn, 1998–; V&A Mus., 2000–. Governor, GSMD, 2000–. *Address:* Central Saint Martins College of Art & Design, Southampton Row, WC1B 4AP. *Clubs:* Chelsea Arts, Union.

BUCK, Sir (Philip) Antony (Fyson), Kt 1983; QC 1974; Barrister-at-Law; *b* 19 Dec. 1928; *yr s* of late A. F. Buck, Ely, Cambs; *m* 1st, 1955, Judy Elaine (marr. diss. 1989), *o d* of late Dr C. A. Grant, Cottesloe, Perth, W Australia, and late Mrs Grant; one *d*; 2nd, 1990, Bienvenida Perez-Blanco (marr. diss. 1993); *m* 1994, Tamaro Norashkaryan. *Educ:* King's School, Ely; Trinity Hall, Cambridge. BA History and Law, 1951, MA 1954. Chm. Cambridge Univ. Cons. Assoc. and Chm. Fedn of Univ. Conservative and Unionist Associations, 1951–52. Called to the Bar, Inner Temple, 1954; Legal Adviser, Nat. Association of Parish Councils, 1957–59 (Vice-Pres., 1970–74). MP (C) Colchester, 1961–83, Colchester North, 1983–92. PPS to Attorney-General, 1963–64; Parly Under-Sec. of State for Defence (Navy), MoD, 1972–74. Chm., Select Cttee on Parly Comr for Admin (Ombudsman), 1977–92; Sec., Conservative Party Home Affairs Cttee, 1964–70, Vice-Chm., 1970–72, Chm., Oct./Nov. 1972; Chm., Cons. Parly Defence Cttee, 1979–89; Mem. Exec., 1922 Cttee, Oct./Nov. 1972, 1977–92. Sponsored and piloted through the Limitation Act, 1963. *Recreations:* most sports, reading. *Club:* Oxford and Cambridge.

BUCKERIDGE, Anthony Malcolm; writer; *b* 20 June 1912; *m* 1st, 1936, Sylvia Goulden Broon; one *s* one *d*; 2nd, 1962, Eileen Norah Selby; one *s*. *Educ:* Seaford Coll., Sussex; University Coll. London. Nat. Fire Service, 1940–45; Schoolmaster, St Lawrence Coll., Ramsgate, until 1950; writer of TV and radio plays and musicals; writer, Jennings plays, BBC Children's Hour, 1948–64. *Publications:* A Funny Thing Happened, 1953; Rex Milligan Raises the Roof; Rex Milligan Reporting; Rex Milligan's Busy Term; Rex Milligan Holds Forth; Stories for Boys, No 1, 1957, No 2, 1965; (ed) In and Out of School, 1958; Jennings Goes to School; Take Jennings For Instance; Thanks to Jennings; Trouble with Jennings; According to Jennings; Jennings and Darbishire; Jennings as Usual; Jennings' Diary; Jennings' Little Hut; Jennings Follows a Clue; Our Friend Jennings; Just Like Jennings; Leave it to Jennings; Jennings, of Course; Especially Jennings; Jennings Abounding; Jennings in Particular; The Jennings Report; Trust Jennings; Speaking of Jennings; While I Remember, 1999. *Recreations:* acting, directing plays. *Address:* East Crink, Barcombe Mills, Lewes, Sussex BN8 5BL. *T:* (01273) 400383.

BUCKHURST, Lord; William Herbrand Thomas Sackville; *b* 13 June 1979; *s* and *heir* of Earl De La Warr, *qv*. *Educ:* Eton; Newcastle Univ. *Recreations:* racing, shooting. *Address:* Buckhurst Park, Withyham, E Sussex TN7 4BL.

BUCKINGHAM, Area Bishop of, since 1998; **Rt Rev. Michael Arthur Hill;** *b* 17 April 1949; *s* of Arthur and Hilda Hill; *m* 1972, Anthea Jean Hill (*née* Longridge); one *s* four *d*. *Educ:* N Cheshire Coll. of FE (Dip. in Business Studies); Brasted Place Coll.; Ridley Hall, Cambridge (GOE); Fitzwilliam Coll., Cambridge (Postgrad. Cert. in Theology). Junior Exec. in printing industry, 1968–72. Mem., Scargill House Community, 1972–73; ordained deacon, 1977, priest, 1978; Curate: St Mary Magdalene, Addiscombe, Croydon, 1977–80; St Paul, Slough, 1980–83; Priest in charge, 1983–90, Rector, 1990–92, St Leonard, Chesham Bois; RD, Amersham, 1990–92; Archdeacon of Berkshire, 1992–98. *Publications:* Reaching the Unchurched, 1992; Lifelines, 1997. *Recreations:* playing guitar, listening to music, cricket, soccer, Rugby League and Union, reading. *Address:* Sheridan, Grimms Hill, Great Missenden, Bucks HP16 9BD. *T:* (01494) 862173, *Fax:* (01494) 890508; *e-mail:* bishopbucks@oxford.anglican.org.

BUCKINGHAM, Archdeacon of; *see* Goldie, Ven. D.

BUCKINGHAM, Amyand David, CBE 1997; FRS 1975; Professor of Chemistry, University of Cambridge, 1969–97; Fellow of Pembroke College, Cambridge, 1970–97, now Emeritus; *b* 28 Jan. 1930; 2nd *s* of late Reginald Joslin Buckingham and late Florence Grace Buckingham (formerly Elliot); *m* 1965, Jillian Bowles; one *s* two *d*. *Educ:* Barker Coll., Hornsby, NSW; Univ. of Sydney; Corpus Christi Coll., Cambridge (Shell Postgraduate Schol.). Univ. Medal 1952, MSc 1953, Sydney; PhD 1956, ScD 1985, Cantab. 1851 Exhibn Sen. Studentship, Oxford Univ., 1955–57; Lectr and subseq. Student and Tutor, Christ Church, Oxford, 1955–65; Univ. Lectr in Inorganic Chem. Lab., Oxford, 1958–65; Prof. of Theoretical Chem., Univ. of Bristol, 1965–69. Vis. Lectr, Harvard, 1961; Visiting Professor: Princeton, 1965; Univ. of California (Los Angeles), 1975; Univ. of Illinois, 1976; Univ. of Wisconsin, 1978; ANU, 1996; Vis. Fellow, ANU, 1979 and 1982; Vis. Erskine Fellow, Univ. of Canterbury, NZ, 1990. FRACI 1961 (Masson Meml Schol. 1952; Rennie Meml Medal, 1958); FRSC (formerly FCS) (Harrison Meml Prize, 1959; Tilden Lectr, 1964; Theoretical Chemistry and Spectroscopy Prize, 1970; Faraday Medal and Lectr, 1997; Mem., Faraday Div. (Pres., 1987–89; Mem. Council, 1965–67, 1975–83, 1987–99)); FInstP (Harrie Massey Medal and Prize, 1995); Fellow: Optical Soc. of America; Amer. Phys. Soc.; Mem., Amer. Chem. Soc.; For. Associate, Nat. Acad. Scis, USA, 1992; Foreign Member: Amer. Acad. of Arts and Scis, 1992; Royal Swedish Acad. Scis, 1996. Editor: Molecular Physics, 1968–72; Chemical Physics Letters, 1978–99. Member: Chemistry Cttee, SRC, 1967–70; Adv. Council, Royal Mil. Coll. of Science, Shrivenham, 1973–87; Council, Royal Soc., 1999–. Senior Treasurer: Oxford Univ. Cricket Club, 1959–64; Cambridge Univ. Cricket Club, 1977–90 (Pres., 1990–). Hon. Dr: Univ. de Nancy I, 1979; Sydney, 1993. Hughes Medal, Royal Soc., 1996. *Publications:* The Laws and Applications of Thermodynamics, 1964; Organic Liquids, 1978; Principles of Molecular Recognition, 1993; papers in scientific jls. *Recreations:* walking, woodwork, cricket, tennis, travel. *Address:* Crossways, 23 The Avenue, Newmarket CB8 9AA.

BUCKINGHAM, Ven. Hugh Fletcher; Archdeacon of the East Riding, 1988–98, now Archdeacon Emeritus; *b* 13 Sept. 1932; *s* of Rev. Christopher Leigh Buckingham and Gladys Margaret Buckingham; *m* 1967, Alison Mary Cock; one *s* one *d*. *Educ:* Lancing College; Hertford Coll., Oxford (MA Hons). Curate: St Thomas', Halliwell, Bolton, 1957–60; St Silas', Sheffield, 1960–65; Vicar of Hindolveston and Guestwick, dio. Norwich, 1965–70; Rector of Fakenham, 1970–88. Hon. Canon of Norwich Cathedral, 1985–88. *Publications:* How To Be A Christian In Trying Circumstances, 1985; Feeling Good, 1989; Happy Ever After, 2000. *Recreations:* pottery, gardening. *Address:* Orchard Cottage, Rectory Corner, Brandsby, York YO61 4RJ.

BUCKINGHAMSHIRE, 10th Earl of, *cr* 1746; **George Miles Hobart-Hampden;** Bt 1611; Baron Hobart 1728; Partner, Watson Wyatt Partners, consulting actuaries, since 1995; company director; *b* 15 Dec. 1944; *s* of Cyril Langel Hobart-Hampden (*d* 1972) (*g g s* of 6th Earl), and Margaret Moncrieff Hilborne Hobart-Hampden (*née* Jolliffe) (*d* 1985); *S* cousin, 1983; *m* 2nd, 1975, Alison Wightman, JP, DL (*née* Forrest); two step *s*. *Educ:* Clifton College; Exeter Univ. (BA Hons History); Birkbeck Coll. and Inst. of Commonwealth Studies, Univ. of London (MA Area Studies). With Noble Lowndes and Partners Ltd, 1970–81; Dir, Scottish Pension Trustees Ltd, 1979–81, resigned; Director: Antony Gibbs Pension Services Ltd, 1981–86; Wardley Investment Services (UK) Ltd, 1986–91; Wardley Investment Services International Ltd (Man. Dir, 1988–91); Wardley Investment Services Ltd, 1988–91; Wardley Unit Trust Managers Ltd (Chm.), 1988–91; Wardley Fund Managers (Jersey) Ltd (Chm.), 1988–91; Wardley Investment Services (Luxembourg) SA, 1988–91; Wardley Asia Investment Services (Luxembourg) SA, 1989–91; Wardley Global Selection, 1989–91; Gota Global Selection, 1988–95; Korea Asia Fund, 1990–91; Wyatt Co. (UK) Ltd, 1991–95; Dir, Russian Pension Trust Co. Ltd, 1994–2001. House of Lords, 1984–99: Member: Sub-Cttee C, 1985–90, Sub-Cttee A, 1990–93, H of L Select Cttee on European Affairs; H of L Sub-Cttee on Staffing of Community Instns, 1987–88. Pres., Buckingham Cons. Constituency Assoc., 1989–. President: John Hampden Soc., 1993–; Friends of the Vale of Aylesbury, 1994–. Mem. Council, Buckinghamshire Chilterns UC, 2001–. Gov., Clifton Coll., Bristol, 1991–; Pres., Old Cliftonian Soc., 2000–. FInstD 1983. Patron: Hobart Town (1804) First Settlers Assoc., 1984–. Sleep Apnoea Trust, 1997. *Recreations:* music, squash, fishing, Real tennis, Rugby football. *Heir: kinsman* Sir John Vere Hobart, Bt, *qv*. *Address:* 1 Falcon Way, Shire Park, Welwyn Garden City, Herts AL7 1TW. *T:* (01707) 607503, *Fax:* (01707) 607563. *Clubs:* Western (Glasgow); West of Scotland Football; Leamington Tennis, Hatfield Tennis.

BUCKLAND, Maj.-Gen. Ronald John Denys Eden, CB 1974; MBE 1956; DL; Chief Executive, Adur District Council, 1975–85; *b* 27 July 1920; *s* of late Geoffrey Ronald Aubert Buckland, CB and Lelgarde Edith Eleanor (*née* Eden); *m* 1968, Judith Margaret Coxhead, MBE, DL; two *d*. *Educ:* Winchester; New College, Oxford (MA). Commissioned into Coldstream Gds, Dec. 1940. Served War of 1939–45: NW Europe, with 4th Coldstream Gds, 1944–45 (wounded twice). GSO3, Gds Div., BAOR, 1946; Adjt, 1st Bn Coldstream Gds, Palestine and Libya, 1948; DAA&QMG, 2nd Guards Bde and 18th Inf. Bde, Malaya, 1950–52 (Dispatches); DAAG, 3rd Div., Egypt, 1954; jssc 1956; Bde Major, 1st Gds Bde, Cyprus, 1958; Bt Lt-Col 1959; Bde Major, 51st Inf. Bde, 1960; commanded 1st Bn, Coldstream Gds, 1961, British Guiana, 1962; GSO1, 4th Div., BAOR, 1963; Brig. 1966; Comdr, 133 Inf. Bde (TA), 1966; ACOS, Joint Exercises Div., HQ AFCENT, Holland, 1967; idc 1968; DA&QMG, 1st British Corps, BAOR, 1969; Maj.-Gen. 1969; Chief of Staff, HQ Strategic Command, 1970; Maj.-Gen. i/c Admin, UKLF, 1972–75. DL W Sussex, 1986. *Recreations:* travel, watching cricket, bricklaying. *Clubs:* MCC; Leander; Sussex.

BUCKLAND, Sir Ross, Kt 1997; Chief Executive and Director, Unigate plc, 1990–2001; *b* 19 Dec. 1942; *s* of William Arthur Haverfield Buckland and Elizabeth Buckland; *m* 1966, Patricia Ann Bubb; two *s*. *Educ:* Sydney Boys' High Sch. Various positions in cos engaged in banking, engrg and food ind., 1958–66; Dir, Finance and Admin, Elizabeth Arden Pty Ltd, 1966–73; Kellogg (Australia) Pty Ltd, 1973–77, Man. Dir, 1978; Pres. and Chief Exec., Kellogg Salada Canada Inc., 1979–80; Chm., Kellogg Co. of GB Ltd and Dir, European Ops and Vice-Pres., Kellogg Co., USA, 1981–90. Director: RJB Mining, 1997–99; Allied Domecq, 1998–; Nat. Australia Bank Europe, 1999–. Fellow, Australian Soc. Certified Practising Accountants; FCIS; FIGD. *Recreation:* walking. *Address:* #2503 Quay West, 100 Gloucester Street, The Rocks, Sydney, NSW 2000, Australia. *Clubs:* Royal Automobile; Sydney Cricket, Stadium Australia (Sydney).

BUCKLAND, Yve Helen Elaine, (Mrs Stephen Freer); Chair, Health Development Agency, since 2000; *b* 29 Nov. 1956; *d* of George Robert Jones and Margaret Ann Jones (*née* O'Hanlon); *m* 1999, Stephen Freer; two *d*. *Educ:* Our Lady of Mercy Grammar Sch., Wolverhampton; Leeds Univ. (BA Hons 1977); Univ. of Liverpool (DipArch 1978); Univ. of Central Lancashire (DMS 1984). Archivist, 1979–83, Dep. County Archivist, 1983–85, Cheshire CC; Team Leader, Mgt Effectiveness Unit, 1985–88, Asst Dir, Social Services, 1988–92, Birmingham CC; Dep. Chief Exec., Nottingham CC, 1992–99; Chm., Health Educn Authy for England, 1999–2000. Non-exec. Dir, Warwicks HA, 1998–. Chm., Pharmacy Health Care Scheme, 2001–. Patron, Foundn for Sustainability, 1999–; Trustee, Community Educn Develt Centre, 2000–. *Recreations:* gardening, bell ringing. *Address:* (office) Trevelyan House, 30 Great Peter Street, SW1P 2HW.

BUCKLE, (Christopher) Richard (Sandford), CBE 1979; writer; critic; exhibition designer; *b* 6 Aug. 1916; *s* of late Lieut-Col C. G. Buckle, DSO, MC, Northamptonshire Regt, and Mrs R. E. Buckle (*née* Sandford). *Educ:* Marlborough; Balliol. Founded "Ballet", 1939. Served Scots Guards, 1940–46; in action in Italy (despatches, 1944). Started "Ballet" again, 1946; it continued for seven years. Ballet critic of the Observer, 1948–55: ballet critic of the Sunday Times, 1959–75; advised Canada Council on state of ballet in Canada, 1962; advised Sotheby & Co. on their sales of Diaghilev Ballet material, 1967–69. Co-founder, Theatre Mus., 1968–83. First play, Gossip Column, prod Q Theatre, 1953; Family Tree (comedy), prod Connaught Theatre, Worthing, 1956. *Organised:* Diaghilev Exhibition, Edinburgh Festival, 1954, and Forbes House, London, 1954–55; The Observer Film Exhibition, London, 1956; Telford Bicentenary Exhibition, 1957; Epstein Memorial Exhibition, Edinburgh Festival, 1961; Shakespeare Exhibition, Stratford-upon-Avon, 1964–65; a smaller version of Shakespeare Exhibition, Edinburgh, 1964; Treasures from the Shakespeare Exhibition, National Portrait Gallery, London, 1964–65; The Communities on the March area in the Man in the Community theme pavilion, Universal and Internat. Exhibition of 1967, Montreal; Exhibition of Beaton Portraits, 1928–68, National Portrait Gallery, 1968; Gala of ballet, Coliseum, 1971; exhibn of Ursula Tyrwhitt, Ashmolean Mus., Oxford, 1974; exhibn Omaggio ai Disegnatori di Diaghilev, Palazzo Grassi, Venice, 1975; exhibn of ballet, opera and theatre costumes, Salisbury Fest., 1975; exhibn Happy and Glorious, 130 years of Royal photographs, Nat. Portrait Gallery, 1977; presented Kama Dev in recital of Indian dancing, St Paul's Church, Covent Garden, 1970; *designed:* new Exhibition Rooms, Harewood House, Yorks, 1959; redesigned interior of Dundee Repertory Theatre, 1963 (burnt down 3 months later). *Publications:* John Innocent at Oxford (novel), 1939; The Adventures of a Ballet Critic, 1953; In Search of Diaghilev, 1955; Modern Ballet Design, 1955; The Prettiest Girl in England, 1958; Harewood (a guide-book), 1959 and (re-written and re-designed), 1966; Dancing for Diaghilev (the memoirs of Lydia Sokolova), 1960; Epstein Drawings (introd. only), 1962; Epstein: An Autobiography (introd. to new edn only), 1963; Jacob Epstein: Sculptor, 1963; Monsters at Midnight: the French Romantic Movement as a background to the ballet Giselle (limited edn), 1966; Nijinsky, 1971, 10th edn 1998; Nijinsky on Stage: commentary on drawings of Valentine Gross, 1971; (ed) U and Non-U revisited, 1978; Diaghilev, 1979; (ed) Self Portrait with Friends, selected diaries of Cecil Beaton, 1979;

Buckle at the Ballet, 1980; (with Roy Strong and others) Designing for the Dancer, 1981; (contrib.) The Englishman's Room, ed A. Lees-Milne, 1986; (contrib.) Sir Iain Moncreiffe of that Ilk, ed J. Jolliffe, 1986; L'Après-midi d'un faune, Vaslav Nijinski (introd. only), 1983; (with John Taras) George Balanchine, Ballet Master, 1988; *autobiography:* 1, The Most Upsetting Woman, 1981; 2, In the Wake of Diaghilev, 1982. *Recreations:* caricature, light verse. *Address:* Roman Road, Gutch Common, Semley, Shaftesbury, Dorset SP7 9BE.

BUCKLE, Richard; *see* Buckle, C. R. S.

BUCKLE, Simon James, DPhil; Senior Manager (Research), Market Infrastructure Division, Bank of England; *b* 29 Feb. 1960; *s* of Roy Thomas Buckle and Muriel May Buckle; *m* 1990, Dr Rajeshree Bhatt; one *d. Educ:* Univ. of Bristol (BSc 1st Cl. Jt Hons Physics and Philosophy 1982); Univ. of Sussex (DPhil Theoretical Physics 1985). Res. Asst, Dept of Physics, Imperial Coll., London, 1985–86; joined HM Diplomatic Service, 1986; Far East Dept, FCO, 1986–88; MoD, 1988–89; Private Sec., MoD, 1989–91; Head of Iran Section, Middle East Dept, FCO, 1992–94; First Sec., Dublin, 1994–97; Political Counsellor and Consul Gen., Seoul, 1997–98; Bank of England, 1998–. *Recreations:* hill walking, music. *Address:* c/o Bank of England, Threadneedle Street, EC2R 8EU.

BUCKLE, Rt Rev. Terrence Owen; *see* Yukon, Bishop of.

BUCKLER, Rev. Canon Philip John Warr; Canon Residentiary, since 1999, and Treasurer, since 2000, St Paul's Cathedral; *b* 26 April 1949; *s* of Ernest and Cynthia Buckler; *m* 1977, Linda Marjorie; one *d. Educ:* Highgate Sch.; St Peter's Coll., Oxford (BA, MA); Cuddesdon Theol Coll. Ordained deacon, 1972, priest, 1973; Asst Curate, St Peter's, Bushey Heath, 1972–75; Chaplain, Trinity Coll., Cambridge, 1975–81; Sacrist and Minor Canon, St Paul's Cathedral, 1981–86; Vicar of Hampstead, 1987–99; Area Dean of N Camden, 1993–98. Chaplain, Actors' Church Union, 1983–92; Hon. Chaplain: Scriveners' Co., 1984–; Merchant Taylors' Co., 1986–87; Spectacle Makers' Co., 2000–01; Mem. Court, Corp. of Sons of Clergy, 1996–. *Recreations:* cricket, walking, gardening. *Address:* 2 Amen Court, EC2M 7BU. *T:* (020) 7248 3312. *Clubs:* Athenæum, MCC.

BUCKLES, Nicholas Peter; Group Chief Executive, Securicor, since 2002; *b* 1 Feb. 1961; *s* of Ronald Peter Buckles and Sylvia Mary Buckles; *m* 1988, Loraine Salter; one *s* two *d. Educ:* Coventry Univ. (BA Hons Business Studies). Dowty Engrg Gp, 1979–83; Business Analyst, Avon Cosmetics, 1983–85; joined Securicor, 1985: Project Accountant, 1985–88; Commercial Manager, 1988–91; Dir, Securicor Cash Services, 1991–93; Dep. Man. Dir, Securicor Guarding, 1993–96; Man. Dir, Securicor Cash Services, 1996–98; Chief Executive: Securicor Europe, 1998–99; Security Div., 1999–2002. *Recreations:* soccer, tennis, walking. *Address:* Securicor, Sutton Park House, 15 Carshalton Park Road, Sutton, Surrey SM1 4LD. *T:* (020) 8770 7000.

BUCKLEY, family name of **Baron Wrenbury**.

BUCKLEY, Edgar Vincent, CB 1999; PhD; Assistant Secretary General for Defence Planning and Operations, North Atlantic Treaty Organisation, since 1999; *b* 17 Nov. 1946; *s* of Michael Joseph Buckley and Mary Buckley; *m* 1972, Frances Jacqueline Cheetham; two *s* three *d. Educ:* St Ignatius Coll., London; North-Western Poly., London (BA Hons 1967); Birkbeck Coll., London (PhD 1974). Teacher, Redbridge, 1970–73; joined MoD, 1973; Administration Trainee, 1974–76; Private Sec. to Vice Chief of Air Staff, 1976–78; Principal, 1978–79; Assistant Director: Strategic Systems Finance, 1980–84; Nuclear Policy, 1984–85; Head of Resources and Programmes (Navy), 1985–89; rcds, 1990; Efficiency Study, Cabinet Office, 1991 (on secondment); Head of Defence Arms Control Unit, 1991–92; Defence Counsellor, UK Delegn to NATO, 1992–96 (on secondment); Asst Under-Sec. of State (Home and Overseas), 1996–99. *Recreations:* running, swimming, reading, home maintenance. *Address:* NATO HQ, 1110 Brussels, Belgium.

BUCKLEY, Eric Joseph, MA; FIOP; Printer to the University of Oxford, 1978–83; Emeritus Fellow of Linacre College, Oxford, 1983 (Fellow, 1979–83); *b* 26 June 1920; *s* of Joseph William Buckley and Lillian Elizabeth Major (*née* Drake); *m* 1st, 1945, Joan Alice Kirby (*d* 1973); one *s* one *d*; 2nd, 1978, Harriett (*d* 1995), *d* of Judge and Mrs Robert Williams Hawkins, Caruthersville, Mo, USA. *Educ:* St Bartholomew's, Dover. MA Oxon 1979 (by special resolution; Linacre College). Served War, RAOC and REME, ME and UK, 1939–45. Apprentice, Amalgamated Press, London, 1935; Dir, Pergamon Press Ltd, 1956–74; joined Oxford Univ. Press as Dir, UK Publishing Services, 1974. Liveryman, Stationers and Newspaper Makers Co., 1981; Freeman, City of London, 1980. *Recreations:* reading, theatre, cats. *Address:* 43 Sandfield Road, Oxford OX3 7RN. *T:* (01865) 760588.

BUCKLEY, George Eric; Counsellor, Atomic Energy, British Embassy, Tokyo, 1976–81; *b* 4 Feb. 1916; *s* of John and Florence Buckley; *m* 1941, Mary Theresa Terry (*d* 1994); one *s* one *d. Educ:* Oldham High Sch.; Manchester Univ. BSc (Hons) Physics; MInstP. Lectr in Physics, Rugby Coll. of Technol., 1938. War service, Sqdn Ldr, RAF, 1940–46. Manager, Health Physics and Safety, Windscale Works, 1949; Works Manager, Capenhurst Works, 1952; Chief Ops Physicist, Risley, 1956; Chief Tech. Manager, Windscale and Calder Works, 1959; Superintendent: Calder Hall and Windscale Advanced Gas Cooled Reactors, 1964; Reactors, and Head of Management Services, 1974. *Recreations:* travel, good food, golf. *Address:* G42 Longueville Court, The Village Green, Orton Longueville, Peterborough PE2 7DN.

BUCKLEY, James; Chief Executive, Baltic Exchange, since 1992; *b* 5 April 1944; *s* of late Harold Buckley and of Mabel Buckley; *m* 1972, Valerie Elizabeth Powles; one *d. Educ:* Sheffield City Grammar Sch.; Imperial College of Science and Technology (BSc, ARCS). RAF Operational Res., 1965. Principal Scientific Officer, 1971; Asst Sec., CSD; Private Secretary: to Lord Privy Seal, Lord Peart, 1979; to Lord President of Council, Lord Soames, 1979; to Chancellor of Duchy of Lancaster, Baroness Young, 1981; Sec., Civil Service Coll., 1982; Chief Exec., BVA, 1985–87; Dep. Dir Gen., GCBS, 1987–91. *Recreations:* photography, tennis. *Address:* Baltic Exchange, St Mary Axe, EC3A 8BH. *T:* (020) 7369 1621.

BUCKLEY, James Arthur, CBE 1975; *b* 3 April 1917; *s* of late James Buckley and of Elizabeth Buckley; *m* 1939, Irene May Hicks; two *s. Educ:* Christ's Hosp., Horsham, Sussex; Westminster Technical Coll.; Bradford Technical Coll. RAFVR, 1940–46. Gas Light & Coke Co.; Gas Supply Pupil, 1934; Actg Service Supervisor, 1939; Service Supervisor, 1946; North Thames Gas Board: Divisional Man., 1954; Commercial Man., 1962; Commercial Man. and Bd Mem., 1964; East Midlands Gas Board: Dep. Chm., 1966–67; Chm., 1967–68; Mem., Gas Council, later British Gas Corp., 1968–76. Pres., IGasE, 1971–72.

BUCKLEY, Martin Christopher Burton; Chief Registrar in Bankruptcy, Companies Court, High Court of Justice, 1997–2001, and Clerk of Restrictive Practices Court, 1988–2001; *b* 5 Oct. 1936; *s* of late Hon. Dr Colin Burton Buckley and Evelyn Joyce Buckley (*née* Webster); *m* 1964, Victoria Gay, *d* of Dr Stanhope Furber; two *s* three *d. Educ:* Rugby School; Trinity College, Oxford (MA). Called to the Bar, Lincoln's Inn, 1961, Bencher, 1996; practised at Chancery Bar, 1962–88; Registrar in Bankruptcy, 1988–97. *Publication:* (ed jtly) Buckley on the Companies Acts, 14th edn 1981 (1st edn 1873—9th edn 1909 by grandfather, Henry Burton Buckley, later 1st Baron Wrenbury). *Recreations:* amateur theatre, choral singing. *Address:* Crouchers, Rudgwick, Horsham, W Sussex RH12 3DD.

BUCKLEY, Michael Sydney; Parliamentary Commissioner for Administration, and Health Service Commissioner for England, Scotland and Wales, since 1997; Scottish Parliamentary Commissioner for Administration and Welsh Administration Ombudsman, since 1999; *b* 20 June 1939; *s* of Sydney Dowsett Buckley and Grace Bew Buckley; *m* 1st, 1972, Shirley Stordy (*d* 1991); one *s* one *d*; 2nd, 1992, Judith Cartmell (*née* Cobb); two step *s* one step *d. Educ:* Eltham College; Christ Church, Oxford (MA; Cert. of Stats). Asst Principal, Treasury, 1962; Asst Private Sec. to Chancellor of Exchequer, 1965–66; Principal: Treasury, 1966–68 and 1971–74; CSD, 1968–71; Assistant Secretary: Treasury, 1974–77 and 1980–82; DoI, 1977–80; Under Secretary: Cabinet Office, 1982–85; Dept of Energy, 1985–91; Chm., Dartford and Gravesham NHS Trust, 1995–96. Mem., CS Appeal Bd, 1991–96. *Recreations:* photography, listening to music, reading. *Address:* Millbank Tower, Millbank, SW1P 4QP.

BUCKLEY, Peter Neville; Chief Executive, since 1987, and Chairman, since 1994, Caledonia Investments PLC (Deputy Chairman, 1987–94); *b* 23 Sept. 1942; *s* of Maj. Edward Richard Buckley and Ina Heather (*née* Cayzer); *m* 1967, Mary Barabel Stewart; two *d. Educ:* Eton; Manchester Business Sch. (DipBA). Served articles with McClelland Moores & Co. (later Ernst & Young); qualified as Chartered Accountant, 1966; joined Brit. & Commonwealth Shipping Co., later Brit. & Commonwealth Hldgs PLC, 1968; Exec. Dir, 1974–88. Chairman: English & Scottish Investors, 1988–; Sterling Inds, 1988–; Bristow Helicopter Gp, 1991–; Bristow Aviation Hldgs, 1996–; Dir, Cayzer Trust Co., 1982–; non-executive Director: RHS Enterprises, 1993–; Sun International Hotels, 1994–; Close Brothers Gp, 1995–; Telegraph Group, 1996–; Offshore Logistics Inc., 1996–. *Recreations:* gardening, golf, shooting. *Address:* Caledonia Investments PLC, Cayzer House, 1 Thomas More Street, E1W 1YB. *T:* (020) 7481 4343.

BUCKLEY, Lt-Comdr Sir (Peter) Richard, KCVO 1982 (CVO 1973; MVO 1968); *b* 31 Jan. 1928; 2nd *s* of late Alfred Buckley and Mrs E. G. Buckley, Crowthorne, Berks; *m* 1958, Theresa Mary Neve; two *s* one *d. Educ:* Wellington Coll. Cadet, RN, 1945. Served in HM Ships: Mauritius, Ulster, Contest, Defender, and BRNC, Dartmouth. Specialised in TA/S. Invalided from RN (Lt-Comdr), 1961. Private Sec. to the Duke and Duchess of Kent, 1961–89; Extra Equerry to the Duke of Kent, 1989–. Director: Vickers Internat., 1981–89; Malcolm McIntyre Consultancy, 1989–92. Governor: Wellington Coll., 1989–98; Eagle House Sch., 1989–98 (Chm. of Govs, 1992–98). *Recreations:* fishing, sailing, bee keeping. *Address:* Coppins Cottages, Iver, Bucks SL0 0AT. *T:* (01753) 653004. *Clubs:* Army and Navy; All England Lawn Tennis and Croquet; Royal Yacht Squadron; Royal Dart Yacht.

BUCKLEY, Hon. Sir Roger (John), Kt 1989; **Hon. Mr Justice Buckley;** a Judge of the High Court of Justice, Queen's Bench Division, since 1989; *b* 26 April 1939; *s* of Harold and Marjorie Buckley; *m* 1965, Margaret Gillian, *d* of Robert and Joan Cowan; one *s* one *d. Educ:* Mill Hill Sch.; Manchester Univ. (LLB (Hons)). Called to the Bar, Middle Temple, 1962 (Harmsworth Schol.); Bencher, Middle Temple, 1987; QC 1979; a Recorder, 1986–89; a Judge of the Employment Appeal Tribunal, 1994–; Pres., Restrictive Practices Court, 1994–. *Recreations:* golf, theatre. *Address:* Royal Courts of Justice, WC2A 2LL. *Club:* Old Mill Hillians.

BUCKMASTER, family name of **Viscount Buckmaster**.

BUCKMASTER, 3rd Viscount *cr* 1933, of Cheddington; **Martin Stanley Buckmaster,** OBE 1979; Baron 1915; HM Diplomatic Service, retired; *b* 11 April 1921; *s* of 2nd Viscount Buckmaster and Joan, Viscountess Buckmaster (*d* 1976), *d* of Dr Garry Simpson; *S* father, 1974. *Educ:* Stowe. Joined TA, 1939; served Royal Sussex Regt (Captain) in UK and Middle East, 1940–46. Foreign Office, 1946; Middle East Centre for Arab Studies, Lebanon, 1950–51; qualified in Arabic (Higher Standard); served in Trucial States, Sharjah (1951–53) and Abu Dhabi (Political Officer, 1955–58) and subsequently in Libya, Bahrain, FO, Uganda, Lebanon and Saudi Arabia, 1958–73; First Sec., FCO, 1973–77; Head of Chancery and Chargé d'Affaires, Yemen Arab Republic, 1977–81. Deputy Chairman: Council for the Advancement of Arab-British Studies; Christian Broadcasting Council. FRGS 1954. *Recreations:* walking, music, railways; Arab and African studies. *Heir:* *b* Hon. Colin John Buckmaster [*b* 17 April 1923; *m* 1946, May, *o d* of late Charles Henry Gibbon; three *s* two *d*]. *Address:* 90 Cornwall Gardens, SW7 4AX. *Club:* Travellers.

BUCKNILL, Thomas Michael, RD 1983; FRCS; Consultant Orthopaedic Surgeon, St Bartholomew's Hospital, since 1977 and Royal London Hospital, since 1995; *b* 11 Jan. 1942; *m* 1968, Rachael Offer; one *s* three *d. Educ:* Douai Sch.; St Bartholomew's Hosp. Med. Coll., London (MB BS 1964). FRCS 1970. House Surgeon, 1965–66, Anatomy Demonstrator, 1966–67, St Bartholomew's Hosp.; Surgical Registrar, St Stephen's Hosp., Chelsea, 1968–70; Registrar, Royal Nat. Orthopaedic Hosp., Stanmore, 1970–76; Clin. Fellow, Harvard Med. Sch., 1976; Cons. Orthopaedic Surgeon, King Edward VII Hosp., London, 1981–. MO, RNR London Div., 1967–93; Surgeon Comdr, RNR, 1987–93, retd; PMO, Royal Marines Reserve, London, 1988–91. FRSocMed 1995. *Publication:* (contrib.) Textbook of General Surgery, 1980. *Recreations:* sailing, golf. *Address:* 134 Harley Street, W1N 1AH. *T:* (020) 7486 2622. *Clubs:* Naval; Moor Park Golf, Royal Southampton Yacht, Royal Air Force Yacht.

BUCKWELL, Prof. Allan Edgar; Director of Policy, Country Land and Business Association, since 2000; *b* 10 April 1947; *s* of George Alfred Donald Buckwell and Jessie Ethel Buckwell (*née* Neave); *m* 1967, Susan Margaret Hopwood (marr. diss. 1990); two *s*; *m* 1997, Elizabeth Gay Mitchell. *Educ:* Wye Coll., Univ. of London (BSc Agric.); Manchester Univ. (MA Econ.). Research Associate, Agricl Adjustment Unit, Newcastle Univ., 1970–73; Lectr in Agricl Economics, Newcastle Univ., 1973–84; Prof. of Agricl Econs, Wye Coll., Univ. of London, 1984–99. Kellogg Res. Fellow, Univ. of Wisconsin, Madison, 1974–75; Vis. Prof., Cornell Univ., 1983. Auxilliare, DG VI, EC, 1995–96. *Publications:* (jtly) The Cost of the Common Agricultural Policy, 1982; Chinese Grain Economy and Policy, 1989; Privatisation of Agriculture in New Market Economies: lessons from Bulgaria, 1994; articles in Jl Agricl Economics. *Recreations:* walking, gardening, cycling. *Address:* 51 Joy Lane, Whitstable, Kent CT5 4DE. *T:* (01227) 265684; *e-mail:* Allanb@cla.org.uk.

BUCZACKI, Dr Stefan Tadeusz; biologist, broadcaster and author; *b* 16 Oct. 1945; *o s* of Tadeusz Buczacki and Madeleine Mary Cato Buczacki (*née* Fry); *m* 1970, Beverley Ann Charman; two *s. Educ:* Ecclesbourne Sch., Duffield; Univ. of Southampton (BSc 1968); Linacre Coll., Oxford (DPhil 1971). FIHort 1986; CBiol, FIBiol; ARPS; FLS. Research Biologist, Nat. Vegetable Res. Station, 1971–84; freelance broadcaster, writer and consultant, 1984–. *Radio:* Gardeners' Question Time, 1982–94; Classic Gardening Forum, 1994–97; The Gardening Quiz (originator and writer), 1988–93; *television:* Gardeners' Direct Line, 1983–85; That's Gardening, 1989–90, 1992; Bazaar, 1989–93; Gardeners' World, 1990–91; Chelsea Flower Show, 1990–91; Good Morning, 1992–96; Stefan Buczacki's Gardening Britain, 1996; At Home, 1997–98; Stefan's Garden Roadshow, 1998–; Open House, 1998–; Learn to Garden with Stefan Buczacki, 1999. President: W Midlands ASE, 1996–97; British Mycological Soc., 1999–2000 (Vice-Pres., 1994); Mem. Council, Gardeners' Royal Benevolent Soc., 1990–98. Trustee: Brogdale Horticultural Trust, 1990–95; Hestercombe Gardens Trust, 1996–. Patron: Parrs Wood Rural Trust, 1990–; Dawlish Gardens Trust, 1990–; Warwick Castle Gdns Trust, 1992–; Nat. Amateur Gardening Show, 1996–98; Southport Flower Show, 1997–. Hon. Prof., Plant Pathology, Liverpool John Moores Univ., 1994–. Benefactors' Medal, British Mycological Soc., 1996. *Publications:* (jtly) Collins Guide to the Pests, Diseases and Disorders of Garden Plants, 1981 (shorter Guide, 1983), 2nd edn (Photoguide), 1998; Gem Guide to Mushrooms and Toadstools, 1982; (ed) Zoosporic Plant Pathogens, 1983; Beat Garden Pests and Diseases, 1985; Gardeners' Questions Answered, 1985; (jtly) Three Men in a Garden, 1986; Ground Rules for Gardeners, 1986; Beginners Guide to Gardening, 1988; Creating a Victorian Flower Garden, 1988; Garden Warfare, 1988; New Generation Guide to the Fungi of Britain and Europe, 1989; A Garden for all Seasons, 1990; Understanding Your Garden, 1990; The Essential Gardener, 1991; Dr Stefan Buczacki's Gardening Hints, 1992; Mushrooms and Toadstools of Britain and Europe, 1992; The Plant Care Manual, 1992; (ed) The Gardener's Handbook, 1993; The Budget Gardening Year, 1993; Stefan Buczacki's Gardening Britain, 1996; (jtly) Classic FM Garden Planner, 1996; Stefan Buczacki's Gardening Dictionary, 1998; Stefan Buczacki's Plant Dictionary, 1998; Plant Problems: prevention and control, 2000; Stefan Buczacki's Best Gardening *series:* Climbers, 1994; Soft Fruit, 1994; Shade Plants, 1994; Foliage Shrubs, 1994; Herbs, 1995; Water Plants, 1995; Roses, 1996; Container Plants, 1996; Garden Doctor, 1997; Summer Flowering Shrubs, 1997; Winter Plants, 1997; Clematis, 1998; Geraniums, 1998; Pruning, 1998; Fuchsias, 1999; Evergreen Trees and Shrubs, 1999; First Time Gardener, 2000; Kitchen Herbs, 2000; Water Gardens, 2000; Ground Cover Plants, 2000; Rock Garden Plants, 2000; articles in magazines and newspapers; numerous scientific papers in professional jls. *Recreations:* own garden, photography, riding, fishing, natural history, book collecting, theatre, kippers, Derbyshire porcelain, fine music, travelling and then returning to appreciate the British countryside. *Address:* c/o Knight Ayton Management, 114 St Martin's Lane, WC2N 4AZ. *T:* (020) 7836 5333. *Club:* Garrick.

BUD, Dr Robert Franklin; Head, Information and Research (formerly Life and Communications Technologies, and Research (Collections)), Science Museum, since 1994; *b* 21 April 1952; *s* of Martin Bud and Hanna Bud (*née* Loebl); *m* 1979, Lisa Frierman; one *s*. *Educ:* University Coll. Sch.; Univ. of Manchester (BSc 1st Cl. Liberal Studies in Sci. 1973); Univ. of Pennsylvania (PhD 1980). Science Museum: Asst Keeper, Industrial Chem., 1978–85; Dep. Keeper, Dept of Physical Scis, 1985–89; Hd, Collections Services, 1989–91; Hd, Life and Envmtl Scis, 1991–94. Associate Sen. Res. Fellow, Centre for Evaluation of Public Policy and Practice, Brunel Univ., 1990–; Adjunct Prof., Univ. of Va, 1993. Associate Editor, Outlook on Sci. Policy, 1989–91; Member Editorial Board: Brit. Jl for Hist. of Sci., 1982–; History and Technol., 1993–; Mem., Editl Adv. Bd, Oxford Companion to the History of Science, 1998–. Member of Council: Brit. Soc. for Hist. of Sci., 1985–88; Soc. for Hist. of Technol., 1996–98; Mem. Steering Cttee, Hist. of Twentieth Century Medicine Gp, Wellcome Trust, 1998–. Trustee, RN Submarine Mus., 1994–99. FWAAS 1989; FRHistS 1999. (Jtly) Bunge Prize, Hans Jenemann Stiftung, 1998. *Publications:* (with G. K. Roberts) Science versus Practice: chemistry in Victorian Britain, 1984; (jtly) Chemistry in America 1876–1976: historical indicators, 1984; The Uses of Life: a history of biotechnology, 1993 (trans. German 1995); edited jointly: Invisible Connections: instruments, institutions and science, 1992; Guide to the History of Technology in Europe, 1992, 3rd edn 1996; Instruments of Science: an historical encyclopedia, 1998; Manifesting Medicine: bodies and machines, 1999; Cold War, Hot Science: applied research in British defence laboratories 1945–1990, 1999; (jtly) Inventing the Modern World: technology since 1750, 2000; articles in learned jls. *Recreations:* family life, walking, second-hand bookshops. *Address:* Science Museum, Exhibition Road, SW7 2DD. *T:* (020) 7938 8041.

BUDD, Sir Alan (Peter), Kt 1997; Provost, The Queen's College, Oxford, since 1999; *b* 16 Nov. 1937; *s* of late Ernest and Elsie Budd; *m* 1964, Susan (*née* Millott); three *s*. *Educ:* Oundle Sch. (Grocers' Co. Schol.); London School of Economics (Leverhulme Schol.; BScEcon); Churchill Coll., Cambridge (PhD). Lectr, Southampton Univ., 1966–69; Ford Foundn Vis. Prof., Carnegie-Mellon Univ., Pittsburgh, 1969–70; Sen. Economic Advr, HM Treasury, 1970–74; Williams & Glyn's Sen. Res. Fellow, London Business Sch., 1974–78; High Level Cons., OECD, 1976–77; Special Advr, Treasury and CS Cttee, 1979–81; Dir, Centre for Economic Forecasting, 1980–88, Prof. of Econs, 1981–91, Fellow, 1997, London Business Sch.; Gp Economic Advr, Barclays Bank, 1988–91; Chief Economic Advr to HM Treasury, and Head of Govt Economic Service, 1991–97; Mem., Monetary Policy Cttee, Bank of England, 1997–99. Reserve Bank of Aust. Vis. Prof., Univ. of New South Wales, 1983. Member: Securities and Investments Board, 1987–88; ABRC, 1991; Chm., Gambling Rev. Body, 2000–. Member: UK-Japan 2000 Gp, 1984–; Council, Inst. for Fiscal Studies, 1988–91; Council, REconS, 1988–93. Chm., British Performing Arts Medicine Trust, 1998–. Governor: LSE, 1994–; NIESR, 1998–. Econs columnist, The Independent, 1991. *Publications:* The Politics of Economic Planning, 1978; articles in professional jls. *Recreations:* music, gardening. *Address:* The Queen's College, Oxford OX1 4AW. *Club:* Reform.

BUDD, Bernard Wilfred, MA; QC 1969; *b* 18 Dec. 1912; *s* of late Rev. W. R. A. Budd; *m* 1944, Margaret Alison, MBE, *d* of late Rt Hon. E. Leslie Burgin, PC, LLD, MP; two *s*. *Educ:* Cardiff High Sch.; W Leeds High Sch.; Pembroke Coll., Cambridge (schol. in natural sciences). Joined ICS, 1935; various Dist appts incl. Dep. Comr, Upper Sind Frontier, 1942–43; Collector and Dist Magistrate, Karachi, 1945–46; cont. in Pakistan Admin. Service, 1947; Dep. Sec., Min. of Commerce and Works, Govt of Pakistan, 1947; Anti-corruption Officer and Inspector-Gen. of Prisons, Govt of Sind, 1949. Called to Bar, Gray's Inn, 1952; ceased practice, 1982. Contested (L), Dover, 1964 and 1966, Folkestone and Hythe, Feb. and Oct. 1974 and 1979. Chm., Assoc. of Liberal Lawyers, 1978–82. Vice-Pres., Internat. Assoc. for the Protection of Industrial Property (British Group), 1978–92. Methodist Local (lay) Preacher, 1933–. *Recreations:* birds, hill walking. *Address* Highlands, Elham, Canterbury, Kent CT4 6UG. *T:* (01303) 840350. *Clubs:* Oxford and Cambridge, National Liberal.

See also C. R. Budd.

BUDD, Colin Richard, CMG 1991; HM Diplomatic Service; Ambassador to the Netherlands, since 2001; *b* 31 Aug. 1945; *s* of Bernard Wilfred Budd, *qv*; *m* 1971, Agnes Smit; one *s* one *d*. *Educ:* Kingswood Sch., Bath; Pembroke Coll., Cambridge. Entered HM Diplomatic Service, 1967; CO, 1967–68; Asst Private Sec. to Minister without Portfolio, 1968–69; Warsaw, 1969–72; Islamabad, 1972–75; FCO, 1976–80; The Hague, 1980–84; Asst Private Sec. to Sec. of State for Foreign and Commonwealth Affairs, 1984–87; European Secretariat, Cabinet Office, 1987–88; Counsellor (Political), Bonn, 1989–92; Chef de Cabinet to Sir Leon Brittan, Vice Pres. of EC, 1993–96; Dep. Sec., Cabinet Office (on secondment), 1996–97; Dep. Under-Sec. of State, FCO, 1997–2001. *Recreations:* running, mountains, music (Mozart, chansons, Don McLean). *Address:* Foreign and Commonwealth Office, SW1A 2AH.

BUDD, Rt Rev. Mgr Hugh Christopher; *see* Plymouth, Bishop of, (RC).

BUDD, Prof. Malcolm John, PhD; FBA 1995; Grote Professor of Philosophy of Mind and Logic, University College London, 1998–2001; *b* 23 Dec. 1941; *s* of Edward Charles Budd and Hilare (*née* Campbell). *Educ:* Latymer Upper Sch.; Jesus Coll., Cambridge (BA 1964; MA 1967; PhD 1968). William Stone Research Fellow, Peterhouse, Cambridge, 1966–70; University College London: Lectr in Philosophy, 1970–87; Reader, 1987–90; Prof. of Philosophy, 1990–98. Editor, Aristotelian Soc., 1989–94. *Publications:* Music and the Emotions, 1985; Wittgenstein's Philosophy of Psychology, 1989; Values of Art, 1995. *Address:* 12 Hardwick Street, Cambridge CB3 9JA.

BUDDEN, Julian Medforth, OBE 1991; FBA 1987; *b* 9 April 1924; *s* of Prof. Lionel Bailey Budden and Dora Magdalene (*née* Fraser). *Educ:* Stowe Sch.; Queen's Coll., Oxford (MA); Royal Coll. of Music; Trinity Coll. of Music (BMus 1955). Joined BBC Music Dept, 1951, as clerk; Music Producer, 1956–70; Chief Producer, Opera (Radio), 1970–76; External Services Music Organiser, 1976–83. *Publications:* The Operas of Verdi, vol. I 1973, vol. II 1978, vol. III 1981; Verdi, 1985; Puccini, 2002; contribs to various musicological periodicals. *Address:* (March, April, July–Sept.) 94 Station Road, N3 2SG. *T:* (020) 8349 2954; (Oct.–Feb., May, June) Via Fratelli Bandiera, 9, 50137 Firenze, Italy. *T:* (55) 678471.

BUDDEN, Kenneth George, FRS 1966; MA, PhD; Reader in Physics, University of Cambridge, 1965–82, now Emeritus; Fellow of St John's College, Cambridge, since 1947; *b* 23 June 1915; *s* of late George Easthope Budden and Gertrude Homer Rea; *m* 1947, Nicolette Ann Lydia de Longesdon Longsdon; no *c*. *Educ:* Portsmouth Grammar Sch.; St John's College, Cambridge (MA, PhD). Telecommunications Research Establishment, 1939–41; British Air Commn., Washington, DC, 1941–44; Air Command, SE Asia, 1945. Research at Cambridge, 1936–39 and from 1947. *Publications:* Radio Waves in the Ionosphere, 1961; The Wave-Guide Mode Theory of Wave Propagation, 1961; Lectures on Magnetoionic Theory, 1964; The Propagation of Radio Waves, 1985; numerous papers in scientific jls, on the propagation of radio waves. *Recreation:* gardening. *Address:* 15 Adams Road, Cambridge CB3 9AD. *T:* (01223) 354752.

BUDGE, Keith Joseph; Head, Bedales School, since 2001; *b* 24 May 1957; *s* of William and Megan Budge; *m* 1983, Caroline Ann Gent; two *s* one *d*. *Educ:* Rossall Sch.; University Coll., Oxford (MA Hons English, PGCE). Asst Master, Eastbourne Coll., 1980–84; Marlborough College: Asst Master, 1984–88 and 1989–91; Housemaster, Cotton Hse, 1991–95; Instructor in English, Stevenson Sch., Pebble Beach, CA, 1988–89; Headmaster, Loretto Sch., 1995–2000. *Recreations:* hill-walking, trout-fishing, gadgets, theatre. *Address:* Bedales School, Petersfield, Hants GU32 2DG. *Club:* Vincent's (Oxford).

BUENO, Antonio de Padua Jose Maria; QC 1989; a Recorder, since 1989; *b* 28 June 1942; *s* of late Antonio and Teresita Bueno; *m* 1966, Christine Mary Lees; three *d*. *Educ:* Downside School; Salamanca Univ. Called to the Bar, Middle Temple, 1964, NSW, Ireland and Gibraltar (Bencher 1998), An Asst Recorder, 1984–89. *Publications:* (ed jtly) Banking section, Atkin's Encyclopaedia of Court Forms, 2nd edn 1976; (Asst Editor, 24th edn 1979 and 25th edn 1983, Jt Editor, 26th edn 1988) Byles on Bills of Exchange; (Asst Editor) Paget's Law of Banking, 9th edn 1982. *Recreations:* fishing, shooting. *Address:* Hammoon House, Hammoon, Sturminster Newton, Dorset DT10 2DB. *T:* (01258) 861704; 4 Paper Buildings, Temple, EC4Y 7EX. *T:* (020) 7353 3366. *Clubs:* East India, MCC; Kildare Street (Dublin).

BUERK, Michael Duncan; foreign correspondent and newscaster, television; *b* 18 Feb. 1946; *s* of Betty Mary Buerk and Gordon Charles Buerk; *m* 1968, Christine Lilley; two *s*. *Educ:* Solihull School. Thomson Newspapers, Cardiff, 1967–69; reporter, Daily Mail, 1969–70; producer, BBC radio, 1970–71; reporter: HTV (West), 1971–72; BBC TV (South), 1972–73; BBC TV London, 1973–76; correspondent, BBC TV: industrial, 1976–77; energy, 1977–79; Scotland, 1979–81; special corresp. and newscaster, 1981–83; Southern Africa, 1983–87; presenter, BBC TV News, 1988–. Hon. MA Bath, 1991; Hon. LLD Bristol, 1994. RTS TV Journalist of the Year and RTS News Award, 1984; UN Hunger Award, 1984; numerous other awards, UK and overseas, 1984, 1985; BAFTA News Award, 1985; James Cameron Meml Award, 1988; Science Writer of the Year Award, 1989; Mungo Park Award, RSGS, 1994. *Recreations:* travel, oenophily. *Address:* c/o BBC Television, W12 7RJ. *T:* (020) 8576 7771. *Club:* Reform.

BUFORD, William Holmes; Literary and Fiction Editor, The New Yorker, since 1995; *b* 6 Oct. 1954; *s* of late William H. Buford and of Helen Shiel; *m* 1991, Alicja Kobiernicka (marr. diss. 2000). *Educ:* Univ. of California, Berkeley (BA); King's College, Cambridge (MA). Editor, Granta, 1979–95; former Chm., Granta Publications Ltd. *Publications:* (as Bill Buford): Among the Thugs, 1991; (ed) The Best of Granta Travel, 1991; (ed) The Best of Granta Reportage, 1993; (ed) The Granta Book of the Family, 1995. *Address:* New Yorker Magazine, 4 Times Square, New York, NY 10036, USA.

BUHARI, Alhaji Haroun Madani; High Commissioner for Sierra Leone in London, and Ambassador for Sierra Leone to Sweden, Denmark, Norway, Spain, Portugal, Greece, India and Tunisia, 1995–96; *b* 23 Aug. 1945; *s* of Alhaji Mohammed Buhari and Haja Fatmatta M'balu (*née* Tejan-Sie); *m* 1st, 1975, Haja Sakinatu Onikeh Adams; three *s*; 2nd, 1990, Máriam Zainab Koroma; one *s* one *d*. *Educ:* St Helena Secondary Sch., Freetown; Islamic Missions Inst. at Al-Azhar Univ., Cairo; El Nasr Boys' Coll., Cairo; Univ. of Alexandria, Egypt (BA Hons 1970); Inst. of Social Studies, Univ. of Alexandria; SW London Coll.; Internat. Inst. for Journalism, W Berlin; Diplomatic Acad., Univ. of Westminster (MA 1997). Ministry of Information and Broadcasting, Sierra Leone: Inf. Officer, 1971–78; Sen. Inf. Officer, 1978–82 (Press. Sec., Office of Pres., 1981–82); Asst Controller/Principal Inf. Officer, 1982–90; Editor-in-Chief, Sierra Leone News Agency, 1986–87; Controller, Govt Inf. Services, 1990–91; Asst Dir of Inf., 1991–92 (Press Sec., Office of Pres., 1987–92); High Comr to Gambia and Ambassador to Senegal, Mauritania and Morocco, 1992–95. Founder Mem., Sierra Leone Assoc. of Journalists, 1971 (Chm., Interim Exec., 1992–93). Sec.-Gen., Sierra Leone Islamic Foundn, 1982–85; Exec. Sec. Federation of Sierra Leone Muslim Orgns, 1987. Governor: Commonwealth Foundn, 1995–96; Commonwealth Inst., 1995–96. Vice-Pres., Royal Over-Seas League, 1996–. *Publications:* articles on literary, political, social and religious issues for Sierra Leone and internat. press. *Recreations:* football, reading, music. *Address:* c/o 92 Grayson House, Radnor Street, EC1V 3SR.

BUIST, John Latto Farquharson, (Ian), CB 1990; Under Secretary, Foreign and Commonwealth Office (Overseas Development Administration), retired; *b* 30 May 1930; *s* of late Lt-Col Thomas Powrie Buist, RAMC, and Christian Mary (*née* Robertson); partner, 1981, J. E. Regensburg, (Dennis Regensburg) (*d* 1988). *Educ:* Dalhousie Castle

Sch.; Winchester Coll.; New Coll., Oxford (MA). Asst Principal, CO, 1952–54; seconded Kenya Govt, 1954–56; Principal, CO, 1956–61; Dept of Tech. Cooperation, 1961–62; Brit. High Commn, Dar-es-Salaam, 1962–64; Consultant on Admin, E African Common Services Org./Community, 1964–69; Sec., Commn on E African Cooperation and related bodies, 1966–69; Asst Sec., Min. of Overseas Develt, 1966–76; Under Sec., FCO (ODA), 1976–90. Director: PLAN International (UK), 1990–; Foster Parents PLAN Inc., 1991–. Co-founder, Classical Assoc. of Kenya; Member: Thames Philharmonic (formerly John Bate) Choir; United Reformed Church; Lesbian and Gay Christian Movement. *Recreations:* singing and other music-making. *Address:* 9 West Hill Road, SW18 1LH.

BUITER, Willem Hendrik, CBE 2000; PhD; FBA 1998; Chief Economist, European Bank for Reconstruction and Development, since 2000; *b* 26 Sept. 1949; *s* of Harm Geert Buiter and Hendrien Buiter, *née* van Schooten; *m* 1st, 1973, Jean Archer (marr. diss. 1998); one *s* one *d*; 2nd, 1998, Prof. Anne Sibert. *Educ:* Cambridge Univ. (BA 1971); Yale Univ. (PhD 1975). Asst Prof., Princeton Univ., 1975–76; Lectr, LSE, 1976–77; Asst Prof., Princeton Univ., 1977–79; Prof. of Economics, Univ. of Bristol, 1980–82; Cassel Prof. of Economics, LSE, Univ. of London, 1982–85; Prof. of Econs, 1985–90, Juan T. Trippe Prof. of Internat. Econs, 1990–94, Yale Univ.; Prof. of Internat. Macroecons, and Fellow of Trinity Coll., Cambridge Univ., 1994–2000. Consultant: IMF, 1979–80; World Bank, 1986–; Inter-American Develt Bank, 1992–; EBRD, 1994–2000; Specialist Advr, House of Commons Select Cttee on the Treasury and CS, 1980–84; Advr, Netherlands Min. of Educn and Science, 1985–86; External Mem., Monetary Policy Cttee, Bank of England, 1997–2000. Mem. Council, Royal Economic Soc., 1997–. Associate Editor, Econ. Jl, 1980–84. *Publications:* Temporary and Long Run Equilibrium, 1979; Budgetary Policy, International and Intertemporal Trade in the Global Economy, 1989; Macroeconomic Theory and Stabilization Policy, 1989; Principles of Budgetary and Financial Policy, 1990; International Macroeconomics, 1990; (jtly) Financial Markets and European Monetary Co-operation: the lessons of the 1992–93 ERM crisis, 1998; articles in learned jls. *Recreations:* tennis, poetry, music. *Address:* 2 St David's Square, E14 3WA.

BUKHT, Mirza Michael John, (Michael Barry), OBE 1996; food journalist; Programme Controller, Classic FM Radio, 1992–97; *b* 10 Sept. 1941; *s* of Mirza Jawan Bukht and Lilian Ray Bukht (*née* Oaten); *m* 1964, Jennie Mary Jones; one *s* three *d*. *Educ:* Haberdashers' Aske's Sch.; King's Coll. London (BA Hons). BBC general trainee, 1963; Producer, Tonight prog., 1965; Prog. Controller, JBC, Jamaica, 1967; Dep. Editor, 24 Hours, BBC TV, 1969; Editor, Special Projects, BBC TV, 1970; Prog. Controller, Capital Radio, 1972; Principal, Nat. Broadcasting Sch., 1979; Man. Dir, Invicta Radio, 1985; Gp Prog. Dir, GWR Gp, 1988. Chm., Kentish Fare Bd, 1994–. Mem. Cttee, Early Dance Circle, 1991–. Chm., Masterclass Charitable Trust, 1997–2000. Gov., St Edmund's Sch., Canterbury, 1997–. FRSA 1995; Fellow, Radio Acad, 1996. *Publications:* (as Michael Barry) 5 Food and Drink books, 1984–89; Food Processor Cookery, 1985; Complete Crafty Cook Book, 1988; Exotic Food, 1989, 2nd edn 1996; Michael Barry's Cook Book, 1991; Big Food and Drink Book, 1993; Great House Cookery, 1993; Classic Recipes, 1993; The Radio Times Cookery Guide, 1994; Entertaining with Food and Drink, 1995; Crafty French Cooking, 1995; Italian Food, 1997; The Classic FM Recipes, 2000. *Recreations:* music, dance, sailing, gardening, military history, food. *Address:* The Manor House, St Stephen's, Canterbury, Kent CT2 7JT. *Club:* East India.

BULFIELD, Prof. Grahame, CBE 2001; PhD; FRSE; FIBiol; Director and Chief Executive, Roslin Institute, BBSRC, since 1993; *b* 12 June 1941; *s* of Frederick Bulfield and Madge (*née* Jones). *Educ:* King's Sch., Macclesfield; Univ. of Leeds (BSc 1964); Univ. of Edinburgh (Dip. Animal Genetics 1965; PhD 1968). FRSE 1992; FIBiol 1995. Fulbright Fellow and NIH Postdoctoral Fellow, Dept of Genetics, Univ. of Calif., Berkeley, 1968–70; SRC Resettlement Fellow, 1970–71, Res. Associate, 1971–76, Inst. of Animal Genetics, Univ. of Edinburgh; Lectr and Convenor of Med. Genetics, Dept of Genetics, Med. Sch. and Sch. of Biol Scis, Univ. of Leicester, 1976–81; Hd, Genetics Gp, AFRC Poultry Res. Centre, Roslin, 1981–86; Hd, Gene Expression Gp, 1986–88, and Hd of Station and Associate Dir, 1988–93, Edinburgh Res. Station of Inst. of Animal Physiology and Genetic Res., Roslin; Chm., Roslin Bio Centre, 1999–. Hon. Fellow, 1981–90, Hon. Prof., 1990–, Div. of Biol Scis, Univ. of Edinburgh. Chm., Roslin Nutrition Ltd, 1997–; Advr, Burrill & Co. Animal Health Fund, 1999–. Pres., Agric. and Food Section, BAAS, 1999–2000. Hon. FRASE 1999. Hon. DSc Edinburgh, 2000. *Publications:* res. papers, reviews and book chapters on biochemical and molecular genetics. *Recreations:* fell-walking, cricket. *Address:* Roslin Institute, Roslin, Midlothian EH25 9PS. *T:* (0131) 527 4200.

BULFIELD, Peter William, CA; Deputy Chairman, Yamaichi Bank (UK) PLC, 1991–94 (Managing Director and Chief Executive, 1988–91); *b* 14 June 1930; *s* of Wilfred Bulfield and Doris (*née* Bedford); *m* 1958, Pamela June Beckett; two *d*. *Educ:* Beaumont Coll., Old Windsor. Peat Marwick Mitchell & Co., 1947–59; J. Henry Schroder Wagg & Co., 1959–86, Dir, 1967–86; Director: Schroder Finance, 1966–73; Schroder Darling Hldgs, Sydney, 1973–80; Vice-Chm., Mitsubishi Trust & Banking Corporation (Europe) SA, 1973–84; Jt Dep. Chm., Schroder Internat., 1977–86; Dep. Chm., Crown Agents for Oversea Govts and Admin, 1982–85 (Mem., 1978–85); Director: Yamaichi Internat. PLC, 1986–87; London Italian Bank, 1989–91. Member: Overseas Projects Board, 1983–86; Overseas Promotions Cttee, BIEC, 1984–86; Export Guarantees Adv. Council, 1985–88. Mem., Finance Cttee, CAFOD, 1994–; Hon. Treas., W Sussex Assoc. for the Blind, 1998–99. KSG 2001. *Recreations:* sailing, music, painting. *Address:* Snow Goose Cottage, Sandy Lane, East Ashling, W Sussex PO18 9AT. *T:* and *Fax:* (01243) 575298. *Clubs:* Sloane, Royal Thames Yacht.

BULFORD, Anne Judith; *see* Weyman, A. J.

BULKELEY, Sir Richard Thomas W.; *see* Williams-Bulkeley.

BULL, Anthony, CBE 1968 (OBE 1944); Transport Consultant: Kennedy and Donkin, 1971–85; Freeman Fox and Partners, 1971–87; *b* 18 July 1908; 3rd *s* of Rt Hon. Sir William Bull, 1st Bt, PC, MP, JP, FSA (*d* 1931), and late Lilian, 2nd *d* of G. S. Brandon, Oakbrook, Ravenscourt Park; *m* 1946, Barbara (*d* 1947), *er d* of late Peter Donovan, Yonder, Rye, Sussex; one *d*. *Educ:* Gresham's Sch., Holt; Magdalene Coll., Cambridge (Exhibitioner; MA). Joined Underground Group of Cos, 1929; served in Staff, Publicity and Public Relations Depts and Chairman's Office. Sec. to Vice-Chm. London Passenger Transport Board, 1936–39. Served War, 1939–45; RE; Transportation Br., War Office, 1939–42; Trans-Africa L of C, 1942–43; GHQ, Middle East, 1943; Staff of Supreme Allied Comdr, SE Asia (end of 1943); Col 1944; Transp. Div., CCG, 1945–46. Returned to London Transport as Chief Staff and Welfare Officer, 1946; Member: LTE, 1955–62; LTB, 1962–65; Vice-Chm., LTE (formerly LTB), 1965–71. Advr to House of Commons Transport Cttee, 1981–82. Institute of Transport: served on Council, 1956–59; Vice-Pres., 1964–66; Hon. Librarian, 1966–69; Pres., 1969–70. Mem. Regional Advisory Council for Technological Educn, 1958–62 (Transp. Adv. Cttee, 1950–62; Chm. Cttee, 1953–62). CStJ 1969. Bronze Star (USA), 1946. *Publications:* contrib. to transport journals. *Recreation:* travel. *Address:* 35 Clareville Grove, SW7 5AU. *T:* (020) 7373 5647. *Club:* Oxford and Cambridge.

See also Sir S. G. Bull, Bt, Sir Robin Chichester-Clark.

BULL, Anthony; *see* Bull, P. A.

BULL, Christopher John; Director, Benefit Fraud Inspectorate, Department for Work and Pensions (formerly Department of Social Security), since 1999; *b* 26 July 1954; *s* of George William and Kathleen Bull; *m* 1983, Alison Jane Hughes; two *d*. *Educ:* UCW, Aberystwyth (BA). CPFA 1983. With Nat. Audit Office, 1977–97; Inspector, Benefit Fraud Inspectorate, DSS, 1997–99. FRSA 2000. *Recreations:* books, wood. *Address:* Benefit Fraud Inspectorate, 12a North Park Road, Harrogate HG1 5QA. *T:* (01423) 832908.

BULL, David Neill; Executive Director, UK Committee for UNICEF, since 1999; *b* 21 June 1951; *s* of Denis Albert and Doreen Lilian Bull; *m* 1978, Claire Grenger; one *d*. *Educ:* Sussex Univ. (BA Econ); Bath Univ. (MSc Develt Studies). Public Affairs Unit Officer, Oxfam, 1979–84; Dir, Environment Liaison Centre, Nairobi, 1984–87; Gen. Sec., World University Service (UK), 1987–90; Dir, Amnesty Internat. (UK Sect.), 1990–99. Trustee: Refugee Council, 1987–90; Pesticides Trust, 1987–99; Mem., Exec. Cttee, ACENVO, 1994–98. *Publications:* A Growing Problem: pesticides and the Third World Poor, 1982; The Poverty of Diplomacy: Kampuchea and the outside world, 1983. *Recreations:* swimming, walking, reading, esp. science fiction. *Address:* UK Committee for UNICEF, Africa House, 64-78 Kingsway, WC2B 6NB. *T:* (020) 7405 5592.

BULL, Deborah Clare, CBE 1999; first Artistic Director, Linbury Studio Theatre and Clore Studio Upstairs, Royal Opera House, since 2002; *b* 22 March 1963; *d* of Rev. Michael John Bull and Doreen Audrey Franklin (*née* Plumb). *Educ:* Royal Ballet Sch. Joined Royal Ballet, 1981; Principal Dancer, 1992–2001; Nutrition Teacher, Royal Ballet Sch., 1996–99; Director, Clore Studio Upstairs, Royal Opera House, 1999–2001; Artists' Develt Initiative, Royal Opera House. Has danced a wide range of work, incl. leading rôles in: Swan Lake; Sleeping Beauty; Don Quixote; particularly noted for modern rôles, incl. Steptext, and Symbiont(s) (Time Out Outstanding Achievement Award); appeared in Diamonds of World Ballet Gala, Kremlin Palace, Moscow, 1996. Mem., Arts Council, 1998– (Mem., Dance Panel, 1996–; Annual Lecture, 1996); Gov., S Bank Centre, 1997–. Columnist, The Telegraph, 1999–; contributing editor, Harpers & Queen, 2000–. Wrote and presented: Dance Ballerina Dance, BBC2, 1998; Leaving Barons Court, Radio 4, 1999; Travels with my Tutu, BBC2, 2000. Hon. Dr Derby, 1998. Prix de Lausanne, 1980. *Publications:* The Vitality Plan, 1998; Dancing Away, 1998; articles in jls and newspapers. *Recreations:* mountain pursuits, food and wine, reading, writing, kayaking, cycling. *Address:* Royal Opera House, Covent Garden, WC2E 9DD. *T:* (020) 7240 1200. *Club:* Two Brydges.

BULL, Sir George (Jeffrey), Kt 1998; Chairman, J Sainsbury PLC, since 1998; *b* 16 July 1936; *s* of late William Perkins Bull and of Hon. Noreen Bull (*née* Hennessy); *m* 1960, Jane Fleur Thérèse Freeland; four *s* one *d*. *Educ:* Ampleforth Coll.; IDV Ltd: Dir, 1972; Dep. Man. Dir, 1982–84; Chief Exec., 1984–92; Chm., 1988–92; Chm. and Chief Exec., Grand Metropolitan Food Sector, 1992–93; Gp Chief Exec., 1993–96, Chm., 1996–98, Grand Metropolitan PLC; Jt Chm., Diageo, 1997–98. Non-Executive Director, United Newspapers, 1993–98; BNP Paribas, 2000–. Formerly Dir, BOTB; Dir, Marketing Council, 1996–2000. Pres., Advertising Assoc., 1996–2000. FRSA 1992. *Recreations:* golf, shooting, photography. *Address:* The Old Vicarage, Arkesden, Saffron Walden, Essex CB11 4HB. *T:* (01799) 550445. *Clubs:* Cavalry and Guards; Royal Worlington and Newmarket Golf (Suffolk).

BULL, John Michael; DL; QC 1983; **His Honour Judge John Bull;** a Circuit Judge, since 1991; *b* 31 Jan. 1934; *s* of John Godfrey Bull and Eleanor Bull (*née* Nicholson); *m* 1959, Sonia Maureen, *d* of Frank Edward Woodcock; one *s* three *d*. *Educ:* Norwich Sch. (State Schol.); Corpus Christi Coll., Cambridge (Parker Exhibnr in Modern History; BA 1958; LLM 1959; MA 1963). Called to the Bar, Gray's Inn, 1960; Dep. Circuit Judge, 1972; Standing Counsel to the Board of Inland Revenue, Western Circuit, 1972–83; a Recorder, 1980–91; Resident Judge, Crown Court at Guildford, 1992–2000. Judge, Employment Appeal Tribunal, 1993–2000. Hon. Recorder of Guildford, 1998. Hon. Vis. Prof., Surrey Univ., 1999. DL Surrey, 1996.

BULL, Dr John Prince, CBE 1973; Director of MRC Industrial Injuries and Burns Unit, 1952–82; *b* 4 Jan. 1917; *s* of Robert James Bull and Ida Mary Bull; *m* 1939, Irmgard Bross; four *d*. *Educ:* Burton-on-Trent Grammar Sch.; Cambridge Univ.; Guy's Hospital. MA, MD, BCh Cantab; MRCS, FRCP. Casualty Res. Officer, Min. of Home Security, 1941; RAMC, 1942–46; Mem. Research Staff 1947, Asst Dir 1948, MRC Unit, Birmingham Accident Hosp. Member: MRC, 1971–75; Med. Commn on Accident Prevention, 1975– (Chm., Transport Cttee, 1981–94); Chairman: Regional Res. Cttee, West Midlands RHA, 1966–82; Inst. of Accident Surgery, 1980–83. Mem., Med. Res. Soc. FRSocMed. *Publications:* contrib. scientific and med. jls. *Recreation:* bricolage. *Address:* 73 Reddings Road, Moseley, Birmingham B13 8LP. *T:* (0121) 449 0474.

BULL, (Oliver) Richard (Silvester); Headmaster, Rugby School, 1985–90; *b* 30 June 1930; *s* of Walter Haverson Bull and Margaret Bridget Bull; *m* 1956, Anne Hay Fife; two *s* four *d*. *Educ:* Rugby Sch.; Brasenose Coll. Oxford (MA). Mil. Service (1st Beds and Herts), 1949–51. Asst Master, Eton Coll., 1955–77 (Housemaster, 1968–77); Headmaster, Oakham Sch., Rutland, 1977–84. *Recreations:* music, walking, reading, ball games. *Address:* Broken Bank Cottage, Gladestry, Kington, Herefords HR5 3NY.

BULL, (Peter) Anthony; JP; FRICS; Proprietor, Walter Bull & Co., 1987–97; *b* 8 July 1937; *s* of Sir Walter Edward Avenon Bull, KCVO; *m* 1964, Susan Mary Battersby. *Educ:* Rugby Sch.; Coll. of Estate Management. Partner, Vigers, 1965–87. City of London: Mem., Court of Common Council, 1968–; Alderman, Ward of Cheap, 1984–. Mem., City and Hackney Jt Consultative Cttee, 1998–. Church Comr, 1986–98; Churchwarden, St Lawrence Jewry, 1984–. Mem., ESU, 1984. Mem., Co. of Parish Clerks, 1993–; Liveryman: Merchant Taylors' Co., 1965; Chartered Surveyors' Co., 1977 (Master, 1990–91); Mem., Guild of Freemen, 1998. Vice Chm., City of London Br., RNLI, 1992–. Member, Council: City of London Br., Royal Soc. of St George; C&G, 1998–; Gov., Westminster City Sch.; Trustee, United Westminster Schs. Patron, Ward of Cheap Club, 1984–; Pres., Associate Ward Clubs, 1997–. Mem., Assoc. of Lancastrians in London. JP City of London, 1984. *Recreations:* clocks, golf, wine, gardening, City of London. *Address:* 58 Burnt Ash Road, Lee, SE12 8PY. *T:* (020) 8297 2855. *Clubs:* Guildhall, City Livery, MCC.

BULL, Prof. Roger John; Vice-Chancellor and Chief Executive, University of Plymouth, since 1992 (Director and Chief Executive, Polytechnic South West, Plymouth, 1989–92); *b* 31 March 1940; *s* of William Leonard Bull and Margery Bull (*née* Slade); *m* 1964, Margaret Evelyn Clifton; one *s* one *d*. *Educ:* Churchers' Coll.; LSE (BSc Econ). FCCA. Research Fellow, DES/ICA, 1967–68; Principal Lectr in Accounting, Nottingham Poly., 1968–72; Head, Sch. of Accounting and Applied Econs, Leeds Poly., 1972–85; Dep. Dir (Academic), Plymouth Poly., 1986–89. Chm., Open Learning

Foundn, 1994–97; Dir, HEQC, 1994–97; Hon. Treas., UUK (formerly CVCP), 1994–. Non exec. Dir, Plymouth Hosps NHS Trust, 1993–; Dir, Plymouth Chamber of Commerce, 1994–97. Member: Council, CNAA, 1981–87; Council for Industry and Higher Educn, 1993–. *Publications:* Accounting in Business, 1969, 6th edn 1990; articles in professional jls. *Recreations:* tennis, music. *Address:* c/o Office of the Vice-Chancellor, University of Plymouth, Drake Circus, Plymouth PL4 8AA. *T:* (01752) 232000.

BULL, Sir Simeon (George), 4th Bt *cr* 1922, of Hammersmith; Senior Partner in legal firm of Bull & Bull; *b* 1 Aug. 1934; *s* of Sir George Bull, 3rd Bt and of Gabrielle, *d* of late Bramwell Jackson, MC; *S* father, 1986; *m* 1961, Annick Elizabeth Renée Geneviève (*d* 2000), *d* of late Louis Bresson and Mme Bresson, Chandai, France; one *s* two *d*. *Educ:* Eton; Innsbruck; Paris. Admitted solicitor, 1959. *Heir:* s Stephen Louis Bull, *b* 5 April 1966. *Address:* Beech Hanger, Beech Road, Shepherd's Hill, Merstham, Surrey RH1 3AE; Pen Enez, Pont l'Abbé, France. *Clubs:* MCC; Royal Thames Yacht.
See also A. Bull.

BULL, Tony Raymond, FRCS; Consultant Surgeon: Charing Cross Hospital; Royal National Throat Nose and Ear Hospital; King Edward VII's Hospital for Officers; *b* 21 Dec. 1934; *m* 1958, Jill Rosemary Beresford Cook; one *s* two *d*. *Educ:* Monkton Combe School; London Hosp. (MB BS 1958). FRCS 1962. President: Eur. Acad. of Facial Plastic Surgery, 1989–96; Section of Otology, RSocMed, 1993–94; Internat. Fedn of Facial Plastic Surgeons, 1997. Yearsley Lectr, 1982, Semon Lectr, 2000, RSocMed. Sir William Wilde Medal, Irish Otolaryngol Soc., 1993. Editor, Facial Plastic Surgery (Quarterly Monographs), 1983–. *Publications:* Atlas of Ear, Nose and Throat Diagnosis, 1974, 3rd edn 1995; Recent Advances in Otolaryngology, 1978; Plastic Reconstruction in the Head and Neck, 1986; Diagnostic Picture Test, Ear, Nose and Throat, 1990. *Recreations:* tennis, golf. *Address:* 107 Harley Street, W1N 1DG. *T:* (020) 7935 3171; 25 Pembroke Gardens Close, W8 6HR. *T:* (020) 7602 4362. *Clubs:* MCC, Hurlingham, Queen's.

BULLARD, Sir Julian (Leonard), GCMG 1987 (KCMG 1982 CMG 1975); HM Diplomatic Service, retired; Fellow of All Souls College, Oxford, 1950–57 and since 1988; *b* 8 March 1928; *s* of late Sir Reader Bullard, KCB, KCMG, CIE, and late Miriam, *d* of late A. L. Smith, Master of Balliol Coll., Oxford; *m* 1954, Margaret Stephens; two *s* two *d*. *Educ:* Rugby; Magdalen Coll., Oxford. Army, 1950–52; HM Diplomatic Service, 1953–88: served at: FO, 1953–54; Vienna, 1954–56; Amman, 1956–59; FO, 1960–63; Bonn, 1963–66; Moscow, 1966–68; Dubai, 1968–70; Head of E European and Soviet Dept, FCO, 1971–75; Minister, Bonn, 1975–79; Dep. Under-Sec. of State, 1979–84 and Dep. to Perm. Under Sec. of State and Political Dir, 1982–84, FCO; Ambassador, Bonn, 1984–88. Birmingham University: Mem. Council, 1988–97; Chm. Council and Pro-Chancellor, 1989–94; Hon. LLD 1994. *Publication:* (ed with Margaret Bullard) Inside Stalin's Russia: the diaries of Reader Bullard 1930–34, 2000. *Address:* 18 Northmoor Road, Oxford OX2 6UR. *T:* (01865) 512981.

BULLEN, Air Vice-Marshal Reginald, CB 1975; GM 1945; MA; Senior Bursar and Fellow, Gonville and Caius College, Cambridge, 1976–87, Life Fellow and Property Developments Consultant, since 1988; *b* 19 Oct. 1920; *s* of Henry Arthur Bullen and Alice May Bullen; *m* 1952, Christiane (*née* Phillips); one *s* one *d*. *Educ:* Grocers' Company School. 39 Sqdn RAF, 458 Sqdn RAAF, 1942–44; Air Min., 1945–50; RAF Coll. Cranwell, 1952–54; psa 1955; Exchange USAF, Washington, DC, 1956–58; RAF Staff Coll., Bracknell, 1959–61; Admin. Staff Coll., Henley, 1962; PSO to Chief of Air Staff, 1962–64; NATO Defence Coll., Paris, 1965; Adjutant General, HQ Allied Forces Central Europe, 1965–68; Dir of Personnel, MoD, 1968–69; idc 1970; Dep. AO i/c Admin, HQ Maintenance Comd, 1971; AOA Training Comd, 1972–75. Chm., Huntingdon DHA, 1981–92. MA Cantab, 1975. FIMgt (FBIM 1979; MBIM 1971). *Publications:* various articles. *Address:* Gonville and Caius College, Cambridge CB2 1TA. *Club:* Royal Air Force.

BULLER; *see* Manningham-Buller, family name of Viscount Dilhorne.

BULLER; *see* Yarde-Buller, family name of Baron Churston.

BULLER, Prof. Arthur John, ERD 1969; FRCP; Emeritus Professor of Physiology, University of Bristol, since 1982; *b* 16 Oct. 1923; *s* of Thomas Alfred Buller, MBE, and Edith May Buller (*née* Wager); *m* 1946, Helena Joan (*née* Pearson); one *s* one *d* (and one *d* decd). *Educ:* Duke of York's Royal Military Sch., Dover; St Thomas's Hosp. Med. Sch. (MB, BS; BSc); PhD Bristol 1992; BA Open Univ., 1996. FRCP 1976; FIBiol 1978; FRSA 1979. Kitchener Scholar, 1941–45; Lectr in Physiology, St Thomas' Hosp., 1946–49. Major, RAMC (Specialist in Physiology; Jt Sec., Military Personnel Research Cttee), 1949–53. Lectr in Medicine, St Thomas' Hosp., 1953–57. Royal Society Commonwealth Fellow, Canberra, Aust., 1958–59. Reader in Physiology, King's Coll., London, 1961–65; Gresham Prof. of Physic 1963–65; Prof. of Physiology, Univ. of Bristol, 1965–82, Dean, Fac. of Medicine, 1976–78, on secondment as Chief Scientist, DHSS, 1978–81. Res. Develt Dir, subseq. Dir of Res. and Support Services, Muscular Dystrophy Gp of GB, 1982–90. Hon. Consultant in Clinical Physiology, Bristol Dist Hosp. (T), 1970–82. Vis. Scholar, UCLA, 1966; Visiting Prof., Monash Univ., Aust., 1972. Lectures: Long Fox Meml, Bristol, 1978; Milroy, RCP, 1983; Haig Gudenian Meml, Muscular Dystrophy Gp, 1993. Member: Bd of Governors, Bristol Royal Infirmary, 1968–74; Avon Health Authority (T), 1974–78; MRC, 1975–81; BBC, IBA Central Appeals Adv. Cttee, 1983–88; Neurosciences and Mental Health Bd, MRC, 1973–77 (Chm., 1975–77); Chm., DHSS Working Party on Clinical Accountability, Service Planning and Evaluation, 1981–86; Trustee, Health Promotion Res. Trust, 1983–90. External Scientific Advisor, Rayne Inst., St Thomas' Hosp., 1979–85. *Publications:* contribs to books and various jls on normal and disordered physiology. *Recreations:* clarets and conversation. *Address:* Lockhall Cottage, Cow Lane, Steeple Aston, Bicester, Oxon OX25 4SG. *T:* (01869) 347502.

BULLERS, Ronald Alfred, CBE 1988; QFSM 1974; FIFireE; consultant fire prevention engineer; Chief Executive Officer, London Fire and Civil Defence Authority, 1986–87; *b* 17 March 1931; *m* 1954, Mary M. Bullers. *Educ:* Queen Mary's Grammar Sch., Walsall. Deputy Asst Chief Officer, Lancashire Fire Brigade, 1971; Dep. Chief Officer, Greater Manchester Fire Brigade, 1974, Chief Officer, 1977; Chief Officer, London Fire Bde, 1981–86. Adviser: Nat. Jt Council for Local Authority Fire Brigades, 1977; Assoc. of Metropolitan Authorities, 1977. FIMgt. OStJ. *Recreations:* gardening, travel. *Address:* 31 Pavillion Close, Aldridge, Walsall WA9 8LS.

BULLIMORE, John Wallace MacGregor; His Honour Judge Bullimore; a Circuit Judge, since 1991; *b* 4 Dec. 1945; *s* of late James Wallace Bullimore and Phyllis Violet Emily Bullimore (*née* Brandt); *m* 1975, Rev. Christine Elizabeth Kinch; two *s* (one *d* decd). *Educ:* Queen Elizabeth Grammar School, Wakefield; Univ. of Bristol (LLB). Called to the Bar, Inner Temple, 1968; Chancellor, Diocese of Derby, 1980, of Blackburn, 1990. Mem., Gen. Synod of the Church of England, 1970–. *Address:* c/o North Eastern Circuit Administrator, West Riding House, Albion Street, Leeds LS1 5AA.

BULLMORE, Prof. Edward Thomas, PhD; Professor of Psychiatry, University of Cambridge, since 1999; Hon. Consultant Psychiatrist, Addenbrooke's Hospital, Cambridge, since 1999; *b* 27 Sept. 1960; *s* of (John) Jeremy David Bullmore, *qv* and Pamela Audrey (*née* Green); *m* 1992, Mary Pitt, *d* of late Arthur Pitt and of Elizabeth Pitt; two *s*. *Educ:* Westminster Sch.; Christ Church, Oxford (BA); St Bartholomew's Hosp. Med. Coll. (MB BS); PhD London 1997; MA Cantab 2000. MRCP 1989; MRCPsych 1992. Lectr in Medicine, Univ. of Hong Kong, 1987–88; SHO in Psychiatry, St George's Hosp., London, 1989–90; Registrar in Psychiatry, Bethlem Royal and Maudsley Hosps, 1990–93; Wellcome Trust Res. Trng Fellow, 1993–96; Advanced Res. Trng Fellow, 1996–99; Hon. Consultant Psychiatrist, Maudsley Hosp., London, 1996–99. Vis. Prof., Inst. of Psychiatry, KCL, 2000–. *Publications:* papers on anatomical and functional brain imaging methods and applications to psychiatry and psycho-pharmacology. *Recreation:* running. *Address:* Department of Psychiatry, University of Cambridge, Addenbrooke's Hospital, Cambridge CB2 2QQ. *T:* (01223) 336582.

BULLMORE, (John) Jeremy David, CBE 1985; Chairman, J. Walter Thompson Co. Ltd, 1976–87; Director: The Guardian Media Group (formerly The Guardian and Manchester Evening News plc), 1988–2001; WPP Group plc, 1988–2001; *b* 21 Nov. 1929; *s* of Francis Edward Bullmore and Adeline Gabrielle Bullmore (*née* Roscow); *m* 1958, Pamela Audrey Green; two *s* one *d*. *Educ:* Harrow; Christ Church, Oxford. Military service, 1949–50. Joined J. Walter Thompson Co. Ltd, 1954: Dir, 1964; Dep. Chm., 1975; Dir, J. Walter Thompson Co. (USA), 1980–87. Mem., Nat. Cttee for Electoral Reform, 1978–. Chm., Advertising Assoc., 1981–87; Pres., Nat. Advertising Benevolent Soc., 1999–2001. *Publication:* Behind the Scenes in Advertising, 1991, 2nd edn 1998. *Address:* 17/20 Embankment Gardens, SW3 4LW. *T:* (020) 7351 2197. *Club:* Arts.
See also E. T. Bullmore.

BULLOCK, family name of **Baron Bullock**.

BULLOCK, Baron *cr* 1976 (Life Peer), of Leafield, Oxon; **Alan Louis Charles Bullock,** Kt 1972; FBA 1967; Founding Master, 1960, and Hon. Fellow, since 1980, St Catherine's College, Oxford (Master, 1960–80); Vice-Chancellor, Oxford University, 1969–73; *b* 13 Dec. 1914; *s* of Frank Allen Bullock; *m* 1940, Hilda Yates, *d* of Edwin Handy, Bradford; three *s* one *d* (and one *d* decd). *Educ:* Bradford Grammar Sch.; Wadham Coll., Oxford (Scholar). MA; 1st Class Lit Hum, 1936; 1st Class, Modern Hist., 1938. DLitt Oxon, 1969. Fellow, Dean and Tutor in Modern Hist., New Coll., 1945–52; Censor of St Catherine's Soc., Oxford, 1952–62; Chairman: Research Cttee of RIIA, 1954–78; Nat. Advisory Council on the Training and Supply of Teachers, 1963–65; Schools Council, 1966–69; Cttee on Reading and Other Uses of English Language, 1972–74 (Report, A Language for Life, published 1975); Trustees, Tate Gallery, 1973–80; Friends of Ashmolean Museum; Cttee of Enquiry on Industrial Democracy, 1976 (Report publ. 1977); Member: Arts Council of Great Britain, 1961–64; SSRC, 1966; Adv. Council on Public Records, 1965–77; Organising Cttee for the British Library, 1971–72. Joined Social Democratic Party, 1981. Sen. Fellow, Aspen Inst., USA; Trustee: Aspen Inst., Berlin; The Observer, 1957–69; Dir, The Observer, 1977–81. Raleigh Lectr, British Acad., 1967; Stevenson Meml Lectr, LSE, 1970; Leslie Stephen Lectr, Cambridge, 1976. Hon. Fellow, Merton Coll., Wadham Coll., Linacre Coll., Wolfson Coll., New Coll. and St Antony's Coll., Oxford. For. Mem., Amer. Acad. Arts and Sciences, 1972; Mem., Academia Europaea, 1990. Hon. FRIBA; Hon. FRA. Hon. Dr Univ. Aix-Marseilles; Hon. DLitt: Bradford; Reading; Newfoundland; Leicester; Sussex; Warwick; Essex; DUniv Open; Hon. Dr Leeds, 2000. Chevalier Légion d'Honneur, 1970; Grosse Verdienstkreuz (Germany), 1995. *Publications:* Hitler, A Study in Tyranny, 1952, rev. edn 1964; The Liberal Tradition, 1956; The Life and Times of Ernest Bevin, Vol. I, 1960, Vol. II, 1967, Vol III (Ernest Bevin, Foreign Secretary), 1983; (ed) The Twentieth Century, 1971; (ed with Oliver Stallybrass) Dictionary of Modern Thought, 1977, new edn (with S. Trombley), 1999; (ed) The Faces of Europe, 1980; (ed with B. R. Woodings) Fontana Dictionary of Modern Thinkers, 1983; The Humanist Tradition in the West, 1985; Hitler and Stalin: parallel lives, 1991, rev. edn 1998; Building Jerusalem, 2000; Gen. Editor (with Sir William Deakin) of The Oxford History of Modern Europe. *Address:* St Catherine's College, Oxford OX1 3UJ; Gable End, 30 Godstow Road, Oxford OX2 8AJ. *T:* (01865) 513380.

BULLOCK, Edward Anthony Watson; HM Diplomatic Service, retired; *b* 27 Aug. 1926; *yr s* of late Sir Christopher Bullock, KCB, CBE, and late Lady Bullock (*née* Barbara May Lupton); *m* 1953, Jenifer Myrtle, *er d* of late Sir Richmond Palmer, KCMG, and late Lady Palmer (*née* Margaret Isabel Abel Smith); two *s* one *d*. *Educ:* Rugby Sch. (Scholar; Running VIII); Trinity Coll., Cambridge (Exhibitioner; MA). Chm., Cambridge Univ. Cons. Assoc. Served The Life Guards, 1944–47. Joined Foreign Service, 1950; served: FO, 1950–52; Bucharest, 1952–54; Brussels, 1955–58; FO, 1958–61; La Paz, 1961–65; ODM, 1965–67; FCO, 1967–69; Havana, 1969–72; HM Treasury, 1972–74; Head of Pacific Dependent Territories Dept, FCO, 1974–77; Consul-Gen., Marseilles, 1978–83; Counsellor, FCO, 1983–85. Chm., Buckhorn Weston and Kington Magna Parish Council, 1993–95. *Recreations:* walking, gardening, tree-planting, reading, charity work. *Address:* Weston House, Buckhorn Weston, Gillingham, Dorset SP8 5HG. *Clubs:* Oxford and Cambridge; Union (Cambridge).

BULLOCK, John; Director, Kingfisher, since 1993; Joint Senior Partner and Deputy Chairman, Coopers & Lybrand (formerly Coopers & Lybrand Deloitte), 1989–92; Chairman, Coopers & Lybrand Europe, 1989–92; *b* 12 July 1933; *s* of Robert and Doris Bullock; *m* 1960, Ruth Jennifer (*née* Bullock); two *s* (and one *s* decd). *Educ:* Latymer Upper School. FCA; FCMA; FIMC. Smallfield Fitzhugh Tillet & Co., 1949–56 and 1958–61; RAF Commission, 1956–58; Robson Morrow, 1961, Partner, 1965–70; Robson Morrow merged with Deloitte Haskins & Sells; Partner in charge, Deloitte Haskins & Sells Management Consultants, 1971–79; Deloitte Haskins & Sells: Managing Partner, 1979–85; Dep. Senior Partner, 1984–85; Sen. Partner, 1985–90; Vice Chm., Deloitte Haskins & Sells Internat., 1985–89; Chm., Deloitte Europe, 1985–89. Director: Brightreasons, 1993–96; Nuclear Electric, 1993–98; British Energy, 1995–99; More Gp, 1997–98. Mem., UKAEA, 1981–93. Mem., Co. of Chartered Accountants' of England and Wales, 1989–. Chm. Govs, Latymer Upper Sch., 2001–. *Recreations:* ski-ing, walking, opera, ballet. *Address:* Braddocks, Oak Avenue, Sevenoaks, Kent TN13 1PR.

BULLOCK, Michael; Director, and Chairman, 1979–98, Morgan Grenfell Investment Services; Director, 1979–98, Chief Investment Officer, 1988–98, Morgan Grenfell Asset Management; *b* 1 Nov. 1951; *m* Felicity Hammond; two *s*. *Educ:* Caterham Sch.; Imperial Coll., London (BSc Hons). ARCS 1973. Joined Morgan Grenfell, as Mem., UK Research Dept, 1973; Mem., Internat. Equity Team (specialised in Japan and Far Eastern mkts), 1975–79; Dir, Morgan Grenfell Capital Mgt Inc., 1985–98. *Recreations:* art, scuba-diving. *Club:* Royal Automobile.

BULLOCK, Stephen Michael; Chairman, University Hospital Lewisham NHS Trust, since 1997 (Director, 1993–97); Head of Labour Group Office, Local Government Association, since 1997; *b* 26 June 1953; *s* of Fred George Bullock and Florence (*née* Gott); *m* 1992, Kristyne Margaret Hibbert. *Educ:* Sir William Turner's Sch., Redcar; Leeds Univ. (BA Hons); Goldsmiths' Coll. (PGCE). Greater London Council: Admin. Officer,

1977–79; Dep. Hd, Labour Gp Office, 1979–83; Asst Dir, Public Relns, 1983–86; Chief Officer, Greenwich CHC, 1986–90. London Borough of Lewisham: Councillor (Lab), 1982–98; Leader of Council, 1988–93. Chm., ALA, 1992–93; Dep. Chm., AMA, 1992–94. Board Member: London Pension Fund Authy, 1989–98; London First, 1993–96; Independent Housing Ombudsman Ltd, 1997–; Chm., Deptford City Challenge Ltd, 1992–93; Vice-Chm., Local Govt Management Bd, 1994–95 (Chm., 1992–93); Dir, Civic Skills Consultancy, 1994–95; Prin. Consultant, Capita Gp, 1995–97. Mem., Commn for Local Democracy, 1994–96. Trustee, Horniman Mus. and Gdns, 1999–. *Publications:* (contrib.) A Transatlantic Policy Exchange, 1993; (with R. Hambleton) Revitalising Local Democracy: the leadership options, 1996; contrib. Local Govt Chronicle, Municipal Jl. *Recreations:* inland waterways, watching Middlesbrough FC lose, seeking the "Moon under Water". *Address:* Garden Flat, 9 Tyson Road, Forest Hill, SE23 3AA. *T:* (020) 8291 5030, *Fax:* (020) 8291 2064; *e-mail:* steve.bullock@lga.lgorgs.gov.uk.

BULLOCK, Susan Margaret, FRAM; soprano; *b* 9 Dec. 1958; *d* of late John Robert Bullock and Mair Bullock (*née* Jones); *m* 1983, Lawrence Archer Wallington. *Educ:* Cheadle Hulme Sch.; Royal Northern Coll. of Music Jun. Sch.; Royal Holloway Coll., Univ. of London (BMus Hons); Royal Acad. of Music (LRAM; FRAM 1997); Nat. Opera Studio. Mem., Glyndebourne Fest. Opera Chorus, 1983–84; Principal Soprano, ENO, 1985–89; freelance internat. soprano, 1989–; *rôles* include: Madama Butterfly (title rôle) with ENO, Houston Grand Opera, Oper der Stadt, Bonn, New Israeli Opera, Portland Opera, USA, NYC Opera and Teatro Colon, Buenos Aires; Jenůfa (title rôle) with ENO, New Israeli Opera, Glyndebourne and Spoleto Fest., USA; Magda Sorel in The Consul with Teatro Colon, Buenos Aires and Spoleto Fest., Italy; Isolde, in Tristan and Isolde, with Opera North and Bochum Symphony; Brünnhilde, in Die Walküre, Tokyo; appears with all major British orchestras and also in Europe, N and S America, and Australia. Frequent broadcasts; has made recordings. *Recreations:* playing the piano, cooking, theatre. *Address:* c/o Harrison Parrott Ltd, 12 Penzance Place, W11 4PA.

BULLOUGH, Prof. Donald Auberon, FSA, FRHistS; Professor of Mediaeval History, University of St Andrews, 1973–91, now Emeritus; *b* 13 June 1928; *s* of late William Bullough and of Edith Shirley (*née* Norman); *m* 1st, 1963, Belinda Jane Turland (marr. diss.); two *d*; 2nd, 1995, Dr Alice Harting-Correa; one step *s* three step *d*. *Educ:* Newcastle-under-Lyme High Sch.; St John's Coll., Oxford (BA 1950, MA 1952). FRHistS 1958; FSA 1968; FRPSL 1993. National Service, 1946–48: commnd RA (attached RHA). Harmsworth Scholar, Merton Coll., Oxford, 1951; Medieval Scholar, British Sch. at Rome, 1951; Fereday Fellow, St John's Coll., Oxford, 1952–55; Lectr, Univ. of Edinburgh, 1955–66; Prof. of Med. History, Univ. of Nottingham, 1966–73; Dean, Faculty of Arts, Univ. of St Andrews, 1984–88. Vis. Prof., Southern Methodist Univ., Dallas, Tex, 1965–66; British Acad. Overseas Vis. Fellow, Max-Planck-Inst. für Gesch., 1972–73; Lilly Endowment Fellow, Pennsylvania Univ., 1980–81; Vis. Prof., Rutgers Univ., NJ, 1991–92, 1993–94; Visitor, IAS, Princeton, 1994–95; Vis. Prof., Univ. of Auckland, NZ, 1996. Lectures: Ford's, in English Hist., Univ. of Oxford, 1979–80; Scott-Hawkins, Southern Methodist Univ., Dallas, 1980; Andrew Mellon, Catholic Univ., Washington, 1980; Raleigh, British Acad., 1985; (Inaugural) Hector Munro Chadwick, Univ. of Cambridge, 1990. Corresponding Fellow, Monumenta Germaniae Historica, 1983–; Hon. Fellow, British Sch. at Rome, 1998 (Mem. Council, Exec., Finance Cttee, 1975–95; Acting Dir, 1984). Mem., Nottingham Univ. Hosp. Management Cttee, 1971–74. Dir, Paul Elek Ltd, 1968–79. Mem., Gen. Synod of Scottish Episcopal Church, 1998–. Major RA (TA); seconded OTC, 1957–67. *Publications:* The Age of Charlemagne, 1965 (2nd edn 1974; also foreign trans); (ed with R. L. Storey) The Study of Medieval Records, 1971; Carolingian Renewal: sources and heritage, 1991; contrib. Settimane di Studi del Centro ital. di St. sull'Alto Medioevo, TLS, British and continental hist. jls, philatelic jls. *Recreations:* talk, looking at buildings, postal history, cooking. *Address:* 14 Queens Gardens, St Andrews, Fife KY16 9TA. *T:* (01334) 478802. *Club:* Athenæum.

BULLOUGH, Dr Ronald, FRS 1985; consultant in UK and USA; Chief Scientist, UK Atomic Energy Authority, 1988–93, and Director for Corporate Research, Harwell, 1990–93; *b* 6 April 1931; *s* of Ronald Bullough and Edna Bullough (*née* Morrow); *m* 1954, Ruth Corbett; four *s*. *Educ:* Univ. of Sheffield. BSc, PhD, DSc. FIM 1964; FInstP 1962. Res. Scientist, AEI Fundamental Res. Lab., Aldermaston Court, Aldermaston, 1956–63; Theoretical Physicist and Group Leader, Harwell Res. Lab., Didcot, Berks, 1963–84; Hd, Materials Develt Div., Harwell, 1984–88; Dir for Underlying Res., Harwell, 1988–90. Visiting Professor: Univ. of Illinois, USA, 1964, 1973, 1979; Univ. of Wisconsin, USA, 1978; Rensselaer Polytechnical Inst., USA, 1968; UCL, 1994–; Univ. of Liverpool, 1994–; Visiting Scientist: Nat. Bureau of Standards, USA, 1965; Oak Ridge Nat. Lab., USA, 1969, 1979; Comisión Nacional de Energía Atómica, Buenos Aires, Argentina, 1977. Hon. Citizen of Tennessee, 1967. *Publications:* articles in learned jls such as Proc. Roy. Soc., Phil. Mag., Jl of Nucl. Materials etc., on defect properties in crystalline solids, particularly in relation to the irradiation and mechanical response of materials. *Recreations:* golf, walking, reading, music. *Address:* 4 Long Meadow, Manor Road, Goring-on-Thames, Reading, Berkshire RG8 9EQ. *T:* (01491) 873266.

BULLOUGH, Prof. William Sydney, PhD, DSc Leeds; Professor of Zoology, Birkbeck College, University of London, 1952–81, now Emeritus; *b* 6 April 1914; *o s* of Rev. Frederick Sydney Bullough and Letitia Anne Cooper, both of Leeds; *m* 1942, Dr Helena F. Gibbs (*d* 1975), Wellington, NZ; one *s* one *d*. *Educ:* William Hulme Grammar Sch., Manchester; Grammar Sch., Leeds; Univ. of Leeds. Lecturer in Zoology, Univ. of Leeds, 1937–44, McGill Univ., Montreal, 1944–46; Sorby Fellow of Royal Society of London, 1946–51; Research Fellow of British Empire Cancer Campaign, 1951–52; Hon. Fellow: Soc. for Investigative Dermatology (US); AAAS, 1981. Vice-Pres., Zoological Soc., 1983–84. *Publications:* Practical Invertebrate Anatomy, 1950; Vertebrate Sexual Cycles, 1951; (for children) Introducing Animals, 1953; Introducing Animals-with-Backbones, 1954; Introducing Man, 1958; The Evolution of Differentiation, 1967; The Dynamic Body Tissues, 1983; scientific papers on vertebrate reproductive cycles, hormones, and chalones published in a variety of journals. *Recreation:* gardening. *Address:* 75 Hillfield Court, Belsize Avenue, NW3 4BG. *T:* (020) 7435 4558.

BULMER, Esmond; *see* Bulmer, J. E.

BULMER, Dr Gerald; Rector of Liverpool Polytechnic, 1970–85 (sabbatical leave, 1984–85), retired; *b* 17 Nov. 1920; *s* of Edward and Alice Bulmer; *m* 1943, Greta Lucy Parkes, MA; two *d*. *Educ:* Nunthorpe Sch., York; Selwyn Coll., Cambridge. BA 1941; PhD 1944; MA 1945. Asst Master, King's Sch., Canterbury, 1945–49; Sen. Lecturer, Woolwich Polytechnic, 1949–53; Head of Dept of Science and Metallurgy, Constantine Technical Coll., Middlesbrough, 1954–57; Vice-Principal, Bolton Technical Coll., 1958–59; Principal, West Ham Coll. of Technology, 1959–64; Dir, Robert Gordon's Inst. of Technology, Aberdeen, 1965–70. Mem. Council CNAA, 1967–78. Freeman City of York, 1952. Hon. DSc CNAA, 1986. *Publications:* papers on organic sulphur compounds in Jl Chem. Soc. and Nature. *Address:* 11 Capilano Park, Winifred Lane, Aughton, Ormskirk, Lancs L39 5HA.

BULMER, (James) Esmond; Director, H. P. Bulmer Holdings plc, since 1962 (Deputy Chairman, 1980; Chairman, 1982–2000); *b* 19 May 1935; *e s* of late Edward Bulmer and Margaret Rye; *m* 1st, 1959, Morella Kearton; three *s* one *d*; 2nd, 1990, Susan Elizabeth Bower (*née* Murray). *Educ:* Rugby; King's Coll., Cambridge (BA); and abroad. Commissioned Scots Guards, 1954. Dir (non-exec.), Wales and W Midlands Regional Bd, National Westminster Bank PLC, 1982–92. Chm., Hereford DHA, 1987–94. MP (C): Kidderminster, Feb. 1974–1983; Wyre Forest, 1983–87. PPS to Minister of State, Home Office, 1979–81. Mem. Council, CBI, 1998–. Mem. Exec. Cttee, Nat. Trust, 1977–87. *Recreations:* gardening, fishing. *Clubs:* Boodle's, Beefsteak.

BULMER, Dr Michael George, FRS 1997; Professor, Department of Biological Sciences, Rutgers University, 1991–95; *b* 10 May 1931; *s* of Dr Ernest and Dr Eileen Mary Bulmer; *m* 1966, Sylvia Ann House. *Educ:* Rugby Sch.; Merton Coll., Oxford (MA, DPhil 1957; DSc 1985). Lectr in Med. Stats, Univ. of Manchester, 1957–59; Lectr in Biomaths, 1959–91, Fellow of Wolfson Coll., 1965–91, now Emeritus, Univ. of Oxford. *Publications:* Principles of Statistics, 1965; The Biology of Twinning in Man, 1970; The Mathematical Theory of Quantitative Genetics, 1980; Theoretical Evolutionary Ecology, 1994; articles in scientific jls on biometry and evolutionary biology. *Recreation:* walking. *Address:* The Old Vicarage, Chittlehampton, Umberleigh, Devon EX37 9RQ. *T:* (01769) 540201.

BULMER-THOMAS, Prof. Victor Gerald, OBE 1998; DPhil; Director, Royal Institute of International Affairs (Chatham House), since 2001; London University, Emeritus Professor, since 1998; *b* 23 March 1948; *s* of late Ivor Bulmer-Thomas, CBE and of Margaret Joan Bulmer-Thomas; *m* 1970, Barbara Ann Swasey; two *s* one *d*. *Educ:* Westminster Sch.; New Coll., Oxford (MA); St Antony's Coll., Oxford (DPhil). Research Fellow, Fraser of Allander Inst., Strathclyde Univ., 1975–78; Queen Mary, subseq. Queen Mary and Westfield, College, London University: Lectr in Econs, 1978–87; Reader in Econs of Latin America, 1987–90; Prof. of Econs, 1990–98; Institute of Latin American Studies, London University: Dir, 1992–98; Sen. Res. Fellow, 1998–2001. Dir, Schroders Emerging Countries Fund, 1996–. Editor, Jl of Latin American Studies, 1986–97. Comdr, Order of San Carlos (Colombia), 1998; Comdr, Order of Southern Cross (Brazil), 1998. *Publications:* Input-Output Analysis for Developing Countries, 1982; The Political Economy of Central America since 1920, 1987; Studies in the Economics of Central America, 1988; (ed) Britain and Latin America, 1989; (jtly) Central American Integration, 1992; (ed jtly) Mexico and the North American Free Trade Agreement: Who Will Benefit?, 1994; The Economic History of Latin America since Independence, 1994; (jtly) Growth and Development in Brazil: Cardoso's *real* challenge, 1995; (ed) The New Economic Model in Latin America and its Impact on Income Distribution and Poverty, 1996; (jtly) Rebuilding the State: Mexico after Salinas, 1996; (ed) Thirty Years of Latin American Studies in the United Kingdom, 1997; (jtly) US-Latin American Relations: the new agenda, 1999; (ed) Regional Integration in Latin America and the Caribbean: the political economy of open regionalism, 2001. *Recreations:* tennis, hill-walking, canoeing, music (viola), underwater photography. *Club:* Athenæum.

BULPITT, Cecil Arthur Charles, (Philip Bulpitt); Director, BIM Foundation Ltd, 1977–84 (Chairman, 1979–82); *b* 6 Feb. 1919; *s* of A. E. Bulpitt; *m* 1943, Joyce Mary Bloomfield; one *s* one *d*. *Educ:* Spring Grove Sch., London; Regent Street Polytechnic. Territorial Army, to rank of Staff Capt., RA, 1937–45. Carreras Ltd: joined firm, 1935; Gen. Manager, 1960; Asst Managing Dir, 1962; Dep. Chm. and Chief Exec., 1968; Chm. 1969–70. Dir, Thomas Tilling, 1973–81; Chairman: Tilling Construction Services Ltd, 1978–81; InterMed Ltd, 1978–81; Graham Building Services Ltd, 1979–81; Newey & Eyre Gp Ltd, 1979–81. Member: London Reg. Council, CBI, 1978–81; BBC Consultative Gp on Industrial and Business Affairs, 1980–84. MIPM 1955; CIMgt (FBIM 1963; Vice-Chm. Council, and Dir, Bd of Companions, BIM, 1979–83). Freeman, City of London, 1969. *Publication:* The Chief Executive, 1971. *Recreations:* golf, swimming, reading, travelling. *Address:* La Casa Tranquila, 35C, Calle 6D, Nueva Andalucia 29660, Málaga, Spain. *T:* (52) 811180. *Clubs:* El Madronal Country, Las Brisas Golf (Nueva Andalucia, Spain).

BUMBRY, Grace; opera singer and concert singer; *b* St Louis, Mo, 4 Jan. 1937. *Educ:* Boston Univ.; Northwestern Univ.; Music Academy of the West (under Lotte Lehmann). Début: Paris Opera, 1960; Bayreuth Fest., 1961; Royal Opera, Covent Gdn, London, 1963; Vienna State Opera, 1963; Salzburg Festival, 1964; Metropolitan Opera, 1965; La Scala, 1964; has also appeared in opera houses in Europe, S America and USA. Film, Carmen, 1968. Richard Wagner Medal, 1963. Hon. Dr of Humanities, St Louis Univ., 1968; Hon. doctorates: Rust Coll., Holly Spring, Miss; Rockhurst Coll., Kansas City; Univ. of Missouri at St Louis. Has made numerous recordings. *Recreations:* psychology, entertaining. *Address:* c/o J. F. Mastroianni Associates, 161 West 61st Street, Suite 17E, New York, NY 10032, USA.

BUNBURY; *see* McClintock-Bunbury, family name of Baron Rathdonnell.

BUNBURY, Bishop of, since 2000; **Rt Rev. William David Hair McCall;** *b* 29 Feb. 1940; *s* of late Rt Rev. Theodore Bruce McCall, ThD, Bishop of Wangaratta, and Helen Christie McCall; *m* 1969, Marion Carmel le Breton; two *s* three *d*. *Educ:* Launceston and Sydney Grammar Schools; Saint Michael's House, Crafers. Deacon 1963, priest 1964, dio. Riverina; Assistant Curate: St Alban's, Griffith, 1963–64; St Peter's, Broken Hill, 1965–67; Priest-in-charge, Barellan-Weethalle, 1967–73; Rector: St John's, Corowa, 1973–78; St George's, Goodwood, 1978–87; Pastoral Chaplain, St Barnabas' Theol Coll., 1980–87; Bishop of Willochra, 1987–2000. *Recreations:* reading, walking. *Address:* Bishopscourt, PO Box 15, Bunbury, WA 6231, Australia. *T:* (office) (8) 9721 2100, *Fax:* (8) 9791 2300.

BUNBURY, Sir Michael; *see* Bunbury, Sir R. D. M. R.

BUNBURY, Sir Michael (William), 13th Bt *cr* 1681, of Stanney Hall, Cheshire; company director, landowner and farmer; Consultant, Smith & Williamson, since 1997 (Partner, 1974–97; Chairman, 1986–93); *b* 29 Dec. 1946; *s* of Sir John William Napier Bunbury, 12th Bt, and of Pamela, *er d* of late Thomas Alexander Sutton; *S* father, 1985; *m* 1976, Caroline Anne, *d* of Col A. D. S. Mangnall, OBE; two *s* one *d*. *Educ:* Eton; Trinity College, Cambridge (MA). Buckmaster & Moore, 1968–74. Chm., Fleming High Income Investment Trust plc, 1996–97 (Dir, 1995–97); Director: Fleming Claverhouse Investment Trust plc, 1996–; Foreign & Colonial Investment Trust plc, 1998–. Mem. Council, Duchy of Lancaster, 1993– (Dep. Chm., 1995–2000, Chm., 2000–). Mem. Exec. Cttee, CLA, 1992–97 and 1999– (Chm., Taxation Cttee, 1999–; Chm. Cttee, Suffolk Br., 1995–97). Trustee, Calthorpe Edgbaston Estate, 1991–. *Heir: s* Henry Michael Napier Bunbury, *b* 4 March 1980. *Address:* Naunton Hall, Rendlesham, Woodbridge, Suffolk IP12 2RD. *T:* (01394) 460235. *Clubs:* Boodle's; Aldeburgh Yacht.

BUNBURY, Lt-Comdr Sir (Richard David) Michael (Richardson-), 5th Bt, *cr* 1787; RN; *b* 27 Oct. 1927; *er s* of Richard Richardson-Bunbury (*d* 1951) and Florence Margaret Gordon (*d* 1993), *d* of late Col Roger Gordon Thomson, CMG, DSO, late RA; *S* kinsman 1953; *m* 1961, Jane Louise, *d* of late Col Alfred William Pulverman, IA; one *s* (and one *s* decd). *Educ:* Royal Naval College, Dartmouth. Midshipman (S), 1945; Sub-Lieut (S), 1947; Lieut (S), 1948; Lieut-Comdr, 1956; retd 1967. Dir, Sandy Laird Ltd, 1988–96. Pres., HMS Sussex Assoc., 1991–. *Publication:* A Short History of Crowcombe, 1999. *Heir: s* Thomas William Richardson-Bunbury, *b* 4 Aug. 1965. *Address:* Upper House, Crowcombe, Taunton, Somerset TA4 4AG. *T:* (01984) 618223.

BUNCE, Michael John, OBE 2001; Director, since 1997, and Chairman, since 1999, International Broadcasting Convention (Member, Management Committee, 1992–94); *b* 24 April 1935; *er s* of late Roland John Bunce, ARIBA, and Dorrie Bunce (*née* Woods); *m* 1961, Tina Sims; two *s* two *d*. *Educ:* St Paul's Sch; Kingston Coll. Nat. Service, RAF. Joined BBC as engineer; subseq. Studio Manager; Producer, People and Politics (World Service); Dir, Gallery; Producer: A Man Apart—The Murderer, 1965; Minorities in Britain; The Younger Generation; Italy and the Italians; Editor: The Money Programme, 1968–70; Nationwide, 1970–75; Chief Asst, TV Current Affairs and Editor, Tonight, 1975–78; Head: Information Services TV, 1978–82; Information Div., 1982–83; Controller, Information Services, 1983–91; Exec. Dir, RTS, 1991–2000. Member: Francis Cttee, 1977; EBU Working Party on Direct Elections, 1978; Adv. Bd, Univ. of Salford Media Centre, 1992–99; Comité d'Honneur, Internat. Television Symposium and Technical Exhibn, Montreux, 1995–98; Chm., Nat. Industries PR Officers Group, 1991–92. Marshall Fund Vis. Fellow, USA, 1975. FRTS 1989. Shell Internat. Television Award, 1969. *Recreations:* gardening, visiting fine buildings, fishing. *Address:* International Broadcasting Convention, Aldwych House, 81 Aldwych, WC2B 4EL. *Club:* Groucho.

BUNCE, Rev. Dr Michael John, FSAScot; Chaplain, Santa Margarita, Menorca, since 2000; *b* 5 Dec. 1949; *s* of Harold Christopher and Kathleen June Bunce; *m* 1973, Frances Sutherland; one *s* one *d*. *Educ:* St Andrew's Univ. (MTh); Westcott House and Trinity Hall, Cambridge; Greenwich Univ. (PhD). Glazing clerk, Middleton Glass Merchant, 1965–69; Personnel Labour Controller, Bird's Eye Unilever, 1969–75. Ordained deacon, 1980, priest, 1981; Curate, 1980–83, Hosp. Chaplain and Team Vicar, 1983–85, Grantham Parish Church; Rector, St Andrew's, Brechin with St Drostan's, Tarfside and St Peter's, Auchmithie (Angus), 1985–92; Provost, St Paul's Cathedral, Dundee, 1992–97. FRSA. *Recreations:* tennis, ski-ing, art, antiques. *Address:* 5 Cidhmore House, 492 Perth Road, Dundee DD2 1LR. *Club:* Edinburgh Angus.

BUNCH, Sir Austin (Wyeth), Kt 1983; CBE 1978 (MBE 1974); Vice-Patron, British Limbless Ex-Servicemen's Association, 1992 (National President, 1983–92); *b* 1918; *s* of Horace William and Winifred Ada Bunch; *m* 1944, Joan Mary Peryer; four *d*. *Educ:* Christ's Hospital. FCA. CompIEE. Deloitte, Plender, Griffiths, 1935–48; Southern Electricity Board, 1949–76: Area Man., Newbury, 1962; Area Man., Portsmouth, 1966; Dep. Chm., 1967; Chm., 1974; Dep. Chm., Electricity Council, 1976–81, Chm., 1981–83; Chm., British Electricity Internat. Ltd, 1977–83; retd. Chm., Queen Mary's Roehampton Hosp. Trust, 1983–89. *Recreation:* sports for the disabled. *Address:* Sumner, School Lane, Cookham, Berks SL6 9QJ.

BUNCH, Dr Christopher, FRCP, FRCPE; Medical Director and Consultant Physician, Oxford Radcliffe Hospitals NHS Trust, 1994–2000; *b* 25 Feb. 1947; *s* of Douglas Campbell Bunch and Barbara Bunch (*née* Hall); *m* 1977, Kathleen Josie Andrew; two *d*. *Educ:* King's School, Worcester; Birmingham Univ. (MB ChB 1969). FRCP 1984; FRCPE 1988. University of Oxford: Clinical Lectr in Medicine, 1975–81; Clinical Reader in Medicine, 1981–94; Professorial Fellow, Wolfson Coll., Oxford, 1981–94, Fellow Emeritus 1994–. Goulstonian Lectr, RCP, 1985. Chm., British Assoc. Medical Managers, 2001– (Dir, 1995). Mem. Council, RCP, 1999–. *Publications:* (ed) Horizons in Medicine I, 1989; contrib. various scientific and medical articles in haematology, especially control of erythropoiesis. *Recreations:* cooking (and eating) SE Asian, French and Italian food, music. *Address:* Bayswater Farm House, Headington, Oxford OX3 8BY. *T:* (office) (01865) 221343.

BUNCLE, Thomas Archibald; Managing Director, Yellow Railroad; *b* 25 June 1953; *s* of Thomas Edgar Buncle and Helen Elizabeth Buncle; *m* 1979, Janet Michelle Louise Farmer; two *s*. *Educ:* Trinity Coll., Glenalmond; Exeter Univ. (BA Sociology and Law 1975); Sheffield Univ. (MA Criminology 1978). Various posts, incl. Law Tutor, Sheffield Univ., and tour guide, Amer. Leadership Study Gps and Voyages Sans Frontières, 1975–77; British Tourist Authority: graduate trainee, 1978–79; Asst Internat. Advertising Manager, 1979–80; Asst Manager, Western USA, 1981–84; Manager, Norway, 1984–86; Regl Dir, SE Asia, 1986–91; Scottish Tourist Board: Internat. Mktg Dir, 1991–96; Chief Exec., 1996–2000. Dir, Edinburgh Festival Council, 1997–2000; Board Member: Scotland the Brand, 1996–2000; Cairngorm Partnership, 1997–2000; Mem. Exec. Council, Scottish Council for Develt and Industry, 1998–2000. *Recreations:* windsurfing, sailing, scuba diving, Rugby, hill walking, cycling. *Address:* 73 Morningside Park, Edinburgh EH10 5EZ. *Club:* Boroughmuir Rugby.

BUNDRED, Stephen; Chief Executive, London Borough of Camden, since 1995; *b* 12 Dec. 1952; *s* of George Bundred, CBE, JP, DL and Theresa Bundred (*née* Hynes); *m* 1976, Kathleen McVeigh; one *s*. *Educ:* St Catherine's Coll., Oxford (BA PPE); Birkbeck Coll., London (MSc Econs); Liverpool Poly. (CPFA). Res. Asst to Eric Varley, MP, 1973–74; Special Advr to Sec. of State for Energy, 1974–75; Hd, Res. Dept, NUM, 1975–83; Principal Technical Accountant, Hackney LBC, 1983–87; Chief Accountant, Lewisham LBC, 1987–88; Financial Sec., Birkbeck Coll., Univ. of London, 1988–90; Dep. Dir of Finance, Hackney LBC, 1990–92; Dir of Finance and Dep. Chief Exec., 1992–95, Chief Finance Officer, 1995–99, Camden LBC; Clerk, N London Waste Authy, 1995–. Member: TEC Assessors Cttee, 1998–99; Rethinking Construction Local Govt Task Force, DETR, 1999–; Bd, HEFCE, 1999–; London Central Learning and Skills Council, 2001–. Member (Lab): Islington LBC, 1975–78; GLC, 1981–86; ILEA, 1981–90. Mem. Council, City Univ., 1999–. Specialist correspondent, Local Govt Chronicle, 1994–. *Publications:* (contrib.) Policing the Riots, 1982; contribs to jls. *Address:* Chief Executive's Office, London Borough of Camden, Town Hall, Judd Street, WC1H 9JE. *T:* (020) 7974 5686, *Fax:* (020) 7974 5998; 3 Colebrooke Row, Islington, N1 8DB.

BUNDY, Prof. Alan Richard, PhD; Professor of Automated Reasoning, University of Edinburgh, since 1990 (Head of Division of Informatics, 1998–2001); *b* 18 May 1947; *s* of Stanley Alfred Bundy and Joan Margaret Bundy; *m* 1967, D. Josephine A. Maule; one *d*. *Educ:* Univ. of Leicester (BSc 1st Cl. Maths 1968; PhD Mathematic Logic 1971). Teaching Asst, Dept of Maths, Univ. of Leicester, 1970–71; University of Edinburgh: Res. Fellow, Metamathematics Unit, 1971–74; Department of Artificial Intelligence: Lectr, 1974–84; Reader, 1984–87; Professorial Fellow, 1987–90. FAAAI 1990; FRSE 1996; Fellow: Soc. for Study of Artificial Intelligence and Simulation of Behaviour, 1997; Eur. Co-ordinating Cttee for Artificial Intelligence, 1999. FRSA 1988. *Publications:* Artificial Intelligence: an introductory course, 1978; The Computer Modelling of Mathematical Reasoning, 1983, 2nd edn 1986; The Benefits and Risks of Knowledge Based Systems, 1989; Eco-logic: logic based approaches to ecological modelling, 1991; Catalogue of Artificial Intelligence Techniques, 1984, 4th edn 1996. *Recreations:* bridge, wine-making, valley walking. *Address:* Division of Informatics, University of Edinburgh, 80 South Bridge, Edinburgh EH1 1HN.

BUNDY, Prof. Colin James, DPhil; Director and Principal, School of Oriental and African Studies, University of London, since 2001; *b* 4 Oct. 1944; *s* of Guy Stanhope Bundy and Winifred Constance Bundy (*née* Tooke); *m* 1st, 1969, Carol Ann Neilson (marr. diss. 1993); one *s* one *d*; 2nd, 2001, Evelyn Jeannette Bertelsen. *Educ:* Graeme Coll., Grahamstown; Univ. of Natal (BA); Univ. of Witwatersrand (BA Hons); Merton Coll., Oxford (Rhodes Schol., 1968); MPhil 1970, DPhil 1976, Oxon. Beit Sen. Res. Scholar, St Antony's Coll., Oxford, 1971–73; Lectr and Sen. Lectr in Hist., Manchester Poly., 1973–78; Res. Fellow, Queen Elizabeth House, Oxford, 1979–80; Tutor in Hist., Dept for External Studies, Oxford Univ., 1980–84; Prof. of Hist., Univ. of Cape Town, 1985–86; Prof. of Hist., concurrently Univs of Cape Town and Western Cape, 1987–90; University of Western Cape: Prof. of Hist., 1991–95; Dir, Inst. of Histl Res., 1992–94; Actg Vice-Rector, 1994–95; Vice-Rector (Academic), 1995–97; Vice-Chancellor and Principal, Univ. of Witwatersrand, Johannesburg, 1998–2001. Chm., South African Nat. Commn for UNESCO. Mem. Council, Robben Island Mus., 1997–2001. Hon. Fellow, Kellogg Coll., Oxford, 1998. Hon. DLitt Manchester Metropolitan, 1999. *Publications:* The Rise and Fall of a South African Peasantry, 1979, 2nd edn 1988; (jtly) Hidden Struggles in Rural South Africa, 1988; (contrib.) Encyclopedia Britannica, other books, and periodicals. *Recreations:* hiking, cricket, chess, music. *Address:* 30 Torrington Square, WC1E 7JL. *T:* (020) 7898 4014.

BUNGEY, Michael; Chairman and Chief Executive Officer, Bates Worldwide (formerly BSB Worldwide), since 1994; Chief Executive Officer, Cordiant Communications Group, since 1997; *b* 18 Jan. 1940; *s* of William Frederick George and Irene Edith Bungey; *m* 1976, Darleen Penelope Cecilia Brooks; one *s* two *d*. *Educ:* St Clement Danes Grammar Sch.; LSE (BSc Econ). Marketing with Nestlé, 1961–65; Associate Dir, Crawfords Advertising, 1965–68; Account Dir, S. H. Benson Advertising, 1969–71; Chm., Michael Bungey & Partners, 1972–84; Dep. Chm., Dorland Advertising, 1984; Chm., Bates Dorland Advertising Ltd, 1987–96; Chairman and Chief Executive Officer: DFS Dorland, 1987; Bates Dorland, 1988; Bates Europe, 1989; Pres. and Chief Operating Officer, BSB Worldwide, 1993–94; Chairman: Bates Americas' Reg., 1993–; Bates USA, 1993–. Dir, Cordiant plc (formerly Saatchi & Saatchi), 1995. *Address:* c/o Bates UK, 121–141 Westbourne Terrace, W2 6JR. *Club:* Hurlingham.

BUNKER, Very Rev. Michael; Dean of Peterborough, since 1992; *b* 22 July 1937; *s* of Murray Bunker and Nora Bunker; *m* 1957, Mary Helena Bunker; four *s*. *Educ:* Acton Technical Coll. and Brunel Coll., Acton (ONC and HNC in Engineering); Oak Hill Theol Coll. Work Study Engr, Napiers of Acton, London, 1956–60. Ordained deacon, 1963, priest, 1964; Assistant Curate: St James' Church, Alperton, Middlesex, 1963–66; Parish Church of St Helen, Merseyside, 1966–70; Incumbent: St Matthew's Church, Muswell Hill, London, 1970–78; St James with St Matthew, Muswell Hill, 1978–92. Prebendary of St Paul's Cathedral, 1990. Chm., Habitat for Humanity GB, 2000–. Trustee, Nat. Kidney Res. Fund, 1999–. *Publication:* The Church on the Hill, 1988. *Recreations:* flyfishing, walking. *Address:* The Deanery, Peterborough, Cambs PE1 1XS. *T:* (01733) 562780.

BUNN, Douglas Henry David; Chairman: All England Jumping Course, Hickstead; White Horse Caravan Co. Ltd; *b* 1 March 1928; *s* of late George Henry Charles Bunn and Alice Ann Bunn; *m* 1st, 1952, Rosemary Pares Wilson; three *d*; 2nd, 1960, Susan Dennis-Smith; two *s* one *d*; 3rd, 1979, Lorna Kirk (*d* 1995); one *s* two *d*. *Educ:* Chichester High Sch.; Trinity Coll., Cambridge (MA). Called to Bar, Lincoln's Inn; practised at Bar, 1953–59; founded Hickstead, 1960; British Show Jumping Team, 1957–68; Pres., BSJA, 2001– (Chm., 1969, 1993–96; Vice-Chm., 1969–93; Vice-Pres., 1996–2001); Mem. British Equestrian Fedn; founded White Horse Caravan Co. Ltd, 1958; Chm., Southern Aero Club, 1968–72. Jt Master, Mid Surrey Drag Hounds, 1976–. *Recreations:* horses, flying, books, wine. *Address:* Hickstead Place, Sussex RH17 5NU. *T:* (01273) 834666; (office) (01273) 834315, *Fax:* (01273) 834452. *Clubs:* Saints and Sinners (Chm., 1989–90), Annabel's.

BUNTING, Prof. Arthur Hugh, CMG 1971; Professor of Agricultural Development Overseas, Reading University, 1974–82, now Emeritus; *b* 7 Sept. 1917; *e s* of S. P. and R. Bunting; *m* 1941, Elsie Muriel Reynard; three *s*. *Educ:* Athlone High Sch., Johannesburg, S Africa; Univ. of the Witwatersrand, Johannesburg; Oriel Coll., University of Oxford. BSc 1937. BSc (Hons Botany), MSc 1938, Witwatersrand; Rhodes Scholar for the Transvaal, 1938; DPhil Oxford, 1941; CBiol, FIBiol; FLS 1993. Asst Chemist, Rothamsted Experimental Station, 1941–45; Member Human Nutrition Research Unit, Medical Research Council, 1945–47; Chief Scientific Officer, Overseas Food Corporation, 1947–51; Senior Research Officer, Sudan Min. of Agriculture, 1951–56; Prof. of Agricultural Botany, 1956–73, Dean, Faculty of Agriculture, 1965–71, Univ. of Reading. Pres., Assoc. of Applied Biologists, 1963–64, Hon. Mem., 1979–; Jt Editor, Journal of Applied Ecology, 1964–68. Foundn Mem., 1968–72, and Mem., 1974–80, Vice-Chm. 1975–77, and Chm. 1978–80, Board of Trustees, Internat. Inst. of Tropical Agriculture, Ibadan, Nigeria; Member: UK Council for Scientific Policy, 1970–72; UN Adv. Cttee on the Applications of Science and Technology to Develt (ACAST), 1972–75; Governing Bodies, Grassland Res. Inst., Hurley, 1959–77, Plant Breeding Inst., Cambridge, 1960–76; Consultant and then Mem., Scientific Cttee, Cotton Res. Corp., 1958–76 (Chm., 1972–76); Member: Panel of Scientific Advisers, CDC, 1967–94; Meteorological Cttee, MoD, 1973–88; Foundn Mem., Internat. Bd for Plant Genetic Resources, 1974–78. LLD *hc* Ahmadu Bello Univ., 1968. *Publications:* (ed) Change in Agriculture, 1970; (ed jtly) Policy and Practice in Rural Development, 1976; (ed jtly) Advances in Legume Science, 1980; (ed) Agricultural Environments, 1987; numerous papers in scientific and agricultural journals. *Recreation:* music. *Address:* 27 The Mount, Caversham, Reading, Berks RG4 7RU. *T:* (0118) 947 2487; *e-mail:* a.h.bunting@reading.ac.uk, ahbunting@netscapeonline.co.uk.

BUNTING, Martin Brian, FCA; company director; *b* 28 Feb. 1934; *s* of late Brian and Renee Bunting; *m* 1959, Veronica Mary Cope; two *s* one *d*. *Educ:* Rugby School. Director, Courage Ltd, 1972, Man. Dir, later Dep. Chm., 1974–84; Dir, Imperial Group plc, 1975–84; Chief Executive, Clifford Foods PLC, 1990–93. Non-executive Director: George Gale & Co. Ltd, 1984–; Longman Cartermill Ltd, 1985–90; Norcros plc, 1986–93; Shepherd Neame Ltd, 1986–; NAAFI, 1993–98; Hobson plc, 1994–96; Chairman: Inn Business Gp plc, 1996–97; Select Catalogues Ltd, 1996–98; Bluebird Toys plc, 1996–98 (Dir, 1991–98). Member, Monopolies and Mergers Commission, 1982–88. Chm. Trustees and Gov., Lord Wandsworth Coll., 2000–. *Address:* The Long House, 41 High Street, Odiham, Basingstoke, Hants RG29 1LF. *T:* (01256) 703585, *Fax:* (01256) 703562.

See also Earl of Southesk.

BUNYAN, Dr Peter John; Chief Scientific Adviser to Ministry of Agriculture, Fisheries and Food, 1990–95; *b* London, 13 Jan. 1936; *o s* of Charles and Jenny Bunyan; *m* 1961, June Rose Child; two *s*. *Educ:* Raynes Park County Grammar Sch.; University Coll., Durham Univ. (BSc, DSc); King's Coll., Univ. of London (PhD). FRSC; CChem; FIBiol; FIFST. Research at KCL, 1960–62, at UCL, 1962–63; Ministry of Agriculture, Fisheries and Food: Sen. Scientific Officer, Infestation Control Lab., 1963–69; PSO, Pest Infestation Control Lab., 1969–73, Head of Pest Control Chemistry Dept, 1973–80; Head of Food Science Div., 1980–84; Head of Agricl Sci. Service, ADAS, 1984–87; Dir of R & D Service, ADAS, 1987–90; Dir. Gen., ADAS and Regl Orgn, 1990–91. Member: AFRC, 1990–94; BBSRC, 1994–95; NERC, 1991–95; Chm., British Crop Protection Council, 1998–. Special Advr to Vice-Chancellor, Surrey Univ., 1996–. Hon. Sec., Inst. of Biol., 1996–2001. Vis. Prof., Sch. of Agriculture, De Montfort Univ., 1996–. *Publications:* numerous scientific papers in wide variety of scientific jls. *Recreations:* gardening, jogging. *Address:* Flushings Meadow, Church Road, Great Bookham, Surrey KT23 3JT. *T:* (01372) 456798. *Club:* Farmers'.

BUNYARD, Sir Robert (Sidney), Kt 1991; CBE 1986; QPM 1980; DL; Commandant, Police Staff College, Bramshill and HM Inspector of Constabulary, 1988–93; *b* 20 May 1930; *s* of Albert Percy Bunyard and Nellie Maria Bunyard; *m* 1948, Ruth Martin; two *d*. *Educ:* Queen Elizabeth Grammar Sch., Faversham; Regent Street Polytechnic Management Sch. (Dip. in Man. Studies). BA (Hons) Open Univ. MIPD; CIMgt. Metropolitan Police, 1952; Asst Chief Constable, Leics, 1972; rcds, 1977; Dep. Chief Constable, 1977, Chief Constable, 1978–87, Essex Police. Man. Editor, Police Jl, 1981–88. Member: Royal Commn on Criminal Justice, 1991–93; Parole Bd, 1994–98. Chm., Essex Reg., Royal Assoc. in Aid of Deaf People, 1994–95; Dir, Addaction, 1998–. DL Essex, 1997. *Publications:* Police: organization and command, 1978; Police Management Handbook, 1979; contrib. police jls. *Recreations:* music, opera, painting. *Address:* Bellmans, Mounthill Avenue, Springfield, Essex CM2 6DB.

BURBIDGE, (Eleanor) Margaret, (Mrs Geoffrey Burbidge), FRS 1964; Professor of Astronomy, 1964–90, University Professor, 1984–90, now Emeritus, and Research Professor, Department of Physics, since 1990, University of California at San Diego; *d* of late Stanley John Peachey, Lectr in Chemistry and Research Chemist, and of Marjorie Peachey; *m* 1948, Geoffrey Burbidge, *qv*; one *d*. *Educ:* Francis Holland Sch., London; University Coll., London (BSc); Univ. of London Observatory (PhD). Asst Director, 1948–50, Actg Director, 1950–51, Univ. of London Observatory; fellowship from Internat. Astron. Union, held at Yerkes Observatory, Univ. of Chicago, 1951–53; Research Fellow, California Inst. of Technology, 1955–57; Shirley Farr Fellow, later Associate Prof., Yerkes Observatory, Univ. of Chicago, 1957–62; Research Astronomer, 1962–64, Dir, Center for Astrophysics and Space Scis, 1979–88, Univ. of California at San Diego; Dir, Royal Greenwich Observatory, 1972–73. Abby Rockefeller Mauzé Vis. Prof., MIT, 1968. Member: American Acad. of Arts and Scis, 1969; US Nat. Acad. of Scis, 1978; Nat. Acad. of Scis Cttee on Science and Public Policy, 1979–81; Pres., Amer. Astronomical Soc., 1976–78; Chairwoman Bd of Dirs, Amer. Assoc. for Advancement of Science, 1983 (Pres., 1982); Mem., Amer. Philosophical Soc., 1980. Fellow University Coll., London, 1967; Hon. Fellow: Girton Coll., Cambridge, 1970; Lucy Cavendish Collegiate Soc., Cambridge, 1971. Hon. DSc: Smith Coll., Massachusetts, USA, 1963; Sussex, 1970; Bristol, 1972; Leicester, 1972; City, 1974; Michigan, 1978; Massachusetts, 1978; Williams Coll., 1979; State Univ. of NY at Stony Brook, 1984; Rensselaer Poly. Inst., 1986; Notre Dame Univ., 1986; Chicago, 1991. Catherine Wolfe Bruce Medal, Astr. Soc. of the Pacific, 1982; Nat. Medal of Science (awarded by President of USA), 1984; Sesquicentennial Medal, Mt Holyoke Coll., 1987; Einstein Medal, World Cultural Council, 1988. *Publications:* Quasi-Stellar Objects (with Geoffrey Burbidge), 1967 (also USA, 1967); contribs to learned jls (mostly USA), Handbuch der Physik, etc. *Address:* Center for Astrophysics and Space Sciences, 0424, University of California, San Diego, La Jolla, CA 92093, USA. *T:* (858) 5344477.

BURBIDGE, Prof. Geoffrey, FRS 1968; Professor of Physics, University of California, San Diego, 1963–84 and since 1988 (Associate Professor, 1962–63, Emeritus Professor, 1984–88); *b* 24 Sept. 1925; *s* of Leslie and Eveline Burbidge, Chipping Norton, Oxon; *m* 1948, Margaret Peachey (*see* E. M. Burbidge); one *d*. *Educ:* Chipping Norton Grammar Sch.; Bristol University; Univ. Coll., London. BSc (Special Hons Physics) Bristol, 1946; PhD London, 1951. Asst Lectr, UCL, 1950–51; Agassiz Fellow, Harvard Univ., 1951–52; Research Fellow, Univ. of Chicago, 1952–53; Research Fellow, Cavendish Lab., Cambridge, 1953–55; Carnegie Fellow, Mount Wilson and Palomar Observatories, Caltech, 1955–57; Asst Prof., Dept of Astronomy, Univ. of Chicago, 1957–58; Assoc. Prof., 1958–62. Dir, Kitt Peak Nat. Observatory, Arizona, 1978–84. Phillips Vis. Prof., Harvard Univ., 1968. Elected Fellow: UCL, 1970; Amer. Acad. of Arts and Scis, 1970. Pres., Astronomical Soc. of the Pacific, 1974–76 (Catherine Wolfe Bruce Medal, 1999); Trustee, Assoc. Universities Inc., 1973–82; Editor, Annual Review Astronomy and Astrophysics, 1973–; Scientific Ed., Astrophysical Jl, 1996–. *Publications:* (with Margaret Burbidge) Quasi-Stellar Objects, 1967; (with Sir Fred Hoyle and J. V. Narlikar) A Different Approach to Cosmology, 2000; scientific papers in Astrophysical Jl, Nature, Rev. Mod. Phys, Handbuch der Physik, etc. *Address:* Department of Physics and Center for Astrophysics and Space Sciences, 0424 University of California, San Diego, La Jolla, CA 92093, USA. *T:* (858) 5346626.

BURBIDGE, Sir Herbert (Dudley), 5th Bt *cr* 1916; *b* 13 Nov. 1904; *s* of Herbert Edward Burbidge (*d* 1945) 2nd *s* of 1st Bt, and Harriet Georgina (*d* 1952), *d* of Henry Stuart Hamilton, Londonderry; *S* cousin, 1974; *m* 1933, Ruby Bly (*d* 1994), *d* of Charles Ethelbert Taylor; one *s*. *Educ:* University Sch., Victoria, BC, Canada. Harrods Ltd, Knightsbridge, 1923–28; R. P. Clarke (Stock Brokers), Vancouver, BC, 1929–31; Merchandising Manager, Silverwood Industries of Vancouver, BC, 1931–70; retired 1970. President: Vancouver Executive Club, 1942; Vancouver Sales Executive Club, 1948. Mem. Bd of Referees, Workmen's Compensation Bd, 1943–61. *Recreation:* landscape gardening. *Heir: s* Peter Dudley Burbidge [*b* 20 June 1942; *m* 1967, Peggy Marilyn, *d* of Kenneth Anderson, Ladner, BC; one *s* one *d*]. *Address:* 3809 West 24th Avenue, Vancouver, BC V6S 1L9, Canada. *Club:* Vancouver Executive.

BURBIDGE, Margaret, (Mrs Geoffrey Burbidge); *see* Burbidge, E. M.

BURBIDGE, Very Rev. (John) Paul, MA Oxon and Cantab; FSA; Dean of Norwich, 1983–95, now Emeritus; *b* 21 May 1932; *e s* of late John Henry Gray Burbridge and Dorothy Vera Burbridge; *m* 1956, Olive Denise Grenfell; four *d*. *Educ:* King's Sch., Canterbury; King's Coll., Cambridge; New Coll., Oxford; Wells Theolog. Coll. Nat. Service Commn in RA, 1957. Jun. Curate, 1959, Sen. Curate, 1961, Eastbourne Parish Church; Vicar Choral of York Minster, 1962–66; Chamberlain, 1962–76; Canon Residentiary, 1966–76; Succentor Canonicorum, 1966; Precentor, 1969–76; Archdeacon of Richmond and Canon Residentiary of Ripon Cathedral, 1976–83; Canon Emeritus, 1998. *Recreation:* model engineering. *Address:* The Old School House, High Fremington, Richmond, N Yorks DL11 6AS. *T:* (01748) 884440.

See also S. N. Burbridge.

BURBRIDGE, Stephen Nigel, CB 1992; MA; Secretary, Monopolies and Mergers Commission, 1986–93; *b* 18 July 1934; *s* of late John Henry Gray Burbridge and late Dorothy Vera (*née* Pratt). *Educ:* King's Sch., Canterbury; Christ Church, Oxford. National Service, 2 Lieut, RA, 1953–55. Asst Principal, Bd of Trade, 1958–62; Trade Commissioner, Karachi, 1963–65; 1st Secretary (Economic), Rawalpindi, 1965–67; Principal, BoT, 1967–71; CS Selection Bd, 1971; Department of Trade and Industry: Asst Sec., 1971–80; Under Sec., 1980–86. *Recreations:* hiking, books. *Address:* Chesil Cottage, Brede Hill, Brede, near Rye, E Sussex TN31 6HH. *Clubs:* Reform; Rye Golf; West Sussex Golf.

See also J. P. Burbridge.

BURCH, Rear Adm. Jonathan Alexander, CBE 1991; CEng; Executive Secretary, Royal Academy of Engineering, since 2000; *b* 18 June 1949; *s* of late Lt Comdr Walter H. Burch and of Mary Angela Burch; *m* 1976, Ursula Georgette Victoria Maria Villiers Bear (*née* Villiers); one step *s*. *Educ:* Chorister Sch., Durham; Durham Sch.; BRNC, Dartmouth; RNEC Manadon (BSc). CEng 1972. HM Submarines, 1972–84; Australian Staff Coll., 1984; Assistant Director: Dockyard Privatisation, 1985–88; Commitments (Middle East), 1989–92; Superintendent Ships, Devonport, 1992–94; rcds 1995; Naval Base Comdr, Devonport (Cdre), 1996–98; DG Aircraft (Navy), 1998–2000 and Chief Naval Engr Officer, 1999. FIMgt 1989; CRAeS 1999; FIMarE 2000. President: Devonport Field Gun, 1996–98; RN Volleyball, 1998–2000. *Recreations:* travel, walking, history, music. *Address:* (office) Royal Academy of Engineering, 29 Great Peter Street, Westminster, SW1P 3LW. *T:* (020) 7222 2688.

BURCH, Maj.-Gen. Keith, CB 1985; CBE 1977 (MBE 1965); Director Personnel, Defence Staff, Ministry of Defence, 1985, retired; Chapter Clerk, York Minster, 1985–95; *b* 31 May 1931; *s* of Christopher Burch and Gwendoline Ada (*née* James); *m* 1957, Sara Vivette Hales; one *s* two *d*. *Educ:* Bedford Modern Sch.; Royal Military Acad., Sandhurst. Commnd Essex Regt, 1951; DS Staff Coll., Camberley, 1968–69; Comd 3rd Bn Royal Anglian Regt, 1969–71; Asst Sec., Chiefs of Staff Cttee, MoD, 1972–75; Col GS HQ 2nd Armoured Div., 1975–78; Dir, Admin. Planning (Army), MoD, 1978–80; Indian National Defence Coll., New Delhi, 1981; Dep. Dir, Army Staff Duties, MoD, 1981–83; ACDS (Personnel and Logistics), 1984. Pres., N Yorks, RBL, 1999–. *Recreations:* country pursuits, cooking. *Address:* Mayfield, Sandy Lane, Stockton on the Forest, York YO32 9US.

BURCH, Rt Rev. William Gerald, DD; *b* Winnipeg, Manitoba, 5 March 1911; *m* 1942, Carroll Borrowman; four *d*. *Educ:* University of Toronto (BA); Wycliffe Coll., Toronto. Deacon, 1936; Priest, 1938. Curate, Christ Church, Toronto, 1936–40; Incumbent, Scarborough Junction with Sandown Park, 1940–42; Rector: St Luke, Winnipeg, 1942–52; All Saints, Windsor, 1952–56; Exam. Chaplain to Bishop of Huron, 1955–56; Canon of Huron, 1956; Dean and Rector, All Saints Cathedral, Edmonton, 1956–60; Suffragan Bishop of Edmonton, 1960–61; Bishop of Edmonton, 1961–76. *Address:* 901 Richmond Avenue, Victoria, BC V8S 3Z4, Canada. *T:* (250) 5984369.

BURCHAM, Prof. William Ernest, CBE 1980; FRS 1957; Emeritus Professor of Physics, Birmingham University, since 1981; *b* 1 Aug. 1913; *er s* of Ernest Barnard and Edith Ellen Burcham; *m* 1st, 1942, Isabella Mary (*d* 1981), *d* of George Richard Todd and of Alice Louisa Todd; one *d* (and one *d* decd); 2nd, 1985, Patricia Newton, *er d* of Frank Harold Newton Marson and Miriam Eliza Marson. *Educ:* City of Norwich Sch.; Trinity Hall, Cambridge. Stokes Student, Pembroke Coll., Cambridge, 1937; Scientific Officer, Ministry of Aircraft Production, 1940, and Directorate of Atomic Energy, 1944; Fellow of Selwyn Coll., Cambridge, 1944; Univ. Demonstrator in Physics, Cambridge, 1945; Univ. Lecturer in Physics, Cambridge, 1946; Oliver Lodge Prof. of Physics, Univ. of Birmingham, 1951–80. Member: SRC, 1974–78; Council, Royal Soc., 1977–79. Hon. Life Fellow, Coventry Polytechnic, 1984. *Publications:* Nuclear Physics: an Introduction, 1963; Elements of Nuclear Physics, 1979; (with M. Jobes) Nuclear and Particle Physics, 1994; papers in Nuclear Physics A, Phys. Letters B, Phys. Rev. Letters. *Address:* 95 Witherford Way, Birmingham B29 4AN. *T:* (0121) 472 1226.

BURCHELL, Andrew; Finance Director, Department for Environment, Food and Rural Affairs, since 2001; *b* 26 March 1955; *s* of Joseph Fredrick Bertram Burchell and Myrtle Miriam Burchell; *m* 1974, Susan Margaret Hewing; one *s* one *d*. *Educ:* London School of Economics and Political Science (BSc (Econ) 1976; MSc 1980). Economist, DHSS, 1976–84; Economic Advr, National Audit Office, 1984–85; Economic Advr, 1985–89, Sen. Economic Advr, 1989–90, Dept of Health; Department of Transport, later Department of the Environment, Transport and the Regions: Sen. Economic Advr, Railways, 1990–96; Director: Strategy and Analysis, 1996; Transport Strategy, 1997; Envmt Protection Strategy, 1998–2001; Dir, Envmt Protection Strategy, DEFRA, 2001. *Publications:* articles on health economics. *Recreations:* golf, playing the guitar, spectating football, reading. *Address:* (office) Ashdown House, 123 Victoria Street, SW1E 6DE. *T:* (020) 7890 6450.

BURCHFIELD, Dr Robert William, CBE 1975; Editor, A Supplement to the Oxford English Dictionary, 1957–86; Chief Editor, The Oxford English Dictionaries, 1971–84; Senior Research Fellow, St Peter's College, Oxford, 1979–90, now Emeritus Fellow (Tutorial Fellow, 1963–79); *b* Wanganui, NZ, 27 Jan. 1923; *s* of Frederick Burchfield and Mary Burchfield (*née* Blair); *m* 1949, Ethel May Yates (marr. diss. 1976); one *s* two *d*; *m* 1976, Elizabeth Austen Knight. *Educ:* Wanganui Technical Coll., New Zealand, 1934–39; Victoria University Coll., Wellington, NZ, 1940–41, 1946–48; MA (NZ) 1948; Magdalen Coll., Oxford, 1949–53; BA (Oxon) 1951, MA 1955. Served War, Royal NZ Artillery, NZ and Italy, 1941–46. NZ Rhodes Scholar, 1949. Junior Lectr in English Lang., Magdalen Coll., Oxford, 1952–53; Lectr in English Lang., Christ Church, Oxford, 1953–57; Lectr, St Peter's Coll., Oxford, 1955–63. Hon. Sec., Early English Text Society, 1955–68 (Mem. Council, 1968–80); Editor, Notes and Queries, 1959–62; Pres., English Assoc., 1978–79. Hon. For. Mem., American Acad. of Arts and Scis, 1977–; Hon. Fellow, Inst. of Linguists, 1984–. Hon. DLitt, Liverpool, 1978; Hon. LitD Victoria Univ. of Wellington, NZ, 1983. Freedom of City of Wanganui, 1986. Shakespeare Prize, FVS Foundn, Hamburg, 1994. *Publications:* (with C. T. Onions and G. W. S. Friedrichsen) The Oxford Dictionary of English Etymology, 1966; A Supplement to the Oxford English Dictionary, vol. I (A-G), 1972, vol. II (H-N), 1976, vol. III (O-Scz), 1982, vol. IV (Se–Z), 1986; (with D. Donoghue and A. Timothy) The Quality of Spoken English on BBC Radio, 1979; The Spoken Language as an Art Form, 1981; The Spoken Word, 1981; The English Language, 1985; The New Zealand Pocket Oxford Dictionary, 1986; (ed) Studies in Lexicography, 1987; Unlocking the English Language, 1989; Points of View, 1992; (ed) The Cambridge History of the English Language, vol. V, 1994; (ed) The New Fowler's Modern English Usage, 3rd edn, 1996; contribs to: Times Lit. Supp., Trans Philological Soc., Encounter, etc. *Recreations:* investigating English grammar, travelling, gardening. *Address:* 14 The Green, Sutton Courtenay, Oxon OX14 4AE. *T:* (01235) 848645. *Club:* Athenæum.

BURCHILL, Julie; columnist, The Guardian, since 1998; *b* 3 July 1959; *d* of Thomas William Burchill and Bette Doreen Burchill (*née* Thomas); *m*; two *s*. *Educ:* Brislington

Comprehensive Sch., Bristol. Columnist: New Musical Express, 1976–80; The Face, 1980–84; Sunday Times, 1984–86; Mail on Sunday, 1986–98. *Publications:* The Boy Looked at Johnny, 1979; Love It or Shove It, 1985; Girls on Film, 1986; Damaged Gods, 1986; Ambition, 1989; Sex and Sensibility, 1992; No Exit, 1993; I Knew I Was Right (autobiog.), 1998; Diana, 1998; Married Alive, 1999; The Guardian Columns 1998–2000, 2001. *Recreations:* sex and shopping. *Address:* Simpson Fox, 52 Shaftesbury Avenue, W1V 7OE. *Club:* Sussex Arts (Brighton).

BURDEKIN, Prof. Frederick Michael, FRS 1993; FREng; Professor of Civil and Structural Engineering, University of Manchester Institute of Science and Technology, since 1977; *b* 5 Feb. 1938; *s* of Leslie and Gwendoline Burdekin; *m* 1965, Jennifer Meadley; two *s*. *Educ:* King's School, Chester; Trinity Hall, Cambridge (MA, PhD). MSc Manchester. FICE, FIMechE, FIStructE, FWeldI, FInstNDT. Welding Inst., 1961–68; Associate, Sandberg, Consulting Engineers, 1968–77. Vice-Principal External Affairs, UMIST, 1983–85. Chm., Manchester Science Park Ltd, 1988–95. Mem., Engrg Council, 1990–93. Brooker Medal, Welding Inst., 1996; James Alfred Ewing Medal, ICE, 1997; Gold Medal, IStructE, 1998. *Publications:* numerous papers on fracture, fatigue and welded structures. *Recreations:* music, sport, countryside. *Address:* 27 Springbank, Bollington, Macclesfield, Cheshire SK10 5LQ.

BURDEN, family name of **Baron Burden**.

BURDEN, 3rd Baron *cr* 1950, of Hazlebarrow, Derby; **Andrew Philip Burden;** *b* 20 July 1959; *e s* of 2nd Baron Burden and of Audrey Elsworth, *d* of Maj. W. E. Sykes; *S* father, 1995. *Heir: b* Hon. Fraser William Elsworth Burden, *b* 6 Nov. 1964.

BURDEN, Maj.-Gen. David Leslie, CB 1996; CBE 1988; Chapter Clerk and Receiver General, Westminster Abbey, since 1999; *b* 14 July 1943; *s* of Jack Leslie Burden and Elizabeth Mary Burden (*née* Attkins); *m* 1974, Susan Stuart Watson; two *d*. *Educ:* Portsmouth Grammar School. FILT. Commissioned RASC 1964, RAOC 1965. Served England, Berlin, W Germany, NI, Cyprus and Hong Kong; NDC, 1981; Chief, Personnel and Logistics, UN Force in Cyprus, 1981–83; CO, 1 Ordnance Bn, 1983–85; ACOS, British Forces, Hong Kong, 1985–87; RCDS, 1988; ACOS, BAOR, 1989–91; Dir-Gen., Resettlement, MoD, 1991–92; Dir-Gen., Logistic Support (Army), 1992–95; Dir Gen., Army Manning and Recruiting, 1995; Dir Gen., Army Personnel Centre, 1996–97; Mil. Sec., and Chief Exec. of Army Personnel Centre, 1997–99. Freeman, City of London; Liveryman, Carmen's Co. *Recreations:* golf, cricket, walking. *Address:* c/o Barclays Bank, 54 Highgate High Street, N6 5JD. *Clubs:* Army and Navy, MCC; Walker's Cricket Circus; Tidworth Garrison Golf.

BURDEN, Derrick Frank; HM Diplomatic Service, retired; Counsellor and Head of Claims Department, Foreign and Commonwealth Office, 1973–78; *b* 4 June 1918; *s* of late Alfred Burden and Louisa Burden (*née* Dean); *m* 1942, Marjorie Adeline Beckley; two *d*. *Educ:* Bec Sch., London. Crown Agents, 1936. Served War, King's Royal Rifle Corps, 1939–41. Joined Foreign Office, 1945; Comr-Gen.'s Office, Singapore, 1950–53; 2nd Sec., Moscow, 1954–56; 2nd Sec., Tokyo, 1957–59; HM Consul, Lourenço Marques, 1959–61; FO, 1962–67 (Asst Head of Protocol Dept, 1965); HM Consul, Khorramshahr (Iran), 1967–69; 1st Sec., Nairobi, 1969–71; HM Consul, Luanda (Angola), 1972–73. *Recreations:* golf, gardening. *Address:* 12 Strathmore Drive, Charvil, Reading, Berks RG10 9QT. *T:* (0118) 934 0564. *Clubs:* Travellers; Nairobi (Nairobi); Phyllis Court (Henley-on-Thames).

BURDEN, Richard Haines; MP (Lab) Birmingham Northfield, since 1992; *b* 1 Sept. 1954; *s* of Kenneth Rodney Burden and late Pauline Langan Burden (*née* Ronnan); partner, Jane Slowey. *Educ:* Wallasey Technical Grammar Sch.; Bramhall Comprehensive Sch.; St John's Coll. of Further Educn, Manchester; York Univ. (BA Politics); Warwick Univ. (MA Indust. Relations). Pres., York Univ. Students' Union, 1976–77. Br. Organiser, 1979–81, Dist Officer, 1979–92, NALGO; whilst working for NALGO led Midlands campaign against water privatisation. Founder and Sec., Joint Action for Water Services, 1985–90. Contested (Lab) Meriden, 1987. PPS to Minister of State: MAFF, 1997–99; DSS, 1999–2001. Secretary: All Party Parly Water Gp, 1994–97; PLP Trade and Industry Cttee, 1996–97 (Vice-Chm., 1995–96); Birmingham Gp of Labour MPs, 1997–. Exec. Mem., Labour ME Council, 1995–. Chairman: All Party Parly Gp on Electoral Reform, 1997–; All Party Parly Motor Gp, 1998–; Labour Campaign for Electoral Reform, 1996–98 (Vice-Chm., 1998–). Mem., Austin Br., RBL. *Publications:* Tap Dancing: water, the environment and privatisation, 1988; contribs to Tribune, Chartist and other jls. *Recreations:* motor racing, cinema, reading, food. *Address:* House of Commons, SW1A 0AA. *T:* (020) 7219 3000; (0121) 475 9295. *Clubs:* Austin Sports and Social, Kingshurst Labour, 750 Motor, House of Commons Motor (Chm., 1997–), Historic Sports Car.

BURDEN, Roger Francis, FCIB; Managing Director, Cheltenham & Gloucester plc, since 1997; *b* 3 June 1946; *s* of Henry A. Burden and Rose Burden, SRN; *m* 1970, Julie Hopkins; two *s*. *Educ:* Cheltenham Technical High Sch. MBCS 1975; FCIB 1983. Martins Bank, 1963–67; Dowty Rotol, 1967–69; Cheltenham & Gloucester Building Society, later Cheltenham & Gloucester plc: Programmer/Analyst, 1969–77; Data Processing Manager, 1977–79; Asst Gen. Manager, 1979–87; Gen. Manager, 1987–89; Ops Dir and Dep. Chief Exec., 1989–97. Chm., Exec. Cttee, Council of Mortgage Lenders, 2001– (Mem., 1997–). Mem. Council, FA, 1995–; Dep. Chm., 1990–, Dir, 1999–, Glos FA. *Recreation:* football (class 1 Association Football referee). *Address:* Cheltenham & Gloucester plc, Barnett Way, Gloucester GL4 3RL.

BURDETT, Sir Savile (Aylmer), 11th Bt *cr* 1665; Managing Director, Rapaway Energy Ltd, 1977–99; retired; *b* 24 Sept. 1931; *s* of Sir Aylmer Burdett, 10th Bt; *S* father, 1943; *m* 1962, June E. C. Rutherford; one *s* one *d*. *Educ:* Wellington Coll.; Imperial Coll., London. *Heir: s* Crispin Peter Burdett, *b* 8 Feb. 1967. *Address:* 2 Knapp Cottages, Gore Lane, Kilmington, Axminster, Devon EX13 7NU. *T:* (01297) 34200; *e-mail:* Rapaway@btinternet.com.

BURDUS, (Julia) Ann; non-executive Director: Next, since 1993; Prudential Corporation, since 1996; *b* 4 Sept. 1933; *d* of Gladstone Beaty and Julia W. C. Booth; *m* 1st, 1956, William Burdus (marr. diss. 1961); 2nd, 1981, Ian B. Robertson (*d* 1996). *Educ:* Durham Univ. (BA Psychology). Clinical psychologist, 1956–60; Res. Exec., Ogilvy, Benson & Mather, 1961–67; Res. Dir, McCann Erickson, 1971–75, Vice Chm., 1975–77; Senior Vice-Pres., McCann Internat., 1977–79; Chm., McCann & Co., 1979–81; Director: Strategic Planning and Development, Interpublic, 1981–83; Audits of Great Britain Ltd, 1983–86; AGB Research, 1986–89; Dir of Communications and Marketing, Olympia & York, Canary Wharf, 1989–92. Non-executive Director: Dawson Internat., 1992–98; Argyll Gp, later Safeway, 1993–99. Chairman: Advertising Assoc., 1980–81; EDC for Distributive Trades, 1983–87. Jt Dep. Chm. and Mem., Health Educn Authority, 1987–90; Member: Sen. (formerly Top) Salaries Rev. Bd, 1991–94; Adv. Council on Business and the Envmt, 1993–96; part-time Mem., CAA, 1993–97. Member: Cttee, Automobile Assoc., 1995–99; Council, Inst. of Dirs, 1995–. *Recreation:* home building.

BURFORD, Earl of; Charles Francis Topham de Vere Beauclerk; *b* 22 Feb. 1965; *s* and *heir* of Duke of St Albans, *qv*; *m* 1994, Louise Anne, *e d* of Col Malcolm Vernon Robey; one *s*. *Educ:* Sherborne; Hertford Coll., Oxford. Created Brigadier-General of Louisiana, USA, on staff of Governor Edwin Edwards, 1986. Trustee, Shakespearean Authorship Trust; Pres., De Vere Soc.; Vice-Pres., Royal Stuart Soc., 1989–. Freeman, City of London 1986; Liveryman, Drapers' Co., 1990. *Heir: s* Lord Vere of Hanworth, *qv*. *Address:* 125 Benton Street, Hadleigh, Suffolk IP7 5AY. *Club:* Brooks's.

BURFORD, Jeremy Michael Joseph; QC 1987; **His Honour Judge Burford;** a Circuit Judge, since 1993; *b* 3 June 1942; *s* of Alexander Joseph Burford and Arlene Burford. *Educ:* Rondebosch Boys' High Sch.; Diocesan Coll., Cape Town; BA Cape Town; MA, LLB Cantab; LLM Harvard. Called to the Bar, Inner Temple, 1968; a Recorder, 1991–93.

BURG, Gisela Elisabeth, Hon. CBE 1987 (for services to exports); Managing Director, GEB Enterprises Ltd, since 1995; *b* 12 Oct. 1939; *d* of Friedrich and Gerda Schlüsselburg. *Educ:* Gymnasium Philippinum, Weilburg, Germany; Ladies Coll., Wetzlar, Germany; Polytechnic of Central London. Founded Expotus Ltd, 1968, Man. Dir, 1968–96. Vice-Pres., Fedn of British Audio, 1979–85 (Chm., 1976); Member: NEDO, 1979–84 (Mem. Electronic Sector Working Party); BOTB, 1982–89. Non-exec. Dir, Royal Mint, 1993–2001. Mem., Jockey Club of S Africa. CIEx 1992. The Times/Veuve Clicquot Business Woman of the Year, 1981. *Recreations:* golf, horseracing. *Address:* 82 Kensington Heights, Campden Hill Road, W8 7BD. *T:* (020) 7727 8884. *Clubs:* Carlton; Woburn Golf and Country (Beds), Erinvale Golf (Somerset West, S Africa).

BURGE, Richard David Arthur; Chief Executive, Countryside Alliance, since 1999; *b* 5 April 1958; *s* of Col Arthur Burge and Elsie (*née* Kimberley); *m* 1980, Karen Jayne Bush; one *s* one *d*. *Educ:* Adams Grammar Sch., Newport; Univ. of Durham (BSc Hons Zoology 1980). Biology Master and Asst Housemaster, King Edward's Sch., Witley, 1980–83; Commonwealth Res. Schol., Dept of Zoology, Univ. of Peradeniya, Sri Lanka, 1983–86; British Council: Asst Dir, Nigeria, 1986–90; Projects Dir, Develt and Trng, 1990–93; Hd, Africa and ME Develt, 1993–95; Dir Gen., Zoological Soc. of London, 1995–99. Trustee: Television Trust for the Envmt, 1996–; Charles Darwin Centre, 1998–. Member: Exec. Cttee, Assoc. of Chief Execs, 1997–; Council, Shropshire and W Midlands Agricl Soc., 1997–. *Recreations:* pigs, theatre, gardening. *Address:* Countryside Alliance, Old Town Hall, 367 Kennington Road, SE11 4PT. *T:* (020) 7840 9206.

BURGE, Prof. Ronald Edgar, CPhys; FInstP; Wheatstone Professor of Physics, King's College, London, since 1989; Director, Leverhulme Trust Grant to Cavendish Laboratory, University of Cambridge, 1994–98; *b* 3 Oct. 1932; *s* of John Henry Burge and Edith Beatrice Burge (*née* Thompson); *m* 1953, Janet Mary (*née* Pitts); two *s*. *Educ:* Canton High Sch., Cardiff; King's Coll. London (BSc, PhD; FKC 1989); DSc London 1975. FInstP 1963. King's College London: Asst Lectr in Physics, 1954–58; Lectr in Physics, 1958–62; Reader in Biophysics, 1962–63, Prof. and Head of Dept of Physics, Queen Elizabeth Coll., Univ. of London, 1963–84; Prof. of Physics, 1984–89, Head of Dept of Physics, 1984–92, Vice Principal, 1988–92, KCL. Vis. Fellow, 1992, Life Mem., 1993, Clare Hall, Cambridge. Member: Swinnerton-Dyer Cttee concerning Academic Governance of Univ. of London, 1979–82; Computer Bd for Univs and Res. Councils (responsible for computer develt in univs in Scotland and, latterly, SW England), 1978–82. MRI 1988. Rodman Medal, RPS, 1993. *Publications:* papers in sci. jls on theory of scattering (electrons, x-rays and radar) and develts in electron microscopy and x-ray microscopy. *Recreations:* gardening, music. *Address:* 5 Toft Lane, Great Wilbraham, Cambridge CB1 5JH. *T:* (01223) 881378.

BURGE, Stuart, CBE 1974; freelance director and actor; *b* 15 Jan. 1918; *s* of late H. O. Burge and K. M. Haig; *m* 1949, Josephine Parker; three *s* two *d*. *Educ:* Eagle House, Sandhurst; Felsted Sch., Essex. Served War of 1939–45, Intell. Corps. Actor; trained Old Vic, 1936–37; Oxford Rep., 1937–38; Old Vic and West End, 1938–39; Bristol Old Vic, Young Vic, Commercial Theatre, 1946–49; 1st Dir, Hornchurch, 1951–53; productions for theatre and TV, 1953–; Dir, Nottingham Playhouse, 1968–74; Artistic Dir, Royal Court Theatre, 1977–80. *Theatre:* Lulu, 1970; Measure for Measure, The Devil is an Ass, Edinburgh Fest. and Nat. Theatre, 1977; Another Country, Greenwich 1981 and Queen's 1982; (actor) The Seagull, Royal Court, 1981; The London Cuckolds, Royal Court and Lyric Hammersmith, 1985; Curtains, Hampstead, 1987, Whitehall, 1988; The Black Prince, Aldwych, 1989; Sunsets and Glories, Leeds Fest., 1990; The Provoked Wife, Touring Partnership, 1994; Last Dance at Dum Dum, Royal Court at New Ambassadors, 1999; *opera:* La Colombe, Buxton and Sadler's Wells, 1983. *Television:* Luther, Bill Brand, Sons and Lovers, The Old Men at the Zoo, Much Ado About Nothing (BBC Shakespeare), Breaking Up, Naming the Names, The Rainbow, House of Bernarda Alba, After the Dance, The Wexford Trilogy, The Writing Game, Talking Heads, etc; *films:* Othello, 1964; Julius Caesar, 1969. Vis. Prof., UC Davis, USA; Hon. Prof. of Drama, Nottingham Univ. *Publication:* (ed) King John (Folio Society), 1973. *Address:* c/o Harriet Cruickshank, 97 Old South Lambeth Road, SW8 1XU.

BURGEN, Sir Arnold (Stanley Vincent), Kt 1976; FRCP 1969; FRS 1964; Master of Darwin College, Cambridge, 1982–89 (Hon. Fellow, 1989); Deputy Vice-Chancellor, Cambridge University, 1985–89; *b* 20 March 1922; *s* of late Peter Burgen and Elizabeth Wolfers; *m* 1st, 1946, Judith Browne (*d* 1993); two *s* one *d*; 2nd, 1993, Dr Olga Kennard, *qv*. *Educ:* Christ's Coll., Finchley. Student, Middlesex Hospital Med. Sch., 1939–45; MRCP 1946. Ho. Phys., Middlesex Hospital, 1945; Demonstrator, 1945–48, Asst Lectr, 1948–49, in Pharmacology, Middlesex Hospital Med. Sch. Prof. of Physiology, McGill Univ., Montreal, 1949–62; Dep. Dir, Univ. Clinic, Montreal Gen. Hospital, 1957–62; Sheild Prof. of Pharmacology, Univ. of Cambridge, 1962–71; Fellow of Downing Coll., Cambridge, 1962–71, Hon. Fellow 1972; Dir, Nat. Inst. for Med. Res., 1971–82. Medical Research Council: Member, 1969–71, 1973–77; Hon. Dir, Molecular Pharmacology Unit, 1967–72; Chm., Tropical Medicine Res. Bd, 1977–81; Assessor, 1985–86. Pres., Internat. Union of Pharmacology, 1972–75; Member: Council, Royal Soc., 1972–73, 1980–86 (Vice Pres., 1980–86; Foreign Sec., 1981–86); Nat. Biol. Standards Bd, 1975–78; Med. Cttee, British Council, 1973–77; Gen. Cttee, ICSU, 1982–88; Exec. Cttee, Eur. Science Foundn, 1985–90; Bureau, European Science and Technol. Assembly, 1994–; Chm., Adv. Cttee on Irradiated and Novel Foods, 1982–87. Dir, Amersham Internat., 1985–92. Trustee, CIBA Foundn, 1985–. Editor, European Review, 1993–. Pres., Academia Europaea, 1988–94. Founder FMedSci 1998. Academico Correspondiente, Royal Acad. of Spain, 1983; Mem., Deutsche Akad. der Naturforscher Leopoldina, 1984; For. Associate, US Nat. Acad. of Scis, 1985; For. Mem., Ukraine Acad. of Scis. Hon. Fellow, Wolfson Coll., Oxford, 1990. Hon. FRCP (C); Hon. Mem., Amer. Assoc. of Physicians; Academician of Finland, 1990. Hon. DSc: Leeds, 1973; McGill, 1973; Liverpool, 1989; Hon. MD: Utrecht, 1983; Zürich, 1983; DUniv. Surrey, 1983. Gold Medal, British Pharmacol Soc, 1999. *Publications:* Physiology of Salivary Glands, 1961;

papers in Journals of Physiology and Pharmacology. *Address:* Keelson, 8a Hills Avenue, Cambridge CB1 4XA.

BURGES, Alan; *see* Burges, N. A.

BURGES, (Norman) Alan, CBE 1980; MSc, PhD; FIBiol; FLS; Vice-Chancellor, New University of Ulster, Coleraine, Northern Ireland, 1966–76; *b* 5 Aug. 1911; *s* of late Lieut J. C. Burges, East Maitland, NSW; *m* 1940, Florence Evelyn (*née* Moulton); three *d. Educ:* Sydney Univ., Australia (represented Sydney and Combined Australian Univs at athletics, 1932); Emmanuel Coll., Cambridge. Graduated, Sydney, BSc Hons., 1931; MSc, 1932; PhD Cambridge, 1937. Senior 1851 Scholar, 1937. Research Fellow, Emmanuel Coll., 1938; Prof. of Botany, Sydney Univ., 1947–52; Dean of Faculty of Science and Fellow of Senate, 1949–52; Holbrook Gaskell Prof. of Botany, Univ. of Liverpool, 1952–66, Acting Vice-Chancellor, 1964–65; Pro-Vice-Chancellor, 1965–66. Hon. Gen. Sec., ANZAAS, 1947–52; President: British Ecological Soc., 1958, 1959; British Mycological Soc., 1962; Mem. Cttee, Nature Conservancy, England, 1959–66; Mem., Waste Management Adv. Council; Joint Editor, Flora Europæa Project, 1956–. Chm., NI Adv. Council for Education, 1966–75; Chairman: Ulster American Folk Park, 1975–88; NI American Bicentennial Cttee, 1975–77; Scots Irish Trust, 1977–92; Chm., Nat. Trust NI Cttee, 1978–81. Mem., Acad. Adv. Cttee, Loughborough Univ., 1967–71. Served War of 1939–45, RAF Bomber Command (despatches). Hon. LLD QUB, 1973; Hon. DTech Loughborough, 1975; Hon. DSc Ulster, 1977. *Publications:* Micro-organisms in the Soil, 1958; (with F. Raw) Soil Biology, 1967; reports: Primary Educn in Northern Ireland, 1968; Existing Selection Procedure for Secondary Educn in Northern Ireland, 1971; Reorganisation of Secondary Educn in Northern Ireland, 1973; various in scientific journals on plant diseases and fungi. *Recreation:* sailing. *Address:* Tokes Cottage, Semley, Wilts SP7 8BP. *T:* (01747) 830297. *Club:* Royal Air Force.

BURGES, Maj.-Gen. Rodney Lyon Travers, CBE 1963; DSO 1946; *b* 19 March 1914; *s* of Richard Burges and Hilda Christine Burges (*née* Lyon); *m* 1946, Sheila Marion Lyster Goldby (*d* 1991), *d* of H. L. Goldby; one *d* (one *s* decd). *Educ:* Wellington; RMA, Woolwich. 2nd Lieut RA, 1934; war service in Burma, 1942 and 1944–45; CO The Berkshire Yeomanry (145 Fd Regt, RA), 1945; Comdr, E Battery, RHA, 1949–51; Bt Lt-Col 1953; 2nd in comd, 1 RHA, 1954–55; CO 3 RHA, 1955–57; CRA 3 Div., 1958–59; IDC, 1960; Brig. Q (Ops) WO, 1961–63; CCRA, 1 Corps, BAOR, 1963–64; Maj.-Gen. 1964; GOC, Cyprus District, 1964–66; VQMG, MoD, 1966–67. Joined Grieveson, Grant & Co., 1968, Partner 1971, retd 1978; Consultant to Pat Simon Wines Ltd, 1978–85; Dir, Caroline Fine Wines Ltd, 1982–85. Freeman and Liveryman, Fishmongers' Co., 1974. *Recreations:* racing, drinking wine in the sun. *Address:* Freemantle, Over Wallop, Hants SO20 8JE. *Clubs:* Buck's, Army and Navy.

BURGES WATSON, Richard Eagleson Gordon; *see* Watson.

BURGESS, Anthony Reginald Frank, (Tony), CVO 1983; consultant on Third World development; HM Diplomatic Service, retired; *b* 27 Jan. 1932; *s* of Beatrice Burgess; *m* 1960, Carlyn Shawyer; one *s. Educ:* Ealing Grammar Sch.; University College London (BScEcon). National Service, 1953–55; TA, 16 Airborne Div., 1955–57. Journalism, 1955–62; European Community Civil Service, 1962–65; HM Diplomatic Service, 1966–89: 1st Sec., European Economic Organisations Dept, FCO, 1966–67; 1st Sec. (Political), Dhaka, 1967–69; 1st Sec., SE Asia Dept, FCO, 1970–72; 1st Sec. (Economic), Ottawa, 1972–76; Head of Chancery and HM Consul, Bogota, 1976–79; 1st Sec., Rhodesia Dept, FCO, 1979–80; Asst Head of Information Dept, FCO, 1980–82; Dep. High Comr, Dhaka, 1982–86; Counsellor and Hd of Chancery, Havana, 1989–89. *Publication:* (jtly) The Common Market and the Treaty of Rome Explained, 1967. *Recreations:* travel, photography, shooting, riding. *Address:* 16 Langford Green, Champion Hill, SE5 8BX. *Club:* Brooks's.

BURGESS, Averil, OBE 1994; Chairman, Independent Schools Inspectorate, Independent Schools Council (formerly Accreditation Review and Consultancy Service, Independent Schools Joint Council), 1993–2000; *b* 8 July 1938; *d* of David and Dorothy Evans (*née* Owen); *m* 1959, Clifford Burgess (marr. diss. 1973). *Educ:* Ashby-de-la-Zouch Girls' Grammar Sch.; Queen Mary Coll., Univ. of London. BA Hons History. Assistant Mistress: Langleybury Secondary Modern Sch., 1959–60; Ensham Sch., 1960–62; Hatfield Sch., 1963–65; Fulham County Sch., 1965–69; Wimbledon High Sch., GPDST, 1969–74 (Head of History and Second Mistress); Headmistress, South Hampstead High School, GPDST, 1975–93. Chm., Camden and Islington FHSA, 1993–96. Chm., Policy Gp, ISJC, 1990–97; Member: Council for Accreditation of Teacher Educn, 1990–93; Nat. Commn on Educn, 1991–93. Adv. Panel on Public Appointments, DCMS, 1997–; Lay Mem., Professional Conduct Cttee, Bar Council, 1996–. Pres., GSA, 1988–89. Governor: Central Sch. of Speech and Drama, 1981–95; Mus. of London, 1994–2000. *Recreations:* many, including Wales, Welsh, watercolours, birdwatching and good meals. *Address:* 123 North Hill, Highgate, N6 4DP.

BURGESS, Cyril Duncan, CB 1989; ERD 1970; Chairman, Council for Registered Gas Installers, 1991–94; *b* 18 Oct. 1929; *s* of John Arthur Burgess and Doris (*née* Sedgwick); *m* 1954, Jean Kathleen Whitney; one *s* one *d. Educ:* Southgate County Grammar Sch.; Univ. of London (BSc). CChem; MRSC. National Service, Royal Signals, 1950. Asst Engineer, English Electric Co., 1952; HM Factory Inspectorate, 1953; served in London and Huddersfield; Sup. Inspector, Scotland, 1974; Sec., Adv. Cttee on Asbestos, 1976; Dir, Hazardous Substances Div., HSE, 1978–89. Chm., Adv. Cttees on Dangerous Substances, 1982, on Toxic Substances, 1985. *Address:* 108 Gravel Lane, Hemel Hempstead, Herts HP1 1SB. *T:* (01442) 392734.

BURGESS, Rev. David John, FSA; Guild Vicar of St Lawrence Jewry Next Guildhall, The Church of the Corporation of London, since 1987; a Chaplain to The Queen, since 1987; *b* 4 Aug. 1939; *e s* of Albert Burgess and Mary Burgess (*née* Kelsey); *m* 1976, Dr Kathleen Louise, *d* of Philip Lindsay Costeloe; one *s* one *d. Educ:* King's School, Peterborough; Trinity Hall, Cambridge; Cuddesdon Theological Coll. FSA 1992. Orthodox Studentship, Halki, Istanbul, 1963–64. Curate, All Saints, Maidstone, 1965; Assistant Chaplain, University Coll., Oxford, 1966; Fellow, 1969; Chaplain, 1970; Domestic Bursar, 1971; Canon of St George's Chapel, Windsor, 1978–87. Hon. Fellow, Inst. of Clerks of Works, 1978; Churchill Hon. Fellow, Westminster Coll., Fulton, Miss, 1989. *Publications:* articles and reviews. *Recreations:* opera, art, cooking. *Address:* The Vicarage, St Lawrence Jewry Next Guildhall, EC2V 5AA. *T:* (020) 7600 9478.

BURGESS, Dilys Averil; *see* Burgess, A.

BURGESS, Gen. Sir Edward (Arthur), KCB 1982; OBE 1972; Deputy Supreme Allied Commander, Europe, 1984–87; Aide-de-Camp General to the Queen, 1985–87; *b* 30 Sept. 1927; *s* of Edward Burgess and Alice Burgess; *m* 1954, Jean Angelique Leslie Henderson; one *s* one *d. Educ:* All Saints Sch., Bloxham; Lincoln Coll., Oxford; RMA, Sandhurst. Commnd RA 1948; served Germany and ME, 1949–59; psc 1960; GSO 2 WO, 1961–63; served Germany and Far East, 1963–65; jssc 1966; Mil. Asst to C-in-C BAOR, 1966–67; GSO I (DS) Staff Coll., 1968–70; CO 25 Light Regt, RA, 1970–72; CRA 4th Div., 1972–74; Dir of Army Recruiting, 1975–77; Dir, Combat Development (Army), 1977–79; GOC Artillery Div., 1979–82; Comdr, UK Field Army, and Inspector Gen. TA, 1982–84. Gentleman Usher to the Sword of State, 1988–97. Col Comdt, RA, 1982–92. Hon. Colonel: 6/7 (V) Bn Queen's Regt, 1991–92; 6/7 (V) Bn Princess of Wales's Royal Regt, 1992–97. Dep. Grand Pres., British Commonwealth Ex-Services League, 1996–; President: Royal British Legion, 1987–93; Army Football Assoc., 1982–88; Hon. Vice Pres., FA, 1982–88. Freeman, City of London, 1988; Liveryman, Glaziers' Co., 1989; Hon. Liveryman, Haberdashers' Co., 1990. *Publications:* articles in military jls. *Recreations:* fishing, music, reading, gardening. *Address:* c/o Lloyds TSB, Haslemere, Surrey GU27 2JG. *Club:* Army and Navy.

BURGESS, Geoffrey Harold Orchard; Chief Scientist (Agriculture and Horticulture), Ministry of Agriculture, Fisheries and Food, 1982–86; *b* 28 March 1926; *s* of late Harold Frank and Eva M. F. Burgess, Reading; *m* 1952, Barbara Vernon, *y d* of late Rev. Gilbert Vernon Yonge; two *s. Educ:* Reading Sch.; Univ. of Reading; UC Hull. BSc Reading, 1951 (Colin Morley Prizewinner 1950); PhD London, 1955. Special research appt, Univ. of Hull, 1951; Sen. Scientific Officer, DSIR, Humber Lab., Hull, 1954; PSO, Torry Res. Stn, Aberdeen, 1960; Officer i/c, Humber Lab., Hull, 1962; Director, Torry Res. Station, 1969–79; Head of Biology Div., Agrictl Science Service, and Officer i/c Slough Lab., MAFF, 1979–82. Hon. Res. Lectr in Fish Technology, Univ. of Aberdeen, 1969–79; Buckland Lectr, 1964; Hon. Lectr in Fish Technology, Univ. of Leeds, 1966–69; Mem. Adv. Cttee on Food Science, Univ. of Leeds, 1970–86; Mem., Panel of Fish Technology Experts, FAO, 1962–79. *Publications:* Developments in the Handling and Processing of Fish, 1965; (with Lovern, Waterman and Cutting) Fish Handling and Processing, 1965; The Curious World of Frank Buckland, 1967; scientific and technical papers, reviews, reports etc concerning handling, processing, transport and preservation for food, of fish, from catching to consumption. *Recreations:* music, book collecting, walking. *Address:* Stoneleghe, Croxton, Stafford ST21 6NL. *T:* (01630) 620202.

BURGESS, Geoffrey Kelsen; Chief Executive and Clerk, Cornwall County Council, 1982–93 (Deputy Clerk, 1969–82); *b* 4 June 1935; *s* of Monty and Edith Burgess; *m* 1959, Brenda (*née* Martin); three *s. Educ:* Central Foundn Boys' Grammar Sch.; London Sch. of Econs and Pol Science (LLB). Admitted solicitor, 1959. Articled with Simon, Haynes, Barlas & Cassels, London, 1956–59; Assistant Solicitor: East Ham CBC, 1960–62; Worcs CC, 1962–63; Northumberland CC, 1963–65; Asst Clerk, Berks CC, 1965–69; Clerk: Cornwall Magistrates' Courts Cttee, 1982–93; Cornwall Sea Fisheries Cttee, 1982–93; Devon and Cornwall Police Authy, 1988–93; Secretary: Adv. Cttee on appt of Magistrates in Cornwall, 1982–93; Cornwall Probation Cttee, 1982–93. Chairman: Jeffrey Kelson Foundn, 1994–2000; Promoting Effective Parenting, 1999–; Cornwall Bd for Young Enterprise, 1999–. *Recreations:* music, walking.

BURGESS, Rear-Adm. John, CB 1987; LVO 1975; CEng; Director, Rolls-Royce and Associates, since 1987; *b* 13 July 1929; *s* of Albert Burgess and Winifred (*née* Evans); *m* 1952, Avis (*née* Morgan); two *d. Educ:* RN Engineering College; Advanced Engineering RN College, Greenwich; nuclear courses, RN College. HM Ships Aisne, Maidstone, Theseus, Implacable, Cumberland, Caprice; Lectr in Thermodynamics, RNEC, 1962–65; HMS Victorious; nuclear reactor design and manufacture at Rolls Royce, 1968–70; Naval Staff, Washington, DC, 1970–72; Royal Yacht Britannia, 1972–75; Head, Forward Design Group, Ship Dept, 1975–77; Naval Asst to Controller of the Navy, 1977–79; in Command, HMS Defiance, 1979–81; in Command, HMS Sultan, 1981–83; Man. Dir, HM Dockyard, Rosyth, 1984–87. Chm., Maker with Rame Parish Council; occasional involvement with urban develt and waterfront management cttees. *Publications:* papers to professional bodies. *Recreations:* golf, sailing.

BURGESS, Ven. John Edward; Archdeacon of Bath, 1975–95, now Emeritus; *b* 9 Dec. 1930; *s* of Herbert and Dorothy May Burgess; *m* 1958, Jonquil Marion Bailey; one *s* one *d. Educ:* Surbiton County Gram. Sch.; London Univ. (St John's Hall). BD (2nd Cl.), ALCD (1st Cl.). Shell Chemicals Ltd, 1947–53. Asst Curate, St Mary Magdalen, Bermondsey, 1957–60; Asst Curate, St Mary, Southampton, 1960–62; Vicar of Dunston with Coppenhall, Staffs, 1962–67; Chaplain, Staffordshire Coll. of Technology, 1963–67; Vicar of Keynsham with Queen Charlton and Burnett, Somerset, 1967–75; Rural Dean of Keynsham, 1971–74. Mem. Council, Univ. of Bath, 1990– (Chm., Buildings Cttee, 1992–); Chm. Trustees, Partis Coll., Bath, 1996–. *Recreation:* history of railways. *Address:* 12 Berryfield Road, Bradford-on-Avon, Wilts BA15 1SX. *T:* (01225) 868905.

BURGESS, Sir (Joseph) Stuart, Kt 1994; CBE 1984; PhD; FRSC; Chairman: Haemonetics Corp., since 1998 (Director, since 1992); Finsbury Worldwide Pharmaceutical Trust plc, since 1995; *b* 20 March 1929; *s* of late Joseph and Emma Burgess (*née* Wollerton); *m* 1955, Valerie Ann Street; one *s* one *d. Educ:* Barnsley Holgate Grammar School; University College London (1st Class Hons BSc Chem, PhD; Fellow, 1994). Amersham International plc (formerly The Radiochemical Centre), 1953–89: Chief Exec., 1979–89; Pres., Amersham Corp. USA, 1975–77; Advr, Immuno Internat. AG, 1990–96; Dir, Anagen plc, 1993–96. Chairman: Oxford RHA, 1990–94; Anglia and Oxford RHA, subseq. Anglia and Oxford Reg., NHS Exec., DoH, 1994–97; Mem., NHS Policy Board, 1994–97. Dir, American Chamber of Commerce (UK), 1988–90. Member: Innovation Adv. Bd, DTI, 1988–93; ACOST Med. Res. and Health Cttee, 1991–92; Chm., CBI Res. and Manufacturing Cttee, 1990–93; Mem., CBI Nat. Manufacturing Council, 1991–92. Vice-Chm., Nat. Asthma Campaign, 2000–. CIMgt (CBIM 1986; Mem., 1996, Chm., 1998–, Bd of Companions). *Recreations:* golf, music, travel. *Address:* Barrington, Hearn Close, Penn, Bucks HP10 8JT. *T:* (01494) 816387.

BURGESS, Keith, PhD; Executive Chairman, Skillsgroup, since 2000; *b* 1 Sept. 1946; *s* of Bert Burgess and Mary Burgess; *m* 1970, Patricia Mitchell; two *d. Educ:* Pengam Sch. for Boys, Gwent; Univ. of Bristol (BSc 1967; PhD 1971). Joined Arthur Andersen & Co., 1971: Partner, 1980–2000; Managing Partner, Andersen Consulting, UK and Ireland, 1989–94; Global Managing Partner: Practice Competency, 1994–97; Business Process Mgt & Enterprises, 1997–99; Sen. Partner, Andersen Consulting UK, 2000. Pres., Mgt Consultancies Assoc., 1994–95. Chm., Corporate Action for the Homeless, 1993–96. Patron, Univ. of Bristol Campaign for Resource, 1991–. FIMC 1995. Master, Guild of Mgt Consultants, 1998–99 (Mem., 1994–); Liveryman, Co. of Inf. Technologists. *Publication:* (jtly) Foundations of Business Systems, 1989, 2nd edn 1992. *Recreations:* shooting, Rugby, cricket. *Address:* Skillsgroup plc, Bridgford House, Heyes Lane, Alderley Edge, Cheshire SK9 7JP. *Club:* Reform.

BURGESS, Prof. Robert George, PhD; Vice-Chancellor, University of Leicester, since 1999; *b* 23 April 1947; *s* of George Burgess and Olive (*née* Andrews); *m* 1974, Hilary Margaret Mary Joyce. *Educ:* Univ. of Durham (Teacher's Cert. 1968; BA 1971); Univ. of Warwick (PhD 1981). University of Warwick: Lectr in Sociol., 1974–84; Sen. Lectr in Sociol., 1984–88; Chair of Dept of Sociol., 1985–88; Dir, Centre for Educnl Develt, Appraisal and Res., 1987–99; Prof. of Sociology, 1988–99; Chair, Faculty of Social Studies, 1988–91; Founding Chair, Graduate Sch., 1991–95; Sen. Pro-Vice-Chancellor, 1995–99. Founding Chair, UK Council for Graduate Educn, 1994–99. Economic and

Social Research Council: Member: Res. Resources Bd, 1991–96; Council, 1996–2000; Chair, Trng Bd, 1997–2000 (Mem., 1989–93). Chairman: E Midlands Univs Assoc., 2001–; HCFCE Quality Assessment Cttee, 2001–. President: British Sociological Assoc., 1989–91; Assoc. for Teaching of Social Scis, 1991–99. Hon. DLitt Staffordshire, 1998. *Publications:* Experiencing Comprehensive Education, 1983; In the Field, 1984; Education, Schools and Schooling, 1985; Sociology, Education and Schools, 1986; (jtly) Implementing In-Service Education, 1993; Research Methods, 1993; ed. of twenty books; numerous contribs to social sci. jls. *Recreations:* walking, listening to music, some gardening. *Address:* University of Leicester, University Road, Leicester LE1 7RH. *T:* (0116) 252 2322.

BURGESS, Sally; classical singer; *b* 9 Oct. 1953; *d* of Edna Rushton (formerly Burgess; *née* Sharman) and Douglas Burgess; *m* 1988, Neal Scott Thornton; one *s*. *Educ:* Royal College of Music. ARCM. Joined ENO 1977; for ENO as a soprano, rôles incl. Zerlina, Cherubino, Pamina, Mimi, Micaela; for ENO as a mezzo, rôles incl. Composer (Ariadne), Sextus (Julius Caesar), Charlotte (Werther), Carmen, Fennimore (Fennimore and Gerda), 1990; Judith (Duke Bluebeard's Castle), 1991; Octavian (Rosenkavalier), 1994; Mrs Begbick (Mahagonny), 1995; Herodias (Salome), 1996; Dulcinée (Don Quixote), 1996; Amelia (Twice Through the Heart), 1997; Opera North: Amneris (Aida), Dido (Trojans), Julie (Showboat), 1989–90; Orfeo (Glück), 1990; Laura (La Gioconda), 1993; Azucena (Trovatore), 1994; Eboli (Don Carlos), 1998; Margaretha (Genoveva), 2000; Royal Opera, Covent Garden: Siebel (Faust), Maddalena (Rigoletto), 1989; Scottish Opera: Fricka (Die Walküre), Amneris (Aida), 1991; New York Metropolitan: Carmen, 1995; Queen Isabella (The Voyage), 1996; Glyndebourne: Smeraldina (Love for Three Oranges); Welsh National Opera: Ottavia (Coronation of Poppea), 1998; Mother Marie (The Carmelites), Kabanicha (Katya Kabanova), Munich, 1999; Fricka (Das Rheingold), 1999, (Die Walküre), 2000, Geneva; Amneris, Strasbourg, Wiesbaden, Lausanne and Nancy; Carmen, Munich, Oregon, Zürich, Berlin, Paris and NZ; Delilah, Nantes; Sally Burgess' Women (one-woman show), Lyric Th., Hammersmith, 1997; numerous concert appearances; numerous recordings, incl. Liverpool Oratorio, and jazz. *Recreations:* family, cooking, walking, reading, singing jazz, theatre. *Address:* AOR Management, West Wood, Lorraine Park, Harrow Weald, Middx HA3 6BX.

BURGESS, Sir Stuart; *see* Burgess, Sir J. S.

BURGESS, Rev. Stuart John; President, Methodist Conference, 1999–2000; Chairman, York and Hull Methodist District, since 1989; *b* 18 March 1940; *s* of Frederick John Burgess and Winifred May (*née* Gowan); *m* 1965, Elisabeth Maud Fowler; two *d*. *Educ:* Moseley Grammar Sch., Birmingham; Univ. of London (BD ext.); Univ. of Nottingham (MEd; MTh). Minister: Headingley Methodist Church, 1965–68; Nottingham W Circuit, and Chaplain, Univ. of Nottingham, 1968–81; Birmingham SW Circuit, and Chaplain, Univ. of Birmingham, 1981–89. Hon. MA Birmingham, 1989; Hon. DD Hull. *Publications:* Seeds of Joy, 1985; Spiritual Journey of John Wesley, 1988; Stations of the Cross, 1991; Making Connections, 1998; Coming of Age: challenges and opportunities for the 21st century, 1999. *Recreations:* music, tennis. *Address:* 13 Lawn Way, York YO31 1JD. *T:* (01904) 424739.

BURGESS, Tony; *see* Burgess, A. R. F.

BURGH, 7th Baron, *cr* 1529 (title called out of abeyance, 1916; by some reckonings he is 9th Baron (from a *cr* 1487) and his father was 8th and grandfather 7th); **Alexander Peter Willoughby Leith;** *b* 20 March 1935; *s* of 6th (or 8th) Baron Burgh; *S* father 1959; *m* 1st, 1957, Anita Lorna Eldridge (marr. diss. 1982); two *s* one *d*; 2nd, 1984, Wilma Schramm; one *d*. *Educ:* Harrow; Magdalene Coll., Cambridge (BA). *Heir: s* Hon. Alexander Gregory Disney Leith [*b* 16 March 1958; *m* 1st, 1984, Catherine Mary (marr. diss. 1999), *d* of David Parkes; two *s*; 2nd, 1999, Emma Jane Burdick].

BURGH, Sir John (Charles), KCMG 1982; CB 1975; President, Trinity College, University of Oxford, 1987–96 (Hon. Fellow, 1997); Chairman, Associated Board of the Royal Schools of Music, 1987–94; Director-General, British Council, 1980–87; *b* 9 Dec. 1925; *m* 1957, Ann Sturge; two *d*. *Educ:* Friends' Sch., Sibford; London Sch. of Economics (BSc Econ.; Leverhulme post-intermediate Schol.; Pres. of Union, 1949; Hon. Fellow, 1983). Asst Principal, BoT, 1950; Private Sec. to successive Ministers of State, BoT, 1954–57; Colonial Office, 1959–62; Mem., UK Delegation to UN Conf. on Trade and Develt, 1964; Asst Sec., DEA, 1964; Principal Private Sec. to successive First Secretaries of State and Secretaries of State for Econ. Affairs, 1965–68; Under-Sec., Dept of Employment, 1968–71; Dep.-Chm., Community Relations Commn, 1971–72; Deputy Secretary: Cabinet Office (Central Policy Rev. Staff), 1972–74; Dept of Prices and Consumer Protection, 1974–79; Dept of Trade, 1979–80. Member: Executive, PEP, 1972–78; Council, Policy Studies Inst., 1978–85; Council, RSA, 1982–85; Council, VSO, 1980–87; Acad. Council, Wilton Park, 1984–87; Exec. Cttee, Anglo-Austrian Soc., 1987–2000; Council, RIIA, 1993–95. Chairman: Nat. Opera Co-ordinating Cttee, 1991– (Sec., 1972–91); Oxford Educnl Trust for Develt of the Arts, 1990–96; Dir, English Shakespeare Co., 1988–94. Chm. Ct of Governors, LSE, 1985–87 (Gov., 1980–); Vice-Chm., Yehudi Menuhin Sch., 1994–. FRCM 1994. Hon. RNCM 1986. Hon. LLD Bath, 1987. *Recreations:* friends, music, the arts generally. *Address:* 2 Oak Hill Lodge, Oak Hill Park, NW3 7LN. *Club:* Royal Over-Seas League.

BURGHLEY, Lord; Anthony John Cecil; *b* 9 Aug. 1970; *s* and *heir* of Marquess of Exeter, *qv*; *m* 1996, Holly Stewart. *Educ:* Eton; Oxford Univ.

BURGON, Colin; MP (Lab) Elmet, since 1997; *b* 22 April 1948; *s* of Thomas and Winifred Burgon; *m* (marr. diss.); one *d*. *Educ:* St Michael's Coll., Leeds; Carnegie Coll., Leeds; Huddersfield Poly. Teacher; Local Govt Policy and Res Officer. Contested (Lab) Elmet, 1987, 1992. *Address:* House of Commons, SW1A 0AA.

BURGON, Geoffrey; composer; *b* 15 July 1941; *s* of Alan Wybert Burgon and Ada Vera Isom; *m* 1st, 1963, Janice Elizabeth Garwood (marr. diss.); one *s* one *d*; 2nd, 1992, Jacqueline Krofchak; one *s*. *Educ:* Pewley Sch., Guildford; Guildhall School of Music and Drama; studied composition with Peter Wishart, trumpet with Bernard Brown. Freelance trumpeter, 1964–71: Royal Opera House (stage band), Philomusica, London Mozart Players, Northern Sinfonia, Jacques and Capriol Orchestras, also session work, theatres and jazz bands. Full time composer and conductor, 1971–; work in almost every musical genre, particularly orchestral, choral, and music for dance, film & TV; commissions from many Festivals, incl. Bath, Edinburgh, Cheltenham, Southern Cathedrals, Three Choirs, and Camden; also many works for Dance, incl. Ballet Rambert and London Contemporary Dance Theatre; work performed internationally. *Major works:* Gending; Alleluia Nativitas; The World Again; Acquainted with Night; Think on Dreadful Domesday; Canciones del Alma; Requiem; Revelations; Title Divine; Short Mass; The Golden Eternity; The Fire of Heaven, Dos Coros; A Hymn to the Creatures; The Golden Fish; The Calm; Running Figures; Goldbergs Dream; Songs, Lamentations and Praises; Mass; The Trials of Prometheus; Hymn to Venus; Five Sonnets of John Donne; Four Guitars; Six Studies for Solo Cello; Worldes Blisse; Trumpet Concerto: the Turning World; First Was the World; City Adventures; Merciless Beauty; The Wanderer; Piano Concerto; A Different Dawn; *opera:* Hard Times; *film scores:* Life of Brian; Dogs of War; Turtle Diary; Robin Hood; *television scores:* Tinker, Tailor, Soldier, Spy; Brideshead Revisited; Bleak House; Happy Valley; Chronicles of Narnia; Children of the North; Martin Chuzzlewit; Silent Witness; Cider with Rosie; Longitude. Prince Pierre of Monaco Award, 1969; Ivor Novello Award, 1979, 1981; Gold Disc for Brideshead record, 1986. *Recreations:* playing jazz, cricket, Bristol motor cars, sleeping. *Address:* c/o Chester Music, 8/9 Frith Street, W1V 5TZ. *T:* (020) 7434 0066.

BURGOYNE, Rear-Adm. Robert Michael, CB 1982; *b* 20 March 1927; *s* of Robert and Elizabeth Burgoyne; *m* 1951, Margaret (Hilda) McCook; one *s* one *d*. *Educ:* Bradfield College; Magdalene College, Cambridge. Joined RN 1945; CO HMS Cleopatra, 1967–68; Captain 2nd Frigate Sqdn and CO HMS Undaunted, 1972–73; Dir, Maritime Tactical Sch., 1974–75; CO HMS Antrim, 1975–77; Comdr, British Navy Staff, Washington and UK Rep. to SACLANT, 1977–80; Senior Naval Member, Directing Staff, RCDS, 1980–82. Dir, RIN, 1983–92. Vice-Pres., Sea Safety Gp (UK), 1992–96. Chm., W Dorset Dist Scout Council, 1995–97.

BURK, Prof. Kathleen Mildred, DPhil; Professor of Modern and Contemporary History, University College London, since 1995; *b* 5 March 1946; *d* of Wayne Eliot Burk and Martha Ann Burk (*née* Ankney); *m* 1980, Dr Michael Jewess; one *d*. *Educ:* Sanger Union High Sch., California; Univ. of California, Berkeley (BA 1969); St Hugh's Coll., Oxford (MA, DPhil 1977). Tutorial Asst in Mod. Hist., Univ. of Dundee, 1976–77; Rhodes Res. Fellow for N America and Caribbean, St Hugh's Coll., Oxford, 1977–80; Lectr in Hist. and Politics, Imperial Coll., London, 1980–90; University College London: Lectr in Hist., 1990–93; Reader in Mod. and Contemp. Hist., 1993–95. Visiting Professor: Kyung Hee Univ., Seoul, Korea, 1986; Univ. of Tübingen, 1999; Vis. Fellow, All Souls Coll., Oxford, 1998. Chm., Historians' Press, 1983–99; Founding Co-Editor, Contemporary European History, 1989–2001. FRHistS 1989. *Publications:* (ed and contrib.) War and the State: the transformation of British Government 1914–1919, 1982; Long Wittenham 1800–1920, 1984; Britain, America and the Sinews of War 1914–1918, 1985; The First Privatisation: the politicians, the city and the denationalisation of steel, 1988; Morgan Grenfell 1838–1988: the biography of a merchant bank, 1989; (with Alec Cairncross) Goodbye, Great Britain: the 1976 IMF crisis, 1992; (with Manfred Pohl) The Deutsche Bank in London 1873–1998, 1998; (ed with Melvyn Stokes) The United States and the Western Alliance since 1945, 1999; Troublemaker: the life and history of A. J. P. Taylor, 2000; articles in Histl Jl, Econ. Hist. Rev. Internat. Hist. Rev., etc. *Recreations:* collecting antiquarian history books, playing early music, wine. *Address:* The Long Barn, Townsend, Harwell, Oxon OX11 0DX. *T:* (01235) 835637. *Club:* Academy.

BURKE, Most Rev. Austin-Emile; *see* Halifax (NS), Archbishop of, (RC).

BURKE, Hon. Brian Thomas; Australian Ambassador to Republic of Ireland and to the Holy See, 1988–91; *b* 25 Feb. 1947; *s* of late Thomas Burke (Federal ALP Member for Perth, 1942–55), and Madelaine Burke; *m* 1965, Susanne May Nevill; four *s* two *d*. *Educ:* Brigidine Convent; Marist Brothers' Coll.; Univ. of Western Australia. FAMI. Former journalist. MLA (Lab) Balga, WA, 1973–88; Opposition Shadow Minister, 1976–81; Leader of the Opposition, 1981–83; Premier and Treasurer of WA, 1983–88. AC 1988. *Recreations:* reading, stamp-collecting, writing poetry, swimming, fishing. *Address:* PO Box 668, Scarborough, WA 6019, Australia.

BURKE, David Thomas, (Tom), CBE 1997; Environmental Policy Adviser: Rio Tinto plc, since 1997; BP Amoco, since 1997; *b* 5 Jan. 1947; *s* of J. V. Burke, DSM, and Mary (*née* Bradley). *Educ:* St Boniface's, Plymouth; Liverpool Univ. (BA (Hons) Philosophy). Great George's Community Arts Project, 1969–70; Lecturer: West Cheshire Coll., 1970–71; Old Swan Technical Coll., 1971–73; Friends of the Earth: Local Groups Co-ordinator, 1973–75; Executive Director, 1975–79; Dir of Special Projects, 1979–80; Vice-Chm., 1980–81; Dir, The Green Alliance, 1982–91; Special Advr to Sec. of State for the Envmt, 1991–97. Press Officer, European Environment Bureau, 1979–87; Sec., Ecological Studies Inst., 1987–92. Member: Bd of Dirs, Earth Resources Research, 1975–87; Waste Management Adv. Council, 1976–81; Packaging Council, 1978–82; Exec. Cttee, NCVO, 1984–89; UK Nat. Cttee, European Year of the Environment, 1986–88; Exec. Cttee, European Environment Bureau, 1987–91; Council, English Nature, 1999–. Contested (SDP): Brighton Kemptown, 1983; Surbiton, 1987. Vis. Fellow, Cranfield, 1991–94; Vis. Prof., Imperial Coll., 1997–. Hon. Vis. Fellow, Manchester Business Sch., 1984. FRSA 1988 (Mem. Council, 1990–92). Royal Humane Society Testimonials: on Vellum, 1966; on Parchment, 1968; Global 500 Laureate, UNEP, 1993. *Publications:* Europe: environment, 1981; (jtly) Pressure Groups in the Global System, 1982; (jtly) Ecology 2000, 1984; (jtly) The Green Capitalists, 1987; (jtly) Green Pages, 1988. *Recreations:* photography, birdwatching. *Address:* Studio 2, Clink Wharf Studios, Clink Street, SE1 9DG. *T:* (020) 7357 9146. *Club:* Reform.

BURKE, Prof. Derek Clissold, CBE 1994; DL; Vice-Chancellor, University of East Anglia, 1987–95; *b* 13 Feb. 1930; *s* of late Harold Burke and Ivy Ruby (*née* Clissold); *m* 1955, Mary Elizabeth Dukeshire, New York; one *s* three *d*. *Educ:* Univ. of Birmingham (BSc, PhD, Chemistry). Res. Fellow, Yale Univ., 1953–55; Scientist, Nat. Inst. for Med. Res., London, 1955–60; Lectr and Sen. Lectr, Dept of Biochemistry, Univ. of Aberdeen, 1960–69; Prof. of Biol Scis, 1969–82, Pro-Vice-Chancellor, 1971–73, Univ. of Warwick; Vice-Pres. and Scientific Dir, Allelix Inc., Toronto, 1982–86. Specialist Advr, H of C Select Cttee on Sci. and Technol., 1995–. Member: MRC Cell Bd, 1976–79; Scientific Cttee, Cancer Res. Campaign, 1979–82 and of CRC Council, 1987–97; Europ. Molecular Biol Org., 1980–; Adv. Cttee on Genetic Modification, HSE, 1987–95; Steering Gp, Technol. Foresight Initiative, OST, 1993–95; Sci. and Engrg Base Bd, 1994–97, Technol. Interaction Bd, 1994–97, BBSRC; EU Life Scis High Level Gp, 2000–; EU-US Biotechnol. Consultative Forum, 2000–. Chm., Adv. Cttee on Novel Foods and Processes, Dept of Health and MAFF, 1989–97. Chm. Council, Paterson Inst. for Cancer Res., 1992–97; Dir, Babraham Inst., Cambridge, 1995–99; Mem. Governing Body, BBSRC Inst. of Food Res., 1995– (Mem. Adv. Bd, AFRC Inst. of Food Res., 1989–95). Chm., Genome Research Ltd, 1997–98. Mem., Archbishops' Med. Ethics Adv. Gp, 1995–. Pres., Soc. for Gen. Microbiology, 1987–90. Hon. Mem., Soc. for Gen. Microbiol., 2001. Editor and Editor in Chief, Journal of General Virology, 1976–87. Trustee, Norfolk and Norwich Fest., 1988–98; Wingfield Arts, 1995–98. Hon. Fellow, St Edmund's Coll., Cambridge, 1997–. Hon. FIBiol 2001. Hon. LLD Aberdeen 1982; Hon. ScD UEA, 1995. DL Norfolk, 1992. *Publications:* Creation and Evolution (ed and contrib.), 1985; (with R. Gill) Strategic Church Leadership, 1996; (ed and contrib.) Cybernauts Awake!, 1999; numerous sci. papers on interferon and animal viruses. *Recreations:* music, walking. *Address:* 13 Pretoria Road, Cambridge CB4 1HD. *Club:* Royal Over-Seas League.

BURKE, Ian; *see* Burke, M. I.

BURKE, Sir James (Stanley Gilbert), 9th Bt *cr* 1797 (Ire.), of Marble Hill, Galway; *b* 1 July 1956; *s* of Sir Thomas Stanley Burke, 8th Bt and Susanne Margaretha (*d* 1983), *er d* of Otto Salvisberg, Thun, Switzerland; *S* father, 1989; *m* 1980, Laura, *d* of Domingo Branzuela; one *s* one *d*. *Heir:* *s* Martin James Burke, *b* 22 July 1980. *Address:* Sous-Géronde 89, 3960 Sierre, Switzerland.

BURKE, Jeffrey Peter; QC 1984; a Recorder of the Crown Court, since 1983; *b* 15 Dec. 1941; *s* of Samuel and Gertrude Burke; *m* 1994, Joanna Mary Heal; one *s* one *d*. *Educ:* Shrewsbury Sch.; Brasenose Coll., Oxford (BA 1963). Called to the Bar, Inner Temple, 1964, Bencher, 1997. Legal Mem., Mental Health Review Tribunal, 1994–; Judge, Employment Appeal Tribunal, 2000–. *Recreations:* sport, wine, charity triathlons, fighting stinging nettles. *Address:* Devereux Chambers, Devereux Court, Temple, WC2R 3JJ. *Clubs:* Economicals AFC; Flamstead Cricket.

BURKE, John Joseph; Vice Chairman, Bristol & West plc, since 1999; *b* 18 Sept. 1942; *m* 1967, Sally Elliott; three *s*. *Educ:* Bridlington Grammar Sch.; Sutton High Sch., Plymouth. Family retail business, 1958–64; Bristol & West Building Society, subseq. Bristol & West plc, 1964–: Gen. Manager, Retail Ops, 1988–90, Business Develt, 1990–91; Main Bd Dir, 1991–; Business Develt Dir, 1991–93; Man. Dir and Chief Exec., 1993–99. Pres., Bristol Chamber of Commerce and Initiative, 2000–. *Recreations:* fishing, Rugby supporter. *Address:* Bristol & West plc, PO Box 27, One Temple Quay, Bristol BS99 7AX; Lea Farm, Sutton Wick, Bishop Sutton, Bristol BS39 5XR. *T:* (01761) 221242.

BURKE, John Kenneth, QC 1985; **His Honour Judge Burke;** a Circuit Judge, since 1995; *b* 4 Aug. 1939; *s* of Kenneth Burke and Madeline Burke; *m* 1962, Margaret Anne (*née* Scattergood); three *d*. *Educ:* Stockport Grammar Sch. Served Cheshire Regt, 1958–60; TA Parachute Regt, 1962–67. Called to the Bar, Middle Temple, 1965, Bencher, 1992. A Recorder, 1980–95. *Recreations:* painting and drawing, walking.

BURKE, Hon. Sir Kerry; *see* Burke, Hon. Sir T. K.

BURKE, (Michael) Ian; Chief Executive, Thistle Hotels plc, since 1998; *b* 21 June 1956; *s* of Ronald and Rosemary Burke; *m* 1979, Jane McGuinness; one *s* one *d*. *Educ:* Imperial Coll., London (BSc Maths); London Business Sch. (MSc Business Admin). ACMA 1981. With Lever Bros, 1978–81; finance and planning, Esso UK, 1981–86; Gp Planning Manager, Gateway Corp., 1986–90; Bass plc: Commercial Dir, Bass Leisure, 1990–92; Man. Dir, Gala Clubs, 1992–95; Exec. Vice Pres. and Man. Dir, Holiday Inn Worldwide, Europe, ME and Africa, 1995–98. Dir, London Tourist Bd, 1998–; Bd Mem., BTA. *Recreations:* fell-walking, cycling. *Address:* (office) Capital House, 25 Chapel Street, Marylebone, NW1 5JJ. *T:* (020) 7723 0101.

BURKE, Peter; *see* Burke, U. P.

BURKE, Prof. Philip George, CBE 1993; FRS 1978; MRIA 1974; Professor of Mathematical Physics, Queen's University of Belfast, 1967–98, now Emeritus; *b* 18 Oct. 1932; *s* of Henry Burke and Frances Mary Burke (*née* Sprague); *m* 1959, Valerie Mona Martin; four *d*. *Educ:* Wanstead County High Sch.; Univ. Coll. of SW of England, Exeter (BSc London (ext.) 1953, 1st cl. Hons Physics); University Coll. London (PhD 1956, Fellow 1986). Res. Fellow, UCL, 1956–57; Asst Lectr, Univ. of London Computer Unit, 1957–59; Res. Associate, Alvarez Bubble Chamber Gp and Theory Gp, Lawrence Berkeley Lab., Calif, 1959–62; Res. Fellow, then Principal Scientific Officer, later SPSO, Theoretical Physics Div., AERE, Harwell, 1962–67; Queen's University of Belfast: Head, Dept of Applied Maths and Theoretical Physics, 1974–77; Chm., Sch. of Physics and Math. Scis, 1985–86; Dir, Sch. of Maths and Physics, 1988–90. Science, subseq. Science and Engineering, Research Council: Mem., Physics Cttee, 1967–71; Chm., Synchrotron Radiation Panel, 1969–71; Mem., Atlas Comp. Cttee, 1973–76; Hd, Div. of Theory and Computational Sci., Daresbury Lab., 1977–82; Chm., Science Bd Computer Cttee, 1976–77 and 1984–86; Chm., Scientific Computing Adv. Panel, 1989–94; Mem., 1989–94; Chairman: Internat. Conf. on Physics of Electronic and Atomic Collisions, 1973–75; Computational Physics Gp, Europ. Physical Soc., 1976–78; Atomic, Molecular and Optical Physics Div., Inst. of Physics, 1987–90; Allocations and Resources Panel, Jt Res. Councils Supercomputer Cttee, 1988–90; Supercomputing Management Cttee, 1991–94; Inter-Council High Performance Computing Mgt Cttee, 1996–98; Mem., ABRC Supercomputing Sub-cttee, 1991–94. Mem., Council, Royal Soc., 1990–92. Co-ordinator, EU Human Capital and Mobility Network of nine EU labs and three E European labs, 1993–96. Dir, 1969–2000, Hon. Dir, 2001–, Computer Physics Communications Internat. Program Library. Hon. Editor, Computer Physics Communications, 1986– (founding and principal editor, 1969–79). Hon. DSc: Exeter, 1981; QUB, 1999. Guthrie Medal, 1994, Sir David Bates Prize, 2000, Inst. of Physics. *Publications:* (with H. Kleinpoppen) series editor, Physics of Atoms and Molecules; many papers in learned journals. *Recreations:* walking, swimming, books, music. *Address:* c/o Department of Applied Mathematics and Theoretical Physics, Queen's University of Belfast, Belfast BT7 1NN. *T:* (028) 9033 5047, *Fax:* (028) 9023 9182; *e-mail:* p.burke@qub.ac.uk; (home) Brook House, Norley Lane, Crowton, Northwich, Cheshire CW8 2RR. *T:* (01928) 788301.

BURKE, Richard; President, Canon Foundation in Europe, 1988–98; *b* 29 March 1932; *s* of David Burke and Elisabeth Burke; *m* 1961, Mary Freeley; two *s* three *d*. *Educ:* University Coll., Dublin (MA). Called to the Bar, King's Inns. Mem., Dublin Co. Council, 1967–73 (Chm., 1972–73); Mem. Dail Eireann, for South County Dublin, 1969–77, for Dublin West, 1981–82; Fine Gael Chief Whip and spokesman on Posts and Telegraphs, 1969–73; Minister for Education, 1973–76. Commission of the European Communities: Member with special responsibility for Transport, Taxation, Consumer Protection, Relations with European Parlt, Research, Educ. and Sci., 1977–81, for Greenland, Greek Memorandum, Personnel and Admin, Jt Interpretation and Conf. Service, Statistical Office and Office of Publications, 1982–85; Vice Pres., 1984–85. Associate Fellow, Center for Internat. Affairs, Harvard Univ., 1980–81. Member: Conseil d'Administration, FIDEPS, UNESCO, 1990–98; Develt Council, HEC, Paris, 1990–. Mem., Academia Scientiarum et Artium Europaea, Salzburg, 1996. Chieftain, Burke Clan, 1990, Hon. Life Pres., 1992. Pro Merito Europa Medal, 1980. Grand Croix, Leopold II (Belgium), 1981; Grand Croix, Phoenix (Greece), 1983. *Recreations:* music, golf, travel. *Address:* 67 Ailesbury Road, Dublin 4, Ireland. *T:* 2692520.

BURKE, Hon. Sir (Thomas) Kerry, Kt 1990; Member, Canterbury Regional Council (Environment Canterbury), Christchurch, since 1998; *b* 24 March 1942; *m* 1st, 1968, Jennifer Shiel (marr. diss. 1984); two *s*; 2nd, 1984, Helen Paske (*d* 1989); one *s*; 3rd, 1997, Fahimeh Rastar; one *s* two *d*. *Educ:* Linwood High Sch.; Univ. of Canterbury (BA); Christchurch Teachers' Coll. (Dip. Teaching). General labourer, Auckland, 1965–66; factory deleg., Auckland Labourers' Union; teacher: Rangiora High Sch., 1967–72; Greymouth High Sch., 1975–78; lang. consultant, Vienna, 1991–98. Chm., Rangiora Post-Primary Teachers' Assoc., 1969–71. MP (Lab) Rangiora, NZ, 1972–75, West Coast, 1978–90; Minister of Regional Develt, and of Employment and Immigration, 1984–87; Speaker, NI House of Reps, 1987–90. *Recreations:* ski-ing, swimming.

BURKE, Tom; *see* Burke, D. T.

BURKE, Trevor Michael; QC 2001; *b* 16 Oct. 1958; *s* of Michael George Burke and Philomena Burke. *Educ:* Handsworth Grammar Sch.; South Bank Univ., (BA Hons Law). Called to the Bar, Middle Temple, 1981. *Recreation:* golf. *Address:* 2 Bedford Row, WC1R 4BU. *T:* (020) 440 8888. *Club:* Brocket Hall Golf.

BURKE, Prof. (Ulick) Peter, FBA 1994; Professor of Cultural History, since 1996, and Fellow of Emmanuel College, since 1979, University of Cambridge; *b* 16 Aug. 1937; *s* of John Burke and Jennie Burke (*née* Colin); *m* 1st, 1972, Susan Patricia Dell (marr. diss. 1983); 2nd, 1989, Maria Lúcia Garcia Pallares. *Educ:* St John's Coll., Oxford; St Antony's Coll., Oxford (MA). Asst Lectr, then Lectr in History, subseq. Reader in Intellectual History, Sussex Univ., 1962–78; Reader in Cultural History, Univ. of Cambridge, 1988–96. *Publications:* The Renaissance Sense of the Past, 1969; Culture and Society in Renaissance Italy, 1972, 3rd edn 1986; Venice and Amsterdam: a study of Seventeenth Century elites, 1974, 2nd edn 1994; Popular Culture in Early Modern Europe, 1978, 2nd edn 1994; Sociology and History, 1980; Montaigne, 1981; Vico, 1985; Historical Anthropology in Early Modern Italy: essays on perception and communication, 1987; The Renaissance, 1987; The French Historical Revolution: the Annales School 1929–89, 1990; The Fabrication of Louis XIV, 1992, 2nd edn 1994; History and Social Theory, 1992; Antwerp, a Metropolis in Europe, 1993; The Art of Conversation, 1993; The Fortunes of the Courtier, 1995; Varieties of Cultural History, 1997; The European Renaissance, 1998; A Social History of Knowledge, 2000; Eyewitnessing, 2001. *Recreation:* travel. *Address:* Emmanuel College, Cambridge CB2 3AP. *T:* (01223) 334272. *Club:* Paineras de Morumbi (São Paulo).

BURKE-GAFFNEY, John Campion; Director-General, The British Red Cross Society, 1985–90; *b* 27 Feb. 1932; *s* of late Dr Henry Joseph O'Donnell Burke-Gaffney, OBE and Constance May (*née* Bishop); *m* 1956, Margaret Mary Jennifer (*née* Stacpoole); two *s* two *d*. *Educ:* Douai School. Called to the Bar, Gray's Inn, 1956. Served: RAC, 1950–52; E Riding of Yorks Imperial Yeomanry (Wenlock's Horse), 1952–56. Shell-Mex and BP Ltd, 1956–75; Shell UK Ltd, 1976–77; Man. Dir, Shell and BP Zambia Ltd, 1977–81; Gp Public Affairs, Shell Internat. Petroleum Co. Ltd, 1981–85. *Address:* c/o Coutts & Co., Park Lane Branch, 1 Old Park Lane, W1A 4AL.

BURKETT, Mary Elizabeth, OBE 1978; FRGS; FMA; Director of Abbot Hall Art Gallery, and Museum of Lakeland Life and Industry, 1967–86, and Borough Museum, Kendal, 1977–86; retired; *d* of Ridley Burkett and Mary Alice Gaussen. *Educ:* Univ. of Durham (BA, Teachers' Cert.). FRGS 1978; FMA 1980. Taught art, craft, maths, etc, at Wroxall Abbey, 1948–54; Art and Craft Lectr, Charlotte Mason Coll., Ambleside, 1954–62; seven months in Turkey and Iran, 1962; Asst Dir, Abbot Hall, 1963–66. Formerly part-time Teacher of Art, Bela River Prison. Member: numerous cttees including National Trust (NW Region), 1978–85; Carlisle Diocesan Adv. Cttee, 1980–1996; Carlisle Cathedral Fabric Cttee, 1991–2001. Dir, Border Television, 1982–93. Round the World trip, lecturing in Hong Kong, Perth (WA), NY as well as seeing the Great Wall of China, 1986. FRSA 1983; Fellow, Huguenot Soc., 1986. Hon. MA Lancaster, 1997. Leverhulme Award (to continue research on Lake District portraits), 1986–88. *Publications:* The Art of the Felt Maker, 1979; Kurt Schwitters (in the Lake District), 1979; (with David Sloss) William Green of Ambleside, 1984; (with David Sloss) Read's Point of View, 1995; (with Val Rickerby) Percy Kelly: a Cumbrian artist, 1997; contrib. art and archaeol jls, and gall. and museum catalogues. *Recreations:* travel, bird watching, photography, writing, doing research into more Cumbrian artists, lecturing, picking up stones. *Address:* Isel Hall, Cockermouth, Cumbria CA13 0QG.

BURLAND, James Alan, RIBA; architect; Principal Partner, burlandtm, since 2000; *b* 25 Sept. 1954; *s* of James Glyn Burland and late Elizabeth Beresford Thompson. *Educ:* King Henry VIII Sch., Coventry; Bath Univ. (BSc 1978; BArch 1980). RIBA 1983. Joined Arup Associates, 1978, Dir and Principal, 1994–2000; projects include: Stockley Park, Heathrow, 1983–2000; Eton Coll. Labs, 1984; Bedford High Sch. Sen. Sch., 1984–85; (with Philip Cox Architects, Sydney) Sydney Olympics 2000 Stadium Studies, 1985–90; Manchester Stadium, 1992–2000 (Consultant, 2000–); Plantation House, Fenchurch Street, London, 1993–2000; Johannesburg Athletics Stadium, 1993–94; new coll., Durham Univ., 1994–2000; Crystal Palace Sports Complex, 1998; BP Solar Showcase G8 Summit, Arup campus building, Birmingham, 1998; private commn, design for Body Shop, including Bath and Brighton, 1982; burlandtm projects include: Ealing Studios, 2000–; Bermondsey Market, 2000–; Spitalfields Refuge and Convent restoration, 2000–. Bovis/Architects' Jl RA Summer Exhibn Grand Award, 1998. *Recreations:* music, sport, art, architecture. *Address:* (office) 43–45 Charlotte Street, W1P 1HA. *T:* (020) 7255 2070; *e-mail:* jb@burlandtm.com. *Club:* Chelsea Arts.

BURLAND, Prof. John Boscawen, FRS 1997; FREng; Professor of Soil Mechanics in the University of London, at Imperial College of Science, Technology and Medicine (formerly Imperial College of Science and Technology), since 1980; *b* 4 March 1936; *s* of John Whitmore Burland and Margaret Irene Burland (*née* Boscawen); *m* 1963, Gillian Margaret, *d* of J. K. Miller; two *s* one *d*. *Educ:* Parktown Boys' High Sch., Johannesburg; Univ. of the Witwatersrand (BSc Eng, MSc Eng, DSc Eng); Univ. of Cambridge (PhD). MSAICE; FICE; FIStructE; FREng (FEng 1981). Res. Asst, Univ. of the Witwatersrand, 1960; Engineer, Ove Arup and Partners, London, 1961–63; Res. Student, Cambridge Univ., 63–66; Building Research Station: SSO and PSO, 1966–72; Head of Geotechnics Div., 1972–79; Asst Dir and Head of Materials and Structures Dept, 1979–80. Visiting Prof., Dept of Civil Engineering, Univ. of Strathclyde, 1973–82. Member: Adv. Panel to Sec. of State for Environment on Black Country Limestone, 1983–95; Italian Prime Minister's Commn for stabilising the Leaning Tower of Pisa, 1990–. Mem. Council, CIRIA, 1987–95 (Vice Pres., 1995–98); Official Visitor, BRE, 1990–97. Chm., Wheathampstead Churches Together, 1990–97. Mem. Council, Royal Acad. of Engrg, 1994–97; Institution of Structural Engineers: Mem. of Council, 1979–82; Murray Buxton Silver Medal, 1977; Oscar Faber Bronze Medal, 1979; Gold Medal, 1998; named in Special Award to DoE for Underground Car Park at Palace of Westminster, 1975; Oscar Faber Diploma, 1982; Instn of Civil Engineers: Telford Premium, 1972, 1985, 1987; Coopers Hill War Meml Medal, 1985; Baker Medal, 1986; Kelvin Medal, for outstanding contribn to engrg, 1989; Brit. Geotechnical Soc. Prize, 1968, 1971, 1974 and 1986; Kevin Nash Gold Medal, Internat. Soc. of Soil Mechanics and Foundn Engrs, 1994; H. Bolton Seed Medal, ASCE, 1996; Gold Medal, World Fedn of Engrg Orgns, 1997. Hon. DEng Heriot-Watt, 1994; Hon. DSc Nottingham, 1998; Hon. DEng Glasgow, 2001. *Publications:* numerous papers on soil mechanics and civil engineering. *Recreations:* sailing, golf, painting, classical guitar.

BURLEIGH, Prof. Michael Christopher Bennet, PhD; FRHistS; William R. Kenan Jnr Professor of History, Washington & Lee University, Lexington, since 2000; *b* 3 April 1955; *s* of late Wing Comdr B. G. S. Bennet Burleigh and C. Burleigh; *m* 1990, Linden Mary Brownbridge. *Educ:* University Coll. London (BA 1st Cl. Hons 1977); Bedford Coll., London (PhD 1982). FRHistS 1988. Weston Jun. Res. Fellow, New Coll., Oxford, 1984–87; British Acad. Post-doctoral Fellow, QMC, 1987–88; London School of

Economics and Political Science: Lectr, 1988–93; Reader in Internat. Hist., 1993–95; Dist. Res. Prof. in Modern European History, Cardiff Univ., 1995–2000. Raoul Wallenberg Vis. Prof. of Human Rights, Rutgers Univ., 1999–2000. Award for Archival Achievement, BFI, 1991; Bronze Medal, NY Film and TV Fest., 1994. *Publications:* Prussian Society and the German Order, 1984; Germany Turns Eastwards, 1988; The Racial State: Germany 1933–45, 1991 (trans. Italian); Death and Deliverance: euthanasia in Germany, 1994 (trans. German); (ed) Confronting the Nazi Past, 1996 (trans. Hungarian); Ethics and Extermination: reflections on Nazi genocide, 1997; The Third Reich: a new history, 2000 (Samuel Johnson Prize, 2001) (trans. German, Italian, French, Spanish). *Recreation:* gardening. *Address:* c/o David Godwin Associates, 55 Monmouth Street, WC2H 9DG. *Club:* Athenæum.

BURLEY, Helen; *see* Boaden, H.

BURLEY, Prof. Jeffery, CBE 1991; PhD; Professor of Forestry, since 1996, Director, Oxford Forestry Institute, since 1985, Oxford University; Professorial Fellow, Green College, Oxford, since 1981; *b* 16 Oct. 1936; *s* of Jack Burley and Eliza Burley (*née* Creese); *m* 1961, Jean Shirley (*née* Palmer); two *s*. *Educ:* Portsmouth Grammar Sch.; New College, Oxford (BA 1961); Yale (MF 1962; PhD 1965). Lieut, Royal Signals, 1954–57. O i/c and Unesco Expert, Forest Genetics Res. Lab., ARC of Central Africa, 1965–69; Sen. Res. Officer, Commonwealth Forestry Inst., Oxford, 1969–76; Univ. Lectr, 1976–83, Head of Dept of Forestry, 1983–85, Oxford. Pres., Internat. Union of Forestry Res. Orgns, 1996–Dec. 2000. *Publications:* (ed jtly) Multipurpose tree germplasm, 1984; (ed jtly) Increasing productivity of multipurpose species, 1985; many book chapters resulting from conference papers; many contribs to periodicals and learned jls on forestry, agroforestry and forest tree breeding. *Recreations:* beekeeping, cricket, gardening. *Address:* Oxford Forestry Institute, South Parks Road, Oxford OX1 3RB. *T:* (01865) 275050.

BURLEY, Sir Victor (George), Kt 1980; CBE 1969; FIEAust; FIEE, FIMechE, FIProdE; Chairman: Advisory Council of Commonwealth Scientific and Research Organization (CSIRO), 1979–81; Allied Industries Pty Ltd, 1984–2000; *b* 4 Dec. 1914; *s* of G. H. Burley and M. A. Luby; *m* 1941, Alpha Loyal Lord; one *s* three *d*. *Educ:* High Sch., Tasmania; Univ. of Tasmania (BE). FIFST; FInstD, FAIM. Cadbury-Fry-Pascall Pty Ltd, Australia, 1938–71: Chief Engr, Director and Vice-Chm.; Director, Cadbury Schweppes Aust Ltd, 1971–78; Cons. Dir, Cadbury Fry Hudson NZ; Technical Cons., Cadbury Schweppes UK, 1978–82. Member, Adv. Council, CSIRO, 1961–78; Chm., State Cttee, Tas. CSIRO, 1964–78; Foundn Mem., Commonwealth Adv. Cttee on Advanced Educn, 1965–71; Foundn Chm., Council of Advanced Educn, Tasmania, 1968–76; Mem., Sci. and Industry Forum, Aust. Acad. of Science, 1967–81. Director: Productivity Promotion Council, Australia, 1983–88; University Research Co., 1985–90. University of Tasmania: Warden of Convocation, 1964–74; Mem., Faculty of Engrg, 1968–93; Mem. Council, 1982–84. *Recreations:* music, reading. *Address:* Montaigne, 553 Sandy Bay Road, Hobart, Tas 7005, Australia. *T:* (3) 62252583. *Clubs:* Melbourne (Melbourne); Tasmanian (Hobart).

BURLIN, Prof. Terence Eric; Rector, University of Westminster (formerly Polytechnic of Central London), 1984–95, Professor Emeritus, 1996; *b* 24 Sept. 1931; *s* of Eric Jonas Burlin and Winifred Kate (*née* Thomas); *m* 1957, Plessey Pamela Carpenter; one *s* one *d*. *Educ:* Acton County School; University of Southampton (BSc), Univ. of London (DSc, PhD). CPhys, FInstP 1969; FIBiotech 1992. Physicist, Mount Vernon Hosp. and Radium Inst., 1953–57; Sen. Physicist, Hammersmith Hosp., 1957–62; Principal Physicist, St John's Hosp. for Diseases of the Skin, 1960–90; Polytechnic of Central London: Sen. Lectr, 1962; Reader, 1969; Pro-Director, 1971; Sen. Pro-Rector, 1974; Acting Rector, 1982. British Cttee on Radiation Units and Measurements: Mem., 1966–74 and 1979–95; Vice-Chm., 1983–84; Chm., 1984–95; Member: Council, Inst. for Study of Drug Dependence, 1974–86; various Boards, CNAA; Cttee on Practical Determination of Dose Equivalent, Internat. Commn on Radiation Units and Measurements (Chm.), 1979–87; Adv. Council on Adult and Continuing Educn, DES, 1980–83; Cttee on Effects of Ionising Radiation, Physics and Dosimetry Sub-Cttee, MRC, 1983–86; Science Bd, SERC, 1986–89. Mem. Council, BTEC, 1984–86. Member: Council, Westminster Chamber of Commerce, 1994–95; Employment Affairs Cttee, 1994–95, Commercial Educn Trust, 1996–, London Chamber of Commerce and Industry. Mem. Bd, Bournemouth Univ., 1996–. Hon. FCP 1990. Hon. DSc Westminster, 1996. *Publications:* chapters in Radiation Dosimetry, 1968, 2nd edn 1972; papers on radiation dosimetry, radiological protection, biomechanical properties of skin, radiobiology. *Recreations:* music, swimming. *Club:* Athenæum.

BURLINGTON, Earl of; William Cavendish; *b* 6 June 1969; *s* and *heir* of Marquess of Hartington, *qv*. *Address:* Beamsley Hall, Skipton, North Yorks BD23 6HD.

BURLISON, family name of **Baron Burlison**.

BURLISON, Baron *cr* 1997 (Life Peer), of Rowlands Gill in the co. of Tyne and Wear; **Thomas Henry Burlison;** DL; *b* 23 May 1936; *s* of Robert Burlison and Georgina (*née* Doige); *m* 1981, Valerie Stephenson; two *s* one *d*. *Educ:* Edmondsley, Co. Durham. Panel beater, 1951–57; professional footballer, 1953–65; RAF, 1959–61; General and Municipal Workers' Union, then General, Municipal, Boilermakers and Allied Trades Union, later GMB: Regl Officer, 1965–78; Regl Sec., 1978–91; Dep. Gen. Sec., 1991–96. Treas., Labour Party, 1992–96. A Lord in Waiting, (Govt Whip), 1999–2001. Exec. Mem., British North American Cttee, 1994–97. DL Tyne and Wear, 1997. *Recreation:* gardening. *Address:* House of Lords, SW1A 0PW.

BURMAN, Roger Stephen, CBE 1991; DL; Chairman, since 1976, and Managing Director, since 1973, Teledictor; *b* 3 April 1940; *s* of Sir Stephen France Burman, CBE and Lady (Joan Margaret) Burman; *m* 1964, Felicity Jane Crook; four *s*. *Educ:* Oundle Sch.; Univ. of Birmingham (BSc Hon.). Burman & Sons, 1961–72 (Dir, 1965–72); Teledictor, 1972–. Chm., Nat. Exhibn Centre, 1989– (Dir, 1984–); Dir, Black Country Develt Corp., 1992–98. Gen. Tax Comr, 1973–. Member: British Hallmarking Council, 1980– (Chm., 1989–97); BOTB, 1990–94 and 1996–99; Council, ICC, 1990–; Pres., Birmingham Chamber of Commerce, 1984–85; Chm., Assoc. of British Chambers of Commerce, 1988–90. University of Birmingham: Life Governor, 1983–; Pro-Chancellor, 1994–2001. Liveryman, Goldsmiths' Co., 1993–. DL 1991, High Sheriff 1999, W Midlands. Hon. LLD Birmingham, 1994. *Recreation:* golf. *Address:* Morton Hall, Holberrow Green, Redditch, Worcs B96 6SJ. *T:* (01386) 793298.

BURN, Adrian; *see* Burn, B. A. F.

BURN, Angus Maitland P.; *see* Pelham Burn.

BURN, (Bryan) Adrian (Falconer); non-executive Chairman: Atlas Group Holdings Ltd, since 1999; Search Holdings Ltd, since 2000; *b* 23 May 1945; *s* of Peter and Ruth Burn; *m* 1968, Jeanette Carol; one *s* three *d*. *Educ:* Abingdon Sch. FCA. Whinney Murray, 1963–72; joined Binder Hamlyn, 1972; seconded to DTI, 1975–77; Partner, 1977, Managing Partner, 1988–94, Binder Hamlyn; Partner, Arthur Andersen, 1994–99. Non-executive Director: Sinclair-Stevenson Ltd, 1990–92; Brent Internat. plc, 1994–99; GE Capital Bank Ltd, 1999–; Pinewood Studios, 2000–; Wolff Olins Ltd, 1999–; Strutt and Parker, 1999–; Richards Butler, 1999–. Mem., Financial Adjudication Panel, Second Severn Crossing, 1991–98. Trustee and Treas., NSPCC, 1999–. *Address:* 13 Woodthorpe Road, Putney, SW15 6UQ. *T:* (020) 8788 6383; *e-mail:* email@adrianburn.com. *Club:* Roehampton.

BURN, Michael Clive, MC 1945; writer; *b* 11 Dec. 1912; *s* of late Sir Clive Burn and Phyllis Stoneham; *m* 1947, Mary Booker (*née* Walter) (*d* 1974); no *c*. *Educ:* Winchester; New Coll., Oxford (open scholar); Hons Degree in Soc. Scis, Oxford, 1945, with distinction in all subjects (awarded whilst POW at Colditz). Journalist, The Times, 1936–39; Lieut 1st Bn Queens Westminsters, KRRC, 1939–40; Officer in Independent Companies, Norwegian Campaign, 1940, subseq. Captain No. 2 Commando; taken prisoner in raid on St Nazaire, 1942; prisoner in Germany, 1942–45. Foreign Correspondent for The Times in Vienna, Jugoslavia and Hungary, 1946–49. Keats Poetry First Prize, 1973. *Plays:* The Modern Everyman (prod. Birmingham Rep., 1947); Beyond the Storm (Midlands Arts Co., and Vienna, 1947); The Night of the Ball (prod. New Theatre, 1956). *Publications: novels:* Yes, Farewell, 1946, repr. 1975; Childhood at Oriol, 1951; The Midnight Diary, 1952; The Trouble with Jake, 1967; *sociological:* Mr Lyward's Answer, 1956; The Debatable Land, 1970; *poems:* Poems to Mary, 1953; The Flying Castle, 1954; Out On A Limb, 1973; Open Day and Night, 1978; *play:* The Modern Everyman, 1948; *non-fiction:* Mary and Richard, 1988. *Address:* Beudy Gwyn, Minffordd, Gwynedd, N Wales LL48 6EN.

BURN, Rear Adm. Richard Hardy, CB 1992; AFC 1969; CEng; FRAeS; Director General Aircraft (Navy), Ministry of Defence, 1990–92; *b* 26 May 1938; *s* of Margaret (*née* Hardy) and Douglas Burn; *m* 1967, Judith Sanderson (*née* Tigg); one *s* one *d* and one step *s* one step *d*. *Educ:* Berkhamsted; BRNC Dartmouth; RNEC Manadon. MIMechE. HMS Broadsword 1958, fighter pilot, 890 Naval Air Sqdn, HMS Ark Royal, 1961–62; test flying work (incl. 3 years exchange, US Navy), NDC Latimer, to 1975; develt of Sea Harrier, MoD (PE), 1975–78; Ops Officer, A&AEE, 1978–79; Air Eng. Officer, RNAS Yeovilton, 1980; Asst Dir Eng. (N), MoD, 1981–84; RCDS 1985; Dir, Aircraft Maint. and Repair, MoD (N), 1986–87; Dir, Helicopter Projects, MoD (PE), and ADC, 1988–90. Mem., Soc. of Experimental Test Pilots. FIMgt. Commendation, US Navy, 1974; Médaille d'Honneur, Soc. d'Encouragement au Progrès, 1989. *Recreations:* skiing, golf, painting.

BURNE, Dr Yvonne Ann; Head, City of London School for Girls, since 1995; *b* 29 Aug. 1947; *d* of Archibald Ford and Florence Louise Ford (*née* Knott); *m* 1968, Anthony Richard Burne; one *s* one *d*. *Educ:* Redland High Sch. for Girls, Bristol; Westfield Coll., Univ. of London (BA Hons; PhD). School teacher: Harrow Co. Grammar Sch. for Girls, 1971–74; Lowlands Sixth Form Coll., 1974–77; Hd, Mod. Langs and Careers Guidance, Northwood Coll., 1984–87; Headmistress, St Helen's Sch. for Girls, Northwood, 1987–95. Editor: Educnl Challenges Inc. (VA, USA), 1978–82; Mary Glasgow Pubns, 1983–84; Heinemann Educnl Books, 1984. Mem., Hillingdon FHSA, 1990–96. FRSA 1991. *Publications:* Tomorrow's News, 1979; The Circus Comes to Town, 1979; articles and children's stories. *Recreations:* theatre, entertaining friends, walking. *Address:* City of London School for Girls, Barbican, EC2Y 8BB.

BURNELL, (Susan) Jocelyn B.; *see* Bell Burnell.

BURNELL-NUGENT, Rear Adm. James Michael, CBE 1999; Commander UK Maritime Force, and Commander Anti Submarine Warfare Striking Force, since 2001; *b* 20 Nov. 1949; *s* of late Comdr Anthony Frank Burnell-Nugent, DSC, RN and of Gian Burnell-Nugent; *m* 1973, Henrietta Mary, *d* of Rt Rev. R. W. Woods, KCMG, KCVO; three *s* one *d*. *Educ:* Stowe Sch.; Corpus Christi Coll., Cambridge (MA Hons). Joined RN, 1971; CO HMS Olympus, 1979–80; CO HMS Conqueror, 1984–86; Comdr, 1985; Captain, 1990; Captain, F2 and CO HMS Brilliant, 1992–93; Cdre, 1994; on secondment to HM Treasury, 1996; CO HMS Invincible, 1997–99; Rear Adm., 1999; ACNS, MoD, and Mem., Admiralty Bd, 1999–2001. Freeman, City of London, 1999. *Publications:* pamphlets incl. Leadership in the Office, Keeping an Eye on the Cost of Government; numerous articles in Naval Review and RUSI Jl. *Recreation:* living in the country. *Address:* Ministry of Defence, Whitehall, SW1A 2HB. *Club:* Cychod Trefdraeth.

BURNER, Edward Alan; HM Diplomatic Service; Ambassador to Senegal and, concurrently, to Guinea Bissau and Cape Verde, since 2000; *b* 26 Sept. 1944; *s* of late Douglas Keith Burner and of Mary Burner; *m* 1969, Jane Georgine Du Port; one *s* two *d*. *Educ:* Uppingham Sch., Rutland; Emmanuel Coll., Cambridge (MA Hons Mod. Langs). Volunteer, Nigeria, VSO, 1966–67; joined HM Diplomatic Service, 1967: Sofia, 1970–72; Bonn, 1972–74; Bridgetown, 1974–78; N America Dept, FCO, 1979; Asst Private Sec. to Minister for Overseas Develt, 1979–82; Dep. Head of Recruitment, FCO, 1982–84; Dep. Hd of Mission, Sofia, 1984–87; on loan to ODA, 1987–90; Hd, Med. Welfare Unit, FCO, 1990–92; Commercial Counsellor, then Dep. Hd of Mission, Lagos, 1992–95; Consul-Gen., Munich, 1995–99. *Recreations:* tennis, walking. *Address:* c/o Foreign and Commonwealth Office, SW1A 2AH; 12 Hillside Road, Sevenoaks, Kent TN13 3XJ. *T:* (01732) 453885.

BURNET, George Wardlaw, LVO 1981; JP; Lord-Lieutenant of Midlothian, since 1992; *b* 26 Dec. 1927; *s* of late Sheriff John Rudolph Wardlaw Burnet, KC and Lucy Margaret Ord Burnet (*née* Wallace); *m* 1951, Jane Elena Moncrieff, *d* of late Malcolm Moncrieff Stuart, CIE, OBE; two *s* one *d*. *Educ:* Edinburgh Acad.; Lincoln Coll., Oxford (BA); Edinburgh Univ. (LLB). Served Black Watch (RHR) TA, retired as Captain, 1957. WS 1954; Partner, Murray Beith and Murray, 1956–90. County Councillor, Midlothian, 1967–76; Convener, Church of Scotland Gen. Finance Cttee, 1980–83. Chairman: Life Assoc. of Scotland, 1985–93; Caledonian Res. Foundn, 1989–99. Brig., Royal Company of Archers, Queen's Body Guard for Scotland, 1985–. Hon. FRIAS 1980. DL 1975, JP 1991, Midlothian. KStJ. *Recreations:* country pursuits, architecture, gardening. *Address:* Rose Court, Inveresk, Midlothian EH21 7TD. *T:* (0131) 665 2689. *Club:* New (Edinburgh).

BURNET, Sir James William Alexander, (Sir Alastair Burnet), Kt 1984; journalist; *b* 12 July 1928; *s* of late Alexander and Schonaid Burnet, Edinburgh; *m* 1958, Maureen Campbell Sinclair. *Educ:* The Leys Sch., Cambridge; Worcester Coll., Oxford. Sub-editor and leader writer, Glasgow Herald, 1951–58; Commonwealth Fund Fellow, 1956–57; Leader writer, The Economist, 1958–62; Political editor, Independent Television News, 1963–64; Editor, The Economist, 1965–74; Editor, Daily Express, 1974–76; broadcaster with ITN, 1976–91; Assoc. Editor, News at Ten, 1982–91. Ind. Dir, Times Newspapers Hldgs Ltd, 1982–; Dir, United Racecourses Hldgs Ltd, 1985–94. Member: Cttee of Award, Commonwealth Fund, 1969–76; Cttee on Reading and Other Uses of English Language, 1972–75; Monopolies Commn specialist panel on newspaper mergers, 1973–91; Council, Banking Ombudsman, 1985–96; Hon. Vice-Pres., Inst. of Journalists, 1990. Richard Dimbleby Award, BAFTA, 1966, 1970, 1979; Judges' Award, 1981, Hall of Fame, 1999, RTS. *Address:* 43 Hornton Court, Campden Hill Road, W8 7NT. *T:* (020) 7937 7563.

BURNET, John Elliot; Chief Executive, Cumbria County Council, 1991–97; *b* 13 Jan. 1947; *m* 1991, Deirdre Eleanor Elizabeth Burton. *Educ:* Barnard Castle Sch.; Nottingham Univ. (BA Law); College of Law, London. Articled, S Shields CBC (Clerk/Asst Solicitor), 1969–73; Sen. Asst Solicitor, S Tyneside MBC, 1973–74; Asst County Clerk, Tyne and Wear CC, 1974–82; Cumbria County Council: Sen. Asst Clerk and Dep. Co. Solicitor, 1982–86; Dir, Econ. Develt and Corporate Policy, 1986–90; Asst Chief Exec., 1990–91. *Recreations:* watching sport, archaeology, historic buildings.

BURNETT, of Leys; *see* Baronetcy of (unclaimed); *see under* Ramsay, Sir Alexander William Burnett, 7th Bt.

BURNETT, Prof. Alan Kenneth; MD; FRCPGlas, FRCPE, FRCP, FRCPath, FMedSci; Professor of Haematology, University of Wales College of Medicine, since 1992; *b* 27 May 1946; *s* of George Binnie Burnett and Janet Maloch Burnett (*née* Henderson); *m* 1971, Alison Forrester Liddell; two *s*. *Educ:* Glasgow Acad.; Univ. of Glasgow (ChB; MD Hons 1988). FRCPGlas 1984; FRCPath 1986; FRCPE 1988; FRCP 1993. Res. Fellow, Univ. of Chicago, 1975–76; Consultant Haematologist, Glasgow Royal Infirmary, 1979–92. Visiting Professor: Univ. of Miami, 1994; Northwestern Univ., Chicago, 1999; Univ. of Kuwait, 2000. Chm., MRC Adult Leukaemia Wkg Party, 1990–; Mem., Med. Advisory Panel, Leukaemia Res. Fund, 1989–93. Pres., British Soc. of Haematol., 1998-99. FMedSci 2000. *Publications:* contrib. papers to medical literature on the subject of leukaemia and bone marrow transplantation. *Recreations:* golf, DIY, irritating NHS overheads. *Address:* 1 Minorca Cottages, Michaelston-Y-Fedw, Cardiff CF3 9XX.

BURNETT, Dr Andrew Michael, FSA; Keeper of Coins and Medals, British Museum, since 1992; *b* 23 May 1952; *s* of Sir John (Harrison) Burnett, *qv*; *m* 1978, Susan Jennifer Allix; two *d*. *Educ:* Fettes Coll., Edinburgh; Balliol Coll., Oxford (BA, MA); Inst. of Archaeology, Univ. of London (PhD). Department of Coins and Medals, British Museum: Res. Assistant, 1974–79; Asst Keeper, 1979–90; Dep. Keeper, 1990–92. Secretary: RNS, 1983–90 (Vice-Pres., 1999–); Internat. Numismatic Commn, 1992–97 (Pres., 1997–). Corresp. Mem., Amer. Numismatic Soc., 1982. FSA 1982. Norwegian Numismatic Soc. Medal, 1991; Silver Medal, RNS, 1993; Prix Allier de Hauteroche, Acad. des Inscriptions et Belles-Lettres, 1999. *Publications:* Coinage in the Roman World, 1987; Interpreting the Past: Coins, 1991; Roman Provincial Coinage, Vol. 1, 1992, Vol. 2, 1999; Behind the Scenes at the British Museum, 2001; contrib. Numismatic Chronicle, Schweizerische Numismatisches Rundschau, Quaderni Ticinesi, Jl Roman Studies, Britannia, etc. *Address:* Department of Coins and Medals, British Museum, WC1B 3DG. *T:* (020) 7323 8170; 19 Almorah Road, N1 3ER. *T:* (020) 7359 2949.

BURNETT, Air Chief Marshal Sir Brian (Kenyon), GCB 1970 (KCB 1965; CB 1961); DFC 1942; AFC 1939; RAF, retired; Chairman, All England Lawn Tennis Club, Wimbledon, 1974–83; *b* 10 March 1913; *s* of late Kenneth Burnett and Anita Catherine Burnett (*née* Evans); *m* 1944, Valerie Mary (*née* St Ludger); two *s*. *Educ:* Charterhouse; Wadham Coll., Oxford (BA 1934; Hon. Fellow, 1974). Joined RAFO 1932; RAF 1934; Long Distance Record Flight of 7,158 miles from Egypt to Australia, Nov. 1938. Served War of 1939–45, in Bomber Command, incl. CO 51 Sqdn, 1942, and FTC; Directing Staff, RAF Staff Coll., 1945–47; UN Military Staff Cttee, New York, 1947–48; Joint Planning Staff, 1949–50; SASO HQ No. 3 (Bomber) Group, 1951–53; CORAF Gaydon, 1954–55; ADC to the Queen, 1953–57; Director of Bomber and Reconnaissance Ops, Air Ministry, 1956–57; Imperial Defence Coll., 1958; Air Officer Administration, HQ Bomber Command, 1959–61; AOC No 3 Gp, Bomber Command, 1961–64; Vice-Chief of the Air Staff, 1964–67; Air Secretary, MoD, 1967–70; C-in-C, Far East Command, Singapore, 1970–71; retired 1972. Air ADC to the Queen, 1969–72. Pres., Squash Rackets Assoc., 1972–75. *Recreations:* tennis, golf, ski-ing. *Address:* Heather Hill, Littleworth Cross, Seale, Farnham, Surrey GU10 1JN. *Clubs:* Royal Air Force; Vincent's (Oxford); All England Lawn Tennis; Jesters Squash; International Lawn Tennis Club of Great Britain.

BURNETT, Charles John, FSAScot; Ross Herald, since 1988 (Dingwall Pursuivant, 1983); *b* 6 Nov. 1940; *s* of Charles Alexander Urquhart Burnett and Agnes Watt; *m* 1967, Aileen Elizabeth McIntyre; two *s* one *d*. *Educ:* Fraserburgh Academy; Gray's Sch. of Art, Aberdeen (DA); Aberdeen Coll. of Education (Teaching Cert.); MLitt Edinburgh 1992. AMA; FHS Scot. House of Fraser, 1963–64; COI, 1964–68; Asst Dir, Letchworth Mus., 1968–71; Head of Design, Nat. Mus. of Antiquities of Scotland, 1971–85; Curator of Fine Art, Scottish United Services Mus., Edinburgh Castle, 1985–96; Chamberlain, Duff House Country House Gall., Banff, 1997–. Heraldic Adviser, Girl Guide Assoc. in Scotland, 1978–; Vice-Patron, Geneal. Soc. of Queensland, 1986–; Vice-President: Heraldry Soc. of Scotland, 1987–; Soc. of Antiquaries of Scotland, 1992–95. Trustee, Bield Retirement Housing Trust, 1992–96. Convenor, Companions of the Order of Malta, 1991–94. KStJ 1991; Librarian, Priory of Order of St John in Scotland, 1987–99. Kt, Order of St Maurice and St Lazarus, 1999. Hon. Citizen, Oklahoma, 1989. *Publications:* Scotland's Heraldic Heritage, 1997; The Order of St John in Scotland, 1997; numerous articles on Scottish heraldry. *Recreations:* reading, visiting places of historical interest. *Address:* Seaview House, Portsoy, Banffshire AB45 2RS. *T:* (01261) 843378.

BURNETT, Prof. Charles Stuart Freeman, PhD; FBA 1998; Professor of the History of Islamic Influences in Europe, Warburg Institute, University of London, since 1999 (Lecturer, 1985–99); *b* 26 Sept. 1951; *m* 1st, 1985, Mitsuri Kamachi (marr. diss. 1991); 2nd, 1995, Tamae Nakamura; two *s*. *Educ:* Manchester Grammar Sch.; St John's Coll., Cambridge (BA 1972; PhD 1976). LGSM 1980. Jun. Res. Fellow, St John's Coll., Cambridge, 1975–79; Sen. Res. Fellow, Warburg Inst., Univ. of London, 1979–82; Leverhulme Res. Fellow, Dept of History, Univ. of Sheffield, 1982–84, 1985; Mem., Inst. for Advanced Study, Princeton, 1984–85. Corresp. Mem., Internat. Acad. of History of Science. *Publications:* (with Masahiro Takenaka) Jesuit Plays on Japan and English Recusancy, 1995; Magic and Divination in the Middle Ages: texts and techniques in the Islamic and Christian worlds, 1996; The Introduction of Arabic Learning into England, 1997; several edns of Latin and Arabic texts; over 100 articles in learned jls. *Recreations:* playing music (viola, piano, viola da gamba, shakuhachi), hill walking, religious activities (Iona community, Japanese Buddhist and Shinto traditions). *Address:* Warburg Institute, Woburn Square, WC1H 0AB. *T:* (020) 7862 8920.

BURNETT, Sir David Humphery, 3rd Bt *cr* 1913; MBE 1945; TD; one of HM Lieutenants of the City of London; *b* 27 Jan. 1918; *s* of Sir Leslie Trew Burnett, 2nd Bt, CBE, TD, DL, and Joan (*d* 1994), *d* of late Sir John Humphery; *S* father, 1955; *m* 1948, Geraldine Elizabeth Mortimer, *d* of Sir Godfrey Arthur Fisher, KCMG; two *s* (and one *s* decd). *Educ:* Harrow; St John's Coll., Cambridge, MA. Served War of 1939–45 (despatches, MBE), in France, N Africa, Sicily and Italy; Temp. Lt-Col GSO1, 1945. Partner, David Burnett & Son, Chartered Surveyors, 1947–50; Director: Proprietors of Hay's Wharf Ltd, 1950–80 (Chm., 1965–80); Guardian Royal Exchange Assurance, 1967–88. Chairman: South London Botanical Institute, 1976–81 (Pres., 1985); London Assoc. of Public Wharfingers, 1964–71. Mem. PLA, 1962–75. Mem. Council, Brighton Coll., 1971–93. Master: Company of Watermen and Lightermen of the River Thames, 1964; Girdlers Company, 1970. FRICS 1970 (ARICS 1948); FIMgt (FBIM 1968); FLS 1979. *Heir: s* Charles David Burnett [*b* 18 May 1951; *m* 1st, 1989, Victoria Joan (marr. diss.), *d* of James Simpson; one *d*; 2nd, 1998, Kay Rosemary Naylor]. *Address:* Tandridge Hall, near Oxted, Surrey RH8 9NJ; Twizel Millhouse, Cornhill-on-Tweed, Northumberland TD12 4UX. *Clubs:* Turf, Oxford and Cambridge.

BURNETT, Ian Duncan; QC 1998; barrister; a Recorder, since 2000; *b* 28 Feb. 1958; *yr s* of David John Burnett and Maureen Burnett (*née* O'Brien); *m* 1991, Caroline Ruth Monks; one *s*. *Educ:* St John's Coll., Southsea; Pembroke Coll., Oxford (MA). Called to the Bar, Middle Temple, 1980, Bencher, 2001; Jun. Crown Counsel, Common Law, 1992–98; Asst Recorder, 1998–2000. *Recreations:* history, music, silver, wine. *Address:* 1 Temple Gardens, EC4Y 9BB. *T:* (020) 7583 1315. *Club:* Carlton.

BURNETT, Sir John (Harrison), Kt 1987; Chairman, Co-ordinating Commission for Biological Recording, since 1989; Chairman, National Biodiversity Network Trust, since 2000; *b* 21 Jan. 1922; *s* of Rev. T. Harrison Burnett, Paisley; *m* 1945, E. Margaret, *er d* of Rev. Dr E. W. Bishop; two *s*. *Educ:* Kingswood Sch., Bath; Merton Coll., Oxford (BA, MA 1947; DPhil 1953; Christopher Welch Scholar, 1947; Hon. Fellow, 1997). FRSE 1957; FIBiol 1969. Served 1942–46 as Lieut RNVR (despatches). Lecturer, Lincoln Coll., 1948–49; Fellow (by Exam.) Magdalen Coll., 1949–53; Univ. Lecturer and Demonstrator, Oxford, 1949–53; Lecturer, Liverpool Univ., 1954–55; Prof. of Botany: Univ. of St Andrews, 1955–60; King's Coll., Newcastle, Univ. of Durham, 1961–63, Univ. of Newcastle, 1963–68; Dean of Faculty of Science, St Andrews, 1958–60, Newcastle, 1966–68; Public Orator, Newcastle, 1966–68; Regius Prof. of Botany, Univ. of Glasgow, 1968–70; Oxford University: Sibthorpian Prof. of Rural Economy and Fellow, St John's Coll., 1970–79; Member: Gen. Bd of Faculties, 1972–77 (Vice-Chm, 1974–76); Hebdomodal Council, 1974–79; Prin. and Vice-Chancellor, Univ. of Edinburgh, 1979–87. Exec. Sec., World Council for the Biosphere, 1987–93; Chm. and Founder, Internat. Orgn for Plant Inf., 1991–96. Lectures: Delgarno, Univ. of Manitoba, 1979–80; Bewley Meml, 1982; Peacock Meml, Dundee Univ., 1982; St Leonard's, Univ. of St Andrews, 1988. Chm., Scottish Horticultural Research Inst., 1959–74; Member: Nature Conservancy Scottish Cttee, 1961–66, English Cttee, 1966–69; Nature Conservancy Council, 1987–89 (Dep. Chm. and Acting Chm., 1988–89; Mem. Scottish Cttee, 1980–87); Nuffield Foundn Biol. Project, 1962–68 (Chm., 1965–68); British Mycological Soc. (Pres., 1982–83); Trustee, The New Phytologist, 1962–85, Advr, 1985–99; Member: Academic Adv. Council, Univs of St Andrews and Dundee, 1964–66; Council, Univ. of Buckingham, 1989–96. Member: Newcastle Reg. Hosp. Bd, 1964–68; Kingswood Assoc. (Pres., 1989). Hon. Consultant: Nat. Grid Co., 1990–99; Heritage Lottery Fund, 1995–99. Hon. Res. Prof., Open Univ., 1996–99. Hon. Fellow: RCSE, 1983; Green Coll., Oxford, 1988. Hon. DSc: Buckingham, 1981; Pennsylvania, 1983; Hon. LLD: Dundee, 1982; Strathclyde, 1983; Glasgow, 1987; Dr *hc* Edinburgh, 1988. Commendatore, Order of Merit (Italy), 1990. *Publications:* Vegetation of Scotland, ed and contrib., 1964; Fundamentals of Mycology, 1968, 3rd edn 1994; Mycogenetics, 1975; Fungal Walls and Hyphal Growth, ed and contrib., 1979; Edinburgh University Portraits II, 1986; Speciation and Evolution in Fungi, 1989; (jt ed. and contrib.) The Maintenance of the Biosphere, 1989; Surviving with the Biosphere, 1994; Biological Recording in the UK: present practice and future development, 1996; papers in various books and scientific journals. *Recreations:* walking, writing, gardens. *Address:* 13 Field House Drive, Oxford OX2 7NT. *Clubs:* Athenæum, Royal Over-Seas League.

See also A. M. Burnett.

BURNETT, John Patrick Aubone; MP (Lib Dem) Devon West and Torridge, since 1997; farmer, since 1976; *b* 19 Sept. 1945; *s* of late Lt-Col Aubone Burnett, OBE and Joan (*née* Bolt); *m* 1971, Elizabeth Sherwood, *d* of Sir Arthur de la Mare, KCMG, KCVO; two *s* two *d*. *Educ:* Ampleforth Coll., Yorks; Britannia RNC, Dartmouth; Coll. of Law, London. Served RM, 1964–70. Admitted Solicitor, 1975; Partner, then Sen. Partner, Burd Pearse, Okehampton, 1976–97. Mem., Law Soc. Revenue Law Cttee, 1984–96. Contested (Lib Dem) Devon West and Torridge, 1987. Lib Dem spokesman on legal affairs, 1997–. Mem. Council, Devon Cattle Breeders' Assoc., 1985–97. *Address:* House of Commons, SW1A 0AA.

BURNETT, Prof. Keith, DPhil; FRS 2001; FInstP; Professor, since 1996, and Head of Atomic and Laser Physics, since 1999, Oxford University; Fellow, St John's College, Oxford, since 1988; *b* 30 Sept. 1953; *s* of Royston Ifor Burnett and Jean Marion Burnett; *m* 1975, Elizabeth Anne Mustoe; one *s* one *d*. *Educ:* Brynteg Comprehensive Sch.; Jesus Coll., Oxford (BA 1975; DPhil 1979). FInstP 1996. Asst Prof., Univ. of Colorado, 1980–84; Fellow, Jt Inst. for Lab. Astrophysics, Colorado Univ. and Nat. Inst. of Standards and Technol., 1981–84; Lecturer in Physics: Imperial Coll., London, 1984–88; Oxford Univ., 1988–96. Mem., EPSRC, 1999–. Fellow: APS, 1996; Optical Soc. of America, 1996. *Publications:* articles in learned jls, incl. Physical Review, Jl Physics B. *Recreations:* reading, music. *Address:* Department of Physics, Clarendon Laboratory, Parks Road, Oxford OX1 3PU. *T:* (01865) 272372.

BURNETT, Sir Walter (John), Kt 1988; President, Royal National Agricultural and Industrial Association of Queensland, since 1983; *b* 15 Jan. 1921; *s* of William Henry and Minna Anna Burnett; *m* 1945, Mabel Nestor Dalton; two *d*. *Educ:* Maleny Primary School; Church of England Grammar School; Pharmacy College, Queensland. Conducted own pharmacy business in Maleny for 32 years. Director: Geriatric Med. Foundn of Qld (also Founder Mem.); Sunshine Coast Hosps Bd, 1958–. Past Chm., Maleny Br., Qld Ambulance Transport Bde; Vice Patron, Schizophrenia Fellowship of S Qld, 1987. Mem., Electoral Re-distribution Commn, Brisbane City Council, 1984–85. Grand Master, United Grand Lodge of Qld, 1983–86. Past Pres., Maroochy Dist Bowls Assoc. *Recreation:* lawn bowls. *Address:* 28 Tamarind Street, Maleny, Qld 4552, Australia. *T:* (7) 54942290.

BURNETT-STUART, Joseph; Chairman, Robert Fleming Holdings Ltd, 1981–90 (Director, 1963–90); *b* 11 April 1930; *s* of late George Eustace Burnett-Stuart, CBE and Etheldreda Cecily (*née* Edge); *m* 1954, Mary Hermione, *d* of late John A. M. Stewart of Ardvorlich, TD; three *s* one *d*. *Educ:* Eton Coll.; Trinity Coll., Cambridge (BA). Bankers Trust Co., 1953–62. A Church Commissioner, 1984–94. *Recreations:* gardening, shooting, fishing. *Club:* New (Edinburgh).

BURNEY, Sir Cecil (Denniston), 3rd Bt *cr* 1921; *b* 8 Jan. 1923; *s* of Sir Charles Dennistoun Burney, 2nd Bt, CMG, and Gladys (*d* 1982), *d* of George Henry High; *S* father, 1968; *m* 1957, Hazel Marguerite de Hamel, *yr d* of late Thurman Coleman; two *s*. *Educ:* Eton; Trinity Coll., Cambridge. Man. Dir, 1951–68, Chm., 1968–72, Northern Motors Ltd; Chairman: Hampton Trust PLC, 1975–87; JMD, subseq. Rhino, Group plc, 1988–92; Director: Security Building Soc., 1959–71; Mount Martin Gold Mines NL, 1985–87. Member of Legislative Council, N Rhodesia, 1959–64; MP Zambia, 1964–68; Chairman, Public Accounts Cttee, Zambia, 1963–67. *Recreations:* tennis, skiing. *Heir: s* Nigel Dennistoun Burney [*b* 6 Sept. 1959; *m* 1992, Lucy Brooks; two *s* one *d*]. *Address:*

PO Box 32037, Lusaka, Zambia; 5 Lyall Street, SW1X 8DW. *T:* (020) 7235 4014. *Clubs:* White's, Carlton, Turf, Buck's; Leander; Harare, Bulawayo (Zimbabwe); Ndola (Zambia).

BURNHAM, 6th Baron *cr* 1903, of Hall Barn, Beaconsfield, Bucks; **Hugh John Frederick Lawson;** Bt 1892; *b* 15 Aug. 1931; *yr s* of 4th Baron Burnham, CB, DSO, MC, TD and (Marie) Enid Burnham, CBE (*d* 1979), *d* of Hugh Scott Robson, Buenos Aires; *S* brother, 1993; *m* 1955, Hilary Margaret, *yr d* of Alan Hunter, Perth; one *s* two *d. Educ:* Eton Coll.; Balliol Coll., Oxford (MA). Commissioned Scots Guards, 1950. Daily Telegraph, 1955–86 (Dep. Man. Dir, 1984–86). Dir Gen., King George's Fund for Sailors, 1988–93. A Dep. Speaker, H of L, 1995–; Opposition spokesman on defence, H of L, 1997–; Opposition Dep. Chief Whip, H of L, 1997–2001; elected Mem., H of L, 1999. Younger Brother, Trinity House, 1998–. *Recreations:* sailing, shooting. *Heir: s* Hon. Harry Frederick Alan Lawson, *b* 22 Feb. 1968. *Address:* Woodlands Farm, Beaconsfield, Bucks HP9 2SF. *Clubs:* Pratt's, Royal Ocean Racing; Royal Yacht Squadron.

BURNHAM, Rt Rev. Andrew; *see* Ebbsfleet, Bishop Suffragan of.

BURNHAM, Andrew Murray; MP (Lab) Leigh, since 2001; *b* Liverpool, 7 Jan. 1970; *s* of Kenneth Roy Burnham and Eileen Mary (*née* Murray); *m* 2000, Marie-France van Heel; one *s. Educ:* St Aelred's RC High Sch., Merseyside; Fitzwilliam Coll., Cambridge (MA Hons Eng.). Researcher to Tessa Jowell, MP, and Labour Health Team, 1994–97; Parly Officer, NHS Confedn, 1997; Advr to Football Task Force, 1997–98; Special Advr to Rt Hon. Chris Smith, MP, DCMS, 1998–2001. Mem., Health Select Cttee, 2001–. *Recreations:* football (Everton FC season ticket holder), Rugby league (Leigh RLC), cricket. *Address:* House of Commons, SW1A 0AA. *T:* (020) 7219 8250; (constituency office) 10 Market Street, Leigh WN7 1DS. *T:* (01942) 682353. *Club:* Lowton Labour.

BURNHAM, Rev. Anthony Gerald; Moderator, Free Churches Group (formerly Free Churches' Council), since 1999; a President, Churches Together in England, since 1999; *b* 2 March 1936; *s* of Selwyn and Sarah Burnham; *m* 1961, Valerie Florence Cleaver; one *s* two *d. Educ:* Silcoates Sch.; Manchester Univ. (BA Admin); Northern Coll., Manchester. Minister: Brownhill Congregational Church, Blackburn, 1961–66; Poulton-le-Fylde and Hambleton Congregational Churches, 1966–69; Lectr, Northern Coll., Manchester, 1969–77; Minister, SW Manchester United Reformed Churches, 1973–81; Synod Moderator, NW Synod URC, 1981–92; Gen. Sec., URC, 1992–2001. Chm. of Corps, Council for World Mission, 1995–99. Religious broadcasting for radio and TV. *Publications:* In The Quietness, 1981; Say One For Me, 1990. *Recreations:* theatre, jazz. *Address:* 30 Sandhurst Road, Didsbury, Manchester M20 5LR.

BURNHAM, Peter Michael; chartered accountant; Partner, Coopers & Lybrand, 1970–93; *b* 13 May 1935; *s* of late Frank Burnham and Winifred Eileen Burnham (*née* Fyson); *m* 1963, Jill, *d* of Comdr Langton Gowlland, RN; two *d. Educ:* Eltham Coll.; Bristol Univ. (BA 1956). FCA, FCMA, JDipMA. With Sturges Fraser Cave & Co., 1956–59; served as Pilot Officer, RAF, 1959–61; with Coopers & Lybrand, 1961–95: Dep. Man. Dir, Consulting Practice, 1981–88. Bd Mem., Historic Bldgs and Monuments Commn (English Heritage), 1984–88; Dir, UK Council for Computing Develt, 1984–88; Dir and Dep. Chm., E London TEC, 1989–93; Dir, Satellite Observing Systems Ltd, 1993–95, 1998–; Mem., Adv. Cttee, HM Inspectorate of Pollution, 1994–95; Mem. Adv. Cttee, 1994–95, Bd Mem., 1995–97, Environment Agency. Member: Archbps' Commn on Cathedrals, 1992–94; Synod Follow-up Gp, 1995–96. *Publications:* various articles in professional jls. *Recreations:* sailing, travelling, listening to music. *Address:* Church Hill House, Church Hill, Midhurst, W Sussex GU29 9NX. *T:* (01730) 812841,. *Fax:* (01730) 817142; La Cumbre, Camino del Morro, 18697 La Herradura, Spain. *T:* and *Fax:* (958) 827426. *Clubs:* Royal Air Force, Royal Thames Yacht.

BURNINGHAM, John Mackintosh; free-lance author-designer; *b* 27 April 1936; *s* of Charles Burningham and Jessie Mackintosh; *m* 1964, Helen Gillian Oxenbury, *qv*; one *s* two *d. Educ:* Summerhill School, Leiston, Suffolk; Central School of Art, Holborn, 1956–59 (Diploma). Now free-lance: illustration, poster design, exhibition, animated film puppets, and writing for children. Wall friezes: Birdland, Lionland, Storyland, 1966; Jungleland, Wonderland, 1968; Around the World, 1972. *Publications:* Borka, 1963 (Kate Greenaway Medal, 1963); John Burningham's ABC, 1964; Trubloff, 1964; Humbert, 1965; Cannonball Simp, 1966 (filmed, 1967); Harquin, 1967; The Extraordinary Tug-of-War, 1968; Seasons, 1969; Mr Gumpy's Outing, 1970 (Kate Greenaway Award, 1971); Around the World in Eighty Days, 1972; Mr Gumpy's Motor Car, 1973; "Little Books" series: The Baby, The Rabbit, The School, The Snow, 1974; The Blanket, The Cupboard, The Dog, The Friend, 1975; The Adventures of Humbert, Simp and Harquin, 1976; Come Away from the Water, Shirley, 1977; Time to Get Out of the Bath, Shirley, 1978; Would You Rather, 1978; The Shopping Basket, 1980; Avocado Baby, 1982; John Burningham's Number Play Series, 1983; First Words/Granpa, 1984 (filmed, 1989); Play and Learn Books: abc, 123, Opposites, Colours, 1985; Where's Julius, 1986; John Patrick Norman McHennessy—the Boy who is Always Late, 1987; Rhymetime: A Good Job, The Car Ride, 1988, Animal Chatter, A Grand Band, 1989; Oi! Get off our Train, 1989; Aldo, 1991; England, 1992; Harvey Slumfenburger's Christmas Present, 1993 (jt winner, W. H. Smith Award, 1994); Courtney, 1994; Cloudland, 1996; France, 1998; Whadayamean, 1999; *illustrated:* Chitty Chitty Bang Bang, 1964; The Wind in the Willows, 1983. *Address:* c/o Jonathan Cape Ltd, 20 Vauxhall Bridge Road, SW1V 2FA.

BURNLEY, Bishop Suffragan of, since 2000; **Rt Rev. John William Goddard;** *b* 8 Sept. 1947; *s* of Rev. Canon William and Anna Elizabeth Goddard; *m* 1970, Vivienne Goddard; two *s. Educ:* Durham Univ. (BA Hons Theol 1969; DipTh 1970). Ordained deacon, 1970, priest, 1971; Curate: St John, Southbank, 1970–74; Cayton with Eastfield, 1974–75; Vicar: Ascension, Middlesbrough, 1975–82; All Saints, Middlesbrough, 1982–88; RD, Middlesbrough, 1981–87; Canon and Prebend, York Minster, 1987–88, now Canon Emeritus; Vice-Principal, Edin. Theol Coll., 1988–92; Team Rector, Ribbleton, 1992–2000. *Recreations:* restoring old houses and working with wood, hill walking, swimming, golf. *Address:* Dean House, 449 Padiham Road, Burnley BB12 6TD. *T:* (01282) 470360.

BURNLEY, Christopher John; Burnley and Evans, Chartered Accountants, Halesowen, since 1989; *b* 1 May 1936; *s* of John Fox Burnley and Helena Burnley; *m* 1960, Carol Joan Quirk; two *d. Educ:* King William's College, Isle of Man. Chartered Accountant. Articled Clerk, 1953–59; Military service, 1959–62; Computer Systems Analyst, IBM, 1962–66; Management Consultant, Peat Marwick, 1966–67; Systems Planning Manager, Castrol, 1967–68; Sen. Planner, IBM, 1969–72; Financial Dir, Foseco FS, 1972–74; Group Treasurer, Foseco Minsep, 1974–75; Financial Dir, BAA, 1975–86; Finance Dir, Dan Air Engrg, 1987–88. *Recreation:* railway enthusiast. *Address:* Thirlmere, 173 Worcester Road, West Hagley, West Midlands DY9 0PB. *T:* (01562) 883592.

BURNS, family name of **Baron Burns**.

BURNS, Baron *cr* 1998 (Life Peer), of Pitshanger in the London Borough of Ealing; **Terence Burns,** GCB 1995; Kt 1983; Permanent Secretary, HM Treasury, 1991–98; *b* 13 March 1944; *s* of Patrick Owen and Doris Burns; *m* 1969, Anne Elizabeth Powell; one *s* two *d. Educ:* Houghton-Le-Spring Grammar Sch.; Univ. of Manchester (BAEcon Hons). London Business School: research posts, 1965–70; Lecturer in Economics, 1970–74; Sen. Lectr in Economics, 1974–79; Prof. of Economics, 1979; Director, LBS Centre for Economic Forecasting, 1976–79, Fellow, 1989; Chief Econ. Advr to the Treasury and Hd of Govt Econ. Service, 1980–91. Member, HM Treasury Academic Panel, 1976–79. Chm., Financial Services and Mkts Jt Cttee, 1999. Chm., Cttee of Inquiry into Hunting with Dogs, 2000. Chm., Nat. Lottery Commn, 2000–01. Non-executive Director: Legal & General Group plc, 1999–; Pearson plc, 1999–. Vis. Prof., Durham Univ., 1995–. Pres., Soc. of Business Economists, 1999– (Vice-Pres., 1985–99); Vice-Pres., REconS, 1992–. CIMgt 1992. Bd Mem., Manchester Business Sch., 1992–98. Dir, Queens Park Rangers FC, 1996–. Governor, Royal Acad. of Music, 1998–. Trustee, Monteverdi Choir and Orch., 1998–. Hon. degrees: Manchester Univ.; Sunderland Univ.; Durham Univ. *Publications:* various articles in economic jls. *Recreations:* music, golf. *Address:* House of Lords, SW1A 0PW. *T:* (020) 7219 0312; *e-mail:* burnst@parliament.uk. *Clubs:* Reform; Ealing Golf.

BURNS, Sir Andrew; *see* Burns, Sir R. A.

BURNS, David Allan, CMG 1993; HM Diplomatic Service, retired; Founder Chairman, Foreign and Commonwealth Office Association, since 1999; *b* 20 Sept. 1937; *s* of Allan Robert Desmond Burns, GM, and Gladys Frances Dine; *m* 1971, Inger Ellen Kristiansson; one *s* one *d. Educ:* Sir Anthony Browne's Sch., Brentwood, Essex. Served HM Forces, 1956–58. Language student and Third Secretary, British Embassy, Belgrade, 1962–65; Second Secretary, Bangkok, 1966–68; First Secretary, Washington, 1969–72; Head of Chancery, Belgrade, 1973–76; Asst Head of Arms Control Dept, FCO, 1976–79; Counsellor, Bangkok, 1979–83; Consul General, Boston, 1983–87; Hd of N America Dept, FCO, 1988–91; Ambassador to Cambodia, 1991–94; Ambassador to Finland, 1995–97. Retirement Liaison Officer, FCO, 1998–99. Mem., Finland's Adv. Bd on Northern Dimension of Common Foreign and Security Policy of EU, 1998–. Mem., Marshall Scholarships Selection Cttee for New England, 1983–87. Chm., UK Bd, Pathfinder Fund Internat., 1998–. *Recreation:* cinema. *Club:* Travellers.

BURNS, Gerry, MBE 1968; Chairman, Review Body on Post Primary Education, since 2000; Assembly Ombudsman for Northern Ireland and Commissioner for Complaints, 1996–2000; *b* 15 Nov. 1934; *s* of Bernard and Sarah Ellen Burns; *m* 1962, Moyra Connolly; three *s* two *d. Educ:* St Mary's Christian Brothers Grammar Sch.; Queen's Univ., Belfast. Divl Inspector, Trading Standards, NI, 1954–68; Lectr in Business Studies, Armagh Coll. of Further and Higher Educn, 1968–76; Chief Exec., Fermanagh DC, 1976–96. Dir, Irish Times Ltd, 1997–; Gov., Irish Times Trust Ltd, 1997. Mem., Solicitors' Disciplinary Tribunal, NI, 1989–. Dir, Fermanagh Training Ltd, 1990–. Chm., Fermanagh Univ. Foundn, 1998–; Trustee, Spirit of Enniskillen Trust, 1988–. Patron: Marie Curie Nursing Gp, Co. Fermanagh, 1998–; Fermanagh Co. Museum, 1999–. DUniv QUB, 1996. *Recreations:* walking, swimming, the arts. *Address:* Old Rossorry Road, Enniskillen, Northern Ireland BT74 7LF.

BURNS, Dr Henry James Gerard, FRCS; Director of Public Health, Greater Glasgow Health Board, since 1994; *b* 25 Jan. 1951; *s* of Henry Burns and Mary (*née* Boyle); *m* 1983, Agnes Capaldi; two *s* four *d. Educ:* St Aloysius Coll., Glasgow; Glasgow Univ. (MB, ChB). FRCS 1979. MPH 1990; MFPHM 1993. Glasgow University: Lectr in Surgery, 1975–83; Sen. Lectr, 1983–89. *Recreations:* participating in and, increasingly, watching sport. *Address:* Greater Glasgow Health Board, Dalian House, 350 St Vincent Street, Glasgow G3 8YZ. *T:* (0141) 201 4602.

BURNS, Ian Morgan, CB 1990; Director-General, Policy (formerly Director of Policy), Lord Chancellor's Department, 1995–99; *b* 3 June 1939; *s* of late Donald George Burns and Margaret Brenda Burns; *m* 1965, Susan Rebecca (*née* Wheeler); two *d. Educ:* Bootham, York. LLB, LLM London. HM Forces, 1957–59. Examiner, Estate Duty Office, 1960; Asst Principal, 1965, Principal, 1969, Home Office; Principal, 1972, Asst Sec., 1974, NI Office; Asst Sec., Home Office, 1977; Under Sec., NI Office, 1979–84; Under Sec. (Finance), 1985, and Gen. Manager, Disablement Services, 1986, DHSS; Deputy Under Secretary of State: NI Office, 1987–90; Police Dept, Home Office, 1990–95. FRSA 1993. *Recreations:* listening to music, adventurous gardening, collecting siurells. *Address:* c/o Lord Chancellor's Department, Selborne House, 54–60 Victoria Street, SW1E 6QW. *Clubs:* Athenæum, Royal Commonwealth Society.

BURNS, James; JP; DL; Member, Strathclyde Regional Council, 1974–95 (Convener, 1982–86); *b* 8 Feb. 1931; *s* of late James Burns and of Mary Burns (*née* Magee); *m* 1959, Jean Ward; two *s. Educ:* St Patrick's Sch., Shotts; Coatbridge Tech. Coll. Engineer with NCB, 1966–71. Member: Lanark CC, 1967–75; Lanarks Health Bd, 1973–77; Strathclyde Regional Council: Chm., Gen. Purposes Cttee, 1975–82; Vice-Convener, 1978–82. Chm. Vis. Cttee, HM Prison, Shotts, 1980–; Member: Commonwealth Games Council for Scotland, 1982–86; Main Organising Cttee, Commonwealth Games 1986, 1982–86. Vice President: Glasgow Western St Andrew's Youth Club, 1982–86; St Andrew's Ambulance Assoc., 1984–86. Hon. President: Strathclyde CRC, 1982–86; Princess Louise Scottish Hosp. (Erskine Hosp.), 1982–86; Strathclyde Charities Band Assoc., 1982–86; Scottish Retirement Council, 1984–86; Hon. Vice Pres., SNO Chorus, 1982–86; Patron: Strathclyde Youth Club Assoc., 1982–86; YMCA Sports Centre, 1982–86; Scottish Pakistani Assoc., 1984–86. Trustee, The Pearce Institute, 1983–86. JP Motherwell, 1972. DL Monklands, Motherwell, Hamilton, E Kilbride and Clydesdale, 1989. *Recreations:* fishing, golf. *Address:* 57 Springhill Road, Shotts ML7 5JA. *T:* (01501) 820187. *Club:* Royal Scottish Automobile (Glasgow).

BURNS, Prof. James Henderson, FBA 1992; Professor of the History of Political Thought, University College London, 1966–86, now Emeritus; *b* 10 Nov. 1921; *yr s* of late William Burns and Helen Craig Tait Henderson; *m* 1947, Yvonne Mary Zéla Birnie, *er d* of late Arthur Birnie, MA, and Yvonne Marie Aline Louis; two *s* (and one *d* decd). *Educ:* George Watson's Boys' Coll., Edinburgh; Univ. of Edinburgh (MA); Balliol Coll., Oxford (MA); PhD Aberdeen. Sub-Editor, Home News Dept, BBC, 1944–45; Lectr in Polit. Theory, Univ. of Aberdeen, 1947–60; Head of Dept of Politics, 1952–60; University College London: Reader in the History of Political Thought, 1961–66; Head of History Dept, 1970–75; Hon. Fellow, 1999. John Hinkley Vis. Prof., Dept of History, Johns Hopkins Univ., Baltimore, 1987; Lectures: Creighton, London Univ., 1986; Carlyle, Oxford Univ., 1988; Gifford, Aberdeen Univ., 1994. Gen. Editor, The Collected Works of Jeremy Bentham, 1961–79; Vice-Chm., Bentham Cttee, 1983–92 (Sec., 1966–78); Pres., Internat. Bentham Soc., 1986–92. FRHistS 1962; Hon. Vice-Pres., RHistS, 1986– (Hon. Sec., 1965–70; Vice-Pres., 1978–82). *Publications:* Scottish University (with D. Sutherland Graeme), 1944; Scottish Churchmen and the Council of Basle, 1962; Lordship, Kingship and Empire: the idea of monarchy 1400–1525, 1992; The True Law of Kingship: concepts of monarchy in early-modern Scotland, 1996; *contributor to:* (with S. Rose) The British General Election of 1951, by D. E. Butler, 1952; Essays on the Scottish Reformation, ed D. McRoberts, 1962; Mill: a collection of critical essays, ed J. B. Schneewind, 1968; Bentham on Legal Theory, ed M. H. James, 1973; Jeremy Bentham: ten critical essays, ed B. Parekh, 1974; Absolutism in Seventeenth Century Europe, ed J. Miller, 1990; The Church and Sovereignty c 590–1918, ed D. Wood, 1991; Political Discourse in Early Modern Britain, ed N. Phillipson and Q. Skinner, 1993; Politics, Ideology and the Law in Early Modern Europe, ed A. E. Bakos, 1994; *edited* (with H. L. A. Hart): Jeremy Bentham, An Introduction in the Principles of Morals and Legislation, 1970; Jeremy Bentham, A Comment on the Commentaries and A Fragment on Government, 1977; (with F. Rosen) Jeremy Bentham, Constitutional Code, vol. I, 1983; The Cambridge History of Medieval Political Thought c350–c1450, 1988; The Cambridge History of Political Thought 1450–1700, 1991; (with T. M. Izbicki) Conciliarism and Papalism, 1997; articles and reviews in: English Historical Review, Scottish Historical Review, Innes Review, Political Studies, History, Trans of RHistSoc, Historical Jl, Jl of Eccles. History, etc. *Address:* 6 Chiltern House, Hillcrest Road, Ealing, W5 1HL. *T:* (020) 8998 9515.

BURNS, Julian Delisle; Managing Director, Operations, Granada plc, since 2000; *b* 18 Sept. 1949; *s* of Benedict Delisle Burns, FRS and of Angela Hughesdon (*née* Ricardo); *m* 1976, Cheryl Ann Matthews; one *s* one *d*. *Educ:* Betteshanger Prep. Sch., Kent; Haberdashers' Aske's Sch., Elstree. Manager, Mendel's Garage, Hampstead, 1968–71; musician, various musical groups, 1972–75; Granada Television Ltd, 1976–: Prodn Manager, Regl Progs, 1976–80; Manager, Prog. Services, 1980–86; Hd, Business Affairs, 1986–90; Dir, Business and Legal Affairs, 1990–94; Jt Man. Dir, 1994–96; Jt Man. Dir, Granada Production, 1996–2000. Dir, Royal Exchange Theatre, Manchester, 1995–. Member: Adv. Cttee on Film Finance, DNH, 1996–; Adv. Cttee on TV Production, DCMS, 1999–; Bd, 2002 Commonwealth Games, 1998–; Bd, Liverpool FC, 1999–. *Recreations:* walking, reading, music, television, art, the Lake District. *Address:* Granada plc, London Television Centre, Upper Ground, SE1 9LT.

BURNS, Kevin Francis Xavier, CMG 1984; HM Diplomatic Service, retired; *b* 18 Dec. 1930; *s* of late Frank Burns and Winifred Burns (*née* O'Neill); *m* 1st, 1963, Nan Pinto (*d* 1984); one *s* two *d*; 2nd, 1992, Elizabeth Hassell. *Educ:* Finchley Grammar Sch.; Trinity Coll., Cambridge (BA 1953). CRO, 1956–58; Asst Private Sec. to Sec. of State, 1958; 2nd Sec., 1959, 1st Sec., 1960–63, Colombo; CRO/FO, 1963–67; 1st Sec., Head of Chancery and Consul, Montevideo, 1967–70; FCO, 1970–73; Counsellor, UK Mission, Geneva, 1973–79; RCDS, 1979; Head of SE Asian Dept, FCO, 1980–83; High Comr, Ghana, and Ambasssador, Togo, 1983–86; High Comr, Barbados and Eastern Caribbean States, 1986–90; Personnel Assessor, FCO, 1991–99. *Address:* 11 Wentworth Hall, The Ridgeway, Mill Hill, NW7 1RJ.

BURNS, Michael; Chairman, South Yorkshire County Association, since 1986; *b* 21 Dec. 1917; *s* of Hugh Burns and Jane Ellin Burns; *m* 1939, Vera Williams (*d* 1984); two *d*. *Educ:* Thorne Grammar Sch. Served War, 1940–46: 1939–45 Star, France and Germany Star, War Medal, Defence Medal. Miner, Hatfield Main Colliery, 1934–40 and 1946–66; Thorpe Marsh Power Stn, 1966–70; Sch. Caretaker, Hatfield Travis Sch., 1970–81 (due to wife's illness); retd 1981. Mem., Nat. Cttee, NUPE, 1979–81; Chm., Health and Safety Local Govt Nat. Cttee, NUPE, 1979–81. Member: S Yorks CC, 1973–86 (Chm., 1982–83); Hatfield Town Council, 1995– (Dep. Mayor, 1995–96; Dep. Ldr, 1995; Mayor, 1996–97; Ldr, 2000–). Chairman: Hatfield and Innscroft Lab Party, 1965–86 (Vice Chm., 1997–); Goole CLP, 1977–83; Doncaster CVS, 1984–90 (Mem., 1977); Thorne No 2 Sub-Div., Police Community Liaison Forum, 1987–; Founder Chm., Doncaster Victim Support Scheme, 1984–95 (Life Pres., 1995); Exec. Mem., Doncaster Intermediate Treatment Orgn, 1990–99; Member: S Yorks Valuation Panel, 1974–89; S Yorks Charity Information Service, 1983–90; Nat. Exec., CVSNA, 1985–87; Doncaster FPC, 1985–86; Doncaster Jt Consultative Cttee, 1985–89; Yorks Local Council Assoc., 1995. Trustee: S Yorks Foundn Charity, 1986–90; Hatfield Church Bldg Trust, 1997–; Chm., Friends of S Yorks Training Trust, 1988–. Pres., Hatfield Br., Arthritic Care, 1980–86. Governor, Hatfield High Sch., 1974–88; Chairman: Hatfield Ash Hill Sch. Bd of Governors, 1974–88 and 1989– (Vice-Chm., 1988–89); Govs, Hatfield Sheepdip Lane Sch., 1974–92; Hatfield Chase Sch. (ESNS), 1984–. Hatfield Spiral Youth Club Cttee, 1974–99; Hatfield/Thorne Moors Forum, 1996–. Church Warden, Christ Church, Dunscroft, 1964–79. *Recreations:* DIY, oil painting, politics. *Address:* 1 Grange Avenue, Hatfield, Doncaster, South Yorks DN7 6RH. *T:* (01302) 846666.

BURNS, Sir (Robert) Andrew, KCMG 1997 (CMG 1992); HM Diplomatic Service; High Commissioner to Canada, since 2000; *b* 21 July 1943; *e s* of late Robert Burns, CB, CMG and Mary Burns (*née* Goodland); *m* 1973, Sarah Cadogan, JP; two *s* one *d*. *Educ:* Highgate Sch.; Trinity Coll., Cambridge. BA (Classics), MA. Entered Diplomatic Service, 1965; UK Mission to UN, NY, 1965; FO 1966; Sch. of Oriental and African Studies, 1966–67; Univ. of Delhi, 1967; served New Delhi, FCO, and UK Delegation to CSCE, 1967–76; First Secretary and Head of Chancery, Bucharest, 1976–78; Private Sec. to Perm. Under Sec. and Head of Diplomatic Service, FCO, 1979–82; Fellow, Center for Internat. Affairs, Harvard Univ., 1982–83; Counsellor (Information), Washington, and Head of British Information Services, NY, 1983–86; Head of S Asian Dept, FCO, 1986–88; Head of News Dept, FCO, 1988–90; Asst Under-Sec. of State (Asia), FCO, 1990–92; Ambassador to Israel, 1992–95; Dep. Under Sec. of State, FCO, 1995–97; Consul-Gen., Hong Kong and Macau, 1997–2000. FRSA 1997. *Publication:* Diplomacy, War and Parliamentary Democracy, 1985. *Recreations:* music, theatre, fishing, walking. *Address:* c/o Foreign and Commonwealth Office, SW1A 2AH. *Clubs:* Garrick, Royal Automobile; Hong Kong; Dublin Lake (New Hampshire, USA).

BURNS, Sandra Pauline, CB 1989; Parliamentary Counsel, 1980–91, retired; *b* 19 June 1938; *d* of John Burns and Edith Maud Burns. *Educ:* Manchester Central High Sch.; Somerville Coll., Oxford (BCL, MA). Called to the Bar, Middle Temple, 1964. *Recreation:* photography. *Address:* 997 Finchley Road, Golders Green, NW11 7HB.

BURNS, Simon Hugh McGuigan; MP (C) Chelmsford West, since 1997 (Chelmsford, 1987–97); *b* 6 Sept. 1952; *s* of late Brian Stanley Burns, MC, and of Shelagh Mary Nash; *m* 1982, Emma Mary Clifford (marr. diss. 2000); one *s* one *d*. *Educ:* Christ the King Sch., Accra, Ghana; Stamford Sch.; Worcester Coll., Oxford (BA Hons Modern History). Political Adviser to Rt Hon. Sally Oppenheim, 1975–81; Dir, What to Buy Ltd, 1981–83; Policy Exec., Inst. of Dirs, 1983–87. PPS to Minister of State: Dept of Employment, 1989–90; Dept of Educn, 1990–92; DTI, 1992–93; PPS to Minister of Agric., Fisheries and Food, 1993–94; an Asst Govt Whip, 1994–95; a Lord Comr of HM Treasury (Govt Whip), 1995–96; Parly Under-Sec. of State, DoH, 1996–97; Opposition spokesman on: social security, 1997–98; envmt, housing and planning, 1998–99. Member: Health Select Cttee, 1999–; 1922 Cttee, (Treas., 1999). *Recreations:* American politics, reading, swimming, travelling. *Address:* House of Commons, SW1A 0AA. *T:* (020) 7219 3000. *Clubs:* Essex, Chelmsford Conservative (Patron).

BURNS, Rev. Mgr Tom Matthew, SM; QHC 1998; VG; Principal Roman Catholic Chaplain to Royal Navy, and Director, Manning (formerly Training and Programmes), Naval Chaplaincy Service, Ministry of Defence, since 1998; *b* 3 June 1944; *s* of late William James Burns and Louisa Mary Burns (*née* McGarry). *Educ:* Heythrop Coll., London Univ. (BD Hons 1973); BA Open Univ. 1984. Joined SM, 1965; ordained, 1971; Curate, St Anne's, Whitechapel, 1973–74; Head of Econs, St Mary's GS, Sidcup, 1974–78; Head of Econs and Social Scis, St Mary's Sixth-Form Coll., Blackburn, 1979–86; Chaplain, RN, 1986–92; Bursar General, Marist Fathers, Rome, 1992–94; Chaplain, RN, 1994–98; VG 1998. MIMgt (MBIM 1980). *Publication:* pamphlet, Index to the Laws of Rugby Football, 1997. *Recreations:* Rugby (advisor to referees), action novels, film-going. *Address:* Naval Chaplaincy Service, Room 203, Victory Building, Portsmouth, Hants PO1 3LS. *T:* (023) 9272 7903.

BURNS, Prof. William, CBE 1966; Emeritus Professor of Physiology, University of London; Professor of Physiology, Charing Cross Hospital Medical School, 1947–77; Hon. Consultant Otologist, Charing Cross Group of Hospitals; *b* 15 Oct. 1909; *e s* of late Charles Burns, MB, ChB, JP and Mary Sillars, lately of Stonehaven, Scotland; *m* 1936, Margaret, *o d* of late W. A. Morgan, Glasgow; one *s* one *d*. *Educ:* Mackie Acad., Stonehaven; Aberdeen Univ. BSc 1932, MB ChB 1935, DSc 1943 Aberdeen. FRCP 1973. Asst in Physiology, Aberdeen, 1935; Lectr in Physiology, Aberdeen, 1936; War-time duty with Admiralty, 1942; established in RN Scientific Service, 1946; Supt RN Physiological Laboratory, 1947; Chm., Flying Personnel Res. Cttee, RAF, 1978–80; Emeritus Civil Consultant to RN in Audiology; Hon. Consultant to RAF in Acoustic Science; pt-time activity for MRC, 1977–84. Member: Council, BAAS, 1956–61 (Pres., Sect. I, Cardiff, 1960); Scientific Adv. Cttee, Inst. of Sound and Vibration Res., Univ. of Southampton, 1964–74; Noise Adv. Council, 1977–81; BMA; formerly: Mem., Cttee on Hearing, Bio-acoustics and Bio-mechanics, Nat. Res. Council, USA; Mem. or Chm., cttees of BSI, ISO, DHSS, MRC, on various aspects of hearing; Member: Physiol Soc.; British Inst. of Acoustics; Hon. Life Mem., British Soc. Audiology. *Publications:* Noise and Man, 1968, 2nd edn 1973; (with D. W. Robinson) Hearing and Noise in Industry, 1970; articles on various aspects of hearing, in Journal of the Acoustical Soc. of America, Annals of Occupational Hygiene, Proc. Assoc. of Industrial Med. Officers, etc. *Recreations:* working in wood and metal; interested in engineering in general.

BURNSIDE, David Wilson Boyd; MP (UU) South Antrim, since 2001; *b* 24 Aug. 1951; *s* of Jack and Betty Burnside; *m* 1999, Fiona Rennie; one *d* by a previous marriage. *Educ:* Coleraine Academical Instn; Queen's Univ. Belfast (BA). Teacher, 1973–74; Press Officer, Vanguard Unionist Party, 1974–76; PR Dir, Inst. of Dirs, 1979–84; Public Affairs Dir, British Airways, 1984–93; Chairman: D. B. Assocs, 1993–; New Century Holdings Ltd, 1995–. Mem., RBL, Antrim. *Recreations:* fishing, shooting, motorcycling. *Address:* The Hill, Secon, Ballymoney, Co Antrim; House of Commons, SW1A 0AA. *T:* (020) 7219 8493. *Clubs:* Carlton; Portballintrae Boat; Coleraine and District Motor.

BURNSTOCK, Prof. Geoffrey, FRS 1986; FAA 1971; Professor of Anatomy, University of London, since 1975, and Director, Autonomic Neuroscience Institute, Royal Free and University College Medical School; Convener, Centre for Neuroscience, University College London, since 1979; *b* 10 May 1929; *s* of James Burnstock and Nancy Green; *m* 1957, Nomi Hirschfeld; three *d*. *Educ:* King's Coll., London; Melbourne Univ. BSc 1953, PhD 1957 London; DSc Melbourne 1971. National Inst. for Medical Res., Mill Hill, 1956–57; Dept of Pharmacology, Oxford Univ., 1957–59; Rockefeller Travelling Fellowship, Univ. of Ill, 1959; University of Melbourne: Sen. Lectr, 1959–62, Reader, 1962–64; Dept. of Zoology; Prof. of Zoology and Chm. of Dept, 1964–75; Associate Dean (Biological Sciences), 1969–72; Prof. Emeritus, Dept of Pharmacology, 1993; Head, Dept of Anatomy and Embryology, then Anatomy and Developmental Biology, UCL, 1975–97. Vis. Prof., Dept of Pharmacology, Univ. of Calif, LA, 1970. Chm., Scientific Adv. Bd, Eisai London Ltd, 1990–; mem. editl bd of over 20 jls. Vice-Pres., Anatomical Soc. of GB and Ireland, 1990. Fellow, UCL, 1996. Member: Academia Europaea, 1992; Russian Soc. of Neuropathology, 1993. Founder FMedSci 1998. Hon. MRCP 1987, Hon. FRCP 2000; Hon. FRCS 1999. Hon. MSc Melbourne 1962. Silver Medal, Royal Soc. of Victoria, 1970; Special Award, NIH Conf., Bethesda, USA, 1989; Royal Medal, Royal Sco., 2000; Janssen Award in Gastroenterol., 2000. *Publications:* (with M. Costa) Adrenergic Neurons: their Organisation, Function and Development in the Peripheral Nervous System, 1975; (with Y. Uehara and G. R. Campbell) An Atlas of the Fine Structure of Muscle and its Innervation, 1976; (ed) Purinergic Receptors, 1981; (ed with G. Vrbová and R. O'Brien) Somatic and Autonomic Nerve-Muscle Interactions, 1983; (ed with S. G. Griffith) Nonadrenergic Innervation of Blood Vessels, 1988; (ed with S. Bloom) Peptides: a target for new drug development, 1991; series editor, The Autonomic Nervous System, vols 1–14, 1992–2001; (ed jtly) Nitric Oxide in Health and Disease, 1997; (ed jtly) Cardiovascular Biology of Purines, 1998; papers on smooth muscle and autonomic nervous system, incl. purinergic signalling in health and disease; in sci. jls. *Recreations:* tennis, wood sculpture. *Address:* Autonomic Neuroscience Institute, Royal Free and University College Medical School, University College London, Royal Free Campus, Rowland Hill Street, NW3 2PF.

BURNTON, Hon. Sir Stanley Jeffrey, Kt 2000; **Hon. Mr Justice Burnton;** a Judge of the High Court of Justice, Queen's Bench Division, since 2000; *b* 25 Oct. 1942; *s* of Harry and Fay Burnton; *m* 1971, Gwenyth Frances Castle; one *s* two *d*. *Educ:* Hackney Downs Grammar Sch.; St Edmund Hall, Oxford. MA. Called to the Bar, Middle Temple, 1965, Bencher, 1991; QC 1982; a Recorder, 1994–2000. *Recreations:* music, theatre, wine, travel. *Address:* Royal Courts of Justice, Strand, WC2A 2LL.

BURNYEAT, Myles Fredric, FBA 1984; Senior Research Fellow in Philosophy, All Souls College, Oxford, since 1996; *b* 1 Jan. 1939; *s* of Peter James Anthony Burnyeat and Cynthia Cherry Warburg; *m* 1st, 1971, Jane Elizabeth Buckley (marr. diss. 1982); one *s* one *d*; 2nd, 1984, Ruth Sophia Padel (marr. diss. 2000); one *d*. *Educ:* Bryanston Sch.; King's Coll., Cambridge (BA). Assistant Lecturer in Philosophy 1964, Lecturer in Philosophy 1965, University Coll. London; Cambridge University: Lectr in Classics, 1978–84; Laurence Prof. of Ancient Philosophy, 1984–96; Fellow, 1978–96, and Lectr in Philosophy, 1978–84, Robinson Coll. For. Hon. Mem., Amer. Acad. of Arts and Scis, 1992. *Publications:* The Theaetetus of Plato, 1990; co-editor: Philosophy As It Is, 1979; Doubt and Dogmatism, 1980; Science and Speculation, 1982; The Original Sceptics, 1997; (ed) The Skeptical Tradition, 1983; contribs to classical and philosophical jls. *Recreation:* travel. *Address:* All Souls College, Oxford OX1 4AL.

BURR, Michael Rodney; His Honour Judge Burr; a Circuit Judge, since 1992; *b* 31 Aug. 1941; *s* of Frank Edward Burr and Aileen Maud Burr; *m* 1963, Rhoda Rule; four *s* one *d*. *Educ:* Brecon County Grammar Sch.; King Edward VI Sch., Chelmsford; Coll. of Law. Solicitor, 1964. Asst Solicitor, Hilliard & Ward, Chelmsford, 1964–69; Sen. Partner, Peter Williams & Co., Swansea, 1972–92; Recorder, 1988. Sec., Incorp. Law Soc. of Swansea and Dist, 1980–83; Law Society: non-Council Member: Professional Purposes Cttee, 1985–86; Adjudication Cttee, 1986–89. *Recreations:* flying, travel.

BURR, Timothy John; Deputy Comptroller and Auditor General, National Audit Office, since 2000; *b* 31 March 1950; *s* of Eric Cyril Burr and Myrtle Burr (*née* Waters); *m* 1975, Gillian Heather Croot; two *s*. *Educ:* Dulwich Coll. Entered HM Treasury, 1968; Cabinet Office, 1984; Asst Sec., HM Treasury, 1985; Under-Sec., Cabinet Office, 1990; Treasury

Officer of Accounts, 1993–94; Asst Auditor Gen., Nat. Audit Office, 1994–2000. *Address:* c/o National Audit Office, Buckingham Palace Road, SW1W 9SP.

BURRELL, Diana Elizabeth Jane; composer; Composition Professor, Guildhall School of Music and Drama, since 1999; *b* 25 Oct. 1948; *d* of Bernard Burrell and Audrey (*née* Coleman); *m* 1971, Richard Fallas; one *s* one *d*. *Educ:* Norwich High Sch.; Girton Coll., Cambridge Univ. (BA Hons Music). Music teacher, Sutton High Sch., 1971–75; freelance viola player and teacher, 1978–90; pianist, Holy Trinity Ch, Mile End, 1985–; part-time Lectr in Composition and 20th Century Studies, Goldsmiths' Coll., London, 1989–93; Composer-in-residence, Pimlico Sch., London, 1990–91; Living Composer, Eastern Orchestral Bd, 1993–95; Composer-in-Association, City of London Sinfonia, 1994–96. Recordings of own works (Classic CD Award, 1998, for Viola Concerto and other works). Hon. FTCL 1997. *Compositions* include: The Albatross (opera), 1987; commissions: Landscape, 1988; Resurrection, 1992; Dunkelhvide Månestråler, 1996; Clarinet Concerto (for Northern Sinfonia), 1996; Symphonies of Flocks, Herds and Shoals (for BBC SO), 1997; Flute Concerto (for London Schools SO), 1998. *Recreations:* birdwatching, walking, gardening, 20th Century architecture. *Address:* c/o United Music Publishers, 42 Rivington Street, EC2A 3BN. *T:* (020) 7729 4700.

BURRELL, (Francis) Gary; QC 1996; a Recorder, since 1996; *b* 7 Aug. 1953; *s* of Francis Ivan George Burrell and Louisa Shane Burrell; *m* 1979, Heather Young; three *s*. *Educ:* Belfast Boys' Model Sch.; Univ. of Exeter (LLB). Called to the Bar, Inner Temple, 1977; Asst Recorder, 1992–96. Mem., Bar Council, 1995–. Pres., S Yorks Medico-Legal Soc., 1991–92; NE Circuit Rep., Personal Injury Bar Assoc., 1995–. *Publications:* various articles on personal injury litigation in Quantum. *Recreations:* sailing, fly fishing, poultry farming. *Address:* 26 Paradise Square, Sheffield S1 2DA. *T:* (0114) 273 8951; 9 Gough Square, EC4A 3DE. *T:* (020) 7353 5371.

BURRELL, Sir (John) Raymond, 9th Bt *cr* 1774; *b* 20 Feb. 1934; *s* of Sir Walter Raymond Burrell, 8th Bt, CBE, TD, and Hon. Anne Judith (OBE) (*d* 1987), *o d* of 3rd Baron Denman, PC, GCMG, KCVO; *S* father, 1985; *m* 1st, 1959, Rowena Frances (marr. diss. 1971), *d* of late M. H. Pearce; one *s*; 2nd, 1971, Margot Lucy, *d* of F. E. Thatcher, Sydney, NSW; one *s* one *d*. *Educ:* Eton; Royal Agricultural Coll., Cirencester. *Heir:* *s* Charles Raymond Burrell [*b* 27 Aug. 1962; *m* 1993, Isabella Elizabeth Nancy, adopted *d* of M. L. Tree]. *Address:* Baynton House, Coulston, Westbury, Wiltshire BA13 4NY. *Club:* Boodle's.

See also M. W. Burrell.

BURRELL, Mark William; Director, Pearson plc, 1977–97; *b* 9 April 1937; *s* of Sir Walter Burrell, 8th Bt, CBE, TD and Hon. Anne Judith, OBE, *o d* of 3rd Baron Denman, PC, GCMG, KCVO; *m* 1966, Margot Rosemary Pearce; two *s* one *d*. *Educ:* Eton; Pembroke Coll., Cambridge (BA 1st Cl. Hons Engrg). With Sir Alexander Gibb & Partners, 1959, then Vickers, 1960–61; joined Pearson plc, 1963; Whitehall Petroleum: Dir, 1964–88; Chm., 1987–88; joined Lazard Brothers, 1970; Dir, 1974; Man. Dir, 1984–86; non-exec. Dir, 1986–97; Director: BSB Holdings, 1987–99; BSkyB Group plc, 1991–94; Dir, then Chm., Royal Doulton plc, 1993–98; Chm., Millbank Financial Services Ltd, 1986–; non-executive Director: RM plc, 1997–; Merlin Communications Internat., 1997– (Chm.); Conafex SA, 1999– (Chm.). Mem. Ct, Sussex Univ. *Recreations:* hunting, polo, tennis, golf, ski-ing. *Address:* c/o 1st Floor, Pollen House, 10–12 Cork Street, W1X 1PD. *Club:* Boodle's.

BURRELL, Michael Peter; Hon. Mr Justice Burrell; Judge of the Court of First Instance of the High Court (formerly Judge, Supreme Court), Hong Kong, since 1995; *b* 18 July 1948; *s* of Peter Burrell and Gwynneth Burrell; *m* 1975, Anne Hughes; two *d*, and one step *s*. *Educ:* Birkenhead Sch.; Magdalene Coll., Cambridge (MA). Called to the Bar, Inner Temple, 1971; in practice on Northern Circuit, 1972–86 (Junior, 1973); Hong Kong: Perm. Magistrate, 1986–90; Dist Judge, 1991–95. Mem., Hong Kong Judicial Studies Bd, 1992–95; Chm., Hong Kong Insider Dealing Tribunal, 1996–98. *Recreations:* sport, reading, walking. *Address:* c/o High Court, Queensway, Hong Kong. *Clubs:* Artists' (Liverpool); Royal Liverpool Golf (Hoylake); Oxton Cricket (Wirral); Hong Kong, Hong Kong Cricket (Hong Kong).

BURRELL, Sir Raymond; *see* Burrell, Sir J. R.

BURRETT, (Frederick) Gordon, CB 1974; Deputy Secretary, Civil Service Department, 1972–81; *b* 31 Oct. 1921; *s* of Frederick Burrett and Marion Knowles; *m* 1943, Joan Giddins; one *s* two *d*. *Educ:* Emanuel Sch.; St Catharine's Coll., Cambridge. Served in Royal Engrs, N Africa, Italy, Yugoslavia, Greece, 1942–45 (despatches). HM Foreign, subseq. Diplomatic, Service, 1946; 3rd Sec., Budapest, 1946–49; FO, 1949–51; Vice-Consul, New York, 1951–54; FO, 1954–57; 1st Sec., Rome, 1957–60; transf. to HM Treasury, 1960; Private Sec. to Chief Sec., Treasury, 1963–64; Asst Secretary: HM Treasury, 1964; Cabinet Office, 1967–68; Secretary: Kindersley Review Body on Doctors' and Dentists' Remuneration; Plowden Cttee on Pay of Higher Civil Service, 1967–68; Civil Service Dept, 1968, Under-Sec. 1969. Mem., Civil Service Pay Res. Unit Bd, 1978–81; conducted govt scrutiny of V&A and Sci. Museums, 1982; Adviser to Govt of Oman on CS reorganisation, 1984; led govt review of policies and operations of Commonwealth Inst., 1986; leader of review team to examine responsibilities and grading of dirs of nat. museums and galls, 1987; conducted review of sen. posts of Arts Council and BFI, 1987–88; Chm., Cttee of Inquiry into CS Pay, Hong Kong, 1988–89. Chairman: Redundant Churches Fund, later Churches Conservation Trust, 1982–95; Wagner Soc., 1984–88. FSA 1985. Cross of St Augustine, 1995. *Publication:* article on the watercolours of John Massey Wright (1777–1866) in vol. 54 of the Old Water-Colour Society's Club Annual. *Recreations:* music, walking, reading. *Address:* 25 Dalmore Avenue, Claygate, Surrey KT10 0HQ. *T:* (01372) 462783. *Club:* Athenæum.

BURRIDGE, Alan; Certification Officer for Trade Unions and Employers' Associations, 1981–85; *b* 15 Feb. 1921; *m* 1961, Joan Edith Neale; one *s*. *Educ:* William Ellis Sch.; Bristol Univ. (BA 1st Cl. Hons 1950). Served War, Army, 1939–46. Northern Assurance Co., 1936–39; Bristol Univ., 1947–50; Swinton Coll., 1950–53; London Municipal Soc., 1953–56; General Electric Co., 1956–67; Dept of Employment, 1967–81. *Address:* 1 Castle Hill Avenue, Berkhamsted, Herts HP4 1HJ. *T:* (01442) 865276.

BURRIDGE, Rev. Dr Richard Alan; Dean, King's College London, since 1994; *b* 11 June 1955; *s* of Alan Burridge and Iris Joyce (*née* Coates); *m* 1979, Susan Morgan; two *d*. *Educ:* University Coll., Oxford (Exhibnr; BA Lit.Hum. 1st Cl. Hons, MA 1981); Univ. of Nottingham (PGCE 1978; Postgrad. DTh 1983; PhD 1989); St John's Coll., Nottingham. Classics Master and House Tutor, Sevenoaks Sch., 1978–82; ordained deacon 1985, priest 1986; Curate, St Peter and St Paul, Bromley, Kent, 1985–87; Lazenby Chaplain, Univ. of Exeter and part-time Lectr, Depts of Theol. and of Classics and Ancient Hist., 1987–94; Hon. Lectr in NT Studies, Dept of Theol. and Religious Studies, KCL, 1994–. Mem., Gen. Synod of C of E, 1994–. Member: Council of Mgt, St John's Coll., Nottingham, 1986–99; Council of Ref., Monarch Pubns, Tunbridge Wells, 1992–. Mem., Academic Bd (formerly Bd of Studies), N Thames Ministerial Trng Course, 1994–; Ext. Examr, SW Ministerial Trng Course, 1995–99. Member: SNTS, 1995–; Soc. for Study of Theol., 1995–; Soc. of Biblical Lit., 1996–. Expert Advr (Faith Zone, Greenwich Dome), Nat. Millennium Experience Co., 1998–. Trustee: Christian Evidence Soc., 1994–; Foundn of St Catherine, Cumberland Lodge, 1998–. *Publications:* Sex Therapy: some ethical considerations, 1985; What are the Gospels?: a comparison with Graeco-Roman biography, 1992; Four Gospels, One Jesus?: a symbolic reading, 1994 (also US and Australian edns); John (People's Bible Commentary), 1998; Faith Odyssey: a journey through Lent, 2000; *contributor to:* A Dictionary of Biblical Interpretation, 1990; The New Dictionary of Christian Ethics and Pastoral Theology, 1995; A Handbook of Classical Rhetoric in the Hellenistic Period 330 BC–AD 400, 1997; The Gospels for all Christians: rethinking the gospel audiences, 1998; Where Shall We Find God?, 1998; The Lion Handbook to the Bible, 1999; The Story of Christian Spirituality, 2001; articles in Theology, Church Times, St John the Evangelist Mag., C of E Newspaper, THES. *Recreations:* golf, cycling, playing guitar and bass. *Address:* Dean's Office, King's College London, Strand, WC2R 2LS. *T:* (020) 7848 2333/2063, *Fax:* (020) 7848 2344; *e-mail:* richard.burridge@kcl.ac.uk.

BURRILL, Timothy; Managing Director, Burrill Productions, since 1966; Chairman, Film Asset Developments Plc, 1987–94; *b* 8 June 1931; *yr s* of L. Peckover Burrill, OBE and Marjorie S. Burrill; *m* 1st, 1959, Philippa (marr. diss. 1966), *o d* of Maurice and Margot Hare; one *d*; 2nd, 1968, Santa (marr. diss. 1993), *e d* of John and Betty Raymond; one *s* two *d*. *Educ:* Eton Coll.; Sorbonne Univ. Served Grenadier Guards, 1949–52: commnd 1950; served 2nd Bn, 1950–52. Jun. management, Cayzer Irvine & Co., 1952–56; entered film industry, 1956; joined Brookfield Prodns, 1965; Dir, World Film Services, 1967–69; first Prodn Administrator, National Film and TV Sch., 1972; Man. Dir, Allied Stars (resp. for Chariots of Fire), 1979–80; Director: Artistry Ltd, 1982–87 (resp. for Superman and Supergirl films); Pathé (formerly Chargeurs) Productions Ltd, 1994–99; Pathé Pictures, 1994–99; Consultant: National Film Develt Fund, 1980–81; Really Useful Group, 1989–90; Script Factory, 1998–. UK Rep., Eurimages, 1994–96. Chairman: BAFTA, 1981–83 (Vice-Chm., 1979–81); First Film Foundn, 1989–98; Producer Mem., Cinematograph Films Council, 1980–85; Member: Gen. Council, ACTT, 1975–76; Exec. Council, British Film and Television Producers Assoc., 1981–89; Exec. Council, The Producers Assoc., 1989–91; Exec. Council, Producers' Alliance for Cinema and Television, 1991– (Vice-Chm., 1993–94); Sir Peter Middleton's Adv. Cttee of Film Finance, 1996–97; Dir, British Film Commn, 1998–2000. Chm., Impact Campaign, 1994–95. Governor: National Film and Television Sch., 1981–92; National Theatre, 1982–88. Films include Tess, The Fourth Protocol, The Pirates of Penzance etc. *Recreation:* theatre. *Address:* 19 Cranbury Road, SW6 2NS. *T:* (020) 7736 8673, *Fax:* (020) 7731 3921; *e-mail:* timothy_burrill@email.nsm.com.

BURRINGTON, Ernest; *b* 13 Dec. 1926; *s* of late Harold Burrington and of Laura Burrington; *m* 1950, Nancy Crossley; one *s* one *d*. Self-educated. Reporter, Oldham Chronicle, 1941–43; Army service, 1945–47; reporter and sub-editor, Oldham Chronicle, 1947–49; sub-editor, Bristol Evening World, 1950; Daily Herald: sub-editor, Manchester, 1950, night editor, 1955; London night editor, 1957; IPC Sun: night editor, 1964; Asst Editor, 1965; Asst Editor and night editor, News International Sun, 1969; dep. night editor, Daily Mirror, 1970; Dep. Editor, 1971, Associate Editor, 1972, Sunday People; Editor, The People, 1985–88 and 1989–90; Dep. Chm. and Asst Publisher, 1988–91, Man. Dir, 1989–91, Mirror Gp Newspapers; Chm., Syndication Internat., 1989–92; Dep. Chm., Mirror Publishing Co., 1989–91; Director: Mirror Group Magazine and Newsday Ltd, 1989–92; Legionstyle Ltd, 1991–92; Mirror Colour Print Ltd, 1991–92; (non-exec.) Sunday Correspondent, 1990; The European, 1990–91; IQ Newsgraphics, 1990–92; Sygma Picture Agency, Paris, 1990–91; Marketing Consultant, Atlantic Media, 1996–97. Member: Council, NPA, 1988–92; IPI (Mem., British Exec., 1988–92); Foreign Press Assoc.; Trustee, Internat. Centre for Child Studies, 1986–90. Life Mem., NUJ, 1996; marketing and publishing consultant; Deputy Publisher, 1993–95, Vice President, 1995, Globe Communications, USA; Director, 1985–92, Chairman, 1991–92, Mirror Group Newspapers. *Recreations:* travel, bridge, Manchester United FC (Hon. Red Devil, 1985). *Address:* 17499 Tiffany Trace Drive, Boca Raton, FL 33487, USA. *T:* (561) 9959897; South Hall, Dene Park, Shipbourne, near Tonbridge TN11 9NS. *T:* (01732) 368517. *Club:* East India.

BURROUGH, Alan, CBE 1970; Director, 1946–87, President, 1983–87, James Burrough plc (Chairman, 1968–82); Chairman: London Tideway Harbour Co. Ltd, since 1988; Albion Quay (1992) Ltd, since 1992; *b* 22 Feb. 1917; *s* of Ernest James Burrough and Sophie (*née* Burston); *m* 1st, 1939, Rosemary June Bruce (*d* 1993); two *s* one *d*; 2nd, 1995, Sheila Vivien van Dam. *Educ:* St Paul's Sch., London; Jesus Coll., Cambridge Univ. (MA). Joined James Burrough Ltd, 1935. War of 1939–45: 91st Field Regt, RA, and 5th RHA (Captain). Rejoined James Burrough Ltd, 1945: Director, 1946; Deputy Chairman, 1967; Chairman, 1968; Director: Corby Distilleries Ltd, Montreal, 1968–82; Hawks Co. Ltd, 1989–97. Dep. Pres., Oxon Br., British Red Cross, 1982–86. *Clubs:* Naval and Military; Hawks (Cambridge); Royal Channel Islands Yacht, Royal Lymington Yacht.

BURROUGH, Rt Rev. John Paul, MBE 1946; MA Oxon; *b* 5 May 1916; *s* of Canon E. G. Burrough; *m* 1962, Elizabeth (Bess) (*d* 1991), *widow* of Stephen John White; one step *d*. *Educ:* St Edward's Sch.; St Edmund Hall, Oxford; Ely Theol. College. Coach, Tigre Boat Club, Buenos Aires, 1938–39. Captain, Royal Signals, Malaya Campaign (POW), 1940–45. Asst, Aldershot Parish Church, 1946–51; Mission Priest, Dio. of Korea, 1951–59; Anglican Chaplain to Overseas Peoples in Birmingham, 1959–68; Canon Residentiary of Birmingham, 1967–68; Bishop of Mashonaland, 1968–81; Rector of Empingham and Hon. Asst Bishop, Diocese of Peterborough, 1981–85. Chaplain and Sub-Prelate, Order of St John of Jerusalem, 1969–. *Publications:* Lodeleigh, 1946; God and Human Chance, 1984; Angels Unawares, 1988. *Recreation:* rowing (Oxford crews, 1937 and 1938). *Address:* 6 Mill Green Close, Bampton, Oxon OX18 2HF. *T:* (01993) 850952. *Clubs:* Leander (Henley); Vincent's (Oxford).

BURROW, Prof. John Anthony, FBA 1986; Winterstoke Professor of English, University of Bristol, 1976–98, now Emeritus; *b* 3 Aug. 1932; *s* of William and Ada Burrow; *m* 1956, Diana Wynne Jones; three *s*. *Educ:* Buckhurst Hill County High Sch., Essex; Christ Church, Oxford (BA, MA). Asst Lectr, King's Coll., London, 1955–57; Lectr in English, Christ Church, 1957–61, and Brasenose Coll., 1957–59, Oxford; Fellow in English, Jesus Coll., Oxford, 1961–75; Dean of Faculty of Arts, Univ. of Bristol, 1990–93. Vis. Prof., Yale Univ., 1968–69. Hon. Dir, EETS, 1983–. *Publications:* A Reading of Sir Gawain and the Green Knight, 1965; Geoffrey Chaucer (critical anthology), 1969; Ricardian Poetry, 1971; (ed) English Verse 1300–1500, 1977; Medieval Writers and their Work, 1982; Essays on Medieval Literature, 1984; The Ages of Man, 1986; (with Thorlac Turville-Petre) A Book of Middle English, 1992; Langland's Fictions, 1993; Thomas Hoccleve, 1994; (ed) Hoccleve's Complaint and Dialogue, 1999; The Gawain-Poet, 2001; articles and reviews in learned jls. *Recreation:* music. *Address:* 9 The Polygon, Clifton, Bristol BS8 4PW. *T:* (0117) 9277845.

BURROW, John Halcrow, CBE 1993 (OBE 1987); QPM 1998; DL; Chief Constable of Essex Police, 1988–98; *b* 1935; *s* of John and Florence Burrow; *m* 1958, Ruth (*née* Taylor); two *s* one *d*. *Educ:* Ulverston Grammar School; University College London (LLB Hons). Lieut, 3rd Kenya Bn, King's African Rifles, 1953–55. Metropolitan Police, 1958–77; Asst/Dep. Chief Constable, Merseyside Police, 1977–88; RCDS, 1979. Pres., ACPO, 1992–93; Chairman: Technical and Res. Cttee, ACPO, 1990–92; ACPO No 5 (SE) Region Cttee, 1991–98; Shotley Training Centre Cttee, 1990–92. Co. Comdr, St John Ambulance, Essex, 1999–. DL Essex, 1998. *Recreation:* walking. *Address:* Acorns, Church End, Shalford, Braintree, Essex CM7 5HA. *T:* (01371) 850577.

BURROW, Prof. John Wyon, FBA 1986; FRHistS 1971; Professor of European Thought, and Fellow of Balliol College, University of Oxford, 1995–2000, Emeritus Fellow, since 2001; Research Professor of Intellectual History, Sussex University, since 2000; *b* 4 June 1935; *s* of Charles and Alice Burrow; *m* 1958, Diane Dunnington; one *s* one *d*. *Educ:* Exeter School; Christ's College, Cambridge (MA, PhD). Research Fellow, Christ's College, Cambridge, 1959–62; Fellow, Downing Coll., Cambridge, 1962–65; Lectr, Sch. of European Studies, Univ. of East Anglia, 1965–69; Reader in History, 1969–82, Prof. of Intellectual History, 1982–95, Univ. of Sussex. Vis. Prof., Univ. of California, Berkeley, 1981 and 1989; Visiting Fellow: History of Ideas Unit, ANU, 1983; All Souls Coll., Oxford, 1994–95. Carlyle Lectr, Oxford, 1985; Christian Gauss Seminars, Princeton Univ., 1988. Hon. Dr Scienze Politiche, Bologna, 1988. *Publications:* Evolution and Society, 1966; A Liberal Descent, 1981 (Wolfson Prize); (with S. Collini and D. Winch) That Noble Science of Politics, 1983; Gibbon, 1985; Whigs and Liberals, 1988; The Crisis of Reason, 2000. *Recreation:* cooking. *Address:* Graduate Centre for the Humanities, Sussex University, Falmer, Brighton BN1 9QN; 22 Bridge Street, Witney, Oxon OX8 6HY. *T:* (01993) 700306.

BURROWES, Edmund Spencer Stanley, CMG 1959; Financial Secretary, Barbados, 1951–66; *b* 16 Dec. 1906; *m* 1st, 1934, Mildred B. Jackson (decd); one *s* three *d*; 2nd, 1965, Gwen Searson. *Educ:* Queen's Coll., British Guiana. British Guiana Colonial Secretariat, 1924; Inspector of Labour, 1940; Deputy Commissioner, 1945; Labour Commissioner, Barbados, 1947. *Publication:* Occupational Terms on Sugar Estates in British Guiana, 1945. *Recreation:* wild life watching. *Address:* 18B Butler's Way, Great Yeldham, Halstead, Essex CO9 4QN.

BURROWES, Norma Elizabeth; opera and concert singer; *d* of Henry and Caroline Burrowes; *m* 1st, 1969, Steuart Bedford, *qv* (marr. diss.); 2nd, 1987, Emile Belcourt; one *s* one *d*. *Educ:* Sullivan Upper Sch., Holywood, Co. Down; Queen's Univ., Belfast (BA); Royal Academy of Music (FRAM 1992). Operas include: Zerlina in Don Giovanni, Glyndebourne Touring Opera (début); Blöndchen in Die Entführung aus dem Serail, Salzburg Festival, and again Blöndchen, Paris Opera, 1976 (début); Fiakermili, Royal Opera House (début), also Oscar, Despina, Nanetta, Woodbird; Entführung aus dem Serail, Ballo in Maschera, Der Rosenkavalier, Metropolitan, NY; Daughter of the Regiment, Midsummer Night's Dream, Elisir d'Amore, Canada; Cosi Fan Tutte, Romeo and Juliet, France; Marriage of Figaro, Germany; Gianni Schicchi, Switzerland; Marriage of Figaro, La Scala. Television operas include: Nanetta in Falstaff; Susanna in Marriage of Figaro and Lauretta in Gianni Schicchi. Sings regularly with major opera companies, gives concerts and recitals, GB and abroad; many recordings. Hon. DMus Queen's Univ. Belfast, 1979. *Recreations:* swimming, gardening, needlework. *Address:* 56 Rochester Road, NW1 9JG. *T:* (020) 7485 7322.

BURROWS, Prof. Andrew Stephen; Norton Rose Professor of Commercial and Financial Law, and Fellow of St Hugh's College, University of Oxford, since 1999; a Recorder, since 2000; *b* 17 April 1957; *s* of William George Burrows and Dora Burrows; *m* 1982, Rachel Jane Gent; three *s* one *d*. *Educ:* Prescot Grammar Sch.; Brasenose Coll., Oxford (Schol.; Martin Wronker Prize 1978; MA; BCL); Harvard Law Sch. (LLM). Called to the Bar, Middle Temple, 1985 (Hon. Bencher, 2000); Mem., Fountain Court Chambers, Temple. Lectr in Law, Merton Coll., Oxford, 1979–80; Harkness Fellow, Harvard Law Sch., 1980–81; Lectr in Law, Univ. of Manchester, 1981–86; Fellow and CUF Lectr in Law, 1986–94, Hon. Res. Fellow, 1994–, LMH, Oxford; Prof. of English Law, UCL, 1994–99; Law Comr for England and Wales, 1994–99. Jt winner, Prize for Outstanding Legal Scholarship, SPTL, 1993. *Publications:* Remedies for Torts and Breach of Contract, 1987, 2nd edn 1994; (ed jtly) Clerk and Lindsell on Torts, 16th edn 1989, 17th edn 1995; Essays on the Law of Restitution (ed Burrows), 1991; The Law of Restitution, 1993; (ed jtly) Chitty on Contracts, 28th edn 1999; (ed jtly) Scrutton on Charterparties, 20th edn 1996; (jtly) Cases and Materials on the Law of Restitution, 1997; Understanding the Law of Obligations, 1998; (jtly) English Private Law, 2000; numerous articles in legal jls. *Recreations:* sport (esp. football), mountain walking. *Address:* St Hugh's College, Oxford OX2 6LE.

BURROWS, Sir Bernard (Alexander Brocas), GCMG 1970 (KCMG 1955; CMG 1950); *b* 3 July 1910; *s* of Edward Henry Burrows and Ione, *d* of Alexander Macdonald; *m* 1944, Ines (*d* 1997), *d* of late John Walter; one *s* one *d*. *Educ:* Eton; Trinity Coll., Oxford. Entered HM Foreign Service (later Diplomatic Service), 1934; served at HM Embassy, Cairo, 1938–45; Foreign Office, 1945–50; Counsellor HM Embassy, Washington, 1950–53; Political Resident in the Persian Gulf, 1953–58; Ambassador to Turkey, 1958–62; Dep. Under-Secretary of State, FO, 1963–66; Permanent British Representative to N Atlantic Council, 1966–70, retired 1970. Dir-Gen., Federal Trust for Educn and Res., 1973–76. *Publications:* (with C. Irwin) Security of Western Europe, 1972; Devolution or Federalism, 1980; (with G. Edwards) The Defence of Western Europe, 1982; Footnotes in the Sand, 1990; A Myth for our Time, 2001; contributed to: A Nation Writ Large, 1973; Federal Solutions to European Issues, 1978; The Third World War 1985, 1978; The Third World War: the untold story, 1982; articles and reviews in New Europe, etc. *Address:* Durford Wood House, Upper Durford Wood, Petersfield GU31 5AN. *Club:* Travellers.

BURROWS, General Eva, AC 1994 (AO 1986); General of the Salvation Army, 1986–93, retired; *b* 15 Sept. 1929; *d* of Robert John Burrows and Ella Maria Burrows (*née* Watson). *Educ:* Brisbane State High School; Queensland Univ. (BA); London Univ. (PGCE); Sydney Univ. (MEd). Salvation Army: Missionary Educator, Howard Inst., Zimbabwe, 1952–67; Principal, Usher Inst., Zimbabwe, 1967–69; Vice-Principal 1970–73, Principal 1974–75, Internat. Coll. for Officers, London; Leader, Women's Social Services in GB and Ireland, 1975–77; Territorial Commander: Sri Lanka, 1977–79; Scotland, 1979–82; Australia, 1982–86. Hon. Dr of Liberal Arts, Ewha Woman's Univ., Seoul, S. Korea, 1988; Hon. LLD: Asbury Coll., USA, 1988; Univ. of NSW, 1996; Hon. DD Olivet Univ., USA, 1993; Hon. DPhil Queensland, 1993; DUniv Griffith, 1994. *Recreations:* classical music, reading, travel. *Address:* Unit 102, 193 Domain Road, South Yarra, Melbourne, Vic 3141, Australia. *T:* (3) 98209701.

BURROWS, Fred, CMG 1981; PhD; international law consultant, since 1990; *b* 10 Aug. 1925; *s* of late Charles Burrows; *m* 1955, (Jennifer) Winsome Munt; two *s*. *Educ:* Altrincham Grammar Sch.; Trinity Hall, Cambridge (MA). PhD Cantab, 1988. Served in RAF, 1944–47. Called to Bar, Gray's Inn, 1950; Asst Legal Adviser, Foreign Office, 1956–65; Legal Adviser, British Embassy, Bonn, 1965–67; returned to FO, 1967; Legal Counsellor, FCO, 1968–77; Counsellor (Legal Adviser), Office of UK Perm. Rep. to European Communities, 1977–80; Legal Counsellor, FCO, 1980–85; Law Officer (Special Duties), then (International Law), Hong Kong, 1985–90. JP Hong Kong, 1986–90. *Publication:* Free Movement in European Community Law, 1985. *Recreations:* sailing, trombone. *Address:* c/o Foreign and Commonwealth Office, SW1A 2AL.

BURROWS, (George) Richard (William); Chief Executive since 1977, and Chairman, since 1991, Irish Distillers Group; *b* 16 Jan. 1946; *m* 1970, Sherril Dix; one *s* three d. *Educ:* Wesley College, Dublin; Rathmines College of Commerce. FICA. Articled Stokes Bros & Pim, 1963–70; Asst to Man. Dir, Edward Dillon & Co., 1970; Man. Dir, Old Bushmills Distillery Co., 1972; Gen. Manager, Irish Distillers, 1976; Man. Dir, Irish Distillers Group, 1978. *Recreations:* sailing, Rugby. *Address:* Irish Distillers Group, Bow Street Distillery, Smithfield, Dublin 7, Ireland.

BURROWS, Jonathan; choreographer and ballet dancer; Artistic Director, Jonathan Burrows Group. Joined Royal Ballet, 1979; *principal rôles* include: Nutcracker, 1986; La Fille Mal Gardée; *works choreographed* include: Dull morning cloudy mild, 1989; Stoics, 1991; Stoics II; Very, 1992; Our, 1994; The Stop Quartet, 1996; Quintet, 1997; Weak Dance, Strong Questions, 2001. Choreographer-in-Residence, South Bank, 1998. Frederick Ashton Choreographic Award, 1991; Prudential Award for Dance, 1995.

BURROWS, Lionel John, CBE 1974; Chief Inspector of Schools, Department of Education and Science, 1966–73; Educational Adviser, Methodist Residential Schools, 1974–84; *b* 9 March 1912; *s* of H. L. Burrows, HM Inspector of Schools, and Mrs C. J. Burrows; *m* 1939, Enid Patricia Carter; one *s* one *d*. *Educ:* King Edward VI Sch., Southampton; Gonville and Caius Coll., Cambridge. BA Cantab (1st cl. hons Mod. Langs Tripos) 1933. West Buckland Sch., Devon, Tiffin Sch., Kingston-upon-Thames and primary schools in London and Surrey, 1934–41; HM Forces (RASC and Intell. Corps), 1941–46; Commendation from US Army Chief of Staff, 1945; HM Inspector of Schools, 1946; Divisional Inspector, Metropolitan Div., 1960. Vice-Pres., Nat. Assoc. for Gifted Children, 1975–88. *Publication:* The Middle School: high road or dead end?, 1978. *Recreations:* natural history, fell-walking. *Address:* 34 Groby Road, Ratby, Leicester LE6 0LJ. *Club:* English-Speaking Union.

BURROWS, Prof. Malcolm, FRS 1985; Professor of Zoology, University of Cambridge, since 1996, and Fellow of Wolfson College, Cambridge, since 1991; *b* 28 May 1943; *s* of William Roy Burrows and Jean Jones Burrows; *m* 1966, Christine Joan Ellis; one *s* one *d*. *Educ:* Cambridge Univ. (MA; ScD 1983); St Andrews Univ. (PhD 1967). Reader in Neurobiology, 1983–86, Prof. of Neurosci., 1986–96, Univ. of Cambridge. Vis. Prof., Konstanz Univ., 1987; Cornelius Wiersma Vis. Prof., CIT, 1991; Distinguished Vis. Prof., Univ. of California, Davis, 1992. Pres., Internat. Soc. for Neuroethology, 1998–2001. MAE 1992. Mem., Bayerische Akad. der Wissenschaften, 1996. Scientific Medal, Zoological Soc., 1980; Alexander von Humboldt award, 1993. *Publication:* The Neurobiology of an Insect Brain, 1996.

BURROWS, Margaret Ann; *see* Buck, M. A.

BURROWS, Reginald Arthur, CMG 1964; HM Diplomatic Service, retired; *b* 31 Aug. 1918; *s* of late Arthur Richard Burrows, first Dir of Programmes, BBC; *m* 1952, Jenny Louisa Henriette Campiche (*d* 1985); one *s* one *d*. *Educ:* Mill Hill Sch.; St Catharine's Coll., Cambridge (Chancellor's Medal for English Verse, 1939; MA 1947). Served with Royal Air Force, Bomber Comd, SE Asia and Italy, 1941–45; comd No 13 (bomber) Sqdn, 1945. Entered the Foreign Service (now the Diplomatic Service), 1947; served in: Paris; Karachi; Tehran; Saigon; The Hague; Istanbul; Foreign Office; Minister, Islamabad, 1970–72; Univ. of Leeds, 1972–73; on secondment as Under-Sec., Civil Service Selection Bd, 1974–75; Asst Under-Sec. of State, 1975–78. *Recreations:* walking, studying Roman history. *Address:* Flat 9, Summer Court, Summer Hill, Harbledown, near Canterbury, Kent CT2 8NP. *T:* (01227) 457394.

BURROWS, Richard; *see* Burrows, G. R. W.

BURROWS, Rt Rev. Simon Hedley; Hon. Assistant Bishop, diocese of Winchester, since 1994; Bishop Suffragan of Buckingham, 1974–85, Area Bishop, 1985–94; *b* 8 Nov. 1928; *s* of late Very Rev. H. R. Burrows, and Joan Lumsden, *d* of Rt Rev. E. N. Lovett, CBE; *m* 1960, Janet Woodd; two *s* three *d*. *Educ:* Eton; King's Coll., Cambridge (MA); Westcott House, Cambridge. Curate of St John's Wood, 1954–57; Chaplain of Jesus Coll., Cambridge, 1957–60; Vicar of Wyken, Coventry, 1960–67; Vicar of Holy Trinity, Fareham, 1967–74, and Rector of Team Ministry, 1971–74. Hon. DLitt Buckingham, 1992. Sub-Prelate, Order of St John, 1992–96. *Address:* 8 Quarry Road, Winchester, Hants SO23 0JF. *T:* (01962) 853332.

BURSELL, Rev. Canon Rupert David Hingston, QC 1986; **His Honour Judge Bursell;** a Circuit Judge, since 1988; *b* 10 Nov. 1942; *s* of Henry and Cicely Mary Bursell; *m* 1967, Joanna Ruth Gibb; two *s* one *d*. *Educ:* St John's School, Leatherhead; Univ. of Exeter (LLB); St Edmund Hall, Oxford (MA, DPhil). Called to the Bar, Lincoln's Inn, 1968; Sir Thomas More Bursary and Hubert Greenland Studentship, Lincoln's Inn, 1969; a Recorder, 1985–88; an Official Referee, 1992–98; a nominated Judge of the Technology and Construction Court, 1998–; Designated Civil Judge, 1999–. Chancellor, Vicar-General and Official Principal, Diocese of Durham, 1989–; Chancellor, Dio. of Bath and Wells, 1992; Chancellor, VG and Official Principal, Dio. of St Albans, 1992–; Dep. Chancellor, Dio. of York, 1994–. Mem., Legal Adv. Commn, Gen. Synod, 1990–. Deacon, 1968; Priest, 1969; Hon. Curate: St Marylebone, 1968–69; St Mary the Virgin, Almondsbury, 1969–71; St Francis, Bedminster, 1971–83; Christ Church, and St Stephen, Bristol, 1983–88; St Andrew, Cheddar, 1993–. Hon. Canon, St Albans Cathedral, 1996–. Hon. Chaplain, 3rd (Vol.) Military Intelligence Bn, 1996–. *Publications:* (contrib.) Atkin's Court Forms, 1972, 2nd edn 1985; (contrib.) Halsbury's Laws of England, 1975; (jtly) Crown Court Practice, 1978; (contrib.) Principles of Dermatitis Litigation, 1985; Liturgy, Order and the Law, 1996; articles in legal jls. *Recreations:* Church music, military history, archaeology of Greece, Turkey and Holy Land, silversmithing. *Address:* The Crown Court, Small Street, Bristol BS1 1DA. *Clubs:* MCC, Army and Navy.

BURSLEM, Alexandra Vivien, OBE 1993; Vice-Chancellor, Manchester Metropolitan University, since 1997; *b* Shanghai, China, 6 May 1940; *d* of Stanley Morris Thornley, CA and Myrra Thornley (*née* Kimberley); *m* 1st, 1960 (marr. diss. 1971); two *s*; 2nd, 1977, Richard Waywell Burslem, MD, FRCOG (*d* 2001); one *d*. *Educ:* Arnold High Sch. for Girls, Blackpool; Manchester Univ. (BA 1st Cl. Hons Politics and Modern Hist. 1971); Manchester Business Sch. (DipBA 1986). Manchester Polytechnic, later Manchester Metropolitan University: Lectr, 1973, Sen. Lectr, 1975–80 and Principal Lectr, 1980–82, Dept of Social Sci., 1973–82; Hd, Dept of Applied Community Studies, 1982–86; Dean, Faculty of Community Studies and Educn, 1986–88; Academic Dir, 1988–92; Dep. Vice-Chancellor, 1992–97. Vice-Chm., Manchester FPC, 1974–89. Chm., BBC Regl Adv. Council, 1983–92. Member: Council, FEFC, 2000–01; Nat. Learning and Skills Council,

2000–; Gen. Teaching Council, 2000–. Mem. Bd, Anchor Trust, 1995–97; Chm., Manchester and Cheshire Anchor Trust, 1995–97. Gov., Eccles Coll., 1996–98. Mem., Manchester Literary and Philosophical Soc., 1988–. FRSA 1989. JP Inner Manchester, 1981. *Recreations:* opera, theatre, reading, travel. *Address:* Manchester Metropolitan University, All Saints, Manchester M15 6BH. *T:* (0161) 247 1020; Lone Oak, Mereside Road, Mere, Knutsford, Cheshire WA16 6QR. *T:* (01565) 830100.

BURSTALL, Dr Clare, FBPsS; Director, National Foundation for Educational Research in England and Wales, 1983–93 (Deputy Director, 1972–83); *b* 3 Sept. 1931; *d* of Alfred and Lily Wells; *m* 1955, Michael Lyle Burstall (marr. diss. 1977); one *s* one *d. Educ:* King's Coll. and Birkbeck Coll., Univ. of London (BA Hons French, BA Hons Psychology, PhD Psychology); La Sorbonne, Paris. FBPsS 1975. Project Leader of team evaluating teaching of French in British primary schs, NFER, 1964–72. Charter Fellow, Coll. of Preceptors, 1988; FRSA 1990; Mem., Soc. of Authors, 2000; Hon. Mem., CGLI, 1987. Hon. DSc Hull, 1988; Hon. DEd De Montford, 1993. *Publications:* French from Eight: a national experiment, 1968; French in the Primary School: attitudes and achievement, 1970; Primary French in the Balance, 1974; French from Age Eight or Eleven?, 1975; (trans. with Vladimir Kisselnikov) Zhitinsky, The Staircase, and Cheops and Nefertiti, 2000; jl articles on various aspects of educnl research (eg, second language learning, large-scale assessment of achievement, class size, and management of educnl res.). *Recreations:* sailing, art collection, music, needlework. *Address:* Painannekatu 1, 15340 Lahti, Finland. *T:* and *Fax:* 37331166; *e-mail:* clare.burstall@phnet.fi.

BURSTEIN, Hon. Dame Rose; *see* Heilbron, Hon. Dame R.

BURSTON, Sir Samuel (Gerald Wood), Kt 1977; OBE 1966; Grazier at Noss Estate, Casterton, Victoria, 1945–85; President, Australian Woolgrowers and Graziers Council, 1976–79; *b* 24 April 1915; *s* of Maj.-Gen. Sir Samuel Burston, KBE, CB, DSO, VD, late RAAMC, and late Lady Burston; *m* 1st, 1940, Verna Helen Peebles (*d* 1980); one *s* one *d*; 2nd, 1995, Phyllis Elaine Irwin. *Educ:* St Peter's Coll., Adelaide (Sch. Captain, 1933). Major, AIF, 1939–45 (despatches). Chm., Country Fire Authority, Vic, 1964–65; Pres., Graziers Assoc. of Vic, 1973–76; Councillor, Nat. Farmers Fedn, 1979–82; Vice-Pres., Confedn of Aust. Industry, 1978–82; Member: Nat. Employers Policy Cttee, 1970–78; Australian Wool Industry Policy Cttee, 1976–78; Aust. Sci. and Technol. Council, 1976–85 (acting Chm., 1982); Aust. Stats Adv. Council, 1976–80; Aust. Govt Econ. Consultative Gp, 1976–82; Nat. Labour Consultative Council, 1976–82; Reserve Bank Bd, 1977–87. Aust. Trade Develt Council, 1979–85; Trade Practices Cons. Council, 1979–82; Aust. Manufacturing Council, 1979–84; Chm., Perpetual Executors & Trustee Co. of Australia, 1981–87. Mem., Victorian Selection Cttee, Winston Churchill Meml Trust, 1967–81; Chm., Aust. Pastoral Res. Trust, 1988–92. *Recreations:* golf, swimming. *Address:* 112 Brougham Place, North Adelaide, SA 5006, Australia. *T:* (8) 82672152. *Clubs:* Adelaide, Naval, Military and Air Force of South Australia (Adelaide); Royal Adelaide Golf.

BURSTOW, Paul Kenneth; MP (Lib Dem) Sutton and Cheam, since 1997; *b* 13 May 1962; *s* of Brian Seymour Burstow and Sheila Burstow; *m* 1995, Mary Everdell Kemm. *Educ:* Poly. of South Bank (BA Hons Business Studies). Buying asst, Allied Shoe Repairs, 1985–86; print sales, Kallkwik Printers, 1986–87; research asst (part time), London Borough of Hounslow, 1987–89; Association of Social Democrat, then Liberal Democrat Councillors: Organising Sec. (part time), 1987–89; Councillors Officer, 1989–92; Campaigns Officer, 1992–96; Actg Political Sec., 1996–97. Council, London Borough of Sutton: Mem., 1986–; Chm., Envmtl Service Cttee, 1988–91 and 1993–96; Dep. Leader, 1994–97. Contested (Lib Dem) Sutton and Cheam, 1992. Lib Dem spokesman on older people, 1999–. Lib Dem Local Govt Team Leader, 1997–. *Recreations:* walking, cooking, gym work. *Address:* House of Commons, SW1A 0AA. *T:* (020) 7219 1196. *Club:* National Liberal.

BURT, Alistair James Hendrie; MP (C) Bedfordshire North East, since 2001; *b* 25 May 1955; *s* of James Hendrie Burt, med. practitioner and Mina Christie Robertson; *m* 1983, Eve Alexandra Twite; one *s* one *d. Educ:* Bury Grammar Sch.; St John's Coll., Oxford (BA Hons Jurisprudence, 1977). Pres., OU Law Soc., Michaelmas term, 1976. Articled Slater Heelis & Co., Manchester, 1978–80; solicitor, Watts, Vallance & Vallance, 1980–92; Consultant, Teeman, Levine and Co. (Solicitors), Leeds, 1992. Councillor, Archway Ward, London Bor. of Haringey, 1982–84. MP (C) Bury North, 1983–97; contested (C) same seat, 1997. Parliamentary Private Secretary: to Sec. of State for the Environment, 1985–86; to Sec. of State for Educn and Science, 1986–89; to Chancellor of Duchy of Lancaster and Chm. of Cons. Party, 1989–90; Parly Under-Sec. of State, DSS, 1992–95; Minister of State (Minister for Disabled People), DSS, 1995–97. Vice-Chm., Tory Reform Gp, 1985–88. Secretary: NW Cons. MPs Group, 1984–88; Parly Christian Fellowship, 1984–97. Consultant, Whitehead Mann plc, 1997–2001. Chm., Enterprise Forum, 1998–. *Recreations:* reading left-wing publications, sport (scored a goal at Wembley, playing for northern MPs football team, Nov. 1991), modern art, astronomy. *Address:* c/o House of Commons, SW1A 0AA.

BURT, Hon. Sir Francis (Theodore Page), AC 1988; KCMG 1977; QC 1960; Governor of Western Australia, 1990–93 (Lieutenant-Governor, 1977–90); *b* Perth, WA, 14 June 1918; *s* of A. F. G. Burt; *m* 1943, Margaret, *d* of Brig. J. E. Lloyd; two *s* two *d. Educ:* Guildford Grammar Sch.; Univ. of Western Australia (LLB, LLM); Hackett Schol., 1941; admitted to Bar of WA, 1941. Served War, RAN and RAAF, 1940–45. A Judge of Supreme Ct, WA, 1969–88; Chief Justice, WA, 1977–88. President: Law Soc. of WA, 1960–62; WA Bar Assoc., 1963–65. Visiting Lectr in Law, Univ. of WA, 1945–65. Chairman: Inst. of Radiotherapy, WA, 1960–62; Bd of Management, Sir Charles Gairdner Hosp., Hollywood, WA, 1962–72; Queen Elizabeth II Medical Centre Trust, 1966–85; Mem., Senate of Univ. of WA, 1968–76. Hon. LLD Univ. of WA, 1987. *Recreations:* tennis, fishing. *Address:* 64 Leake Street, Peppermint Grove WA 6011, Australia. *Club:* Weld (Perth).

BURT, Gerald Raymond, OBE 1984; BEM 1947; FCIT; Chief Secretary, British Railways Board, 1976–84; *b* 15 Feb. 1926; *s* of Reginald George Burt and Lilian May Burt; *m* 1948, Edna Ivy Elizabeth Sizeland; two *s. Educ:* Latymer Upper Sch. FCIT 1971. Joined GWR as Booking Clerk, 1942: RE (Movement Control), 1944–47; BR Management Trainee, 1951–54; Gen. Staff, British Transport Commn, 1956–59; Divl Planning Officer, Bristol, 1959–62; Planning Officer, LMR, 1962–64; Divl Man., St Pancras, 1965; Traffic Man., Freightliners, 1967–70; Principal Corporate Planning Officer, British Railways Bd, 1970–76. Member: Council, Chartered Inst. of Transport, 1967–70, 1981–84; British Transport Police Cttee, 1984–88. Governor, British Transport Staff Coll., 1976–82; Trustee, 1984–99, Vice Pres., 2000–, Rly Benevolent Instn. FRSA 1983. Scouting Medal of Merit, 1978. *Recreations:* gardening, the countryside. *Address:* 16 Ravens Court, Benningfield Gardens, Berkhamsted, Herts HP4 2GX. *T:* (01442) 871725.

BURT, Maurice Edward; Deputy Director, Building Research Establishment, 1975–81, retired; *b* 17 Nov. 1921; *s* of Reginald Edward Burt and Bertha Winifred Burt; *m* 1947, Monica Evelyn Amy; one *s* three *d. Educ:* Victoria Coll., Jersey; Taunton's Sch., Southampton; BA Hons London, 1948. CEng, MICE; FRAeS. Aircraft industry, 1938–48; RAE, 1948–66 (Supt, Airworthiness, 1961–66); Head of Structures Dept, Transport and Road Res. Lab., 1966–73; Head of Res. Management, Dept of Environment, 1973–75. *Publications:* technical reports and articles. *Recreations:* golf, walking, gardening.

BURT, Peter Alexander; Deputy Chairman, HBOS, since 2001; *b* 6 March 1944; *s* of Robert W. Burt and May H. Rodger; *m* 1971, Alison Mackintosh Turner; three *s. Educ:* Merchiston Castle Sch., Edinburgh; Univ. of St Andrews (MA); Univ. of Pennsylvania (MBA). FCIBS (FIB (Scot.) 1987). Hewlett Packard Co., Palo Alto, 1968–70; CSL, Edinburgh, 1970–74; Edward Bates & Sons Ltd, Edinburgh, 1974; joined Bank of Scotland, 1975: Internat. Div., 1975–88; Asst Gen. Manager, 1979–84; Divisional Gen. Manager, 1984–85; Jt Gen. Manager, 1985–88; Treas. and Chief Gen. Manager, 1988–96; Dir, 1995–2001; Chief Exec., 1996–2001. Mem., High Constables and Guard of Honour of Holyroodhouse, Edinburgh. *Recreations:* golf, ski-ing, gardening, reading. *Clubs:* New (Edinburgh); Hon. Co. of Edinburgh Golfers (Muirfield); Royal & Ancient (St Andrews); Gullane Golf (Gullane); Pine Valley Golf.

BURTON, 3rd Baron *cr* 1897; **Michael Evan Victor Baillie;** *b* 27 June 1924; *er s* of Brig. Hon. George Evan Michael Baillie, MC, TD (*d* 1941) and *g s* of Baroness Burton (2nd in line); *S* grandmother, 1962; *m* 1st, 1948, Elizabeth Ursula Forster (marr. diss. 1977; she *d* 1993), *er d* of late Capt. A. F. Wise; two *s* four *d*; 2nd, 1978, Coralie Denise, 2nd *d* of late Claud R. Cliffe. *Educ:* Eton. Lieut, Scots Guards, 1944. Mem., CC, 1948–75, JP 1961–75, DL 1963–65, Inverness-shire; Mem., Inverness Dist Council, 1984–92. Grand Master Mason, 1994–99. *Heir: s* Hon. Evan Michael Ronald Baillie [*b* 19 March 1949; *m* 1970, Lucinda (marr. diss.), *e d* of Robert Law, Newmarket; two *s* one *d*]. *Address:* Dochgarroch Lodge, Inverness IV3 6JX. *T:* (01463) 861252. *Clubs:* Cavalry and Guards; New (Edinburgh).

BURTON, Air Vice-Marshal Andrew John, OBE 1991 (MBE 1986); FCIS; Air Officer Administration and Air Officer Commanding Directly Administered Units, Personnel and Training Command, since 2001; *b* 11 Nov. 1950; *s* of Walter Joseph Burton and Phyllis Jane Burton (*née* Flear); *m* 1977, Sheila Hanson; two *s. Educ:* Llanelli Boys' Grammar Sch.; Univ. of Wales Inst. of Sci. and Technol. (BScEcon 1972). FCIS 1993 (ACIS 1982); FCIPD 2000. Commnd RAF, 1972; Sqn Leader, 1980; Wing Comdr, 1986; Defence Staff, British Embassy, Washington, 1988–90; Gp Capt., 1991; Station Comdr, RAF Uxbridge, 1994–95; Air Cdre, 1996; Dir of Personnel (RAF), 1995–98; Air Vice-Marshal, 1998; AOA and AOC Directly Administered Units, HQ Strike Comd, 1998–2001. *Recreations:* golf, sport, theatre. *Address:* Personnel and Training Command, RAF Innsworth, Gloucester GL3 1EZ. *T:* (01452) 712612. *Club:* Royal Air Force.

BURTON, (Anthony) David, CBE 1992; Chairman, Marshalls Finance Ltd, 1989–98; Director, LIFFE, 1981–94 (Chairman, 1988–92); *b* 2 April 1937; *s* of Leslie Mitchell Burton and Marion Burton (*née* Marsh); *m* 1964, Valerie (*née* Swire); one *s* two *d. Educ:* Arnold Sch., Blackpool. FCIB; FCT. Bank of America National Trust and Savings Assoc., 1966–72; S. G. Warburg & Co. Ltd, 1972–92. Chm., Ludgate 181 plc, 1999–. *Recreations:* antique glass, German pottery, music, opera, sport (participating and spectator). *Club:* MCC.

BURTON, Anthony George Graham; author and broadcaster, since 1968; *b* 24 Dec. 1934; *s* of Donald Graham Burton and Irene Burton; *m* 1959, Pip Sharman; two *s* one *d. Educ:* King James's Grammar Sch., Knaresborough; Leeds Univ. National Service, RAF, 1955–57. Research chemist, 1958–60; publishing, 1960–68. *Publications:* A Programmed Guide to Office Warfare, 1969; The Jones Report, 1970; The Canal Builders, 1972, 3rd edn 1993; Canals in Colour, 1974; Remains of a Revolution, 1975, 2nd edn 2001; Josiah Wedgwood, 1976; (jtly) Canal, 1976; The Miners, 1976; Back Door Britain, 1977; Industrial Archaeological Sites of Britain, 1977; (jtly) The Green Bag Travellers, 1978; The Past At Work, 1980; The Rainhill Story, 1980; The Past Afloat, 1982; The Changing River, 1982; The Shell Book of Curious Britain, 1982; The National Trust Guide to Our Industrial Past, 1983; The Waterways of Britain, 1983; The Rise and Fall of King Cotton, 1984; (ed jtly) Canals: a new look, 1984; Walking the Line, 1985; Wilderness Britain, 1985; (jtly) Britain's Light Railways, 1985; The Shell Book of Undiscovered Britain and Ireland, 1986; (jtly) Landscape Detective, 1986; Britain Revisited, 1986; Opening Time, 1987; Steaming Through Britain, 1987; Walking Through History, 1988; Walk the South Downs, 1988; The Great Days of the Canals, 1989; Cityscapes, 1990; Astonishing Britain, 1990; Slow Roads, 1991; The Railway Builders, 1992; Canal Mania, 1993; (jtly) The Grand Union Canal Walk, 1993; The Railway Empire, 1994; The Rise and Fall of British Shipbuilding, 1994; The Cotswold Way, 1995; The Dales Way, 1995; The West Highland Way, 1996; The Southern Upland Way, 1997; William Cobbett: Englishman, 1997; The Caledonian Canal, 1998; The Wye Valley Walk, 1998; Best Foot Forward, 1998; The Cumbria Way, 1999; The Wessex Ridgeway, 1999; Thomas Telford, 1999; Weekend Walks Dartmoor and Exmoor, 2000; Weekend Walks the Yorkshire Dales, 2000; Traction Engines, 2000; Richard Trevithick, 2000; Weekend Walks The Peak District, 2001; The Orient Express, 2001; *novels:* The Reluctant Musketeer, 1973; The Master Idol, 1975; The Navigators, 1976; A Place to Stand, 1977. *Recreations:* walking and travelling in search of steam engines and good beer; cinema. *Address:* c/o Sara Menguc, Literary Agent, 4 Hatch Place, Kingston upon Thames KT2 5NB. *T:* (020) 8541 1202.

BURTON, Rt Rev. Anthony John; *see* Saskatchewan, Bishop of.

BURTON, Anthony Philip; Senior Research Fellow in Museology and Museum History, Research Department, Victoria and Albert Museum, since 1997; *b* 25 Oct. 1942; *s* of late Frank Burton and Lottie Burton (*née* Lax); *m* 1985, Carol Deborah Baker. *Educ:* King's Sch., Macclesfield; Wadham Coll., Oxford (BLitt, MA). Res. Asst, Dept of English, Birkbeck Coll., Univ. of London, 1965–68; Victoria and Albert Museum: Asst Keeper, Nat. Art Liby, 1968–79; Asst Keeper, Directorate, 1979–81; Hd, Bethnal Green Mus. of Childhood, 1981–97. *Publications:* (with S. Haskins) European Art in the Victoria and Albert Museum, 1983; Children's Pleasures: books, toys and games from the Bethnal Green Museum of Childhood, 1996; Vision & Accident: the story of the Victoria and Albert Museum, 1999; articles on liby and mus. subjects. *Recreations:* cultural pursuits, reading crime fiction. *Address:* 59 Arlington Avenue, N1 7BA. *T:* (020) 7226 0394.

BURTON, Sir Carlisle (Archibald), Kt 1979; OBE 1968; Barbados High Commissioner to the Bahamas, 1978–93; *b* 29 July 1921; *m* 1946, Hyacinth Marjorie Adelle Barker. *Educ:* Harrison Coll., Barbados, WI; Univ. of London (BA); School of Librarianship, Leeds (ALA); Univ. of Pittsburgh (MS). Assistant Master, Harrison Coll., Barbados, 1943–50; Sen. Asst Master, Bishop's High Sch., Tobago, 1950–51; Public Librarian, Barbados, 1953–58; Permanent Secretary: Min. of Educn, 1958–63; Min. of Health, 1963–71; Perm. Sec., Prime Minister's Office, and Head of Civil Service, 1972–81; Chm., Public Services Commn, Barbados, 1981–87, Turks and Caicos Islands, 1988–90. Member: Commonwealth Observer Gp at elections in Southern Rhodesia (Zimbabwe), 1980 and in Malaysia, 1990; Caribbean Community Review Team, 1989–91. Director: Barbados National Bank, 1978–86 (Dep. Chm., 1982–86); Insurance Corp. of Barbados, 1978–86

(Chm., 1981–86). Chm., Cave Hill Campus Council, Univ. of the WI, Barbados, 1984–94; Mem. Council, Barbados Mus. and Historical Soc. Life Mem., Barbados Nat. Trust. Chm., Barbados Assoc. of Retired Persons, 1995–98. Hon. LLD Univ. of WI, 1995. FRSA 1953. *Recreations:* (active) table tennis, swimming, bridge, reading; (spectator) cricket (Life Member, Barbados Cricket Assoc.), athletics (Life Member, Barbados Amateur Athletic Assoc.), soccer. *Address:* Caradelle, Mountjoy Avenue, Pine Gardens, St Michael, Barbados, West Indies. *T:* 4293724.

BURTON, David; *see* Burton, A. D.

BURTON, David Harold; Managing Director, West Anglia Great Northern Railway, 1996–99; *b* 28 Jan. 1947; *s* of George and Helen Burton; *m* 1973, Patricia Burton; one *s*. *Educ:* Bridlington Sch.; Leeds Univ. (BA (Hons) Geography). British Rail: Network Man., S Central Network SE, 1986; Dep. Gen. Man., Southern Region, 1988; Gen. Man., Anglia Region, 1989–91; Gp Dir North, Network SouthEast, 1991–92; Director: Express Parcels, BR Parcels, 1992–93; Restructuring, Network SouthEast, 1993–94; Dir, Product Quality, and Dep. Man. Dir (S & E), BRB, 1994–96. *Recreations:* spectator sport, lousy golf.

BURTON, Lt-Gen. Sir Edmund Fortescue Gerard, KBE 1999 (OBE); Chairman, Police Information Technology Organisation, since 2000; *b* 20 Oct. 1943. *Educ:* Trinity Hall, Cambridge (BA 1968; MA 1972). Commissioned RA, 1963; Brig., 1987; Mil. Attaché, Washington, 1990; Maj.-Gen., 1991; Comdt, RMCS, 1991–94; ACDS, Operational Requirements (Land), 1994–97; DCDS (Systems), 1997–99. Vis. Prof., Cranfield Univ., 2000–. Hon. Col, OTC (Cambridge), 1996–; Col Comdt, RA, 1998–; Hon. Regtl Col, 26 Regt RA, 1999–.

BURTON, Dr Frank Patrick; QC 1998; a Recorder, since 2000; *b* 19 June 1950; *s* of Ronald and Ita Burton; *m* 1983, Caroline Reid; two *s* one *d*. *Educ:* Salesian Coll., Farnborough; Univ. of Kent at Canterbury (BA 1st Cl. Hons 1971); London School of Economics and Political Science (PhD 1974). Lecturer in Social Science: Brunel Univ., 1976–79; City Univ., 1979–82; called to the Bar, Gray's Inn, 1982; in practice at the Bar, 1982–. *Publications:* Medical Negligence Case Law, 1990, 2nd edn 1995; Personal Injury Limitation Law, 1994. *Recreations:* sport, reading, Suffolk. *Address:* 12 King's Bench Walk, Temple, EC4Y 7EL.

BURTON, Sir George (Vernon Kennedy), Kt 1977; CBE 1972 (MBE (mil.) 1945); DL; Chairman, Fisons plc, 1973–84 (Chief Executive, 1966–76, Senior Vice-Chairman, 1966–71, Deputy Chairman, 1971–72); *b* 21 April 1916; *s* of late George Ethelbert Earnshaw Burton and Francesca (*née* Holden-White); *g s* of Sir Bunnell Burton, Ipswich; *m* 1st, 1945, Sarah Katherine Tcherniavsky (marr. diss.); two *s*; 2nd, 1975, Priscilla Margaret Gore (MBE 1996), *d* of late Cecil H. King. *Educ:* Charterhouse; Germany. Served RA, 1939–45, N Africa, Sicily, Italy, Austria. Director: Barclays Bank Internat. plc, 1976–82; Thomas Tilling, 1976–83; Rolls-Royce Ltd, 1976–84. Member: Export Council for Europe, 1965–71 (Dep. Chm., 1967–71); Council, CBI, 1970–84 (Chm., CBI Overseas Cttee, 1975–81); BOTB, 1972–73 (BOTB European Trade Cttee, 1972–81; British Overseas Trade Adv. Council, 1975–79); Investment Insce Adv. Cttee, ECGD, 1971–76; Council on Internat. Develt of ODM, 1977–79; Council, BIM, 1968–70 (FBIM); NEDC, 1975–79; Whitford Cttee to Consider Law on Copyright and Designs, 1974–77; Ipswich County Borough Council, 1947–51; Ipswich Gp HMC; Assoc. for Business Sponsorship of the Arts, 1978–84; Governing Body, British National Cttee of Internat. Chamber of Commerce, 1979–86; Governor, Sutton's Hosp. in Charterhouse, 1979–92; Chm., Ipswich Conservative Assoc., 1982–84. FRSA 1978. DL Suffolk, 1980. Commander: Order of Ouissam Alaouite, Morocco, 1968; Order of Léopold II, Belgium, 1974. *Recreation:* music. *Address:* Aldham Mill, Hadleigh, Suffolk IP7 6LE.

BURTON, Sir Graham (Stuart), KCMG 1999 (CMG 1987); HM Diplomatic Service, retired; High Commissioner, Nigeria, also concurrently Ambassador (non-resident) to the Republic of Benin, 1997–2001; *b* 8 April 1941; *s* of late Cyril Stanley Richard Burton and of Jessie Blythe Burton; *m* 1965, Julia Margaret Lappin; one *s* one *d*. *Educ:* Sir William Borlase's Sch., Marlow. Foreign Office, 1961; Abu Dhabi, 1964; Middle East Centre for Arabic Studies, 1967; Kuwait, 1969; FCO, 1972; Tunis, 1975; UK Mission to United Nations, 1978; Counsellor, Tripoli, 1981; Head, Security Co-ordination Dept, FCO, 1984; Consul General, San Francisco, 1987; Ambassador: UAE, 1990; Indonesia, 1994. *Recreations:* golf, watching cricket, baseball and most other sports; opera. *Club:* MCC.

BURTON, Humphrey McGuire, CBE 2000; writer and broadcaster; *b* 25 March 1931; *s* of Harry (Philip) and Kathleen Burton; *m* 1st, 1957, Gretel (*née* Davis); one *s* one *d*; 2nd, 1970, Christina (*née* Hellstedt); one *s* one *d*. *Educ:* Long Dene Sch., Chiddingstone; Judd Sch., Tonbridge; Fitzwilliam House, Cambridge (BA; Hon. Fellow, Fitzwilliam Coll., 1997). BBC Radio, 1955–58; BBC TV, 1958–67: Editor, Monitor, 1962; Exec. Producer, Music Programmes, 1963; Head of Music and Arts Programmes, 1965–67, productions inc. Workshop, Master Class, In Rehearsal, Britten at 50, Conversations with Glenn Gould; London Weekend TV: Head of Drama, Arts and Music, 1967–69; Editor/Introducer, Aquarius, 1970–75, programmes incl. Mahler Festival, Verdi Requiem, Trouble in Tahiti, The Great Gondola Race, Anatomy of a Record, etc; Head of Music and Arts, BBC TV, 1975–81; Presenter: Omnibus, 1976–78, 1984–85 (Producer, West Side Story documentary, 1985; RAI Prize, Prix Italia, BAFTA Robert Flaherty Best Documentary Award, 1985); In Performance, 1978–82; Young Musician of the Year, biennially 1978–94; Producer/Director: TV Proms with Giulini and Solti, 1981, and with others, 1982–95; Walton 80th Birthday Concert (Previn); Verdi Requiem (Abbado), and Call me Kiri (Te Kanawa), 1982; Candide, Scottish Opera, Glasgow, 1988 and Barbican (conducted by Leonard Bernstein), 1989; Covent Garden opera relays, incl. Die Fledermaus (Joan Sutherland farewell), 1990; Artistic Dir, 1988–90, Artistic Advr, 1990–93, Barbican Centre. Other productions include: 5 Glyndebourne operas, adapted and produced, Southern TV, 1972–74; The Beach at Falesa, World Première, Harlech TV, 1974; Channel 4 operas include: Eugene Onegin, 1994; Ermione, 1995; Lulu, 1996; The Damnation of Faust, Manon Lescaut, 1997; Rodelinda, Hansel and Gretel, 1998; Pelléas et Mélisande, Flight, 1999; BBC2 opera, Falstaff, 1999; UN Day Concert with Pablo Casals, 1971, and subseq. UN days, 1972–92; Berlioz' Requiem at Les Invalides, French TV, 1975; many free-lance prodns in Austria, Czechoslovakia, Germany, Hungary, Italy, Israel, Poland, Russia and USA, including: Mahler, Brahms, Schumann and Beethoven Cycles with Bernstein and Vienna Philharmonic; concerts with von Karajan and Berlin and Vienna Philharmonic, Giulini and LA Philharmonic, Mehta and NY Philharmonic, Maazel and Bayerisches Rundfunk Orch., Solti and Chicago SO; world première, Epitaph, by Charles Mingus, NY, 1989; Director: Boris Godounov, Kirov, 1990; War and Peace, Kirov, 1991; Mozart Requiem, Vienna Bicentennial 1991; Producer: Leonard Bernstein's 70th Birthday Gala Season, Tanglewood, 1988; Bernstein Meml Concert, Carnegie Hall, 1990; Guest Dir, 1983 Hollywood Bowl Summer Music Fest.; *radio:* writer/presenter of series, incl. Life of Leonard Bernstein, Menuhin-Master Musician, Classic FM, Danube Week, etc, BBC. Columnist: Classic FM Magazine, 1995–98; BBC Music Magazine, 1998–99. Chairman: EBU Music Experts Gp, 1976–82; EBU TV Music Working Party, 1982–86; Mem., New Music Sub-Cttee, Arts Council, 1981–83; Advr, Manchester Olympic Fest., 1990; Administrator, Royal Philharmonic Soc.'s Music Awards, 1989–91. Hon. Professorial Fellow, University Coll., Cardiff, 1983–87. Hon. FCSD 1990. Desmond Davis Award, SFTA, 1966; Royal TV Soc. Silver Medal, 1971; Emmy, 1971 for 'Beethoven's Birthday' (CBS TV); Peabody Award, 1972; SFTA Best Specialised Series, 1974; Christopher Award, 1979; Emmy, 1988, for 'Celebrating Gershwin' (BBC TV). Chevalier de l'Ordre des Arts et des Lettres, 1975. *Publications:* Leonard Bernstein, 1994 (trans. German, Chinese and Japanese; ASCAP book award, 1995); Menuhin: a life, 2000; William Walton: a life in pictures, 2001. *Recreations:* music-making, tennis, travel. *Address:* 123 Oakwood Court, W14 8LA. *Club:* Vanderbilt.

BURTON, Iris Grace; Editor-in-Chief: Woman's Realm, 1991–99; Woman's Weekly, 1992–99; Eva, 1994–97; Chat, 1997–99; *d* of Arthur Burton and late Alice Burton; *m*; one *s* one *d*. *Educ:* Roan Girls' Grammar Sch., Greenwich; City of London Coll. Local newspaper, SE London Mercury, until 1966; Writer, then Features Editor, Woman's Own, 1966–78; Asst Editor, TV Times, 1978–80; Editor, Woman's Own, 1980–86; Editor-in-Chief: Prima magazine, 1986–87; Best magazine, 1987–88; Editorial Dir, G+J of the UK publications, 1988–91; Launch Ed., Now mag., 1996. Mem., Press Complaints Commn, 1993–99. *Address:* Anerley, SE20.

BURTON, Prof. John Lloyd, MD; FRCP; Professor of Dermatology, University of Bristol, 1992–98; *b* 29 Aug. 1938; *s* of Lloyd Burton and Dorothy Mary Burton (*née* Pacey); *m* 1964, Patricia Anne Crankshaw, DRCOG, FRCPath; one *s* two *d*. *Educ:* Heanor Grammar Sch., Derbys; Manchester Univ. (BSc; MD 1971). FRCP 1978. Trng posts in hosps in Manchester, London, Edinburgh and Newcastle upon Tyne, 1964–73; Consultant Dermatologist, Bristol Royal Infirmary, 1973–96. Numerous guest lectures, including: Dowling Oration, 1980, Deville, 1995, RSM; Parkes-Weber, RCP, 1988; Long-Fox, Bristol Univ., 1994. Advr in Dermatol. to CMO, DoH, 1988–94. Examr, RCP, 1987–92. Chm., Dermatol. Cttee, RCP, 1993–95; President: Dermatol. Sect., RSocMed, 1994–95; Brit. Assoc. Dermatologists, 1995–96. Editor, Brit. Jl Dermatol., 1981–85. *Publications:* Aids to Postgraduate Medicine, 1970, 6th edn 1994; Aids to Undergraduate Medicine, 1973, 6th edn 1997; Essentials of Dermatology, 1979, 3rd edn 1990; (ed jtly) Textbook of Dermatology (4 Vols), 4th edn 1986 to 6th edn 1998; numerous chapters and scientific papers. *Recreations:* painting, book-binding. *Address:* Norland House, 33 Canynge Road, Clifton, Bristol BS8 3LD. *T:* (0117) 973 3933.

BURTON, John Michael, RIBA; Principal Partner, Purcell Miller Tritton & Partners, Architects, since 1978; Surveyor to the Fabric, Canterbury Cathedral, since 1991; Surveyor of the Fabric of Westminster Abbey, since 1999; *b* 21 May 1945; *s* of Gerald Victor Burton and Kathleen Blodwen (*née* Harper); *m* 1971, Sally Bason; one *s* one *d*. *Educ:* Duston Secondary Mod. Sch., Northampton; Northampton Coll. of Further Educn; Oxford Sch. of Architecture (DipArch). RIBA 1972. Asst to Surveyor to Ely Cathedral, 1971–73; Parish Architect to numerous churches in E Anglia incl. Long Melford and Thaxted, 1973–; Commissioned Architect to English Heritage, 1983–; Architect to NT, Melford Hall, Lavenham Guildhall and Flatford Mill, 1973–96; work on restoration of Colchester Castle, 1984–90; Architect, American Ambassador's Residence, London, 1998–. Chm., Cathedral Architects' Assoc., 1997–99. Member: Cathedrals Fabric Commn for England, 1996–; Redundant Churches Cttee, Church Comrs, 1999–; Places of Worship Adv. Cttee, English Heritage, 2000–; Chm., Redundant Churches Uses Cttee, Chelmsford, 1990–. Mem., DAC for Chelmsford, 1977–, St Edmundsbury and Ipswich, 1986–98. Dir, Mercury Theatre, Colchester, 1999–. Mem., Colchester Trinity Rotary Club. Judge, Stone Awards, 1995 and 1997. Freeman, City of London, 1996; Liveryman, Co. of Masons, 1996–. *Recreations:* cycling, sail boarding, woodwork. *Address:* St Mary's Hall, Rawstorn Road, Colchester, Essex CO3 3JH. *T:* (01206) 244844.

BURTON, Prof. Kenneth, FRS 1974; Professor of Biochemistry, 1966–88, now Emeritus, and Dean of Faculty of Science, 1983–86, University of Newcastle upon Tyne; *b* 26 June 1926; *s* of Arthur and Gladys Burton; *m* 1955, Hilda Marsden; one *s* one *d*. *Educ:* High Pavement Sch., Nottingham; Wath-upon-Dearne Grammar Sch.; King's Coll., Cambridge (MA, PhD). Asst Lectr in Biochem., Univ. of Sheffield, 1949, Lectr 1952; Res. Associate, Univ. of Chicago, 1952–54; MRC Unit for Research in Cell Metabolism, Oxford, 1954–66. Vis. Lectr in Medicine, Harvard, 1964; William Evans Vis. Prof., Univ. of Otago, 1977–78. *Publications:* scientific articles, especially on nucleic acids. *Recreations:* music, hill-walking. *Address:* Byways, The Broadway, Alfriston, Polegate, East Sussex BN26 5XH.

BURTON, Hon. Mark; *see* Burton, R. M.

BURTON, Hon. Sir Michael (John), Kt 1998; **Hon. Mr Justice Burton;** a Judge of the High Court of Justice, Queen's Bench Division, since 1998; Judge of the Employment Appeal Tribunal, since 1999; *b* 12 Nov. 1946; *s* of late Henry Burton, QC, and Hilda Burton; *m* 1972, Corinne Ruth (*d* 1992), *d* of late Dr Jack Cowan, MC, and Dorothy Cowan; four *d*. *Educ:* Eton Coll. (KS, Captain of the School); Balliol Coll., Oxford (MA). President, Balliol JCR, 1967; First President, Oxford Univ. SRC, 1968. Called to Bar, Gray's Inn, 1970, Bencher, 1993; Law Lectr, Balliol Coll., Oxford, 1972–74; QC 1984; Head of Chambers, 1991–98; a Recorder, 1989–98. Chm., Central Arbitration Cttee, 2000–; Pres., Interception of Communications Tribunal, 2000–; Vice-Pres., Investigatory Powers Tribunal, 2000–. Contested: (Lab) RBK&C (local elections), 1971; (Lab) Stratford upon Avon, Feb. 1974; (SDP) Putney, GLC, 1981. Hon. Fellow, Goldsmiths Coll., London, 1998. *Publication:* (contrib.) Bullen & Leake & Jacob's Precedents of Pleadings, 13th edn 1990. *Recreations:* amateur theatricals, lyric writing, singing, bridge, watching Wimbledon Football Club. *Address:* Royal Courts of Justice, Strand, WC2A 2LL.

BURTON, Sir Michael (St Edmund), KCVO 1992 (CVO 1979); CMG 1987; HM Diplomatic Service, retired; *b* 18 Oct. 1937; *s* of late Brig. G. W. S. Burton, DSO (and two Bars), and of Barbara Burton (*née* Kemmis Betty); *m* 1967, Henrietta Jindra Hones; one *s* one *d* (and one *d* decd). *Educ:* Bedford Sch.; Magdalen Coll., Oxford. MA. 2nd Lt, Rifle Brigade, 1955–57. Foreign Office, 1960; Asst Political Agent, Dubai, Trucial States, 1962–64; Private Sec. to Minister of State, FO, 1964–67; Second (later First) Sec. (Information), Khartoum, 1967–69; First Sec. (Inf.), Paris, 1969–72; Asst, Science and Technology Dept, FCO, 1972–75; First Sec. and Head of Chancery, Amman, 1975–77; Counsellor, Kuwait, 1977–79; Head of Maritime, Aviation and Environment Dept, FCO, 1979–81; Head of S Asian Dept, FCO, 1981–84; on secondment to BP as Head of Policy Rev. Unit, 1984–85; Berlin: Minister, 1985–92; Dep. Comdt, BMG, 1985–90; Head of Embassy Office, 1990–92; Asst Under-Sec. of State (ME), FCO, 1993; Ambassador to Czech Republic, 1994–97. *Recreations:* tennis, opera, theatre, music, travel, wine, allotment. *Address:* 6 Napier Court, Ranelagh Gardens, SW6 3UT. *Clubs:* Oxford and Cambridge, Hurlingham.

BURTON, Richard Hilary; Chairman, Cable Authority, 1984–90; *b* 28 Dec. 1923; *s* of Robert Claud and Theodora Constance Helen Burton; *m* 1962, Priscilla Jane Coode-Adams; one *s* one *d*. *Educ:* Lancing; Brasenose Coll., Oxford (MA 2nd Cl. Hons Jurisprudence). Served War, 1942–46, 60th Rifles, Captain (mentioned in despatches);

Mem., Military Courts, Palestine, 1946. Called to the Bar, Inner Temple, 1951; practised at Bar, 1951–54. Gillette Industries Ltd: Manager, Legal Dept, 1954–65; Legal Dir, 1965–78; Chm., 1978–84; Dep. to the Chm., The Gillette Company (USA), 1984–88; Chm., Nestor-BNA plc, 1986–89. Chm., W Mddx Arts Develt Trust, 1978–86. Freeman: City of London, 1974; Co. of Information Technologists, 1988. FRSA. *Recreations:* cricket, real tennis, shooting, ornithology, lepidoptery. *Address:* Danmoor House, Heckfield, Hook, Hants RG27 0JY. *T:* (0118) 932 6233. *Clubs:* Boodle's, MCC (Mem. Cttee, 1989–92).

BURTON, Hon. (Richard) Mark; MP (Lab) Taupo, since 1996; Deputy Leader of the House, Minister of Defence, Minister of State Owned Enterprises, Minister of Tourism and Minister of Veterans' Affairs, New Zealand, since 1999; *b* 16 Jan. 1956; *m* 1977, Carol Botherway; two *s* one *d. Educ:* Waikato Univ. (Cert. Contg Educn); Massey Univ. (Cert. Social Service Supervision); NZ Council of Recreation and Sport (Dip.). Residential Social Worker, Dept of Social Welfare, 1976–78; Community Recreation Advr, Palmerston North City Corp., 1978–82; Community Educn Organiser, Central Plateau Rural Educn Activities Prog., 1982–93. MP (Lab) Tongariro, 1993–96; Lab. Party spokesman for adult and community educn, 1994–99; Sen. Labour Party Whip, 1996–99. Various posts with NZ Assoc. for Community and Contg Educn, 1983–93; Member: Bd of Studies, Contg Educn, Waikato Univ., 1985–86; Bd, NZ Career Develt and Transition Educn Service, 1990–92. NZ Medal, 1990. *Address:* Parliament House, Wellington, New Zealand.

BURTON, Richard St John Vladimir, CBE 1996; Partner, Ahrends Burton & Koralek, since 1961; *b* 3 Nov. 1933; *s* of Percy Basil Harmsworth Burton and Vera (*née* Poliakoff Russell); *m* 1956, Mireille, *d* of Joseph Dernbach-Mayen; three *s* one *d. Educ:* Bryanston; AA Sch. of Architecture (AA Dip Hons). ARIBA 1957. Founding Partner, Ahrends Burton & Koralek, 1961. Principal works: TCD Library and Arts Bldg, 1967 and 1979; Chalvedon and Northlands Housing, Basildon, 1968 and 1980; Templeton Coll., Oxford, 1969–; Nebenzahl House, 1972; extension, Keble Coll., Oxford, 1976; W. H. Smith Head Office Marketing, Swindon, 1985; Burton House, 1987, 1993; Hooke Park Coll., 1990; John Lewis, Kingston-on-Thames, 1991; St Mary's Isle of Wight Low Energy Hosp., 1991; Docklands Light Railway extension, 1993; British Embassy, Moscow, 2000. Chairman: Arts Council Percent for Art Steering Gp, 1989; RIBA Steering Gp on Educn, 1991; Arts Council Adv. Gp on Architecture, 1994–98; 20/20 Vision Jt Report of Nuffield Foundn, RIBA and MARU, 2000–01. FRSA. *Publication:* Ahrends Burton and Koralek, 1991. *Recreations:* building, writing. *Address:* Ahrends Burton & Koralek, 7 Chalcot Road, NW1 8LH. *T:* (020) 7586 3311.

BURTON, Roger; Director of Finance (formerly City Treasurer, then Director of Resources), Birmingham City Council, 1990–97; *b* 12 Oct. 1946; *s* of Norman Burton and Marjorie Rose (*née* Burgin); *m* 1st, 1968, Dorothy May Hey (marr. diss.); one *s* one *d*; 2nd, 1984, Susan Jane Griffiths (marr. diss. 1988); 3rd, 1991, Janet Elizabeth Mauchlen (*née* Davies); two step *s* one step *d. Educ:* Doncaster Grammar Sch.; Lanchester Polytechnic (BSc Econs 1968). CIPFA 1972; IRRV 1990. Coventry CC, 1968–79; Birmingham CC, 1979–97. A Public Works Loan Comr, 1996–. *Recreations:* sport, walking, photography, Real Ale. *T:* (024) 7640 7480.

BURTON, Sydney Harold; JP; FCIB; Director, Gateway Building Society, 1981–88 (Managing Director, 1975–81); *b* 6 April 1916; *s* of Sydney Collard Burton and Maud Burton; *m* 1st, 1941, Jean Cowling (*d* 1985); one *d*; 2nd, 1986, Irene Robertson. *Educ:* Belle Vue High Sch., Bradford. Various appts with Bradford Equitable Building Soc. (excl. war years), 1932–63; joined Temperance Permanent Building Soc., 1963; Jt Gen. Manager, 1965; Gen. Man. and Sec., 1972; following merger of Temperance Permanent and Bedfordshire Bldg Socs became Chief Gen. Man. and Sec. of Gateway Bldg Soc., 1974. Pres., Building Societies Inst., 1976–77; Mem. Council, Building Societies Assoc., 1971–81. JP Worthing, 1974. *Recreations:* music and theatre, social and religious work. *Address:* Cherry Trees, 52 Beehive Lane, Ferring, Sussex BN12 5NR. *T:* (01903) 244704.

BURTON, Tim; film director and producer; *b* Burbank, Calif, 25 Aug. 1958; *s* of late Bill Burton and of Jean Burton; *m* 1989, Lena Gieseke. *Educ:* Calif Inst. of the Arts. Formerly apprentice animator, Walt Disney Studios (projects incl. The Fox and the Hound, 1981; The Black Cauldron, 1985). Animator and dir, Vincent (short film), 1982; *films include: director:* Hansel and Gretel (TV), 1982; Aladdin (TV), 1984; Frankenweenie (short), 1984; Pee-wee's Big Adventure, 1985; Beetlejuice, 1988; Batman, 1989; Sleepy Hollow, 2000; Planet of the Apes, 2001; *director and producer:* Edward Scissorhands, 1991; Batman Returns, 1992; Ed Wood, 1994; Mars Attacks!, 1997; *producer:* The Nightmare Before Christmas, 1993; Cabin Boy, 1994; Batman Forever, 1996; James and the Giant Peach, 1996. *Publications:* My Art and Films, 1993; The Melancholy Death of Oyster Boy and Other Stories, 1997. *Address:* Chapman, Bird & Grey, Suite 200, 1990 South Bundy Drive, Los Angeles, CA 90025, USA.

BURTON, Victoria Geraldine, (Mrs A. M. Burton); *see* Bruce, V. G.

BURTON-CHADWICK, Sir Joshua (Kenneth), 3rd Bt *cr* 1935, of Bidston; Trainer, The International Academy of Human Relations; *b* 1 Feb. 1954; *s* of Sir Robert Burton-Chadwick, (Sir Peter), 2nd Bt, and of Beryl Joan, *d* of Stanley Frederick J. Brailsford; *S* father, 1983. *Heir:* none.

BURTON-PAGE, Piers John; Executive Producer, BBC Radio 3, since 1998; *b* 25 July 1947; *s* of John Garrard Burton-Page and Audrey Ruth Burton-Page (*née* Marley); *m* 1976, Patricia Margaret Cornish; two *s. Educ:* Harrow Sch.; Wadham Coll., Oxford (MA); Univ. of Sussex (MA in Russian Studies). Joined BBC, 1971: studio manager, 1971–75; announcer and newsreader, Radio 4, 1975–77; Producer, Gramophone Dept, 1977–83; External Services Music Organiser, 1983–85; Radio 3: Presentation Editor, 1985–90; presenter/producer, 1990–97. Acting Editor, Opera, 1997. (Jtly) Ohio State Award, for series The Elements of Music, 1984. *Publication:* Philharmonic Concerto: the life and music of Sir Malcolm Arnold, 1994. *Recreations:* cricket, theatre, travel, languages, the open air. *Address:* c/o BBC, Broadcasting House, W1A 1AA. *T:* (020) 7580 4468. *Club:* Bushmen.

BURY, (Anne) Carolyn; *see* Hayman, A. C.

BURY, Lindsay Claude Neils; Chairman, South Staffordshire Group (formerly South Staffordshire Waterworks Co.), since 1992 (Director, since 1981); *b* 13 Feb. 1939; *s* of Frank James Lindsay Bury and Diana Mary Lewis; *m* 1968, Sarah Ann Ingall; one *s* one *d. Educ:* Eton; Trinity College, Cambridge (BA History). J. Henry Schroder Wagg, 1960–66; Singer & Friedlander, 1966–73; Dunbar & Co., 1973–83. Director: ACT (formerly Apricot Computers), 1968–95 (Chm., 1972–89); Portals Holdings, 1973–95; Christie Group, 1989–94; Roxboro Gp, 1993–; Sage Gp, 1995–; Chairman: Unicorn Internat., 1995–97; Henderson Electric & Gen. Investment Trust, 2001– (Dir, 1995–). Trustee, City of Birmingham Touring Opera, 1989–92. Chm. of Govs, Moor Park Sch., 1982–90; Trustee, Millichope Foundn, 1984–; Chm., Fauna and Flora Internat., 1994–. High Sheriff, Shropshire, 1998. *Recreations:* music, country pursuits. *Address:* Millichope Park, Munslow, Craven Arms, Shropshire SY7 9HA. *T:* (01584) 841234; Ruantallain Lodge, Island of Jura, Scotland. *Clubs:* Turf, Pratt's, MCC.

BURY, Michael Oswell, OBE 1968; Consultant, Education and Training, Confederation of British Industry, 1986–87; *b* 20 Dec. 1922; *o s* of Lt-Col Thomas Oswell Bury, TD, and Constance Evelyn Bury; *m* 1954, Jean Threlkeld Wood, *d* of late William Threlkeld Wood; two *s* one *d. Educ:* Charterhouse; London Sch. of Economics. Served War of 1939–45: The Rifle Brigade (ranks of Rifleman to Captain), 1941–47. Steel Company of Wales, 1947–49; British Iron and Steel Fedn, 1949–64 (Dep. Dir, Labour and Trng, 1962–64); Dir, Iron and Steel Industry Trng Bd, 1964–70; Confederation of British Industry: Director, Educn, Trng and Technol., 1970–81; Dir, Corporate Affairs, 1981–84; Dir, Educn, Trng and Technol., 1985–86. Mem., Manpower Services Commn, 1974–81, 1985–87. *Recreations:* gardening, fishing, travel. *Club:* Reform.

BURY, Very Rev. Nicholas Ayles Stillingfleet; Dean of Gloucester, since 1997; *b* 8 Jan. 1943; *s* of Major John J. S. Bury, MC, RA and Joan A. M. Bury; *m* 1973, Jennifer Anne Newbold; two *s* one *d. Educ:* King's Sch., Canterbury; Queens' Coll., Cambridge (MA 1969); MA Oxon 1971; DipEd Oxon; Cuddesdon Theol Coll. Ordained deacon, 1968, priest, 1969; Asst Curate, Our Lady & St Nicholas, Liverpool, 1968–71; Chaplain, Christ Church, Oxford, 1971–75; Vicar: St Mary's, Shephall, Stevenage, Herts, 1975–84; St Peter in Thanet, Broadstairs, 1984–97. *Recreations:* golf, water-colour painting. *Address:* The Deanery, Miller's Green, Gloucester GL1 2BP. *T:* (01452) 524167.

BURY, Air Cdre Thomas Malcolm Grahame, CB 1972; OBE 1962; retired as Head of Technical Training and Maintenance, British Aircraft Corporation, Saudi Arabia; *b* 11 Sept. 1918; *s* of late Ernest Bury, OBE; *m* 1951, Dillys Elaine Jenkins, MBE, *d* of Dr Aneurin Jenkins, Swansea; two *s* one *d. Educ:* Forest Sch., E17. Served War, 1939–45, NW Europe, Arabia. Joined RAF, 1935; STSO, HQ, 1 Gp, 1961–64; DDME, MoD, 1965–66; Senior Engr Officer, Air Forces Gulf, 1967–68; Command Mech. Engr, HQ Strike Command, 1968–73; retired 1973. *Address:* 45 Abbey Mill, Church Street, Bradford on Avon, Wilts BA15 1AB.

BUSCH, Constantinus Albertus Maria; Member Supervisory Board: Roto Smeets De Boer NV, since 1993; Parcom Ventures BV, since 1995; *b* 17 Aug. 1937; *m* 1963, Ingrid (*née* Haaksma); two *s* two *d. Educ:* in The Netherlands; Amsterdam Univ. (Economics degree). 1st Lieut, Dutch Army, 1962–64; Corporate Finance Dept, NV Philips Eindhoven, 1964–66; Manager, Philips Internat. Finance, Luxembourg, 1966–70; Naarden International NV: Treasurer, 1970–72; Dir of Finance and Mem. Bd of Management, 1973–80; Financial Dir, Philips Electronics UK, 1981–85; Corporate Finance Dir, NV Philips Eindhoven, 1985–87; UK Vice-Chm. and Financial Dir, Philips Electronics, 1988; Chm. and Man. Dir, Philips Electronics and Associated Industries, 1989–90; Corporate Finance Dir, Philips Internat. BV, 1991–92; Mem. Bd of Dirs, Verenigde Nederlandse Uitgeversbedryven BV, 1993–97. Chm., Supervisory Bd, Airspray Internat. NV, 1998–; Advr, Holland Corporate Finance, 1997–. *Recreations:* music, particularly piano, clarinet and saxophone; tennis, golf, ski-ing. *Address:* Dirck van Homelaan 23, Waalre 5581 CZ, Netherlands.

BUSCH, Rolf Trygve; Comdr, Order of St Olav; Hon. GCVO 1988; Norwegian Ambassador to the Court of St James's, 1982–88; *b* 15 Nov. 1920; *s* of Aksel Busch and Alette (*née* Tunby); *m* 1950, Solveig Helle; one *s. Educ:* Oslo Univ. (degree in Law); National Defence Coll. Dep. Judge, 1946–47; entered Norwegian Foreign Service, 1947; Min. of For. Affairs, 1947–50; Sec., Cairo, 1950–52; Vice-Consul, New York, 1952–54; Min. of For. Affairs, 1954–56; National Def. Coll., 1956–57; First Sec., Norwegian Delegn to NATO, Paris, 1957–60; Min. of For. Affairs, 1960–65; Counsellor and Dep. Perm. Rep., Norwegian Delegn to NATO, Paris and Brussels, 1965–70; Dir-Gen., Min. of For. Affairs, 1970–71; Perm. Rep. to N Atlantic Council, 1971–77; Ambassador to Fed. Republic of Germany, 1977–82. Officer, Order of the Nile, Egypt; Comdr with Star, Order of the Falcon, Iceland; Grand Cross, Order of Merit, Fed. Republic of Germany. *Address:* 2 Hafrsfjords Gt, 0273 Oslo 2, Norway. *T:* 22431791.

BUSCOMBE, family name of **Baroness Buscombe**.

BUSCOMBE, Baroness *cr* 1998 (Life Peer), of Goring in the co. of Oxfordshire; **Peta Jane Buscombe;** *b* 12 March 1954; *m* 1980, Philip John Buscombe; twin *s* one *d. Educ:* Hinchley Wood Sch.; Rosebery Grammar Sch., Epsom; Inns of Ct Sch. of Law. Called to the Bar, Inner Temple, 1977. Legal Advr, Dairy Trade Fedn, 1979–80; lawyer, Barclays Bank International, NY, then Hd Office Lawyer and Inspector, Barclays Bank plc, UK, 1980–84; Asst Sec., Inst. of Practitioners in Advertising, 1984–87. Mem. (C) S Oxfordshire DC, 1995–99. Opposition front bench spokesman, H of L, on trade and industry, social security and legal affairs, 1999–2001, on Cabinet Office affairs, 2000, on home and legal affairs, 2001–. Vice Chm., All Party Gp for Mgt Consultants, 2001–; Mem., All Party Gp for Corporate Social Responsibility, 2001–. Vice Chm. resp. for Develt, Cons. Party, 1997–99; Founder, Cons. Network and Cons. Cultural Unit; Vice Chm., S Oxfordshire Cons. Assoc., 1995–98; Pres., Slough Cons. Assoc., 1997–. Contested (C) Slough, 1997. Chm., Goring and Streatley Amenity Assoc., 1995–98; Mem., Assoc. of Rural Businesses in Oxfordshire. Patron: Foundn for Internat. Commercial Arbitration and Alternative Dispute Resolution, 1999–; Inns of Ct Sch. of Law Cons. Assoc.; Vice Patron, Abbeyfield House Appeal; Ambassador, Guide Assoc. Vice Pres., Henley Soc.; Mem., Chiltern Soc. *Recreations:* theatre, opera, boating, swimming. *Address:* House of Lords, SW1A 0PW. *Club:* Rock Sailing (N Cornwall).

BUSH, Bryan; His Honour Judge Bush; a Circuit Judge, since 1983; *b* 28 Nov. 1936; *s* of Maurice and Hetty Bush; *m* 1963, Jacqueline (*née* Rayman); two *s* one *d. Educ:* Leeds Grammar Sch.; Keble Coll., Oxford (MA). Called to the Bar, Gray's Inn, 1961; practising on NE Circuit, 1961–83; a Recorder of the Crown Court, 1978–83. *Recreations:* theatre, lawn tennis. *Address:* c/o Leeds Crown Court, Leeds LS1 3BE.

BUSH, Charles Martin Peter, MA; Headmaster, Eastbourne College, since 1993; *b* 28 June 1952; *s* of late Dr John Peter Bush and of Edith Mary (*née* Farnsworth); *m* 1977, Rosalind Mary Nevin; three *s. Educ:* Melbourne C of E Grammar Sch.; Univ. of Melbourne; Trinity Coll., Oxford (MA). Aylesbury Grammar Sch., 1975–78, Hd of Pure Maths, 1977–78; Hd of Maths, Abingdon Sch., 1978–82; Marlborough College, 1982–93: Hd of Maths, 1982–89; Housemaster, B1 House, 1988–93. *Publication:* (co-author in SMP Team) Revised Advanced Mathematics (Book 1), 1988. *Recreations:* golf, cricket, mathematics, fell walking. *Address:* The Headmaster's House, Old Wish Road, Eastbourne, E Sussex BN21 4JX. *T:* (01323) 737655. *Clubs:* MCC; Melbourne Cricket.

BUSH, Geoffrey Hubert, CB 1998; Deputy Chairman, Board of Inland Revenue, 1998–99, retired; *b* 5 April 1942; *s* of late Sidney Arthur Bush and Dorothy Elizabeth Bush; *m* 1965, Sylvia Mary Squibb; one *s* one *d. Educ:* Cotham Grammar Sch., Bristol. Tax Officer, 1959; Inspector of Taxes, 1968; Dist Inspector of Taxes, 1973; Principal Inspector of Taxes, 1981; Board of Inland Revenue: Under Sec., 1988–94; Dir Gen.,

1994–98. Advr, Office of Govt Commerce. Chm. Council, Order of St John, Devon, 2001–. *Recreations:* travel, golf, gardening. *Address:* (home) Lympstone, Devon. *Clubs:* Exeter Golf and Country (Devon); Knowle Lawn Tennis (Bristol).

BUSH, George Herbert Walker, Hon. GCB 1993; President of the United States of America, 1989–93; *b* Milton, Mass, 12 June 1924; *s* of late Prescott Sheldon Bush and Dorothy (*née* Walker); *m* 1945, Barbara, *d* of Marvin Pierce, NY; four *s* one *d*. *Educ:* Phillips Acad., Andover, Mass; Yale Univ. (BA Econs 1948). Served War, USNR, Lieut, pilot (DFC, three Air Medals). Co-founder and Dir, Zapata Petroleum Corp., 1953–59; Founder, Zapata Offshore Co., Houston, 1954, Pres., 1956–64, Chm. Bd, 1964–66. Chm., Republican Party, Harris Co., Texas, 1963–64; Delegate, Republican Nat. Convention, 1964, 1968; Republican cand. US Senator from Texas, 1964, 1970; Mem., 90th and 91st Congresses, 7th District of Texas, 1967–71; US Perm. Rep. to UN, 1971–73; Chm., Republican Party Nat. Cttee, 1973–74; Chief, US Liaison Office, Peking, 1974–75; Dir, US Central Intelligence Agency, 1976–77; Vice-President of the USA, 1981–89. Cand. for Republican Presidential nomination, 1980. Hon. degrees from many colleges and univs. *Publications:* (with Victor Gold) Looking Forward: an autobiography, 1988; (with Gen. Brent Scowcroft) A World Transformed, 1998; All the Best: my life in letters and other writings, 2000. *Recreations:* tennis, jogging, golf, boating, fishing. *Address:* Suite 900, 10000 Memorial Drive, Houston, TX 77024, USA.

See also G. W. Bush.

BUSH, George Walker; President of the United States of America, since 2001; *b* 6 July 1946; *e s* of George Herbert Walker Bush, *qv*; *m* 1977, Laura Welch; twin *d*. *Educ:* Phillips Acad., Andover; Yale Univ. (BA History 1968); Harvard Business Sch. (MBA 1975). F-102 Pilot, Texas Air Nat. Guard. Founded Bush Exploration, 1975; merged with Spectrum 7 Energy Corp., 1984 (Pres.), subseq. Harken Energy Corp., 1986 (Consultant); advr and speechwriter to father during Presidential campaign, 1986–88; Governor of Texas, 1995–2000. Republican. Part-owner, Texas Rangers baseball team, 1989–98. *Publication:* A Charge to Keep, 1999. *Address:* The White House, Washington, DC 20500, USA.

BUSH, Dr Harry John, CB 2000; Director (formerly Deputy Director), Head of Enterprise and Growth Unit, HM Treasury, since 1997; *b* 26 Aug. 1953; *s* of Harold Leslie Bush and Bridget Bush (*née* Gorman). *Educ:* Quintin Grammar Sch.; Quintin Kynaston Sch.; Merton Coll., Oxford (BA Mod. Hist. and Econs 1974); DPhil Oxon 1980. Nuffield College, Oxford: Student, 1974–77; Prize Res. Fellow, 1977–79; Jun. Dean, 1978–79; HM Treasury, 1979–: Private Sec. to Minister of State, 1981–82; Principal, 1982; Dep. Press Sec., 1987–89; Asst Sec., 1989; Head of Privatisation, 1993–97. Chm., OECD Privatisation Network, 1996–98. *Recreations:* political biography, travel, food, wine, moderate exercise. *Address:* HM Treasury, Parliament Street, SW1P 3AG. *T:* (020) 7270 6325.

BUSH, Janet Elizabeth; Director, New Europe, since 1999; *b* Lytham-St-Annes 2 June 1960; *d* of Arthur and Mary Bush; partner, Nick de Cent; one *d*. *Educ:* Berkhamsted Sch. for Girls; Somerville Coll., Oxford (BA Eng. Lang. and Lit.); Centre for Journalism Studies, Cardiff (Reuters schol., postgrad. degree in journalism). Frankfurt Correspondent, 1983–84, Econs writer, 1984–86, Reuters; Dep. Econs Correspondent, 1986–87, NY Correspondent, 1987–90, Financial Times; Presenter, economic documentaries, Money Prog., BBC, 1990–92; Econs Correspondent, 1992–96, Economics Editor, 1997–99, The Times. Harold Wincott Young Financial Journalist of the Year, 1987. *Publications:* (ed) Everything You Always Wanted to Know About the Euro But Were Afraid to Ask a Tory, 1999; other New Europe publications. *Recreations:* good conversation, wine, gardening, women's and development issues, campaigning and family life. *Address:* Blackacre, Colyton, Devon EX24 6SF. *T:* (01404) 871238; *e-mail:* janetbush@myisp.co.uk.

BUSH, Adm. Sir John (Fitzroy Duyland), GCB 1970 (KCB 1965 CB 1963); DSC 1941, and Bars, 1941, 1944; Vice-Admiral of the United Kingdom and Lieutenant of the Admiralty, 1979–84; *b* 1 Nov. 1914; *s* of late Fitzroy Bush, Beach, Glos; *m* 1938, Ruth Kennedy Horsey; three *s* two *d*. *Educ:* Clifton Coll. Entered Navy, 1933; served in Destroyers throughout War. Commanded HM Ships: Belvoir, 1942–44; Zephyr, 1944; Chevron, 1945–46. Comdr Dec. 1946; Plans Div., Admiralty, 1946–48; graduated Armed Forces Staff Coll., USA, 1949; Comd, HMS Cadiz, 1950–51; Capt. June 1952; Dep. Sec. Chiefs of Staff Cttee, 1953–55; Capt. (F) Sixth Frigate Sqdn, 1955–56; Cdre, RN Barracks, Chatham, 1957–59; Dir. of Plans, Admiralty, 1959–60; Rear-Adm. 1961; Flag Officer Flotillas (Mediterranean), 1961–62; Vice-Adm. 1963; Comdr, British Naval Staff and Naval Attaché, Washington, 1963–65; Vice-Chief of the Naval Staff, Ministry of Defence, 1965–67; C-in-C Western Fleet, C-in-C Eastern Atlantic, and C-in-C Channel (NATO), 1967–70; Admiral 1968; retd, 1970. Rear-Admiral of the UK, 1976–79. Dir, Gordon A. Friesen International Inc., Washington, DC, 1970–73. Adm., Texas (USA) Navy. Governor, Clifton Coll., 1973– (Chm. Council, 1978–81; Pres., 1982–87). Pres., Old Cliftonians Soc., 1967–69; Vice-Pres., Eighth Army Veterans Assoc., 1984–. Mem., E Hants District Council, 1974–76. *Recreations:* wood turning, gardening.

BUSH, Maj.-Gen. Peter John, OBE 1968; Controller, Army Benevolent Fund, 1980–87; *b* 31 May 1924; *s* of Clement Charles Victor Bush and Kathleen Mabel Peirce; *m* 1948, Jean Mary Hamilton; two *s* one *d*. *Educ:* Maidenhead County Sch. Commnd Somerset LI, 1944; comd LI Volunteers, 1966; GSO 1 HQ 14 Div./Malaya Dist, 1968; Comdr 3 Inf. Bde, 1971 (mentioned in despatches, 1973); Asst Comdt RMA Sandhurst, 1974; Chief of Staff and Head of UK Delegn to Live Oak, SHAPE, 1977–79, retd. Col, The Light Infantry, 1977–82. *Recreations:* natural history, walking, reading. *Address:* c/o Barclays Bank, High Street, Maidenhead, Berks SL6 1PX.

BUSH, Prof. Ronald Lee, PhD; Drue Heinz Professor of American Literature and Fellow of St John's College, Univeristy of Oxford, since 1997; *b* 16 June 1946; *s* of Raymond J. Bush and Esther Schneyer Bush; *m* 1969, Marilyn Wolin; one *s*. *Educ:* Univ. of Pennsylvania (BA 1968); Pembroke Coll., Cambridge (BA 1970); Princeton Univ. (PhD 1974). Asst Prof., later Associate Prof. of English, Harvard Univ., 1974–82; Associate Prof., later Prof. of Literature, CIT, 1982–97. NEH Fellow, 1977–78, 1992–93; Vis. Fellow, Exeter Coll., Oxford, 1994–95. *Publications:* The Genesis of Ezra Pound's Cantos, 1976; T. S. Eliot: a study of character and style, 1984; (ed) T. S. Eliot: the modernist in history, 1991; (ed) Prehistories of the Future, 1995. *Recreation:* tennis. *Address:* St John's College, Oxford OX1 3JP. *T:* (01865) 277300.

BUSHBY, Frederick Henry; Director of Services, Meteorological Office, 1978–84; *b* 10 Jan. 1924; *s* of Mr and Mrs Frederick George Bushby; *m* 1945, Joan Janet Gates (*d* 1996); one *s*; *m* 2000, Margaret Joan (*née* Atkins). *Educ:* Portsmouth Southern Secondary Sch.; Imperial Coll. of Science and Technol. (BSc 1st Cl. Hons Special Maths). ARCS. Meteorol Br., RAF, 1944–48; Meteorol Office, 1948–84; Asst Dir (Forecasting Res.), 1965–74; Dep. Dir (Dynamical Res.), 1974–77, (Forecasting), 1977–78. *Recreations:* bridge, bowls. *Address:* 25 Holmes Crescent, Wokingham, Berks RG41 2SE. *T:* (0118) 978 4930.

BUSHE, Frederick Joseph William, OBE 1994; RSA 1986 (ARSA 1977); Founder, 1979, and Director, 1979–96, Scottish Sculpture Workshop; *b* 1 March 1939; *s* of Frederick M. C. Bushe and Kathleen Welch; *m* 1st, 1956, Rosemary R. Beattie; three *s* one *d*; 2nd, 1984, Fiona M. S. Marr; one *d*. *Educ:* Out Lady's High Sch., Motherwell; Glasgow Sch. of Art (DA). Temp. Captain RAEC, 1954–58. Art teacher, Midlothian, 1958–60, Berwickshire, 1960–62; Lectr in Art Educn, Notre Dame, Liverpool, 1962–69, Aberdeen Coll. of Educn, 1969–79. Curator, Scandex, 15th anniv. touring exhibn of Scottish sculpture, 1994–95. Governor, Edinburgh Coll. of Art, 1983–88. Invited Artist: Formaviva Internat. Symposium of Sculptors, Yugoslavia, 1988; Terra Internat. Symposium, Kikinda, Yugoslavia, 1990. Work in numerous public collections; one man exhibitions: Edinburgh, 1962, 1971, 1982; Liverpool, 1966; Glasgow, 1974; Manchester, 1975; Stirling, 1978; group exhibns. *Recreations:* listening to music, cooking. *Address:* Rose Cottage, Lumsden, Huntly, Aberdeenshire AB54 4JJ. *T:* (01464) 861394.

BUSHILL-MATTHEWS, Philip Rodway; Member (C) West Midlands, European Parliament, since 1999; *b* 15 Jan. 1943; *s* of William Bushill-Matthews, MBE and Phyllis Bushill-Matthews, OBE; *m* 1967, Angela Loveday Bingham; one *s* two *d*. *Educ:* Malvern Coll.; University Coll., Oxford (MA); Harvard Business Sch. (AMP 1987). Joined Birds Eye Foods Ltd, 1965; seconded to Thomas Lipton Inc., USA, 1976; Nat. Accounts Dir, Birds Eye Sales Ltd, 1977–80; Man. Dir, Iglo industries de gelados, Lisbon, 1980–81; Sales Dir, then Sales and Distribution Dir, Birds Eye Wall's Ltd, 1981–88; Managing Director: Craigmillar Ltd, 1988–91 (also Dir, Van den Bergh & Jurgens Ltd); Red Mill Snack Foods Ltd, 1991–99; Red Mill Co., BV, Netherlands, 1993–99. FInstD 1994. *Recreations:* bridge, the theatre, enjoying the countryside. *Address:* The Manor House, Harbury, Leamington Spa, Warwicks CV33 9HX. *T:* (01926) 612476; *e-mail:* bushillm@aol.com. *Club:* Harbury Working Men's.

BUSHNELL, Alexander Lynn, CBE 1962; County Clerk and Treasurer, Perth County Council, 1946–75, retired; *b* 13 Aug. 1911; *s* of William and Margaret Bushnell; *m* 1939, Janet Braithwaite Porteous; two *d*. *Educ:* Dalziel High Sch., Motherwell; Glasgow University. *Recreation:* golf. *Address:* 18 Fairies Road, Perth PH1 1NB. *T:* (01738) 622675.

BUSK, Maj.-Gen. Leslie Francis Harry, CB 1990; Director General, British Heart Foundation, since 1990; *b* 12 Sept. 1937; *s* of late Lt-Col Charles William Francis Busk and Alice (*née* van Bergen); *m* 1st, 1960, Jennifer Helen Ring (*d* 1992); three *s*; 2nd, 1993, Glennis McElwain. *Educ:* Wellington Coll.; RMA, Sandhurst; RMCS, Shrivenham (BSc (Eng) London Univ.). Commnd RE, 1957; served in UK, NI, BAOR, India and Singapore; Defence Services Staff Coll., India, 1969; OC 25 Field Sqn, 1971–73; Instr, Staff Coll., Camberley, 1975–77; CO 35 Engr Regt, 1977–79; C of S 2nd Armoured Div., 1979–81; Bde Comd 11 Engr Bde, 1981–83; RCDS, 1984; DMO, MoD, 1985–86; Army Pilots Course, 1986–87; Dir, AAC, 1987–89, retd. Hon. Col, RE Volunteers (Sponsored Units), 1986–91; Col Comdt, RE, 1990–95. Chairman: AMRC, 1991–95, 1999–; Eur. Heart Network, 1998–. *Recreations:* golf, tennis. *Address:* British Heart Foundation, 14 Fitzhardinge Street, W1H 4DH. *Club:* Naval and Military.

BUSQUIN, Philippe; Member, European Commission, since 1999; *b* 6 Jan. 1941; *m*. *Educ:* Univ. Libre de Bruxelles (Licence in Phys. Scis 1962; Cand. in Philosophy 1971; post-grad. in Envmt 1976). Asst in Physics, Faculty of Medicine, Univ. Libre de Bruxelles, 1962–77; Prof., Teachers' Coll., Nivelles, 1962–77; Pres., Bd of Dirs, IRE, 1978–80. Deputy: Province of Hainaut, 1977–78; Chamber of Reps, Belgium, 1978–95; Senator, Belgium, 1995–99; Minister of Educn, 1980; Minister for the Interior, 1981; Walloon Minister for Budget and for Energy, 1982–85; Walloon Minister for Economy, 1988; Minister of Social Affairs, 1988–92; Minister of State, 1992–. Mayor of Seneffe, 1995–99. Mem., Community Exec., 1980–81. Pres., Socialist Party, Belgium, 1992–; Vice-President: Internat. Socialists, 1992–; European Socialist Party, 1995–97. *Address:* European Commission, 200 rue de la Loi, 1049 Brussels, Belgium.

BUSS, Barbara Ann, (Mrs Lewis Boxall); freelance journalist, since 1976; Editor-in-Chief, Woman magazine, 1974–75; Consultant, IPC Magazines Ltd, 1975–76; *b* 14 Aug. 1932; *d* of late Cecil Edward Buss and Victoria Lilian (*née* Vickers); *m* 1966, Lewis Albert Boxall (*d* 1983); no *c*. *Educ:* Lady Margaret Sch., London. Sec., Conservative Central Office, 1949–52; Sec./journalist, Good Taste magazine, 1952–56; Journalist: Woman and Beauty, 1956–57; Woman, 1957–59; Asst Editor, Woman's Illustrated, 1959–60; Editor, Woman's Illustrated, 1960–61; Journalist, Daily Herald, 1961; Associate Editor, Woman's Realm, 1961–62; Editor: Woman's Realm, 1962–64; Woman, 1964–74. *Recreations:* reading, theatre, cinema. *Address:* 1 Arlington Avenue, N1 7BE. *T:* (020) 7226 3265.

BUSSELL, Darcey Andrea, OBE 1995; Principal Ballerina, Royal Ballet, since 1989; *b* 27 April 1969; *d* of Philip Michael Bussell and Andrea Pemberton (*née* Williams); *m* 1997, Angus Forbes; one *d*. *Educ:* Arts Educnl Sch.; Royal Ballet Sch. Joined Sadler's Wells Royal Ballet (later Birmingham Royal Ballet), 1987; joined Royal Ballet, 1988: soloist, 1988; first soloist, 1989. *Leading rôles in:* Giselle; Swan Lake; Sleeping Beauty; La Bayadère (also with Kirov and Australian Ballet, 1998); Laurentia pas de six; Song of the Earth; Requiem; Galanteries; Spirit of Fugue; Pursuit; first Royal Ballet perf. of Ballanchine's Rubies; Cinderella; Enigma Variations; Nutcracker; McMillan's Elite Syncopations; Raymonda; Monotones; Symphony in C; first Royal Ballet perf. of Ballanchine's Stravinsky Violin Concerto; Agon; Bloodlines; Les Biches; Tchaikovsky pas de deux; first perf. of William Forsythe's In the middle somewhat elevated; Romeo and Juliet; *rôles created:* Princess Rose in Prince of the Pagodas, Royal Opera House, 1989; pas de deux (Farewell to Dreams) for HM Queen Mother's 90th Birthday Tribute, Palladium and Royal Opera House, 1990. Prix de Lausanne, 1986; Variety Club of GB Award for most promising newcomer, 1990; Dancer of Year Award, Dance and Dancers Mag., 1990; Evening Standard Award for dance, 1990. *Publication:* (with Judith Mackrell) Life in Dance (autobiog.), 1998. *Recreations:* art and painting, reading, swimming. *Address:* The Royal Opera House, Covent Garden, WC2E 9DD.

BUSVINE, Prof. James Ronald; Professor of Entomology as applied to Hygiene in the University of London, 1964–76, Emeritus Professor 1977; *b* 15 April 1912; *s* of William Robert and Pleasance Dorothy Busvine; *m* 1960, Joan Arnfield; one *s* one *d*. *Educ:* Eastbourne Coll.; Imperial Coll. of Science and Technology, London Univ. BSc Special (1st Class Hons) 1933; PhD 1938; DSc 1948, London. Imperial Chemical Industries, 1936–39; MRC Grants, 1940–42; Entomological Adviser, Min. of Health, 1943–45; London Sch. of Hygiene and Tropical Medicine: Lecturer 1946; Reader 1954; Professor 1964. Member: WHO Panel of Experts on Insecticides, 1956– (Cttee Chm. 1959 and 1968); FAO Panel of Experts on Pest Resistance, 1967– (Cttee Rapporteur). Has travelled professionally in Malaya, Ceylon, Africa, USA, India, etc. *Publications:* Insects and Hygiene, 1951 (3rd edn 1980); A Critical Review of the Techniques for Testing Insecticides, 1957, 2nd edn 1971; Anthropod Vectors of Disease, 1975; Insects, Hygiene and History, 1976; I warmed both Hands, 1986; Discovery of Disease Transmission by Arthropods and 90 Years of Attempts to stop it, 1993; numerous scientific articles. *Recreations:* painting, bridge. *Address:* Musca, 26 Braywick Road, Maidenhead, Berks SL6 1DA. *T:* (01628) 622888.

BUTCHER, Anthony John; QC 1977; a Recorder, 1985–97; *b* 6 April 1934; *s* of late F. W. Butcher and O. M. Butcher (*née* Ansell); *m* 1959, Maureen Workman (*d* 1982); one *s* two *d.* *Educ:* Cranleigh Sch.; Sidney Sussex Coll., Cambridge (MA, LLB). Called to the Bar, Gray's Inn, 1957, Bencher, 1986; in practice at English Bar, 1957–97. Mem., Bar Council, 1989–91, and 1993–97; Chm., Official Referees Bar Assoc., 1986–92. *Recreations:* enjoying the arts and acquiring useless information. *Address:* Anthony Cottage, Polecat Valley, Hindhead, Surrey GU26 6BE. *T:* (01428) 609053; 1 Atkin Building, Gray's Inn, WC1R 5BQ. *T:* (020) 7404 0102. *Clubs:* Garrick, Beefsteak.
See also C. J. Butcher.

BUTCHER, Christopher John; QC 2001; *b* 14 Aug. 1962; *o s* of Anthony John Butcher, *qv*; *m* 1992, Fiona, *y d* of Prof. Maxwell Gaskin, *qv*; one *s* one *d.* *Educ:* Charterhouse (Sen. Schol.); Magdalen Coll., Oxford (Demy; Gibbs Prize in Mod. Hist. 1982; BA 1st Cl. Hons Mod. Hist; MA); City Univ. (Dip. Law); King's Coll., London (Dip. EC Law). Fellow, All Souls Coll., Oxford, 1983-98 (Jun. Dean, 1988-90 and 1992-98); Eldon Law Schol., Univ. of Oxford, 1987; called to the Bar, Gray's Inn, 1986 (Bacon Schol., Atkin Schol.). *Publications:* contrib. to various legal pubns. *Recreations:* history, literature, travel, the arts. *Address:* 7 King's Bench Walk, Temple, EC4Y 7DS. *T:* (020) 7583 0404.

BUTCHER, John Patrick; Director: Pertemps Group, since 1997; Phoenix Telecom, since 1999; Partner, J. & A. Butcher Associates, since 1996. *Educ:* Huntingdon Grammar Sch.; Birmingham Univ. (BSocSc). Marketing exec. and Product Manager, computer industry, 1968–79. Mem., Birmingham City Council, 1972–78 (Vice-Chm., Educn Cttee). Vis. Lectr, Manufg Gp, Warwick Univ., 1996–. Chairman: Texas Instruments Ltd, 1990–98; Media Square, 2000–; Fullard Pertemps, 2000–; non-exec. Dir, Finelist Group plc, 1999–. MP (C) Coventry SW, 1979–97; Parly Under Sec. of State, DoI, 1982–83, DTI, 1983–88, DES, 1988–89. Co-Chm., All-Party Manufacturing Industry Gp. Chm., Inst. of Dirs, 1997–2001. CompIEE. Bicentenary Medal, RSA, 1986. *Recreations:* the Lake District, fell-walking, pre-Conquest history, remote places, occasional journalism.

BUTCHER, Richard James; Under Secretary (Legal), Department of Health and Social Security, 1983–87, retired; *b* 5 Dec. 1926; *s* of late James Butcher, MBE and Kathleen Butcher; *m* 1954, Sheila Joan Windridge; one *s* two *d.* *Educ:* City of London Sch.; Peterhouse, Cambridge (BA 1948, MA 1961). Called to the Bar, Lincoln's Inn, 1950. Served Educn Br., RAF, 1948–50 (Flying Officer). Entered Legal Civil Service as Legal Asst, 1951; Sen. Legal Asst, 1960; Asst Solicitor, 1971. *Recreation:* gardening. *Address:* The Knoll, Park View Road, Woldingham, Surrey CR3 7DN. *T:* (01883) 652275.

BUTCHER, Willard Carlisle; Chairman, and Chief Executive Officer, Chase Manhattan Bank (formerly Chase National Bank), New York City, 1981–90, retired; *b* Bronxville, NY, 25 Oct. 1926; *s* of Willard F. Butcher and Helen Calhoun; *m* 1st, 1949, Sarah C. Payne (*d* 1955); two *d*; 2nd, 1956, Elizabeth Allen (*d* 1978); one *s* one *d*; 3rd, 1979, Carole E. McMahon; one *s.* *Educ:* Scarsdale High School, New York; Middlebury Coll., Vermont; Brown Univ., Rhode Island (BA; Fellow, 1981, now Emeritus). Served with USNR, 1944–45. Joined Chase National Bank, 1947; Asst Vice-Pres., 1956; Vice-Pres., 1958; Sen. Vice-Pres., 1961; assigned Internat. Dept, 1968; Exec. Vice-Pres. in charge of Dept, 1969; Vice-Chm. 1972; Pres. 1972–81; Chief Exec. Officer, 1979. Trustee, Amer. Enterprise Inst. (Chm., 1986–90). Director: Texaco Inc., 1981–; Asarco Inc., 1974–. Hon. LLD: Brown Univ.; Pepperdine Univ.; Tulane Univ.; Hon. HLD Pace Univ. *Address:* 101 Park Avenue, Suite 2700, New York, NY 10178, USA.

BUTE, 7th Marquess of, *cr* 1796; **John Colum Crichton-Stuart, (Johnny Bute);** Viscount Ayr, 1622; Bt (NS), 1627; Earl of Dumfries, Lord Crichton of Sanquhar and Cumnock, 1633; Earl of Bute, Viscount Kingarth, Lord Mountstuart, Cumrae and Inchmarnock, 1703; Baron Mountstuart, 1761, Baron Cardiff, 1776; Earl of Windsor, Viscount Mountjoy, 1796; Hereditary Sheriff of Bute; Hereditary Keeper of Rothesay Castle; *b* 26 April 1958; *s* of 6th Marquess of Bute, KBE and of his 1st wife, Nicola (*née* Weld-Forester); *S* father, 1993; *m* 1st, 1984, Carolyn E. R. M. (marr. diss. 1993), *d* of late Bryson Waddell; one *s* two *d*; 2nd, 1999, Serena Solitaire Wendell; one *d.* British Formula Three Champion, 1984; European Formula Three Championship runner-up, 1984; Formula One Ferrari test driver, 1985; JPS Lotus Grand Prix Driver, 1986; Works Driver for World Champion Sports Prototype Team Silk Cut Jaguar, 1988 (Jt Winner, 24 hr Le Mans sports car race, 1988); Lead Driver for Toyota GB, World Sports Prototype Championship, 1989, 1990. *Heir: s* Lord Mountstuart, *qv.*

BUTHELEZI, Mangosuthu Gatsha; Minister of Home Affairs, Republic of South Africa, since 1994; President, Inkatha Freedom Party; *b* 27 Aug. 1928; *s* of Chief Mathole Buthelezi and Princess Magogo; *m* 1952, Irene Audrey Thandekile Mzila; three *s* four *d.* *Educ:* Fort Hare Univ. (BA). Chief of Buthelezi Tribe, 1953–; involved in admin of Zulu people, 1953–68; Chief Minister, KwaZulu, 1976–94. Numerous foreign awards and orders. *Publication:* South Africa: my vision of the future, 1990. *Address:* Ministry of Home Affairs, Private Bag X741, Pretoria 0001, South Africa.

BUTLER, family name of **Earl of Carrick, Viscount Mountgarret, Baron Butler of Brockwell** and **Baron Dunboyne.**

BUTLER OF BROCKWELL, Baron *cr* 1998 (Life Peer), of Herne Hill in the London Borough of Lambeth; **Frederick Edward Robin Butler,** GCB 1992 (KCB 1988); CVO 1986; Master, University College, Oxford, since 1998; Secretary of the Cabinet and Head of the Home Civil Service, 1988–98; *b* 3 Jan. 1938; *s* of late Bernard Butler and of Nora Butler; *m* 1962, Gillian Lois Galley; one *s* two *d.* *Educ:* Harrow Sch.; University Coll., Oxford (BA Lit. Hum., 1961). Joined HM Treasury, 1961; Private Sec. to Financial Sec. to Treasury, 1964–65; Sec., Budget Cttee, 1965–69; seconded to Cabinet Office as Mem., Central Policy Rev. Staff, 1971–72; Private Secretary: to Rt Hon. Edward Heath, 1972–74; to Rt Hon. Harold Wilson, 1974–75; returned to HM Treasury as Asst Sec. i/c Gen. Expenditure Intell. Div., 1975; Under Sec., Gen. Expenditure Policy Gp, 1977–80; Prin. Establishments Officer, 1980–82; Principal Private Sec. to Prime Minister, 1982–85; Second Perm. Sec., Public Expenditure, HM Treasury, 1985–87. Mem., Royal Commn on H of L reform, 1999. Governor, Harrow Sch., 1975–91 (Chm. of Govs, 1988–91); Chm. Govs, Dulwich Coll., 1997–. *Recreation:* competitive games. *Address:* University College, Oxford OX1 4BH. *Clubs:* Athenæum, Brooks's, Beefsteak, Royal Anglo-Belgian.

BUTLER, Rt Hon. Sir Adam (Courtauld), Kt 1986; PC 1984; Vice Lord-Lieutenant, Warwickshire, since 1998; Director, H. P. Bulmer Holdings plc, 1988–97; *b* 11 Oct. 1931; *s* of late Baron Butler of Saffron Walden, KG, CH, PC and late Sydney, *o c* of late Samuel Courtauld; *m* 1955, Felicity Molesworth-St Aubyn; two *s* one *d.* *Educ:* Eton; Pembroke College, Cambridge. National Service, 2nd Lieut KRRC, 1949–51. Cambridge (BA History/Economics), 1951–54. ADC to Governor-General of Canada, 1954–55; Courtaulds Ltd, 1955–73; Director: Aristoc Ltd, 1966–73; Kayser Bondor Ltd, 1971–73; Capital and Counties Property Co., 1973–79; Dep. Chm., CMW Gp, 1989–93. MP (C) Bosworth, 1970–87. PPS to: Minister of State for Foreign Affairs, 1971–72; Minister of Agriculture, Fisheries and Food, 1972–74; PPS to Leader of the Opposition, 1975–79; an Asst Govt Whip, 1974; an Opposition Whip, 1974–75; Minister of State: DoI, 1979–81; NI Office, 1981–84; Defence Procurement, 1984–85. Chm., British Hallmarking Council, 1998–. Mem. NFU. Mem. Court of Assistants, Goldsmiths' Co. 1987–. Chairman: Samuel Courtauld Trustees, 1989–; Airey Neave Trust, 1989–99. Mem. Council, RSA, 1986–90. Pres., BHS, 1990–92. DL Warwicks, 1993. *Recreations:* field sports, music, pictures. *Address:* The Old Rectory, Lighthorne, Warwick CV35 0AR. *T:* (01926) 651214.
See also Hon. Sir R. C. Butler.

BUTLER, Allan Geoffrey Roy; HM Diplomatic Service, retired; Director, Park South Ltd, since 1996; *b* 25 Aug. 1933; *s* of Frederick William Butler and Florence May Butler; *m* 1965, Pauline Rosalind Birch, SRN; three *d.* *Educ:* Chatham House School, Ramsgate. RAF, 1952–54. Colonial Office, 1954–66; served in Aden and Washington; Asst Private Sec. to Colonial Sec., 1965–66; HM Diplomatic Service, 1966; Birmingham University, 1966; Consul, Athens, 1967; First Sec., Athens, 1969, Georgetown, 1972, FCO, 1975; Head of Chancery, Dakar, 1977; Nat. Defence Coll., Latimer, 1981; Head of Parly Relations, FCO, 1981; Ambassador to Mongolian People's Republic, 1984; Dep. Perm. Rep., UK Delegn to the Council of Europe, 1987–89. Director: Strategy, subseq. Saatchi & Saatchi Govt Communications, 1989–92; Park South Management, 1991–99; Hexagon Communications, 1991–93. Chm., Anglo-Mongolian Soc., 1990–93. *Recreations:* walking, listening to music. *Address:* Cringle Cottage, Snow Street, Roydon, Diss, Norfolk IP22 5SB.

BUTLER, Anthony John; Director, Oxford University Careers Service, since 1996; Fellow, New College, Oxford, since 1996; *b* 30 Jan. 1945; *s* of Martin Edward and Freda Alice Butler; *m* 1967, Margaret Ann, *d* of George and Margaret Randon; one *s* one *d.* *Educ:* Maidstone Grammar Sch.; University Coll., Oxford (Exhibnr, Mod. Hist.; MA); Inst. of Criminology and Trinity Hall, Cambridge (Dip. Crim.); Cambridge–Columbia Fellow, Columbia Law Sch., NY. FIPD. Joined Home Office as Asst Principal, 1969; Police and Criminal Depts, 1969–72; Private Sec. to Minister of State, Home Office, 1972–74; Principal, Gen. Dept, Sex Discrimination and Race Relations Legislation Units and Broadcasting Dept, 1974–79; Private Sec. to Sec. of State for the Home Dept, 1979–80; Asst Sec., Broadcasting, Finance and Prisons Depts, 1980–88; Asst Under-Sec. of State, seconded to DoE, 1988 as Dir, Inner Cities; Principal Finance Officer, Home Office, 1990; Dir of Personnel and Finance, then of Personnel, later of Services, HM Prison Service, 1990–96. Ind. Assessor, DCMS, 2000–. Trustee, University Coll. Oxford Old Members' Trust, 1988–94 (Chm. Trustees, 1991–94). *Recreations:* music, walking, under-gardening. *Address:* Oxford University Careers Service, 56 Banbury Road, Oxford OX2 6PA.

BUTLER, Hon. Sir Arlington Griffith, KCMG 1996; Bahamas Ambassador to the United States of America; *b* 2 Jan. 1938; *s* of late James and Lovinia Butler; *m* 1965, Sheila Paulette Smith; two *s.* *Educ:* Loughborough Coll. (Dip. 1964). Teacher, 1957–67: Headmaster, Public Schs, Deep Creek, Eleuthera, West End, Grand Bahama, and Kemps Bay, Andros; Maths Master, Govt High Sch., Nassau; Dep. Head, Prince William High Sch., Nassau; Educn Trg Welfare Officer, Bahamas Electricity Corp., 1967. Formerly: Chm., Progressive Liberal Party, Bahamas; Dep. Speaker, House of Assembly; Minister for Public Safety and Immigration, 1992–94; Minister of Public Works, 1994. Vice-Pres., Olympic Bahamas Assoc.; Life Vice-Pres., Bahamas AAA. *Address:* Bahamas Embassy, 2220 Massachusetts Avenue NW, Washington, DC 20008, USA.

BUTLER, Arthur William, ERD 1964; consultant on parliamentary relations; Secretary, Parliamentary & Scientific Committee, 1979–95, Hon. Life Member 1996; *b* 20 Jan. 1929; *s* of late F. Butler and E. Butler; *m* 1958, Evelyn Mary Luetchford; one *d.* *Educ:* Wanstead High Sch.; LSE (BSc (Econ)). Universities' Prize Essayist, RAS, 1950. Nat. Service, India Cadet Co., Queen's Royal Regt, RAOC, 1946–48, 2nd Lt; Lt, AER, RAOC, 1953, Capt., 1957–64. Trainee, Kemsley Newspapers Graduate Trng Course, Middlesbrough Evening Gazette, 1951–55; Political Correspondent, News Chronicle, 1956–60; Political Ed., Reynolds News, 1960–62; Political Correspondent, Daily Express, 1963–69; Political Ed., Daily Sketch, 1969–71; Man. Dir, Partnerplan Public Affairs, 1971–74; Dir, Public Affairs Div., John Addey Associates, 1974–77; Vice-Chm., Charles Barker Watney & Powell, 1988–89 (Jt. Man. Dir, 1978–87). Dir, CSM Parly Consultants Ltd, 1995–. Secretary: Roads Campaign Council, 1974–86; All-Party Roads Study Gp, 1974–86; Founder Secretary: Parly All-Party Motor Industry Gp, 1978–90; Parly IT Cttee, 1981–84; Associate Parly Gp on Meningitis, 1999–. Consultant on Parly Relns, McAvoy Wreford Bayley, 1989–92, GCI London, 1992–93. Jt Managing Editor, Science in Parliament, 1989–98; Editor, Free Romanian (English edn), 1985–95. Freeman, City of London, 1976; Liveryman, Co. of Tobacco Pipe Makers, 1977. Governor, Shelley Sch., Kennington, 1999–. *Publications:* No Feet to Drag (with Alfred Morris, MP), 1972; (with C. Powell) The First Forty Years: a history of the Parliamentary & Scientific Committee, 1980; (with D. Smith) Lobbying in the British Parliament, 1986; articles in newspapers and various pubns. *Recreations:* travel, collecting books and militaria, gardening. *Address:* 30 Chester Way, Kennington, SE11 4UR. *T:* (020) 7587 5170. *Club:* Royal Automobile.

BUTLER, Mrs Audrey Maude Beman, MA; Headmistress, Queenswood (GSA), Hatfield, Herts, 1981–96; *b* 31 May 1936; *d* of Robert Beman Minchin and Vivien Florence Fraser Scott; *m* 1959, Anthony Michael Butler (marr. diss. 1981); two *d.* *Educ:* Queenswood, Hatfield; St Andrews Univ., Scotland (1st Cl. MA Hons, Geography and Polit. Economy; Scottish Univs Medal, RSGS, 1957–58). Asst Geography Teacher, Queenswood, 1958–59; part-time teacher, Raines Foundn Sch. for Girls, Stepney, 1959–61; Head of Geography, S Michael's, Burton Park, 1970–73, VI Form Tutor/Geography asst, 1974–78; first House Mistress of Manor House, Lancing Coll., 1978–81. Chm., Boarding Schs Assoc., 1989–91 (Hon. Life Mem., 1996); Mem. Exec. Cttee, GSA, 1987–90 (Hon. Life Mem., GSA, 1996). Governor: Duncombe Sch., 1982–97; Tockington Manor Sch., 1984–97 (Chm., 1995–97); Aldenham Sch., 1987–; Maltman's Green Sch., 1988–98; St Mary's, Ascot, 1995–; St Leonard's, Mayfield, 1999–. Trustee, Bloxham Project, 1999– (Vice-Chm., 1992–99). Dir, British Tennis Foundn, 1997–. Hon. Vice-Pres., Sussex County Ladies Golf Assoc., 1996–; Vice-Pres., Herts LTA, 1986–. FRGS. Freeman, City of London, 1997. *Recreations:* golf (Sussex County Colours, 1970), travel. *Address:* Chandlers Cottage, Lodsworth Common, Petworth, W Sussex GU28 9DT. *T:* (01798) 861750.

BUTLER, Basil Richard Ryland, CBE 1997 (OBE 1976); FREng; FIMM; Chairman, KS Biomedix plc, since 1995; Director, Murphy Oil Corp., Arkansas, since 1991; *b* 1 March 1930; *s* of Hugh Montagu Butler and Annie Isabel (*née* Wiltshire); *m* 1954, Lilian Joyce Haswell; one *s* two *d.* *Educ:* Denstone Coll., Staffs; St John's Coll., Cambridge (MA). Reservoir Engr, Trinidad Leaseholds Ltd, 1954; Petroleum Engr to Chief Petroleum Engr and Supt Prodn Planning Div., Kuwait Oil Co., 1958–68; transf. to BP, Operations Man., Colombia, 1968; Ops Man., BP Alaska Inc., Anchorage, 1970; seconded to Kuwait Oil Co. as Gen. Man. Ops, 1972; Manager: Ninian Develts, BP Petroleum Development Co. Ltd, London, 1975; Sullom Voe Terminal, Shetland Is, 1976; BP Petroleum Development Ltd: Gen. Man., Exploration and Prodn, Aberdeen, 1978; Chief Exec., London, 1980;

Dir, BP Internat. Ltd; Chm., BP Exploration Co. Ltd, 1986–89 (Man. Dir and Chief Exec., 1986); Man. Dir, British Petroleum Co. plc, 1986–91; Dir, BP Solar Internat., 1991–98 (Chm., 1991–95). Chairman: Devonport Management, 1992–94; Brown and Root Ltd, 1993–98 (Dir, 1991–98). Chm., Europ. Council of Applied Scis and Engrg, 1992–97. Mem., Cttee for ME Trade, 1985–93. Pres., Inst. of Petroleum, 1990–92; Mem. Council, Royal Acad. of Engrg, 1994– (Hon. Sec. for Internat. Affairs, 1995–98; Sen. Vice Pres., 1996–99). FInstPet 1965; Hon. FIChemE 1991. Liveryman, Shipwrights' Co., 1988. *Recreations:* sailing, music. *Address:* KS Biomedix plc, Miller House, Bedford Road, Guildford GU1 4SJ.

BUTLER, Brian; Director of Communication, Home Office, since 1998; *b* 3 May 1949; *s* of Joseph and Alice Eileen Butler; *m* 1978, Margaret Ruth Anne Macdonald (marr. diss. 1990). *Educ:* Hunslet Carr Primary Sch., Leeds; Cockburn High Sch., Leeds; Univ. of Birmingham (BA). Journalist, Westminster Press, 1971–75; Central Office of Information: Information Officer, Newcastle upon Tyne, 1975–79; Sen. Information Officer, Birmingham, 1979–86; Sen. Information Officer, then Grade 7, DoH, 1986–88; Media and Govt Relns Manager, Lloyds Bank, 1988–94; Co-ordinator, Deregulation Task Forces, DTI, 1993–94; Head: of Information Services, Benefits Agency, 1994–96; of News, Home Office, 1996–98. FRSA 2000. *Publications:* (ed jtly and contrib.) Oxford Dictionary of Finance, 1993; (ed jtly and contrib.) Oxford Dictionary of Finance and Banking, 1997. *Recreations:* acting, writing, singing, directing, the USA, the works of Stephen Sondheim. *Address:* (office) 50 Queen Anne's Gate, SW1H 9AT. *T:* (020) 7273 3757. *Clubs:* Two Brydges; Meanwood Working Men's (Leeds) (Life Mem.).

BUTLER, Christine Margaret; *b* 14 Dec. 1943; *d* of late Cecil and Gertrude Smith; *m* 1964, Robert Patrick Butler; three *s*. *Educ:* Middlesex Univ. (BA Hons). MP (Lab) Castle Point, 1997–2001; contested (Lab) same seat, 2001. Mem., Envmt, Transport and Regl Affairs Select Cttee, 1997–2001. *Recreations:* walking, music, art.

BUTLER, (Christopher) David, CB 1995; Research Manager, International Commission on Holocaust Era Insurance Claims, since 1999; *b* 27 May 1942; *s* of Major B. D. Butler, MC (killed in action, 1944) and H. W. Butler (*née* Briggs); *m* 1967, Helen Christine, *d* of J. J. Cornwell and G. Cornwell (*née* Veysey); two *d*. *Educ:* Christ's Hospital; Jesus College, Oxford (BA). Joined HM Treasury, 1964; Asst Private Sec. to Chancellor of Exchequer, 1967–69; Sec., Cttee to Review Nat. Savings (Page Cttee), 1970–72; Head of public expenditure divs, HM Treasury, 1978–82; Head of corporate planning div., Central Computer and Telecoms Agency, 1982–85; HM Treasury: Under-Sec., 1985–89; Head of running costs, manpower and superannuation group, 1985–86; Principal Estabt and Finance Officer, 1987–89; Dep. Dir, 1989–91, Dir, 1991–95, Dept for Nat. Savings; Chief Exec., The Princess Royal Trust for Carers, 1996–99. Governor, Sadler's Wells Foundn, 1989–94; Dir, Sadler's Wells Trust Ltd, 1989–95. *Recreations:* ballet, opera, reading, family activities. *Club:* Civil Service (Chm., 1994–96).

BUTLER, Christopher John; Director, Butler Kelly Ltd, since 1998; *b* 12 Aug. 1950; *s* of Dr John Lynn Butler and late Eileen Patricia Butler; *m* 1989, Jacqueline Clair, *d* of Mr and Mrs R. O. F. Harper, Lymm, Cheshire; one *s*. *Educ:* Emmanuel Coll., Cambridge (MA). Market Research Consultant, 1975–77; Cons. Res. Dept, 1977–80; Political Office, 10 Downing Street, 1980–83; Special Advr, Sec. of State for Wales, 1983–85; Market Res. Consultant, 1985–86; Special Advr, Minister for the Arts, and of the Civil Service, 1986–87; Consultant in Public Policy, Public Policy Unit, 1992–95; Dir, Grandfield Public Affairs, 1995–97. MP (C) Warrington South, 1987–92; contested (C) Warrington South, 1992; contested (C) Wales, Eur. Parly elecns, 1999. Mem., Select Cttee on Employment, 1990–92. Vice Chm., All Party Leasehold Reform Gp, 1989–92; Secretary: All Party Drugs Misuse Cttee, 1989–92; All Party Penal Affairs Cttee, 1990–92. Mem., Exec. Cttee, CPA, 1991–92. *Recreations:* writing, deltiology, book collecting. *Address:* Longwall House, Seven Mile Lane, Borough Green, Kent TN15 8QY.

BUTLER, Dr Colin Gasking, OBE 1970; FRS 1970; retired as Head of Entomology Department, Rothamsted Experimental Station, Harpenden, 1972–76 (Head of Bee Department, 1943–72); *b* 26 Oct. 1913; *s* of Rev. Walter Gasking Butler and Phyllis Pearce; *m* 1937, Jean March Innes; one *s* one *d*. *Educ:* Monkton Combe Sch., Bath; Queens' Coll., Cambridge. MA 1937, PhD 1938, Cantab. Min. of Agric. and Fisheries Research Schol., Cambridge, 1935–37; Supt Cambridge Univ. Entomological Field Stn, 1937–39; Asst Entomologist, Rothamsted Exper. Stn, 1939–43. Hon. Treas., Royal Entomological Soc., 1961–69, Pres., 1971–72, Hon. FRES, 1984; Pres., Internat. Union for Study of Social Insects, 1969–73; Mem., NT Regional Cttee for Devon and Cornwall, 1982–89. FRPS 1957; FIBiol. Hon. Fellow, British Beekeepers' Assoc., 1983. Silver Medal, RSA, 1945. *Publications:* The Honeybee: an introduction to her sense physiology and behaviour, 1949; The World of the Honeybee, 1954; (with J. B. Free) Bumblebees, 1959; scientific papers. *Recreations:* nature photography, fishing. *Address:* 1 Redwood Lodge, Grange Road, Cambridge CB3 9AR. *T:* (01223) 352455.

BUTLER, David; *see* Butler, C. D.

BUTLER, David; Chairman, Butler Cox & Partners, since 1977–92; Senior Advisor, Computer Sciences Corporation, since 1994; *b* 1 Feb. 1936; *s* of James Charles Butler and Ethel Violet (*née* Newell); *m* 1st, 1956, Catherine Anita Harry (marr. diss. 1974); one *s* two *d*; 2nd, 1975, Frances Mary McMahon; one *d*. *Educ:* Mill Hill Sch.; Keble Coll., Oxford (BA Lit. Hum.). Management Trainee, Herts CC, 1960–64; Computer Manager, NW Metropolitan Hosp. Bd, 1964–65; Management Consultant, Urwick Gp, 1965–72; Dir, Diebold Europe, 1972–76; Chm., Butler Cox Foundn, 1977–92. Director: Istel, 1983–92; Octagon Services, 1986–92; JMI Advisory Services, 1986–92; Investment Advr, United Bank of Kuwait, 1985–92; Chm., The Publishing Hub Ltd, 1999–. Mem., Fraud Trials Cttee, 1984–85; Vice Pres., BCS, 1981–83; Chm., Humanitec Foundn for the disabled, 1986–92. *Publications:* The Convergence of Technologies, 1977; Britain and the Information Society, 1981; A Director's Guide to Information Technology, 1982; Trends in Information Technology, 1984; Information Technology and Realpolitik, 1986; The Men who Mastered Time (novel), 1986; Senior Management IT Education, 1987; Measuring Progress in IT, 1995; numerous press articles. *Recreations:* cricket, Rugby, ancient history. *Address:* 12 Laurel Road, SW13 0EE. *T:* (020) 8876 1810.

BUTLER, David Edgeworth, CBE 1991; FBA 1994; Fellow of Nuffield College, Oxford, since 1954; *b* 1924; *yr s* of late Professor Harold Edgeworth Butler and Margaret, *d* of Prof. A. F. Pollard; *m* 1962, Marilyn Speers Evans (*see* M. S. Butler); three *s*. *Educ:* St Paul's; New Coll., Oxford (MA, DPhil). J. E. Procter Visiting Fellow, Princeton Univ., 1947–48; Student, Nuffield Coll., 1949–51; Research Fellow, 1951–54; Dean and Senior Tutor, 1956–64. Served as Personal Assistant to HM Ambassador in Washington, 1955–56. Chm., Hansard Soc., 1993–2001. Hon. DUniv Paris, 1978; Hon. DSSc QUB, 1985; Dr *hc* Essex, 1993; Hon. Dr: Plymouth, 1994; Teesside, 1999. Co-editor, Electoral Studies, 1982–92. *Publications:* The British General Election of 1951, 1952; The Electoral System in Britain 1918–51, 1953; The British General Election of 1955, 1955; The Study of Political Behaviour, 1958; (ed) Elections Abroad, 1959; (with R. Rose) The British General Election of 1959, 1960; (with J. Freeman) British Political Facts, 1900–1960, 1963; (with A. King) The British General Election of 1964, 1965; The British General Election of 1966, 1966; (with D. Stokes) Political Change in Britain, 1969; (with M. Pinto-Duschinsky) The British General Election of 1970, 1971; The Canberra Model, 1973; (with D. Kavanagh) The British General Election of February 1974, 1974; (with D. Kavanagh) The British General Election of October 1974, 1975; (with U. Kitzinger) The 1975 Referendum, 1976; (ed) Coalitions in British Politics, 1978; (ed with A. H. Halsey) Policy and Politics, 1978; (with A. Ranney), Referendums, 1978; (with A. Sloman) British Political Facts 1900–79, 1980; (with D. Kavanagh) The British General Election of 1979, 1980; (with D. Marquand) European Elections and British Politics, 1981; (with A. Ranney) Democracy at the Polls, 1981; (with V. Bogdanor) Democracy and Elections, 1983; Governing without a Majority, 1983; (with D. Kavanagh) The British General Election of 1983, 1984; A Compendium of Indian Elections, 1984; (with P. Jowett) Party Strategies in Britain, 1985; (with G. Butler) British Political Facts 1900–85, 1986; (with D. Kavanagh) The British General Election of 1987, 1988; British Elections since 1945, 1989; (with P. Roy) India Decides, 1989, 3rd edn as India Decides 1952–1991, 1995; (with A. Low) Sovereigns and Surrogates, 1991; (with B. Cain) Congressional Redistricting, 1991; (with D. Kavanagh) The British General Election 1992, 1992; (with A. Ranney) Electioneering, 1992; Failure in British Government, 1994; (with G. Butler) British Political Facts 1900–94, 1994; (with D. Kavanagh) The British General Election of 1997, 1997; (with M. Westlake) British Politics and European Elections 1994, 1999; (jtly) Law and Politics, 1999; (with G. Butler) British Political Facts 1900–2000, 2000. *Address:* Nuffield College, Oxford OX1 1NF. *T:* (01865) 278500.

BUTLER, Denis William Langford; Comptroller and City Solicitor to the City of London, 1981–89; *b* 26 Oct. 1926; *s* of late William H. Butler, Shrewsbury and Kitty Butler; *m* 1953, Marna (*née* Taylor); three *d*. *Educ:* Repton. RM, 1945–47. Admitted Solicitor, 1951. Assistant Solicitor: Norfolk CC, 1953–54; Shropshire CC, 1954–57; Sen. Asst Solicitor, Lindsey (Lincs) CC, 1957–60; Dep. Clerk, 1960–74, County Solicitor and Clerk, 1974–81, Wilts CC. Chm., County Secs Soc., 1974–76. Freeman, City of London, 1981; Liveryman, City of London Solicitors' Co., 1983–. *Recreations:* travel, gardening. *Club:* Guildhall.

BUTLER, Eamonn Francis, PhD; Director, Adam Smith Institute, since 1978; *b* 3 Jan. 1952; *s* of Richard Henry Bland Butler and Janet Provan Butler (*née* MacDonald); *m* 1986, Christine Anna Pieroni; two *s*. *Educ:* Univ. of Aberdeen; Univ. of St Andrews (MA 1973, MA Hons 1974; PhD 1978). Research Associate, US House of Representatives, 1976–77; Asst Prof. of Philosophy, Hillsdale Coll., Michigan, 1977–78. Editor, The Broker, 1979–87. *Publications:* Hayek: his contribution to the social and economic thought of our time, 1983; Milton Friedman: a guide to his economic thought, 1985; Ludwig von Mises: fountainhead of the modern microeconomics revolution, 1989; (with R. L. Schuettinger) Forty Centuries of Wage and Price Controls, 1979; with M. Pirie: Test Your IQ, 1983; Boost Your IQ, 1990; The Sherlock Holmes IQ Book, 1995; IQ Puzzlers, 1995; contrib. articles to various newspapers and jls. *Recreations:* archaeology, antiquarian books and prints. *Address:* The Adam Smith Institute, 23 Great Smith Street, SW1P 3BL; *e-mail:* info@adamsmith.org.uk.

BUTLER, George William P.; *see* Payne-Butler.

BUTLER, His Honour Gerald Norman; QC 1975; a Circuit Judge, 1982–97; Senior Judge at Southwark Crown Court, 1984–97; *b* 15 Sept. 1930; *s* of Joshua Butler and Esther Butler (*née* Lampel); *m* 1959, Stella, *d* of Harris and Leah Isaacs; one *s* two *d*. *Educ:* Ilford County High Sch.; London Sch. of Economics; Magdalen Coll., Oxford. LLB London 1952, BCL Oxon 1954. 2nd Lieut, RASC, 1956–57. Called to Bar, Middle Temple, 1955; a Recorder of the Crown Court, 1977–82. Inquiry and Report into: English RFU, 1997; Central Casework at CPS, 1999; prosecution of R. *v* Doran and others, 2000; Treasury Counsel instructed by CPS, 2000. *Recreations:* Rugby, opera, Japanese pottery, walking. *Address:* 1 Essex Court, Temple, EC4Y 9AR. *Clubs:* Garrick, MCC.

BUTLER, Maj.-Gen. Hew Dacres George, CB 1975; DL; *b* 12 March 1922; *s* of late Maj.-Gen. S. S. Butler, CB, CMG, DSO; *m* 1954, Joanna, *d* of late G. M. Puckridge, CMG, ED; two *s* one *d*. *Educ:* Winchester. Commnd Rifle Bde, 1941; Western Desert, 1942–43; POW, 1943–45; psc 1951; BM 7th Armd Bde, 1951–53; Kenya, 1954–55; Instructor, Staff Coll., 1957–60; CO 1 RB, 1962–64; Cyprus (despatches, 1965); comd 24 Inf. Bde, Aden, 1966–67; idc 1969; ACOS G3 Northag, 1970–72; GOC Near East Land Forces, 1972–74. Chief of Staff (Contingencies Planning), SHAPE, 1975–76; retired 1977. Sec., Beit Trust, 1978–93. DL 1980, High Sheriff 1983, Hants. *Recreations:* shooting, racing, horticulture. *Address:* Bury Lodge, Hambledon, Hants PO7 4QL. *Clubs:* Army and Navy, MCC.

BUTLER, Sir James; *see* Butler, Sir P. J.

BUTLER, (James) Pearse; Chief Executive, Royal Liverpool and Broadgreen University Hospitals NHS Trust, since 1999; *b* 27 Jan. 1957; *s* of James and Nancy Butler; *m* 1979, Deborah Veronica Downing; one *s* one *d*. *Educ:* St Mary's Coll., Crosby; Keble Coll., Oxford (BA). Community Worker, Liverpool CVS, 1979–80; Hosp. Admin, S Birmingham HA, 1980–83; Dep. Adminr, then Adminr, Bolton Gen. Hosp., 1983–85; Mgt Consultant, HAY-MSL Mgt Consultants, 1985–86; Gen. Manager, Obst. and Gyn. Service, Liverpool HA, 1986–88; Dist Gen. Manager, Chester HA, 1988–89; Chief Executive: Royal Liverpool Children's NHS Trust, 1990–93; Wirral HA, 1993–97; Wigan and Leigh NHS Trust, 1997–99. *Recreations:* family, Everton FC, golf. *Address:* Royal Liverpool University Hospital, Prescot Street, Liverpool L7 8XP. *T:* (0151) 706 2259. *Clubs:* West Lancashire Golf, Campion Lawn Tennis.

BUTLER, James Walter, RA 1972 (ARA 1964); RWA; FRBS; *b* 25 July 1931; *m* (marr. diss.); one *d*; *m* 1975, Angela, *d* of Col Roger Berry, Johannesburg, South Africa; four *d*. *Educ:* Maidstone Grammar Sch.; Maidstone Coll. of Art; St Martin's Art Sch.; Royal Coll. of Art. National Diploma in Sculpture, 1950. Worked as Architectural Carver, 1950–53, 1955–60. Tutor, Sculpture and Drawing, City and Guilds of London Art School, 1960–75. Major commissions include: *portrait statues:* Pres. Kenyatta, Nairobi, 1973; Sir John Moore, Sir John Moore Barracks, Winchester, 1987; John Wilkes, New Fetter Lane, 1988, Wilkes Univ., USA, 1995; Thomas Cook, Leicester, 1994; Billy Wright, Molineux Stadium, Wolverhampton, 1996; James Brindley, Coventry Canal Basin, 1998; Duncan Edwards, Dudley, 1999; portrait busts: Sir Frank Whittle, RAF Club, 1995; Robert Beldam, Corpus Christi Coll., Cambridge, 2000; *memorial statues:* Richard III, Leicester, 1980; Field Marshal Earl Alexander of Tunis, Wellington Barracks, London, 1985; Reg Harris, Manchester, 1994; *other:* Monument to Freedom Fighters of Zambia, Lusaka, 1974; The Burton Cooper, Burton-on-Trent, 1977; Dolphin Fountain, Dolphin Square, London, 1988; Skipping girl, Harrow, 1988; The Leicester Seamstress, Leicester, 1990; James Henry Greathead, Cornhill, 1994; The Stratford Jester, Stratford-upon-Avon, 1995; D-day Memorial for Green Howards, Crépon, Normandy, 1996; Seagull Sculpture, Anchorpoint, Singapore, 1997; Memorial to Fleet Air Arm, Victoria Embankment Gdns, London, 2000; Great Seal of the Realm, 2001. Silver Medal, RBS, 1988. *Recreations:*

interested in astronomy, golf. *Address:* Valley Farm, Radway, Warwick CV35 0UJ. *T:* (01926) 641938. *Club:* Arts.

BUTLER, John Manton, MSc; *b* 9 Oct. 1909; *m* 1940, Marjorie Smith, Melbourne; one *s* one *d.* *Educ:* Southland, NZ; Univ. of Otago (Sen. Schol., NZ, Physics; BSc 1929; Smeaton Schol. Chemistry, 1930, John Edmond Fellow, 1930; MSc 1st class Hons). Pres., Students' Union; Graduate Rep. Univ. Council. Joined Shell, NZ, 1934; served various Shell cos in UK, Australia and S Africa until 1957; Man. Dir, Lewis Berger (GB) Ltd, 1957; Dir, Berger, Jenson & Nicholson Ltd, 1969–74. Chm., BNEC Cttee for Exports to NZ, 1967 (Dep. Chm., 1965). Pres., NZ Soc., 1971. Member: Cttee, Spastics Soc.; St David's Cttee, Conservative Assoc., 1979–80; Aust. Inst. of Internat. Affairs, 1981–. Consultant. *Recreations:* travel, golf, photography. *Address:* Osborne, 28 Ranfurlie Crescent, Glen Iris, Victoria 3146, Australia. *T:* (3) 998859458. *Club:* Royal Melbourne Golf.

BUTLER, John Michael, CPFA, FCCA; Director of Finance and Information Technology, East Riding of Yorkshire Council, since 1995; *b* 12 Sept. 1943; *s* of Reginald Butler and late Kathleen (*née* Garside); *m* 1964, Daphne Ann Head (*d* 1999); two *s.* *Educ:* Beckenham and Penge Grammar Sch. CPFA 1966; IRRV 1974; FCCA 1980. Audit Asst, Beckenham BC, 1960–61; Accountancy Assistant: Sevenoaks UDC, 1961–63; Caterham UDC, 1963–64; Sen. Accountant, Dorking UDC, 1964–66; Asst Treas., Esher UDC, 1966–70; Asst Borough Treas., Greenwich LBC, 1970–74; Chief Finance Officer, Lambeth LBC, 1974–79; City Treas., Swansea CC, 1979–95. National President: IRRV, 1989–90; Soc. of Dist Council Treasurers, 1992–93; Mem. Council, CIPFA, 1994–. FIMgt 1969. *Recreations:* orienteering, ski-ing, windsurfing, squash. *Address:* County Hall, Beverley, ER Yorks HU17 9BA. *T:* (01482) 884630. *Clubs:* Swansea Bay Orienteering, Humberside and Lincolnshire Orienteering; Beverley Squash; Beverley Athletic; York Cross Country Ski.

BUTLER, Prof. John Nicholas, (Nick), OBE 1988; RDI 1981; FCSD; industrial designer; Chairman and Joint Managing Director, BIB Design Consultants, since 1989; *b* 21 March 1942; *s* of William and Mabel Butler; *m* 1967, Kari Ann Morrison (marr. diss. 1999); two *s.* *m* 2001, Mary Thompson. *Educ:* Leeds Coll. of Art (NDD); Royal Coll. of Art (DesRCA, 1st Cl. Hons). FCSD (FSIAD 1975). Founded BIB Design Consultants, 1967; Sen. Partner, 1967–89. Prof. of Industrial Design, RCA, 1987–90; Vis. Prof., Massey Univ., 1993–. Chm., British Design Export Gp, 1980–81; Member: Design Bd, RSA, 1987–; Design Council, 1988–93 (Mem., Chairman's Review Team, 1993–); Chairman's Design Bd, BAA, 1992–; Royal Fine Art Commn, 1998–99. Master, RDI, 1995–97. Hon. Sec., SIAD, 1978–81, Treasurer 1981–84. FRSA 1983 (Vice Pres., 1995–). *Recreations:* reading, music, country pursuits, watching Rugby, drawing. *Address:* BIB Design Consultants, 11 St Gabriel's Manor, Myatts Fields, Lambeth, SE5 9RH.

BUTLER, Keith Stephenson, CMG 1977; HM Diplomatic Service, retired; Appeal Director for various charities, since 1978; *b* 3 Sept. 1917; *s* of late Raymond R. Butler and Gertrude Stephenson; *m* 1st, 1952, Geraldine Marjorie Clark (*d* 1979); 2nd, 1979, Mrs Priscilla Wittels; no *c.* *Educ:* King Edward's Sch., Birmingham; Liverpool Coll.; St Peter's Coll., Oxford (MA). HM Forces, 1939–47 (despatches): served, RA, in Egypt, Greece and Crete; POW, Germany, 1941–45. Foreign Correspondent for Sunday Times and Kemsley Newspapers, 1947–50. Joined HM Foreign Service, 1950; served: First Sec., Ankara and Caracas; Canadian Nat. Defence Coll.; Paris, Montreal. HM Consul-General: Seville, 1968; Bordeaux, 1969; Naples, 1974–77. *Publications:* contrib. historical and political reviews. *Recreation:* historical research. *Address:* Sheilings, 10 Station Road, Kintbury, near Newbury, Berks RG17 9UP. *T:* (01488) 658350.

BUTLER, Prof. Marilyn Speers, DPhil; Rector, Exeter College, since 1993, and Titular Professor of English Language and Literature, since 1998, University of Oxford; *b* 11 Feb. 1937; *d* of Sir Trevor Evans, CBE and Margaret (*née* Gribbin); *m* 1962, David Edgeworth Butler, *qv*; three *s.* *Educ:* Wimbledon High Sch.; St Hilda's Coll., Oxford (MA; DPhil). Trainee and talks producer, BBC, 1960–62; Oxford University: full-time res. and teaching, 1962–70, Jun. Res. Fellow, 1970–73, St Hilda's Coll.; Fellow and Tutor, St Hugh's Coll., 1973–85; Lectr, 1985–86; King Edward VII Prof. of English Lit., 1986–93, and Fellow of King's Coll., 1988–93, Univ. of Cambridge. Pt-time Lectr, ANU, 1967; British Academy Reader, 1982–85. Mem., HEFCE, 1997–2000. *Publications:* Maria Edgeworth: a literary biography, 1972; Jane Austen and the War of Ideas, 1975; Peacock Displayed, 1979; Romantics, Rebels and Reactionaries, 1981, 2nd edn 1985; (ed) Burke, Paine, Godwin and the Revolution Controversy, 1984; (ed with J. Todd) Works of Mary Wollstonecraft, 1989; (ed) Maria Edgeworth, Castle Rackrent, and Ennui, 1992; (ed) Frankenstein, the 1818 edition, 1993; (ed) Northanger Abbey, 1995; (ed) Works of Maria Edgeworth, 1999. *Address:* The Rector's Lodgings, Exeter College, Oxford OX1 3DP.

BUTLER, Sir Michael; *see* Butler, Sir R. M. T.

BUTLER, Sir Michael (Dacres), GCMG 1984 (KCMG 1980 CMG 1975); HM Diplomatic Service, retired; Chairman, International Advisory (formerly European Strategy) Board, ICL, since 1988; *b* 27 Feb. 1927; *s* of T. D. Butler, Almer, Blandford, and Beryl May (*née* Lambert); *m* 1951, Ann, *d* of Rt Hon. Lord Clyde; two *s* two *d.* *Educ:* Winchester; Trinity Coll., Oxford. Joined HM Foreign Service, 1950; served in: UK Mission to UN, New York, 1952–56; Baghdad, 1956–58; FO, 1958–61 and 1965–68; Paris, 1961–65; Counsellor, UK Mission in Geneva, 1968–70; Fellow, Center for Internat. Affairs, Harvard, 1970–71; Counsellor, Washington, 1971–72; Head of European Integration Dept, FCO, 1972–74; Asst Under-Sec. in charge of European Community Affairs, FCO, 1974–76; Dep. Under-Sec. of State, FCO, 1976–79; Ambassador and Perm. UK Rep. to EC, Brussels, 1979–85. Hambros PLC and Hambros Bank Ltd: Dir, 1986–94; non-executive Dir, 1994–97; Consultant, 1997–98; Dir, Eurosynergies (France), 1990–98. Lab. Party's Special Envoy on EU Enlargement, 1996–97; Advr to Sec. of State for Foreign and Commonwealth Affairs, 1997–98. Advr, Govt of Ukraine, 1991–94. Chairman: City European Cttee, British Invisibles (formerly BIEC), 1988–93; Oriental Art Magazine, 1988–95; European Unification Bd, Hercules Europe, 1989–94; Business Link–Dorset, 1994–; Halo Ltd, 1994–96; Pathway Gp Ltd, 1995–2000; Guidephone Ltd, 1997–; Treasury Mgt Internat. Editl Adv. Panel, 1992–; Member: Standing Cttee on Internat. Relations, ACOST, 1987–90; Panel of Conciliators, Internat. Centre for the Settlement of Investment Disputes, 1987–94; Bank of Montreal Internat. Adv. Council, 1992–98; Adv. Council, Foreign Policy Centre, 1997–. Dir, Wellcome Foundn, 1986–95; Pro-Provost and Chm. Council, RCA, 1991–96 (Sen. Fellow, 1997); Mem. Council, Oriental Ceramic Soc., 1977–80, 1985–88 and 1995–98; Dep. Chm., Bd of Trustees, V&A Museum, 1985–97. Hon. DBA Bournemouth, 1998. Knight Grand Cross, Order of Merit (Portugal), 1998. *Publications:* Chinese Porcelain, The Transitional Period 1620–82: a selection from the Michael Butler Collection, 1986; Europe: More than a Continent, 1986; The Butler Family Collection, 17th Century Chinese Porcelain, 1990; contribs to Trans Oriental Ceramic Soc. *Recreations:* collecting Chinese porcelain, ski-ing. *Address:* 36A Elm Park Road, SW3 6AX. *Club:* Brooks's.

BUTLER, Prof. Michael Gregory, PhD, LittD; Professor of Modern German Literature, University of Birmingham, since 1986; *b* 1 Nov. 1935; *s* of Maurice Gregory Butler and Winifred May Butler (*née* Barker); *m* 1960, Jean Mary Griffith; one *s* one *d.* *Educ:* High Pavement Sch., Nottingham; Fitzwilliam Coll., Cambridge (MA; LittD 1999); Trinity Coll., Oxford (DipEd); CNAA (PhD 1974). Assistant Master: King's Sch., Worcester, 1958-61; Reuchlin Gymnasium, Pforzheim, FRG, 1961-62; Hd of German, Ipswich Sch., 1962-70; University of Birmingham: Lectr, 1970-80; Sen. Lectr, 1980-86; Head: Dept of German Studies, 1984-2001; Sch. of Mod. Langs, 1988-93; Professorial Fellow, Inst. for German Studies, 1997–; Public Orator, 1997–. Vis. Fellow, Humanities Res. Centre, ANU, 1979. Vice-Pres., 1994-96, Pres., 1996-99, Conf. of Univ. Teachers of German in GB and Ireland. Editor, Samphire, New Poetry, 1968-81. Cross, Order of Merit (FRG), 1999. *Publications:* The Novels of Max Frisch, 1975; (ed) Englische Lyrik der Gegenwart, 1981; The Plays of Max Frisch, 1985; Frisch: Andorra, 1985, 2nd edn 1994; (ed) Rejection and Emancipation: writing in German-speaking Switzerland 1945-1991, 1991; (ed) The Narrative Fiction of Heinrich Böll: social conscience and literary achievement, 1995; (ed) The Challenge of German Culture, 2000; (ed) The Making of Modern Switzerland 1848-1998, 2000; contrib. articles to many learned jls, incl. Text+Kritik (Germany), Forum for Mod. Lang. Studies, New German Studies, German Life and Letters, and Publications of the English Goethe Soc. *Recreations:* walking, talking, watching. *Address:* 45 Westfields, Catshill, Bromsgrove B61 9HJ. *T:* (01527) 874189; Department of German Studies, University of Birmingham, Edgbaston, Birmingham B15 2TT. *T:* (0121) 414 6173.

BUTLER, Michael Howard, OBE, FCA; Finance Director, British Coal (formerly National Coal Board), 1985–93, Member of the Board, 1986–93; *b* 13 Feb. 1936; *s* of Howard Butler and Constance Gertrude Butler; *m* 1961, Christine Elizabeth Killer; two *s* one *d.* *Educ:* Nottingham High School. Articled pupil, H. G. Ellis Kennewell & Co., Nottingham, 1952–58; Stewarts & Lloyds Gp, 1960–62; National Coal Board: various posts, NCB HQ, W Midlands Div. and NE Area, 1962–68; Chief Accountant, Coal Products Div., 1968; Dep. Treas., NCB HQ, 1970; Treas. and Dep. Dir Gen. of Finance, 1978; Dir Gen. of Finance, 1981; Chm., British Fuels Co., 1992–93. Director: British Coal Enterprises, 1988–96; Edinburgh Fund Managers, 1993–95; Chairman: CIN Management Ltd, 1993–96; British Investment Trust, 1993–97. Trustee, Mineworkers Pension Fund (formerly British Coal Pension Funds), 1981–2000 (Chm., 1995–2000). *Recreations:* gardening, listening to music, playing tennis. *Address:* Banstead Down, Chorleywood Road, Rickmansworth, Herts WD3 4EH. *T:* (01923) 778001.

BUTLER, Prof. Neville Roy, MD; FRCP; FRCOG; Director, International Centre for Child Studies, since 1983; Professor of Child Health, Bristol University, 1965–85, Emeritus Professor, since 1985; Visiting Fellow, Institute of Education, London University, since 1998; *b* Harrow, 6 July 1920; *o s* of late Dr C. J. Butler, MRCS, LRCP and Ida Margaret Butler; *m* 1954, Jean Ogilvie (decd), *d* of late John McCormack; two *d.* *Educ:* Epsom Coll.; Charing Cross Hosp. Med. Sch. MB BS 1942, MD 1949; MRCP 1946, FRCP 1965; DCH 1949; FRCOG 1979. Served RAMC, 1942–44, temp. Captain. First Assistant to Paediatric Unit, UCH, 1950; Med. Registrar and Pathologist, Hosp. for Sick Children, Gt Ormond St, 1953; Consultant Paediatrician, Oxford and Wessex RHB, 1957–63; Dir, Perinatal Mortality Survey, Birthday Trust Fund, 1958; Consultant Physician, Hosp. for Sick Children, Gt Ormond St and Sen. Lectr, Inst. of Child Health, London Univ., 1963–65; Hon. Cons. Paediatrician, Bristol & Weston Teaching Dist and Southmead Dist, 1965–85. Co-Dir, Nat. Child Develt Study (1958 cohort), 1965–69; Dir, Child Health and Educn Study (1970 cohort), and Youthscan UK, 1975–89. Harding Meml Lect., RIBA, 1983. Member: BPA, 1958–; Neonatal Soc., 1961–; Cuban Paediatric Soc., 1973–; Hungarian Paediatric Soc., 1979–. Hon. FRCPCH 1996. *Publications:* jointly: Perinatal Mortality, 1963; 11,000 Seven Year Olds, 1966; Perinatal Problems, 1969; From Birth to Seven, 1972; ABO Haemolytic Diseases of the Newborn, 1972; The Social Life of Britain's Five Year Olds, 1984; Ethnic Minority Children, 1985; The Health of Britain's Five Year Olds, 1986; papers in scientific and med. jls. *Address:* International Centre for Child Studies, 86 Cumberland Road, Bristol BS1 6UG. *T:* (0117) 925 0835, *Fax:* (0117) 909 3739; Centre for Longitudinal Studies, Institute of Education, University of London, 20 Bedford Way, WC1H 0AL, *T:* (020) 7612 6899, *Fax:* (020) 7612 6880. *Club:* Savage.

BUTLER, Nick; *see* Butler, J. N.

BUTLER, Norman John Terence, CBE 1993; Director of Social Services, Hampshire, since 1988; *b* 18 Feb. 1946; *s* of Arthur Reginald Butler and Lucy Mary Butler; *m*; two *d.* *Educ:* Peveril Bilateral Sch., Nottingham; Trent Polytechnic, Nottingham (Cert. in Social Work); Nat. Inst. of Social Work, London; Brunel Univ. (MA Public and Social Admin). Mental Welfare Officer, Nottingham, 1965–71; Sen. Social Worker, Nottingham, 1971–73; Area Man., Haringey, 1974–81; Asst Dir of Social Services, Royal Bor. of Kingston upon Thames, 1981–83; Dep. Dir of Social Services, E Sussex, 1983–88. Member: Firth Cttee, examining public expenditure on residential care, 1987; Algebra Gp, 1992–93; Data Protection Tribunals Bd, 1996–; Standing Gp for Service Delivery and Orgn, NHS R & D Directorate, 1997–; Co-Leader, Community Care Support Force, providing practical support to local and health authorities in implementation of NHS and Community Care Act, 1992–93; Mem. Adv. Bd for Restricted Patients, 1995–; Vice-Pres., Relatives Assoc., 1995–. Hon. Treas., Assoc. of Dirs of Social Services, 1997. *Publications:* articles in various jls, incl. Social Work Today, Insight and Community Care. *Recreations:* travel, tennis, swimming, entertaining, being entertained. *Address:* (office) Trafalgar House, The Castle, Winchester, Hants SO23 8UQ. *T:* (01962) 841841; Edgar House, 9 Lansdowne Avenue, St Cross, Winchester, Hants SO23 9TJ.

BUTLER, Patricia; *see* Ferguson, P.

BUTLER, Pearse; *see* Butler, J. P.

BUTLER, Sir (Percy) James, Kt 2001; CBE 1981; DL; FCA; Deputy Chairman, since 1995 and Director, since 1994, Camelot PLC; farmer, since 1974; *b* 15 March 1929; *s* of late Percy Ernest Butler and Phyllis Mary Butler (*née* Bartholomew); *m* 1954, Margaret Prudence Copland; one *s* two *d.* *Educ:* Marlborough Coll.; Clare Coll., Cambridge (MA). Joined Peat, Marwick, Mitchell & Co. (later KPMG Peat Marwick), 1952; qualified, 1955; Partner, 1965; Gen. Partner, 1971; Managing Partner, London Reg., 1981–85; Dep. Sen. Partner, 1985–86; Sen. Partner, 1986–93; Mem. of KPMG Exec. Cttee and Council, 1987–93; Chm., KPMG Internat., 1991–93. Director: Mersey Docks and Harbour Co., 1972–90 (Dep. Chm., 1987–90); Tompkins PLC, 1994–95; Wadworth and Co. Ltd, 1994–; Nicholson, Graham & Jones, 1994–; Chairman: European Passenger Services Ltd, 1994–96; Union Railways, 1995–96. Mem. (part time), BRB, 1994–95. Business Advr to Treasury and CS Cttee, 1980–82; Member: Cttee on review of Railway Finance, 1982; Cadbury Cttee on Financial Aspects of Corporate Governance, 1990–95. Member: Council, Business in the Community, 1988–90; ICAEW Council, 1992–94; Council, CBI, 1989–94; Governing Body, City Res. Project, 1991–95; Adv. Council, Prince's Youth Business Trust, 1993–; Council, SCF, 1994–2000 (Chm., SCF Private Appeal, 1994–2000). Treasurer, Pilgrims Soc., 1982–97; Trustee, Royal Opera House Trust, 1991–99 (Chm., 1993–95; Vice Chm., 1995–99); Dir, Royal Opera House, 1994–98; Trustee: Winchester Cathedral Trust, 1991– (Chm., Cathedral Appeal, 1991–94); RA,

1997– (Mem., Mgt Cttee, 1997–); Chm. Trustees, Music at Winchester, 1999–. Mem., Marlborough Coll. Council, 1975–2001 (Chm., 1992–2001). Liveryman: Worshipful Co. of Cutlers, 1965– (Mem. Court, 1985–; Master, 1995–96); Worshipful Co. of Chartered Accountants in England and Wales, 1977–. DL Hants, 1994. *Recreations:* bridge, shooting, opera, ballet, farming. *Address:* Littleton House, Crawley, Winchester SO21 2QF. *T:* (01962) 880206. *Club:* Boodle's.

BUTLER, Peter; Chief Executive: Milton Keynes Business Services Ltd; Flying Scotsman plc; Chairman: Law Express Ltd; Snowstorm Developments Ltd; *b* 10 June 1951; *s* of late Kenneth Jonathan Butler and of Barbara Butler; *m* 1973, Peggy Mary, *d* of Richard Nott; three *d. Educ:* Adams Grammar Sch., Newport, Shropshire; St Edmund Hall, Oxford (MA English Lit.; PGCE 1974). Admitted Solicitor, 1978; Solicitor, Thames Valley Police, 1978–80; Partner, 1981–92, Consultant, 1992–, Linnells, solicitors, Oxford. Nat. Chm., Trainee Solicitors, England and Wales, 1976. Mem. (C) Oxfordshire CC, 1985–89. MP (C) Milton Keynes North East, 1992–97; contested (C) same seat, 1997. PPS to Minister of State, DoH, 1994–95, to Chancellor of Exchequer, 1995–97. Mem., Home Affairs Select Cttee, 1992. Non-executive Director: Penmarric PLC; Continental Trustees Ltd. Non-exec Dir, Milton Keynes Chamber of Commerce. Sch. Gov., 1985–92. *Recreations:* music, trying to keep up with three energetic children, avoiding organised exercise. *Address:* Castle Farm, Lavendon, Olney, Bucks MK46 4JG. *T:* (01234) 240046. *Clubs:* Royal Automobile; Vintage Sports Car; Bentley Drivers'.

BUTLER, Sir (Reginald) Michael (Thomas), 3rd Bt *cr* 1922; QC (Ont); Barrister and Solicitor, retired; sometime Partner of Butler, Angus, Victoria, BC; Director, Teck Corporation; *b* 22 April 1928; *s* of Sir Reginald Thomas, 2nd Bt, and Marjorie Brown Butler; *S* father, 1959; *m* Marja McLean (marr. diss.); three *s*; one *s* adopted; *m* Judith Ann Blackwell, LLB, *d* of Harold Blackwell. *Educ:* Brentwood Coll., Victoria, BC; Univ. of British Columbia (BA). Called to Bar (Hons) from Osgoode Hall Sch. of Law, Toronto, Canada, 1954. *Heir: s* (Reginald) Richard (Michael) Butler [*b* 3 Oct. 1953; *m* 1982, Dale Karen Piner (marr. diss.); three *s*]. *Address:* Old Park Cottage, 634 Avalon Road, Victoria, BC V8V 1N7, Canada.

BUTLER, Hon. Sir Richard (Clive), Kt 1981; DL; Chairman, County Natwest Investment Management, 1989–96; Life Member, Council, National Farmers' Union, since 1962 (President, 1979–86); farmer since 1953; *b* 12 Jan. 1929; *e s* of late Baron Butler of Saffron Walden, KG, CH, PC and late Sydney, *o c* of late Samuel Courtauld; *m* 1952, Susan Anne Maud Walker; twin *s* one *d. Educ:* Eton Coll.; Pembroke Coll., Cambridge (MA). 2nd Lieut, Royal Horse Guards, 1947–49. Vice-Pres. 1970–71, Dep. Pres., 1971–79, NFU. Member: Agricultural Adv. Council, 1968–72; Central Council for Agricultural and Horticultural Co-operation, 1970–79. Director: National Westminster Bank, 1986–96; Agroceres & Co. (formerly Ferruzzi Trading (UK)), 1986–98; Agricola (UK), 1986–92; Barton Bendish Farms, 1986–92; County Natwest Group (formerly Natwest Investment Bank), 1989–92; National Farmers' Union Mutual Insurance Soc. Ltd, 1985–96; Avon Insurance, 1990–96. Mem. Ct of Assts, Farmers' Co. (Master, 1997–98); Master, Skinners' Co., 1994–95. DL Essex, 1972. *Recreations:* hunting, shooting, DIY. *Address:* Gladfen Hall, Halstead, Essex CO9 1RN. *T:* (01787) 472828. *Club:* Farmers'.

See also Rt Hon. Sir A. C. Butler.

BUTLER, Richard Edmund, AM 1988; telecommunication policy adviser; Secretary-General, International Telecommunication Union, United Nations, Specialised Agency, Geneva, 1983–89 (Deputy Secretary-General, 1968–82); *b* 25 March 1926; *m* 1951, Patricia Carmel Kelly; three *s* two *d. Educ:* A, DPA; AASA; CPA; FRIPA. Posts in Australian Post Office, incl. Chief Industrial Officer, 1955–60; Exec. Officer, Dep. Asst Dir-Gen., 1960–68 (Ministerial and External Relations), 1960–68; apptd (in absentia) Sec., Aust. Telecommunications Commn, 1975 and later Dir, Corporate Planning Directorate. Formerly Member Australian delegations: for Internat. Telecommunication Satellite Consortium, Plenipotentiary Conf. 1965 (Dep. Leader; Mem. Administrative Council and Plan Cttees, 1962–68); to UN Conf. on Peaceful Uses of Outer Space, Vienna, 1968 (Dep. Leader). Mem., Admin. Cttee of Co-ordination for UN and Heads of Specialized Agencies; Chairman: Ad-Hoc UN Common System subsid. gps; ITU (Tripartite) Staff Pension Cttee, 1968–83; Member: Ministerial Adv. Cttee, Implementation of Australian Telecommns Reform decisions, 1990–91; Adv. Bd, Centre for Internat. Res. on Communication and ITs, Melbourne, 1991–; Associate Mem., Austr. Telecommn Authy), 1990–91. Chairman: Asiaspace Ltd, 1999– (Mem. Bd, 1997–); Sky Station Australia Pty Ltd, 1999– (Mem. Bd, 1996–); Mem. Internat. Adv. Bd, Sky Station Internat. Inc., 1995–. Member, Advisory Board: Pacific Telecommns Council, Hawaii, 1993–; Telematics, India, 1994–; Mem. Bd, Volunteers in Technical Assistance, 1993–. Governor, Internat. Computer Commns Conf., 1975–85; UN System co-ordinator, Develt of Commns Infrastructure prog., world commns year, 1983. Hon. Mem., Greek Soc. of Air and Space Law, 1984. FRIPA; Hon. Fellow, Instn of Electronic and Telecommunications Engrs, New Delhi, 1988. Fellow, Telecommns Soc. of Aust., 1995. Philipp Reis Medal, Germany, 1987. Grand Insignia, Order of Merit for Telecommunications, Spain, 1983. *Publications:* papers on changing telecommunication environment and on multi-dimensional consequences of telecommunications for economic development of nations. *Recreations:* golf, reading. *Address:* 40 Barrington Avenue, Kew, Vic 3101, Australia. *Clubs:* Royal Over-Seas League; CTA NSW (Sydney); Melbourne Cricket; Greenacres Golf (Kew).

BUTLER, Sir Richard (Pierce), 13th Bt *cr* 1628 (Ire.), of Cloughgrenan, Co. Carlow; *b* 22 July 1940; *s* of Col Sir Thomas Pierce Butler, 12th Bt, CVO, DSO, OBE and Rosemary Liège Woodgate Davidson-Houston (*d* 1997); *S* father, 1994; *m* 1965, Diana, *yr d* of Col S. J. Borg; three *s* one *d. Educ:* Eton; NY Univ. MBA. FCA 1963. Partner, Charles Wakeling & Co., 1964–66; Director: The First Boston Corp. (NY), 1967–78; PaineWebber Inc. (NY), 1978–88 (Management Council, 1985–88); PaineWebber International Bank, 1986–89; Emesco Industrial Equity Co. SA, 1987–; The Transportation Gp Ltd, 1989–94; RP&C Internat. (formerly Rauscher Pierce & Clark) Inc., 1992–2000. Mem. Council, Pestalozzi Children's Village Trust, 1983– (Chm., 1985–94); Founder, Pestalozzi Overseas Children's Trust, 1995. Treas., GAPAN, 1963–66. *Heir: s* Thomas Pierce [*b* 9 Oct. 1966; *m* 1993, Lucinda Pamela Murphy; one *s* two *d*].

BUTLER, Rosemary Jane; Director of Statistics, Department of Health, 1991–98; *b* 15 July 1946; *d* of Samuel Laight Medlar and Rosemary Peggy Medlar; *m* 1971, Anthony David Butler. *Educ:* Maynard School, Exeter; LSE (BSc Econ). Central Statistical Office, 1967–73; Unit for Manpower Studies, 1973–77; Dept of Employment, 1977–80; Statistician and Chief Statistician, MoD, 1980–85; Chief Statistician, HM Treasury, 1985–89; Asst Sec., DSS, 1989–91. FRSA 1993. *Recreations:* theatre, music, birdwatching. *Address:* 16 Maidenstone Hill, Greenwich, SE10 8SX.

BUTLER, Rosemary Janet Mair; Member (Lab) Newport West, National Assembly for Wales, since 1999; *b* 21 Jan. 1943; *d* of Godfrey McGrath and late Gwyneth Jones; *m* 1966, Derek Richard Butler; two *d. Educ:* St Julian's High Sch., Newport. Qualified chiropodist, 1962; in practice, 1962–75. Dir, Tourism S and W Wales, 1993–99. Mem. (Lab) Newport BC, subseq. CBC, 1973–99 (Chm., Leisure Services, 1983–97); Mayor of Newport, 1989–90. Sec. for Educn and Children, Nat. Assembly for Wales, 1999–2000. Member: Sports Council for Wales, 1993–99; Museums and Galls Commn, 1996–2000; Broadcasting Council for Wales, 1997–99. Founder and Chair: Newport Internat. Comp. for Young Pianists, 1979–; Newport–Kutaisi (Republic of Georgia) Twinning Assoc., 1989–99. Hon. Citizen, Kutaisi, Republic of Georgia, 1997. *Recreations:* museums, galleries, the arts, foreign travel. *Address:* National Assembly for Wales, Cardiff Bay, Cardiff CF99 1NA; 13 Highfield Close, Caerleon, Newport NP18 3DW. *T:* (01633) 421081.

BUTLER, Rt Rev. Thomas Frederick; *see* Southwark, Bishop of.

BUTLER, Vincent Frederick, RSA 1977; RGI 1989; figurative sculptor; works in bronze; *b* Manchester, 1933; *m* 1961, Camilla Luisa Meazza; two *s. Educ:* Acad. of Fine Art, Milan. Regular exhibitor at major exhibitions in Scotland; work in RA and several private galleries in Edinburgh, Glasgow and London. Prof. of Sculpture, Univ. of Northern Nigeria, 1998–. *Publication:* Casting for Sculptors, 1997. *Address:* 17 Deanpark Crescent, Edinburgh EH4 1PH. *T:* (0131) 332 5884; *e-mail:* vincent.butler@virgin.net.

BUTLER, Prof. William Elliott; Professor of Comparative Law in the University of London, since 1976; Director, Vinogradoff Institute (formerly Centre for the Study of Socialist Legal Systems), University College London, since 1982; Professor of International and Comparative Law, Moscow Higher School of Social and Economic Sciences, since 1993 (Dean of the Faculty of Law, 1993–98); *b* 20 Oct. 1939; *s* of late William Elliott Butler and of Maxine Swan Elmberg; *m* 1st, 1961, Darlene Mae Johnson (*d* 1989); two *s*; 2nd, 1991, Maryann Elizabeth Gashi. *Educ:* The American Univ. (BA); Harvard Law School (JD); Acad. Law Sch., Russian Acad. of Scis (LLM); The Johns Hopkins Univ. (MA, PhD); London Univ. (LLD). FSA 1989. Res. Asst, Washington Centre of Foreign Policy Res., Sch. of Advanced Internat. Studies, The Johns Hopkins Univ., 1966–68; Res. Associate in Law, and Associate, Russian Res. Centre, Harvard Univ., 1968–70; University of London: Reader in Comparative Law, 1970–76; Mem., SSEES, 1973–93 (Vice-Chm., 1983–88); Dean of Faculty of Laws, UCL, 1977–79; Vice Dean, 1986–88, Dean, 1988–90, Faculty of Laws, London Univ; Mem., Cttee of Management, Inst. of Advanced Legal Studies, 1985–88. Visiting Scholar: Faculty of Law, Moscow State Univ., 1972, 1980; Inst. of State and Law, USSR Acad. of Scis, 1976, 1981, 1983, 1984, 1988; Mongolian State Univ., 1979; Harvard Law Sch., 1982; Visiting Professor: NY Univ. Law Sch., 1978; Ritsumeikan Univ., 1985; Harvard Law Sch., 1986–87; Lectr, Hague Acad. of Internat. Law, 1985. Associé, Internat. Acad. of Comparative Law, 1982–; Member, Bar: Dist of Columbia; US Supreme Court; Union of Jurists, 1990; Mem., Russian Ct of Internat. Commercial Arbitration, 1995–. Chm., Civil Rights in Russia Adv. Panel, Univ. of London, 1983–87; Co-ordinator, UCL-USSR Acad. of Sciences Protocol on Co-operation, 1981–; Special Counsel, Commn on Econ. Reform, USSR Council of Ministers, 1989–91; Of Counsel, Clifford Chance, London, Moscow and Almaty, 1992–94; Partner: White & Case, 1994–96; PricewaterhouseCoopers, 1997–; Member: EC Joint Task Force on Law Reform in CIS, 1992–93; Working Gp on Commercial Law, Govt of Russian Fedn, 1992; Advr, State Property Fund, Rep. of Kyrgyzstan, 1992; Consultant, World Bank, 1992–. Mem., Secretariat, Internat. Assoc. of Mongolists (Ulan Bator), 1987–92; Hon. Member: All-Union Soc. of Bibliophiles, USSR, 1989; Soviet Assoc. of Maritime Law, 1990. Mem., Court of Governors, City of London Polytechnic, 1985–89. Sec., The Bookplate Soc., 1978–86 (Foreign Sec., 1988–94); Exec. Sec., Féd. Internat. des Sociétés d'Amateurs d'Ex-Libris, 1986– (Vice-Pres., 1984–86). Academician: Internat. Acad. of the Book and Art of the Book, Russia, 1992; Russian Acad. of Natural Scis (Russian Encyclopedia Section), 1992; Nat. Acad. of Scis of Ukraine, 1992; Russian Acad. of Legal Scis, 1999. Editor, Year Book on Socialist Legal Systems, 1985–90; Co-editor, The Bookplate Jl, 1989–91 (Editor, 1983–86); Editor: Bookplate Internat., 1994–; Sudebnik, 1996–; Russian Law: theory and practice, 1999–; Mem., editorial bds of learned jls, incl. Marine Policy, 1988–, European Business Law Rev., 1990–; editor of looseleaf services and microfiche projects. FRSA 1986. *Publications:* more than 800 books, articles, translations, and reviews, including: The Soviet Union and the Law of the Sea, 1971; Russian Law, 1977; (with others) The Soviet Legal System, 3rd and 4th edns, 1977–84; A Source Book on Socialist International Organizations, 1978; Northeast Arctic Passage, 1978; International Law in Comparative Perspective, 1980; Basic Documents on Soviet Legal System, 1983, 2nd edn 1991; Chinese Soviet Republic 1931–1934, 1983; Soviet Law, 1983, 2nd edn 1988; Comparative Law and Legal System, 1985; The Law of the Sea and International Shipping, 1985; The Golden Era of American Bookplate Design, 1986; Justice and Comparative Law, 1987; International Law and the International System, 1987; The Non-Use of Force and International Law, 1989; Perestroika and International Law, 1990; The History of International Law in Russia 1647–1917, 1990; (with D. J. Butler) Modern British Bookplates, 1990; Sherlockian Bookplates, 1992; The Butler Commentaries: USSR Law on Ownership, 1991; USSR Fundamental Principles on Investment Activity, 1991; Foreign Investment Legislation in the Republic of the Former Soviet Union, 1993; (with M. E. Gashi-Butler) Doing Business in Russia, 1994; Russian–English Legal Dictionary, 1995; Russian Law, 1999; Tadzhikistan Legal Texts, 1999; Uzbekistan Legal Texts, 1999; American Bookplates, 2000; *translations of:* G. I. Tunkin, Theory of International Law, 1974; A. Kuznetsov, The Journey, 1984; Kazakhstan Civil Code, 1995; Uzbekistan Civil Code, 1998; Russian Civil Legislation, 1999. *Recreations:* book collecting, bookplate collecting. *Address:* Stratton Audley Park, Oxon OX6 9AB. *T:* (01869) 278960. *Clubs:* Cosmos (Washington, DC); Grolier (New York).

BUTLER, William Gerard; Member (Lab) Glasgow Anniesland, Scottish Parliament, since Nov. 2000; *b* 30 March 1956; *s* of William Muir Butler and Mary Butler (*née* Watters); *m* 1988, Patricia Josephine Ferguson, *qv. Educ:* St Mungo's Acad., Glasgow; Univ. of Stirling (BA Hons); Notre Dame Coll. of Educn (PGCE 1980). Teacher of English: Greenock High Sch., 1980–83; Port Glasgow High Sch., 1983–84; Castlehead High Sch., 1984–85; John Street Secondary Sch., 1985–86; Stonelaw High Sch., 1986–2000. Member (Lab) Glasgow CC, 1987–2001 (Convener: Property Services, 1995–98, Policy Formulation, 1998–99; Vice-Convener, Policy and Resources, 1998–2000). Sec., Glasgow City Labour Gp, 1998–2000. *Recreations:* reading, theatre, film, visiting Italy, following Partick Thistle FC. *Address:* Scottish Parliament, Edinburgh EH99 1SP; Constituency Advice Office, 129 Dalsetter Avenue, Glasgow G15 8SZ. *T:* (0141) 944 9441.

BUTLER-BOWDON, Humphrey Anthony Erdeswick, (Humphrey Ocean); painter; *b* 22 June 1951; *s* of late Capt. Maurice Erdeswick Butler-Bowdon, OBE, RN, and Anne (*née* Darlington); *m* 1982, Miranda Argyle; two *d. Educ:* Ampleforth; Tunbridge Wells Art Sch.; Brighton Coll. of Art; Canterbury Coll. of Art (DipAD). Bass player, Kilburn and the Highroads, 1971–73. Res. Fellow, Camberwell Coll. of Art, 1999–2002; Artist in Residence, Dulwich Picture Gall., 2002. Mem., Artistic Records Cttee, Imperial War Mus., 1985–98. Work includes: The First of England, for Neptune Court, Nat. Maritime Mus., 1999; project for Port Authy, Bruges-Zeebrugge, Belgium, 2000; *portrait commissions* for National Portrait Gallery: Tony Benn; William Whitelaw; A. J. Ayer;

Philip Larkin; Paul McCartney; *one-man exhibitions:* Nat. Portrait Gall., 1984; Ferens Art Gall., Hull and touring, 1987; Double-Portrait, Dulwich Picture Gallery, Tate Gall., Liverpool, 1992; urbasuburba, Whitworth Art Gall., Manchester and touring, 1997; The Painter's Eye, Nat. Portrait Gall., 1999; *group exhibitions* include: Haus der Kunst, Munich, 1986; Picturing People 1945–1989, British Council, touring Far East, 1989; Die Kraft der Bilder, Martin Gropius Bau, Berlin, 1996; Treasures from NPG, British Council, touring Japan, 1996; Painting the Century, NPG, 2000–01; Best of British, NPG, Canberra, 2001; *work in collections:* Ferens Art Gall., Hull; Imperial War Mus.; Magdalen Coll., Oxford; Nat. Maritime Mus.; NPG; Royal Liby, Windsor Castle; Royal Opera House, Covent Gdn; Royal Soc. Chemistry; Scottish NPG; Southwark Collection; Univ. of Birmingham; Wellcome Trust; Wolverhampton Art Gall. Imperial Tobacco Portrait Award, 1982; Wellcome Trust Sci-Art Award, 1998. *Publications:* The Ocean View, 1982; (with S. Nugent) Big Mouth: the Amazon speaks, 1990. *Recreation:* carrying binoculars. *Address:* 22 Marmora Road, SE22 0RX. *T:* (020) 8693 8387; (studio) *T:* and *Fax:* (020) 7820 7764.

BUTLER-SLOSS, Rt Hon. Dame (Ann) Elizabeth (Oldfield), DBE 1979; PC 1988; President of the Family Division, since 1999; *b* 10 Aug. 1933; *d* of late Sir Cecil Havers, QC, and late Enid Snelling; *m* 1958, Joseph William Alexander Butler-Sloss, *qv*; two *s* one *d*. *Educ:* Wycombe Abbey Sch. Called to Bar, Inner Temple, Feb. 1955, Bencher, 1979, Treasurer, 1998; practice at Bar, 1955–70; Registrar, Principal Registry of Probate, later Family, Division, 1970–79; a Judge of the High Court, Family Div., 1979–88; a Lord Justice of Appeal, 1988–99. Chm., Cleveland Child Abuse Inquiry, 1987–88. Contested (C), Lambeth, Vauxhall, 1959. Member: Medico-Legal Soc.; Judicial Studies Bd, 1985–89; Pres., Commonwealth and Ethnic Bar Assoc. Pres., Honiton Agricultural Show, 1985–86; Chancellor, Univ. of West of England, 1993–. Hon. Fellow, St Hilda's Coll., Oxford, 1988; Fellow, KCL, 1991. FRSocMed 1992, Hon. FRSocMed 1997; Hon. FRCP 1992; Hon. FRCPsych 1993; Hon. FRCPCH 1996 (Hon. Mem., BPA, 1988). Hon. LLD: Hull, 1988; Keele, Bristol, 1991; Exeter, Brunel, 1992; Manchester, 1995; Cantab, Greenwich, 2000; Liverpool, 2001; Hon. DLitt Loughborough, 1992; DUniv Central England, 1994. *Publications:* Joint Editor: Phipson on Evidence (10th edn); Corpe on Road Haulage (2nd edn); a former Editor, Supreme Court Practice, 1976 and 1979. *Address:* c/o Royal Courts of Justice, Strand, WC2A 2LL. *Club:* Lansdowne.

BUTLER-SLOSS, Joseph William Alexander; Chairman, 1992 Delimitation Commission, Botswana, 1992–93; *b* 16 Nov. 1926; 2nd and *o* surv. *s* of late Francis Alexander Sloss and Alice Mary Frances Violet Sloss (*née* Patchell); *m* 1958, Ann Elizabeth Oldfield Havers (*see* Rt Hon. Dame (Ann) Elizabeth (Oldfield) Butler-Sloss); two *s* one *d*. *Educ:* Bangor Grammar Sch., Co. Down; Hertford Coll., Oxford. Ordinary Seaman, RN, 1944; Midshipman 1945, Sub-Lieut 1946, RNVR. MA (Jurisprudence) Hertford Coll., Oxford, 1951. Called to Bar, Gray's Inn, 1952; joined Western Circuit, 1954; joined Inner Temple; a Recorder, 1972–84; a Judge of High Court, Kenya, 1984–90. Joint Master, East Devon Foxhounds, 1970–76. Hon. Editor, The Irish Genealogist, 1993–. *Recreations:* racing, the violin. *Address:* Higher Marsh Farm, Marsh Green, Rockbeare, Exeter EX5 2EX. *Clubs:* Carlton; Nairobi.

BUTLER-WHEELHOUSE, Keith Oliver; Chief Executive, Smiths Group (formerly Smiths Industries), since 1996; *b* 29 March 1946; *s* of late Kenneth Butler-Wheelhouse and May (*née* Page); *m* 1973, Pamela Anne Bosworth Smith; two *s*. *Educ:* Queen Mary's, Walsall; Grey Sch., Port Elizabeth; Witwatersrand Univ. (BCom); Cape Town Univ. Grad. Sch. Mfg, Product Develt, Finance and Mktg Depts, Ford Motor Co., 1965–85; General Motors, 1985–96 (led mgt buy-out of GMSA to form Delta, 1985–92); Pres., Saab Automobile, Sweden, 1992–96. Non-exec. Dir, J. Sainsbury plc, 1999–. Citizen of Year, Port Elizabeth, 1987. *Recreations:* golf, jogging, tennis, surfing. *Address:* Smiths Group, 765 Finchley Road, NW11 8DS. *T:* (020) 8458 3232. *Clubs:* Moor Park Golf, Wentworth Golf; Harrow Tennis; Humewood St Francis Golf, Fancourt Golf (S Africa).

BUTLIN, Martin Richard Fletcher, CBE 1990; FBA 1984; Keeper of Historic British Collection, Tate Gallery, 1967–89; Consultant, Christie's, since 1989; *b* 7 June 1929; *s* of late Kenneth Rupert Butlin and Helen Mary (*née* Fletcher), MBE, JP; *m* 1969, Frances Caroline Chodzko. *Educ:* Rendcomb Coll.; Trinity Coll., Cambridge (MA); Courtauld Inst. of Art, London Univ. (BA). DLit London 1984. Asst Keeper, Tate Gall., 1955–67. *Publications:* A Catalogue of the Works of William Blake in the Tate Gallery, 1957, 3rd edn 1990; Samuel Palmer's Sketchbook of 1824, 1962; Turner Watercolours, 1962; (with Sir John Rothenstein) Turner, 1964; (with Mary Chamot and Dennis Farr) Tate Gallery Catalogues: The Modern British Paintings, Drawings and Sculpture, 1964; The Later Works of J. M. W. Turner, 1965; William Blake, 1966; The Blake-Varley Sketchbook of 1819, 1969; (with E. Joll) The Paintings of J. M. W. Turner, 1977, 2nd edn 1984 (jtly, Mitchell Prize for the History of Art, 1978); The Paintings and Drawings of William Blake, 1981; Aspects of British Painting 1550–1800, from the Collection of the Sarah Campbell Blaffer Foundation, 1988; (with Mollie Luther and Ian Warrell) Turner at Petworth, 1989; (with Ted Gott and Irena Zdanowicz) William Blake in the Collection of the National Gallery of Victoria, 1989; selected paintings and prepared catalogues for following exhibitions: (with Andrew Wilton and John Gage) Turner 1775–1851, 1974; William Blake, 1978; (with Gert Schiff) William Blake, Tokyo, 1990; (ed jtly) The Oxford Companion to J. M. W. Turner, 2001; articles and reviews in Burlington Mag., Connoisseur, Master Drawings, Blake Qly, Blake Studies, Turner Studies. *Recreations:* music, travel. *Address:* 74c Eccleston Square, SW1V 1PJ.

BUTLIN, Prof. Robin Alan, DLitt; Professor of Historical Geography, University of Leeds, 2000; *b* 31 May 1938; *s* of late Rowland Henry Butlin and Mona Butlin; *m* 1961, Norma Coroneo; two *s* one *d*. *Educ:* Liverpool Univ. (BA, MA); DLitt Loughborough, 1987. Demonstrator, University Coll. of N Staffordshire, 1961–62; Lectr in Geography, UC Dublin, 1962–71; Queen Mary College, University of London: Lectr in Geography, 1971; Sen. Lectr, 1975; Reader in Historical Geography, 1977–79; Loughborough University: Prof. of Geography, 1979–95; Hd of Dept, 1979–91; Dean, Sch. of Human and Environmental Studies, 1983–86; Principal, and Prof. of Historical Geography, UC of Ripon and York St John, 1995–98. Vis. Associate Prof. of Geography, Univ. of Nebraska, 1969–70; Vis. Professorial Fellow and Leverhulme Res. Fellow, Wolfson Coll., Cambridge, 1986–87; Vis. Prof., Leeds Univ., 1998–2000. FRGS 1972 (Vice-Pres., RGS/IBG, 1995–98). Victoria Medal, RGS, 1999. *Publications:* (ed with A. R. H. Baker) Studies of Field Systems in the British Isles, 1973; (ed) The Development of the Irish Town, 1977; (ed with R. A. Dodgshon) An Historical Geography of England and Wales, 1978, 2nd edn 1990; (ed with H. S. A. Fox) Change in the Countryside: essays on rural England 1500–1900, 1979; The Transformation of Rural England c. 1580–1800, 1982; Historical Geography: through the gates of space and time, 1993; (ed jtly) Geography and Imperialism 1820–1940, 1995; (ed with N. Roberts) Ecological Relations in Historical Times, 1995; (ed with R. A. Dodgshon) Historical Geography of Europe, 1999. *Recreations:* music, walking, reading. *Address:* 15 Lawnway, Stockton Lane, York YO31 1JD. *T:* (01904) 416544.

BUTROS, Prof. Albert Jamil; Istiqlal Order First Class, Jordan, 1987; Professor of English, University of Jordan, 1967–79 and since 1985; *b* 25 March 1934; *s* of Jamil Issa and Virginie Antoine (Albina); *m* 1962, Ida Maria Albina; four *d*. *Educ:* Univ. of London (BA Hons English 1958); Univ. of Exeter (BA *ad eundem* 1958); Columbia Univ. (PhD English 1963). Teacher, Amman, 1950–55; Instructor in English, Teacher's Coll., Amman, 1958–60; Lectr, Hunter Coll., City Univ., NY, 1961; Instructor, Miami Univ., Oxford, Ohio, 1962–63; University of Jordan: Asst Prof., English, 1963–65; Associate Prof., 1965–67; Acting Chm., Dept of English, 1964–67; Chm., Dept of English, 1967–73, 1974–76; Dean, Research and Graduate Studies, 1973–76; Ambassador to UK, 1987–91, and (non-res.) to Ireland, 1988–91, and to Iceland, 1990–91. Special Advr to HRH Crown Prince Hassan of Jordan, 1984–85. Dir Gen./Pres., Royal Sci. Soc., Amman, 1976–84. Vis. Prof., Ohio Wesleyan Univ., 1971–72; Sen. Res. Fellow, Internat. Develt Res. Centre, Canada, 1983–84. Rapporteur, Cttee on Jordan Incentive State Prize in Translation, 2001. Formerly Member: Arab Thought Forum; World Affairs Council, Amman. Gov., Internat. Develt Res. Centre, Canada, 1986–98; Mem., Bd of Trustees, Philadelphia Univ., Amman, 1995–. Fellow, World Acad. of Art and Sci., 1986. KStJ 1991. Order of Merit, Italy, 1983. *Publications:* Tales of the Caliphs, 1965; Leaders of Arab Thought, 1969; articles and translations. *Recreations:* reading, writing, translation, art, world affairs, application of science and technology to development, walking. *Address:* PO Box 309, Jubeiha, Amman 11941, Jordan.

BUTT, Geoffrey Frank; Principal Assistant Solicitor, Inland Revenue, 1993–96; *b* 5 May 1943; *s* of late Frank Thomas Woodman Butt and Dorothy Rosamond Butt; *m* 1972, Lee Anne Davey; two *s* one *d*. *Educ:* Royal Masonic Sch., Bushey; Univ. of Reading (BA). Solicitor 1970. Joined Solicitor's Office, HM Customs and Excise as Legal Asst, 1971; Sen. Legal Asst, 1974; Asst Solicitor, 1982; Prin. Asst Solicitor, 1986–93. *Recreations:* family life, classical music, literature and art, gardening. *Address:* 14 Richmond Close, Wellswood, Torquay, Devon TQ1 2PW.

BUTT, Michael Acton; Director, XL Capital Ltd, since 1998; *b* Thruxton, 25 May 1942; *s* of Leslie Acton Kingsford Butt and Mina Gascoigne Butt; *m* 1st, 1964, Diana Lorraine Brook; two *s*; 2nd, 1986, Zoé Benson. *Educ:* Rugby; Magdalen Coll., Oxford (MA History); INSEAD, France (MBA 1967). Bland Welch Gp, 1964; Dir, Bland Payne Holdings, 1970; Chm., Sedgwick Ltd, 1983–87; Dep. Chm., Sedgwick Gp plc, 1985–87; Chm. and Chief Exec., Eagle Star Hldgs, 1987–91; President and Chief Executive Officer, Mid Ocean Ltd, 1993–98; Director: Marceau Investissements, Paris, 1987–94; Phoenix International (Bermuda), 1992–97; INA, 1994–97; Bank of N. T. Butterfield & Son Ltd, 1996–. Board Mem., Internat. Adv. Council, INSEAD, 1982–. *Recreations:* travel, tennis, opera, reading, family, the European movement. *Address:* Leamington House, 50 Harrington Sound Road, Hamilton Parish CR 04, Bermuda. *T:* (441) 2931378, *Fax:* (441) 2938511. *Clubs:* Travellers; Royal Bermuda Yacht, Mid Ocean, Coral Beach (Bermuda).

BUTT, Richard Bevan; Chief Executive, Rural Development Commission, 1989–99; *b* 27 Feb. 1943; *s* of Roger William Bevan and Jean Mary (*née* Carter); *m* 1975, Amanda Jane Finlay (CBE 2001); two *s*. *Educ:* Magdalen Coll., Oxford (BA Hist.); Lancaster Univ. (MA Regional Econs). Asst Principal, Min. of Housing, 1965–68; Sen. Res. Associate, Birmingham Univ., 1969–72; Consultant, 1972; HM Treasury: Principal, 1973–78; Asst Sec., 1978–86; seconded as Financial Counsellor, UK Perm. Repn to EC, 1981–84, Head of Conservation, English Heritage, 1986–89. Specialist Advr to Agriculture Select Cttee, 1998–99. Member: Policy Council, TCPA; Churches Conservation Trust, 1999–; Trustee, Action for Market Towns, 1998–; Hon. Rural Advr, Civic Trust, 1998–. *Recreations:* ceramics, architecture, gardening, travel. *Address:* 35 Gloucester Circus, SE10 8RY.

BUTTER, Major Sir David (Henry), KCVO 1991; MC 1941; JP; landowner and farmer; company director; HM Lord-Lieutenant of Perth and Kinross, 1975–95; *b* 18 March 1920; *s* of late Col Charles Butter, OBE, DL, JP, Pitlochry, and Agnes Marguerite (Madge), *d* of late William Clark, Newark, NJ, USA; *m* 1946, Myra Alice (CVO 1992), *d* of Hon. Maj.-Gen. Sir Harold Wernher, 3rd Bt, GCVO, TD; one *s* four *d*. *Educ:* Eton; Oxford. Served War of 1939–45: 2nd Lieut Scots Guards, 1940, Western Desert and North Africa, Sicily (Staff), 1941–43; Italy (ADC to GOC 8th Army, Gen. Sir Oliver Leese, 1944); Temp. Major, 1946; retd Army, 1948. Lieut, Queen's Body Guard for Scotland (Royal Company of Archers); Pres., Highland T&AVR, 1979–84. County Councillor, Perth, 1955–74; DL Perthshire, 1956, Vice-Lieutenant of Perth, 1960–71; HM Lieutenant of County of Perth, 1971–75, and County of Kinross, 1974–75. *Recreations:* shooting, golf, ski-ing, travel. *Address:* Cluniemore, Pitlochry, Scotland PH16 5NE. *T:* (01796) 472006; 64 Rutland Gate, SW7 1PJ. *T:* (020) 7589 6731. *Clubs:* Turf; Royal and Ancient (St Andrews).

See also Earl of Dalhousie.

BUTTER, John Henry, CMG 1962; MBE 1946; Financial Director to Government of Abu Dhabi, 1970–83; *b* 20 April 1916; *s* of late Captain A. E. Butter, CMG, and late Mrs Baird; *m* 1950, Joyce Platt; three *s*. *Educ:* Charterhouse; Christ Church, Oxford. Indian Civil Service, 1939–47; Pakistan Admin. Service, 1947–50 (served in Punjab, except for period 1942–46 when was Asst to Political Agent, Imphal, Manipur State). HM Overseas Civil Service, Kenya, 1950–65 (Perm. Sec. to the Treasury, 1959–65); Financial Adviser, Kenya Treasury, 1965–69. *Publication:* Uncivil Servant, 1989. *Recreations:* golf, bridge. *Address:* PO Box 16526, Nairobi, Kenya; Whitehill, Gordon, Berwickshire TD3 6LQ. *Club:* East India.

BUTTER, His Honour Neil (McLaren), CBE 2001; QC 1976; a Circuit Judge, 1982–2001; a Judge of Central London County Court, 1994–2001; Designated Civil Judge, London County Court Group, 1998–2001; Senior Circuit Judge, 1998–2001; *b* 10 May 1933; *y s* of late Andrew Butter, MA, MD and late Ena Butter, MB, ChB; *m* 1974, Claire Marianne Miskin. *Educ:* The Leys Sch.; Queens' Coll., Cambridge (MA). Called to Bar, Inner Temple, 1955, Bencher, 1994; an Asst and Dep. Recorder of Bournemouth, 1971; Recorder of the Crown Court, 1972–82; a Judge of Bow County Court, 1986–94; occasional Judge of Employment Appeal Tribunal, 1995–98. Member: Senate of the Inns of Court and the Bar, 1976–79; County Court Rule Cttee, 1993–99; Clinical Disputes Forum, 1997–2001; Chm., Court Mediation Scheme Cttee, 1996–2001. Inspector, for Dept of Trade, Ozalid Gp Hldgs Ltd, 1977–79. A Legal Assessor to GMC and GDC, 1979–82; Mem., Mental Health Review Tribunal, 1983–92. Chm., London County Court Assoc. of Circuit Judges, 1998–2001. Trustee, Kingdon-Ward Speech Therapy Trust, 1980–87. *Recreations:* writing for amusement, browsing through Who's Who. *Club:* Royal Over-Seas League.

BUTTER, Peter Joseph Michael, CB 1992; Deputy Managing Director, Property Services Agency, Building Management, Department of the Environment, 1992, retired; *b* 9 Dec. 1932; *s* of Joseph Butter and Kathleen (*née* Woodward); *m* 1956, Pamela Frances Roberts; three *s*. *Educ:* Brighton, Hove and Sussex Grammar School. Served Royal Signals, 1951–53. BR, 1953–67; Principal, Min. of Transport, 1967–73; Private Sec. to Minister of Transport, 1973; joined PSA, 1974: Hd, Defence Secretariat (Navy), 1974–79; Asst Dir, Estate Surveying Services, 1979–84; Dir, SE Region, 1984–88; Dir, Home Regional Services, 1988–90; Dir. of Ops, PSA, Bldg Management, DoE, 1990–91. Sec.,

Sussex Cricket League, 1999–. *Recreations:* cricket administration and umpiring, listening to music, exploring Britain. *Address:* 6 Scarletts Close, Uckfield, E Sussex TN22 2BA. *Club:* Sussex CC.

BUTTERFIELD, Hon. Sir (Alexander) Neil (Logie), Kt 1995; **Hon. Mr Justice Butterfield;** a Judge of the High Court of Justice, Queen's Bench Division, since 1995. *Educ:* Sidney Sussex Coll., Cambridge (BA 1964). Called to the Bar, Inner Temple, 1965; a Recorder, 1978–95; QC 1985. Leader, 1992–95, Presiding Judge, 1997–2000, Western Circuit. *Address:* Royal Courts of Justice, Strand, WC2A 2LL. *Club:* Athenæum.

BUTTERFIELD, Charles Harris; QC (Singapore) 1952; HMOCS, retired; *b* 28 June 1911; 2nd *s* of William Arthur Butterfield, OBE, and Rebecca Butterfield; *m* 1st, 1938, Monica, *d* of Austin Harrison, London; one *d*; 2nd, by special permission of the Holy See, Ellen, *d* of Ernest John Bennett, Singapore and *widow* of J. E. King, Kuala Lumpur, Singapore and Hooe. *Educ:* Downside; Trinity Coll., Cambridge. Barrister-at-law, Middle Temple, 1934. Entered Colonial Legal Service, 1938; Crown Counsel, Straits Settlements, 1938. Served Singapore RA (Volunteer) and RA, 1941–46; POW, 1942–45. Solicitor-General, Singapore, 1948–55, Attorney-General, 1955–57; Legal Adviser's Dept CRO and FCO, 1959–69; DoE and Sec. of State's Panel of Inspectors (Planning), 1969–74. *Recreations:* beagling, walking. *Address:* 18 Kewhurst Avenue, Cooden, Bexhill on Sea, E Sussex TN39 3BJ.

BUTTERFIELD, Jeremy Nicholas, PhD; FBA 1996; Senior Research Fellow, All Souls College, Oxford, since 1998; *b* 23 Dec. 1954; *s* of Baron Butterfield, OBE, DM, FRCP and of Isobel-Ann Foster Butterfield (*née* Kennedy); *m* 1978, Sally Damon Snell; one *s* one *d*. *Educ:* Trinity Coll., Cambridge (BA 1976; PhD 1984). Cambridge University: Asst Lectr in Philosophy, 1981–85; Lectr, 1985–97; Reader in Philosophy, 1997; Fellow of Jesus Coll., 1981–97. Vis. Prof., Princeton Univ., 1989. *Publications:* articles in learned jls. *Address:* All Souls College, Oxford OX1 4AL. *T:* (01865) 279379.

BUTTERFIELD, John Michael; Chief Executive, National Association of Youth Clubs, 1975–86; *b* 2 July 1926; *s* of late John Leslie Butterfield and Hilda Mary Butterfield (*née* Judson); *m* 1955, Mary Maureen (*d* 1998), *d* of John Martin; one *s* twin *d* (and one *s* decd). *Educ:* Leeds Modern Sch.; Leeds Univ. John Butterfield & Son, Leeds, 1949–60; John Atkinson & Sons (Sowerby Bridge) Ltd, 1960–61. Youth Officer, Coventry Cathedral, 1961–68; Liverpool Council of Social Service: Head of Youth and Community Dept, 1968–72; Operations Dir, 1972–75. Mem., BCC, 1954–73 (Mem., 1952–68; Chm., Exec. Cttee, 1962–67, Youth Dept); Vice-Chairman: Nat. Council for Voluntary Youth Services, 1977–83; UK Adv. Cttee, SCF, 1990–93; Chairman: Leics Council of Voluntary Youth Services, 1985–98; Youthaid, 1986–90; Youth Club Leics, 1987–99; UK Grants Cttee, Charity Projects later Comic Relief, 1992–98; Hinckley and Bosworth CVS, 1997–. Merseyside Advr, Baring Foundn, 1987–96; UK Rep., Amer. Youth Work Center, 1987–98. *Recreations:* music, reading, walking, railways. *Address:* 4 Church Farm Court, Aston Flamville, near Hinckley, Leics LE10 3AF. *T:* (01455) 611027.

BUTTERFIELD, Stewart David; Managing Director, Granada UK Broadcasting, since 1997; *b* 10 Sept. 1947; *s* of Bernard and Moray Butterfield. *Educ:* Mount St Mary's Coll., Spinkhill, Derbys; London Sch. of Econs (BSc Econ). McCann-Erickson, 1973–91, European Media Dir, 1989–91; Dir of Advertising Sales and Mktg, Channel Four, 1991–97. *Address:* Granada Broadcasting, London Television Centre, Upper Ground, SE1 9LT. *Club:* Royal Automobile.

BUTTERFILL, John Valentine; MP (C) Bournemouth West, since 1983; *b* 14 Feb. 1941; *s* of George Thomas Butterfill and Elsie Amelia (*née* Watts); *m* 1965, Pamela Ross-Symons; one *s* three *d*. *Educ:* Caterham Sch.; Coll. of Estate Management. FRICS 1974. Valuer, Jones, Lang, Wootton, 1961–64; Sen. Exec., Hammerson Gp, 1964–69; Dir, Audley Properties Ltd (Bovis Gp), 1969–71; Man. Dir, St Paul's Securities Gp, 1971–76; Sen. Partner, Curchod & Co., 1977–91, Consultant, 1992–. Chm., Conservative Investments, 1984–; Director: Micro Business Systems, 1977–79; John Lelliott Developments, 1984–88; ISLEF Building and Construction, 1984–91; Pavilion Services Gp, 1992–94; Delphi Gp, 1996–99. Pres., European Property Associates, 1979–. Parliamentary Private Secretary: to Sec. of State for Energy, 1988–89; to Sec. of State for Transport, 1989–90; to Minister of State for NI, 1991–92. Vice Chm., 1922 Cttee, 1997–2001; Mem., Trade and Industry Select Cttee, 1992–2001; Chm., All Party Gp on Occupational Pensions, 1992–; Hon. Sec., All Party Gp on Bldg Socs, 1996–; Vice-Chm., All Party Parly Gp on Bldg Socs, 1997–; Jt Sec., All Party Parly Gp on Insurance and Financial Services, 1997–; Member: Cttee on Unopposed Bills, 1995–; Speaker's Panel of Chairmen, 1996–; Vice-Chairman: Backbench Tourism Cttee, 1986–88; Backbench Finance Cttee, 1992–2000; Chm., Backbench Europ. Affairs Cttee, 1995–97; Sec., Backbench Trade and Industry Cttee, 1987–88, and 1991; Vice Pres., Cons. Gp for Europe, 1992–95 (Chm., 1989–92); Vice-Chm., Parly Gp, Cons. Friends of Israel, 1995–. Mem., Council of Management, PDSA, 1990–. *Publications:* occasional contribs to property, insurance and financial publications. *Recreations:* ski-ing, tennis, bridge, music. *Address:* House of Commons, SW1A 0AA.

BUTTERSS, Rt Rev. Robert Leopold; Bishop of the Eastern Region (Assistant Bishop of the Diocese of Melbourne), 1985–94; *b* 17 Jan. 1931; *s* of A. L. Butterss; *m* 1956, Margaret (*née* Hayman); two *s* one *d*. *Educ:* Haileybury; Brighton and Ridley Coll., Melbourne. Ordained: deacon, 1955; priest, 1956; Curate, St Andrew's, Brighton, 1955–56; Vicar, Holy Trinity, Lara, 1956–60; Priest in charge, Popondetta, PNG, 1960–64; Vicar: Holy Trinity, Pascoe Vale, 1964–66; St Stephen's, Mt Waverley, 1970–76; Canon, St Peter and St Paul's Cathedral, PNG, 1976–83; Dean, St John's Cathedral, Brisbane, 1983–85. Chm., Australian Bd of Missions, Sydney, 1976–83 (Victorian Sec., 1966–70). *Recreation:* music. *Address:* Dayspring, Stroud, NSW 2425, Australia.

BUTTERWORTH, family name of **Baron Butterworth**.

BUTTERWORTH, Baron *cr* 1985 (Life Peer), of Warwick in the County of Warwickshire; **John Blackstock Butterworth,** CBE 1982; JP; DL; First Vice-Chancellor, University of Warwick, 1963–85; *b* 13 March 1918; *o s* of John William and Florence Butterworth; *m* 1948, Doris Crawford Elder; one *s* two *d*. *Educ:* Queen Elizabeth's Grammar Sch., Mansfield; The Queen's Coll., Oxford. Royal Artillery, 1939–46. MA 1946. Called to Bar, Lincoln's Inn, 1947, Hon. Bencher, 1989. New Coll., Oxford: Fellow, 1946–63; Dean, 1952–56; Bursar, 1956–63; Sub Warden, 1957–58. Junior Proctor, 1950–51; Faculty Fellow of Nuffield Coll., 1953–58; Member of Hebdomadal Council, Oxford Univ., 1953–63. Managing Trustee 1964–85, Trustee, 1985–, Nuffield Foundation; Chairman: Inter-Univ. Council for Higher Educn Overseas, 1968–77; Universities Cttee for Non-teaching Staffs, 1970–85; Inquiry into work of Probation Officers and Social Workers in Local Authorities and Nat. Service, 1971–73; Standing Cttee on Internat. Co-operation in Higher Educn, British Council, 1981–85; Inter-Univ. and Polytechnic Council, 1981–85; Pres., Foundn for Sci. and Technol., 1997– (Chm., 1990–97). Univ. Comr (Under Educn Reform Act 1988), 1988–; Member: Royal Commn on the Working of the Tribunals of Inquiry (Act), 1921, 1966; Intergovernmental Cttee on Law of Contempt in relation to Tribunals of Inquiry, 1968; Jarratt Cttee on University Efficiency, 1986; Cttee on the review of UGC, 1987; Noise Advisory Council, 1974–81; Bd, British Council 1981–85; British delegn to Commonwealth Educn Conferences in Lagos, 1968, Canberra, 1971, Kingston, 1974, Accra, 1977, Colombo, 1980. Governor, Royal Shakespeare Theatre, 1964–99, now Hon. Emeritus Governor. DL Warwickshire, 1967–74, DL West Midlands 1974–; JP City of Oxford, 1962, Coventry, 1963–. Hon. DCL Univ. of Sierra Leone, 1976; Hon. DSc Univ. of Aston, 1985; Hon. LLD Warwick, 1986. *Address:* The Barn, Barton, Guiting Power, Glos GL54 5US. *T:* (01451) 850297. *Club:* Athenæum.

See also Hon. A. E. B. Walker.

BUTTERWORTH, Anthony; *see* Butterworth, C. A.

BUTTERWORTH, Anthony Edward, PhD; FRS 1994; MRC External Scientific Staff, 1979–95, retired; Hon. Professor of Medical Parasitology, University of Cambridge, 1993–95; *b* 8 July 1945; *s* of late Edward Alexander Butterworth and Sylvia (*née* Hardy); *m* 1972, Margot Lois Hudson (marr. diss. 1999); one *s* one *d*. *Educ:* Harrow Sch.; Trinity Hall, Cambridge (BA); St Mary's Hosp. Med. Sch., London (MB, BChir); Clare Coll., Cambridge (PhD). Wellcome Trust Research Fellow: Nairobi, Kenya, 1973–77; Harvard Med. Sch., Boston, 1977–79; University of Cambridge: Associate Lectr, 1980–89; Hon. Reader, 1989–93. Frederick Murgatroyd Prize, RCP, 1979; Bernhard Nocht Medal, 1987; King Faisal Internat. Prize in Medicine, 1990; Chalmers Medal, RSTM&H, 1990. *Publications:* papers and book chapters on immunology and parasitology. *Recreations:* African sculpture, travel, bird-watching, sailing. *Address:* Biomedical Research and Training Institute, PO Box CY 1753, Causeway, Harare, Zimbabwe.

BUTTERWORTH, Prof. (Charles) Anthony, CBE 1996; PhD; FRCN; Professor of Community Nursing, Queen's Nursing Institute, since 1987, and Pro-Vice Chancellor, since 1999, University of Manchester; *b* 14 March 1947; *s* of Norman Butterworth and Anne Alison Butterworth; *m* 1971, Jacqueline; one *s* one *d*. *Educ:* Univ. of Aston, Birmingham (MSc; PhD 1986); Storthes Hall Hosp., Huddersfield (RMN); Manchester Royal Infirmary (RGN); Univ. of Manchester (RNT). Clinical nurse, Yorks and Gtr Manchester, 1968–75; Lectr, then Sen. Lectr, 1975–80, Principal Lectr and Hd of Nursing, 1980–86, Manchester Poly. FRCN 1996; Founder FMedSci 1998. Hon. FRCPsych 1999. FRSA 1996. *Publications:* Community Psychiatric Nursing, 1980; Caring for the Mentally Ill in the Community, 1981; Clinical Supervision and Mentorship in Nursing, 1992, 2nd edn 1999. *Recreations:* gardening, walking, travel, motor-cycling. *Address:* Coupland III Building, University of Manchester, Oxford Road, Manchester M13 9PL. *T:* and *Fax:* (0161) 275 5336.

BUTTERWORTH, Prof. Ian, CBE 1984; FRS 1981; Senior Research Fellow, Imperial College, since 1991; Professor of Physics, University of London, 1971–91, now Emeritus; *b* 3 Dec. 1930; *s* of Harry and Beatrice Butterworth; *m* 1964, Mary Therese (*née* Gough); one *d*. *Educ:* Bolton County Grammar Sch.; Univ. of Manchester. BSc 1951; PhD 1954. Sen. Scientific Officer, UK Atomic Energy Authority, 1954–58; Lectr, Imperial Coll., 1958–64; Vis. Physicist, Lawrence Radiation Laboratory, Univ. of California, 1964–65; Sen. Lectr, Imperial Coll., 1965–68; Group Leader, Bubble Chamber Research Gp, Rutherford High Energy Laboratory, 1968–71; Professor, 1971–86, Head of Dept, 1980–83, Dept of Physics, Imperial Coll.; on leave of absence as Res. Dir, CERN, 1983–86; Principal, QMC, then QMW, 1986–91; Pro Vice-Chancellor for Eur. Affairs, London Univ., 1989–91. Science and Engineering Research Council (formerly Science Research Council): Mem., 1979–83 (Mem., Nuclear Physics Bd, 1972–75 and 1978–83, Chm., 1979–83; Mem., Particle Physics Cttee, 1978–79; Chm., Film Analysis Grants Cttee, 1972–75); UK deleg. on Council, CERN, 1979–82 (Mem., Research Bd, 1976–82; Chm., Super Proton Synchroton Cttee, 1976–79). Member: Physics Res. Cttee, Deutsches Elektronen Synchroton, Hamburg, 1981–85; Sci. Policy Cttee, Stanford Linear Accelerator Center, Calif, 1984–88; Sci. Adv. Cttee, British Council, 1986–91; Science Cttee, UK Nat. Commn for UNESCO, 2000–; Physical Scis and Engrg Standing Cttee, ESF, 2000–; IUPAP deleg. to Internat. Council for Scientific and Technical Inf., 1999–. Council Member: Royal Soc., 1989–90; Inst. of Physics, 1989–92 (Vice Pres., 1993–97; Chm., IOP Publishing Ltd, 1993–97); MAE 1989 (Vice Pres., 1997–). Hon. Mem., Manchester Lit. and Phil. Soc., 1987. Fellow, Imperial Coll., 1988. Dr *hc* Soka Univ., 1989. Glazebrook Prize and Medal, Inst. of Physics, 1993. *Publications:* numerous papers in learned jls (on experimental particle physics). *Recreations:* reading, history of art. *Address:* Blackett Laboratory, Imperial College, Prince Consort Road, SW7 2AZ; 48 Burntwood Grange Road, SW18 3JX. *Club:* Arts.

BUTTFIELD, Dame Nancy (Eileen), DBE 1972; formerly Senator for South Australia; *b* 12 Nov. 1912; *d* of Sir Edward Wheewall Holden and Hilda May Lavis; *m* 1936, Frank Charles Buttfield; two *s*. *Educ:* Woodlands Church of England Girls' Grammar Sch., Adelaide; Composenea; Paris; Univ. of Adelaide, SA. Senator for South Australia, Oct. 1955–June 1965, re-elected July 1968–74. Exec. Mem., Commonwealth Immigration Adv. Council, 1955–; Vice-President: Good Neighbour Council of SA, 1956–62; Phoenix Soc. for the Physically Handicapped, 1959–. Dir, Co-operative Building Soc. of SA, 1959, now Emeritus Dir. Mem. Council, Bedford Industries, 1965–. Mem., Nat. Council of Women of SA. *Recreations:* farming, dress-making, gourmet cooking, music. *Address:* 52 Strangeways Terrace, North Adelaide, SA 5006, Australia. *Clubs:* Queen Adelaide, Lyceum, Royal Adelaide Golf (all SA).

BUTTLE, Eileen, CBE 1995; PhD; FIBiol; Member Scientific Committee, European Environment Agency, since 1994; *b* 19 Oct. 1937; *d* of late George Ernest Linford and of Mary Stewart Linford; *m* 1970, Hugh Langley Buttle. *Educ:* Harrow Weald County Grammar Sch.; Univ. of Southampton (BSc (Hons); PhD). FIBiol 1990. Post-doctoral Res. Fellow, Univ. of Southampton, 1963–65; Research Scientist: Nat. Inst. of Res. in Dairying, 1965–71; Cattle Breeding Centre, MAFF, 1971–76; Policy Administrator, MAFF, 1976–89; Sec., NERC, 1989–94; Dir, World Humanity Action Trust, 1994–97. Dir, Shell Transport and Trading Co. plc, 1998–. Trustee: Buckland Foundn, 1994–; Horniman Mus. of Gdns, 1994–98; Onyx Envmtl Trust, 1997–; Earthwatch Europe, 1997–. Gov. and Mem. Council, ICSTM, 1999–. *Recreations:* golf, fly fishing. *Address:* Willows Farm, Cleverton, Chippenham, Wilts SN15 5BT. *T:* (01666) 825618. *Club:* Farmers'.

BUTTON, Henry George; author; *b* 11 Aug. 1913; *e s* of late Rev. Frank S. and Bertha B. Button; *m* 1938, Edith Margaret Heslop (*d* 1972); two *d*. *Educ:* Manchester Grammar Sch.; Christ's Coll., Cambridge (Scholar). Mod. and Medieval Langs Tripos, Part II, 1st Class (with dist.) 1934; MLitt 1977; Tiarks German Scholar (research at Univ. of Bonn), 1934–35; Sen. Studentship of Goldsmiths' Company, 1935–36. Entered Civil Service, 1937; Board of Trade, 1937–57 (served in Min. of Production, 1942; Counsellor, UK Delegn to OEEC, Paris, 1952–55; on staff of Monopolies Commn, 1955–56); transf. Min. of Agriculture, Fisheries and Food, 1957; Under-Sec., Min. of Agriculture, Fisheries and Food, 1960–73 (Principal Finance Officer, 1965–73). Res. Student, 1974–76, Fellow-Commoner, 1982–, Christ's Coll., Cambridge. Mem. Agricultural Research Council,

1960–62. Leader of various UK Delegns to FAO in Rome. BBC Brain of Britain for 1962; rep. Great Britain in radio quiz in Johannesburg, 1966; Bob Dyer's TV show, Sydney, 1967. *Publications:* The Guinness Book of the Business World (with A. Lampert), 1976; contribs to various jls both learned and unlearned, and to newspapers. *Recreations:* reading, writing, studying old businesses (hon. review ed., Business Archives Council, 1966–75; Hon. Sec., Tercentenarians' Club, 1970–2001), showing visitors round the colleges. *Address:* 7 Amhurst Court, Grange Road, Cambridge CB3 9BH. *T:* (01223) 355698. *Club:* Civil Service.

See also Air Marshal Sir T. Garden.

BUTTRESS, Donald Reeve, LVO 1997; FSA; architect; Partner, Buttress Fuller Alsop, Manchester, since 1974; Surveyor of the Fabric of Westminster Abbey, 1988–99, now Surveyor Emeritus; *b* 27 April 1932; *s* of Edward Crossley Buttress and Evelyn Edna Reeve-Whaley; *m* 1956, Elsa Mary Bardsley; two *s* three *d*. *Educ:* Stockport Sch.; Univ. of Manchester (MA, DipArch). ARIBA. Flying Officer, RAF, 1958–61. Lectr, Manchester Univ., 1964–78; Vis. Prof. and Fulbright Travelling Scholar, Univ. of Florida, 1967–68. Architect to: Bangor and Sheffield Cathedrals, 1978–88; Leeds (RC) Cathedral, 1983–95; Llandaff Cathedral, 1986–97; Surveyor to the Fabric, Chichester Cathedral, 1984–. Principal works: Stockport SS Community Centre, 1973; extn, St Matthew, Hayfield, 1978; St George's Chapel, Sheffield Cathedral, 1981; rebldg, St Matthew, Westminster, 1982; repair of spire, All Souls, Halifax, 1984; repair of nave, North transept and West front, Chichester Cath., 1985–95; reconstruction, Tonbridge Sch. Chapel, 1992–95; restoration of West front and Henry VII Chapel, Westminster Abbey, 1989–95. Member: Cathedrals and Churches Adv. Cttee (formerly Churches Sub-Cttee, English Heritage), 1988–94; Council for the Care of Churches, 1976–86, 1991–96; Council, Royal Archaeological Inst., 1991–94; Chester DAC, 1970–88; St Albans DAC, 1998–. President: Ecclesiol Soc., 1995– (Vice Pres., 1992–95); Surveyors' Club, 1994–95; Mem., Baconian Club. Gov., Sutton's Hosp. in Charterhouse, 2001–. Master, Art Workers' Guild, 2000 (Brother, 1989). Mem., Editl Bd, Church Building magazine, 1982–. DLitt Lambeth, 2001. *Publications:* Manchester Buildings, 1967; Gawthorpe Hall (NT guide), 1971; articles in learned jls. *Recreations:* ecclesiology, 18th Century furniture, stained glass, heraldry. *Address:* 95 Fishpool Street, St Albans AL3 4RU. *T:* (01727) 810753. *Club:* Royal Air Force.

BUTTREY, Prof. Theodore Vern, PhD; FSA; Keeper, Department of Coins, Fitzwilliam Museum, Cambridge, 1988–91, now Keeper Emeritus; *b* 29 Dec. 1929; *s* of Theodore Vern Buttrey and Ruth Jeanette Scoutt; *m* 1st, 1954, Marisa Macina (marr. diss. 1967); three *s* one *d*; 2nd, 1967, Ann Elizabeth Johnston. *Educ:* Phillips Exeter Acad.; Princeton Univ. (BA 1950; PhD 1953). Instr, 1954–58, Asst Prof., 1958–64, Yale Univ.; University of Michigan: Associate Professor, 1964–67; Prof. of Greek and Latin, 1967–85; Prof. Emeritus, 1985–; Chm., Dept of Classical Studies, 1968–71, 1983–84; Dir, Kelsey Mus. of Archaeology, 1969–71. Member: Clare Hall, Cambridge, 1971–; Faculty of Classics, Cambridge Univ., 1975–. Pres., RNS, 1989–94; Sec., UK Numismatic Trust, 1994–98. Corresp. Mem., Royal Danish Acad. of Scis and Letters, 1995. Medal, RNS, 1985; Medal, Amer. Numismatic Soc., 1996. *Publications:* (jtly) Greek, Roman and Islamic Coins from Sardis, 1981; (jtly) Morgantina Studies: the coins, 1989; numerous publications in ancient and modern numismatics. *Recreations:* Ernest Bramah, P. G. Wodehouse, travel. *Address:* 6 de Freville Avenue, Cambridge CB4 1HR. *T:* (01223) 351156.

BUXTON, family name of **Barons Buxton of Alsa** and **Noel-Buxton**.

BUXTON OF ALSA, Baron *cr* 1978 (Life Peer), of Stiffkey in the County of Norfolk; **Aubrey Leland Oakes Buxton,** KCVO 1996; MC 1943; DL; Director, Anglia Television, since 1958 (Chairman, 1986–88); *b* 15 July 1918; *s* of Leland Wilberforce Buxton and Mary, *d* of Rev. Thomas Henry Oakes; *m* 1st, 1946, Pamela Mary (*d* 1983), *d* of Sir Henry Birkin, 3rd Bt; two *s* four *d*; 2nd, 1988, Mrs Kathleen Peterson, Maine, USA. *Educ:* Ampleforth; Trinity Coll., Cambridge. Served 1939–45, RA; combined ops in Arakan, 1942–45 (despatches, 1944). Extra Equerry to Duke of Edinburgh. A Trustee of the British Museum (Natural History), 1971–73. Member: Countryside Commn, 1968–72; Royal Commission on Environmental Pollution, 1970–74; British Vice Pres., World Wildlife Fund; Trustee, Wildfowl Trust; Treasurer, London Zoological Soc., 1978–83; Former Pres., Royal Television Soc.; Chairman: Independent Television Cos Assoc., 1972–75; UPITN Inc., USA, 1981–83; ITN, 1981–86. Wildlife Film Producer, Anglia TV. Golden Awards, Internat. TV Festival, 1963 and 1968; Silver Medal, Zoological Society of London, 1967; Silver Medal, Royal TV Society, 1968; Queen's Award to Industry, 1974; Gold Medal, Royal TV Soc., 1977. High Sheriff of Essex 1972; DL Essex, 1975–85. *Publications:* (with Sir Philip Christison) The Birds of Arakan, 1946; The King in his Country, 1955. *Recreations:* travel, natural history, painting, sport. *Address:* Old Hall Farm, Stiffkey, Norfolk NR23 1QJ. *Club:* White's.

BUXTON, Adrian Clarence, CMG 1978; HM Diplomatic Service, retired; Ambassador to Bolivia, 1977–81, and to Ecuador, 1981–85; *b* 12 June 1925; *s* of Clarence Buxton and Dorothy (*née* Lintott); *m* 1st, 1958, Leonora Mary Cherkas (*d* 1984); three *s*; 2nd, 1985, June Samson. *Educ:* Christ's Hosp., Horsham; Trinity Coll., Cambridge. RNVR, 1944–46; FO, 1947; Bangkok, 1948–52; FO, 1952–53; Khartoum, 1953–55; Bonn, 1955–58; Bogota, 1958–62; FO, 1962–64; Saigon, 1964–67; Havana, 1967–69; Geneva, 1969–73; sabbatical, Univ. of Surrey, 1973–74; FCO, 1974–77. *Recreations:* golf, choral singing. *Address:* 89 Glenferness Avenue, Bournemouth BH3 7ES.

BUXTON, Andrew Robert Fowell; Deputy Chairman, FI Group plc, since 1999; *b* 5 April 1939; *m* 1965, Jane Margery Grant; two *d*. *Educ:* Winchester Coll.; Pembroke Coll., Oxford. Joined Barclays Bank, 1963; Man. Dir, 1988–92; Chief Exec., 1992–93; Chm., 1993–99. Mem. Court, Bank of England, 1997–2001. Pres., British Bankers' Assoc., 1997–2001. *Club:* Royal Automobile.

BUXTON, Sir Jocelyn (Charles Roden), 7th Bt *cr* 1840, of Belfield, Dorset; VRD 1975; *b* 8 Aug. 1924; *er s* of Captain Roden H. V. Buxton, CBE, RN (*d* 1970) and Dorothy Alina St John Buxton (*d* 1956); *S* cousin, 1996; *m* 1960, Ann Frances, *d* of late Frank Smitherman, MBE; three *d*. *Educ:* Eton. Served RNVR, 1942–45 (despatches); Korea, 1952. *Heir: b* Lieut-Comdr Gerard St John Roden Buxton, RN [*b* 28 Sept. 1927; *m* 1954, Judith Averil, *d* of Hon. Angus Campbell, CBE; one *s* two *d*]. *Address:* Rodwell House, Loddon, Norfolk.

BUXTON, Prof. John Noel, FBCS; CEng; Chairman, Room Underwriting Systems Ltd, 1993–97; Professor of Information Technology, King's College, London, 1984–94; *b* 25 Dec. 1933; *s* of John William Buxton and Laura Frances Buxton; *m* 1958, Moira Jean O'Brien; two *s* two *d*. *Educ:* Bradford Grammar Sch.; Trinity Coll., Cambridge (BA 1955, MA 1959). FBCS 1968. Flight Trials Engr, De Havilland Propellers, 1955–59; Ops Res. Scientist, British Iron and Steel Res. Assoc., 1959–60; Applied Science Rep., IBM UK, 1960–62; Lectr, Inst. of Computer Science, Univ. of London, 1962–66; Chief Software Consultant, CEIR (now Scicon Ltd) 1966–68; Prof. of Computer Science, Univ. of Warwick, 1968–84. UNDP Proj. Manager, Internat. Computing Educn Centre, Budapest, 1975–77; Vis. Scholar, Harvard Univ., 1979–80; Dir of Systems Engrng, DTI, 1989–91 (on secondment). Hon. Vice-Pres. (Engrg), BCS, 1997–. *Publications:* (ed) Simulation Programming Languages, 1968; (ed jtly) Software Engineering Concepts and Techniques (Procs of NATO Confs 1968 and 1969), 1976; (jtly) The Craft of Software Engineering, 1987; three computer programming languages; papers in professional jls. *Recreations:* mountaineering, music, ancient houses, genealogy, local history. *Address:* The Guildhall, Church Street, Eye, Suffolk IP23 7BD.

BUXTON, Hon. Margaret Evelyn; *see* Aston, Hon. M. E.

BUXTON, Prof. Neil Keith; Vice-Chancellor, University of Hertfordshire, since 1992; *b* 2 May 1940; *s* of William F. A. Buxton and Janet A. Buxton; *m* 1962, Margaret G. Buxton (*née* Miller); two *s* one *d*. *Educ:* Aberdeen Univ. (MA Hons Political Econs); PhD Heriot-Watt. Asst Lectr, Dept of Political Econ., Aberdeen Univ., 1962–64; Lectr, Dept of Econ., Univ. of Hull, 1964–69; Lectr and Sen. Lectr, 1969–78, Prof., 1979–83, Heriot-Watt Univ.; Depute Dir, Glasgow Coll. of Technology, 1983–87; Dir, Hatfield Poly., 1987–92. Vis. Prof. in Econs and Public Admin, Lewis and Clark Coll., Oregon, 1982. Dir, Herts TEC, 1989–; Member: Board: Businesslink, Herts, 1993–; Herts Learning and Skills Council; Herts Prosperity Forum; Regl Bd, GWR (Chiltern) Radio. *Publications:* (with T. L. Johnston and D. Mair) Structure and Growth of the Scottish Economy, 1971; (with D. I. Mackay) British Employment Statistics, 1977; Economic Development of the British Coal Industry, 1978; (ed) British Industry Between the Wars, 1979; articles in professional jls. *Recreations:* sport, bridge, overseas travel, pipe smoking. *Address:* University of Hertfordshire, College Lane, Hatfield, Herts AL10 9AB. *T:* (01707) 284000.

BUXTON, Paul William Jex; Northern Ireland Office, 1974–85 (Under Secretary, 1981–85); *b* 20 Sept. 1925; *s* of of late Denis Buxton and Emily Buxton (*née* Hollins); *m* 1st, 1950, Katharine Hull (marr. diss. 1971, she *d* 1977); two *s* one *d*; 2nd, 1971, Hon. Margaret Aston (*née* Bridges) (*see* M. E. Aston); two *d*. *Educ:* Rugby Sch.; Balliol Coll., Oxford (MA). Coldstream Guards, 1944–47. HM Foreign, later Diplomatic, Service, 1950–71; served Delhi, UN, Guatemala and Washington, latterly as Counsellor. Investment banking, 1972–74; on staff of Monopolies and Mergers Commn, 1985–91. Treasurer: Anti-Slavery International (formerly Anti-Slavery Soc.), 1986–; Howard League for Penal Reform, 1991–97 (Mem. Council, 1985–99); Hon. Treas., Prisoners' Advice Service, 1991–96. *Recreation:* forestry. *Address:* Castle House, Chipping Ongar, Essex CM5 9JT. *T:* (01277) 362642. *Club:* Brooks's.

BUXTON, Raymond Naylor, OBE 1975; BEM 1957; QPM 1971; *b* 16 Sept. 1915; *s* of late Tom Bird Buxton and Ethel Buxton, Rushall, Walsall; *m* 1939, Agatha, *d* of late Enoch and Elizabeth Price, Essington, Wolverhampton; three *s*. *Educ:* King Edward VI Grammar Sch., Stafford. Constable to Chief Supt in Staffordshire Co. Police. Served War, RAF, Navigator, 1943–45 (FO). Police Coll. Staff, 1958–61; Asst Chief Constable, then Dep. Chief Constable of Herts, 1963–69, Chief Constable, 1969–77; HM Inspector of Constabulary, 1977–79. *Address:* Mannicotts, Radford Rise, Weeping Cross, Stafford ST17 4PS.

BUXTON, Rt Hon. Sir Richard (Joseph), Kt 1994; PC 1997; **Rt Hon. Lord Justice Buxton;** a Lord Justice of Appeal, since 1997; *b* 13 July 1938; *o s* of late Bernard Buxton, DSO, chartered mechanical engineer, and of Sybil (*née* Hurley), formerly of Burton-upon-Trent; *m* 1987, Mary Tyerman, JP, *y d* of late Donald Tyerman, CBE and Margaret Tyerman. *Educ:* Brighton Coll. (Schol.); Exeter Coll., Oxford (Schol.; First Cl. Final Hon. Sch. of Jurisprudence 1961, First Cl. BCL 1962; Vinerian Schol. 1962; MA; Hon. Fellow, 1998). FCIArb 1992. Lectr, Christ Church, 1962–63; Lectr 1963–64, Fellow and Tutor 1964–73, Sub-Rector 1966–71, Exeter Coll., Oxford. Called to the Bar, Inner Temple, 1969; Bencher, 1992; in practice, 1972–88; QC 1983; a Recorder, 1987–93; a Law Comr, 1989–93; a Judge of the High Court, QBD, 1994–97; a Judge, Restrictive Practices Court, 1994–97. Second Lieut RAOC, 1957–58. Councillor, Oxford CC, 1966–69. Chm. of Governors, Penton I and JM Sch., N1, 1986–91. Hon. LLD Nottingham, 2000. Médaille de la Ville de Paris (échelon argent), 1999. *Publications:* Local Government, 1970, 2nd edn 1973; articles in legal periodicals. *Address:* Royal Courts of Justice, Strand, WC2A 2LL.

BUXTON, Ronald Carlile, MA Cantab; *b* 20 Aug. 1923; *s* of Murray Barclay Buxton and Janet Mary Muriel Carlile; *m* 1959, Phyllida Dorothy Roden Buxton; two *s* two *d*. *Educ:* Eton; Trinity Coll., Cambridge. Chartered Structural Engineer (FIStructE). Director of H. Young & Co., London and associated companies. MP (C) Leyton, 1965–66. *Recreations:* travel, music, riding. *Address:* Kimberley Hall, Wymondham, Norfolk NR18 0RT; 67 Ashley Gardens, SW1P 1QG. *Club:* Carlton.

BUYERS, Thomas Bartlett, OBE 1975; HM Chief Inspector of Prisons for Scotland, 1985–89, retired; *b* 21 March 1926; *s* of Charles Stuart Buyers and Bessie Heywood Buyers; *m* 1951, Agnes Lodge Alexander; three *d*. *Educ:* Glasgow Acad., Glasgow; Glasgow Univ. (BSc); BA Open Univ. 1998. MIChemE. Res. Chemist, Shell, 1947–50; professional and management posts, BP Chemicals, Grangemouth and Baglan Bay, 1951–73; Dir, Scottish Petroleum Office, 1973–74; Dir of Engrg, Offshore Supplies Office, Dept of Energy, 1974–75; BP Rep./Commissioning Man., Sullom Voe Terminal, Shetland, 1975–80; Special Projects Man., BP Chemicals, London, 1980–84. *Recreations:* gardening, hill walking, voluntary work. *Address:* 24 Kinord Drive, Aboyne, Aberdeenshire AB34 5JZ.

BUZAN, Prof. Barry, PhD; FBA 1998; Research Professor of International Studies, University of Westminster, since 1995; *b* 28 April 1946; *s* of Gordon and Jean Buzan; *m* 1973, Deborah Skinner. *Educ:* Univ. of British Columbia (BA Hons 1968); London Sch. of Econs (PhD 1973). Computer trainee, Honeywell UK, 1970; Res. Fellow, Inst. of Internat. Relns, Univ. of BC, 1973–75; University of Warwick: Lectr, 1976–83, Sen. Lectr, 1983–88, Reader, 1988–90, Dept of Internat. Studies; Prof., Dept of Politics and Internat. Studies, 1990–95. Vis. Prof., Internat. Univ. of Japan, 1993; Olof Palme Vis. Prof., Sweden, 1997–98. Dir, project on European security, Copenhagen Peace Res. Inst., 1988–; Consultant: Swedish Min. for Foreign Affairs, 1984–86; ESRC, 1987; London Business Sch., 1987–89. External Examiner: Sussex Univ., 1983–86; Open Univ., 1984–85, 1995–96; LSE, 1985–87; Bristol Univ., 1990–93. Chm., British Internat. Studies Assoc., 1988–90; Internat. Vice-Pres., Internat. Studies Assoc., 1993–94. Member, International Advisory Board: Jl of Peace Res., 1986–; Eur. Jl of Internat. Relns, 1994–99; Co-operation and Conflict, 1997–; Co-Ed., The New International Relations series, 1991–. Francis Deak Prize, Amer. Jl of Internat. Law, 1982. *Publications:* Seabed Politics, 1976; (ed with R. J. Barry Jones) Change and the Study of International Relations: the evaded dimension, 1981; People, States and Fear: the national security problem in international relations, 1983, 2nd edn as An Agenda for International Security Studies in the Post-Cold War Era, 1991; (jtly) South Asian Insecurity and the Great Powers, 1986; An Introduction to Strategic Studies: military technology and international relations, 1987; (ed) The International Politics of Deterrence, 1987; (jtly) The European Security Order Recast: scenarios for the post-cold war era, 1990; (jtly) The Logic of Anarchy: neorealism to structural realism, 1993; (jtly) Identity, Migration and the New Security Agenda in Europe, 1993; (with T. Buzan) The Mind Map Book, 1993; (jtly) Security: a new framework for analysis, 1998; (with G. Segal) Anticipating the Future: twenty millennia of human progress, 1998; (with E. Herring) The Arms Dynamic in World Politics, 1998; (with R. Little) International Systems in World History: remaking the study of international relations, 2000; contrib. numerous articles in learned jls incl. Survival, American Jl Internat. Law, Jl Peace Res., Internat. Orgn, Internat. Affairs, Rev. Internat. Studies, Internat. Pol Sci. Rev. and World Policy Jl. *Recreations:* chess, motorcycle touring, gardening. *Address:* Garden Flat, 17 Lambolle Road, NW3 4HS. *T:* (020) 7433 1431.

BUZEK, Dr Jerzy Karol; Prime Minister of Poland, 1997–2001; *b* 3 July 1940; *s* of Paweł and Bronisława Buzek; *m* 1974, Ludgarda; one *d*. *Educ:* Silesian Poly.; Dr Tech. Scis Polish Acad. of Scis. Chemical Engineering Institute, Polish Academy of Sciences: scientific res.; Dir for Scientific Affairs, 1963–97; Lecturer: Silesian Technical Univ., 1975–80; Technical Univ., Opole, 1993–97. Chm., Cttee of European Integration, 1998. Mem., Solidarity, 1980–: Chm., 1st, 4th, 5th and 6th Nat. Congress; Chm., Econ. Sub-Cttee, Election Cttee. Golden Cross of Commitment (Poland), 1989. *Publications:* books, patents, numerous sci. articles and papers. *Recreations:* poetry, theatre, horse riding, tennis, sailing, canoeing. *Address:* c/o Office of the Prime Minister, Aleje Ujazdowskie 1/3, 00–567 Warsaw, Poland.

BUZZARD, Sir Anthony (Farquhar), 3rd Bt *cr* 1929; Lecturer in Theology, Atlanta Bible (formerly Oregon Bible) College, since 1982; *b* 28 June 1935; *s* of Rear-Admiral Sir Anthony Wass Buzzard, 2nd Bt, CB, DSO, OBE, and Margaret Elfreda (*d* 1989), *d* of Sir Arthur Knapp, KCIE, CSI, CBE; *S* father, 1972; *m* 1970, Barbara Jean Arnold, Mendon, Michigan, USA; three *d*. *Educ:* Charterhouse; Christ Church, Oxford (MA 1960); Ambassador Coll., Pasadena, USA (BA); MA Th Bethany Theol Seminary, 1990. ARCM. Lecturer in French, Ambassador Coll., Pasadena, 1962–65; Peripatetic Music Teacher for Surrey County Council, 1966–68; Lectr in French and Hebrew, Ambassador Coll., Bricket Wood, Herts, 1969–74; teacher of mod. langs, American Sch. in London, 1974–81. Founded Restoration Fellowship, 1981. *Publications:* The Coming Kingdom of the Messiah: a Solution to the Riddle of the New Testament, 1988; The Doctrine of the Trinity: Christianity's Self-Inflicted Wound, 1994; Our Fathers who Aren't in Heaven: the forgotten Christianity of Jesus the Jew, 1995; articles on eschatology and Christology in various jls. *Recreations:* tennis, squash, music. *Heir: b* Timothy Macdonnell Buzzard [*b* 28 Jan. 1939; *m* 1970, Jennifer Mary, *d* of late Peter Patching; one *s* one *d*]. *Address:* (home) 175 West Lake Drive, Fayetteville, GA 30214, USA. *T:* (770) 9641571; (office) Box 100,000, Morrow, GA 30260, USA. *T:* (404) 3620052.

BYAM SHAW, Nicholas Glencairn; Deputy Chairman, Macmillan Ltd, since 1998 (Chairman, 1990–97); *b* 28 March 1934; *s* of Lieut. Comdr David Byam Shaw, RN, OBE (killed in action, 19 Dec. 1941) and Clarita Pamela Clarke; *m* 1st, 1956, Joan Elliott; two *s* one *d*; 2nd, 1974, Suzanne Filer (*née* Rastello); 3rd, 1987, Constance Wilson (*née* Clarke). *Educ:* Royal Naval Coll., Dartmouth. Commnd RN, 1955 (Lieut). Joined William Collins Sons & Co. Ltd, Glasgow, as salesman, 1956; Sales Manager, 1960; Macmillan and Co., subseq. Macmillan Publishers Ltd: Sales Manager, 1964; Sales Dir, 1965; Dep. Man. Dir, 1967; Man. Dir, 1969–90. Director: St Martins Press, 1980– (Dep. Chm., 1997–); Pan Books, 1983– (Chm., 1986–); Gruppe Georg von Hotzbrinck, Stuttgart, 1996–. *Recreations:* gardening, travel. *Address:* 9 Kensington Park Gardens, W11 3HB. *T:* (020) 7221 4547.

BYATT, Dame Antonia (Susan), (Dame Antonia Duffy), DBE 1999 (CBE 1990); FRSL 1983; writer; *b* 24 Aug. 1936; *d* of His Honour John Frederick Drabble, QC and late Kathleen Marie Bloor; *m* 1st, 1959, Ian Charles Rayner Byatt (*see* Sir I. C. R. Byatt) (marr. diss. 1969); one *d* (one *s* decd); 2nd, 1969, Peter John Duffy; two *d*. *Educ:* Sheffield High Sch.; The Mount Sch., York; Newnham Coll., Cambridge (BA Hons; Hon. Fellow 1999); Bryn Mawr Coll., Pa, USA; Somerville Coll., Oxford. Extra-Mural Lectr, Univ. of London, 1962–71; Lectr in Literature, Central Sch. of Art and Design, 1965–69; Lectr in English, 1972–81, Sen. Lectr, 1981–83, UCL. Associate of Newnham Coll., Cambridge, 1977–82. Member: Social Effects of Television Adv. Gp, BBC, 1974–77; Bd of Communications and Cultural Studies, CNAA, 1978–84; Bd of Creative and Performing Arts, CNAA, 1985–87; Kingman Cttee on English Language, 1987–88; Management Cttee, Soc. of Authors, 1984–88 (Dep. Chm., 1986; Chm., 1986–88); Bd, British Council, 1993–98 (Mem., Literature Adv. Panel, 1990–98). Broadcaster, reviewer; judge of literary prizes (Hawthornden, Booker, David Higham, Betty Trask). FRSL. Hon. Fellow, London Inst., 2000. Hon. DLitt: Bradford, 1987; Durham, 1991; Nottingham, 1992; Liverpool, 1993; Portsmouth, 1994; London, 1995; Sheffield, 2000; Hon. LittD Cambridge, 1999; DUniv York, 1991. *Publications:* Shadow of the Sun, 1964; Degrees of Freedom, 1965 (reprinted as Degrees of Freedom: the early novels of Iris Murdoch, 1994); The Game, 1967; Wordsworth and Coleridge in their Time, 1970 (reprinted as Unruly Times: Wordsworth and Coleridge in their Time, 1989); Iris Murdoch, 1976; The Virgin in the Garden, 1978; (ed) George Eliot, The Mill on the Floss, 1979; Still Life, 1985 (PEN/Macmillan Silver Pen of Fiction, 1986); Sugar and Other Stories, 1987; (ed) George Eliot: selected essays, 1989; Possession: a romance, 1990 (Booker Prize, 1990; Irish Times/Aer Lingus Internat. Fiction Prize, 1990; Eurasian section of Best Book in Commonwealth Prize, 1991); (ed) Robert Browning's Dramatic Monologues, 1990; Passions of the Mind (essays), 1991; Angels and Insects (novellae), 1992; The Matisse Stories (short stories), 1993; The Djinn in the Nightingale's Eye: five fairy stories, 1994; (jtly) Imagining Characters, 1995; (ed jtly) New Writing 4, 1995; Babel Tower, 1996; (ed jtly) New Writing 6, 1997; (ed) The Oxford Book of English Short Stories, 1998; Elementals: stories of fire and ice (short stories), 1998; The Biographer's Tale, 2000; On Histories and Stories (essays), 2000. *Address:* 37 Rusholme Road, SW15 3LF.

BYATT, Sir Hugh Campbell, KCVO 1985; CMG 1979; HM Diplomatic Service, retired; Director, EFM Japan Trust PLC, 1992–97; Chairman: EFM Java Trust, 1990–98; EFM Dragon Trust, 1992–98 (Director, 1987–98); *b* 27 Aug. 1927; *e s* of late Sir Horace Byatt, GCMG, and Lady Byatt (*née* Olga Margaret Campbell), MBE; *m* 1954, Fiona, *d* of Ian P. Coats, DL, and May Coats, MBE; two *s* one *d*. *Educ:* Gordonstoun; New College, Oxford (MA 1951). Served in Royal Navy, 1945–48 (Sub-Lieut RNVR); HMOCS Nigeria, 1952–57; Commonwealth Relations Office, 1958; Bombay, 1961–63; CRO, 1964–65; seconded to Cabinet Office, 1965–67; Head of Chancery, Lisbon, 1967–70; Asst Head, South Asian Dept, FCO, 1970–71; Consul-General, Mozambique, 1971–73; Inspector, HM Diplomatic Service, 1973–75; RCDS, 1976; Dep. High Comr, Nairobi, 1977–78; Ambassador to Angola, 1978–81, to São Tomé, 1980–81, to Portugal, 1981–86. Advr, RTZ, 1986–96; Special Advr, Scottish Financial Enterprise, 1986–92. Mem., Parole Bd for Scotland, 1990–92. Chm., Cttee for Scotland, Malcolm Sargent Cancer Fund for Children, 1991–96. Chm. of Govs, Centre for Inf. on Lang. Teaching and Res., 1986–90. FSAScot 1989. Hon. Sheriff, Campbeltown, 1994. Knight Grand Cross, Mil. Order of Christ (Portugal), 1985. *Recreation:* living in Argyll. *Address:* Leargnahension, Tarbert, Argyll PA29 6YB. *T:* (01880) 820644. *Clubs:* Royal Ocean Racing, RNVR Yacht; New (Edinburgh); Royal Highland Yacht (Oban).

See also R. A. C. Byatt.

BYATT, Sir Ian (Charles Rayner), Kt 2000; Senior Associate, Frontier Economics, since 2001; Director General of Water Services, 1989–2000; *b* 11 March 1932; *s* of Charles Rayner Byatt and Enid Marjorie Annie Byatt (*née* Howat); *m* 1st, 1959, A. S. Byatt (*see* Dame A. S. Byatt) (marr. diss. 1969); one *d* (one *s* decd); 2nd, 1997, Dr Deirdre Anne Kelly; two step *s*. *Educ:* Kirkham Grammar Sch.; Oxford University. Commonwealth Fund Fellow, Harvard, 1957–58; Lectr in Economics, Durham Univ., 1958–62; Economic Consultant, HM Treasury, 1962–64; Lectr in Economics, LSE, 1964–67; Sen. Economic Adviser, Dept of Educn and Science, 1967–69; Dir of Econs and Stats, Min. of Housing and Local Govt, 1969–70; Dir Economics, DoE, 1970–72; Under Sec., 1972–78, Dep. Chief Econ. Advr, 1978–89, HM Treasury. Chm., Economic Policy Cttee of the European Communities, 1982–85 (Mem., 1978–89); Member: Central Council of Educn (England), 1965–66; Economics Cttee, CNAA, 1968–70; ESRC, 1983–89; Urban Motorways Cttee, 1970; Cttee on Water Services: Econ. and Financial Objectives, 1970–73; Chm., Adv. Cttee to HM Treasury on Accounting for Econ. Costs and Changing Prices, 1986. Member: Bd, Public Finance Foundn, 1984–89; Bd of Mgt, Internat. Inst. of Public Finance, 1987–90, 2000–; Council of Mgt, NIESR, 1996–; Council, REconS, 1983–92 (Mem. Exec. Cttee, 1987–89); Governing Body, Birkbeck Coll., 1997–; Bd of Advisors, St Edmund Hall, 1998–. President: Econs and Business Educn Assoc., 1998–2001; Human City Inst., 1999–; Vice-Pres., Strategic Planning Soc., 1993–; Co-Sec.-Gen., Foundn for Internat. Studies in Social Security, 2000–. Treas., Holy Cross Centre Trust, 1988–. Chm., Friends of Birmingham Cathedral, 1999–. CIMgt 1993. DUniv: Brunel, 1994; Central England, 2000. *Publications:* The British Electrical Industry 1875–1914, 1979; articles on economics in books and learned jls; official reports. *Recreation:* painting. *Address:* Frontier Economics, 150 Holborn, EC1N 2NS. *T:* (020) 7611 9494, *Fax:* (020) 7611 9495; 34 Frederick Road, Birmingham B15 1JN. *T:* (0121) 689 7946, *Fax:* (0121) 454 6438; *e-mail:* ianbyatt@blueyonder.co.uk. *Club:* Oxford and Cambridge.

BYATT, Ronald Archer Campbell, (Robin), CMG 1980; HM Diplomatic Service, retired; High Commissioner in New Zealand and concurrently to Western Samoa, and Governor (non-resident), Pitcairn Islands, 1987–90; *b* 14 Nov. 1930; *s* of late Sir Horace Byatt, GCMG and late Olga Margaret Campbell, MBE; *m* 1954, Ann Brereton Sharpe, *d* of C. B. Sharpe; one *s* one *d*. *Educ:* Gordonstoun; New Coll., Oxford; King's Coll., Cambridge. Served in RNVR, 1949–50. Colonial Admin. Service, Nyasaland, 1955–58; joined HM Foreign (now Diplomatic) Service, 1959; FO, 1959; Havana, 1961; FO, 1963; UK Mission to UN, NY, 1966; Kampala, 1970; Head of Rhodesia Dept, FCO, 1972–75; Vis. Fellow, Glasgow Univ., 1975–76; Counsellor and Head of Chancery, UK Mission to UN, NY, 1977–79; Asst Under Sec. of State, FCO, 1979–80; High Comr in Zimbabwe, 1980–83; Mem, Directing Staff, RCDS, 1983–84; Ambassador to Morocco, 1985–87. CSSB Panel Chm., 1992–95. Mem., HGTAC, 1993–98 (Chm., Envmt Sub-Cttee, 1993–98). Trustee: Beit Trust, 1987–; UK Antarctic Heritage Trust, 1992–. Order of the Throne, 1st cl. (Morocco), 1987. *Recreations:* sailing, gardening, watching and painting birds. *Address:* Drim-na-Vullin, Lochgilphead, Argyll PA31 8LE. *Club:* Oxford and Cambridge.

See also Sir H. C. Byatt.

BYCROFT, Prof. Barrie (Walsham), PhD; CChem, FRSC; Professor of Pharmaceutical Chemistry, since 1979, and Head, Department of Pharmaceutical Sciences and School of Pharmacy, 1985–89 and since 1995, University of Nottingham; *b* 26 Jan. 1939; *s* of Henry Thomas Bycroft and Cissie Bycroft; *m* 1962, Jean Skinner (separated); one *s* one *d*. *Educ:* Univ. of Nottingham (BSc Chem.; PhD 1963). CChem 1982; FRSC 1982. NATO Fellow, Univ. of Zurich, 1963–65; University of Nottingham: Lectr, then Reader, Dept of Chemistry, 1965–79; Pro-Vice Chancellor (Research), 1990–94; Dean, Grad. Sch., 1994–96. Vis. Prof., Med. Sch., Federal Univ., Rio de Janeiro, 1973. Mem., Food Adv. Cttee, MAFF, 1988–92. Non-exec. Mem., Nottingham HA, 1990–94. Biotechnology and Biological Sciences Research Council: Mem., Sci. and Engrg Bd, 1993–96; Chm., Postgrad. Trng Award Panel, 1994–. Vice-Chm., UK Council for Grad. Educn, 1993–96. Hon. MPharmS 1990. *Publications:* numerous contribs to learned jls. *Recreations:* tennis, golf, good food and wine, travel. *Address:* 14 The Cloisters, Beeston, Nottingham NG9 2FR. *T:* (0115) 925 9415; 8 Rydon Street, Islington, N1 7AL. *T:* (020) 7226 4104.

BYE, Christopher Harwood; Editor, Yorkshire Evening Post, 1987–98; Director, Yorkshire Post Newspapers Ltd, 1987–98; *b* 6 Feb. 1952; *s* of John Harwood Bye and Joan Alice (*née* Cushing). *Educ:* Tadcaster Grammar Sch. News Editor, Yorkshire Post, 1980–82; Editor, Yorkshire Post Colour Magazine, 1981–83; Dep. Editor, Yorkshire Post, 1982–87. British Press award for investigative journalism, 1986. *Recreations:* classical music, antiques, wine, food, travel, walking, sport.

BYE, Ruby; *see* Wax, R.

BYERS, Hon. Charles William; His Honour Judge Byers; a Circuit Judge, since 1999; *b* 24 March 1949; *o s* of Baron Byers, PC, OBE and Joan Elizabeth Byers (*née* Oliver); *m* 1972, Suzan Mary Stone (marr. diss. 1995); two *s*. *Educ:* Westminster Sch.; Christ Church, Oxford. Called to the Bar, Gray's Inn, 1973; Recorder, 1993–99. Dep. Chm., Gray's Inn Continuing Education Cttee, 1997–98; Mem., Adv. Panel, Coll. of Law, 1996–. Gov., Hurstpierpoint Coll., 1993–. *Recreations:* gardening, agriculture, sport, aquatics, acquiring practical skills. *Address:* Crown Court, Pocock Street, SE1 0BT. *Club:* National Liberal.

BYERS, Dr Paul Duncan; Reader Emeritus in Morbid Anatomy, University of London; Head of Department of Morbid Anatomy, Institute of Orthopaedics, University of London, 1980–87, retired (Dean of Institute, 1971–79); *b* Montreal, 3 July 1922; *s* of A. F. Byers and Marion Taber; *m* 1959, Valery Garden (*d* 1999); *m* 1999, Mea Brown. *Educ:* Bishops College Sch., PQ, Canada; McGill Univ. (BSc, MD, CM); Univ. of London (DCP, PhD). FRCPath. Alan Blair Memorial Fellow, Canadian Cancer Soc., 1955–57. Asst Morbid Anatomist, Inst. of Orthopaedics, 1960; Reader in Morbid Anatomy, Univ. of London, 1974. Hon. Consultant, Royal National Orthopaedic Hosp., 1965; Hon. Senior Lectr, Royal Postgrad. Med. Sch., 1969. Chm., Osteosarcoma Histopathol. Panel, MRC/EORTC, 1983–86; Member: Osteosarcoma Wkg Party, MRC, 1982–86; Soft Tissue Sarcoma Wkg Party, MRC, 1983–84. Mem., Management Cttee, Courtauld Inst. of Art, Univ. of London, 1979–82. *Publications:* (jtly) Diseases of Bones and Joints, 1994; articles in medical press on arthritis, metabolic bone disease, bone tumours, medical education. *Recreation:* arts. *Address:* 2 Manorside, Barnet, Herts EN5 2LD. *T:* (020) 8440 3376.

BYERS, Rt Hon. Stephen (John); PC 1998; MP (Lab) Tyneside North, since 1997 (Wallsend, 1992–97); Secretary of State for Transport, Local Government and the Regions, since 2001; *b* Wolverhampton, 13 April 1953; *s* of late Robert Byers. *Educ:* Chester City Grammar Sch.; Chester Coll. of Further Educn; Liverpool Polytechnic (LLB). Sen. Lectr in Law, Newcastle Polytechnic, 1977–92. Mem. (Lab) North Tyneside MBC, 1980–92 (Dep. Leader, 1985–92; Chm. Educn Cttee, 1982–85). Contested (Lab) Hexham, 1983. An Opposition Whip, 1994–95; frontbench spokesman on educn and employment, 1995–97; Minister of State, DfEE, 1997–98; Chief Sec. to HM Treasury, 1998; Sec. of State for Trade and Industry, 1998–2001. Mem., Select Cttee on Home Affairs, 1994. Chm., PLP Home Affairs Cttee, 1992–94. Leader, Council of Local Educn Authorities, 1990–92; Chairman: Nat. Employers' Orgn for Teachers, 1990–92; Educn Cttee, AMA, 1990–92; Mem., BTEC, 1985–89. FRSA 1991. *Address:* House of Commons, SW1A 0AA. *T:* (020) 7219 4085.

BYFORD, family name of **Baroness Byford**.

BYFORD, Baroness *cr* 1996 (Life Peer), of Rothley in the county of Leicestershire; **Hazel Byford,** DBE 1994; *b* 14 Jan. 1941; *d* of Sir Cyril Osborne, MP and Lady Osborne; *m* 1962, C. Barrie Byford, CBE; one *d* (one *s* decd). *Educ:* St Leonard's Sch., St Andrews; Moulton Agricl Coll., Northampton. WRVS Leics, 1961–93, County Organiser, 1972–76. An Opposition Whip, H of L, 1997–98; Opposition spokesman on agriculture and rural affairs, H of L, 1998–. Chm., Nat. Cttee, Conservative Women, 1990–93; Vice Pres., 1993–96, Pres., 1996–97, Nat. Union of Cons. and Unionist Assocs. Member: Transport Users' Consultative Cttee, 1989–94; Rail Users' Consultative Cttee, 1994–95. Patron: Virsa, 1998–; Inst. of Agricl Secs and Adminrs, 2000. *Recreations:* golf, bridge, reading. *Club:* Farmers'.

BYFORD, Sir Lawrence, Kt 1984; CBE 1979; QPM 1973; DL; management consultant, since 1987; HM Chief Inspector of Constabulary, 1983–87; *b* 10 Aug. 1925; *s* of George Byford and Monica Irene Byford; *m* 1950, Muriel Campbell Massey; two *s* one *d*. *Educ:* Univ. of Leeds (LLB Hons). Barrister-at-Law. Joined W Riding Police, 1947; served on Directing Staff of Wakefield Detective Sch., 1959–62, and Police Staff Coll., Bramshill, 1964–66; Divl Comdr, Huddersfield, 1966–68; Asst Chief Constable of Lincs, 1968, Dep. Chief Constable 1970, Chief Constable, 1973–77; HM Inspector of Constabulary for: SE Region, 1977–78; NE Region, 1978–82. Lecture tour of univs, USA and Canada, 1976; Headed: British Police Mission to Turkey, 1978–79; official review into Yorkshire Ripper case, 1981. DL: Lincs, 1987; N Yorks, 1998. Hon. LLD Leeds, 1987. *Recreations:* cricket, Pennine walking and travel. *Clubs:* Royal Over-Seas League (Chm., 1989–92, Vice-Pres., 1992–), MCC; Yorks County Cricket (Hon. Life Mem.; Chm., 1991–98; Pres., 1991–2000).
See also M. J. Byford.

BYFORD, Mark Julian; Director, BBC World Service, since 1998; *b* 13 June 1958; *s* of Sir Lawrence Byford, *qv*; *m* 1980, Hilary Bleiker; two *s* three *d*. *Educ:* Lincoln Sch.; Univ. of Leeds (LLB 1979); Wharton Business Sch., USA. BBC Television: Look North, Leeds, 1979–82; producer, South Today and Inquiry, Southampton, 1982–87; editor, Points West, Bristol, 1987–88; Home Editor, BBC News and Current Affairs, 1988–89; Head of Centre, Leeds, 1989–90; Asst Controller, 1991, Controller, 1991–94, Dep. Man. Dir, 1995–96, Dir, 1996–98, BBC Regl Broadcasting. Director: BARB, 1993–96; Radio Joint Audience Research Ltd, 1993–96. Trustee, BBC Children in Need Appeal, 1993–96. Fellow, Radio Acad., 2000. *Recreations:* family, football (Leeds United and Southampton), cricket, travel, the seaside especially Scarborough and the Solent, the New Forest, cathedrals, fell-walking, rock music, swimming. *Address:* Bolberry House, 1 Clifton Hill, Winchester, Hants SO22 5BL. *T:* (01962) 860197, *Fax:* (01962) 860944; BBC World Service, Room 313 CB, Bush House, PO Box 76, Strand, WC2B 4PH, *T:* (020) 7557 2057, *Fax:* (020) 7557 1900; *e-mail:* mark.byford@bbc.co.uk. *Club:* Yorkshire County Cricket.

BYGRAVES, Max Walter, OBE 1983; entertainer; *b* 16 Oct. 1922; *s* of Henry and Lilian Bygraves, Rotherhithe, SE16; *m* 1942, Gladys Blossom Murray; one *s* two *d*. *Educ:* St Joseph's, Rotherhithe. Began in advertising agency, carrying copy to Fleet Street, 1936. Volunteered for RAF, 1940; served 5 years as fitter. Performed many shows for troops; became professional, 1946; has appeared in venues all over English-speaking world, incl. 19 Royal Command Performances; best selling record artist (31 Gold Discs). Host, Family Fortunes, TV, 1983–85. Freeman, City of London, 1994. *Publications:* I Wanna Tell You a Story (autobiog.), 1976; The Milkman's on his Way (novel), 1977; After Thoughts (autobiog.), 1988; I Wanna Tell You a Funny Story, 1992; In His Own Words (autobiog.), 1997. *Recreations:* golf, painting, reading, writing. *Address:* Roebuck House, Victoria, SW1E 5BE. *T:* (020) 7828 4595. *Clubs:* St James's, East India.

BYLES, Timothy John; Chief Executive, Norfolk County Council, since 1996; *b* 7 Dec. 1958; *s* of Charles Humphrey Gilbert Byles and Pamela Beatrice Byles; *m* 1985, Shirley Elizabeth Rowland; three *s*. *Educ:* Univ. of Kent (BA Hons); Mid Kent Coll. of Further Educn (DMS London). British Gas, 1980–84: mgt trainee; Marketing Dept; Corporate Planning; English Tourist Board, 1984–88: Manager, Mgt Services, 1984–85; Asst Dir of Develt, 1985–88; Dir of Economic Develt, Kent CC, 1988–96. *Recreations:* music, swimming, church. *Address:* County Hall, Martineau Lane, Norwich NR1 2DH. *T:* (01603) 222000.

BYNG, family name of **Earl of Strafford,** and of **Viscount Torrington**.

BYNOE, Dame Hilda Louisa, DBE 1969; in General Medical Practice, Port of Spain, Trinidad, 1974–89, retired; *b* Grenada, 18 Nov. 1921; *d* of late Thomas Joseph Gibbs, CBE, JP, Estate Proprietor, and Louisa Gibbs (*née* La Touche); *m* 1947, Peter Cecil Alexander Bynoe, ARIBA, Dip. Arch., former RAF Flying Officer; two *s*. *Educ:* St Joseph's Convent, St George's, Grenada; Royal Free Hospital Medical Sch., Univ. of London. MB, BS (London), 1951, MRCS, LRCP, 1951. Teacher, St Joseph's Convents, Trinidad and Grenada, 1939–44; hospital and private practice, London, 1951–53; public service with Govt of Trinidad and Tobago, 1954–55, with Govt of Guyana (then British Guiana), 1955–58, with Govt of Trinidad and Tobago, 1958–65; private practice, Trinidad, 1961–68; Governor of Associated State of Grenada, WI, 1968–74. Mem. YWCA. Patron: Caribbean Women's Assoc., 1970–; John Hayes Meml Kidney Foundn, 1979–; Music Foundn of Trinidad and Tobago, 1986–; African Assoc. of Trinidad and Tobago. *Recreations:* swimming, music, reading, poetry-writing. *Address:* 5A Barcant Avenue, Maraval, Trinidad. *Club:* Soroptimist (Port of Spain).

BYRNE, David; Member, European Commission, since 1999; *b* 26 April 1947; *m* 1972, Geraldine Fortune; two *s* one *d*. *Educ:* Dominican Coll., Newbridge, Co. Kildare; University Coll. Dublin (BA). FCIArb 1998. Called to the Bar, King's Inns, Dublin, 1970; called to Inner Bar, 1985; Attorney General, Ireland, 1997–99. Member: Govt Review Body on Social Welfare Law, 1989; Constitution Review Gp, 1995–96. Member: Nat. Cttee, ICC, 1988–97; ICC Internat. Court of Arbitration, Paris, 1990–97. Ext. Examr for arbitration and competition law, King's Inns, 1995–97. Member: Bar Council, 1974–87 (Hon. Treas., 1982–83); Barristers' Professional Practices and Ethics Cttee, 1995–97. Hon. FRCPI 2000. *Address:* European Commission, Rue de la Loi 200, 1049 Brussels, Belgium.

BYRNE, Douglas Norman; Head of Marine Directorate, Department of Transport (formerly Marine Division, Department of Trade), 1980–84; *b* 30 Jan. 1924; *s* of Leonard William Byrne and Clarice Evelyn Byrne; *m* 1949, Noreen Thurlby Giles; one *s* one *d*. *Educ:* Portsmouth Grammar Sch.; St John's Coll., Cambridge (MA). RAF, 1942–46. Asst Principal, Min. of Supply, 1949; BoT, 1956; Cabinet Office, 1961–64; Asst Sec., 1964; on staff of Monopolies Commn, 1966–68; Under-Sec., Dept of Industry, 1974–77; Hd of Fair Trading Div., Dept of Prices and Consumer Protection, 1977–79; Under-Sec., Dept of Trade, 1979–83, Dept of Transport, 1983–84. *Recreations:* hill walking, natural history. *Club:* Royal Air Force.

BYRNE, John Anthony; teacher, lecturer and writer; Head of Ballet and Dance, Sydney Church of England Co-educational Grammar School (Redlands), since 1997; *b* Sydney, Australia, 14 Dec. 1945; *s* of Reginald Thomas Byrne and Mary Ida (*née* Sinclair). *Educ:* Scully-Borovansky Sch. of Ballet, Sydney; Univ. of Sydney (BA); Polytechnic of Central London (Dip. Arts Admin 1977); Royal Acad. of Dancing (ARAD; Dip. PDTC 1979). Professional dancer with various companies in ballet, opera-ballet and musicals, Australia, NZ, Germany, UK and Hong Kong, 1970–76; teaching dance in Australia, 1979–90; Royal Academy of Dancing: Major Examr, 1987–; Tutor, Sydney and London HQ, 1990–91; Artistic Dir and Chm., Bd of Examrs, 1991–93. *Publications:* (jtly) Body Basics, 1992; Classical syllabus for boys, 1992; contrib. articles on dance criticism, etc to Dance Australia Mag., 1981–90. *Recreations:* walking, reading, gardens. *Address:* 729 Forest Road, Bexley South, NSW 2207, Australia.

BYRNE, John Keyes; *see* Leonard, Hugh.

BYRNE, Lavinia; Tutor, Westcott House, Cambridge, since 1997; *b* 10 March 1947; *d* of Basil James Byrne and (Edith Marion) Josephe Byrne. *Educ:* St Mary's Convent, Shaftesbury; Queen Mary College, London (BA Modern Langs); Hughes Hall, Cambridge (PGCE). Entered Inst. of Blessed Virgin Mary, 1964, resigned 2000. Associate Sec., CCBI, 1990–95. Co-Editor, The Way, 1985–90. Hon. DD Birmingham, 1997. *Publications:* Women Before God, 1988; Sharing the Vision, 1989; (ed) The Hidden Tradition, 1990; (ed) The Hidden Journey, 1992; (ed) The Hidden Voice, 1994; Woman at the Altar, 1995; A Time to Receive, 1997; (ed) The Daily Service, 1997; The Dome of Heaven, 1999; The Journey is My Home, 2000. *Recreations:* computers, cookery. *Address:* 8 Park Street, Cambridge CB5 8AS.

BYRNE, Rev. Father Paul Laurence, OMI; OBE 1976; Director, Irish Episcopal Commission for Emigrants, since 1994; *b* 8 Aug. 1932; *s* of late John Byrne and Lavinia Byrne. *Educ:* Synge Street Christian Brothers' Sch. and Belcamp Coll., Dublin; University Coll., Dublin (BA, Hons Phil.); Oblate Coll., Piltown. Ordained, 1958. Teacher, Belcamp Coll., 1959–65; Dean of Belcamp Coll., 1961–65; Dir, Irish Centre, Birmingham, 1965–68; Dir, Catholic Housing Aid Soc. (Birmingham) and Family Housing Assoc., Birmingham, 1965–69; Nat. Dir, Catholic Housing Aid Soc., and Dir, Family Housing Assoc., London, 1969–70; Dir, SHAC (a housing aid centre), 1969–76; Sec. Gen., Conf. of Major Religious Superiors of Ire., 1980–87; Provincial Superior, Anglo-Irish Prov. of Missionary OMI, 1988–94. Board Member: Threshold Centre; Servite Houses; Housing Corp., 1974–77. Hon. Mem., Inst. of Housing, 1972. *Recreations:* golf, theatre-going. *Address:* 57 Parnell Square West, Dublin 1. *T:* (1) 8723655. *Club:* Foxrock Golf.

BYRNE, Terence Niall; HM Diplomatic Service; Consul-General and Director of Trade Promotion, Auckland, since 1999; *b* 28 April 1942; *e s* of late Denis Patrick Byrne and of Kathleen Byrne (*née* Carley); *m* 1st, 1966, Andrea Dennison (marr. diss. 1977); one *s* one *d*; 2nd, 1981, Susan Haddow Neill; two *d*. *Educ:* Finchley Catholic Grammar Sch.; Open Univ. (BA Hons). Min. of Housing and Local Govt, 1964–68; Prime Minister's Office, 1968–70; MAFF, 1971–78 (Private Sec. to Parly Sec., MAFF, 1974–75); First Sec. (Agriculture), The Hague, 1978–82; Commonwealth Co-ordination Dept, FCO, 1982–84; Asst Head, UN Dept, FCO, 1984–85; Head of Chancery and Consul, Quito, 1986–89; Counsellor and Dep. High Comr, Lusaka, 1990–93; Dir of Trade Promotion, Canberra, 1993–94; Dep. High Comr, Kuala Lumpur, 1994–98. *Recreations:* running, golf, cinema. *Address:* c/o Foreign and Commonwealth Office, King Charles Street, SW1A 2AH.

BYRNE, Terrance Dennis; a Commissioner, and Director, Law Enforcement (formerly Fraud and Intelligence), HM Customs and Excise, since 1999; *b* 26 Nov. 1944; *s* of Thomas Edward Byrne and Sybil Elizabeth Byrne; *m* 1966, Pamela Ashley; one *s* one *d*. *Educ:* Downham Market Grammar Sch., Norfolk. Joined Civil Service, 1962; HM Customs and Excise, 1964–: specialist investigator, 1971–84; Mgt Consultant, 1984–88; Dep. Chief Investigation Officer, 1988–91; Head, Customs Enforcement Policy, 1991–99. *Recreations:* horticulture, sport (mainly golf), reading. *Address:* (office) New King's Beam House, 22 Upper Ground, SE1 9PJ. *T:* (020) 7865 5025.

BYRNE, Timothy Russell, FCA; Chief Executive, Airtours plc, since 2000; *b* 16 March 1959; *s* of late Russell Vincent Byrne and of Barbara Ann Byrne; *m* 1986, Caroline Margaret Lander; three *d*. *Educ:* Stanney High Sch. FCA 1994. With Lowndes McLintock, 1980–84; Accountancy Tuition Centre, 1984–85; Granada TV Div., 1985–92; Airtours plc, 1993–: Group Financial Controller, 1993–97; Group Finance Dir, 1998–2000. *Recreations:* country pursuits. *Address:* Airtours plc, Parkway 1, 300 Princess Parkway, Manchester M14 7QU. *T:* (0161) 232 6519.

BYROM, Peter Craig, OBE 1987; self-employed textile consultant, since 1985; non-executive Director, Parry Murray & Co. Ltd, since 1992; *b* 4 Dec. 1927; *s* of Robert Hunter Byrom, Master Cotton Spinner and Winifred Agnes Byrom (*née* Goodwin); *m* 1st, 1952, Norma Frances Mawdesley Harris (marr. diss. 1984); three *s* three *d*; 2nd, 1984, Gillian Elizabeth Hoyte. *Educ:* Virginia Episcopal Sch., Lynchburg, USA; St Edward's Sch., Oxford; Univ. of Liverpool, Sch. of Architecture; Salford Royal Tech. Coll.; Admin. Staff Coll., Henley; Open Univ. (BA). CText; FTI 1986. RNVR, 1945–48. Asst Gen. Manager, Robert Byrom (Stalybridge), cotton spinners, 1951–59; Merchandising Manager, British Nylon Spinners, 1959–64; Marketing Manager and Adv. and Promotions Manager, ICI Fibres, 1964–71; Dir, Deryck Healey Internat., 1972–74; Man. Dir, Dartington Hall Tweeds, 1975–85. Lay Inspector of Schs, OFSTED, 1993–98. Consultant to: ODA, Nepal, 1980; Intermediate Tech. Gp, India, 1986; Chm., British Colour Council, 1971–73; Mem., Textile and Fashion Bd, CNAA, 1974–77; Chm. Council, RCA, 1981–86 (Mem., 1973–86; Sen. Fellow, 1983); Mem. Council, Textile Inst., 1986–96 (Service Medal, 1992); External Assessor, Manchester Metropolitan Univ., 1992–95. Governor: Dartington Coll. of Arts, 1979–89; Loughborough Coll. of Art and Design, 1993–98 (Vice-Chm., Govs, 1996–98). FRSA 1970 (Mem. Council, 1987–93; Mem. Design Bd, 1986–91; Chm., Textiles, Young Designers into Industry, 1985–90). *Publications:* Textiles: product design and marketing, 1987; contrib. to Young Designers into the Textile Industry. *Recreations:* walking, cycling, swimming, theatre, music, books. *Address:* Barton House, Woodland, Ashburton, Devon TQ13 7LN. *T:* (01364) 653926.

BYRON, 13th Baron *cr* 1643, of Rochdale, Co. Lancaster; **Robert James Byron;** Partner, Holman Fenwick & Willan, since 1984; *b* 5 April 1950; *o* surv. *s* of 12th Baron Byron, DSO and Dorigen Margaret (*d* 1985), *o d* of Percival Kennedy Esdaile; *S* father, 1989; *m* 1979, Robyn Margaret, *d* of John McLean, Hamilton, NZ; one *s* three *d*. *Educ:* Wellington Coll.; Trinity Coll., Cambridge (MA). Called to the Bar, Inner Temple, 1974; admitted solicitor, 1978. *Heir:* *s* Hon. Charles Richard Gordon Byron, *b* 28 July 1990. *Address:* Marlow House, Lloyds Avenue, EC3N 3AL.

BYRON, Sir (Charles Michael) Dennis, Kt 2000; Chief Justice, Eastern Caribbean Supreme Court, since 1999; *b* 4 July 1943; *s* of late Vincent Fitzgerald Byron, MBE and Pearl Eulalie Byron (*nee* O'Loughlin); *m* 1966, Monika Botfeldt; four *s*. *Educ:* Fitzwilliam Coll., Cambridge (MA, LLB 1966). Called to the Bar, Inner Temple, 1965; barrister-at-law, W Indies (Leeward Is), 1966–82; Eastern Caribbean Supreme Court: High Ct Judge, 1982–90; Justice of Appeal, 1990–96; Actg Chief Justice, 1996–99. *Recreations:* tennis, golf. *Address:* Eastern Caribbean Supreme Court, PO Box 1093, Castries, St Lucia, West Indies. *T:* 4522574/4527998, *Fax:* 4525475; *e-mail:* appeal@candw.lc.

BYRT, His Honour (Henry) John; QC 1976; a Circuit Judge, 1983–99; *b* 5 March 1929; *s* of Dorothy Muriel Byrt and Albert Henry Byrt, CBE; *m* 1957, Eve Hermione Bartlett; one *s* two *d*. *Educ:* Charterhouse; Merton Coll., Oxford (BA, MA). Called to the Bar, Middle Temple, 1953; called within the Bar, 1976; a Recorder of the Crown Court, 1976–83. First Pres., Social Security Appeal Tribunals and Medical Appeal Tribunals, 1983–90. Judge, Mayors and City of London Court, 1990–99 (Sen. Judge, 1994–99). Vice-Principal, Working Mens' Coll., London, 1978–82, Principal, 1982–87; Mem. Council, Queen's Coll., London, 1982–99. Freeman, City of London, 1999. *Recreations:* building, gardening, travel, music. *Address:* 13 Springalls Wharf, 25 Bermondsey Wall West, SE16 4TL. *T:* (020) 7740 1358. *Club:* Leander.

BYWATER, Air Cdre David Llewellyn, FRAeS, FIMgt; Director, Airport and Flight Operations, Marshall Aerospace, since 1993; Commandant, Aeroplane and Armament Experimental Establishment, Boscombe Down, 1988–92, retired; *b* 16 July 1937; *s* of Stanley and Gertrude Bywater; *m* 1960, Shelagh May Gowling; one *s* one *d*. *Educ:* Liverpool Inst. High Sch.; RAF Coll., Cranwell. No XV Sqdn, 1958–63; Empire Test Pilots Sch., 1964; A&AEE Test Pilot, 1965–68; RAF Staff Coll., 1969; HQ Germany, 1970–73; Wing Comdr Flying, RAE Farnborough, 1974–78; MoD Operational Requirements, 1979–81; Gp Captain, Superintendent of Flying, A&AEE, 1982–85; RAF Staff Coll., Bracknell, 1985–88. *Recreations:* sailing, ski-ing. *Club:* Royal Air Force.

BYWATERS, Eric George Lapthorne, CBE 1975; MB (London); FRCP; Professor of Rheumatology, Royal Postgraduate Medical School, University of London, 1958–75, now Emeritus; Hon. Consultant Physician, Hammersmith Hospital and Wexham Park Hospital, Slough, Bucks; Hon. Librarian, Heberden Library, Royal College of Physicians, 1970–90; *b* 1 June 1910; *s* of George Ernest Bywaters and Ethel Penney; *m* 1935, Betty Euan-Thomas (*d* 1998); three *d*. *Educ:* Sutton Valence Sch., Kent; Middx Hosp. (Sen. Broderip Schol., Lyell Gold Medallist). McKenzie McKinnon Fellow, RCP, 1935; Asst Clin. Pathologist, Bland Sutton Inst., 1936; Rockefeller Travelling Fellow and Harvard Univ. Research Fellow in Med., 1937–39; Beit Memorial Fellow, 1939; Actg Dir, MRC Clin. Res. Unit (Shock), 1943; Lectr in Med., Postgrad. Med. Sch., 1945; Dir, MRC Rheumatism Res. Unit, Taplow, 1958–75; Sen. MRC Res. Fellow, Bone and Joint Unit, London Hosp., 1977–. Pres., European League against Rheumatism, 1977 (Hon. Mem. 1981); Councillor, Internat. League against Rheumatism. Fellow, RPMS, 1993. Hon. Mem., Heberden Soc., 1977; Hon. FACP, 1973; Hon. FRCP&S (Canada), 1977; Hon. FRSocMed, 1983. Hon. MD Liège, 1973. Gairdner Foundation Medical Award, 1963; Heberden Orator and Medallist, 1966; Croonian Lectr, RCP, 1968; Bunim Lectr and Medallist, 1973; Ewart Angus Lectr, Toronto, 1974; Samuel Hyde Lectr, RSocMed, 1986. Hon. Mem. Dutch, French, Amer., German, Czech, Spanish, Portuguese, Aust., Indian, Canadian, Chilean, Peruvian, Jugoslav, Egyptian, Turkish, Greek, S African and Argentine Rheumatism Assocs. *Publications:* papers on rheumatism, Crush Syndrome, etc. *Recreations:* painting, gardening. *Address:* 53 Burkes Road, Beaconsfield, Bucks HP9 1PW.

C

CABALLÉ, Montserrat; Cross of Lazo de Dama of Order of Isabel the Catholic, Spain; opera and concert singer; *b* Barcelona, 12 April 1933; *d* of Carlos and Ana Caballé; *m* 1964, Bernabé Marti, tenor; one *s* one *d*. *Educ:* Conservatorio del Liceo, Barcelona. Continued to study singing under Mme Eugenia Kemeny. Carnegie Hall début as Lucrezia Borgia, 1965; London début in this role, with the London Opera Society, at the Royal Festival Hall, 1968. Has sung at Covent Garden, Glyndebourne, La Scala, Vienna, Metropolitan Opera, San Francisco and most major opera venues. Major roles include Maria Stuarda, Luisa Miller, Queen Elizabeth in Roberto Devereux, Imogene in Il Pirata, Violetta in La Traviata, Marguerite in Faust, Desdemona in Otello, Norma, Tosca, Turandot, Leonora in La Forza del Destino, Semiramide, Salome, Il Viaggio a Reims, Tristan und Isolde, and also those of contemporary opera. Over 120 roles sung and recorded. Numerous hon. degrees, awards and medals.

CABLE, Dr (John) Vincent; MP (Lib Dem) Twickenham, since 1997; *b* 9 May 1943; *s* of John Leonard Cable and Edith Cable; *m* 1968, Olympia Rebelo (*d* 2001); two *s* one *d*. *Educ:* Fitzwilliam Coll., Cambridge (BA Hons; Pres., Cambridge Union); Glasgow Univ. (PhD). Finance Officer, Kenya Treasury, 1966–68; Lectr in Econs, Univ. of Glasgow, 1968–74; First Sec., FCO, 1974–76; Dep. Dir, ODI, 1976–83; Special Advr (Dir), Econs, Commonwealth Secretariat, 1983–90; Gp Planning Dept, Shell, 1990–93; Hd of Economic Prog., Chatham House, 1993–95; Chief Economist, Shell, 1995–97. Advr to Chm., World Commn on Envmt and Devclt, UN, 1975–77; Special Advr to Sec. of State for Trade, 1979. Mem (Lab), Glasgow CC, 1971–74. Contested: (Lab) Glasgow, Hillhead, 1970; (SDP/L Alliance) York, 1983, 1987; (Lib Dem) Twickenham, 1992. Lib Dem spokesman on finance and EMU, 1997–99, on Trade and Industry, 1999–. Mem., Treasury Select Cttee, 1998–99. Vis. Fellow, Nuffield Coll., Oxford. *Publications:* Protectionism and Industrial Decline, 1983; (with B. Persaud) Foreign Investment and Development, 1985; Global Super Highways, 1994; The New Giants: China and India, 1994; The World's New Fissures, 1994; Globalisation and Global Governance, 2000. *Recreations:* walking, dancing. *Address:* 102 Whitton Road, Twickenham TW1 1BS. *T:* (020) 8892 3212. *Club:* Lensbury (Teddington).

CABLE-ALEXANDER, Lt-Col Sir Patrick (Desmond William), 8th Bt *cr* 1809, of the City of Dublin; Director of Administration, Institute of Optometry, since 1999; *b* 19 April 1936; *s* of Sir Desmond William Lionel Cable-Alexander, 7th Bt and of Mary Jane, *d* of James O'Brien, Enniskillen; *S* father, 1988; *m* 1st, 1961, Diana Frances Rogers (marr. diss. 1976); two *d*; 2nd, 1976, Jane Mary Weekes (*née* Lewis); one *s*. *Educ:* Downside School; RMA Sandhurst. Commnd 3rd Carabiniers (POWDG), 1956; Lt-Col Royal Scots Dragoon Guards, 1976; comd Duke of Lancaster's Own Yeomanry, 1978–80; Chief of Staff, HQ North West District, 1980–83; retd, 1984. Sec. to the Council and Bursar, Lancing Coll., 1984–98. *Recreations:* cricket, gardening, visiting France, art. *Heir:* *s* Fergus William Antony Cable-Alexander, *b* 19 June 1981. *Address:* 15 Cambridge Road, Worthing, West Sussex BN11 1XD.

CABORN, Rt Hon. Richard (George); PC 1999; MP (Lab) Sheffield, Central, since 1983; Minister of State (Minister for Sport), Department for Culture, Media and Sport, since 2001; *b* 6 Oct. 1943; *s* of late George and of Mary Caborn; *m* 1966, Margaret Caborn; one *s* one *d*. *Educ:* Hurlfield Comprehensive Sch.; Granville Coll. of Further Educn; Sheffield Polytechnic. Engrg apprentice, 1959–64; Convenor of Shop Stewards, Firth Brown Ltd, 1967–79. Mem. (Lab) Sheffield, European Parlt, 1979–84. Minister of State: (Minister for the Regions, Regeneration and Planning), DETR, 1997–99; DTI, 1999–2001. Chm., Select Cttee on Trade and Industry, 1992–95. *Recreation:* amateur football. *Address:* House of Commons, SW1A 0AA; 29 Quarry Vale Road, Sheffield S12 3EB. *T:* (0114) 239 3802. *Club:* Carlton Working Men's (Sheffield).

CABRERA, Pablo; Ambassador of Chile to the Russian Federation, since 2000; *b* Santiago, 18 Jan. 1948; *m* 1973, Cecilia Pérez Walker; two *s* one *d*. *Educ:* Catholic Univ. of Chile (Lic. Juridical and Social Scis). Lawyer; entered Foreign Service, Chile, 1970: Consul, 1974, Second Sec., 1975–76, La Paz; Second Sec., Carácas, 1977–78; Consul Gen., Toronto, 1981–82; Chargé d'Affaires, Bucarest, 1983–85; Counsellor and Minister Counsellor, London, 1987–91; Minister Counsellor, Madrid, concurrent with Greece, 1991–93; Dep. Head, 1993, Head, 1994, Special Policy Dept, Min. of Foreign Affairs, Santiago; Under-Sec. of State for Navy, MoD, Santiago, 1995–99; Ambassador of Chile to UK and Ireland, 1999–2000. Formerly Head, Chilean Delegns to internat confs. Vis. Prof., Nat. Acad. for Political and Strategic Studies, 1993–. Mem., Internat. Law Soc. of Chile, 1963–. Mem., Christian Democratic Party, 1963–. Official, 1980, and Great Cross, 1995, Order of Rio Branco (Brazil); Great Cross, Order of Civil Merit (Spain), 1996; Comdr First Cl., Polar Star Royal Order (Sweden), 1996. *Recreations:* golf, tennis, football. *Address:* ul. Yunosty 11, str. 1, 111395 Moscow, Russia. *T:* (095) 3739571, 3739576, *Fax:* (095) 3737725. *Club:* Los Leones Golf (Santiago).

CACHELIN, Commissioner Francy; International Evangelist, The Salvation Army, 1987–89, retired; *b* 4 Aug. 1923; *s* of Maurice Cachelin and France Hauswirth; *m* 1951, Geneviève Irène Catherine Booth; two *s* two *d*. *Educ:* Lausanne School of Arts. Commissioned Salvation Army Officer, 1944; served in Switzerland as Corps Officer; Editor, The War Cry, in Belgium, 1951; responsible for youth work, France, 1957; Field Secretary, Switzerland, 1966; Chief Secretary, France, 1975, British Territory, 1977; Territorial Commander, Germany, 1979; British Comr, 1984. Federal Cross of Merit (FRG), 1984. *Recreations:* reading, languages.

CACOYANNIS, Michael; director, stage and screen, since 1954; *b* 11 June 1922; *s* of late Sir Panayotis Cacoyannis and Angeliki, *d* of George M. Efthyvoulos and Zoe Constantinides, Limassol, Cyprus. *Educ:* Greek Gymnasium; Gray's Inn and Old Vic Sch., London. Radio Producer, BBC, Greek Service, 1941–50. Actor on English stage, 1946–51; parts included: Herod, in Salome, 1946; Caligula, in Caligula, 1949, etc. *Directed films:* Windfall in Athens, 1953; Stella, 1954; Girl in Black, 1956; A Matter of Dignity, 1958; Our Last Spring, 1960; The Wastrel, 1961; Electra, 1962; Zorba the Greek, 1964; The Day the Fish Came Out, 1967; The Trojan Women, 1971; Attila '74, 1975; Iphigenia, 1977; Sweet Country, 1986; Up, Down and Sideways, 1992; The Cherry Orchard, 2000; directed *plays:* produced several of these in Athens for Ellie Lambetti's Company, 1955–61; The Trojan Women, New York, 1963–65, Paris, 1965; Things That Go Bump in the Night, and The Devils, New York, 1965; Iphigenia in Aulis, New York, 1968; King Oedipus, Abbey Theatre, Dublin, 1973; Miss Margarita, Athens, 1975; The Bacchae, Comédie Française, 1977, New York, 1980; The Glass Menagerie, Nat. Theatre, Athens, 1978; Antony and Cleopatra, Athens, 1979; Zorba (musical), USA, 1983; Electra, Epidaurus, 1984; Naked, Athens, 1989; Henceforward, Athens, 1990; The Trojan Women, Epidaurus, 1995; Master Class, Athens, 1997; directed *operas:* Mourning Becomes Electra, Metropolitan Opera, NY, 1967; La Bohème, Juillard, NY, 1972; La Traviata, Athens, 1983; Iphigenia in Aulis and in Tauris, Frankfurt State Opera, 1987; La Clemenza di Tito, Aix-en-Provence, 1988; Medea, Athens, 1995. Hon. DH Columbia Coll., Chicago, 1981. Silver Medal for Life Achievement, Greek Acad., 1995. Order of the Phœnix (Greece), 1965; Commandeur des Arts et des Lettres, 1987. *Publications:* Collected Writings, 1990; *translations:* (into English) The Bacchae, 1982; (into Greek) Antony and Cleopatra, 1980, Hamlet, 1985; Coriolanus, 1990; Othello, 2001; (into modern Greek) The Trojan Women, 1995. *Recreations:* walking, swimming. *Address:* 15 Mouson Street, Athens 117–41, Greece.

CADBURY, Sir Adrian; *see* Cadbury, Sir G. A. H.

CADBURY, Sir Dominic; *see* Cadbury, Sir N. D.

CADBURY, Sir (George) Adrian (Hayhurst), Kt 1977; DL; a Director of the Bank of England, 1970–94; *b* 15 April 1929; *s* of late Laurence John Cadbury, OBE and Joyce Cadbury, OBE, *d* of Lewis O. Mathews, Birmingham; *m* 1st, 1956, Gillian Mary (*d* 1992), *d* of late E. D. Skepper, Neuilly-sur-Seine; two *s* one *d*; 2nd, 1994, Susan Jacqueline, *d* of late D. B. Sinclair. *Educ:* Eton Coll.; King's Coll., Cambridge (MA Economics). Coldstream Guards, 1948–49; Cambridge, 1949–52. Cadbury Schweppes: Dep. Chm. and Man. Dir, 1969–74; Chm., 1975–89; Director: Cadbury Bros Ltd, 1958; IBM UK Ltd, 1975–94; Nat. Exhibition Centre, 1989–2001. Mem., Panel on Takeovers and Mergers, 1990–94. Chancellor, Univ. of Aston in Birmingham, 1979–. Chairman: West Midlands Economic Planning Council, 1967–70; CBI Econ. & Financial Policy Cttee, 1974–80; Food & Drink Industries Council, 1981–83; Promotion of Non-Exec. Dirs, 1984–95; Cttee on Financial Aspects of Corporate Governance, 1991–95; Pres., Birmingham Chamber of Industry and Commerce, 1988–89. High Sheriff, 1994–95, DL 1995, W Midlands. Freeman, City of Birmingham, 1982. Hon. DSc: Aston, 1973; Cranfield, 1985; Birmingham, 1996; Hon. LLD: Bristol, 1986; Birmingham, 1989; Lancaster, 1993; Cambridge, 1994. Albert Medal, RSA, 1995. *Publication:* The Company Chairman, 1990, 2nd edn 1995. *Fax:* (01564) 771130. *Clubs:* Boodle's; Hawks (Cambridge); Leander (Henley).

See also Sir N. D. Cadbury.

CADBURY, Sir (Nicholas) Dominic, Kt 1997; Chairman: The Wellcome Trust, since 2000; Cadbury Schweppes plc, 1993–2000 (Chief Executive, 1984–93); *b* 12 May 1940; *s* of late Laurence John Cadbury, OBE and Joyce Cadbury, OBE; *m* 1972, Cecilia Sarah Symes; three *d*. *Educ:* Eton Coll. (Fellow, 1996); Trinity Coll., Cambridge; Stanford Univ. (MBA). Chairman: Economist Gp, 1994– (Dir, 1990–); Transense Technologies plc, 2000–; Dep. Chm., Guinness PLC, 1994–97; Jt Dep. Chm., EMI Gp plc, 1999– (Bd Mem., 1998–). Dir, Misys plc, 2000–. Mem., President's Cttee, 1989–94 and 1998–2000, Chm., Educn and Trng Affairs Cttee, 1993–97, CBI; Dep. Chm., Qualifications and Curriculum Authority, 1997–2000; Member: Royal Mint Adv. Cttee, 1986–94; Stanford Adv. Council, 1989–95; Food Assoc., 1989–2000; NACETT, 1993–95; Marketing Council, 1997–2000; Council of Mgt, NIESR, 1998–2000. Pres., Food and Drink Fedn, 1998–99. Vice Pres., Edgbaston High Sch. for Girls, Birmingham, 1987–; Gov., Tudor Hall Sch., 1993–96. CIMgt (CBIM 1984); FCIM (Pres., 1996–97). *Recreations:* tennis, golf, shooting.

See also Sir G. A. H. Cadbury.

CADBURY, Nigel Robin; Stipendiary Magistrate, Leeds, since 1997; *b* 6 July 1956; *s* of Robin Norman Cadbury, JP, and Rosemary Jayne Cadbury; *m* 1982, Julie Ann Dean; two *s* one *d*. *Educ:* Rugby Sch.; Kent Univ. (BA Law 1978). Called to the Bar, Middle Temple, 1979; in practice at the Bar, 1979–97; Mem., Midland and Oxford Circuit, 1979–97. Mem., Criminal Bar Assoc., 1990–97. Trustee, Edward Cadbury Charitable Trust, 1991–. *Recreations:* squash, ski-ing, gardening, cinema. *Address:* Leeds Magistrates Court, PO Box 97, Westgate, Leeds LS1 3JP. *T:* (0113) 245 9653. *Club:* Edgbaston Priory Tennis and Squash.

CADBURY, Peter (Egbert); Chairman, Preston Publications Ltd, since 1985; *b* Great Yarmouth, Norfolk, 6 Feb. 1918; *s* of late Sir Egbert Cadbury, DSC, DFC; *m* 1st, 1947, Eugenie Benedicta (marr. diss. 1968), *d* of late Major Ewen Bruce, DSO, MC and of Mrs Bruce; one *s* one *d*; 2nd, 1970, Mrs Jennifer Morgan-Jones (*see* J. M. V. d'Abo) (marr. diss. 1976), *d* of Major Michael Hammond Maude, Ramsden, Oxon; one *s*; 3rd, 1976, Mrs Jane Mead; two *s*. *Educ:* Leighton Park Sch.; Trinity Coll., Cambridge (BA, MA 1939). Called to Bar, Inner Temple, 1946; practised at Bar, 1946–54. Served Fleet Air Arm, 1940, until released to Ministry of Aircraft Production, 1942, as Prodn, Research and Experimental Test Pilot. Contested (L) Stroud (Glos), 1945. Member, London Travel Cttee, 1958–60; Chm. and Man. Dir, Keith Prowse Group, 1954–71; Chairman: Alfred Hays Ltd, 1955–71; Ashton & Mitchell Ltd and Ashton & Mitchell Travel Co. Ltd,

1959–71; Air Westward Ltd, 1977–79; Air West Ltd, 1977–79; Educational Video Index Ltd, 1981–83; Westward Travel Ltd, 1982–84; Testworth Ltd, 1996–; Exec. Chm., Westward Television Ltd, 1960–80; Chm., Preston Estates, 1973–90; Director: Independent Television News Ltd, 1972–79; Willett Investments Ltd, 1955–. Chm., George Cadbury Trust, 1979–; Trustee: Help the Aged, 1986–; Mus. of Army Flying, 1986–; Winchester Cathedral Trust, 1986–. Freeman of City of London, 1948. *Recreations:* theatre, racing, flying, golf, tennis, sailing. *Address:* Upton Grey Lodge, Upton Grey, near Basingstoke, Hants RG25 2RE. *T:* (01256) 862374, *Fax:* (01256) 862988; (car) 0836 220214. *Clubs:* Royal Thames Yacht, Buck's, XL (Forty), MCC (Hon. Life Mem.), Lord's Taverners; Hawks (Cambridge); Island Sailing, Royal Motor Yacht, RAF Yacht.

CADBURY-BROWN, Henry Thomas, OBE 1967; TD; RA 1975 (ARA 1971); FRIBA; Professor of Architecture, Royal Academy, 1975–88; architect, in partnership with John F. Metcalfe and Elizabeth R. Cadbury-Brown, 1962–84; *b* 20 May 1913; *s* of Henry William Cadbury-Brown and Marion Ethel Sewell; *m* 1953, Elizabeth Romeyn, *d* of Prof. A. Elwyn, Croton on Hudson, NY. *Educ:* Westminster Sch.; AA Sch. of Architecture (Hons Diploma). Architect in private practice since winning competition for British Railways Branch Offices, 1937. Work includes pavilions for "The Origins of the People", main concourse and fountain display at Festival of Britain; schools, housing, display and interiors. Architect for new civic centre at Gravesend and halls for residence for Birmingham Univ. and, with Sir Hugh Casson and Prof. Robert Goodden, for new premises for Royal College of Art; awarded London Architecture Bronze Medal, 1963; lecture halls for Univ. of Essex; for RBK & C: Tavistock Cres. housing; World's End redevelt (in gp partnership Eric Lyons, Cadbury-Brown, Metcalfe & Cunningham); interior alterations in Burlington House for RA. Taught at Architectural Association Sch., 1946–49; Tutor at Royal Coll. of Art, 1952–61. Invited as Visiting Critic to Sch. of Architecture, Harvard Univ., 1956. Member: RIBA Council, 1951–53; MARS (Modern Architectural Research) group. Pres. Architectural Assoc., 1959–60. TA and military service, 1931–45; Major RA (TD). Hon. Fellow: RCA; Kent Inst. of Art and Design, 1992. DU Essex, 1989. *Recreations:* numerous, including work. *Address:* 3 Church Walk, Aldeburgh, Suffolk IP15 5DU. *T:* (01728) 452591.

CADELL, Patrick Moubray, CBE 2001; FSAScot; Keeper of the Records of Scotland, 1991–2000; *b* 17 March 1941; *s* of late Col H. M. Cadell of Grange, OBE and Christina Rose Nimmo; *m* 1968, Sarah Margaret Florence King (*d* 1996); two *s* one *d*. *Educ:* Merchiston Castle Sch.; Trinity Coll., Cambridge (BA 1962); Toulouse Univ. FSAScot 1985. British Museum: guide lectr, Dept of Admin, 1964–66; Asst Keeper, Dept of Manuscripts, 1966–68; National Library of Scotland: Asst Keeper, Dept of Manuscripts, 1968–83; Keeper, Dept of Manuscripts, 1983–90. Bailie, Abbey Court of Holyrood, 1995–. *Publications:* The Iron Mills at Cramond, 1973; (contrib.) The Water of Leith, 1984; The Abbey Court and High Constables of Holyrood, 1985; (contrib.) A Sense of Place: studies in Scottish Local history, 1988; (contrib.) For the Encouragement of Learning: Scotland's National Library 1689–1989, 1989; The Third Statistical Account of Scotland, Vol. for West Lothian, 1992; contribs on historical subjects to books and jls. *Recreations:* walking, the French language. *Address:* 27 Ellen's Glen Road, Edinburgh EH17 7QL. *T:* (0131) 658 1432.

CADELL of Grange, William Archibald; RIBA; FRIAS; Vice Lord–Lieutenant of West Lothian, since 2001; *b* 9 March 1933; *s* of late Col Henry Moubray Cadell of Grange, OBE, RE and Christina Rose Cadell (*née* Nimmo); *m* 1960, Mary-Jean Carmichael; three *s*. *Educ:* Merchiston Castle Sch.; Trinity Coll., Cambridge (BA 1956; MA); Regent St Poly., London (DipArch). RIBA 1961. Founded William A. Cadell Architects, 1968, retired, 1995; manager, Grange Estate, 1971–2000. Chm., Drum Housing Develt, 1991–. Comr, Royal Fine Art Commn for Scotland, 1992–2000; Trustee, Architectural Heritage Fund, 1997–. DL West Lothian, 1982. *Recreations:* gardening, forestry, the Arts. *Address:* Grange, Linlithgow, West Lothian, EH49 7RH. *T:* (01506) 842946.

See also P. M. Cadell.

CADIEUX, Hon. Léo; PC 1965; OC 1975; Ambassador of Canada to France, 1970–75; *b* 28 May 1908; *s* of Joseph E. Cadieux and Rosa Paquette, both French Canadian; *m* 1962, Monique, *d* of Placide Plante; one *s*. *Educ:* Commercial Coll. of St Jerome and Seminary of Ste Thérèse de Blainville, Quebec. Editorial staff of La Presse, Montreal, Quebec, 1930–41; Associate Dir of Public Relations, Can. Army, 1941–44; War Corresp. for La Presse, Montreal, 1944; Mayor of St Antoine des Laurentides, Que., 1948. First elected to House of Commons, gen. elec., 1962; re-elected gen. elec., 1963, 1965, 1968; apptd Associate Minister of Nat. Defence, 1965; Minister of National Defence, Canada, 1967–70. *Address:* 20 Driveway, Appt 1106, Ottawa, ON K2P 1C8, Canada.

CADMAN, family name of **Baron Cadman**.

CADMAN, 3rd Baron *cr* 1937, of Silverdale; **John Anthony Cadman;** farmer, 1964–85; *b* 3 July 1938; *s* of 2nd Baron Cadman and Marjorie Elizabeth Bunnis; *S* father, 1966; *m* 1975, Janet Hayes; two *s*. *Educ:* Harrow; Selwyn Coll., Cambridge; Royal Agricultural Coll., Cirencester. *Heir: s* Hon. Nicholas Anthony James Cadman, *b* 18 Nov. 1977. *Address:* 3 Court Farm Road, Willsbridge, Bristol BS30 9AA.

CADMAN, Surg. Rear-Adm. (D) (Albert) Edward, CB 1977; Director of Naval Dental Services, 1974–77; *b* 14 Oct. 1918; *m* 1st, 1946, Margaret Henrietta Tomkins-Russell (*d* 1974); one *s* one *d*; 2nd, 1975, Mary Croil Macdonald (*d* 1987), Superintendent, WRNS; 3rd, 1988, Irene Davies (*née* Lowther). *Educ:* Dover Grammar Sch.; Guy's Hosp. Dental Sch. LDS RCS 1941. Surg. Lieut (D) RNVR, 1942; transf. to RN, 1947; served as Asst to Dir, Naval Dental Services, 1967–70; Comd Dental Surgeon on staff of Flag Officer, Naval Air Comd, 1970–74. QHDS 1974–77. *Address:* Dore View, 3 The Glebe Close, Ewyas Harold, Herefordshire HR2 0EY. *T:* (01981) 240173.

CADOGAN, family name of **Earl Cadogan**.

CADOGAN, 8th Earl *cr* 1800; **Charles Gerald John Cadogan;** DL; Baron Cadogan 1718; Viscount Chelsea 1800; Baron Oakley 1831; *b* 24 March 1937; *o s* of 7th Earl Cadogan, MC and his 1st wife, Hon. Primrose Lilian Yarde-Buller (*d* 1970), *yr d* of 3rd Baron Churston; *S* father, 1997; *m* 1st, 1963, Lady Philippa Wallop (*d* 1984), *d* of 9th Earl of Portsmouth; two *s* one *d*; 2nd, 1989, Jennifer Jane Greig Rae (marr. diss. 1994), *d* of J. E. K. Rae and Mrs S. Z. de Ferranti; 3rd, 1994, Dorothy Ann Shipsey, MVO, *yr d* of late Dr W. E. Shipsey. *Educ:* Eton. Chm., Leukaemia Research Fund, 1985–. Freeman, City of London, 1979; Liveryman, GAPAN. DL Greater London, 1996. *Heir: s* Viscount Chelsea, *qv*. *Clubs:* White's, Royal Automobile.

CADOGAN, Prof. Sir John (Ivan George), Kt 1991; CBE 1985; PhD, DSc London; FRS 1976; FRSE; CChem, FRSC; first Director General, Research Councils, 1994–98; Visiting Professor of Chemistry, Imperial College, since 1979; Professorial Fellow, University College of Swansea, University of Wales, since 1979; Chairman, DNA Research Innovations Ltd, since 1999; Science Policy Adviser, Science Foundation Ireland, since 2000; *b* Pembrey, Carmarthenshire, 8 Oct. 1930; *er s* of late Alfred Cadogan and of Dilys Cadogan, MBE; *m* 1st, 1955, Margaret Jeanne (*née* Evans) (*d* 1992); one *s* one *d*; 2nd, 1997, Elizabeth Purnell. *Educ:* Grammar Sch., Swansea; King's Coll., London (State Scholar, 1948; 1st cl. Hons Chem. 1951). Research at KCL, 1951–54. Civil Service Research Fellow, 1954–56; Lectr in Chemistry, King's Coll., London, 1956–63; Purdie Prof. of Chemistry and Head of Dept, St Salvator's Coll., Univ. of St Andrews, 1963–69; Forbes Prof. of Organic Chemistry, Edinburgh Univ., 1969–79; Chief Scientist, BP Res. Centre, 1979–81; Dir of Res., BP, 1981–92. Chm., BP Vencap, 1988–92; Director: BP Gas International, 1983–87; BP Ventures, 1981–90 (Chief Exec., 1988–90); BP Chemicals, 1983–92; BP Venezuela, 1985–92; BP Solar International, 1988–92 (Chm., 1988–90); Chm., Kaldair Internat., 1988–90. Advr to EC Comr for Sci., R&D, 1993–94. Mem., Royal Commn on Criminal Justice, 1991–93. Chairman: Defence Sci. Adv. Council, 1985-91; Nuclear Weapons Safety Cttee, 1992–98; Nuclear Powered Warships Safety Cttee, 1992–98; Defence Nuclear Safety Cttee, 1998–2000. Member: Chemistry Cttee, SRC, 1967–71 (Chm. 1972–75); Council, SERC, 1981–85 (Chm., Science Bd, 1981–85; Mem., Science Bd, SRC, 1972–75); ACORD, Dept of Energy, 1987–89; HEFCW, 1992–95 (Chm., Res. Gp, 1992–94); HEFCE, 1994–98; Hong Kong Technol. Review Bd, 1992–95. Member: Council, Chem. Soc., 1966–69, 1973–76; Council, RIC, 1979–80; Chem. Soc.-RIC Unification Cttee, 1975–80; Council, RSC, 1980–85, 1989–92 (Pres. RSC, 1982–84); Council of Management, Macaulay Inst. for Soil Res., Aberdeen, 1969–79; Council, St George's Sch. for Girls, 1974–79; Council, RSE, 1975–80 (Vice-Pres., 1978–80); Council, Royal Soc., 1989–91, 1993–95 (Mem., Royal Soc. Sci. Inquiry, 1990–92); COPUS, 1994–97; Conseil d'Admin, Fondation de la Maison de la Chemie, 1994–; Vice-Pres., Royal Instn, 1986–87 (Mem. Council, 1984–87). Member: Bd of Trustees, Royal Observatory Trust, Edinburgh, 1979–86; Adv. Bd, RCDS, 1989–; Adv. Bd, Eur. Business Management Sch., UC Swansea, 1990–95; Adv. Council, RMCS, 1992–; Res. Cttee, Univ. of Newcastle upon Tyne, 1992–94; Ind. Adv. Cttee, Univ. of Durham, 1992–94; Trustee: Overseas Students Trust, UC Swansea, 1989–; RSE Scotland Foundn, 1998–. Governor: Jt Res. Centre, EC, 1994–2000; Salters' Inst. of Industrial Chem., 1999–. Pres., Chem. Sect., BAAS, 1981. Chemistry Advr, Carnegie Trust Univ. of Scotland, 1985–. Pres., Techniquest, 1997–99. Fellow: KCL, 1976 (Mem. Council, 1980–94; Vice-Chm., 1990–94); UC, Swansea, 1992; Cardiff Univ., 1998; FIC 1992. Hon. FREng (Hon. FEng 1992); Hon. FRSC 1999. First RSE Schs Christmas Lectures, 1980; lectures: Tilden, Chem. Soc., 1971; David Martin Royal Soc. BAYS, 1981; Humphry Davy, Royal Instn, 1982; Holroyd Meml, Soc. Chem. Ind., 1984; Salters' Co., Royal Instn, 1984; Philips, Royal Soc., 1985; Pedler, RSC, 1986; Dalton, RSC, 1989; BGS Dist., 1995; Irvine Meml, St Andrews, 1995; Salters' Millennium, 2000. Freeman, City of London; Liveryman, Salters' Co., 1993. Hon. DSc: St Andrews, 1983; Wales, 1984; Edinburgh, 1986; Aberdeen, 1991; Durham, 1992; Leicester, 1992; London, 1992; Sunderland, 1994; Cranfield, 1995; Glamorgan, 1996; Nottingham, 1999; Nottingham Trent, 1999; DUniv Stirling, 1984; Hon. Dr l'Univ Aix-Marseille, 1984. Samuel Smiles Prize, KCL, 1950; Millar Thomson Medallist, KCL, 1951; Meldola Medallist, Soc. of Maccabaeans and Royal Inst. of Chemistry, 1959; Corday-Morgan Medallist, Chem. Soc., 1965; SCI Medal, 2001. *Publications:* Principles of Free Radical Chemistry, 1971; Organophosphorus Reagents in Organic Synthesis, 1979; about 300 scientific papers, mainly in Jl RSC, and patents. *Recreations:* being in France, music, gardening, supporting Rugby football (Vice-Pres., Crawshay's Welsh RFC, London Welsh RFC; Patron, Swansea RFCC). *Address:* Department of Chemistry, Imperial College, South Kensington, SW7 2AY. *T:* (020) 7594 5864, *Fax:* (020) 7594 5800; *e-mail:* d.pappoe@ic.ac.uk. *Clubs:* Athenæum; Cardiff and County.

CADOGAN, Peter William; lecturer, writer and campaigner; Secretary, Northern Ireland Project, Gandhi Foundation, since 1988; *b* 26 Jan. 1921; *s* of Archibald Douglas Cadogan and Audrey Cadogan (*née* Wannop); *m* 1949, Joyce (marr. diss. 1969), *d* of William Stones, MP; one *d*. *Educ:* Tynemouth Sch., Tynemouth; Univ. of Newcastle, 1946–51 (BA (Hons) History, DipEd; Joseph Cowen Meml Prize, 1951). Served War, Air Sea Rescue Service, RAF, 1941–46. Teaching, Kettering and Cambridge, 1951–65. Committed to the Far Left, 1945–60; broke with Marxism, 1960. Founding Secretary, East Anglian Committee of 100: exploring theory and practice of non-violent direct action, 1961; Sec., Internat. Sub-Cttee of Cttee of 100, 1962; Sec. (full-time), National Cttee of 100, 1965–68. Mem., Nat. Council of CND, mix-sixties; Founding Sec., Save Biafra Campaign, 1968–70; Gen. Sec., South Place Ethical Soc., 1970–81; Co-Founder: Turning Point, 1975; Peace Anonymous, Action '84 and Summit '84, 1983–84; Co-Chm., Anglo-Afghan Circle, 1987–92. Founder Mem., New Consensus/New Dialogue, 1990; Co-founder: Values and Vision, 1991; Kilburn 2000, 1995 (Press Officer, 1996–); Chm., London Alliance, 1998–. Chm., Blake Soc. of St James', 1988–94 (Vice-Pres., 1994). *Publications:* Extra-Parliamentary Democracy, 1968; Direct Democracy, 1974, rev. 1975; Early Radical Newcastle, 1975; Six Ballads for the Seventies, 1976; many articles in learned jls, periodicals and elsewhere. *Recreations:* reading, gardening, social invention. *Address:* 3 Hinchinbrook House, Greville Road, NW6 5UP. *T:* (020) 7328 3709; *e-mail:* petercadogan@aol.com.

CÆSAR, Rev. Canon Anthony Douglass, CVO 1991 (LVO 1987); an Extra Chaplain to the Queen, since 1991; *b* 3 April 1924; *s* of Harold Douglass and Winifred Kathleen Cæsar. *Educ:* Cranleigh School; Magdalene Coll., Cambridge; St Stephen's House, Oxford. MA, MusB, FRCO. Served War with RAF, 1943–46. Assistant Music Master, Eton Coll., 1948–51; Precentor, Radley Coll., 1952–59; Asst Curate, St Mary Abbots, Kensington, 1961–65; Asst Sec., ACCM, 1965–70; Chaplain, Royal School of Church Music, 1965–70; Deputy Priest-in-Ordinary to the Queen, 1967–68, Priest-in-Ordinary, 1968–70; Resident Priest, St Stephen's Church, Bournemouth, 1970–73; Precentor and Sacrist, Winchester Cathedral, 1974–79; Sub-Dean of HM Chapels Royal, Dep. Clerk of the Closet, Sub-Almoner and Domestic Chaplain to the Queen, 1979–91; Hon. Canon of Winchester Cathedral, 1975–76 and 1979–91, Residentiary Canon, 1976–79, Canon Emeritus, 1991–; Chaplain, St Cross Hosp., Winchester, 1991–93. *Publications:* (jt ed.) The New English Hymnal, 1986; part songs, church music. *Recreation:* other people. *Address:* Flat 2, Old Kiln, Yarbridge, Brading, Isle of Wight PO36 0BP. *T:* (01983) 406435.

CAFFERTY, Michael Angelo; HM Diplomatic Service; Consul-General, Melbourne, Australia, 1983–87; *b* 3 March 1927; *m* 1950, Eileen E. Geer; two *s* three *d*. *Educ:* Univ. of London. BoT, 1951; Asst Trade Comr, Johannesburg, 1955, Pretoria, 1957; seconded to FO, Buenos Aires, 1958; Trade Comr, Singapore, 1964; FCO, 1968; Consul (Commercial), Milan, 1974; First Sec. and Head of Chancery, Rome (Holy See), 1977; Ambassador and Consul-Gen., Santo Domingo, 1979–83. *Address:* 12 Brackendale Way, Earley, Reading RG6 1DZ.

CAGIATI, Dr Andrea; Grand Cross, Italian Order of Merit, 1979; Hon. GCVO; Ambassador, retired 1988; *b* Rome, 11 July 1922; *m* 1968, Sigrid von Morgen; one *s* one *d*. *Educ:* University of Siena (Dr of Law). Entered Foreign Service, 1948. Served: Secretary, Paris, 1950; Principal Private Sec. to Minister of State, 1951; Vice-Consul-General, New York, 1953; Prin. Private Sec. to Minister of State and subsequently Dept of Political Affairs, 1955; Counsellor, Athens, 1957; Counsellor, Mexico City, 1960; Delegate, Disarmament Cttee, Geneva, March-Dec. 1962; Italian Delegation, UN, June 1962; Head, NATO Dept, Dec. 1962; Minister-Counsellor, Madrid, 1966; Ambassador,

Bogotá, 1968; Inst for Diplomatic Studies, 1971; Diplomatic Adviser to Prime Minister, 1972; Ambassador, Vienna, 1973; Ambassador, Court of St James's, 1980; Ambassador to the Holy See and to the Order of Malta, 1985. Vice Chm., 1989–94, Dir, 1987–94, Alitalia. President: Circolo di Studi Diplomatici, 1989–98 (now Hon. Pres.); Centro Conciliazione Internazionale, 1989–97; Fondazione Cagiati von Morgen, 1990–; Eurodéfence (Italia), 1994–99 (now Hon. Pres.); Vice-Pres., Fondazione De Gasperi, 1993–. Hon. GCVO during State Visit to Italy of HM The Queen, Oct. 1980; KM, 1953; Grand Cross: Order of Merit, Austria, 1980; Order of Merit, Malta, 1987; Order of Pius IX, Holy See, 1988. *Publications:* La Diplomazia dalle origini al XVII secolo, 1944; Verso quale avvenire?, 1958; I Sentieri della Vita, ricordi di un diplomatico, 1990; Scritti di Politica Estera, 4 vols 1991–2000; articles in quarterlies on foreign and defence affairs. *Recreations:* sculpture, golf, shooting. *Address:* Largo Olgiata, 15 (49D)–00123 Rome, Italy. *T:* and *Fax:* (6) 30888135. *Club:* Nuovo Circolo Scacchi (Rome).

CAHILL, Frances Rebecca; *see* Gibb, F. R.

CAHILL, Kevin James Patrick; Chief Executive, Comic Relief, since 1997 (Deputy Director, 1993–97); *b* 4 March 1952; *s* of James and Jean Cahill; *m* 1975, Shân Jones (marr. diss. 1982); one *s* one *d*; partner, Becky Webb; one *s*. *Educ:* Manchester Univ. (BA Hons English and Drama); PGCE Liberal Studies; RSA Dip. TEFL. Head of Educn, Nat. Theatre, later Royal Nat. Theatre, 1982–91; Dir of Educn, 1991–92, of Communications, 1992–93, Comic Relief. Patron, Nxt Theatre Co., 1999–. Chair, Gate Theatre, 1988–; Mem. Bd, Young Vic Theatre, 1993–. *Recreations:* football (Manchester United supporter), France, food. *Address:* Comic Relief, 89 Albert Embankment, SE1 7TP. *Club:* Groucho.

CAHILL, Teresa Mary; opera and concert singer; *b* 30 July 1944; *d* of Florence and Henry Cahill; *m* 1971, John Anthony Kiernander (marr. diss. 1978). *Educ:* Notre Dame High Sch., Southwark; Guildhall School of Music and Drama; London Opera Centre (LRAM Singing, AGSM Piano). Glyndebourne début, 1969; Covent Garden début, 1970; La Scala Milan, 1976, Philadelphia Opera, 1981, specialising in Mozart, Strauss and Elgar; concerts: all London orchestras; Boston Symphony Orch., Chicago Symphony Orch., Rotterdam Philharmonic Orch., West Deutscher Rundfunk, Warsaw Philharmonic, RAI Turin, Frankfurt Radio Orch.; Promenade concerts; Festivals: Vienna, 1983; Berlin, 1987; Bath, 2000; BBC radio and TV; recordings, incl. Strauss, Elgar and Mahler, for all major companies; master classes: Dartington Fest., 1984, 1986; Oxford Univ., 1995–; S'Hertogenbosch Vocal Concours, 1998 (Mem. Internat. Jury), 2000; Peabody Inst., Baltimore, 1999; recitals and concerts throughout Europe, USA, Far East. Professor: Royal Northern Coll. of Music; Trinity Coll. of Music. Artistic Advr, Nat. Mozart Competition, 1997–. Mem. Jury, Kathleen Ferrier Comp., 1988; Adjudicator, 1988–, Music Advr, 2000–, Live Music Now; Adjudicator: Young Concert Artists' Trust, 1989–; annual music comp., Royal Over-Seas League, 1985–89, 1992, 1995, 2000. Gov., Royal Soc. of Musicians, 2000–. Silver Medal, Worshipful Co. of Musicians, 1966; John Christie Award 1970. *Recreations:* cinema, theatre, travel, reading, collecting things, sales from car boots to Sotheby's, photography. *Address:* 65 Leyland Road, SE12 8DW. *Club:* Royal Over-Seas League (Hon. Mem.).

CAHN, Sir Albert Jonas, 2nd Bt *cr* 1934; marital, sexual and family therapist; *b* 27 June 1924; *s* of Sir Julien Cahn, 1st Bt, and Phyllis Muriel, *d* of A. Wolfe, Bournemouth; *S* father, 1944; *m* 1948, Malka, *d* of late R. Bluestone; two *s* two *d*. *Educ:* Headmaster's House, Harrow. Dir, Elm Therapy Centre, New Malden, 1983–93. *Recreations:* cricket, horse riding, photography. *Heir:* *s* Julien Michael Cahn [*b* 15 Jan. 1951; *m* 1987, Marilynne Janelle, *d* of Frank Owen Blyth; one *s* one *d*]. *Address:* 6 Fairacres, Roehampton Lane, SW15 5LX.

CAHN, Andrew Thomas, CMG 2001; Director, British Airways plc, since 2000; *b* 1 April 1951; *s* of Robert Wolfgang Cahn, *qv* and of Pat (*née* Hanson); *m* 1976, Virginia Beardshaw; two *s* one *d*. *Educ:* Bedales Sch.; Trinity Coll., Cambridge (BA 1st Cl. Hons). MAFF, 1973–77; FCO, 1977–78; Private Sec. to Perm Sec., MAFF, 1978–79; 1st Sec., Office of UK Perm. Repn to EC, FCO, 1982–84, Cabinet of Vice Pres., CEC, 1984–88; Asst Sec., MAFF, 1988–92; Principal Private Secretary to: Chancellor of Duchy of Lancaster, 1992–94; Minister of Agriculture, 1994–95; Dep. Head, European Secretariat, Cabinet Office, 1995–97; Chef de Cabinet to Rt Hon. Neil Kinnock, EC, Brussels, 1997–2000. Non-exec. Dir, Cadbury Ltd, 1990–92. Gov., Bedales Sch., 1993–98. Trustee, Gatsby Charitable Foundn, 1996–. FRSA 1979. *Recreations:* family, reading, mountains, squash. *Address:* British Airways, Waterside, PO Box 365, Harmondsworth, Middx UB7 0GB. *T:* (020) 8738 7594; 91 Patshull Road, NW5 2LE. *Club:* Royal Automobile.

CAHN, Prof. Robert Wolfgang, PhD, ScD; FRS 1991; FIM; FInstP; Distinguished Research Fellow (formerly Senior Associate), Department of Materials Science and Metallurgy, Cambridge University, since 1986; *b* 9 Sept. 1924; *s* of Martin and Else Cahn; *m* 1947, Patricia Lois Hanson; two *s* two *d*. *Educ:* Cambridge Univ. (BA 1945; PhD 1950; ScD 1963). FIM 1962; FInstP 1959. SO, later SSO, Harwell, 1947–51; Lectr, Sen. Lectr, then Reader, Physical Metallurgy Dept, Birmingham Univ., 1951–62; Professor of Materials Technol., UCNW, 1962–64; Prof. of Materials Sci., Sussex Univ., 1965–81, now Prof. Emeritus (Dean of Engrg, 1973–78); Prof. of Physical Metallurgy, Université de Paris–Sud, 1981–83; Fairchild Distinguished Scholar, CIT, 1985–86. Commonwealth Vis. Prof., Monash Univ., Melbourne, 1976; Visiting Professor: Univ. of Surrey, 1986–92; Univ. Autónoma de Barcelona, 1993. Editor, several scientific jls and book series. MAE 1989; Foreign Member: Göttingen Acad. Arts and Scis, 1987; Chinese Acad. of Sci., 1996; Foreign Corresp. Mem., Real Academia de Ciencias Exactas, Fisicas y Naturales, Madrid, 1995; Foreign Fellow, Indian Nat. Sci. Acad., 1997; Fellow: Amer. Soc. for Materials Internat., 1997; Minerals, Metals and Materials Soc., USA, 2000; Hon. Member: Indian Inst. of Metals, 1972; Materials Res. Soc. of India, 1991. FRSA. Ste Claire Deville Medal, Société Française de Métallurgie, 1978; A. A. Griffith Medal, Materials Science Club, 1983; Heyn Medal, Deutsche Ges. für Materialkunde, 1996; Luigi Losana Gold Medal, Assoc. Italiana di Metallurgia, 2001. *Publications:* (ed) Physical Metallurgy, 1965, 4th edn 1996; (ed) Processing of Metals and Alloys, 1991; Artifice and Artefacts—100 Essays in Materials Science, 1992; (contrib.) Twentieth Century Physics, ed B. R. Pippard *et al*, 1995; The Coming of Materials Science, 2001; contrib. scientific jls incl. Nature and Acta Metallurgica. *Recreations:* composing English prose, literature, looking at and collecting pictures, mountains and alpine flowers, music. *Address:* Department of Materials Science and Metallurgy, Pembroke Street, Cambridge CB2 3QZ. *T:* and *Fax:* (01223) 334381; 6 Storey's Way, Cambridge CB3 0DT. *T:* (01223) 360143; *e-mail:* rwc12@cam.ac.uk.
See also A. T. Cahn.

CAIE, Andrew John Forbes; HM Diplomatic Service; High Commissioner, Brunei, since 2002; *b* 25 July 1947; *s* of Norman Forbes Caie and Joan Margaret Caie (*née* Wise); *m* 1976, Kathie-Anne Williams; one *s* one *d*. *Educ:* St Dunstan's Coll., Catford; Sidney Sussex Coll., Cambridge (MA). Joined FCO, 1969; Manila, 1976–80; FCO, 1980–84; Dep. Head of Mission, Bogotá, 1984–88; FCO, 1988–93; Dep. High Comr, Islamabad, 1993–96; FCO Resident Chair, CSSB, 1996–97; FCO, 1997–98; Ambassador to Guatemala, 1998–2001. *Address:* c/o Foreign and Commonwealth Office, SW1A 2AH.

CAILLARD, Air Vice-Marshal (Hugh) Anthony, CB 1981; retired 1982; Director General, Britain-Australia Society, and Hon. Secretary, Cook Society, 1982–89; *b* 16 April 1927; *s* of late Col F. Caillard, MC, and Mrs M. Y. Caillard; *m* 1957, Margaret-Ann Crawford, Holbrook, NSW, Australia; four *s*. *Educ:* Downside; Oriel Coll., Oxford. Cranwell, 1947–49; served, 1949–65: 13 Sqdn, Egypt; ADC to C-in-C MEAF, and to AOC-in-C Tech. Trng Comd; 101 Sqdn, Binbrook; RAAF No 2 Sqdn; 49 Sqdn (Sqdn Ldr) and 90 Sqdn; RN Staff Coll.; HQ Bomber Comd (Wg Cdr); OC 39 Sqdn, Malta, 1965–67; Jt Services Staff Coll., 1967; Planning Staffs, MoD, 1967–70; Asst Air Attaché, Washington (Gp Captain), 1970–73; OC Marham, 1974–75; Def. Intell. Staff (Air Cdre), 1975–79; Dep. Chief of Staff, Ops and Intelligence, HQ Allied Air Forces, Central Europe, 1979–82. Specialist Air Advr, H of C Defence Cttee, 1985–92. Chairman: Ex Forces Fellowship Centre, 1987–93; Ex Services Mental Welfare Soc., 1990–93; Member: Grants and Appeals Cttee, RAF Benevolent Fund, 1987–93; Britain-Australia Bicentennial Cttee, 1984–88; Council, British Atlantic Cttee, 1988–92; Lord Mayor of Sydney's Sister City Cttee, 1994–; Trustee, Australian Arts Foundn, 1985–89. *Address:* 58 Hilltop Road, Clareville, NSW 2107, Australia. *Clubs:* Royal Air Force; Union (Sydney).

CAIN; *see* Nall-Cain, family name of Baron Brocket.

CAIN, Sir Edney; *see* Cain, Sir H. E. C.

CAIN, Sir (Henry) Edney (Conrad), Kt 1986; OBE 1975 (MBE 1965); FCCA; CA (Belize); first Governor, Central Bank of Belize, 1982–83, reappointed 1991; *b* 2 Dec. 1924; *s* of Henry Edney Conrad Cain I and Rhoda Cain (*née* Stamp); *m* 1951, Leonie (*née* Locke). *Educ:* St George's Coll., Belize; St Michael's Coll., Belize; Balham and Tooting Coll. of Commerce, London. FCCA 1977 (ACCA 1961); CA Belize 1984. Belize Government Service, 1940–: Examr of Accts, Audit Dept, 1954; Auditor, Audit Dept, 1959; Asst Accountant Gen., 1961; Accountant Gen., 1963; Man. Dir, Monetary Authority of Belize, 1976; Ambassador to USA, 1983; High Comr to Canada (resident in Washington, DC), 1984; Financial Sec., Ministry of Finance, Belize, 1985–87; High Comr to UK, 1987–90. Chm., Belize Bank Ltd, 1995–; Dir, Carlisle Hldgs Ltd (formerly Belize Holdings Inc., then BHI Corp.), 1992–. *Publication:* When the Angel says 'Write' (verse), 1948. *Recreations:* music, reading, current affairs. *Address:* PO Box 238, 936 Orchid Gardens, Belmopan, Belize. *T:* (501) 822492.

CAIN, James Crookall, FCA; Speaker, House of Keys, Isle of Man, 1991–96; Deputy President of Tynwald, 1992–96; *b* Douglas, IOM, 19 March 1927; *s* of James Mylchreest Cain, OBE, JP, formerly MHK and Jean (*née* Crookall); *m* 1959, Muriel Duckworth; two *d*. *Educ:* King William's Coll., IOM. Nat. Service, 1945–48, SSC, E Lancs, 1946. Qualified as Chartered Accountant with W. H. Walker & Co. (Liverpool), 1953; returned to Douglas office, 1954; Partner, 1959–71; Pannell Kerr Forster, 1971–86: Sen. IOM Partner, 1974; retd 1986. Mem., House of Keys, 1986–96; Member: Treasury, 1986–88; Dept of Highways Posts & Properties, 1989; Minister for Health and Social Security, 1989–91. Pres., Hospice Care, 1990 (Chm., 1983–89). *Recreations:* walking, reading. *Address:* Maughold, Alexander Drive, Douglas, Isle of Man IM2 3QZ. *T:* (01624) 675068.

CAIN, Hon. John; MLA (Lab) for Bundoora, 1976–92; Premier of Victoria, 1982–90; Professorial Associate, Department of Political Science, University of Melbourne, since 1991; *b* 26 April 1931; *s* of late Hon. John Cain; *m* 1955, Nancye Williams; two *s* one *d*. *Educ:* Melbourne Univ. (LLB). Practised as barrister and solicitor. Mem., Law Reform Commn, 1975–77. Pres., Law Inst. of Victoria, 1972–73 (Treasurer, 1969–70; Chm. of Council, 1971–72); Mem. Exec., Law Council of Australia, 1973–76. Vice-Chm., Vic. Br., Australian Labor Party, 1973–75; Mem., Parly Labor Exec., 1977–90; Leader, State Labor Party, 1981–90; Leader of Opposition, 1981–82; Minister: for Fed. Affairs, 1982; for Women's Affairs, 1982–90; Attorney-General of Vic, 1982–83. Commonwealth Observer, S African elecns, Apr. 1994. Trustee, Melbourne Cricket Ground, 1982–98, 1999–. *Address:* 9 Magnolia Road, Ivanhoe, Vic 3079, Australia.

CAIN, John Clifford; broadcasting research historian; Controller, Public Affairs, BBC, 1981–84; Hon. Vice-President, Broadcasting Support Services, since 1989 (Chairman, 1980–85; Trustee, 1985–89); *b* 2 April 1924; *s* of William John Cain and Florence Jessie (*née* Wood); *m* 1954, Shirley Jean Roberts; two *d*. *Educ:* Emanuel Sch.; Imperial Coll., Borough Road Coll., London Univ. (BSc); University Coll., London Univ. (MSc); Open Univ. (BA (Hons) 1988; PhD 1996). Served RAF (aircrew), 1944–47. Maths and science teacher in grammar, secondary modern and comprehensive schs and in polytechnic, 1950–59; Lectr, Science Museum, 1959–61; Asst Head of Sch. Broadcasting, Associated-Rediffusion, 1961–63; BBC Television: Producer, 1963–71; Asst Head of Further Educn Dept, 1971–72, Head, 1972–77; Asst Controller, Educn Br., BBC, 1977–80. Dir, Broadcasters' Audience Res. Bd, 1982–84. Mem., Health Educn Council, 1978–83. FRSA 1990. *Publications:* Talking Machines, 1961; (jtly) Mathematics Miscellany, 1966; (contrib.) Culture, Education and the State, 1988; The BBC: 70 years of broadcasting, 1992; (jtly) In a Class of its Own: BBC education 1924–1994, 1994; articles in EBU Review, Adult Educn, etc. *Recreations:* reading, gardening, music, theatre. *Address:* 63 Park Road, Chiswick, W4 3EY. *T:* (020) 8994 2712.

CAIN, Steven Anthony; Chief Executive, Carlton Communications plc, 1999–2000; *b* 30 Sept. 1964; *s* of Peter and Patricia Cain; *m* 1993; two *s* one *d*. *Educ:* Imperial Coll., London (MEng Chem. Engrg); Harvard; London Business Sch. Consultant, Bain & Co., 1987–89; Gp Develt Manager, Kingfisher plc, 1989–92; Asda plc: Mktg Controller, 1992–94; Grocery Trading Dir, 1994–95; Store Develt Dir, 1995–97; Mktg Dir, 1997–99. *Recreations:* football, tennis, squash, snow-boarding, golf. *Club:* Moor Allerton Golf (Leeds).

CAIN, Thomas William; QC 1989; **His Honour Deemster Cain;** HM's First Deemster and Clerk of the Rolls, Isle of Man, since 1998; *b* 1 June 1935; *s* of late James Arthur Cain and Mary Edith Cunningham (*née* Lamb); *m* 1961, Felicity Jane, *d* of late Rev. Arthur Stephen Gregory; two *s* one *d*. *Educ:* King's College Choir Sch., Cambridge; Marlborough Coll.; Worcester Coll., Oxford (BA 1958, MA 1961). National Service, 2nd Lieut RAC, 1953–55. Called to the Bar, Gray's Inn, 1959; Advocate, Manx Bar, 1961. Attorney-General, Isle of Man, 1980–93; Second Deemster, 1993–98. Pres., I of M Law Soc., 1985–89. Hon. Fellow, Soc. for Advanced Legal Studies, 2000. *Recreations:* sailing; Chairman, Manx Wildlife Trust. *Address:* Ivie Cottage, Kirk Michael, Isle of Man IM6 1AU. *T:* (01624) 878266.

CAINE, Sir Michael, Kt 2000; CBE 1992; actor; *b* Old Kent Road, London, 14 March 1933 (Maurice Joseph Micklewhite); *s* of late Maurice and of Ellen Frances Marie Micklewhite; *m* 1st, 1955, Patricia Haines (marr. diss.); one *d*; 2nd, 1973, Shakira Baksh; one *d*. *Educ:* Wilson's Grammar Sch., Peckham. Began acting in youth club drama gp. Served in Army, Berlin and Korea, 1951–53. Asst Stage Manager, Westminster Rep., Horsham, Sx, 1953; actor, Lowestoft Rep., 1953–55; Theatre Workshop, London, 1955;

numerous TV appearances (over 100 plays), 1957–63; *play:* Next Time I'll Sing for You, Arts, 1963; *films:* A Hill in Korea, 1956; How to Murder a Rich Uncle, 1958; Zulu, 1964; The Ipcress File, 1965; Alfie, The Wrong Box, Gambit, 1966; Hurry Sundown, Woman Times Seven, Deadfall, 1967; The Magus, Battle of Britain, Play Dirty, 1968; The Italian Job, 1969; Too Late the Hero, 1970; The Last Valley, Get Carter, 1971; Zee & Co., Kidnapped, Pulp, 1972; Sleuth, 1973; The Black Windmill, Marseilles Contract, The Wilby Conspiracy, 1974; Fat Chance, The Romantic Englishwoman, The Man who would be King, Harry and Walter Go to New York, 1975; The Eagle has Landed, A Bridge Too Far, Silver Bears, 1976; The Swarm, 1977; California Suite, 1978; Ashanti, Beyond the Poseidon Adventure, The Island, Dressed to Kill, 1979; Escape to Victory, 1980; Death Trap, 1981; Jigsaw Man, Educating Rita, The Honorary Consul, 1982; Blame it on Rio, 1984; Water, The Holcroft Covenant, 1985; Hannah and Her Sisters (Academy Award), Half Moon Street, Mona Lisa, 1986; The Fourth Protocol, The Whistle Blower, Surrender, Jaws The Revenge, 1987; Without a Clue, Dirty Rotten Scoundrels, 1989; A Shock to the System, Bullseye, Mr Destiny, 1990; Noises Off, Blue Ice, The Muppet Christmas Carol, 1992; On Deadly Ground, 1993; Bullet to Beijing, 1994; Mandela and de Klerk, 1996; Blood & Wine, Curtain Call, Shadowrun, 1997; The Debtors, 1998; Little Voice, 1999; The Cider House Rules (Academy Award), Quills, Last Orders, Quick Sands, 2000; Miss Congeniality, Shiner, 2001; *films for TV:* Jack The Ripper, 1988; Jekyll and Hyde, 1989; World War II: When Lions Roared, 1994. Fellow, BAFTA, 2000. *Publications:* Not Many People Know That, 1985; Not Many People Know This Either, 1986; Moving Picture Show, 1988; Acting in Film, 1990; What's It All About (autobiog.), 1992. *Recreations:* cinema, theatre, travel, gardening. *Address:* c/o International Creative Management, Oxford House, 76 Oxford Street, W1N 0AX.

CAINES, Eric, CB 1993; Professor of Health Service Management, Nottingham University, 1993–96; *b* 27 Feb. 1936; *s* of Ernest and Doris Caines; *m* 1st, 1958 (marr. diss. 1984); three *s*; 2nd, 1984, Karen Higgs; two *s*. *Educ:* Rothwell Grammar School, Wakefield; Leeds Univ. (LLB Hons). Dip. Hist. Art, London Univ., 1984. Short Service Commission, RAEC, 1958–61. NCB, 1961–65; BBC, 1965–66; as Principal, Min. of Health, Management Side Sec., General Whitley Council, 1966–70; Sec., NHS Reorganisation Management Arrangements Study, 1970–73; Assistant Sec., DHSS, 1973–77; IMF/World Bank, Washington, 1977–79; Under Sec., DHSS, 1979, Dir, Regl Organisation, 1981–84; Dir, Personnel and Finance, Prison Dept, Home Office, 1984–87; Dir, Operational Strategy, DHSS, then DSS, 1987–90; Dir of Personnel, NHS, DoH, 1990–93. Mem., Sheehy Inquiry into Police Responsibilities and Rewards. Director: Trebor Ltd, 1985–90; Premier Prisons, 1994–. FIPM. *Recreation:* travelling on foot with a book. *Address:* Mill Farm, Church Road, Brasted, Westerham, Kent TN16 1HZ. *T:* (01959) 564478. *Club:* Athenæum.

CAINES, Sir John, KCB 1991 (CB 1983); Permanent Secretary, Department for Education (formerly of Education and Science), 1989–93; *b* 13 Jan. 1933; *s* of late John Swinburne Caines and Ethel May Stenlake; *m* 1963, Mary Large; one *s* two *d*. *Educ:* Sherborne Prep. Sch.; Westminster Sch.; Christ Church, Oxford (MA). Asst Principal, Min. of Supply, 1957; Asst Private Sec., Min. of Aviation, 1960–61; Principal, Min. of Aviation, 1961–64; Civil Air Attaché in Middle East, 1964–66; Manchester Business Sch., 1967; Asst Sec., BoT, 1968; Sec., Commn on Third London Airport, 1968–71; Asst Sec., DTI, 1971–72; Principal Private Sec. to Sec. of State for Trade and Industry, 1972–74; Under-Sec., Dept of Trade, 1974–77; Sec., 1977–80, Mem. and Dep. Chief Exec., 1979–80, NEB; Dep. Sec., Dept of Trade, and Chief Exec., BOTB, 1980–82; Dep. Sec., Central Policy Review Staff, Cabinet Office, 1983; Dep. Sec., DTI, 1983–87; Permanent Sec., ODA, FCO, 1987–89. Director: Investors Compensation Scheme, 1993–2001 (Dep. Chm., 1997–2001); Norsk Hydro (UK) Ltd, 1994–2000; Medical Defence Union, 1998–; Chm., European Capital, 1995–2000. Mem., Gibraltar Financial Services Commn, 1995–. Ind. Reviewer for ASA, 1999–. Member of Council: Southampton Univ., 1993–2000; Open Univ., 1993–2001 (Chm., Audit Cttee, 1993–2001). DUniv Open, 1993. *Address:* 13 Hambleden Place, SE21 7EY.

CAIRD, Most Rev. Donald Arthur Richard; Archbishop of Dublin and Primate of Ireland, 1985–96; *b* Dublin, 11 Dec. 1925; *s* of George Robert Caird and Emily Florence Dreaper, Dublin; *m* 1963, Nancy Ballantyne, *d* of Prof. William Sharpe, MD, and Gwendolyn Hind, New York, USA; one *s* two *d*. *Educ:* Wesley Coll., Dublin, 1935–44; Trinity Coll., Dublin Univ., 1944–50. Sen. Exhibn, TCD, 1946; elected Schol. of the House, TCD, 1948; 1st cl. Moderatorship in Mental and Moral Science, 1949; Prizeman in Hebrew and Irish Language, 1946 and 1947; Lilian Mary Luce Memorial Prize for Philosophy, 1947; BA 1949; MA and BD 1955; HDipEd 1959. Curate Asst, St Mark's. Dundela, Belfast, 1950–53; Chaplain and Asst Master, Portora Royal Sch., Enniskillen, 1953–57; Lectr in Philosophy, University Coll. of St. David's, Lampeter, 1957; Rector, Rathmichael Parish, Shankill, Co. Dublin, 1960–69; Asst Master, St Columba's Coll., Rathfarnham, Co. Dublin, 1960–67; Dept Lectr in Philosophy, Trinity Coll., Dublin, 1962–63; Lectr in the Philosophy of Religion, Church of Ireland Theol Coll., Dublin, 1964–70; Dean of Ossory, 1969–70; Bishop of Limerick, Ardfert and Aghadoe, 1970–76; Bishop of Meath and Kildare, 1976–85. Fellow of St Columba's Coll., Dublin, 1971. Vis. Prof., Gen. Theol Seminary of ECUSA, 1997. Mem., Bord na Gaeilge, 1974; Hon. Life Mem., Royal Dublin Soc., 1996. Hon. DD TCD, 1988; Hon. LLD: NCEA, 1993; NUI, 1995. *Publication:* The Predicament of Natural Theology since the Criticism of Kant, in Directions, 1970 (Dublin). *Recreations:* swimming, tennis, walking. *Address:* 3 Crofton Avenue, Dun Laoghaire, Co. Dublin.

CAIRD, John Newport; director and writer of plays, musicals, opera and film; Hon. Associate Director, Royal Shakespeare Company; *b* 22 Sept. 1948; *s* of late Rev. George Bradford Caird, DPhil, DD, FBA and Viola Mary Newport, MA; *m* 1st, 1972, Helen Frances Brammer (marr. diss. 1982); 2nd, 1982, Ann Dorszynski (marr. diss. 1990); two *s* one *d*; 3rd, 1990, Frances Ruffelle (marr. diss. 1997); one *s* one *d*; 4th, 1998, Maoko Imai; one *s* one *d*. *Educ:* Selwyn House Sch., Montreal; Magdalen Coll. Sch., Oxford; Bristol Old Vic Theatre Sch. Associate Dir, Contact Theatre, Manchester, 1974–76; directed, Contact: Look Back in Anger, Downright Hooligan, Twelfth Night; Resident Dir, 1977–82, Associate Dir, 1983–90, RSC; directed, RSC: Dance of Death, 1977; Savage Amusement, Look Out, Here Comes Trouble, 1978; Caucasian Chalk Circle, 1979; (co-dir, with Trevor Nunn) Nicholas Nickleby, London, New York and Los Angeles, 1980, 1982, 1986 (SWET Award, 1980, Tony Award, 1982, for Best Dir; televised, 1981, Emmy Award, 1983); Naked Robots, Twin Rivals, 1981; Our Friends in the North, 1982; Peter Pan (co-dir with Trevor Nunn), 1982–84; Twelfth Night, Romeo and Juliet, 1983; The Merchant of Venice, Red Star, 1984; Philistines, 1985; Les Misérables (co-dir with Trevor Nunn), London, 1985 and worldwide, 1985–2001 (Tony Award for Best Dir, 1986, 1987); Every Man in his Humour, Misalliance, 1986; A Question of Geography, The New Inn, 1987; As You Like It, A Midsummer Night's Dream, 1989; Columbus and the Discovery of Japan, Antony and Cleopatra, 1992; directed, RNT: Trelawny of the 'Wells', 1993; The Seagull, 1994; Stanley, 1996, NY, 1997 (Outer Critics Circle Award for Best Dir); Peter Pan, 1997; Money, Candide (a new version with music by Leonard Bernstein), 1999 (Olivier Award, 2000); Hamlet, 2000. Directed: Song and Dance, London, 1982; As You Like It, Stockholm, 1984 (also for TV, 1985); Zaïdé by Mozart, Battignano, 1991; Life Sentences, NY, 1993; The Millionairess (UK tour), 1995; Murder in the Red Barn, Tiller-Clowes Marionettes, Theatre Mus., 1999; Midsummer Night's Dream, Stockholm, 2000. Devised and dir., Intimate Letters (a series of concerts for actors and string quartet); staged: WWF Religion and Interfaith Ceremony, Assisi, 1986; WWF Sacred Gifts for a Living Planet Ceremony, Bakhtapur, Nepal, 2000; wrote and directed: The Kingdom of the Spirit, London, 1986; Siegfried & Roy at the Mirage, Las Vegas, 1989; Children of Eden, a musical (with music and lyrics by Stephen Schwartz), London, 1991, and worldwide, 1991–2001; The Beggar's Opera (a new version with music by Ilona Sekacz), RSC, 1992; Jane Eyre, a musical (music by Paul Gordon), Canada and USA, 1995–2000; Toronto, 1996; adapted and dir., Henry IV (BBC TV), 1995. Recordings: Beggar's Opera; Children of Eden; Jane Eyre; Candide. Dir, Mountview Theatre Sch., 2000; Trustee, Friends of Highgate Cemetery Ltd., 1999. Hon. FWCMD. Hon. Fellow, Mansfield Coll., Oxford, 2000. *Publications:* (with Trevor Nunn) Peter Pan, by J. M. Barrie (new versions), 1993, 1998; (with Stephen Schwartz) Children of Eden, 1996; The Beggar's Opera (new version), 1999. *Recreation:* music. *Address:* Church House, 10 South Grove, Highgate, N6 6BS. *T:* (020) 8348 1996, *Fax:* (020) 8340 5030.

CAIRNCROSS, Frances Anne, (Mrs Hamish McRae); Management Editor, The Economist, since 1999; Chairman, Economic and Social Research Council, since 2001; *b* 30 Aug. 1944; *d* of Sir Alexander Kirkland Cairncross, KCMG, FBA and late Mary Frances (*née* Glynn); *m* 1971, Hamish McRae, *qv*; two *d*. *Educ:* Laurel Bank Sch., Glasgow; St Anne's Coll., Oxford (MA History; Hon. Fellow 1993); Brown Univ., Rhode Island (MAEcon). On Staff of: The Times, 1967–69; The Banker, 1969; The Observer, 1970–73; Economics Correspondent 1973–81, Women's Page Editor 1981–84, The Guardian; The Economist: Britain Ed., 1984–89; Envmt Ed., 1989–94; Media Ed., 1994–97; Public Policy Ed., 1997–98. Member: SSRC Economics Cttee, 1972–76; Newspaper Panel, Monopolies Commn, 1973–80; Council, Royal Economic Soc., 1980–85; Council, PSI, 1987–90; Cttee of Inquiry into Proposals to Amend the Shops Act, 1983–84; Inquiry into British Housing, 1984–85; School Teachers Review Body, 1991–94; Council, Inst. for Fiscal Studies, 1995–2001. Director: Prolific Gp plc, 1988–89; Alliance & Leicester Gp plc (formerly Alliance & Leicester Building Soc.), 1990–. Gov., NIESR, 1995–2001. Vis. Fellow, Nuffield Coll., Oxford, 2001–. Hon. Treas., Nat. Council for One Parent Families, 1980–83; Trustee, Kennedy Memorial Trust, 1974–90. *Publications:* Capital City (with Hamish McRae), 1971; The Second Great Crash (with Hamish McRae), 1973; The Guardian Guide to the Economy, 1981; Changing Perceptions of Economic Policy, 1981; The Second Guardian Guide to the Economy, 1983; Guide to the Economy, 1987; Costing the Earth, 1991; Green, Inc, 1995; The Death of Distance, 1997. *Recreation:* home life. *Address:* 6 Canonbury Lane, N1 2AP. *T:* (020) 7359 4612.

CAIRNCROSS, Neil Francis, CB 1971; Deputy Under-Secretary of State, Home Office, 1972–80; *b* 29 July 1920; *s* of late James and Olive Hunter Cairncross; *m* 1947, Eleanor Elizabeth Leisten; two *s* one *d*. *Educ:* Charterhouse; Oriel Coll., Oxford. Royal Sussex Regt, 1940–45. Called to the Bar, 1948. Home Office, 1948; a Private Sec. to the Prime Minister, 1955–58; Sec., Royal Commn on the Press, 1961–62; Dep. Sec., Cabinet Office, 1970–72; Dep. Sec., NI Office, March-Nov. 1972. Member: Parole Bd, 1982–85; Home Grown Timber Adv. Cttee, 1981–90; (co-opted) Avon Probation Cttee, 1983–89. *Recreation:* painting. *Address:* Little Grange, The Green, Olveston, Bristol BS35 4EJ. *T:* (01454) 613060. *Club:* Oxford and Cambridge.

CAIRNS, family name of **Earl Cairns**.

CAIRNS, 6th Earl *cr* 1878; **Simon Dallas Cairns,** CVO 2000; CBE 1992; Baron Cairns 1867; Viscount Garmoyle 1878; Chairman: CDC Group plc (formerly Commonwealth Development Corporation), since 1995; Commonwealth Business Council, since 1997; *b* 27 May 1939; *er s* of 5th Earl Cairns, GCVO, CB and Barbara Jeanne Harrisson, *y d* of Sydney H. Burgess; *S* father, 1989; *m* 1964, Amanda Mary, *d* of late Major E. F. Heathcoat Amory, and Mrs Roderick Heathcoat Amory; three *s*. *Educ:* Eton; Trinity Coll., Cambridge. Man. Dir, 1981–84, a Vice-Chm., 1984–86, Mercury Securities plc.; S. G. Warburg & Co.: Man. Dir, 1979–85; Dir, 1985–95; a Vice-Chm., 1985–87; Jt Chm., 1987–91; Chief Exec. and Dep. Chm., 1991–95; Chairman: BAT Industries, 1996–98 (Dir, 1990–); Allied Zurich, 1998–2000; Vice-Chairman: Zurich Financial Services, 1998–2000; Zurich Allied AG, 1998–2000. Receiver-General, Duchy of Cornwall, 1990–2000. Mem., City Capital Markets Cttee, 1989–94. Chairman: VSO, 1981–92; ODI, 1995–. Curator, Oxford Univ. Chest, 1995–2000. *Heir: s* Viscount Garmoyle, *qv*. *Address:* (office) 1 Bessborough Gardens, SW1V 2JQ. *T:* (020) 7828 4488. *Club:* Turf.

CAIRNS, Alun Hugh; Member (C) South Wales West, National Assembly for Wales, since 1999; *b* 30 July 1970; *s* of Hewitt and Margaret Cairns; *m* 1996, Emma Elizabeth Turner. *Educ:* Ysgol Gyfun Ddwyieithog Ystalyfera. Joined Lloyds Bank Gp, 1989; Business Develt Consultant, Lloyds TSB (formerly Lloyds Bank), 1993–. Joined Conservative Party, 1987 (economic spokesman, Wales, 1997–). Contested (C) Gower, 1997. *Address:* National Assembly for Wales, Cardiff Bay, Cardiff CF99 1NA.

CAIRNS, Andrew Ruaraidh A.; *see* Adams-Cairns.

CAIRNS, David; MP (Lab) Greenock and Inverclyde, since 2001; *b* 7 Aug. 1996; *s* of John Cairns and Teresa Cairns (*née* Harkins). *Educ:* Gregorian Univ., Rome; Franciscan Study Centre, Canterbury. Priest, 1991–94; Dir, Christian Socialist Movement, 1994–97; researcher for Siobahn McDonagh, MP, 1997–2001. *Recreations:* cinema, reading (US history). *Address:* House of Commons, SW1A 0AA.

CAIRNS, David Adam; Music Critic, Sunday Times, 1985–92; *b* 8 June 1926; *s* of Sir Hugh William Bell Cairns, KBE, FRCS and Barbara Cairns, *d* of A. L. Smith, sometime Master of Balliol; *m* 1959, Rosemary, *d* of Aubrey and Hilary Goodwin; three *s*. *Educ:* Trinity Coll., Oxford (1st Cl. Mod. History). Nat. Service, Intell. Corps, 1949–50. Co-Founder, Chelsea Opera Gp, 1950; Jane Eliza Procter Fellow, Princeton, 1950–51; Liby Clerk, H of C, 1951–53; TES, 1955–58; Music Critic, Evening Standard, and Spectator, 1958–62; Arts Editor, Spectator, 1961–62; Asst Music Critic, Financial Times, 1962–67; Music Critic, New Statesman, 1967–70; Classical Programme Co-ordinator, Philips Records, 1968–73; freelance music critic, 1973–85; founder and conductor, Thorington Players, 1983. Dist. Vis. Prof., Univ. of California, Davis, 1985; Vis. Scholar, Getty Center for History of Art and Humanities, 1992; Vis. Res. Fellow, Merton Coll., Oxford, 1993. FRSL 2001. Hon. RAM 2000. Hon. DLitt Southampton, 2001. CBE 1997; Officier de l'Ordre des Arts et des Lettres, 1991 (Chevalier, 1975). *Publications:* The Memoirs of Hector Berlioz (ed and trans.), 1969, 5th edn 2002; Responses: musical essays and reviews, 1973; Berlioz, vol. 1, The Making of an Artist 1803–1832, 1989 (Yorkshire Post Prize; Royal Phil. Soc. Award; Derek Allen Meml Prize, British Acad.), vol. 2, Servitude and Greatness 1832–1869 (Whitbread Award for Biography; Royal Phil. Soc. Award; Samuel Johnson Non-fiction Prize), 1999; (jtly) English National Opera Guides: The Magic Flute, 1980; Falstaff, 1982. *Recreations:* conducting, cinema, France and the French. *Address:* 49 Amerland Road, SW18 1QA. *T:* (020) 8870 4931.

CAIRNS, Air Vice-Marshal Geoffrey Crerar, CBE 1970; AFC 1960; FRAeS 1979; Consultant, FLS Aerospace (Lovaux) Ltd, 1992–94; *b* 21 May 1926; *s* of late Dr J. W. Cairns, MD, MCh, DPH and Marion Cairns; *m* 1948, Carol (*d* 1985), *d* of H. I. F. Evernden, MBE; four *d. Educ:* Loretto School, Musselburgh; Cambridge Univ. Joined RAF, 1944; served: Sqdns 43 and 93, Italy; Sqdn 73, Malta, 1946–49; Sqdn 72, UK, 1949–51; Adjutant, Hong Kong Auxiliary Air Force; test pilot A&AEE, Boscombe Down, 1957–60; Jt Planning Staff, MoD, 1961; Chief Instructor, Helicopters, CFS, RAF Ternhill, 1963; JSSC 1966; Supt Flying A&AEE 1968; Dir, Defence Operational Requirements Staffs, MoD, 1970; Commandant, Boscombe Down, 1972–74; ACAS (Op. Requirements), MoD, 1974–76; Comdr, Southern Maritime Air Region, 1976–78; Chief of Staff No 18 Group, Strike Command, 1978–80. Consultant, Marconi Avionics, 1980–81. Dir, Trago Aircraft Ltd, 1982–87. *Recreations:* golf, railways. *Club:* Royal Air Force.

CAIRNS, Hugh John Forster, DM; FRS 1974; Professor of Microbiology, Harvard School of Public Health, 1980–91; *b* 21 Nov. 1922; *er s* of Prof. Sir Hugh Cairns, KBE, DM; *m* 1948, Elspeth Mary Foster; two *s* one *d. Educ:* Balliol Coll., Oxford Univ. (BA 1943; BM, BCh 1946; DM 1952). Surg. Registrar, Radcliffe Infirmary, Oxford, 1945; Med. Intern, Postgrad. Med. Sch., London, 1946; Paediatric Intern, Royal Victoria Infirmary, Newcastle, 1947; Chem. Pathologist, Radcliffe Infirmary, 1947–49; Virologist, Hall Inst., Melbourne, Aust., 1950–51; Virus Research Inst., Entebbe, Uganda, 1952–54; Research Fellow, then Reader, Aust. Nat. Univ., Canberra, 1955–63; Rockefeller Research Fellow, California Inst. of Technology, 1957; Nat. Insts of Health Fellow, Cold Spring Harbor, NY, 1960–61; Dir, Cold Spring Harbor Lab. of Quantitative Biology, 1963–68; Prof of Biology (Hon.), State Univ. of New York, Stony Brook, 1968–73, Amer. Cancer Soc. Prof. 1968–73; Head of Imperial Cancer Research Fund Mill Hill Laboratories, 1973–80. *Address:* Holly Grove House, Wilcote, Chipping Norton, Oxon OX7 3EA. *T:* (01993) 868706; *e-mail:* j.cairns@ctsu.ox.ac.uk.

CAIRNS, Dr James Ford; MHR (ALP) for Lalor, 1969–78 (for Yarra, 1955–69); *b* 4 Oct. 1914; *s* of James John Cairns and Letitia Cairns (*née* Ford); *m* 1939, Gwendolyn Olga Robb; two *s. Educ:* Melton/Sunbury State Sch.; Northcote High Sch.; Melbourne Univ. MComm and PhD (Melb.). Australian Estates Co. Ltd, 1932; Victoria Police Force, 1935. Served War, AIF, 1945. Melbourne University: Sen. Tutor, Lectr, Sen. Lectr (Economic Hist.), 1946–55; Nuffield Dominion Fellow, Oxford Univ., 1951–52. Minister for Overseas Trade, 1972–74; Treasurer of Australia, 1974–75; Dep. Prime Minister, 1974–75; Minister for the Environment, Australia, 1975. Chifley Meml Lect., 2001. *Publications:* Australia, 1951 (UK); Living with Asia, 1965; The Eagle and the Lotus, 1969; Tariffs or Planning, 1970; Silence Kills, 1970; The Quiet Revolution, 1972; Oil in Troubled Waters, 1976; Vietnam: Scorched Earth Reborn, 1976; Growth to Freedom, 1979; Survival Now, the Human Transformation, 1983; Human Growth: its source ... and potential, 1985; Strength Within: towards an end to violence, 1988; The Untried Road, 1990; Towards a New Society: a new day has begun, 1993; Reshaping the Future, 1997; On the Horizon, 1999; numerous articles in jls and press, incl. title Australia: History in Enc. Brit. *Recreations:* sleeping, reading, listening to music.

CAIRNS, Very Rev. John Ballantyne; Minister of Riverside Parish Church, Dumbarton, since 1985; Chaplain to the Queen, since 1997; Moderator of the General Assembly of the Church of Scotland, 1999–2000; *b* 15 March 1942; *s* of William Cairns and Isobel Margaret (*née* Thom); *m* 1968, Elizabeth Emma Bradley; three *s. Educ:* Sutton Valence Sch., Kent; Bristol Univ. (LLB); Edinburgh Univ. (LTh). Messrs Richards, Butler & Co., Solicitors, 1964–68; E Lothian CC, 1968–69; Asst Minister, St Giles, Elgin, 1973–75; ordained, 1974; Minister, Langholm, Ewes and Westerkirk, 1975–85, also linked with Canonbie, 1981–85. Moderator, Presbytery of Dumbarton, 1993–94. General Assembly of the Church of Scotland: Convener: Cttee on Maintenance of the Ministry and Bd of Ministry and Mission, 1984–88; Cttee on Chaplains to HM Forces, 1993–98; Chm., Judicial Commn, 1993–98; Chaplain to the Moderator, 1995–96. Gen. Trustee, Church of Scotland, 1996–. *Publications:* Keeping Fit for Ministry, 1988; articles in various theol jls. *Recreations:* golf, gardening. *Address:* Riverside Church, High Street, Dumbarton G82 1NB. *T:* (01389) 742551.

CAIRNS, Patricia Rose Marie R.; *see* Roberts Cairns.

CAIRNS, Robert; Chairman, East of Scotland Water, 1998–April 2002; *b* 16 July 1947; *s* of William and Mary Cairns; *m* 1972, Pauline Reidy (marr. diss. 1995); two *s. Educ:* Morgan Acad., Dundee; Univ. of Edinburgh (MA Hons); Moray House Coll. (DipEd). Asst Ed., Scottish Nat. Dictionary, 1969–74; teacher, James Gillespie's High Sch., 1975–96. Mem. (Lab), Edinburgh CC, 1974– (Convenor, Planning Cttee, 1986–). Contested (Lab) N Edinburgh, Nov. 1973, Feb. 1974. *Recreations:* theatre, food and drink, walking. *Address:* 70 Ratcliffe Terrace, Edinburgh EH9 1ST. *T:* (0131) 667 1741.

CAITHNESS, 20th Earl of, *cr* 1455; **Malcolm Ian Sinclair;** PC 1990; FRICS; Lord Berriedale, 1455; Bt 1631; consultant and trustee to various companies and trusts, since 1994; Chief Executive, Clan Sinclair Trust, since 1999; *b* 3 Nov. 1948; *s* of 19th Earl of Caithness, CVO, CBE, DSO, DL, JP; *S* father, 1965; *m* 1975, Diana Caroline (*d* 1994), *d* of Major Richard Coke, DSO, MC, DL; one *s* one *d. Educ:* Marlborough; Royal Agricl Coll., Cirencester. Savills, land and estate agents, 1972–78; Brown and Mumford, 1978–80; property developer and other small businesses, 1980–84. A Lord in Waiting (Govt Whip), 1984–85; parly spokesman on health and social security, 1984–85, on Scotland, 1984–86; Parly Under-Sec. of State, Dept of Transport, 1985–86; Minister of State: Home Office, 1986–88; DoE, 1988–89; Paymaster Gen. and Minister of State, HM Treasury, 1989–90; Minister of State: FCO, 1990–92; Dept of Transport, 1992–94; elected Mem., H of L, 1999. Dir, 1995–98, Consultant, 1998–, Victoria Soames, Residential Property Consultants. *Heir: s* Lord Berriedale, *qv. Address:* c/o House of Lords, SW1A 0PW.

CALATRAVA-VALLS, Dr Santiago; architect; *b* Valencia, 28 July 1951; *m* 1976, Robertina Calatrava-Maragoni; three *s. Educ:* art sch., Valencia; Escuela Technica Superior de Arquitectura de Valencia; Swiss Fed. Inst. of Technol., Zürich (studies in civil engrg; Dr Tech. Sci.). Asst, Inst. for Bldg Statics and Construction and for Aerodynamics and Light Weight Constructions, Zürich, 1979–81; Founder: architectural and civil engrg practice, Zürich, 1981; architectural practice, Paris, 1989, and Valencia, 1991. Major projects include: Stadelhofen Rly Stn, Zürich, 1983–90; Lucerne Stn Hall, 1983–89; BCE Place, Toronto, 1987–92; Alamillo Bridge and La Cartuja Viaduct, Seville, 1987–92; Lusitania Bridge, Merida, 1988–91; Montjuic Communication Tower, Barcelona, 1989–92; Lyon Airport Rly Stn, 1989–94; Kuwait Pavilion, Expo '92, Seville, 1991–92. Exhibitions of work include: Mus. of Architecture, Basel, 1987; Design Mus., Zürich, 1991; Mus. of Modern Art, NY, 1992; retrospective, RIBA, London, 1992; Deutsches Mus., Munich, 1993; Valencia, Lübeck and Copenhagen, 1993. Member: Union of Swiss Architects, 1987; Internat. Acad. of Architecture, 1987; European Acad., 1992. Hon. FRIBA 1993. Hon. Mem., Union of German Architects, 1989. Dr *hc* Valencia, 1993; Seville, 1994. Numerous international prizes and awards including: Internat. Assoc. for Bridge and Structural Engrg Award, 1988; Gold Medal, IStructE, 1992. *Address:* Höschgasse 5, 8008 Zürich, Switzerland. *T:* (1) 4227500, *Fax:* (1) 4225600.

CALCUTT, Sir David (Charles), Kt 1991; QC 1972; Chairman: City Panel on Takeovers and Mergers, 1989–2000; Council of the Banking Ombudsman, 1994–2001; a Judge of the Courts of Appeal of Jersey and Guernsey, 1978–2000; Chancellor of the Dioceses of Exeter and of Bristol, since 1971 and in Europe (formerly Gibraltar in Europe), since 1983; *b* 2 Nov. 1930; *s* of late Henry Calcutt; *m* 1969, Barbara, JP and Freeman, City of London, *d* of late Vivian Walker. *Educ:* Christ Church, Oxford (chorister); Cranleigh Sch. (music schol.); King's Coll., Cambridge (choral schol.; Stewart of Rannoch Schol., 1952; prizeman; MA, LLB, MusB). Called to the Bar, Middle Temple, 1955 (Bencher, 1981; Treas., 1998); Harmsworth Law Schol., Garraway Rice Prize, 1956; Chm. of the Bar, 1984–85 (Vice-Chm., 1983–84). Dep. Chm., Somerset QS, 1970–71; a Recorder, 1972–89. Fellow Commoner, 1980–85, Master, 1986–94, Magdalene Coll., Cambridge (Hon. Fellow, 1994–). Dept of Trade Inspector, Cornhill Consolidated Gp Ltd, 1974–77; Chairman: CS Arbitration Tribunal, 1979–94; Falkland Is Commn of Enquiry, 1984; Inst. of Actuaries' Appeal Bd, 1985–94; Dep. Pres., 1983–87, Pres., 1987–97, Lloyds of London Appeal Tribunal; Member: Criminal Injuries Compensation Bd, 1977–97; Council on Tribunals, 1980–86; conducted: Cyprus Service Police Inquiry, 1985–86; Colin Wallace Inquiry, 1990; Review of Press Self-Regulation, 1992–93; Member: Interception of Communications Tribunal, 1986–2001 (Vice-Pres., 1996–2001); Investigatory Powers Tribunal, 2000–; Pres., Interception of Communications Tribunal (Guernsey), 1998–; Arbitrator, Internat. Centre for the Settlement of Investment Disputes, Washington, 1992– (Conciliator, 1986–92); Indep. Mem., Diplomatic Service Appeal Bd, 1986–92; Assessor of Compensation for Miscarriages of Justice, Home Office, 1989–2001, MoD, 1993–; Chm., Cttee on Privacy and Related Matters, 1989–90; Judicial Chm., City Disputes Panel, 1994–; Chm., Legal Services Commn, IoM, 2000–01. UK Deleg., Consultative Cttee, Bars and Law Socs, EEC, 1979–83. Gresham Prof. of Law, 1992–95. Fellow, Internat. Acad. of Trial Lawyers (NY), 1978–; Hon. Member: American Bar Assoc., 1985–; Canadian Bar Assoc., 1985–; Cambridge Union Soc., 1994–. Dir, Edington Music Fest., 1956–64. Dep. Chm., RCM, 1988–90 (FRCM 1988). Chairman: Council, Cranleigh and Bramley Schs, 1987–93 (Vice-Chm., 1983–87); Septemviri, Cambridge Univ., 1988–95; Gov., Ditchley Foundn, 1992–. Trustee, Winchester Cathedral, 1992–. Fellow, Winchester Coll., 1992. Hon. LLD: Exeter, 1996; Staffordshire, 1997; Southampton, 1998; UWE, 1998. *Recreation:* living on Exmoor. *Address:* 35 Essex Street, Temple, WC2R 3AR. *T:* (020) 7353 6381. *Clubs:* Athenæum; New (Edinburgh); Hawks (Cambridge).

CALCUTTA, Archbishop of, (RC), since 1986; **Most Rev. Henry Sebastian D'Souza;** *b* 20 Jan. 1926; *s* of George William and Aurelia Clotilde D'Souza. *Educ:* Papal Atheneum, Kandy (LPH, LD); Urban Univ., Rome (DCL). Nominated Archbishop of Cuttack-Bhubaneswar, 1974. Secretary General: Catholic Bishops' Conference of India, 1979–82; Federation of Asian Bishops' Confs, 1983–93. Pres., Conf. of Catholic Bishops of India (Latin Rite), 1988–94, 1998–. *Address:* Archbishop's House, 32 Park Street, Calcutta 700016, India. *T:* (33) 2471960, (33) 2474666.

CALDECOTE, 3rd Viscount *cr* 1939, of Bristol, co. Gloucester; **Piers James Hampden Inskip;** *b* 20 May 1947; *o s* of 2nd Viscount Caldecote, KBE, DSC and of Jean Hamilla, *d* of Rear-Adm. H. D. Hamilton; *S* father, 1999; *m* 1st, 1970, Susan Bridget (*née* Mellen); 2nd, 1984, Kristine Elizabeth, *d* of Harvey Holbrooke-Jackson; one *s. Educ:* Eton; Magdalene Coll., Cambridge. Group Exec., Carlton Communications. *Heir: s* Hon. Thomas James Inskip, *b* 22 March 1985. *Address:* 72 Erpingham Road, SW15 1BG.

CALDECOTT, Andrew Hilary; QC 1994; *b* 22 June 1952; *s* of Andrew Caldecott, CBE and Zita (*née* Belloc); *m* 1977, Rosamond Ashton Shuttleworth; two *s* two *d. Educ:* Eton Coll.; New Coll., Oxford (BA Hons Mod. Hist.). Called to the Bar, Inner Temple, 1975. Play: Higher than Babel, Bridewell Theatre, 1999. *Address:* 1 Brick Court, Temple, EC4Y 9BY. *T:* (020) 7353 8845.

CALDER, Elisabeth Nicole; Publisher (formerly Publishing Director), Bloomsbury Publishing, since 1986; *b* 20 Jan. 1938; *d* of Florence Mary Baber and Ivor George Baber; *m* 1958, Richard Henry Calder (marr. diss. 1972); one *d* one *s. Educ:* Broadfields, Edgware; Palmerston North Girls' High Sch., NZ; Canterbury Univ., NZ (BA 1958). Reader, Metro-Goldwyn-Mayer story dept, 1969–70; Publicity Manager, Victor Gollancz, 1971–74; Editorial Director: Victor Gollancz, 1975–78; Jonathan Cape, 1979–86. *Recreations:* reading, thinking about gardening, junking. *Address:* Bloomsbury Publishing, 38 Soho Square, W1V 5DF. *T:* (020) 7494 2111.

CALDER, Dr Ian Maddison, TD 1973; MD; FRCPath; FFOM; consultant adviser on occupational medicine to Ministry of Defence, since 1994; *b* 22 March 1937; *s* of late Walter James Calder, MIMechE, and Alice (*née* Maddison); *m* 1964, Dorothy Joan Hubbard, MBE, RGN; one *s* one *d. Educ:* Norwich Sch.; Univ. of St Andrews (MB ChB 1962; State Scholar); Univ. of Dundee (MD 1977; DSc 1992). MRCPath 1981, FRCPath 1996; FFOM 1990; FCPath (HK) 1993; MRCP 1996. Served RA, 1955 (2nd Lieut); Hon. Col, 254 Field Ambulance, RAMC (V), 1991–; Mem., E Anglia TAVRA Cttee, 1990. Lectr in Forensic Medicine, St George's Hosp. Med. Sch., Univ. of London, 1972–76; Lectr, London Hosp. Med. Coll., 1976–81, then Hon. Lectr. Visiting Fellow: St Edmund's Coll., Cambridge, 1978–; Wellcome Inst. of Comparative Neurology, Univ. of Cambridge, 1978–; Travelling Scholar, UCLA, 1976; Advr to Nat. Undersea Res. Centre, Univ. of N Carolina. Ext. Examnr, Univ. of Hong Kong, 1985–90; Advr to Labour Dept, Hong Kong, 1991–94. Member: MoD Ethical Cttee, 1983–; MRC Hyperbaric Scis Panel; MRC Long Term Health Effects Cttee; DoH Dangerous Pathogens Working Party. Mem., Physicians for Human Rights. *Publications:* chapters in textbooks of pathology and occupational medicine; papers on diving and hyperbaric medicine research. *Recreations:* sailing, boat-building, antique furniture and cabinet making, rowing, church music. *Address:* Thorpe, Huntingdon Road, Girton, Cambridge CB3 0LG. *T:* (01223) 277220. *Club:* Athenæum.

CALDER, John Mackenzie; Managing Director: John Calder (Publishers) Ltd, 1950–91; Calder Publications Ltd, since 1991; President, Riverrun Press Inc., New York, since 1978; *b* 25 Jan. 1927; *e s* of James Calder, Ardargie, Forgandenny, Perthshire, and Lucianne Wilson, Montreal, Canada; *m* 1st, 1949, Mary Ann Simmonds; one *d*; 2nd, 1960, Bettina Jonic (marr. diss. 1975); one *d. Educ:* Gilling Castle, Yorks; Bishops College Sch., Canada; McGill Univ.; Sir George Williams Coll.; Zürich Univ. Studied political economy; subseq. worked in Calders Ltd (timber co.), Director; founded John Calder (Publishers) Ltd, 1949; Man. Dir, Calder & Boyars, 1964–75. Organiser of literary confs for Edinburgh Festival, 1962 and 1963, and Harrogate Festival, 1969. Founded Ledlanet Nights, 1963, in Kinross-shire (music and opera festival, closed 1974). Active in fields related to the arts and on many cttees; Co-founder, Defence of Literature and the Arts Society; Chm., Fedn of Scottish Theatres, 1972–74. Contested (L): Kinross and W Perthshire, 1970; Hamilton, Oct. 1974; (European Parlt) Mid Scotland and Fife, 1979. FRSA 1974. Chevalier des Arts et des Lettres (France), 1975; Chevalier, 1983, Officier, 1997, de l'Ordre nationale de mérite (France). *Publications:* (ed) A Samuel Beckett Reader, 1967; (ed) Beckett at 60,

1967; (ed) William Burroughs Reader, 1982; (ed) New Samuel Beckett Reader, 1983; (ed) Henry Miller Reader, 1985; (ed) The Nouveau Roman Reader, 1986; (ed) As No Other Dare Fail: for Samuel Beckett on his 80th birthday, 1986; The Garden of Eros, 1997; The Philosophy of Samuel Beckett, 1997; What's Wrong, What's Right (poems), 1999; Pursuit (autobiog.), 2001; (ed) Gambit International Drama Review, etc; obituaries and reviews for newspapers; articles in many jls. *Recreations:* writing (several plays, stories; criticism, etc; translations); music, theatre, opera, reading, chess, lecturing, conversation; travelling, promoting good causes, fond of good food and wine. *Address:* c/o Calder Publications Ltd, 51 The Cut, SE1 8LF. *Clubs:* Caledonian; Scottish Arts (Edinburgh).

CALDER, Julian Richard; Director of Statistical Support Services (formerly Survey and Statistical Services) Group, Office for National Statistics, 1996–2000; *b* 6 Dec. 1941; *s* of Donald Alexander and Ivy O'Nora Calder; *m* 1965, Avril Tucker; two *s*. *Educ:* Dulwich College; Brasenose College, Oxford; Birkbeck College, London. Statistician, 1973, Chief Statistician, 1978, Central Statistical Office; Chief Statistician, 1981, Dir of Stats, 1985–94, Board of Inland Revenue; Hd of Div., Govt Statistical Service and Gen. Div., Central Statistical Office, 1994–96. *Recreations:* cycling, listening to music.

CALDER, Nigel David Ritchie, MA; science writer; *b* 2 Dec. 1931; *e s* of Baron Ritchie-Calder, CBE; *m* 1954, Elisabeth Palmer; two *s* three *d*. *Educ:* Merchant Taylors' Sch.; Sidney Sussex Coll., Cambridge. Physicist, Mullard Research Laboratories, 1954–56; Editorial staff, New Scientist, 1956–66; Science Editor, 1960–62; Editor, 1962–66. Science Correspondent, New Statesman, 1959–62 and 1966–71; Chairman, Assoc. of British Science Writers, 1962–64. Mem., Initiative Group, Foundn Scientific Europe, 1987–90; Consultant on public inf., ESA, 1994–. FRAS; FRGS. (Jtly) UNESCO Kalinga Prize for popularisation of science, 1972. *Publications:* Electricity Grows Up, 1958; Robots, 1958; Radio Astronomy, 1958; (ed) The World in 1984, 1965; The Environment Game, 1967; (ed) Unless Peace Comes, 1968; Technopolis: Social Control of the Uses of Science, 1969; Living Tomorrow, 1970; (ed) Nature in the Round: a Guide to Environmental Science, 1973; Timescale, 1983; 1984 and After, 1983; The English Channel, 1986; The Green Machines, 1986; (ed) Future Earth, 1988; (ed) Scientific Europe, 1990; Giotto to the Comets, 1992; Hubble Space Telescope, 1993; Beyond this World, 1995; The Manic Sun, 1997; *books of own TV programmes:* The Violent Universe, 1969; The Mind of Man, 1970; The Restless Earth, 1972; The Life Game, 1973; The Weather Machine, 1974; The Human Conspiracy, 1975–76; The Key to the Universe, 1977; Spaceships of the Mind (TV series), 1978; Einstein's Universe, 1979; Nuclear Nightmares, 1979; The Comet is Coming!, 1980; Spaceship Earth, 1991 (TV series). *Recreation:* sailing. *Address:* 26 Boundary Road, Northgate, Crawley, W Sussex RH10 2BT. *T:* (01293) 549969. *Club:* Cruising Association (Vice-Pres., 1981–84).

CALDERWOOD, Sir Robert, Kt 1990; Chairman, Greater Glasgow Health Board, 1993–97; Chief Executive, Strathclyde Regional Council, 1980–92; Director, GEC (Scotland) Ltd, 1991–99; *b* 1 March 1932; *s* of Robert Calderwood and Jessie Reid (*née* Marshall); *m* 1958, Meryl Anne (*née* Fleming); three *s* one *d*. *Educ:* William Hulme's Sch., Manchester; Manchester Univ. (LLB (Hons)). Admitted solicitor, 1956; Town Clerk: Salford, 1966–69; Bolton, 1969–73; Manchester, 1973–79. Dir, Glasgow Garden Fest. 1988 Ltd, 1985–88; Chm., Strathclyde Buses, 1989–93. Member: Parole Bd for England and Wales, 1971–73; Soc. of Local Authority Chief Execs, 1974–92 (Pres., 1989–90); Scottish Consultative Cttee, Commn for Racial Equality, 1981–88; Employers Panel, Industrial Tribunals in Scotland, 1992–98; Local and Central Govt Relations Res. Cttee, Joseph Rowntree Foundn, 1992–97. Director: European Summer Special Olympic Games 1990 (Strathclyde) Ltd, 1989–90; Scottish Opera, 1991–96 (Dep. Chm., 1992–96); Quality Scotland Foundn, 1991–92. Mem. Council, Industrial Soc., 1983–92. Gov., Glasgow Caledonian Univ., 1994–96. Chm., Clyde Heritage Trust, 1997–98. Hon. Mem., Incorporation of Coopers, Trades House of Glasgow, 1994–; Hon. Patron, Scottish Overseas Aid, 1993–98. Hon. FIWEM 1992. *Recreations:* theatre, watching Rugby. *Address:* 6 Mosspark Avenue, Milngavie, Glasgow G62 8NL.

CALDICOTT, Dame Fiona, DBE 1996; FRCP, FRCPsych; Principal, Somerville College, Oxford, since 1996; *b* 12 Jan. 1941; *d* of Joseph Maurice Soesan and Elizabeth Jane (*née* Ransley); *m* 1965, Robert Gordon Woodruff Caldicott; one *d* (one *s* decd). *Educ:* City of London Sch. for Girls; St Hilda's Coll., Oxford (MA, BM, BCh; Hon. Fellow 1996). DPM; FRCPsych 1985; FRCP 1995; FRCPI 1996; FRCGP 1996. House Surgeon and Physician, Coventry Hosps, 1966–67; General Practice, Family Planning and Child Welfare, 1968–70; training in Psychiatry, Walsgrave Hosp., Coventry and Central Hosp., Warwick, 1970–76; Sen. Registrar in Psychiatry, W Midlands Regl Trng Scheme, 1977–79; Consultant Psychiatrist, Univ. of Warwick, 1979–85; Consultant Psychotherapist, Uffculme Clinic, Birmingham, 1979–96; Sen. Clinical Lectr in Psychotherapy, Univ. of Birmingham, 1982–96; Unit General Manager, Mental Health, Central Birmingham, 1989–91; Clin. Dir, Adult Psychiatric and Psychotherapy Service, Mental Health Unit, S Birmingham, 1991–94; Med. Dir, S Birmingham Mental Health NHS Trust, 1994–96 (Hon. Consultant Psychiatrist, 1996–). Non-exec. Dir, Coventry Building Soc., 1997–2001. Chm., Cttee to Review Patient-Identifiable Information, reported 1997; Mem., Sec. of State's Standing Adv. Cttee, on Med. Workforce (formerly Manpower) Planning, 1991–; Mem., Broadcasting Standards Commn (formerly Council), 1996–2001. Pres., Section for Psychiatry, 1995–99 (Sec., 1991–95), Sec., European Bd of Psychiatry, 1992–96, Union of European Med. Specialists; Member: Council: BMA, 1996–2000 (Chm., Bd of Med. Educn, 1996–2000); RSocMed, 1996–99; Acad. Med. Sci., 1998–; GMC, 1999–; Mem., Hebdomadal Council, 1998–2000, Council, 2000–, Oxford Univ., 1998–. Sub-Dean 1987–90, Dean 1990–93, Pres., 1993–96, RCPsych; Chm., Acad. of Med. Royal Colls, 1995–96. Pres., British Assoc. of Counselling, 2000–. Consultant Advr to Commissioning Bd for High Security Psychiatric Care, 1996–2000. Trustee: Zito Trust, 1994–; Bethlem Art and History Collections Trust, 1995–99; Nuffield Trust, 1998–. Patron: Oxford Healthy Living Centre, 1996–; Family Nurturing Network, Oxford, 1997–; Hon. Pres., Guild of Health Writers, 1996–99. Founder FMedSci 1998; Fellow, Acad. of Medicine, Singapore, 1994; Mem., Czech Psychiatric Soc., 1994. Hon. DSc Warwick, 1997; Hon. MD Birmingham, 1997. Chevalier du Tastevin, 1991. *Publications:* contrib. Discussing Doctors' Careers (ed Isobel Allen), 1988; papers in Bull. RCPsych, Current Opinion in Psychiatry, Postgraduate Psychiatry. *Recreations:* family, friends, reading, wine. *Address:* Somerville College, Oxford OX2 6HD; The Old Rectory, Manor Farm Lane, Balscote, Banbury OX15 6JJ. *T:* (01295) 730293, *Fax:* (01295) 730549. *Clubs:* Reform, Royal Society of Medicine.

CALDOW, William James, CMG 1977; Consultant, ICI plc, 1981–86; *b* 7 Dec. 1919; *s* of William Caldow and Mary Wilson Grier; *m* 1950, Monique Henriette Hervé, *d* of Gaétan Hervé, Chevalier de la Légion d'Honneur and Croix de Guerre (member of French Resistance, executed 1944); one *s* (and one *s* decd). *Educ:* Marr College (Dux Medallist); Glasgow University (Scholar; MA Hons); Sorbonne. Captain, Intelligence Corps, 1940–45. Colonial Administrative Service, Gold Coast, later Ghana, 1947–59; War Office, later Ministry of Defence, 1959–80. *Recreations:* reading, music, bird watching. *Address:* 3 Pilgrims Way, Guildford, Surrey GU4 8AB. *T:* (01483) 562183.

CALDWELL, Edward George, CB 1990; First Parliamentary Counsel, since 1999 (Parliamentary Counsel, 1981–99); *b* 21 Aug. 1941; *s* of Arthur Francis Caldwell and Olive Caldwell (*née* Riddle); *m* 1992, Dr Helen Beynon. *Educ:* St Andrew's, Singapore; Clifton College; Worcester College, Oxford. Law Commission, 1967–69, 1975–77, 1986–88; joined Office of Parly Counsel, 1969. *Address:* Office of the Parliamentary Counsel, 36 Whitehall, SW1A 2AY. *T:* (020) 7210 6640.

CALDWELL, Maj.-Gen. Frank Griffiths, OBE 1953 (MBE 1945); MC 1941 and Bar 1942; retired; *b* 26 Feb. 1921; *s* of William Charles Francis and Violet Marjorie Kathleen Caldwell; *m* 1945, Betty, *d* of Captain Charles Palmer Buesden; one *s* one *d*. *Educ:* Elizabeth Coll., Guernsey. Commnd Royal Engrs, 1940; served Western Desert RE, 1940–43 (MC and Bar; dispatches); Special Air Service NW Europe, 1944–45 (MBE); Malaya, 1951–53 (OBE); Comdr RE, 2 Div. BAOR, 1961–63; Corps Comdr RE, 1 (BR) Corps, 1967–68; Dir Defence Operational Plans, MoD, 1970; Engineer in Chief (Army), 1970–72; Asst CGS (Operational Requirements), 1972–74. Col Comdt, RE, 1975–80. Director: Scout Insurance (Guernsey) Ltd, 1990–2000; Guernsey Envmtl Services, 2001–. President: RBL, Guernsey, 1986–; La Société Guernesiaise, 1994–96; Chm., Guernsey Scout Council, 1987–99. Belgian Croix de Guerre, 1940, and Croix Militaire, 1945. *Recreation:* ornithology. *Address:* Le Courtil Tomar, Rue des Pres, St Pierre du Bois, Guernsey GY7 9AQ.

CALDWELL, Prof. John Anthony, DPhil; Titular Professor of Music, University of Oxford, since 1999; Senior Research Fellow, Jesus College, Oxford, since 1999; *b* 6 July 1938; *s* of George Wilfrid Caldwell and Susannah Marion Caldwell (*née* Haywood); *m* 1967, Janet Susan Kellar; one *s* one *d*. *Educ:* Birkenhead Sch.; Keble Coll., Oxford (BA 1960; BMus 1961; MA 1964; DPhil 1965). FRCO 1957. Asst Lectr in Music, Bristol Univ., 1963–66; Oxford University: Lectr in Music, 1966–96, Reader in Music, 1996–99; Keble College: Lectr in Music, 1966–67; Res. Fellow, 1967–75; Official Fellow, 1975–92; Lecturer in Music: Balliol Coll., 1966–; Jesus Coll., 1970–; Lincoln Coll., 1972–. General Editor: Corpus of Early Keyboard Music, 1982–; Early English Church Music, 1995–; Co-editor, Plainsong and Medieval Music, 1992–96; Mem., Editl Bd and Trustee, Music and Letters, 1995–. Organist: St Luke's, Tranmere, Birkenhead, 1955–57; St Giles', Oxford (also Choirmaster), 1966–67; SS Philip and James, Oxford, 1968–77. *Compositions:* Good Friday (opera), prod Oxford, 1998; Divertimento for orch., 1999; The Word (opera), prod Oxford, 2001. *Publications:* (ed) Early Tudor Organ Music I, 1966; English Keyboard Music before the Nineteenth Century, 1973; Medieval Music, 1978, rev. trans. as La música medieval, 1984; Editing Early Music, 1985, 2nd edn 1996; The Oxford History of English Music, Vol i 1991, Vol. ii 1999; (ed) Tudor Keyboard Music, 1995. *Recreation:* visiting churches and archaeological sites. *Address:* Faculty of Music, St Aldate's, Oxford OX1 1DB. *T:* (01865) 276125.

CALDWELL, Prof. John Bernard, OBE 1979; PhD; FREng, FRINA; Emeritus Professor of Naval Architecture, University of Newcastle upon Tyne, since 1991; *b* 26 Sept. 1926; *s* of John Revie Caldwell and Doris (*née* Bolland); *m* 1955, Jean Muriel Frances Duddridge; two *s*. *Educ:* Bootham Sch., York; Liverpool Univ. (BEng); Bristol Univ. (PhD). CEng; FRINA 1963; FREng (FEng 1976). Res. Fellow, Civil Engrg, Bristol Univ., 1953; Sen. Scientific Officer 1955, Principal Sci. Off. 1958, Royal Naval Scientific Service; Asst Prof. of Applied Mechanics, RNC Greenwich, 1960–66; Newcastle upon Tyne University: Prof. of Naval Architecture, 1966–91; Hd of Dept of Naval Architecture, 1966–83; Hd, Sch. of Marine Technol., 1975–80, 1986–88; Dean of Faculty of Engrg, 1983–86. Director: Nat. Maritime Inst. Ltd, 1983–85; Marine Design Consultants Ltd, 1985–89; Newcastle Technology Centre, 1985–90; Northern Engrg Centre, 1989–92. Vis. Prof. of Naval Arch., MIT, 1962–63. President: N-E Coast Instn of Engrs and Shipbuilders, 1976–78; RINA, 1984–87 (Vice-Pres., 1977–84). Mem., Engineering Council, 1988–94 (Chm., Bd for Engrs' Registration, 1990–92). FRSA 1982. Hon. DSc Gdansk Tech. Univ., 1985. Froude Medal, RINA, 1984; David W. Taylor Medal, SNAME, 1987. *Publications:* numerous papers on research and educn in naval arch. *Address:* Barkbooth, Winster, Windermere, Cumbria LA23 3NZ. *T:* (01539) 568222.

CALDWELL, Marion Allan; QC (Scot.) 2000; *d* of late Henry Moffat Caldwell and of Elizabeth Bloomer Smith or Caldwell. *Educ:* Eastbank Acad., Glasgow; Aberdeen Univ. (LLB Hons); European Univ. Inst., Florence; Glasgow Univ. (DipLP). Journalist, 1970–77; trainee Solicitor, 1983–84; Solicitor, 1984–85; admitted to Faculty of Advocates, 1986; called to the Bar, Inner Temple, 1991; Standing Jun. Counsel to Accountant of Court and Accountant in Bankruptcy, Scotland, 1991–2000. Legal chm., Pensions Appeal Tribunals for Scotland, 2001–. *Recreations:* swimming, ski-ing, walking, social tennis, reading. *Address:* Advocates' Library, Parliament House, Edinburgh EH1 1RF. *T:* (0131) 667 5391.

CALDWELL, Philip; Chief Executive Officer, 1979–85, and Chairman of Board, 1980–85, Ford Motor Company; *b* Bourneville, Ohio, 27 Jan. 1920; *s* of Robert Clyde Caldwell and Wilhelmina (*née* Hemphill); *m* 1945, Betsey Chinn Clark; one *s* two *d*. *Educ:* Muskingum Coll. (BA Econs 1940); Harvard Univ. Graduate Sch. of Business (MBA Indust. Management, 1942). Served to Lieut, USNR, 1942–46. With Navy Dept, 1946–53, as civilian (Dep. Dir, Procurement Policy Div., 1948–53); joined Ford Motor Co., 1953: Vice Pres. and Gen. Man. Truck Ops, 1968–70; Pres. and Dir, Philco-Ford Corp. (subsid. of Ford Motor Co.), 1970–71; Vice Pres. Manufg Gp, N Amer. Automotive Ops, 1971–72; Chm. and Chief Exec. Officer, Ford of Europe, Inc., 1972–73; Dir, Ford Motor Co., 1973–90; Exec. Vice Pres., Internat. Automotive Ops, 1973–77; Vice Chm. of Bd, 1977–79; Dep. Chief Exec. Officer, 1978–79; Pres., 1978–80; Director: Ford of Europe, 1972–85; Ford Latin America, 1973–85; Ford Mid-East and Africa, 1973–85; Ford Asia-Pacific, 1973–85; Ford Motor Credit Co., 1977–85; Ford of Canada, 1977–85; Mem., Eur. Adv. Council, 1976–88 (Chm., 1987–88). Sen. Man. Dir, Lehman Brothers Inc., 1985–98. Director: Digital Equipment Corp., 1980–95; Chase Manhattan Corp., and Chase Manhattan Bank, NA, 1982–85 (Mem., Chase Manhattan Bank Internat. Adv. Cttee, 1979–85); Federated Dept Stores, 1984–88; Russell Reynolds Associates, Inc., 1984–; Kellogg Co., 1985–92; Shearson Lehman Brothers Hldgs Inc., 1985–93; Amer. Guarantee and Liability Insce Co., 1986–99; Zurich Reinsurance Co. of New York, 1987–90; Zurich-American Insurance Gp, 1989–99; Mexico Fund, 1991–; Specialty Coatings Internat., 1991–93; Zurich Reinsurance Centre Holdings, 1993–97; Waters Corp., 1994–; Castech Aluminium Gp, 1994–96; Mettler-Toledo Inc., 1996– (Chm., 1996–98); Detroit Symphony Orch., 1974–85; Harvard Business Sch. Associates, 1977–93. Vice Chairperson, New Detroit, Inc., 1977–85; Vice Chm., Japan Soc., 1987–89 (Mem., 1983–89; Chm. Exec. Cttee, 1987–89); Member: US Chamber of Commerce Transportation Cttee, 1968–77; US Council, Internat. Chamber of Commerce, 1973–77; US Council for Internat. Business, 1977–85; Soc. of Automotive Engrs, 1969–85; Engrg Soc. of Detroit, 1970–85; Motor Vehicle Manufrs Assoc. of US, 1978–85 (Chm., 1978 and 1983; Mem., Motor Truck Cttee, 1964–70); Econ. Club of Detroit, 1977–86; Highway Users Fedn, 1977–85; INSEAD, 1978–81 (Chm., US Adv. Bd, 1979–84; Mem., Internat. Council, 1983–); Conf. Bd, 1979–; Cttee for Econ. Develt, 1979–; (Charter Mem.) Business Higher Educn Forum, 1979–83; Business Council,

1980–2002; Policy Cttee, Business Roundtable, 1980–85; Trilateral Commn, 1980–86; Citizens Res. Council of Mich, 1980–85; Adv. Council on Japan–US Econ. Relations, 1981–85; US Trade Representative Adv. Cttee for Trade Negotiations, 1983–85; President's Export Council, 1985–89; Council on Foreign Relations, 1985–; Mexico-US Bus. Com., 1985–. Bd of Advrs, Jerome Levy Econs Inst., 1988–. Trustee: Muskingum Coll., 1967–; Winterthur Mus. and Gdns, 1986–2000. Philip Caldwell Professorship of Business Admin, Harvard Business Sch., established 1989. Hon. HHD Muskingum, 1974; Hon. DBA Upper Iowa Univ., 1978; Hon. LLD: Boston Univ. and Eastern Mich Univ., 1979; Miami Univ., 1980; Davidson Coll., 1982; Univ. of Mich, 1984; Ohio Univ., 1984; Lawrence Inst. of Technol., 1984. 1st William A. Jump Meml Award, 1950; Meritorious Civilian Service Award, US Navy, 1953; Muskingum Coll. Alumni Dist. Service Award, 1978; Brigham Young Univ. Sch. of Management Internat. Exec. of the Year Award, 1983; Automotive Industry Leader of the Year, 1984; Club of Greater NY Business Statesman Award, 1984; Alumni Achievement Award, Harvard Business Sch., 1985; Club of Columbus Businessman of the Year, Columbus, Ohio, 1984; Automotive Hall of Fame, 1990; Statesman of the Year, Detroit, 1991. *Address:* Ford Motor Co., 225 High Ridge Road, West Building, Stamford, CT 06905, USA. *T:* (203) 3578880, *Fax:* (203) 3578241. *Clubs:* Links, River (New York).

CALDWELL-MOORE, Sir Patrick; *see* Moore.

CALEDON, 7th Earl of, *cr* 1800; **Nicholas James Alexander;** Baron Caledon, 1790; Viscount Caledon, 1797; Lord Lieutenant of County Armagh, since 1989; *b* 6 May 1955; *s* of 6th Earl of Caledon, and Baroness Anne (*d* 1963), *d* of late Baron Nicolai de Graevenitz; *S* father, 1980; *m* 1st, 1979, Wendy (marr. diss.), *d* of Spiro Coumantaros and Mrs Suzanne Dayton; 2nd, 1989, Henrietta, *d* of John Newman, Compton Chamberlayne, Wilts; one *s* one *d*. *Educ:* Sandroyd School, Gordonstoun School (Round-Square House). *Recreations:* ski-ing, tennis, swimming, photography, travel. *Heir: s* Viscount Alexander, *qv*. *Address:* Caledon Castle, Caledon, Co. Tyrone, Northern Ireland. *T:* (028) 3756 8232; 3 Petyt Place, SW3 5DJ.

CALGARY, Bishop of, since 2000; **Rt Rev. Barry Craig Bates Hollowell;** *b* Boston, Mass, 14 April 1948; *m* 1976, Linda Barry; two *s* one *d*. *Educ:* Valparaiso Univ., Indiana (BA 1970); Westcott House and Fitzwilliam Coll., Cambridge (BA 1972, MA 1976); Episcopal Divinity Sch., Cambridge, Mass (MDiv 1973); St Paul Univ., Ottawa (MPastStudies 1979); Univ. of NB (MA Psychol. 1986). Ordained deacon, 1973, priest, 1974; Deacon, All Saints', Chelmsford, Mass, 1973–74; Asst Curate, Christ Church Cath., Fredericton, NB, 1974–75; pastoral and liturgical work, Christ Church Cath., and Anglican Chaplain, Univ. of NB, 1975–86; pastoral work, St Barnabas, Ottawa, 1978–79; interim Priest-in-charge, St Margaret's Chapel-of-Ease, 1983; Rector, St George's Anglican Ch, St Catharines, Niagara, 1986–2000; Archdeacon, Lincoln, Niagara, 1991–2000. Mem., Gen. Synod, 1989– (Chm., Faith, Worship and Ministry Cttee, 1995–). Rep. Anglican Ch of Canada at signing of Porvoo Agreement, Westminster Abbey, 1996. *Recreations:* photography, music, downhill ski-ing. *Address:* (home) 137 Citadel Circle NW, Calgary, AB T3G 4C2, Canada. *T:* (403) 208 6475; (office) 560, 1207-11th Avenue SW, Calgary, AB T3C 0M5, Canada. *T:* (403) 243 3673, *Fax:* (403) 243 2182; *e-mail:* hollowell@calgary.anglican.ca.

CALIGARI, Prof. Peter Douglas Savaria, PhD, DSc; CBiol, FIBiol, Professor of Agricultural Botany, University of Reading, since 1986 (Head of Department, 1987–98); *b* 10 Nov. 1949; *s* of Kenneth Vane Savaria Caligari, DFM, RAF retd, and Mary Annette (*née* Rock); *m* 1973, Patricia Ann (*née* Feeley); two *d*. *Educ:* Hereford Cathedral Sch.; Univ. of Birmingham (BSc Biol Sci., 1971; PhD Genetics, 1974; DSc Genetics, 1989). CBiol 1997; FIBiol 1997. Res. Asst, 1971–74, Res. Fellow, 1974–81, Dept of Genetics, Univ. of Birmingham; SSO, 1981–84, PSO, 1984–86, Scottish Crop Res. Inst. Managing Director: BioHybrids International Ltd, 1996–; BioMarkers Ltd, 1997–. Member: Exec. Cttee, XVIIth Internat. Congress of Genetics, 1991–93; Governing Body, Plant Science Research Ltd, 1991–94; Governing Council, John Innes Centre, 1994–99; European Council, Volcani Centre, 1999–; Bd, Internat. Lupin Assoc., 1999–; Chm., Sci. Prog., Triennial EUCARPIA Congress, 1999–2001. Vice Pres., Inst. of Biology, 1999– (Chm., Sci. Policy Bd, 1999–). FRSA 1990. Editor, Heredity, 1987–90 (Jun. Editor, 1985–87); Mem. Editl Bd, Euphytica, 1991–. *Publications:* (contrib.) The Potato Crop, 1991; (contrib.) Applications of Synthetic Seeds to Crop Improvement, 1992; (jtly) Selection Methods in Plant Breeding, 1995; (ed jtly) Compositae: biology and utilization, 1996; (contrib.) Lupins: production and utilization, 1998; (ed jtly) Cashew and Coconuts: trees for life, 1998; scientific papers and reports on genetics, plant breeding and biotechnology (*c* 230 papers, *c* 45 reports). *Address:* Department of Agricultural Botany, School of Plant Sciences, University of Reading, Whiteknights, PO Box 221, Reading RG6 6AS. *T:* and *Fax:* (0118) 931 6684; *e-mail:* p.d.s.caligari@reading.ac.uk.

CALLADINE, Prof. Christopher Reuben, ScD; FRS 1984; FREng; Professor of Structural Mechanics, University of Cambridge, since 1986; Fellow of Peterhouse, since 1960; *b* 19 Jan. 1935; *s* of Reuben and Mabel Calladine (*née* Boam); *m* 1964, Mary R. H. Webb; two *s* one *d*. *Educ:* Nottingham High Sch.; Peterhouse, Cambridge; Massachusetts Inst. of Technology. Development engineer, English Electric Co., 1958; Demonstrator in Engrg, Univ. of Cambridge, 1960, Lectr, 1963; Reader, 1978. Vis Research Associate, Brown Univ., 1963; Vis. Prof., Stanford Univ., 1969–70. FREng (FEng 1994). James Alfred Ewing Medal, ICE, 1998. *Publications:* Engineering Plasticity, 1969; Theory of Shell Structures, 1983; (with H. R. Drew) Understanding DNA, 1992, 2nd edn 1997; papers in engrg and biological jls. *Recreations:* music, architecture. *Address:* 25 Almoners Avenue, Cambridge CB1 8NZ. *T:* (01223) 246742.

CALLAGHAN, family name of **Baron Callaghan of Cardiff**.

CALLAGHAN OF CARDIFF, Baron *cr* 1987 (Life Peer), of the City of Cardiff in the County of South Glamorgan; **Leonard James Callaghan,** KG 1987; PC 1964; *b* 27 March 1912; *s* of James Callaghan, Chief Petty Officer, RN; *m* 1938, Audrey Elizabeth Moulton; one *s* two *d*. *Educ:* Elementary and Portsmouth Northern Secondary Schs. Entered Civil Service as a Tax Officer, 1929; Asst Sec., Inland Revenue Staff Fed., 1936–47 (with an interval during the War of 1939–45, when served in Royal Navy). Joined Labour Party, 1931. MP (Lab): S Cardiff, 1945–50; SE Cardiff, 1950–83; Cardiff S and Penarth, 1983–87. Parly Sec., Min. of Transport, 1947–50; Chm. Cttee on Road Safety, 1948–50; Parliamentary and Financial Sec., Admiralty, 1950 51; Opposition Spokesman: Transport, 1951–53; Fuel and Power, 1953–55; Colonial Affairs, 1956–61; Shadow Chancellor, 1961–64; Chancellor of the Exchequer, 1964–67; Home Secretary, 1967–70; Shadow Home Sec., 1970–71; Opposition Spokesman on Employment, 1971–72; Shadow Foreign Sec., 1972–74; Sec. of State for Foreign and Commonwealth Affairs, 1974–76; Minister of Overseas Develt, 1975–76; Prime Minister and First Lord of the Treasury, 1976–79; Leader, Labour Party, 1976–80; Leader of the Opposition, 1979–80. Father, House of Commons, 1983–87. Deleg. to Council of Europe, Strasburg, 1948–50 and 1954. Mem., Labour Party NEC, 1957–80; Treasurer, Labour Party, 1967–76, Vice-Chm. 1973, Chm. 1974. Consultant to Police Fedn of England and Wales and to Scottish Police Fedn, 1955–64. President: Adv. Cttee on Protection (formerly Pollution) of the Sea, 1963– (Chm., 1952–63); United Kingdom Pilots Assoc., 1963–76; Jt Pres., RIIA, 1983–. Hon. Pres., Internat. Maritime Pilots Assoc., 1971–76. Pres., Univ. of Wales, Swansea (formerly UC Swansea), 1986–95 (Hon. Fellow, 1993). Visiting Fellow, Nuffield Coll., Oxford, 1959–67, Hon. Life Fellow, 1967; Hon. Fellow: UC Cardiff, 1978; Portsmouth Polytechnic, 1981; Cardiff Inst. of Higher Educn, 1991. Hon. LLD: Wales, 1976; Sardar Patel Univ., India, 1978; Birmingham, 1981; Sussex, 1989; Westminster, 1993; Liverpool, 1996; Hon. PhD Meisei Univ., Tokyo, 1984; DUniv Open, 1996. Hon. Bencher, Inner Temple, 1976. Freeman: City of Portsmouth, 1991; City of Swansea, 1993; Hon. Freeman: City of Cardiff, 1974; City of Sheffield, 1979. Hubert H. Humphrey Internat. Award, 1978. Grand Cross, 1st class, Order of Merit of Federal Republic of Germany, 1979. *Publications:* A House Divided: the dilemma of Northern Ireland, 1973; Time and Chance (autobiog.), 1987. *Address:* House of Lords, SW1A 0PW.

See also Baroness Jay of Paddington.

CALLAGHAN, Rev. Brendan Alphonsus, SJ; Lecturer in Psychology, Heythrop College, University of London, since 1980 (Principal, 1985–97; Acting Principal, 1998–99); Superior, Wimbledon Jesuit Community, since 1998; *b* 29 July 1948; *s* of Dr Kathleen Callaghan (*née* Kavanagh) and Dr Alphonsus Callaghan. *Educ:* Stonyhurst; Heythrop, Oxon; Campion Hall, Oxford (MA 1977); Univ. of Glasgow (MPhil 1976); Heythrop Coll., Univ. of London (MTh 1979). AFBPsS; CPsychol. Joined Society of Jesus, 1967; Clinical Psychologist, Glasgow, 1974–76; Middx Hosp., 1976–79; ordained priest, 1978; curate, St Aloysius, Glasgow, 1979–80; Lectr in Psychology, Allen Hall, Chelsea, 1981–87. Superior, Brixton Jesuit Community, 1993–94; Merrivale Jesuit Community, KwaZulu-Natal, 1998. University of London: Chm., Bd of Examrs, Theol and Religious Studies, 1987–89; Schools Examn Bd, 1987–97; Collegiate Council and Senate, 1989–94; Council, 1994–97; Institute of Medical Ethics: Hon. Asst/Associate Dir, 1976–89; Governing Body, 1989–; Gen. Sec., 1999–. Visiting Lecturer: St Joseph's Theol Inst., KwaZulu-Natal, 1987 and 1997–98; (in Med. Ethics), Imperial Coll., London, 1990–; KCL, 1991–94; Vis. Prof., Fordham Univ., NY, 1990; Vis. Scholar, Weston Sch. of Theol., Cambridge, Mass, 1992. Member: Conf. of Seminary Rectors, 1987–97; Cttee of Catholic Principals, 1985–97; Ethics Cttee, St Thomas' Hosp., 1990–; Higher Educn Cttee, RC Bps Conf. of England and Wales, 1986–97; Academic Bd, and Governing Body, Heythrop Coll., 1982–97; Academic Adv. Cttee, Jews' Coll., 1993–97. Chm. Govs, Digby Stuart Coll., 1998–, Mem. Council, 1998–, Univ. of Surrey Roehampton (formerly Roehampton Inst.); Member, Advisory Boards: Campion Hall, Oxford, 1985–95; Syon House, Angmering, 1985–97; Centre for the Study of Communication and Culture (Chm.), 1990–; Inst. of St Anselm, Westgate (Chm.), 1991 98; Mem., Management Cttee, Family Res. Trust, 1991–. Vice Pres., Catholic Students Trust Appeal. Consultant Psychologist to Marriage Care (formerly Catholic Marriage Adv. Council), 1981–, and to religious congregations and orders. Hon. FCP 1996. Member: Catholic Inst. for Internat. Relations; British and Irish Assoc. for Practical Theol.; Soc. for Study of Religions; Amnesty; CND; Royal African Soc. FRSocMed. Broadcaster, BBC and World Service radio, Channel Four. Member, Editorial Board: Law and Justice, 1986–; Jl of Contemp. Religion, 1994–97; Mental Health, Religion and Culture, 1997–. *Publications:* Life Before Birth (with K. Boyd and E. Shotter), 1986; articles, reviews and verse in Br. JL Psych, Jl Med. Ethics, Heythrop Jl, The Way and magazines. *Recreations:* photography, long distance walking, poetry. *Address:* Heythrop College, Kensington Square, W8 5HQ. *T:* (020) 7795 6600, *Fax:* (020) 7795 4200.

CALLAGHAN, James; *b* 28 Jan. 1927. Lectr, Manchester Coll., 1959–74. Metropolitan Borough Councillor, 1971–74. MP (Lab) Middleton and Prestwich, Feb. 1974–1983, Heywood and Middleton, 1983–97. *Recreations:* sport and art. *Address:* 17 Towncroft Avenue, Middleton, Manchester M24 3DA.

CALLAGHAN, Prof. Paul Terence, DPhil, DSc; FRS 2001; FRSNZ; Alan Macdiarmid Professor of Physical Sciences, Victoria University of Wellington, New Zealand, since 2001; *b* 19 Aug. 1947; *s* of Ernest Edward Callaghan and Mavis Eileen Callaghan; *m* 1969, Susan Audrey Roberts; one *s* one *d*. *Educ:* Victoria Univ. of Wellington (BSc Hons); Wolfson Coll., Oxford (DPhil 1974); DSc Oxon 1995. Massey University, NZ: Lectr in Physics, 1974–84; Prof. of Physics, 1984-2001; Sir Neil Waters Dist. Prof., 2001–. FRSNZ 1991. Cooper Medal, 1991, Hector Medal, 1998, Royal Soc. of NZ; Mechaelis Medal, Otago Univ., 1995. *Publications:* Principles of Nuclear Magnetic Resonance Microscopy, 1991; contrib. numerous articles to learned jls. *Recreations:* music, walking. *Address:* School of Chemical and Physical Sciences, Victoria University of Wellington, Wellington, New Zealand. *T:* (4) 4721000.

CALLAGHAN, William Henry; Chairman, Health and Safety Commission, since 1999; *b* 19 May 1948; *s* of Henry William Callaghan and Constance Callaghan; one *s*. *Educ:* St John's Coll., Oxford (BA PPE); Univ. of Kent at Canterbury (MA Econs). Trades Union Congress: Asst, 1971–74, Asst Sec., 1974–77, Head, 1978–93, Econ. Dept; Head, Econ. and Social Affairs, and Chief Economist, 1994–99. Member: Low Pay Commn, 1997–2000; Res. Priorities Bd, ESRC, 1994–99. Former Mem. Bd, BITC; Mem. Bd, Basic Skills Agency. Vis. Fellow Nuffield Coll. Oxford, 1999–. *Publications:* numerous TUC pubns on econ. and social affairs. *Recreations:* sailing, cycling, walking, listening to music. *Address:* 71 Fairfield Road, Kingston upon Thames, Surrey KT1 2PZ. *T:* (020) 8547 2911.

CALLAN, Hilary Margaret West; Director, Royal Anthropological Institute of Great Britain and Ireland, since 2000; *b* 27 Oct. 1942; *d* of John Sydney Flashman and late Marion Louise Flashman (*née* Thornton) (Silver Laurel Leaf Emblem and King's Commendation for Brave Conduct in Civil Defence, 1941); *m* 1965, Ivan Roy Callan (marr. diss. 1987); one *d*. *Educ:* Marsden Sch., NZ; St Paul's Girls Sch.; Somerville Coll., Oxford (MA, MLitt, Dip. Social Anthropol.). Sen. Res. Associate, Birmingham Univ., 1968–70; Asst Prof., American Univ. of Beirut, Lebanon, 1971–75; Lecturer: Univ. of Kent at Canterbury, 1977–80; Trent Univ., Canada, 1981–84 (Harry Frank Guggenheim Res. Award, 1982–84; Oxford Poly., 1987–88; Brunel Univ., 1988–89; Asst dir, UKCOSA: Council for Internat. Educn, 1989–93; Exec. Dir, Eur. Assoc. for Internat. Educn, 1993–2000 (Hon. Life Mem., 2000). Hon. Prof. Associate, Brunel Univ., 2001–. Mem., Editl Bd, Jl Studies in Internat. Educn, 2000–. Contested (SDP/LAll) Scarborough, 1987. *Publications:* Ethology and Society: towards an anthropological view, 1970; (ed jtly) The Incorporated Wife, 1984; (ed) International Education: towards a critical perspective, 2000; numerous articles in books and jls in anthropology and internat. educn. *Recreations:* reading, music, family and friends. *Address:* Royal Anthropological Institute, 50 Fitzroy Street, W1T 5BT. *T:* (020) 7387 0455.

CALLAN, Sir Ivan, KCVO 1998; CMG 1990; HM Diplomatic Service; Ambassador to Oman, 1999–April 2002; *b* 6 April 1942; *s* of Roy Ivan Callan and (Gladys) May Callan (*née* Coombe); *m* 1st, 1965, Hilary Flashman; one *d*; 2nd, 1987, Mary Catherine Helena Williams; two step *s* one step *d*. *Educ:* Reading Sch.; University Coll., Oxford. BA, Dip. Soc. Anthrop., BLitt, MA. Entered FCO, 1969; Middle East Centre for Arab Studies, 1970–71; Second, later First Sec., Beirut, 1971–75; FCO, 1975–80; First Sec. and Head of Chancery, Ottawa, 1980–83; Counsellor, Hd of Chancery and Consul-General, Baghdad, 1983–87; Consul-General, Jerusalem, 1987–90; Counsellor, FCO, 1991–94; High Comr, Brunei, 1994–98. *Recreations:* fine arts, painting, craftsmanship. *Address:* c/o Foreign and Commonwealth Office, King Charles Street, SW1A 2AH. *Club:* Reform.

CALLAN, Maj.-Gen. Michael, CB 1979; President, and Chairman of Board of Trustees, Royal Army Ordnance Corps Charitable Trust, 1993–96; *b* 27 Nov. 1925; *s* of Major John Callan and Elsie Dorothy Callan (*née* Fordham); *m* 1948, Marie Evelyn Farthing; two *s*. *Educ:* Farnborough Grammar Sch., Hants. rcds, jssc, psc. Enlisted Hampshire Regt, 1943; commnd 1st (KGV's Own) Gurkha Rifles (The Malaun Regt), 1944; resigned commn, 1947; re-enlisted, 1948; re-commnd, RAOC, 1949; overseas service: India, Burma, French Indo China, Netherlands East Indies, 1944–47; Kenya, 1950–53; Malaya/Singapore, 1958–61; USA, 1966–68; Hong Kong, 1970–71; Comdr, Rhine Area, BAOR, 1975–76; Dir Gen., Ordnance Services, 1976–80. Col Comdt, RAOC, 1981–89; Hon. Col, SW London ACF, 1982–89. Registrar, Corporation of the Sons of the Clergy, 1982–83; consultant in defence logistics and admin, 1984–89. *Recreations:* sailing, DIY, gardening. *Address:* c/o Royal Bank of Scotland, Drummonds Branch, 49 Charing Cross, SW1A 2DX.

CALLANAN, Martin John; Member (C) North East Region, England, European Parliament, since 1999; *b* 8 Aug. 1961; *s* of John and Ada Callanan; *m* 1997, Jayne Burton; one *s*. *Educ:* Newcastle Poly. (BSc Electrical and Electronic Engrg). Project Engr, Scottish & Newcastle Breweries, 1986–99. *Recreations:* squash, reading. *Address:* (office) 22 Osborne Road, Jesmond, Newcastle upon Tyne NE2 2AD. *T:* (0191) 240 2600; European Parliament, Rue Wiertz, 1047 Brussels, Belgium. *T:* (2) 2845701.

CALLANDER, Maj. (John) Henry; landowner and farmer; Vice Lord-Lieutenant, Midlothian, since 1996; *b* 9 May 1948; *s* of Maj. John David Callander, MC and Mary Callander (*née* Crampton-Roberts); *m* 1987, Jacqueline Hulda (*née* Crocker); two *s* one *d*. *Educ:* Eton Coll. Royal Scots Greys; Royal Scots Dragoon Guards; retd 1991. DL Midlothian. *Recreation:* field sports. *Address:* Prestonhall, Pathhead, Midlothian, EH37 5UG. *T:* (01875) 320949. *Club:* New (Edinburgh).

CALLAWAY, Betty; *see* Callaway-Fittall, B. D.

CALLAWAY, Sir Frank (Adams), Kt 1981; AO 1995; CMG 1975; OBE 1970; Professor and Head of Department of Music, University of Western Australia, 1959–84, Professor Emeritus, since 1985; *b* 16 May 1919; *s* of Archibald Charles Callaway and Mabel Callaway (*née* Adams); *m* 1942, Kathleen Jessie, *d* of R. Allan; two *s* two *d*. *Educ:* West Christchurch High Sch.; Dunedin Teachers' Coll., NZ; Univ. of Otago, NZ (MusB); Royal Academy of Music. FRAM, ARCM, FTCL; FACE. Head, Dept of Music, King Edward Tech. Coll., Dunedin, NZ, 1942–53; Reader in Music, Univ. of WA, 1953–59. Mem., RNZAF Band, 1940–42. Conductor: King Edward Tech. Coll. Symphony Orchestra, 1945–53; Univ. of WA Orchestral Soc., 1953–64; Univ. of WA Choral Soc., 1953–79; Guest Conductor: WA Symphony Orchestra; S Australia Symphony Orchestra; Adelaide Philharmonic Choir; Orpheus Choir, Wellington, NZ. Member: Australian Music Exams Bd, 1955–84 (Chm., 1964–66 and 1977–79); Adv. Bd, Commonwealth Assistance to Australian Composers, 1966–72; Australian Nat. Commn for UNESCO, 1968–82; Exec. Bd, Internat. Music Council of UNESCO, 1976–82 (Pres., 1980–81; Individual Mem., 1982–85, Life Mem. of Honour, 1986); Music Bd, Australia Council, 1969–74; Chairman: WA Arts Adv. Bd, 1970–73; WA Arts Council, 1973–79; Organizing Cttees, Aust. Nat. Eisteddfod 1979, Indian Ocean Fests, 1979, 1984; Indian Ocean Arts Assoc., 1980–85 (Pres., 1985–). Founding Pres. and Life Mem., Australian Soc. for Music Educn, 1966–71; Mem., Bd of Dirs, Internat. Soc. for Music Educn, 1958– (Pres., 1968–72, Treasurer, 1972–88, Hon. Pres., 1988–). External Examiner (Music), Kenyatta Univ., Nairobi, 1985–87; Consultant, Callaway Internat. Resource Centre for Music Educn (Univ. of WA), 1988–. Patron, Music Council of Australia, 1994. Foundn Mem., 1983, Pres., 1984–97, WA Br., Lord's Taverners Australia. Founding Editor: Australian Jl of Music Educn, 1967–82; Studies in Music, 1967–84; Internat. Jl of Music Educn, 1983–85; also General Editor, Music Series and Music Monographs. W Australian Citizen of the Year, 1975. Hon. Fellowship in Music, Australian Music Exams Bd, 1997. Hon. MusD: W Australia, 1975; Melbourne, 1982. Aust. Nat. Critics' Circle Award for Music, 1977; Sir Bernard Heinze Award for Service to Australian Music, 1988; Internat. Percy Grainger Medal, 1991; Internat. Music Council/UNESCO Music Prize, 1997. *Publications:* (General Editor) Challenges in Music Education, 1975; (ed with D. E. Tunley) Australian Composition in the Twentieth Century, 1978; (compiled) Percy Grainger Symposium, 1982; (ed) Essays in Honour of David Evatt Tunley, 1995; articles on music and music education. *Recreations:* reading, gardening, cricket. *Address:* 1 Sambell Close, Churchlands, WA 6018, Australia. *T:* and *Fax:* (8) 92443733.

CALLAWAY-FITTALL, Betty Daphne, (Betty Callaway), MBE 1984; trainer of skaters; skating consultant to Ice Arena, Slough, since 1986; *b* 22 March 1928; *d* of William A. Roberts and Elizabeth T. Roberts; *m* 1st, 1949, E. Roy Callaway; 2nd, 1980, Captain W. Fittall (*d* 1990), British Airways, retd. *Educ:* Greycoat Sch., and St Paul's Convent, Westminster. Started teaching, Richmond Ice Rink, 1952; Nat. Trainer, W Germany, 1969–72; retired from full-time teaching, 1972. Commentator, ITV, 1984–. Pupils include: Angelika and Erich Buck (European Champions and 2nd in World Championship, 1972); Chrisztine Regoczy and Andras Sally (Hungarian and World Champions and Olympic silver medallists, 1980); Jayne Torvill and Christopher Dean (World Champions, 1981, 1982, 1983, 1984, European Champions, 1981, 1982, and Olympic gold medallists, 1984). Pres., British Ice Teachers Assoc., 1985–. Hon. Citizen, Ravensburg, Germany, 1972. Gold Medal, Nat. Skating Assoc., 1955; Hungarian Olympic Medal, 1980; Coach of the Year Award, Nat. Coaching Foundn, 1995. *Recreations:* music, water ski-ing, gardening. *Address:* 35 Long Grove, Seer Green, Beaconsfield, Bucks HP9 2YN.

CALLBECK, Hon. Catherine Sophia; Senator, Senate of Canada, since 1997; with Callbeck's Ltd, family business, 1978–88 and since 1996; *b* 25 July 1939; *d* of Ralph Callbeck and Ruth Callbeck (*née* Campbell), Central Bedeque, PEI. *Educ:* Mt Allison Univ. (BComm 1960); Dalhousie Univ. (BEd 1963); Syracuse Univ. Prince Edward Island: MLA (L) Fourth Dist, 1974–78; Minister of Health and Social Services and Minister responsible for Disabled, 1974–78; MP (L) Malpeque, 1988–93; Official Opposition Critic for Consumer and Corporate Affairs, Energy, Mines and Resources and Financial Instns, 1988–93; Associate Critic for Privatization and Regulatory Affairs; Vice-Chm., Caucus Cttee on sustainable develt; MLA (L) First Dist of Queens, and Premier of PEI, 1993–96; Leader, Liberal Party of PEI, 1993–96. Dir, Mutual Fund Dealers Assoc. Mem., Child Alliance Adv. Cttee, PEI. Hon. Mem. Bd, Glaucoma Res. Soc. of Canada. *Address:* Central Bedeque, PE C0B 1G0, Canada. *T:* (902) 6288560.

CALLENDER, Dr Maurice Henry; Ministry of Defence, 1977–80; retired, 1980; *b* 18 Dec. 1916; *s* of Harry and Lizbeth Callender; *m* 1941, Anne Kassel; two *s*. *Educ:* Univ. of Durham (MA, PhD). Commissioned: Royal Northumberland Fusiliers, 1939–41; RAF, 1941–45. Lectr, Huddersfield Technical Coll., 1945–47; Research, Univ. of Durham, 1947–49; Lectr, Bristol Univ. Extra-Mural Dept, 1949–53; MoD, 1953–62; Joint Services Staff Coll., 1959–60; Cabinet Office, 1962–64; MoD, 1964–70; Cabinet Office, 1970–73; Counsellor, Canberra, 1973–77. *Publications:* Roman Amphorae, 1965; various articles in archaeological jls. *Recreations:* oil painting, golf, bridge. *Address:* 24 Glanleam Road, Stanmore, Middx HA7 4NW. *T:* (020) 8954 1435. *Club:* Aldenham Golf and Country.

CALLER, Maxwell Marshall; Managing Director, London Borough of Hackney, since 2000; *b* 9 Feb. 1951; *s* of Abraham Leon Caller and Cynthia Rachel Caller; *m* 1972, Linda Ann Wohlberg; three *s* one *d*. *Educ:* Newport High Sch.; University Coll. London (BSc Hons Engrg). CEng, MICE; MCIWEM; CDipAF. GLC, 1972–74; Thames Water Authority, 1974–75; London Boroughs of: Hammersmith, 1975–78; Newham, 1978–81; Merton, 1981–85 (Asst Dir of Development); Barnet: Controller of Engrg Services, 1985–87; Dir of Technical Services, 1987–89; Chief Exec., 1989–2000. Technical Advr, N London Waste Authy, 1985–87; Adviser, Highways Cttee 1987–89, Public Works Cttee 1990–97, AMA. Founder Mem., 1990, and Vice Chm., Steering Cttee, 1990–2000, Barnet Crime Reduction Partnership; Director: Enfield Enterprise Agency, 1994–99; N London TEC, 1995–2000; Prospects Careers Services Ltd, 1999–2000; Chm., Barfield Group Ltd, 1995–98. Trustee, Barnet War Memorials Initiative, 1994–. Freeman, City of London, 1991. DUniv Middlesex, 2000. *Recreations:* watching Welsh Rugby Union, work. *Address:* Town Hall, Mare Street, E8 1EA. *T:* (020) 8356 3210; *e-mail:* mcaller@gw.hackney.gov.uk.

CALLICOTT, Richard Kenneth; Chief Executive, UK Sport, since 1999; *b* 18 Sept. 1946; *s* of Ernest Victor Callicott and Joan Alfreda Callicott (*née* Furley); *m* 1st, 1972, Diane Lesley Kidd (marr. diss. 1984); two *s*; 2nd, 1985, Jacqueline Steele (marr. diss. 1995); one *s*. *Educ:* Colston's Sch., Bristol; City of Birmingham Coll. of Educn (Cert Ed); Univ. of Birmingham (BPhil Ed). Teacher, jun. schs, Smethwick and Warley, 1968–74; Warden, Churchbridge Teachers' Centre, 1974–80; Community Educn and Recreation Officer, Birmingham CC, 1980–83; Vice Principal, Central Inst., Birmingham, 1983–85; Area Manager, Recreation and Community, Birmingham CC, 1985; Co-ordinator, Birmingham's Olympic Bid, 1985–86; Develt Manager, Sport and Leisure, Birmingham CC, 1988–89; Dir of Sport, NEC Gp, 1989–99, and Hd of Sport, City of Birmingham, 1996–99. Dir, Saga Radio, 2001–. *Recreations:* golf, cycling, reading, gardening, theatre, insatiable appetite for sport. *Address:* 40 Thornhill Road, Streetly, Sutton Coldfield B74 3EH.

CALLIL, Carmen Thérèse; Founder, 1972, and Chairman, 1972–95, Virago Press; *b* 15 July 1938; *d* of Frederick Alfred Louis Callil and Lorraine Clare Allen. *Educ:* Star of the Sea Convent, Gardenvale, Melbourne; Loreto Convent, Mandeville Hall, Melbourne; Melbourne Univ. (BA). Buyer's Asst, Marks & Spencer, 1963–65; Editorial Assistant: Hutchinson Publishing Co., 1965–66; B. T. Batsford, 1966–67; Publicity Manager, Panther Books, later also of Granada Publishing, 1967–70; André Deutsch, 1971–72; publicity for Ink newspaper, 1972; founded Carmen Callil Ltd, book publicity co., 1972; founded Virago Press, 1972, incorp. as co., 1973, Man. Dir, 1972–82. Man. Dir, Chatto & Windus: The Hogarth Press, 1983–93; Publisher-at-Large, Random House UK, 1993–94; Ed.-at-Large, Knopf, NY, 1993–94. Mem. Bd, Channel 4, 1985–91. FRSA. Hon. LittD Sheffield, 1994; Oxford Brookes, 1995; DUniv: York, 1995; Open, 1997. *Publications:* (ed with Craig Raine) New Writing 7, 1998; (with Colm Tóibín) The Modern Library: the 200 best novels in England since 1950, 1999. *Recreations:* friends, reading, animals, television, politics, films, gardening, France.

CALLMAN, His Honour Clive Vernon; a Circuit Judge, 1973–2000, assigned to South-Eastern Circuit; a Deputy Circuit Judge, since 2000; a Deputy High Court Judge, 1976–2000; *b* 21 June 1927; *o s* of Felix Callman, DMD, LDS, RCS and Edith Callman, Walton-on-Thames, Surrey; *m* 1967, Judith Helen Hines, BA, DipSocStuds (Adelaide), *o d* of Gus Hines, OBE, JP, and Hilde Hines, St George's, Adelaide, S Aust.; one *s* one *d*. *Educ:* Ottershaw Coll.; St George's Coll., Weybridge; LSE, Univ. of London. BSc(Econ), Commercial Law. Called to the Bar, Middle Temple, 1951; Blackstone Pupillage Prizeman, 1951; practised as Barrister, London and Norwich, 1952–73 (Head of London chambers, 1963), South-Eastern Circuit; Hon. Mem., Central Criminal Court Bar Mess; Dep. Circuit Judge in Civil and Criminal Jurisdiction, 1971–73. Legal Assessor: GMC, 2000–; GDC, 2000–. Dir, Woburn Press, Publishers, 1971–73; dir of finance cos, 1961–73; non-executive Director, Frank Cass & Co. Ltd and Vallentine Mitchell & Co. Ltd, 2000–. University of London: Fac. Mem., Standing Cttee of Convocation, 1954–79; Senator, 1978–94; Mem. Careers Adv. Bd, 1979–92; Mem., Commerce Degree Bureau Cttee, 1980; Mem., Adv. Cttee for Magistrates' Courses, 1979; Mem., Univ. Governing Council, 1994–2001; Vice-Pres., Graduates' Soc.; Governor: Birkbeck Coll., 1982–2000; LSE, 1990–; Hebrew Univ. of Jerusalem, 1992–; Mem. Court, City Univ., 1991–. Mem. Exec. Cttee, Soc. of Labour Lawyers, 1958; Chm., St Marylebone Constituency Labour Party, 1960–62. Mem. Council, Anglo-Jewish Assoc., 1956–. Editor, Clare Market Review, 1947; Member Editorial Board: Professional Negligence, 1985–; Jl of Child Law, 1989–95; Child and Family Law Qly, 1995–. *Recreations:* reading, travelling, the arts. *Address:* 11 Constable Close, NW11 6UA. *T:* (020) 8458 3010. *Club:* Bar Yacht.

CALLOW, Maj. Gen. Christopher George, CB 2001; OBE 1984; Chief Executive, Defence Secondary Care Agency, 1998–2000; *b* 12 July 1941; *s* of George Alexander Callow and Barbara Callow (*née* Tannahill); *m* 1967, Elizabeth Anne Macmillan Hynd; one *s* two *d*. *Educ:* Duke of York Sch., Nairobi; Univ. of Edinburgh (MB ChB 1966); DPhysMed 1971; MSc London 1984. MFCM 1987, FFPHM 1996. RMO, 1st Bn, Green Howards, 1968–69; Army Staff Coll., 1976; Dep. Asst Dir Gen. AMS, MoD, 1977–79; CO, Armd Field Amb., 1979–83; Col, Med. Ops & Plans, MoD, 1985–88; Comdr Med., 1 Armd Div., 1988–90; Chief, Med. Plans & Policy, SHAPE, 1990–93; Comdr Med., BAOR, subseq. UKSC (Germany), 1993–96; Dir Gen., Defence Med. Trng, 1996–99. QHP 1995–2000. Consultant in Army Occupnl and Public Health Medicine, 1987–2000. OStJ 1995. *Publications:* articles on noise-induced hearing loss. *Recreations:* golf, music, travel, computing.

CALLOW, His Honour Henry William, CBE 1994; HM Second Deemster, Isle of Man, 1988–93; *b* 16 May 1926; 2nd *s* of Frederick Henry Callow and Elizabeth Callow (*née* Cowley); *m* 1952, Mary Elaine Corlett. *Educ:* Douglas High Sch.; King William's Coll., IOM. Served Army, 1945–48. Advocate, Manx Bar, 1950; High Bailiff and Coroner of Inquests, IOM, 1969–88; Chairman: IOM Criminal Injuries Compensation Tribunal, 1988–93; IOM Licensing Appeal Court, 1988–93. Police Complaints Comr, IOM, 1994–. Chairman of Trustees: Noble's Hosp., IOM, 1987–98; Ellan Vannin Home, 1988–97; Trustee, Grest Home, 1995–. Pres., Ramsey Male Choir, 1997–; Chm., IOM Church Music Assoc., 1997–2000. *Recreations:* music, walking. *Address:* 8 Marlborough Crescent, Clifton Park, Ramsey, Isle of Man IM8 3NE. *T:* (01624) 815929. *Clubs:* Manx Automobile (Douglas); Laxey Sailing (Laxey).

CALLOW, Prof, James Arthur, PhD; CBiol, FIBiol; Mason Professor of Botany, University of Birmingham, since 1983; *b* 17 Jan. 1945; *s* of James and Olive Callow; *m* 1968, Dr Maureen Elizabeth Wood; one *s*. *Educ:* Barrow-in-Furness Grammar Sch. for Boys; Univ. of Sheffield (BSc 1st cl. Hons Botany 1966; PhD 1969). Lectr in Botany,

Univ. of Leeds, 1969–83. *Publications:* numerous, including books, professional academic jl articles. *Recreations:* golf, gardening, antiques, photography, travel. *Address:* School of Biosciences, University of Birmingham, Birmingham B15 2TT. *T:* (0121) 414 5559.

CALLOW, Simon Phillip Hugh, CBE 1999; actor and director; *b* 15 June 1949; *s* of Neil Callow and Yvonne Mary Callow. *Educ:* London Oratory Grammar Sch.; Queen's Univ. Belfast; Drama Centre. London productions include: Schippel, 1975; A Mad World My Masters, 1977; Arturo Ui, Mary Barnes, 1978; As You Like It, Amadeus, NT, 1979; The Beastly Beatitudes of Balthazar B, Total Eclipse, Restoration, 1981; The Relapse, 1983; On the Spot, 1984; Kiss of the Spider Woman, 1985; Faust I and II, Lyric, Hammersmith, 1988; Single Spies (double bill: A Question of Attribution (also dir); An Englishman Abroad), NT, 1988, Queen's, 1989; The Destiny of Me (also dir), Leicester Haymarket, 1994; The Alchemist, RNT, 1996; The Importance of Being Oscar, Savoy, 1997; In Defence of Fairies, Criterion, 1997; Chimes at Midnight, Chichester, 1998; The Mystery of Charles Dickens, Comedy, transf. Albery, 2000; *directed:* Loving Reno, Bush, 1984; The Passport, 1985, Nicolson Fights, Croydon, 1986, Offstage; Amadeus, Theatr Clwyd, 1986; The Infernal Machine, 1986; Così fan Tutte, Switzerland, 1987; Jacques and his Master, LA, 1987; Shirley Valentine, Vaudeville, 1988, NY, 1989; Die Fledermaus, Theatre Royal, Glasgow, 1988, 1989; Stevie Wants to Play the Blues, LA Theater Center, 1990; Carmen Jones, Old Vic, 1991; Ballad of the Sad Café (film), 1991; Shades, 1992; My Fair Lady, 1992; Les Enfants du Paradis, Barbican, 1996; Stephen Oliver Trilogy, 1996; Calisto, NY, 1996; Il Turco in Italia, Broomhill Opera, 1997; HRH, Playhouse, 1997; The Consul, Holland Park, 1999; The Pajama Game, Victoria Palace, 1999. *Films:* Amadeus, 1983; A Room with a View, 1986; The Good Father, 1986; Maurice, 1987; Manifesto, 1988; Mr & Mrs Bridge, 1991; Postcards from the Edge, 1991; Crucifer of Blood, 1991; Soft Top, Hard Shoulder, 1993; Don't Look Away, 1993; Four Weddings and a Funeral, 1994; Jefferson in Paris, 1995; Ace Ventura: when Nature calls, 1996; James and the Giant Beanstalk, 1996; The Scarlet Tunic, 1998; Bedrooms and Hallways, 1999; Shakespeare in Love, 1999. *Television series:* Chance in a Million, 1983, 1985–86; David Copperfield, 1986; *other television includes:* Cariani and the Courtesans, 1987; Charles Laughton (documentary), 1987; Old Flames, 1989; Revolutionary Witness, 1989; Femme Fatale, 1993; The Purcell Film, 1995; An Audience with Charles Dickens, 1996; The Woman in White, 1997; A Christmas Dickens, 1997. *Publications:* Being an Actor, 1984; A Difficult Actor: Charles Laughton, 1987; trans. Jacques et son Maître, by Kundera, 1986; Acting in Restoration Comedy, 1990; Shooting the Actor, 1990; Orson Welles: the road to Xanadu, 1995; Snowdon on Stage: with a personal view of the British theatre 1954–1996, 1997; The National, 1997; Love is Where it Falls, 1999; Shakespeare On Love, 2000; Oscar Wilde and his Circle, 2000; The Night of the Hunter, 2001. *Address:* c/o BAT, 180 Wardour Street, W1V 3AA.

CALLWAY, Eric Willi; HM Diplomatic Service, retired; Consul General, Frankfurt, 1997–2001; *b* 30 Jan. 1942; *s* of Edward and Auguste Callway; *m* 1965, Gudrun Viktoria Granström; two *s.* Joined HM Foreign, later Diplomatic, Service, 1960: FO, 1960–61; CRO, 1961–63; New Delhi, 1963–66; Georgetown, Guyana, 1966–70; Second Sec., FCO, 1970–72; RAF Staff Coll., Bracknell, 1972; UK Mission, Geneva, 1973–77; First Secretary: FCO, 1977–79; on loan to MoD, 1979–80; FCO, 1980–81; (Commercial), E Berlin, 1981–84; (Labour), 1984–86, then (Commercial), Stockholm, 1986–88; on loan to ODA, 1988; FCO, 1989–94; Counsellor, and Dep. High Comr, Karachi, 1994–97. *Address:* 5 Bradbourne Street, SW6 3TF.

CALMAN, Sir Kenneth (Charles), KCB 1996; DL; MD; FRCP, FRCS; FRSE; Vice-Chancellor and Warden, Durham University, since 1998; *b* 25 Dec. 1941; *s* of Arthur McIntosh Calman and Grace Douglas Don; *m* 1967, Ann Wilkie; one *s* two *d. Educ:* Allan Glen's Sch., Glasgow; Univ. of Glasgow (BSc, MD, PhD). FRCSGlas 1971; FRCP 1985, FRCPE 1989; FRCGP 1989; FFPHM (FFCM 1989); FRSE 1979. Hall Fellow in Surgery, Western Infirmary, Glasgow, 1968; Lectr in Surgery, Univ. of Glasgow, 1969; MRC Clinical Res. Fellow, Inst. of Cancer Res., London, 1972; University of Glasgow: Prof. of Clinical Oncology, 1974; Dean of Postgrad. Medicine and Prof. of Postgrad. Med. Educn, 1984–88; Chief Medical Officer: Scottish Office Home and Health Dept, 1989–91; DES, later DFE, then DFEE, based at DoH, 1991–98. Mem., Statistics Commn, 2000–. Lectures include: Honeyman Gillespie, Edinburgh Royal Infirmary, first annual Douglas, Liverpool Univ., Neil Wates Meml, RSocMed, Stanley Melville Meml, ICE, Wade, Keele Univ., 1993; Sir William Weipers Meml, Glasgow Univ., 1994; Frank Lowe, Liverpool Univ., 1995; Calman Muir Meml, RCPE, Brough, Paisley Univ., 1996; Dow Meml, Dundee Univ., 1997; Harben, RIPHH, 1998; Finlayson, RCPSGlas, Meriel, Academic Vet. Soc., first Hastings, Oxford, 1999; Henry Cohen, Hebrew Univ., Jerusalem, 2000. Hon. FRCR 1990; Hon. FRCSE 1991; Hon. FRCPath 1992; Hon. FFPM 1992; Hon. FFOM 1993; Hon. FRCS 1995; Hon. FRCOG 1996; Hon. FRCSI 1997; Hon. FRSocMed 1997; Founder FMedSci 1998; Hon. FRCOphth 1999; Hon. Fellow, Inst. of Cancer Res., 1999. DUniv: Stirling, 1992; Open, 1996; Paisley, 1997; Hon. DSc: Strathclyde, 1993; Westminster, 1995; Glasgow Caledonian, 1995; Glasgow, 1996; Brighton, 2000; Hon. MD: Nottingham, 1994; Newcastle, 1995; Birmingham, 1996. Medals include: Sir Thomas and Lady Dixon, Belfast, 1994; Francis Bissett Hawkins, RCP, 1995; Crookshanks, RCR, 1995; Alexander Hutchison, RSocMed, 1995; Gold, Macmillan Cancer Relief, 1996; Heberden (also Orator), British Soc. of Rheumatol., 1996; Silver, RCSI, 1997; Allwyn Smith, FPHM, 1998; Bradlaw, RCS Dental Faculty, 1999; Thomas Graham, Royal Philosophical Soc., Glasgow, 1999. DL Durham, 2000. *Publications:* Basic Skills for Clinical Housemen, 1971, 2nd edn 1983; Basic Principles of Cancer Chemotherapy, 1982; Invasion, 1984; Healthy Respect, 1987, 2nd edn 1994; The Potential for Health, 1998; Risk Communication and the Public Health, 1999; Storytelling, Humour and Learning in Medicine, 2001. *Recreations:* gardening, golf, collecting cartoons, Scottish literature. *Address:* Old Shire Hall, Durham DH1 3HP.

CALNAN, Prof. Charles Dermod, MA, MB, BChir Cantab; FRCP; Director, Department of Occupational Dermatoses, St John's Hospital for Diseases of the Skin, 1974–82, retired; Honorary Consultant Dermatologist: Royal Free Hospital, 1958–82; St John's Hospital for Diseases of the Skin, London, 1958–82; *b* 14 Dec. 1917; *s* of James Calnan, Eastbourne, Sussex; *m* 1950, Josephine Gerard Keane, *d* of late Lt-Col Michael Keane, RAMC; three *s* one *d. Educ:* Stonyhurst Coll.; Corpus Christi Coll., Cambridge; London Hospital. 1st Cl. Hons Nat. Sci. Trip., Cambridge 1939. RAMC Specialist in Dermatology, Major, 1942–46; Marsden Prof., Royal Free Hosp., 1958; Visiting Research Associate, Univ. of Pennsylvania, 1959; Prof. of Dermatology, Inst. of Dermatology, 1960–74. WHO Cons. Adviser to Nat. Inst. of Dermatology of Thailand, 1971–82. Editor: Transactions of the St John's Hosp. Dermatological Soc., 1958–75; Contact Dermatitis, 1975–87. Hon. Fellow, Brit. Assoc. of Dermatology; Hon. FRSocMed (Mem. Dermatological Section). Order of the White Elephant (Thailand), 1986. *Publications:* Atlas of Dermatology, 1974; The Life and Times of Geoffrey Barrow Dowling, 1992; various papers in med. and dermatological jls. *Recreations:* books, theatre. *Address:* West Claydon House, Lechlade, Glos GL7 3DS.

CALNAN, Prof. James Stanislaus, FRCP; FRCS; Professor of Plastic and Reconstructive Surgery, University of London, at the Royal Postgraduate Medical School and Hammersmith Hospital, 1970–81, now Emeritus; *b* 12 March 1916; *e s* of James and Gertrude Calnan, Eastbourne, Sussex; *m* 1949, Joan (formerly County Councillor for Great Berkhamsted and Dacorum District Councillor, and Town Councillor, Berkhamsted), *e d* of George Frederick and Irene Maud Williams, Roath Park, Cardiff; one *d. Educ:* Stonyhurst Coll.; Univ. of London at London Hosp. Med. Sch. LDS RCS 1941; MRCS, LRCP 1943; DA 1944; DTM&H 1948; MRCP (London and Edinburgh) 1948; FRCS 1949; FRCP 1971. Served War of 1939–45, F/Lt RAF, UK, France, India. RMO, Hosp. for Tropical Diseases, 1948; Sen. Lectr, Nuffield Dept of Plastic Surgery, Oxford, 1954; Hammersmith Hospital and Royal Postgraduate Med. Sch.: Lectr in Surgery, 1960; Reader, 1965; Professor, 1970. Hunterian Prof. RCS, 1959. Vis. Prof. in Plastic Surgery, Univ. of Pennsylvania, 1959. Member: BMA, 1941–82; British Assoc. of Plastic Surgeons, 1949–71; Sen. Mem., Surgical Research Soc., 1962–. Fellow, Royal Soc. of Medicine, 1943; FCST 1966. Mem., Soc. of Authors, 1985–. Clemson Award for Bioengineering, 1980. *Publications:* Speaking at Medical Meetings, 1972, 2nd edn 1981; Writing Medical Papers, 1973; How to Speak and Write: a practical guide for nurses, 1975; One Way to do Research, 1976; Talking with Patients, 1983; Coping with Research: the complete guide for beginners, 1984; The Hammersmith 1935–1985: the first 50 years of the Royal Postgraduate Medical School, 1985; Principles of Surgical Research, 1989; contribs to medical and scientific jls and chapters in books, on cleft palate, wound healing, lymphatic diseases, venous thrombosis, research methods and organisation. *Recreations:* gardening, carpentry, reading and writing. *Address:* White Haven, 23 Kings Road, Berkhamsted, Herts HP4 3BH. *T:* (01442) 862320; Royal Postgraduate Medical School, Ducane Road, W12 0HS. *T:* (020) 8743 2030.

See also Prof. C. D. Calnan.

CALNE, Sir Roy (Yorke), Kt 1986; MA, MS; FRCS; FRS 1974; Professor of Surgery, University of Cambridge, 1965–98; Fellow of Trinity Hall, Cambridge, 1965–98, now Emeritus; Yeoh Ghim Seng Professor of Surgery, National University of Singapore, since 1998; *b* 30 Dec. 1930; *s* of Joseph Robert and Eileen Calne; *m* 1956, Patricia Doreen Whelan; two *s* four *d. Educ:* Lancing Coll.; Guy's Hosp. Med. Sch. MB, BS London with Hons (Distinction in Medicine), 1953. House Appts, Guy's Hosp., 1953–54; RAMC, 1954–56 (RMO to KEO 2nd Gurkhas); Deptl Anatomy Demonstrator, Oxford Univ., 1957–58; SHO Nuffield Orthopædic Centre, Oxford, 1958; Surg. Registrar, Royal Free Hosp., 1958–60; Harkness Fellow in Surgery, Peter Bent Brigham Hosp., Harvard Med. Sch., 1960–61; Lectr in Surgery, St Mary's Hosp., London, 1961–62; Sen. Lectr and Cons. Surg., Westminster Hosp., 1962–65; Hon. Consulting Surgeon, Addenbrooke's Hosp., Cambridge, 1965–98. Royal Coll. of Surgeons: Hallet Prize, 1957; Jacksonian Prize, 1961; Hunterian Prof., 1962; Cecil Joll Prize, 1966; Mem. Ct of Examiners, 1970–76; Mem. Council, 1981–90; Vice-Pres., 1986–89; Hunterian Orator, 1989. Founder FMedSci 1998. Fellow Assoc. of Surgeons of GB; Mem. Surgical Research Soc.; Pres., European Soc. for Organ Transplantation, 1983–84; Corresp. Fellow, Amer. Surgical Assoc., 1972, Hon. Fellow 1981; Hon. FRCP 1989; Hon. FRCS Thailand, 1992; Hon. FRCSE 1993. Hon. MD: Oslo, 1986; Athens, 1990; Hanover, 1991; QUB, 1994; Karachi, 1994. Prix de la Société Internationale de Chirurgie, 1969; Faltin Medal, Finnish Surgical Soc., 1977; Lister Medal, 1984; Fothergill Gold Medal, Med. Soc. of London, 1989; Cameron Prize, Edinburgh Univ., 1990; Ellison-Cliffe Medal, 1990; Ernst Jung Preis, 1992; Medawar Prize, Transplantation Soc., 1992; Medal of Helsinki Univ., 1993; Gold Medal, Catalan Transplantation Soc., 1996; King Faisel Internat. Prize for Medicine, 2001. Grand Officer, Order of Merit (Republic of Italy), 2000. *Publications:* Renal Transplantations, 1963, 2nd edn 1967; (with H. Ellis) Lecture Notes in Surgery, 1965, 7th edn 1987; A Gift of Life, 1970; (ed and contrib.) Clinical Organ Transplantation, 1971; (ed and contrib.) Immunological Aspects of Transplantation Surgery, 1973; (ed and contrib.) Liver Transplantation, 1983; (ed and contrib.) Transplantation Immunology, 1984; Surgical Anatomy of the Abdomen in the Living Subject, 1988; (ed) Operative Surgery, 1992; Too Many People, 1994; Art Surgery and Transplantation, 1996; The Ultimate Gift, 1998; papers on tissue transplantation and general surgery; sections in several surgical text-books. *Recreations:* tennis, squash, painting. *Address:* 22 Barrow Road, Cambridge CB2 2AS. *T:* (01223) 359831.

CALOW, Prof. Peter, OBE 2000; PhD, DSc; CBiol, FIBiol; FLS; Professor of Zoology, University of Sheffield, since 1984; *b* 23 May 1947; *s* of late Harry Calow and Norah K. Calow; *m* 1971, Lesley Jane Chapman (marr. diss. 1991); one *s* one *d. Educ:* William Rhodes Sch., Chesterfield; Univ. of Leeds (BSc; PhD 1972; DSc 1984). CBiol, FIBiol 1985; FLS 1987. Lectr, then Reader, Univ. of Glasgow, 1972–84; Warden, Wolfson Hall of Residence, 1975–84. Founding Editor (with J. Grace), Functional Ecology, 1986–98; Editor, Integrated Environmental Management, 1991–95. Chairman: UK Govt Adv. Cttee on Hazardous Substances, 1991–2000; Jt Govt/Business Task Force on Application of Risk Benefit Analysis to Chemical Controls, 1993–95; Member: NE Regl Envmtl Adv. Cttee, Envmt Agency, 1996–2000; Adv. Cttee on Pesticides, 1997– (Chm., Envmtl Panel, 1999–); Expert Panel, Res. Inst. for Fragrance Materials, 1999–; External Sci. Adv. Panel, European Chemical Industry Long-range Res. Initiative, 1999–; Scientific Cttee on Toxicity, Ecotoxicity and Envmt, EC, 2000–. Vice-Pres., European Soc. of Evolutionary Biol., 1988–89; Pres., Soc. of Envmtl Toxicol. and Chemistry (UK), 1990–91, (Europe) 1991–92. Mem., Bd of Trustees, Health and Envmtl Scis Inst., 1996–; Member Council: Freshwater Biol Assoc., 1988–92 and 1995–99; Univ. of Buckingham, 1997– (Chm., Acad. Adv. Council, 1999–). FRSA 1992. *Publications:* Biological Machines, 1976; Life Cycles, 1979; Invertebrate Biology, 1981; Evolutionary Principles, 1983; (with R. Sibly) Physiological Ecology of Animals, 1986; (with R. S. K. Barnes and P. J. W. Olive) The Invertebrates: a new synthesis, 1988, 2nd edn 1993; (ed) Handbook of Ecotoxicology, vol. 1 1993, vol. 2 1994; Controlling Environmental Risks from Chemicals, 1997; Handbook of Environmental Risk Assessment and Management, 1998; (Ed.-in-Chief) The Encyclopedia of Ecology & Environmental Management, 1998; numerous contribs to learned jls. *Recreations:* reading, writing, tennis. *Address:* Department of Animal and Plant Sciences, University of Sheffield, Sheffield S10 2TN; 4 Daleside, Riverdale Road, Sheffield S10 3FA.

CALTHORPE; *see* Anstruther-Gough-Calthorpe.

CALTON, Patsy; MP (Lib Dem) Cheadle, since 2001; *b* 19 Sept. 1948; *d* of John Gordon and Joan Yeldon; *m* 1969, Clive Roger Calton; one *s* two *d. Educ:* Wymondham Coll., Norfolk; UMIST (BSc Biochem.); Univ. of Manchester (PGCE). Chemistry teacher, 1971-79 and 1987-2001. Mem. (Lib Dem) Stockport MBC, 1994- (Dep. Leader, 1999-2001). *Recreations:* running (marathons, 1999 and 2001), gardening, reading. *Address:* House of Commons, SW1A 0AA. *T:* (020) 7219 8471; 30 Melbourne Road, Bramhall, Stockport, Cheshire SK7 1LS. *Club:* National Liberal.

CALVERLEY, 3rd Baron *cr* 1945; **Charles Rodney Muff;** *b* 2 Oct. 1946; *s* of 2nd Baron Calverley and of Mary, *d* of Arthur Farrar, Halifax; *S* father, 1971; *m* 1972, Barbara Ann, *d* of Jonathan Brown, Kelbrook, near Colne; two *s. Educ:* Fulneck School for Boys. Police Officer, City of Bradford Police, 1963–74, W Yorks Police, 1974–97 (RUC secondment, 1979–80). *Heir: s* Hon. Jonathan Edward Muff, *b* 16 April 1975. *Address:* 110 Buttershaw Lane, Wibsey, Bradford, W Yorks BD6 2DA.

CALVERLEY, Prof. Peter Martin Anthony, FRCP, FRCPE; Professor of Medicine (Pulmonary Rehabilitation), University of Liverpool, since 1995; *b* 27 Nov. 1949; *s* of Peter Calverley and Jennifer (*née* Taylor); *m* 1973, Margaret Tatam; four *s*. *Educ:* Univ. of Edinburgh (MB ChB). FRCP 1990; FRCPE 1990. Jun. physician posts in Edinburgh and Leicester, 1973–76; MRC Clinical Fellow, 1976–79, Sen. Registrar, 1979–85, Dept of Medicine, Royal Infirmary, Edinburgh; Consultant Physician, Aintree NHS Trust, Liverpool, 1988–95 (Hon. Consultant Physician, 1995–). Travelling Fellow, Meakin-Christie Labs, McGill Univ., Montreal, 1982–83. *Publications:* (ed jtly) Chronic Obstructive Pulmonary Disease, 1994; papers on pathophysiology and treatment of chronic obstructive pulmonary disease and sleep-related breathing disorders. *Recreations:* sailing, ski-ing, travel, family. *Address:* University Clinical Department, Aintree NHS Trust, Longmoor Lane, Liverpool L9 7AZ. *T:* (0151) 529 2933.

CALVERT, Barbara Adamson, (Lady Lowry); QC 1975; barrister-at-law; a Recorder of the Crown Court, 1980–98; *b* 30 April 1926; *d* of late Albert Parker, CBE; *m* 1st, 1948, John Thornton Calvert, CBE (*d* 1987); one *s* one *d*; 2nd, 1994, Baron Lowry, PC (*d* 1999). *Educ:* St Helen's, Northwood; London Sch. of Economics (BScEcon). Called to Bar: Middle Temple, 1959 (Bencher 1982); NI, 1978 (QC 1978; Hon. Bencher, 1995). Admin. Officer, City and Guilds of London Inst., 1961; practice at Bar, 1962–. Full-time Chm., Industrial Tribunals, London, 1986–96 (part-time Chm., 1974–86); Mem., Matrimonial Causes Rules Cttee, 1983–85. Freeman, City of London, 1989. *Recreations:* gardening, swimming, poetry. *Address:* (home) 158 Ashley Gardens, SW1P 1HW; (chambers) 4 Brick Court, Temple, EC4Y 7AN. *Clubs:* Sloane; Royal Fowey Yacht.

CALVERT, Denis; *see* Calvert, L. V. D.

CALVERT, Florence Irene, (Mrs W. A. Prowse); Principal, St Mary's College, University of Durham, 1975–77; *b* 1 March 1912; *d* of Ernest William Calvert and Florence Alice (*née* Walton); *m* 1977, William Arthur Prowse (*d* 1981). *Educ:* Univ. of Sheffield (BA, 1st Cl. Hons French and Latin, MA). Asst Language Teacher, Accrington Grammar Sch., 1936–39; Head, Modern Langs Dept, Accrington Girls' High Sch., 1939–48; Univ. of Durham: Lectr in Educn, 1948; Sen. Lectr, 1964–75. *Publications:* French Plays for the Classroom, 1951; L'Homme aux Mains Rouges, 1954; Contes, 1957; French by Modern Methods in Primary and Secondary Schools, 1965. *Address:* 7 St Mary's Close, Shincliffe, Durham DH1 2ND. *T:* (0191) 386 5502.

CALVERT, John Raymond; Chairman, Worcestershire Community and Mental Health NHS Trust, since 1999; *b* 14 June 1937; *s* of Matthew and Eva Mary Calvert; *m* 1962, Elspeth Sarah Naish; one *s* one *d*. *Educ:* Bootham, York; Manchester Univ. (BA Econs). FIPD (FIPM 1986). Cadbury Schweppes Ltd, 1961–70; Delta Metals Ltd, 1970–73; Pilkington Bros Ltd, 1973–84: Personnel Dir, Triplex Safety Glass Ltd, 1973–80; Dir, Chance Bros Ltd, 1973–80; Gp Employee Relations Manager, 1980–84; Dir, Industrial Relations, ITCA, 1984–88; Gp Personnel Dir, Yorkshire Tyne Tees TV Hldgs plc, 1988–93; Man. Dir, 1993–97, Dep. Chm., 1996–97, Tyne Tees TV. Director: Northern Sinfonia, 1993–; Newcastle Initiative, 1994–. Council Member: Industrial Soc., 1994–; NE Chamber of Commerce, 1995–. Chm., Newcastle Educn Business Partnership, 1995–. Trustee, Cleveland Community Foundn, 1995–. Gov., Newcastle Coll., 1994–. FRSA 1989. *Recreations:* church organist and choirmaster, fell walking, tennis. *Address:* (office) Isaac Maddox House, Shrub Hill Road, Worcester WR4 9RW. *T:* (01905) 681514; Dorset Cottage, Droitwich Road, Feckenham, near Redditch, Worcs B96 6HX. *T:* (01527) 892387.

CALVERT, (Louis Victor) Denis, CB 1985; Comptroller and Auditor General for Northern Ireland, 1980–89, retired; *b* 20 April 1924; *s* of Louis Victor Calvert, Belfast and Gertrude Cherry Hobson, Belfast; *m* 1949, Vivien Millicent Lawson; two *s* one *d*. *Educ:* Belfast Royal Academy; Queen's Univ., Belfast (BScEcon); Admin. Staff Coll., Henley-on-Thames. Served with RAF, 1943–47, navigator (F/O). Northern Ireland Civil Service, 1947–80: Min. of Agriculture, 1947–56; Dep. Principal 1951; Principal, Min. of Finance, 1956–63; Min. of Health and Local Govt, 1963–65; Asst Sec. 1964; Min. of Development, 1965–73; Sen. Asst Sec. 1970; Dep. Sec. 1971; Min. of Housing, Local Govt and Planning, 1973–76; DoE for NI, 1976–80. Mem. Bd, Internat. Fund for Ireland, 1989–92. *Recreations:* gardening, golf, reading.

CALVERT, Michael, OBE 1998; FRAgS; Chief Executive, Royal Agricultural Society of England, since 2000; *b* 22 May 1950; *s* of Noel Calvert and Nancy Winifred Calvert (*née* Warkup); *m* 1972, Josephine Mary McGinty; three *s*. *Educ:* Edinburgh Univ. (BSc Hons 1972). FRAgS 1998. Tech. Rep., ICI, 1972–74; Partner, Northwold Agricl Services, 1974–80; General Manager: Farmplan Pty, 1980–81; Sentry Farm Mgt, 1981–85; CWS Farms Gp, 1985–2000. Dir, Rothamsted Exptl Stn, 2000–. Member: Council, BBSRC, 1998–; Sci. Cttee, MAFF, later DEFRA, 2000–; Chm., LINK Sustainable Livestock Prodn Prog., 1996–. *Recreations:* walking, tennis, gardening, in France. *Address:* Iscennen House, 8 Chapel Lane, Gaddesby, Leics LE7 4WB. *T:* (01664) 840780. *Club:* Farmers.

CALVERT, Norman Hilton; retired; Deputy Secretary, Departments of the Environment and of Transport, 1978–80; *b* 27 July 1925; *s* of Clifford and Doris Calvert; *m* 1st, 1949, May Yates (*d* 1968); one *s* one *d*; 2nd, 1971, Vera Baker (*d* 1996). *Educ:* Leeds Modern Sch.; Leeds Univ.; King's Coll., Durham Univ. BA Hons 1st cl. Geography, 1950. Served Royal Signals, 1943–47: 81 (W African) Div., India, 1945–47. Min. of Housing and Local Govt: Asst Principal, 1950–55; Principal, 1956–64; Asst Sec., 1964–71; Sec., Water Resources Bd, 1964–68; Principal Regional Officer, Northern Region, 1969–71; Regional Dir, Northern Region, and Chm, Northern Econ. Planning Bd, 1971–73; Under Sec., DoE, 1971–78. *Recreations:* fell walking, listening to music, motoring. *Address:* 6 Monmouth Gardens, Beaminster, Dorset DT8 3BT. *T:* (01308) 863366.

CALVERT, Rev. Canon Peter Noel; Vicar of Todmorden, West Yorkshire, since 1982; Chaplain to the Queen, since 1998; *b* 20 Dec. 1941; *s* of Harry and Beatrice Annie Calvert; *m* 1980, Stella Christine Horrocks; two *s* one *d*. *Educ:* Queen Elizabeth GS, Wakefield; Arnold Sch., Blackpool; Christ's Coll., Cambridge (BA 1963; MA 1967). Ordained deacon, 1966, priest, 1967; Curate, Brighouse, 1966–71; Vicar, Heptonstall, 1971–82; Priest-in-charge, Cross Stone, 1983–93; Rural Dean, Calder Valley, 1984–; Hon. Canon, Wakefield Cathedral, 1992–. *Recreations:* photography, philately, walking, interest in transport. *Address:* The Vicarage, Todmorden, Lancs OL14 7BS. *T:* (01706) 813180.

CALVERT, Phyllis; actress; *b* 18 Feb. 1915; *d* of Frederick and Annie Bickle; *m* 1941, Peter Murray Hill (*d* 1957); one *s* one *d*. *Educ:* Margaret Morris Sch.; Institut Français. Malvern Repertory Company, 1935; Coventry, 1937; York, 1938. First appeared in London in A Woman's Privilege, Kingsway Theatre, 1939; Punch Without Judy, Embassy, 1939; Flare Path, Apollo, 1942; Escapade, St James's, 1953; It's Never Too Late, Strand, 1954; River Breeze, Phoenix, 1956; The Complaisant Lover, Globe, 1959; The Rehearsal, Globe, 1961; Ménage à Trois, Lyric, 1963; Portrait of Murder, Savoy, Vaudeville, 1963; A Scent of Flowers, Duke of York's, 1964; Present Laughter, Queen's, 1965; A Woman of No Importance, Vaudeville, 1967; Blithe Spirit, Globe, 1970; Crown Matrimonial, Haymarket, 1973; Dear Daddy, Ambassadors, 1976; Mrs Warren's Profession, Worcester, 1977; She Stoops to Conquer, Old World, Exeter, 1978; Suite in Two Keys, tour, 1978; Before the Party, Queen's, 1980; Smithereens, Theatre Royal, Windsor, 1985; The Heiress, Chichester Fest., 1989. Started films, 1939. *Films include:* Kipps, The Young Mr Pitt, Man in Grey, Fanny by Gaslight, Madonna of the Seven Moons, They were Sisters, Time out of Mind, Broken Journey, My Own True Love, The Golden Madonna, A Woman with No Name, Mr Denning Drives North, Mandy, The Net, It's Never Too Late, Child in the House, Indiscreet, The Young and The Guilty, Oscar Wilde, Twisted Nerve, Oh! What a Lovely War, The Walking Stick, Mrs Dalloway. *Television* series and serials: Kate, 1970; Cover her Face, 1985; All Passion Spent, 1986; A Killing on the Exchange, 1987; Boon, 1987; Sophia and Constance, 1988; The Woman He Loved, 1988; Capsticks Law, 1989; Victoria Wood, 1989; After Henry, 1990; Lime Grove, 1991; Jute City, 1991; Woof, 1991; House of Elliot, 1993; Sherlock Holmes, 1994; Casualty, 1996; Midsomer Murders, 1999; plays: Death of a Heart, 1985; Across the Lake, 1988. *Recreations:* swimming, gardening, collecting costume books. *Address:* 1 Sandringham Court, Westleigh Avenue, SW15 6RE.

CALVERT-SMITH, David; QC 1997; Director of Public Prosecutions, since 1998; *b* 6 April 1945; *s* of Arthur and late Stella Calvert-Smith; *m* 1971, Marianthe Phoca. *Educ:* Eton; King's Coll., Cambridge (MA). Called to the Bar, Middle Temple, 1969, Bencher, 1994; a Recorder, 1986–98; Jun. Treasury Counsel, 1986; Sen. Treasury Counsel, 1991; First Sen. Treasury Counsel, 1995. Vice-Chm., 1997–98, Chm., 1998, Criminal Bar Assoc.; Mem., Criminal Cttee, Judicial Studies Bd, 1997–98. *Recreations:* music, sports. *Address:* Crown Prosecution Service, 50 Ludgate Hill, EC4M 7EX. *T:* (020) 7796 8098.

CALVET, Jacques; President, Peugeot SA, 1984–97; Referendary Councillor, Cour des Comptes (Audit Office), since 1963; *b* 19 Sept. 1931; *s* of Prof. Louis Calvet and Yvonne Calvet (*née* Olmières); *m* 1956, Françoise Rondot; two *s* one *d*. *Educ:* Lycée Janson-de-Sailly; Law Faculty, Paris (Licencié en droit; Dipl. Inst. d'Etudes Politiques; Dipl. d'Etudes Supérieures d'Economie Politique et des Sciences Economiques). Trainee, l'Ecole Nationale d'Administration, 1955–57; Audit Office, 1957–59; Office of Sec. of State for Finance, 1959–62, of Minister of Finance, 1962–66; Dep. Dir, 1964, Head of Dept, 1967, Central Finance Admin; Head of Finance Dept, Paris Préfecture, 1967–69; Asst Dir, later Dir, Office of Minister of Economy and Finance, 1969–74; Dir in Ministry of Finance, 1973; Asst Dir Gen., 1974, Dir Gen., 1976, Pres., 1979–82, Banque Nationale de Paris; Vice-Prés. du Conseil d'Administration, 1984, Prés, 1990, Automobiles Peugeot; Président du Conseil d'Administration: Automobiles Citroën, 1983–97; Publicité Française, 1991–97. Administrateur: Chaussures André; Galeries Lafayette; Bazar de l'hôtel de Ville; Société Générale; AXA; Cottin Frères; Société Foncière Lyonnaise. Consulting Advr, Banque de France; Mem., Internat. Adv. Council, Allianz. Commandeur, Légion d'Honneur, 1996; Officier: Ordre Nat. du Mérite, 1970; Ordre Nat. du Mérite Agricole, 1970; Chevalier des Palmes académiques, 1964; Grande Ufficiale, Ordine al Merito della Repubblica Italiana, 1995. *Address:* 31 avenue Victor Hugo, 75116 Paris, France; 7 rue de Tilsitt, 75017 Paris, France.

CALVIN, Michael; Chief Sports Feature Writer, Mail on Sunday, since 1998; *b* 3 Aug. 1957; *s* of Charles Calvin and Margaret Calvin (*née* Platts); *m* 1977, Lynn Goss; three *s* one *d*. *Educ:* Watford Grammar Sch. Reporter: Watford Observer, 1975–77; Hayters Sports Agency, 1977–79; writer and broadcaster, Thames TV, 1983–84; Chief Sports Writer, Westminster Press, 1979–83; Feature Writer, 1984–86, Chief Sports Writer, 1986–96, Daily Telegraph; Sen. Sports Writer, The Times, 1997–98. Segrave Trophy for Outstanding Achievement, 1990; Sports Journalist of the Year, English Sports Council, 1992; Sports Reporter of the Year, British Press Awards, 1992, 1999; Award for Services to Yachting Journalism, RYA, 1993; led winning team for coverage of disabled sport, British Sports Assoc. for Disabled, 1994, 1995, 1996. *Publications:* Captaincy, 1977; Only Wind and Water, 1998. *Recreation:* long distance sailing. *Address:* Broomwood, Higher Rads End, Eversholt MK17 9ED. *T:* (01525) 280300. *Clubs:* Royal Ocean Racing; Cape Horners.

CALVOCORESSI, Peter (John Ambrose); author; *b* 17 Nov. 1912; *s* of Pandia Calvocoressi and Irene (Ralli); *m* 1938, Barbara Dorothy Eden, *d* of 6th Baron Henley; two *s*. *Educ:* Eton (King's Scholar); Balliol Coll., Oxford. Called to Bar, 1935. RAF Intelligence, 1940–45; Wing Comdr. Trial of Major War Criminals, Nuremberg, 1945–46. Contested (L) Nuneaton, 1945. Staff of Royal Institute of International Affairs, 1949–54 (Mem. Council, 1955–70); Dir of Chatto & Windus Ltd and The Hogarth Press Ltd, 1954–65; Editorial Dir, 1972–76, Publisher and Chief Exec., 1973–76, Penguin Books. Chm., Open Univ. Educnl Enterprises Ltd, 1979–88. Reader (part time) in International Relations, Univ. of Sussex, 1965–71; Member: Council, Inst. for Strategic Studies, 1961–71; Council, Inst. of Race Relations, 1970–71; UN Sub-Commn on the Prevention of Discrimination and Protection of Minorities, 1962–71; Chm., The Africa Bureau, 1963–71; Mem., Internat. Exec., Amnesty International, 1969–71; Chm., The London Library, 1970–73; Dep. Chm., N Metropolitan Conciliation Cttee, 1967–71. DUniv Open, 1990. *Publications:* Nuremberg: The Facts, the Law and the Consequences, 1947; Surveys of International Affairs, vol. 1, 1947–48, 1950; vol. 2, 1949–50, 1951; vol. 3, 1951, 1952; vol. 4, 1952, 1953; vol. 5, 1953, 1954; Middle East Crisis (with Guy Wint), 1957; South Africa and World Opinion, 1961; World Order and New States, 1962; World Politics since 1945, 1968, 8th edn as World Politics 1945–2000, 2000; (with Guy Wint) Total War, 1972, 2nd rev. edn (with John Pritchard) 1989; The British Experience 1945–75, 1978; Top Secret Ultra, 1980; Independent Africa and the World, 1985; A Time for Peace, 1987; Who's Who in the Bible, 1987; Resilient Europe 1870–2000, 1991; Threading My Way (memoirs), 1994; Fall Out: World War II and the shaping of Europe, 1997. *Address:* 1 Queen's Parade, Bath BA1 2NJ. *T:* (01225) 333903. *Club:* Garrick.

CALVOCORESSI, Richard Edward Ion; Director (formerly Keeper), Scottish National Gallery of Modern Art, since 1987; Keeper, Dean Gallery, since 1999; *b* 5 May 1951; *s* of Ion Melville Calvocoressi and Katherine (*née* Kennedy); *m* 1976, Francesca Temple Roberts; one *s* two *d*. *Educ:* Eton; Brooke House, Market Harborough; Magdalen Coll., Oxford (Exhibnr; BA (Hons) English Lang. and Lit.); Courtauld Inst. of Art (MA Hist. of Art, 19th and 20th centuries). Research Assistant: Scottish Nat. Gall. of Modern Art, Edinburgh, 1977–79; Modern Collection, Tate Gall., 1979–82; Asst Keeper, Tate Gall., 1982–87. Art Advr, Chelmsford Mus., 1980–86; Member: Cttee, British Council, Scotland, 1989–98; Visual Arts Adv. Cttee, British Council, 1991– (Chm., 1999–); Visual Arts Cttee, Scottish Arts Council, 1993–95. Dir, Grimsthorpe and Drummond Castle Trust, 1993–. Governor, Glasgow Sch. of Art, 1988–91. *Publications:* Magritte, 1979, 5th edn 1998; numerous exhibn catalogues, reviews and articles. *Address:* Scottish National Gallery of Modern Art, Belford Road, Edinburgh EH4 3DR.

CAMBRIDGE, Alan John; HM Diplomatic Service, retired; *b* 1 July 1925; *s* of Thomas David Cambridge and Winifred Elizabeth (*née* Jarrett); *m* 1947, Thelma Elliot; three *s* one *d*. *Educ:* Beckenham Grammar Sch. Served War, FAA and RAFVR, 1943–47 (Air Gunner, Bomber Comd). War Pensions Office and MPNI, 1948–55; entered CRO,

1955; Chief Clerk: Madras, 1956–58; Kuala Lumpur, 1959–62; 2nd Sec., Salisbury, Fedn of Rhodesia and Nyasaland, 1962–65; 1st Sec. (Political), Freetown, 1965–66; UN Dept, FCO, 1966–68; 1st Sec., Prague, 1969; 1st Sec. (Consular/Aid), Suva, 1970–72; HM Consul, Milan, 1972–74; Asst Head of Inf. Dept, FCO, 1974–78; 1st Sec., Ankara, 1978–81; Asst Head, 1981–82, Head and Counsellor, 1983–85, Migration and Visa Dept, FCO; Assessor, FCO, 1985–90. *Recreations:* photography, swimming. *Address:* 9 The Ferns, Carlton Road, Tunbridge Wells TN1 2JT. *T:* (01892) 531223. *Club:* Civil Service.

CAMBRIDGE, Sydney John Guy, CMG 1979; CVO 1979; HM Diplomatic Service, retired; *b* 5 Nov. 1928; *o s* of late Jack and Mona Cambridge; unmarried. *Educ:* Marlborough; King's Coll., Cambridge. Entered HM Diplomatic Service, Sept. 1952; Oriental Sec., British Embassy, Jedda, 1953–56; Foreign Office, 1956–60; First Sec., UK Delegn to United Nations, at New York, 1960–64; Head of Chancery, British Embassy, Djakarta, 1964–66; FO, 1966–70; Counsellor, British Embassy, Rome, 1970–73; Head of Financial Relations Dept, FCO, 1973–75; Counsellor, British High Commn, Nicosia, 1975–77; Ambassador: to Kuwait, 1977–82; to Morocco, 1982–84. *Address:* Saint Peter's House, Filkins, Lechlade, Glos GL7 3JQ.

CAMDEN, 6th Marquess *cr* 1812; **David George Edward Henry Pratt;** Baron Camden, 1765; Earl Camden, Viscount Bayham, 1786; Earl of Brecknock, 1812; *b* 13 Aug. 1930; *o s* of 5th Marquess Camden and Marjorie, Countess of Brecknock, DBE (*d* 1989); *S* father, 1983; *m* 1961, Virginia Ann (marr. diss. 1984), *o d* of late F. H. H. Finlaison, Arklow Cottage, Windsor, Berks; one *s* one *d* (and one *s* decd). *Educ:* Eton. Late Lieutenant, Scots Guards. Dir, Clive Discount Co. Ltd, 1958–69. *Heir: s* Earl of Brecknock, *qv*. *Address:* Wherwell House, Andover, Hants SP11 7JP. *T:* (01264) 860020.

CAMDESSUS, Michel Jean; Managing Director, International Monetary Fund, 1987–2000; *b* 1 May 1933; *s* of Alfred Camdessus and Madeleine Camdessus (*née* Cassembon); *m* 1957, Brigitte d'Arcy; two *s* four *d*. *Educ:* Inst. of Political Studies, Paris; Diploma, Nat. Sch. of Administration. Administrateur Civil, French Treasury, 1960; Financial Attaché, Permt French Delegn to European Communities, 1966–68; Asst Dir, Treasury, 1971, Dep. Dir, 1974, Dir, 1982; Dep. Governor, Bank of France, Aug. 1984, Governor, Nov. 1984. Chm., Paris Club, 1978–84. Officier de la Légion d'Honneur; Chevalier de l'Ordre National du Mérite; Croix de la valeur militaire. *Address:* 27 rue de Valois, 75001 Paris, France.

CAME, Nicholas John Gard, FICS; Director, Australian, New Zealand and Papua New Guinea Chambers of Commerce (UK), 1993–96; *b* Swansea, 10 March 1937; *s* of Victor Henry Thomas Came and Dorothy Edith Came (*née* Prestidge); *m* 1961, Edelgard Elise Irma Meyer; two *d*. *Educ:* Bromsgrove Sch. FICS 1984; MCIT 1988. Officer Cadet Trng Vessel, Rakaia, 1954–57; Bethell Gwyn & Co., 1958–59; Nat. Service, commnd RA, 1959–61; Exec., Dowie & Marwood Ltd, 1961–66; Manager: NZ Shipping Co. Ltd, London, 1967–71; P&OSN Co., 1971–78; Dir, Shipping Corp. of NZ (UK) Ltd, 1978–91. Director: Internat. Shipping Fedn, 1983–91; Shipowners Refrigerated Cargo Res. Assoc., 1984–91; Mem. Council, Internat. Chamber of Shipping, 1983–92. Pres., NZ Soc., 1990–91. *Recreations:* walking, music, languages, travel. *Club:* Royal Over-Seas League.

CAMERON, family name of **Baron Cameron of Lochbroom.**

CAMERON OF LOCHBROOM, Baron *cr* 1984 (Life Peer), of Lochbroom in the District of Ross and Cromarty; **Kenneth John Cameron;** PC 1984; a Senator of the College of Justice in Scotland, since 1989; *b* 11 June 1931; *s* of Hon. Lord Cameron, KT, DSC; *m* 1964, Jean Pamela Murray; two *d*. *Educ:* The Edinburgh Academy; Corpus Christi Coll., Oxford (MA 1955; Hon. Fellow, 1989); Edinburgh Univ. (LLB). Served RN, 1950–52; commissioned RNVR, 1951 (Lt). Admitted Faculty of Advocates, 1958; QC (Scot.) 1972; Standing Junior to Dept of Transport, 1964–71; to DoE, 1971–72; Chairman of Industrial Tribunals in Scotland, 1966–81; Advocate Depute, 1981–84; Lord Advocate, 1984–89. Chm. of Pensions Appeal Tribunal (Scotland), 1975, Pres. 1976–84. Chairman: Cttee for Investigation in Scotland of Agricultural Marketing Schemes, 1980–84; Scottish Civic Trust, 1989–95; Edinburgh New Town Conservation Cttee, 1991–94; Royal Fine Art Commn for Scotland, 1995–. Pres., Scottish Council for Voluntary Orgns, 1989–. Hon. Bencher, Lincoln's Inn, 1984. FRSE 1990. Hon. FRIAS 1994. *Recreations:* fishing, sailing, music. *Address:* Stoneyhill House, Musselburgh EH21 6RP. *T:* (0131) 665 1081. *Clubs:* Scottish Arts, New (Edinburgh).

CAMERON, Prof. Alan Douglas Edward, FBA 1975; Anthon Professor of Latin Language and Literature, Columbia University, New York, since 1977; *b* 13 March 1938; *er s* of A. D. Cameron, Egham; *m* 1st, 1962, Averil Sutton (marr. diss. 1980. *see* Averil Cameron); one *s* one *d*; 2nd, 1987, Charlotte Innes (marr. diss. 1992); 3rd, 1998, Carla Asher. *Educ:* St Paul's Sch. (Schol.); New Coll., Oxford (Schol.). Craven Scholar 1958; 1st cl. Hon. Mods 1959; De Paravicini Scholar 1960; Chancellor's Prize for Latin Prose 1960; 1st cl. Lit. Hum. 1961; N. H. Baynes Prize 1967; John Conington Prize 1968. Asst Master, Brunswick Sch., Haywards Heath, 1956–57; Asst Lectr, then Lectr, in Humanity, Glasgow Univ., 1961–64; Lectr in Latin, 1964–71, Reader, 1971–72, Bedford Coll., London; Prof. of Latin, King's Coll., London, 1972–77. Visiting Professor: Columbia Univ., NY, 1967–68; UCLA, 1989; Visiting Fellow: Humanities Research Centre, ANU, 1985; Inst. for Advanced Study, Princeton, 1990. Fellow: Amer. Acad. of Arts and Sciences, 1979; Amer. Philosophical Soc., 1992. Charles J. Goodwin Award, 1996. *Publications:* Claudian: Poetry and Propaganda at the Court of Honorius, 1970; (contrib.) Prosopography of the Later Roman Empire, ed Jones, Morris and Martindale, i, 1971, ii, 1980; Porphyrius the Charioteer, 1973; Bread and Circuses, 1974; Circus Factions, 1976; Literature and Society in the Early Byzantine World, 1985; (jtly) The Consuls of the Later Roman Empire, 1985; (with J. Long) Barbarians and Politics at the Court of Arcadius, 1993; The Greek Anthology: from Meleager to Planudes, 1993; Callimachus and his Critics, 1995; The Last Pagans of Rome, 2002; Greek Mythography in the Roman World, 2002; articles and reviews in learned jls. *Recreation:* the cinema. *Address:* 450 Riverside Drive, New York, NY 10027, USA.

CAMERON, Alan John; Consultant, Andersen, and Andersen Legal, Australia, since 2001; *b* 9 Feb. 1948; *s* of John and Norma Cameron; *m* 1971, Susan Patricia Sanders; two *s*. *Educ:* Sydney Univ. (BA, LLB, LLM). Principal Solicitor, NSW Aboriginal Legal Service, 1973–75; Lectr in Law, Univ. of N Sumatra, 1975–77; Dawson Waldron, Solicitors, later Blake Dawson Waldron: Partner, 1979–91; Man. Partner, 1982–85, 1989–91; Commonwealth Ombudsman (Australia), 1991–92; Chm., Australian Securities & Investments Commn, 1993–2000. Dir, SFE Corp. Ltd. *Recreations:* tennis, walking, reading. *Address:* (office) Andersen, 363 George Street, Sydney, NSW 2000, Australia.

CAMERON, Major Allan John, MBE 1988; JP; Vice Lord-Lieutenant, Highland Region (Ross and Cromarty), 1977–92; *b* 25 March 1917; *s* of Col Sir Donald Cameron of Lochiel, KT, CMG (*d* 1951), and Lady Hermione Cameron (*d* 1978), *d* of 5th Duke of Montrose; *m* 1945, Mary Elizabeth Vaughan-Lee, Dillington, Somerset; two *s* two *d* (and one *s* decd). *Educ:* Harrow; RMC Sandhurst. Served QO Cameron Highlanders, 1936–48; Major, Retd (POW Middle East, 1942). County Councillor, Ross-shire, 1955–75 (Chm. Educn Cttee, 1962–75); Councillor, 1975–96, Convener, 1991–96, Ross and Cromarty DC. Former Member: Red Deer Commn; Countryside Commn for Scotland; Broadcasting Council for Scotland. *Recreations:* curling (Past Pres. Royal Caledonian Curling Club), gardening, golf. *Address:* Allangrange, Munlochy, Ross-shire IV8 8NZ. *T:* (01463) 811249. *Club:* Naval and Military.

See also Col Sir Donald Cameron of Lochiel.

CAMERON, Most Rev. Andrew Bruce; *see* Aberdeen and Orkney, Bishop of.

CAMERON, Prof. Averil Millicent, CBE 1999; MA, PhD; FBA 1981; FSA 1982; Warden, Keble College, since 1994, and Professor of Late Antique and Byzantine History, since 1998, University of Oxford; *b* 8 Feb. 1940; *d* of T. R. Sutton, Leek, Staffs; *m* 1962, Alan Douglas Edward Cameron, *qv* (marr. diss. 1980); one *s* one *d*. *Educ:* Westwood Hall Girls' High Sch., Leek, Staffs; Somerville Coll., Oxford (Passmore Edwards Schol. 1960; Rosa Hovey Schol. 1962; MA); Univ. of Glasgow; University Coll. London (PhD; FKC 1987). King's College London: Asst Lectr, 1965; Lectr, 1968; Reader in Ancient History, 1970; Prof. of Ancient History, 1978–89; Head of Dept of Classics, 1984–89; Prof. of Late Antique and Byzantine Studies, and Dir, Centre for Hellenic Studies, 1989–94. Visiting Professor: Columbia Univ., 1967–68; Collège de France, 1987; Sather Prof., Univ. of Calif. at Berkeley, 1985–86; Vis. Member, Inst. of Advanced Study, Princeton, 1977–78; Summer Fellow, Dumbarton Oaks Center for Byzantine Studies, 1981; British Acad. Wolfson Res. Reader in Hist., 1990–92. Chm., British Nat. Byzantine Cttee, 1983–89; Pres., Roman Soc., 1995–98 (Vice-Pres., 1983–95, 1999–); Mem., British Acad. Council, 1983–86. Chm., Cathedrals Fabric Commn for England, 1999–. Editor, Jl of Roman Studies, 1985–90. Hon. DLitt: Warwick, 1996; St Andrews, 1997; QUB, 2000; Lund, 2001. *Publications:* Procopius, 1967; Agathias, 1970; Corippus: In laudem Iustini minoris, 1976; Change and Continuity in Sixth-Century Byzantium, 1981; (ed jtly) Images of Women in Antiquity, 1983, 2nd edn 1993; (ed jtly) Constantinople in the Eighth Century: the Parastaseis Syntomoi Chronikai, 1984; Procopius and the Sixth Century, 1985; (ed) History as Text: the writing of ancient history, 1989; Christianity and the Rhetoric of Empire, 1991; (ed jtly) The Byzantine and Early Islamic Near East, vol. I: Problems in the Literary Source Material, 1992, vol. II: Land Use and Settlement Patterns, 1994, vol. III: States, Resources and Armies, 1995; The Later Roman Empire, 1993; The Mediterranean World in Late Antiquity, AD 395–600, 1993; Changing Cultures in Early Byzantium, 1996; (ed with P. D. Gainsey) Cambridge Ancient History, vol. XIII, 1998; (ed with S. G. Hall) Eusebius, Life of Constantine, 1999; (ed jtly) Cambridge Ancient History, vol. XIV, 2001; numerous articles in learned jls. *Address:* Keble College, Oxford OX1 3PG.

CAMERON, Colin Neil; Head of Network Programmes, BBC Scotland, and Head of Network Development, BBC Nations and Regions, since 2000; *b* 30 March 1950; *s* of Hector MacDonald Cameron and Frances (*née* Majury); *m* 1978, Christine Welsh Main; two *s*. *Educ:* Glasgow Acad.; Duke of York, Nairobi; Poly. of Central London (Dip. Communication Studies). Journalist, BBC Scotland, 1973–76; BBC TV: Film Dir, That's Life, 1976–77; Producer/Dir, Everyman and Heart of the Matter, 1977–85; Editor, Features and Documentaries, BBC North, 1985–88; Hd, Documentary Features, BBC TV, 1988–91; Hd of TV, 1991–96, Hd of Production, 1996–2000, BBC Scotland. Chm., BAFTA Scotland, 1993–98. Mem., Adv. Gp, Glasgow Common Purpose, 1994–. Mem. Bd, Balfron High Sch., 1997–. Mem., RTS, 1984–. UNA Media Peace Prize, 1984. *Recreations:* sailing, cycling, cinema, Scottish art. *Address:* BBC Scotland, Queen Margaret Drive, Glasgow G12 8DG. *T:* (0141) 338 2424.

CAMERON, David William Donald; MP (C) Witney, since 2001; *b* 9 Oct. 1966; *s* of Ian Donald Cameron and Mary Fleur Cameron; *m* 1996, Samantha Gwendoline Sheffield. *Educ:* Eton Coll.; Brasenose Coll., Oxford (BA 1st Cl. Hons PPE). Cons. Res. Dept, 1988–92; Special Adviser: HM Treasury, 1992–93; Home Office, 1993–94; Hd, Corporate Affairs, Carlton Communications plc, 1994–2001. *Recreations:* tennis, bridge, cooking. *Address:* House of Commons, SW1A 0AA. *T:* (020) 7219 3000.

CAMERON OF LOCHIEL, Colonel Sir Donald (Hamish), KT 1973; CVO 1970; TD 1944; JP; 26th Chief of the Clan Cameron; Lord-Lieutenant of County of Inverness, 1971–85 (Vice-Lieutenant, 1963–70); Chartered Accountant; *b* 12 Sept. 1910; *s* of Col Sir Donald Walter Cameron of Lochiel, KT, CMG, 25th Chief of the Clan Cameron, and Lady Hermione Emily Graham (*d* 1978), 2nd *d* of 5th Duke of Montrose; *S* father, as 26th Chief, 1951; *m* 1939, Margaret, *o d* of Lieut-Col Hon. Nigel Gathorne-Hardy, DSO; two *s* two *d*. *Educ:* Harrow; Balliol Coll., Oxford. Joined Lovat Scouts, 1929; Major 1940; Lieut-Col 1945; Lieut-Col comdg 4/5th Bn (TA) QO Cameron Highlanders, 1955–57; Col 1957 (TARO). Hon. Colonel: 4/5th Bn QO Cameron Highlanders, 1958–67; 3rd (Territorial) Bn Queen's Own Highlanders (Seaforth and Camerons), 1967–69; 2nd Bn, 51st Highland Volunteers, 1970–75. Member (part-time): British Railways Bd, 1962–64; Scottish Railways Bd, 1964–72 (Chm. Scottish Area Bd, BTC, 1959–64); Transport Holding Co., 1962–65; Director: Royal Bank of Scotland, 1954–80 (Vice-Chm., 1969–80); Save & Prosper Gp, 1968–84; Culter Guard Bridge Holdings Ltd, 1970–77 (Chm., 1970–76); Scottish Widows Life Assurance Soc., 1955–81 (Chm., 1964–67). Crown Estate Comr, 1957–69. Chm., Scottish Cttee, Malcolm Sargent Cancer Fund for Children, 1975–91. President: Scottish Landowners Fedn, 1979–84; Royal Highland and Agricultural Soc. of Scotland, 1971, 1979 and 1987. Governor, Harrow Sch., 1967–77. *Heir: s* Donald Angus Cameron, younger of Lochiel [*b* 2 Aug. 1946; *m* 1974, Lady Cecil Kerr, *d* of Marquess of Lothian, *qv*; one *s* three *d*]. *Address:* Achnacarry, Spean Bridge, Inverness-shire PH34 4EJ. *T:* (01397) 712708. *Clubs:* Pratt's; New (Edinburgh).

See also Major A. J. Cameron.

CAMERON, Donald William; Canadian Consul General to New England, 1993–97; *b* 20 May 1946; *m* 1969, Rosemary Simpson; one *s* two *d*. *Educ:* East Pictou Rural High Sch.; Nova Scotia Agricl Coll.; McGill Univ. (BSc). Dairy farmer; MLA (PC) Pictou East, 1974–93; Minister of: Recreation, 1978–79; Fisheries, 1978–80; Industry, Trade and Technology, 1988–91; Leader, Nova Scotia Progressive Cons. Party, 1991; Premier of Nova Scotia, 1991–93. *Recreations:* ski-ing, boating, hockey, tennis. *Address:* RR #1, New Glasgow, NS B2H 5C4, Canada.

CAMERON, Rt Rev. Douglas Maclean; *see* Argyll and the Isles, Bishop of.

CAMERON, Ellen; *see* Malcolm, E.

CAMERON, Rt Rev. Ewen Donald; Assistant Bishop, Diocese of Sydney, 1975–93; *b* 7 Nov. 1926; *s* of Ewen Cameron, Balranald, NSW, and Dulce M. Cameron, Sydney, NSW; *m* 1952, Joan R., *d* of T. Wilkins, Mosman, NSW; one *s* two *d*. *Educ:* Sydney C of E Grammar Sch., N Sydney; Moore Theological Coll., Sydney. ACA (Aust.); BD (London); ThSchol (Aust. Coll. of Theol.). Public Accountancy, 1945–57. Lectr, Moore Theological Coll., 1960–63; Rector, St Stephen's, Bellevue Hill, 1963–65; Federal Secretary, CMS of Aust., 1965–72; Archdeacon of Cumberland with Sydney, 1972–75; Bishop of North Sydney, 1983–90; Registrar, dio. of Sydney, 1990–93. Mem., ARCIC,

1983–90. *Address:* Unit 1, Gowrie Village, 10 Edward Street, Gordon, NSW 2072, Australia. *T:* (2) 94992493. *Club:* Union (Sydney).

CAMERON, Ewen James Hanning; DL; FRICS; Chairman: Countryside Agency, since 1999; Lets Go Travel Ltd, since 1998; Government's Rural Advocate, since 2000; *b* 24 Nov. 1949; *s* of Maj. Allan John Cameron and Elizabeth Cameron (*née* Vaughan-Lee); *m* 1975, Caroline Anne Ripley; three *s* one *d*. *Educ:* Christ Church, Oxford (MA). FRICS 1992; FRAgS 1995. Manager, Dillington Estate, Somerset, 1971–. Founding Chm., Orchard Media Ltd, 1989–99. Mem., Minister of Agriculture's CAP rev. gp, 1995. Dir, Village Retail Services Assoc. for Village Shops, 1992–2000. Nat. Pres., CLA, 1995–97. Mem., UK Round Table for Sustainable Develt, 1997–2000. Pres., Somerset Young Farmers, 1990–91; Mem., Mgt Bd, Nat. Fedn of Young Farmers, 1998–2000. FRSA 1996. High Sheriff, 1986–87, DL 1989, Somerset. *Recreations:* golf, windsurfing. *Address:* Dillington Farms, Ilminster, Som TA19 9EQ.

CAMERON, Francis (Ernest), MA, DipEth (Oxon); FRCO(CHM), ARAM; organist and ethnomusicologist; Choirmaster and Organist, City Church of St Michael at the North Gate, Oxford, 1988–94; *b* London, 5 Dec. 1927; *er s* of Ernest and Doris Cameron; *m* 1952, Barbara Minns; three *d*. *Educ:* Mercers' Sch.; Caerphilly Boys' Secondary Sch.; Royal Acad. of Music; University Coll., Oxford. Henry Richards Prizewinner, RAM, 1946. Organist, St Peter's, Fulham, 1943; Pianist, Canadian Legion, 1944; Organist, St Luke's, Holloway, 1945; Sub-organist, St Peter's, Eaton Square, 1945; Organist, St James-the-Less, Westminster, 1946; commissioned RASC, 1948; Organ Scholar, University Coll., Oxford, 1950; Organist: St Anne's, Highgate, 1952; St Barnabas', Pimlico, 1953; St Mark's, Marylebone Road, 1957–58; Choirmaster, St Aloysius, Somers Town, 1959; Master of Music, Westminster Cathedral, 1959; Visiting Organist, Church of St Thomas of Canterbury, Rainham, Kent, 1961; Organist and Choirmaster, Church of Our Lady of the Assumption and St Gregory, Warwick Street, W1, 1962–68. Travel for UNESCO, 1952–55; Dep. Dir of Music, LCC (subsequently GLC), 1954–68; Asst-Dir of Music, Emanuel Sch., 1954; Music Master, Central Foundation Boys' Grammar Sch., 1956; Prof. of Organ and Composition, RAM, 1959–68; *locum tenens* Dir of Music, St Felix Sch., Southwold, 1963 and 1964; Asst Dir, 1968, Chm. of Musicology, 1974–79, NSW State Conservatorium of Music; Organist, Church of St Mary the Virgin, Iffley, 1980–88; Sen. Lectr, Musical Studies, Oxford Poly., 1982–86; Demonstrator: Oxford Univ. Computing Services, 1988–96; computing, Univ. of Oxford Dept for Continuing Educn, 1994–96; computer programming tutor, Oxford Centre for Adult Learning, 1992–96. Inaugural Conductor, Witan Operatic Soc., 1957–58; Conductor: "I Cantici", 1961–65; Francis Cameron Chorale, 1965–68; Singers of David, 1973–76; British Adjudicator, Fedn of Canadian Music Festivals, 1965; Examr Associated Bd of Royal Schools of Music, 1965–68; Dep. Chm., NSW Adv. Bd, Aust. Music Exams Bd, 1969–74. Field Officer, Deep Creek Aboriginal Monuments res. and recording prog., 1973; Mem., Lancefield Archaeol Expedn, 1975. President: "Open Score", 1946–68; Musicol Soc. of Aust., 1971–75 (jt leader, ethnomusicol expedn to New Hebrides, 1971–72); Sydney Univ. Anthropol Soc., 1974–75; Phoenix Photographic Circle, 1977–79; Conservatorium Professional Staff Assoc., 1978–79; Vice-Pres., Aust. Chapter, ISCM, 1970–77; Ed., INFO, European Seminar in Ethnomusicology, 1986–90. Beethoven Commemorative Medal, Fed. Repub. of Germany, 1970. *Publications:* editor (with John Steele) Musica Britannica vol. xiv (The Keyboard Music of John Bull, part I), 1960; Old Palace Yard, 1963; Eight dances from Benjamin Cosyn's Second Virginal Book, 1964; I Sing of a Maiden, 1966; John Bull, ausgewählte Werke, 1967; I Believe, 1969; incidental music for film The Voyage of the New Endeavour, 1970; songs and incidental music for Congreve's Love for Love, 1972; Alleluia, 1990; contributor to: Church Music; Composer; The Conductor; Liturgy; Musical Times; Australian Jl of Music Education; Studies in Music; Music in Tertiary Educn; Con Brio; Musicology IV; Aust. Nat. Hist.; Nation Review; Quanta; ICTM (UK) Bulletin; Eur. Studies in Ethnomusicol. *Address:* 12 Norreys Avenue, Oxford OX1 4SS. *T:* (01865) 240058.

CAMERON, Sir (Hugh) Roy (Graham), Kt 1999; QPM 1994; Chief Constable, Lothian and Borders Police, since 1996; *b* 14 April 1947; *s* of Angus and May Cameron; *m* 1969, Margaret Scott; two *s*. *Educ:* Bearsden Acad.; Univ. of Strathclyde (BA 1976; MPhil 1992). Cadet, Dunbartonshire Constabulary, 1964–66; Constable, 1966, Asst Chief Constable, 1990–94, Strathclyde Police; Chief Constable, Dumfries and Galloway Constabulary, 1994–96. *Recreations:* hillwalking, swimming, golf, music, cinema, reading. *Address:* Police Headquarters, Fettes Avenue, Edinburgh EH4 1RB. *T:* (0131) 311 3131.

CAMERON, Prof. Iain Thomas, MD; Professor of Obstetrics and Gynaecology, University of Southampton, since 1999; *b* 21 Feb. 1956; *s* of late James David Cameron and Stella (*née* Turner); *m* 1st, 1983 (marr. diss.); two *d*; 2nd, 1992, Heidi Wade; one *s* one *d*. *Educ:* Hutton Grammar Sch.; Univ. of Edinburgh (BSc Med. Sci. 1977; MB ChB 1980; MD 1988); MA Cantab 1992. MRCOG 1986, FRCOG 1999; MRACOG 1987. House Officer and Sen. House Officer, Western Infirmary, Glasgow, Royal Infirmary, Edinburgh and Simpson Meml Maternity Pavilion, Edinburgh, 1980–82; University of Edinburgh: Research Fellow, Dept of Obstetrics and Gynaecology, 1982–84; Lectr and Registrar, 1984–86; Monash University: Clinical Res. Fellow, 1986–88; Lectr, 1987–88; Sen. Registrar, Royal Women's Hosp., Melbourne, 1988–89; University of Cambridge: Lectr, 1989–92; Sen. Registrar, 1989–91; Consultant, 1991–92; Regius Prof. of Obstetrics and Gynaecology, Glasgow Univ., 1993–99; Mem., HFEA, 2001–. Chm., Blair Bell Res. Soc., 1999–Dec. 2002, Chm., Meetings Cttee, and Convenor, Postgrad. Meetings, 2000–, RCOG. Specialist Advr, Menorrhagia, NICE, 2000. Ed.-in-Chief, Reproductive Medicine Rev., 1999–. *Publications:* articles and other contribs on menstrual disorders, endometrium, and reproductive medicine. *Recreations:* reading, solo piping. *Address:* Obstetrics and Gynaecology, Level F (815), Princess Anne Hospital, Coxford Road, Southampton SO16 5YA.

CAMERON, Ian Alexander; Sheriff of Grampian, Highland and Islands at Wick, Dornoch and Stornoway, since 1993; *b* 5 Nov. 1938; *s* of late James Cameron and Isabella Cameron; *m* 1968, Dr Margaret Anne Innes; one *s*. *Educ:* Elgin Acad.; Edinburgh Univ. (MA); Aberdeen Univ. (LLB with dist.). Qualified as solicitor, 1961; Partner, Stewart & McIsaac, Solicitors, Elgin, 1962–87; Sheriff of Lothian and Borders at Edinburgh, 1987–93. *Recreations:* travel, railway history. *Address:* Braemoray, Elgin, Moray IV30 4NJ. *T:* (01343) 542731; 19/4 Damside, Dean Village, Edinburgh EH4 3BB. *T:* (0131) 220 1548.

CAMERON, Prof. Ian Rennell, CBE 1999; DM; FRCP; Vice-Chancellor, University of Wales College of Medicine, 1994–2001; *b* 20 May 1936; *s* of James and Frances Mary Cameron; *m* 1st, 1964, Jayne Bustard (marr. diss.); one *s* one *d*; 2nd, 1980, Jennifer, *d* of Stewart and Josephine Cowin. *Educ:* Westminster Sch.; Corpus Christi Coll., Oxford (BA 1958 1st Cl. Hons Animal Physiol; MA 1961; DM 1969; Hon. Fellow, 2000); St Thomas's Hosp. Med. Sch. (BM BCh 1961). FRCP 1976. Jun. med. appts, St Thomas' Hosp., 1961–64; Res. Asst, Dept of Physiol., UCL, 1966–68; Lectr 1967, Sen. Lectr 1969, Reader 1975, St Thomas's Hosp. Med. Sch.; Prof. of Medicine, UMDS of Guy's and St Thomas' Hosps, 1979–94 (Dean, St Thomas', 1986–89; Principal, UMDS, 1989–92, Hon. Fellow, 1997); Hon. Consultant Physician, St Thomas' Hosp., 1970–94. NIH Postdoctoral Fellowship at Cedars-Sinai Med. Center, LA, and Asst Prof., Dept of Physiol, UCLA, 1968–69. Mem., Medway HA, 1981–86; non-exec. Dir, Bro Taf HA, 1996–99; Dir, R & D, SE Thames RHA, 1993–94. Examiner, Univ. of London Final MB, 1980–94; Mem. Senate, Univ. of London, 1989–92. Member: Med. Res. Soc., 1966–; Physiol Soc., 1974–; Assoc. of Physicians of GB and Ire., 1979–; Council, RCP, 1992–95; GMC, 1994– (Treas., 1997–); Univs UK (formerly CVCP), 1994–2001; Commn for Health Improvement, 1999. Chm., UK Centre for Advancement of Inter-professional Educn, 1998–99. Mem. Council, KCL, 1993–99. Hon. FKC 1998; Founder FMedSci 1998. *Publications:* Respiratory Disorders (with N. T. Bateman), 1983; papers in various med. and physiol jls. *Recreation:* collecting (books, paintings and ceramics). *Club:* Athenæum.

CAMERON, Ivor Gill S.; *see* Smith-Cameron.

CAMERON, Prof. J(ames) Malcolm, MD, PhD; FRCSGlas, FRCPath, DMJ; Professor of Forensic Medicine, University of London, at The London Hospital Medical College, 1973–92, now Professor Emeritus; Consulting Editor of Medicine, Science and Law (Editor, 1970–95); *b* 29 April 1930; *s* of late James Cameron and Doris Mary Robertson; *m* 1956, Primrose Agnes Miller McKerrell, MCST (decd); one *d*. *Educ:* The High Sch. of Glasgow; Univ. of Glasgow (MB, ChB, MD, PhD). The London Hospital Medical College: Lectr in Forensic Med., 1963–65; Sen. Lectr in Forensic Med., 1965–70; Reader in Forensic Med., 1970–72; Sen. Lectr in Forensic Med. at St Bartholomew's Hosp. Med. Coll., 1971–92; Ver Heyden De Lancey Reader in Forensic Medicine, Council of Legal Educn, 1978–92. Hon. Consultant: London, subseq. Royal London Hosp., 1967–92; in Forensic Medicine, to Army, 1971–92, and RN, 1972–92; RAF, 1990–92; Emeritus Consultant to Army, 1999–; Hon. Med. Advr to Amateur Swimming Assoc., 1985-2000 (Hon. Life Mem., 1997). Formerly: Examiner in Forensic Med. to Univ. of Dublin; Convenor for Exams of Dip. in Med. Jurisp. of Honourable Soc. of Apothecaries of London; Mem. Council, Royal Coll. of Pathologists. Chm. and Hon. Sec., Med. Cttee, Ligue Européenne de Natation, 1990–2000. Member: BMA; Council, Brit. Assoc. in Forensic Med. (Pres., 1985–87); British Acad. of Forensic Sciences (Sec. Gen., 1970–85; Pres., 1978–79); FINA Med. Cttee (Hon. Sec., 1986–2000); Assoc. of Police Surgeons of GB (Hon. Fellow); Forensic Science Soc.; Assoc. of Clinical Pathologists; Pathological Soc. of GB and Ire.; Research Defence Soc.; Sen. Fellow, Amer. Acad. of Forensic Sciences; Mem., Academic Internationalis Medicinae Legalis et Medicinae Socialis. Hon. Dip. in Forensic Odontology, London Hosp. Med. Coll., 1985. *Publications:* scientific papers in numerous learned jls, both med. and forensic. *Recreations:* sports medicine and legal medicine. *Clubs:* Savage, Royal Naval Medical.

CAMERON, John Alastair; *see* Abernethy, Hon. Lord.

CAMERON, John Bell, CBE 1982; Chairman, World Meats Group, International Federation of Agricultural Producers, since 1984; Director, South West Trains, since 1996; *b* 14 June 1939; *s* of John and Margaret Cameron; *m* 1964, Margaret (*née* Clapperton). *Educ:* Dollar Academy. AIAgrE; FRAgS. Studied agriculture in various countries, Scandinavia, S America and Europe, 1956–61; farmed in Scotland, 1961–64. National Farmers' Union of Scotland: Mem. National Council, 1964; Vice-Pres., 1976; Pres., 1979–84 (first long-term Pres.). Mem., Agricultural Praesidium of EEC, 1979–89; Chairman: EEC Adv. Cttee for Sheep Meat, 1982–89; UK Sheep Consultative Cttee, 1986–87; Scottish Beef Council, 1997–. Chm., BR (Scotland) and Scottish Mem., BRB, 1988–93. Chm. Governors, Dollar Acad., 1984–. Hon. DTech Napier, 1998. Winner: George Headley Award to the UK Sheep Industry, 1986; Sir William Young Award to the Scottish Livestock Industry, 1986. *Recreations:* flying, shooting, travelling. *Address:* Balbuthie Farm, By Leven, Fife, Scotland KY9 1EX. *T:* (01333) 730210.

CAMERON, John Charles Finlay; Member, London Transport Executive, 1975–84; *b* 8 Feb. 1928; *s* of Robert John and Nancy Angela Cameron; *m* 1st, Ruth Thompson, Sydney, Australia; two *s* two *d*; 2nd, Nancy Foy, author, Redlands, Calif. *Educ:* privately; University Coll., Southampton. CEng, MICE, FCIT, CIMgt. Royal Marines, 1946–48. British Railways, Southern Region, Civil Engineering, 1948; BR Transport Commn, 1957; BR Rlys Workshops, 1962; Rank Organisation, 1968–75. Dir-Gen. and Sec., CIT, 1984–88 (Hon. Vice Pres., 1988–91; Chm., Scot. Sect., 1995–96); Dir, BURA, 1989–93; Chm., Highland Perthshire Develt Co., 1990–94. Member: Management Cttee, Abbotstone, Ag. Prop. Unit Trust, 1982–91; Westminster Br., IMgt (Chm., 1985–88; Vice-Pres., 1988–91). Gov., Pitlochry Fest. Theatre, 1991–98. Major, Engr and Transport Staff Corps, RE (TA), 1985–98. Liveryman, Carmen's Co., 1984. *Recreations:* book collecting, binding and dealing. *Address:* Clunemore Farm, Killiecrankie, Pitlochry, Perthshire PH16 5LS. *T:* (01796) 473470, *Fax:* (01796) 473030; *T:* (020) 7249 1177. *Club:* Oriental.

CAMERON, Prof. John Robinson; Regius Professor of Logic, University of Aberdeen, since 1979; *b* 24 June 1936; *s* of Rev. George Gordon Cameron and Mary Levering (*née* Robinson); *m* 1st, 1959, Mary Elizabeth Ranson (*d* 1984); one *s* two *d*; 2nd, 1987, Barbara Elizabeth Blair. *Educ:* Dundee High Sch.; Univ. of St Andrews (MA 1st Cl. Hons Maths, BPhil Philosophy); Univ. of Calif, Berkeley; Cornell Univ. Harkness Fellow, Berkeley and Cornell, USA, 1959–61; University of Dundee (formerly Queen's College): Asst in Phil., 1962–63; Lectr in Phil., 1963–73; Sen. Lectr in Phil., 1973–78. *Publications:* articles in phil jls. *Recreation:* bricolage. *Address:* 70 Cornhill Road, Aberdeen AB25 2EH. *T:* (01224) 486700.

CAMERON, John Taylor; *see* Coulsfield, Rt Hon. Lord.

CAMERON, Lewis; Sheriff of South Strathclyde, Dumfries and Galloway at Hamilton, since 1994; *b* 12 Aug. 1935; *s* of James Aloysius Cameron and Marie Isobel McKenzie; *m* 1962, Sheila Colette Gallacher; two *s* two *d*. *Educ:* Blairs Coll., Aberdeen; St Sulpice, Paris; Glasgow Univ. (MA, LLB). Admitted Solicitor, 1962. RAF (Nat. Service), 1954–56. Chm., Social Security Appeal Tribunals, 1983–88; Mem., Legal Aid Central Cttee, 1970–80; Legal Aid Sec., Airdrie, 1978–87; Dean, Airdrie Soc. of Solicitors, 1984–85; Tutor, Strathclyde Univ., 1981–88; Sheriff of S Strathclyde, Dumfries and Galloway at Dumfries, 1988–94. Treas., Monklands Victim Support Scheme, 1983–88; Chairman: Dumfries and Galloway Family Conciliation Service, 1988–92; Dumfries and Galloway Scottish Assoc. for Study of Delinquency, 1989–92. Mem., Scotland Cttee, Nat. Children's Homes, 1991–94; Chm., Phew (Parental Help Evenings/Weekends, Mentally Handicapped), 1994–2000. Trustee, Oscar Marzaroli Trust, 1990–93. *Publications:* occasional articles and journalism. *Recreations:* cinema, theatre, tennis, travel. *Address:* Sheriff Court House, 4 Beckford Street, Hamilton ML3 6AA. *T:* (01698) 282957. *Clubs:* New (St Andrews); Glasgow Art; Ross Priory (Gartocharn, Loch Lomond).

CAMERON, Sir Roy; *see* Cameron, Sir H. R. G.

CAMERON, Roy James, CB 1982; PhD; Australian Statistician, 1977–85; *b* 11 March 1923; *s* of Kenneth Cameron and Amy Jean (*née* Davidson); *m* 1951, Dorothy Olive

Lober; two *s* one *d*. *Educ:* Univ. of Adelaide (BEc 1st Cl. Hons, MEc); PhD Harvard. Lecturer in Economics, Canberra University College, 1949–51; Economist, World Bank, 1954–56; Australian Treasury official, 1956–73; Australian Ambassador to OECD, Paris, 1973–77. Chairman: ACT Taxi Fares Adv. Cttee, 1987–89; Cttee of Inquiry into Distribution of Federal Roads Grants, 1985–86. Associate Commr, Industries Assistance Commn, 1989–90. Mem. Council, Canberra Coll. of Advanced Educn, 1986–89. *Recreation:* lawn bowls. *Address:* PO Box 305, Curtin, ACT 2605, Australia. *T:* (2) 62814522.

CAMERON, Sheila Morag Clark, (Mrs G. C. Ryan); QC 1983; Dean, Arches Court of Canterbury and Auditor, Chancery Court of York, since 2001; *b* 22 March 1934; *d* of Sir James Clark Cameron, CBE, TD, and Lady (Irene M.) Cameron; *m* 1960, Gerard Charles Ryan, *qv*; two *s*. *Educ:* Commonweal Lodge Sch., Purley; St Hugh's Coll., Oxford (MA). Called to the Bar, Middle Temple, 1957, Harmsworth Law Scholar, 1958, Bencher, 1988; Part-time Lectr in Law, Southampton Univ., 1960–64; part-time Tutor, Council of Legal Educn, 1966–71; a Recorder, 1985–99. Mem., Bar Council, 1967–70. Comr, Boundary Commn for England, 1989–96 (Asst Comr, 1981–89). Official Principal, Archdeaconry of Hampstead, 1968–86; Chancellor: Dio. of Chelmsford, 1969–2001; Dio. of London, 1992–2001; Vicar-Gen., Province of Canterbury, 1983–2001. Chairman: Archbishops' Group on the Episcopate, 1986–90; Ecclesiastical Judges Assoc., 1997–; Member: Legal Adv. Commn, Gen. Synod of C of E, 1975–; Gen. Synod Marriage Commn, 1975–78; Council on Tribunals, 1986–90. Mem. Council, Wycombe Abbey Sch., 1972–86. *Address:* 2 Harcourt Buildings, Temple, EC4Y 9DB. *T:* (020) 7353 8415.

CAMERON, Stuart Gordon, MC 1943; Chairman and Chief Executive, Gallaher Ltd, 1980–89; *b* 8 Jan. 1924; *s* of late James Cameron and Dora Sylvia (*née* Godsell); *m* 1946, Joyce Alice, *d* of Roland Ashley Wood; three *s* one *d*. *Educ:* Chigwell School, Essex. Served War, 2nd Gurkha Rifles, 1942–46 (MC). Managing Dir, 1976–78, Dep. Chm., 1978–80, Gallaher Ltd. Director: American Brands Inc., 1980–89; Royal Mint, 1989–94; Saatchi & Saatchi Ltd, 1990–94. *Club:* Royal Thames Yacht.

CAMERON, Susan Ruth; Headmistress, North Foreland Lodge, since 1996; *b* Edinburgh; *e d* of James Norval Cameron and Ruth Scott Doig (*née* Nicolson). *Educ:* Wycombe Abbey Sch.; Westfield Coll., London (Exhibnr; BA Hons; Pres., Students' Union). VSO, Oguta, Eastern Nigeria; Housemistress, Godstowe Sch., High Wycombe; teacher, Housemistress, then Dep. Head, Woodford House, Hawkes Bay, NZ; Housemistress: Queenswood Sch., 1977–78; Sherborne Sch. for Girls, 1978–84; Headmistress: Cobham Hall, 1985–89; Downe House, 1989–96. Governor: Queen Margaret's Sch., York, 1986–95; Farlington Sch., Horsham, 1987–95; Repton Sch., 1995–; Gordonstoun Schs, 2000–; Pres., Seniors' Assoc., Wycombe Abbey Sch., 1996–. *Recreations:* music, sport (mostly non-active now), walking the dogs, language, creative thinking. *Address:* North Foreland Lodge, Sherfield-on-Loddon, Hook, Hants RG27 0HT. *T:* (01256) 884801. *Club:* Lansdowne.

CAMERON, Thomas Anthony, (Tony); Chief Executive, Scottish Prison Service, since 1999; *b* 3 Feb. 1947; *o s* of late Thomas Alexander and Olive Cameron; *m* 1970, Elizabeth Christine Sutherland; two *s*. *Educ:* Stranraer High Sch. Dept of Agric. and Fisheries for Scotland, Scottish Office, 1966–72; Private Secretary: to Dep. Under Sec. of State, 1972; to Perm. Under Sec. of State, 1973–74; Department of Agriculture and Fisheries for Scotland: HEO(D), 1974–77, Principal, 1977–82; Asst Sec., 1982–87; Scottish Office Finance Div., 1987–92; Under Sec., 1992; Head of Food and Agric., Scottish Office, 1992–99. Mem., Duke of Edinburgh's Sixth Commonwealth Study Conf., Australia, 1986. *Recreations:* reading, mountaineering, cycling. *Address:* Scottish Prison Service, Calton House, 5 Redheughs Rigg, Edinburgh EH12 9HW. *T:* (0131) 556 8400, *Fax:* (0131) 244 8563.

CAMERON-RAMSAY-FAIRFAX-LUCY; *see* Fairfax-Lucy.

CAMERON WATT, Prof. Donald, FBA 1990; Stevenson Professor of International History in the University of London, 1981–93, now Professor Emeritus; *b* 17 May 1928; *s* of late Robert Cameron Watt and Barbara, *d* of late Rt Rev. E. J. Bidwell, former Bishop of Ontario; *m* 1st, 1951, Marianne Ruth Grau (*d* 1962); one *s*; 2nd, 1962, Felicia Cobb Stanley (*d* 1997); one step *d*. *Educ:* Rugby Sch.; Oriel Coll., Oxford (BA 1951; MA 1954; DLitt 1991; Hon. Fellow, 1998). FRHistS. Asst Editor, Documents on German Foreign Policy, 1918–1945, in Foreign Office, 1951–54; Asst Lectr, Lectr, Sen. Lectr in Internat. History, LSE, 1954–66; Reader in Internat. History in Univ. of London, 1966; Titular Prof. of Internat. History, 1972–81. Editor, Survey of Internat. Affairs, Royal Inst. of Internat. Affairs, 1962–71; Rockefeller Research Fellow in Social Sciences, Inst of Advanced Internat. Studies, Washington, 1960–61; Official Historian, Cabinet Office Historical Section, 1978–. Sec., 1967, Chm., 1976–87, Assoc. of Contemporary Historians; Mem. Bd, Inst. of Contemporary British History, 1987–2001; Chm., Greenwich Forum, 1974–84; Sec.-Treasurer, Internat. Commn for the Hist. of Internat. Relations, 1982–95 (Hon. Vice-Pres., 1995–). Member Editorial Board: Political Quarterly, 1969–2000; Marine Policy, 1978–94; Internat. History Rev., 1984–94; Intelligence and National Security, 1986–; Review of Internat. Studies, 1989–95; Gen. Ed. British Documents on Foreign Affairs, 1985–97. FRSA 1990. Foreign Mem., Polish Acad. of Arts and Scis, Krakow, 1993. *Publications:* (ed jtly) Oxford Poetry, 1950; Britain and the Suez Canal, 1956; (ed) Documents on the Suez Crisis, 1957; Britain looks to Germany, 1965; Personalities and Policies, 1965; (ed) Survey of International Affairs 1961, 1966; (ed) Documents on International Affairs 1961, 1966; (ed, with K. Bourne) Studies in International History, 1967; A History of the World in the Twentieth Century, Pt I, 1967; (ed) Contemporary History in Europe, 1969; (ed) Hitler's Mein Kampf, 1969, 2nd edn 1992; (ed) Survey of International Affairs 1962, 1969; (ed, with James Mayall): Current British Foreign Policy 1970, 1971; Current British Foreign Policy 1971, 1972; Current British Foreign Policy 1972, 1973; Too Serious a Business, 1975, 2nd edn 1993; (ed) Survey of International Affairs 1963, 1977; Succeeding John Bull: America in Britain's place 1900–1975, 1984; How War Came, 1989; (ed with Guido Di Tella): Argentina between the Great Powers, 1990. *Recreations:* exploring London, cats. *Address:* c/o London School of Economics and Political Science, Houghton Street, WC2A 2AE. *Club:* Players Theatre.

CAMILLERI, Victor; Ambassador and Permanent Representative for Malta to Belgium, since 1997; *b* 8 Oct. 1942; *s* of John Camilleri and Esther (*née* Casingena); *m* 1967, Elizabeth Bernadette Heaney; two *s*. *Educ:* Lyceum, Malta; Birmingham Univ. (BA Hons English). Joined Min. of Foreign Affairs, Malta, 1968: 2nd Sec., 1968–74; 1st Sec., 1974–86; Counsellor, 1986–90; 1st Counsellor, 1990; postings in Rome, Brussels, NY and London; Ambassador: to UNIDO and UNESCO, 1981–85; to CSCE, 1985–86; Actg Sec., Min. of Foreign Affairs, 1986–87; Dep. High Comr, 1987–90, High Comr, 1991 and 1996, London; Ambassador to UN, 1991–93. *Recreations:* reading, swimming. *Address:* Maltese Embassy, Rue Belliard 65–67, 1040 Brussels, Belgium.

CAMM, Prof. A(lan) John, MD; FRCP, FACC, FESC; QHP; Prudential Professor of Clinical Cardiology, since 1986, and Chairman, Department of Medicine, 1991–94, St George's Hospital Medical School, London University; *b* 11 Jan. 1947; *s* of John Donald and Joan Camm; *m* 1987, Joy-Maria Frappell; one *s* one *d*. *Educ:* Guy's Hosp. Med. Sch., London Univ. (BSc 1968; MB BS 1971; MD 1981). LRCP, MRCS 1971; FACC 1981; FRCP 1984; FESC 1988. Guy's Hospital: House Surgeon, 1971; House Physician, 1971–72; Jun. Registrar, 1972; Jun. Lectr in Medicine, 1972–73; Registrar in Cardiology, 1973–74; Clin. Fellow in Cardiology, Univ. of Vermont, USA, 1974–75; St Bartholomew's Hospital: British Heart Foundn Res. Registrar, 1975–76, Sen. Registrar 1977–79; Wellcome Sen. Lectr and Hon. Consultant Cardiologist, 1979–83; Sir Ronald Bodley Scott Prof. of Cardiovascular Medicine, 1983–86. Convener of Medicine, London Univ., 1994–. Member, Council: RCP, 1994–; British Cardiac Soc., 1997–98 (Pres. elect, 1998–2001, Pres., 2001–). QHP 1992–. Trustee, N. American Soc. of Pacing and Electrophysiology, 1998–. Freeman, City of London, 1984. CStJ 1990. *Publications:* First Aid, Step by Step, 1978; Pacing for Tachycardia Control, 1983; Heart Disease in the Elderly, 1984, 2nd edn 1994; Clinical Electrophysiology of the Heart, 1987; Heart Disease in Old Age, 1988; Clinical Aspects of Cardiac Arrhythmias, 1988; Diseases of the Heart, 1989, 2nd edn 1996; Heart Disease in Old Age, 1990; Heart Rate Variability, 1998; Evidence Based Cardiology, 1998; approx. 900 papers in major jls. *Recreations:* collector of prints, watercolours and other antiques, model railway enthusiast. *Address:* St George's Hospital Medical School, Cranmer Terrace, Tooting, SW17 0RE. *Clubs:* Athenæum, Oriental, Royal Society of Medicine.

CAMMELL, John Ernest; Consultant: Warwick Manufacturing Group, Warwick University, since 1993; British Standards Institution, since 2000 (a Director, 1992–2000); *b* 14 Nov. 1932; *s* of Ernest Alfred Cammell and Gladys Clara (*née* Burroughes); *m* 1976, Janis Linda Moody. *Educ:* Highfield Coll., Leigh-on-Sea, Essex. Mil. Service, Royal Signals. Joined Victualling Dept, Admiralty, 1952; DSIR, 1963; Min. of Technology, 1964; DTI, 1967; Dept of Industry, 1973; Dir, National Maritime Inst., 1981–84; Hd, Mech. Engrg and Manufg Technol. Div., subseq. Manufg Technol. Div., DTI, 1986–92. CompIEE (Companion, IProdE, 1988); FRSA. *Recreations:* amateur theatre, golf, cricket, eating. *Address:* 41 Cunnington Street, Chiswick, W4 5ER. *T:* (020) 8995 6937.

CAMOYS, 7th Baron *cr* 1264 (called out of abeyance, 1839); **Ralph Thomas Campion George Sherman Stonor,** GCVO 1998; PC 1997; DL; Lord Chamberlain of HM Household and Chancellor of Royal Victorian Order, 1998–2000; a Permanent Lord in Waiting to the Queen, since 2000; *b* 16 April 1940; *s* of 6th Baron Camoys and Mary Jeanne (*d* 1987), *d* of late Captain Herbert Marmaduke Joseph Stourton, OBE; *S* father, 1976; *m* 1966, Elisabeth Mary Hyde, *d* of Sir William Stephen Hyde Parker, 11th Bt; one *s* three *d*. *Educ:* Eton Coll.; Balliol Coll., Oxford (MA). Chm., Jacksons of Piccadilly, 1968–85; Gen. Manager and Director, National Provincial and Rothschild (London) Ltd, 1968; Man. Director, Rothschild Intercontinental Bank Ltd, 1969; Chief Exec. Officer and Man. Dir, 1975–77, Chm., 1977–78, Amex Bank Ltd; Man. Dir, 1978–84, Exec. Vice-Chm., 1984–86, Barclays Merchant Bank; Chief Exec., 1986–88, Dep. Chm., 1987–98, Barclays de Zoete Wedd (BZW); Dep. Chm., Sotheby's, 1993–97. Director: Barclays Bank Internat. Ltd, 1980–84; Barclays Bank PLC, 1984–94; Mercantile Credit Co. Ltd, 1980–84; National Provident Instn, 1982–93; Administrative Staff Coll., 1989–2000; 3i Group, 1991–; Perpetual, 1994–2000. A Lord in Waiting, 1992–97. Member: House of Lords EEC Select Cttee, 1979–81; Historic Bldgs and Monuments Commn for England, 1985–87, Royal Commn on Historical MSS, 1987–94. Pres., Mail Users' Assoc., 1977–84. Consultor, Extraordinary Section of Administration of Patrimony of Holy See, 1991–. Mem. Court of Assistants, Fishmongers' Co., 1980– (Prime Warden, 1992–93). DL Oxfordshire, 1993. Order of Gorkha Dakshina Bahu, 1st class (Nepal), 1981. *Recreations:* the arts, shooting. *Heir:* *s* Hon. (Ralph) William (Robert Thomas) Stonor, *b* 10 Sept. 1974. *Address:* Stonor Park, Henley-on-Thames, Oxon RG9 6HF. *Clubs:* Boodle's, Pratt's; Leander (Henley-on-Thames).

CAMP, Anthony John, MBE 1999; Director, Society of Genealogists, 1979–97; *b* 27 Nov. 1937; *s* of late Henry Victor Camp and Alice Emma Camp (*née* Doidge); *m* 1976, Deborah Mary (marr. diss. 1978), *d* of D. J. Jeavons; one *s*. *Educ:* Alleyne's Sch., Stevenage; University College London (BA Hons). Society of Genealogists: Res. Assistant, 1957; Librarian, 1959; Dir of Res., 1962; Hon. Fellow, 1982. Member Council: Assoc. of Genealogists and Record Agents, 1968–75 (Chm., 1973–75; Vice-Pres., 1980–); British Record Soc., 1967–71, 1983–; British Records Assoc. (Record Preservation Sect.), 1980–83, 1985–88; English Genealogical Congress, 1975–90 (Pres., 1991–92); Friends of Public Record Office, 1988–94; Marc Fitch Fund, 1991–; Fedn of Family History Socs, 1992–98 (Pres., 1998–2000); Pres., Herts Family and Population Hist. Soc., 1982–. Lecturer: yearly Nat. Geneal. Soc. Confs, USA, 1981–; Australasian Congress, Canberra, 1986; Sesquicentennial Conf., Auckland, 1990; First Irish Genealogical Congress, 1991. Fellow, Utah Geneal. Assoc., 1989. Freeman, City of London, 1984. Award of Merit, Nat. Geneal. Soc., USA, 1984. *Publications:* (with P. Spufford) Genealogists Handbook, 1961; Wills and their Whereabouts, 1963; Tracing Your Ancestors, 1964; Everyone has Roots, 1978; Index to Wills proved in the Prerogative Court of Canterbury 1750–1800, 6 vols, 1976–92; (contrib.) My Ancestor series, 1987–; (contrib.) The Records of the Nation, 1990; articles to Family Tree and other jls. *Recreation:* genealogy. *Address:* 65 Fursecroft, George Street, W1H 5LG. *T:* (020) 7723 3758.

CAMP, Jeffery Bruce, RA 1984 (ARA 1974); artist; Lecturer, Slade School of Fine Art, 1963–88; *b* 1923. *Educ:* Edinburgh Coll. of Art. DA (Edin.). One-man exhibitions include: Galerie de Seine, 1958; Beaux Arts Gallery, 1959, 1961, 1963; New Art Centre, 1968; S London Art Gall., 1973 (retrospective); Serpentine Gall., 1978; Bradford City Art Gallery, 1979; Browse and Darby, 1984, 1993, 1997; Aldeburgh Fest., 1986; Nigel Greenwood Gall., 1986, 1990, 1993; Royal Acad., 1988 (retrospective); other exhibitions include: Hayward Annual, 1974, 1982, 1985; Serpentine Gall., 1974, 1987; Narrative Painting, ICA and Arts Council tour, 1979; British Council touring exhibns to China and Edinburgh, 1982, to India, 1985, to Kuala Lumpur, 1988; Chantrey Bicentenary, Tate Gall., 1981; The Hardwon Image, Tate Gall., 1984; group exhibn, Twining Gall., NY, 1985; Peter Moores exhibn, Liverpool, 1986; Athena Art Awards, 1987; represented in public collections including Arts Council, British Council, Tate Gall. and Royal Acad. *Publications:* Draw, 1981; Paint, 1996. *Address:* 27 Stirling Road, SW9 9EF; c/o Browse & Darby, 19 Cork Street, W1X 2LP. *T:* (020) 7734 7984.

CAMP, William Newton Alexander; writer and political and corporate adviser, retired; *b* 12 May 1926; *s* of I. N. Camp, OBE, Colonial Administrative Service, Palestine, and Freda Camp; *m* 1st, 1950, Patricia Cowan (marr. diss. 1973); two *s* one *d*; 2nd, 1975, Juliet Schubart, *d* of late Hans Schubart, CBE; four step *s*. *Educ:* Bradfield Coll.; Oriel Coll., Oxford (Classical Scholar, MA). Served in Army, 1944–47. Asst Res. Officer, British Travel and Holidays Assoc., 1950–54; Asst Sec., Consumer Adv. Council, BSI, 1954–59; Asst Sec., Gas Council, 1960–63; Public Relations Adviser, Gas Council (British Gas Corp.), 1963–67; Dir of Information Services, British Steel Corp., 1967–71; Mem., British Nat. Oil Corp., 1976–78. Special Adviser: milling and baking industries, 1972–90; British Leyland Motor Corp., 1975; railway trades unions, 1975–76; C. A. Parsons & Co. Ltd, 1976–77; Prudential Corp. (formerly Prudential Assurance Co.), 1978–88; Northern Engineering Industries plc, 1978–84; Corporate Advr, British Railways Bd, 1977–90.

Director: Quartet Books, 1973–76; Westminster Communications Gp Ltd, 1989–90; Chm., Camden Consultants Ltd, 1975–91. Mem. Exec. Cttee, Labour Euro-Safeguards Campaign, 1999–. Trustee, Transport 2000, 1997–. Mem. Cttee, Foundn for Al Quds Med. Sch., Jerusalem, 1997–. Chm., Oxford Univ. Labour Club, 1949; contested (Lab) Solihull, 1950; Mem., Southwark Borough Council, 1953–56; Press Adviser (unpaid) to Prime Minister, Gen. Election, 1970. Founder Mem., Public Enterprise Group. *Publications: novels:* Prospects of Love, 1957; Idle on Parade, 1958 (filmed, 1959); The Ruling Passion, 1959; A Man's World, 1962; Two Schools of Thought, 1964; Flavour of Decay, 1967; The Father Figures, 1970; Stroke Counterstroke, 1986; *biography:* The Glittering Prizes (F. E. Smith), 1960. *Address:* 61 Gloucester Crescent, NW1 7EG. *T:* (020) 7482 5112; Keeper's Cottage, Marshfield, near Chippenham, Wilts SN14 8PD. *T:* (01225) 891211. *Clubs:* Garrick, Beefsteak.

CAMPBELL, family name of **Duke of Argyll,** of **Earl Cawdor,** and of **Barons Campbell of Alloway, Campbell of Croy, Colgrain** and **Stratheden.**

CAMPBELL OF ALLOWAY, Baron *cr* 1981 (Life Peer), of Ayr in the District of Kyle and Carrick; **Alan Robertson Campbell,** ERD 1996; QC 1965; a Recorder of the Crown Court, 1976–89; *b* 24 May 1917; *s* of late J. K. Campbell; *m* 1957, Vivien, *y d* of late Comdr A. H. de Kantzow, DSO, RN. *Educ:* Aldenham; Ecole des Sciences Politiques, Paris; Trinity Hall, Cambridge. Called to Bar, Inner Temple, 1939, Bencher, 1972; Western Circuit. Commissioned RA (Suppl. Res.), 1939; served France and Belgium, 1939–40; POW, 1940–45. Consultant to sub-cttee of Legal Cttee of Council of Europe on Industrial Espionage, 1965–74; Chm., Legal Res. Cttee, Soc. of Conservative Lawyers, 1968–80. Member: H of L Cttee for Privileges, 1982–2000; H of L Select Cttee on Murder and Life Imprisonment, 1988–89; Ecclesiastical Cttee, 2000–. Member: Law Adv. Cttee, British Council, 1974–82; Management Cttee, UK Assoc. for European Law, 1975–90. Vice Pres., Assoc. de Juristes Franco-Britanniques, 1989–90. Pres., Colditz Assoc., 1998–. Patron, Inns of Court Sch. of Law Conservatives, 1996–2000. *Publications:* (with Lord Wilberforce) Restrictive Trade Practices and Monopolies, 1956, 2nd edn, 1966, Supplements 1 and 2, 1973; Restrictive Trading Agreements in the Common Market, 1964, Supplement, 1965; Common Market Law, vols 1 and 2, 1969, vol. 3, 1973 and Supplement, 1975; Industrial Relations Act, 1971; EC Competition Law, 1980; Trade Unions and the Individual, 1980. *Address:* 2 King's Bench Walk, Temple, EC4Y 7DE. *T:* (020) 7353 9276. *Clubs:* Carlton (Mem., Political Cttee, 1967–79), Pratt's, Beefsteak.

CAMPBELL OF CROY, Baron *cr* 1974 (Life Peer), of Croy in the County of Nairn; **Gordon Thomas Calthrop Campbell;** PC 1970; MC 1944, and Bar, 1945; DL; Vice-Lord-Lieutenant, Highland Region (Nairn), 1988–99; *b* 8 June 1921; *s* of late Maj.-Gen. J. A. Campbell, DSO and bar; *m* 1949, Nicola Elizabeth Gina Madan; two *s* one *d. Educ:* Wellington and Hospital. War of 1939–45: commissioned in Regular Army, 1939; Captain, 1940; instructor OCTU, Larkhill; RA, Major, 1942; commanded 320 Field Battery in 15 Scottish Div.; wounded and disabled, 1945. Entered HM Foreign Service, 1946; served, until 1957, in FO, UK Delegn to the UN (New York), Cabinet Office (Private Sec. to Sec. of Cabinet) and Vienna; Sec., first Conf. of Privy Councillors on Security, 1955. MP (C) Moray and Nairn, 1959–Feb. 1974; Asst Govt Whip, 1961–62; a Lord Comr of the Treasury and Scottish Whip, 1962–63; Joint Parly Under-Sec. of State, Scottish Office, 1963–64; Opposition Spokesman on Defence and Scottish Affairs, 1966–70; Sec. of State for Scotland, 1970–74. Vice-Pres., Parly Maritime Gp, 1986–. Oil industry consultant, 1975–95; Partner in Holme Rose Farms and Estate, 1969–; Chm., Scottish Bd, 1976–94, Dir, 1983–91, Alliance and Leicester (formerly Alliance) Building Soc.; Chm., Stoic Financial Services (formerly Stoic Insurance Services), 1979–93; Advisory Committee on Pollution of Sea: Vice-Pres., 1976–84; Acting Chm., 1980–82; Chm., 1987–89. Chm., Scottish Cttee, Internat. Year of Disabled, 1981; Mem., RA Council, Scotland, 1980–91; Pres., Anglo-Austrian Soc., 1991–. Trustee, Thomson Foundn, 1980–; First Fellow, Nuffield Provincial Hospitals Trust Queen Elizabeth The Queen Mother Fellowship, 1980. DL Nairn, 1985. *Publication:* Disablement: Problems and Prospects in the UK, 1981. *Recreations:* music, birds. *Address:* Holme Rose, Cawdor, Nairnshire IV12 5XT. *T:* (01667) 493223.

CAMPBELL, Alan; MP (Lab) Tynemouth, since 1997; *b* 8 July 1957; *s* of Albert Campbell and Marian Campbell (*née* Hewitt); *m* 1991, Jayne Lamont; one *s* one *d. Educ:* Univ. of Lancaster (BA Hons); Univ. of Leeds (PGCE); Newcastle Poly. (MA). Teacher: Whitley Bay High Sch., 1980–89; Hirst High Sch., Ashington, 1989–97. *Address:* House of Commons, SW1A 0AA.

CAMPBELL, Alan Grant; Chief Executive, Aberdeenshire Council, since 1995; *b* 4 Dec. 1946; *s* of late Archie and Catherine Campbell; *m* 1974, Susan Marion Black; one *s* two *d. Educ:* Aberdeen GS; Aberdeen Univ. (LLB 1968). Admitted Solicitor, Scotland, 1970; legal appts, Aberdeen CC, 1968–75; Grampian Regional Council: Asst Dir, 1975–79, Depute Dir, 1979–84, Dir, 1984–91, of Law and Admin; Chief Exec., 1991–95. Chm., SOLACE (Scotland), 1997–99. Mem., Cttee of Inquiry into professional conditions of service for teachers, 2000. *Recreations:* competitive cycling and following the Tour de France, gardening, photography, the enjoyment of red wine. *Address:* Woodhill House, Westburn Road, Aberdeen AB16 5GB. *T:* (01224) 665400.

CAMPBELL, Sir Alan (Hugh), GCMG 1979 (KCMG 1976; CMG 1964); HM Diplomatic Service, retired; *b* 1 July 1919; *y s* of late Hugh Campbell and Ethel Campbell (*née* Warren); *m* 1947, Margaret Taylor (*d* 1999); three *d. Educ:* Sherborne Sch.; Caius Coll., Cambridge. Served in Devonshire Regt, 1940–46. 3rd Sec., HM Foreign (now Diplomatic) Service, 1946; appointed to Lord Killearn's Special Mission to Singapore, 1946; served in Rome, 1952, Peking, 1955; UK Mission to UN, New York, 1961; Head of Western Dept, Foreign Office, 1965; Counsellor, Paris, 1967; Ambassador to Ethiopia, 1969–72; Asst Under-Sec. of State, FCO, 1972–74; Dep. Under-Sec. of State, FCO, 1974–76; Ambassador to Italy, 1976–79; Foreign Affairs adviser to Rolls Royce Ltd, 1979–81. Director: National Westminster Bank, 1979–89; Mercantile and General Reinsurance Co., 1979–89; H. Clarkson (Hldgs), 1979–89; Agricola (UK) Ltd, 1987–92. Chairman: Soc. of Pension Consultants, 1982–87; British-Italian Soc., 1983–90; British Sch. at Rome, 1987–94 (Mem. Council, 1982–94); Mem. Council, London Philharmonic Orchestra, 1982–90. Governor, Sherborne Sch., 1973–87 (Chm. of Governors, 1982–87). *Publications:* Colleagues and Friends (autobiog.), 1988; articles in Internat. Affairs, contrib. to New DNB. *Recreation:* painting in watercolour. *Address:* 45 Carlisle Mansions, Carlisle Place, SW1P 1HY. *Clubs:* Brooks's, Beefsteak.

CAMPBELL, Alastair John; Director of Communications and Strategy, Prime Minister's Office, since 2001(Head, Strategic Communications Unit, 2000–01); *b* 25 May 1957; *s* of Donald Campbell and Elizabeth (*née* Caldwell); partner, Fiona Millar; two *s* one *d. Educ:* City of Leicester Boys Sch.; Gonville and Caius Coll., Cambridge (MA). Trainee reporter, Tavistock Times and Sunday Independent, 1980–82; freelance reporter, London, 1982–83; reporter, Daily Mirror, 1982–85; news editor, Sunday Today, 1985–86; reporter, Daily Mirror, 1986; Sunday Mirror: Political Corresp., 1986–87; Political Editor, 1987–89; Columnist, 1989–91; Daily Mirror: Political Editor, 1989–93; Columnist, 1991–93; Asst Editor and Columnist, Today, 1993–95; Press Sec. to Leader of Opposition, 1994–97, to PM, 1997–2001. *Recreations:* family, bagpipes, Burnley Football Club. *Address:* Prime Minister's Office, 10 Downing Street, SW1A 2AA.

CAMPBELL, Alastair Peter; QC (Scot.) 1995; *b* 18 Sept. 1949; *s* of Rev. Donald Campbell and Margaret Campbell (*née* Montgomery); *m* 1973, Flora Beaton; one *s* two *d. Educ:* George Watson's Coll.; Aberdeen Univ. (MA); Strathclyde Univ. (LLB). Teacher of English, 1973–75; Solicitor, Procurator Fiscal Service, 1979–84; Advocate, 1985; Advocate Depute, 1990–93; called to the Bar, Inner Temple, 1990; Standing Jun. Counsel in Scotland to HM Customs and Excise, 1995; Home Advocate Depute, 1997–98. Member: Criminal Justice Forum, 1996–97; Scottish Criminal Rules Council, 1996–98; Criminal Injuries Compensation Bd, 1997. *Recreations:* walking, sailing, golf. *Address:* Cerna, 69 Dirleton Avenue, North Berwick EH39 4QL. *T:* (01620) 894288.

CAMPBELL, Prof. Alastair Vincent; Professor of Ethics in Medicine, University of Bristol, since 1996; *b* 16 April 1938; *s* of William Lee Campbell and Jean Graham Dow; *m* 1st, 1959, Paula Barker (marr. diss.); one *s* four *d*; 2nd, 1979, Sally Barbara Forbes; two *s. Educ:* Hamilton Acad.; Univ. of Edinburgh (MA, BD); San Francisco Theol Seminary (ThD). Ordained Minister, Church of Scotland, 1963. Associate Chaplain, Univ. of Edinburgh, 1964–69; Lectr in Ethics, RCN, Scotland, 1966–72; University of Edinburgh: Lectr and Sen. Lectr, Dept of Christian Ethics and Practical Theology, 1969–90; Head of Dept, 1987–90; Associate Dean, Faculty of Divinity, 1978–81; Prof. of Biomedical Ethics, Otago Med. Sch., and Dir, Bioethics Res. Centre, Dunedin, Univ. of Otago, NZ, 1990–96. Foundn Editor, Jl of Medical Ethics, 1975–80. Milligan Soc. Medallion, 1980; H. K. Beecher Award, Hastings Center, NY, 1999. *Publications:* Moral Dilemmas in Medicine, 1972; Medicine, Health and Justice, 1978; Rediscovering Pastoral Care, 1981; (with R. Higgs) In That Case, 1982; Moderated Love, 1984; Paid to Care?, 1985; The Gospel of Anger, 1986; The Dictionary of Pastoral Care, 1987; (with G. R. Gillett and D. G. Jones) Practical Medical Ethics, 1992; Health as Liberation, 1995; articles in learned jls. *Recreations:* music, ski-ing, walking. *Address:* Centre for Ethics in Medicine, University of Bristol, 73 St Michael's Hill, Bristol BS2 8BH. *T:* (0117) 928 9843.

CAMPBELL, Hon. Alexander Bradshaw; PC (Canada) 1967; Judge, Supreme Court of Prince Edward Island, 1978–94; *b* 1 Dec. 1933; *s* of Dr Thane A. Campbell and late Cecilia B. Campbell; *m* 1961, Marilyn Gilmour; two *s* one *d. Educ:* Dalhousie Univ. (BA, LLB). Called to Bar of Prince Edward Island, 1959; practised law with Campbell & Campbell, Summerside, PEI, 1959–66; QC (PEI) 1966. MLA, Prince Edward Island, 1965–78; Leader of Liberal Party, Dec. 1966–78; Premier, 1966–78; served (while Premier) as Attorney-Gen., 1966–69, Minister of Development, 1969–72, Minister of Agriculture, 1972–74, and Minister of Justice, 1974–78. Dir, Inst. of Man and Resources, 1976–80. Pres., Summerside YMCA, 1981–91; Founder Pres., Summerside Area Historical Soc., 1983; Founder Chm., PEI Council, Duke of Edinburgh Awards (Canada), 1984. Mem., Wyatt Foundn, 1993–. Mem., Heedless Hoarsemen Men's Chorus, Largo, Fla, 1996–. Elder of Trinity United Church, Summerside. Sigma Chi Fraternity. Hon. LLD: McGill 1967; PEI, 1978. *Recreations:* golf, boating, gardening. *Address:* Stanley Bridge, Kensington, RR #6, PE C0B 1M0, Canada. *T:* (902) 8862081. *Club:* Y's Men's (Summerside).

CAMPBELL, Alexander Buchanan, ARSA; FRIBA; architect; Senior Partner, A. Buchanan Campbell and Partners, Glasgow, 1949–90; *b* 14 June 1914; *s* of Hugh Campbell and Elizabeth Flett; *m* 1939, Sheila Neville Smith; one *s* one *d. Educ:* Royal Technical Coll., Glasgow; Glasgow School of Art; Univ. of Strathclyde (BArch). ARSA 1973; PPRIAS. Assistant: Prof. T. Harold Hughes, 1937; G. Grey Wornum, 1938; City Architect, Glasgow, 1939; served War, Royal Engineers, 1940–46; Inspector, Inspectorate of Elect. and Mech. Equipment, 1947; Chief Technical Officer, Scottish Building Centre, 1948, Dep. Dir, 1949. Principal works include: Dollan Swimming Baths and Key Youth Centre, East Kilbride; Whittingehame Court, Ascot; Flats, Great Western Road, Glasgow; St Christopher's Church, Glasgow; Priesthill Church, Glasgow; St James Primary Sch., Renfrew; Callendar Park Coll. and Craigie College of Education at Falkirk and Ayr (Civic Trust Awards); High Rise Flats, Drumchapel. President: Glasgow Inst. of Architects, 1974–76; Royal Incorporation of Architects in Scotland, 1977–79. *Recreations:* music, art, golf. *Address:* 19 Lochan Avenue, Kirn, Dunoon, Argyll PA23 8HT. *T:* (01369) 703674. *Club:* Glasgow Art (President, 1972–74).

CAMPBELL, Prof. Alexander Elmslie, PhD; FRHistS; Professor of American History, University of Birmingham, 1972–87 (part-time, 1984–87; Director of American Studies, 1972–84); now Emeritus Professor; *b* 12 May 1929; *s* of Rev. John Young Campbell and Emma (*née* Wickert); *m* 1st, 1956, Sophia Anne Sonne (*d* 1972); one *s* one *d*; 2nd, 1983, Juliet Jeanne d'Auvergne Collings (*see* J. J. d'A. Campbell). *Educ:* Paisley Grammar Sch.; Perse Sch., Cambridge; St John's Coll., Cambridge (MA; PhD 1956). MA Oxon 1959. FRHistS 1970. Smith-Mundt Student, Harvard Univ., 1953–54; Fellow, King's Coll., Cambridge, 1955–59; Second Sec., HM Foreign Service, 1958–60; Fellow and Tutor in Mod. Hist., Keble Coll., Oxford, 1960–72, Emeritus Fellow 1981–. Vis. Professor: Hobart and William Smith Colls, NY, 1970; Columbia Univ., 1975; Univ. of Kansas, 1976; Stanford Univ., 1977. Mem., Inst. for Advanced Study, Princeton, 1975. *Publications:* Great Britain and the United States, 1895–1903, 1960; (ed) Expansion and Imperialism, 1970; America Comes of Age: the era of Theodore Roosevelt, 1971; (ed) The USA in World Affairs, 1974; articles and reviews in collections and jls. *Address:* 3 Belbroughton Road, Oxford OX2 6UZ. *T:* (01865) 558685. *Clubs:* Athenæum; Cosmos (Washington, DC).

CAMPBELL, Sir Alexander Thomas C.; *see* Cockburn-Campbell.

CAMPBELL, Andrew Neville; QC 1994; a Recorder, since 1989; *b* 17 June 1949; *s* of Archibald Campbell, CMG and of Peggie Campbell (*née* Hussey); *m* 1980, Rebecca Thornton; two *s* one *d. Educ:* Berkhamsted Sch.; New Coll., Oxford (BA Hons Jurisprudence). Called to the Bar, Middle Temple, 1972. *Recreations:* fishing, shooting, cricket, squash, ski-ing, walking. *Address:* 10 Park Square, Leeds, W Yorks LS1 2LH. *T:* (0113) 245 5438. *Club:* Harrogate Cricket (Pres.).

CAMPBELL, Anne; MP (Lab) Cambridge, since 1992; *b* 6 April 1940; *d* of late Frank Lucas and Susan (*née* Chadwick); *m* 1963, Archibald MacRobert Campbell; one *s* two *d. Educ:* Newnham Coll., Cambridge (Maths Tripos Pt II, 1962; MA 1965). FSS 1985; FIS 1985. Sen. Lectr in Statistics, Cambs Coll. of Arts and Technol., 1970–83; Head of Stats and Data Processing, Nat. Inst. of Agricl Botany, Cambridge, 1983–92. PPS to Minister for E-commerce and Small Businesses, 1999–2001, to Sec. of State for Trade and Industry, 2001–. Mem., Cambs CC, 1985–89. FRSA 1992. *Publication:* Calculation for Commercial Students, 1972. *Recreations:* tennis, ski-ing, gardening, mountain walking. *Address:* Alex Wood Hall, Norfolk Street, Cambridge CB1 2LD. *T:* (01223) 506500.

CAMPBELL, Hon. Sir Anthony; *see* Campbell, Hon. Sir W. A.

CAMPBELL, Arthur McLure, CBE 1990; Principal Clerk of Session and Justiciary, Scotland, 1982–89, retired; *b* 15 Aug. 1932; *s* of late Hector Brownlie Campbell, MBE,

AIPA and Catherine Smylie (*née* Renwick). *Educ:* Queen's Park Sch., Glasgow; Open Univ. (BA Hons; DipEurHum). Deptl Legal Qual., Scottish Court Service, 1956. National Service, FAA, 1950–52. Admiralty Supplies Directorate, 1953–54; entered Scottish Court Service (Sheriff Clerk Br.), 1954; Sheriff Clerk Depute, Kilmarnock, 1957–60; Sheriff Clerk of Orkney, 1961–65; seconded HM Treasury (O & M), 1965–69; Principal Sheriff Clerk Depute, Glasgow, 1969; Sheriff Clerk, Airdrie, 1969–72; Principal, Scottish Court Service Staff Trng Centre, 1973–74; Asst Sheriff Clerk of Glasgow, 1974–81. Clerk of Cttees, H of L (temp.), 1991. Secretary: Lord Chancellor's Cttee on Re-sealing of Probates and Confirmations, 1967–68; Scottish Office Cttee on Money Transfer Services, 1968–69; Chm., Simplified Divorce (Scotland) Implementation Gp, 1981–82 (Scottish Consumer Council's Consumer Champion Award, 1983); Mem., Review Body on Use of Judicial Time in Superior Courts in Scotland, 1985–86. Chm., Sheriff Clerks' Assoc., 1971–72. *Recreation:* opsimathy. *Address:* 1 Westhill, Lord Street West, Southport PR8 2BJ; Flat 17, Herriet Court, 37 Herriet Street, Glasgow G41 2JY; Calle Maestro Nicolau 8, 07181 Palma Nova-Calvia, Mallorca. *Clubs:* National Liberal, Civil Service.

CAMPBELL, Rt Hon. Avril Phaedra; *see* Campbell, Rt Hon. Kim.

CAMPBELL, Maj.-Gen. (Charles) Peter, CBE 1977; Director, Quicks (formerly H. & J. Quick) Group Plc, 1982–91; *b* 25 Aug. 1926; *s* of late Charles Alfred Campbell and Blanche Campbell; *m* 1st, 1949, Lucy Kitching (*d* 1986); two *s*; 2nd, 1986, Elizabeth Tristram. *Educ:* Gillingham Grammar Sch.; Emmanuel Coll., Cambridge. FIMgt. Commnd RE, 1945 (despatches, Palestine, 1948); psc 1957; DAA&QMG Trng Bde, RE, 1958–60; OC 11 Indep. Field Sqdn, RE, 1960–62; Jt Services Staff Coll., 1963; DAAG WO, 1963–65; Co. Comd, RMA Sandhurst, 1965–67; CO 21 Engr Regt, 1967–70; GSOI MoD, 1970–71; CRE 3 Div., 1971; Comd 12 Engr Bde, 1972–73; RCDS, 1974; COS HQ NI, 1975–77; Engineer-in-Chief (Army), 1977–80. Col Comdt, RE, 1981–86, Rep. Col Comdt, 1982; Hon. Colonel: RE (Vol.) (Explosive Ordnance Disposal), 1986–88; 101 (London) Engr Regt (Explosive Ordnance Disposal) (V), 1988–91. Chm., RE Assoc., 1983–89. Gov., Gordon's Sch., 1993–96; Mem., Foundn of Gordon's Sch., 1991– (Vice-Chm., 1996–99). *Recreations:* painting and collecting militaria. *Club:* Naval and Military.

CAMPBELL, Cheryl Anne; actress. *Educ:* London Acad. of Music and Dramatic Art (Rodney Millington Award). Acted at Glasgow Citizens Theatr, Watford Rep., Birmingham Rep., King's Head, National Theatre and Theatre Clwyd; Blanche Dubois in A Streetcar Named Desire (Best Actress, Regl Theatre Awards); Nora in A Doll's House (SWET Award, 1983, for best actress of 1982 in a revival), RSC; title rôle in Miss Julie, Lyric, Hammersmith, and Duke of York's, 1983; title rôle in Daughter-in-Law, Hampstead, 1985; The Sneeze, Aldwych, 1988; Betrayal, Almeida, 1991; The Changeling, RSC, 1992; Misha's Party, Macbeth, RSC, 1993; The Strip, Royal Court, 1995; Some Sunny Day, Hampstead, 1996; The Last Yankee, Mercury Th., Colchester, 1996; The Seagull, Donmar, 1997; What the Butler Saw, Sheffield Crucible, 1997; Passion Play, Donmar, 2000. *Television* serials: Pennies from Heaven, 1978; Testament of Youth (Best Actress Award, BAFTA, and British Broadcasting Press Guild Award, 1979); Malice Aforethought; Centrepoint; The Secret Agent, 1992; Monsignor Renard, 2000. *Films* include: Chariots of Fire, 1981; Greystoke, 1983; The Shooting Party, 1985. *Address:* c/o Rebecca Blond Associates, 69a King's Road, SW3 4NX. *T:* (020) 7351 4100.

CAMPBELL, Christopher James, CBE 1993; Chairman, British Shipbuilders, since 1989; *b* 2 Jan. 1936; *s* of David Heggie Campbell and Nettie Phyllis (*née* Burgess). *Educ:* Epsom College. FCA. Served RAPC, 1959–61. Debenhams and subsidiaries, 1966–86, incl. Man. Dir, Hardy Amies, 1978–79; former Director: Debenhams dept stores; Harvey Nichols; Lotus; Debenhams Finance; Debenhams (M & S). Mem., and chief negotiator, 1986–88, non-exec. Mem., 1988–91, National Bus Co.; Finance Dir, Nat. Rivers Authy Adv. Cttee, 1988–89; Director: Harrods Bank Ltd, 1991–2000; Crown Timber plc, 1996–2000; Riverside Mental Health NHS Trust, 1993–96; Mem., BRB, 1994–97 (Vice-Chm., 1994–96). Mem. Council, Technology Colls Trust. Gov., United World Coll. of the Atlantic, 1993–. Trustee, Cobbe collection of ancient keyboard instruments, 1998–. Captain Paymaster, HAC Inf. Bn, 1960–63. *Recreations:* politics, opera, entertaining, visual arts. *Address:* 19 Morpeth Mansions, Morpeth Terrace, SW1P 1ER. *T:* (020) 7630 7527. *Clubs:* Brooks's, Garrick.

CAMPBELL, Colin Donald Norman; Master of the Supreme Court Costs (formerly Taxing) Office, since 1996; *b* 26 Nov. 1952; *s* of Maj. Gregory Campbell, TD and Myra Campbell (*née* Robertson); *m* 1985, Jacqueline Merete Mollett; one *s* one *d*. *Educ:* Oundle; Univ. of London (BA). Admitted as solicitor, 1983; Partner, Brown Cooper Solicitors and Privy Council Agents, 1987–96; Dep. Taxing Master, 1993–96. *Recreations:* Rugby Union, ski-ing, fly-fishing. *Address:* The Old Vicarage, Syleham, near Eye, Suffolk IP21 4LN. *T:* (01379) 668306. *Club:* MCC.

CAMPBELL, Colin MacIver; Member (SNP) Scotland West, Scottish Parliament, since 1999; *b* 31 Aug. 1938; *s* of Archibald James Campbell, MB ChB, DPH, and Christina Ellen Campbell (*née* MacIver); *m* 1963, Evelyn Jean Marcella George; three *s* (and one *s* decd). *Educ:* Paisley Grammar Sch.; Glasgow Univ. (MA Hons); Jordanhill Coll. of Educn. Teacher: Hillhead High Sch., 1961–63; Paisley GS, 1963–67; Principal Teacher, Greenock Acad., 1967–73; Depute Head, Merksworth High Sch., 1973–77; Head, Westwood Secondary Sch., 1977–89; Tutor, Sen. Studies Inst., Strathclyde Univ., 1995–98. Mem., Renfrewshire Council, 1995–99. Nat. Sec., SNP, 1997–99 (Defence Spokesperson, 1995–). *Recreation:* military history of the Great War. *Address:* Scottish Parliament, Edinburgh EH99 1SP. *T:* (0131) 348 5723; Braeside, Shuttle Street, Kilbarchan, Renfrewshire PA10 2PR.

CAMPBELL, Colin Malcolm; QC (Scot.) 1990; *b* 1 Oct. 1953; *s* of Malcolm Donald Campbell and Annabella Ferguson or Campbell; *m* 1977, Fiona Anderson; one *s* one *d* (and one *d* decd). *Educ:* Grove Acad., Broughty Ferry; Univ. of Dundee (LLB). Passed Advocate, 1977. Lectr, Dept of Scots Law, Univ. of Edinburgh, 1977–79; Standing Junior Counsel: to Scottish Develt Dept (all matters other than Planning), 1984–86; to Scottish Develt Dept (Planning), 1986–90. Vice Dean, Faculty of Advocates, 1997–. Part-time Mem., Mental Welfare Commn for Scotland, 1997–. Gov., Fettes Coll, 1991–. *Publications:* articles in Scots Law Times and Jl of Law Soc. of Scotland. *Recreation:* golf. *Address:* Advocates' Library, Parliament House, Edinburgh EH1 1RF. *T:* (0131) 226 5071. *Clubs:* New, Hon. Co. of Edinburgh Golfers, Bruntsfield Links (Edinburgh).

CAMPBELL, Sir Colin (Murray), Kt 1994; DL; Vice-Chancellor, University of Nottingham, since 1988; Professor Emeritus, Queen's University, Belfast; First Commissioner for Judicial Appointments, since 2001; *b* 26 Dec. 1944; *s* of late Donald Campbell and of Isobel Campbell; *m* 1974, Elaine Carlisle (marr. diss. 1999); one *s* one *d*. *Educ:* Robert Gordon's Coll., Aberdeen; Univ. of Aberdeen (LLB 1st Cl. Hons). Lecturer: Faculty of Law, Univ. of Dundee, 1967–69; Dept of Public Law, Univ. of Edinburgh, 1969–73; Prof. of Jurisprudence, 1974–88, Dean of Faculty of Law, 1977–80, Pro-Vice-Chancellor, 1983–87, QUB. Member: Council, Soc. for Computers and Law, 1973–88; Standing Adv. Commn on Human Rights, 1977–80; Legal Aid Adv. Cttee, NI, 1978–82; Mental Health Legislation Rev. Cttee, NI, 1978–82; UGC, 1987–88; Nottingham Develt Enterprise, 1988–91; UFC Scottish Cttee, 1989–93; HEFCE, 1992–97; Inquiry into Police Responsibilities and Rewards, 1992–93; Trent RHA, 1992–96. Chairman: QUBIS Ltd, 1983–88; Zeton Ltd, 1990; Ind. Adv. Gp on Consumers Protection in NI, 1984; NI Economic Council, 1987–94 (Mem., 1985–94); Lace Market Develt Co., 1989–97; Human Fertilisation and Embryology Authy, 1990–94; Med. Workforce Standing Adv. Cttee, 1991–; Food Adv. Cttee, 1994–; Human Genetics Adv. Commn, 1996–99. Non-exec. Dir, Swiss Re GB, 1999–. DL Notts, 1996. *Publications:* (ed jtly) Law and Society, 1979; (ed) Do We Need a Bill of Rights?, 1980; (ed) Data Processing and the Law, 1984; numerous articles in books and jls. *Recreations:* sport, walking, music, reading. *Address:* University of Nottingham, Nottingham NG7 2RD.

CAMPBELL, David Ian; HM Diplomatic Service; Deputy Head of Mission, Manila, since 2000; *b* 9 July 1958; *s* of Ian Flett Campbell and Irene Joyce Campbell (*née* Cook). *Educ:* St Nicholas Grammar Sch., Northwood; Univ. of Bristol (LLB Hons 1980). Joined FCO, 1981; served: Budapest, 1984–85; Georgetown, 1985–87; FCO, 1987–89; First Sec., UK Mission to UN, Geneva, 1989–93; Deputy Head: of Mission, Belgrade, 1994; Human Rights Policy Dept, FCO, 1995–99. *Recreations:* books, theatre, travel. *Address:* c/o Foreign and Commonwealth Office, King Charles Street, SW1A 2AH.

CAMPBELL, David Ross, CBE 2000; Member, since 1991, Chairman, since 1995, Health Education Board for Scotland; *b* 27 Sept. 1943; *s* of William Pancost Clyde Campbell and Davidina (née Ross); *m* 1968, Moira Bagley Donald. *Educ:* Educ: Whitehill Sch.; James Watt Meml Coll. Radio Officer, MN, 1961-67; Sales Exec., Remington Rand, 1967-69; various posts, Glasgow Herald & Evening Times, 1969-75; Man. Dir, Scottish & Universal Newspapers, 1975-79; Exec. Dir, Scottish & Universal Investments, 1978-83; Dir, Clyde Cablevision Hldgs Ltd, 1983-87; Chm. and Chief Exec., West Independent Newspapers Ltd, 1984-94. Chairman: Saltire Hldgs Ltd, 1990-93; Clansman Leisure Ltd, 1990-93; Dep. Chm., Enterprise Ayrshire, 1991-2000. Member: PPITB, 1976-78; Press Council, 1988-90; Bd Scotland, New Opportunities Fund, 1998-. Pres., Glasgow Chamber of Commerce, 1988-90. Also holds various other public and private sector chm. and dir positions. FInstD 1980. Scottish Free Enterprise Award, Aims of Industry, 1990. *Recreations:* golf, theatre, travel, reading. *Address:* Summerlea, Summerlea Road, Seamill, W Kilbride KA23 9HP. *Club:* Western (Glasgow).

CAMPBELL, Sir Donald, Kt 1994; CBE 1987; FRCA; FRCS; FRCSE; FFARCSI; FRCPGlas; FRCPE; Professor of Anaesthesia, University of Glasgow, 1976–92, now Emeritus (Dean of Faculty of Medicine, 1987–91); President, Royal College of Physicians and Surgeons of Glasgow, 1992–94; *b* 8 March 1930; *s* of Archibald Peter and Mary Campbell; *m* 1st, 1954, Nancy Rebecca McKintosh (decd); one *s* one *d*, 2nd, 1975, Catherine Conway Bradburn; two *d*. *Educ:* Hutchesons' Boys' Grammar Sch.; Univ. of Glasgow (MB, ChB). Lectr in Anaesthesia, 1959–60, Cons. Anaesthetist, 1960–76, Royal Inf., Glasgow. Vice-Dean, 1981–82, Dean, 1982–85, Faculty of Anaesthetists, RCS; Vice-Pres., RCS, 1985–87; Visitor, RCPSG, 1990–92. Chm., Scottish Council for Postgrad. Med. Educn, 1985–90. FACP; FRACP. *Publications:* A Nurse's Guide to Anaesthetics, Resuscitation and Intensive Care, 1964, 7th edn 1983; Anaesthetics, Resuscitation and Intensive Care, 1965, 8th edn 1996; contribs to med. jls, mainly on anaesthesia and intensive therapy. *Recreation:* angling. *Address:* Novar, 27 Tannoch Drive, Milngavie, Glasgow G62 8AR. *T:* (0141) 956 1736.

CAMPBELL, Donald le Strange, MC 1944; *b* 16 June 1919; *s* of late Donald Fraser Campbell and Caroline Campbell; *m* 1952, Hon. Shona Catherine Greig Macpherson, *y d* of 1st Baron Macpherson of Drumochter; one *s* one *d*. *Educ:* Winchester Coll.; Clare Coll., Cambridge. Served War, 1939–45, Major RA (MC). EFCO Ltd, 1947–55; MEECO Ltd, 1955–61; Davy-Ashmore Ltd, 1961–67; Dep. Chm. and Man. Dir, Davy-Ashmore Internat., 1965–69; Dir, Hovair Ltd, 1970–78; farming, Berks and Devon, 1979–96. Chm., BNEC Latin America, 1967. *Recreations:* farming, sailing, field sports, music. *Address:* Clarendon Grange, Alderbury, Salisbury, Wilts SP5 3AG. *Clubs:* Boodle's; Royal Yacht Squadron.

CAMPBELL, Duncan; Director of Communications, Scottish Natural Heritage, 1992–95; *b* 23 Sept. 1935; *s* of late Duncan Campbell, sometime Manager, Chartered Bank of India and Australasia, and Mary Beryl Campbell; *m* 1959, Morny Key; two *s*. *Educ:* Merchiston Castle Sch., Edinburgh; Edinburgh Univ.; Newcastle upon Tyne Univ. Nat. service, RHA, 1954–56. Forestry Commission: Forest Manager, 1960–73; Landscape Architect, 1973–80; Head of Design and Recreation Br., 1980–85; Head of Environment Br., 1985–88; Dir, Countryside Commission for Scotland, 1988–92. *Publications:* articles in Landscape Design and Jl of RASE. *Recreations:* landscape appreciation, fishing. *Address:* 15 Torphin Bank, Colinton, Edinburgh EH13 0PH.

CAMPBELL, Gordon Arden, FREng; Chairman, Babcock International Group, since 2001; *b* 16 Oct. 1946; *s* of late Hugh Eric Campbell and Jessie Campbell; *m* 1970, Jennifer Vaughan; two *d*. *Educ:* Churchill Coll., Cambridge (MA). Joined Courtaulds Research, 1968; Dir, British Celanese, 1976; Managing Director: Courtaulds Chemicals, 1980; SAICCOR, S Africa, 1985; Dir, 1987, Dep. Chief Exec., 1995, Chief Exec., 1996–98, Courtaulds. Mem., UKAEA, 1994–96; non-executive Director: AEA Technol., 1996–97; Argos plc, 1997–98; non-executive Chairman: International Process Technologies, 1999–; Wade-Allied Hldgs, 1999–. President: Comité Internat. de Rayon et Fibres Synthétiques, 1995–98; IChemE, 1998–99 (Vice-Pres., 1992–94). Member: President's Council, CBI, 1995–2000; Council, British Heart Foundn, 1999–. Mem. Court, Cranfield Univ., 1999–. FREng (FEng 1993). *Recreations:* Rugby, golf, ski-ing. *Address:* The Parks, Eastcote Lane, Hampton in Arden, Warwicks B92 0AS.

CAMPBELL, Graham Gordon, CB 1984; Under-Secretary, Department of Energy, 1974–84; *b* 12 Dec. 1924; *s* of late Lt-Col and Mrs P. H. Campbell; *m* 1955, Margaret Rosamond Busby; one *d*. *Educ:* Cheltenham Coll.; Caius Coll., Cambridge (BA Hist.). Served War, Royal Artillery, 1943–46. Asst Principal, Min. of Fuel and Power, 1949; Private Sec. to Parly Sec., Min. of Fuel and Power, 1953–54; Principal, 1954; Asst Sec., Min. of Power, 1965; Under-Sec., DTI, 1973. *Recreations:* watching birds, music, hill-walking, clearing scrub. *Address:* 3 Clovelly Avenue, Warlingham, Surrey CR6 9HZ. *T:* (01883) 624671.

CAMPBELL, Gregor Bruce Loudoun; Secretary-General, Institute of Actuaries, and Chief Executive (Joint Affairs), Faculty of Actuaries and Institute of Actuaries, since 1997; *b* 22 April 1942; *s* of Donald and Alison Campbell; *m* 1966, Suzanne Elizabeth Austin; one *s* two *d*. *Educ:* Glasgow Acad.; London Univ. (BScEng). Corps of Royal Engineers, 1962–92; retd as Brig.; Dep. Sec., Inst. of Actuaries, 1993–97. *Recreations:* family, travel, gardening, motor cycles. *Address:* Institute of Actuaries, Staple Inn Hall, High Holborn, WC1V 7QJ. *T:* (020) 7632 2100.

CAMPBELL, Gregory Lloyd; MP (DemU) Londonderry East, since 2001; Member (DemU) Londonderry East, Northern Ireland Assembly, since 1998; Minister for

Regional Development, since 2000; *b* 15 Feb. 1953; *m* Frances; one *s* three *d*. *Educ:* Ebrington Primary Sch.; Londonderry Tech. Coll.; Magee Coll. Civil Servant, 1972-82 and 1986-94; businessman, 1994-. Mem. (DemU), NI Assembly, 1982-86; Mem., NI Forum for Political Dialogue, 1996-98. Mem. (DemU) Londonderry CC, 1981-. Contested (DemU): Foyle, 1992; E Londonderry, 1997. *Publications:* Discrimination: the truth, 1987; Discrimination: where now?, 1993; Ulster's Verdict on the Joint Declaration, 1994; Working Toward 2000, 1998. *Recreations:* soccer, music, reading. *Address:* House of Commons, SW1A 0AA.

CAMPBELL, Harold Edward; Director, Greater London Secondary Housing Association, 1978–83; Chairman, Sutton (Hastoe) Housing Association, 1975–85; *b* 28 Feb. 1915; *s* of Edward Inkerman Campbell and Florence Annie Campbell. *Educ:* Southbury Road Elementary Sch.; Enfield Central Sch. Asst Sec., 1946–64, Sec., 1964–67, Cooperative Party; Mem., 1967–73, Dep. Chm., 1969–73, Housing Corp. Gen. Manager, Newlon Housing Trust, 1970–76; Chairman: Cooperative Planning Ltd, 1964–74; Co-Ownership Develt Soc. Ltd, 1966–76; Sutton Housing Trust, 1973–80 (Trustee, 1967–86); Dir, Co-op. Housing Centre, and S British Housing Assoc., 1976–78; Dep. Chm., Stevenage Develt Corp., 1968–80; Mem., Cooperative Develt Agency, 1978–81; Pres., Enfield Highway Cooperative Soc. Ltd, 1976–85 (Dir, 1965–85); Dir, CWS Ltd, 1968–73. Chairman: DoE Working Party on Cooperative Housing, 1973–75; DoE Working Group on New Forms of Housing Tenure, 1976–77; Housing Assoc. Registration Adv. Cttee, 1974–79; Hearing Aid Council, 1970–71. Borough Councillor, Enfield, 1959–63. *Recreations:* music, theatre, cinema. *Address:* 31 Epperstone Court, West Bridgford, Nottingham NG2 7QR.

CAMPBELL, Dr Henrietta, CB 2000; FRCP, FRCPGlas, FFPHM; Chief Medical Officer for Northern Ireland, since 1995; *b* 2 Nov. 1948; *d* of Thomas James Hanna and Jean Hanna; *m* 1972, William McBride Campbell; one *s* two *d*. *Educ:* Queen's Univ., Belfast (MD 1998). FFPHM 1996; FRCP 1997; FRCPGlas 2000. GP, NI, 1974–79; civilian medical practitioner, BAOR, 1979–83; SMO, 1983–90, Dep. CMO, 1990–95, Dept of Health and Social Services, NI. *Recreations:* gardening, water-colour painting, hill-walking. *Address:* 1A The Rookery, Killinchy, Co. Down, Northern Ireland BT23 6SY. *T:* (028) 9754 2800.

CAMPBELL, Hugh Hall; QC (Scot.) 1983; FCIArb; *b* 18 Feb. 1944; *s* of William Wright Campbell and Marianne Doris Stuart Hutchison or Campbell; *m* 1969, Eleanor Jane Hare; three *s*. *Educ:* Glasgow Acad.; Trinity Coll., Glenalmond (Alexander Cross Scholar); Exeter Coll., Oxford (Open Scholar in Classics; BA Hons, MA); Edinburgh Univ. (LLB Hons). FCIArb 1986. Called to the Scottish Bar, 1969; Standing Jun. Counsel to Admiralty, 1976. *Recreations:* carnival, wine, music. *Address:* 12 Ainslie Place, Edinburgh EH3 6AS. *T:* (0131) 225 2067. *Club:* Hon. Company of Edinburgh Golfers.

CAMPBELL, Prof. Iain (Donald), PhD; FRS 1995; Professor of Structural Biology, University of Oxford, since 1992; Tutorial Fellow in Biochemistry, St John's College, Oxford, since 1989; *b* 24 April 1941; *s* of Daniel Campbell and Catherine Campbell (*née* Lauder); *m* 1967, Karin C. Wehle; one *s* two *d*. *Educ:* Perth Acad.; St Andrews Univ. (BSc 1963; PhD 1967); MA Oxon 1987. University Lectr, Dept of Biochem., Oxford, 1976–92. Member: Molecular and Cellular Medicine Bd, MRC, 1992–96; Wellcome Trust Molecular Cell Bd, 1997–. Mem., EMBO, 1990. Delegate, OUP, 1996–. Mem., various editl bds of scientific jls. Education in Partnership with Industry Award, DTI, 1982; BDH Medal, Biochem. Soc., 1990. *Publications:* numerous scientific papers and reviews. *Address:* Department of Biochemistry, Oxford University, South Parks Road, Oxford OX1 3QU. *T:* (01865) 275346, *Fax:* (01865) 275253.

CAMPBELL, Ian; JP; *b* 26 April 1926; *s* of William Campbell and Helen Crockett; *m* 1950, Mary Millar; two *s* three *d*. *Educ:* Dumbarton Academy; Royal Technical Coll., Glasgow (now Strathclyde Univ.). Formerly CEng, MIMechE. Engineer with South of Scotland Electricity Board for 17 years. Councillor, Dumbarton, 1958–70; Provost of Dumbarton, 1962–70. MP (Lab): Dunbartonshire W, 1970–83; Dumbarton, 1983–87. PPS to Sec. of State for Scotland, 1976–79. Member: Dumbarton Dist Enterprise Trust, 1987–98; Strathclyde Region Local Valuation Panel, 1988–2000. *Address:* The Shanacles, Gartocharn, Alexandria, Dunbartonshire G83 8NB. *T:* (01389) 752286.

CAMPBELL, Ian Burns; His Honour Judge Ian Campbell; a Circuit Judge, since 1984; Deputy High Representative for Legal Affairs, and Head, Legal Affairs Department, Office of High Representative, Sarajevo, since 2000 (on secondment); *b* 7 July 1938; *s* of late James Campbell and of Laura W. Campbell; *m* 1967, Mary Elisabeth Poole, BArch, MCD Liverpool; two *s* one *d*. *Educ:* Tiffin Boys' Sch.; Cambridge Univ. (MA, LLM, PhD); Diplôme d'Etudes Supérieures de Droit Comparé, Strasbourg, 1964. Called to the Bar, Middle Temple, 1966. French Govt Scholar, Univ. of Paris, 1961–62; Asst Lectr in Law, Liverpool Univ., 1962–64, Lectr 1964–69; a Recorder, 1981–84; Liaison Judge, N and S Sefton Benches, 1988–2000; seconded to Legal Dept, Office of High Rep., Sarajevo, 1999–2000. Mem., Franco-British Judicial Co-operation Cttee, 1996–. Hon. Mem., Albanian Nat. Judicial Conf., 1999–. Hon. Vis. Prof., Liverpool Univ., 1995–. Member, Editorial Board: Liverpool Law Review, 1996–; Judicial Studies Bd Jl, 1996–. *Publications:* (contrib.) Legal Visions of the New Europe, 1993; contrib. legal jls. *Recreation:* journeying.

CAMPBELL, Ian Dugald, FRCPE, FFCM; Treasurer, Royal College of Physicians of Edinburgh, 1981–85; *b* Dornie, Kintail, 22 Feb. 1916; *s* of John Campbell and Margaret Campbell; *m* 1943, Joan Carnegie Osborn; one *s* two *d*. *Educ:* Dingwall Acad.; Edinburgh Univ. (MB, ChB 1939). FRCPE 1973, FFCM 1974. Served War, 1941–46: UK, BAOR, MEF, RAMC; final appt OC Field Amb. (Lt-Col). Med. Supt, St Luke's Hosp., Bradford, 1946–49; Asst SMO, Leeds Reg. Hosp. Bd, 1949–57; Dep. Sen. Admin. MO, S-Eastern Reg. Hosp. Bd, Scotland, 1957–72, Sen. Admin. MO, 1972–73; Chief Admin. MO, Lothian Health Bd, 1973–80. QHP 1977–80. WHO assignments, SE Asia, 1969, 1971, 1975. *Publications:* various medical. *Recreations:* fishing, shooting, golf. *Address:* 5 Succoth Park, Edinburgh EH12 6BX. *T:* (0131) 539 5965. *Clubs:* New (Edinburgh); Hon. Company of Edinburgh Golfers (Muirfield). *Address:* Royal Burgess Golfing Society (Barnton, Edinburgh).

CAMPBELL, Ian H.; *see* Hay-Campbell.

CAMPBELL, Ian James; Director General Research Maritime, Ministry of Defence, 1978–81; *b* 9 June 1923; *s* of Allan and Elizabeth Campbell; *m* 1946, Stella Margaret Smith (*d* 2001). *Educ:* George Heriot's Sch.; Edinburgh Univ. (MA Hons, Maths and Natural Phil.). Op. Res. Sect., HQ Bomber Comd, 1943–46; Asst Lectr in Astronomy, St Andrews Univ., 1946–48; joined Royal Naval Scientific Service, 1948; Dept of Aeronaut. and Eng Res., Admiralty, 1948–49; Admiralty Res. Lab., 1949–59; Admiralty Underwater Weapons Estab., 1959–68 (leader of res. team which established concept and technol. base for Stingray torpedo, 1962–68); Chief Scientist, Naval Construction Res. Estab., 1969–73; Head of Weapons Dept, Admiralty Underwater Weapons Estab., 1973–76; Ministry of Defence: Dir of Res. (Ships), 1976–78; Scientific Advr to Ship Dept, 1976–81. Defence sci. consultant, 1982–92; Technical Dir, CAP Scientific, 1983–87; Dir of Studies, Centre for Operational Res. and Defence Analysis, 1987–88. Chm., Res. Adv. Cttee, Electronic Engrg Assoc., 1989–91. *Publications:* papers on fluid mechanics in scientific jls. *Address:* 6 Queens Avenue, Dorchester, Dorset DT1 2EW. *T:* (01305) 264270. *Club:* Sloane.

CAMPBELL, Air Vice-Marshal Ian Robert, CB 1976; CBE 1964; AFC 1948; *b* 5 Oct. 1920; *s* of late Major and Hon. Mrs D. E. Campbell; *m* 1st, 1953, Beryl Evelyn Newbigging (*d* 1982); one *s*; 2nd, 1984, Elisabeth Lingard-Guthrie. *Educ:* Eton; RAF Coll., Cranwell. Anti-Shipping Ops, 1940–42; POW, Italy and Germany, 1942–45; 540 Sqdn, Benson, 1946; psa 1949; PSO to C-in-C Far East, 1950; 124 (F) Wing Oldenburg, 1953; OC, RAF Sandwich, 1956; pfc 1957; OC 213 Sqdn, Bruggen, 1958; ACOS Plans HQ 2ATAF, 1959; OC, RAF Marham, 1961; MoD (Air) DASB, 1964; SASO, HQ No 1 Group, 1965; Air Attaché, Bonn, 1968; Dir of Management and Support Intell., MoD, 1970–73; C of S, No 18 (M) Group, Strike Command, 1973–75, retired. *Recreations:* shooting, travel. *Address:* Pike Farm, Fossebridge, Cheltenham, Glos GL54 3JR. *Clubs:* Boodle's, Royal Air Force.

CAMPBELL, Sir Ian (Tofts), Kt 1988; CBE 1984; VRD 1961; JP; Director, Conservative Board of Finance, 1978–90; Director of Finance and Administration, Scottish Conservative Party, 1988–90; *b* 3 Feb. 1923; *o s* of John Walter Campbell and Mary Hardie Campbell (*née* Scott); *m* 1961, Marion Kirkhope Paterson (*née* Shiel); one *d*. *Educ:* Daniel Stewart's College, Edinburgh. FInstD 1964. RN 1942–46, RNR 1946–65 (Comdr). Man. Dir, MacGregor Wallcoverings, 1966–78. Chm., Select Assured Properties, Glasgow, 1989–96; Dep. Chm., Heath (Scotland) Ltd, 1988–95 (Dir, 1987–96; consultant, 1996–2000); Director: Travel System, 1987–89; Hermiston Securities, 1990–. Mem., Transport Users' Cons. Cttee for Scotland, 1981–87. Councillor, City of Edinburgh District Council, 1984–88. JP Edinburgh, 1987. Freeman, City of Glasgow, 1992. OStJ 1987. KLJ 1984. *Recreations:* golf, water colour painting, vintage cars. *Address:* Merleton, 10 Boswall Road, Edinburgh EH5 3RH. *T:* (0131) 552 4825. *Club:* New (Edinburgh).

CAMPBELL of Succoth, Sir Ilay (Mark), 7th Bt *cr* 1808, of Succoth, Dunbartonshire; *b* 29 May 1927; *o s* of Sir George Ilay Campbell, 6th Bt; *S* father, 1967; *m* 1961, Margaret Minette Rohais, *o d* of J. Alasdair Anderson; two *d*. *Educ:* Eton; Christ Church, Oxford. BA 1952; MA 1970. Chm., Christie's Scotland, 1978–96. Dir., High Craigton Farming Co. Member: Historic Buildings Council for Scotland, 1989–98; Gardens Cttee, Nat. Trust for Scotland, 1994–. Pres., Assoc. for Protection of Rural Scotland, 1978–90. Mem., C of S Cttee for Artistic Matters, 1984–91 (Covener, 1987–91); Convener, Church Bldgs Renewal Trust, Glasgow, 1995–98. Hon. Vice Pres., Scotland's Gardens Scheme, 1960–; Trustee, Crarae Gardens Charitable Trust, 1978–. *Recreations:* heraldry, collecting heraldic bookplates, horticulture. *Heir:* none. *Address:* Crarae Lodge, Inveraray, Argyll PA32 8YA. *T:* (01546) 886274, *Fax:* (01546) 886262. *Club:* Turf.

See also Sir Gregor MacGregor of MacGregor, Bt.

CAMPBELL, Prof. James, FBA 1984; FSA 1971; Professor of Medieval History, University of Oxford, 1996–Sept. 2002; Fellow of Worcester College, Oxford, since 1957; *b* 26 Jan. 1935. *Educ:* Mill Road Mixed Infants, Clowne, Derbyshire and other primary schools; Lowestoft Grammar School; Magdalen College (Exhibitioner; BA 1955, MA). Oxford University: Junior Research Fellow, Merton College, 1956–57; Tutorial Fellow, 1957, Fellow Librarian, 1977–Sept. 2002, Sen. Tutor, 1989–93, Worcester College; Lectr in Modern History, 1958–90; Reader in Medieval History, 1990–96; Senior Proctor, 1973–74. Visiting Professor: Univ. of South Carolina, 1969; Univ. of Rochester, 1986–87. Creighton Lectr, Univ. of London, 1995; Ford's Lectr, Univ. of Oxford, 1996. *Publications:* Norwich, 1975; (ed) The Anglo-Saxons, 1982; Essays in Anglo-Saxon History, 1986; The Anglo-Saxon State, 2000; articles in learned jls. *Recreation:* topography. *Address:* Worcester College, Oxford OX1 2HB. *T:* (01865) 278340; 9 The Willows, Newland Mill, Witney, Oxon OX8 6HN. *Club:* Oxford and Cambridge.

CAMPBELL, James Alastair G.; *see* Graham-Campbell.

CAMPBELL, Sir James (Alexander Moffat Bain), 9th Bt *cr* 1667, of Aberuchill, Perthshire; independent insurance consultant, since 2001; *b* 23 Sept. 1956; *er s* of Sir Colin Campbell, 8th Bt and of Mary Campbell (*née* Bain); *S* father, 1997; *m* 1993, Carola Jane Denman; one *s* two *d*. *Educ:* Stowe. Scots Guards (Capt.), 1975–83. Motorcycle despatch rider, 1984; insurance broker: Bain Dawes Ltd, Bain Clarkson plc, Bain Hogg plc, Aon Corp., 1984–97; R. K. Harrison Ltd, 1997. *Recreations:* shooting, trees, gardening. *Heir:* *s* Colin George Denman Bain Campbell, *b* 1 Oct. 1999. *Address:* Kilbryde Castle, Dunblane, Perthshire FK15 9NF. *T:* (01786) 824897.

CAMPBELL, James Hugh; Consultant, Bird Semple Fyfe Ireland, WS, Glasgow, Edinburgh and London, 1991–93; *b* 13 Nov. 1926; *s* of William Campbell and Agnes Wightman Campbell; *m* 1953, Iris Burnside (*née* Hercus); two *s* one *d*. *Educ:* Univ. of Glasgow, 1944–45 and 1948–50 (BL). Service in RAF, Japan, 1946–48. Solicitor; Partner, Bird Son & Semple, 1952–73, Sen. Partner, 1965–73; Sen. Partner, Bird Semple & Crawford Herron, subseq. Bird Semple Fyfe Ireland, 1973–91. President: Glasgow Juridical Soc., 1951–52; Law Soc. of Scotland, 1991–92 (Mem. Council, 1986–95; Vice-Pres., 1990–91). Hon. Mem., Royal Faculty of Procurators, Glasgow, 1997. Deacon, Incorp. of Wrights, Glasgow, 1980–81. *Recreations:* music, reading, golf. *Address:* 24 Woodvale Avenue, Giffnock, Glasgow G46 6RQ. *T:* (0141) 638 2630. *Clubs:* Royal Scottish Automobile, Western (Glasgow); Glasgow Golf, East Renfrewshire Golf.

CAMPBELL, Jim; *see* Campbell, R. J.

CAMPBELL, John Davies, CVO 1980; CBE 1981 (MBE 1957); MC 1945, and bar 1945; company director; HM Diplomatic Service, retired; Consul-General, Naples, 1977–81; *b* 11 Nov. 1921; *s* of late William Hastings Campbell and of late The Hon. Mrs Campbell (Eugenie Anne Westenra, subsequently Harbord), *d* of 14th Baron Louth; *m* 1959, Shirley Bouch; one *s* two *d*. *Educ:* Cheltenham Coll.; St Andrews Univ. Served War, HM Forces, Argyll and Sutherland Highlanders and Popski's Private Army, 1940–46. HM Colonial Service (subseq. HMOCS), 1949–61 (despatches, 1957); HM Foreign (subseq. HM Diplomatic) Service, 1961; First Secretary, 1961; Counsellor, 1972; Counsellor (Information) Ottawa, 1972–77. Commendatore dell'ordine al merito della Repubblica Italiana, 1980. *Recreations:* travel, walking. *Address:* Townsend House, Luston, Leominster, Herefordshire HR6 0DZ. *T:* (01568) 612446. *Clubs:* Special Forces; Muthaiga Country (Nairobi) (Life Mem.); Mombasa.

CAMPBELL, Prof. John Joseph, DPhil; Wilde Professor of Mental Philosophy, University of Oxford, since 2001; Fellow, Corpus Christi College, Oxford, since 2001; *b* 2 Nov. 1956; *s* of Roderick Campbell and Catriona (*née* MacKinnon); *m* 1978, Patricia Carrol (marr. diss. 1986). *Educ:* Univ. of Stirling (BA); Univ. of Calgary (MA); Wolfson Coll., Oxford (BPhil, DPhil 1986). University of Oxford: Res. Lectr, Christ Church, 1983–86; Fellow and Tutor in Philosophy, New Coll., 1986–2001; British Acad. Res.

Reader, 1995–97; Reader in Philosophy, 1997–2001. Visiting posts at: UCLA, 1998; Univ. of Cambridge, 1990–91; ANU 1991–92; Cornell Univ., 1998. *Publication:* Past, Space and Self, 1994. *Recreations:* gardening, country pubs. *Address:* Corpus Christi College, Oxford OX1 4JP. *T:* (01865) 276700.

CAMPBELL, (John) Quentin; His Honour Judge Quentin Campbell; a Circuit Judge, since 1996; *b* 5 March 1939; *s* of late John McKnight Campbell, OBE, MC, and late Katharine Margaret Campbell; *m* 1st, Penelope Jane Redman (marr. diss. 1976); three *s* one *d*; 2nd, 1977, Ann Rosemary Beeching, DL, a District Judge; one *s* one *d*. *Educ:* Loretto Sch., Musselburgh, Scotland; Wadham Coll., Oxford (MA). Admitted as Solicitor, 1965; private practice, Linnell & Murphy, Oxford (Partner, 1968–80); Metropolitan Stipendiary Magistrate, 1981–96; a Recorder, 1989–96. A Pres., Mental Health Review Tribunals, 1996–; Mem., Parole Bd, 2000–. Chairman, Bd of Governors, Bessels Leigh Sch., near Oxford, 1979–96. *Recreations:* opera, gardening. *Address:* The Crown Court, Inner London Sessions House, Newington Causeway, SE1 6AZ. *T:* (020) 7234 3100. *Clubs:* Travellers; Frewen (Oxford).

CAMPBELL, Juliet Jeanne d'Auvergne, CMG 1988; HM Diplomatic Service, retired; Mistress of Girton College, Cambridge, 1992–98, now Life Fellow; Deputy Vice-Chancellor, Cambridge University, 1993–98; *b* 23 May 1935; *d* of Maj.-Gen. Wilfred d'Auvergne Collings, CB, CBE and of Nancy Draper Bishop; *m* 1983, Prof. Alexander Elmslie Campbell, *qv*. *Educ:* a variety of schools; Lady Margaret Hall, Oxford (BA; Hon. Fellow, 1992). Joined Foreign Office 1957; Common Market Delegation, Brussels, 1961–63; FO, 1963–64; Second, later First Secretary, Bangkok, 1964–66; News Dept, FO, 1967–70; Head of Chancery, The Hague, 1970–74; European Integration Dept, FCO, 1974–77; Counsellor (Inf.), Paris, 1977–80; RCDS, 1981; Counsellor, Jakarta, 1982–83; Head of Training Dept, FCO, 1984–87; Ambassador to Luxembourg, 1988–91. Member: Cambridge Univ. Council of Senate (later Council), 1993–97; Wilton Park Academic Council, 1993–2000. Trustee: Changing Faces, 1992–; Cambridge European Trust, 1994–98; Kurt Hahn Trust, 1995–98; Cambridge Overseas Trust, 1995–98; Henry Fellowships, 1997–. Governor: Queen's Coll., Harley St, 1992–; Marlborough Coll., 1999–. *Address:* 3 Belbroughton Road, Oxford OX2 6UZ. *Club:* Oxford and Cambridge.

CAMPBELL, Air Vice-Marshal Kenneth Archibald, CB 1989; consulting engineer; Air Officer Maintenance, RAF Support Command, 1987–89; *b* 3 May 1936; *s* of John McLean and Christina Campbell; *m* 1959, Isobel Love Millar; two *d*. *Educ:* George Heriot's Sch.; Glasgow Univ. (BSc); College of Aeronautics, Cranfield (MSc). Various engrg appts, RAF, 1959–90; Air Officer, Wales, 1977–79; Dir, Engrg Policy (RAF), 1981–83; AO, Engrg and Supply, RAF Germany, 1983–85; DG Personal Services (RAF), 1985–87. *Recreations:* golf, skiing. *Club:* Royal Air Force.

CAMPBELL, Rt Hon. Kim; PC (Canada) 1989; QC (BC) 1990; Canadian Consul General, Los Angeles (California, Utah, Nevada, Hawaii, Guam), since 1996; *b* 10 March 1947. *Educ:* Univ. of British Columbia (BA 1969; LLB 1983); LSE (Hon. Fellow, 1994). Called to the Bar of BC, 1984. Lectr in Pol Sci., Univ. of BC, 1975–78; Lectr in Pol Sci. and Hist., Vancouver Community Coll., 1978–81; Articled student, 1983–84, Associate, Gen. Litigation, 1984–85, Ladner Downs Vancouver; Exec. Dir, Office of Premier of BC, 1985–86; MLA Vancouver Point Grey, 1986–88; MP (PC) Vancouver Centre, 1988–93; Minister of State, Indian Affairs and Northern Develt, 1989–90; Minister of Justice and Attorney Gen., 1990–93; Minister of Nat. Defence and Minister of Veterans' Affairs, 1993; Prime Minister of Canada, 1993. Fellow, John F. Kennedy Sch. of Govt, Harvard Univ., 1994. Dir, KPMG Centre for Govt Foundn, 1996. Mem. Vis. Cttee, Center for Internat. Affairs, Harvard Univ., 1995–; Sen. Fellow, Sch. of Public Policy and Social Res., UCLA, 1998–. *Publication:* Time and Chance (memoirs), 1996.

CAMPBELL, Sir Lachlan (Philip Kemeys), 6th Bt *cr* 1815; *b* 9 Oct. 1958; *e s* of Col Sir Guy Campbell, 5th Bt, OBE, MC and of Lizbeth Webb, *d* of late Frederick Holton; *S* father, 1993; *m* 1986, Harriet Jane Sarah, *o d* of F. E. J. Girling; two *s* one *d*. *Educ:* Temple Grove; Eton; RMA Sandhurst. The Royal Greenjackets (Lieut); served NI. *Recreations:* golf, Rugby, cricket, painting. *Heir: s* Archibald Edward FitzGerald Campbell, *b* 13 June 1990. *Address:* 32 Malwood Road, SW12 8EN. *Clubs:* Army and Navy, Royal Greenjackets, MCC; London Scottish Golf and Rugby.

CAMPBELL, Rev. Laurence Jamieson; Methodist Minister, supernumerary; Minister, Trinity Church, Newport, Gwent Circuit, 1987–94; *b* 10 June 1927; *er s* of George S. Campbell and Mary P. Paterson; *m* 1954, Sheena E. Macdonald; two *s* one *d*. *Educ:* Hillhead High Sch., Glasgow; Aberdeen Univ., Edinburgh Univ. (MA). Lieut RA, 1945–48. Housemaster, Alliance High Sch., Kenya, 1952–56; Presbyterian Church of E Africa, 1957–61: Tumutumu Coll., 1957–60; Supervisor of Schs, 1960–61; Educn Sec., Christian Council of Kenya, 1962; Headmaster: Alliance High Sch., Kenya, 1963–70; Kingswood Sch., Bath, 1970–87. Methodist minister, ordained 1988. Contested North Kenya Constituency, Kenya General Election, 1961. Mem. Council, Univ. of East Africa, 1963–69; Chm., Heads Assoc. of Kenya, 1965–69; Official of Kenya Commonwealth Games Team, 1970. Schoolmaster Fellow, Balliol Coll., Oxford, 1970. Chairman: Christians Abroad, 1977–81; Bloxham Project, 1981–84. *Recreations:* golf, athletics, church. *Address:* 1A Edward VII Avenue, Newport, Gwent NP9 4NF.

CAMPBELL, Rt Hon. Menzies; *see* Campbell, Rt Hon. W. M.

CAMPBELL, Sir Niall (Alexander Hamilton), 8th Bt *cr* 1831, of Barcaldine and Glenure; 15th Chieftain, Hereditary Keeper of Barcaldine Castle; Clerk to Justices of N Devon Divisions of Barnstaple, Bideford and Great Torrington and South Molton, 1976–90; *b* 7 Jan. 1925; *o s* of Sir Ian Vincent Hamilton Campbell, 7th Bt, CB, and Madeline Lowe Reid (*d* 1929), *e d* of late Hugh Anglin Whitelocke, FRCS; *S* father, 1978; *m* 1st, 1949, Patricia Mary (marr. diss. on his petition, 1956), *d* of R. G. Turner; 2nd, 1957, Norma Joyce, *d* of W. N. Wiggin; two *s* one *d* (including twin *s* and *d*) (and one *d* decd). *Educ:* Cheltenham College (Scholar); Corpus Christi Coll., Oxford. Called to the Bar, Inner Temple. Served War, 1943–46, Lieut Royal Marines; in Inf. bn, NW Europe campaign and on staff of Comdr RM training bde. Appts as Hosp. Administrator, 1953–70, inside and outside NHS, including St Mary's, Paddington, London Clinic, and Royal Hosp. and Home for Incurables, Putney (Chief Exec.); Dep. Chief Clerk, Inner London Magistrates' Courts, 1970–76, and Dep. Coroner, Inner London (South), Southwark. Mem. Exec. Cttee, N Devon Community Health Council; Governor, Grenville Coll., Bideford; Mem. Management Cttee, N Devon Cheshire Home. *Publication:* Making the Best Use of Bed Resources—monograph based on lecture sponsored by King Edward's Hospital Fund, 1965. *Recreations:* garden labour; writing letters to the Times, with little success; keeping a golden retriever; birds. *Heir: er s* Roderick Duncan Hamilton Campbell, of Barcaldine, Younger [*b* 24 Feb. 1961; *m* 1989, Jean Caroline, *d* of Laurie Bicknell, Braunton, Devon; two *d*]. *Address:* (seat) Barcaldine Castle, Ledaig, Oban, Argyllshire PA37 1SA. *Club:* Marshalls (Barnstaple).

CAMPBELL, Niall Gordon; Under Secretary, Civil and Criminal Law Group, Scottish Executive Justice (formerly Scottish Office Home) Department, since 1997; *b* 9 Nov. 1941; *s* of Ian M. Campbell and Jean G. Sanderson; *m* 1975, Alison Margaret Rigg; three *s*. *Educ:* Edinburgh Academy; Merton College, Oxford (BA). Entered Scottish Office, 1964; Asst Sec., 1978; posts in Scottish Educn and Scottish Develt Depts; Under Sec., Social Work Services Gp, SHHD, then Scottish Office Home Dept, 1989–97. *Address:* 15 Warriston Crescent, Edinburgh EH3 5LA. *T:* (0131) 556 2895.

CAMPBELL, Nicholas Charles Wilson; QC 2000; a Recorder, since 2000; *b* 8 May 1954; *s* of late Prof. Wilson William Campbell and of Pearl Campbell (*née* Ackrill); *m* 1987, Hon. Nicole Montagu. *Educ:* King's Sch., Canterbury; Trinity Coll., Cambridge (BA). Called to the Bar, Inner Temple, 1978. *Address:* 11 King's Bench Walk, EC4Y 7EQ. *T:* (020) 7353 3337.

CAMPBELL, Maj.-Gen. Peter; *see* Campbell, Maj.-Gen. C. P.

CAMPBELL, Prof. Peter Nelson; Courtauld Professor of Biochemistry, and Director of the Courtauld Institute, Middlesex Hospital Medical School, London University, 1976–87, now Emeritus Professor; Editor in Chief, Biotechnology and Applied Biochemistry, 1981–95; *b* 5 Nov. 1921; *s* of late Alan A. Campbell and Nora Nelson; *m* 1946, Mollie (*née* Manklow); one *s* one *d* (and one *s* decd). *Educ:* Eastbourne Coll.; Univ. Coll. London (Fellow, 1981). BSc, PhD, DSc, London; FIBiol. Research and Production Chemist with Standard Telephones and Cables, Ltd, 1942–46; PhD Student, UCL; 1946–47; Asst Lectr UCL, 1947–49; staff of Nat. Inst. for Med. Research, Hampstead and Mill Hill, 1949–54; Asst, Courtauld Inst. of Biochem., Middx Hosp. Med. Sch., 1954–57; Sen. Lectr, Middx Hosp. Med. Sch., 1957–64; Reader in Biochem., Univ. of London, 1964–67; Prof. and Head of Dept of Biochem., Leeds Univ., 1967–75. Hon. Consulting Chemical Pathologist to Middlesex Hosp., 1987–. Butland Vis. Prof., Univ. of Auckland, 1988. Chm., Assoc. of Researchers in Medicine and Sci., 1987–95. Hon. Lectr, Dept of Biochem., UCL, 1954–67. Hon. Mem., Biochemical Soc., 1988. Convenor, FEBS Scientific Apparatus Recycling Scheme, 1990–. Foreign Mem., Lithuanian Acad. of Scis. Diplôme d'Honneur, FEBS, 1981; Dist. Service Award, IUBMB, 2000. *Publications:* Structure and Function of Animal Cell Components, 1966; (ed with B. A. Kilby) Basic Biochemistry for Medical Students, 1975; (ed) Biology in Profile, 1981; (with A. D. Smith) Biochemistry Illustrated, 1982, 4th edn 2000; (ed) Oxford Dictionary of Biochemistry and Molecular Biology, 1997, rev. edn 2000; many scientific papers in Biochem. Jl. *Recreations:* theatre, travelling, conversation. *Address:* Department of Biochemistry and Molecular Biology, University College London, WC1E 6BT. *T:* (020) 7679 2169; *e-mail:* pcampbell@biochemistry.ucl.ac.uk.

CAMPBELL, Prof. Peter (Walter); Professor of Politics, Reading University, 1964–91, now Emeritus; *b* 17 June 1926; *o s* of late W. C. H. and L. M. Campbell. *Educ:* Bournemouth Sch.; New Coll., Oxford. 2nd class PPE, 1947; MA 1951; Research Student, Nuffield Coll., Oxford, 1947–49. Asst Lecturer in Govt, Manchester Univ., 1949–52; Lectr, 1952–60; Vice-Warden Needham Hall, 1959–60; Visiting Lectr in Political Science, Victoria Univ. Coll., NZ, 1954; Prof. of Political Economy, 1960–64, Dean, Faculty of Letters, 1966–69, Chm., Graduate Sch. of Contemporary European Studies, 1971–73, Reading University. Hon. Sec. Political Studies Assoc., 1955–58; Chm., Inst. of Electoral Research, 1959–65; Mem. Council, Hansard Soc. for Parly Govt, 1962–77; Editor of Political Studies, 1963–69; Hon. Treas., Joint Univ. Council for Social and Public Administration, 1965–69; Chm., Reading Romilly Assoc., 1965–69; Vice-Chm., Reading and District Council of Social Service, 1966–71; Vice-Pres., Electoral Reform Soc., 1972–97; Mem., Nat. Cttee for Electoral Reform, 1976–93; Trustee, Ballot Services (ERS) Ltd, 1988–92; Hon. Treas., CAER, 1990–94. Member: Adv. Panel, Commonwealth Scholarship Commn, 1964–73; Political Science Cttee, SSRC, 1968–72; CNAA Bds and Panels, 1971–78; Social Studies Sub-Cttee, UGC, 1973–83. Co-Pres., Reading Univ. Cons. Assoc., 1961–91. Mem. Council, Campaign for Homosexual Equality, 1978–79; Convenor, Reading CHE, 1979–80; Mem. Council of Management, Albany Soc., 1988–91; Vice-Pres., Cons. Gp for Homosexual Equality, 1988–91 (Chm., 1982–88); Chm., Exec. Cttee, Soc. for Individual Freedom, 1992–93; Trustee, Civic Educn and Res. Trust, 1993–95. Patron, Univ. of Buckingham, 1984–. *Publications:* (with W. Theimer) Encyclopædia of World Politics, 1950; French Electoral Systems and Elections, 1789–1957, 1958; (with B. Chapman) The Constitution of the Fifth Republic, 1958. Articles in British, French and New Zealand Jls of Political Science. *Recreations:* ambling, idling. *Address:* 6 Treyarnon Court, 37 Eastern Avenue, Reading RG1 5RX. *T:* (0118) 966 1888. *Clubs:* Athenæum, Oxford and Cambridge.

CAMPBELL, Philip Henry Montgomery, PhD; Editor, Nature, since 1995; Editor in Chief, Nature Publications, since 1995; *b* 19 April 1951; *s* of Hugh and Mary Montgomery Campbell; *m* 1980, Judie Yelton (*d* 1992); two *s*. *Educ:* Shrewsbury Sch.; Bristol Univ. (BSc Aeronautical Engrg 1972); Queen Mary Coll., Univ. of London (MSc Astrophysics 1974); Leicester Univ. (PhD Ionospheric Physics 1978). FInstP 1995. Res., Leicester Univ., 1977–79; Asst Editor, 1979–82, Physical Scis Editor, 1982–88, Nature; Founding Editor, Physics World, 1988–95. Dir, Nature Publishing Gp, 1997–. Broadcasts on BBC World Service. FRAS 1979. Hon. DSc Leicester, 1999. *Publications:* papers and articles in learned jls, magazines and newspapers. *Recreation:* music. *Address:* Nature, 4 Crinan Street, N1 9XW. *T:* (020) 7833 4000.

CAMPBELL, Quentin; *see* Campbell, J. Q.

CAMPBELL, Robert, MSc; FICE; management consultant; Chairman and Chief Executive, Rem Campbell Management Ltd, 1987–2000; *b* 18 May 1929; *s* of Robert Stewart Campbell and Isobella Frances Campbell; *m* 1950, Edna Maud Evans. *Educ:* Emmanuel IGS; Loughborough Univ. (DLC (Hons), MSc). MIWES. Member of Gray's Inn, 1960. Contracts Engineer, Wyatts, Contractors, 1954–56; Chief Asst Engr, Stirlingshire and Falkirk Water Board, 1956–59; Water Engr, Camborne, 1959–60; Chief Asst City Water Engr, Plymouth, 1960–65; Civil Engr, Colne Valley Water Co., 1965–69; Engrg Inspector, Min. of Housing and Local Govt/DoE, 1969–74; Asst Dir, Resources, Planning, Anglian Water Authority, 1974–77; Chief Executive, Epping Forest Dist Council, 1977–79; Sec., ICE, 1979–81, and Man. Dir, Thomas Telford Ltd, Dir, Watt Cttee on Energy, and Hon. Sec., ICE Benevolent Fund, 1979–81; Chm., Rem Campbell Internat., 1981–87. Freeman of City of London, 1977; Liveryman of Horners' Co., 1977–. *Publication:* The Pricing of Water, 1973. *Recreations:* golf, music, caravanning, cricket. *Address:* Bronafon, Pen-y-Banc, Llechryd, near Cardigan, Dyfed SA43 2NR. *Club:* MCC.

CAMPBELL, Prof. Robert James, (Jim); Professor of Education, since 1992, and Director, Institute of Education, since 1996, University of Warwick; *b* 19 Dec. 1938; *s* of William Campbell and Elsie Campbell (*née* O'Connor); *m* 1st, 1964, Jennifer Rhodes (marr. diss. 1970); 2nd, 1972, Sarah Miranda Frankland; two *d*. *Educ:* Hull Univ. (BA Upper 2nd Cl. Classics 1959; PGCE 1960); Bradford Univ. (MSc Educnl Res. 1971). Teacher: Westgate Primary Sch., Newcastle upon Tyne, 1959; Nettleswell Comprehensive Sch., Harlow, 1960–62; Mkt Res. Officer, Mkt Res. Associates, London, 1962–63; Teacher, Latton Bush Comprehensive Sch., Harlow, 1963–64; Lectr, W Suffolk Coll. of Further Educn, Bury St Edmunds, 1964–67; Res. Student, Univ. of Bradford,

1967–68; Res. Officer, Curriculum Res. Unit, Inst. of Educn, Univ. of London, 1968–70; Lectr, Coventry Coll. of Educn, 1970–78; University of Warwick: Lectr, 1978–86; Sen. Lectr, 1986–89; Reader, 1989–92. FRSA 1998. Phi Delta Kappa, 1974. *Publications:* Developing the Primary School Curriculum, 1985; Humanities in the Primary School, 1989; Breadth and Balance in the Primary School Curriculum, 1991; Primary Teachers at Work, 1994; Secondary Teachers at Work, 1994; The Meaning of Infant Teachers' Work, 1994; Curriculum Reform at Key Stage 1: teacher commitment and policy failure, 1994; contrib. numerous articles to jls. *Recreations:* wine, whisky, women, jazz. *Address:* Institute of Education, University of Warwick, Coventry CV4 7AL. *T:* (024) 7652 3850.

CAMPBELL, Sir Robin Auchinbreck, 15th Bt *cr* 1628 (NS); *b* 7 June 1922; *s* of Sir Louis Hamilton Campbell, 14th Bt and Margaret Elizabeth Patricia (*d* 1985), *d* of late Patrick Campbell; *S* father, 1970; *m* 1st, 1948, Rosemary, (Sally) (*d* 1978), *d* of Ashley Dean, Christchurch, NZ; one *s* two *d*; 2nd, 1978, Mrs Elizabeth Gunston, *d* of Sir Arthur Colegate, Bembridge, IoW. Formerly Lieut (A) RNVR. *Heir: s* Louis Auchinbreck Campbell [*b* 17 Jan. 1953; *m* 1976, Fiona Mary St Clair, *d* of Gordon King; two *d*]. *Address:* 287A Waikawa Road, Picton, New Zealand.

CAMPBELL, Ronald, (Ronnie); MP (Lab) Blyth Valley, since 1987; *b* 14 Aug. 1943; *m* 1967, Deirdre (*née* McHale); five *s* one *d*. *Educ:* Ridley High Sch., Blyth. Miner, 1958–86. Member: Blyth Borough Council, 1969–74; Blyth Valley Council, 1974–88 (Chm., Environmental Health Cttee; Vice-Chm., Housing Cttee). Mem., NUM. *Address:* 68 Broadway, Blyth, Northumberland NE24 2PR; House of Commons, SW1A 0AA.

CAMPBELL, Ross, DSC 1944; President, InterCon Consultants Ltd, Ottawa, since 1996 (Senior Partner, 1983–96); *b* 4 Nov. 1918; *s* of late William Marshall Campbell and of Helen Isabel Harris; *m* 1945, Penelope Grantham-Hill; two *s*. *Educ:* Univ. of Toronto Schs; Trin. Coll., Univ. of Toronto. BA, Faculty of Law, 1940. Served RCN, 1940–45. Joined Dept. of Ext. Affairs, Canada, 1945; Third Sec., Oslo, 1946–47; Second Sec., Copenhagen, 1947–50; European Div., Ottawa, 1950–52; First Sec., Ankara, 1952–56; Head of Middle East Div., Ottawa, 1957–59; Special Asst to Sec. of State for Ext. Aff., 1959–62; Asst Under-Sec. of State for Ext. Aff., 1962–64; Adviser to Canadian Delegns to: UN Gen. Assemblies, 1958–63; North Atlantic Coun., 1959–64; Ambassador to Yugoslavia, 1964–67, concurrently accredited Ambassador to Algeria, 1965–67; Ambassador and Perm. Rep. to NATO, 1967–73 (Paris May 1967, Brussels Oct. 1967); Ambassador to Japan, 1973–75, and concurrently to Republic of Korea, 1973. Chm., Atomic Energy of Canada Ltd, 1976–79; President: Atomic Energy of Canada International, 1979–80; Canus Technical Services Corp., Ottawa, 1981–83; Dir, Adopac Ltd, 1992–. *Recreation:* gardening. *Address:* Rivermead House, 890 Aylmer Road, Aylmer, QC J9H 5T8, Canada; (office) Suite 1610, 350 Albert Street, Ottawa K1R 1A4, Canada. *Club:* Rideau (Ottawa).

CAMPBELL, Dr Simon Fraser, FRS 1999; FRSC; Senior Vice-President, Worldwide Discovery and Medicinals R&D Europe, Pfizer Central Research, 1996–98; Director and Board Member, Pfizer Ltd, 1996–98, retired; *b* 27 March 1941; *s* of William Fraser Campbell and Ellen Mary Campbell; *m* 1966, Jill Lewis; two *s*. *Educ:* Birmingham Univ. (BSc 1st Cl. Hons 1962; PhD 1965). FRSC 1985. Postdoctoral Fellow: Univ. Tecnica Santa Maria, Valparaiso, 1966–67; Stanford Univ., Calif, 1968–70; Vis. Prof., Univ. do São Paulo, 1970–72; joined Pfizer Central Research, Sandwich, 1972: staff chemist, 1972–78; Manager, 1978–83, Dir, 1983–92, Discovery Chemistry; Gp Dir, 1992–93, Vice-Pres., 1993–96, Medicinals Discovery. Visiting Professor: Birkbeck Coll., Univ. of London, 1987–90; Univ. of Leeds, 1996–99. Chm., WHO Expert Scientific Adv. Cttee for Medicine, 1999–. Jt-Ed., Current Opinion in Drug Discovery and Develt, 1998–. Member: Acad. Adv. Bd, Dept of Chem., Bristol Univ., 1998–2001; Council, Univ. of Kent, 1999–. Award for Medicinal Chem., RSC, 1989; E. B. Hershberg Award, ACS, 1997; Achievement Award, Industrial Res. Inst. (US), 1997. *Publications:* contribs to learned jls; patents. *Recreations:* gardening, travel, wine, active sports player.

CAMPBELL, Hon. Sir Walter (Benjamin), AC 1989; Kt 1979; QC (Qld) 1960; Governor of Queensland, Australia, 1985–92; *b* 4 March 1921; *s* of Archie Eric Gordon Campbell and Leila Mary Campbell; *m* 1942, Georgina Margaret Pearce; one *s* one *d* (and one *s* decd). *Educ:* Univ. of Queensland (MA, LLB; Hon. LLD 1980). Served War, RAAF, 1941–46 (pilot). Called to the Qld Bar, 1948; Judge, Supreme Court, Qld, 1967; Chief Justice, Qld, 1982–85. Chairman: Law Reform Commn of Qld, 1969–73; Remuneration Tribunal (Commonwealth), 1974–82; sole Mem., Academic Salaries Tribunal (Commonwealth), 1974–78. President: Qld Bar Assoc., 1965–67; Australian Bar Assoc., 1966–67; Mem. Exec., Law Council of Aust., 1965–67. Dir, Winston Churchill Meml Trust, 1969–80; Chm., Utah Foundn, 1977–85. Mem. Senate 1963–85, and Chancellor 1977–85, Univ. of Qld. Hon. Life Vice Pres., Aircrew Assoc. (UK), 1993. Trustee, Gowrie Scholarship Trust Fund, 1984–. Patron, Soc. of St Andrew of Scotland, 1986–. Fellow Aust. Inst. Judicial Admin., 1986. KStJ 1986. Freeman, City of London, 1987; Liveryman, GAPAN, 1988. Hon. DLitt James Cook Univ., 1988; DUniv: Queensland Univ. of Technology, 1991; Griffith Univ., 1992. *Recreations:* golf, reading. *Address:* 6 Dennison Street, Ascot, Brisbane, Qld 4007, Australia. *Clubs:* Queensland, Brisbane (Hon. Life Mem.), United Service (Hon. Life Mem.), Royal Queensland Golf (Brisbane); Australasian Pioneers (Sydney).

CAMPBELL, Rt Hon. (Walter) Menzies, CBE 1987; PC 1999; QC (Scot.) 1982; MP Fife North East, since 1987 (L 1987–88, Lib Dem since 1988); *b* 22 May 1941; *s* of George Alexander Campbell and Elizabeth Jean Adam Phillips; *m* 1970, Elspeth Mary Urquhart or Grant-Suttie, *d* of Maj.-Gen. R. E. Urquhart, CB, DSO. *Educ:* Hillhead High School, Glasgow; Glasgow Univ. (MA 1962, LLB 1965; President of the Union, 1964–65); Stanford Univ., Calif. Advocate, Scottish Bar, 1968; Advocate Depute, 1977–80; Standing Jun. Counsel to the Army, 1980–82. Member: Clayson Cttee on licensing reform, 1971; Legal Aid Central Cttee, 1983–87; Scottish Legal Aid Bd, 1987; Broadcasting Council for Scotland, 1984–87. Part-time Chairman: VAT Tribunal, 1984–87; Medical Appeal Tribunal, 1985–87. Chm., Scottish Liberal Party, 1975–77; contested (L): Greenock and Port Glasgow, Feb. 1974 and Oct. 1974; E Fife, 1979; NE Fife, 1983; Lib. spokesman on arts, broadcasting and sport, 1987–88; Lib Dem spokesman on arts, broadcasting and sport, 1988, on sport and defence, 1988–94, on foreign affairs and defence, 1994–97, chief spokesman on foreign affairs, 1997–, on Europe, 1997–2001, on defence, 1997–2001; Mem., Jt Cabinet Cttee on Constitutional Reform, 1997–. Member: Select Cttee on Members Interests, 1987–90; Select Cttee on Trade and Industry, 1990–92; Defence Select Cttee, 1992–99. Member: UK Delegn to N Atlantic Assembly, 1989–; UK Delegn to Parly Assembly, OSCE, 1992–97 and 1999–. Mem. Bd, British Council, 1998–; Gov., Ditchley Foundn, 1999–. Chm., Royal Lyceum Theatre Co., Edinburgh, 1984–87. Member: UK Sports Council, 1965–68; Scottish Sports Council, 1971–81. Governor, Scottish Sports Aid Foundn, 1981–90; Trustee: Scottish Internat. Educn Trust, 1984–; London Marathon, 1997–2000. AAA 220 Yards Champion, 1964 and 1967; UK 100 Metres Record Holder, 1967–74; competed at Olympic Games, 1964 and Commonwealth Games, 1966; Captain, UK Athletics Team, 1965 and 1966. *Recreations:* all sports, reading, music, theatre. *Address:* c/o House of Commons, SW1A 0AA. *T:* (020) 7219 4446. *Club:* Reform.

CAMPBELL, Rt Hon. Sir (William) Anthony, Kt 1988; PC 1999; **Rt Hon. Lord Justice Campbell;** a Lord Justice of Appeal, Supreme Court of Northern Ireland, since 1998; *b* 30 Oct. 1936; *s* of late H. E. Campbell and of Marion Wheeler; *m* 1960, Gail, *e d* of F. M. McKibbin; three *d*. *Educ:* Campbell Coll., Belfast; Queens' Coll., Cambridge. Called to the Bar, Gray's Inn, 1960, Hon. Bencher, 1995; called to the Bar of NI, 1960 (Bencher, 1983; Chm., Exec. Council, 1985–87). Jun. Counsel to Attorney-Gen. for NI, 1971–74; QC (NI) 1974; Senior Crown Counsel in NI, 1984–88; Judge of the High Ct of Justice, NI, 1988–98. Chairman: Council of Legal Educn in NI, 1994–; Judicial Studies Bd, NI, 1995–. Governor, Campbell Coll., 1976–98 (Chm., 1984–86); Mem. Council, St Leonards Sch., St Andrews, 1985–94. Hon. Fellow, Amer. Bar Foundn, 1997. *Recreations:* sailing, hill walking. *Address:* Royal Courts of Justice, Belfast BT1 3JY. *Clubs:* New (Edinburgh); Royal Ulster Yacht.

See also J. E. P. Grigg.

CAMPBELL-GRAY, family name of **Lord Gray.**

CAMPBELL-JOHNSTON, Very Rev. Michael Alexander Ninian, SJ; Director, Servicio Jesuita para el Desarrollo, since 1994; *b* 27 Sept. 1931; *s* of Ninian Campbell-Johnston and Marguerite Antoinette Shakespear. *Educ:* Beaumont College; Séminaire Les Fontaines, France (Lic Phil); LSE (BSc Econ, DipEd); Col. Max. Christi Regis, Mexico (STL). Dir, Guyana Inst. for Social Research and Action, 1967–75; Dir, Social Secretariat, Jesuit Generalate, Rome, 1975–84; Regional Co-ordinator, Jesuit Refugee Service for Mexico and Central America, El Salvador, 1984–87; Provincial, British Province, SJ, 1987–93. Editor: Gisra; Promotio Justitiae. *Recreations:* reading, motorbike riding. *Address:* Servicio Jesuita para el Desarrollo, Apartado Postal 01-34, San Salvador, El Salvador. *T:* 2620002, *Fax:* 2434753; *e-mail:* macjsj@es.com.sv.

CAMPBELL-ORDE, Sir John A.; *see* Orde.

CAMPBELL-PRESTON, Dame Frances (Olivia), DCVO 1990 (CVO 1977); Woman of the Bedchamber to HM Queen Elizabeth the Queen Mother, since 1965; *b* 2 Sept. 1918; *d* of Lt-Col Arthur Grenfell and Hilda Margaret Grenfell (*née* Lyttelton); *m* 1938, Lt-Col George Patrick Campbell-Preston (*d* 1960), The Black Watch; two *s* two *d*. *Educ:* St Paul's Girls' Sch. WRNS, 1941–43. Mem., Argyll CC, 1960–64; Chm., Children's Panel, Argyle and Argyll and Bute, 1970–80. *Address:* 93 Whitelands House, Cheltenham Terrace, SW3 4RA.

CAMPBELL-SAVOURS, family name of **Baron Campbell-Savours.**

CAMPBELL-SAVOURS, Baron *cr* 2001 (Life Peer), of Allerdale in the County of Cumbria; **Dale Norman Campbell-Savours;** *b* 23 Aug. 1943; *s* of late John Lawrence and of Cynthia Lorraine Campbell-Savours; *m* 1970, Gudrun Kristin Runolfsdottir; three *s*. *Educ:* Keswick Sch.; Sorbonne, Paris. Dir, manufacturing co., 1969–77. Member, Ramsbottom UDC, 1972–73. Mem., TGWU and UNISON (formerly COHSE), 1970–. Contested (Lab): Darwen Division of Lancashire, gen. elections, Feb. 1974, Oct. 1974; Workington, by-election, 1976. MP (Lab) Workington, 1979–2001. *Address:* House of Lords, SW1A 0PW.

CAMPBELL-WHITE, Martin Andrew; Joint Chief Executive, Askonas Holt Ltd, since 1999; *b* 11 July 1943; *s* of late John Vernon Campbell-White and Hilda Doris (*née* Ash); *m* 1969, Dr Margaret Mary Miles; three *s*. *Educ:* Dean Close Sch., Cheltenham; St John's Coll., Oxford; Univ. of Strasbourg. Thomas Skinner & Co. Ltd (Publishers), 1964–66; Ibbs & Tillett Ltd (Concert Agents), 1966–72, Dir, 1969–72; Harold Holt Ltd (Concert Agents), subseq. Askonas Holt Ltd, 1972–: Dir, 1973–; Dep. Chm., 1989–92; Chief Exec., 1992–99. Chm., Brit. Assoc. of Concert Agents, 1978–81. Council Mem., London Sinfonietta, 1973–86; Dir, Chamber Orchestra of Europe, 1983–93; Mem. Bd, Première Ensemble, 1991–. Asst Dir, Fest. of German Arts, 1987; Founding Dir, Japan Fest. 1991, 1991. Trustee: Abbado Trust for Young Musicians, 1987–; Salzburg Fest. Trust, 1996–2000; Mem. Bd, Riverside Studios, 1988–2000. FRSA 1980. Sebetia Ter Prize for Culture, Naples, 1999. *Recreations:* tennis, watching cricket, classical music, travel. *Address:* c/o Askonas Holt Ltd, Lonsdale Chambers, 27 Chancery Lane, WC2A 1PF. *T:* (020) 7400 1700, *Fax:* (020) 7400 1799. *Clubs:* Arts, MCC.

CAMPDEN, Viscount; Anthony Baptist Noel; *b* 16 Jan. 1950; *s* and *heir* of 5th Earl of Gainsborough, *qv*; *m* 1972, Sarah Rose (LVO 1996, DL), *er d* of Col T. F. C. Winnington; one *s*. *Educ:* Ampleforth; Royal Agricultural Coll., Cirencester. *Heir: s* Hon. Henry Robert Anthony Noel, *b* 1 July 1977. *Address:* Exton Park, Oakham, Rutland, Leics LE15 8AN. *T:* (01572) 812209; 105 Earls Court Road, W8 6QH. *T:* (020) 7370 5650. *Clubs:* White's, Pratt's.

See also Sir F. S. W. Winnington, Bt.

CAMPION, Peter James, DPhil; FInstP; technical consultant; *b* 7 April 1926; *s* of Frank Wallace Campion and Gertrude Alice (*née* Lambert); *m* 1st, 1950, Beryl Grace Stanton (*d* 1995), *e d* of John and Grace Stanton; one *s* one *d* (and one *s* decd); 2nd, 1997, Rev. Patricia Adele Houseman (*née* O'Brien); three step *d*. *Educ:* Westcliff High Sch., Essex; Exeter Coll., Oxford (MA, DPhil). FInstP 1964. RNVR, 1943. Nuffield Res. Fellow, Oxford, 1954; Chalk River Proj., Atomic Energy of Canada Ltd, 1955; National Physical Lab., Teddington, 1960–86: Supt, Div. of Radiation Science, 1964; Supt, Div. of Mech. and Optical Metrology, 1974; Dep. Dir, 1976. Mem., Comité Consultatif pour les Etalons de Mesure des Rayonnements Ionisante, 1963–79; Chm., Sect. II, reconstituted Comité Consultatif, Mesure des radionucléides, 1970–79; Mem., NACCB, 1984–86. Editor, Internat. Jl of Applied Radiation and Isotopes, 1968–71. *Publications:* A Code of Practice for the Detailed Statement of Accuracy (with A. Williams and J. E. Burns), 1973; A Campion Saga, 2000; technical and rev. papers in learned jls on neutron capture gamma rays, measurement of radioactivity, and on metrology generally. *Recreations:* watercolour painting, genealogy.

CAMPLING, Very Rev. Christopher Russell; Dean of Ripon, 1984–95; *b* 4 July 1925; *s* of Canon William Charles Campling; *m* 1953, Juliet Marian Hughes; one *s* two *d*. *Educ:* Lancing Coll.; St Edmund Hall, Oxford (MA; Hons Theol. cl. 2); Cuddesdon Theol. Coll. RNVR, 1943–47. Deacon 1951, priest 1952; Curate of Basingstoke, 1951–55; Minor Canon of Ely Cathedral and Chaplain of King's School, Ely, 1955–60; Chaplain of Lancing Coll., 1960–67; Vicar of Pershore with Pinvin and Wick and Birlingham, 1968–76; RD of Pershore, 1970–76; Archdeacon of Dudley and Director of Religious Education, Diocese of Worcester, 1976–84. Mem., General Synod of Church of England, 1970–95; Chm., House of Clergy, Diocese of Worcester, 1981–84; Chm., Council for the Care of Churches, 1988–94. Lectr, Leeds Parish Church, 1988–. *Publications:* The Way, The Truth and The Life: Vol. 1, The Love of God in Action, 1964; Vol. 2, The People of God in Action, 1964; Vol. 3, The Word of God in Action, 1965; Vol. 4, God's Plan in Action, 1965; also two teachers' volumes; Words of Worship, 1969; The Fourth Lesson,

Vol. 1 1973, Vol. 2 1974; The Food of Love, 1997. *Recreations:* music, drama, golf. *Address:* Pebble Ridge, Aglaia Road, Worthing, West Sussex BN11 5SW. *Club:* Naval.

CAMPORA, Dr Mario; Argentine Ambassador to Belgium and Luxembourg, 1996–99; *b* 3 Aug. 1930; *m* 1972, Magdalena Teresa María Díaz Gavier; one *s* two *d*. *Educ:* Nat. Univ. of Rosario, Argentina (Dr in Diplomacy). Argentine Foreign Service, 1955–71 and 1973–75; Internat. Orgns Dept, Foreign Policy Bureau, and Legal Dept, Ministry for Foreign Affairs; has served in Geneva, Washington, The Hague, New Delhi, and as deleg. to UN and OAS; Mem., Justicialist Party, active in politics, 1971–73, 1975–; Ambassador Extraordinary, Argentine Special Mission for Disarmament, Geneva, 1985; Sec. of State, Ministry for Foreign Affairs, 1989–90; Argentine Ambassador to UK, 1990–94. *Publications:* articles on foreign policy and international relations.

CAMPOS, Prof. Christophe Lucien, OBE 1994; Director, British Institute in Paris, since 1978; *b* 27 April 1938; *s* of Lucien Antoine Campos and Margaret Lilian (*née* Dunn); *m* 1977, Lucy Elizabeth Mitchell; one *s* two *d*; two *d* by former marriage. *Educ:* Lycée Lamoricière, Oran; Lycée Français de Londres; Lycée Henri IV, Paris; Gonville and Caius Coll., Cambridge. LèsL (Paris), PhD (Cantab). Lector in French, Gonville and Caius Coll., 1959; Lecturer in French: Univ. of Maryland, 1963; Univ. of Sussex, 1964; Lectr in English, Univ. i Oslo, 1969; Prof. of French, University Coll., Dublin, 1974. Gen. Editor, Franco-British Studies, 1988–. Chevalier de l'Ordre des Arts et des Lettres (France), 1988. *Publications:* The View of France, 1964; L'Enseignement de la civilisation française, 1988; contribs to Th. Qly, TLS, Univs Qly, Franco-British Studies. *Recreations:* bees, football, gastronomy, navigation. *Address:* L'Hocherie, 86230 Sossay, France.

CAMRE, Henning Niels Juel; Chief Executive, Danish Film Institute, since 1998; *b* 15 Nov. 1938; *s* of Sigfred N. J. Camre and Carna (*née* Petersen); *m* 1st, 1967, Merete Friis (marr. diss.); one *d*; 2nd, 1978, Janne Giese (marr. diss.); one *d* and one adopted *d*; partner, Regitze Oppenhejm. *Educ:* Univ. of Copenhagen; Nat. Film Sch. of Denmark (Dip. in Cinematography). Dir of Photography (feature and documentary film), 1968–88; Director: Nat. Film Sch. of Denmark, 1975–92; Nat. Film and TV Sch., UK, 1992–98. Chairman: Nordic Film Council, 1979–89; Danish State Film Studio, 1989–92; Centre International de Liaison des Ecoles de Cinéma et de Télévision: Mem., Exec. Council, 1980–86; Chm., Programme for Developing Countries, 1982–; Vice-Pres., 1986–. Chevalier de l'Ordre des Arts et des Lettres (France), 1990. *Publications:* Bridging the Gap, 1982; Film and Television Training in Indonesia, 1985; Asia-Pacific Film and Television Schools, 1991. *Recreation:* cycling. *Address:* Callisensvej 25, 2900 Hellerup, Denmark; Danish Film Institute, Vognmagergade 10, 1120 Copenhagen K, Denmark.

CAMROSE, 4th Viscount *cr* 1941, of Hackwood Park, Southampton; **Adrian Michael Berry;** Bt 1921; Baron 1929; *b* 15 June 1937; *er s* of Baron Hartwell (Life Peer), MBE, TD (who disclaimed his hereditary peerages for life, 1995); *S* father, 2001; *m* 1967, Marina Beatrice, *d* of Cyrus Sulzberger; one *s* one *d*. *Educ:* Eton; Christ Church, Oxford. Science Corresp., Daily Telegraph, 1977–96; Consulting Editor (Science), Daily Telegraph, 1996–. *Publications:* The Next Ten Thousand Years, 1974; The Iron Sun, 1977; From Apes to Astronauts, 1980; High Skies and Yellow Rain, 1983; The Super-Intelligent Machine, 1983; Koyama's Diamond, 1984; Ice With Your Evolution, 1986; Labyrinth of Lies, 1986; Harrap's Book of Scientific Anecdotes, 1989; (ed) Eureka!: The Book of Scientific Anecdotes, 1993; The Next 500 Years, 1995; Galileo and the Dolphins, 1996; The Giant Leap, 1999. *Heir: s* Hon. Jonathan William Berry [*b* 26 Feb. 1970; *m* 1996, Aurélie E. C. Molin; one *s* two *d*]. *Address:* 11 Cottesmore Gardens, W8 5PR. *T:* (020) 7937 5354.

See also N. W. Berry.

CANADA, Primate of All; *see* Peers, Most Rev. M. G.

CANADA, Primate of; *see* Quebec, Archbishop of, (RC).

CANADA, Metropolitan of the Ecclesiastical Province of; *see* Nova Scotia, Archbishop of.

CANAVAN, Dennis Andrew; Member (Ind.) Falkirk West, Scottish Parliament, since 1999; *b* 8 Aug. 1942; *s* of late Thomas and Agnes Canavan. *Educ:* St Columba's High Sch., Cowdenbeath; Edinburgh Univ. (BSc Hons, DipEd). Head of Maths Dept, St Modan's High Sch., Stirling, 1970–74; Asst Head, Holy Rood High Sch., Edinburgh, 1974. District Councillor, 1973–74; Leader of Labour Gp, Stirling District Council, 1974; Member: Stirling Dist Educn Sub-cttee, 1973–74; Stirlingshire Youth Employment Adv. Cttee, 1972–74. Sec., W Stirlingshire Constituency Labour Party, 1972–74; Labour Party Agent, Feb. 1974; Treasurer, Scottish Parly Lab. Gp, 1976–79, Vice-Chm., 1979–80, Chm., 1980–81. MP (Lab 1974–99, Ind. 1999–2000) W Stirlingshire, Oct. 1974–1983, Falkirk W, 1983–2000. Member: H of C Select Cttee on For. Affairs, 1982–97, on Internat. Develt, 1997–99; Chair: PLP NI Cttee, 1989–97; Parly Br, EIS, 1983–2000; Vice-Chm., All-Party Hospice Gp, 1992–2000; Founder and Convener, All-Party Parly Scottish Sports Gp, 1987–99; Mem., British-Irish Inter-Parly Body, 1992–2000. Scottish Parliament: Mem., European Cttee, 1999–; Founder and Convener, Sports Gp, 1999–. *Publications:* contribs to various jls on educn and politics. *Recreations:* hill walking, running, swimming, reading, football (Scottish Univs football internationalist, 1966–67 and 1967–68; Hon. Pres., Milton Amateurs FC). *Address:* Ardsonas, Sauchieburn, Bannockburn, Stirlingshire FK7 9PZ. *T:* (01786) 812581; Scottish Parliament, Edinburgh EH99 1SP. *T:* (0131) 348 5630. *Clubs:* Bannockburn Miners' Welfare (Bannockburn); Camelon Labour (Falkirk).

CANAVAN, Vincent Joseph; Sheriff of South Strathclyde, Dumfries and Galloway at Hamilton, since 1987; *b* 13 Dec. 1946; *s* of James Canavan and Catherine Ludivine Brogan; *m* 1973, Mary Allison; three *s* three *d*. *Educ:* St Aloysius Coll., Glasgow; Univ. of Glasgow (LLB Hons 1968). Qualified as Solicitor, 1970; passed Advocate, 1980. Member: Victim Support (Scotland) Hamilton Court Project Working Party, 1990–94; Strathclyde Regl Council Cons. Cttee on Social Work in criminal justice system, 1991–96. Chm., Lanarks Br., Scottish Assoc. for Study of Delinquency, 1992–95 (Vice-Chm., 1991–92). *Recreations:* reading history, Italian cuisine, visiting art exhibitions. *Address:* Sheriff Court, Almada Street, Hamilton, Lanarks ML3 0HF. *Club:* Glasgow Art.

CANBERRA AND GOULBURN, Archbishop of, (RC), since 1983; **Most Rev. Francis Patrick Carroll;** *b* 9 Sept. 1930; *s* of P. Carroll. *Educ:* De La Salle Coll., Marrickville; St Columba's Coll., Springwood; St Patrick's Coll., Manly; Pontifical Urban Univ. De Propaganda Fide. Ordained priest, 1954; Asst Priest, Griffith, NSW, 1955–59; Asst Inspector of Catholic Schs, dio. of Wagga, 1957–61; Asst Priest, Albury, 1959–61; Bishop's Sec., Diocesan Chancellor, Diocesan Dir of Catholic Educn, 1965–67; consecrated Co-Adjutor Bishop, 1967; Bishop of Wagga Wagga, 1968–83. Chm., Nat. Catholic Educn Commn, 1974–78; Mem., Internat. Catechetical Council, Rome, 1974–93; Pres., Australian Catholic Bishops' Conf., 2000–. Hon. DLitt Charles Sturt Univ., NSW, 1994. *Publication:* The Development of Episcopal Conferences, 1965. *Address:* Archbishop's House, GPO Box 89, Canberra, ACT 2601, Australia.

CANBERRA AND GOULBURN, Bishop of, since 1993; **Rt Rev. George Victor Browning;** *b* 28 Sept. 1942; *s* of John and Barbara Browning; *m* 1965, Margaret Rowland; three *s*. *Educ:* Ardingly Coll.; Lewes County Grammar Sch., Sussex; St John's Coll., Morpeth, NSW (ThL 1st cl. Hons 1965). Curate: Inverell, 1966–68; Armidale, 1968–69; Vicar, Warialda, 1969–73; Vice Warden and Lectr in Old Testament Studies and Pastoral Theol., St John's Coll., Morpeth, 1973–75 (Acting Warden, 1974); Rector of Singleton, Rural Dean and Archdeacon of the Upper Hunter, 1976–84; Rector of Woy Woy and Archdeacon of the Central Coast, 1984–85; Bishop of the Northern Reg., Brisbane, 1985–92; Principal, St Francis' Theol Coll., 1988–92; Bishop of the Coastal Reg., and Asst Bishop, dio. of Brisbane, 1992–93. *Recreations:* reading, running (anything that presents a challenge). *Address:* 51 Rosenthal Street, Campbell, Canberra, ACT 2612, Australia. *T:* (2) 62480716, 62480811, *Fax:* (2) 62476829; *e-mail:* george.browning@anglican.org.au.

CANDLIN, Prof. Christopher Noel; Chair Professor of Applied Linguistics and Director, Centre for English Language Education and Communication Research, City University of Hong Kong, since 1998; *b* 31 March 1940; *s* of Edwin Frank Candlin and Nora Candlin (*née* Letts); *m* 1964, Sally (*née* Carter); one *s* three *d*. *Educ:* Jesus Coll., Oxford (MA); Univ. of London (PGCE); Yale Univ. (MPhil). Research Associate, Univ. of Leeds, 1967–68; University of Lancaster: Lectr, 1968, later Sen. Lectr; Prof. of Linguistics and Modern English Language, 1981–87; Macquarie University, Sydney: Prof. and Chm., Linguistics Dept, 1987–98; Exec. Dir, Nat. Centre for Eng. Lang. Teaching and Res., 1988–98; Dir, Centre for Lang. in Social Life, 1993–98; Adjunct Prof. of Linguistics, 1998. Visiting Professor: Univ. of Giessen, 1975; Ontario Inst. for Studies in Educn, Toronto, 1983; East-West Centre, Honolulu, 1978; Univ. of Hawaii at Manoa, 1984; Univ. of Melbourne, 1985; Jyväskylä Univ., Finland, 1993; Univ. of Wales, Cardiff, 1995 (Hon. Prof., 1995); Adjunct Prof., Univ. of Technol., Sydney, 1998. General Editor: Applied Linguistics and Language Study; Language in Social Life; Language Teacher Educn Scheme; Language Teaching Methodology Series; Applied Linguistics in Action; Advances in Applied Linguistics. Pres., Internat. Assoc. of Applied Linguistics, 1996–. FRSA. Hon. PhD Jyväskylä, 1996. *Publications:* Challenges, 1978; The Communicative Teaching of English, 1981; Computers in English Language Teaching and Research, 1985; Language Learning Tasks, 1986; Language, Learning and Community, 1989; English at Work, vol. 1, 1991, vol. 2, 1992; (ed jtly) Australian Learners' Dictionary, 1997; Writing: texts, processes and practices, 1999. *Recreations:* theatre, concerts, sailing, cooking. *Address:* Department of English, City University of Hong Kong, Tatchee Avenue, Kowloon Tong, Hong Kong SAR.

CANDLISH, Thomas Tait, FREng; Managing Director, George Wimpey PLC, 1978–85 (Director, 1973–85); *b* 26 Nov. 1926; *s* of John Candlish and Elizabeth (*née* Tait); *m* 1964, Mary Trinkwon; two *s*. *Educ:* Perth Acad.; Glasgow Univ. (BSc Eng). FICE 1971; FREng (FEng 1980). Served RE, 1946–49 (commnd). Student Engr, George Wimpey & Co. Ltd, 1944–46; rejoined Wimpey, 1951; served in: Borneo, 1951–54; Papua New Guinea, 1955–57; Arabian Gulf area, 1958–62; W Africa, 1962–65; Director: Wimpey Internat., 1973–85 (Chm., 1979–85); Wimpey ME & C, 1973–85; Wimpey Marine Ltd, 1975–85 (Chm., 1979–85); Brown & Root-Wimpey Highlands Fabricators, 1974–89 (Chm., 1981–86); British Smelter Constructions Ltd, 1977–83 (Chm., 1977–83); Hill Samuel Developments, 1978–85; A & P Appledore Holdings, 1979–85; Brown & Root (UK) Ltd, 1985–89; OGC Internat., 1993–97; Chairman: Howard Humphreys Gp Ltd, 1987–89; Historic Cars Ltd, 1989–97. Chm., Export Gp for Constructional Industries, 1983–85; Member: EDC for Civil Engrg, 1979–82; British Overseas Trade Bd, 1984–87. *Recreations:* motor sport, golf. *Address:* Tithe Cottage, Dorney Wood Road, Burnham, Bucks SL1 8EQ. *Clubs:* Royal Automobile; Denham Golf.

CANDY, Elizabeth Mary; Head Mistress, The Lady Eleanor Holles School, Hampton, since 1981; *b* 12 Oct. 1942; *d* of late Donald Glen Candy and Phyllis Mary Candy (*née* Denbury). *Educ:* Merrywood Grammar Sch., Bristol; Westfield Coll., London (BSc 1965). Chemistry Mistress then Jt Head of Science, Bromley High Sch., 1965–71; Head of Science then Second Mistress, Putney High Sch., 1971–81. Mem. Council, Royal Holloway, London Univ., 1995–. FRSA 1994. Dame Chevalier, Ordre des Coteaux de Champagne, 1998. *Recreations:* opera, reading, France and French wine, photography, cycling, tennis, golf. *Address:* The Lady Eleanor Holles School, Hanworth Road, Hampton, Middx TW12 3HF. *T:* (020) 8979 1601. *Club:* Cripplegate Ward.

CANDY, Lorraine A.; Editor, Cosmopolitan, since 2000; *b* 8 July 1968; *d* of A. R. Butler and V. S. Butler; *m* C. James Candy. *Educ:* Liskeard Comprehensive Sch., Cornwall. Formerly: Feature writer, Daily Mirror; Woman's Editor: Sun; Today; Deputy Editor: Marie Claire mag.; Times Saturday Mag.; Ed., B mag.; Features Ed., The Times. *Recreations:* riding, shopping. *Address:* Cosmopolitan, 72 Broadwick Street, W1V 2BP.

CANE, Prof. Violet Rosina; Professor of Mathematical Statistics, University of Manchester, 1971–81, now Emeritus; *b* 31 Jan. 1916; *d* of Tubal George Cane and Annie Louisa Lansdell. *Educ:* Newnham Coll., Cambridge (MA, Dipl. in Math. Stats). BoT, 1940; Univ. of Aberdeen, 1941; FO, 1942; Min. of Town and Country Planning, 1946; Statistician to MRC Applied Psychol. Unit, 1948; Queen Mary Coll., London, 1955; Fellow, Newnham Coll., Cambridge, 1957; Lectr, Univ. of Cambridge, 1960. Mem., UGC, 1974–79. Mem., Cambridge CC, 1965–72, 1982–90 (Hon. Councillor, 1990–). Hon. MSc Manchester, 1974. *Publications:* (contrib.) Current Problems in Animal Behaviour, 1961; (contrib.) Perspectives in Probability and Statistics, 1975; papers in Jl of Royal Stat. Soc., Animal Behaviour, and psychol jls. *Recreation:* supporting old houses. *Address:* 13/14 Little St Mary's Lane, Cambridge CB2 1RR. *T:* (01223) 357277; Statistical Laboratory, University of Cambridge, 16 Mill Lane, Cambridge CB2 1SB.

CANHAM, Paul George, LVO 1991; JP; Official Secretary to Governor-General of New Zealand, 1985–90; *b* 25 Oct. 1933; *s* of George Ernest Canham and Ella Mary (*née* Mackenzie); *m* 1964, Diane Alderton; one *s* one *d*. *Educ:* Timaru Boys' High Sch.; Victoria Univ. of Wellington (BA, MA Hons History). Teacher: Pomfret Sch., Conn., 1957; Matamata Coll., NZ, 1960; Hauraki Plains Coll., 1967; Heretaunga Coll., 1969; Dep. Prin., Hutt Valley High Sch., 1973; Prin., Wanganui High Sch., 1979. JP Hawkes Bay, 1991. *Publication:* The Return (novel), 1999. *Recreation:* bridge. *Address:* 6 Gresham Place, Taradale 4001, Hawkes Bay, New Zealand. *T:* (6) 8445823.

CANN, Charles Richard, CB 1996; Deputy Secretary, Ministry of Agriculture, Fisheries and Food, 1991–96; *b* 3 Feb. 1937; *s* of Charles Alfred Cann and Grace Elizabeth Cann; *m* 1979, Denise Ann Margaret Love; two *s*. *Educ:* Merchant Taylors' Sch., Northwood, Mddx; St John's Coll., Cambridge (MA). Asst Principal, MAFF, 1960, Principal 1965; Cabinet Office, 1969–71; Asst Sec., MAFF, 1971; Under Sec., 1981; Fisheries Sec., MAFF, 1987–91. Mem. Policy Cttee, CPRE, 1996–. *Address:* 50 St Peters Street, N1 8JT.

CANN, James Charles; MP (Lab) Ipswich, since 1992; *b* 28 June 1946; *s* of Charles George Cann and Brenda Julia Cann; *m* 1970, Rosemary Lovitt; two *s*. *Educ:* Barton on Humber Grammar Sch.; Kesteven Coll. of Education. Schoolteacher, 1967–92; Dep. Head, Handford Hall Primary Sch., Ipswich, 1981–92. Leader, Ipswich Council,

1979–91. *Recreations:* snooker, squash, badminton, walking, reading, history. *Address:* 79 Woodbridge Road East, Ipswich IP4 5QL. *Clubs:* various Ipswich sports and social.

CANN, Prof. Johnson Robin, ScD; FRS 1995; Professor of Earth Sciences, University of Leeds, since 1989; *b* 18 Oct. 1937; *er s* of Johnson Ralph Cann and (Ethel) Mary (*née* Northmore); *m* 1st, 1963, Janet (*d* 1994), *d* of late Prof. Charles John Hamson, QC; two *s*; 2nd, 2001, Helen Dunham. *Educ:* St Alban's Sch.; St John's Coll., Cambridge (MA, PhD, ScD). Research fellow, St John's Coll., 1962–66; post-doctoral work in Depts of Mineralogy and Petrology, and Geodesy and Geophysics, Cambridge, 1962–66; Dept of Mineralogy, British Museum (Natural History), 1966–68; Lectr, then Reader, School of Environmental Sciences, Univ. of East Anglia, 1968–77; J. B. Simpson Prof. of Geology, Univ. of Newcastle upon Tyne, 1977–89; current research in hot springs of mid-ocean ridges, seafloor volcanoes, rocks of ocean floor, creation of oceanic crust, obsidian in archaeology. Member, then Chm., ocean crust panel, 1975–78, UK rep. on planning cttee, 1978–84, Jt Oceanographic Instns for Deep Earth Sampling; co-chief scientist on Glomar Challenger, 1976 and 1979; Adjunct Scientist, Woods Hole Oceanographic Instn, 1987–; Chief Scientist, British Mid-Ocean Ridge Initiative, 1992–. Chm., UK Ocean Drilling Program Grants Cttee, 1987–90. Mem., UGC physical sciences sub-cttee, 1982–88. Murchison Medal, Geol Soc. of London, 1990. *Publications:* papers in jls of earth science and archaeology. *Address:* Department of Earth Sciences, University of Leeds, Leeds LS2 9JT. *T:* (0113) 233 5204; *e-mail:* j.cann@earth.leeds.ac.uk.

CANN, Paul Lewis; Chief Executive, National Autistic Society, since 1997; *b* 29 Aug. 1953; *s* of John Samuel Jones Cann and Eileen Dorothy Jean (*née* Daymond John); *m* 1981, Phillippa Terese Cook; one *s* one *d.* *Educ:* Tiffin Sch.; King's Coll., Cambridge (BA Hons 1975; MA 1979); Westminster Coll., Oxford (Cert Ed 1976). Schoolmaster: Christchurch Cathedral Sch., 1976–78; Abingdon Sch., 1978–81; Civil Service, 1981–88: Asst Private Secretary to: Lord Privy Seal, 1982–83; Minister for Arts, 1983–84; Principal, Cabinet Office, 1985–88; Sen. Consultant, Hay Mgt Consultants, 1988–90; Hd of Personnel, Newspaper Publishing plc, 1990–92; Exec. Dir, British Dyslexia Assoc., 1992–97. Corporate Mem., Inst. Personnel and Develt, 1986. *Recreations:* singing, drinking wine, enjoying Hook Norton village. *Address:* 7 Bell Hill, Hook Norton, Oxon OX15 5NG. *T:* (01608) 737282.

CANNADINE, Prof. David Nicholas, DPhil, LittD; FRHistS; FBA 1999; FRSL; Director, Institute of Historical Research, and Professor of History, University of London, since 1998; *b* 7 Sept. 1950; *s* of Sydney Douglas Cannadine and Dorothy Mary Cannadine (*née* Hughes); *m* 1982, Linda Jane Colley, *qv*; one *d* decd. *Educ:* King Edward's Five Ways Sch., Birmingham; Clare Coll., Cambridge (schol.; BA 1st cl. Hons 1972; MA 1975; LittD 1993); Princeton Univ. (Jane Eliza Procter Vis. Fellow); St John's Coll., Oxford (Sen. Schol.; DPhil 1975). FRHistS 1981. Cambridge University: Res. Fellow, St John's Coll., 1975–77; Asst Lectr, 1976–80, Lectr, 1980–88, in Hist.; Christ's College: Fellow, 1977–88; Dir of Studies in Hist., 1977–83; Tutor, 1979–81; Prof. of History, 1988–92, Moore Collegiate Prof. of History, 1992–98, Columbia Univ. Vis. Mem., Inst. for Advanced Study, Princeton, 1980–81; Vis. Prof., Birkbeck Coll., London Univ., 1995–97; Vis. Fellow, Whitney Humanities Center, Yale Univ., 1995–98; Vis. Scholar, Pembroke Coll., Cambridge, 1997. Lectures: Motitz, Kalamazoo, 1992; first Leonard Hastings Schoff, Columbia Univ., 1993; Hayes Robinson, RHC, 1994; Raleigh, British Acad., 1997; Charles Edmonson, Baylor Univ., 1997; George Orwell Meml, Sheffield Univ., 1997; Curtis, Univ. of Central Lancs, 1998; Earl, Keele, 1999; Beall-Russell, Baylor Univ., 1999; Esmée Fairbairn, Lancaster Univ., 1999; London Liby, 2001; Carnochan, Stanford Univ., 2001; Throckmorton, Lewis and Clark Coll., 2001; Burrows, Univ. of Essex, 2002; Rothschild Archive, 2002. Fellow: Berkeley Coll., Yale Univ., 1985–; ACLS, 1990–91; J. P. Morgan Liby, NY, 1992–98. Regular broadcaster on wireless and television. Member: Eastern Regl Cttee, Nat. Trust, 2001–; Cttee of Mgt, Centre for Res. in the Arts, Social Scis and Humanities, 2001–. Vice-President: British Records Soc., 1998–; RHistS, 1998–; Pres., Worcs Historical Soc., 1999–. Member Advisory Board: Centre for Study of Soc. and Politics, Kingston Univ., 1998–; ICBH, 1998–; Member Advisory Council: Warburg Inst. (formerly Adv. Bd), 1998–; Inst. of US Studies, 1999–; PRO, 1999–; Inst. of English Studies, 2000–, Inst. of Latin Amer. Studies, 2000–, London Univ. Trustee: Kennedy Meml Trust, 2000–; Nat. Portrait Gall., 2000–. Gov., Ipswich Sch., 1982–88. General Editor: Studies in Modern Hist., 1979–; Penguin Hist. of Britain, 1989–; Penguin Hist. of Europe, 1991–; Historical Res., 1998–; Reviews in History, 1998–; Member, Editorial Board: Urban Hist. Yearbook, 1979–83; Past and Present, 1983– (Vice Chm., 2000–); Midland Hist., 1985–88; Twentieth Century British Hist., 1990–; Rural Hist., 1995–; Prospect, 1995–; Library Hist., 1998–. FRSA 1998; FRSL 1999. Hon. DLitt: UEA, 2001; South Bank, 2001. T. S. Ashton Prize, Econ. Hist. Soc., 1977; Silver Jubilee Prize, Agricl Hist. Soc., 1977; Dean's Dist. Award in the Humanities, Columbia Univ., 1996. *Publications:* Lords and Landlords: the aristocracy and the towns 1774–1967, 1980; (ed and contrib.) Patricians, Power and Politics in Nineteenth-Century Towns, 1982; (ed jtly and contrib.) H. J. Dyos, Exploring the Urban Past, 1982; (ed jtly and contrib.) Rituals of Royalty: power and ceremonial in traditional societies, 1987; The Pleasures of the Past, 1989; (ed and contrib.) Winston Churchill's Famous Speeches, 1989; (ed jtly and contrib.) The First Modern Society: essays in English history in honour of Lawrence Stone, 1989; The Decline and Fall of the British Aristocracy (Lionel Trilling Prize), 1990; G. M. Trevelyan: a life in history, 1992; Aspects of Aristocracy: grandeur and decline in modern Britain, 1994; (ed jtly and contrib.) History and Biography: essays in honour of Derek Beales, 1996; Class in Britain, 1998; History in Our Time, 1998; Making History Now, 1999; Ornamentalism: how the British saw their Empire, 2001; Churchill and After: the present and the past in twentieth-century Britain, 2002; numerous contribs to other books and learned jls. *Recreations:* life, laughter. *Address:* Institute of Historical Research, Senate House, Malet Street, WC1E 7HU. *T:* (020) 7862 8740. *Club:* Athenæum.

CANNAN, Hon. David; *see* Cannan, Hon. J. D. Q.

CANNAN, Denis; dramatist and script writer; *b* 14 May 1919; *s* of late Captain H. J. Pullein-Thompson, MC, and late Joanna Pullein-Thompson (*née* Cannan); *m* 1st, 1946, Joan Ross (marr. diss.); two *s* one *d*; 2nd, 1965, Rose Evansky; he changed name to Denis Cannan, by deed poll, 1964. *Educ:* Eton. A Repertory factotum, 1937–39. Served War of 1939–45, Queen's Royal Regt, Captain (despatches). Actor at Citizens' Theatre, Glasgow, 1946–48. *Publications: plays:* Max (prod. Malvern Festival), 1949; Captain Carvallo (Bristol Old Vic and St James's Theatres), 1950; Colombe (trans. from Anouilh), New Theatre, 1951; Misery Me!, Duchess, 1955; You and Your Wife, Bristol Old Vic, 1955; The Power and The Glory (adaptation from Graham Greene), Phoenix Theatre, 1956, and Phœnix Theatre, New York, 1958; Who's Your Father?, Cambridge Theatre, 1958; US (original text), Aldwych, 1966; adapted Ibsen's Ghosts, Aldwych, 1966; One at Night, Royal Court, 1971; The Ik (adaptation and collaboration), 1975; Dear Daddy, Oxford Festival and Ambassadors, 1976 (Play of the Year award, 1976); the screenplays of several films; plays for TV and radio, adaptations for TV series. *Address:* 43 Osmond Road, Hove, Sussex BN3 1TF.

See also D. L. A. Farr, J. M. W. Pullein-Thompson.

CANNAN, Hon. (John) David (Qualtrough), Speaker, House of Keys, Isle of Man, since 2000; MHK (Ind.) Michael, since 1982; *b* 24 Aug. 1936; *s* of Rev. Canon Charles Alfred Cannan and Mary Eleanor Cannan (*née* Qualtrough); *m* 1966, Patricia Mary, *d* of Bernard and Jean Roberts, Taranaki, NZ; three *s* one *d.* *Educ:* King William's Coll., IOM. Martin's Bank, IOM, 1953–54; Nat. Service, RA, 1954–56; tea and rubber industries., Ceylon, 1956–61, Malaya, 1961–67; business interests, Berks, 1967–79. Mem. (C), Bradfield DC, 1970–74; returned to IOM, 1980; Minister for Treasury, 1986–89; Chm., Financial Supervision Commn, 1987–89; Vice-Chm., Public Accounts Commn, 1997–2000. *Recreations:* gardening, bee-keeping, Manx history. *Address:* Legislative Buildings, Douglas, Isle of Man IM1 3PW. *T:* (01624) 685500; White Gables, Curragh Road, Ballaugh, Isle of Man IM7 5BG. *T:* and *Fax:* (01624) 897926.

CANNELL, Prof. Robert Quirk; Director, Virginia Agricultural Experiment Station and Associate Dean for Research, Virginia Polytechnic Institute and State University, since 1994; *b* 20 March 1937; *s* of William Watterson Cannell and Norah Isabel Corjeag; *m* 1962, Edwina Anne Thornborough; two *s.* *Educ:* King's Coll., Newcastle upon Tyne; Univ. of Durham (BSc, PhD). FIBiol 1986. Shell Chemical Co., London, 1959; School of Agriculture, Univ. of Newcastle upon Tyne, 1961; Dept of Agronomy and Plant Genetics, Univ. of Minnesota, 1968–69; Letcombe Lab., AFRC, Oxon, 1970; Dir, Welsh Plant Breeding Station, Aberystwyth, 1984–87; Head of Crop and Soil Envmtl Scis Dept, Virginia Polytech. Inst. and State Univ., 1987–94. *Publications:* papers in agricultural science jls. *Address:* College of Agriculture and Life Sciences, Virginia Polytechnic Institute and State University, Blacksburg, VA 24061, USA. *T:* (540) 2316336.

CANNING, family name of **Baron Garvagh**.

CANNING, Hugh Donaldson; Music Critic, The Sunday Times, since 1989; *b* 28 May 1954; *s* of David Donaldson Canning and Olga Mary Canning (*née* Simms). *Educ:* Oakham Sch.; Pembroke Coll., Oxford (BA). Freelance music critic, 1979–87; Music Critic: London Daily News, 1987; The Guardian, 1987–89; Opera Critic, The Listener. Critic of Year Award, Brit. Press Awards, 1994. *Recreations:* music, theatre, tennis, food, gossip. *Address:* c/o the Sunday Times, 1 Pennington Street, E1 9XN.

CANNON, Prof. John Ashton, CBE 1985; PhD; Professor of Modern History, University of Newcastle upon Tyne, 1976–92, now Professor Emeritus; Pro-Vice Chancellor, 1983–86; *b* 8 Oct. 1926; *s* of George and Gladys Cannon; *m* 1st, 1948, Audrey Elizabeth, *d* of G. R. Caple (marr. diss. 1953); one *s* one *d*; 2nd, 1953, Minna, *d* of Frederick Pedersen, Denmark; one *s* two *d.* *Educ:* Hertford Grammar Sch.; Peterhouse, Cambridge (MA 1955). PhD Bristol, 1958. Served RAF, 1947–49 and 1952–55. History of Parlt Trust, 1960–61; Univ. of Bristol: Lectr, 1961; Sen. Lectr, 1967; Reader, 1970; Dean, Faculty of Arts, Univ. of Newcastle upon Tyne, 1979–82. Member: UGC, 1983–89 (Vice-Chm., 1986–89; Chm., Arts Sub-Cttee, 1983–89); Open Univ. Vis. Cttee, 1988–92. Lectures: Wiles, Queen's Univ. Belfast, 1982; Raleigh, British Acad., 1982; Prothero, RHistS, 1985; Stenton, Reading Univ., 1986; James Ford Special, Oxford, 1996. Chm., Radio Bristol, 1970–74. FRHistS 1980; FRSA 1990. *Publications:* The Fox-North Coalition: crisis of the constitution, 1970; Parliamentary Reform, 1640–1832, 1973; (ed with P. V. McGrath) Essays in Bristol and Gloucestershire History, 1976; (ed) The Letters of Junius, 1978; (ed) The Historian at Work, 1980; (ed) The Whig Ascendancy, 1981; Aristocratic Century, 1984; (ed jtly) The Blackwell Dictionary of Historians, 1988; (with R. Griffiths) The Oxford Illustrated History of the British Monarchy, 1988; Samuel Johnson and the politics of Hanoverian England, 1994; (ed) The Oxford Companion to British History, 1997. *Recreations:* music, losing at tennis. *Address:* 35a Osborne Road, Jesmond, Newcastle upon Tyne NE2 2AH. *T:* (0191) 281 4096.

CANNON, John Francis Michael; Keeper of Botany, Natural History Museum (formerly British Museum (Natural History)), 1978–90; *b* 22 April 1930; *s* of Francis Leslie Cannon and Aileen Flora Cannon; *m* 1954, Margaret Joy (*née* Herbert); two *s* one *d.* *Educ:* Whitgift Sch., South Croydon, Surrey; King's Coll., Newcastle upon Tyne, Univ. of Durham (BSc 1st Cl. Hons Botany). Dept of Botany, British Museum (Nat. History), 1952, Dep. Keeper 1972. President: Botanical Soc. of the British Isles, 1983–85; Ray Soc., 1986–88. *Publications:* papers in scientific periodicals and similar pubns. *Recreations:* travel, music, gardening. *Address:* Barn Croft, Rodmell, near Lewes, E Sussex BN7 3HF.

CANNON, Richard Walter, CEng, FIEE; Joint Managing Director, 1977–83, Managing Director, 1983, Cable and Wireless plc; retired; *b* 7 Dec. 1923; *s* of Richard William Cannon and Lily Harriet Cannon (*née* Fewins); *m* 1949, Dorothy (formerly Jarvis); two *d.* *Educ:* Eltham Coll. Joined Cable and Wireless Ltd, 1941; Exec. Dir, 1973. Director: Batelco (Bahrain), 1981–90; Teletswana (Botswana), 1984–86. *Publications:* telecommunications papers for IEE and IERE.

CANNON, Thomas; Chief Executive: Management Charter Initiative, since 1995; MDE Services, since 1982; *b* 20 Nov. 1945; *s* of Albert and Bridget Cannon; *m* 1971, Frances Cannon (*née* Constable); one *s* one *d.* *Educ:* St Francis Xavier's Grammar Sch., Liverpool; Borough Polytechnic. BSc (Hons) Sociology (London Univ. external degree). Res. Associate, Warwick Univ., 1969–71; Lectr, Middlesex Poly., 1971–72; Products Man., Imperial Gp, 1972–74; Lectr, Durham Univ., 1975–81; Prof., Univ. of Stirling, 1981–89; Dir, 1989–92, Vis. Prof., 1992–95, Manchester Business Sch.; Associate Rector, Hajioannion Univ., Cyprus, 1993–94. Visiting Professor: Kingston Univ., 1993–; Bradford Univ., 1997–; Middlesex Univ., 1997–; Mercers' Sch. Meml Prof. of Commerce, Gresham Coll., 1996–. Dir, Stirling Gp. Member: ESRC; Industry, Environment and Economy R&D Gp, 1990–92; Jt Cttee, ESRC/SERC, 1990–94; Business Links Gp, 1993–94; Chairman: Jt Working Party, Scottish Examinations Bd, 1988–90; Rail Users Consultative Cttee for NW, 1996–97; Dep. Chm., Management Develt to the Millennium, Inst. of Management, 1992–95. Member: Quality Standard Cttee, NCVO, 1997–; BBC Educn Council, 1998–. FCGI; FRSA; FCIM; CIMgt. *Publications:* Advertising Research, 1972; Distribution Research, 1973; Advertising: the economic implications, 1974; Basic Marketing, 1976, 4th edn 1995; How to Win Profitable Business, 1983; How to Win Business Overseas, 1984; Enterprise, 1991; The World of Business, 1991; Women as Entrepreneurs, 1992; Corporate Responsibility, 1993; (ed jtly) The Times Good University Guide, 1994; How to Get Ahead in Business, 1994; The Guinness Book of Business Records, 1996; Welcome to the Revolution, 1996; papers in learned jls. *Recreations:* soccer, supporting Everton FC, walking, writing. *Address:* 13 Old Broadway, Manchester M20 3DH. *T:* (0161) 434 2989.

CANNON-BROOKES, Peter, PhD; FMA, FIIC; international museum consultant; *b* 23 Aug. 1938; *s* of Victor Montgomery Cannon Brookes and late Nancy Margaret (*née* Markham Carter); *m* 1966, Caroline Aylmer, *d* of John Aylmer Christie-Miller; one *s* one *d.* *Educ:* Bryanston; Trinity Hall, Cambridge (MA); Courtauld Inst. of Art, Univ. of London (PhD). FMA 1975. Gooden and Fox Ltd, London, 1963–64; Keeper, Dept of Art, City Museums and Art Gall., Birmingham, 1965–78; Sessional Teacher in History of Art, Courtauld Inst. of Art, London, 1966–68; Keeper of Dept of Art, Nat. Mus. of Wales, Cardiff, 1978–86; Mus. Services Dir, STIPPLE Database Services, 1986–90. Internat. Council of Museums: Mem. Exec. Bd, UK Cttee, 1973–81; Pres., Internat. Art Exhibns

Cttee, 1977–79 (Dir, 1974–80; Sec., 1975–77); Dir, Conservation Cttee, 1975–81 (Vice Pres., 1978–81). Member: Town Twinning Cttee, Birmingham Internat. Council, 1968–78; Birm. Diocesan Synod, 1970–78; Birm. Diocesan Adv. Cttee for Care of Churches, 1972–78; Edgbaston Deanery Synod, 1970–78 (Lay Jt Chm., 1975–78); Society of Authors, 1972–; Art and Design Adv. Panel, Welsh Jt Educn Cttee, 1978–86; Welsh Arts Council, 1979–84 (Member: Art Cttee, 1978–84; Craft Cttee, 1983–87); Projects and Orgns Cttee, Crafts Council, 1985–87. President: Welsh Fedn of Museums and Art Galleries, 1980–82; S Wales Art Soc., 1980–87. Trustee, Welsh Sculpture Trust, 1981–94; Consultant Curator, Tabley House Collection, 1988–. Editor, Museum Management and Curatorship, 1981–. Freeman 1969, Liveryman 1974, Worshipful Co. of Goldsmiths. FRSA. JP Birmingham, 1973–78, Cardiff, 1978–82. Prize, Masaryk Acad. of Arts, Prague, 1998. *Publications:* (with H. D. Molesworth) European Sculpture, 1964; (with C. A. Cannon-Brookes) Baroque Churches, 1969; Omar Ramsden, 1973; Lombard Painting, 1974; After Gulbenkian, 1976; The Cornbury Park Bellini, 1977; Michael Ayrton, 1978; Emile Antoine Bourdelle, 1983; Ivor Roberts-Jones, 1983; Czech Sculpture 1800–1938, 1983; Paintings from Tabley, 1989; The Painted Word, 1991; William Redgrave, 1998; contrib. Apollo, Art Bull., Arte Veneta, Burlington Mag., Connoisseur, Internat. Jl of Museum Management and Curatorship, and Museums Jl. *Recreations:* photography, growing vegetables, cooking. *Address:* Thrupp House, Abingdon, Oxon OX14 3NE. *T:* (01235) 520595, *Fax:* (01235) 534817. *Club:* Athenæum.

CANT, Rev. Harry William Macphail; Minister of St Magnus Cathedral, Kirkwall, Orkney, 1968–90; Chaplain to the Queen in Scotland, 1972–91, and Extra Chaplain, since 1991; *b* 3 April 1921; *s* of late J. M. Cant and late Margaret Cant; *m* 1951, Margaret Elizabeth Loudon; one *s* two *d*. *Educ:* Edinburgh Acad.; Edinburgh Univ. (MA, BD); Union Theological Seminary, NY (STM). Lieut, KOSB, 1941–43; Captain, King's African Rifles, 1944–46; TA Chaplain, 7th Argyll and Sutherland Highlanders, 1953–61. Asst Minister, Old Parish Church, Aberdeen, 1950–51; Minister of Fallin Parish Church, Stirling, 1951–56; Scottish Sec., Student Christian Movt, 1956–59; Minister of St Thomas' Parish Church, 1960–68. *Publications:* Preaching in a Scottish Parish Church: St Magnus and Other Sermons, 1970; Springs of Renewal in Congregational Life, 1980; (ed jtly) Light in the North, 1989; Pilgrimage of a Pupil, Preacher and Pastor: the mystery and the miracle of the Church, 1999. *Recreations:* angling, golf. *Address:* Quoylobs, Holm, Orkney KW17 2RY.

CANTACUZINO, Sherban, CBE 1988; FSA; FRIBA; Secretary, Royal Fine Art Commission, 1979–94; *b* 6 Sept. 1928; *s* of late Georges M. Cantacuzino and Sanda Stirbey; *m* 1954, Anne Mary Trafford; two *d* (one *s* decd). *Educ:* Winchester Coll.; Magdalene Coll., Cambridge (MA). Partner, Steane, Shipman & Cantacuzino, Chartered Architects, 1956–65; private practice, 1965–73; Asst Editor, Architectural Review, 1967–73, Exec. Editor, 1973–79. Sen. Lectr, Dept of Architecture, College of Art, Canterbury, 1967–70. Trustee: Thomas Cubitt Trust, 1978–98; Design Museum, 1981–98; Member: Arts Panel, Arts Council, 1977–80; Steering Cttee, Aga Khan Award for Architecture, 1980–83 (Mem., Master Jury, 1980); Council, RSA, 1980–85; Design Cttee, London Transport, 1981–82; Adv. Panel, Railway Heritage Trust, 1985–; Fabric Cttee, Canterbury Cathedral, 1987–; Adv. Cttee, Getty Grant Prog., 1993–98; Design Panel, Plymouth Develt Corp., 1994–98; Bd, Landscape Foundn, 1995–. Advr, Earth Centre, 1995–. Dir, Taylor Warren Ltd, 1995–2001. Pres., UK Cttee, ICOMOS, 1987–93 (Mem., Exec. Cttee, 1990–99). Chm., Princess Margarita of Roumania Trust, 1995–98; Trustee, Wallingford Arts Park Gallery Trust, 1995–98. FSA 1995. DUniv York, 1996. *Publications:* Modern Houses of the World, 1964, 3rd edn 1966; Great Modern Architecture, 1966, 2nd edn 1968; European Domestic Architecture, 1969; New Uses for Old Buildings, 1975; (ed) Architectural Conservation in Europe, 1975; Wells Coates, a monograph, 1978; (with Susan Brandt) Saving Old Buildings, 1980; The Architecture of Howell, Killick, Partridge and Amis, 1981; Charles Correa, 1984; (ed) Architecture in Continuity: building in the Islamic world today, 1985; Re/Architecture: old buildings/New uses, 1989; What makes a good building?: an inquiry by Royal Fine Art Commission, 1994; articles in Architectural Rev. *Recreations:* music, cooking. *Address:* 140 Iffley Road, W6 0PE. *T:* (020) 8748 0415. *Club:* Garrick.

CANTER, Prof. David Victor, PhD; FBPsS; Professor of Psychology, University of Liverpool, since 1994; *b* 5 Jan. 1944; *s* of late Hyman Victor Canter and Coralie Lilian Canter (*née* Hyam); *m* 1967, Sandra Lorraine Smith; one *s* two *d*. *Educ:* Liverpool Collegiate Grammar Sch.; Liverpool Univ. (BA Hons 1964; PhD 1969). Research Associate, Liverpool Univ., 1964–65; Strathclyde University: Res. Associate, 1966; Res. Fellow, Building Performance Res. Unit, 1967–70; Lectr, 1971–72; University of Surrey: Lectr, 1972–78; Reader, 1978–83; Prof. of Applied Psychology, 1983–87; Prof. of Psychology, 1987–94; Hd of Dept of Psychology, 1987–91. CPsychol 1988; FBIM; FAPA. Mem., Forensic Sci. Soc. Hon. Mem., Japanese Inst. of Architects, 1971. Man. Ed., Jl of Envmtl Psychology, 1981–. *Publications:* Architectural Psychology, 1970; Psychology for Architects, 1974; (ed jtly) Psychology and the Built Environment, 1974; Environmental Interaction, 1975; (with P. Stringer) Psychology of Place, 1977; (ed jtly) Designing for Therapeutic Environments, 1979; (ed) Fires and Human Behaviour, 1980, 2nd edn 1990; (ed jtly) Psychology in Practice, 1982; (ed) Facet Theory, 1985; (ed jtly) The Research Interview, 1985; (ed jtly) Environmental Perspectives, 1988; (ed jtly) Environmental Policy, Assessment and Communication, 1988; (ed jtly) New Directions in Environmental Participation, 1988; (ed jtly) Environmental Social Psychology, 1988; (with M. Comber and D. Uzzell) Football in its Place, 1989; (ed jtly) Empirical Approaches to Social Representations, 1992; Criminal Shadows: inside the mind of the serial killer, 1994; (jtly) The Faces of Homelessness, 1995; Psychology in Action, 1996; (ed jtly) Criminal Detection and the Psychology of Crime, 1997; Assessing Accounts of Crime, 1998; (ed jtly) Profiling in Policy and Practice, 1999; Interviewing and Deception, 1999; The Social Psychology of Crime, 2000; Profiling Property Crimes, 2000; Profiling Rape and Murder, 2001; contribs to learned jls, newspapers, radio, TV. *Recreations:* clarinet, musical composition. *Address:* Department of Psychology, University of Liverpool, Liverpool L69 7ZA. *T:* (0151) 794 3910, *Fax:* (0151) 794 3938; *e-mail:* canter@liverpool.ac.uk.

CANTERBURY, Archbishop of, since 1991; **Most Rev. and Rt Hon. George Leonard Carey;** PC 1991; *b* 13 Nov. 1935; *s* of George and Ruby Carey; *m* 1960, Eileen Harmsworth Hood, Dagenham, Essex; two *s* two *d*. *Educ:* Bifrons Secondary Modern Sch., Barking; London College of Divinity; King's College, London. BD Hons, MTh, PhD London. National Service, RAF Wireless Operator, 1954–56. Deacon, 1962; Curate, St Mary's, Islington, 1962–66; Lecturer: Oak Hill Coll., Southgate, 1966–70; St John's Coll., Nottingham, 1970–75; Vicar, St Nicholas' Church, Durham, 1975–82; Principal, Trinity Coll., Stoke Hill, Bristol, 1982–87; Hon. Canon, Bristol Cathedral, 1983–87; Bishop of Bath and Wells, 1987–91. FKC, 1994. Hon. doctorates from UK and USA univs. *Publications:* I Believe in Man, 1975; God Incarnate, 1976; (jtly) The Great Acquittal, 1980; The Church in the Market Place, 1984; The Meeting of the Waters, 1985; The Gate of Glory, 1986, 2nd edn 1992; The Message of the Bible, 1988; The Great God Robbery, 1989; I Believe, 1991; (jtly) Planting New Churches, 1991; Sharing a Vision, 1993; Spiritual Journey, 1994; My Journey, Your Journey, 1996; Canterbury–Letters to the Future, 1998; Jesus 2000, 1999; contributor to numerous jls. *Recreations:* reading, writing, walking. *Address:* Lambeth Palace, SE1 7JU. *T:* (020) 7898 1200.

CANTERBURY, Dean of; *see* Willis, Very Rev. R. A.

CANTERBURY, Archdeacon of; *see* Evans, Ven. P. A. S.

CANTLE, Edward Francis; Associate Director, Performance Support, Improvement and Development Agency, since 2001; *b* 12 Feb. 1950; *s* of John Victor Cantle and Isabel Ruth Cantle; *m* 1974, Heather Ann Welburn; two *d*. *Educ:* Shooters Hill Grammar Sch., London; Portsmouth Poly. (BSc Hons); Dip. Housing 1978; FCIH 1986. Housing Advr, 1972–73, Area Improvement Officer, 1973–74, Manchester CC; Asst. Chief Housing Officer, 1974–80, Chief Housing Officer, 1980–83, City of Wakefield; Under Sec., AMA, 1983–88; Dir of Housing, Leicester City, 1988–90; Chief Exec., City of Nottingham, 1990–2001. Chm., DETR Local Govt Construction Task Force, 1999–; Mem. Bd, EA, 2000–. Chm., Queen's Medical Centre, Nottingham Univ. Hosp. NHS Trust, 2001–. Chm., Sustainability First (charity), 1999–. *Publications:* contrib. AMA studies, incl. Defects in Housing series; numerous contribs to local govt and construction press. *Recreations:* sports, including walking, tennis and golf. *Address:* Improvement and Development Agency, Layden House, 76–86 Turnmill Street, EC1M 5LG.

CANTOR, Anthony John James; HM Diplomatic Service; Ambassador to Paraguay, since 2001; *b* 1 Feb. 1946; *s* of late John Stanley Frank Cantor and of Olive Mary Cantor (*née* McCartney); *m* 1968, Patricia Elizabeth Naughton; one *s* two *d*. *Educ:* Bournemouth Grammar Sch. Joined Diplomatic Service, 1965; FCO, 1965–68; Rangoon, 1968–71; Japanese lang. trng, Sheffield Univ., 1971–72, Tokyo, 1972–73; Third, then Second, Sec., Tokyo, 1973–76; Accra, 1977–80; Aid Policy Dept, 1980–82, W Indian and Atlantic Dept, 1982–83, FCO; Consul (Commercial), Osaka, 1983–89; Dep. Hd of Mission, Hanoi, 1990–92; Dep. Dir, Invest UK, 1992–94; First Sec., Tokyo, 1994–95; Dep. Consul-Gen., Osaka, 1995–98; EU Dept (Bilateral), FCO, 1999–2000; Dep. Comr-Gen., UK Pavilion, Hanover, 2000; Public Diplomacy Dept, FCO, 2000–01. Mem., Britain-Burma Soc. *Recreations:* travel, languages, horse-riding, World War II in Asia. *Address:* c/o Foreign and Commonwealth Office, SW1A 2AH. *Clubs:* Royal Commonwealth Society; Kobe (Japan).

CANTOR, Prof. Brian, PhD; FREng; FIM; FInstP; FRMS; Cookson Professor of Materials, since 1995, and Head, Division of Mathematical and Physical Sciences, since 2000, Oxford University; Fellow, St Catherine's College, Oxford, since 1995; *b* 11 Jan. 1948; *s* of Oliver Horace Cantor and Gertrude Mary Cantor (*née* Thompson); *m* 1st, 1967, Margaret Elaine Pretty (marr. diss. 1979); two *s*; 2nd, 1981, Anne Catherine Sharry (*d* 1993). *Educ:* Manchester Grammar Sch.; Christ's Coll., Cambridge (BA, MA, PhD 1972). CEng 1979, FREng (FEng 1998); FIM 1989; FRMS 1993; FInstP 1999. Res. Fellow, Sch. of Engrg, Sussex Univ., 1972–81; Lectr, 1981–91, Reader in Materials Processing, 1991–95, Head, 1995–2000, Dept of Materials, Oxford Univ.; Sen. Res. Fellow, Jesus Coll., Oxford, 1987–95; Dir, Oxford Centre for Advanced Materials and Composites, 1990–95. Industrial Fellow, GE Corporate Labs, Schenectady, NY, 1982. Consultant, Rolls-Royce, 1996–. Editl Advr, Inst. of Physics Press, 1983–. Consultant, Alcan Internat., Banbury Labs, Oxon, 1986–94. Jt Ed., Progress in Materials Science, 1988–; Chm. Eds, Internat. Jl of Cast Metals, 1997–. *Publications:* (ed) Rapidly Quenched Metals III, 1978; (ed with P. B. Hirsch) Tribute to J. W. Christian, 1992; (jtly) Stability of Microstructure in Metallic Systems, 1997. *Recreations:* mountain walking, guitar. *Address:* Department of Materials, Oxford University, Parks Road, Oxford OX1 3PH. *T:* (01865) 273737.

CANTY, Brian George John, CBE 1993 (OBE 1988); HM Diplomatic Service, retired; Governor of Anguilla, 1989–92; *b* 23 Oct. 1931; *s* of George Robert Canty and Phœbe Charlotte Canty (*née* Cobb); *m* 1954, Maureen Kathleen Kenny; one *s* one *d*. *Educ:* South West Essex Technical College; external student, London University (Social Studies); RAF Staff College (psc 1970). RN 1950; Air Ministry, 1957; Financial Adviser's Office, Cyprus, 1960; MoD (Air), 1963; FCO, 1971; served Oslo, 1973, Kingston, 1977, Vienna, 1979; FCO, 1984; Dep. Governor, Bermuda, 1986. Dir, A. S. Trust Ltd, 1993–. JP Bermuda, 1986. *Recreations:* sailing, ski-ing, DIY.

CAPE, Donald Paul Montagu Stewart, CMG 1977; CBE 1998; HM Diplomatic Service, retired; Ambassador and UK Permanent Representative to the Council of Europe, Strasbourg, 1978–83; *b* 6 Jan. 1923; *s* of late John Scarvell and Olivia Millicent Cape; *m* 1948, Cathune Johnston; four *s* one *d*. *Educ:* Ampleforth Coll.; Brasenose Coll., Oxford. Scots Guards, 1942–45. Entered Foreign Service, 1946. Served: Belgrade, 1946–49; FO, 1949–51; Lisbon, 1951–55; Singapore, 1955–57; FO, 1957–60; Bogota, 1960–61; Holy See, 1962–67; Head of Information Administration Dept, FCO, 1968–70; Counsellor, Washington, 1970–73; Counsellor, Brasilia, 1973–75; Ambassador to Laos, 1976–78. Administrator, Anglo-Irish Encounter, 1983–98; Chm., Anglo-Portuguese Soc., 1988–91. *Recreations:* tennis, walking, swimming. *Address:* Hilltop, Wonersh, Guildford, Surrey GU5 0QT.

CAPE, Maj.-Gen. Timothy Frederick, CB 1972; CBE 1966; DSO; idc, jssc, psc; *b* Sydney, 5 Aug. 1915; *s* of C. S. Cape, DSO, Edgecliff, NSW; *m* 1961, Elizabeth (*d* 1985), *d* of Brig. R. L. R. Rabett; one *d*. *Educ:* Cranbrook Sch., Sydney; RMC Duntroon. Served with RAA, 1938–41; Bde Major Sparrow Force, Timor, 1942; GS01: (Air) New Guinea Force, 1942–43; (Ops) Melbourne, 1944; (Air) Morotai, 1945; (Ops) Japan, 1946–47; (Plans) Melbourne, 1948–49; Instructor, Staff Coll., Camberley, UK, 1950–52; Comdt, OCS, Portsea, 1954–56; Dep. Master-Gen. Ordnance, 1957–59; COS Northern Comd, Brisbane, 1961; Dir of Staff Duties, Army HQ, Canberra, 1962–63; Comdr, Adelaide, 1964; GOC Northern Comd, Brisbane, 1965–68; Master-General of the Ordnance, 1968–72; retd 1972. Nat. Chm., Royal United Services Inst. of Australia, 1980–83; Chm., Nat. Disaster Relief Cttee and Mem., Nat. Council, Australian Red Cross Soc., 1975–85. Bronze Star (US). *Address:* Unit 311, The Grange, 67 Macgregor Street, Deakin, ACT 2600, Australia. *Clubs:* Melbourne (Melbourne); Commonwealth (Canberra); Union (Sydney); Royal Sydney Golf.

CAPE TOWN, Archbishop of, and Metropolitan of Southern Africa, since 1996; **Most Rev. (Winston Hugh) Njongonkulu Ndungane;** *b* Kokstad, 2 April 1941; *s* of Foster Tunyiswa Ndungane and Tingaza (*née* Gcanca); *m* 1st, 1972, Nosipho Ngcelwane (*d* 1986); one *s* one *d*; 2nd, 1987, Nomahlubi Vokwana. *Educ:* Lovedale High Sch., Alice, E Cape; Federal Theol Seminary, Alice (Associate, 1973); King's Coll., London (AKC, BD 1978; MTh 1979; FKC 1997). Ordained deacon, 1973, priest, 1974; Assistant Priest: St Mark's, Athlone, Cape Town, 1973–75; St Mark, Mitcham, 1975–76; St Peter's, Hammersmith, 1976–77; St Mary the Virgin, Primrose Hill, 1977–79; Asst Chaplain, St George's, Paris, 1979; Rector, St Nicholas, Elsies River, Cape Town, 1980–81; Provincial Liaison Officer, CPSA, 1981–84; Principal, St Bede's Coll., Umtata, 1985–86; Provincial Canon, 1987; Chief Exec. Officer, CPSA, 1987–91; Bishop of Kimberley and Kuruman, 1991–96. Vis. Scholar, Ch Divinity Sch. of the Pacific, Berkeley, 1990–91. Chairman:

SACC Church Leaders' Forum, 1997–98; Nat. Poverty Hearings, 1998; Member: Budget Gp, USPG, 1981–86; ACC, and its Standing Cttee, 1981–90; Bd, SABC, 1993– (Chm., Religious Broadcasting Panel, 1995–). Hon. DD Rhodes Univ., 1997. *Publications* include: The Commuter Population for Claremont, Cape, 1973; Human Rights and the Christian Doctrine of Man, 1979; contributions to: Peace and Peacemaking, 1984; Open to the Spirit, 1987; Doing Ethics in Context, 1994; Ethics and Values: a global perspective, 1997; Change and Challenge, 1998; articles in periodicals. *Address:* Bishopscourt, Claremont, Cape 7700, South Africa.

CAPE TOWN, Bishops Suffragan of; *see* Castle, Rt Rev. M. E.; Gregorowski, Rt Rev. C. J.

CAPEL CURE, (George) Nigel, TD; JP; DL; *b* 28 Sept. 1908; *o s* of late Major George Edward Capel Cure, JP, Blake Hall, Ongar; *m* 1935, Nancy Elizabeth, *d* of late William James Barry, Great Witchingham Hall, Norwich; two *s* one *d*. *Educ:* Eton; Trinity Coll., Cambridge. DL and JP, 1947, High Sheriff, 1951, Essex; Vice-Lieutenant, later Vice Lord-Lieutenant, Essex, 1958–78; late of Blake Hall, Ongar. *Recreations:* shooting, cricket. *Address:* Ashlings, Moreton Road, Ongar, Essex CM5 0EZ. *T:* (01277) 362634. *Clubs:* MCC, City University.

CAPELL, family name of **Earl of Essex**.

CAPELLA, Josephine Marie; *see* Durning, J. M.

CAPELLAS, Michael D.; President and Chief Executive Officer, Compaq Computer Corporation, since 1999; *m* Marie; two *c*. *Educ:* Kent State Univ. (BBA 1976). CPA. Systems analyst and manufg posts, Republic Steel Corp., 1976-81; Schlumberger Ltd, 1981-96: posts included Dir for Inf. Systems; Controller and Treas., Asia Pacific; Chief Financial Officer, Dowell Schlumberger Inc.; Ops Manager, Fairchild Semiconductor Unit; Founder, and Man. Partner, Benchmarking Partners,1996; Dir of Supply Chain Mgt, SAP America, 1996-97; Sen. Vice-Pres. and Gen. Manager, Oracle Corp., 1997-98; Chief Inf. Officer, 1998-99, Chief Operating Officer, 1999, Compaq Computer Corp. *Address:* Compaq Computer Corporation, PO Box 692000, 20555 State Highway 249, Houston, TX 77269-2000, USA.

CAPEWELL, Vasanti Emily Indrani; *see* Selvaratnam, V. E. I.

CAPEY, Montague Martin; Under Secretary and Director of Establishments and Organisation, Department for Education (formerly Department of Education and Science), 1988–93; *b* 16 July 1933; *s* of Ernest Paton Capey and Lettice Isabel Capey; *m* 1960, Diana Mary Barnes; one *s* one *d*. *Educ:* The Leys Sch., Cambridge; Clare Coll., Cambridge (MA); Didsbury Coll., Bristol; Univ. of Bristol (BA). Methodist Minister, 1958–71. Principal 1971–76, Asst Sec. 1976–88, DES. *Recreations:* gardening, music, enjoying Cornwall. *Address:* Bramble Cottage, West Kitty, St Agnes, Cornwall TR5 0SU.

CAPLAN, Hon. Lord; Philip Isaac Caplan; a Senator of the College of Justice in Scotland, 1989–2000; *b* 24 Feb. 1929; *s* of Hyman and Rosalena Caplan; *m* 1st, 1953; two *s* one *d*; 2nd, 1974, Joyce Ethel Stone; one *d*. *Educ:* Eastwood Sch., Renfrewshire; Glasgow Univ. (MA, LLB). Solicitor, 1952–56; called to Bar, 1957; Standing Junior Counsel to Accountant of Court, 1964–70; QC (Scot.) 1970; Sheriff of Lothian and Borders, 1979–83; Sheriff-Principal of North Strathclyde, 1983–89. Member: Sheriff Court Rules Council, 1984–89; Adv. Council on Messengers-at-Arms and Sheriff Officers, 1987–89. Chairman: Plant Varieties and Seeds Tribunal, Scotland, 1977–79; Scottish Assoc. for Study of Delinquency, 1985–89 (Hon. Vice-Pres., 1990–); Family Mediation Scotland (formerly Scottish Assoc. of Family Conciliation Services), 1989–94 (Hon. Pres., 1994–); Bd of Trustees, CommunicAbility, 1992–. FRPS 1988; AFIAP 1985. Hon. LLD Glasgow, 1996. *Recreations:* photography, reading, music. *Club:* New (Edinburgh).

CAPLAN, Prof. (Ann) Patricia (Bailey), PhD; FRAI; Professor of Social Anthropology, Goldsmiths College, University of London, 1989–97 and since 2001; *b* 13 March 1942; *d* of Sylvester Launcelot Bailey and Marjorie Bailey (*née* Parr); *m* 1967, Prof. Lionel Caplan; one *s* one *d*. *Educ:* Sch. of Oriental and African Studies, Univ. of London (BA Hons African Studies 1963; MA Social Anthropology 1965; PhD 1968). Tutor: Birkbeck Coll., Univ. of London, 1964–65 and 1968–69; Open Univ., 1970–71 and 1974–75; Postdoctoral Fellow, SOAS, 1968–70 and 1974–76; Lectr, then Sen. Lectr, in Anthropology, Goldsmiths Coll., Univ. of London, 1977–89; Prof. of Anthropology, and Dir, Inst. of Commonwealth Studies, Univ. of London, 1998–2000. Chair, Assoc. of Social Anthropologists, 1997–2001. *Publications:* Priests and Cobblers: social change in a Hindu village in Western Nepal, 1972; Choice and Constraint in a Swahili Community: property, hierarchy and cognatic descent on the East African Coast, 1975; (ed with J. Bujra) Women United, Women Divided: cross cultural perspectives on female solidarity, 1978; Class and Gender in India: women and their organisations in a South Indian city, 1985; (ed) The Cultural Construction of Sexuality, 1987; (ed with F. le Guennec-Coppens) Les Swahili entre Afrique et Arabie, 1992; (ed jtly) Gendered Fields: women, men and ethnography 1993; (ed) Understanding Disputes: the politics of law, 1995; African Voices, African Lives: personal narratives from a Swahili village, 1997; (ed) Food, Health and Identity: approaches from the social sciences, 1997; (ed) Risk Revisited, 2000; numerous articles in learned jls. *Recreations:* swimming, walking, classical music, gardening. *Address:* Department of Anthropology, Goldsmiths College, SE14 6NW. *T:* (020) 7919 7800, 7803, *Fax:* (020) 7919 7813; *e-mail:* p.caplan@gold.ac.uk.

CAPLAN, Jonathan Michael; QC 1991; a Recorder, since 1995; *b* 11 Jan. 1951; *s* of Dr Malcolm Denis Caplan and late Jean Hilary Caplan, JP; *m* 1993, Selena Lennard (*née* Peskin); one *s*, and one step *s* one step *d*. *Educ:* St Paul's Sch.; Downing Coll., Cambridge (MA). Called to Bar, Gray's Inn, 1973, Bencher, 2000; Asst Recorder, 1989–95. Mem., General Council of Bar, 1986–90; Chairman: Bar Council Report on Televising the Courts, 1989; Public Affairs Cttee, Bar Council, 1991–92. Member: Appeal Cttee, Wiener Liby, 1996–; BBC Ind. Rev. Panel on documentaries, 1997; Develt Bd, Royal Court Theatre, 1997–. Mem., BAFTA. FRSA 1992. Mem. Editl Bd, Jl of Criminal Law, 1988–. *Publications:* The Confait Confessions, 1977; (contrib.) Disabling Professions, 1978. *Recreations:* writing, tennis, collecting historical newspapers and manuscripts, Khmer and Thai sculpture, cinema, books, flat horseracing. *Address:* 5 Paper Buildings, Temple, EC4Y 7HB. *T:* (020) 7583 6117. *Clubs:* Queen's; Royal Ascot Racing.

CAPLAN, Patricia; *see* Caplan, A. P. B.

CAPLAN, Philip Isaac; *see* Caplan, Hon. Lord.

CAPLAT, Moran Victor Hingston, CBE 1968; General Administrator, Glyndebourne Festival Opera, retired; *b* 1 Oct. 1916; *s* of Roger Armand Charles Caplat and Norah Hingston; *m* 1943, Diana Murray Downton; one *s* two *d* (and one *s* decd). *Educ:* privately; Royal Acad. of Dramatic Art. Actor, etc., 1934–39. Royal Navy, 1939–45. Glyndebourne: Asst to Gen. Man., 1945; Gen. Man., later known as Gen. Administrator, 1949–81. *Publication:* Dinghies to Divas (autobiog.), 1985. *Address:* Mermaid Cottage, 6 Church Road, Newick, Lewes, East Sussex BN8 4JU. *T:* (01825) 722964. *Clubs:* Garrick, Royal Ocean Racing; Royal Yacht Squadron (Cowes).

See also D. N. O. Sekers.

CAPLIN, Dianne; *see* Hayter, D.

CAPLIN, Ivor Keith; MP (Lab) Hove, since 1997; an Assistant Government Whip, since 2001; *b* 8 Nov. 1958; *s* of late Leonard Caplin and of Alma Caplin (*née* Silver); *m* 1985, Maureen Whelan; two *s* one *d*. *Educ:* King Edward's Sch., Witley; Brighton Coll. of Technol. (Nat. Cert. Business Studies 1979). Joined Legal & General Assurance Society, 1978: various mgt posts, 1989–94; Quality Manager, Sales Div., 1994–97. Nat. Sec., ASTMS, 1983–88. Hove Borough Council: Mem. (Lab), 1991–97; Leader, 1995–97; Mem., Brighton and Hove UA, 1996–98. PPS to Leader of H of C, 1998–2001. Treas., All Party Animal Welfare Gp, 1997–; Sec., Parly Lab. Local Govt Gp, 1997–99; Officer, All Party Football Gp, 1998–. Mem. Exec., Lab. Friends of Israel, 1997–. Trustee, Old Market Trust, Brunswick, Hove, 1997–. *Recreations:* supporter Brighton and Hove Albion FC and Sussex CCC, music, reading. *Address:* House of Commons, SW1A 0AA; Parliamentary Office, Town Hall, Hove BN3 4AH. *T:* (01273) 292933.

CAPRON, (George) Christopher; independent television producer; Director, Capron Productions, 1987–99; *b* 17 Dec. 1935; *s* of late Lt-Col George Capron and Hon. Mrs (Edith) Christian Capron (*née* Hepburne-Scott); *m* 1958, Edna Naomi Goldrei; one *s* one *d*. *Educ:* Wellington Coll.; Trinity Hall, Cambridge (BA Hons Mod. Langs). Served Army, 12th Royal Lancers (Prince of Wales's), 1954–56. British Broadcasting Corporation: radio producer, 1963–67; television producer, 1967–76; Editor, Tonight, 1976–77; Editor, Panorama, 1977–79; Asst Head, 1979–81, Head, 1981–85, TV Current Affairs Programmes; Head of Parly Broadcasting, 1985–87. FRTS 1996. *Recreations:* village cricket, tennis, golf. *Address:* 32 Amerland Road, SW18 1PZ; Southwick Hall, Oundle, Northants PE8 5BL.

CAPSTICK, His Honour Brian Eric; QC 1973; a Circuit Judge, 1985–98; *b* 12 Feb. 1927; *o s* of late Eric and Betty Capstick; *m* 1960, Margaret Harrison; one *s* one *d*. *Educ:* Sedbergh; Queen's Coll., Oxford (Scholar) (MA). Served HM Forces, 1945–48: 17/21st Lancers, Palestine, 1947–48. Tancred Student, and called to Bar, Lincoln's Inn, 1952; Bencher, 1980; a Recorder, 1980–85. Dep. Chm., Northern Agriculture Tribunal, 1976–; Asst Boundary Comr, 1978–85; Member: Parole Bd, 1995–; Mental Health Review Tribunal, 1999–2000. Appeal Steward, British Board of Boxing Control, 1985–. *Recreations:* shooting, reading, cooking. *Address:* 71 South End Road, NW3 2RJ. *Club:* Garrick.

CAPSTICK, Charles William, CB 1992; CMG 1972; Deputy Secretary, Food Safety Directorate, Ministry of Agriculture, Fisheries and Food, 1989–94; *b* 18 Dec. 1934; *s* of late William Capstick and Janet Frankland; *m* 1962, Joyce Alma Dodsworth; two *s*. *Educ:* King's Coll., Univ. of Durham (BSc (Hons)); Univ. of Kentucky, USA (MS). MAFF: Asst Agricl Economist, 1961; Principal Agricl Economist, 1966; Senior Principal Agricl Economist, 1968; Sen. Econ. Advr and Head, Milk and Milk Products Div., 1976; Under Sec., 1977, Dir of Econs and Statistics, 1977. Pres., Agricultural Economics Soc., 1983. Pres., Old Clitheronians Assoc., 2001. *Recreations:* gardening, golf. *Address:* 7 Dellfield Close, Radlett, Herts WD7 8LS.

CARBERRY, Kay; Head, Equal Rights Department, Trades Union Congress, since 1988; *b* 19 Oct. 1950; *d* of Sean and Sheila Carberry; one *s* by Peter Ashby. *Educ:* Royal Naval Sch., Malta; Sussex Univ. (BA Hons English); QTS. Secondary sch. teacher, 1972–75; Researcher, NUT, 1975–78; Policy Officer, 1978–84, Sen. Policy Officer, 1984–88, TUC. Member: Women's Nat. Commn, 1987–92; EOC, 1999–. Member: Nat. Adv. Body for Public Sector Higher Educn, 1984–87; Adv. Cttee for Women's Employment, Dept of Employment, 1987–90; Race Relations Employment Adv. Gp, Dept of Employment, then DfEE, 1990–96; Ministerial Adv. Cttee on Work-Life Balance Employment, DfEE, 2000–; Ministerial Adv. Gp on Age, DfEE, 2001–. Trustee, NCOPF, 1990–. *Recreations:* theatre, swimming. *Address:* Trades Union Congress, Congress House, Great Russell Street, WC1B 3LS. *T:* (020) 7467 1266.

CARBERY, 11th Baron *cr* 1715; **Peter Ralfe Harrington Evans-Freke;** Bt 1768; *b* 20 March 1920; *o s* of Major the Hon. Ralfe Evans-Freke, MBE (*yr s* of 9th Baron) (*d* 1969), and Vera (*d* 1984), *d* of late C. Harrington Moore; *S* uncle, 1970; *m* 1941, Joyzelle Mary, *o d* of late Herbert Binnie; three *s* two *d*. *Educ:* Downside School. MICE. Served War of 1939–45, Captain RE, India, Burmah. Member of London Stock Exchange, 1955–68. *Recreations:* hunting, tennis, winter sports. *Heir: e s* Hon. Michael Peter Evans-Freke [*b* 11 Oct. 1942; *m* 1967, Claudia Janet Elizabeth, *o d* of Captain P. L. C. Gurney; one *s* three *d*]. *Address:* 2 Hayes Court, Sunnyside, Wimbledon, SW19 4SH.

CARBERY, Prof. Thomas Francis, OBE 1983; Emeritus Professor, University of Strathclyde, since 1990; Chairman, Board of Studies, Huron University in London, since 1995; *b* 18 Jan. 1925; *o c* of Thomas Albert Carbery and Jane Morrison; *m* 1954, Ellen Donnelly; one *s* two *d*. *Educ:* St Aloysius Coll., Glasgow; Univ. of Glasgow and Scottish Coll. of Commerce. Cadet Navigator and Meteorologist, RAFVR, 1943–47; Min. of Labour, 1947–61; Lectr, then Sen. Lectr, in Govt and Econs, Scottish College of Commerce, Glasgow, 1961–64; University of Strathclyde: Sen. Lectr in Govt-Business Relations, 1964–75; Head of Dept of Office Organisation, 1975–79, and Prof., 1979–85; Prof., Dept of Inf. Science, 1985–88, and Chm. of Dept, 1985–86; Prof. (part-time), Dept. of Marketing, 1988–90. Member: IBA (formerly ITA), 1970–79 (Chm., Scottish Cttee, 1970–79); Royal Commn on Gambling, 1976–78; Central Transport Users' Consultative Cttee, 1976–80 (Chm., Scottish Transport Users' Consultative Cttee, 1976–80); European (later International) Adv. Council, Salzburg Seminar, 1980–91; Broadcasting Complaints Commn, 1981–86; Data Protection Tribunal, 1984–98; Scottish Legal Aid Bd, 1986–92; Press Council, 1987–90; Dep. Chm., Scottish Consumer Council, 1980–84 (Mem. 1977–80); Chairman: S of Scotland Electricity Consumers' Cttee, 1990–95; Scottish Cttee, Information Technology, 1982–85; Ombudsman to Mirror Gp Newspapers Scottish titles, 1990–91; Special Adviser, H of C Select Cttee on Scottish Affairs, 1982. Mem. Bd, Energy Action Scotland, 1996–. Academic Governor, Richmond Coll., 1983–95; Governor, 1984–2000, Trustee, 1991–, St Aloysius' Coll., Glasgow. Editor, Approaches to Information Technology (Plenum Press series), 1984–90. KSG 1995. *Publications:* Consumers in Politics, 1969; (jtly) An Introduction to Office Management and Automation, 1991. *Recreations:* golf, conversation, spectating at Association football, listening to Radio 4, watching television. *Address:* 24 Fairfax Avenue, Glasgow G44 5AL. *T:* (0141) 637 0514. *Clubs:* University of Strathclyde, Glasgow Art, Ross Priory (Glasgow).

CARDEN, (Sir) Christopher Robert, (5th Bt *cr* 1887, of Molesey, Surrey; but does not use the title); tropical forest management consultant; conservationist; *b* 24 Nov. 1946; *o s* of Sir Henry Carden, 4th Bt, OBE and of his 1st wife, Jane St Clare Daniell; *S* father, 1993; *m* 1st, 1972, Sainimere Rokotuibau (marr. diss. 1979), Suva, Fiji; 2nd, 1981, Clarita

Eriksen (marr. diss. 1996), Manila, Philippines. *Educ:* Eton; Univ. of Aberdeen (BSc Forestry, 1970). Guide, Internat. Raëlian Movement. *Address:* Casilla 1341, Santa Cruz, Bolivia.

CARDEN, Derrick Charles, CMG 1974; HM Diplomatic Service, retired; Ambassador, Sudan, 1977–79; *b* 30 Oct. 1921; *s* of Canon Henry Craven Carden and Olive (*née* Gorton); *heir pres.* to Sir John Craven Carden, 7th Bt, *qv*; *m* 1952, Elizabeth Anne Russell; two *s* two *d*. *Educ:* Marlborough; Christ Church, Oxford. Sudan Political Service, 1942–54. Entered HM Diplomatic Service, 1954; Foreign Office, 1954–55; Political Agent, Doha, 1955–58; 1st Sec., Libya, 1958–62; Foreign Office, 1962–65; Head of Chancery, Cairo, 1965; Consul-General, Muscat, 1965–69; Dir, ME Centre of Arab Studies, 1969–73; Ambassador, Yemen Arab Republic, 1973–76. Governor, IDS, Sussex Univ., 1981–87. Mem. Bd, CARE Britain, 1988–90. JP Fareham, 1980–91. *Recreation:* pleasures of the countryside. *Address:* Apartment 47, The King's House, Peninsula Square, Winchester SO23 8GJ. *Club:* Vincent's (Oxford).

CARDEN, Sir John Craven, 7th Bt *cr* 1787; *b* 11 March 1926; *s* of Capt. Sir John V. Carden, 6th Bt and Dorothy Mary, *d* of Charles Luckrart McKinnon; *S* father, 1935; *m* 1947, Isabel Georgette, *y d* of late Robert de Hart; one *d*. *Educ:* Eton. *Heir: cousin* Derrick Charles Carden, *qv*. *Address:* PO Box 66, St Helier, Jersey, CI JE4 8PZ. *Club:* White's.

CARDEN, Richard John Derek, CB 1998; Director-General, Trade Policy, Department of Trade and Industry, since 2000; *b* 12 June 1943; *s* of late John and Hilda Carden; *m* 1971, Pamela Haughton; one *s* one *d*. *Educ:* Merchant Taylors' Sch., Northwood; St John's Coll., Oxford (Craven Scholar, 1964; Derby Scholar, 1966; MA Lit. Hum. 1969; DPhil 1970); Freie Universität, Berlin. Research for Egypt Exploration Soc., 1969–70; entered Civil Service, MAFF, 1970; HM Treasury, 1977–79; MAFF, 1979–93 and 1994–2000: Chief Regional Officer, Midlands and Western Region, 1983–86; Under Sec., European Community and Ext. Trade Policy, 1987–91; Fisheries Sec., 1991–93; Dep. Hd, Eur. Secretariat, Cabinet Office, 1993–94; Dep. Sec., Food Safety Directorate, 1994–96; Hd, Food Safety and Envmt Directorate, 1996–2000; actg Perm. Sec., Feb.–May 2000. Dir (non-exec.), Golden Wonder Ltd, 1985–86. *Publications:* The Papyrus Fragments of Sophocles, 1974; (contrib.) The Oxyrhynchus Papyri, vol. LIV, 1987; articles on Greek literature. *Address:* Department of Trade and Industry, Kingsgate House, Victoria Street, SW1E 6SW.

CARDEW, Anthony John; Chairman, Cardew & Co. Ltd, since 1991; *b* 8 Sept. 1949; *s* of Dr Martin Philip Cardew and Anne Elizabeth Cardew (*née* Foster); *m* 1971, Janice Frances Smallwood; one *s* one *d*. *Educ:* Marlborough. Work on local newspapers, 1967–70; United Press Internat., 1970–71; Financial Corresp., Reuters, 1971–74; Charles Barker City, 1974–83; Dir, 1976–83; Hd, Financial Public Relns, 1979–83; Dep. Chm., 1983–85, Chm., 1985–91, Grandfield Rork Collins Financial. Chm., London Cttee, Sarum Coll., 1997 . *Recreations:* book collecting, walking, shooting. *Address:* Cardew & Co. Ltd, 12 Suffolk Street, SW1Y 4HQ. *T:* (020) 7930 0777. *Club:* Reform.

CARDIFF, Archbishop of, (RC), since 2001; **Most Rev. Peter David Smith;** *b* 21 Oct. 1943. *Educ:* Clapham Coll.; Univ. of Exeter (LLB 1966); St John's Seminary, Wonersh; Angelicum Univ., Rome (JCD *summa cum laude* 1977). Coutts Bank, London, 1962–63; ordained priest, 1972; Asst Priest, Larkhall Lane, London, 1972 74; Prof. of Canon Law, St John's Seminary, Wonersh, 1977–84; Parish Priest, St Andrew's, Thornton Heath, 1984–85; Rector, St John's Seminary, Wonersh, 1985–95; Bishop of E Anglia, 1995–2001. Vice-Officialis and Judge, Diocesan Marriage Tribunal, 1977; Officialis, Metropolitan Tribunal, 1980–85. Bishops' Conference: Mem., Cttee for Ministerial Formation, 1989–95; Chairman: Cttee for Marriage and Family Life, 1995–; Dept for Christian Responsibility and Citizenship, 1998–. Chairman: Catholic Trust Soc., 1993–; Catholic Assoc. Pilgrimage Trust, 1998–; Vice-Chm., Catholic Agency for Social Concern, 1996–. Mem. Mgt Cttee, Catholic Educn Service, 1998–. *Address:* Archbishop's House, 41–43 Cathedral Road, Cardiff CF1 9HD.

CARDIFF, Jack, OBE 2000; film director and cameraman; *b* 18 Sept. 1914; *s* of John Joseph and Florence Cardiff; *m*. *Educ:* various schools, incl. Medburn Sch., Herts. Started as child actor, 1918; switched to cameras, 1928. World travelogues, 1937–39. Photographed, MOI Crown Film Unit: Western Approaches, 1942; best known films include: A Matter of Life and Death, Black Narcissus, The Red Shoes, Scott of the Antarctic, Under Capricorn, Pandora and the Flying Dutchman, African Queen, War and Peace. Started as Director, 1958. *Films include: directed:* Sons and Lovers, My Geisha, The Lion, The Long Ships, Young Cassidy, The Mercenaries, The Liquidator, Girl on a Motorcycle, The Mutation; *photographed:* Ride a Wild Pony, The Prince and the Pauper, Behind the Iron Mask, Death on the Nile, Avalanche Express, The Awakening, The Dogs of War, Ghost Story, The Wicked Lady, Scandalous, The Far Pavilions, The Last Days of Pompeii, Conan II, First Blood II, Catseyes, Million Dollar Mystery, Showscan Hollywood, Journey into Space, Magic Balloon; *directed and photographed:* music documentaries, Delius, Vivaldi's Four Seasons. FRPS 1945. Hon. Member: Assoc. Française de Cameramen, 1971; BAFTA, 1995. Hon. Dr of Art: Rome, 1953; RCA, 2000; Hon. DLitt Bradford, 1996; Hon. PhD APU, 2001. Academy Award for photography, Black Narcissus, 1947; Golden Globe Award, 1947; Coup Ce Soir (France), 1951; Film Achievement Award, Look Magazine; British Acad. of Cinematographers Award, War and Peace; New York Critics Award for best film direction, Golden Globe Award, outstanding directorial award (all for Sons and Lovers); Internat. Award for Outstanding Achievement, 1944, Hollywood Internat. Life Achievement Award, 1995, Amer. Soc. of Cinematographers; Contribn to Art of Photography award, British Acad. of Cinematographers, 1996; London Film Critics Life Achievement Award, 1997; Lumière Award, RPS, 1999; Academy Award for Lifetime Achievement, 2001; BAFTA Special Award, 2001. *Publication:* Magic Hour (autobiog.), 1996. *Recreations:* tennis, cricket, painting. *Club:* MCC.

CARDIGAN, Earl of; David Michael James Brudenell-Bruce; Manager, since 1974, owner, and 31st Hereditary Warden, since 1987, Savernake Forest; *b* 12 Nov. 1952; *s* and *heir* of 8th Marquess of Ailesbury, *qv*; *m* 1980, Rosamond Jane, cookery author, *er d* of Captain W. R. M. Winkley, Wyke Champflower Manor, near Bruton, Somerset, and Mrs Jane Winkley; one *s* one *d*. *Educ:* Eton; Rannoch; Royal Agricultural Coll., Cirencester. Sec., Marlborough Conservatives, 1985–; Mem. Exec., Devizes Constituency Cons. Assoc., 1988–. *Heir: s* Viscount Savernake, *qv*. *Address:* Savernake Lodge, Savernake Forest, Marlborough, Wilts SN8 3HP.

CARDIN, Pierre; Commandeur de la Légion d'Honneur, 1997; couturier; *b* 2 July 1922. Designer: Paquin, Paris, 1945–46; Dior, Paris, 1946–50; founded own fashion house, 1950. Founder and Dir, Théâtre des Ambassadeurs, now Espace Pierre Cardin complex, 1970–; Chm., Maxim's Restaurant, 1981–. Designed costumes for films, including: Cocteau's La Belle et la Bête, 1946; The Yellow Rolls Royce, 1965. Retrospective exhibition, V & A, 1990. Dé d'Or, 1977, 1979, 1982; Fashion Oscar, 1985; prize of Foundn for Advancement of Garment and Apparel Res., Japan, 1988. Grand Officer, Order of Merit (Italy), 1988. *Address:* 59 rue du Faubourg Saint-Honoré, 75008 Paris, France.

CARDOSO E CUNHA, António José Baptista; Commissioner General, EXPO '98, 1993–98; Chairman, PARQUE EXPO '98 SA, 1993–98; *b* 28 Jan. 1934; *s* of Arnaldo and Maria Beatriz Cardoso e Cunha; *m* 1958, Dea Cardoso e Cunha; four *s*. *Educ:* Instituto Superior Tecnico; Lisbon Univ. MSc Chem. Engrg. Professional engineer, Lisbon, 1957–65; Man. Dir/Chief Exec. Officer of private cos, Sa da Bandeira, Angola, 1965–77; in business, director of private cos, Lisbon, 1977–78 and 1982–85. Mem. Portuguese Parlt, 1979–83 and 1985–89; Mem. Portuguese Government: Sec. of State for Foreign Trade, 1978, for Industry, 1979; Minister for Agriculture/Fisheries, 1980–82; Mem., European Commn, 1986–92. Grand Croix, Leopold II, Belgium, 1980; Gran Cruz, Merito Agricola, Spain, 1981; Grã-Cruz, Ordem Infant D. Henrique, Portugal, 1993.

CARDOZO, Lydia Helena L.; *see* Lopes Cardozo.

CARDROSS, Lord; Henry Thomas Alexander Erskine; *b* 31 May 1960; *s* and *heir* of 17th Earl of Buchan, *qv*; *m* 1987, Charlotte, *d* of Hon. Matthew Beaumont and Mrs Alexander Maitland; two *s*.

CARDY, Prof. John Lawrence, PhD; FRS 1991; Professor of Physics, University of Oxford, since 1996; Senior Research Fellow, All Souls College, Oxford, since 1993; *b* 19 March 1947; *s* of late George Laurence Cardy and Sarah Cardy; *m* 1985, Mary Ann Gilreath. *Educ:* Downing Coll., Cambridge (BA 1968; PhD 1971). Research Associate: European Orgn for Nuclear Res., Geneva, 1971–73; Daresbury Lab., 1973–74; Res. Associate, 1974–76, Prof. of Physics, 1977–93, Univ. of California, Santa Barbara; Fellow: European Orgn for Nuclear Res., 1976–77; Alfred P. Sloan Foundn, 1978; Guggenheim Foundn, 1986. Paul Dirac Medal, Inst. of Physics, 2000. *Publications:* Finite-Size Scaling, 1988; Scaling and Renormalization in Statistical Physics, 1996; contrib. to learned jls. *Recreation:* mountaineering. *Address:* All Souls College, Oxford OX1 4AL.

CARDY, Peter John Stubbings; Chief Executive, Macmillan Cancer Relief, since 2001; *b* 4 April 1947; *s* of Gordon Douglas Stubbings and Eva Stubbings (*née* Walker), assumed name of Cardy, 1987; *m* 1987, Christine Mary Cardy. *Educ:* University Coll., Durham (BA); Cranfield Inst. of Technol. (MSc). Adult Educn Principal, Cromwell Community Coll., Cambs, 1968–71; Dist Sec., WEA N of Scotland, 1971–77; Dep. Dir, Volunteer Centre, UK, 1977–87; Dir, Motor Neurone Disease Assoc., 1987–94; Chief Exec., Multiple Sclerosis Soc. of GB and NI, 1994–2001. Chm., Nat. Assoc. of Volunteer Bureaux, 1988–91; Mem., Charities Effectiveness Rev. Trust, 1990–93; Sec.-Gen., Internat. Alliance of MND/ALS Assocs, 1991–94; Chm., Neurological Alliance, 1998–; Comr, Medicines Commn, 1998–. Non-exec. Dir, Northampton Healthcare NHS Trust, 1993–97. *Publications:* numerous articles in voluntary sector and medical jls. *Recreations:* sailing, conversation, travel. *Address:* Macmillan Cancer Relief, 89 Albert Embankment, SE1 7UQ. *Club:* Reform.

CAREW, 7th Baron (UK) *cr* 1838; **Patrick Thomas Conolly-Carew;** Baron Carew (Ire.) 1834; *b* 6 March 1938; *er s* of 6th Baron Carew, CBE and Lady Sylvia Maitland (*d* 1991), *o d* of 15th Earl of Lauderdale; *S* father, 1994; *m* 1962, Celia Mary, *d* of Col Hon. (Charles) Guy Cubitt, CBE, DSO, TD; one *s* three *d*. *Educ:* Harrow Sch.; RMA Sandhurst. RHG (The Blues), 1958–65 (Captain); served UK, Cyprus, Germany. Mem., Irish Olympic Three Day Event Team, Mexico 1968, Munich 1972, Montreal 1976. President: Equestrian Fedn of Ireland, 1979–84; Irish Horse Trials Soc., 1998–. Mem. Bureau, Fédération Equestre Internationale, 1989–97 (Hon. Mem., 1997; Chm., 3 Day Event Cttee, 1989–97). *Recreations:* all equestrian sports, cricket, shooting, bridge. *Heir: s* Hon. William Patrick Conolly-Carew [*b* 27 March 1973; *m* 2000, Jane Anne, *d* of Joseph Cunningham, Dublin; one *d*]. *Address:* Donadea House, Naas, near Donadea, Co. Kildare, Ireland. *T:* (45) 868204, *Fax:* (45) 861105. *Club:* Kildare Street and University (Dublin).

CAREW, Sir Rivers (Verain), 11th Bt *cr* 1661; journalist; *b* 17 Oct. 1935; *s* of Sir Thomas Palk Carew, 10th Bt, and Phyllis Evelyn (*d* 1976), *o c* of Neville Mayman; *S* father, 1976; *m* 1st, 1968, Susan Babington (marr. diss. 1991), *yr d* of late H. B. Hill, London; one *s* three *d* (and one *s* decd); 2nd, 1992, Siobhán, 2nd *d* of late C. MacCárthaigh, Cork. *Educ:* St Columba's Coll., Rathfarnham, Co. Dublin; Trinity Coll., Dublin. MA, BAgr (Hort.). Asst Editor, Ireland of the Welcomes (Irish Tourist Bd magazine), 1964–67; Joint Editor, The Dublin Magazine, 1964–69; Irish Television, 1967–87; BBC World Service, 1987–93. *Publication:* (with Timothy Brownlow) Figures out of Mist (verse). *Recreations:* reading, music, reflection. *Heir: s* Gerald de Redvers Carew, *b* 24 May 1975. *Address:* Cherry Bounds, Hicks Lane, Girton, Cambridge CB3 0JS.

CAREW POLE, Sir (John) Richard (Walter Reginald), 13th Bt *cr* 1628, of Shute House, Devonshire; OBE 2000; DL; farmer and chartered surveyor; *b* 2 Dec. 1938; *s* of Sir John Gawen Carew Pole, 12th Bt, DSO, TD and Cynthia Mary (*d* 1977), OBE, *o d* of Walter Burns; *S* father, 1993; *m* 1st, 1966, Hon. Victoria Marion Ann Lever (marr. diss. 1974), *d* of 3rd Viscount Leverhulme, KG, TD; 2nd, 1974, Mary (MVO 1983), *d* of Lt-Col Ronald Dawnay; two *s*. *Educ:* Eton Coll.; Royal Agricultural Coll., Cirencester. ARICS 1967. Lieut, Coldstream Guards, 1958–63. Asst Surveyor, Laws & Fiennes, Chartered Surveyors, 1967–72. Director: South West Venture Capital, 1985–87; Eden Project Ltd, 1999–; Mem. Regional Bd, West of England, subseq. Portman, Bldg Soc., 1989–91. Chm., Devon and Cornwall Police Authority, 1985–87 (Mem., 1973–89); Member: SW Area Electricity Bd, 1981–90; NT Cttee for Devon and Cornwall, 1979–83. President: Surf Life Saving Assoc. of GB, 1976–86; Royal Cornwall Agricultural Show, 1981; RHS, 2001– (Mem. Council, 1999–); Trustee: Nat. Heritage Meml Fund, 1991–2000; Countryside Commission, 1991–96; Tate Gall., 1993–. Governor: Seale Hayne Agric. Coll., 1979–89; Plymouth Coll., 1985–96; Mem. Bd, Theatre Royal, Plymouth, 1985–97. Trustee: Eden Trust, 1996–; Trusthouse Charitable Foundn, 1999–; Pilgrim Trust, 2000–. County Councillor, Cornwall, 1973–93 (Chairman: Planning Cttee, 1980–84; Finance Cttee, 1985–89; Property Cttee, 1989–93); High Sheriff of Cornwall, 1979; DL Cornwall, 1988. Liveryman, Fishmongers' Co., 1960 (Mem. Court of Assistants, 1993–). *Recreations:* gardening, daydreaming, contemporary art. *Heir: s* Tremayne John Carew Pole, *b* 22 Feb. 1974. *Address:* Antony House, Torpoint, Cornwall PL11 2QA. *T:* (01752) 814914.

CAREY, Group Captain Alban Majendie, CBE 1943; owner/farmer Church Farm, Great Witchingham, since 1973; *b* 18 April 1906; *m* 1934, Enid Morten Bond; one *s*. *Educ:* Bloxham. Commissioned RAF 1929; served in night bombers, flying boats and as flying boat and landplane instructor; Pilots Cert. no 5283 for Public Transport; Navigator's Licence no 175, 1936; Sen. Op. Trng Officer, Coastal Command, 1939–42; Station Commander: Pembroke Dock, 1942–43; Gibraltar, 1943–45; Haverfordwest, 1945; St Eval, 1945–46. Chairman: Shaw & Sons Ltd, 1946–79; Jordan & Sons Ltd, 1953–68; Hadden Best Ltd, 1957–72; Shaw & Blake Ltd, 1960–68; H. T. Woodrow & Co., 1961–68; Chirit Investment Co., 1970–; Leutromedia Computers Internat., 1971–; Maden Park Property Investment Co., 1975–; East Coast Plastics, 1984–; Viking Opticals, 1986–; Dep. Chm., Trident Group Printers plc 1972–78; Sen. Partner, Park Farm

Syndicate, Snettisham, 1988–. Pres., Nat. Assoc. of Engravers and Die Stampers, 1954; Pres., Central London Br., British Fedn of Printing Industries, 1963; Chm., Nat. Assoc. of Law Stationers, 1963–68; Pres., Egham and Thorpe, Royal Agr. Assoc., 1961, 1962; Chm., Egham and Dist Abbeyfield Assoc., 1970–82. Trustee: Pensthorpe Waterfowl Trust, 1986–; Thursford Collection of Steam Engines, 1990–. *Recreations:* shooting, fishing, yachting. *Address:* Church Farm, Great Witchingham, Norfolk NR9 5PQ. *T:* (01603) 872511. *Clubs:* Royal Air Force; Royal Air Force Yacht.

CAREY, Charles John, CMG 1993; Member, European Communities' Court of Auditors, 1983–92; *b* 11 Nov. 1933; *s* of Richard Mein Carey and Celia Herbert Amy (*née* Conway); *m* 1990, Elizabeth Dale (*née* Slade). *Educ:* Rugby; Balliol Coll., Oxford. HM Treasury: Asst Principal, 1957; Principal, 1962; Asst Sec., 1971; seconded to HM Diplomatic Service as Counsellor (Econs and Finance), Office of UK Perm. Rep. to EEC, Brussels, 1974–77; Under Sec., HM Treasury, 1978–83. Chm., EC Conciliation Body for clearance of European Agricl Guidance and Guarantee Fund accounts, 1994–2001. Mem., CIPFA, 1988. Grand Croix de l'ordre de Merite (Luxembourg), 1992. *Publications:* (contrib.) Encyclopaedia of the European Union, 1998; articles on audit and financial mgt of EC funds in jls in UK, France and Netherlands. *Recreations:* mountaineering, Bavarian baroque churches, Trollope novels. *Club:* Oxford and Cambridge.

CAREY, Prof. Christopher, PhD; Professor of Classics, Royal Holloway and Bedford New College, University of London, since 1991 (Dean of Arts, 1998–2000); *b* 14 Sept. 1950; *s* of Christopher and Alice Carey; *m* 1969, Pauline Hemmings; two *s* one *d.* *Educ:* Alsop High Sch., Liverpool; Jesus Coll., Cambridge (BA 1972, MA; PhD 1976). Res. Fellow, Jesus Coll., Cambridge, 1974–77; Lectr in Greek, St Andrews Univ., 1977–91. Visiting Professor: Univ. of Minn, 1987–88; Carleton Coll., Minn, 1988; British Acad./Leverhulme Sen. Res. Fellow, 1996–97. Mem., Postgrad. Panel (Classics), AHRB, 1998–2001; Chm., Classics, Ancient History, Byzantine and Modern Greek Panel, 2001 RAE. *Publications:* A Commentary on Five Odes of Pindar, 1981; (with R. A. Reid) Demosthenes: Selected Private Speeches, 1985; Lysias: Selected Speeches, 1989; Apollodoros Against Neaira: [Demosthenes] 59, 1992; Trials from Classical Athens, 1997; The Speeches of Aeschines, 2000; Democracy in Classical Athens, 2000; articles on Greek lyric, epic, drama, oratory and law. *Address:* Royal Holloway, University of London, Egham, Surrey TW20 0EX. *T:* (01784) 443417.

CAREY, Brig. Conan Jerome; Chief Executive, The Home Farm Trust, since 1988; *b* 8 Aug. 1936; *s* of late Dr James J. Carey and Marion Carey; *m* 1966, Elizabeth Gay Docker, *d* of late Lt-Col L. R. Docker, OBE, MC, TD and Cynthia (*née* Washington); one *s* two *d.* *Educ:* Belvedere College, Dublin; RMA Sandhurst; RMCS Shrivenham; Staff Coll., Camberley (psc). FIPD. Enlisted Royal Hampshire Regt, 1954; Commissioned RASC, 1956; qualified aircraft pilot, 1960; seconded Army Air Corps, 1960–65; flying duties Malaya, Brunei, Borneo, Hong Kong, BAOR; transf. to RCT, 1965; Comdr 155 (Wessex) Regt RCT(V), 1976–78; Defence Staff, British Embassy, Washington DC, 1979–82; HQ BAOR, 1982; Dep. Dir-Gen., Transport and Movements, MoD, 1985; Comdr Training Gp, RCT, 1988. MInstD; FRSA. *Recreations:* golf, walking, cooking, wine. *Address:* HFT, Merchants House, Bristol BS1 4RW. *Clubs:* Army and Navy; Tracy Park Golf and Country (Bath).

CAREY, de Vic Graham; Bailiff of Guernsey, since 1999; a Judge of the Court of Appeal, Jersey, since 1999; *b* 15 June 1940; *s* of Victor Michael de Vic Carey and Jean Burnett (*née* Bullen); *m* 1968, Bridget Lindsay Smith; two *s* two *d.* *Educ:* Cheam Sch.; Bryanston Sch.; Trinity Hall, Cambridge (BA 1962; MA 1967); Univ. of Caen (Cert. des études juridiques françaises et normandes 1965). Admitted Solicitor, 1965; Advocate, Royal Court of Guernsey, 1966; QC (Guernsey) 1989. People's Dep., States of Guernsey, 1976; Solicitor-Gen. for Guernsey, 1977–82; Attorney-Gen., 1982–92; Receiver-Gen., 1985–92; Dep. Bailiff, 1992–99. Mem., Gen. Synod of C of E, 1982–98; Chm., House of Laity, Winchester Dio. Synod, 1993–97. *Address:* c/o Royal Court House, Guernsey GY1 2PB. *T:* (01481) 726161, *Fax:* (01481) 263687.

CAREY, Most Rev. and Rt Hon. George Leonard; *see* Canterbury, Archbishop of.

CAREY, Godfrey Mohun Cecil; QC 1991; a Recorder of the Crown Court, since 1986; *b* 31 Oct. 1941; *s* of Dr Godfrey Fraser Carey, LVO and Prudence Loveday (*née* Webb); *m* 1st, 1965, Caroline Jane Riggall (marr. diss. 1975); one *s* one *d* (and one *s* decd); 2nd, 1978, Dorothy May Sturgeon (marr. diss. 1983); one *d.* *Educ:* Highfield, Liphook; Eton. Legal Advr, Small Engine Div., Rolls Royce Ltd, 1964–70. Called to the Bar, Inner Temple, 1969, Bencher, 2000; in practice at the Bar, 1971–. *Recreations:* music, tennis. *Address:* 5 Paper Buildings, EC4Y 7HB. *T:* (020) 7583 6117. *Club:* Boodle's.

CAREY, Hugh Leo; former Executive Vice-President, W. R. Grace and Co.; *b* Brooklyn, NY, 11 April 1919; *s* of Denis Carey and Margaret (*née* Collins); *m* 1947, Helen Owen Twohy (*d* 1974); seven *s* four *d*, and one step *d* (and two *s* decd). *Educ:* St Augustine's Academy and High School, Brooklyn; St John's Coll.; St John's Law School. JD 1951. Served War of 1939–45 (Bronze Star, Croix de Guerre with Silver Star); with US Army in Europe, 1939–46, rank of Lt-Col. Joined family business (petrochemicals), 1947. Called to Bar, 1951. Member US House of Reps, rep. 12th District of Brooklyn, 1960–75 (Democrat); Deputy Whip; Governor of New York State, 1974–83.

CAREY, Prof. John, FBA 1996; FRSL 1982; Merton Professor of English Literature, Oxford University, 1976–2001; Fellow of Merton College, Oxford, 1976–2001; *b* 5 April 1934; *s* of Charles William Carey and Winifred Ethel Carey (*née* Cook); *m* 1960, Gillian Mary Florence Booth; two *s.* *Educ:* Richmond and East Sheen County Grammar Sch.; St John's Coll., Oxford (MA, DPhil; Hon. Fellow, 1991). 2nd Lieut, East Surrey Regt, 1953–54; Harmsworth Sen. Scholar, Merton Coll., Oxford, 1957–58; Lectr, Christ Church, Oxford, 1958–59; Andrew Bradley Jun. Research Fellow, Balliol, Oxford, 1959–60; Tutorial Fellow: Keble Coll., Oxford, 1960–64; St John's Coll., Oxford, 1964–75. Principal book reviewer, Sunday Times, 1977–. Chm., Booker Prize Judges, 1982; W. H. Smith Prize Judge, 1990–; Irish Times Lit. Prize Judge, 1993. Mem. Council, RSL, 1989–95. Hon. Fellow, Balliol Coll., Oxford, 1992. *Publications:* The Poems of John Milton (ed with Alastair Fowler), 1968, 2nd edn 1997; Milton, 1969; (ed) Andrew Marvell, 1969; (ed) The Private Memoirs and Confessions of a Justified Sinner, by James Hogg, 1969, 2nd edn 1981; The Violent Effigy: a study of Dickens' imagination, 1973, 2nd edn 1991; (trans.) Milton, Christian Doctrine, 1973; Thackeray: Prodigal Genius, 1977; John Donne: Life, Mind and Art, 1981, 2nd edn 1990; (ed) William Golding—the Man and his Books: a tribute on his 75th birthday, 1986; Original Copy: selected journalism and reviews, 1987; (ed) The Faber Book of Reportage, 1987; (ed) Donne, 1990; The Intellectuals and the Masses, 1992; (ed) Saki, Short Stories, 1994; (ed) The Faber Book of Science, 1995; (ed) The Faber Book of Utopias, 1999; Pure Pleasure, 2000; articles in Rev. of English Studies, Mod. Lang. Rev., etc. *Recreations:* swimming, gardening, bee-keeping. *Address:* Brasenose Cottage, Lyneham, Oxon OX7 6QL; 57 Stapleton Road, Headington, Oxford OX3 7LX. *T:* (01865) 764304.

CAREY, Dr Nicholas Anthony Dermot; Chairman, Alzheimer's Society, since 2001; *b* 4 May 1939; *s* of Eustace Dermot Carey and Audrey Mabel Carey (*née* Grenfell); *m* 1964, Helen Margaret Askey; two *s.* *Educ:* Shrewsbury Sch.; Trinity Coll., Dublin (BA, MA); King's Coll., Cambridge (PhD). ICI, 1968–93: Gen. Manager, Chlorine and derivatives, 1980–87; Man. Dir, Petrochemicals and Plastics, 1987–92; Planning Manager, Millbank, 1992–93; Dir Gen., C&G, 1993–2001. Director: Nalfloc, 1981–89; Phillips Imperial Petroleum, 1987–92; Teeside Power, 1991–92. Chm., Sir Isaac Pitman Ltd, 1993–2001; Dir, Opera Restor'd, 2001–. Governor, Reaseheath Coll., 2001–. Member: Court, Imperial Coll., 1993–2001; Council, City Univ., 1995–2001. Liveryman: Vintners' Co., 1960–; Tallow Chandlers' Co., 1995–. *Recreations:* opera, reading, an occasional game of golf. *Address:* Gorse House, Lower Whitley, Cheshire WA4 4ER. *T:* (01925) 730329. *Clubs:* Athenæum, MCC.

CAREY, Peter Philip, FRSL; writer; *b* 7 May 1943; *s* of Percival Stanley Carey and Helen Jean Carey; *m* 1st, 1964, Leigh Weetman; 2nd, Alison Margaret Summers; two *s.* *Educ:* Geelong Grammar Sch., Vic, Aust. FRSL 1988. Hon. DLitt Queensland, 1989. *Publications:* Fat Man in History, 1980; Bliss, 1981; Illywhacker, 1985; Oscar and Lucinda, 1988 (Booker Prize, 1988; filmed, 1998); The Tax Inspector, 1991; The Unusual Life of Tristan Smith, 1994; Collected Stories, 1995; The Big Bazoohley, 1995; Jack Maggs, 1997; True History of the Kelly Gang, 2000 (Commonwealth Writers' Prize, Booker Prize, 2001); 30 Days in Sydney, 2001. *Recreation:* sleeping. *Address:* c/o Rogers, Coleridge & White, Powis Mews, W11 1JN.

CAREY, Sir Peter (Willoughby), GCB 1982 (KCB 1976; CB 1972); Senior Adviser, Morgan Grenfell Group, 1990–96; Chairman, Dalgety PLC, 1986–92 (Director, 1983–92); Director: BPB Industries PLC, 1983–95; NV Philips Electronics, 1984–95; *b* 26 July 1923; *s* of Jack Delves Carey and Sophie Carey; *m* 1946, Thelma Young; three *d.* *Educ:* Portsmouth Grammar Sch.; Oriel Coll., Oxford; Sch. of Slavonic Studies. Served War of 1939–45: Capt., Gen. List, 1943–45. Information Officer, British Embassy, Belgrade, 1945–46; FO (German Section), 1948–51; Bd of Trade, 1953; Prin. Private Sec. to successive Presidents, 1960–64; IDC, 1965; Asst Sec., 1963–67, Under-Sec., 1967–69, Bd of Trade; Under-Sec., Min. of Technology, 1969–71; Dep. Sec., Cabinet Office, 1971–72; Dep. Sec., 1972–73, Second Permanent Sec., 1973–74, DTI; Second Permanent Sec., 1974–76, Permanent Sec., 1976–83, DoI. Director: Morgan Grenfell Hldgs, then Morgan Grenfell Gp, 1983–90 (Chm., 1987–89); Cable and Wireless, 1984–94; Westland Gp, 1986–88. Hon. LLD Birmingham, 1983; Hon. DSc Cranfield Inst. of Tech., 1984; Hon. DCL City, 1991. *Recreations:* music, theatre, travel. *Address:* 5 Rushmere Place, Marryat Road, Wimbledon, SW19 5RP. *T:* (020) 8947 5222. *Club:* Oxford and Cambridge.

CAREY EVANS, David Lloyd, OBE 1984; JP; DL; farmer; *b* 14 Aug. 1925; *s* of Sir Thomas Carey Evans, MC, FRCS and Lady Olwen Carey Evans, DBE; *m* 1959, Annwen Williams; three *s* one *d.* *Educ:* Rottingdean Sch.; Oundle Sch.; Univ. of Wales, Bangor. BSc (Agric) 1950. Sub-Lieut, RNVR, 1943–46; farming 1947–; Chm., Welsh Council, NFU, 1976–79; Welsh Representative and Chm., Welsh Panel, CCAHC, 1974; Chm., WAOS. JP Portmadoc, Gwynedd, 1969. DL Gwynedd 1988. *Address:* Eisteddfa, Criccieth, Gwynedd LL52 0PT. *T:* (01766) 522104. *Club:* Sloane.

CAREY-HUGHES, Richard John; QC 2000; a Recorder, since 2000; *b* 18 Dec. 1948; *s* of John Carey-Hughes and Esme (*née* Klein); m 1st, 1972, Elizabeth Blackwood (marr. diss. 1976); one *d*; 2nd, 1987, Sophia Bayne-Powell (marr. diss. 1998); one *s* two *d.* *Educ:* Rugby Sch. Airline pilot with BOAC, then British Airways, 1969-76; called to the Bar, Gray's Inn, 1977; specialist in crime cases. Member, Committee: Criminal Bar Assoc., 1991-98 (Hon. Sec., 1996-98); S Eastern Circuit, 1998-2001. *Recreations:* gardening, cycling, cinema. *Address:* 9 Bedford Row, WC1R 4AZ. *T:* (020) 7489 2727. *Club:* Chelsea Arts.

CARINE, Rear-Adm. James; Chief of Staff to Commander-in-Chief Naval Home Command, 1989–91; Registrar, Arab Horse Society, 1992–2000; *b* 14 Sept. 1934; *s* of Amos Carine and Kathleen Prudence Carine (*née* Kelly); *m* 1961, (Carolyn) Sally Taylor; three *s* one *d* (and two *s* decd). *Educ:* Victoria Road Sch., Castletown, IoM; King William's Coll., IoM. FCIS 1971. Joined Royal Navy 1951; Captain 1980; Sec., Second Sea Lord, 1979–82; SACLANT HQ, Norfolk, Va, 1982–85; Naval Home Staff, 1985–88; Commodore in Comd, HMS Drake, 1988–89. Pres., RN Assoc. (IOM), 1992–2000. Member: London Campaign Cttee for Multiple Sclerosis, 1993–95; Cttee, Ex-Services Mental Welfare Soc., 1997–; Copyright Tribunal, 1999–. Dir, United Services Trust, 1995–. Governor, St Antony's-Leweston Sch., 1996–. Chartered Secretaries' & Administrators' Co.: Liveryman, 1988; Mem., Court of Assistants, 1989; Jun. Warden, 1995–96; Sen. Warden, 1996–97; Master, 1997–98. KSG. *Recreations:* dinghy sailing, horse racing. *Address:* 5 Little Sands, Yatton Keynell, Chippenham, Wilts SN14 7BA.

CARINGTON, family name of **Baron Carrington**.

CARLESS, Hugh Michael, CMG 1976; HM Diplomatic Service, retired; Chairman, GEECO International, since 1997; *b* 22 April 1925; *s* of late Henry Alfred Carless, CIE, and Gwendolen Pattullo; *m* 1956, Rosa Maria, *e d* of Martino and Ada Frontini, São Paulo; two *s.* *Educ:* Sherborne; Sch. of Oriental Studies, London; Trinity Hall, Cambridge. Served in Paiforce and BAOR, 1943–47; entered Foreign (subseq. Diplomatic) Service, 1950; 3rd Sec., Kabul, 1951; 2nd Sec., Rio de Janeiro, 1953; Tehran, 1956; 1st Sec., 1957; FO, 1958; Private Sec. to Minister of State, 1961; Budapest, 1963; Civil Service Fellow, Dept of Politics, Glasgow Univ., 1966; Counsellor and Consul-Gen., Luanda, 1967–70; Counsellor, Bonn, 1970–73; Head of Latin American Dept, FCO, 1973–77; Minister and Chargé d'Affaires, Buenos Aires, 1977–80; on secondment to Northern Engineering Industries International Ltd, 1980–82; Ambassador to Venezuela, 1982–85. Exec. Vice Pres., Hinduja Foundn (UK), 1986–97; Vice Chm., S Atlantic Council, 1987–97. Chm. British Cttee, Argentine-British Confs, 1994–96. An Hon. Vice Pres., RSAA, 1992–95. *Recreations:* golf, history. *Address:* 15 Bryanston Square, W1H 2DN. *Clubs:* Travellers; Royal Mid Surrey Golf.

CARLETON, Air Vice-Marshal Geoffrey Wellesley, CB 1997; Director, Royal Air Force Legal Services, Ministry of Defence, 1992–97; Head of RAF Prosecuting Authority, 1997, retired; *b* 22 Sept. 1935; *s* of Gp Capt. Cyril Wellesley Carleton and Francis Beatrice (*née* Hensman); *m* 1985, Dianne Margaret Creswick; one *s.* *Educ:* Sherborne Sch. Admitted solicitor, 1959; commnd RAF, 1959, Pilot Officer, 1959–61; Asst Solicitor, Herbert Smith & Co., 1961–65; re-joined RAF, 1965 as Flt Lieut; Legal Officer, HQ MEAF, Aden, HQ NEAF, Cyprus, HQ FEAF, Singapore, HQ RAF, Germany, 1965–78; Deputy Director of Legal Services: HQ RAF, Germany, 1979–82 and 1985–88; MoD, 1988–92. Non-exec. Dir, Poole Hospital NHS Trust, 1998–. *Publications:* articles in professional and service jls and pubns. *Recreations:* sailing, ski-ing, equitation, opera. *Address:* c/o National Westminster Bank, 8 Christchurch Road, Bournemouth BH1 3LZ. *Clubs:* Royal Air Force, Royal Ocean Racing.

CARLETON-SMITH, Maj.-Gen. Sir Michael (Edward), Kt 1998; CBE 1980 (MBE 1966); DL; Chairman, Suzy Lamplugh Trust, since 2000; *b* 5 May 1931; *s* of late Lt-Col D. L. G. Carleton-Smith and Mrs B. L. C. Carleton-Smith (*née* Popham); *m* 1963, Helga Katja Stoss (*d* 1993); three *s*. *Educ:* Radley Coll.; RMA, Sandhurst. Graduate: Army Staff Coll.; JSSC; NDC; RCDS. Commissioned into The Rifle Brigade, 1951; Rifle Bde, Germany, 1951–53; active service: Kenya, 1954–55; Malaya, 1957; Exchange PPCLI, Canada, 1958–60; GSO2 General Staff, HQ1(BR) Corps, 1962–63; Rifle Brigade: Cyprus, Hong Kong, active service, Borneo, 1965–66; Sch. of Infantry Staff, 1967–68; Comd Rifle Depot, 1970–72; Directing Staff NDC, 1972–74; Col General Staff, HQ BAOR, 1974–77; Commander Gurkha Field Force, Hong Kong, 1977–79; Dep. Director Army Staff Duties, MoD, 1981; Defence Advr and Head of British Defence Liaison Staff, Canberra, Australia, also Mil. Advr, Canberra, and Wellington, NZ, and Defence Advr, PNG, 1982–85, retd. Dir-Gen., Marie Curie Meml Foundn, then Marie Curie Cancer Care, 1985–96; Chm., Marie Curie Trading Co., 1990–95. Chm., Leicester Royal Infirmary NHS Trust, 1998–2000. Vice-Chm., Nat. Council for Hospice and Specialist Palliative Care Services, 1992–96. Trustee, Progressive Supra Nuclear Palsy Assoc. (Europe), 1992–. Gov., Royal Star and Garter Home, 1998–. FRSA. DL Leics, 1992. *Recreations:* travel, current affairs, history. *Address:* Plough Cottage, Drayton, Market Harborough, Leics LE16 8SD.

CARLIER, Maj.-Gen. Anthony Neil, CB 1992; OBE 1982; Director, Haig Homes, since 1992; *b* 11 Jan. 1937; *s* of Geoffrey Anthony George and Sylvia Maude Carlier; *m* 1974, Daphne Kathleen Humphreys; one *s* one *d*. *Educ:* Highgate Sch.; RMA Sandhurst; RMCS. BSc(Eng) London. Troop Comdr, Cyprus, 1962–64; GSO3, 19 Inf. Bde, Borneo, 1965–66; Instructor, RMA Sandhurst, 1967–70; Staff Course: RMCS Shrivenham, 1971; BRNC Greenwich, 1972; GSO2, Staff of Flag Officer, Carriers and Amphibious Ships, 1973–74; Sqn Comdr, 1975–76; Regtl Comdr, 1977–80; Mil. Asst to Army Bd Mem., 1980–83; Engr Gp Comdr, 1983–85; rcds, 1986; Comdr British Forces, Falkland Is, 1987–88; Chief, Jt Services Liaison Organisation, Bonn, 1989–90; Team Leader, QMG's Logistic Support Review, 1991–92. Col Comdt, RE, 1993–2000. President: Officers' Christian Union, 1992–97; Mission to Mil. Garrisons, 1992–; Chm., UK Appeal Cttee for Christ Church Cathedral, Falkland Is, 1989–2000. Trustee: Cornelius Trust; Royal Engineer Yacht Club, 1992–. Gov., Monkton Combe Sch., 1996–. *Recreations:* offshore sailing, fishing, gardening, DIY. *Club:* International Association of Cape Horners (St Malo).

CARLILE, family name of **Baron Carlile of Berriew**.

CARLILE OF BERRIEW, Baron *cr* 1999 (Life Peer), of Berriew in the County of Powys; **Alexander Charles Carlile;** QC 1984; a Recorder, since 1986; *b* 12 Feb. 1948; *s* of Erwin Falik, MD and Sabina Falik; *m* 1968, Frances, *d* of Michael and Elizabeth Soley; three *d*. *Educ:* Epsom Coll.; King's Coll., London (LLB; AKC). Called to the Bar, Gray's Inn, 1970, Bencher, 1992. Hon. Recorder, City of Hereford, 1995–. Contested (L) Flint E, Feb. 1974, 1979. MP (L) 1983–88, (Lib Dem) 1988–97, Montgomery. Chm., Welsh Liberal Party, 1980–82; Leader, Welsh Lib Dems, 1992–97. Non-executive Director: UNICEF UK Ltd, 1997–; Wynnstay & Clwyd Farmers plc, 1998–; Mid Wales Opera Ltd, 1999–. Member: Adv. Council on Public Records, 1989–95; GMC, 1989–99; Council, Justice, 1993–; Council, NACRO, 1997–; Bd, Crime Concern, 1997–99. Fellow, Industry and Parlt Trust, 1985. *Recreations:* reading, theatre. *Address:* 9–12 Bell Yard, WC2A 2LF.

CARLILE, Thomas, CBE 1975; FREng; Chairman, Burnett and Hallamshire Holdings, 1985–88; *b* 9 Feb. 1924; *s* of late James Love Carlile and Isobel Scott Carlile; *m* 1955, Jessie Davidson Clarkson; three *d*. *Educ:* Minchenden County Sch.; City & Guilds Coll., London. Joined Babcock & Wilcox Ltd, 1944; Man. Dir, 1968–84, Dep. Chm., 1978–84, Babcock Internat. plc. Chm., Shipbuilding Industry Training Board, 1967–70; Dep. Chm., Police Negotiating Bd, 1987–95. Mem., Energy Commn, 1977–79. Pres., Engineering Employers' Fedn, 1972–74, a Vice-Pres., 1979–84. Director: Chubb & Son plc, 1976–84; French Kier Hldgs Plc, 1985–86. Chm., British Soc. of Master Glass Painters, 1995–2000. FCGI 1978; FREng (FEng 1979). *Address:* 8 Aldenham Grove, Radlett, Herts WD7 7BW. *T:* (01923) 857033.

CARLILL, Rear Adm. John Hildred, OBE 1969; DL; Royal Navy, retired 1982; *b* 24 Oct. 1925; *o s* of late Dr and Mrs H. B. Carlill; *m* 1955, (Elizabeth) Ann, *yr d* of late Lt Col and Mrs W. Southern; three *d*. *Educ:* RNC Dartmouth. psc 1961; jssc 1967. Served War 1939–45. Joined RN as Exec. Cadet 1939, transferred to Accountant Branch 1943; HMS Mauritius 1943–45. Comdr 1963, Captain 1972 (Sec. to FO Naval Air Comd, Dir Naval Manning and Training (S), Sec. to Second Sea Lord, Admty Interview Board, Cdre HMS Drake); Rear Admiral 1980; Adm. President, RNC Greenwich, 1980–82. Sec., Engineering Council, 1983–87. Chm., ABTA Appeal Bd, 1996–. President: Guildford Br., RN Assoc., 1989–; Guildford Sea Cadets, 1998–. Freeman: City of London, 1980; Drapers' Co., 1983. DL Surrey, 1994. *Recreations:* walking, short story writing, water colour painting. *Address:* Crownpits Barn, Crownpits Lane, Godalming, Surrey GU7 1NY. *T:* (01483) 415022.

CARLING, William David Charles, OBE 1991; Rugby football commentator, ITV, since 1997; *b* 12 Dec. 1965; *s* of Pamela and Bill Carling; *m* 1999, Lisa Cooke. *Educ:* Sedbergh School; Durham Univ. (BA Psych.). Played for Harlequins, 1987–97 and 1999–2000; international career, 1988–97: 1st cap for England, 1988; 72 caps, 59 as Captain; Captain of England, 1988–96 (centre three-quarter); captained: two Grand Slam sides, 1991, 1992; World Cup final, 1991; Barbarians, in Hong Kong 7's, 1991; England tour, South Africa, 1994; World Cup, South Africa, 1995; Mem., British Lions, NZ tour, 1993. *Publications:* Captain's Diary, 1991; Rugby Skills, 1994; (with R. Heller) The Way to Win, 1995; (with P. Ackford) Will Carling: my autobiography, 1998. *Recreations:* theatre, sketching, golf. *Address:* c/o Wentworth & Associates, White Hart House, Silwood Road, Ascot, Berks SL5 0PY. *Clubs:* Special Forces, Groucho; Harlequins, Harbour.

CARLISLE, family name of **Baron Carlisle of Bucklow**.

CARLISLE, 13th Earl of *cr* 1661; **George William Beaumont Howard;** Viscount Howard of Morpeth, Baron Dacre of Gillesland 1661; Lord Ruthven of Freeland 1651; *b* 15 Feb. 1949; *s* of 12th Earl of Carlisle, MC, and of Hon. Ela Hilda Aline Beaumont, *o d* of 2nd Viscount Allendale, KG, CB, CBE, MC; *S* father, 1994. *Educ:* Eton Coll.; Balliol Coll., Oxford; Army Staff Coll., Camberley. 9th/12th Royal Lancers, 1967–87; Lieut 1970, Captain 1974, Major 1981. Lectr, Estonian Nat. Defence and Public Service Acad., 1995–96. Sec., British-Estonian All-Party Parly Gp, 1997–99. Contested: (L/Alliance) Easington, 1987; (Lib Dem): Northumbria, European parly elecn, 1989; Leeds West, 1992. Order of Marjamac, 1st class, 1998. *Recreations:* reading, travel, learning Estonian. *Heir:* *b* Hon. Philip Charles Wentworth Howard [*b* 25 March 1963; *m* 1992, Elizabeth Harrison (*née* Moore); one *s* one *d*]. *Clubs:* Beefsteak, Pratt's.

CARLISLE OF BUCKLOW, Baron *cr* 1987 (Life Peer), of Mobberley in the County of Cheshire; **Mark Carlisle;** PC 1979; QC 1971; DL; Chairman, Criminal Injuries Compensation Board, 1989–2000; a Judge of the Courts of Appeal, Jersey and Guernsey, 1990–99; *b* 7 July 1929; 2nd *s* of late Philip Edmund and Mary Carlisle; *m* 1959, Sandra Joyce Des Voeux; one *d*. *Educ:* Radley Coll.; Manchester Univ. LLB (Hons) Manchester, 1952. Called to the Bar, Gray's Inn, 1953, Bencher 1980; Northern Circuit; a Recorder, 1976–79, 1981–98. Mem., Home Office Advisory Council on the Penal System, 1966–70. MP (C): Runcorn, 1964–83; Warrington S, 1983–87. Joint Hon. Secretary, Conservative Home Affairs Cttee, 1965–69; Conservative Front Bench Spokesman on Home Affairs, 1969–70; Parly Under-Sec. of State, Home Office, 1970–72; Minister of State, Home Office, 1972–74; Sec. of State for Educn and Science, 1979–81. Chairman: Cons. Home Affairs Cttee, 1983–87; Parole Review Cttee, 1987–88; Prime Minister's Adv. Cttee on Business Appts of Crown Servants, 1988–99; Soc. of Cons. Lawyers, 1996–. Treas., CPA, 1982–85, Dep. Chm., UK Br., 1985–87. Mem., Adv. Council, BBC, 1975–79. DL Cheshire, 1983. *Recreation:* golf. *Address:* Queen Elizabeth Building, Temple, EC4Y 9BS. *T:* (020) 7583 5766; 3 Holt Gardens, Mobberley, Cheshire WA16 7LH. *T:* (0156587) 2275. *Clubs:* Garrick; St James's (Manchester).

CARLISLE, Bishop of, since 2000; **Rt Rev. Geoffrey Graham Dow;** *b* 4 July 1942; *s* of Ronald Graham Dow and Dorothy May Dow (*née* Christie); *m* 1966, Molly Patricia (*née* Sturges); three *s* one *d*. *Educ:* St Alban's Sch.; Queen's Coll., Oxford (BA 1963; BSc 1965; MA 1968); Clifton Theol Coll.; Birmingham Univ. (Dip. Pastoral Studies 1974); Nottingham Univ. (MPhil 1982). Ordained deacon, 1967, priest, 1968; Asst Curate, Tonbridge Parish Church, 1967–72; Chaplain-Student, St John's Coll., Oxford, 1972–75; Lectr in Christian Doctrine, St John's Coll., Nottingham, 1975–81; Vicar, Holy Trinity, Coventry, 1981–92; Canon Theologian, Coventry Cathedral, 1988–92; Area Bp of Willesden, 1992–2000. *Publications:* Dark Satanic Mills? Shaftesbury Project, 1979; The Local Church's Political Responsibility, 1980; St John's College Extension Studies B1—God and the World, 1980; Whose Hand on the Tiller?, 1983; Those Tiresome Intruders, 1990; Explaining Deliverance, 1991; Christian Renewal in Europe, 1992; A Christian Understanding of Daily Work, 1994; Pathways of Prayer, 1996. *Recreations:* steam and narrow gauge railways, model railways, travel, music. *Address:* Rose Castle, Dalston, Carlisle CA5 7BZ.

CARLISLE, Dean of; *see* Knowles, Very Rev. G. P.

CARLISLE, Archdeacon of; *no new appointment at time of going to press.*

CARLISLE, Brian Apcar, CBE 1974; DSC 1945; Chairman, Saxon Oil PLC, 1980–85; *b* 27 Dec. 1919; 2nd *s* of Captain F. M. M. Carlisle, MC; *m* 1953, Elizabeth Hazel Mary Binnie, 2nd *d* of Comdr J. A. Binnie, RN; one *s* three *d*. *Educ:* Harrow Sch.; Corpus Christi Coll., Cambridge. Royal Navy, 1940–46, served in N Atlantic, Channel and Mediterranean in HMS Hood and destroyers; Sudan Political Service, 1946–54, served in Kassala, Blue-Nile and Bahr-el-Ghazal Provinces; Royal Dutch/Shell Group, 1955–74: served in India with Burmah Shell, 1960–64; Regional Co-ordinator, Middle East, and Dir, Shell International Petroleum, 1970–74; participated in pricing negotiations with OPEC states, 1970–73; Dir, Home Oil Co. Ltd, 1977–80; Oil Consultant to Lloyds Bank International, 1975–81. Chm., Bd of Governors, Gordon's Sch. (formerly Gordon Boys' Sch.), 1985–95. Chm., Sudan Church Assoc., 1982–99. *Recreations:* gardening, crosswords, golf. *Address:* Heath Cottage, Hartley Wintney, Hants RG27 8RE. *T:* (01252) 842224.

CARLISLE, Hugh Bernard Harwood; QC 1978; a Recorder of the Crown Court, since 1983; *b* 14 March 1937; *s* of late W. H. Carlisle, FRCS (Ed), FRCOG, and Joyce Carlisle; *m* 1964, Veronica Marjorie, *d* of late G. A. Worth, MBE; one *s* one *d*. *Educ:* Oundle Sch.; Downing Coll., Cambridge. Nat. Service, 2nd Lt, RA. Called to the Bar, Middle Temple, 1961, Bencher, 1985. Jun. Treasury Counsel for Personal Injuries Cases, 1975–78. Dept of Trade Inspector: Bryanston Finance Ltd, 1978–87; Milbury plc, 1985–87. Pres., Transport Tribunal, 1997–. Member: Criminal Injuries Compensation Bd, 1982–2000; Bar Council, 1989–92 (Chm., Professional Conduct Cttee, 1991–92). *Recreations:* fly fishing, woodworking, croquet. *Address:* 1 Temple Gardens, EC4Y 9BB. *T:* (020) 7583 1315. *Clubs:* Garrick, Hurlingham (Chm., 1982–85).

CARLISLE, Sir James (Beethoven), GCMG 1993; Governor-General of Antigua and Barbuda, since 1993; *b* 5 Aug. 1937; *s* of late James Carlisle and of Jestina Jones; *m* 1st, 1963, Umilta Mercer (marr. diss. 1973); one *s* one *d*; 2nd, 1973, Anne Jenkins (marr. diss. 1984); one *d*; 3rd, 1984, Nalda Amelia Meade; one *s* one *d*. *Educ:* Univ. of Dundee (BDS). General Dentistry, 1972–92. Chief Scout of Antigua and Barbuda. Chm., Nat. Parks Authority, 1986–90. Member: BDA; Amer. Acad. of Laser Dentistry; Internat. Assoc. of Laser Dentistry. Hon. FDSRCSE 1995. Hon. LLD Andrews Univ., USA, 1995. Kt Grand Cross, Order of Queen of Sheba (Ethiopia), 1995. *Recreation:* gardening. *Address:* Governor-General's Residence, St John's, Antigua, West Indies. *T:* (809) 4620003.

CARLISLE, Sir (John) Michael, Kt 1985; DL; CEng, FIMechE, FIMarE; Chairman, Trent Regional Health Authority, 1982–94; *b* 16 Dec. 1929; *s* of John Hugh Carlisle and Lilian Amy (*née* Smith); *m* 1957, Mary Scott Young; one *s* one *d*. *Educ:* King Edward VII Sch., Sheffield; Sheffield Univ. (BEng). Served Royal Navy (Lieut), 1952–54. Production Engr, Lockwood & Carlisle Ltd, 1954–57, Man. Dir, 1958–70, Chm. and Man. Dir, 1970–81; Dir of several overseas subsid. cos; Director: Eric Woodward (Electrical) Ltd, 1965–85; Diesel Marine Internat., 1981–89; Torday & Carlisle, 1981–94. Chairman: N Sheffield Univ. HMC, 1971–74; Sheffield AHA(T), 1974–82; Community Health Sheffield NHS Trust, 1994–99; Member: Sheffield HMC, 1969–71; Bd of Governors, United Sheffield Hosps, 1972–74; MRC, 1991–95; NHS Policy Bd, 1993–94. Member Council: Sheffield Chamber of Commerce, 1967–78; Production Engrg Res. Assoc., 1968–73; Chm., Sheffield Productivity Assoc., 1970; Pres., Sheffield Jun. Chamber of Commerce, 1967–68; non-executive Director: Fenchurch Midlands Ltd, 1986–94; Norhomes plc, 1989–97; Welpac plc, 1991–95; Residences at York plc, 1992–97; York Science Park Ltd, 1992–; York Science Park (Innovation) Centre Ltd, 1995–; Headrow Northern plc, 1992–97; Headrow Western plc, 1993–97; CBAMS Ltd, 1997–; SE Sheffield Primary Care Gp, 1999–2001. Governor: Sheffield City Polytechnic, 1979–82 (Hon. Fellow, 1977); Sheffield High Sch., 1977–87; Member: Sheffield Univ. Court, 1968–; Sheffield Univ. Careers Adv. Bd, 1974–82; Nottingham Univ. Court, 1982–94; Council and Court, York Univ., 1991– (Pro-Chancellor, 1996–). CIMgt. Freeman, City of London, 1989; Freeman, Co. of Cutlers in Hallamshire. DL S Yorks, 1996. Hon. LLD: Sheffield, 1988; Nottingham, 1992; DUniv York, 1998. *Recreations:* golf, country walking, water colour painting, genealogy. *Address:* St Ovin, Lastingham, N Yorks YO6 6TL. *T:* (01751) 417341; 4 Broad Elms Lane, Sheffield S11 9RQ. *T:* (0114) 236 5988. *Clubs:* Royal Society of Medicine; Sickleholme Golf; Kirkbymoorside Golf.

CARLISLE, John Russell; Executive Director, Tobacco Manufacturers' Association, since 1997; *b* 28 Aug. 1942; *s* of Andrew and Edith Carlisle; *m* 1964, Anthea Jane Lindsay May; two *d*. *Educ:* Bedford Sch.; St Lawrence Coll.; Coll. of Estate Management, London. Sidney C. Banks Ltd, Sandy, 1964–78; Consultant: Louis Dreyfus plc, 1982–87; Barry

Simmons PR, 1987–97; non-executive Director: Bletchley Motor Gp, 1988–95; Charles Sidney plc, 1995–97; Member: London Corn Exchange, 1987–97; Baltic Exchange, 1991–97. Chm., Mid Beds Cons. Assoc., 1974–76. MP (C) Luton West, 1979–83, Luton North, 1983–97. Chm., Cons Parly Cttee on Sport, 1981–82, 1983–84, 1985–97; Vice Chm., All-Party Football Cttee, 1987–97; Mem., Commons Select Cttee on Agriculture, 1985–88. Chm., British–S Africa Gp, 1987 (Sec., 1983–87); Treas., Anglo-Gibraltar Gp, 1981–82. Governor, Sports Aid Foundn (Eastern), 1985–96. President: Luton 100 Club; Luton Band; Bedfordshire CCC, 1993–97. *Recreations:* sport, music, shooting. *Address:* (office) 55 Tufton Street, SW1P 3QF. *Clubs:* Carlton, Farmers', MCC.

CARLISLE, Sir Kenneth (Melville), Kt 1994; *b* 25 March 1941; *s* of late Kenneth Ralph Malcolm Carlisle, TD and of Hon. Elizabeth Mary McLaren, *d* of 2nd Baron Aberconway; *m* 1986, Carla, *d* of A. W. Heffner, Md, USA; one *s. Educ:* Harrow; Magdalen Coll., Oxford (BA History). Called to Bar, Inner Temple, 1965. Brooke Bond Liebig, 1966–74; farming in Suffolk, 1974–. MP (C) Lincoln, 1979–97. PPS to: Minister of State for Energy, 1981–83; Minister of State for Home Office, 1983–84; Sec. of State for NI, 1984–85; Home Secretary, 1985–87; an Asst Govt Whip, 1987–88; a Lord Comr of HM Treasury, 1988–90; Parly Under-Sec. of State, MoD, 1990–92, Dept of Transport, 1992–93. Mem. Council, RHS, 1996–. *Recreations:* botany, gardening, history. *Address:* Wyken Hall, Stanton, Bury St Edmunds, Suffolk IP31 2DW.

CARLISLE, Sir Michael; *see* Carlisle, Sir J. M.

CARLOW, Viscount; Charles George Yuill Seymour Dawson-Damer; *b* 6 Oct. 1965; *s* and *heir* of 7th Earl of Portarlington, *qv. Educ:* Eton College; Univ. of Edinburgh (MA Hons 1988). A Page of Honour to the Queen, 1979–80. *Address:* c/o Yuills Ltd, Bride House, 18–20 Bride Lane, EC4Y 8JT. *Club:* Royal Sydney Golf (Sydney).

CARLOWAY, Hon. Lord; Colin John MacLean Sutherland; a Senator of the College of Justice in Scotland, since 2000; *b* 20 May 1954; *s* of Eric Alexander Cruickshank Sutherland and Mary Macaulay or Sutherland; *m* 1988, Jane Alexander Turnbull; two *s. Educ:* Hurst Grange Prep. Sch., Stirling; Edinburgh Acad.; Edinburgh Univ. (LLB Hons). Advocate, 1977; Advocate Depute, 1986–89; QC (Scot.) 1990. Treas., Faculty of Advocates, 1994–2000. *Address:* Supreme Courts, Parliament House, Edinburgh EH1 1RQ. *T:* (0131) 225 2595. *Club:* Scottish Arts (Edinburgh).

CARLTON, Viscount; Reed Montagu Stuart Wortley; *b* 5 Feb. 1980; *s* and heir of Earl of Wharncliffe, *qv.*

CARLUCCIO, Antonio Mario Gaetano; restaurateur, broadcaster and author; *b* 19 April 1937; *s* of Giovanni Carluccio and Maria (*née* Trivellone); *m* 1981, Priscilla Marion Conran. *Educ:* Roland Matura Schule, Vienna. Reporter, Gazzetta del Popolo, and La Stampa, Turin, 1953–54; wine merchant, Germany, 1963–75, England, 1975–81; restaurateur, 1981–89, Proprietor, 1989–, The Neal Street Restaurant; Jt Proprietor, Carluccio's Italian Food Shop, 1991–. *Television:* various appearances, BBC2, 1986–; *series:* Italian Feast, BBC2, 1996; Southern Italian Feast, BBC2, 1998. *Publications:* Invitation to Italian Cooking (Bejam Cookery Book of the Year), 1986; Passion for Mushrooms, 1989; Passion for Pasta, 1993; Italian Feast (Best Cookery Book, Good Food mag.), 1996; Carluccio's Complete Italian Food, 1997; Southern Italian Feast, 1998; Antonio Carluccio's Vegetables, 2000. *Address:* The Neal Street Restaurant, 26 Neal Street, WC2H 9PS. *T:* (020) 7836 8368.

CARLYLE, Joan Hildred; soprano; *b* 6 April 1931; *d* of late Edgar James and Margaret Mary Carlyle; *m*; two *d. Educ:* Howell's Sch., Denbigh, N Wales. Became Principal Lyric Soprano, Royal Opera House, Covent Garden, 1955; Oscar in Ballo in Maschera, 1957–58 season; Sophie in Rosenkavalier, 1958–59; Micaela in Carmen, 1958–59; Nedda in Pagliacci (new Zeffirelli production), Dec. 1959; Mimi in La Bohème, Dec. 1960; Titania in Gielgud production of Britten's Midsummer Night's Dream, London première, Dec. 1961; Pamina in Klemperer production of The Magic Flute, 1962; Countess in Figaro, 1963; Zdenko in Hartman production of Arabella, 1964; Sœur Angelica (new production), 1965; Desdemona in Otello, 1965, 1967; Sophie in Rosenkavalier (new production), 1966; Pamina in Magic Flute (new production), 1966; Arabella in Arabella, 1967; Marschallin in Rosenkavalier, 1968; Jenifer, Midsummer Marriage (new prod.), 1969; Donna Anna, 1970; Reiza, Oberon, 1970; Adrianna Lecouvreur, 1970; Russalka, for BBC, 1969; Elizabeth in Don Carlos, 1975; now teaching privately, giving masterclass workshops, promoting concerts for young singers, and performing in staged prodns. Roles sung abroad include: Oscar, Nedda, Mimi, Pamina, Zdenko, Micaela, Desdemona, Donna Anna, Arabella, Elizabeth. Has sung in Buenos Aires, Belgium, Holland, France, Monaco, Naples, Milan, Berlin, Capetown, Munich. Has made numerous recordings; appeared BBC, TV (in film). *Recreations:* gardening, cooking, interior decorating, countryside preservation. *Address:* Laundry Cottage, Hanmer, N Wales SY13 4QX.

CARLYLE, Robert, OBE 1990; actor; *b* Glasgow, 14 April 1961; *s* of Joseph and Elizabeth Carlyle; *m* 1997, Anastasia Shirley. *Educ:* North Kelvinside Secondary Sch.; RSAMD. Founder, Rain Dog Theatre Co., 1990; dir of prodns incl. Wasted, One Flew Over the Cuckoo's Nest, Conquest of the South Pole, Macbeth. *Theatre includes:* Twelfth Night; Dead Dad Dog; Nae Problem; City; No Mean City; Cuttin' a Rug; Othello. *Television includes:* The Part of Valour, 1981; Hamish Macbeth, 1995; Cracker, 1993, 1997; 99–01; Safe, 1993; The Advocates; Arena; Byrne on Byrne; Taggart; Looking After Jo Jo, 1998. *Films include:* Riff Raff, 1990; Silent Scream, 1990; Safe, 1993; Being Human, 1993; Priest, 1994; Go Now, 1995; Trainspotting, 1996; Carla's Song, 1996; Face, 1997; The Full Monty, 1997 (Best Actor, BAFTA, 1998); Ravenous, 1999; Plunkett & Macleane, 1999; The World is Not Enough, 1999; Angela's Ashes, 2000; The Beach, 2000; There's Only One Jimmy Grimble, 2000; To End All Wars, 2000; 51st State, 2001. Best Actor: Evening Standard Film Awards, 1998; Film Critics' Circle Awards, 1998; Bowmore Whisky/Scottish Screen Awards, 2001; Michael Elliott Awards, 2001; David Puttnam Patrons Award. *Address:* c/o ICM, Oxford House, 76 Oxford Street, W1N 0AX.

CARMICHAEL, Alexander Morrison, (Alistair); MP (Lib Dem) Orkney and Shetland, since 2001; *b* 15 July 1965; *s* of Alexander C. Carmichael and Mina Neil McKay or Carmichael; *m* 1987, Kathryn Jane Eastham; two *s. Educ:* Port Ellen Primary Sch.; Islay High Sch.; Aberdeen Univ. (LLB 1992; DipLP 1993). Hotel Manager, Glasgow and Orkney, 1984–89; Procurator Fiscal Depute, Crown Office, Edinburgh and Aberdeen, 1993–96; solicitor in private practice, Aberdeen and Macduff, 1996–2001. Elder, Church of Scotland. *Recreations:* music, theatre. *Address:* House of Commons, SW1A 0AA. *T:* (020) 7219 3000; Torshavn, Finstown, Orkney KW17 2EG.

CARMICHAEL, Catherine McIntosh, (Kay); social worker; *b* 22 Nov. 1925; *d* of John D. and Mary Rankin; *m* 1948, Neil George Carmichael (later Baron Carmichael of Kelvingrove) (marr. diss.; he *d* 2001); one *d*; *m* 1987, David Vernon Donnison, *qv. Educ:* Glasgow and Edinburgh. Social worker, 1955–57; psychiatric social work, 1957–60; Dep. Dir, Scottish Probation Training Course, 1960–62; Lectr, 1962, Sen. Lectr, 1974–80, Dept of Social Administration and Social Work, Univ. of Glasgow. Mem., 1969–75, Dep. Chm., 1975–80, Supplementary Benefits Commn. *Recreation:* Alexander technique. *Address:* 23 Bank Street, Glasgow G12 8JQ. *T:* (0141) 334 5817.

CARMICHAEL, Sir David William G. C.; *see* Gibson-Craig-Carmichael.

CARMICHAEL, Ian (Gillett); actor; *b* 18 June 1920; *s* of Arthur Denholm Carmichael, Cottingham, E Yorks, and Kate Gillett, Hessle, E Yorks; *m* 1st, 1943, Jean Pyman Maclean (*d* 1983), Sleights, N Yorks; two *d*; 2nd, 1992, Kate Fenton, novelist. *Educ:* Scarborough Coll.; Bromsgrove Sch. Studied at RADA, 1938–39. Served War of 1939–45 (despatches). First professional appearance as a Robot in "RUR", by Karel and Josef Capek, The People's Palace, Stepney, 1939; *stage appearances* include: The Lyric Revue, Globe, 1951; The Globe Revue, Globe, 1952; High Spirits, Hippodrome, 1953; Going to Town, St Martin's, 1954; Simon and Laura, Apollo, 1954; The Tunnel of Love, Her Majesty's, 1958; The Gazebo, Savoy, 1960; Critic's Choice, Vaudeville, 1961; Devil May Care, Strand, 1963; Boeing-Boeing, Cort Theatre, New York, 1965; Say Who You Are, Her Majesty's, 1965; Getting Married, Strand, 1968; I Do! I Do!, Lyric, 1968; Birds on the Wing, O'Keefe Centre, Toronto, 1969; Darling I'm Home, S African tour, 1972; Out on a Limb, Vaudeville, 1976; Overheard, Theatre Royal, Haymarket, 1981; Pride and Prejudice, Theatre Royal, York and nat. tour, 1987; The Circle, nat. tour, 1990; The School for Scandal, Chichester, 1995. *Films* include: (from 1955) Simon and Laura; Private's Progress; Brothers in Law; Lucky Jim; Happy is the Bride; The Big Money; Left, Right and Centre; I'm All Right Jack; School for Scoundrels; Light Up The Sky; Double Bunk; The Amorous Prawn; Hide and Seek; Heavens Above!; Smashing Time; The Magnificent Seven Deadly Sins; From Beyond the Grave; The Lady Vanishes. *TV series* include: The World of Wooster; Bachelor Father; Lord Peter Wimsey; All For Love; Obituaries; Strathblair; Wives and Daughters, 1999. Hon. DLitt Hull, 1987. *Publication:* Will the Real Ian Carmichael . . . (autobiog.), 1979. *Recreations:* cricket, gardening, photography and reading. *Address:* c/o London Management, 2–4 Noel Street, W1F 8GB. *Club:* MCC.

CARMICHAEL, Prof. Ian Stuart Edward, PhD; FRS 1999; Professor of Geology, University of California, Berkeley, since 1967; *b* 29 March 1930; *s* of Edward Arnold Carmichael and Jeanette Carmichael; *m* Kathleen Elizabeth O'Brien; two *s* two *d* by previous marriages. *Educ:* Trinity Hall, Cambridge (BA 1954); Imperial Coll., London Univ. (PhD 1958). Lectr in Geology, Imperial Coll., London Univ., 1958-63; NSF Fellow, Univ. of Chicago, 1964; University of California, Berkeley: Mem. Faculty, 1964–; Chm., Dept of Geology, 1972-76, 1980-82; Associate Dean, 1976-78, 1985-2000; Associate Provost for Res., 1986-2000; Dir, Lawrence Hall of Sci., 1996–. Day Medal, Geol Soc. Amer., 1991; Schlumberger Medal, Mineralol Soc., 1992; Murchison Medal, Geol Soc., 1995; Roebling Medal, Mineralol Soc. Amer., 1997. *Publications:* Igneous Petrology, 1974; contribs to jls. *Address:* Department of Earth and Planetary Science, University of California, Berkeley, CA 94720, USA.

CARMICHAEL, Kay; *see* Carmichael, C. M.

CARMICHAEL, Keith Stanley, CBE 1981; FCA; chartered accountant in practice, 1969–81 and since 1990; *b* 5 Oct. 1929; *s* of Stanley and Ruby Dorothy Carmichael; *m* 1958, Cynthia Mary (née Jones); one *s. Educ:* Charlton House Sch.; Bristol Grammar Sch.; qualified as Chartered Accountant, 1951; FTII 1951, FCA 1961. Partner, Wilson Bigg & Co., 1957–69; Man. Partner, Longcrofts, 1981–90. Director: H. Foulks Lynch & Co. Ltd, 1957–69; Radio Rentals Ltd, 1967–69. Member: Monopolies and Mergers Commn, 1983–92; Council, Share and Business Valuers, 1995–; Soc. of Trust and Estate Practitioners, 1996–. Lloyd's Underwriter, 1976–90. Pres., Hertsmere Cons. Assoc. Chm. Bd of Governors, and Trustee, Rickmansworth Masonic Sch., 1984–. Freeman, City of London, 1960; Liveryman, Co. of Chartered Accountants in England and Wales. FInstD. Mem., Editl Bd, Simon's Taxes, 1970–82. CStJ 2001. *Publications:* Spicer and Pegler's Income Tax (ed), 1965; Corporation Tax, 1966; Capital Gains Tax, 1968; Ranking Spicer and Pegler's Executorship Law and Accounts (ed), 1969, 1987; (with P. Wolstenholme) Taxation of Lloyd's Underwriters, 1980, 4th edn 1993; contribs to Accountancy. *Recreations:* gardening, reading, golf. *Address:* 117 Newberries Avenue, Radlett, Herts WD7 7EN. *T:* (01923) 855098. *Clubs:* Carlton (Dep. Chm., 1989–95; Trustee, 1999–), MCC, Lord's Taverners.

CARNAC; *see* Rivett-Carnac.

CARNARVON, 8th Earl of, *cr* 1793; **George Reginald Oliver Molyneux Herbert;** Baron Porchester 1780; *b* 10 Nov. 1956; *er s* of 7th Earl of Carnarvon, KCVO, KBE; *S* father, 2001; *m* 1st, 1989, Jayne (marr. diss. 1997), *d* of K. A. Wilby, Cheshire; one *s* one *d*; 2nd, 1999, Fiona, *e d* of late R. Aitken; one *s. Educ:* St John's Coll., Oxford (BA). A Page of Honour to the Queen, 1969–73. *Heir: s* Lord Porchester, *qv. Address:* The Field House, Highclere Park, Newbury RG15 9RN. *Club:* White's.

CARNE, Dr Stuart John, CBE 1986 (OBE 1977); FRCGP; Senior Partner, Grove Health Centre, 1967–91; *b* 19 June 1926; *s* of late Bernard Carne and Millicent Carne; *m* 1951, Yolande (*née* Cooper); two *s* two *d. Educ:* Willesden County Grammar Sch.; Middlesex Hosp. Med. Sch. MB BS; MRCS; LRCP; DCH. House Surgeon, Middlesex Hosp., 1950–51; House Physician, House Surgeon and Casualty Officer, Queen Elizabeth Hosp. for Children, 1951–52; Flight Lieut, Med. Branch, RAF, 1952–54; general practice in London, 1954–91; Sen. Tutor in General Practice, RPMS, 1970–91. DHSS appointments: Chm., Standing Med. Adv. Cttee, 1982–86 (Mem., 1974–86); Member: Central Health Services Council, 1976–79; Children's Cttee, 1978–81; Personal Social Services Council, 1976–80; Chm., Jt Cttee on Contraception, 1983–86 (Mem., 1975–86). Hon. Civil Consultant in Gen. Practice to RAF, 1974–. Royal College of General Practitioners: Mem. Council, 1961–91; Hon.Treasurer, 1964–81; Pres., 1988–91; President: Section of General Practice, 1973–74, United Services Sect., 1985–87, RSocMed; Mem. Council, World Orgn of Nat. Colls and Acads of Gen. Practice and Family Medicine,1970–80 (Pres., 1976–78); Mem. Exec. Council, British Diabetic Assoc., 1981–87. Examnr in medicine, Soc. of Apothecaries, 1980–88. Chm., St Mary Abbots Court Ltd, 1981–. Hon. MO, 1959–89, Vice-Pres., 1989–96, Queens Park Rangers FC. Hon. Fellow, Royal NZ Coll. of GPs, 1989; Hon. FRCPCH 1996; Hon. Mem., BPA, 1982. *Publications:* Paediatric Care, 1976; (jtly) DHSS Handbook on Contraceptive Practice, 3rd edn 1984, 4th edn 1988; numerous articles in Lancet, BMJ and other jls. *Recreations:* music, theatre, photography, philately. *Address:* 5 St Mary Abbots Court, Warwick Gardens, W14 8RA. *T:* (020) 7602 1970. *Club:* Royal Air Force.

CARNEGIE, family name of **Duke of Fife** and **Earl of Northesk**.

CARNEGIE, Lord; Charles Duff Carnegie; *b* 1 July 1989; *s* and *heir* of Earl of Southesk, *qv.*

CARNEGIE, Lt-Gen. Sir Robin (Macdonald), KCB 1979; OBE 1968; DL; Director General of Army Training, 1981–82, retired; *b* 22 June 1926; *yr s* of late Sir Francis Carnegie, CBE; *m* 1955, Iona, *yr d* of late Maj.-Gen. Sir John Sinclair, KCMG, CB, OBE; one *s* two *d. Educ:* Rugby. Commnd 7th Queen's Own Hussars, 1946; comd The Queen's

Own Hussars, 1967–69; Comdr 11th Armd Bde, 1971–72; Student, Royal Coll. of Defence Studies, 1973; GOC 3rd Div., 1974–76; Chief of Staff, BAOR, 1976–78; Military Secretary, 1978–80. Col, The Queen's Own Hussars, 1981–87. Non-Service Mem., Police, Prison and Fire Service Selection Bds, 1987–96. DL Wilts, 1990.

CARNEGIE, Sir Roderick (Howard), Kt 1978; FTS; Chairman: Hudson Conway Ltd, since 1987; Valiant Consolidated Ltd, since 1993; GEC Plessey Telecom (Australia) Ltd, since 1994; Adacel Techs Ltd, since 1998; *b* 27 Nov. 1932; *s* of late Douglas H. Carnegie and of Margaret F. Carnegie, AO; *m* 1959, Carmen, *d* of W. J. T. Clarke; three *s*. *Educ:* Geelong Church of England Grammar Sch.; Trinity Coll., Univ. of Melbourne; New Coll., Oxford Univ.; Harvard Business Sch., Boston. BSc; Dip. Agricl Economics, MA Oxon; MBA Harvard; FTS 1985. McKinsey & Co., New York, 1954–70: Principal, 1964–68, Director, 1968–70; Man. Dir, 1971–83, Chm. and Chief Exec., 1974–86, CRA Ltd; Chm., GIO Australia Hldgs Ltd, 1992–94. Dir, Aust. Mining Industry Council, 1974 (a Sen. Vice-Pres., 1985); former Dir, ANZ Banking Gp Ltd; Mem., IBM Asia Pacific Gp. Member: General Motors Aust. Adv. Council, 1979; Chm., Consultative Cttee on Relations with Japan, 1984–87; Pres., Business Council of Aust., 1987–88; International Councillor: Morgan Guaranty Trust; The Brookings Instn. Mem., CSIRO Bd, 1986–91. Hon. DSc Newcastle, 1985. *Recreations:* surfing, tennis, reading. *Address:* Hudson Conway Ltd, Level 1, 99 Queensbridge Street, Southbank, Qld 3006, Australia; The Domain, 1 Albert Road, South Melbourne, Vic 3205, Australia. *Clubs:* Melbourne (Victoria, Aust.); Links (New York).

CARNEGY OF LOUR, Baroness *cr* 1982 (Life Peer), of Lour in the District of Angus; **Elizabeth Patricia Carnegy of Lour;** DL; formerly a farmer; *b* 28 April 1925; *e d* of late Lt Col U. E. C. Carnegy, DSO, MC, DL, JP, 12th of Lour, and Violet Carnegy, MBE. *Educ:* Downham Sch., Essex. Served Cavendish Lab., Cambridge, 1943–46. With Girl Guides Association, 1947–89: County Comr, Angus, 1956–63; Trng Adviser, Scotland, 1958–62; Trng Adviser, Commonwealth HQ, 1963–65; Pres. for Angus, 1971–79, for Scotland, 1979–89. Co-opted to Educn Cttee, Angus CC, 1967–75; Tayside Regional Council: Councillor, 1974–82; Convener: Recreation and Tourism Cttee, 1974–76; Educn Cttee, 1977–81. Chairman: Working Party on Prof. Trng for Community Education in Scotland, 1975–77; Scottish Council for Community Educn, 1981–88 (Mem., 1978–88); Tayside Cttee on Med. Res. Ethics, 1990–93. Member: MSC, 1979–82 (Chm., Cttee for Scotland, 1981–83); Council for Tertiary Educn in Scotland, 1979–84; Scottish Economic Council, 1981–93; H of L Scrutiny Cttees on European Community, 1983–97; Council, Open Univ., 1984–96; Admin. Council, Royal Jubilee Trusts, 1985–88; Court, St Andrews Univ., 1991–96; Trustee, Nat. Museums of Scotland, 1987–91. Hon. Sheriff, 1969–84; DL Angus, 1988. Hon. LLD: Dundee, 1991; St Andrews, 1997; DUniv Open, 1998. *Address:* Lour, by Forfar, Angus DD8 2LR. *T:* (01307) 820237; 33 Tufton Court, Tufton Street, SW1P 3QH. *Clubs:* Lansdowne; New (Edinburgh).

CARNELL, Rev. Canon Geoffrey Gordon, Chaplain to The Queen, 1981–88; Non-Residentiary Canon of Peterborough Cathedral, 1965–85, Canon Emeritus since 1985; *b* 5 July 1918; *m* 1945, Mary Elizabeth Boucher Smith; two *s*. *Educ:* City of Norwich Sch.; St John's Coll., Cambridge (Scholar, 1937; BA 1940; Naden Divinity Student, 1940; Lightfoot Scholar, 1940; MA 1944); Cuddesdon Coll., Oxford. Ordained deacon, Peterborough Cathedral, 1942; priest, 1943. Asst Curate, Abington, Northampton, 1942–49, Chaplain and Lectr in Divinity, St Gabriel's Coll., Camberwell, 1949–53; Rector of Isham with Great and Little Harrowden, Northants, 1953–71; Rector of Boughton, Northampton, 1971–85. Examining Chaplain to Bishop of Peterborough, 1962–86; Dir, Post-Ordination Trng and Ordinands, 1962–86; Peterborough Diocesan Librarian, 1968–93. Chaplain: to High Sheriff of Northants, 1972–73; to Mayor of Kettering, 1988–89. Member: Ecclesiastical History Soc., 1979–; Church of England Record Soc., 1992–; a Vice-Chm., Northants Record Soc., 1982–89. *Publication:* The Bishops of Peterborough 1541–1591, 1993. *Recreations:* walking, music, art history, local history. *Address:* 52 Walsingham Avenue, Barton Woods, Kettering, Northamptonshire NN15 5ER. *T:* (01536) 511415.

CARNELLEY, Ven. Desmond; Archdeacon of Doncaster, 1985–94, now Archdeacon Emeritus; *b* 28 Nov. 1929; *m* 1st, 1954, Dorothy Frith (*d* 1986); three *s* one *d*; 2nd, 1988, Marjorie Freeman. *Educ:* St John's Coll., York; St Luke's Coll., Exeter; William Temple Coll., Rugby; Ripon Hall, Oxford. BA (Open Univ.); Cert. Ed. (Leeds); Cert. Rel. Ed. (Exon). Curate of Aston, 1960–63; Priest-in-charge, St Paul, Ecclesfield, 1963–67; Vicar of Balby, Doncaster, 1967–72; Priest-in-charge, Mosborough, 1973; Vicar of Mosborough, 1974–85; RD of Attercliffe, 1979–84; acting Dir of Educn, dio. of Sheffield, 1991–92. *Recreations:* reading, theatre, walking in Derbyshire. *Address:* 7 Errwood Avenue, Buxton, Derbyshire SK17 9BD. *T:* (01298) 71460.

CARNEY, Michael; Secretary, Water Services Association (formerly Water Authorities Association), 1987–92; *b* 19 Oct. 1937; *s* of Bernard Patrick Carney and Gwyneth (*née* Ellis); *m* 1963, Mary Patricia (*née* Davies) (marr. diss. 2000); two *s* one *d*. *Educ:* University College of North Wales, Bangor (BA). Administrative Officer, NCB, 1962–65; Staff Officer to Dep. Chm., NCB, 1965–68; Electricity Council: Administrative Officer, 1968–71; Asst Sec. (Establishments), 1971–74; Sec., S Western Region, CEGB, 1974–80, Personnel Man., Midlands Region, 1980–82; Personnel Dir, Oxfam, 1982–87. *Publications:* Britain in Pictures: a history and bibliography, 1995; Stoker: the life of Hilda Matheson, OBE, 1888–1940, 1999. *Recreations:* reading, book collecting, music, theatre. *Address:* Pencaedu, Llangynog SY10 0HA. *T:* and *Fax:* (01691) 860486; *e-mail:* michael.carney@care4free.net.

CARNLEY, Most Rev. Peter Frederick; *see* Perth (Australia), Archbishop of.

CARNOCK, 4th Baron *cr* 1916, of Carnock; **David Henry Arthur Nicolson;** Bt (NS) of that Ilk and Lasswade 1629, of Carnock 1637; Chief of Clan Nicolson; solicitor; *b* 10 July 1920; *s* of 3rd Baron Carnock, DSO, and Hon. Katharine (*d* 1968), *e d* of 1st Baron Roborough; *S* father, 1982. *Educ:* Winchester; Balliol Coll., Oxford (MA). Admitted Solicitor, 1949; Partner, Clifford-Turner, 1953–86. Served War of 1939–45, Royal Devon Yeomanry and on staff, Major. *Recreations:* shooting, fishing, gardening. *Heir: cousin* Nigel Nicolson, *qv*. *Address:* 90 Whitehall Court, SW1A 2EL; Ermewood House, Harford, Ivybridge, S Devon PL21 0JE. *Clubs:* Travellers, Beefsteak.

CARNWATH, Francis Anthony Armstrong, CBE 1997; Director, Greenwich Foundation for the Royal Naval College, since 1997; *b* 26 May 1940; *s* of Sir Andrew Hunter Carnwath, KCVO, DL and Kathleen Marianne (*née* Armstrong); *m* 1975, Penelope Clare Rose; one *s* one *d* (and one *d* decd). *Educ:* Eton (Oppidan Schol.); Cambridge (BA Econs). With Baring Brothers & Co., 1962–89: postings to S Africa, 1965–66, USA, 1969, France, 1972–73; Chief Exec. and Dir, Pertanian Baring Sanwa Multinational, Malaysia, 1977–79; Dir, 1979–89; Chm., Ravensbourne Registration Services Ltd, 1981–89. Dep. Dir, Tate Gall., 1990–94; Actg Dir, 1995, Advr, 1996–97, Nat. Heritage Meml Fund/Heritage Lottery Fund. English Heritage: Mem., London Adv. Cttee, 1990–99; Chm., Commemorative Plaques Panel, 1995–. Trustee and later Dep. Chm., Shelter, 1968–76; Treas., VSO, 1979–84. Chm., Spitalfields Historic Buildings Trust, 1984–2000; Trustee: Phillimore Estates, 1983–; Whitechapel Art Gall., 1994–2000 (Dep. Chm., 1996–2000); Royal Armouries, 2000–. Master, Musicians' Co., 1995–96. *Recreations:* music, gardening, walking. *Address:* 213 South Lambeth Road, SW8 1XR. *T:* (020) 7735 3360. *Club:* Garrick.

See also Rt Hon. Sir R. J. A. Carnwath.

CARNWATH, Rt Hon. Sir Robert John Anderson, Kt 1994; CVO 1995; PC 2002; **Rt Hon. Lord Justice Carnwath;** a Lord Justice of Appeal, since 2002; Chairman, Law Commission, since 1999; *b* 15 March 1945; *s* of Sir Andrew Carnwath, KCVO; *m* 1974, Bambina D'Adda. *Educ:* Eton; Trinity Coll., Cambridge (MA, LLB). Called to the Bar, Middle Temple, 1968, Bencher 1991; QC 1985. Junior Counsel to Inland Revenue, 1980–85; Attorney Gen. to the Prince of Wales, 1988–94; a Judge of the High Court, Chancery Div., 1994–2002. Chairman: Shepherds Bush Housing Assoc., 1988–93; Administrative Law Bar Assoc., 1993–94; Tabernacle Trust, 1996–99. Governor, RAM, 1989– (Hon. Fellow 1994). Trustee, 1996–, Chm., 2001–, Britten-Pears Foundn. *Publications:* Knight's Guide to Homeless Persons Act, 1977; (with Rt Hon. Sir Frederick Corfield) Compulsory Acquisition and Compensation, 1978; Enforcing Planning Control (report commnd for DoE), 1989; various legal texts and reports on planning and local govt law. *Recreations:* viola, singing (Bach Choir), tennis, golf, etc. *Address:* Law Commission, Conquest House, 37/38 John Street, Theobalds Road, WC1N 2BQ.

See also F. A. A. Carnwath.

CARO, Sir Anthony (Alfred), OM 2000; Kt 1987; CBE 1969; sculptor; *b* 8 March 1924; *s* of late Alfred and Mary Caro; *m* 1949, Sheila May Girling; two *s*. *Educ:* Charterhouse; Christ's Coll., Cambridge (Hon. Fellow, 1981); Regent Street Polytechnic; Royal Acad. Schs, London (Landseer Schol., 1st Landseer Award). Served FAA, 1944–46. Asst to Henry Moore, 1951–53; taught part-time, St Martin's Sch. of Art, 1953–79; taught sculpture at Bennington Coll., Vermont, 1963–65. Initiated and taught at Triangle Workshop, Pine Plains, NY, 1982–89. Visiting Artist, 1989: Univ. of Alberta; Red Deer Coll., Alberta. *One-man exhibitions include:* Galleria del Naviglio, Milan, 1956; Gimpel Fils, London, 1957; Whitechapel Art Gall., 1963; Andre Emmerich Gall., NY, 1964, 1966, 1968, 1970, 1972, 1973, 1974, 1977, 1978, 1979, 1982, 1984, 1986, 1988, 1989; Washington Gall. of Modern Art, Washington, DC, 1965; Kasmin Ltd, London, 1965, 1967, 1971, 1972; David Mirvish Gall., Toronto, 1966, 1971, 1974; Galerie Bischofberger, Zurich, 1966; Rijkmuseum, Kröller-Müller, Holland, 1967; Hayward Gall., 1969; Norfolk and Norwich Triennial Fest., 1973; Kenwood House, Hampstead, 1974, 1981, 1994; Galleria dell'Ariete, Milan, 1974; Galerie Andre Emmerich, Zürich, 1974, 1978, 1985; Mus. of Modern Art, NY, 1975 (toured to Walker Art Center, Minn, Mus. of Fine Arts, Houston, Mus. of Fine Arts, Boston); Richard Gray Gall., Chicago, 1976, 1978, 1986, 1989; Watson/de Nagy Gall., Houston, 1976; Lefevre Gall., London, 1976; Galerie Wentzel, Hamburg, 1976, 1978, Cologne, 1982, 1984, 1985, 1988; Galerie Piltzer-Rheims, Paris, 1977; Waddington & Tooth Galls, London, 1977; Waddington Galls, London, 1983, 1986; Harkus Kracow Gall., Boston, 1978, 1981, 1985; Knoedler Gall., London, 1978, 1982, 1983, 1984, 1986, 1989, 1991; Ace Gall., Venice, Calif, 1978, Vancouver, 1979; Kunsthalle Mannheim, 1979; Kunstverein Braunschweig, 1979; Kunstverein Frankfurt, 1979; Städtische Galerie im Lenbachhaus, Munich, 1979; Gall Kasahara, Osaka, Japan, 1979, 1990; York Sculptures, Christian Science Center, Boston, 1980; Acquavella Galls, NY, 1980, 1984, 1986; Galerie Andre, Berlin, 1980; Downstairs Gall., Edmonton, Alta, 1981; Storm King Art Center, Mountainville, NY, 1981; Städtische Galerie im Stadel, Frankfurt, 1981; Saarland Mus., Saarbrücken, 1982; Gallery One, Toronto, 1982, 1985, 1987–88, 1990; Galerie de France, Paris, 1983; Martin Gerard Gall., Edmonton, 1984; Serpentine Gall., 1984; Whitworth Art Gall., Manchester, 1984; Leeds City Art Gall., 1984; Ordrupgaard Samlingen, Copenhagen, 1984; Kunstmuseum Düsseldorf, 1985; Joan Miró Foundn, Barcelona, 1985; C. Grimaldis Gall., Baltimore, 1985, 1987, 1989; Galerie Blanche, Stockholm , 1985; Galleri Lang, Malmö, 1985; Galerie Artek, Helsinki, 1985; Galleria Stendhal, Milan, 1985; Norrköpings Kunstmuseum, Sweden, 1985; Galerie Joan Prats, Barcelona, 1986; Comune di Bogliasco, Genoa, 1986; Iglesia de San Esteban, Spain, 1986; La Lonja, Spain, 1987; Soledad Lorenzo Galerie, Madrid, 1987; Northern Centre for Contemp. Art, Sunderland, 1987; Sylvia Cordish Fine Art, Baltimore, 1988; Elisabeth Franck Gall., Belgium, 1988; Galerie Renée Ziegler, Zürich, 1988; Annely Juda Fine Art, 1989, 1991, 1994 (retrospective), 1998; Walker Hill Art Center, Seoul, 1989; Galeria Fluxis, Porto, 1989; Galerie Lelong, Paris, 1990; Baugre Palace, Antwerp, 1990; Tate Gall., 1991; Mus. of Contemp. Art, Tokyo, 1995; Marlborough Gall., NY, 1997, 1998, 2001, Boca Raton, 1999; Nat. Gall., 1998. British Council touring exhibn, 1977–79: Tel Aviv, NZ and Australia; 1993–1995: Hungary, Romania, Turkey, Greece, Holland and Germany. *Group shows:* exhibited in over 180, many widely toured, in UK, USA, Canada, Europe, Australia and Far East, incl. Biennale in Venice, 1958, 1966, 1968, 1972, 1986, 1988 and 1999, Carrara, 1959, Paris, 1959 and 1977, Antwerp, 1959 and 1983, São Paolo, 1969, Arese, 1980, and Monte Carlo, 1989. Sculpture commnd by Nat. Gall. of Art, Washington, 1978. Co-Designer, Millennium Bridge, London, 1996–2000. Member: Council, RCA, 1981–83 (Hon. Fellow 1986); Council, Slade Sch. of Art, 1982–92; Trustee, Tate Gall., 1982–89. Hon. Mem., Amer. Acad. and Inst. of Arts and Letters, 1979; For. Hon. Mem., Amer. Acad. of Arts and Sciences, 1988. Lectures: William Townsend Meml, UCL, 1982; Delia Heron Meml, Falmouth Sch. of Art, 1985; Annual, Clore Gall., London, 1987. Hon. Fellow, Wolfson Coll., Oxford, 1992. Hon. DLitt: East Anglia, 1968; York Univ., Toronto, 1979; Brandeis Univ., Mass, 1981; Hon. LittD Cambridge, 1985; DUniv Surrey, 1987; Hon. DFA Yale, 1989; Hon. Dr RCA, 1994, etc. Given key to City of New York, 1974. Henry Moore Grand Prize, 1991; Praemium Imperiale, 1992; Internat. Sculpture Centre Lifetime Achievement Award, 1997. *Relevant publications:* Anthony Caro, by R. Whelan *et al*, 1974; Anthony Caro, by W. S. Rubin, 1975; Anthony Caro, by D. Waldman, 1982; Anthony Caro, by Terry Fenton, 1986; Caro, by Karen Wilkin, 1991. *Recreation:* listening to music. *Address:* 111 Frognal, Hampstead, NW3 6XR.

CARO, Prof. David Edmund, AO 1986; OBE 1977; MSc, PhD; FInstP, FAIP, FACE; Chancellor, University of Ballarat, since 1998; Vice-Chancellor: University of Melbourne, 1982–87; (interim), Northern Territory University, 1988–89; *b* 29 June 1922; *s* of George Alfred Caro and Alice Lillian Caro; *m* 1954, Fiona Macleod; one *s* one *d*. *Educ:* Geelong Grammar Sch.; Univ. of Melbourne (MSc); Univ. of Birmingham (PhD). FInstP 1960, FAIP 1963, FACE 1982. Served War, RAAF, 1941–45. Demonstrator, Univ. of Melbourne, 1947–49; 1851 Overseas Res. Scholar, Birmingham, 1949–51; University of Melbourne: Lectr, 1952; Sen. Lectr, 1954; Reader, 1958; Foundn Prof. of Exper. Physics, 1961; Dean, Faculty of Science, 1970; Dep. Vice-Chancellor, 1972–77; Vice-Chancellor, Univ. of Tasmania, 1978–82. Chairman: Antarctic Res. Policy Adv. Cttee, 1979–85; Aust. Vice-Chancellors Cttee, 1982–83; Melbourne Theatre Co., 1982–87; Pres., Victorian Coll. of the Arts, 1989–91. Chairman: SSAU Nominees Ltd, 1984–89; UniSuper Ltd, 1990–94; Sarou Pty Ltd, 1991–. Member: Management Cttee, Royal Melbourne Hosp., 1982–92; Council, Univ. of South Australia, 1990–94; Council, Univ. of Ballarat, 1994–. Hon. LLD: Melbourne, 1978; Tasmania, 1982; Hon. DSc Melbourne, 1987. *Publication:* (jtly) Modern Physics, 1961 (3rd edn 1978). *Recreations:* skiing, gardening, theatre. *Address:* 17 Fairbairn Road, Toorak, Vic 3142, Australia. *Clubs:* Melbourne (Melbourne); Peninsula Golf (Vic); Tasmanian (Hobart).

CAROL, Sister; *see* Griese, Sr Carol.

CAROLIN, Prof. Peter Burns, CBE 2000; ARIBA; Professor and Head of Department of Architecture, University of Cambridge, 1989–2000, now Professor Emeritus, and Fellow of Corpus Christi College, since 1989; *b* 11 Sept. 1936; *s* of late Joseph Sinclair Carolin and Jean Bell Carolin (*née* Burns); *m* 1964, Anne-Birgit Warning; three *d*. *Educ:* Radley Coll.; Corpus Christi Coll., Cambridge (MA); University Coll. London (MA Architecture). Served RNR, Lieut, 1955–61. Asst to John Voelcker, 1960–63; Architect: with Colin St John Wilson, 1965–70; with Sir John Burnet, Tait and Partners, 1970–71; Associate, 1971–73, and Partner, 1973–80, Colin St John Wilson and Partners; Partner, Cambridge Design, 1980–81; Technical Ed., 1981–84, Editor, 1984–89, Architects' Jl; Co-founder, Facilities Newsletter, 1983; Chm. Editl Bd, and Editor, arq (Architectural Res. Qly), 1995–. Magazine of Year Award (jtly), 1985; (jtly) numerous publishing awards, 1985–87. *Publications:* articles in professional jls in UK and Germany. *Recreation:* sailing. *Address:* 34 Selwyn Gardens, Cambridge CB3 9AY. *T:* (01223) 352723; Martin Centre for Architectural and Urban Studies, University of Cambridge, Department of Architecture, 6 Chaucer Road, Cambridge CB2 2EB. *T:* (01223) 331700, *Fax:* (01223) 331701; *e-mail:* pc207@hermes.cam.ac.uk.

CAROLUS, Cheryl Anne; Chief Executive Officer, South Africa Tourism, since 2001; *b* 27 May 1958; *m* 1990, Graeme Bloch. Former teacher; Dep. Sec. Gen., 1994–98, acting Sec.-Gen., March 1998, ANC; High Comr for S Africa in the UK, 1998–2001. *Address:* Private Bag X10012, Sandton 2146, South Africa.

CARON, Leslie (Claire Margaret); film and stage actress; *b* 1 July 1931; *d* of Claude Caron and Margaret Caron (*née* Petit); *m* 1st, 1951, George Hormel (marr. diss.); 2nd, 1956, Peter Reginald Frederick Hall (marr. diss. 1965); one *s* one *d*; 3rd, 1969, Michael Laughlin (marr. diss.). *Educ:* Convent of the Assumption, Paris. With Ballet des Champs Elysées, 1947–50, Ballet de Paris, 1954. *Films:* American in Paris, 1950; The Man With a Cloak, 1951; Lili, Story of Three Loves, 1953; Glory Alley, The Glass Slipper, 1954; Daddy Long Legs, 1955; Gaby, 1956; Gigi, The Doctor's Dilemma, 1958; The Man Who Understood Women, 1959; The Subterraneans, Austerlitz, 1960; Fanny, 1961; The L-Shaped Room, 1962; Guns of Darkness, 1963; Father Goose, A Very Special Favour, 1964; Les Quatres Vérités, Is Paris Burning?, 1965; Promise Her Anything, 1966; Head of the Family, 1968; Madron, 1970; Chandler, 1971; QB VII; Valentino, Sérail, 1975; L'homme qui aimait les femmes, 1976; Goldengirl, 1978; Tous Vedettes, 1979; The Contract, 1980; Imperatif, 1981; The Unapproachable, 1982; La Diagonale du Fou, 1983; Le Génie du Faux, 1984; Le Train de Lenine, 1987; Courage Mountain, Guerriers et Captives, 1988; Master of the Game; Damage, 1992; Funny Bones, Let it be Me, 1994; The Ring, 1995; The Reef, 1996; The Last of the Blonde Bombshells, 1999; Chocolat, 2001; Crime on the Orient Express, 2001. *Plays:* Orvet, Paris, 1955; La Sauvage (TV), England; Gigi, (title rôle), New Th., 1956; 13 rue de l'Amour, USA and Australia; Ondine (title rôle), RSC, Aldwych, 1961; Carola (TV), USA; The Rehearsal, UK tour, 1983; On Your Toes, US tour, 1984; One for the Tango, USA tour, 1985; L'Inaccessible, Paris, 1985; George Sand, Greenwich Fest., 1995; Nocturne for Lovers, Chichester, 1997. *Musical:* Grand Hotel, Berlin, 1991. *Television:* Tales of the Unexpected, 1982. *Publication:* Vengeance (short stories), 1982. *Recreation:* collecting antiques. *Address:* c/o Maureen Vincent, Peters, Fraser & Dunlop, Drury House, 34–43 Russell Street, WC2B 5HA. *T:* (020) 7344 1000.

CARPANINI, Prof. David Lawrence, RE 1982 (ARE 1979); RWA 1983 (ARWA 1977); RBA 1976; NEAC 1983; RCA 1992; painter and etcher; Professor of Art, University of Wolverhampton School of Education, 1992–2000, retired; President, Royal Society of Painter Printmakers, since 1995; *b* Abergwynfi, W Glam, 22 Oct. 1946; *o s* of Lorenzo Carpanini and Gwenllian (*née* Thomas); *m* 1972, Jane Allen, RWS, RBA, RWA; one *s*. *Educ:* Glanafan Grammar Sch., Port Talbot; Glos Coll. of Art & Design, Cheltenham (DipAD 1968); Royal Coll. of Art (MA 1971); Univ. of Reading (ATC 1972). Dir, Bankside Gall. Ltd, 1995–. Royal Society of British Artists: Hon. Treas., 1979–82; Vice-Pres., 1982–88; Mem. Council, 1993–95; Mem. Council, RWA, 1987–90. Has exhibited at: RA, RBA, RWA, NEAC, Bankside Gall., Piccadilly Gall., Attic Gall., Agnews, Albany Gall., New Acad. Gall., Tegfryn; numerous one-man exhibitions, 1972–, including: Welsh Arts Council Gall., 1980; Warwick Arts Fest., 1986; Mostyn Gall., 1988; Rhondda Heritage Park, 1989, 1994; Walsall Mus., 1989; Swansea Arts Fest., 1994. Work in collections, including: Nat. Mus. of Wales; Contemporary Art Soc. for Wales: Nat. Liby of Wales; Newport Mus. and Art Gall.; Govt Art Collection, DoE; Fitzwilliam Mus., Cambridge; BNOC; Univ. of Wales; Ashmolean Mus., Oxford. Gov., Fedn of British Artists, 1982–86. De Lazlo Medal, RBA, 1980; Agnews Drawing Prize, NEAC, 1992; Catto Gall. Award, 1993, First Prize, Daler Rowney Award, 1995, RWS Open. Hon. RWS 1996. *Publications:* Vehicles of Pictorial Expression, 1982; numerous articles and illustrations for instructional books and art periodicals. *Recreations:* opera, cycling, ballroom dancing. *Address:* Fernlea, 145 Rugby Road, Milverton, Leamington Spa, Warwicks CV32 6DJ. *T:* (01926) 430658. *Club:* Arts.

CARPENTER; *see* Boyd-Carpenter.

CARPENTER, Ven. Frederick Charles; Archdeacon of the Isle of Wight, 1977–86, Archdeacon Emeritus since 1986; Chaplain, Godolphin School, Salisbury, 1989–95; *b* 24 Feb. 1920; *s* of Frank and Florence Carpenter; *m* 1952, Rachel Nancy (*d* 1994), *widow* of Douglas H. Curtis. *Educ:* Sir George Monoux Grammar Sch., Walthamstow; Sidney Sussex Coll., Cambridge (BA 1947, MA 1949); Wycliffe Hall, Oxford; MPhil Exeter, 1993. Served with Royal Signals, 1940–46; Italy, 1944 (despatches). Curate of Woodford, 1949–51; Asst Master, 1951–62, and Asst Chaplain, 1951–58, then Chaplain, 1958–62, Sherborne School, Dorset; Vicar of Moseley, Birmingham, 1962–68; Director of Religious Education, Diocese of Portsmouth, 1968–75; Canon Residentiary of Portsmouth, 1968–77; Priest-in-charge of the Holy Cross, Binstead, IoW, 1977–86. *Recreations:* music, conversation. *Address:* 21 Gracey Court, Woodland Road, Broadclyst, Exeter, Devon EX5 3LP. *T:* (01392) 462445.

CARPENTER, Harry Leonard, OBE 1991; sports commentator, BBC, 1949–94; *b* 17 Oct. 1925; *s* of Harry and Adelaide May Carpenter; *m* 1950, Phyllis Barbara Matthews; one *s*. *Educ:* Ashburton School, Shirley; Selhurst Grammar School, Croydon. Greyhound Express, 1941; RN, 1943–46; Greyhound Owner, 1946–48; Speedway Gazette, 1948–50; Sporting Record, 1950–54; Daily Mail, 1954–62; BBC TV, full-time 1962–94. Sports Personality of the Year, TV and Radio Industries, 1989; Internat. Award, Amer. Sportscasters' Assoc., 1989. *Publications:* Masters of Boxing, 1964; Illustrated History of Boxing, 1975; The Hardest Game, 1981; Where's Harry? My Story, 1992. *Recreations:* golf, chess, classical music. *Address:* Sommerfield Holdings plc, 35 Old Queen Street, SW1H 9JD.

CARPENTER, Humphrey William Bouverie, FRSL; author, broadcaster, musician; *b* 29 April 1946; *s* of late Rt Rev. Harry James Carpenter and of Urith Monica Trevelyan; *m* 1973, Mari Christina Prichard; two *d*. *Educ:* Dragon Sch., Oxford; Marlborough Coll.; Keble Coll., Oxford (MA, DipEd). FRSL 1983. BBC general trainee, 1968–70; staff producer, BBC Radio Oxford, 1970–74; freelance writer and broadcaster, 1975–. Founded: 1983, the band Vile Bodies, playing 1920s and 1930s dance music and jazz, resident at the Ritz Hotel, London, 1987–94; 1984, Mushy Pea Theatre Co., children's theatre group. Prog. dir, Cheltenham Fest. of Lit., 1994–96. *Plays:* Father Ignatius, Edinburgh Fest. fringe, 1974; Mr Majeika, the Musical, Oxford, 1991, Shaw Theatre, 1993; Secret Gardens trilogy, BBC Radio, 1992; Babes (musical), Oxford, 1992, Shaw Theatre, 1993; Over the Rainbow, BBC Radio, 1995; Gulliver's Travels, Theatr Clywd, 1995; (adapted) Listen to the Wind, King's Head, 1996. *Publications:* A Thames Companion (with Mari Prichard), 1975; J. R. R. Tolkien: a biography, 1977; The Inklings (Somerset Maugham Award), 1978; Jesus (Past Masters series), 1980; (ed with Christopher Tolkien) The Letters of J. R. R. Tolkien, 1981; W. H. Auden: a biography, 1981 (E. M. Forster Award, Amer. Acad. of Arts and Letters, 1984); (with Mari Prichard) The Oxford Companion to Children's Literature, 1984; OUDS: a centenary history of the Oxford University Dramatic Society, 1985; Secret Gardens: the golden age of children's literature, 1985; Geniuses Together: American writers in Paris, 1987; A Serious Character: the life of Ezra Pound (Duff Cooper Meml Prize), 1988; The Brideshead Generation: Evelyn Waugh and his friends, 1989; Benjamin Britten: a biography, 1992 (Royal Philharmonic Soc. award); The Envy of the World: fifty years of the BBC Third Programme and Radio 3, 1996; Robert Runcie: the reluctant archbishop, 1996; Dennis Potter, a biography, 1998; That Was Satire That Was, 2000; *children's books:* The Joshers, 1977; The Captain Hook Affair, 1979; Mr Majeika, 1984; Mr Majeika and the Music Teacher, 1986; Mr Majeika and the Haunted Hotel, 1987; The Television Adventures of Mr Majeika, 1987; More Television Adventures of Mr Majeika, 1988; Mr Majeika and the Dinner Lady, 1989; Further Television Adventures of Mr Majeika, 1990; Mr Majeika and the School Play, 1991; Mr Majeika and the School Book Week, 1992 (Mr Majeika books serialised on television, 1988–90); (with Jenny McDade) Wellington and Boot, 1991; What Did You Do At School Today?, 1992; Charlie Crazee's Teevee, 1993; Mr Majeika and the School Inspector, 1993; Mr Majeika and the Ghost Train, 1994; Shakespeare Without the Boring Bits, 1994; Mr Majeika and the School Caretaker, 1996; (ed) The Puffin Book of Classic Children's Stories, 1996; Mr Majeika Vanishes, 1997; More Shakespeare Without the Boring Bits, 1997; Mr Majeika and the School Trip, 1999; Mr Majeika on the Internet, 2000. *Recreations:* sleep, exploring decayed railway junctions. *Address:* 6 Farndon Road, Oxford OX2 6RS.

CARPENTER, John; *see* Carpenter, V. H. J.

CARPENTER, Leslie Arthur; Chief Executive, 1982–86, Chairman, 1985–87, Reed International PLC; *b* 26 June 1927; *s* of William and Rose Carpenter; *m* 1st, 1952; one *d*; 2nd, 1989, Louise Botting, *qv*. *Educ:* Hackney Techn. Coll. Director: Country Life, 1965; George Newnes, 1966; Odhams Press Ltd (Managing), 1968; International Publishing Corp., 1972; Reed International Ltd, 1974; IPC (America) Inc., 1975; Chairman: Reed Hldgs Inc. (formerly Reed Publishing Hldgs Inc.), 1977; Reed Publishing Hldgs Ltd, 1981; Chm. and Chief Exec., IPC Ltd, 1974; Chief Exec., Publishing and Printing, Reed International Ltd, 1979. Dir, Watmoughs (Hldgs) plc, 1988–98. *Recreations:* racing, gardening. *Address:* Gable House, High Street, Broadway, Worcs WR12 7DP.

CARPENTER, Louise, (Mrs L. A. Carpenter); *see* Botting, Louise.

CARPENTER, Michael Alan; Chairman and Chief Executive Officer, Salomon Smith Barney, New York City, since 1998; *b* 24 March 1947; *s* of Walter and Kathleen Carpenter; *m* 1975, Mary A. Aughton; one *s* one *d*. *Educ:* Univ. of Nottingham (BSc 1968); Harvard Business Sch. (MBA 1973). Business analyst, Mond Div., ICI, Runcorn, 1968-71; Consultant, 1973-78, Vice-Pres., 1978-83, Boston Consulting Gp; joined General Electric Co., 1983: Vice-Pres., Corporate Business Develt and Planning, 1983-86; Exec. Vice-Pres., GE Capital Corp., 1986-89; Chm., Pres. and CEO, Kidder, Peabody Gp Inc., 1989-94; Chm. and CEO, Travelers Life and Annuity Co., and Vice-Chm., Travelers Gp, Inc., 1994-98. *Address:* Salomon Smith Barney, 388 Greenwich Street, 39th Floor, New York, NY 10013, USA. *T:* (212) 8168864.

CARPENTER, Michael Stephen Evans; Legal Commissioner, Charity Commission, since 1998; *b* 7 Oct. 1942; *s* of Ernest Henry Carpenter and Eugenie Carpenter (*née* Evans); *m* 1968, Gabriel Marie Lucie Brain; one *s* one *d*. *Educ:* Eastbourne Coll.; Bristol Univ. (LLB). Admitted Solicitor, 1967; Slaughter and May, 1967–94 (Partner, 1974–94); Withers, 1994–97 (Partner, 1994–96; Consultant, 1997). Sec., Garfield Weston Foundn, 1997. *Recreations:* hill-walking, golf, Scottish islands, the church. *Address:* (office) Harmsworth House, 13–15 Bouverie Street, EC4Y 8DP.

CARPENTER, Maj.-Gen. (Victor Harry) John, CB 1975; MBE 1945; FCIT, FILT; Senior Traffic Commissioner, Western Traffic Area and Licensing Authority, 1990–91; *b* 21 June 1921; *s* of Harry and Amelia Carpenter; *m* 1946, Theresa McCulloch; one *s* one *d*. *Educ:* Army schools; Apprentice Artificer RA; RMC Sandhurst. Joined the Army, Royal Artillery, 1936; commissioned into Royal Army Service Corps as 2nd Lieut, 1939. Served War of 1939–45 (Dunkirk evacuation, Western Desert, D-Day landings). Post-war appts included service in Palestine, Korea, Aden, and Singapore; also commanded a company at Sandhurst. Staff College, 1951; JSSC, 1960; served WO, BAOR, FARELF, 1962–71; Transport Officer-in-Chief (Army), MoD, 1971–73; Dir of Movements (Army), MoD, 1973–75; Chm., Traffic Comrs, NE Traffic Area (formerly Yorks Traffic Area), 1975–85; Traffic Comr, W Traffic Area, 1985–90. Col Comdt, 1975–87, Representative Col Comdt, 1976, 1978 and 1985, RCT. Nat. Pres., 1940 Dunkirk Veterans Assoc., 1991–2000; President: Artificers Royal Artillery Assoc., 1974–2001; RASC/RCT Assoc., 1977–87; Somerset Br., Normandy Veterans Assoc., 1994–. Chm., Yorkshire Section, CIT, 1980–81; Pres., Taunton Gp, IAM. Hon. FIRTE 1987. Commander, Order of Leopold II (Belgium), 1992. *Recreation:* gardening. *Club:* Royal Over-Seas League.

CARR, family name of **Baron Carr of Hadley**.

CARR OF HADLEY, Baron *cr* 1975 (Life Peer), of Monken Hadley; **(Leonard) Robert Carr;** PC 1963; FIC; *b* 11 Nov. 1916; *s* of late Ralph Edward and of Katie Elizabeth Carr; *m* 1943, Joan Kathleen, *d* of Dr E. W. Twining; two *d* (and one *s* decd). *Educ:* Westminster Sch. (Hon. Fellow, 1991); Gonville and Caius Coll., Cambridge, BA Nat. Sci. Hons, 1938; MA 1942. FIM 1957. Joined John Dale Ltd, 1938 (Dir, 1948–55; Chm., 1958–63); Director: Metal Closures Group Ltd, 1964–70 (Dep. Chm., 1960–63 and Jt Man. Dir, 1960–63); Carr, Day & Martin Ltd, 1947–55; Isotope Developments Ltd, 1950–55; Metal Closures Ltd, 1959–63; Scottish Union & National Insurance Co. (London Bd), 1958–63; S. Hoffnung & Co., 1963, 1965–70, 1974–80; Securicor Ltd and Security Services PLC, 1961–63, 1965–70, 1974–85; SGB Gp PLC, 1974–86; Prudential Assurance Co., 1976–85 (Dep. Chm., 1979–80, Chm., 1980–85); Prudential Corporation PLC, 1978–89 (Dep. Chm., 1979–80, Chm., 1980–85); Cadbury Schweppes PLC, 1979–87; Chm., Strategy

Ventures, 1988–; Mem., London Adv. Bd, Norwich Union Insurance Gp, 1965–70, 1974–76; Member, Advisory Board: PA Strategy Partners, 1985–87; LEK Partnership, 1987–95. Mem. Council, CBI, 1976–87 (Chm., Educn and Trng Cttee, 1977–82); Chm., Business in the Community, 1984–87. MP (C) Mitcham, 1950–74, Sutton, Carshalton, 1974–76; PPS to Sec. of State for Foreign Affairs, Nov. 1951–April 1955, to Prime Minister, April-Dec. 1955; Parly Sec., Min. of Labour and Nat. Service, Dec. 1955–April 1958; Sec. for Technical Co-operation, 1963–64; Sec. of State for Employment, 1970–72; Lord President of the Council and Leader of the House of Commons, April-Nov. 1972; Home Secretary, 1972–74. Governor: St Mary's Hosp., Paddington, 1958–63; Imperial Coll. of Science and Technology, 1959–63 and 1976–87 (Fellow 1985); St Mary's Medical Sch. Council, 1958–63; Hon. Treas., Wright Fleming Inst. of Microbiology, 1960–63. Duke of Edinburgh Lectr, Inst. of Building, 1976. Pres., Surrey CCC, 1985–86. CIMgt (CBIM 1982); CIPD (CIPM 1975). *Publications:* (jt) One Nation, 1950; (jt) Change is our Ally, 1954; (jt) The Responsible Society, 1958; (jt) One Europe, 1965; articles in technical jls. *Recreations:* lawn tennis, music, gardening. *Address:* 14 North Court, Great Peter Street, SW1P 3LL. *Club:* Brooks's.

CARR, Alan Michael; Senior Partner, Simmons & Simmons, 1992–96; *b* 1 Sept. 1936; *m* 1963, Dalia Lebhar; two *s* one *d. Educ:* Gresham's Sch., Holt; King's Coll., Cambridge (MA). Articled Simmons & Simmons, 1957; admitted solicitor, 1961; Partner, 1966–96. FRGS 1989. *Recreation:* travel among remote people.

CARR, Sir (Albert) Raymond (Maillard), Kt 1987; DLitt (Oxon); FRHistS; FRSL; FBA 1978; Warden of St Antony's College, Oxford, 1968–87 (Sub-Warden, 1966–68); Fellow since 1964; *b* 11 April 1919; *s* of Reginald and Marion Maillard Carr; *m* 1950, Sara Strickland; three *s* one *d. Educ:* Brockenhurst Sch.; Christ Church, Oxford (Hon. Student 1986). Gladstone Research Exhnr, Christ Church, 1941; Lectr, UCL, 1945–46; Fellow of All Souls' Coll., 1946–53; Fellow of New Coll., 1953–64. Director, Latin American Centre, 1964–68. Chm. Soc. for Latin American Studies, 1966–68. Prof. of History of Latin America, Oxford, 1967–68. Distinguished Prof., Boston Univ., 1980; King Juan Carlos Prof. of Spanish History, NY Univ., 1992. Mem., Nat. Theatre Bd, 1968–77. Hon. Fellow: Exeter Univ., 1987; St Antony's Coll., Oxford, 1988. Corresp. Mem., Royal Acad. of History, Madrid. Hon. DLitt Madrid, 1999. Award of Merit, Soc. for Spanish Hist. Studies of the US, 1987; Leimer Award for Spanish Studies, Univ. of Augsburg, 1990; Prince of Asturias Award in Social Scis, Prince of Asturias Foundn, 1999. Grand Cross of the Order of Alfonso el Sabio (Spain), 1983; Order of Infante Dom Henrique (Portugal), 1989. *Publications:* Spain 1808–1939, 1966; Latin America (St Antony's Papers), 1969; (ed) The Republic and the Civil War in Spain, 1971; English Fox Hunting, 1976; The Spanish Tragedy: the Civil War in Perspective, 1977; (jtly) Spain: Dictatorship to Democracy, 1979; Modern Spain, 1980; (with Sara Carr) Fox-Hunting, 1982; Puerto Rico: a colonial experiment, 1984; (ed) The Spanish Civil War, 1986; (ed) The Chances of Death: a diary of the Spanish Civil War, 1995; Visiones de fin de siglio, 1999; (ed) Spain: a history, 2000; articles on Swedish, Spanish and Latin American history. *Recreation:* fox hunting. *Address:* Burch, North Molton, South Molton EX36 3JU. *T:* (01769) 550267. *Clubs:* Beefsteak, Oxford and Cambridge.

CARR, Andrew Jonathan, FRCS; Nuffield Professor of Orthopaedic Surgery, University of Oxford, and Fellow, Worcester College, Oxford, since 2001; *b* 18 June 1958; *s* of John Malcolm Carr and Patricia (*née* Hodgson); *m* 1985, Clare Robertson; one *s* three *d. Educ:* Bradford Grammar Sch.; Bristol Univ. (MB ChB 1982; ChM 1989). FRCS 1986. House surgeon and physician, 1982-83, anatomy demonstrator, 1983-84, Bristol Univ.; Surgical Lectr, Sheffield Univ., 1984-85; Metabolic Medicine Res. Fellow, Univ. of Oxford, 1985-87; Orthopaedic Registrar and Sen. Registrar, Nuffield Orthopaedic Centre and John Radcliffe Hosp., Oxford, 1988-92; Consultant Orthopaedic Surgeon, Nuffield Orthopaedic Centre, Oxford, 1993-2001. Research Fellow: Seattle, 1992; Melbourne, 1992; Hunterian Prof., RCS, 2000. Robert Jones Gold Medallist and British Orthopaedic Assoc. Prize Winner, 2000. *Publications:* (jtly) Outcomes in Orthopaedic Surgery, 1993; (jtly) Outcomes in Trauma, 1995; (jtly) Assessment Methodology in Orthopaedic Surgery, 1997; (jtly) Orthopaedics in Primary Care, 1999; (jtly) Classification in Trauma, 1999; (jtly) Oxford Textbook of Orthopaedic Surgery, 2001; contrib. to learned jls etc on shoulder and elbow surgery, genetics and osteoarthritis. *Recreations:* rowing, tennis, cooking, trampolining. *Address:* Nuffield Department of Orthopaedic Surgery, Nuffield Orthopaedic Centre NHS Trust, Oxford OX3 7LD; Worcester College, Oxford OX1 2HB. *Club:* Leander (Henley-on-Thames).

CARR, Annabel; *see* Carr, E. A.

CARR, Very Rev. (Arthur) Wesley, PhD; Dean of Westminster, since 1997; *b* 26 July 1941; *s* of Arthur and Irene Carr; *m* 1968, Natalie Gill; one *d. Educ:* Dulwich College; Jesus Coll., Oxford (MA); Jesus Coll., Cambridge (MA); Ridley Hall, Cambridge; Univ. of Sheffield (PhD). Curate, Luton Parish Church, 1967–71; Tutor, Ridley Hall, Cambridge, 1970–71, Chaplain 1971–72; Sir Henry Stephenson Fellow, Dept of Biblical Studies, Univ. of Sheffield, 1972–74; Hon. Curate, Ranmoor, 1972–74; Chaplain, Chelmsford Cathedral, 1974–78; Dep. Director, Chelmsford Cathedral Centre for Research and Training, 1974–82; Dir of Training, Diocese of Chelmsford, 1976–82; Canon Residentiary, Chelmsford Cathedral, 1978–87; Dean of Bristol, 1987–96. Mem., Gen. Synod of C of E, 1980–87, 1989–2000. Select Preacher, Univ. of Oxford, 1984–85; Hon. Fellow, New Coll., Edinburgh, 1986–94. Hon. DLitt UWE, 1997. *Publications:* Angels and Principalities, 1977; The Priestlike Task, 1985; Brief Encounters, 1985; The Pastor as Theologian, 1989; Ministry and the Media, 1990; Lost in Familiar Places, 1991; (with E. R. Shapiro) Manifold Wisdom, 1991; (ed) Say One for Me, 1992; A Handbook of Pastoral Studies, 1997; articles in Theology, etc. *Recreations:* music, reading, writing, gardening. *Address:* The Deanery, Westminster Abbey, SW1P 3PA. *T:* (020) 7654 4801, *Fax:* (020) 7654 4883; *e-mail:* wesley.carr@westminster-abbey.org.

CARR, Christopher; QC 1983; barrister; *b* 30 Nov. 1944; *s* of Edwin Wilfred Carr and Kathleen Carr; *m*; two *d* one *s. Educ:* Skegness Grammar Sch.; London Sch. of Economics; Clare Coll., Cambridge. Called to the Bar, Lincoln's Inn, 1968, Bencher, 1991. Lectr in Law, LSE, 1968–69 and 1972–73; Asst Prof. of Law, Univ. of British Columbia, 1969–72; Associate Prof. of Law, Univ. of Toronto, 1973–75; part-time Lectr, QMC, London, 1975–78; in practice at the Bar, 1975–. *Publications:* articles and notes in English and Canadian law jls. *Recreations:* mathematics, philosophy, history. *Address:* 1 Essex Court, Temple, EC4Y 9AR. *Club:* Athenæum.

CARR, Donald Bryce, OBE 1985; Secretary, Cricket Council and Test and County Cricket Board, 1974–86, retired; *b* 28 Dec. 1926; *s* of John Lillingston Carr and Constance Ruth Carr; *m* 1953, Stella Alice Vaughan Simpkinson; one *s* one *d. Educ:* Repton Sch.; Worcester Coll., Oxford (MA). Served Army, 1945–48 (Lieut Royal Berks Regt). Asst Sec., 1953–59, Sec., 1959–62, Derbyshire CCC; Asst Sec., MCC, 1962–74. *Recreations:* golf, following most sports. *Address:* 28 Aldenham Avenue, Radlett, Herts WD7 8HX. *T:* (01923) 855602. *Clubs:* MCC, British Sportsman's, Lord's Taverners; Vincent's, Oxford University Cricket (Oxford).

CARR, Edward Arthur John, CBE 1995; heritage and tourism consultant, since 1995; Chief Executive, CADW, Welsh Historic Monuments Executive Agency, 1991–95 (Director, 1985–91); *b* 31 Aug. 1938; *s* of Edward Arthur Carr, CMG and Margaret Alys Carr (*née* Willson); *m* 1st, 1960, Verity Martin (marr. diss.); two *d*; 2nd, 1980, Patrice Metro; one *s* one *d. Educ:* Leys Sch., Cambridge; Christ's Coll., Cambridge (BA 1960; MA 1963). Journalist: Thomson Regional Newspapers, 1960–65; Financial Times, 1965–67; Sunday Times, 1967–70; Manager, Times Newspapers, 1970–81; Chief Executive, Waterlow & Sons, 1981; Dir, Neath Develt Partnership, 1982–84. Non-exec. Dir, Bro Morgannwg NHS Trust, 1999–. Trustee, UK Buildings Preservation Trust, 1996–; Chm., Assoc. of Preservation Trusts (Wales). *Recreations:* family, newspapers. *Address:* 2 East Cliff, Southgate, Swansea SA3 2AS. *T:* (01792) 232800.

CARR, (Elizabeth) Annabel; QC 1997; **Her Honour Judge Annabel Carr;** a Circuit Judge, since 2001; *b* 14 Nov. 1954; *d* of William John Denys Carr and Norah Betty Carr; one *s* one *d. Educ:* Queenswood Sch., Hatfield; Sheffield Univ. (LLB Hons 1975). Called to the Bar, Gray's Inn, 1976; in practice at the Bar, 1977–2001; Recorder, 1995–2001. *Recreations:* travelling, family, theatre. *Address:* Sheffield Combined Court Centre, 50 West Bar, Sheffield S3 8PH.

CARR, Dr Eric Francis, FRCP, FRCPsych; Lord Chancellor's Medical Visitor, 1979–89; Member: Mental Health Act Commission, since 1983; Parole Board, since 1988; *b* 23 Sept. 1919; *s* of Edward Francis Carr and Maude Mary Almond; *m* 1954, Janet Gilfillan (marr. diss. 1980); two *s* one *d. Educ:* Mill Hill Sch.; Emmanuel Coll., Cambridge. MA, MB BChir; FRCP, 1971, FRCPsych, 1972; DPM. Captain, RAMC, 1944–46. Consultant Psychiatrist: St Ebba's Hosp., 1954–60; Netherne Hosp., 1960–67; Epsom and West Park Hosps, 1967–76; Hon. Consultant Psychiatrist, KCH, 1960–76; SPMO, DHSS, 1976–79. Fellow, RSocMed. *Recreations:* reading, listening to music, cooking. *Address:* 116 Holly Lane East, Banstead, Surrey SM7 2BE. *T:* (01737) 353675.

CARR, Glyn; *see* Styles, F. S.

CARR, Henry James; QC 1998; *b* 31 March 1958; *s* of Malcolm Carr and Dr Sara Carr; *m* 1988, Jan Dawson; three *s* one *d. Educ:* Hertford Coll., Oxford (BA 1st cl. Hons Jurisp.); Univ. of British Columbia (LLM). Called to the Bar, Gray's Inn, 1982; in practice at the Bar, 1982–. Chm., Council of Experts, Intellectual Property Inst. *Publication:* Computer Software: legal protection in the United Kingdom, 1987, 2nd edn (jtly) 1992. *Recreations:* tennis, swimming, theatre. *Address:* 11 South Square, Gray's Inn, WC1R 5EU. *T:* (020) 7405 1222. *Clubs:* Royal Automobile, Hurlingham, Harbour.

CARR, Ian Henry Randell; freelance trumpeter, composer, author and broadcaster, since 1960; Associate Professor, Guildhall School of Music and Drama, since 1982; *b* 21 April 1933; *s* of late Thomas Randell Carr and Phyllis Harriet Carr; *m* 1963, Margaret Blackburn Bell (*d* 1967); one *d*; 2nd, 1972, Sandra Louise Major (marr. diss. 1993). *Educ:* Barnard Castle Sch.; King's Coll., Newcastle upon Tyne (BA Hons English Lang. and Lit. 1955). Nat. Service, 2nd Lieut, Royal Northumberland Fusiliers, 1956–58. Member: Emcee Five Quintet, 1960–62; Don Rendell/Ian Carr Quintet, 1963–69; Ian Carr's Nucleus, 1969–88 (toured world-wide); Founder Mem., United Jazz and Rock Ensemble, 1975–. *Compositions:* Solar Plexus, 1970; Labyrinth, 1973; Will's Birthday Suite, 1974 (for Globe Theatre Trust); Out of the Long Dark, 1978, Old Heartland, 1988; Sounds and Sweet Airs, for trumpet and Cathedral organ, 1992; many broadcasts for BBC Radio 3. Mem., Royal Soc. of Musicians of GB, 1982. Calabria Award for outstanding contrib. in the field of jazz (Italy), 1982. *Publications:* Music Outside, 1973; Miles Davis: a critical biography, 1982, 3rd edn 1998 (as Miles Davis: the definitive biography); (jtly) Jazz: the essential companion, 1987; Keith Jarrett: the man and his music, 1991; (jtly) The Rough Guide to Jazz, 1995; contrib. BBC Music mag. *Recreations:* music, the visual arts, world literature, travel. *Address:* Flat 1, 34 Brailsford Road, SW2 2TE. *T:* (020) 8671 7195. *Club:* Ronnie Scott's.

CARR, John Roger, CBE 1991; JP; Chairman, Countryside Commission for Scotland, 1986–92 (Member, 1979–84; Vice-Chairman, 1984–85); *b* 18 Jan. 1927; *s* of James Stanley Carr and Edith Carr (*née* Robinson); *m* 1951, Catherine Elise Dickson Smith; two *s. Educ:* Ackworth and Ayton (Quaker Schools). FRICS. Royal Marines, 1944–47; Gordon Highlanders (TA), 1950–54. Factor, Walker Scottish Estates Co., 1950–54; Factor, 1954–67, Dir and Gen. Man., 1967–88, Dir, 1988–90, Moray Estates Develt Co. Dir, Strathearn Tourism Develt Co., 1959–98. Mem., Wkg Party, Management Training for Leisure and Recreation in Scotland, 1986; Chm., Countryside around Towns Forum, 1991–95; Vice Pres., Farming and Wildlife Adv. Gp for Scotland, 1992–98; Director: Macaulay Land Use Res. Inst., 1987–97; UK 2000 Scotland, 1991–93. Mem., Moray DC, 1974–80. JP Moray, 1975. *Recreations:* most countryside pursuits. *Address:* Goosehill, Invererne Road, Forres, Moray IV36 1DZ.

CARR, Maurice Chapman; His Honour Judge Carr; a Circuit Judge, since 1986; *b* 14 Aug. 1937; *s* of John and Elizabeth Carr; *m* 1959, Caryl Olson; one *s* one *d. Educ:* Hookergate Grammar Sch.; LSE (LLB); Harvard Univ. (LLM). Lectr in Law, 1960–62, Asst Prof. of Law, 1963–64, Univ. of British Columbia; Lecturer in Law: UCW, 1964–65; Univ. of Newcastle upon Tyne, 1965–69. Called to the Bar, Middle Temple, 1966. *Recreations:* walking, music. *Address:* 33 Broad Chare, Newcastle upon Tyne NE1 3DQ. *T:* (0191) 232 0541.

CARR, Michael; teacher; *b* 31 Jan. 1946; *s* of James and Sheila Mary Carr; *m* 1st (wife *d* 1979); one *s*; 2nd, 1980, Georgina Clare; four *s* two *d. Educ:* St Joseph's Coll., Blackpool; Catholic Coll., Preston; Margaret McMillan Coll. of Educn, Bradford (CertEd); Bradford and Ilkley Community Coll. (DPSE). Engrg apprentice, 1962–63; Local Govt Officer, 1964–68; partner in family retail newsagency, 1968–70; Teacher of Geography: Brookside Sec. Sch., Middlesbrough, 1973–74; Stainsby Sch., Middlesbrough, 1974–75; Head of Geog., St Thomas Aquinas RC High Sch., Darwen, Lancs, 1975–82; Head of Gen. Studies, Blackthorn County Sec. Sch. and Blackthorn Wing of Fearns CS Sch., Bacup, 1982–87; Mem., Lancs Educn Cttee Sch. Support Team (Disruptive Behaviour), 1988–91. Mem., Sabden Parish Council, 1976–78, 1979–83; Mem. (C 1979–81, SDP 1981–83), Ribble Valley BC, 1979–83. Joined SDP, 1981; contested (SDP/Lib Alliance) Ribble Valley, 1983, 1987; MP (Lib Dem) Ribble Valley, March 1991–1992; contested (Lib Dem) Ribble Valley, 1992, 1997, 2001. Mem., NAS/UWT (Dist Sec., Rossendale Assoc., 1983–87; Press Officer, Lancs Fedn, 1983–87, 1988–90). *Recreations:* hill walking, cooking, music.

CARR, Peter Derek, CBE 1989; DL; Chairman: County Durham Development Co., since 1990; Newcastle and North Tyne Health Authority, since 1998; Northern Screen Commission, since 1990; Durham County Waste Management Co., since 1993; Acorn Energy Supplies Ltd, since 1998; *b* 12 July 1930; *s* of George William Carr and Marjorie (*née* Tailby); *m* 1958, Geraldine Pamela (*née* Ward); one *s* one *d. Educ:* Fircroft Coll., Birmingham; Ruskin Coll., Oxford. National Service, RAF, 1951–53. Carpenter and joiner, construction industry, 1944–51 and 1953–56; college, 1956–60; Lectr, Percival Whitley Coll., Halifax, 1960–65; Sen. Lectr in Indust. Relations, Thurrock Coll., and part-time Adviser, NBPI, 1965–69; Director: Commn on Industrial Relations, 1969–74; ACAS, 1974–78; Diplomatic Service, Washington, 1978–83; Regl Dir, Northern Regl Office, Dept of Employment, and Leader, City Action Team, 1983–89; Chairman: Northern RHA, 1990–94; Occupational Pensions Bd, 1994–97. Chm., Premier Waste Mgt, 1997–99. Vis. Fellow, Durham Univ., 1989–. DL Durham, 1997. *Publications:* directed study for CIR on worker participation and collective bargaining in Europe, and study for ACAS on industrial relations in national newspaper industry. *Recreations:* cycling, cooking, furniture-making. *Address:* 4 Corchester Towers, Corbridge, Northumberland NE45 5NP. *T:* (01434) 632841, *Fax:* (01434) 633726; *e-mail:* petercarr@aol.com.

CARR, Sir Raymond; *see* Carr, Sir A. R. M.

CARR, Reginald Philip; Director, University Library Services, and Bodley's Librarian, University of Oxford, since 1997; Fellow, Balliol College, Oxford, since 1997; *b* 20 Feb. 1946; *s* of Philip Henry Carr and Ida Bayley Carr; *m* 1968, Elizabeth Whittaker; one *s* three *d. Educ:* Manchester Grammar Sch.; Univ. of Leeds (BA 1968); Univ. of Manchester (MA 1971); MA Cantab 1983; MA Oxon 1997. English lang. teaching asst, Lycée Fontenelle, Rouen, 1966–67; Asst Librarian, John Rylands Univ. Liby, Manchester, 1970–72; Librarian-in-Charge, Sch. of Educn Liby, Univ. of Manchester, 1972–76; Sub-Librarian, Univ. of Surrey, 1976–78; Deputy Librarian: Univ. of Aston, 1978–80; Univ. of Cambridge, 1980–86; University of Leeds: Univ. Librarian and Keeper, Brotherton Collection, 1986–96; Dean, Information Strategy, 1996. Mem., Jt Information Systems Cttee, 1997–. Chm., Res. Libraries Gp Inc., 1999–. FRSA 1996. Hon. DLitt Leicester, 2000. Hon. Citizen, Toyota City, 1998. *Publications:* Anarchism in France: the case of Octave Mirbeau, 1977; (jtly) Spirit in the New Testament, 1985; The Mandrake Press, 1985; (jtly) An Introduction to University Library Administration, 1987; contribs to professional and learned jls. *Recreations:* Bible study, book collecting. *Address:* The Bodleian Library, Broad Street, Oxford OX1 3BG. *T:* (01865) 277166.

CARR, Hon. Robert John; MP (ALP) Maroubra, NSW, since 1983; Premier of New South Wales, and Minister for the Arts and for Ethnic Affairs, since 1995; *b* 28 Sept. 1947; *s* of Edward and Phyllis Carr; *m* 1973, Helena John. *Educ:* Univ. of NSW (BA Hons). Journalist, ABC Current Affairs Radio, 1969–72; Educn Officer, Labour Council, NSW, 1972–78; Journalist, The Bulletin, 1978–83. Minister for: Planning and Envmt, 1984–88; Consumer Affairs, 1986; Heritage, 1986–88; Leader of the Opposition, NSW, 1988–95. *Address:* Governor Macquarie Tower, 1 Farrer Place, Sydney, NSW 2000, Australia. *T:* (2) 92285239, *Fax:* (2) 92283935.

CARR, Roger Martyn; Chairman, Chubb plc, since 2000; Chief Executive, Williams plc, 1994–2000; *b* 22 Dec. 1946; *s* of John and Kathleen Carr; *m* 1973, Stephanie Elizabeth; one *d. Educ:* Nottingham High Sch.; Nottingham Poly. Dir, Williams Hldgs plc, 1988–2000. Non-executive Director: Bass plc, 1996–; Centrica plc, 2001–; Cadbury Schweppes, 2001–. *Recreations:* theatre, opera, golf, tennis. *Address:* Pentagon House, Sir Frank Whittle Road, Derby DE21 4XA. *Clubs:* London Capital, Royal Automobile; China (Hong Kong).

CARR, Very Rev. Wesley; *see* Carr, Very Rev. A. W.

CARR, Prof. Wilfred; Professor, since 1994, and Head of School of Education (formerly Department of Educational Studies), since 1996, University of Sheffield; *b* 18 March 1943; *s* of Wilfred and Leah Carr; *m* 1976, Marisse Evans; three *d. Educ:* Xaverian Coll., Manchester; Shenstone Coll. of Educn, Worcs (DipEd); Warwick Univ. (BA, MA). History teacher, Oldbury Tech. Sch., Warley, Worcs, 1966–70; Lectr, Sch. of Educn, UCNW, 1974–88; Sen. Lectr, Dept of Educnl Studies, 1988–90, Reader 1990–94, Univ. of Sheffield. Ed., Pedagogy, Culture and Society, 1993–. Chm., Philosophy of Educn Soc. of GB, 1996–99. *Publications:* (with S. Kemmis) Becoming Critical: education knowledge and action research, 1986 (trans. Spanish, 1988); For Education: towards critical educational inquiry, 1995 (trans. Spanish, 1996, Chinese, 1997). *Recreations:* cookery, reading, walking. *Address:* School of Education, University of Sheffield, 388 Glossop Road, Sheffield S10 2JA. *T:* (0114) 222 8085; *e-mail:* w.carr@sheffield.ac.uk.

CARR, William Compton; *b* 10 July 1918; *m*; two *s* one *d. Educ:* The Leys Sch., Cambridge. MP (C) Barons Court, 1959–64; PPS to Min. of State, Board of Trade, 1963; PPS to Financial Sec. to the Treasury, 1963–64. *Recreations:* reading, theatre-going, skin diving, eating, dieting.

CARR-ELLISON, Sir Ralph (Harry), KCVO 1999; Kt 1973; TD; DL; Lord-Lieutenant of Tyne and Wear, 1984–2000; *b* 8 Dec. 1925; *s* of late Major John Campbell Carr-Ellison; *m* 1st, 1951, Mary Clare (*d* 1996), *d* of late Major Arthur McMorrough Kavanagh, MC; three *s* one *d*; 2nd, 1998, Louise Gay Dyer (*née* Walsh), *widow* of Simon Dyer, CBE. *Educ:* Eton. Served Royal Glos Hussars and 1st Royal Dragoons, 1944–49; Northumberland Hussars (TA), (Lt-Col Comdg), 1949–69; TAVR Col, Northumbrian Dist, 1969–72; Col, Dep. Comdr (TAVR), NE Dist, 1973; Chm., N of England TA&VRA, 1976–80 (Pres. 1987–90; Vice-Pres., 1990–2000); ADC (TAVR) to HM the Queen, 1970–75; Hon. Colonel: Northumbrian Univs OTC, 1982–86; QOY, 1988–90 (Northumberland Hussars Sqn, 1986–88); Col Comdt, Yeomanry RAC TA, 1990–94. Chairman: Northumbrian Water Authy, 1973–82; Tyne Tees Television Ltd, 1974–97 (Dir, 1966–97); Director: Newcastle & Gateshead Water Co., 1964–73; Trident Television, 1972–81 (Dep. Chm., 1976–81); Yorkshire–Tyne Tees Television Hldgs, 1992–97. Co. Comr, Northumberland Scouts, 1958–68; Mem. Cttee of Council, 1960–67, Mem. Council, 1982–, Scout Assoc. Chm., Berwick-on-Tweed Constituency Cons. Assoc., 1959–62, Pres., 1973–77; Northern Area Cons. Assocs: Treas., 1961–66, Chm., 1966–69; Pres., 1974–78; Vice-Chm., Nat Union of Cons. and Unionist Assocs, 1969–71. Chm., North Tyne Area, Manpower Bd, MSC, 1983–84. Vice Pres., Automobile Assoc., 1995–99 (Vice-Chm., 1985–86; Chm., 1986–95). Mem. Council, The Wildfowl Trust, 1981–88. Chm., Newcastle Univ. Develt Trust, 1978–81 (Mem., 1992–98); Mem. Ct, Newcastle Univ., 1979–; Governor, Swinton Conservative College, 1967–81. FRSA 1983. High Sheriff, 1972, JP 1953–75, DL 1981–85, Vice Lord-Lieut, 1984, Northumberland; DL Tyne and Wear, 2001. Hon. DCL Newcastle, 1989; Hon. LLD Sunderland, 1998. KStJ 1984. *Recreation:* Jt Master, West Percy Foxhounds, 1950–90. *Address:* Beanley Hall, Beanley, Alnwick, Northumberland NE66 2DX. *T:* (01665) 578273. *Clubs:* Cavalry and Guards, White's, Pratt's; Northern Counties (Newcastle upon Tyne).

CARR-GOMM, Richard Culling, OBE 1985; *b* 2 Jan. 1922; *s* of Mark Culling Carr-Gomm and Amicia Dorothy (*née* Heming); *m* 1957, Susan, *d* of Ralph and Dorothy Gibbs; two *s* three *d. Educ:* Stowe School. Served War: commnd Coldstream Guards, 1941; served 6th Guards Tank Bde, NW Europe (twice wounded, mentioned in despatches); Palestine, 1945; ME; resigned commn, 1955. Founded: Abbeyfield Soc., 1956; Carr-Gomm Soc., 1965; Morpeth Soc. (charity socs), 1972. Templeton UK Project Award, 1984. Croix de Guerre (Silver Star), France, 1944. KStJ. *Publications:* Push on the Door (autobiog.), 1979; Loneliness—the wider scene, 1987. *Recreations:* golf, backgammon, painting. *Address:* 9 The Batch, Batheaston, Somerset BA1 7DR. *T:* (01225) 858434.

CARR LINFORD, Alan; artist, antique dealer; *b* 15 Jan. 1926; *m* 1948, Margaret Dorothea Parish; one *s* one *d. Educ:* Royal College of Art (ARCA 1946), and in Rome. ARE 1946; ARWS 1949, RWS 1955. Prix de Rome, 1947. *Recreation:* shooting.

CARR-SMITH, Maj.-Gen. Stephen Robert; Ombudsman for Estate Agents, since 1999; Chairman, Applied Systems International plc, since 1999; *b* 3 Dec. 1941; *s* of Charles Carr-Smith and Elizabeth Carr-Smith (*née* Marsh); *m* 1967, Nicole Bould; two *s* one *d. Educ:* Welbeck College; RMA; RMCS; BA Open Univ., 1992. Commissioned Royal Signals, 1962; served in UK, Germany, Aden and Belgium; Mil. Sec., 1973–74, Operational Requirements, 1978–79, MoD; CO, 1st Armoured Div. HQ and Signal Regt, 1979–82; Instructor, Army Staff Coll., 1982–84; Comdt, Army Apprentices Coll., Harrogate, 1984–86; Col MGO Secretariat, MoD, 1986–88; Chief CIS Policy Branch, SHAPE, Mons, 1988–91; Dep. Dir Gen., NATO CIS Agency, Brussels, 1992–95; Dir of Special Projects, Defence Systems Ltd, 1995–98; Sen. Mil. Advr, CORDA, BAe and SEMA, 1995–99. Hon. Col, FANY, Princess Royal's Volunteer Corps, 1996–; Col Comdt, RCS, 1996–. FIMgt. *Recreations:* cricket, golf, bridge, politics, international affairs. *Address:* c/o Cox's & King's, PO Box 1190, 7 Pall Mall, SW1Y 5NA.

CARRELL, Prof. Robin Wayne, FRSNZ 1980; FRCP; Professor of Haematology, University of Cambridge, since 1986; Fellow of Trinity College, Cambridge, since 1987; *b* 5 April 1936; *s* of Ruane George Carrell and Constance Gwendoline Carrell (*née* Rowe); *m* 1962, Susan Wyatt Rogers; two *s* two *d. Educ:* Christchurch Boys' High School, NZ; Univ. of Otago (MB ChB 1959); Univ. of Canterbury (BSc 1965); Univ. of Cambridge (MA, PhD 1968). FRACP 1973; FRCPath 1976; MRCP 1985, FRCP 1990. Mem., MRC Abnormal Haemoglobin Unit, Cambridge, 1965–68; Dir, Clinical Biochemistry, Christchurch Hosp., NZ, 1968–75; Lectr and Consultant in Clinical Biochem., Addenbrooke's Hosp. and Univ. of Cambridge, 1976–78; Prof. of Clinical Biochem., Christchurch Sch. of Clinical Medicine, Univ. of Otago, 1978–86. Pres., British Soc. of Thrombosis and Haemostasis, 1999. Member: Gen. Bd, Univ. of Cambridge, 1989–92; Court, Imperial Coll., London, 1997–. Commonwealth Fellow, St John's Coll. and Vis. Scientist, MRC Lab. of Molecular Biol., 1985. Founder FMedSci 1998. Pharmacia Prize for biochem. res., NZ, 1984; Hector Medal, Royal Soc., NZ, 1986. *Publications:* articles in sci. jls, esp. on genetic abnormalities of human proteins. *Recreations:* gardening, walking. *Address:* 19 Madingley Road, Cambridge CB3 0EG. *T:* (01223) 312970.

CARRERAS, José; tenor; *b* 5 Dec. 1946; *s* of José and Antonia Carreras; *m*; one *s* one *d.* Opera début as Gennaro in Lucrezia Borgia, Barcelona, 1970; US début in Madama Butterfly, NY City Opera, 1972; Tosca, NY Met, 1974; Covent Garden début in La Traviata, 1974; Un Ballo In Maschera, La Scala, 1975; after break owing to illness, concerts in Barcelona, 1988, Covent Gdn, 1989; Music Dir, Barcelona Olympics, 1992; first UK perf., Stiffelio, Covent Gdn, 1993; appears at all major opera houses and festivals in Europe, USA and S America; has made many recordings. *Films:* Don Carlos, 1980; West Side Story (TV), 1985. RAM 1990. Personality of the Year, Classical Music Awards, 1994. Pres., José Carreras Internat. Leukaemia Foundn, 1988–. *Address:* c/o FIJC, Muntaner 383, 2°, 08021 Barcelona, Spain.

CARRICK, 10th Earl of *cr* 1748; **David James Theobald Somerset Butler;** Viscount Ikerrin 1629; Baron Butler (UK) 1912; *b* 9 Jan. 1953; *s* of 9th Earl of Carrick, and his 1st wife, (Mary) Belinda (*d* 1993), *e d* of Major David Constable-Maxwell, TD; *S* father, 1992; *m* 1975, Philippa V. J., *yr d* of Wing Commander L. V. Craxton; three *s* (including twin *s*). *Educ:* Downside. *Heir:* s Viscount Ikerrin, *qv. Address:* Pant yr Eos, Moelfre, Llansilin, Oswestry, Shropshire SY10 7QR.

CARRICK, Hon. Sir John (Leslie), KCMG 1982; Senator, Commonwealth Parliament of Australia, 1971–87, retired; *b* 4 Sept. 1918; *s* of late A. J. Carrick and of E. E. Carrick; *m* 1951, Diana Margaret Hunter; three *d. Educ:* Univ. of Sydney (BEc; Hon. DLitt 1988). Res. Officer, Liberal Party of Aust., NSW Div., 1946–48, Gen. Sec., 1948–71; Minister: for Housing and Construction, 1975; for Urban and Regional Develt, 1975; for Educn, 1975–79; Minister Assisting Prime Minister in Fed. Affairs, 1975–78; Minister for Nat. Develt and Energy, 1979–83; Dep. Leader, 1978, Leader, 1978–83, Govt in the Senate. Vice-Pres., Exec. Council, 1978–82. Chairman: NSW Govt Cttee of Review of Schs, 1988–89; Gas Council of NSW, 1990–95. Pres., Univ. of Sydney Dermatology Res. Foundn, 1989–; Mem. Adv. Council, Inst. of Early Childhood, Macquarie Univ., 1990–; Chm., Adv. Cttee, GERRIC (Gifted Children), Univ. of NSW, 1998–. Mem. Exec. Cttee, Foundn for Aged Care, 1989–2001. Mem., Commonwealth Roundtable (Indigenous), 2000–. Hon. FACE 1994. Hon. DLitt Macquarie, 2000. *Recreations:* swimming, reading. *Address:* 21 Cambridge Apartments, 162E Burwood Road, Concord, NSW 2137, Australia. *Clubs:* Australian (Sydney); Commonwealth (Canberra).

CARRICK, Mervyn; *see* Carrick, W. M.

CARRICK, Sir Roger (John), KCMG 1995 (CMG 1983); LVO 1972; HM Diplomatic Service, retired; international consultant; Chairman, cmb Ltd, since 2001; *b* 13 Oct. 1937; *s* of John H. and Florence M. Carrick; *m* 1962, Hilary Elizabeth Blinman; two *s. Educ:* Isleworth Grammar Sch.; Sch. of Slavonic and East European Studies, London Univ. Served RN, 1956–58. Joined HM Foreign (subseq. Diplomatic) Service, 1956; SSEES, 1961; Sofia, 1962; FO, 1965; Paris, 1967; Singapore, 1971; FCO, 1973; Counsellor and Dep. Head, Personnel Ops Dept, FCO, 1976; Vis. Fellow, Inst. of Internat. Studies, Univ. of Calif, Berkeley, 1977–78; Counsellor, Washington, 1978–82; Hd, Overseas Estate Dept, FCO, 1982–85; Consul-Gen., Chicago, 1985–88; Asst Under-Sec. of State (Economic), FCO, 1988–90; Ambassador, Republic of Indonesia, 1990–94; High Comr, Australia, 1994–97. Dep. Chm., The D Gp, 1999–; non-executive Director: etms, 2000–; cmb technologies, 2001–. Churchill Fellow (Life), Westminster Coll., Fulton, Missouri, 1987. Chm., Britain–Australia Soc., 1999–. Member: RSAA; Anglo-Indonesian Soc.; Cook Soc.; Bd of Trustees, Chevening Estate, 1998–. Jt Founder, WADE. *Publications:* East-West Technology Transfer in Perspective, 1978; RolleroundOz, 1998. *Recreations:* sailing, travel, reading, enjoying music and avoiding gardening. *Address:* 43 Dornden Drive, Langton Green, Tunbridge Wells, Kent TN3 0AE. *Clubs:* Royal Over-Seas League, Pilgrims; Primary (Australia).

CARRICK, (William) Mervyn; Member (DemU) Upper Bann, Northern Ireland Assembly, since 1998; *b* 13 Feb. 1946; *s* of late William and of Margaret Carrick; *m* 1969, Ruth Cardwell; three *s* one *d. Educ:* Portadown Technical Coll. Accountant, 1961–. Mem., NI Forum for Political Dialogue, 1996–98. Mem. (DemU), Craigavon BC, 1990– (Dep. Mayor, 1997–98, Mayor, 1998–99). *Recreation:* gardening. *Address:* 72 Dungannon Road, Portadown, Co. Armagh BT62 1LQ. *T:* (028) 3833 6392.

CARRIER, Dr John Woolfe; Chairman, Royal Free Hampstead NHS Hospital Trust, since 1997; Senior Lecturer in Social Policy, London School of Economics and Political Science, since 1974; *b* 26 Sept. 1938; *s* of Louis Carrier and Rachel Carrier; *m* 1964, Sarah Margaret Dawes; two *s* two *d. Educ:* Regent's Park Central Sch.; Chiswick Poly.; London Sch. of Econs (BSc (Soc) 1965; MPhil 1969; PhD 1983); Univ. of Westminster (LLB Hons. 1994). Principal Lectr, Goldsmiths' Coll., Univ. of London, 1967–74. Lectures:

William Marsden, Royal Free Hosp., 1996; Richard Titmuss Meml, Hebrew Univ. of Jerusalem, 1997. Jt Ed., Internat. Jl Sociol. of Law, 1993–; Member, Editorial Board: Jl Social Policy, 1975–81; Ethnic and Racial Studies, 1990–96. Mem. (Lab) Camden BC, 1971–78. Mem. and Vice-Chm., Hampstead HA, 1982–91; Vice-Chm., Royal Free Hampstead NHS Hosp. Trust, 1991–97. Vice-Chm. and Trustee, Centre for Advancement of Inter-professional Educn, 1990–99; Trustee, William Ellis and Birkbeck Schs Trust, 1996–. Mem. Council, Royal Free Hosp. Med. Sch., 1988–98; Trustee, RNTNEH, 1997–99; Special Trustee, Royal Free Hosp., 1999–. Chairman: Camden Victim Support Scheme, 1978–83; Highgate Cemetery Trust, 1983–97. Governor: Gospel Oak Primary Sch., 1972–80 (Chm., 1977–80); Brookfield Primary Sch., 1974–89 (Chm., 1981–87); William Ellis Sch., 1971–96 (Chm., 1987–96). JP Highbury, 1983–90. Hon. FRSocMed 1999; FRSA 1999. *Publications:* with Ian Kendall: Medical Negligence: complaints and compensation, 1990; (ed) Socialism and the NHS, 1990; Health and the National Health Service, 1998; (ed jtly) Interprofessional Issues in Community and Primary Health Care, 1995; (ed jtly) Asylum in the Community, 1996; contrib. articles to learned jls. *Recreations:* running, tennis, walking, films, art galleries. *Address:* 37 Dartmouth Park Road, NW5 1SU. *T:* (020) 7267 1376.

CARRINGTON, 6th Baron (Ireland) *cr* 1796, (Great Britain) *cr* 1797; **Peter Alexander Rupert Carington,** KG 1985; GCMG 1988 (KCMG 1958); CH 1983; MC 1945; PC 1959; Baron Carington of Upton (Life Peer), 1999; Chairman, Christies International plc, 1988–93; Director, The Telegraph plc, since 1990; Chancellor, Order of the Garter, since 1994; *b* 6 June 1919; *s* of 5th Baron and Hon. Sibyl Marion (*d* 1946), *d* of 2nd Viscount Colville; *S* father, 1938; *m* 1942, Iona, *yr d* of late Sir Francis McClean; one *s* two *d. Educ:* Eton Coll.; RMC Sandhurst. Served NW Europe, Major Grenadier Guards. Parly Sec., Min. of Agriculture and Fisheries, 1951–54; Parly Sec., Min. of Defence, Oct. 1954–Nov. 1956; High Comr for the UK in Australia, Nov. 1956–Oct. 1959; First Lord of the Admiralty, 1959–63; Minister without Portfolio and Leader of the House of Lords, 1963–64; Leader of the Opposition, House of Lords, 1964–70 and 1974–79; Secretary of State: for Defence, 1970–74; for Energy, 1974; for For. and Commonwealth Affairs, 1979–82; Minister of Aviation Supply, 1971–74. Chm., Cons. Party Organisation, 1972–74. Chm., GEC, 1983–84; Sec.-Gen., NATO, 1984–88. Chm., EC Conf. on Yugoslavia, 1991–92. Sec. for Foreign Correspondence and Hon. Mem., Royal Acad. of Arts, 1982–; Chm., Bd of Trustees, V & A Museum, 1983–88. Chancellor, Univ. of Reading, 1992–. President: The Pilgrims, 1983–; VSO, 1993–. Hon Bencher, Middle Temple, 1983; Hon. Elder Brother of Trinity House, 1984. Chancellor, Order of St Michael and St George, 1984–94. JP 1948, DL Bucks. Fellow of Eton Coll., 1966–81; Hon. Fellow, St Antony's Coll., Oxford, 1982. Hon. LLD: Cambridge, 1981; Leeds, 1981; Aberdeen, 1985; Nottingham, 1993; Birmingham, 1993; Newcastle, 1998; Hon. Dr Laws: Univ. of Philippines, 1982; Univ. of S Carolina, 1983; Harvard, 1986; Reading, 1989; Sussex, 1989; Hon. DCL Newcastle, 1989; DUniv: Essex, 1983; Buckingham, 1989; Hon. DSc Cranfield, 1988. *Publication:* Reflect on Things Past (autobiog.), 1988. *Heir: s* Hon. Rupert Francis John Carington [*b* 2 Dec. 1948; *m* 1989, Daniela, *d* of Mr and Mrs Flavio Diotallevi; one *s* two *d*]. *Address:* 32a Ovington Square, SW3 1LR. *T:* (020) 7584 1476; The Manor House, Bledlow, Princes Risborough, Bucks HP27 9PB. *T:* (01844) 343499. *Clubs:* Pratt's, White's.

CARRINGTON, Prof. Alan, CBE 1999; FRS 1971; Royal Society Research Professor, Southampton University, 1979–84 and since 1987, Oxford University, 1984–87; *b* 6 Jan. 1934; *o s* of Albert Carrington and Constance (*née* Nelson); *m* 1959, Noreen Hilary Taylor; one *s* two *d. Educ:* Colfe's Grammar Sch.; Univ. of Southampton. BSc, PhD; MA Cantab, MA Oxon. FRSC 1989; FInstP 1993. University of Cambridge: Asst in Research, 1960; Fellow of Downing Coll., 1960, Hon. Fellow, 1999; Asst Dir of Res., 1963; Prof. of Chemistry, Univ. of Southampton, 1967; Fellow, Jesus Coll., Oxford, 1984–87. Sen. Fellowship, SRC, 1976. Tilden Lectr, Chem. Soc., 1972; George Pimental Meml Lectr, Univ. of Calif at Berkeley, 1996. Pres., Faraday Div., RSC, 1997–99. FRSA 1999. Foreign Hon. Mem., Amer. Acad. of Arts and Scis, 1987; Foreign Associate, Nat. Acad. of Scis, USA, 1994. Hon. DSc Southampton, 1985. Harrison Mem. Prize, Chem. Soc., 1962; Meldola Medal, Royal Inst. of Chemistry, 1963; Marlow Medal, Faraday Soc., 1966; Corday Morgan Medal, Chem. Soc., 1967; Chem. Soc. Award in Structural Chemistry, 1970; Faraday Medal, RSC, 1985; Davy Medal, Royal Soc., 1992. *Publications:* (with A. D. McLachlan) Introduction to Magnetic Resonance, 1967; Microwave Spectroscopy of Free Radicals, 1974; numerous papers on topics in chemical physics in various learned jls. *Recreations:* family, music, fishing, golf, sailing. *Address:* 46 Lakewood Road, Chandler's Ford, Hants SO53 1EX. *T:* (023) 8026 5092.

CARRINGTON, Maj.-Gen. Colin Edward George, CB 1991; CBE 1983; Commander, Army Security Vetting Unit, since 1991; *b* 19 Jan. 1936; *s* of Edgar John Carrington and Ruth Carrington (*née* West); *m* 1967, Joy Bracknell; one *s* one *d. Educ:* Royal Liberty Sch.; RMA Sandhurst. FCIT 1988. Troop Comdr, BAOR, 1956–59; Air Despatch duties, 1960–64; Instructor, RMA, 1964–68; Sqdn Comdr, BAOR, 1972–74; Directing Staff, Staff Coll., 1975–77; CO 1 Armd Div. Transport Regt, 1977–79; DCOS 1 Armd Div., 1979–82; RCDS 1983; Dir, Manning Policy (Army), 1984–86; Comd Transport 1 (BR) Corps, 1986–88; Dir Gen. Transport and Movements (Army), MoD, 1988–91, retd. Freeman, City of London, 1988. *Recreations:* gardening, reading.

CARRINGTON, Matthew Hadrian Marshall; Chairman, Outdoor Advertising Association, since 1998; *b* 19 Oct. 1947; *s* of Walter Carrington, *qv* and Dilys Carrington; *m* 1975, Mary Lou Darrow; one *d. Educ:* London Lycée; Imperial Coll. of Science and Technol., London (BSc Physics); London Business Sch. (MSc). Prodn Foreman, GKN Ltd, 1969–72; banker: with The First National Bank of Chicago, 1974–78; with Saudi Internat. Bank, 1978–87. MP (C) Fulham, 1987–97; contested (C) Hammersmith and Fulham, 1997, 2001. PPS to Rt Hon. John Patten, MP, 1990–94; an Asst Govt Whip, 1996–97. Mem., Treasury and Civil Service Select Cttee, 1994–96; Chm., Treasury Select Cttee, 1996. *Recreations:* cooking, political history. *Address:* 34 Ladbroke Square, W11 3NB.

CARRINGTON, Ruth; *see* James, M. L.

CARRINGTON, Walter Hadrian Marshall; Director, Constructive Teaching Centre Ltd, since 1960; Teacher, F. Matthias Alexander Technique, since 1939; *b* 4 May 1915; *s* of Rev. Walter Marshall Carrington and Hannah Carrington (*née* Robinson); *m* 1940, Dilys Mary Gwyneth Jones; three *s. Educ:* Choir Sch. of All Saints; St Paul's Sch.; completed F. Matthias Alexander's trng course for teachers of his Alexander Technique. Served War of 1939–45: RAF Pilot trng, 1941; with 614 (Pathfinder) Sqn, MAAF, 1944 (Pathfinder Award); Flight Lieut. Asst to F. Matthias Alexander, 1939–41, 1946–55. Mem., Pathfinder Assoc., 1945–. MInstD 1960. *Publications:* (with Dr Séan Carey) Explaining the Alexander Technique, 1992; Thinking Aloud, 1994; A Time to Remember, 1996; The Art of Living, 1999. *Recreations:* riding, dressage, classical horsemanship. *Address:* 18 Lansdowne Road, W11 3LL. *T:* (020) 7727 7222.
See also M. H. M. Carrington.

CARROL, Charles Gordon; Director, Commonwealth Institute, Scotland, 1971–97; *b* 21 March 1935; *s* of Charles Muir Carrol and Catherine Gray Napier; *m* 1970, Frances Anne, *o d* of John A. and Flora McL. Sinclair; three *s. Educ:* Melville Coll., Edinburgh; Edinburgh Univ. (MA); Moray House Coll. (DipEd). Education Officer: Govt of Nigeria, 1959–65; Commonwealth Inst., Scotland, 1965–71. Lay Member, Press Council, 1978–82. *Recreations:* walking, reading, cooking. *Address:* 11 Dukehaugh, Peebles, Scotland EH45 9DN. *T:* (01721) 721296.

CARROLL, Ven. Charles William Desmond; Archdeacon of Blackburn, 1973–86; Archdeacon Emeritus since 1986; Vicar of Balderstone, 1973–86; *b* 27 Jan. 1919; *s* of Rev. William and Mrs L. Mary Carroll; *m* 1945, Doreen Daisy Ruskell; three *s* one *d. Educ:* St Columba Coll.; Trinity Coll., Dublin. BA 1943; Dip. Ed. Hons 1945; MA 1946. Asst Master: Kingstown Grammar Sch., 1943–45; Rickerby House Sch., 1945–50; Vicar of Stanwix, Carlisle, 1950–59; Hon. Canon of Blackburn, 1959; Dir of Religious Education, 1959; Hon. Chaplain to Bishop of Blackburn, 1961; Canon Residentiary of Blackburn Cathedral, 1964. *Publication:* Management for Managers, 1968. *Address:* 11 Assheton Road, Blackburn BB2 6SF. *T:* (01254) 251915. *Club:* Rotary (Blackburn).

CARROLL, Most Rev. Francis Patrick; *see* Canberra and Goulburn, Archbishop of, (RC).

CARROLL, Prof. John Edward, FREng; Professor of Engineering, University of Cambridge, since 1983; Fellow of Queens' College, Cambridge, since 1967; *b* 15 Feb. 1934; *s* of Sydney Wentworth Carroll and May Doris Carroll; *m* 1958, Vera Mary Jordan; three *s. Educ:* Oundle Sch.; Queens' Coll., Cambridge (Wrangler; Foundn Schol., 1957). BA 1957; PhD 1961; ScD 1982. FIEE; FREng (FEng 1985). Microwave Div., Services Electronic Res. Lab., 1961–67; Cambridge University: Lectr, 1967–76; Reader, 1976–83; Dep. Hd of Engrg Dept, 1986–90; Head of Electrical Div., 1992–99; Chm. Council, Sch. of Technol., 1996–99. Vis. Prof., Queensland Univ., 1982. Editor, IEE Jl of Solid State and Electron Devices, 1976–82. *Publications:* Hot Electron Microwave Generators, 1970; Physical Models of Semiconductor Devices, 1974; Solid State Devices (Inst. of Phys. vol. 57), 1980; Rate Equations in Semiconductor Electronics, 1986; Distributed Feedback Semiconductor Lasers, 1998; contribs on microwaves, semiconductor devices and optical systems to learned jls. *Recreations:* swimming, piano, walking, reading thrillers, carpentry. *Address:* Engineering Department, Cambridge University, Trumpington Street, Cambridge CB2 1PZ. *T:* (01223) 332799, *Fax:* (01223) 332662.

CARROLL, Michael John; His Honour Judge Carroll; a Circuit Judge, since 1996; *b* 26 Dec. 1948; *s* of Matthew Carroll and Gladys Carroll; *m* 1974, Stella Reilly; two *s* two *d* (and one *d* decd). *Educ:* Shebbear Coll., N Devon; City of London Business Sch. (BA Hons); Inns of Court Sch. of Law. Called to the Bar, Gray's Inn, 1973. Factory worker, 1964; shop asst, 1967; fastfood chef, 1968; public service vehicle conductor, 1968–72, and driver, 1973; part-time PO counter clerk, 1968–73. Asst Recorder, 1990–94; Recorder, 1994–96. *Recreations:* reading, antiques, football. *Address:* The Crown Court at Woolwich, 2 Belmarsh Road, SE28 0EY. *T:* (020) 8312 7000.

CARROLL, Rt Rev. Mgr Philip; Parish Priest, St Bede's Church, Washington, since 1996; *b* 30 Nov. 1946; *s* of Joseph Carroll and Jean Carroll (*née* Graham). *Educ:* Venerable English College, Rome (PhL, STL). Ordained 1971; Assistant Priest, Our Blessed Lady Immaculate, Washington, 1972–78; Hexham and Newcastle Diocesan Religious Educn Service, 1979–88; Asst Gen. Sec., 1988–91, Gen. Sec., 1992–96, Catholic Bishops' Conf. *Recreations:* cricket, fell walking. *Address:* St Bede's, Coach Road Estate, Washington, Tyne and Wear NE37 2HE. *T:* (0191) 416 3805. *Clubs:* Ryton Cricket; Tyneside Golf.

CARROLL, Terence Patrick, (Terry); Managing Director, Hollins Consulting, since 1994; *b* 24 Nov. 1948; *s* of George Daniel Carroll and Betty Doreen Carroll (*née* Holmes); *m* 1st, 1971, Louise Mary (*née* Smith) (marr. diss. 1984); one *s*; 2nd, 1984, Penelope Julia, (Penny) (*née* Berry) (marr. diss. 1994); 3rd, 1994, Heather Carmen (*née* Summers). *Educ:* Gillingham Grammar Sch.; Univ. of Bradford (BSc Business Studies). FCA 1980; FCT 1990 (MCT 1985); FCIB (FCBSI 1986). Auditor and Computer Auditor, Armitage & Norton, 1970–76; Management Accountant, Bradford & Bingley Building Soc., 1976–80; Exec. and Mem. Stock Exchange, Sheppards & Chase, 1980–82; Treasurer, Halifax Building Soc., 1982–85; National & Provincial Building Society: Gen. Manager Finance, 1985–86; Acting Chief Exec., 1986–87; Finance Dir, 1987–90; Treasury Dir, 1990–91; Finance Dir, United Leeds Teaching Hosps NHS Trust, 1991–94; Man. Dir, Portland Internat. HR Consultants Ltd, 1996–97. Chairman: Bradford Breakthrough Ltd, 1989–91; Central Yorks Inst. of Mgt, 1996–98. *Publications:* The Role of the Finance Director, 1997, 3rd edn 2002; Moving Up, 1998; Understanding Swaps in a Day, 1999; NLP for Traders, 2000; The Risk Factor, 2001; How to Be Your Best, 2001. *Recreations:* golf, tennis, bridge. *Address:* Hollins House, Bishop Thornton, Harrogate, N Yorks HG3 3JZ. *Club:* Ilkley Golf.

CARRUTHERS, Alwyn Guy; Director of Statistics, Department of Employment, 1981–83 (Deputy Director, 1972–80); *b* 6 May 1925; *yr s* of late John Sendall and of Lily Eden Carruthers, Grimsby; *m* 1950, Edith Eileen, *o d* of late William and Edith Addison Lumb; no *c. Educ:* Wintringham Grammar Sch., Grimsby; King's Coll., London Univ. BA First Cl. Hons in Mathematics, Drew Gold Medal and Prize, 1945. RAE, Farnborough, 1945–46; Instructor Lieut, RN, 1946–49; Rothamsted Experimental Station, 1949. Postgraduate Diploma in Mathematical Statistics, Christ's Coll., Cambridge, 1951. Bd of Trade and DTI Statistics Divisions, 1951–72. Lay Reader, Church of England, 1994–. *Publications:* articles in official publications and learned jls. *Recreations:* gardening, music. *Address:* 24 Red House Lane, Bexleyheath, Kent DA6 8JD. *T:* (020) 8303 4898.

CARRUTHERS, Colin Malcolm, CMG 1980; HM Diplomatic Service, retired; *b* 23 Feb. 1931; *s* of late Colin Carruthers and Dorothy Beatrice Carruthers; *m* 1954, Annette Audrey Buckton; three *s* one *d. Educ:* Monkton Combe School; Selwyn College, Cambridge (MA). Royal Signals, 1950–51; joined HMOCS Kenya, 1955; District Officer, Kenya, 1955–63; Dep. Civil Sec., Rift Valley Region, Kenya, 1963–65; Field Dir, Oxfam, Maseru, Lesotho, 1965–67; joined HM Diplomatic Service, 1968; First Sec. (Economic), Islamabad, 1969–73; First Sec., Ottawa, 1973–77; Counsellor and Hd of Chancery, Addis Ababa, 1977–80 (Chargé d'Affaires, 1978–79); Asst Election Comr, Zimbabwe-Rhodesia elecns, 1980; Head of South Pacific Dept, FCO, 1980–83, retired. UK Comr, British Phosphate Comrs, 1981–87; Govt and Internat. Relns Consultant, World Vision Internat., 1985–97; Dir and Trustee, World Vision UK, 1997–2001. Governor, Monkton Combe Sch., 1984–91. Churchwarden, St Alban's, Frant, 1992–97; Lay Reader, Chichester Dio., 1994–. *Recreations:* golf, family. *Address:* 6 Lime Close, Frant, near Tunbridge Wells, Kent TN3 9DP. *T:* (01892) 750238. *Club:* Hawks (Cambridge).

CARRUTHERS, James Edwin; Assistant Secretary, Royal Hospital Chelsea, 1988–94; *b* 19 March 1928; *er s* of James and Dollie Carruthers; *m* 1955, Phyllis Williams (*d* 1996); one *s. Educ:* George Heriot's Sch.; Edinburgh Univ. (MA; Medallist in Scottish Hist.). FSAScot. Lieut, The Queen's Own Cameron Highlanders, 1949–51, and TA, 1951–55. Air Ministry: Asst Principal, 1951; Private Sec. to DCAS, 1955; Asst Private Sec. to Sec.

of State for Air, 1956; Principal, 1956; Min. of Aviation, 1960–62; Private Secretary: to Minister of Defence for RAF, 1965–67; to Parly Under Sec. of State for RAF, 1967; Asst Sec., 1967; Chief Officer, Sovereign Base Areas Admin, Cyprus, 1968–71; Dep. Chief of Public Relations, MoD, 1971–72; Private Sec. to Chancellor of Duchy of Lancaster, Cabinet Office, 1973–74; Sec., Organising Cttee for British Aerospace, DoI, 1975–77; Under-Sec., 1977; seconded as Asst to Chm., British Aerospace, 1977–79; Dir Gen., Royal Ordnance Factories (Finance and Procurement), 1980–83; Chm., C S Selection Bd, 1983–84; Asst Under Sec. of State, MoD, 1984–88. *Recreations:* painting, travel. *Address:* 11 John's Lee Close, Loughborough, Leics LE11 3LH.

CARRUTHERS, Hon. Norman Harry; Hon. Mr Justice Carruthers; Chief Justice of the Supreme Court of Prince Edward Island, since 1985; *b* 25 Oct. 1935; *s* of Lorne C. H. Carruthers and Jean R. Webster; *m* 1970, Diana C. Rodd; one *s* two *d. Educ:* Prince of Wales Coll.; Mount Allison Univ. (BSc, BEd); Dalhousie Law Sch. (LLB). Canadian Industries Ltd, 1956–59; schoolteacher, 1961–64; Lawyer, Foster, MacDonald and Carruthers, 1968–80; Chief Judge, Provincial Court, PEI, 1980–85. *Address:* 16 Trafalgar Street, Charlottetown, PE C1A 3Z1, Canada. *T:* (902) 5663007; (office) (902) 3686023.

CARRUTHERS, William Buttrick; part-time Chairman, Industrial Tribunals, then Employment Tribunals, 1995–99; *b* 1 Aug. 1929; *s* of Alexander Norman and Olive Carruthers; *m* 1961, Jennifer Stevens; one *s* two *d. Educ:* Middlesex School, Concord, Mass; Radley College; Clare College, Cambridge (BA Hons, LLB). Called to the Bar, Lincoln's Inn, 1954; practised in N Rhodesia (later Zambia), 1956–70; part time Chm., Industrial Tribunals, 1970; Chm., 1975, Regl Chm., 1990–95, Industrial Tribunals, Bedford. *Recreations:* tennis, bridge. *Address:* Worndith Hall, Kimbolton, Huntingdon, Cambs PE18 0JW. *T:* (01480) 860203.

CARSBERG, Sir Bryan (Victor), Kt 1989; Secretary-General, International Accounting Standards Committee, 1995–2001; *b* 3 Jan. 1939; *s* of Alfred Victor Carsberg and Maryllia (*née* Collins); *m* 1960, Margaret Linda Graham; two *d. Educ:* Berkhamsted Sch.; London Sch. of Econs and Polit. Science (MScEcon; Hon. Fellow, 1990). Chartered Accountant, 1960. Sole practice, chartered accountant, 1962–64; Lectr in Accounting, LSE, 1964–68; Vis. Lectr, Grad. Sch. of Business, Univ. of Chicago, 1968–69; Prof. of Accounting, Univ. of Manchester, 1969–81 (Dean, Faculty of Econ. and Social Studies, 1977–78); Arthur Andersen Prof. of Accounting, LSE, 1981–87; Dir of Res., ICA, 1981–87; Dir Gen. of Telecommunications, 1984–92; Dir Gen. of Fair Trading, 1992–95. Visiting Professor: of Business Admin, Univ. of Calif, Berkeley, 1974; of Accounting, LSE, 1988–89. Asst Dir of Res. and Technical Activities, Financial Accounting Standards Bd, USA, 1978–81; Mem., Accounting Standards Bd, 1990–94 (Vice-Chm., 1990–92). Mem. Council, ICA, 1975–79. Director: Economists Adv. Gp, 1976–84; Economist Bookshop, 1981–91; Philip Allan (Publishers), 1981–92, 1995–; Cable & Wireless Communications, 1997–2000; Chm., MLL Telecoms Ltd, 1999–; Mem. Bd, Radiocommunications Agency, 1990–92. Member, Council: Univ. of Surrey, 1990–92; Loughborough Univ., 1999–. Mem., Royal Swedish Acad. of Engrg Scis, 1994. Hon. MAEcon Manchester, 1973; Hon. ScD UEA, 1992; Hon. DLitt Loughborough, 1994; DUniv Essex, 1995; Hon. LLD Bath, 1996. Chartered Accountants Founding Societies Centenary Award, 1988. *Publications:* An Introduction to Mathematical Programming for Accountants, 1969; (with H. C. Edey) Modern Financial Management, 1969; Analysis for Investment Decisions, 1974; (with E. V. Morgan and M. Parkin) Indexation and Inflation, 1975; Economics of Business Decisions, 1975; (with A. Hope) Investment Decisions under Inflation, 1976; (with A. Hope) Current Issues in Accountancy, 1977, 2nd edn 1984; (with J. Arnold and R. Scapens) Topics in Management Accounting, 1980; (with S. Lumby) The Evaluation of Financial Performance in the Water Industry, 1983; (with M. Page) Current Cost Accounting, 1984; (with M. Page *et al*) Small Company Financial Reporting, 1985. *Recreations:* road running, theatre, music, opera.

CARSON, Hugh Christopher Kingsford; Headmaster, Malvern College, since 1997; *b* 29 Dec. 1945; *s* of late Lt-Col James Kingsford Carson and of Elsie Adeline Carson (*née* Cockersell); *m* 1972, Penelope Susan Elizabeth Hollingbury, PhD. *Educ:* Tonbridge Sch.; Royal Holloway Coll., London Univ. (BA Mod. Hist., Hist. of Econs and Politics, 1979); Reading Univ. (PGCE); RMA, Sandhurst. Commnd RTR, 1967–76. Asst Master, then Housemaster, Epsom Coll., 1980–90; Headmaster, Denstone Coll., 1990–96. *Recreations:* photography, historical research, hill-walking. *Address:* Headmaster's House, College Road, Malvern, Worcs WR14 3HW. *T:* (01684) 581500.

CARSON, Joan; *see* Carson, M. J.

CARSON, John, CBE 1981; draper; Member (OUP) for Belfast North, Northern Ireland Assembly, 1982–86; *b* 1934. Member, Belfast District Council, (formerly Belfast Corporation), 1971–; Official Unionist Councillor for Duncairn; Lord Mayor of Belfast, 1980–81, 1985–86. MP (UU) Belfast North, Feb. 1974–1979. Dir, Laganside Corp., 1989; non-exec. Dir, Royal Gp of Hosps & Dental Hosp. HSS Trust, 1992–. Vice-Chm., NI Youth Council, 1985. Mem., Adv. Bd, Salvation Army. High Sheriff, Belfast, 1978. *Address:* 16A Cardy Road, Greyabbey, Co. Down, N Ireland BT22 2LS.

CARSON, (Margaret) Joan; Member (UU) Fermanagh and South Tyrone, Northern Ireland Assembly, since 1998; *b* 29 Jan. 1935; *d* of Charles Patterson and Gladys Patterson (*née* Irvine); *m* 1957, James Carson; two *s* one *d. Educ:* Stranmillis Coll., Belfast. Teacher: Enniskillen Model Primary Sch., 1956–62; Granville Primary Sch., 1972–79; Dungannon Primary Sch., 1979–82; Principal, Tamnamore Primary Sch., 1982–88. Mem. (UU), Dungannon DC, 1997–. Constituency Sec., Fermanagh and S Tyrone, UUP. *Recreations:* ornithology, painting, reading. *Address:* Drumgold House, 115 Moy Road, Dungannon, Co. Tyrone BT71 7DX. *T:* (028) 8778 4285.

CARSON, Robert Andrew Glendinning, FBA 1980; Keeper, Department of Coins and Medals, British Museum, 1978–83; *b* 7 April 1918; *s* of Andrew and Mary Dempster Carson; *m* 1949, Meta Fransisca De Vries; one *s* one *d. Educ:* Kirkcudbright Acad.; Univ. of Glasgow (MA (1st Cl. Hons Classics) 1940; Foulis Schol. 1940; Hon. DLitt 1983). FSA 1965. Served War, RA, 1940–46, NW Europe; 2nd Lieut 1941, Captain 1945. Asst Keeper, 1947, Dep. Keeper, 1965, Dept of Coins and Medals, British Museum. Pres., Internat. Numismatic Commn, 1979–86. Editor, Numismatic Chronicle, 1966–73; Mem., Adv. Cttee on Historic Wreck Sites, 1973–80; Pres., Royal Numismatic Soc., 1974–79 (Medallist, 1972; Hon. Fellow, 1980); Patron, Australian Numismatic Soc., 1984–. Hon. Vis. Fellow, Univ. of Tasmania, 1990. Hon. Assoc., Powerhouse Mus., Sydney, 1986. Hon. Member: Romanian Numismatic Soc., 1977; British Numismatic Soc., 1979; Corresponding Member: Amer. Numismatic Soc., 1967; Austrian Numismatic Soc., 1971; Foreign Mem., Finnish Soc. of Science and Letters, 1986. Medallist: Soc. française de Numismatique, 1970; Luxembourg Museum, 1971; Amer. Numismatic Soc., 1978. Silver Jubilee Medal, 1977. *Publications:* (with H. Mattingly and C. H. V. Sutherland) Roman Imperial Coinage, 1951–; ed, Essays in Roman Coinage presented to Harold Mattingly, 1956; (with P. V. Hill and J. P. C. Kent) Late Roman Bronze Coinage, 1960; Coins, ancient, mediæval and modern, 1962, 2nd edn 1972; Catalogue of Roman Imperial Coins in the British Museum, vol. VI, 1962; ed, Mints, Dies and Currency, 1971; Principal Coins of the Romans, vol. I, 1978, vol. II, 1980, vol. III, 1981; ed, Essays presented to Humphrey Sutherland, 1978; History of the Royal Numismatic Society, 1986; Coins of the Roman Empire, 1990; articles in Numismatic Chron., Rev. Numismatique, etc. *Address:* 2/2A Queen's Parade, Newport, NSW 2106, Australia.

CARSON, William Hunter Fisher, OBE 1983; jockey, retired 1997; racing pundit, BBC, since 1997; Manager, Thoroughbred Corp., Europe, since 1997; *b* 16 Nov. 1942; *s* of Thomas Whelan Carson and Mary Hay; *m* 1963, Carole Jane Sutton (marr. diss. 1979); three *s*; *m* 1982, Elaine Williams. *Educ:* Riverside, Stirling, Scotland. Apprenticed to Captain G. Armstrong, 1957; 1st winner, Pinkers Pond, Catterick, 1962; trans. to Fred Armstrong, 1963–66; First Jockey to Lord Derby, 1967; first classic win, High Top, 1972; Champion Jockey, 1972, 1973, 1978, 1980 and 1983; became First Jockey to W. R. Hern, 1977; also appointed Royal Jockey, riding Dunfermline to the Jubilee Oaks and St Leger wins in the colours of HM the Queen; won the 200th Derby on Troy, trained by W. R. Hern, 1979; the same combination won the 1980 Derby, with Henbit, and the 1980 Oaks, with Bireme; also won King George VI and Queen Elizabeth Stakes, on Troy, 1979, on Ela-Mana-Mou, 1980, on Petoski, 1985, on Nashwan, 1989; 1983 Oaks and St Leger, with Sun Princess; Ascot Gold Cup, on Little Wolf, 1983; St Leger, on Minster Son, 1988 (only jockey ever to breed and ride a Classic winner); Derby, on Nashwan, 1989; 1,000 Guineas, Oaks and Irish Derby, on Salsabil, 1990; 1,000 Guineas and Oaks, on Shadayid, 1991; Derby, on Erhaab, 1994. During the 1989 season rode 50th Group One winner in England; by 1997 had ridden 3,828 winners including 18 Classics. DUniv Stirling, 1998. *Address:* Minster House, Barnsley, Cirencester, Glos GL7 5DZ.

CARSS-FRISK, Monica Gunnel Constance; QC 2001. *Educ:* UCL (LLB); UC Oxford (BCL). Called to the Bar, Gray's Inn, 1985; in practice at the Bar, 1986–. Part-time tutor in law, UCL, 1984–87. Mem., HM Treasury Solicitor's Supplementary Common Law Panel, 1997–99; Jun. Counsel to the Crown (A Panel), 1999–2001. Mem. Bd, Internat. Centre for Legal Protection of Human Rights. *Publications:* contributor: Human Rights Law and Practice, 1999; European Employment Law in the UK, 2001; Halsbury's Laws of England. *Recreation:* literature. *Address:* Blackstone Chambers, Blackstone House, Temple, EC4Y 9BW.

CARSWELL, Rt Hon. Sir Robert (Douglas), Kt 1988; PC 1993; Lord Chief Justice of Northern Ireland, since 1997; *b* 28 June 1934; *er s* of late Alan E. Carswell and of Nance E. Carswell; *m* 1961, Romayne Winifred Ferris (*see* R. W. Carswell); two *d. Educ:* Royal Belfast Academical Instn; Pembroke Coll., Oxford (Schol.; 1st Cl. Honour Mods, 1st Cl. Jurisprudence, MA; Hon. Fellow, 1984); Univ. of Chicago Law Sch. (JD). Called to Bar of N Ireland, 1957 (Bencher, 1979), and to English Bar, Gray's Inn, 1972 (Hon. Bencher, 1993); Counsel to Attorney-General for N Ireland, 1970–71; QC (NI), 1971; Sen. Crown Counsel in NI, 1979–84; Judge of High Court of Justice, NI, 1984–93; Lord Justice of Appeal, Supreme Court of Judicature, NI, 1993–97. Chancellor, Dios of Armagh and of Down and Dromore, 1990–97. Chairman: Council of Law Reporting for NI, 1987–97; Law Reform Adv. Cttee for NI, 1989–97. Pres., NI Scout Council, 1993–. Governor, Royal Belfast Academical Instn, 1967–, Chm. Bd of Governors, 1986–97; Pro-Chancellor and Chm. Council, Univ. of Ulster, 1984–94. Hon. Bencher, King's Inns, Dublin, 1997. Hon. DLitt Ulster, 1994. *Publications:* Trustee Acts (Northern Ireland), 1964; articles in legal periodicals. *Recreations:* golf, hill walking. *Address:* Royal Courts of Justice, Belfast BT1 3JF. *Club:* Ulster Reform (Belfast).

CARSWELL, Romayne Winifred, (Lady Carswell), OBE 1988; JP; Lord-Lieutenant, County Borough of Belfast, since 2000; *d* of late James Ferris, JP, Greyabbey, Co. Down and of Eileen Ferris, JP; *m* 1961, Robert Douglas Carswell (*see* Rt Hon. Sir R. D. Carswell); two *d. Educ:* Victoria Coll., Belfast; Queen's Univ., Belfast (BA, LLB). Asst Principal, NICS, 1959–61; Mem., 1977–83, Dep. Chm., 1983–94, Police Complaints Bd for NI, subseq. Ind. Commn for Police Complaints; Member: Standing Adv. Commn on Human Rights, 1984–86; Industrial Tribunals, 1987–97. Mem., Bd of Govs, Victoria Coll., Belfast, 1979–99 (Dep. Chm., 1995–99). Pres., Friends of Ulster Mus., 1996–; Trustee, Ulster Histl Foundn, 1991– (Dep. Chm., 1997–2000). DL Belfast, 1997; JP 2000. CStJ 2000. *Recreations:* heritage, conservation, hillwalking. *Address:* c/o Lord Chief Justice's Office, Royal Courts of Justice, Belfast BT1 3JF. *T:* (028) 9023 5111.

CARTER; *see* Bonham-Carter and Bonham Carter.

CARTER, family name of **Baron Carter**.

CARTER, Baron *cr* 1987 (Life Peer), of Devizes in the County of Wiltshire; **Denis Victor Carter;** PC 1997; Captain of the Hon. Corps of Gentlemen at Arms (Government Chief Whip in the House of Lords), since 1997; agricultural consultant and farmer, since 1957; *b* 17 Jan. 1932; *s* of Albert William and Annie Julia Carter; *m* 1957, Teresa Mary Greengoe; one *d* (one *s* decd). *Educ:* Xaverian Coll., Brighton; East Sussex Inst. of Agriculture; Essex Inst. of Agriculture (NDA, Queen's Prize); Oxford Univ. (BLitt). Nat. Service, Canal Zone, GHQ MELF, 1950–52. Audit clerk, 1949–50 and 1952–53; farmworker, 1953–54; student of agriculture, 1954–57. Founded AKC Ltd, Agricultural Accounting and Management, 1957; commenced farming, Oxfordshire, Hants and Wilts, 1975. Sen. Research Fellowship in Agricultural Marketing, MAFF, 1970–72. Opposition frontbench spokesman on agric. and rural affairs, 1987–97, also on social security, 1988–90, and health, 1989–92; Dep. Chief Opposition Whip, H of L, 1990–92. Contested (Lab) Basingstoke, 1970. Exec. Prod., LINK, 1988–97. Chairman: UK Co-operative Council, 1993–97; BBC Rural Affairs and Agricl Adv. Cttee, 1987–90; President: British Inst. of Agricl Consultants, 1992–97; Guild of Agricl Journalists, 1994–96; Inst. of Agricl Mgt, 1996–97. Trustee: Rural Housing Trust, 1992–97; John Arlott Meml Trust, 1993–97. Vice-Pres., Shaw Trust, 1991–97. *Recreations:* walking, reading, supporting Southampton Football Club. *Clubs:* Farmers' (Chm., 1982; Trustee, 1986–97; Vice-Pres., 1997–); Turners (Stockbridge); Grasshoppers (Amesbury).

CARTER, Andrew, CMG 1995; HM Diplomatic Service; UK Permanent Representative to Council of Europe, Strasbourg (with personal rank of Ambassador), since 1997; *b* 4 Dec. 1943; *s* of Eric and Margaret Carter; *m* 1st, 1973, Anne Caroline Morgan (marr. diss. 1986); one *d*; 2nd, 1988, Catherine Mary Tyler; one *s* one *d. Educ:* Latymer Upper Sch., Hammersmith; Royal Coll. of Music; Jesus Coll., Cambridge (Scholar 1962; MA). FRCO; LRAM; ARCM. Asst Master, Marlborough Coll., 1965–70. Joined HM Diplomatic Service, 1971; Warsaw, 1972; Geneva, 1975; Bonn, 1975; FCO, 1978; Brussels, 1986; Dep. Gov., Gibraltar, 1990–95; Minister, Moscow, 1995–97. *Recreation:* music. *Address:* c/o Foreign and Commonwealth Office, SW1A 2AH.

CARTER, Bernard Thomas; Hon. RE 1975; full-time artist (painter and etcher), since 1977; *b* 6 April 1920; *s* of Cecil Carter and Ethel Carter (*née* Darby); *m* Eugenie Alexander, artist and writer; one *s. Educ:* Haberdashers' Aske's; Goldsmith's College of Art, London Univ. NDD, ATD. RAF, 1939–46. Art lectr, critic and book reviewer, 1952–68; National Maritime Museum: Asst Keeper (prints and drawings), 1968; Dep. Keeper (Head of Picture Dept), 1970; Keeper (Head of Dept of Pictures and Conservation), 1972–77.

One-man exhibns in London: Arthur Jeffress Gall., 1955; Portal Gall., 1963, 1965, 1967, 1969, 1974, 1978, 1979, 1981, 1984, 1987, 1990 and 1993; mixed exhibns: Royal Academy, Arts Council, British Council and galleries in Europe and USA; works in public collections, galleries abroad and British educn authorities, etc. TV and radio include: Thames at Six, Pebble Mill at One, Kaleidoscope, London Radio, etc. *Publication:* Art for Young People (with Eugenie Alexander), 1958. *Recreations:* reading, listening to music, gardening, theatre. *Address:* 56 King George Street, Greenwich, SE10 8QD. *T:* (020) 8858 4281.

CARTER, Dr Brandon, FRS 1981; Directeur de Recherche (Centre National de la Recherche Scientifique), Observatoire de Paris-Meudon, since 1986; *b* Sydney, Australia, 26 May 1942; *s* of Harold Burnell Carter and Mary (*née* Brandon Jones); *m* 1969, Lucette Defrise; three *d.* *Educ:* George Watson's Coll., Edinburgh; Univ. of St Andrews; Pembroke Coll., Cambridge (MA, PhD 1968, DSc 1976). Res. Student, Dept of Applied Maths and Theoretical Physics, Cambridge, 1964–67; Res. Fellow, Pembroke Coll., Cambridge, 1967–68; Staff Mem., Inst. of Astronomy, Cambridge, 1968–73; Univ. Asst Lectr, 1973–74, Univ. Lectr, 1974–75, Dept of Applied Maths and Theoretical Physics, Cambridge; Maître de Recherche, co-responsable Groupe d'Astrophysique Relativiste (CNRS), Paris-Meudon, 1975–86. *Recreation:* wilderness. *Address:* 19 rue de la Borne au Diable, 92310 Sèvres, France. *T:* (1) 45344677.

CARTER, Sir Charles (Frederick), Kt 1978; FBA 1970; Vice-Chancellor, University of Lancaster, 1963–79; *b* Rugby, 15 Aug. 1919; *y s* of late Frederick William Carter, FRS; *m* 1944, Janet Shea (*d* 2000); one *s* two *d.* *Educ:* Rugby Sch.; St John's Coll., Cambridge. Friends' Relief Service, 1941–45; Lectr in Statistics, Univ. of Cambridge, 1945–51; Fellow of Emmanuel Coll., 1947–51 (Hon. Fellow, 1965–); Prof. of Applied Economics, The Queen's Univ., Belfast, 1952–59; Stanley Jevons Prof. of Political Economy and Cobden Lectr, Univ. of Manchester, 1959–63. Chairman: Science and Industry Cttee, RSA, British Assoc. and Nuffield Foundn, 1954–59; Schools' Broadcasting Council, 1964–71; Joint Cttee of the Univs and the Accountancy Profession, 1964–70; Adv. Bd of Accountancy Educn, 1970–76; North-West Economic Planning Council, 1965–68; Centre for Studies in Social Policy, 1972–78; PO Rev. Cttee, 1976–77; NI Economic Council, 1977–87; Sec.-Gen., Royal Econ. Soc., 1971–75; Member: UN Expert Cttee on Commodity Trade, 1953; Capital Investment Advisory Cttee, Republic of Ireland, 1956; British Assoc. Cttee on Metric System, 1958; Council for Scientific and Industrial Research, 1959–63; Commn on Higher Education, Republic of Ireland, 1960–67; Heyworth Cttee on Social Studies, 1963; Advisory Council on Technology, 1964–66; North Western Postal Bd, 1970–73; President: Manchester Statistical Soc., 1967–69; BAAS, 1981–82; Pres., 1989–91, Jt Pres., 1991–97, Policy Studies Inst. Joint Editor: Journal of Industrial Economics, 1955–61; Economic Journal, 1961–70; Editor, Policy Studies, 1980–88. Chm. Council, Goldsmiths' Coll., Univ. of London, 1988–94. Hon. MRIA; Comp OR; Trustee: Joseph Rowntree Meml Trust, 1966–94 (Vice-Chm., 1981–94); Sir Halley Stewart Trust, 1969– (Chm., 1986–97); Chairman: Rosehill Theatre Trust, 1984–98; Learning from Experience Trust, 1986–92 and 1994–98. Hon. DEconSc, NUI, 1968; Hon. DSc: NUU, 1979; Lancaster, 1979; QUB, 1980; Hon. LLD: TCD, 1980; Liverpool, 1982. *Publications:* The Science of Wealth, 1960, 3rd edn 1973; (with W. B. Reddaway and J. R. N. Stone) The Measurement of Production Movements, 1948; (with G. L. S. Shackle and others) Uncertainty and Business Decisions, 1954; (with A. D. Roy) British Economic Statistics, 1954; (with B. R. Williams) Industry and Technical Progress, 1957; Investment in Innovation, 1958; Science in Industry, 1959; (with D. P. Barritt) The Northern Ireland Problem, 1962, 2nd edn 1972; Wealth, 1968; (with G. Brosan and others) Patterns and Policies in Higher Education, 1971; On Having a Sense of all Conditions, 1971; (with J. L. Ford and others) Uncertainty and Expectation in Economics, 1972; Higher Education for the Future, 1980; (with J. H. M. Pinder) Policies for a Constrained Economy, 1982; (with P. John) A New Accord, 1992; Members One of Another, 1996; articles in Economic Journal, etc. *Recreation:* gardening. *Address:* 1 Gosforth Road, Seascale, Cumbria CA20 1PU. *T:* (019467) 28359; *e-mail:* sircart@aol.com. *Club:* National Liberal.

See also C. P. Carter.

CARTER, (Christopher) Peter, MBE 1971; Deputy Director-General, Office of Electricity Regulation, 1993–99; Chief Operating Officer, Office of Gas and Electricity Markets, 1999; *b* 10 Dec. 1945; *s* of Sir Charles Frederick Carter, *qv*; *m* 1st, 1971, Pamela Joy Waddilove (marr. diss. 1985); two *s* one *d*; 2nd, 1986, Andrea Rigby; one *s* one *d.* *Educ:* Methodist Coll., Belfast; Manchester Grammar Sch.; St Catharine's Coll., Cambridge (BA Geography 1967). HM Diplomatic Service, 1967–78; served MECAS, Amman, Copenhagen and European Integration Dept, FCO; Department of Energy: Community and Internat. Policy Div., 1978–80; Energy Conservation Div., 1980–81; Coal Div., 1981–85; Gas Div., 1985–86; Dir, R&D, Offshore Supplies Office, 1986–93; Dep. Dir-Gen. (Scotland), Office of Electricity Regulation, 1993. *Recreations:* playing the violin, gardening, recreational cycling. *Address:* 100 Trafalgar Road, Moseley, Birmingham B13 8BU. *T:* (0121) 449 0490; *e-mail:* peter@carterandrigby.freeserve.co.uk.

CARTER, David; *see* Carter, R. D.

CARTER, Dr David, CVO 1995; HM Diplomatic Service; High Commissioner, Bangladesh, since 2000; *b* 4 May 1945; *s* of John Carter and Kathleen Carter (*née* Oke); *m* 1968, Susan Victoria Wright; one *s* two *d.* *Educ:* Zambia; Univ. of Wales (BA Jt Hons); Univ. of Durham (PhD 1978). Joined HM Diplomatic Service, 1970; FCO, 1970–71; Accra, 1971–75; FCO, 1975–80; Hd of Chancery, Manila, 1980–83; 1st Sec., S Africa Desk, later Dep. Hd, SE Asia Dept, FCO, 1983–86; Dep. High Comr and Counsellor, Lusaka, 1986–90; Counsellor and Overseas Inspector, FCO, 1990–92; Counsellor and Dep. Hd of Mission, Cape Town/Pretoria, 1992–96; Minister and Dep. Head of Mission, New Delhi, 1996–99. *Publications:* contrib. jls on Southern Africa. *Recreations:* distant travel, music, reading, walking, manual labour. *Address:* c/o Foreign and Commonwealth Office, King Charles Street, SW1A 2AH. *Club:* Royal Commonwealth Society.

CARTER, Sir David (Craig), Kt 1996; FRCS, FRCSE, FRCSGlas, FRCPE, FFPHM; FRSE; Vice-Principal, Edinburgh University, since 2000; Chief Medical Officer, Scottish Executive (formerly Scottish Office) Department of Health, 1996–2000; *b* 1 Sept. 1940; *s* of Horace Ramsay Carter and Mary Florence Carter (*née* Lister); *m* 1967, Ilske Ursula Luth; two *s.* *Educ:* Cockermouth Grammar Sch.; St Andrews Univ. (MB ChB, MD). FRCSE 1967; FRCSGlas 1980; FRCPE 1993; FRCS 1995; FFPHM 1998. FRSE 1995. British Empire Cancer Campaign Fellow, 1967; Lecturer in Surgery: Edinburgh Univ., 1969; Makerere Univ., Uganda, 1972; Wellcome Trust Sen. Lectr, Edinburgh Univ., 1974, seconded for 12 months to Center for Ulcer Res. and Educn, LA, 1976; Sen. Lectr in Surgery, Edinburgh Univ., 1974–79; St Mungo Prof. of Surgery, Glasgow Univ., 1979–88; Regius Prof. of Clinical Surgery, Edin. Univ., 1988–96. Hon. Consultant Surgeon, Royal Infirmary, Edin., 1988–96; Hon. Consultant Surgeon and Chm., Scottish Liver Transplantation Unit, 1992–96; Surgeon to the Queen in Scotland, 1993–97. External Examiner at univs incl. London, Oxford, Leeds, Dundee, Newcastle, Hong Kong, Nairobi, Penang and Kuwait. Chairman: Scottish Foundn for Surgery in Nepal, 1988–; Scottish Council for Postgrad. Med. Educn, 1990–96; Scientific Adv. Cttee, CRC, 2000–; Dir, Scottish Cancer Foundn, 2000–; Mem., Jt Med. Adv. Cttee, HEFC, 1993–96. President: Internat. Hepatobiliary-Pancreatic Assoc., 1988–89; Surgical Res. Soc., 1996–97; Assoc. of Surgeons of GB and Ire., 1996–97; BMA, 2001–July 2002. Member: Council, RCSE, 1980–90; James IV Assoc. of Surgeons, 1981–; Internat. Surgical Gp, 1984–. Mem., Broadcasting Council, BBC Scotland, 1989–94. Non-exec. Dir, Lothian Health Bd, 1994–96. Company Sec., British Jl of Surgery Soc., 1991–95; Co-Editor, British Journal of Surgery, 1986–91; General Editor, Operative Surgery, 1983–. Mem. Court, St Andrews Univ., 1997–2000; Governor: Beatson Inst. for Cancer Res., 1997–2000; PPP Healthcare Med. Trust, 2001–. Mem., Amer. Surgical Assoc., 1997; Founder FMedSci 1998. Hon. FACS 1996; Hon. FRCSI 1996; Hon. FRACS 1998; Hon. FRCGP 1999; Hon. Fellow, Deutsche Ges. für Chirurgie, 1994; Hon. Mem., Soc. of Surgeons of Nepal, 1994; For. Associate Mem., Inst. of Medicine, USA, 1998. Hon. DSc: St Andrews, 1997; Queen Margaret Coll., 1997; Aberdeen, 2000; Hon. LLD Dundee, 1997. William Leslie Prize in Surgery, Univ. of Edinburgh, 1968; Moynihan Prize in Surgery, Assoc. of Surgeons of GB and Ire., 1973; Gold Medal, RCSE, 2000. Gorka Dakshim Bahu (Nepal), 1999. *Publications:* Peptic Ulcer, 1983; Principles and Practice of Surgery, 1985; Pancreatitis, 1988; Surgery of the Pancreas, 1993, 2nd edn 1997; numerous contribs to surgical and gastroenterological jls. *Recreations:* music, golf. *Address:* 19 Buckingham Terrace, Edinburgh EH4 3AD. *T:* (0131) 332 5554. *Clubs:* New (Edinburgh); Royal & Ancient Golf (St Andrews); Luffness Golf.

CARTER, (Edward) Graydon; Editor in Chief, Vanity Fair, since 1992; *b* 14 July 1949; *s* of E. P. Carter and Margaret Ellen Carter; *m* 1982, Cynthia Williamson; three *s* one *d.* *Educ:* Carleton Univ. (incomplete); Univ. of Ottawa (incomplete). Editor, The Canadian Review, 1973–77; writer, Time, 1978–83; Writer, Life, 1983–86; Founder and Editor, Spy, 1986–91; Editor, New York Observer, 1991–92. Hon. Editor, Harvard Lampoon, 1989. *Recreation:* fly fishing. *Address:* Condé Nast Building, 4 Times Square, New York, NY 10036, USA. *Club:* Washington (Washington, Connecticut).

CARTER, Elizabeth Angela; *see* Shaw, E. A.

CARTER, Elliott (Cook), DrMus; composer; *b* New York City, 11 Dec. 1908; *m* 1939, Helen Frost-Jones; one *s.* *Educ:* Harvard Univ. (MA); Ecole Normale, Paris (DrMus). Professor of Greek and Maths, St John's Coll., Annapolis, 1940–42; Professor of Music: Columbia Univ., 1948–50; Yale Univ., 1960–61. *Compositions include:* First Symphony, 1942–43; Quartet for Four Saxophones, 1943; Holiday Overture, 1944; Piano Sonata, 1945; Ballet, The Minotaur, 1946–47; Woodwind Quintet, 1947; Sonata for Cello and Piano, 1948; First String Quartet, 1950–51; Sonata for Flute, Oboe, Cello and Harpsichord, 1952; Variations for Orchestra, 1953; Second String Quartet, 1960 (New York Critics' Circle Award; Pulitzer Prize; Unesco 1st Prize); Double Concerto for Harpsichord and Piano, 1961 (New York Critics' Circle Award); Piano Concerto, 1967; Concerto for Orchestra, 1970; Third String Quartet, 1971 (Pulitzer Prize); Duo for Violin and Piano, 1973–74; Brass Quintet, 1974; A Mirror on which to Dwell (song cycle), 1976; A Symphony of Three Orchestras, 1977; Syringa, 1979; Night Fantasies (for piano), 1980; In Sleep in Thunder, 1982; Triple Duo, 1983; Penthode, 1985; Fourth String Quartet, 1986; Oboe Concerto, 1988; Three Occasions for Orchestra, 1989; Violin Concerto, 1991; Partita, 1992; Adagio Tenebroso, 1993; Fifth String Quartet, 1995; Figment, 1996; Allegro Scorrevolo, 1996; Clarinet Concerto, 1996; Luimen, 1997, What Next? (opera), 1998; Tempo e tempi, 1999; Statement, 1999; Fantasy, 1999; Asko Concerto, 2000; Cello Concerto, 2000; Oboe Quartet, 2001. Member: Nat. Inst. of Arts and Letters, 1956 (Gold Medal for Music, 1971); Amer. Acad. of Arts and Sciences (Boston), 1962; Amer. Acad. of Arts and Letters, 1971; Akad. der Kunste, Berlin, 1971. Hon. degrees incl. MusD Cantab, 1983. Sibelius Medal (Harriet Cohen Foundation), London, 1961; Premio delle Muse, City of Florence, 1969; Handel Medallion, New York City, 1978; Mayor of Los Angeles declared Elliott Carter Day, 27 April 1979; Ernst Von Siemens Prize, Munich, 1981; Gold Medal, MacDowell Colony, 1983; National Medal of Arts, USA, 1985. Commandeur, Ordre des Arts et des Lettres (France) 1987; Commander, Order of Merit (Italy), 1991. *Publications:* The Writings of Elliott Carter, 1977; Collected Essays and Lectures 1937–1995, 1997; *relevant publications:* The Music of Elliott Carter, by David Schiff, 1983; Elliot Carter ou le temps fertile, by Max Noubel, 2001. *Address:* c/o Boosey & Hawkes, 295 Regent Street, W1R 8JH.

CARTER, Eric Stephen, CBE 1986; Convener, Standing Conference on Countryside Sports, since 1988; *b* 23 June 1923; *s* of Albert Harry Carter, MBE and Doris Margaret (*née* Mann); *m* 1948, Audrey Windsor; one *s.* *Educ:* Grammar Sch., Lydney; Reading Univ. BSc (Agric) 1945. Techn. Officer, Gloucester AEC, 1945–46; Asst District Officer, Gloucester NAAS, 1946–49, Dist Off. 1949–57; Sen. Dist Off., Lindsey (Lincs) NAAS, 1957–63, County Agric. Off. 1963–69; Yorks and Lancs Region: Dep. Regional Dir, NAAS, 1969–71; Regional Agric. Off., ADAS, 1971–73; Regional Off. (ADAS), 1973–74; Chief Regional Off., MAFF, 1974–75; Dep. Dir-Gen., Agricl Develt and Advisory Service, 1975–81; Adviser, Farming and Wildlife Adv. Gp, 1981–88. Pres., Lincs Agricl Soc., 1998–99; Member: Nuffield Farming Scholarships Trust Selection Cttee, 1981–92 (Hon. Nuffield Farming Scholar, 1992); Adv. Cttee, Welsh Plant Breeding Station, 1987–89; Governing Body, AFRC Inst. for Grassland and Envmtl Res., 1989–91. FIBiol 1974, CBiol 1974 (Vice-Pres., 1993–96); FRAgS 1985; Hon. FRASE 1988 (Hon. Vice-Pres., 1997–). FRSA 1998. Editor, Jl of Royal Agricl Soc. of England, 1985–94. *Publications:* (with M. H. R. Soper) Modern Farming and the Countryside, 1985, 2nd edn (with M. H. R. Soper) as Farming and the Countryside, 1991; (with J. M. Stansfield) British Farming: changing policies and production systems, 1994; contrib. agric. and techn. jls. *Recreations:* travel, reading, music, countryside. *Address:* 15 Farrs Lane, East Hyde, Luton, Beds LU2 9PY. *T:* (01582) 760504. *Club:* Farmers'.

CARTER, Maj. Gen. Sir Evelyn John W.; *see* Webb-Carter.

CARTER, His Honour Frederick Brian; QC 1980; a Circuit Judge, 1985–2001; *b* 11 May 1933; *s* of late Arthur and Minnie Carter; *m* 1960, Elizabeth Hughes, JP, *d* of late W. B. Hughes and Mrs B. M. Hughes; one *s* three *d* (and one *s* decd). *Educ:* Stretford Grammar Sch.; King's Coll., London (LLB). Called to Bar, Gray's Inn, 1955, practised Northern Circuit, 1957–85; Prosecuting Counsel for Inland Revenue, Northern Circuit, 1973–80; a Recorder, 1978–85. *Recreations:* golf, travel. *Address:* 23 Lynton Park Road, Cheadle Hulme, Cheadle, Cheshire SK8 6JA. *Clubs:* Big Four (Manchester); Chorlton-cum-Hardy Golf.

CARTER, George; *see* Carter, W. G. K.

CARTER, His Eminence G(erald) Emmett, Cardinal, CC 1983; Archbishop Emeritus of Toronto (Archbishop, 1978–90); *b* Montreal, Quebec, 1 March 1912; *s* of Thomas Carter and Mary Kelty. *Educ:* Univ. of Montreal (BA, MA, PhD); Grand Seminary of Montreal (STL). Founder, Director and Teacher at St Joseph's Teachers' Coll., Montreal, 1939–61; Auxiliary Bishop of London, Ont., 1961; Bishop of London, 1964. Cardinal, 1979. Chairman, Internat. Cttee for English in the Liturgy, 1971; President, Canadian Catholic Conf. of Bishops, 1975–77. Elected Member, Permanent

Council of the Synod of Bishops in Rome, 1977. Hon. LLD: Univ. of W Ontario, 1964; Concordia Univ., 1976; Univ. of Windsor, 1977; McGill Univ., Montreal, 1980; Notre Dame Univ., 1981; St Francis Xavier Univ., 1998; Assumption Univ., Windsor, 1999; Hon. DD Huron Coll., Univ. of W Ont., 1978; Hon. DHL Duquesne Univ., Pittsburg, 1965; Hon. DLitt: St Mary's Univ., Halifax, 1980; (in Medieval Studies), Pontifical Inst. of Medieval Studies, Toronto, 1995 (also Hon. Licence in Med. Studies); Hon. DSL Univ. of St Michael's Coll., Toronto, 1998. *Publications:* The Catholic Public Schools of Quebec, 1957; Psychology and the Cross, 1959; The Modern Challenge, 1961. *Recreations:* tennis, skiing. *Address:* Catholic Pastoral Centre, 1155 Yonge Street, Toronto, ON M4T 1W5, Canada. *T:* (416) 9340606, *Fax:* (416) 9343437.

CARTER, Godfrey James, CBE 1984; Parliamentary Counsel, 1972–79; *b* 1 June 1919; *s* of Captain James Shuckburgh Carter, Grenadier Guards (killed in action, 1918), and Diana Violet Gladys Carter (*née* Cavendish); *m* 1946, Cynthia, *e d* of Eric Strickland Mason; three *s*. *Educ:* Eton (KS); Magdalene Coll., Cambridge (BA 1945, MA 1948; LLM 1946). War Service (Rifle Bde), Middle East, 1940–43 (twice wounded). Called to Bar, Inner Temple, 1946; Asst Parly Counsel, 1949–56; commercial dept, Bristol Aeroplane Co. Ltd, and Bristol Siddeley Engines Ltd, 1956–64; re-joined Parly Counsel Office, 1964; Dep. Counsel, 1970. *Address:* Old Bournstream House, Wotton-under-Edge, Glos GL12 7PA. *T:* (01453) 843246.

CARTER, Graydon; *see* Carter, E. G.

CARTER, Imelda Mary Philomena Bernadette; *see* Staunton, I. M. P. B.

CARTER, James Earl, Jr, (Jimmy); President of the United States of America, 1977–81; *b* Plains, Georgia, USA, 1 Oct. 1924; *s* of late James Earl Carter and Lillian (*née* Gordy); *m* 1946, Rosalynn Smith; three *s* one *d*. *Educ:* Plains High Sch.; Georgia Southwestern Coll.; Georgia Inst. of Technology; US Naval Acad. (BS); Union Coll., Schenectady, NY (post grad.). Served in US Navy submarines and battleships, 1946–53; Ensign (commissioned, 1947); Lieut (JG) 1950, (SG) 1952; retd from US Navy, 1953. Became farmer and warehouseman, 1953, farming peanuts at Plains, Georgia, until 1977. Member: Sumter Co. (Ga) School Bd, 1955–62 (Chm. 1960–62); Americus and Sumter Co. Hosp. Authority, 1956–70; Sumter Co. (Ga) Library Bd, 1961; President: Plains Develt Corp., 1963; Georgia Planning Assoc., 1968; Chm., W Central Georgia Area Planning and Develt Commn, 1964; Dir, Georgia Crop Improvement Assoc., 1957–63 (Pres., 1961). State Chm., March of Dimes, 1968–70; Dist Governor, Lions Club, 1968–69. State Senator (Democrat), Georgia, 1963–67; Governor of Georgia, 1971–75. Chm., Congressional Campaign Cttee, Democratic Nat. Cttee, 1974; Democratic Candidate for the Presidency of the USA, 1976. Founder, Carter Center, Emory Univ, 1982. Mem., Bd of Dirs, Habitat for Humanity, 1984–87; Chairman, Board of Trustees: Carter Center, Inc., 1986–; Carter-Menil Human Rights Foundn, 1986–; Global 2000 Inc., 1986–; Chairman: Council of Freely-Elected Heads of Government, 1986–; Council of Internat. Negotiation Network, 1991–. Distinguished Prof., Emory Univ., 1982–. Baptist. Hon. LLD: Morehouse Coll., and Morris Brown Coll., 1972; Notre Dame, 1977; Emory Univ., 1979; Kwansei Gakuim Univ., Japan, and Georgia Southwestern Coll., 1981; New York Law Sch., and Bates Coll., 1985; Centre Coll., and Creighton Univ., 1987; Hon. DE Georgia Inst. Tech., 1979; Hon. PhD: Weizmann Inst. of Science, 1980; Tel Aviv Univ., 1983; Haifa Univ., 1987; Hon. DHL Central; Connecticut State Univ., 1985. Awards include: Gold Medal, Internat. Inst. for Human Rights, 1979; Internat. Mediation Medal, American Arbitration Assoc., 1979; Harry S. Truman Public Service Award, 1981; Ansel Adams Conservation Award, Wilderness Soc., 1982; Distinguished Service Award, Southern Baptist Convention, 1982; Human Rights Award, Internat. League for Human Rights, 1983; Albert Schweitzer Prize for Humanitarianism, 1987; Jefferson Award, Amer. Inst. of Public Service, 1990. *Publications:* Why Not the Best?, 1975; A Government as Good as its People, 1977; Keeping Faith: memoirs of a President, 1982; The Blood of Abraham, 1985; (with Rosalynn Carter) Everything to Gain: making the most of the rest of your life, 1987; An Outdoor Journal, 1988; Always a Reckoning (poetry), 1995. *Address:* (office) The Carter Center, One Copenhill Avenue NE, Atlanta, GA 30307–1400, USA.

CARTER, Sir John, Kt 1966; QC (Guyana) 1962; Guyana Diplomatic Service, retired; *b* 27 Jan. 1919; *s* of Kemp R. Carter; *m* 1959, Sara Lou (formerly Harris); two *s* three *d*. *Educ:* University of London and Middle Temple, England. Called to English Bar, 1942; admitted to Guyana (late British Guiana) Bar, 1945; Member of Legislature of Guyana, 1948–53 and 1961–64; Pro-Chancellor, Univ. of Guyana, 1962–66; Ambassador of Guyana to US, 1966–70; High Comr for Guyana in UK, 1970–76; Ambassador to China and Korea, 1976–81 and to Japan, 1979–81; High Comr to Jamaica, 1981–83. *Recreations:* cricket, swimming. *Address:* 3603 East West Highway, Chevy Chase, MD 20815, USA. *Clubs:* MCC; Georgetown (Guyana).

CARTER, Sir John (Alexander), Kt 1989; Chairman, Stock Land & Estates Ltd, since 1987; *b* 2 Nov. 1921; *s* of Allan Randolph Carter and Beatrice Alice Carter; *m* 1954; two *d*. *Educ:* Duke of York's Royal Military Sch., Dover, Kent. Served Territorial Army, 1939–45: Warwicks Yeo., RA and Loyal N Lancs Regt. Founder Chm., Carter Holdings PLC, 1964–89. Co-opted Mem., Conservative Central Bd of Finance, 1983–87; Conservative Party, East of England: Chm., Industrial Council, 1983–87; Chm., Property Adv. Bd, 1986–87. KStJ 1992; Chm. Council, Order of St John for Essex, 1988–94. *Recreations:* golf, swimming, reading. *Address:* Cobblers, Mill Road, Stock, near Ingatestone, Essex CM4 9RG. *T:* (01277) 840580. *Club:* Carlton.

CARTER, Sir John (Gordon Thomas), Kt 1998; FIA; Chief Executive, Commercial Union plc, 1994–98; *b* 28 Dec. 1937; *s* of Gordon Percival Carter and Mary Ann Carter (*née* Edgington); *m* 1961, Margaret Elizabeth Dobson; three *s*. *Educ:* City of Oxford High Sch.; Jesus Coll., Oxford (Lawrence Exhibnr; MA Maths; Hon. Fellow, 1998). FIA 1966. Nat. Service, MEAF, 1956–58. Joined Commercial Union, 1961: Life Manager, 1978–80; Dep. Gen. Manager, 1981–82; Gen. Manager, 1983–86; Dir, 1987–98. Director: Trade Indemnity plc, 1991–95; Credito Italiano Bank, 1994–99; NHBC, 1998–; Canary Wharf Gp plc, 1999–; Mem., UK Bd Cttee, CGU plc, 1998–2000. Mem., Council for Industry and Higher Educn, 1993–98. Chairman: Mgt Cttee, Motor Insurers Bureau, 1985–90; Loss Prevention Council, 1991–94; Assoc. of British Insurers, 1995–97; Policyholders Protection Bd, 2000–. Adviser: HSBC Investment Bank, 1998–; Munich Reinsurance Co. Ltd, 1999–. Curator, Univ. Chest, 1998–2000, Mem. Investment Cttee, 2000–, Oxford Univ.; Gov., London Guildhall Univ., 1998– (Chm. Govs, 1999–). *Recreations:* golf, ski-ing, hill walking, opera, theatre. *Address:* 42 Wolsey Road, Moor Park, Northwood, Middx HA6 2EN. *Club:* Moor Park Golf.

CARTER, Dr (John) Timothy, FRCP, FFOM; Chief Medical Adviser (Transport Safety), Department for Transport, Local Government and the Regions (formerly Department of the Environment, Transport and the Regions), since 1999; Hon. Senior Clinical Lecturer, University of Birmingham, since 1995; *b* 12 Feb. 1944; *s* of Reginald John Carter and Linda Mary (*née* Briggs); *m* 1967, Judith Ann Lintott; one *s* two *d*. *Educ:* Dulwich Coll.; Corpus Christi Coll., Cambridge (MB, MA); University Coll. Hosp., London. FFOM 1984; FRCP 1987. London Sch. of Hygiene, 1972–74 (MSc). MO, British Petroleum, 1974–78; SMO, BP Chemicals, 1978–83; Health and Safety Executive: Dir of Med. Services, 1983–92, and of Health Policy, 1989–92; Dir of Field Ops Div., 1992–96; Med. Advr, 1996–97. Member: MRC, 1983–96; Bd, Faculty of Occupnl Medicine, 1982–88 (Vice Dean, 1996–98); Hon. Sec., Occupnl Medicine Section, RSM, 1979–83; Pres., British Occupnl Hygiene Soc., 1987–88. *Publications:* articles on investigation and control of occupnl health hazards and med. history. *Recreation:* history—natural, medical and local. *Address:* Department for Transport, Local Government and the Regions, 2/14C Great Minster House, 76 Marsham Street, SW1P 4DR.

CARTER, Matthew, RDI 1981; Principal, Carter & Cone Type Inc., Cambridge, Mass, since 1992; *b* London, 1 Oct. 1937; *s* of late Harry Graham Carter, OBE and Ella Mary Carter (*née* Garratt). Punch Cutter, Netherlands, 1956; freelance designer of lettering and type, London, 1957–63; typographical advr, Crosfield Electronics, 1963–65; type designer: MergenthalerLinotype, NY, 1965–71; Linotype Cos, London, 1971–81; Co-founder, Sen. Vice Pres. and Dir, Bitstream Inc., 1981–92. Typographical Advr, HMSO, 1980–84; Consultant, Printer Planning Div., IBM, 1980–81. Typefaces designed include: Snell Roundhand, 1966; Olympian, 1970; Galliard, 1978; Bell Centennial, 1978; Bitstream Charter, 1987; Mantinia, 1993; Verdana, and Georgia, 1996; Miller, 1997. Hon. DFA Art Inst. of Boston, 1992. Middleton Award, Amer. Center for Design, 1995; Chrysler Award for Innovation in Design, 1996; Amer. Inst. of Graphic Arts Medal, 1996; Vadim Award, Moscow Acad. of Graphic Design, 1998. *Address:* 36-A Rice Street, Cambridge, MA 02140, USA.

CARTER, Peter; *see* Carter, C. P.

CARTER, Peter; QC 1995; *b* 8 Aug. 1952; *s* of Tom Carter and Winifred (*née* Fox); *m* 1973, Caroline Ann Adams; one *s*. *Educ:* University Coll. London (LLB 1973). Called to the Bar, Gray's Inn, 1974. *Publication:* (jtly) Offences of Violence, 1991, supplement 1994. *Recreations:* poetry, cricket, walking. *Address:* 18 Red Lion Court, EC4A 3EB. *T:* (020) 7520 6000.

CARTER, Peter Basil; QC 1990; Emeritus Fellow, Wadham College, Oxford, since 1988 (Fellow, 1949–88); *b* 10 April 1921; *s* of Albert George Carter and Amy Kathleen FitzGerald (*née* Arthur); *m* 1st, 1960, Elizabeth Maxwell (*née* Ely) (decd); 2nd, 1982, Lorna Jean (*née* Sinclair). *Educ:* Loughborough GS; Oriel Coll., Oxford (BA 1st Cl. Hons Jurisprudence; BCL 1st Cl. Hons; Vinerian Scholar, 1949; MA). War Service, RAC, 1941–46 (Croix de Guerre, 1944). Called to the Bar, Middle Temple, 1947; Hon. Bencher, 1981. Curator, Bodleian Library, Oxford, 1963–90; Sen. Bursar, Wadham Coll., Oxford, 1965–77. Inns of Court School of Law: Lectr in Conflict of Laws, 1960–89; Lectr in Evidence, 1971–95; Hon. Reader, 1985. Visiting Professor of Law: Univ. of Melbourne, 1953; Univ. of Florida, 1955; New York Univ., 1961 and 1969; Osgoode Hall Law Sch., Ont, 1971, 1973, 1978 and 1982; Walter S. Owen Prof., Univ. of British Columbia, 1986; Canada Commonwealth Vis. Fellow, Faculty of Law, Univ. of Toronto, 1970; delivered Gen. Course of Lectures on Private Internat. Law, The Hague Acad. of Internat. Law, 1981. Rapporteur, Cttee on Transnational Recognition and Enforcement of Foreign Public Laws, Internat. Law Assoc., 1984–88. Gen. Comr for Income Tax Appeals, E Oxfordshire, 1965–95 (Chm., 1991–95). Dir (non-exec.), University Life Assurance Soc., 1969–91 (Chm., 1980–91). FInstD 1984. Hon. LLD: Victoria (BC), 1995; Pace, NY, 1997. JP Oxon, 1959–88. Jt Editor, International and Comparative Law Qly, 1961–2000; Gen. Editor, Oxford Monographs in Private Internat. Law, 1992–2001. *Publications:* Essays on the Law of Evidence (with Sir Zelman Cowen), 1956; Cases and Statutes on Evidence, 1981, 2nd edn 1990, supplement 1992; articles, mostly on private internat. law or law of evidence, in British Yearbook of Internat. Law, Internat. and Comparative Law Qly, Law Qly Rev., Cambridge Law Jl, Modern Law Rev., etc. *Recreation:* appreciating architecture. *Address:* Wadham College, Oxford OX1 3PN. *T:* (01865) 277900. *Club:* Oxford and Cambridge.

CARTER, Peter Leslie; HM Diplomatic Service; Deputy Head of Mission and Consul General, Tel Aviv, since 2001; *b* 19 Nov. 1956; *s* of late Leonard Arthur Carter and of Evelyn Joyce Carter; *m* 1985, Rachelle Rain Hays; one *d*. *Educ:* Skinners' Sch., Tunbridge Wells; New Coll., Oxford (BA Modern Langs). Trainee mgt consultant, Arthur Andersen, 1979–80; freelance lang. consultant, Italy, 1980–84; joined HM Diplomatic Service, 1984: Maritime, Aviation and Envmt Dept, FCO, 1984–85; Hindi language trng, 1985–86; Second, later First Sec., New Delhi, 1986–89; Hd of Indo-China Section, SE Asia Dept, FCO, 1989–92; Hd of Recruitment, Personnel Policy Dept, FCO, 1992–94; Principal Adminr, Common Foreign and Security Policy Unit, Gen. Secretariat, Council of EU, 1994–98; Hd, NE Asia and Pacific Dept, FCO, 1998–2001. *Recreations:* travel, reading, cinema, theatre. *Address:* c/o Foreign and Commonwealth Office, King Charles Street, SW1A 2AH. *T:* (020) 7270 1500.

CARTER, Sir Philip (David), Kt 1991; CBE 1982; Managing Director, Littlewoods Organisation, 1976–83; *b* 8 May 1927; *s* of Percival Carter and Isobell (*née* Stirrup); *m* 1946, Harriet Rita (*née* Evans); one *s* two *d*. *Educ:* Waterloo Grammar Sch., Liverpool. Volunteered for Fleet Air Arm, 1945. Professional career in Littlewoods Organisation, 1948–83. Chm., Forminster plc, 1995–. Chm., Mail Order Traders Assoc. of GB, 1979–83; Pres., European Mail Order Traders Assoc., 1983; Chm., Man Made Fibres Sector Wkg Party, 1980–82; Member: Jt Textile Cttee, NEDO, 1979–82; Distributive Trades EDC, 1980–83; Merseyside Develt Corp., 1981–91 (Chm., 1987–91); Merseyside Residuary Body, 1986–89. Chm., Merseyside Tourism Bd, 1986–93. Chairman: Empire Theatre Trust, Liverpool, 1986–; Liverpool John Moores Univ. Trust, 1993–; Pro-Chancellor, 1994–, and Chm. Bd of Govs, 1997–, Liverpool John Moores Univ. Chm., Liverpool Conservative Assoc., 1985–95. Dir, Everton FC, 1975– (Chm., 1978–91, 1998–); Pres., Football League, 1986–88. Chm., Roy Castle Lung Cancer Foundn, 1998–. *Recreations:* football, private flying, music, theatre. *Address:* Oak Cottage, Noctorum Road, Noctorum, Wirral, Cheshire CH43 9UQ. *T:* (0151) 652 4053.

CARTER, Raymond John, CBE 1991; Executive, since 1980, Director, since 1983, Marathon Oil Co.; *b* 17 Sept. 1935; *s* of late John Carter and Nellie Carter (*née* Woodcock); *m* 1959, Jeanette Hills; one *s* two *d*. *Educ:* Mortlake Co. Secondary Sch.; Reading Technical Coll.; Staffordshire Coll. of Technology. National Service, Army, 1953–55. Sperry Gyroscope Co.: Technical Asst, Research and Development Computer Studies, 1956–65. Electrical Engineer, Central Electricity Generating Bd, 1965–70, Mem., CEGB Management, 1979–80. Mem., Gen. Adv. Council, BBC, 1974–76. Mem., Interim Adv. Cttee (Teachers' Pay and Conditions), DES, 1987–91; Dep. Chm., School Teachers' Review Body, 1991–93. Mem. Easthampstead RDC, 1963–68. Contested: Wokingham, Gen. Elec., 1966; Warwick and Leamington, By-elec., March 1968; MP (Lab) Birmingham, Northfield, 1970–79; Parly Under-Sec. of State, Northern Ireland Office, 1976–79. Member: Public Accounts Cttee, 1973–74; Parly Science and Technology Cttee, 1974–76; author of Congenital Disabilities (Civil Liability) Act, 1976. Delegate: Council of Europe, 1974–76; WEU, 1974–76. Trustee: BM (Nat. Hist.), 1986–96; Guild of Handicraft Trust, 1991–. Mem., Develt Cttee, Arvon Foundn, 1995–. Co-cataloguer and exhibitor, works of Sir John Betjeman, 1983. *Recreations:* running, reading, book collecting. *Address:* 1 Lynwood Chase, Warfield Road, Bracknell, Berkshire RG12 2JT. *T:* (01344) 420237.

CARTER, Sir Richard (Henry Alwyn), Kt 1992; Chairman: Ports of Auckland Ltd, since 1993; Carter Holt Harvey Ltd, 1984–92; *b* 24 April 1935; *s* of Kenneth Clifford Alwyn Carter, OBE and Stella Grace (*née* Dedman); *m* 1960, June Doreen White; one *d.* *Educ:* Waitaki Boys' High Sch.; Auckland Univ. FCA. With Carter Consolidated, subseq. Carter Holt Hldgs, then Carter Holt Harvey Ltd, 1953–92: Gen. Manager, Admin, 1960; Associate Dir, 1961; Dir, 1966; Jt Man. Dir, 1974. Chm., Council, NZ Timber Industry, 1976–78; Member: NZ Timber Merchants Fedn Inc., 1960–78 (Pres., 1976–78); NZ Business Roundtable, 1974–92. *Recreations:* field shooting, farming. *Address:* Waytemore Farm, Ararimu Road, Drury RD 3, S Auckland, New Zealand. *T:* (9) 2925892.

CARTER, Prof. Richard Lawrance, CBE 1997; DM, DSc; Professorial Fellow and Visiting Professor, University of Surrey, 1994–2000; *b* 5 Sept. 1934; *o s* of Thomas Lawrance Carter and Rhoda Edith Carter (*née* Horton). *Educ:* St Lawrence Coll., Ramsgate; Corpus Christi Coll., Oxford (MA 1960; DM 1966); UCH, London (DSc 1978). FRCPath 1978; FFPM 1994. Med. posts, Radcliffe Infirmary, Oxford, Yale Univ., UCH; Reader in Pathology, Inst. of Cancer Research, and Consultant Histopathologist, Royal Marsden Hosp., Sutton, 1975–99. Former chm. or mem. of govt adv. cttees and wkg parties, DoH, DoE, MAFF; former examr, RCPath, RCS, RCSI; Fellow or Mem., RSocMed, UK Children's Cancer Study Gp. *Publications:* author, jt author or editor of books and papers on lab. and experimental aspects of human cancers, mainly of the head and neck, tumours in children, and human carcinogenesis. *Recreations:* gardening, birds, books, music. *Address:* Pine Cottage, Hascombe, Surrey GU8 4JN. *Club:* Athenæum.

CARTER, Air Commodore Robert Alfred Copsey, CB 1956; DSO 1942; DFC 1943; Royal Air Force, retired; *b* 15 Sept. 1910; *s* of S. H. Carter and S. Copsey; *m* 1947, Sally Ann Peters, Va, USA; two *s* one *d.* *Educ:* Portsmouth Grammar Sch.; RAF Coll., Cranwell. Cranwell Cadet, 1930–32; commissioned in RAF, 1932; served in India, 1933–36; grad. RAF School of Aeronautical Engineering, 1938; served in Bomber Command, 1940–45; commanded 103 and 150 Sqdns; Station Comdr, RAF, Grimsby; grad. RAF Staff Coll., 1945; attended US Armed Forces Staff Coll., Norfolk, Va, USA, 1947; attached to RNZAF, 1950–53; comd. RAF Station, Upwood, 1953–55; SASO, RAF Transport Command, 1956–58; Director of Personal Services, Air Ministry, 1958–61; AO i/c Admin, HQ, RAF Germany, 1961–64; retired 1964. MRAeS 1960; CEng, 1966. *Club:* Royal Air Force.

CARTER, Roland; retired; Visiting Fellow, 1990–91, Visiting Senior Research Fellow, 1991–92, Institute for Research in the Social Sciences, York University; *b* 29 Aug. 1924; *s* of Ralph Carter; *m* 1950, Elisabeth Mary Green; one *s* two *d.* *Educ:* Cockburn High Sch., Leeds; Leeds Univ. Served War of 1939–45: Queen's Royal Regt, 1944; 6th Gurkha Rifles, 1945; Frontier Corps (South Waziristan and Gilgit Scouts), 1946. Seconded to Indian Political Service, as Asst Political Agent, Chilas, Gilgit Agency, 1946–47; Lectr, Zurich Univ. and Finnish Sch. of Economics, 1950–53. Joined Foreign Service, 1953: FO, 1953–54; Third Sec., Moscow, 1955; Germany, 1956–58; Second Sec., Helsinki, 1959 (First Sec., 1962); FO, 1962–67; Kuala Lumpur, 1967–69; Ambassador to People's Republic of Mongolia, 1969–71; seconded to Cabinet Office, 1971–74; Counsellor: Pretoria, 1974–77; FCO, 1977–80, retired. Area Appeals Manager, N and NE England, Nat. Soc. for Cancer Relief, 1981–89. *Publication:* Näin Puhutaan Englantia (in Finnish; with Erik Erämetsä), 1952. *Recreations:* music, linguistics, Iranian history and culture. *Address:* 4 Feversham Road, Helmsley, N Yorks YO62 5HN.

CARTER, (Ronald) David, CBE 1980; RDI 1975; Founder, DCA Design International Ltd, 1975 (Chairman, 1975–95; Director, 1995–99); Professor of Industrial Design Engineering, Royal College of Art, and Imperial College of Science, Technology and Medicine, 1991–95; *b* 30 Dec. 1927; *s* of H. Miles Carter and Margaret Carter; *m* 1953, Theo (Marjorie Elizabeth), *d* of Rev. L. T. Towers; two *s* two *d.* *Educ:* Wyggeston Sch., Leicester; Central Sch. of Art and Design, London. Served RN, 1946–48. Appts in industry, 1951–60; Principal, David Carter Associates, 1960–75. Visiting Lectr, Birmingham Coll. of Art and Design, 1960–65. Examnr, RCA, 1976–79 and 1987–90. Mem., Design Council, 1972–84 (Dep. Chm., 1975–84; Chm., Report on Industrial Design Educn in UK, 1977). Pres., Soc. of Industrial Artists and Designers, 1974–75; Chm., DATEC, 1977–82; Royal Fine Arts Comr, 1986–98. Vice-Chm., Design Mus. (formerly Conran Foundn), 1992– (Chm., 1986–92; Trustee, 1981–95); Moderator, Hong Kong Polytechnic, 1981–86; Mem., Prince of Wales Award for Indust. Innovation, 1981–85. Governor, London Inst., 1988–91. Design Awards, 1961, 1969, 1983; Duke of Edinburgh Prize for Elegant Design, 1967. FCSD (FSIA 1967); Sen. FRCA 1995. FRSA 1975. Hon. DDes De Montfort, 1993; DUniv UCE, 2000. *Recreations:* dry stone walls, boats, County Cork. *Address:* The Old Parsonage, Compton Abdale, near Cheltenham, Glos GL54 4DS. *T:* (01242) 890340. *Club:* Reform.

CARTER, Ronald Louis, OBE 1999; DesRCA; RDI 1971; FCSD (FSIAD 1961); private consultancy design practice, 1974–96, then formed Ron Carter Design Ltd, 1996; *b* 3 June 1926; *s* of Harry Victor Carter and Ruth Allensen; *m* 1st (marr. diss.); three *d*; 2nd, 1985, Ann McNab; one step *s* two step *d.* *Educ:* Birmingham Central College of Art: studied Industrial and Interior Design (NDD; Louisa Anne Ryland Schol. for Silver Design), 1946–49; Royal College of Art: studied Furniture Design (1st Cl. Dip.; Silver Medal for work of special distinction; Travelling Schol. to USA), 1949–52; DesRCA; Fellow, RCA, 1966; Hon. Fellow, 1974; Sen. Fellow, 1994. Staff Designer with Corning Glass, 5th Avenue, NY City, 1952–53; freelance design practice, Birmingham and London, 1954; Tutor, School of Furniture, RCA, 1956–74; Partner: Design Partners, 1960–68; Carter Freeman Associates, 1968–74; Dir, Miles-Carter, 1980–92. *Recreations:* fishing, painting, walking. *Address:* 35 Great Queen Street, WC2B 5AA. *T:* (020) 7242 2291.

CARTER, (Thomas) Sebastian; designer and printer; Partner, since 1971, and owner, since 1991, Rampant Lions Press; *b* 20 Feb. 1941; *s* of late William Nicholas Carter, OBE and Barbara Ruth Carter (*née* Digby); *m* 1966, Penelope Ann Bowes Kerr; one *s* one *d.* *Educ:* Christ's Hosp.; King's Coll., Cambridge (MA). Designer: John Murray, 1962–63; The Trianon Press, Paris, 1963–65; Ruari McLean Associates, 1965–66; joined Rampant Lions Press, 1966. Mem., Internat. Acad. of the Book and Art of the Book, Russia, 1995. Francis Minns Meml Prize (for Shades by David Piper), NBL, 1971. *Publications:* The Book Becomes, 1984; Twentieth Century Type Designers, 1987, 2nd edn 1995; contribs to Matrix. *Recreations:* gardening, food, listening to music. *Address:* Swan House, Over, Cambridge CB4 5ND. *T:* (01954) 231003.

CARTER, Timothy; *see* Carter, J. T.

CARTER, Prof. Timothy, PhD; Professor of Music, Royal Holloway, University of London, since 1995; *b* 3 July 1954; *s* of Thomas Carter and Thais (*née* Epifantseff); *m* 1995, Annegret Fauser. *Educ:* Univ. of Durham (BA); Univ. of Birmingham (PhD 1980). Lectr in Music, Univ. of Lancaster, 1980–87; Lectr, 1987–92, Reader in Music, 1992–95, RHBNC, Univ. of London. Fellow, Harvard Center for Italian Renaissance Studies, Villa I Tatti, Florence, 1984–85. Ed., Music & Letters, 1992–99. Has made broadcasts. *Publications:* W. A. Mozart: Le Nozze di Figaro, 1987; Jacopo Peri (1561–1633): his life and works, 1989; Music in Late Renaissance and Early Baroque Italy, 1992; articles and essays in Jl Royal Musical Assoc., Early Music Hist., Jl Amer. Musicological Soc. *Address:* Music Department, Royal Holloway, Egham, Surrey TW20 0EX.

CARTER, (William) George (Key), CBE 1994; DL; FCA; Chairman, Black Country Development Corporation, 1994–98; *b* 29 Jan. 1934; *s* of late William Tom Carter, OBE, JP and Georgina Margaret Carter (*née* Key); *m* 1965, Anne Rosalie Mary Flanagan; one *s* one *d.* *Educ:* Warwick School. FCA 1957. Articled with Loarridge Beaven & Co., 1951–56; joined Price Waterhouse, 1956; Nat. Service, 2nd Lieut, 16/5th Queen's Royal Lancers, 1958–60; returned to Price Waterhouse, 1960: Manager, 1963–66; Partner, London, 1966–82; Dir of Finance, 1966–70; Sen. Partner, W Midlands, 1982–94. Dir, W Midlands Develt Agency, 1989–95 (Chm., 1991–95); Mem., NW Worcs HA, 1994–96. Mem., Pharmacists Rev. Panel, 1981–97. Member: CBI W Midlands Regl Council, 1988–98; DTI Industry '96 Steering Gp, 1993–97. Pres., Birmingham Chamber of Industry and Commerce, 1993–94; Vice-Chm., Birmingham Mkting Partnership, 1993–95; Non-executive Director: Birmingham Econ. Devel Partnership, 1991–95; Birmingham Children's Hosp. NHS Trust, 1996–. Institute of Chartered Accountants: Member: Insce Industry Cttee (Chm., 1974–80); Party and Law Cttee, 1978–83; Co-Chm., Auditors and Actuaries Cttee, 1975–80; Courses Cttee 1978–81. Member: Birmingham Univ. Business Sch. Adv. Bd, 1989–99; Council, Aston Univ., 1995–98. Pres., ESU, Worcs, 1998–. Gov. and Feoffee, Old Swinford Hosp. Sch., 1986–2000. FRSA 1993. DL W Midlands, 1996; High Sheriff, W Midlands, 1998–99. CStJ 1998 (Chm., Council, W Midlands, 1994–2001; Mem., Chapter Gen., 1996–99; Mem., Priory of England Chapter, 1999–). *Publication:* (jtly) Institute of Chartered Accountants Guide to Investigations, 1978. *Recreations:* gardening, golf, shooting. *Address:* The Old Rectory, Elmley Lovett, Droitwich, Worcs WR9 0PS. *T:* (01299) 851459; 28 Westmoreland Terrace, Pimlico, SW1V 4AF. *T:* (020) 7630 0597; *e-mail:* georgecarter@elmleylovett.freeserve.co.uk. *Club:* Cavalry and Guards.

CARTER, Prof. Yvonne Helen, (Mrs M. J. Bannon), OBE 2000; MD; FRCGP; Professor and Head of Department of General Practice and Primary Care, Bart's and The London, Queen Mary's School of Medicine and Dentistry (formerly St Bartholomew's and Royal London School of Medicine and Dentistry, Queen Mary and Westfield College), University of London, since 1996; *b* 16 April 1959; *d* of Percival Anthony Daniel Carter and Ellen Carter (*née* Bore); *m* 1988, Dr Michael Joseph Bannon; one *s.* *Educ:* Notre Dame High Sch., Liverpool; St Mary's Hosp. Med. Sch., Univ. of London (BSc, MB BS, MD 1994; DRCOG, DCH). FRCGP 1994. S Sefton Vocational Trng Scheme, Liverpool, 1984–87; General Practitioner: Liverpool, 1987–90; Newcastle-under-Lyme, 1990–93; Sen. Lectr, Dept of General Practice, Univ. of Birmingham, 1992–96; GP Tutor, Queen Elizabeth Postgrad. Med. Centre, Birmingham, 1994–96. Hon. Res. Fellow, Keele Univ., 1990–92. Chm. of Res., RCGP, 1996–2000. Founder FMedSci 1998. *Publications:* (ed with C. Thomas) Research Methods in Primary Care, 1996; (ed jtly) Handbook of Palliative Care, 1998; (ed jtly) Handbook of Sexual Health in Primary Care, 1998; (ed jtly) Research Opportunities in Primary Care, 1999; papers in med. jls on injury prevention (accidents to children and older people; child protection and aggression and violence in general practice and primary care). *Recreations:* reading, theatre, interior design. *Address:* Department of General Practice and Primary Care, Medical Sciences Building, Queen Mary's School of Medicine and Dentistry, Mile End Road, E1 4NS. *T:* (020) 7295 7904. *Club:* Royal Society of Medicine.

CARTER-JONES, Lewis, CBE 1995; *b* Gilfach Goch, S Wales, 17 Nov. 1920; *s* of Tom Jones, Kenfig Hill, Bridgend, Glam.; *m* 1945, Patricia Hylda, *d* of late Alfred Bastiman, Scarborough, Yorks; two *d.* *Educ:* Bridgend County Sch.; University Coll. of Wales, Aberystwyth (BA; Chm. Student Finance Cttee; Capt, Coll., Univ. and County Hockey XI). Served War of 1939–45 (Flight Sergeant Navigator, RAF). Head of Business Studies, Yale Grammar Technical Sch., Wrexham, 1950–64. Contested (Lab) Chester, by-election, 1956, and general election, 1959. MP (Lab) Eccles, 1964–87. Chairman: Cttee for Research for Apparatus for Disabled, 1973–80; Anglo-Columbian Gp, 1975–87; PLP Disablement Gp, 1975–81; PLP Aviation Gp, 1978–87. Exec. Mem., UK Br., CPA, 1983–87; Secretary: Indo-British Parly Gp, 1966–87; All-Party BLESMA Gp, 1973–87; All Party Aviation Gp, 1980–87. Hon. Parliamentary Adviser: RNIB, 1973–87; British Assoc. of Occupational Therapists; Soc. of Physiotherapists, until 1987. Mem., Gen. Adv. Council, IBA, 1982–87. Chairman: British Cttee, Rehabilitation International, 1978–92; Adv. Gp on Artificial Limbs to DoH, 1993–; Vice-President: Wales Council for the Disabled, 1981–; RADAR, 1987– (Chm., Access to the Skies Cttee, 1992–); Member: Disablement Services Authority, 1987–91; Disabled Persons Transport Adv. Cttee, Dept of Transport, 1988– (Chm., Airport Sub Cttee, 1988–); Adv. Gp on Rehabilitation to Sec. of State for Health, 1991–; Trustee, Granada Telethon, 1987. Dir, Possum Controls Ltd, 1974–92. *Address:* Cader Idris, 5 Cefn Road, Rhosnesni, Wrexham, Clwyd LL13 9NF.

CARTER-MANNING, Jeremy James; QC 1993; a Recorder, since 1993; *b* 25 Dec. 1947; *s* of Landon and Nancie Carter-Manning; *m* 1970, Bridget Mary Simpson; one *s* one *d.* *Educ:* St Paul's Sch. Solicitor 1971; called to the Bar, Middle Temple, 1975. *Recreation:* tennis. *Address:* 9–12 Bell Yard, WC2A 2LF. *T:* (020) 7400 1800.

CARTER-RUCK, Peter Frederick; Founder, 1981, Senior Partner, 1981–98, now Media and Trust Consultant, Peter Carter-Ruck and Partners, Solicitors; *b* 26 Feb. 1914; *s* of Frederick Henry Carter-Ruck and Nell Mabel Carter-Ruck; *m* 1940, Pamela Ann, *o d* of late Gp Capt. Reginald Stuart Maxwell, MC, DFC, AFC, RAF; one *d* (one *s* decd). *Educ:* St Edward's, Oxford; Law Society; Solicitor of the Supreme Court (Hons). Admitted Solicitor, 1937; served RA, 1939–44, Captain Instr in gunnery. Sen. Partner, Oswald Hickson, Collier & Co., 1945–81. Specialist Member, Council of Law Soc., 1971–84; Chairman: Law Soc. Law Reform Cttee, 1980–83; Media Cttee, Internat. Bar Assoc., 1983–85; Mem., Council of Justice (Internat. Commn of Jurists), 1968–; President: City of Westminster Law Soc., 1975–76; Council, Media Soc., 1981–82 and 1984–86 (Hon. Life Vice Pres., 1988). Fellow, Soc. for Advanced Legal Studies, 1998–. Governor, St Edward's Sch., Oxford, 1950–78; past Chm. and Founder Governor, Shiplake Coll., Henley, 1960–73; Gov., St Bartholomew Charitable Foundn, 1996–. Mem. Livery, City of London Solicitors' Co., 1949–. *Publications:* Libel and Slander, 1953, 5th edn 1997; (with Ian Mackrill) The Cyclist and the Law, 1953; (with Edmund Skone James) Copyright: modern law and practice, 1965; Memoirs of a Libel Lawyer, 1990. *Address:* Carlton Mansions, York Buildings, Adelphi, WC2N 6LS. *T:* (020) 7839 7515, *Fax:* (020) 7839 1240; Latchmore Cottage, Great Hallingbury, Bishop's Stortford, Herts CM22 7PJ. *T:* (01279) 654357, *Fax:* (01279) 504921; *e-mail:* peter-carter-ruck@dial.pipex.com; Eilagadale, N Ardnamurchan, Argyll PH36 4LG. *T:* (01972) 510267. *Clubs:* Garrick, Press, Royal Ocean Racing; Royal Yacht Squadron, Lloyd's Yacht, Law Society Yacht (past Commodore), Ocean Cruising (past Commodore).

CARTER-STEPHENSON, George Anthony; QC 1998; *b* 10 July 1952; *s* of Raymond M. Stephenson and Brenda S. Stephenson; *m* 1974, Christine Maria; one *s* one *d*. *Educ:* Leeds Univ. (LLB Hons). Called to the Bar, Inner Temple, 1975; in practice at the Bar, 1975–. *Recreations:* motorcycling, theatre, cinema, music. *Address:* 3 Gray's Inn Square, Gray's Inn, WC1R 5AH. *T:* (020) 7520 5600.

CARTIER-BRESSON, Henri; photographer, draughtsman; *b* France, 22 Aug. 1908. Studied painting with André Lhote, 1927–28. Asst Dir to Jean Renoir, 1936–39; Co-founder, Magnum Photos, 1947. Photographs exhibited: Mexico; Japan; Mus. of Modern Art, NY, 1947, 1968, 1987; Villa Medicis, Rome; Louvre, 1955, 1967, Grand Palais, 1970, Paris; V&A, 1969; Manege, Moscow, 1972; Edinburgh Festival, 1978; Hayward Gall., London, 1978; drawings exhibited: Carlton Gall., NY, 1975; Bischofberger Gall., Zürich, 1976; Forcalquier Gall., France, 1976; Mus. of Modern Art, Paris, 1981; Mus. of Modern Art, Mexico, 1982; French Inst., Stockholm, 1983; Pavilion of Contemporary Art, Milan, 1983; Mus. of Modern Art, Oxford, 1984; Palace Liechtenstein, Vienna, Salzburg, 1985; Herstand Gall., NY, 1987; Ecole des Beaux Arts, Paris, 1989; Le Printemps, Tokyo, 1989; Fondation Gianadda, Switzerland, 1990; Villa Medicis, Rome, 1990; Musée de Louvain, Belgium, 1991; Mus. of Modern Art, Taiwan, 1991; Palazzo Sanvitale, Parma, 1992; Museo Camon Aznar, Zaragoza, 1992; Hamburg, 1994; Tokyo, Barcelona, 1995; Minneapolis Art Inst., 1996; Berggruen Gall., 1996; Hayward and Nat. Portrait Galls, 1998; Landscapes, Tokyo, Kyoto, 1999, Paris, 2000. Collection of 390 photographs at DeMenil Foundn, Houston, USA, V&A, Univ. of Fine Arts, Osaka, Japan, Bibliothèque Nationale, Paris. Drawings exhibited: Galerie Claude Bernard, Paris, 1997; RCA, 1998; Mus. of Contemporary Art, Kyoto, 1998; Künsthaus, Zürich, 1998; Palazzo Medici Riccardi, Florence, then travelling, 1999–. Documentary films: on hosps, Spanish Republic, 1937; (with J. Lemare) Le Retour, 1945; (with J. Boffety) Impressions of California, 1969; (with W. Dombrow) Southern Exposures, 1970. Mem., Amer. Acad. of Arts and Scis, 1974. Hon. Prof., Acad. of Fine Arts, China, 1996. Hon. DLitt Oxon, 1975. Awards: US Camera, 1948; Overseas Press Club of America, 1949; Amer. Soc. of Magazine Photography, 1953; Photography Soc. of America, 1958; Overseas Press Club, 1954 (for Russia), 1960 (for China), 1964 (for Cuba); German Photographic Soc.; Hasselblad, 1983; Novecento, Palermo, 1986; Japanese Photographic Soc., 1989. *Publications:* (ed) Images à la Sauvette (The Decisive Moment), 1952; The Europeans, Moscow, 1955; From One China to the Other, 1956; Photographs by Cartier-Bresson; Flagrants Délits (The World of Henri Cartier-Bresson, 1968); (with F. Nourrissier) Vive la France, 1970; Cartier-Bresson's France, 1971; (jtly) L'Homme et la Machine, 1972 (Man and Machine, 1969) for IBM; Faces of Asia, 1972; A Propos de l'URSS, 1973 (About Russia, 1974); Henri Cartier-Bresson Pocket Book, 1985; Henri Cartier-Bresson in India, 1988; Traits pour Traits (Line by Line), 1989 (drawings); L'Amérique Furtivement (America in Passing), 1991; A Propos de Paris, 1994 (also German, American and Japanese edns); Carnets mexicains (text by Carlos Fuentes), 1995 (also German and Italian edns); André Breton, roi soleil, 1995; L'imaginaire d'après nature, 1996 (also German and US edns); Dessins 1974–1997 (text by Jean Leymarie), 1997; Europeans, 1998; Tête à Tête (text by E. H. Gombrich), 1998 (also French, German and US edns); The Mind's Eye, 1999; *relevant publications:* Yves Bonnefoy, Henri Cartier-Bresson, Photographer, 1979, rev. edn 1992; André P. de Mandiargues, Photoportrait, 1985; Peter Galassi, Early Work, USA 1987 (French edn 1991); Jean Pierre Montier, L'Art sans Art, 1995. *Address:* c/o Magnum Photos, 19 rue Hégesippe Moreau, 75018 Paris, France; c/o Helen Wright, 135 East 74th Street, New York, NY 10021, USA.

CARTLAND, Sir George (Barrington), Kt 1963; CMG 1956; BA; Vice-Chancellor of the University of Tasmania, 1968–77; Chairman, Australian National Accreditation Authority for Translators and Interpreters, 1977–83; *b* 22 Sept. 1912; *s* of William Arthur and Margaret Cartland, West Didsbury; *m* 1937, Dorothy Rayton (*d* 1993); two *s*. *Educ:* Manchester Central High Sch.; Manchester Univ.; Hertford Coll., Oxford. Entered Colonial Service, Gold Coast, 1935; served Colonial Office, 1944–49; Head of African Studies Br. and Founding Ed. Jl of Afr. Adminis., 1945–49; Sec. London Afr. Conf., 1948; Admin. Sec., Uganda, 1949; Sec. for Social Services and Local Govt, Uganda, 1952; Min. for Social Services, Uganda, 1955; Min. of Education and Labour, Uganda, 1958; Chief Sec., Uganda, 1960; Deputy Gov. of Uganda, 1961–62 (Acting Gov., various occasions, 1952–62); Registrar of Univ. of Birmingham, 1963–67. Part-time Mem., West Midlands Gas Bd, 1964–67. Member: Exec. Cttee, Inter Univ. Council for Higher Educn Overseas (UK), 1963–67; Commonwealth Scholarship Commn (UK), 1964–67. Dep. Chm., Australian Vice-Chancellors' Cttee, 1975 and 1977. Chairman: Adv. Cttee on National Park in SW Tasmania, 1976–78; Tasmanian Council of Australian Trade Union Trng Authority, 1979. Appointed to review: Library and Archives Legislation of Tasmania, 1978; Tasmanian Govt Admin, 1979. Mem., Australian Nat. Cttee of Hoover Awards for Marketing, 1968–82. Chm., St John Council, Uganda, 1958–59; Pres., St John Council, Tasmania, 1969–78. Member Council: Makerere Coll., 1952–60; Royal Tech. Coll., Nairobi, 1952–60; UC of Rhodesia, 1963–67; Univ. of S Pacific, 1972–76. FACE 1970. Hon. LLD Univ. of Tasmania, 1978. KStJ 1972; awarded Belgian Congo medal, 1960. *Publication:* (jtly) The Irish Cartlands and Cartland Genealogy, 1978. *Recreation:* fly fishing. *Address:* 5 Aotea Road, Sandy Bay, Hobart, Tasmania 7005, Australia. *Clubs:* Athenæum; Tasmanian, Royal Tasmanian Yacht (Hobart).

CARTLEDGE, Sir Bryan (George), KCMG 1985 (CMG 1980); Principal of Linacre College, Oxford, 1988–96 (Hon. Fellow, 1996); *b* 10 June 1931; *s* of Eric Montague George Cartledge and Phyllis (*née* Shaw); *m* 1st, 1960, Ruth Hylton Gass (marr. diss. 1994; she *d* 1998), *d* of John Gass; one *s* one *d*; 2nd, 1994, Dr Freda Gladys Newcombe (*d* 2001). *Educ:* Hurstpierpoint; St John's Coll., Cambridge (Hon. Fellow, 1985). Queen's Royal Regt, 1950–51. Commonwealth Fund Fellow, Stanford Univ., 1956–57; Research Fellow, St Antony's Coll., Oxford, 1958–59 (Hon. Fellow, 1987). Entered HM Foreign (subseq. Diplomatic) Service, 1960; served in FO, 1960–61; Stockholm, 1961–63; Moscow, 1963–66; DSAO, 1966–68; Tehran, 1968–70; Harvard Univ., 1971–72; Counsellor, Moscow, 1972–75; Head of E European and Soviet Dept, FCO, 1975–77; Private Sec. (Overseas Affairs) to Prime Minister, 1977–79; Ambassador to Hungary, 1980–83; Asst Under-Sec. of State, FCO, 1983–84; Dep. Sec. of the Cabinet, 1984–85; Ambassador to the Soviet Union, 1985–88. *Publications:* (ed) Monitoring the Environment, 1992; (ed) Energy and the Environment, 1993; (ed) Health and the Environment, 1994; (ed) Population and the Environment, 1995; (ed) Transport and the Environment, 1996; (ed) Mind, Brain and Environment, 1997. *Address:* Jasmine House, Holton, Oxon OX33 1PU. *Club:* Reform.

CARTTISS, Michael Reginald Harry; *b* Norwich, 11 March 1938; *s* of Reginald Carttiss and Doris Culling. *Educ:* Filby County Primary Sch.; Great Yarmouth Tech. High Sch.; Goldsmiths' Coll., London Univ. (DipEd); LSE (part time, 1961–64). Nat. Service, RAF, 1956–58. Teacher: Orpington, Kent, and Waltham Cross, Herts, 1961–64; Oriel Grammar Sch., 1964–69; Cons. Party Agent, Gt Yarmouth, 1969–82. Member: Norfolk CC, 1966–85 (Vice-Chm., 1972, Chm., 1980–85, Educn Cttee); Gt Yarmouth BC, 1973–82 (Leader, 1980–82). MP (C) Great Yarmouth, 1983–97; contested (C) same seat, 1997. Chm., Norfolk Museums Service, 1981–85; Mem., E Anglian RHA, 1981–85; Comr, Gt Yarmouth Port and Haven Commn, 1982–86. *Recreations:* reading, writing, talking, walking, theatre. *Address:* Main Road, Filby, Great Yarmouth, Norfolk NR29 3HN.

CARTWRIGHT, David Edgar, DSc; FRS 1984; Assistant Director, Institute of Oceanographic Sciences, Bidston Observatory, Birkenhead, 1973–86, retired; *b* 21 Oct. 1926; *s* of Edgar A. Cartwright and Lucienne Cartwright (*née* Tartanson); *m* 1952, Anne-Marie Guerin; two *s* two *d*. *Educ:* St John's Coll., Cambridge (BA); King's Coll., London (BSc, DSc). Dept of Naval Construction, Admiralty, Bath, 1951–54; Nat. Inst. of Oceanography (later Inst. of Oceanographic Sciences), Wormley, Surrey: Sci. Officer, rising to Individual Merit SPSO, 1954–73; Research Associate, Univ. of California, La Jolla, 1964–65, 1993, 1994; Sen. Res. Associate, NASA–Goddard Space Flight Center, Greenbelt, Md, 1987–89; Consultant, NASA, 1990–92. Fellow: Royal Astronomical Soc., 1975; Amer. Geophysical Union, 1991. Dr (*hc*) Toulouse, 1992. *Publications:* Tides–a Scientific History, 1999; over 80 papers on marine sci. research; reviews, etc, in various learned jls. *Recreations:* music, walking, travel. *Address:* 3 Borough House, Borough Road, Petersfield, Hants GU32 3LF. *T:* (01730) 267195.

CARTWRIGHT, Harry, CBE 1979 (MBE 1946); MA, CEng, MIMechE, MIEE; Director, Atomic Energy Establishment, Winfrith, 1973–83; *b* 16 Sept. 1919; *s* of Edwin Harry Cartwright and Agnes Alice Cartwright (*née* Gillibrand); *m* 1950, Catharine Margaret Carson Bradbury; two *s*. *Educ:* William Hulme's Grammar Sch., Manchester; St John's Coll., Cambridge (Schol.). 1st cl. Mechanical Sciences Tripos, 1940. Served War, RAF, 1940–46: Flt Lt, service on ground radar in Europe, India and Burma. Decca Navigator Co., 1946–47; English Electric Co., 1947–49; joined Dept of Atomic Energy, Risley, as a Design and Project Engr, 1949; Chief Engr, 1955; Dir in charge of UKAEA consultancy services on nuclear reactors, 1960–64; Dir, Water Reactors, 1964–70, and as such responsible for design and construction of Winfrith 100 MW(e) SGHWR prototype power station; Dir, Fast Reactor Systems, 1970–73. Pres., British Nuclear Energy Soc., 1979–82; Pres., European Nuclear Soc., 1983–85 (Vice-Pres., 1980–83). Chm. of Trustees, Corfe Castle Charities, 1991–98. Chm. of Govs, Purbeck Sch., 1985–88. *Publications:* various techn. papers. *Recreations:* walking, gardening. *Address:* Tabbit's Hill House, Corfe Castle, Wareham, Dorset BH20 5HZ. *T:* (01929) 480582. *Club:* Oxford and Cambridge.

CARTWRIGHT, John Cameron; JP; Deputy Chairman, Police Complaints Authority, 1993–99 (Member, 1992–99); *b* 29 Nov. 1933; *s* of Aubrey John Randolph Cartwright and Ivy Adeline Billie Cartwright; *m* 1959, Iris June Tant; one *s* one *d*. *Educ:* Woking County Grammar School. Exec. Officer, Home Civil Service, 1952–55; Labour Party Agent, 1955–67; Political Sec., RACS Ltd, 1967–72; Director, RACS Ltd, 1972–74. Leader, Greenwich Borough Council, 1971–74. Mem., Labour Party Nat. Exec. Cttee, 1971–75 and 1976–78. MP Greenwich, Woolwich East, Oct. 1974–1983, Woolwich, 1983–92 (Lab, 1974–81; SDP, 1981–90; Soc. Dem., 1990–92); contested (Soc. Dem.) Woolwich, 1992. PPS to Sec. of State for Education and Science, 1976–77; Chm., Parly Labour Party Defence Group, 1979–81; Mem., Select Cttee on Defence, 1979–82 and 1986–92; SDP party spokesman on environment, 1981–87, on defence and foreign affairs, 1983–87; SDP/Liberal Alliance spokesman on defence, 1987; SDP Parly Whip, 1983–92; Vice Pres., SDP, 1987–88, Pres., 1988–91. Jt Chm., Council for Advancement of Arab British Understanding, 1983–87; Vice-Chm., GB-USSR Assoc., 1983–91. Mem., Calcutt Cttee on Privacy and Related Matters, 1989–90. Non-executive Director: Lambeth, Southwark and Lewisham HA, 1995–2000; Maidstone and Tunbridge Wells NHS Trust, 2000–. Vice-Pres., Assoc. of Metropolitan Authorities, 1974–. Trustee, Nat. Maritime Museum, 1976–83. JP Inner London, 1970. *Publication:* (jtly) Cruise, Pershing and SS20, 1985. *Recreations:* do-it-yourself, listening to jazz, supporting Lincoln City FC. *Address:* 24 Juniper Close, Maidstone, Kent ME16 0XP. *T:* (01622) 691324.

CARTWRIGHT, Prof. Nancy Lynn Delaney, (Lady Hampshire), PhD; FBA 1996; Professor of Philosophy, Logic and Scientific Method, since 1991, and Director, Centre for the Philosophy of Natural and Social Science, since 1993, London School of Economics and Political Science, London University; *b* 24 June 1944; *m* 1985, Sir Stuart Hampshire, *qv*; two *d*. *Educ:* Pittsburgh Univ. (BS Maths 1966); Illinois Univ. (PhD 1971). Asst Prof. of Philosophy, Maryland Univ., 1971–73; Stanford University: Asst Prof., 1973–77; Associate Prof., 1977–83; Prof. of Philosophy, 1983–91. Vis. Lectr, Cambridge Univ., 1974; Visiting Professor: UCLA, 1976; Princeton Univ., 1978; Pittsburgh Univ., 1984; Oslo Univ., 1993, 1994; Univ. of Calif, San Diego, 1995; Old Dominion Fellow, Princeton Univ., 1996; Prof. of Philosophy, Univ. of Calif, San Diego, 1997–. Mem., Acad. Leopoldina, 1999. *Publications:* How the Laws of Physics Lie, 1983; Nature's Capacities and their Measurement, 1989; (jtly) Otto Neurath: philosophy between science and politics, 1995. *Address:* London School of Economics and Political Science, Houghton Street, WC2A 2AE. *T:* (020) 7955 7330.

CARTWRIGHT, Rt Rev. Richard Fox; Assistant Bishop, Diocese of Exeter, since 1988; *b* 10 Nov. 1913; *s* of late Rev. George Frederick Cartwright, Vicar of Plumstead, and Constance Margaret Cartwright (*née* Clark); *m* 1947, Rosemary Magdalen, *d* of Francis Evelyn Bray, Woodham Grange, Surrey; one *s* three *d*. *Educ:* The King's School, Canterbury; Pembroke Coll., Cambridge (BA 1935, MA 1939); Cuddesdon Theological Coll. Deacon, 1936; Priest, 1937; Curate, St Anselm, Kennington Cross, 1936–40; Priest-in-Charge, Lower Kingswood, 1940–45; Vicar, St Andrew, Surbiton, 1945–52; Proctor in Convocation, 1950–52; Vicar of St Mary Redcliffe, Bristol (with Temple from 1956 and St John Bedminster from 1965), 1952–72; Hon. Canon of Bristol, 1960–72; Suffragan Bishop of Plymouth, 1972–81; Asst Bishop, dio. of Truro, 1982–91. Sub-Chaplain, Order of St John, 1957–; Director: Ecclesiastical Insurance Office Ltd, 1964–85; Allchurches Trust Ltd, 1985–91. Chm. Governors, Kelly Coll., 1973–88. Hon. DD Univ. of the South, Tennessee, 1969. *Recreations:* fly-fishing, gardening, water-colour painting. *Address:* 5 Old Vicarage Close, Ide, near Exeter, Devon EX2 9RT. *T:* (01392) 211270. *Club:* Army and Navy.

CARTWRIGHT, Lt-Col Robert Guy; Secretary, Central Chancery of Orders of Knighthood and Assistant Comptroller, Lord Chamberlain's Office, since 1999; Extra Equerry to the Queen, since 2000; *b* 6 Aug. 1950; *s* of Major Robin Vivian Cartwright and Loveday Elizabeth Cartwright (*née* Leigh-Pemberton); *m* 1972, Caroline, *d* of late Gilbert Stephenson and Eleanor Stephenson; two *s*. *Educ:* Wellington Coll.; RMA Sandhurst; RMCS Shrivenham; RN Staff Coll. Commissioned Grenadier Guards, 1970; CO, 1st Bn Grenadier Guards, 1990–92; Directing Staff, RN Staff Coll., 1993–94; MoD, 1995–96; retired, 1996. *Recreations:* running, reading, wine. *Address:* 151 Wakehurst Road, SW11 6BW. *Club:* HAC.

CARTWRIGHT, Hon. Dame Silvia (Rose), PCNZM 2001; DBE 1989; Governor-General of New Zealand, since 2001; *b* 7 Nov. 1943; *d* of Monteith Poulter and Eileen Jane Poulter, both of Dunedin, NZ; *m* 1969, Peter John Cartwright. *Educ:* Univ. of Otago, NZ (LLB). Partner, Harkness Henry & Co., Barristers and Solicitors, Hamilton, NZ, 1971–81; Dist Court and Family Court Judge, 1981–89; Chief Dist Court Judge, 1989–93; Judge of the High Court, NZ, 1993–2001. Mem., Commn for the Future, 1975–80; conducted Inquiry into: Soc. Sci. Funding in NZ, 1986–87; Treatment of

Cervical Cancer at Nat. Women's Hosp., Auckland, NZ, 1987–88. Mem. Cttee, UN Human Rights Convention to eliminate discrimination against women, 1992–2000. F. W. Guest Meml Lectr, Univ. of Otago, 1993. Hon. LLD: Otago, 1993; Waikato, 1994. *Address:* Government House, Wellington, New Zealand. *T:* (4) 3898055, *Fax:* (4) 3895536.

CARTWRIGHT, Sonia Rosemary Susan, (Mrs C. Cartwright); *see* Proudman, S. R. S.

CARTY, Hilary; Director of Dance, Arts Council, since 1994; *b* 26 May 1962; *d* of Solomon Carty and Catherine (*née* Bailey). *Educ:* Leicester Poly. (BA Hons Performing Arts, 1983); Cultural Trng Centre, Jamaica (Cert. in Dance Educn, 1984); Univ. of Westminster (MBA 1994). Community Arts Officer, Leics Expressive Arts, 1985; Community Arts Develt Officer, The Cave, Birmingham, 1985; Arts Officer (Dance and Mime), E Midlands Arts, 1986–90; Gen. Manager, Adzido Pan African Dance Ensemble, 1990–94. *Publication:* Folk Dances of Jamaica, 1988. *Recreations:* squash, badminton, theatre, dance. *Address:* 296 Crystal Palace Road, Dulwich, SE22 9JJ. *T:* (020) 7973 6489.

CARUANA, Hon. Peter Richard; QC (Gibraltar) 1998; MP (GSD) Gibraltar, since 1991; Chief Minister of Gibraltar, since 1996; *b* 15 Oct. 1956; *s* of John Joseph Caruana and Maria Teresa Caruana (*née* Vasquez); *m* 1982, Cristina Maria Triay; two *s* three *d* (and one *s* decd). *Educ:* Ratcliffe Coll., Leicester; Queen Mary Coll., London Univ.; Council of Legal Educn, London. Called to the Bar, Inner Temple, 1979; with law firm Triay & Triay, Gibraltar, 1979–95, Partner specialising in commercial and shipping law, 1990–95. Joined GSD, 1990, Leader, 1991–; Leader of the Opposition, Gibraltar, 1992–96. *Recreation:* golf. *Address:* 10/3 Irish Town, Gibraltar; (home) 6 Convent Place, Gibraltar. *T:* 70071, *Fax:* 76396.

CARUS, Louis Revell, Hon. RAM, FRSAMD, FRCM, FBSM; Consultant to Benslow Music Trust, since 1987; Principal, Birmingham School of Music, 1975–87; *b* Kasauli, India, 22 Oct. 1927; *s* of Lt-Col Martin and Enid Carus-Wilson; *m* 1951, Nancy Reade Noell; two *s* one *d*. *Educ:* Rugby Sch.; Brussels Conservatoire (Premier Prix); Peabody Conservatory, USA. LRAM. Scottish National Orchestra, 1950; solo violinist and chamber music specialist, 1951–; Head of Strings, Royal Scottish Academy of Music, 1956; Scottish Trio and Piano Quartet, New Music Group of Scotland, 1956–75; Northern Sinfonia, Monteverdi Orchestras, 1963–73; Orchestra Da Camera, 1975; Artistic Dir, Internat. String Quartet Week, 1985–. Adjudicator, 1960–; Examr, Associated Bd of Royal Schs of Music, 1976–. Pres., ISM, 1986–87; FRSAMD 1976; Hon. RAM 1977; FRCM 1983; FBSM 1988. FUCEB (Fellow, Birmingham Poly., 1988). *Publications:* various musical journalism, eg, daily press, Strad Magazine, ISM Jl, Gulbenkian Report. *Recreations:* painting, gardening, travel. *Address:* 15 Kings End Road, Powick, Worcester WR2 4RA. *T:* (01905) 831715. *Clubs:* Royal Society of Musicians, Incorporated Society of Musicians, European String Teachers Association; Rotary (Worcester).

CARUS, Roderick; QC 1990; a Recorder, since 1990; *b* 4 June 1944; *s* of Anthony and Kathleen Carus; *m* 1972, Hilary Mary (*née* Jones); two *s* two *d*. *Educ:* Wirral GS, Merseyside; University Coll., Oxford (BA Law); Manchester Business Sch. (Postgrad. Diploma in Advanced Business Studies). Called to the Bar, Gray's Inn, 1971. Merchant bank, investments, 1966–70. Asst Recorder, 1987–90. *Recreations:* chess, crosswords, fishing, gardening. *Address:* Midways, Back Lane, Ashley, Altrincham, Cheshire WA15 0QH. *Club:* Hale Conservative.

CARVEL, John Douglas; Social Affairs Editor, The Guardian, since 2000; *b* 26 May 1947; *s* of late Robert Burns Carvel and of Florence Annie Carvel (*née* Wilson); marr. diss.; two *s*. *Educ:* Merchant Taylors' Sch., Northwood; Exeter Coll., Oxford (BA Hons PPE). Reporter, Newcastle Jl, 1969–72; The Guardian, 1973–: Business Reporter, 1973–75; News Ed., Financial Guardian, 1975–76; Industrial Corresp., 1976–79; Dep. Features Ed., 1979–81; Local Govt Corresp., 1981–85; Political Corresp., 1985–89; Associate Ed., 1989–; Home Affairs Ed., 1989–92; Eur. Affairs Ed., 1992–95; Educn Ed., 1995–2000. Commendation, British Press Awards, 1984 and 1990; Local Govt Journalist of Year, Local Govt Inf. Services, 1985; Legal Affairs Journalist of Year, Bar Council, 1991; Freedom of Information Award, Campaign for Freedom of Inf., 1995. *Publications:* Citizen Ken, 1984, 2nd edn 1986; An Account of the Guardian Case, in Openness and Transparency in the EU, ed V. Deckmyn and I. Thomson, 1998; Turn Again Livingstone, 1999. *Recreations:* tennis, gardening, being with my sons. *Address:* The Guardian, 119 Farringdon Road, EC1R 3ER. *T:* (020) 7278 2332, *Fax:* (020) 7713 4154.

CARVER, family name of **Baron Carver**.

CARVER, Baron *cr* 1977 (Life Peer); **Field-Marshal (Richard) Michael (Power) Carver,** GCB 1970 (KCB 1966; CB 1957); CBE 1945; DSO 1943 and Bar 1943; MC 1941; designated British Resident Commissioner in Rhodesia, 1977–78; *b* 24 April 1915; 2nd *s* of late Harold Power Carver and late Winifred Anne Gabrielle Carver (*née* Wellesley); *m* 1947, Edith, *d* of Lt-Col Sir Henry Lowry-Corry, MC; two *s* two *d*. *Educ:* Winchester Coll.; Sandhurst. 2nd Lieut Royal Tank Corps, 1935; War of 1939–45 (despatches twice); GSO1, 7th Armoured Div., 1942; OC 1st Royal Tank Regt, 1943; Comdr 4th Armoured Brigade, 1944; Tech. Staff Officer (1), Min. of Supply, 1947; Joint Services Staff Coll., 1950; AQMG, Allied Land Forces, Central Europe, 1951; Col GS, SHAPE 1952; Dep. Chief of Staff, East Africa, 1954 (despatches); Chief of Staff, East Africa, 1955; idc 1957; Dir of Plans, War Office, 1958–59; Comdr 6th Infty Brigade, 1960–62; Maj.-Gen. 1962; GOC, 3 Div., 1962–64, also Comdr Joint Truce Force, Cyprus, and Dep. Comdr United Nations' Force in Cyprus, 1964; Dir, Army Staff Duties, Min. of Defence, 1964–66; Lt-Gen. 1966; comd FE Land Forces, 1966–67; Gen., 1967; C-in-C, Far East, 1967–69; GOC-in-C, Southern Command, 1969–71; Chief of the General Staff, 1971–73; Field-Marshal 1973; CDS, 1973–76. Col Commandant: REME 1966–76; Royal Tank Regt, 1968–72; RAC, 1974–77; ADC (Gen.) 1969–72. Hon. DLitt Southampton, 1991. *Publications:* Second to None (History of Royal Scots Greys, 1919–45), 1954; El Alamein, 1962; Tobruk, 1964; (ed) The War Lords, 1976; Harding of Petherton, 1978; The Apostles of Mobility, 1979; War Since 1945, 1980; A Policy for Peace, 1982; The Seven Ages of the British Army, 1984; Dilemmas of the Desert War, 1986; Twentieth Century Warriors, 1987; Out of Step: memoirs of Field-Marshal Lord Carver, 1989; Tightrope Walking: British defence policy since 1945, 1992; (ed) Letters of a Victorian Army Officer: Edward Wellesley 1840–1854, 1995; Britain's Army in the 20th Century, 1998; National Army Museum Book of the Boer War, 1999. *Address:* Wood End House, Wickham, Fareham, Hants PO17 6JZ. *T:* (01329) 832143. *Club:* Royal Anglo-Belgian.

CARVER, James, CB 1978; CEng, FIMM; consulting mining engineer; *b* 29 Feb. 1916; *s* of late William and Ellen Carver; *m* 1944, Elsie Sharrock; one *s* two *d* (of whom one *s* one *d* are twins). *Educ:* Wigan Mining and Technical Coll. Certificated Mine Manager. Asst Mine Manager, Nos 5, 6 and 7 mines, Garswood Hall, Lancs, 1941–43; HM Jun. Inspector Mines and Quarries, W Midlands Coalfields, 1943; Dist Inspector, Mines and Quarries, N Staffordshire, 1951; Senior District Inspector: M&Q, London Headquarters, 1957; M&Q, Doncaster Dist (in charge), 1962; Principal Inspector, M&Q, London Headquarters, 1967; Dep. Chief, M&Q, 1973; Chief Inspector, M&Q, 1975–77; Member, Health and Safety Exec., 1976–77. *Publications:* author or co-author, papers in Trans IMinE; several papers to internat. mining confs. *Recreation:* golf. *Address:* 196 Forest Road, Tunbridge Wells, Kent TN2 5JB. *T:* (01892) 526748. *Club:* Nevill Golf (Tunbridge Wells).

CARVER, Peter William John; JP, DL; landowner and farmer; Commissioner-in-Chief, 1995–99, Chief Commissioner, Operations and Member, Board of Trustees, 1999–2000, St John Ambulance; *b* 18 June 1938; *s* of late John Henton Carver and Juliet Carver (*née* Clitherow); *m* 1963, Jacqueline Boyce; one *s*. *Educ:* Uppingham Sch. Nat. Service, 2nd Lt, DCLI, 1957–59. Staff broadcaster, British Forces Network, Germany and Radio Luxembourg, 1959–64. Mem., ER Yorks CC, 1971–74. Contested (C) Kingston-upon-Hull, Feb. and Oct. 1974. Chm. and Pres., Humberside Euro Constituency, 1979–88. County Commissioner: Humberside Scouts, 1983–90 (Chm., 1978–83; Pres., 1991–); Council, Scout Assoc., 1986–90; St John Ambulance (Humberside), 1991–95. Underwriting Mem., Lloyd's, 1971–98. Mem., Yorks Regl Cttee, NT, 1985–91. Patron, living of N Cave, E Yorks, 1969–. JP 1973, DL 1983, Humberside, now ER Yorks; High Sheriff, ER Yorks, 1997–98. KStJ 1995. *Recreations:* gardens, historic houses. *Address:* Manor House, North Cave, E Yorks HU15 2LW. *T:* (01430) 422203.

CARVILL, Patrick, CB 1994; Permanent Secretary, Department of Finance and Personnel, Northern Ireland, since 1998; *b* 13 Oct. 1943; *s* of Bernard and Susan Carvill; *m* 1965, Vera Abbott; two *s*. *Educ:* St Mary's Christian Brothers Grammar School, Belfast; Queen's Univ., Belfast (BA Hons). Min. of Fuel and Power, Westminster, 1965; Min. of Development, Stormont, 1967; Min. of Community Relations, 1969; Asst Sec., Dept of Educn, 1975–83; Under-Secretary: Dept of Finance and Personnel, 1983–88; Dept of Econ. Develt, 1988–89; Dept of Finance and Personnel, 1989–90; Perm. Sec., Dept of Educn for NI, 1990–98. *Recreations:* reading, hill-walking, diving. *Address:* c/o Department of Finance and Personnel, Rathgael House, Balloo Road, Bangor, Co. Down BT19 7PR.

CARY, family name of **Viscount Falkland**.

CARY, Anthony Joyce, CMG 1997; HM Diplomatic Service; on loan as Chef de Cabinet to Rt Hon. Christopher Patten, Member of the European Commission, since 1999; *b* 1 July 1951; *s* of Sir Michael Cary, GCB and Isabel Cary; *m* 1975, Clare Elworthy; three *s* one *d*. *Educ:* Eton; Trinity Coll., Oxford (MA English); Stanford Business Sch. (MBA). Joined FCO, 1973: BMG Berlin, 1974–77; Policy Planning Staff, FCO, 1978–80; Harkness Fellow, Stanford Business Sch., 1980–82; EC Dept, FCO, 1982–84; Private Sec. to Minister of State, FCO, 1984–86; Head of Chancery, Kuala Lumpur, 1986–88; on loan to Cabinet of Sir Leon Brittan, EC, Brussels, 1989–92; Head of EU Dept (Internal), FCO, 1993–96; Counsellor, Washington, 1997–99. *Address:* CHAR 15/139, European Commission, Rue de la Loi 200, 1049 Brussels, Belgium.

CARY, Sir Roger Hugh, 2nd Bt *cr* 1955; a consultant to BBC's Director-General, since 1986; *b* 8 Jan. 1926; *o s* of Sir Robert (Archibald) Cary, 1st Bt, and Hon. Rosamond Mary Curzon (*d* 1985), *d* of late Col Hon. Alfred Nathaniel Curzon; *S* father, 1979; *m* 1st, 1948, Marilda (marr. diss. 1951), *d* of Major Pearson-Gregory, MC; one *d*; 2nd, 1953, Ann Helen Katharine, *e d* of Hugh Blair Brenan, OBE (formerly Asst Sec., Royal Hosp., Chelsea); two *s* one *d*. *Educ:* Ludgrove; Eton; New Coll., Oxford (BA Mod. Hist. 1949). Enlisted Grenadier Guards, 1943; Lieut 1945; Staff Captain and Instr, Sch. of Signals, Catterick, 1946; Signals Officer, Guards Trng Bn, 1946–47; R of O 1947. Sub-editor and Leader-writer, The Times, 1949–50; Archivist, St Paul's Cathedral, 1950; joined BBC, 1950: attached Home Talks, 1951; Producer, Overseas Talks, 1951–56; Asst, European Talks, 1956–58; Dep. Editor, The Listener, 1958–61; Man. Trng Organiser, 1961–66; Asst, Secretariat, 1966–72, Sen. Asst, 1972–74; Sec., Central Music Adv. Cttee, 1966–77, 1982–83; Special Asst (Public Affairs), 1974–77; Special Asst to Alasdair Milne, when Man. Dir, BBC TV, 1977–82; Chief Asst to Sec., BBC, 1982–83; Chief Asst to Dir of Progs, BBC TV, 1983–86; Research, Richard Cawston's documentary film, Royal Family, 1969; Secretary: Sims Cttee on portrayal of violence on TV, 1979, Wyatt Cttee revision 1983; Wenham Cttee on Subscription Television, 1980–81; Cotton Cttee on Sponsorship and BBC TV, 1981; British Deleg., Internat. Art-Historical Conf., Amsterdam, 1952; Salzburg Scholar in Amer. Studies, 1956. Associate, RHistS. Trustee, Kedleston, 1988–. *Recreation:* looking at pictures. *Heir:* *s* Nicolas Robert Hugh Cary [*b* 17 April 1955; *m* 1979, Pauline Jean, *d* of Dr Thomas Ian Boyd; three *s*]. *Address:* 36 Magnolia Road, Chiswick, W4 3QW. *Clubs:* Pratt's, First Guards; The Bushmen.

CASALE, Roger Mark; MP (Lab) Wimbledon, since 1997; *b* 22 May 1960; *s* of Edward Casale and Jean Casale (*née* Robins); *m* 1997, Fernanda Miucci; one *d*. *Educ:* King's Coll. Sch., Wimbledon; Hurstpierpoint Coll., Sussex (Scholar); Brasenose Coll., Oxford (BA Hons); Bologna Centre, Johns Hopkins Univ. (MA). Head, trng inst., Germany, 1986–92; Lectr in Politics, Greenwich Univ., 1994–97. Mem., Select Cttee on Eur. Legislation, 1997–; Chm., All Party British-Italian Gp, 1998–; Hon. Sec., PLP Foreign Affairs Cttee, 1999–. Hon. Pres., London and SE Direct Aid to Kosovo. Governor, Wimbledon Sch. of Art. *Recreation:* spending time with family and friends. *Address:* House of Commons, SW1A 0AA. *T:* (020) 7219 4565.

CASE, Anthea Fiendley, (Mrs D. C. Case); Director, National Heritage Memorial Fund (Heritage Lottery Fund), since 1995; *b* 7 Feb. 1945; *d* of Thomas Fiendley Stones and of late Bess Stones (*née* Mackie); *m* 1967, David Charles Case; two *d*. *Educ:* Christ's Hospital, Hertford; St Anne's Coll., Oxford (BA). HM Treasury: Asst Principal, 1966–70; Private Sec. to Financial Sec., 1970–71; Principal, 1971–79; Asst Sec., 1980–88; Under Sec., 1988–95 (with Fiscal Policy Gp, 1993–95); Asst Dir, Budget & Public Finances Directorate, 1995. *Address:* National Heritage Memorial Fund, 7 Holbein Place, SW1W 8NR. *T:* (020) 7591 6000.

CASE, Humphrey John; Keeper, Department of Antiquities, Ashmolean Museum, 1973–82; *b* 26 May 1918; *s* of George Reginald Case and Margaret Helen (*née* Duckett); *m* 1st, 1942, Margaret Adelia (*née* Eaton); 2nd, 1949, Jean Alison (*née* Orr); two *s*; 3rd, 1979, Jocelyn (*née* Herickx). *Educ:* Charterhouse; St John's Coll., Cambridge (MA); Inst. of Archaeology, London Univ. Served War, 1939–46. Ashmolean Museum: Asst Keeper, 1949–57; Sen. Asst Keeper, 1957–69; Dep. Keeper, Dept of Antiquities, 1969–73. Vice-Pres., Prehistoric Soc., 1969–73; has directed excavations in England, Ireland and France. FSA 1954. *Publications:* in learned jls (British and foreign): principally on neolithic in Western Europe, prehistoric metallurgy and regional archaeology. *Recreations:* drawing, reading, music, gardening. *Address:* Pitt's Cottage, 187 Thame Road, Warborough, Wallingford, Oxon OX10 7DH.

CASE, Janet Ruth; Her Honour Judge Case; a Circuit Judge, since 2001; *b* 29 June 1943; *d* of James and Cathleen Simpson; *m* 1965, Jeremy David Michael Case (marr. diss. 1982); one *s* one *d*. *Educ:* Univ. of Durham (LLB 1965). Called to the Bar, Inner Temple,

1975; barrister, Wales and Chester Circuit, 1975–2001; Chm., Med. Appeals Tribunals, 1988–96; a Recorder, 1995–2001. *Recreations:* gardening, opera, travel. *Address:* Croeswylan, Oswestry, Shropshire SY11 2AN. *T:* (01691) 653726. *Club:* Lansdowne.

CASE, Richard Ian, FREng, FRAeS; Managing Director, Agusta-Westland and Chairman, Westland Helicopters, since 2001; *b* 14 June 1945; *m* 1975, Denise Margaret Mills; one *s* one *d*. *Educ:* Cranfield Inst. of Technology (MSc Aircraft Propulsion). FRAeS 1985; FREng (FEng 1993). Technical Manager, Arab British Helicopters, Egypt, 1978–82; Westland Helicopters Ltd: Chief Designer, 1982–85; Engrg Dir, 1985–88; EH101 Project Dir and Engrg Dir, 1988–92; Man. Dir, 1992–95; Chief Exec., GKN Westland Helicopters Ltd, 1995–2001. RAeS Gold Medal, 1998. Cavaliere dell 'Ordine al Merito (Italy), 1995. *Recreations:* golf, opera. *Address:* Westland Helicopters Ltd, Lysander Road, Yeovil, Somerset BA20 2YB. *T:* (01935) 702505.

CASE, Stephen M.; Chairman, AOL Time Warner Inc., since 2001; *b* Honolulu, 21 Aug. 1958; *s* of Dan and Carol Case; *m* 1st, 1985, Joanne (marr. diss.); three *d*; 2nd; two *c*. *Educ:* Punahou Sch., Honolulu; Williams Coll., Mass. (BA Pol Sci. 1980). Marketing Dept, Procter & Gamble, 1980-82; Manager, new pizza develt, Pizza Hut Div., PepsiCo, 1982-83; joined Control Video Corp., 1983, co. renamed Quantum Computer Services, 1985, and became America Online, (AOL), 1991; CEO, 1991-2001, and Chm., 1995-2001, when merged with Time Warner. *Address:* AOL Time Warner Inc, 22000 AOL Way, Dulles, VA 20166-9302, USA.

CASEBOURNE, Michael Victor, CEng, FICE; Chief Executive and Secretary, Institution of Civil Engineers, 1999–2001; *b* 7 Oct. 1945; *s* of Eric Thomas Casebourne and Marjorie May Casebourne (*née* Chapman); *m* 1972, Margaret Dunlop; one *s* one *d*. *Educ:* Harrow Co. Grammar Sch.; Nottingham Univ. (BSc). CEng 1967; FICE 1984. With Costain Civil Engrg, 1967–73; Trafalgar House Construction, 1973–90 (Dir, 1984–90); Managing Director: Wimpey Engrg & Construction UK, 1990–96; GT Railway Maintenance, 1996–99. *Recreations:* sailing, motor boating. *Address:* The Boundary, Ballards Farm Road, S Croydon CR2 7JA.

CASEY, Derek Grant; international consultant; Chief Executive, Sport England (formerly English Sports Council), 1997–2001; *b* 19 Feb. 1950; *s* of Andrew Casey and Jean Grant. *Educ:* St Aloysius' Coll., Glasgow; Univ. of Glasgow (MA Hons). Dir of Ops, Scottish Sports Council, 1979–88; GB Sports Council: Dir of Nat. Services, 1988–93; Chief Exec., 1993–96. Chm., Cttee for Development of Sport, Council of Europe, 1993–95. Hon. DSc Southampton, 1996. *Publications:* contribs on sport, recreation and physical activity, to jls and periodicals. *Recreations:* walking, theatre, American literature. *Address:* 42/5 Barnton Park Avenue, Edinburgh EH4 3EY. *Club:* Royal Scottish Automobile (Glasgow).

CASEY, Most Rev. Eamonn, DD; RC Bishop of Galway and Kilmacduagh, 1976–92; Apostolic Administrator of Kilfenora, 1976–92; *b* Firies, Co. Kerry, 23 April 1927; *s* of late John Casey and late Helena (*née* Shanahan). *Educ:* St Munchin's Coll., Limerick; St Patrick's Coll., Maynooth. LPh 1946; BA 1947. Priest, 1951; Curate, St John's Cath., Limerick, 1951–60; Chaplain to Irish in Slough, 1960–63; set up social framework to re-establish people into new environment; started social welfare scheme; set up lodgings bureau and savings scheme; invited by Cardinal Heenan to place Catholic Housing Aid Soc. on national basis; founded Family Housing Assoc., 1964; Dir, British Council of Churches Housing Trust; Trustee, Housing the Homeless Central Fund; Founder-Trustee of Shelter (Chm. 1968); Mem. Council, Nat. Fedn of Housing Socs; Founder Mem., Marian Employment Agency; Founder Trustee, Shelter Housing Aid Soc., 1963–69; Bishop of Kerry, 1969–76. Missionary work, Ecuador, 1992–98. Exec. Chm., Trocaire, 1973–92; Mem. Bd, Siamsa Tire, Nat. Folk Th. of Ireland. Launched Meitheal, 1982; estab. Galway Adult Educn Centre, 1985, Galway Family Guidance Inst., 1986. Chm., Nat. Youth Resource Gp, 1979–86. Member: Commn for Social Welfare, 1971–74; Maynooth Coll. Exec. Council, 1974–84; Episcopal Commn for Univs, 1976–92; Governing Body, University Coll., Galway, 1976–92. *Publications:* (with Adam Ferguson) A Home of Your Own; Housing—A Parish Solution; contribs to journals, etc. *Recreations:* music, theatre, concerts, films when time, conversation, motoring. *Address:* Priest's House, Staplefield, Hayward's Heath, West Sussex RH16 6ET.

CASEY, Gavin Frank, FCA; Corporate Finance Consultant, PricewaterhouseCoopers, since 2001; *b* 18 Oct. 1946; *s* of Frank Frederick Casey and Diana Casey; *m* 1970, Lesley Riding; two *s* one *d*. Chartered Accountant, 1970; Harmood Banner & Co., 1965–70; Coopers & Lybrand, 1970–71; County Bank, later County NatWest, 1972–89; Smith New Court, later Merrill Lynch International, 1989–96; Chief Exec., London Stock Exchange plc, 1996–2000. Dir, Kinetic Inf. Systems Services Ltd, 2001–; Mem. Adv. Bd, Strathdon Investments Ltd, 2001–. Chm. of Treasurers, USPG, 1991–96. *Recreations:* theatre, horse racing, shooting. *Club:* City of London.

CASEY, Rt Hon. Sir Maurice (Eugene), Kt 1991; PC 1986; Judge of Court of Appeal of New Zealand, 1986–95; Judge of the Court of Appeal: Fiji, Samoa, and Cook Islands, since 1995; Niue, since 1996; Solomon Islands, since 1999; *b* 28 Aug. 1923; *s* of Eugene Casey and Beatrice (*née* Nolan); *m* 1948, Stella Katherine Wright (Dame Stella Casey, DBE; she *d* 2000); three *s* six *d*. *Educ:* St Patrick's Coll., Wellington; Victoria Univ. (LLM Hons). Served War, Naval Officer, 1943–45. Barrister and Solicitor, 1946; Vice Pres., Auckland Dist Law Soc., 1974; Judge, Supreme (later High) Court, 1974. Chm., Penal Policy Review Cttee, 1981. *Publications:* Hire Purchase Law in New Zealand, 1961; Garrow and Casey's Principles of the Law of Evidence, 8th edn 1996; (contrib.) Laws of New Zealand, 1999. *Address:* 5/144 Oriental Parade, Wellington, New Zealand. *T:* (4) 3843258. *Clubs:* Wellington; Northern (Auckland).

CASEY, Michael Bernard; Chairman, Michael Casey & Associates, 1993–2000; *b* 1 Sept. 1928; *s* of late Joseph Bernard Casey, OBE, and Dorothy (*née* Love); *m*; two *s* two *d*. *Educ:* Colwyn Bay Grammar Sch.; LSE (Scholar in Laws, 1952; LLB 1954). RAF, 1947–49. Principal, MAFF, 1961; Office of the Minister for Science, 1963–64; Asst Sec., DEA, 1967; DTI (later Dept of Prices and Consumer Protection), 1970; Under Sec., DoI, 1975–77; a Dep. Chm. and Chief Exec., British Shipbuilders, 1977–80; Chm. and Man. Dir, Mather & Platt, 1980–81; Chm., Sallingbury Casey Ltd, later Rowland Sallingbury Casey, 1982–92. *Recreations:* golf, chess, bridge. *Address:* Apartado Solbank, San Pedro de Alcantara, Málaga, Spain. *T:* (95) 2799029. *Club:* Reform.

CASEY, Michael Vince, OBE 1990; BSc(Eng); FREng, FIMechE; Chief Engineer, Channel Tunnel Rail Link, British Rail, 1989–90; *b* 25 May 1927; *s* of Charles John Casey and May Louise Casey; *m* 1954, Elinor Jane (*née* Harris) (*d* 1987); two *s* two *d*. *Educ:* Glossop Grammar Sch.; The College, Swindon. BSc(Eng) Hons London. Premium Apprentice, GWR Locomotive Works, Swindon, 1944–49; Univ. of London External Degree Course, 1949–52; British Rail Western Region: Locomotive Testing and Experimental Office, Swindon, 1952–58; Supplies and Contracts Dept, Swindon, 1958–61; Chief Mechanical and Electrical Engr's Dept, Paddington, 1961–63; Area Maintenance Engr, Old Oak Common, 1963–66; Chief Mech. and Elec. Engr's Dept, Paddington, 1966–71; Chief Mech. and Elec. Engineer: Scottish Region, Glasgow, 1971–76; Eastern Region, York, 1976–78; Engrg Dir, British Rail Engrg Ltd, 1978–82; Dir, Mechanical and Electrical Engrg, BRB, 1982–87; Project Dir (BR Engrg), 1987–89. FREng (FEng 1985). *Recreations:* gardening, philately. *Address:* Anakiwa, Wards Road, Chipping Norton, Oxon OX7 5BU. *T:* (01608) 642644.

CASEY, Dr Raymond, FRS 1970; retired; Senior Principal Scientific Officer (Special Merit), Institute of Geological Sciences, London, 1964–79; *b* 10 Oct. 1917; *s* of Samuel Gardiner Casey and Gladys Violet Helen Casey (*née* Garrett); *m* 1943, Norah Kathleen Pakeman (*d* 1974); two *s*. *Educ:* St Mary's, Folkestone; Univ. of Reading. PhD 1958; DSc 1963. Geological Survey and Museum: Asst 1939; Asst Exper. Officer 1946; Exper. Officer 1949; Sen. Geologist 1957; Principal Geologist 1960. *Publications:* A Monograph of the Ammonoidea of the Lower Greensand, 1960–80; (ed, with P. F. Rawson) The Boreal Lower Cretaceous, 1973; numerous articles on Mesozoic palaeontology and stratigraphy in scientific press. *Recreation:* research into early Russian postal and military history (Past Pres., British Soc. of Russian Philately). *Address:* 38 Reed Avenue, Orpington, Kent BR6 9RX. *T:* (01689) 851728.

CASH, Sir Gerald (Christopher), GCMG 1980; GCVO 1985 (KCVO 1977); OBE 1964; JP; Governor-General, Commonwealth of the Bahamas, 1979–88 (Acting Governor-General, 1976–79); Consultant Counsel, Cash, Fountain & Co., Nassau, since 1989; *b* Nassau, Bahamas, 28 May 1917; *s* of late Wilfred Gladstone Cash and of Lillian Cash; *m* Dorothy Eileen (*née* Long); two *s* one *d*. *Educ:* Govt High Sch., Nassau. Called to the Bar, Middle Temple, 1948. Counsel and Attorney, Supreme Court of Bahamas, 1940. Member: House of Assembly, Bahamas, 1949–62; Exec. Council, 1958–62; Senate, 1969–73 (Vice-Pres., 1970–72; Pres., 1972–73). Chm., Labour Bd, 1950–52. Member: Bd of Educn, 1950–62; Police Service Commn, 1964–69; Immigration Cttee, 1958–62; Road Traffic Cttee, 1958–62. Rep. Bahamas, Independence Celebrations of Jamaica, Trinidad and Tobago, 1962. Chairman: Vis. Cttee, Boys Indust. Sch., 1952–62; Bd of Governors, Govt High Sch., 1949–63 and 1965–76; Bahamas National Cttee, United World Colls, 1977–. Formerly: Hon. Vice-Consul for Republic of Haiti; Vice-Chancellor, Anglican Dio.; Admin. Adviser, Rotary Clubs in Bahamas to Pres. of Rotary Internat.; Treasurer and Dir, YMCA; Treas., Bahamas Cricket Assoc.; Chm., Boy Scouts Exec. Council; Mem. Board: Dirs of Central Bank of Bahamas; Dirs of Bahamas Assoc. for Mentally Retarded. Formerly: President: Rotary Club of E Nassau; Gym Tennis Club; Florida Tennis Assoc.; Bahamas Lawn Tennis Assoc.; Bahamas Table Tennis Assoc.; Vice-President: Boy Scouts Assoc.; Olympic Assoc., Amateur Athletic Assoc., Swimming Assoc., Football Assoc., Bahamas. JP Bahamas, 1940. Coronation Medal, 1953; Silver Jubilee Medal, 1977; Silver Medal, Olympic Order, 1983. *Recreations:* golf, tennis, table tennis, swimming. *Address:* 4 Bristol Street, PO Box N-476, Nassau, Bahamas. *T:* 3934767, 3932062. *Clubs:* Royal Commonwealth Society; Kingston Cricket (Jamaica); Lyford Cay, Gym Tennis (Nassau).

CASH, Prof. John David, CBE 1998; PhD; FRCP, FRCPE, FRCPath, FRCSE, FRCPGlas; National Medical and Scientific Director, Scottish National Blood Transfusion Service, 1988–96; *b* 3 April 1936; *s* of John Henry Cash and May Annie Cash (*née* Taylor); *m* 1962, Angela Mary Thomson; one *s* one *d*. *Educ:* Ashville College, Harrogate; Edinburgh Univ. (BSc 1959, MB ChB 1961, PhD 1967). FRCPE 1970; FRCPath 1986; FRCPGlas 1994; FRCSE 1995; FRCP 1997. Regional Transfusion Centre Dir, Edinburgh and SE Scotland, 1974–79; Nat. Med. Dir, Scottish Nat. Blood Transfusion Service, 1979–88. Pres., RCPE, 1994–97 (Vice-Pres., 1992–94); Pres., British Blood Transfusion Soc., 1997–99. Mem., Nat. Biol Standards Bd, 1997–. Hon. Prof., Edinburgh Univ., 1986. Governor, Fettes Coll., Edinburgh, 1988–. *Publication:* Progress in Transfusion Medicine, 1988. *Recreations:* fishing, gardening, golf. *Address:* 1 Otterburn Park, Edinburgh EH14 1JX.

CASH, William Nigel Paul; MP (C) Stone, since 1997 (Stafford, 1984–97); *b* 10 May 1940; *s* of Paul Trevor Cash, MC (killed in action Normandy, July 13, 1944) and Moyra Roberts (*née* Morrison); *m* 1965, Bridget Mary Lee; two *s* one *d*. *Educ:* Stonyhurst Coll.; Lincoln Coll., Oxford (MA History). Qualified as Solicitor, 1967; William Cash & Co. (constitutional and administrative lawyer), 1979–. Shadow Attorney-General, 2001–. Mem., Select Cttee on European Legislation, 1985–; Chairman: Cons. Backbench Cttee on European Affairs, 1989–91; All Party Cttee on E Africa, 1988–; All Party Gp, Jubilee 2000, 1997–; Jt Chm., All Party Jazz Gp, 1991–. Founder, and Chm., European Foundn, 1993–. Vice Pres., Cons. Small Business Bureau, 1986–. *Publications:* Against a Federal Europe—The Battle for Britain, 1991; Europe: the crunch, 1992. *Recreations:* history, cricket, jazz. *Address:* Upton Cressett Hall, near Bridgnorth, Shropshire WV16 6UH. *T:* (01746) 714307. *Clubs:* Carlton, Beefsteak; Vincent's (Oxford).

CASHEL AND EMLY, Archbishop of, (RC), since 1988; **Most Rev. Dermot Clifford,** DD; *b* 25 Jan. 1939. *Educ:* St Brendan's Coll., Killarney, Co. Kerry; St Patrick's Coll., Maynooth (BSc 1960); Irish Coll., Rome; Lateran Coll., Rome (STL 1964); NUI (HDipE 1966); LSE (MSc 1974); Loughborough (PhD 1989). Ordained priest, Rome, 1964; Dean of Studies, St Brendan's Coll., Killarney, 1964–72; Diocesan Sec., Kerry, 1974–86; Lectr, Univ. Coll., Cork, 1975–81; Chaplain, St Mary of the Angels Home for Handicapped Children, Beaufort, Co. Kerry, 1976–86; ordained Archbishop, Thurles, 1986; Coadjutor Archbishop of Cashel and Emly, 1986–88. Chm., Council for R&D of Irish Episcopal Commn, 1991–. Mem. Governing Body, NUI, Cork, 2000–. Trustee: Mary Immaculate Teachers' Trng Coll., Limerick, 1987–; Bothar, Third World Aid Orgn, 1991–. Patron, Gaelic Athletic Assoc., 1989–. *Publication:* The Social Costs and Rewards of Caring, 1990. *Recreations:* reading, walking, sport. *Address:* Archbishop's House, Thurles, Co. Tipperary, Ireland. *T:* (504) 21512, *Fax:* (504) 22680.

CASHEL AND OSSORY, Bishop of, since 1997; **Rt Rev. John Robert Winder Neill;** *b* 17 Dec. 1945; *s* of Eberto Mahon Neill and Rhoda Anne Georgina Neill; *m* 1968, Betty Anne (*née* Cox); three *s*. *Educ:* Sandford Park School, Dublin; Trinity Coll., Dublin (Foundation Schol., BA 1st Cl., MA); Jesus Coll., Cambridge (MA, Gardiner Memorial Schol., Univ. of Cambridge); Ridley Hall, Cambridge (GOE). Curate Asst, St Paul's, Glenageary, Dublin, 1969–71; Lectr (Old Testament) in Divinity Hostel, 1970–71; Bishop's Vicar and Dio. Registrar, Kilkenny, 1971–74; Rector of Abbeystrewry, Skibbereen, Co. Cork, 1974–78; Rector of St Bartholomew's, and Leeson Park, Dublin, 1978–84; Lectr (Liturgy) in Theological Coll., 1982–84; Exam. Chaplain to Archbishop of Dublin, 1982–84; Dean of Christ Church Cathedral, Waterford, 1984–86; Archdeacon of Waterford, 1984–86; Bishop of Tuam, Killala and Achonry, 1986–97. Sec., Irish House of Bishops, 1988–95; Mem., Central Cttee, WCC, 1994–; Pres., CTBI, 1999–. *Publications:* contribs to Theology, New Divinity, Search, Doctrine and Life and Intercom. *Recreations:* photography, travel. *Address:* The Palace, Kilkenny, Ireland. *T:* (56) 21560, *Fax:* (56) 64399; *e-mail:* bishop@cashel.anglican.org.

CASHMAN, John Prescott; Under-Secretary, Department of Health (formerly of Health and Social Security), 1973–88; *b* 19 May 1930; *s* of late John Patrick Cashman and late Mary Cashman (*née* Prescott). *Educ:* Balliol Coll., Oxford (MA (English Lang. and Lit.)). Army (Intell. Corps), 1948–49. Entered Min. of Health, 1951; Principal 1957; Private Sec.

to Minister, 1962–65; Asst Sec. 1965; Nuffield Foundn Trav. Fellow, 1968–69; Private Sec. to Sec. of State, 1969. Trustee, Macfarlane Trust, 1989–97; Dir, Bd, Hospital Saving Assoc., 1999–2000 (Mem. Exec. Council, 1989–99). *Address:* 3 Paul Gardens, Croydon, Surrey CR0 5QL. *T:* (020) 8681 6578.

CASHMAN, Michael Maurice; Member (Lab) West Midlands Region, European Parliament, since 1999; *b* 17 Dec. 1950; *s* of John Cashman and Mary Cashman (*née* Clayton); partner, Paul Cottingham. *Educ:* St Mary's and St Joseph's Primary Sch.; Cardinal Griffin Secondary Modern Sch., London; Gladys Dare's Sch., Surrey; Borlands Tutorial, London. Actor, director and playwright, 1963–99; work includes: actor: *stage:* Oliver, Albery, 1963; Bent, RNT, 1990, transf. Garrick; Noises Off, Mobil Touring Theatre, nat. tour, 1995; Merchant of Venice, and Gypsy, W Yorks Playhouse, 1996; The Tempest, internat. tour, 1997; *television:* Eastenders, 1986–89; director: Kiss of the Spiderwoman, New Victoria Th., Newcastle-under-Lyme, 1998; playwright: Before your very Eyes; Bricks 'n' Mortar. Mem. Council and Hon. Treas., Equity, 1994–98; Mem., Labour Party NEC, 1998–2000 and 2001–. Founding Chm., Stonewall Gp, 1988–96. FRSA 1996. Special Service Award, Amer. Assoc. Physicians for Human Rights and Gay Med. Assoc., 1988. *Recreations:* travel, writing, photography, theatre. *Address:* (constituency office) 67 Birmingham Road, Bromwich B70 6PY. *T:* (0121) 553 6642.

CASHMORE, Prof. Roger John, DPhil; FRS 1998; FInstP; Research Director for Collider Programmes, CERN, since 1999; Professor of Experimental Physics, University of Oxford, since 1991 (on leave); *b* 22 Aug. 1944; *e s* of C. J. C. and E. M. Cashmore; *m* 1971, Elizabeth Ann, *d* of Rev. S. J. C. Lindsay; one *s*. *Educ:* Dudley Grammar Sch.; St John's Coll., Cambridge (schol.; BA 1965; MA); Balliol Coll., Oxford (DPhil 1969). FInstP 1985. Weir Jun. Res. Fellow, University Coll., Oxford, 1967–69; 1851 Res. Fellow, 1968; Res. Associate, Stanford Linear Accelerator Centre, Calif, 1969–74; Oxford University: Res. Officer, 1974–79; Lectr, Christ Church, 1976–78; Fellow, Balliol Coll., 1979–; Sen. Res. Fellow, Merton Coll., 1977–79; Tutor, Balliol Coll., and Univ. Lectr in Physics, 1979–90; Reader in Experimental Physics, 1990–91; Chm. of Physics, 1996–98. SERC Sen. Res. Fellow, 1982–87; Vis. Prof., Vrije Univ., Brussels, 1982; Guest Scientist, Fermilab, Chicago, 1986. Mem., policy and prog. cttees, CERN, Deutsches Electronen-Synchrotron, Hamburg, and SERC. Gov., Ludlow Coll., 1995–98. MAE 1992. FRSA 1996. C.V. Boys Prize, Inst. of Physics, 1983; Humboldt Res. Award, Alexander Von Humboldt Stiftung, 1995. *Publications:* contrib. Nuclear Physics, Physics Letters, Phys. Rev., Phys. Rev. Letters. *Recreations:* sports, wine. *Address:* CERN, 1211 Geneva 23, Switzerland.

CASIDA, John Edward, PhD; William Muriece Hoskins Professor of Chemical and Molecular Entomology, University of California at Berkeley, since 1996; *b* 22 Dec. 1929; *s* of Lester Earl Casida and Ruth Casida (*née* Barnes); *m* 1956, Katherine Faustine Monson; two *s*. *Educ:* Univ. of Wisconsin (BS 1951; MS 1952; PhD 1954). Served USAF, 1953. University of Wisconsin: Res. Asst, 1951–53; Mem. Faculty, 1954–63; Prof. of Entomology, 1959–63; University of California at Berkeley: Prof. of Entomology, 1964–; Dir, Envmtl Chemistry and Toxicology Lab., 1964–; Faculty Res. Lectr, 1998. Schol.-in-Res., Bellagio Study and Conf. Centre, Rockefeller Foundn, Lake Como, 1978; Sterling B. Hendricks Lectr, US Dept of Agric., and ACS, 1992–. Mem., US Nat. Acad. of Sci., 1991; Foreign Mem., Royal Soc., 1998. Wolf Prize in Agriculture, 1993; Founder's Award, Soc. Envmt, Toxicology and Chemistry, 1994; Kôrô-sho Prize, Pesticide Sci. Soc., Japan, 1995. *Address:* (home) 1570 La Vereda Road, Berkeley, CA 94708-2036, USA; (office) University of California, Department of Environment Science Policy Management, Wellman Hall, Berkeley, CA 94720-3112, USA.

CASKEN, Prof. John, DMus; composer; Professor of Music, University of Manchester, since 1992; *b* 15 July 1949. *Educ:* Birmingham Univ. (BMus, MA); DMus Durham, 1992. FRNCM 1996. Polish Govt Scholarship, Warsaw, 1971–72. Lectr, Birmingham Univ., 1973–79; Res. Fellow, Huddersfield Poly., 1980–81; Lectr, Durham Univ., 1981–92. Northern Electric Performing Arts Award, 1990. *Compositions include: orchestral:* Tableaux des Trois Ages, 1977; Masque, 1982; Orion over Farne, 1984; Maharal Dreaming, 1989; Cello Concerto, 1991; Still Mine (for baritone and orch.), 1992 (Prix de Composition Musicale, Prince Pierre de Monaco, 1993); Darting the Skiff, 1993; Violin Concerto, 1995; Sortilège, 1996; Distant Variations (for saxophone quartet and wind orchestra), 1997; *ensemble and instrumental:* Amarantos, 1978; Firewhirl (for soprano and ensemble), 1980; String Quartet No 1, 1982; Vaganza, 1985; Salamandra, 1986; Piano Quartet, 1990; String Quartet No 2, 1994; Infanta Marina, 1994; Après un silence, 1998; *vocal and choral:* Ia Orana Gauguin, 1978; To Fields We Do Not Know, 1984; Sharp Thorne, 1992; *opera:* Golem, 1988 (first Britten Award, 1990; Gramophone Award for best contemp. recording, 1991); God's Liar, 2000; *electronic:* Piper's Linn, 1984. *Address:* Department of Music, University of Manchester, Denmark Road, Manchester M15 6HY; *e-mail:* John.Casken@man.ac.uk.

CASLEY, Henry Roberts; non-executive Director, Scottish and Southern Energy plc, since 1998; *s* of Benjamin Rowe Casley and May Casley; *m* 1960, Sheila Laity; one *s* one *d*. MCIM. Eastern Electricity: Energy Mkting Manager, 1975–78; Supplies Manager, 1978–82; Mkting Dir, 1982–86; Southern Electric plc: Dep. Chm., 1986–89; Man. Dir, 1989–93; Chief Exec., 1993–96; non-exec. Dir, 1996–98. *Recreations:* sport, gardening. *Address:* Scottish and Southern Energy plc, 200 Dunkeld Road, Perth PH1 3AQ. *Club:* Phyllis Court (Henley-on-Thames).

CASS, Edward Geoffrey, CB 1974; OBE 1951; Alternate Governor, Reserve Bank of Rhodesia, 1978–79; *b* 10 Sept. 1916; *s* of Edward Charles and Florence Mary Cass; *m* 1941, Ruth Mary Powley; four *d*. *Educ:* St Olave's; Univ. Coll., London (Scholar); BSc (Econ.) London (1st Cl.) 1937; The Queen's Coll., Oxford (Scholar); George Webb Medley Scholarship, 1938; BA Oxon (1st Cl. PPE) 1939, MA 1987. Lecturer in Economics, New Coll., Oxford, 1939. From 1940 served in Min. of Supply, Treasury, Air Ministry, MoD; Private Sec. to the Prime Minister, 1949–52; Chief Statistician, Min. of Supply, 1952; Private Sec. to Min. of Supply, 1954; Imperial Defence Coll., 1958; Asst Under-Sec. of State (Programmes and Budget), MoD, 1965–72; Dep. Under-Sec. of State (Finance and Budget), MoD, 1972–76. Mem., Review Bd for Govt Contracts, 1977–84; Chm., Verbatim Reporting Study Gp, 1977–79. *Address:* 60 Rotherwick Road, NW11 7DB. *T:* (020) 8455 1664.

CASS, Sir Geoffrey (Arthur), Kt 1992; MA; CIMgt; Chairman: Royal Shakespeare Company, 1985–2000; Royal Shakespeare Theatre Trust, since 1983; President, and Chairman of the Council, Lawn Tennis Association, 1997–99; Chief Executive, Cambridge University Press, 1972–92; Fellow of Clare Hall, Cambridge, since 1979; *b* 11 Aug. 1932; *o c* of late Arthur Cass and Jessie Cass (*née* Simpson), Darlington and Oxford; *m* 1957, Olwen Mary, *o c* of late William Leslie Richards and of Edith Louisa Richards, Llanelli and Brecon; four *d*. *Educ:* Queen Elizabeth Grammar Sch., Darlington (Head of Sch.); Jesus Coll., Nuffield Coll., and Dept of Social and Admin. Studies, Oxford Univ. (BA 1954; MA 1958; Hon. Fellow, Jesus Coll., 1998); MA Cantab, 1972. FInstD 1968; FIWM, FIIM 1979; CIMgt (CBIM 1980). Commnd RAFVR, fighter control, 1954; served RAF, 1958–60: Air Min. Directorate of Work Study; Pilot Officer, 1958; Flying Officer, 1960. Consultant: PA Management Consultants Ltd, 1960–65; British Communications Corp., and Controls and Communications Ltd, 1965; Dir, Controls and Communications Ltd, 1966–69; Managing Director, George Allen and Unwin Ltd, 1967–71; Cambridge University Press: Sec., Press Syndicate, 1974–92; Univ. Printer, 1982–83, 1991–92; Consultant, 1992–; Director: Weidenfeld (Publishers) Ltd, 1972–74; Chicago Univ. Press (UK), 1971–86; Mem., Jesus Coll., Cambridge, 1972–. Member: Univ. of Cambridge Cttee of Management of Fenner's (and Exec. Cttee), 1976–; Univ. of Cambridge Careers Service Syndicate (formerly Appts Bd), 1977– (Exec. Cttee, 1982–); Governing Syndicate, Fitzwilliam Mus., Cambridge, 1977–78; Chm. Governors, Perse Sch. for Girls, Cambridge, 1978–88 (Governor, 1977–); Trustee, Univ. of Cambridge Foundn, 1998–; Chm., Univ. of Cambridge ADC Theatre Appeal, 2000–. Founder Mem. Council, Royal Shakespeare Theatre Trust, 1967–; Gov., 1975–, Dep. Pres., 2000–, RSC (Mem., Council, 1975–2000; Mem., 1976–2000, Chm. 1982–2000, Exec. Cttee, Council); Trustee and Guardian, Shakespeare Birthplace Trust, 1982– (Life Trustee, 1994); Founder Mem., Inigo Productions, 1996. Director: Newcastle Theatre Royal Trust, 1984–89; American Friends of the Royal Shakespeare Theatre, 1985–2000; Method & Madness (formerly Cambridge Theatre Co.), 1986–95; Theatres Trust, 1991–2000; Marc Sinden Productions. Pres., Macmillan Cancer Relief Cambs and Peterborough Project, 1998–. The All England LTC (Wimbledon) Ltd, 1997–2000; The All England Lawn Tennis Ground PLC, 1997–2000. Cambridgeshire LTA: Mem. Exec., 1974–84; Chm., F and GP Cttee 1982–84; Captain 1974–78; Pres., 1980–82; Hon. Life Vice-Pres., 1982–; The Lawn Tennis Association of GB: Dep. Pres., 1994–96; Member: Council, 1976–; Management Bd, 1985–90, 1993–2000; Nat. Trng and Internat. Match Cttee (Davis Cup, Fedn Cup, Wightman Cup, etc), 1982–90, 1992–93 (Chm., 1985–90); Internat. Events Cttee, 1991–93; Chm., Nat. Ranking Cttee, 1990–99; Wimbledon Championships: Member: Cttee of Management, 1990–; Jt Finance Bd, 1989–93; Jt Finance Cttee, 1993– (Chm., 1997–99); British Jun. Championships Cttee of Management, 1983–90 (Chm., 1985–90); Nat. Championships Cttee of Management, 1988–89; Rules and Internat. Cttee, 1980–81; Re-orgn Wkg Party, 1984–85; Chm., Reconstruction Wkg Gp, 1994–99. Tennis singles champion: Durham County, 1951; Cambridgeshire, 1976; Oxford University: tennis Blue, 1953, 1954, 1955 (Sec., 1955); badminton, 1951, 1952 (Captain, 1952); Chm., Cambridge Univ. Lawn Tennis Club, 1977– (Hon. Cambridge tennis Blue, 1980); played in Wimbledon Championships, 1954, 1955, 1956, 1959; played in inter-county lawn tennis championships for Durham County, then for Cambridgeshire, 1952–82; represented RAF, 1958–59; Brit. Veterans (over 45) singles champion, Wimbledon, 1978; Mem., Brit. Veterans' Internat. Dubler Cup Team, Barcelona, 1978, Milano Marittima, 1979 (Captain). FRSA 1991. Chevalier, Ordre des Arts et des Lettres (France), 1982. *Recreations:* lawn tennis, theatre. *Address:* Middlefield, Huntingdon Road, Cambridge CB3 0LH. *Clubs:* Hurlingham, Institute of Directors, All England Lawn Tennis and Croquet (Hon.), Queen's (Hon.), International Lawn Tennis of GB, The 45 (Hon.), Veterans' Lawn Tennis of GB; Hawks (Cambridge); Cambridge University Lawn Tennis; West Hants Lawn Tennis (Hon.).

CASS, John, QPM 1979; National Co-ordinator of Regional Crime Squads, 1981–84; Security Consultant; *b* 24 June 1925; *m* 1948, Dilys Margaret Hughes, SRN; three *d*. *Educ:* Nelson Sch., Wigton, Cumbria; UCW, Lampeter (DipTh 1997; BA Hons (Theol.) 1999). Served no 40 RM Commando, 1944–45. Joined Metropolitan Police, 1946; Comdt, Detective Training Sch., Hendon, 1974; Commander: CID, New Scotland Yard, 1975; Complaints Bureau, 1978; Serious Crime Squads, New Scotland Yard, 1980. UK Rep., Interpol Conf. on crime prediction, Paris, 1976. Student in Criminology, Cambridge Univ., 1966. Adviser, Police Staff Coll., on multi-Force major investigations, 1982–83; Chief Investigator, War Crimes Inquiry, Home Office, 1988–89. Mem., British Acad. of Forensic Scis, 1965. Member: Association of Chief Police Officers; Metropolitan Police Commanders' Assoc.; Internat. Police Assoc. Lay preacher. Mem., Lampeter Soc. Freeman, City of London, 1979. *Recreations:* Lakeland, walking, wild life; and Janet (BA), Anne (BDS), Sarah (LLB), James (MB BS), Gwilym, Bryn, Elizabeth, Ieuan Jack and Catherine Olivia. *Address:* Bryn Eryl, Peniel, Carmarthenshire SA32 7HT. *T:* (01267) 236948, *T:* (020) 8521 1580. *Club:* Special Forces.

CASSANI, Barbara Ann; Chief Executive Officer, Go Fly Ltd, since 1997; *b* 22 July 1960; *d* of James and Noreen Cassani; *m* 1985, Guy Davis; one *s* one *d*. *Educ:* Mount Holyoke Coll., USA (BA Hons *magna cum laude* Internat. Relns); Woodrow Wilson Sch. of Public and Internat. Affairs, Princeton Univ. (MPA). Mgt Consultant, Coopers & Lybrand, in Washington and London, 1984–87; various mgt rôles with British Airways in UK and USA, 1987–97. *Recreations:* reading, horse-riding, travel. *Address:* Go Fly Ltd, Stansted Airport, Essex CM24 1SB. *T:* (01279) 666303.

CASSAR, Francis Felix Anthony; Director, Omnirace Ltd, 1990–2000; *b* 10 May 1934; *s* of Carmelo and Filomena Cassar; *m* 1969, Doreen Marjorie; two *s*. *Educ:* Primary Sch., Malta; Lyceum, Malta. Emigrated to UK, 1953. Studied mech. engrg, 1953–58; Man. Dir of own motor engrg co., 1959–74; Co. Sec., Malta Drydocks (UK) Ltd, 1975–80. Represented Malta Labour Party in the UK, also at meetings of the Bureau of the Socialist International, 1960–80; Acting High Comr for Malta in London and Cyprus, 1981–85, High Comr, 1985–87; Chargé d'Affaires, Baghdad, 1988–90. Administrator, St Mark's Res. Foundn, 1991–; Financial Controller, St Mark's Educnl Trust, 1995–. Mem., Inst of Management, 1977. JP: Brentford and Ealing, Tottenham, 1972–80; Enfield, 1990. *Recreations:* music, football, DIY, cooking.

CASSEL, family name of **Baroness Mallalieu**.

CASSEL, Sir Timothy Felix Harold, 4th Bt *cr* 1920; QC 1988; *b* 30 April 1942; *s* of Sir Harold Cassel, 3rd Bt, TD, QC; *S* father, 2001; *m* 1st, 1971, Jenifer Puckle (marr. diss. 1976); one *s* one *d*; 2nd, 1979, Ann Mallalieu (*see* Baroness Mallalieu); two *d*. *Educ:* Eton College. Called to the Bar, Lincoln's Inn, 1965, Bencher, 1994; Jun. Prosecuting Counsel at Central Criminal Court, 1978, Sen. Prosecuting Counsel, 1986–88; Asst Boundaries Comr, 1979–85. *Heir: s* Alexander James Felix Cassel, *b* 25 May 1974. *Address:* Studdridge Farm, Stokenchurch, Bucks HP14 3XS. *T:* (01494) 482303. *Clubs:* Garrick, Turf.

CASSELL, Frank, CB 1987; Chairman, Crown Agents Pension Scheme, since 1997 (Member, Board of Crown Agents, 1991–97); Economic Minister, Washington, and UK Executive Director, International Monetary Fund and World Bank, 1988–90; *b* 21 August 1930; *s* of Francis Joseph Cassell and Ellen Blanche Cassell (*née* Adams); *m* 1957, Jean Seabrook; two *s* one *d*. *Educ:* Borden Grammar School; LSE (BSc Econ). Asst City Editor, News Chronicle, 1953–58; Dep. Editor, The Banker, 1958–65; HM Treasury: Economic Adviser, 1965; Senior Economic Adviser, 1968; Under Sec., 1974; Deputy Sec., 1983–88. Chm., Stats Cttee, Internat. Financial Services, London, 1994–. Vis. Scholar, Federal Reserve Bank of Minneapolis, 1970. *Publications:* Gold or Credit?, 1965; articles on economic policy, 1953–65. *Recreations:* walking, watching cricket, reading history. *Address:* Crown Agents, St Nicholas House, Sutton, Surrey SM1 1EL.

CASSELL, Michael Robert; writer; *b* 2 June 1946; *s* of Donald and Joyce Cassell; *m* 1995, Linda Radway. *Educ:* Lode Heath High Sch.; Solihull Coll. Reporter, W Midlands Press, 1964–67; Business Reporter, Birmingham Post, 1967–69; City Reporter, Daily Express,

1969–70; Financial Times, 1970–2000: successively Property, Political, Industry, and Business Correspondent; Ed., Observer column, 1996–2000. *Publications:* One Hundred Years of Co-operation, 1984; Readymixers, 1986; Dig it, Burn it, Sell it!, 1990; Long Lease, 1991. *Recreations:* horse riding, walking, watercolours. *Address:* Gunridge House, Clunton, Shropshire SY7 0HX.

CASSELS, Sir John (Seton), Kt 1988; CB 1978; Chairman, UK SKILLS, 1990–2000; *b* 10 Oct. 1928; *s* of Alastair Macdonald Cassels and Ada White Cassels (*née* Scott); *m* 1956, Mary Whittington; two *s* two *d.* *Educ:* Sedbergh Sch., Yorkshire; Trinity Coll., Cambridge (1st cl. Hons, Classics, 1951). Rome Scholar, Classical Archaeology, 1952–54. Entered Ministry of Labour, 1954; Secretary of the Royal Commission on Trade Unions and Employers' Associations, 1965–68; Under-Sec., NBPI, 1968–71; Managing Directors' Office, Dunlop Holdings Ltd, 1971–72; Chief Exec., Training Services Agency, 1972–75; Dir, Manpower Services Commn, 1975–81; Second Permanent Sec., MPO, 1981–83; Dir Gen., NEDO, 1983–88. Dir, Nat. Commn on Educn, 1991–97. Chm., Ind. Inquiry into the Role and Responsibilities of the Police, 1994–96. Member Council: Inst. of Manpower Studies, subseq. Inst. of Employment Studies, 1982– (Pres., 1989–95); Policy Studies Inst., 1983–88; Industrial Soc., 1984–93; Assoc. for Consumer Res., 1989–94; NIESR, 1993–. Chm., Internat. Comparisons in Criminal Justice, 1990–95; Mem., Prince's Trust Volunteers Mgt Adv. Bd, 1998–; Chairman: Sussex Careers Services, 1995–98; Modern Apprenticeship Adv. Cttee, Dept for Educn and Skills (formerly DfEE). Non-exec. Dir, Ealing HA, 1990–91. Chm., Richmond Adult and Community Coll., 1996–2001. Dist. Vis. Fellow, 1989, Sen. Fellow, 1990, PSI. FIPD; FRSA. Hon. Dr: Sussex, 1995; Heriot-Watt, 1996; Brunel, 1997; Companion, De Montfort Univ., 1995. Hon. CGIA 1989. *Publication:* Britain's Real Skill Shortage—and what to do about it, 1990. *Address:* 10 Beverley Road, Barnes, SW13 0LX. *T:* (020) 8876 6270; UK SKILLS, 18 Park Square East, NW1 4LH. *T:* (020) 7543 7488. *Club:* Reform.

CASSELS, Prof. John William Scott, FRS 1963; FRSE 1981; MA, PhD; Sadleirian Professor of Pure Mathematics, Cambridge University, 1967–84; Head of Department of Pure Mathematics and Mathematical Statistics, 1969–84; *b* 11 July 1922; *s* of late J. W. Cassels (latterly Dir of Agriculture in Co. Durham) and late Mrs M. S. Cassels (*née* Lobjoit); *m* 1949, Constance Mabel Merritt (*née* Senior) (*d* 2000); one *s* one *d.* *Educ:* Neville's Cross Council Sch., Durham; George Heriot's Sch., Edinburgh; Edinburgh and Cambridge Univs. MA Edinburgh, 1943; PhD Cantab, 1949. Fellow, Trinity, 1949–; Lecturer, Manchester Univ., 1949; Lecturer, Cambridge Univ., 1950; Reader in Arithmetic, 1963–67. Mem. Council, Royal Society, 1970, 1971 (Sylvester Medal, 1973); Vice Pres., 1974–78, Mem. Exec., 1978–82, Internat. Mathematical Union; Pres., London Mathematical Soc., 1976–78. Dr (*hc*) Lille Univ., 1965; Hon. ScD Edinburgh, 1977. De Morgan Medal, London Mathematical Soc., 1986. *Publications:* An Introduction to Diophantine Approximation, 1957; An Introduction to the Geometry of Numbers, 1959; Rational Quadratic Forms, 1978; Economics for Mathematicians, 1981; Local Fields, 1986; Lectures on Elliptic Curves, 1991; (with E. V. Flynn) Prolegomena to a Middlebrow Arithmetic of Curves of Genus 2, 1996; papers in diverse mathematical journals on arithmetical topics. *Recreations:* arithmetic (higher only), gardening (especially common vegetables). *Address:* 3 Luard Close, Cambridge CB2 2PL. *T:* (01223) 246108.

CASSELS, Adm. Sir Simon (Alastair Cassillis), KCB 1982; CBE 1976; *b* 5 March 1928; *o s* of late Comdr A. G. Cassels, RN, and Clarissa Cassels (*née* Motion); *m* 1962, Jillian Francies Kannreuther; one *s* one *d.* *Educ:* RNC, Dartmouth. Midshipman 1945; Commanding Officer: HM Ships Vigilant, Roebuck, and Tenby, 1962–63; HMS Eskimo, 1966–67; HMS Fearless, 1972–73; Principal Staff Officer to CDS, 1973–76; CO HMS Tiger, 1976–78; Asst Chief of Naval Staff (Op. Requirements), 1978–80; Flag Officer, Plymouth, Port Adm. Devonport, Comdr Central Sub Area Eastern Atlantic and Comdr Plymouth Sub Area Channel, 1981–82; Second Sea Lord, Chief of Naval Personnel and Adm. Pres., RNC, Greenwich, 1982–86. Dir Gen., TSB Foundn for Eng. and Wales, 1986–90. Younger Brother of Trinity House, 1963. Pres., Regular Forces Employment Assoc., 1990–93 (Chm., 1989). Freeman, City of London, 1983; Liveryman, Shipwrights' Co., 1984. FRGS 1947. *Publication:* Peninsular Portrait 1811–1814, 1963. *Recreations:* archaeology, historical research, water colours. *Address:* c/o Lloyds TSB, Bishop's Waltham, Southampton SO32 1GS. *Club:* Army and Navy.

CASSELTON, Prof. Lorna Ann, (Mrs W. J. D. Tollett), PhD, DSc; FRS 1999; Professor of Fungal Genetics, University of Oxford, since 1997; Fellow, St Cross College, Oxford, since 1993; *b* 18 July 1938; *d* of William Charles Henry Smith and Cecille Smith (*née* Bowman); *m* 1st, 1961, Peter John Casselton (marr. diss. 1978); 2nd, 1981, William Joseph Dennis Tollett. *Educ:* Southend High Sch. for Girls; University Coll. London (BSc; PhD 1964; DSc 1993); MA Oxon. Royal Commn for Exhibn of 1851 Sen. Student, 1963–65; Asst Lectr, RHC, 1966–67; Lectr, 1967–76, Reader, 1976–89, QMC; Prof. of Genetics, QMW, 1989–91; AFRC/BBSRC Postdoctoral Fellow, 1991–95, BBSRC Sen. Res. Fellow, 1995–2001, Univ. of Oxford. Vis. Prof. of Genetics, QMW, 1997–. Hon. Fellow, St Hilda's Coll., Oxford, 2000. *Publications:* numerous res. and rev. articles. *Recreations:* reading, classical music, dancing. *Address:* 83 St Bernard's Road, Oxford OX2 6EJ. *T:* (01865) 559997.

CASSEN, Prof. Robert Harvey; Visiting Professor, London School of Economics, since 1997; Professor of the Economics of Development, Queen Elizabeth House, International Development Centre, University of Oxford, 1986–97, and Professorial Fellow, St Antony's College, 1986–97, now Emeritus; *b* 24 March 1935; *s* of John and Liliane Cassen; *m* 1988, Sun Shuyun. *Educ:* Bedford School; New Coll., Oxford (BA LitHum, MA); Univ. of California, Berkeley; Harvard (PhD Econ). Dept of Economics, LSE, 1961–69; Sen. Economist, ODM, 1966–67; First Sec. (Econ.), New Delhi, 1967–68; Sen. Economist, World Bank, Washington, 1969–72 and 1980–81; Fellow, Inst. of Develt Studies, Sussex Univ., 1972–86; Sen. Res. Fellow, Centre for Population Studies, LSHTM, 1976–77; Dir, Queen Elizabeth House, Internat. Develt Centre, Oxford Univ., 1986–93. Special Adviser, H of C Select Cttee on Overseas Develt, 1973–74; Secretariat, Brandt Commn, 1978–79 and 1981–82; Mem., Bd of Trustees, Population Council, NY, 1978–87; UK Mem., UN Cttee for Develt Planning, 1982–84. *Publications:* India: Population, Economy, Society, 1978; (ed and contrib.) Planning for Growing Populations, 1979; (ed and contrib.) World Development Report, 1981; (ed and contrib.) Rich Country Interests and Third World Development, 1982; (ed) Soviet Interests in the Third World, 1985; Does Aid Work? (report), 1986, 2nd edn 1994; (ed) Poverty in India, 1992; (ed and contrib.) Population and Development: old debates, new conclusions, 1994; (ed) India: the future of economic reform, 1995; contribs to learned jls. *Recreations:* music, walking. *Address:* LSE, Houghton Street, WC2A 2AE. *T:* (020) 7955 6352.

CASSIDI, Adm. Sir (Arthur) Desmond, GCB 1983 (KCB 1978); President, Royal Naval Association, 1987–96; Deputy Grand President, British Commonwealth Ex-Services League, 1986–96; *b* 26 Jan. 1925; *s* of late Comdr Robert A. Cassidi, RN and late Clare F. (*née* Alexander); *m* 1st, 1950, Dorothy Sheelagh Marie (*née* Scott) (*d* 1974); one *s* two *d*; 2nd, 1982, Dr Deborah Marion Pollock (*née* Bliss), FRCS. *Educ:* RNC Dartmouth. Qual. Pilot, 1946; CO, 820 Sqdn (Gannet aircraft), 1955; 1st Lieut HMS Protector, 1955–56; psc 1957; CO, HMS Whitby, 1959–61; Fleet Ops Officer Home Fleet, 1962–64; Asst Dir Naval Plans, 1964–67; Captain (D) Portland and CO HMS Undaunted, 1967–68; idc 1969; Dir of Naval Plans, 1970–72; CO, HMS Ark Royal, 1972–73; Flag Officer Carriers and Amphibious Ships, 1974–75; Dir-Gen., Naval Manpower and Training, 1975–77; Flag Officer, Naval Air Command, 1978–79; Chief of Naval Personnel and Second Sea Lord, 1979–82; C-in-C Naval Home Comd, 1982–85; Flag ADC to the Queen, 1982–85. Mem. Adv. Council, Science Museum, 1979–84, Trustee, 1984–92; Pres., FAA Museum, 1985–95. FRSA 1986. *Recreation:* country pursuits. *Address:* c/o Barclays Bank, 2 Victoria Street, SW1H 0ND.

CASSIDY, Bryan Michael Deece; *b* 17 Feb. 1934; *s* of late William Francis Deece Cassidy and Kathleen Selina Patricia Cassidy (*née* Geraghty); *m* 1960, Gillian Mary Isobel Bohane; one *s* two *d.* *Educ:* Ratcliffe College; Sidney Sussex College, Cambridge. MA (Law). Commissioned RA, 1955–57 (Malta and Libya); HAC, 1957–62. With Ever Ready, Beecham's and Reed International (Dir, European associates). Mem. Council, CBI, 1981–84. Dir Gen., of a trade assoc., 1981–84. Contested (C) Wandsworth Central, 1966; Mem. GLC (Hendon North), 1977–86 (opposition spokesman on industry and employment, 1983–84). MEP (C), Dorset E and Hampshire W, 1984–94, Dorset and E Devon, 1994–99; contested (C) SW Reg., 1999. Vis. Woodrow Wilson Fellow, American Univs, 2000. Dir of Studies, Hawksmere Brussels Brielinge, 2001. *Publication:* Hawksmere European Lobbying Guide, 2000. *Recreations:* history, country sports, theatre. *Address:* 11 Esmond Court, Thackeray Street, W8 5HB. *T:* (020) 7937 3558, *Fax:* (020) 7937 3789; *e-mail:* bcassidy@europundit.co.uk.

CASSIDY, His Eminence Cardinal Edward; *see* Cassidy, His Eminence Cardinal I. E.

CASSIDY, Elizabeth Grace; Command Secretary to Second Sea Lord and Commander-in-Chief Naval Home Command, and Assistant Under-Secretary of State (Naval Personnel), Ministry of Defence, 1999–2001; *b* 6 July 1951; *er d* of late William Charles Cassidy and Mildred Joan Cassidy (*née* Ross); *m* 1984, Edward Roy Dolby. *Educ:* Girls' Grammar Sch., Prescot, Lancs; Girton Coll., Cambridge (MA); Wye Coll., Univ. of London (MSc). Ministry of Defence: Admin Trainee, 1978; Private Sec. to Chief of Defence Procurement, 1983; Principal, 1984; Private Sec. to CAS, 1990–93; Asst Sec., Hd, IT Business Systems, then IT Strategy, 1993–95; Advr to Jt Services Comd and Staff Coll. Project, 1995–97; Dir, Finance Policy, 1997–99. Chm. Adv. Panel, Greenwich Hosp., 1999–. *Recreations:* music, reading, travel, sailing. *Address:* c/o HSBC, Whitefriars, Gravel Walk, Canterbury, Kent CT1 2JP.

CASSIDY, Rt Rev. George Henry; *see* Southwell, Bishop of.

CASSIDY, Very Rev. Herbert; Dean of Armagh and Keeper of the Library, since 1989; *b* 25 July 1935; *s* of Herbert Cassidy and Frederica Jane Somerville; *m* 1961, Elizabeth Ann Egerton; one *s* two *d.* *Educ:* Cork Grammar Sch.; Trinity Coll., Dublin (BA 1957; MA 1965). Curate Assistant: Holy Trinity, Belfast, 1958–60; Christ Church, Londonderry, 1960–62; Rector: Aghavilly and Derrynoose, 1962–65; St Columba's, Portadown, 1965–85; Dean of Kilmore, 1985–89. Hon. Sec., Gen. Synod, Ch. of Ireland, 1990–. *Publications:* various pamphlets. *Recreations:* music, travel. *Address:* The Library, Abbey Street, Armagh BT61 7DY. *T:* (028) 3752 3142.

CASSIDY, His Eminence Cardinal (Idris) Edward, AC 1990; President, Pontifical Council for Promoting Christian Unity, and Commission for Religious Relations with the Jews, 1989–2001; *b* 5 July 1924; *s* of Harold George Cassidy and Dorothy May Philipps. *Educ:* Parramatta High Sch.; St Columba Seminary, Springwood; St Patrick's Coll., Manly; Lateran Univ., Rome (DCnL 1955); Diploma of Pontifical Eccl. Acad., Rome, 1955. Ordained priest, 1949; Asst Priest, Parish of Yenda, NSW, Australia, 1950–52; Secretary, Apostolic Nunciature, India, 1955–62 and Ireland, 1962–67; El Salvador, 1967–69; Counsellor, Apostolic Nunciature, Argentina, 1969–70; ordained Archbishop, Rome, 1970; Apostolic Pro-Nuncio: to Republic of China, 1970–79; to Bangladesh, 1973–79; to Lesotho, 1979–84, and Apostolic Delegate to Southern Africa; to the Netherlands, 1984–88; Substitute of Vatican Secretariat of State, 1988–89. Cardinal, 1991. Orders from El Salvador, China, Netherlands, Italy, France, Sweden and Germany. *Recreations:* tennis, golf. *Address:* 16 Coachwood Drive, Warabrook, NSW 2304, Australia.

CASSIDY, Most Rev. Joseph; Archbishop of Tuam, 1987–95; pastor, Moore; *b* 29 Oc 1933; *s* of John Cassidy and Mary Gallagher. *Educ:* St Nathy's College, Maynoot University College, Galway. Professor, Garbally College, Ballinasloe, 1959–77, Presider 1977–79; Coadjutor Bishop of Clonfert, 1979–82; Bishop of Clonfert, 1982–8 Spokesman for Irish Bishops' Conference, 1980–88. *Publications:* plays, articles anc homilies. *Address:* Moore, Ballydangan, Athlone, Co. Roscommon, Ireland.

CASSIDY, Michael John; Senior Partner, Maxwell Batley, solicitors, since 1991; *b* 14 Jan. 1947; *s* of Frank and Vera Cassidy; *m* 1st, 1974, Amanda (marr. diss. 1988); one *s* two *d*; 2nd, 1997, Amelia Simpson; one *d.* *Educ:* Downing Coll., Cambridge (BA); MBA (with distinction), City Univ. Business Sch., 1985. Qualified Solicitor, 1971; Partner, Maxwell Batley, 1971–. Chairman: London Infrastructure Consortium, 1999–; Lighthouse Consulting Services Ltd, 2001–; Director: British Land Plc, 1996–; UBS Warburg, 2000–. Corporation of London: Mem., Common Council, 1980–; Chairman: Planning Cttee, 1986–89; Policy and Resources Cttee, 1992–97; Chm., Barbican Arts Centre, 2000–. Chairman: Estates Cttee, London Inst., 2000–; Develt Bd, City Univ., 2000–. Liveryman: Fletchers' Co.; Solicitors' Co. (Master, 2001–June 2002). Hon. Fellow, London Business Sch., 1995; Hon. FRIBA 1995. Hon. LLD South Bank, 1995; Hon. DCL City, 1996. *Publications:* articles on City matters and pension fund investment. *Recreations:* boating, Barbican concerts. *Address:* 202 Cromwell Tower, Barbican EC2Y 8DD. *T:* (020) 7628 5687; (office) 27 Chancery Lane, WC2A 1PA. *Club:* London Capital.

CASSIDY, Seamus John; Senior Producer, Comedy and Entertainment, Planet 24, since 1997; *b* 20 Nov. 1958; *s* of late Michael Cassidy and of Patricia Cassidy. *Educ:* St Columb's Coll., Derry; Queen's Univ., Belfast (LLB Hons). Researcher, 1982–84; Asst Ed., 1984–87; Commissioning Ed., Comedy and Entertainment, Channel 4 TV, 1987–97. *Address:* Planet 24 Ltd, Planet Building, 195 Marsh Wall, Thames Quay, E14 9SG.

CASSIDY, Dr Sheila Anne; Specialist in Psychosocial Oncology, Plymouth Oncology Centre, since 1993; *b* 18 Aug. 1937; *d* of late Air Vice-Marshal John Reginald Cassidy and Barbara Margaret Cassidy. *Educ:* Univ. of Sydney; Somerville Coll., Oxford (BM BCh 1963; MA). Worked in Oxford and Leicester to 1971; went to Chile to work, 1971; arrested for treating wounded revolutionary, 1975; tortured and imprisoned 2 months, released Dec. 1975; lectured on human rights; in monastic religious order, 1978–80; returned to medicine, 1980; Medical Dir, St Luke's Hospice, Plymouth, 1982–93; Palliative Care Physician, Plymouth Gen. Hosp., 1993; lecturer in UK and overseas, preacher, writer, broadcaster. Freedom, City of Plymouth, 1998. Hon. DSc Exeter, 1991; Hon. DLitt CNAA, 1992. Valiant for Truth Media Award, 1977. *Publications:* Audacity to Believe, 1977; Prayer for Pilgrims, 1979; Sharing the Darkness, 1988; Good Friday People, 1991 (Collins Religious Book Award Special Prize, 1991); Light from the Dark Valley,

1994; The Loneliest Journey, 1995. *Recreations:* writing, sewing, creative pursuits, reading, TV. *Address:* Plymouth Oncology Centre, Derriford Hospital, Plymouth PL6 8DH.

CASSIDY, Stuart; ballet dancer; founder member, Kumakawa Ballet Co., since 1999; *b* 26 Sept. 1968; *s* of John and Jacqueline Cassidy; *m* 1993, Nicola Searchfield; one *s*. *Educ:* Royal Ballet Sch. (Hons 1987). Principal, Royal Ballet Co., 1991–99. *Principal rôles with Royal Ballet Company include:* Romeo and Mercutio, in Romeo and Juliet, Albrecht in Giselle, Siegfried in Swan Lake, Solor in La Bayadère, Jean de Brienne in Raymonda, Daphnis in Daphnis and Chloë, Florimund in Sleeping Beauty, Prince in Prince of the Pagodas, Prince in Nutcracker, Prince in Cinderella, Colas in La Fille Mal Gardée, Lescaut in Manon, Basilio in Don Quixote; Thaïs Pas de Deux, Tchaikovsky Pas de Deux. Nora Roche Award, 1986; Prix de Lausanne Prof. Prize, 1987. *Recreations:* golf, gardening, antiques. *Address:* 23 Devonshire Road, Chiswick, W4 2EX. *T:* (020) 8995 6820.

CASSIRER, Nadine, (Mrs Reinhold Cassirer); *see* Gordimer, N.

CASSON, Prof. Andrew John, FRS 1998; Professor of Mathematics, University of California, Berkeley. *Educ:* Trinity Coll., Cambridge (BA 1965). Formerly Lectr in Maths, and Fellow, Trinity Coll., Cambridge. *Publication:* (with S. A. Bleiler) Automorphisms of Surfaces after Nielsen and Thurston, 1988. *Address:* Department of Mathematics, University of California, Berkeley, CA 94720, USA.

CASSON, (Frederick) Michael, OBE 1983; self-employed potter, since 1945 (first workshop, 1952); *b* 2 April 1925; *s* of William and Dorothy Casson; *m* 1955, Sheila Wilmot; one *s* two *d*. *Educ:* Tollington Grammar Sch.; Hornsey Coll. of Art (Art Teachers Dip.). First pots made 1945; has continued to make functional pots from opening of first workshop, 1952; at present making stoneware and porcelain pots fired with wood. Teacher part-time, all ages, 1946–95: taught history of ceramics and lectured in USA. Founder member: Craftsmen Potters Assoc., 1958 (Chm., 1963–67); Harrow Studio Pottery Course, 1963; Vice-Chm., Crafts Council of GB, 1986–88. Presenter, The Craft of the Potter, BBC TV series, 1975. Hon. DA Wolverhampton, 2000. Gold Medal, Prague Internat. Acad. of Ceramic Art, 1964. *Publications:* Pottery in Britain Today, 1967; The Craft of the Potter, 1976, 2nd edn, 1980; many articles in Crafts, Ceramic Review, Ceramics Monthly (USA). *Recreation:* history - particularly the history of crafts. *Address:* Wobage Farm, Upton Bishop, near Ross-on-Wye, Herefordshire HR9 7QP. *T:* (01989) 780233.

CASSON, Prof. Mark Christopher; Professor of Economics, University of Reading, since 1981; *b* 17 Dec. 1945; *s* of Stanley Christopher Casson and Dorothy Nowell Barlow; *m* 1975, Janet Penelope Close; one *d*. *Educ:* Manchester Grammar Sch.; Univ. of Bristol (BA 1st cl. hons 1966); Churchill Coll., Cambridge (graduate student). University of Reading: Lecturer in Economics, 1969; Reader, 1977; Head, Dept of Econs, 1987–94. Vis. Prof. of Internat. Business, Univ. of Leeds, 1995–. Mem. Council, REconS, 1985–90. Chm., Business Enterprise Heritage Trust. Fellow, Acad. of Internat. Business, 1993; FRSA 1996. *Publications:* Introduction to Mathematical Economics, 1973; (jtly) The Future of the Multinational Enterprise, 1976; Alternatives to the Multinational Enterprise, 1979; Youth Unemployment, 1979; Unemployment: a disequilibrium approach, 1981; The Entrepreneur: an economic theory, 1982; Economics of Unemployment: an historical perspective, 1983; (ed) The Growth of International Business, 1983; (jtly) The Economic Theory of the Multinational Enterprise: selected papers, 1985; (jtly) Multinationals and World Trade: vertical integration and the division of labour in world industries, 1986; The Firm and the Market: studies in multinational enterprise and the scope of the firm, 1987; Enterprise and Competitiveness: a systems view of international business, 1990; (ed) Entrepreneurship, 1990; (ed) Multinational Corporations, 1990; Economics of Business Culture: game theory, transaction costs and economic performance, 1991; (ed) Global Research Strategy and International Competitiveness, 1991; (ed) International Business and Global Integration, 1992; (ed jtly) Multinational Enterprise in the World Economy: essays in honour of John Dunning, 1992; (ed jtly) Industrial Concentration and Economic Inequality: essays in honour of Peter Hart, 1993; Entrepreneurship and Business Culture, 1995; The Organization of International Business, 1995; (ed) The Theory of the Firm, 1996; Information and Organization: a new perspective on the theory of the firm, 1997; (ed) Culture, Social Norms and Economic Performance, 1997; (ed jtly) Institutions and the Evolution of Modern Business, 1997; (ed jtly) The Economics of Marketing, 1998; (ed jtly) Cultural Factors in Economic Growth, 2000; Economics of International Business, 2000; Enterprise and Leadership, 2000. *Recreations:* collecting old books, studying old railways, visiting old churches. *Address:* 6 Wayside Green, Woodcote, Reading RG8 0QJ. *T:* (home) (01491) 681483; (office) (0118) 931 8227.

CASSON, Michael; *see* Casson, F. M.

CASTALDI, Dr Peter; Chief Medical Officer, UNUM Ltd, since 1999; *b* 13 Jan. 1942; *s* of Frank and Sarah Jane Castaldi; *m* 1967, Joan Sherratt; one *s* one *d*. *Educ:* Grammar Sch. for Boys, Neath; Welsh Nat. Sch. of Medicine (MB, BCh 1966). Resident hosp. posts, N Wales, 1966–69; Principal in General Practice, Bangor, Gwynedd, 1969–79; MO 1979–84, SMO 1984–86, DHSS; PMO, DSS, 1986–92. Chief Med. Advr, DSS, and Dir of Med. Services, Benefits Agency, 1992–95. Med. Dir, Mediprobe, 1997–; Company Medical Officer: UNUM UK, 1996–99; Guardian Royal Exchange, 1997–; Med. Assessor, Indep. Tribunal Service, 1996–. CStJ 1993. *Recreations:* squash, swimming, armchair Rugby critic, St John Ambulance Brigade. *Address:* 24 Cavendish Road, Lytham St Annes, Lancs FY8 2PX.

CASTELL, Sir William (Martin), Kt 2000; FCA; Chief Executive, Nycomed Amersham (formerly Amersham International) plc, since 1990; *b* 10 April 1947; *s* of William Gummer Castell and Gladys (*née* Doe); *m* 1971, Renice Mendelson; one *s* two *d*. *Educ:* St Dunstan's Sch.; City of London Coll. (BA). ACA 1974, FCA 1980. Various posts in marketing, finance and admin, Wellcome Foundn, 1975–86; Co-founding Dir, Biomedical Res. Centre, Vancouver, 1983; Man. Dir, Wellcome Biotech., 1984–87; Commercial Dir, Wellcome plc, 1987–89. Non-exec. Dir, Marconi (formerly GEC), 1997–. Chairman: Cttee on Design Bursaries Health and Envmt, RSA, 1986–88; Design Dimension, 1994–99 (Dep. Chm., 1988–94); Regeneration Through Heritage, BITC, 1997–; Prince's Trust, 1998–. Vis. Fellow, Green Coll., Oxford, 1993–. Hon. Mem., Russian Academia Europaea, 1996. *Recreations:* international affairs, shooting, ski-ing, tennis. *Address:* Nycomed Amersham plc, Amersham Place, Little Chalfont, Bucks HP7 9NA. *T:* (01494) 544000. *Club:* Athenæum.

CASTILLO, Rudolph Innocent, MBE 1976; Secretary, National Advisory Commission on Belize–Guatemala Relations, since 2000; *b* 28 Dec. 1927; *s* of late Justo S. and Marcelina Castillo; *m* 1947, Gwen Frances Powery; three *s* four *d*. *Educ:* St John's Coll., Belize. Training Assignments with BBC and COI, London. Lectr in Maths, Spanish and Hist., St John's Coll., 1946–52; Radio Belize: Announcer, 1952–53; Sen. Announcer, 1953–55; Asst Prog. Organizer, 1955–59; Govt Information Services: Information Officer, 1959–62; Chief Information Officer, 1962–74; Permanent Secretary: Agriculture, 1974–76; Education, 1976–79; Sec. to Cabinet, 1980–83; Chief of Protocol, 1981–83; first High Comr for Belize in London, and first Belize Ambassador to France, Fed. Republic of Germany, Holy See, EEC and Unesco, 1983–85; retired from public service, 1985; first resident High Comr for Belize in Canada, 1990–93; Rep. to ICAO, 1991–93; business consultant, 1994–2000. TV Commercial Productions (voicing commentary). Citation Award, Audubon Soc., 1994. *Recreations:* photography, theatre, watercolour painting. *Address:* 29 Mahogany Street, Belmopan, Belize, Central America.

CASTLE, family name of **Baroness Castle of Blackburn**.

CASTLE OF BLACKBURN, Baroness *cr* 1990 (Life Peer), of Ibstone in the County of Buckinghamshire; **Barbara Anne Castle;** PC 1964; BA; Member (Lab) Greater Manchester West, European Parliament, 1984–89 (Greater Manchester North, 1979–84); Leader, British Labour Group, 1979–85, Vice-Chairman of Socialist Group, 1979–86, European Parliament; *b* 6 Oct. 1910; *d* of Frank and Annie Rebecca Betts; *m* 1944, Edward Cyril Castle (later Baron Castle) (*d* 1979); no *c*. *Educ:* Bradford Girls' Grammar Sch.; St Hugh's Coll., Oxford. Elected to St Pancras Borough Council, 1937; Member Metropolitan Water Board, 1940–43; Editor, Town and County Councillor, 1936–40; Administrative Officer, Ministry of Food, 1941–44; Housing Correspondent and Affairs Adviser, Daily Mirror, 1944–45. MP (Lab) Blackburn, 1945–50, Blackburn East, 1950–55, Blackburn, 1955–79. Member of National Executive Cttee of Labour Party, 1950–79; Chm., Labour Party, 1958–59 (Vice-Chm. 1957–58). Minister of: Overseas Development, 1964–65; Transport, 1965–68; First Secretary of State and Sec. of State for Employment and Productivity, 1968–70; Sec. of State for Social Services, 1974–76. Hon. Fellow: St Hugh's Coll., Oxford, 1966; Bradford and Ilkley Community Coll., 1985; UMIST, 1991; Humberside Poly., 1991; York Univ., 1992. Hon. DTech: Bradford, 1968; Loughborough, 1969; Hon. LLD: Lancaster, 1991; Manchester, 1993; Cambridge, 1998; Hon. DLitt De Montfort, 1998; Hon. Dr North London, 1998. Cross of Order of Merit (FRG), 1990. *Publications:* part author of Social Security, edited by Dr Robson, 1943; The Castle Diaries 1974–76, 1980, vol. II, 1964–70, 1984, repr. in one vol., 1990; Sylvia and Christabel Pankhurst, 1987; Fighting All the Way (autobiog.), 1993. *Recreations:* poetry and walking. *Address:* House of Lords, SW1A 0PW.

CASTLE, Rt Rev. Brian Colin; *see* Tonbridge, Bishop Suffragan of.

CASTLE, Enid, OBE 1997; JP; Principal, The Cheltenham Ladies' College, 1987–96; *b* 28 Jan. 1936; *d* of Bertram and Alice Castle. *Educ:* Hulme Grammar Sch. for Girls, Oldham; Royal Holloway Coll., Univ. of London. BA Hons History. Colne Valley High Sch., Yorks, 1958–62; Kenya High Sch., Nairobi, 1962–65; Queen's Coll., Nassau, Bahamas, 1965–68; Dep. Head, Roundhill High Sch., Leicester, 1968–72; Headmistress: High Sch. for Girls, Gloucester, 1973–81; Red Maids' Sch., Bristol, 1982–87. Pres., GSA, 1990–91. JP Glos, 1989. *Recreations:* travel, tennis, bridge, music.

CASTLE, John Christopher, FIM; Director, Farraxton Martlet Ltd, since 1998; *b* 4 Nov. 1944; *s* of George Frederick Castle and Winifred Mary Castle; *m* 1966, Susan Ann Neal; one *s* two *d*. *Educ:* Royal Grammar Sch., Guildford; Pembroke Coll., Cambridge (MA). With BP, 1963–68; Associated Industrial Consultants, 1968–73; Alcan Aluminium UK Ltd: Divl Dir of Industrial Relns, 1973–77; Chief Personnel Officer, 1977–80; Dir of Ops, 1980–82; Man. Dir, Base Internat. Ltd, 1982–86; Man. Dir, Thermalite, 1986–89, Gp Man. Dir, 1989–93, Marley plc; President: Avdel Textron, 1994–97; Textron Europe, 1995–97; Chief Exec., Taylor Woodrow plc, 1997. Non-executive Director: GKR Gp, 1993–99; ER Consultants Ltd, 1998–; Chm., Xternal Dimensions Ltd, 1999–. *Recreations:* tennis, bridge, restoration. *Address:* Flat 6, 10 Windmill Street, W1P 1HF. *T:* (020) 7580 7791.

CASTLE, Rt Rev. Merwyn Edwin; a Bishop Suffragan of Cape Town (Bishop of False Bay, since 1998); *b* 2 Nov. 1942; *s* of Ernest Edwin and Catherine Castle. *Educ:* Federal Theol Seminary, Alice (DipTh). Ordained deacon, 1969, priest, 1970; Rector, Christ the King, Coronationville, 1977–82; Dean, Johannesburg, 1982–87; Rector: Gambleville, Uitenhage, 1987–90; Matroosfontein, Cape Town, 1990–92; Chaplain, Archbishop of Cape Town, 1992–93; Rector, St Saviour's, Claremont, 1993–94; Bishop Suffragan of Cape Town, Southern Reg., 1994–98. *Recreations:* gardening, music, reading. *Address:* Bishopsholme, 2 Slabbert Street, Somerset West, 7130, South Africa. *T:* (office) (21) 8525243; (home) (21) 8521686, *Fax:* (21) 8529430; *e-mail:* mcastle@cpsa.org.za.

CASTLE STEWART, 8th Earl, *cr* 1800 (Ireland); **Arthur Patrick Avondale Stuart;** Viscount Stuart, 1793; Baron, 1619; Bt 1628; *b* 18 Aug. 1928; 3rd but *e* surv. *s* of 7th Earl Castle Stewart, MC, and Eleanor May (*d* 1992), *er d* of late S. R. Guggenheim, New York; *S* father, 1961; *m* 1952, Edna Fowler; one *s* one *d*. *Educ:* Brambletye; Eton; Trinity Coll., Cambridge (BA). Lieut Scots Guards, 1949. FIMgt. *Heir:* *s* Viscount Stuart, *qv*. *Address:* Manor Farm, Babcary, Somerton, Somerset TA11 7DT. *T:* (01458) 223040; Stuart Hall, Stewartstown, Co. Tyrone BT71 5AE. *T:* (028) 8773 8208. *Club:* Carlton.

CASTLEMAINE, 8th Baron *cr* 1812; **Roland Thomas John Handcock,** MBE (mil.) 1981; *b* 22 April 1943; *s* of 7th Baron Castlemaine and Rebecca Ellen (*d* 1978), *o d* of William T. Soady, RN; *S* father, 1973; *m* 1st, 1969, Pauline Anne (marr. diss.), *e d* of John Taylor Bainbridge; 2nd, 1989, Lynne Christine, *e d* of Maj. Justin Michael Gurney, RAEC; one *s*. *Educ:* Campbell Coll., Belfast. psc, ph (cfs). Lt-Col, AAC, retd 1992. *Heir:* *s* Hon. Ronan Michael Edward Handcock, *b* 27 March 1989.

CASTLEMAN, Christopher Norman Anthony; corporate adviser; Executive Director, Standard Chartered Bank, 1991–2001; *b* 23 June 1941; *s* of late S. Phillips and Mrs Joan S. R. Pyper; *m* 1st, 1965, Sarah Victoria (*née* Stockdale) (*d* 1979); one *s* one *d*; 2nd, 1980, Caroline Clare (*née* Westcott) (marr. diss. 1990); two *d*; 3rd, 1990, Suzy M. Diamond (*née* Twycross); one *s* one *d*. *Educ:* Harrow; Clare Coll., Cambridge (MA Law). Joined M. Samuel & Co. Ltd, 1963; General Manager, Hill Samuel Australia Ltd, 1970–72; Director, Hill Samuel & Co. Ltd, 1972; Man. Dir, Hill Samuel Group (SA) Ltd and Hill Samuel (SA) Ltd, 1978–80; Chief Executive: Hill Samuel Gp Plc, 1980–87; Blue Arrow PLC, 1987–88; Director: Macquarie Bank Ltd, 1985–92; Consolidated Gold Fields plc, 1988–89; Christopher Castleman & Co., 1988–89; Chairman: Nat. Investment Hldgs, 1988–90; Johnson Fry PLC (formerly LIT Holdings), 1991–95 (Chief Exec., 1989–91); ABP Holdings, 1991–94. *Recreations:* sport, travel. *Address:* Standard Chartered Bank, 4th Floor, 22 Billiter Street, EC3M 2RY. *T:* (020) 7280 7008, *Fax:* (020) 7280 7522.

CASTLEREAGH, Viscount; Frederick Aubrey Vane-Tempest-Stewart; *b* 6 Sept. 1972; *s* and *heir* of 9th Marquess of Londonderry, *qv*.

CASTON, Geoffrey Kemp, CBE 1990; Vice-Chancellor, University of the South Pacific, 1983–92; *b* 17 May 1926; *s* of late Reginald and Lilian Caston, West Wickham, Kent; *m* 1st, Sonya Chassell; two *s* one *d*; 2nd, Judith Roizen, Berkeley, Calif; two step *s* one step *d*. *Educ:* St Dunstan's Coll.; (Major Open Scholar) Peterhouse, Cambridge (MA). First Cl. Pt 1 History; First Cl. Pt II Law (with distinction) and Geo. Long Prize for Jurisprudence, 1950; Harvard Univ. (Master of Public Admin. 1951; Frank Knox Fellow, 1950–51). Sub-Lt, RNVR, 1945–47. Colonial Office, 1951–58; UK Mission to UN,

New York, 1958–61; Dept of Techn. Co-op., 1961–64; Asst Sec., Dept of Educn and Sci. (Univs and Sci. Branches), 1964–66; Jt Sec., Schools Council, 1966–70; Under-Secretary, UGC, 1970–72; Registrar of Oxford Univ. and Fellow of Merton Coll., Oxford, 1972–79; Sec.-Gen., Cttee of Vice-Chancellors and Principals, 1979–83. Project Manager, GAP, 1993–. Sec., Assoc. of First Div. Civil Servants, 1956–58; Adv. to UK Delegn to seven sessions of UN Gen. Assembly, 1953–63; UK Rep. on UN Cttee on Non-Self-Governing Territories, 1958–60; UN Techn. Assistance Cttee, 1962–64; Mem., UN Visiting Mission to Trust Territory of Pacific Islands, 1961; Consultant, Commonwealth Secretariat, 1992–. Chm., SE Surrey Assoc. for Advancement of State Educn, 1962–64; UK Delegn to Commonwealth Educn Confs, Ottawa, 1964, Gaborone, 1997. Ford Foundn travel grants for visits to schools and univs in USA, 1964, 1967, 1970. Vis. Associate, Center for Studies in Higher Educn, Univ. of Calif, Berkeley, 1978–. Chairman: Planning Cttee, 3rd and 4th Internat. Curriculum Confs, Oxford, 1967, New York, 1968; Ford Foundn Anglo-American Primary Educn Project, 1968–70; Library Adv. Council (England), 1973–78; Nat. Inst. for Careers Educn and Counselling, 1975–83; DES/DHSS Working Gp on Under 5s Res., 1980–82; Commonwealth Scholarship Commn in the UK, 1996–; Vice-Chm., Educnl Res. Bd, SSRC, 1973–77; Member: Steering Gp, OECD Workshops on Educnl Innovation, Cambridge 1969, W Germany, 1970, Illinois 1971; Exec. Cttee, Inter-Univ. Council for Higher Educn Overseas, 1977–83; Council, Univ. of Papua New Guinea, 1984–92; Council, ACU, 1987–88; Governor, Centre for Educnl Development Overseas, 1969–70; Dep., Admin. Bd, Internat. Assoc. of Univs, 1990–96. Bank of Hawaii Distinguished Lectr, Univ. of Hawaii, 1992. Hon. LLD Dundee, 1982; Hon. DLitt Deakin, 1991. *Publications:* The Management of International Co-operation in Universities, 1996; contribs to educnl jls. *Address:* 3 Pennsylvania Park, Exeter EX4 6HB. *T:* (01392) 421360.

CASTRO, Rev. Emilio Enrique; Pastor, Methodist Church, Montevideo; *b* Uruguay, 2 May 1927; *s* of Ignacio Castro and Maria Pombo; *m* 1951, Gladys Nieves; one *s* one *d*. *Educ:* Union Theol. Seminary, Buenos Aires (ThL); University of Basel (post graduate work, 1953–54); University of Lausanne (ThD 1984). Ordained, 1948; Pastor: Durazno and Trinidad (Uruguay), 1951–53; Central Methodist Church, La Paz, 1954–56; Central Methodist Church, Montevideo, 1957–65; concurrently Prof. of Contemp. Theol. Thought, Mennonite Seminary, Montevideo; Coordinator, Commn for Evangelical Unity in Latin America, 1965–72; Exec. Sec., S American Assoc. of Theol. Schools, 1966–69; Pres., Methodist Church in Uruguay, 1970–72; Dir, WCC Commn on World Mission and Evangelism, 1973–83; Gen. Sec., WCC, 1985–92. Chm., Fellowship of Christians and Jews in Uruguay, 1962–66; Moderator, Conf. on future of CCIA, Netherlands, 1967; Chm., WCC's Agency for Christian Literature Develt, 1970–72. Hon. DHL: Westmar Coll., USA, 1984; Holy Cross, Boston, 1988; Hon. DTh Geneva, 1992. *Publications:* Jesus the Conqueror, 1956; When Conscience Disturbs, 1959; Mission, Presence and Dialogue, 1963; A Pilgrim People, 1965; Reality and Faith, 1966; Amidst Evolution, 1975; Towards a Latin American Pastoral Perspective, 1973; Sent Free: Mission and Unity in the Perspective of the Kingdom, 1985; When we pray together, 1989; (ed and contrib.) Christian Century, 1971–75; (ed and contrib.) International Review of Mission, 1973–83; (ed) To the Wind of God's Spirit: Reflections on the Canberra Theme, 1990; A Passion for Unity, 1992; numerous articles in several languages. *Recreation:* basket ball. *Address:* Chemin Briquet 22, 1209 Geneva, Switzerland. *Fax:* (22) 7333533.

CASTRO RUZ, Dr Fidel; Head of State, Cuba, since 1976; *b* 13 Aug. 1927; *s* of Angel Castro y Argiz and Lina Ruz de Castro (*née* González); *m* 1948, Mirta Diaz-Balart (marr. diss. 1955); one *s*. *Educ:* Colegio Lassalle; Colegio Dolores; Colegio Belén; Univ. of Havana (Pres., Students' Fedn; Dr Law 1950). Lawyer, Havana, 1950–53; imprisoned, 1953–55; C-in-C, Armed Forces, Cuba, 1959; Prime Minister of Cuba, 1959–76; Head, Nat. Defence Council, 1992–. Chm., Agrarian Reform Inst., 1965–. First Sec., Partido Comunista (formerly Partido Unido de la Revolución Socialista), 1963–. *Publications:* Ten Years of Revolution, 1964; History Will Absolve Me, 1968; Major Speeches, 1968; (jtly) Fidel, 1987; (jtly) How Far We Slaves Have Come, 1991. *Address:* Palacio del Gobierno, Havana, Cuba.

CATCHPOLE, Nancy Mona, OBE 1987; Chairman of Governors, BFWG Charitable Foundation (formerly Crosby Hall), 1995–98 (Vice-Chairman, 1992–95); *b* 6 Aug. 1929; *d* of George William Page and Mona Dorothy Page (*née* Cowin), New Eltham; *m* 1959, Geoffrey David Arthur Catchpole; one *s* one *d*. *Educ:* Haberdashers' Aske's Hatcham Girls' Sch.; Bedford Coll., Univ. of London. BA Hons (History). Asst mistress, Gravesend Grammar Sch. for Girls, 1952–56; i/c History, Ipswich High Sch. GPDST, 1956–62; part time lectr in History and General Studies, Bath Tech. Coll., 1977–96. Sec., Bath Assoc. of University Women, 1970–75; Regional Rep. on Exec., BFUW, 1975–77, Vice-Pres., 1977–80, Pres., 1981–84. Women's National Commission: Co-Chairman, 1983–85; Immediate Past Co-Chairman, 1985–86; part-time Sec. with special responsibility for Women's Trng Roadshow prog., 1985–88; Actg Sec., March–Dec. 1988; Consultant for Women's Trng Roadshow prog. to RSA Women's Adv. Gp/Industry Matters, 1989–90; Vice-Chm., RSA Women's Adv. Gp, (formerly Women's Working Group for Industry Year 1986), 1985–95. Chm., U3A, Bath, 2001–. Chm., Bath Branch, Historical Assoc., 1993–96 (Sec., 1975–79; Hon. Treas., 2001–); Trustee, Bath Royal Literary and Scientific Inst., 1997–. A Governor, Weston Infants' Sch., Bath, 1975–85 (Chm., 1981–83; Vice-Chm., 1983–86); Member: Managers, Eagle House Community Sch., Somerset CC, 1979–82; Case Cttee, Western Nat. Adoption Soc., 1975–77; Wessex RHA, 1986–90; Avon FHSA Service Cttee, 1990–96; Discipline Cttee, Avon HA, 1997–. FRSA 1986. *Recreations:* listening, viewing, talking, writing. *Address:* 66 Leighton Road, Weston, Bath BA1 4NG. *T:* (01225) 423338.

CATER, Antony John E.; *see* Essex-Cater.

CATER, Sir Jack, KBE 1979 (CBE 1973; MBE 1956); JP; Consultant, Hong Kong Nuclear Investment Co., since 1990 (Managing Director, 1987–89); Director, Guangdong Nuclear Power Joint Venture Co. Ltd, 1986–89 (First Deputy General Manager, 1985–86); *b* 21 Feb. 1922; *yr s* of Alfred Francis Cater and Pamela Elizabeth Dukes; *m* 1950, Peggy Gwenda Richards; one *s* two *d*. *Educ:* Sir George Monoux Grammar Sch., Walthamstow. Served War of 1939–45, Sqdn Ldr, RAFVR; British Military Administration, Hong Kong, 1945; joined Colonial Administrative Service, 1946, appointed Hong Kong; attended 2nd Devonshire Course, Oxford (The Queen's Coll.), 1949–50; various appts, incl. Registrar of Co-operative Societies and Director of Marketing, Dir of Agriculture and Fisheries, Dep. Economic Sec.; IDC 1966; Defence Sec./Special Asst to Governor/Dep. Colonial Sec. (Special Duties), 1967; Executive Dir, HK Trade Development Council, 1968–70; Director, Commerce and Industry, 1970–72; Secretary for Information, 1972; for Home Affairs and Information, 1973; Founding Commissioner, Independent Commn Against Corruption, 1974–78; Chief Secretary, Hong Kong, 1978–81; actg Governor and Dep. Governor on several occasions; MEC and MLC, variously 1970–81; Hong Kong Comr in London, 1982–84; Adviser to Consultative Cttee for the Basic Law, Hong Kong, 1986–90. Chairman: HG (Asia) Ltd, 1992–95 (Director: Hoare Govett (Asia), 1990–92; HG (Asia), then ABN AMRO HG (Asia), now ABN AMRO, 1995–2001); Oriental Develt Co. Ltd, 1992–2001; Director: Hong Kong Cable Communications Ltd, 1990–92; The Scottish Asian Development Co. Ltd, 1990–2000; Hong Kong Inst. of Biotechnol./Syntex Ltd, 1991–95; Television Broadcasts Ltd, 1992–; Television Entertainment (Holdings) Ltd, 1992–96; Springfield Bank and Trust, 1994–99; Consultant: Philips & Co., China and Hong Kong, 1990–92; Internat. Bechtel Inc., 1990–97; DAO Heng Bank Ltd, 1996–2001. Pres., Agency for Volunteer Service, Hong Kong, 1982–99; Member: Internat. Bd of Dirs, United World Colls, UK, 1981–92; Court, Univ. of Hong Kong, 1982–2000; Bd of Govs, Hong Kong Baptist Univ., 1991–99; Dir, Li Po Chun United World Coll. of Hong Kong, 1991–2001. Hon. DSSc Univ. of Hong Kong, 1982; Hon. LLD Bath, 1995. *Recreations:* walking, bridge, reading, watching television. *Club:* Hong Kong.

CATESBY, (William) Peter; Chief Executive, Swallow Group plc, 1999–2000; former Chairman, Swallow Hotels Ltd; *b* 11 Sept. 1940; *s* of R. C. Catesby, MBE; *m* 1972, Cynthia Nixon; two *d*. *Educ:* Battersea Coll. of Advanced Technol. (ACT). Joined Grosvenor House Ltd, 1962; Hotel Manager, 1962–65; Hotels Trng Manager, Trust House Hotels Ltd, 1968–70; Dist Manager (SE), 1970–72, Asst Regl Dir (S), 1972–73, Trust House Forte Ltd; joined Swallow Hotels, 1973: Gen. Manager, Swallow Hotels Div., Vaux Breweries Ltd, 1973–75; Man. Dir, Swallow Hotels Ltd, 1975–77; Vaux Group plc: Main Bd Dir, 1977; Gp Dep. Chm., 1990–92; Jt Man. Dir, 1992–99; Vaux Gp plc renamed Swallow Gp, 1999. FHCIMA 1974. Dir, BHA Ltd, 1998– (Chm., Finance Cttee). Hon. Dep. Col, C(DLI) Co., Tyne-Tees Regt. Vice Chm., N of England, RFCA. *Address:* Badgers Green, West End, Sedgefield, Co. Durham TS21 2BS.

CATFORD, Sir (John) Robin, KCVO 1993; CBE 1990; Secretary for Appointments to the Prime Minister and Ecclesiastical Secretary to the Lord Chancellor, 1982–93; *b* 11 Jan. 1923; *er s* of late Adrian Leslie Catford and Ethel Augusta (*née* Rolfe); *m* 1948, Daphne Georgina, *o d* of late Col J. F. Darby, CBE, TD; three *s* one *d*. *Educ:* Hampton Grammar Sch.; Univ. of St Andrews (BSc); St John's Coll., Cambridge (DipAgric). Sudan Civil Service: Dept of Agriculture and Forests: Kordofan Province, 1946; Equatoria Province, 1948; Blue Nile Province (secondment to White Nile Schemes Bd), 1952–55; various posts in industry and commerce, mainly in UK, 1955–66; Home Civil Service: Principal, MAFF, 1966; sec. to Cttee of Inquiry on Contract Farming, 1971; Asst Sec., 1972; Under-Sec. (Agricultural Resources Policy and Horticulture), 1979; transferred to PM's Office, 1982. Member: Economic Development Cttee for Hotels and Catering, 1972–76; EDC for Agriculture, 1979–82. Mem. Chichester Dio. Synod, 1979–84 and 1988–90. Crafts Advr, Radcliffe Trust, 1993–. *Recreations:* sailing, theatre, travel, arts, avoiding gardening. *Address:* Priory Cottage, Priory Road, Chichester, West Sussex PO19 1NS. *T:* (01243) 783197. *Club:* Oxford and Cambridge.

CATHCART, family name of **Earl Cathcart**.

CATHCART, 7th Earl, *cr* 1814; **Charles Alan Andrew Cathcart;** Lord Cathcart (Scot.) 1447; Viscount Cathcart, Baron Greenock 1807; ACA; Chairman, Equator Group plc, since 1996; *b* 30 Nov. 1952; *s* of 6th Earl Cathcart, CB, DSO, MC and Rosemary (*d* 1980), *yr d* of Air Cdre Sir Percy Smyth-Osbourne, CMG, CBE; *S* father, 1999; *m* 1981, Vivien Clare, *o d* of F. D. McInnes Skinner; one *s* one *d*. *Educ:* Eton. Commnd Scots Guards, 1972–75. Whinney Murray, 1976–79; Ernst & Whinney, 1979–83; Gardner Mountain and Capel-Cure Agencies Ltd, 1983–94; Director: Murray Lawrence Members Agencies Ltd, 1995–96; RGA Holdings Ltd, 1996–; RGA Capital Ltd, 1996–. Mem., Queen's Bodyguard for Scotland, Royal Co. of Archers. Liveryman, Merchant Taylors' Co. *Recreations:* ski-ing, sailing, country pursuits. *Heir:* *s* Lord Greenock, *qv*. *Address:* Gateley Hall, Norfolk. *Club:* Pratt's.

CATHCART, Samuel; Floating Sheriff, Glasgow and Strathkelvin, since 2000; *b* 5 March 1950; *s* of Samuel Cathcart and Margaret Gordon or Cathcart; *m* 1985, Sandra Fullarton; one *s* one *d*. *Educ:* Dalry High Sch.; Edinburgh Univ. (LLB). Admitted Solicitor, 1974, in practice, 1974–77; Procurator Fiscal Depute, 1977–88; called to the Scottish Bar, 1989; Advocate, 1989–99; Advocate Depute, Crown Office, 1996–99. *Recreations:* sailing, fishing, triathlon. *Address:* 43 Douglas Street, Largs, Ayrshire KA30 8PT. *T:* (01475) 672478.

CATHERWOOD, Sir (Henry) Frederick (Ross), Kt 1971; President, Evangelical Alliance, since 1992; Member (C) Cambridge and North Bedfordshire, European Parliament, 1984–94 (Cambridgeshire, 1979–84); *b* 30 Jan. 1925; *s* of late Stuart and of Jean Catherwood, Co. Londonderry; *m* 1954, Elizabeth, *er d* of late Rev. Dr D. M. Lloyd Jones, Westminster Chapel, London; two *s* one *d*. *Educ:* Shrewsbury; Clare Coll., Cambridge (Hon. Fellow, 1992). Articled Price, Waterhouse & Co.; qualified as Chartered Accountant, 1951; Secretary, Laws Stores Ltd, Gateshead, 1952–54; Secretary and Controller, Richard Costain Ltd, 1954–55; Chief Executive, 1955–60; Asst Managing Director, British Aluminium Co. Ltd, 1960–62; Managing Director, 1962–64; Chief Industrial Adviser, DEA, 1964–66; Dir-Gen., NEDC, 1966–71; Managing Dir and Chief Executive, John Laing & Son Ltd, 1972–74. European Parliament: Chm., Cttee for External Economic Relations, 1979–84; a Vice-Pres., 1989–91; Vice Pres., Foreign Affairs Cttee, 1992–94. British Institute of Management, subseq. Institute of Management: Mem. Council, 1961–66, 1969–79; Vice-Chm., 1972; Chm., 1974–76. Member of Council: NI Development Council, 1963–64; RIIA, 1964–77; BNEC, 1965–71; NEDC, 1964–71; Chm., BOTB, 1975–79. Pres., Fellowship of Independent Evangelical Churches, 1977; Chm. of Council, 1971–77, Pres., 1983–84, Univs and Colls Christian Fellowship (formerly Inter-Varsity Fellowship); Mem., Central Religious Adv. Cttee to BBC and IBA, 1975–79. Hon. DSc Aston, 1972; Hon. DSc (Econ.) QUB, 1973; Hon. DUniv Surrey, 1979. *Publications:* The Christian in Industrial Society, 1964, rev. edn 1980 (On the Job, USA, 1983); Britain with the Brakes Off, 1966; The Christian Citizen, 1969; A Better Way, 1976; First Things First, 1979; God's Time God's Money, 1987; Pro Europe?, 1991; David: Poet, Warrior, King, 1993; At the Cutting Edge (memoirs), 1995; Jobs & Justice, Homes & Hope, 1997; It Can be Done, 2000. *Recreations:* music, gardening, reading. *Address:* Sutton Hall, Balsham, Cambridgeshire CB1 6DX. *T:* (01223) 894017. *Club:* Oxford and Cambridge.

CATHERWOOD, Herbert Sidney Elliott, CBE 1979; Chairman of Ulsterbus and Citybus, 1967–89; *b* 8 March 1929. *Educ:* Belfast Royal Academy, N Ireland. Chairman, Ulsterbus Ltd, from inception, 1967; Member, NI Transport Holding Co., 1968–73; Director of Merger of Belfast Corporation Transport with Ulsterbus, 1972. Director: Sea Ferry Parcels, 1972–99; RMC Catherwood, 1974–96; Chm., Lombard Ulster Bank Ltd, 1989–97. *Address:* Boulderstone House, 917 Antrim Road, Templepatrick, Co. Antrim, N Ireland BT39 0AT.

CATLIN, Brian Ernest Frederick; His Honour Judge Catlin; a Circuit Judge, since 1995; *b* 7 Feb. 1937; *s* of Ernest William Catlin and Winifred May Catlin (*née* White); *m* 1962, Patricia Ann Wheeldon; two *s* one *d*. *Educ:* Welwyn Garden City Grammar Sch. Served RN, 1955–57. Clerk, Bower Cotton & Bower, 1953–60; Clerk, Kidd Rapinet, 1960–67; admitted solicitor, 1967; Partner, Kidd Rapinet, 1969–84; Dist Judge, 1984–95; a Recorder, 1991–95. *Recreations:* golf, grandchildren, gardening, steeplechasing. *Address:*

c/o Reading County Court, 160/163 Friar Street, Reading RG1 1HE. *T:* (0118) 950 5815. *Club:* Springs Golf.

CATLIN, John Anthony; Under-Secretary (Legal), Departments of Health and for Work and Pensions (formerly of Social Security), since 1996; *b* 25 Nov. 1947; *s* of John Vincent Catlin and Kathleen Glover Catlin (*née* Brand); *m* 1974, Caroline Jane Goodman; one *s* two *d*. *Educ:* Ampleforth Coll., York; Birmingham Univ. (LLB 1969). Solicitor of the Supreme Court, 1972. Articled Clerk, 1970–72, Asst Solicitor, 1972–75, Gregory Rowcliffe & Co.; Legal Asst, 1975–78, Sen. Legal Asst, 1978–84, Treasury Solicitor's Dept; Asst Solicitor, 1984–89, Dep. Solicitor, 1989–96, DoE. *Recreations:* history, music, computers. *Address:* Office of the Solicitor, Departments of Health and for Work and Pensions, New Court, 48 Carey Street, WC2A 2LS. *T:* (020) 7412 1465.

CATLING, Hector William, CBE 1989 (OBE 1980); MA, DPhil, FSA; Director of the British School at Athens, 1971–89, retired; *b* 26 June 1924; *s* of late Arthur William Catling and Phyllis Norah Catling (*née* Vyvyan); *m* 1948, Elizabeth Anne (*née* Salter) (*d* 2000); two *s* one *d*. *Educ:* The Grammar Sch., Bristol; St John's Coll., Oxford (Hon. Fellow 1986). Casberd Exhbr, 1948, BA 1950, MA 1954, DPhil 1957. Served War, RNVR, 1942–46. At Univ.: undergrad. 1946–50, postgrad. 1950–54. Goldsmiths' Travelling Schol., 1951–53. Archaeological Survey Officer, Dept of Antiquities, Cyprus, 1955–59; Asst Keeper, Dept of Antiquities, Ashmolean Museum, Univ. of Oxford, 1959–64, Sen. Asst Keeper, 1964–71. Fellow, 1967–71, Supernumerary Fellow, 1991–, Linacre Coll., Oxford. Sanders Meml Lectr, Sheffield, 1979; Myres Meml Lectr, Oxford, 1987; Mitford Meml Lectr, St Andrews, 1989. Corresp. Mem., German Archaeological Inst., 1961; Hon. Mem., Greek Archaeological Soc., 1975 (Vice-Pres., 1998–). Hon. Dr Athens, 1987. *Publications:* Cypriot Bronzework in the Mycenaean World, 1964; (with J. N. Coldstream) Knossos, the North Cemetery: early Greek tombs, 4 vols, 1996; contribs to jls concerned with prehistoric and classical antiquity in Greek lands. *Recreation:* ornithology. *Address:* Dunford House, Langford, Lechlade, Glos GL7 3LN. *Club:* Athenæum.

CATLING, Sir Richard (Charles), Kt 1964; CMG 1956; OBE 1951; KPM 1945; *b* 22 Aug. 1912; *y s* of late William Catling, Leiston, Suffolk; *m* 1951, Mary Joan Feyer (*née* Lewis) (*d* 1974). *Educ:* The Grammar School, Bungay, Suffolk. Palestine Police, 1935–48; Federation of Malaya Police, 1948–54; Commissioner of Police, Kenya, 1954–63 (despatches); Inspector General of Police, Kenya, 1963–64; Police Advr to Jordan Govt, 1971–75. Security/Safety Consultant to Guthrie Corp., London, 1965–88. Officer Brother, OStJ, 1956. Freeman, City of London, 1979. *Recreations:* reading, gardening. *Address:* Hall Fen House, Irstead, Norfolk NR12 8XT. *Club:* East India.

CATLOW, Prof. Charles Richard Arthur, FRSC, FInstP; Wolfson Professor of Natural Philosophy, since 1989 and Director of Davy Faraday Laboratory, since 1998, Royal Institution of Great Britain; *b* 24 April 1947; *s* of Rolf M. Catlow and Constance Catlow (*née* Aldred); *m* 1978, Carey Anne Chapman; one *s*; *m* 2000, Nora de Leeuw. *Educ:* Clitheroe Royal Grammar School; St John's College, Oxford (MA, DPhil). FRSC 1990; FInstP 1995. Research Fellow, Oxford Univ., 1973–76; Lectr, Dept of Chemistry, UCL, 1976–85; Prof. of Physical Chemistry, Univ. of Keele, 1985–89. Medal for Solid State Chem., 1992, Award for Interdisciplinary Science, 1998, RSC. *Publications:* (jtly) Point Defects in Materials, 1988; ed jtly and contrib. to works on computational and materials sciences; 600 papers in learned jls. *Recreations:* reading, music, walking. *Address:* Royal Institution of Great Britain, 21 Albemarle Street, W1X 4BS. *T:* (020) 7409 2992. *Club:* Athenæum.

CATO, Brian Hudson; Full-time Chairman of Industrial Tribunals, 1975–92, Regional Chairman, Newcastle upon Tyne, 1989–92; *b* 6 June 1928; *s* of Thomas and Edith Willis Cato; *m* 1963, Barbara Edith Myles; one *s*. *Educ:* LEA elem. and grammar schs; Trinity Coll., Oxford; RAF Padgate. MA Oxon, LLB London. RAF, 1952–54. Called to Bar, Gray's Inn, 1952; in practice NE Circuit, 1954–75; a Recorder of the Crown Court, 1974–75. Special Lectr (part-time) in Law of Town and Country Planning, King's Coll., now Univ. of Newcastle, 1956–75; Hon. Examnr, Inst. of Landscape Architects, 1960–75. Pres., N of England Medico-legal Soc., 1973–74. Corresp. Sec., Berwickshire Naturalists Club, 1992–96. Freeman of City of Newcastle upon Tyne by patrimony; Founder Mem. Scriveners' Co., Newcastle upon Tyne (Clerk, 1992–); Freeman, City of London, 1985. Hon. ALI. *Recreations:* bibliomania, antiquarian studies, family life. *Address:* 2 Croft Place, Newton-by-the-Sea, Alnwick, Northumberland NE66 3DL. *T:* (01665) 576334.

CATON, Martin Philip; MP (Lab) Gower, since 1997; *b* 15 June 1951; *s* of William John Caton and Pauline Joan Caton; *m* 1996, Bethan, *d* of late Hermus Evans and of Menai Evans; two step *d*. *Educ:* Newport Grammar Sch., Essex; Norfolk Sch. of Agriculture; Aberystwyth Coll. of FE (HNC). Scientific Officer, Welsh Plant Breeding Stn, Aberystwyth, 1974–84; Political Researcher, David Morris, MEP, 1984–97. Mem. (Lab) Swansea CC, 1988–97. *Address:* House of Commons, SW1A 0AA.

CATON, Dr Valerie, (Mrs D. M. Harrison); HM Diplomatic Service; Senior Associate Member, St Antony's College, Oxford, since 2001; *b* 12 May 1952; *d* of Robert Caton and Florence Amy Caton (*née* Aspden); *m* 1987, David Mark Harrison; one *s* one *d*. *Educ:* Blackburn High Sch. for Girls; Bristol Univ. (BA, PhD); Grad. Sch. of European Studies, Univ. of Reading (MA). Lectrice, Univ. of Sorbonne, Paris, 1977–78; Tutor in French, Exeter Univ., 1978–80; joined HM Diplomatic Service, 1980: FCO, 1980–82; Second, later First Sec., EC Affairs, Brussels, 1982–84; First Sec. (Chancery), Paris, 1988–92; Dep. Head of Mission, Stockholm, 1993–96; Counsellor (Financial and European), Paris, 1997–2001. *Publications:* various articles in jls on works of French writer, Raymond Queneau. *Recreations:* reading, theatre, collecting humorous books, walking, riding. *Address:* c/o Foreign and Commonwealth Office, King Charles Street, SW1A 2AH.

CATOVSKY, Prof. Daniel, MD, DSc; FRCP, FRCPath, FMedSci; Professor of Haematology, Institute of Cancer Research, since 1988; Hon. Consultant, Royal Marsden Hospital, since 1988; *b* 19 Sept. 1937; *s* of Felix Catovsky and Ana Kabanchik; *m* 1960, Julia Margarita Polak, *qv*; two *s* one *d*. *Educ:* Faculty of Medicine, Buenos Aires Univ. (MD 1961); London Univ. (DSc Med. 1985). FRCPath 1986; FRCP 1990. Royal Postgraduate Medical School: Fellow, 1967–76; Hon. Sen. Lectr in Haematol. and Medicine, 1976–87; Prof. of Haematol Oncology, 1987–88; Consultant, Hammersmith Hosp., 1976–88. Vis. Prof., Mount Sinai Med. Sch., NY, 1981. Ham–Wasserman Lecture (first annual), Amer. Soc. of Hematology, 1984. FMedSci 1999. *Publications:* The Leukemic Cell, 1981, 2nd edn 1991; (with A. Polliack) Chronic Lymphocytic Leukaemia, 1988; (with R. Foa) The Lymphoid Leukaemias, 1990. *Recreations:* walking, squash, films, theatre. *Address:* Royal Marsden Hospital, Fulham Road, SW3 6JJ. *T:* (020) 7352 8171.

CATOVSKY, Julia Margaret, (Mrs Daniel Catovsky); *see* Polak, J. M.

CATTANACH, Bruce Macintosh, PhD, DSc; FRS 1987; Senior Scientist, MRC, 1970–98; *b* 5 Nov. 1932; *s* of James and Margaretta Cattanach; *m* 1st, 1966, Margaret Bouchier Crewe (*d* 1996); two *d*; 2nd, 1999, Josephine Peters. *Educ:* King's Coll., Univ. of Durham (BSc, 1st Cl. Hons); Inst. of Animal Genetics, Univ. of Edinburgh (PhD, DSc). Scientific Staff, MRC Induced Mutagenesis Unit, Edinburgh, 1959–62, 1964–66; NIH Post Doctoral Res. Fellow, Biology Div., Oak Ridge Nat. Lab., Tenn, USA, 1962–64; Sen. Scientist, City of Hope Med. Centre, Duarte, Calif, 1966–69; Scientific Staff, 1969–86, Hd of Genetics Div., 1987–96, MRC Radiobiology Unit, Chilton, Oxon; Actg Dir, MRC Mammalian Genetics Unit, Harwell, 1996–97. *Publications:* contribs to several learned jls on X-chromosome inactivation, sex determination, mammalian chromosome imprinting, and genetics generally. *Recreations:* squash; breeding, showing and judging pedigree dogs; investigating inherited disease in dogs and devising control schemes for elimination. *Address:* Downs Edge, Reading Road, Harwell, Oxon OX11 0JJ. *T:* (01235) 835410.

CATTERALL, Dr John Ashley, OBE 1995; FIM, FInstP; Senior Executive, Engineering Council, 1997–99; *b* 26 May 1928; *s* of John William Catterall and Gladys Violet Catterall; *m* 1960, Jennifer Margaret Bradfield; two *s*. *Educ:* Imperial Coll. of Science and Technol., London (BSc, PhD, DIC). ARSM; FIM 1964; FInstP 1968; CEng 1978. National Physical Lab., 1952–74; Dept of Industry, 1974–81; Head, Energy Technology Div., and Dep. Chief Scientist, Dept of Energy, 1981–83; Sec., SERC, 1983–88; Sec., Inst. of Metals, 1988–91, then Sec. and Chief Exec., Inst. of Materials, 1991–97. Inst. of Metals Rosenhain Medal for Physical Metallurgy, 1970. *Publications:* (with O. Kubaschewski) Thermochemical Data of Alloys, 1956; contrib. Philos. Mag., Jl Inst. of Physics, Jl Inst. of Metals. *Recreation:* reading. *Address:* Hill House, The Doward, Whitchurch, Ross-on-Wye, Herefordshire HR9 6DU. *T:* (01600) 890341.

CATTERALL, John Stewart; Managing Director, Conferences and Training Ltd, since 1993; *b* 13 Jan. 1939; *s* of John Bernard and Eliza Catterall; *m* 1965, Ann Beryl Hughes; two *s*. *Educ:* Blackpool Tech. Coll. and Sch. of Art. Mem. CIPFA. Posts in local authorities, 1961–70; Management Accountant, Cambridgeshire and Isle of Ely CC, 1970–72, Chief Accountant, 1972–73; Asst County Treasurer, Financial Planning and Accounting, Cambs CC, 1973–76; Dist. Treasurer, Southampton and SW Hants DHA, 1976–78, Area Treasurer, 1978–82; Regional Treasurer, NE Thames RHA, 1982–85; Dep. Dir, Finance, NHS Mgt Bd, 1985–89; Head of Health Services, 1985–89, Head of Health Adv. Services, 1989, CIPFA. Chm. and Chief Exec., C International Ltd, 1990–92; Dir, Capita PLC, 1992–93. *Publications:* contribs to professional jls. *Recreations:* golf, swimming, reading. *Address:* Birkdale, Green Lane, Chilworth, Southampton SO1 7JW. *T:* (023) 8076 9402.

CATTERMOLE, Joan Eileen, (Mrs James Cattermole); *see* Mitchell, Prof. J. E.

CATTO, family name of **Baron Catto**.

CATTO, 3rd Baron *cr* 1936, of Cairncatto, co. Aberdeen; **Innes Gordon Catto;** Bt 1921; *b* 7 Aug. 1950; *e s* of 2nd Baron Catto; *S* father, 2001. *Educ:* Grenville Coll.; Shuttleworth Agric. Coll. *Heir:* *b* Hon. Alexander Gordon Catto [*b* 22 June 1952; *m* 1981, Elizabeth Scott, twin *d* of Maj. T. P. Boyes; two *s* one *d*].

CATTO, Gay; *see* Catto, P. G. W.

CATTO, Prof. Graeme Robertson Dawson, MD; DSc; FRCP, FRCPE, FRCPGlas, FMedSci; FRSE; Vice Principal, King's College London, and Dean, Guy's, King's and St Thomas' Medical and Dental School of King's College London, since 2000; *b* 24 April 1945; *s* of William Dawson Catto and Dora Elizabeth (*née* Spiby); *m* 1967, Joan Sievewright; one *s* one *d*. *Educ:* Robert Gordon's Coll., Aberdeen; Univ. of Aberdeen (MB ChB Hons 1969; MD Hons 1975; DSc 1988). FRCPGlas 1982; FRCP 1984; FRCPE 1988; FRSE 1996. House Officer, Aberdeen Royal Infirmary, 1969–70; Res. Fellow, then Lectr, Univ. of Aberdeen, 1970–75; Harkness Fellow, Commonwealth Fund of NY; Fellow in Medicine, Harvard Univ., 1975–77; University of Aberdeen: Sen. Lectr, then Reader, 1977–88; Dean, Faculty of Medicine and Med. Scis, 1992–98; Prof. of Medicine and Therapeutics, 1988–2000; Vice Principal, 1995–2000; Hon. Consultant Physician and Nephrologist, Aberdeen Royal Infirmary, 1977–2000. Vice-Chm., Aberdeen Royal Hosps NHS Trust, 1992–99. Chief Scientist, Scottish Executive (formerly Scottish Office) Health Dept, 1997–2000. Member: GMC, 1994– (Chm. Educn Cttee, 1999–); SHEFC, 1996–; Specialist Trng Authority, 1999–. Mem., Lambeth, Southwark and Lewisham HA, 2000–. Founder FMedSci 1998 (Treas., 1998–). Chm., Robert Gordon's Coll., Aberdeen, 1995–. Hon. FRCGP 2000. FRSA 1996. *Publications:* (ed) Clinical Transplantation: current practice and future prospects, 1987; (with D. A. Power) Nephrology, 1988; (ed) Calculus Disease, 1988; (ed) Chronic Renal Failure, 1988; (ed) Haemodialysis, 1988; (ed) Management of Renal Hypertension, 1988; (ed) Pregnancy and Renal Disorders, 1988; (ed) Drugs and the Kidney, 1989; (ed) Glomerulo-nephritis, 1989; Multisystem Diseases, 1989; Transplantation, 1989; (ed) Urinary Tract Infections, 1989; (with A. W. Thomson) Immunology of Renal Transplantation, 1993; contrib. to learned jls on aspects of renal disease. *Recreation:* hills and glens. *Address:* 4 Woodend Avenue, Aberdeen AB15 6YL. *T:* (01224) 310509; Maryfield, Glenbuchat, Aberdeenshire AB36 8TS. *T:* (01975) 641317; Vice Principal's Office, King's College, James Clerk Maxwell Building, Waterloo Road, SE1 8WA. *Clubs:* Athenæum; Royal Northern and University (Aberdeen).

CATTO, Prof. Henry Edward; Professor of Political Science, University of Texas (San Antonio), since 1993; *b* 6 Dec. 1930; *s* of Henry E. Catto and Maurine H. Catto; *m* 1958, Jessica Hobby; two *s* two *d*. *Educ:* Williams Coll. (BA). Businessman, San Antonio, Texas, 1952–69; Dep. US Rep., Orgn of American States, 1969–71; US Ambassador to El Salvador, 1971–73; US Chief of Protocol, 1974–76; Consultant, Washington DC, 1977–81; Asst Sec. of Defense, 1981–83; Vice-Chm., H & C Communications, 1983–89; US Ambassador to UK, 1989–91; Dir, US Inf. Agency, 1991–93. *Recreations:* tennis, hiking, running, ski-ing, golf. *Address:* 110 East Crockett Street, San Antonio, TX 78205, USA.

CATTO, (Patricia) Gay (Warren); Ceremonial Officer, Cabinet Office, since 2000; *b* 16 Nov. 1940; *d* of late Rt Rev. (William) Warren Hunt and of Mollie Hunt (*née* Green); *m* 1971, Alistair William Gillespie Catto (separated); one *s* one *d*. *Educ:* Sherborne Sch. for Girls; St Hugh's Coll., Oxford (BA). Asst Principal, Min. of Pensions and Nat. Insce, 1963–66; Private Sec. to Perm. Sec., Home Office, 1966–67; Principal: Home Office, 1967–73; Dept of Employment, 1978–83; Assistant Secretary: Resources and Planning Div., HSE, 1983–88; Police Dept, 1988–96, Constitutional Unit, 1996–2000, Home Office. *Address:* Ceremonial Branch, Cabinet Office, Ashley House, 2 Monck Street, SW1P 2BQ. *T:* (020) 7276 2770.

CAU, Antoine Emond André; Chief Executive, Forte Hotels, since 1998; *b* 26 Aug. 1947; *s* of Henri and Laure Cau; *m* 1978, Patricia Stamm. *Educ:* Lycée Mignet, Aix-en-Provence; Institut d'Etudes Commerciales de Grenoble (diplôme de direction et de gestion des entreprises; maîtrise de gestion). Hertz: Station Manager, Avignon, 1970–75; station manager posts, 1975–77; District Manager: Nice, 1977; Côte d'Azur, 1978–80; Zone Manager, S of France, 1980–82; Ops Manager, Italy, 1982–84; Corporate Accounts

Manager, Hertz Europe, 1984; Ops Manager, France, 1985–90; Vice Pres., Ops, Hertz Europe, 1990; Vice Pres., Hertz Corp., and Pres., Hertz International, 1990–97. Chevalier de l'Ordre National du Mérite (France), 1992. *Recreations:* tennis, motorsport, music. *Address:* (office) 166 High Holborn, WC1V 6TT. *T:* (020) 7301 2170.

CAULCOTT, Thomas Holt; Chairman, Royal Shrewsbury Hospitals NHS Trust, since 1998; Chief Executive, Birmingham City Council, 1982–88; *b* 7 June 1927; *s* of late L. W. Caulcott and Doris Caulcott; *m* 1st, 1954, C. Evelyn Lowden (marr. diss. 1987); one *d* (and one *s* decd); 2nd, 1988, Jane Marguerite Allsopp. *Educ:* Solihull Sch.; Emmanuel Coll., Cambridge. Asst Principal, Central Land Bd and War Damage Commn, 1950–53; transferred to HM Treasury, 1953; Private Sec. to Economic Sec. to the Treasury, 1955; Principal, Treasury supply divs, 1956–60; Private Sec. to successive Chancellors of the Exchequer, Sept. 1961–Oct. 1964; Principal Private Sec. to First Sec. of State (DEA), 1964–65; Asst Sec., HM Treasury, 1965–66; Min. of Housing and Local Govt, 1967–69; Civil Service Dept, 1969–70; Under-Sec., Machinery of Govt Gp, 1970–73; Principal Finance Officer, Local Govt Finance Policy, DoE, 1973–76; Sec., AMA, 1976–82. Mem., S Shropshire DC, 1991–95 (Chm., Policy and Resources Cttee, 1993–95). Mem. Cttee of Mgt, Hanover Housing Assoc., 1988–94. Mem. Bd, W Midlands Arts, 1996–97. Harkness Fellowship, Harvard and Brookings Instn, 1960–61; Vis. Fellow, Dept of Land Economy, Univ. of Cambridge, 1984–85; Hon. Fellow: Inst. of Local Govt Studies, Univ. of Birmingham, 1979–; Univ. of Central England (formerly Birmingham Polytechnic), 1990–. *Publication:* Management and the Politics of Power, 1996. *Address:* 12 Dinham, Ludlow, Shropshire SY8 1EJ. *T:* (01584) 875154, *Fax:* (01584) 874764.

CAULFEILD, family name of **Viscount Charlemont**.

CAULFIELD, Ian George, CBE 2000; Clerk of the Council and Chief Executive, Warwickshire County Council, and Clerk to the Warwickshire Lieutenancy, since 1986; *b* 14 Dec. 1942; *s* of William and Elizabeth Caulfield; *m* 1967, Geraldine Mary Hind; three *s*. *Educ:* Liverpool Inst. High Schs for Boys; Univ. of Manchester (BA Hons Geography); Liverpool Poly. (DipTP). Jun. Planning Assistant, Liverpool City, 1964–65; Planning Assistant, Lancs CC, 1965–69; Sen. Planning Officer, Hants CC, 1969–74; Asst Hd, Res. and Intelligence Unit, 1974–76, Prin. Assistant to Chief Exec., 1976–78, Oxford CC; Asst Exec., 1978–83, Dep. Clerk and Asst Chief Exec., 1983–86, Warwicks CC. *Publication:* (jtly) Planning for Change: strategic planning and local government, 1989. *Recreation:* sport, particularly soccer. *Address:* Shire Hall, Warwick CV34 4RR. *T:* (01926) 410410.

CAULFIELD, Patrick Joseph, CBE 1996; RA 1993; artist; *b* London, 29 Jan. 1936; *s* of Patrick and Annie Caulfield; *m* 1st, 1968, Pauline Jacobs (marr. diss. 1999); three *s*; 2nd, 1999, Janet Nathan. *Educ:* Acton Central Secondary Modern Sch.; Chelsea Sch. of Art; RCA (Sen. FRCA 1993). Served RAF, 1953–56. Taught at Chelsea Sch. of Art, 1963–71. First exhibited, FBA Galls, 1961; group exhibitions include: Whitechapel, Tate, Hayward, Waddington and Tooth Galls, and ICA, in London; Walker Art Gall., Liverpool; and exhibns in Paris, Brussels, Milan, NY, São Paulo, Berlin, Lugano, Dortmund, Bielefeld and Helsinki. One-man exhibitions include: Robert Fraser Gall., London, 1965, 1967; Robert Elkon Gall., NY, 1966, 1968; Waddington Galls, 1969, 1971, 1973, 1975, 1979, 1981, 1985, 1997, 1998; Tate Gall. (retrospective), 1981; Serpentine Gall. (retrospective), 1992; Hayward Gall. (retrospective), 1999; also in Italy, France, Australia, Belgium, USA and Japan. Designs for ballets, Covent Garden: Party Game, 1984; Rhapsody, 1995. Work in public collections incl. Tate Gall.; V&A; Walker Art Gall., Liverpool; Whitworth Art Gall., and Manchester City Art Gall.; and museums and galls in GB, Australia, USA, W Germany and Japan. Hon. Fellow, London Inst., 1996. *Address:* 19 Belsize Square, NW3 4HT; c/o Waddington Galleries, 2 Cork Street, W1X 1PA.

CAUSLEY, Charles Stanley, CBE 1986; poet; broadcaster; *b* Launceston, Cornwall, 24 Aug. 1917; *o s* of Charles Causley and Laura Bartlett. *Educ:* Launceston National Sch.; Horwell Grammar Sch.; Launceston Coll.; Peterborough Training Coll. Served on lower-deck in Royal Navy (Communications Branch), 1940–46. Literary Editor, 1953–56, of BBC's West Region radio magazines Apollo in the West and Signature. Awarded Travelling Scholarships by Society of Authors, 1954 and 1966. Mem., Arts Council Poetry Panel, 1962–66. Hon. Vis. Fellow in Poetry, Univ. of Exeter, 1973. FRSL 1958. Hon. DLitt Exeter, 1977; Hon. MA Open, 1982. Awarded Queen's Gold Medal for Poetry, 1967; Cholmondeley Award, 1971; Kurt Maschler Award, 1987; Ingersoll Prize, 1990. *Publications:* Hands to Dance (short stories), 1951, rev. edn as Hands to Dance and Skylark, 1979; *poetry:* Farewell, Aggie Weston, 1951; Survivor's Leave, 1953; Union Street, 1957; Peninsula (ed), 1957; Johnny Alleluia, 1961; Dawn and Dusk (ed), 1962; Penguin Modern Poets 3 (with George Barker and Martin Bell), 1962; Rising Early (ed), 1964; Modern Folk Ballads (ed), 1966; Underneath the Water, 1968; Figure of 8, 1969; Figgie Hobbin, 1971; The Tail of the Trinosaur, 1973; (ed) The Puffin Book of Magic Verse, 1974; Collected Poems 1951–1975, 1975; The Hill of the Fairy Calf, 1976; (ed) The Puffin Book of Salt-Sea Verse, 1978; The Animals' Carol, 1978; (ed) Batsford Book of Stories in Verse for Children, 1979; (trans.) 25 Poems by Hamdija Demirovíc, 1980; (ed) The Sun, Dancing, 1982; Secret Destinations, 1984; 21 Poems, 1986; (trans.) Kings' Children, 1986; Early in the Morning, 1986; Jack the Treacle Eater, 1987; A Field of Vision, 1988; The Young Man of Cury, 1991; Bring in the Holly, 1992; Collected Poems, 1992; All Day Saturday, 1994; Going to the Fair, 1994; Collected Poems for Children, 1996; (jtly) Penguin Modern Poets, 1996; Collected Poems 1951–1997, 1997; Selected Poems for Children, 1997; Collected Poems 1951–2000, 2000; *children's stories:* Three Heads made of Gold, 1978; The Last King of Cornwall, 1978; The Merrymaid of Zennor, 1999; *verse plays:* The Gift of a Lamb, 1978; The Ballad of Aucassin and Nicolette, 1981; *libretti:* Jonah (music by William Mathias), 1990; St Martha and the Dragon (music by Phyllis Tate), 1991; contrib. to many anthologies of verse in Great Britain and America. *Recreations:* the theatre; European travel; the re-discovery of his native town; playing the piano with expression. *Address:* 2 Cyprus Well, Launceston, Cornwall PL15 8BT. *T:* (01566) 772731.

CAUTE, (John) David; JP; MA, DPhil; writer; *b* 16 Dec. 1936; *m* 1st, 1961, Catherine Shuckburgh (marr. diss. 1970); two *s*; 2nd, 1973, Martha Bates; two *d*. *Educ:* Edinburgh Academy; Wellington; Wadham Coll., Oxford. Scholar of St Antony's Coll., 1959. Spent a year in the Army in the Gold Coast, 1955–56, and a year at Harvard Univ. on a Henry Fellowship, 1960–61. Fellow of All Souls Coll., Oxford, 1959–65; Visiting Professor, New York Univ. and Columbia Univ., 1966–67; Reader in Social and Political Theory, Brunel Univ., 1967–70. Regents' Lectr, Univ. of Calif., 1974; Vis. Prof., Bristol Univ., 1985. Literary Editor, New Statesman, 1979–80. Co-Chm., Writers' Guild, 1981–82; Chm., Sinclair Fiction Prize, 1984. FRSL 1998. JP Inner London, 1993. *Plays:* Songs for an Autumn Rifle, staged by Oxford Theatre Group at Edinburgh, 1961; The Demonstration, Nottingham Playhouse, 1969; The Fourth World, Royal Court, 1973; Brecht and Company, BBC TV, 1979; BBC Radio: Fallout, 1972; The Zimbabwe Tapes, 1983; Henry and the Dogs, 1986; Sanctions, 1988; Animal Fun Park, 1995. *Publications:* At Fever Pitch (novel), 1959 (Authors' Club Award and John Llewelyn Rhys Prize, 1960); Comrade Jacob (novel), 1961; Communism and the French Intellectuals, 1914–1960, 1964; The Left in Europe Since 1789, 1966; The Decline of the West (novel), 1966; Essential Writings of Karl Marx (ed), 1967; Fanon, 1970; The Confrontation: a trilogy, 1971 (consisting of The Demonstration (play), 1970; The Occupation (novel), 1971; The Illusion, 1971); The Fellow-Travellers, 1973, rev. edn 1988; Collisions, 1974; Cuba, Yes?, 1974; The Great Fear: the anti-communist purge under Truman and Eisenhower, 1978; Under the Skin: the Death of White Rhodesia, 1983; The K-Factor (novel), 1983; The Espionage of the Saints, 1986; News from Nowhere (novel), 1986; Sixty Eight: the year of the barricades, 1988; Veronica or the Two Nations (novel), 1989; The Women's Hour (novel), 1991; Joseph Losey, 1994; Dr Orwell and Mr Blair (novel), 1994; Fatima's Scarf (novel), 1998; *as John Salisbury: novels:* The Baby-Sitters, 1978; Moscow Gold, 1980. *Address:* 41 Westcroft Square, W6 0TA.

CAUTHEN, Stephen Mark; jockey; *b* Covington, Kentucky, 1 May 1960; *e s* of Ronald (Tex) Cauthen and Myra Cauthen; *m* Amy Kathrine Roth Fuss; one *d*. Apprentice jockey, 1976, Churchill Downs, Kentucky; first win, Red Pipe, 1976; raced at Aqueduct and Santa Anita; champion jockey, USA, 1977; won US Triple Crown on Affirmed, 1978; moved to Lambourn, 1979; champion jockey, UK, 1984, 1985, 1987; races won include: with Tap on Wood, 2,000 Guineas, 1979; with Slip Anchor, Derby, 1985; with Oh So Sharp, Oaks, 1,000 Guineas and St Leger, 1985; with Reference Point, Derby, St Leger and King George V and Queen Elizabeth Diamond Stakes, 1987; with Diminuendo, Oaks, 1988; with Michelozzo, St Leger, 1989; with Old Vic, French Derby and Irish Derby, 1989; Champion Stakes 3 times (Cormorant Wood, Indian Skimmer, In the Groove); Grand Prix de St Cloud (Atcatanango, Diamond Shoal); Prix de Diane (Indian Skimmer). *Address:* 167 S Main Street, Walton, KY 41094, USA.

CAUTLEY, (Edward) Paul (Ronald), CMG 2001; DL; Founder Chairman, The D Group, since 1993; *b* 1 March 1940; *s* of Ronald Lockwood Cautley and Ena Lily Medwin; *m* 1966, Sandra Elizabeth Baker; two *d*. *Educ:* Downside Sch. Syndication Manager, Central Press Features, 1958–60; Marketing Manager, ICI Paints, 1960–62; Finance Negotiator, GDM Finance, 1960–62; General Manager, Marling Industries, 1963–66; Account Dir, S. H. Benson, 1966–70; Dir, New Product Development, BRB, 1971–73; Chief Exec. and founder Chm., Strategy Ltd, 1974–. Founder Director: Settle and Carlisle Railway Develt Co.; Team First Ltd; Founder, Royal Marine Business Liaison Gp. HAC, 1958–60; RM Reserve, 1961–68. Hon. Col, RM, London, 1999–; Pres., Chatham Marine Cadets, 2000–; Col, Marine Cadets, Sea Cadets Corps, 2001–. Trustee: RM Mus.; Industrial Trust, NT. DL Greater London, 2001. FRGS; Member: Royal Philatelic Soc.; RPS; Founder Mem., Foundn and Friends, Royal Botanic Gardens, Kew; life mem., 15 railway preservation socs. *Publication:* The Cautley Chronicle, 1986. *Recreations:* philately (British Commonwealth), photography (mainly landscapes), 00 gauge model railway enthusiast. *Address:* (office) 13 The Ivory House, St Katharine Docks, E1W 1BN. *T:* (020) 7480 5652. *Clubs:* Army and Navy, Honourable Artillery Company, Special Forces.

CAVALIER-SMITH, Prof. Thomas, PhD; FRS 1998; FRSC 1997; NERC Professorial Fellow, Department of Zoology, since 1999 and Professor of Evolutionary Biology, since 2000, University of Oxford; Fellow, Canadian Institute for Advanced Research (Evolutionary Biology Programme), since 1988; *b* 21 Oct. 1942; *s* of Alan Hailes Spencer Cavalier-Smith and Mary Maude Cavalier-Smith; *m* 1st, 1964, Gillian Glaysher; one *s* one *d*; 2nd, 1991, Ema E-Yung Chao; one *d*. *Educ:* Kenninghall Primary Sch.; Norwich Sch.; Gonville and Caius Coll., Cambridge (MA 1967); King's Coll., London (PhD 1967); Open Univ. (BA). FLS; FIBiol. Tutorial Student, King's Coll., London, 1964–67; Guest Investigator, and Damon Runyon Meml Res. Fellow, Rockefeller Univ., NY, 1967–69; Lectr, 1969–82, Reader, 1982–89, in Biophysics, King's Coll., London; Prof. of Botany, Univ. of BC, 1989–99. Vis. Fellow, Res. Sch. of Biol. Scis, ANU, 1981, 1985–86; Vis. Scientist, Univ. of Cape Town, 1995–96. FRSA. *Publications:* (ed with J. P. Hudson) Biology, Society and Choice, 1982; (ed) The Evolution of Genome Size, 1985; over 140 scientific articles in jls, contribs to books. *Recreations:* reading, natural history, travel. *Address:* Department of Zoology, University of Oxford, South Parks Road, Oxford OX1 3PS. *T:* (01865) 281065.

CAVALIERO, Roderick; Deputy Director General, British Council, 1981–88 (Assistant Director General, 1977–81); *b* 21 March 1928; *s* of Eric Cavaliero and Valerie (*née* Logan); *m* 1957, Mary McDonnell; one *s* four *d*. *Educ:* Tonbridge School; Hertford Coll., Oxford. Teaching in Britain, 1950–52; teaching in Malta, 1952–58; British Council Officer, 1958–88 (service in India, Brazil, Italy). Chm., Educnl and Trng Export Cttee, 1979–88; Dir, Open Univ. Educnl Enterprises, 1980–88; Pres., British Educnl Equipment Assoc., 1987–92. Mem., British Section, Franco-British Council, 1981–88. Trustee, Charles Wallace India Trust, 1981–2000. Mem. Council, British Sch. at Rome, 1989–96 (Chm., Management Cttee, 1991–95); Trustee, St George's English Sch., Rome, 1979–96. *Publications:* Olympia and the Angel, 1958; The Last of the Crusaders, 1960; The Independence of Brazil, 1993; Admiral Satan: the life and campaigns of Suffren, 1994. *Address:* 10 Lansdowne Road, Tunbridge Wells, Kent TN1 2NJ. *T:* (01892) 533452.

CAVAN, 13th Earl of, *cr* 1647 (Ire.); **Roger Cavan Lambart;** Baron Cavan 1618; Baron Lambart 1618; Viscount Kilcoursie 1647; *b* 1 Sept. 1944; *s* of Frederick Cavan Lambart (*d* 1963) and Audrey May, *d* of Albert Charles Dunham. *Educ:* Wilson's School, Wallington, Surrey.

[Has not yet established his right to the peerage.]

CAVANAGH, Diana Lesley; Director of Educational Studies (formerly Strategic Director of Education), City of Bradford Metropolitan District Council, since 1996; *b* 19 Nov. 1944; *d* of Arthur and Nellie Eggleston; *m* 1973, Michael Cavanagh. *Educ:* Fairfield High Sch.; Westfield Coll., London (BA Hons 1966); Univ. of Liverpool (PGCE 1967); Univ. of Edinburgh (Dip. Applied Linguistics 1973); Sheffield Poly. (MSc 1982). German Teacher, Cumberland, 1967–70; English Teacher, Sulingen Gymnasium, W Germany, 1970–73; Lectr in English Lang./Educn, Univ. of Birmingham, 1973–75; British Council Project Co-ordinator, Medical Coll., Jeddah, 1975–77; Section Hd, ESOL, Abraham Moss Centre, Manchester, 1977–83; Professional Asst, and Dep. Area Educn Officer, Derbyshire, 1983–85; Asst Educn Officer (Reorgn and Curriculum), Rochdale, 1985–89; Institute of Citizenship Studies: Chief Asst Exec. Officer (Policy Develt), 1989–91; CEO, 1991–96. Chair, NW Reg., 1993, Council Mem., 1994, Soc. of Educn Officers; Mem. and Chair of the Board, NEAB, 1996; Dep. Chair, Assessment and Qualifications Alliance, 1999–; Dir, Careers Bradford, 1996–. FRSA 1991. *Publications:* Introducing PET, 1980; Power Relations in the Further Education College, 1983; Staff Development in the Further Education College, 1984. *Recreations:* hill walking, polar travel, reading. *Address:* Bradford Education, Flockton House, Flockton Road, Bradford, W Yorks BD4 7RY. *T:* (01274) 751700, *Fax:* (01274) 740612.

CAVANAGH, John Bryan; Dress Designer; Chairman and Managing Director, John Cavanagh Ltd, retired 1974; *b* 28 Sept. 1914; *s* of Cyril Cavanagh and Anne (*née* Murphy). *Educ:* St Paul's School. Trained with Captain Edward Molyneux in London and Paris, 1932–40. Joined Intelligence Corps, 1940, Captain (GS, Camouflage), 1944. On demobilisation, 1946, travelled throughout USA studying fashion promotion. Personal Assistant to Pierre Balmain, Paris, 1947–51; opened own business, 1952; opened John Cavanagh Boutique, 1959. Elected to Incorporated Society of London Fashion Designers,

1952 (Vice-Chm., 1956–59). Took own complete Collection to Paris, 1953; designed clothes for late Princess Marina and wedding dresses for the Duchess of Kent and Princess Alexandra. Gold Medal, Munich, 1954. *Recreations:* the theatre, swimming, travelling. *Address:* Nazareth House, Hammersmith Road, W6 8DB.

CAVANAGH, John Patrick; QC 2001; *b* 17 June 1960; *s* of Dr Gerry Cavanagh and Anne Cavanagh (*née* Kennedy); *m* 1989, Suzanne Tolley; one *s* three *d*. *Educ:* Mt Carmel Convent Sch., Stratford-on-Avon; Warwick Sch.; New Coll., Oxford (MA); Clare Coll., Cambridge (LLM); Univ. of Illinois Coll. of Law. Residential social worker, St Philip's Sch., Airdrie, 1979–80; Instructor in Law, Univ. of Illinois Coll. of Law, Urbana–Champaign, 1983–84; part-time Lectr in Law, New Coll., Oxford, 1984–87; called to the Bar, Middle Temple, 1985; in practice at the Bar, 1986–; Jun. Counsel to Crown, B Panel, 1997–2001. *Publications:* (ed and contrib.) Tolley's Employment, 9th edn 1985 to 14th edn 2000; (contrib.) Butterworth's Local Government Law, 1998; (ed jtly and contrib.) Harvey on Industrial Relations and Employment Law, annually 2000–. *Recreations:* family, reading, football (Celtic from afar), avoiding gardening. *Address:* 11 King's Bench Walk, Temple, EC4Y 7EQ. *T:* (020) 7632 8500.

CAVE, Charles Anthony H.; *see* Haddon-Cave.

CAVE, Sir John (Charles), 5th Bt *cr* 1896, of Sidbury Manor, Sidbury, co. Devon; DL; farmer and landowner; *b* 8 Sept. 1958; *e s* of Sir Charles Cave, 4th Bt and of (Mary) Elizabeth, Lady Cave, *yr d* of late John Francis Gore, CVO, TD; *S* father, 1997; *m* 1984, Carey Diana (*née* Lloyd); two *s* one *d*. *Educ:* Eton; RAC, Cirencester. DL Devon, 2001. *Heir: s* George Charles Cave, *b* 8 Sept. 1987. *Address:* Sidbury Manor, Sidmouth, Devon EX10 0QE. *Club:* MCC.

CAVE, Prof. Martin Edward, DPhil; Professor of Economics, since 1986, and Vice-Principal, since 1996, Brunel University; *b* 13 Dec. 1948; *s* of D. T. and S. M. Cave; *m* 1972, Kathryn Wilson; one *s* two *d*. *Educ:* Balliol Coll., Oxford (BA 1969); Nuffield Coll., Oxford (BPhil 1971; DPhil 1977). Res. Fellow, Birmingham Univ., 1971–74; Brunel University: Lectr, 1974–81; Sen. Lectr, 1981–86. Economic Consultant: HM Treasury, 1986–90; OFTEL, 1990–; Postal Services Commn, 2000–. Mem., Competition (formerly Monopolies and Mergers) Commn, 1996–. *Publications:* Computers and Economic Planning: the Soviet experience, 1980; (with Paul Hare) Alternative Approaches to Economic Planning, 1981; (jtly) The Use of Performance Indicators in Higher Education, 1988, 3rd edn 1997; (ed jtly) Output and Performance Measurement in Government, 1990; (ed with Saul Estrin) Competition and Competition Policy: a comparative analysis of Central and Eastern Europe, 1993; (ed jtly) Reconstituting the Market: the political economy of microeconomic transformation, 1999; (with Robert Baldwin) Understanding Regulation, 1999; contrib. to jls on regulatory economics and other subjects. *Recreations:* tennis, cinema. *Address:* Brunel University, Uxbridge UB8 3PH. *T:* (01895) 203320.

CAVE, Prof. Terence Christopher, FBA 1991; Professor of French Literature, Oxford University, since 1989; Fellow and Tutor in French, St John's College, Oxford, since 1972; *b* 1 Dec. 1938; *s* of Alfred Cyril Cave and Sylvia Norah (*née* Norman); *m* 1965, Helen Elizabeth Robb (marr. diss. 1990); one *s* one *d*. *Educ:* Winchester Coll.; Gonville and Caius Coll., Cambridge (MA; PhD; Hon. Fellow 1997). University of St Andrews: Assistant, 1962–63; Lectr, 1963–65; University of Warwick: Lectr, 1965–70; Sen. Lectr, 1970–72. Visiting Professor: Cornell Univ., 1967–68; Univ. of California, Santa Barbara, 1976; Univ. of Virginia, Charlottesville, 1979; Univ. of Toronto, 1991; Univ. of Alberta, 1992; Univ. of Paris VII, 1995; UCLA, 1997; Visiting Fellow: All Souls Coll., Oxford, 1971; Princeton Univ., 1984; Royal Norwegian Soc. of Scis and Letters, Trondheim, 1991 (Mem., 1993); Hon. Sen. Res. Fellow, Inst. of Romance Studies, Univ. of London, 1990. Mem., Academia Europaea, 1990. *Publications:* Devotional Poetry in France, 1969; Ronsard the Poet, 1973; The Cornucopian Text: problems of writing in the French Renaissance, 1979; Recognitions: a study in poetics, 1988; (trans.) Madame de Lafayette, The Princesse de Clèves, 1992; (ed) George Eliot, Daniel Deronda, 1995; (ed) George Eliot, Silas Marner, 1996; Pré-histoires: textes troublés au seuil de la modernité, 1999; articles and essays in learned jls, collective vols, etc. *Recreations:* music, languages. *Address:* St John's College, Oxford OX1 3JP. *T:* (01865) 277345.

CAVE-BROWNE-CAVE, Sir Robert, 16th Bt *cr* 1641; President of Seaboard Chemicals Ltd; *b* 8 June 1929; *s* of 15th Bt, and Dorothea Plewman, *d* of Robert Greene Dwen, Chicago, Ill; *S* father, 1945; *m* 1st, 1954, Lois Shirley (marr. diss. 1975), *d* of John Chalmers Huggard, Winnipeg, Manitoba; one *s* one *d*; 2nd, 1977, Joan Shirley, d of Dr Kenneth Ashe Peacock, West Vancouver, BC. *Educ:* University of BC (BA 1951). KSJ 1986. *Heir: s* John Robert Charles Cave-Browne-Cave, *b* 22 June 1957. *Address:* 20901–83 Avenue, RR11, Langley, BC V3A 6Y3, Canada.

CAVELL, John James; His Honour Judge Cavell; a Circuit Judge, since 1994; *b* 1 Oct. 1947; *s* of Eric Essery Cavell and Edith Emma Doreen (*née* Jose); *m* 1977, Philippa Julia Frances (*née* Kelly); one *s* one *d*. *Educ:* King Edward's Sch., Stourbridge; Churchill Coll., Cambridge (MA). Called to the Bar, Middle Temple, 1971. Practising Barrister on Midland and Oxford Circuit, 1971–94; a Recorder, 1991–94. *Recreations:* playing the piano, music generally, walking, bridge, gardening. *Address:* c/o Midland and Oxford Circuit Secretariat Judicial Team, 6th Floor, The Priory Courts, 33 Bull Street, Birmingham B4 6DW.

CAVELL, Rt Rev. John Kingsmill; Assistant Bishop, Diocese of Salisbury, since 1988; Hon. Canon, Salisbury Cathedral, since 1988; *b* 4 Nov. 1916; *o s* of late William H. G. Cavell and Edith May (*née* Warner), Deal, Kent; *m* 1942, Mary Grossett (*née* Penman) (*d* 1988), Devizes, Wilts; one *d*. *Educ:* Sir Roger Manwood's Sch., Sandwich; Queens' Coll., Cambridge (MA; Ryle Reading Prize); Wycliffe Hall, Oxford. Ordained May 1940; Curate: Christ Church, Folkestone, 1940; Addington Parish Church, Croydon, 1940–44; CMS Area Secretary, dio. Oxford and Peterborough, and CMS Training Officer, 1944–52; Vicar: Christ Church, Cheltenham, 1952–62; St Andrew's, Plymouth, 1962–72; Rural Dean of Plymouth, 1967–72; Prebendary of Exeter Cathedral, 1967–72; Bishop Suffragan of Southampton, 1972–84; Bishop to HM Prisons and Borstals, 1975–85. Hon. Canon, Winchester Cathedral, 1972–84. Proctor in Convocation; Member of General Synod (Mem., Bd for Social Responsibility, 1982–84); Surrogate. Chm., Home Cttee, CMS London; Chm., Sarum Dio. Readers' Bd, 1984–88. Chaplain, Greenbank and Freedom Fields Hosps, Plymouth; Member: Plymouth City Educn Cttee, 1967–72; City Youth Cttee; Plymouth Exec. Council NHS, 1968–72; Chairman: Hants Assoc. for the Deaf, 1972–84; Salisbury Diocesan Assoc. for the Deaf, 1988–91; Pres., Hants Genealogical Soc., 1979–84; Vice-Pres., Soc. of Genealogists. Life Fellow, Pilgrim Soc., Massachusetts, 1974. Patron, Southampton RNLI Bd, 1976–84. Governor: Cheltenham Colls of Educn; King Alfred's College of Educn, 1973–84; Croft House Sch., Shillingstone, 1986–88; Chairman: St Mary's Coll., Cheltenham, Building Cttee, 1957–62; Talbot Heath Sch., Bournemouth, 1975–84; Queensmount Sch., Bournemouth, 1980–84. *Recreations:* historical research, genealogy, philately. *Address:* Strathmore, 5 Constable Way, West Harnham, Salisbury, Wilts SP2 8LN. *T:* (01722) 334782.

CAVENAGH, Prof. Winifred Elizabeth, OBE 1977; PhD, BScEcon; Professor of Social Administration and Criminology, University of Birmingham, 1972–76, now Emeritus; Barrister-at-Law; *b* 12 Nov. 1908; *d* of Arthur Speakman and Ethel Speakman (*née* Butterworth); *m* 1938, Hugh Cavenagh; one step *s*. *Educ:* London Sch. of Economics, Univ. of London (BSc Econ); PhD Birmingham. Called to the Bar, Gray's Inn, 1964. With Lewis's Ltd, 1931–38; Min. of Labour, 1941–45. Univ. of Birmingham, 1946–. Birmingham: City Educn Cttee (co-opted expert), 1946–66; City Magistrate, 1949– (Dep. Chm., 1970–78; supplemental list, 1978–); Police Authority, 1970–78. Governor, Birmingham United Teaching Hosps (Ministerial appt, 1958–64); W Midlands Economic Planning Council, 1967–71; Indep. Mem. of Wages Councils; Home Office Standing Advisory Cttee on Probation, 1958–67; Lord Chancellor's Standing Adv. Cttee: on Legal Aid, 1960–71; on Training of Magistrates, 1965–73. Nat. Chm., Assoc. of Social Workers, 1955–57; Council, Magistrates Assoc. (co-opted expert), 1965–78; BBC Gen. Adv. Council, 1977–80; Chm., Industrial Tribunal, 1974–77; Hon. Mem., Internat. Assoc. of Juvenile and Family Courts (Vice-Pres., 1978–91). Visiting Prof., Univ of Ghana, 1971; Eleanor Rathbone Meml Lectr, 1976; Moir Cullis Lectr Fellowship, USA, 1977, Canada, 1980. *Publications:* Four Decades of Students in Social Work, 1953; The Child and the Court, 1959; Juvenile Courts, the Child and the Law, 1967; contrib. articles to: Public Administration, Brit. Jl Criminology, Justice of the Peace, Social Work To-day, etc. *Recreations:* theatre, music, films. *Address:* Flat 20, Lingfield Court, 60 High Street, Harborne, Birmingham B17 9NE. *T:* (0121) 428 2400. *Club:* University Women's.

CAVENAGH-MAINWARING, Captain Maurice Kildare, DSO 1940; Royal Navy; Simpson (Piccadilly) Ltd, 1961–91; *b* 13 April 1908; *yr s* of Major James Gordon Cavenagh-Mainwaring, Whitmore Hall, Whitmore, Staffordshire; *m* Iris Mary, *d* of late Colonel Charles Denaro, OBE; one *s*. *Educ:* RN College, Dartmouth. Joint Services Staff College, 1951–52; HMS St Angelo and Flag Captain to Flag Officer, Malta, 1952–54; President, Second Admiralty Interview Board, 1955–56; Naval Attaché, Paris, 1957–60. ADC to the Queen, 1960. Retired from RN, 1960. Cross of Merit Sovereign Order, Knights of Malta, 1955; Comdr Légion d'Honneur, 1960. *Address:* 47 Cadogan Gardens, SW3 2TH. *T:* (020) 7584 7870. *Club:* Naval and Military.

CAVENDISH, family name of **Barons Cavendish of Furness, Chesham,** of **Duke of Devonshire,** and of **Baron Waterpark**.

CAVENDISH OF FURNESS, Baron *cr* 1990 (Life Peer), of Cartmel in the County of Cumbria; **Richard Hugh Cavendish;** Chairman, Holker Estate Group of Companies (interests including agricultural and urban property, leisure, mineral extraction, export, construction and forestry), since 1971; *b* 2 Nov. 1941; *s* of late Richard Edward Osborne Cavendish and of Pamela J. Lloyd Thomas; *m* 1970, Grania Mary Caulfeild; one *s* two *d*. *Educ:* Eton. International banking, 1961–71. Dir, UK Nirex Ltd, 1993–99. A Lord in Waiting (Govt Whip), 1990–92. Mem., H of L Select Cttee on Croydon Tramlink Bill, 1992–93. Mem., Hist. Buildings and Monuments Commn for England, 1992–98. Chm., Lancs & Cumbria Foundn for Med. Res., 1994–. Chm., Morecambe and Lonsdale Conservative Assoc., 1975–78. Chm. Governors, St Anne's Sch., Windermere, 1983–89. Mem., Cumbria CC, 1985–90. High Sheriff 1978, DL 1988, Cumbria. FRSA. *Recreations:* gardening, National Hunt racing, collecting drawings, reading, travel. *Address:* Holker Hall, Cark-in-Cartmel, Cumbria LA11 7PL. *T:* (015395) 58220. *Clubs:* Brooks's, Pratt's, White's, Beefsteak.

CAVENDISH, Lady Elizabeth (Georgiana Alice), CVO 1997 (LVO 1976); Extra Lady-in-Waiting to Princess Margaret, since 1951; Chairman, Cancer Research Campaign, 1981–96; Member, Press Complaints Commission, 1991–96; *b* 24 April 1926; *d* of 10th Duke of Devonshire, KG, and Lady Mary Cecil, GCVO, CBE (*d* 1988), *d* of 4th Marquess of Salisbury, KG, GCVO. *Educ:* private. Member: Advertising Standards Authority, 1981–91; Marre Cttee on Future of Legal Profession, 1986–89; Lay Mem., Disciplinary Cttee of Gen. Council of the Bar (formerly Senate of Inns of Court's Professional Conduct Cttee of Bar Council and Disciplinary Cttee Tribunal), 1983–. Chm., Bd of Visitors, Wandsworth Prison, 1970–73; Mem. Council, St Christopher's Hospice, Sydenham, 1991–. JP London, 1961; Chairman: N Westminster Magistrates' Court PSD, 1980–83; Inner London Juvenile Courts, 1983–86. *Address:* 19 Radnor Walk, SW3 4BP. *T:* (020) 7352 0774; Moor View, Edensor, Bakewell, Derbyshire DE45 1PH. *T:* (01246) 582204.

See also Duke of Devonshire.

CAVENDISH, Maj.-Gen. Peter Boucher, CB 1981; OBE 1969; DL; retired; Chairman, Military Agency for Standardisation and Director, Armaments Standardisation and Interoperability Division, International Military Staff, HQ NATO, 1978–81; *b* 26 Aug. 1925; *s* of late Brig. R. V. C. Cavendish, OBE, MC (killed in action, 1943) and Helen Cavendish (*née* Boucher); *m* 1952, Marion Loudon (*née* Constantine); three *s*. *Educ:* Abberley Hall, Worcester; Winchester Coll.; New Coll., Oxford. Enlisted 1943; commnd The Royal Dragoons, 1945; transf. 3rd The King's Own Hussars, 1946; Staff Coll., Camberley, 1955; served Palestine, BAOR, Canada and N Africa to 1966; CO 14th/20th King's Hussars, 1966–69; HQ 1st British Corps, 1969–71; Comdt RAC Centre, 1971–74; Canadian Defence Coll., 1975; Sec. to Mil. Cttee and Internat. Mil. Staff, HQ NATO, 1975–78. Colonel, 14th/20th King's Hussars, 1976–81; Hon. Col, The Queen's Own Mercian Yeomanry, TAVR, 1982–87; Col Comdt, Yeomanry RAC TA, 1986–90. Mem., Peak Park Jt Planning Bd, 1982–91 (Vice-Chm., 1987–91). Chairman: SSAFA/FHS Derbyshire, 1987–96; Derbys Forces Link, 1990–. FIMgt (FBIM 1979). High Sheriff, 1986–87, DL 1989, Derbys. *Recreations:* shooting, country pursuits, computers, DIY. *Address:* The Rock Cottage, Middleton-by-Youlgrave, Bakewell, Derbys DE45 1LS. *T:* (01629) 636225, *Fax:* (01629) 636325; *e-mail:* pbcav@aol.com.

CAWDOR, 7th Earl *cr* 1827; **Colin Robert Vaughan Campbell;** Baron Cawdor, 1796; Viscount Emlyn, 1827; DL; *b* 30 June 1962; *s* of 6th Earl and of his 1st wife, Cathryn, *d* of Maj.-Gen. Sir Robert Hinde, KBE, CB, DSO; *S* father, 1993; *m* 1994, Lady Isabella Stanhope, *y d* of Earl of Harrington, *qv*; one *s* one *d*. *Educ:* Eton; St Peter's College, Oxford. Member, James Bridal Meml Soc., London. DL Nairn, 1996. *Heir: s* Viscount Emlyn, *qv*. *Address:* Carnoch, The Streens, Nairn IV12 5RQ.

CAWDRON, George Edward; District Judge (Magistrates' Courts) (formerly Provincial Stipendiary Magistrate), North East London, since 1993; *b* 24 Feb. 1943; 3rd *s* of William Edward Cawdron and Louise Kathleen (*née* Walker); *m* 1965, Linda Margaret Preest; two *d*. *Educ:* Arnos Sch. Called to the Bar, Inner Temple, 1974. Dep. Clerk to the Justices, Willesden Div., London, 1975–77; Clerk to the Justices, Dacorum Div., 1977–91, Dacorum and Watford Divs, 1991–93, Herts; County Trng Officer for magistrates and staff, Herts, 1980–93. *Recreations:* classic cars, swimming, golf, gardening. *Address:* Croft End, 23 Barncroft Road, Berkhamsted, Herts HP4 3NL. *T:* (01442) 871112.

CAWLEY, family name of **Baron Cawley**.

CAWLEY, 4th Baron *cr* 1918; **John Francis Cawley;** Bt 1906; *b* 28 Sept. 1946; *s* of 3rd Baron Cawley and of Rosemary Joan (*née* Marsden); *S* father, 2001; *m* 1979, Regina

Sarabia, *d* of late Marqués de Hazas, Madrid; three *s* one *d*. *Educ:* Eton. *Heir: s* Hon. William Robert Harold Cawley, *b* 2 July 1981. *Address:* Castle Ground, Ashton, Leominster, Herefordshire HR6 0DN. *T:* (01584) 711209.

CAWLEY, Stephen Ingleby, FCA; Director of Finance, Property Services and Royal Travel, Royal Household, since 1996; *b* 14 March 1947; *s* of Joe Cawley and Madge (*née* Ingleby); *m* 1971, Mariquet Scott; two *s*. *Educ:* Hull Grammar Sch.; Edinburgh Univ. (MA 1970). FCA 1973. Joined KPMG, 1970; Partner, 1984–94; Sen. Partner, Sussex, 1992–94; financial consultancy and Lectr, Univ. of Brighton, 1994–96. *Recreations:* opera, wine, gardening, sports. *Address:* (office) Buckingham Palace, SW1A 1AA. *T:* (020) 7930 4832.

CAWSEY, Ian Arthur; MP (Lab) Brigg and Goole, since 1997; *b* 14 April 1960; *s* of Arthur Henry Cawsey and Edith Morrison Cawsey; *m* 1987, Linda Mary, *d* of Henry and Joy Kirman; one *s* two *d*. *Educ:* Wintringham Sch. Computer operator, 1977–78; computer programmer, 1978–82; systems analyst, 1982–85; IT consultant, 1985–87; PA to Elliot Morley, MP, 1987–97. Member (Lab): Humberside CC, 1989–96; N Lincs Unitary Council, 1995–97 (Leader, 1995–97); Chm., Humberside Police Authy, 1993–97. PPS to Leader of House of Lords, 2001–. Chm., All Party Gp on Animal Welfare, 1998–. *Address:* House of Commons, SW1A 0AA.

CAWSON, Prof. Roderick Anthony, MD; FDS, RCS and RCPS Glasgow; FRCPath; Professor (Hon. Consultant) and Head of Department of Oral Medicine and Pathology, United Medical and Dental Schools, Guy's Hospital, 1966–86, now Emeritus; *b* 23 April 1921; *s* of Capt. Leopold Donald Cawson and Ivy Clunies-Ross; *m* 1949, Diana Hall, SRN; no *c*. *Educ:* King's College Sch. Wimbledon; King's College Hosp. Med. Sch. MD (London); MB, BS, BDS (Hons) (London); FDS, RCS; FDS, RCPS Glasgow; MRCPath; LMSSA. Served RAF, 1944–48; Nuffield Foundn Fellow, 1953–55; Dept of Pathology, King's Coll. Hosp., Sen. Lectr in Oral Pathology, King's Coll. Hosp. Med. Sch., 1955–62; Sen. Lectr in Oral Pathology, Guy's Hosp. Med. Sch., 1962–66. Examinerships: Pathology (BDS) London, 1965–69; Univ. of Wales, 1969–71; Dental Surgery (BDS), Glasgow, 1966–70; BChD Leeds, 1966–70; Newcastle, 1967–71; FDS, RCPS Glasgow, 1967–86; BDS Lagos, 1975–78; RCPath, 1984–87. Chairman: Dental Formulary Sub-cttee (BMA); Dental and Surgical Materials Cttee, Medicines Division, 1976–80; recently First Chm, Univ. Teachers' Gp (BDA). *Publications:* Essentials of Dental Surgery and Pathology 1962, 5th edn 1991, 6th edn as Oral Pathology and Oral Medicine (with E. W. Odell), 1998; Medicine for Dental Students (with R. H. Cutforth), 1960; (with R. G. Spector) Clinical Pharmacology in Dentistry, 1975, 5th edn 1989; Aids to Oral Pathology and Diagnosis, 1981; (with C. Scully) Medical Problems in Dentistry, 1982, 4th edn 1998; (with A. W. McCracken and P. B. Marcus) Pathology: the mechanisms of disease, 1982, 2nd edn 1989; (with A. W. McCracken) Clinical and Oral Microbiology, 1982; (with J. W. Eveson) Oral Pathology and Diagnosis, 1987, 2nd edn as Oral Disease: clinico-pathological correlations, 1993; (jtly) Lucas's Pathology of Tumours of the Oral Tissues, 5th edn 1998; numerous papers, etc, in med. and dental jls. *Recreations:* reading, music, gardening (reluctantly). *Address:* 40 Court Lane, Dulwich, SE21 7DR. *T:* (020) 8693 5781.

CAWTHRA, Rear-Adm. Arthur James, CB 1966; Admiral Superintendent, HM Dockyard, Devonport, 1964–66; *b* 30 Sept. 1911; *s* of James Herbert Cawthra, MIEE, and Margaret Anne Cawthra; *m* 1959, Adrien Eleanor Lakeman Tivy, *d* of Cecil B. Tivy, MCh, Plymouth; one *s* (and one *s* decd). *Educ:* abroad. Joined Royal Navy, 1930; Imperial Defence Course, 1956; HMS Fisgard, 1958–59; Dir Underwater Weapons, Admiralty, 1960–63. Capt. 1955; Rear-Adm. 1964.

CAWTHRA, David Wilkinson, CBE 1997; FREng; FICE; Principal, Cawthra & Co., since 1995; *b* 5 March 1943; *s* of Jack and Dorothy Cawthra; *m* 1967, Maureen Williamson; one *s* one *d*. *Educ:* Heath Grammar Sch., Halifax; Univ. of Birmingham (BSc Hons). Mitchell Construction Co., 1963–73; Tarmac Construction, 1973–78; Balfour Beatty Ltd, 1979–91; Chief Executive: Balfour Beatty, 1988–91; Miller Group, 1992–94. Dir, BICC, 1988–91. Chm., Nat. Rail Contractors' Gp, 1999–. Vice-Pres., ICE, 1996–99. FREng (FEng 1990). *Recreation:* hill walking. *Address:* Redhurst, 68 Ravelston Dykes, Edinburgh EH12 6HF. *Club:* Royal Automobile.

CAYGILL, Hon. David Francis; Partner, Buddle Findlay, Barristers and Solicitors, New Zealand, since 1996; *b* 15 Nov. 1948; *s* of Bruce Allott Caygill and Gwyneth Mary Caygill; *m* 1974, Eileen Ellen Boyd; one *s* three *d*. *Educ:* St Albans Primary Sch.; Christchurch Boys' High Sch.; Univ. of Canterbury (BA, LLB). Pres., Univ. of Canterbury Students' Assoc., 1971. Barrister and Solicitor, 1974–78; Christchurch City Councillor, 1971–80; MP (Lab) St Albans, NZ, 1978–96; Minister of Trade and Industry, Minister of Nat. Develt, Associate Minister of Finance, 1984–87; Minister of Health, Dep. Minister of Finance, 1987–88; Minister of Finance, 1988–90; Dep. Leader of the Opposition, 1994–96. *Recreations:* collecting and listening to classical records, following American politics. *Address:* c/o Buddle Findlay, PO Box 322, Christchurch, New Zealand. *Club:* St Albans Shirley.

CAYLEY, Sir Digby (William David), 11th Bt *cr* 1661; MA; Master i/c Shooting, Marlborough College, since 1994; *b* 3 June 1944; *s* of Lieut-Comdr W. A. S. Cayley, RN (*d* 1964) (*g g s* of 7th Bt), and Natalie Maud Cayley, BA (*d* 1994); *S* kinsman, 1967; *m* 1st, 1969, Christine Mary Gaunt (marr. diss. 1987); two *d*; 2nd, 1993, Cathryn Mary Russell, MA Cantab; two *s*. *Educ:* Malvern Coll.; Downing Coll., Cambridge (MA). Assistant Classics Master: Portsmouth Grammar Sch., 1968–73; Stonyhurst Coll., 1973–81; dealer in antiques, 1981–89; Assistant Classics Master: Marlborough Coll., 1989–90 and 1994–97; Abingdon Sch., 1990–94. *Recreations:* target rifle shooting, travel. *Heir: s* Thomas Theodore William Cayley, *b* 17 Feb. 1997. *Address:* Morris House, Marlborough College, Marlborough, Wilts SN8 1PA. *T:* (01672) 513188.

CAYLEY, Michael Forde; Director, Personnel and Support Services, Department of Social Security, 1998–2000; *b* 26 Feb. 1950; *s* of Forde Everard De Wend Cayley and Eileen Lilian Cayley; *m* 1987, Jennifer Athalie Jeffcoate Lytle. *Educ:* Brighton Coll.; St John's Coll., Oxford (MA English). Admin Trainee, Inland Revenue, 1971–73; Private Sec. to Chm., Price Commn, 1973–75; Inland Revenue: Principal, 1975; Asst Sec., 1982; Under Sec., 1991; Dir, Financial Instns Div., 1994–98, Company Tax Div., 1995–98. *Publications: poems:* Moorings, 1971; (ed) Selected Poems of Richard Crashaw, 1972; The Spider's Touch, 1973; poems and articles on modern poets in various mags. *Recreations:* piano-playing, choral singing, languages, walking, art, history, crosswords.

CAYTON, William Henry Rymer, (Harry), OBE 2001; Chief Executive, Alzheimer's Society (formerly Executive Director, Alzheimer's Disease Society), since 1991; *b* 27 March 1950; *s* of late Dr Henry Rymer Cayton and Marion Cromie (*née* Young). *Educ:* Bristol Cathedral Sch.; New Univ. of Ulster (BA Hons 1971); Univ. of Durham (Dip. Anth. 1973); Univ. of Newcastle upon Tyne (BPhil 1979). Teacher: King's Sch., Rochester, 1972; Dame Allan's Sch., Newcastle upon Tyne, 1973–76; Northern Counties Sch. for the Deaf, 1976–80; National Deaf Children's Society: Educn Officer, 1980–82; Dir, 1982–91. Canadian Commonwealth Fellow, 1983. Member: Sec. of State for Health's Adv. Gp on Youth Treatment Service, 1991–96; Central R&D Cttee, NHS, 1999–; NHS Modernisation Bd, 2000; Vice Chm., Consumers in NHS Research, 1996–. Chm., Voluntary Council for Handicapped Children, 1986–91. Trustee: Hearing Res. Trust, 1985–; Nat. Children's Bureau, 1987–91; Age Concern England, 1992–94. Mem. Bd, Alzheimer Europe, 1998–. Pres. and Hon. Life Mem., European Fedn of Deaf Children's Assocs, 1990–91. Frequent broadcasts. FRSA 1995. *Publications:* chapters in: Clinical Developments in Cochlear Implants, 1990; Managing Alzheimer's Disease, 1992; Options For Long Term Care, 1996; Alzheimer's at your Fingertips, 1997; Psychiatry in the Elderly, 2001; numerous articles in jls. *Recreations:* modern British art, music, food. *Address:* 24 Barlby Gardens, North Kensington, W10 5LW. *T:* (office) (020) 7306 0606.

CAYZER, family name of **Baron Rotherwick**.

CAYZER, Sir James Arthur, 5th Bt *cr* 1904; *b* 15 Nov. 1931; *s* of Sir Charles William Cayzer, 3rd Bt, MP (*d* 1940), and Beatrice Eileen (*d* 1981), *d* of late James Meakin and Emma Beatrice (later wife of 3rd Earl Sondes); *S* brother, 1943. *Educ:* Eton. *Heir:* cousin Baron Rotherwick, *qv*. *Address:* Kinpurnie Castle, Newtyle, Angus PH12 8TW. *T:* (01828) 650207. *Club:* Carlton.

CAZALET, Hon. Lady; Camilla Jane; *b* 12 July 1937; *d* of 6th Viscount Gage, KCVO, and Hon. Alexandra Imogen Clare Grenfell (*d* 1969); *m* 1965, Hon. Sir Edward Stephen Cazalet, *qv*; two *s* one *d*. *Educ:* Benenden Sch. Dir, Lumley Cazalet, 1967–. Trustee, Glyndebourne Arts Trust, 1978–; Member: Royal Nat. Theatre Bd, 1991–97; Exec. Cttee, Friends of Covent Garden, 1994–; Royal Nat. Theatre Develt Council, 1996–; Gov., Royal Ballet, 2000–. *Recreations:* theatre, music, tennis. *Address:* 58 Seymour Walk, SW10 1NF. *T:* (020) 7352 0401; Shaw Farm, Plumpton Green, near Lewes, Sussex BN7 3DG. *T:* (01273) 890207.

CAZALET, Hon. Sir Edward (Stephen), Kt 1988; DL; a Judge of the High Court of Justice, Family Division, 1988–2000; *b* 26 April 1936; *s* of late Peter Victor Ferdinand Cazalet and Leonora Cazalet (*née* Rowley); *m* 1965, Camilla Jane (*née* Gage) (*see* Hon. Lady Cazalet); two *s* one *d*. *Educ:* Eton Coll. (Fellow, 1989); Christ Church, Oxford (MA Jurisprudence). Called to the Bar, Inner Temple, 1960, Bencher, 1985. QC 1980; a Recorder, 1985–88; Family Division Liaison Judge for SE Circuit, 1990–96. Chairman: Horserace Betting Levy Appeal Tribunal, 1977–88; Sussex Assoc. for Rehabilitation of Offenders, 1991–98; CAB, Royal Courts of Justice, 1992–98; British Agencies for Adoption and Fostering, 2000–. Chm. Trustees, Charles Douglas-Home Award, 1986–96. Trustee, Injured Jockeys' Fund, 1987–. DL E Sussex, 1989. *Recreations:* riding, ball games, chess. *Address:* 58 Seymour Walk, SW10 9NF. *Club:* Garrick.

CAZALET, Sir Peter (Grenville), Kt 1989; Chairman, Seascope Shipping Holdings plc, since 2000 (Director since 1997); *b* 26 Feb. 1929; *e s* of Vice-Adm. Sir Peter (Grenville Lyon) Cazalet, KBE, CB, DSO, DSC, and Lady (Elise) Cazalet (*née* Winterbotham); *m* 1957, Jane Jennifer, *yr d* of Charles and Nancy Rew, Guernsey, CI; three *s*. *Educ:* Uppingham Sch., Uppingham, Rutland (schol.); Magdalene Coll., Cambridge (Schol.; MA Hons). General Manager, BP Tanker Co. Ltd, 1968; Regional Co-ordinator, Australasia and Far East, 1970; Pres., BP North America Inc., 1972–75; Director: Standard Oil Co. of Ohio, 1973–75; BP Trading Ltd, 1975–81; Peninsular & Oriental Steam Navigation Co., 1980–99; Man. Dir, 1981–89, Dep. Chm., 1986–89, BP; Chm., BP Oil International, 1981–89. Chm., APV plc, 1989–96; Dep. Chm., GKN, 1989–96; Chm., Hakluyt and Co., 1998–99 (Mem., Hakluyt Foundn, 1997–2000). Dir, De La Rue Co., 1983–95. Chm., Armed Forces Pay Review Body, 1989–93; Mem., Top Salaries Review Body, 1989–94. Pres., China Britain Trade Gp, 1996–98 (Vice-Pres., 1993–96); a Vice-Pres., ME Assoc., 1982–; Hon. Sec., King George's Fund for Sailors, 1989–2000; Gov., Wellcome Trust Ltd, 1992–96 (Trustee, Wellcome Trust, 1989–92); Trustee, Uppingham Sch., 1976–95; Mem., Gen. Cttee, Lloyd's Register of Shipping, 1981–99 (Mem. Bd, 1981–86). CIMgt (CBIM 1982). Liveryman: Tallow Chandlers' Co. (Master, 1991–92); Shipwrights' Co. *Recreations:* theatre, fishing. *Address:* c/o 22 Hill Street, W1X 7FU. *T:* (020) 7496 4423. *Clubs:* Brooks's, Royal Wimbledon Golf, MCC.

CECIL; *see* Gascoyne-Cecil, family name of Marquess of Salisbury.

CECIL, family name of **Baron Amherst of Hackney, Marquess of Exeter** and **Baron Rockley**.

CECIL, Baron; *see* Viscount Cranborne.

CECIL, Desmond Hugh, CMG 1995; Senior Advisor: British Nuclear Fuels, since 1996; Marconi (formerly GEC/Marconi Communications), since 1998; *b* 19 Oct. 1941; *s* of Dr Rupert Cecil, DFC, and Rosemary Cecil (*née* Luker); *m* 1964, Ruth Elizabeth Sachs; three *s* one *d*. *Educ:* Headington Co. Primary Sch.; Magdalen Coll. Sch., Oxford; Queen's Coll., Oxford (MA); studied violin/viola and oboe with Max Rostal, Berne and Joy Boughton, London. Violinist and oboist in Switzerland; Leader, Neuchâtel Chamber Orchestra, 1965–70; joined HM Diplomatic Service, 1970; Second Sec., FCO, 1970–73; First Secretary: Bonn, 1973–74; FCO, 1974–76; also Press Officer, Mission to UN, Geneva, 1976–80; FCO, 1980–85; Counsellor and Chargé d'Affaires, Vienna, 1985–89; FCO, 1989–92; on secondment with Board of P&O European Ferries, 1992; Under Sec., FCO, 1992–95. Sen. Advr, British Telecom, 1996–97. Antiquarian book dealer, 1997–. Council Mem., Britain Russia Centre, 1998–2000; Member Board: Germany Project, Panel 2000, 1999–2000; Internat. Mendelssohn Foundn, Leipzig, 2001–. Council Mem., Royal Philharmonic Soc., 1995– (Chm., Sponsorship Cttee, 1998–; Hon. Co-Treas., 1999–); Dir and Trustee, Jupiter Orch., 1996–; Advr, Internat. Menuhin Fest., Gstaad, 2001–; Trustee: Russia Arts Help Charity, Moscow, 2000–; Voices for Hospices, 2000–. Member: Mensa, 1968–; Sherlock Holmes Soc. of London, 1970–; Kingston Chamber Music Soc., 1990; British–German Assoc., 2001–. *Recreations:* playing music and cricket, downhill ski-ing, chess, antiquarian travel books. *Address:* 38 Palace Road, East Molesey, Surrey KT8 9DL. *T:* (020) 8783 1998. *Clubs:* Athenæum (Chm., Wine Cttee), MCC (Eur. Cricket Advr, 1998–); Claygate Cricket (Captain).

CECIL, Henry Richard Amherst; trainer of racehorses; *b* 11 Jan. 1943; *s* of late Hon. Henry Kerr Auchmuty Cecil and of Elizabeth Rohays Mary (who; *m* 2nd, Sir Cecil Boyd-Rochfort, KCVO), *d* of Sir James Burnett, 13th Bt, CB, CMG, DSO; *m* 1st, 1966, Julia (marr. diss. 1990), *d* of Sir Noel Murless; one *s* one *d*; 2nd, 1992, Natalie Payne; one *s*. *Educ:* Canford School. Commenced training under flat race rules, 1969; previously Assistant to Sir Cecil Boyd-Rochfort. Leading Trainer, 1976, 1978, 1979, 1982, 1984, 1985, 1987, 1988, 1990, 1993. *Publication:* On the Level (autobiog.), 1983. *Recreation:* gardening. *Address:* Warren Place, Newmarket, Suffolk CB8 8QQ. *T:* (01638) 662387.

CECIL, Rear-Adm. Sir (Oswald) Nigel (Amherst), KBE 1979; CB 1978; *b* 11 Nov. 1925; *s* of Comdr the Hon. Henry M. A. Cecil, OBE, RN, and the Hon. Mrs Henry Cecil; *m* 1961, Annette (CStJ 1980), *d* of Maj. Robert Barclay, TD, Bury Hill, near Dorking, Surrey; one *s*. *Educ:* Ludgrove; Royal Naval Coll., Dartmouth. Joined Navy, 1939; served World War II, Russian convoys, Western approaches and English Channel, 1943–45; HMS Swiftsure, British Pacific Fleet, 1945–46; in comd HM MTB 521, 1947–48; Flag Lieut to Admiral, BJSM, Washington, 1950–52; Comdr, 1959; Chief Staff

Officer, London Div. RNR, 1959–61; in comd: HMS Corunna, 1961–63; HMS Royal Arthur, 1963–66; Captain 1966; Central Staff, MoD, 1966–69; Captain (D) Dartmouth Trng Sqdn and in comd HMS Tenby and HMS Scarborough, 1969–71; Senior British Naval Officer, S Africa, Naval Attaché, Capetown, and in command HMS Afrikander, as Cdre, 1971–73; Dir, Naval Operational Requirements, 1973–75; Naval ADC to the Queen, 1975; Rear-Adm., 1975; NATO Comdr SE Mediterranean, 1975–77; Comdr British Forces Malta, and Flag Officer Malta, 1975–79; Lieut Gov., Isle of Man, and Pres. of Tynwald, 1980–85. Pres., St John Council, IoM, 1980–85, IoW, 1996–; County Pres., IoW, St John Ambulance, 1991–96; Vice Pres., RUKBA, 1991–; Vice Patron, Naval Officers Assoc. of S Africa, 1973–. FIMgt (FBIM 1980). KStJ 1980 (OStJ 1971). *Address:* The Old Rectory, Shorwell, Isle of Wight PO30 3JL. *Clubs:* White's, MCC.

CELA, Camilo José; Grand Cross, Order of Isabel la Católica; Spanish writer; *b* 11 May 1916; *s* of Camilo Cela and Camila (*née* Trulock Bertorini); *m* 1991, Marina Castaño; one *s* by former marriage. *Educ:* Univ. of Madrid. Has held various jobs including those of actor, bull fighter, painter, journalist and civil servant. Senator, Cortés, 1977–78. Founder, 1956, and Editor, 1956–79, Papeles de Son Armadans (literary jl). Asturias Prize, 1987; Nobel Prize for Literature, 1989. Grand Cross, Order of the Sun (Peru). *Publications: fiction:* La familia de Pascal Duarte, 1942; Pabellón de reposo, 1943; Nuevas andanzas y desventuras del Lazarillo de Tormes, 1944; La colmena, 1951; Timoteo el incomprendido, 1952; Santa Balbina, 37, gas en cada piso, 1952; Mrs Cadwell habla con su hijo, 1952; Café des artistas, 1953; La catira, 1955; El molino de viento, 1956; Tobogán de hambrientos, 1962; El ciudadano Iscariote Reclús, 1965; La familia del héroe o Discurso histórico de los últimos restos, 1965; Víspera, festividad y octava de San Camilo 1936 en Madrid, 1969; Oficio de tinieblas 5, 1973; Mazurca para dos muertos, 1983 (Nat. Literature Prize, 1984); Cristo Versus Arizona, 1988; Los Caprichos de Francisco de Goya y Lucientes, 1989; El asesinato del perdedor, 1994; La cruz de San Andrés, 1994; Madera de boj, 1999; *short stories:* Esas nubes que pasan, 1945; El bonito crimen del carabinero, 1947; El gallego y su cuadrilla, 1949; Nuevo retablo de Don Cristobita, 1957; Los viejos amigos, 1960; Gavillas de fábulas sin amor, 1962; Toreo de salón: farsa con acompañamiento de clamor y murga, 1963; El solitario y los sueños de Quesada de Rafael Zabaleta, 1963; Once cuentos de fútbol, 1963; Izas, rabizas y colipoterras: drama con acompañamiento de cachondeo y dolor de corazón, 1964; Nuevas escenas matritenses, 1965; Rol de cornudos, 1976; El espejo y otros cuentos, 1981; La bandada de palomas, 1987; El hombre y el mar, 1990; La sima de las penúltimas inocencias, 1993; *poetry:* Pisando la dudosa luz del día, 1945; El monasterio y las palabras, 1945; Cancionero de la Alcarria, 1948; Tres poemas galegos, 1957; Reloj de arena, reloj de sol, reloj de sangre, 1989; Poesía completa, 1996; *ballads:* La verdadera historia de Gumersinda Cosculluela, moza que prefirió la muerte a la deshonva, 1959; Encarnación Toledano o la Perdición de los hombres, 1959; Viaje a USA, 1965; *plays:* Maria Sabina, 1967; El carro de heno o el inventor de la guillotina, 1969; Homenaje al Bosco II, 1999; *travel:* Viaje a la Alcarria, 1948; Avila, 1952; Del Miño al Bidasoa, 1952; Judíos, moros y cristianos, 1956; Primer viaje andaluz, 1959; Páginas de geografía errabunda, 1965; Viaje al Pirineo de Lérida, 1965; Madrid, 1966; Barcelona, 1970; Nuevo viaje a la Alcarria, 1986; Galicia, 1990; *non-fiction:* Diccionario secreto, 1968; Enciclopedia del erotismo, 1976; Diccionario geográfico popular, vol. I, 1998; *essays:* Mesa revuelta, 1945; Cajón de sastre, 1957; La rueda de los ocios, 1957; Cuatro figuras del 98, 1959; Garito de hospicianos o guirigay de imposturas y bambollas, 1963; Las compañías convenientes y otros fingimientos y cegueras, 1963; Al servicio de algo, 1969; Los sueños vanos, los ángeles curiosos, 1979; Vuelta de hoja, 1981; Los vasos comunicantes, 1981; El juego de los tres madroños, 1983; El asno de Buridán, 1986; Cachondeos, escarceos y otros meneos, 1991; Desde el palomar de Hita, 1991; El camaleón soltero, 1992; El huevo del juicio, 1993; A bote pronto, 1994; *memoirs:* La rosa, 1959; Memorias, entendimientos y voluntades, 1993; *adaptations and translations:* Poema del Cid, Cantar 1, 1957–59; Ruperto de No la, Libro de guisados manjares y potajes, 1969; Bertolt Brecht, La resistible ascensión de Arturo Ui, 1975; La Celestina, 1979; El Quijote, 1981. *Address:* c/o Agencia Literaria Carmen Balcells, Diagonal 580, 08021 Barcelona, Spain.

CELAC, Sergiu; Chairman, EmC Emission Control Ltd, since 2000; Senior Research Fellow, Romanian Institute of International Studies, since 2000; *b* Bucharest, 26 May 1939; *s* of Nicolae and Elena Celac; *m* 1964, Rea-Silvia Casu. *Educ:* Bucharest Univ. Romanian Foreign Service, 1961–2000: Private Sec. to Dep. Foreign Minister, 1963–69; Dep. Dir, then Dir, Policy Planning, Min. of Foreign Affairs, 1969–74; interpreter at Presidency, 1974–78; reader, Scientific and Encyclopaedic Publishing House, 1978–89; Minister of Foreign Affairs, Dec. 1989–June 1990; Romanian Ambassador to the UK, 1990–96, and to Ireland, 1991–96. Co-Chm., CEPS Caucasus Task Force. Member: Nat. Council, Romanian Writers' Union, 1990–2000; Journalists' Soc. of Romania, 1991–2000; European Atlantic Gp, 1991–2000; Atlantic Council of UK, 1993–2000; IISS, 1994–2000. Vice-Pres., Black Sea Univ. Foundn. Mem. Nat. Exec., Romanian Shooting and Fishing Sports Union, 1990–2000 (Past Pres.). *Publications:* studies and essays on political sci.; trans. novels and poetry from and into Russian and English. *Recreation:* shooting. *Address:* Aleea Alexandru 10, 71273 Bucharest 1, Romania. *T:* (1) 2301935, *Fax:* (1) 2312068; *e-mail:* sergiu.celac@emcrom.ro.

CERF, Vinton Gray, PhD; Senior Vice-President for Internet Architecture and Technology, WorldCom Corporation, since 1998; *b* New Haven, Conn, 23 June 1943; *s* of Vinton Thruston Cerf and Muriel Cerf (*née* Gray); *m* 1966, Sigrid L. Thorstenberg; two *s*. *Educ:* Van Nuys High Sch., Calif; Stanford Univ. (BS 1965); UCLA (MS 1970; PhD 1972). Systems Engr, IBM Corp., 1965-67; Principal Programmer, Computer Sci. Dept, UCLA, 1967-72; Asst Prof. of Elec. Engrg and Computer Sci., Stanford Univ., 1972-76; Prog. Manager, 1976-81, Principal Scientist, 1981-82, Defense Advanced Res. Projects Agency; Vice-Pres. of Engrg, MCI Digital Inf. Services Co., 1982-86; Vice-Pres., Corp. for Nat. Res. Initiatives, 1986-94; Sen. Vice-Pres. for Data Architecture, MCI Telecoms Corp., 1994-95; Sen. Vice-Pres. for Internet Architecture and Engrg, MCI Communications Corp., 1996-98. Dist. Vis. Scientist, Jet Propulsion Lab., CIT, 1998-. Internet Society: Founder Mem., 1992-; Founder Pres., 1992-95; Chm., 1998-99; Trustee, 1992-; Chm., Internet Societal Task Force, 1999-2000. FAAAS, 1990. *Address:* WorldCom Corporation, 22001 Loudoun County Parkway, Ashburn, VA 20147, USA.

CESARANI, Prof. David, DPhil; Director, AHRB Parkes Centre for the Study of Jewish/non-Jewish Relations and Professor of Modern Jewish History, Southampton University, since 2000; *b* 13 Nov. 1956; *s* of Henry Cesarani and late Sylvia Cesarani (*née* Packman); *m* 1991, Dawn Waterman; one *s* one *d*. *Educ:* Latymer Upper Sch.; Queens' Coll., Cambridge (BA Hist.); Columbia Univ., NY (MA Jewish Hist.); St Antony's Coll., Oxford (DPhil 1986). Montague Burton Fellow in Modern Jewish Hist., Univ. of Leeds, 1983–86; part-time Lectr, Oxford Centre for Postgrad. Hebrew Studies, 1986–87; Barnett Shine Sen. Res. Fellow and Lectr in Politics, Dept of Political Studies, QMC, 1986–89; Dir of Studies and Educnl Activities, 1989–92, Dir, 1992–95 and 1996–2000, Inst. of Contemporary Hist. and Wiener Liby, London; Adjunct Lectr, Dept of Hebrew and Jewish Studies, UCL, 1990–95; Alliance Family Prof. of Modern Jewish Studies, Dept of Religions and Theol., Univ. of Manchester, 1995–96; Parkes-Wiener Prof. of Twentieth Century European Jewish Hist. and Culture, Southampton Univ., 1996–2000. *Publications:* (ed) The Making of Modern Anglo-Jewry, 1990; Justice Delayed: how Britain became a refuge for Nazi war criminals, 1992; (ed with T. Kushner) The Internment of Aliens in Twentieth Century Britain, 1993; (ed) The Final Solution: origins and implementation, 1994; The Jewish Chronicle and Anglo-Jewry 1841–1991, 1994; (ed with M. Fulbrook) Citizenship, Nationality and Migration in Europe, 1996; (ed) Genocide and Rescue: the Holocaust in Hungary 1944, 1997; (ed jtly) Belsen in History and Memory, 1997; Arthur Koestler: the homeless mind, 1998. *Recreations:* walking, badminton, food, films, friends and family. *Address:* Department of History, University of Southampton, Highfield, Southampton SO17 1BJ.

CHADLINGTON, Baron *cr* 1996 (Life Peer), of Dean in the county of Oxfordshire; **Peter Selwyn Gummer;** Director, Huntsworth plc, since 2000; *b* 24 Aug. 1942; *s* of late Rev. Canon Selwyn Gummer and Sybille (*née* Mason); *m* 1982, Lucy Rachel, *er d* of A. Ponsonby Dudley-Hill; one *s* three *d*. *Educ:* King's Sch., Rochester, Kent; Selwyn Coll., Cambridge (BA, MA). Portsmouth and Sunderland Newspaper Gp, 1964–65; Viyella International, 1965–66; Hodgkinson & Partners, 1966–67; Industrial & Commercial Finance Corp., 1967–74; Chairman, Shandwick Internat. plc, 1974–2000; Internat. Public Relations, 1998–2000. Non-executive Director: CIA Group PLC, 1990–94; Halifax plc (formerly Halifax Building Soc.), 1994–2001 (non-exec. Mem., London Bd, 1990–94); Black Box Music Ltd, 1999–; Oxford Resources, 1999–; hotcourses.com, 2000–. Chm., Royal Opera House, Covent Gdn, 1996–97. Member: NHS Policy Bd, 1991–95; Arts Council of England (formerly of GB), 1991–96 (Chm., Nat. Lottery Adv. Bd for Arts and Film, 1994–96). Mem., EU Select Sub-Cttee B (Energy, Industry and Transport), H of L, 2000–. Chm., Action on Addiction, 2000–. Chm., Understanding Industry Trust, 1991–96; Trustee, Atlantic Partnership, 1999–; Mem. Bd of Trustees, Amer. Univ., 1999–2001; Mem. Council, Cheltenham Ladies' Coll., 1998–. Dir, Walbrook Club, 1999–2001. FRSA. Hon. Fellow, Bournemouth Univ., 1999–. *Publications:* various articles and booklets on public relations and marketing. *Recreations:* opera, Rugby, cricket. *Address:* c/o House of Lords, SW1A 0PW. *T:* (020) 7408 2232. *Clubs:* Garrick, White's, Carlton, MCC.

See also Rt Hon. J. S. Gummer.

CHADWICK, Charles McKenzie, CBE 1992 (OBE 1984); British Council Director (formerly Representative), Poland, 1989–92; *b* 31 July 1932; *s* of late Trevor McKenzie Chadwick and of Marjorie Baron; *m* 1st, 1965, Evelyn Ingeborg Ihlenfeldt (marr. diss.); one *s*; 2nd, 1999, Mary Christina Beatrice Teale; one *s*. *Educ:* Charterhouse School; Trinity Coll., Toronto (BA). Army service, 1950–52; HMOCS Provincial Administration, Northern Rhodesia, 1958–64; Lectr, 1964–66, and Head, Administrative Training, 1966–67, Staff Trng Coll., Lusaka; British Council Officer, 1967–92; service in Kenya, Nigeria, Brazil, London; British Election Supervisor, Zimbabwe, 1980; British Council Rep., Canada, 1981–88. Member: Commonwealth Observer Gp, Ghanaian Presidential elections, 1992, Pakistan National elections, 1993, Cameroon Parly elections, 1997; EU observer team, S African election, 1994; FCO Observer, Uganda elections, 1996; OSCE Supervisor, Bosnia elections, 1996. Gov., Hampstead Sch., 1992–2000. *Address:* 25A Denning Road, NW3 1ST.

CHADWICK, Derek James, DPhil; CChem, FRSC; Director, Novartis (formerly Ciba) Foundation, since 1988; *b* 9 Feb. 1948; *s* of Dennis Edmund and Ida Chadwick; *m* 1980, Susan Reid; two *s*. *Educ:* St Joseph's Coll., Blackpool; Keble Coll., Oxford (BA, BSc, MA, DPhil). FRSC 1982; MACS 1989. ICI Fellow, Cambridge Univ., 1972–73; Prize Fellow, Magdalen Coll., Oxford, 1973–77; Lectr and Sen. Lectr, Liverpool Univ., 1977–88. Vis. Prof., Univ. of Trondheim, Norway, 1995–. Member: Sci. Cttee, Louis Jeantet Foundn, Geneva, 1989–98; Hague Club of European Foundn Dirs, 1989– (Sec., 1993–97); Sci. Adv. Cttee, 1990–96, Exec. Council, 1991–2000 (Vice-Chm., 1994–2000), Assoc. of Med. Res. Charities. Mem., Soc. of Apothecaries, 1990. *Publications:* chapters in: Aromatic and Heteroaromatic Chemistry, 1979; Comprehensive Heterocyclic Chemistry, 1984; The Research and Academic Users' Guide to the IBM PC, 1988; Pyrroles, Pt 1, 1990; ed many vols in Novartis (formerly Ciba) Foundn symposium series; many papers in chemistry jls, eg, Jl Chem. Soc., Tetrahedron, Tet. Letters, etc. *Recreations:* music, gardening. *Address:* 4 Bromley Avenue, Bromley, Kent BR1 4BQ. *T:* (020) 8460 3332; The Novartis Foundation, 41 Portland Place, W1B 1BN. *T:* (020) 7636 9456; *e-mail:* dchadwick@novartisfound.org.uk.

CHADWICK, Fiona Jane; Ballet Administrator, Royal Ballet School, since 1996; *b* 13 May 1960; *d* of late William Chadwick and of Anne Chadwick; *m* 1st, 1990, Anthony Peter Dowson (marr. diss.); one *d*; 2nd, 1996, Robert Cave. *Educ:* Royal Ballet Sch. Joined Royal Ballet Co., 1978; Soloist, 1981–84; Principal, 1984–96. Leading rôles included: Swan Lake, Romeo and Juliet, Sleeping Beauty, Cinderella, La Fille Mal Gardée, Giselle, Prince of the Pagodas, La Bayadère, Pursuit, Firebird. *Address:* Royal Ballet School, 153 Talgarth Road, W14 9DE.

CHADWICK, Rt Rev. Graham Charles; Principal, then Director, Institute for Christian Spirituality, Sarum College, Salisbury, 1995–98; *b* 3 Jan. 1923; *s* of William Henry and Sarah Ann Chadwick; *m* 1955, Jeanne Suzanne Tyrell; one *s*. *Educ:* Swansea Grammar School; SOAS; Keble Coll., Oxford (MA); St Michael's Coll., Llandaff. RNVR, 1942–46. Deacon 1950, priest 1951; Curate, Oystermouth, Dio. Swansea and Brecon, 1950–53; Diocese of Lesotho, 1953–63; Chaplain, University Coll., Swansea, 1963–68; Senior Bursar, Queen's Coll., Birmingham, 1968–69; Diocesan Missioner, Lesotho, and Warden of Diocesan Training Centre, 1970–76; Bishop of Kimberley and Kuruman, 1976–82; Chaplain, St Asaph Cathedral, and Advr on Spirituality, Dio. of St Asaph, 1983–90; Asst Bishop of Liverpool, 1990–95. *Address:* 66 Hulse Road, Salisbury SP1 3LY. *T:* (01722) 505801, *Fax:* (01722) 505802; *e-mail:* Gcchadwick@aol.com.

CHADWICK, Professor Henry, KBE 1989; DD; FBA 1960; MRIA; Master of Peterhouse, Cambridge, 1987–93 (Hon. Fellow, 1993); Regius Professor Emeritus of Divinity, University of Cambridge, 1983 (Regius Professor, 1979–83); *b* 23 June 1920; 3rd *s* of late John Chadwick, Barrister, Bromley, Kent, and Edith (*née* Horrocks); *m* 1945, Margaret Elizabeth, *d* of late W. Pemell Browning; three *d*. *Educ:* Eton (King's Scholar); Magdalene Coll., Cambridge (Music Schol.). John Stewart of Rannoch Scholar, 1939. MusB. Asst Master, Wellington Coll., 1945; University of Cambridge: Fellow of Queens' Coll., 1946–58; Hon. Fellow, 1958; Junior Proctor, 1948–49. Regius Professor of Divinity and Canon of Christ Church, Oxford, 1959–69; Dean of Christ Church, Oxford, 1969–79 (Hon. Student, 1979); Pro-Vice-Chancellor, Oxford Univ., 1974–75; Delegate, OUP, 1960–79; Fellow, Magdalene Coll., Cambridge, 1979–87 (Hon. Fellow 1962). Fellow, Eton, 1976–79; Hon. Fellow: St Anne's Coll., Oxford, 1979; Trinity Coll., Cambridge, 1987. Gifford Lectr, St Andrews Univ., 1962–64; Birkbeck Lectr, Cambridge, 1965; Burns Lectr, Otago, 1971; Sarum Lectr, Oxford, 1982–83. Editor, Journal of Theological Studies, 1954–85. Member, Anglican-Roman Catholic International Commn, 1969–81 and 1983–90. Mem., Amer. Philosophical Soc.; For. Hon. Mem., Amer. Acad. Arts and Sciences; Correspondant de l'Académie des Inscriptions et des Belles Lettres, Institut de France; Mem., Société des Bollandistes, Brussels; Corresponding Member: Göttingen Acad. of Scis; Rhineland Acad. of Scis; Erfurt Acad. Hon. DD, Glasgow, Yale, Harvard, Surrey, Manchester, Jena and Lateran

(Augustinianum); Hon. Teol Dr, Uppsala; D Humane Letters, Chicago. Humboldt Prize, 1983; Lucas Prize, Tübingen, 1991. Order pour le mérite (Germany), 1993. *Publications:* Origen, Contra Celsum, 1953, 3rd edn 1980; Alexandrian Christianity (with J. E. L. Oulton), 1954; Lessing's Theological Writings, 1956; The Sentences of Sextus, 1959; Early Christian Thought and the Classical Tradition, 1966; The Early Church (Pelican), 1967, 2nd edn 1993; The Treatise on the Apostolic Tradition of St Hippolytus of Rome, ed G. Dix (rev. edn), 1968; Priscillian of Avila, 1976; Boethius, 1981; History and Thought of the Early Church, 1982; Augustine, 1986; (ed) Atlas of the Christian Church, 1987; Augustine's Confessions, 1991; Heresy and Orthodoxy in the Early Church, 1991; Tradition and Exploration, 1994; (contrib.) Oxford History of the Classical World, 1986; (contrib.) Oxford Illustrated History of Christianity, 1990; (contrib.) Cambridge Ancient History, vol. XIII, 1997. *Recreation:* music. *Address:* 46 St John Street, Oxford OX1 2LH. *T:* (01865) 512814.

See also Priscilla Chadwick, W. O. Chadwick.

CHADWICK, Rear Adm. John, CB 2001; CEng, FIEE; Flag Officer Training and Recruiting, since 1998; *b* 26 March 1946; *s* of Alec and Elsie Chadwick; *m* 1970, Jacqueline Cosh; two *s*. *Educ:* Cheadle Hulme Sch. CEng 1973; FIEE 1996. BRNC Dartmouth, 1966; RNC Greenwich (electronic engrg), 1967–69; submarine service, 1970; served in HM Submarines Otter, Ocelot, Spartan, 1970–82; Sqdn Weapon Engr, 3rd Submarine Sqdn, 1984–86; Submarine Weapon System Manager, MoD(PE), 1987–89; Captain 1989; Asst Dir, Operational Requirements, MoD, 1990–93; Dir, Underwater Weapons, MoD(PE), 1993–96; i/c HMS Collingwood, 1996–98; Chief Naval Engr Officer, 1999–2001. Pres., RN Rugby League, 1997–2001. *Recreations:* walking, gardening, house renovation. *Address:* c/o Naval Secretary, Victory Building, HM Naval Base, Portsmouth PO1 3LS.

CHADWICK, Rt Hon. Sir John (Murray), Kt 1991; ED; PC 1997; **Rt Hon. Lord Justice Chadwick;** a Lord Justice of Appeal, since 1997; *b* 20 Jan. 1941; *s* of Hector George Chadwick and Margaret Corry Chadwick (*née* Laing); *m* 1975, Diana Mary Blunt; two *d*. *Educ:* Rugby School; Magdalene Coll., Cambridge (MA). Called to the Bar, Inner Temple, 1966, Bencher, 1986. Standing Counsel to DTI, 1974–80; QC 1980; Judge of Courts of Appeal of Jersey and Guernsey, 1986–93; a Recorder, 1989–91; Judge of the High Court, Chancery Div., 1991–97; Chancery Supervising Judge, Birmingham, Bristol and Cardiff, 1995–97. *Recreation:* sailing. *Address:* Royal Courts of Justice, Strand, WC2A 2LL. *Clubs:* Athenæum, Beefsteak; Royal Yacht Squadron (Cowes).

CHADWICK, Sir Joshua Kenneth B.; *see* Burton-Chadwick.

CHADWICK, Lynn Russell, CBE 1964; sculptor since 1948; *b* 24 Nov. 1914; *s* of late Verner Russell Chadwick and Margery Brown Lynn; *m* 1942, Charlotte Ann Secord (*d* 1997); one *s*; *m* 1959, Frances Mary Jamieson (*d* 1964); two *d*; *m* 1965, Eva Reiner; one *s*. *Educ:* Merchant Taylors' Sch. Architectural Draughtsman, 1933–39; Pilot, FAA, 1941–44. Exhibitions have been held in London, in various galleries, by the Arts Council and British Council; his works have also been shown in numerous international exhibitions abroad, including Venice Biennale, 1956 (Internat. Sculpture Prize). *Works in public collections:* Great Britain: Tate Gallery, London; British Council, London; Arts Council of Great Britain; Victoria and Albert Museum; Pembroke Coll., Oxford; City Art Gallery, Bristol; Art Gallery, Brighton; Whitworth Art Gallery, University of Manchester; France: Musée National D'Art Moderne, Paris; Holland: Boymans van Beuningen Museum, Rotterdam; Germany: Municipality of Recklinghausen; Staatliche Graphische Sammlung, Munich; Staatische Kunstmuseum, Duisburg; Sweden: Art Gallery, Gothenburg; Belgium: Musées Royaux des Beaux-Arts de Belgique, Brussels; Italy: Galleria D'Arte Moderna, Rome; Museo Civico, Turin; Australia: National Gallery of SA, Adelaide; Canada: National Gallery of Canada, Ottawa; Museum of Fine Arts, Montreal; USA: Museum of Modern Art, New York; Carnegie Institute, Pittsburgh; University of Michigan; Albright Art Gallery, Buffalo; Art Institute, Chicago; Chile: Inst. de Artes Contemporáneas, Lima. Hon. Fellow: Cheltenham and Gloucester Coll. of Higher Educn, 1995; Bath Spa UC, 1998; Associate, Académie Royale de Belgique, 1995. Commandeur des Arts et des Lettres (France), 1993; Order of Andres Bello, First Class (Venezuela), 1988. *Address:* Lypiatt Park, Stroud, Glos GL6 7LL.

CHADWICK, Owen; *see* Chadwick, W. O.

CHADWICK, Peter, PhD, ScD; FRS 1977; Professor of Mathematics, University of East Anglia, 1965–91, now Emeritus; *b* 23 March 1931; *s* of late Jack Chadwick and Marjorie Chadwick (*née* Castle); *m* 1956, Sheila Gladys Salter, *d* of late Clarence F. and Gladys I. Salter; two *d*. *Educ:* Huddersfield Coll.; Univ. of Manchester (BSc 1952); Pembroke Coll., Cambridge (PhD 1957, ScD 1973). Scientific Officer, then Sen. Scientific Officer, Atomic Weapons Res. Estabt, Aldermaston, 1955–59; Lectr, then Sen. Lectr, in Applied Maths, Univ. of Sheffield, 1959–65; Dean, Sch. of Maths and Physics, 1979–82, Leverhulme Emeritus Fellow, 1991–93, UEA. Vis. Prof., Univ. of Queensland, 1972. Member: Exec. Cttee, Internat. Soc. for Interaction of Mechanics and Maths, 1982–88; British Nat. Cttee for Theoretical and Applied Mechanics, 1969–75, 1985–89. Hon. Mem., British Soc. of Rheology, 1991. Jt Exec. Editor, Qly Jl of Mechanics and Applied Maths, 1965–72, Trustee, 1977–91. Hon. DSc Glasgow, 1991. *Publications:* Continuum Mechanics: concise theory and problems, 1976, repr. 1999; numerous papers on theoretical solid mechanics and the mechanics of continua in various learned journals and books. *Address:* 8 Stratford Crescent, Cringleford, Norwich NR4 7SF. *T:* (01603) 451655; *e-mail:* p.chadwick@uea.ac.uk.

CHADWICK, Dr Priscilla; Principal, Berkhamsted Collegiate School, since 1996; *b* 7 Nov. 1947; *d* of Prof. Henry Chadwick, *qv*. *Educ:* Oxford High Sch.; Clarendon Sch., N Wales; Girton Coll., Cambridge (BA Theol Tripos 1970); Oxford Univ. (PGCE); London Univ. (MA Curriculum Studies 1983; PhD 1993). Head of Religious Education: St Helen's Sch., Northwood, 1971–73; Putney High Sch., 1973–78; St Bede's C of E/RC Comprehensive, Redhill, 1979–82; Dep. Head, Twyford C of E High Sch., Acton, 1982–85; Headteacher, Bishop Ramsey C of E Sch., Ruislip, 1986–91; Dean, Educnl Develt, South Bank Univ., 1992–96. Member: English Anglican/RC Cttee, 1981–; BBC/ITC Central Religious Adv. Cttee, 1983–93; Youth Crime Cttee, NACRO, 1988–94; Goldsmiths' Coll. Council, 1991–97. Chm., St Gabriel's Trust, 1987–. Gov., Westminster Sch., 1997–. FRSA 1992. *Publications:* Schools of Reconciliation, 1994; Shifting Alliances: the partnership of Church and State in English education, 1997; articles in various educnl jls. *Recreations:* music and the arts, world travel. *Address:* Wilson House, Berkhamsted Collegiate School, Berkhamsted, Herts HP4 2BE. *T:* (01442) 864827. *Club:* East India.

CHADWICK, (William) Owen, OM 1983; KBE 1982; FBA 1962; *b* 20 May 1916; 2nd *s* of John Chadwick and Edith (*née* Horrocks); *m* 1949, Ruth, *e d* of B. L. Hallward, *qv*; two *s* two *d*. *Educ:* Tonbridge; St John's Coll., Cambridge, and took holy orders. Fellow of Trinity Hall, Cambridge, 1947–56; Master of Selwyn Coll., Cambridge, 1956–83; Dixie Professor of Ecclesiastical History, 1958–68; Regius Prof. of Modern History, 1968–83; Vice-Chancellor, Cambridge Univ., 1969–71; Chancellor, UEA, 1985–94. Pres., British Academy, 1981–85. Chm., Archbishops' Commn on Church and State, 1966–70; Mem., Royal Commn on Historical MSS, 1984–91. Trustee, Nat. Portrait Gall., 1978–94 (Chm., 1988–94). Hon. Mem., American Acad. of Arts and Scis, 1977. Hon. Freeman, Skinners' Co., 2000. Hon. FRSE. Hon. DD: St Andrews; Oxford; Wales; Hon. DLitt: Kent; Bristol; London; Leeds; Hon. LittD: UEA; Cambridge; Hon. Dr of Letters, Columbia; Hon. LLD Aberdeen. *Publications include:* John Cassian, 1950; From Bossuet to Newman, 1957; Victorian Miniature, 1960; The Reformation, 1964; The Victorian Church, 1966, 1971; The Secularization of the European Mind in the 19th Century, 1976; The Popes and European Revolution, 1981; Britain and the Vatican during the Second World War, 1986; Michael Ramsey, 1990; The Spirit of the Oxford Movement, 1990; The Christian Church in the Cold War, 1992; A History of Christianity, 1995; A History of the Popes 1830–1914, 1998. *Address:* 67 Grantchester Street, Cambridge CB3 9HZ.

See also Henry Chadwick.

CHADWICK-JONES, Prof. John Knighton, PhD, DSc(Econ); Research Professor, University of Fribourg, Switzerland, since 1993; *b* 26 July 1928; *s* of Thomas Chadwick-Jones and Cecilia Rachel (*née* Thomas); *m* 1965, Araceli Carceller y Bergillos, PhD; two *s* one *d*. *Educ:* Bromsgrove Sch.; St Edmund Hall, Oxford (MA). PhD Wales, 1960; DSc(Econ) Wales, 1981. FBPsS. Scientific Staff, Nat. Inst. of Industrial Psychol., London, 1957–60; Lectr, then Sen. Lectr, in Industrial Psychol., UC, Cardiff, 1960–66; Reader in Social Psychol., Flinders Univ. of South Australia, 1967–68; Dir, Occupational Psychol. Res. Unit, UC, Cardiff, 1968–74; Prof. of Psychology, Saint Mary's Univ., Halifax, Canada, 1974–93, now Emeritus (Mem., Exec. Cttee, Bd of Governors, 1975–78). Canada Soc. Scis and Humanities Res. Council Leave Fellow: Darwin Coll., Cambridge, 1980–81; MRC Unit on Develt and Integration of Behaviour, Cambridge, 1984–85; Visiting Fellow: Clare Hall, Cambridge, 1982; Wolfson Coll., Cambridge, 1984–85; Wolfson Coll., Oxford, 1988–89; St Edmund's Coll., Cambridge, 1990–91. Dir, Cambridge Canadian Trust (Toronto), 1988–94. Fellow: Amer. Psychol Assoc.; Canadian Psychol Assoc. *Publications:* Automation and Behavior: a social psychological study, 1969; Social Exchange Theory: its structure and influence in social psychology, 1976; (jtly) Brain, Environment and Social Psychology, 1979; Absenteeism in the Canadian Context, 1979; (jtly) Social Psychology of Absenteeism, 1982; Developing a Social Psychology of Monkeys and Apes, 1998; articles in academic jls. *Address:* Department of Psychology, University of Fribourg, 2 rue de Faucigny, Fribourg 1700, Switzerland.

CHADWYCK-HEALEY, Sir Charles (Edward), 5th Bt *cr* 1919, of Wyphurst, Cranleigh, Co. Surrey and New Place, Luccombe, Somerset; Chairman, Chadwyck-Healey Ltd, 1973–99; President, Chadwyck-Healey Inc., 1975–99; Chairman, ANT Ltd, since 1999; *b* 13 May 1940; *s* of Sir Charles Arthur Chadwyck-Healey, 4th Bt, OBE, TD, and of Viola, *d* of late Cecil Lubbock; *S* father, 1986; *m* 1967, Angela Mary, *e d* of late John Metson; one *s* two *d*. *Educ:* Eton; Trinity Coll., Oxford (MA). Mem., Lord Chancellor's Adv. Council on Public Records, 2001. Member: Adv. Council, Inst. of English Studies, Univ. of London, 1999; Ely Cathedral Council, 2001. *Heir: s* Edward Alexander Chadwyck-Healey [*b* 2 June 1972; *m* 1999, Denise Suzanne, (Denny), *e d* of Caroline Osborne; one *d*]. *Address:* Manor Farm, Bassingbourn, Cambs SG8 5NX. *T:* (01763) 242447. *Clubs:* Athenæum, Brooks's.

CHAILLY, Riccardo; conductor; Principal Conductor: Royal Concertgebouw Orchestra, Amsterdam, since 1988; Orchestra Giuseppe Verdi, Milan, since 1999; *b* 20 Feb. 1953; *m* 1987, Gabriella Terragni; two *s*. *Educ:* Conservatory of Music, Perugia; St Cecilia, Rome; Giuseppe Verdi, Milan. Chief Conductor, Berlin Radio Symph. Orch., 1982–89; Principal Conductor and Music Dir, Teatro Comunale, Bologna, 1986–93; has conducted world's leading orchestras, including Vienna and Berlin Philharmonic, Chicago Symphony, Philadelphia and Cleveland; has performed in major opera houses, including: La Scala, Milan, Vienna State Opera, Covent Garden, Munich, Metropolitan Opera, NY. Hon. RAM 1996. Numerous recordings. Grand Prix du Disque, Acad. Charles Cros, 1984, 1985, 1987, 1992, and other recording awards. Grande Ufficiale, Italian Republic, 1994. *Address:* Royal Concertgebouw Orchestra, Jacob Obrechtstraat 51, 1071 KJ Amsterdam, The Netherlands.

CHAISTY, Paul; QC 2001; a Recorder, since 2000; *b* 12 March 1958; *s* of Dora Cranston (*née* Preston); *m* 1987, Margaret Judith Lewis; one *s* one *d*. *Educ:* Parrswood High Sch., Manchester; Nottingham Univ. (LLB); Exeter Coll., Oxford (BCL). Called to the Bar, Lincoln's Inn, 1982; in practice as barrister, Manchester, 1982–, specialising in commercial and Chancery law. Mem., Goostrey Gooseberry Soc. *Recreations:* fishing, family, football, friends. *Address:* (chambers) 40 King Street, Manchester M2 6BA. *T:* (0161) 832 9082. *Club:* Smeatons (Southport).

CHAKAIPA, Most Rev. Patrick; *see* Harare, Archbishop of, (RC).

CHAKRABARTI, Sumantra; Director General for the Regional Programmes, Department for International Development, since 2001; *b* 12 Jan. 1959; *s* of Hirendranath Chakrabarti and Gayatri Chakrabarti (*née* Rudra); *m* 1983, Mari Sako, *qv*; one *d*. *Educ:* City of London Sch. for Boys; New Coll., Oxford (BA PPE 1981); Sussex Univ. (MA Econ 1984). ODI Fellow and Economist, Govt of Botswana, 1981–83; Sen. Economic Asst and Economic Advr, ODA, 1984–88; Asst to UK Exec. Dir, IMF and World Bank, Washington, 1988–90; Private Sec. to Rt Hon. Lynda Chalker, 1990–92; Assistant Secretary: Aid Policy and Resources Dept, ODA, 1992–96; Envmt, Transport, and Regions Team, Spending Directorate, HM Treasury, 1996–98; Dep. Dir, Budget and Public Finances, HM Treasury, 1998; Dir, Performance and Innovation Unit, 1998–2000, Head, Econ. and Domestic Affairs Secretariat, 2000–01, Cabinet Office. *Recreations:* Indian history, soul music, football. *Address:* Department for International Development, 1 Palace Street, SW1E 5HE.

CHALFONT, Baron, *cr* 1964 (Life Peer); **Alun Arthur Gwynne Jones;** PC 1964; OBE 1961; MC 1957; Chairman: Marlborough Stirling Group, since 1994; Southern Mining Corp., 1997–99; *b* 5 Dec. 1919; *s* of Arthur Gwynne Jones and Eliza Alice Hardman; *m* 1948, Dr Mona Mitchell, MB ChB; one *d* decd. *Educ:* West Monmouth Sch. Commissioned into South Wales Borderers (24th Foot), 1940; served in: Burma 1941–44; Malayan campaign 1955–57; Cyprus campaign 1958–59; various staff and intelligence appointments; Staff Coll., Camberley, 1950; Jt Services Staff Coll., 1958; Russian interpreter, 1951; resigned commission, 1961, on appt as Defence Correspondent, The Times; frequent television and sound broadcasts and consultant on foreign affairs to BBC Television, 1961–64; Minister of State, Foreign and Commonwealth Office, 1964–70; UK Permanent Rep. to WEU, 1969–70; Foreign Editor, New Statesman, 1970–71. Dep. Chm., IBA, 1989–90; Chm., Radio Authy, 1991–94. Director: W. S. Atkins International, 1979–83; IBM UK Ltd, 1973–90 (Mem. IBM Europe Adv. Council, 1973–90); Lazard Bros & Co. Ltd, 1983–90; Shandwick plc, 1985–95; Triangle Holdings, 1986–90; Television Corp. plc, 1996–; Chairman: Industrial Cleaning Papers, 1979–86; Peter Hamilton Security Consultants Ltd, 1984–86; VSEL Consortium, later VSEL, 1987–95; President: Abington Corp. (Consultants) Ltd, 1981–; Nottingham Bldg Soc., 1983–90. Pres., All Party Defence Gp, H of L, 1995– (Chm., 1980–94). President:

Hispanic and Luso Brazilian Council, 1975–80; RNID, 1980–87; Llangollen Internat. Music Festival, 1979–90; Freedom in Sport, 1982–88; Chairman: UK Cttee for Free World, 1981–89; Eur. Atlantic Gp, 1983–; Member: Nat. Defence Industries Council, 1992–; IISS; Bd of Governors, Sandle Manor Sch. MRI; MInstD. FRSA. Hon. Fellow UCW Aberystwyth, 1974. Hon. Col, Univ. of Wales OTC, 1991–94. Liveryman, Worshipful Co. of Paviors. Freeman, City of London. *Publications:* The Sword and The Spirit, 1963; The Great Commanders, 1973; Montgomery of Alamein, 1976; (ed) Waterloo: battle of three armies, 1979; Star Wars: suicide or survival, 1985; Defence of the Realm, 1987; By God's Will: a portrait of the Sultan of Brunei, 1989; The Shadow of My Hand (autobiog.), 2000; contribs to The Times, and other national and professional journals. *Recreations:* formerly Rugby football, cricket, lawn tennis; now music and theatre. *Address:* House of Lords, SW1A 0PW. *Clubs:* Garrick, MCC, City Livery.

CHALKER OF WALLASEY, Baroness *cr* 1992 (Life Peer), of Leigh-on-Sea in the County of Essex; **Lynda Chalker;** PC 1987; independent consultant on Africa and development to business and the World Bank; company director; *b* 29 April 1942; *d* of late Sidney Henry James Bates and Marjorie Kathleen Randell; *m* 1st, 1967, Eric Robert Chalker (marr. diss. 1973); no *c*; 2nd, 1981, Clive Landa. *Educ:* Heidelberg Univ.; London Univ.; Central London Polytechnic. Statistician with Research Bureau Ltd (Unilever), 1963–69; Dep. Market Research Man. with Shell Mex & BP Ltd, 1969–72; Chief Exec. of Internat. Div. of Louis Harris International, 1972–74. MP (C) Wallasey, Feb. 1974–1992; Opposition Spokesman on Social Services, 1976–79; Parly Under-Sec. of State, DHSS, 1979–82, Dept of Transport, 1982–83; Minister of State, Dept of Transport, 1983–86; Minister of State, 1986–97, and Minister for Overseas Develt, 1989–97, FCO. Non-executive Director: Freeplay Power Gp, 1997–; Capital Shopping Centres plc, 1997–2000; Landell Mills Ltd, 1999–; Adv. Dir, Unilever plc and Unilever NV, 1998–. Member: BBC Gen. Adv. Cttee, 1975–79; RIIA, 1977–. Pres. and Chm., BESO, 1998–; Pres., Southern African Business Assoc., 1998–. Chm. Mgt Bd, LSHTM, 1998–. Hon. Col, 156(NW) Transport Regt, RLC(V), 1995–2000. *Publications:* (jtly) Police in Retreat (pamphlet), 1967; (jtly) Unhappy Families (pamphlet), 1971; (jtly) We are Richer than We Think, 1978; Africa: turning the tide, 1989. *Recreations:* music, cooking, theatre, driving. *Address:* House of Lords, SW1A 0PW.

CHALLEN, Colin Robert; MP (Lab) Morley and Rothwell, since 2001; *b* 12 June 1953; *s* of Grenfell Stephen William Challen and Helen Mary Challen (*née* Swift). *Educ:* Hull Univ. (BA Hons Philosophy 1982). Served RAF, 1971–74. Postman, 1974–78; publisher and printer, Hull, 1983–94; Labour Party Organiser, Leeds and W Yorks, 1994–2000. *Publication:* Price of Power: the secret funding of the Conservative Party, 1998. *Recreations:* rambling, art, music. *Address:* House of Commons, SW1A 0AA. *T:* (020) 7219 3000. *Clubs:* Rothwell Labour, Ackroyd Street Working Mens (Morley).

CHALLEN, David John; Co-Chairman, Schroder Salomon Smith Barney, since 2000; *b* 11 March 1943; *s* of Sydney Albert Challen and Doris Ellen Challen (*née* Hardy); *m* 1967, Elizabeth McCartney; one *s* one *d*. *Educ:* The High Sch., Dublin; Trinity Coll., Dublin; Harvard Univ. (MBA). With J. Walter Thompson, 1964–72; J. Henry Schroder & Co. Ltd, 1972–2000: Dir, 1979–; Hd, Corporate Finance, 1990–94; Vice Chm., 1995–97; Chm., 1997–2000. Non-executive Director: Anglian Water PLC, 1993–; Thomson Travel Group plc, 1998–2000. Chm., Financial Services Practitioner Forum, 1998–2001; Member: Adv. Cttee on Business and the Envmt, 1991–92; Panel on Takeovers and Mergers, 1993–94, 1999–; Financial Reporting Council, 1995–. Gov., Morley Coll., 1993–99. *Address:* 32 Lebanon Park, Twickenham, Middx TW1 3DG. *Club:* Harvard (NYC).

CHALLEN, Rt Rev. Michael Boyd, AM 1988; Executive Director, Brotherhood of St Laurence, 1991–99; Adjunct Professor, Curtin University of Technology, Perth; *b* 27 May 1932; *s* of late B. Challen; *m* 1961, Judith, *d* of A. Kelly; two *d*. *Educ:* Mordialloc High School; Frankston High School; Univ. of Melbourne (BSc 1955); Ridley College, Melbourne (ThL 1956). Deacon 1957, priest 1958; Curate of Christ Church, Essendon, 1957–59; Member, Melbourne Dio. Centre 1959–63; Director, 1963–69; Priest-in-charge, St Luke, Fitzroy, 1959–61; St Alban's, N Melbourne, 1961–65; Flemington, 1965–69; Dir, Anglican Inner-City Ministry, 1969; Dir, Home Mission Dept, Perth, 1971–78; Priest-in-charge, Lockridge with Eden Hill, 1973; Archdeacon, Home Missions, Perth, 1975–78; Asst Bp, dio. of Perth, WA, 1978–91; Exec. Dir, Anglican Health and Welfare Service, Perth, 1977–78. *Address:* 8A John Street, North Fremantle, WA 6159, Australia. *T:* and *Fax:* (8) 94336784.

CHALLENS, Wallace John, CBE 1967 (OBE 1958); Director, Atomic Weapons Research Establishment, Aldermaston, 1976–78; *b* 14 May 1915; *s* of late Walter Lincoln Challens and Harriet Sybil Challens (*née* Collins); *m* 1st, 1938, Winifred Joan Stephenson (*d* 1971); two *s*; 2nd, 1973, Norma Lane. *Educ:* Deacons Sch., Peterborough; University Coll., Nottingham; BSc (Hons) London. Research Dept, Woolwich, 1936; Projectile Develt Estabt, Aberporth, 1939. British Commonwealth Scientific Office, Washington, 1946; Armament Research Estabt, Fort Halstead, 1947; Atomic Weapons Research Estabt: Fort Halstead, 1954; Aldermaston, 1955–78. Scientific Dir of trials at Christmas Island, 1957. Appointed: Chief of Warhead Develt, 1959; Asst Dir, 1965; Dep. Dir, 1972. FInstP 1944. US Medal of Freedom (Bronze) 1946. *Recreation:* golf. *Address:* Far End, Crossborough Hill, Basingstoke, Hampshire RG21 4AG. *T:* (01256) 464986.

CHALMERS, Sir Iain (Geoffrey), Kt 2000; DSc; FRCPE, FFPHM; Director, UK Cochrane Centre, since 1992; *b* 3 June 1943; *s* of Hamish and Lois Chalmers; *m* 1972, Jan; two *s*. *Educ:* Middlesex Hosp. Med. Sch., London Univ. (MB BS 1966; MSc Social Medicine 1975; DSc 1999). MRCS 1966; LRCP 1966; DCH 1973; MRCOG 1973, FRCOG 1985; FFPHM 1986; FRCPE 1996. House Physician, House Surgeon, Middlesex Hosp.; House Physician, Welsh Nat. Sch. of Medicine; House Surgeon, Raigmore Hosp., Inverness; MO, UNRWA for Palestinian Refugees, Gaza; Registrar, Dept of Obst. and Gynaecol., then MRC Fellow, Dept of Med. Stats, Welsh Nat. Sch. of Medicine, Cardiff; Oxford University: Dir, Nat. Perinatal Epidemiology Unit, 1978–92; Clin. Lectr in Obst. and Gynaecol., 1978–92; Archie Cochrane Res. Fellow, Green Coll., 1992–94; Hon. Consultant in Public Health Medicine, Oxfordshire HA, 1978–. Visiting Professor: Univ. of Liverpool, 1993–; Inst. of Child Health, 1997–, Sch. of Public Policy, 1998–, UCL; Exeter Univ., 2000–. Ed., Oxford Database of Perinatal Trials, 1988–92. FMedSci 1999. *Publications:* (ed jtly) Effectiveness and Satisfaction in Antenatal Care, 1982; (ed jtly) Effective Care in Pregnancy and Childbirth, 1989; (ed jtly) Systematic Reviews, 1995; (ed jtly) Non-random Reflections on Health Services Research, 1997. *Address:* UK Cochrane Centre, NHS R & D Programme, Summertown Pavilion, Middle Way, Oxford OX2 7LG. *T:* (01865) 516300.

CHALMERS, Ian Pender, CMG 1993; OBE 1980; HM Diplomatic Service, retired; Counsellor, Foreign and Commonwealth Office, 1987–98; *b* 30 Jan. 1939; *s* of John William Pender Chalmers and Beatrice Miriam Emery; *m* 1962, Lisa Christine Hay; two *s* two *d* (and one *d* decd). *Educ:* Hordle House, Harrow; Trinity College Dublin. Joined HM Diplomatic Service, 1963; Second Sec., Beirut, 1966–68; FCO, 1968–70; First Sec., Warsaw, 1970–72; FCO, 1972–76; First Sec., Paris, 1976–80; FCO, 1980–84; Counsellor, UK Mission to UN, Geneva, 1984–87. *Recreations:* golf, reading, walking. *Address:* The Croft, Packhorse Lane, Marcham, Oxon OX13 6NT. *Clubs:* Frilford Heath Golf, Huntercombe Golf.

CHALMERS, Prof. John Philip, AC 1991; FAA; Professor of Medicine, since 1996, and Chairman, Research Development for Faculty of Medicine, since 2000, University of Sydney; *b* 12 Jan. 1937; *m* 1977, Dr Alexandra Bune; four *s* one *d*. *Educ:* King's Sch., Parramatta; St Paul's Coll., Univ. of Sydney (BSc, MB BS); Univ. of NSW (PhD). FRCP, FRCPG, FRCPE, FACP, FRACP, FRACMA. Medical appts, Royal Prince Alfred Hosp., to 1968; Research Fellow: Nat. Heart Foundn, Univ. of NSW, 1965–66; MIT, 1969–70; RPMS, 1970–71; University of Sydney: Sen. Lectr, 1971–72; Assoc. Prof. of Medicine, 1973–75; Prof. of Medicine, Flinders Univ., 1975–96. Hon. Physician, Royal Prince Alfred Hosp., 1971–75; Vis MO, Repatriation Gen. Hosp., Concord, 1972–75; Mem., Bd of Management, Flinders Med. Centre, 1977–; Dean, Sch. of Medicine, Flinders Univ., 1991–92; Res. Chm., Royal N Shore Hosp., 1996–2000. Royal Australian College of Physicians: Chm., State Cttee for SA, 1982–86; Chm., Bd of Censors, 1984–88; Vice-Pres., 1988–90; Pres., 1990–92; Pres., Internat. Soc. of Hypertension, 1992–94; Chm., Scientific Adv. Bd, Internat. Soc. and Fedn of Cardiology, 1997–; former mem. and chm., numerous sci. adv. cttees and govt med. bodies. FAA 1987; Hon. FRACS. Hon. MD: Queensland, 1991; NSW, 1994; Flinders, 1999. Wellcome Medal for contrib. to Med. Res., 1981; Volhard Award, Internat. Soc. of Hypertension, for contrib. to Hypertension Res., 1998. Mem., editl bds of learned jls. *Publications:* numerous contribs to medical jls, on pharmacology, physiology, blood pressure, hypertension and other medical research. *Recreations:* cricket, cooking, theatre, travel. *Address:* Institute for International Health, University of Sydney, PO Box 576, Newtown, Sydney, NSW 2042, Australia; 3A Dettmann Avenue, Longueville, NSW 2066, Australia.

CHALMERS, Sir Neil (Robert), Kt 2001; Director, The Natural History Museum (formerly British Museum (Natural History)), since 1988; *b* 19 June 1942; *s* of William King and Irene Margaret Chalmers (*née* Pemberton); *m* 1970, Monica Elizabeth Byanjeru (*née* Rusoke); two *d*. *Educ:* King's College Sch., Wimbledon; Magdalen Coll., Oxford (BA); St John's Coll., Cambridge (PhD). Lectr in Zoology, Makerere University Coll., Kampala, 1966–69; Scientific Dir, Nat. Primate Res. Centre, Nairobi, 1969–70; Open University: Lectr, subseq. Sen. Lectr, then Reader in Biology, 1970–85; Dean of Science, 1985–88. *Publications:* Social Behaviour in Primates, 1979; numerous papers on animal behaviour in Animal Behaviour and other learned jls. *Recreations:* music, squash. *Address:* The Natural History Museum, Cromwell Road, SW7 5BD.

CHALMERS, Patrick Edward Bruce; JP; Director, Scottish Ensemble, since 1995; *b* Chapel of Garioch, Aberdeenshire, 26 Oct. 1939; *s* of L. E. F. Chalmers, farmer, Lethenty, Inverurie, and Helen Morris Campbell; *m* 1963, Ailza Catherine Reid, *d* of late William McGibbon, Advocate in Aberdeen; three *d*. *Educ:* Fettes Coll., Edinburgh; N of Scotland Coll. of Agriculture (NDA); Univ. of Durham (BScA). Joined BBC as radio talks producer, BBC Scotland, 1963; television producer, 1965; sen. producer, Aberdeen, 1970; Head of Television, Scotland, 1979–82; Gen. Man., Co-Productions, London, 1982; Controller, BBC Scotland, 1983–92; Dir, BBC World Service Television, Asia, 1992–93, retd 1994. Director: Hutchvision News Ltd, 1992–93; Grampian Venture Capital Fund, 1996–. President: Edinburgh Television Fest., 1984–92; BAFTA, Scotland, 1990–92. Dir, Scottish Film Production Fund, 1988–91. Mem., Aberdeenshire Council, 1995–99 (Chm., Lib Dem Gp); Convenor, Grampian Police Bd, 1998–99. Chm., Marr Area Cttee, 1996–99. Mem., Grampian Region Children's Panel, 1974–79. FRSA 1990. Bailie of Bennachie, 1975. JP Aberdeenshire, 1996. *Recreations:* ski-ing, gardening. *Address:* Corblelack, Logie Coldstone, Aboyne, Aberdeenshire AB34 5PR. *T:* and *Fax:* (013398) 81439. *Clubs:* New (Edinburgh); Royal Northern (Aberdeen); Foreign Correspondents (Hong Kong); Kandahar Ski.

CHALMERS, William Gordon, CB 1980; MC 1944; Crown Agent for Scotland, 1974–84; *b* 4 June 1922; *s* of Robert Wilson Chalmers and Mary Robertson Chalmers (*née* Clark); *m* 1948, Margaret Helen McLeod (*d* 1997); one *s* one *d*. *Educ:* Robert Gordon's Coll., Aberdeen; Aberdeen Univ. (BL). University, 1940–42 and 1947–48; served with Queen's Own Cameron Highlanders, 1942–47; Solicitor in Aberdeen, 1948–50; Procurator Fiscal Depute at Dunfermline, 1950–59; Senior Procurator Fiscal Depute at Edinburgh, 1959–63; Asst in Crown Office, 1963–67; Deputy Crown Agent, 1967–74. Jt Hd, War Crimes Enquiry in UK, 1988–89. *Recreations:* golf, bridge. *Address:* 3/4 Rocheid Park, East Fettes Avenue, Edinburgh EH4 1RP. *T:* (0131) 332 7937.

CHALONER; family name of **Baron Gisborough**.

CHALONER, Prof. William Gilbert, FRS 1976; Hildred Carlile Professor of Botany and Head of School of Life Sciences, Royal Holloway (formerly Royal Holloway and Bedford New College), University of London, 1985–94 (at Bedford College, 1979–85), Emeritus Professor, 1994, and engaged in research, Department of Geology, since 1994; *b* London, 22 Nov. 1928; *s* of late Ernest J. and L. Chaloner; *m* 1955, Judith Carroll; one *s* two *d*. *Educ:* Kingston Grammar Sch.; Reading Univ. (BSc, PhD). 2nd Lt RA, 1955–56. Lectr and Reader, University Coll., London, 1956–72. Visiting Prof., Pennsylvania State Univ., USA, 1961–62; Prof. of Botany, Univ. of Nigeria, 1965–66; Prof. of Botany, Birkbeck Coll., Univ. of London, 1972–79. Wilmer D. Barrett Prof. of Botany, Univ. of Mass, 1988–91. Vis. Prof., UCL, 1995–. Member: Senate, Univ. of London, 1983–91; Bd of Trustees, Royal Botanic Gardens, Kew, 1983–96. Mem., NERC, 1991–94. President: Palaeontological Assoc., 1976–78; Internat. Orgn of Palaeobotany, 1981–87; Linnean Soc., 1985–88; Vice-Pres., Geol Soc. London, 1985–86. Corresponding Mem., Botanical Soc. of Amer., 1987–. Associé Etranger de l'Acad. des Scis, Inst. de France, 1989. Linnean Medal (Botany), Linnean Soc., 1991; Lyell Medal, Geol. Soc., 1994. *Publications:* papers in Palaeontology and other scientific jls, dealing with fossil plants. *Recreations:* swimming, tennis, visiting USA. *Address:* 20 Parke Road, SW13 9NG. *T:* (020) 8748 3863.

CHALSTREY, Sir (Leonard) John, Kt 1996; MD; FRCS; JP; Lord Mayor of London, 1995–96; Consultant Surgeon, St Bartholomew's Hospital, 1969–96; Senior Lecturer, St Bartholomew's Hospital Medical College, University of London, 1969–96; *b* 17 March 1931; *s* of late Leonard Chalstrey and Frances Mary (*née* Lakin); *m* 1958, Aileen Beatrice Bayes; one *s* one *d*. *Educ:* Dudley Sch., Worcs; Queens' Coll., Cambridge (BA Hons 1954; MA 1958); Med. Coll., St Bartholomew's Hosp. (MB, BChir 1957; MD 1967). MRCS, LRCP 1957; FRCS 1962. Nat. Service, RAEC, 1949–51. Jun. med. and surgical posts, St Bartholomew's Hosp., 1958–59; Lectr in Anatomy, Middx Hosp. Med. Sch., 1959–61; Jun. Surgical Registrar, St Bartholomew's Hosp., 1962; Registrar, then Sen. Surgical Registrar, Royal Free Hosp., 1963–69; Hon. Consultant Surgeon, St Luke's Hosp. for Clergy, 1975–93. Examiner in Surgery: Univ. of London, 1976–95; Univ. of Cambridge, 1989–94. Non-exec. Mem., City and Hackney HA, 1992–93. City University: Mem. Court, 1986–92; Mem. Council, 1992–; Chancellor, 1995–96. Maj., 357 Field Surgical Team, RAMC(V), TA, 1991–96; Hon. Col, 256 (City of London) Field Hosp., RAMC(V), 1996–2000; Member: City of London TAVRA, 1992–2000; Gtr London TAVRA, 1992–2000. Governor, Corp. of Sons of the Clergy, 1992–. Mem., Court of Common Council, City of London Corp., 1981–84; Alderman (Vintry Ward), City of

London, 1984–; Sheriff, City of London, 1993–94; HM Lieut, City of London, 1995; JP 1984. Member, Court of Assistants: Soc. of Apothecaries (Sen. Warden, 1992–93 and 1993–94; Master, 1994–95); Barbers' Co. (Master, 1998–99); Member: Parish Clerks' Co., 1993–; HAC, 1995– (Hon. Mem., Ct of Assts, 1984–). Vice-Pres., City of London Sect., BRCS, 1992–. Trustee, Morden Coll., 1995–; Special Trustee: St Bartholomew's Hosp., 1998–; Royal London Hosp., 1999–. FRSocMed 1965; Fellow, Assoc. of Surgeons of GB and Ireland, 1969; FRSA 1996. Hon. GSM 1996; Hon. FRSH 1996; Hon. Fellow, QMW, 1996. Hon. DSc City, 1995. KStJ 1995 (Mem., Chapter-Gen., 1994–99); Surgeon-in-Chief, and Chm., Med. Bd, St John Ambulance, 1993–99; Hospitaller, Priory of England, 1999– (Mem., Priory Council and Chapter, 1999–). Grand Officier, Ordre National du Merité (France), 1996. *Publications:* (with Coffman and Smith-Laing) Gastro-Intestinal Disorders, 1986; (contrib.) Cancer in the Elderly, 1990; (contrib.) Maingot's Abdominal Operations, 7th edn 1980, 8th edn 1986; papers on surgical subjects in Brit. Jl Surgery, Brit. Jl Cancer and Jl RSM. *Recreations:* painting in oils, history of City of London. *Address:* Danebury, 113 The Chine, N21 2EG. *T:* (020) 8360 8921. *Clubs:* Oxford and Cambridge, City Livery, East India.

CHAMBERLAIN, Prof. Geoffrey Victor Price, RD 1974; MD; FRCS, FRCOG; Professor and Chairman, Obstetrics and Gynaecology, St George's Hospital Medical School, 1982–95, now Emeritus Professor; *b* 21 April 1930; *s* of late Albert Chamberlain and Irene Chamberlain (*née* Price); *m* 1956, Jocelyn Olivia Kerley, *d* of late Sir Peter Kerley, KCVO, CBE; three *s* two *d*. *Educ:* Llandaff Cathedral Sch.; Cowbridge; University Coll. and UCH, London (Goldsmith Schol. 1948; MB 1954; Fellow, UCL, 1987); MD 1968; FRCS 1960; FRCOG 1978. Residencies at RPMS, Gt Ormond St, Queen Charlotte's and Chelsea Hosps, KCH, 1955–69; Tutor, George Washington Med. Sch., Washington DC, 1965–66; Consultant Obstetrician and Gynaecologist, Queen Charlotte's and Chelsea Hosps, 1970–82. RNR, 1955–74, Surgeon Comdr. Member: Council, RSocMed, 1977–84 (Council, Obst. Sect., 1970–93; Council, Open Sect., 1987–95); Council, RCOG, 1971–77, 1982–87, 1990–94 (Vice-Pres., 1984–87; Pres., 1993–94); Chairman: Med. Cttee, Nat. Birthday Trust, 1982–95; Blair Bell Res. Soc., 1977–80; Assoc. of Profs of Obstetrics and Gynaecology, 1989–92. Fulbright Fellow, 1966; Thomas Eden Fellow, RCOG, 1966; Visiting Professor: Beckman, USA, 1984; Daphne Chung, Hong Kong, 1985; Edwin Tooth, Brisbane, 1987; Peshwar, Pakistan, 1993; Chicago Medical Sch., 1996. S African Representative Cttee, 1988. Hon. FACOG 1990; Hon. FSLCOG 1994; Hon. FFFP 1996. Hon. Mem., Polish Acad. of Medicine, 1992. Freeman, City of London, 1982. Foundn Prize, Amer. Assoc. of Obstetricians, 1967; James Simpson Gold Medal, RCSE, 1993. Editor: Contemporary Reviews in Obstetrics and Gynaecology, 1987–2000; British Jl of Obstetrics and Gynaecology, 1992–95. *Publications:* Safety of the Unborn Child, 1969; Lecture Notes in Obstetrics, 1975, 8th edn 1999; British Births, 1970; Placental Transfer, 1979; Clinical Physiology in Obstetrics, 1980, 4th edn 1997; Tubal Infertility, 1982; Pregnant Women at Work, 1984; Prepregnancy Care, 1985; (ed) Obstetrics by Ten Teachers, 14th edn, 1985, to 16th edn, 1994; (ed) Gynaecology by Ten Teachers, 14th edn, 1985, to 16th edn, 1994; Birthplace, 1987; Lecture Notes in Gynaecology, 6th edn 1988 to 8th edn 1999; Manual of Obstetrics, 1988; Obstetrics, 1989, 3rd edn 1999; ABC of Antenatal Care, 1991, 4th edn 2000; Pregnancy in the 1990s, 1992; Relief of Pain in Labour, 1993; Homebirth, 1997; ABC of Labour Care, 1999; A Practice of Obstetrics and Gynaecology, 1999; The Life of Victor Bonney, 2000; contribs to BMJ, Lancet, UK and overseas Jls of Obst. and Gyn. *Recreations:* history of medicine, carpentry. *Address:* Sycamores, Llanmadoc, Gower, Glamorgan SA3 1DB.

CHAMBERLAIN, Rev. George Ford, (Leo), OSB; Headmaster, Ampleforth College, since 1993; *b* 13 Aug. 1940; *s* of Brig. Noel Joseph Chamberlain, CBE and Sarah (Sally) (*née* Ford). *Educ:* Ampleforth Coll.; University Coll., Oxford (BA 1961; MA 1965). Novitiate, Ampleforth Abbey, 1961, solemn profession, 1964; ordained priest, 1968; Housemaster, St Dunstan's House, 1972–92; Sen. History Master, Ampleforth Coll., 1974–92. Member: Council of Management, Keston Inst. (formerly Keston Coll.), 1985–; Catholic Bishops' Cttee for European Affairs, 1992–; HMC, 1993–; Catholic Ind. Schs Conf., 1993– (Mem. Cttee, 1995–99). *Recreation:* assisting Christians in Central and Eastern Europe. *Address:* Ampleforth College, York YO62 4ER. *T:* (01439) 766800, *Fax:* (01439) 788330. *Club:* East India.

CHAMBERLAIN, Kevin John, CMG 1992; barrister; Deputy Legal Adviser, Foreign and Commonwealth Office, 1990–99; *b* 31 Jan. 1942; *s* of late Arthur James Chamberlain and of Gladys Mary (*née* Harris); *m* 1967, Pia Rosita Frauenlob; one *d*. *Educ:* Wimbledon Coll.; King's Coll., London (LLB). Called to the Bar, Inner Temple, 1965. HM Diplomatic Service, 1965–99: Asst Legal Adviser, FCO, 1965–74; Legal Adviser: British Mil. Govt, Berlin, 1974–76; British Embassy, Bonn, 1976–77; Asst Legal Adviser, FCO, 1977–79; Legal Counsellor, FCO, 1979–83; Counsellor (Legal Advr), Office of UK Perm. Rep. to EC, Brussels, 1983–87; Legal Counsellor, FCO, 1987–90. *Recreations:* opera, tennis, choral singing. *Address:* Fairfield, Warren Drive, Kingswood, Tadworth, Surrey KT20 6PY.

CHAMBERLAIN, (Leslie) Neville, CBE 1990; Chairman, The Company Hub plc, since 2000; Deputy Chairman, British Nuclear Fuels plc, 1995–99 (Chief Executive, 1986–96); *b* 3 Oct. 1939; *s* of Leslie Chamberlain and Doris Anne Chamberlain (*née* Thompson); *m* 1971, Joy Rachel Wellings; one *s* three *d*. *Educ:* King James Grammar School, Bishop Auckland; King's College, Univ. of Durham (BSc 1961; MSc 1962). FInstP. UKAEA, 1962–71; Urenco Ltd, 1971–77; British Nuclear Fuels: Fuel Production, 1977–81; Enrichment Business Manager, 1981–84; Dir, Enrichment Div., 1984–86. Non-executive Director: Dennis Gp plc, 1994–98; Urenco Ltd, 1999–; Manchester 2002 Ltd, 1999–; New East Manchester Ltd, 1999–. Chm., Nat Council, TEC, 1999–2001; Mem., NACETT, 1999–2001. Chairman: British Energy Assoc., 1999–; Internat. Nuclear Energy Acad., 2001–. Mem., Council, Salford Univ., 2000–. Freeman, City of London, 1997; Liveryman, Fuellers' Co., 1997–. CIMgt; FRSA. Hon. FINucE 1994; Hon. Fellow, European Nuclear Soc., 1994. Hon. DSc Salford, 1989. Melchett Lectr and Medal, Inst. of Energy, 1989. *Recreations:* horse racing, swimming, music. *Address:* Oaklands, 2 The Paddock, Hinderton Road, Neston, South Wirral, Cheshire CH64 9PH. *T:* (0151) 353 1980. *Club:* Athenæum.

CHAMBERLAIN, Michael Aubrey, FCA; Consultant, KPMG, Leicester, since 1994; *b* 16 April 1939; *s* of George Thomas Everard Chamberlain and Doris (*née* Arden). *Educ:* Repton Sch., Derbys. FCA 1963. Sen. partner, KPMG Peat Marwick, 1974–93. Pres., Inst. of Chartered Accountants in England and Wales, 1993–94 (Vice-Pres., 1991–92; Dep. Pres., 1992–93). Chm., Leicester Diocesan Bd of Finance, 1983–98; Mem., Archbishops' Council, 1999– (Chm. Finance Cttee, 1999–). Mem. Council, Univ. of Leicester, 1996– (Treas., 1999–). Hon. LLD Leicester, 1993. *Address:* 1 Waterloo Way, Leicester LE1 6LP. *T:* (0116) 256 6000.

CHAMBERLAIN, Rt Rev. Neville; *see* Brechin, Bishop of.

CHAMBERLAIN, Neville; *see* Chamberlain, L. N.

CHAMBERLAIN, Prof. Owen, AB, PhD; Professor of Physics, University of California, 1958–89, now Emeritus; *b* San Francisco, 10 July 1920; *s* of W. Edward Chamberlain and Genevieve Lucinda Owen; *m* 1st, 1943, Babette Copper (marr. diss. 1978); one *s* three *d*; 2nd, 1980, June Greenfield Steingart (*d* 1991); 3rd, 1998, Senta Pugh (*née* Gaiser). *Educ:* Philadelphia; Dartmouth Coll., Hanover, NH (AB). Atomic research for Manhattan District, 1942, transferred to Los Alamos, 1943; worked in Argonne National Laboratory, Chicago, 1947–48, and studied at University of Chicago (PhD); Instructor in Physics, University of California, 1948; Asst Professor, 1950; Associate Professor, 1954. Guggenheim Fellowship, 1957; Loeb Lecturer in Physics, Harvard Univ., 1959. Fellow: American Phys. Soc.; Amer. Acad. of Arts and Scis; Mem., Nat. Acad. of Sciences, 1960; Berkeley Fellow, 1992. Nobel Prize (joint) for Physics, 1959; Berkeley Citation, 1989. *Publications:* papers in Physical Review, Physical Review Letters, Nature, Nuovo Cimento. *Address:* Department of Physics, University of California, Berkeley, CA 94720, USA.

CHAMBERLAIN, Paul Arthur; Headmaster, Cheltenham College, since 1997; *b* 10 June 1948; *s* of Arthur and Lilian Amy Chamberlain; *m* 1970, Kathleen Eleanor Hopley; one *s* one *d*. *Educ:* Verdin Grammar Sch., Winsford, Cheshire; Univ. of Durham (BSc Hons Zoology 1969; PGCE 1970). Haileybury College: Asst Master, 1970–83; Housemaster, 1983–88; Headmaster, St Bees Sch., Cumbria, 1988–97. *Recreations:* fell walking, fly-fishing, music, photography. *Address:* College House, Thirlestaine Road, Cheltenham, Glos GL53 7AH. *T:* (01242) 265622. *Clubs:* East India, Lansdowne.

CHAMBERLAIN, Peter Edwin, FREng; FRINA; Director: Timely Solutions Ltd, since 2000; Xienta Ltd, since 2001; *b* 25 July 1939; *s* of Dr Eric Alfred Charles Chamberlain, OBE, FRSE, and late Winifred Louise, (Susan) (*née* Bone); *m* 1963, Irene May Frew; two *s* one *d*. *Educ:* Royal High Sch.; Edinburgh Univ. (Keasby Schol., BSc); RN Colls Manadon and Greenwich. RCNC. Asst Constructor, ship and submarine design, ME and Bath, 1963–68; Constructor: submarine design, Bath, 1968–69; submarine construction, Birkenhead, 1969–72; ship structures R&D, Dunfermline, 1972–74; postgrad. programmes in Naval Architecture, UCL, 1974–77; ship design, Bath, 1977–78; Chief Constructor: Hd of Secretariat, Bath, 1978–80; Surface Ship Forward Design, Bath, 1980–82; RCDS 1983; Asst Sec., Hd of Secretariat to Master Gen. of Ordnance, London, 1984–85; Under Sec., Dir Gen. Future Material Programmes (Naval), London, 1985–87; Dep. Controller Warship Equipments, MoD, 1987–88; Chief Underwater Systems Exec., MoD, 1988–89; creation of Defence Res. Agency, MoD, 1989–92; Engr Dir, System and Services Div., BAe, 1992–98; Dir, ANZAC WIP Project, BAe Australia, 1999. Mem., Internat. Council on Systems Engrg, 1995–. FREng (FEng 1988); FRINA 1988. *Recreations:* music, visual arts, poetry, computing. *Address:* 33 Cromwell Tower, Barbican, EC2Y 8DD; *e-mail:* peter_e_chamberlain@compuserve.com.

CHAMBERLAIN, Richard, TD 1949; Chief Master of the Supreme Court, Chancery Division, 1985–86 (Master, 1964–84); *b* 29 Jan. 1914; *o s* of late John Chamberlain and Hilda (*née* Poynting); *m* 1938, Joan (*d* 1997), *d* of late George and Eileen Kay; two *s* one *d*. *Educ:* Radley Coll.; Trinity Coll., Cambridge (MA). Admitted Solicitor, 1938. Served War, 1939–45: Devon Regt, TJFF, Staff Coll., Haifa. Partner, Kingsford Dorman & Co., 1948–64. Asst, Worshipful Co. of Solicitors of the City of London, 1966, Warden, 1973–74, Master, 1975. *Publication:* Asst Editor, Supreme Court Practice, 1967. *Recreations:* gardening, photography, travel, grandparental duties. *Address:* 3 Fitzwarren House, Highgate, N6 5LX. *T:* (020) 7281 2289.

See also P. A. Penney.

CHAMBERLAIN, William Richard Frank, DL; Chairman: Cricket Council, 1990–96; Test and County Cricket Board, 1990–94; *b* 13 April 1925; *s* of Lt-Comdr Richard Chamberlain and Elizabeth Chamberlain (*née* Robson); *m* 1960, Gillian Diarmid Castle; one *s* one *d*. *Educ:* Uppingham School. Served Fleet Air Arm 1943–46. Played cricket for Northants CCC, 1946. Joined W. W. Chamberlain (Assoc. Cos) Ltd, subseq. Chamberlain Phipps, 1947: Dir, 1953; Jt Man. Dir, 1957; Chm. and Jt Man. Dir, 1963–69; Dep. Chm. and Man. Dir, 1969, Chm. and Man. Dir, 1972, Chm., 1975–87, Chamberlain Phipps Ltd; Chm., Stead & Simpson, 1984–89; Regional Dir, Nat. Westminster Bank, 1983–90; Dir, Kingsgrange, 1989–91; Mem. Council, CBI, 1982–87. Pres., Northants CCC, 1990– (Chm., 1985–90). Freeman, City of London; Master, Patternmaker's Co., 1987. High Sheriff, 1990, DL 1991, Northants. *Recreations:* cricket, shooting. *Address:* Manor House, Swineshead, Bedford MK44 2AF. *T:* (01234) 708283. *Clubs:* Naval and Military, East India, MCC, Lord's Taverners.

CHAMBERLEN, Nicholas Hugh; Chairman, Clive Discount Company, 1977–93; *b* 18 April 1939; *s* of late Rev. Leonard Saunders Chamberlen, MC, and Lillian Margaret (*née* Webley); *m* 1962, Jane Mary Lindo (*d* 1998); three *s* one *d*. *Educ:* Sherborne Sch.; Lincoln Coll., Oxford (BA Hons). Nat. Cash Register Co., 1962–67; Clive Discount Co. Ltd, 1967–93. *Recreations:* shooting, golf, cricket. *Address:* Church Farm House, Berwick, Polegate, East Sussex BN26 6SB. *Clubs:* Turf; Royal and Ancient Golf (St Andrews).

CHAMBERS, Prof. Andrew David; Director, Management Audit Ltd, since 1991; Academic Director, FTMS, since 1999; *b* 7 April 1943; *s* of Lewis Harold and Florence Lilian Chambers; *m* 1st, 1969, Mary Elizabeth Ann Kilbey (marr. diss. 1984); two *s*; 2nd, 1987, Celia Barrington (*née* Pruen); two *s* two *d* (incl. twin *s* and *d*), and one step *s*. *Educ:* St Albans Sch.; Hatfield Coll., Univ. of Durham (BA Hons). CEng; FCA, FBCS, FCCA, FIIA. Arthur Andersen & Co., 1965–69; Barker & Dobson, 1969–70; United Biscuits, 1970–71; City University Business School: Lectr in Computer Applications in Accountancy, 1971–74; Leverhulme Sen. Res. Fellow in Internal Auditing, 1974–78; Sen. Lectr in Audit and Management Control, 1978–83; Prof. of Internal Auditing, 1983–93, then Emeritus; Administrative Sub-Dean, 1983–86; Acting Dean, 1985–86; Dean, 1986–91; Head of Dept of Business Studies, 1986–89; Warden, Northampton Hall, City Univ., 1983–86 (Dep. Warden, 1972–76); Prof. of Audit and Control, Univ. of Hull, 1994–98. Vis. Prof. in Computer Auditing, Univ. of Leuven, Belgium, 1980–81, 1992–93. Chm., Harlequin IT Services Ltd, 1998–99. Consultant: MacIntyre Hudson, Chartered Accountants, 1987–89; BBHW, Chartered Accountants, 1990–92; Director: Paragon Gp of Cos (formerly Nat. Home Loans Hldgs), 1991–; Nat. Mortgage Bank, 1991–92; IIA Inc., 1993–96 (Mem. Internat. Standards Bd, 1992–95); Pilgrim Health NHS Trust, 1996–99; FTMS Online, 1999–. Institute of Internal Auditors-UK: Mem. Council, 1985–86; Mem., Professional Standards and Guidelines Cttee (Chm., 1991–95). Member: BCS, 1979–82 (Mem., Tech. Bd; Chm., Meetings Cttee); IT Cttee, ICA, 1986–91; Educn, Training and Technol. Transfer Cttee, British Malaysian Soc., 1987–90; MBA Adv. Bd, Ashridge Management Coll., 1986–92; Dir, Council of Univ. Management Schs, 1988–92; Hon. Auditor, RSAA, 1986–91. MInstD 1986; FRSA. Gov., Islington Green Comprehensive Sch., 1989–91. Member, Editorial Board: Computer Fraud and Security, 1981–87; Managerial Auditing Jl, 1986–94; Gen. Editor, Internat. Jl of Auditing, 1995–; Editor: Internal Control, 1997–; Corporate Governance, 1998–; Fraud, 2000–01. *Publications:* (with O. J. Hanson) Keeping Computers Under Control, 1975; (ed) Internal Auditing: developments and horizons, 1979; Internal Auditing: theory and practice, 1981, 2nd edn (with G. M. Selim and G. Vinten) 1987;

Computer Auditing, 1981, 3rd edn (with J. M. Court) 1991; Effective Internal Audits: how to plan and implement, 1992; (with G. Rand) Auditing the IT Environment, 1994; (with G. Rand) Auditing Contracts, 1994; (ed) Internal Auditing, 1996; (with G. Rand) The Operational Auditing Handbook: auditing business processes, 1997; (with J. Ridley) Leading Edge Internal Auditing, 1998; papers in learned jls. *Recreation:* family. *Address:* Management Audit Ltd, 6 Market Street, Sleaford, Lincs NG34 7SF. *T:* (01529) 413344, *Fax:* (01529) 413355; *e-mail:* profadc@aol.com. *Clubs:* Reform, Travellers.

CHAMBERS, Dr Douglas Robert; HM Coroner, City of London, since 1994; *b* 2 Nov. 1929; *s* of Douglas Henry Chambers and Elizabeth Paterson; *m* 1955, Barbara June Rowe; one *s* two *d. Educ:* Shene Grammar Sch.; King's College, London. MB BS; AKC 1953; LLB 1960; MA Univ. of Wales, 1989. FIBiol 1992. Called to the Bar, Lincoln's Inn, 1965. RAF Med. Br., 1955–58; Med. Advr, Parke Davis, 1959–61, Nicholas Laboratories, 1961–63, Pharmacia, 1964–65; Med. Dir, Hoechst Pharmaceuticals, 1965–70; Dep. Coroner, West London, 1969–70; HM Coroner, Inner North London, 1970–94. Vis. Lectr, City Univ., 1976–; Hon. Sen. Clin. Lectr in med. law, UCL, 1978–96; Hon. Sen. Lectr, medical law, Royal Free Hosp., 1978–. Chairman: Richmond Div., BMA, 1969–70; Animal Research and Welfare Panel, Biological Council, 1986–92; Animal Welfare in Res. and Educn Cttee, Inst. of Biology, 1992–95; Pres., Library (sci. research) section, RSocMed, 1979–80; Pres., British sect., Anglo-German Med. Soc., 1980–84; Pres., Coroners' Soc., 1985–86. Hon. Mem., British Micro-circulation Soc., 1986 (Hon. Treas., 1968–86). Dist Comr, Richmond & Barnes Dist Scouts, 1976–85 (Silver Acorn 1984). Pres., Kensington Rowing Club, 1973–78. Baron C. ver Heyden de Lancey Prize for services to law and medicine, RSocMed, 1990. *Publications:* (jtly) Coroners' Inquiries, 1985; (consultant editor with Dr J. Burton) Jervis on Coroners, 11th edn, 1993; papers on medico-legal subjects. *Recreation:* local history of coroners and of scouting. *Address:* 4 Ormond Avenue, Richmond, Surrey TW10 6TN. *T:* (home) (020) 8940 7745, (court) (020) 7332 1598. *Club:* Auriol-Kensington Rowing.

CHAMBERS, Ernest George Wilkie; Chief Executive, West of Scotland Water, 1995–2001; *b* 10 May 1947; *s* of Ernest and Ada Chambers; *m* 1971, Jeanette; one *s* one *d. Educ:* Harris Acad., Dundee; Dundee Univ. (BSc 1st Cl. Hons Applied Sci. 1969); Strathclyde Univ. (MBA 1987). Graduate civil engr, E of Scotland Water Bd, 1969–73; Asst Engr, Lower Clyde Water Bd, 1973–75; Area Engr (Renfrew), 1975–78; Lower Clyde Division: Divl Ops Engr, 1978–84; Asst Divl Manager, 1984–86; Asst Dir (Ops and Maintenance), 1986–88; Dir of Water, 1988–94; Dir, Water Services, Strathclyde Regl Council, 1994–95. *Recreations:* DIY, gardening, sailing.

CHAMBERS, Fredrick Rignold H.; *see* Hyde-Chambers.

CHAMBERS, John T.; President and Chief Executive Officer, Cisco Systems Inc., since 1995; *m* Elaine; two *c. Educ:* West Virginia Univ. (BS/BA business; JD); Indiana Univ. (MBA). Formerly posts with IBM (incl. Exec. Vice-Pres.), and Wang Labs (latterly Sen. Vice-Pres. of US Ops); Sen. Vice-Pres. for Worldwide Ops, 1991-94, Exec. Vice-Pres., 1994-95, Cisco Systems Inc. Formerly Mem., US President's Cttee for Trade Policy. *Address:* Cisco Systems Inc., 170 West Tasman Drive, San Jose, CA 95134, USA.

CHAMBERS, Nicholas Mordaunt; QC 1985; **His Honour Judge Chambers;** a Circuit Judge, since 1999; Mercantile Judge for Wales and Chester, since 1999; *b* 25 Feb. 1944; *s* of Marcus Mordaunt Bertrand Chambers and Lona Margit Chambers (*née* Gross); *m* 1966, Sarah Elizabeth, *er d* of T. H. F. (Tony) Banks; two *s* one *d. Educ:* King's School, Worcester; Hertford College, Oxford (BA 1965). Called to the Bar, Gray's Inn, 1966, Bencher, 1994; a Recorder, 1987–99; a Dep. High Court Judge, 1994–99. Mem., Civil Procedure Rule Cttee, 1997–99. *Recreation:* sketching. *Address:* Civil Justice Centre, 2 Park Street, Cardiff CF10 1ET. *Clubs:* Garrick, Lansdowne.

CHAMBERS, Maj.-Gen. Peter Antony, MBE 1982; Deputy Chief of Staff, HQ Land Command, since 1998; *b* 23 April 1947; *s* of Mary Eugenie Chambers and Vincent Gerard Chambers; *m* 1968, Valerie Anne Straker; two *d. Educ:* De La Salle Grammar Sch.; Liverpool Univ. (BA Hons). FCIPS, FCIT, FILT. Commissioned RAOC, 1969; Staff Coll., 1979 (psc); OC 51 Ordnance Co., 1980–83; CO 1 Ordnance Bn, 1985–88; Col Ordnance 1, 1988–90; Higher Comd and Staff Course, 1990; Comdr Supply, 1st (BR) Corps, 1990–93; Sen. Army Mem., RCDS, 1993; Dir, Logistic Support Policy, 1995–97; Sen. Army Mem., RCDS, 1997–98. FIMgt. *Recreations:* walking, dinghy sailing, family. *Address:* RHQ, Royal Logistic Corps, Princess Royal Barracks, Deepcut, Camberley, Surrey GU16 6RW.

CHAMBERS, Prof. Richard Dickinson, PhD, DSc; FRS 1997; Professor of Chemistry, University of Durham, since 1976; *b* 16 March 1935; *s* of Alfred and Elizabeth Chambers; *m* 1959, Anne Boyd; one *s* one *d. Educ:* Stanley Grammar Sch.; Univ. of Durham (BSc; PhD 1959; DSc 1968). Research Fellow, UBC, Vancouver, 1959–60; University of Durham: Lectr, 1960–69; Reader, 1969–76; Head of Dept, 1983–86; Sir Derman Christopherson Res. Fellow, 1988–89. Vis. Lectr and Fulbright Fellow, Case-Western Reserve Univ., Cleveland, Ohio, 1966–67; Tarrant Vis. Prof., Univ. of Florida, Gainesville, 1999. Non-exec. Dir, F2 Chemicals Ltd, 1995–2000. Internat. Award for Creative Work in Fluorine Chemistry, ACS, 1991. *Publications:* Fluorine in Organic Chemistry, 1973; contribs to jls on many aspects of organo-fluorine compounds. *Recreations:* opera, golf, soccer. *Address:* Department of Chemistry, University of Durham, South Road, Durham DH1 3LE. *T:* (0191) 374 3120; *e-mail:* R.D.Chambers@durham.ac.uk; 5 Aykley Green, Whitesmocks, Durham DH1 4LN. *T:* (0191) 386 5791.

CHAMBERS, Robert Alexander H.; *see* Hammond-Chambers.

CHAMBERS, Prof. Robert Guy; Professor of Physics, University of Bristol, 1964–90, Emeritus 1990; *b* 8 Sept. 1924; *s* of A. G. P. Chambers; *m* 1st, 1950, Joan Brislee (marr. diss. 1981); one *d*; 2nd, 1988, Susan Eden. *Educ:* King Edward VI Sch., Southampton; Peterhouse, Cambridge. Work on tank armament (Ministry of Supply), 1944–46; Electrical Research Association, 1946–47; Royal Society Mond Laboratory, Cambridge, 1947–57; Stokes Student, Pembroke Coll., 1950–53; PhD 1952; ICI Fellow, 1953–54; NRC Post-doctoral Fellow, Ottawa, 1954–55; University Demonstrator, Cambridge, 1955–57; Bristol University: Sen. Lectr, 1958–61; Reader in Physics, 1961–64; Dean of Science, 1973–76, 1985–88; Pro-Vice-Chancellor, 1978–81. Member: Physics Cttee, 1967–71, Nuclear Physics Bd, 1971–74, Sci. Bd, 1975–78, SRC; Physical Sci. Sub-Cttee, UGC, 1974–81. Institute of Physics: Mem., Publications Cttee, 1969–81 (Chm., 1977–81); Vice-Pres., 1977–81. Chm., Standing Conf. of Physics Profs, 1987–89. Chairman: SLS (Information Systems) Ltd, 1986–89; Track Analysis Systems Ltd, 1986–92. Hon. Fellow, Univ. of Bristol, 1994. Hughes Medal, Royal Soc., 1994. *Publications:* Electrons in Metals and Semiconductors, 1990; various papers in learned journals on the behaviour of metals at low temperatures. *Recreation:* hill-walking. *Address:* 9 Apsley Road, Clifton, Bristol BS8 2SH. *T:* (0117) 973 9833.

CHAMBERS, Timothy Lachlan; JP; FRCP; Physician, Royal Hospital for Sick Children, Bristol, since 1979; Consultant Paediatrician, Southmead Hospital, Bristol, and Weston-super-Mare General Hospital, since 1979; *b* 11 Feb. 1946; adopted *s* of late Victor Lachlan Chambers and Elsie Ruth (*née* Reynolds); *m* 1971, (Elizabeth) Joanna Ward, FRCP; one *s* two *d. Educ:* Wallington County Grammar Sch.; King's College London; King's Coll. Hosp. Med. Sch. (MB BS 1969). FRCP 1983; FRCPE 1985; FRCPI 1995; FRCPCH 1997. Jun. med. posts, London and SE England, 1969–73; Tutor in paed. and child health, Univ. of Leeds, 1973–76 (Sen. Registrar in medicine, St James's Hosp., Leeds, 1974–75); Physician, Derbyshire Children's Hosp. and other Derby and Nottingham Hosps, 1976–79; University of Bristol: Sen. Clinical Lectr in Child Health, 1979–; Clinical Dean, Southmead Hosp., 1983–90; Mem. Governing Body, Inst. of Child Health, 1987–97; Mem. Court, 1994–99. Dep. Med. Dir, Southmead Health Services NHS Trust, 1994–96. Consultant in paediatrics: MoD, 1985–; RN, 1993–. Medicines Control Agency: Member: Cttee on Safety of Medicines, 1999–; Adv. Bd on Registration of Homoeopathic Products, 2000–. Royal College of Physicians: Mem. Council, 1990–92; Censor, 1992–94; Regl (SW England) Advr, RCPE, 1996–2001; Mem., BMA 1979 (Chm., Paed. Sub-Cttee, Central Consultants and Specialists Cttee, 1989–94); Hon. Sec., Internat. Bd, RCPCH, 1998–2000 (Mem., 1976–96, Hon. Sec., 1984–90, BPA); FRSocMed 1977 (a Vice-Pres., 2001–; Mem. Council, 1995–; Pres., Sect. of Paediatrics, 1994–95; Hon. Editor, 1997–2001; Pres., United Services Section, 2001–); President: Union of Nat. Eur. Paed. Socs and Assocs, 1990–94; Bristol Medico-Chirurgical Soc., 1996–97; Bristol Div., BMA, 1999–2000. Examnr to med. bodies and univs at home and abroad; Chm. and Mem., prof. and govtl cttees and adv. bodies in UK and Europe. Member: Bristol Medico-Legal Soc.; Philosophical Soc., Oxford; British Assoc. for Paed. Nephrology; Corresp. Mem., Société Française de Pédiatrie, 1994. Patron, Lifeline Charity, 1985–; Trustee: St John's Home, Bristol, 1985–93; Royal Med. Benevolent Fund, 1988–. Mem., Bd of Govs, Hosps for Sick Children (London) SHA, 1993–94. Lt Col, RAMC(V), (commnd Captain, 1984). Eucharistic Minister and Reader, RC Cathedral Church of SS Peter and Paul, Clifton, 1991–. Freeman, City of London; Liveryman, Apothecaries' Soc., 1985 (Mem. Court, 2000–). JP Bristol, 1993. *Publications:* Fluid Therapy in Childhood, 1987; contribs to med. and lay jls and collective works. *Recreation:* basking in reflected glory. *Address:* 4 Clyde Park, Bristol BS6 6RR. *T:* (0117) 974 2814. *Clubs:* Athenæum, Naval and Military; Clifton (Bristol); Galle Face Hotel (Colombo).

CHAMIER, Anthony Edward Deschamps; Under Secretary, Department of Education and Science, 1980–92; *b* 16 Aug. 1935; *s* of late Brig. George Chamier, OBE and of Marion (*née* Gascoigne), Achandunie, Alness, Ross-shire; *m* 1962, Anne-Carole Tweeddale Dalling, *d* of William and Kathleen Dalling, Transvaal, S Africa; one *s* one *d. Educ:* Stowe, Buckingham; Trinity Hall, Cambridge; Yale Univ. (Henry Fellow). Military service, 1st Bn Seaforth Highlanders, 1953–55. HM Foreign (later Diplomatic) Service, 1960; Third Secretary, Foreign Office, 1960–62; Second Sec., Rome, 1962–64; Asst Political Adviser, HQ Middle East Comd, Aden, 1964–66; First Sec., FCO, 1966–71; Head of Chancery, Helsinki, 1971–72; seconded, later transf. to Dept of Educn and Science; Principal, 1972–73; Principal Private Sec. to Sec. of State for Educn and Science, 1973–74; Asst Sec., 1974–79; Prin. Estabt Officer, 1980–84. Director, Clan Munro Heritage Ltd, 1994–; Partner, Highland Hospitality (tour operators), 1993–2000. *Recreations:* walking, shooting, gardening. *Address:* Achandunie House, Ardross, by Alness, Ross shire IV17 0YB. *T:* and *Fax:* (01349) 883255. *Club:* Royal Over-Seas League.

CHAMIER, Michael Edward Deschamps, FCA; Director of Finance, European Parliament, since 1983; *b* 4 Feb. 1941; *s* of Saunders Edward Chamier and Mary Frances (*née* Chapman); *m* 1977, Deborah Mary Unwin; one *s* two *d. Educ:* Ampleforth Coll., York. FCA 1975. Sen. Audit Mgr, Arthur Young, Paris, 1965–68; Dep. Dir, Finance and Admin, Reckitt & Coleman, France, 1968–72; Asst Financial Controller for Europe, Squibb Europe, 1972–77; Dep. Dir of Financial Admin, Europe, CABOT Europe, 1977–83. *Publication:* Property Purchasing in France, 1981. *Recreations:* travel, music. *Address:* European Parliament, Batîment KAD 4A007, 2929 Luxembourg. *T:* 430022762.

CHAMP, Andrea Helen; *see* Quinn, A. H.

CHAN, Baron *cr* 2001 (Life Peer), of Oxton in the County of Merseyside; **Michael Chew Koon Chan,** MBE 1991; MD; FRCP, FRACP, FRCPCH; part-time Advisor on Ethnic Health, North West Regional Office, NHS, since 2000; Visiting Professor in Ethnic Health, University of Liverpool, since 1996; *b* 6 March 1940; *s* of James Chieu Kim Chan and Rosie Chan; *m* 1965, Irene Wei-Len Chee; one *s* one *d. Educ:* Raffles Instn, Singapore; Guy's Hosp. Med. Sch. London Univ. (MB BS); MD Singapore 1969. FRCP 1986; FRACP 1975; FRCPCH 1996; MFPHM 1996. Lectr, Dept of Paediatrics, 1970–73, Sen. Lectr and Consultant Paediatrician, 1973–76, Univ. of Singapore; BPA Heinz Res. Fellow, Inst. of Child Health, Univ. of London and Gt Ormond St Hosp. for Sick Children, 1974–75; Sen. Lectr and Consultant Paediatrician, Liverpool Sch. of Tropical Medicine, 1976–94; Dir, NHS Ethnic Health Unit, 1994–97. Non-exec. Dir, Wirral and W Cheshire Community NHS Trust, 1999–. *Publications:* (ed jtly) Diseases of Children in the Subtropics and Tropics, 1991; (contrib.) The Future of Multi Ethnic Britain: the Parekh Report, 2000; contrib. learned jls. *Recreations:* overseas travel, Chinese cooking, community involvement, preaching, gardening. *Address:* 1 Rathmore Drive, Oxton, Wirral CH43 2HD. *T:* (0151) 653 6956; House of Lords, SW1A 0PW.

CHAN, Cho-chak John, GBS 1999; CBE 1993 (OBE 1985); LVO 1986; JP; Managing Director, The Kowloon Motor Bus Co. (1933) Ltd, since 1993; *b* 8 April 1943; *s* of late Kai Kit Chan and Yuk Ying Wong; *m* 1965, Wai-chun Agnes Wong; one *s* one *d. Educ:* St Rose of Lima's Sch.,; Wah Yan Coll., Kowloon; La Salle Coll., Univ. of Hong Kong (BA (Hons), DMS). Commerce and Industry Dept, 1964; Economic Br., Govt Secretariat, 1970; Private Sec. to Gov., 1973; City Dist Comr (Hong Kong), 1975; Asst Dir of Home Affairs, 1976; Dep. Dir of Trade, 1977; Exec. Dir and Gen. Man., Sun Hung Kai Finance Co. Ltd, 1978; Principal Assistant Secretary: for Security, Govt Secretariat, 1980; for CS, 1982; Dep. Dir of Trade, 1983; Dep. Sec. (Gen. Duties), 1984; Dir of Inf. Services, 1986; Dep. Chief Sec., 1987; Sec. for Trade and Industry, 1989; Sec. for Educn and Manpower, 1991. JP Hong Kong, 1984. Hon. Fellow, Univ. of Hong Kong, 2000. Hon. DBA Internat. Management Centres, 1997. *Recreations:* swimming, ten-pin bowling, music, reading. *Address:* The Kowloon Motor Bus Co. (1933) Ltd, 1 Po Lun Street, Lai Chi Kok, Kowloon, Hong Kong. *T:* 27868833. *Clubs:* Hong Kong Jockey; Hong Kong.

CHAN FANG, Anson Maria Elizabeth, (Mrs Anson Chan), CBE 1992; JP; Chief Secretary for Administration, Government Secretariat, Hong Kong Special Administrative Region, 1997–2001; *b* 17 Jan. 1940; *d* of Howard Fang and Fang Zhao Ling; *m* 1963, Archibald John Chan Tai-wing, MBE, QPM, CPM; one *s* one *d. Educ:* Univ. of Hong Kong (BA Hons). Admin. Officer, Hong Kong Govt, 1962–70; Asst Financial Sec., 1970–72; Asst Sec. for New Territories, 1972–75; Principal Asst Sec. for Social Services, 1975–79; Dep. Dir, 1979–84, Dir, 1984–87, Social Welfare; Sec. for Econ. Services, 1987–93; Sec. for CS, April–Nov. 1993; Chief Sec., 1993–97. JP Hong Kong, 1975. *Recreation:* music. *Address:* Chief Secretary for Administration's Office, Government Secretariat, Lower Albert Road, Hong Kong. *T:* 28102406. *Clubs:* Zonta (Hong Kong East); Hong Kong, Hong Kong Jockey, American (Hong Kong).

CHAN, Rt Hon. Sir Julius, GCMG 1994; KBE 1980 (CBE 1975); PC 1981; Parliamentary Leader, People's Progress Party, Papua New Guinea, 1970–97; Prime Minister and Minister for Foreign Affairs, 1994–97; *b* 29 Aug. 1939; *s* of Chin Pak and Tingoris Chan; *m* 1966, Stella Ahmat. *Educ:* Marist Brothers Coll., Ashgrove, Qld; Univ. of Queensland, Australia (Agricl Science). Co-operative Officer, Papua New Guinea Admin, 1960–62; private business, coastal shipping and merchandise, 1963–70. MP PNG, 1968–97; Minister for Finance, 1972–77; Dep. Prime Minister and Minister for Primary Industry, 1977–78; Prime Minister, 1980–82; Minister for Finance and Planning, 1985–86; Dep. Prime Minister, 1985–88; Minister for Trade and Industry, 1986–88; Dep. Opposition Leader, 1988–92; Dep. Prime Minister and Minister for Finance and Planning, 1992–94. Hon. Dr Technol., Univ. of Technol., PNG, 1983. *Recreations:* swimming, walking, boating. *Address:* PO Box 6030, Boroko, Papua New Guinea.

CHAN, Nai Keong, (Kenneth), CBE 1985; JP; FREng; Chairman, Leighton (Asia) Ltd, since 1997; Chairman Emeritus, Parsons Brinckerhoff (Asia) Ltd, since 1992; *b* 17 Nov. 1931; two *s* one *d.* FICE. FIStructE, FHKIE, FHKAES; FREng (FEng 1986). Public Works Dept, Hong Kong: pupil engineer, Roads Office, 1952; Civil Engineering Office, 1960; Senior Engineer, 1964; Highways Office, 1969; Principal Govt Engineer, 1973, i/c Tuen Mun New Town develt; Dir, Engineering Dept, 1980; Dep. Dir, Public Works, 1981; Dep. Sec. for Lands and Works, 1982; Sec. for Lands and Works, 1983–86; Gp Man. Dir, Cavendish Internat. Holdings Ltd, 1987–89; Dir, Parsons Brinckerhoff (Asia) Ltd, 1989–92. JP Hong Kong, 1972. Hon. DTech Loughborough, 1984. *Recreations:* bridge, swimming, yoga, music. *Address:* c/o Parsons Brinckerhoff (Asia) Ltd, 23/F AIA Tower, 183 Electric Road, North Point, Hong Kong. *T:* 25798899, *Fax:* 28569908. *Clubs:* Hongkong, Hong Kong Jockey, Chinese, Chinese Recreation, China (Hong Kong).

CHAN, Siu-Oi, Patrick; Hon. Mr Justice Chan; Permanent Judge, Court of Final Appeal, Hong Kong, since 2000; *b* 21 Oct. 1948; *s* of late Chan Chu-Yau and of Li Man-Yee; *m* 1990, Lisa Chiang Miu-Chu. *Educ:* Univ. of Hong Kong (LLB 1974; Postgrad. Cert. in Laws, 1975). Barrister in private practice, Hong Kong, 1977–87; Judge of District Court, 1987–91; Dep. Registrar of Supreme Court, 1991–92; Judge, 1992–97, Chief Judge, 1997–2000, High Court of Hong Kong. *Address:* Court of Final Appeal, 1 Battery Path, Central, Hong Kong. *T:* 21230033.

CHAN, Dr Stephen Ming Tak; HM Coroner, Inner North London, since 1995; *b* 16 Oct. 1948; *s* of late Kwok Kong Chan and Fun Ching Cheung; *m* 1972, Margaret Ann Small, *y d* of Francis Shadrack Small and Edith May Small. *Educ:* Bishop Hall Jubilee Sch., Hong Kong; RMN 1970; Kent Univ.; Charing Cross Hosp. Med. Sch., Univ. of London (MB, BS 1978; DMJ 1988); Cardiff Law Sch., Univ. of Wales (LLM 1992). Psychiatric nurse, St Augustine's Hosp., near Canterbury, 1967–70; jun. med. posts, Radcliffe Infirmary and John Radcliffe Hosp., Oxford and Charing Cross Hosp., 1979–80; postgrad. medical trng, Hammersmith Hosp., RPMS, Univ. of London, 1980–83; Principal in general practice, Epsom, 1983–86; Forensic Medical Examnr, 1984–90, Sen. Forensic Medical Examnr, 1990–94, Metropolitan Police; Forensic Medical Consultant in private practice, 1986–94; Asst Dep. Coroner, 1989–93, Dep. Coroner, 1993–94, Southern Dist, Gtr London; Asst Dep. Coroner, City of London, 1990–93. Member: Coroners' Soc. for England & Wales, 1989–; Council, Medico-Legal Soc., 1994– (Hon. Treas., 1990–94); British Acad. Forensic Sci., 1988–; RIIA, 1993–; RSAA, 1992–. *Publications:* Suicide Verdict: the coroner's dilemma, 1992; papers on medico-legal subjects. *Recreations:* Italian opera, Victorian antiques, Chinese history, gardening. *Address:* St Pancras Coroner's Court, Camley Street, NW1 0PP. *T:* (020) 7387 4884. *Clubs:* Lansdowne, Royal Over-Seas League.

CHANCE, Sqdn Ldr Dudley Raymond, FRGS; a Recorder of the Crown Court, 1980–86; *b* 9 July 1916; *s* of Captain Arthur Chance, Sherwood Foresters, and Byzie Chance; *m* 1958, Jessie Maidstone, widow, *d* of John and Alice Dewing. *Educ:* Nottingham High Sch.; London Univ. (BA Oriental Religions and Philosophies, LLB 1969); BA Hons Internat. Politics and For. Policy, Open Univ., 1980. Called to Bar, Middle Temple, 1955; Dep. Circuit Judge, 1973–80. Commissioned in Royal Air Force, 1936; served Egypt, Transjordan, 1936–37; Bomber Comd (4 Gp), 1938; served in Bomber Comd Nos 97 and 77 Sqdns; took part in first raids on Norway; crashed off Trondheim; picked up later from sea by HMS Basilisk, later sunk at Dunkirk; Air Ministry, Whitehall, 1941–42, later in 2 Group, Norfolk, 21 Sqdn; also served in SEAC, Bengal/Burma. Sqdn Ldr, RAFO, until March 1961; gazetted to retain rank of Sqdn Ldr from that date. Member: panel of Chairmen of Medical Appeal Tribunals (DHSS), 1978–88; panel of Independent Inspectors for motorway and trunk road inquiries for DoE, 1978–83. Contested (C) Norwich North, 1959. FRGS 1979. *Recreations:* violin, painting. *Address:* Lamb Buildings, Temple, EC4Y 7AS; Fenners Chambers, 4 Madingley Road, Cambridge CB3 0EE. *Club:* Goldfish (RAF aircrew rescued from sea).

CHANCE, Sir (George) Jeremy (ffolliott), 4th Bt *cr* 1900, of Grand Avenue, Hove; retired; *b* 24 Feb. 1926; *s* of Sir Roger James Ferguson Chance, 3rd Bt, MC and Mary Georgina (*d* 1984), *d* of Col William Rowney; *S* father, 1987; *m* 1950, (cousin) Cecilia Mary Elizabeth, *d* of Sir William Hugh Stobart Chance, CBE; two *s* two *d. Educ:* Gordonstoun School; Christ Church, Oxford (MA). Sub-Lieut RNVR, 1944–47. Harry Ferguson Ltd, 1950–53; Massey-Ferguson, 1953–78; Director, Massey-Ferguson (UK) Ltd, 1973–78; farmer, 1978–87. *Recreations:* choral singing, painting. *Heir: s* (John) Sebastian Chance [*b* 2 Oct. 1954; *m* 1977, Victoria Mary, *d* of Denis McClean; two *s* one *d*]. *Address:* Hafod-y-Bryn, Criccieth, Gwynedd LL52 0AH.

CHANCE, Michael Edward Ferguson; counter-tenor; *b* Penn, Bucks, 7 March 1955; *s* of John Wybergh Chance and Wendy Muriel (*née* Chance); *m* 1991, Irene, *d* of Hon. Francis Edward Noel-Baker, *qv*; one *s* one *d. Educ:* St George's Sch., Windsor; Eton Coll.; King's Coll., Cambridge (MA English 1977; Mem., King's Coll. Choir, 1974–77). Stockbroker, Mullens & Co., 1977–80. Founder Mem., The Light Blues, 1977–83; Mem., Monteverdi Choir, 1980–83; solo career, 1983–: operatic débuts: Buxton Fest., 1983; Kent Opera, Opéra de Lyon, Göttingen Handel Fest., 1985; Paris Opera, 1988; Glyndebourne Fest., 1989; ENO, Netherlands Opera, 1991; Covent Garden, Scottish Opera, 1992; Australian Opera, 1993; Buenos Aires, 1996; WNO, 1997; San Francisco Opera, 1998; Maggio Musicale, Florence, 1999; rôles include: Oberon in A Midsummer Night's Dream; Apollo in Death in Venice; Julius Caesar; Andronico in Tamerlano; Bertarido in Rodelinda; Orfeo in Orfeo ed Euridice; Ottone in Agrippina; Ottone in L'incoronazione di Poppea; Military Governor in A Night at the Chinese Opera; Orpheus in The Second Mrs Kong; concert performances in Europe, USA and Japan. Visiting Professor: RCM, 1996–; Scuola di Musica di Fiesole, 1997. Numerous recordings of oratorio, opera and recitals. *Recreations:* racquet sports, hill-walking, olive cultivation. *Address:* c/o Ingpen & Williams, 26 Wadham Road, SW15 2LR. *T:* (020) 8874 3222, *Fax:* (020) 8877 3113. *Club:* Garrick.

CHANCE, Michael Spencer; Executive Counsel, Joint Disciplinary Scheme, 1993–97; *b* 14 May 1938; *s* of Florence and Ernest Horace Chance; *m* 1962, Enid Mabel Carter; three *d. Educ:* Rossall School. Solicitor. With Challinor & Roberts, Warley, 1962–70; Senior Asst Prosecuting Solicitor, Sussex Police Authy, 1970–72; Office of Director of Public Prosecutions, 1972–86: Asst Dir, 1981–86; Chief Crown Prosecutor, North London, 1986–87; Asst Head of Legal Services, Crown Prosecution Service, 1987; Dep. Dir, Serious Fraud Office, 1987–90; Consultant, Cameron Markby Hewitt, 1991–93. *Address:* Box Tree Cottage, Arkesden, Saffron Walden, Essex CB11 4EX.

CHANCELLOR, Alexander Surtees; columnist: The Guardian, since 1996; The Daily Telegraph, since 1998; *b* 4 Jan. 1940; *s* of Sir Christopher Chancellor, CMG and Sylvia Mary, OBE, *e d* of Sir Richard Paget, 2nd Bt and Lady Muriel Finch-Hatton, *d* of 12th Earl of Winchilsea and Nottingham; *m* 1964, Susanna Elisabeth Debenham; two *d. Educ:* Eton College; Trinity Hall, Cambridge. Reuters News Agency, 1964–74; ITN, 1974–75; Editor: The Spectator, 1975–84; Time and Tide, 1984–86; Dep. Editor, Sunday Telegraph, 1986; US Editor, The Independent, 1986–88; Editor: The Independent Magazine, 1988–92; The New Yorker's Talk of the Town, 1992–93; columnist, The Times, 1992–93; Associate Ed., Sunday Telegraph, 1994–95; Founding Ed., Sunday Telegraph Mag., 1995. Comr, English Heritage, 1990–92. *Publication:* Some Times in America, 1999. *Address:* 1 Souldern Road, W14 0JE. *Clubs:* Garrick, Beefsteak.

CHANDLER, Sir Colin (Michael), Kt 1988; FRAeS; Chairman: Vickers Defence Systems Ltd, since 2000; Vickers plc, 1997–2000 (Managing Director, 1990–92; Chief Executive, 1992–98); *b* 7 Oct. 1939; *s* of Henry John Chandler and Mary Martha (*née* Bowles); *m* 1964, Jennifer Mary Crawford; one *s* one *d. Educ:* St Joseph's Acad.; Hatfield Polytechnic. FCMA; FRAeS 1994. Commercial Apprentice, De Havilland Aircraft Co., 1956; Hawker Siddeley Aviation, later British Aerospace, Kingston: Commercial Manager, 1967–72; Exec. Dir, Commercial, 1973–78; Divl Man. Dir., 1978–82; Gp Marketing Dir, 1983–85; Hd of Defence Export Services, MoD, 1985–89. Non-executive Director: Siemens Plessey Electronic Systems, 1990–95; TI Group, subseq. Smiths Group, 1992–; Guardian Royal Exchange, 1995–99; Racal Electronics plc, 1999–2000 (Chm., 2000–); Thaler plc, 2000–. Vice Pres., EEF, 1991; Member: NDIC, 1992–; Cttee, DTI Priority Japan Campaign, 1992–. Commander, Order of the Lion of Finland, 1982. *Recreations:* playing tennis, reading, gardening, listening to music. *Address:* c/o Rolls-Royce plc, 65 Buckingham Gate, SW1E 6AT. *Clubs:* Reform, Mark's; Harbour.

CHANDLER, Dr David Geoffrey; author; lecturer and military historian, Royal Military Academy Sandhurst; *b* 15 Jan. 1934; *s* of late Rev. Geoffrey Edmund Chandler and Joyce Mary Chandler; *m* 1961, Gillian Dixon; three *s. Educ:* Marlborough Coll.; Keble Coll., Oxford (BA 1955; Cert Ed 1956; MA 1960; DLitt 1991). Captain, RAEC, Royal W Africa Frontier Force, Nigeria, 1956–60; Royal Military Academy Sandhurst: Lectr, Dept of Modern Subjects, 1960–61; Lectr, 1961–64, Sen. Lectr, 1964–69, Dept of Mil. History; Dep. Head, 1969–80, Head, 1980–94, Dept of War Studies. Visiting Professor: Mershon, in Mil. History, Ohio State Univ., 1970; Mary Ann Northen, in Humanities, Virginian Mil. Inst., 1988; Mil. Studies, US Marine Corps Univ., 1991. Trustee, Royal Armouries, HM Tower of London, and Leeds, 1989–95. Hon. President: European Union of Re-enactments Soc., 1990–95 (Founder, 1990); Napoleonic Assoc. (UK), 1994–. Mil. advr, War and Peace, BBC TV, 1971–73; question setter, Mastermind, 1990–94; mil. history cons., Great Military Leaders, Channel 4, 1992–93; Cons., From Hoplites to Harrier—a Radio History of War, BBC, 1993–94. FRHistS 1966; FRGS 1971. Golden Cross of Merit (Polish govt in exile), 1979. *Publications* include: The Campaigns of Napoleon, 1967 (Internat. Napoleonic Soc. Lit Award, 1995); The Marlborough Wars: Robert Parker and Count de Mérode-Westerloo, 1968; Marlborough as Military Commander, 1973; The Art of War on Land, 1973; The Art of Warfare in the Age of Marlborough, 1976; A Dictionary of the Napoleonic Wars, 1979; Waterloo: The Hundred Days, 1984; An Atlas of Military Strategy, 1618–1868, 1980; Sedgemoor, 1685, 1985; (ed) Napoleon's Marshals, 1987; (ed) Military Maxims of Napoleon, 1987; Battles and Battlescenes of World War Two, 1989; Austerlitz, 1805, 1990; The Illustrated Napoleon, 1990; (ed) The Great Battles of the British Army, 1991; (ed) Sandhurst—the Royal Military Academy: 250 years, 1991; Jena, 1806, 1993; (sen. ed.) D-Day Encyclopaedia, 1993; On the Napoleonic Wars (Napoleonic Soc. of Amer. Lit. Award), 1994; (sen. ed.) The Oxford Illustrated History of the British Army, 1995; (ed) A Traveller's Guide to the Battlefields of Europe, 1998; contribs to DNB. *Recreations:* battlefield visits, wargaming, military re-enactment societies, rowing, naval model-making, drawing. *Address:* Hindford, Monteagle Lane, Yateley, Hants GU46 6LT. *T:* (01252) 872175.

See also P. G. Chandler.

CHANDLER, Sir Geoffrey, Kt 1983; CBE 1976; Chairman, Business Group, Amnesty International UK, since 1991 (Member of Board, 1996–98); *b* 15 Nov. 1922; *s* of Frederick George Chandler, MD, FRCP, and Marjorie Chandler; *m* 1955, Lucy Bertha Buxton; four *d. Educ:* Sherborne; Trinity Coll., Cambridge (MA History). Military Service, 1942–46: Captain 60th Rifles; Political Warfare Exec., Cairo; Special Ops Exec. (Force 133), Greece; Anglo-Greek Information Service, W Macedonia, 1945; Press Officer, Volos and Salonika, 1946. Cambridge Univ., 1947–49; Captain, Univ. Lawn Tennis, 1949. BBC Foreign News Service, 1949–51; Leader Writer and Features Editor, Financial Times, 1951–56; Commonwealth Fund Fellow, Columbia Univ., New York, 1953–54; Shell Internat. Petroleum Co.: Manager, Econs Div., 1957–61; Area Co-ordinator, W Africa, 1961–64; Chm. and Man. Dir, Shell Trinidad Ltd, 1964–69; Shell Internat. Petroleum Co.: Public Affairs Co-ordinator, 1969–78; Dir, 1971–78; Dir, Shell Petroleum Co., and Shell Petroleum NV, 1976–78; initiator, Shell's first Statement of Gen. Business Principles, 1976; Dir Gen., NEDO, and Mem., NEDC, 1978–83; Dir, Industry Year 1986, 1984–86; Leader, RSA Industry Matters team, 1987–89; Industry Advr, RSA, 1987–92. Pres., Inst. of Petroleum, 1972–74. Member: Council and Exec. Cttee, Overseas Develt Inst., 1969–78; British Overseas Trade Adv. Council, 1978–82; Council and Exec. Cttee, VSO, 1980–96; Chm., NCVO, 1989–96. Chm., BBC Consultative Group on Industrial and Business Affairs, and Mem. BBC Gen. Adv. Council, 1983–88; Chm., Consultative Council, Soc. of Educn Officers Schools Curriculum Award, 1984–96; Member: Wilton Park Academic Council, 1983–87; Council for Charitable Support, 1990–96; Associate, Ashridge Management Coll., 1983–89; Pres., Assoc. for Management & Business Educn, 1986–90. Trustee, Charities Aid Foundn, 1990–96; UK Trustee, Council on Economic Priorities (Europe), 1997–99. FRSA. Hon. Mem., CGLI, 1988. Hon. Fellow: Sheffield City Polytechnic, 1981; Girton Coll., Cambridge, 1986; Hon. FInstPet 1982. Hon. DBA Internat. Management Centre from Buckingham, 1986; Hon. DSc: CNAA, 1986; Bradford, 1987; Aston, 1987; Hon. CGIA 1987. *Publications:* The Divided Land: an Anglo-Greek Tragedy, 1959, 2nd edn 1994; (jtly) The State of the Nation: Trinidad & Tobago in the later 1960s, 1969; (contrib.) Britain's Economic Performance, 1994, 2nd edn 1998; Corporate Citizenship, 1998; Human Rights Standards and the Responsibility of Transnational Corporations, 1999; Human Rights and the Oil Industry, 2000; articles on oil, energy, trans-national corporations, human rights and corporate responsibility; numerous speeches and articles, urging employee participation, coherent British indust. policy and the need for clearly articulated business principles. *Recreations:* working in woodland, gardening, music, observing butterflies. *Address:* Little Gaterounds, Parkgate Road, Newdigate, Surrey RH5 5AJ. *T:* (01306) 631612. *Club:* Hawks (Cambridge).

CHANDLER, Paul Geoffrey; Chief Executive, Traidcraft, since 2001; *b* 13 Oct. 1961; *s* of David Geoffrey Chandler, *qv* and Gillian Chandler; *m* 1993, Sarah Gillian Munro-Faure; three *d. Educ:* Wellington Coll., Berks; St John's Coll., Oxford (Stanhope Histl Essay Prize, 1983; BA Mod. Hist. 1983; MA 1987); Henley Mgt Coll. (MBA 1987). ACIB 1985. Joined Barclays Bank, 1983: Manager, Moorgate Br., 1986–87; on secondment to Church Urban Fund, 1987; Manager, Gp Strategic Planning, 1987–89; Asst Personal Sector Dir, London Western Reg., 1990–92; Gen. Sec., SPCK, 1992–2001. Member: Council, Overseas Bishoprics Fund, 1992–2001; Bd of Mission, C of E, 1994–2001; Exec. Cttee, Feed the Minds, 1996–2001; Trustee, C of E Pensions Bd, 1998–2001. Trustee, SPCK-USA, 1992–2001; Member: Cttee of Mgt, Assoc. for Promoting Christian Knowledge (Ireland), 1995–2001; Exec. Cttee, Indian SPCK, 1998–2001. St Stephen's Church Warden, S Lambeth, 2000–01 (Mem. PCC, 1984–94, 1996–2001). Gov., St Martin-in-the-Fields High Sch. for Girls, 1992–2001 (Vice-Chm., 1993–2001). Trustee, All Saints Educnl Trust, 1992–2001. *Recreations:* playing with my daughters, reading, history, walking on Yorkshire Moors, collecting works of John Buchan. *Address:* The Hermitage, Sunderland Bridge Village, Durham DH6 5HD.

CHANDLER, Tony John; Hon. Research Fellow, University College London, since 1989; Visiting Professor, King's College, London, since 1989; *b* 7 Nov. 1928; *s* of Harold William and Florence Ellen Chandler; *m* 1954, Margaret Joyce Weston; one *s* one *d. Educ:* King's Coll., London. MSc. PhD, AKC, MA. Lectr, Birkbeck Coll., Univ. of London, 1952–56; University Coll. London: Lectr, 1956–65; Reader in Geography, 1965–69; Prof. of Geography, 1969–73; Prof. of Geography, Manchester Univ., 1973–77; Master of Birkbeck Coll., Univ. of London, 1977–79. Sec., Royal Meteorological Soc., 1969–73, Vice-Pres., 1973–75. Member: Council, NERC; Health and Safety Commn; Cttee of Experts on Major Hazards; Royal Soc. Study Gp on Pollution in the Atmosphere, 1974–77; Clean Air Council; Royal Commn on Environmental Pollution, 1973–77; Standing Commn on Energy and the Environment 1978. *Publications:* The Climate of London, 1965; Modern Meteorology and Climatology, 1972, 2nd edn 1981; contribs to: Geographical Jl, Geography, Weather, Meteorological Magazine, Bulletin of Amer. Meteorological Soc., etc. *Recreations:* horology, music, reading, travel. *Address:* 15 Durrell Close, Langney, Eastbourne, East Sussex BN23 7AN.

CHANDLER, Wendy; *see* Hall, W.

CHANDOS, 3rd Viscount *cr* 1954, of Aldershot; **Thomas Orlando Lyttelton;** Baron Lyttelton of Aldershot (Life Peer) 2000; Chairman, Lopex plc, since 1997; *b* 12 Feb. 1953; *s* of 2nd Viscount Chandos and of Caroline Mary (who *m* 1985, Hon. David Hervey Erskine), *d* of Rt Hon. Sir Alan Lascelles, GCB, GCVO, CMG, MC; *S* father, 1980; *m* 1985, Arabella Sarah, *d* of Adrian Bailey and Lady Mary Russell; two *s* one *d. Educ:* Eton; Worcester College, Oxford (BA). Banker, 1974–93, Dir, 1985–93, Kleinwort Benson. Opposition spokesman on Treasury matters, 1995–97. Chief Exec., Northbridge Ventures Ltd; Chm., Capital & Regional plc; Director: Botts Co. Ltd, 1993–97; Cine-UK Ltd; Middlesex Hldgs; ENO; Nat. Film and Television Sch.; Education 2000. *Heir: s* Hon. Oliver Antony Lyttelton, *b* 21 Feb. 1986. *Address:* 149 Gloucester Avenue, NW1 8LA. *T:* (020) 7722 8329.

CHANDRACHUD, Hon. Yeshwant Vishnu; Chief Justice of India, 1978–85; *b* Poona (Maharashtra), 12 July 1920; *s* of Vishnu Balkrishna Chandrachud and Indira; *m* Prabha; one *s* one *d. Educ:* Bombay Univ. (BA, LLB). Advocate of Bombay High Court, 1943, civil and criminal work; part-time Prof. of Law, Government Law Coll., Bombay, 1949–52; Asst Govt Pleader, 1952; Govt Pleader, 1958; Judge, Bombay High Court, 1961–72; one-man Pay Commn for Bombay Municipal Corporation officers, later Arbitrator in dispute between Electricity Supply and Transport Undertaking and its employees' union; one-man Commn to inquire into circumstances leading to death of Deen Dayal Upadhyaya; Judge, Supreme Court of India, 1972–78. President: Internat. Law Assoc. (India Branch), 1978–; Indian Law Inst., 1978–. *Address:* (official) 7–B Samata, General Bhosale Marg, Bombay 400021, India. *T:* (22) 2042474.

CHANDRASEKHAR, Prof. Sivaramakrishna, FRS 1983; Director, Centre for Liquid Crystal Research, Bangalore, since 1991; *b* 6 Aug. 1930; *s* of S. Sivaramakrishnan and Sitalaxmi; *m* 1954, Ila Pinglay; one *s* one *d. Educ:* Nagpur Univ. (MSc, DSc); Pembroke Coll., Cambridge (PhD 1958; ScD 1987). Res. Schol., Raman Res. Inst., Bangalore, 1950–54; 1851 Exhibn Schol., Cavendish Lab., Cambridge, 1954–57; DSIR Fellow, Dept of Crystallography, UCL, 1957–59; Res. Fellow, Davy Faraday Res. Lab., Royal Instn, 1959–61; Prof. and Hd of Dept of Physics, Univ. of Mysore, 1961–71; Prof., Raman Res. Inst., Bangalore, 1971–90. Nehru Vis. Prof., and Fellow Pembroke Coll., Cambridge, 1986–87; Bhatnagar Fellow, CSIR, 1990–95. India Corresp., 1987–, Royal Medal, 1994, Royal Soc.; Niels Bohr—UNESCO Gold Medal, 1998. Chevalier, Ordre des Palmes Académiques (France), 1999. *Publications:* Liquid Crystals, 1977, 2nd edn, 1992; editor of several books; contrib. scientific papers to learned jls. *Address:* Centre for Liquid Crystal Research, PO Box 1329, Jalahalli, Bangalore 560013, India.

CHANEY, Hon. Sir Frederick (Charles), KBE 1982 (CBE 1969); AFC 1945; Chairman, Home Building Society, 1974–87; *b* 12 Oct. 1914; *s* of Frederick Charles Chaney and Rose Templar Chaney; *m* 1938; four *s* three *d. Educ:* Aquinas Coll.; Claremont Coll. Served War, RAAF, 1940–45. Teacher, 1936–40 and 1946–55. MHR (L) Perth, 1955–69; Govt Whip, 1961–63; Minister for the Navy, 1963–66; Administrator, Northern Territory, 1970–73. Lord Mayor of Perth, WA, 1978–82. Dep. Pres., King's Park Bd, 1981–84. Freeman, City of Perth, 1998. *Address:* 9A Melville Street, Claremont, WA 6010, Australia. *T:* (9) 3840596. *Clubs:* West Australian Cricket Assoc., East Perth Football (Perth).

CHANG-HIM, Rt Rev. French Kitchener; *see* Seychelles, Bishop of.

CHANNING, (Raymond) Alastair, FCIT, FILT; Managing Director, Associated British Ports, 1995–97; *b* 2 May 1943; *s* of late Geoffrey Channing, FRCS and Kathleen Channing; *m* 1976, Victoria Margaret Nish. *Educ:* Clifton Coll.; Clare Coll., Cambridge (MA; athletics Blue, 1965, and competed for Oxford and Cambridge against various American Univs, 1965). Various posts in Depts of Transport and Envmt, incl. Asst Private Sec. to successive Ministers of Transport; British Transport Docks Board, later Associated British Ports: Sec., 1979–84; Dir, 1984; Dep. Man. Dir, 1991–95; Dir, ABP Hldgs plc, 1992–97. FCIT 1994 (Chm., 1996–98); CIMgt 1995. *Recreations:* listening to music, making furniture, the countryside, athletics (now vicarious). *Address:* The Old Manor House, Hampnett, Cheltenham, Glos GL54 3NW. *T:* (01451) 860795. *Club:* Reform.

CHANNON, family name of **Baron Kelvedon**.

CHANNON, Prof. Derek French, DBA; FCIM; Professor of Management, Imperial College of Science, Technology and Medicine, 1990–97; *b* 4 March 1939; *s* of John French and Betty Blanche Channon; *m* 1963, Ann Lesley (marr. diss. 1986); one *s* one *d. Educ:* University Coll. London (BSc); Manchester Business Sch. (MBA); Harvard Graduate Sch. of Business (DBA). FCIM 1985. Marketing management, Royal Dutch Shell Gp, 1960–68; Lectr in Marketing, Manchester Business Sch., 1968–70; Ford Foundn European Doctoral Fellow, Harvard Bus. Sch., 1968–71; Manchester Business School: Sen. Res. Fellow, 1971–76; Prof. of Strategic Management and Marketing, 1977–89; Associate Dir, 1985–87. Jt Man. Dir, Evode Holdings PLC, 1976–77. Director: Strategic Management Soc., 1982– (Pres. 1985–88); Bray Technologies, 1983–92; Royal Bank of Scotland, 1988–95. *Publications:* Strategy and Structure of British Enterprise, 1973; (with J. Stopford and B. Norburn) Business Policy, 1975; British Banking Strategy and the International Challenge, 1977; The Service Industries, 1978; (with R. M. Jalland) Multinational Strategic Planning, 1979; British Transnational Bank Strategy, 1979; (with J. Stopford and J. Constable) Cases in Strategic Management, 1980; (with P. Rushton) Retail Electronic Banking and Point of Sale, 1982; Bank Strategic Management and Marketing, 1986; Global Banking Strategy, 1988; (ed) Blackwell Encyclopedic Dictionary of Strategic Management, 1997. *Recreations:* golf, tennis, painting.

CHANT, (Elizabeth) Ann, CB 1997; a Commissioner and Director General, Board of Inland Revenue, since 2000; *b* 16 Aug. 1945; *d* of late Capt. Harry Charles Chant and Gertrude Chant (*née* Poel). *Educ:* Blackpool Collegiate Sch. for Girls. Nat. Assistance Bd, Lincoln, 1963–66; Min. of Social Security, Lincoln, 1966–70; NHS Whitley Council, DHSS London, 1970–72; DHSS, Lincoln, 1972–74; DHSS Regl Office, Nottingham, 1974–82; Manager, DHSS Sutton-in-Ashfield, 1982–83; DHSS HQ, London, 1983–85; Prin. Private Sec. to Permanent Sec., DHSS, 1985–87; Head: Records Br., DSS, Newcastle upon Tyne, 1987–89; Contribns Unit, 1990–91; Chief Executive: Contributions Agency, DSS, 1991–94; Child Support Agency, DSS, 1994–97; Man. Dir for Corporate Social Responsibility, BITC, 1997–99; Reviews of Public Trust Office and Legal Services Ombudsman's Office for Lord Chancellor's Dept, 1999. Exec. Council Mem., Industrial Soc., 1993–. FRSA 1991. *Recreations:* friends, music (especially opera), theatre. *Address:* Inland Revenue, Somerset House, Strand, WC2R 1LB.

CHANTLER, Sir Cyril, Kt 1996; MD; FRCP; Chairman, Great Ormond Street Hospital for Sick Children NHS Trust, since 2000; Children Nationwide Medical Research Fund Professor of Paediatric Nephrology, London University, 1990–2000; Emeritus Professor, University of London, since 2001; Senior Associate, King Edward VII Hospital Fund for London and King's College London, since 2001; *b* 12 May 1939; *s* of Fred Chantler and Marjorie Chantler (*née* Clark); *m* 1963, Shireen Saleh; two *s* one *d. Educ:* Wrekin Coll.; St Catharine's Coll., Cambridge (BA 1960; MB BChir 1963; MD 1973); Guy's Hosp. Med. Sch. FKC 1998. MRC Travelling Fellow, Univ. of California, 1971; Guy's Hospital: Sen. Lectr and Consultant Paediatrician, 1972–80; Prof. of Paediatric Nephrology, 1980–2000; General Manager, 1985–88; Clinical Dean, Principal, 1989–92, 1992–98, UMDS, Guy's and St Thomas' Hosps; Vice Principal, KCL, and Dean, GKT Hosps' Med. and Dental Sch. of KCL, 1998–2000; Pro-Vice-Chancellor, London Univ., 1997–2000. Mem., NHS Policy Bd, 1989–95. Chairman: Sci. Adv. Cttee, Foundn for the Study of Infant Deaths, 1988–90; Standards Cttee, GMC, 1997–; Council of Heads of UK Med. Schs, 1998–99. Non-executive Director: Guy's and Lewisham NHS Trust, 1991–92; Guy's and St Thomas' NHS Trust, 1993–97; Lambeth, Southwark, Lewisham HA, 1998–2000; Inst. of Health Management Consultants, 1990–94; Pres., British Assoc. of Medical Managers, 1991–97. Teale Lectr, 1987, Censor, 1989–90, RCP. Founder FMedSci 1998. Mem., Inst. of Medicine, Nat. Acad. of Scis, USA, 1999; Hon. Mem., Amer. Paed. Assoc., 1992. Co-Editor, Pediatric Nephrology Jl, 1986–96. *Recreations:* golf, opera, reading. *Address:* 6 Charlton Park House, Charlton Park, near Malmesbury, Wilts SN16 9DG; 22 Benbow House, 24 New Globe Walk, Bankside, SE1 9DS. *T:* (020) 7401 3246, *Fax:* (020) 7401 3250. *Club:* Athenæum.

CHANTRY, Dr George William, CEng, FIEE; CPhys, FInstP; Director, European Operations, 1990–93, Senior Vice-President Europe, 1994–99, Carnahan & Associates; Consultant to Ministry of Defence on Strategic Defence Initiative Technology Transfer, 1990–98; *b* 13 April 1933; *s* of George William Chantry and Sophia Veronica (*née* Johnston); *m* 1956, Diana Margaret Rhodes (*née* Martin); two *s* one *d. Educ:* Christ Church, Oxford (DPhil 1959, MA 1960). CEng, FIEE 1976; FInstP 1974. Res. Associate, Cornell Univ., 1958; National Physical Lab., Dept of Industry: Sen. Res. Fellow, 1960; Sen. Scientific Officer, 1962; Principal Sci. Officer, 1967; Sen. Principal Sci. Officer, 1973; Dep. Chief Sci. Officer, DoI HQ, 1982, seconded to FCO; Counsellor (Sci. and Tech.), Bonn and Berne, 1982; Res. and Technol. Policy Div., DTI, 1985; seconded to MoD as Asst Dir for Industry in SDI Participation Office, 1985. Past Chm., European Molecular Liquids Gp; Mem., Science Educn and Technol. Bd, IEE, 1980–82. Editor, Proc. IEE, Science, Measurement and Technology (formerly Part A), 1981–. *Publications:* Submillimetre Spectroscopy, 1971; High-Frequency Dielectric Measurement, 1972; Submillimetre Waves and their Applications, 1978; Modern Aspects of Microwave Spectroscopy, 1980; Long-Wave Optics, 1983; papers in learned literature. *Recreations:* philately, bridge, gardening, music.

CHAPLAIS, Pierre Théophile Victorien Marie, Médaille de la Résistance, 1946; FBA 1973; Reader in Diplomatic in the University of Oxford, 1957–87, now Reader Emeritus; Professorial Fellow, Wadham College, Oxford, 1964–87, now Emeritus Fellow; *b* Châteaubriant, Loire-Atlantique, France, 8 July 1920; *s* of late Théophile Chaplais and Victorine Chaplais (*née* Roussel); *m* 1948, Mary Doreen Middlemast; two *s. Educ:* Collège St-Sauveur, Redon, Ille-et-Vilaine; Univ. of Rennes, Ille-et-Vilaine (Licence en Droit, Licence ès-Lettres); Univ. of London (PhD). Editor, Public Record Office, London, 1948–55; Lectr in Diplomatic, Univ. of Oxford, 1955–57; Literary Dir, Royal Hist. Soc., 1958–64. Corresp. Fellow, Mediaeval Acad. of America, 1979. *Publications:* Some Documents regarding . . . The Treaty of Brétigny, 1952; The War of St Sardos, 1954; Treaty Rolls, vol. I, 1955; (with T. A. M. Bishop) Facsimiles of English Royal Writs to AD 1100 presented to V. H. Galbraith, 1957; Diplomatic Documents, vol. I, 1964; English Royal Documents, King John-Henry VI, 1971; English Medieval Diplomatic Practice, Part II, 1975, Part I, 1983; Essays in Medieval Diplomacy and Administration, 1981; Piers Gaveston, Edward II's Adoptive Brother, 1994; articles in Bulletin of Inst. of Historical Research, English Hist. Review, Jl of Soc. of Archivists, etc. *Recreations:* gardening, fishing. *Address:* Lew Lodge, Lew, Bampton, Oxfordshire OX18 2BE. *T:* (01993) 850613.

CHAPLIN, Edward Graham Mellish, OBE 1988; HM Diplomatic Service; Ambassador to the Hashemite Kingdom of Jordan, since 2000; *b* 21 Feb. 1951; *s* of James and Joan Chaplin; *m* 1983, Nicola Helen Fisher; one *s* two *d. Educ:* Queens' Coll., Cambridge (BA 1st Cl. Hons Oriental Studies 1973). Entered FCO, 1973; Muscat, 1975–77; Brussels, 1977–78; Ecole Nat. d'Admin, Paris, 1978–79; on secondment to CSD as Private Sec. to Lord Pres. of the Council and Leader of H of L, 1979–81; FCO, 1981–84; Head of Chancery, Tehran, 1985–87; FCO, 1987–89; on secondment to Price Waterhouse Management Consultants, 1990–92; Dep. Perm. Rep., UKMIS Geneva, 1992–96; Hd, ME Dept, FCO, 1997–99. *Recreations:* music, tennis, hill/mountain walking. *Address:* c/o Foreign and Commonwealth Office, SW1A 2AH.

CHAPLIN, John Cyril, CBE 1988; FREng; FRAeS; Member, Civil Aviation Authority and Group Director, Safety Regulation (formerly Safety Services), 1983–88; *b* 13 Aug.

1926; *s* of late Ernest Stanley Chaplin and Isabel Chaplin; *m* 1949, Ruth Marianne Livingstone; two *s* two *d*. *Educ:* Keswick School. Miles Aircraft, 1946; Vickers-Supermarine, 1948; Handley Page, 1950; Somers-Kendall Aircraft, 1952; Heston Aircraft, 1956; Air Registration Board, 1958; Civil Aviation Authority, 1972, Dir-Gen. Airworthiness, 1979. FREng (FEng 1987). *Publications:* papers to RAeS. *Recreations:* sailing, photography, travel. *Address:* 18 Cromwell Gardens, Steeple Drive, Alton, Hants GU34 1TR. *T:* (01420) 84103. *Club:* Cruising Association (Vice-Pres., 1995–98).

CHAPLIN, Sir Malcolm (Hilbery), Kt 1991; CBE 1984; FRICS; Senior Partner, Hilbery Chaplin & Hilbery Chaplin Porter, chartered surveyors, Romford and London, W1; *b* 17 Jan. 1934; *s* of Sir George Chaplin, CBE, FRICS and Lady Chaplin, (Doris Evelyn, *née* Lee); *m* 1959, Janet Gaydon; three *s*. *Educ:* Summerfields, Oxford; Rugby Sch.; Trinity Hall, Cambridge (MA Est. Man. 1961; Athletics Blue, 440 yds). Former Member: Barking, Havering and Brentwood DHA; Essex AHA. Treasurer: Billericay Cons. Assoc., 1970–73; Brentwood and Ongar Cons. Assoc., 1973–79 (Pres., 1988–92); Eastern Area Cons. Assocs, 1980–88 (Vice Pres., 1988–98); Mem., Nat. Union Exec. and Gen. Purposes Cttees, 1980–98; Chm., Cons. Bd of Finance, 1993– (Dep. Chm., 1988–93); Conservative Party: Mem. Bd of Mgt, 1993–98; Treasurer, 1993–; Association Chm., 1994–; Trustee, Cons. Agents Superannuation and Benevolent Funds, 1992–. Former Governor: Brentwood Sch.; St Martins Schs, Hutton. Trustee, Romford War Meml Old Folks Club and other trusts. Freeman, City of London. Mem., Innholders' Co. (Master, 1992–93); Liveryman, Chartered Surveyors' Co. *Recreations:* dairy farming, golf, watching cricket and Rugby. *Address:* c/o 7 Upper Grosvenor Street, W1X 0LL. *Clubs:* Carlton, Bucks, Oxford and Cambridge, MCC; Hawks (Cambridge); Gentlemen of Essex CC.

CHAPMAN, family name of **Baron Northfield**.

CHAPMAN, Angela Mary, (Mrs I. M. Chapman); Headmistress, Central Newcastle High School (GDST), 1985–99; *b* 2 Jan. 1940; *d* of Frank Dyson and Mary Rowe; *m* 1959, Ian Michael Chapman; two *s*. *Educ:* Queen Victoria High Sch., Stockton; Univ. of Bristol (BA Hons French); Sorbonne (Dip. de Civilisation Française). Teacher of French, Bede Sch., Sunderland, 1970–80; Dep. Headmistress, Newcastle upon Tyne Church High Sch., 1980–84. FRSA 1989. *Recreations:* military history, walking, tennis. *Address:* 14 Alpine Way, Sunderland, Tyne and Wear SR3 1TN.

CHAPMAN, Ben; *see* Chapman, J. K.

CHAPMAN, Charles Cyril Staplee; corporate development consultant; Member for Corporate Development and Finance, UK Atomic Energy Authority, 1988–90; *b* 9 Aug. 1936; *s* of Thomas John Chapman and Gertrude Gosden Chapman; *m* 1963, Lorraine Dorothy Wenborn; two *s*. *Educ:* St Peter's Sch., York; Univ. of Sheffield (BSc Hons). British Petroleum Co., 1958, Manager, Chemicals, Corporate Planning, Minerals, 1962–85; Senior Strategy Advisor, British Telecom, 1986–88. *Recreation:* growing rhododendrons.

CHAPMAN, Christine; Member (Lab) Cynon Valley, National Assembly for Wales, since 1999; *b* 7 April 1956; *d* of John Price and Edith Jean Price; *m* 1981, Dr Michael Chapman; one *s* one *d*. *Educ:* Porth County Girls' Sch.; UCW, Aberystwyth (BA Hons); South Bank Poly. (Dip. Careers Guidance 1989); UWCC (MSc Econ 1992); Univ. of Wales Swansea (PGCE 1995). Mid Glamorgan County Council: Community Services Agency, 1979–80; Careers, 1980–93; Educn Business Partnership (on secondment), 1993–94; teaching and consultancy posts, 1995–96; Co-ordinator, Torfaen Educn Business Partnership, 1996–99. Mem. (Lab) Rhondda Cynon Taff Council, 1995–99. *Recreations:* keeping fit, playing the piano, women's history. *Address:* National Assembly for Wales, Cardiff Bay, Cardiff CF99 1NA. *T:* (029) 2089 8364; (office) Midland Bank Chambers, 28a Oxford Street, Mountain Ash, Rhondda Cynon Taff CF45 3EU. *T:* (01443) 478098.

CHAPMAN, Prof. Christopher Hugh; Scientific Advisor, Schlumberger Cambridge Research, since 1991; *b* 5 May 1945; *s* of late John Harold Chapman and of Margaret Joan Weeks; *m* 1974, Lillian Tarapaski; one *s* one *d*. *Educ:* Latymer Upper School; Christ's College, Cambridge (MA); Dept of Geodesy and Geophysics, Cambridge (PhD). Asst Prof., Univ. of Alberta, 1969–72, Associate Prof., 1973–74; Asst Prof., Univ. of California, Berkeley, 1972–73; University of Toronto: Associate Prof., 1974–80; Prof., 1980–84; Killam Research Fellow, 1981–83; Adjunct Prof., 1984–88; Prof. of Physics, 1988–90; Prof. of Geophysics, Dept of Earth Scis, and Fellow, Christ's Coll., Cambridge, 1984–88. Green Scholar, Univ. of California, San Diego, 1978–79, 1986. *Publications:* research papers in sci. jls. *Recreations:* sailing, photography, woodwork. *Address:* Schlumberger Cambridge Research, High Cross, Madingley Road, Cambridge CB3 0EL. *T:* (01223) 315576.

CHAPMAN, His Honour Cyril Donald; QC 1965; a Circuit Judge, 1972–86; *b* 17 Sept. 1920; *s* of Cyril Henry Chapman and Frances Elizabeth Chapman (*née* Braithwaite); *m* 1st, 1950, Audrey Margaret Fraser (*née* Gough) (marr. diss. 1959); one *s*; 2nd, 1960, Muriel Falconer Bristow; one *s*. *Educ:* Roundhay Sch., Leeds; Brasenose Coll., Oxford (MA). Served RNVR, 1939–45. Called to Bar, 1947; Harmsworth Scholar, 1947; North Eastern Circuit, 1947; Recorder of Huddersfield, 1965–69, of Bradford, 1969–71. Contested (C) East Leeds 1955, Goole 1964, Brighouse and Spenborough, 1966. *Recreation:* walking. *Address:* Hill Top, Collingham, Wetherby, W Yorks LS22 5BB. *T:* (01937) 572813. *Club:* Leeds (Leeds).

CHAPMAN, Daniel Ahmling; *see* Chapman Nyaho.

CHAPMAN, Sir David (Robert Macgowan), 3rd Bt *cr* 1958, of Cleadon, Co. Durham; DL; First Vice-President and Senior Relationship Manager for North East England, Merrill Lynch International Bank, since 1999; *b* 16 Dec. 1941; *s* of Sir Robert Macgowan Chapman, 2nd Bt, CBE, TD and of Barbara May, *d* of Hubert Tonks; *S* father, 1987; *m* 1965, Maria Elizabeth de Gosztonyi-Zsolnay, *o d* of Dr N. de Mattyasovsky-Zsolnay; one *s* one *d*. *Educ:* Marlborough; McGill Univ., Montreal (BCom). Wise Speke Ltd, then Wise Speke Div., Brewin Dolphin Securities Ltd, stock and share brokers, Newcastle upon Tyne: Partner, 1971–87; Dir, 1987–99. Chm., Team General Partner Ltd, 1994–; Director: Northern Rock plc, then Northern Rock Building Soc. (formerly North of England Building Soc.), 1974–; Breathe North Appeal Ltd, 1988–2001; British Lung Foundation Ltd, 1989–95; Gordon Durham & Co. Ltd, 1994–98; High Gosforth Park Ltd, 1999–; Zytronic plc, 2000–. Stock Exchange: Mem. Council, 1979–88; Chairman: Northern Unit, 1988–91; NE Reg. Adv Gp, 1991–98. MSI 1991 (NE Pres., 1993–). Chm., NE Reg., CBI, 2001–. Chm., Northumbria Coalition Against Crime, 1995–2000. Mem., Greenbury Cttee, 1995. Dir, Shrievalty Assoc. Ltd, 1999–2001. Governor: St Aidan's Coll., Durham, 1987–97; UC, Durham, 1998–2000; Mem. Council, Univ. of Durham, 1997–. Tyne and Wear: High Sheriff, 1993–94; DL 1997. *Heir: s* Michael Nicholas Chapman [*b* 21 May 1969; *m* 1998, Eszter, *y d* of Dr Attila Perlényi]. *Address:* Westmount, 14 West Park Road, Cleadon, Sunderland, Tyne and Wear SR6 7RR; Merrill Lynch International Bank Ltd, Quayside House, 110 Quayside, Newcastle upon Tyne NE1 3DX.

CHAPMAN, (Francis) Ian, CBE 1988; Chairman, Radiotrust PLC, 1997–2001; Chairman, 1991–96, Deputy Chairman, 1997–99, Guinness Publishers Ltd; Chairman, Scottish Radio Holdings (formerly Radio Clyde) PLC, 1972–96 (Hon. President, since 1996); *b* 26 Oct. 1925; *s* of late Rev. Peter Chapman and Frances Burdett; *m* 1953, Marjory Stewart Swinton; one *s* one *d*. *Educ:* Shawlands Academy, Glasgow; Ommer Sch. of Music, Glasgow. Served RAF, 1943–44; worked in coal mines as part of national service, 1945–47. Joined Wm Collins Sons & Co. Ltd, 1947 as management trainee; Sales Manager, 1955; Gp Sales Dir, 1960; Jt Man. Dir, 1968–76; Dep. Chm., William Collins Hldgs, 1976–81; Chm., William Collins Publishers Ltd, 1979–81; Chm. and Gp Chief Exec., William Collins Hldgs plc, 1981–89. Chairman: Harvill Press Ltd, 1976–89; Hatchards Ltd, 1976–89; Ancient House Bookshop (Ipswich) Ltd, 1976–89; Co-Chm. and Actg Chief Exec., Harper & Row, NY, 1987–89; Chm. and Man. Dir, Chapmans Publishers, 1989–94. Chm., The Listener Publications PLC, 1988–93; Dep. Chm., Orion Publishing Gp, 1993–94; Director: Independent Radio News, 1984–85; Pan Books Ltd, 1962–84 (Chm., 1974–76); Book Tokens Ltd, 1981–94; Stanley Botes Ltd, 1985–89; (non-exec.) Guinness PLC, 1986–91; (non-exec.) United Distillers PLC, 1987–91; Pres.-Dir Gen., Guinness Media SAS, Paris, 1996–99. Publishers' Association: Mem. Council, 1963–76, 1977–82; Vice Pres., 1978–79 and 1981–82; Pres., 1979–81; Trustee, 1993–97. Chm., Nat. Acad. of Writing, 2000–; Member: Bd, Book Develt Council, 1967–73; Governing Council, Scottish Business in the Community, 1983–98; Dir, Scottish Opera, Theatre Royal Ltd, 1974–79; Trustee, Book Trade Benevolent Soc., 1982–. Chm. Council, Strathclyde Univ. Business School, 1985–88. FRSA 1985; CIMgt (CBIM 1982). Hon. DLitt Strathclyde, 1990. Scottish Free Enterprise Award, 1985. *Publications:* various articles on publishing in trade jls. *Recreations:* music, golf, reading, grandchildren. *Address:* Kenmore, 46 The Avenue, Cheam, Surrey SM2 7QE. *T:* (020) 8642 1820, *Fax:* (020) 8770 0225; *e-mail:* fic@onetel.net.uk. *Clubs:* Garrick, Groucho, MCC; Royal Wimbledon Golf; Walton Heath Golf.

CHAPMAN, Frank Arthur; His Honour Judge Chapman; a Circuit Judge, since 1992; *b* 28 May 1946; *s* of Dennis Arthur Chapman and Joan Chapman; *m* 1968, Mary Kathleen Jones; one *s* one *d*. *Educ:* Newton-le-Willows Grammar School; University College London (LLB, LLM). Called to the Bar, Gray's Inn, 1968; practice at Birmingham. Practising Anglican. *Recreations:* travel, mountaineering, angling.

CHAPMAN, Frank Joseph, CEng, FIMechE; Chief Executive, BG Group plc, since 2000; *b* 17 June 1953; *s* of Frank William Chapman and Clara Mini Chapman; *m* 1st, 1975, Evelyn Mary Hill (marr. diss. 1995); two *d*; 2nd, 1996, Kari Elin Theodorsen; one *s*. *Educ:* East Ham Tech. Coll. (OND (Dist.) 1971); Queen Mary Coll., London Univ. (BSc 1st Cl. Hons Mech. Engrg 1974). CEng 1999; FIMechE 1999. Engr, BP, 1974–78; various engrg and mgt appts, Shell, 1978–96; joined British Gas, 1996; Man. Dir, BG Exploration and Production, 1996–99; Dir, BG Gp (formerly BG) plc, 1997–; Pres., BG Internat., 1999–2000. FRSA 2000. *Recreations:* yachting, ski-ing, music. *Address:* BG Group plc, 100 Thames Valley Park Drive, Reading, Berks RG6 1PT. *T:* (0118) 929 2006.

CHAPMAN, Frederick John; Group Treasurer, LucasVarity, 1996–98; *b* 24 June 1939; *s* of late Reginald John Chapman and Elizabeth Chapman; *m* 1964, Paula Brenda Waller; one *s* two *d*. *Educ:* Sutton County Grammar Sch. Joined ECGD, 1958; Principal, 1969; Asst Sec., 1977; Under Sec., 1982; Principal Estabt and Finance Officer, 1985–88; Varity Corporation: Treas. (Europe), 1988–89; Treas. and Vice-Pres., 1990–96. *Recreations:* reading, music. *Address:* 812 Chestnut Hill, East Aurora, NY 14052, USA.

CHAPMAN, Prof. Garth; Professor of Zoology, Queen Elizabeth College, University of London, 1958–82, now Emeritus (Vice Principal, 1974–80; Acting Principal, Sept. 1977–March 1978; Fellow, 1984); *b* 8 Oct. 1917; *o s* of E. J. Chapman and Edith Chapman (*née* Attwood); *m* 1941, Margaret Hilda Wigley; one *s* one *d* (and one *s* decd). *Educ:* Royal Grammar Sch., Worcester; Trinity Hall, Cambridge (Major Scholar); ScD Cantab 1977. FIBiol 1963; FKC 1985. Telecommunications Research Establishment, Ministry of Aircraft Production, 1941–45; Asst Lectr in Zoology, 1945–46, Lectr in Zoology, 1946–58, QMC, Univ. of London; Dean, Faculty of Science, Univ. of London, 1974–78. Vis. Prof., Univ. of California, Berkeley, 1967, Los Angeles, 1970–71. Member: Cttee for Commonwealth Univ. Interchange, British Council, 1978–80; Inter-Univ. Council for Higher Educn Overseas, 1973–83; Council, Westfield Coll., Univ. of London, 1978–84; Central Research Fund Cttee B, 1978–82; Management Cttee of Univ. Marine Biological Station, Millport, 1975–82. *Publications:* Zoology for Intermediate Students (with W. B. Barker), 1964; Body Fluids and their Functions, 1967; various on structure and physiology of marine invertebrates. *Recreations:* gardening, wood-engraving. *Address:* The Grove, Callis Street, Clare, Suffolk CO10 8PX. *T:* (01787) 277235. *Club:* Athenæum.

CHAPMAN, Geoffrey Lloyd; Vice Judge Advocate General, 1984–94; *b* 20 Oct. 1928; *o s* of Sydney Leslie Chapman and Dora Chapman (*née* Lloyd); *m* 1958, Jean, *er d* of Valentine Harry Coleman and Marjorie Coleman (*née* Poston); one *s* two *d*. *Educ:* Latymer Upper School; Christ Church, Oxford (BCL, MA). National Service, 1947–49 (2nd Lieut, RASC). Called to the Bar, Inner Temple, 1953; practised London and Western Circuit; Legal Asst, Min. of Labour and Nat. Service, 1957; Legal Asst, JAG's Office, 1958; Dep. Judge Advocate, 1961 (Germany, 1963–66, Cyprus, 1969–72); Asst JAG, 1971 (Germany, 1972–76); Dep. JAG, British Forces in Germany, 1979–82. *Recreations:* beagling, reading. *Address:* The Myrtles, Alma Road, Reigate, Surrey RH2 0DH. *T:* (01737) 247860.

CHAPMAN, Sir George (Alan), Kt 1982; FCA; FCIS; Senior Partner, Chapman Upchurch, Chartered Accountants, retired 2000; *b* 13 April 1927; *s* of late Thomas George Chapman and Winifred Jordan Chapman; *m* 1950, Jacqueline Sidney (*née* Irvine); two *s* five *d*. *Educ:* Trentham Sch.; Hutt Valley High Sch.; Victoria University. Fellow, Chartered Inst. of Secretaries, 1969 (Mem., 1948–); Fellow, Inst. of Chartered Accountants of NZ (formerly NZ Soc. of Accountants), 1969 (Mem., 1948–). Joined Chapman Ross & Co., subseq. Chapman Upchurch, 1948. Chairman: Norwich Union General Insurance (formerly Norwich Winterthur) (NZ), 1985–92 (Dir, 1982–92); BNZ Finance, 1979–88 (Dir, 1977–88); Mitel Telecommunications, 1984–91; Pilkington (formerly Pilkington Brothers) (NZ), 1989–94 (Dir, 1982–94); Director: Bank of New Zealand, 1968–86 (Dep. Chm., 1976–86); Maui Developments Ltd, 1979–85; Offshore Mining Co. Ltd, 1979–85; Liquigas Ltd, 1981–85 (Chm., 1982–84); NZ Bd, Norwich Union Life Insurance Soc., 1982–92; Skellerup Industries Ltd, 1982–90 (Dep. Chm., 1984–87); Skellerup Industries, Malaysia, 1986–90; State Insurance Ltd, 1990–99 (Vice Chm., 1992–99); Norwich Union Holdings (NZ) Ltd, 1990–99 (Vice Chm., 1992–99); Vice Chm., Norwich Union Life Insurance (NZ) Ltd, 1993–98. Chairman: NZ Building Industry Authority, 1992–2000; Housing New Zealand Ltd, 1992–95 (Chm. Housing Corp. of NZ and Housing NZ Estabt Bd, April–July 1992). NZ National Party: Member, 1948–; Vice-Pres., 1966–73; Pres., 1973–82. Councillor, Upper Hutt Bor. Council, 1952–53, Deputy Mayor, Upper Hutt, 1953–55; Member: Hutt Valley Drainage Bd, 1953–55; Heretaunga Bd of Governors, 1953–55; Pres., Upper Hutt Chamber of

Commerce, 1956–57. FInstD 1979. *Publication:* The Years of Lightning, 1980. *Recreations:* golf, reading, tennis. *Address:* 53 Barton Avenue, Heretaunga, Wellington, New Zealand. *T:* (4) 5283512. *Clubs:* Wellington Golf, Wellington Racing.

CHAPMAN, Honor Mary Ruth, CBE 1997; FRICS; a Crown Estate Commissioner, since 1997; International Director, Jones Lang LaSalle (formerly International Partner, Jones Lang Wootton), since 1979; *b* 29 July 1942; *d* of Alan Harry Woodland and Frances Evelyn (*née* Ball); *m* 1966, David Edwin Harold Chapman (marr. diss. 1997). *Educ:* Coll. of Estate Mgt, London Univ. (BSc Estate Mgt 1963); University Coll. London (MPhil Town Planning 1966). MRTPI 1971; FRICS 1979. Surveyor, Valuation Dept, LCC, 1963–64; with Nathaniel Lichfield & Partners (Econ. and Planning Consultants), 1966–76 (Partner, 1971–76); freelance Consultant, 1976–79; Sloan Fellow, London Bus. Sch., 1977; Chm., Research, Jones Lang Wootton, 1979–95; Chief Exec. (on secondment half-time), London First Centre, 1993–95 (Dir, 1993–99). Dir, Legal and General plc, 1993–. Vice-Chm., London Develt Agency, 2000–. Board Member: English Estates, 1984–92; Cardiff Bay Urban Develt Corp., 1987–94. Gov. and Mem., Exec. Cttee, Centre for Economic Policy Res., 1988–96. FRSA 1992. *Recreations:* dairy farming, watching people do things well. *Address:* c/o Jones Lang LaSalle, 22 Hanover Square, W1A 2BN. *Club:* University Women's.

CHAPMAN, Ian; *see* Chapman, F. I.

CHAPMAN, James Keith, (Ben); MP (Lab) Wirral South, since Feb. 1997; *b* 8 July 1940; *s* of John Hartley and Elsie Vera Chapman; *m* 1st (marr. diss); three *d*; 2nd, 1999, Maureen Ann (*née* Byrne). *Educ:* Appleby Grammar Sch., Appleby in Westmorland. Pilot Officer, RAFVR, 1959–61. Min. of Pensions and Nat. Insce, 1958–62; Min. of Aviation/BAA, 1962–67; Rochdale Cttee of Inquiry into Shipping, 1967–70; BoT, 1970–74; First Sec. (Commercial), Dar es Salaam, 1974–78; First Sec. (Econ.), Accra, 1978–81; Asst Sec., DTI, 1981–87; Commercial Counsellor, Peking, 1987–90; Dep. Regl Dir, NW, and Dir, Merseyside, 1991–93, Regl Dir, Northwest, 1993–94, DTI; Dir, Trade and Industry, Govt Office for NW, 1994–95. Founder Consultant, Ben Chapman Associates, 1995–97. PPS to Minister of State, DETR, 1997–99, DTI, 1999–2001, DCMS, 2001–. Chairman, All-Party Parliamentary Groups: Britain-China, 1997–; Britain-Turkey, 1998–2001; Soap and Detergents Industry, 1999–2001; UK Cleaning Products Industry, 2001–. Chairman: Adv. Bd, China Gateway-North West, 1996–97. Hon. Ambassador: for Cumbria, 1995–; for Merseyside, 1997–. *Recreations:* opera, music, walking. *Address:* House of Commons, SW1A 0AA.

CHAPMAN, Leslie Charles; Founder and Chairman, Campaign to Stop Waste in Public Expenditure, since 1981; *b* 14 Sept. 1919; *e s* of Charles Richard Chapman and Lilian Elizabeth Chapman; *m* 1947, Beryl Edith England; (one *s* decd). *Educ:* Bishopshalt Sch. Served War, Army, 1939–45. Civil Service, 1939 and 1945–74; Regional Dir, Southern Region, MPBW and PSA, 1967–74. Chm. and mem., various cttees; Mem. (pt-time), LTE, 1979–80. *Publications:* Your Disobedient Servant, 1978, 2nd revised edn 1979; Waste Away, 1982. *Recreations:* reading, music, gardening. *Address:* Cae Caradog, Ffarmers, Llanwrda, Dyfed SA19 8NQ. *T:* (01558) 650504.

CHAPMAN, Mark Fenger, CVO 1979; HM Diplomatic Service, retired; Member, Police Complaints Authority, 1991–95; *b* 12 Sept. 1934; *er s* of late Geoffrey Walter Chapman and Esther Maria Fenger; *m* 1959, Patricia Mary Long; three *s* (and one *s* decd). *Educ:* Cranbrook Sch.; St Catharine's Coll., Cambridge. Entered HM Foreign Service, 1958; served in: Bangkok, 1959–63; FO, 1963–67; Head of Chancery, Maseru, 1967–71; Asst Head of Dept, FCO, 1971–74; Head of Chancery, Vienna, 1975–76; Dep. High Comr and Counsellor (Econ. and Comm.), Lusaka, 1976–79; Diplomatic Service Inspector, 1979–82; Counsellor, The Hague, 1982–86; Ambassador to Iceland, 1986–89. *Club:* Royal Commonwealth Society.

CHAPMAN, Mary Madeline, (Mrs A. R. Pears); Director General, Institute of Management, since 1998; *b* 9 March 1949; *d* of Kenneth F. Chapman, MBE and Agnes G. B. Chapman (*née* Thompson); *m* 1st, 1976, Robert Henry Lomas (marr. diss. 1986); 2nd, 1990, Andrew Roger Pears; one *d*. *Educ:* Sutton High Sch.; Univ. of Bristol (BA Hons). Dip CIM 1975. Mkting Exec., BTA, 1971–76; Mkting Manager, L'OREAL (Golden Ltd), 1976–82; General Manager: Nicholas Labs Ltd, 1982–86; Biotherm, 1986–88; Man. Dir, Helena Rubinstein, 1988–90; Dir, Personnel Ops, L'OREAL (UK), 1990–93; Chief Exec., Investors in People UK, 1993–98. *Recreations:* walking, sailing, theatre, church and community projects.

CHAPMAN, Ven. Michael Robin; Archdeacon of Northampton, since 1991; *b* 29 Sept. 1939; *s* of Frankland and Kathleen Chapman; *m* 1973, Bernadette Taylor; one *s* one *d*. *Educ:* Lichfield Cathedral Sch.; Ellesmere Coll.; Leeds Univ. (BA 1961); Coll. of the Resurrection, Mirfield. Ordained, dio. of Durham, deacon, 1963, priest, 1964; curate, St Columba, Sunderland, 1963–68; Chaplain, RN, 1968–84; Vicar, St John the Evangelist, Farnham, 1984–91; Rural Dean of Farnham, 1988–91. *Recreations:* flying light aircraft, music, hill walking. *Address:* 11 The Drive, Northampton NN1 4RZ. *T:* (01604) 714015.

CHAPMAN, Nicholas John; Managing Director, The Irish Times Ltd, since 1999; *b* 17 June 1947; *s* of Frank and Elizabeth Chapman; *m* 1995, Louise Shaxson; two *d*. *Educ:* Merchant Taylors' Sch.; Clare Coll., Cambridge (MA). With Hodder and Stoughton: Graduate Trainee, 1969; European Sales, 1970; Editor, 1973; Publishing Dir, Associated Business Press, 1975; Editor-in-Chief, Futura Paperbacks, 1979; Publishing Director: Macdonald Futura, 1980; Macmillan London, 1983; Head of BBC Books and Educn, 1986–89, Dir, Consumer Products Gp, 1989–94, BBC Enterprises; Man. Dir, BBC Worldwide Publishing, 1994–97; Director: BBC Worldwide Ltd, 1994–97; BBC Americas Inc., 1994–97; Mem., BBC Bd of Management, 1994–96; Man. Dir & Publisher, Orion Military, subseq. Cassell Mil. Publishing, Orion Publishing Gp, 1998–99. Pres., Publishers Assoc., 1994–96. Gov., Norwood Sch., 1998–99. *Recreations:* walking, natural history, reading. *Address:* The Irish Times Ltd, 10–16 D'Olier Street, Dublin 2, Ireland.

CHAPMAN, Nigel Conrad; Deputy Director, BBC World Service, since 2000; *b* 14 Dec. 1955; *s* of Norman Bellamy Chapman, *qv*; *m* 1984, Margaret Farrar; two *d*. *Educ:* Hymers Coll., Hull; Magdalene Coll., Cambridge (MA Hons English Lit.). Joined BBC, 1977: researcher and producer, BBC News and Current Affairs, incl. Nationwide, Newsnight and Breakfast News, 1979–89; Editor, Public Eye, 1989–92; Head: Regl and Local Progs, SE, 1992–94; Broadcasting, Midlands and East, 1994–96; Controller, English Regions, 1996–98; Dir, BBC Online, 1999–2000. *Recreations:* sport (football and cricket), classical music, walking, reading. *Address:* BBC World Service, Bush House, PO Box 76, WC2B 4PH.

CHAPMAN, Prof. Norman Bellamy, MA, PhD; CChem, FRSC; G. F. Grant Professor of Chemistry, Hull University, 1956–82, now Emeritus; Pro-Vice-Chancellor, 1973–76; *b* 19 April 1916; *s* of Frederick Taylor Chapman and Bertha Chapman; *m* 1949, Fonda Maureen Bungey; one *s* one *d*. *Educ:* Barnsley Holgate Grammar Sch.; Magdalene Coll., Cambridge (Entrance Scholar). 1st Cl. Parts I and II Nat. Sciences Tripos, 1937 and 1938; BA 1938, MA 1942, PhD 1941. Bye-Fellow, Magdalene Coll., 1939–42; Univ. Demonstrator in Chemistry, Cambridge, 1945; Southampton Univ.: Lectr, 1947; Senior Lectr, 1949; Reader in Chemistry, 1955. R. T. French Visiting Prof., Univ. of Rochester, NY, 1962–63; R. J. Reynolds Vis. Prof., Duke Univ., N Carolina, 1971; Cooch Behar Prof., Calcutta, 1982. Universities Central Council on Admissions: Dep. Chm., 1979–83; Chm., Technical Cttee, 1974–79; Chm., Statistics Cttee, 1983–89. Hon. DSc Hull, 1984. *Publications:* (ed with J. Shorter) Advances in Free Energy Relationships, 1972; (ed) Organic Chemistry, Series One, vol. 2: Aliphatic Compounds (MTP Internat. Review of Science), 1973, Series Two, vol 2, 1976; Correlation Analysis in Chemistry: recent advances, 1978; contribs to Jl Chem. Soc., Analyst, Jl Medicinal Chem., Tetrahedron, Jl Organic Chemistry, Chemistry and Industry. *Recreations:* music, gardening, cricket, Rugby football. *Address:* 5 The Lawns, Molescroft, Beverley HU17 7LS. *T:* (01482) 860553.

See also N. C. Chapman.

CHAPMAN, Rev. Canon Rex Anthony; Residentiary Canon of Carlisle Cathedral, since 1978; Diocesan Director of Education, since 1985; Chaplain to the Queen, since 1997; *b* 2 Sept. 1938; *s* of Charles Arthur and Doris Chapman; *m* 1964, Margaret Anne (*née* Young); one *s* one *d*. *Educ:* Leeds Grammar Sch.; UCL (BA); St Edmund Hall, Oxford (MA); Univ. of Birmingham (DPS); Wells Theol Coll. National Service, RAF, 1957–59. Ordained deacon, 1965, priest, 1966; Asst Curate, St Thomas', Stourbridge, 1965–68; Associate Chaplain, Univ. of Aberdeen, 1968–78; Hon. Canon, St Andrew's Cathedral, Aberdeen, 1976–78; Bishop's Advr for Educn, dio. of Carlisle, 1978–85; Bishops' Selector for Ministry in C of E, 1985– (Sen. Selector, 1997–). Chm., Vacancy-in-See Cttee, dio. of Carlisle, 1997–; Mem., Crown Appts Commn for See of Carlisle, 1988, 2000. Mem., Gen. Synod of C of E, 1985–2000 (Mem., Bd of Educn, 1985–96; Chm., Schs Cttee, 1990–96); Chm., House of Clergy, dio. of Carlisle, 1996–. Member: Cumbria Educn Cttee, 1978–98; Cumbria Educn Forum, 1999–; Standing Adv. Council for Religious Educn, Cumbria, 1978– (Chm., 1989–); Standing Cttee, Nat. Soc. for Promoting Religious Educn, 1982–97; Chm. Orgn Cttee, Cumbria Schs, 2001– (Vice-Chm., 1999–2001). Governor: Trinity Sch., Carlisle, 1978– (Chm., 1989–); Carlisle and Blackburn (formerly Carlisle) Dio. Trng Inst., 1979–; St Martin's Coll. (formerly UC of St Martin), Lancaster, 1985–; St Chad's Coll., Durham, 1989–94. Trustee, Carlisle Educnl Charity, 1978– (Chm. of Trustees, 1998–99). *Publications:* A Kind of Praying, 1970; Out of the Whirlwind, 1971; A Glimpse of God, 1973; The Cry of the Spirit, 1974; The Glory of God, 1978; contrib. to A Dictionary of Christian Spirituality, 1983. *Recreations:* travel, photography, hill-walking, malt whisky. *Address:* 1 The Abbey, Carlisle CA3 8TZ. *T:* (01228) 597614. *Club:* Royal Over-Seas League.

CHAPMAN, Hon. Rhiannon Elizabeth, FIPM; Managing Director, Plaudit, since 1994; Chairman, Fleming Managed Growth plc, since 1999; *b* 21 Sept. 1946; *d* of 2nd Viscount St Davids and Doreen Guinness Jowett; *m* 1974, Donald Hudson Chapman (marr. diss. 1992); two step *s*. *Educ:* Tormead Sch., Guildford; King's Coll., London Univ. (LLB Hons 1967; AKC). FIPM 1972. Industrial Soc., 1968; LWT, 1968–70; Philips Electronics Industries, 1970–77; CPI Data Peripherals Ltd, 1977–80; Personnel Dir, London Stock Exchange, 1980–90; business consultant, 1990–91; Dir, Industrial Soc., 1991–93; Mem., WDA, 1994–98. Chm., National Australia CIF Trustee Ltd, 1994–96; non-exec. Dir, S. R. Gent plc, 1994–97. Member: UFC, 1989–93; Employment Appeal Tribunal, 1991–; Council, PSI, 1993–; Technical Mem., BUPA, 1997–. External Reviewer of Complaints, TTA, 1998–. CIMgt. *Recreations:* circuit training, handcrafts, opera, travel. *Address:* 3 Church Green, Great Wymondley, Hitchin, Herts SG4 7HA. *T:* (01438) 759102.

CHAPMAN, Roy de Courcy; Headmaster of Malvern College, 1983–96; *b* 1 Oct. 1936; *s* of Edward Frederic Gilbert Chapman and Aline de Courcy Ireland; *m* 1959, Valerie Rosemary Small; two *s* one *d*. *Educ:* Dollar Academy; St Andrews Univ. (Harkness Schol.: MA 1959); Moray House Coll. of Educn, Edinburgh. Asst Master, Trinity Coll., Glenalmond, 1960–64; Marlborough College: Asst Master, 1964–68; Head of Mod. Langs, 1968–75; OC CCF, 1969–75; Rector of Glasgow Acad., 1975–82. Chairman: Common Entrance Bd, 1988–93; HMC, 1994. *Publications:* Le Français Contemporain, 1971; (with D. Whiting) Le Français Contemporain: Passages for translation and comprehension, 1975. *Recreations:* France, snorkelling. *Address:* 41 North Castle Street, St Andrews, Fife KY16 9BG.

CHAPMAN, Roy John, FCA; Chairman: Consignia (formerly Post Office) Pension Fund, since 1995; AEA Technology Pension Fund, since 1996; Director, Eurotunnel plc, since 1995; *b* 30 Nov. 1936; *s* of William George Chapman and Frances Harriet Chapman; *m* 1961, Janet Gibbeson Taylor; two *s* one *d*. *Educ:* Kettering Grammar Sch.; St Catharine's Coll., Cambridge (Athletics Blue; MA). CIMgt, FRSA. Joined Arthur Andersen & Co., Chartered Accountants, 1958; consulting, UK and abroad, incl. France, USA, Algeria, Greece, Turkey, Thailand and Switzerland, 1964–84; admitted to Partnership, 1970; Hd of Financial Services Practice, 1970–84; Man. Partner, London, 1984–89; Sen. Partner, 1989–93; Mem., Internat. Bd, 1988–93. Director: Halifax Bldg Soc., then Halifax plc, 1994–2001; Westminster Forum Ltd, 1989–99. Member: Adv. Council, London Enterprise Agency, 1985–88; Jt Disciplinary Scheme for Accounting Profession, 1994–. Mem. Governing Body, SOAS, London, 1990–2000. Council Mem., BITC, 1991–93. London Marathon, 1983 (Save the Children). Pres., St Catharine's Coll. Cambridge Soc., 1994–95; Chm., St Catharine's Coll. Develt Campaign, 1994–2000. Liveryman, Farriers' Co., 1992–. *Publications:* contribs to professional jls. *Recreations:* walking, reading, travel. *Address:* 9 Chislehurst Road, Bickley, Kent BR1 2NN. *T:* (020) 8467 3749. *Clubs:* Athenæum, Oxford and Cambridge, MCC; Hawks (Cambridge).

CHAPMAN, Prof. Stephen Jonathan, DPhil; Professor of Mathematics and its Applications, and Fellow of Mansfield College, University of Oxford, since 1999; *b* 31 Aug. 1968; *s* of Stephen Cyril Chapman and Pauline Mary Chapman; *m* 1996, Aarti Chand; one *s*. *Educ:* Merton Coll., Oxford (BA Maths 1989); St Catherine's Coll., Oxford (DPhil Applied Maths 1991). Research Fellow: Stanford Univ., Calif, 1992–93; St Catherine's Coll., Oxford, 1993–95; Royal Soc. Res. Fellow, Univ. of Oxford, 1995–99. Richard C. Diprima Prize, SIAM, 1994; Jun. Whitehead Prize, London Mathematical Society, 1998. *Publications:* papers in learned jls. *Recreations:* squash, golf, drinking with Paul. *Address:* Mathematical Institute, 24–29 St Giles, Oxford OX1 3LB. *T:* (01865) 270507.

CHAPMAN, Sir Sydney (Brookes), Kt 1995; RIBA; FRTPI; MP (C) Chipping Barnet, since 1979; Chartered Architect and Chartered Town and Country Planner; private planning consultant (non-practising); freelance writer; *b* 17 Oct. 1935; *m* 1976, Claire Lesley McNab (*née* Davies) (marr. diss. 1987); two *s* one *d*. *Educ:* Rugby Sch.; Manchester University. DipArch 1958; ARIBA 1960; DipTP 1961; AMTPI 1962; FFB 1980. Nat. Chm., Young Conservatives, 1964–66 (has been Chm. and Vice-Chm. at every level of Movt); Sen. Elected Vice-Chm., NW Area of Nat. Union of C and U Assocs, 1966–70. Contested (C) Stalybridge and Hyde, 1964; MP (C) Birmingham, Handsworth,

1970–Feb. 1974; PPS to Sec. of State for Transport, 1979–81, to Sec. of State for Social Services, 1981–83; an Asst Govt Whip, 1988–90; a Lord Comr of HM Treasury (Govt Whip), 1990–92; Vice-Chamberlain of HM Household, 1992–95. Member, Select Committee: on Environment, 1983–87; on Public Service, 1995–97; on Accommodation and Works, 1995– (Chm., 1997–); Member: House of Commons Services Cttee, 1983–87; Jt Cttee on Private Bill Procedure, 1987–88; Co-Chairman: Parly Road Transport Study Gp, 1997–; All Party Built Envmt Gp, 1997–. Chm., Parly Consultants Gp, British Consultants Bureau, 1980–88. Lectr in Arch. and Planning at techn. coll., 1964–70; Dir (Information), British Property Fedn, 1976–79; Dir (non-exec.), Capital and Counties plc, 1980–88; consultant to YJ Lovell (Holdings) plc, 1982–88. Originator of nat. tree planting year, 1973; President: Arboricultural Assoc., 1983–89; London Green Belt Council, 1985–89; Chm., Queen's Silver Jubilee London Tree Group, 1977; Vice-Chm., Wildlife Link, 1985–89; Patron, Tree Council. RIBA: Vice-Pres., 1974–75; Chm., Public Affairs Bd, 1974–75; Mem. Council, 1972–77. President: Friends of Barnet Hosps, 1981–; Friends of Tamarisk Trust (formerly Peter Pan Homes), 1981–; Barnet Soc., 1990–. Hon. Assoc. Mem., BVA, 1983–; Hon. ALI; FRSA; Hon. FBEng (Hon. FIAAS 1987); Hon. FFB 1989 (Pres., 1999–2000); Hon. FSVA 1997; Hon. RICS 2000. *Publications:* Town and Countryside: future planning policies for Britain, 1978; regular contributor to bldg and property jls and to political booklets. *Recreation:* tree spotting. *Address:* House of Commons, SW1A 0AA.

CHAPMAN, Maj.-Gen. Sir Timothy John G.; *see* Granville-Chapman.

CHAPMAN, William Edward; Secretary for Appointments to the Prime Minister, and Ecclesiastical Secretary to the Lord Chancellor, since 1999; *b* 20 March 1952; *s* of late Philip Chapman and Pam Chapman. *Educ:* High Wych Primary Sch.; Bishop's Stortford Coll.; St Peter's Coll., Oxford (MA); Hertford Coll., Oxford (MLitt). Joined DoE (subseq. DETR), 1976: Private Sec. to two Ministers, 1980–83; mem., a Rayner Efficiency Scrutiny team, 1984; Branch head: Radioactive Waste Policy, 1984–87; Housing Policy, 1987–88; Information Directorate and speech writer for two Secs of State, 1988–91; Private Sec. for Home Affairs, then Parly Affairs, to the Prime Minister, 1991–94; Head: Planning Policies Div., 1994–98; Regeneration Div., 1998–99. Trustee: S Hackney Parochial Sch. Charity; Mitzvah Trust. *Recreations:* books, pictures, music, liming. *Address:* c/o 10 Downing Street, SW1A 2AA.

CHAPMAN NYAHO, Daniel Ahmling, CBE 1961; Director: Pioneer Tobacco Co. Ltd, Ghana (Member of British-American Tobacco Group), 1967–89; Standard Bank Ghana Ltd, 1970–75; *b* 5 July 1909; *s* of William Henry Chapman and Jane Atsiamesi (*née* Atriki); *m* 1941, Jane Abam (*née* Quashie); two *s* four *d* (and two *d* decd). *Educ:* Bremen Mission Schs, Gold Coast and Togoland; Achimota Coll., Ghana; St Peter's Hall, Oxford. Postgraduate courses at Columbia Univ. and New York Univ.; Teacher, Government Senior Boys' School, Accra, 1930; Master, Achimota Coll., 1930–33, 1937–46. Area Specialist, UN Secretariat, Lake Success and New York, 1946–54; Sec. to Prime Minister and Sec. of Cabinet, Gold Coast/Ghana, 1954–57; Ghana's Ambassador to USA and Permanent Representative at UN, 1957–59; Headmaster, Achimota Sch., Ghana, 1959–63; Dir, UN Div. of Narcotic Drugs, Geneva, 1963–66; Ambassador (Special Duties), Min. of External Affairs, Ghana, 1967. Gen. Sec., All-Ewe Conf., 1944–46; Commonwealth Prime Ministers' Conf., 1957; Mem., Ghana delegn to the conf. of indep. African States, Accra, 1958. First Vice-Chm., Governing Council of UN Special Fund, 1959; Chairman: Mission of Indep. African States to Cuba, Dominican Republic, Haiti, Venezuela, Bolivia, Paraguay, Uruguay, Brazil, Argentina, Chile, 1958; Volta Union, 1968–69. Vice-Chairman: Commn on Univ. Educn in Ghana, 1960–61; Ghana Constituent Assembly, 1978–79. Member: Board of Management, UN Internat. Sch., New York, 1950–54, 1958–59; UN Middle East and N Africa Technical Assistance Mission on Narcotics Control, 1963; Dir, UN Consultative Gp on Narcotics Control in Asia and Far East, Tokyo, 1964; Member: Political Cttee of Nat. Liberation Council, 1967; Board of Trustees of General Kotoka Trust Fund, 1967–83; Chairman: Arts Council of Ghana, 1968–69; Council of Univ. of Science and Technology, Kumasi, 1972; Bd of Directors, Ghana Film Industry Corporation, 1979–80; Ghana National Honours and Awards Cttee, 1979–80. Darnforth Vis. Lectr, Assoc. Amer. Colls, 1969, 1970. Hon. LLD Greenboro Agric. and Techn. Coll., USA, 1958. Fellow, Ghana Acad. of Arts and Sciences. *Publications:* Human Geography of Eweland, 1946; Our Homeland—Book I: South-East Gold Coast, 1945; (Ed.) The Ewe News-Letter, 1945–46. *Recreations:* music, gardening, walking. *Address:* 7 Tenth Avenue, Tesano, Accra, Ghana. *T:* 227180.

CHAPPLE, family name of **Baron Chapple**.

CHAPPLE, Baron *cr* 1985 (Life Peer), of Hoxton in Greater London; **Francis Joseph Chapple;** General Secretary, Electrical, Electronic, Telecommunication and Plumbing Union, 1966–84; *b* Shoreditch, 1921; *m*; two *s*. *Educ:* elementary school. Started as Apprentice Electrician; Member ETU, 1937–83; Shop Steward and Branch Official; Member Exec. Council, 1958; Asst General Secretary, 1963–66. Mem., Gen. Council of TUC, 1971–83, Chm. 1982–83; Gold Badge of Congress, 1983. Member: National Exec. Cttee of Labour Party, 1965–71; Cttee of Inquiry into Shipping, 1967; Royal Commn on Environmental Pollution, 1973–77; Horserace Totalisator Bd, 1976–90; Energy Commn, 1977–79; NEDC, 1979–83; Nat. Nuclear Corp., 1980–86; Southern Water Authority, 1983–89; Director: Inner City Enterprises, 1983–88; N. G. Bailey Orgn, 1989–. *Publication:* (autobiog.) Sparks Fly, 1984. *Recreation:* racing pigeons. *Address:* c/o Amalgamated Engineering and Electrical Union, Hayes Court, West Common Road, Bromley BR2 7AU.

CHAPPLE, Field Marshal Sir John, GCB 1988 (KCB 1985); CBE 1980 (MBE 1969); Vice Lord-Lieutenant of Greater London, since 1997; *b* 27 May 1931; *s* of C. H. Chapple; *m* 1959, Annabel Hill; one *s* three *d*. *Educ:* Haileybury; Trinity Coll., Cambridge (MA). Joined 2nd KEO Goorkhas, 1954; served Malaya, Hong Kong, Borneo; Staff Coll., 1962; jssc 1969; Commanded 1st Bn 2nd Goorkhas, 1970–72; Directing Staff, Staff Coll., 1972–73; Services Fellow, Fitzwilliam Coll., Cambridge, 1973; Commanded 48 Gurkha Infantry Bde, 1976; Gurkha Field Force, 1977; Principal Staff Officer to Chief of Defence Staff, 1978–79; Comdr, British Forces Hong Kong, and Maj.-Gen., Brigade of Gurkhas, 1980–82; Dir of Military Operations, 1982–84; Dep. Chief of Defence Staff (Progs and Personnel), 1985–87; C-in-C, UKLF, 1987–88; CGS, 1988–92; Gov. and C-in-C, Gibraltar, 1993–95. ADC Gen. to the Queen, 1987–92. Col, 2nd Goorkhas, 1986–94. Hon. Col, Oxford Univ. OTC, 1988–95. Chm., King Mahendra UK Trust, 1993–; Trustee, King Mahendra Trust, Nepal, 1993–. Member, Council: WWF UK, 1984–99 (Trustee, 1988–93; Amb., 1999–); and Trustee: Gurkha Mus., 1973–; Nat. Army Mus., 1981–; President: Indian Mil. Hist. Soc., 1991–; Mil. Hist. Soc., 1992–; Soc. for Army Histl Res., 1993–; BSES; Trekforce; Sir Oswald Stoll Foundn, 1998–. Pres., Combined Services Polo Assoc. FZS (Pres., 1992–94), FLS, FRGS (Mem. Council). DL Greater London, 1996. KStJ. *Club:* Beefsteak.

CHAPPLE, Keith, FIEE; Chairman, Alliance for Electronic Business, since 2001; *b* 11 Aug. 1935; *s* of Reginald Chapple and Gladys Evelyn (*née* Foster); *m* 1962, Patricia Margaret Aitchison; one *s* two *d*. *Educ:* City of Bath Boys' Sch.; Rugby Coll. of Technol. FIEE 1984; MIMgt 1976. Engrg Manager, Gen. Precision Systems Ltd, 1961–66; Sales Engr, SGS-Fairchild Ltd, 1966–69; Mktg Manager, SGS-Fairchild SpA (Italy), 1969–70; Sales Manager, Intel Corp. (Belgium), 1970–72; Chm. and Man. Dir, Intel Corp. (UK) Ltd, 1972–2000. President: Fedn of Electronics Industry, 1996–97 (Vice-Pres., 1997–99); Swindon Chamber of Commerce, 1996–98; Chm., EU Cttee, American Chamber of Commerce in Belgium, 1998–2001. Mem., Oxford Isis Br., Rotary Club. FRSA 1999. Hon. DTech Loughborough, 1986. *Recreations:* music, family. *Club:* Clarendon (Oxford).

CHAPPLE, Air Vice-Marshal Robert, CB 1994; Principal Medical Officer, Royal Air Force Support Command, 1991–94, retired; *b* 2 May 1934; *s* of Kevin Chapple and Florence Elsie (*née* Cann); *m* 1960, Barbara Ann (*née* Webster); one *s* one *d*. *Educ:* Finchley Catholic Grammar Sch.; St Mary's Hosp. Med. Sch. (MB, BS 1958). MRCS, LRCP 1958; DPH 1973; MFPHM 1978; MFOM 1980. Joined RAF Med. Br., 1960; served in UK, Singapore, Gibraltar, Germany and Cyprus; Officer Commanding: Princess Mary Hosp., Cyprus, 1982–85; Princess Mary's RAF Hosp., Halton, 1987–89; Princess Alexandra Hosp., Wroughton, 1989–91; Commandant, RAF Central Med. Estabt, 1991. QHP, 1992–94. MIMgt (MBIM 1974). *Recreations:* golf, watching most sports, archaeology, visiting old churches, matters of general interest. *Address:* Hazel House, Withington, Cheltenham, Glos GL54 4DA.

CHARD, Prof. Timothy, MD; FRCOG; Professor, Obstetrics and Gynaecology, Bart's and The London, Queen Mary's School of Medicine and Dentistry (formerly St Bartholomew's and Royal London School of Medicine and Dentistry, Queen Mary and Westfield College), University of London, since 1996; *b* 4 June 1937; *s* of Henry Francis and Dorothea Elaine Chard; *m* 1st, 1965, Marty Jane Batten (marr. diss.); two *s*; 2nd, 1977, Linda Kay Elmore (marr. diss.); 3rd, 2000, Mary Christina Munro Macintosh. *Educ:* Merchant Taylors' School; St Thomas's Hosp. Med. Sch. Junior med. posts, 1960–65; MRC Clinical Research Fellow, 1965–68; Sen. Lectr, St Bartholomew's Hosp. Med. Coll., 1968–73; Prof. of Reproductive Physiol., St Bartholomew's Hosp. Med. Coll., 1973–96. *Publications* (jointly): Radioimmunoassay, 1978, 5th edn 1995; Placental Function Tests, 1982; Basic Sciences for Obstetrics, 1984, 5th edn 1998; Computing for Clinicians, 1988, 2nd edn 1995. *Recreations:* fine arts, venture capital. *Address:* 171 Lauderdale Tower, EC2Y 8BY. *T:* (020) 7628 5662; *e-mail:* timchard@waitrose.com.

CHARING CROSS, Archdeacon of; *see* Jacob, Ven. W. M.

CHARKHAM, Jonathan Philip; director of companies; Adviser to the Governors, Bank of England, 1988–93 (Chief Advr, 1985–88); *b* 17 Oct. 1930; *s* of late Louis Charkham and Phoebe Beatrice Barquet (*née* Miller); *m* Moira Elizabeth Frances, *d* of late Barnett A. Salmon and Molly Salmon; twin *s* one *d*. *Educ:* St Paul's Sch.; Jesus Coll., Cambridge (BA 1952). Called to Bar, Inner Temple, 1953. Morris Charkham Ltd, 1953–63 (Man. Dir, 1957–63); Div. Dir, Rest Assured Ltd, 1963–68. Civil Service Department: Principal, Management Services, later Pay, 1969–73; Asst Sec., 1973–78, Personnel Management, 1973–75; Dir, Public Appts Unit, 1975–82; Under Sec., 1978, Management and Organisation, 1980–82; on secondment from Bank of England as Dir, PRO NED, 1982–85. Director: Great Universal Stores, 1993–2001; CrestaCare, 1993–99; CLM, 1993–99; Leopold Joseph Hldgs, 1994–2001; PRS Ltd, 1996–97; Rostrum plc, 2001–; Consultant, Pensions and Investment Research Consultants, 1994–2000; Mem., London Adv. Bd, Industrial Bank of Japan, 1997–. Member: Council, Royal Inst. of Public Admin., 1981–82; Industry and Finance Cttee, NEDC, 1988–90; Steering Cttee, Corporate Takeovers Inquiry, 1990–91; Instnl Investors Project Adv. Bd, Columbia Univ. of NY Center for Law and Econ. Studies, 1989–93; City Transportation Task Force, 1990–92; Cttee on Financial Aspects of Corporate Governance, 1991–93; US subcouncil on Corporate Governance and Financial Mkts, 1992–94; CIT Working Party on Financing Transport Infrastructure, 1992–93; Steering Cttee on Corporate Governance in NHS, 1993–94; Adv. Bd, Centre of Bd Leadership (USA), 1997; Fabian Soc. Commn on Taxation and Citizenship, 1998–2000; Global Corp. Governance Forum, World Bank, 1999–. Vis. Prof., City Univ. Business Sch., 1997–. Mem., Duke of Edinburgh's 7th Commonwealth Study Conf., 1990–92; Chm., Knightsbridge Assoc., 1998– (Mem. Cttee, 1989–). Chm., CU Labour Club, 1952. Master, Worshipful Co. of Upholders, 1979–80, 1980–81; Sheriff, City of London, 1994–95; Mem., Court of Common Council, 1997–. CIMgt. *Publications:* Keeping Good Company: a survey of corporate governance in five countries, 1994; Conversations with a Silent Friend, 1998; (with Anne Simpson) Fair Shares, 1999; booklets and pamphlets on non-executive directors, boards and shareholders. *Recreations:* music, playing golf, antique furniture, wine. *Address:* The Yellow House, 22 Montpelier Place, SW7 1HL. *T:* (020) 7589 9879, *Fax:* (020) 7581 8520. *Clubs:* Athenæum, MCC.

See also F. S. Shackleton.

CHARKIN, Richard Denis Paul; Chief Executive, Macmillan Ltd, since 1998; *b* 17 June 1949; *s* of Frank Charkin and Mabel Doreen Charkin (*née* Rosen); *m* 1972, Susan Mary Poole; one *s* two *d*. *Educ:* Haileybury and ISC; Trinity College, Cambridge (MA); Harvard Bus. Sch. (AMP). Science Editor, Harrap & Co., 1972; Sen. Publishing Manager, Pergamon Press, 1973; Oxford University Press: Medical Editor, 1974; Head of Science and Medicine, 1976; Head of Reference, 1980; Managing Dir, Academic and General, 1984; Octopus Publishing Group (Reed International Books), 1988; Chief Exec., Reed Consumer Books, 1989–94; Exec. Dir, 1988–96 and Chief Exec., 1994–96, Reed Internat. Books; CEO, Current Science Gp, 1996–97. Mem., Bd of Mgt, John Wisden & Son, 1995–; non-executive Director: Scoot.com plc, 2000–; X-Refer Ltd, 2000–. Vis. Fellow, Green College, Oxford, 1987. Chairman of Trustees: Whitechapel Art Gall., 1997–2000; Common Purpose UK, 1998–. *Recreations:* music, cricket. *Address:* 3 Redcliffe Place, SW10 9DB.

CHARLEMONT, 14th Viscount *cr* 1665 (Ire.); **John Day Caulfeild;** Baron Caulfeild of Charlemont 1620 (Ire.); *b* 19 March 1934; *s* of Eric St George Caulfeild (*d* 1975) and Edith Evelyn, *d* of Frederick William Day, Ottawa; *S* uncle, 1985; *m* 1st, 1964, Judith Ann (*d* 1971), *d* of James E. Dodd; one *s* one *d*; 2nd, 1972, Janet Evelyn, *d* of Orville R. Nancekivell. *Heir: s* Hon. John Dodd Caulfeild [*b* 15 May 1966; *m* 1991, Nadea Stella, *d* of Wilson Fortin; one *s*]. *Address:* 820 Burnhamthorpe Road, Apt 1009, Etobicoke, Ontario M9C 4W2, Canada.

CHARLES, Rt Rev. Adrian Owen, AM 1994; RFD 1983; ED 1976; Bishop of Western Region (Assistant Bishop of Diocese of Brisbane), 1984–92; Bishop to Australian Defence Force, 1989–94; *b* 31 July 1926; *s* of Robert Charles and Alice (*née* Donovan); *m* 1955, Leonie Olive (*née* Robinson); one *s* one *d*. *Educ:* Slade Sch., Warwick, Qld; St Francis Coll., Univ. of Qld; Anglican Central Coll., Canterbury (ThL, Diploma in Divinity). Ordained priest, 1952; Royal Australian Army Chaplains Dept, 1955–83; Rector: Christ Church, St Lucia, Brisbane, 1958–66; St Paul's, Ipswich, 1966–71; Dir, Religious Studies, Christ Church Grammar Sch., Perth, 1971–72; Dean, St James' Cathedral, Townsville, 1972–77; Rector, St David's, Chelmer, Brisbane, 1977–83; Sen. Chaplain, 1st Mil. Dist, 1981–83; Archdeacon and Chaplain to Archbishop of Brisbane, 1981–83; Bishop of Southern Region, 1983–84. Mem., Brisbane Cricket Ground Trust. *Recreations:* reading, cricket, golf, theatre. *Address:* 16 Sandalwood Street, Sinnamon Park, Qld 4073, Australia. *Club:* Brisbane Golf.

CHARLES, Hon. Sir (Arthur) William (Hessin), Kt 1998; **Hon. Mr Justice Charles;** a Judge of the High Court of Justice, Family Division, since 1998; *b* 25 March 1948; *s* of late Arthur Attwood Sinclair Charles and of May Davies Charles (*née* Westerman); *m* 1974, Lydia Margaret Ainscow; one *s* one *d.* *Educ:* Malvern College; Christ's College, Cambridge (MA Hons). Called to the Bar, Lincoln's Inn, 1971; Junior Counsel to the Crown (Chancery), 1986; First Junior Counsel to HM Treasury on Chancery Matters, 1989–98. *Recreations:* golf, tennis. *Address:* Royal Courts of Justice, Strand, WC2A 2LL. *Clubs:* Hawks (Cambridge); Denham Golf.

CHARLES, (Bernard) Leopold; QC 1980; **His Honour Judge Charles;** a Circuit Judge, since 1990; Senior Circuit Judge, since 1998; *b* 16 May 1929; *s* of Chaskiel Charles and Mary Harris; *m* 1st, 1958, Margaret Daphne Abel (marr. diss. 1993); one *s* two *d*; 2nd, 1994, Judith Lynda Orus. *Educ:* King's Coll., Taunton. Called to the Bar, Gray's Inn, 1955. Practised in London and on South Eastern Circuit, 1956–90; a Recorder, 1985–90. *Recreations:* music, politics. *Address:* Lamb Building, Temple, EC4Y 7AS. *T:* (020) 7797 8300; 12 East 41st Street, New York, NY 10017, USA.

CHARLES, Caroline, (Mrs Malcolm Valentine); fashion designer; Founder, Caroline Charles, 1963; *b* 18 May 1942; *m* 1966, Malcolm Valentine; one *s* one *d.* *Educ:* Sacred Heart Convent, Woldingham; Swindon Art Sch. *Recreations:* gardening, tennis, theatre, travel. *Address:* 56/57 Beauchamp Place, SW3 1NY. *T:* (020) 7225 3197.

CHARLES, Dame Eugenia; *see* Charles, Dame M. E.

CHARLES, Sir George (Frederick Lawrence), KCMG 1998; CBE 1972; JP; Chief Minister, St Lucia, 1960–64; *b* 7 June 1916; *s* of James Luke Charles and Marie Philomene Jean Baptiste; *m* 1942, Amelia Charles (*née* Francois); two *s* three *d.* *Educ:* Soufriere RC Boys' Sch.; Dennery RC Boys' Sch.; St Mary's Coll. Secondary Sch. Mem., St Lucia Volunteer Force, 1940–43. Trade unionist, 1946–79: Sec., 1949–54, Pres., 1954–68, St Lucia Workers' Union; Pres., St Lucia Agriculture and General Workers' Union, 1968–79. Mem. (Lab), Castries CC, 1949–52, 1954–57. MHA (Lab) S Castries, St Lucia, 1951–74; Minister of Social Services, 1956–60; Leader of the Opposition, 1964–69. Labour Advr to govt, 1979–82. Editor, St Lucia Workers' Clarion, 1950–57. JP St Lucia, 1950. St Lucia Cross, 1986. *Publication:* History of the Labour Movement in Saint Lucia (1946–1974), 1995. *Recreations:* reading, bridge, games, TV, conversationalist. *Address:* Summersdale, Castries, Saint Lucia. *T:* 4527265.

CHARLES, Hampton; *see* Martin, R. P.

CHARLES, Jack; Director of Establishments, Greater London Council, 1972–77, retired; *b* 18 Jan. 1923; *o s* of late Frederick Walter Charles and Alice Mary Charles; *m* 1959, Jean (*d* 1991), *d* of late F. H. Braund, London; one *s* one *d.* *Educ:* County High Sch., Ilford. Air Min., 1939–42; RAF, 1942–46; Min. of Supply, 1947–59 (Private Sec. to Minister of Supply, 1952–54); War Office, 1959–60; UKAEA, 1960–68 (Authority Personnel Officer, 1965–68); Dep. Dir of Estabs, GLC, 1968–72. *Recreations:* gardening, walking. *Address:* Kings Warren, Enborne Row, Wash Water, Newbury, Berks RG20 0LY. *T:* (01635) 30161.

CHARLES, James Anthony, ScD; FREng; Reader in Process Metallurgy, University of Cambridge, 1978–90, now Emeritus; Fellow, St John's College, Cambridge, since 1963; *b* 23 Aug. 1926; *s* of John and Winifred Charles; *m* 1951, Valerie E. King (*d* 2001); two *s.* *Educ:* Imperial College of Science and Technology, Royal School of Mines (BScEng, ARSM); MA, ScD Cantab; FIM; FREng (FEng 1983). J. Stone & Co. Ltd, 1947–50; British Oxygen Ltd, 1950–60; Dept of Metallurgy and Materials Science, Univ. of Cambridge, 1960–90. Vis. Prof., UCL (Inst. of Archaeology), 1991–; Special Prof., Univ. of Nottingham, 1993–99. Hon. Keeper of Metalwork, Fitzwilliam Museum, 1996– (Syndic., 1986–96). Sir George Beilby Medal and Prize, RIC, Soc. Chem. Ind. and Inst. of Metals, 1965; Sir Robert Hadfield Medal, Metals Soc., 1977; Kroll Medal, Inst. of Metals, 1989; Elegant Work Prize, Inst. of Materials, 1992. *Publications:* Oxygen in Iron and Steel Making, 1956; Selection and Use of Engineering Materials, 1984, 3rd edn 1997; Out of the Fiery Furnace: recollections and meditations of a metalurgist, 2000; numerous papers on the science and technology of metals and archaeometallurgy. *Recreations:* philately, listening to music, archaeology. *Address:* New Lodge, 22 Mingle Lane, Stapleford, Cambridge CB2 5BG. *T:* (01223) 843812.

CHARLES, Jonathan James; District Judge (Magistrates' Courts), Wolverhampton, since 2001; *b* 4 Sept. 1946; *s* of William Robert Charles and Elizabeth Charles; *m* 1970, Linda Ann Llewellyn; two *s* one *d.* *Educ:* Bridgend Boys' Grammar Sch.; Bristol Poly. Admitted Solicitor, 1980; Justices Clerk: Merthyr Tydfil, 1981–1985; Lower Rhymney Valley, 1985–88; Bridgend, 1988–97; Consultant Solicitor, Keith Evans & Co., Newport, 1997–2001. Sec., Lord Chancellor's Adv. Cttee for Mid-Glamorgan, 1995–97. *Recreations:* travel, Rugby football, cricket. *Address:* Law Courts, North Street, Wolverhampton WV1 1RA. *T:* (01902) 773151.

CHARLES, Leopold; *see* Charles, B. L.

CHARLES, Dame (Mary) Eugenia, DBE 1991; Prime Minister and Minister of Finance, Commonwealth of Dominica, 1980–95; MP (Dominica Freedom Party) Roseau, 1970–95 (Nominated MP, 1970–75); *b* 15 May 1919; *d* of John Baptiste Charles and Josephine (*née* Delauney). *Educ:* Convent High Sch., Roseau, Dominica; St Joseph's Convent, St George's, Grenada; University Coll., Univ. of Toronto (BA); London Sch. of Econs and Pol. Science. Called to the Bar, Inner Temple, 1947; admitted to practice, Dominica, 1949. Entered Parlt, 1970; Leader of the Opposition, 1975–79; Minister of Foreign Affairs, 1980–90. *Recreations:* reading, gardening, travelling. *Address:* PO Box 121, 1 Cross Lane, Roseau, Commonwealth of Dominica. *T:* 4482855, (office) 4482876.

CHARLES, Michael Geoffrey A.; *see* Audley-Charles.

CHARLES, Sir Robert (James), KNZM 1999; CBE 1992 (OBE 1972); golf professional, since 1960; *b* 14 March 1936; *s* of Albert Ivor Charles and Phyllis Irene Charles; *m* 1962, Verity Joan Aldridge; one *s* one *d.* *Educ:* Wairarapa Coll. Nat. Bank of NZ, 1954–60. Golf tournament victories include: NZ Open, 1954 (amateur), 1966, 1970, 1973; NZ PGA, 1961, 1979, 1980; Swiss Open, 1962, 1974; British Open, 1963; Atlanta Classic, USA, 1967; Canadian Open, 1968; Piccadilly World Match Play, England, 1969; John Player Classic and Dunlop Masters, England, 1972; S African Open, 1973; joined Senior Tour, 1986: 75 victories incl. Sen. British Open, 1989 and 1993. *Publications:* Left Handed Golf, 1965; The Bob Charles Left Handers Golf Book, 1985, 2nd edn 1993; Golf for Seniors, 1994. *Recreations:* farming, golf course architecture, tennis, boating. *Address:* Lytham, Burnt Hill Road, Oxford 8253, New Zealand. *Club:* Christchurch Golf (New Zealand).

CHARLES, Hon. Sir William; *see* Charles, Hon. Sir A. W. H.

CHARLES-EDWARDS, Prof. Thomas Mowbray, DPhil; FBA 2001; Jesus Professor of Celtic, and Fellow of Jesus College, University of Oxford, since 1997; *b* 11 Nov. 1943; *s* of Thomas Charles-Edwards and Imelda Charles-Edwards (*née* Bailey); *m* 1975, Davina Gifford Lewis (pen name Gifford Lewis); two *s.* *Educ:* Ampleforth Coll.; Corpus Christi Coll., Oxford (BA, MA, DPhil, Dip. Celtic Studies). Scholar, Dublin Inst. for Advanced Studies, 1967–69; P. S. Allen Jun. Res. Fellow in History, 1969–71, Fellow and Tutor in Modern Hist., 1971–96, Corpus Christi Coll., Oxford. *Publications:* Bechbretha (with Fergus Kelly), 1983; The Welsh Laws, 1989; Early Irish and Welsh Kinship, 1993; Early Christian Ireland, 2000. *Recreations:* sailing, dog-walking. *Address:* 31 First Turn, Upper Wolvercote, Oxford OX2 8AH. *T:* (01865) 556168; Jesus College, Oxford OX1 3DW. *T:* (01865) 279739; *e-mail:* thomas.charles-edwards@jesus.ox.ac.uk.

CHARLESWORTH, Prof. Brian, PhD; FRS 1991; Royal Society Research Professor, Institute of Cell, Animal and Population Biology, University of Edinburgh, since 1997; *b* 29 April 1945; *s* of Francis Gustave Charlesworth and Mary (*née* Ryan); *m* 1967, Deborah Maltby; one *d.* *Educ:* Queens' Coll., Cambridge (BA Natural Scis; PhD Genetics). Post-Doctoral Fellow, Univ. of Chicago, 1969–71; Lectr in Genetics, Univ. of Liverpool, 1971–74; Lectr, 1974–82, Reader, 1982–84, in Biology, Univ. of Sussex; Prof., 1985–92, Chm., 1986–91, G. W. Beadle Distinguished Service Prof., 1992–97, Dept of Ecology and Evolution, Univ. of Chicago. Pres., Soc. for Study of Evolution, 1999. Fellow, Amer. Acad. of Arts and Scis, 1996. Darwin Medal, Royal Soc., 2000. *Publications:* Evolution in Age-Structured Populations, 1980, 2nd edn 1994; papers in Nature, Science, Genetics, Genetical Res., Evolution, Amer. Naturalist, Procs Roy. Soc. *Recreations:* reading, listening to classical music, walking. *Address:* Institute of Cell, Animal and Population Biology, University of Edinburgh, West Mains Road, Edinburgh EH9 3JT.

CHARLESWORTH, Peter James; His Honour Judge Charlesworth; a Circuit Judge, since 1989; *b* 24 Aug. 1944; *s* of late Joseph William Charlesworth and Florence Mary Charlesworth; *m* 1967, Elizabeth Mary Postill; one *s* one *d.* *Educ:* Hull Grammar Sch.; Leeds Univ. (LLB 1965, LLM 1966). Called to the Bar, Inner Temple, 1966. In practice on North-Eastern Circuit, 1966–89; a Recorder, 1982–89. Mem., Rugby Football League Disciplinary Cttee, 1994–. *Recreations:* tennis, reading, Rugby League football (spectating), walking in the Yorkshire dales. *Address:* Daleswood, Creskeld Gardens, Bramhope, Leeds LS16 9EN. *Clubs:* Hull Rugby League Football (Vice-Pres.); Leeds YMCA Tennis.

CHARLTON, Alan, CMG 1996; HM Diplomatic Service; Director, South East Europe, Foreign and Commonwealth Office, since 2001; *b* 21 June 1952; *s* of Henry and Eva Charlton; *m* 1974, Judith Angela Carryer; two *s* one *d.* *Educ:* Nottingham High Sch.; Gonville and Caius Coll., Cambridge (MA); Leicester Univ. (PGCE); Manchester Univ. (BLing). Teacher, Gesamtschule, Gelsenkirchen, Germany, 1975–77; West Africa Dept, FCO, 1978–79; Amman, 1981–84; Near East and North Africa Dept, FCO, 1984–86; BMG Berlin, 1986–90; Dep. Chief, Assessments Staff, Cabinet Office, 1991–93; Head, Eastern Adriatic Unit, FCO, 1993–95; Bosnia Contact Group Rep., 1995–96; Political Counsellor, 1996–98, Dep. Hd of Mission, 1998–99, Bonn; Dep. Hd of Mission, Berlin, 1999–2001. *Recreations:* chess, football, cricket, dancing. *Address:* c/o Foreign and Commonwealth Office, SW1A 2AH.

CHARLTON, Sir Bobby; *see* Charlton, Sir Robert.

CHARLTON, Graham; *see* Charlton, T. A. G.

CHARLTON, Prof. Graham, MDS; FDSRCSE; Professor of Conservative Dentistry, University of Edinburgh, 1978–91, now Emeritus Professor (Dean of Dental Studies, 1978–83); *b* 15 Oct. 1928; *s* of Simpson R. Charlton and Georgina (*née* Graham); *m* 1956, Stella Dobson; two *s* one *d.* *Educ:* Bedlington Grammar Sch., Northumberland; St John's Coll., York (Teaching Cert.); King's Coll., Univ. of Durham (BDS); Univ. of Bristol (MDS). Teacher, Northumberland, 1948–52; National Service, 1948–50; Dental School, 1952–58; General Dental Practice, Torquay, 1958–64; University of Bristol: Lecturer, 1964–72; Cons. Sen. Lectr, 1972–78; Dental Clinical Dean, 1975–78. *Address:* 10 Pear Tree Court, Aldwark, York YO1 7DF. *T:* (01904) 655619.

CHARLTON, Henry Marshall, DPhil; FRS 1994; Reader in Neuroendocrinology, since 1990, and Fellow of Linacre College, since 1970, University of Oxford; *b* 10 March 1939; *s* of Joseph Douglass Charlton and Lilian Charlton; *m* 1965, Margaret Jeffrey; one *s* one *d.* *Educ:* Corpus Christi Coll., Oxford (MA, DPhil). Mem., MRC Neuroendocrinology Unit, Oxford, 1964–68; Lectr, Oxford Univ., 1968–90. Founder FMedSci 1998. *Publications:* contrib. scientific jls. *Recreations:* Real tennis, hill walking, gardening. *Address:* 61 Plantation Road, Oxford OX2 6JE. *T:* (01865) 554248.

CHARLTON, John, (Jack), OBE 1974; DL; Manager, Republic of Ireland Football Team, 1986–95; broadcaster; *b* 8 May 1935; *s* of late Robert and Elizabeth Charlton; *m* 1958, Patricia; two *s* one *d.* *Educ:* Hirst Park Sch., Ashington. Professional footballer, Leeds United, 1952–73; 35 England caps, 1965–70; Manager: Middlesbrough, 1973–77; Sheffield Wednesday FC, 1977–83; Newcastle United FC, 1984–85. Mem., Sports Council, 1977–82. DL Northumberland, 1997. *Publications:* Jack Charlton's American World Cup Diary, 1994; The Autobiography, 1996. *Recreations:* shooting, fishing, gardening.

See also Sir Robert Charlton.

CHARLTON, Prof. Kenneth; Emeritus Professor of History of Education, King's College, University of London, since 1983; *b* 11 July 1925; 2nd *s* of late George and Lottie Charlton; *m* 1953, Maud Tulloch Brown, *d* of late P. R. Brown, MBE and M. B. Brown; one *s* one *d.* *Educ:* City Grammar Sch., Chester; Univ. of Glasgow. MA 1949, MEd 1953, Glasgow. RNVR, 1943–46. History Master, Dalziel High Sch., Motherwell, and Uddingston Grammar Sch., 1950–54; Lectr in Educn, UC N Staffs, 1954–64; Sen. Lectr in Educn, Keele Univ., 1964–66; Prof. of History and Philosophy of Educn, Birmingham Univ., 1966–72; Prof. of History of Educn and Head of Dept of Educn, King's Coll., Univ. of London, 1972–83. *Publications:* Recent Historical Fiction for Children, 1960, 2nd edn 1969; Education in Renaissance England, 1965; Women, Religion and Education in Early Modern England, 1999; contrib. Educnl Rev., Brit. Jl Educnl Psych., Year Bk of Educn, Jl Hist. of Ideas, Brit. Jl Educnl Studies, Internat. Rev. of Educn, Trans Hist. Soc. Lancs and Cheshire, Irish Hist. Studies, Northern Hist., Hist. of Educn, Hist. of Educn Quarterly. *Recreations:* gardening, listening to music. *Address:* 128 Ridge Langley, Sanderstead, Croydon CR2 0AS.

See also P. Charlton.

CHARLTON, Philip, OBE 1987; FCIB; CIMgt; Co-Founder, and Chairman, 1991–96, Charlton Associates; *b* 31 July 1930; *s* of George and Lottie Charlton; *m* 1953, Jessie Boulton; one *s* one *d.* *Educ:* Chester Grammar School. Entered service of Chester Savings Bank, 1947; Gen. Manager, Chester, Wrexham and N Wales Savings Bank, 1966–75; Gen. Manager, TSB Wales & Border Counties, 1975–81; TSB Group Central Executive: Dep. Chief Gen. Manager, 1981–82; Chief Gen. Manager, 1982–85; Gp Man. Dir,

1986–88; Chief Exec., 1988–89; Dep. Chm., 1990–91; Mem., TSB Central Bd, 1976–77, 1981–90; Director: TSB Computer Services (Wythenshawe) Ltd, 1976–81; TSB Trust Co. Ltd, 1979–82; TSB Gp Computer Services Ltd, 1981–86; Central Trustee Savings Bank, later TSB Bank, 1982–89; TSB (Holdings) Ltd, 1982–86; Hill Samuel Gp, 1987–89. Council Mem., 1968–71, Hon. Treasurer, 1975–77, Savings Bank Inst.; Vice Pres., Internat. Savings Banks Inst. (Geneva), 1988–91; Mem., Bd of Admin, European Savings Banks Gp, Brussels, 1989–91. Chm., TSB Nat. Sports Council, 1979–82. FCIB (FIB 1977; Mem. Council, 1982–; Dep. Chm., 1989–91; Pres., 1990–92); CIMgt (CBIM 1983). *Recreations:* music, swimming, sport. *Address:* 62 Quinta Drive, Arkley, near Barnet, Herts EN5 3BE. *T:* (020) 8440 4477. *Clubs:* Royal Automobile; City (Chester).

See also Prof. K. Charlton.

CHARLTON, Richard McKenzie, AM 1996; FTS; FInstPet; Chairman: South East Water Ltd, since 1995; Neptunus Pharmaceuticals Inc., since 1995; *b* 20 March 1935; *s* of Richard Rutherford Charlton and Yvonne Gladys Charlton (*née* McKenzie); *m*; two *s* two *d*. *Educ:* Sydney Univ. (BE Mining 1957; MESc 1959). Joined Shell as trainee petroleum engr, 1959: various posts in The Hague, UK, Nigeria, Kuwait, Trinidad and Brunei, 1959–75; Shell Australia: Gen. Manager, Exploration & Prodn, 1975–76; Exec. Dir, NW Shelf Project, 1976–80; Dir Ops, Shell UK Exploration & Prodn, Aberdeen, 1980–83; Chm., Shell Cos in Malaysia, 1983–86; Hd, Exploration & Prodn Ops & Liaison, The Hague, 1986–91; Chm. and Chief Exec. Officer, Shell Gp of Cos in Australia, 1991–95, retd. Director: Fujitsu Australia Ltd, 1994–97; Coles-Myer Ltd, 1995–; Hongkong Bank of Australia, 1996–2001; Chm., Adcorp Australia Ltd, 1999–. Chancellor, Univ. of Newcastle, NSW, 1994–. Chairman: Art Foundn, Victoria, 1994–97 (Dep. Chm., 1992–94); Hunter Symphony Orch., 1995–97; Australia-Malaysia Soc., 1995–. Chm., Nat. Basketball League, 1997–. Mem., Soc. Petroleum Engrs, 1971; FAICD; FInstD; FAIM. *Publications:* papers on petroleum industry. *Recreations:* horse racing, Rugby, snow ski-ing, surfing, tennis. *Address:* c/o Level 5, 1 Spring Street, Melbourne, Vic 3000, Australia. *T:* (3) 96668850. *Clubs:* Melbourne, Australia (Melbourne); Victoria Racing, Moonee Valley Racing.

CHARLTON, Sir Robert, (Sir Bobby), Kt 1994; CBE 1974 (OBE 1969); Director, Manchester United Football Club, since 1984; *b* 11 Oct. 1937; *s* of late Robert and Elizabeth Charlton; *m* 1961, Norma; two *d*. *Educ:* Bedlington Grammar Sch., Northumberland. Professional Footballer with Manchester United, 1954–73, for whom he played 751 games and scored 245 goals; FA Cup Winners Medal, 1963; FA Championship Medals, 1956–57, 1964–65 and 1966–67; World Cup Winners Medal (International), 1966; European Cup Winners medal, 1968. 100th England cap, 21 April 1970; 106 appearances for England, 1957–73. Manager, Preston North End, 1973–75. Mem., Cttee, FIFA. Hon. Fellow, Manchester Polytechnic, 1979. Hon. MA Manchester Univ. Sir Stanley Matthews Award, 2000. *Publications:* My Soccer Life, 1965; Forward for England, 1967; This Game of Soccer, 1967; Book of European Football, Books 1–4, 1969–72. *Recreation:* golf. *Address:* Garthollerton, Chelford Road, Ollerton, near Knutsford, Cheshire WA16 8RY.

See also John Charlton.

CHARLTON, (Thomas Alfred) Graham, CB 1970; Secretary, Trade Marks, Patents and Designs Federation, 1973–84; *b* 29 Aug. 1913; 3rd *s* of late Frederick William and Marian Charlton; *m* 1940, Margaret Ethel, *yr d* of A. E. Furst; three *d*. *Educ:* Rugby School; Corpus Christi Coll., Cambridge. Asst Principal, War Office, 1936; Asst Private Secretary to Secretary of State for War, 1937–39; Principal, 1939; Cabinet Office, 1947–49; Asst Secretary, 1949; International Staff, NATO, 1950–52; War Office, later MoD, 1952–73; Asst Under-Sec. of State, 1960–73. Coronation Medal, 1953. *Recreation:* gardening. *Address:* 2A Sandelswood End, Beaconsfield, Bucks HP9 2NY. *T:* (01494) 672837.

CHARMLEY, Prof. John Denis, DPhil; FRHistS; Professor of Modern History, University of East Anglia, since 1998; *b* 9 Nov. 1955; *s* of John Charmley and Doris Charmley; *m* 1st, 1977, Ann Dorothea Bartlett (marr. diss. 1992); three *s* (incl. twins); 2nd, 1992, Lorraine Fegan. *Educ:* Rock Ferry High Sch., Birkenhead; Pembroke Coll., Oxford (BA 1977; MA 1982; DPhil 1982). FRHistS 1987. University of East Anglia: Lectr in English Hist., Sch. of English and American Studies, 1979–92; Sen. Lectr in Hist., Sch. of Hist., 1992–96; Reader in Hist., 1996–98. Fulbright Prof., Westminster Coll., Fulton, Mo, 1992–93. *Publications:* Duff Cooper, 1986; Lord Lloyd and the Decline of the British Empire, 1987; (ed) Descent to Suez: the diaries of Sir Evelyn Shuckburgh, 1987; Chamberlain and the Lost Peace, 1989; Churchill: the end of glory, 1993; Churchill's Grand Alliance, 1995; A History of Conservative Politics 1990–1996, 1996; Splendid Isolation?: Britain and the balance of power 1874–1914, 1999. *Recreations:* reading, walking, dining out. *Address:* School of History, University of East Anglia, Norwich NR4 7TJ. *T:* (01603) 592790. *Club:* Norfolk (Norwich).

CHARNLEY, Helen; *see* Dunmore, H.

CHARNLEY, Sir (William) John, Kt 1981; CB 1973; MEng, FREng, FRAeS, FRIN; consultant in advanced technology; *b* 4 Sept. 1922; *s* of George and Catherine Charnley; *m* 1945, Mary Paden; one *s* one *d*. *Educ:* Oulton High Sch., Liverpool; Liverpool Univ. MEng 1945; FREng (FEng 1982); FRIN 1963; FRAeS 1966. Aerodynamics Dept, RAE Farnborough, 1943–55; Supt. Blind Landing Experimental Unit, 1955–61; Imperial Defence Coll., 1962; Head of Instruments and Electrical Engineering Dept, 1963–65, Head of Weapons Dept, 1965–68, RAE Farnborough; Head of Research Planning, 1968–69, Dep. Controller, Guided Weapons, Min. of Technology, later MoD, 1969–72; Controller, Guided Weapons and Electronics, MoD (PE), 1972–73; Chief Scientist (RAF), 1973–77, and Dep. Controller, R&D Establishments and Res. C, MoD, 1975–77; Controller, R&D Establishments and Res., MoD, 1977–82. Director: Fairey Holdings Ltd, 1983–86; Winsdale Investments Ltd, 1985–88. Technical Advr, Monopolies and Mergers Commn, 1982; Specialist Advr to House of Lords Select Cttee on Science and Technology, 1986. Chm., Civil Aviation Res. and Develt Programme Bd, 1984–92; Mem., Air Traffic Control Bd, 1985–96. President: Royal Inst. of Navigation, 1987–90; European Orgn for Civil Aviation Equipment, 1993–97. Trustee, Richard Ormonde Shuttleworth Remembrance Trust, 1987–98. Hon. FRAeS 1992. Hon. DEng Liverpool, 1988. Bronze Medal, RIN, 1960; Silver Medal, 1973, Gold Medal, 1980, RAeS. *Publications:* papers on subjects in aerodynamics, aircraft all weather operation, aircraft navigation, defence R&D. *Address:* Kirkstones, 29 Brackendale Close, Camberley, Surrey GU15 1HP. *T:* (01276) 22547. *Club:* Royal Air Force.

CHARPAK, Georges; Physicist, Organisation européenne pour la recherche nucléaire (CERN); *b* Poland, 1 Aug. 1924; *s* of Anne Szapiro and Maurice Charpak; *m* 1953, Dominique Vidal; three *c*. *Educ:* Ecole des Mines de Paris. Went to France at age 7; served in French Resistance; imprisoned for 1 year in Dachau. Centre national de la recherche scientifique (CNRS), 1948; CERN, Geneva, 1959; in 1968 invented multiwire proportional chamber (linked to computers) for detecting particles in atom smashers. Mem., Acad des Sciences, France, 1985; Foreign Associate of Nat. Acad. of Sciences, USA, 1986. Nobel Prize for Physics, 1992. *Recreations:* ski-ing, travel, music. *Address:* CERN, 1211 Geneva 23, Switzerland. *T:* (22) 7672144, *Fax:* (22) 7677555.

CHARTERIS, family name of **Earl of Wemyss.**

CHARTRES, Rt Rev. and Rt Hon. Richard John Carew; *see* London, Bishop of.

CHARVET, Richard Christopher Larkins, RD 1972; JP; Consultant: Tyser & Co., since 1999; Johnson Stevens Agencies, since 1999; General Manager, Morline Ltd (formerly Associate Director, Anglo Soviet Shipping Co. Ltd), 1988–94; *b* 12 Dec. 1936; *s* of late Patrice and Eleanor Charvet; *m* 1990; two *s* one *d* by a previous marriage. *Educ:* Rugby. FITT, ACIArb; FCIS; FIMgt; MIFF; MIEx. FRSA 1985. National Service, Royal Navy, 1955–57; Mem., London Div., RNR, 1955–. Union Castle Line, 1957–58; Killick Martin & Co. Ltd, Shipbrokers, 1958–81; Vogt and Maguire Ltd, Shipbrokers, 1981–88. Consultant, Howden Marine Ltd, then AON Gp, 1994–99. Mem., Court of Common Council for Aldgate Ward, City of London, 1970–76; Alderman, Aldgate Ward, 1976–85; Sheriff, 1983–84. Prime Warden, Worshipful Co. of Shipwrights, 1985–86 (Renter Warden, 1984–85); Master, Guild of World Traders, 1991. President: City of London Sea Cadet Unit, 1994–; NE Area (London), St John Ambulance, POW Dist, 1997–; Chairman: City Br., St John Ambulance Appeal, 1985–92; City Br., RNLI, 1986–98. JP 1976. CStJ 1989. Hon. JSM, Malaysia, 1974. *Publication:* Peter and Tom in the Lord Mayor's Show, 1982. *Recreations:* gardening, travel, sailing. *Clubs:* Aldgate Ward, Lime Street Ward, Little Ship.

CHASE, Robert John; HM Diplomatic Service, retired; Secretary General, International Aluminium Institute (formerly International Primary Aluminium Institute), since 1997; *b* 13 March 1943; *s* of late Herbert Chase and of Evelyn Chase; *m* 1966, Gillian Ann Chase (*née* Shelton); one *s* two *d*. *Educ:* Sevenoaks Sch.; St John's Coll., Oxford. MA (Mod. Hist.). Entered HM Diplomatic Service, 1965; Third, later Second Sec., Rangoon, 1966–69; UN Dept, FCO, 1970–72; First Sec. (Press Attaché), Brasilia, 1972–76; Hd Caribbean Section, Mexico and Caribbean Dept, FCO, 1976–80; on secondment as a manager to Imperial Chemical Industries PLC, 1980–82; Asst Hd, S American Dept, FCO, 1982–83; Asst Hd, Maritime, Aviation and Environment Dept, FCO, 1983–84; Counsellor (Commercial), Moscow, 1985–88; Overseas Inspector, FCO, 1988–89; Hd, Resource Mgt Dept, FCO, 1989–92; Consul-Gen., Chicago, 1993–96; Dir Gen. of Trade and Investment, and Consul-Gen., Milan, 1996–97. MInstD. *Recreations:* military history, visiting historic sites, swimming. *Address:* IAI, New Zealand House, Haymarket, SW1Y 4TE. *T:* (020) 7930 0528; 71 South Cliff, Bexhill on Sea, E Sussex TN39 3EE. *T:* (01424) 217611.

CHASE, Rodney Frank, CBE 2000; Deputy Group Chief Executive, BP plc, since 1998; *b* 12 May 1943; *s* of Norman Maxwell Chase and Barbara Chase (*née* Marshall); *m* 1968, Diana Mary Lyle; one *s* one *d*. *Educ:* Liverpool Univ. (BA Hons Hist.). Joined British Petroleum, 1964: various posts in marketing, oil trading and shipping distribn, 1964–81; Dir (Exploration and Prodn), BP Australia, 1982–85; Gp Treas, BP Co. plc, 1986–89; Chief Exec. Officer, BP Exploration (USA) Inc., 1989–92; a Man. Dir, BP, 1992–98; Chm. and Chief Exec. Officer, BP America Inc., 1992–94. Non-executive Director: Diageo, 1999–; Computer Scis Corp., 2000–. Chm., UK Emissions Trading Gp, 1998–; Mem., Adv. Cttee on Business and the Envmt, 1993–. Mem., Amer. Petroleum Inst., 2000–. *Recreations:* golf, ski-ing. *Address:* BP plc, Britannic House, 1 Finsbury Circus, EC2M 7BA. *T:* (020) 7496 4000.

CHASE, Roger Robert; Director of Personnel, BBC, 1989–91; *b* 19 Sept. 1928; *s* of Robert Joseph Chase and Lillian Ada (*née* Meredith); *m* 1958, Geraldine Joan Whitlamsmith; three *d*. *Educ:* Gosport Grammar Sch. Served RN, 1947–49. Joined BBC, 1944; Engrg Div., 1944–47 and 1949–67; Television Personnel Dept, 1967–74; Head, Central Services Dept, 1974–76; Controller, Personnel, Television, 1976–82; Dep. Dir of Personnel, 1982–89. Chm., BBC Club, 1979–91. *Recreation:* sailing. *Address:* Vernons, Vernons Road, Chappel, Colchester, Essex CO6 2AQ. *T:* (01206) 240143. *Club:* Royal Naval Sailing Association.

CHASKALSON, Hon. Arthur; President, Constitutional Court of South Africa, since 1994; *b* Johannesburg, 24 Nov. 1931; *s* of Harry and Mary Chaskalson; *m* 1961, Lorraine Dianne Ginsberg; two *s*. *Educ:* Hilton Coll., Natal; Univ. of Witwatersrand (BCom 1952; LLB *cum laude* 1955). Called to Johannesburg Bar, 1956; SC 1971; in practice as barrister, 1956–94: defence counsel for mems of liberation movements at several major political trials, incl. that of Nelson Mandela, 1963–64. Jt Founder, 1978, and Dir, 1978–93, Legal Resources Centre. Member: Legal Aid Bd, 1992–2000; Judicial Service Commn, 1994–; Comr, Internat. Commn of Jurists, 1995–. Consultant to Namibian Constituent Assembly on drafting of Constitution of Namibia, 1989–90. Mem., Johannesburg Bar Council, 1967–71 and 1973–84 (Chm., 1976, 1982); Vice-Chm., Gen. Council of Bar of S Africa, 1982–87 (Jt Hon. Pres., 1994–); Vice-Chm., Internat. Legal Aid Div., Internat. Bar Assoc., 1983–93. Mem., Nat. Council of Lawyers for Human Rights, 1980–91. Hon. Prof. of Law, Univ. of Witwatersrand, 1981–95. Hon. LLD: Natal, 1986; Witwatersrand, 1990; Rhodes, 1997. Numerous awards, incl. (jtly) Human Rights Award, Foundn for Freedom and Human Rights, Berne, 1990. *Address:* Constitutional Court, Private Bag X32, Braamfontein 2017, S Africa.

CHATAWAY, Rt Hon. Sir Christopher (John), Kt 1995; PC 1970; Chairman, Bletchley Park Trust, since 2000; *b* 31 Jan. 1931; *m* 1st, 1959, Anna Lett (marr. diss. 1975); two *s* one *d*; 2nd, 1976, Carola Walker; two *s*. *Educ:* Sherborne Sch.; Magdalen Coll., Oxford (BA Hons PPE). Rep. Great Britain, Olympic Games, 1952 and 1956; briefly held world 5,000 metres track record in 1954. Arthur Guinness Son & Co., 1953–55; Independent Television News, 1955–56; BBC Television, 1956–59. Elected for N Lewisham to LCC, 1958–61; Leader, Educn Cttee, ILEA, 1967–69. MP (C): Lewisham North, 1959–66; Chichester, May 1969–Sept. 1974; PPS to Minister of Power, 1961–62; Joint Parly Under-Secretary of State, Dept of Education and Science, 1962–64; Minister of Posts and Telecommunications, 1970–72; Minister for Industrial Develt, DTI, 1972–74. Chairman: LBC, 1981–93; CAA, 1991–96. Man. Dir, Orion Royal Bank, 1974–88; Director: BET, 1974–96; Credito Italiano Internat., 1992–96; Macquarie Securities Ltd, 1994–; 1975–92: Chm., United Med. Enterprises, Isola 2000, Kitcat & Aitken, RBC CI, Crown Communications; Dir, Fisons, Plessey Telecommunications, Dorchester Hotel, UK subsids of Honeywell, GE of America and Petrofina. Treasurer, Nat. Cttee for Electoral Reform, 1976–84. Chairman: Groundwork Foundn, 1985–90; UK Athletics, 1998–. Chm., CIT, 1994–96. Pres., Adv. Council, Action Aid, 2000– (Treas., 1976–86; Chm., 1986–92). Trustee, Foundn for Sport and the Arts, 1993–. Hon. DLitt: Loughborough, 1985; Macquarie, 2000; Hon. DSc Cranfield, 1994. Nansen Medal, 1960. *Club:* Garrick.

CHATER, Dr Anthony Philip John; Editor, Morning Star, 1974–95; parents both shoe factory workers; *m* 1954, Janice (*née* Smith); three *s*. *Educ:* Northampton Grammar Sch. for Boys; Queen Mary Coll., London. BSc (1st cl. hons Chem.) 1951, PhD (Phys.Chem.) 1954. Fellow in Biochem., Ottawa Exper. Farm, 1954–56; studied biochem. at Brussels

Univ., 1956–57; Teacher, Northampton Techn. High Sch., 1957–59; Teacher, Blyth Grammar Sch., Norwich, 1959–60; Lectr, subseq. Sen. Lectr in Phys. Chem., Luton Coll. of Technology, 1960–69; Head of Press and Publicity of Communist Party, 1969–74; Nat. Chm. of Communist Party, 1967–69. Contested (Com) Luton, Nov. 1963, 1964, 1966, 1970. Mem. Presidential Cttee, World Peace Council, 1969–74. *Publications:* Race Relations in Britain, 1966; numerous articles. *Recreations:* walking, swimming, music, camping.

CHATER, Prof. Keith Frederick, PhD; FRS 1995; Head, Department of Molecular Microbiology, John Innes Centre, since 2001; *b* 23 April 1944; *s* of Frederick Ernest Chater and Marjorie Inez Chater (*née* Palmer); *m* 1966, Jean Wallbridge; three *s* one *d*. *Educ:* Trinity Sch. of John Whitgift, Croydon; Univ. of Birmingham (BSc 1st Cl. Hons Bacteriol. 1966; PhD Genetics 1969). John Innes Institute, later John Innes Centre: research scientist in Streptomyces genetics, 1969–; Dep. Head, 1989–98, Head, 1998–2001, Dept. of Genetics. Fulbright Scholar, Harvard Univ., 1983; Hon. Professor: UEA, 1988–; Chinese Acad. of Scis, 1999; Huazhong Agricl Univ., Wuhan, 2000. *Publications:* (jtly) Genetic Manipulation of Streptomyces: a laboratory manual, 1985; (ed jtly) Genetics of Bacterial Diversity, 1989; (jtly) Practical Streptomyces Genetics, 2000. *Recreations:* painting, gardening, bird-watching. *Address:* John Innes Centre, Norwich Research Park, Colney, Norwich NR4 7UH. *T:* (01603) 450000, *Fax:* (01603) 450045; *e-mail:* keith.chater@bbsrc.ac.uk.

CHATFIELD, family name of **Baron Chatfield**.

CHATFIELD, 2nd Baron *cr* 1937, of Ditchling; **Ernle David Lewis Chatfield;** *b* 2 Jan. 1917; *s* of 1st Baron Chatfield, PC, GCB, OM, KCMG, CVO (Admiral of the Fleet Lord Chatfield), and Lillian Emma St John Matthews (*d* 1977); *S* father, 1967; *m* 1969, (Felicia Mary) Elizabeth, *d* of late Dr John Roderick Bulman, Hereford. *Educ:* RNC Dartmouth; Trinity Coll., Cambridge. ADC to Governor-General of Canada, 1940–44. *Heir:* none. *Address:* 535 Island Road, Victoria, BC V8S 2T7, Canada.

CHATFIELD, Sir John (Freeman), Kt 1993; CBE 1982; DL; Chairman, Association of County Councils, 1989–92; Consultant Solicitor in private practice, 1989–95; *b* 28 Oct. 1929; *s* of Cecil Freeman Chatfield and Florence Dorothy Chatfield; *m* 1954, Barbara Elizabeth Trickett. *Educ:* Southdown Coll., Eastbourne; Roborough Sch., Eastbourne; Lawrence Sheriff Sch., Rugby; Lewes Grammar Sch.; Law Soc. Sch. (Final, 1951). Solicitor, 1952; Sen. Partner, Hart Reade & Co., Eastbourne, 1976–89; Dep. Registrar, County Court, 1965–78. Mem., E Sussex CC, 1972–93 (Leader, 1981–85; Chm., 1985–87); Chairman: Sussex Police Authy, 1982–85; Police Cttee, ACC, 1982–85; Official Side, Police Negotiating Bd, 1982–85; Mem., Police Adv. Bd, England and Wales, 1980–85; Vice-Chm., ACC, 1986–89; Chm., UK Local Authorities Internat. Bureau, 1989–92; first Chm., Internat. Council for Local Envmt Initiatives, 1990–93; Pres., Consultative Council of Local and Regional Authorities in Europe, 1990–93; a Vice-President: CEMR, 1989–93; British Section, IULA/CEMR, 1993–97; Leader, UK Delegn, 1989–92, Mem., Standing Cttee, 1990–93, CLRAE. Mem. Ct and Council, Sussex Univ., 1981–85 and 1991–2001 (Vice-Chm. Council, 1996–99); Gov., Ravensbourne Coll. of Design and Communication, 1999–. Pres., Eastbourne Law Soc., 1972–73. Freeman, City of London, 1994; Liveryman, Co. of Basketmakers, 1995–. DL E Sussex, 1986. *Recreations:* music, theatre, travel. *Address:* Underhill House, East Dean, Eastbourne, E Sussex BN20 0DB. *T:* (01323) 423397.

CHATTEN, Harold Raymond Percy, CB 1975; RCNC; Chief Executive, Royal Dockyards, 1975–79, and Head of Royal Corps of Naval Constructors, Apr.-Sept. 1979, Ministry of Defence. Production Manager, HM Dockyard, Chatham, 1967–70; General Manager, HM Dockyard, Rosyth, Fife, 1970–75. MA Cambridge 1946.

CHATTERJEE, Krishna; *see* Chatterjee, V. K. K.

CHATTERJEE, Dr Satya Saran, OBE 1971; JP; FRCP, FRCPE; Consultant Chest Physician and Physician in Charge, Department of Respiratory Physiology, Wythenshawe Hospital, Manchester, 1959–88; *b* 16 July 1922; *m* 1948, Enid May (*née* Adlington); one *s* two *d*. *Educ:* India, UK, Sweden and USA. MB, BS; FCCP (USA). Asst Lectr, Dept of Medicine, Albany Med. Coll. Hosp., NY, 1953–54; Med. Registrar, Sen. Registrar, Dept of Thoracic Medicine, Wythenshawe Hosp., Manchester, 1954–59. Mem., NW RHA, 1976–. Chairman: NW Conciliation Cttee, Race Relations Board, 1972–77; Overseas Doctors Assoc., 1975–81 (Pres., 1981–87); Manchester Area Cttee on Ethnic Minority Health, 1993–94; Member: Standing Adv. Council on Race Relations, 1977–86; GMC, 1979–92; NW Adv. Council, BBC, 1987–92; Vice-Pres., Manchester Council for Community Relations, 1974–. Chm., ODA News Review, 1986–. President: Rotary Club, Wythenshawe, 1975–76; Indian Assoc., Manchester, 1962–71. Mem. Bd and Trustee, Community Technical Aid Centre, Manchester, 1998–99 (Dir, 1992–97). *Publications:* research papers in various projects related to cardio/pulmonary disorders. *Address:* 15 Hunters Mews, Macclesfield Road, Wilmslow, Cheshire SK9 2AR. *T:* (01625) 522559.

CHATTERJEE, Prof. (Vengalil) Krishna (Kumar), FRCP; Professor of Endocrinology, University of Cambridge, since 1998; Fellow of Churchill College, Cambridge, since 1990; *b* 23 April 1958. *Educ:* Wolfson Coll., Oxford (BA, BM BCh). FRCP 1996. SHO, Hammersmith, Brompton and St Thomas' Hosps., 1983–85; Registrar, Hammersmith Hosp., 1985–87; Res. Fellow, Massachusetts Gen. Hosp., 1987–90; Wellcome Sen. Fellow and Hon. Cons. Physician, Addenbrooke's Hosp., 1994–. *Recreations:* travel, music. *Address:* Department of Medicine, University of Cambridge, Addenbrooke's Hospital, Hills Road, Cambridge CB2 2QQ.

CHATTO, Beth, VMH 1988; Creator and Managing Director of The Beth Chatto Gardens; *b* 27 June 1923; *d* of William George and Bessie Beatrice Little; *m* 1943, Andrew Edward Chatto (*d* 1999); two *d*. *Educ:* Colchester County High Sch.; Hockerill Training Coll. for Teachers. No formal horticultural educn; parents enthusiastic gardeners; husband's lifelong study of natural associations of plants was original inspiration in use of species plants in more natural groupings, thus introducing ecology into garden design; Sir Cedric Morris' knowledge and generosity with many rare plants from his rich collection at Benton End, Suffolk, became basis for gdns at Elmstead Market; began career demonstrating flower arranging; Beth Chatto Gardens, 1960–, Nursery, 1967–; a keen advocate of organic gardening and diet for over 40 yrs. Founder Mem., Colchester Flower Club (2nd Flower Club in England). Lectures throughout UK; lecture tours and talks: USA, 1983, 1984 and 1986; Holland and Germany, 1987; Australia and Toronto, 1989. DUniv Essex, 1988. Lawrence Meml Medal, RHS, 1988. *Publications:* The Dry Garden, 1978; The Damp Garden, 1982; Plant Portraits, 1985; The Beth Chatto Garden Notebook, 1988; The Green Tapestry, 1989 (also USA); (with Christopher Lloyd) Dear Friend and Gardener: letters exchanged between Beth Chatto and Christopher Lloyd, 1998; The Gravel Garden, 2000; articles in The Garden, The English Garden, Horticulture, Amer. Jl of Hort., Sunday Telegraph, and Hortus. *Recreations:* family, cooking, entertaining, music, reading—and always creating the garden. *Address:* The Beth Chatto Gardens, Elmstead Market, Colchester, Essex CO7 7DB. *T:* (01206) 822007.

CHATWANI, Jaswanti; Legal Chairman, Immigration Appeal Tribunal, since 2000 (Vice President, 1992–2000); *b* 23 Nov. 1933; *d* of Keshavji Ramji Tanna and Shantaben Tanna; *m* 1953, Rajnikant Popatlal Chatwani; one *s* one *d*. *Educ:* Government Sch., Dar-es-Salaam, Tanzania. Called to the Bar, Lincoln's Inn, 1959; attached to Chopra & Chopra, Legal Practice, Mwanza, Tanzania, 1959–60; in private practice, Zanzibar, 1960–65; Sec. and Legal Aid Counsel, Tanganyika Law Soc., 1965–68; in private practice, Dar-es-Salaam, Tanzania, 1968–70; Sen. Immigration Counsellor, UKIAS, 1971–78; Legal Officer, then Sen. Complaints Officer, CRE, 1979–87; part-time Adjudicator, Immigration Appeals, 1980–87, full-time Adjudicator 1987–92. Mem., Judicial Studies Bd, Ethnic Minorities Adv. Cttee, 1991–94. *Recreations:* walking, travel, reading.

CHATWIN, (John) Malcolm, CEng, FIEE; Chief Executive, Yorkshire Electricity Group, 1992–97; *b* 19 July 1945; *s* of John Edward Chatwin and Louie Valery Chatwin; *m* 1969, Elizabeth Joy West; one *s* two *d*. *Educ:* City of London Sch.; University College London (BSc(Eng) Elect. Eng.). Operations Engr, LEB, 1969–73; Commercial Economist, Seeboard, 1973–77; Pricing Policy Manager, Electricity Council, 1977–79; Dep. Commercial Dir and Commercial Dir, N of Scotland Hydro-Electric Bd, 1980–87; Yorkshire Electricity: Dir, Business Planning, 1987–90; Commercial Dir, 1990–92. Dir, Electricity Assoc., 1992–97; Chm., Regional Power Generators, 1992–94, 1996–97. Dir, Century Inns, 1995–99. CIMgt. *Recreations:* ski-ing, sailing.

CHAUDHRY, Mahendra Pal; MP, Fiji, 1987, 1992–99 and since 2001; Prime Minister of Fiji, 1999–2000; Minister for Finance, Public Enterprises, Sugar Industry and Information, 1999–2000; *b* 2 Sept. 1942; *m* Virmati Frank; two *s* one *d*. *Educ:* Tavua Indian Sch.; Shri Vivekananda High Sch. Assistant, Res. Lab., Emperor Gold Mines, 1959–60; Office of the Auditor Gen., 1960–75 (Sen. Auditor, 1973–75); General Secretary: Fiji Public Service Assoc., 1970–99; Nat. Farmers' Union, 1978–99. Asst Nat. Sec., 1975–87, Nat. Sec., 1988–92, Fiji TUC. Minister of Finance, April–May 1987. Fiji Labour Party: Founder Mem., 1985; Asst Sec.-Gen., 1985–94; Sec.-Gen. and Parly Leader, 1994–2001.

CHAUDHURI, Prof. Kirti Narayan, PhD; FBA 1990; FRHistS; Director: Centre of Comparative Studies, Provence, since 1999; Gallery Schifanoia, Mas de San Vitale, since 1999; *b* 8 Sept. 1934; *s* of late Nirad C. Chaudhuri, CBE, FRSL, FRAS; *m* 1961, Surang Chaudhuri; one *s*. *Educ:* privately in India; London Univ. (BA Hons Hist., 1959; PhD 1961). Derby Postgrad. Schol., London Univ., 1959–61; School of Oriental and African Studies, London University: Res. Fellow in Econ. Hist., 1961–63; Lectr in Econ. Hist. of Asia, 1963–74; Reader, 1974–81; Prof. of Econ. Hist. of Asia, 1981–91; Chairman: S Asia Area Studies Centre, 1982–85; History Exam. Bd, 1982–87; Vasco da Gama Prof. of Hist. of European Expansion, European Univ. Inst., Florence, 1991–99. FRHistS 1993; MAE 1994. D. João de Castro Internat. History Prize. *Publications:* The English East India Company: the study of an early joint-stock company 1600–1640, 1965; The Economic Development of India under the East India Company 1814–58: a selection of contemporary writings, 1971; The Trading World of Asia and the English East India Company 1660–1760, 1978; Trade and Civilisation in the Indian Ocean: an economic history from the rise of Islam to 1750, 1985; Asia before Europe: the economy and civilisation in the Indian Ocean from the rise of Islam to 1750, 1990; From the Atlantic to the Arabian Sea, 1995; The Dream of the Unicorn in the Year of Geneviève, 1996; A Mediterranean Triptych, 1998; The Landscape of the Corvo, 1998; (ed jtly) Historia Expansão Portuguesa, 5 vols, 1998–99; The Sacrifice, 2000; Venezia, the Vision of the Blind Gladiator, 2000; Interlace, Variations on Ornamental Space, 2001; contribs to Econ. Hist. Rev., Eng. Histl Rev., Jl of European Econ. Hist., Jl of RAS, Modern Asian Studies, TLS. *Recreations:* mountain walking, sailing, exploration, collecting modern prints and vintage watches, photography, wine tasting. *Address:* Centre of Comparative Studies, 14 Le Clos des Arts, rue du Crucifix, 84000 Avignon, France; Flat 8, 155 Arlington Road, NW1 7ET; *e-mail:* chaudhuri@mailandnews.co.uk. *Club:* Athenæum.

CHAUNY de PORTURAS-HOYLE, Gilbert; Ambassador of Peru to the Court of St James's, and to Ireland, 2000–01; *b* Lima, 8 March 1944; *m* 1971, Carmen Loreto; two *s* one *d*. *Educ:* UNI (BA Arch 1966); Pontificia Universidad Católica, Peru (BA Arts 1967); Peruvian Diplomatic Acad. (Dip. and Licentiate Internat. Relns 1969). Joined Peruvian Diplomatic Service, 1970: Third Secretary: Under-Secretariat for Political and Diplomatic Affairs, Dept of Europe, Africa, Asia and Oceania, Min. of Foreign Affairs, Lima, 1970–72; Bogotá, 1972–75; Second Sec., Perm. Representation to Internat. Orgns, Geneva, and Consul Gen., Geneva and Vaud, 1975–78; First Secretary: Head: of Ceremonials, Protocol Dept, 1978–79; OAS Dept, Dept for Internat. Orgns and Confs, 1979–80; Counsellor, Hd of Political Dept, Washington, 1980–84; Minister Counsellor: and Consul Gen., Toronto, 1984–86; Asst Dir for America, Min. of Foreign Affairs, 1986–88; Minister, Dir of Aeronautical and Space Affairs, Min. of Foreign Affairs, 1988–89 (Delegate to Internat. Civil Aviation Orgn, Montreal); Minister and Hd of Chancery, London, and Perm. Rep. to IMO, 1989–93 (Chargé d'Affaires, March–June 1989 and March–Nov. 1993); Ambassador: Dir Gen. of Special Pol Affairs, Min. of Foreign Affairs, 1993–95; to Austria, and concurrently to Slovenia, Slovakia and Turkey, 1995–2000; Perm. Rep. of Peru to UN Office, Vienna, UNIDO, IAEA and Comp. Nuclear Test-Ban Treaty Orgn, 1995–2000. President, National Commission: for Antarctic Affairs, 1993–95; for Biol Diversity, 1993–95; for Climatic Changes and Ozone, 1993–95. Member: Peruvian Inst. for Genealogical Res., 1962–; Peruvian Inst. Aerospace Law, 1994–2000. Mem., Confrérie des Chevaliers du Tastevin. Dir (Counsellor), Peruvian Assoc. of Kts of SMO, Malta. Kt, SMO (Malta), 1988; Kt Comdr, Orden de Bogotá (Colombia), 1974; Official: Order of San Carlos (Colombia), 1975; Orden de Isabel la Católica (Spain), 1978; Grand Cross, Orden del Condor de los Andes (Bolivia), 1995; Gold Grand Cross, Honour Badge for Merit (Austria), 2000. *Publications:* contrib. books and periodicals on internat. diplomatic relns, protocol, hist. of art, hist., and genealogy. *Recreations:* art and old map collecting, historical and genealogical research, tennis, bridge. *Address:* c/o Embassy of Peru, 52 Sloane Street, SW1X 9SP. *Clubs:* Canning, Naval and Military, Travellers, Brooks's, Carlton; Nacional, Regatas (Lima); St Johanns (Vienna).

CHAUVIRÉ, Yvette, Commandeur de la Légion d'Honneur, 1988 (Officier, 1974); Commandeur des Arts et des Lettres, 1975; Grand Croix, Ordre National du Mérite, 1998 (Officier, 1972; Commandeur, 1981); ballerina assoluta, since 1950; *b* Paris, 22 April 1917. *Educ:* Ecole de la Danse de l'Opéra, Paris. Paris Opera Ballet, 1931; first major rôles in David Triomphant and Les Créatures de Prométhée; Danseuse étoile 1942; danced Istar, 1941; Monte Carlo Opera Ballet, 1946–47; returned to Paris Opera Ballet, 1947–49. Has appeared at Covent Garden, London; also danced in the USA, and in cities of Rome, Moscow, Leningrad, Berlin, Buenos Aires, Johannesburg, Milan, etc; official tours: USA 1948; USSR 1958, 1966, 1969; Canada 1967; Australia. Leading rôles in following ballets: Les Mirages, Lac des Cygnes, Sleeping Beauty, Giselle, Roméo et Juliette, Suite en Blanc, Le Cygne (St Saens), La Dame aux Camélias, etc; Giselle, Moscow, 1966 (guest for 125th anniversary celebration); acting rôle, Reine Léda, Amphitryon 38, Paris, 1976–77; La

Comtessa de Doris in Raymonda, Paris, 1983. Choreographer: La Péri, Roméo et Juliette, Le Cygne; farewell performances: Paris Opera, Giselle, Nov. 1972, Petrouchka and The Swan, Dec. 1972; Berlin Opera, Giselle, 1973; Artistic and Tech. Adviser, Paris Opera, 1963–72, teacher of dance for style and perfection, 1970–; Acad. Internat. de la Danse, Paris, 1972–76; Artistic Dir, Acad. ARIMA, Kyoto, Japan, 1980–81. *Films:* La Mort du Cygne, 1937 (Paris); Carrousel Napolitain, 1953 (Rome); Dominique Delouche présente un grand portrait sur Yvette Chauviré, une Etoile pour l'exemple, 1988. *Publication:* Je suis Ballerine. *Recreations:* painting and drawing, collections of swans. *Address:* 21 Place du Commerce, Paris 75015, France.

CHAVASSE, Christopher Patrick Grant; *b* 14 March 1928; *s* of late Grant Chavasse and of Maureen Shingler (*née* Whalley); *m* 1955, Audrey Mary Leonard; two *s* one *d*. *Educ:* Bedford Sch.; Clare Coll., Cambridge (Exhibitioner; MA). Commissioned The Rifle Brigade, 1947; served in Palestine (despatches), 1948; RAFVR 1949. Admitted Solicitor, 1955; Partner: Jacobs & Greenwood, 1960; Woodham Smith, 1970; President, Holborn Law Soc., 1977–78. Clerk, 1981–88, Hon. Liveryman, 1988–, Grocers' Co. Chairman: NADFAS Tours Ltd, 1986–92; Totnes DFAS, 1993–96; Vice-President: NADFAS, 1992–97; Chiltern DFAS, 1986–. Hon. Steward of Westminster Abbey, 1950–; Treasurer, St Mary-le-Bow Church, 1981–88. Secretary: Governing Body of Oundle and Laxton Schs, 1981–88; The Grocers' Charity, 1981–88. Mem. Ct, Corp. of Sons of the Clergy, 1985–. *Publications:* Conveyancing Costs, 1971; Non-Contentious Costs, 1975; The Discretionary Items in Contentious Costs, 1980; various articles in Law Society's Gazette, New Law Jl, Solicitors Jl, and others. *Address:* Duncannon House, Stoke Gabriel, Totnes, Devon TQ9 6QY. *T:* (01803) 782291. *Clubs:* Royal Air Force; Leander.

CHÁVEZ FRÍAS, Hugo Rafael; President of Venezuela, since 1999; *b* 28 July 1954; *s* of Hugo de los Reyes Chávez and Elena de Chávez; *m* Maria Isabel Rodriguez; two *s* three *d*. *Educ:* Liceo O'Leary, Barinas State; Venezuelan Military Acad., Caracas (grad. 1975); Univ. Simón Bolívar, Caracas. Paratrooper, Venezuelan Army (Lt-Col). Jt Founder, Movimiento Revolucionario Bolivariano 200, 1982; led failed mil. coup against Pres. Carlos Pérez, 1992 (imprisoned); Founder, Movimiento Quinta República, 1997. *Address:* Central Information Office of the Presidency, Torre Oeste 18°, Parque Central, Caracas 1010, Venezuela.

CHAYTOR, David Michael; MP (Lab) Bury North, since 1997; *b* 3 Aug. 1949; *m*; one *s* two *d*. *Educ:* Bury Grammar Sch.; Royal Holloway Coll., London (BA Hons 1970); Leeds Univ. (PGCE 1976); London Univ. (MPhil 1979). Sen. Staff Tutor, Manchester Coll. of Adult Educn, 1983–90; Hd, Dept of Continuing Educn, Manchester Coll. of Arts and Technology, 1993–97. Mem., Calderdale DC, 1982–97. Contested (Lab) Calder Valley, 1987, 1992. *Address:* House of Commons, SW1A 0AA.

CHAYTOR, Sir George Reginald, 8th Bt *cr* 1831; *b* 28 Oct. 1912; *s* of William Richard Carter Chaytor (*d* 1973) (*g s* of 2nd Bt) and Anna Laura (*d* 1947), *d* of George Fawcett; *S* cousin, Sir William Henry Clervaux Chaytor, 7th Bt, 1976. *Heir: cousin* (Herbert) Gordon Chaytor [*b* 15 June 1922; *m* 1947, Mary Alice, *d* of Thomas Craven; three *s*].

CHAZOT, Georges-Christian; international consultant; *b* 19 March 1939; *s* of late Raymond Chazot, banker and Suzanne Monnet; *m* 1962, Marie-Dominique Tremois, painter; one *s* two *d*. *Educ:* Lycée Gauthier; Lycée Bugeaud Algiers; Ecole Polytechnique, Paris; Univ. of Florida (MSEE 1964); Internat. Marketing Inst., Harvard, 1972. Joined Schlumberger Group, 1962; Electro-Mechanical Research, USA, 1962–65; Schlumberger Instrument and Systems, 1965–76; Alcatel Alsthom, 1977–92; Saft, 1977–88; Chairman and Chief Executive: Saft, 1984; Alcatel Business Systems, 1990; Adia France, 1992–93; Gp Man. Dir, Eurotunnel, 1994–2000. Director: Actim, Paris, 1988–92; Fondn Franco Japonaise Sasakawa, 1990–; Dir and former Dir, internat. cos. Mem., Adv. Council, World Economic Forum, Switzerland, 1983–87; Vice-Pres., French Chamber of Commerce in London, 1995. FCIT 1995. Chevalier, Légion d'honneur, 1990; Officier, Ordre National du Mérite (France), 1996. *Recreations:* sailing, ski-ing.

CHECKETTS, Sir David (John), KCVO 1979 (CVO 1969; MVO 1966); Squadron Leader, retired; an Extra Equerry to the Prince of Wales, since 1979; *b* 23 Aug. 1930; 3rd *s* of late Reginald Ernest George Checketts and late Frances Mary Checketts; *m* 1958, Rachel Leila Warren Herrick; one *s* three *d*. Flying Training, Bulawayo, Rhodesia, 1948–50; 14 Sqdn, Germany, 1950–54; Instructor, Fighter Weapons Sch., 1954–57; Air ADC to C-in-C Malta, 1958–59; 3 Sqdn, Germany, 1960–61; Equerry to Duke of Edinburgh, 1961–66, to the Prince of Wales, 1967–70; Private Sec. to the Prince of Wales, 1970–79. Chm., Rainbow Boats Trust. *Recreation:* ornithology. *Address:* Church Cottage, Winkfield, Windsor, Berks SL4 4SF. *T:* (01344) 890517. *Club:* Whitefriars.

CHECKETTS, Guy Tresham, CBE 1982; Deputy Chairman and Managing Director, Hawker Siddeley International, 1975–90, retired; *b* 11 May 1927; *s* of John Albert and Norah Maud Checketts; *m* 1957, Valerie Cynthia Stanley; four *s*. *Educ:* Warwick Sch.; Birmingham Univ. (BScEng Hons). British Thompson Houston Co., Rugby, 1948–51; Brush Group, 1951–57; Hawker Siddeley International, 1957–90. Chm., SE Asia Trade Adv. Gp, 1979–83; Mem., BOTB, 1981–84. *Recreation:* sailing. *Club:* Royal Over-Seas League.

CHECKLAND, Sir Michael, Kt 1992; Director-General, BBC, 1987–92; Chairman, Higher Education Funding Council for England, 1997–2001; *b* 13 March 1936; *s* of Leslie and Ivy Florence Checkland; *m* 1st, 1960, Shirley Frances Corbett (marr. diss. 1983); two *s* one *d*; 2nd, 1987, Sue Zetter. *Educ:* King Edward's Grammar Sch., Fiveways, Birmingham; Wadham Coll., Oxford (BA Modern History; Hon. Fellow, 1989). FCMA; CIMgt. Accountant: Parkinson Cowan Ltd, 1959–62; Thorn Electronics Ltd, 1962–64; BBC: Senior Cost Accountant, 1964; Head of Central Finance Unit, 1967; Chief Accountant, Central Finance Services, 1969; Chief Accountant, Television, 1971; Controller, Finance, 1976; Controller, Planning and Resource Management, Television, 1977; Director of Resources, Television, 1982; Dep. Dir-Gen., 1985; Director: BBC Enterprises, 1979–92 (Chm., 1986–87); Visnews, 1980–85; Nynex Cable Communications, 1995–97. President: Commonwealth Broadcasting Assoc., 1987–88; Birmingham & Midland Inst., 1994; Vice-President: RTS, 1985–94 (FRTS 1987); EBU, 1991–92; Mem., ITC, 1997–. Chairman: NCH Action for Children, 1991–2001; Brighton Internat. Fest., 1993–; CBSO, 1995–2001; Dir, Nat. Youth Music Theatre, 1992–; Trustee, Reuters, 1994–. Governor: Westminster Coll., Oxford, 1993–97; Birkbeck Coll., 1993–97; Brighton Univ., 1996–97. *Recreations:* sport, music, travel. *Address:* Orchard Cottage, Park Lane, Maplehurst, near Horsham, West Sussex RH13 6LL.

CHECKLEY, Prof. Stuart Arthur, FRCPsych; Consultant Psychiatrist, Maudsley Hospital, since 1981; Dean, 1989–2001, and Professor of Psychoneuroendocrinology, 1994–2001, now Emeritus, Institute of Psychiatry; *b* 15 Dec. 1945; *s* of Arthur William George Checkley and Hilda Dorothy Checkley; *m* 1971, Marilyn Jane Evans, BA; one *s* one *d*. *Educ:* St Albans Sch.; Brasenose Coll., Oxford (BA, BM BCh). FRCP, FRCPsych. House appts, London Hosp. and St Charles Hosp., 1970–73; Registrar in Psych., London Hosp., 1973–74; Maudsley Hospital: Registrar, 1974–76; Hon. Sen. Registrar, 1977–78; Hon. Consultant, 1980–81; research worker, supported by Wellcome Trust, 1978–81; Mapother Travelling Fellow, USA, 1979; Institute of Psychiatry: Sen. Lectr, 1979–81; Sen. Lectr, Metabolic Unit, 1985–94. Non-exec. Dir, S London and Maudsley NHS Trust, 1999–. FKC. *Publications:* (ed) The Management of Depression, 1998; papers on treatment of depression and hormones in relation to depression. *Recreation:* bird watching. *Address:* Institute of Psychiatry, De Crespigny Park, SE5 8AF. *T:* (020) 7836 5454.

CHEDLOW, Barry William; QC 1969; a Recorder of the Crown Court, 1974–96; Member, Criminal Injuries Compensation Board, 1976–96; *b* Macclesfield, 8 Oct. 1921; *m* Anne Sheldon, BA; one *s* one *d*. *Educ:* Burnage High Sch.; Manchester Univ.; Birkbeck Coll., London (BA Hons German 1997). Served RAF, 1941–46: USAAF, Flying Instructor, 1942; Flt-Lt 1943. Called to Bar, Middle Temple, 1947, Bencher, 1976; Prizeman in Law of Evidence. Practises in London, Midland and Oxford Circuit; arbitrator in aviation disputes. *Publications:* author and editor of various legal text-books. *Recreations:* flying (private pilot's licence, singles, twins, helicopters), languages, sailing. *Address:* Little Kimblewick Farm, Finch Lane, Amersham, Bucks HP7 9NB. *T:* (01494) 762156. *Club:* Royal Air Force.

CHEESEMAN, Prof. Ian Clifford, PhD; ARCS; CEng, FRAeS; Professor of Helicopter Engineering, University of Southampton, 1970–82, now Emeritus; consultant in aeronautical, acoustic and general engineering matters; *b* 12 June 1926; *s* of Richard Charles Cheeseman and Emily Ethel Clifford; *m* 1957, Margaret Edith Pither; one *s* two *d*. *Educ:* Andover Grammar Sch.; Imperial Coll. of Science and Technology. Vickers Supermarine Ltd, 1951–53; Aeroplane and Armament Estab., 1953–56; Atomic Weapons Res. Estab., 1956–58; Nat. Gas Turbine Estab., 1958–70. Res. Dir, 1983–87, Dir and Consultant, 1987–88, Stewart Hughes Ltd, Southampton. Pres., Airship Assoc., 1986–94. *Publications:* (contrib.) Airship Technology, 1999; contribs to Jl RAeS, Jl CIT, Jl Sound and Vibration, Procs Phys. Soc. 'A', Vertica. *Recreations:* dog breeding, gardening, photography, historical research. *Address:* Abbey View, Tarrant Keynston, Blandford Forum, Dorset DT11 9JE. *T:* (01258) 456877.

CHEESMAN, Colin; Chief Executive and County Clerk, Cheshire County Council, since 1998; *b* 8 Nov. 1946; *s* of John Hamilton Cheesman and Elsie Louisa Cheesman; *m* 1969, Judith Mary Tait; one *s* three *d*. *Educ:* Alleyn's Sch., Dulwich; Liverpool Univ. (LLB Hons). Admitted Solicitor, 1971. Portsmouth County BC, 1969–71; Notts CC, 1971–73; joined Cheshire CC, 1973; Group Director: Support Services, 1991–94; Information and Leisure Services, 1994–97. Clerk, Cheshire Lieutenancy and Sec. to Cheshire Adv. Cttee, 1998–; Sec. and Solicitor, Cheshire Fire Authy, 1998–; Sec., Cheshire Probation Cttee, 1998–. Mem. Court, Univ. of Liverpool, 1999–. *Recreations:* reading, hill walking, keeping fit, squash, theatre. *Address:* County Hall, Chester CH1 1SF. *T:* (01244) 602101; 7 Radnor Drive, Westminster Park, Chester CH4 7PS. *T:* (01244) 678866.

CHEETHAM, Anthony John Valerian; Chief Executive, Orion Publishing Group Ltd (formerly Orion Books), since 1991; *b* 12 April 1943; *s* of Sir Nicolas Cheetham, *qv*; *m* 1st, 1969, Julia Rollason (marr. diss.); two *s* one *d*; 2nd, 1979, Rosemary de Courcy (marr. diss.); two *d*; 3rd, 1997, Georgina Capel. *Educ:* Eton Coll.; Balliol Coll., Oxford (BA). Editorial Dir, Sphere Books, 1968; Managing Director: Futura Publications, 1973; Macdonald Futura, 1979; Chm., Century Publishing, 1982–85; Man. Dir, Century Hutchinson, 1985; Chm. and Chief Exec., Random Century Gp, 1989–91. *Publication:* Richard III, 1972. *Recreations:* walking, tennis, gardening. *Address:* Orion Publishing Group Ltd, Orion House, 5 Upper St Martin's Lane, WC2H 9EA. *T:* (020) 7240 3444.

CHEETHAM, Prof. Anthony Kevin, FRS 1994; FRSC; Director, Materials Research Laboratory, since 1992, Professor of Materials, since 1991, and Professor of Chemistry, since 1992, University of California at Santa Barbara; Professor of Solid State Chemistry, Royal Institution, since 1986; Emeritus Student, Christ Church, Oxford, since 1991; *b* 16 Nov. 1946; *s* of Norman James Cheetham and Lilian Cheetham; *m* 1984, Janet Clare (*née* Stockwell); one *s* one *d*, and one *s* one *d* from a previous marriage. *Educ:* Stockport Grammar Sch.; St Catherine's Coll., Oxford (Hon. Scholar); Wadham Coll., Oxford (Sen. Scholar). BA (Chem.) 1968; DPhil 1971. University of Oxford: Cephalosporin Fellow, Lincoln Coll., 1971–74; Lectr in Inorganic Chem., St Hilda's Coll., 1971–85; Lectr in Chemical Crystallography, 1974–90; Tutor in Inorganic Chem., Christ Church, 1974–91; Reader in Inorganic Materials, 1990–91. Visiting Professor: Arizona State Univ., 1977; Univ. of California, Berkeley, 1979; Blaise Pascal Internat. Res. Prof., Paris, 1997–99; Vis. Foreign Scientist, Amer. Chem. Soc., 1981. Mem. Scientific Council, Institut Laue-Langevin, Grenoble, 1988–90. Dir, Gen. Funds Investment Trust plc, 1984–87. Foreign Mem., Indian Nat. Acad. of Scis, 1998; Foreign Fellow, Pakistan Acad. of Scis, 1997; Distinguished Fellow, Nehru Center for Advanced Scientific Res., Bangalore, 1999. Corday-Morgan Medal and Prize, 1982, Solid State Chemistry Award, 1988, Structural Chemistry Award, 1996, RSC. *Publications:* Solid State Chemistry: techniques (with P. Day), 1986; Solid State Chemistry: compounds (with P. Day), 1992; contribs to sci. jls. *Recreations:* cricket, stock market. *Address:* Materials Research Laboratory, University of California, Santa Barbara, CA 93106, USA. *T:* (805) 8938767, *Fax:* (805) 8938797; *e-mail:* cheetham@mrl.ucsb.edu. (home) 1695 East Valley Road, Montecito, CA 93108, USA. *T:* (805) 5651211.

CHEETHAM, Francis William, OBE 1979; FMA; arts and museums consultant, since 1991; Director, Norfolk Museums Service, 1974–90; *b* 5 Feb. 1928; *s* of Francis Cheetham and Doris Elizabeth Jones; *m* 1954, Monica Fairhurst; three *s* one *d*. *Educ:* King Edward VII Sch., Sheffield; Univ. of Sheffield (MA). Dep. Art Dir and Curator, Castle Museum, Nottingham, 1960–63; Dir, City of Norwich Museums, 1963–74. Winston Churchill Fellow, 1967. Member: Management Cttee, Norfolk and Norwich Triennial Fest., 1966–89; Crafts Council, 1978–81; Management Cttee, Eastern Arts Assoc., 1978–79, 1987–89; Bd, Norwich Puppet Theatre, 1981–87; Founder Mem., National Heritage, 1970; Chairman: Norfolk and Norwich Film Theatre, 1968–70; Norfolk Contemporary Crafts Soc., 1972–85 and 1991–94 (Life Pres., 1985); Melton Arts Trust, 1990–92. Museums Association: AMA 1959; FMA 1966; Hon. Treasurer, 1970–73; Vice-Pres., 1977–78, 1979–80; Pres., 1978–79; Chm., Soc. of County Museum Dirs, 1974–77; Museum Advr to ACC, 1976–84. Member: Exec. Bd, ICOM (UK), 1981–84; Bd, Radio Broadland (ILR Station), 1983–96. FRSA 1986. *Publications:* Medieval English Alabaster Carvings in the Castle Museum, Nottingham, 1962, revd edn 1973; English Medieval Alabasters, 1984; contrib. Jl of Museums Assoc. *Recreations:* hill-walking, listening to music, especially early and baroque. *T:* (01603) 434091.

CHEETHAM, Prof. Juliet, OBE 1995; Social Work Commissioner, Mental Welfare Commission for Scotland, since 1998; *b* 12 Oct. 1939; *d* of Harold Neville Blair and Isabel (*née* Sanders); *m* 1965, Christopher Paul Cheetham; one *s* two *d*. *Educ:* St Andrews Univ. (MA); Oxford Univ. (Dip. in Social and Admin. Studies). Qual. social worker. Probation Officer, Inner London, 1960–65; Lectr in Applied Social Studies, and Fellow of Green Coll., Oxford Univ., 1965–85; Prof. and Dir, Social Work Res. Centre, Stirling Univ., 1986–95, now Prof. Emeritus; Contract Res. Co-ordinator, SHEFC, 1996–97; Devlt Officer, E Lothian Council, 1998. Member: Cttee of Enquiry into Immigration and

Youth Service, 1966–68; Cttee of Enquiry into Working of Abortion Act, 1971–74; NI Standing Adv. Commn on Human Rights, 1974–77; Central Council for Educn and Trng in Social Work, 1973–89; Commn for Racial Equality, 1977–84; Social Security Adv. Cttee, 1983–88; CNAA Social Scis Cttee, 1989–91; ESRC Res. Resources Bd, 1993–96. Vice-Chm., Social Policy and Social Work Panel, HEFCE Res. Assessment Exercise, 1996. *Publications:* Social Work with Immigrants, 1972; Unwanted Pregnancy and Counselling, 1977; Social Work and Ethnicity, 1982; Social Work with Black Children and their Families, 1986; (jtly) Evaluating Social Work Effectiveness, 1992; (jtly) The Working of Social Work, 1998; contrib. collected papers and prof. jls. *Recreation:* canal boats. *Address:* Peffermill House, 91 Peffermill Road, Edinburgh EH16 5UX. *T:* (0131) 661 0948.

CHEETHAM, Sir Nicolas (John Alexander), KCMG 1964 (CMG 1953); *b* 8 Oct. 1910; *s* of late Sir Milne Cheetham, KCMG, and late Mrs Nigel Law, CBE, DStJ; *m* 1st, 1937, Jean Evison Corfe (marr. diss. 1960); two *s*; 2nd, 1960, Lady Mabel Brooke (*née* Jocelyn). *Educ:* Eton College; Christ Church, Oxford. Entered HM Diplomatic Service, 1934; served in Foreign Office and at Athens, Buenos Aires, Mexico City and Vienna; UK Deputy Permanent Representative on North Atlantic Council, 1954–59; HM Minister to Hungary, 1959–61; Assistant Under-Secretary, Foreign Office, 1961–64; Ambassador to Mexico, 1964–68. *Publications:* A History of Mexico, 1970; New Spain, 1974; Mediaeval Greece, 1981; Keepers of the Keys: the Pope in history, 1982. *Address:* 50 Cadogan Square, SW1X 0JW. *T:* (020) 7589 5624. *Club:* Travellers.
See also A. J. V. Cheetham.

CHEETHAM, Ven. Dr Richard Ian; Archdeacon of St Albans, since 1999; *b* 18 Aug. 1955; *s* of John Brian Margrave Cheetham and Mollie Louise Cheetham; *m* 1977, Felicity Mary Loving; one *s* one *d*. *Educ:* Kingston Grammar Sch.; Corpus Christi Coll., Oxford (MA, PGCE); Ripon Coll., Cuddesdon (Cert. Theol. 1987); Kings Coll., London (PhD 1999). Science Teacher, Richmond Sch., N Yorks, 1978–80; Physics Master, Eton Coll., 1980–83; Investment Analyst, Legal & General, London, 1983–85; ordained deacon, 1987, priest 1988; Asst Curate, Holy Cross, Fenham, Newcastle upon Tyne, 1987–90; Vicar, St Augustine of Canterbury, Luton, 1990–99; RD of Luton, 1995–98. *Recreations:* hockey, squash, tennis, walking, theatre, cinema. *Address:* 6 Sopwell Lane, St Albans, Herts AL1 1RR. *T:* (01727) 847212.

CHEEVERS, William Harold; Director of Engineering, Granada Television, 1970–73, retired; *b* 20 June 1918; *m* 1964, Shirley Cheevers; one *s*; *m* 1999, Marion Cheevers. *Educ:* Christ's Coll., London. Engineer, BBC Television, 1938–39. War Service, Army, PoW, 1941–45. Sen. Engr, BBC Television, 1946–54; Planning Engr, Radio-Corp. of America, in USA and Canada, 1954–55; Head of Engineering, Associated Rediffusion, 1955–60; Gen. Manager, Westward Television, Jt Man. Dir, 1963–67, Man. Dir, 1967–70; Dir, ITN News, 1967–70, and of IT Publications; also Director: Keith Prowse, 1963–70; Direct Line Services, 1964–87; Prowest, 1967–70; Penwell Ltd, 1971–88. Chm., British Regional Television Assoc., 1968–69. Fellow British Kinematograph Soc.; MInstD; MIMgt; AssIEE. *Publications:* articles for most TV Jls, and Symposiums, at home and abroad. *Recreations:* boating, golf, reading. *Address:* 52 Preston Down Road, Paignton, Devon TQ3 1DU. *T:* (01803) 524455. *Club:* Royal Western Yacht Club of England (Plymouth).

CHEFFINS, Prof. Brian Robert; S. J. Berwin Professor of Corporate Law, and Fellow of Trinity Hall, University of Cambridge, since 1998; *b* 21 Jan. 1961; *s* of Ronald Ian Cheffins and Sylvia Joy Cheffins; *m* 1992, Joanna Hilary Thurstans; one *d*. *Educ:* Univ. of Victoria, BC (BA, LLB); Trinity Hall, Cambridge (LLM). Faculty of Law, University of British Columbia, Vancouver: Asst Prof., 1986–91; Associate Prof., 1991–97; Prof., 1997. Vis. Fellow, Duke Univ., 2000. *Publication:* Company Law: theory, structure and operation, 1997 (SPTL Prize, 1998). *Address:* Faculty of Law, University of Cambridge, 10 West Road, Cambridge CB3 9DZ. *T:* (01223) 330084; *e-mail:* brc21@cam.ac.uk.

CHELMSFORD, 4th Viscount *cr* 1921, of Chelmsford, co. Essex; **Frederic Corin Piers Thesiger;** Baron Chelmsford 1858; *b* 6 March 1962; *o s* of 3rd Viscount Chelmsford and of Clare Rendle, *d* of Dr G. R. Rolston; *S* father, 1999. *Heir:* (to Barony only) *kinsman* Sir Wilfred Thesiger, *qv*. *Address:* 4/4 Hampstead Hill Gardens, NW3 2PL.

CHELMSFORD, Bishop of, since 1996; **Rt Rev. John Freeman Perry;** *b* 15 June 1935; *s* of Richard and Elsie Perry; *m* 1959, Gay Valerie Brown; three *s* two *d*. *Educ:* Mill Hill School; London College of Divinity (ALCD). LTh St John's Coll., Nottingham, 1974; MPhil Westminster Coll., Oxford, 1986. Assistant Curate: Christ Church, Woking, 1959–62; Christ Church, Chorleywood, 1962–63; Vicar, St Andrew's, Chorleywood, 1963–77; RD of Rickmansworth, 1972–77; Warden, Lee Abbey, Lynton, Devon, 1977–89; RD of Shirwell, 1980–84; Suffragan Bishop of Southampton, 1989–96. Hon. Canon, Winchester Cathedral, 1989–96. *Publication:* Christian Leadership, 1983. *Recreations:* a large family, walking, sport, travel, classical music, film reviews. *Address:* Bishopscourt, Margaretting, Ingatestone, Essex CM4 0HD.

CHELMSFORD, Dean of; *see* Judd, Very Rev. P. S. M.

CHELSEA, Viscount; Edward Charles Cadogan; *b* 10 May 1966; *s* and *heir* of 8th Earl Cadogan, *qv*; *m* 1990, Katharina Johanna Ingeborg, *d* of Rear-Adm. D. P. A. Hülsemann; two *s* one *d*. *Educ:* St David's Coll., Llandudno. Joined RAF, 1987; served Germany, UK and Cyprus; Flt Lt. Gulf War Medal with Clasp, 1991. *Recreations:* country pursuits, ski-ing, rock climbing, hill walking. *Heir:* *s* Hon. George Edward Charles Diether Cadogan, *b* 24 Sept. 1995. *Club:* Royal Air Force.

CHELTENHAM, Archdeacon of; *see* Ringrose, Ven. H. S.

CHELTON, Captain Lewis William Leonard, RN; Secretary, Engineering Council, 1987–97; *b* 19 Dec. 1934; *s* of Lewis Walter Chelton and Doris May Chelton (*née* Gamblin); *m* 1957, Daphne Joan Landon; three *s*. *Educ:* Royal Naval College, Dartmouth. Called to the Bar, Inner Temple, 1966. Entered RN as Cadet, 1951; served in ships and shore estabts, home and abroad; Fleet Supply Officer, 1979–81; Captain, 1981; Chief Naval Judge Advocate, 1982–84; retired (voluntarily), 1987. Dep. Chm., Taunton Constituency Cons. Assoc., 1999–. Vice-Chm., R. S. Surtees Soc. Gov., Bruton Sch. for Girls, 1999–. *Recreations:* shooting, gardening, country life. *Address:* Palmers Green House, Hatch Beauchamp, near Taunton, Som TA3 6AE. *T:* (01823) 480221. *Club:* Farmers'.

CHENERY, Peter James; Director and Cultural Counsellor, British Council, Canada, since 2000; *b* 24 Oct. 1946; *s* of Dudley James Chenery and Brenda Dorothy (*née* Redford); *m* 1979, Alice Blanche Faulder; three *d*. *Educ:* Forest Sch.; Christ Church, Oxford (MA); SOAS, London Univ. Teacher, Ghana Teaching Service, 1967–70; joined British Council, 1970: Amman, 1971–73; Middle East Dept, 1973–76; Riyadh, 1977; Freetown, 1978–80; Jedda, 1981–84; Sana'a, 1984–88; Munich, 1988–90; Sec. and Hd of Public Affairs, 1990–97; Dir and Cultural Counsellor, Greece, 1997–2000. Associate Mem., St Antony's Coll., Oxford, 2000. FRSA 1996. *Recreations:* amusing conversation, beers of the world, early English coins. *Address:* c/o Foreign and Commonwealth Office, King Charles Street, SW1A 2AH. *Club:* Leander.

CHENEY, Richard Bruce; Vice-President of the United States of America, since 2001; *b* 30 Jan. 1941; *s* of Richard H. Cheney and Marjorie Dickey Cheney; *m* 1964, Lynne Ann Vincent; two *d*. *Educ:* Casper Elementary Sch.; Natrona County High Sch.; Univ. of Wyoming (BA 1965; MA 1966); Univ. of Wisconsin. Public service, Wyoming, 1965–69; Federal service, 1969–73; Vice-Pres., Bradley Woods, 1973–74; Dep. Asst to Pres. Ford, 1974–75; Asst to Pres. Ford and White House Chief of Staff, 1975–77; Mem. (Republican) for Wyoming House of Representatives, 1978–89; Chm., Repub. Policy Cttee, 1981, Repub. House Conf., 1987; Repub. House Whip, 1988; Sec. of Defense, USA, 1989–93; Mem., Cttees on Interior and Insular Affairs, Intelligence, Iran Arms Deals. Sen. Fellow, Amer. Enterprise Inst., 1993–95. Chm. Bd, and CEO, Halliburton Co., 1995–2000. *Publication:* (with Lynne V. Cheney) Kings of the Hill, 1983. *Address:* The White House, Washington, DC 20501, USA.

CHERNAIK, Judith Sheffield, PhD; writer; Founder, Secretary, and Co-Editor, Poems on the Underground, since 1986; *b* 24 Oct. 1934; *d* of Reuben Sheffield and Gertrude Lapidus; *m* 1956, Warren Lewis Chernaik; one *s* two *d*. *Educ:* Cornell Univ. (BA); Yale Univ. (PhD). Instr in English, Columbia Univ., 1963–65; Asst Prof. of English, Tufts Univ., 1965–69 (Scholar, Radcliffe Inst., 1966–68); Lectr, QMW, Univ. of London, 1975–88. Writer: features and documentaries for BBC Radio; The Two Marys (play), perf. in London and Bologna, 1997. Fellow, Amer. Council of Learned Socs, 1972. *Publications:* The Lyrics of Shelley, 1972; *novels:* Double Fault, 1975; The Daughter, 1979; Leah, 1987; Mab's Daughters, 1991 (US title, Love's Children, 1992; trans Italian, 1997); *poetry anthologies:* (ed jtly) 100 Poems on the Underground, 1991, (ed) 9th edn, Poems on the Underground, 1999; (ed) Reflecting Families, 1995; reviews and essays in TLS, London Magazine, The Times, New York Times, Guardian, etc. *Recreations:* chamber music, tennis. *Address:* 124 Mansfield Road, NW3 2JB.

CHERRY, Alan Herbert, MBE 1984; FRICS; Founder Director, 1971, and Chairman, since 1981, Countryside Properties plc; *b* 4 Aug. 1933; *s* of William Alfred Cherry and Helen Grace (*née* Parrish); *m* 1976, Fay Angela Robbins; two *s*. *Educ:* Mayfield Sch. Founder Partner, Bairstow Eves, 1958–81; Dep. Chm., Workspace Gp plc, 1987–. Member: Inquiry into British Housing, 1985–87; Urban Task Force, 1998–99. Dir, E of England Investment Agency, 1997–; Mem. Bd, E of England Develt Agency, 1998–. Nat. Pres., House Builders' Fedn, 1988. Chm. Govs, Anglia Poly. Univ., 1988–. Hon. MRTPI 1991. *Recreations:* ski-ing, walking, swimming. *Address:* (office) Countryside House, The Drive, Brentwood, Essex CM13 3AT. *T:* (01277) 260000.

CHERRY, Bridget Katherine, FSA; Editor: Buildings of England, since 1983; Buildings of Scotland, Ireland and Wales, since 1991; *b* 17 May 1941; *d* of Norman Stayner Marsh, *qv*; *m* 1966, John Cherry, *qv*; one *s* one *d*. *Educ:* Oxford High Sch. for Girls; Lady Margaret Hall, Oxford (BA Modern Hist.); Courtauld Inst. of Art, Univ. of London (Dip. Hist. of Art). FSA 1980. Asst Librarian, Conway Library, Courtauld Inst., 1964–68; Res. Asst to Sir Nikolaus Pevsner, Buildings of England, 1968–83. Mem., Royal Commn on Historical Monuments of England, 1987–94; English Heritage. Commr, 1992–2001; Mem., London Adv. Cttee, 1985–99; Mem., Historic Buildings Adv. Cttee, 1986–. Trustee, Sir John Soane's Mus., 1994–. Hon. FRIBA 1993. *Publications:* reviser or part author, 2nd edns, Buildings of England series, incl. Wiltshire, 1975, Hertfordshire, 1977, London 2: South, 1983, Devon, 1989, London 3: North West, 1991, London 4: North, 1998; articles and reviews on arch. subjects in learned jls. *Recreation:* walking. *Address:* Buildings of England, Penguin Books, 27 Wrights Lane, W8 5TZ. *T:* (020) 7416 3201.

CHERRY, Colin; Director of Operations, Inland Revenue, 1985–90; *b* 20 Nov. 1931; *s* of late Reginald Cherry and Dorothy (*née* Brooks); *m* 1958, Marjorie Rose Harman; two *d*. *Educ:* Hymers Coll., Hull. Joined Inland Revenue, 1950; HM Inspector of Taxes, 1960; Under Sec., 1985. Fiscal Advr, IMF, 1994–99. Chm., CS Retirement Fellowship, 1992–94. *Recreations:* music, chrysanthemums, photography.

CHERRY, John, FSA, FRHistS; Keeper, Department of Medieval and Modern Europe (formerly of Medieval and Later Antiquities), British Museum, since 1998; *b* 5 Aug. 1942; *s* of Edwin Lewis Cherry and Vera Edith Blanche (*née* Bunn); *m* 1966, Bridget Katherine Marsh (*see* B. K. Cherry); one *s* one *d*. *Educ:* Portsmouth Grammar Sch.; Christ Church, Oxford (Open Scholar 1960, MA). British Museum: Asst Keeper, Dept of British and Medieval Antiquities, 1964–69; Asst Keeper, 1969–81, Dep. Keeper, 1981–98, Dept of Medieval and Later Antiquities. Dir, British Archaeological Assoc., 1977–82; Vice Pres., Soc. of Antiquaries of London, 1996–2000 (Sec., 1986–96). *Publications:* (jtly) The Ring from Antiquity to the 20th Century, 1981; (ed with I. H. Longworth) Archaeology in Britain since 1945, 1986; Medieval Decorative Art, 1991; Goldsmiths, 1992; The Middleham Jewel and Ring, 1994; (ed) Mythical Beasts, 1995; (ed with M. Caygill) Sir Augustus Wollaston Franks: Collecting and the British Museum, 1997; articles in learned jls on topics of archaeology and collecting. *Address:* 58 Lancaster Road, N4 4PT. *T:* (020) 7272 0578.

CHERRY, John Mitchell; QC 1988; a Recorder, since 1987; *b* 10 Sept. 1937; *s* of John William and Dorothy Mary Cherry; *m* 1972, Eunice Ann Westmoreland; one *s* two *d* (and one *s* decd). *Educ:* Cheshunt Grammar Sch.; Council of Legal Education. Called to the Bar, Gray's Inn, 1961. Mem., Criminal Injuries Compensation Bd, 1989–. *Recreations:* cricket, Rugby, food, wine. *Address:* Winterton, Turkey Street, Bulls Cross, Enfield, Middx EN1 4RJ. *T:* (01992) 719018.

CHERRYMAN, John Richard; QC 1982; *b* 7 Dec. 1932; *s* of Albert James and Mabel Cherryman; *m* 1963, Anna Greenleaf Collis; three *s* one *d*. *Educ:* Farnham Grammar Sch.; London School of Economics (LLB Hons); Harvard Law Sch. Called to Bar, Gray's Inn, 1955, Bencher, 1988. *Recreations:* restoring old houses in Italy, music, theatre. *Address:* 4 Breams Buildings, EC4A 1AQ. *Club:* Travellers'.

CHESHAM, 6th Baron, *cr* 1858; **Nicholas Charles Cavendish;** *b* 7 Nov. 1941; *s* of 5th Baron Chesham, TD, PC and of Mary Edmunds, *d* of late David G. Marshall; *S* father, 1989; *m* 1st, 1965, Susan Donne Beauchamp (marr. diss. 1969); 2nd, 1973, Suzanne Adrienne, *d* of late Alan Gray Byrne; two *s*. *Educ:* Eton. Chartered Accountant. Capt. of the Yeoman of the Guard (Dep. Govt Chief Whip in H of L), 1995–97. *Recreations:* tennis, ski-ing, shooting. *Heir:* *s* Hon. Charles Gray Compton Cavendish, *b* 11 Nov. 1974. *Address:* The Old Post House, Church Street, Ropley, Alresford, Hants SO24 0DR. *Clubs:* Pratt's; Australian (Sydney); Royal Sydney Golf.

CHESHER, Prof. Andrew Douglas, FBA 2001; Professor of Economics, University College London, since 1999; *b* 21 Dec. 1948; *s* of late Douglas George Chesher and of Eileen Jessie Chesher (*née* Arnott); *m* 1st, 1971, Janice Margaret Elizabeth Duffield (marr. diss.); two *s*; 2nd, 2000, Valérie Marie Rose Jeanne Lechene. *Educ:* Whitgift Sch.; Univ. of Birmingham (BSocSc Maths, Econs and Stats). Res. Associate, Acton Soc., 1970–71; Lectr in Econometrics, Univ. of Birmingham, 1972-83; Prof. of Econometrics, 1984-99,

Hd, Dept of Econs, 1987-90 and 1996-98, Univ. of Bristol; Dir, Centre for Microdata Methods and Practice, Inst. for Fiscal Studies and Dept of Econs, UCL, 2000-. Vis. Prof., Univ. of Bristol, 2000-; Associate Mem., Nuffield Coll., Oxford, 2000-. Mem. Council, ESRC, 2001- (Mem., 1996-2000, Vice-Chm., 1997-2000, Res. Resources Bd; Chm., Res. Grants Bd, 2001-). Mem. Cttee, Nat. Food Survey, 1987-. Mem. Council, REconS, 1998-. Fellow, Econometric Soc., 1999. Associate Editor: Econometrica, 1990-96 and 2000-; Jl Econometrics, 1995-; Econ. Jl, 1997-2000; Jl Royal Statistical Soc., Series A, 1999-; Co-Ed., Econometric Soc. Monograph Series, 2001-. *Publications:* (with R. Harrison) Vehicle Operating Costs in Developing Countries, 1987; contribs to learned jls in stats, econs, nutrition and highway engrg. *Address:* Woodcroft, Foxcombe Lane, Boars Hill, Oxford OX1 5DH.

CHESHIRE, Dr Christopher Michael, FRCP; Consultant Physician, Manchester Royal Infirmary, since 1983; Director of Education, Central Manchester Healthcare NHS Trust, since 1997 (Medical Director, 1993–97); *b* 18 July 1946; *s* of Gordon Sydney Cheshire and Vera Cheshire; *m* 1970, Jane Mary Cordle; one *s* one *d*. *Educ:* Manchester Univ. (BSc Hons 1969; MB ChB Hons 1976). DCH 1979; FRCP 1990. House Officer, Medicine and Surgery, Manchester Royal Infirmary, 1976–77; Senior House Officer: Cardiothoracic Medicine, Wythenshawe, 1977–78; Paediatrics, Univ. Hosp., S Manchester, 1978–79; Medicine, Manchester Royal Infirmary, 1979–80; Lectr in Geriatric Medicine, Univ. Hosp., S Manchester, 1980–83. Chairman: NW, British Geriatrics Soc., 1998–; Educn Gp, British Assoc. of Med. Managers, 1998–. *Publications:* contribs on topics of medicine and management. *Recreations:* running, swimming, reading novels, garden, family. *Address:* 38 The Crescent, Davenport, Stockport SK3 8SN. *T:* (0161) 483 2972.

CHESHIRE, Lt Col Colin Charles Chance, OBE 1993; Chief Executive, National Rifle Association, since 1995; *b* 23 Aug. 1941; *s* of Air Chief Marshal Sir Walter Graemes Cheshire, GBE, KCB and Mary Cheshire (*née* Chance), DL; *m* 1st, 1968, Cherida Evelyn (marr. diss. 1975), *d* of Air Chief Marshal Sir Wallace Hart Kyle, GCB, KCVO, CBE, DSO, DFC; one *s* one *d*; 2nd, 1976, Angela, *d* of D. Fulcher. *Educ:* Worksop Coll. Royal Tank Regiment: served Borneo, Singapore, Malaysia, BAOR, NI, UK; Armour Sch., Bovington Camp, 1968; RMCS, 1972–73; psc† 1974; Bde Major, RAC, HQI (BR) Corps, 1978–80; Lt Col, 1980; retd 1981. Sales and Marketing Manager: Vickers Instruments Ltd, 1981–83; Army Systems, Ferranti Computer Systems, 1983–85; Sales and Mktg Dir, Wallop Gp, and Man. Dir, Walloptronics Ltd, 1985–87; Bursar, Oundle Sch., 1987–95. Mem., Exec. Cttee, Independent Schs Bursars Assoc., 1992–95. Chm., GB Target Shooting Fedn, 1994–97; Mem., British Rifle Team, 1971– (Captain, 1991, 1992, 1994, 1995, Vice Captain, 1982, 1999); Winner, World Long Range Rifle Team Championships, Palma Team, 1992, 1995. Mem., HAC, 1960–. Mem., Guild of Sports Internationalists, 1998– (Lower Warden, 1999–). FIMgt 1985. *Publication:* History and Records of the Palma Match 1876 to date, 1992. *Recreations:* rifle shooting, golf. *Address:* The Barn, Bisley Camp, Brookwood, Woking, Surrey GU24 0NY. *T:* (01483) 799852.
See also Sir J. A. Cheshire.

CHESHIRE, Air Chief Marshal Sir John (Anthony), KBE 1995 (CBE 1991; OBE 1982); CB 1994; FRAeS; Lieutenant-Governor and Commander-in-Chief, Jersey, since 2000; *b* 4 Sept. 1942; *s* of Air Chief Marshal Sir Walter Cheshire, GBE, KCB and Lady Cheshire; *m* 1964, Shirley Ann Stevens; one *s* one *d*. *Educ:* Ipswich Sch.; Worksop Coll.; RAF Coll., Cranwell. Operational Flying Duties, UK and Singapore, 1964–70; Air Ops Officer, Special Forces, 1971–73; Canadian Forces Staff Coll., 1973–74; Operational Flying Duties, Special Forces, 1975–76; Air Plans, MoD, 1976–79; Commander: Air Wing, Brunei, 1980–82; RAF Lyneham, 1983–85; Plans Br., HQ Strike Command, 1986–87; Defence and Air Attaché, Moscow, 1988–90; Dep. Comdt, RAF Staff Coll., 1991–92; ACOS (Policy), SHAPE, 1992–94; UK Mil. Rep., HQ NATO, 1995–97; C-in-C, Allied Forces NW Europe, 1997–2000. *Recreations:* squash, tennis, golf, field shooting. *Club:* Royal Air Force.
See also C. C. C. Cheshire.

CHESSELLS, Sir Arthur David, (Sir Tim), Kt 1993; Chairman of Trustees, British Telecommunications Pension Scheme, since 1999; *b* 15 June 1941; *s* of late Brig. Arthur Chessells and Carmel Mary (*née* McGinnis); *m* 1966, Katharine, *d* of Dick and Rachel Goodwin; two *s* two *d*. *Educ:* Stonyhurst Coll. CA 1965. Partner, Arthur Young, 1972–89; Mem., Kent AHA, 1979–82; Vice-Chm., Tunbridge Wells HA, 1982–88; Mem., SE Thames RHA, 1988–90; Chairman: NE Thames RHA, 1990–92; London Implementation Gp, 1992–95; Legal Aid Bd, 1995–2000. Non-exec. Mem., NHS Policy Bd, 1992–95. Director: Odgers and Co. Ltd, 1989–95; Price and Pierce Inc., 1993–97; Dixons Gp, 1995–; Care UK, 1995–, and other cos; Chm., Hermes Pension Management, 1999–. Chm., Nat. Approval Council for Security Systems, 1995–99. Mem. Council, St Christopher's Hospice, 1989–92. Trustee: Kent Community Housing Trust, 1990–95; Stonyhurst Charitable Fund, 1980–93; Chatham Historic Dockyard, 1992–97; Charities Aid Foundn, 1998–; Chm. Trustees, Horder Centre for Arthritis, 2000; Chm. Special Trustees, Guy's and St Thomas' Charitable Foundn, 1996–. *Recreations:* reading, shooting, gardening. *Address:* British Telecommunications Pension Scheme, Lloyds Chambers, 1 Portsoken Street, E1 8HZ. *T:* (020) 7680 2304. *Club:* Carlton.
See also J. M. Chessells.

CHESSELLS, Prof. Judith Mary, MD; FRCP, FRCPath; Leukaemia Research Fund Professor of Haematology and Oncology, Institute of Child Health, London University, since 1988; *b* 30 Dec. 1938; *d* of late Brig. Arthur Edgar Chessells and Carmel Mary Chessells (*née* McGinnis); *m* 1969, Dr Gerald McEnery; one *d*. *Educ:* Sacred Heart Convent, Brighton; London Hosp. Med. Coll., London Univ. (MB BS Hons; MD). Lectr in Haematology, Inst. of Child Health, 1972–73; Consultant Haematologist, Hosp. for Sick Children, Great Ormond St, 1973–87, Hon. Consultant, 1988–. FRCPCH 1997. *Publications:* contrib. to learned jls. *Recreations:* theatre, literature. *Address:* Institute of Child Health, 30 Guildford Street, WC1N 1EH. *T:* (020) 7813 8190.
See also Sir A. D. Chessells.

CHESSELLS, Sir Tim; *see* Chessells, Sir A. D.

CHESSHYRE, (David) Hubert (Boothby), LVO 1988; FSA; Clarenceux King of Arms, since 1997; Secretary, Most Noble Order of the Garter, since 1988; Registrar of the College of Arms, 1992–2000; *b* 22 June 1940; *e s* of late Col Hubert Layard Chesshyre and Katharine Anne (*née* Boothby), Canterbury, Kent. *Educ:* King's Sch., Canterbury; Trinity Coll., Cambridge (Choral Clerk; MA); Christ Church, Oxford (DipEd 1967). FSA 1977; FHS 1990. Taught French in England and English in France, at intervals 1962–67; wine merchant (Moët et Chandon and Harvey's of Bristol), 1962–65; Hon. Artillery Co., 1964–65 (fired salute at funeral of Sir Winston Churchill, 1965); Green Staff Officer at Investiture of the Prince of Wales, 1969; Rouge Croix Pursuivant, 1970–78, and on staff of Sir Anthony Wagner, Garter King of Arms, 1971–78; Chester Herald of Arms, 1978–95; Norroy and Ulster King of Arms, 1995–97. Mem., Westminster Abbey Fabric Commn (formerly Architectural Adv. Panel), 1985–. Member: Council, Heraldry Soc., 1973–85; Bach Choir, 1979–93; Madrigal Soc., 1980–. Hon. Genealogist to Royal Victorian Order, 1987–. Lectr, NADFAS, 1982–. Lay Clerk, Southwark Cathedral, 1971–. Freeman: City of London, 1975; Musicians' Co., 1994 (Liveryman, 1995–). *Publications:* (Eng. lang. editor) C. A. von Volborth, Heraldry of the World, 1973; The Identification of Coats of Arms on British Silver, 1978; (with A. J. Robinson) The Green: a history of the heart of Bethnal Green, 1978; (with Adrian Ailes) Heralds of Today, 1986, 2nd edn 2001; (ed with T. Woodcock) Dictionary of British Arms, vol. I, 1992; Garter Banners of the Nineties, 1998; (with P. J. Begent) The Most Noble Order of the Garter, 650 Years, 1999; genealogical and heraldic articles in British Heritage and elsewhere. *Recreations:* singing, gardening, mountain walking, motorcycling. *Address:* Hawthorn Cottage, 1 Flamborough Walk, E14 7LY. *T:* (020) 7790 7923; College of Arms, Queen Victoria Street, EC4V 4BT. *T:* (020) 7248 1137.

CHESSUN, Ven. Christopher Thomas James; Archdeacon of Northolt, since 2001; *b* 5 Aug. 1956; twin *s* of Thomas Frederick and Joyce Rosemary Chessun. *Educ:* Hampton Grammar Sch.; University Coll., Oxford (BA Hons Modern Hist. 1978; MA 1982); Trinity Hall, Cambridge (BA Hons Pt II Theol. Tripos 1982); Westcott House Theol Coll., Cambridge. Ordained deacon, 1983, priest, 1984; Asst Curate, St Michael and All Angels, Sandhurst, 1983–87; Sen. Curate, St Mary, Portsea, 1987–89; Chaplain and Minor Canon, St Paul's Cathedral, 1989–93; Vocations Advr, Dio. London, 1991–93; Rector of St Dunstan and All Saints', Stepney, 1993–2001; Area Dean, Tower Hamlets, 1997–2001. *Recreations:* music, history, travel, overseas church links. *Address:* 247 Kenton Road, Kenton, Middlesex HA3 0HQ. *T:* (020) 8907 5941, *Fax:* (020) 8909 2368; *e-mail:* archdeacon.northolt@london.anglican.org.

CHESTER, Bishop of, since 1996; **Rt Rev. Peter Robert Forster;** *b* 16 March 1950; *s* of Thomas and Edna Forster; *m* 1978, Elisabeth Anne Stevenson; two *s* two *d*. *Educ:* Merton Coll., Oxford (MA 1973); Edinburgh Univ. (BD 1977; PhD 1985); Edinburgh Theol Coll. Ordained deacon, 1980, priest, 1981; Asst Curate, St Matthew and St James, Mossley Hill, Liverpool, 1980–82; Senior Tutor, St John's Coll., Durham, 1983–91; Vicar, Beverley Minster and Asst Curate, Routh, 1991–96. *Recreations:* tennis, woodcrafts, family. *Address:* Bishop's House, Abbey Square, Chester CH1 2JD. *T:* (01244) 350864, *Fax:* (01244) 314187.

CHESTER, Dean of; *no new appointment at time of going to press.*

CHESTER, Archdeacon of; *see* Hewetson, Ven. C.

CHESTER, Maj.-Gen. John Shane, OBE 1982; Chief Executive (formerly Secretary), Chartered Institute of Management Accountants, 1995–2001; *b* 21 April 1944; *s* of late Hugh Chester and of Stella Florence Mary Chester (*née* Turner); *m* 1970, Amanda Gay, *d* of late Wing Comdr Stanley Graham Pritchard; two *s*. *Educ:* St Joseph's Coll., Ipswich. 2nd Lieut, RM, 1963; served 40, 41, 43 and 45 Commandos RM (Borneo, Norway, NI), 1964–88 (despatches 1981); BM, 3 Commando Brigade, 1981–83 (incl. Falklands Campaign); CO 40 Commando RM, 1987–89 (despatches 1988); COS, HQ Special Forces, 1989–91; Brig. Comdg Training and Reserve Forces, RM, 1991–92; Sen. Directing Staff (Navy), RCDS, 1993–95. Gov., Royal Naval Scholarship Fund, 1996–. FIPD 1992; FIMgt; FRSA. *Recreations:* sailing, golf, ski-ing, military history. *Address:* c/o Lloyds TSB, Budleigh Salterton, Devon EX9 6NQ. *Clubs:* Army and Navy; Royal Marines Sailing; Royal Southern Yacht.

CHESTER, Dr Peter Francis, FREng; FInstP; FIEE; Chairman, National Wind Power Ltd, 1991–95; *b* 8 Feb. 1929; *s* of late Herbert and of Edith Maud Chester (*née* Pullen); *m* 1953, Barbara Ann Collin; one *s* four *d*. *Educ:* Gunnersbury Grammar Sch.; Queen Mary College, London (BSc 1st Physics 1950); PhD London 1953. Post-doctoral Fellow, Nat. Research Council, Ottawa, 1953–54; Adv. Physicist, Westinghouse Res. Labs, Pittsburgh, 1954–60; Head of Solid State Physics Section, CERL, 1960–65; Head of Fundamental Studies Section, CERL, 1965–66; Res. Man., Electricity Council Res. Centre, 1966–70; Controller of Scientific Services, CEGB NW Region, 1970–73; Dir, Central Electricity Res. Labs, 1973–82; a Dir, Technol. Planning and Res., Div., CEGB, 1982–86; Dir, Environment, CEGB, 1986–89; Exec. Dir, Technology and Environment, Nat. Power, 1990–92. Science Research Council: Mem., 1976–80; Mem., Science Bd, 1972–75; Chm., Energy Round Table and Energy Cttee, 1975–80. Mem., ACORD, DTI, 1992–93. Vice-Pres., Inst. of Physics, 1972–76. A Dir, Fulmer Res. Inst., 1976–83. Faraday Lectr, IEE, 1984–85. Robens Coal Science Medal, 1985. *Publications:* original papers in solid state and low temperature physics, reports on energy and the environment, acid rain, clean technology, renewable energy and windpower.

CHESTERFIELD, Archdeacon of; *see* Garnett, Ven. D. C.

CHESTERMAN, Rev. Canon (George) Anthony, PhD; Continuing Ministerial Education Adviser to Bishop of Derby and Residentiary Canon, Derby Cathedral, since 1989; Chaplain to the Queen, since 1998; *b* 22 Aug. 1938; *s* of late Francis John Chesterman and Frances Annie Chesterman; *m* 1964, Sheila Valerie Wilkinson; one *s* one *d*. *Educ:* Lancaster Royal Grammar Sch.; Univ. of Manchester (BSc); Nottingham Univ. (DipAE 1974; PhD 1989); Coll. of the Resurrection, Mirfield. Ordained deacon, 1964, priest, 1965; Curate, St John the Evangelist, Newbold, Chesterfield, 1964–67; Litchurch Gp Ministry, Derby (youth and adult educn specialist), 1967–70; Rector, All Saints, Mugginton and Kedleston, 1970–89; Diocesan Adult Educn Officer, Derby, 1970–79; Vice-Principal, E Midlands Ministry Trng Course, 1979–88. Mem., Gen. Synod, 1990–95. *Publications:* occasional articles and book reviews. *Recreations:* cooking, gardening, beekeeping, the visual arts. *Address:* Derby Church House, Full Street, Derby DE1 3DR. *T:* (01332) 382233; (home) 13 Newbridge Road, Ambergate, Derby DE56 2GR. *T:* (01773) 852236.

CHESTERS, Rt Rev. Alan David; *see* Blackburn, Bishop of.

CHESTERTON, David, CB 1999; Chief Executive, UK Sports Council, 1998–99 (on secondment); *b* 30 Nov. 1939; *s* of Raymond and Joyce Chesterton; *m* 1st, 1965, Ursula Morgan; one *s* three *d*; 2nd, 1977, Lindsay Fellows; three step *d*. *Educ:* Reading Sch.; St Catherine's Coll., Oxford (BA). Editorial Assistant: Financial World, 1961–62; Fleet Street Letter, 1962–65; Producer, BBC External Services, 1965–68, Exec. Producer, 1968–74; Northern Ireland Office: Principal, 1974–80; Asst Sec., 1980–85; Under Sec., 1985–92; Hd of Heritage and Tourism Gp, DNH, 1992–96; Head of Sport, Tourism, Millennium and Nat. Lotteries Charities Bd Gp, DNH, then DCMS, 1996–98. *Recreations:* walking, food and drink.

CHESTERTON, Dame Elizabeth (Ursula), DBE 1987 (OBE 1977); architect and town planner; *b* 12 Oct. 1915; *d* of late Maurice Chesterton, architect, and Dorothy (*née* Deck). *Educ:* King Alfred Sch.; Queen's Coll., London; Architectural Assoc. Sch. of Architecture, London. AA Dipl. (Hons) 1939; ARIBA 1940; DistTP 1968; FRTPI 1967 (AMTPI 1943). Asst County Planning Officer, E Suffolk CC, 1940–47; Develt Control Officer, Cambs CC Planning Dept, 1947–51; Mem. Staff: Social Res. Unit, Dept of Town Planning, UCL, 1951–53; Architectural Assoc. Sch. of Architecture, 1954–61. Member: Council, Architectural Assoc., 1964–67; Royal Fine Art Commn, 1970–93;

Historic Buildings Council, 1973–84; Royal Parks Review Gp, 1991–96. English Heritage: Member: Historic Bldgs Adv. Cttee, 1984–88, Historic Areas Adv. Cttee, 1984–91; Historic Bldgs and Areas Adv. Cttee, 1991–; British Rail: Member: Envmt Panel, 1983–88; Architecture Panel, 1988–91; Architecture and Design Panel, 1991–93; National Trust: Member: Architecture Panel, 1978–90; Council, 1984–90; Mem., Fabric Adv. Cttee, Exeter Cathedral, 1994–97. FRSA 1982. Reports prepared: Report on Local Land Use for the Dartington Hall Trustees, 1957; (jtly) The Historic Core of King's Lynn: study and plan, 1964; Plan for the Beaulieu Estate, 1966; North West Solent Shore Estates Report, 1969; (jtly) Snowdon Summit Report for Countryside Commission, 1974; Plans for Quarries and Rail Distribution Depots, Foster Yeoman and Yeoman (Morvern), 1974–81; Central Area Study, Chippenham, for North Wiltshire District Council, 1975–80; The Crumbles, Eastbourne, for Chatsworth Settlement, 1976; Aldeburgh, Suffolk, for Aldeburgh Soc., 1976; Old Market Conservation and Redevelopment Study, for City of Bristol and Bristol Municipal Charities, 1978; Uplands Landscape Study, for Countryside Commission, 1980. *Recreations:* gardening, travel. *Address:* 12 The Mount, NW3 6SZ. *T:* (020) 7435 0666.

CHESTERTON, Sir Oliver (Sidney), Kt 1969; MC 1943; Consultant, Chestertons, Chartered Surveyors, London, since 1980 (Partner, 1936, Senior Partner, 1945–80); *b* 28 Jan. 1913; *s* of Frank and Nora Chesterton; *m* 1944, Violet Ethel Jameson; two *s* one *d*. *Educ:* Rugby Sch. Served War of 1939–45, Irish Guards. Director: Woolwich Equitable Building Soc., 1962–86 (Chm., 1976–83); Property Growth Assurance, 1972–85; London Life Assoc., 1975–84; Estates Property Investment Co., 1979–88. Vice-Chm., Council of Royal Free Med. Sch., 1964–77; Crown Estate Comr, 1969–82. Past Pres., Royal Instn of Chartered Surveyors, Hon. Sec., 1972–79; Pres., Commonwealth Assoc. Surveying and Land Economy, 1969–77; first Master, Chartered Surveyors' Co., 1977–78. Governor, Rugby Sch., 1972–88. *Recreations:* golf, fishing, National Hunt racing. *Address:* Hookfield House, Abinger Common, Dorking, Surrey RH5 6JF. *Club:* New Zealand Golf.

CHESWORTH, Air Vice-Marshal George Arthur, CB 1982; OBE 1972; DFC 1954; JP; Lord-Lieutenant of Moray, since 1994; Chairman, Moray, Badenoch and Strathspey Enterprise Co., 1996–2000 (Deputy Chairman, 1991–96); *b* 4 June 1930; *s* of Alfred Matthew Chesworth and Grace Edith Chesworth; *m* 1951, Betty Joan Hopkins; two *d* (one *s* decd). *Educ:* Carshalton and Wimbledon. Joined RAF, 1948; commissioned, 1950; 205 Flying boat Sqdn, FEAF, 1951–53 (DFC 1954); RAF Germany, RAF Kinloss, RAF St Mawgan, 1956–61; RN Staff Coll., 1963; MoD, 1964–67; OC 201 Nimrod Sqdn, 1968–71 (OBE); OC RAF Kinloss, 1972–75; Air Officer in Charge, Central Tactics & Trials Orgn, 1975–77; Director, RAF Quartering, 1977–80; C of S to Air Comdr CTF 317 during Falkland Campaign, Apr.–June 1982 (CB); C of S, HQ 18 Gp, RAF, 1980–84. Chief Exec., Glasgow Garden Fest. (1988), 1985–89; Dir, SEC Ltd, 1989–95. Hon. Col, 76 Engr Regt (Vols), 1992–97. Chm., ATC Council for Scotland and NI, 1989–95; Pres., Highland TAVR, 1998– (Vice-Chm. (Air), 1990–98). Develt Dir, Military and Aerospace Mus. (Aldershot) Trust, 1990–91; Trustee, MacRobert Trusts, 1994–2000; Mem. Management Bd, RAF Benevolent Fund Home, Alastrean House, Tarland, Aberdeenshire, 1990– (Chm., 1994–). Hon. Air Cdre, No 2622 (Highland) Sqdn, RAuxAF Regt, 2000–. DL Moray, 1992; JP Moray, 1994. *Address:* Pindlers Croft, Lower Califer, Forres, Moray IV36 2RQ. *T:* (01309) 674136. *Club:* Royal Air Force.

CHESWORTH, John, FCA; Chairman, Bodycote International plc, since 2002 (Managing Director, 1980–2002); *b* 8 June 1937; *m* Elizabeth Ann; two *s* three *d*. *Educ:* Burnage Grammar Sch., Manchester. FCA 1964. Articled clerk, Burne Phillips & Co., 1958–63; Chartered Accountant, Deloitte & Co., 1964–67; Financial Accountant, Kellog Co. of GB Ltd, 1967–68; Gp Accountant, Nemo Heat Treatments Ltd, 1968–71; Chief Exec., Bodycote (UK) Gp, 1972. Director: HIP Ltd; Metallurgical Testing Services International; Industrial Materials Technology Inc.; non-exec. Chm., Zinc Alloy Ltd, 1980–. Harold Moore Meml Lectr, Royal Soc., 1995. Member: ICAEW; Adv. Gp, Dept of Materials and Metallurgy, Univ. of Birmingham, 1995–. *Publications:* papers on metallurgical heat treatment in jls. *Recreations:* sailing, swimming, soccer (represented Lancashire). *Address:* Oulton Manor, Rushton Spencer, Macclesfield, Cheshire SK11 0RS. *T:* (01260) 226314. *Clubs:* Tytherington; Royal Yacht.

CHETWODE, family name of **Baron Chetwode**.

CHETWODE, 2nd Baron *cr* 1945, of Chetwode; **Philip Chetwode;** Bt, 1700; *b* 26 March 1937; *s* of Capt. Roger Charles George Chetwode (*d* 1940; *o s* of Field Marshal Lord Chetwode, GCB, OM, GCSI, KCMG, DSO) and Hon. Molly Patricia Berry, *d* of 1st Viscount Camrose (she *m* 2nd, 1942, 1st Baron Sherwood, from whom she obtained a divorce, 1948, and *m* 3rd, 1958, late Sir Richard Cotterell, 5th Bt, CBE); *S* grandfather, 1950. *m* 1st, 1967, Mrs Susan Dudley Smith (marr. diss. 1979); two *s* one *d*; 2nd, 1990, Mrs Fiona Holt. *Educ:* Eton. Commissioned Royal Horse Guards, 1956–66. *Heir:* s Hon. Roger Chetwode [*b* 29 May 1968; *m* 1998, Miranda, *d* of Comdr Graeme Rowan-Thomson; one *d*]. *Address:* The Mill House, Chilton Foliat, Hungerford, Berks RG17 0TG. *Club:* White's.

CHETWOOD, Sir Clifford (Jack), Kt 1987; FCIOB, FRSH; Chairman, Chetwood Associates Ltd, since 1988; *b* 2 Nov. 1928; *s* of Stanley Jack Chetwood and Doris May Palmer; *m* 1953, Pamela Phyllis Sherlock; one *s* three *d*. George Wimpey & Co. Ltd, later George Wimpey PLC: Director, 1969; Chm., Bd of Management, 1975–79; a Gp Man. Dir, 1978–82; Chief Exec., 1982–90; Chm., 1984–92; Chairman: Wimpey Construction UK, 1979–83; Wimpey Homes Holdings, 1981–83; Broadgate Properties, 1994–96 (Dir, 1993–94). Pres., Building Employers' Confedn, 1989–92; Chm., Construction ITB, 1990–96. Mem. Council, Imperial Soc. of Knights Bachelor, 1988–95; Trustee: V&A Museum, 1985–97; London Zoological Soc. Develt Trust, 1986–90; Chm. of Trustees, Develt Trust, ICE, 1988–96; Pres., Bldg Industry Youth Trust, 1990–95; Vice-President: C&G, 1992–97; Tennis and Rackets Assoc., 1992–. Master, Guild of Freemen, City of London, 1993–94. FRSA; Hon. FICE 1990; Hon. FCGI 1991. Prince Philip Medal, CGLI, 1987. Man of the Year, Architects and Surveyors Inst., 1989. *Recreations:* Real tennis (Pres., Royal Court Club, 1991–), lawn tennis. *Address:* Wineberry House, The Drive, Eaton Park, Cobham, Surrey KT11 2JQ.

CHETWYN, Robert; *b* 7 Sept. 1933; *s* of Frederick Reuben Suckling and Eleanor Lavinia (*née* Boffee). *Educ:* Rutlish, Merton, SW; Central Sch. of Speech and Drama. First appeared as actor with Dundee Repertory Co., 1952; subseq. in repertory at Hull, Alexandra Theatre, Birmingham, 1954; Birmingham Repertory Theatre, 1954–56; various TV plays, 1956–59; 1st prodn, Five Finger Exercise, Salisbury Playhouse, 1960; Dir of Prodns, Opera Hse, Harrogate, 1961–62; Artistic Dir, Ipswich Arts, 1962–64; Midsummer Night's Dream, transf. Comedy (London), 1964; Resident Dir, Belgrade (Coventry), 1964–66; Assoc. Dir, Mermaid, 1966, The Beaver Coat, three one-act plays by Shaw; There's a Girl in My Soup, Globe, 1966 and Music Box (NY), 1967; A Present for the Past, Edinburgh Fest., 1966; The Flip Side, Apollo, 1967; The Importance of Being Earnest, Haymarket, 1968; The Real Inspector Hound, Criterion, 1968; What the Butler Saw, Queens, 1968; The Country Wife, Chichester Fest., 1968; The Bandwaggon, Mermaid, 1968 and Sydney, 1970; Cannibal Crackers, Hampstead, 1969; When We are Married, Strand, 1970; Hamlet, in Rome, Zurich, Vienna, Antwerp, Cologne, then Cambridge (London), 1971; Parents Day, Globe, 1972; Restez Donc Jusq'au Petit Déjeuner, Belgium, 1973; Who's Who, Fortune, 1973; At the End of the Day, Savoy, 1973; Chez Nous, Globe, 1974; Qui est Qui, Belgium, 1974; The Doctor's Dilemma, Mermaid, 1975; Getting Away with Murder, Comedy, 1976; Private Lives, Melbourne, 1976; It's All Right If I Do It, Mermaid, 1977; A Murder is Announced, Vaudeville, 1977; Arms and The Man, Greenwich, 1978; LUV, Amsterdam, 1978; Brimstone and Treacle, Open Space, 1979; Bent, Royal Court and Criterion, 1979; Pygmalion, National Theatre of Belgium, 1979; Moving, Queen's, 1980; Eastward Ho!, Mermaid, 1981; Beethoven's 10th, Vaudeville, 1983 (also Broadway, New York); Number One, Queen's, 1984; Why Me?, Strand, 1985; Selling The Sizzle, Hampstead, 1988; Independent State, Sydney Opera House, 1995. Has produced and directed for BBC (incl. series Private Shulz, by Jack Pullman, film, That Uncertain Feeling, Born In the Gardens) and ITV (Irish RM first series, Small World, Case of the Late Pig). Trustee, Dirs' Guild of GB, 1984–. *Publication:* (jtly) Theatre on Merseyside (Arts Council report), 1973. *Recreations:* tennis, films, gardening. *Address:* 1 Wilton Court, Eccleston Square, SW1V 1PH.

CHETWYND, family name of **Viscount Chetwynd**.

CHETWYND, 10th Viscount *cr* 1717 (Ireland); **Adam Richard John Casson Chetwynd;** Baron Rathdowne, 1717 (Ireland); Life Assurance Agent, Liberty Life Association of Africa Ltd, Sandton Branch, Johannesburg; *b* 2 Feb. 1935; *o s* of 9th Viscount and Joan Gilbert (*d* 1979), *o c* of late Herbert Alexander Casson, CSI, Ty'n-y-coed, Arthog, Merioneth; *S* father, 1965; *m* 1st, 1966, Celia Grace (marr. diss. 1974), *er d* of Comdr Alexander Robert Ramsay, DSC, RNVR, Fasque, Borrowdale, Salisbury, Rhodesia; twin *s* one *d*; 2nd, 1975, Angela May, *o d* of Jack Payne McCarthy, 21 Llanberis Grove, Nottingham. *Educ:* Eton. Fellow, Inst. of Life and Pension Advrs, 1982. 2nd Lieut Cameron Highlanders, 1954–56. With Colonial Mutual Life Assurance Soc. Ltd, Salisbury, Rhodesia, then Johannesburg, 1968–78; Liberty Life Assoc. of Africa (formerly Prudential Assurance Co. of South Africa), 1978–. Liveryman, GAPAN. Qualifying Mem., Million Dollar Round Table, 1979–94; qualified Top of the Table, 1984–99; Holder, Internat. Quality Award, 1979–99. *Recreations:* astronomy, travel. *Heir: s* Hon. Adam Douglas Chetwynd, *b* 26 Feb. 1969. *Address:* c/o M. J. G. Fletcher, Esq., Lee Bolton & Lee, 1 The Sanctuary, Westminster, SW1P 3JT. *Club:* Rotary (Morningside).

CHETWYND, Sir Arthur (Ralph Talbot), 8th Bt *cr* 1795; Chairman: Brocton Hall Communications Ltd, Toronto (President, 1978–88); Board of Directors, Chetwynd Productions Inc. (formerly Chetwynd Films Ltd), Toronto, since 1977 (Founder, President and General Manager, 1950–76); *b* Walhachin, BC, 28 Oct. 1913; *o s* of Hon. William Ralph Talbot Chetwynd, MC, MLA (*d* 1957) (*b* of 7th Bt), and Frances Mary (*d* 1986), *d* of late James Jupe; *S* uncle, 1972; *m* 1940, Marjory May McDonald, *er d* of late Robert Bruce Lang, Vancouver, BC, and Glasgow, Scotland; two *s*. *Educ:* Vernon Preparatory School, BC; University of British Columbia (Physical Education and Recreation). Prior to 1933, a rancher in interior BC; Games Master, Vernon Prep. School, BC, 1936–39, also Instructor, Provincial Physical Education and Recreation; Chief Instructor, McDonald's Remedial Institute, Vancouver, 1939–42; Director of Remedial Gymnastics, British Columbia Workmen's Compensation Board, 1942; RCAF, 1943–45; Associate in Physical and Health Education, Univ. of Toronto, also Publicity Officer, Univ. of Toronto Athletic Assoc., 1946–52. Former Dir, NZ Lamb Co. Ltd. Former Chairman: Canterbury Cathedral Appeal in Canada; Codrington Coll. (Barbados) Appeal in Canada; Toronto Branch, Royal Commonwealth Soc.; Pres., Empire Club of Canada, 1974–75; Chairman: Nat. Council, Royal Commonwealth Soc. of Canada, 1993–95; Royal Commonwealth Soc. Toronto Foundn; Member: Monarchist League of Canada; Military and Hospitaller Order of St Lazarus of Jerusalem, Canada. CMLJ. Hon. Mem., Order of Barbados (SCM), 1984. *Recreations:* photography, travelling, swimming. *Heir: er s* Robin John Talbot Chetwynd [*b* 21 Aug. 1941; *m* 1st, 1967, Heather Helen (marr. diss. 1986), *d* of George Bayliss Lothian; one *s* one *d*; 2nd, 1986, Donna (*née* Davey)]. *Address:* #1–117 King Street East, Cobourg, ON K9A 1L2, Canada. *Club:* Albany (Toronto).

CHETWYND-TALBOT, family name of **Earl of Shrewsbury and Waterford**.

CHEUNG, Sir Oswald (Victor), Kt 1987; CBE 1976 (OBE 1972); QC (Hong Kong) 1965; Member, Executive Council, Hong Kong, 1974–86; *b* 22 Jan. 1922; *s* of Cheung U Pui and Elizabeth Ellis; *m* 1963, Pauline Cheng; one *s*. *Educ:* Diocesan Boys' Sch.; Hong Kong Univ.; University Coll., Oxford (BA 1949, MA 1963). Called to the Bar, Lincoln's Inn, 1951; Bencher, 1987. Magistrate, 1951–52; Hong Kong Bar, 1952–; Mem., Legislative Council, Hong Kong, 1970–81 (Senior Unofficial Mem., 1978–81); Chairman: Criminal Injuries Compensation Bd; Law Enforcement Injuries Compensation Bd. Director: Mass Transit Railway Corp., 1975–89; Hong Kong Electric (Holdings) Ltd, 1985–94; Ciba-Geigy (HK) Ltd, 1981–96; Wing On Company Internat. Ltd, 1994–. Member: Univ. and Polytechnic Grants Cttee, 1970–78; Court, Hong Kong Univ. Trustee, Croucher Foundn, 1986–92; Chm., Children's Meals Soc., 1966–81; Steward, Royal Hong Kong Jockey Club, 1977–92 (Chm. of Stewards, 1986–89). Captain, Royal Hong Kong Regt, 1956–62, Hon. Col, 1977–82. Fellow, Internat. Acad. of Trial Lawyers. Hon. LLD Hong Kong, 1979; Hon. DSocSc City Univ. of Hong Kong, 1999. *Recreations:* photography, racing, travel. *Address:* New Henry House, 10th Floor, 10 Ice House Street, Hong Kong. *T:* 25242156. *Clubs:* Hong Kong Jockey, Hong Kong, Hong Kong Golf, Chinese.

CHEW, (Victor) Kenneth, TD 1958; Research Fellow of the Science Museum, London, 1977–95; *b* 19 Jan. 1915; *yr s* of Frederick and Edith Chew. *Educ:* Christ's Hospital; Christ Church, Oxford (Scholar). 1st class, Final Honours School of Natural Science (Physics), 1936; BA (Oxon) 1936, MA 1964. Asst Master, King's Sch., Rochester, 1936–38; Winchester Coll., 1938–40. Served War: Royal Signals, 1940–46. Asst Master, Shrewsbury Sch., 1946–48 and 1949–58; Lecturer in Education, Bristol Univ., 1948–49. Entered Science Museum as Asst Keeper, 1958; Deputy Keeper and Sec. to Advisory Council, 1967; Keeper, Dept of Physics, 1970–78. *Publications:* official publications of Science Museum. *Recreations:* hill walking, photography. *Address:* 701 Gilbert House, Barbican, EC2Y 8BD.

CHEWTON, Viscount; Edward Robert Waldegrave; *b* 10 Oct. 1986; *e s* of 13th Earl Waldegrave, *qv*.

CHEYNE, Iain Donald, CBE 1995; Director of Private Affairs to HM the Aga Kha[illegible] since 2000; *b* 29 March 1942; *s* of Andres Delporte Gordon Cheyne and Florence M[illegible] Cheyne; *m* 1969, Amelia Martinez Vara; two *s* one *d*. *Educ:* Hertford Coll., Oxford [illegible] English Lit.); London Univ. (Dip. Archaeol.); Stanford Univ., Calif; London Busine[illegible] Articled Clerk, Droogleever and Co., Solicitors, 1964–68; admitted solicito[illegible] Partner, Alfille and Co., Solicitors, 1968–72; Lloyds Bank, subseq Lloyds TSB, [illegible] Advr, 1972–86; General Manager: Corporate Communications, 1986–88[illegible] Planning, 1988–91; Corporate and Instnl Banking, 1991–97; Man. Dir, Interna[illegible] 1997–2000. *Recreations:* archaeology, game shooting, vintage car racing. *Ad*[illegible] Secrétariat de Son Altesse l'Aga Khan, Aiglemont, 60270 Gouvieux, France[illegible]

CHEYNE, Major Sir Joseph (Lister Watson), 3rd Bt *cr* 1908; OBE 1976; Curator, Keats Shelley Memorial House, Rome, 1976–90; *b* 10 Oct. 1914; *e s* of Sir Joseph Lister Cheyne, 2nd Bt, MC, and Nelita Manfield (*d* 1977), *d* of Andrew Pringle, Borgue; *S* father, 1957; *m* 1st, 1938, Mary Mort (marr. diss. 1955; she *d* 1959), *d* of late Vice-Adm. J. D. Allen, CB; one *s* one *d*; 2nd, 1955, Cicely, *d* of late T. Metcalfe, Padiham, Lancs; two *s* one *d*. *Educ:* Stowe Sch.; Corpus Christi Coll., Cambridge. Major, The Queen's Westminsters (KRRC), 1943; served Africa, 1943–44 (African Star); Italian Campaign. 2nd Sec. (Inf.), British Embassy, Rome, 1968, 1st Sec., 1971, 1st Sec. (Inf.), 1973–76. *Heir: s* Patrick John Lister Cheyne [*b* 2 July 1941; *m* 1968, Helen Louise Trevor, *yr d* of Louis Smith, Southsea; one *s* three *d*]. *Address:* The Haa, Gloup, Cullivoe, Yell, Shetland ZE2 9DD. *Club:* Circolo della Caccia (Rome).

CHEYSSON, Claude, Commander Legion of Honour; Croix de Guerre (5 times); Hon. GCMG 1984; Member, European Parliament, 1989–94; Town Councillor, Bargemon, 1983–89 and since 1995; *b* 13 April 1920; *s* of Pierre Cheysson and Sophie Funck-Brentano; *m* 1969, Danièle Schwarz; one *s* two *d* (and two *s* one *d* by former marrs). *Educ:* Coll. Stanislas, Paris; Ecole Polytechnique; Ecole Nationale d'Administration. Escaped from occupied France, 1943; Tank Officer, Free French Forces, France and Germany, 1944–45. Liaison Officer with German authorities, Bonn, 1948–52; Political Adviser to Viet Nam Govt, Saigon, 1952–53; Personal Adviser: to Prime Minister of France, Paris, 1954–55; to French Minister of Moroccan and Tunisian Affairs, 1956; Sec.-Gen., Commn for Techn. Cooperation in Africa, Lagos, Nairobi, 1957–62; Dir-Gen., Sahara Authority, Algiers, 1962–66; French Ambassador in Indonesia, 1966–69; Pres., Entreprise Minière et Chimique, 1970–73; European Comr (relations with Third World), 1973–81, 1985–89; Minister for External Relations, 1981–84. Bd Mem., Le Monde, 1978–92. President: Institut Pierre Mendès-France, 1988–91; Arche de la Fraternité, 1989–93. Grand Cross, Grand Officer and Comdr of many national orders; US Presidential Citation. Dr *hc* Univ. of Louvain; Joseph Bech Prize, 1978; Luderitz Prize, 1983. *Publications:* Une idée qui s'incarne, 1978; articles on Europe, and develt policies. *Address:* 52 rue de Vaugirard, 75006 Paris, France. *T:* and *Fax:* 143264665.

CHIANG KAI-SHEK, Madame (Mayling Soong Chiang); Chinese sociologist; *y d* of C. J. Soong; *m* 1927, Generalissimo Chiang Kai-Shek (*d* 1975). *Educ:* Wellesley Coll., USA. First Chinese woman appointed Mem. Child Labor Commn; Inaugurated Moral Endeavor Assoc.; established schools in Nanking for orphans of Revolutionary Soldiers; former Mem. Legislative Yuan; served as Sec.-General of Chinese Commission on Aeronautical Affairs; formerly: Member Chinese Commission on Aeronautical Affairs; Director-General of the New Life Movement and Chairman of its Women's Advisory Council; Founder and Director: National Chinese Women's Assoc. for War Relief; National Assoc. for Refugee Children; Chinese Women's Anti-Aggression League; Huashing Children's Home; Cheng Hsin Medical Rehabilitation Center for Post Polio Crippled Children. Chm., Fu Jen Catholic University. Governor, Nat. Palace Museum. Frequently made inspection tours to all sections of Free China where personally trained girl workers carry on war area and rural service work; accompanied husband on military campaigns; first Chinese woman to be decorated by National Govt of China. Recipient of highest military and Civil decorations; formerly: Hon. Chm., British United Aid to China Fund, China; Hon. Chm., Soc. for the Friends of the Wounded; Hon. President, American Bureau for Medical Aid to China; Patroness, International Red Cross Commn; Hon. President, Chinese Women's Relief Assoc. of New York; Hon. Chairman, Canadian Red Cross China Cttee; Hon. Chairman, Board of Directors, India Famine Relief Cttee; Hon. Mem., New York Zoological Soc.; Hon. Pres., Cttee for the Promotion of the Welfare of the Blind; Life Mem., San Francisco Press Club and Associated Countrywomen of the World; Mem., Phi Beta Kappa, Eta Chapter; first Hon. Member, Bill of Rights Commemorative Society; Hon. Member: Filipino Guerrillas of Bataan Assoc.; Catherine Lorillard Wolf Club. Hon. FRCS. Hon. LHD: John B. Stetson Univ., Deland, Fla, Bryant Coll., Providence, RI, Hobart and William Smith Colls, Geneva, NY; Hon. LLD: Rutgers Univ., New Brunswick, NJ, Goucher Coll., Baltimore, Wellesley Coll., Wellesley, Mass, Loyola Univ., UCLA, Russell Sage Coll., Troy, NY, Hahnemann Medical Coll., Philadelphia, Pa, Wesleyan Coll., Macon, Ga, Univ. of Michigan, Univ. of Hawaii, Boston Univ., Mass. Medal of Honour, New York City Federation of Women's Clubs; YWCA Emblem; Gold Medal, New York Southern Soc.; Chi Omega Nat. Achievement Award for 1943; Gold Medal for distinguished services, National Institute for Social Sciences; Distinguished Service Award, Altrusa Internat. Assoc.; Churchman Fifth Annual Award, 1943; Distinguished Service Citation, All-American Conf. to Combat Communism, 1958; Hon. Lieut-Gen. US Marine Corps. *Publications:* China in Peace and War, 1939; China Shall Rise Again, 1939; This is Our China, 1940; We Chinese Women, 1941; Little Sister Su, 1943; Ten Eventful Years, for Encyclopædia Britannica, 1946; Album of Reproduction of Paintings, vol. I, 1952, vol. II, 1962; The Sure Victory, 1955; Madame Chiang Kai-Shek Selected Speeches, 1958–59; Madame Chiang Kai-shek Selected Speeches, 1965–66; Album of Chinese Orchid Paintings, 1971; Album of Chinese Bamboo Paintings, 1972; Album of Chinese Landscape Paintings, 1973; Album of Chinese Floral Paintings, 1974; Conversations with Mikhail Borodin, 1977; Religious Writings 1934–63, 1964.

CHIASSON, Most Rev. Donat; RC Archbishop of Moncton, 1972–95; *b* Paquetville, NB, 2 Jan. 1930; *s* of Louis Chiasson and Anna Chiasson (*née* Godin). *Educ:* St Joseph's Univ., NB; Holy Heart Seminary, Halifax, NS; Theological and Catechetical studies, Rome and Lumen Vitae, Belgium. *Address:* PO Box 119, Rogersville, NB E0A 2T0, Canada.

CHIBA, Kazuo, Hon. KCMG 1998; Statutory Auditor, Toshiba Corporation, since 1997 (Adviser, 1991–96); *b* 19 April 1925; *s* of Shin-ichi and Miyoko Chiba; *m* 1954, Keiko Okamoto; one *s* one *d*. *Educ:* Univ. of Tokyo (LLB 1949); Fletcher Sch. of Law and Diplomacy, Medford, Mass, USA (MA 1951). Joined Min. of Foreign Affairs, Tokyo, 1948; Geneva, 1956; Iran, 1958; Min. of For. Affairs, 1959; Washington, DC, 1964; Dir, N America Div., N American Affairs Bureau, Min. of For. Affairs, 1967; Minister, Moscow, 1972; Consul-Gen., Atlanta, Ga, 1974; Consul-Gen., West Berlin, 1976; Dir Gen., Middle Eastern and African Affairs Bureau, Min. of For. Affairs, 1978; Ambassador: Sri Lanka, 1980; in Geneva (Perm. Mission of Japan to internat. orgns), 1982–87; to [illegible] 88–91. Counselor, Mitsui & Co. Ltd, 1991–98; Dir, Foreign & Colonial Pacific [illegible] Trust, London, 1993–97. Chairman: GATT Council, 1984–85; GATT [illegible] rties, 1985–86. Vis. Centennial Prof., LSE, 1992–94. Order of the Rising [illegible] 7. *Recreations:* reading (history), travel. *Address:* Toshiba Corp., 1-1 [illegible] Minato-ku, Tokyo 105-8001, Japan.

[illegible] **Callum,** MA, DPhil; FSA; FBA 1978; Fellow of Clare Hall, [illegible] Sept. 1915; *d* of J. C. Morgan, MBE; *m* 1947, Prof. Albert [illegible] 988); one *s* one *d* and two step *d*. *Educ:* Shrewsbury Priory [illegible] Margaret Hall, Oxford; Sorbonne, Paris. BLitt, MA, DPhil [illegible] Amy Mary Preston Read Scholar, Oxford, 1937–38; Goldsmiths' [illegible]; Nursing Auxiliary, 1939; Susette Taylor Research Fellow, Lady [illegible] rd, 1940–41; Asst Lectr, University Coll., Southampton, 1941–43; Asst Lectr, 1943–45, Lectr, 1945–47, in Medieval History, Univ. of Aberdeen; Lectr in History, later Fellow of Girton Coll., Cambridge, 1947–65; Research Fellow, Clare Hall, Cambridge, 1969–75; Leverhulme Emeritus Fellowship, 1982. Dir, Battle Conf. on Anglo-Norman Studies, 1989–93. Prothero Lectr, RHistS, 1987. Vice-Pres., Selden Soc., 1987–90. Corresp. Fellow, Medieval Acad. of America, 1983. Hon. Fellow, Girton Coll., Cambridge, 1988. Hon. DLitt Birmingham, 1979. *Publications:* The English Lands of the Abbey of Bec, 1946; Select Documents of the English Lands of the Abbey of Bec, 1951; The *Historia Pontificalis* of John of Salisbury, 1956; The Ecclesiastical History of Orderic Vitalis, 6 vols, 1969–80; Charters and Custumals of the Abbey of Holy Trinity Caen, 1982; The World of Orderic Vitalis, 1984; Anglo-Norman England 1066–1166, 1986; (ed) Anglo-Norman Studies, XII, 1990, XIII, 1991, XIV, 1992, XV, 1993, XVI, 1994; The Empress Matilda, 1991; (ed with Leslie Watkiss) The Waltham Chronicle, 1994; (ed with R. H. C. Davis) The *Gesta Guillelmi* of William of Poitiers, 1998; The Debate on the Norman Conquest, 1999; Piety, Power and History in Medieval England and Normandy, 2000; The Normans, 2000; numerous articles and reviews, principally in English and French historical jls. *Address:* Clare Hall, Cambridge CB3 9AL. *T:* (01223) 353923. *Club:* University Women's.

CHICHESTER, family name of **Marquess of Donegall.**

CHICHESTER, 9th Earl of, *cr* 1801; **John Nicholas Pelham;** Bt 1611; Baron Pelham of Stanmer, 1762; *b* (posthumous) 14 April 1944; *s* of 8th Earl of Chichester (killed on active service, 1944) and Ursula (*d* 1989) (she *m* 2nd, 1957, Ralph Gunning Henderson; marr. diss. 1971), *o d* of late Walter de Pannwitz, de Hartekamp, Bennebroek, Holland; *S* father, 1944; *m* 1975, Mrs June Marijke Hall; one *d*. *Recreations:* music, flying. *Heir: kinsman* Richard Anthony Henry Pelham [*b* 1 Aug. 1952; *m* 1987, Georgina, *d* of David Gilmour; two *s*]. *Address:* Little Durnford Manor, Salisbury, Wilts SP4 6AH.

CHICHESTER, Viscount; James Chichester; *b* 19 Nov. 1990; *s* and *heir* of Earl of Belfast, *qv*.

CHICHESTER, Bishop of, since 2001; **Rt Rev. John William Hind;** *b* 19 June 1945; *s* of late Harold Hind and Joan Mary Hind; *m* 1966, Janet Helen McLintock; three *s*. *Educ:* Watford Grammar Sch.; Leeds Univ. (BA 1966). Asst Master, Leeds Modern Sch., 1966–69; Asst Lectr, King Alfred's Coll., Winchester, 1969–70; Cuddesdon Theol Coll.; Deacon 1972, Priest 1973; Asst Curate, St John's, Catford, 1972–76; Vicar, Christ Church, Forest Hill, 1976–82 and Priest-in-Charge, St Paul's, Forest Hill, 1981–82; Principal, Chichester Theol Coll., 1982–91; Area Bishop of Horsham, 1991–93; Bishop of Gibraltar in Europe, 1993–2001. Canon Residentiary and Bursalis Preb., Chichester Cathedral, 1982–90. Chm., Faith and Order Adv. Gp, C of E, 1991–; Mem., Faith and Order Commn, WCC, 1999–. *Recreations:* cooking, gardening, languages. *Address:* The Palace, Chichester, W Sussex PO19 1PY.

CHICHESTER, Dean of; *no new appointment at time of going to press.*

CHICHESTER, Archdeacon of; *see* Brotherton, Ven. J. M.

CHICHESTER, Sir (Edward) John, 11th Bt *cr* 1641; *b* 14 April 1916; *s* of Comdr Sir Edward George Chichester, 10th Bt, RN, and late Phyllis Dorothy, *d* of late Henry F. Compton, Minstead Manor, Hants; *S* father, 1940; *m* 1950, Hon. Mrs Anne Rachel Pearl Moore-Gwyn, JP, *widow* of Capt. Howel Moore-Gwyn, Welsh Guards, and *d* of 2nd Baron Montagu of Beaulieu and late Hon. Mrs Edward Pleydell-Bouverie; two *s* two *d* (and one *d* decd). *Educ:* Radley; RMC Sandhurst. Commissioned RSF, 1936. Patron of one living. Served throughout War of 1939–45. Was employed by ICI Ltd, 1950–60. A King's Foreign Service Messenger, 1947–50. Formerly Capt., Royal Scots Fusiliers and Lieut RNVR. *Heir: s* James Henry Edward Chichester [*b* 15 Oct. 1951; *m* 1990, Anne, *d* of late Major J. W. Chandos-Pole; two *s*]. *Address:* Battramsley Lodge, Boldre, Lymington, Hants SO41 8PT. *Club:* Naval.

CHICHESTER, Giles Bryan; Member (C) South West Region, England, European Parliament, since 1999 (Devon and East Plymouth, 1994–99); *b* 29 July 1946; *s* of Sir Francis Chichester, KBE and Sheila Mary (*née* Craven); *m* 1979, Virginia Ansell; two *s* one *d*. *Educ:* Westminster Sch.; Christ Church, Oxford (BA Hons Geography; MA). FRGS 1972. Trainee, Univ. of London Press and Hodder & Stoughton, publishers, 1968–69; Francis Chichester Ltd: Production Manager, 1969–71; Co. Sec., 1970–89; Dir, 1971–; Man. Dir, 1983–; Chm., 1989–. Chm., Foreign Affairs Forum, 1987–90. Cons. spokesman: on Research, Technol Develt and Energy Cttee, EP, 1994–99; on Industry, External Trade, Res. and Energy Cttee, EP, 1999–. Vice-Pres., European Energy Foundn, 1995–. Mem. Council, Air League, 1995–99. *Publication:* pamphlet on nuclear energy. *Recreations:* rowing, sailing, snooker, vegetarian cooking. *Address:* (constituency office) 48 Queen Street, Exeter EX4 3SR. *T:* (01392) 491815; (office) 9 St James's Place, SW1A 1PE. *T:* (020) 7493 0931; Longridge, West Hill, Ottery St Mary, Devon EX11 1UX. *Clubs:* Pratt's, United and Cecil; London Rowing; Royal Western Yacht (Plymouth); Royal Yacht Squadron (Cowes).

CHICHESTER, Sir John; *see* Chichester, Sir E. J.

CHICHESTER-CLARK, family name of **Baron Moyola.**

CHICHESTER-CLARK, Sir Robert, (Sir Robin), Kt 1974; *b* 10 Jan. 1928; *s* of late Capt. J. L. C. Chichester-Clark, DSO and Bar, DL, MP, and Mrs C. E. Brackenbury; *m* 1st, 1953, Jane Helen Goddard (marr. diss. 1972); one *s* two *d*; 2nd, 1974, Caroline, *d* of Anthony Bull, *qv*; two *s*. *Educ:* Royal Naval Coll.; Magdalene Coll., Cambridge (BA Hons Hist. and Law). Journalist, 1950; Public Relations Officer, Glyndebourne Opera, 1952; Asst to Sales Manager, Oxford Univ. Press, 1953–55. MP (UU) Londonderry City and Co., 1955–Feb. 1974; PPS to Financial Secretary to the Treasury, 1958; Asst Government Whip (unpaid), 1958–60; a Lord Comr of the Treasury, 1960–61; Comptroller of HM Household, 1961–64; Chief Opposition Spokesman on N Ireland, 1964–70, on Public Building and Works and the Arts, 1965–70; Minister of State, Dept of Employment, 1972–74. Dir, Instn of Works Managers, 1968–72. Chairman: Restoration of Appearance and Function Trust, 1988–2000; Arvon Develt Cttee, 1995–; Arvon Foundn, 1997–; Trustee, Royal Philharmonic Orchestra Develt Trust, 1993–95. Hon. FIWM 1972. *Recreations:* fishing, reading. *Club:* Brooks's.
See also P. Hobhouse, Baron Moyola.

CHICK, John Stephen; educational consultant; HM Diplomatic Service, retired; *b* 5 Aug. 1935; *m* 1966, Margarita Alvarez de Sotomayor; one *s* three *d*. *Educ:* St John's Coll., Cambridge (BA 1959); Univ. of Pennsylvania (MA 1960). Entered FO, 1961; Madrid, 1963–66; First Sec., Mexico City, 1966–69; FCO, 1969–73; First Sec. and Head of Chancery, Rangoon, 1973–76; Head of Chancery, Luxembourg, 1976–78; Commercial Counsellor and Consul-Gen., Buenos Aires, 1978–81; Head of Arms Control Dept, FCO, 1981–83; Head of S Pacific Dept, FCO, 1983–85. Consul-Gen., Geneva, 1985–89. Dir of Internat. Affairs, Sallingbury Casey Ltd, 1990–91; Associate Dir, Rowland Public Affairs, 1991. *Address:* 24 Beverley Road, SW13 0LX. *T:* (020) 8876 5916.

CHIDGEY, David William George, CEng, FICE, FIHT; MP (Lib Dem) Eastleigh, since June 1994; *b* 9 July 1942; *s* of Cyril Cecil Chidgey and Winifred Hilda Doris Chidgey (*née* Weston); *m* 1965, April Carolyn Idris-Jones; one *s* two *d*. *Educ:* Royal Naval Coll., Portsmouth; Portsmouth Poly. CEng 1971; MCIT 1985; FIHT 1990; FIEI 1990; FICE 1993; MConsEI 1993. Mech. and aeronautical engr, Admiralty, 1958–64; Highways and Civil Engr, Hants CC, 1965–72; Brian Colquhoun and Partners: Chartered Engr and Project Manager, UK, ME and W Africa, 1973–80; Associate Partner and Man. Dir, Ireland, 1981–88; Associate Partner, Central Southern England, 1988–93; Thorburn Colquhoun: Associate Dir, Southern England and Project Dir, Engrg Facilities Management, mil. estabts in Hants, 1994–. Contested: (SLD) Hampshire Central, Eur. Parlt, Dec. 1988 and 1989; (Lib Dem) Eastleigh, 1992. Lib Dem spokesman for: employment, 1994–95; transport, 1995–97; trade and industry, 1997–99. Mem., Foreign Affairs Cttee. CRAeS; CompIMechE. *Publications:* papers in technical jl, Traffic Engineering and Control. *Recreations:* golf, reading. *Address:* c/o House of Commons, SW1A 0AA. *Club:* National Liberal.

CH'IEN Kuo Fung, Dr Raymond, GBS 1999; CBE 1994; JP; Executive Chairman, chinadotcom corporation, since 1999; *b* 26 Jan. 1952; *s* of James Ch'ien and Ellen Ma; *m* Whang Hwee Leng; one *s* two *d*. *Educ:* Rockford Coll., Illinois (BA 1973); Univ. of Pennsylvania (PhD Econs 1978). Gp Man. Dir, Lam Soon Hong Kong Gp, 1984–97; Non-executive Chairman: Inchcape Greater China, 1997–; HSBC Private Equity (Asia) Ltd, 1997–. MEC, Hong Kong, then HKSAR, 1992–. JP Hong Kong, 1993. Young Industrialist Award, Hong Kong, 1988; Global Leader for Tomorrow Award, World Econ. Forum, 1993. *Recreation:* scuba diving. *Address:* 22/F Citicorp Centre, 18 Whitfield Road, North Point, Hong Kong. *T:* 28801328. *Clubs:* Hong Kong, Hong Kong Jockey, Hong Kong Cricket, Hong Kong Golf.

CHIENE, John; Chairman, Gartmore Capital Strategy Fund, since 1996; *b* 27 Jan. 1937; *s* of John and Muriel Chiene; *m* 1st, 1965, Anne; one *s* one *d*; 2nd, 1986, Carol; one *d*. *Educ:* Rugby; Queen's Coll., Cambridge (BA). Wood Mackenzie: joined, 1962; Man. Partner, 1969; Sen. Partner, 1974; Jt Chief Exec., Hill Samuel & Co. Ltd (who had merged with Wood Mackenzie), 1987; Chm., County NatWest Securities, on their merger with Wood Mackenzie, 1988–89; Dep. Chm., County NatWest Ltd, 1989–90. Director: The Gartmore Scotland Investment Trust plc, 1991–; Henderson Japanese Smaller Cos Trust plc, 1993–. *Recreations:* golf, opera, ski-ing. *Address:* 7 St Leonard's Terrace, SW3 4QB. *Clubs:* Cavalry and Guards, City of London; New (Edinburgh).

CHIEPE, Hon. Gaositwe Keagakwa Tibe, PH 1996; PMS 1975; MBE 1962; FRSA; Minister for Education, Botswana, 1995–99; *b* 20 Oct. 1922; *d* of late T. Chiepe. *Educ:* Fort Hare, South Africa (BSc, EdDip); Bristol Univ., UK (MA (Ed)). Asst Educn Officer, 1948–53; Educn Officer and Schools Inspector, 1953–62; Sen. Educn Officer, 1962–65; Dep. Dir of Educn, 1965–67; Dir of Educn, 1968–70; High Comr to UK and Nigeria, 1970–74; Ambassador: Denmark, Norway, Sweden, France and Germany, 1970–74; Belgium and EEC, 1973–74; Minister of Commerce and Industry, 1974–77; Minister for Mineral Resources and Water Affairs, 1977–84; Minister for External Affairs, 1984–95. Chairman: Africa Region, CPA, 1981–83; Botswana Branch, CPA, 1981–. Member: Botswana Society; Botswana Girl Guide Assoc.; Internat. Fedn of University Women. Hon. Pres., Kalahari Conservation Soc.; Patron, Botswana Forestry Assoc. Hon. LLD Bristol, 1972, Hon. DLitt de Paul Univ., Chicago, 1994; Hon. DEd Fort Hare Univ., SA, 1996. FRSA 1973. *Recreations:* gardening, a bit of swimming (in Botswana), reading. *Address:* PO Box 186, Gaborone, Botswana.

CHIGNELL, Anthony Hugh, FRCS, FRCOphth; Consulting Ophthalmic Surgeon: St Thomas' Hospital, 1973–99; King Edward VII Hospital, 1985–2000; *b* 14 April 1939; *s* of Thomas Hugh Chignell and Phyllis Una (*née* Green); *m* 1962, Phillippa Price Brayne-Nicholls; one *s* two *d*. *Educ:* Worth Sch.; Downside Sch.; St Thomas' Hosp. (MB BS 1962). DO 1966; FRCS 1968. Registrar, Moorfields Eye Hosp., 1966–69; Sen. Registrar, Retinal Unit, Moorfields Eye Hosp. and St Thomas' Hosp., 1969–73; Teacher in Ophthalmology, London Univ., 1980–99. Civilian Consultant in Ophthalmology to Army, 1983–99; Consultant Advr in Ophthalmology to Metropolitan Police, 1988–99. Scientific Advr, Nat. Eye Inst., 1991–99. Gov., Royal Nat. Coll. for Blind, 1987–97; Mem. Council, GDBA, 1989–. Mem., Jules Gonin Club, 1972. Trustee: Ridley Foundn, 1988–; Fight for Sight, 1992–95. Mem. Court, Spectacle Makers' Co., 1988– (Master, 1999–2000). OStJ 1987. *Publications:* Retinal Detachment Surgery, 1979, 2nd edn 1988; Vitreo-Retinal Surgery, 1998; numerous articles related to retinal detachment surgery. *Recreations:* fly-fishing, golf, the theatre, Herefordshire. *Address:* 3 Tedworth Square, SW3 4DU. *Clubs:* Royal Anglo-Belgian, MCC; New Zealand Golf (Weybridge).

CHIKETA, Stephen Cletus; Ambassador of Zimbabwe to State of Kuwait, since 1995, also to Bahrain, Oman, Qatar and United Arab Emirates; *b* 16 Sept. 1942; *s* of Mangwiro S. Chiketa and Mary Magdalene (*née* Chivero); *m* 1976, Juliet Joalane; one *s* two *d*. *Educ:* Univ. of South Africa (BA Hons); Univ. of Basutoland, Botswana and Swaziland (BA, PGCE). Asst Teacher, Swaziland schs, 1967–73; part-time Lectr, Univ. of Botswana, Lesotho and Swaziland, 1972–73; Principal, High School in Lesotho, 1974–80; Under Sec., Min. of Foreign Affairs, 1982; Dep. Perm. Rep., UN, 1982–86; Dep. Sec., Min. of Foreign Affairs, 1986–87; Ambassador to Romania and Bulgaria, 1987–90; High Comr for Zimbabwe in London, 1990–93; Dep. Sec., Ministry of Foreign Affairs, Harare, 1993–95. *Publications:* history articles in Swaziland weekly newspapers. *Recreations:* photography, tennis, reading, table tennis, cards. *Address:* Embassy of Zimbabwe, Salwa Area 9, Street 105 House no 8, PO Box 36484, Airaas 24755, Kuwait City, Kuwait.

CHILCOT, Sir John (Anthony), GCB 1998 (KCB 1994; CB 1990); Staff Counsellor for Security and Intelligence Services, since 1999; *b* 22 April 1939; *s* of Henry William Chilcot and Catherine Chilcot (*née* Ashall); *m* 1964, Rosalind Mary Forster. *Educ:* Brighton Coll. (Lyon Scholar); Pembroke Coll., Cambridge (Open Scholar; MA; Hon. Fellow, 1999). Joined Home Office, 1963; Asst Private Sec. to Home Secretary (Rt Hon. Roy Jenkins), 1966; Private Sec. to Head of Civil Service (late Baron Armstrong of Sanderstead), 1971–73; Principal Private Secretary to Home Secretary (Rt Hon. Merlyn Rees; Rt Hon. William Whitelaw), 1978–80; Asst Under-Sec. of State, Dir of Personnel and Finance, Prison Dept, 1980–84; Under-Sec., Cabinet Office (MPO), 1984–86; Asst Under Sec. of State, 1986 (seconded to Schroders, 1986–87), Dep. Under Sec. of State, 1987–90, Home Office; Permanent Under Sec. of State, NI Office, 1990–97. Member: Indep. Commn on the Voting System, 1997–98; Lord Chancellor's Adv. Council on Public Records, 1999–. Director: RTZ Pillar, 1986–90; Abraxa Ltd, 1998–. Chm., B & CE Benefit Schemes, 1999–. Pres., First Div. Pensioners' Gp, 1998–. Chm., Police Foundn, 2001 (Trustee, 1998–; Chm., Res. Cttee, 1999–). *Recreations:* reading, music and opera, travel. *Address:* c/o Cabinet Office, Whitehall, SW1A 2AS. *Club:* Travellers.

CHILD, Christopher Thomas; National President, Bakers' Union, 1968–77; former Consultant to Baking Industry, Industrial Relations Officer and Training Officer, Baking Industry and Health Food Products, 1970–85; *b* 8 Jan. 1920; *s* of late Thomas William and Penelope Child; *m* 1943, Lilian Delaney; two *s* one *d*. *Educ:* Robert Ferguson Sch., Carlisle; Birmingham Coll. of Food and Domestic Science. Apprenticed baker, 1936; gained London City and Guilds final certificates in Breadmaking, Flour Confectionery and Bakery Science, 1951, and became Examiner in these subjects for CGLI. Full-time trade union official in Birmingham, 1958. Member: Birmingham Trades Council Exec., 1958–68; Adv. Council, Midland Regional TUC, 1959–68; Disablement Adv. Cttee, Birmingham, 1959–68. Former Chairman: Nat. Council Baking Education; Nat. Joint Apprenticeship Council for Baking. Mem., Industrial Training Bd, Food, Drink and Tobacco, 1968–78; former Vice-Pres., EEC Food Group and Mem., EEC Cttees on Food Products, Vocational Training, and Food Legislation; former Sec., Jt Bakers' Unions of England, Scotland and Ireland. Mem., TEC C4 programme Cttee, Hotel, Food, Catering and Institutional Management. *Recreations:* fishing, gardening, climbing in English Lake District. *Address:* Moss Cottages, 14 Hodwell, Ashwell, Baldock, Herts SG7 5QG. *T:* (01462) 743454.

CHILD, Sir (Coles John) Jeremy, 3rd Bt *cr* 1919; actor; *b* 20 Sept. 1944; *s* of Sir Coles John Child, 2nd Bt, and Sheila (*d* 1964), *e d* of Hugh Mathewson; *S* father, 1971; *m* 1971, Deborah Jane (*née* Snelling) (marr. diss. 1976); one *d*; *m* 1978, Jan (marr. diss. 1986), *y d* of B. Todd, Kingston upon Thames; one *s* one *d*; *m* 1987, Libby, *y d* of Rev. Grenville Morgan, Canterbury, Kent; one *s* one *d*. *Educ:* Eton; Univ. of Poitiers (Dip. in French). Trained at Bristol Old Vic Theatre Sch., 1963–65; Bristol Old Vic, 1965–66; repertory at Windsor, Canterbury and Colchester; Conduct Unbecoming, Queen's, 1970; appeared at Royal Court, Mermaid and Bankside Globe, 1973; Oh Kay, Westminster, 1974; Donkey's Years, Globe, 1977; Hay Fever, Lyric, Hammersmith, 1980; Out of Order, Far and Middle East tour, 1995; Plenty, Albery, 1999; Pride and Prejudice, UK tour, 2000; *films include:* Privilege, 1967; Oh What a Lovely War!, 1967; The Breaking of Bumbo, 1970; Young Winston, 1971; The Stud, 1976; Quadrophenia, 1978; Sir Henry at Rawlinson's End, 1979; Chanel Solitaire, 1980; High Road to China, 1982; Give my Regards to Broad Street, 1983; Taffin, 1987; A Fish called Wanda, 1989; The Madness of King George, 1994; Regeneration, 1996; Don't Go Breaking My Heart, 1997; Whatever Happened to Harold Smith?, 1999; Lagaan, 2000; Laisser Passer, 2001; *television includes:* T'is Pity She's a Whore; Diana, Her True Story; Love in a Cold Climate; *series:* Father, Dear Father, Edward and Mrs Simpson, The Jewel in the Crown, Bergerac, The Glittering Prizes, Wings, Fairly Secret Army, Oxbridge Blues, Edge of Darkness, First Among Equals, Game, Set and Match, Lovejoy, Perfect Scoundrels, Gravy Train Goes East, Headhunters, Harnessing Peacocks, Sharpe's Enemy, Frank Stubbs Promotes, A Dance to the Music of Time, Mosley, Getting Hurt, A Touch of Frost. *Recreations:* gardening, cooking, travel. *Heir: s* Coles John Alexander Child, *b* 10 May 1982. *Club:* Garrick.

CHILD, Denis Marsden, CBE 1987; Chairman, IBM UK Pensions Trust, 1994–97 (Member, 1984–97); *b* 1 Nov. 1926; *s* of late Percival Snowden Child and Alice Child (*née* Jackson); *m* 1973, Patricia Charlton; two *s* one *d* by previous marr. *Educ:* Woodhouse Grove Sch., Bradford. Joined Westminster Bank, Leeds, 1942; RN, 1944–48; rejoined Westminster Bank; National Westminster Bank: Asst Area Manager, Leeds, 1970; Area Manager, Wembley, 1972; Chief Manager, Planning and Marketing, 1975; Head, Management Inf. and Control, 1977; Gen. Manager, Financial Control Div., 1979; Dir, NatWest Bank, 1982–96; Dep. Gp Chief Exec., 1982–87; Dir, Coutts & Co., 1982–97; Chm., Lombard North Central, 1991–96. Chairman: Exec. Cttee, BBA, 1986–87; Council, Assoc. for Payment Clearing Services, 1985–86; Financial Markets Cttee, Fedn Bancaire, EC, 1985–87; Director: Internat. Commodities Clearing House, 1982–86 (Chm., 1990–93); Eurotunnel Gp, 1985–98; Investors Compensation Scheme Ltd, 1988–92. Bd Mem., CAA, 1986–90. Member: Accounting Standards Cttee, 1985–90; Securities and Investments Bd, 1986–92. FCIB; FCT; FCIS. *Recreations:* golf, gardening. *Address:* Fairways, Park Road, Farnham Royal, Bucks SL2 3BQ. *T:* (01753) 648096. *Club:* Stoke Poges Golf.

CHILD, Sir Jeremy; *see* Child, Sir C. J. J.

CHILD, Prof. John; Professor of Commerce, University of Birmingham, since 2000; *b* 10 Nov. 1940; *s* of late Clifton James Child, OBE and Hilde Child (*née* Hurwitz); *m* 1965, Elizabeth Anne Mitchiner; one *s* one *d*. *Educ:* St John's College, Cambridge (scholar; MA, PhD, ScD). Rolls-Royce, 1965–66; Aston Univ., 1966–68; London Business Sch., 1968–73; Prof. of Organizational Behaviour, Aston Univ., 1973–91 (Dean, Aston Business Sch., 1986–89); Dean and Dir, China-Europe Management Inst., Beijing, 1989–90; Diageo Prof. of Mgt Studies, Univ. of Cambridge, and Fellow of St John's Coll., Cambridge, 1991–2000. Vis. Fellow, Nuffield Coll., Oxford, 1973–78; Vis. Prof., Univ. of Hong Kong, 1998–. Editor-in-Chief, Organization Studies, 1992–96. *Publications include:* British Management Thought, 1969; The Business Enterprise in Modern Industrial Society, 1969; Organization, 1977; (jtly) Lost Managers, 1982; (ed) Reform Policy and the Chinese Enterprise, 1990; (jtly) Reshaping Work, 1990; (jtly) New Technology in European Services, 1990; Management in China, 1994; (jtly) Co-operative Strategy, 1998; (jtly) The Management of International Acquisitions, 2001; numerous contribs to learned jls. *Recreations:* sailing, mountain walking, bridge. *Address:* University of Birmingham, Birmingham B15 2TT. *T:* (0121) 414 6701; *e-mail:* J.Child@bham.ac.uk. *Club:* Earlswood Sailing.

CHILD, Prof. Mark Sheard, PhD; FRS 1989; Coulson Professor of Theoretical Chemistry, University of Oxford, since 1994, and Fellow of University College, Oxford, since 1994; *b* 17 Aug. 1937; *s* of George Child and Kathleen (*née* Stevenson); *m* 1964, Daphne Hall; one *s* two *d*. *Educ:* Pocklington Sch., Yorks; Clare Coll., Cambridge (BA, PhD). Vis. Scientist, Berkeley, California, 1962–63; Lectr in Theoretical Chem., Glasgow Univ., 1963–66; Oxford University: Lectr in Theoretical Chem., 1966–89; Aldrichian Praelector in Chemistry, Oxford Univ., 1989–92; Prof. of Chemical Dynamics, 1992–94; Fellow, St Edmund Hall, 1966–94. *Publications:* Molecular Collision Theory, 1974; Semiclassical Methods with Molecular Applications, 1991. *Recreations:* gardening, walking. *Address:* University College, Oxford OX1 4BH. *T:* (01865) 271532.

CHILD VILLIERS, family name of **Earl of Jersey**.

CHILSTON, 4th Viscount *cr* 1911, of Boughton Malherbe; **Alastair George Akers-Douglas;** Baron Douglas of Baads, 1911; film producer; *b* 5 Sept. 1946; *s* of Ian Stanley Akers-Douglas (*d* 1952) (*g s* of 1st Viscount) and of Phyllis Rosemary (who *m* 2nd, John Anthony Cobham Shaw, MC), *d* of late Arthur David Clere Parsons; *S* cousin, 1982; *m* 1971, Juliet Anne, *d* of Lt-Col Nigel Lovett, Glos Regt; three *s*. *Educ:* Eton College; Madrid Univ. *Recreation:* sailing. *Heir: s* Hon. Oliver Ian Akers-Douglas, *b* 13 Oct. 1973. *Address:* The Old Rectory, Twyford, near Winchester, Hants SO21 1NS. *T:* (01962) 712300.

CHILTON, Brig. Sir Frederick Oliver, Kt 1969; CBE 1963 (OBE 1957); DSO 1941 and bar 1944; Chairman, Repatriation Commission, Australia, 1958–70; *b* 23 July 1905. *Educ:* Univ. of Sydney (BA, LLB). Solicitor, NSW, 1929. Late AIF; served War of 1939–45, Libya, Greece, New Guinea and Borneo (despatches, DSO and bar); Controller of Joint Intelligence, 1946–48; Asst Sec., Dept of Defence, Australia, 1948–50; Dep. Sec., 1950–58. *Address:* Box 129, Avalon PO, NSW 2107, Australia. *Clubs:* Melbourne, Union, Naval and Military (Melbourne).

CHILTON, John James; jazz musician, since 1958; *b* 16 July 1932; *s* of Thomas William Chilton and Eileen Florence (*née* Burke); *m* 1963, Teresa McDonald; two *s* one *d*. *Educ:* Yardley Gobion Sch., Northants; Claremont Sch., Kenton, Middx. Nat. Service, RAF, 1950–52. Worked in an advertising agency and for nat. newspaper before becoming professional musician, leading own band, 1958; played in a ship's orchestra, 1960; with Bruce Turner's Jump Band, 1960–63; jt-leader with Wally Fawkes, 1969–72; formed The Feetwarmers, 1972, regular accompanists for George Melly, 1972–. Recording, composing and arranging, 1972–. Grammy Award, USA, for best album notes, 1983; ARSC Award, USA, for best researched jazz or blues book, 1992; Jazz Writer of the Year, British Jazz award, 2000. *Publications:* Who's Who of Jazz, 1970, 5th edn 1989; Billie's Blues, 1974, 5th edn 1990; McKinney's Music, 1978; Teach Yourself Jazz, 1979, 2nd edn 1980; A Jazz Nursery, 1980; Stomp Off, Let's Go, 1983; Sidney Bechet: the wizard of jazz, 1987, 2nd edn 1996; The Song of the Hawk, 1990; Let the Good Times Roll, 1992; Who's Who of British Jazz, 1996; Ride, Red, Ride, 1999; articles on jazz in books and newspapers. *Recreations:* watching cricket, soccer, collecting modern first editions.

CHILVER, family name of **Baron Chilver**.

CHILVER, Baron *cr* 1987 (Life Peer), of Cranfield in the County of Bedfordshire; **Henry Chilver,** Kt 1978; FRS 1982; FREng; CIMgt; Chairman, Chiroscience Group plc, 1995–98; *b* 30 Oct. 1926; *e s* of A. H. Chilver and A. E. Mack; *m* 1959, Claudia M. B. Grigson, MA, MB, BCh, *o d* of Sir Wilfrid Grigson; three *s* two *d*. *Educ:* Southend High Sch.; Bristol Univ. (Albert Fry Prize 1947). Structural Engineering Asst, British Railways, 1947; Asst Lecturer, 1950, Lecturer, 1952, in Civil Engineering, Bristol Univ.; Demonstrator, 1954, Lectr, 1956, in Engineering, Cambridge Univ.; Fellow of Corpus Christi Coll., Cambridge, 1958–61 (Hon. Fellow, 1981); Chadwick Prof. of Civil Engineering, UCL, 1961–69; Vice-Chancellor, Cranfield Inst. of Technology, 1970–89; Director: Centre for Environmental Studies, 1967–69; Node Course (for civil service and industry), 1974–75. Chairman: English China Clays, 1989–95 (Dir, 1973–95); RJB Mining plc, 1993–97; Director: SKF (UK), 1972–80; De La Rue Co., 1973–81; SE Reg., Nat. Westminster Bank, 1975–83; Delta Gp, 1977–84; Powell Duffryn, 1979–89; TR Technology Investment Trust, 1982–88; Hill Samuel Gp, 1983–87; Britoil, 1986–88; ICI, 1990–93; Zeneca Group, 1993–95. Chairman: Milton Keynes Develt Corp., 1983–92; Plymouth Develt Corp., 1996–98. Chairman: PO, 1980–81; Higher Educn Review Body, NI, 1978–81; Univs' Computer Bd, 1975–78; RAF Trng and Educn Adv. Cttee, 1976–80; Adv. Council, RMCS, Shrivenham, 1978–83; Working Gp on Advanced Ground Transport, 1978–81; Electronics EDC, 1980–85; ACARD, 1982–85; Interim Adv. Cttee on Teachers' Pay, 1987–91; UFC, 1988–91; Innovation Adv. Bd, DTI, 1989–93. Member: Ferrybridge Enquiry Cttee, 1965; Management Cttee, Inst. of Child Health, 1965–69; ARC, 1967–70 and 1972–75; SRC, 1970–74; Beds Educn Cttee, 1970–74; Planning and Transport Res. Adv. Council, 1972–79; Cttee for Ind. Technologies, 1972–76; ICE Special Cttee on Educn and Trng, 1973 (Chm.); CNAA, 1973–76; Royal Commn on Environmental Pollution, 1976–81; Standing Commn on Energy and the Environment, 1978–81; Adv. Bd for Res. Councils, 1982–85; Bd, Nat. Adv. Body for Local Authority Higher Educn, 1983–85. Dep. Pres., Standing Conf. on Schools Sci. and Technol.; Assessor, Inquiry on Lorries, People and the Envt, 1979–80. President: Inst. of Management Services, 1982–2000; Inst. of Logistics, 1993–95; Vice-Pres., ICE, 1981–83; Mem., Smeatonian Soc. of Civil Engrs (Pres., 1997). Member Council: Birkbeck Coll., 1980–82; Cheltenham Coll., 1980–88. Lectures: STC Communications, 1981; O'Sullivan, Imperial Coll., 1984; Lady Margaret Beaufort, Bedford, 1985; Fawley, Southampton Univ., 1985; Lubbock, Oxford, 1990. Telford Gold Medal, ICE, 1962; Coopers Hill War Meml Prize, ICE, 1977. FREng (FEng 1977). Hon. DSc: Leeds, 1982; Bristol, 1983; Salford, 1983; Strathclyde, 1986; Bath, 1986; Cranfield, 1989; Buckingham, 1990; Compiègne, 1990. *Publications:* Problems in Engineering Structures (with R. J. Ashby), 1958; Strength of Materials (with J. Case), 1959, 3rd edn as Strength of Materials and Structures (with J. Case and C. T. Ross), 1993, 4th edn 1999; Thin-walled Structures (ed), 1967; papers on structural theory in engineering journals. *Clubs:* Athenæum, Oxford and Cambridge.

CHILVER, Brian Outram; Chairman, Eskmuir Properties plc, since 1990; *b* 17 June 1933; *s* of late Bertram Montagu Chilver and of Edith Gwendoline Chilver; *m* 1956, Erica Mary; two *s* two *d*. *Educ:* University College Sch. FCA 1965; FCMA 1993. Temple Gothard & Co., 1949–55 (articled clerk); National Service, RAF, 1955–57; Barton Mayhew & Co., 1957–59; Temple Gothard & Co., 1959–85 (Partner, 1960, Senior Partner, 1975); Chairman: Laing Properties, 1987–90; Seafield plc, 1990–96; Forward Technology Industries plc, 1991–2000; Dir (non-exec.), John Laing plc, 1988–. Chm., Tear Fund, 1990–99. *Recreations:* walking, swimming, reading, music. *Address:* Bretaye, Limbourne Lane, Fittleworth, West Sussex RH20 1HR; (office) 8 Queen Anne Street, W1M 9LD.

CHILVER, Elizabeth Millicent, (Mrs R. C. Chilver); Principal of Lady Margaret Hall, Oxford, 1971–79, Honorary Fellow, 1979; *b* 3 Aug. 1914; *o d* of late Philip Perceval Graves and late Millicent Graves (*née* Gilchrist); *m* 1937, Richard Clementson Chilver, CB (*d* 1985). *Educ:* Benenden Sch., Cranbrook; Somerville Coll., Oxford (Hon. Fellow, 1977). Journalist, 1937–39; temp. Civil Servant, 1939–45; Daily News Ltd, 1945–47; temp. Principal and Secretary, Colonial Social Science Research Council and Colonial Economic Research Cttee, Colonial Office, 1948–57; Director, Univ. of Oxford Inst. of Commonwealth Studies, 1957–61; Senior Research Fellow, Univ. of London Inst. of Commonwealth Studies, 1961–64; Principal, Bedford Coll., Univ. of London, 1964–71, Fellow, 1974. Mem. Royal Commn on Medical Education, 1965–68. Trustee, British Museum, 1970–75; Mem. Governing Body, SOAS, Univ. of London, 1975–80. Médaille de la Reconnaissance française, 1945. *Publications:* articles on African historical subjects. *Address:* 47 Kingston Road, Oxford OX2 6RH. *T:* (01865) 553082.

CHILVERS, Prof. Clair Evelyn Druce; Director of Research and Development, Trent Region, NHS Executive, Department of Health, since 1999; *b* 8 Feb. 1946; *d* of Air Cdre Stanley Edwin Druce Mills, CB, CBE and of Joan Mary Mills (*née* James); *m* 1st, 1965, Antony Stuart Chilvers, MA, MChir, FRCS (marr. diss. 1995); one *s* one *d*; 2nd, 1998, Bill Crampin. *Educ:* Cheltenham Ladies' Coll.; LSE (BSc Econ); LSHTM (MSc); DSc Nottingham 1995. Scientist, Inst. of Cancer Res., 1979–90; Prof. of Epidemiology, Med. Sch., 1990–99, now Emeritus, and Dean of Grad. Sch., 1996–99, Nottingham Univ.; Director: Trent Inst. for Health Services Res., Nottingham, 1994–99; Trent Cancer Registry, 1994–96. Mem., Royal Commn on Envmtl Pollution, 1994–98. Mem., Cttee on Carcinogenicity of Chemicals in Food, Consumer Products and Envmt, DoH, 1993–2000. Non-executive Director: Nottingham Community Health NHS Trust, 1991–96; Learning and Skills Develt Agency, 1998–. Mem. Council, Nottingham Univ., 1994–99; Chm. Council, Southwell Cathedral, 2000–. Hon. MFPHM 1991. *Publications:* numerous in learned jls, mainly in field of cancer epidemiology. *Recreations:* music, walking, cinema, theology. *Club:* Royal Automobile.

CHILVERS, Prof. Edwin Roy, PhD; FRCP, FRCPE; Professor of Respiratory Medicine, University of Cambridge, since 1998, and Fellow of St Edmund's College, Cambridge, since 1999; *b* 17 March 1959; *s* of Derek John Chilvers and Marjorie Grace Chilvers; *m* 1982, Rowena Joy Tyssen; two *s* one *d*. *Educ:* Univ. of Nottingham Med. Sch. (BMedSci 1980; BM BS Hons 1982); PhD London 1991. MRCP 1985, FRCP 1999; FRCPE 1995. Registrar, Ealing and Hammersmith Hosps, 1985–87; MRC Clinical Trng Fellow, 1987–90; Edinburgh University: Lectr in Respiratory Medicine, 1990–92; Wellcome Trust Sen. Res. Fellow in Clinical Sci., 1992–98; Reader in Medicine, 1997–98. Hon. Consultant Physician: Royal Infirmary, Edinburgh, 1992–98; Addenbrooke's and Papworth Hosps, 1998–. Mem., Comberton Baptist Church. *Publications:* (ed jtly) Davidson's Principles and Practice of Medicine, 17th edn 1995, 18th edn 1999; contrib. scientific papers on inflammatory cell biol. and intracellular signalling. *Recreations:* modern literature, spectator sport, wine. *Address:* 4 Mallows Close, Comberton, Cambridge CB3 7GN. *T:* (01223) 762007.

CHILWELL, Hon. Sir Muir Fitzherbert, Kt 1989; **Hon. Mr Justice Chilwell;** Judge of the Court of Appeal, Cook Islands, since 1990; Judge of the High Court, Cook Islands, 1991–94; *b* 12 April 1924; *s* of Benjamin Charles Chilwell and Loris Madeleine Chilwell; *m* 1947, Lynette Erica Frances Cox; two *d* (one *s* decd). *Educ:* Auckland University Coll., Univ. of New Zealand (LLB 1949; LLM Hons 1950). Law Clerk, 1941–49; admitted Barrister and Solicitor, 1949; Partner, Haddow, Haddow & Chilwell, later Haddow Chilwell Pain & Palmer, 1949–65; QC 1965; admitted Victorian Bar (Aust.) and QC Vict. 1970; Judge of the Supreme, later High, Court of NZ, 1973–91; Admin. Div., High Court, 1982–91. Lectr, Univ. of Auckland, 1950 and 1953–60. Member: Contracts and Commercial Law Reform Cttee, 1966–68 (Chm., 1968–73); Law Revision Commn, 1968–73; Disciplinary Cttee, NZ Law Soc., 1971–73; Council, Legal Educn, NZ, 1985–91 (Assessor in Law of Contract, 1964–67); Chm., Legal Res. Foundn, 1977–81; Mem. Council, Auckland Dist Law Soc., 1960–67, Pres., 1967–68; Pres., Auckland Medico-Legal Soc., 1969–70, Life Mem., 1989. Silver Jubilee Medal, 1977; Commemoration Medal, NZ, 1990. *Recreation:* boating. *Address:* 87 St Heliers Bay Road, Auckland 1005, New Zealand. *T:* (9) 5757999. *Club:* Royal New Zealand Yacht Squadron.

CHINERY, David John; District Judge (Magistrates' Courts) (formerly Stipendiary Magistrate), West Midlands, since 1998; *b* 10 Aug. 1950; *s* of Oliver John Chinery and Gladys Alberta Chinery; *m* 1973, Jeannette Elizabeth Owens; two *d*. *Educ:* Alleyne's Sch., Stevenage; Coll. of Law. Justices' Clerk's Asst, Hitchin Magistrates' Court, 1969–75; Asst Clerk to Justices, Northampton Magistrates' Court, 1975–79; admitted solicitor, 1979; Asst Solicitor, 1979–82, Partner, 1982–90, Borneo, Martell & Partners, Northampton; sole practitioner, 1990–98. Deputy Stipendiary Magistrate: Nottingham, 1993–98; Doncaster, 1996–98; Birmingham, 1997–98. *Recreations:* Rugby Union football, cricket, music, Victorian poetry. *Address:* Victoria Law Courts, Corporation Street, Birmingham B4 6QA.

CHING, Henry, CBE 1982; Secretary General, Caritas–Hong Kong, 1990–91; *b* 2 Nov. 1933; *s* of Henry Ching, OBE and Ruby Irene Ching; *m* 1963, Eileen Frances Peters; two *d*. *Educ:* Diocesan Boys' School, Hong Kong; Hong Kong Univ. (BA Hons); Wadham Coll., Oxford (MA, DipEd). Schoolmaster, 1958–61; Hong Kong Civil Service: various appts, 1961–73; Principal Asst Financial Sec., 1973–76; Dep. Financial Sec., 1976–83; Sec. for Health and Welfare and MLC, Hong Kong, 1983–85, retired. Chief Administrator, Hong Kong Foundn, 1989. *Recreations:* cricket, rowing. *Address:* 39 Saiala Road, East Killara, NSW 2071, Australia.

CHINN, Sir Trevor (Edwin), Kt 1990; CVO 1989; Chairman, Lex Service PLC, since 1973 (Director, since 1959); *b* 24 July 1935; *s* of late Rosser and Susie Chinn; *m* 1965, Susan Speelman; two *s*. *Educ:* Clifton Coll.; King's Coll., Cambridge. Man. Dir, 1968–73, Chief Exec., 1973–96, Lex Service. Vice-Chm., Commn for Integrated Transport, 1999–; Chm., Motorists' Forum, 2000–; non-exec. Chm., ITIS, 2000–. President: United Jewish Israel Appeal; Norwood Ravenswood; Vice Chm., Wishing Well Appeal, Gt Ormond St Hosp. for Sick Children, 1985–89. Trustee, Royal Acad. Trust, 1989– (Dep. Chm., 1996–); Dir, Hampstead Theatre, 1990– (Vice Chm., 1997–). Trustee, Duke of Edinburgh's Award, 1978–88. Freeman of the City of London. Chief Barker, Variety Club of GB, 1977, 1978. *Address:* Lex House, 17 Connaught Place, W2 2EL. *T:* (020) 7705 1212.

CHINNERY, (Charles) Derek; Controller, Radio 1, BBC, 1978–85; *b* 27 April 1925; *s* of Percy Herbert and Frances Dorothy Chinnery; *m* 1953, Doreen Grace Clarke. *Educ:* Gosforth Grammar School. Youth in training, BBC, 1941; RAF Cadet Pilot, 1943. BBC: Technical Asst, 1947; Programme Engineer, 1948; Studio Manager, 1950; Producer, 1952; Executive Producer, 1967; Head of Radio 1, 1972. *Recreations:* DIY, travelling. *Address:* 13 Cliffhouse, Chesterfield Road, Eastbourne BN20 7NU.

CHINO, Yoshitoki, Hon. KBE 1992; Hon. Chairman, Daiwa Securities Co. Ltd, since 1991; *b* 18 March 1923; *s* of Hisakichi Chino and Tokiyo Chino; *m* 1950, Sachiko Kawabata; one *s* one *d*. *Educ:* Keio Univ. (BA Law 1946). Joined Daiwa Securities Co. Ltd, 1946: Gen. Manager, Sales and Foreign Depts, 1959–61; Dir, 1961–65; Man. Dir, 1966–70; Sen. Man Dir, 1970–72; Exec. Vice-Pres., 1972–81; Vice-Chm., 1981–82; Chm., 1982–91. Commendatore dell'Ordine al Merito (Italy), 1994. *Publication:* Internationalization by Feel, 1988. *Recreations:* personal computer, reading books, fishing. *Address:* Daiwa Securities Co. Ltd, 6–4 Otemachi 2-chome, Chiyoda-ku, Tokyo 100, Japan.

CHIONA, Most Rev. James; *see* Blantyre, Archbishop of, (RC).

CHIPIMO, Elias Marko Chisha; Ambassador of Zambia to Japan, also accredited to Indonesia, Korea and the Philippines, and as High Commissioner, Australia and New Zealand, since 2000; *b* 23 Feb. 1931; *s* of Marko Chipimo, Zambia (then Northern Rhodesia); *m* 1959, Anna Joyce Nkole Konie; four *s* three *d*. *Educ:* St Canisius, Chikuni, Zambia; Munali; Fort Hare Univ. Coll., SA; University Coll. of Rhodesia and Nyasaland; Univ. of Zambia (LLB 1985). Schoolmaster, 1959–63; Sen. Govt Administrator, 1964–67; High Comr for Zambia in London, and Zambian Ambassador to the Holy See, 1968–69; Perm. Sec., Min. of Foreign Affairs, 1969; Hon. Minister, Lusaka Province, 1991–96; MP (MMD) Kantanshi, 1991–96; Nat. Chm., 1991–96, and Mem., Nat. Exec. Cttee, until 1996, MMD; Ambassador to Germany, 1997–2000. Chairman: Zambia Stock Exchange Council, 1970–72; Zambia Nat. Bldg Soc., 1970–71; Dep. Chm., Development Bank of Zambia Ltd, 1973–75; Dep. Chm., 1975, Chm., 1976–80, Standard Bank Zambia Ltd; Director: Zambia Airways Corp., 1975–81; Zambia Bata Shoe Co. Ltd, 1977–92. Mem., Nat Council for Sci. Res., 1977–80. Pres., Zambia Red Cross, 1990–95 (Vice-Pres., 1976–90; Life Mem., 1995; Pres., Lusaka Br., 1970–75); Mem., Zambia Univ. Council, 1970–76; Dir, Internat. Sch. of Lusaka, 1970–76. Cllr, Lusaka City Council, 1974–80. Rep., Commonwealth Soc., 1979–88. *Publications:* Our Land and People, 1966; Tied Loans and the Role of Banks (vol. 2 of International Financing of Economic Development), 1978; articles in Univ. of Zambia Jl. *Recreations:* gardening, reading, general literature, linguistics, philosophy, politics, economics, discussions, chess. *Address:* Zambian Embassy, 10-2 Ebara 1-chome, Shinagawa-ku, Tokyo 142-0063, Japan.

CHIPMAN, Dr John Miguel Warwick, CMG 1999; Director: International Institute for Strategic Studies, since 1993; IISS-US and IISS (Asia), since 2001; Arundel House Enterprises, since 1999; *b* 10 Feb. 1957; *s* of Lawrence Carroll Chipman and Maria Isabel (*née* Prados); *m* 1997, Lady Theresa Helen Margaret Manners, *yr d* of 10th Duke of Rutland, CBE; twin *s. Educ:* Harvard Coll. (BA Hons); London Sch. of Economics (MA Dist.); Balliol Coll., Oxford (MPhil, DPhil). Research Associate: IISS, 1983–84; Atlantic Inst. for Internat. Affairs, Paris, 1985–87; International Institute for Strategic Studies: Asst Dir for Regl Security, 1987–91; Dir of Studies, 1991–93. Mem. Bd, Aspen Inst., Italy, 1995–. Founder, Strategic Comments jl, 1995. *Publications:* V ième République et Défense de l'Afrique, 1986; (ed and jt author) NATO's Southern Allies, 1988; French Power in Africa, 1989; numerous contribs to edited vols, learned jls and newspapers. *Recreations:* tennis, ski-ing, scuba diving, riding, collecting travel books. *Address:* International Institute for Strategic Studies, Arundel House, 13–15 Arundel Street, Temple Place, WC2R 3DX. *T:* (020) 7379 7676. *Clubs:* Brooks's, Beefsteak; Harvard (New York).

CHIPP, David Allan; Editor in Chief, Press Association, 1969–86; *b* 6 June 1927; *s* of late Thomas Ford Chipp and late Isabel Mary Ballinger; unmarried. *Educ:* Geelong Grammar Sch., Australia; King's Coll., Cambridge (MA). Served with Middlesex Regt, 1944–47; Cambridge, 1947–50. Joined Reuters as Sports Reporter, 1950; Correspondent for Reuters: in SE Asia, 1953–55; in Peking, 1956–58; various managerial positions in Reuters, 1960–68; Editor of Reuters, 1968. An Indep. Dir, The Observer, 1985–93; Director: Reuter Foundn, 1986–90; TV-am News Co., 1986–92; Lloyds of London Press, 1990–93; Teletext UK, 1992–; Talk Radio UK, 1994–95; Chm., News World, 1994–96. Mem., Press Complaints Commn, 1991–93. *Recreations:* reading, opera. *Address:* 2 Wilton Court, 59/60 Eccleston Square, SW1V 1PH. *T:* (020) 7834 5579. *Clubs:* Garrick, Beefsteak; Leander (Henley-on-Thames). *Address:* Hawks (Cambridge).

CHIPPERFIELD, David Alan, RIBA; Principal, David Chipperfield Architects, since 1984; *b* 18 Dec. 1953; *s* of Alan John Chipperfield and Peggy Chipperfield (*née* Singleton); partner, Dr Evelyn Stern; two *s* one *d*, and one *s* from previous relationship. *Educ:* Wellington Sch., Somerset; Kingston Poly.; Architectural Assoc. (AA Dip). RIBA 1982. Designer, Douglas Stephens & Partners, 1977–78; Architect, Richard Rogers & Partners, 1978–79; Project Architect, Foster Associates, 1981–84. Projects include: private museum, Japan, 1987; TAK Design Centre, Kyoto, Japan, 1989; Matsumoto Corp. HQ, Okayama, Japan, 1990; Grassimus., Leipzig, 1995; Landeszentralbank HQ, Gera, Germany, 1996; River and Rowing Mus., Henley-on-Thames, 1996–97 Best Building in England, RFAC/BSkyB Award, 1999); Neues Mus., Berlin, and Shore Club Hotel, Miami, 1997; Ernsting Service Centre, Munster, Berlin Museum Is Masterplan, and Bryant Park Hotel, NY, 1998; Salerno Palace of Justice, and Davenport Mus. of Art, Iowa, 1999. Founder and Dir, 9H Gall., London. Design Tutor, RCA, 1988–89; Prof. of Architecture, Staatliche Akad. der Bildenden Künste, Stuttgart, 1995–; Visiting Professor: Harvard Univ., 1987–88; Graz Univ., 1992; Naples Univ., 1992; Ecole Polytechnique, Lausanne, 1993–94. Trustee, Architecture Foundn, 1992–97. Special Mention, Financial Times Award, 1991; Palladio Award, 1993; Regl Award, RIBA, 1996, 1998; RIBA Award, 1998; Tessanow Gold Medal, 1999; Civic Trust Award, 1999. *Publication:* Theoretical Practice, 1994; *relevant publications:* Gustavo Gili: monograph, 1992; Blueprint Extra Equipment Stores, 1993; 2G: recent work (monograph), 1997; El Croquis (monograph), 1998. *Recreations:* reading, drawing, swimming. *Address:* (office) Cobham Mews, Agar Grove, NW1 9SB. *T:* (020) 7267 9422. *Club:* Royal Automobile.

CHIPPERFIELD, Sir Geoffrey (Howes), KCB 1992 (CB 1985); Deputy Chairman, since 1999, and Director, since 1993, Pennon Group (formerly South West Water plc); *b* 20 April 1933; *s* of Nelson Chipperfield and Eleanor Chipperfield; *m* 1959, Gillian James; two *s. Educ:* Cranleigh; New Coll., Oxford. Called to the Bar, Gray's Inn, 1955. Joined Min. of Housing and Local Govt, 1956; Harkness Fellow, Inst. of Govtl Studies, Univ. of Calif, Berkeley, 1962–63; Principal Private Sec., Minister of Housing, 1968–70; Sec., Greater London Develt Plan Inquiry, 1970–73; Under Sec., 1976, Dep. Sec., 1982–87, DoE; Dep. Sec., Dept of Energy, 1987–89; Perm. Under-Sec. of State, Dept of Energy, 1989–91; Perm. Sec. and Chief Exec., PSA Services, 1991–93. Chairman: DTI Energy Adv. Panel, 1996–; British Cement Assoc., 1996–. Pro-Chancellor, Univ. of Kent, 1998–. *Recreations:* reading, gardening. *Club:* Oxford and Cambridge.

CHIPPINDALE, Christopher Ralph, PhD; Senior Assistant Curator, Cambridge University Museum of Archaeology, since 1993 (Assistant Curator, 1988–93); *b* 13 Oct. 1951; *s* of Keith and Ruth Chippindale; *m* 1976, Anne Lowe; two *s* two *d. Educ:* Sedbergh School; St John's College, Cambridge (BA Hons); Girton Coll., Cambridge (PhD). MIFA. Editor, freelance, Penguin Books, Hutchinson Publishing Group, 1974–82; Res. Fellow in Archaeology, 1985–88, Bye-Fellow, 1988–91, Girton Coll., Cambridge. Editor, Antiquity, 1987–97. *Publications:* Stonehenge Complete, 1983, 2nd edn 1994; (ed jtly) The Pastmasters, 1989; (jtly) Who owns Stonehenge?, 1990; A High Way to Heaven, 1998; (ed jtly) The Archaeology of Rock Art, 1999; articles in jls. *Recreations:* work, worrying. *Address:* 85 Hills Road, Cambridge CB2 1PG.

CHIRAC, Jacques René; President of the French Republic, since 1995; *b* Paris, 29 Nov. 1932; *s* of François Chirac, company manager and Marie-Louise (*née* Valette); *m* 1956, Bernadette Chodron de Courcel; two *d. Educ:* Lycée Carnot and Lycée Louis-le-Grand, Paris; Diploma of Inst. of Polit. Studies, Paris, and of Summer Sch., Harvard Univ., USA. Served Army in Algeria. Ecole Nat. d'Admin, 1957–59; Auditor, Cour des Comptes, 1959; Head Dept: Sec.-Gen. of Govt, 1962; Private Office of Georges Pompidou, 1962–67; Counsellor, Cour des Comptes, 1965; State Secretary: Employment Problems, 1967–68; Economy and Finance, 1968–71; Minister for Parly Relations, 1971–72; Minister for Agriculture and Rural Development, 1972–74; Home Minister, March-May 1974; Prime Minister, 1974–76 and 1986–88. Deputy from Corrèze, elected 1967, 1968, 1973, 1976 (UDR), 1978 (RPR), 1981, 1986, 1988 and 1993; Sec.-Gen., UDR, Dec. 1974–June 1975; Pres., Rassemblement pour la République, 1976–81 and 1982–94. Mayor of Paris, 1977–95. Member from Meymac, Conseil Général of Corrèze, 1968–, Pres. 1970–79. Mem., European Parlt, 1979–80. Treasurer, Claude Pompidou Foundn (charity for elderly and for handicapped children), 1969–. Grand-Croix, Ordre national du Mérite; Croix de la valeur militaire; Chevalier du Mérite agricole, des Arts et des Lettres, de l'Etoile noire, du Mérite sportif, du Mérite touristique; Médaille de l'Aéronautique. *Publications:* a thesis on development of Port of New Orleans, 1954; Discours pour la France à l'heure du choix, 1978; La lueur d'espérance: réflexion du soir pour le matin, 1978; Une Nouvelle France, 1994; La France pour Tous, 1995. *Address:* Palais de l'Elysée, 75008 Paris, France.

CHISHOLM, Prof. Alexander William John; Professor Emeritus, University of Salford, since 1994; *b* 18 April 1922; *s* of Thomas Alexander Chisholm and Maude Mary Chisholm (*née* Robinson); *m* 1945, Aline Mary (*née* Eastwood) (*d* 1995); one *s* (one *d* decd). *Educ:* Brentwood Sch., Essex; Northampton Polytechnic; Manchester Coll. of Science and Technology; Royal Technical Coll., Salford (BSc(Eng) London). CEng, FIMechE, FIEE. Section Leader, Res. Dept, Metropolitan Vickers Electrical Co. Ltd, 1944–49; Sen. Scientific Officer, then Principal Scientific Officer, Nat. Engrg Lab., 1949–57; UK Scientific Mission, British Embassy, USA, 1952–54; Head of Dept of Mechanical Engrg, then Prof. of Mechanical Engrg, Royal Coll. of Advanced Technology, Salford, 1957–67; University of Salford: Prof. of Mech. Engineering, 1967–82; Research Prof. in Engrg., 1982–87; Professorial Fellow, 1987–94; Chm., Salford Univ. Industrial Centre, subseq. Salford Univ. Industrial Centre Ltd, 1968–82. Visitor, Cambridge Univ. Engrg Dept and Vis. Fellow, Wolfson Coll., 1973–74. Chm., Engrg Profs Conf., 1976–80; Dir, Prog. for Improvement of Quality of Engrg Educn, 1990–95 (Hon. Chm., 1995–96). Chm., Industrial Admin and Engrg Prodn Gp, IMechE, 1960–62. Nat. Council for Technological Awards: Chm., Mechanical/Prodn Engrg Cttee, 1960–63; Vice-Chm., Bd of Studies in Engrg and Governor, 1963–65. Member: Technology Cttee, UGC, 1969–74; Engrg Processes Cttee, SERC, 1980–83. Pres., CIRP, 1983–84 (Chm., UK Bd, 1977–88; Hon. Life Mem. 1987). Mem., Court, Cranfield Inst. of Technology, 1974–91. Whitworth Prize, IMechE, 1965. *Publications:* numerous on production process technology, manufacturing systems, industrial research, educn and training of engineers, human factors in manufacturing. *Recreations:* hill walking, sailing, tree planting. *Address:* 12 Legh Road, Prestbury, Macclesfield, Cheshire SK10 4HX. *T:* (01625) 829412. *Club:* Athenæum.

CHISHOLM, Sir John (Alexander Raymond), Kt 1999; FREng; Chief Executive, Defence Evaluation and Research (formerly Defence Research) Agency, since 1991; *b* 27 Aug. 1946; *s* of Ruari Ian Lambert Chisholm and Pamela Harland Chisholm; *m* 1969, Catherine Alexandra (*née* Pana); one *s* one *d. Educ:* Univ. of Cambridge (MA). CEng 1974, FREng (FEng 1996); FIEE 1995; FRAeS 1996; FInstP. Vauxhall Motors, 1964–69; Scicon Ltd, 1969–79; Cap Scientific Ltd, 1979–91: Man. Dir, 1981–86; Chm., 1986–91; Chm., Yard Ltd, 1986–91; UK Man. Dir, Sema Group plc, 1988–91. Non-executive Director: Expro Internat. plc, 1994–; Bespak plc, 1999–. Mem., UK Foresight Steering Gp, 1993–2000. Pres., Electronic and Business Equipment Assoc., 1989–90. Mem. Council, Cranfield Univ., 1995–. *Recreations:* participative sports, old cars. *Address:* Batchworth Hill House, London Road, Rickmansworth WD3 1JS.

CHISHOLM, Malcolm George Richardson; Member (Lab) Edinburgh North and Leith, Scottish Parliament, since 1999; *b* 7 March 1949; *s* of Olive and George Chisholm; *m* 1975, Janet Broomfield, writer; two *s* one *d. Educ:* George Watson's Coll.; Edinburgh Univ. (MA Hons, Dip Ed). Formerly Teacher of English, Castlebrae High School and Broughton High School. MP (Lab) Edinburgh, Leith, 1992–97, Edinburgh North and Leith, 1997–2001. Parly Under-Sec. of State, Scottish Office, 1997. Dep. Minister for Health and Community Care, Scottish Exec., 2000–. *Recreations:* reading, cinema. *Address:* Scottish Parliament, George IV Bridge, Edinburgh EH99 1SP. *T:* (020) 7219 4613.

CHISHOLM, Prof. Malcolm Harold, FRS 1990; Distinguished Professor of Mathematical and Physical Sciences, Ohio State University, since 2000; *b* 15 Oct. 1945; *s* of Angus and Gweneth Chisholm; *m* 1st, 1969, Susan Sage (marr. diss.); one *s*; 2nd, 1982, Cynthia Brown; two *s. Educ:* London Univ. (BSc 1966; PhD 1969). Sessional Lectr, Univ. of W Ontario, 1970–72; Asst Prof. of Chemistry, Princeton Univ., 1972–78; Indiana University: Associate Prof., 1978–80; Prof., 1980–85; Distinguished Prof. of Chemistry, 1985–99. Guggenheim Fellow, 1985–86. Editor, Polyhedron, 1983 ; Associate Editor, Dalton Trans, 1988–; Chemical Communications, 1995–99. FAAAS 1987. Hon. DSc London, 1980. RSC Award for Chem. and Electrochem. of Transition Elements, 1987; Alexander von Humboldt Sen. Scientist Award, 1988; (jtly) ACS Nobel Laureate Signature Award, 1988; ACS Award in Inorganic Chm., 1989; Centenary Medal and Lectr, RSC, 1995; ACS Distinguished Service to Inorganic Chemistry, 1999; Davy Medal, Royal Soc., 1999; Ludwig Mond Medal and Lectr., RSC, 2000. *Publications:* Reactivity of Metal-Metal Bonds, 1982; Inorganic Chemistry: towards the 21st century, 1983; Early Transition Metal Clusters with π-Donor Ligands, 1995; numerous articles, mostly in chem. jls. *Recreations:* squash, gardening. *Address:* 100 Kenyon Brook Drive, Worthington, OH 43085, USA. *T:* (614) 9850942; 38 Norwich Street, Cambridge CB2 1NE. *T:* (01223) 312392.

CHISHOLM, Prof. Michael Donald Inglis; Professor of Geography, University of Cambridge, 1976–96, now Emeritus; Professorial Fellow, St Catharine's College, Cambridge, 1976–96; *b* 10 June 1931; *s* of M. S. and A. W. Chisholm; *m* 1st, 1959, Edith Gretchen Emma (*née* Hoof) (marr. diss. 1981); one *s* two *d*; 2nd, 1986, Judith Carola Shackleton (*née* Murray). *Educ:* St Christopher Sch., Letchworth; St Catharine's Coll., Cambridge (MA; ScD 1996). Nat. Service Commn, RE, 1950–51. Deptl Demonstrator, Inst. for Agric. Econs, Oxford, 1954–59; Asst Lectr, then Lectr in Geog., Bedford Coll., London, 1960–64; Vis. Sen. Lectr in Geog., Univ. of Ibadan, 1964–65; Lectr, then Reader in Geog., Univ. of Bristol, 1965–72; Prof. of Economic and Social Geography, Univ. of Bristol, 1972–76. Associate, Economic Associates Ltd, consultants, 1965–77; Mem. SSRC, and Chm. of Cttees for Human Geography and Planning, 1967–72; Member: Local Govt Boundary Commn for England, 1971–78; Rural Develt Commn, 1981–90; English Adv. Cttee on Telecommunications, 1990–92; Local Govt Commn for England, 1992–95. Mem. Council, Inst. of British Geographers, 1961 and 1962, Junior Vice-Pres., 1977, Sen. Vice-Pres., 1978, Pres. 1979. Conservator of River Cam, 1979– (Chm., 1991–). Vice-Chm. Cambs ACRE, 2001–. Gill Memorial Prize, RGS, 1969. Geography Editor for Hutchinson Univ. Lib., 1973–82. *Publications:* Rural Settlement and Land Use: an essay in location, 1962; Geography and Economics, 1966; (ed jtly) Regional Forecasting, 1971; (ed jtly) Spatial Policy Problems of the British Economy, 1971; Research in Human Geography, 1971; (ed) Resources for Britain's Future, 1972; (jtly) Freight Flows and Spatial Aspects of the British Economy, 1973; (jtly) The Changing Pattern of Employment, 1973; (ed jtly) Studies in Human Geography, 1973; (ed jtly) Processes in Physical and Human Geography: Bristol Essays, 1975; Human Geography: Evolution or Revolution?, 1975; Modern World Development, 1982; Regions in Recession and Resurgence, 1990; (ed jtly) Shared Space: Divided Space, 1990; Britain on the Edge of Europe, 1995; (ed jtly) A Fresh Start for Local Government, 1997; Structural Reform of British Local Government: rhetoric and reality, 2000; papers in Farm Economist, Oxford Econ. Papers, Trans Inst. British Geographers, Geography, Geographical Jl, Applied Statistics, Area, Envmt and Planning, Jl of Local Govt Law, etc. *Recreations:* gardening, theatre, opera, interior design. *Address:* 5 Clarendon Road, Cambridge CB2 2BH.

CHISHOLM, Nicolas; *see* Chisholm, P. N.

CHISHOLM, (Peter) Nicolas; Headmaster, Yehudi Menuhin School, since 1988; *b* 7 Dec. 1949; *s* of David Whitridge Chisholm and Marjorie Chisholm; *m* 1977, Auriol Mary Oakeley. *Educ:* Christ's Hospital, Horsham; St John's Coll., Cambridge (MA). Tenor Lay Vicar, Chichester Cathedral, 1972–76; Asst Master, Prebendal Sch., Chichester, 1972–76; Hurstpierpoint College: Hd Classics, 1976–88; Housemaster, Eagle Hse, 1982–88. Chairman: Sussex Assoc. of Classical Teachers, 1982–88; Trustees, SE Music Schemes, 1996–; Educn Cttee, SHMIS, 1996–. Gov., Royal Ballet Sch., 1997–; Mem., Performing Arts Panel, SE Arts Bd, 1990–96. Pres., Surrey Philharmonic Orch., 2000–01. FRSA.

Recreations: music, classic cars, walking, photography, archaeology. *Address:* Yehudi Menuhin School, Stoke D'Abernon, Cobham, Surrey KT11 3QQ. *T:* (01932) 584418.

CHISLETT, Derek Victor; Warden, Sackville College, 1988–96; *b* 18 April 1929; *s* of Archibald Lynn Chislett and Eva Jessie Chislett (*née* Collins); *m* 1954, Joan Robson; two *d. Educ:* Christ's Hospital. Admiralty, 1946–53; HM Forces, 1947–49; Nat. Assistance Board, 1953–66; Min. of Social Security, 1966–68; Department of Health and Social Security, 1968–88: Under Sec., 1983; Controller, Newcastle Central Office, 1983–86; Dir of Finance (Social Security), 1986–88. Mem. Exec. Cttee, Nat. Assoc. of Almshouses, 1989– (Vice-Chm., 1995–). Trustee, Motability Tenth Anniversary Trust, 1989–2000. Freeman, City of London, 1998; Mem., Guild of Freemen, City of London, 1999. *Publication:* Sackville College: a short history and guide, 1995. *Recreations:* opera, playing and listening to the 'cello, bee-keeping. *Address:* Greensands, Ripe, Lewes, East Sussex BN8 3AX. *T:* (01323) 811525.

CHISWELL, Rt Rev. Peter; Bishop of Armidale, 1976–99; *b* 18 Feb. 1934; *s* of Ernest and Florence Ruth Chiswell; *m* 1960, Betty Marie Craik; two *s* one *d. Educ:* Univ. of New South Wales (BE); Moore Theological College (BD London, Th. Schol.). Vicar of Bingara, 1961–68; Vicar of Gunnedah, 1968–76; Archdeacon of Tamworth, 1971–76. Chm., Fed. Exec., CMS, Australia. *Address:* 93 Trelawney Road, Armidale, NSW 2350, Australia. *T:* (2) 67713919.

CHISWELL, Maj.-Gen. Peter Irvine, CB 1985; CBE 1976 (OBE 1972; MBE 1965); DL; Chairman, Buckland Leadership Development Centre, since 1996 (Director, since 1989); *b* 19 April 1930; *s* of late Col Henry Thomas Chiswell, OBE (late RAMC) and Gladys Beatrice Chiswell; *m* 1958, Felicity Philippa, *d* of R. F. Martin; two *s. Educ:* Allhallows School; RMA Sandhurst. Commissioned Devonshire Regt, 1951; transf. Parachute Regt, 1958; DAAG HQ Berlin Inf. Bde, 1963–65; Brigade Major, 16 Para Bde, 1967–68; GSO1 (DS), Staff Coll., 1968–69; CO 3 PARA, 1969–71; Col GS (Army Training), 1971–74; Comd British Contingent DCOS UN Force Cyprus, 1974–76; Comd, 44 Para Bde, 1976–78; ACOS (Operations), HQ Northern Army Gp, 1978–81; Comd, Land Forces NI, 1982–83; GOC Wales, 1983–85. Hon. Chief Exec., Airborne Forces Charities, 1996–. Gov., Christ Coll., Brecon, 1987–. FRSA 1994. DL Powys, 1994. *Recreation:* travel.

CHITNIS, family name of **Baron Chitnis**.

CHITNIS, Baron *cr* 1977 (Life Peer), of Ryedale, N Yorks; **Pratap Chidamber Chitnis;** Chairman, British Refugee Council, 1986–89; *b* 1 May 1936; *s* of late Chidamber N. Chitnis and Lucia Mallik; *m* 1964, Anne Brand; one *s* decd. *Educ:* Penryn Sch.; Stonyhurst Coll.; Univs of Birmingham (BA) and Kansas (MA). Admin. Asst, Nat. Coal Board, 1958–59; Liberal Party Organisation: Local Govt Officer, 1960–62; Agent, Orpington Liberal Campaign, 1962; Trng Officer, 1962–64; Press Officer, 1964–66; Head of Liberal Party Organisation, 1966–69. Sec., 1969–75, Chief Exec. and Dir, 1975–88, Joseph Rowntree Social Service Trust. Mem., Community Relations Commn, 1970–77; Chm., BBC Immigrants Programme Adv. Cttee, 1979–83 (Mem., 1972–77). Chm., Refugee Action, 1981–86. Reported on elections in: Zimbabwe, 1979; (jtly) Guyana, 1980; El Salvador, 1982, 1984, 1988 and 1989; Nicaragua, 1984. *Address:* Quartier des Trois Fontaines, 84490 Vaucluse, France.

CHITTICK, Carolyn Julie; *see* Fairbairn, C. J.

CHITTY, Alison Jill; theatre designer; *b* 16 Oct. 1948; *d* of late Ernest Hedley Chitty, Prebendary of St Paul's Cathedral and of Irene Joan Waldron. *Educ:* King Alfred School, London; St Martin's School of Art; Central School of Art and Design (Degree in Theatre Design); Arts Council Scholarship. Victoria Theatre, Stoke-on-Trent, 1970–79 (designed over 40 productions; Head of Design 4 years); designer, 1970–, for *theatre:* Hampstead Theatre, Riverside studios, Sheffield, RSC (Hamlet, 2000), Haymarket, Stratford East, Playhouse (Rose Tattoo, 1991); RNT (Cardiff East, 1997; Remembrance of Things Past, 2000 (Best Costume Designer, Laurence Olivier Awards, 2001)); for *opera:* Opera North, Houston Grand Opera, Royal Opera House (Gawain, 1991; Billy Budd, Arianna, 1995; The Bartered Bride, 1998); Opera Theatre, St Louis (The Vanishing Bridegroom, 1991); Gotenborg Music Theatre (Falstaff, 1993); Dallas Opera (Jenufa, 1993); ENO (Khovanshchina, 1994); Geneva Opera (Billy Budd, 1994; Aida, 1999); Santa Fe Opera (Blond Eckbert, 1994; Modern Painters, 1995; Dialogues of the Carmelites, 1999); Danish Royal Opera (Die Mëistersinger, 1996); Bastille Opera, Paris (Turandot, 1997); Bordeaux Opera (Julius Caesar, 1999); Bavarian State Opera (Otello, 1999); Glyndebourne Touring Opera (The Last Supper, 2000); Almeida Opera (Ion, 2000); Seattle Opera, and Tel Aviv Opera (Billy Budd, 2001); San Francisco Opera (Jenufa, 2001); for *films:* Blue Jean, Aria, Life is Sweet, 1991; A Sense of History, 1992; Naked, 1993; Secrets & Lies, 1995 (Palme d'Or, 1996). Co-Dir, Motley Theatre Design Sch., 1992–. *Publication:* (contrib.) Theatre in a Cool Climate. *Address:* c/o Curtis Brown Group, 4th Floor, Haymarket House, 28/29 Haymarket, SW1Y 4SP.

CHITTY, Dr Anthony; retired; Director of Corporate Engineering, Rolls-Royce Power Engineering Ltd (formerly Northern Engineering Industries, R-R Industrial Power Group), 1989–93 (Deputy Director, 1988–89); *b* 29 May 1931; *s* of Ashley George Chitty and Doris Ellen Mary Buck; *m* 1956, Audrey Munro; two *s* one *d. Educ:* Glynn Grammar Sch., Epsom; Imperial Coll., London. BSc, PhD, DIC; CEng. GEC Res. Labs, 1955; Hd, Creep of Steels Lab., ERA, 1959; GEC Power Gp, 1963; Chief Metallurgist (Applications), C. A. Parsons, 1966; Dir, Advanced Technol. Div., Clarke Chapman-John Thompson, 1973; Internat. Res. and Develt, 1978; Gen. Manager, Engrg Products, N.E.I. Parsons, 1979; Regional Industrial Adviser, NE Region, DTI, 1984–88. Vis. Prof., Univ. of Aston in Birmingham, 1977–84. Chairman: Bd of Newcastle Technol. Centre, 1988–90 (Dep. Chm., 1985–88); Centre for Adhesive Technol, 1990–93; Member, Board: Newcastle Univ. New Ventures Ltd, 1989–93; Newcastle Polytechnic Products Ltd, 1989–93. *Publications:* research publications in the fields of materials and welding for power generation. *Recreations:* hill walking, gardening. *Address:* 1 Willow Way, Darras Hall, Ponteland, Northumberland NE20 9RJ.

CHITTY, (Margaret) Beryl, (Mrs Henry Fowler), CMG 1977; HM Diplomatic Service, retired; *b* 2 Dec. 1917; *d* of Wilfrid and Eleanor Holdgate; *m* 1st, 1949, Keith Chitty, FRCS (*d* 1958); 2nd, 1989, Henry Fowler, CD, Kingston, Jamaica. *Educ:* Belvedere Sch. (GPDST), Liverpool; St Hugh's Coll., Oxford (BA, MA; Hon. Fellow, 1982). Dominions Office, 1940; Private Sec. to Party Under-Sec. of State, 1943–45; Principal, 1945; CRO, 1947–52; First Sec., Commonwealth Office, 1958; Jt Sec., First Commonwealth Educn Conf., 1959; UK Mission to UN, New York, 1968–70; FCO, 1970–71; Dep. (and Acting) British High Comr in Jamaica, 1971–75; Head of Commonwealth Co-ord. Dept, FCO, 1975–77. Appeal Sec., St Hugh's Coll., Oxford, 1978–81; Appeal Dir, St Peter's Coll., Oxford, 1982–88. Non-Press Mem., Press Council, 1978–80. Mem., Governing Body, Queen Elizabeth House, Oxford, 1977–80. *Address:* 79 Bainton Road, Oxford OX2 7AG. *T:* (01865) 553384.

CHITTY, Susan Elspeth, (Lady Chitty); author; *b* 18 Aug. 1929; *d* of Rudolph Glossop and Mrs E. A. Hopkinson (writer, as Antonia White); *m* 1951, Sir Thomas Willes Chitty, Bt, *qv;* one *s* three *d. Educ:* Godolphin Sch., Salisbury; Somerville Coll., Oxford. Mem. editorial staff, Vogue, 1952–53; subseq. journalist, reviewer, broadcaster and lecturer. *Publications: novels:* Diary of a Fashion Model, 1958; White Huntress, 1963; My Life and Horses, 1966; *biographies:* The Woman who wrote Black Beauty, 1972; The Beast and the Monk, 1975; Charles Kingsley and North Devon, 1976; Gwen John 1876–1939, 1981; Now to My Mother, 1985; That Singular Person Called Lear, 1988; Playing the Game, 1997; *non-fiction:* (with Thomas Hinde) On Next to Nothing, 1976; (with Thomas Hinde) The Great Donkey Walk, 1977; The Young Rider, 1979; *edited:* The Intelligent Woman's Guide to Good Taste, 1958; The Puffin Book of Horses, 1975; As Once in May, by Antonia White, 1983; Antonia White: Diaries 1926–1957, vol. I, 1991, vol. II, 1992. *Recreations:* riding, travel. *Address:* Bow Cottage, West Hoathly, Sussex RH19 4QF. *T:* (01342) 810269.

CHITTY, Sir Thomas Willes, 3rd Bt *cr* 1924; author (as Thomas Hinde); *b* 2 March 1926; *e s* of Sir (Thomas) Henry Willes Chitty, 2nd Bt, and Ethel Constance (*d* 1971), *d* of S. H. Gladstone, Darley Ash, Bovingdon, Herts; *S* father, 1955; *m* 1951, Susan Elspeth (*see* S. E. Chitty); one *s* three *d. Educ:* Winchester; University Coll., Oxford. Royal Navy, 1944–47. Shell Petroleum Co., 1953–60. Granada Arts Fellow, Univ. of York, 1964–65; Visiting Lectr, Univ. of Illinois, 1965–67; Vis. Prof., Boston Univ., 1969–70. *Publications:* novels: Mr Nicholas, 1952; Happy as Larry, 1957; For the Good of the Company, 1961; A Place Like Home, 1962; The Cage, 1962; Ninety Double Martinis, 1963; The Day the Call Came, 1964; Games of Chance, 1965; The Village, 1966; High, 1968; Bird, 1970; Generally a Virgin, 1972; Agent, 1974; Our Father, 1975; Daymare, 1980; *non-fiction:* (with wife, as Susan Hinde) On Next to Nothing, 1976; (with Susan Chitty) The Great Donkey Walk, 1977; The Cottage Book, 1979; Stately Gardens of Britain, 1983; Forests of Britain, 1985; (ed) The Domesday Book: England's heritage, then and now, 1986; Courtiers: 900 years of court life, 1986; Tales from the Pumproom: an informal history of Bath, 1988; Imps of Promise: a history of the King's School, Canterbury, 1990; Looking Glass Letters, 1991; Paths of Progress: a history of Marlborough College, 1993; A History of Highgate School, 1993; A History of King's College School, 1994; Carpenter's Children: a history of the City of London School, 1995; The University of Greenwich, 1996; The Martlet and the Griffen: a history of Abingdon School, 1997; *autobiography:* Sir Henry and Sons, 1980; *biography:* A Field Guide to the English Country Parson, 1983; Capability Brown, 1986; *anthology:* Spain, 1963. *Heir: s* Andrew Edward Willes Chitty, *b* 20 Nov. 1953. *Address:* Bow Cottage, West Hoathly, Sussex RH19 4QF. *T:* (01342) 810269.

CHOI SUNG-HONG; Ambassador of the Republic of Korea to the Court of St James's, 1999–2001; *b* 24 Dec. 1938; *m* 1968, Wha-boo; one *s* two *d. Educ:* Coll. of Law, Seoul Nat. Univ. (degree in Law). Entered Diplomatic Service, 1970: Third Sec., Bonn, 1970–74; First Sec., Rome, 1974–78; Dir for Legal Affairs, Office of Planning and Mgt, Seoul, 1978–80; Dir, Treaties Div. 1, Treaties Bureau, Min. of Foreign Affairs, 1980–81; Counsellor, Abu Dhabi, 1981–84; Dir, Internat. Econ. Orgns Div., Internat. Econ. Affairs Bureau, Min. of Foreign Affairs, 1984–85; Protocol Sec. to Pres., 1985–89; Consul-Gen., Montreal, 1989–93; Dir-Gen., Eur. Affairs Bureau, Min. of Foreign Affairs, 1992–93; Ambassador to Hungary, 1993–96; Ambassador and Dep. Perm. Rep., Korean Perm. Mission to UN, 1996–98; Dep. Minister for Foreign Affairs, Min. of Foreign Affairs and Trade, 1998–99. Service Medal, 1986, Meritorious Service Medal, 1988 (Korea); Diplomatic Medal (Hungary), 1995. *Recreations:* painting, golf. *Address:* c/o Embassy of the Republic of Korea, 60 Buckingham Gate, SW1E 6AJ. *T:* (020) 7227 5512. *Clubs:* Athenæum, Travellers; Coombe Hill Golf, Wentworth Golf.

CHOLERTON, Frederick Arthur, CBE 1978; *b* 15 April 1917; *s* of Frederick Arthur Cholerton and Charlotte (*née* Wagstaffe); *m* 1939, Ethel (*née* Jackson); one *s* decd. *Educ:* Penkhull Secondary Sch., Stoke-on-Trent. Locomotive driver, British Rail, 1934–77; Trade Union work with ASLEF, 1934–71. City of Stoke-on-Trent: Councillor, 1951–87; Leader of Council, 1976–81; Lord Mayor, 1971–72; Staffordshire County Council: Councillor, 1973–89; Vice-Chm., 1973–76; Chm., 1977 and 1981–89; Opposition Leader, 1977–81. Chm., Poplar Resource Management Co. Ltd, 1992–96; Director: North Staffordshire South Cheshire Broadcasting (Signal Radio), Ltd, 1982–88; Longton Enterprise Ltd, 1980–87; 1986 Nat. Garden Festival, Stoke-on-Trent, Staffordshire Ltd, 1983–88; W Midlands Industrial Develt Bd, 1983–89; Staffordshire Cable, 1988–93. Chairman: Bereavement Care Centre, Potteries and N Staffs, 1988–95; Staffs Sports for Disabled Trust, 1992–; Trustee, Central Telephon, 1990–. JP Stoke-on-Trent, 1956–74. MUniv Keele, 1988. *Recreations:* sports, gardening, politics, voluntary work for charities. *Address:* 12 Werburgh Drive, Trentham, Stoke-on-Trent ST4 8JP. *T:* (01782) 657457.

CHOLMELEY, Sir Frederick; *see* Cholmeley, Sir H. J. F. S.

CHOLMELEY, Sir (Hugh John) Frederick (Sebastian), 7th Bt *cr* 1806, of Easton, Lincolnshire; *b* 3 Jan. 1968; *o s* of Sir Montague Cholmeley, 6th Bt and of Juliet Auriol Sally (*née* Nelson); *S* father, 1998; *m* 1993, Ursula Anne, *d* of Hon. Sir H. P. D. Bennett, *qv;* one *s* one *d. Educ:* Eton Coll.; RAC Cirencester. ARICS 1992. *Recreation:* the countryside. *Heir: s* Montague Hugh Peter Cholmeley, *b* 19 May 1997.

CHOLMONDELEY, family name of **Marquess of Cholmondeley,** and of **Baron Delamere**.

CHOLMONDELEY, 7th Marquess of, *cr* 1815; **David George Philip Cholmondeley;** DL; Bt 1611; Viscount Cholmondeley (Ire.), 1661; Baron Cholmondeley of Namptwich (Eng.), 1689; Earl of Cholmondeley, Viscount Malpas, 1706; Baron Newborough (Ire.), 1715; Baron Newburgh (Gt Brit.), 1716; Earl of Rocksavage, 1815; Joint Hereditary Lord Great Chamberlain of England (acting for the reign of Queen Elizabeth II); *b* 27 June 1960; *s* of 6th Marquess of Cholmondeley, GCVO, MC and of Lavinia Margaret, *d* of late Col John Leslie, DSO, MC; *S* father, 1990. DL Cheshire, 1992. *Heir: cousin* Charles George Cholmondeley, *b* 18 March 1959. *Address:* Cholmondeley Castle, Malpas, Cheshire.

CHOLMONDELEY CLARKE, Marshal Butler; Master of the Supreme Court of Judicature (Chancery Division), 1973–92; *b* 14 July 1919; *s* of Major Cecil Cholmondeley Clarke and Fanny Ethel Carter; *m* 1947, Joan Roberta Stephens; two *s. Educ:* Aldenham. Admitted a solicitor, 1943; Partner, Burton Yeates & Hart, Solicitors, London, WC2, 1946–72. Pres., City of Westminster Law Soc., 1971–72; Mem. Council, Law Soc., 1966–72; Chm., Family Law Cttee, 1970–72; Chm., Legal Aid Cttee, 1972; Chancery Procedure Cttee, 1968–72. *Publication:* The Supreme Court Practice (Chancery ed.), 1985, 1991, 1993. *Recreations:* reading, genealogy. *Address:* 44 Pelham Court, Fulham Road, SW3 6SH. *Club:* Turf.

CHOMSKY, Prof. (Avram) Noam, PhD; Institute Professor, Massachusetts Institute of Technology, since 1976 (Ferrari P. Ward Professor of Modern Languages and Linguistics, 1966–76); *b* Philadelphia, 7 Dec. 1928; *s* of late William Chomsky and of Elsie

Simonofsky; *m* 1949, Carol Doris Schatz; one *s* two *d*. *Educ:* Central High Sch., Philadelphia; Univ. of Pennsylvania (PhD); Society of Fellows, Harvard, 1951–55. Massachusetts Institute of Technology: Asst Prof., 1955–58; Associate Prof., 1958–61; Prof. of Modern Langs, 1961–66. Res. Fellow, Harvard Cognitive Studies Center, 1964–65. Vis. Prof., Columbia Univ., 1957–58; Nat. Sci. Foundn Fellow, Inst. for Advanced Study, Princeton, 1958–59; Linguistics Soc. of America Prof., Univ. of Calif, LA, 1966; Beckman Prof., Univ. of Calif, Berkeley, 1966–67; Vis. Watson Prof., Syracuse Univ., 1982; Lectures: Shearman, UCL, 1969; John Locke, Oxford, 1969; Bertrand Russell Meml, Cambridge 1971; Nehru Meml, New Delhi, 1972; Whidden, McMaster Univ., 1975; Huizinga Meml, Leiden, 1977; Woodbridge, Columbia, 1978; Kant, Stanford, 1979. Member: Nat. Acad. of Scis; Amer. Acad. of Arts and Scis; Linguistic Soc. of America; Amer. Philosophical Assoc.; Bertrand Russell Peace Foundn; Utrecht Soc. of Arts and Scis; Deutsche Akademie der Naturforscher Leopoldina; Corresp. Mem., British Acad., 1974; Hon. Mem., Ges. für Sprachwissenschaft, Germany, 1990. Fellow, Amer. Assoc. for Advancement of Science; William James Fellow, Amer. Psychological Assoc., 1990. Hon. FBPsS; Hon. FRAI 1990. Hon. DLitt: London, 1967; Visva-Bharati, West Bengal, 1980; Cambridge, 1995; Hon. DHL: Chicago, 1967; Loyola Univ., Chicago, 1970; Swarthmore Coll., 1970; Bard Coll., 1971; Delhi, 1972; Massachusetts, 1973; Pennsylvania, 1985; Maine, 1992; Gettysburg Coll., 1992; Amherst Coll., 1995; Buenos Aires, 1996; Rovira i Virgili, Tarragona, 1998; Guelph, 1999; Columbia, 1999; Connecticut, 1999; Scuola Normale Superiore, Pisa, 1999; Toronto, 2000; Western Ontario, 2000; Harvard, 2000; Distinguished Scientific Contribution Award, Amer. Psychological Assoc., 1984; Kyoto Prize in Basic Science, Inamori Foundn, 1988; Orwell Award, Nat. Council of Teachers of English, 1987, 1989; Killian Award, MIT, 1992; Lannan Literary Award, for non-fiction, 1992; Homer Smith Award, New York Univ. Sch. of Medicine, 1994; Loyola Mellon Humanities Award, Loyola Univ., Chicago, 1994; Helmholtz Medal, Berlin-Brandenburgische Akad. Wissenschaften, 1996. *Publications:* Syntactic Structures, 1957; Current Issues in Linguistic Theory, 1964; Aspects of the Theory of Syntax, 1965; Cartesian Linguistics, 1966; Topics in the Theory of Generative Grammar, 1966; Language and Mind, 1968; (with Morris Halle) Sound Pattern of English, 1968; American Power and the New Mandarins, 1969; At War with Asia, 1970; Problems of Knowledge and Freedom, 1971; Studies on Semantics in Generative Grammar, 1972; For Reasons of State, 1973; The Backroom Boys, 1973; Peace in the Middle East?, 1974; (with Edward Herman) Bains de Sang, 1974; Reflections on Language, 1975; The Logical Structure of Linguistic Theory, 1975; Essays on Form and Interpretation, 1977; Human Rights and American Foreign Policy, 1978; Language and Responsibility, 1979; (with Edward Herman) Political Economy of Human Rights, 1979; Rules and Representations, 1980; Radical Priorities, 1981; Lectures on Government and Binding, 1981; Towards a New Cold War, 1982; Some Concepts and Consequences of the Theory of Government and Binding, 1982; Fateful Triangle: the United States, Israel and the Palestinians, 1983; Modular Approaches to the Study of the Mind, 1984; Turning the Tide, 1985; Barriers, 1986; Pirates and Emperors, 1986; Knowledge of Language: its nature, origin and use, 1986; Generative Grammar: its basis, development and prospects, 1987; On Power and Ideology, 1987; Language in a Psychological Setting, 1987; Language and Problems of Knowledge, 1987; The Chomsky Reader, 1987; The Culture of Terrorism, 1988; (with Edward Herman) Manufacturing Consent, 1988; Necessary Illusions, 1989; Deterring Democracy, 1991; Chronicles of Dissent, 1992; Year 501: the conquest continues, 1993; Rethinking Camelot: JFK, the Vietnam war, and US political culture, 1993; Letters from Lexington: reflections on propaganda, 1993; World Orders, Old and New, 1994; The Minimalist Program, 1995; Powers and Prospects, 1996; Class Warfare (interviews), 1996; The Common Good (interviews), 1998; Profit Over People, 1998; The New Military Humanism, 1999; New Horizons in the Study of Language and Mind, 2000; Rogue States, 2000; A New Generation Draws the Line, 2000. *Recreation:* gardening. *Address:* Department of Linguistics and Philosophy, Massachusetts Institute of Technology, E39-219, 77 Massachusetts Avenue, Cambridge, MA 02139–4307, USA. *T:* (781) 2537819.

CHOPE, Christopher Robert, OBE 1982; MP (C) Christchurch, since 1997; barrister; *b* 19 May 1947; *s* of late His Honour Robert Charles Chope and of Pamela Durell; *m* 1987, Christo Hutchinson; one *s* one *d*. *Educ:* St Andrew's Sch., Eastbourne; Marlborough Coll.; St Andrews Univ. (LLB Hons). Called to the Bar, Inner Temple, 1972. Mem., Wandsworth Borough Council, 1974–83; Chm., Housing Cttee, 1978–79; Leader of Council, 1979–83. Consultant, Ernst & Young, 1992–98. MP (C) Southampton, Itchen, 1983–92; contested (C) Southampton, Itchen, 1992. PPS to Minister of State, HM Treasury, 1986; Parly Under-Sec. of State, DoE, 1986–90; Parly Under-Sec. of State (Minister for Roads and Traffic), Dept of Transport, 1990–92; front bench spokesman on trade and industry, 1998–99. Jt Sec., Cons. Backbench Environment Cttee, 1983–86; Member: Select Cttee on Procedure, 1984–86; Select Cttee on Trade and Industry, 1999–. Chm., Cons. Parly Candidates Assoc., 1995–97. A Vice Chm., Cons. Party, 1997–98. Member: HSC, 1993–97; Local Govt Commn for England, 1994–95; Vice-Pres., LGA, 2000. Mem. Exec. Cttee, Soc. of Cons. Lawyers, 1983–86. *Address:* 63 Roupell Street, Waterloo, SE1 8SS. *T:* (020) 7633 9129. *Clubs:* Royal Southampton Yacht; Christchurch Conservative.

CHORLEY, family name of **Baron Chorley**.

CHORLEY, 2nd Baron *cr* 1945, of Kendal; **Roger Richard Edward Chorley,** FCA; Chairman, National Trust, 1991–96; *b* 14 Aug. 1930; *er s* of 1st Baron Chorley, QC, and Katharine Campbell (*d* 1986), *d* of late Edward Hopkinson, DSc; *S* father, 1978; *m* 1964, Ann, *d* of late A. S. Debenham; two *s*. *Educ:* Stowe Sch.; Gonville and Caius Coll., Cambridge (BA). Pres., CU Mountaineering Club. Expedns to Himalayas, 1954 (Rakaposhi), 1957 (Nepal); joined Cooper Brothers & Co. (later Coopers & Lybrand), 1955; New York office, 1959–60; Pakistan (Indus Basin Project), 1961; Partner, 1967–89; seconded to Nat. Bd for Prices and Incomes as accounting adviser, 1965–68; Visiting Prof., Dept of Management Sciences, Imperial Coll. of Science and Technology, Univ. of London, 1979–82. National Trust: Member: Finance Cttee, 1970–90; Exec. Cttee, 1989–96; Council, 1989–98; British Council: Mem. Rev. Cttee, 1979–80; Bd Mem., 1981–99; Dep. Chm., 1990–99. Member: Royal Commn on the Press, 1974–77; Finance Act 1960 Tribunal, 1974–79; Ordnance Survey Rev. Cttee, 1978–79; British Council Rev. Cttee, 1979–80; Nat. Theatre Bd, 1980–91; Top Salaries Review Body, 1981–90; Ordnance Survey Adv. Bd, 1983–85; H of L Select Cttee on Sci. and Technology, 1983, 1987, 1988, 1989, 1993, 1994, and Select Cttee on Sustainable Develt, 1994–95; NERC, 1988–94; Council, City and Guilds of London Inst., 1977–90; Council, RGS, 1984–93 (Pres., 1987–90); Council, RSA, 1987–89; Chm., Cttee into Handling of Geographic Information, 1985–87; Vice Pres., Council for Nat. Parks, 1997–. Hon. Sec., Climbers Club, 1963–67; Mem. Management Cttee, Mount Everest Foundn, 1968–70; Pres., Alpine Club, 1983–85; Hon. Pres., Assoc. for Geographic Inf., 1993–. Hon. Fellow, Central Lancs Univ., 1993; Hon. FRICS 1995. Hon. DSc: Reading, 1990; Kingston, 1992; Hon. LLD Lancaster, 1995. *Recreation:* mountains. *Heir:* *s* Hon. Nicholas Rupert Debenham Chorley, *b* 15 July 1966. *Address:* 50 Kensington Place, W8 7PW. *Club:* Alpine.

CHORLEY, Prof. Richard John; Professor of Geography, University of Cambridge, 1974–94, now Emeritus; Fellow of Sidney Sussex College, Cambridge, 1962–94, now Emeritus (Vice-Master, 1990–93); *b* 4 Sept. 1927; *s* of Walter Joseph Chorley and Ellen Mary Chorley; *m* 1965, Rosemary Joan Macdonald More; one *s* one *d*. *Educ:* Minehead Grammar Sch.; Exeter Coll., Oxford. MA (Oxon), ScD (Cantab). Lieut, RE, 1946–48. Fulbright Schol., Columbia Univ., 1951–52; Instructor: in Geography, Columbia Univ., 1952–54; in Geology, Brown Univ., 1954–57; Cambridge University: Demonstrator in Geography, 1958–62; Lectr in Geography, 1962–70, Reader, 1970–74. British rep. on Commn on Quantitative Techniques of Internat. Geographical Union, 1964–68; Dir, Madingley Geog. Courses, 1963–78. First Hon. Life Mem., British Geomorphological Res. Gp, 1974; Corresponding Mem., Italian Geographical Soc.; Emeritus Hon. Fellow, Internat. Assoc. of Geomorphologists, 1997. Hon. DSc Bristol, 1996. Gill Meml Medal, 1967, Patron's Medal, 1987, RGS; Hons Award, Assoc. of Amer. Geographers, 1981; David Linton Award, 1984. *Publications:* co-author of: The History of the Study of Landforms, Vols I, II and III, 1964, 1973, 1991; Atmosphere, Weather and Climate, 1968, 7th edn 1997; Network Analysis in Geography, 1969; Physical Geography, 1971; Environmental Systems, 1978; Geomorphology, 1984; co-editor of: Frontiers in Geographical Teaching, 1965; Models in Geography, 1967; editor of: Water, Earth and Man, 1969; Spatial Analysis in Geomorphology, 1972; Directions in Geography, 1973; contribs to: Jl of Geology, Amer. Jl of Science, Bulletin of Geolog. Soc. of Amer., Geog. Jl, Geol. Magazine, Inst. of Brit. Geographers, etc. *Recreations:* theatre, grave renovation. *Address:* 76 Grantchester Meadows, Newnham, Cambridge CB3 9JL.

CHOTHIA, Cyrus Homi, PhD; FRS 2000; Member of Scientific Staff, MRC Laboratory of Molecular Biology, Cambridge, since 1990; *b* 19 Feb. 1942; *s* of Homi and Betty Chothia; *m* 1967, Jean Sandham; one *s* one *d*. *Educ:* Alleyn's Sch., London; Univ. of Durham (BSc 1965); Birkbeck Coll., London Univ. (MSc 1967); UCL (PhD 1970). Mem., Scientific Staff, MRC Lab. of Molecular Biology, Cambridge, 1970–73; EMBO Fellow, Dept of Molecular Biochemistry and Biophysics, Yale Univ., and Dept of Chemical Physics, Weizmann Inst. of Science, Israel, 1974; Chargé de Recherche, Service du Biochimie Cellulaire, Institut Pasteur, Paris, 1974–76; Res. Associate, Dept of Chemistry, UCL, 1976–80; Royal Soc. EPA Cephalosporin Fund Sen. Res. Fellow, MRC Lab. of Molecular Biology, Cambridge, and Dept of Chemistry, UCL, 1980–90; Mem., Scientific Staff, Cambridge Centre for Protein Engrg, 1990–93. Mem., EMBO, 1988. *Publications:* papers on molecular biology in scientific jls. *Recreations:* cinema, books, conversation. *Address:* MRC Laboratory of Molecular Biology, Hills Road, Cambridge CB2 2QH. *T:* (01223) 402221; 26 Clarendon Street, Cambridge CB1 1JX.

CHOUFFOT, Geoffrey Charles, CBE 1983 (MBE 1965); Director and Treasurer, St Wilfrid's Hospice (South Coast) Ltd, 1987–93; Deputy Chairman, Civil Aviation Authority, 1980–83, retired; *m* 1941, June Catherine, *d* of Rev. W. Peebles Fleming; one *s* two *d*. Group Director, Safety Services, Civil Aviation Authority, 1978–80. *Club:* Royal Air Force.

CHOW, Sir Chung Kong, Kt 2000; FREng; Chief Executive, GKN plc, 1997–2001; *b* 9 Sept. 1950. *Educ:* Univ. of Wisconsin (BS Chem. Engrg 1972); Univ. of California (MS Chem. Engrg 1974); Chinese Univ. of Hong Kong (MBA 1981); Harvard (AMP 1991). FIChemE 1997; FREng 2001. Res. Engr, Climax Chemical Co., New Mexico, 1974–76; Process Engr, Sybron Asia Ltd, Hong Kong, 1976–77; with BOC Group, 1977–96: Hong Kong Oxygen, Hong Kong and BOC, Australia, 1977–84; Man. Dir, Hong Kong Oxygen, 1984–86; Pres., BOC Japan, 1986–89; Gp Manager, Gases Business Develt, BOC Gp plc, England and USA, 1989–91; Regl Dir, N Pacific, based in Tokyo and Hong Kong, 1991–93; Chief Exec., Gases, 1993–96; joined Main Bd, 1994; Man. Dir, 1994–97. Non-exec. Dir, Standard Chartered plc, 1997–. Pres., 1999–2000, Dep. Pres., 2000–2001, SBAC. *Address:* GKN plc, 7 Cleveland Row, SW1A 1DB. *T:* (020) 7930 2424.

CHRÉTIEN, Rt Hon. Jean; PC (Canada); QC (Canada) 1980; MP (L) Beauséjour, New Brunswick, since 1990; Prime Minister of Canada, since 1993; *b* 11 Jan. 1934; *s* of Wellie Chrétien and Marie Boisvert Chrétien; *m* 1957, Aline Chaîné; two *s* one *d*. *Educ:* Trois-Rivières; Joliette; Shawinigan; Laval Univ. (BA, LLL). Called to the Bar, and entered Shawinigan law firm of Chrétien, Landry, Deschênes, Trudel and Normand, 1958; Counsel, Lang Michener Lawrence and Shaw, 1986–90; Director: Shawinigan Sen. Chamber of Commerce, 1962; Bar of Trois-Rivières, 1962–63. Govt of Canada: MP (L) St Maurice, 1963–86; Parly Sec. to Prime Minister, 1965, and to Minister of Finance, 1966; Minister of State, 1967; Minister of National Revenue, Jan. 1968; Minister of Indian and Northern Affairs, July 1968; Pres., Treasury Bd, 1974; Minister of Industry, Trade and Commerce, 1976; Minister of Finance, 1977–79; Minister of Justice, responsible for constitutional negotiations, Attorney General, Minister of State for Social Develt, 1980–82; Minister of Energy, Mines and Resources, 1982–84; Deputy Prime Minister and External Affairs Minister, 1984; External Affairs Critic for official Opposition, 1984–86; Leader of the Opposition, 1990–93. Elected Leader, Liberal Party of Canada, June 1990. Hon LLD: Wilfred Laurier Univ., 1981; Laurentian Univ., 1982; Univ. of W Ontario, 1982; York Univ., Ont., 1986; Univ. of Alberta, 1987; Lakehead Univ., 1988. *Recreations:* ski-ing, fishing, golf, reading, classical music. *Address:* Office of the Prime Minister, Langevin Block, Parliament Buildings, Ottawa, ON K1A 0A2, Canada.

CHRIMES, Neil Roy; HM Diplomatic Service; Counsellor (Trade and Economic), Ottawa, since 2001; *b* 10 June 1954; *er s* of Geoffrey Richard Chrimes and Dorothy Enid Chrimes (*née* Wyatt); *m* 1982, Anne Margery, (Henny), Barnes; one *s* one *d*. *Educ:* Queen Mary's Grammar Sch., Basingstoke; Univ. of Exeter (BA 1975); MIT (SM 1979). Economic Assistant, MAFF, 1975–77; Harkness Fellow, MIT, 1977–79; Sen Economic Assistant, MAFF, 1979–81; Economic Advr, FCO, 1981–87; Economist, Res. Dept, IMF, Washington DC, 1987–89; Sen. Econ. Advr, FCO, 1989–94; Dep. UK Perm. Rep. and Counsellor (Econ. and Financial), OECD, Paris, 1994–98; Economic Counsellor, Jakarta, 1998; Hd, African Dept (Southern), FCO, 1999–2001. *Address:* c/o Foreign and Commonwealth Office, SW1A 2AH. *Club:* MCC.

CHRIST CHURCH, Dublin, Dean of; *see* Paterson, Very Rev. J. D. F.

CHRIST CHURCH, Oxford, Dean of; *see* Heaton, Very Rev. E. W.

CHRISTCHURCH, Bishop of, since 1990; **Rt Rev. Dr David John Coles;** *b* 23 March 1943; *s* of Samuel Arthur and Evelyn Ann Coles; *m* 1970, Ceridwyn Mary Parr; one *s* one *d*. *Educ:* Auckland Grammar Sch.; Univ. of Auckland (MA Hons 1967); Univ. of Otago (BD 1969; MTh 1971); Univ. of Manchester (PhD 1974); Melbourne Coll. of Divinity (Dip. Religious Educn). Deacon 1968, priest 1969; Curate, St Mark, Remuera, Auckland, 1968–70; Asst Chaplain, Selwyn Coll., Dunedin, 1970–71; Curate, Fallowfield, 1972–73; Chaplain, Hulme Hall, Univ. of Manchester, 1973–74; Vicar of: Glenfield, 1974–76; Takapuna, 1976–80; Examining Chaplain to Bp of Auckland, 1974–80; Dean and Vicar of St John's Cathedral, Napier, dio. Waiapu, 1980–84; Dean of Christchurch and Vicar-General, dio. Christchurch, 1984–90. Pres., Conf. of Churches of Aotearoa–NZ, 1991. *Recreations:* music, ski-ing, tramping. *Address:* The Anglican Centre, PO Box 4438, Christchurch 8001, New Zealand. *T:* (3) 3630913.

CHRISTENSEN, Jayne, (Mrs P. L. Christensen); *see* Torvill, J.

CHRISTENSEN, Jens; Commander First Class, Order of the Dannebrog; Hon. GCVO; Ambassador of Denmark to Organization for Economic Co-operation and Development, 1989–91; *b* 30 July 1921; *s* of Christian Christensen and Sophie Dorthea Christensen; *m* 1st, 1950, Tove (*née* Jessen) (*d* 1982); one *s* two *d*; 2nd, 1983, Vibeke Pagh. *Educ:* Copenhagen Univ. (MPolSc 1945). Joined Danish Foreign Service, 1945; Head of Section, Econ. Secretariat of Govt, 1947; Sec. to OEEC Delegn in Paris, 1949 and to NATO Delegn, 1952; Hd of Sect., Min. of Foreign Affairs, 1952, Actg Hd of Div., 1954; Chargé d'Affaires *a.i.* and Counsellor of Legation, Vienna, 1957; Asst Hd of Econ.-Polit. Dept, Min. of For. Affairs, 1960; Dep. Under-Sec., 1961; Under-Sec. and Hd of Econ.-Polit. Dept, 1964–71; Hd of Secretariat for Europ. Integration, 1966; Ambassador Extraord. and Plenipotentiary, 1967; State Sec. for Foreign Econ. Affairs, 1971; Ambassador to the Court of St James's, 1977–81; Pres., Danish Oil and Natural Gas Co., 1980–84; Ambassador to Austria, 1984–89. Governor for Denmark, The Asian Development Bank, 1967–73. Knight Grand Cross: Order of Icelandic Falcon; Order of Northern Star, Sweden; Order of St Olav, Norway; Royal Victorian Order; Austrian Order of Honour. *Address:* Strandvejen 647, 2930 Klampenborg, Denmark.

CHRISTIAN, Prof. Reginald Frank; Professor of Russian, St Andrews University, 1966–92, Emeritus Professor 1992; *b* Liverpool, 9 Aug. 1924; *s* of late H. A. Christian and late Jessie Gower (*née* Scott); *m* 1952, Rosalind Iris Napier; one *s* one *d*. *Educ:* Liverpool Inst.; Queen's Coll., Oxford (Open Scholar; MA). Hon. Mods Class. (Oxon), 1943; 1st cl. hons Russian (Oxon), 1949. Commnd RAF, 1944; flying with Atlantic Ferry Unit and 231 Sqdn, 1943–46. FO, British Embassy, Moscow, 1949–50; Lectr and Head of Russian Dept, Liverpool Univ., 1950–55; Sen. Lectr and Head of Russian Dept, Birmingham Univ., 1956–63; Vis. Prof. of Russian, McGill Univ., Canada, 1961–62; Prof. of Russian, Birmingham Univ., 1963–66; Exchange Lectr, Moscow, 1964–65. Mem. Univ. Ct, 1971–73 and 1981–85, Associate Dean, Fac. of Arts, 1972–73, Dean, Fac. of Arts, 1975–78, St Andrews Univ. Pres., British Univs Assoc. of Slavists, 1967–70; Member: Internat. Cttee of Slavists, 1970–75; UGC Atkinson Cttee, 1978–81. *Publications:* Korolenko's Siberia, 1954; (with F. M. Borras) Russian Syntax, 1959, 2nd rev. edn, 1971; Tolstoy's War and Peace: a study, 1962; (with F. M. Borras) Russian Prose Composition, 1964, 2nd rev. edn, 1974; Tolstoy: a critical introduction, 1969; (ed and trans.) Tolstoy's Letters, 2 vols, 1978; (ed and trans.) Tolstoy's Diaries, 2 vols, 1985, abridged edn, Tolstoy's Diaries, 1994; Alexis Aladin: the tragedy of exile, 1999; numerous articles and reviews in Slavonic and E European Review, Slavonic and E European Jl, Mod. Languages Review, Survey, Forum, Birmingham Post, Times Lit. Supp., Oxford Slavonic Papers, etc. *Recreations:* fell-walking, violin. *Address:* Culgrianach, 48 Lade Braes, St Andrews KY16 9DA. *T:* (01334) 474407; Scioncroft, Knockard Road, Pitlochry, Perthshire PH16 5HJ. *T:* (01796) 472993.

CHRISTIANI, Alexander, Dr jur; Ambassador of Austria to the Court of St James's, since 2000; *b* 31 May 1940; *s* of Dr Alfred Christiani-Kronwald, (Baron von Christiani-Kronwald), and Rose Christiani-Kronwald; *m* 1968, Renate Sedlmayer, PhD; one *s* one *d*. *Educ:* Univ. of Vienna (Dr jur 1964); Diplomatic Acad., Vienna. Federal Ministry for Foreign Affairs, Austria: Political Dept, 1966–69; Asst to Sec.-Gen. for Foreign Affairs, 1969; UN Mission, NY, 1970–75; Alternate Rep. of Austria to Security Council, 1973–74; Dir, Div. i/c of Vienna Internat. Centre, 1976–81; Consul Gen., Austrian Delegn, Berlin, 1981–86; Ambassador to South Africa, 1986–90; Dir, Dept for ME and Africa, 1990–96; Ambassador to the Netherlands, 1996–2000. Mem., Austrian Delegns to UN Gen. Assemblies, 1967–81. Cross, KM. Grand Cross: Order of Oranje-Nassau (Netherlands), 2000; Al-Istiglal Order (Jordan); Grand Officer, Order of Merit (Syria); Comdr, Order of Oak Crown (Luxembourg); Grand Decoration of Honour (Austria). *Recreations:* music, travelling, theatre. *Address:* 18 Belgrave Square, SW1X 8HU. *T:* (office) (020) 7235 3731. *Clubs:* White's; Rotary, St Johann's (Vienna); Haag'sche (The Hague).

CHRISTIANSON, Alan, CBE 1971; MC 1945; Deputy Chairman, South of Scotland Electricity Board, 1967–72; retired; *b* 14 March 1909; *s* of Carl Robert Christianson; *m* 1936, Gladys Muriel Lewin, *d* of William Barker; two *d*. *Educ:* Royal Grammar Sch., Newcastle upon Tyne; FCA, CompIEE. Served as Major, RA, 1939–45: comd Field Battery, 1943–45. Central Electricity Bd, 1934–48; Divisional Sec., British Electricity Authority, SW Scotland Div., 1948–55; Dep. Sec., S of Scotland Electricity Bd, 1955–62; Chief Financial Officer, 1962–65; Gen. Man., Finance and Administration, 1965–67. *Recreation:* golf. *Address:* Tynedale, Lennox Drive East, Helensburgh, Dunbartonshire G84 9JD. *T:* (01436) 74503.

CHRISTIANSON, Rev. Canon Rodney John, (Bill); Secretary General, Mission to Seafarers, since 2001; *b* S Africa, 19 March 1947; *s* of late Kenneth Alfred John Christianson and Jessie Winifred Nelson (*née* Kelly). *Educ:* Glenwood High Sch., Durban; Officer Trng Sch., S Africa; St Paul's Theol Coll., Grahamstown (DipTh); Open Univ. Ordained deacon 1972, priest 1973; Curate, Pietermaritzberg, SA, 1972–75; Missions to Seamen, subseq. Mission to Seafarers: Asst Chaplain, Gravesend, 1976–81; Sen. Chaplain, Port of London, 1981–82; Port Chaplain, Richards Bay, SA, 1982–91; also Parish Priest, St Andrew, Richards Bay and St Aidan, Kwambonambi, 1982–91; Trng Chaplain, Hull, 1991–93; Ministry Sec., 1993–2000. Mem., Archbp of Cape Town's Commn to conduct investigation into work amongst young people in the Church of SA, 1974. Guild Chaplain, St Bride's Ch, London, 1990; Hon. Canon, Bloemfontein Cathedral, SA, 1993. Hon. Master Mariner, SA, 1988. *Recreations:* painting/art, music, theatre, photography. *Address:* Mission to Seafarers, St Michael Paternoster Royal, College Hill, EC4R 2RL. *T:* (020) 7248 5202.

CHRISTIE, Ann Philippa; *see* Pearce, A. P.

CHRISTIE, Augustus Jack; Executive Chairman, Glyndebourne Productions Ltd, since 2000 (Director, since 1989); *b* 4 Dec. 1963; *s* of Sir George William Langham Christie, *qv*; *m* 1993, Imogen Lycett Green; three *s*. *Educ:* St Aubyns, Rottingdean; Eton Coll.; King's Coll., London (2nd Cl. Hons Zool.). Worked in various theatres, incl. Tricycle, NT, Batignano Opera, Robert Fox Associates, 1987; asst ed. and asst cameraman, Partridge Films, 1989–91; freelance cameraman, 1991–; documentaries include: A Puffin's Tale, Halloween, 1991; A New Fox in Town, 1993; The Lion's Share, Lions, 1994; Hugo's Diary, 1995; Red Monkeys of Zanzibar, 1996; The Battle of the Sexes, The Tale of Two Families, 1998; Buffalo: the African boss, Triumph of Life, 1999. *Recreations:* sport, music, nature. *Address:* Glyndebourne, Lewes, E Sussex BN8 5UU.

CHRISTIE, Campbell, CBE 1997; General Secretary, Scottish Trades Union Congress, 1986–98; *b* 23 Aug. 1937; *s* of Thomas Christie and Johnina Rolling; *m* 1962, Elizabeth Brown Cameron; two *s*. *Educ:* Albert Sen. Secondary Sch., Glasgow. Civil Service, 1954–72: Admiralty, 1954–59; DHSS, 1959–72; Society of Civil and Public Servants, 1972–85: Asst Sec., 1972–73; Asst Gen. Sec., 1973–75; Dep. Gen. Sec., 1975–85. Mem., EU Economic and Social Cttee, 1986–. Dir, Scottish Coal Co. Ltd, 1994–; Board Member: Scottish Enterprise, 1998–; British Waterways, 1998–; South West Trains Ltd, 1998–. Trustee, Forth Valley Acute Hosps NHS Trust, 1999–. Mem. Bd, Falkirk FC, 1996– (Chm., 1993–94). FEIS; FSQA. Hon. DLitt: Napier, 1992; Stirling, 2000; St Andrews, 2001; Hon. DLit: Queen Margaret Coll., Edinburgh, 1998; Glasgow Caledonian, 1999. *Address:* 31 Dumyat Drive, Falkirk, Stirlingshire FK1 5PA. *T:* (01324) 624555.

CHRISTIE, David; Warden, St Edward's School, Oxford, since 1988; *b* 22 Feb. 1942; *s* of William and Jean Christie, Bannockburn; *m* 1969, Elsa Margaret Shearer; one *s* two *d*. *Educ:* Dollar Acad.; Univ. of Strathclyde; Univ. of Glasgow. Lektor, British Centre, Folkuniversity of Sweden, 1965–66; Asst Master, George Watson's Coll., 1966–71; Lectr in Economics, Moray House Coll., Edinburgh, 1971–77; Res. Associate (part-time), Esmée Fairbairn Research Centre, Heriot-Watt Univ., 1972–77; Teacher, European Sch., Luxembourg, 1977–83; pt-time Faculty Mem., Miami Univ. European Center, Luxembourg, 1980–83; Head of Econs, Winchester Coll., 1983–88. Member: Econs and Business Studies Panel, Scottish Cert. of Educn Exam. Bd, 1973–77 (Convenor, 1975–77); Scottish Cttee, IBA, 1973–77; Dep. Chm., HMC Wkg Party on Inspection, 1993–97; Chm., Oxford Conf. in Educn, 1997–. Governor, Abingdon Sch., 2001–. Editor, Educn Sect., Economics, 1973–80. FRSA 1994. *Publications:* (contrib.) Curriculum Development in Economics, 1973; (contrib.) Teaching Economics, 1975; (with Prof. A. Scott) Economics in Action, 1976; articles, reviews and entries in jls and in Cambridge Guide to Literature, Golfers' Handbook. *Recreations:* books, golf, hills. *Address:* St Edward's School, Oxford OX2 7NN. *T:* (01865) 319323. *Clubs:* East India; Royal & Ancient (St Andrews).

CHRISTIE, Elizabeth Mary, (Mrs Stuart Christie); *see* Steel, E. M.

CHRISTIE, Sir George (William Langham), Kt 1984; DL; Director, Glyndebourne Productions Ltd (Chairman, 1956–99); *b* 31 Dec. 1934; *o s* of John Christie, CH, MC, and Audrey Mildmay Christie; *m* 1958, Patricia Mary Nicholson; three *s* one *d*. *Educ:* Eton. Asst to Sec. of Calouste Gulbenkian Foundation, 1957–62. Chm. of various family companies. Mem., Arts Council of GB, 1988–92 (Chm., Adv. Panel on Music, 1988–92). Founder Chm., The London Sinfonietta, 1968–88. DL E Sussex, 1983. Hon. FRCM 1986; Hon. FRNCM 1986; Hon. GSM 1991. DUniv Sussex, 1990; Hon. DMus: Keele, 1993; Exeter, 1994. Cavaliere al Merito della Repubblica Italiana, 1977. *Address:* Glyndebourne, Lewes, E Sussex BN8 5UU. *T:* (01273) 812250.

See also A. J. Christie.

CHRISTIE, Herbert; Director General, European Investment Bank, 1995–99, now Hon. Director General (Director, Research Department, 1983–95); *b* 26 Sept. 1933; *s* of Brig.-Gen. H. W. A. Christie, CB, CMG, and Mary Ann Christie; *m* 1982, Gilberte F. M. V. Desbois; one *s*. *Educ:* Methodist Coll., Belfast; Univ. of St Andrews (MA). Asst Lectr, Univ. of Leeds, 1958–60; Econ. Asst, HM Treasury, 1960–63; First Sec., Washington, DC, 1963–66; Econ. Adviser, J. Henry Schroder Wagg and Co. Ltd, 1966–71, with secondment as Econ. Adviser, NBPI, 1967–71; Sen. Econ. Adviser, Min. of Posts and Telecommunications, 1971–74, and Dept of Prices and Consumer Protection, 1974–76; Econ. Adviser, EEC Commn, Brussels, 1976–78; Under Sec., HM Treasury, 1978–83. Hon. Vis. Prof., Middlesex Univ., 1990–95. *Publications:* contrib. to books and learned jls. *Recreations:* languages, foreign travel. *Address:* 47 Rue J-B Esch, 1473 Luxembourg. *Club:* Reform.

CHRISTIE, Prof. Ian Leslie, FBA 1994; Professor of Film and Media History, Birkbeck College, University of London, since 1999; 23 Feb. 1945; *s* of Robert Christie and late Ethel Christie; *m* 1989, Patsy Nightingale; one *s* three *d*. *Educ:* Belfast Royal Acad.; Queen's Univ., Belfast (BA 1966). Lectr in Complementary Studies, Derby Coll. of Art, 1969–73; Sen. Lectr in Art Hist. and Film Studies, Derby Coll. of Higher Educn, 1973–75; British Film Institute: Regl Prog. Advr, then Hd of Programming, 1976–84; Hd of Distbn, 1984–92; Head of Special Projects, 1993–94; Associate Ed., Sight and Sound, 1995–97; Prof. of Film Studies, Univ. of Kent at Canterbury, 1997–99. Vis. Dir, Film Centre, Art Inst. of Chicago, 1985–86; Vis. Prof., Univ. of S Florida, 1989; Dist. Vis. Fellow, European Humanities Res. Centre, 1995–98, Vis. Lectr in Film, and Fellow, Magdalen Coll., 1995–98, Oxford Univ. Dir, Connoisseur Video, 1990–97. Vice-Pres., Europa Cinemas, 1993–. Mem. Exec. Cttee, GB-USSR Assoc., 1983–89. Co-curator of exhibitions: Eisenstein: his life and art, MOMA, Oxford, and Hayward Gall., 1988; Spellbound: art and film, Hayward Gall., 1996; The Director's Eye, MOMA, Oxford, 1996. Frequent radio and television broadcaster on cinema. *Publications:* Powell, Pressburger and Others, 1978; Arrows of Desire: the films of Michael Powell and Emeric Pressburger, 1985, 2nd edn 1994; (ed) The Life and Death of Col Blimp, 1994; The Last Machine, 1995; (ed) Gilliam on Gilliam, 1999; A Matter of Life and Death, 2000; *edited jointly:* FEKS, Formalism, Futurism, 1978; The Film Factory, 1988, 2nd edn 1994; Eisenstein at 90, 1988; Scorsese on Scorsese, 1989, 2nd edn 1996; Inside the Film Factory, 1991; Eisenstein Rediscovered, 1993; Protazanov and the Continuity of Russian Cinema, 1993. *Recreations:* running, ski-ing, coarse carpentry, affordable wine. *Address:* 131 Mount View Road, N4 4JH. *T:* (020) 8348 3656.

CHRISTIE, John Belford Wilson, CBE 1981; Sheriff of Tayside, Central and Fife (formerly Perth and Angus) at Dundee, 1955–83; *b* 4 May 1914; *o s* of late J. A. Christie, Advocate, Edinburgh; *m* 1939, Christine Isobel Syme, *o d* of late Rev. J. T. Arnott; four *d*. *Educ:* Merchiston Castle Sch.; St John's Coll., Cambridge; Edinburgh Univ. Admitted to Faculty of Advocates, 1939. Served War of 1939–45, in RNVR, 1936–48. Sheriff-Substitute of Western Div. of Dumfries and Galloway, 1948–55. Mem., Parole Bd for Scotland, 1967–73; Mem., Queen's Coll. Council, Univ. of St Andrews, 1960–67; Mem. Univ. Court, 1967–75, and Hon. Lectr, Dept of Private Law, Univ. of Dundee. Hon. LLD Dundee, 1977. KCHS 1994 (KHS 1988). *Recreations:* curling, golf. *Address:* Glebe House, Ashlar Lane, Cupar, Fife KY15 5BA. *T:* (01334) 653999. *Clubs:* New (Edinburgh); Royal and Ancient (St Andrews).

CHRISTIE, John Rankin, CB 1978; Deputy Master and Comptroller of the Royal Mint, 1974–77; *b* 5 Jan. 1918; *s* of Robert Christie and Georgina (*née* Rankin); *m* 1941, Constance May, *d* of Henry Gracie; one *s* two *d*. *Educ:* Ormskirk Gram. Sch.; London Sch. of Economics. Royal Ordnance Factories, 1936–43; Royal Artillery, 1943–47 (Captain); Min. of Supply, 1947; Admin. Staff Coll., 1949; Air Ministry, 1954; Private Sec. to Ministers of Supply, 1955–57; Asst Sec., 1957; British Defence Staffs, Washington, 1962–65; Under-Sec., Min. of Aviation, 1965–67, Min. of Technology, 1967–70, Min. of Aviation Supply, 1970–71; Asst Under-Sec. of State, MoD, 1971–74. *Recreations:* travel, bird-watching. *Address:* Twitten Cottage, East Hill, Oxted, Surrey RH8 9AA. *T:* (01883) 713047.

CHRISTIE, Julie (Frances); actress; *b* 14 April 1940; *d* of Frank St John Christie and Rosemary Christie (*née* Ramsden). *Educ:* Convent; Brighton Coll. of Technology; Central Sch. of Speech and Drama. *Films:* Crooks Anonymous, 1962; The Fast Lady, 1962; Billy Liar, 1963; Darling, 1964 (Oscar, NY Film Critics Award, Br. Film Academy Award, etc); Young Cassidy, 1964; Dr Zhivago, 1965 (Donatello Award); Fahrenheit 451, 1966; Far from the Madding Crowd, 1966; Petulia, 1967; In Search of Gregory, 1969; The Go-Between, 1971; McCabe and Mrs Miller, 1972; Don't Look Now, 1973; Shampoo, 1974;

Heaven Can Wait, 1978; Memoirs of a Survivor, 1981; The Animals Film, 1982; Return of the Soldier, 1982; Heat and Dust, 1983; The Gold Diggers, 1984; Power, 1987; Miss Mary, 1987; The Railway Station Man, 1992; Hamlet, 1997; Afterglow, 1998; *stage:* Old Times, Wyndham's, 1995; Suzanna Andler, Chichester, 1997. Fellow, BAFTA, 1997. Motion Picture Laurel Award, Best Dramatic Actress, 1967; Motion Picture Herald Award, Best Dramatic Actress, 1967. *Address:* c/o ICM Ltd, 76 Oxford Street, W1N 0AX.

CHRISTIE, Linford, OBE 1998 (MBE 1990); athlete; Managing Director, Nuff Respect, sports management company; *b* Jamaica, 2 April 1960; *s* of James and late Mabel Christie. *Educ:* Wandsworth Tech. Coll. Has competed over 50 times for Great Britain, 1980–97. *European indoor championships:* Gold medal (200 m), 1986; Gold medal (60 m), 1988 and 1990; *European championships:* Gold medal (100 m), 1986 and 1990; *Commonwealth Games:* Silver medal (100 m), 1986; Gold medal (100 m), 1990 and 1994; *European Cup:* Gold medals (100 and 200 m), 1987; Gold medal (100 m), 1991, 1992 and 1994; Gold medals (100 and 200m), 1997 (Men's Team Captain); *Olympic Games:* Silver medal (100 m), 1988; Gold medal (100 m), 1992 (British Men's Team Captain); *World indoor championships:* Silver medals (60 and 200 m), 1991; *World Cup:* Silver medal (200 m), 1992; Gold medal (100 m), 1989 and 1992; *World championships:* Gold medal (100 m), 1993; Silver medal (100 m relay), 1993. British and European 100 m record (9.92 seconds), and British 200 m record (20.09 seconds), 1988; British 100 yards record (9.30 seconds), Edinburgh, 1994; European 60 m record (6.47 seconds) and World indoor 200 m record (20.25 seconds), 1995. British Athletics Writers' Assoc., Male Athlete of the Year, 1988 and 1992. Hon. MSc Portsmouth Univ., 1993. *Publications:* Linford Christie (autobiog), 1989; To Be Honest With You (autobiog.), 1995. *Address:* Nuff Respect, The Coach House, 107 Sherland Road, Twickenham, Middlesex TW1 4HB. *T:* (020) 8891 4145. *Club:* Thames Valley Harriers.

CHRISTIE, Prof. Thomas; Professor of Educational Assessment and Evaluation, since 1994, and Director, Centre for Educational Leadership, since 1996, School of Education, and Dean, Faculty of Education, and Director, School of Education, since 1997, University of Manchester; *b* 12 May 1939; *s* of John Frew Christie and Margaret Watson Christie; *m* 1962, Patricia Ray Bozie; two *s* one *d*. *Educ:* Univ. of Edinburgh (MA, BEd). Res. Associate, 1963-66, Lectr in Educn, 1966-73, Sen. Lectr, 1973–76 and 1978–86, Dept of Educn, Univ. of Manchester; Sen. Lectr in Educnl Res., Dept of Educn, Univ. of Guyana, and Commonwealth Fund for Tech. Co-operation Consultant to Caribbean Exams Council, Barbados, 1976-78; Dir, Centre for Formative Assessment Studies, Sch. of Educn, Univ. of Manchester, 1986-96. Hon. DSc National Univ. of Mongolia, 1998. *Publications:* (jtly) Creativity: a selective review of research, 1968, 2nd edn 1971; (with G. M. Forrest) Standards at GCE A Level: 1963 and 1973, 1980; (with G. M. Forrest) Defining Public Examination Standards, 1981; A Guide to Teacher Assessment (3 vols), 1990; (ed with B. Boyle) Issues in Setting Standards: establishing comparabilities, 1996. *Recreations:* reading, crossword puzzles, desert travel. *Address:* 284 Bramhall Lane South, Bramhall, Stockport SK7 3DJ. *T:* T: (0161) 439 1518.

CHRISTIE, Sir William, Kt 1975; MBE 1970; JP; Lord Mayor of Belfast, 1972–75; a Company Director; *b* 1 June 1913; *s* of Richard and Ellen Christie, Belfast; *m* 1935, Selina (*née* Pattison); one *s* two *d* (and one *s* decd). *Educ:* Ward Sch., Bangor, Northern Ireland. Belfast City Councillor, 1961; High Sheriff of Belfast, 1964–65; Deputy Lord Mayor, 1969; Alderman, 1973 77. JP Belfast, 1951; DL Belfast, 1977. Freeman, City of London, 1975. Salvation Army Order of Distinguished Auxiliary Service, 1973. *Recreations:* travel, walking, boating, gardening.

CHRISTIE, William James; Sheriff of Tayside, Central and Fife at Kirkaldy, 1979–97; *b* 1 Nov. 1932; *s* of William David Christie and Mrs Anne Christie; *m* 1957, Maeve Patricia Gallacher; three *s*. *Educ:* Holy Cross Acad., Edinburgh; Edinburgh Univ. (LLB). Nat. Service, 1954–56; commnd Royal Scots. Private Practice, 1956–79. Mem. Council, Law Soc. of Scotland, 1975–79; President: Soc. of Procurators of Midlothian, 1977–79; Soc. of Solicitors in the Supreme Court, 1979. *Recreations:* music, reading, shooting. *Address:* c/o Sheriff Court House, Whytescauseway, Kirkcaldy, Fife KY1 1XQ. *Club:* New (Edinburgh).

CHRISTIE, William Lincoln; harpsichord player, organist and conductor; Founder and Director, Les Arts Florissants, since 1979; *b* New York, 19 Dec. 1944; *s* of William Lincoln Christie and Ida Jones Christie; adopted French citizenship. *Educ:* Harvard Coll. (BA 1966); Yale Univ. (MusM 1969). Student of piano and harpsichord in US, 1957–70; Asst in Hist. of Music and Dir, Collegium Musicum, Dartmouth Coll., USA, 1970–71; moved to France, 1971; Collaborator, Soc. de musique d'autrefois, Paris, 1972–75; Visiting Professor: Conservatoires of Paris, Lyon and The Hague, and GSMD, 1977–81; Sommer Akademie für Musik, Innsbrück, 1978–83; Prof., Paris Conservatoire, 1982–95. Musical Dir, Hyppolite et Aricie, L'Opéra de Paris, 1985; regularly conducts orchs in France, Switzerland, UK and USA; Glyndebourne début, Handel's Theodora, 1996. Mem., Vis. Cttee for Music, Harvard Univ., 1993–96. Has made numerous recordings, 1976–, esp. works for harpsichord, and vocal works of 17th and 18th centuries with Les Arts Florissants. Hon. DMus NY at Buffalo, 1997. Officier des Arts et des Lettres (France); Chevalier de la Légion d'Honneur (France), 1993. *Publications:* Sonate Baroque, 1989; Purcell au Coeur du Baroque, 1995. *Recreation:* gardening. *Address:* Les Arts Florissants, 2 rue de St Petersbourg, 75008 Paris, France. *T:* (1) 43879888; Le Logis, 85210 Thiré, France.

CHRISTO AND JEANNE-CLAUDE; artists; Christo Javacheff; *b* Gabrovo, Bulgaria, 13 June 1935 and Jeanne-Claude (*née* de Guillebon), *b* Casablanca, 13 June 1935; *m*; one *s*. Emigrated to USA 1964. Completed works include: Wrapped Objects, 1958; Stacked Oil Barrels and Dockside Packages, Cologne Harbour, 1961; Iron Curtain-Wall of Oil Barrels, blocking Rue Visconti, Paris, 1962; Store Fronts, NYC, 1964; Wrapped Kunsthalle, Berne, and Wrapped Fountain and Wrapped Medieval Tower, Spoleto, Italy, 1968; 5,600 Cubicmeter Package, Documenta 4, Kassel, 1968; Wrapped Floor and Stairway, Mus. of Contemporary Art, Chicago, 1969; Wrapped Coast, Little Bay, Sydney, Australia, 1969; Wrapped Monuments, Milan, 1970; Wrapped Floors and Covered Windows and Wrapped Walk Way, Krefeld, Germany, 1971; Valley Curtain, Grand Hogback, Rifle, Colo, 1970–72; The Wall, Wrapped Roman Wall, Via V. Veneto and Villa Borghese, Rome, 1974; Ocean Front, Newport, RI, 1974; Running Fence, Sonoma and Marin Counties, Calif, 1972–76; Wrapped Walk Ways, Kansas City, Mo, 1977–78; Surrounded Islands, Biscayne Bay, Miami, Fla, 1980–83; The Pont Neuf Wrapped, Paris, 1975–85; The Umbrellas, Japan–USA, 1984–91; Wrapped Floors and Stairways and Covered Windows, Mus. Würth, Künzelsau, Germany, 1995; Wrapped Reichstag, Berlin, 1971–95; Wrapped Trees, Switzerland, 1997–98. *Address:* 48 Howard Street, New York, NY 10013, USA.

CHRISTODOULOU, Anastasios, CBE 1978; Secretary-General, Association of Commonwealth Universities, 1980–96; Secretary-General (formerly Joint Secretary), UK Commonwealth Scholarship Commission, 1980–96; Executive Secretary, Marshall Scholarships Commemoration Commission, 1980–96; *b* Cyprus, 1 May 1932; *s* of Christodoulos and Maria Haji Yianni; *m* 1955, Joan P. Edmunds; two *s* two *d*. *Educ:* St Marylebone Grammar Sch.; The Queen's Coll., Oxford (MA). Colonial Administrative Service, Tanganyika (Tanzania), 1956–62; served as District Commissioner and Magistrate. Univ. of Leeds Administration, 1963–68: Asst Registrar, 1963–65; Dep. Sec., 1965–68; Secretary, Open Univ., 1969–80. Chm., Surrey Univ. Centre for Commonwealth and European Educnl Develt, 1990–96; Vice-Chm., Commonwealth Inst., 1981–89; Member: Bd of Trustees, Harlow Campus, Meml Univ. of Newfoundland, 1980–97; Exec. Cttee, Council for Educn in Commonwealth, 1980–99 (Chm., 1996–99); Fulbright Commn, 1980–96; Bd of Trustees, Richmond Coll., London, 1988–; Bd of Trustees, Internat. Extension Coll., 1994–99 (Chm., 1996–99); Bd of Govs, Commonwealth of Learning, 1988–93. Member, Court: Exeter Univ., 1980–96; Hull Univ., 1980–96; RCA, 1980–96. FRSA. Hon. Prof., Univ. of Mauritius, 1986; Hon. Vis. Prof., Surrey, 1991–. Hon. FCP 1995. DUniv: Open, 1981; Athabasca, 1981; Brunel, 1996; Ottawa, 1998; Hon. LLD Auckland, 1992; Hon. DCL Acadia, 1992. Univ. of Lesotho 50th Anniversary Award for Distinguished Service to African Educn, 1995. *Recreations:* sport, music, bridge; international and Commonwealth relations. *Address:* 246 Lauderdale Mansions, Lauderdale Road, W9 1NQ. *T:* (020) 7286 0011, *Fax:* (020) 7289 3309. *Club:* Royal Commonwealth Society.

CHRISTOPHER, Baron *cr* 1998 (Life Peer), of Leckhampton in the co. of Gloucestershire; **Anthony Martin Grosvenor Christopher,** CBE 1984; Chairman, TU Fund Managers Ltd (formerly Trades Union Unit Trust), since 1983 (Director, since 1981); public and political affairs consultant, since 1989; General Secretary, Inland Revenue Staff Federation, 1976–88; *b* 25 April 1925; *s* of George Russell Christopher and Helen Kathleen Milford Christopher (*née* Rowley); *m* 1962, Adela Joy Thompson. *Educ:* Cheltenham Grammar Sch.; Westminster Coll. of Commerce. Articled Pupil, Agric. Valuers, Gloucester, 1941–44; RAF, 1944–48; Inland Revenue, 1948–57; Asst Sec. 1957–60, Asst Gen. Sec. 1960–74, Jt Gen. Sec. 1975, Inland Revenue Staff Fedn; Member: TUC General Council, 1976–89 (Chm., 1988–89); TUC Economic Cttee, 1977–89; TUC Education Cttee, 1977–85; TUC Educn and Training Cttee, 1985–86; TUC Employment Policy and Orgn Cttees, 1985–89; TUC International Cttee, 1982–89; TUC Finance and General Purposes Cttee, 1983–89; TUC Media Working Group, 1979–89 (Chm., 1985–89); TUC Employment Policy and Orgn Cttee, 1979–85; TUC Social Insurance Cttee, 1986–89; Mems Auditor, ICFTU, 1984–. Member: Tax Reform Cttee, 1974–80; Tax Consultative Cttee, 1980–88; Royal Commn on Distribution of Income and Wealth, 1978–79; IBA, 1978–83; Council, Inst. of Manpower Studies, 1984–89; ESRC, 1985–88; GMC, 1989–94. Chm., Tyre Industry EDC, 1983–86; Vice Pres., Building Socs Assoc., 1985–90; Director: Civil Service Building Soc., 1958–87 (Chm., 1978–87); Birmingham Midshires Building Soc., 1987–88; Policy Studies Inst. Council, 1983–91; Member: Bd, Civil Service Housing Assoc., 1958–96 (Vice-Chm., 1988–96); Council, NACRO, 1956–98 (Chm., 1973–98); Home Sec.'s Adv. Council for Probation and After-care, 1967–77; Inner London Probation and After-care Cttee, 1966–79; Audit Commn, 1989–95; Broadcasting Complaints Commn, 1989–97; Council, 1985–90, Assembly, 1990–, SCF; Chm., Alcoholics Recovery Project, 1970–76; Member: Home Sec.'s Working Party on Treatment of Habitual Drunken Offenders, 1969–71; Inquiry into Rover Cowley Works Closure, 1990. Trustee: Commonwealth Trades Union Council Charitable Trust, 1985–89; Inst. for Public Policy Res., 1989–94 (Treas., 1990–94). Vis. Fellow, Univ. of Bath, 1981–; Mem. Council, Royal Holloway and Bedford New Coll., 1985–89. FRSA 1989. *Publications:* (jtly) Policy for Poverty, 1970; (jtly) The Wealth Report, 1979; (jtly) The Wealth Report 2, 1982. *Recreations:* gardening, reading, walking dogs. *Address:* c/o TU Fund Managers Ltd, Congress House, Great Russell Street, WC1B 3LQ. *Clubs:* Beefsteak, Wig and Pen, Royal Automobile.

CHRISTOPHER, Ann, RA 1989 (ARA 1980); RWA; FRBS; sculptor; *b* 4 Dec. 1947; *d* of William and Phyllis Christopher; *m* 1969, Kenneth Cook. *Educ:* Harrow School of Art (pre-Diploma); West of England College of Art (DipAD Sculpture). RWA 1983; FRBS 1992. Prizewinner, Daily Telegraph Young Sculptors Competition, 1971; Arts Council grants, 1973–76; Silver Medal for Sculpture of Outstanding Merit, RBS, 1994. *Exhibitions include:* Oxford Gallery, Oxford, 1973, 1974, 1978; Dorset County Mus. and Art Gall. (retrospective), 1989; Victoria Art Gall., Bath, 1992; Courcoux & Courcoux, 1991, 1999; Sculpture 93, London, 1993; Summer Exhibns, Redfern Gall., 1995, 1996; solo exhibn, Redfern Gall., 1997; Royal Academy, Summer Exhibns, 1971–. *Work in Collections:* Bristol City Art Gallery; Contemporary Arts Soc.; Chantrey, London; Glynn Vivian Art Gall., Swansea; RWA. *Commissions:* 3½m bronze, Tower Bridge Rd, London, 1990; 4½m bronze, Castle Park, Bristol, 1993; 2·3m bronze, Washington, USA, 1994; 4·8m corten steel, Plymouth, 1996; 2·3m bronze, Linklaters & Paines, London, 1997; 3m bronze, Great Barrington, Mass, USA, 1998; 5·5m corten steel, Portmarine, 2001. *Recreation:* cinema. *Address:* The Stable Block, Hay Street, Marshfield, near Chippenham, Wilts SN14 8PF.

CHRISTOPHER, Colin Alfred; National Secretary, Construction, Furniture, Timber and Allied Section, GMB, 1993–96; *b* 6 Nov. 1932; *s* of Alfred and Ivy Christopher; *m* 1952, Mary (*née* Wells); one *s* one *d*. *Educ:* Woodland Secondary Modern Sch., Gillingham, Kent. Apprentice upholsterer, furniture industry, 1947–52. Nat. Service, RAOC, 1952–54. Furniture, Timber and Allied Trades Union: Dist Organiser for Kent/Sussex/Hampshire area, 1968; Nat. Trade Organiser for Soft Furnishing and Bedding Sect., 1978; Gen. Sec., 1986–93. Mem. Bd, FIRA, 1986–; Mem., Exec. Cttee, IFBWW, 1989–. Active Mem, British Labour Party, at Constituency and Nat. Level, 1960–. *Recreations:* gardening, reading, classical music, ballet. *Address:* c/o GMB, 22–24 Worple Road, Wimbledon, SW19 4DD.

CHRISTOPHER, Sir (Duncan) Robin (Carmichael), KBE 2000; CMG 1997; HM Diplomatic Service; Ambassador to Argentina, since 2000; *b* 13 Oct. 1944; *m* 1980, Merril Stevenson; two *d*. FCO, 1970; Second, then First, Sec., New Delhi, 1972; First Sec., FCO, 1976; Hd of Chancery, Lusaka, 1980; First Sec., FCO, 1983; on secondment to Cabinet Office, 1985; Counsellor: Madrid, 1987; FCO, 1991; Ambassador: to Ethiopia, 1994–97; to Indonesia, 1997–2000. *Recreations:* ski-ing, music, family life. *Address:* c/o Foreign and Commonwealth Office, SW1A 2AH.

CHRISTOPHER, John; *see* Youd, S.

CHRISTOPHER, John Anthony, CB 1983; BSc; FRICS; Chief Valuer, Valuation Office, Inland Revenue, 1981–84, retired; *b* 19 June 1924; *s* of John William and Dorothy Christopher; *m* 1947, Pamela Evelyn Hardy; one *s* one *d* (and one *s* decd). *Educ:* Sir George Monoux Grammar Sch., Walthamstow; BSc Estate Management (London). Chartered Surveyor; LCC Valuation Dept, 1941. Served War, RAF, 1943–47. Joined Valuation Office, 1952; District Valuer and Valuation Officer, Lincoln, 1965; Superintending Valuer, Darlington, 1972; Asst Chief Valuer, 1974; Dep. Chief Valuer, Valuation Office, Inland Revenue, 1978. *Recreation:* golf. *Address:* 40 Svenskaby, Orton Wistow, Peterborough, Cambs PE2 6YZ. *T:* (01733) 238199.

CHRISTOPHER, Sir Robin; *see* Christopher, Sir D. R. C.

CHRISTOPHER, Warren; lawyer; Secretary of State, United States of America, 1993–97; *b* 27 Oct. 1925; *s* of Ernest and Catharine Christopher; *m* 1956, Marie Wyllis; three *s* one *d*. *Educ:* Univ. of Southern California; Stanford Law Sch. USNR, 1943–45. Joined O'Melveny and Myers, LA, 1950, partner, 1958–67, 1969–76, 1981–92. Dep. Attorney-Gen., USA, 1967–69; Dep. Sec. of State, 1977–81. US Medal of Freedom, 1981. *Address:* Suite 700, 1999 Avenue of the Stars, Los Angeles, CA 90067–6035, USA.

CHRISTOPHERS, Richard Henry Tudor, (Harry); conductor; *b* 26 Dec. 1953; *s* of Richard Henry Christophers and Constance Clavering Christophers (*née* Thorp); *m* 1979, Veronica Mary Hayward; two *s* two *d*. *Educ:* Canterbury Cathedral Choir Sch.; King's Sch., Canterbury; Magdalen Coll., Oxford (Mods Classics, BA Music). Founder and Conductor, The Sixteen Choir and Orchestra, then The Sixteen and the Symphony of Harmony and Invention, 1977–; débuts: BBC Prom. concert, 1990; Salzburg Fest., 1989; Lisbon Opera, 1994; ENO, 2000; freelance conductor: Scottish Chamber Orch., Avanti!, BBC Philharmonic, City of London Sinfonia, Concertgebouw Chamber Orch., English Chamber Orch., Beethoven Academie, Northern Sinfonia, etc. Numerous recordings. Grand Prix du Disque, 1988; Deutschen Schallplattenkritik, 1992 and 1993; Gramophone Award, 1992; Diapason d'or, 1995 and 1996. *Recreations:* cooking, Arsenal FC. *Address:* The Sixteen, Enslow House, Station Road, Enslow, Kidlington, Oxon OX5 3AX.

CHRISTOPHERSEN, Henning; Managing Director, Epsilon SPRL, since 1995; *b* Copenhagen, 8 Nov. 1939; *m* Jytte Risbjerg Christophersen; one *s* two *d*. *Educ:* Copenhagen University (MA Econs, 1965). Head, Economic Div., Danish Fedn of Crafts and Smaller Industries, 1965–70; economics reporter for periodical NB, 1970–71, for weekly Weekendavisen, 1971–78. MP (L) for Hillerød, 1971–84; Nat. Auditor, 1976–78; Minister for Foreign Affairs, 1978–79; Pres., Liberal Party Parly Gp, 1979–82; Dep. Prime Minister and Minister for Finance, 1982–84; a Vice-Pres., EC (formerly CEC), 1985–95). Mem., parly finance and budget cttee, 1972–76 (Vice-Chm., 1975); Chm., parly foreign affairs cttee, 1979–81; Mem., Nordic Council, 1981–82. Dep. Leader, Danish Liberal Party, Venstre, 1972–77; Political spokesman of Liberal MPs, 1973–78; Acting Leader, Liberal Party, 1977, Party Leader, 1978–84. Vice-Pres., Fedn of European Liberals and Democrats, 1980–84. Sen. Advr to Czech Govt, 1996–99; Chm., Örestad Co., 1999–; Vice-Chm., Scania Danmark AS, 2000–. Director: Danish Central Bank, 1979–82; Scancem AB, 1998–99; Den Danske Bank, 1995–; Mem. Bd, KS Consult AS, 1999–. Member: Danish Council for Eur. Policy, 1995–; Prime Minister's Adv. Council for Baltic Sea Co-operation, Sweden, 1996–; EC Adv. Cttee on Opening-up of Public Procurement, 1997–; Pres., Energy Charter Conf., Brussels, 1998–. Mem. Bd, Rockwool Foundn, 1995–. Chm., Eur. Inst. of Public Admin, Maastricht, 1996–. *Publications:* books and articles on political and economic subjects. *Address:* Epsilon SPRL, Rue de Toulouse 49, 1040 Brussels. *T:* (2) 2300081, *Fax:* (2) 2301086; *e-mail:* epsilon@epsilon-consulting.be.

CHRISTOPHERSON, Harald Fairbairn, CMG 1978; Commissioner of Customs and Excise, 1970–80, retired; *b* 12 Jan. 1920; *s* of late Captain H. and Mrs L. G. L. Christopherson; *m* 1947, Joyce Winifred Emmett (*d* 1979); one *s* two *d*. *Educ:* Heaton Grammar Sch., Newcastle upon Tyne; King's Coll., Univ. of Durham (BSc and DipEd). Served in RA, 1941–46, Captain 1945. Teacher and lecturer in mathematics, 1947–48. Entered administrative class, Home CS, Customs and Excise, 1948; seconded to Trade and Tariffs Commn, W Indies, 1956–58; Asst Sec., 1959; seconded to Treasury, 1965–66; Under Sec., 1969. Senior Clerk, Committee Office: House of Commons, 1980–85; House of Lords, 1985–86. Mem. Cttee for Southern Region, Nat. Trust, 1986–94. *Recreations:* music, museums and galleries, books, travel. *Address:* 57a York Road, Sutton, Surrey SM2 6HN. *T:* (020) 8642 2444. *Club:* Reform.

CHRISTOPHERSON, Romola Carol Andrea, CB 1998; Associate Director, Media Strategy, since 1999; non-executive Director, Primary Care Group Ltd, since 1999; *b* 10 Jan. 1939; *d* of late Albert Edward Christopherson and Kathleen Christopherson (*née* Marfitt). *Educ:* Collegiate School for Girls, Leicester; St Hugh's College, Oxford (BA Hons English). DSIR, Min. of Technology, 1962; DoE, 1970; Min. of Agriculture, Fisheries and Food, 1978; N Ireland Office, 1981; Dep. Press Sec. to Prime Minister, 1983; Head of Inf., Dept of Energy, 1984; Dir of Information, then of Press and Publicity, DHSS, later DoH, 1986–98. *Recreations:* amateur dramatics, antiques. *Address:* 28 Wharton Street, WC1X 9PJ.

CHRUSZCZ, Charles Francis; QC 1992; a Recorder, since 1990; *b* 19 Nov. 1950; *s* of Janick Francis Chruszcz and Kathleen Whitehurst Chruszcz; *m* 1972, Margaret Olivia Chapman; three *s*. *Educ:* Queen Mary Coll., London (LLB Hons). Called to the Bar, Middle Temple, 1973; Asst Recorder, 1985. *Recreations:* reading, music, building renovation, the outdoors. *Address:* 28 St John Street Chambers, Manchester M3 4DJ. *T:* (0161) 834 8418.

CHU, Prof. Steven, PhD; Professor of Physics and Applied Physics, since 1987, Theodore and Frances Geballe Professor of Physics and Applied Physics, since 1990, Stanford University, California; *b* 28 Feb. 1948; *s* of Ju Chin Chu and Ching Chen Li; two *s*. *Educ:* Univ. of Rochester (AB Maths 1970, BS Physics 1970); Univ. of Calif, Berkeley (PhD Physics 1976). Postdoctoral Res. Fellow, Univ. of Calif, Berkeley, 1976–78; Mem., Technical Staff, Bell Labs, Murray Hill, 1978–83; Hd, Quantum Electronics Res. Dept, AT&T Bell Labs, Holmdel, 1983–87; Chm., Physics Dept, Stanford Univ., 1990–93. Vis. Prof., Collège de France, 1990. Fellow: APS, 1987; Optical Soc. of America, 1988; Amer. Acad. Arts and Scis, 1992. Member: NAS, 1993; Academica Sinica, 1994; Amer. Philosophical Soc., 1998; Foreign Member: Chinese Acad. Scis, 1998; Korean Acad. Scis and Technol., 1998. Broida Prize for Laser Spectroscopy, 1987, Schawlow Prize for Laser Sci., 1994, APS; King Faisal Internat. Prize for Sci., 1993; Meggers Award for Spectroscopy, Optical Soc. of America, 1994; Humboldt Sen. Scientist Award, 1995; Science for Art Prize, LVMH, 1995; (jtly) Nobel Prize for Physics, 1997. *Recreations:* swimming, cycling, tennis. *Address:* Varian Physics, Room 230, Stanford, CA 94305–4060, USA; 636 Alvarado Row, Stanford, CA 94305, USA. *T:* (650) 7233571.

CHUA, Nam-Hai, FRS 1988; Andrew W. Mellon Professor and Head of Laboratory of Plant Molecular Biology, Rockefeller University, since 1981; *b* 8 April 1944; *m* 1970, Suat Choo Pearl; two *d*. *Educ:* Univ. of Singapore (BSc Botany and Biochem.); Harvard Univ. (AM, PhD Biol.). Lectr, Biochem. Dept, Univ. of Singapore, 1969–71; Rockefeller University, Cell Biology Department: Res. Associate, 1971–73; Asst Prof., 1973–77; Associate Prof., 1977–81. Chm., Management Bd, 1995–, Scientific Adv. Bd, 1995–, Inst. of Molecular Agrobiology, Nat. Univ. of Singapore. Fellow, Acad. Sinica, Taipei, 1988; Associate Fellow, Third World Acad. of Scis, 1988; Hon. Mem., Japanese Biochemical Soc., 1992. Nat. Sci. and Technol. Medal, Singapore, 1998. *Publications:* Methods in Chloroplast Molecular Biology, 1982; Plant Molecular Biology, 1987; Methods in Arabidopsis Research, 1992; 308 pubns in professional jls. *Recreations:* squash, skiing. *Address:* Rockefeller University, 1230 York Avenue, New York, NY 10021–6399, USA. *T:* (212) 3278126, *Fax:* (212) 3278327; *e-mail:* chua@rockvax.rockefeller.edu.

CHUAN LEEKPAI; MHR, Trang Province, Thailand, since 1969; Prime Minister 1992–95 and since 1997, and Minister of Defence, since 1997, Thailand; *b* 28 July 1938. *Educ:* Trang Wittaya Sch.; Silpakorn Pre-Univ.; Thammasat Univ. (LLB 1962). Barrister-at-Law, Thai Bar, 1964; lawyer. Thailand, Dep. Minister of Justice, 1975; Minister to Prime Minister's Office, 1976; Minister: of Justice, 1976 and 1980–81; of Commerce, 1981; of Agric. and Co-operatives, 1982–83; of Educn, 1983–86; Speaker, House of Reps, 1986–88; Minister of Public Health, 1988–89; Dep. Prime Minister and Minister of Agric. and Co-operatives, 1990–92; Leader of Opposition, 1995–97. Leader, Democrat Party. Vis. Lectr, Forensic Medicine Dept, Faculty of Medicine, Chulalongkorn Univ. Hon. Dr Political Science: Srinakharinwirot, 1985; Ramkhamhaeng, 1987; Hon. LLD: Philippines, 1993; Vongchavalitkul, 1998; Hon. LitD: (Painting) Silpakorn, 1994; Nat. Univ. of San Marcos, Lima, 1999. Kt Grand Cross (First Cl.), 1979, Kt Grand Cordon, 1981, Order of Crown (Thailand); Kt Grand Cross (First Cl.), 1980, Kt Grand Cordon (Special Cl.), 1982, Order of White Elephant (Thailand). *Address:* Office of the Prime Minister, Government House, Bangkok 10300, Thailand.

CHUBB, family name of **Baron Hayter**.

CHUBB, Anthony Gerald Trelawny, FCA; Chairman, Foseco (formerly Foseco Minsep) PLC, 1986–90; *b* 6 April 1928; *s* of Ernest Gerald Trelawny Chubb and Eunice Chubb; *m* 1951, Beryl Joyce (*née* Cross); two *s*. *Educ:* Wylde Green Coll., Sutton Coldfield. FCA 1962 (ACA 1951); ACMA 1956. CBIM 1981. Joined Foundry Services Ltd, 1951; Man. Dir, Foseco UK, 1964–69; Dir, Foseco Ltd, 1966; Man. Dir, Foseco International, 1969–78; Dep. Gp Man. Dir, 1974–79, Gp Man. Dir, 1979–86, Foseco Minsep PLC; Chm., Electrocomponents PLC, 1986–90 (Dep. Chm., 1983–86; Dir, 1980–90). *Recreations:* golf, gardening, reading.

CHUBB, Dr Frederick Basil, MA, DPhil, LittD; Professor of Political Science, 1960–91, now Fellow Emeritus, Trinity College, Dublin; *b* 8 Dec. 1921; *s* of late Frederick John Bailey Chubb and Gertrude May Chubb, Ludgershall, Wilts; *m* 1st, 1946, Margaret Gertrude Rafther (*d* 1984); no *c*; 2nd, 1985, Orla, *d* of Seán and Veronica Sheehan; one *d*. *Educ:* Bishop Wordsworth's Sch., Salisbury; Merton Coll., Oxford. BA 1946; MA Oxon; MA Dublin; DPhil Oxon 1950; LittD Dublin 1976. Lecturer in Political Science, Trinity Coll., Dublin, 1948; Fellow in Polit. Sci., 1952; Reader in Polit. Sci., 1955; Bursar, 1957–62. Chm., Comhairle na n-Ospidéal, 1972–78; Chm., Employer-Labour Conf., 1970–. MRIA 1969. *Publications:* The Control of Public Expenditure, 1952; (with D. E. Butler (ed) and others) Elections Abroad, 1959; A Source Book of Irish Government, 1964, 2nd edn 1983; (ed with P. Lynch) Economic Development and Planning, 1969; The Government and Politics of Ireland, 1970, 3rd edn 1992; Cabinet Government in Ireland, 1974; The Constitution and Constitutional Change in Ireland, 1978; The Politics of the Irish Constitution, 1991; articles in learned jls. *Recreation:* fishing. *Address:* 19 Clyde Lane, Ballsbridge, Dublin 4. *T:* (1) 6684625.

CHUNG, Kyung-Wha, Korean Order of Merit; concert violinist; *b* 26 March 1948; *d* of Chun-Chai Chung and Won-Sook (Lee) Chung; *m*; two *s*. *Educ:* Juilliard Sch. of Music, New York. Moved from Korea to New York, 1960; 7 years' study with Ivan Galamian, 1960–67; New York début with New York Philharmonic Orch., 1967; European début with André Previn and London Symphony Orch., Royal Festival Hall, London, 1970. First prize, Leventritt Internat. Violin Competition, NY, 1967. *Address:* c/o Harrison/Parrott Ltd, 12 Penzance Place, W11 4PA.

CHUNG Se Yung, Hon. CBE 1982; Hon. Chairman, Hyundai Motor Company, since 1996; *b* 6 Aug. 1928; *m* 1958, Young Ja Park; one *s* two *d*. *Educ:* Korea Univ. (BA); Miami Univ. of Ohio (MA). Joined Hyundai Construction Co., 1957: Pres., Hyundai Motor Co., 1967–87; Chm., Hyundai Business Gp, 1987–96. Vice-Chm., Fedn of Korean Industry; Dep. Chm., Korea–Japan Econ. Assoc. Hon. LLD Miami Univ. of Ohio, 1983. *Address:* 140-2 Kye-dong, Chongro-ku, Seoul, Korea. *T:* (2) 7441231.

CHUNG, Sir Sze-yuen, GBE 1989 (CBE 1975; OBE 1968); Kt 1978; PhD; FREng; JP; Pro-Chancellor, Hong Kong University of Science and Technology, since 1999 (Founding Chairman, 1988–99); Chairman, Kowloon Motor Bus Holdings Ltd, since 1999; *b* 3 Nov. 1917; *m* 1942, Nancy Cheung (*d* 1977); one *s* two *d*. *Educ:* Hong Kong Univ. (BScEng 1st Cl. Hons, 1941); Sheffield Univ. (PhD 1951). FREng (FEng 1983); FIMechE 1957, Hon. FIMechE 1983; Hon. FHKIE 1976; FIEE (FIProdE 1958); CBIM (FBIM 1978). Consulting engr, 1952–56; Gen. Man., Sonca Industries (now Sonca Products), 1956–60, Man. Dir 1960–77, Chm. 1977–88. Director: CLP Hldgs (formerly China Light & Power Co.), 1968–; Wheelock & Co., 1983–. Mem., Hong Kong Legislative Council, 1965–74, Sen. Mem., 1974–78; Mem., Hong Kong Exec. Council, 1972–80, Sen. Mem., 1980–88; Advr to Govt of People's Republic of China on Hong Kong affairs, 1992–97; Mem., Chinese Govt's Preparatory Cttee for establishment of HKSAR, 1996–97; Convenor, HKSAR Exec. Council, 1997–99. Chairman: Standing Commn on CS Salaries and Conditions of Service, 1980–88; Hong Kong Productivity Council, 1974–76; Asian Product. Orgn, 1969–70; Hong Kong Industrial Design Council, 1969–75; Fedn of Hong Kong Industries, 1966–70 (Hon. Life Pres. 1974); Hong Kong Metrication Cttee, 1969–73; Hong Kong–Japan Business Co-operation Cttee, 1983–88; Hong Kong–US Econ. Co-operation Cttee, 1984–88. Founding Chairman: Hong Kong Polytechnic, 1972–86; City Polytechnic of Hong Kong, 1984 (Founding Fellow, 1986); Hong Kong Hosp. Authy, 1991–95 (Chm., Provisional Hosp. Authy, 1988–90). Founding Pres., Hong Kong Acad. of Engrg Scis, 1994–97; Pres., Engrg Soc. of Hong Kong, 1960–61. LLD (*hc*): Chinese Univ. of Hong Kong, 1983; Sheffield, 1985; DSc (*hc*) Hong Kong Univ., 1976; DEng (*hc*) Hong Kong Polytechnic, 1989; DBA (*hc*) City Polytechnic of Hong Kong, 1989. JP Hong Kong, 1964. Man of the Year, Hong Kong Business Today magazine, 1985. Defence Medal, 1948; Silver Jubilee Medal, 1977; Gold Medal, Asian Productivity Orgn, 1980; HKSAR Grand Bauhinia Medal, 1997. Japanese Order of Sacred Treasure (3rd cl.), 1983. *Publications:* contrib. Proc. IMechE, Jl Iron and Steel Inst., and Jl Engrg Soc. of Hong Kong. *Recreation:* swimming. *Address:* House 25, Bella Vista, Silver Terrace Road, Clear Water Bay, Kowloon, Hong Kong. *T:* Hong Kong 27610281, 27192857, *Fax:* Hong Kong 27607493, 23580689. *Clubs:* Hong Kong, Hong Kong Jockey, Kowloon Cricket (Hong Kong); Pacific (Kowloon).

CHURCH, Ian David; Editor, Official Report (Hansard), House of Commons, since 1989; *b* 18 Oct. 1941; *s* of John Jasper and Violet Kathleen Church; *m* 1964, Christine Stevenson; one *d*. *Educ:* Roan School. Journalist with: Dundee Courier and Advertiser, 1958–64; Press Association, 1964; The Scotsman, 1966; The Times, 1968; joined Hansard, 1972; Dep. Editor, 1988. Sec., Commonwealth Hansard Editors Assoc., 1990– (Pres., 1996–99). *Address:* Department of the Official Report, House of Commons, SW1A 0AA.

CHURCH, James Anthony, (Tony); Dean, National Theatre Conservatory, Denver, USA, 1989–96, now Emeritus; *b* 11 May 1930; *s* of Ronald Frederic and Margaret Fanny Church; *m* 1958, Margaret Ann Blakeney; one *s* two *d*. *Educ:* Hurstpierpoint Coll.; Clare Coll., Cambridge. MA 1954. First perf. as professional, Arts Theatre, London, 1953; frequent television, radio, regional theatre perfs; founder mem., RSC, 1960, and Associate

Artist, 1960–; roles there include: Henry IV; Polonius (twice); King Lear; John of Gaunt; Friar Laurence; Ulysses; Pandarus; York in Richard II; Trelawney in Maydays; Horsham in Waste; Director of Nuclear Plant in Sarcophagus; Wizard in Wizard of Oz, 1987; Cymbeline, Gonzalo and Antigonus in the late Shakespeares, NT, 1988. Extensive tours of USA, 1974–: King Lear, 1982; Falstaff (Santa Cruz), 1984; Prospero, Shylock (Colorado), 1987; Denver Center Theatre Company: Scrooge, 1990; Malvolio, 1991; Uncertainty, 1992; The Quick Change Room, King Lear, 1995; Sir in The Dresser, 1995; Valley Song, Taking Leave, Travels with my Aunt, Prospero, 1998; Give 'em a Bit of Mystery (solo devised performance), 1999, 2000. Recorded 26 Shakespeare roles, 1956–66. Founder dir, Northcott Theatre, Exeter, 1967–71; Dir of Drama, GSMD, 1982–88; Drama Advr, Hong Kong Govt, 1982–85. Member: Arts Council, 1982–85 (Chm., Drama Panel, 1982–85); British Council Drama Cttee, 1985–88. Hon. MA Exeter, 1971; Hon. DHL Denver, 1998. *Recreations:* listening to music, narrowboats, travel. *Address:* 38 Rosebery Road, N10 2LJ; c/o National Theatre Conservatory, 1050 13th Street, Denver, CO 80204, USA. *T:* (303) 8934200.

CHURCH, John Carver, CMG 1986; CVO 1988; MBE 1970; HM Diplomatic Service, retired; *b* 8 Dec. 1929; *s* of Richard Church, CBE, FRSL, and Catherina Church; *m* 1953, Marie-Geneviève Vallette; two *s* two *d. Educ:* Cranbrook Sch., Kent; Ecole Alsacienne, Paris; Christ's Coll., Cambridge (MA 1953). Reuters News Agency, 1953–59; Central Office of Information, 1959–61; Commonwealth Relations Office: Information Officer, Calcutta, 1961–65; Foreign and Commonwealth Office: Second Secretary (Commercial) Rio de Janeiro, 1966–69; First Sec. (Information) Tel Aviv, 1969–74; First Sec., News Dept, FCO, 1974–77; Consul (Commercial) Milan, 1977–78; Consul-General: São Paulo, 1978–81; Naples, 1981–86; Barcelona, 1986–89. *Address:* 41 rue de Rochechouart, 75009 Paris, France. *T:* 148745419; La Métairie, Le Maine, 24510 Ste Alvère, France.

CHURCH, John George, CBE 1998; DL; FCA; President, Church & Co. plc, since 2001 (Chairman, 1991–2001); *b* 14 May 1936; *s* of Dudley Ross Church and Louise Elizabeth Church; *m* 1965, Rhona Elizabeth Gibson; one *s* one *d. Educ:* Stowe Sch. FCA 1959. Mgt Consultant, Annan Impey Morrish, 1961–64; joined Church & Co. plc, 1964: Asst Co. Sec., 1964–67; Co. Sec., 1967–76; Dir, 1968–; Man. Dir, 1976–97. Non-executive Director: Babers Ltd, 1972– (Chm., 1996 -); James Southall and Co. Ltd, 1985–98 and 2000–; Start Rite Ltd, 1985–98 and 2000–; Kingsley Park Properties (formerly St Matthew's Hosp.) Ltd, 1981–. President: British Footwear Mfrs Fedn, 1988–89; Boot Trade Benevolent Soc., 1984–85. Mem. Ct, UC of Northampton (formerly Nene Coll., Northampton), 1994–; Gov., 1995–, Mem. Bd Mgt, 1999–, St Andrew's Hosp., Northampton. Mem., Bd of Mgt, Cordwainers' Coll. until 2000. Liveryman, Cordwainers' Co., 1958– (Master, 1998–99). FRSA 1995. High Sheriff, Northants, 1993–94; DL Northants, 1997. *Recreation:* country pursuits. *Address:* The Old Rectory, Farthingstone, Towcester, Northants NN12 8EZ. *T:* (01327) 361227. *Club:* Royal Automobile.

CHURCH, Judith Ann; *b* 19 Sept. 1953; *d* of late Edmund Church and of Helen Church; two *s. Educ:* Leeds Univ. (BA Hons Maths and Phil.); Huddersfield Poly. (PGCE Technical); Aston Univ. (Postgrad. Dip. Occupational Health and Safety); Thames Valley Coll. (DMS). Teacher, VSO, 1975–77; Process Research, Mars UK, 1979–80; HM Inspector of Factories, HSE, 1980–86; Nat. Health and Safety Officer, MSF, 1986–91. Contested (Lab) Stevenage, 1992; MP (Lab) Dagenham, June 1994–2001. *Recreation:* keeping fit.

CHURCH, Tony; *see* Church, J. A.

CHURCHHOUSE, Prof. Robert Francis, CBE 1982; PhD; Professor of Computing Mathematics, University of Wales, College of Cardiff (formerly University College, Cardiff), 1971–95; *b* 30 Dec. 1927; *s* of Robert Francis Churchhouse and Agnes Howard; *m* 1954, Julia McCarthy; three *s. Educ:* St Bede's Coll., Manchester; Manchester Univ. (BSc 1949); Trinity Hall, Cambridge (PhD 1952). Royal Naval Scientific Service, 1952–63; Head of Programming Gp, Atlas Computer Lab., SRC, 1963–71. Vis. Fellow, St Cross Coll., Oxford, 1972–90. Chm., Computer Bd for Univs and Res. Councils, 1979–82; Mem., Welsh Cttee, UFC, 1989–93. Pres., IMA, 1986–87. Hon. DSc South Bank, 1993. KSG 1988. *Publications:* (ed jtly) Computers in Mathematical Research, 1968; (ed jtly) The Computer in Literary and Linguistic Studies, 1976; Numerical Analysis, 1978; papers in math. and other jls. *Recreations:* cricket, astronomy. *Address:* 15 Holly Grove, Lisvane, Cardiff CF14 0UJ. *T:* (029) 2075 0250.

CHURCHILL; *see* Spencer-Churchill.

CHURCHILL, 3rd Viscount *cr* 1902; **Victor George Spencer,** OBE 2001; Baron 1815; Managing Director, CCLA Investment Management Ltd, 1988–99; *b* 31 July 1934; *s* of 1st Viscount Churchill, GCVO, and late Christine Sinclair (who *m* 3rd, Sir Lancelot Oliphant, KCMG, CB); *S* half-brother, 1973. *Educ:* Eton; New Coll., Oxford (MA). Lieut, Scots Guards, 1953–55. Morgan Grenfell & Co. Ltd, 1958–74; Investment Manager: Central Bd of Finance, C of E, 1974–99; Charities Official Investments Fund, 1974–95. A Church Comr, 2001–. Director: Local Authorities' Mutual Investment Fund, 1974–99; Schroder Split Fund; Foreign & Colonial Income and Growth Investment Trust; Charter European Trust. *Heir* (to Barony only): Richard Harry Ramsay Spencer [*b* 11 Oct. 1926; *m* 1958, Antoinette Rose-Marie de Charrière; two *s*]. *Address:* 6 Cumberland Mansions, George Street, W1H 5TE.

CHURCHILL, Caryl, (Mrs David Harter); playwright; *b* 3 Sept. 1938; *d* of Robert Churchill and Jan (*née* Brown); *m* 1961, David Harter; three *s. Educ:* Trafalgar Sch., Montreal; Lady Margaret Hall, Oxford (BA 1960). Student prodns of early plays, 1958–61; *radio plays:* The Ants, 1962; Lovesick, 1966; Identical Twins, 1968; Abortive, 1971; Not... not... not... not... not enough oxygen, 1971; Schreiber's Nervous Illness, 1972; Henry's Past, 1972; Perfect Happiness, 1973; *television plays:* The Judge's Wife, 1972; Turkish Delight, 1973; The After Dinner Joke, 1978; The Legion Hall Bombing, 1978; Crimes, 1981; (with Ian Spink) Fugue, 1987; *stage plays:* Owners, 1972; Moving Clocks Go Slow, 1975; Objections to Sex and Violence, 1975; Light Shining in Buckinghamshire, 1976; Vinegar Tom, 1976; Traps, 1977; (contrib.) Floorshow, 1977; Cloud Nine, 1979; Three More Sleepless Nights, 1980; Top Girls, 1982; Fen, 1983; Softcops, 1983; (collaborator) Midday Sun, 1984; (with David Lan and Ian Spink) A Mouthful of Birds, 1986; Serious Money, 1987; Ice cream, 1989; Hot Fudge, 1989; Mad Forest, 1990; (with Ian Spink and Orlando Gough) Lives of the Great Poisoners, 1991; The Skriker, 1994; (trans.) Seneca's Thyestes, 1994; Blue Heart, 1997; This is a Chair, 1997, Far Away, 2000. *Publications:* Owners, 1973; Light Shining, 1976; Traps, 1977; Vinegar Tom, 1978; Cloud Nine, 1979; Top Girls, 1982; Fen, 1983; Fen and Softcops, 1984; A Mouthful of Birds, 1986; Serious Money, 1987; Plays I, 1985; Plays II, 1988; Objections to Sex and Violence in Plays by Women, vol. 4, 1985; Light Shining, 1989; Traps, 1989; Cloud Nine, 1989; Ice cream, 1989; Mad Forest, 1990; Lives of the Great Poisoners, 1992; The Skriker, 1994; Thyestes, 1994; Blue Heart, 1997; This is a Chair, 1999; Faraway, 2000; anthologies. *Address:* c/o Casarotto Ramsay Ltd, National House, 60–66 Wardour Street, W1V 3HP. *T:* (020) 7287 4450.

CHURCHILL, Winston Spencer; author; journalist; parliamentarian; *b* 10 Oct. 1940; *s* of late Hon. Randolph Frederick Edward Spencer Churchill, MBE and Hon. Mrs Averell Harriman, sometime US Ambassador to France; *m* 1st, 1964, Mary Caroline, (Minnie), d'Erlanger (marr. diss. 1997); two *s* two *d*; 2nd, 1997, Luce Engelen. *Educ:* Eton; Christ Church, Oxford (MA). War correspondent in Yemen, Congo and Angola, 1963; Correspondent: Borneo and Vietnam, 1966; Middle East, 1967; Chicago, Czechoslovakia, 1968; Nigeria, Biafra and Middle East, for The Times, 1969–70; Special Correspondent: China, for The Observer, 1972; Portugal, for The Daily Telegraph, 1975. Presenter, This Time of Day, BBC Radio, 1964–65. Lecture tours of the US and Canada, 1965–99. Contested Gorton Div. of Manchester, Nov. 1967. MP (C) Stretford, 1970–83, Davyhulme, Manchester, 1983–97. PPS to Minister of Housing and Construction, 1970–72, to Minister of State, FCO, 1972–73; Sec., Cons. Foreign and Commonwealth Affairs Cttee, 1973–76; Conservative Party front-bench spokesman on Defence, 1976–78. Member: Select Cttee on Defence, 1983–97; Select Cttee on H of C (Services), 1985–86. Vice-Chm., Cons. Defence Cttee, 1979–83; Cons. Party Co-ordinator for Defence and Multilateral Disarmament, 1982–84; Mem. Exec., 1922 Cttee, 1979–85, Treas., 1987–88. Sponsored Motor Vehicles (Passenger Insce) Act 1972, Crown Proceedings (Armed Forces) Act 1987. Pres., Trafford Park Indust. Council, 1971–97. Member, Council: Consumers' Assoc., 1990–93; British Kidney Patients Assoc., 1990–. President: Friends of Airborne Forces, 1996–; Friends of War Memorials, 1997–; Chm., Nat. Benevolent Fund for the Aged, 1994– (Trustee, 1974–); Trustee: Winston Churchill Meml Trust, 1968–; Sandy Gall's Afghanistan Appeal, 1995–. Governor, English-Speaking Union, 1975–80; Vice-Pres., British Technion Soc., 1976–. Hon. Fellow, Churchill Coll., Cambridge, 1969. Hon. FSE 1989. Hon. LLD Westminster Coll., Fulton, Mo, USA, 1972; Hon. DSc Technion, Israel, 1997. *Publications:* First Journey, 1964; Six Day War, 1967; Defending the West, 1981; Memories and Adventures, 1989; His Father's Son, 1996; The Great Republic, 1999. *Recreations:* tennis, sailing, ski-ing. *Clubs:* White's, Buck's, Press; Air Squadron; St Moritz Tobogganing.

CHURSTON, 5th Baron *cr* 1858; **John Francis Yarde-Buller;** Bt 1790; *b* 29 Dec. 1934; *s* of 4th Baron Churston, VRD and Elizabeth Mary (*d* 1951), *d* of late W. B. du Pre; *S* father, 1991; *m* 1973, Alexandra Joanna, *d* of A. G. Contomichalos; one *s* two *d. Educ:* Eton Coll. 2nd Lt RHG, 1954. A Freemason. *Heir: s* Hon. Benjamin Anthony Francis Yarde-Buller [*b* 13 Sept. 1974; *m* 2000, Sophie Frances, *e d* of Brian Duncan]. *Address:* Yowlestone House, Puddington, Tiverton, Devon EX16 8LN. *T:* (01884) 860328. *Clubs:* Buck's, White's.

CHYNOWETH, David Boyd; Chief Executive, Universities Superannuation Scheme Ltd, since 1994; *b* 26 Dec. 1940; *s* of Ernest and Blodwen Chynoweth; *m* 1968, Margaret Slater; one *s* two *d. Educ:* Simon Langton Sch., Canterbury; Univ. of Nottingham (BA). CPFA (IPFA 1966); FCCA 1983. Public Finance posts with Derbs CC, 1962 and London Borough of Ealing, 1965; Asst County Treas., Flints CC, 1968; Dep. County Treas., West Suffolk CC, 1970; County Treasurer, S Yorks CC, 1973; Dir of Finance, Lothian Regl Council, 1985–94. Vice-Chairman: UK-American Properties Inc., 1980–86; American Properties Unit Trust, 1980–86; Mem. Bd, Lazards Small Cos Exempt Unit Trust, 1979–97. Mem. Council, CIPFA, 1983–99 (Vice Pres., 1991–92; Pres., 1992–93); Mem. Investment Protection Cttee, 1976–80, 1982–86 and 1999–, Council Mem., 1998–, Nat. Assoc. of Pension Funds; Mem. Bd, Foundn for Regulation of Accountancy Profession, 1999–. Pres., Assoc. of Public Service Finance Officers, 1981–82. *Recreations:* walking, photography. *Address:* (office) Royal Liver Building, Liverpool L3 1PY. *T:* (0151) 227 4711. *Club:* Royal Over-Seas League.

CHYNOWETH, Rt Rev. Neville James, AM 1996; ED 1966; *b* 3 Oct. 1922; *s* of Percy James and Lilian Chynoweth; *m* 1951, Joan Laurice Wilson; two *s* two *d. Educ:* Manly High School; Sydney Univ. (MA); Melbourne Coll. of Divinity (BD); Moore Theological Coll. (ThL). ARSCM 1993. Assistant, St Michael's, Sydney, 1950; Rector, Kangaroo Valley, 1951–52; Chaplain, Royal Prince Alfred Hospital, 1952–54; Rector: St John's, Deewhy, 1954–63; St Anne's, Strathfield, 1963–66; All Saints, Canberra, 1966–71; St Paul's, Canberra, 1971–74; Archdeacon of Canberra, 1973–74; Assistant Bishop of Canberra and Goulburn, 1974–80; Bishop of Gippsland, 1980–87. *Recreations:* music, biography. *Address:* 10 Fortitude Street, Red Hill, Canberra, ACT 2603, Australia. *T:* (2) 62397056.

CIAMPI, Dr Carlo Azeglio; President of the Republic of Italy, since 1999; *b* Livorno, 9 Dec. 1920; *s* of Pietro and Marie Ciampi; *m* 1946, Franca Pilla; one *s* one *d. Educ:* Scuola Normale Superiore, Pisa; Univ. of Pisa (BA, LLB 1946). Served Italian Army, 1941–44 (MC). Joined Bank of Italy, Rome, 1946: work in various branches, 1946–60; Economist and Hd, Res. Dept, 1960–73; Sec.-Gen., 1973–76; Dep. Dir Gen., 1976–78; Dir Gen., 1978; Gov., and Chm., Ufficio Italiano dei Cambi, 1979–83 (Hon. Gov., 1993–); Gov. for Italy, IBRD, IDA, IFC, Washington, and ADB, Manila, 1979–93; Pres., Council of Ministers, Rome, 1993–94; Vice-Pres., BIS, Basle, 1994–96 (Dir, 1979–93); Chm., Competitiveness Adv. Gp, EU, 1995–96; Minister of the Treasury, Budget and Econ. Programming, 1996–99; Chm., Interim Cttee, IMF, Washington, 1998–99. Pres., Venice Internat. Univ., 1996–99. *Publications:* Un Metodo per Governare, 1996; contrib. numerous reports and articles. *Address:* Palazzo del Quirinale 00187 Rome, Italy.

CICCONE, Madonna Louise Veronica, (Madonna); singer and actress; *b* 16 Aug. 1958; *d* of Sylvio, (Tony), Ciccone and late Madonna Ciccone; *m* 1st, 1985, Sean Penn (marr. diss. 1989); one *d* by Carlos Leon; 2nd, Guy Ritchie, 2000; one *s. Educ:* Adams High Sch.; Univ. of Michigan (dance scholarship); Alvin Alley Studios, NY. Formed Maverick Records Co.; *recordings* include: first hit single, Holiday, 1983; albums: Like a Virgin, 1985; True Blue, 1986; Like a Prayer, 1989; Erotica, 1992; Bedtime Stories, 1994; Something to Remember, 1995; Ray of Light, 1998; Music, 2000. *Films:* A certain Sacrifice, 1979; Vision Quest, 1985; Desperately seeking Susan, 1985; Shanghai Surprise, 1986; Who's that Girl?, 1987; Bloodhounds of Broadway, 1989; Dick Tracy, 1989; Soap-Dish, 1990; Shadows and Fog, 1991; A League of their Own, 1991; In Bed with Madonna, 1991; Truth or Dare, 1991; Body of Evidence, 1992; Snake Eyes, 1994; Dangerous Game, 1994; Blue in the Face, 1995; Girl 6, 1996; Evita (Golden Globe Award for best actress), 1996; Four Rooms, 1996; The Next Best Thing, 2000. *Publication:* Sex, 1992. *Address:* Maverick Recording Co., 9348 Civic Center Drive, Beverly Hills, CA 90210, USA.

CICUTTO, Francis John; Managing Director and Chief Executive Officer, National Australia Bank Ltd, since 1999 (Chief General Manager, 1996–99); *b* 9 Nov. 1950; *s* of Francesco Cicutto and Ultima (*née* Margaritta); *m* 1982, Christine Bates; one *s. Educ:* Univ. of NSW. Chief Manager, Central Business Dist, Victoria Nat. Australia Bank Ltd, 1986–88; Exec. Vice Pres., Americas, NAB, USA, 1988–89; NAB Australia: Gen. Manager, Credit Bureau, 1989–92; State Manager, NSW and ACT, 1992–94; Dir and Chief Exec., Clydesdale Bank PLC, 1994–96. *Recreations:* Rugby, golf, cricket, theatre. *Address:* National Australia Bank Ltd, 500 Bourke Street, Melbourne, Vic 3000, Australia. *Clubs:* Union, Killara Golf (Sydney); Australian (Melbourne).

CITARELLA, Victor Thomas; social care and management consultant; *b* 8 May 1951; *s* of Thomas and Evelyn R. M. Citarella; *m* 1975, Jacqueline Hopley; three *s* one *d*. *Educ:* Sweyne Grammar Sch., Essex; University Coll., Cardiff (BSc Hons Econs 1973, Cert. Social Work 1978). Residential Child Care Officer, S Glamorgan, 1974–80; Team Manager, Hillingdon Social Services, 1980–82; Day and Residential Care Officer, W Sussex, 1982–85; Area Manager, Bristol, Avon, 1985–88; Dep. Dir of Social Services, 1988–91, Dir of Social Services, 1991–2000, City of Liverpool. Pres., Social Care Assoc., 1992. *Address:* 5 New Acres, Newburgh, Wigan, Lancs WN8 7TU. *T:* (01257) 462698.

CITRINE, family name of **Baron Citrine**.

CITRINE, 3rd Baron *cr* 1946, of Wembley; **Dr Ronald Eric Citrine,** MRCS, LRCP; *b* 19 May 1919; *yr s* of 1st Baron Citrine, GBE, PC and Doris Helen (*d* 1973), *d* of Edgar Slade; *S* brother, 1997 but does not use the title; *m* 1945, Mary, (*d* 1995), *d* of Reginald Williams. *Heir:* none. *Address:* 1 Rosella Place, Maunu, Whangarei, New Zealand. *T:* (9) 4380872.

CLAES, Willy; Secretary General, NATO, 1994–95; *b* Hasselt, Belgium, 24 Nov. 1938; *m* 1965, Suzanne Meynen; one *s* one *d*. *Educ:* Free Univ., Brussels. Asst Sec., then Provincial Sec., De Voorzorg, 1962–65; Local Councillor, Hasselt, 1964–94; MHR (Socialist), Hasselt, 1968–94; Minister of: Nat. Educn, Flemish Reg., 1972–73; Econ. Affairs, 1973–74 and 1977–79; Deputy Prime Minister and Minister of: Econ. Affairs, 1979–81; Econ. Affairs and Planning and Nat. Educn, 1987; Foreign Affairs, 1992–94. Belgian Socialist Party: Mem., Exec. Cttee, 1965–94; Co-Pres., 1975–77. Numerous decorations from Europe, Mexico and Bolivia. *Publications:* Tussen droom en werkelijkheid: bouwstenen voor en ander Europa, 1979; La Chine et l'Europe, 1980; Livre Blanc de l'Energie, 1980; Quatre Années aux Affaires Economiques, 1980; Elementen voor een nieuw energiebeleid, 1980; Belgie … quo vadis?: un conte moderne, 1980; De Derde Weg: beschouwingen over de Wereldcrisis, 1987. *Recreations:* piano music, conducting orchestras. *Address:* Berkenlaan 62, 3500 Hasselt, Belgium.

CLAGUE, Joan; Director of Nursing Services, Marie Curie Memorial Foundation, 1986–90; *b* 17 April 1931; *d* of James Henry Clague and Violet May Clague (*née* Johnson). *Educ:* Malvern Girls' Coll.; Guy's Hosp.; Hampstead Gen. Hosp.; Simpson Meml Maternity Pavilion. Asst Regional Nursing Officer, Oxford Regional Hosp. Bd, 1965–67; Principal, then Chief Nursing Officer, St George's Hosp. Bd of Governors, 1967–73; Area Nursing Officer, Merton, Sutton and Wandsworth AHA, 1973–81; Regl Nursing Officer, NE Thames RHA, 1981–86. Pres., Assoc. of Nurse Administrators, 1983–85. Trustee, WRVS Trustees Ltd, 1991–96. WHO Fellow, 1969; Smith and Nephew EEC Scholar, 1981. *Recreations:* walking, domestic pursuits. *Address:* 7 Tylney Avenue, SE19 1LN. *T:* (020) 8670 5171.

CLANCARTY, 9th Earl of, *cr* 1803; **Nicholas Power Richard Le Poer Trench;** Baron Kilconnel 1797; Viscount Dunlo 1801; Baron Trench (UK) 1815; Viscount Clancarty (UK) 1823; Marquess of Heusden (Kingdom of the Netherlands) 1818; *b* 1 May 1952; *o s* of Hon. Power Edward Ford Le Poer Trench (*d* 1975), *y s* of 5th Earl of Clancarty, and Jocelyn Louise Courtney (*d* 1962); S uncle, 1995. *Educ:* Ashford Grammar Sch.; Plymouth Polytech.; Univ. of Colorado.

CLANCHY, Joan Lesley, (Mrs Michael Clanchy); Headmistress, North London Collegiate School, 1986–97; *b* 26 Aug. 1939; *d* of Leslie and Mary Milne; *m* 1962, Dr Michael Clanchy; one *s* one *d*. *Educ:* St Leonard's Sch., St Andrews; St Hilda's Coll., Oxford. MA; DipEd. Schoolteacher: Woodberry Down Sch., London, 1962–63; The Park Sch., Glasgow, 1967–76; Headmistress, St George's Sch., Edinburgh, 1976–85. *Address:* 28 Hillfield Road, NW6 1PZ.

CLANCY, Deirdre V., (Mrs M. M. Steer); set and costume designer; portrait painter; *b* 31 March 1943; adopted *d* of Julie M. Clancy; *m* 1975, Michael Maxwell Steer; one *s* two *d*. *Educ:* Convent of Sacred Heart, Tunbridge Wells; Birmingham Coll. of Art (NDD 1st Cl. Hons). Arts Council Asst, Lincoln Rep., 1965; House Designer, Royal Court Theatre, 1966–68: productions include costumes for D. H. Lawrence Trilogy, 1966; sets and costumes for: Early Morning, 1967; The Sea, 1973; has designed for RNT, RSC, ENO, Scottish Opera, New Sadlers Wells Opera, Chichester Fest. Theatre; numerous prodns in Europe, N America, Japan and Australia. *Films* include: The Virgin and The Gypsy, 1969; Mrs Brown, 1997 (Best Film Costumes, BAFTA Award, 1998); Tom's Midnight Garden, 1998; *television:* Wives and Daughters, 1999. Has exhibited designs. Portrait Painter. Green Room Award, Vic, Australia, for Best Costume (opera), 1990 and 1991; Olivier Award for Best Costume Design (for A Month in the Country, Triumph Prodns, and Loves Labours Lost, RSC) 1997. *Publication:* Costume since 1945, 1996. *Recreations:* infrequent domesticity, family pursuits, more painting. *Address:* c/o KCPM, 6 Ganton Street, W1V 1LJ. *T:* (020) 7734 7304.

CLANCY, His Eminence Cardinal Edward Bede, AC 1992 (AO 1984); Archbishop of Sydney, (RC), 1983–2001; *b* 13 Dec. 1923; *s* of John Bede Clancy and Ellen Lucy Clancy (*née* Edwards). *Educ:* Marist Brothers Coll., Parramatta, NSW; St Patrick's Coll., Manly, NSW; Biblical Inst., Rome (LSS); Propaganda Fide Univ., Rome (DD). Ordained to priesthood, 1949; parish ministry, 1950–51; studies in Rome, 1952–54; parish ministry, 1955–57; seminary staff, 1958–61; studies in Rome, 1962–64; seminary staff, Manly, 1966–73; Auxiliary Bishop, Sydney, 1974–78; Archbishop of Canberra and Goulburn, 1979–82. Cardinal, 1988. Chancellor, Aust. Catholic Univ., 1990–2001. *Publications:* The Bible—The Church's Book, 1974; contribs to Australian Catholic Record. *Recreation:* golf. *Address:* c/o Chancery Office, 13th Floor, Polding House, 276 Pitt Street, Sydney, NSW 2000, Australia.

CLANCY, Richard Francis Stephen; District Judge (Magistrates' Courts), Birmingham, since 2001; *b* 2 Sept. 1948; *s* of Francis Gerrard Clancy and Evaline Margaret Clancy; *m* 1976, Anne Margaret Lawless; one *s* one *d*. *Educ:* St Ambrose Coll., Altrincham; Coll. of Law, Guildford. Articled to John Arthur Wheeler, OBE, Solicitor, Warrington, 1969–74; admitted solicitor, 1974; prosecuted, W Midlands and Merseyside, 1974–83; in private practice as partner, Ridgway Greenall, Warrington, and E. Rexmakin & Co., Liverpool, 1983–2000. *Recreations:* sport, piano, accordian, history, literature. *Address:* The Law Courts, Corporation Street, Birmingham B4 6QA. *T:* (0121) 212 6600.

CLANCY, Thomas L., Jr, (Tom); writer; *b* 12 March 1947; *m* 1969, Wanda Thomas; one *s* three *d*. *Educ:* Loyola Coll., Baltimore, Md. Served USAR OTC. Former insurance agent, Baltimore, Md and Hartford, Conn; joined O. F. Bowen Agency, insurance firm, Owings, Md, 1973, owner (with wife), 1980–. Co-founder, Red Storm Entertainment. *Publications:* (as Tom Clancy): *novels:* The Hunt for Red October, 1984 (filmed); Red Storm Rising, 1986; Patriot Games, 1987; Cardinal of the Kremlin, 1988; Clear and Present Danger, 1989; The Sum of all Fears, 1991; Without Remorse, 1993; Debt of Honor, 1994; Reality Check, 1995; Executive Orders, 1996; Balance of Power, 1998; Rainbow Six, 1998; Carrier, 1999; The Bear and the Dragon, 2000; Net Force series (with Steve Pieczevik): Net Force; The Deadliest Game; End Game; The Great Race; One is the Loneliest Number; The Ultimate Escape; Cyberspy; Hidden Agendas; Gameprey; Deathworld; Night Moves; Breaking Point; Private Lives; Virtual Vandals; Op Centre series (with Steve Pieczevik): Op Centre, 1995; Mirror Image, 1995; Games of State, 1996; Acts of War, 1997; State of Siege; Balance of Power; Divide and Conquer; Power Plays series (with M. H. Greenberg): Politika; Ruthless.com; Shadow Watch; Bio-Strike, 2000; *non-fiction:* Submarine, 1993; Fighter Wing, 1995; Armored Warfare, 1996; Marine, 1996; Airborne, 1997; Carrier; (with Fred Franks Jr) Into the Storm, 1997; (with J. B. Alexander) Future War; War in the Boats; Every Man a Tiger, 1999. *Address:* c/o Michael Ovitz, Artists Management Group, Suite 212, 9465 Wilshire Boulevard, Beverly Hills, CA 90212-2604, USA.

CLANFIELD, Viscount; Ashton Robert Gerard Peel; *b* 16 Sept. 1976; *s* and *heir* of 3rd Earl Peel, *qv*. *Educ:* Ampleforth; Durham Univ. (BA Hons 1999). With Cazenove Fund Management, 2000–.

CLANMORRIS, 8th Baron *cr* 1800 (Ire.); **Simon John Ward Bingham,** MA; FCA; *b* 25 Oct. 1937; *s* of 7th Baron Clanmorris and of Madeleine Mary, *d* of late Clement Ebel; *S* father, 1988; *m* 1971, Gizella Maria, *d* of Sandor Zverkó; one *d*. *Educ:* Downside; Queens' College, Cambridge (MA). ACA 1965, FCA 1975. *Heir:* *cousin* Robert Derek de Burgh Bingham [*b* 29 Oct. 1942; *m* 1969, Victoria Mary, *yr d* of P. A. Pennant-Rea; three *d*]. *Address:* c/o Child & Co., 1 Fleet Street, EC4Y 1BD.
See also Hon. Charlotte Bingham.

CLANWILLIAM, 7th Earl of, *cr* 1776 (Ire.); **John Herbert Meade;** Bt 1703; Viscount Clanwilliam, Baron Gillford 1766; Baron Clanwilliam (UK) 1828; *b* 27 Sept. 1919; 2nd *s* of Adm. Hon. Sir Herbert Meade-Fetherstonhaugh, GCVO, CB, DSO (*d* 1964) (3rd *s* of 4th Earl) and Margaret Ishbel Frances (*d* 1977), *d* of Rt. Rev. Hon. Edward Carr Glyn, DD; *S* cousin, 1989; *m* 1956, Maxine, *o d* of late J. A. Hayden-Scott; one *s* two *d*. *Educ:* RNC Dartmouth. *Heir:* *s* Lord Gillford, *qv*. *Address:* Blundells House, Tisbury, Wilts SP3 6HA. *Club:* Turf.

CLAPHAM, Michael; MP (Lab) Barnsley West and Penistone, since 1992; *b* 15 May 1943; *s* of late Thomas Clapham and of Eva Clapham; *m* 1965, Yvonne Hallsworth; one *s* one *d*. *Educ:* Leeds Polytechnic (BSc); Leeds Univ. (PGCE); Bradford Univ. (MPhil). Miner, 1958–70; Lectr, 1974–77; Dep. Head, Yorks NUM Compensation Dept, 1977–83; Head of Industrial Relations, NUM, 1983–92. PPS to Minister of State for Health, 1997. Mem., Trade and Industry Cttee, 1992–97; Vice Chm., back-bench Trade and Industry Gp, 1996–97; Chairman, All-Party Group: on Occupational Safety and Health, 1996–; on Coalfield Communities, 1997–; on Fire Safety, 2001–. Chairman: Barnsley Community Safety Partnership (formerly Barnsley Crime Prevention Partnership), 1995–; Multi Agency Panel, 1999–. *Recreations:* reading, walking, gardening, squash. *Address:* (office) 18 Regent Street, Barnsley, Yorks S70 2HG. *T:* (01226) 730692.

CLAPHAM, Sir Michael (John Sinclair), KBE 1973; Chairman: IMI Ltd, 1974–81; BPM Holdings Ltd, 1974–81; *b* 17 Jan. 1912; *s* of late Sir John Clapham, CBE and Lady Clapham, Cambridge; *m* 1935, Hon. Elisabeth Russell Rea (*d* 1994), *d* of 1st Baron Rea of Eskdale; two *s* one *d* (and one *s* decd). *Educ:* Marlborough Coll.; King's Coll., Cambridge (MA). Apprenticed as printer with University Press, Cambridge, 1933–35; Overseer and later Works Man., Percy Lund Humphries & Co. Ltd, Bradford, 1935–38; joined ICI Ltd as Man., Kynoch Press, 1938; seconded, in conseq. of developing a diffusion barrier, to Tube Alloys Project (atomic energy), 1941–45; Personnel Dir, ICI Metals Div., 1946; Midland Regional Man., ICI, 1951; Jt Man. Dir, ICI Metals Div., 1952; Chm. 1959; Dir, ICI, 1961–74, Dep. Chm. 1968–74; served as Overseas Dir; Dir, ICI of Austr. & NZ Ltd, 1961–74; Director: Imp. Metal Industries Ltd, 1962–70; Lloyds Bank Ltd, 1971–82 (Dep. Chm., 1974–80); Grindlay's Bank Ltd, 1975–84; Associated Communications Corp., 1982–88; Heytesbury (UK) Ltd, 1988–90. Mem., General Motors European Adv. Council, 1975–82. Dep. Pres., 1971–72, Pres., 1972–74, CBI. Member: IRC, 1969–71; Standing Adv. Cttee on Pay of Higher Civil Service, 1968–71; Review Body on Doctors' and Dentists' Remuneration, 1968–70; Birmingham Educn Cttee, 1949–56; W Mids Adv. Coun. for Techn., Commercial and Art Educn, and Regional Academic Bd, 1952; Life Governor, Birmingham Univ., 1955 (Mem. Coun., 1956–61); Member: Court, Univ. of London, 1969–85; Govt Youth Service Cttee (Albemarle Cttee), 1958; CNAA, 1964–77 (Chm., 1971–77); NEDC, 1971–76; Pres., Inst. of Printing, 1980–82. Hon. DSc Aston, 1973; Hon. LLD: CNAA, 1978; London, 1984. *Publications:* Printing, 1500–1730, in The History of Technology, Vol. III, 1957; Multinational Enterprises and Nation States, 1975; Perishable Collections, 1997; various articles on printing, personnel management and education. *Recreations:* sailing, cooking. *Address:* 26 Hill Street, W1J 5NN. *T:* (020) 7499 1240. *Clubs:* Naval, Royal Yacht Squadron.
See also B. D. Till.

CLAPHAM, Peter Brian, CB 1996; PhD; CEng, FInstP; Consultant on technology and public administration reform, since 1996; Director, National Physical Laboratory, 1990–95; *b* 3 Nov. 1940; *s* of Wilfred Clapham and Una Frances (*née* Murray); *m* 1965, Jean Margaret (*née* Vigil); two *s*. *Educ:* Ashville Coll., Harrogate; University Coll. London (BSc, PhD; Fellow, 1996). Research in optics and metrology, NPL, 1960–70; Sec., Adv. Cttee on Res. on Measurements and Standards, 1970–71; res. management and head of marketing, NPL, 1972–81; Res. and Technology Policy, DoI, 1981–82; Supt of Div. of Mech. and Optical Metrology, NPL, 1982–84; Dir 1985, Chief Exec. 1989, Nat. Weights and Measures Lab. Chm., W European Legal Metrology Cooperation, 1989–90; Member: Presidential Council of Internat. Orgn of Legal Metrology, 1985–90; Internat. Cttee of Weights and Measures, 1991–96; British Hallmarking Council, 2001–. Dir, Bushy Park Water Gardens Trust, 1997–. *Publications:* numerous sci. contribs to learned jls. *Recreations:* peregrination, crafts.

CLAPP, Captain Michael Cecil, CB 1982; RN retired; *b* 22 Feb. 1932; *s* of Brig. Cecil Douglas Clapp, CBE and Mary Elizabeth Emmeline Palmer Clapp; *m* 1975, Sarah Jane Alexander; one *s* two *d*. *Educ:* Chafyn Grove Sch., Salisbury; Marlborough College. Joined Royal Navy, 1950; commanded HM Ships Puncheston, Jaguar and Leander, and 801 Sqdn; Commander, Falklands Amphibious Task Gp, 1982. Mem., Stock Exchange, 1987–95. Governor: Kelly Coll., 1985–; St Michael Sch., Tavistock, 1985–. *Publication:* Amphibious Assault, Falklands, 1996. *Recreations:* sailing, shooting, fishing, country life. *Club:* Royal Cruising.

CLAPP, Susannah; Theatre Critic, The Observer, since 1997; *b* 9 Feb. 1949; *d* of Ralph James Clapp and Marion (*née* Heeremans). *Educ:* Ashford Co. Grammar Sch.; Univ. of Bristol (BA Hons). Sub-editor, The Listener, 1970–74; reader and ed., Jonathan Cape, 1974–79; radio critic, Sunday Times, 1978–80; Asst Ed., London Rev. of Books, 1979–92; Theatre Critic: Nightwaves, Radio 3, 1994–; New Statesman, 1996–97. *Publication:* With Chatwin: portrait of a writer, 1997. *Address:* 37 Granville Square, WC1X 9PD. *T:* (020) 7837 1686. *Club:* Groucho.

CLAPPISON, (William) James; MP (C) Hertsmere, since 1992; *b* 14 Sept. 1956; *m* 1984, Helen Margherita Carter; one *s* three *d*. *Educ:* St Peter's Sch., York; Queen's Coll., Oxford (Schol.; PPE). Called to the Bar, Gray's Inn, 1981. Contested (C): Barnsley E, 1987; Bootle, May and Nov. 1990. Parly Under-Sec. of State, DoE, 1995–97; Opposition frontbench spokesman on home affairs, 1997–2001; Shadow Minister for Work, 2001–. *Recreations:* bridge, walking. *Address:* House of Commons, SW1A 0AA. *Clubs:* Carlton, Oxford and Cambridge.

CLARE, Prof. Anthony Ward, MD; FRCPsych; FRCPI; Clinical Professor of Psychiatry, Trinity College, Dublin, since 1989; Consultant Psychiatrist, St Patrick's Hospital, Dublin, since 1989 (Medical Director, 1989–2000); *b* 24 Dec. 1942; *s* of late Bernard Joseph Clare and Mary Agnes (*née* Dunne); *m* 1966, Jane Carmel Hogan; three *s* four *d*. *Educ:* Gonzaga Coll., Dublin; University Coll., Dublin. MB, BCh, BAO 1966, MD 1982; MPhil 1972; FRCPsych 1985 (MRCPsych 1973), FRCPI 1983 (MRCPI 1971). Auditor, Literary and Historical Soc., 1963–64. Internship, St Joseph's Hosp., Syracuse, New York, 1967; psychiatric training, St Patrick's Hosp., Dublin, 1967–69; Psychiatric Registrar, Maudsley Hosp., London, 1970–72, Sen. Registrar, 1973–75; research worker, General Practice Research Unit, Inst. of Psychiatry, 1976–79, Sen. Lectr, 1980–82; Prof. and Head of Dept of Psychol Medicine, St Bartholomew's Hosp. Med. Coll., 1983–88. Radio series: In the Psychiatrist's Chair, 1982–; All in the Mind, 1988–; Men in Crisis, 2000; TV series: Motives, 1983; The Enemy Within, 1995. Hon. FRCP 1998. *Publications:* Psychiatry in Dissent, 1976, 2nd edn 1980; (ed with P. Williams) Psychosocial Disorders in General Practice, 1979; (with S. Thompson) Let's Talk About Me, 1981; (ed with R. Corney) Social Work and Primary Health Care, 1982; (ed with M. Lader) Psychiatry and General Practice, 1982; In the Psychiatrist's Chair, 1984, 1992, 1995, 1998; Lovelaw, 1986; (with S. Milligan) Depression and How To Survive It, 1993; On Men: masculinity in crisis, 2000. *Recreations:* tennis, broadcasting, theatre, family life. *Address:* 87 Coper's Cope Road, Beckenham, Kent BR3 1NR. *T:* (020) 8650 1784; St Patrick's Hospital, PO Box No 136, James's Street, Dublin 8, Ireland; Delville, Lucan, Co. Dublin. *T:* 6798055. *Club:* Garrick.

CLARE, Herbert Mitchell N.; *see* Newton-Clare.

CLARE, James Paley S.; *see* Sabben-Clare.

CLARE, John Charles; Chief Executive, Dixons Group plc, since 1994; *b* 2 Aug. 1950; *s* of Sidney Charles and Joan Mildred Clare; *m* 1974, Anne Ross; two *s*. *Educ:* Edinburgh Univ. (BSc Hons Applied Maths). Sales and marketing roles in UK, Switzerland, Denmark, Sweden, Mars Ltd, 1972–82; Business Develt Dir and Marketing Dir, Racing Div., Ladbroke Gp plc, 1982–85; Dixons Group plc, 1985–: Marketing Dir 1985–86, Man. Dir 1986–88, Dixons Ltd; Gp Dir, 1988–92; Man. Dir, Dixons Stores Gp, 1988–92; Gp Man. Dir, 1992–94. *Recreations:* cricket, music, family, Tottenham Hotspur supporter. *Address:* Dixons House, Maylands Avenue, Hemel Hempstead, Herts HP2 7TG. *T:* (01442) 353000.

CLARE, John Robert; Education Editor, Daily Telegraph, since 1988; *b* 19 Aug. 1941; *s* of late John Arnold Clare and of Ludmilla Clare (*née* Nossoff); *m* 1996, Leigh Maxina James; two *s* one *d* by previous marriages. *Educ:* St George's Grammar Sch., Cape Town; Univ. of Cape Town. Reporter: Post, Johannesburg, 1963–64; The Journal, Newcastle upon Tyne, 1965–66; sub-editor, Daily Mirror, 1966–67; sub-editor, then reporter, The Times, 1967–72; reporter, ITN, 1972–73; Dep. Ed., LBC, 1973–74; Labour Corresp., The Observer, 1974–76; Social Services Corresp., Evening Standard, 1976–77; Community Relns Corresp., then Educn Corresp., BBC, 1977–86; Educn Corresp., The Times, 1986–88. Ed., Daily Telegraph Schools Guide, 1992–. Reporter of Year, BPA, 1971. *Recreation:* daydreaming. *Address:* Daily Telegraph, 1 Canada Square, E14 5DT. *T:* (020) 7538 5000.
See also Rear-Adm. R. A. G. Clare.

CLARE, Pauline Ann, QPM 1996; DL; Chief Constable of Lancashire, since 1995; *b* 26 July 1947; *d* of Kathleen and Thomas Rostron; *m* 1983, Reginald Stuart Clare; two step *d*. *Educ:* St Mary's Secondary Modern Sch., Leyland, Lancs; Open Univ. (BA Hons). CIMgt 1996. Lancashire Constabulary: Police Cadet, 1964; Constable to Inspector, Policewomen's Dept, Juvenile Liaison, 1966; Merseyside Police: Inspector Uniform Patrol and Computer Project Team, 1973; Chief Inspector, Uniform Patrol, Community Services Dept, 1983; Supt, Community Services Dept, Sub Divl and Dep. Divl Comd, Sefton, 1987; Chief Supt, Divl Comd, Sefton, 1991; Asst Chief Constable, Crime and Ops, 1992–94; Dep. Chief Constable, Cheshire Constabulary, 1994–95. Hon. Col, Lancs ACF, 1996–. Pres., Lancs Assoc. of Clubs for Young People (formerly Lancs Assoc. of Boys' Clubs), 1995–. DL Lancs 1998. Hon. Fellow, Univ. of Central Lancashire, 1994. Police Long Service and Good Conduct Medal, 1988; Lancashire Woman of the Year, 1993. SSStJ 1985 (Mem. Council, Lancs, 1998–). *Recreations:* gardening, horse riding, tapestry, reading novels, entertaining at home. *Address:* Lancashire Police HQ, Hutton, Preston PR4 5SB. *Club:* Soroptimist International (Ormskirk).

CLARE, Rear Adm. Roy Alexander George; Director, National Maritime Museum, since 2000; *b* 30 Sept. 1950; *s* of late John Arnold Clare and of Ludmilla Clare (*née* Nossoff); *m* 1st, 1979, Leonie (Mimi) Hutchings (*d* 1979); 2nd, 1981, Sarah Catherine Jane Parkin; one *s* two *d*. *Educ:* St George's Grammar Sch., Cape Town; BRNC, Dartmouth (Queen's Sword, 1972). Joined Royal Navy, 1966; jun. rating, HMS Ganges and HMS Decoy, 1966–68; Upperyardman Cadet, Dartmouth, 1968; Midshipman, HMS Ashanti, 1970–71; Sub-Lieut, Yacht Adventure, Whitbread Round The World Race, 1973–74; Lieut, HMS Diomede, 1974–75; First Lieut, HMS Bronington (HRH The Prince of Wales), 1975–77; Principal Warfare Officer, HMS Juno, 1978–80; CO, HMS Bronington, 1980–81; Ops Officer, HMS Glamorgan (Lt Comdr), 1982–83; Staff of Flag Officer Sea Trng, 1984–85; msc, Greenwich (Comdr), 1985–86; CO, HMS Birmingham, 1987–89; MA to Minister of State for Armed Forces, 1989–91; CO, HMS York and Capt., Third Destroyer Sqdn, 1991–92; rcds, 1993; Asst Dir, Naval Plans and Programmes Div., MoD, 1993–96; CO, HMS Invincible, 1996–97; Commodore, BRNC, 1998–99; Rear-Adm. 1999; Dir Operational Mgt, NATO Regl Comd North, 1999–2000. Trustee: Bronington Trust, 1990–99 (Vice Pres., 1999–); Naval Review, 2000–; Britannia Assoc., 2001–. Chm., Midland Naval Officers' Assoc., 2000–; Member: Greenwich Forum, 2000–; Univ. of Greenwich Assembly, 2000–; RNSA. CIMgt 2001. Freeman, City of London, 2001; Mem., Shipwrights' Co., 2001–. *Publications:* (ed) HMS Bronington: a tribute to one of Britain's last wooden walls, 1996; contrib. to Naval Rev. *Recreations:* family, sailing, walking. *Address:* National Maritime Museum, Greenwich, SE10 9NF. *Club:* Royal Yacht Squadron (Naval Mem.).
See also J. R. Clare.

CLARENDON, 7th Earl of, 2nd *cr* 1776; **George Frederick Laurence Hyde Villiers;** Managing Director, 1962–93, and Chairman, 1985–93, Seccombe Marshall and Campion plc; *b* 2 Feb. 1933; *o s* of Lord Hyde (*d* 1935) and Hon. Marion Féodorovna Louise Glyn, Lady Hyde (*d* 1970), *er d* of 4th Baron Wolverton; *S* grandfather, 1955; *m* 1974, Jane Diana, *d* of late E. W. Dawson; one *s* one *d*. Page of Honour to King George VI, 1948–49; Lieut RHG, 1951–53. Mem. Ct of Assts, Fishmongers' Co., 1988– (Prime Warden, 1999–2000). *Heir:* *s* Lord Hyde, *qv*. *Address:* Holywell House, Swanmore, Hants SO32 2QE. *T:* (01489) 896090.

CLARFELT, Jack Gerald; Chairman, Heathcourt Properties Ltd, since 1987; *b* 7 Feb. 1914; *s* of Barnett Clarfelt and Rene (*née* Frankel); *m* 1948, Baba Fredman; one *s* one *d*. *Educ:* Grocers' Co. Sch.; Sorbonne. Qualified as Solicitor, 1937; Man. Dir, Home Killed Meat Assoc., 1940–43 and 1945–54; Queen's Royal Surreys, 1943–45; Man. Dir, Fatstock Marketing Corp., 1954–60; Chm., Smithfield & Zwanenberg Gp Ltd, 1960–75; Exec. Dep. Chm., 1975–79, Dir, 1979–83, FMC Ltd. Dir, S. and W. Berisford Ltd, 1973–75; Chm., Linhay Frizzell Insurance Brokers Ltd, 1984–88. Farming, Hampshire. Master, Worshipful Co. of Butchers, 1978. *Recreations:* golf, swimming. *Address:* Linhay Meads, Timsbury, Romsey, Hants SO51 0LA. *T:* (01794) 368243. *Clubs:* City Livery, Farmers'.
See also R. E. Rhodes.

CLARIDGE, Prof. Michael Frederick; Emeritus Professor of Entomology, Cardiff University; *b* 2 June 1934; *s* of Frederick William Claridge and Eva Alice (*née* Jeffrey); *m* 1967, Lindsey Clare Hellings; two *s* one *d*. *Educ:* Lawrence Sheriff Sch., Rugby; Keble Coll., Oxford (MA, DPhil). Lectr in Zoology 1959–74, Sen. Lectr in Zoology 1974–77, Univ. Coll., Cardiff; Reader in Entomology 1977–83, Prof. of Entomology, 1983–99, Head of Sch. of Biol., 1989–94, Univ. of Wales, Cardiff. President: Linnean Soc. of London, 1988–91; Systematics Assoc., 1991–94; Royal Entomol Soc., 2000–June 2002. Linnean Medal for Zool., Linnean Soc., 2000. *Publications:* Handbook for the Identification of Leafhoppers and Planthoppers of Rice, 1991; chapters in: The Leafhoppers and Planthoppers, 1985; Organization of Communities – Past and Present, 1987; Prospects in Systematics, 1988; The Biodiversity of Micro-organisms and Invertebrates, 1991; Evolutionary Patterns and Processes, 1993; Planthoppers: their ecology and management, 1993; Identification of Pest Organisms, 1994; Species—the Units of Biodiversity, 1997; papers in Biol Jl of Linnean Soc., Ecological Entomology, Amer. Naturalist. *Recreations:* classical music, cricket, natural history. *Address:* School of Biosciences, Cardiff University, Cardiff CF1 3TL; *e-mail:* claridge@cardiff.ac.uk.

CLARK; *see* Chichester-Clark.

CLARK, family name of **Barons Clark of Kempston** and **Clark of Windermere**.

CLARK OF KEMPSTON, Baron *cr* 1992 (Life Peer), of Kempston in the County of Bedfordshire; **William Gibson Clark,** Kt 1980; PC 1990; *b* 18 Oct. 1917; *m* 1944, Irene Dorothy Dawson Rands; two *s* (and one *s* one *d* decd). *Educ:* London. Mem., Chartered Association (formerly Association) of Certified Accountants, 1941. Served in Army, 1941–46 (UK and India), Major. Mem. Wandsworth Borough Council, 1949–53 (Vice-Chm. Finance Cttee). Contested (C) Northampton, 1955; MP (C): Nottingham South, 1959–66; East Surrey, 1970–74; Croydon South, 1974–92. Opposition Front Bench Spokesman on Economics, 1964–66; Chairman: Select Cttee on Tax Credits, 1973; Cons. Back-bench Finance Cttee, 1979–92. Jt Deputy Chm., Conservative Party Organisation, 1975–77 (Jt Treasurer, 1974–75). Pres., City Gp for Smaller Cos, 1993–98. Chm., Anglo-Austrian Soc., 1983–98 (Patron, 1998–). Hon. Nat. Dir, Carrington £2 million Appeal, 1967–68. Freeman, City of London, 1987. Grand Gold Cross (Austria), 1989; Grand Decoration of Honour in Gold with Star (Austria), 1994. *Recreation:* reading. *Address:* The Clock House, Box End, Bedford MK43 8RT. *T:* (01234) 852361; 3 Barton Street, SW1P 3NG. *T:* (020) 7222 5759. *Clubs:* Carlton, Buck's.

CLARK OF WINDERMERE, Baron *cr* 2001 (Life Peer), of Windermere in the County of Cumbria; **David George Clark;** PC 1997; *b* 19 Oct. 1939; *s* of George and Janet Clark; *m* 1970, Christine Kirkby; one *d*. *Educ:* Manchester Univ. (BA(Econ), MSc); Sheffield Univ. (PhD 1978). Forester, 1956–57; Laboratory Asst in Textile Mill, 1957–59; Student Teacher, 1959–60; Student, 1960–63; Pres., Univ. of Manchester Union, 1963–64; Trainee Manager in USA, 1964; University Lecturer, 1965–70. Non-executive Director: Homeowners Friendly Soc., 1999–; Thales plc. Contested Manchester (Withington), 1966; MP (Lab) Colne Valley, 1970–Feb. 1974; contested same seat, Oct. 1974; MP (Lab) South Shields, 1979–2001. Opposition spokesman on Agriculture and Food, 1973–74, on Defence, 1980–81, on the Environment, 1981–86; Opposition front bench spokesman on: environmental protection and develt, 1986–87; food, agriculture and rural affairs, 1987–92; defence, disarmament and arms control, 1992–97; Chancellor, Duchy of Lancaster, 1997–98. Mem., Parly Assembly, NATO, 1981–; Chm., Atlantic Council of UK, 1998–. Pres., Open Spaces Soc., 1979–88. Freedom, Borough of S Tyneside, 1989. *Publications:* The Industrial Manager, 1966; Colne Valley: Radicalism to Socialism, 1981; Victor Grayson, Labour's Lost Leader, 1985; We Do Not Want The Earth, 1992; various articles on Management and Labour History. *Recreations:* fell-walking, ornithology, watching football, gardening. *Address:* House of Lords, SW1A 0PW.

CLARK, Rt Rev. Alan Charles; RC Bishop of East Anglia, 1976–94, Former Bishop, since 1995; *b* 9 Aug. 1919; *s* of William Thomas Durham Clark and Ellen Mary Clark (*née* Compton). *Educ:* Westminster Cathedral Choir Sch.; Ven. English Coll., Rome, Italy. Priest, 1945; Curate, St Philip's, Arundel, 1945–46; postgrad. studies, Rome, 1946–48; Doctorate in Theol., Gregorian Univ., Rome, 1948; Tutor in Philosophy, English Coll., Rome, 1948–53, Vice-Rector, 1954–64; Parish Priest, St Mary's, Blackheath, SE3, 1965–69; Auxiliary Bishop of Northampton, 1969–76; Titular Bishop of Elmham, 1969–76. *Peritus* at Vatican Council, 1962–65; Jt Chm., The Anglican/Roman Catholic Internat. Commn, 1969–81 (Lambeth Cross); Chm., Dept for Mission and Unity, Bishops' Conf. of Eng. and Wales, 1984–94; Co-Moderator, Jt Working Group of RC Church and WCC, 1984–93. Freeman, City of London, 1969. *Recreation:* music. *Address:* 19 Upgate, Poringland, Norwich NR14 7SH.

CLARK, Alan Richard; HM Diplomatic Service, retired; *b* 4 Sept. 1939; *s* of George Edward Clark and Norah Ivy Maria Clark (*née* Hope); *m* 1961, Ann Rosemary (*née* Hosford); one *s*. *Educ:* Chatham House Grammar Sch., Ramsgate. Foreign Office, 1958; HM Forces, 1960–62; FO 1962; served Tehran, 1964–66; Jedda, 1966–68; Second Sec. (Economic), later First Sec., Paris, 1969–71; FCO, 1972–76; Dep. Hd of Mission, Freetown, 1976–80; FCO, 1980–84; secondment (with rank of Counsellor) to Vickers Shipbuilding and Engineering Ltd, 1984–86; Counsellor and Head of Chancery, Bucharest, 1986–89; Consul-Gen., Montreal, 1990–93; Sen. Overseas Inspector, FCO, 1994–96. Vice-Chm., Thanet Community Housing Assoc, 1999–. Trustee, Michael Joakley's Charity, 2000–. *Recreations:* swimming, walking, reading. *Address:* Dane End, 103 Sea Road, Westgate-on-Sea, Kent CT8 8QE. *Club:* Royal Commonwealth Society.

CLARK, Alistair Campbell; WS; Consultant, Blackadder Reid Johnston (formerly Reid Johnston Bell & Henderson), Solicitors, Dundee, 1995–99 (Partner, 1961–95); *b* 4 March 1933; *s* of Peter Campbell Clark and Janet Mitchell Scott or Clark; *m* 1960, Evelyn M. Johnston; three *s*. *Educ:* St Andrews Univ. Admitted solicitor, 1957. WS 1991. Hon. Sheriff, Tayside Central and Fife, 1986–. Mem. Council, Law Soc. of Scotland, 1982–91 (Pres., 1989–90); Dean, Faculty of Procurators and Solicitors, Dundee, 1979–81 (Hon. Mem., 1991). Chm., Scottish Conveyancing and Executry Services Bd, 1996–. Chm.,

Dovetail Enterprises. Founder Chm., Broughty Ferry Round Table; Founder Pres., Claverhouse Rotary Club, Dundee. *Recreations:* family, travel, erratic golf. *Address:* Blythehill, 16 Balmyle Road, West Ferry, Dundee DD5 1JJ. *T:* (01382) 477989. *Clubs:* New (Edinburgh); Royal and Ancient (St Andrews); Panmure Angus Golf.

CLARK, Brian Robert, FRSL 1985; playwright; *b* 3 June 1932; *s* of Leonard and Selina Clark; *m* (marr. diss.); two *s*; *m* 1990, Cherry Potter. *Educ:* Merrywood Grammar Sch., Bristol; Redland Coll. of Educn, Bristol; Central Sch. of Speech and Drama, London; Nottingham Univ. BA Hons English. Teacher, 1955–61, and 1964–66; Staff Tutor in Drama, Univ. of Hull, 1966–70. Since 1971 has written some thirty television plays, incl. Whose Life Is It Anyway? and The Saturday Party; television film, (with Cherry Potter) House Games; also series: Telford's Change; Late Starter. Stage plays: Whose Life Is It Anyway? (SWET award for Best Play, 1977; filmed, 1982); Can You Hear Me At the Back?, 1978; Campions Interview; Post Mortem; Kipling, London and NY, 1985; The Petition, NY and Nat. Theatre, 1986; (with Kathy Levin) Hopping to Byzantium, Germany 1989, Sydney, Aust., 1990; In Pursuit of Eve (also acted), London, 2001. Founded Amber Lane Press, publishing plays and books on the theatre, 1978. *Publications:* Group Theatre, 1971; Whose Life Is It Anyway?, 1978; Can You Hear Me At the Back?, 1979; Post Mortem, 1979; The Petition, 1986; In Pursuit of Eve, 2001. *Address:* c/o Judy Daish Associates, 2 St Charles Place, W10 6EG. *T:* (020) 8964 8811.

CLARK, Rt Rev. Bruce Quinton; *see* Riverina, Bishop of.

CLARK, Charles Anthony, (Tony), CB 1994; Director, Student Support, Department for Education and Employment, 1999–2000; *b* 13 June 1940; *s* of late Stephen and Winifred Clark; *m* 1968, Penelope Margaret (*née* Brett); one *s* two *d*. *Educ:* King's Coll. Sch., Wimbledon; Pembroke Coll., Oxford (MA Nat. Sci.). Pressed Steel Co., 1961; Hilger & Watts Ltd, 1962–65; DES, subseq. DFE, later DFEE, 1965–2000; seconded to UGC, 1971–73; Under Sec., 1982; Hd of Finance Br. and Prin. Finance Officer, 1987–89; Dir (formerly Under Sec.), Higher Educn, 1989–99. Chm., Nat. Centre for Work Experience, 2001–. Advr, e-loft, 2000–. Mem. Council, Surrey Univ., 1999–; Governor: Surrey Inst. of Art and Design, 1999–; Southampton Inst., 2000–. Mem. Gen. Council, British Univs N American Club, 2000–. Hon. LLD 2000. *Recreations:* gardening, golf, travel. *Address:* The Paddock, Guildford Road, Effingham, Surrey KT24 5QA; *e-mail:* caclark@post.com.

CLARK, Charles David Lawson; Adviser, Freedom to Publish, Publishers' Association, since 2000; Legal Adviser: Publishers' Association, 1984–99; Copyright Licensing Agency, 1988–99 (Chairman, 1985–88); General Counsel, International Publishers Copyright Council, 1990–99; Copyright Representative, Federation of European Publishers, 1990–99; *b* 12 June 1933; *s* of Alec Fulton Charles Clark, CB, and of Mary Clark; *m* 1960, Fiona McKenzie Mill; one *s* three *d*. *Educ:* Edinburgh Acad.; Jesus Coll., Oxford (Exhibnr; MA). Called to the Bar, Inner Temple, 1960. Second Lieut 4th Regt RHA. Editor: Sweet and Maxwell, 1957–60; Penguin Books, 1960–66; Managing Director: Penguin Educn, 1966–72; Allen Lane the Penguin Press, 1967–69; Dir, LWT (Holdings) Ltd, 1982–84. Chairman: Bookrest, 1975–78; Book Marketing Council, 1979–81; Hutchinson Publishing Group, 1972–80 (Man. Dir, 1972); Chief Exec., Hutchinson Ltd, 1980–84. Member: Book Trade Working Party, 1970–72; Brit. Copyright Council, 1976–79 and 1984–99 (Treas. 1987–93); Legal Adv. Bd, EC, 1990–99; Council of Management, CLIP, 1990–94; Council of Management, MIND, the Nat. Assoc. of Mental Health, 1970–79 (Chm. MIND, 1976–79, Vice-Pres., 1980–). *Publications:* (ed) Publishing Agreements, 1980, 5th edn 1997; articles on publishing topics. *Recreations:* music, golf. *Address:* 19 Offley Road, SW9 0LR. *T:* (020) 7735 1422. *Clubs:* Groucho, Le Beaujolais.

CLARK, Rt Hon. Charles Joseph, (Joe), CC 1995; PC (Canada) 1979; President, Joe Clark & Associates (Principal Partner, 1994); Leader, Progressive Conservative Party of Canada, 1976–83 and since 1998; *b* 5 June 1939; *s* of Charles and Grace Clark; *m* 1973, Maureen McTeer (she retained her maiden name); one *d*. *Educ:* High River High Sch.; Univ. of Alberta (BA History; MA Polit. Sci.). Journalist, Canadian Press, Calgary Herald, Edmonton Jl, High River Times, 1964–66; Prof. of Political Science, Univ. of Alberta, Edmonton, 1966–67; Exec. Asst to Hon. Robert L. Stanfield, Leader of the Opposition, 1967–70. MP (Progressive C) Rocky Mountain, later Yellowhead, Constituency, 1972–93; Leader of the Opposition, Canada, 1976–79; Prime Minister of Canada, 1979–80; Leader of the Opposition, 1980–83; Sec. of State for External Affairs, 1984–91; Minister for Constitutional Affairs, 1991–93. UN Special Rep. for Cyprus, 1993–95. Pres., Queen's Privy Council for Canada, 1991–93. Hon. LLD: New Brunswick, 1976; Calgary, 1984; Alberta, 1985; King's Coll., Halifax, 1994; Concordia, 1994; St Thomas, Minn, 1999. Alberta Award of Excellence, Alberta Univ., 1983. *Recreations:* riding, reading, walking, film going. *Address:* (office) Suite 1050, 155 Queen Street, Ottawa, ON K1A 0A6, Canada.

CLARK, Christopher Harvey; QC 1989; a Recorder, since 1986; *b* 20 Dec. 1946; *s* of Harvey Frederick Beckford Clark and Winifred Julia Clark; *m* 1972, Gillian Elizabeth Ann Mullen; one *s* two *d*. *Educ:* Taunton's Grammar Sch., Southampton; The Queen's Coll., Oxford (BA 1968; MA 1987). Called to the Bar, Gray's Inn, 1969, Bencher, 2000; Mem., Western Circuit, 1969–; Asst Recorder, 1982. Chancellor, dio. of Winchester, 1993–; Deputy Chancellor: dio. of Portsmouth, 1994–; dio. of Chichester, 1995–; dio. of Salisbury, 1997–. Lay Reader, C of E, 1998–. *Recreations:* amateur dramatics, golf, cricket, gardening, youth club work, local community affairs, ski-ing. *Address:* 3 Pump Court, Temple, EC4Y 7AJ. *T:* (020) 7353 0711; 31 Southgate Street, Winchester, Hants SO23 9EE. *T:* (01962) 868161.

CLARK, Christopher Richard Nigel; Chief Executive, Johnson Matthey plc, since 1998; *b* 29 Jan. 1942; *s* of late Rev. Vivian George Clark and Aileen Myfanwy Clark (*née* Thompson); *m* 1964, Catherine Ann Mather; two *s* one *d* (and one *s* decd). *Educ:* Marlborough Coll.; Trinity Coll., Cambridge; Brunel Univ. MIM 1967. Johnson Matthey plc, 1962–: Mem. Bd, 1990–; Chief Operating Officer, 1996–98. Non-executive Director: Trinity Holdings (Dennis), 1993–98; FKI plc, 2000–. MInstD 1990. *Recreations:* shooting, golf, opera, ballet, watching Rugby and cricket. *Address:* 30 Marryat Road, SW19 5BD. *T:* (020) 8946 5887. *Clubs:* Travellers; Jesters.

CLARK, Prof. Colin Whitcomb, PhD; FRS 1997; FRSC 1988; Professor of Mathematics, University of British Columbia, 1969–94, Professor Emeritus, since 1994; *b* 18 June 1931; *s* of George Savage Clark and Irene (Stewart) Clark; *m* 1955, Janet Arlene Davidson; one *s* two *d*. *Educ:* Univ. of BC (BA 1953); Univ. of Washington (PhD 1958). Instructor, Univ. of Calif, Berkeley, 1958–60; Asst Prof., then Associate Prof. of Maths, Univ. of BC, 1960–69. Regent's Lectr in Maths, Univ. of Calif, Davis, 1986; Visiting Professor: of Ecology and Systematics, Cornell Univ., 1987; of Ecology and Evolutionary Biol., Princeton Univ., 1997. Hon. DSc 2000. *Publications:* Mathematical Bioeconomics, 1976, 2nd edn 1990; Bioeconomic Modelling and Fisheries Management, 1985; (with M. Mangel) Dynamic Modelling in Behavioral Ecology, 1988; (with M. Mangel) Dynamic State Variable Models in Ecology, 2000. *Recreations:* natural history, ski-ing, hiking. *Address:* Institute of Applied Mathematics, University of British Columbia, Vancouver, BC V6T 1Z2, Canada. *T:* (604) 8223262.

CLARK, David Beatson, CBE 1986; TD 1966; DL; Chairman, Rotherham District Health Authority, 1993–96 (Member, 1985–96); *b* 5 May 1933; *s* of late Alec Wilson Clark, OBE, JP, DSc(Tech) and Phyllis Mary Clark; *m* 1959, Ann Morgan Mudford; two *s* one *d*. *Educ:* Wrekin College; Keele Univ. (BA Hons Physics and Econs). Beatson Clark: joined 1958; Managing Dir, 1971; Chm. and Managing Dir, 1979; Exec. Chm., 1984–88. Non-Executive Director: Royal Bank of Scotland, 1988–91; Yorkshire Electricity Gp, 1990–94 (Mem., Yorkshire Electricity Bd, 1980–90); Rotherham TEC, 1990–92. President: Rotherham Chamber of Commerce, 1975–76; Sheffield Br., BIM, 1983–86; Glass Manufacturers' Fedn, 1982–83; Mem. Council, Univ. of Sheffield, 1984–2000. Liveryman, Glass Sellers' Co., 1967; Freeman, Cutlers' Co. in Hallamshire, 1980. DL S Yorks, 1990; High Sheriff, S Yorks, 1992. Hon. Fellow, Sheffield City Polytechnic, 1988. *Address:* Sorrelstan, 154 Moorgate Road, Rotherham, South Yorks S60 3AZ. *T:* (01709) 365539. *Club:* Army and Navy.

CLARK, David John; Head of Resource Management Division, Department of Health, since 1999; *b* 20 Sept. 1947; *m* 1970, Caroline Russell; two *s* three *d*. *Educ:* Univ. of Kent at Canterbury (MA). Department of Health and Social Security, later Departments of Health and of Social Security: Asst Principal, 1969; Principal, 1973; Asst Sec., 1983; Under Sec., 1990; Dir of Personnel, Personnel Services Div., DoH, 1994–99. *Address:* Department of Health, Eileen House, 80–94 Newington Causeway, SE1 6EF.

CLARK, Denis; His Honour Judge Denis Clark; a Circuit Judge, since 1988; *b* 2 Aug. 1943; twin *s* of John and Mary Clark; *m* 1967, Frances Mary (*née* Corcoran); four *d*. *Educ:* St Anne's RC Primary, Rock Ferry, Birkenhead; St Anselm's Coll., Birkenhead; Sheffield Univ. LLB. Called to the Bar, Inner Temple, 1966; practised Northern Circuit, 1966–88; a Recorder, 1984–88. *Recreations:* medieval history, cricket, theatre. *Address:* c/o The Queen Elizabeth II Law Courts, Derby Square, Liverpool L2 1XA.

CLARK, Derek John, FCIS; Principal, DJC Services, since 1994; *b* 17 June 1929; *s* of Robert Clark and Florence Mary (*née* Wise); *m* 1949, Edna Doris Coome; one *s* one *d*. *Educ:* Selhurst Grammar Sch., Croydon; SE London Technical Coll. FCIS 1982 (ACIS 1961). National Service, RAF, 1948–49. Corp. of Trinity House, 1949–66; RICS, 1966–71; ICMA, 1971–82; Sec., IStructE, 1982–94. Sec. and Dir, Detecnicks (Property) Ltd, 1999–; Sec., Detecnicks Ltd, 1999; Sec. and Dir, Detecnicks (Finance) Ltd, 2000–. Hon. FIStructE 1994. *Recreations:* athletics (until 1961), squash (until 1994). *Address:* 24 North Way, Felpham, Bognor Regis, W Sussex PO22 7BT. *T:* (01243) 822585.

CLARK, Desmond; *see* Clark, John D.

CLARK, Sir Francis (Drake), 5th Bt *cr* 1886, of Melville Crescent, Edinburgh; *b* 16 July 1924; *yr s* of Sir Thomas Clark, 3rd Bt and Ellen Mercy (*d* 1987), *d* of late Francis Drake; *S* brother, 1991; *m* 1958, Mary (*d* 1994), *yr d* of late John Alban Andrews, MC, FRCS; one *s*. *Educ:* Edinburgh Acad. RN 1943–46. Dir, Clark Travel Service Ltd, London, 1948–80. *Recreations:* tennis, cricket, music, gardening. *Heir: s* Edward Drake Clark, *b* 27 April 1966. *Address:* Woodend Cottages, Burgh-next-Aylsham, Norfolk NR11 6TS.

CLARK, Frank, CBE 1991; Director, Strathcarron Hospice, since 1996; *b* 17 Oct. 1946; *m*; two *d*. MHSM 1974; DipHSM 1974. Clerical Trainee, Bd of Mgt for Royal Cornhill and Associated Hosps, 1965–67; Higher Clerical Officer, Kingseat Hosp., 1967–69; Dep. Hosp. Sec., 1969–70, Hosp. Sec., 1970–71, Canniesburn and Schaw Hosps; Dep. Hosp. Sec., Glasgow Royal Infirmary and Sub-Gp, 1971–74; Administrator, Glasgow Royal Infirmary, 1974–77; Greater Glasgow Health Board Eastern District: Asst Dist Administrator, 1977–81; Dist Gen. Administrator, 1981–83; Hamilton and E Kilbride Unit, Lanarkshire Health Board: Dist Administrator, 1983–84; Dir of Admin. Services, June–Sept. 1984; Sec. to Bd, Lanarks Health Bd, 1984–85; General Manager: Lanarks Health Bd, 1985–96; Lothian Health Bd, May–Dec. 1990. Vis. Prof., Health Fac., Glasgow Caledonian Univ., 1993–; Hon. Prof., Human Scis Faculty, Univ. of Stirling, 1997–. Chairman: W of Scotland Health Service Res. Network, 1990–95; Lanarks Drugs Action Team, 1995–96; Scottish Hospices Forum, 1998–; Central Scotland Health Care NHS Trust, Jan.–March 1999; Forth Valley Primary Care Trust, April–Sept. 1999; Ministerial Task Force, NHS Tayside, 2000; Vice Chairman: Scottish Health Bd Gen. Managers Gp, 1995–96; Scottish Partnership Agency for Palliative and Cancer Care, 1998–; Member: Chief Scientist's Health Service Res. Cttee, 1989–93; Scottish Health Service Adv. Council, 1990–93; Scottish Overseas Health Support Policy Bd, 1990–96; Jt Wkg Gp on Purchasing, 1992–96; Scottish Implementation Gp, Jun. Doctors' and Dentists' Hours of Work, 1992–96; Scottish Council for Postgrad. Med. and Dental Educn, 1993–96; Implementation Gp, Scottish Health Services Mgt Centre, 1993–96; Strategy Gp, R&D Strategy for NHS in Scotland, 1994–96; Indep. Hospices Representative Cttee, Help the Hospices, 1998–. Mem. Bd, New Lanarkshire Ltd, 1992–98. Non-exec. Dir, Voluntary Assoc. for Mental Welfare, 1997–. Mem. Edtl Adv. Bd, Health Bulletin, 1993–96. Pres., Cumbernauld Rotary Club, 2000–. *Address:* Ash Lea, 5 Gullane Crescent, Westerwood Green, Cumbernauld G68 0HR.

CLARK, Gerald, CBE 1990; Inspector of Companies, Head of Companies Investigation Branches, Department of Trade and Industry, 1984–90; *b* 18 Sept. 1933; *s* of John George and Elizabeth Clark (*née* Shaw); *m* 1958, Elizabeth McDermott; one *s*. *Educ:* St Cuthbert's Grammar School, Newcastle upon Tyne. Chartered Secretary. National Health Service, Northumberland Exec. Council, 1949–55; National Coal Board 1955–60; Board of Trade, Official Receiver's Service, 1960–71; Companies Investigation Branch, 1971–79; Official Receiver, High Court of Justice, 1981–83; Principal Examiner, Companies Investigation Branch, 1983–84. Mem., Herts Area Cttee, Sanctuary Housing Assoc., 1990– (Chm., 1992–2000). *Recreations:* music, photography.

CLARK, Gerald Edmondson, CMG 1989; General Secretary, ESCL, since 2001; *b* 26 Dec. 1935; *s* of Edward John Clark and Irene Elizabeth Ada Clark (*née* Edmondson); *m* 1967, Mary Rose Organ; two *d*. *Educ:* Johnston Grammar School, Durham; New College, Oxford (MA). FInstE 1998. HM Diplomatic Service, 1960–93: Foreign Office, 1960; Hong Kong, 1961; Peking, 1962–63; FO, 1964–68; Moscow, 1968–70; FCO, 1970–73; Head of Chancery, Lisbon, 1973–77; Asst Sec., Cabinet Office, 1977–79; seconded to Barclays Bank International, 1979–81; Commercial Counsellor, Peking, 1981–83; FCO, 1984–87; UK Perm. Rep to IAEA, UNIDO, and to UN in Vienna, 1987–92; Sen. DS, RCDS, 1993; Sec. Gen., Uranium Inst., 1994–2000. Patron, New London Orchestra, 1993–. Chm., London Gp, Henley Alumni Assoc., 1997–. *Publications:* articles and speeches about all aspects of the civil nuclear fuel cycle. *Recreations:* architecture, economics, the spread of scientific thinking. *Address:* Lew Hollow, Beer Hill, Seaton, Devon EX12 2PY. *T:* and *Fax:* (01297) 22001; *e-mail:* GeraldEClark@aol.com. *Club:* Athenæum.

CLARK, Hon. Glen David; MLA (NDP) Vancouver-Kingsway, since 1991 (Vancouver-East, 1986–91); Premier of British Columbia, 1996–99; *b* 22 Nov. 1957; *m* 1980, Dale

Babish; one *s* one *d*. *Educ:* Simon Fraser Univ. (BA Pol Sci. & Canadian Studies); Univ. of BC (MA Community & Regl Planning). Minister of: Finance and Corporate Relns, 1991–93; Employment and Investment, 1993–96; Leader, NDP, BC, 1996–. *Recreation:* spending time with family. *Address:* Parliament Buildings, Victoria, BC V8V 1P5, Canada. *T:* (250) 3873655.

CLARK, Prof. Gordon Leslie, PhD; Halford Mackinder Professor of Geography, University of Oxford, since 1995; Professorial Fellow: St Peter's College, Oxford, since 1995; Said Business School, University of Oxford, since 2000; *b* 10 Sept. 1950; *s* of Bryan Clark and Florence Lesley Clark (*née* Cowling); *m* 1972, Shirley Anne Spratling; one *s*. *Educ:* Monash Univ. (BEcon, MA); Univ. of Oxford (MA); McMaster Univ. (PhD 1978; Dist. Alumni Award, 1998). Asst Prof., Harvard Univ., 1978–83; Associate Prof., Univ. of Chicago, 1983–85; Prof., Carnegie Mellon Univ., 1985–91; Monash University: Prof., 1989–95; Hd of Dept, 1990–93; Associate Dean, 1991–94; Actg Dean, 1993–94; Dir, Inst. of Ethics and Public Policy, 1991–95; Chm., Faculty Bd of Anthropology and Geography, Univ. of Oxford, 1999–. Nat. Research Council Fellow, US Nat. Acad. of Sci., 1981–82; Fellow, Lincoln Land Inst., 1981–82. FASSA 1993. Chancellor's Medal, UCSB. *Publications:* Interregional Migration, National Policy and Social Justice, 1983; (jtly) State Apparatus, 1984; Judges and the Cities, 1985; (jtly) Regional Dynamics, 1986; Unions and Communities Under Siege, 1989; Pensions and Corporate Restructuring in American Industry, 1993; (ed jtly) Multiculturalism, Difference and Postmodernism, 1993; (ed jtly) Management Ethics, 1995; (ed jtly) Asian Newly Industrialised Economies in the Global Economy, 1996; (ed jtly) Accountability and Corruption: public sector ethics, 1997; Pension Fund Capitalism, 2000; (ed jtly) Oxford Handbook of Economic Geography, 2000. *Recreations:* walking, reading, holidays. *Address:* School of Geography, University of Oxford, Mansfield Road, Oxford OX1 3TB.

CLARK, Gregor Munro; Scottish Parliamentary Counsel, Edinburgh, since 1999; Counsel to the Scottish Law Commission, 1995–2000; *b* 18 April 1946; *s* of late Ian Munro Clark and Norah Isobel Joss; *m* 1st, 1974, Jane Maralyn Palmer (*d* 1999); one *s* two *d*; 2nd, 2000, Alexandra Plumtree (*née* Miller). *Educ:* Queen's Park Senior Secondary Sch., Glasgow; St Andrews Univ. (LLB Hons). Admitted Faculty of Advocates, 1972; entered Lord Advocate's Dept, 1974; Asst Parly Draftsman, then Dep. Parly Draftsman, 1974–79; Asst Legal Sec. to Lord Advocate, and Scottish Parly Counsel, London, 1979–99; Scottish Exec., 1999–. *Recreations:* music, opera, Scandinavian languages and literature. *Address:* 18 Rocheid Park, Inverleith, Edinburgh EH4 1RU. *T:* (0131) 3154634.

CLARK, Rt Hon. Helen Elizabeth; PC 1990; MP (Lab) Mount Albert, New Zealand, 1981–96 and since 1999 (Owairaka, 1996–99); Prime Minister of New Zealand, since 1999; *b* 26 Feb. 1950; *d* of George and Margaret Clark; *m* 1981, Dr Peter Byard Davis. *Educ:* Epsom Girls' Grammar School; Auckland Univ. (BA 1971; MA Hons 1974). Junior Lectr in Political Studies, Auckland Univ., 1973–75; UGC Post Graduate Scholar, 1976; Lectr, Political Studies Dept, Auckland Univ., 1977–81. Minister: of Housing, of Conservation, 1987–89; of Health, of Labour, 1989–90; Dep. Prime Minister, 1989–90; Dep. Leader of the Opposition, 1990–93, Leader, 1993–99. *Recreations:* theatre, music, ski-ing, trekking, reading. *Address:* Parliament House, Wellington, New Zealand. *T:* (4) 4719999.

CLARK, Henry Maitland; journalist; with Avon Advertiser, 1989–97; *b* 11 April 1929; *s* of Major H. F. Clark, Rockwood, Upperlands, Co. Londonderry; *m* 1972, Penelope Winifred Tindal (*d* 1994); one *s* two *d*. *Educ:* Shrewsbury Sch.; Trinity Coll., Dublin; Trinity Hall, Cambridge. Entered Colonial Service and appointed District Officer, Tanganyika, 1951; served in various Districts of Tanganyika, 1951–59; resigned from Colonial Service, 1959. Wine merchant, IDV Ltd and Cock Russell Vintners, 1972–76; Hd of Information, CoSIRA, 1977–89. MP (UU) Antrim North (UK Parliament), Oct. 1959–1970; Chm. Conservative Trade and Overseas Develt Sub-Cttee; Member: British Delegation to Council of Europe and WEU, 1962–65; Advisory Council Food Law Res. Centre, Univ. of Brussels; Exec. Cttee, Lepra (British Leprosy Relief Assoc.); Select Cttee on Overseas Aid and Develt, 1969–70; Grand Jury, Co. Londonderry, 1970. A Commonwealth Observer, Mauritius General Election, 1967. Vice-Pres., Dublin Univ. Boat Club. *Recreations:* rowing coach, sailing, shooting, golf, collecting old furniture. *Address:* Rockwood, Upperlands, Co. Derry, Northern Ireland BT46 5SB. *T:* (028) 7964 2237; Staddles, Hindon Lane, Tisbury, Wilts SP3 6PU. *T:* (01747) 870330. *Clubs:* Kildare Street and University (Dublin); Royal Portrush Golf.
See also H. W. S. Clark.

CLARK, (Henry) Wallace (Stuart), MBE 1970; DL; Vice Lord-Lieutenant of County Londonderry, 1993–2001; Director, Wm Clark & Sons, Linen Manufacturers, since 1972, non-executive Director, since 1987; *b* 20 Nov. 1926; *s* of Major H. F. Clark, MBE, JP, RA, Rockwood, Upperlands, and Sybil Emily (*née* Stuart); *m* 1957, June Elisabeth Lester Deane; two *s*. *Educ:* Shrewsbury School. Lieut, RNVR, 1945–47 (bomb and mine disposal); Cattleman, Merchant Navy, 1947–48. District Comdt, Ulster Special Constabulary, 1955–70; Major, Ulster Defence Regt, 1970–81. Foyle's Lectr, USA tour, 1964. Led Church of Ireland St Columba commemorative curragh voyage, Derry to Iona, 1963; Dir and Skipper, Lord of the Isles Voyage, Galway to Stornaway in 16th century galley, 1991. Mem., Cttee of Management, RNLI, 1990–2001. DL 1962, High Sheriff 1969, Co. Londonderry. *Publications:* (jtly) North and East Coasts of Ireland, 1957; (jtly) South and West Coasts of Ireland, 1962, 2nd edn 1970; Guns in Ulster, 1967; Rathlin Disputed Island, 1972; Sailing Round Ireland, 1976; Linen on the Green, 1982; Lord of the Isles Voyage, 1993; Upperlands History and Visitors Guide, 1998; Sailing Round Russia: the story of Miles Clark's unique voyage, 1999. *Recreation:* sailing to islands. *Address:* Gorteade Cottage, Upperlands, Co. Londonderry, N Ireland BT46 5SB. *T:* (028) 8674 2737. *Clubs:* Royal Cruising, Irish Cruising (Cdre 1962).
See also H. M. Clark.

CLARK, Prof. Ian, PhD; FBA 1999; Professor of International Politics, University of Wales, Aberystwyth, since 1998; *b* 14 March 1949; *m* 1970, Janice (*née* Cochrane); one *s* one *d*. *Educ:* Glasgow Univ. (MA); Australian National Univ. (PhD 1975). Lectr, 1974–81, Sen. Lectr, 1981–84, Univ. of Western Australia; Fellow, Selwyn Coll., Cambridge, 1985–97, Hon. Fellow, 2000; Dep. Dir, Centre of Internat. Studies, Cambridge, 1993–97. *Publications* include: The Hierarchy of States, 1989; Globalization and Fragmentation: international relations in the twentieth century, 1997; Nuclear Diplomacy and the Special Relationship, 1994; Globalization and International Relations Theory, 1999; The Post-Cold War Order, 2001. *Recreations:* hill walking, grandfather. *Address:* Department of International Politics, University of Wales, Aberystwyth, Penglais, Aberystwyth SY23 3DA. *T:* (01970) 621767.

CLARK, Ian Robertson, CBE 1979; *b* 18 Jan. 1939; *s* of Alexander Clark and Annie Dundas Watson; *m* 1961, Jean Scott Waddell Lang; one *s* one *d*. *Educ:* Dalziel High Sch., Motherwell. FCCA, CPFA. Trained with Glasgow Chartered Accountant; served in local govt, 1962–76, this service culminating in the post of Chief Executive, Shetland Islands Council; full-time Mem., BNOC, from 1976 until privatisation in 1982; Jt Man. Dir, Britoil plc, 1982–85; Chm., Ventures Div., Costain Gp, subseq. Urban Enterprises Ltd, 1987–93. Hon. LLD Glasgow, 1979. *Publications:* Reservoir of Power, 1980; contribs to professional and religious periodicals. *Recreations:* theology, general reading, walking. *Address:* Bellfield House, Askomil Road, Campbeltown, Argyll PA28 6EN. *T:* (01586) 553905.

CLARK, Jacqueline; *see* Davies, J.

CLARK, James Leonard; Under Secretary, Establishment Personnel Division, Departments of Industry and Trade Common Services, 1980–83 (Under Secretary, Department of Trade, 1978–80); *b* 8 Jan. 1923; *s* of James Alfred and Grace Clark; *m* 1st, 1954, Joan Pauline Richards (*d* 1992); 2nd, 1997, Helga Thomas. *Educ:* Mercers' School. Lieut (A), Fleet Air Arm, 1942–46. Clerical Officer, HM Treasury, 1939; Private Sec. to successive First Secs of State, 1964–67; Cabinet Office, 1969–71; Asst Sec., Price Commn, 1973–75; Dept of Industry, 1975–78. CBI, 1983–85; Hd of Administration, SIB, 1985–89. *Address:* 4 Westcott Way, Cheam, Surrey SM2 7JY. *T:* (020) 8393 2622.

CLARK, Dame Jill M.; *see* Macleod Clark.

CLARK, Rt Hon. Joe; *see* Clark, Rt Hon. C. J.

CLARK, Sir John (Allen), Kt 1971; retired; Chief Executive Officer, The Plessey Company plc, 1962–89; Chairman, GEC-Plessey Telecommunications Holdings, 1988–89; *b* 14 Feb. 1926; *e s* of late Sir Allen Clark and Lady (Jocelyn) Clark, *d* of late Percy and Madeline Culverhouse; *m* 1952, Deirdre Kathleen (marr. diss. 1962), *d* of Samuel Herbert Waterhouse and Maeve Murphy Waterhouse; one *s* one *d*; *m* 1970, Olivia, *d* of H. Pratt and of late Mrs R. S. H. Shepard; twin *s* one *d*. *Educ:* Harrow; Cambridge. Served War of 1939–45; commnd RNVR (2nd Lieut). Received early industrial training with Metropolitan Vickers and Ford Motor Co.; spent over a year in USA, studying the electronics industry. Asst to Gen. Manager, Plessey International Ltd, 1949; Dir and Gen. Man., Plessey (Ireland) Ltd, and Wireless Telephone Co. Ltd, 1950; appointed to main board, The Plessey Co. Ltd, 1953; Gen. Man., Plessey Components Group, 1957; Dep. Chm., The Plessey Co. Ltd, 1967–70, Chm., 1970–89. Director: International Computers Ltd, 1968–79; Banque Nationale de Paris Ltd, 1976–89. Pres., Telecommunication Engineering and Manufacturing Assoc., 1964–66, 1971–73; Vice-President: Inst. of Works Managers; Engineering Employers' Fedn. Member: Nat. Defence Industries Council; Engineering Industries Council, 1975–89. CompIEE; FIM. Order of Henry the Navigator, Portugal, 1973. *Recreations:* horseriding, shooting. *Address:* Redenham Park, Redenham, near Andover, Hants SP11 9AQ. *Club:* Boodle's.
See also Michael W. Clark.

CLARK, Prof. John Benjamin; Professor of Neurochemistry, since 1990, Academic Vice Dean, since 1996, Institute of Neurology, University of London, at University College London; Hon. Consultant Neurochemist, National Hospital of Neurology and Neurosurgery, since 1990; *b* 30 Jan. 1941; *e s* of P. B. Clark and J. E. Clark (*née* Smith); *m* 1965, Joan Gibbons; one *s* one *d* (and one *s* decd). *Educ:* Southend High Sch. for Boys; University College London (BSc 1962; PhD 1964; DSc 1982). St Bartholomew's Hospital Medical College, University of London: Lectr, Sen. Lectr and Reader in Biochemistry, 1965–86; Prof. of Cell Biochemistry, 1986–90. MRC Travelling Fellow, Johnson Res. Foundn, Univ. of Pennysylvania, 1969–70; Vis. Prof., Dept of Biochem. and Molecular Biol., UCL, 1991–. *Publications:* numerous contribs to sci. jls on mitochondrial metabolism and brain development. *Recreations:* walking, fine wines, reading. *Address:* Miriam Marks Department of Neurochemistry, Institute of Neurology, Queen Square, WC1N 3BG. *T:* (020) 7829 8722.

CLARK, Prof. J(ohn) Desmond, CBE 1960; PhD, ScD; FBA 1961; FSA 1952; FRSSAf 1959; Professor of Anthropology, University of California, Berkeley, USA, 1961–86, now Emeritus Professor; *b* London, 10 April 1916; *s* of late Thomas John Chown Clark and Catharine (*née* Wynne); naturalised American, 1993; *m* 1938, Betty Cable, *d* of late Henry Lea Baume and late Frances M. S. (*née* Brown); one *s* one *d*. *Educ:* Monkton Combe Sch.; Christ's Coll., Cambridge. PhD in Archaeology (Cambridge), 1950; ScD Cantab 1975. Dir, Rhodes-Livingstone Museum, Livingstone, N Rhodesia, 1938–61. Has conducted excavations in Southern, East and Equatorial Africa, the Sahara, Ethiopia, Syria, 1938–, India, 1980–82, China, 1990–. Military Service in East Africa, Abyssinia, The Somalilands and Madagascar, 1941–46. Founder Mem. and Sec., N Rhodesia Nat. Monuments Commn, 1948–61. Corr. Mem. Scientific Coun. for Africa South of the Sahara, 1956–64, etc. Lectures: Faculty Res. Berkeley, 1979; Raymond Dart, Johannesburg, 1979; Mortimer Wheeler, British Acad., 1981; John Mulvaney, ANU, 1991; Distinguished, Amer. Anthropol Assoc., 1992. Fellow, Amer. Acad. of Arts and Sciences, 1965; Mem., Nat. Acad. of Science, USA, 1993. Hon. DSc: Univ. of the Witwatersrand, 1985; Univ. of Cape Town, 1985. Huxley Medal, RAI, 1974; Gold Medal, Soc. of Antiquaries of London, 1985; Fellows Medal, Calif. Acad. of Scis, 1987; Gold Medal, Archaeological Inst. of America, 1989; L. S. B. Leakey Prize, 1996; Grahame Clark Medal for Prehistory, British Acad., 1997. Comdr, Nat. Order of Senegal, 1968. *Publications:* The Prehistoric Cultures of the Horn of Africa, 1954; The Prehistory of Southern Africa, 1959; The Stone Age Cultures of Northern Rhodesia, 1960; Prehistoric Cultures of Northeast Angola and their Significance in Tropical Africa, 1963; (ed) Proc. 3rd Pan-African Congress on Pre-history, 1957; (comp.) Atlas of African Pre-history, 1967; (ed with W. W. Bishop) Background to Evolution in Africa, 1967; Kalambo Falls Prehistoric Site, vol. I, 1969, vol. II, 1973, vol. III, 2000; The Prehistory of Africa, 1970; (ed) Cambridge History of Africa, vol I, 1982; (ed with G. R. Sharma) Palaeoenvironment and Prehistory in the Middle Son Valley, India, 1983; (ed with Steven A. Brandt) From Hunters to Farmers: the causes and consequences of food production in Africa, 1984; (ed) Cultural Beginnings, 1991; 295 contribs to learned journals on prehistoric archaeology. *Recreations:* gardening, walking, photography. *Address:* Grand Lake Gardens, 401 Santa Clara Avenue, Apt 223–24, Oakland, CA 94610, USA. *T:* (510) 6250444, *Fax:* (510) 6250555. *Clubs:* Royal Commonwealth Society, Oxford and Cambridge.

CLARK, John Edward, OBE 1995; Secretary, National Association of Local Councils, 1978–95; *b* 18 Oct. 1932; *s* of Albert Edward Clark and Edith (*née* Brown); *m* 1969, Judith Rosemary Lester; one *s* (one *d* decd). *Educ:* Royal Grammar Sch., Clitheroe; Keble Coll., Oxford (MA, BCL). Called to the Bar, Gray's Inn, 1957; practised at the Bar, 1957–61. Dep. Sec., National Assoc. of Local (formerly Parish) Councils, (part-time) 1959–61, (full-time) 1961–78. Hon. Consultant, Assoc. of Burial Authorities, 1998–. Co-ordinator, Friends of All Saints', W Dulwich, 2000–. *Publications:* chapters on local govt, public health, and theatres, in Encyclopaedia of Court Forms, 2nd edn 1964 to 1975. *Recreations:* walking, indoor games, collecting detective fiction, fortifications, rough ecclesiastical carpentry. *Address:* 113 Turney Road, Dulwich SE21 7JB. *T:* (020) 7274 1381.

CLARK, John Mullin; Chief Secretary for Mission to Archbishops' Council, Church of England, since 2000; *b* 19 April 1946; *s* of James and Margaret Clark; *m* 1975, Jenny Brown; one *s*. *Educ:* St Peter's Coll., Oxford (MA); Inst. of Educn, London Univ. (PGCE 1974); King's Coll., London (MA 1999). Operation Mobilisation, Iran, 1967–73; Iran Literature Assoc., Tehran, 1976–80; Church Missionary Society: Regl Sec., ME and

Pakistan, 1980–86; Communications Sec., 1987–91; Overseas Sec., Bishoprics' Fund, and Partnership Sec., Bd of Mission, C of E, 1992–2000. *Recreations:* walking, church history, T. E. Lawrence, Iran. *Address:* 32 Weigall Road, Lee, SE12 8HE. *T:* (020) 8852 2741.

CLARK, Sir John S.; *see* Stewart-Clark.

CLARK, Prof. Jonathan Charles Douglas, PhD; Hall Distinguished Professor of British History, University of Kansas, since 1995; *b* 28 Feb. 1951; *s* of Ronald James Clark and Dorothy Margaret Clark; *m* 1996, Katherine Redwood Penovich. *Educ:* Downing Coll., Cambridge (BA 1972); Corpus Christi Coll., Cambridge (MA 1976); Peterhouse, Cambridge (PhD 1981). Research Fellow: Peterhouse, Cambridge, 1977–81; Leverhulme Trust, 1983; All Souls Coll., Oxford, 1986–95 (Sen. Res. Fellow, 1995). Vis. Prof., Cttee on Social Thought, Univ. of Chicago, 1993; Dist. Vis. Lectr, Univ. of Manitoba, 1999; Vis. Fellow, Forschungszentrum Europäische Aufklärung, Potsdam, 2000; Vis. Prof., Univ. of Northumbria, 2001–. Initiated Oxford American Inst. (now Rothermere Amer. Inst.), 1990. Gov., Pusey House, Oxford, 1991–98. *Publications:* The Dynamics of Change, 1982; English Society 1688–1832, 1985, 2nd edn, as English Society 1660–1832, 2000; Revolution and Rebellion, 1986; (ed) The Memoirs and Speeches of James, 2nd Earl Waldegrave, 1988; (ed) Ideas and Politics in Modern Britain, 1990; The Language of Liberty 1660–1832, 1994; Samuel Johnson, 1994; (ed) Edmund Burke, Reflections on the Revolution in France, 2001; (ed jtly) Samuel Johnson in Historical Context, 2001; articles in learned jls. *Recreation:* more history. *Address:* Hall Centre for the Humanities, University of Kansas, Lawrence, KS 66045–2967, USA. *T:* (785) 8644798. *Club:* Beefsteak.

CLARK, Sir Jonathan (George), 5th Bt *cr* 1917, of Dunlambert, City of Belfast; Managing Director, Paragon Homes Ltd, since 1992; *b* 9 Oct. 1947; *o s* of Sir Colin Douglas Clark, 4th Bt and of Margaret Coleman Clark (*née* Spinks); *S* father, 1995; *m* 1971, Susan Joy, *d* of Brig. T. I. G. Gray; one *s* two *d. Educ:* Eton. Royal Green Jackets, 1966–78. Various appts within private health care industry, 1978–92. *Recreations:* horse trials, hunting. *Heir: s* Simon George Gray Clark, *b* 3 Oct. 1975. *Address:* Somerset House, Threapwood, Malpas, Cheshire SY14 7AW. *T:* (01948) 770205.

CLARK, Prof. Jonathan William, (Jon); Professor of Industrial Relations, University of Southampton, 1990–99, now Emeritus; Chair: UK Police Negotiating Board, since 2000; Police Advisory Board for England and Wales, since 2001; *b* 1 June 1949; *s* of late Ernest Roy Clark and Hazel Lucy Clark (*née* Lucas). *Educ:* Royal Grammar Sch., High Wycombe; Univ. of Birmingham (BA); Free Univ. of West Berlin; Univ. of Bremen (DrPhil). Res. Officer, LSE, 1976–77; Res. Fellow, Groupe de Sociologie du Travail, Univ. of Paris VII, 1977–78; University of Southampton: Lectr, 1978–86; Sen. Lectr. 1986–90; Dean of Soc. Scis. 1994–97; Dir, New College, 1998; Professorial Res. Fellow, Univ. of Warwick, 1991–93. Mem., ACAS Nat. Panel of Trade Disputes Arbitrators, 1990–. Dir, Bournemouth SO, 2000–. FRSA 2000. *Publications:* (with R. Lewis) Labour Law and Politics in the Weimar Republic, 1981; (with Lord Wedderburn and R. Lewis) Labour Law and Industrial Relations: building on Kahn-Freund, 1983; (jtly) The Process of Technological Change, 1988; (with I. McLoughlin) Technological Change at Work, 1988, 2nd edn 1994; (with R. Lewis) Employment Rights, Industrial Tribunals and Arbitration: the case for alternative dispute resolution, 1993; Human Resource Management and Technical Change, 1993; (with C. Barnard and R. Lewis) The Exercise of Individual Employment Rights in the Member States of the European Community, 1995; Managing Innovation and Change, 1995; James S Coleman, 1996. *Recreations:* classical music, opera, travel. *Address:* 16 Holt Road, Fitzhugh, Southampton, Hants SO15 2HU.

CLARK, Dame June; *see* Clark, Dame M. J.

CLARK, Keith; International General Counsel, and Member, European Executive Committee, Morgan Stanley, since 2002; *b* 25 Oct. 1944; *s* of Douglas William Clark and Evelyn Lucy (*née* Longlands); *m* 1974, Linda Sue Woodger; one *s* one *d. Educ:* Chichester High Sch. for Boys; St Catherine's Coll., Oxford (MA Jurisprudence; BCL). Joined Clifford Chance, 1971; Partner, 1976; Sen. Partner, 1993; Chm., 2000–02. *Publications:* (jtly) Syndicated Lending Practice Documentation, 1993; articles on banking and financial topics. *Recreations:* walking, ballet, theatre, novels. *Address:* 5 Alwyne Place, Canonbury, N1 2NL.

CLARK, Ven. Kenneth James, DSC 1944; Archdeacon of Swindon, 1982–92; *b* 31 May 1922; *er s* of Francis James Clark and Winifred Adelaide Clark (*née* Martin); *m* 1948, Elisabeth Mary Monica Helen Huggett; three *s* three *d. Educ:* Watford Grammar School; St Catherine's Coll., Oxford (MA); Cuddesdon Theological Coll. Midshipman RN, 1940; Lieutenant RN, 1942; served in submarines, 1942–46. Baptist Minister, Forest Row, Sussex, 1950–52; Curate of Brinkworth, 1952–53; Curate of Cricklade with Latton, 1953–56; Priest-in-Charge, then Vicar (1959), of Holy Cross, Inns Court, Bristol, 1956–61; Vicar: Westbury-on-Trym, 1961–72; St Mary Redcliffe, Bristol, 1972–82; Hon. Canon of Bristol Cathedral, 1974. Member, Gen. Synod of C of E, 1980–92. *Recreations:* music, travel, gardening. *Address:* 6 Saxon Road, Harnham, Salisbury, Wilts SP2 8JZ. *T:* (01722) 421410.

CLARK, Luther Johnson, (L. John Clark); Founding Partner, Compass Partners International LLC Ltd, since 1997; *b* 27 Aug. 1941; *s* of E. T. Clark and Mary Opal Clark; *m* 1965, Judith Dooley; one *s* one *d. Educ:* Wharton Sch. of Finance & Commerce, Univ. of Pennsylvania (BS Econs/Finance 1963); Wharton Graduate Sch. of Finance & Commerce (MBA Marketing/Finance 1968). Captain, US Marine Corps, 1963–66. Singer Co.: joined 1968; Corp. Vice-Pres., 1978–81; Pres. and Chief Exec., Europe, Africa and Middle East, 1982–85; Exec. Vice-Pres., V. F. Corp., 1986–87; Chm. and Chief Exec., Coremark Internat. Inc., 1988–91; Chief Exec. and Man. Dir, BET PLC, 1991–96. Non-exec. Director: Yale and Nutone, 1988–91; Rolls-Royce PLC, 1993–96; Kvaerner ASA, 1997–. Overseer, Wharton Sch., 1989–; Trustee, Univ. of Pennsylvania, 1996–.

CLARK, Dr Lynda Margaret; QC (Scot.) 1989; MP (Lab) Edinburgh Pentlands, since 1997; Advocate General for Scotland, since 1999; *b* 26 Feb. 1949. *Educ:* St Andrews Univ. (LLB Hons); Edinburgh Univ. (PhD). Lectr, Univ. of Dundee, 1973–76; admitted Advocate, Scots Bar, 1977; called to the English Bar, Inner Temple, 1988, Bencher, 2000. Contested (Lab) Fife North East, 1992. Mem. Court, Edinburgh Univ., 1995–97. *Address:* House of Commons, SW1A 0AA; (office) Dover House, Whitehall, SW1A 2AU. *T:* (020) 7270 6720.

CLARK, Malcolm, CB 1990; Inspector General, Insolvency Service, Department of Trade and Industry, 1984–89, retired; *b* 13 Feb. 1931; *s* of late Percy Clark and Gladys Helena Clark; *m* 1956, Beryl Patricia Dale; two *s. Educ:* Wheelwright Grammar Sch., Dewsbury, Yorks. FCCA 1980. Department of Trade and Industry Insolvency Service: Examiner, 1953–62; Sen. Examiner, 1962–66; Asst Official Receiver, Rochester, 1966–70; Official Receiver, Lytham St Annes, 1970–79; Principal Inspector of Official Receivers, 1979–81; Dep. Inspector Gen., 1981–84. *Recreations:* theatre, gardening, reading. *Address:* Teak Cottage, 37 The Avenue, Poole, Dorset BH13 6LJ.

CLARK, Rev. Canon Malcolm Aiken; Dean, Collegiate Church of St Vincent since 1982, Dean of Edinburgh, 1983–85, Hon. Canon, since 1985; *b* 3 Oct. 1905; *s* of Hugh Aiken Clark, MB, CM, and Agnes Roberta Douglas Baxter; *m* 1936, Margherita Felicinna Columba Gannaway (*d* 1973); two *s* one *d. Educ:* Drax, Yorks; High School of Glasgow; Lichfield Theological College. Deacon 1934, priest 1935, Glasgow; Curate, St John's, Greenock; Rector, All Saints, Lockerbie, 1938–49, with All Saints, Langholm, 1939–42. Chaplain, RAFVR, 1942–46. Priest-in-charge, St Mary's, Dalkeith, 1949–56; Rector, Good Shepherd, Murrayfield, 1956–77; retired; warrant to officiate, dio. Edinburgh. Chaplain of St Vincent, Edinburgh, Order of St Lazarus of Jerusalem, 1977–99; Canon 1980, Dean 1982; also Canon of Cathedral Church of St Mary, Edinburgh and Dean, 1983. FSA (Scot.) 1979. *Address:* 12 St Vincent Street, Edinburgh EH3 6SH. *T:* (0131) 557 3662.

CLARK, Dr Malcolm Brian, OBE 2001; Chairman, Grant & Cutler, since 2000; Director, Queen Elizabeth's Foundation for Disabled People, 1980-2001; *b* 17 May 1934; *s* of Herbert Clark and Doris May Clark (*née* Waples); *m* 1st, 1960, Jennifer Anne Thonger (*d* 1985); one *s* one *d*; 2nd, 1988, Lorna Stephanie Killick (marr. diss. 1995). *Educ:* Univ. of Birmingham (BSc Chem. Engrg; PhD 1958). Chemical Engineer: Albright & Wilson, 1958-62; A. Boake Roberts, 1962-66; Marketing Manager, Bush Boake Allen, 1966-68; Albright & Wilson: Res. Manager, 1968–70; Personnel Dir, 1970–72; Personnel and Prodn Dir, 1972–74; Man. Dir, Bush Boake Allen, 1975-80. *Recreations:* books, walking, theatre, music, wine. *Address:* 2 Howard Close, Leatherhead, Surrey KT22 8PH.

CLARK, Dame (Margaret) June, DBE 1995; FRCN; Professor of Community Nursing, University of Wales, Swansea, since 1997; *b* 31 May 1941; *d* of Ernest Harold Hickery and Marion Louise Hickery (*née* Walters); *m* 1966, Roger Michael Geoffrey Clark; one *s* one *d. Educ:* Pontywaun Grammar Sch.; University College London (BA Hons Classics 1962); University College Hosp. (SRN 1965); Royal College of Nursing (RHV 1967); Univ. of Reading (MPhil 1972); PhD South Bank Polytechnic 1985. FRCN 1982. Nurse, 1965; health visitor, 1967; clinical nursing appts, combined with teaching and research while bringing up a family; resumed as health visitor, Berks, 1981; Senior Nurse (Research), 1983; Health Authority posts: Special Projects Co-ordinator, Lewisham and N Southwark, 1985–86; Dir, Community Nursing Services, W Lambeth, 1986–88; Chief Nursing Adviser, Harrow, 1988–90; Prof. of Nursing, Middlesex Poly., later Univ., 1990–96. Mem., Royal Commn on Long Term Care of the Elderly, 1997–98. Pres., RCN, 1990–94. Council of Europe Fellow, 1981; Churchill Fellow, 1996. *Publications:* A Family Visitor, 1973; (with R. Hiller) Community Care, 1975; What Do Health Visitors Do?, 1981; (with S. Parsonage) Infant Feeding and Family Nutrition, 1981; (with J. Henderson) Community Health, 1983; (with M. Baly) District Nursing, 1981; many papers in med. and nursing jls. *Recreation:* travel. *Address:* School of Health Science, University of Wales, Swansea, Singleton Park, Swansea SA2 8PP.

CLARK, Maxwell Robert Guthrie Stewart S.; *see* Stafford-Clark.

CLARK, Dr Michael; *b* 8 Aug. 1935; *s* of late Mervyn Clark and of Sybilla Norma Clark (*née* Winscott); *m* 1958, Valerie Ethel, *d* of C. S. Harbord; one *s* one *d. Educ:* King Edward VI Grammar School, East Retford; King's College London (BSc (1st cl. Hons) Chemistry, 1956; FKC 1987); Univ. of Minnesota (Fulbright Scholar, 1956–57); St John's College, Cambridge (PhD 1960). FRSC 1988. Research Scientist, later Factory Manager, ICI, 1960–66; Smith's Industries Ltd, 1966–69; PA International Management Consultants, 1969–73; Marketing Manager, St Regis Paper Co., 1973–78; Dir, Courtenay Stewart International, 1978–81; PA International Management Consultants, 1981–93 (Trustee, 1994–2000). Treasurer, 1975–78, Chm., 1980–83, Cambs Cons. Assoc.; Cons. Eastern Area Exec., 1980–83. Contested (C) Ilkeston, 1979; MP (C) Rochford, 1983–97, Rayleigh, 1997–2001. Chm., Sci. and Technol. Select Cttee, 1997–2001; Member: Select Cttee for Energy, 1983–92 (Chm., 1989–92); Select Cttee on Trade and Industry, 1992–94; Council, Parly IT Cttee, 1984–90; Speaker's Panel of Chairmen, 1997–2001; Chairman: All Party Gp for the Chemical Industry, 1994–97 (Hon. Sec. 1985–90; Vice-Chm., 1990–94); Parly Gp for Energy Studies, 1992–97; Bd, Parly Office of Sci. and Technol., 1993–97; Parly British-Russian Gp., 1994–2001; Parly British-Venezuelan Gp, 1995–2001; Hon. Secretary: Parly and Scientific Cttee, 1985–88; Parly Anglo-Nepalese Soc., 1985–90; Parly Anglo-Malaŵi Gp, 1987–90; Parly Space Cttee, 1989–91; Cons. Backbench Energy Cttee, 1986–87 (Vice-Chm., 1987–90); Mem., 1922 Exec. Cttee, 1997–2001; Chm., IPU, 1990–93 (Mem. Exec., 1987–94). Mem., Adv. Panel, Conservation Foundn, 1995–. Mem., Adv. Bd, Fulbright Commn, 1995–. Governor, Melbourn Village Coll., 1974–83 (Chm., 1977–80). *Publication:* The History of Rochford Hall, 1990. *Recreations:* gardening, golf, grandchildren. *Address:* 3 The Old Steam Laundry, Higher Wharf, Bude, Cornwall EX23 8LW. *T:* (01702) 542042. *Clubs:* Rochford Conservative; Rayleigh Conservative.

CLARK, Michael William, CBE 1977; DL; landowner; Deputy Chairman and Deputy Chief Executive, Plessey Co. plc, 1970–87; *b* 7 May 1927; *yr s* of late Sir Allen Clark and late Jocelyn Anina Maria Louise Clark (*née* Emerson Culverhouse); *m* 1st, 1955, Shirley (*née* MacPhadyen) (*d* 1974); two *s* one *d* (and one *d* decd); 2nd, 1985, Virginia, Marchioness Camden. *Educ:* Harrow. 1st Foot Guards, Subaltern, 1945–48. Plessey Co. plc, 1950–87: founded and built Electronics Div., 1951; Main Bd Dir, 1953; Dir, Corporate Planning, 1965, Man. Dir, Telecommunications Gp, 1967; Chief. Exec., Defence Electronics, 1970–87. Member: Electronics EDC, 1975–80; Council, Inst. of Dirs; Nat. Electronics Council; Ct of Univ. of Essex. President: Essex Br., SSAFA, 1988–99; Essex Br., Grenadier Guards Assoc., 1988–99. CompIEE, 1964; CompIERE, 1965. FIMgt (FBIM 1974). DL Essex, 1988, High Sheriff, 1991–92. *Recreations:* fishing, shooting, forestry. *Address:* Braxted Park, Witham, Essex CM8 3EN. *Clubs:* Boodle's, Pratt's.

See also Sir J. A. Clark.

CLARK, Oswald William Hugh, CBE 1978; Assistant Director-General, Greater London Council, 1973–79; *b* 26 Nov. 1917; *s* of late Rev. Hugh M. A. Clark and Mabel Bessie Clark (*née* Dance); *m* 1966, Diana Mary (*née* Hine); one *d. Educ:* Rutlish Sch., Merton; Univ. of London (BA; BD Hons); Univ. of Wales (LLM). Local Govt Official, LCC (later GLC), 1937–79. Served War, HM Forces, 1940–46: Major, 2nd Derbyshire Yeo., Eighth Army, Middle East, NW Europe. Member: Church Assembly (later General Synod), 1948–90; Standing and Legislative Cttees, 1950–90; Standing Orders Cttee (Chm.), 1950–90; Crown Appts Commn, 1987–90; Chm., House of Laity, 1979–85 (Vice-Chm., 1970–79); a Church Commissioner, 1958–88 (Mem. Bd of Governors, 1966–68, 1969–73, 1977–88); a Reader, 1951–96. Vice-Pres., Corp. of Church House, 1981–98. Principal, Soc. of the Faith, 1987–92. Parish Clerk, 1992–, and Churchwarden, 1990–2000, St Andrew by the Wardrobe. Co. of Parish Clerks, 1986– (Master, 1997–98); Liveryman, Upholders' Co., 1999–. Life Fellow, Guild of Guide Lectrs, 1982. *Recreations:* London's history and development, Goss china, heraldry. *Address:* 5 Seaview Road,

Highcliffe, Christchurch, Dorset BH23 5QJ. *T:* (01425) 280823. *Clubs:* Cavalry and Guards, Pratt's.

CLARK, Paul Anthony Mason; a District Judge (Magistrates' Courts) (formerly Metropolitan Stipendiary Magistrate), since 1996; *b* 19 Aug. 1952; *s* of Thomas James, (Tony), Clark and Winifred Mary Clark (*née* Mason); *m* 1979, Jane Ann Knapp; one *s* two *d. Educ:* John Leggott GS, Scunthorpe; Jesus Coll., Oxford (MA). Called to the Bar, Middle Temple, 1975 (Astbury Schol.); in practice, 1975–96. Chm., Inner London Youth Courts, 1997–. Mem., Family Proceedings Court, 1999–. Mem., Council of Dist Judges for England and Wales, 2001–. Lectr, Gen. Council of the Bar, 1998. Vice Pres., David Isaacs Fund, 1998–. *Recreations:* cricket, painting, gardening, book and china collecting. *Address:* Principal Chief Clerk's Office, Secretariat Department, 65 Romney Street, SW1P 3RD.

CLARK, Air Vice-Marshal Paul Derek, CB 1993; CEng, FRAeS; Vice President, C-130 AMP Program, BAE SYSTEMS Aerospace Sector, Austin, Texas, since 2000; *b* 19 March 1939; *s* of John Hayes Clark and Kathleen Clark; *m* 1963, Mary Elizabeth Morgan; two *d. Educ:* Orange Hill Grammar Sch.; RAF Henlow Technical Coll. BA Open Univ., 1985. CEng 1970; FRAeS 1987. Commnd Engr Br., RAF, 1961; RAF Wittering, 1961–63, Topcliffe, 1963, Wittering, 1964–69, Cranwell, 1969–70; RAF Staff Coll., Bracknell, 1971; HQ Logistics Comd, USAF, 1972–74; HQ Strike Comd, 1974–76; Nat. Defence Coll., 1977; OC Engrg Wing, RAF Leuchars, 1977–79; HQ No 1 Gp, RAF Bawtry, 1980–81; Stn Comdr No 30 Maintenance Unit, RAF Sealand, 1981–83; RCDS, 1984; MoD, 1985–86; Directorate Electronics Radar Air, MoD (PE), 1986–87; Dir, European Helicopter 101 Project, MoD (PE), 1987–89; Comdt RAF Signals Engrg Estabt, 1990–91; AO, Engrg and Supply, HQ Strike Comd, 1991–93; retd, 1994; Dir of Mil. Support, Support Div., GEC–Marconi Avionics, 1994–95; RMPA Prog. Dir, GEC-Marconi Aerospace Systems Ltd, 1995–97; Pres. and CEO, GEC-Marconi Avionics Inc., Atlanta, 1997–98; Vice Pres., GEC Account Dir for Lockheed Martin, 1998–99. *Recreations:* theatre, art, high handicap golfing. *Club:* Royal Air Force.
See also Prof. T. J. H. Clark.

CLARK, Paul Gordon; MP (Lab) Gillingham, since 1997; *b* 29 April 1957; *s* of Gordon Thomas Clark and Sheila Gladys Clark; *m* 1980, Julie Hendrick; one *s* one *d. Educ:* Gillingham Grammar Sch.; Keele Univ. (BA Hons 1980; Sec., Students' Union, 1977–78); Univ. of Derby (DMS 1996). Res. Assistant to Pres., then Educn Adminr, AEU, 1980–86; Admin. Asst Sec., then Manager, Nat. Educn Centre, TUC, 1986–97. Mem., Gillingham BC, 1982–90 (Leader, Lab. Gp, 1989–90). Contested (Lab) Gillingham, 1992. PPS, LCD, 1999–2001, to Minister for Housing and Planning, 2001–. Mem. Bd, Thames Gateway Kent Partnership, 2000–. *Address:* House of Commons, SW1A 0AA.

CLARK, Paul Nicholas Rowntree; His Honour Judge Paul Clark; a Circuit Judge, since 1985; *b* 17 Aug. 1940; *s* of late Henry Rowntree Clark and Gwendoline Victoria Clark; *m* 1st, 1967, Diana Barbara Bishop (marr. diss.); two *s* one *d*; 2nd, 1997, Jacqueline Davies, *qv. Educ:* Bristol Grammar Sch.; New Coll., Oxford (Open Schol.; MA (Lit. Hum.)). Called to the Bar, Middle Temple, 1966 (Harmsworth Schol.), Bencher 1982; in practice on Midland and Oxford (formerly Oxford) Circuit, 1966–85; a Recorder, 1981–85. Pres., Council of HM Circuit Judges, 1998. Chm., Friends of the Ashmolean Mus., 1996–. Pres., Old Bristolians' Soc., 1999–2000. *Address:* 2 Harcourt Buildings, Temple, EC4Y 9DB. *T:* (020) 7353 6961. *Club:* Garrick.

CLARK, Peter Charles Lister; His Honour Judge Peter Clark; a Circuit Judge, since 1995; *b* 16 June 1948; *s* of Charles Lister Clark and Mary Isobel Clark; *m* 1973, Josephine Neilson Hogg; one *s* one *d. Educ:* Repton Sch.; Southampton Univ. (LLB). Called to the Bar, Gray's Inn, 1970; in practice at the Bar, 1971–95; a Recorder, Midland and Oxford Circuit, 1994–95. *Recreations:* various. *Address:* Devereux Chambers, Devereux Court, WC2R 3JJ. *T:* (020) 7353 7534. *Club:* Reform.

CLARK, Petula, (Sally Olwen), CBE 1998; singer, actress; *b* 15 Nov. 1932; *d* of Leslie Clark; *m* 1961, Claude Wolff; one *s* two *d*. Own BBC radio series, Pet's Parlour, 1943; early British films include: Medal for the General, 1944; I Know Where I'm Going, 1945; Here Come the Huggetts, 1948; Dance Hall, 1950; White Corridors, 1951; The Card, 1951; Made in Heaven, 1952; The Runaway Bus, 1953; That Woman Opposite, 1957. Began career as singer in France, 1959. Top female vocalist, France, 1962; Bravos du Music Hall award for outstanding woman in show business, France, 1965; Grammy awards for records Downtown and I Know A Place. Numerous concert and television appearances in Europe and USA including her own BBC TV series; world concert tour, 1997. *Films:* Finian's Rainbow, 1968; Goodbye Mr Chips, 1969; Second to the Right and Straight on till Morning, 1982; *musicals:* The Sound of Music, Apollo Victoria, 1981; (also composer and creator) Someone Like You, Strand, 1990; Blood Brothers, NY, 1993, nat. tour, 1994–95; Sunset Boulevard, Adelphi, 1995, 1996, NY, 1998, nat. US tour, 1998–2000. *Address:* c/o John Ashby, PO Box 288, Woking, Surrey GU22 0YN.

CLARK, Ramsey; lawyer in private practice, New York City, since 1969; *b* Dallas, Texas, 18 Dec. 1927; *s* of late Thomas Clark, and of Mary Ramsey; *m* 1949, Georgia Welch, Corpus Christi, Texas; one *s* one *d. Educ:* Public Schs, Dallas, Los Angeles, Washington; Univ. of Texas (BA); Univ. of Chicago (MA, JD). US Marine Corps, 1945–46. Engaged private practice of law, Dallas, 1951–61; Asst Attorney Gen., Dept of Justice, 1961–65; Dep. Attorney Gen., 1965–67, Attorney Gen., 1967–69. *Address:* 37 West 12th Street, New York, NY 10011–8503, USA.

CLARK, Richard David; Clerk to Devon and Cornwall Police Authority, 1993–97 (Associate Clerk, 1989–93); *b* 2 Sept. 1934; *s* of David and Enid Clark; *m* 1958, Pamela Mary (*née* Burgess); two *d. Educ:* Keele Univ. (BA, DipEd); Univ. de Paris, Sorbonne. Teaching, Woodberry Down Comprehensive School, 1957–61; Education Admin., Herts CC, 1961–69; Asst Educn Officer, Lancs CC, 1969–71; Second Dep. County Educn Officer, Hants CC, 1972–76; Chief Educn Officer, Glos CC, 1976–83; County Educn Officer, Hants CC, 1983–88; Chief Exec., and Clerk to the Lieutenancy, Devon CC, 1989–95. Dir, Devon and Cornwall TEC, 1989–95. Mem., Adv. Cttee on Supply and Educn of Teachers. Adviser to: Burnham Cttee, 1982–87; Educn Cttee, ACC, 1982–89, 1990–95; Council of Local Educn Authorities, 1983–89. Governor: Plymouth Univ., 1995–2000; Sidmouth Coll., 1995–2000. Fellow Commoner, Churchill Coll., Cambridge, 1983; Vis. Fellow, Southampton Univ., 1986–88; Hon. Fellow, Exeter Univ., 1992–. FRSA 1977. *Recreations:* books, gardening, wood turning, croquet. *Address:* Glendale House, Rannoch Road, Crowborough, East Sussex TN6 1RB. *T:* (01892) 663453.

CLARK, Sir Robert (Anthony), Kt 1976; DSC 1944; Chairman, RP & C International (formerly Rauscher Pierce & Clark), since 1992; *b* 6 Jan. 1924; *yr s* of John Clark and Gladys Clark (*née* Dyer); *m* 1949, Andolyn Marjorie Lewis; two *s* one *d. Educ:* Highgate Sch.; King's Coll., Cambridge. Served War, Royal Navy, 1942–46. Partner with Slaughter and May, Solicitors, 1953–61; Director: Alfred McAlpine plc (formerly Marchwiel plc), 1957–96; Hill Samuel Bank Ltd, merchant bankers (formerly Philip Hill, Higginson, Erlangers Ltd, then Hill Samuel & Co. Ltd), 1961–91 (Chm., 1974–87); Bank of England, 1976–85; Eagle Star Holdings Ltd, 1976–87; BL, subseq. Rover Gp plc, 1977–88; Shell Transport and Trading Co., plc, 1982–94; SmithKline Beecham plc, 1987–95 (Vice-Chm.); Vodafone Group plc (formerly Racal Telecom PLC), 1988–98; Chairman: Hill Samuel Gp plc, 1980–88 (Chief Exec., 1976–80); IMI plc, 1981–89; Marley plc, 1985–89; Mirror Group (formerly Mirror Group Newspapers) plc, 1992–98; Lambert Fenchurch Gp (formerly Lowndes Lambert Group Hldgs) plc, 1995–98 (Dep. Chm., 1992–95); Dep. Chm., TSB Gp, 1989–91 (Dir, 1987–91). Chairman: Industrial Development Adv. Bd, 1973–80; Review Body on Doctors' and Dentists' Remuneration, 1979–86; Council, Charing Cross and Westminster Med. Sch., 1982–96; Dir, ENO, 1983–87. Hon. DSc Cranfield Inst. of Technol., 1982. *Recreations:* reading, music, collecting antiquarian books, the garden at Munstead Wood. *Address:* Munstead Wood, Godalming, Surrey GU7 1UN. *T:* (01483) 417867; RP & C International, 56 Green Street, W1Y 3RH. *T:* (020) 7491 2434, *Fax:* (020) 7491 9081. *Club:* Pratt's.
See also T. N. Clark.

CLARK, Prof. Robert Bernard, DSc, PhD; FIBiol, FRSE; Professor of Zoology, University of Newcastle upon Tyne, 1966–89, now Emeritus; *b* 13 Oct. 1923; *s* of Joseph Lawrence Clark and Dorothy (*née* Halden); *m* 1st, 1956, Mary Eleanor (*née* Laurence) (marr. diss.); 2nd, 1970, Susan Diana (*née* Smith); one *s* one *d. Educ:* St Marylebone Grammar Sch.; Chelsea Polytechnic (BSc London 1944); University Coll., Exeter (BSc 1950); Univ. of Glasgow (PhD 1956); DSc London 1965. FIBiol 1966, FLS 1969, FRSE 1970. Asst Experimental Officer, DSIR Road Research Laboratory, 1944; Asst to Prof. of Zoology, Univ. of Glasgow, 1950; Asst Prof., Univ. of California (Berkeley), 1953; Lectr in Zoology, Univ. of Bristol, 1956; Head of Dept of Zoology and Dir of Dove Marine Laboratory, Univ. of Newcastle upon Tyne, 1966–77, Dir of Research Unit on Rehabilitation of Oiled Seabirds, 1967–76; Dir of NERC Research Unit on Rocky Shore Biology, 1981–87. Member: NERC, 1971–77 and 1983–86; Royal Commn on Environmental Pollution, 1979–83; Adv. Cttee on Pesticides, 1986–90; Mem. Council, Nature Conservancy, 1975. *Publications:* Neurosecretion (ed jtly), 1962; Dynamics in Metazoan Evolution, 1964, corrected repr. 1967; Practical Course in Experimental Zoology, 1966; (jtly) Invertebrate Panorama, 1971; (jtly) Synopsis of Animal Classification, 1971; (ed jtly) Essays in Hydrobiology, 1972; (ed) The Long-Term Effects of Oil Pollution on Marine Populations, Communities and Ecosystems, 1982; Marine Pollution, 1986, 5th edn 2001; The Waters Around the British Isles: their conflicting uses, 1987; (ed jtly) Environmental Effects of North Sea Oil and Gas Development, 1987; Founder, 1968, and ed, Marine Pollution Bulletin; numerous papers in learned jls. *Recreations:* architecture, music, unambitious gardening, cooking. *Address:* Department of Marine Sciences, Ridley Building, University of Newcastle upon Tyne, Newcastle upon Tyne NE1 7RU. *T:* (0191) 222 6661; Highbury House, Highbury, Newcastle upon Tyne NE2 3LN. *T:* (0191) 281 4672.

CLARK, Robert Joseph, CBE 2000; Circuit Administrator, South Eastern Circuit, Lord Chancellor's Department, 1997–2001; *b* 29 March 1942; *s* of late Edward Clark and Elsie Clark (*née* Bush); *m* 1970, Elke Agnes, *d* of late Hans Schmidt and Herma Schmidt; two *d. Educ:* state schools in London. Lord Chancellor's Department: Official Solicitor's Dept, 1960–70; Nat. Industrial Relns Court, 1970–74; HQ, 1974–77; Trng Centre, 1977–79; Chief Clerk, Court of Protection, 1979–83; S Eastern Circuit Office, 1983–88; Head: Civil Business Div., 1988–91; Judicial Appointments Div. II, 1991–93; Circuit Administrator, Western Circuit, 1993–97. *Recreations:* theatre, walking. *Address:* 36 Kayemoor Road, Sutton, Surrey SM2 5HT.

CLARK, Prof. Robin Jon Hawes, FRS 1990; Sir William Ramsay Professor of Chemistry, University College London, since 1989; *b* 16 Feb. 1935; *s* of Reginald Hawes Clark, JP, BCom and Marjorie Alice Clark (*née* Thomas); *m* 1964, Beatrice Rawdin Brown, JP; one *s* one *d. Educ:* Christ's Coll., NZ; Canterbury University Coll., Univ. of NZ (BSc 1956; MSc (1st cl. hons) 1958); University Coll. London (British Titan Products Scholar and Fellow; PhD 1961); DSc London 1969. FRSC 1969. University College London: Asst Lectr in Chemistry, 1962; Lectr 1963–71; Reader 1972–81; Prof., 1982–89; Dean of Faculty of Science, 1988–89; Hd, Dept of Chemistry, 1989–99; Mem. Council, 1991–94; Fellow, 1992. Mem., Senate and Academic Council, Univ. of London, 1988–93. Visiting Professor: Columbia, 1965; Padua, 1967; Western Ontario, 1968; Texas A&M, 1978; Bern, 1979; Fribourg, 1979; Auckland, 1981; Odense, 1983; Sydney, 1985; Bordeaux, 1988; Pretoria, 1991; Würzburg, 1996; Indiana, 1998; Thessaloniki, 1999; Lectures: Kresge-Hooker, Wayne State, 1965; John van Geuns, Amsterdam, 1979; Carman, SA Chemical Inst., 1994; Moissan, Paris, 1998; Leermakers, Wesleyan Univ., 2000; Hassel, Oslo, 2000. Mem. Council, Royal Soc., 1993–94; Royal Society of Chemistry: Mem., Dalton Divl Council, 1985–88, Vice-Pres., 1988–90; Lectures: Tilden, 1983–84; Nyholm, 1989–90; Thomas Graham, 1991; Harry Hallam, 1993, 2000; UK-Canada Rutherford, Royal Soc., 2000. Member: SRC Inorganic Chem. Panel, 1977–80; SERC Post-doctoral Fellowships Cttee, 1983; SERC Inorganic Chem. Sub-Cttee, 1993–94; Chairman: XI Internat. Conf. on Raman Spectroscopy, London, 1988; Steering Cttee, Internat. Confs on Raman Spectroscopy, 1990–92 (Mem., 1988–). Mem. Council, Royal Instn of GB, 1996– (Vice-Pres., 1997–98; Sec., 1998–). Trustee, Ramsay Meml Fellowships Trust, 1993– (Chm. Adv. Council, 1989–). MAE 1990; FRSA 1992. Hon. FRSNZ, 1989. Hon. DSc Canterbury, 2001. Joannes Marcus Marci Medal, Czech Spectroscopy Soc., 1998. *Publications:* The Chemistry of Titanium and Vanadium, 1968; (jtly) The Chemistry of Titanium, Zirconium and Hafnium, 1973; (jtly) The Chemistry of Vanadium, Niobium and Tantalum, 1973; (ed jtly) Advances in Spectroscopy, vols 1–26, 1975–98; (ed jtly) Raman Spectroscopy, 1988; (ed) nine monographs on Inorganic Chemistry, 1978–; over 430 contribs to learned jls, in fields of transition metal chem. and spectroscopy. *Recreations:* golf, long distance walking, travel, bridge, music, theatre, wine. *Address:* Christopher Ingold Laboratories, University College London, 20 Gordon Street, WC1H 0AJ. *T:* (020) 7679 7457, *Fax:* (020) 7679 7463; 3a Loom Lane, Radlett, Herts WD7 8AA. *T:* (01923) 857899. *Clubs:* Athenæum, Porters Park Golf (Radlett).

CLARK, Prof. Ronald George, FRCSE, FRCS; Professor of Surgery, 1972–93, now Emeritus, and Pro-Vice-Chancellor, 1988–93, University of Sheffield; Consultant Surgeon: Northern General Hospital, 1966–93; Royal Hallamshire Hospital, since 1966; *b* 9 Aug. 1928; *s* of late George Clark and of Gladys Clark; *m* 1960, Tamar Welsh Harvie; two *d. Educ:* Aberdeen Acad.; Univ. of Aberdeen (MB, ChB); MD Sheffield 1996. FRCSE 1960; FRCS 1980. House appts, Aberdeen Royal Infirmary, 1956–57; Registrar, Western Infirmary, Glasgow, 1958–60; Surgical Res. Fellow, Harvard, USA, 1960–61; Lectr in Surgery, Univ. of Glasgow, 1961–65; Sheffield University: Sen. Lectr in Surgery, 1966–72; Dean, Faculty of Medicine and Dentistry, 1982–85. Examiner, Universities of: Aberdeen, Glasgow, Edinburgh, Liverpool, Newcastle, Leicester, London, Southampton, Malta, Ibadan, Jos. Chm., European Soc. for Parenteral and Enteral Nutrition, 1982–; Council Mem., Nutrition Soc., 1982–85; Scientific Governor, British Nutrition Foundn, 1982–; Member: GMC, 1983–93; GDC, 1990–; Assoc. of Surgeons of GB and Ireland, 1968–; Surgical Res. Soc., 1969–. Mem., Editorial Bd, Scottish Medical Jl, 1962–65; Editor-in-Chief, Clinical Nutrition, 1980–82. *Publications:* contribs to books and jls on surgical topics and metabolic aspects of acute disease. *Recreation:* golf. *Address:* Brookline, 15 Comerton Place, Drumoig, Leuchars, St Andrews, Fife KY16 0NG. *T:* and *Fax:* (01382) 540058.

CLARK, Sir Terence (Joseph), KBE 1990; CMG 1985; CVO 1978; HM Diplomatic Service, retired; Senior Consultant, MEC, since 1995; *b* 19 June 1934; *s* of Joseph Clark and Mary Clark; *m* 1960, Lieselotte Rosa Marie Müller; two *s* one *d*. *Educ:* Thomas Parmiter's, London. RAF (attached to Sch. of Slavonic Studies, Cambridge), 1953–55; Pilot Officer, RAFVR, 1955. HM Foreign Service, 1955; ME Centre for Arab Studies, 1956–57; Bahrain, 1957–58; Amman, 1958–60; Casablanca, 1961–62; FO, 1962–65; Asst Polit. Agent, Dubai, 1965–68; Belgrade, 1969–71; Hd of Chancery, Muscat, 1972–73; Asst Hd of ME Dept, FCO, 1974–76; Counsellor (Press and Information), Bonn, 1976–79; Chargé d'Affaires, Tripoli, Feb.-March 1981; Counsellor, Belgrade, 1979–82. Dep. Leader, UK Delegn, Conf. on Security and Co-operation in Europe, Madrid, 1982–83; Hd of Information Dept, FCO, 1983–85; Ambassador to Iraq, 1985–89; Ambassador to Oman, 1990–94. Dir, Internat. Crisis Gp Bosnia Project, Sarajevo, 1996. Chm., Anglo-Omani Soc., 1995–. Member: Council, Soc. for Arabian Studies; Exec. Cttee of Mgt, ME Assoc., 1998–. Member: RGS, 1991; RSAA, 1993; RIIA, 1995. Commander's Cross, Order of Merit (Fed. Republic of Germany), 1978. *Publications:* (jtly) The Saluqi: coursing hound of the East, 1996; articles on Salukis and coursing in magazines. *Recreations:* Salukis, walking. *Address:* 29 Westleigh Avenue, SW15 6RQ. *Club:* Hurlingham.

CLARK, Thomas Alastair; Executive Director, Bank of England, since 1997; *b* 27 Feb. 1949; *s* of late Andrew Evans Clark and of Freda (*née* Seal); *m* 1986, Shirley Anne Barker; one *s* (one *d* decd). *Educ:* Stockport Grammar Sch.; Emmanuel Coll., Cambridge (MA Maths); London Sch. of Econs (MSc Econs). Bank of England, 1971–: PA to Dep. Governor, 1980–81; UK Alternate Exec. Dir, IMF, 1983–85; UK Alternate Dir, EIB, 1986–88; Head: Financial Markets and Instns Div., 1987–93; European Div., 1993–94; Dep. Dir, 1994–97. Director: International Financial Services, London (formerly British Invisibles), 1997–; Crestco, 1998–. *Recreations:* joinery, hill-walking. *Address:* Bank of England, Threadneedle Street, EC2R 8AH. *T:* (020) 7601 4444.

CLARK, Sir Thomas (Edwin), Kt 1986; retired director; farming since 1986; *b* 6 Aug. 1916; *s* of Thomas Edwin and Margaret Clark; *m* 1st, 1938, Joan Mary Hodgson (marr. diss. 1954); one *s* two *d* (and one *d* decd); 2nd, 1954, Josephine Mary Buckley (*d* 1962); one *s* two *d*; 3rd, 1963, Patricia Mary France; two *s* one *d*. *Educ:* King's College, Auckland. General labourer, Amalgamated Brick and Pipe Co., 1932; Asst Factory Manager, 1937; Associate Director, 1939; Manager, R & D, 1938; Gen. Manager, 1942; Director and Jt Gen. Manager, 1946 (with brother M. M. Clark); Jt Man. Dir, 1954; company name changed to Ceramco, 1964; Man. Dir, 1972, retired 1984. Chm., West Auckland Hospice Trust. *Recreations:* yachting, gardening. *Address:* Aotea Farms, South Kaipara Heads, RDI Helensville, New Zealand. *T:* (9) 4202854. *Clubs:* Auckland; Royal NZ Yacht Squadron, Titirangi Golf, Helensville Golf.

CLARK, Prof. Timothy John Hayes, FRCP; Professor of Pulmonary Medicine, Imperial College School of Medicine at the National Heart and Lung Institute, since 1990; Pro-Rector and Provost, Imperial College at Wye, since 2000; *b* 18 Oct. 1935; *s* of John and Kathleen Clark; *m* 1961, Elizabeth Ann Day; two *s* two *d*. *Educ:* Christ's Hospital; Guy's Hospital Medical Sch. BSc 1958; MB BS (Hons) 1961, MD 1967 London. FRCP 1973 (LRCP 1960, MRCP 1962); MRCS 1960. Fellow, Johns Hopkins Hosp., Baltimore USA, 1963; Registrar, Hammersmith Hosp., 1964; Lecturer and Sen. Lectr, Guy's Hospital Med. Sch., 1966; Consultant Physician: Guy's Hosp., 1968–90; Royal Brompton Hosp., 1970–98; Prof. of Thoracic Med., Guy's Hosp. Med. Sch., later UMDS, 1977–89; Dean: Guy's Hosp., 1984–89; UMDS, 1986–89; Pro-Vice-Chancellor for Medicine and Dentistry, Univ. of London, 1987–89; Dean, Nat. Heart and Lung Inst., 1990–97; Pro-Rector (Medicine), 1995–97, (Educnl Qly), 1997–2000, Imperial Coll. Mem., Council of Governors, UMDS, 1982–89, 1990–. Specialist Adviser to Social Services Cttee, 1981 and 1985. Special Trustee, Guy's Hosp., 1982–86. Pres., British Thoracic Soc., 1990–91; Vice-Chairman: Nat. Asthma Campaign, 1993–2000; ICRF, 1997–. *Publications:* (jtly) Asthma, 1977, 4th edn 2000; (ed) Small Airways in Health and Disease, 1979; (jtly) Topical Steroid Treatment of Asthma and Rhinitis, 1980; (ed) Clinical Investigation of Respiratory Disease, 1981; (jtly) Practical Management of Asthma, 1985, 3rd edn 1998; articles in British Medical Jl, Lancet, and other specialist scientific jls. *Recreation:* cricket. *Address:* 8 Lawrence Court, NW7 3QP. *T:* (020) 8959 4411. *Club:* MCC.
See also Air Vice-Marshal P. D. Clark.

CLARK, Timothy Nicholas; Senior Partner, Slaughter and May, since 2001; *b* 9 Jan. 1951; *s* of Sir Robert Anthony Clark, *qv*; *m* 1974, Caroline Moffat; two *s*. *Educ:* Sherborne Sch.; Pembroke Coll., Cambridge (MA Hist.). Admitted solicitor, 1976; with Slaughter and May (Solicitors), 1974–, Partner, 1983–. *Recreations:* flying, football, cricket, theatre. *Address:* Slaughter and May, 35 Basinghall Street, EC2V 5DB. *T:* (020) 7710 3086. *Clubs:* Air Squadron, Lowtonians.

CLARK, Tony; *see* Clark, C. A.

CLARK, Wallace; *see* Clark, H. W. S.

CLARK, Gen. Wesley K., Hon. KBE 2000; Supreme Allied Commander, Europe, 1997–2000; Commander-in-Chief, United States European Command, 1997–2000. *Educ:* US Military Acad.; Univ. of Oxford (Rhodes Schol.). Served in Vietnam (Silver and Bronze Stars); Sen. Military Asst to Gen. Alexander Haig; Head, Nat. Army Trng Centre; Dir of Strategy, Dept of Defense; Mem., American negotiating team, Bosnian peace negotiations, Dayton, Ohio, 1995; Head, US Southern Comd, Panama. *Publication:* Waging Modern War, 2001.

CLARK, William P.; Chief Executive Officer, Clark Co., since 1958; Counsel, McCann Fitzgerald, Dublin, since 1990; Senior Counsel, Clark, Cali and Negranti, since 1997; *b* 23 Oct. 1931; *s* of William and Bernice Clark; *m* 1955, Joan Brauner; three *s* two *d*. *Educ:* Stanford Univ., California; Loyola Law Sch., Los Angeles, California. Admitted to practice of law, California, 1958; Sen. Member, law firm, Clark, Cole & Fairfield, Oxnard, Calif, 1958–67. Served on Cabinet of California, Governor Ronald Reagan, first as Cabinet Secretary, later as Executive Secretary, 1967–69; Judge, Superior Court, State of California, County of San Luis Obispo, 1969–71; Associate Justice: California Court of Appeal, Second District, Los Angeles, 1971–73; California Supreme Court, San Francisco, 1973–81; Dep. Secretary, Dept of State, Washington, DC, 1981–82; Assistant to Pres. of USA for Nat. Security Affairs, 1982–83; Sec. of the Interior, 1983–85. Chairman: Presidential Task Force on Nuclear Weapons Program Management, 1985; USA-ROC (Taiwan) Business Council; Member: Commn on Defense Management, 1985–86; Commn on Integrated Long-Term Strategy, 1987. Counselor, Standing Cttee on Law and Nat. Security, American Bar Assoc. Dir, Mus. of Flying, Santa Monica, California. *Publications:* judicial opinions in California Reports, 9 Cal. 3d through 29 Cal. 3d. *Recreations:* ranching, horseback riding, outdoor sports, flying. *Address:* Clark Company, Clark Building, 1031 Pine Street, Paso Robles, CA 93446, USA. *Clubs:* Bohemia (San Francisco); California Cattleman's Association; Rancheros Visitadores (California).

CLARK HUTCHISON, Sir George Ian; *see* Hutchison.

CLARKE, family name of **Baron Clarke of Hampstead**.

CLARKE, Hon. Lord; Matthew Gerard Clarke; a Senator of the College of Justice in Scotland, since 2000; *s* of Thomas Clarke and Ann (*née* Duddy). *Educ:* Holy Cross High Sch., Hamilton; Univ. of Glasgow (MA; LLB). Solicitor, 1972. Lectr, Dept of Scots Law, Edinburgh Univ., 1972–78; admitted to Faculty of Advocates, 1978; Standing Junior Counsel to Scottish Home and Health Dept, 1983–89; QC (Scot.) 1989; a Judge of the Courts of Appeal of Jersey and Guernsey, 1995–2000. Member: Consumer Credit Licensing Appeal Tribunal, 1976–2000; Estate Agents Tribunals, 1980–2000; Trademarks Tribunal, 1995–2000; Chm. (part-time), Industrial Tribunals, 1987–2000. Leader, UK Delegn, Council of the Bars and Laws Socs of EC, 1992–96 (Mem., 1989–99). British Council: Mem., Scottish Cttee, 2001–; Chm., Scottish Law Cttee, 2001. Hon. Fellow, Europa Inst., Univ. of Edinburgh, 1995–. *Publications:* (Scottish Editor) Sweet & Maxwell's Encyclopaedia of Consumer Law, 1980; (contrib.) Corporate Law: the European dimension, 1991; (contrib.) Butterworth's EC Legal Systems, 1992; (contrib.) Green's Guide to European Laws in Scotland, 1995; (contrib.) McPhail, Sheriff Court Practice, 1999. *Recreations:* opera, chamber music, the music of Schubert, travel. *Address:* Parliament House, Parliament Square, Edinburgh EH1 1RQ. *Club:* Athenæum.

CLARKE OF HAMPSTEAD, Baron *cr* 1998 (Life Peer), of Hampstead in the London Borough of Camden; **Anthony James Clarke,** CBE 1998; *b* 17 April 1932; *s* of Henry Walter and Elizabeth Clarke; *m* 1954, Josephine Ena (*née* Turner); one *s* one *d*. *Educ:* New End Primary Sch., Hampstead; St Dominic's RC Sch., Kentish Town; Ruskin Coll., Oxford (TU educn course, 1954). Nat. Service, Royal Signals, 1950–52; TA and AER, 1952–68. Joined PO as Telegraph Boy at 14; worked as Postman until elected full-time officer, Union of Post Office Workers, 1979; Nat. Editor, The Post, UPW jl, 1979–82; Dep. Gen. Sec., UPW, later CWU, 1982–93. Member: Hampstead Lab Party, 1954–86; St Albans Lab Party, 1986–; Lab Party NEC, 1983–93; Chm., Lab Party, 1992–93. Mem. (Lab) Camden LBC, 1971–78. Contested (Lab) Camden, Hampstead, Feb. and Oct. 1974. Member: Exec. Cttee, Camden Cttee for Community Relns, 1974–81; Camden Council of Social Services, 1978–87. Mem., Labour Friends of Israel, 1972–. Governor, Westminster Foundn for Democracy, 1992–98. Trustee, Wells and Campden Charitable Trust; Founder Mem., and Trustee, One World Action (formerly One World), 1984–. KSG 1994. *Recreations:* Arsenal FC, The Archers, reading. *Address:* 83 Orchard Drive, St Albans, Herts AL2 2QH. *T:* (01727) 874276; House of Lords, SW1A 0PW.

CLARKE, Prof. Adrienne Elizabeth, AO 1991; PhD; FTSE, FAA; Professor, Personal Chair in Botany, University of Melbourne, since 1985; *b* 6 Jan. 1938; *d* of A. L. Petty; *m* (marr. diss.); two *d* one *s*. *Educ:* Ruyton Grammar Sch.; Univ. of Melbourne (PhD). Melbourne University: Reader in Botany, 1981; Dir, Plant Cell Biol. Res. Centre, 1982–99; Dep. Head, Sch. of Botany, 1992. Chm., CSIRO, 1991–96; Mem., Sci. Adv. Bd, Friedrich Meischer Inst., 1991. Director: Alcoa of Australia, 1993–96; AMP Soc., 1994–; Woolworths Ltd, 1994–; WMC Ltd, 1996–. Lt-Governor, Victoria, 1997–2001. Pres., Internat. Soc. for Plant Molecular Biology, 1997–98. Foreign Associate, Nat. Acad. of Scis, USA; Comp., Inst. of Engrs, Australia. *Publications:* (ed with I. Wilson) Carbohydrate–Protein Recognition, 1988; (with B. A. Stone) Chemistry and Biology of Glucans, 1992; chapters in numerous books; contribs to learned jls. *Recreations:* swimming, bush walking. *Address:* Plant Cell Biology Research Centre, School of Botany, University of Melbourne, Parkville, Vic 3052, Australia. *T:* (3) 93445043.

CLARKE, Alan; Chief Executive, Northumberland County Council, since 2000; *b* 18 Aug. 1953; *s* of Neville Clarke and (late) Jean Clarke; *m* 1977, Deborah Anne Hayes; one *s* two *d*. *Educ:* Univ. of Lancaster (BA Hons Econs 1974); Univ. of Liverpool (MCD 1977) MRTPI 1980. Policy Officer, South Ribble BC, 1974–75; Planning Asst, S Tyneside Council, 1977–79; Newcastle City Council: Planning Asst, 1979–83; Sen. Econ. Develt Asst, 1983–86; Hd, Econ. Develt, 1986–91; Chief Econ. Develt Officer, 1991–95; Asst Chief Exec., Sunderland CC, 1995–2000. *Recreations:* cycling, football, hill-walking. *Address:* Northumberland County Council, County Hall, Morpeth, Northumberland NE61 2EF. *T:* (01670) 533100.

CLARKE, Prof. Alan Douglas Benson, CBE 1974; Professor of Psychology, University of Hull, 1962–84, now Emeritus; *b* 21 March 1922; *s* of late Robert Benson Clarke and late Mary Lizars Clarke; *m* 1950, Prof. Ann Margaret (*née* Gravely); two *s*. *Educ:* Lancing Coll.; Univs of Reading and London. 1st cl. hons BA Reading 1948; PhD London 1950; FBPsS. Reading Univ., 1940–41 and 1946–48. Sen. Psychol., 1951–57 and Cons. Psychol., 1957–62, Manor Hosp., Epsom. Dean of Faculty of Science, 1966–68, and Pro-Vice-Chancellor 1968–71, Univ. of Hull. Vis. Prof., Univ. of Hertfordshire, 1992–98. Rapporteur, WHO Expert Cttee on Organization of Services for Mentally Retarded, 1967; Mem. WHO Expert Adv. Panel on Mental Health, 1968–85; Chm., Trng Council for Teachers of Mentally Handicapped, 1969–74; Hon. Vice-Pres., Nat. Assoc. for Mental Health, 1970–; President: Internat. Assoc. for Sci. Study of Mental Deficiency, 1973–76 (Hon. Past-Pres., 1976–88; Hon. Life Pres., 1988–); BPsS, 1977–78. Member: Personal Social Services Council, 1973–77; DHSS/SSRC Organizing Gp Transmitted Deprivation, 1974–83 (Chm. 1978–83); Cons., OECD/NZ Conf. on Early Childhood Care and Educn, 1978; Chairman: Sec. of State's Adv. Cttee on Top Grade Clinical Psychologist Posts and Appts, NHS, 1981–82; Adv. Cttee, Thomas Coram Res. Unit, Univ. of London Inst. of Educn, 1981–98. Lectures: Maudsley, RMPA, 1967; Stolz, Guy's Hosp., 1972; Tizard Meml, Assoc. for Child Psychol. and Psychiatry, 1983. Hon. Life Mem., Amer. Assoc. on Mental Deficiency, 1975 (Research award, 1977, with Ann M. Clarke). Hon. FRCPsych 1989. Hon. DSc Hull, 1986. (With Ann M. Clarke) Distinguished Achievement Award for Scientific Lit., Internat. Assoc. for Scientific Study of Mental Deficiency, 1982. Editor, Brit. Jl Psychol., 1973–79; Mem., Editorial Bds of other jls. *Publications* (with Ann M. Clarke): Mental Deficiency: the Changing Outlook, 1958, 4th edn 1985; Mental Retardation and Behavioural Research, 1973; Early Experience: myth and evidence, 1976; (with B. Tizard) Child Development and Social Policy: the life and work of Jack Tizard, 1983; (with P. Evans) Combating Mental Handicap, 1991; (with Ann M. Clarke) Early Experience and the Life Path, 2000; numerous in psychol and med. jls. *Address:* 109 Meadway, Barnet, Herts EN5 5JZ. *T:* (020) 8441 9690.

CLARKE, Prof. Alan Maxwell, CMG 1995; FRACS; Executive Director, New Zealand Spinal Trust, since 1995; *b* 12 Dec. 1932; *s* of John Maxwell Clarke and Daisy Martha Clarke; *m* 1956, Jane Malloch; three *s* one *d*. *Educ:* King's Coll., Auckland; Otago Univ., Dunedin (MB ChB 1956; ChM 1969). FRACS 1961. Otago University: Sen. Lectr in Surgery, 1964–69; Prof. of Surgery, 1970–85; Dean, Christchurch Sch. of Medicine, 1986–93; Dir, Spinal Injuries Unit, Burwood Hosp., Christchurch, 1993–99. James IV Traveller in Surgery, 1970; Nuffield Travelling Fellow, 1963–64. Amer. Cancer Soc. Award, 1968 and 1976. *Publications:* Understanding Cancer, 1982; Cancer Consensus

Manual, 1984; numerous papers in learned jls. *Recreations:* art, reading, flying light aeroplanes. *Address:* New Zealand Spinal Trust, Burwood Hospital, Private Bag 4708, Christchurch, New Zealand. *T:* (3) 3836850, *Fax:* (3) 3836851.

CLARKE, Allen; *see* Clarke, C. A. A.

CLARKE, Andrew Bertram; QC 1997; *b* 23 Aug. 1956; *s* of Arthur Bertram Clarke and Violet Doris Clarke; *m* 1981, Victoria Clare Thomas; one *s* two *d.* *Educ:* Crewe Grammar Sch.; King's Coll., London (LLB; AKC); Lincoln Coll., Oxford (BCL). Called to the Bar, Middle Temple, 1980; in practice at the Bar, 1981–. Gov., Goffs Grant Maintained Sch., Cheshunt, 1996–. Chm., Friends of St Mary's Church, Cheshunt, 1994–. *Recreations:* supporter of Crewe Alexander FC, Gloucestershire CCC; collector of European ceramics and modern prints. *Address:* 38 Albury Ride, Cheshunt, Herts EN8 8XF. *T:* (020) 7797 8600.

CLARKE, Rt Hon. Sir Anthony (Peter), Kt 1993; PC 1998; **Rt Hon. Lord Justice Clarke;** a Lord Justice of Appeal, since 1998; *b* 13 May 1943; *s* of Harry Alston Clarke and Isobel Clarke; *m* 1968, Rosemary (*née* Adam); two *s* one *d.* *Educ:* Oakham Sch.; King's Coll., Cambridge (Econs Pt I, Law Pt II; MA). Called to the Bar, Middle Temple, 1965, Bencher, 1987; QC 1979; a Recorder, 1985–92; a Judge of the High Court of Justice, QBD, 1993–98; Admiralty Judge, 1993–98. *Recreations:* golf, tennis, holidays. *Address:* Royal Courts of Justice, Strand, WC2A 2LL.

CLARKE, Anthony Richard; MP (Lab) Northampton South, since 1997; *b* 6 Sept. 1963; *s* of Walter Arthur Clarke and Joan Ada Iris Clarke; *m* Carole Chalmers; one *s* one *d.* *Educ:* Lings Upper Sch., Northampton. Social Work Trainer, Northamptonshire CC; Disability Trg Officer. *Address:* House of Commons, SW1A 0AA.

CLARKE, Sir Arthur (Charles), Kt 1998; CBE 1989; *b* 16 Dec. 1917; *s* of Charles Wright Clarke and Nora Mary Willis; *m* 1953, Marilyn Mayfield (marr. diss. 1964). *Educ:* Huish's Grammar Sch., Taunton; King's Coll., London (BSc); FKC 1977; FRAS. HM Exchequer and Audit Dept, 1936–41. Served RAF, 1941–46. Instn of Electrical Engineers, 1949–50. Techn. Officer on first GCA radar, 1943; originated communications satellites, 1945. Chm., British Interplanetary Soc., 1946–47, 1950–53. Asst Ed., Science Abstracts, 1949–50. Since 1954 engaged on underwater exploration on Gt Barrier Reef of Australia and coast of Ceylon. Extensive lecturing, radio and TV in UK and US. Chancellor, Moratuwa Univ., Sri Lanka, 1979–; Vikram Sarabhai Prof., Physical Research Lab., Ahmedabad, 1980; Marconi Internat. Fellowship, 1982; Hon. Fellow, AIAA, 1976 (Aero-space Communications Award, 1974). Hon. DSc: Beaver Coll., Pa, 1971; Univ. of Moratuwa, Sri Lanka, 1979; Hon. DLitt: Bath, 1988; Liverpool, 1995; Baptist Univ., Hong Kong, 1996. Freeman of Minehead, 1992. Unesco, Kalinga Prize, 1961; Acad. of Astronautics, 1961; World Acad. of Art and Science, 1962; Stuart Ballantine Medal, Franklin Inst., 1963; Westinghouse-AAAS Science Writing Award, 1969; Nebula Award, Science Fiction Writers of America, 1972, 1974, 1979; John Campbell Award, 1974; Hugo Award, World Science Fiction Convention, 1974, 1980; Vidya Jyothi Medal (Presidential Science Award), 1986; Grand Master, SF Writers of America, 1986; Charles Lindbergh Award, 1987; Lord Perry Award, 1992; von Karman Award, Internat. Acad. of Astronautics, 1996. *Publications: non-fiction:* Interplanetary Flight, 1950; The Exploration of Space, 1951; The Young Traveller in Space, 1954 (publ. in USA as Going into Space); The Coast of Coral, 1956; The Making of a Moon, 1957; The Reefs of Taprobane, 1957; Voice Across the Sea, 1958; The Challenge of the Spaceship, 1960; The Challenge of the Sea, 1960; Profiles of the Future, 1962; Voices from the Sky, 1965; (with Mike Wilson): Boy Beneath the Sea, 1958; The First Five Fathoms, 1960; Indian Ocean Adventure, 1961; The Treasure of the Great Reef, 1964; Indian Ocean Treasure, 1964; (with R. A. Smith) The Exploration of the Moon, 1954; (with Editors of Life) Man and Space, 1964; (ed) The Coming of the Space Age, 1967; The Promise of Space, 1968; (with the astronauts) First on the Moon, 1970; Report on Planet Three, 1972; (with Chesley Bonestell) Beyond Jupiter, 1973; The View from Serendip, 1977; (with Simon Welfare and John Fairley) Arthur C. Clarke's Mysterious World, 1980 (also TV series); (with Simon Welfare and John Fairley) Arthur C. Clarke's World of Strange Powers, 1984 (also TV series); Ascent to Orbit, 1984; 1984: Spring, 1984; (with Peter Hyams) The Odyssey File, 1985; (with editors of OMNI) Arthur C. Clarke's July 20, 2019, 1986; (with Simon Welfare and John Fairley) Arthur C. Clarke's Chronicles of the Strange and Mysterious, 1987; Astounding Days, 1988; How the World was One, 1992; (with Simon Welfare and John Fairley) Arthur C. Clarke's A–Z of Mysteries, 1993; By Space Possessed, 1993; The Snows of Olympus, 1994; Greetings, Carbon-based Bipeds!, 1999; *fiction:* Prelude to Space, 1951; The Sands of Mars, 1951; Islands in the Sky, 1952; Against the Fall of Night, 1953; Childhood's End, 1953; Expedition to Earth, 1953; Earthlight, 1955; Reach for Tomorrow, 1956; The City and the Stars, 1956; Tales from the White Hart, 1957; The Deep Range, 1957; The Other Side of the Sky, 1958; A Fall of Moondust, 1961; Tales of Ten Worlds, 1962; Dolphin Island, 1963; Glide Path, 1963; (with Stanley Kubrick) novel and screenplay, 2001: A Space Odyssey, 1968; The Lost Worlds of 2001, 1972; The Wind from the Sun, 1972; Rendezvous with Rama, 1973; Imperial Earth, 1975; The Fountains of Paradise, 1979; 2010: Space Odyssey II, 1982 (filmed 1984); The Songs of Distant Earth, 1986; 2061: Odyssey III, 1988; (with Gentry Lee) Cradle, 1988; Rama II, 1989; The Ghost from the Grand Banks, 1990; The Garden of Rama, 1991; (with Gregory Benford) Beyond the Fall of Night, 1991; The Hammer of God, 1993; (with Gentry Lee) Rama Revealed, 1993; (with Mike McQuay) Richter 10, 1996; 3001: The Final Odyssey, 1997; (with Michael Kube-McDowell) The Trigger, 1999; (with Stephen Baxter) The Light of Other Days, 2000; *anthologies:* Across the Sea of Stars, 1959; From the Ocean, From the Stars, 1962; Prelude to Mars, 1965; The Nine Billion Names of God, 1967; Of Time and Stars, 1972; The Best of Arthur C. Clarke, 1973; The Sentinel, 1983; A Meeting with Medusa, 1988; Tales from Planet Earth, 1990; More than One Universe, 1991; The Collected Short Stories, 2001; papers in Electronic Engineering, Wireless World, Wireless Engineer, Aeroplane, Jl of British Interplanetary Soc., Astronautics, etc. *Recreations:* diving, table-tennis. *Address:* 25 Barnes Place, Colombo 7, Sri Lanka. *T:* 699757, 694255, *Fax:* 698730; c/o David Higham Associates, 5 Lower John Street, Golden Square, W1R 3PE. *Clubs:* British Sub-Aqua; Colombo Swimming, Otters.

CLARKE, Dr Arthur S.; Keeper, Department of Natural History, Royal Scottish Museum, 1980–83, retired; *b* 11 Feb. 1923; *yr s* of late Albert Clarke and Doris Clarke (*née* Elliott); *m* 1951, Joan, *er d* of Walter Andrassy; one *s* one *d.* *Educ:* Leeds Boys' Modern School; Aireborough Grammar School; Leeds Univ. (BSc 1948, PhD 1951). Pilot, RAF, 1943–46. Assistant Lecturer, Glasgow Univ., 1951; Asst Keeper, Royal Scottish Museum, 1954; Deputy Keeper, 1973. *Address:* Rose Cottage, Yarrow, Selkirk TD7 5LB.

CLARKE, Brian; *see* Clarke, J. B.

CLARKE, Prof. Bryan Campbell, DPhil; FRS 1982; Foundation Professor of Genetics, 1971–93, Research Professor, 1993–97, now Professor Emeritus and Leverhulme Emeritus Research Fellow, University of Nottingham; *b* 24 June 1932; *s* of Robert Campbell Clarke and Gladys Mary (*née* Carter); *m* 1960, Ann Gillian, *d* of late Prof. John Jewkes, CBE; one *s* one *d.* *Educ:* Fay Sch., Southborough, Mass, USA; Magdalen Coll. Sch., Oxford; Magdalen Coll., Oxford (MA, DPhil). FLS 1980. National Service, 1950–52 (Pilot Officer, RAF). Nature Conservancy Res. Student, Oxford Univ., 1956; Asst 1959, Lectr 1963, Reader 1969, Dept of Zoology, Univ. of Edinburgh. Res. Fellow, Stanford Univ., 1973; SRC Sen. Res. Fellow, 1976–81; Hon. Res. Fellow, Natural Hist. Mus., 1993–. Joint Founder, Population Genetics Gp, 1967; Pres., Section D (Biology), BAAS, 1989; Vice-President: Genetical Soc., 1981; Linnean Soc., 1985–87; Soc. for Study of Evolution, USA, 1990–91; Zool Soc. of London, 1998–99; Chairman: Terrestrial Life Sciences Cttee, NERC, 1984–87; Molecular Biology and Genetics Sub-Cttee, SERC, 1990–93; Biol Scis Sub-Cttee, HEFCE, 1992–. Mem., Council, Royal Soc., 1994–96. Scientific expeditions to: Morocco, 1955; Polynesia, 1962, 1967, 1968, 1980, 1982, 1986, 1991, 1994, 2000. Editor: Heredity, 1978–85; Proceedings of the Royal Society, Series B, 1989–93. *Publications:* Berber Village, 1959; contrib. scientific jls, mostly on ecological genetics and evolution. *Recreations:* sporadic painting and gardening; archaeology, computing. *Address:* Linden Cottage, School Lane, Colston Bassett, Nottingham NG12 3FD. *T:* (01949) 81243. *Club:* Royal Air Force.

CLARKE, Sir (Charles Mansfield) Tobias, 6th Bt *cr* 1831; *b* Santa Barbara, California, 8 Sept. 1939; *e s* of Sir Humphrey Orme Clarke, 5th Bt, and Elisabeth (*d* 1967), *d* of Dr William Albert Cook; *S* father, 1973; *m* 1971, Charlotte (marr. diss. 1979), *e d* of Roderick Walter; *m* 1984, Teresa L. A. de Chair, *d* of late Somerset de Chair; one *s* two *d.* *Educ:* Eton; Christ Church, Oxford (MA); Univ. of Paris; New York Univ. Graduate Business Sch. Bankers Trust Co., NY, 1963–80 (Vice-Pres., 1974–80). Associate Dir, Swiss Bank Corp., London, 1992–94. Underwriting Mem., Lloyds, 1984–; MSI 1993. Chm., Standing Council of the Baronetage, 1993–96 (Vice-Chm., 1990–92; Hon. Treas., 1980–92); Editor and founder, The Baronets Journal, 1987–99; Chm. Trustees, Baronets Trust, 1996– (Trustee, 1989–); Publisher, The Official Roll of the Baronetage, 1997. Lord of the Manor of Bibury. *Recreations:* accidental happenings, riding, gardening, photography, stimulating conversation; Pres., Bibury Cricket Club. *Heir:* *s* (Charles Somerset) Lawrence Clarke, *b* 12 March 1990. *Address:* South Lodge, 80 Campden Hill Road, W8 7AA. *T:* (020) 7938 2955; The Church House, Bibury, Cirencester, Glos GL7 5NR. *T:* (01285) 740293. *Clubs:* White's, Boodle's, Beefsteak, Pratt's, Pilgrims', MCC; Jockey (Paris); The Brook, Racquet & Tennis (New York).

CLARKE, Rt Hon. Charles (Rodway); PC 2001; MP (Lab) Norwich South, since 1997; Minister without Portfolio and Chairman of the Labour Party, since 2001; *b* 21 Sept. 1950; *s* of Sir Richard Clarke, KCB, OBE and Brenda Clarke (*née* Skinner); *m* 1984, Carol Marika Pearson; two *s.* *Educ:* Highgate Sch.; King's Coll., Cambridge (BA Hons 1973). Pres., NUS, 1975–77; various admin. posts, 1977–80; Head, Office of Rt Hon. Neil Kinnock, MP, 1981–92; Chief Exec., Quality Public Affairs, 1992–97. Mem. (Lab) Hackney LBC, 1980–86. Parly Under-Sec. of State, DfEE, 1998–99; Minister of State, Home Office, 1999–2001. Mem., Treasury Select Cttee, 1997–98. *Recreations:* chess, reading, walking. *Address:* House of Commons, SW1A 0AA. *T:* (020) 7219 3000. *Club:* Norwich Labour.

CLARKE, (Christopher) Michael; Director, National Gallery of Scotland, since 2001; *b* 29 Aug. 1952; *s* of Patrick Reginald Clarke and Margaret Catherine Clarke (*née* Waugh); *m* 1978, Deborah Clare Cowling; two *s* one *d.* *Educ:* Felsted; Manchester Univ. (BA (Hons) History of Art). Art Asst, York City Art Gall., 1973–76; Res. Asst, British Mus., 1976–78; Asst Keeper in Charge of Prints, Whitworth Art Gall., Manchester Univ., 1978–84; Asst Keeper, 1984–87, Keeper, 1987–2000, Nat. Gall. of Scotland. Vis. Fellow, Yale Center for British Art, 1985. *Publications:* Pollaiuolo to Picasso: Old Master prints in the Whitworth Art Gallery, 1980; The Tempting Prospect: a social history of English watercolours, 1981; (ed with N. Penny) The Arrogant Connoisseur: Richard Payne Knight, 1982; The Draughtsman's Art: Master Drawings in the Whitworth Art Gallery, 1983; Lighting up the Landscape: French Impressionism and its origins, 1986; Corot and the Art of Landscape, 1991; Eyewitness Art: watercolour, 1993; (ed jtly) Corot, Courbet und die Maler von Barbizon, 1996; Oxford Concise Dictionary of Art Terms, 2001; articles, reviews, etc, in Apollo, Art Internat., Burlington Magazine, Museums Jl. *Recreations:* golf, travel. *Address:* 9A Summerside Street, Trinity, Edinburgh EH6 4NT.

CLARKE, Christopher Simon Courtenay Stephenson; QC 1984; a Recorder, since 1990; a Deputy High Court Judge, since 1993; a Judge of the Courts of Appeal of Jersey and Guernsey, since 1998; *b* 14 March 1947; *s* of late Rev. John Stephenson Clarke and of Enid Courtenay Clarke; *m* 1974, Caroline Anne Fletcher; one *s* two *d.* *Educ:* Marlborough College; Gonville and Caius College, Cambridge (MA). Called to the Bar, Middle Temple, 1969, Bencher, 1991; Attorney of Supreme Court of Turks and Caicos Islands, 1975–. Councillor, Internat. Bar Assoc., 1988–90; Chm., Commercial Bar Assoc., 1993–95; Mem., Bar Council, 1993–99. FRSA 1995. *Address:* 42 The Chase, SW4 0NH. *T:* (020) 7622 0765; Brick Court Chambers, 7–8 Essex Street, WC2R 3LD. *T:* (020) 7379 3550. *Clubs:* Brooks's, Hurlingham.

CLARKE, (Cyril Alfred) Allen, MA, DLitt; Headmaster, Holland Park Secondary School, 1957–71; *b* 21 Aug. 1910; *s* of late Frederick John Clarke; *m* 1934, Edna Gertrude Francis (decd); three *s.* *Educ:* Langley Sch., Norwich; Culham Coll. of Educn, Oxon; Birkbeck Coll., Univ. of London; King's Coll., Univ. of London. DLitt Knightsbridge Univ., Copenhagen, 1993. Entered London Teaching Service, 1933; Royal Artillery, 1940–46; Staff Officer (Major) in Educn Br. of Mil. Govt of Germany, 1945–46; Asst Master, Haberdashers' Aske's Hatcham Boys' Sch., 1946–51; Headmaster: Isledon Sec. Sch., 1951–55; Battersea Co. Sec. Sch., 1955–57. Hon. Gov., Langley Sch., 1994–. *Recreations:* photography, writing, reading, archaeology. *Address:* 16 Plasset Drive, Attleborough, Norfolk NR17 2NU. *T:* (01953) 454518.

CLARKE, David Clive; QC 1983; **His Honour Judge David Clarke;** a Senior Circuit Judge, and Hon. Recorder of Liverpool, since 1997; *b* 16 July 1942; *s* of Philip George Clarke and José Margaret Clarke; *m* 1969, Alison Claire, *d* of Rt Rev. Percy James Brazier; two *s* (and one *s* decd). *Educ:* Winchester Coll.; Magdalene Coll., Cambridge. BA 1964, MA 1968. Called to the Bar, Inner Temple, 1965, Bencher, 1992. In practice, Northern Circuit, 1965–93 (Treas., 1988–92); a Recorder, 1981–93; a Circuit Judge, 1993–97. Mem., Criminal Justice Consultative Council, 1999–. Chm., Merseyside Area Criminal Justice Strategy Cttee, 1997–. *Recreations:* walking, sailing, swimming, canals. *Address:* Queen Elizabeth II Law Courts, Derby Square, Liverpool L2 1XA. *T:* (0151) 473 7373. *Clubs:* Trearddur Bay Sailing (Anglesey); Oxton Cricket and Sports (Birkenhead).

CLARKE, David Stuart, AO 1992; Executive Chairman, Macquarie Bank Ltd, since 1985; Chairman, Brian McGuigan Wines Ltd, since 1991; *b* 3 Jan. 1942; *s* of Stuart Richardson Clarke and Ailsie Jean Talbot Clarke; *m* 1st, 1964, Margaret Maclean Partridge (marr. diss. 1994); two *s*; 2nd, 1995, Jane Graves. *Educ:* Knox Grammar Sch.; Sydney Univ. (BEcon Hons); Harvard Univ. (MBA). Hill Samuel Australia Ltd: Jt Man. Dir, 1971–77; Man. Dir, 1977–84; Exec. Chm., 1984–85; Director: Darling & Co. Ltd (now Schroder Australia Ltd), 1966–71; Babcock Aust. Holdings Ltd, 1972–81; Chairman: Accepting Houses Assoc. of Aust., 1974–76; Sceggs Darlinghurst Ltd, 1976–78; Barlile Corp. Ltd, 1986–93; Goodman Fielder Ltd, 1995–; Director: Hill Samuel & Co. Ltd (London), 1978–84; Hooker Corp. Ltd, 1984–86; Reil Corp. Ltd, 1986–87. Member:

Lloyds of London, 1983–97; Aust. Stock Exch. Ltd, 1987–; Fed. Govt Cttee under Financial Corporations Act, 1975–85; Exec. Cttee, Cttee for Econ. Develt of Australia, 1982–98. Chairman: Australian Opera, 1986–95; Aust. Wool Realisation Commn, 1991–93. Member: Council, Royal Agricl Soc. of NSW, 1986– (Chm., Wine Cttee, 1990–); Harvard Business Sch. Alumni Council, 1986–89; Investment Adv. Cttee, Australian Olympic Foundn, 1996–; Stage II Project, Nat. Inst. for Dramatic Art, 1996–; Asia Adv. Cttee, Harvard Business Sch., 1997–. Hon. Fed. Treas., Liberal Party of Aust., 1987–89. Member: Bd Trustees, Financial Markets Foundn for Children, 1989–2000 (Hon. Life Mem.); Sydney Adv. Bd, Salvation Army, 1990– (Chm., 1999–); Corporate Citizens Cttee, Children's Cancer Inst. of Australia, 1992–; Chairman: Salvation Army Red Shield Appeal, 1990–92 (Cttee Mem., 1985–88; Dep. Chm., 1989–90); Menzies Res. Centre, 1994–97; Campaign Chm., (NSW), Salvation Army Educn Foundn, 1996–98. Mem., Cook Soc., 1979– (Co-Convener, 1988–97). Pres., Nat. Council, Opera Australia, 1996– (Chm., Opera Australia Capital Fund, 1996–). Chairman: NSW Rugby Union, 1989–95 (Treas., 1989); Australian Rugby Union, 1998– (Dep. Chm., 1997–98). Confrère des Chevaliers du Tastevin. *Recreations:* opera, ski-ing, tennis, golf, bridge, philately, personal computers, ballet, wine. *Address:* 5 Keltie Bay, 15 Sutherland Crescent, Darling Point, NSW 2027, Australia. *T:* (2) 93634966. *Clubs:* Australian, Harvard of Australia (Pres. 1977–79), Royal Sydney Golf, Elanora Country, Cabbage Tree (Sydney).

CLARKE, Prof. David William, DPhil; FRS 1998; FREng, FIEE; Professor of Control Engineering, Oxford University, since 1992; Fellow, New College, Oxford, since 1969; *b* 31 May 1943; *s* of Norman William Clarke and Laura (*née* Dewhurst); *m* 1967, Lynda Ann Weatherhead; two *s. Educ:* Balliol Coll., Oxford. MA, DPhil Oxon. FIEE 1984; FREng (FEng 1989). Oxford University: Astor Res. Fellow, New Coll., 1966–69; Lectr, 1969–86; Reader in Information Engrg, 1986–92; Hd, Dept of Engrg Sci., 1994–99. Dir, Invensys UTC for Advanced Instrumentation. Sir Harold Hartley Silver Medal, Inst. of Measurement and Control, 1983. *Publications:* Advances in Model-Based Predictive Control, 1994; papers in learned jls. *Recreation:* gardening. *Address:* New College, Oxford OX1 3BN. *T:* (01865) 279507.

CLARKE, Donald Roberts; Finance Director, 3i (formerly Investors in Industry) Group plc, 1988–91; *b* 14 May 1933; *s* of Harold Leslie Clarke and Mary Clarke; *m* 1959, Susan Charlotte Cotton; one *s* three *d. Educ:* Ealing Grammar Sch.; The Queen's Coll., Oxford (MA). Articled Peat Marwick Mitchell & Co., 1957–62; Accountant, The Collingwood Group, 1962–64; Industrial and Commercial Finance Corporation: Investigating Accountant, 1964; Controller, 1964–67; Br. Manager, 1967–68; Co. Sec., 1968–73; Investors in Industry Gp (formerly Finance for Industry): Sec./Treasurer, 1973–76; Asst Gen. Man., 1976–79; Gen. Man., Finance, 1979–88. Dir, Consumers' Assoc. Ltd, 1990–92. Member: UGC, 1982–85; Industrial, Commercial and Prof. Liaison Gp, National Adv. Body for Local Authority Higher Educn, 1983–85; Continuing Educn Standing Cttee, Nat. Adv. Body for Local Authority Higher Educn and UGC, 1985–89; Council, Royal Holloway, Univ. of London (formerly RHBNC), 1987–. *Publication:* (jtly) 3i: 50 years investing in industry, 1995. *Recreations:* music, gardening, photography. *Club:* Oxford and Cambridge.

CLARKE, Most Rev. Edwin Kent, DD; *b* 21 Jan. 1932. *Educ:* Bishop's Univ., Lennoxville (BA 1954, LST 1956); Union Seminary, NY (MRE 1960); Huron Coll., Ontario (DD). Deacon 1956, priest 1957, Ottawa. Curate of All Saints, Westboro, 1956–59; Director of Christian Education, Diocese of Ottawa, 1960–66; Rector of St Lambert, Montreal, 1966–73; Diocesan Sec., Diocese of Niagara, 1973–76; Archdeacon of Niagara, 1973–76; Bishop Suffragan of Niagara, 1976–79; Bishop of Edmonton, 1980; Archbishop of Edmonton and Metropolitan of Rupert's Land, 1986–87. *Address:* RR#3, Pembroke, Ontario K8A 6W4, Canada.

CLARKE, Sir Ellis (Emmanuel Innocent), TC 1969; GCMG 1972 (CMG 1960); Kt 1963 (but does not use the title within Republic of Trinidad and Tobago); President of Trinidad and Tobago, 1976–86 (Governor General and C-in-C, 1973–76); *b* 28 Dec. 1917; *o c* of late Cecil Clarke and of Mrs Elma Clarke; *m* 1952, Eyrmyntrude (*née* Hagley); one *s* one *d. Educ:* St Mary's Coll., Trinidad (Jerningham Gold Medal, 1936, and other prizes). London Univ. (LLB 1940); called to the Bar, Gray's Inn, 1940. Private practice at Bar of Trinidad and Tobago, 1941–54; Solicitor-Gen., Oct. 1954; Dep. Colonial Sec., Dec. 1956; Attorney-Gen., 1957–62; Actg Governor, 1960; Chief Justice designate, 1961; Trinidad and Tobago Perm. Rep. to UN, 1962–66; Ambassador: to United States, 1962–73; to Mexico, 1966–73; Rep. on Council of OAS, 1967–73. Chm. of Bd, British West Indian Airways, 1968–72. KStJ 1973. *Address:* (office) 16 Frederick Street, Port of Spain, Trinidad, West Indies. *T:* 6272150. *Clubs:* Queen's Park Cricket (Port of Spain); Trinidad Turf, Arima Race (Trinidad); Tobago Golf (President, 1969–75).

CLARKE, Eric Lionel; *b* 9 April 1933; *s* of late Ernest and Annie Clarke; *m* 1955, June Hewat; two *s* one *d. Educ:* St Cuthbert's Holy Cross Acad.; W. M. Ramsey Tech. Coll.; Esk Valley Tech. Coll. Coalminer: Roslin Colliery, 1949–51; Lingerwood Colliery, 1951–69; Bilston Glen Colliery, 1969–77; Trade Union Official, 1977–89; Gen. Sec., NUM Scotland; redundant, unemployed, 1989–92. Mem., Midlothian CC and then Lothian Regl Council, 1962–78. MP (Lab) Midlothian, 1992–2001. An Opposition Whip, 1994–97. *Recreations:* fly fishing, gardening, carpentry, football spectator. *Address:* 32 Mortonhall Park Crescent, Edinburgh EH17 8SY. *T:* (0131) 664 8214. *Clubs:* Mayfield Labour; Morris Working Men's; Danderhall Miners' Welfare.

CLARKE, Frederick, BSc; FBCS; Director: DS Information Systems, since 1991; DS Group Holdings Ltd; *b* 8 Dec. 1928; *s* of George and Edna Clarke; *m* 1955, Doris Thompson (marr. diss. 1987); two *d*; *m* 1988, Dorothy Sugrue. *Educ:* King James I Grammar Sch., Bishop Auckland; King's Coll., Durham Univ. (BSc 1951). FBCS 1972. Served RAF, 1951–54. Schoolmaster, 1954–57; IBM, 1957–82 (final appts, Gen. Man. and Dir); Chm., Royal Ordnance plc (formerly Royal Ordnance Factories), 1982–85. Chm., Lingfield Park Racecourse, 1988–90; Dir, Leisure Investments, 1985–90. Freeman, City of London, 1987. *Recreations:* golf, cricket, racing, reading. *Address:* Arran, Bute Avenue, Petersham, Richmond, Surrey TW10 7AX.

CLARKE, Garth Martin; Chief Executive, Transport Research Laboratory, since 1997; *b* 1 Feb. 1944; *s* of Peter Oakley Clarke and Ella Audrey (*née* Jenner); *m* 1966, Carol Marian Trimble; three *d. Educ:* Duke's Grammar Sch., Alnwick, Northumberland; Liverpool Univ. (BSc Hons). FIHT 1996; FILT (FCIT 1996). Research Physicist, 1966–73, Ops Dir, 1983–87, Plessey Research (Caswell) Ltd; Dir, Commercial Ops, Plessey Res. and Technology Ltd, 1987–89; Business Develt Dir, Business Systems Gp, GPT Ltd, 1990–93; Business Dir, TRL, 1993–97. Chief Exec., Transport Res. Foundn, 1997–; Chm., Viridis, 1999–. *Recreations:* birdwatching, water colour painting, photography. *Address:* Transport Research Laboratory, Old Wokingham Road, Crowthorne, Berks RG45 6AU. *T:* (01344) 770001. *Club:* Royal Automobile.

CLARKE, Geoffrey, RA 1976 (ARA 1970); ARCA; artist and sculptor; *b* 28 Nov. 1924; *s* of John Moulding Clarke and Janet Petts; two *s. Educ:* Royal College of Art (Hons). Exhibitions: Gimpel Fils Gallery, 1952, 1955; Redfern Gallery, 1965; Taranman Gallery, 1975, 1976, 1982; Yorkshire Sculpture Park, Chappel Gall., Colchester, and Friends Room, Royal Acad., 1994; touring exhibitions: Christchurch Mansions, Ipswich, 1994; Herbert Art Gall., Coventry, and Pallant House, Chichester, 1995. Works in public collections: Victoria and Albert Museum; Tate Gallery; Arts Council; Museum of Modern Art, NY; etc. Prizes for engraving: Triennial, 1951; London, 1953, Tokyo, 1957. Commissioned work includes: mosaics, Liverpool Univ. Physics Block; stained glass windows for Treasury, Lincoln Cathedral; bronze sculpture, Thorn Electric Building, Upper St Martin's Lane; 3 stained glass windows, high altar, cross and candlesticks, the flying cross and crown of thorns, all in Coventry Cathedral; sculpture, Nottingham Civic Theatre; UKAEA Culham; Univs of Liverpool, Exeter, Cambridge, Oxford, Manchester, Lancaster, Loughborough and Warwick; screens in Royal Military Chapel, Birdcage Walk. Further work at Chichester, Newcastle, Manchester, Plymouth, Ipswich, Canterbury, Taunton, Winchester, St Paul, Minnesota, Lincoln, Nebraska, Newcastle Civic Centre, Wolverhampton, Leicester, Churchill Coll., Aldershot, Suffolk Police HQ, All Souls, W1, The Majlis, Abu Dhabi, York House, N1.

CLARKE, Giles Colin Scott, PhD; Head, Department of Exhibitions and Education, Natural History Museum, since 1994; *b* 9 Jan. 1944; *s* of Colin Richard Clarke and Vera Joan, (Georgie), Clarke (*née* Scott); *m* 1967, Helen Parker (*see* Helen Clarke); one *s. Educ:* Sevenoaks Sch.; Keble Coll., Oxford (MA 1970); Birmingham Univ. (PhD 1970). VSO, Gambia, 1963; Mem., Internat. Biological Prog. Bipolar Expeditions, 1967–68; Asst Keeper of Botany, Manchester Mus., 1970–73; Head, Pollen Section, 1973–79, Dep. Head, Dept of Public Services, 1979–94, British Mus. (Natural History), later Natural History Mus. Member: Council, British Bryological Soc., 1971– (Pres, 1998–99); Cttee, Wildlife Photographer of the Year, 1984–; Cttee, Trends in Leisure and Entertainment Conf. and Exhibn, 1993– (Chair, 1998). Trustee, Eureka! Children's Mus., 1999–. FLS 1971; FMA 1996; FRSA 1997. *Publications:* numerous papers in prof. jls on botany and museums. *Recreations:* opera, organ music, art galleries, reading, making things. *Address:* Department of Exhibitions and Education, Natural History Museum, Cromwell Road, SW7 5BD. *T:* (020) 7942 5216.

CLARKE, Graham Neil; Development Editor, since 1999 and Editorial Manager, since 2000, Guild of Master Craftsman Publications Ltd; Editor: Water Gardening, since 1999; Exotic & Greenhouse Gardening, since 2000; Garden Calendar, since 2000; *b* 23 July 1956; *s* of late Henry Charles Owen Clarke, RVM and of Doris May Clarke; *m* 1980, Denise Carole (*née* Anderson); two *d. Educ:* Rutherford Sch., N London; Wisley School of Horticulture (WisCertHort). Staff gardener, Buckingham Palace, 1975–76; Nurseryman, Hyde Park, 1976; Amateur Gardening: Sub-Editor, 1976–79; Chief Sub-Editor, 1979–81; Dep. Editor, 1981–86; Editor, 1986–98; Editor, Home Plus Magazine, 1984–85; IPC gardening titles: Gp Editor, 1993–95; Special Projects Editor, 1995–98; Editor-at-Large, 1998–99. FLS 1990; MIHort 1995 (AIHort 1991). *Publications:* Step by Step Pruning, 1985; Autumn and Winter Colour in the Garden, 1986; Complete Book of Plant Propagation, 1990; The Ultimate House Plant Handbook, 1997; Beginner's Guide to Water Gardening, 2002. *Recreations:* genealogy, philately, collecting toast racks, gardening. *Address:* c/o Guild of Master Craftsman Publications Ltd, 86 High Street, Lewes, East Sussex BN7 1XN. *T:* (01273) 477374. *Club:* Royal Horticultural Society Garden (Surrey).

CLARKE, Gregory; Chief Executive Officer, ICO Global Communications, since 2000; *b* 27 Oct. 1957; *s* of George and Mary Clarke; *m* 1984, Anne Wilson; four *d. Educ:* Gateway Grammar Sch., Leicester; Wolverhampton Poly (BA Hons 1980); City Univ. Business Sch. (MBA 1983). Vice Pres., Global Cellular, Nortel, 1992–95; Chief Exec., Cable & Wireless Mobile, 1995–97; CEO, 1997–99, Chief Exec., 1999–2000, Cable & Wireless Communications plc. *Recreations:* family, Leicester City FC, opera, Rugby, reading. *Address:* ICO Global Communications, Symphony House, Cowley Business Park, Uxbridge, Middlesex UB8 2AD.

CLARKE, Guy Hamilton, CMG 1959; HM Ambassador to Nepal, 1962–63, retired; *b* 23 July 1910; 3rd *s* of late Dr and Mrs Charles H. Clarke, Leicester. *Educ:* Wyggeston Grammar Sch., Leicester; Trinity Hall, Cambridge. Probationer Vice-Consul, Levant Consular Service, Beirut, 1933; transf. to Ankara, 1936; Corfu, 1940; Adana, 1941; Baltimore, 1944; has since served at: Washington, Los Angeles (Consul 1945), Bangkok, Jedda, Kirkuk (Consul 1949), Bagdad, Kirkuk (Consul-Gen. 1951); Ambassador to the Republic of Liberia, 1957–60, and to the Republic of Guinea, 1959–60; Mem. United Kingdom Delegation to United Nations Gen. Assembly, New York, 1960; HM Consul-General, Damascus, Feb. 1961, and Chargé d'Affaires there, Oct. 1961–Jan. 1962. *Address:* 10 Fairlawn House, Christchurch Road, Winchester, Hants SO23 9SR.

CLARKE, Dr Helen, FSA; Director, Society of Antiquaries, 1990–94; *b* 25 Aug. 1939; *d* of George Parker and Helen (*née* Teare); *m* 1967, Giles Colin Scott Clarke, *qv*; one *s. Educ:* Univ. of Birmingham (BA; PhD); Univ. of Lund, Sweden. FSA 1972. Dir of Excavations, King's Lynn, 1963–67; Res. Fellow, Sch. of History, Birmingham Univ., 1965–67; Lecturer in Medieval Archaeology: Glasgow Univ., 1967–69; UCL, 1976–90. Visiting Professor in Medieval Archaeology: Lund Univ., Sweden, 1991; Århus Univ., Denmark, 1992; Kiel Univ., Germany, 1993. Editor and Translator: Royal Swedish Acad. of History and Antiquities, 1975–; Bd of National Antiquities, Sweden (also Consultant), 1990–95; Consultant, English Heritage, 1987–94. Member: Svenska Arkeologiska Samfundet, 1988; Vetenskapssocieten i Lund, 1988. Hon. Fil Dr Lund, 1991. *Publications:* Regional Archaeologies: East Anglia, 1971; Excavations in King's Lynn, 1963–1970, 1977; The Archaeology of Medieval England, 1984, 2nd edn 1986; Towns in the Viking Age, 1991, 2nd edn 1995. *Recreations:* attending opera, watching cricket, looking at the landscape.

CLARKE, Henry Benwell; Director, People and Places International, since 1993; *b* 30 Jan. 1950; *yr s* of late Stephen Lampard Clarke and Elinor Wade Clarke (*née* Benwell); *m* 1973, Verena Angela Lodge; four *s* one *d. Educ:* St John's Sch., Leatherhead; South Bank Polytechnic (BSc Estate Management 1972); Imperial College London (MSc Management Science 1977; DIC 1977). ARICS 1973, FRICS 1986; ACIArb 1979. British Rail Property Board: S Region, 1972–78; NW Region, 1978–82; E Region, 1982–85; Regional Estate Surveyor and Manager, Midland Region, 1985–86; Chief Estate Surveyor, HQ, 1986–87; Nat. Develt Manager, 1987–88; Dep. Chief Exec., Crown Estate Comrs, 1988–92, Acting Chief Exec. and Accounting Officer, 1989. Mem., Gen. Council, British Property Fedn, 1989–92. Member: Council, Christian Union for Estate Profession, 1983–88; Bd, Youth with a Mission (England), 1990–; Bd, Mercy Ships (UK), 1995–; Bd, Moggerhanger House Preservation Trust, 1997–; advisor to various Christian trusts. Member Board: Rail Estate Consultancy, 1998–; Telecom Property Ltd, 1999–; The Greater Bristol Light Railway Co. Ltd, 1999–. *Recreations:* reading, walking, transport, architecture, Church. *Address:* 42 Wordsworth Road, Harpenden, Herts AL5 4AF. *Club:* National.

CLARKE, (James) Brian; author and journalist; Fishing Correspondent, The Times, since 1991; *b* 28 May 1938; *s* of Thomas Clarke and Annette Clarke (*née* Vickers); *m* 1968, Anne Farley; three *d. Educ:* St Mary's Grammar Sch., Darlington. Reporter and sub-ed., Northern Echo, Darlington, 1955–59; Dep. Features Ed., Evening Gazette,

Middlesbrough, 1959–61; home news sub-ed., Scottish Daily Mail, Edinburgh, 1961–62; home news and Parly sub-ed., The Guardian, 1962–67; Nat. Press Officer, IBM UK, 1967–68; Public Affairs Advr, Nat. Computing Centre, 1968–69; indep. mgt consultant, 1969–74; various corporate communications and envmtl mgt posts, IBM UK, 1974–91 (on secondment to BBC, 1988–90: series producer, In the Name of the Law (television), 1988–89; Consultant, BBC Bd of Mgt, 1989–90); consultant, envmtl progs, IBM UK, 1990–91; Fishing Corresp., Sunday Times, 1975–96. *Publications:* The Pursuit of Stillwater Trout, 1975, 7th edn 2001; The Trout and the Fly, 1980, 6th edn 1995; Flyfishing for Trout (US), 1993; Trout etcetera: selected writings 1982–1996, 1996; The Stream (novel) 2000 (BP Natural World Book Prize, Authors' Club Best First Novel Award, 2000). *Recreations:* fishing, walking, photography, sitting still in the countryside watching and listening. *Address:* c/o Watson, Little Ltd, Capo di Monte, Windmill Hill, NW3 6RJ. *Clubs:* Arts, Flyfishers.

CLARKE, James Samuel, MC 1943 and Bar 1944; Under-Secretary and Principal Assistant Solicitor, Inland Revenue, 1970–81, retired; Managing Director, Bishop and Clarke Ltd, 1981–96; *b* 19 Jan. 1921; *s* of James Henry and Deborah Florence Clarke; *m* 1949, Ilse Cohen; two *d. Educ:* Reigate Grammar Sch.; St Catharine's Coll., Cambridge (MA). Army Service, 1941–45: Royal Irish Fusiliers; served 1st Bn N Africa and Italy; Major 1943. Called to Bar, Middle Temple, 1946. Entered Legal Service (Inland Rev.), 1953; Sen. Legal Asst, 1958; Asst Solicitor, 1965. *Recreation:* gardening. *Address:* Dormers, The Downs, Givons Grove, Leatherhead, Surrey KT22 8LH. *T:* (01372) 378254. *Clubs:* National Liberal, Royal Automobile.

CLARKE, Jane; Head, Broadcast and Allied Media Section, Public Diplomacy Department, Foreign and Commonwealth Office, since 1999; *b* 14 Oct. 1951; *d* of Michael David Hilborne-Clarke and Margaret Lythell; one *d* by Howard Austin Trevette. *Educ:* Norwich High Sch. for Girls; University College London (BA Hons English Lang. and Lit. 1975); Slade Sch. of Fine Art. Film Programmer, BFI, 1980–82; Features Prod., TV-am, 1982–88: Ed., Henry Kelly Saturday Show, 1984–85; Features Ed., Good Morning Britain, 1985–87; Ed., After Nine, 1987–88; Independent Prod., Pithers, Clarke and Ferguson, 1988–89 (prod., Children First, 1989; Series Ed., New Living, 1990–91); Controller, Features, West Country TV, 1992–95; Dep. Dir, BFI, 1995–97; Chief Exec., BAFTA, 1998. Dir, London Fest. of Literature, 2000–. *Publication:* Move Over Misconceptions: Doris Day reappraised, 1981. *Recreations:* reading, walking, cinema, theatre, visual arts, music, poetry. *Address:* 38A St Augustine's Road, NW1 9RN.

CLARKE, Prof. John, FRS 1986; Professor of Physics, since 1973, and Luis W. Alvarez Memorial Chair for Experimental Physics, since 1994, University of California, Berkeley; *b* 10 Feb. 1942; *s* of Victor Patrick and Ethel May Clarke; *m* 1979, Grethe F. Pedersen; one *d. Educ:* Christ's Coll., Cambridge (BA, MA 1968; Hon. Fellow, 1997); Darwin Coll., Cambridge (PhD 1968). Postdoctoral Scholar, 1968, Asst Prof., 1969, Associate Prof., 1971–73, Univ. of California, Berkeley. Alfred P. Sloan Foundn Fellow, 1970; Adolph C. and Mary Sprague Miller Inst. for Basic Research into Science Prof., 1975, 1994; John Simon Guggenheim Fellow, 1977; Vis. Fellow, Clare Hall, Cambridge, 1989; By-Fellow, Churchill Coll., Cambridge, 1998. FAAAS 1982; Fellow, Amer. Phys. Soc., 1985; FInstP 1999. Charles Vernon Boys Prize, Inst. of Physics, 1977; Calif. Scientist of the Year, 1987; Fritz London Meml Award for Low Temperature Physics, 1987; Joseph F. Keithley Award, APS, 1998; Comstock Prize for Physics, NAS, 1999. *Publications:* numerous contribs to learned jls. *Address:* Department of Physics, University of California, Berkeley, CA 94720–7300, USA. *T:* (510) 6423069.

CLARKE, Prof. John Frederick, FRS 1987; Professor of Theoretical Gas Dynamics, Cranfield Institute of Technology, 1972–91, Professor Emeritus, since 1992; *b* 1 May 1927; *s* of Frederick William Clarke and Clara Auguste Antonie (*née* Nauen); *m* 1953, Jean Ruth Gentle; two *d. Educ:* Warwick School; Queen Mary Coll., Univ. of London (BSc Eng 1st Cl. Hons, David Allan Low Prize, PhD; Hon. Fellow, 1992). FIMA 1965; FRAeS 1969; FInstP 1999. Qualified Service Pilot, RN, 1946–48; Aerodynamicist, English Electric Co., 1956–57; Lectr, Coll. of Aeronautics, 1958–65 (Vis. Associate Prof. and Fulbright Scholar, Stanford Univ., 1961–62); Reader, Cranfield Inst. of Technology, 1965–72. Vis. Prof. at univs in USA, Australia and Europe; Vis. Res. Fellow, Centre for Non-linear Studies, Univ. of Leeds, 1987–; Benjamin Meaker Vis. Prof., Univ. of Bristol, 1988–89; first G. C. Steward Vis. Fellow, Gonville and Caius Coll., Cambridge, 1992. Member: NATO Collaborative Research Grants Panel, 1987–90; Esso Energy Award Cttee, 1988–93; Maths Cttee, SERC, 1990–91. Member, Editorial Board: Qly Jl Mech. Appl. Math., 1982–; Combustion Theory & Modelling, 1997–; Philosophical Trans A, Royal Soc., 1997–. *Publications:* (with M. McChesney) The Dynamics of Real Gases, 1964; (with M. McChesney) Dynamics of Relaxing Gases, 1976; contribs to professional jls on gas dynamics and combustion theory. *Recreation:* Sunday painter. *Address:* Field House, Green Lane, Aspley Guise MK17 8EN. *T:* (01908) 582234.

CLARKE, Prof. John Innes, DL; Chairman, NE Regional Awards Committee, National Lottery Charities Board, since 1997; *b* 7 Jan. 1929; *s* of late Bernard Griffith Clarke and Edith Louie (*née* Mott); *m* 1955, Dorothy Anne Watkinson; three *d. Educ:* Bournemouth Sch.; Univ. of Aberdeen (MA 1st cl., PhD); Univ. of Paris (French Govt scholar). FRGS 1963. RAF 1952–54 (Sword of Merit, 1953). Asst Lectr in Geog., Univ. of Aberdeen, 1954–55; Prof. of Geog., Univ. Coll. of Sierra Leone, 1963–65; University of Durham: Lectr in Geog., 1955–63; Reader in Geog., 1965–68; Prof. of Geog., 1968–90, now Emeritus; Acting Principal, Trevelyan Coll., 1979–80; Pro-Vice-Chancellor and Sub-Warden, 1984–90; Leverhulme Emeritus Fellow, 1990–92. Visiting Professor: Univ. of Wisconsin, 1967–68; Cameroon, 1965, 1966, 1967; Clermont-Ferrand, 1974; Cairo, 1982; Shanghai, 1986. Acting Chm., Human Geog. Cttee, SSRC, 1975; RGS rep. on British Nat. Cttee for Geography, 1976–81, 1988–89; Chairman: IGU Commn on Population Geography, 1980–88; Higher Educn Support for Industry in the North, 1987–89; Cttee on Population and Environment, Internat. Union for Scientific Study of Population, 1990–95; Durham, then N Durham DHA, 1990–96. Bd Mem., Co. Durham Foundn, 1995–. Vice-President: Eugenics Soc., 1981–84; RGS, 1991–95. DL Durham, 1990. FRSA 1990. Silver Medal, RSGS, 1947; Victoria Medal, RGS, 1991. *Publications:* Iranian City of Shiraz, 1963; (jtly) Africa and the Islands, 1964, 4th edn 1977; Population Geography, 1965, 2nd edn 1972; (with B. D. Clark) Kermanshah: an Iranian Provincial City, 1969; Population Geography and the Developing Countries, 1971; (jtly) People in Britain: a census atlas, 1980; The Future of Population, 1997; The Human Dictionary, 2000; *edited:* Sierra Leone in Maps, 1966, 2nd edn 1969; An Advanced Geography of Africa, 1975; Geography and Population: approaches and applications, 1984; *co-edited:* Field Studies in Libya, 1960; Populations of the Middle East and North Africa: a geographical approach, 1972; Human Geography in France and Britain, 1976; Régions Géographiques et Régions d'Aménagements, 1978; Change and Development in the Middle East, 1981; Redistribution of Population in Africa, 1982; Population and Development Projects in Africa, 1985; Population and Disaster, 1989; Mountain Population Pressure, 1990; Environment and Population Change, 1994; Population-Environment-Development Interactions, 1995; Population and Environment in Arid Regions, 1997; author of many learned articles. *Recreations:* travel, sports (now vicariously), countryside, family history. *Address:* Tower Cottage, The Avenue, Durham DH1 4EB. *T:* (0191) 384 8350.

CLARKE, Rev. Canon John Martin; Principal of Ripon College, Cuddesdon, since 1997; Canon and Prebendary of Lincoln Cathedral, since 2000; *b* 20 Feb. 1952; *s* of Roland Ernest Clarke and Edna Lucy Hay; *m* 1985, Constance Elizabeth Cressida Nash; two *s* one *d. Educ:* West Buckland Sch.; Hertford Coll., Oxford (MA); Edinburgh Theol Coll. (BD). Ordained deacon, 1976, priest, 1977; Asst Curate, The Ascension, Kenton, Newcastle, 1976–79; Precentor, St Ninian's Cathedral, Perth, 1979–82; Information Officer and Communications Advr to the Gen. Synod of the Scottish Episcopal Church, 1982–87; Philip Usher Scholarship, Greece, 1987–88; Vicar, St Mary, Battersea, 1989–96. *Recreations:* walking, reading, music, cricket. *Address:* Ripon College, Cuddesdon, Oxford OX44 9EX; The Old Vicarage, Cuddesdon, Oxford OX44 9HP. *T:* (01865) 874427.

CLARKE, (John) Neil; Chairman, British Coal, 1991–97; *b* 7 Aug. 1934; *s* of late George Philip Clarke and Norah Marie Clarke (*née* Bailey); *m* 1958, Sonia Heather Beckett; three *s. Educ:* Rugby School; King's College London (LLB). FICA 1959. Partner, Rowley, Pemberton, Roberts & Co., 1960–69; Charter Consolidated, 1969–88: Dir, 1973; Exec. Dir, 1974; Man. Dir, 1979; Chief Exec., 1980; Dep. Chm. and Chief Exec., 1982–88; Chairman: Johnson Matthey, 1984–89; Molins, 1989–91 (Dir, 1987–91); Genchem Holdings, 1989–; Director: Anglo American Corp. of SA, 1976–90; Consolidated Gold Fields, 1982–89; Travis Perkins, 1990–. *Recreations:* music, tennis, golf. *Address:* High Willows, 18 Park Avenue, Farnborough Park, Orpington, Kent BR6 8LL. *T:* (01689) 851651. *Clubs:* MCC; Royal West Norfolk Golf, Addington Golf.

CLARKE, Rear-Adm. John Patrick, CB 1996; LVO 1986; MBE 1978; Chief Executive, British Marine Industries Federation, since 2001; Hydrographer of the Navy and Chief Executive, United Kingdom Hydrographic Office (formerly Hydrographic Agency) 1996–2001; *b* 12 Dec. 1944; *s* of Frank and Christine Clarke; *m* 1st, 1969, Ann Parham (marr. diss. 1997); one *s* two *d*; 2nd, 1998, Mrs Jeffy J. Salt. *Educ:* Epsom Coll.; BRNC. Commanding Officer, HM Ships: Finwhale, 1976; Oberon, 1977; Dreadnought, 1979–80; CO, Submarine CO's Qualifying Course, 1983–84; Exec. Officer, HM Yacht Britannia, 1985–86; Captain: Submarine Sea Training, 1986–89; Seventh Frigate Squadron, 1989–90; Asst Dir, Naval Staff Duties, 1990–92; Dir, Naval Welfare, 1992; Dir, Naval Management, Communications and Inf. Systems, 1993–94; Flag Officer Trng and Recruiting, 1994–96. Younger Brother, Trinity House, 1997. FIMgt; FRGS. Hon. Mem., RICS. *Recreations:* golf, sailing. *Address:* British Marine Industries Federation, Marine House, Thorpe Lea, Egham, Surrey TW20 8BF. *Clubs:* Lansdowne; Yeovil Golf; Royal Southern Yacht.

CLARKE, Rt Rev. John Robert; *see* Athabasca, Bishop of.

CLARKE, His Honour Sir Jonathan (Dennis), Kt 1981; a Circuit Judge, 1982–93; *b* 19 Jan. 1930; *e s* of late Dennis Robert Clarke, Master of Supreme Court, and of Caroline Alice (*née* Hill); *m* 1956, Susan Margaret Elizabeth (*née* Ashworth); one *s* three *d. Educ:* Kidstones Sch.; University Coll. London. Admitted Solicitor, 1956; partner in Townsends, solicitors, 1959–82; a Recorder of the Crown Court, 1972–82. Mem. Council, Law Soc., 1964 82, Pres., 1980–81; Sec., Nat. Cttee of Young Solicitors, 1962–64; Member: Matrimonial Causes Rule Cttee, 1967–78; Legal Studies Bd, CNAA, 1968–75; Judicial Studies Bd, 1979–82; Criminal Injuries Compensation Bd, 1993–; Criminal Injuries Compensation Appeals Panel, 1996–. Governor, College of Law, 1970–90, Chm. of Governors, 1982. *Recreations:* sailing, ski-ing. *Address:* c/o HSBC, The Forum, Marlborough Road, Swindon, Wilts SN3 1QT. *Clubs:* Garrick, Farmers'; Royal Western Yacht.

CLARKE, Rt Hon. Kenneth Harry; PC 1984; QC 1980; MP (C) Rushcliffe, since 1970; *b* 2 July 1940; *e c* of Kenneth Clarke and Doris (*née* Smith), Nottingham; *m* 1964, Gillian Mary Edwards; one *s* one *d. Educ:* Nottingham High Sch.; Gonville and Caius Coll., Cambridge (BA, LLB; Hon. Fellow, 1997). Chm., Cambridge Univ. Conservative Assoc., 1961; Pres., Cambridge Union, 1963; Chm., Fedn Conservative Students, 1963. Called to Bar, Gray's Inn 1963, Hon. Bencher, 1989, Bencher, 1998; Mem., Midland Circuit. Chairman: Savoy Asset Mgt plc; British American Racing (Hldgs) Ltd, 2001–; Dep. Chm., British American Tobacco plc, 1998–; Director: Foreign & Colonial Investment Trust, 1997–; Independent News & Media (UK) Ltd, 1999–; Alliance UniChem, 2001– (Chm., 1997–2001). Research Sec., Birmingham Bow Group, 1965–66. Contested Mansfield, 1964 and 1966. PPS to Solicitor General, 1971–72; an Asst Govt Whip, 1972–74 (Govt Whip for Europe, 1973–74); a Lord Comr, HM Treasury, 1974; Parly Sec., DoT, later Parly Under Sec. of State for Transport, 1979–82; Minister of State (Minister for Health), DHSS, 1982–85; entered Cabinet as Paymaster General and Minister for Employment, 1985–87; Chancellor of Duchy of Lancaster and Minister for Trade and Industry (with additl responsibility to co-ordinate Govt policy on Inner Cities), 1987–88; Secretary of State: for Health, 1988–90; for Educn and Science, 1990–92; for the Home Dept, 1992–93; Chancellor of the Exchequer, 1993–97. Mem., Parly delegn to Council of Europe and WEU, 1973–74; Sec., Cons. Parly Health and Social Security Cttee, 1974; Opposition Spokesman on: Social Services, 1974–76; Industry, 1976–79. Liveryman, Clockmakers' Co. Hon. LLD: Nottingham, 1989; Huddersfield, 1993; DUniv Nottingham Trent, 1996. *Publications:* New Hope for the Regions, 1969; pamphlets published by Bow Group, 1964–. *Recreations:* modern jazz music; watching Association Football and cricket, bird-watching. *Address:* House of Commons, SW1A 0AA. *Clubs:* Garrick; Nottinghamshire CC.

CLARKE, Rt Rev. Kenneth Herbert; *see* Kilmore, Elphin and Ardagh, Bishop of.

CLARKE, Prof. Malcolm Alistair, PhD; Professor of Commercial Contract Law, Cambridge University, since 1999; Fellow, St John's College, Cambridge, since 1970; *b* 1 April 1943; *s* of Kenneth Alfred William Clarke and Marian Florence Clarke (*née* Rich); *m* 1968, Eva Olga Bergman; two *s. Educ:* Kingswood Sch., Bath; L'Ecole des Roches, Verneuil-sur-Avre, France; St John's Coll., Cambridge (LLB 1965; MA 1968; PhD 1973). Asst, Institut de Droit Comparé, Paris, 1965–66; Research Fellow, Fitzwilliam Coll., Cambridge, 1966–68; Lectr, Univ. of Singapore, 1968–70; Cambridge University: Asst Lectr in Law, 1970–75; Lectr, 1975–93; Reader in Commercial Contract Law, 1993–99; Dir of Studies, St John's Coll., Cambridge, 1972–92. *Publications:* Aspects of the Hague Rules, 1976; (jtly) Shipbuilding Contracts, 1981, 2nd edn 1992; The International Carriage of Goods by Road: CMR, 1982, 3rd edn 1997; The Law of Insurance Contracts, 1989, 3rd edn 1997, and bi-annually, 1999–; (jtly) Contracts for the Carriage of Goods, annually 1993–; Policies and Perceptions of Insurance, 1997. *Recreations:* cycling, music, photography, more or less concurrently. *Address:* St John's College, Cambridge CB2 1TP. *T:* (01223) 338600, *Fax:* (01223) 337720.

CLARKE, Prof. Malcolm Roy, FRS 1981; Senior Principal Scientific Officer, Marine Biological Association of the UK, 1978–87; *b* 24 Oct. 1930; *s* of Cecil Dutfield Clarke and Edith Ellen Woodward; *m* 1958, Dorothy Clara Knight; three *s* one *d. Educ:* eleven schools and finally Wallingford County Grammar Sch.; Hull Univ. BSc 1955, PhD 1958,

DSc 1978. National Service, Private, RAMC, 1949–50. Teacher, 1951; Hull Univ., 1951–58; Whaling Inspector in Antarctic, 1955–56; Scientific Officer, later PSO, Nat. Inst. of Oceanography, 1958–71; led Oceanographic Expedns on RRS Discovery, RRS Challenger, RRS Frederick Russell and RV Sarsia; PSO, Marine Biol Assoc. of UK, 1972–78. Visiting Professor: in Zoology, Liverpool Univ., 1987–; in Marine Biol., Azores Univ., 1994–. *Publications:* (ed jtly) Deep Oceans, 1971; Identification of Cephalopod Beaks, 1986; (ed jtly) Evolution, vol. 10, The Mollusca, 1986, vol. 11, Form and Function, 1987, vol. 12, Palaeontology and Neontology of the Cephalopoda, 1987; (ed jtly) Identification of "Larval" Cephalopods, 1987; (ed jtly) Cephalopod Diversity, Ecology and Evolution, 1998; papers on squids and whales in Jl of Marine Biol Assoc., Nature etc, and a Discovery Report, 1980. *Recreations:* boating, painting. *Address:* Ancarva, Southdown, Millbrook, Torpoint, Cornwall PL10 1EZ. *T:* (01752) 823054.

CLARKE, Marshal Butler C.; *see* Cholmondeley Clarke.

CLARKE, Prof. Martin Lowther; *b* 2 Oct. 1909; *s* of late Rev. William Kemp Lowther Clarke; *m* 1942, Emilie de Rontenay Moon (*d* 1991), *d* of late Dr R. O. Moon; two *s*. *Educ:* Haileybury Coll.; King's Coll., Cambridge. Asst, Dept of Humanity, Edinburgh Univ., 1933–34; Fellow of King's Coll., Cambridge, 1934–40; Asst Lecturer in Greek and Latin, University Coll., London, 1935–37. Foreign Office, 1940–45. Lecturer, 1946–47, and Reader, 1947–48, in Greek and Latin, University Coll., London; Prof. of Latin, University Coll. of North Wales, 1948–74, Vice-Principal, 1963–65, 1967–74. *Publications:* Richard Porson, 1937; Greek Studies in England, 1700 to 1830, 1945; Rhetoric at Rome, 1953; The Roman Mind, 1956; Classical Education in Britain, 1500–1900, 1959; George Grote, 1962; Bangor Cathedral, 1969; Higher Education in the Ancient World, 1971; Paley, 1974; The Noblest Roman, 1981. *Address:* 61 Ilges Lane, Cholsey, Wallingford OX10 9PA. *T:* (01491) 651389.

CLARKE, Martin Peter; consultant, Associated Newspapers; *b* 26 Aug. 1964; *s* of Robert William Clarke and Doris May (*née* Snowden); *m* 1998, Veronica (*née* Gilfedder). *Educ:* Gravesend Grammar Sch. for Boys; Bristol Univ. (BA Hons). Daily Mail Executive, 1988–94; News Ed., Daily Mirror, 1995; Editor: Scottish Daily Mail, 1995–97; The Scotsman, 1997–98; Ed.-in-Chief, Daily Record and Sunday Mail Ltd, 1998–2000. *Address:* c/o Associated Newspapers Ltd, Northcliffe House, 2 Derry Street, W8 5TT.

CLARKE, Mary; Editor, Dancing Times, since 1963; *b* 23 Aug. 1923; *d* of Frederick Clarke and Ethel Kate (*née* Reynolds); unmarried. *Educ:* Mary Datchelor Girls' School. London Corresp., Dance Magazine, NY, 1943–55; London Editor, Dance News, NY, 1955–70; Asst Editor and Contributor, Ballet Annual, 1952–63; joined Dancing Times as Asst Editor, 1954. Dance critic, The Guardian, 1977–94, retired. Queen Elizabeth II Coronation Award, Royal Acad. of Dancing, 1990; Nijinsky Medal, Poland, 1996. Kt, Order of Dannebrog (Denmark), 1992. *Publications:* The Sadler's Wells Ballet: a history and an appreciation, 1955; Six Great Dancers, 1957; Dancers of Mercury: the story of Ballet Rambert, 1962; ed (with David Vaughan) Encyclopedia of Dance and Ballet, 1977; (with Clement Crisp): Ballet, an Illustrated History, 1973, 2nd edn 1992; Making a Ballet, 1974; Introducing Ballet, 1976; Design for Ballet, 1978; Ballet in Art, 1978; The History of Dance, 1981; Dancer, Men in Dance, 1984; Ballerina, 1987; contrib. Encycl. Britannica, New DNB. *Address:* 54 Ripplevale Grove, N1 1HT. *T:* (020) 7607 3422. *Club:* Gautier.

CLARKE, Matthew Gerard; *see* Clarke, Hon. Lord.

CLARKE, Michael; *see* Clarke, C. M.

CLARKE, Prof. Michael, FRCP, FRCPE, FFPHM; Professor of Epidemiology, University of Leicester, since 1981; Hon. Consultant, Leicestershire Health, since 1974; *b* 2 Nov. 1940; *s* of Leslie Frederick Clarke and late Gertrude Mary Clarke (*née* Dring); *m* 1966, Susan Jenkins Thompson (marr. diss. 1994); one *s* one *d*. *Educ:* Middlesex Hosp. Med. Sch., Univ. of London (MB BS 1965). MRCS, LRCP 1965; DPH 1968; MFPHM 1974, FFPHM 1979; FRCP 1991; FRCPE 1996. Lectr, St Thomas' Hosp., London, 1968–74; Vis. Scientist, R&D, Nat. Centre for Health Services, 1972–73; Sen. Lectr, Dept of Community Health, Univ. of Leicester, 1974–80. Dir, Trent Inst. for Health Services Res., 1993–; non-exec. Dir, Leics Gen. Hosp., 1992–. Vis. Prof., Univ. of Colorado, 1982. Member: MRC Public Health & Health Services Res. Bd, 1990–94; Chair: Heads of Academic Depts of Public Health, 1990–92; Strategic Review of the NHS R&D Levy, 1998–2000. Vice Pres., FPHM, 1995–2000. *Publications:* articles on epidemiology and health services res., particularly in relation to reproduction, care of the elderly and urinary incontinence. *Recreations:* cooking, interior design. *Address:* Department of Epidemiology and Public Health, University of Leicester, 22–28 Princess Road West, Leicester LE1 6TP. *T:* (0116) 252 3201.

CLARKE, Prof. Michael Gilbert, CBE 2000; DL; Professor, School of Public Policy, since 1993, and Pro-Vice-Chancellor, since 1998, University of Birmingham; *b* 21 May 1944; *s* of Rev. Canon Reginald Gilbert Clarke and Marjorie Kathleen Clarke; *m* 1967, Angela Mary Cook; one *s* two *d*. *Educ:* Queen Elizabeth Grammar Sch., Wakefield; Sussex Univ. (BA 1966; MA 1967). Teaching Assistant, Essex Univ., 1967–69; Lectr and Dir of Studies in Politics, Edinburgh Univ., 1969–75; Asst Dir and Depute Dir, Policy Planning, Lothian Regl Council, 1975–81; Dir, LGTB, 1981–90; Chief Exec., Local Govt Mgt Bd, 1990–93; Head, Sch. of Public Policy, Univ. of Birmingham, 1993–98. Mem., Local Govt Commn for England, 1993– (Dep. Chm., 1998–). Member: Gen. Synod of C of E, 1990–93, 1995–; Council, Queen's Foundn, Birmingham, 1997–; W Midlands Regl Chamber, 1999–; Bd, Commonwealth Local Govt Forum, 1998–; Bd, Ikon Gall., Birmingham, 1999–. Trustee: Inst. for Citizenship Studies, 1992–; Civic Trust, 1998–. Lay Canon and Mem. Chapter, Worcester Cathedral, 2001–. DL Worcs, 2000. *Publications:* articles on UK public policy and management issues esp. local govt and central-local relns. *Recreations:* books, family, gardening. *Address:* Millington House, 15 Lansdowne Crescent, Worcester WR3 8JE. *T:* (01905) 617634. *Club:* Reform.

CLARKE, Maj.-Gen. Michael Hugo Friend; Immigration Appeals Adjudicator, since 1994, Special Adjudicator, since 1999; *b* 22 Sept. 1936; *s* of Patrick Joseph Clarke and Catherine Amy Clarke (*née* Friend); *m* 1962, Gerritje van der Horst; one *s* one *d*. *Educ:* Rutland House Sch.; Allhallows Sch. Called to the Bar, Lincoln's Inn, 1959; enlisted RASC, 1959; commissioned 2nd Lieut RASC, 1960; Captain, Army Legal Services, 1961; served BAOR, Singapore, Nairobi, Hong Kong, Cyprus, N Ireland; HQ Army Legal Aid, 1981; MoD, 1983; Army Legal Aid, BAOR, 1986; Army Legal Group UK, 1987; Brig., Legal HQ BAOR, 1989; Dir, Army Legal Services, 1992–94. Trustee, Inst. of Obs and Gyn., 1995–. *Recreations:* gardening, walking, sport. *Address:* c/o Lloyds TSB, Cox's and King's Branch, PO Box 1190, 7 Pall Mall, SW1Y 5NA.

CLARKE, Neil; *see* Clarke, J. N.

CLARKE, Nicholas Campbell, (Nick); Presenter, World at One, BBC Radio Four, since 1994; *b* 9 June 1948; *s* of John Campbell Clarke and Ruth Wilda (*née* McNeile); *m* 1st, 1973, Sue Armstrong (marr. diss. 1990); two *s* one *d*; 2nd, 1991, Barbara Want. *Educ:* Bradfield Coll., Berks; Fitzwilliam Coll., Cambridge (BA Hons). Yorkshire Evening Post, 1970–72; Reporter and Industrial Corresp., BBC North-West, 1973–79; Reporter, Money Prog., BBC, 1980–85; Political Corresp. and Presenter, Newsnight, BBC, 1986–89; Presenter, World This Weekend, Radio 4, 1989–94. Pres., Fitzwilliam Soc., 2001–02. Best Individual Contributor to Radio, Voice of the Listener and Viewer, 1999; Radio Broadcaster of the Year, BPG, 2000. *Publication:* Alistair Cooke: The Biography, 1999. *Recreations:* cricket, cooking, wine, worrying. *Address:* c/o BBC News Centre, Wood Lane, W12 7RJ. *T:* (020) 8624 9730. *Club:* Groucho.

CLARKE, Nicky; hair stylist; Founder and Co-Director, Nicky Clarke Salon, Mayfair, and Nicky Clarke Haircare Products; *b* 17 June 1958; *m* 1982, Lesley Anne Gale; one *s* one *d*. Director: Kasmare Ltd; Southern Tropics Ltd; Nicky Clarke Products Ltd. Has made numerous TV appearances as expert and spokesperson on matters related to hair. Numerous awards, including: British Hairdresser of Year Award; London Hairdresser of Year Award. *Publications:* Hair Power, 1999; contribs to newspapers and magazines, incl. Vogue, Tatler, Marie Claire and Harpers Bazaar. *Recreations:* ski-ing, water ski-ing, contemporary music, riding Harley Davidson. *Address:* 130 Mount Street, W1Y 5HA. *T:* (020) 7355 4575.

CLARKE, Norman, OBE 1982; Secretary and Registrar, Institute of Mathematics and its Applications, from its foundation, 1964–87, now Emeritus; *b* 21 Oct. 1916; *o s* of late Joseph Clarke and of Ellen Clarke, Oldham; *m* 1940, Hilda May Watts; two *d*. *Educ:* Hulme Grammar Sch., Oldham; Univ. of Manchester (BSc). FInstP; FIMA, Hon. FIMA 1990. Pres., Manchester Univ. Union, 1938–39. External Ballistics Dept, Ordnance Bd, 1939–42; Armament Res. Estabt, Br. for Theoretical Res., 1942–45; Dep. Sec., Inst. Physics, 1945–65; Hon. Sec., Internat. Commn on Physics Educn, 1960–66. Southend-on-Sea County Borough Council: Mem., 1961–74; Alderman, 1964–74; Chm. of Watch Cttee, 1962–69 and of Public Protection Cttee, 1969–78; Vice-Chm., Essex Police Authority, 1969–85; Member: Essex CC, 1973–85; Southend-on-Sea Borough Council, 1974– (Mayor, 1975–76; Chm., Highways Cttee, 1980–84; Leader, 1984–87, 1990–93; Leader, Cons. Gp, 1984–93). Hon. Freeman, Southend-on-Sea, 1996. *Publications:* papers on educn; editor and contributor: A Physics Anthology: (with S. C. Brown) International Education in Physics; Why Teach Physics; The Education of a Physicist; contributor: A Survey of the Teaching of Physics in Universities (Unesco); Metrication. *Recreations:* cricket, gastronomy, photography. *Address:* 106 Olive Avenue, Leigh-on-Sea, Essex SS9 3QE. *T:* (01702) 558056. *Club:* MCC.

CLARKE, Prof. Patricia Hannah, DSc; FRS 1976; Emeritus Professor, University of London, since 1984; *b* 29 July 1919; *d* of David Samuel Green and Daisy Lilian Amy Willoughby; *m* 1940, Michael Clarke; two *s*. *Educ:* Howells Sch., Llandaff; Girton Coll., Cambridge (BA). DSc London. Armament Res. Dept, 1940–44; Wellcome Res. Labs, 1944–47; National Collection of Type Cultures, 1951–53; University College London: Lectr, Dept of Biochemistry, 1953; Reader in Microbial Biochemistry, 1966; Prof. of Microbial Biochemistry, 1974–84; Hon. Fellow, 1995. Leverhulme Emer. Fellow, 1984–87; Hon. Professorial Fellow, UWIST, Univ. of Wales, 1984–90; Kan Tong-Po Prof., Chinese Univ. of Hong Kong, 1986. Chm., Inst. for Biotechnological Studies, 1986–87. Hon. Gen. Sec., Soc. for General Microbiology, 1965–70 (Hon. Mem., 1996); Mem., CNAA, 1973–79. Gov., Cirencester Deer Park Comprehensive Sch., 1988–99. Lectures: Royal Soc. Leeuwenhoek, 1979; Marjory Stephenson, Soc. for Gen. Microbiology, 1981; A. J. Kluyver, Netherlands Soc. for Microbiology, 1981. A Vice-Pres., Royal Soc., 1981–82. Hon. DSc: Kent, 1984; CNAA, 1990. *Publications:* Genetics and Biochemistry of Pseudomonas (ed with M. H. Richmond), 1975; papers on genetics, biochemistry and enzyme evolution in Jl of Gen. Microbiol. and other jls. *Recreations:* walking, gardening, travelling. *Address:* 7 Corinium Gate, Cirencester, Glos GL7 2PX.

CLARKE, Paul Robert Virgo, FRICS; Chief Executive, Clerk of the Council, Keeper of the Records and Surveyor General, Duchy of Lancaster, since 2000; *b* 13 Aug. 1953; *s* of Robert Charles Houghton Clarke and Joan Clarke (*née* Stanton); *m* 1978, Vanessa Carol Pike; two *d*. *Educ:* Abingdon Sch.; W London Coll. FRICS 1988. Valuation Surveyor and Tech. Asst to Exec. Trustee, Grosvenor Estate, 1974–82; Equity Partner, Clarke & Green, Chartered Surveyors, 1982–96; Property Investment Manager, Wellcome Trust, 1996–2000. *Recreations:* ski-ing, walking, horse riding, painting, travel. *Address:* Duchy of Lancaster Office, 1 Lancaster Place, Strand, WC2E 7ED. *T:* (020) 7836 8277.

CLARKE, Peter, CBE 1983; PhD, CChem, FRSC, FInstPet; Principal, Robert Gordon's Institute of Technology, Aberdeen, 1970–85, retired; Chairman, Scottish Vocational Education Council, 1985–91; *b* 18 March 1922; *er s* of Frederick John and Gladys May Clarke; *m* 1947, Ethel Jones; two *s*. *Educ:* Queen Elizabeth's Grammar Sch., Mansfield; University Coll., Nottingham (BSc). Industrial Chemist, 1942; Sen. Chemistry Master, Buxton Coll., 1947; Lectr, Huddersfield Technl Coll., 1949; British Enka Ltd, Liverpool, 1956; Sen. Lectr, Royal Coll. of Advanced Tech., Salford, 1962; Head of Dept of Chemistry and Biology, Nottingham Regional Coll. of Technology, 1963; Vice-Principal, Huddersfield Coll. of Technology, 1965–70. Member: SERC (formerly SRC), 1978–82; Council for Professions Supplementary to Medicine, 1977–85; Scottish Technical Educn Council, 1982–85; CNAA, 1982–87 (Chm., Cttee for Scotland, 1983). Chm., Assoc. of Principals of Colleges (Scotland), 1976–78; President: Assoc. of Principals of Colleges, 1980–81; Assoc. for Educnl and Trng Technol., 1993–95. Chairman: Aberdeen Enterprise Trust, 1984–92; Industrial Trng Centre Aberdeen Ltd, 1989–95; Gordon Cook Foundn, 1997–99 (Trustee, 1989–). FRSA 1986. Burgess of Guild, City of Aberdeen, 1973. Hon. LLD Aberdeen, 1985; Hon. DEd: CNAA, 1992; Robert Gordon, 1999. *Publications:* contribs to Jl of Chem. Soc., Chemistry and Industry. *Recreation:* walking. *Address:* 108 Whinhill Gate, Aberdeen AB11 7WF.

CLARKE, Major Sir Peter Cecil, KCVO 1992 (CVO 1969; LVO 1964); Chief Clerk, Duchy of Lancaster, 1969–92; Extra Equerry to HRH Princess Alexandra, the Hon. Lady Ogilvy; *b* 9 Aug. 1927; *s* of late Captain E. D. Clarke, CBE, MC, Binstead, Isle of Wight; *m* 1950, Rosemary Virginia Margaret Harmsworth, *d* of late T. C. Durham, Appomattox, Virginia, USA; one *s* two *d*. *Educ:* Eton; RMA, Sandhurst. 3rd The King's Own Hussars and 14th/20th King's Hussars, 1945–64; Adjt 3rd The King's Own Hussars, GSO2 2 Inf. Div., psc 1959. Seconded as Asst Private Secretary to HRH Princess Marina, Duchess of Kent, 1961–64; Comptroller, 1964–68; Comptroller to HRH Princess Alexandra, 1964–69. Mem. Court of Assts, Corp. of Sons of the Clergy, 1987–98. JP Hants, 1971–81. *Recreations:* golf, fishing. *Address:* 6 Gordon Place, W8 4JD. *T:* (020) 7937 0356. *Club:* Cavalry and Guards.

CLARKE, Prof. Peter Frederick, LittD; FBA 1989; Master of Trinity Hall, Cambridge, since 2000; Professor of Modern British History, Cambridge University, since 1991; *b* 21 July 1942; *s* of late John William Clarke and of Winifred Clarke (*née* Hadfield); *m* 1st, 1969, Dillon Cheetham (marr. diss. 1990); two *d*; 2nd, 1991, Dr Maria Tippett, FRS(Can), Vancouver. *Educ:* Eastbourne Grammar Sch.; St John's Coll., Cambridge (BA 1963; MA 1967; PhD 1967; LittD 1989). FRHistS 1972. Asst Lectr and Lectr in History, 1966–78, Reader in Modern Hist., 1978–80, UCL; Cambridge University: Fellow, St John's Coll., 1980–2000 (Tutor, 1982–87); Lectr in History, 1980–87; Reader in Modern

History, 1987–91; Sec., Faculty Bd of Hist., 1985–86. Vis. Prof. of Modern British Hist., Harvard Univ., 1974; Vis. Fellow, Res. Sch. of Social Scis, ANU, 1983. Creighton Lectr, London Univ., 1998. Member: Council, RHistS, 1979–83; Adv. Council on Public Records, 1995–; Royal Commn on Historical MSS, 2000–. Chm., S Cambs Area Party, SDP, 1981–82. Jt Review Ed., History, 1967–73; Chm., Editl Bd, Twentieth Century British History, 1988–98. *Publications:* Lancashire and the New Liberalism, 1971, 2nd edn 1993; Liberals and Social Democrats, 1978, 3rd edn 1993; The Keynesian Revolution in the Making, 1988, 2nd edn 1990; A Question of Leadership: from Gladstone to Thatcher, 1991, 2nd edn 1992, new edn, from Gladstone to Blair, 1999; Hope and Glory: Britain 1900–1990, 1996, 2nd edn 1997; The Keynesian Revolution and its Economic Consequences, 1998; articles in learned jls; contribs to TLS, London Rev. of Books, etc. *Recreations:* walking, cooking. *Address:* The Master's Lodge, Trinity Hall, Cambridge CB2 1TJ. *T:* (01223) 332540. *Club:* Royal Over-Seas League.

CLARKE, Peter Henry, FRICS; Member of the Lands Tribunal, since 1993 (part time, 1993–96, full time, since 1996); *b* 22 September 1935; *s* of late Henry George Clarke and Winifred Eva Clarke (*née* Sharp); *m* 1964, May Connell; one *d*. *Educ:* Ealing Technical Coll.; Coll. of Estate Management; LLB 1972, MPhil 1993, London. ARICS 1957, FRICS 1973; ACIArb 1976. With G. L. Hearn & Partners, 1952–57, 1959–60; Cubitt Estates, 1960–64; Eldonwall Ltd, 1964–69; Donaldsons, 1969–96 (Partner, 1972–96). *Publications:* (jtly) Land Values, 1965; (jtly) Valuation: Principles into Practice, 1980, 5th edn 2000; The Surveyor in Court, 1985; articles on compensation and rent reviews in various jls. *Recreations:* music, opera, reading, walking, dogs. *Address:* Lands Tribunal, 48/49 Chancery Lane, WC2A 1JR. *T:* (020) 7947 7166.

CLARKE, Peter James, CBE 1993; Secretary of the Forestry Commission, 1976–94, retired; *b* 16 Jan. 1934; *s* of Stanley Ernest Clarke and Elsie May (*née* Scales); *m* 1966, Roberta Anne, *y d* of Robert and Ada Browne; one *s* one *d*. *Educ:* Enfield Grammar Sch.; St John's Coll., Cambridge (MA). Exec. Officer, WO, 1952–62 (univ., 1957–60), Higher Exec. Officer, 1962; Sen. Exec. Officer, Forestry Commn, 1967, Principal 1972; Principal, Dept of Energy, 1975. *Recreations:* gardening, walking, travel. *Address:* 5 Murrayfield Gardens, Edinburgh EH12 6DG. *T:* (0131) 337 3145.

CLARKE, Peter William; QC 1997; a Recorder, since 1991; *b* 29 May 1950; *s* of His Honour Edward Clarke, QC, and Dorothy May Clarke (*née* Leask); *m* 1978, Victoria Mary, *d* of Michael Francis Gilbert, *qv*; one *s* one *d*. *Educ:* Sherborne Sch.; Inns of Court Sch. of Law. Called to the Bar, Lincoln's Inn, 1973; in practice at the Bar, specialising in criminal law, 1974–; Asst Recorder, 1987–91. *Recreations:* losing at tennis to my children, ski-ing, golf (winner, Bar golfing tournament, 1985), photography, enjoying my wife's paintings. *Address:* 3rd Floor, Queen Elizabeth Building, Temple, EC4Y 9BS. *T:* (020) 7583 5766. *Clubs:* Garrick; Royal Mid Surrey Golf.

CLARKE, Richard Ian; High Commissioner to Tanzania, since 2001; *b* 7 Sept. 1955; *s* of Sydney Thomas Reginald Clarke and Joan Clarke; *m* 1st, 1978, Anne Elizabeth Menzies (marr. diss. 1993); one *s*; 2nd, 1993, Sheenagh Marie O'Connor; two *s*. *Educ:* Market Harborough Upper Sch.; Univ. of E Anglia (BSc). Joined FCO, 1977: 3rd, later 2nd, Sec., Caracas, 1978–83; 2nd, later 1st, Sec., FCO, 1983–87; 1st Sec., Washington, 1987–91; Asst Hd, Planning Staff, FCO, 1991–93; Dep. Hd, UN Dept, FCO, 1993–96; Counsellor and Dep. Hd of Mission, Dublin, 1996–98, Hd, Policy Planning Staff, FCO, 1998–2001. Ian St James Award for short fiction, 1991. *Publication:* (contrib.) Midnight Oil, 1991. *Recreations:* Leicester City, reading, Wars of the Roses, American Civil War, Glamrock, crisps, early 20th century art. *Address:* c/o Foreign and Commonwealth Office, King Charles Street, SW1A 2AH.

CLARKE, Most Rev. Richard Lionel; *see* Meath and Kildare, Bishop of.

CLARKE, Sir Robert (Cyril), Kt 1993; Chairman, Thames Water Plc, 1994–99 (non-executive Director, since 1988); *b* 28 March 1929; *s* of Robert Henry Clarke and Rose Lilian (*née* Bratton); *m* 1952, Evelyn (Lynne) Mary, *d* of Cyrus Harper and Ann Ellen (*née* Jones); three *s* (incl. twin *s*) one *d*. *Educ:* Dulwich Coll.; Pembroke Coll., Oxford (MA Hist.; Hon. Fellow, 1993). Served Royal West Kent Regt, 1947–49. Joined Cadbury Bros, as trainee, 1952; Gen. Manager, John Forrest, 1954; Marketing Dir, Cadbury Confectionary, 1957; Man. Dir, 1962–69, Chm., 1969–71, Cadbury Cakes; Dir, Cadbury Schweppes Foods, 1969–71; Man. Dir, McVitie & Cadbury Cakes, 1971–74; Dir, 1974–95, Chm. and Man. Dir, 1984–95, United Biscuits UK Ltd; Man. Dir, UB Biscuits, 1977–84; Dir, 1984–95, Gp Chief Exec., 1986–90, Chm., 1990–95, United Biscuits (Holdings). Member: Council, Cake and Biscuit Alliance, 1965–83; Council, ISBA, 1977–84; Resources Cttee, Food and Drink Fedn, 1984–86; Bd of Dirs, Grocery Manufrs of America, 1991–95. Gov., World Economic Forum, 1990–. Special Trustee, Gt Ormond St Hosp. for Children NHS Trust, 1991–99 (Chm., Special Trustees, 1994–99; non-exec. Mem., Trust Bd, 1994–99). Hon. Fellow, Inst. of Child Health, 1997. FIGD; CIMgt. *Recreations:* reading, walking, renovating old buildings, planting trees.

CLARKE, Rev. Robert Sydney, OBE 2000; Secretary and Director of Training, Hospital Chaplaincies Council, since 1994; Chaplain to HM the Queen, since 1987; *b* 31 Oct. 1935; *s* of George Sydney and Elizabeth Clarke. *Educ:* St Dunstan's College; King's Coll., Univ. of London (AKC 1964; MA 1965). Chaplain: New Cross Hospital, Wolverhampton, 1970–74; Herrison and West Dorset County Hosp., Dorchester, 1974–79; Westminster Hosp. and Westminster Medical School, Univ. of London, 1979–85; Winchester HA, 1985–94. Sen. Hon. Chaplain, Winchester and Eastleigh Health Care Trust, 1994–. *Recreations:* breeding and showing dogs, music, travel, DIY. *Address:* Fielden House, Little College Street, Westminster SW1P 3SH. *T:* (020) 7222 5090. *Club:* Kennel.

CLARKE, Robin Mitchell, MC 1944; JP; DL; Chairman, Gatwick Airport Consultative Committee, 1982–90; *b* 8 Jan. 1917; *e s* of Joseph and Mary Clarke; *m* 1946, Betty Mumford; twin *s* and *d*. *Educ:* Ruckholt Central Sch., Leyton. Middleton and St Bride's Wharf, Wapping, 1932–34; Town Clerk's Office, City of Westminster, 1935–40. War of 1939–45: 12th Regt, RHA (HAC) and 142 (Royal Devon Yeomanry) Fd Regt, RA; Major, 1944; served Sicily and Italy (wounded, despatches, MC). Town Clerk's Office, Westminster, 1946–48; Crawley Development Corporation, 1948–62; Manager, Crawley, Commn for the New Towns, 1962–78; Chief Exec., New Towns Commn, 1978–82. Vice-Pres., St Catherine's Hospice, Crawley, 1989– (Chm., 1983–89). Master, Worshipful Co. of Chartered Secs and Administrators, 1984–85. ACIS 1949; FCIS 1959 (Mem. Nat. Council, 1968–87; Pres., 1978). JP Crawley, 1971; DL West Sussex, 1982. FRSA 1980. *Address:* Mayford Cottage, 89 Golden Avenue, East Preston, W Sussex BN16 1QT. *T:* (01903) 771739.

CLARKE, Roger Eric; Maritime consultant; literary translator; Director of Shipping and Ports, Department of the Environment, Transport and the Regions, 1997–99; *b* 13 June 1939; *s* of Frederick Cuérel Clarke and late Hilda Josephine Clarke; *m* 1983, Elizabeth Jane, *d* of Gordon W. Pingstone and Anne Ellen Pingstone; one *d*. *Educ:* UCS, Hampstead; Corpus Christi Coll., Cambridge (MA). FCIArb 1999. Various posts in civil aviation divs of Min. of Aviation, BoT and Depts of Trade and Transport, 1961–72 and 1980–85; Air Traffic Rights Advr to Govt of Fiji, 1972–74; Asst Sec., Insce and Overseas Trade Divs, Dept of Trade, 1975–80; Under Sec., Civil Aviation Policy Directorate, 1985–89, Public Transport Directorate, 1989–91, Shipping Policy Directorate, 1991–97, Dept of Transport. *Publications:* (trans.) Pushkin, Eugene Onegin, 1999; (trans.) Pushkin, Boris Godunov, 1999; The Trawler Gaul: why was no search made for the wreck?, 2000; The Trawler Gaul: the search for bodies of the crew in northern Russia, 2000. *Recreations:* family, friends, church, philately, garden, walking, theatre, music, languages, travel. *Address:* 64 Scotts Lane, Shortlands, Bromley, Kent BR2 0LX. *Club:* Reform.

CLARKE, Roger Howard, PhD; Director, National Radiological Protection Board, since 1987; *b* 22 Aug. 1943; *s* of late Harold Pardoe and Laurie Gwyneth Clarke; *m* 1966, Sandra Ann (*née* Buckley); one *s* one *d*. *Educ:* King Edward VI Sch., Stourbridge; Univ. of Birmingham (BSc, MSc); Polytechnic of Central London (PhD). Res. Officer, Berkeley Nuclear Laboratories, CEGB, 1965–77; Hd of Nuclear Power Assessments, NRPB, 1978–83; Bd Sec., 1983–87. Deleg. to UN Sci. Cttee on the Effects of Atomic Radiation, 1979–; Chairman: OECD Nuclear Energy Agency Cttee on Radiation Protection and Public Health, 1987–92; Internat. Commn on Radiol Protection, 1993– (Mem., 1989–93); Mem., Gp of Experts, Article 31, Euratom, 1988–. Visiting Professor: Imperial Coll. of Science, Technol. and Medicine, 1993–; Univ. of Surrey, 1994–. Lindell Lectr, Swedish Risk Kollegiat, 1999. Hon. FRCR 1994; Hon. FSRP 1995. G. William Morgan Award, US Health Physics Soc., 1994; Ellison-Cliffe Medal, RSocMed, 1996. *Publications:* Carcinogenesis and Radiation Risk (with W. V. Mayneord), 1975; numerous papers in sci. and technical literature. *Recreations:* gardening, theatre, travel. *Address:* Corner Cottage, Woolton Hill, Newbury, Berks RG20 9XJ. *T:* (01635) 253957.

CLARKE, Roy; writer, since 1965; *b* 28 Jan. 1930; *s* of Austin and Alice Clarke; *m* 1953, Enid Kitching; one *s* one *d*. *Educ:* badly during World War II. Soldier, salesman, policeman and teacher until I was able to persuade people I was actually a writer. *Television series:* The Misfit, 1970–72; Last of the Summer Wine, 1972–; Open All Hours, 1975–82; Potter, 1979–83; Pulaski, 1987; Single Voices, 1990; The World of Eddie Weary, 1990; Keeping Up Appearances, 1990–96; Ain't Misbehaving, 1994; *films:* Hawks, 1988; A Foreign Field, 1993. Freeman of Doncaster, 1994. Hon. DLitt: Bradford, 1988; Huddersfield, 1997. Best Series Award, Writers' Guild, 1970; Pye TV Award, 1982, Denis Potter Award, 1996, BAFTA. *Publications:* Summer Wine Chronicles, 1986; The Moonbather, 1987; Harborne, 1994; Summer Wine Country, 1995; (with J. Rice) Hyacinth Bucket's Hectic Social Calendar, 1995. *Recreations:* walking, reading, hiding. *Address:* c/o The Agency, 24 Pottery Lane, Holland Park, W11 4LZ. *T:* (020) 7727 1346.

CLARKE, Major Sir Rupert William John, 3rd Bt *cr* 1882; AM 1999; MBE 1943; late Irish Guards; Chairman: United Distillers Co., 1960–88; National Australia Bank Ltd (formerly National Bank of Australasia), 1986–92 (Director, since 1955); International Ranch Management Services Pty Ltd; P & O Australia Ltd, 1983–96 (Director, since 1980; Hon. President, since 1996); *b* 5 Nov. 1919; *s* of 2nd Bt and Elsie Florence (who *m* 2nd, 1928, 5th Marquess of Headfort), *d* of James Partridge Tucker, Devonshire; *S* father, 1926; *m* 1st, 1947, Kathleen (*d* 1999), *d* of P. Grant Hay, Toorak, Victoria, Australia; two *s* one *d* (and one *s* decd); 2nd, 2000, Mrs Gillian de Zoete. *Educ:* Eton; Magdalen Coll., Oxford (MA). Hon. Fellow, Trinity Coll., Melbourne, 1981. Served War of 1939–45 (despatches, MBE). Chm., Cadbury Schweppes Australia Ltd (formerly Schweppes (Australia)), 1955–89; Dir, Cadbury Schweppes, 1977–85; Chairman: Bank of South Pacific, 1986–92; First National Ltd, 1986–92; Vice Chm., Conzinc, 1970–87; Director: Riotinto of Australia, 1962–87; Custom Credit Corp.; Morganite Australia Pty (Chm., 1976–84); National Australia Gp (UK), 1990–92. Vice Pres., Howard Florey Inst. of Exptl Physiology and Medicine, 1997–2000 (Mem. Bd, 1994–2000). Pres., Royal Humane Soc. of Australasia Inc., 1992–99. Mem. Cttee, Vict. Amateur Turf Club (Chm., 1972–88); Councillor, Royal Agricl Soc. of Vic, 1965–. Hon. Consul General for Monaco, 1975– (Hon. Consul, 1961). Officier de la Légion d'Honneur, 1998; Comdr, Ordre des Grimaldi (Monaco); Officer, Order of Leopold (Belgium), 1989. *Publication:* At War with Alex (memoirs), 2000. *Heir: s* Rupert Grant Alexander Clarke, LLB (Hons) [*b* 12 Dec. 1947; *m* 1978, Susannah, *d* of Sir Robert Law-Smith, *qv*; one *s* two *d*]. *Address:* Bolinda Vale, Clarkefield, Vic 3430, Australia; Fairlie, 4/54 Anderson Street, South Yarra, Vic 3141. *Fax:* (3) 96702629. *Clubs:* Cavalry and Guards, Lansdowne; Melbourne, Athenæum, Australian (Melbourne); Union (Sydney).

CLARKE, Samuel Laurence Harrison, CBE 1988; CEng, FIEE; Assistant Technical Director, GEC plc, 1981–91; Director: Sira Ltd, 1989–95; Filtronic Ltd, 1989–93; *b* 16 Dec. 1929; *s* of late Samuel Harrison Clarke, CBE; *m* 1952, Ruth Joan Godwin, *yr d* of Oscar and Muriel Godwin; one *s* three *d*. *Educ:* Westminster Sch.; Trinity Coll., Cambridge (BA). Technical Dir, GEC-Elliott Automation Ltd, 1970–74; Technical Dir (Automation), GEC-Marconi Electronics Ltd, 1974–81; Director, GEC Computers Ltd, 1971–83. Dep. Dir, 1983–87, Dir, 1987, Alvey Programme, DTI. *Publications:* various papers in learned and technical jls. *Recreations:* ski-ing, Scottish dancing, conservation. *Address:* Sarum End, Salisbury Road, Southwold, Suffolk IP18 6LG. *T:* (01502) 725116.

CLARKE, Stanley George, CBE 1975; Chief Inspector of the Prison Service, 1971–74; Member: Prisons Board, 1971–74; Parole Board, 1975–78; *b* Dunfermline, 5 May 1914; *s* of Stanley and Catherine Clarke; *m* 1940, Mary Preston Lewin; one *s* one *d*. *Educ:* Sutton High Sch., Plymouth (school colours: cricket, Rugby, soccer). Civil Service Clerk: Dartmoor Prison, 1931; Lowdham Grange Borstal, 1933; North Sea Camp, 1935; Borstal Housemaster: Portland, 1937; North Sea Camp, 1939. Served War, 1941–45 (despatches): Sqdn Ldr, RAF. Borstal Housemaster: Hollesley Bay Colony, 1945; Gaynes Hall, 1946. Dep. Governor, Manchester Prison, 1947; Governor: Norwich Prison, 1949; Nottingham Prison, 1952; Eastchurch Prison, 1955; Liverpool Prison, 1959. Asst Dir of Prisons, in charge of North Region, 1964; Asst Controller, Prison Dept, 1970.

CLARKE, Sir Stanley (William), Kt 2001; CBE 1990; Chairman, St Modwen Properties PLC, since 1986; *b* 7 June 1933; *s* of Victor Raymond Clarke and Mabel Ellen Clarke (*née* Royall); *m* 1958, Hilda Joan Leavesley; one *s* three *d*. *Educ:* St Peter's Sch., Stapenhill, Burton upon Trent; Burton upon Trent Tech. High Sch.; Burton Tech. Coll. Founded plumbing business, 1954, later S. W. Clarke (Contractors) Ltd, then Clarke Homes; estabd St Modwen Properties Ltd, 1966 (all part of Clarke Gp); estabd St Modwen Properties PLC, 1986, following sale of Clarke Gp. Founder and Chm., Northern Racing Ltd, 1994–; non-exec. Chm., British Bloodstock Agency, 2001– . DUniv Staffordshire, 1998. *Recreations:* horse racing, breeding racehorses. *Address:* The Knoll, Barton-under-Needwood, Staffs DE13 8AB. *T:* (01283) 712294.

CLARKE, Mrs Stella Rosemary, CBE 1997; JP; DL; Chairman, Community Self Build Agency, since 1989; *b* 16 Feb. 1932; *d* of John Herbert and Molly Isabel Bruce King; *m* 1952, Charles Nigel Clarke; four *s* one *d*. *Educ:* Cheltenham Ladies' Coll.; Trinity Coll. Dublin. Long Ashton RDC: Councillor, Chm. Council, Housing and Public Health Cttees, 1955–73; Mem., Woodspring Dist Council, 1973–76; co-opted Mem., Somerset CC, Social Services and Children's Cttee, 1957–73. A Governor, BBC, 1974–81. Purchased and restored Theatre Royal, Bath, with husband, 1974–76. Dir, Fosters Rooms

Ltd, 1975–96. Member: Housing Corp., 1988–95; Bristol Develt Corp., 1989–96; Lord Chancellor's Lay Interviewers Panel for Judges, 1994–; Nat. Lottery Charities Bd, 1995–99 (Chm., England Cttee, 1997–99). Member, Board: Knightstone Housing Assoc., 1976–2000 (Chm., 1997–2000); @Bristol, 2000–. Pro-Chancellor, Bristol Univ., 1997– (Chm. Council, 1987–97). JP Bristol, 1968 (Chm., Bench, 1991–95); DL Bristol (formerly Avon), 1986. *Recreations:* family and the variety of life. *Address:* Gatcombe Court, Flax Bourton, Bristol BS48 3QT. *T:* (01275) 393141, *Fax:* (01275) 394274.

CLARKE, Stephen Patrick; His Honour Judge Stephen Clarke; a Circuit Judge, since 1995; *b* 23 March 1948; *s* of Leslie Clarke and Anne Mary Clarke; *m* 1974, Margaret Roberta Millar; two *s*. *Educ:* Rostrevor Coll., Adelaide, SA; Univ. of Hull (LLB Hons). Called to the Bar, Inner Temple, 1971; practised as barrister on Wales and Chester Circuit, 1971–95; Circuit Junior, 1988–89; Asst Recorder, 1988–92; Recorder, 1992–95. Asst Parly Boundary Comr for Wales, 1994–95. *Recreations:* golf, watching cricket, theatre. *Address:* The Crown Court, The Castle, Chester CH1 2AN. *T:* (01244) 317606. *Clubs:* City (Chester); Upton by Chester Golf.

CLARKE, Rt Hon. Thomas, CBE 1980; PC 1997; JP; MP (Lab) Coatbridge and Chryston, since 1997 (Coatbridge and Airdrie, June 1982–1983, Monklands West, 1983–97); *b* 10 Jan. 1941; *s* of James Clarke and Mary (*née* Gordon). *Educ:* All Saints Primary Sch., Airdrie; Columba High Sch., Coatbridge; Scottish College of Commerce. Started working life as office boy with Glasgow Accountants' firm; Asst Director, Scottish Council for Educational Technology, before going to Parliament. Councillor: (former) Coatbridge Council, 1964; (reorganised) Monklands District Council, 1974; Provost of Monklands, 1975–77, 1977–80, 1980–82. Vice-President, Convention of Scottish Local Authorities, 1976–78, President, 1978–80. Opposition front bench spokesman on: Scottish Affairs, 1987; health and social security (personal social services), 1987–90; Scotland, 1992–93; overseas aid, 1993–94; disabled people's rights, 1994–95; Minister of State (Minister for Film and Tourism), Dept of Culture, Media and Sport, 1997–98. Chm., PLP Foreign Affairs Cttee, 1983–86. Author and main sponsor, Disabled Persons (Consultation, Representation and Services) Act, 1986. Director, award winning amateur film, Give Us a Goal, 1972; former President, British Amateur Cinematographers' Central Council. JP County of Lanark, 1972. *Recreations:* films, reading, walking. *Address:* 37 Blairhill Street, Coatbridge, Lanarkshire ML5 1PG. *T:* (01236) 600800. *Clubs:* Coatbridge Municipal Golf, Easter Moffat Golf.

CLARKE, Sir Tobias; *see* Clarke, Sir C. M. T.

CLARKE, William Malpas, CBE 1976; Chairman, Central Banking Publications Ltd, since 1990; *b* 5 June 1922; *o s* of late Ernest and Florence Clarke; *m* 1st, 1946, Margaret Braithwaite; two *d*; 2nd, 1973, Faith Elizabeth Dawson. *Educ:* Audenshaw Grammar Sch.; Univ. of Manchester (BA Hons Econ). Served Royal Air Force, 1941–46; Flying Instructor, Canada, 1942–44; Flight-Lieut, 1945. Editorial Staff, Manchester Guardian, 1948–55; The Times, 1955–66: City Editor, 1957–62; Financial and Industrial Editor, 1962–66; Editor, The Banker, March-Sept. 1966, Consultant 1966–76. Dir, 1968–76, Dep. Chm. and Dir Gen., 1976–87, British Invisible Exports Council (formerly Cttee on Invisible Exports); Deputy Chairman: City Communications Centre, 1976–87; Trade Indemnity Co. Ltd, 1980–86; Chairman: Grindlays Bank (Jersey), 1981–92; ANZ Merchant Bank, 1987–91 (Dir, 1985–91); Transatlantic Capital (Biosciences) Ltd, 1989–92; Director: ANZ Grindlays Bank (formerly Grindlays Bank), 1966–85, 1987–92; Euromoney Ltd, 1969–84; Trade Indemnity plc, 1971–87; Swiss Reinsurance Co. (UK) plc, 1977–93; ANZ Holdings, 1985–87. Chm., Harold Wincott Financial Journalist Press Award Panel, 1971–92. Governor, The Hospitals for Sick Children, 1984–90; Chm., Great Ormond Street Wishing Well Redevelt Appeal Trust, 1985–94. Hon. DLitt London Guildhall Univ., 1992. *Publications:* The City's Invisible Earnings, 1958; The City in the World Economy, 1965; Private Enterprise in Developing Countries, 1966; (ed, as Director of Studies) Britain's Invisible Earnings, 1967; (with George Pulay) The World's Money, 1970; Inside the City, 1979, rev. edn 1983; How the City of London Works, 1986, 5th edn 1999; The Secret Life of Wilkie Collins, 1988, rev. edn 1996; Planning for Europe: 1992, 1989; The Lost Fortune of the Tsars, 1994 (US and German edns, 1995; Argentine edn, 1996; Polish and Romanian edns, 1998), 3rd edn 2000; (ed) Letters of Wilkie Collins, 1999; The Golden Thread, 2001. *Recreations:* books, theatre. *Address:* 37 Park Vista, Greenwich, SE10 9LZ. *T:* (020) 8858 0979. *Club:* Reform.

CLARKE-HACKSTON, Fiona; Director, British Screen Advisory Council, since 1990 (Secretary, 1987–90); *b* 30 April 1954; *d* of Donald Gordon Hackston and Muriel Lesley Hackston (*née* Glover); *m* 1984, Norman Malcolm Clarke; one *s* one *d*. *Educ:* UC of S Wales and Monmouthshire, Cardiff (BA Hons); Univ. of Southampton (MA 1977). Sec. to Marketing Dir, Grants of St James, 1978–79; Editor, and Head of Book Dept, Truman & Knightley, 1979–81; Personnel Advr, Ernst & Whinney, Middle East, 1981–84; Asst, Film, TV and Video, British Council, 1986. *Recreations:* golf, film, walking, music, family. *Address:* 353 Wimbledon Park Road, SW19 6NS.

CLARKE HALL, Denis; architect; President, Architectural Association, 1958–59; Chairman, Architects Registration Council of the UK, 1963–64; *b* 4 July 1910; *s* of Sir William Clarke Hall and Edna (*née* Waugh); *m* 1936, Mary Garfitt; one *s* two *d*. *Educ:* Bedales. AA Dip. Own practice, 1937–71. *Address:* Moorhouse, Iping, Midhurst, W Sussex GU29 0PJ.

CLARKSON, Rt Hon. Adrienne; PC (Can.); CC (OC 1992); CMM; CD; Governor General of Canada, since 1999; *b* Hong Kong, 10 Feb. 1939; naturalised Canadian citizen; *m* John Ralston Saul, writer. *Educ:* Univ. of Toronto (BA Hons English Lit.; MA 1961); Sorbonne, Univ. of Paris. Agent-Gen. for Ontario, Paris, 1982–87; Pres. and Publisher, McClelland & Stewart, 1987–88; Presenter, Writer and Producer: Take Thirty, Adrienne at Large, The Fifth Estate, CBC TV, 1965–82; Adrienne Clarkson's Summer Festival, 1988–98; Adrienne Clarkson Presents, 1988–98; Exec. Prod. and Presenter, Something Special. Chair, Bd of Trustees, Canadian Mus. of Civilization, Quebec, 1995–99; formerly Pres., Exec. Bd, IMZ, Vienna. Lay Bencher, Law Soc. of Upper Canada. Hon. Fellow: Royal Conservatory of Music, Toronto, 1993; Univ. of Trinity Coll., Toronto, 1996. Hon. LLD: Dalhousie, 1991; Univ, of PEI, 1996. *Publications:* three books; numerous articles in newspapers and jls. *Address:* Government House, 1 Promenade Sussex Drive, Ottawa, ON K1A 0A1, Canada. *T:* (613) 9938195, *Fax:* (613) 9931967.

CLARKSON, Ven. Alan Geoffrey; Archdeacon of Winchester, 1984–99, Archdeacon Emeritus, since 1999; Vicar of Burley, Ringwood, 1984–99; *b* 14 Feb. 1934; *s* of Instructor Captain Geoffrey Archibald Clarkson, OBE, RN and Essie Isabel Bruce Clarkson; *m* 1959, Monica Ruth (*née* Lightburne); two *s* one *d*. *Educ:* Sherborne School; Christ's Coll., Cambridge (BA 1957, MA 1961); Wycliffe Hall, Oxford. Nat. Service Commn, RA, 1952–54. Curate: Penn, Wolverhampton, 1959–60; St Oswald's, Oswestry, 1960–63; Wrington with Redhill, 1963–65; Vicar, Chewton Mendip with Emborough, 1965–74; Vicar of St John Baptist, Glastonbury with Godney, 1974–84; Priest in Charge: West Pennard, 1981–84; Meare, 1981–84; St Benedict, Glastonbury, 1982–84. Proctor in Convocation, 1970–75, 1990–95. Hon. Canon, Winchester Cathedral, 1984–99. *Recreations:* music, gardening, carpentry, wood-turning. *Address:* 4 Harefield Rise, Linton, Cambridge CB1 6LS. *T:* and *Fax:* (01223) 892988.

CLARKSON, Prof. Brian Leonard, DSc; FREng; Principal, University College of Swansea, 1982–94; Vice-Chancellor, University of Wales, 1987–89; *b* 28 July 1930; *s* of L. C. Clarkson; *m* 1953, Margaret Elaine Wilby; three *s* one *d*. *Educ:* Univ. of Leeds (BSc, PhD). FREng (FEng 1986); FRAeS; Hon. FInst Acoustics. George Taylor Gold Medal, RAeS, 1963. Dynamics Engineer, de Havilland Aircraft Co., Hatfield, Herts, 1953–57; Southampton University: Sir Alan Cobham Research Fellow, Dept of Aeronautics, 1957–58; Lectr, Dept of Aeronautics and Astronautics, 1958–66; Prof. of Vibration Studies, 1966–82; Dir, Inst. of Sound and Vibration Res., 1967–78; Dean, Faculty of Engrg and Applied Science, 1978–80; Deputy Vice-Chancellor, 1980–82. Sen. Post Doctoral Research Fellow, Nat. Academy of Sciences, USA, 1970–71 (one year's leave of absence from Southampton). Chm., ACU, 1992–93 (Vice-Chm., 1990–92). Sec., Internat. Commn on Acoustics, 1975–81. Pres., Fedn of Acoustical Socs of Europe, 1982–84. Member: SERC, 1984–88; CNAA, 1988–91. Hon. DSc: Leeds, 1984; Southampton, 1987; Universiti Sains Malaysia, 1990; Hon. LLD Wales, 1996. *Publications:* author of sections of three books: Technical Acoustics, vol. 3 (ed Richardson) 1959; Noise and Acoustic Fatigue in Aeronautics (ed Mead and Richards), 1967; Noise and Vibration (ed White and Walker), 1982; (ed) Stochastic Problems in Dynamics, 1977; technical papers on Jet Noise and its effect on Aircraft Structures, Jl of Royal Aeronautical Soc., etc. *Recreations:* walking, gardening, travelling, golf. *Address:* Highmead, 17 Southgate Road, Southgate, Swansea SA3 2BT.

CLARKSON, His Honour Derek Joshua; QC 1969; a Circuit Judge, 1977–95; Middlesex Liaison Judge, 1985–95; *b* 10 Dec. 1929; *o s* of Albert and Winifred Charlotte Clarkson (*née* James); *m* 1960, Peternella Marie-Luise Ilse Canenbley; one *s* one *d*. *Educ:* Pudsey Grammar Sch.; King's Coll., Univ. of London. LLB (1st cl. Hons) 1950. Called to Bar, Inner Temple, 1951; Nat. Service, RAF, 1952–54 (Flt Lt). In practice as Barrister, 1954–77; Prosecuting Counsel to Post Office on North-Eastern Circuit, 1961–65; Prosecuting Counsel to Inland Revenue on North-Eastern Circuit, 1965–69; Recorder of Rotherham, 1967–71; Recorder of Huddersfield, 1971; a Recorder of the Crown Court, 1972–77. Mem., Gen. Council of the Bar, 1971–73. Inspector of companies for the Department of Trade, 1972–73, 1975–76. Pres., Middlesex Magistrates' Assoc., 1994–95. *Recreations:* theatre-going, walking, book collecting. *Address:* Millbank Court, 24 John Islip Street, Westminster, SW1P 4LG; 72A Cornwall Road, Harrogate HG1 2NE.

CLARKSON, Prof. Geoffrey Peniston Elliott, PhD; Chairman, Circle L Ltd, since 1990; *b* 30 May 1934; *s* of George Elliott Clarkson and Alice Helene (*née* Manneberg); *m* 1960, Eleanor M. (*née* Micenko); two *d*. *Educ:* Carnegie-Mellon Univ., Pittsburgh, Pa (BSc, MSc, PhD). Asst Prof., Sloan Sch. of Management, MIT, 1961–65, Associate Prof., 1965–67, Vis. Prof., 1975–77. Vis. Ford Foundn Fellow, Carnegie-Mellon Univ., 1965–66; Vis. Prof., LSE, 1966–67; Nat. Westminster Bank Prof. of Business Finance, Manchester Business Sch., Univ. of Manchester, 1967–77; Prof. of Business Admin, 1977–89, and Dean, Coll. of Business Admin, 1977–79, Northeastern Univ., Boston. Dir of and consultant to public and private manufng and financial services cos, 1969–; Chairman: Polymerics Inc., 1983–89; Sealcorp Ltd, 1990–94. MInstD 1973. *Publications:* Portfolio Selection: a simulation of trust investment, USA 1962 (Ford Dissertation Prize, 1961); The Theory of Consumer Demand: a critical appraisal, USA 1963; Managerial Economics, 1968; (with B. J. Elliott) Managing Money and Finance, 1969 (3rd edn 1982); Jihad, 1981; Day Trader, 2000. *Recreations:* fishing, sailing, reading. *Address:* 8635 W Sahara Avenue, Suite 50, Las Vegas, NV 89117, USA.

CLARKSON, Gerald Dawson, CBE 1990; QFSM 1983; Chief Fire Officer and Chief Executive, London Fire and Civil Defence Authority, 1987–91, retired; Chairman, Dawson Usher International Ltd, since 1994; *b* 4 June 1939; *s* of Alexander Dickie Clarkson and Agnes Tierney Price; *m* 1959, Rose Lilian Hodgson; one *s* one *d*. *Educ:* Westminster Technical Coll.; Polytechnic of Central London (BA Hons). FIMS, FIMgt, FRSH. Served Royal Engineers, 1960–61. Joined London Fire Bde, 1961; Dep. Chief Officer, 1983; Reg. Fire Comdr No 5, Greater London Region, 1987–91. Member: Central Fire Bdes Adv. Council, 1987–91; Fire Service Central Examinations Bd, 1987–; Ind. Mem., Kent Police Authy, 1995–; Adviser: Nat. Jt Council for Local Authorities Fire Bdes, 1987–91; Assoc. of Metropolitan Authorities, 1987–91; Chairman: Fedn of British Fire Orgns, 1990–91; London Fire Brigade Retired Members Association, 1991–; President: London Fire Brigade Widows' and Orphans' Friendly Soc., 1987–91; Commonwealth and Overseas Fire Service Assoc., 1990–; Dir, Nat. Fire Protection Assoc., USA, 1990–93. Founder Chm., Firefighters Meml Charitable Trust, 1990–. Freeman, City of London, 1985; Founder Master, Guild of Firefighters, 1988; Founder Mem., Firefighters' Co., 1995– (Sen. Past Master). OStJ 1989. Hon. FIFireE, 1989. *Recreations:* reading, golf, sailing, fishing. *Address:* Field Mill, Field Mill Lane, Egerton, Kent TN27 9AU. *Club:* East India.

CLARKSON, Jeremy Charles Robert; journalist and broadcaster, since 1978; *b* 11 April 1960; *m* 1993, Frances Catherine Cain, *d* of Major Robert Henry Cain, VC and Mary Denise Addison; one *s* two *d*. *Educ:* Repton Sch. Rotherham Advertiser, 1978–81; family co-selling Paddington Bears, 1981–84; established Motoring Press Agency, 1984–94; columnist: Performance Car magazine, 1986–93; Top Gear magazine, 1993–; Esquire magazine, 1992–93; Sunday Times, 1993–; The Sun, 1996–; *television:* presenter, Top Gear, 1989–99; Jeremy Clarkson's Motorworld, 1995, 1996; Extreme Machines, 1998; Robot Wars, 1998; Clarkson, 1998, 1999, 2000; Clarkson's Car Years, 2000. *Publications:* Clarkson on Cars, 1996; Clarkson Hot 100, 1997; Planet Dagenham, 1998; Born to be Riled, 1999; Jeremy Clarkson on Ferrari, 2000. *Recreation:* smoking.

CLARKSON, Patrick Robert James; QC 1991; a Recorder, since 1996; *b* 1 Aug. 1949; *s* of Commander Robert Anthony Clarkson, LVO, RN and Sheelagh Clarissa Neale; *m* 1975, Bridget Cecilia Doyne; two *s* one *d*. *Educ:* Winchester. Called to the Bar, Lincoln's Inn, 1972. *Recreation:* country. *Address:* 1 Serjeants Inn, EC4Y 1NH. *T:* (020) 7583 1355. *Clubs:* Boodle's, MCC.

CLARKSON, Dr Peter David; Executive Secretary, Scientific Committee on Antarctic Research, since 1989; *b* 19 June 1945; *s* of late Maurice Roland Clarkson and of Jessie Yoxall (*née* Baker); *m* 1974, Rita Margaret Skinner; one *d*. *Educ:* Epsom Coll.; Univ. of Durham (BSc 1967); Univ. of Birmingham (PhD 1977). FGS 1980. Geologist with British Antarctic Survey, 1967–89: wintered in Antarctica, Halley Bay, 1968 and 1969; Base Comdr, 1969; Antarctic field seasons in Shackleton Range (leader 3 times), 1968–78; in S Shetland Is, 1974–75; in Antarctic Peninsula, 1985–86 (leader). UK adviser to PROANTAR, Brazil, 1982. Trustee, Trans-Antarctic Assoc., 1996– (Hon. Sec., 1980–93; Grants Sec., 1993–96). Polar Medal, 1976. *Publications:* (jtly) Natural Wonders of the World: 100 spectacular wonders of the natural world, 1995; Volcanoes, 2000; articles on Antarctic geology. *Recreations:* walking, woodwork, photography, music, all matters Antarctic. *Address:* SCAR Secretariat, Scott Polar Research Institute, Lensfield Road, Cambridge CB2 1ER. *T:* (01223) 362061; 35 King's Grove, Barton, Cambridge CB3 7AZ. *T:* (01223) 263417. *Club:* Antarctic.

CLARRICOATS, Prof. Peter John Bell, CBE 1996; FRS 1990; FREng; Professor of Electronic Engineering, Queen Mary and Westfield (formerly Queen Mary) College, University of London, 1968–97, now Emeritus Professor, Queen Mary, University of London (Head of Department, 1979–97); *b* 6 April 1932; *s* of John Clarricoats and Cecilia (*née* Bell); *m* 1st, 1955, Gillian (*née* Hall) (marr. diss. 1962); one *s* one *d*; 2nd, 1968, Phyllis Joan (*née* Lloyd); two *d* one step *s* one step *d*. *Educ:* Minchenden Grammar Sch.; Imperial College. BSc (Eng), PhD, DSc (Eng) 1968; FInstP 1964; FIEE 1967; FIEEE 1967; FCGI 1980; FREng (FEng 1983). Scientific Staff, GEC, 1953–58; Lectr, Queen's Univ. Belfast, 1959–62; Sheffield Univ., 1962–63; Prof. of Electronic Engineering, Univ. of Leeds, 1963–67. Mem., Governing Body, QMC, 1976–79, Dean of Engineering, 1977–80; Fellow, QMW, 1999. Chm., British Nat. Cttee for Radio Sci., subseq. UK Panel for URSI, 1985–93; Vice-Pres., URSI, 1993–99. Chairman: 1st Internat. Conf. on Antennas and Propagation, IEE, 1978; European Microwave Conf., 1979; Mil. Microwaves Conf., 1988; Microwaves and RF Conf., 1994. Distinguished Lectr, IEEE, 1987–88. Institution of Electrical Engineers: Vice-Pres., 1989–91; Mem. Council, 1964–67, 1977–80; Chm., Electronics Div., 1978–79; Hon. Fellow, 1993; awards: Premia, Electronics Section, 1960, 1961; Marconi, 1974; Oliver Lodge, 1992; Coopers Hill Meml Prize, 1964; IEEE Cert. of Appreciation, 1989; European Microwave Prize, 1989; IEE Measurement Prize, 1989; J. J. Thomson Medal, IEE, 1989; Distinguished Achievement Award, IEEE. Hon DSc: Kent, 1993; Aston, 1995. Co-Editor, Electronics Letters (IEE Jl), 1964–. *Publications:* Microwave Ferrites, 1960; (with A.D. Olver) Corrugated Horns for Microwave Antennas, 1984; (with A. D. Olver) Microwave Horns and Feeds, 1994; papers on antennas and waveguides. *Recreations:* music, history. *Address:* The Red House, Grange Meadows, Elmswell, Suffolk IP30 9GE. *T:* (01359) 240585, *Fax:* (01359) 242665.

CLARY, Prof. David Charles, FRS 1997; Professor of Chemistry, and Director, Centre for Theoretical and Computational Chemistry, University College London, since 1996; *b* Halesworth, Suffolk, 14 Jan. 1953; *s* of late Cecil Raymond Clary and of Mary Mildred Clary (*née* Hill); *m* 1975, Heather Ann Vinson; three *s*. *Educ:* Colchester Royal Grammar Sch.; Sussex Univ. (BSc 1974); Corpus Christi Coll., Cambridge (PhD 1977); ScD Cantab 1998. CChem, FRSC 1997; CPhys, FInstP 1997. IBM World-Trade Postdoctoral Fellow, San Jose, Calif, 1977–78; Postdoctoral Fellow, Manchester Univ., 1978–80; Research Lectr in Chemistry, UMIST, 1980–83; Department of Chemistry, Cambridge University: Demonstrator, 1983–87; Lectr, 1987–93; Reader in Theoretical Chem., 1993–96; Magdalene College, Cambridge: Fellow, 1983–96; Dir of Studies in Natural Scis, 1988–96; Sen. Tutor, 1989–93; Fellow Commoner, 1996–. Visiting Fellow: Univ. of Colo, 1987–88; Canterbury Univ., NZ, 1992; Univ. of Sydney, Australia, 1994; Hebrew Univ. of Jerusalem, 1994; Université de Paris Sud, 1995; Miller Vis. Prof., Univ. of Calif at Berkeley, 2001. Royal Society of Chemistry: Mem. Council, 1990–93 and 1994–2001, Vice-Pres., 1997–2001, Faraday Div.; Meldola Medal, 1981; Marlow Medal, Faraday Div., 1986; Corday-Morgan Medal, 1989; Tilden Medal and Lectr, 1998; Chemical Dynamics Prize, 1998. Annual Medal, Internat. Acad. of Quantum Molecular Scis, 1989 (Mem., 1998–). Editor, Chemical Physics Letters, 2000–. *Publications:* papers on chemical physics and theoretical chemistry in learned jls. *Recreations:* family, football (Ipswich Town), foreign travel. *Address:* Department of Chemistry, University College London, WC1H 0AJ. *T:* (020) 7679 1488; *e-mail:* d.c.clary@ucl.ac.uk.

CLASPER, Michael, CBE 1995; Deputy Chief Executive, BAA plc, since 2001; *b* 21 April 1953; *s* of Douglas and Hilda Clasper; *m* 1975, Susan Rosemary Shore; two *s* one *d*. *Educ:* Bede Sch., Sunderland; St John's Coll., Cambridge (1st cl. Hons Engineering). British Rail, 1974–78; joined Procter & Gamble 1978, Advertising Dir, 1985–88; Gen. Manager, Procter & Gamble Holland, 1988–91; Man. Dir and Vice-Pres., Procter & Gamble UK, 1991–95; Regl Vice-Pres., Laundry Products, Procter & Gamble Europe, 1995–99; Pres., Global Home Care and New Business Develt, Procter & Gamble, 1999–2001. Member: Adv. Council on Business and the Envmt, 1993–99; Mgt Cttee, Business and Envmt Prog., Univ. of Cambridge Prog. for Industry, 2000–. *Recreations:* swimming, cycling, ski-ing, tennis, golf. *Address:* BAA plc, 130 Wilton Road, SW1V 1LQ.

CLATWORTHY, Robert, RA 1973 (ARA 1968); sculptor; *b* 31 Jan. 1928; *s* of E. W. and G. Clatworthy; *m* 1954, Pamela Gordon (marr. diss.); two *s* one *d*. *Educ:* Dr Morgan's Grammar Sch., Bridgwater. Studied West of England Coll. of Art, Chelsea Sch. of Art, The Slade. Teacher, West of England Coll. of Art, 1967–71. Visiting Tutor, RCA, 1960–72; Mem., Fine Art Panel of Nat. Council for Diplomas in Art and Design, 1961–72; Governor, St Martin's Sch. of Art, 1970–71; Head of Dept of Fine Art, Central Sch. of Art and Design, 1971–75. Exhibited: Hanover Gall., 1954, 1956; Waddington Galls, 1965; Holland Park Open Air Sculpture, 1957; Battersea Park Open Air Sculpture, 1960, 1963; Tate Gallery, British Sculpture in the Sixties, 1965; British Sculptors 1972, Burlington House; Basil Jacobs Fine Art Ltd, 1972; Diploma Galls, Burlington House, 1977; Photographers Gall., 1980; Quinton Green Fine Art, London, 1986; British Sculpture 1950–65, New Art Centre, 1986; Chapman Gall., 1988, 1989; Keith H. Chapman Gall., 1988, 1992, 1994, 1996; Austin Desmond Fine Art, 1991, 1998; UK Modern Art, 2001. Work in Collections: Arts Council, Contemporary Art Soc., Tate Gallery, Victoria and Albert Museum, Greater London Council, Nat. Portrait Gall. (portrait of Dame Elisabeth Frink, 1985). Public sculptures include: Large Bull, Roehampton, SW15; Monumental Horse and Rider, Finsbury Avenue, London, 1984. *Address:* Moelfre, Cynghordy, Llandovery, Carms SA20 0UW. *T:* (01550) 720201. *Club:* Chelsea Arts.

CLAUSEN, Alden Winship, (Tom); Chairman, and Chief Executive Officer, BankAmerica Corporation, 1986–90; *b* 17 Feb. 1923; *s* of Morton and Elsie Clausen; *m* 1950, Mary Margaret Crassweller; two *s*. *Educ:* Carthage Coll. (BA 1944); Univ. of Minnesota (LLB 1949); Grad. Harvard Advanced Management Program, 1966. Admitted to Minnesota Bar, 1949. Joined Bank of America, 1949: Vice-Pres., 1961–65; Sen. Vice-Pres., 1965–68; Exec. Vice-Pres., 1968–69; Vice-Chm. of Bd, 1969; Pres. and Chief Exec. Officer, 1970–81; Pres., The World Bank, 1981–86. President: Fed. Adv. Council, 1972; Internat. Monetary Conf., Amer. Bankers' Assoc., 1977. Former Director: US-USSR Trade and Econ. Council, 1974–81; Nat. Council for US-China Trade, 1974–81; Co-Chm., Japan-California Assoc., 1973–80. Hon. LLD: Carthage, 1970; Lewis and Clark, 1978; Gonzaga Univ., 1978; Univ. of Notre Dame, 1981; Hon. DPS Univ. Santa Clara, 1981. *Address:* c/o BankAmerica Corporation, 555 California Street, San Francisco, CA 94104, USA.

CLAY, Edward, CMG 1994; HM Diplomatic Service; High Commissioner, Kenya, since 2001; *b* 21 July 1945; *m* 1969, Anne Stroud; three *d*. FO, later FCO, 1968; Nairobi, 1970; Second, later First, Sec., Sofia, 1973; FCO, 1975; First Secretary: Budapest, 1979; FCO, 1982; Counsellor: Nicosia, 1985; FCO, 1989; Ambassador (non-resident) to Rwanda, 1994–95, to Burundi, 1994–96; High Comr to Uganda, 1993–97; Dir, Public Diplomacy and Public Services, FCO, 1997–99; High Comr to Cyprus, 1999–2001. *Address:* c/o Foreign and Commonwealth Office, SW1A 2AH.

CLAY, His Honour John Lionel, TD 1961; a Circuit Judge, 1977–88; *b* 31 Jan. 1918; *s* of Lionel Pilleau Clay and Mary Winifred Muriel Clay; *m* 1952, Elizabeth, *d* of Rev. Canon Maurice Ponsonby, MC and Lady Phyllis Ponsonby, OBE, *d* of 1st Earl Buxton, GCMG, PC; one *s* three *d*. *Educ:* Harrow Sch.; Corpus Christi Coll., Oxford (MA). Served War of 1939–45 (despatches): in 1st Bn Rifle Bde, N Africa (8th Army), Italy, 1941–44; Instr, Infantry Heavy Weapons Sch., 1944–45; 1st Bn Rifle Bde, Germany, 1945–46. London Rifle Bde Rangers (TA); Major (2nd i/c Bn) and 23 SAS (TA), 1948–60. Called to the Bar, Middle Temple, 1947; a Recorder of the Crown Court, 1975–77. Chm., Horserace Betting Levy Appeal Tribunal for England and Wales, 1974–77. Freeman of City of London, 1980; Liveryman, Gardeners' Co., 1980. *Recreations:* gardening, fishing. *Address:* Newtimber Place, Hassocks, Sussex BN6 9BU.

CLAY, John Martin; Deputy Chairman: Hambros plc, 1986–90; Hambros Bank Ltd, 1972–84 (Director, 1961–84); *b* 20 Aug. 1927; *s* of late Sir Henry Clay and Gladys Priestman Clay; *m* 1952, Susan Jennifer (*d* 1997), *d* of Lt-Gen. Sir Euan Miller, KCB, KBE, DSO, MC; four *s*. *m* 2001, Ann Monica, *widow* of Martin Beale, OBE, JP and *d* of Eric Barnard, CB, CBE, DSO. *Educ:* Eton; Magdalen Coll., Oxford. Chairman: Johnson & Firth Brown Ltd, 1973–93; Hambro Life Assurance Ltd, 1978–84. Dir, Bank of England, 1973–83. Mem., Commonwealth Develt Corp., 1970–88. FIMgt (FBIM 1971). *Recreation:* sailing. *Club:* Royal Thames Yacht.

CLAY, Prof. Dame Marie (Mildred), DBE 1987; FRSNZ 1994; Professor of Education, University of Auckland, New Zealand, 1975–91, now Emeritus, and Head of Department of Education, 1975–78 and 1986–88; *b* 3 Jan. 1926; *d* of Donald Leolin Irwin and Mildred Blanche Irwin (*née* Godier); *m* 1951, Warwick Victor Clay; one *s* one *d*. *Educ:* Wellington East Girls' College; Wellington Teachers' College; Univ. of New Zealand (MA Hons, DipEd); Univ. of Minnesota; Univ of Auckland (PhD). Teacher Training, 1943–45; Teacher of Retarded Children, 1945; Asst Psychologist, 1948–50; Fulbright Scholar, Univ. of Minnesota, 1950–51; Teacher, 1953–54; Psychologist, 1955–59; University of Auckland: Univ. Lectr, 1960–67; Sen. Lectr, 1968–72; Associate Prof., 1973–74. Distinguished Vis. Prof., Ohio State Univ., 1984–85; Vis. Fellow, Wolfson Coll., Oxford, 1987–88; George A. Miller Vis. Prof., Univ. of Illinois, 1991; Sen. Fulbright Fellow, Ohio State Univ., 1991; Vis. Prof, Univ. of London, 1991–93; President's Scholar, Texas Woman's Univ., 1994. Pres., Internat. Reading Assoc., 1992–93. FNZPsS 1978; Hon. FNZEI 1976. Hon. LHD Lesley Coll., Mass., 1994; Hon. DHL Ohio State Univ., 1998. David H. Russell Award, Nat. Council of Teachers of English, USA, 1979; Internat. Citation of Merit, 1978, William S. Gray Citation of Merit, 1995, Internat. Reading Assoc.; Mackie Medal, ANZAAS, 1983. *Publications:* What Did I Write, 1975; Reading: the patterning of complex behaviour, 1972, 2nd edn 1979; The Early Detection of Reading Difficulties, 1972, 3rd edn 1985; Children of Parents Who Separate, 1978; (jtly) Reading Begins at Home, 1979; Observing Young Readers, 1982; Round About Twelve, 1983; Record of Oral Language, 1983; Writing Begins at Home, 1987; Quadruplets and Higher Multiple Births, 1989; Becoming Literate: the Construction of Inner Control, 1991; An Observation Survey, 1993; Reading Recovery: guidelines for teachers in training, 1993; By Different Paths to Common Outcomes, 1998; Change Over Time in Children's Literacy Development, 2001.

CLAY, Sir Richard (Henry), 7th Bt *cr* 1841, of Fulwell Lodge, Middlesex; *b* 2 June 1940; *s* of Sir Henry Felix Clay, 6th Bt, and Phyllis Mary (*d* 1997), *yr d* of late R. H. Paramore, MD, FRCS; *S* father, 1985; *m* 1963, Alison Mary, *d* of late Dr James Gordon Fife; three *s* two *d*. *Educ:* Eton. FCA 1966. *Recreation:* sailing. *Heir: s* Charles Richard Clay, *b* 18 Dec. 1965. *Address:* The Copse, Shiplate Road, Bleadon, N Somerset BS24 0NX.

CLAY, Robert Alan; Partner, Roots Music, since 1993; *b* 2 Oct. 1946; *s* of Albert Arthur Clay, OBE and Joyce Doris (*née* Astins); *m* 1980, Uta Christa. *Educ:* Bedford Sch.; Gonville and Caius Coll., Cambridge. Busdriver, Tyne and Wear PTE, 1975–83. Branch Chm., GMBATU, 1977–83. MP (Lab) Sunderland North, 1983–92. Treas., 1983–86, Sec., 1986–87, Campaign Gp of Labour MPs. Chief Exec., Pallion Engrg Ltd, 1992–93. *Recreations:* walking, reading.

CLAYDON, Geoffrey Bernard, CB 1990; Member, Legal Directorate, Department of Transport, 1990–95; *b* 14 Sept. 1930; *s* of Bernard Claydon and Edith Mary (*née* Lucas); unmarried. *Educ:* Leeds Modern; King Edward's, Birmingham; Birmingham Univ. (LLB). Articled at Pinsent & Co., Birmingham, 1950; admitted Solicitor, 1954. Legal Asst, 1959, Sen. Legal Asst, 1965, Treasury Solicitor's Dept; Asst Solicitor, DTI, 1973; Asst Treasury Solicitor, 1974; Principal Asst Treasury Solicitor and Legal Advr, Dept of Energy, 1980. Mem., Editorial Bd, Jl of Energy and Natural Resources Law, 1983–90. Sec., National Tramway Museum, 1958–84 (Vice-Chm., 1969–99); Vice-Pres., Light Rail Transit Assoc. (formerly Light Railway Transport League), 1968– (Chm. of League, 1963–68); Pres., Tramway and Light Railway Soc., 1996–2001 (Chm., 1967–93; Vice-Pres., 1993–96); Vice-Pres., Tramway Mus. Soc., 1998–; Chm., Consultative Panel for Preservation of British Transport Relics, 1982–; Member: Inst. of Transport Admin, 1972–; Legislation Cttee, Heritage Railway Assoc., 1995–; Fixed Track Section, Confedn of Passenger Transport, 1996–; CIT Working Party on transport legislation, 1996–98. MCIT 1997; MILT 1999. *Publication:* (contrib. on tramways) Halsbury's Laws of England, 2000. *Recreations:* rail transport, travel. *Address:* 23 Baron's Keep, W14 9AT. *T:* (020) 7603 6400. *Club:* Royal Automobile.

CLAYMAN, David, CEng, FIChemE; Managing Director, Esso UK plc, 1986–95; *b* 28 May 1934; *s* of Maurice and Nancy Clayman; *m* 1956, Patricia Moore; two *s*. *Educ:* Purley Grammar Sch.; University College London (BSc Chem. Engrg). Joined Esso Petroleum Co., 1956; Supply Manager, London, 1966–67, Esso Europe Inc., 1970–71; Marketing Div. Dir, 1971–79; Exec. Asst to Chm., Exxon Corp., 1979–80; Dir, Esso Petroleum Co., 1982–83; Pres., Esso Africa Inc., 1983–86; Director: Esso Europe Inc., 1983–86; Esso Exploration and Production UK, 1986–95; Esso Pension Trust, 1986–95; Chm., Mainline Pipeline, 1986–95. Mem., Sen. Salaries Review Body, 1997–. Council Member: GCBS, 1986–87; Foundn for Management Educn, 1986–95; Pres., UKPIA, 1988–90 and 1992–94 (Vice Pres., 1986–88); Vice-Pres., Oil Industries Club, 1988–95. *Clubs:* Royal Automobile; Burhill Golf.

CLAYSON, Christopher William, CBE 1974 (OBE 1966); President, Royal College of Physicians of Edinburgh, 1966–70; retired; *b* 11 Sept. 1903; *s* of Christopher Clayson and Agnes Lilias Montgomerie Hunter; *m* 1st, 1933, Elsie Webster Breingan; 2nd, 1988, Anne Dorothy Miller or Middlemiss. *Educ:* George Heriot's Sch.; Edinburgh University. MB, ChB 1926; DPH 1929; MD (Gold Medal) Edinburgh 1936; FRCPE 1951; FRCP 1967. Physician: Southfield Hosp., Edinburgh, 1931–44; Edinburgh City Hosp., 1939–44; Lectr in Tuberculosis Dept, Univ. of Edinburgh, 1939–44; Med. Supt, Lochmaben Hosp., 1944–48; Consultant Phys. in Chest Medicine, Dumfries and Galloway, 1948–68; retd from clinical practice, 1968. Served on numerous Govt and Nat. Health Service cttees, 1948–; Chairman: Scottish Licensing Law Cttee, 1971–73; Scottish Council for Postgrad. Med. Educn, 1970–74. Hon. Mem., Scottish Soc. of Physicians; Mem., Thoracic Soc.; Hon. FACP 1968; Hon. FRACP 1969; Hon. FRCPGlas 1970; Hon. FRCGP 1971; Hon. FRCPE 1990. William Cullen Prize, RCPE, 1978. *Publications:* various papers on tuberculosis problem and on alcoholism in leading medical jls. *Recreations:* gardening, fishing. *Address:* Cockiesknowe, Lochmaben, Lockerbie, Dumfriesshire DG11 1RL. *T:* (01387) 810231. *Clubs:* Caledonian; New (Edinburgh).

CLAYTON, Prof. Dame Barbara (Evelyn), (Dame Barbara Klyne), DBE 1988 (CBE 1983); MD, PhD; FRCP, FRCPath; Hon. Research Professor in Metabolism, Faculty of Medicine, University of Southampton, since 1987 (Professor of Chemical Pathology and Human Metabolism, 1979–87, and Dean of the Faculty of Medicine, 1983–86); *b* 2 Sept. 1922; *m* 1949, William Klyne (*d* 1977); one *s* one *d. Educ:* Univ. of Edinburgh (MD, PhD). FRCP 1972; FRCPath 1971; FRCPE 1985. Consultant in Chem. Pathology, Hosp. for Sick Children, London, 1959–70; Prof. of Chem. Pathology, Inst. of Child Health, Univ. of London, 1970–78. Leverhulme Emeritus Fellow, 1988–90. Hon Consultant, 1979–92, Mem., 1983–87, Southampton and SW Hants HA. Member: Commonwealth Scholarship Commn, 1977–93; Royal Commn on Environmental Pollution, 1981–96. Chm., Task Force on Nutrition, DoH, 1992–95; Member: Study Gp on Long Term Toxicity, Royal Soc., 1976–78; Standing Med. Adv. Cttee (DHSS), 1981–87; Cttee on Toxicity of Chemicals in Food, Consumer Products and the Environment, DoH (formerly DHSS), 1977–93; Systems Bd, MRC, 1974–77; British Nat. Cttees on Chemistry and Biochemistry, 1977–78; British Nat. Cttee on Problems of the Environment, 1988–89; COMA Panel on Dietary Reference Values, 1987–91; WHO Expert Adv. Panel on Nutrition, 1989–97; DoH Steering Gp on Undergrad. Med. and Dental Educn and Res., 1989–; Adv. Gp on Medical Educn, Trng and Service, DoH, 1995–; Chairman: Adv. Cttee on Borderline Substances, 1971–83; MRC Adv. Gp on Lead and Neuropsychol Effects in Children, 1983–88; Cttee on Med. Aspects of Contaminants in Air, Soil and Water, 1984–90; Standing Cttee on Postgrad. Med. and Dental (formerly Med.) Educn, 1988–99; Med. and Scientific Panel, Leukaemia Res. Fund, 1989–; MRC Cttee on Toxic Hazards in the Workplace and the Environment, 1989–95. Council, RCPath, 1974–77 and 1982– (Pres., 1984–87); GMC, 1983–87. President: Assoc. of Clinical Biochemists, 1977, 1978; Soc. for Study of Inborn Errors of Metabolism, 1981–82; Biomedical Scis Sect., BAAS, 1989–90; British Dietetic Assoc., 1989–; Nat. Soc. for Clean Air and Envmtl Protection, 1995–97 (Vice Pres., 1999–); Hon. Pres., British Nutrition Foundn, 1999– (Gov., 1987–99). Member: Bd of Govs, Hosps for Sick Children, London, 1968–78; Scientific Adv. Cttee, Assoc. of Med. Res. Charities, 1990–97. Lectures: Stanley Davidson, RCPE, 1973; Harben, RIPH&H, 1988; Wellcome, Assoc. of Clinical Biochemists, 1988; Osler, 1989; Ireland, Liverpool, 1990; Hartley, Southampton Univ., 1990; G. H. Foote Meml, Southampton Med. Soc., 1991; Wilfred Fish Meml, GDC, 1993; British Nutrition Foundn Annual, 1997; Osler Annual Oration, 1997. Hon. Member: Soc. for Study of Inborn Errors of Metabolism, 1988; Assoc. of Clinical Biochemists, 1990; Corresponding Member: Société Française Pédiatric, 1975; Gesellschaft für Laboratoriumsmedizin, 1990. Member, Editorial Board: Archives of Diseases in Childhood; Clin. Sci.; Jl Endocrinol.; Clin. Endocrinol. Hon. Fellow: British Dietetic Assoc., 1976; Faculty of Pathology, RCPI, 1986; Amer. Soc. of Clin. Pathologists, 1987; Hon. FIBiol 2000; Hon. FRCPCH 1997 (Hon. Mem., BPA, 1963); FMedSci 2000. Hon. DSc: Edinburgh, 1985; Southampton, 1992; London, 2000. Jessie MacGregor Prize for Med. Sci., RCPE, 1955 and 1985; Wellcome Prize, Assoc. of Clin. Biochemists, 1988; BMA Gold Medal for Distinguished Merit, 1999. *Publications:* contrib. learned jls, incl. Jl Endocrinol., Arch. Dis. Childhood, and BMJ. *Recreations:* natural history, walking. *Address:* 16 Chetwynd Drive, Bassett, Southampton SO16 3HZ. *T:* (023) 8076 9937.

CLAYTON, Captain Sir David (Robert), 12th Bt *cr* 1732, of Marden; Shipmaster since 1970; Director, Oceanic Lines (UK) Ltd, since 1989; *b* 12 Dec. 1936; *s* of Sir Arthur Harold Clayton, 11th Bt, DSC, and of Alexandra, Lady Clayton, *d* of late Sergei Andreevsky; *S* father, 1985; *m* 1971, Julia Louise, *d* of late Charles Henry Redfearn; two *s. Educ:* HMS Conway. Joined Merchant Service, 1953; promoted to first command as Captain, 1970. *Recreations:* shooting, sailing. *Heir: s* Robert Philip Clayton, *b* 8 July 1975. *Address:* Rock House, Kingswear, Dartmouth, Devon TQ6 0BX. *T:* (01803) 752433. *Club:* Royal Dart Yacht (Kingswear).

CLAYTON, Prof. George; Newton Chambers Professor of Applied Economics, University of Sheffield, 1967–83, Pro-Vice-Chancellor, 1978–82, now Emeritus Professor; *b* 15 July 1922; *s* of late William Clayton and Gertrude Alison Clarke Clayton; *m* 1948, Rhiannon Jones, JP; two *s* two *d. Educ:* Liverpool Collegiate Sch.; King's Coll., Cambridge (Exhibnr). Served War of 1939–45: Pilot, RAF, 1941–45; Pilot, Fleet Air Arm, 1945. Univ. of Liverpool: Asst Lectr, 1947–50; Lectr, 1950–57; Sen. Lectr, 1957–60 and 1961–63; Sen. Simon Res. Fellow, Univ. of Manchester, 1960–61; Prof. and Head of Dept of Econs, UCW Aberystwyth, 1963–67; Luis Olariaga Lectr, Madrid Univ., 1959; Special Univ. Lectr, London, 1970; Page Fund Lectr, UC Cardiff, 1970. Member: Council, Royal Econ. Soc., 1965–68; Commn on Rating and Taxation in IoM (report published, 1967); (part-time) East Midland Gas Bd, 1967–70; Crowther Cttee on Consumer Credit, 1968–70; Scott Cttee on Property Bonds and Equity-linked Insce, 1970–72; Econs Cttee, SSRC, 1978–82 (Vice-Chm., 1979–82). Non-exec. Dir, Pioneer Mutual Assurance Co., 1976–90; Consultant, Eastern Caribbean Central Bank, 1987–. Chm., British, Canadian and Amer. Mission to British Honduras, 1966; Econ. Adviser: Govt of Tanzania, 1965–66; Govt of Gibraltar, 1974–82. Chm., Assoc. of Univ. Teachers of Economics, 1973–78. *Publications:* (contrib.) A New Prospect of Economics, ed G. L. S. Shackle, 1956; (contrib.) Banking in Western Europe, ed R. S. Sayers, 1959; Insurance Company Investment, 1965; Problems of Rail Transport in Rural Wales: Two Case Studies, 1967; Monetary Theory and Monetary Policy in the 1970s, 1971; British Insurance, 1971; articles in Econ. Jl, etc. *Recreations:* tennis, sailing, theatre, fell walking. *Address:* 40 Ranmoor Crescent, Sheffield S10 3GW. *T:* (0114) 263 0531, *Fax:* (0114) 263 0386. *Club:* Hawks (Cambridge).

CLAYTON, John Pilkington, CVO 1986 (LVO 1975); MA, MB, BChir; Apothecary to HM Household at Windsor, 1965–86; Surgeon Apothecary to HM Queen Elizabeth the Queen Mother's Household at the Royal Lodge, Windsor, 1965–86; Senior Medical Officer, Eton College, 1965–86 (MO, 1962–65); *b* 13 Feb. 1921; *s* of late Brig.-Gen. Sir Gilbert Clayton, KCMG, KBE, CB, and Enid, *d* of late F. N. Thorowgood. *Educ:* Wellington Coll.; Gonville and Caius Coll., Cambridge; King's Coll. Hospital. RAFVR, 1947–49; Sqdn Ldr 1949. Senior Resident, Nottingham Children's Hosp., 1950. MO, Black and Decker Ltd, 1955–70; MO, 1953–62, SMO 1962–81, Royal Holloway Coll. *Address:* Knapp House, Market Lavington, near Devizes, Wilts SN10 4DP.

CLAYTON, Prof. Keith Martin, CBE 1984; Professor of Environmental Sciences, 1967–93, now Emeritus; *b* 25 Sept. 1928; *s* of Edgar Francis Clayton and Constance Annie (*née* Clark); *m* 1st, 1950 (marr. diss. 1976); three *s* one *d*; 2nd, 1976. *Educ:* Bedales Sch.; Univ. of Sheffield (MSc). PhD London. Demonstrator, Univ. of Nottingham, 1949–51. Served RE, 1951–53. Lectr, London Sch. of Economics, 1953–63; Reader in Geography, LSE, 1963–67; Univ. of E Anglia: Founding Dean, Sch. of Environmental Scis, 1967–71 and 1987–93; Pro-Vice-Chancellor, 1971–73; Dir, Centre of E Anglian Studies, 1974–81; Vis. Professor, State Univ. of New York at Binghamton, 1960–62. Chm., Adv. Cttee, Document Supply Centre, British Library, 1986–93; Member: NERC, 1970–73; UGC, 1973–84; Nat. Radiological Protection Bd, 1980–85; Nat. Adv. Bd for Local Authority Higher Educn, 1982–84; Cttee on Med. Aspects of Radiation in Environment, DHSS, 1985–; Ministerial Adv. Cttee on Envmt and Energy, MoD, 1990–; Broads Authy, 1994–98. Chm., Broadland Housing Assoc., 1995–. Councillor, Broadland DC, 1994–98. Pres., IBG, 1984. Hon. DSc Lancaster, 1995. Patron's Medal, RGS, 1989. *Publications:* Editor and publisher, Geo Abstracts, 1960–85. *Recreations:* gardening, work. *Address:* Well Close, Pound Lane, Thorpe, Norwich NR7 0UA. *T:* (01603) 433780.

CLAYTON, Margaret Ann; Chairman: Mental Health Act Commission, since 1999; Farriers Registration Council, since 2001; *b* 7 May 1941; *d* of late Percy Thomas Clayton and of Kathleen Clayton (*née* Payne). *Educ:* Christ's Hospital, Hertford; Birkbeck Coll., London (BA, MSc). Entered Home Office, 1960; Executive Officer/Asst Principal, 1960–67; Asst Private Secretary to Home Secretary, 1967–68; Principal, 1968–75 (seconded to Cabinet Office, 1972–73); Asst Sec., 1975–82; Asst Under Sec. of State, 1983–96; Resident Chm., CSSB, 1983; Dir of Services, Prison Service, 1986–90; Police Dept, 1990–93; Personnel Dept, 1994. Dir, Butler Trust, 1996–99. Mem., Lambeth, Southwark and Lewisham HA, 1995–99. Freeman, City of London, 1984; Liveryman, Farriers' Co., 1984–. *Recreations:* equitation, gardening, theatre. *Club:* Reform.

CLAYTON, Michael Aylwin; Editor of Horse and Hound, 1973–96; Editor-in-Chief, IPC country titles, 1994–97; *b* 20 Nov. 1934; *s* of late Aylwin Goff Clayton and Norah (*née* Banfield); *m* 1st, 1959, Mary L. B. Watson (marr. diss.); one *s* one *d*; 2nd, 1979, Barbara Jane Ryman (*née* Whitfield) (marr. diss. 1988); 3rd, 1988, Marilyn Crowhurst (*née* Orrin. *Educ:* Bournemouth Gammar School. National Service, RAF, 1954–56. Reporter: Lymington Times and New Milton Advertiser, 1951–54; Portsmouth Evening News, 1956–57; London Evening News, 1957–61; reporter/feature writer, New Zealand Herald, 1961; reporter, London Evening Standard, 1961, Dep. News Editor, 1962–64; News Editor, Southern Ind. Television, 1964–65; staff correspondent, BBC TV and radio (incl. Vietnam, Cambodia, India, Pakistan and Middle East), 1965–73; Presenter, Today, BBC Radio 4, 1973–75. Dir, IPC Magazines, 1994–97. Chm., British Soc. of Magazine Editors, 1986. Mem., Press Complaints Commn, 1991–93. Chairman: BHS, 1998–; British Horse Industry Confedn, 1999–. *Publications:* A Hunting We Will Go, 1967; (with Dick Tracey) Hickstead—the First Twelve Years, 1972; (ed) The Complete Book of Showjumping, 1975; (ed) Cross-Country Riding, 1977; The Hunter, 1980; The Golden Thread, 1984; Prince Charles: horseman, 1987; The Chase: a modern guide to foxhunting, 1987; Foxhunting in Paradise, 1993. *Recreations:* foxhunting, music. *Address:* Stable Lodge, Burley-on-the-Hill, Oakham, Rutland LE15 7SU.

CLAYTON, Prof. Robert Norman, FRS 1981; Professor, Departments of Chemistry and of the Geophysical Sciences, University of Chicago, since 1966; *b* 20 March 1930; *s* of Norman and Gwenda Clayton; *m* 1971, Cathleen Shelburne Clayton; one *d. Educ:* Queen's Univ., Canada (BSc, MSc); California Inst. of Technol. (PhD). Res. Fellow, Calif. Inst. of Technol., 1955–56; Asst Prof., Pennsylvania State Univ., 1956–58; University of Chicago: Asst Prof., 1958–62; Associate Prof., 1962–66. *Publications:* over 200 papers in geochemical journals. *Address:* 5201 South Cornell, Chicago, IL 60615, USA. *T:* (773) 6432450; Enrico Fermi Institute, University of Chicago, 5640 South Ellis Avenue, Chicago, IL 60637, USA.

CLAYTON, Stanley James; Town Clerk of the City of London 1974–82; *b* 10 Dec. 1919; *s* of late James John Clayton and late Florence Clayton; *m* 1955, Jean Winifred, *d* of late Frederick Etheridge; one *s* one *d. Educ:* Ensham Sch.; King's Coll., London (LLB). Served War of 1939–45, commnd RAF. Admitted Solicitor 1958. City of Westminster, 1938–52; Camberwell, 1952–60; Asst Solicitor, Holborn, 1960–63; Deputy Town Clerk: Greenwich, 1963–65; Islington, 1964–69; City of London, 1969–74. Comdr, Order of Dannebrog (Denmark); holds other foreign orders. *Address:* 15 Andrew Court, 68 Wickham Road, Beckenham, Kent BR3 6RG. *Club:* Royal Air Force.

CLEALL, Charles; author; *b* 1 June 1927; *s* of Sydney Cleal and Dorothy (*née* Bound); *m* 1953, Mary, *yr d* of G. L. Turner, Archery Lodge, Ashford, Mddx; two *d. Educ:* Hampton Sch.; Univ. of London (BMus); Univ of Wales (MA); Jordanhill Coll. of Educn, Glasgow. ADCM, GTCL, FRCO(CHM), LRAM, HonTSC. Command Music Adviser, RN, Plymouth Command, 1946–48; Prof. of Singing and Voice Production, TCL, 1949–52; Conductor, Morley Coll. Orch., 1949–51; Choral Scholar, Westminster Abbey, 1949–52; Organist and Choirmaster, Wesley's Chapel, City Road, EC4, 1950–52; Conductor, Glasgow Choral Union, 1952–54; BBC Music Asst, Midland Region, 1954–55; Music Master, Glyn County Sch., Ewell, 1955–66; Conductor, Aldeburgh Festival Choir, 1957–60; Organist and Choirmaster: St Paul's, Portman Sq., W1, 1957–61; Holy Trinity, Guildford, 1961–65; Lectr in Music, Froebel Inst., 1967–68; Adviser in Music, London Borough of Harrow, 1968–72; Warden, Education Section, ISM, 1971–72; music specialist, N Div., HM Inspectorate of Schs in Scotland, 1972–87; Tutor in Speech-Training, Scottish Congregational Coll. and Scottish Churches' Open Coll., Napier Univ., 1996–. Regd Teacher, Sch. of Sinus Tone, 1985–. Editor, Jl of Ernest George White Soc., 1983–88. Presented papers at: study-conf. of teachers of singing, The Maltings, Snape, 1976; Nat. Course on Develt of Young Children's Musical Skills, Univ. of Reading Sch. of Educn, 1979; annual conf., Scottish Fedn of Organists, 1980; Nat. Conf., Assoc. of Music Advisers in Scotland, 1987; Edinburgh Centre of ISM, 1993. Internat. Composition Prizeman of Cathedral of St John the Divine, NY; Limpus Fellowship Prizeman of RCO. *Publications:* Voice Production in Choral Technique, 1955, rev. edn 1970; The Selection and Training of Mixed Choirs in Churches, 1960; Sixty Songs from Sankey, 1960; (ed) John Merbecke's Music for the Congregation at Holy Communion, 1963; Music and Holiness, 1964; Plainsong for Pleasure, 1969; Authentic Chanting, 1969; Guide to Vanity Fair, 1982; Walking round the Church of St James the Great, Stonehaven, 1993; A Jewel of a Church: Laleham-All Saints', 2001. *Recreations:* reading, writing, walking. *Address:* 14 Heathfields Way, Shaftesbury, Dorset SP7 9JZ.

CLEARY, Jon Stephen; novelist; *b* 22 Nov. 1917; *s* of Matthew Cleary and Ida (*née* Brown); *m* 1946, Constantine Lucas; one *d* (and one *d* decd). *Educ:* Marist Brothers' Sch., Randwick, NSW. Variety of jobs, 1932–40; served with AIF, 1940–45; freelance writer, 1945–48; journalist with Australian News and Information Bureau: London, 1948–49; New York, 1949–51; subseq. full-time writer. Jt winner, Nat. Radio Play Contest, ABC, 1945; second prize, Sydney Morning Herald Novel Comp., 1946; Australian Lit. Soc. Gold Medal, 1950; regional winner, NY Herald Tribune World Short Story Contest, 1950; First Lifetime Award, Aust. Crime Writers' Soc., 1998. *Publications:* These Small Glories (short stories), 1946; You Can't See Round Corners, 1947 (2nd Prize, Novel Contest, Sydney Morning Herald); The Long Shadow, 1949; Just Let Me Be, 1950 (Crouch Gold Medal for best Australian novel); The Sundowners, 1952; The Climate of Courage, 1953; Justin Bayard, 1955; The Green Helmet, 1957; Back of Sunset, 1959; North from Thursday, 1960; The Country of Marriage, 1962; Forests of the Night, 1963; A Flight of Chariots, 1964; The Fall of an Eagle, 1964; The Pulse of Danger, 1966; The High Commissioner, 1967; The Long Pursuit, 1967; Season of Doubt, 1968; Remember Jack Hoxie, 1969; Helga's Web, 1970; Mask of the Andes, 1971; Man's Estate, 1972; Ransom, 1973; Peter's Pence (Edgar Award for best crime novel; Mystery Writers of

America, Best Crime Novel), 1974; The Safe House, 1975; A Sound of Lightning, 1976; High Road to China, 1977; Vortex, 1977; The Beaufort Sisters, 1979; A Very Private War, 1980; The Golden Sabre, 1981; The Faraway Drums, 1981; Spearfield's Daughter, 1982; The Phoenix Tree, 1984; The City of Fading Light, 1985; Dragons at the Party, 1987; Now and Then, Amen, 1988; Babylon South, 1989; Murder Song, 1990; Pride's Harvest, 1991; Dark Summer, 1992; Bleak Spring, 1993; Autumn Maze, 1994; Winter Chill, 1995; Endpeace, 1996; A Different Turf, 1997; Five Ring Circus, 1998; Dilemma, 1999; Bear Pit, 2000; Yesterday's Shadow, 2001. *Recreations:* tennis, reading. *Address:* c/o HarperCollins, 77–85 Fulham Palace Road, W6 8JB.

CLEASBY, Very Rev. Thomas Wood Ingram; Dean of Chester, 1978–86, Dean Emeritus, since 1986; *b* 27 March 1920; *s* of T. W. Cleasby, Oakdene, Sedbergh, Yorks, and Jessie Brown Cleasby; *m* 1st, 1956, Olga Elizabeth Vibert Douglas (*d* 1967); one *s* one *d* (and one *d* decd); 2nd, 1970, Monica, *e d* of Rt Rev. O. S. Tomkins; one *d*. *Educ:* Sedbergh Sch., Yorks; Magdalen Coll., Oxford; Cuddesdon Coll., Oxford. BA, MA (Hons Mod. History) 1947. Commissioned, 1st Bn Border Regt, 1940; served 1st Airborne Div., 1941–45, Actg Major. Ordained, Dio. Wakefield, 1949 (Huddersfield Parish Church). Domestic Chaplain to Archbishop of York, 1952–56; Anglican Chaplain to Univ. of Nottingham, 1956–63; Archdeacon of Chesterfield, 1963–78; Vicar of St Mary and All Saints, Chesterfield, 1963–70; Rector of Morton, Derby, 1970–78. *Recreations:* fell-walking, bird-watching, gardening, fishing, local history. *Address:* Low Barth, Dent, Cumbria LA10 5SZ. *T:* (01539) 625476.

CLEAVE, Brian Elseley, CB 1995; Solicitor of Inland Revenue, 1990–99; *b* 3 Sept. 1939; *s* of Walter Edward Cleave and Hilda Lillian Cleave (*née* Newman); *m* 1979, Celia Valentine Williams. *Educ:* Eastbourne Coll. (Duke of Devonshire's schol.); Exeter Univ. (LLB 1961); Kansas Univ.; Manchester Univ. Admitted Solicitor, 1966; called to the Bar, Gray's Inn, 1999. Asst Solicitor, Wilkinson Howlett and Durham, 1966–67; Inland Revenue Solicitor's Office, 1967–99: Asst Solicitor, 1978; Prin. Asst Solicitor, 1986. Hon. QC 1999. FRSA 1995. *Recreations:* theatre, travel, walking. *Address:* Gray's Inn Tax Chambers, Third Floor, Gray's Inn Chambers, Gray's Inn, WC1R 5JA.

CLEAVER, Sir Anthony (Brian), Kt 1992; FBCS; Chairman: AEA Technology plc, since 1996; IX Holdings (formerly IX Europe) Ltd, since 1999; SThree, since 2000; Chairman, Medical Research Council, since 1998; *b* 10 April 1938; *s* of late William Brian Cleaver and Dorothea Early Cleaver (*née* Peeks); *m* 1st, 1962, Mary Teresa Cotter (*d* 1999); one *s* one *d*; 2nd, 2000, Mrs Jennifer Guise Lloyd Graham, widow. *Educ:* Berkhamsted Sch.; Trinity Coll., Oxford (Schol.; MA; Hon. Fellow 1989). Joined IBM United Kingdom, 1962; IBM World Trade Corp., USA, 1973–74; Dir, DP Div., IBM UK, 1977; Vice-Pres. of Marketing, IBM Europe, Paris, 1981–82; Gen. Man., 1984, Chief Exec., 1986–91, Chm., 1990–94, IBM United Kingdom Holdings Ltd; Chm., General Cable PLC, 1995–98 (Dir, 1994–98). Chm., UKAEA, 1993–96. Chairman: The Strategic Partnership Ltd, 1997–2000; Baxi Partnership, 1999–2000; Chm., Asia Pacific Advisers (Trade Partners UK), 2000–. Director: General Accident plc (formerly General Accident, Fire & Life Assurance Corp.), 1988–98; Smith & Nephew PLC, 1993–; Loral Europe Ltd, 1995–96; Cable Corp., 1995–96; Lockheed Martin Tactical Systems UK Ltd, 1996–99; Lockheed Martin UK Ltd, 1999–. Dir, Nat. Computing Centre, 1976–80. Member Board: UK Centre for Econ. and Environmental Develt, 1985–98 (Dep. Chm., 1992–98), DITC, 1985–2000 (Chm., Business in the Envmt Target Team, 1988–99; Mem., President's Cttee, 1988–91; Dep. Chm., 1991–2000); RIPA, 1985–90; Mem., Council, ABSA, 1985–97 (Dir, 1991–97); Pres., Involvement and Participation Assoc., 1997–. Chairman: Industrial Develt Adv. Bd, DTI, 1993–99; TEC Ind. Assessors Cttee, 1994–98; Council for Excellence in Mgt and Leadership, 2000–; Member: Nat. Adv. Council for Educn and Trng Targets, 1993–98; Electronics EDC, NEDO, 1986–92; CBI, 1986–97 (Mem., President's Cttee, 1988–92); BOTB, 1988–91; Nat. Trng Task Force, 1989–92; Adv. Council, Centre for Dispute Resolution, 1996–; Partnership Korea, 1997–99; PPARC Appointments Cttee, 1996–; Cttee on Standards in Public Life, 1997–; British Government Panel on Sustainable Develt, 1998–2000; Singapore British Business Council, 1999–2000. Chm., Asia Pacific Advisers (Trade Partners UK), 2000–. Dir, American Chamber of Commerce, 1989–91. Member: HRH Duke of Edinburgh's Seventh Commonwealth Study Conf. Council, 1990–92; Council for Industry and Higher Educn, 1991–94; Carnegie Inquiry into Third Age, 1991–93. Chm., Portsmouth Univ. Business Adv. Bd, 1992–99; Member: Oxford Univ. Adv. Council on Continuing Educn, 1993–99; Oxford Univ. Develt Prog. Adv. Bd, 1999–; President's Cttee, Oxford Univ. Appeal, 1988; Appeal Chm., Trinity Coll., Oxford, 1989–98; Chm., RCM, 1999– (Mem. Council, 1998–); Member Council: Templeton Coll., Oxford, 1982–93; PSI, 1985–88; Pres., Inst. of Mgt, 1999–2000; Chm. Govs, Birkbeck Coll., 1989–98; Mem., Cttee of Chm. of Univ. Councils, 1992–98; Trustee, Oxford Univ. Higher Studies Fund, 1994–. Dep. Chm., ENO, 1998–2000 (Dir, 1988–2000). Pres., Classical Assoc., 1995–96. Freeman, City of London, 1987; Co. of Information Technologists, 1985– (Liveryman, 1994). Hon. FCIM 1989 (Hon. Vice-Pres., 1991–; Pres., London Br., 1993–2000); Hon. FCIPS 1996; FRSA 1987 (Chm., RSA Inquiry into Tomorrow's Co., 1993–95). Mem. Council, WWF, 1988–92. Patron, Friends of Classics, 1991–. Hon. Fellow, Birkbeck Coll., London, 1999. Hon. LLD: Nottingham, 1991; Portsmouth, 1996; Hon. DSc Cranfield, 1995. UN Envmt Program Global 500 Roll of Honour, 1989. *Recreations:* music, especially opera; sport, especially cricket, golf. *Address:* AEA Technology plc, Central House, Upper Woburn Place, WC1H 0JN. *T:* (020) 7554 5553. *Clubs:* Royal Automobile, MCC.

CLEAVER, William Benjamin, CEng, FIMinE; JP; Deputy Director, South Wales Area, National Coal Board, 1969–85; *b* 15 Sept. 1921; *s* of David John Cleaver and Blodwen (*née* Miles); *m* 1943, Mary Watkin (*née* James); one *s* two *d*. *Educ:* Pentre (Rhondda) Grammar Sch.; University Coll. Cardiff (BSc Hons). National Coal Board: Manager: N Celynen Collieries, Gwent, 1947; Oakdale Colliery, Gwent, 1950; Production Manager (Group), S Wales, 1953; Area General Manager, No 2 S Wales Area, 1958. Sec., Contemporary Art Soc. for Wales, 1972–91; Member: Welsh Arts Council, 1977–83 (Vice-Chm., 1980–83); Arts Council of GB, 1980–83; Council, Nat. Museum of Wales, 1982–2000; Exec. Cttee, Council of Museums in Wales, 1983–97 (Chm., 1986–97). Founder Pres., Cardiff Jun. Ch. of Commerce, 1953. Rugby Union Football: Cardiff RFC, 1940–50; Welsh Rugby International, 1947–50 (14 caps); British Lion to NZ and Aust., 1950; Barbarian Rugby Club, 1946; Founder Chm., Welsh Youth Rugby Union, 1949–57. JP Cardiff 1973. OStJ 1961. *Recreations:* theatre, fine arts. *Address:* 29 Lon-y-deri, Rhiwbina, Cardiff CF4 6JN. *T:* (029) 2069 3242. *Club:* Cardiff and County (Cardiff).

CLEERE, Henry Forester, OBE 1992; FSA; Director, Council for British Archaeology, 1974–91 (Hon. Vice-President, 1994); World Heritage Co-ordinator, International Council on Monuments and Sites, 1991–2002; *b* 2 Dec. 1926; *s* of late Christopher Henry John Cleere and Frances Eleanor (*née* King); *m* 1st, 1950, Dorothy Percy (marr. diss.); one *s* one *d*; 2nd, 1975, Pamela Joan Vertue; two *d*. *Educ:* Beckenham County Sch.; University Coll. London (BA Hons 1951; Fellow 1992); Univ. of London Inst. of Archaeology (PhD 1981). FSA 1967. Commissioned Royal Artillery, 1946–48. Successively, Production Editor, Asst Sec., Man. Editor, Dep. Sec., Iron and Steel Inst., 1952–71; Industrial Development Officer, UN Industrial Develt Org., Vienna, 1972–73. Archaeol Advr, GLC Historic Buildings Panel, 1979–84. Member: Exec. Cttee, ICOMOS, 1981–90; Duchy of Cornwall Archaeol Adv. Panel, 1983–90; Scientific Cttee, Centro Universitario Europeo per i Beni Culturali, 1985–95; NT Archaeol. Panel, 1990–94. President: Sussex Archaeol Soc., 1987–91 (Vice Pres., 1994); Europ. Forum of Heritage Assocs, 1991–93; Sec., Europ. Assoc. of Archaeologists, 1991–96. MIFA 1982, Hon. MIFA 1991; FIMgt; Hon. Foreign Mem., Archaeol Inst. of America, 1995. Winston Churchill Fellow, 1979; Hon. Vis. Fellow, Univ. of York, 1988–92; Vis. Res. Fellow, Univ. de Paris I (Sorbonne), 1989; UK Trust Sen. Fellow, Indian Nat. Trust for Art and Cultural Heritage, 1990. Vis. Prof., Inst. of Archaeology, UCL, 1998–. Hon. DLitt Sussex, 1993. Editor, Antiquity, 1992. *Publications:* Approaches to the Archaeological Heritage, 1984; (with D. W. Crossley) The Iron Industry of the Weald, 1985; Archaeological Heritage Management in the Modern World, 1988; Oxford Archaeological Guide to Southern France, 2001; papers in British and foreign jls on heritage mgt, early ironmaking, Roman fleets, etc. *Recreations:* gardening, cookery. *Address:* Acres Rise, Lower Platts, Ticehurst, Wadhurst, East Sussex TN5 7DD. *T:* (01580) 200752; *e-mail:* henry.cleere@talk21.com. *Club:* Athenæum.

CLEESE, John Marwood; writer and actor; *b* 27 Oct. 1939; *s* of late Reginald and Muriel Cleese; *m* 1st, 1968, Connie Booth (marr. diss. 1978); one *d*; 2nd, 1981, Barbara Trentham (marr. diss. 1990); one *d*; 3rd, 1993, Alyce Faye Eichelberger. *Educ:* Clifton Sports Acad.; Downing College, Cambridge (MA). Founder and former Dir, Video Arts Ltd. Started making jokes professionally, 1963; started on British television, 1966; TV series have included: The Frost Report, At Last the 1948 Show, Monty Python's Flying Circus, Fawlty Towers, The Human Face (documentary). Films include: Interlude, 1968; And Now For Something Completely Different, 1970; The Magic Christian, 1971; Monty Python and the Holy Grail, 1974; Romance with a Double Bass, 1974; Life of Brian, 1978; Privates on Parade, 1982; The Meaning of Life, 1982; Yellowbeard, 1983; Silverado, 1985; Clockwise, 1986; A Fish Called Wanda, 1988; Erik the Viking, 1989; Splitting Heirs, 1993; Mary Shelley's Frankenstein, 1994; Rudyard Kipling's The Jungle Book, 1995; Fierce Creatures, 1997; The Out of Towners, 1998; Isn't She Great, 1998; The World Is Not Enough, 1999; Quantum Project, 2000; Pluto Nash, 2000; Rat Race, 2001. Andrew D. White Prof.-at-Large, Cornell Univ., 1999–. Hon. LLD St Andrews. *Publications:* (with Robin Skynner) Families and How to Survive Them, 1983; The Golden Skits of Wing Commander Muriel Volestrangler FRHS and Bar, 1984; The Complete Fawlty Towers, 1989; (with Robin Skynner) Life and How to Survive It, 1993. *Recreations:* gluttony, sloth. *Address:* c/o David Wilkinson, 115 Hazlebury Road, SW6 2LX.

CLEGG, Brian George Herbert; management consultant and company director; *b* 10 Dec. 1921; *s* of Frederic Bradbury Clegg and Gladys Butterworth; *m* 1st, 1949, Iris May Ludlow (marr. diss. 1976); one *s* one *d*; 2nd, 1976, Anne Elizabeth Robertson (marr. diss. 1996); one *s*; 3rd, 1997, Banjit, (Joom,) Sawaengdee (marr. diss. 1999); 4th, 1999, Christine Lawino. *Educ:* Manchester Grammar Sch.; Trinity Coll., Cambridge (Open Math. Schol., MA). FIS, FIM, CEng, FIGasE. Sci. Officer, Min. of Supply, 1942; Hon. Flt-Lt, RAFVR. Statistician, Liverpool Gas Co., 1946; Market and Operational Res. Man., Southern Gas Bd, 1957; Commercial Man., Southern Gas Bd, 1961; Dep. Dir of Marketing, Gas Council, 1968; Dir of Marketing, British Gas Corp., 1972; Chm., Northern Region of British Gas Corp., 1975–82, retired. Dir (nominee), Midland Montagu Ventures Ltd, 1984–92. *Publications:* numerous articles and papers on marketing and fuel matters. *Recreations:* swimming, ice-skating, electronic organ. *Address:* 30 The Pines, 40 The Avenue, Poole, Dorset BH13 6HJ.

CLEGG, Prof. Edward John, MD, PhD; FIBiol; Regius Professor of Anatomy, University of Aberdeen, 1976–89; Professor of Biological Anthropology, University of Aberdeen, 1990–91, now Emeritus; *b* 29 Oct. 1925; *s* of Edward Clegg and Emily Armistead; *m* 1958, Sheila Douglas Walls; two *d* (and one *d* decd). *Educ:* High Storrs Grammar Sch., Sheffield; Univ. of Sheffield (MB, ChB Hons 1948, MD 1964). PhD Liverpool, 1957; FIBiol 1974. RAMC, 1948–50 and RAMC (TA), 1950–61; late Major, RAMC (RARO). Demonstr, Asst Lectr and Lectr in Anatomy, Univ. of Liverpool, 1952–63; Lectr, Sen. Lectr and Reader in Human Biology and Anatomy, Univ. of Sheffield, 1963–77. MO, British Kangchenjunga Expedn, 1955; Sci. Mem., Chogolungma Glacier Expedn, 1959; Leader, WHO/IBP Expedn, Simien Mountains, Ethiopia, 1967. Pres., Anat. Soc. of GB and Ire, 1988–89; Chm., Soc. for the Study of Human Biology, 1988–92. *Publications:* The Study of Man: an introduction to human biology, 1968 (2nd edn 1978); papers on anatomy, endocrinology and human biology. *Recreations:* mountaineering, fishing, sailing, music. *Address:* 22 Woodburn Avenue, Aberdeen AB15 8JQ; c/o School of Biomedical Sciences, Marischal College, Aberdeen AB9 1AS. *T:* (01224) 274324. *Clubs:* Alpine; Wayfarers (Liverpool).

CLEGG, Prof. John Brian, PhD; FRS 1999; Professor of Molecular Medicine, University of Oxford, since 1996; *b* 9 April 1936; *s* of John Richard and Phyllis Clegg. *Educ:* Arnold Sch., Blackpool; Fitzwilliam House, Cambridge (MA 1963; PhD 1963). Univ. of Washington, Seattle, 1963; Johns Hopkins Univ., 1964–65; MRC Lab. of Molecular Biology, 1965; Department of Medicine, University of Liverpool: Lectr, 1966–68; Sen. Lectr, 1969–74; University of Oxford: Lectr, Dept of Medicine, 1974–79; Reader in Molecular Haematology, 1987–96; Asst Dir, Inst. of Molecular Medicine, 1989; MRC Sen. Scientific Staff, 1979–. Hon. MRCP 1986, Hon. FRCP 1999. *Publications:* (with D. J. Weatherall) The Thalassaemia Syndromes, 1965, 4th edn 2001; scientific contribs to learned jls. *Recreations:* gardening, travel in France. *Address:* Institute of Molecular Medicine, John Radcliffe Hospital, Oxford OX3 9DS. *T:* (01865) 222378.

CLEGG, Nicholas William Peter; Member (Lib Dem) East Midlands, European Parliament, since 1999; *b* 7 Jan. 1967; *s* of Nicholas P. Clegg and Hermance Eulalie Van den Wall Bake; *m* 2000, Miriam Gonzalez Durantez. *Educ:* Westminster Sch.; Robinson Coll., Cambridge (MA Anthropol.); Univ. of Minnesota (post grad. res., Political Theory); Coll. of Europe, Bruges (MA European Studies). Trainee journalist, The Nation mag., NY, 1990; Consultant, GJW Govt Relns, London, 1992–93; Official, Relns with New Independent States, EC, 1994–96; Mem. of Cabinet, Office of Sir Leon Brittan, EC, 1996–99. David Thomas Prize, Financial Times, 1993. *Recreations:* ski-ing, mountaineering, theatre. *Address:* 23 The Green, Ruddington, Notts NG11 6HH. *Club:* National Liberal.

CLEGG, Philip Charles; His Honour Judge Clegg; a Circuit Judge, since 1987; Resident Judge, Basildon Combined Court Centre, since 1996; *b* 17 Oct. 1942; *s* of Charles and Patricia Clegg; *m* 1st, 1965, Caroline Frances Peall (marr. diss. 1996); one *s* two *d*; 2nd, 1997, Fiona Cameron. *Educ:* Rossall; Bristol Univ. (LLB Hons). Called to the Bar, Middle Temple, 1966; in practice on Northern Circuit; Asst Recorder, 1980–83; a Recorder, 1983–87. *Recreations:* sailing, model engineering.

CLEGG, Richard Ninian Barwick; QC 1979; a Recorder of the Crown Court, 1978–93; *b* 28 June 1938; *o s* of Sir Cuthbert Clegg, TD; *m* 1963, Katherine Veronica, *d* of A. A. H. Douglas; two *s* one *d*. *Educ:* Aysgarth; Charterhouse; Trinity Coll., Oxford

(MA). Captain of Oxford Pentathlon Team, 1959. Called to Bar, Inner Temple, 1960, Bencher, 1985. Chm., NW section of Bow Group, 1964–66; Vice-Chm., Bow Group, 1965–66; Chm., Winston Circle, 1965–66; Pres., Heywood and Royton Conservative Assoc., 1965–68. *Publication:* (jtly) Bow Group pamphlet, Towards a New North West, 1964. *Recreations:* sport, music, travel. *Address:* Ford Farm, Wootton Courtenay, Minehead, Somerset TA24 8RW. *T:* (01643) 841669. *Club:* Lansdowne.

CLEGG, Simon Paul, OBE 2001; Chief Executive, British Olympic Association, since 1997; *b* 11 Aug. 1959; *s* of Peter Vernon Clegg and Patricia Anne Clegg (*née* Long); *m* 1985, Hilary Anne Davis; one *s* one *d. Educ:* Stowe Sch. Commnd RA, 1981; OC Battery, 7th Parachute Regt, RHA, 1989. Manager, British Biathlon Team, 1984–85; British Olympic Association, 1989–: Asst Gen. Sec., 1989–91; Dep. Gen. Sec., 1991–96; Olympic Quartermaster, Summer and Winter Olympic Games, 1988 (on secondment); Great Britain Team: Dep. Chef de Mission, Olympic Games, 1992 and 1996, Olympic Winter Games, 1994; Chef de Mission: Olympic Winter Games, 1998 and 2002; Olympic Games, 2000; Chief Exec., European Youth Olympic Games, Bath, 1995. *Address:* British Olympic Association, 1 Wandsworth Plain, SW18 1EH. *T:* (020) 8871 2677. *Club:* Cavalry and Guards.

CLEGG, William; QC 1991; a Recorder, since 1992; *b* 5 Sept. 1949; *s* of Peter Hepworth Clegg and Sheila Clegg; *m* 1974, Wendy Doreen Chard; one *s* one *d. Educ:* St Thomas More High School; Bristol Univ. (LLB). Called to the Bar, Gray's Inn, 1972; in practice, SE Circuit. Head of Chambers, 1995–. *Recreations:* squash, cricket. *Address:* 2 Bedford Row, WC1R 4BU. *T:* (020) 7440 8888. *Clubs:* Garrick, Our Society.

CLEGG-HILL, family name of **Viscount Hill**.

CLEGHORN, Bruce Elliot; HM Diplomatic Service; Minister and Deputy Permanent Representative, UK Delegation to NATO, Brussels, since 1997; *b* 19 Nov. 1946; *s* of Ivan Robert Cleghorn and Margaret (*née* Kemplen); *m* 1976, Sally Ann Robinson; three *s. Educ:* Sutton Valence Sch., Kent; St John's Coll., Cambridge (BA Hons). Commonwealth Fellow, Panjab Univ., 1970–72; Jun. Res. Fellow, Inst. of Commonwealth Studies, Univ. of London, 1972–74; joined HM Diplomatic Service, 1974; Delegn to CSCE, 1974–75; FCO, 1975–76; First Secretary: Delegn to NATO, 1976–79; New Delhi, 1980–83; FCO, 1983–87; Counsellor, CSCE Delegn, Vienna, 1987–89; Dep. Hd, UK Delegn to negotiations on conventional arms control, Vienna, 1989–91; Dep. High Comr and Counsellor (Econ. and Commercial), Kuala Lumpur, 1992–94; Head of Non-Proliferation Dept, FCO, 1995–97. *Publication:* (with V. N. Datta) A Nationalist Muslim and Indian Politics, 1974. *Recreations:* swimming, walking, studying British 20th century painters. *Address:* c/o Foreign and Commonwealth Office, King Charles Street, SW1A 2AH.

CLELAND, Helen Isabel, (Mrs Robin Hoult); Headteacher, Woodford County High School, since 1991; *b* 3 July 1950; *d* of John Douglas Cleland and Hilda Malvina Cleland; *m* 1973, Dr Robin Hoult (*d* 2001); one *s* one *d. Educ:* King Edward VI High Sch. for Girls, Birmingham; Exeter Univ. (BA Hons English); Homerton Coll., Cambridge (PGCE). English Teacher, Dame Alice Owen's Sch., London, 1972–76; English Teacher, 1976–79, Sen. Teacher, 1979–86, Haverstock Sch., London; Dep. Head, Edmonton Sch., Enfield, 1986–91. *Recreations:* reading, theatre, hill walking. *Address:* Woodford County High School, High Road, Woodford Green, Essex IG8 9LA. *T:* (020) 8504 0611.

CLELAND, Dame Rachel, DBE 1980 (CBE 1966; MBE 1959); *b* Peppermint Grove, Jan. 1906; *d* of W. H. Evans, Perth, WA; *m* 1928, Sir Donald Cleland, *s* of E. D. Cleland; two *s. Educ:* Methodist Ladies' Coll., Perth, WA; Kindergarten Training Coll. Pres., Girl Guide Assoc., Papua and New Guinea, 1952–66; President: Red Cross, Papua and New Guinea, 1952–66; Branch of Aust. Pre-Sch. Assoc. (TPNG), 1952–66. *Publications:* Pathways to Independence: official and family life in Papua New Guinea 1951–1976, 1984, 2nd edn 1985; Grassroots to Independence and Beyond: contribution by women in Papua New Guinea, 1996. *Recreations:* music, theatre, reading. *Address:* 2/24 Richardson Avenue, Claremont, WA 6010, Australia. *Club:* Queen's (Sydney).

CLELAND, William Paton, FRCP, FRCS, FACS; Consulting Surgeon, National Heart and Chest Hospital; Consulting Thoracic Surgeon, King's College Hospital; Emeritus Consultant to the RN; late Adviser in Thoracic Surgery to the Department of Health and Social Security; *b* 30 May 1912; *o s* of late Sir John Cleland, CBE; *m* 1940, Norah, *d* of George E. Goodhart; two *s* one *d. Educ:* Scotch Coll., Adelaide; Univ. of Adelaide, S Australia. MB, BS (Adelaide). Resident appts, Royal Adelaide and Adelaide Children's Hosps, 1935–36; MRCP 1939; House Physician and Resident Surgical Officer, Brompton Chest Hosp., 1939–41. Served in EMS as Registrar and Surgeon, 1939–45. FRCS 1946. Consultant Thoracic Surg., King's Coll. Hosp., 1948; Surgeon, Brompton Chest Hospital, 1948; Sen. Lectr in Thoracic Surgery, Royal Postgrad. Med. Sch., 1949; Dir, Dept of Surgery, Cardio-Thoracic Inst., Brompton Hosp. Member: Assoc. Thoracic Surgeons of Gt Brit. and Ire.; Thoracic Soc.; British Cardiac Soc.; Amer. Coll. of Surgeons. Editor, Jl of Cardiovascular Surgery, 1978–83. Comdr, Order of Lion of Finland; Comdr, Order of Falcon of Iceland. *Publications:* (jt author) Medical and Surgical Cardiology, 1969; chapters on thoracic surgery in British Surgical Practice, Diseases of the Chest (Marshall and Perry), Short Practice of Surgery (Bailey and Love), and Operative Surgery (Rob and Rodney Smith); articles on pulmonary and cardiac surgery in medical literature. *Recreations:* fishing, gardening, beekeeping. *Address:* Green Meadows, Goodworth Clatford, Andover, Hants SP11 7HH. *T:* (01264) 324327.

CLELLAND, David Gordon; MP (Lab) Tyne Bridge, since Dec. 1985; *b* 27 June 1943; *s* of Archibald and Ellen Clelland; *m* 1965, Maureen (separated 1998); two *d. Educ:* Kelvin Grove Boys' School, Gateshead; Gateshead and Hebburn Technical Colleges. Apprentice electrical fitter, 1959–64; electrical tester, 1964–81. Gateshead Borough Council: Councillor, 1972–86; Recreation Chm., 1976–84; Leader of Council, 1984–86. Nat. Sec., Assoc. of Councillors, 1981–85. An Asst Govt Whip 1997–2000; a Lord Comr of HM Treasury (Govt Whip), 2000–01. Member: Home Affairs Select Cttee, 1986–88; Energy Select Cttee, 1989–90. Chairman: Backbench Envmt Cttee, 1990–97; PLP Regl Govt Gp, 1992–97; PLP Trade Union Gp, 1994–97; Sec., Northern Gp of Lab MPs, 1990–98. *Recreation:* golf, music, reading. *Address:* 19 Ravensworth Road, Dunston, Gateshead NE11 9AB. *T:* (0191) 420 0300.

CLEMENS, Clive Carruthers, CMG 1983; MC 1946; HM Diplomatic Service, retired; High Commissioner in Lesotho, 1981–84; *b* 22 Jan. 1924; British; *s* of late M. B. Clemens, Imperial Bank of India, and late Margaret Jane (*née* Carruthers); *m* 1947, Philippa Jane Bailey; three *s. Educ:* Blundell's Sch.; St Catharine's Coll., Cambridge. War Service 1943–46: commissioned in Duke of Cornwall's Light Infantry; served in India and Burma, 1944–45. Entered HM Foreign Service and apptd to FO, 1947; Third Sec., Rangoon, 1948; Third (later Second) Sec., Lisbon, 1950; FO, 1953; First Sec., Budapest, 1954; Brussels, 1956; Seoul, 1959; FO, 1961; Strasbourg (UK Delegn to Council of Europe), 1964; Counsellor, Paris, 1967; Principal British Trade Comr, Vancouver, 1970–74; Dep. Consul-Gen., Johannesburg, 1974–78; Consul-Gen., Istanbul, 1978–81. *Recreations:* birdwatching, photography. *Address:* 9 Saxonhurst, Downton, Salisbury, Wilts SP5 3JN.

CLEMENT, David James; Chairman, Systems Network, since 1997; *b* 29 Sept. 1930; *s* of James and Constance Clement; *m* 1958, Margaret Stone; two *s* one *d. Educ:* Chipping Sodbury Grammar Sch.; Univ. of Bristol (BA). CPFA 1957. Internal Audit Asst, City of Bristol, 1953–56; Accountancy/Audit Asst, 1956–60, Chief Accountancy Asst, 1960–65, City of Worcester; Dep. Chief Finance Officer, Runcorn Develt Corp., 1965–68; Chief Finance Officer, Antrim and Ballymena Develt Commn, 1968–72; Asst Sec., Dept of Finance, NI, 1972–75, Dep. Sec., 1975–80; Under Sec., DoE, NI, 1980–84. Financial consultant, 1985–90; Chm., HELM Corp., 1990–98. Chm. Trustees, Ulster Historical Foundn, 2000–. *Recreations:* lawn tennis, Association football, contract bridge, philately.

CLEMENT, David Morris, CBE 1971; FCA; Hon. FCGI; Chairman, Joint Mission Hospital Equipment Board Ltd, 1978–85; *b* 6 Feb. 1911; 2nd *s* of Charles William and Rosina Wannell Clement, Swansea; *m* 1938, Kathleen Mary (*d* 1991), *o d* of Ernest George Davies, ACA, Swansea; one *d. Educ:* Bishop Gore's Grammar Sch., Swansea. Mem. Inst. Chartered Accountants, 1933. A. Owen John & Co., Swansea, and Sissons Bersey Gain Vincent & Co., London, Chartered Accts, 1928–35; ICI Ltd, Lime Gp, 1935–40; Chloride Electrical Storage Co. Ltd, 1941–46; National Coal Board: Sec., North Western Div., 1946–49; Chief Acct, Northern and Durham Divs, 1950–55; Dep. Dir-Gen. of Finance, 1955–61; Dir-Gen. of Finance, 1961–69; Bd Mem., 1969–76; Chairman: NCB (Ancillaries) Ltd, 1973–79; Redwood-Corex Services Ltd, 1978–82. Chm., Staff and Mineworkers Pension Schemes Jt Investment Cttee, 1961–76. Chm., Public Corporations Finance Gp, 1975–76. Dep. Chm., Horizon Exploration Ltd, 1978–80. Underwriting Member of Lloyd's, 1978–96. Member: Aircraft and Shipbuilding Industries Arbitration Tribunals, 1980–83; Council, CIPFA, 1975–76; Council, CGLI (Hon. Treas.), 1978–82. *Recreations:* golf, photography. *Address:* The Old Hall, Mulbarton, Norfolk NR14 8JS. *T:* (01508) 578655. *Clubs:* Directors'; Norfolk (Norwich).

See also D. J. Mellor.

CLEMENT, John; Chairman: Culpho Consultants, since 1991; Tuddenham Hall Foods, since 1991; *b* 18 May 1932; *s* of Frederick and Alice Eleanor Clement; *m* 1956, Elisabeth Anne (*née* Emery); two *s* one *d. Educ:* Bishop's Stortford College. Howards Dairies, Westcliff on Sea, 1949–64; United Dairies London Ltd, 1964–69; Asst Managing Director, Rank Leisure Services Ltd, 1969–73; Chairman, Unigate Foods Div., 1973; Chief Executive, 1976–90, Chm., 1977–91, Unigate Group. Non-executive Chairman: The Littlewoods Organisation, 1982–90; Nat. Car Auctions Ltd, 1995–98; Director: NV Verenigde Bedrijven Nutricia, 1981–92; Eagle Star Holdings plc, 1981–86; Eagle Star Insce Co., 1981–84; Anglo American Insce Co., 1991–94 (Chm., 1993–94); Ransomes plc, 1991– 98 (Chm., 1993–98); Dresdner RCM Second Endowment Policy Trust plc (formerly Kleinwort Second Endowment Trust plc), 1993– (Chm., 1998–); Jarvis Hotels Ltd, 1994–. Mem., Securities and Investments Bd, 1986–89. Chairman: King's Coll., Cambridge I-IV (business expansion scheme), 1993–98; Govs, Framlingham Coll., 1991–2001 (Gov., 1982–2001). Chairman: Children's Liver Disease Foundn, 1979–95; British Liver Trust, 1992–99. High Sheriff, Suffolk, 2000–01. CIMgt (FBIM 1977); FIGD 1979. *Recreations:* shooting, sailing, bridge, Rugby, tennis. *Address:* Tuddenham Hall, Tuddenham, Ipswich, Suffolk IP6 9DD. *T:* (01473) 785217, *Fax:* (01473) 785405. *Clubs:* Farmers'; Cumberland Lawn Tennis. *Address:* Royal Harwich Yacht.

See also R. Clement.

CLEMENT, John Handel, CB 1980; *b* 24 Nov. 1920; *s* of late William and Mary Hannah Clement; *m* 1946, Anita Jones; one *d* (and one *d* decd). *Educ:* Pontardawe Grammar Sch. RAF, 1940–46, Flt Lt (despatches). Welsh Board of Health: Clerical Officer, 1938; Exec. Officer, 1946; Higher Exec. Officer, 1948; Sen. Exec. Officer, 1956; Principal, Welsh Office, Min. of Housing and Local Govt, 1960, Asst Sec., 1966; Private Sec. to Sec. of State for Wales, 1966; Under-Sec., 1971–81, Dir of Industry Dept, 1976–81, Welsh Office. Sec., Council for Wales, 1955–59; Chm., Welsh Planning Bd, 1971–76. Member: Wales Tourist Bd, 1982–88; Midland Bank Adv. Council for Wales, 1985–94. Hon. MA Wales, 1982. *Recreations:* Welsh Rugby, fishing.

CLEMENT, Richard, (Dick); freelance writer, director and producer; *b* 5 Sept. 1937; *s* of Frederick and Alice Eleanor Clement; *m* 1st, Jennifer F. Sheppard (marr. diss. 1981); three *s* one *d*; 2nd, 1982, Nancy S. Campbell; one *d. Educ:* Bishop's Stortford Coll.; Westminster Sch., Conn, USA. Co-writer (with Ian La Frenais): *television:* The Likely Lads, 1964–66; Whatever Happened to the Likely Lads, 1972–73; Porridge, 1974–76; Thick as Thieves, 1974; Going Straight, 1978; Auf Wiedersehen, Pet, 1984; Freddie and Max, 1990; Full Stretch, 1993; *films:* The Jokers, 1967; Otley, 1968; Hannibal Brooks, 1968; Villain, 1971; Porridge, 1979; Water, 1984; Vice Versa, 1987; The Commitments, 1991; Still Crazy, 1998; Honest, 2000; Director: *films:* Otley, 1968; A Severed Head, 1969; Porridge, 1979; Bullshot, 1983; Water, 1984; co-producer (with Ian La Frenais) Vice Versa, 1987; The Commitments, 1991 (jtly, Evening Standard Peter Sellers Award, 1992); *stage:* Billy, 1974; Anyone for Denis?, 1981. *Recreations:* work, tennis, dinner; supporting Essex CCC, Chelsea FC and Los Angeles Dodgers. *Address:* 9700 Yoakum Drive, Beverly Hills, CA 90210, USA.

See also John Clement.

CLEMENT-JONES, family name of **Baron Clement-Jones**.

CLEMENT-JONES, Baron *cr* 1998 (Life Peer), of Clapham in the London Borough of Lambeth; **Timothy Francis Clement-Jones,** CBE 1988; Chairman: DLA Upstream, public affairs practice of DLA (formerly Dibb Lipton Alsop), since 1999; Environmental Context Ltd, since 1997; *b* 26 Oct. 1949; *s* of late Maurice Llewelyn Clement-Jones and of Margaret Jean Clement-Jones (*née* Hudson); *m* 1st, 1973, Dr Vicky Veronica Yip (*d* 1987); 2nd, 1994, Jean Roberta Whiteside; one *s. Educ:* Haileybury; Trinity Coll., Cambridge (Economics Pt I, Law Tripos Pt II; MA). Admitted Solicitor, 1974. Articled Clerk, Coward Chance, 1972–74; Associate, Joynson-Hicks, 1974–76; Corporate Lawyer, Letraset Internat. Ltd, 1976–80; Hd Legal Services, LWT, 1980–83; Legal Dir, Grand Metropolitan Retailing, 1984–86; Gp Co. Sec. and Legal Advr, Woolworth Hldgs, then Kingfisher plc, 1986–95; Dir, Political Context Ltd, 1996–99. Lib Dem spokesman on health, H of L, 1998–. Chm., Assoc. of Liberal Lawyers, 1982–86. Chairman: Liberal Party, 1986–88; Lib Dem Finance Cttee, 1991–98; Dir, Lib Dem EP election campaign, 1994; Chm., Lib Dem Mayoral and Assembly campaign, London, 2000. Trustee and Dir, Cancer BACUP (founded by Dr V. V. Clement-Jones), 1986–. Chm., Crime Concern, 1991–95. FRSA; MInstD. *Recreations:* reading, eating, talking, travelling, walking. *Address:* 10 Northbourne Road, SW4 7DJ. *T:* (020) 7622 4205; *e-mail:* timcj@atlas.co.uk.

CLEMENTI, David Cecil; Deputy Governor, Bank of England, since 1997; *b* 25 Feb. 1949; *s* of Air Vice-Marshal Cresswell Montagu Clementi, CB, CBE and Susan (*née* Pelham); *m* 1972, Sarah Louise, (Sally), Cowley; one *s* one *d. Educ:* Winchester Coll.; Lincoln Coll., Oxford; Harvard Business Sch. (MBA 1975). With Arthur Andersen & Co., 1970–73; qualified as CA 1973; with Kleinwort Benson Ltd, 1975–97: Dir, 1981–97; Man. Dir, KB Securities, 1987–89; Head, Corporate Finance, 1989–94; Chief Exec.,

1994–97; Vice Chm., 1997. *Recreation:* sailing. *Address:* Bank of England, EC2R 8AH. *Clubs:* Royal Ocean Racing; Royal Yacht Squadron.

CLEMENTS, Alan William, CBE 1990; Director, Capital Valve Brokers Ltd, since 1999; *b* 12 Dec. 1928; *s* of William and Kathleen Clements; *m* 1953, Pearl Dorling (*d* 1993); two *s* one *d*. *Educ:* Culford School, Bury St Edmunds; Magdalen College, Oxford (BA Hons). HM Inspector of Taxes, Inland Revenue, 1952–56; ICI: Asst Treasurer, 1966; Dep. Treasurer, 1971; Treasurer, 1976; Finance Director, 1979–90. Chairman: David S. Smith (Hldgs), 1991–99; Cementone, 1994–97; Non-executive Director: Trafalgar House, 1980–95 (Chm., 1992–93); Cable & Wireless, 1985–91; Guinness Mahon Hldgs, 1988–92; Granada Gp, 1990–94; Mirror Gp (formerly Mirror Gp Newspapers), 1991– 99 (Dep. Chm., 1992–); Brent Walker Gp, 1991–93. Lay Mem., Internat. Stock Exchange, 1984–88. Founder Pres., Assoc. of Corp. Treasurers. *Publications:* articles on finance in jls. *Recreations:* golf, music, reading.

CLEMENTS, Andrew Joseph; Chief Music Critic, Guardian, since 1993; *b* 15 Sept. 1950; *s* of Joseph George Clements and Linda Helen Clements; *m* 1977, Kathryn Denise Coltman; two *d*. *Educ:* Crypt Sch., Gloucester; Emmanuel Coll., Cambridge (BA). Music Critic: New Statesman, 1977–88; Financial Times, 1979–93; Editor, Musical Times, 1987–88. Dir, Holst Foundn, 1992–. *Publication:* Mark–Anthony Turnage, 2000. *Recreation:* birding. *Address:* c/o Guardian, 119 Farringdon Road, EC1R 3ER.

CLEMENTS, John Rodney, FCA; Secretary of the Chest, then Director of Finance and Secretary of the Chest, University of Oxford, since 1995; Fellow of Merton College, Oxford, since 1995; *b* 19 Jan. 1947; *s* of late Peter Larby Clements and of Ethel Blanche Lillian Clements (*née* Steele); *m* 1st, 1969, Janet Sylvia Mallender (marr. diss 1992); two *d*; 2nd, 1999, Georgina Margaret Eckles. *Educ:* Univ. of Manchester (BA Hons Mod. Hist. with Econs and Politics 1968). ACA 1973, FCA 1978. Auditor, KPMG Peat Marwick, Accountants, 1968–73; Financial Accountant, Co-operative Bank, 1973–74; Asst to Chief Accountant, Stock Exchange, 1974–79; Dep. Finance Officer, UCL, 1979–85; Dep. Dir of Finance, Univ. of Sheffield, 1985–92; Dir of Finance, Univ. of Leeds, 1992–94; independent consultant, 1994–95. *Recreations:* history, literature, hill walking, model railways. *Address:* University Offices, University of Oxford, Wellington Square, Oxford OX1 2JD. *T:* (01865) 270150.

CLEMENTS, Judith M.; Chief Executive and National Director, National Association for Mental Health, since 1992; *b* 27 June 1953; *d* of Robert and Margaret Dunn; *m* 1st, 1975, Paul Clements (marr. diss. 1979); 2nd, 1998, Rex Hewitt. *Educ:* Birmingham Univ. (LLB Hons 1974); Brunel Univ. (MA Public and Social Admin 1979). Dip. Inst. Housing 1976. London Borough of Camden: Estate Manager, 1974–76; Sen. Estate Manager, 1976–79; Tenancy Services Officer, 1979–81; Business System Analyst, 1981–82; Asst Dir of Housing, 1982–87; Dep. Chief Housing Officer, Brighton BC, 1987–91; Hd of Management Practice, Local Govt Management Bd, 1991–92. Hon. DSocSci Brunel, 1997. *Recreations:* reading, especially crime fiction and feminist fiction, aerobic exercise, scuba diving. *Address:* (office) Granta House, 15–19 The Broadway, E15 4BQ. *T:* (020) 8519 2122; Studio 1, Limehouse Cut, Morris Road, E14 6NQ.

CLEMENTS, Julia; *see* Seton, Lady, (Julia).

CLEMENTS, Kirsty Anne; *see* Wark, K. A.

CLEMENTS, Richard Harry; author and journalist; Director, Citizens Income Trust, 1993–96; *b* 11 Oct. 1928; *s* of Harry and Sonia Clements; *m* 1952, Bridget Mary MacDonald; two *s*. *Educ:* King Alfred Sch., Hampstead; Western High Sch., Washington, DC; Regent Street Polytechnic. Middlesex Independent, 1949; Leicester Mercury, 1951; Editor, Socialist Advance (Labour Party Youth paper), 1953; industrial staff, Daily Herald, 1954; joined Tribune, 1956, Editor, 1961–82; Political Adviser to the Leader of the Opposition, Rt Hon. Michael Foot, 1982–83; Exec. Officer to Leader of the Opposition, Rt Hon. Neil Kinnock, 1983–87. *Publication:* Glory without Power: a study of trade unions, 1959. *Recreation:* woodwork. *Address:* 68 Strafford Road, High Barnet, Herts EN5 4LR.

CLEMENTS, Prof. Ronald Ernest; Samuel Davidson Professor of Old Testament Studies, King's College, University of London, 1983–92, now Professor Emeritus; *b* 27 May 1929; *m* 1955, Valerie Winifred (*née* Suffield); two *d*. *Educ:* Buckhurst Hill County High Sch.; Spurgeon's Coll.; Christ's Coll., Cambridge; Univ. of Sheffield. MA, DD Cantab. Asst Lectr 1960–64, Lectr 1960–67, Univ. of Edinburgh; Lectr, Univ. of Cambridge, 1967–83. Hon. For. Sec., SOTS, 1973–83 (Pres., 1985–); Hon. Mem., OTWSA, 1979–. Hon. DLitt Acadia, Nova Scotia, 1982. *Publications:* God and Temple, 1965; Prophecy and Covenant, 1965; Old Testament Theology, 1978; Isaiah 1–39, 1979; A Century of Old Testament Study, 1976, 2nd edn 1983; Prayers of the Bible, 1986; Jeremiah, 1988; (ed) The World of Ancient Israel, 1989; Wisdom in Theology, 1993; Old Testament Prophecy: from oracles to canon, 1996; contrib. Vetus Testamentum, Jl of Semitic Studies. *Recreations:* reading, travel, photography, aeromodelling. *Address:* 8 Brookfield Road, Coton, Cambridge CB3 7PT.

CLEMINSON, Sir James (Arnold Stacey), KBE 1990; Kt 1982; MC 1945; DL; Deputy Chairman, J. H. Fenner plc, 1993–97 (Director, 1989–97); *b* 31 Aug. 1921; *s* of Arnold Russel Cleminson and Florence Stacey; *m* 1950, Helen Juliet Measor; one *s* two *d*. *Educ:* Rugby Sch. Served War, 1940–46, mainly in Parachute Regt. Reckitt & Colman, 1946–86: Chief Exec., 1973–80; Chm., 1977–86; Chairman: Jeyes Hygiene, 1986–89; Riggs A P Bank, 1987–91 (Dir, 1985–); Director: Norwich Union, 1979–92 (Vice-Chm., 1981–92); United Biscuits, 1982–89; Eastern Counties Newspaper Gp, 1987–93; Riggs Nat. Bank of Washington, 1991–93; Member: Council, CBI, 1978– 86 (Dep. Pres., 1983; Pres., 1984–86); London Cttee, Toronto Dominion Bank, 1982–90; NEDC, 1984–86. Jt Chm., Netherlands British Chamber of Commerce Council, 1978–84; Chairman: Food and Drink Industries Council, 1983–84; Nurses' Independent Pay Review Body, 1986–90; BOTB, 1986–90. Pres., Endeavour Trng, 1984–98; Trustee, Airborne Forces Security Fund. Chm., Theatre Royal Norwich Trust, 1991–98. Pro-Chancellor, Hull Univ., 1985–94. Hon. LLD Hull, 1985. DL Norfolk, 1983. *Recreations:* field sports, golf. *Address:* Loddon Hall, Hales, Norfolk NR14 6TB. *Clubs:* Sloane; Norfolk (Norwich).

CLEMITS, John Henry, RIBA; Managing Director, PSA Projects Cardiff, 1990–92; *b* 16 Feb. 1934; *s* of late Cyril Thomas Clemits and Minnie Alberta Clemits; *m* 1958, Elizabeth Angela Moon; one *s* one *d*. *Educ:* Sutton High Sch.; Plymouth College of Art. ARIBA 1962 (Dist. in Thesis). National Service, RAF, 1959–61; Captain, RE (TA), 43 Wessex Div. and Royal Monmouthshire RE (Militia), 1964–69. Plymouth City Architects Dept, 1954–59; Watkins Gray & Partners, Architects, Bristol, 1961–63; SW RHB, 1963–65; Architect, MPBW, Bristol, 1965–69; Sen. Architect, MPBW, Regional HQ, Rheindahlen, Germany, 1969–71; Naval Base Planning Officer, MPBW, Portsmouth, 1971–73; Suptg Architect, PSA, Directorate of Bldg Develt, 1973–75; Suptg Planning Officer, PSA, Rheindahlen, 1975–79; Dir of Works (Army), PSA, Chessington, 1979–85; Dir for Wales, PSA, Central Office for Wales, DoE, 1985–90. Chairman: Cowbridge Choral Soc., 1988–90; Vale of Glamorgan Buildings Preservation Trust, 1994–97; Dewi Sant Housing Assoc., 1995–2000. Mem. Nat. Council, Welsh Fedn of Housing Assocs, 1996–99. *Recreations:* music, DIY, painting, travel. *Address:* The Lodge, Hendrescythan, Creigiau, Cardiff CF15 9NN. *T:* (029) 2089 1786.

CLEMMOW, Jana Eve; *see* Bennett, J. E.

CLEOBURY, Nicholas Randall, MA; FRCO; conductor; *b* 23 June 1950; *s* of John and Brenda Cleobury; *m* 1978, Heather Kay; one *s* one *d*. *Educ:* King's Sch., Worcester; Worcester Coll., Oxford (MA Hons). Assistant Organist: Chichester Cathedral, 1971–72; Christ Church, Oxford, 1972–76; Chorus Master, Glyndebourne Opera, 1977–79; Asst Director, BBC Singers, 1977–79; Conductor: main BBC, provincial and London orchestras and opera houses, also in Australia, Austria, Belgium, Canada, Denmark, France, Germany, Holland, Italy, Norway, Singapore, Spain, Sweden, Switzerland, USA; regular BBC, TV appearances; numerous CD recordings. Principal Opera Conductor, Royal Academy of Music, 1981–88; Artistic Director: Aquarius, 1983–92; Cambridge Symphony Soloists, 1990–92; Britten Sinfonia, 1992–; Sounds New, 1997–; Music Dir, Oxford Bach Choir, 1997–; Principal Guest Conductor, Gävle, Sweden, 1989–91; Guest Conductor, Zürich Opera, 1993–. Music Dir, Broomhill Arts, 1990–94; Artistic Dir, Cambridge Fest., 1992. Hon. RAM 1985. *Recreations:* reading, food, wine, theatre, walking, cricket. *Address:* China Cottage, Church Lane, Petham, Canterbury CT4 5RD. *T:* (01227) 700584, *Fax:* (01227) 700827; *e-mail:* nicholascleobury@aol.com. *Clubs:* Savage, MCC, Lord's Taverners.

See also S. J. Cleobury.

CLEOBURY, Stephen John, FRCM; FRCO; Fellow, Director of Music and Organist, King's College, Cambridge, since 1982; Conductor, Cambridge University Musical Society, since 1983; Organist, Cambridge University, since 1991; Chief Conductor, BBC Singers, since 1995; *b* 31 Dec. 1948; *s* of John Frank Cleobury and Brenda Julie (*née* Randall); *m* 1971, Penelope Jane (*née* Holloway); two *d*. *Educ:* King's Sch., Worcester; St John's Coll., Cambridge (MA, MusB). FRCO 1968; FRCM 1993. Organist, St Matthew's, Northampton, 1971–74; Sub-Organist, Westminster Abbey, 1974–78; Master of Music, Westminster Cathedral, 1979–82. President: IAO, 1985–87; Cathedral Organists' Assoc., 1988–90; RCO, 1990–92 (Hon. Sec., 1981–90); Mem. Council, RSCM, 1982–. *Recreation:* reading. *Address:* King's College, Cambridge CB2 1ST. *T:* (01223) 331224.

See also N. R. Cleobury.

CLERIDES, Glafcos John; President of Cyprus, since 1993; *b* Nicosia, 24 April 1919; *s* of Yiannis Clerides, CBE, QC and Elli Clerides; *m* 1946, Lilla Erulkar; one *d*. *Educ:* Pancyprium Gymnasium, Nicosia; King's Coll., London (LLB 1948). Served in RAF, 1939–45; shot down and taken prisoner, 1942–45 (mentioned in despatches). Called to the Bar, Gray's Inn, 1951; practised in Cyprus, 1951–60; Head, Greek Cypriot Delegn, Jt Constitutional Cttee, 1959–60; Minister of Justice, 1959–60; Mem. for Nicosia, House of Representatives, 1960–76, 1981–93; First Pres. of House, 1960–76; Leader, Greek Cypriot Delegn to London Conf., 1964; Rep. of Greek Cypriots to intercommunal talks, 1968–76; Actg Pres., July–Dec. 1974 (after Turkish invasion of Cyprus). Founder and Leader: Unified Party, 1969–76; Democratic Rally Party, 1976–93. Cert. of Honour and Life Mem., Cyprus Red Cross (Pres., 1961–63). Gold Medal, Order of the Holy Sepulchre, 1961. Grand Cross of the Redeemer (Greece), 1993. *Publication:* My Deposition, 4 vols. *Address:* Presidential Palace, Nicosia, Cyprus.

CLERK of Penicuik, Sir John Dutton, 10th Bt *cr* 1679; CBE 1966; VRD; FRSE 1977; JP; Lord-Lieutenant of Midlothian, 1972–92 (Vice-Lieutenant, 1965–72); Cdre RNR; retd; *b* 30 Jan. 1917; *s* of Sir George James Robert Clerk of Penicuik, 9th Bt, and Hon. Mabel Honor (*d* 1974), *y d* of late Col Hon. Charles Dutton and *sister* of 6th Baron Sherborne, DSO; *S* father, 1943; *m* 1944, Evelyn Elizabeth Robertson; two *s* two *d*. *Educ:* Stowe. Brig., 1973–89, Ensign, 1989–96, Lieut, 1996–, Queen's Body Guard for Scotland, Royal Company of Archers. JP 1955, DL 1956, Midlothian. *Heir:* *s* Robert Maxwell Clerk, Younger of Penicuik OBE [*b* 3 April 1945; *m* 1970, Felicity Faye, *yr d* of George Collins, Bampton, Oxford; two *s* one *d*. *Educ:* Winchester Coll.; London Univ. (BSc (Agric)). FRICS]. *Address:* Penicuik House, Penicuik, Midlothian EH26 9LA. *T:* (01968) 674318. *Clubs:* Royal Over-Seas League; New (Edinburgh).

CLERKE, Sir John Edward Longueville, 12th Bt *cr* 1660; Captain Royal Wilts Yeomanry, RAC, TA; *b* 29 Oct. 1913; *er s* of Francis William Talbot Clerke (killed in action, 1916), *e s* of 11th Bt, and late Albinia Mary, *er d* of Edward Henry Evans-Lombe (who *m* 3rd, 1923, Air Chief Marshal Sir Edgar Rainey Ludlow-Hewitt, GCB, GBE, CMG, DSO, MC); *S* grandfather, 1930; *m* 1948, Mary (marr. diss. 1987; she *d* 1998), *d* of late Lt-Col I. R. Beviss Bond, OBE, MC; one *s* two *d*. *Heir:* *s* Francis Ludlow Longueville Clerke [*b* 25 Jan. 1953; *m* 1982, Vanessa Anne, *o d* of late Charles Cosman Citron and of Mrs Olga May Citron, Mouille Point, Cape Town; one *s* two *d*]. *Address:* Sampford House, 27 Shurnhold, Bath Road, Melksham, Wilts SN12 8DD. *T:* (01225) 703994.

CLEVELAND, Archdeacon of; *see* Ferguson, Ven. P. J.

CLEVELAND, Alexis Jane; Chief Executive, Benefits Agency, Department for Work and Pensions (formerly Department of Social Security), 2001–April 2002; *b* 28 Jan. 1954; *d* of Arthur and Peggy Cleveland. *Educ:* Brighton and Hove High Sch.; Univ. of Salford. Business Develt Dir, IT Services Agency, 1989–93; Benefits Agency: Territorial and Jobseekers Allowance Dir, 1993–97; Ops Support Dir, 1997–2000. *Recreations:* travel, walking, swimming, cinema, theatre. *Address:* Benefits Agency, Quarry House, Quarry Hill, Leeds, LS2 7UA. *T:* (0113) 232 7845. *Club:* Durham Working Men's.

CLEVELAND, Harlan; President, World Academy of Art and Science, 1991–2000, now President Emeritus; Professor, 1980–88 and Dean, 1980–87, Hubert H. Humphrey Institute of Public Affairs, University of Minnesota, now Professor Emeritus; *b* 19 Jan. 1918; *s* of Stanley Matthews Cleveland and Marian Phelps (*née* Van Buren); *m* 1941, Lois W. Burton; one *s* two *d*. *Educ:* Phillips Acad., Andover, Mass; Princeton Univ.; Oxford Univ. (Rhodes Scholar). Farm Security Admin., Dept of Agric., 1940–42; Bd of Econ. Warfare (subseq. Foreign Econ. Admin.), 1942–44; Exec. Dir Econ. Sect., 1944–45, Actg Vice-Pres., 1945–46, Allied Control Commn, Rome; Mem. US Delegn, UNRRA Council, London, 1945; Dept Chief of Mission, UNRRA Italian Mission, Rome, 1946–47; Dir, UNRRA China Office, Shanghai, 1947–48; Dir, China Program, Econ. Coop. Admin., Washington, 1948–49; Dept Asst Adminstr, 1949–51; Asst Dir for Europe, Mutual Security Agency, 1952–53; Exec. Editor, The Reporter, NYC, 1953–56, Publisher, 1955–56; Dean, Maxwell Sch. of Citizenship and Pub. Affairs, Syracuse Univ., 1956–61; Asst Sec. for Internat. Orgn Affairs, State Dept, 1961–65; US Ambassador to NATO, 1965–69; Pres., Univ. of Hawaii, 1969–74; Dir, Program in Internat. Affairs, Aspen Inst. for Humanistic Studies, 1974–80. Distinguished Vis. Tom Slick Prof. of World Peace, Univ. of Texas at Austin, 1979. Delegate, Democratic National Convention, 1960. Chairman: Weather Modification Adv. Bd, US Dept of Commerce, 1977–78; Nat.

Retiree Volunteer Coalition, 1989–92; Volunteers in Technical Assistance, 1994–96. Holds hon. degrees and foreign orders; US Medal of Freedom, 1946. Woodrow Wilson Award, Princeton Univ., 1968; Prix de Talloires, Groupe de Talloires, 1981. *Publications:* Next Step in Asia (jtly), 1949; (ed jtly) The Art of Overseasmanship, 1957; (jtly) The Overseas Americans, 1960; (ed) The Promise of World Tensions, 1961; (ed jtly) The Ethic of Power, 1962; (ed jtly) Ethics and Bigness, 1962; The Obligations of Power, 1966; NATO: the Transatlantic Bargain, 1970; The Future Executive, 1972; China Diary, 1976; The Third Try at World Order, 1977; (jtly) Humangrowth: an essay on growth, values and the quality of life, 1978; (ed) Energy Futures of Developing Countries, 1980; (ed jtly) Bioresources for Development, 1980; (ed) The Management of Sustainable Growth, 1981; The Knowledge Executive, 1985; The Global Commons, 1990; Birth of a New World, 1993; Leadership and the Information Revolution, 1997. *Address:* 46891 Grissom Street, Sterling, VA 20165, USA. *T:* (703) 4500428, *Fax:* (703) 4500429. *Clubs:* Century (NY); International (Washington).

CLEVERDON, Julia Charity, (Mrs John Garnett), CBE 1996; Chief Executive, Business in the Community, since 1992; *b* 19 April 1950; *d* of late Thomas Douglas James Cleverdon, BBC producer and of Elinor Nest Lewis; *m* 1st, 1973, Martin Christopher Ollard (marr. diss. 1978); 2nd, 1985, (William) John (Poulton Maxwell) Garnett, CBE (*d* 1997); two *d*. *Educ:* Newnham Coll., Cambridge (BA Hons History). Communication Adviser, British Leyland and Anglo-American Mining Corp., S Africa, 1972–75; Industrial Society: Head, Eastern and Public Services Dept, 1975–77; Head, Common Purpose Campaign, 1977–79; Dir, Communication and Publicity Div., 1979–81; founded Pepperell Dept for Inner Cities and Educn work, 1981–88; Man. Dir, Develt, BITC, 1988–92. *Publication:* Why Industry Matters, 1978. *Recreations:* children, gardening, collecting pink lustre. *Address:* (office) 137 Shepherdess Walk, N1 7RQ. *T:* (0870) 600 2482; 8 Alwyne Road, Islington, N1 2HH.

CLEWS, Michael Arthur; Master of the Supreme Court Taxing Office, 1970–87; *b* Caudebec, France, 16 Sept. 1919; *s* of late Roland Trevor Clews and late Marjorie (*née* Baily); *m* 1947, Kathleen Edith Hollingworth; one *s* two *d*. *Educ:* Epworth Coll., Rhyl; Clare Coll., Cambridge (MA). Served in Indian Army (Major, RA and V Force), 1940–46. Solicitor, 1953; Partner, W. H. House & Son, and Knocker & Foskett, Sevenoaks, 1957–70. Mem., Lord Chancellor's Adv. Cttee on Legal Aid, 1977–84. *Address:* Hameau de Coriolan 9, 83120 Plan de la Tour, Var, France.

CLIBBORN, John Donovan Nelson dalla Rosa, CMG 1997; HM Diplomatic Service; Foreign and Commonwealth Office, since 1995; *b* 24 Nov. 1941; *s* of Donovan Harold Clibborn, CMG, and Margaret Mercedes Edwige (*née* Nelson); *m* 1968, Juliet Elizabeth Pagden; one *s* two *d*. *Educ:* Downside Sch., Stratton-on-the-Fosse, Bath; Oriel Coll., Oxford (1st Cl. Hon. Mods and Lit.Hum. BA, MA). Joined HM Diplomatic Service, 1965; FCO, 1965–67; 3rd, subseq. 2nd Sec., Nicosia, 1967–69; FCO, 1970–72; 1st Secretary: Bonn, 1972–75; UK Mission to EC, Brussels, 1975–78; Jt Res. Centre, EEC, 1978–81; FCO, 1981–88; Counsellor, Washington, 1988–91; FCO, 1991–93; Counsellor, Washington, 1994–95. Member: Soc. for the Promotion of Roman Studies, 1963–; Soc. for the Promotion of Hellenic Studies, 1964–; Palestine Exploration Fund, 1965–. *Recreations:* classical literature, ancient history. *Address:* c/o Foreign and Commonwealth Office, SW1A 2AH. *Club:* Athenæum.

CLIBURN, Van, (Harvey Lavan Cliburn Jr); pianist; *b* Shreveport, La, 12 July 1934; *o c* of Harvey Lavan Cliburn and late Rildia Bee (*née* O'Bryan). *Educ:* Kilgore High Sch., Texas; Juilliard Sch. of Music, New York. Made début in Houston, Texas, 1947; subsequently has toured extensively in N and S America, Europe and Asia. Awards include first International Tchaikovsky Piano Competition, Moscow, 1958, and every US prize, for pianistic ability. *Recreation:* swimming. *Address:* c/o McClain Asset Management, PO Box 470217, Fort Worth, TX 76147, USA.

CLIFF, Prof. Andrew David, FBA 1996; FSS; Professor of Theoretical Geography, University of Cambridge, since 1997; Fellow, Christ's College, Cambridge, since 1974; *b* 26 Oct. 1943; *s* of Alfred Cliff and Annabel Cliff (*née* McQuade); *m* 1964, Margaret Blyton; three *s*. *Educ:* King's Coll. London (BA 1964); Northwestern Univ. (MA 1966); Univ. of Bristol (PhD 1969; DSc 1982); MA Cantab 1973. FSS 1968. Teaching Asst in Geog., Northwestern Univ., 1964–66; Res. Associate in Geog., 1968–69, Lectr, 1969–72, Bristol Univ.; Lectr in Geog., 1973–91, Reader in Theoretical Geog., 1991–97, Univ. of Cambridge. *Publications:* jointly: Spatial Autocorrelation, 1973; Elements of Spatial Structure: a quantitative approach, 1975; Locational Analysis in Human Geography, 2nd edn 1977; Locational Models, 1977; Locational Methods, 1977; Spatial Processes: models and applications, 1981; Spatial Diffusion: an historical geography of epidemics in an island community, 1981; Spatial Components in the Transmission of Epidemic Waves through Island Communities: the spread of measles in Fiji and the Pacific, 1985; Spatial Aspects of Influenza Epidemics, 1986; Atlas of Disease Distributions: analytical approaches to epidemiological data, 1988; London International Atlas of AIDS, 1992; Measles: an historical geography of a major human viral disease from global expansion to local retreat 1840–1990, 1993; Deciphering Global Epidemics: analytical approaches to the disease records of world cities 1888–1912, 1998; Island Epidemics, 2000. *Recreations:* watching Grimsby Town FC, old roses, theatre. *Address:* Department of Geography, University of Cambridge, Downing Place, Cambridge CB2 3EN. *T:* (01223) 333381.

CLIFF, Ian Cameron, OBE 1991; HM Diplomatic Service; Ambassador to Bosnia and Herzegovina, since 2001; *b* 11 Sept. 1952; *s* of late Gerald Shaw Cliff and Dorothy Cliff; *m* 1988, Caroline Mary Redman; one *s* one *d*. *Educ:* Hampton Grammar Sch.; Magdalen Coll., Oxford (MA Modern Hist.). Asst Master (Hist.), Dr Challoner's GS, Amersham, 1975–79; joined HM Diplomatic Service, 1979: SE Asia Dept, 1979–80; Arabic lang. trng, St Andrews Univ. and Damascus, 1980–82; First Sec., Khartoum, 1982–85; Head, Arabian Peninsula Section, ME Dept, FCO, 1985–87; Perm. Under Sec.'s Dept, FCO, 1987–89; First Sec., UK Mission to UN, NY, 1989–93; Counsellor, on loan to DTI as Dir, Exports to ME, Near East and N Africa, 1993–96; Deputy Hd of Mission, Consul-Gen. and Dir of Trade Promotion, Vienna, 1996–2001. *Publications:* occasional articles in railway magazines. *Recreations:* railways, philately, music. *Address:* c/o Foreign and Commonwealth Office, King Charles Street, SW1A 2AH.

CLIFFORD, family name of **Baron Clifford of Chudleigh**.

CLIFFORD OF CHUDLEIGH, 14th Baron *cr* 1672; **Thomas Hugh Clifford;** Count of The Holy Roman Empire; *b* 17 March 1948; *s* of 13th Baron Clifford of Chudleigh, OBE and Hon. Katharine Vavasseur Fisher, 2nd *d* of 2nd Baron Fisher; *S* father, 1988; *m* 1st, 1980, (Muriel) Suzanne (marr. diss. 1993), *d* of Major Campbell Austin and Mrs Campbell Austin; two *s* one *d*; 2nd, 1994, Clarissa, *er d* of His Honour A. C. Goodall, MC. *Educ:* Downside Abbey. Commnd Coldstream Guards, 1967; stationed British Honduras, 1967–68; Instructor, Guards Depot, 1968–69; Northern Ireland, 1969, 1971, 1972; ADC to Chief of Defence Staff, 1972–73; served with ACE Mobile Force, 1973; Adjutant, Guards Depot, 1973–75. Royal Agricultural College, Cirencester, 1976–78. *Recreations:* shooting, fishing, tennis, croquet. *Heir:* *s* Hon. Alexander Thomas Hugh Clifford, *b* 24 Sept. 1985. *Address:* Ugbrooke Park, Chudleigh, South Devon TQ13 0AD. *T:* (office) (01626) 852179.

CLIFFORD, Most Rev. Dermot; *see* Cashel and Emly, Archbishop of, (RC).

CLIFFORD, Nigel Richard; Chief Executive, Tertio Ltd, since 2000; *b* 22 June 1959; *s* of Dr John Clifford and Barbara Dorothy Clifford; *m* 1989, Jeanette Floyd; two *s* one *d*. *Educ:* Portsmouth Grammar Sch.; Downing Coll., Cambridge (MA 1983); Strathclyde Univ. (MBA 1994); DipCAM 1986; Dip. Inst. Mkting 1984. British Telecom, 1981–92: Head, Internat. Operator Services, 1987–90; Sen. Strategy Advr, Chm's Office, 1990; Head, Business Strategy and Develt, Mobile Communications, 1990–92; Chief Exec., Glasgow Royal Infirmary Univ. NHS Trust, 1992–98; Sen. Vice Pres., Service Delivery, Cable & Wireless Communications, 1998–2000. Founding Dir, Herald Foundn for Women's Health, 1994. FIMgt 1995; FRSA 1996. *Recreations:* family life, walking, running. *Address:* Tertio Ltd, Riverside Buildings, 108 Walcot Street, Bath BA1 5BG. *T:* (01225) 478090. *Club:* Morpeth Comrades Social (Morpeth).

CLIFFORD, Rev. Paul Rowntree, MA; President, Selly Oak Colleges, Birmingham, 1965–79; *b* 21 Feb. 1913; *s* of Robert and Harriet Rowntree Clifford; *m* 1st, 1947, Marjory Jean Tait (*d* 1988); one *s* one *d*; 2nd, 1989, Dorothy Marion White, OBE. *Educ:* Mill Hill Sch.; Balliol Coll., Oxford; Mansfield and Regents Park Colls, Oxford. MA (Oxon) 1939. West Ham Central Mission, London: Asst Minister, 1938–43; Supt Minister, 1943–53; McMaster Univ., Hamilton, Canada: Asst Prof. of Homiletics and Pastoral Theology, 1953–59; Dean of Men and Chm. of Dept of Religion, 1959–64; Prof. of Religion, 1964–65. Hon. Treas., Internat. Assoc. for Mission Studies, 1974–88; Sec., Foundn for Study of Christianity and Society, 1980–90. *Publications:* The Mission of the Local Church, 1953; The Pastoral Calling, 1959; Now is the Time, 1970; Interpreting Human Experience, 1971; The Death of the Dinosaur, 1977; Politics and the Christian Vision, 1984; Government by the People?, 1986; An Ecumenical Pilgrimage, 1994; The Reality of the Kingdom, 1996; Radical Politics, 1996; Expanding Horizons, 1997; articles in Jl of Religion, Metaphysical Review, Dialogue, Canadian Jl of Theology, Scottish Jl of Theology, Foundations, Religious Studies. *Recreations:* reading, writing. *Address:* Honeywood House, Rowhook, Horsham, West Sussex RH12 3QD. *Club:* Reform (Chm., 1987–89; Trustee, 1990–).

CLIFFORD, Sir Roger (Joseph), 7th Bt *cr* 1887; *b* 5 June 1936; *s* of Sir Roger Charles Joseph Gerard Clifford, 6th Bt and Henrietta Millicent Kiver (*d* 1971); *S* father 1982; *m* 1968, Joanna Theresa, *d* of C. J. Ward, Christchurch, NZ; two *d*. *Educ:* Beaumont College, England. *Recreations:* golf, Rugby football. *Heir:* *b* Charles Joseph Clifford [*b* 5 June 1936; *m* 1983, Sally Green]. *Address:* 135 Totara Street, Christchurch 4, New Zealand. *T:* (3) 3485958, *Fax:* (3) 3415958. *Clubs:* Blenheim (Bleinheim, NZ); Christchurch, Christchurch Golf.

CLIFFORD, Susan Merlyn, MBE 1994; Founder Director, 1983, and Joint Co-ordinator, since 1988, Common Ground; *b* 16 April 1944; *d* of Bernard Clifford and Hilda Clifford (*née* Moorley). *Educ:* Brincliffe Grammar Sch., Nottingham; Univ. of Hull (BSc Hons); Edinburgh Coll. of Art (DipTP). Work in planning consultancy, Edinburgh, 1966–68; landscape architecture practice, 1968–69; Lectr in Extra-Mural Studies, Edinburgh Univ., 1968–69; Lectr, then Sen. Lectr in Planning and Natural Resource Mgt, PCL, 1970–74; Lectr, Bartlett Sch. of Architecture and Planning, UCL, 1975–90. Hon. Dir, Friends of the Earth (UK), 1971–82; Founder Trustee, Earth Resources Res., 1972; Hon. Dir, Common Ground, 1983–88 (initiated Apple Day annual fest., 21 Oct.); Hon, Mem., Culture SW (Regl Cultural Consortium) Design Review Cttee, Commn for Architecture and Built Envmt. Has initiated and toured exhibns, including: The Tree of Life, with S Bank Centre, 1989–90; Out of the Wood, with Crafts Council, 1989–90; Leaves by Andy Goldsworthy, Natural Hist. Mus., 1989; from place to PLACE, Barbican Centre, 1996. *Publications:* (ed jtly) Second Nature, 1984; (ed jtly) Pulp!, 1989; Places: the city and the invisible, 1993; with Angela King: Holding Your Ground: an action guide to local conservation, 1985; The Apple Source Book, 1991; Celebrating Local Distinctiveness, 1994; A Manifesto for Fields, 1997; edited with Angela King: Trees Be Company: an anthology of tree poetry, 1989 and 2001; Rivers, Rhymes and Running Brooks, 2000. Local Distinctiveness: place particularity and identity, 1993; from place to PLACE: maps and parish maps, 1996; Field Days: an anthology of poetry about fields, 1998; The River's Voice: an anthology of poetry about rivers, 2000; Rivers, Rhymes and Running Brooks, 2000. *Recreation:* looking at the land. *Address:* c/o Common Ground, PO Box 25309, NW5 1ZA. *T:* (020) 7267 2144.

CLIFFORD, Timothy Peter Plint; Director-General, National Galleries of Scotland, since 2001 (Director, 1984–2000); *b* 26 Jan. 1946; *s* of Derek Plint Clifford and late Anne (*née* Pierson); *m* 1968, Jane Olivia, *yr d* of Sir George Paterson, OBE, QC; one *d*. *Educ:* Sherborne, Dorset; Perugia Univ. (Dip. Italian); Courtauld Inst., Univ. of London (BA Hons, History of Art). Dip. Fine Art, Museums Assoc., 1972; AMA. Asst Keeper, Dept of Paintings, Manchester City Art Galleries, 1968–72, Acting Keeper, 1972; Asst Keeper, Dept of Ceramics, Victoria and Albert Mus., London, 1972–76; Asst Keeper, Dept of Prints and Drawings, British Mus., London, 1976–78; Dir, Manchester City Art Galls, 1978–84. Member: Manchester Diocesan Adv. Cttee for Care of Churches, 1978–84; NACF Cttee (Cheshire and Gtr Manchester Br.), 1978–84; North Western Museum and Art Gall. Service Jt Adv. Panel, 1978–84; Cttee, ICOM (UK), 1980–82; Chm., Internat. Cttee for Museums of Fine Art, ICOM, 1980–83 (Mem., Exec. Cttee, 1983–88); Board Member: Museums and Galleries Commn, 1983–88; British Council, 1987–92 (Fine Arts Adv. Cttee, 1988–92); Founder and Committee Member: Friends of Manchester City Art Galls, 1978–84; Patrons and Associates, Manchester City Art Galls, 1979–; Mem. Exec. Cttee, Scottish Museums Council, 1984–; Mem. Adv. Council, Friends of Courtauld Inst. Cttee Mem., Derby Internat. Porcelain Soc., 1983–86; Vice-Pres., Turner Soc., 1984–86, and 1989–; Pres., NADFAS, 1996–; Mem., Adv. Cttee, Come and See Scotland's Churches, 1989–90. Member Consultative Committee: Sculpture Jl, 1998–; Gazette des Beaux-Arts, 1999–. Vice-Pres., Frigate Unicorn Preservation Soc., 1987–. Trustee: Lake Dist Art Gall. and Mus. Trust, 1989–97; Royal Yacht Britannia, 1998–; Hermitage Develt Trust, 1999–; Stichting Hermitage aan de Amstel, 1999–. Patron, Friends of Sherborne House, 1997–. Member: Accademia Italiana delle Arti Applicate, 1988; Ateneo Veneto, Italy, 1997. FRSA; FRSE 2001; FSAScot 1986. Freeman: Goldsmiths' Co., 1989; City of London, 1989. Hon. LLD St Andrews, 1996; Hon. DLitt Glasgow, 2001. Special Award, BIM, 1991. Commendatore al Ordine della Repubblica Italiana, 1999 (Cavaliere, 1988). *Publications:* (with Derek Clifford) John Crome, 1968; (with Dr Ivan Hall) Heaton Hall, 1972; (with Dr T. Friedmann) The Man at Hyde Park Corner: sculpture by John Cheere, 1974; Vues Pittoresques de Luxembourg … par J. M. W. Turner, (Luxembourg) 1977; Ceramics of Derbyshire 1750–1975 (ed, H. G. Bradley), 1978; J. M. W. Turner, Acquerelli e incisioni, (Rome) 1980; Turner at Manchester, 1982; (with Ian Gow) The National Gallery of Scotland: an architectural and decorative history, 1988; (jtly) Raphael: the pursuit of perfection, 1994; (with Ian Gow) Duff House, 1995; (with A. Weston-Lewis) Effigies and Ecstasies: Roman Baroque sculpture and design in the age of Bernini, 1998; Designs of Desire: architectural and ornament prints and drawings 1500–1850,

2000; contrib. Burlington Magazine, Apollo, etc. *Recreations:* bird watching, entomology. *Address:* National Galleries of Scotland, The Mound, Edinburgh EH2 2EL. *Clubs:* Turf, Beefsteak; New (Edinburgh).

CLIFT, Richard Dennis, CMG 1984; HM Diplomatic Service, retired; *b* 18 May 1933; *s* of late Dennis Victor Clift and Helen Wilmot Clift (*née* Evans); *m* 1st, 1957, Barbara Mary Travis (marr. diss. 1982); three *d*; 2nd, 1982, Jane Rosamund Barker (*née* Homfray). *Educ:* St Edward's Sch., Oxford; Pembroke Coll., Cambridge. BA 1956. FO, 1956–57; Office of British Chargé d'Affaires, Peking, 1958–60; British Embassy, Berne, 1961–62; UK Delegn to NATO, Paris, 1962–64; FO, 1964–68; Head of Chancery, British High Commn, Kuala Lumpur, 1969–71; FCO, 1971–73; Counsellor (Commercial), Peking, 1974–76; Canadian Nat. Defence Coll., 1976–77; seconded to NI Office, 1977–79; Hd of Hong Kong Dept, FCO, 1979–84; High Comr in Freetown, 1984–86; Political Advr, Hong Kong Govt, 1987–89. Student, London Coll. of Furniture, 1989–91. *Recreations:* sailing, walking. *Address:* 18 Langwood Chase, Teddington, Middx TW11 9PH.

CLIFT, Prof. Roland, OBE 1994; FREng; Professor of Environmental Strategy and Director, Centre for Environmental Strategy, University of Surrey, since 1992; *b* 19 Nov. 1942; *s* of Leslie William Clift and Ivy Florence Gertrude Clift (*née* Wheeler); *m* 1st, 1968, Rosena Valory (*née* Davison); one *d*; 2nd, 1979, Diana Helen (*née* Manning); one *s* (and one *s* decd). *Educ:* Trinity Coll., Cambridge (BA 1963; MA 1967); PhD McGill 1970. CEng, FIChemE; FREng (FEng 1986). Technical Officer (Chem. Engr), ICI, 1964–67; Lectr, Asst Prof. and Associate Prof., McGill Univ., 1967–75; Lectr, Imperial Coll., London, 1975–76; Lectr, Univ. of Cambridge, 1976–81; Fellow, Trinity Coll., Cambridge, 1976–81 (Praelector, 1980–81); Prof. of Chem. Engrg, Univ. of Surrey, 1981–92. Visiting Professor: Univ. di Napoli, 1973–74; Chalmers Univ., 1989–. Director: ClifMar Associates, 1986–; Particle Consultants Ltd, 1988–. Chairman: Clean Technology Management Cttee, SERC, 1990–94; Engrg Bd, AFRC, 1992–94; Member: UK Ecolabelling Bd, 1992–; Royal Commn on Envmtl Pollution, 1996–. Mem., Governing Body, Charterhouse Sch., 1982–91. Hon. Citizen of Augusta, Georgia, 1987. Editor in Chief, Powder Technology, 1987–95. *Publications:* (jtly) Bubbles, Drops and Particles, 1978; (ed jtly) Fluidization, 1985; (jtly) Slurry Transport using Centrifugal Pumps, 1992, 2nd edn 1997; (jtly) Processing of Particulate Solids, 1997. *Recreation:* arguing and thinking. *Address:* Centre for Environmental Strategy, University of Surrey, Guildford, Surrey GU2 5XH. *T:* (01483) 259271, *Fax:* (01483) 259394. *Club:* Athenæum.

CLIFTON, Lord; Ivo Donald Stuart Bligh; *b* 17 April 1968; *s* and *heir* of 11th Earl of Darnley, *qv*; *m* 1997, Peta, *d* of A. R. Beard; one *s*. *Educ:* Marlborough Coll.; Edinburgh Univ. *Heir:* *s* Hon. Harry Robert Stuart Bligh, *b* 23 April 1999. *Address:* Netherwood Manor, Worcestershire.

CLIFTON, Bishop of, (RC), since 2001; **Rt Rev. Declan Lang;** *b* 15 April 1950; *s* of Francis and Mai Lang. *Educ:* Ryde Sch., IoW; Allen Hall, St Edmund's Coll., Ware; Royal Holloway Coll., Univ. of London (BA Hons). Ordained priest, 1975; Asst Priest, St John's Cathedral, Portsmouth, 1975–79; Sec. to Bishop of Portsmouth, 1979–82; Diocesan Advr for Adult Religious Educn, 1982–90; Parish Priest: Our Lady of the Apostles, Bishop's Waltham, Hants, 1982–86; Sacred Heart, Bournemouth, 1986–90; Administrator, St John's Cathedral, Portsmouth, 1990–96; VG, Dio. Portsmouth and Parish Priest, St Edmund, Abingdon, 1996–2001. *Publication:* (jtly) Parish Project: a resource book for parishes to review mission, 1992. *Recreations:* walking, travel, cinema, theatre. *Address:* St Ambrose, North Road, Leigh Woods, Bristol BS8 3PW. *T:* (0117) 973 3072.

CLIFTON, Gerald Michael; His Honour Judge Clifton; a Circuit Judge, since 1992; *b* 3 July 1947; *s* of Frederick Maurice Clifton and Jane Clifton; *m* 1973, Rosemary Anne Vera Jackson; two *s*. *Educ:* Liverpool Coll.; Brasenose Coll., Oxford (Open Classical Schol., MA). Called to the Bar, Middle Temple, 1970; joined Northern Circuit, 1970; Asst Recorder, 1982; Recorder, 1988; Mem., Manx Bar, 1992. Pres., NW Area, Mental Health Review Tribunal, 1997–. Life Gov., Liverpool Coll., 1992. *Recreations:* walking, philately, sailing, tennis. *Address:* c/o Circuit Administrator, Northern Circuit, 15 Quay Street, Manchester M60 9FD. *Club:* Bar Yacht.

CLIFTON-BROWN, Geoffrey Robert; MP (C) Cotswold, since 1997 (Cirencester and Tewkesbury, 1992–97); chartered surveyor and farmer; *b* 23 March 1953; *s* of Robert and Elizabeth Clifton-Brown; *m* 1979, Alexandra Peto-Shepherd; one *s* one *d*. *Educ:* Tormore Sch., Kent; Eton Coll.; RAC, Cirencester. ARICS. Chm., N Norfolk Cons. Assoc., 1986–91 (Mem., Eastern Area Exec., 1986–91); Vice Chm., Norfolk Eur. Constituency Council, 1990–91. PPS to Minister of Agric., Fisheries and Food, 1995–97; an Opposition Whip, 1999–2001. Mem., Envmt Select Cttee, 1992–95; Vice Chm., Cons. Backbench Cttee on Eur. Affairs, 1997–99 (Sec., 1992–95); Chm., All Party Gp on Population, Develt and Reproductive Health, 1995–97; Vice Chm., Euro Atlantic Gp, 1996–; Member: Public Accounts Commn, 1997–99; Public Accounts Cttee, 1997–99. Vice Chairman: Charities Property Assoc., 1993–; Small Business Bureau, 1995–. Freeman, City of London, 1981; Liveryman, Farmers' Co., 1984. *Recreations:* fishing, all country pursuits. *Address:* House of Commons, SW1A 0AA. *T:* (020) 7219 3000. *Clubs:* Carlton, Farmers'.

CLINCH, David John, OBE 1997; Consultant, University for Industry, since 2000; Secretary, Open University, 1981–98; *b* 14 Feb. 1937; *s* of Thomas Charles Clinch and Madge Isabel Clinch (*née* Saker); *m* 1963, Hilary Jacques; one *s* one *d*. *Educ:* Nautical Coll., Pangbourne; St Cuthbert's Soc., Univ. of Durham (BA); Indiana Univ. (MBA). National Service, Royal Navy (Sub-Lieut), Supply and Secretariat, 1955–57. Administrator, Univ. of Sussex, 1963–69; Deputy Secretary and Registrar, Open University, 1969–81; Registrar Counterpart, Allama Iqbal Open Univ., Pakistan, 1976–77. Member: Conf. of Univ. Administrators, 1973–99; Conf. of Registrars and Secs, 1981–98 (Chm., 1990–91); Council of Foundn, Internat. Baccalaureate Orgn, 1999– (Treas., 2000–); British Fulbright Scholars Assoc., 1978–. Dir, Nat. Educnl Resources Information Service Trust, 1989–93; Trustee, Open Univ. Superannuation Scheme, 1989–97; Hon. Vice Pres., Open Univ. Students Assoc., 2000–. Dir, Milton Keynes City Orch., 2001–. FRSA 1997. DUniv Open, 2000. *Recreations:* music, natural history, reading, walking. *Address:* 39 Tudor Gardens, Stony Stratford, Milton Keynes MK11 1HX. *T:* (01908) 562475.

CLINES, Prof. David John Alfred; Professor of Biblical Studies, University of Sheffield, since 1985; Director, Sheffield Academic Press, since 1987 (Chairman, 1987–92); *b* 21 Nov. 1938; *s* of Alfred William and Ruby Coral Clines; *m* 1st, 1963, Dawn Naomi Joseph; one *s* one *d*; 2nd, 1989, Heather Ann McKay. *Educ:* Univ. of Sydney (BA Hons 1960); St John's Coll., Cambridge (BA 1963; MA 1967). University of Sheffield: Asst Lectr in Biblical History and Literature, 1964–67; Lectr, 1967–73, Sen. Lectr, 1973–79, Reader, 1979–85, in Biblical Studies. Co-Founder and Partner, JSOT Press, 1976–87. Pres., SOTS, 1996. *Publications:* I, He, We and They: a literary approach to Isaiah 53, 1976; The Theme of the Pentateuch, 1978, 2nd edn 1997; Ezra, Nehemiah, Esther, 1984; The Esther Scroll; the story of the story, 1984; Job 1–20, 1990; What Does Eve Do to Help? and Other Readerly Questions to the Old Testament, 1990; Interested Parties: the ideology of writers and readers of the Hebrew Bible, 1995; The Bible and the Modern World, 1997; The Sheffield Manual for Authors and Editors in Biblical Studies, 1997; On the Way to the Postmodern: Old Testament essays 1967–1998, 1998; *edited:* The Dictionary of Classical Hebrew: vol. 1, 1993, vol. 2, 1995, vol. 3, 1996, vol. 4, 1998; The Poetical Books: a Sheffield reader, 1997; *edited jointly:* Art and Meaning: rhetoric in biblical literature, 1982; Midian, Moab and Edom: the history and archaeology of late Bronze and Iron Age Jordan and North-West Arabia, 1983; The Bible in Three Dimensions (essays), 1990; Telling Queen Michal's Story: an experiment in comparative interpretation, 1991; Among the Prophets: imagery, language and structure in the prophetic writings, 1993; Of Prophets' Visions and the Wisdom of Sages (essays), 1993; The New Literary Criticism and the Hebrew Bible, 1993; The Bible in Human Society (essays), 1995; The World of Genesis: persons, places, perspectives, 1998; Auguries: the Jubilee volume of the Department of Biblical Studies, 1998; articles in learned jls. *Recreations:* congresses, spreadsheets. *Address:* Department of Biblical Studies, University of Sheffield, Sheffield S10 2TN. *T:* (0114) 222 0505; *e-mail:* d.clines@shef.ac.uk.

CLINTON; *see* Fiennes-Clinton, family name of Earl of Lincoln.

CLINTON, 22nd Baron *cr* 1299 (title abeyant 1957–65); **Gerard Nevile Mark Fane Trefusis;** DL; landowner; *b* 7 Oct. 1934; *s* of Capt. Charles Fane (killed in action, 1940); assumed by deed poll, 1958, surname of Trefusis in addition to patronymic; *m* 1959, Nicola Harriette Purdon Coote; one *s* two *d*. *Educ:* Gordonstoun. Took seat in House of Lords, 1965. Mem., Prince of Wales's Councils, 1968–79. JP Bideford, 1963–83; DL Devon, 1977. *Recreations:* shooting, fishing, forestry. *Heir:* *s* Hon. Charles Patrick Rolle Fane Trefusis [*b* 21 March 1962; *m* 1992, Rosanna, *yr d* of John Izat; three *s*]. *Address:* Heanton Satchville, near Okehampton, North Devon EX20 3QE. *T:* (01805) 804224. *Club:* Boodle's.

CLINTON, Alan; *see* Clinton, R. A.

CLINTON, Bill; *see* Clinton, W. J.

CLINTON, (Robert) Alan; Director, 1986–95, Managing Director, 1987–95, Picton House Group of Companies, property development cos; *b* 12 July 1931; *s* of John and Leah Clinton; *m* 1956, Valerie Joy Falconer. *Educ:* George Dixon Grammar Sch., Edgbaston, Birmingham; Manchester Business Sch. On leaving school, joined the Post Office, 1948; Member, North Western Postal Board, 1970; Asst Director (Personnel), London, 1975; Asst Director (Operations), London, 1976; Director of Eastern Postal Region, Colchester, 1978; Director of Postal Operations, London, 1979; Member Post Office Board, 1981–85: for Mails Network and Develt, 1981; for Mails Ops and Estates, 1982; for Corporate Services, 1984–85; Man. Dir, Counter Services, 1984–85. Mem. Mgt Cttee, Royal Assoc. in Aid of Deaf People, 1994–97. Pres., Clacton and NE Essex Arts and Literary Soc., 1992–97. Mem. Cttee, St Osyth Historical Soc., 1995–. Chm., St Osyth Almshouse Charity, 1995–; Consultant, Hampton Discretionary Trust, 1997–. FCIT 1982. Mem., Worshipful Company of Carmen, 1981; Freeman of City of London, 1979. *Recreations:* music, walking, sailing, cooking. *Address:* Summer Cottage, The Quay, St Osyth, Clacton-on-Sea, Essex CO16 8EZ. *T:* (01255) 820368; *e-mail:* summer.quay@amserve.net. *Club:* City of London.

CLINTON, William Jefferson, (Bill), JD; President of the United States of America, 1993–2001; *b* 19 Aug. 1946; *s* of late Virginia Kelly; *m* 1975, Hillary Rodham; one *d*. *Educ:* Georgetown Univ. (BS 1968); University Coll., Oxford (Rhodes Schol.; Hon. Fellow, 1993; DCL by Diploma, 1994); Yale Univ. Law Sch. (JD 1973). Prof., Univ. of Arkansas Law Sch., 1974–76; Attorney Gen., Arkansas, 1977–79; with Wright, Lindsey & Jennings, law firm, 1981–83; Governor of Arkansas, 1979–81 and 1983–92. Chairman: Educn Commn of the States, 1986–87; Nat. Governors' Assoc., 1986–87 (Co-Chm., Task Force on Educn, 1990–91); Democratic Governors' Assoc., 1989–90 (Vice Chm., 1987–88); Democratic Leadership Council, 1990–91. Democrat. Hon. DCL Oxford, 1994. *Publication:* Between Hope and History, 1996.

CLINTON-DAVIS, family name of **Baron Clinton-Davis**.

CLINTON-DAVIS, Baron *cr* 1990 (Life Peer), of Hackney in the London Borough of Hackney; **Stanley Clinton Clinton-Davis;** PC 1998; *b* 6 Dec. 1928; *s* of Sidney Davis; name changed to Clinton-Davis by deed poll, 1990; *m* 1954, Frances Jane Lucas; one *s* three *d*. *Educ:* Hackney Downs Sch.; Mercers' Sch.; King's Coll., London University (LLB 1950; FKC 1996). Admitted Solicitor, 1953; in practice, 1953–70; consultant, S. J. Berwin & Co., 1989–97. Mem. Exec. Council, Nat. Assoc. of Labour Student Organisations, 1949–50. Councillor, London Borough of Hackney, 1959; Mayor of Hackney, 1968. Contested (Lab): Langstone Div. of Portsmouth, 1955; Yarmouth, 1959 and 1964. MP (Lab) Hackney Central, 1970–83; Parly Under-Sec. of State, Dept of Trade, 1974–79; Opposition spokesman on trade, prices and consumer protection, 1979–81, on foreign affairs, 1981–83; Opposition frontbench spokesman on transport, H of L, 1990–97; Minister of State, DTI, 1997–98. Vice Chm., Parly Envmt Gp. Mem., Commn of EC, 1985–89. Chm., Adv. Cttee on Protection of the Sea, 1984–85, 1989–97; Pres., Refugee Council, 1989–97. Pres., AMA, 1992–97. Vice Pres., Lab. Finance and Industry Gp, 1993–. Member: RIIA; Council and Exec. Cttee, Justice; UN Selection Cttee for Sasakawa, Envmt Project; Adv. Bd, Centre of European Law, KCL; formerly Mem., Bd of Deputies of British Jews; Parly Relations Sub-Cttee of the Law Soc.; Hon. Mem., London Criminal Courts Solicitors' Assoc. Mem. Council, British Maritime League, 1989–97. Jt Pres., Soc. of Labour Lawyers, 1991–; President: UK Pilots Assoc. (Marine), 1991–; BALPA, 1994–; Inst. of Travel Management; Aviation Envmt Fedn; Vice-Pres., Chartered Instn of Envmtl Health Officers, 1991–. Pres., Hackney Br., Multiple Sclerosis Soc.; Vice-Pres., Hackney Assoc. for Disabled; Hon. Mem. Rotary Club, Hackney. Hon. Mem., 1979, and former Trustee, NUMAST (formerly Merchant Navy and Airline Officers' Assoc.); Hon. Fellow, QMW, 1993; Hon. FCIWEM; FRSA 1992 (Mem. Acad. Bd for Internat. Trade). Hon. Dr *hc* Polytechnical Inst., Bucharest, 1993. First Medal for Outstanding Services to Animal Welfare in Europe, Eurogroup for Animal Welfare, 1988. Grand Cross, Order of Leopold II, Belgium (for services to EC), 1990. *Recreations:* golf, Association football, reading biographical histories. *Address:* House of Lords, SW1A 0PW.

CLITHEROE, 2nd Baron *cr* 1955, of Downham; **Ralph John Assheton;** Bt 1945; Chairman, Yorkshire Bank, 1990–99; Vice Lord-Lieutenant of Lancashire, 1995–99; *b* 3 Nov. 1929; *s* of 1st Baron Clitheroe, KCVO, PC, FSA, and Sylvia Benita Frances, Lady Clitheroe, FRICS, FLAS, (*d* 1991), *d* of 6th Baron Hotham; *S* father, 1984; *m* 1961, Juliet, *d* of Lt-Col Christopher Lionel Hanbury, MBE, TD; two *s* one *d*. *Educ:* Eton; Christ Church, Oxford (Scholar, MA). FCIB 1991. Served as 2nd Lieut Life Guards, 1948–49. Chairman: RTZ Chemicals Ltd, 1973–87; RTZ Borax Ltd, 1979–89; US Borax and Chemical Corp., 1979–89; RTZ Oil & Gas Ltd, 1983–88; Director: Borax Consolidated, 1960–89; RTZ Corp., 1968–89; First Interstate Bank of California, 1981–89; TR Natural Resources Investment Trust, 1982–87; American Mining Congress, 1982–89; Halliburton Co., Texas, 1987–. Mem., Council, Chemical Industries Assoc., 1984–88. FRSA 1991. Liveryman, Skinners' Co. DL Lancs, 1986. *Heir:* *s* Hon. Ralph Christopher Assheton [*b* 19 March 1962; *m* 1996, Olivia, *o d* of Anthony Warrington]. *Address:* Downham Hall,

Clitheroe, Lancs BB7 4DN. *Clubs:* Boodle's, Pratt's, Royal Automobile.
See also Hon. N. Assheton.

CLIVE, Viscount; Jonathan Nicholas William Herbert; *b* 5 Dec. 1979; *s* and *heir* of Earl of Powis, *qv.*

CLIVE, Eric McCredie, CBE 1999; FRSE; Visiting Professor, University of Edinburgh, since 1999; *b* 24 July 1938; *s* of Robert M. Clive and Mary L. D. Clive; *m* 1962, Kay M. McLeman; one *s* two *d* (and one *d* decd). *Educ:* Univs of Edinburgh (MA, LLB with dist.); Michigan (LLM); Virginia (SJD). Solicitor. Lecturer 1962–69, Sen. Lectr 1969–75, Reader 1975–77, Professor of Scots Law 1977–81, Univ. of Edinburgh; a Scottish Law Comr, 1981–99. FRSE 1999. *Publications:* Law of Husband and Wife in Scotland, 1974, 4th edn 1997; articles and notes in legal jls. *Address:* 14 York Road, Edinburgh EH5 3EH. *T:* (0131) 552 2875.

CLOAKE, John Cecil, CMG 1977; FSA; HM Diplomatic Service, retired; *b* 2 Dec. 1924; *s* of late Dr Cecil Stedman Cloake, Wimbledon, and Maude Osborne Newling; *m* 1956, Margaret Thomure Morris, Washington, DC, USA; one *s*. *Educ:* King's Coll. Sch., Wimbledon; Peterhouse, Cambridge. Served in Army, 1943–46 (Lieut RE). Foreign Office, 1948; 3rd Sec., Baghdad, 1949, and Saigon, 1951; 2nd Sec., 1952; FO, 1954; Private Sec. to Permanent Under-Sec., 1956, and to Parly Under-Sec., 1957; 1st Sec., 1957; Consul (Commercial), New York, 1958; 1st Sec., Moscow, 1962; FO, 1963; DSAO, 1965; Counsellor, 1966; Head of Accommodation Dept, 1967; Counsellor (Commercial), Tehran, 1968–72; Fellow, Centre for International Studies, LSE, 1972–73; Head of Trade Relations and Exports Dept, FCO, 1973–76; Ambassador to Bulgaria, 1976–80. Member: Council, British Inst. of Persian Studies, 1981–95 (Hon. Treas. 1982–90); Cttee of Honour for Bulgarian 1300th Anniv., 1981. Chairman: Richmond Soc. History Section, 1975–76, 1984–85; Richmond Local Hist. Soc., 1985–90 (Pres., 1990–); Richmond Museum Project, 1983–86; Mus. of Richmond, 1986–95; Pres., Richmond upon Thames Soc. of Voluntary Guides, 1997–. FSA 1998. *Publications:* Templer: Tiger of Malaya, 1985; Richmond Past, 1991; Royal Bounty, 1992; Palaces and Parks of Richmond and Kew, Vol. 1, 1995, Vol. 2, 1996; Richmond Past and Present, 1999; Cottages and Common Fields at Richmond and Kew, 2001; articles on local history. *Recreations:* gardening, painting, architecture, local history, genealogy. *Address:* 4 The Terrace, Richmond Hill, Richmond, Surrey TW10 6RN.

CLOGHER, Bishop of, (RC), since 1979; **Most Rev. Joseph Duffy,** DD; *b* 3 Feb. 1934; *s* of Edward Duffy and Brigid MacEntee. *Educ:* St Macartan's College, Monaghan; Maynooth College. MA, BD, HDipEd. Ordained priest, 1958; Teacher, 1960–72; Curate, 1972–79. *Publications:* Patrick in his own words, 1972; Lough Derg Guide, 1980; Monaghan Cathedral, 1992. *Recreations:* local history, travel. *Address:* Tigh an Easpaig, Monaghan, Ireland. *T:* (47) 81019, *Fax:* (47) 84773.

CLOKIE, Hilary Ann; *see* Nicolle, H. A.

CLOSE, Anthony Stephen, CBE 1997; Chairman, Health Education Authority, 1994–99; *b* 9 Aug. 1931; *s* of Steven John Henry Close and Marion Lily Close (*née* Matthews); *m* 1961, Josephine Oakey; one *d*. *Educ:* Colston's Sch.; Queen's Coll., Oxford (MA); Birkbeck Coll., London (MSc). AFBPsS. Shell International Petroleum Co.; BOAC; Beecham Group; Grand Metropolitan, 1973–83; Group Dir of Personnel, Trusthouse Forte, 1983–93. Director: BIOSS Internat., 1993–; EAR Ltd, 1997–. Mem., FEFC, 1992–95. MInstD (Mem. Council, 1985–). *Recreations:* walking, opera, choral singing, cooking. *Address:* Danes, Cox Green Lane, Maidenhead SL6 3EY. *T:* (01628) 622910. *Club:* Savile.

CLOSE, Prof. Francis Edwin, OBE 2000; FInstP; Professor of Theoretical Physics, University of Oxford, since 2001; Fellow, Exeter College, Oxford; *b* 24 July 1945; *s* of Frederick Archibald Close and Frances Moreton Close; *m* 1969, Gillian Matilda Boyce; two *d*. *Educ:* King's Sch., Peterborough; St Andrew's Univ. (BSc 1967); Magdalen Coll., Oxford (DPhil 1970). FInstP 1991. Research Fellow: Stanford Linnear Accelerator, Calif, 1970–72; Daresbury Lab., 1973; CERN, Geneva, 1973–75; Res. Scientist, 1975–2000, and Head of Theoretical Physics Div., 1991–2000, Rutherford Appleton Lab. Dist. Scientist, Oak Ridge Nat. Lab. and Univ. of Tennessee, 1988–90; Vis. Prof., Birmingham Univ., 1996–; Sen. Scientist, CERN, 1997–2000; Gresham Prof. of Astronomy, 2000–. Mem. Council, Royal Instn, 1997– (Christmas Lectr, 1993); Vice-Pres., BAAS, 1993–. Fellow, APS, 1992; Fellow in Public Understanding of Physics, Inst. Physics, 1995–97. Kelvin Medal, Inst. Physics, 1996. *Publications:* Introduction to Quarks and Partons, 1979; The Cosmic Onion, 1983; The Particle Explosion, 1987; End, 1988; Too Hot to Handle, 1991; Lucifer's Legacy, 2000; numerous res. papers on theoretical physics, and articles on science in The Guardian. *Recreations:* writing, singing, travel, squash. *Address:* Department of Theoretical Physics, Keble Road, Oxford OX1 3NP. *Club:* Harwell Squash.

CLOSE, Glenn; actress; *b* 19 March 1947; *d* of William and Bettine Close; *m* 1st, 1969, Cabot Wade (marr. diss.); 2nd, 1984, James Marlas (marr. diss.); one *d* by John Starke. *Educ:* William and Mary Coll. (BA 1974). With New Phoenix Repertory Co., 1974–75; *theatre* includes: New York: Love for Love, 1974; A Streetcar Named Desire; The Crucifer of Blood, 1978–79; Barnum, 1980–81; The Real Thing, 1984 (Tony Award); Benefactors, 1986; Death and the Maiden, 1992 (Tony Award); Sunset Boulevard, LA, 1993–94, NY, 1994–95 (Tony Award); *films* include: The World According to Garp, 1982; The Natural, 1984; Fatal Attraction, 1987; Dangerous Liaisons, 1989; Hamlet, 1991; The House of Spirits, 1994; Serving in Silence: the Margarethe Cammermeyer story, 1995; Air Force One, 1997; Paradise Road, 1997; Cookie's Fortune, 1999; Things You Can Just Tell by Looking at Her, 2000; 102 Dalmatians, 2000; numerous TV appearances. *Address:* c/o CAA, 9830 Wilshire Boulevard, Beverly Hills, CA 90212, USA.

CLOSE, Roy Edwin, CBE 1973; Director General, British Institute of Management, 1976–85; *b* 11 March 1920; *s* of Bruce Edwin and Minnie Louise Close; *m* 1947, Olive Joan Forty; two *s*. *Educ:* Trinity County Sch., N London; MSc Aston 1973. Served Army, 1939–46; RASC, Para Regt and SAS, 1943–46 (Captain). Editorial Staff, The Times; Asst Editor, The Times Review of Industry, 1949–56; Executive, Booker McConnell GP; Dir, Bookers Sugar Estates, 1957–65; Directing Staff, Admin. Staff Coll., Henley, 1965; Industrial Adviser, NEDO, 1966–69; Industrial Dir, NEDO, 1969–73; Chm., Univ. of Aston Management Centre, and Dean of Faculty of Management, 1973–76; Proprietor, Management Adv. Services, 1986–92. Director: Davies and Perfect, 1985–87; Flextech plc, 1985–87; Kepner Tregoe Ltd, 1986–89; Broad Street Group, 1986–91 (Chm., 1986–88); Equity Development Ltd, 1996–2000 (Chm., 1996–99); Equity I Ltd, 2000–. Chairman: Open Univ. Management Educn Sector Bd, 1984–87; Open Business Sch., 1984–87; Mem., Open Univ. Business Sch. Industrial and Professional Adv. Cttee, 1988–93 (Chm., 1988–90). Chm., Conservation Foundn, 1987–98 (Dir, 1986–98). Mem. Council, Farm-Africa, 1987–92. CIMgt (FBIM 1979); FIIM (FIWM 1979); FRSA 1980. DUniv Open, 1987. *Publications:* various articles on industrial, economic subjects. *Recreations:* swimming, walking, reading, listening to music. *Address:* Cathedral Cottage, North Elmham, Dereham, Norfolk NR20 5JU. *Clubs:* Reform, Special Forces.

CLOSE, Seamus Anthony, OBE 1996; Member (Alliance) Lagan Valley, Northern Ireland Assembly, since 1998; *b* 12 Aug. 1947; *s* of James and Kathleen Close; *m* 1978, Deirdre McCann; three *s* one *d*. *Educ:* St Malachy's Coll.; Belfast Coll. of Business Studies. Company Sec., 1970–85; Financial Dir, 1985–. Mem. (Alliance), Lisburn BC, 1973– (Mayor, 1993–94); Mem. (Alliance) NI Assembly, 1982–86; Negotiator: Brooke/Mayhew Talks, 1991–92; Good Friday Agreement, 1998. Dep. Leader, Alliance Party, 1991–. *Recreations:* sports, family, current affairs. *Address:* 123 Moira Road, Lisburn, Northern Ireland BT28 1RJ. *T:* (028) 9267 0639; Parliament Building, Stormont, Northern Ireland BT4 3XX. *T:* (028) 9052 0353.

CLOTHIER, Sir Cecil (Montacute), KCB 1982; QC 1965; Chairman, Council on Tribunals, 1989–92; *b* 28 Aug. 1919; *s* of Hugh Montacute Clothier, Liverpool; *m* 1st, 1943, Mary Elizabeth (*d* 1984), *o d* of late Ernest Glover Bush; one *s* two *d*; 2nd, 1992, Diana Stevenson (*née* Durrant). *Educ:* Stonyhurst Coll.; Lincoln Coll., Oxford (BCL, MA; Hon. Fellow 1984). Served 1939–46, 51 (Highland) Div.; British Army Staff, Washington, DC; Hon. Lt-Col Royal Signals. Called to Bar, Inner Temple, 1950, Bencher, 1973. Recorder of Blackpool, later of the Crown Court, 1965–78; Judge of Appeal, IoM, 1972–78. A Legal Assessor to Gen. Medical and Gen. Dental Councils, 1972–78; Inquiry into Deaths in Devonport Hosp., 1972; Mem., Royal Commn on NHS, 1976–78; Parly Comr for Admin, and Health Service Comr for England, Wales and Scotland, 1979–84; Chm., Police Complaints Authority, 1985–89; Mem., Sen. (formerly Top) Salaries Rev. Body, 1989–95; Vice-Pres., Interception of Communications Tribunal, 1986–96; Chairman: Cttee on Ethics of Gene Therapy, 1990–92; Allitt Inquiry, 1993–94; Review Body on Police Services in Jersey, 1996–97; Review Panel on Machinery of Govt in Jersey, 1999–2001. Mem., Adv. Council, British Library, 1993–98. John Snow Meml Lectr (Assoc. of Anaesthetists of GB and Ireland/Amer. Assoc. of Anaesthesiologists), 1981. Hon. Mem., Assoc. of Anaesthetists of GB and Ireland, 1987; Hon. FRPharmS 1990; Hon. FRCP 1998. Rock Carling Fellow, Nuffield Provincial Hosps Trust, 1987. Hon. LLD Hull, 1982. *Address:* 1 Temple Gardens, Temple, EC4Y 9BB.

CLOTHIER, Richard John; Chief Executive, Plantation & General Investments plc, since 1998; Director, Granada Group PLC, since 1996; *b* 4 July 1945; *s* of J. Neil Clothier and Barbara Clothier; *m* 1st, 1972, Ingrid Hafner (*d* 1994); two *s*; 2nd, 1995, Sarah (*née* Riley). *Educ:* Peterhouse, Zimbabwe; Univ. of Natal (BSc Agric.); Harvard (AMP). Milk Marketing Board, 1971–77; Dalgety Agriculture, 1977–88; Chief Executive: Pig Improvement Co., 1988–92; Dalgety Gp, 1993–97. *Publication:* The Bundu Book, 1969. *Recreations:* yacht racing, field sports. *T:* (020) 7246 0200. *Clubs:* Farmers, Royal Thames Yacht, Royal Ocean Racing.

CLOUDSLEY-THOMPSON, Prof. John Leonard, MA, PhD (Cantab), DSc (London); FRES, FLS, FZS, CBiol, FIBiol, FWAAS; Professor of Zoology, Birkbeck College, University of London, 1972–86, now Emeritus (Reader 1971–72); *b* Murree, India, 23 May 1921; *s* of Dr Ashley George Gyton Thompson, MA, MD (Cantab), DPH, and Muriel Elaine (*née* Griffiths); *m* 1944, Jessie Anne Cloudsley, MCSP, DipBS, LCAD; three *s*. *Educ:* Marlborough Coll.; Pembroke Coll., Univ. of Cambridge. War of 1939–45: commissioned into 4th Queen's Own Hussars, 1941; transf. 4th Co. of Lond. Yeo. (Sharpshooters); N Africa, 1941–42 (severely wounded); Instructor (Capt.), Sandhurst, 1943; rejoined regt for D Day (escaped from Villers Bocage), Caen Offensive, etc, 1944 (Hon. rank of Capt. on resignation). Lectr in Zoology, King's Coll., Univ. of London, 1950–60; Prof. of Zoology, Univ. of Khartoum, and Keeper, Sudan Nat. Hist. Museum, 1960–71. Nat. Science Foundn Sen. Res. Fellow, Univ. of New Mexico, Albuquerque, USA, 1969; Visiting Professor: Univ. of Kuwait, 1978 and 1983; Univ. of Nigeria, Nsukka, 1981; Univ. of Qatar, 1986; Sultan Qaboos Univ., Muscat, 1988; Leverhulme Emeritus Fellow at UCL, 1987–89; Visiting Research Fellow: ANU, 1987; Desert Ecol. Res. Unit of Namibia, 1989. Hon. Consultant: Univ. of Malaya, 1969; Arabian Gulf Univ., Bahrain, 1986; Univ. of Kuwait, 1990; Indo-British Workshop on Biodiversity, 1993. Took part in: Cambridge Iceland Expedn, 1947; Expedn to Southern Tunisia, 1954; univ. expedns with his wife to various parts of Africa, 1960–73, incl. trans-Sahara crossing, 1967. Chairman: British Naturalists' Assoc., 1974–83 (Vice-Pres., 1985–); Biological Council, 1977–82 (Medal, 1985). President: British Arachnological Soc., 1982–85 (Vice-Pres., 1985–86); British Soc. for Chronobiology, 1985–87; Vice-President: Linnean Soc., 1975–76 and 1977–78; 1st World Congress of Herpetology, 1989. Hon. FLS 1997; Hon. Member: Royal African Soc., 1969 (Medal, 1969); British Herpetological Soc., 1983 (Pres., 1991–96); Centre Internat. de Documentation Arachnologique, Paris, 1995. Liveryman, Worshipful Co. of Skinners, 1952. Silver Jubilee Gold Medal and Hon. DSc, Khartoum, 1981. Inst. of Biology K. S. S. Charter Award, 1981; J. H. Grundy Meml Medal, Royal Army Med. Coll., 1987; Foundn for Envmtl Conservation Prize, Geneva, 1989; Peter Scott Meml Award, British Naturalists' Assoc., 1993. Editor-in-Chief (formerly Founding Editor) (assisted by wife), Jl of Arid Environments Vol. 1, 1978–Vol. 37, 1997, now Editor Emeritus; Editor: (with wife) Natural History of the Arabian Gulf (book series), 1981–82; Adaptations of Desert Organisms (book series), 1989–2000 (25 vols). *Publications:* Biology of Deserts (ed), 1954; Spiders, Scorpions, Centipedes and Mites, 1958 (2nd edn 1968); Animal Behaviour, 1960; Rhythmic Activity in Animal Physiology and Behaviour, 1961; Land Invertebrates (with John Sankey), 1961; Life in Deserts (with M. J. Chadwick), 1964; Desert Life, 1965; Animal Conflict and Adaptation, 1965; Animal Twilight: man and game in eastern Africa, 1967; Microecology, 1967; Zoology of Tropical Africa, 1969; The Temperature and Water Relations of Reptiles, 1971; Desert Life, 1974; Terrestrial Environments, 1975; Insects and History, 1976; Evolutionary Trends in the Mating of Arthropoda, 1976; (ed jtly) Environmental Physiology of Animals, 1976; Man and the Biology of Arid Zones, 1977; The Water and Temperature Relations of Woodlice, 1977; The Desert, 1977; Animal Migration, 1978; Why the Dinosaurs Became Extinct, 1978; Wildlife of the Desert, 1979; Biological Clocks: their functions in nature, 1980; Tooth and Claw: defensive strategies in the animal world, 1980; (ed) Sahara Desert, 1984; Guide to Woodlands, 1985; Evolution and Adaptation of Terrestrial Arthropods, 1988; Ecophysiology of Desert Arthropods and Reptiles, 1991; The Diversity of Desert Life, 1993; (novel) The Nile Quest, 1994; Predation and Defence Amongst Reptiles, 1994; Biotic Interactions in Arid Lands, 1996; Teach Yourself Ecology, 1998; The Diversity of Amphibians and Reptiles: an introduction, 1999; contribs to Encyclopædia Britannica, Encyclopedia Americana; shorter monographs and eleven children's books; many scientific articles in learned jls, etc. *Recreations:* music (especially opera), photography, travel. *Address:* 10 Battishill Street, N1 1TE.

CLOUGH, Christopher George, FRCP; Consultant Neurologist, since 1995, and Medical Director, since 1998, King's College Hospital; *b* 30 Aug. 1953; *s* of George and Daisy Clough; *m* 1979, Lyn Sylvia Griffiths; two *s* one *d*. *Educ:* Manchester Univ. (MB ChB). FRCP 1992. Royal Alexandra Hosp., Rhyl, 1975–76; Hull Royal Infirmary, 1976–79; Leeds Gen. Infirmary, 1979–80; Mount Sinai Med. Centre, 1980–81; Queen Elizabeth Med. Centre, Birmingham, and Midlands Centre for Neurology and Neurosurgery, Smethwick, 1981–89; Cons. Neurologist, Brook Regl Neuroscience Centre and Bromley Hosps, 1989–95; Dir, Regl Neuroscis Centre, 1991–98. Member: Fabian Soc.; Labour Party. *Publications:* pubns on Parkinson's Disease, headache and restless legs. *Recreations:* tennis, music, lifelong Spurs fan. *Address:* 17 Blenheim Road, Bickley BR1 2EX.

CLOUGH, (John) Alan, CBE 1972; MC 1945; Chairman, British Mohair Holdings plc (formerly British Mohair Spinners Ltd), 1980–84 (Deputy Chairman, 1970–80, Chief Executive, 1977–80, Joint Managing Director, 1980–83); *b* 20 March 1924; *s* of late John Clough and Yvonne (*née* Dollfus); *m* 1st, 1949, Margaret Joy Catton (marr. diss.); one *s* two *d*; 2nd, 1961, Mary Cowan Catherwood; one *s* one *d*. *Educ:* Marlborough Coll.; Leeds Univ. HM Forces, Queen's Bays, 1942–47, N Africa and Italy (Captain); TA Major, Yorkshire Hussars, 1947–55. Mayor, Co. of Merchants of Staple of England, 1969–70. Chairman: Wool Industries Res. Assoc., 1967–69; Wool Textile Delegn, 1969–72; Textile Res. Council, 1984–89; Member: Wool Textile EDC, 1967–72; Jt Textile Cttee, NEDO, 1972–74; President: Comitextil (Co-ordinating Cttee for Textile Industries in EEC), Brussels, 1975–77; British Textile Confedn, 1974–77; Textile Inst., 1979–81; Confedn of British Wool Textiles, 1982–84. Chm., Instant Muscle Ltd, 1989–94. CompTI 1975. Hon. DSc Bradford, 1987. *Recreations:* fishing, gardening, travel. *Address:* 7 King George Square, Richmond, Surrey TW10 6LF. *Club:* Boodle's.

CLOUGH, Mark Gerard; QC 1999; Partner, Ashurst Morris Crisp, since 1995; *b* 13 May 1953; *s* of Philip Gerard Clough, *qv* and Mary Elizabeth Clough (*née* Carter); one *d*; *m* 1989, Joanne Elizabeth Dishington; two *s*. *Educ:* Ampleforth Coll.; St Andrews Univ. (MA 1976). Called to the Bar, Gray's Inn, 1978; admitted Solicitor, 1995; Solicitor Advocate, 1996. Mem., Editl Bd, Internat. Trade Law and Regulation Jl. *Publications:* EC Competition Law and Shipping, 1990; EC Merger Regulation, 1995; (contrib.) Vaughan's Laws of the European Communities, 1997; articles on EC Law and competition law. *Recreations:* theatre, poetry, tennis, golf. *Address:* Ashurst Morris Crisp, Broadwalk House, 5 Appold Street, EC2A 2HA. *T:* (020) 7638 1111. *Club:* Travellers.

CLOUGH, Philip Gerard; Non permanent Member, Court of Final Appeal, Hong Kong, since 1997; Justice of Appeal: Bermuda, since 1998; Gibraltar, since 1998; *b* 11 March 1924; *s* of Gerard Duncombe Clough and Grace Margaret (*née* Phillips); *m* 1st, Mary Elizabeth Carter (marr. diss.); one *s*; 2nd, Margaret Joy Davies; one *s* one *d*. *Educ:* Dauntsey's Sch.; King's Coll., Cambridge (Exhibnr; MA). War service, Sub Lieut (A) RNVR, 1942–46. Called to the Bar, Inner Temple, 1949; Colonial Legal Service: Federal Counsel, Malaya, 1951–58; Chancery Bar, Lincoln's Inn, 1958–78; Legal Affairs Advr, Brunei, 1978–81; Dist Judge, 1981–83, High Court Judge, 1983–86, Justice of Appeal, 1986–92, Hong Kong. *Address:* Laurel House, Chapel Lane, Urchfont, Devizes, Wiltshire SN10 4QY. *T:* (01380) 840233, *Fax:* (01380) 840025. *Clubs:* Garrick; Hong Kong.
See also M. G. Clough.

CLOUGH, Susanna Patricia; *see* FitzGerald, S. P.

CLOUT, Prof. Hugh Donald, PhD; FBA 1997; Professor of Geography, University College London, since 1987; *b* 29 April 1944; *s* of Donald Clout and Florence (*née* Allwood). *Educ:* University College London (BA, MPhil, PhD); Univ. de Paris I (Dde l'Univ). Lectr, 1967–81, Reader, 1981–87, in Geography, UCL. *Publications:* (ed) Regional Development in Western Europe, 1975, 3rd edn 1987; (ed) Themes in the Historical Geography of France, 1977; Agriculture in France on the Eve of the Railway Age, 1980; The Land of France 1815–1914, 1982; (ed) Western Europe: geographical perspectives, 1985, 3rd edn 1994; (ed) Times London History Atlas, 1991, 3rd edn, as The Times History of London, 1999; After the Ruins: restoring the countryside of northern France after the Great War, 1996. *Address:* Department of Geography, University College London, 26 Bedford Way, WC1H 0AP. *T:* (020) 7679 5549.

CLOWES, Alfred William; General Secretary, Ceramic and Allied Trades Union, 1980–95; *b* 17 Dec. 1931. Joined the Industry on leaving school; Asst Gen. Sec., Ceramic and Allied Trades Union, 1975–80. Hon. Freeman, City of Stoke-on-Trent, 1995. *Address:* 22 Meadow Avenue, Wetley Rocks, Stoke-on-Trent ST9 0BD.

CLUCAS, Sir Kenneth (Henry), KCB 1976 (CB 1969); Permanent Secretary, Department of Trade, 1979–82; Chairman, Nuffield Foundation Committee of Inquiry into Pharmacy, 1983–86; *b* 18 Nov. 1921; *o s* of late Rev. J. H. Clucas and Ethel Clucas (*née* Sim); *m* 1960, Barbara (*d* 1993), *e d* of late Rear-Adm. R. P. Hunter, USN, Washington; two *d*. *Educ:* Kingswood Sch.; Emmanuel Coll., Cambridge. Royal Signals, 1941–46 (despatches). Joined Min. of Labour as Asst Principal, 1948; 2nd Sec. (Labour), British Embassy, Cairo, 1950; Principal, HM Treasury, 1952; Min. of Labour, 1954; Private Sec. to Minister, 1960–62; Asst Sec., 1962; Under-Sec., 1966–68; Sec., Nat. Bd for Prices and Incomes, 1968–71; First Civil Service Comr, and Dep. Sec., CSD, 1971–73; Dep. Sec., DTI, 1974; Permanent Sec., Dept of Prices and Consumer Protection, 1974–79. Member: Council on Tribunals, 1983–89; Adv. Panel, Freedom of Information Campaign, 1984–; RIPA Wkg Gp on Politics and the Civil Service, 1985–86; Chairman: Cttee of Inquiry into Advertising Controls, 1986–87; Monitoring Cttee, ABI Code of Practice, 1989–93; FIMBRA, 1993–98 (Mem. Council, 1986–); Dep. Chm., CIBA Foundn Media Resource Steering Cttee, 1984–93; Chm., Lloyd's Wkg Pty on Consumer Guarantees, 1985; Lloyd's Members Ombudsman, 1988–94. Chm., Nat. Assoc. of Citizens' Advice Bureaux, 1984–89 (Vice Chm., 1983–84; Chm. Surrey and W Sussex Area Cttee, 1982–84); Mem. Management Cttee, Godalming CAB, 1982–85; Vice Pres., and Chm. of Trustees, Friends of CAB, 1991–95. FRSA. Hon. FRPharmS, 1989. *Recreations:* walking, theatre, opera, composing and solving puzzles. *Address:* Cariad, Knoll Road, Godalming, Surrey GU7 2EL. *T:* (01483) 416430.

CLUCKIE, Prof. Ian David, FREng, FCIWEM; FICE; Professor of Hydrology and Water Management, and Director, Water and Environmental Management Research Centre, Bristol University, since 1997; *b* Edinburgh, 20 July 1949; *m* 1972; one *s* one *d*. *Educ:* Univ. of Surrey (BSc); Univ. of Birmingham (MSc, PhD). CEng, FREng (FEng 1997); FIWEM 1983; FICE 1988; FRMetS 1979. W. S. Atkins, Swansea, 1966–72; Central Water Planning Unit, Reading, 1974–76; Lectr, Univ. of Birmingham, 1976–88; Salford University: Prof. of Water Resources, 1988–97; Chm., Dept of Civil Engrg, 1991–96; Dir, Telford Res. Inst., 1993–94, 1996–97; Acad. Dir, Salford Civil Engineering Ltd, 1989–97. Natural Environment Research Council: Mem., AAPS Res. Grants and Trng Awards Cttee, 1988–91; Chm., AAPS Cttee, 1991–94; Mem., Terrestrial and Freshwater Scis, Marine Scis, Atmospheric Scis and Higher Educn Affairs Cttees, 1991–94. FRSA 1993. *Publications:* (with C. G. Collier) Hydrological Applications of Weather Radar, 1991; contribs to learned jls. *Recreations:* sailing, hill walking.

CLUFF, John Gordon, (Algy); Chairman and Chief Executive, Cluff Mining, since 1996; Chairman, The Spectator, since 1985 (Proprietor, 1981–85); *b* 19 April 1940; *o s* of late Harold Cluff and of Freda Cluff, Waldeshare House, Waldeshare, Kent; *m* 1993, Blondel Hodge, Anguilla, WI; two *s*. *Educ:* Stowe Sch. 2/Lieut, Grenadier Guards, 1959; Captain, Guards Independent Parachute Co., 1963; served W Africa, Cyprus, Malaysia, retd 1965. Founded Cluff Oil, subseq. Cluff Resources, 1971, Chief Exec., 1971, Chm., 1979. Trustee: Anglo-Hong Kong Trust, 1989–; Stowe House Preservation Trust, 1999–. A Dir, Centre for Policy Studies, 1998–. Governor: Commonwealth Inst., 1994–; Stowe Sch., 1998–. Chm., Cons. Commn on the Commonwealth, 2000. Contested (C) Ardwick Div. of Manchester, 1966. *Address:* (office) 29 St James's Place, SW1A 1NR. *Clubs:* White's, Beefsteak, Pratt's, City of London; Brook, Racquet and Tennis (New York); Travellers (Paris); Rand (Johannesburg).

CLUNIES ROSS, Prof. Margaret Beryl, (Mrs J. R. Green); McCaughey Professor of English Language and Early English Literature, University of Sydney, since 1990; Director, Centre for Medieval Studies, since 1997; President, National Academies Forum, 1998; *b* 24 April 1942; *d* of Ernest Phillips Tidemann and Beryl Chudleigh Tidemann (*née* Birch); *m* 1st, 1964, Bruce Axel Clunies Ross; 2nd, 1971, Lester Richard Hiatt; one *s* one *d*; 3rd, 1990, John Richard Green. *Educ:* Walford Girls' Grammar Sch., Adelaide; Univ. of Adelaide (BA Hons 1963); Somerville Coll., Oxford (MA 1970; BLitt 1973). George Murray Overseas Scholar, Univ. of Adelaide at Somerville Coll., Oxford, 1963–65; Lectr in Medieval English Lang. and Lit., St Hilda's Coll. and LMH, Oxford, 1965–68; Alice B. Horsman Travelling Fellow, Somerville Coll., Oxford, at Arnamagnaean Inst. for Icelandic Studies, Copenhagen Univ., 1968–69; University of Sydney: Lectr, Dept of Early Eng. Lit. and Lang., 1969–73; Sen. Lectr, English Dept, 1974–83; Associate Prof., 1984–90; Head, Dept of English, 1993–94. Vis. Mem., Linacre Coll., Oxford and Hon. Res. Associate, UCL, 1979–80; Guest researcher, Univ. of Munich, 1986–87; Vis. Scholar, Univ. of N Carolina, Chapel Hill, 1991–92; Vis. Prof., McMaster Univ., Ont and Vis. Scholar, Pontifical Inst. of Mediaeval Studies, Toronto, 1995; Exchange scholar, Kungl. Vitterhetsakademien, Sweden 1996; Quatercentenary Vis. Fellow, Emmanuel Coll., Cambridge, 1997. Mem., Australian Res. Council, 1995–97. Mem., Nat. Bd of Employment, Educn and Trng, 1995–97. Pres., Aust. Acad. of Humanities, 1995–98. *Film:* (jtly) Waiting for Harry, 1980 (1st Prize, RAI film comp., 1982). *Publications:* (with S. A. Wild) Djambidj: an Aboriginal song series from Northern Australia, 1982; (ed jtly) Songs of Aboriginal Australia, 1987; Skáldskaparmál: Snorri Sturluson's ars poetica and medieval theories of language, 1987; (with J. Mundrugmundrug) Goyulan the Morning Star: an Aboriginal clan song series from North Central Arnhem Land, 1988; Prolonged Echoes: Old Norse myths in Medieval northern society, Vol. 1: The Myths, 1994; Vol. 2: The Reception of Myth in Medieval Iceland, 1998; (ed jtly) Old Norse Studies in the New World, 1994; The Norse Muse in Britain 1750–1820, 1998; contrib. numerous articles in learned jls and chapters in books of essays. *Recreations:* gardening, staying at home and on my country property. *Address:* Department of English, University of Sydney, NSW 2006, Australia. *T:* (2) 93516832.

CLUTTERBUCK, Vice-Adm. Sir David Granville, KBE 1968; CB 1965; *b* Gloucester, 25 Jan. 1913; *m* 1937, Rose Mere Vaile, Auckland, NZ; two *d*. Joined RN, 1929. Served War of 1939–45 (despatches twice): navigating officer of cruisers HMS Ajax, 1940–42, HMS Newfoundland, 1942–46 (present Japanese surrender at Tokyo). Subsequently commanded destroyers Sluys and Cadiz, 1952–53; Naval Attaché at British Embassy, Bonn; Capt. (D) of Third Training Squadron in HMS Zest, Londonderry, 1956–58; commanded cruiser HMS Blake, 1960–62; Chief of Staff to C-in-C Home Fleet and C-in-C Allied Forces Eastern Atlantic, 1963–66; Rear-Adm., 1963; Vice-Adm. 1966; Dep. Supreme Allied Comdr, Atlantic, 1966–68. *Address:* Burrard Cottage, Walhampton, Lymington, Hampshire SO41 5SA. *Clubs:* Army and Navy; Royal Lymington Yacht.

CLUTTON, Rafe Henry, CBE 1992; FRICS; Consultant to Cluttons, Chartered Surveyors, London, since 1992 (Partner, 1955–92); *b* 13 June 1929; *s* of late Robin John Clutton and Rosalie Muriel (*née* Birch); *m* 1954, Jill Olwyn Evans; four *s* one *d*. *Educ:* Tonbridge Sch., Kent. FRICS 1959. Director: Legal & General Group PLC (formerly Legal & General Assurance Soc. Ltd), 1972–93; Rodamco (UK) BV (formerly Haslemere Estates), 1990–96. Member: Royal National Theatre Bd, 1976–93; Salvation Army London Adv. Bd, 1971–; Royal Commn for Exhibn of 1851, 1988–99. Governor, Royal Foundn of Grey Coat Hosp., 1967– (Chm., 1981–2001). *Recreations:* grandchildren, books, admiring the view. *Address:* Providence Cottage, Church Road, Barcombe, East Sussex BN8 5TP. *T:* (01273) 400763. *Club:* Royal Thames Yacht.

CLUTTON-BROCK, Prof. Timothy Hugh, PhD; ScD; FRS 1993; Professor of Animal Ecology, University of Cambridge, since 1994 (Reader, 1991–94); *b* 13 Aug. 1946; *s* of Hugh Alan Clutton-Brock and Eileen Mary Stableforth; *m* 1980, Dafila Kathleen Scott; one *s* one *d*. *Educ:* Rugby Sch.; Magdalene Coll., Cambridge (BA, MA, PhD, ScD). NERC res. fellowship, Animal Behaviour Res. Gp, Oxford, 1972; Lectr in Ethology, Univ. of Sussex, 1973; Cambridge University: Sen. Res. Fellow in Behavioural Ecology, King's Coll., 1976; SERC Advanced Fellow, Dept of Zoology, 1981; Royal Soc. Res. Fellow in Biology, 1983; Lectr in Zoology, 1987–91. Chm., IUCN Deer Specialist Gp, 1980–90. Jt Editor, Princeton Monographs in Behavioral Ecology, 1982–. Scientific Medal, 1984, Frink Medal, 1998, Zoological Soc. of London; Hart Merriam Award, Mammal Soc. of America, 1991; Marsh Award, British Ecol Soc., 1998. *Publications:* (ed) Primate Ecology, 1977; (ed) Readings in Sociobiology, 1978; Red Deer: the behaviour and ecology of two sexes, 1982; (ed) Rhum, Natural History of an Island, 1987; (ed) Reproductive Success, 1988; Red Deer in the Highlands, 1989; The Evolution of Parental Care, 1991; approx. 200 sci. papers on animal behaviour, ecology and evolution in Nature, Jl Animal Ecol., Evolution, Amer. Naturalist, Jl of Zoology, Animal Behaviour, Behaviour, Behavioral Ecol. and Sociobiol., Folia Primatologica and other jls. *Recreations:* bird watching, fish watching, fishing. *Address:* White Roses, Reach, Cambridgeshire CB5 0JQ; Department of Zoology, Downing Street, Cambridge CB2 3EJ. *T:* (01223) 336600.

CLWYD, 3rd Baron *cr* 1919; **John Anthony Roberts;** Bt 1908; *b* 2 Jan. 1935; *s* of 2nd Baron Clwyd and Joan de Bois (*d* 1985); *d* of late Charles R. Murray; *S* father, 1987; *m* 1969, Geraldine, *yr d* of Charles Eugene Cannons, Sanderstead; three *s*. *Educ:* Harrow; Trinity College, Cambridge. Called to the Bar, Gray's Inn, 1970. *Heir: s* Hon. John Murray Roberts, *b* 27 Aug. 1971. *Address:* 24 Salisbury Avenue, Cheam, Sutton, Surrey SM1 2DJ.

CLWYD, Ann; MP (Lab) Cynon Valley, since May 1984; journalist and broadcaster; *b* 21 March 1937; *d* of Gwilym Henri Lewis and Elizabeth Ann Lewis; *m* 1963, Owen Dryhurst Roberts, TV director and producer. *Educ:* Halkyn Primary Sch.; Holywell Grammar Sch.; The Queen's Sch., Chester; University Coll., Bangor. Former: Student-teacher, Hope Sch., Flintshire; BBC Studio Manager; freelance reporter, producer, Welsh corresp., The Guardian and The Observer, 1964–79; Vice-Chm., Welsh Arts Council, 1975–79. Member: Welsh Hospital Board, 1970–74; Cardiff Community Health Council, 1975–79; Royal Commn on NHS, 1976–79; Working Party, report, Organisation of Out-Patient Care, for Welsh Hosp. Bd; Working Party, Bilingualism in the Hospital Service; Labour Party Study Gp, People and the Media; Arts Council of Gt Britain, 1975–80; Labour Party NEC, 1983–84; PLP Exec., 1997–; Chm., Cardiff Anti-Racialism Cttee, 1978–80. Chm., Labour back bench cttee on Health and Social Security, 1985–87; Vice-Chm., Labour back bench cttee on Defence, 1985–87; Opposition front bench spokesperson on women, 1987–88, on educn, 1987–88, on overseas develt and co-operation, 1989–92, on Wales, 1992, on Nat. Heritage, 1992–93, on employment, 1993–94, on foreign affairs, 1994–95; Mem., Shadow Cabinet, 1989–93. Chm., All Party Gp on Human Rights, 1997–.

Member: NUJ; TGWU. Contested (Lab): Denbigh, 1970; Gloucester, Oct. 1974; Mem. (Lab) Mid and West Wales, European Parlt, 1979–84. *Address:* (office) 6 Deans Court, Dean Street, Aberdare, Mid Glam CF44 7BN. *T:* (01685) 871394.

CLYDE, family name of **Baron Clyde**.

CLYDE, Baron *cr* 1996 (Life Peer), of Briglands in Perthshire and Kinross; **James John Clyde;** PC 1996; a Lord of Appeal in Ordinary, 1996–2001; *b* 29 Jan. 1932; *s* of Rt Hon. Lord Clyde; *m* 1963, Ann Clunie Hoblyn; two *s*. *Educ:* Edinburgh Academy; Corpus Christi Coll., Oxford (BA; Hon. Fellow, 1996); Edinburgh Univ. (LLB). Called to Scottish Bar, 1959; QC (Scot.) 1971; Advocate-Depute, 1973–74. Chancellor to Bishop of Argyll and the Isles, 1972–85; a Judge of the Courts of Appeal of Jersey and Guernsey, 1979–85; a Senator of the College of Justice in Scotland, 1985–96. Chairman: Med. Appeal Tribunal, 1974–85; Cttee of Investigation for Scotland on Agricl Mktg, 1984–85; Scottish Valuation Adv. Council, 1987–96 (Mem., 1972–96). Mem., UK Delegn to CCBE, 1978–84 (Leader, 1981–84). Hon. Pres., Scottish Young Lawyers' Assoc., 1988–97; Vice-Pres., Royal Blind Asylum and Sch., 1987–; Assessor to Chancellor, 1989–97, Vice-Chm., 1993–96, Court of Edinburgh Univ.; Chm., Europa Inst., Edinburgh Univ., 1990–97; Pres., Scottish Univs Law Inst., 1991–98. Dir, Edinburgh Acad., 1979–88; Trustee: St Mary's Music Sch., 1976–92; Nat. Library of Scotland, 1977–93; Chm. of Govs, St George's Sch. for Girls, 1989–97; Gov., Napier Polytechnic, 1989–93. Chm. Special Trustees, St Mary's Hosp., Paddington, 1997–; Pres., Dumfries Burns Club, 1996–97. Chm., Orkney Children Inquiry, 1991–92. Hon. Bencher, Middle Temple, 1996. DUniv Heriot-Watt, 1991; Dr *hc* Edinburgh, 1997; Hon. DLitt Napier, 1995. *Publications:* (ed jtly) Armour on Valuation, 3rd edn, 1961, 5th edn, 1985; (jtly) Judicial Review, 2000. *Recreations:* music, gardening. *Address:* House of Lords, SW1A 0PW. *Club:* New (Edinburgh).

CLYDE, (Samuel) Wilson; Member (DUP) Antrim South, Northern Ireland Assembly, since 1998; *b* 8 April 1934; *m* 1970, Margaret Evelyn; one *s*. *Educ:* Shane's Castle Primary Sch. Farmer, 1948–98. Mem. (DUP), Antrim BC, 1981–. *Recreations:* stock car racing, motor cycling. *Address:* 21 Groggan Road, Randalstown, Antrim BT41 3HA. *T:* (028) 9447 8370.

CLYDESMUIR, 3rd Baron *cr* 1948, of Braidwood, co. Lanark; **David Ronald Colville;** *b* 8 April 1949; *e s* of 2nd Baron Clydesmuir, KT, CB, MBE, TD and of Joan Marguerita, *d* of late Lt-Col E. B. Booth, DSO; *S* father, 1996; *m* 1978, Aline Frances, *er d* of Peter Merrriam; two *s* two *d*. *Educ:* Charterhouse. *Heir: s* Hon. Richard Colville, *b* 21 Oct. 1980. *Address:* Langlees House, Biggar, Lanarkshire ML12 6NP.

COADY, Aubrey William Burleton, CMG 1959; Chairman, Electricity Commission of NSW, 1959–75 (Member, 1950–75); *b* Singleton, NSW, 15 June 1915; *s* of W. A. Coady, Belmont; *m* 1964, Phyllis K., *d* of late G. W. Mathews. *Educ:* Newcastle High Sch.; Sydney Univ. (BA, BEc). Under-Sec. and Comptroller of Accounts, NSW Treasury, 1955–59.

COADY, Frances Rachel; Vice-President and Publisher, Picador USA, since 2000; *b* 16 June 1958; *d* of Matthew and Patricia Coady. *Educ:* Streatham Hill and Clapham High Sch.; Bromley High Sch.; Univ. of Sussex (BA Hons English Lit. 1980); Univ. of Essex (MA English Lit. 1981). Faber and Faber, 1982–86, Sen. Non-Fiction Commng Editor, 1983–86; Researcher for Alan Yentob, Head of Dept of Music and Arts, BBC TV, 1986; Random House, 1986–95: Editl Dir, Jonathan Cape, 1986–89; Founder Publisher, Vintage Paperbacks, 1989–93; Publisher, overseeing Jonathan Cape, Chatto & Windus, Pimlico and Vintage, 1993–95; Publisher, Granta Books, 1995–99. *Recreations:* theatre, cinema, reading. *Address:* Picador USA, 175 Fifth Avenue, New York, NY 10010, USA. *Club:* Two Brydges.

COAKER, Vernon Rodney; MP (Lab) Gedling, since 1997; *b* 17 June 1953; *s* of Edwin Coaker; *m* 1978, Jacqueline Heaton; one *s* one *d*. *Educ:* Drayton Manor Grammar Sch., London; Warwick Univ. (BA Hons); Trent Poly. (PGCE). Hist. Teacher, Manvers Pierrepont Sch., 1976–82; Hd of Dept, Arnold Hill Sch., 1982–88; Sen. Teacher, Bramcote Pk Sch., 1989–95; Dep. Headteacher, Big Wood Sch., 1995–97. Mem., Rushcliffe BC, 1983–97 (Leader, 1987–97). PPS to Minister of State for Social Security, 1999, to Financial Sec. to HM Treasury, 1999–2001, to Minister of State (Minister for School Standards), DfES, 2001–. Contested (Lab): Rushcliffe, 1983; Gedling, 1987, 1992. *Address:* House of Commons, SW1A 0AA.

COAKLEY, Rev. Prof. Sarah Anne; Edward Mallinckrodt Jr Professor of Divinity, Harvard University, since 1995 (Professor of Christian Theology, 1993–95); *b* 10 Sept. 1951; *d* of Frank Robert Furber, *qv* and Anne Wilson Furber; *m* 1975, Dr James Farwell Coakley; two *d*. *Educ:* Blackheath High Sch.; New Hall, Cambridge (BA 1973; MA, PhD 1982); Harvard Divinity Sch. (ThM 1975). Harkness Fellow, 1973–75; Univ. Lectr in Religious Studies, 1976–90, Sen. Lectr, 1990–91, Lancaster Univ.; Tutorial Fellow in Theology, Oriel Coll., and Univ. Lectr in Theology, Oxford, 1991–93. Select Preacher, Oxford Univ., 1991; Hulsean Lectr, Cambridge Univ., 1991–92; Henry Luce III Fellow, 1994–95; Hulsean Preacher, Cambridge Univ., 1996. Lectures: Samuel Ferguson, Manchester Univ., 1997; Riddell, Newcastle Univ., 1999; Tate-Willson, Southern Methodist Univ., 1999; Prideaux, Exeter Univ., 2000; Jellema, Calvin Coll., Mich, 2001. Ordained deacon, 2000, priest, 2001; Asst Curate, SS Mary and Nicholas, Littlemore, 2000–. Consultant to C of E Doctrine Commn, 1982–84, Mem., 1984–92. *Publications:* Christ Without Absolutes: a study of the Christology of Ernst Troeltsch, 1988; (ed with David A. Pailin) The Making and Remaking of Christian Doctrine, 1993; (ed) Religion and the Body, 1997; Powers and Submissions: spirituality, philosophy and gender, 2002; contrib. to C of E reports and to theol. jls. *Recreations:* musical activities, thinking about the garden. *Address:* Harvard Divinity School, 45 Francis Avenue, Cambridge, MA 02138, USA.

See also R. J. Furber.

COASE, Prof. Ronald Harry, DSc; Professor Emeritus and Senior Fellow in Law and Economics, University of Chicago, since 1982; *b* 29 Dec. 1910; *s* of Henry Joseph Coase and Rosalie Elizabeth (*née* Giles); *m* 1937, Marian Ruth Hartung. *Educ:* Kilburn Grammar Sch.; LSE (BCom 1932; DSc Econ 1951). Assistant Lecturer: Dundee Sch. of Econs, 1932–34; Univ. of Liverpool, 1934–35; later Lectr, then Reader, LSE, 1935–40, 1946–51; War service: Hd of Statistical Div., Forestry Commn, 1940–41; Statistician, later Chief Statistician, Central Statistical Office, Offices of War Cabinet, 1941–46; Professor: Univ. of Buffalo, 1951–58; Univ. of Virginia, 1958–64; Clifford R. Musser Prof., Univ. of Chicago Law Sch., 1964–82. Fellow, Amer. Acad. of Arts and Scis, 1978; Dist. Fellow, Amer. Econ. Assoc., 1980; Membre Titulaire, European Acad., 1992; Corresp. Fellow, British Acad., 1985; Hon. Fellow, LSE. Hon. doctorates: Dr rer. pol. Cologne, 1988; DSocSc Yale, 1989; LLD Washington, St Louis, 1991; LLD Dundee, 1992; DSc Buckingham, 1995; DHL Beloit Coll., 1996; Dr *hc* Paris, 1996. Nobel Prize for Economics, 1991. *Publications:* British Broadcasting: a study in monopoly, 1950; The Firm, the Market and the Law, 1988; Essays on Economics and Economists, 1994. *Address:* University of Chicago Law School, 1111 East 60th Street, Chicago, IL 60637, USA.

COATES, Sir Anthony Robert M.; *see* Milnes Coates.

COATES, David; HM Diplomatic Service; Director, British Trade and Cultural Office, Taipei, since 1998; *b* 13 Nov. 1947; *s* of late Matthew Coates and Margaret Ann Davies Coates (*née* Ross); *m* 1974, Joanna Kay Weil; two *d*. *Educ:* Dame Allan's Boys' Sch., Newcastle; Univ. of Bristol (BA Hist.); Univ. of Hawaii; Joint Univ. Centre, Taiwan. FCO, 1974–77; language training, Hong Kong, 1977–78; First Sec., Peking, 1978–81; Iran Desk, FCO, 1981–83; Asst Head, S America Dept, 1983–86; First Sec., UKMIS, Geneva, 1986–89; Counsellor and Head, Political Section, Peking, 1989–92; Head, Jt Assistance Unit, Central and E Europe, FCO, 1993–95; Head, Far Eastern and Pacific Dept, FCO, 1995–98. *Recreations:* ski-ing, theatre, hill-walking, leeks. *Address:* c/o Foreign and Commonwealth Office, SW1A 2AH.

COATES, Sir David (Charlton Frederick), 3rd Bt *cr* 1921, of Haypark, City of Belfast; *b* 16 Feb. 1948; *o s* of Sir Frederick Gregory Lindsay Coates, 2nd Bt and of Joan Nugent, *d* of Maj.-Gen. Sir Charlton Spinks, KBE, DSO; *S* father, 1994; *m* 1973, Christine Helen, *d* of Lewis F. Marshall; two *s*. *Educ:* Millfield. *Heir: s* James Gregory David Coates, *b* 12 March 1977. *Address:* 30 Hauxton Road, Little Shelford, Cambs CB2 5HJ.

COATES, David Randall, CB 2000; Chief Economic Adviser, and Head of Economics Profession, Department of Trade and Industry, since 1990; *b* 22 March 1942; *m* Julia Hagedorn (*d* 1995); one *s* one *d*. *Educ:* Leeds Grammar Sch.; Queen's Coll., Oxford; LSE. Res. Assistant, Univ. of Manchester and Manchester Business Sch., 1966–68; Economic Advr, Min. of Technology and DTI, 1968–74; Sen. Economic Advr, Dept of Trade and DTI, 1974–82; Asst Sec., DTI, 1982–89; Grade 3, DTI, 1989. *Recreations:* family, gardening, travel, music. *Address:* Department of Trade and Industry, 1 Victoria Street, SW1H 0ET. *T:* (020) 7215 6059.

COATES, Dudley James; consultant; Head of Environment Group, Ministry of Agriculture, Fisheries and Food, 1996–2001; *b* 15 Sept. 1946; *o s* of Edward Coates and late Margot Coates; *m* 1969, Rev. Dr Jean Walsingham; two *d*. *Educ:* Westcliff High School for Boys; Univ. of Sussex (BA (Hons)). Joined MAFF as Asst Principal, 1968; Second Sec., UK Delegn to the EC, Brussels, 1970–72; Principal, MAFF, 1973; Lectr, Civil Service Coll., 1978–81; Head of Animal Health Div. II, 1981–83, Head of Financial Management Team, 1983–87, MAFF; Dir Gen. of Corporate Services, Intervention Bd for Agricultural Produce, 1987–89; Dir, Regl Services, MAFF, 1989–96. Methodist local preacher, 1970–; Mem., Methodist Conf., 1988, 1989, 1993–; Chair, Methodist Publishing House, 1996–. *Publication:* (contrib.) Policies into Practice (ed David Lewis and Helen Wallace), 1984. *Recreations:* Christian activities, cycling, singing. *Address:* 15 Lewcos House, 57-63 Regency Street, SW1P 4AF; *e-mail:* coates@appleonline.net.

COATES, Prof. Geoffrey Edward, MA, DSc; Professor of Chemistry, University of Wyoming, 1968–79, now Emeritus; *b* 14 May 1917; *er s* of Prof. Joseph Edward Coates, OBE; *m* 1951, Winifred Jean Hobbs; one *s* one *d*. *Educ:* Clifton Coll.; Queen's Coll., Oxford. Research Chemist, Magnesium Metal Corp., 1940–45; Univ. of Bristol: Lecturer in Chemistry, 1945–53; Sub-Warden of Wills Hall, 1946–51; Prof. of Chemistry, Univ. of Durham, 1953–68. *Publications:* Organo-metallic Compounds (monograph), 1956, 3rd edn (2 vols), 1967–68; Principles of Organometallic Chemistry, 1968; papers in scientific journals. *Address:* 1801 Rainbow Avenue, Laramie, WY 82070–4318, USA. *Club:* Royal Commonwealth Society.

See also J. F. Coates.

COATES, James Richard, CB 1992; FCIT, FILT; Under Secretary, Urban and Local Transport Directorate, Department of Transport, 1994; *b* 18 Oct. 1935; *s* of William Richard Coates and Doris Coral (*née* Richmond); *m* 1969, Helen Rosamund Rimington; one *s* one *d*. *Educ:* Nottingham High Sch.; Clare Coll., Cambridge (MA). Joined Ministry of Transport, 1959; Private Sec. to Permanent Sec., 1962–63; Principal, 1963; Private Sec. to Secretary of State for Local Govt and Regional Planning, 1969, and to Minister of Transport, 1970–71; Asst Sec., DoE, 1971; Under Secretary, 1977; Dir, London Reg., PSA, 1979–83; Department of Transport: Highways Policy and Prog. Directorate, 1983–85; Rlys Directorate, 1985–91; Urban and Gen. Directorate, 1991–93. FILT (FCIT 1996; Mem., Policies Cttee). *Recreations:* reading, listening to music, looking at buildings, gardening. *Address:* 10 Alwyne Road, N1 2HH.

COATES, John Dowling, AO 1995 (AM 1989); President, Australian Olympic Committee, since 1990; Partner, Greaves Wannan & Williams, Solicitors, since 1991; *b* 7 May 1950; *s* of Sidney Dowling Coates and Valerie Irene Coates; *m* 1981, Pauline Frances Kahl; five *s* one *d*. *Educ:* Homebush Boys' High Sch.; Sydney Univ. (LLB). Joined Greaves Wannan & Williams, 1971: Partner, 1977–87; Consultant, 1987–91. Man. Dir, Austus Properties Ltd, 1987–90 (Dir, 1990–91); Chairman: Reef Casino Trust, 1993–97; Triplecee Retail Investment Trust, 1994–99; Accord Pacific Hldgs Ltd, 1994–; Australian Olympic Foundn Ltd, 1996–; Burson-Marsteller Australia, 2000–; Dep. Chm., Kengfu Properties Pte Ltd, 1997–; Dir, David Jones Ltd, 1995–. Dir, Australian Inst. of Sport, 1985–86 (Dep. Chm., 1986–89); Dep. Chm., Australian Sports Commn, 1989– (Mem., 1987–89); Mem. Council, Internat. Rowing Fedn (FISA), 1992–; Vice-Pres., Internat. Council of Arbitration for Sport, 1994–. Australian Olympic Committee: Mem., Exec. Bd, 1982–85; Vice-Pres., 1985–90; Exec. Dir, 1992 Olympic Games Bid, Brisbane CC, 1985–86; Vice Pres., Sydney Olympics 2000 Bid Ltd, 1991–93; Sen. Vice Pres., Sydney Organising Cttee for Olympic Games, 1999–2000. Dir, Roseville Coll. Foundn Ltd, 1997–. Rowing Manager, Australian Team, Montreal Olympics, 1976; Admin Dir., Australian Team, Moscow Olympics, 1980; Asst Gen. Manager, Australian Team, Los Angeles Olympics, 1984; Chef de Mission and Gen. Manager, Australian Team: Seoul Olympics, 1988; Barcelona Olympics, 1992; Atlanta Olympics, 1996; Sydney Olympics, 2000. Hon. Life Member: NSW Olympic Council Inc., 1990; Australian Rowing Council Inc., 1993; NSW Rowing Assoc. Inc., 1994; Australian Olympic Cttee, 1997. IOC Centennial Trophy, 1994; Olympic Order in Gold, 2000; FISA Medal of Honour, 2000. *Recreations:* golf, swimming, rowing, other sports, the Olympic movement. *Address:* c/o Australian Olympic Committee Inc., Level 27, The Chifley Tower, 2 Chifley Square, Sydney, NSW 2000, Australia. *Clubs:* Sydney Rowing (Hon. Life Mem.), Tattersall's (Hon. Mem.); Royal Sydney Yacht, Cruising Yacht of Australia (Hon. Mem.); Sydney Turf and Carbine (past Chm.).

COATES, John Francis, OBE 1955; Deputy Director, Ship Design, Ministry of Defence, 1977–79, retired; *b* 30 March 1922; *s* of Joseph Edward Coates and Ada Maria Coates; *m* 1954, Jane Waymouth; two *s*. *Educ:* Clifton Coll.; Queen's Coll., Oxford (MA 1946). Entered RCNC, 1943; RCDS, 1971; Supt, Naval Construction Res. Estabt, Dunfermline, 1974. Dir, The Trireme Trust, 1985–. Hon. DSc Bath, 1989. *Publications:* (with J. S. Morrison): The Athenian Trireme, 1986, 2nd edn (with N. B. Rankov) 2000; The Age of the Galley, 1995; Greek and Roman Oared Warships, 1996; papers on naval architecture of ancient ships. *Recreation:* nautical research. *Address:* Sabinal, Lucklands

Road, Bath BA1 4AU. *T:* (01225) 423696.
See also Prof. G. E. Coates.

COATES, Prof. John Henry, FRS 1985; Sadleirian Professor of Pure Mathematics, Cambridge University, since 1986; Professorial Fellow of Emmanuel College, Cambridge, since 1986; *b* 26 Jan. 1945; *s* of J. R. Coates and Beryl (*née* Lee); *m* 1966, Julie Turner; three *s. Educ:* Australian National Univ. (BSc); Trinity Coll., Cambridge (PhD). Assistant Prof., Harvard Univ., 1969–72; Associate Prof., Stanford Univ., 1972–74; Univ. Lectr, Cambridge, and Fellow, Emmanuel Coll., 1974–77; Prof., ANU, 1977–78; Prof. of Maths, Univ. de Paris, Orsay, 1978–86, Ecole Normale Supérieure, Paris, 1985–86; Hd of Dept of Pure Maths and Math. Stats, Cambridge Univ., 1991–97. Pres., London Math. Soc., 1988–90; Vice-Pres., Internat. Mathematical Union, 1991–95; Mem. Council, Royal Soc., 1992–94. Dr *hc* Ecole Normale Supérieure, 1997. *Address:* Emmanuel College, Cambridge CB1 2EA; 104 Mawson Road, Cambridge CB1 2EA. *T:* (01223) 360884.

COATES, Kenneth Sidney; Special Professor in Continuing Education, University of Nottingham, since 1990 (Reader, 1980–89); *b* 16 Sept. 1930; *s* of Eric Arthur Coates and Mary Coates; *m* 1969, Tamara Tura; three *s* three *d* (and one *d* decd). *Educ:* Nottingham Univ. (Mature State Scholar, 1956; BA 1st Cl. Hons Sociology, 1959). Coal miner, Notts Coalfield, 1948–56; student, 1956–60; Asst Tutor, Tutor, and Sen. Tutor in Adult Educn, Univ. of Nottingham, 1960–80. MEP (Lab 1989–98, Ind Lab 1998–99), Nottingham, 1989–94, Notts N and Chesterfield, 1994–99. Chm., Human Rights Subcttee, 1989–94, Rapporteur, Temp. Cttee on Employment, 1994–95, EP. Member: Bertrand Russell Peace Foundn, 1965–; Inst. of Workers' Control, 1968–; Jt Sec., European Nuclear Disarmament Liaison Cttee, 1981–89. *Publications:* (with A. J. Topham) Industrial Democracy in Great Britain, 1967, 3rd edn 1976; (with R. L. Silburn) Poverty, the Forgotten Englishmen, 1970, 4th edn 1983; (with A. J. Topham) The New Unionism, 1972, 2nd edn 1974; (with A. J. Topham) Trade Unions in Britain, 1980, 3rd edn 1988; Heresies, 1982; The Most Dangerous Decade, 1984; (with A. J. Topham) Trade Unions and Politics, 1986; Think Globally, Act Locally, 1988; (with A. J. Topham) The Making of the Transport and General Workers' Union, 1991; Clause IV: common ownership and the Labour Party, 1995; The Right to Work, 1995; (with S. Holland) Full Employment for Europe, 1995; (jtly) Dear Commissioner, 1996; (with M. Barratt Brown) The Blair Revelation, 1996; Community Under Attack, 1998. *Recreations:* walking, reading. *Address:* Russell House, Bullwell Lane, Nottingham NG6 0BT. *T:* (0115) 978 4504.

COATES, Marten Frank; His Honour Judge Coates; a Circuit Judge, since 1997; *b* 26 March 1947; *s* of Frank and Violet Coates; *m* 1973, Susan Anton-Stephens; three *d. Educ:* Pocklington Sch., York; Durham Univ. (BA Hons 1972); Birmingham Univ. (Dip. Biblical Studies). Called to the Bar, Inner Temple, 1972; Asst Recorder, Midland and Oxford Circuit, 1989–93; Recorder, 1993–97. Dep. Chancellor, Dio. Lichfield, 1997–. *Address:* c/o Midland and Oxford Circuit Office, The Priory Court, 33 Bull Street, Birmingham B4 6DW.

COATES, Michael Arthur, FCA; Chairman, Price Waterhouse, World Firm, 1982–88; *b* 12 May 1924; *yr s* of late Joseph Michael Smith Coates, OBE, Elmfield, Wylam, Northumberland, and late Lillian Warren Coates (*née* Murray); *m* 1st, 1952, Audrey Hampton Thorne (marr. diss. 1970); one *s* two *d*; 2nd, 1971, Sally Rogers (marr. diss. 1980). *Educ:* Uppingham Sch. Admitted Mem., Inst. of Chartered Accountants, 1951. Served RA, mainly in ME and Italy, 1942–47. Articled with Price Waterhouse & Co., Newcastle, 1942; returned to Price Waterhouse, 1947; transf. to London, 1954; Partner, Price Waterhouse & Co., 1959–82, Dep. Sen. Partner, 1974–75, Sen. Partner, 1975–82; Chm., Price Waterhouse Internat. Manpower Cttee, 1971–74; Mem., Policy Cttee, 1974–88. *Recreations:* diverse, including music, modern painting, antiques, gardens, reading, railways, photography. *Address:* 20 Wilton Crescent, SW1X 8SA. *T:* (020) 7235 4423; Cantray House, Croy, Inverness-shire IV2 5PW. *T:* (01667) 493204.

COATES, Prof. Nigel Martin; Joint Founder and Co-director, Branson Coates Architecture Ltd, since 1985; Professor of Architectural Design, Royal College of Art, since 1995; *b* 2 March 1949; *s* of Douglas Coates and Margaret Coates (*née* Trigg). *Educ:* Hanley Castle Grammar Sch., Malvern; Univ. of Nottingham (BA Arch Hons); Architectural Assoc. (AA Dip (Year Prize)); Univ. of Rome (Italian Govt Scholar). Unit Master, AA, 1979–89. Founder Partner, Omniate (production co. for own designs), 1987–. Course Master, Bennington Coll., Vt, 1980–81. Founder Mem., Narrative Architecture Today, 1979–89. Mem., Adv. Bd, ICA, 1987–89. Ext. Examr, Bartlett Sch. of Architecture and AA, 1993–94. Presenter, 1989, advr and subject, 1992, TV documentaries. Lectures world-wide. Branson Coates' projects include: Katharine Hamnett shop, London, 1988; Arca di Noe 1988, Hotel Otaru Marittimo 1989, Nishi Azabu Wall 1990 and Art Silo 1993, in Japan; shops for Jigsaw in UK, Ireland and Japan, 1988–96; new depts for Liberty, Regent St, branches and airport shops, 1992–96; La Fôret and Nautilus Restaurants, Schiphol Airport, Amsterdam, 1993; Bargo Bar, Bass Taverns, 1996; (contrib.) Living Bridges Exhibn, RA, 1996; (contrib.) Erotic Design Exhibn, Design Mus., 1997; New Gall. Bldg, Geffrye Mus., 1998; Nat. Centre for Popular Music, Sheffield, 1998; British Expo Pavilion, Lisbon 98; exhibn design, Look Inside! New British Public Interiors, internat. tour, 1997. Nigel Coates designs include: Metropole and Jazz furniture collections, 1986; Noah collection, 1988; Female, He-man and She-woman mannequins, 1988; Tongue chair, 1989; Carpet collection, 1990; Slipper chair, 1994; glass vase collection, 1996; Oxo furniture, Hitch Mylin; Oyster furniture, Lloyd Loom. Exhibitions: Panama City, Air Gall., 1985; (one-person) Dark Albion, AA, 1984; Ecstacity, AA, 1992; work in collections of V&A Mus.; work exhibited in UK, Europe, US and Japan. Inter-Design Award for Contribution to Japanese cities, Japan Inter-Design Forum, 1990. *Publication:* Ecstacity, 1992. *Recreations:* contemporary art, video-making, motorcycling, riding. *Address:* Branson Coates Architecture, 23 Old Street, EC1V 9HL. *T:* (020) 7490 0343. *Clubs:* Groucho, Blacks.

COATES, Reginald Charles, FREng; Emeritus Professor of Civil Engineering, University of Nottingham, since 1983; *b* 28 June 1920; *s* of Wilfrid and Margaret Anne Coates; *m* 1942, Doris Sheila (*née* Sharrad) (*d* 1988); two *s* one *d. Educ:* New Mills Grammar Sch.; The Herbert Strutt Sch., Belper, Derbyshire; University Coll., Nottingham. Served War of 1939–45, Corps of Royal Engineers. Univ. of Nottingham: Lectr in Civil Engineering, 1946; Sen. Lectr, 1953; Prof. and Head of Dept of Civil Engrg, 1958–82; Dep. Vice-Chancellor, 1966–69; Prof. and Hd, Dept of Civil Engrg, Papua New Guinea Univ. of Technol., 1982–85. Member: Council, Instn of Civil Engineers, 1967–72 (Vice-Pres., 1975–78, Pres., 1978–79); Sheffield Regional Hosp. Bd, 1971–74; Notts AHA, 1974–75; Council, Construction Industry Research and Information Assoc., 1978–82; Adv. Cttee, Books for Overseas, British Council, 1974–82; Construction and Housing Res. Adv. Council, DoE, 1976–79. FREng (FEng 1978). *Publications:* (with M. G. Coutie and F. K. Kong) Structural Analysis, 1972, 3rd edn 1987; occasional articles in technical press. *Recreations:* cooking and idling. *Address:* c/o Two Trees, Longford, Ashbourne, Derbys DE6 3DR.

COATES, Suzanne; Her Honour Judge Suzanne Coates; a Circuit Judge, since 1998; *b* 2 Aug. 1949; *d* of late Jack Coates and of Elsie Coates (now Brown); *m* 1980, John Brian Camille Tanzer, *qv*; two *s. Educ:* Skipton Girls' High Sch.; Guy's Hosp.; South Bank Poly. (HVCert 1972); Queen Mary Coll., London Univ. (LLB 1977). SRN, Guy's Hosp., 1968–71; Health Visitor, Bromley LBC, 1972–74; called to the Bar, Gray's Inn, 1978; Asst Recorder, 1992–96; a Recorder, 1996–98. *Recreations:* music, reading, walking, football (watching), gardening, travel, cooking. *Address:* Brighton County Court, John Street, Brighton, Sussex. *T:* (01273) 674421.

COATS, Sir Alastair Francis Stuart, 4th Bt *cr* 1905; *b* 18 Nov. 1921; *s* of Lieut-Col Sir James Stuart Coats, MC, 3rd Bt and Lady Amy Coats (*d* 1975), *er d* of 8th Duke of Richmond and Gordon; *S* father, 1966; *m* 1947, Lukyn, *d* of Capt. Charles Gordon; one *s* one *d. Educ:* Eton. Served War of 1939–45, Coldstream Guards (Capt.). *Heir: s* Alexander James Coats [*b* 6 July 1951; *m* 1999, Clara, *d* of Ernesto Abril de Vivero]. *Address:* Birchwood House, Durford Wood, Petersfield, Hants GU31 5AW. *T:* (01730) 892254.

COATS, Sir William David, Kt 1985; DL; Chairman, Coats Patons PLC, 1981–86 (Deputy Chairman, 1979–81); Deputy Chairman, Clydesdale Bank, 1985–93 (Director, since 1962); *b* 25 July 1924; *s* of Thomas Heywood Coats and Olivia Violet Pitman; *m* 1950, Hon. Elizabeth Lilian Graham MacAndrew; two *s* one *d. Educ:* Eton Coll. Entered service of J. & P. Coats Ltd, later Coats Patons PLC, 1948: Director: The Central Agency Ltd (subsid. co.), 1953–55; Coats Patons PLC, 1960–86; Murray Caledonian Trust Co. Ltd, 1961–81; Weir Group Ltd, 1970–83; Murray Investment Trusts, 1986–92. Mem., S of Scotland Electricity Bd, 1972–81. Hon. LLD Strathclyde, 1977. DL Ayr and Arran, 1986. *Recreation:* golf. *Address:* The Cottage, Symington, Ayrshire KA1 5QG. *T:* (01563) 830287. *Club:* Western (Glasgow).

COBB, Henry Nichols; Partner, Pei Cobb Freed & Partners, Architects, since 1960; *b* 8 April 1926; *s* of Charles Kane Cobb and Elsie Quincy Cobb; *m* 1953, Joan Stewart Spaulding; three *d. Educ:* Harvard College (AB 1947); Harvard Graduate Sch. of Design (MArch 1949). Architectural Div., Webb & Knapp, 1950–60; Pei Cobb Freed & Partners (formerly I. M. Pei & Partners), 1960–. Sch. of Architecture, Yale University: William Henry Bishop Vis. Prof., 1973, 1978; Charlotte Sheperd Davenport Vis. Prof., 1975; Graduate School of Design, Harvard: Studio Prof. and Chm., Dept of Architecture, 1980–85; Adjunct Prof. of Architecture and Urban Design, 1985–88. Hon. DFA Bowdoin Coll., 1985; Dr Technical Scis *hc*, Swiss Fed. Inst. of Technol., 1990. Topaz Medallion for Excellence in Architectural Educn, Assoc. of Collegiate Schs of Architecture/AIA, 1995. *Publications:* Where I Stand, 1980; Architecture and the University, 1985. *Address:* Pei Cobb Freed & Partners, 88 Pine Street, New York, NY 10005-1801, USA. *T:* (212) 8724020.

COBB, Henry Stephen, CBE 1991; FSA; FRHistS; Clerk of the Records, House of Lords, 1981–91; *b* 17 Nov. 1926; *y s* of Ernest Cobb and Violet Kate Cobb (*née* Sleath), Wallasey; *m* 1969, Eileen Margaret Downer. *Educ:* Birkenhead Sch.; London School of Economics (BA, MA); Liverpool Univ. (Dip. Archive Admin). Archivist, Church Missionary Soc., 1951–53; Asst Archivist, House of Lords, 1953–59, Asst Clerk of the Records, 1959–73, Dep. Clerk, 1973–81. Lecturer in Palaeography, School of Librarianship, North London Polytechnic, 1973–77. Pres., Soc. of Archivists, 1992–96 (Mem. Council, 1970–82; Chm., 1982–84); Mem. Council, British Records Assoc., 1978–81; Chm., London Record Soc., 1984–. Mem. Cttee of Management, Inst. of Historical Research, 1986–90. FSA 1967; FRHistS 1970. *Publications:* (ed) The Local Port Book of Southampton 1439–40, 1961; (ed with D. J. Johnson) Guide to the Parliament and the Glorious Revolution Exhibition, 1988; (ed) The Overseas Trade of London: Exchequer Customs Accounts 1480–1, 1990; contribs to Economic History Rev., Jl of Soc. of Archivists, Archives, etc. *Recreations:* music, historical research. *Address:* 1 Child's Way, Hampstead Garden Suburb, NW11 6XU. *T:* (020) 8458 3688.

COBB, Timothy Humphry, MA; *b* 4 July 1909; *s* of Humphry Henry Cobb and Edith Muriel (*née* Stogdon); *m* 1952, Cecilia Mary Josephine, *d* of W. G. Chapman; two *s* one *d. Educ:* Harrow; Magdalene Coll., Cambridge. Asst Master, Middlesex Sch., Concord, Mass, USA, 1931–32; Bryanston Sch., Blandford, Dorset, 1932–47, Housemaster, Head of Classics, Estate Bursar; Headmaster of King's Coll., Budo, Kampala, Uganda, 1947–58; formerly Sec., Uganda Headmasters' Association; Headmaster, Dover College, 1958–73. *Publication:* Certificate English Language Practice, 1958. *Recreations:* music, railways, producing vegetables. *Address:* Parkgate Farm, Framlingham, Woodbridge, Suffolk IP13 9JH. *T:* (01728) 638672. *Clubs:* MCC; Bluemantles Cricket (Tunbridge Wells and W Kent).

COBBETT, David John, TD 1973; ERD 1962; railway and transportation management consultant; *b* 9 Dec. 1928; *m* 1952, Beatrix Jane Ogilvie Cockburn; three *s. Educ:* Royal Masonic Sch. FCIT, FILT. Gen. Railway admin. and managerial positions, 1949–67; Divl Movements Manager, Liverpool Street, 1967; Divl Manager, Norwich (British Railways Bd), 1968–70; Asst Managing Dir, Freightliners Ltd, 1970–73; Dep. Gen. Manager, British Railways Bd Scottish Region, 1973; Gen. Manager, British Railways Scottish Region, 1974–76; Chm., British Transport Ship Management, Scotland, 1974–76; Gen. Manager, BR Eastern Region, 1976–77; British Railways Board: Export Dir (Special Projects), 1977–78; Dir, Strategic Studies, 1978–83; Dir, Information Systems and Technology, 1983–85. Dir, Transmark, 1978. Mem. Bd, Railway Benevolent Instn, 1974–99 (Dep. Chm., 1981–84; Chm., 1984–98; Vice Pres., 2000–). Bt Col, Royal Corps of Transport (RARO), 1974. *Recreations:* military matters, historical reading, games. *Address:* Ballytruim, Newtonmore, Inverness-shire PH20 1DS. *T:* and *Fax:* (01540) 673269. *Clubs:* Army and Navy, MCC.

COBBOLD; *see* Lytton Cobbold, family name of Baron Cobbold.

COBBOLD, 2nd Baron *cr* 1960, of Knebworth; **David Antony Fromanteel Lytton Cobbold;** DL; Chairman and Managing Director, Lytton Enterprises Ltd, Knebworth House, since 1971; *b* 14 July 1937; *s* of 1st Baron Cobbold, KG, GCVO, PC, and of Lady Hermione Bulwer-Lytton, *er d* of 2nd Earl of Lytton, KG, GCSI, GCIE, PC; assumed by deed poll, 1960, additional surname of Lytton; *S* father, 1987; *m* 1961, Christine Elizabeth, 3rd *d* of Major Sir Dennis Frederic Bankes Stucley, 5th Bt; three *s* one *d. Educ:* Eton College; Trinity Coll., Cambridge (BA Hons Moral Sciences). Fellow, Assoc. of Corporate Treasurers. PO, RAF, 1955–57. NATO Flying Training Scheme, Canada 1956–57. Morgan Guaranty Trust Co., New York, 1961–62; Bank of London and South America Ltd, London, Zürich, Barcelona, 1962–72; Treasurer, Finance for Industry Ltd, 1974–79; Manager Treasury Div., BP Finance International, The British Petroleum Co. plc, 1979–87; Gen. Manager Financial Markets, TSB England & Wales plc, 1987–88; Dir, Hill Samuel Bank Ltd, and Head of TSB-Hill Samuel Treasury Div., 1988–89; Man. Dir, Gaiacorp Currency Managers, 1991–94 (Dir, 1989–94); Director: Close Brothers Gp plc, 1993–2000. Stevenage Leisure Ltd, 1999–. Mem., Assoc. for Monetary Union in Europe, 1992–. Pres., Develt Cttee, 1991–, Mem., Bd of Govs, 1993–, Univ. of Hertfordshire (formerly Hatfield Poly.). Mem., Finance and Policy Cttee, HHA, 1973–97 (Hon. Treas., 1988–97); Gov., Union of European HHAs, 1993–97. Chm., Stevenage Community

Trust, 1990–; Trustee, Pilgrim Trust, 1993–; Director: Shuttleworth Trust, 1998–; English Sinfonia Orch. Ltd, 1998–. Elected Mem., H of L, 2000–, crossbencher. Contested (L): Bishop Auckland, Oct. 1974; Hertfordshire, European Parly Election, 1979. DL Herts, 1993. *Recreation:* travel. *Heir:* s Hon. Henry Fromanteel Lytton Cobbold [*b* 12 May 1962; *m* 1987, Martha Frances, *d* of James Buford Boone, Jr; one *s* one *d*]. *Address:* Park Gate House, Knebworth, Herts SG3 6QD. *T:* (01438) 812261, *Fax:* (01438) 811908.

COBBOLD, Rear-Adm. Richard Francis, CB 1994; Director, Royal United Services Institute for Defence Studies, since 1994; *b* 25 June 1942; *s* of Geoffrey Francis and Elizabeth Mary Cobbold; *m* 1975, Anne Marika Hjörne (marr. diss. 1994); one *s* one d. Educ.: Bryanston Sch.; BRNC Dartmouth. Early service, RN: HMS Kent; Staff of FO Naval Flying Training; HMS Juno; HMS Hermes; loan to RAN; RN Staff College 1973; Arctic Flight in comd, 1973–74; 820 Sqdn, Sen. Observer, 1974–75; MoD, 1975–77; HMS Mohawk in comd, 1977–79; MoD, 1979–83; RCDS 1984; HMS Brazen in comd, 1985–86; Dir of Defence Concepts, MoD, 1987–88; Captain 2nd Frigate Sqdn, 1989–90; ACDS Op. Requirements (Sea), 1991–94, and for Jt Systems, 1992–94. Specialist Advr, H of C Defence Cttee, 1997–. FRAeS 1994. Governor, London Nautical Sch., 1997–. *Recreations:* ski-ing, running marathons, gardening, naval and military history. *Address:* Royal United Services Institute for Defence Studies, Whitehall, SW1A 2ET. *Club:* Naval and Military.

COBHAM, 11th Viscount *cr* 1718; **John William Leonard Lyttelton;** Bt 1618; Baron Cobham 1718; Lord Lyttelton, Baron of Frankley 1756 (renewed 1794); Baron Westcote (Ire.) 1776; DL; *b* 5 June 1943; *e s* of 10th Viscount Cobham, KG, PC, GCMG, GCVO, TD, and Elizabeth Alison Viscountess Cobham (*d* 1986), *d* of J. R. Makeig-Jones, CBE; *S* father, 1977; *m* 1974, Penelope Ann (*see* Penelope, Viscountess Cobham) (marr. diss. 1995); *m* 1997, Dr Lisa Clayton. *Educ:* Eton; Christ's College, New Zealand; Royal Agricultural College, Cirencester. DL West Midlands, 2000. *Recreations:* cricket, shooting. *Heir: b* Hon. Christopher Charles Lyttelton [*b* 23 Oct. 1947; *m* 1973, Tessa Mary, *d* of late Col A. G. J. Readman, DSO; one *s* one *d*]. *Address:* Hagley Hall, near Stourbridge, West Midlands DY9 9LG. *T:* (01562) 885823. *Club:* MCC.

COBHAM, Penelope, Viscountess; Penelope Ann Lyttelton; Chairman, Civic Trust, since 1999; *b* 2 Jan. 1954; *d* of late Roy Cooper and of Dorothy Henshall (now Mrs John Turner); *m* 1974, 11th Viscount Cobham, *qv* (marr. diss. 1995). *Educ:* St James's Sch., Malvern. Chm., British Casino Assoc., 1999–. Comr, Museums and Galls Commn, 1993–2000; Trustee, V&A, 1993– (Chm. V&A Audit Cttee, 1999–); Member: LDDC, 1993–98; Historic Royal Palaces Ministerial Adv. Bd, 1990–98; Exec. Council, HHA, 1985–. Vice Pres., Heart of England Tourist Bd, 1997– (Vice-Chm., 1985–90; Pres., 1990). Co. Dir and Consultant incl. Chm., Heart of England Radio Ltd, subseq. Chrysalis Radio Midlands, 1993–. Guardian, Birmingham Assay Office, 1990–. Pres., governor and patron, numerous civic, charitable and educnl bodies. Freeman: City of London; Goldsmiths' Co. DL West Midlands, 1994–95. FRSA. *Address:* 20 Kylestrome House, Cundy Street, SW1W 9JT; (office) Canal House, 42 Gas Street, Birmingham B1 2JT. *T:* (0121) 633 4149. *Club:* Birmingham Press (Pres.).

COBHAM, Sir Michael (John), Kt 1995; CBE 1981; FRAeS; CIMgt; Life President, Cobham plc (formerly Flight Refuelling (Holdings) Ltd, subseq. FR Group plc), (Chief Executive, 1969–92; Chairman, 1969–95); *b* 22 Feb. 1927; *s* of Sir Alan John Cobham, KBE, AFC, and Lady (Gladys) Cobham; *m* 1st, 1954, June Oakes (marr. diss. 1972); 2nd, 1973, Nadine Felicity, *e d* of William Abbott, Wimborne, Dorset; one *d*. *Educ:* Malvern; Trinity Coll., Cambridge (BA 1949, MA 1965). Served RN, 1945–47. Called to the Bar, Inner Temple, 1952; practised, 1952–55. Flight Refuelling Ltd: Dir, 1952; Man. Dir, 1964–77. Pres., 1976–77, Treasurer, 1980–84, SBAC; Mem. Council, Inst. of Dirs, 1976–97. Life Vice-Pres., Air League, 1992 (Chm., 1990–92); Trustee, Fleet Air Arm Museum, 1987–. Hon. DEng Bournemouth, 1994. *Recreations:* ski-ing, sailing. *Address:* The Manor House, Martin, near Fordingbridge, Hants SP6 3LN. *Clubs:* Naval and Military; Royal Thames Yacht; Royal Southern Yacht (Hamble).

COCHRAN, William, PhD, MA; FRS 1962; Professor of Natural Philosophy, University of Edinburgh, 1975–87, now Emeritus; *b* 30 July 1922; *s* of James Cochran and Margaret Watson Cochran (*née* Baird); *m* 1953, Ingegerd Wall; one *s* two *d*. *Educ:* Boroughmuir Sch., Edinburgh; Edinburgh Univ. Asst Lectr, Edinburgh Univ., 1943–46; Demonstrator and Lectr, Univ. of Cambridge, 1948–62; Reader in Physics, Univ. of Cambridge, 1962–64. Fellow of Trinity Hall, Cambridge, 1951–64; University of Edinburgh: Prof. of Physics, 1964–75; Dean, Faculty of Science, 1978–81; Vice-Principal, 1984–87. Research fellowships abroad, 1950–51, 1958–59, 1970. Hon. Fellow, Trinity Hall, Cambridge, 1982. Hon. DSc: Heriot-Watt, 1992; Edinburgh, 1994. Guthrie medallist, Inst. Physics and Phys. Soc., 1966; Hughes medallist, Royal Soc., 1978; Potts medallist, Franklin Inst., 1985. *Publications:* Vol. III of The Crystalline State (with Prof. H. Lipson), 1954, new edn 1966; Dynamics of Atoms in Crystals, 1973; (jtly) 20th Century Physics, 1995. *Recreations:* Scots verse, family history. *Address:* Department of Physics, The University, The King's Buildings, Edinburgh EH9 3JZ; 3 Rustic Cottages, Colinton Road, Edinburgh EH13 0LD.

COCHRANE, family name of **Earl of Dundonald** and **Baron Cochrane of Cults**.

COCHRANE, Lord; Archie Iain Thomas Blair Cochrane; *b* 14 March 1991; *s* and *heir* of Earl of Dundonald, *qv*.

COCHRANE OF CULTS, 4th Baron *cr* 1919; **Ralph Henry Vere Cochrane;** DL; Chairman, Craigtoun Meadows Ltd, since 1972; *b* 20 Sept. 1926; 2nd *s* of 2nd Baron Cochrane of Cults, DSO and Hon. Elin Douglas-Pennant (*d* 1934), *y d* of 2nd Baron Penrhyn; *S* brother, 1990; *m* 1956, Janet Mary Watson, *d* of late William Hunter Watson Cheyne, MB, MRCS, LRCP; two *s*. *Educ:* Eton; King's Coll., Cambridge (MA). Served RE, 1945–47 (Lt). Formerly: Vice-Chm., Cupar-Fife Savings Bank; Dir for Fife, Tayside Savings Bank. Underwriting Mem. of Lloyds, 1965–96. Gen. Comr for Income Tax. Mem., Queen's Body Guard for Scotland (Royal Co. of Archers), 1962–. DL Fife 1976. *Heir: s* Hon. Thomas Hunter Vere Cochrane, LLB, ACII, *b* 7 Sept. 1957. *Address:* Cults, Cupar, Fife KY15 5RD. *Club:* New (Edinburgh).

COCHRANE, (Alexander John) Cameron, MBE 1987; MA; education consultant, since 1996; *b* 19 July 1933; *s* of late Dr Alexander Younger Cochrane and Jenny Johnstone Cochrane; *m* 1958, Rosemary Aline, *d* of late Robert Alexander Ogg and Aline Mary Ogg; one *s* two *d*. *Educ:* The Edinburgh Academy; University Coll., Oxford. National Service in RA, 1952–54. Asst Master, St Edward's Sch., Oxford, 1957–66; Warden, Brathay Hall, Ambleside, Cumbria, 1966–70; Asst Dir of Educn, City of Edinburgh, 1970–74; Headmaster, Arnold Sch., Blackpool, 1974–79; Headmaster, Fettes Coll., Edinburgh, 1979–88; first Principal, Prince Willem-Alexander Coll., Holland, 1988–91; Principal, British Internat. Sch., Cairo, 1992–95. Member: Lancashire CC Educn Cttee, 1976–79; Council, Outward Bound Trust, 1979–88; Scottish Cttee, Duke of Edinburgh's Award, 1981–86; Chairman: Outward Bound Ullswater, 1979–84; Outward Bound Loch Eil, 1984–88; Lothian Fedn of Boys' Clubs, 1981–84. Commandant, XIII Commonwealth Games Village, Edinburgh, 1986. Governor: Aiglon Coll., 1985–94; Pocklington Sch., 1985–. CFM 1988. *Recreations:* games, the countryside, photography, travel, family. *Address:* Gamekeeper's Cottage, Auchtertool, Fife KY2 5XW. *Clubs:* East India, MCC; New (Edinburgh); Vincent's (Oxford).

COCHRANE, Christopher Duncan; QC 1988; *b* 29 Aug. 1938; *s* of Harold Hubert and Joan Cochrane; *m* 1st, 1960, Caroline Beatrice Carey; two *d*; 2nd, 1970, Patricia Joan Godley; 3rd, 1984, Doreen Ann Suffolk; one step *d*. *Educ:* Ampleforth Coll.; Magdalen Coll., Oxford (Schol.; MA). Called to the Bar, Middle Temple, 1965; a Recorder, 1985. *Recreations:* travel, theatre, spectator sport, dining out. *Address:* 2–3 Gray's Inn Square, Gray's Inn, WC1R 5JH. *T:* (020) 7242 4986.

COCHRANE, Sir (Henry) Marc (Sursock), 4th Bt *cr* 1903; *b* 23 Oct. 1946; *s* of Sir Desmond Oriel Alastair George Weston Cochrane, 3rd Bt, and of Yvonne Lady Cochrane (*née* Sursock); *S* father, 1979; *m* 1969, Hala (*née* Es-Said); two *s* one *d*. *Educ:* Eton; Trinity Coll., Dublin (BBS, MA). Director: Hambros Bank Ltd, 1979–85; GT Management PLC, 1986–. Hon. Consul General of Ireland in Beirut, 1979–84. Trustee, Chester Beatty Library and Gall. of Oriental Art, Dublin. *Recreations:* skiing, target shooting, electronics. *Heir: s* Alexander Desmond Cochrane, *b* 7 May 1973. *Address:* Woodbrook, Bray, Co. Wicklow, Ireland. *T:* (1) 2821421; Palais Sursock, PO Box 154, Beirut, Lebanon. *T:* (1) 331607.

COCHRANE, Keith Robertson; Group Chief Executive, Stagecoach Holdings plc, since 2000; *b* 11 Feb. 1965; *m* 1998, Fiona Margaret Armstrong; one *d*. *Educ:* Dunblane High Sch.; Univ. of Glasgow (BAcc 1st Cl. Hons). CA 1989; Audit Manager, Arthur Andersen, 1990–93; Gp Financial Controller and Co. Sec., 1993–96, Gp Financial Dir, 1996–2000, Stagecoach Holdings plc. *Recreations:* golf, music, travel, reading. *Address:* Stagecoach Holdings plc, 10 Dunkeld Road, Perth PH1 5TW. *T:* (01738) 442111.

COCHRANE, Malcolm Ralph; Vice Lord-Lieutenant of Oxfordshire, since 1999; *b* 8 Aug. 1938; *s* of Air Chief Marshal Hon. Sir Ralph Cochrane, GBE, KCB, AFC and Hilda (*née* Wiggin); *m* 1972, Mary Anne Scrope, *d* of Ralph Scrope and Lady Beatrice Scrope, *d* of 6th Earl of Mexborough; one *s* two *d*. *Educ:* Eton Coll.; Balliol Coll., Oxford. Nat. Service, Scots Guards, 1957–58. Design Research Unit, 1962–65; Design Panel, BRB, 1965–72; Director: Cochranes of Oxford Ltd, 1972–; Cults Lime Ltd, 1976–. High Sheriff, 1996, DL 1998, Oxon. *Recreations:* arts, gardening, watching sport. *Address:* Grove Farmhouse, Shipton-under-Wychwood, Oxon OX7 6DG. *T:* (01993) 830742.

COCHRANE, Sir Marc; *see* Cochrane, Sir H. M. S.

COCHRANE, Prof. Peter, OBE 1999; PhD, DSc; FREng, FIEE, FIEEE; Co-Founder and Director, ConceptLabs, California, since 2000; consultant to government and international companies; *b* 11 July 1946; *s* of Colin Cochrane and Gladys Cochrane; *m* 1971, Brenda Cheetham; two *s* two *d*. *Educ:* Trent Poly. (BSc Electrical Engrg 1973); Essex Univ. (MSc Telecommunications 1976; PhD Transmission Systems 1979; DSc Systems Design 1991). CGIA 1975; CEng 1977; FIEE 1987 (MIEE 1977); FIEEE 1992 (MIEEE 1983); FREng (FEng 1994). General Post Office: Technician, System Maintenance, 1962–69; Student Engr, 1969–73; Exec. Engr, GPO Res. Labs, 1973–79; BT Laboratories: Head of Gp, 1979–83; Head of Section, 1983–87; Head, Optical Networks Div., 1987–91; Head, Systems Res., 1991–93; Head, Advance Res., 1993–94; Head of Res., 1994–99; Chief Technologist, BT, 1999–2000. Mem. Adv. Bd, Computer Scis Corp. Vanguard Prog., 1996–98. Visiting Professor: CNET, Lannion Univ., France, 1978; NE London Poly., 1980–90; Essex Univ., 1988–; Southampton Univ., 1991–94; Kent Univ., 1991–96; UCL, 1994–. Mem., NY Acad. of Scis, 1995. FRSA. Hon. DTech Stafford, 1996. Holds 14 original patents. *Publications:* (with J. E. Flood) Transmission Systems, 1991; (with D. J. T. Heatley) Modelling Telecommunication Systems, 1995; numerous professional papers and articles in IEE, IEEE, and other jls. *Recreations:* music, running, mathematics, philosophy, my family, playing with my children, reading, skate boarding. *Address:* ConceptLabs, 2550 Ninth Street, Suite 112, Berkeley, CA 94710, USA.

COCHRANE-DYET, Fergus John; HM Diplomatic Service; temporary duty, Conakry and Freetown, since 2001; *b* 16 Jan. 1965; *s* of Lt-Col Iain Cochrane-Dyet and Rosemary Cochrane-Dyet; *m* 1987, Susie Emma Jane Aram; three *s*. *Educ:* Felsted Sch.; Jesus Coll., Oxford; Durham Univ. (BA Hons). Joined HM Diplomatic Service, 1987; FCO, 1987–90 (Arabic lang. trng, 1988–89); Third, later Second Sec. (Political), Lagos, 1990–93; Second Sec. (Political), Abuja, 1993–94; First Secretary: Hd, N Africa Section, FCO, 1994–96; Hd, British Interests Section, Tripoli, 1996–97; (Commercial), Jakarta, 1998; Dir, Trade and Investment Promotion for Australia, and Dep. Consul Gen., Sydney, 1998–2001. *Recreations:* running, scuba diving, British films. *Address:* c/o Foreign and Commonwealth Office, King Charles Street, SW1A 2AH. *Club:* Lansdowne.

COCKAYNE, Prof. David John Hugh, DPhil; FRS 1999; Professor of the Physical Examination of Materials, University of Oxford, since 2000; Fellow, Linacre College, Oxford, since 2000; *b* 19 March 1942; *s* of John Henry Cockayne and Ivy Cockayne; *m* 1967, Jean Mary Kerr; one *s* two *d*. *Educ:* Geelong C of E Grammar Sch., Australia; Trinity Coll., Univ. of Melbourne (BSc 1964; MSc 1966); Magdalen Coll., Oxford (DPhil 1970). Res. Lectr and Jun. Res. Fellow, Christ Church, and Res. Fellow, Dept of Materials, Univ. of Oxford, 1969–74; Dir, Electron Microscope Unit, 1974–2000, Prof. of Physics, 1992–2000, Univ. of Sydney; Dir, Aust. Key Centre for Microscopy and Microanalysis, 1996–2000. Visiting Research Scientist: Atomic Energy of Canada, 1970; Univ. of Calif at Berkeley, 1979; Royal Soc. Anglo-Australasian Vis. Fellow, Univ. of Oxford, 1982; Visiting Professor: Univ. Sci. and Tech. and Academia Sinica, Beijing, 1988; Univ. of Paris, 1993. General Secretary: Cttee, Asia Pacific Socs, Electron Microscopy, 1984–96; Internat. Fedn of Socs for Electron Microscopy, 1995–; Chm., Nat. Cttee, Electron Microscopy, Australian Acad. of Sci., 1986–94. FAIP; FInstP 1999. *Publications:* over 180 scientific articles. *Recreation:* bushwalking. *Address:* Department of Materials, University of Oxford, Parks Road, Oxford OX1 3PH.

COCKBURN, Prof. Forrester, CBE 1996; MD; FRCPGlas; FRSE; Samson Gemmell Professor of Child Health, University of Glasgow, 1977–96, now Emeritus Professor; Chairman, Yorkhill NHS Trust, since 1997; *b* 13 Oct. 1934; *s* of Forrester Cockburn and Violet E. Bunce; *m* 1960, Alison Fisher Grieve; two *s*. *Educ:* Leith Acad.; Univ. of Edinburgh (MD). DCH Glasgow. FRCPE 1971; FRCPGlas 1978; FRSE 1999. Med. trng, Royal Infirmary of Edinburgh, Royal Hosp. for Sick Children, and Simpson Memorial Maternity Pavilion, Edinburgh, 1959–63; Huntingdon Hertford Foundn Res. Fellow, Boston Univ., Mass, 1963–65; Nuffield Sen. Res. Fellow, Univ. of Oxford, 1965–66; Wellcome Trust Sen. Med. Res. Fellow, Univ. of Edin. and Simpson Meml Maternity Pavilion, 1966–71; Sen. Lectr, Dept of Child Life and Health, Univ. of Edin., 1971–77. Chm., Panel on Child Nutrition and Wkg Gp on Weaning Diet, Cttee on Med. Aspects of Food Policy (Report, 1994). Hon. FRCPCH 1996; Hon. FRCSE 2000. James Spence Medal, RCPCH, 1998. *Publications:* Neonatal Medicine, 1974; The Cultured Cell in Inherited Metabolic Disease, 1977; Inborn Errors of Metabolism in Humans, 1980; (with O. P. Gray) Children—A Handbook for Children's Doctors, 1984; (with J. H. Hutchison) Practical Paediatric Problems, 6th edn 1986; (with T. L. Turner and J. Douglas) Craig's Care of the Newly Born Infant, 8th edn 1988; Fetal and Neonatal Growth, 1988; (ed jtly and contrib.) Diseases of the Fetus and Newborn, 1989, 2nd edn 1995; (jtly) Children's Medicine and Surgery, 1996; contrib. Fetal and Neonatal Nutrition. *Recreation:* sailing. *Address:* University Department of Child Health, Royal Hospital for Sick Children, Yorkhill, Glasgow G3 8SJ. *T:* (0141) 201 0000.

COCKBURN, Sir John (Elliot), 12th Bt of that Ilk, *cr* 1671; *b* 7 Dec. 1925; *s* of Lieut-Col Sir John Cockburn, 11th Bt of that Ilk, DSO and Isabel Hunter (*d* 1978), *y d* of late James McQueen, Crofts, Kirkcudbrightshire; *S* father, 1949; *m* 1949, Glory Patricia, *er d* of Nigel Tudway Mullings; three *s* two *d* (of whom one *s* one *d* are twins). *Educ:* RNC Dartmouth; Royal Agricultural Coll., Cirencester. Served War of 1939–45, joined RAFVR, July 1944. *Recreation:* reading. *Heir: s* Charles Christopher Cockburn [*b* 19 Nov. 1950; *m* 1985, Ruth, *d* of Samuel Bell; two *s* one *d* (of whom one *s* one *d* are twins)]. *Address:* 48 Frewin Road, SW18 3LP.

COCKBURN, William, CBE 1989; TD 1980; Group Managing Director, British Telecommunications UK, 1997–2001; *b* 28 Feb. 1943. Entered Post Office, 1961; held various junior and middle management positions; apptd Mem., PO Board, 1981, Mem. for Finance, Counter Services and Planning, 1982–84; Mem. for Royal Mail Operations, 1984–86; Man. Dir, Royal Mail, 1986–92; Chief Executive: The Post Office, 1992–95; W. H. Smith Gp PLC, 1996–97. Chm., Internat. Post Corp., 1994–95; non-executive Director: Lex Service plc, 1993–; Centrica plc, 1997–99. Member: Bd, BITC, 1990–; Council, Industrial Soc., 1992–. Col, RE Postal and Courier Service (V), 1986–91; Hon. Col, RE Postal and Courier Service, 1992–94; Hon. Col Comdt, RLC, 1996–. FCIT; FRSA; CIMgt 1993. Freeman, City of London. *Address:* 9 Avenue Road, Farnborough, Hants GU14 7BW.

COCKBURN-CAMPBELL, Sir Alexander (Thomas), 7th Bt *cr* 1821, of Gartsford, Ross-shire; Building Operations Supervisor, Knight Frank Facilities Managers, Perth, WA, since 2000; *b* 16 March 1945; *o s* of Sir Thomas Cockburn-Campbell, 6th Bt and of Josephine Zoi Cockburn-Campbell (*née* Forward); *S* father, 1999; *m* 1969, Kerry Ann, *e d* of Sgt K. Johnson; one *s* one *d. Educ:* Edwards Business Coll. (Adv. Cert. Mkting/Mgt). Prodn Mgr, 1980–90; Maintenance Manager, Uniting Church Homes, 1995–2000. Protestant Lay Minister, 1980– (Dip. Ministry). *Recreation:* surf-board riding. *Heir: s* Thomas Justin Cockburn-Campbell, *b* 10 Feb. 1974. *Address:* 25 Davidia Lake Drive, Canning Vale, WA 6155, Australia. *T:* (8) 92561861.

COCKCROFT, John Hoyle; Director, International Conflict Resolution, since 1990; writer and political and corporate adviser; various electronics directorships, since 1977; *b* 6 July 1934; *s* of late Lionel Fielden Cockcroft and of Jenny Hoyle; *m* 1971, Tessa Fay Shepley; three *d. Educ:* Primary, Trearddur House; Oundle; St John's Coll., Cambridge (Sen. Maj. Scholar (History), 1953). MA Hons History and Econs 1958; Pres., Cambridge Union, 1958. Royal Artillery, 2nd Lieut, 1953–55. Feature writer, Financial Times, 1959–61; Economist, GKN, 1962–67 (re-acquisitions, 1962–65); seconded to Treasury, Public Enterprises Div. (transport), 1965–66; Econ. Leader-writer, Daily Telegraph, 1967–74. MP (C) Nantwich, Feb. 1974–1979; Mem. Select Cttee on Nationalised Industries (transport), 1975–79; Company Secretaries Bill (Private Member's), 1978. Duff Stoop & Co., stockbrokers (corporate finance), 1978–86; Laurence Prust, stockbrokers (corporate finance), 1986–90; Dir, BR (Eastern Region), 1984–89; Consultant: GKN, 1971–76; Mail Users' Assoc., 1976–79; Inst. of Chartered Secretaries, 1977–79; Cray Electronics, 1982–84; Dowty, 1983–86; Wedgwood, 1983–84; Crystalate, 1983–86; Commed Ltd, 1983–93; Camden Associates, 1984–88; Cambridge Corp. Consultants, 1989–; Raitt Orr, 1992–95; MAP Securities (corporate finance), 1992–95; Heathmere (UK), 1996–. Consultant, NEI History Archives, 1980–85. Member Council: European Movement, 1973–74, 1983–84; Conservative Gp for Europe, 1980–87. Member: RUSI; UNA/European-Atlantic Gp. Mem., Cambridge Union Soc. MInstD. Trustee, Sanderson Trust (Oundle), 1992–. Columnist: Microscope, 1982–85; electronic money transmission, Banking World, 1984–86; Westminster Watch, Electronics Times, 1985–90. *Publications:* (jtly) Reforming the Constitution, 1968; (jtly) Self-Help Reborn, 1969; Why England Sleeps, 1971; (jtly) An Internal History of Guest Keen and Nettlefolds, 1976; Microtechnology in Banking, 1984; Microelectronics (booklet), 1979 and 1982; Leaders, Sunday Telegraph, 1981–86; articles in The European, The Scotsman, Jl of Contemp. British Hist., 1979–. *Recreations:* walking, reading, writing, entertaining. *Address:* 7 Canterbury Way, Chelmsford CM1 2XN. *T:* (01245) 252611.

COCKE, Dr Thomas Hugh, FSA; Chief Executive, National Association of Decorative and Fine Arts Societies, since 2001; Fellow, Darwin College, Cambridge, since 1987; *b* 19 Feb. 1949; *s* of late J. W. G. Cocke, TD, MA and of E. J. Cocke (*née* Ferguson); *m* 1973, Carolyn Marina Clark, *d* of K. W. Clark (MBE 2000); one *s* one *d. Educ:* Marlborough Coll.; Pembroke Coll., Cambridge (MA); Courtauld Inst. (MA, PhD 1982). FSA 1983. Lectr, History of Art Dept, Univ. of Manchester, 1973–76; Investigator, RCHM for England, 1976–90; Mem., Faculty of Architecture and History of Art, Univ. of Cambridge, 1985–; Sec., Council for the Care of Churches, 1990–2001 (Pres., 2001–). Mem., Adv. Bd for Redundant Churches, 1988–90. Extra Mem. Court, Skinners' Co., 1988–91. *Publications:* Churches of South East Wiltshire, 1987; (with P. Kidson) Salisbury Cathedral: perspectives on the architectural history, 1993; Nine Hundred Years: the restorations of Westminster Abbey, 1995; contribs to British and European learned jls and exhibn catalogues. *Recreations:* gardening, topography, Italian travel. *Address:* NADFAS House, 8 Guilford Street, WC1N 1DT.

COCKELL, Michael Henry; a Deputy Chairman of Lloyd's, 1986; *b* 30 Aug. 1933; *s* of Charles and Elise Seaton; *m* 1961, Elizabeth Janet Meikle; one *s* three *d. Educ:* Harrow School. Underwriter for G. N. Rouse Syndicate 570, 1968–90; Chm., M. H. Cockell & Co., 1978; Senior Partner, M. H. Cockell & Partners, 1986; Chm., Atrium Cockell Underwriting Ltd, 1997–; Dir, Medway plc, 1997–. Dep. Chm., Lloyd's Non-Marine Assoc., 1982, Chm., 1983–; Mem. Council, Lloyd's, 1984–87, 1990–93 and 1995–96. *Recreations:* all sport (especially cricket), ornithology, music (not loud pop), gardening, countryside. *Address:* Court Horeham, Cowbeech, Herstmonceaux, E Sussex BN27 4JN. *T:* (01323) 833171. *Clubs:* City of London, MCC; IZ.

COCKER, Victor, CBE 2000; Group Chief Executive, Severn Trent plc (formerly Chief Executive, Severn Trent Water), 1995–2000; *b* 30 Oct. 1940; *s* of Harold Nathan Cocker and Marjorie Cocker; *m* 1963, Jennifer Nicholls; two *d. Educ:* King Edward VII Sch., Sheffield; Nottingham Univ. (BA Econ Hons). NW Gas Board, 1962–68; West Midlands Gas, 1968–74; Severn Trent Water Authy, 1974–89; Man. Dir, Severn Trent Water Ltd, 1991–95. Non-executive Director: Aquafin NV, 1993–2000; Railtrack, 1999–; AGA Foodservice Gp (formerly Glynwed Internat.), 2000–. Chm., Waste and Resources Action Prog., 2000–. Water Aid: Trustee, 1996–; Vice Chm., 1998–2001; Chm., 2001–; Chm., Severn Trent Region, 1997–2000. Dir, Midlands Excellence, 1996–2000. Member: Adv. Cttee on Business in Environment, 1996–; World Business Council for Sustainable Develt, 1997–2000. Chm., Forward Birmingham RNLI Lifeboat Campaign, 1994–96; Mem., RNLI Cttee of Management, 1996–. *Recreations:* hill walking, National Hunt, cinema, music. *Address:* Tredington Manor, Tredington, Shipston on Stour CV36 4NJ. *T:* (01608) 663779.

COCKERAM, Eric (Paul); JP; *b* 4 July 1924; *er s* of Mr and Mrs J. W. Cockeram; *m* 1949, Frances Irving; two *s* two *d. Educ:* The Leys Sch., Cambridge. Served War, 1942–46: Captain The Gloucestershire Regt; "D Day" landings (wounded and later discharged). MP (C): Bebington, 1970–Feb. 1974; Ludlow, 1979–87. PPS: to Minister for Industry, 1970–72; to Minister for Posts and Telecommunications, 1972; to Chancellor of Exchequer, 1972–74. Mem., Select Cttee on Corporation Tax, 1971, on Industry and Trade, 1979–87; Mem., Public Accounts Cttee, 1983–87. Pres., Menswear Assoc. of Britain, 1964–65. Mem., Bd of Governors, United Liverpool Hosps, 1965–74; Chm., Liverpool NHS Exec. Council, 1970. Chairman: Watson Prickard Ltd, 1966–2001; Johnson Fry (Northern) Ltd, 1988–94; Director: TSB (NW), 1968–83; TSB (Wales & Border Counties), 1983–88; Liverpool Building Soc., 1975–82 (Vice-Chm., 1981–82); Midshires Building Soc., 1982–88; Muller Group (UK) Ltd, 1983–94. Member of Lloyd's. Liveryman, Worshipful Co. of Glovers, 1969–, Mem. Court, 1979–. Freeman: City of London; City of Springfield, Ill. JP, City of Liverpool, 1960. *Recreations:* bridge, golf, shooting, country walking. *Address:* Fairway Lodge, Caldy, Wirral, Cheshire CH48 1NB. *T:* (0151) 625 1100. *Clubs:* Carlton, Army and Navy.

COCKERELL, Michael Roger Lewis; political documentary maker; author; *b* 26 Aug. 1940; *s* of Prof. Hugh Cockerell and Fanny Cockerell (*née* Jochelman); *m* 1st, 1970, Anne Faber (marr. diss. 1980); one *s* one *d*; 2nd, 1984, Bridget Heathcoat-Amory (marr. diss. 1990); two *d*; partner, Anna Lloyd; three *d. Educ:* Kilburn Grammar Sch.; Heidelberg Univ.; Corpus Christi Coll., Oxford (MA PPE). Magazine journalist, 1962–66; Producer, BBC African Service, 1966–68; Current Affairs, BBC TV, 1968–87: Producer, 24 Hours, 1968–72; reporter: Midweek, 1972–75; Panorama, 1975–87; freelance TV reporter and documentary maker, 1987–: *programmes* include: investigations into political lobbying, the Honours system and the Whips; How to Be series; profiles of Alan Clark, James Callaghan, Edward Heath, Enoch Powell, Barbara Castle, Roy Jenkins, Betty Boothroyd, The Rivals (Gordon Brown and Michael Portillo); Tony Blair's Thousand Days, 2000; News from Number Ten: Alastair Campbell and the media, 2000. Vis. Lectr, LSE, 1998–2000. Huw Wheldon Lect., BBC2, 2001. Consultant, New DNB, 2000–. Emmy Award, 1980; Best Documentary Award, RTS, 1982; Golden Nymph Award, Monte Carlo, 1988. *Publications:* (jtly) Sources Close to the Prime Minister, 1984; Live from Number Ten: the inside story of Prime Ministers and TV, 1988; (contrib.) The Blair Effect, 2001. *Recreations:* cricket, tennis, merry-making. *Address:* 27 Arundel Gardens, W11 2LW. *T:* (020) 7727 8035; (office) (020) 7973 6117. *Clubs:* MCC (playing mem.), Lord's Taverners, Bushmen.

COCKERHAM, David, CBE 1995; HM Diplomatic Service, retired; International Director, Invest.UK (formerly Invest in Britain Bureau), 1999–2001; *b* 14 May 1944; *s* of late Henry Cockerham and Eleanor Cockerham (*née* Nicholls); *m* 1967, Ann Lesley Smith; two *s. Educ:* Leeds Central High Sch. Joined FO, 1962; Saigon, 1967–68; Japanese studies, Tokyo, 1969–71; Vice-Consul: Yokohama, 1971–72; Tokyo, 1972–75; FCO, 1975–79; Vice-Consul (Commercial Inf.), British Inf. Services, NY, 1979–81; Consul (Commercial) and Exec. Asst to Dir-Gen. of Trade Devclt, USA, British Trade Devclt Office, NY, 1981–83; First Sec. (Commercial), Tokyo, 1983–87; Hd, Exports to Japan Unit, DTI, 1987–90 (on secondment); Dir of Ops, Migration and Visa Dept, FCO, 1990–91; Dep. High Comr, Madras, 1991–94; Consul-Gen. and Dir of Trade Promotion, Osaka, 1994–98. *Recreations:* golf, jazz clarinet, clocks, cooking.

COCKERILL, Geoffrey Fairfax, CB 1980; Secretary, University Grants Committee, 1978–82; *b* 14 May 1922; *e s* of late Walter B. Cockerill and Mary W. Cockerill (*née* Buffery); *m* 1959, Janet Agnes Walters, JP, MA, *d* of late Archibald J. Walters, MBE, and Elsie Walters; two *s. Educ:* Humberstone Foundation Sch.; UC Nottingham. BA London 1947. Royal Artillery, 1941–45 (Captain). Min. of Labour, 1947; Min. of Educn, 1952; Private Sec. to last Minister of Educn and Secs of State for Educn and Science, 1963–65; Asst Sec., 1964; Sec., Public Schools Commn, 1966–68; Jt Sec., Schools Council for Curriculum and Examinations, 1970–72; Under-Sec., DES, 1972–77; Dep. Sec., 1978. Chairman: Anglo-Amer. Primary Educ. Project, 1970–72; Working Party on Nutritional Aspects of School Meals, 1973–75; Kingston-upon-Thames CAB, 1985–88; Member: Adv. Gp on London Health Services, 1980–81; RCN Commn on Nursing Educn, 1984–85; RCN Strategy Gp, 1985–87; UGC, Univ. of S Pacific, 1984–87; Vice-Pres., Experiment in Internat. Living, 1989–98. Reviewed for Government: Central Bureau for Educational Visits and Exchanges, 1982; Youth Exchanges, 1983; Nat. Youth Bureau, 1983; Consultant to Cttee of Vice-Chancellors and Principals, 1984–85. Hon. Senior Research Fellow, KCL, 1982–86. *Recreations:* gardening, photography. *Address:* 29 Lovelace Road, Surbiton, Surrey KT6 6NS. *T:* (020) 8399 0125. *Clubs:* Athenæum, Royal Commonwealth Society.

COCKERTON, Rev. Canon John Clifford Penn; Rector of Wheldrake with Thorganby, 1985–92 (Rector of Wheldrake, 1978–85); Canon of York (Prebend of Dunnington), 1987–92, Canon Emeritus 1992; *b* 27 June 1927; *s* of late William Penn Cockerton and Eleanor Cockerton; *m* 1974, Diana Margaret Smith (*d* 1987), *d* of Mr and Mrs W. Smith, Upper Poppleton, York. *Educ:* Wirral Grammar Sch.; Univ. of Liverpool; St Catherine's Society, Oxford; Wycliffe Hall, Oxford. Asst Master, Prenton Secondary Sch., 1949–51; Deacon 1954; Priest 1955; Asst Curate, St Helens Parish Church, 1954–58; Tutor 1958–60, Chaplain 1960–63, Cranmer Hall, Durham; Vice-Principal, St John's Coll., Durham, 1963–70; Principal, St John's College and Cranmer Hall, Durham, 1970–78. Examining Chaplain to Bishop of Durham, 1971–73; Proctor in Convocation, 1980–85. *Recreation:* music. *Address:* 42 Lucombe Way, Hartrigg Oaks, New Earswick, York YO32 4DS. *T:* (01904) 765505.

COCKETT, Frank Bernard, MS, FRCS; Consulting Surgeon to: St Thomas' Hospital; King Edward VII Hospital for Officers, London; *b* Rockhampton, Australia, 22 April 1916; *s* of late Rev. Charles Bernard Cockett, MA, DD; *m* 1945, Felicity Ann (*d* 1958), *d* of Col James Thackeray Fisher, DSO, Frieston, near Grantham, Lincs; one *s* two *d*; *m* 1960, Dorothea Anne Newman (MBE 1999); twin *s. Educ:* Bedford Sch.; St Thomas's Hosp. Med. Sch. BSc (1st Cl. Hons), 1936; MRCS, LRCP 1939; MB, BS (London) 1940; FRCS Eng 1947; MS (London) 1953. Sqdn Ldr (Surgical Specialist) RAFVR, 1942–46; Surgical Registrar, St Thomas' Hosp., 1947–48; Resident Asst Surg., St Thomas' Hosp., 1948–50, Consultant, 1954–81; Senior Lecturer in Surgery, St Thomas's Hosp. Med. Sch., 1950–54; Consultant, King Edward VII Hosp. for Officers, 1974–81. Fellow Assoc. of Surgs of Gt Brit.; Mem. European Soc. of Cardiovascular Surgery; Pres., Vascular Surgical Soc. of GB and Ireland, 1980; Chm., Venous Forum, RSM, 1986–87. *Publications:* The Pathology and Surgery of the Veins of the Lower Limb, 1956, 2nd edn 1976; several contribs to Operative Surgery (ed C. G. Rob and Rodney Smith), 1956; The War Diary of St Thomas' Hospital 1939–1945, 1991; Early Sea Painters, 1995; Peter Monamy, 2000; various papers in medical and surgical journals. *Recreations:* sailing, tennis, squash, gardening, marine paintings. *Address:* 14 Essex Villas, Kensington, W8 7BN. *T:* (020) 7937

9883. *Club:* Royal Lymington Yacht.
See also R. D. Hull.

COCKETT, Geoffrey Howard; consultant; Chief Scientific Officer, Ministry of Defence, and Deputy Director, Royal Armament Research and Development Establishment, 1983–86; *b* 18 March 1926; *s* of late William Cockett and Edith (*née* Dinham); *m* 1951, Elizabeth Bagshaw; two *d. Educ:* King Edward VI Sch., Southampton; Univ. of Southampton (BSc, Hons Maths, and Hons Physics). MRI; FInstP; CPhys. Royal Aircraft Establishment, 1948–52; Armament Research Estabt, Woolwich, 1952–62; RARDE, 1962–68; Supt of Physics Div., Chemical Defence Estabt, 1968–71; RARDE: Supt, Optics and Surveillance Systems Div., 1971–76; Head, Applied Physics Group, 1976–83. Chm., Sci. Recruitment Bds, CS Commn, 1985–94; Consultant, Directorate of Sci. (Land), MoD, 1986–98. (Jtly) Gold Medal, Congrès des Materiaux Résistant à Chaud, Paris, 1951. *Publications:* official reports; scientific and technical papers in various learned jls. *Recreations:* the computer, photography, under gardening. *Address:* Defence Research and Evaluation Agency, Fort Halstead, Sevenoaks, Kent TN14 7BP. *T:* (01959) 514000. *Club:* Civil Service.

COCKFIELD, family name of **Baron Cockfield**.

COCKFIELD, Baron *cr* 1978 (Life Peer), of Dover in the County of Kent; **Francis Arthur Cockfield,** Kt 1973; PC 1982; a Vice-President, Commission of the European Communities, 1985–88; *b* 28 Sept. 1916; 2nd *s* of late Lieut C. F. Cockfield (killed on the Somme in Aug. 1916) and Louisa (*née* James); *m* Aileen Monica Mudie (*d* 1992), choreographer. *Educ:* Dover Grammar Sch.; London Sch. of Economics (LLB, BSc (Econ.)). Called to Bar, Inner Temple, 1942. Home Civil Service, Inland Revenue, 1938; Asst Sec. to Board of Inland Revenue, 1945; Commissioner of Inland Revenue, 1951–52; Dir of Statistics and Intelligence to Board of Inland Revenue, 1945–52; Boots Pure Drug Co. Ltd: Finance Dir, 1953–61; Man. Dir, and Chm. Exec. Management Cttee, 1961–67. Chm., Price Commn, 1973–77. Minister of State, HM Treasury, 1979–82; Sec. of State for Trade and Pres., BoT, 1982–83; Chancellor of the Duchy of Lancaster, 1983–84. Mem., NEDC, 1962–64, 1982–83; Advr on Taxation Policy to Chancellor of Exchequer, 1970–73. Mem., Court of Governors, Univ. of Nottingham, 1963–67. Pres., Royal Statistical Soc., 1968–69. Hon. Fellow, LSE, 1972. Hon. LLD Fordham Univ., NY, 1989; Sheffield, 1990; DUniv Surrey, 1989. Grand Cross, Order of Leopold II, Belgium, 1990. *Publication:* The European Union: creating the single market, 1994. *Address:* House of Lords, SW1A 0PW.

COCKING, Prof. Edward Charles Daniel, FRS 1983; Professor of Botany, University of Nottingham, 1969–97, now Professor Emeritus; *b* 26 Sept. 1931; *y s* of late Charles Cocking and Mary (*née* Murray); *m* 1960, Bernadette Keane; one *s* one *d. Educ:* Buckhurst Hill County High Sch., Essex; Univ. of Bristol (BSc, PhD, DSc). FIBiol. Civil Service Commission Research Fellow, 1956–59; Nottingham University: Lectr in Plant Physiology, 1959–66; Reader, 1966–69; Head of Dept of Botany, 1969. Leverhulme Trust Res. Fellow, 1995–97. S. Yoshida Meml Lecture, Hangzhou Univ., China, 1987. Member: Lawes Agricl Trust Cttee, Rothamsted Experimental Stn, 1987–91 (Mem., Governing Body, 1991–; Chm., 1999–); Adv. Cttee on Forest Res., Forestry Commn, 1987–95; Council, Royal Soc., 1986–88; AFRC, 1990–94 (Royal Soc. Assessor, 1988–90). Mem., Bd of Trustees, Royal Botanic Gardens, Kew, 1983–93; Member, Governing Body: Glasshouse Crops Res. Inst., 1983–87; British Soc. Horticultural Res., 1987–89. Pres., Sect. K, BAAS, 1983. Royal Soc. Trustee, Uppingham Sch., 1997–. MAE 1993. Hon. Mem., Hungarian Acad. Scis, 1995; Fellow, Indian Acad. of Agricl Scis, 2000. *Publications:* Introduction to the Principles of Plant Physiology (with W. Stiles, FRS), 3rd edn 1969; numerous scientific papers in botanical/genetics jls on plant genetic manipulations and nitrogen fixation. *Recreations:* walking, travelling, especially by train, occasional chess. *Address:* Centre for Crop Nitrogen Fixation, Plant Science Division, School of Biological Sciences, University of Nottingham, University Park, Nottingham NG7 2RD. *T:* (0115) 951 3056, *Fax:* (0115) 951 3240; 30 Patterdale Road, Woodthorpe, Nottingham NG5 4LQ. *T:* (0115) 926 2452.

COCKRILL, Maurice, RA 1999; artist; *b* Hartlepool, 8 Oct. 1935; *s* of William and Edith Cockrill; *m* 1st, 1957, Pauline Hinds (marr. diss. 1963); one *s*; 2nd, 1963, Elizabeth Ashworth (marr. diss. 1968); one *s*; partner 1974, Helen Moslin; one *s. Educ:* Wrexham Sch. of Art (NDD 1960); Univ. of Reading (ATD 1964). Numerous exhibns in UK, Paris, Düsseldorf, Frankfurt, Stavelot, NY, Sydney 1960–, including: Edward Totah Gall., London, annually 1982–86; Kunstmus., Düsseldorf, 1985; Bernard Jacobson Gall., annually 1986–96; Retrospectives, Walker Art Gall., Liverpool, 1994; RWA, 1998; work in many collections, including: BM; Arts Council; Contemporary Arts Soc.; Walker Art Gall.; Kunstmus., Düsseldorf; Deutsche Bank; Unilever; RA. *Publications:* various exhibn catalogues and bibliography. *Recreations:* walking esp. in Snowdonia (where has a small studio), reading esp. modern poetry, contemporary classical music, jazz, nature. *Address:* 78B Park Hall Road, SE21 8BW. *Club:* Chelsea Arts.

COCKROFT, Peter John; His Honour Judge Cockroft; a Circuit Judge, since 1993; *b* 24 Sept. 1947; *s* of Walter Philip Barron Cockroft and Nora (*née* Collett); *m* 1975, Maria Eugenia Coromina Perandones; one *s* two *d. Educ:* Queen Elizabeth I Grammar Sch., Darlington; Queens' Coll., Cambridge (BA, LLB). Called to the Bar, Middle Temple, 1970 (Astbury Scholar); practised NE Circuit; Asst Recorder, 1985–89; Recorder, 1989–93. *Recreations:* visiting Spain, gardening. *Address:* Brackenwell Cottage, North Rigton, N Yorks LS17 0DG. *T:* (01423) 734585. *Clubs:* Yorkshire County Cricket; Yorkshire Rugby Football Union.

COCKS, family name of **Baron Somers**.

COCKS, Anna Gwenllian S.; *see* Somers Cocks.

COCKS, Freda Mary, CBE 1999 (OBE 1972); JP; Deputy Leader, Birmingham City Council, 1982–86; *b* 30 July 1915; *d* of Frank and Mary Wood; *m* 1942, Donald Francis Melvin, *s* of Melvin J. Cocks; one *d* (and one *d* decd). *Educ:* St Peter's Sch., Harborne; Queen's Coll., Birmingham. Birmingham Council, 1953–78: Alderman, 1965–74; Lord Mayor of Birmingham, 1977–78; Dep. Chm., Housing Cttee, 1968–70, Chm. 1970–72. Founder Sec., Birmingham Sanatoria League of Friends, 1950–68; Founder and Chm., Birm. Hosps Broadcasting Assoc., 1952–78; Member: Little Bromwich Hosp. Management Cttee, 1953–68; West Birmingham Health Authority, 1981–92; Vice-Pres. and Mem., Nat. Careers Assoc., 1985–. Conservative Women's Central Council: Chm., 1968–71; Chm., Gen. Purposes Cttee, 1978; service on housing, finance, policies, and land cttees; Vice Pres., Edgbaston Conservative Assoc., 1992– (Pres., 1980–92). Member: Focus Housing Assoc.; Civic Housing Assoc.; Birmingham Blind Action Forum; Council Mem., Birmingham Rathbone Soc. (Patron, 1998). Pres., Missions to Seamen, Birmingham, 1981–. Patron, Pulse Trust, 1997–. JP Birmingham, 1968. Hon. Freeman: City of Birmingham, 1986; Du-Panne, Belgium, 1978. *Recreations:* hospitals and housing. *Address:* 49 Timber Mill Court, Serpentine Road, Harborne, Birmingham B17 9RD. *T:* (0121) 427 9123.

COCKS, Dr Leonard Robert Morrison, (Dr Robin Cocks), OBE 1999; TD 1979; Keeper of Palaeontology, Natural History Museum (formerly British Museum (Natural History)), 1986–98; *b* 17 June 1938; *s* of late Ralph Morrison Cocks and of Lucille Mary Cocks (*née* Blackler); *m* 1963, Elaine Margaret Sturdy; one *s* two *d. Educ:* Felsted School; Hertford College, Oxford (BA, MA, DPhil, DSc). FGS; CGeol. Commissioned Royal Artillery 1958; active service Malaya, 1958–59; DSIR Research Student, Oxford Univ., 1962–65; British Museum (Nat. Hist.), 1965–; Dep. Keeper of Palaeontology, 1980–86. Geologist, Royal Engineers, 1970–83. Pres., Palaeontographical Soc., 1994–98; Member: Council, Palaeontological Assoc., 1969–82, 1986–88 (Editor, 1971–82, Pres., 1986–88); Council, Geological Soc., 1982–89, 1997–2000 (Sec., 1985–89; Pres., 1998–2000; Coke Medal, 1995); NERC Geological Res. Grants Cttee, 1978–81, 1984. Comr, Internat. Commn on Zoological Nomenclature, 1982–2000. Vis. Fellow, Southampton Univ., 1988–95; Vis. Prof., Imperial Coll., London, 1997–. *Publications:* The Evolving Earth, 1979; papers in sci. jls, on Ordovician-Silurian biostratigraphy and brachiopods, esp. from Britain, Canada, Norway, Sweden, China. *Recreations:* country pursuits. *Address:* c/o Department of Palaeontology, Natural History Museum, Cromwell Road, SW7 5BD. *T:* (020) 7942 5140.

COCKS, Robin; *see* Cocks, L. R. M.

COCKSHAW, Sir Alan, Kt 1992; FREng; FICE; FIHT; Chairman: PCS International Ltd, since 1998; English Partnerships (formerly English Partnerships, and Commission for New Towns), since 1998; *b* 14 July 1937; *s* of John and Maud Cockshaw; *m* 1960, Brenda Payne; one *s* three *d. Educ:* Farnworth Grammar Sch.; Leeds Univ. (BSc). FIHT 1968; FICE 1985; FREng (FEng 1986). Chief Executive: Fairclough Civil Engrg, 1978–85; Fairclough Parkinson–Mining, 1982–85; Fairclough Engrg, 1983–84; Gp Chief Exec., 1984–88, Chm., 1988–97, AMEC plc; Chairman: Manchester Millennium Ltd, 1996–; Roxboro Gp, 1997–; British Airways Regl, 2000–; CapitaLand (formerly Pidemco Land) UK Hldgs, 2000–; New East Manchester, 2000–. Non-exec. Dep. Chm., Norweb plc, 1992–95; non-exec. Dir, New Millennium Experience Co., 1997–2000. Chairman: Overseas Projects Bd, DTI, 1992–95; Oil and Gas Projects and Supplies Office, DTI, 1994–97; Mem., BOTB, 1992–95; Dep. Chm., NW Business Leadership Team, 1990–97. Chm., Major Projects Assoc., 1998–. Pres., ICE, 1997–98. Hon. DEng UMIST, 1997; Hon. DSc Salford, 1998. *Recreations:* Rugby (both codes), cricket, walking, gardening. *Address:* 81 Fountain Street, Manchester M2 2EE. *T:* (0161) 228 0558.

COCKSHUT, Gillian Elise, (Mrs A. O. J. Cockshut); *see* Avery, G. E.

COCKSWORTH, Rev. Canon Christopher John, PhD; Principal, Ridley Hall Theological College, Cambridge, since 2001; *b* 12 Jan. 1959; *s* of Stanley John Cocksworth and Auriol Gwyneth Cocksworth; *m* 1979, Charlotte Mary Pytches; five *s. Educ:* Manchester Univ. (BA (1st cl. Hons) Theol., 1980; PhD 1989); Didsbury Sch. of Educn (PGCE 1981); St John's Theol Coll., Nottingham. Teacher and House Tutor, King Edward's Sch., Witley, Surrey, 1981–84; doctoral res. student, 1986–88. Ordained deacon, 1988, priest, 1989; Asst Curate, Christ Church, Epsom, 1988–92; Chaplain, RHBNC, Univ. of London, 1992–97; Dir, STETS, 1997–2001. Hon. Canon, Guildford Cathedral, 2000–01, now Canon Emeritus. Mem., C of E Liturgical Commn, 1996–. *Publications:* Evangelical Eucharistic Thought in the Church of England, 1993; (with Paul Roberts) Renewing Daily Prayer, 1993; (with Alan Wilkinson) An Anglican Companion, 1996, 2nd edn 2001; Holy, Holy, Holy: worshipping the Trinitarian God, 1997; Prayer and the Departed, 1997; (with Jeremy Fletcher) The Spirit and Liturgy, 1998; various articles in bks and learned jls. *Recreations:* hill-walking, cycling, swimming, film watching. *Address:* The Principal's Lodge, Ridley Hall, Cambridge CB3 9HG. *T:* (01223) 741060.

CODD, Michael Henry, AC 1991; Chancellor, University of Wollongong, since 1997; *b* 26 Dec. 1939; *s* of Ernest Applebee Codd and Nell Gregory (*née* Pavy). *Educ:* Univ. of Adelaide (BEc Hons). Statistician, 1962–69; joined Dept of Prime Minister, Australia, 1969; Under-Sec., Dept of Prime Minister and Cabinet, 1979–81; Sec., Dept of Employment and Ind. Relns, 1981–83; Chm., Industries Assistance Commn, 1983–85; Sec., Dept of Community Services, 1985–86; Head, Dept of Prime Minister and Cabinet and Sec. to Cabinet, 1986–91. Director: Toogoolawa Consulting Pty Ltd, 1993–; Menzies Foundn, 1993–; non-executive Director: Qantas, 1992–; MLC, 1996–; Australian Nuclear Science and Technol. Orgn, 1996–; CitiPower, 1999–. *Address:* RMB 35A Monaro Highway, Williamsdale, NSW 2620, Australia. *T:* (2) 62350160.

CODD, Ronald Geoffrey, CEng; Managing Partner, InterChange Associates, since 1990; *b* 20 Aug. 1932; *s* of Thomas Reuben Codd and Betty Leyster Codd (*née* Sturt); *m* 1960, Christine Ellen Léone Robertson; one *s* two *d. Educ:* Cathedral Sch., Llandaff; The College, Llandovery. FBCS; CEng 1990. Dip. in Company Direction, 1989. Served RAF, Transport Comd, 1952–57. Rolls Royce, Aero-Engine Div., 1957–58; International Computers, 1958–61; Marconi Co., 1961–70; J. Bibby & Sons, Liverpool, 1970–74; Weir Gp, Glasgow, 1974–80; Brooke Bond Gp, 1981–86; Under Sec. and Dir., Information and Risks Management, ECGD, 1986–90. Dir, Randolph Enterprise, 1992–98. Advr to Bd, HM Customs and Excise, 1992–96. Associate, Wentworth Res., 1992–. Mem., ELITE Forum, BCS, 1991–. FInstD. Freeman, City of London, 1990; Liveryman, Co. of Inf. Technologists, 1990. *Publications:* contributor to business magazines. *Recreations:* competitive and leisure sailing, theatre, practical pastimes. *Address:* Chesterton House, Three Gates Lane, Haslemere, Surrey GU27 2LD. *Clubs:* City Livery; Royal Northern and Clyde Yacht.

CODRINGTON, John Ernest Fleetwood, CMG 1968; *b* 1919; *s* of late Stewart Codrington; *m* 1951, Margaret, *d* of late Sir Herbert Hall Hall, KCMG; three *d. Educ:* Haileybury; Trinity Coll., Cambridge. Served RNVR, 1940–42: HMS Enchantress, HMS Vanity; Royal Marines, 1942–46: 42 (RM) Commando; Colonial Administrative Service, 1946: Gold Coast (later Ghana), 1947–58; Nyasaland, 1958–64; Financial Sec., Bahamas, 1964–70; Bahamas Comr in London, 1970–73, acting High Comr, 1973–74; Financial Sec., Bermuda, 1974–77. Consultant, FCO, 1991–94. *Recreation:* sailing. *Address:* 2 Bryn Road, St Davids, Pembs SA62 6SG. *Club:* Army and Navy.

CODRINGTON, Richard John; HM Diplomatic Service; Deputy High Commissioner, Ottawa, since 1999; *b* 18 Dec. 1953; *s* of Capt. Christopher Thomas Codrington, RN and Anna Maria (*née* Hanscomb); *m* 1985, Julia Elizabeth Nolan; two *s. Educ:* Ampleforth; Lincoln Coll., Oxford (BA). MoD, 1975–78; entered HM Diplomatic Service, 1978: FCO, 1978–79; 2nd, later 1st, Sec., Dar es Salaam, 1980–82; FCO, 1983–85; 1st Sec., New Delhi, 1985–88; Asst Hd, S Asian Dept, FCO, 1989–92; on loan to S. G. Warburg & Co. Ltd, 1992–94; on loan, as Hd, Cross-media ownership review team, DNH, 1994; Dir of Trade Promotion and Investment, Paris, 1995–99. *Recreations:* computer games, sightseeing, photography, family history. *Address:* c/o Foreign and Commonwealth Office, SW1A 2AH.

CODRINGTON, Sir Simon (Francis Bethell), 3rd Bt *cr* 1876; *b* 14 Aug. 1923; *s* of Sir Christopher William Gerald Henry Codrington, 2nd Bt, and Joan Mary Hague-Cook (*d* 1961); *S* father, 1979; *m* 1st, 1947, Joanne (marr. diss. 1959), *d* of J. W. Molineaux and *widow* of William Humphrey Austin Thompson; 2nd, 1959, Pamela Joy Halliday Wise (marr. diss. 1979); three *s*; 3rd, 1980, Sarah Gwynne Gaze (*née* Pennell) (marr. diss. 1987); 4th, 1989, Shirley Ann, *d* of Percival Davis. *Educ:* Eton. Late Coldstream Guards. *Heir: s* Christopher George Wayne Codrington [*b* 20 Feb. 1960; *m* 1991, Noelle, *d* of Dale Leverson; one *s* one *d*]. *Address:* Dodington, Chipping Sodbury, Bristol BS37 6SD. *T:* (01454) 312354.

CODRINGTON, Sir William (Alexander), 8th Bt *cr* 1721; FNI; Director, World-Wide Shipping Agency Ltd, 1994–97; Port Captain, Hong Kong, for Worldwide Shipping Agency, 1979–97; *b* 5 July 1934; *e s* of Sir William Richard Codrington, 7th Bt, and Joan Kathleen Birellu, *e d* of Percy E. Nicholas, London, NW; *S* father, 1961. *Educ:* St Andrew Coll., S Africa; S African Naval Coll., General Botha. FNI 1976. Joined Merchant Navy, 1952; joined Union Castle Mail Steamship Co., 1960; Master Mariner's Certificate of Competency, 1961. Joined Worldwide Shipping 1976. Chm., HK Br., Nautical Inst., 1994–97. Mem., Hon. Co. of Master Mariners. *Recreations:* model engineering, sailing. *Heir: b* Giles Peter Codrington [*b* 28 Oct. 1943; *m* 1989, Shirley Linda Duke; two *s* one *d*]. *Address:* 75 Backchurch Lane, E1 1LQ. *Club:* Oriental.

CODRON, Michael Victor, CBE 1989; theatrical producer; *b* 8 June 1930; *s* of I. A. Codron and Lily (*née* Morgenstern). *Educ:* St Paul's Sch.; Worcester Coll., Oxford (MA). Director: Aldwych Theatre; Hampstead Theatre; Theatres Mutual Insurance Co. Cameron Mackintosh Prof. of Contemporary Theatre, Oxford Univ., 1993. Productions include: Share My Lettuce, Breath of Spring, 1957; Dock Brief and What Shall We Tell Caroline?, The Birthday Party, Valmouth, 1958; Pieces of Eight, 1959; The Wrong Side of the Park, The Caretaker, 1960; Three, Stop It Whoever You Are, One Over the Eight, The Tenth Man, Big Soft Nellie, 1961; Two Stars for Comfort, Everything in the Garden, Rattle of a Simple Man, 1962; Next Time I'll sing to You, Private Lives (revival), The Lovers and the Dwarfs, Cockade, 1963; Poor Bitos, The Formation Dancers, Entertaining Mr Sloane, 1964; Loot, The Killing of Sister George, Ride a Cock Horse, 1965; Little Malcolm and his Struggle against the Eunuchs, The Anniversary, There's a Girl in my Soup, Big Bad Mouse, 1966; The Judge, The Flip Side, Wise Child, The Boy Friend (revival), 1967; Not Now Darling, The Real Inspector Hound, 1968; The Contractor, Slag, The Two of Us, The Philanthropist, 1970; The Foursome, Butley, A Voyage Round my Father, The Changing Room, 1971; Veterans, Time and Time Again, Crown Matrimonial, My Fat Friend, 1972; Collaborators, Savages, Habeas Corpus, Absurd Person Singular, 1973; Knuckle, Flowers, Golden Pathway Annual, The Norman Conquests, John Paul George Ringo . . . and Bert, 1974; A Family and A Fortune, Alphabetical Order, A Far Better Husband, Ashes, Absent Friends, Otherwise Engaged, Stripwell, 1975; Funny Peculiar, Treats, Donkey's Years, Confusions, Teeth 'n' Smiles, Yahoo, 1976; Dusa, Stas, Fish & Vi, Just Between Ourselves, Oh, Mr Porter, Breezeblock Park, The Bells of Hell, The Old Country, 1977; The Rear Column, Ten Times Table, The Unvarnished Truth, The Homecoming (revival), Alice's Boys, Night and Day, 1978; Joking Apart, Tishoo, Stage Struck, 1979; Dr Faustus, Make and Break, The Dresser, Taking Steps, Enjoy, 1980; Hinge and Bracket at the Globe, Rowan Atkinson in Revue, House Guest, Quartermaine's Terms, 1981; Season's Greetings, Noises Off, Funny Turns, The Real Thing, 1982; The Hard Shoulder, 1983; Benefactors, 1984; Why Me?, Jumpers, Who Plays Wins, Look, No Hans!, 1985; Made in Bangkok, Woman in Mind, 1986; Three Sisters, A View from the Bridge, 1987; Hapgood, Uncle Vanya, Re: Joyce, The Sneeze, Henceforward, 1988; The Cherry Orchard, 1989; Man of the Moment, Look Look, Hidden Laughter, Private Lives, 1990; What the Butler Saw, 70 Girls 70, The Revengers' Comedies, 1991; The Rise and Fall of Little Voice, 1992; Time of My Life, Jamais Vu, 1993; Kit and the Widow, Dead Funny, Arcadia, The Sisters Rosensweig, 1994; Indian Ink, Dealer's Choice, 1995; The Shakespeare Revue, A Talent to Amuse, 1996; Tom and Clem, Silhouette, Heritage, 1997; Things We Do for Love, Alarms and Excursions, The Invention of Love, 1998; Copenhagen, Comic Potential, 1999; Peggy for You, 2000; *film:* Clockwise, 1986. *Recreation:* collecting Caroline of Brunswick memorabilia. *Address:* Aldwych Theatre Offices, Aldwych, WC2B 4DF. *Club:* Garrick.

COE, family name of **Baron Coe**.

COE, Baron *cr* 2000 (Life Peer), of Ranmore in the co. of Surrey; **Sebastian Newbold Coe,** OBE 1990 (MBE 1982); Private Secretary to Leader of the Conservative Party, 1997–2001 (Deputy Chief of Staff, 1997); *b* 29 Sept. 1956; *s* of Peter and Angela Coe; *m* 1990, Nicola McIrvine; two *s* two *d*. *Educ:* Loughborough University (BSc Hons Economics and Social History). Won gold medal for running 1500m and silver medal for 800m at Moscow Olympics, 1980; gold medal for 1500m and silver medal for 800m at Los Angeles Olympics, 1984; European Champion for 800m, Stuttgart, 1986; set world records at 800m, 1000m and mile, 1981. Research Assistant, Loughborough Univ., 1981–84. Sports Council: Mem., 1983–89; Vice-Chm., 1986–89; Chm., Olympic Review Gp, 1984–85. Member: HEA, 1987–92; Olympic Cttee, Medical Commn, 1987–93; Olympic Cttee, Sport for All Commn, 1997–. Steward, BBBC, 1995–97. Associate Mem., Académie des Sports, France; Mem., Athletes Commn, Internat. Olympic Cttee, Lausanne (first Chm., 1981–92). Chm., Diadora (UK), 1987–94. Sebastian Coe Health Clubs, Jarvis Hotel Group, 1994–. MP (C) Falmouth and Camborne, 1992–97; contested (C) same seat, 1997. PPS to Ministers of State for Defence Procurement and for Armed Forces, MoD, 1994–95, to Dep. Prime Minister, 1995–96; a Govt Whip, 1996–97. Hon. DTech Loughborough, 1985; Hon. DSc Hull, 1988. Principe de Asturias award (Spain), 1987. *Publications:* (with David Miller) Running Free, 1981; (with Peter Coe) Running for Fitness, 1983; (with Nicholas Mason) The Olympians, 1984, 2nd edn 1996. *Recreations:* listening to recorded or preferably live jazz, theatre. *Address:* House of Lords, SW1A 0PW. *Clubs:* East India, Sportsman's.

COE, Albert Henry, (Harry); Chairman, Travelsphere, since 2000; *b* 28 May 1944; *m* Beryl Margaret; two *d*. Supervisor, Coopers & Lybrand, 1967–70; Gp Financial Controller, Aerialite Ltd, 1970–72; Gp Finance Dir, London Scottish Bank, 1972–75; Finance Director: (print and packaging), Smurfit Ltd, 1975–81; Granada TV, 1981–88; Airtours plc: Gp Finance Dir, 1988–96; Dep. Chief Exec., 1996–97; Gp Man. Dir, 1997–99; non-exec. Dir, 1999–2001. *Recreations:* cricket, tennis, golf, ski-ing, stock market, current affairs. *Address:* c/o Airtours plc, Parkway One, Parkway Business Centre, 300 Princess Road, Manchester M14 7QU.

COE, Denis Walter; Founder, 1987 and Executive Chairman, 1987–97, British Youth Opera; *b* 5 June 1929; *s* of James and Lily Coe, Whitley Bay, Northumberland; *m* 1953, Margaret Rae Chambers (marr. diss. 1979); three *s* one *d*; *m* 1979, Diana Rosemary, *d* of Maxwell and Flora Barr. *Educ:* Bede Trng Coll., Durham; London Sch. of Economics. Teacher's Certificate, 1952; BSc (Econ.) 1960; MSc (Econ.) 1966. National Service in RAF, 1947–50; Junior and Secondary Schoolmaster, 1952–59; Dep. Headmaster, Secondary Sch., 1959–61; Lectr in Govt, Manchester Coll. of Commerce, 1961–66. Contested (Lab) Macclesfield, 1964; MP (Lab) Middleton, Prestwich and Whitefield, 1966–70; Parly deleg. to Council of Europe and WEU, 1968–70. Dean of Students, NE London Polytechnic, 1970–74; Asst Dir, Middx Polytechnic, 1974–82; Dir of Cleveland Arts, 1986–89; Founder/Dir., Cleveland Music Fest., 1985–89. Member: Archbishops Cttee, Church and State, 1966–69; Warnock Cttee of Enquiry on Special Educational Needs, 1974–78; Planning Cttee, Arts Council, 1987–90. Vice Pres., NYT, 1989– (Mem., Governing Council, 1968–89); Founder Chm., Nat. Bureau for Handicapped Students, 1975–83. FRSA 1992; Hon. Fellow, South Bank Univ., 1993; Hon. GSM 1993; Hon. FRAM 1998. Hon. PhD Middlesex, 1994. *Recreations:* music, drama, walking.

COE, Harry; *see* Coe, A. H.

COEN, Prof. Enrico Sandro, PhD; FRS 1998; John Innes Professor, School of Biological Sciences, University of East Anglia, since 1999; *b* 29 Sept. 1957; *s* of Ernesto Coen and Dorotea Coen (*née* Cattani); *m* 1984, Lucinda Poliakoff; two *s* one *d*. *Educ:* King's Coll., Cambridge (BA 1979; PhD Genetics 1982). SERC Postdoctoral Fellow, Cambridge, 1982–84; Res. Fellow, St John's Coll., Cambridge, 1982–85; Res. Scientist, John Innes Centre, BBSRC, 1984–99. EMBO Medal, Rome, 1996; Science for Art Prize, LVMH, Moët Hennessy, Paris, 1996; Linnean Medal, 1997. *Publications:* papers in Nature, Cell, Science. *Recreation:* painting. *Address:* Genetics Department, John Innes Centre, Colney Lane, Norwich NR4 7UH. *T:* (01603) 452571.

COEN, Massimo (Aldo), Hon. CBE 1991; Cavaliere al Merito del Lavoro 1982; Grande Ufficiale nell'Ordine al Merito della Repubblica Italiana 1979; Hon. Life President, Italian Chamber of Commerce and Industry for the UK, 1994; President, Etrufin Reserco Ltd, since 1985; *b* Bologna, 29 July 1918; *s* of Cavaliere Ragioniere Terzo Coen and Delia Coen Guetta; *m* 1946, Thelma Doreen Kelley (*d* 1993); one *s* three *d*. *Educ:* Liceo Marco Foscarini, Venice (dipl. 1937); Padua University; London School of Economics. Came to London from Venice because of racial laws, 1939; interned in Isle of Man, June-Dec. 1940; Netherland Shipping & Trading Cttee Ltd, Jan.-April 1941; Italian Section, BBC External Services, 1941–46 (Shift Leader and Senior Announcer Translator); Chairman and Managing Director: Granosa Trading Co. Ltd and subsidiaries (dealing in textiles), 1946–92; Florence (Arts & Crafts) Ltd, 1946–92; Thames Rugs & Tweed Fabrics Ltd, 1959–92; Chm., Britalia Consultants Ltd, 1993–2001. Dir, Business Develt–Italy, Levy Gee Chartered Accountants, 1994–2001; Chief Advr, Internat. Affairs Italy, Simmons & Simmons Solicitors, 1993–2000. Vis. Prof., Dept of Italian, UCL, 1996–. Councillor, 1951–72, Vice-Pres., 1972–78, Pres., 1978–94, Italian Chamber of Commerce for GB; Chm., 1985–99, Life Hon. Chm., 1999, Club di Londra; Mem., Rotary Club, London, 1996–2001. Many radio plays, talks and commentaries during the war years. Acted in Snowbound, 1947, Hotel Sahara, 1951. Hon. LLD Warwick, 1997. Cavaliere 1956, Ufficiale 1968, Commendatore 1972, nell'Ordine al Merito della Repubblica Italiana. *Publications:* Four Lectures, 1996; Another Four Lectures, 1999; contrib. to Italian Studies, Raccordo. *Recreations:* shooting, fishing; formerly golf, competition skiing and fencing. *Address:* 14 Acacia Road, St John's Wood, NW8 6AN. *T:* (020) 7722 2459, *Fax:* (020) 7586 8595.

COEN, Paul; Chief Executive, Surrey County Council, since 1995; *b* 21 Dec. 1953; *s* of Patrick Coen and Anne Coen (*née* O'Neil); *m* 1974, Kate Knox; two *s* two *d*. *Educ:* Manchester Univ. (BA Econ Hons Govt). NCB, later British Coal, 1977–89; Hertfordshire County Council, 1990–95: Dir, Commercial Services, 1990–91; Dir, Business Services, 1991–94; Dep. Chief Exec., 1995. *Recreations:* reading, cycling, walking, cooking. *Address:* Surrey County Council, County Hall, Penrhyn Road, Kingston on-Thames KT1 2DN. *T:* (020) 8541 9008.

COEN, Yvonne Anne, (Mrs John Pini); QC 2000; a Recorder, since 2000; *d* of John and Bernadette Coen; *m* 1991, John Pini; one *s* one *d*. *Educ:* Loreto Coll., St Albans; St Catherine's Coll., Oxford (MA Hons Jurisp.). Called to the Bar, Lincoln's Inn, 1982; criminal practitioner, Midland and Oxford Circuit, 1982–. Mem., Bar Council, 1987–90. *Recreation:* Stamford Shoestring Theatre. *Address:* 7 Bedford Row, WC1R 4BU. *T:* (020) 7242 3555.

COETZEE, Prof. John M.; writer; Distinguished Professor of Literature, University of Cape Town, since 1999; *b* 9 Feb. 1940; one *d* (one *s* decd). *Educ:* Univ. of Cape Town (MA); Univ. of Texas (PhD). FRSL 1988. Assistant Professor of English, State University of New York at Buffalo, 1968–71; Lectr in English, 1972–82, Prof. of Gen. Lit., 1983–98, Univ. of Cape Town. Butler Prof. of English, State Univ. of New York at Buffalo, 1984; Hinkley Prof. of English, Johns Hopkins Univ., 1986, 1989; Visiting Professor of English: Harvard Univ., 1991; Univ. of Texas, 1995; Univ. of Chicago, 1996–99. Hon. Fellow, MLA, 1989. Hon. DLitt: Strathclyde, 1985; SUNY, 1989; Cape Town, 1995; Natal, 1996; Rhodes, 1999. *Publications:* Dusklands, 1974; In the Heart of the Country, 1977 (CNA Literary Award, 1977; filmed as Dust, 1986); Waiting for the Barbarians, 1980 (CNA Literary Award, 1980; James Tait Black Prize, 1980; Geoffrey Faber Award, 1980); Life and Times of Michael K, 1983 (CNA Literary Award, 1983; Booker-McConnell Prize, 1983; Prix Femina Etranger, 1985); Foe, 1986 (Jerusalem Prize, 1987); (ed with André Brink) A Land Apart, 1986; White Writing, 1988; Age of Iron, 1990 (Sunday Express Award, 1990); Doubling the Point, 1992; The Master of Petersburg, 1994 (Irish Times Internat. Fiction Award, 1995); Giving Offence, 1996; Boyhood, 1997; The Lives of Animals, 1999; Disgrace, 1999 (Booker Prize, 1999); essays in Comp. Lit., Jl of Mod. Lit., Linguistics, Mod. Lang. Notes, Pubns of MLA, etc. *Address:* PO Box 92, Rondebosch, 7701, South Africa.

COFFEY, Ann; *see* Coffey, M. A.

COFFEY, Rev. David Roy; General Secretary, Baptist Union of Great Britain, since 1991; *b* 13 Nov. 1941; *s* of Arthur Coffey and Elsie Maud Willis; *m* 1966, Janet Anne Dunbar; one *s* one *d*. *Educ:* Spurgeon's Coll., London (BA). Ordained, 1967; Minister: Whetstone Baptist Church, Leicester, 1967–72; North Cheam Baptist Ch., London, 1972–80; Sen. Minister, Upton Vale Baptist Ch., Torquay, 1980–88; Sec. for Evangelism, BUGB, 1988–91. President: BUGB, 1986–87; European Baptist Fedn, 1997–99; Vice Pres., Baptist World Alliance, 2000–. *Publications:* Build that Bridge – a Study in Conflict and Reconciliation, 1986; Discovering Romans, 2000. *Recreations:* music, walking. *Address:* Baptist House, PO Box 44, 129 Broadway, Didcot, Oxon OX11 8RT. *T:* (01235) 517700.

COFFEY, John Joseph; QC 1996; a Recorder, since 1989; *b* 29 July 1948; *s* of John and Hannah Coffey; *m* 1970, Patricia Anne Long; three *s* (and one *s* decd). *Educ:* Bishop Ward Secondary Modern Sch., Dagenham; Mid-Essex Coll. of Technology (LLB Hons London). Called to the Bar, Middle Temple, 1970; Asst Recorder, 1985. *Recreation:* supporting West Ham United. *Address:* 3 Temple Gardens, Temple, EC4Y 9AU. *T:* (020) 7353 3102.

COFFEY, (Margaret) Ann; MP (Lab) Stockport, since 1992; *b* 31 Aug. 1946; *d* of late John Brown, MBE, and of Marie Brown; *m* 1973 (marr. diss. 1989); one *d*. *Educ:* Poly. of South Bank (BSc); Manchester Univ. (MSc). Trainee Social Worker, Walsall Social Services Dept, 1971–72; Social Worker: Birmingham, 1972–73; Gwynedd, 1973–74; Wolverhampton, 1974–75; Stockport, 1977–82; Cheshire, 1982–88; Team Leader, Fostering, Oldham Social Services Dept, 1988–92. Mem. (Lab) Stockport MBC, 1984–92

(Leader, Labour Group, 1988–92). Contested (Lab) Cheadle, 1987. An Opposition Whip, 1995–96; Opposition spokeswoman on health, 1996–97; PPS to Prime Minister, 1997–98. Mem., Trade and Industry Select Cttee, 1993–95. *Address:* House of Commons, SW1A 0AA.

COFFIN, Cyril Edwin, CBE 1984; Director General, Food Manufacturers' Federation, 1977–84; *b* 29 June 1919; *m* 1947, Joyce Mary Tobitt; one *s* one *d* (and one *d* decd). *Educ:* King's Coll. Sch., Wimbledon; King's Coll., Cambridge. War service, 1939–45, Captain RIASC; jssc 1950. Civil servant, 1946–77; Alternate UK Governor, Internat. Atomic Energy Agency, 1964; Under-Secretary: Min. of Technology, 1966, later DTI; Dept of Prices and Consumer Protection, 1974–77. FRSA 1979. *Publications:* Working with Whitehall, 1987; A Blackmore Vale Family, 1992; articles in various jls. *Recreations:* music, learning languages. *Address:* 54 Cambridge Avenue, New Malden, Surrey KT3 4LE. *T:* (020) 8942 0763.

COFFIN, Rt Rev. Peter Robert; *see* Ottawa, Bishop of.

COGGINS, Prof. John Richard, PhD; FRSE; Professor of Molecular Enzymology, since 1995, Director, and Director of Research, Institute of Biomedical and Life Sciences, since 1998, University of Glasgow; *b* 15 Jan. 1944; *s* of Cecil Rex Coggins and Pamela Mary Coggins (*née* Burnet); *m* 1970, Lesley Frances Watson; one *s* one *d*. *Educ:* Bristol GS; Queen's Coll., Oxford (MA); Univ. of Ottawa (PhD). FRSE 1988. Research Fellow: Brookhaven Nat. Lab., USA, 1970–72; Cambridge Univ., 1972–74; Glasgow University: Lectr, 1974–78; Sen. Lectr, 1978–86; Prof. of Biochemistry, 1986–95; Dir, Grad. Sch. of Biomedical and Life Scis, 1995–97; Hd, Div. of Biochemistry and Molecular Biology, Inst. of Biomed. and Life Scis, 1997–98. Chm., Biochem. and Biophys. Cttee, 1985–88, Mem., Biotechnol. Directorate Management Cttee, 1987–90, SERC; Member: Liby and Inf. Services Cttee, Scotland, 1982–88; Biotechnol. Jt Adv. Bd, 1989–94; Wkg Party on Biotechnol., NEDO, 1990–92; AFRC, 1991–94; Council, Hannah Res. Inst., 1994–; Governing Mem., Caledonian Res. Foundn, 1994–; Advr for Biochem., UFC, 1989–92; Chm., HEFCE RAE Panel for Biochemistry, 1995–96. Chm., Molecular Enzymol. Gp, Biochemical Soc., 1981–85. *Publications:* Multidomain Proteins: structure and evolution, 1986; contribs on enzymes and on plant and microbial biochem. to Biochem. Jl, Jl of Biol Chem., Jl Molecular Biol., etc. *Recreations:* sailing, travel, good food, reading. *Address:* Planning Office, Institute of Biomedical and Life Sciences, West Medical Building, University of Glasgow, Glasgow G12 8QQ. *T:* (0141) 330 3524. *Club:* Clyde Cruising (Glasgow).

COGHILL, Sir Patrick Kendal Farley, 9th Bt *cr* 1778, of Coghill, Yorkshire; *b* 3 Nov. 1960; *o s* of Sir Toby Coghill, 8th Bt; *S* father, 2000. *Heir: cousin* John Kendal Plunket Coghill, OBE [*b* 17 July 1929; *m* 1951, Diana Mary Callen; three *d*].

COGHLAN, Terence Augustine; QC 1993; a Recorder, since 1989; *b* 17 Aug. 1945; *s* of late Austin Frances Coghlan and of Ruby Coghlan (*née* Comrie); *m* 1973, Angela Agatha Westmacott; one *s* two *d*. *Educ:* Downside; Perugia; New Coll., Oxford; Inns of Court. Called to the Bar, Inner Temple, 1968 (Scholar). Pres., Mental Health Review Tribunal, 2000–. Film extra, 1968; Dir, City of London Sinfonia, 1975–. *Publications:* Meningitis, 1998; medico-legal articles. *Recreations:* architecture, wine, windsurfing, cycling, singing in choirs. *Address:* 1 Crown Office Row, Temple, EC4Y 7HH. *T:* (020) 7797 7500. *Clubs:* Omar Khayyam, Les Six.

COGHLIN, Hon. Sir Patrick, Kt 1997; **Hon. Mr Justice Coghlin;** a Judge of the High Court of Justice, Northern Ireland, since 1997; President, Lands Tribunal, Northern Ireland, 1999–March 2002; Deputy Chairman, Boundary Commission, Northern Ireland, 1999–Dec. 2002; *b* 7 Nov. 1945; *s* of late James Edwin Coghlin and Margaret Van Hovenberg Coghlin; *m* 1971, Patricia Ann Elizabeth Young; one *s* three *d*. *Educ:* Royal Belfast Academical Instn; Queen's Univ., Belfast (LLB Hons); Christ's Coll., Cambridge (Dip. Criminology). Called to the Bar: NI, 1970; Gray's Inn, 1975; NSW, 1992; Republic of Ireland, 1995; Jun. Crown Counsel for NI, 1983–85; QC (NI) 1985; Dep. County Court Judge, 1983–94; Sen. Crown Counsel, NI, 1993–97. Vice-Chm., Mental Health Review Tribunal, 1987–97; Mem., Law Reform Adv. Cttee, NI, 1988–93; Vice-Pres., VAT Tribunal, NI, 1990–93. Chm., NI Bar Council, 1991–93. *Recreations:* Rugby, soccer, squash, reading, music, travel. *Address:* Royal Courts of Justice, Belfast, N Ireland BT1 3JY. *Clubs:* Royal Ulster Yacht, Ballyholme Yacht; Bangor Rugby, Perennials Rugby; Ballyholme Bombers FC.

COGMAN, Very Rev. Frederick Walter; Dean of Guernsey, 1967–78; Rector of St Peter Port, Guernsey, 1976–78; *b* 4 March 1913; *s* of William Frederick Cogman and Mabel Cozens; *m* 1940, Rose Hélène Mauger; one *s* one *d*. *Educ:* Rutlish Sch., Merton; King's Coll., London. Asst Priest, Upton-cum-Chalvey, Slough, 1938–42; Chaplain and Housemaster, St George's Sch., Harpenden, 1942–48; Rector of St Martin, Guernsey, 1948–76. *Recreation:* music.

COHAN, Robert Paul, CBE 1989; Founder Artistic Director, Contemporary Dance Trust; *b* 27 March 1925; *s* of Walter and Billie Cohan; British citizen, 1989. *Educ:* Martha Graham Sch., NYC. Joined Martha Graham Co., 1946; Partner, 1950; Co-Dir, Martha Graham Co., 1966; Artistic Dir, Contemporary Dance Trust Ltd, 1967; Artistic Dir and Principal Choreographer, 1969–87, Dir, 1987–89, London Contemporary Dance Theatre; Artistic Advr, Batsheva Co., Israel, 1980; Director: York Univ., Toronto Choreographic Summer Sch., 1977; Gulbenkian Choreographic Summer Sch., Univ. of Surrey, 1978, 1979, 1982; Banff Sch. of Fine Arts Choreographic Seminar, Canada, 1980; New Zealand Choreographic Seminar, 1982; Choreographic Seminar, Simon Frazer Univ., Vancouver, 1985; Internat. Dance Course for Professional Choreographers and Composers, Surrey Univ., 1985, 1989. With London Contemporary Dance Theatre toured Britain, E and W Europe, S America, N Africa and USA; major works created: Cell, 1969 (recorded for BBC TV, 1982); Stages, 1971; Waterless Method of Swimming Instruction, 1974 (recorded for BBC TV); Class, 1975; Stabat Mater, 1975 (recorded for BBC TV); Masque of Separation, 1975; Khamsin, 1976; Nympheas, 1976 (recorded for BBC TV, 1983); Forest, 1977 (recorded by BBC TV); Eos, 1978; Songs, Lamentations and Praises, 1979; Dances of Love and Death, 1981; Agora, 1984; A Mass for Man, 1985 (recorded for BBC TV); Ceremony, 1986; Interrogations, 1986; Video Life, 1986; Phantasmagoria, 1987; A Midsummer Night's Dream, 1993; The Four Seasons, 1996; Aladdin, 2000. Editor, Choreography and Dance, 1988–. Hon. Fellow, York Univ., Toronto. Hon. DLitt: Exeter, 1993; York, 1996; DUniv Middlesex, 1994. Evening Standard Award for most outstanding achievement in ballet, 1975; Soc. of West End Theatres Award for most outstanding achievement in ballet, 1978. *Publication:* The Dance Workshop, 1986. *Recreation:* dancing. *Address:* The Place, 17 Dukes Road, WC1H 9AB. *T:* (020) 7387 0161.

COHEN; *see* Waley-Cohen.

COHEN, family name of **Baroness Cohen of Pimlico**.

COHEN OF PIMLICO, Baroness *cr* 2000 (Life Peer), of Pimlico in the City of Westminster; **Janet Cohen;** Director: Defence Logistics Organisation, since 1999; London Stock Exchange, since 2001; BPP Holdings, since 1994; *b* 4 July 1940; *d* of late George Edric Neel and of Mary Isabel Neel (*née* Budge); *m* 1971, James Lionel Cohen; two *s* one *d*. *Educ:* Newnham Coll., Cambridge (BA Hons Law 1962; Associate Fellow, 1988–91). Articled clerk, Frere Cholmeley, 1963–65; admitted solicitor, 1965; Consultant: ABT Associates, USA, 1965–67; John Laing Construction, 1968–69; Department of Trade and Industry: Principal, 1969–78; Asst Sec., 1978–82; Asst Dir, 1982–88, Dir, 1988–2000, Charterhouse Bank Ltd. Chm., Café Pelican Ltd, 1984–90; Vice Chm., Yorks Building Soc., 1994–99 (Dir, 1991–94); Non-executive Director: Waddington plc (formerly John Waddington), 1994–97; London & Manchester Gp plc, 1997–98; United Assce Gp, 1999–. Mem., Schools Exam. and Assessment Council, 1990–93. Mem. Bd, Sheffield Develt Corp., 1993–97. A Governor, BBC, 1994–99. Hon. Fellow, St Edmund's Coll., Cambridge. Hon. DLitt Humberside, 1995. *Publications:* as Janet Neel: Death's Bright Angel, 1988; Death on Site, 1989; Death of a Partner, 1991; Death among the Dons, 1993; A Timely Death, 1996; To Die For, 1998; O Gentle Death, 2000; as Janet Cohen: The Highest Bidder, 1992; Children of a Harsh Winter, 1994. *Recreation:* restaurants.

COHEN, Prof. Bernard Woolf; Slade Professor, and Chair of Fine Art, University of London, 1988–2000, now Emeritus Slade Professor; *b* 28 July 1933; *s* of Victor and Leah Cohen; *m* 1959, Jean Britton; one *s* one *d*. *Educ:* Slade School of Fine Art, University Coll. London (Dip. Fine Art). Head of Painting, Wimbledon Sch. of Art, 1980–87. Vis. Prof., Univ. of New Mexico, USA, 1969–70. Fellow, UCL, 1992. First one man exhibn, Gimpel Fils Gall., 1958, again in 1960; other exhibitions: Molton Gall., 1962; Kasmin Gall., Bond Street, 1963, 1964, 1967; Waddington Gall., 1974, 1977, 1979, 1990; First New York exhibn, Betty Parsons Gall., 1967; major retrospective, Hayward Gall., 1972; print retrospective, Tate Gall., 1976; drawing retrospective, Ben Uri Gall., 1994; paintings, Tate Gall., 1995; paintings of the 90s, Flowers East Gall., London, 1998, Flowers West Gall., Santa Monica, 1999; Flowers Central, 2001; represented GB at Venice Biennale, 1966. Work in collections of Tate Gall., Mus. of Modern Art, New York; Fogg Mus., Mass; Minneapolis Walker Art Centre; Carnegie Inst., Pittsburgh, and others. *Recreations:* painting, travel, music. *Address:* 80 Camberwell Grove, SE5 8RF.

COHEN, Betty; *see* Jackson, B.

COHEN, Ven. Clive Ronald Franklin; Archdeacon of Bodmin, since 2000; *b* 30 Jan. 1946; *s* of Ronald Arthur Wilfred Cohen and Janet Ruth Lindsay Cohen (*née* Macdonald); *m* 1969, (Elizabeth) June Kingsley Kefford; three *s* one *d* (and one *s* decd). *Educ:* Salisbury and Wells Theol Coll. ACIB 1971. Asst Master, Edinburgh House Sch., 1964–67; Midland Bank plc, 1967–79; ordained deacon, 1981, priest, 1982; Asst Curate, Esher, Surrey, 1981–85; Rector, Winterslow, Wilts, 1985–2000; Rural Dean, Alderbury, Wilts, 1989–93; Non-Residentiary Canon and Prebendary, Salisbury Cathedral, 1992–2000. *Publications:* Crying in the Wilderness, 1994; So Great a Cloud, 1995. *Recreation:* local history. *Address:* Archdeacon's House, Cardynham, Bodmin, Cornwall PL30 4BL. *T:* (01208) 821614.

COHEN, Sir Edward, Kt 1970; company director; solicitor; *b* 9 Nov. 1912; *s* of Brig. Hon. H. E. Cohen; *m* 1939, Meryl D., *d* of D. G. Fink; one *s*. *Educ:* Scotch Coll., Melbourne (Exhibnr in Greek and Roman History); Ormond Coll., Univ. of Melbourne (LLB; Aust. Blue Athletics, Hockey). Served, 1940–45: AIF, 2/12 Fd Regt, 9th Div. Artillery, Captain 1942. Partner, Pavey, Wilson, Cohen & Carter, 1945–76, then, following amalgamation, Consultant, Corrs Chambers Westgarth, solicitors, Melbourne, 1976–98; Director: Carlton and United Breweries, 1947–84 (Chm., 1967–84); Swan Brewery, 1947–57; Associated Pulp & Paper Mills Ltd, 1951–83 (Dep. Chm. 1981–83); Electrolytic Zinc Co., A'asia, 1951–84 (Chm., 1960–84); Glazebrooks Paints and Chemicals Ltd, 1951–61; Standard Mutual Bldg Soc., 1951–64; E. Z. Industries, 1956–84 (Chm., 1960–84, Pres., 1984–); Pelaco Ltd, 1959–68; Commercial Union Assurance, 1960–82 (Chm., 1964–82); Union Assce Soc. of Aust., 1960–75 (Local Advisor, 1951–60); Michaelis Bayley Ltd, 1964–80; Qld Brewery (later CUB Qld), 1968–84; Herald and Weekly Times Ltd, 1974–77 (Vice-Chm., 1976–77); Chairman: Derwent Metals, 1957–84; CUB Fibre Containers, 1963–84; Emu Bay Railway Co., 1967–84; Manufrs Bottle Co., Vic, 1967–84; Northern Aust. Breweries (CUB (N Qld)), 1967–84; Nat. Commercial Union, 1982–84. Past Member: Faculty of Law of Melbourne Univ.; Internat. Hse Council, Melbourne Univ.; Council of Legal Education and Bd of Examiners. Mem. Council Law Inst. of Victoria, 1959–68, Pres. 1965–66. Chairman: Pensions Cttee, Melbourne Legacy, 1961–84 (Mem., 1955–84); Royal Women's Hosp. 1968 Million Dollar Bldg Appeal; Eileen Patricia Goulding Meml Fund Appeal, 1983; Life Governor: Austin, Prince Henry's, Royal Children's, Royal Melbourne, Royal Women's Hosps; Corps of Commissionaires; Adult Deaf and Dumb Soc. of Victoria. Hon. Solicitor, Queens Fund, 1951–94. Twelfth Leonard Ball Orator, Victorian Foundn on Alcoholism and Drug Dependence, 1980. *Address:* 722 Orrong Road, Toorak, Victoria 3142, Australia. *Clubs:* Naval and Military, Victoria Racing, Royal Automobile, Melbourne Cricket, Kooyong Lawn Tennis (Melbourne).

COHEN, Prof. Gerald Allan, FBA 1985; Chichele Professor of Social and Political Theory and Fellow of All Souls, Oxford, since Jan. 1985; *b* 14 April 1941; *s* of Morrie Cohen and Bella Lipkin; *m* 1965, Margaret Florence Pearce (marr. diss. 1996); one *s* two *d*; *m* 1999, Michèle Jacottet. *Educ:* Morris Winchevsky Jewish School, Montreal; Strathcona Academy, Montreal; Outremont High School, Montreal; McGill University (BA 1961); New College, Oxford (BPhil 1963). Lectr in Philosophy, University College London, 1963, Reader, 1978–84. Vis. Asst Prof. of Political Science, McGill Univ., 1965; Vis. Associate Prof. of Philosophy, Princeton Univ., 1975; Vis. Prof., McGill Univ., 2000–. *Publications:* Karl Marx's Theory of History: a defence, 1978, new edn 2000; History, Labour and Freedom: themes from Marx, 1988; Self-ownership, Freedom and Equality, 1995; If You're An Egalitarian, How Come You're So Rich?, 2000; articles in anthologies, philosophical and social-scientific jls. *Recreations:* Guardian crosswords, the visual arts, the politics of India, patience, travel. *Address:* All Souls College, Oxford OX1 4AL. *T:* (01865) 279339.

COHEN, Harry Michael; MP (Lab) Leyton and Wanstead, since 1997 (Leyton, 1983–97); accountant; *b* 10 Dec. 1949; *m* 1978, Ellen Hussain; one step *s* one step *d* and one foster *s*. Mem., Waltham Forest Borough Council, 1972–83 (formerly Chm., Planning Cttee and Sec., Labour Group). Mem., Select Cttee on Defence, 1997–; Mem., All-Party Parly Gp on Race and Community. Mem., N Atlantic Assembly, 1992– (Chm. sub-cttee for Economic Co-operation and Convergence with Central & Eastern Europe, 1996–). Mem., UNISON. Vice Pres., Royal Coll. of Midwives. *Address:* House of Commons, SW1A 0AA.

COHEN, Sir Ivor (Harold), Kt 1992; CBE 1985; TD 1968; Chairman: Remploy Ltd, 1987–93; Japan Electronics Business Association, since 1991; *b* 28 April 1931; *s* of Jack Cohen and Anne (*née* Victor); *m* 1963, Betty Edith, *yr d* of Reginald George and Mabel Appleby; one *d*. *Educ:* Central Foundation Sch., EC2; University Coll. London (BA

(Hons) Mod. Hist.; Fellow, 1987). Nat. Service, Royal Signals, 1952–54 (2nd Lieut); TA, Royal Signals, 1954–69 (Major 1964). Engrg industry, 1954–57; range of managerial posts, Mullard Ltd (subsid. of Philips (UK)), 1957–77; Dir, Philips Lighting, 1977–79; Man. Dir, Mullard Ltd, 1979–87; Dir, Philips Electronics (UK) Ltd, 1984–87. Non-executive Director: AB Electronic Products Gp plc, 1987–93; Océ (UK) Ltd, 1988–2001; PA Holdings Ltd, 1989–2001; Redifon Holdings Ltd, 1989–94; Magnetic Materials Gp plc, 1992; Electron Technologies Ltd, 1994–97; Deltron Electronics, 1995–; Russell Partnership Ltd, 1996–97; Chairman: Optima Group Ltd, 1995–96; Sira Ltd, 1998–2001; Cons., Comet Gp plc, 1987–90; Advr, Apax & Co. Ventures (formerly Alan Patricof Associates), 1987–93; Mem., Adv. Cttee, Mitsubishi Electric (UK) Ltd, 1991–. Member: IT Adv. Panel, 1981–86; Teletext and Viewdata Steering Gp, DTI, 1981–86; Electronic Components EDC, NEDO, 1980–88; Electronics Ind. EDC, NEDO, 1982–86; Steering Cttee, Telecom. Infrastructure, DTI, 1987–88; Computing Software and Communications Requirements Bd, DTI, 1984–88; Steering Bd, Radiocommunications Agency, DTI, 1990–95; Electronics Ind. Sector Gp, NEDO, 1988–92 (Chm., 1990–92); Chairman: Electronic Applications Sector Gp, NEDO, 1988–90; Measurement Adv. Cttee, DTI, 1994–97; Member Council: Electronic Components Ind. Fedn, 1980–87; European Electronic Components Assoc., 1985–87; Dir, Radio Industries Council, 1980–87. Mem., Schs Examinations and Assessment Council, 1988–90; British Schools Technology: Mem. Council of Management, 1984–87, Trustee Dir, 1987–89; Mem., Management Adv. Gp IT Res. Inst., Brighton Poly., 1987–90. CompIEE 1988; CompInstMC 1997; Hon. Mem. CGLI, 1989; FInstD 1988; FRSA 1984; Hon. FREng (Hon. FEng 1992). Freeman, City of London, 1982; Liveryman, Sci. Instrument Makers' Co., 1982– (Master, 1997). Hon. DSc City, 1998. Mem., Editl Bd, Nat. Electronics Review, 1987–90. *Publications:* articles on electronics policy and marketing and use of inf. technology in the technical press. *Recreations:* opera, reading, occasional sculpting, walking in towns. *Address:* 24 Selborne Road, Croydon, Surrey CR0 5JQ. *Clubs:* East India, Reform.

COHEN, Janet; *see* Baroness Cohen of Pimlico.

COHEN, Jonathan Lionel; QC 1997; a Recorder, since 1997; *b* 8 May 1951; *s* of Hon. Leonard Harold Lionel Cohen, *qv* and Eleanor Lucy Quixano Cohen (*née* Henriques); *m* 1983, Bryony Frances Carfrae; two *s* one *d*. *Educ:* Eton Coll.; Univ. of Kent at Canterbury (BA Hons). Called to the Bar, Lincoln's Inn, 1974; SE Circuit. Mem., Mental Health Review Tribunal, 2000–. Liveryman, Skinners' Co., 1978– (Mem., Ct of Assts, 2000–). Gov., Skinners' Co.'s Sch. for Girls, Hackney, 1994–. *Address:* 4 Paper Buildings, Temple, EC4Y 7EX.

COHEN, Laurence Jonathan, FBA 1973; Fellow and Praelector in Philosophy, 1957–90, Senior Tutor, 1985–90, Queen's College, Oxford, now Emeritus Fellow; British Academy Reader in Humanities, Oxford University, 1982–84; *b* 7 May 1923; *s* of Israel and Theresa Cohen; *m* 1953, Gillian Mary Slee; three *s* one *d*. *Educ:* St Paul's Sch., London; Balliol Coll., Oxford (MA 1947, DLitt 1982). Served War: Naval Intell. in UK and SEAC, 1942–45, and Lieut (Sp.) RNVR. Asst in Logic and Metaphysics, Edinburgh Univ., 1947–50; Lectr in Philosophy, St Andrews Univ. at Dundee, 1950–57; Commonwealth Fund Fellow in Logic at Princeton and Harvard Univs, 1952–53. Vis. Lectr, Hebrew Univ. of Jerusalem, 1952; Visiting Professor: Columbia Univ., 1967; Yale Univ., 1972, Northwestern Univ. Law Sch., 1988; Hon. Prof., Northwest Univ., Xian, China, 1987. Vis. Fellow, ANU, 1980. British Acad. Philosophical Lectr, 1975; Fry Lectr, Bristol Univ., 1976; Austin Lectr, UK Assoc. for Legal and Social Philos., 1982. Sec., Internat. Union of History and Philosophy of Science (Div. of Logic, Methodology and Philosophy of Science), 1975–83, Pres., 1987–91; Pres., British Soc. for Philosophy of Science, 1977–79; Chairman: British Nat. Cttee for Logic, Methodology and Philosophy of Science, 1987–91; Section K (Phil.), British Acad., 1994–96; Sec.-Gen., ICSU, 1993–96; Member: Comité Directeur, Fédn Internat. des Socs de Philosophie, 1983–91; Nat. Cttee for Philosophy, 1993–. Governor: Bartholomew Sch., Eynsham, 1989–93; Wood Green Sch., Witney, 1990–93. General Editor, Clarendon Library of Logic and Philosophy, 1973–. *Publications:* The Principles of World Citizenship, 1954; The Diversity of Meaning, 1962; The Implications of Induction, 1970; The Probable and the Provable, 1977; (ed jtly) Applications of Inductive Logic, 1980; (ed jtly) Logic, Methodology and Philosophy of Science, 1982; The Dialogue of Reason, 1986; An Introduction to the Philosophy of Induction and Probability, 1989; An Essay on Belief and Acceptance, 1992; articles in academic jls. *Recreations:* gardening; work for Council for Protection of Rural England. *Address:* Queen's College, Oxford OX1 4AW.

COHEN, Hon. Leonard Harold Lionel, OBE 1995; barrister-at-law; *b* 1 Jan. 1922; *s* of Rt Hon. Lord Cohen, PC (Life Peer), and Adelaide, Lady Cohen (*née* Spielmann); *m* 1949, Eleanor Lucy Quixano Henriques; two *s* one *d*. *Educ:* Eton Coll.; New Coll., Oxford (MA). War Service, Rifle Bde (wounded), Captain, 1941–45. Called to Bar, Lincoln's Inn, 1948, Bencher, 1989; practised at Chancery Bar, 1949–61. Chm., Secure Retirement PLC, 1987–92; Dir, M. Samuel & Co. Ltd (subseq. Hill Samuel & Co. Ltd), 1961–76. Dir-Gen., Accepting Houses Cttee, 1976–82; Chairman: United Services Trustee, 1976–82; Council, Royal Free Hosp. Med. Sch., 1982–92; Community Trust for Berkshire, 1988–93; Pres., Jewish Colonization Assoc., 1976–92. Master of the Skinners' Co., 1971–72. Hon. Col, 39th (City of London) Signal Regt (V), 1973–78. High Sheriff of Berks, 1987–88. *Recreation:* reading. *Address:* Dovecote House, Swallowfield Park, Reading RG7 1TG. *T:* (0118) 988 4775. *Club:* White's.

See also J. L. Cohen.

COHEN, Michael Antony; Chief Executive, The Guinness Trust, 1987–2001; *b* 18 April 1940; *s* of Gerald and Beatrice Cohen; *m* 1967, Jennifer Audrey Price; one *s* two *d*. *Educ:* Quarry Bank Grammar School, Liverpool; Univ. of Liverpool (BA Hons Econ.). FCA; MIH. Articled clerk, 1962–65; Accountant and Planning Manager, Bank of London & S America, 1965–72; posts in European and US banking, Lloyds Bank, 1972–78; Internat. Project Finance Manager, Lloyds Bank, 1978–82; Regional Dir, Housing Corp., 1982–87. Dir, Housing Forum Ltd, 1999–. Mem. Council, London Borough of Barnet, 1972–78. Chairman: St Mungo Community Housing Assoc., 1991–; Barnet Housing Aid Centre, 1990–; Phoenix Cinema Trust Ltd, 1996–; Trustee, Prince's Foundn, 1999–. Chm. Govs, Christ's Coll., Finchley, 1996–. *Recreations:* walking, eating, France, theatre, finding time. *Address:* 6 Talbot Avenue, East Finchley, N2 0LS. *T:* (020) 8883 9433.

COHEN, Lt-Col Mordaunt, TD 1954; DL; Regional Chairman of Industrial Tribunals, 1976–89 (Chairman, 1974–76); *b* 6 Aug. 1916; *s* of Israel Ellis Cohen and Sophie Cohen; *m* 1953, Myrella Cohen (*see* Her Honour Myrella Cohen); one *s* one *d*. *Educ:* Bede Collegiate Sch. for Boys, Sunderland. Admitted solicitor, 1938. Served War, RA, 1940–46: seconded RWAFF; despatches, Burma campaign; served TA, 1947–55: CO 463(M) HAA Regt, RA(TA), 1954–55. Alderman, Sunderland Co. Bor. Council, 1967–74; Chm., Sunderland Educn Cttee, 1970–72; Chm., NE Council of Educn Cttees, 1971; Councillor, Tyne and Wear CC, 1973–74; Dep. Chm., Northern Traffic Comrs, 1973–74. Chm., Mental Health Review Tribunal, 1967–76. Chm. of Governors, Sunderland Polytechnic, 1969–72; Mem. Court, Univ. of Newcastle upon Tyne, 1968–72. Pres., Sunderland Law Soc., 1970; Hon. Life Pres., Sunderland Hebrew Congregation, 1988; Mem., Bd of Deputies of British Jews (Chm., Provincial Cttee, 1985–91; Dir, Central Enquiry Desk, 1990–2000); former Mem., Chief Rabbinate Council; Vice Pres., AJEX, 1995– (Chm., 1993–95); Life Pres., Sunderland Br., AJEX, 1970; Trustee, Ajex Charitable Trust, 1978–; Hon. Treas., AJEX Charitable Foundn, 2000–; Trustee, Colwyn Bay Synagogue Trust, 1978–. Chm. of Govs, Edgware Sch., 1991–96. FRSA 1998. DL Tyne and Wear, 1986. *Recreations:* watching sport, playing bowls; communal service, promoting inter-faith understanding. *Address:* Flat 1, Peters Lodge, 2 Stonegrove, Edgware, Middlesex HA8 7TY. *Clubs:* Ashbrooke Cricket and Rugby Football (Sunderland); Durham County Cricket (Life Mem.).

COHEN, Her Honour Myrella; QC 1970; a Circuit Judge, 1972–95; *b* 16 Dec. 1927; *d* of late Samuel and Sarah Cohen, Manchester; *m* 1953, Lt-Col Mordaunt Cohen, *qv*; one *s* one *d*. *Educ:* Manchester High Sch. for Girls; Colwyn Bay Grammar Sch.; Manchester Univ. (LLB 1948). Called to the Bar, Gray's Inn, 1950. Recorder of Hull, 1971; Dep. High Court Judge, Family Div., 1975–95. Mem., Parole Bd, 1983–86. Dep. Pres., Internat. Assoc. of Jewish Lawyers and Jurists, 1996– (Chm., UK Br., 1996–). Vice-Pres., N of England CRC, 1974–. Life Mem., Council, League of Jewish Women, 1991; Exec. Mem., Jewish Marriage Council. Pres., 1968, 1988, Hon. Mem., 1989, Sunderland Soroptomists. Patron: Sunderland Council for the Disabled; Suzy Lamplugh Trust; Women of North Distaff Cttee; British Emunah. FRSA 1993. Hon. LLD Sunderland, 1992. *Address:* 1 Peters Lodge, 2 Stonegrove, Edgware, Middlesex HA8 7TY. *Club:* Soroptimist of Great Britain.

COHEN, Sir Philip, Kt 1998; PhD; FRS 1984; FRSE 1984; Royal Society Research Professor, since 1984, Director, Medical Research Council Protein Phosphorylation Unit, since 1990, and Director, Wellcome Trust Biocentre, since 1997, University of Dundee; *b* 22 July 1945; *s* of Jacob Davis Cohen and Fanny (*née* Bragman); *m* 1969, Patricia Townsend Wade; one *s* one *d*. *Educ:* Hendon County Grammar Sch.; University Coll. London (BSc 1st Cl. Hons (Biochemistry Special), 1966; PhD Biochem., 1969; Fellow, 1993). SRC/NATO Postdoctoral Res. Fellow, Dept of Biochem., Univ. of Washington, Seattle, USA, 1969–71; Univ. of Dundee: Lectr in Biochem., 1971–78; Reader in Biochem., 1978–81; Prof. of Enzymology, 1981–84. Mem., Eur. Molecular Biology Orgn, 1982–; MAE 1990. Founder FMedSci 1998. Hon. FRCPath 1998. Hon. DSc: Abertay, 1998; Strathclyde, 1999. Anniversary Prize, Fedn of Eur. Biochemical Socs, 1977; Colworth Medal, 1978, CIBA medal and prize, 1992, British Biochem. Soc.; Prix van Gysel, Belgian Royal Acads of Medicine, 1992; Dundee City of Discovery Rosebowl Award, 1993; Bruce Preller Prize, RSE, 1993; Special Achievement Award, Miami Biotech. Winter Symposium, 1996; Louis-Jeantet Prize for Medicine, 1997; Pfizer Award for Innovative Sci., 1999. Man. Editor, Biochimica et Biophysica Acta, 1981–92. *Publications:* Control of Enzyme Activity, 1976, 2nd edn 1983; (ed series) Molecular Aspects of Cellular Regulation: vol. 1, 1980; vol. 2, 1982; vol. 3, 1984; vol. 4, 1985; vol. 5, 1988; vol. 6, 1991; over 400 original papers and revs in scientific jls. *Recreations:* chess, bridge, golf, natural history. *Address:* Inverbay II, Invergowrie, Dundee DD2 5DQ. *T:* (01382) 562328. *Clubs:* Downfield Golf; Dukes Golf; Isle of Harris Golf; Dundee Bridge.

COHEN, Prof. Robert Donald, CBE 1997, MD; FRCP, FMedSci; Professor of Medicine and Director, Academic Medical Unit (Whitechapel), St Bartholomew's and the Royal London School of Medicine and Dentistry, Queen Mary and Westfield College, (formerly London Hospital Medical College), University of London, 1981–99, now Professor Emeritus; *b* 11 Oct. 1933; *s* of Dr Harry H. and Ruby Cohen; *m* 1961, Dr Barbara Joan Boucher; one *s* one *d*. *Educ:* Clifton Coll.; Trinity Coll., Cambridge. MA, MD (Cantab). Hon. Cons. Physician, London Hosp., 1967–; Dir, Academic Unit of Metabolism and Endocrinology, 1974, Prof. of Metabolic Medicine, 1974–81, London Hosp. Med. Coll. Chairman: Adv. Cttee on the Application of Computing Science to Medicine and the Nat. Health Service, 1976–77; DHSS Computer R&D Cttee, 1977–80; DHSS/MRC Monitoring Cttee on Magnetic Resonance Imaging, 1986–89; Review Body, British Diabetic Assoc., 1990–95; Member: Jt Cttee on Higher Med. Trng, 1983–90, 1996–97 (Chm., Special Adv. Cttee on Gen. Internal Medicine, 1983–90); GMC, 1988–96; Physiological Systems Bd, MRC, 1990–92; Health Services Res. Cttee, MRC, 1990–92; Physiological Medicine and Infections Bd, MRC, 1992–94; Health Services and Public Health Bd, MRC, 1992–94; Innovation Grants Cttee, MRC, 1998–2000; Cttee, Nat. Kidney Res. Fund, 1992–98; Council, King Edward VII Hosp., Midhurst, 1997–2000; Chm., ICRF, 1994– (Mem. Council, 1989–; Vice-Chm., 1991–94). Sen. Censor and First Vice-Pres., RCP, 1991–93. Founder FMedSci 1998. Hon. Fellow, QMW, 2001. Chm., Editorial Bd, Clinical Science and Molecular Medicine, 1973–74. *Publications:* Clinical and Biochemical Aspects of Lactic Acidosis (with H. F. Woods), 1976; (jtly) The Metabolic and Molecular Basis of Acquired Disease, 1990; papers in Clin. Sci. and Molecular Med., Jl of Clin. Investigation, Lancet, Biochemical Journal. *Address:* Long Meadow, East Dean, Chichester, W Sussex PO18 0JB. *T:* (01243) 811230; *e-mail:* rcohen@doctors.org.uk.

COHEN, Sir Ronald (Mourad), Kt 2001; Founder, and Chairman, since 1972, Apax Partners & Co. Ltd (formerly MMG Patricof Group); *b* 1 Aug. 1945; *s* of late Michel Mourad Cohen and of Sonia Sophie Cohen (*née* Douek); *m* 1st, 1972, Carol Marylene Belmont (marr. diss. 1975); 2nd, 1983, Claire Whitmore Enders (marr. diss. 1986); 3rd, 1987, Sharon Ruth Harel; one *s* one *d*. *Educ:* Orange Hill GS; Exeter Coll., Oxford (Exhibnr, MA; Hon. Fellow, 2000; Pres., Oxford Union Soc.); Harvard Business Sch. (MBA). Consultant, McKinsey & Co. (UK and Italy), 1969–71; Chargé de mission, Institut de Développement Industriel France, 1971–72. Founder, British Venture Capital Assoc., 1983 (Chm., 1985–86); Founder Director: Eur. Venture Capital Assoc., 1985; City Gp for Smaller Cos, 1992; a Founder and Vice-Chm., Eur. Assoc. Securities Dealers Automated Quotation, 1995–. Chairman: Tech. Stars Steering Cttee, DTI, 1997–; Social Investment Task Force; Member: Finance and Industry Cttee, NEDC, 1988–90; Wider Share Ownership Cttee, 1988–90, City Adv. Gp, 1993–99, CBI; Wkg Party on Smaller Cos, Stock Exchange, 1993; UK Competitiveness Cttee, DTI, 1998–. Member: Exec. Cttee, Centre for Econ. Policy Res., 1996–99; Finance Cttee, Inst. for Social and Econ. Policy in ME, Kennedy Sch., Harvard Univ., 1997–98; Adv. Bd, Fulbright Commn, 1997–99; Franco-British Council, 1997–99; Adv. Council, Foundn for Entrepreneurial Mgt, London Business Sch., 1997–99; RIIA. Mem., Adv. Bd, InterAction, 1986–. Contested (L): Kensington N, 1974; London W, EP elecn, 1979. *Recreations:* music, art, theatre, tennis. *Address:* Apax Partners & Co. Ltd, 15 Portland Place, W1B 1PT. *T:* (020) 7872 6300, *Fax:* (020) 7872 8999. *Clubs:* Royal Automobile, Queen's.

COHEN, Stanley; *b* 31 July 1927; *s* of Thomas and Teresa Cohen; *m* 1954, Brenda P. Rafferty; three *s* one *d*. *Educ:* St Patrick's and St Charles' Schools, Leeds. Served in Royal Navy, 1947–49. Employed in Clothing Industry, 1943–47 and 1949–51; Clerical Officer with British Railways, 1951–70. Mem. Leeds City Council, 1952–71; elected Alderman, 1968. Contested (Lab) Barkston Ash, 1966; MP (Lab) Leeds South East, 1970–83. PPS to Minister of State, DES, 1976–79. Mem., Duke of Edinburgh's Commonwealth Study Conf. to Australia, 1968. *Recreations:* walking, camping, driving. *Address:* 9 Pendil Close,

Whitkirk, Leeds LS15 0NE. *T:* (0113) 264 9568. *Clubs:* Crossgates Recreational; Irish Centre (Leeds).

COHEN, Prof. Stanley, PhD; FBA 1997; Martin White Professor of Sociology, London School of Economics, since 1995; *b* 23 Feb. 1942; *s* of Ray and Sie Cohen; *m* 1963, Ruth Kretzmer; two *d*. *Educ:* Univ. of Witwatersrand, Johannesburg (BA); LSE, Univ. of London (PhD). Psychiatric social worker, 1963–64; Lectr in Sociology: Enfield Coll., 1965–67; Univ. of Durham, 1967–72; Sen. Lectr in Sociol., 1972–74, Prof. of Sociol., 1974–81, Univ. of Essex; Prof. of Criminology, Hebrew Univ., Jerusalem, 1981–95. Vis. Centennial Prof., LSE, 1994–95. Sellin-Glueck Award, Amer. Soc. of Criminology, 1985. *Publications:* Images of Deviance, 1971; Folk Devils and Moral Panics, 1972; Psychological Survival, 1972; The Manufacture of News, 1973; Escape Attempts, 1976; Prison Secrets, 1978; Social Control and the State, 1984; Visions of Social Control: crime, punishment and classification, 1985; Against Criminology, 1988; States of Denial, 2000. *Address:* Department of Sociology, London School of Economics, Houghton Street, WC2A 2AE.

COHEN, Prof. Stanley; Distinguished Professor, Department of Biochemistry, Vanderbilt University School of Medicine, since 1986; *b* 17 Nov. 1922; *s* of Louis Cohen and Fruma Feitel; *m* 1st, 1951, Olivia Larson; three *s*; 2nd, 1981, Jan Elizabeth Jordan. *Educ:* Brooklyn Coll., NY; Oberlin Coll., Ohio; Univ. of Michigan (BA, PhD). Teaching Fellow, Dept of Biochem., Univ. of Michigan, 1946–48; Instructor, Depts of Biochem. and Pediatrics, Univ. of Colorado Sch. of Medicine, 1948–52; Fellow, Amer. Cancer Soc., Dept of Radiology, Washington Univ., St Louis, 1952–53; Associate Prof., Dept of Zoology, Washington Univ., 1953–59; Vanderbilt University School of Medicine, Nashville: Asst Prof. of Biochem., 1959–62; Associate Prof., 1962; Prof. 1967–86. Mem., Editl Bds of learned jls. Mem., Nat. Acad. of Science, and other sci. bodies. Hon. DSc Chicago, 1985. Nobel Prize for Physiology or Medicine, 1986 (jtly); other prizes and awards. *Publications:* papers in learned jls on biochemistry, cell biology, human developmental biology, embryology. *Address:* Department of Biochemistry, Vanderbilt University School of Medicine, 607 Light Hall, Nashville, TN 37232–0146, USA.

COHEN, Prof. Sydney, CBE 1978; FRS 1978; Professor of Chemical Pathology, Guy's Hospital Medical School, 1965–86, now Emeritus Professor, University of London; *b* Johannesburg, SA, 18 Sept. 1921; *s* of Morris and Pauline Cohen; *m* 1st, 1950, June Bernice Adler (*d* 1999); one *s* one *d*; 2nd, 1999, Deirdre Maureen Ann Boyd. *Educ:* King Edward VIIth Sch., Johannesburg; Witwatersrand and London Univs. MD, PhD. Lectr, Dept of Physiology, Witwatersrand Univ., 1947–53; Scientific Staff, Nat. Inst. for Med. Research, London, 1954–60; Reader, Dept of Immunology, St Mary's Hosp. Med. Sch., 1960–65. Mem., MRC, 1974–76; Chm., Tropical Med. Research Bd, MRC, 1974–76; Chm., WHO Scientific Gp on Immunity to Malaria, 1976–81; Mem., WHO expert adv. panel on malaria, 1977–89; Mem. Council, Royal Soc., 1981–83; Royal Soc. Assessor, MRC, 1982–84. Nuffield Dominion Fellow in Medicine, 1954; Founder Fellow, RCPath, 1964. Hon. DSc Witwatersrand, 1987. *Publications:* papers on immunology and parasitic diseases in sci. jls. *Recreations:* golf, gardening, forestry. *Address:* 8 Gibson Place, St Andrews, Fife KY16 9JE; Hafodfraith, Llangurig, Powys SY18 6QG. *Club:* Royal and Ancient (St Andrews).

COHEN, Hon. William S(ebastian); Secretary of Defense, United States of America, 1996–2001; *b* 28 Aug. 1940; *s* of Reuben Cohen and Clara (*née* Hartley); *m*; two *s*. *Educ:* Bangor High Sch.; Bowdoin Coll. (AB 1962); Boston Univ. Law Sch. (LLB 1965). Admitted: Maine Bar; Massachusetts Bar; Dist of Columbia Bar; Partner, Prairie, Cohen, Lynch, Weatherbee and Kobritz, 1966–72; Asst Attorney, Penobscot County, Maine, 1968–70; Instr., Univ. of Maine at Orono, 1968–72; Mem., US Congress, 1972–79; US Senator from Maine, 1979–97. Fellow, John F. Kennedy Inst. of Politics, Harvard, 1972. Mem., Bangor City Council, 1969–72 (Mayor, 1971–72). *Publications:* Of Sons and Seasons, 1978; Roll Call, 1981; (jtly) Getting the Most Out of Washington, 1982; (jtly) The Double Man, 1985; A Baker's Nickel, 1986; (jtly) Men of Zeal, 1988; One-Eyed Kings, 1991; (jtly) Murder in the Senate, 1993.

COHEN-TANNOUDJI, Prof. Claude, PhD; Officier, Légion d'Honneur; Commandeur, Ordre National du Mérite; Professor of Atomic and Molecular Physics, Collège de France, Paris, since 1973; *b* 1 April 1933; *s* of Abraham Cohen-Tannoudji and Sarah Sebbah; *m* 1958, Jacqueline Veyrat; one *s* one *d* (and one *s* decd). *Educ:* Ecole Normale Supérieure, Paris; Univ. of Paris (PhD Physics 1962). Researcher, CNRS, 1960–64; Associate Prof., 1964–67, Prof., 1967–73, Univ. of Paris. Member: Académie des Sciences, Paris, 1981; NAS, USA, 1994. (Jtly) Nobel Prize for Physics, 1997. *Publications:* (jtly) Quantum Mechanics, Vols I and II, 1977; Atoms in Electromagnetic Fields, 1994; with J. Dupont-Roc and G. Grynberg: Photons and Atoms: introduction to Q.E.D., 1989; Atom-photon Interactions, 1992. *Recreation:* music. *Address:* Laboratoire Kastler Brossel, Département de Physique de l'ENS, 24 rue Lhomond, 75231 Paris Cedex 05, France. *T:* (1) 47077783.

COHN, Prof. Norman, MA; DLitt; FBA 1978; FRHistS; Astor-Wolfson Professor of History, University of Sussex, 1973–80, now Professor Emeritus; *b* London, 12 Jan. 1915; *yr s* of August Cohn and Daisy (*née* Reimer); *m* 1941, Vera, *d* of Mark and Eva Broido, St Petersburg; one *s*. *Educ:* Gresham's Sch.; Christ Church, Oxford (Scholar). 1st Class Hons, Sch. of Medieval and Mod. Languages, 1936; DLitt Glasgow, 1957. Served War of 1939–45, Queen's Royal Regt and Intell. Corps. Lectr in French, Glasgow Univ., 1946–51; Professor of French: Magee Univ. Coll. (then associated with TCD), 1951–60; King's Coll., Durham Univ., 1960–63; changed career to become Dir, Columbus Centre, Sussex Univ. and Gen. Editor, Columbus Centre's Studies in the Dynamics of Persecution and Extermination, 1966–73. Professorial Fellow, Sussex Univ., 1966–73; advr on comparative study of genocide, Concordia Univ., Montreal, 1982–85; adviser: Montreal Inst. for Genocide Studies, 1985–; Center for Millennial Studies, Boston Univ., 1999–; Vis. Prof., KCL, 1986–89. Hugh Le May Fellow, Rhodes Univ., 1950; Fellow, Center for Advanced Study in the Behavioral Sciences, Stanford, Calif, 1966; Vis. Fellow, Center for Humanities, Wesleyan Univ., Conn, 1971; Fellow, Netherlands Inst. for Advanced Study, 1975–76; Canadian SSHRC Vis. Fellow, 1982, Canadian Commonwealth Vis. Fellow, 1983. Hon. LLD Concordia Univ., 1985. *Publications:* Gold Khan and other Siberian legends, 1946; The Pursuit of the Millennium: revolutionary millenarians and mystical anarchists of the middle ages, 1957, 4th edn 1993 (trans. German, French, Spanish, Portuguese, Italian, Norwegian, Greek, Hebrew, Dutch and Japanese); Warrant for Genocide: the myth of the Jewish world-conspiracy and the Protocols of the Elders of Zion, 1967, 3rd edn 1996 (Anisfield-Wolf Award in Race Relations, 1967) (trans. German, French, Spanish, Portuguese, Italian, Russian, Serbian, Hebrew and Japanese); Europe's Inner Demons: an enquiry inspired by the great witch-hunt, 1975, 3rd edn 1993 (trans. French, Spanish, Portuguese, Hungarian, Norwegian and Japanese); Cosmos, Chaos and the World to Come: the ancient roots of apocalyptic faith, 1993 (trans. German, Spanish, Portuguese, French and Japanese), 2nd edn 2001; Noah's Flood: the Genesis story in western thought, 1996 (trans. Japanese); contributor to various symposia, learned jls, and reviews. *Recreations:* walking, looking at pictures, butterfly-watching. *Address:* Orchard Cottage, Wood End, Ardeley, Herts SG2 7AZ. *T:* (01438) 869247. *Club:* Athenæum.

COHN, Prof. Paul Moritz, FRS 1980; Emeritus Professor of Mathematics, University of London, and Hon. Research Fellow in Mathematics, University College London, since 1989; *b* Hamburg, 8 Jan. 1924; *o c* of late James Cohn and late Julia Cohn (*née* Cohen); *m* 1958, Deirdre Sonia Sharon; two *d*. *Educ:* Trinity Coll., Cambridge. BA 1948, MA, PhD 1951. Chargé de Recherches, Univ. de Nancy, 1951–52; Lectr, Manchester Univ., 1952–62; Reader, London Univ., at Queen Mary Coll., 1962–67; Prof. of Maths, London Univ. at Bedford Coll., 1967–84, at UCL, 1984–86; Astor Prof. of Maths, UCL, 1986–89. Visiting Professor: Yale Univ., 1961–62; Univ. of California (Berkeley), 1962; Univ. of Chicago, 1964; State Univ. of New York (Stony Brook), 1967; Rutgers Univ., 1967–68; Univ. of Paris, 1969; Tulane Univ., 1971; Indian Inst. of Technology, Delhi, 1971; Univ. of Alberta, 1972, 1986; Carleton Univ., Ottawa, 1973; Technion, Haifa, 1975; Iowa State Univ., 1978; Univ. of Bielefeld, 1979; Bar Ilan Univ., Ramat Gan, 1987; Univ. of Hamburg, 1992. Member: Mathematics Cttee, SRC, 1977–80; Council, Royal Soc., 1985–87; IMU Rep., Royal Soc. Internat. Relns Cttee, 1990–93; London Mathematical Society: Sec., 1965–67; Mem. Council, 1968–71, 1972–75, 1979–84; Pres., 1982–84; Editor, London Math. Soc. Monographs, 1968–77, 1980–93. Lester R. Ford Award (Mathematical Assoc. of America), 1972; Senior Berwick Prize, London Mathematical Soc., 1974. *Publications:* Lie Groups, 1957; Linear Equations, 1958; Solid Geometry, 1961; Universal Algebra, 1965, 2nd edn 1981 (trans foreign langs); Free Rings and their Relations, 1971, 2nd edn 1985; Algebra, vol. I, 1974, 2nd edn 1982, vol. II, 1977, 2nd edn 1989, vol. III, 1990; Skew Field Constructions, 1977; Algebraic Numbers and Algebraic Functions, 1991; Elements of Linear Algebra, 1994; Skew Fields, vol. 57 of Encyclopedia of Mathematics and its Applications, 1995; An Introduction to Ring Theory, 2000; Classic Algebra, 2000; contribs to Encyclopedia Britannica, New DNB; papers on algebra in various mathematical periodicals. *Recreations:* linguistics, etymology. *Address:* Department of Mathematics, University College London, Gower Street, WC1E 6BT. *T:* (020) 7679 4459; *e-mail:* pmc@math.ucl.ac.uk.

COHN-SHERBOK, Rabbi Prof. Dan; Professor of Judaism, University of Wales, Lampeter, since 1997; *b* 1 Feb. 1945; *s* of Dr Bernard Sherbok and Ruth Sherbok (*née* Goldstein), Denver, Colo; *m* 1976, Lavinia Charlotte Heath. *Educ:* Williams Coll., Mass (BA); Hebrew Union Coll., Ohio (BHL, MAHL); Wolfson Coll., Cambridge (MLitt, PhD). Served as rabbi in US, Australia, SA and England, 1970–75; Lectr in Jewish Theology, Univ. of Kent, 1975–97; Dir, Centre for Study of Religion and Society, Univ. of Kent, 1982–90. Visiting Professor: Univ. of Essex, 1993–94; of Inter-Faith Dialogue, Univ. of Middx, 1995–; of Judaism, Univ. of Wales at Lampeter, 1995–97; Vilnius Univ., 2000. Hon. DD Hebrew Union Coll., 1996. *Publications:* On Earth as it is in Heaven, 1987; The Jewish Heritage, 1988; Holocaust Theology, 1989; Jewish Petitionary Prayer, 1989; Rabbinic Perspectives on the New Testament, 1990; (ed) The Canterbury Papers, 1990; (ed) The Salman Rushdie Controversy, 1990; (ed) Using the Bible Today, 1991; (ed) A Traditional Quest, 1991; (ed) The Sayings of Moses, 1991; (ed) Tradition and Unity, 1991; (ed) Problems in Contemporary Jewish Philosophy, 1991; A Dictionary of Judaism and Christianity, 1991; Issues in Contemporary Judaism, 1991; The Blackwell Dictionary of Judaica, 1992; The Crucified Jew, 1992; Israel: the history of an idea, 1992; Exodus, 1992; (ed) Many Mansions, 1992; (ed) World Religions and Human Liberation, 1992; (ed) Religion in Public Life, 1992; (ed) Torah and Revelation, 1992; Atlas of Jewish History, 1993; The Jewish Faith, 1993; Judaism and Other Faiths, 1994; The Future of Judaism, 1994; Jewish and Christian Mysticism, 1994; The American Jew, 1994; Jewish Mysticism, 1995; (ed) Divine Interventions and Miracles, 1996; Medieval Jewish Philosophy, 1996; The Hebrew Bible, 1996; Modern Judaism, 1996; Biblical Hebrew for Beginners, 1996; God and the Holocaust, 1996; Fifty Key Jewish Thinkers, 1997; (ed) Islam in a World of Diverse Faiths, 1997; The Jewish Messiah, 1997; After Noah, 1997; (ed) Theodicy, 1997; Concise Encyclopedia of Judaism, 1998; Understanding the Holocaust, 1999; (ed) The Future of Jewish Christian Dialogue, 1999; (ed) The Future of Religion, 1999; Judaism, 1999; Jews, Christians and Religious Pluralism, 1999; Messianic Judaism, 2000; Holocaust Theology: a reader, 2001; Interfaith Theology, 2001; The Palestine-Israeli Conflict, 2001; numerous articles to learned jls. *Recreations:* keeping cats, walking, drawing cartoons. *Address:* Department of Theology and Religious Studies, University of Wales, Lampeter SA48 7ED. *T:* (01570) 422351. *Clubs:* Athenæum; Williams (New York).

COID, Dr Donald Routledge; Director of Medical Services, Armadale Health Service, Western Australia, since 2001; *b* 13 June 1953; *s* of Charles Routledge Coid and Marjory Macdonald Coid (*née* Keay); *m* 1985, Susan Kathleen Ramus (*née* Crocker); three *d*. *Educ:* Bromley Grammar Sch. for Boys; Harrow County Sch. for Boys; Univ. of Nottingham (BMedSci; BM, BS); LSHTM (MSc 1981). MRCP 1979; MFCM 1985, MFPHM 1989, FFPHM 1996; FRACMA 1985; FAFPHM 1991; FRCPE 1998; FRIPHH 1998. Hse Physician, Nottingham City Hosp., 1976; Hse Surgeon, Nottingham Gen. Hosp., 1977; Sen. Hse Officer, Brook Gen. Hosp., London, 1977–78; Res. Asst, Middlesex Hosp. Med. Sch., 1979; Field Med. Officer, Royal Flying Doctor Service, Australia, Eastern Goldfields Sect., 1979–80; MO, Community Health Services, WA, 1981–82; Regl Dir of Public Health, Eastern Goldfields, WA, 1982–85; Med. Supt, Kalgoorlie Reg. Hosp., WA, 1984–85; Fife Health Board: Cons. in Public Health, 1985–92; Asst Gen. Manager, 1992–93; Chief Admin. MO, Dir of Public Health and Exec. Dir, Tayside Health Bd, 1994–98; Consultant in Health Services Res., Ninewells Hosp. and Med. Sch., Dundee, 1998–2000; Public Health Consultant, Grampian Health Bd, 2000–01. Hon. Sen. Lectr, Dundee Univ., 1994–. Consultant, WHO. Mem. Council, RIPH&H. *Publications:* on public health and related topics in learned jls. *Recreations:* golf, singing, cricket, piano. *Address:* PO Box 799, Cottesloe, WA 6011, Australia. *Clubs:* Royal & Ancient Golf, New Golf (St Andrews).

COKAYNE, family name of **Baron Cullen of Ashbourne**.

COKE, family name of **Earl of Leicester**.

COKE, Viscount; Thomas Edward Coke; *b* 6 July 1965; *er s* and *heir* of Earl of Leicester, *qv*; *m* 1996, Polly, *y d* of David Whately; two *d*. *Educ:* Eton; Univ. of Manchester (BA). Scots Guards, 1987–93. *Address:* Holkham, Wells-next-the-Sea, Norfolk NR23 1AB.

COKER, Paul, FCA; Managing Director, Ranks Hovis McDougall, 1992–93; *b* 27 July 1938; *s* of Leslie and Mabel Coker; *m* 1966, Delphine Rostron Baden; twin *s* one *d*. *Educ:* Merchant Taylors' Sch. Joined Ranks Hovis McDougall (Cerebos Group), 1964: Man. Dir, General Products, 1982–87; Planning Dir, 1987–89; Dep. Man. Dir, 1989–91; Finance Dir, 1991–92. *Recreations:* golf, cricket, gardening, theatre. *Address:* Courtlands, Nightingales Lane, Chalfont St Giles, Bucks HP8 4SL. *T:* (01494) 762040.

COKER, Peter Godfrey, RA 1972 (ARA 1965); ARCA 1953; *b* 27 July 1926; *m* 1951, Vera Joyce Crook; one *s* decd. *Educ:* St Martin's Sch. of Art; Royal Coll. of Art (Royal Schol.). Brit. Inst. Schol., 1954. Arts Council Award to Artists, 1976. Hon. RE 1998. One-man Exhibitions: Zwemmer Gall., 1956, 1957, 1959, 1964, 1967; Magdalene Street

Gall., Cambridge, 1968; Stone Gall., Newcastle, 1969; Thackeray Gall., London, 1970, 1972, 1974, 1975, 1976, 1978; Gallery 10, London, 1980, 1982, 1984, 1986, 1988; Flying Colours Gall., Edinburgh, 1990. Retrospective Exhibitions: Minories, Colchester, 1972; Victoria Gall., Bath, 1972; Morley Gall., London, 1973; Mappin Art Gall., Sheffield, 1973; Chelmsford and Essex Museum, 1978; Royal Acad., 1979; Fitzwilliam Mus., Cambridge, 1989 (working drawings and sketchbooks, 1955–88); Kendal, 1992, then tour to Carlisle, Royal Acad. and Ipswich (landscapes 1956–90); Chris Beetles Gall., 2001. Represented in Group Exhibitions: Tate Gall., 1958; Jordan Gall., Toronto, 1958; John Moores, Liverpool, 1959, 1961; Northampton, 1960; Europaisches Forum, Alpbach, Austria, 1960; Neue Galerie, Linz, 1960; RCA, 1952–62; Painters in E Anglia, Arts Council, 1966; Bicentenary Exhibn, Royal Acad., 1768–1968, 1968; British Painting 1900–1960, Sheffield and Aberdeen, 1975–76; British Painting 1952–77, RA; Recent Chantrey Purchases, Tate Gall., 1981; Acquisitions since 1980, Tate Gall., 1982; The Forgotten Fifties, Sheffield and UK tour, 1984; Exhibition Road, RCA, 1988; The Kitchen Sink Painters, Mayor Gall., 1991; New Displays, Tate Gall., 1992. Works in permanent collections: Tate Gall.; British Museum; Scottish Nat. Gall. of Modern Art; Arts Council; Contemp. Art Soc., GB; Contemp. Art Soc., Wales; Chantrey Bequest; Nat. Portrait Gall.; V&A; Nat. Maritime Museum; Eastern Arts Assoc.; Rugby Library and Museum; Chelmsford and Essex Museum; Castle Museum, Norwich; Fitzwilliam Mus., Cambridge; Art Galls and Museums of Carlisle, Ipswich, Leicester, Rochdale, Doncaster; Art Galls of Bath (Victoria), Batley, Birmingham, Coventry (Herbert), Kendal (Abbot Hall), Kettering, Leeds City, Manchester City, Sheffield City, Southport (Atkinson), Salford; RCA; RA; Minories, Colchester; Beecroft Art Gall., Southend-on-Sea; Educn Cttees of Nottingham, Essex, Derbyshire, Lancs, ILEA; Liverpool Univ.; Stedelijk Mus., Ostend; Berardo Collection, Sintra, Portugal. *Publication:* Etching Techniques, 1976. *Recreations:* 19th century French painters and neoclassicism. *Address:* The Red House, Mistley, Manningtree, Essex CO11 1BX.

COKER, William John; QC 1994; *b* 19 July 1950; *s* of Edgar and Peggy Coker; *m* 1977, Ruth Elaine Pull; one *s* one *d*. *Educ:* Bedford Sch.; Manchester Univ. (LLB). Called to the Bar, Gray's Inn, 1973. *Recreations:* golf, fishing. *Address:* 7 Bedford Row, WC1R 4BU. *T:* (020) 7242 3555.

COLCHESTER, Area Bishop of, since 2001; **Rt Rev. Christopher Heudebourck Morgan;** *b* 23 March 1947; *m* 1975, Anne Musgrave; one *s* one *d*. *Educ:* City of Bath Boys' Sch.; Kelham Theol Coll.; Lancaster Univ. (BA 1973); Heythrop Coll., London (MTh 1991). Ordained deacon, 1973, priest, 1974; Curate, St James the Great, Birstall, 1973–76; Chaplain to EC staff, and Asst Chaplain, Holy Trinity Ch, Brussels, 1976–80; Team Vicar, St George, Redditch, and part-time Industrial Chaplain, 1980–85; Vicar, Sonning, 1985–96; Gloucester Diocesan Officer for Ministry, and a Residentiary Canon, Gloucester Cathedral, 1996–2001. Principal, Berks Christian Trng Scheme, 1985–89; Dir, Pastoral Studies, St Albans and Oxford Diocesan Ministry Course, 1992–96. *Recreations:* hill walking, amateur dramatics, improving at golf, music. *Address:* 1 Fitzwalter Road, Lexden, Colchester, Essex CO3 3SS.

COLCHESTER, Archdeacon of; *see* Wallace, Ven. M. W.

COLCLOUGH, Rt Rev. Michael John; *see* Kensington, Area Bishop of.

COLDSTREAM, Sir George (Phillips), KCB 1955 (CB 1949); KCVO 1968; QC 1960; *b* 20 Dec. 1907; *s* of late Francis Menzies Coldstream; *m* 1st, 1934, Mary Morna (marr. diss. 1948), *o d* of Major and Mrs A. D. Carmichael, Meigle, Perthshire; one *d* (and one *d* decd); 2nd, Sheila Hope, *widow* of Lt-Col J. H. H. Whitty, DSO, MC. *Educ:* Rugby; Oriel Coll., Oxford. Called to the Bar, Lincoln's Inn, 1930. Bencher, 1954; Asst to Parly Counsel to Treasury, 1934–39; Legal Asst, Lord Chancellor's Office, 1939–44; Dep. Clerk of the Crown, 1944–54; Clerk of the Crown in Chancery and Permanent Sec. to the Lord Chancellor, 1954–68. Member: British War Crimes Executive, 1944–46; Anglo-Amer. Legal Exchanges, 1961–69; Royal Commn on Assizes and Quarter Sessions, 1967–70; Top Salaries Review Body, 1971–82. Part-time Chm., Industrial Tribunals, 1975–80. Chm., Council of Legal Educn, 1970–73. Hon. LLD Columbia Univ., 1966. *Address:* The Gate House, Seaford, East Sussex BN25 2AH. *T:* (01323) 892801. *Clubs:* Athenæum; Royal Cruising.

COLDSTREAM, Prof. John Nicolas, FSA; FBA 1977; Yates Professor of Classical Art and Archaeology, 1983–92, now Emeritus, Hon. Fellow, 1993, University College London; *b* 30 March 1927; *s* of Sir John Coldstream and Phyllis Mary Hambly; *m* 1970, Imogen Nicola Carr. *Educ:* Eton; King's College, Cambridge (Class. Tripos, BA 1951, MA 1956). FSA 1964. Nat. Service, Buffs and HLI (Egypt and Palestine), 1945–48. Asst Master, Shrewsbury Sch., 1952–56; Temp. Asst Keeper, Dept of Greek and Roman Antiquities, BM, 1956–57; Macmillan Student, British Sch. at Athens, 1957–60; Bedford College, London: Lectr, 1960–66; Reader, 1966–75; Prof. of Aegean Archaeology, 1975–83. Geddes-Harrower Vis. Prof. of Classical Archaeology, Univ. of Aberdeen, 1983; Vis. Prof., Australian Archaeol Inst., Athens, 1989; T. B. L. Webster Meml Vis. Prof., Stanford Univ., Calif, 1990; Vis. Prof., Univ. of Athens, 1992. Mem., 1966–, Chm., 1987–91, Managing Cttee, British Sch. at Athens. Chm., Nat. Organizing Cttee, XI Internat. Congress of Classical Archaeol., London, 1978. Member: European Acad. of Scis and Arts, Salzburg, 1991; Deutsches Archäologisches Inst., 1978; Corresponding Member: Nordrhein-Westfälische (formerly Rheinisch-Westfälische) Akademie der Wissenschaften, 1984; Acad. of Athens, 1993; Hon. Mem., Archaeol Inst. of America, 1994. Hon. Fellow, Archaiologikē Hetaireia Athenōn, 1987. Editor, Annual of the British School at Athens, 1968–73. *Publications:* Greek Geometric Pottery, 1968; (with G. L. Huxley) Kythera: Excavations and Studies, 1972; Knossos: The Sanctuary of Demeter, 1973; Geometric Greece, 1977; (with H. W. Catling) Knossos, the North Cemetery: early Greek tombs, 4 vols, 1996; (jtly) Knossos, Pottery Handbook II: Greek and Roman, 2001; articles in British and foreign classical and archaeological journals. *Recreations:* music, travel. *Address:* 180 Ebury Street, SW1W 8UP.

COLDSTREAM, John Richard Francis; writer; Literary Editor, The Daily Telegraph, 1991–99; *b* 19 Dec. 1947; *s* of Gerald Coldstream and Marian Gatehouse; *m* 1977, Susan Elizabeth Pealing. *Educ:* Bradfield Coll.; Univ. of Nice; Univ. of Sussex. Evening Echo, Hemel Hempstead, 1971–74; joined Daily Telegraph, Peterborough column, 1974; Dep. Literary Editor, Daily Telegraph, 1984–91 and Sunday Telegraph, 1989–91. *Publication:* (ed) The Daily Telegraph Book of Contemporary Short Stories, 1995. *Recreations:* theatre; eating, France, when possible simultaneously. *Address:* 11 Abbey House, 1a Abbey Road, NW8 9BT. *Club:* Garrick.

COLE, family name of **Earl of Enniskillen**.

COLE, Babette S.; author and illustrator of children's books; *b* Jersey, 10 Sept. 1950. *Educ:* convent, Jersey; Canterbury Coll. of Educn (BA 1st Cl. Hons Illustration and Audio Visual 1973). Worked for BBC Children's TV. Member: BSJA; SSA. Side Saddle Rider of the Year, 1998. *Publications* include: Hairy Book, 1984; Slimy Book, 1985; Smelly Book, 1987; Silly Book, 1989; Trouble with Grandad, 1989; Three Cheers for Errol, 1990; Princess Smartypants, 1992; Mummy Laid an Egg (BRIT Award Best Illustrated Children's Bk of Year), 1993 (trans. 73 languages); Prince Cinders, 1993; Hurrah for Ethelyn, 1993; Tarzanna, 1993; Trouble with Mum, 1993; Trouble with Uncle, 1994; Dr Dog, 1994; Trouble with Dad, 1995; Winni Allfours, 1995; Trouble with Gran, 1997; Two of Everything, 1997; Bad Good Manners Book, 1997; King Change-a-lot, 1998; Bad Habits!, 1999; Animals Scare Me Stiff, 2000; Truelove, 2001. *Recreation:* breeding and showing show hunters. *Address:* c/o Rosemary Sandberg Ltd, 6 Bayley Street, WC1B 3HB. *T:* (020) 7304 4110.

COLE, Caroline Louise; *see* Flint, C. L.

COLE, (Claude Neville) David, CBE 1977; JP; Deputy Managing Director, International Thomson Organisation plc, 1985–86 (Joint Deputy Managing Director, 1980–84); Chairman, Thomson Foundation, since 1986; *b* 4 June 1928; 2nd *s* of late W. J. Cole and of Mrs M. J. Cole; *m* 1951, Alma Gwlithyn Williams (*d* 1990); one *s* one *d* (and one *s* decd); *m* 1992, Mary Agnes Rose Symonds. *Educ:* Royal Masonic School; Harvard Business Sch. Journalist: Merthyr Express; South Wales Echo; Daily Graphic (Manchester); Daily Sketch (London); Daily Recorder; Empire News (Cardiff); Editor, Western Mail, Cardiff, 1956–59; Managing Director: Western Mail and Echo Ltd, 1959–67 (now Chm.); Newcastle Chronicle and Journal Ltd, 1967–69; Thomson Regional Newspapers Ltd: Asst Man. Dir and Editorial Dir, 1969–72; Man. Dir and Chief Exec., 1972–82; Chm., 1980–82; Chm. and Chief Exec., Thomson Information Services, 1982–84. Chairman: Rainbird Publishing Gp, 1980–85; Hamish Hamilton, 1982–85; Thomson Books, 1980–85; Janes Publishing Co., 1981–86; Director: Thomson Organisation (Exec. Bd), 1973–80; Reuters Ltd, 1976–81; Press Assoc. (Chm. 1976–77, 1977–78); Welsh Nat. Opera Co. Ltd, 1960–71; Chairman: Celtic Press Ltd; Cole Cttee on Recruitment of Nurses in Wales, 1961–63; Working Party on Welsh Tourism, 1963–64; Barry Development Partnership, 1986–88; Civic Trust for Wales, 1986–96 (Pres., 1996–); Director: Welsh Develt Agency, 1987–90; Celtic Trees plc. Member: Council, Newspaper Soc., 1974–86 (Pres., 1982); Press Council, 1976–80; PIRA Council, 1984–86; Trustee, Reuters Ltd, 1983–. Chairman: Univ. of Wales Investment Cttee; Univ. of Wales Press, 1992–; Member: Court of Governors of Univ. of Wales, 1962–; Council of Univ. of Wales, 1962–; Council of Welsh National Sch. of Medicine, 1964–67; Council, Univ. of Wales Coll., Cardiff, 1988–92; Governing Body of Cardiff Coll. of Music and Drama, 1963–67; Council of Cardiff New Theatre Trust, 1964–67; Welsh Nat. Theatre Cttee; Aberfan Disaster Fund, 1966–67; Welsh Hospitals Bd, 1962–67. Vice-Patron, Coun. for Wales, Brit. Empire and Commonwealth Games. Pres., Tenovus, 1963–. FIMgt. Hon. LLD Wales, 1989. OStJ. *Publications:* This and Other Worlds (poems), 1975; Meeting Places and other poems, 1977; Mount of Angels (poems), 1978; The New Wales, 1991; Challenges to a Challenging Faith, 1995; The Wells of Life (poems), 1996. *Recreations:* two of the three R's. *Address:* Flat One, Gwentland, Marine Parade, Penarth, S Glam CF64 3BE. *T:* (029) 2070 3487. *Clubs:* East India, Devonshire, Sports and Public Schools; Cardiff and County (Cardiff).

COLE, David; *see* Cole, C. N. D.

COLE, Eileen Marie Lucy, CBE 1987; Chief Executive, Research International (Unilever Ltd), 1973–85 (in Rotterdam, 1973–77), retired 1985; *b* 22 April 1924; *d* of Arthur Walter Cole and Mary Agnes Boyd. *Educ:* grammar schs; Girton Coll., Cambridge (BA Hons Econ.). Joined Unilever as trainee, 1948; with associated cos and market res. div. of Unilever, 1948–60; Market Research Controller, Lever Bros Ltd, 1960–64; Research Bureau Ltd: Dir, 1964–67; Chm. and Man. Dir, 1967–72. Director: (non-exec.) Post Office, 1980–90; (part-time), LRT, 1984–88. Vice-Pres., 1979–, and Full Mem., UK Market Res. Soc. (Chm., 1977–79; Hon. Life Mem., 1985); Council Mem., Women in Management, 1971–; Mem., Careers Advisory Services: Cambridge Univ., 1968–75, 1979–83; Reading Univ., 1970–76, 1979–. FIMgt; Mem., Inst. of Dirs. Freeman: Marketors' Co., 1992; City of London, 1993. *Publications:* various in learned jls connected with market research. *Recreations:* gardening, cooking, reading, theatre. *Address:* Nicholas Farm, Lower Wield, Alresford, Hants SO24 9RX.

COLE, Frank; *see* Cole, (George) Francis.

COLE, George, OBE 1992; actor on stage, screen, radio and television; *b* 22 April 1925; *m* 1st, 1954, Eileen Moore (marr. diss. 1966); one *s* one *d*; 2nd, 1967, Penelope Morrell; one *s* one *d*. *Educ:* Surrey County Council Secondary Sch., Morden. Made first stage appearance in White Horse Inn, tour and London Coliseum, 1939; Cottage to Let, Birmingham, 1940; West End and on tour, 1940–41; subseq. West End plays included Goodnight Children, New, 1942; Mr Bolfry, Playhouse, 1943. Served in RAF, 1943–47. Returned to stage in Dr Angelus, Phoenix, 1947; The Anatomist, Westminster, 1948; Mr Gillie, Garrick, 1950; A Phoenix too Frequent and Thor with Angels, Lyric, Hammersmith, 1951; Misery Me, Duchess, 1955; Mr Bolfry, Aldwych, 1956; Brass Butterfly, Strand, 1958; The Bargain, St Martin's, 1961; The Sponge Room and Squat Betty, Royal Court, 1962; Meet Me on the Fence (tour), 1963; Hedda Gabler, St Martin's, 1964; A Public Mischief, St Martin's, 1965; Too True To Be Good, Strand, 1965; The Waiting Game, Arts, 1966; The Three Sisters, Royal Court, 1967; Doubtful Haunts, Hampstead, 1968; The Passionate Husband, 1969; The Philanthropist, Mayfair, 1971; Country Life, Hampstead, 1973; Déjà Revue, New London, 1974; Motive (tour), 1976; Banana Ridge, Savoy, 1976; The Case of the Oily Levantine, Guildford, 1977; Something Afoot, Hong Kong, 1978; Brimstone and Treacle, Open Space, 1979; Liberty Hall, Greenwich, 1980; The Pirates of Penzance, Drury Lane, 1982; A Month of Sundays, Duchess, 1986; A Piece of My Mind, Apollo, 1987; Peter Pan, Cambridge, 1987; The Breadwinner (tour), 1989; Natural Causes (tour), 1993; Theft (tour), 1995; Lock Up Your Daughters, Chichester, 1996; Heritage, Hampstead, 1997. *Films include:* Cottage to Let, 1941; Morning Departure, Laughter in Paradise, Scrooge, Top Secret, 1949–51; Will Any Gentleman?, The Intruder, 1952; Happy Ever After, Our Girl Friday, 1953; Belles of St Trinian's, 1954; Quentin Durward, 1955; The Weapon, It's a Wonderful World, The Green Man, 1956; Blue Murder at St Trinian's, Too Many Crooks, Don't Panic Chaps, The Bridal Path, 1957–59; The Pure Hell of St Trinian's, Cleopatra, Dr Syn, 1961–62; One Way Pendulum, Legend of Dick Turpin, 1964; Great St Trinian's Train Robbery, 1965; The Green Shoes, 1969; Vampire Lovers, 1970; Girl in the Dark, 1971; The Blue Bird, 1975; Minder on the Orient Express (TV film), 1985; Mary Reilly, 1996; The Ghost of Greville Lodge, 2000. TV Series include Life of Bliss (also radio), A Man of our Times, Don't Forget to Write, Minder (9 series), The Bounder (2 series), Blott on the Landscape, Comrade Dad, Life after Life, Single Voices, My Good Friend (2 series), An Independent Man, Dad (2 series), The Sleeper, Station Jim. *Address:* c/o Joy Jameson, 2.19 The Plaza, 535 King's Road, SW10 0SZ.

COLE, George Francis, (Frank); Founder Director, Frank Cole (Consultancy) Ltd, since 1979; *b* 3 Nov. 1918; *m*; Gwendoline Mary Laver (decd); two *s* one *d*; Barbara Mary Booth (*née* Gornall). *Educ:* Manchester Grammar Sch. Dir and Gen. Manager, Clarkson Engineers Ltd, 1944–53; Gen. Man., Ariel Motors Ltd (BSA Group), 1953–55; Dir, then Man. Dir, Vono Ltd, 1955–67. Past Chairman: Grovewood Products Ltd; Portways Ltd; R. & W. H. Symington Holdings Ltd; National Exhibition Centre Ltd; Crane's Screw

(Hldgs); Stokes Bomford (Holdings) Ltd; Debenholt Ltd; Stokes Bomford (Foods) Ltd; James Cooke (Birmingham) Ltd; Franklin Medical Ltd; Aero Needles Gp plc; Needle Industries Gp Ltd; F. J. Neve & Co. Ltd; Wild Barnsley Engrg Gp Ltd; Past Director: Duport Ltd; Shipping Industrial Holdings Ltd; G. Clancey Ltd; Armstrong Equipment PLC (retd as Dep. Chm., 1989); William Mitchell (Sinkers) Ltd (Chm., 1982–89); Director: Alexander Stenhouse (formerly Reed Stenhouse) UK Ltd, 1981–91; Mitchell-Grieve Ltd, 1989–91. Pres., Birmingham Chamber of Commerce and Industry, 1968–69. Leader of Trade Missions to West Germany, Yugoslavia, Romania and Hungary. CIMgt; Life Governor, Birmingham Univ.; Liveryman of City of London. Radio and Television appearances. *Publications:* press articles on economics, exports, etc. *Recreations:* tennis (competes regularly in Nat. Veteran Championships of GB), oil painting, snooker, gardening. *Address:* 2 Woodcote Drive, Dorridge, Solihull, West Midlands B93 8JR. *T:* (01564) 777795.

COLE, Humphrey John Douglas; retired; Deputy Secretary and Chief Economic Adviser, Department of Transport, and Chief Economic Adviser, Department of the Environment, 1983–87; *b* 30 Jan. 1928; *s* of late G. D. H. Cole and Dame Margaret I. Cole, DBE; *m* 1955, Hilda Annette Robinson; two *s* one *d*. *Educ:* Winchester Coll.; Trinity Coll., Cambridge. Research, Oxford Inst. of Statistics, 1950–61; Head, Economic Indicators and Foreign Trade, OECD Statistics Div., 1961–66; Dept of Economic Affairs: Senior Economic Adviser (Regional), 1966–67; Asst Dir of Economics, 1967–69; Dir of Economics, Min. of Technology, 1969–70; Dir of Econs (Urban and Highways), DoE, 1970–72; Dir Gen., Econs and Resources, DoE, 1972–76; Chief Economic Advr, DoE and Dept of Transport, 1976–82. *Publications:* articles in Bulletin of Inst. of Statistics, 1950–61. *Recreation:* walking. *Address:* 3 The Mead, W13 8AZ. *T:* (020) 8997 8285.

COLE, John Morrison; Political Editor, BBC, 1981–92; *b* 23 Nov. 1927; *s* of George Cole and Alice Jane Cole, Belfast; *m* 1956, Margaret Isobel, *d* of Mr and Mrs John S. Williamson, Belfast; four *s*. *Educ:* Fortwilliam and Skegoneill Primary Schs, Belfast; Belfast Royal Acad.; London Univ. (BA External). Belfast Telegraph, 1945–56: successively reporter, industrial, municipal and political correspondent; The Guardian: reporter, 1956–57; Labour Correspondent, 1957–63; News Editor, 1963–69; Dep. Editor, 1969–75; The Observer: Asst Editor, 1975; Dep. Editor, 1976–81. DUniv Open, 1992; Hon. DSSc QUB, 1992; Hon. DLitt Ulster, 1992; Hon. LLD St Andrews, 1993. *Publications:* The Poor of the Earth, 1976; The Thatcher Years: a decade of revolution in British politics, 1987; As It Seemed To Me: political memoirs, 1995; A Clouded Peace (novel), 2001; contrib. to books on British and Irish politics. *Recreations:* reading, travel. *Address:* c/o BBC Office, House of Commons, Westminster, SW1A 0AA. *T:* (020) 7219 4765. *Club:* Athenæum.

COLE, Prof. John Peter; Professor of Human and Regional Geography (formerly of Regional Geography), University of Nottingham, 1975–94, Emeritus since 1994; *b* Sydney, Australia, 9 Dec. 1928; *s* of Philip and Marjorie Cecelia Cole; *m* 1952, Isabel Jesús Cole (*née* Urrunaga); two *s*. *Educ:* Bromley Grammar Sch.; Univ. of Nottingham (State Schol., BA, MA, PhD, DLitt); Collegio Borromeo, Pavia Univ., Italy (British Council Schol.). Demonstrator, Univ. of Nottingham, 1951–52; Nat. Service with RN, Jt Services Sch. for Linguists, Russian Language Interpreter, 1952–54 (Lt Comdr RNR, retired); Oficina Nacional de Planeamiento y Urbanismo, Lima, Peru, 1954–55; Lectr in Geography, Univ. of Reading, 1955–56; Lectr in Geography, Univ. of Nottingham, 1956–69. Reader, 1969–75; Vis. Lectr or Prof., Univs of Washington, Columbia, Mexico, Valparaiso, Nanjing, Beijing. *Publications:* Geography of World Affairs, 1959, 6th edn 1983; (with F. C. German) Geography of the USSR, 1961, 2nd edn 1970; Italy, 1964; Latin America, 1965, 2nd edn 1975; (with C. A. M. King) Quantitative Geography, 1968; (with N. J. Beynon) New Ways in Geography, 1968, 2nd edn 1982; Situations in Human Geography, 1975; The Development Gap, 1981; Geography of the Soviet Union, 1984; China 1950–2000 Performance and Prospects, 1985; The Poverty of Marxism in Contemporary Geographical Applications and Research, 1986; Development and Underdevelopment, 1987; (with T. Buck) Modern Soviet Economic Performance, 1987; (with F. J. Cole) The Geography of the European Community, 1993, 2nd edn 1997; Geography of the World's Major Regions, 1996; Global 2050: a basis for speculation, 1999; contribs to learned jls, UK and overseas. *Recreations:* travel, languages, pen drawing and painting, gardening. *Address:* 10 Ranmore Close, Beeston, Nottingham NG9 3FR. *T:* (0115) 925 0409.

COLE, Prof. Peter Geoffrey; journalist; Professor of Journalism Studies, University of Sheffield, since 2000; *b* 16 Dec. 1945; *s* of Arthur and Elizabeth Cole; *m* 1982, Jane Ellison; three *s* one *d*. *Educ:* Tonbridge Sch.; Queens' Coll., Cambridge. Reporter, Evening News, 1968–72; Diary Editor, Evening Standard, 1976–78; News Editor, Deputy Editor, The Guardian, 1978–88; Editor, Sunday Correspondent, 1988–90; News Review Editor, The Sunday Times, 1990–93; Prof. of Journalism, Univ. of Central Lancs, 1993–2000. *Publication:* Can You Positively Identify This Man? (with Peter Pringle), 1975. *Address:* Department of Journalism Studies, University of Sheffield, Sheffield S10 2TN. *Clubs:* Plymouth Argyle Supporters' (London Branch); Lancashire County Cricket.

COLE, Richard Raymond Buxton; DL; **His Honour Judge Richard Cole;** a Circuit Judge, since 1984; *b* 11 June 1937; *s* of late Raymond Buxton Cole, DSO, TD, DL, and Edith Mary Cole; *m* 1962, Sheila Joy Rumbold; one *s* one *d*. *Educ:* Dragon School, St Edward's, Oxford. Admitted as Solicitor 1960; Partner in Cole & Cole Solicitors, Oxford, 1962–84; Recorder, 1976–84; Hon. Recorder, City of Coventry, 1999. Mem., Parole Bd, 1981–83. President: Berks, Bucks and Oxon Law Soc., 1981–82; Council of HM Circuit Judges, 2000–. Mem. Governing Body, Dragon Sch., 1975–92, Chm., 1986–92. Chm., Burford Parish Council, 1976–79, first Town Mayor, 1979. Master, Upholders' Co., 1992–93. Hon. Pres., Assoc. of Master Upholsterers, 1993–. DL Warwickshire, 2001. *Recreations:* sport, gardening. *Clubs:* MCC; Frewen (Oxford).

COLE, Robert Templeman, CBE 1981; FREng; DL; Chairman, Conder Group plc, 1979–87; *b* 14 Dec. 1918; *s* of Percival P. Cole and Amy Gladys Cole (*née* Templeman); *m* 1947, Elspeth Lawson; one *s* one *d*. *Educ:* Harrow; Cambridge Univ. (MA). FIStructE; FREng (FEng 1982). Served RAF, 1940–46. Hampshire County Council, 1946–47; Founder Partner, Conder Engineering, 1947; Chairman: Conder Engineering Co. Ltd, 1950; Conder International Ltd, 1964. DL Hants 1988. Hon. DSc Southampton, 1980. *Recreations:* gliding, jogging, travel. *Address:* Chilland Rise, Martyr Worthy, Winchester, Hampshire SO21 1AS. *T:* (01962) 779264.

COLE, Sir (Robert) William, Kt 1981; Director, Legal and General, Australia, 1987–91; *b* 16 Sept. 1926; *s* of James Henry and Rita Sarah Cole; *m* 1956, Margaret Noleen Martin; one *s* one *d*. *Educ:* Univ. of Melbourne (BCom). Joined Australian Public Service, 1952; Res. Officer, Treasury, 1952–57; Technical Asst, IMF, Washington, 1957–59; various positions, Treasury, 1959–70; Dir, Bureau of Transport Econs, Dept of Shipping and Transport, 1970–72; First Asst Sec., Gen. Financial and Economic Policy Div., Treasury, 1972–76; Australian Statistician, 1976; Sec., Dept of Finance, 1977–78; Chm., Public Service Bd, 1978–83; Sec., Defence Dept, 1983–86. Hon. Treas., Winston Churchill Meml Trust. *Recreations:* reading, fishing, wine. *Address:* 14 Macarthur Street, Cottesloe, WA 6011, Australia.

COLE, Stephanie, (Mrs Peter Birrel); actress; *b* 5 Oct. 1941; *d* of June Sheldon; *m* 1st, 1973, Henry Marshall (marr. diss.); one *d*; 2nd, 1998, Peter Birrel. *Educ:* Clifton High Sch., Bristol; Bristol Old Vic Sch. Work in repertory theatre, and with Old Vic, etc; *television:* Soldiering On (Alan Bennett Talking Heads monologue), 1988; *series:* Tenko, 1980–84; Waiting for God, 1989–94; Keeping Mum, 1997–99; Life As We Know It, 2001–; *theatre* includes: A Passionate Woman, Comedy, 1995; Quartet, Albery, 1999; *films* include: Grey Owl, 2000. Best TV Comedy Actress, 1992; Best TV Comedy Performance, 1999. *Publication:* A Passionate Life, 1998. *Recreations:* reading, gardening, painting, walking, theatre-going. *Address:* c/o Ladkin, 1 Duchess Street, W1N 3DE. *T:* (020) 7436 4626.

COLE, Sir William; *see* Cole, Sir R. W.

COLE-HAMILTON, (Arthur) Richard, CBE 1993; BA; CA; FCIBS; Chairman, Stakis PLC, 1995–98 (Deputy Chairman, 1994–95); Chief Executive, Clydesdale Bank PLC, 1982–92; *b* 8 May 1935; *s* of late John Cole-Hamilton, CBE; *m* 1963, Prudence Ann; one *s* two *d*. *Educ:* Ardrossan Academy; Loretto School; Cambridge Univ. (BA). Commissioned Argyll and Sutherland Highlanders, 1960–62. Brechin Cole-Hamilton & Co. (Chartered Accountants), 1962–67; Clydesdale Bank, 1967–92: Manager, Finance Corp. and Money Market, 1971; Asst Manager, Chief London Office, 1971; Supt of Branches, 1974; Head Office Manager, 1976; Asst Gen. Manager, 1978; Gen. Manager, 1979; Dep. Chief Gen. Manager, Feb. 1982; Dir, 1984–92. Chm., Cttee of Scottish Clearing Bankers, 1985–87, and 1991–92; Vice-Pres., Scottish Council for Develt and Industry, 1992–96; Dir, Glasgow Chamber of Commerce, 1985–91; Pres., Ayrshire Chamber of Commerce and Industry, 1992–96. Pres., Inst. of Bankers in Scotland, 1988–90. Mem. Council, Inst. of Chartered Accts of Scotland, 1981–85. Trustee: Nat. Galls of Scotland, 1986–96; Princess Royal Trust for Carers, 1991–98; Mem. Exec. Cttee, Erskine Hosp., 1976–. *Recreation:* golf. *Address:* 28 South Beach, Troon, Ayrshire KA10 6EF. *T:* (01292) 310603. *Clubs:* Western (Glasgow); Highland Brigade; Royal and Ancient Golf, Prestwick Golf.

COLEBROOK, Philip Victor Charles, CEng; retired 1984; Managing Director, Imperial Continental Gas Association, 1973–84 (Director, 1971; Director, CompAir Ltd, 1980–84); Director: Calor Group Ltd, 1969–84; Century Power & Light Ltd, 1980–84; Contibel SA (Belgium), 1978–84; *b* 8 March 1924; *s* of Frederick Charles Colebrook and Florence Margaret (*née* Cooper); *m* 1946, Dorothy Ursula Kemp; one *s* three *d*. *Educ:* Andover Grammar Sch.; Guildford Technical Coll.; Battersea Polytechnic, London. Served War of 1939–45, RNVR. Joined Pfizer as Works and Production Manager, 1952; Dir, 1956, Man. Dir, 1958–69, Pfizer Ltd; Chm. and Man. Dir, Pfizer Gp, 1961–69; Vice-Pres., Pfizer Internat., 1967–69; Man. Dir, Calor Gas Holding Co., 1969–80. Member: NHS Affairs Cttee, Assoc. of the British Pharmaceutical Industry, 1963–67; CBI Cttee on State Intervention in Private Business, 1975–78. Trustee and Mem. of Steering Cttee, Univ. of Kent at Canterbury, 1964–65. *Publication:* Going International, 1972. *Recreations:* sailing, ski-ing, golf.

COLEBY, Anthony Laurie; Executive Director, Bank of England, 1990–94; *b* 27 April 1935; *s* of Dr Leslie James Moger Coleby and Laurie Coleby (*née* Shuttleworth); *m* 1966, Rosemary Melian Elisabeth, *d* of Sir Peter Garran, KCMG; one *s* two *d*. *Educ:* Winchester; Corpus Christi, Cambridge (BAEcon, MA). Bank of England: joined, 1961; Personal Asst to Man. Dir, IMF, 1964–67; Assistant Chief, Overseas Dept, 1969; Adviser, Overseas Dept, 1972; Dep. Chief Cashier, 1973; Asst Dir, 1980–86; Chief Monetary Advr to the Governor, 1986–90; Exec. Dir, 1990–94. Non-executive Director: Halifax Building Soc., subseq. Halifax plc, 1994–2001; Anglo Irish Bank Corp., 1994–2001; Italian Internat. Bank, 1994–99. *Recreations:* choral singing, railways and transport. *Address:* Woodruff Farm, Debden Green, Saffron Walden, Essex CB11 3LZ.

COLECLOUGH, Peter Cecil; Chairman, Howard Machinery Ltd, 1969–82 (Director, 1950–82); Director: National Westminster Bank (Chairman SE Region), 1976–86; NCR Ltd, 1971–87; *b* 5 March 1917; *s* of late Thomas James Coleclough and of Hilda Emma (*née* Ingram); *m* 1944, Pamela Beresford (*née* Rhodes); one *s* (and one *s* decd). *Educ:* Bradfield. Served War, Cheshire Yeomanry, 1939; commnd into Roy. Warwickshire Regt, 1940; served until 1946. Mem., FBI/CBI Council, 1962–72; Chm., E Region, CBI, 1971–72; Leader, OECD/BIAC Investment Gp to Ceylon, 1968 and 1969; Chm., Meat and Livestock Commn, 1971–74; Pres., Agricl Engrs Assoc., 1971–72; Pres., Royal Warrant Holders Assoc., 1971–72. Chm., Appeals and Management Cttee, S Essex Medical Educn and Research Trust, 1969–75. *Recreation:* fishing. *Address:* Longlands Hall, Stonham Aspal, Stowmarket, Suffolk IP14 6AR. *T:* (01449) 711242.

COLEGATE, Isabel Diana, (Mrs Michael Briggs); novelist; *b* 10 Sept. 1931; *d* of Sir Arthur Colegate, sometime MP, and Winifred Mary, *d* of Sir William Worsley, 3rd Bt; *m* 1953, Michael Briggs; two *s* one *d*. *Educ:* Runton Hill Sch., Norfolk. Worked as literary agent at Anthony Blond (London) Ltd, 1952–57. FRSL 1981. Hon. MA Bath, 1988. *Publications:* The Blackmailer, 1958; A Man of Power, 1960; The Great Occasion, 1962 (re-issued as Three Novels, 1983); Statues in a Garden, 1964; Orlando King, 1968; Orlando at the Brazen Threshold, 1971; Agatha, 1973 (re-issued as The Orlando Trilogy, 1984); News from the City of the Sun, 1979; The Shooting Party, 1980 (W. H. Smith Literary Award, 1980; filmed, 1985); A Glimpse of Sion's Glory, 1985; Deceits of Time, 1988; The Summer of the Royal Visit, 1991; Winter Journey, 1995; A Pelican in the Wilderness: hermits and solitaries, 2002. *Recreation:* walking the dog. *Address:* Midford Castle, Bath BA2 7BU.

COLEMAN, Prof. Alice Mary; Professor of Geography, King's College, London, 1987–96, now Emeritus; *b* 8 June 1923; *d* of Bertie Coleman and Elizabeth Mary (*née* White). *Educ:* Clarendon House Sch.; Furzedown Training Coll. (Cert. of Educn); Birkbeck Coll., Univ. of London (BA Hons 1st Cl.); King's Coll., Univ. of London (MA with Mark of Distinction). FKC 1980. Geography Teacher, Northfleet Central Sch. for Girls, 1943–48; Geography Dept, King's Coll., London: Asst Lectr, 1948; Lectr, 1951; Sen. Lectr, 1963; Reader, 1965. Vis. Prof. for Distinguished Women Social Scientists, Univ. of Western Ontario, 1976; BC/Mombusho Prof. of Geog., Hokkaido Univ. of Educn at Asahikawa, 1985. Initiated and directed Second Land Utilisation Survey of Britain, 1960–; Dir, Design Improvement Controlled Experiment, 1988–94. Editor, Graphological Magazine, 1995–. Gill Meml Award, RGS, 1963; The Times-Veuve Clicquot Award, 1974; Busk Award, RGS, 1987. *Publications:* The Planning Challenge of the Ottawa Area, 1969; Utopia on Trial, 1985; Scapes and Fringes: environmental territories of England and Wales, 2000; 120 land-use maps in eleven colours at the scale of 1:25,000; over 300 academic papers. *Recreations:* reading, graphology. *Address:* King's College, Strand, WC2R 2LS; 19 Giles Coppice, SE19 1XF. *T:* (020) 8244 6733.

COLEMAN, Bernard, CMG 1986; HM Diplomatic Service, retired; Ambassador to Paraguay, 1984–86; *b* 3 Sept. 1928; *s* of William Coleman and Ettie Coleman; *m* 1st, 1950,

Sonia Dinah Walters (*d* 1995); two *d*; 2nd, 1996, Georgina Edith Dorndorf; three step *d*. *Educ:* Alsop High Sch., Liverpool. HM Forces (RAEC), 1946–48. Entered Foreign (later Diplomatic) Service, 1950; FO, 1950–53; Lima, 1953–56; Detroit, 1956–59; Second Secretary (Information): Montevideo, 1959–62; Caracas, 1962–64; First Sec. (Inf.), Caracas, 1964–66; FCO, 1967–69; First Sec. (Inf.), Ottawa, 1969–73; FCO, 1973–74; seconded to DTI, 1974–75; Consul-Gen., Bilbao, 1976–78; First Sec. (Commercial), Dublin, 1979–80; High Commissioner, Tonga, 1980–83. *Recreations:* golf, bowls, bridge, reading, walking, travel. *Address:* Apartado de Correos 517, 03730 Javea, Alicante, Spain.

COLEMAN, Brian John; Member (C) Barnet and Camden, London Assembly, Greater London Authority, since 2000; *b* 25 June 1961; *s* of John Francis Coleman and Gladys Coleman (*née* Cramp). *Educ:* Queen Elizabeth Boys' Sch., Barnet. Mills Allen Ltd, advertising co., 1989–99. Mem., Barnet CHC, 1991–94. Mem. (C) Barnet BC, 1998–. Dep. Chair and Cons. Gp Leader, London Fire and Emergency Planning Authy. Governor: Christchurch Secondary Sch., 1993– (Chm., 1999–); Ravenscroft Sch., 1996–. Vice Pres., Friern Barnet Summer Show (Chm., 1995–99); Trustee, Finchley Charities 2000. *Recreations:* opera, theatre. *Address:* 1 Essex Park, Finchley, N3 1ND. *T:* (020) 8349 2024. *Club:* Finchley Rotary.

COLEMAN, Dr Dena; Headteacher, Bushey Meads School, since 1998; *b* 7 Sept. 1952; *d* of Norman and Muriel Friedman; *m* 1974, Gordon David Coleman; one *s* one *d*. *Educ:* Copthall Co. Grammar Sch.; Manchester Univ. (BSc Hons Botany and Zool.; PGCE); Chelsea Coll., London (MA); King's Coll. London (PhD 1991). Sci. teacher, various London schools, 1974–86; Head of Sci., Queenswood Sch., 1986–90; Dep. Headteacher, 1990–95, Headteacher, 1995–98, Hasmonean High Sch. Member: Exec. Cttee, Assoc. Foundn and Vol. Aided (formerly Grant Maintained and Aided) Schools, 1997–; Herts Sch. Orgn Cttee, 1999–. Consultant, York Univ. Nat. Curriculum Sci. QCA Proj., 2000–01. *Publications:* (with R. Gold) Running a School, 2002; contrib. to Hist. of Educn Jl. *Recreations:* foreign travel, piano, clothes shopping. *Address:* Bushey Meads School, Coldharbour Lane, Bushey, Herts WD23 4PA. *T:* (020) 8950 3000.

COLEMAN, Prof. Dulcie Vivien, MD; FRCPath; Professor Emeritus of Cell Pathology, Imperial College School of Medicine, London University, since 1998 (Head of Department of Cytopathology and Cytogenetics, St Mary's Hospital, London, 1972–98; Professor of Cell Pathology, St Mary's Hospital Medical School, 1988–98); *b* 19 Oct. 1932; *d* of Dr Frank Stuart Coleman and Celia Coleman (*née* Walsman); *m* 1957, Jacob Benjamin Poznansky; three *s* one *d*. *Educ:* Bournemouth Sch. for Girls; Roedean Sch.; St Bartholomew's Hosp. Med. Sch. (MB, BS 1956; MD 1972). MRCPath 1980, FRCPath 1992. Hse Surgeon, Churchill Hosp., Oxford, 1956–57; Hse Physician, Plaistow Hosp., Essex, 1957–58; GP locums, 1959–64; Med. Asst (part-time), RPMS, 1967–70; Clin. Asst (part-time) (Cytopathol. and Cytogenetics), St Mary's Hosp., London, 1964–72; St Mary's Hospital Medical School: Sen. Lectr and Hon. Consultant in Cytopathol. and Cytogenetics, 1972–83; Reader in Cell Pathology, 1983–88; Hon. Consultant Cytopathologist, Hammersmith Hosps NHS Trust, 1998–. Member: Wkg Party on Safety of Chronic Villus sampling, MRC, 1987–90; Jt Wkg Party on Cytology Trng, DHSS, Inst. of Med. Lab. Scis and British Soc. for Clin. Cytol., 1988–90; Panel of Advrs, ACU, 1991–; Chairman: Wkg Party on Cervical Cancer Screening, Europe Against Cancer, 1990–; Wkg Party on Eur. Guidelines for Quality Assce in Cervical Screening (report pubd 1993); Cttee for Quality Assce, European Fedn of Cytology Socs, 1993–. Chm., Brit. Soc. for Clinical Cytology, 1989–92; Pres., Oncology section, RSM, 1988. Editor-in-Chief, Cytopathology, 1989–; Member, Editorial Board: Analytical Cellular Pathol.; Prenatal Diagnosis. Examr in Cytopathol. and Cytogenetics, Univs of London and Brunel, and RCPath. Hon. Member: Greek Cytology Soc.; CERDEC, France. Fellow, Internat. Acad. of Cytology. Morgani Medal, Italian Soc. of Pathology and Cytology, 1998. *Publications:* (with L. G. Koss) Advances in Clinical Cytology, Vol. 1 1981, Vol. 2 1984; (with D. M. D. Evans) Biopsy Pathology and Cytology of the Cervix, 1988, 2nd edn, 1999; (with P. C. Chapman) Clinical Cytotechnology, 1989; numerous papers, chapters, reviews on human polyomaviruses, human papillomaviruses, and other virus cytopathol. and prenatal diagnosis, incl. new techniques for cytodiagnosis of malignant disease, also on automated analysis of cervical smears. *Recreations:* gardening, swimming, nature walks. *Address:* Flat 12, 24 Hyde Park Square, W2 2NN. *T:* (020) 7262 0240.

COLEMAN, Iain; MP (Lab) Hammersmith and Fulham, since 1997; *b* 18 Jan. 1958; *m* 1996, Sally Powell (*see* Dame S. A. V. Powell); one *s*. *Educ:* Tonbridge Sch. Former Local Govt Officer. Mem., Hammersmith and Fulham BC, 1986–97 (Leader, 1991–96; Mayor, 1996–97). *Address:* House of Commons, SW1A 0AA.

COLEMAN, Isobel Mary; *see* Plumstead, I. M.

COLEMAN, Jeremy Barrington; a District Judge (Magistrates' Courts) (formerly Metropolitan Stipendiary Magistrate), since 1995; *b* 9 June 1951; *s* of Neville Coleman and Pauline Coleman; *m* 1975, Margot; one *s* one *d*. *Educ:* Coll. of Law, London. LRPS 1982. Admitted solicitor, 1976; Partner in family firm, Samuel Coleman, 1976–. Mem., Law Soc. Children's Panel, 1990. Mem., RPS. *Recreations:* photography, cricket, archaeology. *Address:* Justices' Secretariat Department, 65 Romney Street, SW1P 3RD. *Club:* Middlesex CC.

COLEMAN, John Ennis, CB 1990; Legal Adviser, Department of Education and Science, 1983–90, retired; *b* 12 Nov. 1930; *o s* of late Donald Stafford Coleman and Dorothy Jean Balieff (*née* Ennis); *m* 1958, Doreen Gwendoline Hellinger; one *s* one *d*. *Educ:* Dean Close Sch., Cheltenham; Dulwich Coll.; Worcester Coll., Oxford (MA). Solicitor (Hons), 1957. Legal Asst, Treasury Solicitor's Dept, 1958; Senior Legal Asst, 1964; Asst Solicitor, 1971; Under Sec. (Legal), Depts of Industry and Trade, 1980–83. Jt Editor, The Law of Education, 1993–. *Publication:* (jtly) Butterworth's Education Law, 1997.

COLEMAN, Lucille Madeline; *see* Stone, L. M.

COLEMAN, Nicholas John; His Honour Judge Coleman; a Circuit Judge, since 1998; *b* 12 April 1947; *s* of late Leslie Ernest Coleman and Joyce Coleman; *m* 1971, Isobel Mary Plumstead, *qv*; one *s* two *d*. *Educ:* Royal Pinner Sch.; Liverpool Univ. (LLB Hons). Called to the Bar, Inner Temple, 1970; practised SE Circuit, 1972–98; a Recorder, 1989–98. Lectr, 1970–72, Examr, 1972–76, Inns of Court Sch. of Law. *Recreations:* sport, travel, theatre, cinema. *Address:* c/o Snaresbrook Crown Court, 75 Hollybush Hill, E11 1QW. *T:* (020) 8982 5500. *Clubs:* MCC; Hampstead and Westminster Hockey, Pelicans Hockey (King's Lynn); Hunstanton Golf, Aldeburgh Golf.

COLEMAN, Peter Anthony; Secretary General, European Parliamentary Labour Party, since 1997; *b* 10 Oct. 1945; *s* of late William and of Maggie Coleman; *m* 1966, Dorothy Edith Lawrence; two *d*. *Educ:* Avenue Primary Sch., Wellingborough; Park Road Junior Sch., Kettering; Kettering Sch. for Boys; Kettering Boot and Shoe Tech. Coll. (ABBSI). Progress chaser: Holyoake Footwear, 1961–64; Wilson & Watsons, 1964–66; Labour Party: organiser: Peterborough, 1967–71; Nottingham, 1972–76; SE Derbys, 1976–78; Asst Regl Organiser, E Midland, 1978–83, Regl Organiser, 1983–93; Nat. Dir of Orgn and Develt, 1993–97. Nat. Vice-Pres., Nat. Union of Labour Organisers, 1977–78. Member: Exec. Cttee, Fabian Soc., 1994–95; Mgt Cttee, H. S. Chapman Soc., 2000–. *Publications:* (ed) Labour's Fundraising Guide, 1984; pamphlets on electoral law, Labour Party regeneration and polling-day systems. *Recreations:* theatre, travel, watching cricket and football. *Address:* 2 Queen Anne's Gate, SW1H 9AA. *T:* (020) 7222 1719.

COLEMAN, Rt Rev. Peter Everard; Bishop Suffragan of Crediton, 1984–96; an Assistant Bishop, diocese of Bath and Wells, since 1996; *b* 28 Aug. 1928; *s* of Geoffrey Everard Coleman and Lilian Coleman; *m* 1960, HSH Princess Elisabeth-Donata Reuss; two *s* two *d*. *Educ:* Haileybury; King's Coll., London Univ. (LLB, AKC); Bristol Univ. (MLitt). Mil. Service, RHG and RA, 1947–49. Called to the bar, Middle Temple, 1965. Ordained, Bristol, 1955; Chaplain and Lectr, King's Coll., London, 1960–66; Vicar of St Paul's, Clifton, and Chaplain, Bristol Univ., 1966–71; Canon Residentiary and Dir of Training, Bristol, 1971–81; Archdeacon of Worcester, 1981–84. Clerical Member, Court of Arches, 1980–91; Mem. General Synod, 1974–81, 1990–95. Chm., British Trust for the Ecumenical Inst., Jerusalem, 1991–. Provost, Western Div., Woodard Corp., 1992– (Fellow, 1985–). OStJ 1993. Jt Editor, Theology, 1982–91. *Publications:* Experiments with Prayer, 1961; A Christian Approach to Television, 1968; Christian Attitudes to Homosexuality, 1980; Gay Christians—a moral dilemma, 1989; The Ordination of Women to the Priesthood, 1990. *Recreations:* film making, fishing. *Address:* Boxenwood Cottage, West Bagborough, Bishops Lydeard, Somerset TA4 3HQ. *T:* (01984) 618607. *Club:* Army and Navy.

COLEMAN, Robert John; Director General, Health and Consumer Protection, European Commission, since 1999; *b* 8 Sept. 1943; *s* of Frederick and Kathleen Coleman; *m* 1966, Malinda Tigay Cutler; two *d*. *Educ:* Univ. of Oxford (MA); Univ. of Chicago (JD). Called to the Bar, Inner Temple, 1969. Lectr in Law, Univ. of Birmingham, 1967–70; Barrister at Law, 1970–73; European Commission: Administrator, subseq. principal administrator, 1974–82; Dep. Head of Div., safeguard measures and removal of non-tariff barriers, 1983; Head of Div., Intellectual Property and Unfair Competition, 1984–87; Dir, Public Procurement, 1987–90; Dir, Approximation of Laws, Freedom of Estabt, and Freedom to Provide Services, 1990–91; Dir Gen., Transport, 1991–99. Vis. Prof., Univ. of East London, 1997–. Mem. Adv. Bd, Sch. of Mgt, Univ. of Bath, 2001–. *Publications:* contribs and articles on legal and policy issues, concerning corporate accounting, employee participation, intellectual property and transport. *Recreations:* cycling, music. *Address:* 114 rue des Deux Tours, 1210 Brussels, Belgium. *T:* (2) 2183865.

COLEMAN, Ronald Frederick, CB 1991; DSc; CChem, FRSC; consultant in technology management, since 1992; Chief Engineer and Scientist, Department of Trade and Industry, 1987–92; *b* 10 Nov. 1931; *s* of late Frederick George Coleman and Dorothy Alice Coleman (*née* Smith); *m* 1954, Maureen Mary Salt; one *s* one *d*. *Educ:* King Edward VI Sch., Birmingham; College of Technology, Birmingham (BSc, DSc). Chance Brothers Glassworks, Smethwick, 1949–54; UKAEA: Aldermaston, 1954–71; Harwell, 1972; Laboratory of the Government Chemist, 1973–77; National Physical Laboratory, 1977–81; Government Chemist, 1981–87. Dir, Beard Dove Ltd, 1994–95. Visiting Professor: Kingston Polytechnic, 1981–91; Royal Holloway and Bedford New Coll., 1985–92. Pres., British Acad. of Forensic Sciences, 1982–83. Member: SERC, 1987–92; AFRC, 1987–92. Pres., BioIndustry Assoc., 1992–96. Chm., Bd of Govs, Kingston Univ. (formerly Polytechnic), 1991–95. DUniv Surrey, 1987; Hon. DSc: Poly. of Central London, 1989; Cranfield Inst. of Technology, 1992. *Publications:* various papers on analytical chemistry, nuclear chemistry and forensic science. *Recreations:* music, golf, gardening. *Address:* Lime Cottage, Thames Street, Sonning on Thames, Berks RG4 6UR. *T:* (0118) 969 9837.

COLEMAN, Dame Sally (Ann Vickers); *see* Powell, Dame S. A. V.

COLEMAN, Terry, (Terence Francis Frank); reporter and author; *b* 13 Feb. 1931; *s* of J. and D. I. B. Coleman; *m* 1st, 1954, Lesley Fox-Strangeways Vane (marr. diss.); two *d*; 2nd, 1981, Vivien Rosemary Lumsdaine Wallace; one *s* one *d*. *Educ:* 14 schs. LLB London. Formerly: Reporter, Poole Herald; Editor, Savoir Faire; Sub-editor, Sunday Mercury, and Birmingham Post; Reporter and then Arts Corresp., The Guardian, 1961–70, Chief Feature Writer, 1970–74; Special Writer with Daily Mail, 1974–76; The Guardian: Chief Feature Writer, 1976–79, writing mainly political interviews, inc. last seven British Prime Ministers; NY Correspondent, 1981; special corresp., 1982–89; Associate Editor, The Independent, 1989–91. FRSA. Feature Writer of the Year, British Press Awards, 1982; Journalist of the Year, Granada Awards, 1987. *Publications:* The Railway Navvies, 1965 (Yorkshire Post prize for best first book of year); A Girl for the Afternoons, 1965; (with Lois Deacon) Providence and Mr Hardy, 1966; The Only True History: collected journalism, 1969; Passage to America, 1972; (ed) An Indiscretion in the Life of an Heiress (Hardy's first novel), 1976; The Liners, 1976; The Scented Brawl: collected journalism, 1978; Southern Cross, 1979; Thanksgiving, 1981; Movers and Shakers: collected interviews, 1987; Thatcher's Britain, 1987; Empire, 1993; Nelson: the man and the legend, 2001. *Recreations:* cricket, opera, circumnavigation. *Address:* c/o Peters, Fraser & Dunlop, Drury House, 34–43 Russell Street, WC2B 5HA. *T:* (020) 7344 1000. *Club:* MCC.

COLEMAN, Victor Paul; HM Chief Inspector of Railways, Health and Safety Executive, since 1998; *b* 28 Feb. 1952; *s* of Richard William Coleman and Edna Grace Coleman; *m* 1978, Eleanor Jane Kirkwood. *Educ:* Greenford Co. Grammar Sch.; King's Coll., Cambridge (MA); Univ. of Aston in Birmingham (Dip. Occupational Safety and Health). HM Inspector of Factories, 1973–83; Health and Safety Executive: Principal Inspector of Factories, 1983–92; Hd, Railway Safety Policy, 1992–94; Dep. Chief Inspector of Railways, 1995–98. Chm., Railways Industry Adv. Cttee, HSC, 1998–; Mem., Channel Tunnel Safety Authy, 1995–98. *Recreations:* theatre, walking. *Address:* (office) Rose Court, 2 Southwark Bridge, SE1 9HS. *T:* (020) 7717 6501.

COLENSO-JONES, Maj. (Gilmore) Mervyn (Boyce); one of HM Body Guard, Honourable Corps of Gentlemen-at-Arms, 1982–2000 (Harbinger, 1997–2000); *b* 4 Sept. 1930; *s* of late Dr Gilmore Leonard Colenso Colenso-Jones and Kathleen Edwina Colenso-Jones (*née* Macartney); *m* 1968, Rosamond Anne Bowen. *Educ:* Rugby Sch. Commnd Royal Welch Fusiliers, 1950; served at home and abroad; jssc, Latimer, 1968–69; Brit. Exchange Officer, US Continental Army Comd, Va, 1969–70; retd 1972, in rank of Maj.; Regtl Sec., RWF, 1972–81. Mem., S Glamorgan HA, 1981–84. CStJ 1981 (Priory Sec. for Wales, 1981–84). *Recreations:* country pursuits, water-colour painting. *Address:* Savernake Cottage, E Grafton, Marlborough, Wilts SN8 3DB. *T:* (01672) 810868. *Club:* Army and Navy.

COLERAINE, 2nd Baron *cr* 1954, of Haltemprice; **James Martin Bonar Law;** *b* 8 Aug. 1931; *s* of 1st Baron Coleraine, PC, *y s* of Rt Hon. Andrew Bonar Law, and Mary Virginia (*d* 1978), *d* of A. F. Nellis, Rochester, NY; *S* father, 1980; *m* 1st, 1958, Emma Elizabeth Richards (marr. diss.); two *d*; 2nd, 1966, Anne Patricia, (Tomt) (*d* 1993), *yr d* of Major-Gen. R. H. Farrant, CB; one *s* one *d* (and one *d* decd); 3rd, 1998, Marion Robina,

(Bobbie), *d* of Sir Thomas Ferens, CBE and *widow* of Peter Smyth. *Educ:* Eton; Trinity College, Oxford. Formerly in practice as a solicitor. Hon. Consultant, Fedn of Private Residents' Assocs, 1994–. *Heir: s* Hon. James Peter Bonar Law, *b* 23 Feb. 1975. *Address:* 5 Kensington Park Gardens, W11 3HB. *T:* (020) 7221 4148; The Dower House, Sunderlandwick, Driffield, E Yorks YO25 9AD. *T:* (01377) 253535.
See also Baron Ironside.

COLERIDGE, family name of **Baron Coleridge**.

COLERIDGE, 5th Baron *cr* 1873, of Ottery St Mary; **William Duke Coleridge;** *b* 18 June 1937; *s* of 4th Baron Coleridge, KBE, and Cecilia Rosamund (*d* 1991), *d* of Adm. Sir William Wordsworth Fisher, GCB, GCVO; *S* father, 1984; *m* 1st, 1962, Everild Tania (marr. diss. 1977), *d* of Lt-Col Beauchamp Hambrough, OBE; one *s* two *d*; 2nd, 1977, Pamela, *d* of late G. W. Baker, CBE, VRD; two *d*. *Educ:* Eton; RMA Sandhurst. Commissioned into Coldstream Guards, 1958; served King's African Rifles, 1962–64; commanded Guards Independent Parachute Company, 1970–72. Director: Abercrombie & Kent, 1978–90; Universal Energy Ltd, 1984–90; Larchpark Properties Ltd, 1987–92; European Leisure Estates plc, 1988–90; Advr, Nat. Marine Aquarium, 1990–. Gov., Royal West of England Residential Sch. for the Deaf, 1984–. *Heir:* Hon. James Duke Coleridge, *b* 5 June 1967. *Address:* The Chanters House, Ottery St Mary, Devon EX11 1DQ. *T:* (01404) 812417.

COLERIDGE, David Ean; Chairman of Lloyd's, 1991, 1992 (Deputy Chairman, 1985, 1988, 1989); *b* 7 June 1932; *s* of Guy Cecil Richard Coleridge, MC and Katherine Cicely Stewart Smith; *m* 1955, Susan Senior; three *s*. *Educ:* Eton. Glanvill Enthoven, 1950–57; R. W. Sturge & Co., 1957–95: Dir, 1966–95; Chm., A. L. Sturge (Holdings) Ltd (now Sturge Holdings PLC), 1978–95. Chairman: Oxford Agency Hldgs Ltd, 1987–90; Ockham Hldgs, 1995 (Dir, 1995–); Director: R. A. Edwards (Holdings) Ltd, 1985–90; Wise Speke Hldgs Ltd, 1987–94. Mem., Council and Cttee of Lloyd's, 1983–92. *Recreations:* golf, racing, gardening, family. *Address:* Spring Pond House, Wispers, near Midhurst, W Sussex GU29 0QH. *T:* (01730) 813277; 37 Egerton Terrace, SW3 2BU. *T:* (020) 7581 1756.
See also N. D. Coleridge.

COLERIDGE, Geraldine Margaret, (Gill), (Mrs D. R. Leeming); Partner, Rogers Coleridge and White, Literary Agency, since 1988; *b* 26 May 1948; *d* of Antony Duke Coleridge and June Marian Caswell; *m* 1974, David Roger Leeming; two *s*. *Educ:* Queen Anne's School, Caversham; Marlborough Secretarial College, Oxford. BPC Partworks, Sidgwick & Jackson, Bedford Square Book Bang, to 1971; Publicity Manager, Chatto & Windus, 1971–72; Dir and Literary Agent, Anthony Sheil Associates, 1973–88. Pres., Assoc. of Authors' Agents, 1988–91. *Recreations:* entertaining, reading, music, gardening. *Address:* 113 Calabria Road, N5 1HS. *T:* (020) 7226 5875.

COLERIDGE, Lady (Marguerite) Georgina; *b* 19 March 1916; *d* of 11th Marquess of Tweeddale; *m* 1941, Arthur Coleridge (*d* 1988), *yr s* of John Duke Coleridge; one *d*. *Educ:* home, abroad as a child. Freelance writer, Harpers Bazaar, etc, 1936; joined National Magazine Co.: Circulation Dept, 1937; Advertisement Dept., 1938; joined Country Life, 1945; Editor of Homes and Gardens, 1949–63; Chm., Inst. of Journalists (London District), 1954, Fellow 1970; Chm., Women's Press Club, 1959 (Pres., 1965–67). Dir, Country Life Ltd, 1962–74; Dir, George Newnes Ltd, 1963–69; Publisher: Homes and Gardens; Woman's Journal, 1969–71; Ideal Home, 1970–71; Dir, Special Projects, IPC Women's Magazines, 1971–74; Consultant: IPC Women's Magazines, 1974–82; Public Relations Counsel Ltd, 1974–85 (Dir, 1978–85). Mem., Internat. Assoc. of Women and Home Page Journalists, 1968–74; Associate, Women in Public Relations, 1972; Associate Mem., Ladies Jockeys Assoc. of GB, 1973; Founder Mem., Media Soc. Ltd (Inst. of Journalists Foundn), 1973–76; Member: Information Cttee, Brit. Nutrition Foundn, 1975–79; Information Cttee, RCP, 1977–81; Vice-Pres., Greater London Fund for the Blind, 1981; President: Dale Youth Club, N Kensington, 1978; Friends of Moorfields, 1981–92. Freeman, Worshipful Co. of Stationers and Newspapermakers, 1973. *Publications:* Grand Smashional Pointers (book of cartoons), 1934; I Know What I Like (clichés), 1959; That's Racing, 1978; many features for various jls. *Recreations:* racing, writing, cooking; nothing highbrow. *Address:* 33 Peel Street, W8 7PA.

COLERIDGE, Nicholas David; Managing Director, Condé Nast Publications, since 1992 (Editorial Director, 1989–91); Vice-President, Condé Nast International Inc., since 1999; *b* 4 March 1957; *s* of David Ean Coleridge, *qv*; *m* 1989, Georgia Metcalfe; three *s* one *d*. *Educ:* Eton; Trinity Coll., Cambridge. Associate Editor, Tatler, 1979–81; Columnist, Evening Standard, 1981–84; Features Editor, Harpers and Queen, 1985–86, Editor, 1986–89. Chm., British Fashion Council, 2000–. Council Mem., RCA, 1995–2000. Young Journalist of the Year, British Press Awards, 1983. *Publications:* Tunnel Vision, collected journalism, 1982; Around the World in 78 Days, 1984; Shooting Stars, 1984; The Fashion Conspiracy, 1988; How I Met My Wife and other stories, 1991; Paper Tigers, 1993; With Friends Like These, 1997; Streetsmart, 1999. *Address:* 39 Kensington Park Gardens, W11 2QT. *T:* (020) 7221 4293. *Clubs:* Harry's Bar, Mark's.

COLERIDGE, Hon. Sir Paul (James Duke), Kt 2000; **Hon. Mr Justice Coleridge;** a Judge of the High Court, Family Division, since 2000; *b* 30 May 1949; *s* of James Bernard and Jane Evelina Coleridge; *m* 1973, Judith Elizabeth Rossiter; two *s* one *d*. *Educ:* Cranleigh Sch., Surrey; College of Law, London. Called to the Bar, Middle Temple, 1970, Bencher, 2000; in practice at the Bar, 1970–85; Internat. Legal Advr to Baron Hans Heinrich Thyssen-Bornemisza, Switzerland, 1985–89; private practice, 1989–2000; QC 1993; a Recorder, 1996–2000. *Recreations:* Dorset, gardening, motor-bikes. *Address:* Royal Courts of Justice, Strand WC2A 2LL. *Club:* MCC.

COLES, Adrian Michael; Director-General, Building Societies Association, since 1993; *b* 19 April 1954; *s* of Kenneth Ernest Coles and Constance Mary (*née* Sykes); *m* 1981, Marion Alma Hoare; one *s* one *d*. *Educ:* Holly Lodge Grammar Sch., Smethwick; Univ. of Nottingham (BA Hons); Univ. of Sheffield (MA). Economist, Electricity Council, 1976–79; Building Societies Association: Economist, 1979–81; Head: Econs and Stats, 1981–86; External Relns, 1986–93; Dir-Gen., Council of Mortgage Lenders, 1993–96. Chm., Thames Valley Housing Assoc., 1990–93; Director: Housing Securities Ltd, 1994–; Banking Code Standards Bd Ltd; Parsons Mead Educnl Services Ltd. Trustee, Money Advice Trust, 1994–. *Publications:* (with Mark Boleat) The Mortgage Market, 1987; numerous articles in housing and housing finance jls. *Recreations:* running, cycling, reading, family. *Address:* The Building Societies Association, 3 Savile Row, W1X 1AF. *T:* (020) 7437 0655.

COLES, Sir (Arthur) John, GCMG 1997 (KCMG 1989 CMG 1984); HM Diplomatic Service, retired; Permanent Under-Secretary of State, Foreign and Commonwealth Office, and Head of the Diplomatic Service, 1994–97; *b* 13 Nov. 1937; *s* of Arthur Strixton Coles and Doris Gwendoline Coles; *m* 1965, Anne Mary Sutherland Graham; two *s* one *d*. *Educ:* Magdalen Coll. Sch., Brackley; Magdalen Coll., Oxford (BA 1960, MA). Served HM Forces, 1955–57. Joined HM Diplomatic Service, 1960; Middle Eastern Centre for Arabic Studies, Lebanon, 1960–62; Third Sec., Khartoum, 1962–64; FO (later FCO), 1964–68; Asst Political Agent, Trucial States (Dubai), 1968–71; FCO, 1971–75; Head of Chancery, Cairo, 1975–77; Counsellor (Developing Countries), UK Perm. Mission to EEC, 1977–80; Head of S Asian Dept, FCO, 1980–81; Private Sec. to Prime Minister, 1981–84; Ambassador to Jordan, 1984–88; High Commissioner to Australia, 1988–91; Dep. Under-Sec. of State, FCO, 1991–94. Non-exec. Dir, BG plc, 1998–. Chm., Sight Savers Internat., 2001–. Trustee, Imperial War Mus., 1999–. Vis. Fellow, All Souls Coll., Oxford, 1998–99. Gov., Ditchley Foundn, 1997–; Mem. Council, Atlantic Coll., 2001. *Publications:* British Influence and the Euro, 1999; Making Foreign Policy: a certain idea of Britain, 2000. *Recreations:* walking, cricket, bird-watching, reading, music. *Address:* Kelham, Dock Lane, Beaulieu, Hants SO42 7YH. *Club:* Oxford and Cambridge.

COLES, Bruce; *see* Coles, N. B. C.

COLES, Rt Rev. David John; *see* Christchurch, Bishop of.

COLES, Gerald James Kay, QC 1976; **His Honour Judge Gerald Coles;** a Circuit Judge, since 1985; *b* 6 May 1933; *o s* of James William Coles and Jane Elizabeth Coles; *m* 1958, Kathleen Yolande, *e d* of Alfred John Hobson, FRCS, and Kathleen Elizabeth Hobson; three *s*. *Educ:* Coatham Sch., Redcar; Brasenose Coll., Oxford; Harvard Law Sch., Harvard Univ. Meritorious Award, Hastings Schol., Queen's Coll., Oxford, 1949; Akroyd Open Schol. 1950; BA 1954, BCL 1955, Oxon; Westengard Schol., Harvard Law Sch., 1955; LLM 1956. Called to Bar, Middle Temple, 1957; practised at Bar, London and NE Circuit, 1957–85; Prosecuting Counsel to Inland Revenue, 1971–76; a Recorder, 1972–85; Designated Family Judge, York, 1990–96; Resident Judge, Bradford Crown Court, 1992–2000. A Pres., Mental Health Review Tribunals, 1986–. Mem., Ethnic Minorities Adv. Cttee, Judicial Studies Bd, 1993–98. *Recreations:* Freemasonry (Provincial Grand Master and Grand Supt, Prov. of Yorks, N and E Ridings, 1995–), music, theatre, photography. *Address:* Redwood, Dean Lane, Hawksworth, Guiseley, Leeds, Yorks LS20 8NY. *Clubs:* Oxford and Cambridge; Bradford.

COLES, Sir John; *see* Coles, Sir A. J.

COLES, John David, RCNC; Director General, Equipment Support (Sea), Chief Executive, Warship (formerly Ships) Support Agency, and Head of Royal Corps of Naval Constructors, since 1998; *b* 10 May 1945; *s* of William Frederick Coles and Alice Marie Coles; *m* 1967, Judith Ann Baker (*d* 1992); two *d*. *Educ:* University Coll. London (BSc 1969; MSc 1970). FRINA 1998. RCNC 1971–; Staff Constructor to Flag Officer Submarines, 1978–82; Head of British Admiralty Office, USA, 1982–85; Assistant Director: Future Projects, 1985–88; Dir Gen. Submarines, 1988–92; Dir of Works, Strategic Systems, 1992–94; rcds, 1994; Supt Ships, Devonport, MoD, 1995–97. *Address:* Room 102, B Block, Ministry of Defence, Foxhill, Bath BA1 5AB. *T:* (01225) 883935.

COLES, John Morton, ScD, PhD; FBA 1978; Professor of European Prehistory, University of Cambridge, 1980–86; Fellow of Fitzwilliam College, since 1963, Honorary Fellow, 1987; *b* 25 March 1930; *s* of Edward John Langdon Coles and Alice Margaret (*née* Brown); *m* 1985, Bryony Jean Orme; two *s* two *d* of previous marr. *Educ:* Woodstock, Ontario; Univ. of Toronto (BA); Univ. of Cambridge (MA, ScD); Univ. of Edinburgh (PhD). Research Fellow, Univ. of Edinburgh, 1959–60; Asst Lectr, 1960–65, Lectr, 1965–76, Reader, 1976–80, Univ. of Cambridge. Fellow, McDonald Inst. for Archaeological Res., Univ. of Cambridge, 1992–96; Hon. Res. Prof., Univ. of Exeter, 1993–. President, Prehistoric Soc., 1978–82. Member: Royal Commn on Ancient and Historical Monuments of Scotland, 1992–; Directorate, Discovery Prog. Ireland, 2001–. MAE 1989; Hon. Corresp. Mem., Deutschen Archäologischen Instituts, 1979; Hon. Mem., Inst. of Field Archaeologists, 1991. FSA 1963 (Vice-Pres., 1982–86). Hon. FilDr Uppsala Univ., 1997. Grahame Clark Medal, British Acad., 1995; ICI Medal, British Archaeol Awards, 1998. *Publications:* The Archaeology of Early Man (with E. Higgs), 1969; Field Archaeology in Britain, 1972; Archaeology by Experiment, 1973; (with A. Harding) The Bronze Age in Europe, 1979; Experimental Archaeology, 1979; (with B. Orme) Prehistory of the Somerset Levels, 1980; The Archaeology of Wetlands, 1984; (with B. J. Coles) Sweet Track to Glastonbury: the Somerset Levels in prehistory, 1986; (ed with A. Lawson) European Wetlands in Prehistory, 1987; Meare Village East, 1987; (with B. J. Coles) People of the Wetlands, 1989; Images of the Past, 1990; From the Waters of Oblivion, 1991; (with A. Goodall and S. Minnitt) Arthur Bulleid and the Glastonbury Lake Village 1892–1992, 1992; (with D. Hall) Fenland Survey, 1994; Rock Carvings of Uppland, 1994; (with S. Minnitt) Industrious and Fairly Civilised: the Glastonbury lake village, 1995; (with B. Coles) Enlarging the Past: the contribution of wetland archaeology, 1996; (with S. Minnitt) The Lake Villages of Somerset, 1996; (with D. Hall) Changing Landscapes: the ancient Fenland, 1998; (ed jtly) World Prehistory: studies in memory of Grahame Clark, 1999; (ed jtly) Bog Bodies, Sacred Sites and Wetland Archaeology, 1999; Patterns in a Rocky Land: rock carvings in South West Uppland, Sweden, 2000; (jtly) Ceremony and Display: the South Cadbury Bronze Age shield, 2000; contrib. Proc. Prehist. Soc., Antiquaries Jl, Antiquity, Somerset Levels Papers, etc. *Recreations:* music, ancient art, wetlands, woodlands. *Address:* Fursdon Mill Cottage, Thorverton, Devon EX5 5JS. *T:* (01392) 860125.

COLES, Kenneth George, AM 2000; BE; FIEAust; CEng, FIMechE, FAIM; Chairman, Conveyor Co. of Australia Pty Ltd, 1957–91; *b* Melbourne, 30 June 1926; *s* of Sir Kenneth Coles; *m* 1st, 1950, Thalia Helen (marr. diss. 1980); one *s* two *d*; 2nd, 1985, Rowena Danziger. *Educ:* The King's Sch., Parramatta, NSW; Sydney Univ. (BE 1948). FIE(Aust) 1986; FIMechE 1969; FAIM 1959. Gained engrg experience in appliance manufacturing and automotive industries Nuffield Aust. Pty Ltd, Gen. Motors Holdens Pty Ltd and Frigidaire, before commencing own business manufacturing conveyors, 1955; Chm and Man. Dir, K. G. Coles & Co. Pty Ltd, 1955–76, Chm. 1976–95; Chm. and Man. Dir, KGC Magnetic Tape Pty Ltd, 1973–80. Director: Australian Oil & Gas Corp. Ltd, 1969–89 (Dep. Chm., 1984–89); A. O. G. Minerals Ltd, 1969–87 (Dep. Chm., 1984–87); Coles Myer Ltd (formerly G. J. Coles & Coy Ltd), 1976–94; Electrical Equipment Ltd, 1976–84; Permanent Trustee Co. Ltd, 1978–94 (Vice Chm., 1990–91; Chm., 1991–94); Centre for Industrial Technol. Ltd, 1985–87; Chatham Investment Co. Ltd, 1987–94; NRMA Insurance Ltd, 1989–90; Stockland Trust Group, 1990–95; Chairman: Innovation Council of NSW Ltd, 1984–89 (Dir, 1982–89); Nat. Engrg (now Metal and Engrg) Training Bd, 1988–99. Metal Trades Industry Association: Gen. Councillor, NSW Br., 1976–94; Nat. Councillor, 1988–94; Mem. Bd, Sir William Tyree MTIA Foundn, 1995–. Chm., Lizard Island Reef Res. Foundn, 1994– (Dir, 1992–). Member: Internat. Solar Energy Soc., 1957–; Science & Industry Forum, Australian Academy of Science, 1983–94; Mem. and Employers' Rep., NSW Bd of Secondary Educn, 1987–90. Mem. Council, Nat. Roads and Motorists Assoc., NSW, 1986–90. Councillor and Mem. Bd of Governors, Ascham Sch., 1972–82; Employers' Rep., NSW Secondary Schs Bd, 1979–83. Sydney University: Fellow, Senate, 1983–97; Chairman: Internat. House, 2001– (Mem. Council 1993–); Save Sight Inst., 2001– (Mem. Council, 1998–). Hon. Dr Univ Sydney, 1999. *Address:* 2/24 Rosemont Avenue, Woollahra, NSW 2025, Australia. *T:* and *Fax:* (2) 93286084. *Clubs:* Union, Australian, Sydney Rotary (Sydney); Royal Sydney Golf.

COLES, (Norman) Bruce (Cameron), QC 1984; **His Honour Judge Bruce Coles;** a Circuit Judge, since 1997; *b* 28 Feb. 1937; *s* of Sir Norman Coles and of Dorothy Verna (*née* Deague); *m* 1961, Sally Fenella Freeman; one *s* three *d*. *Educ:* Melbourne Grammar Sch.; Univ. of Melbourne (LLB); Magdalen Coll., Oxford Univ. (BCL). 2nd Lieut, 6th Bn Royal Melbourne Regt, 1956–59. Associate to Sir Owen Dixon, Chief Justice of High Court of Australia, 1959–60; called to English Bar, Middle Temple, 1963, Bencher, 1991; admitted to Bar of Supreme Court of Victoria, 1964. Assistant Recorder, 1982–86; Recorder, 1986–97; Dep. Official Referee, 1992–97. Chm., Bar Race Relations Cttee, 1994–97; Mem., Equal Treatment Adv. Cttee, Judicial Studies Bd, 1999–. Mem. Council, Oxfam, 1985–98. Chm. of Govs, Enstone Co. Primary Sch., 1993–2000. *Recreations:* mountaineering, cycling, theatre, music. *Clubs:* Cyclist Touring (Surrey); Gentian Mountaineering (Glos).

COLES, Sherard Louis C.; *see* Cowper-Coles.

COLEY, Dr Graham Douglas; Business Continuity Director, Defence Evaluation and Research Agency, since 2000; *b* 16 Nov. 1946; *s* of late Douglas Leonard Coley and of Phyllis Adeline Coley (*née* Hughes); *m* 1972, Susan Elizabeth Thackery. *Educ:* Halesowen Grammar Sch.; Birmingham Univ. (BSc 1st Cl. Hons); Darwin Coll., Cambridge (PhD 1971). FIEE 1994; FInstP 1998. Midlands Res. Station, Gas Council, 1967–68; Atomic Weapons Research Establishment, Aldermaston, 1968–87: Supt, Explosives Technol. Br., 1982–85; Head, Chemical Technol. Div., 1985–87; Dir, Nuclear Resources, MoD PE, 1987–90; Dep. Head, Efficiency Unit, Prime Minister's Office, 1990–92; Asst Chief Scientific Advr (Projects), MoD, 1992–94; Man. Dir, Chem. and Biol Defence Estabt, MoD, 1994–96; Man. Dir, Protection and Life Scis Div., 1996–97, Man. Dir, Science, 1997–2000, DERA. *Publications:* papers in technical jls and internat. conf. proc. *Recreations:* flyfishing, shooting, gardening (auriculas). *Address:* Defence Evaluation and Research Agency, Cody Building, Ively Road, Farnborough, Hants GU14 0LX. *Club:* Flyfishers'.

COLFOX, Sir (William) John, 2nd Bt *cr* 1939; JP; DL; *b* 25 April 1924; *yr* and *o* surv. *s* of Sir (William) Philip Colfox, 1st Bt, MC, and Mary (Frances) Lady Colfox (*d* 1973); *S* father, 1966; *m* 1962, Frederica Loveday, *d* of Adm. Sir Victor Crutchley, VC, KCB, DSC; two *s* three *d*. *Educ:* Eton. Served in RNVR, 1942–46, leaving as Lieut. Qualified Land Agent, 1950. Chm., Land Settlement Assoc., 1980–81. Vice-Chm., TSW, 1981–92. JP Dorset, 1962, High Sheriff of Dorset, 1969, DL Dorset, 1977. *Heir: s* Philip John Colfox [*b* 27 Dec. 1962; *m* Julia, *yr d* of G. St G. Schomberg; one *s* three *d* (incl. twins)]. *Address:* Symondsbury House, Bridport, Dorset DT6 6HB. *T:* (01308) 422956.

COLGAN, Samuel Hezlett; His Honour Judge Colgan; a Circuit Judge, since 1990; *b* 10 June 1945; *s* of late Henry George Colgan and of Jane Swan Hezlett. *Educ:* Foyle College, Londonderry; Trinity College Dublin (MA, LLB). Called to the Bar, Middle Temple, 1969; a Recorder, SE Circuit, 1987. *Recreations:* travelling, the arts, reading, tennis. *Address:* Lord Chancellor's Department, SE Circuit, New Cavendish House, 18 Maltravers Street, WC2R 3EU.

COLGRAIN, 3rd Baron *cr* 1946, of Everlands; **David Colin Campbell;** *b* 24 April 1920; *s* of 2nd Baron Colgrain, MC, and of Margaret Emily (*d* 1989), *d* of late P. W. Carver; *S* father, 1973; *m* 1st, 1945, Veronica Margaret (marr. diss. 1964), *d* of late Lt-Col William Leckie Webster, RAMC; one *s* one *d*; 2nd, 1973, Mrs Sheila M. Hudson. *Educ:* Eton; Trinity Coll., Cambridge. Served War of 1939–45, 9th Lancers. Manager, Grindlays Bank Ltd, India and Pakistan, 1945–49; joined Antony Gibbs and Sons Ltd, 1949, Director, 1954–83, retired. *Heir: s* Hon. Alastair Colin Leckie Campbell [*b* 16 Sept. 1951; *m* 1979, Annabel Rose, *yr d* of Hon. Robin Warrender, *qv*; two *s*]. *Address:* Bushes Farm, Weald, Sevenoaks, Kent TN14 6ND.

COLHOUN, Prof. John; Barker Professor of Cryptogamic Botany, University of Manchester, 1960–80, now Emeritus; Dean, Faculty of Science, 1974 and 1975; Pro-Vice-Chancellor, 1977–80; *b* 15 May 1913; *yr s* of late James and Rebecca Colhoun, Castlederg, Co. Tyrone; *m* 1949, Margaret (*d* 1997), *e d* of late Prof. Gilbert Waterhouse, LittD, and Mary Elizabeth, *e d* of Sir Robert Woods; two *d* (and one *d* decd). *Educ:* Edwards Sch., Castlederg, Co. Tyrone; The Queen's Univ. of Belfast; Imperial Coll. of Science, London Univ. BSc, MAgr (Belfast), PhD, DSc (London), MSc (Manchester), DIC. Min. of Agriculture for Northern Ireland: Research Asst, 1939–46; Senior Scientific Officer, 1946–50; Principal Scientific Officer, 1951–60. The Queen's Univ., Belfast: Asst Lecturer in Agricultural Botany, 1940–42; Asst Lectr 1942–45, Jun. Lectr 1945–46, Lectr 1946–54, Reader 1954–60, in Mycology and Plant Pathology. Warden of Queen's Chambers, 1942–49. FLS 1955. FIBiol 1963. President: British Mycological Soc., 1963; The Queen's Univ. Assoc., 1960–61; The Queen's Univ. Club, London, 1983–85. Chm., Fedn of British Plant Pathologists, 1968; Hon. Mem., British Soc. for Plant Pathology, 1989. Jt Editor, Jl of Phytopathology (Phytopath. Zeitschrift), 1973–91. *Publications:* Diseases of the Flax Plant, 1947; Club Root Disease of Crucifers caused by *Plasmodiophora brassicae* Woron, 1958; numerous papers in Annals of Applied Biology, Annals of Botany, Trans Brit. Mycological Soc., Nature, Phytopath. Z. *Address:* 12 Southdown Crescent, Cheadle Hulme, Cheshire SK8 6EQ. *T:* (0161) 485 2084. *Club:* Athenæum.

COLL, Elizabeth Anne Loosemore E.; *see* Esteve-Coll.

COLLARBONE, Dame Patricia, DBE 1998; EdD; Founder and Director, London Leadership Centre, Institute of Education, University of London, since 1997. MBA 1995; EdD Lincolnshire and Humberside Univ. 1999. Headteacher, Haggerston Sch., Hackney, 1990–96. Manager, London Regl Assessment Centre, 1996–98, London Regl Trng and Development Centre, 1998–, NPQH. Advr, on rôle of the Headteacher, Govt 9th Select Cttee, 1998; Special Advr, on headship and leadership issues, DfEE, 1999–. Former Member: SCAA Key Stage 3 Adv. Gp; DfEE Adv. Cttee on Improving Schs; Educn Summit. Member: DfEE Sch. Improvement Team; NPQH Mgt Develt Gp, TTA. London Pres., NAHT. Fellow: Univ. of Lincolnshire and Humberside; Hull Univ., 2000. FRSA. *Address:* c/o Institute of Education, 10 Woburn Square, WC1H 0NS.

COLLARD, Douglas Reginald, OBE 1976; HM Diplomatic Service, retired; *b* 7 April 1916; *s* of late Hebert Carthew Collard and late Mary Ann (*née* Pugh); *m* 1947 (marr. diss. 1969); two *s* three *d*. *Educ:* Wallasey Grammar Sch.; privately. Army Service, 1940–46 (despatches); UNRRA, Greece, 1946–47; Asst Commercial Adviser, British Econ. Mission to Greece, 1947; Consul, Patras, Greece, 1947–52; Beirut, 1952–54; Khartoum, 1954–56; Copenhagen, 1958–61; Tripoli, 1961–65; Lahore, 1965–67; Montevideo, 1969–71; Algiers, 1971–73; Consul-Gen., Bilbao, 1973–76. Director: Anglo-Arab Assoc., 1976–90; Arab British Centre, 1981–90. *Recreations:* reading, meditation, good company. *Address:* Flat 23, Westminster Court, 23 Cambridge Park, Wanstead, E11 2PU. *T:* (020) 8530 8308.

COLLECOTT, Dr Peter Salmon; HM Diplomatic Service; Director, Resources, Foreign and Commonwealth Office, since 1999; *b* 8 Oct. 1950; *s* of George William Collecott and Nancy Alice Collecott (*née* Salmon); *m* 1982, Judith Patricia Pead. *Educ:* Chigwell Sch., Essex; St John's Coll., Cambridge (MA 1976; PhD 1976); MIT (Kennedy Schol. 1972). Royal Soc. Fellow, Max Planck Inst. for Physics and Astrophysics, Munich, 1976–77; joined HM Diplomatic Service, 1977: FCO, 1977–78; MECAS, Lebanon, later London, 1978–80; 1st Secretary: (Political), Khartoum, 1980–82; (Econ., Commercial, Agricl), Canberra, 1982–86; Head, Iran/Iraq Section, ME Dept, FCO, 1986–88; Asst Head, EC Dept (Ext.), FCO, 1988–89; Counsellor, Head of Chancery and Consul Gen., later Dep. Head of Mission, Jakarta, 1989–93; Counsellor (EU and Econ.), Bonn, 1994–98; Hd, Admin Restructuring Rev. Team, FCO, 1998–99. *Publications:* papers on theoretical physics in learned jls. *Recreations:* walking, reading. *Address:* c/o Foreign and Commonwealth Office, King Charles Street, SW1A 2AH.

COLLEE, Prof. (John) Gerald, CBE 1991; MD; FRCPath; FRCPE; FRSE; Robert Irvine Professor of Bacteriology and Head of Department of Medical Microbiology (formerly Department of Bacteriology), University of Edinburgh, 1979–91, now Emeritus Professor; Chief Bacteriologist to Edinburgh Royal Infirmary and Consultant Bacteriologist, Lothian Health Board, 1979–91; Consultant Adviser in Microbiology to Scottish Home and Health Department, 1986–91; *b* 10 May 1929; *s* of John Gerald Collee and Mary Hay Wilson Kirsopp Cassels; *m* 1st, 1952, Isobel McNay Galbraith (marr. diss. 1995); two *s* one *d*; 2nd, 1995, Anne Ferguson (*d* 1998). *Educ:* Bo'ness Acad.; Edinburgh Acad.; Edinburgh Univ. MB ChB, MD (Gold Medal). Ho. Phys., 1951–52. AMS (Captain RAMC), 1952–54. Lectr in Bacteriology, Edinburgh, 1955–63; WHO Vis. Prof. of Bacteriol., Baroda, 1963–64; Sen. Lectr, Edinburgh, and Hon. Cons. Bacteriologist, 1964–70; Reader in Bacteriol. 1970–74, Personal Prof. of Bacteriol. 1974–79, Edinburgh. Member: Scottish Health Service Planning Council Adv. Gp on Infection, 1981–90; Jt Cttee on Vaccination and Immunisation, 1982–95; Cttee on Safety of Medicines, 1987–89; Cttee on Vaccination and Immunisation Procedures, MRC, 1988–95; Medicines Commn, 1992–95. *Publications:* Applied Medical Microbiology, 1976, 2nd edn 1981; contrib. and ed several textbooks, incl. Mackie and McCartney's Practical Medical Microbiology, 1996; many sci. papers on aspects of infection, anaerobes of clin. importance, antimicrobial drugs and immunization. *Recreations:* woodwork, mechanics, fishing, music, painting. *Address:* 27B Drummond Place, Edinburgh EH3 6PN. *T:* (0131) 557 5234. *Clubs:* Scottish Arts, New (Edinburgh).

COLLENDER, Andrew Robert; QC 1991; a Recorder, since 1993; a Deputy High Court Judge, since 1998; *b* 11 Aug. 1946; *s* of John and Kathleen Collender; *m* 1974, Titia Tybout; two *s*. *Educ:* Mt Pleasant Boys High Sch., Southern Rhodesia, now Zimbabwe; Univ. of Bristol (LLB Hons). Called to the Bar, Lincoln's Inn, 1969, Bencher, 2000. *Recreations:* playing the violin, sailing. *Address:* 2 Temple Gardens, Temple, EC4Y 9AY. *T:* (020) 7822 1200. *Club:* Bosham Sailing.

COLLENETTE, Hon. David Michael; PC (Canada) 1983; MP (L) Don Valley East, since 1993; Minister of Transport, Canada, since 1997; *b* 24 June 1946; *s* of David Henry and Sarah Margaret Collenette; *m* 1975, Penny Hossack; one *s*. *Educ:* Glendon Coll., York Univ. (BA Hons); postgrad. studies in legislative behaviour and urban studies, Carleton and York Univs. Admin. Officer, Marketing Div., Internat. Life Assurance Co., UK, 1970–72; Exec. Vice-Pres., Mandrake Management Consultants, Canada, 1987–93. MP (L) York East, 1974–79 and 1980–84; Minister of State for Multiculturalism, 1983–84; Minister of Nat. Defence and of Veterans' Affairs, 1993–96. Sec.-Gen., Liberal Party of Canada, 1985–87 (Exec. Dir, Toronto, 1969–70, Ontario, 1972–74). *Recreations:* squash, theatre, classical music. *Address:* House of Commons, Ottawa, ON K1A 0A6, Canada. *T:* (613) 9954988. *Club:* University (Toronto).

COLLENS, Rupert; *see* Mackeson, Sir R. H.

COLLETT, Sir Christopher, GBE 1988; JP; Partner in Ernst & Young, Chartered Accountants, London, retired 1993; Lord Mayor of London, 1988–89; *b* 10 June 1931; 2nd *s* of Sir Henry Seymour Collett, 2nd Bt, and Lady (Ruth Mildred) Collett (*née* Hatch) (*d* 1994); *m* 1959, Christine Anne, *d* of Oswald Hardy Griffiths, Nunthorpe, Yorks; two *s* one *d*. *Educ:* Harrow; Emmanuel Coll., Cambridge. MA; FCA. Nat. Service, RA and Surrey Yeomanry; Captain TA (RA). Articled with Cassleton Elliott & Co., Chartered Accountants, 1954; qualified, 1958; Partner, Ghana 1960, London 1963; firm merged to become Josolyne Miles and Cassleton Elliott, Josolyne Layton Bennett & Co., Arthur Young, and then Ernst & Young. Mem., Court of Common Council (Broad Street Ward), City of London, 1973–79; Alderman, 1979–; Sheriff, City of London, 1985–86; HM Lieut, 1988–; Trustee, Temple Bar Trust, 1992– (Chm., 1993–); Chm., Lord Mayor's 800th Anniversary Awards Trust, 1989–. Liveryman: Glovers' Co., 1965 (Master, 1981); Chartered Accts in Eng. and Wales' Co., 1984 (Asst, 1986–93); Haberdashers' Company: Hon. Liveryman, 1990; Asst, 1991; Third Warden, 1993; Hon. Asst, 1994–; Member: Guild of Freemen, 1983–; City of London TAVR Cttee, 1980–92. Non-exec. Mem., Dumfries and Galloway Health Bd, 1997–. Council Mem., Action Research for the Crippled Child, 1984–93. Governor: Haberdashers' Aske's Schs, Elstree, 1982–94; King Edward's Sch., Witley, 1983–94; Music Therapy Gp Ltd, 1986–94; Bridewell Royal Hosp., 1987–94; Hon. Treas., Lee House, Wimbledon, 1950–; Trustee, Morden Coll., 1993–; Chm., Eskdale Foundn, 1996–. Pres., Broad Street Ward Club, 1979–. JP City of London, 1979. Hon. DSc City, 1988. KStJ 1988. Order of Merit (cl. II), State of Qatar, 1985; Orden del Merito Civil (cl. II), Spain, 1986; Commander, Order of Merit, Federal Republic of Germany, 1986; CON, 1st cl. (Nigeria), 1989. *Recreations:* gardening, fishing. *Address:* Broomholm, Langholm, Dumfriesshire DG13 0LJ. *T:* (01387) 380448.

COLLETT, Sir Ian (Seymour), 3rd Bt *cr* 1934; *b* 5 Oct. 1953; *s* of David Seymour Collett (*d* 1962), and of Sheila Joan Collett; (who *m* 1980, Sir James William Miskin, QC), *o d* of late Harold Scott; *S* grandfather, 1971; *m* 1982, Philippa, *o d* of James R. I. Hawkins, Preston St Mary, Suffolk; one *s* one *d*. *Educ:* Lancing College, Sussex. Notary Public, 1985. Mem., Law Society, 1979. *Recreations:* golf, fishing, cricket, shooting. *Heir: s* Anthony Seymour Collett, *b* 27 Feb. 1984. *Clubs:* MCC; Aldeburgh Golf; Aldeburgh Yacht.

COLLEY, Maj.-Gen. (David) Bryan (Hall), CB 1988; CBE 1982 (OBE 1977 MBE 1968); FCIT, FILT; Director-General, Road Haulage Association, 1988–97; *b* 5 June 1934; *s* of Lawson and Alice Colley; *m* 1957, Marie Thérèse (*née* Préfontaine); one *s* one *d*. *Educ:* King Edward's Sch., Birmingham; RMA, Sandhurst. Commissioned: RASC, 1954; RCT, 1965; regimental appts in Germany, Belgium, UK, Hong Kong and Singapore; Student, Staff Coll., Camberley, 1964; JSSC Latimer, 1970; CO Gurkha Transport Regt and 31 Regt, RCT, 1971–74; Staff HQ 1st (British) Corps, 1974–77; Comd Logistic Support Gp, 1977–80; Col AQ (Ops and Plans) and Dir Admin. Planning, MoD (Army), 1980–82; Comd Transport 1st (British) Corps and Comdr Bielefeld Garrison, 1983–86; Dir Gen., Transport and Movts (Army), 1986–88, retired. Col Comdt, RCT, 1988–93; Col Comdt, Royal Logistic Corps, 1993–2000. Freeman, City of London, 1986; Hon. Liveryman, Worshipful Co. of Carmen, 1986. *Recreations:* travel, information technology, walking. *Address:* c/o HSBC, Redditch, Worcs B97 4EA. *Club:* Army and Navy.

COLLEY, Surg. Rear-Adm. Ian Harris, OBE 1963; Member, Committee of Management, Royal National Lifeboat Institution, since 1982; *b* 14 Oct. 1922; *s* of Aubrey James Colley and Violet Fulford Colley; *m* 1952, Joy Kathleen (*née* Goodacre). *Educ:*

Hanley Castle Grammar Sch.; King's Coll., London and King's Coll. Hosp. MB, BS 1948; DPH; MFOM; FFCM. Royal Naval Medical Service, 1948–80: MO HMS Cardigan Bay and HMS Consort, 1949–52; service with Fleet Air Arm, 1955–78: as PMO HMS Centaur; MO i/c Air Med. Sch.; Pres., Central Air Med. Bd; Comd MO to Flag Officer, Naval Air Comd; Surg. Rear Adm. (Ships and Estabs), 1978–80, retired. QHP 1978–80. Consultant in Aviation Medicine; former Examr to Conjoint Bd, Royal College of Surgeons and Royal College of Physicians for DAvMed. Life Vice-Pres., RNLI, 1997 (Vice-Pres., 1989–97; Chm., Med. and Survival Cttee, 1984–88). CStJ 1980. *Publications:* papers in field of aviation medicine. *Address:* c/o Royal Bank of Scotland, Inveraray, Argyll PA32 8TY.

COLLEY, Prof. Linda Jane, PhD; FRHistS; FBA 1999; School Professor in History and Leverhulme Personal Research Professor, European Institute, London School of Economics, London University, since 1998; *b* 13 Sept. 1949; *d* of Roy Colley and Marjorie (*née* Hughes); *m* 1982, David Nicholas Cannadine, *qv*; one *d* decd. *Educ:* Bristol Univ. (BA); Cambridge Univ. (MA, PhD). University of Cambridge: Eugenie Strong Research Fellow, Girton Coll., 1975–78; Fellow: Newnham Coll., 1978–79; Christ's Coll., 1979–81; Yale University: Dir, Lewis Walpole Liby, 1982–96; Asst Prof., History, 1982–85; Associate Prof., 1985–90; Prof., History, 1990–92; Richard M. Colgate Prof. of History, 1992–98. Hooker Distinguished Vis. Prof., McMaster Univ., 1999. Journalism and work on TV. Lectures: Anstey, Univ. of Kent, 1994; William Church Meml, Brown Univ., 1994; Dist. (in British Hist.), Univ. of Texas at Austin, 1995; Trevelyan, Cambridge Univ., 1997; Wiles, QUB, 1997; Hayes Robinson, Royal Holloway, Univ. of London, 1998; Ford Special, Oxford Univ., 1998; Bliss Carnochan, Stanford Humanities Center, 1998; Prime Minister's Millennium, 1999; Ena H. Thompson, Pomona Coll., Calif, 2001. Member: Council, Tate Gall. of British Art, 1999–; BL Bd, 1999–; Adv. Council, Paul Mellon Centre for British Art, 1998–. FRHistS 1988. Hon. DLitt South Bank, 1998. *Publications:* In Defiance of Oligarchy: The Tory Party 1714–60, 1982; Namier, 1989; Crown Pictorial: art and the British monarchy, 1990; Britons: forging the nation 1707–1837, 1992 (Wolfson Prize, 1993); numerous articles and reviews in UK and USA jls. *Recreations:* travel, looking at art. *Address:* European Institute, London School of Economics, Houghton Street, WC2A 2AE; c/o Curtis Brown, Haymarket House, 28–29 Haymarket, SW1Y 4SP. *Club:* Reform.

COLLIER, family name of **Baron Monkswell**.

COLLIER, Andrew James, CB 1976; Deputy Secretary, Department of Health and Social Security, 1973–82; *b* 12 July 1923; *s* of Joseph Veasy Collier and Dorothy Murray; *m* 1950, Bridget, *d* of George and Edith Eberstadt, London; two *d*. *Educ:* Harrow; Christ Church, Oxford (Boulter Exhibnr). Served Army, RHA, 1943–46. Entered HM Treasury, 1948; Private Sec. to: Sir Henry Wilson Smith, 1950; Sir Leslie Rowan, 1951; Chancellors of the Exchequer, 1956–59 (Rt Hon. Harold Macmillan, Rt Hon. Peter Thorneycroft, Rt Hon. Derick Heathcoat Amory); Asst Sec., 1961; Under-Sec., 1967; Under-Secretary: Civil Service Dept, 1968–71; DHSS, 1971–73. Chm., Chelsea Housing Assoc., 1983–95; Member: Special Hosps Services Authy, 1989–93; Mgt Cttee, Battersea Churches and Chelsea Housing Trust, 1995–. *Address:* 10 Lambourne Avenue, SW19 7DW. *T:* (020) 8879 3560. *Club:* Athenæum.

COLLIER, Andrew John, CBE 1995; Schools Adjudicator, since 1999; General Secretary, Society of Education Officers, 1996–99 (Treasurer, 1987–92; President, 1990); *b* 29 Oct. 1939; *s* of Francis George Collier and Margaret Nancy (*née* Nockles); *m* 1964, Gillian Ann (*née* Churchill); two *d*. *Educ:* University College Sch.; St John's Coll., Cambridge (MA). Assistant Master, Winchester Coll., 1962–68; Hampshire County Educn Dept, 1968–71; Buckinghamshire County Educn Dept, 1971–77; Dep. Chief Educn Officer, 1977–80, Chief Educn Officer, 1980–96, Lancashire CC. Member: Open Univ. Vis. Cttee, 1982–88; Council for Accreditation of Teacher Educn, 1984–89; Nat. Training Task Force, 1989–92; Gen. Synod Bd of Educn, 1993–2001; Educn Cttee, Royal Soc., 1995–2000; Chm., County Educn Officers' Soc., 1987–88; Treas., Schools Curriculum Award, 1987–92. Liveryman, Worshipful Company of Wheelwrights, 1972. Mem. Council, Univ. of Lancaster, 1981–86, 1988–94, 1996–99; Gov., Myerscough Coll., 1996–. Pres., Lancs Fedn of Young Farmers' Clubs, 1985–88. *Publications:* (contrib.) New Directions for County Government, 1989; articles in jls. *Recreations:* music, walking, gardening. *Clubs:* Athenæum; Leander (Henley-on-Thames).

COLLIER, John Spencer, FCA; Secretary General, Institute of Chartered Accountants in England and Wales, since 1998; *b* 4 March 1945; *s* of James Bradburn Collier and Phyllis Mary Collier; *m* 1972, Theresa Mary Peers; two *s* one *d*. *Educ:* Trinity Coll., Cambridge (BA Geography 1967). FCA 1973. Joined Price Waterhouse, 1969: various posts, incl. Sen. Manager, 1969–81; Partner, 1981–92; Chief Executive: Newcastle Initiative, 1992–95; Lowes Gp plc, 1995–96; Finance Dir, Earth Centre, 1996–97; acting Sec. and Chief Exec., ICAEW, 1997–98. *Publication:* The Corporate Environment: the financial consequences for business, 1995. *Recreations:* mountains, marathons. *Address:* 147 Queens Road, Richmond, Surrey TW10 6HF. *T:* (020) 8940 1921. *Club:* Northern Counties (Newcastle upon Tyne).

COLLIER, Lesley Faye, CBE 1993; Répétiteur, Royal Ballet, since 2000; Principal Dancer with the Royal Ballet, 1972–95; *b* 13 March 1947; *d* of Roy and Mavis Collier; twin *s*. *Educ:* The Royal Ballet School, White Lodge, Richmond. Joined Royal Ballet, 1965; has danced most principal roles in the Royal repertory; Ballet Mistress, 1995–99, Mem., Classical Ballet Staff, 1999–2000, Royal Ballet Sch. Evening Standard Ballet Award, 1987. *Address:* Royal Ballet, Royal Opera House, Covent Garden, WC2E 9DD.

COLLIER, Prof. Leslie Harold, MD, DSc; FRCP, FRCPath; Professor of Virology, University of London, 1966–86, now Emeritus; Consulting Pathologist, Royal London Hospital (formerly London Hospital), since 1987; *b* 9 Feb. 1921; *s* of late Maurice Leonard Collier and Ruth (*née* Phillips); *m* 1942, Adeline Barnett; one *s*. *Educ:* Brighton Coll.; UCH Med. Sch. MD London 1953; DSc London 1968; MRCP 1969; FRCPath 1975; FRCP 1980. House Phys., UCH, 1943; served RAMC, 1944–47; Asst Pathologist, St Helier Hosp., Carshalton, 1947; Lister Inst. of Preventive Medicine, 1948–78: Head, Dept of Virology, 1955–74; Dep. Dir, 1968–74; Dir, Vaccines and Sera Laboratories, 1974–78; Hon. Dir, MRC Trachoma Unit, 1957–73; Prof. of Virology and Sen. Lectr, Jt Dept of Virology, London Hosp. Med. Coll. and St Bartholomew's Hosp. Med. Coll., 1978–86; Hd, Dept of Virology, London Hosp. Med. Coll., 1982–86. Hon. Consultant in Virology, Tower Hamlets HA, 1978–86. Pres., Sect. of Pathology, RSM, 1986–88, Hon. Mem., 1994. Chibret Gold Medal, Ligue contre le Trachome, 1959; Luys Prize, Soc. de Médecine de Paris, 1963. *Publications:* (ed jtly) Topley and Wilson's Principles of Bacteriology, Virology and Immunity, 8th edn, 1990, 9th edn, as Topley and Wilson's Microbiology and Microbial Infections (Editor in Chief), 1997 (Soc. of Authors and Med. Soc. of London award, 1998); (jtly) Human Virology, 1993, 2nd edn 2000; papers in med. and scientific jls. *Recreations:* various. *Address:* 8 Peto Place, Regent's Park, NW1 4DT. *T:* (020) 7487 4848.

COLLIER, Prof. Melvyn William; Librarian, Tilburg University, Netherlands, since 2001; part-time Professor, Information Management Research Institute, University of Northumbria at Newcastle, since 2000; *b* 31 July 1947; *s* late James Collier and of Jessie Collier (*née* Siddall); *m* 1968, Anne Nightingale; one *s* one *d*. *Educ:* Bolton Sch.; Univ. of St Andrews (MA); Strathclyde Univ. (DipLib). ALA 1981; MIInfSc 1990, FIInfSc 1997. Academic Librarian posts at St Andrews Univ., UC, Cardiff and Hatfield Poly., 1970–79; Dep. Hd, Liby Services, PCL, 1980–84; Librarian, Leicester Poly., 1985–89; Hd, Div. of Learning Develt, and Prof. of Information Mgt, De Montfort Univ., 1989–97; Dir, Strategic and Operational Planning, Dawson Hldgs, 1997–2000. Vis. Prof., De Montfort Univ., 1997–. Mem., Liby and Inf. Commn, 1996– (Chm., Res. Cttee, 1996–); Chairman: Liby and Inf. Adv. Cttee, British Council, 1995–; UK Office for Liby Networking, 1995–97; Mem., Jt Inf. Systems Cttee, HEFCs, 1996–97. Director: Open Learning Foundn, 1995–97; Information For All, 1997–99. Medal, Hungarian Liby Assoc., 1992. *Publications:* Local Area Networks: the implications for library and information science, 1984; (ed) Case Studies in Software for Information Management, 1986; (ed) Telecommunications for Information Management and Transfer, 1987; (jtly) Decision Support Systems in Academic Libraries, 1991; (jtly) Decision Support Systems and Performance Assessment in Academic Libraries, 1993; (ed) Electronic Library and Visual Information Research: ELVIRA 1, 1995, ELVIRA 2, 1996; numerous jl articles and res. reports. *Recreations:* golf, hill-walking. *Address:* The Library, Tilburg University, PO Box 90153, 5000 LE Tilburg, Netherlands. *T:* (13) 4662121. *Club:* Leicestershire Golf.

COLLIER, Prof. Paul, DPhil; Director, Research Department, World Bank, Washington, since 1998; Professor of Economics, since 1993 and Director, Centre for Study of African Economies, since 1991, Oxford University (on leave of absence); Fellow, St Antony's College, Oxford, since 1986; *b* 23 April 1949; *s* of Charles and Doris Collier; *m* 1998, Pauline Boerma; one *s*. *Educ:* King Edward VII Grammar Sch., Sheffield; Trinity Coll., Oxford (MA 1970); Nuffield Coll., Oxford (DPhil 1975). Oxford University: Fellow, Keble Coll. and Research Officer, Inst. of Econs and Stats, 1976–86; Univ. Lectr in Econs, 1986–89; Reader in Econs, 1989–92. Prof. Invité, Centre d'Études et de Recherches sur le Développement Internat., Univ. d'Auvergne, 1989–; Vis. Prof., Kennedy Sch. of Govt, Harvard, 1992–96; Fellow, Centre for Economic Policy Res., 1993–; Associate, Tinbergen Inst., 1994–95. Lectures: Rausig, Moscow, 2000; Summers, Pa, 2001. Member: Overseas Develt Council, Program Associates Gp, Washington, 1994–96; Africa Panel, SSRC, NY, 1993–96; ESCOR Cttee, ODA then DFID, 1996–98. Man. Editor, Jl of African Economies, 1992–. Edgar Graham Prize, SOAS, 1988; Distinction Award, 1996, 1998. *Publications:* Labour and Poverty in Kenya, 1986; Labour and Poverty in Rural Tanzania, 1986, 2nd edn 1991; Peasants and Governments, 1989; Controlled Open Economies, 1990, 2nd edn 1994. *Address:* World Bank, 1818 H Street, NW, Washington, DC 20433, USA.

COLLIER, Peter Neville; QC 1992; a Recorder, since 1988; a Deputy High Court Judge (Family Division), since 1998; *b* 1 June 1948; *s* of late Arthur Neville Collier and of Joan Audrey Collier (*née* Brewer); *m* 1972, Susan Margaret Williamson; two *s*. *Educ:* Hymer's Coll., Hull; Selwyn Coll., Cambridge (MA). Called to the Bar, Inner Temple, 1970. Chancellor: dio. of Wakefield, 1992–; dio. of Lincoln, 1998–. Mem., Bar Council, 2000–. *Recreations:* walking, reading, music. *Address:* 30 Park Square, Leeds LS1 2PF. *T:* (0113) 243 6388.

COLLIER-WRIGHT, John Hurrell, CBE 1966; Member, British Transport Docks Board, 1974–77; *b* 1 April 1915; *s* of John Robert Collier Collier-Wright and Phyllis Hurrell Walters; *m* 1940, Pauline Beatrice Platts; three *s* (and one *s* decd). *Educ:* Bradfield Coll.; Queen's Coll., Oxford (MA). FCIT. Traffic Apprentice, LNER, 1936–39. Served War of 1939–45, RE, France, Iraq and Iran (Lt-Col; US Legion of Merit). East African Railways and Harbours, 1946–64; Chief Commercial Supt; joined British Transport Docks Bd, 1964; Chief Commercial Man., 1964–70; Asst Man. Dir, 1970–72; Dep. Man. Dir, 1972–77; Dir, British Transport Advertising, 1966–81. *Address:* 62 Marygate, York YO3 7BH. *Club:* Nairobi (Kenya).

COLLIN, Maj.-Gen. Geoffrey de Egglesfield, CB 1975; MC 1944; DL; *b* 18 July 1921; *s* of late Charles de Egglesfield Collin and Catherine Mary Collin; *m* 1949, Angela Stella (*née* Young); one *s* three *d*. *Educ:* Wellington Coll., Berks. Served War of 1939–45: commissioned as 2nd Lt, RA, 1941; in India and Burma, 1942–45. Qualified as Army Pilot, 1946; attended Staff Coll., Camberley, 1951; Instructor at RMA, Sandhurst, 1954–56; served Kenya, 1956–58; JSSC, 1958; Instructor at Staff Coll., Camberley, 1960–62; comd 50 Missile Regt, RA, 1962–64; GSO 1 Sch. of Artillery, 1965; CRA, 4th Div., 1966–67; attended Imperial Defence College, London, 1968; Comdt, Royal School of Artillery, 1969–71; Maj.-Gen. RA, HQ BAOR, 1971–73; GOC North East District, York, 1973–76; retired 1976. Col Comdt, RA, 1976–83 (Rep. Col Comdt, 1982). Chairman: CS Selection Bd, 1981–91 (Mem., 1978); Retired Officer Selection Bd, 1979–2001. Hon. Dir, Great Yorks Show, 1976–87; Pres., Yorks Agricl Soc., 1988–89. DL N Yorks, 1977. *Recreations:* fishing, ornithology, music, keeping gun dog and garden under control. *Address:* c/o Lloyds TSB, 8 Cambridge Crescent, Harrogate HG1 1PQ. *Club:* Army and Navy.

COLLIN, Jack, MA, MD; FRCS; Clinical Reader in Surgery, University of Oxford, Consultant Surgeon, John Radcliffe Hospital, Oxford and Fellow of Trinity College, Oxford, since 1980; *b* 23 April 1945; *s* of John Collin and Amy Maud Collin; *m* 1971, Christine Frances Proud; three *s* one *d*. *Educ:* Univ. of Newcastle (MB BS, MD); Mayo Clinic, Minn. University of Newcastle: Demonstrator in Anatomy, 1969–70; Sen. Res. Associate, 1973–75; Registrar in Surgery, Royal Victoria Infirmary, Newcastle, 1971–80; Chm., Faculty of Clin. Medicine, Univ. of Oxford, 1990–92. Mayo Foundn Fellow, Mayo Clinic, Minn, 1977. Moynihan Fellow, Assoc. of Surgeons of GB and Ire., 1980; James IV Fellow, James IV Assoc. of Surgeons Inc., NY, 1993. Royal College of Surgeons: Arris and Gale Lectr, 1976; Jacksonian Prize, 1977; Hunterian Prof., 1988–89. Non-exec. Dir, Nuffield Orthopaedic Centre NHS Trust, 1990–93. Member: Internat. Soc. of Surgery, 1994–; European Surgical Assoc., 1994–. Jobst Prize, Vascular Surgical Soc. of GB and Ireland, 1990. *Publications:* papers on vascular surgery, intestinal myoelectrical activity and absorption, parenteral nutrition and pancreatic and intestinal transplantation. *Recreations:* gardening, walking. *Address:* Nuffield Department of Surgery, John Radcliffe Hospital, Oxford OX3 9DU. *T:* (01865) 221282, 221286.

COLLIN, (John) Richard (Olaf), FRCS; Consultant Surgeon: Moorfields Eye Hospital, since 1981; King Edward VII Hospital for Officers, since 1993; Hon. Consultant Ophthalmic Surgeon, Great Ormond Street Hospital for Sick Children, since 1983; *b* 1 May 1943; *s* of late John Olaf Collin and Ellen Vera (*née* Knudsen); *m* 1st, 1979, Theresa Pedemonte (marr. diss. 1982); 2nd, 1993, Geraldine O'Sullivan; two *d*. *Educ:* Charterhouse; Sidney Sussex Coll., Cambridge (MA); Westminster Med. Sch. (MB BChir). FRCS 1972. House surgeon and house physician, Westminster Hosp., 1967–68; ship's surgeon, P&O, 1969–70; Ophthalmology Registrar, Moorfields Eye Hosp., 1972–75; Fellow in Ophthalmic Plastic and Reconstructive Surgery, Univ. of Calif, San

Francisco, 1976–77; Lectr, then Sen. Lectr, Professorial Unit, Moorfields Eye Hosp., 1978–81. *Publications:* A Manual of Systematic Eyelid Surgery, 1983, 2nd edn 1989; (with A. G. Tyers) A Colour Atlas of Ophthalmic Plastic Surgery, 1995; articles on ophthalmic, plastic and reconstructive surgery topics. *Recreations:* sailing, shooting, tennis, hunting, fishing, theatre, opera. *Address:* 67 Harley Street, W1N 1DE. *T:* (020) 7486 2699; 48 South Eaton Place, SW1W 9JJ. *T:* (020) 7730 9794. *Clubs:* Royal Ocean Racing, Hurlingham; Beaulieu River Sailing (Beaulieu).

COLLING, Rev. Canon James Oliver, MBE 1995; Rector of Warrington, 1973–97; Canon Diocesan of Liverpool Cathedral, 1976–97, now Canon Emeritus; Chaplain to The Queen, 1990–2000; *b* 3 Jan. 1930; *e s* of late Leonard Colling and Dorothy Colling (*née* Atherton); *m* 1957, Jean Wright; one *s* one *d* (one twin *s* decd). *Educ:* Leigh Grammar Sch.; Univ. of Manchester (BA 1950); Cuddesdon Coll., Oxford. Commissioned RAF, 1950–52 (Nat. Service). Deacon 1954; priest 1955; Asst Curate, Wigan Parish Church, 1954–59; Vicar of Padgate, 1959–71, Rector, 1971–73; Rural Dean of Warrington, 1970–82 and 1987–89, Area Dean, 1989–95. Chairman: Warrington CHC, 1974–82; Warrington Community Council, 1974–87; Vice-Chm., Warrington HA, 1982–89. Chairman: Warrington C of E Educnl Trust, 1973–97; Warrington and Dist Soc. for the Deaf, 1974–93; Warrington Charities Trust, 1989–91; Mem., Cheshire Family Health Services Authority, 1990–94. Chairman: Governors, Sir Thomas Boteler High Sch., Warrington, 1988–97; Boteler Educnl Trust, 1995–97. *Recreations:* looking at buildings and places, local history. *Address:* 19 King Street, Chester CH1 2AH. *T:* (01244) 317557.

COLLINGE, Prof. John, MD; Professor of Molecular Neurogenetics and Head, Department of Neurogenetics, Imperial College School of Medicine at St Mary's (formerly St Mary's Hospital Medical School), since 1994; *b* 25 Jan. 1958; *s* of late Robert Collinge and of Edna Collinge; *m* 1986, Donna Anne Keel (marr. diss. 1990). *Educ:* Burnley Grammar Sch.; St John's Coll., Cambridge; Univ. of Bristol (BSc Hons 1981; MB ChB 1984; MD 1992). MRCP 1988, FRCP 1998; FRCPath 1999. Bristol Royal Infirmary: House Surg., 1984–85; House Physician, 1985; Hon. Sen. House Officer in Pathology, 1985–86; Demonstrator in Pathology, Univ. of Bristol, 1985–86; Med. Rotation, Westminster Hosp., 1986–87; Senior House Officer: in Medicine, Hammersmith Hosp., 1987; in Neurology, Nat. Hosp. for Neurology and Neurosurgery, 1987–88; Merck, Sharp and Dohme Fellow, 1988, Clin. Scientic Staff, 1988–90, MRC Div. of Psychiatry, Clin. Res. Centre, Harrow; Hon. Registrar in Psychiatry, Northwick Park Hosp., 1988–90; Clin. Res. Fellow, Dept of Biochemistry and Molecular Genetics, St Mary's Hosp. Med Sch., 1990–91; St Mary's Hospital: Hon. Registrar, 1990–91, Hon. Sen. Registrar, 1991–94, in Neurology; Hon. Consultant in Neurology and Molecular Genetics, 1994–; Wellcome Sen. Res. Fellow, 1992–96, Prin. Res. Fellow, 1996–, in Clin. Scis, Imperial Coll. Sch. of Medicine at St Mary's; Hon. Consultant Neurologist, Nat. Hosp. for Neurology and Neurosurgery, 1996–; Hon. Dir, MRC Prion Unit, 1998–. Member: Neuroscis Panel, Wellcome Trust, 1994–97; Spongiform Encephalopathy Adv. Cttee, 1996–; Dep. Chm., High-level Gp on BSE, EU, 1996–97; Chm., Res. Adv. Panel, MND Assoc., 1997– (Mem., 1994–97). Member: Amer. Acad. of Neurology, 1993; Clin. Genetics Soc., 1993; Assoc. of British Neurologists, 1995. Founder FMedSci 1998. Linacre Medal, 1992, Graham Bull Prize in Clin. Sci., 1993, RCP; Alfred Meyer Medal, British Neuropathol Soc., 1997. *Publications:* (ed jtly) Prion Diseases of Humans and Animals, 1992; (ed jtly) Prion Diseases, 1997; papers on prion diseases and neurogenetics. *Recreations:* mountain walking, flying. *Address:* Department of Neurogenetics, Imperial College School of Medicine at St Mary's, Norfolk Place, W2 1PG. *T:* (020) 7594 3760.

COLLINGE, John Gregory; High Commissioner for New Zealand in the United Kingdom, 1994–97, and concurrently High Commissioner in Nigeria and Ambassador to the Republic of Ireland; *b* 10 May 1939; *s* of Norman Gregory Collinge and Hilary Winifred Fendall; *m* 1st, 1965, Ngaire Jean Main (marr. diss. 1980); 2nd, 1984, Bronwyn Christine Waite (marr. diss. 1994); two *d*. *Educ:* Auckland Univ. (LLB); University Coll., Oxford (MLitt). Called to the Bar, 1963, and admitted Solicitor, 1963, High Court of NZ; called to the Bar, 1966, and admitted Solicitor, 1966, High Court of Australia. Sen. Lectr in Law, Melbourne Univ., 1967–70; Partner, law firm, Melbourne, Wellington and Auckland, 1969–94. Pres., NZ National Party, 1989–94. Chairman: Policy and Finance Cttee, Auckland Regl Authy, 1983–86; Commerce Commn, 1984–89; Alcohol Adv. Council of NZ, 1991–94; Nat. Civil Defence Energy Planning Cttee, 1992–94; Member: Auckland Electric Power Bd, 1977–80, 1992–93 (Chm., 1980–92); Electrical Develt Assoc. of NZ, 1990–91 (Pres., 1991–94); Council, Electricity Supply Assoc. of NZ, 1991–92. Chairman: New Zealand Pelagic Fisheries Ltd, 1975–81; United Distillers (NZ) Ltd, 1991 (Dir, 1986–91). Alternate Gov., EBRD, 1994–97. Comr, Commonwealth War Graves Commn, 1994–97; Gov., Commonwealth Foundn, 1994–97; Mem. Bd of Govs, Commonwealth Inst., 1994–. Vice-Pres., Royal Over-Seas League, 1994–97; Trustee, Waitangi Foundn, 1994–; Patron: Captain Cook Birthplace Trust, 1994–97; Shakespeare Globe Trust, 1994–97; British/NZ Trade Council, 1994–97. Commemoration Medal, NZ, 1990. *Publications:* Restrictive Trade Practices and Monopolies in New Zealand, 1969, 2nd edn 1982; Tutorials in Contract, 1985, 4th edn 1989; The Law of Marketing in Australia and New Zealand, 1989, 2nd edn 1990. *Recreations:* New Zealand history, restoring colonial houses and colonial antiques, Rugby, cricket. *Address:* 13/97 Jervois Road, Herne Bay, Auckland. *T:* 93608951; c/o Frogpond Farm, Ansty, Wilts. *Clubs:* Vincent's (Oxford); Wellington (NZ).

COLLINGRIDGE, Prof. Graham Leon, PhD; FRS 2001; Professor of Neuroscience, Department of Anatomy, since 1994, and Director, MRC Centre for Synaptic Plasticity, since 1999, University of Bristol; *b* 1 Feb. 1955; *s* of Cyril Leon Collingridge and Marjorie May Caesar; *m* 1992, Catherine Rose; one *s* two *d*. *Educ:* Enfield GS; Univ. of Bristol (BSc 1977); Sch. of Pharmacy, London Univ. (PhD 1980). CBiol, FIBiol 1997. Res. Fellow in Physiology, Univ. of British Columbia, 1980–82; Sen. Res. Officer, Dept of Physiology and Pharmacology, Univ. of NSW, 1983; Lectr, 1983–90, Reader, 1990, Dept of Pharmacology, Univ. of Bristol; Prof., and Head of Dept of Pharmacology, Univ. of Birmingham, 1990–94; Head of Dept of Anatomy, Univ. of Bristol, 1996–98. Member: Neurosci. Bd, 1995–99, LINK Panel, 1995–99, MRC; Internat. Interest Gp, Wellcome Trust, 1996–. Founder, European Dana Alliance for the Brain, 1999. Founder FMedSci 1998. Editor-in-Chief, Neuropharmacology, 1993–. *Publications:* numerous papers in scientific jls, such as Nature, Neuropharmacology, on the neural basis of learning and memory and other aspects of neuroscience. *Recreations:* ski-ing, travel. *Address:* Department of Anatomy, University of Bristol, Bristol BS8 1TH. *T:* (0117) 928 7420.

COLLINGRIDGE, Jean Mary; *see* King, J. M.

COLLINGS, Juliet Jeanne d'Auvergne; *see* Campbell, J. J. d'A.

COLLINGWOOD, John Gildas, FREng, FIChemE; Director: Unilever Ltd, 1965–77; Unilever NV, 1965–77; Head of Research Division of Unilever Ltd, 1961–77; *b* 15 June 1917; *s* of Stanley Ernest Collingwood and Kathleen Muriel (*née* Smalley); *m* 1942, Pauline Winifred Jones (*d* 1998); one *s* one *d*. *Educ:* Wycliffe Coll., Stonehouse, Glos; University Coll. London (BSc; Fellow, 1970). English Charcoal, 1940–41; British Ropeway Engrg Co, 1941–44; De Havilland Engines, 1944–46; Olympia Oil and Cake Mills Ltd, 1946–49; British Oil and Cake Mills Ltd, 1949–51; Mem., UK Milling Group of Unilever Ltd, 1951–60; Dir, Advita Ltd, 1951–60; Dir, British Oil & Cake Mills Ltd, 1955–60. Mem. Research Cttee, 1963–68, Mem. Council, 1964–67, IChemE. Member: Council, Univ. of Aston, 1971–83 (Chm., Academic Advisory Cttee, 1964–71); Research Cttee, CBI, 1970–71; Council for Scientific Policy, 1971–72; Exec. Cttee, British Nutrition Foundn, 1978–82 (Council, 1970–85); Food Standards Cttee, 1972–80; Royal Commn on Environmental Pollution, 1973–79; Standing Commn on Energy and the Environment, 1978–81. A Gen. Sec., BAAS, 1978–83, 1986–88. Vice Pres., Nat. Children's Home, 1989– (Chm., F and GP Cttee, 1983–89); Pres., Wycliffe Coll., Stonehouse, Glos, 1997– (Mem. Council, 1967–; Chm., 1985–89; Vice-Pres., 1989–97). Hon. DSc Aston, 1966. *Recreations:* sailing, music. *Address:* 54 Downs Road, Coulsdon, Surrey CR5 1AA. *T:* (01737) 554817. *Club:* Athenæum.

COLLINI, Prof. Stefan Anthony, PhD; FRHistS; FBA 2000; Professor of Intellectual History and English Literature, Cambridge University, since 2000; Fellow, Clare Hall, Cambridge, since 1986; *b* 6 Sept. 1947; *s* of Raymond Collini and Hilda May (*née* Brown); *m* 1971, Ruth Karen Morse. *Educ:* St Joseph's Coll., Beulah Hill; Jesus Coll., Cambridge (BA 1969, MA 1973; Thirlwall Prize and Seeley Medal 1973; PhD 1977); Yale Univ. (MA 1970). FRHistS 1981. Res. Fellow, St John's Coll., Cambridge, 1973–74; University of Sussex: Lectr in Intellectual Hist., 1974–82; Reader, 1982–86; Cambridge University: Asst Lectr in English, 1986–90; Lectr, 1990–94; Reader, 1994–2000. Visiting Fellow: History of Ideas Unit, ANU, 1982–83 and 1987; Clare Hall, Cambridge, 1986; Vis. Prof., Inst. Internacional de Estudios Avanzados, Caracas, 1983; Dir d'études associé, Ecole des Hautes Etudes en Scis Sociales, Paris, 1986 and 1991; Mem., Inst. for Advanced Study, Princeton, 1994–95; British Studies Fellow, Ransom Humanities Res. Center, Austin, Tex., 1995; Sen. Res. Fellowship, British Acad., 1999–2000. Co-ed., Cambridge Rev., 1986–93. *Publications:* Liberalism and Sociology, 1979; (jtly) That Noble Science of Politics, 1983; Arnold, 1988, 2nd edn 1994; (ed) On Liberty, by J. S. Mill, 1989; Public Moralists, 1991; (ed) Interpretation and Overinterpretation, by Umberto Eco, 1992; (ed) Culture and Anarchy, by Matthew Arnold, 1993; (ed) The Two Cultures, by C. P. Snow, 1993; English Pasts: essays in history and culture, 1999; (ed jtly) Economy, Polity, and Society, 2000; (ed jtly) History, Religion, and Culture: British Intellectual History 1750–1950, 2000; contrib. essays and reviews in jls, incl. TLS, London Rev. of Books, etc. *Address:* Faculty of English, Cambridge University, 9 West Road, Cambridge CB3 9DP. *T:* (01223) 335082.

COLLINS, Alan Stanley, CMG 1998; HM Diplomatic Service; Ambassador to the Philippines, 1998–2002; *b* 1 April 1948; *s* of Stanley Arthur Collins and Rose Elizabeth Collins; *m* 1971, Ann Dorothy Roberts; two *s* one *d*. *Educ:* Strand GS; London School of Economics and Political Science (BSc Econs). Joined MoD, 1970; Private Sec. to Vice Chief of Air Staff, 1973–75; joined FCO, 1981; Deputy Head of Mission: Addis Ababa, 1986–90; Manila, 1990–93; Counsellor, FCO, 1993–95; Dir-Gen., British Trade and Cultural Office, Taipei, 1995–98. *Recreations:* sport, antiques, reading, walking. *Address:* c/o Foreign and Commonwealth Office, King Charles Street, SW1A 2AH. *Club:* Royal Commonwealth Society.

COLLINS, Hon. Sir Andrew (David), Kt 1994; **Hon. Mr Justice Collins;** a Judge of the High Court of Justice, Queen's Bench Division, since 1994; President, Immigration Appeal Tribunal, since 1999; *b* 19 July 1942; *s* of late Rev. Canon Lewis John Collins, MA, and of Diana Clavering Collins (*see* Dame D. C. Collins); *m* 1970, Nicolette Anne Sandford-Saville; one *s* one *d*. *Educ:* Eton; King's Coll., Cambridge (BA, MA). Called to the Bar, Middle Temple, 1965, Bencher, 1992; QC 1985; a Recorder, 1986–94. *Address:* Royal Courts of Justice, Strand, WC2A 2LL.

COLLINS, Arthur John, OBE 1973; HM Diplomatic Service, retired; Foreign and Commonwealth Office representative (protocol), since 1988; *b* 17 May 1931; *s* of Reginald and Margery Collins; *m* 1952, Enid Maureen, *d* of Charles Stableford, FRIBA and Sarah Stableford; one *s* one *d*. *Educ:* Purley Grammar Sch. Served RAF, 1949–51. Min. of Health, 1951–68 (Private Sec. to Perm. Sec., 1960–61, and to Parly Sec., 1962–63); transf. to HM Diplomatic Service, 1968; FCO, 1968–69; First Secretary and Head of Chancery: Dhaka, 1970–71; Brasilia, 1972–74; Asst Head of Latin America and Caribbean Depts, FCO, 1974–77; Counsellor, UK Del. to OECD, Paris, 1978–81; High Comr, Papua New Guinea, 1982–85; adviser on management, FCO, 1986–88; Consultant, EBRD, 1991; Assessor, VSO, 1993–99. Pres., Brighton and Hove Archaeol Soc., 1996–99. Chm., Brighton, Hove and Dist, ESU, 1998–. *Publications:* papers on early colonialism in New Guinea. *Recreation:* downland walking. *Address:* 60 Dean Court Road, Rottingdean, Sussex BN2 7DJ. *Clubs:* Royal Over-Seas League, Royal Commonwealth Society.

COLLINS, Basil Eugene Sinclair, CBE 1983; Chairman, Nabisco Group, 1984–89; *b* 21 Dec. 1923; *s* of Albert Collins and Pauline Alicia (*née* Wright); *m* 1942, Doris Slott; two *d*. *Educ:* Great Yarmouth Grammar School. Sales Manager, L. Rose & Co. Ltd, 1945; Export Dir, Schweppes (Overseas) Ltd, 1958; Group Admin Dir, Schweppes Ltd, 1964, Chm. of Overseas Gp 1968; Chm. of Overseas Gp, Cadbury Schweppes Ltd, 1969, Dep. Man. Dir 1972, Man. Dir 1974, Dep. Chm. and Group Chief Exec., Cadbury Schweppes plc, 1980–83; Director: Thomas Cook Gp, 1980–85; British Airways Bd, 1982–88; Royal Mint, 1984–88. Royal College of Nursing: Chm., Finance and General Purposes Cttee, 1970–86; Hon. Treasurer, 1970–86; Vice-Pres., 1972, Life Vice-Pres., 1986. Fellow Inst. of Dirs, 1974, Council Mem., 1982–89; Managing Trustee, Inst. of Economic Affairs, 1987–91; Mem. Council, UEA, 1987–94. FZS 1975; CIMgt (FBIM 1976); Fellow, Amer. Chamber of Commerce, 1979, Dir 1984–89. FRSA 1984. Hon. Fellow, UEA, 1995. *Recreations:* music, languages, travel, English countryside. *Address:* Wyddial Parva, Buntingford, Herts SG9 0EL.

COLLINS, Sir Bryan (Thomas Alfred), Kt 1997; OBE 1989; QFSM 1983; HM Chief Inspector of Fire Services, 1994–98; *b* 4 June 1933; *m* 1959, Terry Skuce; one *s* one *d*. *Educ:* Queen Mary's Sch. RAF, 1951–53; with Fire Service, 1954–98; Chief Fire Officer, Humberside, 1979–89; Inspector of Fire Services: Northern Area, 1989–93; Midlands and Wales, 1993–94. *Address:* Gwelo, Thatcher Stanfords Close, Melbourn, S Cambs SG8 6DT.

COLLINS, Christopher Douglas; Chairman, Hanson PLC, since 1998; *b* 19 Jan. 1940; *s* of Douglas and Patricia Collins; *m* 1976, Susan Anne Lumb; one *s* one *d*. *Educ:* Eton. Chartered Accountant. Articled clerk, Peat Marwick Mitchell, 1958–64; Goya Ltd: Man. Dir, 1968–75; Dir, 1975–80; joined Hanson, 1989: Dir, 1991–; Vice Chm., 1995–97; Dep. Chm., 1997. Chm., Forth Ports PLC, 2000–; Director: Old Mutual plc, 1999–; The Go-Ahead Gp plc, 1999–; Alfred McAlpine PLC, 2000–. Amateur steeplechase jockey, 1965–75; represented GB in 3-day equestrian events, 1974–80; Chm., British Team Selection Cttee, 1981–84; Jockey Club Steward, 1980–81; Mem., Horse Race Betting Levy Bd, 1982–84. Chairman: Aintree Racecourse Ltd, 1983–88; National Stud, 1986–88. *Recreations:* riding, ski-ing. *Address:* Hanson PLC, 1 Grosvenor Place, SW1X 7JH. *T:* (020) 7245 1245. *Clubs:* Jockey, White's.

COLLINS, Crispian Hilary Vincent; Chairman, Phillips & Drew, since 1999; Vice Chairman, UBS Asset Management, since 2000; *b* 22 Jan. 1948; *s* of late Bernard John Collins, CBE, and Gretel Elisabeth Collins (*née* Piehler); *m* 1974, Diane Barbara Bromley; one *s* two *d*. *Educ:* Ampleforth Coll.; University Coll., Oxford (BA Hons Modern History). Joined Phillips & Drew, 1969; Fund Manager, Pension Funds, 1975–98; Partner, 1981–85; Dir, 1985–, Mem., Mgt Cttee, 1994–2000, Phillips & Drew Fund Mgt; Chief Exec., Phillips & Drew, 1998–2000. *Recreations:* golf, watching sport, opera, gardens. *Address:* c/o Phillips & Drew Ltd, Triton Court, 14 Finsbury Square, EC2A 1PD. *T:* (020) 7901 5670.

COLLINS, Dame Diana (Clavering), DBE 1999; *b* 13 Aug. 1917; *d* of Jan Lettsom Elliot and Florence Elizabeth Vere (*née* Fison); *m* 1939, Rev. Canon Lewis John Collins (*d* 1982); four *s*. *Educ:* Bedgebury Park Sch.; Lady Margaret Hall, Oxford. Trustee: Internat. Defence & Aid Fund for Southern Africa, 1982–91; Canon Collins Educn Trust for Southern Africa, 1991–. Hon. DLitt Bradford, 1996. *Publications:* Partners in Protest, 1992; Time and the Priestleys, 1994. *Recreations:* reading, gardening, concert and opera, theatre. *Address:* Mill House, Chappel Road, Mount Bures CO8 5AX. *T:* (01787) 227388.
See also Hon. Sir A. D. Collins.

COLLINS, Gerard; *see* Collins, James G.

COLLINS, Henry Edward, CBE 1948; FREng; Consulting Mining Engineer; *b* 4 Oct. 1903; *s* of James Collins; *m* 1934, Cecilia Harris (*d* 1975); no *c*. *Educ:* Rotherham Grammar Sch.; Univ. of Sheffield (MEng). Sen. Lectr in Mining, Univ. of Sheffield, 1935–38; Manager, Rossington Main Colliery, Doncaster, 1939–42; Agent, Markham Colliery, Doncaster, 1942–44; Chief Mining Agent, Doncaster Amalgamated Collieries Ltd, 1944–45; Dir Coal Production, CCG, 1945–47; British Chm., UK/US Coal Control Gp, Germany (later Combined Coal Control Gp), 1947–50; Production Dir, Durham Div., NCB, 1950–56; Dir-Gen. of Reconstruction, NCB, 1956–57; Board Mem. for Production, NCB, 1957–67; Consultant to NCB, 1967–69. Mem., Govtl Cttee on Coal Derivatives, 1959–60; Chairman: NCB Opencast Executive, 1961–67; NCB Brickworks Executive, 1962–67; Whittlesea Central Brick Co. Ltd, 1966–67; Field Research Steering Cttee, Min. of Power, 1964–67; Past Director: Omnia Concrete Sales Ltd; Bradley's (Concrete) Ltd; Powell Duffryn Technical Services Ltd; Inter-Continental Fuels Ltd. Member: Minister of Power's Adv. Council on Research and Develt, 1963–67; Min. of Power Nat. Jt Pneumoconiosis Cttee, 1964–67; Safety in Mines (Adv.) Bd; Mining Qualifications Bd, 1962–69. Pres., Inst. of Mining Engineers, 1962, Hon. Fellow, 1988. FREng (FEng 1976). *Publications:* Mining Memories and Musings: the autobiography of a mining engineer, 1985; numerous papers on mining engineering subjects. *Address:* St Mary's Nursing Home, Ednaston, Brailsford, Derby DE6 3BA.

COLLINS, Jacqueline Jill, (Jackie); writer; *b* London, 4 Oct.; *d* of late Joseph Collins and Elsa (*née* Bessant); *m* Wallace Austin (marr. diss.); one *d*; *m* 1966, Oscar Lerman (*d* 1992); two *d*. Formerly TV and film actress. *Publications:* The World is Full of Married Men, 1968; The Stud, 1969 (filmed, 1978); Sunday Simmons and Charlie Brick, 1971 (new edn as Sinners, 1984); Lovehead, 1974; The World is Full of Divorced Women, 1975; Lovers and Gamblers, 1977; The Bitch, 1979 (filmed, 1979); Chances, 1981 (televised, 1990); Hollywood Wives, 1983 (televised); Lucky, 1985 (televised); Hollywood Husbands, 1986; Rock Star, 1988; Love Killers, 1989; Lady Boss, 1990 (televised); American Star, 1993; Hollywood Kids, 1994; Vendetta: Lucky's revenge, 1996; Thrill, 1998; LA Connections (four parts), 1998; Dangerous Kiss, 1999; Lethal Seduction, 2000; Hollywood Wives: the new generation, 2001. *Address:* c/o Simon and Schuster, 1230 Avenue of the Americas, New York, NY 10020, USA.
See also Joan H. Collins.

COLLINS, (James) Gerard; Member, European Parliament, since 1994; *b* Abbeyfeale, Co. Limerick, 16 Oct. 1938; *s* of late James J. Collins, TD and Margaret Collins; *m* 1969, Hilary Tattan. *Educ:* University Coll., Dublin (BA). Teacher. Asst Gen. Sec., Fianna Fáil, 1965–67. TD (FF) Limerick W, 1967–97; Parly Sec. to Ministers for Industry and Commerce and for the Gaeltacht, 1969–70; Minister for Posts and Telegraphs, 1970–73; opposition front-bench spokesman on agriculture, 1973–75; spokesman on justice, 1975–77; Minister for Justice, 1977–81; Minister for Foreign Affairs, March-Dec. 1982; opposition front-bench spokesman on foreign affairs, 1983–87; Minister for Justice, 1987–89; Minister for Foreign Affairs, 1989–92. Mem., Consultative Assembly, Council of Europe, 1973–77; Chm., Parly Cttee on Secondary Legislation of European Communities, 1983–87. Mem., Limerick CC, 1974–77. *Address:* The Hill, Abbeyfeale, Co. Limerick.

COLLINS, Dr Jane Elizabeth, (Mrs David Evans), FRCP, FRCPCH; Consultant in Metabolic Medicine, Great Ormond Street Hospital, since 1996; Medical Director, Great Ormond Street Hospital NHS Trust, since 1999; *b* 19 Oct. 1954; *d* of Thomas and Betsy Collins; *m* 1978, David Evans; one *s* one *d*. *Educ:* Portsmouth High Sch.; Univ. of Birmingham (MSc, MD 1988). FRCP 1994; FRCPCH 1996. Consultant Paediatric Neurologist: Guy's Hosp., 1991–94; Gt Ormond St Hosp., 1994–96. Children's Doctor column, The Times, 1999–. *Address:* Great Ormond Street Hospital, WC1N 3JH. *T:* (020) 7405 9200.

COLLINS, Prof. Jeffrey Hamilton, FRSE; FREng; Professor and Specialist Advisor to Vice-Chancellor, Napier University, 1994–97; *b* 22 April 1930; *s* of Ernest Frederick and Dora Gladys Collins; *m* 1956, Sally Parfitt; two *s*. *Educ:* London Univ. (BSc, MSc, DSc). FIEE, CPhys, FInstP, FIEEE; CEng, FREng (FEng 1981). GEC Research Laboratories, London, 1951–56; Ferranti Ltd, Edinburgh, 1956–57; Univ. of Glasgow, 1957–66; Research Engr, Stanford Univ., Calif, 1966–68; Dir of Physical Electronics, Rockwell International, Calif, 1968–70; University of Edinburgh: Research Prof., 1970–73; Prof. of Industrial Electronics, 1973–77; Prof. of Electrical Engrg and Hd of Dept, 1977–84; Emeritus Prof., 1984; Chm., Parallel Computing Centre, 1991–94. Dir, Automation and Robotics Res. Inst., and Prof. of Electrical Engrg, Univ. of Texas at Arlington, 1987–90; Sen. Technical Specialist, Lothian Regl Council, 1991–93. Member: Electronics Res. Council, 1979; Computer Bd for Univs and Res. Councils, 1985–86; Information Systems Cttee, UFC, 1992–93; Jt Information Systems Cttee, HEFCs, 1993–94. Director: MESL, 1970–79; Racal-MESL, 1979–81; Advent Technology, 1981–86; Filtronics Components, 1981–85; Burr-Brown Ltd, 1985; River Bend Bank, Fort Worth, 1987–90. Member Honour Societies: Eta Kappa Nu; Tau Beta Pi; Upsilon Pi Epsilon; Phi Beta Delta. Hon. DEng Napier, 1997. *Publications:* Computer-Aided Design of Surface Acoustic Wave Devices, 1976; 197 articles in learned soc. electrical engrg jls. *Recreations:* music, DIY, tennis.

COLLINS, Joan Henrietta, OBE 1997; actress; *b* 23 May 1933; *er d* of late Joseph Collins and Elsa (*née* Bessant); *m* 1st, 1954, Maxwell Reed (marr. diss. 1957; he *d* 1974); 2nd, 1963, (George) Anthony Newley (marr. diss. 1970; he *d* 1999); one *s* one *d*; 3rd, 1972, Ronald S. Kass (marr. diss. 1983); one *d*; 4th, 1985, Peter Holm (marr. diss. 1987). *Educ:* Francis Holland Sch.; RADA. *Films include:* Lady Godiva Rides Again, I Believe in You, 1952; Our Girl Friday, The Square Ring, 1953; The Good Die Young, Turn the Key Softly, 1954; Land of the Pharaohs, The Virgin Queen, The Girl in the Red Velvet Swing, 1955; The Opposite Sex, 1956; The Wayward Bus, Island in the Sun, Sea Wife, 1957; The Bravados, 1958; Rally Round the Flag, Boys, 1959; Esther and the King, Seven Thieves, 1960; Road to Hong Kong, 1962; Warning Shot, The Subterfuge, 1967; Can Hieronymous Merkin Ever Forget Mercy Humppe and Find True Happiness?, Drive Hard Drive Fast, 1969; Up in the Cellar, The Executioner, 1970; Quest for Love, Revenge, 1971; Tales from the Crypt, Fear in the Night, 1972; Tales that witness Madness, 1973; Dark Places, Alfie Darling, 1974; The Call of the Wolf, I don't want to be born, 1975; The Devil within Her, 1976; Empire of the Ants, 1977; The Big Sleep, 1978; Sunburn, The Stud, 1979; The Bitch, 1980; The Nutcracker, 1984; The Cartier Affair, 1985; Decadence, 1994; In the Bleak Midwinter, 1995; The Clandestine Marriage, 1998; The Flintstones in Viva Rock Vegas, 2000; Those Old Broads, 2000; *stage includes:* The Last of Mrs Cheyney, Cambridge Th., 1980; Private Lives, Aldwych, 1990, US tour and NY, 1992; Love Letters, US, 2000; Over the Moon, Old Vic, 2001; *television includes:* serials: Dynasty, 1981–89; Sins, 1986; Monte Carlo, 1986; series: Tonight at 8.30, 1991; film: Annie: A Royal Adventure, 1995; also appearances in plays and series. Awards: Best TV Actress, Golden Globe, 1982; Hollywood Women's Press Club, 1982; Favourite TV Performer, People's Choice, 1985. *Publications:* Past Imperfect (autobiog.), 1978; The Joan Collins Beauty Book, 1980; Katy: a fight for life, 1982; Prime Time, 1988; Love and Desire and Hate, 1990; My Secrets, 1994; Too Damn Famous, 1995; Second Act (autobiog.), 1996; My Friends' Secrets, 2000; Star Quality, 2001. *Address:* c/o Paul Keylock, 16 Bulbecks Walk, South Woodham Ferrers, Essex CM3 5ZN. *T:* (01245) 328367, *Fax:* (01245) 328625.

COLLINS, Sir John (Alexander), Kt 1993; Deputy Chairman, 2001–Sept. 2002, Chairman, from Sept. 2002, Dixons Group plc; *b* 10 Dec. 1941; *s* of John Constantine Collins and Nancy Isobel Mitchell; *m* 1965, Susan Mary Hooper. *Educ:* Campbell Coll., Belfast; Reading Univ. Joined Shell International Chemicals, 1964; various appointments in Shell in Kenya, Nigeria, Columbia and UK, until 1989; Supply and Marketing Co-ordinator, and Dir, Shell Internat. Petroleum Co. Ltd, 1989–90; Chm. and Chief Exec., Shell UK, 1990–93; Chief Exec., Vestey Gp, 1994–2001; Chm., National Power, 1997–2000. Director: BSkyB, 1994–97; N. M. Rothschild & Sons, 1995–; LSO, 1997–; P&O, 1998–; Stoll Moss Theatres Ltd, 1999–2000. Chm., Cantab Pharmaceuticals plc, 1996–99. Chm., Adv. Cttee on Business and Envmt, 1991–93; Mem., PM's Adv. Cttee for Queen's Awards for Export, Technological and Envmtl Achievement, 1992–99. Gov., Wellington Coll., 1995–99. *Recreations:* opera, theatre, sailing, riding, golf, tennis, a love of the New Forest. *Address:* Dixons Group plc, 29 Farm Street, W1X 7RD.

COLLINS, John Ernest Harley, MBE 1944; DSC 1945 and Bar 1945; Chairman: Morgan Grenfell Holdings Ltd, 1974–79; Guardian Royal Exchange Assurance, 1974–88; *b* 24 April 1923; *o s* of late G. W. Collins, Taynton, Glos; *m* 1st, 1946, Gillian (*d* 1981), *e d* of 2nd Baron Bicester; one *s* one *d*; 2nd, 1986, Jennifer Faith, *widow* of Capt. A. J. A. Cubitt. *Educ:* King Edward's Sch., Birmingham; Birmingham Univ. Royal Navy, 1941–46. Morgan Grenfell & Co. Ltd, 1946, Dir 1957. Director: Royal Exchange Assce, 1957; Rank Hovis McDougall Ltd, 1965–91; Charter Consolidated Ltd, 1966–83; Hudson's Bay Co., 1957–74. Chm. United Services Trustee, 1968–76. DL Oxon, 1975–96; High Sheriff, Oxon, 1975. KStJ 1983. *Recreation:* fishing. *Address:* Chetwode Manor, Buckingham MK18 4BB. *T:* (01280) 848333. *Club:* White's.

COLLINS, (John) Martin; QC 1972; Commissioner, Royal Court, Jersey, since 2000; a Judge of the Courts of Appeal of Jersey, 1984–99, and of Guernsey, 1984–2000; *b* 24 Jan. 1929; *s* of John Lissant Collins and Marjorie Mary Collins; *m* 1957, Daphne Mary, *d* of George Martyn Swindells, Prestbury; two *s* one *d*. *Educ:* Uppingham Sch.; Manchester Univ. (LLB). Called to Bar, Gray's Inn, 1952 (Bencher, 1981; Chm., Mgt Cttee, 1990; Vice-Treas., 1998; Treas., 1999); called to the Bar of Gibraltar, 1990. Dep. Chm., Cumberland QS, 1969–72; a Recorder, 1972–88. Member: Senate of Inns of Court and Bar, 1981–84; Gen. Council of the Bar, 1991. *Address:* 10 Essex Street, Outer Temple, WC2R 3AA; 19 avenue Messine, 75008 Paris, France; 12 Gray's Inn Square, WC1R 5JP. *T:* (020) 7404 6299; Les Grandes Masses, 50580 Denneville, France. *Clubs:* Athenæum, Carlton.

COLLINS, John Morris; a Recorder of the Crown Court, 1980–98; *b* 25 June 1931; *s* of late Emmanuel Cohen, MBE, and Ruby Cohen; *m* 1968, Sheila Brummer; one *d*. *Educ:* Leeds Grammar Sch.; The Queen's Coll., Oxford (MA LitHum). Called to Bar, Middle Temple, 1956, Member of North Eastern Circuit; Hd of Chambers, 1966–2001, Jt Hd of Chambers, 2001–; a Deputy Circuit Judge, 1970. Pres., Leeds Jewish Representative Council, 1986–89. *Publications:* Summary Justice, 1963; various articles in legal periodicals, etc. *Recreation:* walking. *Address:* (home) 14 Sandhill Oval, Leeds LS17 8EA. *T:* (0113) 268 6008; (chambers) Zenith Chambers, 10 Park Square, Leeds LS1 2LH. *T:* (0113) 245 5438, *Fax:* (0113) 242 3515.

COLLINS, John Vincent, MD; FRCP; Consultant Physician, Royal Brompton Hospital, since 1976; Consultant Physician, since 1979, and Medical Director, since 1994, Chelsea and Westminster Hospital; *b* 16 July 1938; *s* of Thomas Ernest Vincent Collins and Zillah Phoebe Collins; *m* 1963, Helen Eluned Cash; one *s* one *d*. *Educ:* Guy's Hosp. Med. and Dental Sch. (BDS 1961; MD 1974). FRCP 1981. Dental and Medical Schs, Guy's Hosp., 1956–66; Guy's, St Mary's, Royal Brompton and Westminster Hosps, 1967–72; Hon. Consultant Physician and Sen. Lectr, St Bartholomew's Hosp. Med. Sch., London, 1973–76; Cons. Physician, St Stephen's Hosp., 1979–89; Hon. Consultant, In Pensioners, Royal Hosp., Chelsea, 1980–. Mem., Soc. of Apothecaries. *Publications:* more than 140 papers and contribs to books. *Recreations:* painting, travel, tennis. *Address:* Chelsea and Westminster Healthcare NHS Trust, 369 Fulham Road, SW10 9NH. *T:* (020) 8852 9496.

COLLINS, Judith, (Mrs R. J. H. Collins); *see* McClure, J.

COLLINS, Kathleen Joyce, (Kate), (Mrs D. A. L. Cooke); Deputy Director General, Organised and International Crime Directorate, Home Office, since 2000; *b* 12 March 1952; *d* of Norman Jeffrey Collins and Phyllis Laura Collins (*née* Yardley); *m* 1984, David Arthur Lawrence Cooke, *qv*. *Educ:* Lady Margaret Hall, Oxford (BA Mod. Langs 1973; MA 1974). Joined Home Office as Immigration Officer, 1975; Admin Trainee, 1977; Principal, 1982; Dep. Chief Insp., 1988–91, Dir (Ports), 1991–94, Immigration Service; Cabinet Office, 1994–96; Police Dept, Home Office, 1997; Dep. Dir Gen., Immigration and Nationality Directorate, 1998–2000. *Recreations:* music, reading, countryside. *Address:* c/o Home Office, 50 Queen Anne's Gate, SW1H 9AT.

COLLINS, Kenneth Darlingston; Chairman, Scottish Environment Protection Agency, since 1999; *b* 12 Aug. 1939; *s* of Nicholas Collins and Ellen Williamson; *m* 1966, Georgina Frances Pollard; one *s* one *d*. *Educ:* St John's Grammar Sch.; Hamilton Acad.; Glasgow Univ. (BSc Hons); Strathclyde Univ. (MSc). FRSGS 1993. Left school, 1956; steelworks apprentice, 1956–59; univ., 1960–65; planning officer, 1965–66; WEA Tutor-Organiser, 1966–67; Lecturer: Glasgow Coll. of Bldg, 1967–69; Paisley Coll. of Technol., 1969–79. MEP (Lab) Strathclyde E, 1979–99. European Parliament: Dep. Leader, Labour Gp, 1979–84; Socialist spokesman on envmt, public health and consumer protection, 1984–89;

Chm., Cttee on Envmt, Public Health and Consumer Protection, 1979–84 and 1989–99 (Vice Chm., 1984–87); Chm., Conf. of Cttee Chairmen, 1993–99. Dir, Inst. for Eur. Envmt Policy, London, 1991–99. Member: East Kilbride Town and Dist Council, 1973–79; Lanark CC, 1973–75; East Kilbride Develt Corp., 1976–79; Bd, Forward Scotland, 1996–; Bd, EEA, 2000–; Chairman: NE Glasgow Children's Panel, 1974–76; Central Scotland Countryside Trust, 1998–. Hon. Sen. Res. Fellow, Dept of Geography, Lancaster Univ., 1991–98; Associate Fellow, Eur. Centre for Public Affairs, 1999–. Member: Fabian Soc.; Amnesty Internat.; Labour Movement in Europe; Howard League; Hon. Vice-President: Royal Envmtl Health Inst. of Scotland, 1983; Internat. Fedn on Envmtl Health, 1987; Inst. of Trading Standards Admin; Inst. of Environmental Health Officers; Energy Action Scotland; Nat. Soc. for Clean Air; Town and Country Planning Assoc. Fellow, Industry and Parlt Trust, 1984. *Publications:* contributed to European Parliament reports; various articles on European envmt policy. *Recreations:* Labour Party, music, boxer dogs, cycling. *Address:* 11 Stuarton Park, East Kilbride, Lanarkshire G74 4LA. *T:* and *Fax:* (01355) 237282.

COLLINS, Hon. Sir Lawrence (Antony), Kt 2000; LLD; FBA 1994; **Hon. Mr Justice Lawrence Collins;** a Judge of the High Court of Justice, Chancery Division, since 2000; Fellow of Wolfson College, Cambridge, since 1975; *b* 7 May 1941; *s* of late Sol Collins and Phoebe (*née* Barnett); *m* 1982, Sara Shamni, psychotherapist; one *s* one *d. Educ:* City of London Sch.; Downing Coll., Cambridge (BA, George Long Prize, McNair Schol., 1963; LLB, Whewell Schol., 1964; LLD 1994; Hon. Fellow, 2000); Columbia Univ. (LLM 1965). Mem. Inst de Droit Internat., 1989. Admitted solicitor, 1968; Partner, Herbert Smith, solicitors, 1971–2000 (Hd, Litigation and Arbitration Dept, 1995–98); QC 1997; a Dep. High Court Judge, 1997–2000. Bencher, Inner Temple, 2001. Vis. Prof., QMC, then QMW, 1982–; Lectr, Hague Acad. of Internat. Law, 1991, 1998; Graveson Meml Lectr, KCL, 1995; F. A. Mann Lectr, British Inst. of Internat. and Comparative Law, 2001. Member: Lord Chancellor's Wkg Party on Foreign Judgments, 1979–81; Bar and Law Soc. Jt Wkg Party on UK-US Judgments Convention, 1980–82; Law Commn Jt Wkg Party on Torts in Private Internat. Law, 1982–84. Hon. Sec., British Br., 1983–88, Chm., Cttee on Internat. Securities Regulation, 1988–94, Internat. Law Assoc. Member: Adv. Council, Centre for Commercial Law Studies, QMW, 1989–; Council of Management, and Chm., Adv. Bd, Private Internat. Section, British Inst. of Internat. and Comparative Law, 1992–; Adv. Bd, Cambridge Univ. Centre for European Legal Studies, 1993–97. Hon. Member: SPTL, 1993; Law Soc., 2000. Member: Editl Adv. Cttee, Law Qly Rev., 1988–; Bd of Eds, Internat. and Comparative Law Qly, 1988–; Editl Cttee, British Yearbook of Internat. Law, 1991–. *Publications:* European Community Law in the United Kingdom, 1975, 4th edn 1990; Civil Jurisdiction and Judgments Act 1982, 1983; Essays in International Litigation and the Conflict of Laws, 1994; (Gen. Ed.) Dicey & Morris, Conflict of Laws, 11th edn 1987, 13th edn 2000. *Address:* Chancery Division, Royal Courts of Justice, Strand, WC2A 2LL.

COLLINS, Lesley Elizabeth; *see* Appleby, L. E.

COLLINS, Margaret Elizabeth, CBE 1983; RRC; Matron-in-Chief, Queen Alexandra's Royal Naval Nursing Service, 1980–83; *b* 13 Feb. 1927; *d* of James Henry Collins and Amy Collins. *Educ:* St Anne's Convent Grammar Sch., Southampton. RRC 1978 (ARRC 1965). Royal Victoria Hosp., Bournemouth, SRN 1949; West Middlesex Hosp., CMB Part 1, entered QARNNS as Nursing Sister, 1953; accepted for permanent service, 1958; Matron, 1972; Principal Matron, 1976. SSStJ 1978. QHNS, 1980–83. *Recreations:* gardening, theatre-going. *Address:* Lancastria, First Marine Avenue, Barton-on-Sea, Hants BH25 6DP. *T:* (01425) 612374.

COLLINS, Martin; *see* Collins, J. M.

COLLINS, Michael; aerospace consultant; Vice President, LTV Aerospace and Defense Company (formerly Vought Corporation), 1980–85; former NASA Astronaut; Command Module Pilot, Apollo 11 rocket flight to the Moon, July 1969; *b* Rome, Italy, 31 Oct. 1930; *s* of Maj.-Gen. and Mrs James L. Collins, Washington, DC, USA; *m* 1957, Patricia M. Finnegan, Boston, Mass; one *s* two *d. Educ:* St Albans Sch., Washington, DC (grad.). US Mil. Academy, West Point, NY (BSc); advanced through grades to Colonel; Harvard Business Sch. (AMP), 1974. Served as an experimental flight test officer, Air Force Flight Test Center, Edwards Air Force Base, Calif; he was one of the third group of astronauts named by NASA in Oct. 1963; served as backup pilot for Gemini 7 mission; as pilot with John Young on the 3-day 44-revolution Gemini 10 mission, launched 18 July 1966, he shared record-setting flight (successful rendezvous and docking with a separately launched Agena target vehicle; completed two periods of extravehicular activity); Command Module Pilot for Apollo flight, first lunar landing, in orbit 20 July 1969, when Neil Armstrong and Edwin Aldrin landed on the Moon. Asst Sec. of State for Public Affairs, US, 1970–71; Dir, Nat. Air and Space Museum, Smithsonian Institution, 1971–78; Under Sec., Smithsonian Inst., 1978–80. Maj. Gen. Air Force Reserve, retired. Member: Bd of Trustees, Nat. Geographic Soc.; Soc. of Experimental Test Pilots; Fellow, Amer. Astronautical Soc. Member, Order of Daedalians. Hon. degrees from: Stonehill Coll.; St Michael's Coll.; Northeastern Univ.; Southeastern Univ. Presidential Medal of Freedom, NASA; FAI Gold Space Medal; DSM (NASA); DSM (AF); Exceptional Service Medal (NASA); Astronaut Wings; DFC. *Publications:* Carrying the Fire (autobiog.), 1974; Flying to the Moon and Other Strange Places (for children), 1976; Liftoff, 1988; Mission to Mars, 1990. *Recreations:* fishing, painting. *Clubs:* Alfalfa, Alibi (Washington, DC).

COLLINS, Michael Brendan, OBE 1983 (MBE 1969); HM Diplomatic Service, retired; HM Consul-General, Istanbul, 1988–92; *b* 9 Sept. 1932; *s* of Daniel James Collins, GM and Mary Bridget Collins (*née* Kennedy); *m* 1959, Maria Elena Lozar. *Educ:* St Illtyd's College, Cardiff; University College London. HM Forces, 1953–55. FO 1956; Santiago, Chile, 1959; Consul, Santiago, Cuba, 1962; FO, 1964; Second, later First, Sec. (Admin.) and Consul, Prague, 1967; Dep. High Comr, Bathurst, The Gambia, 1970; Head of Chancery, Algiers, 1972; First Sec., FCO, 1975; Consul Commercial, Montreal, 1978; Consul for Atlantic Provinces of Canada, Halifax, 1981; Counsellor (Economic and Commercial), Brussels, 1983. *Recreations:* fishing, golf, walking, reading, music. *Address:* 1 Talbot Place, Blackheath, SE3 0TZ. *Club:* Army and Navy.

COLLINS, Michael Geoffrey; QC 1988; *b* 4 March 1948; *s* of late Francis Geoffrey Collins and Margaret Isabelle Collins; *m* 1985, Bonnie Gayle Bird. *Educ:* Peterhouse, Rhodesia (now Zimbabwe); Exeter Univ. (LLB). Called to the Bar, Gray's Inn, 1971, Bencher, 1999. A Recorder, 1997–2001. *Publication:* contributor, Private International Litigation, 1988. *Recreations:* golf, tennis, watercolours, amateur dramatics. *Address:* Essex Court Chambers, 24 Lincoln's Inn Fields, WC2A 3ED. *T:* (020) 7813 8000.

COLLINS, Michael John; clarinettist; Professor, Royal College of Music, since 1983; *b* 27 Jan. 1962; *s* of Gwendoline Violet and Fred Allenby Collins; *m* 1997, Isabelle van Keulen; one *s* one *d. Educ:* Royal Coll. of Music (ARCM, Clarinet and Piano with Hons). BBC Young Musician of the Year, 1978. Principal clarinet: London Sinfonietta, 1982–; Nash Ensemble, 1982–88; Philharmonia Orchestra, 1988–; Dir, London Winds Ensemble. Many solo recordings. Hon. RAM 1997. Musicians' Co. Medal, 1980; competition winner: Leeds, 1980; Concert Artists' Guild, NY, 1982 (Amcon Award); Internat Rostrum of Young Performers, Unesco, 1985; Tagore Gold Medal, 1982. *Recreations:* walking, driving, wildlife. *Address:* Monks Park, Luddington Avenue, Virginia Water, Surrey GU25 4DF. *T:* (01344) 841263.

COLLINS, Neil Adam; City Editor, Daily Telegraph, since 1986; *s* of Clive and Joan Collins; *m* 1981, Vivien Goldsmith (marr. diss. 1994); one *d*; *m* 1999, Julia Frances Barnes. *Educ:* Uppingham School; Selwyn College, Cambridge (MA). City Editor: Evening Standard, 1979–84; Sunday Times, 1984–86. *Recreations:* walking, wine, fly fishing, opera. *Address:* 12 Gertrude Street, SW10 0JN. *T:* (office) (020) 7538 6900.

COLLINS, Nina; *see* Lowry, Noreen Margaret.

COLLINS, Paul Howard, CBE 1999; **His Honour Judge Collins;** a Circuit Judge, since 1992; *b* 31 Jan. 1944; *s* of Michael and Madie Collins; *m* 1987, Sue Fallows; one step *s. Educ:* Orange Hill Grammar Sch.; St Catherine's Coll., Oxford (MA). Called to the Bar, Lincoln's Inn, 1966 (Bencher, 2000); a Recorder, 1989. Dir of Studies, Judicial Studies Bd, 1997–99. *Recreations:* theatre, cycling, the internet. *Address:* c/o SE Circuit Administrator, New Cavendish House, 18 Maltravers Street, WC2R 3EU. *Club:* Questors.

COLLINS, Pauline, OBE 2001; actress (stage and television); *b* Exmouth, Devon, 3 Sept. 1940; *d* of William Henry Collins and Mary Honora Callanan; *m* John Alderton, *qv*; two *s* one *d. Educ:* Convent of the Sacred Heart, Hammersmith, London; Central Sch. of Speech and Drama. *Stage:* 1st appearance in A Gazelle in Park Lane, Theatre Royal, Windsor, 1962; 1st London appearance in Passion Flower Hotel, Prince of Wales, 1965; The Erpingham Camp, Royal Court, 1967; The Happy Apple, Hampstead, 1967, and Apollo, 1970; Importance of Being Earnest, Haymarket, 1968; The Night I chased the Women with an Eel, 1969; Come As You Are (3 parts), New, 1970; Judies, Comedy, 1974; Engaged, National Theatre, Old Vic, 1975; Confusions, Apollo, 1976; Rattle of a Simple Man, Savoy, 1980; Romantic Comedy, Apollo, 1983; Shirley Valentine, Vaudeville, 1988, NY, 1989 (Tony Award, Best Actress, 1989); Shades, Albery, 1992; *television*, 1962–: series: Upstairs Downstairs; No Honestly; P. G. Wodehouse; Thomas and Sarah; The Black Tower; Forever Green; The Ambassador; plays: Long Distance Information, 1979; Knockback, 1984; *films:* Shirley Valentine, 1989 (Evening Standard Film Actress of the Year, 1989; BAFTA Best Actress Award, 1990); City of Joy, 1992; My Mother's Courage, 1997; Paradise Road, 1997. Dr *hc* Liverpool Poly., 1991. *Publication:* Letter to Louise, 1992.

COLLINS, Peter; *see* Collins, V. P.

COLLINS, Peter G., RSA 1974 (ARSA 1966); painter in oil; *b* Inverness, 21 June 1935; *s* of E. G. Collins, FRCSE; *m* 1959, Myra Mackintosh (marr. diss. 1978); one *s* one *d. Educ:* Fettes Coll., Edinburgh; Edinburgh Coll. of Art. Studied in Italy, on Andrew Grant Major Travelling Scholarship, 1957–58. Work in permanent collections: Aberdeen Civic; Glasgow Civic; Scottish Arts Council. Hon. Librarian, RSA. *Recreations:* music, art-historical research. *Address:* Royal Scottish Academy, The Mound, Edinburgh EH2 2EL; The Cottage, Hilltown of Ballindean, Inchture, Perthshire PH14 9QS.

COLLINS, Air Vice-Marshal Peter Spencer, CB 1985; AFC 1961; *b* 19 March 1930; *s* of Frederick Wildbore Collins and Mary (*née* Spencer); *m* 1953, Sheila Mary (*née* Perks) (*d* 2000); three *s* one *d. Educ:* Royal Grammar Sch., High Wycombe; Univ. of Birmingham (BA (Hons) History). CIMgt (FBIM 1979). Joined RAF, 1951; flying tours incl. service on squadron nos: 63, 141, 41, AWDS, AFDS; RAF Handling Sqdn, nos 23 and 11; commanded: 111 Sqdn, 1970–72; RAF Gütersloh, 1974–76; staff tours include: Air Ministry, 1962–64; Strike Comd HQ, 1968–70 and 1972–74; Dir of Forward Policy (RAF), 1978–81; SASO, HQ 11 Gp, 1981–83; DG, Communications, Inf. Systems and Orgn (RAF), 1983–85; psc 1965, rcds 1977; retired 1985. Marconi Radar Systems: Dir, Business Develt, 1986–88; Consultant Dir, 1988–95; Consultant, GEC-Marconi Res. Centre, 1989–95. Hon. Pres., Essex Wing, ATC; Vice-Pres., Chelmsford Br., RAFA. *Publications:* contribs to service jls and to Seaford House Papers, 1978. *Recreations:* golf, music, gardening. *Address:* Babylon, Boreham, Essex CM3 3EJ. *Club:* Royal Air Force.

COLLINS, Philip, LVO 1994; singer, drummer, songwriter, actor and record producer; Trustee, Prince's Trust, since 1983; patron of numerous charities; *b* 30 Jan. 1951; *s* of Greville and June Collins; *m* 1st, 1976 (marr. diss.); one *s* one *d*; 2nd, 1984, Jill Tavelman (marr. diss. 1995); one *d*; 3rd, 1999, Orianne Cevey; one *s. Educ:* primary and secondary schs; Barbara Speake Stage Sch. Played parts in various television, film and stage productions, 1965–67; mem. of various rock groups, 1967–70; drummer, 1970–96, lead singer, 1975–96, Genesis; started writing songs, 1976; toured Japan, USA and Europe, 1978, 1987; first solo album, 1981; solo world tours, 1985, 1990; started producing records for other artists, 1981. *Albums* include: *with Genesis:* Nursury Crime, 1971; Foxtrot, 1972; Genesis Live, 1973; Selling England by the Pound, 1973; The Lamb Lies Down on Broadway, 1974; A Trick of the Tail, 1976; Genesis Rock Roots, 1976; Wind and Wuthering, 1977; Genesis Seconds Out, 1977; And Then There Were Three, 1978; Duke, 1980; Abacab, 1981; Three Sides Live, 1982; Genesis, 1983; Invisible Touch, 1986; We Can't Dance, 1991; *solo:* Face Value, 1981; Hello … I must be Going, 1982; No Jacket Required, 1985; But Seriously, 1989; Both Sides, 1993; Dance into the Light, 1996; Hits, 1998. *Films:* Buster (lead role), 1988; Frauds, 1993. Numerous awards, incl. Grammy (eight), Ivor Novello (six), Brit (four), Variety Club of GB (two), Silver Clef (two), Academy Award, and Elvis awards.

COLLINS, Prof. Philip Arthur William; Emeritus Professor of English, University of Leicester, since 1982; *b* 28 May 1923; *er s* of Arthur Henry and Winifred Nellie Collins; *m* 1st, 1952, Mildred Lowe (marr. diss. 1963); 2nd, 1965, Joyce Dickins; two *s* one *d. Educ:* Brentwood Sch.; Emmanuel Coll., Cambridge (Sen. Schol.). MA 1948. Served War (RAOC and Royal Norfolk Regt), 1942–45. Leicester: Staff Tutor in Adult Educn, 1947; Warden, Vaughan Coll., 1954; Sen. Lectr in English, 1962–64; Prof., 1964–82; Head, English Dept, 1971–76, 1981–82; Public Orator, 1975–78, 1980–82. Visiting Prof.: Univ. of California, Berkeley, 1967; Columbia, 1969; Victoria Univ., NZ, 1974. Sec., Leicester Theatre Trust Ltd, 1963–87; Member: Drama Panel, Arts Council of Gt Britain, 1970–75; National Theatre Bd, 1976–82; British American Drama Acad. Bd, 1983–97; Pres., Dickens Fellowship, 1983–85; Chm. Trustees, Dickens House Museum, 1984–92; Chm., Tennyson Soc., 1984–97. Many overseas lecture-tours; performances, talks and scripts for radio and television. *Publications:* James Boswell, 1956; (ed) English Christmas, 1956; Dickens and Crime, 1962; Dickens and Education, 1963; The Canker and the Rose (Shakespeare Quater-centenary celebration) perf. Mermaid Theatre, London, 1964; The Impress of the Moving Age, 1965; Thomas Cooper the Chartist, 1969; A Dickens Bibliography, 1970; Dickens's Bleak House, 1971; (ed) Dickens, the Critical Heritage, 1971; (ed) A Christmas Carol: the public reading version, 1971; Reading Aloud: a Victorian Métier, 1972; (ed) Dickens's Public Readings, 1975; Dickens's David Copperfield, 1977; (ed) Dickens: Interviews and Recollections, 1981; (ed) Thackeray: Interviews and Recollections, 1983; Trollope's London, 1983; (ed) Dickens: Sikes and

Nancy and other Readings, 1983; Tennyson, Poet of Lincolnshire, 1984; (co-ed) The Annotated Dickens, 1986; contrib. to: Encyclopaedia Britannica, Listener, TLS, sundry learned journals. *Recreations:* theatre, music. *Address:* 26 Knighton Drive, Leicester LE2 3HB. *T:* (0116) 270 6026.

COLLINS, Terence Bernard; Chairman, 1984–87, Vice Chairman, 1976–84, Group Managing Director, 1975–86, Berger Jenson Nicholson; *b* 3 March 1927; *s* of George Bernard Collins and Helen Theresa Collins; *m* 1956, Barbara (*née* Lowday); two *s* two *d.* *Educ:* Marist Coll., Hull; Univ. of St Andrews (MA Hons). Trainee, Ideal Standard, 1951–52; Blundell Spence: Area Manager, 1953–55; Regl Manager, 1955–57; UK Sales Manager, 1957–59; Berger Jenson Nicholson: Sales Manager, 1959–62; Man. Dir, Caribbean, 1962–69; Overseas Regl Exec., 1969–70; Gp Dir UK, 1970–74. Chairman: Cranfield Conf. Services Ltd, 1987–93; Cranfield Ventures Ltd, 1990–93; CIT Hldgs Ltd, 1991–92 (Dir, 1989–93); Interact Design and Print Ltd (formerly Interact Ltd), 1994–; Director: A. G. Stanley Hldgs, 1977–87; Hoechst UK, 1979–87; Hoechst Australia Investments, 1980–87; Mayborn Gp PLC, 1986–91; Phoenix Develts Ltd, 1987–94, 1995– (Chm., 2000–); Aldehurst Consultants Ltd, 1987–94; Cranfield Precision Engineering Ltd, 1990–95; Chm., Management Bd, Kingline Consultants Ltd, 1989–90. Mem., Duke of Edinburgh's Award Internat. Panel, 1978–86; Trustee, Atlas Econ. Foundn UK, 1986–93. Cranfield University (formerly Institute of Technology): Mem. Court, 1977–98; Mem. Council, 1981–93; Treasurer, 1991–92; Chm., Finance Cttee, 1991–92; University of Buckingham: Vice-Chm. Council, 1987–95; Chm., F and GP Cttee, 1987–94. DUniv Buckingham, 1994. *Recreations:* golf, music, gardening. *Address:* Aldehurst, Church Walk, Aldeburgh, Suffolk IP15 5DX. *Club:* Directors.

COLLINS, Most Rev. Thomas; *see* Edmonton (Alberta), Archbishop of, (RC).

COLLINS, Timothy William George, CBE 1996; MP (C) Westmorland and Lonsdale, since 1997; *b* 7 May 1964; *s* of late William and of Diana Collins; *m* 1997, Clare, *d* of Geoffrey and Auriel Benson. *Educ:* Chigwell Sch., Essex; LSE (BSc); KCL (MA). Cons. Res. Dept, 1986–89; Advr to Secs of State for the Envmt, 1989–90, for Employment, 1990–92; Press Sec. to Prime Minister, 1992; Dir of Communications, Cons. Party, 1992–95; Mem., Prime Minister's Policy Unit, 1995; Media Consultant to Chm. of Cons. Party, 1995–97. Sen. Strategy Consultant, WCT Ltd, 1995–97. An Opposition Whip, 1998–99; Shadow Minister for the Cabinet, 2001–. Vice-Chm., Cons. Party, 1999–2001. *Address:* House of Commons, SW1A 0AA; *e-mail:* listening@timcollins.co.uk.

COLLINS, Prof. (Vincent) Peter, MD; FRCPath; Professor of Histopathology, University of Cambridge, since 1997; Hon. Consultant Pathologist, Addenbrooke's Hospital, since 1997; *b* 3 Dec. 1947; *s* of James Vincent Collins and Mary Ann Collins (*née* Blanche). *Educ:* University Coll., Dublin (MB, BCh, BAO 1971); Karolinska Hosp., Stockholm (MD 1978). MRCPath 1988, FRCPath 1996. House appts, Mater Hosp., Dublin, 1972–73; junior appts, 1974–82, Cons. Pathologist, 1982–90, Sen. Cons. Pathologist, 1994–97, Karolinska Hosp.; Head of Clin. Res., Ludwig Inst. for Cancer Res., Stockholm Br., 1986–98; Prof. of Neuropathology, Univ. of Gothenburg, 1990–94; Sen. Cons. Pathologist, Sahlgrenska Univ. Hosp., Gothenburg, 1990–94; Prof. of Tumour Pathology, Karolinska Inst., 1994–97. Foreign Adjunct Prof., Karolinska Inst., 1998–. *Publications:* over 200 papers on human brain tumours. *Recreations:* sailing, ski-ing, music. *Address:* Department of Histopathology, Box 235, Addenbrooke's Hospital, Cambridge CB2 2QQ. *T:* (01223) 336072.

COLLINS, William Janson; Chairman, William Collins Sons & Co. (Holdings) Ltd, 1976–81; *b* 10 June 1929; *s* of late Sir William Alexander Roy Collins, CBE, and Lady Collins (Priscilla Marian, *d* of late S. J. Lloyd); *m* 1951, Lady Sara Elena Hely-Hutchinson, *d* of 7th Earl of Donoughmore; one *s* three *d.* *Educ:* Magdalen Coll., Oxford (BA). Joined William Collins Sons & Co. Ltd, 1952; Dir, then Man. Dir, 1967; Vice-Chm., 1971; Chm., 1976. *Recreations:* Royal tennis, shooting, fishing, tennis, golf. *Address:* High Coodham, Symington, Kilmarnock, Ayrshire KA1 5SJ. *T:* (01563) 830253, *Fax:* (01563) 830673. *Club:* All England Lawn Tennis and Croquet.

COLLINSON, Rev. Nigel Thomas; Secretary, Methodist Conference, since 1998 (President, 1996–97); *b* 14 March 1941; *m* 1964, Lorna Ebrill; two *d.* *Educ:* Forster Street Sch., Tunstall; Hanley High Sch., Stoke on Trent; Hull Univ. (BA Theol); Wesley House, Cambridge (MA Theol). Methodist Minister: Clifton and Redland Circuit, Bristol, 1964–67; Stroud and Cirencester Circuit, 1967–72; Wolverhampton Trinity Circuit, 1972–80; Supt, Oxford Circuit, 1980–88; Chm., Southampton Dist, 1988–98. Hon. DD Hull, 1998. *Publications:* The Opening Door, 1986; (with David Matthews) Facing Illness, 1986; The Land of Unlikeness, 1996. *Recreations:* a wide range of sports and the arts, caravanning. *Address:* Methodist Church House, 25 Marylebone Road, NW1 5JR. *T:* (020) 7486 5502.

COLLINSON, Prof. Patrick, CBE 1993; PhD; FBA 1982; FRHistS, FAHA; Regius Professor of Modern History, University of Cambridge, 1988–96, now Emeritus; Fellow of Trinity College, Cambridge, since 1988; *b* 10 Aug. 1929; *s* of William Cecil Collinson and Belle Hay (*née* Patrick); *m* 1960, Elizabeth Albinia Susan Selwyn; two *s* two *d.* *Educ:* King's Sch., Ely; Pembroke Coll., Cambridge (Exhibnr 1949, Foundn Scholar 1952; BA 1952, 1st Cl. Hons Hist. Tripos Pt II; Hadley Prize for Hist., 1952). PhD London, 1957; FRHistS 1967 (Mem. Council, 1977–81, Vice-Pres., 1983–87 and 1994–98); FAHA 1974. University of London: Postgrad. Student, Royal Holloway Coll., 1952–54; Res. Fellow, Inst. of Hist. Res., 1954–55; Res. Asst, UCL, 1955–56; Lectr in Hist., Univ. of Khartoum, 1956–61; Asst Lectr in Eccles. Hist., King's Coll., Univ. of London, 1961–62, Lectr, 1962–69 (Fellow 1976); Professor of History: Univ. of Sydney, 1969–75; Univ. of Kent at Canterbury, 1976–84; Prof. of Modern Hist., Sheffield Univ., 1984–88. Vis. Fellow, All Souls Coll., Oxford, 1981; Andrew W. Mellon Fellow, Huntington Library, California, 1984; Douglas S. Freeman Vis. Prof., Richmond Univ., Va, 1999; Vis. Hon. Prof., Univ. of Warwick, 2000–. Lectures: Ford's, in Eng. Hist., Univ. of Oxford, 1978–79; Birkbeck, Univ. of Cambridge, 1981; Stenton Meml, Univ. of Reading, 1985; Neale Meml, Univ. of Manchester, 1986; Anstey Meml, Univ. of Kent, 1986; Neale Meml, UCL, 1987; F. D. Maurice, KCL, 1990; Homer J. Crotty, Huntington Liby, 1990; Sir D. Owen Evans Meml, UCW Aberystwyth, 1992; A. H. Dodd Meml, UCNW Bangor, 1992; Raleigh, British Academy, 1993; S. T. Bindoff Meml, QMW, 1995; Douglas S. Freeman, Richmond Univ., Va, 1999; Eberhard L. Faber, Princeton Univ., 1999. Chm., Adv. Editorial Bd, Jl of Ecclesiastical History, 1982–93. President: Ecclesiastical Hist. Soc., 1985–86; C of E Record Soc., 1991–; Mem. Council, British Acad., 1986–89. Mem., Academia Europaea, 1989; Corresp. Mem., Massachusetts Historical Soc., 1990. DUniv York, 1988; Hon. DLitt: Kent at Canterbury, 1989; Oxford, 1997; Essex, 2000; Hon. LittD: TCD, 1992; Sheffield, 1995. Medlicott Medal, Histl Assoc., 1998. *Publications:* The Elizabethan Puritan Movement, 1967 (USA 1967; repr. 1982); Archbishop Grindal 1519–1583: the struggle for a Reformed Church, 1979 (USA 1979); The Religion of Protestants: the Church in English Society 1559–1625 (Ford Lectures, 1979), 1982; Godly People: essays on English Protestantism and Puritanism, 1983; English Puritanism, 1983; The Birthpangs of Protestant England: religious and cultural change in the 16th and 17th centuries, 1988; Elizabethan Essays, 1994; (jtly) A History of Canterbury Cathedral, 1995; (ed jtly) The Reformation in English Towns 1500–1640, 1998; (jtly) A History of Emmanuel College, Cambridge, 1999; (ed) Short Oxford History of the British Isles: The Sixteenth Century, 2001; articles and revs in Bull. Inst. Hist. Res., Eng. Hist. Rev., Jl of Eccles. Hist., Studies in Church Hist., TLS, London Rev. of Books. *Recreations:* hills, music, gardening. *Address:* The Winnats, Cannonfields, Hathersage, Hope Valley S32 1AG; Trinity College, Cambridge CB2 1TQ.

COLLIS, Ian; His Honour Judge Collis; a Circuit Judge, since 2000; *b* 21 Feb. 1946; *s* of late Harold Collis and Florence Collis; *m* 1968; Julia Georgina Cure; three *s.* *Educ:* Dartford Grammar Sch.; Coventry Univ. (LLB Hons). Admitted Solicitor, 1970; District Judge, 1987–2000; a Recorder, 1996–2000. *Recreations:* gardening, music, piano.

COLLIS, Peter George; Chief Land Registrar and Chief Executive, HM Land Registry, since 1999; *b* 13 Oct. 1953; *s* of Martin Arthur Collis and Margaret Sophie Collis; *m* 1978, Linda Jean Worssam (marr. diss. 1999); one *s* one *d;* *m* 2000, Jan Morgan; one step *s.* *Educ:* Univ. of Aston in Birmingham (BSc 1st Cl. Hons Communication Sci. and Linguistics 1975). Joined Civil Service, 1975; admin trainee, Depts of Trade, Industry and Prices and Consumer Protection, 1975–78; Personal Asst to Chm. and Dep. Chm., NEB, 1978–80; Principal, Dept of Trade, 1980–83; Mktg Exec., Balfour Beatty, 1983–85 (on secondment); Principal, Dept of Transport, 1985–88; Head, Driver Licensing Div., DVLA, 1988–91; Head, Finance Exec. Agencies 2 Div., 1991–92, Highways Resource Mgt Div., 1992–94, Dept of Transport; Strategy and Private Finance Dir, Highways Agency, 1994–97; Business Develt Dir, Dept of Transport, 1997; Finance and Commercial Policy Dir, Employment Service, 1997–99. *Recreations:* family, travelling, enjoying the countryside. *Address:* HM Land Registry, Lincoln's Inn Fields, WC2A 3PL. *T:* (020) 7917 5980.

COLLIS, Simon Paul; HM Diplomatic Service; Consul General, Dubai, since 2000; *b* 23 Feb. 1956; *s* of Arthur Albert Collis and Sheelah Collis (*née* Findlay); *m* 1974 (marr. diss.); one *s* one *d;* partner, 1994, Sandra Kelly. *Educ:* King Edward VII Sch., Sheffield; Christ's Coll., Cambridge (BA Hons). Joined HM Diplomatic Service, 1978: FCO, 1978–80; Arabic lang. trng, 1980–81; 3rd, later 2nd, Sec., Bahrain, 1981–83; 1st Secretary: FCO, 1984–85; UK Mission to UN, NY, 1986; Head, India Section, S Asia Dept, FCO, 1987–88; Head of Chancery, Tunis, 1988–90; Gulf War Emergency Unit, FCO, 1990–91; New Delhi, 1991–94; Asst Head, Near East and N Africa Dept, FCO, 1994–96; Dep. Hd of Mission, Amman, 1996–99; on secondment to BP, 1999–2000. *Recreation:* R&B music. *Address:* c/o Foreign and Commonwealth Office, King Charles Street, SW1A 2AH. *Clubs:* Rodent's Return (Pres.), Dubai Country (Dubai).

COLLUM, Hugh Robert, FCA; Chairman, British Nuclear Fuels PLC, since 1999; *b* 29 June 1940; *s* of late Robert Archibald Hugh Collum and Marie Vivien Collum (*née* Skinner); *m* 1965, Elizabeth Noel Stewart; two *d.* *Educ:* Eton. FCA 1964. With Coopers & Lybrand, 1959–64; Dir, Plymouth Breweries Ltd and Courage Western, 1965–72; Financial Director: Courage Ltd, 1973–81; Cadbury Schweppes PLC, 1981–86; Beecham Gp, 1987–89; Exec. Vice Pres. and Chief Financial Officer, SmithKline Beecham, 1989–98. Non-executive Director: Imperial Tobacco, 1978–81; Sedgwick Gp, 1987–92; M & G Gp, 1992–98; Ladbroke Grove Gp, 1994–96; Safeway, 1997–; Whitehead Mann Gp, 1997–; Invensys, 1998–; Celltech Gp, 1999–; S African Breweries, 1999–; Chm., Chiroscience Gp, 1998–99. Chm., Hundred Gp of Finance Dirs, 1990–92. Mem., Cadbury Cttee on Financial Aspects of Corporate Governance, 1991–95. Liveryman, Co. of Wax Chandlers, 1963–; Mem., Ct of Assts, Co. of Chartered Accountants, 1992–. *Recreations:* sport, opera, travel, shooting. *Address:* Clinton Lodge, Fletching, E Sussex TN22 3ST. *T:* (01825) 722952. *Clubs:* Boodle's, MCC.

COLLYEAR, Sir John (Gowen), Kt 1986; FREng; Chairman, USM Texon Ltd (formerly United Machinery Group), 1987–95; *b* 19 Feb. 1927; *s* of John Robert Collyear and late Amy Elizabeth Collyear (*née* Gowen); *m* 1953, Catherine Barbara Newman; one *s* two *d.* *Educ:* Leeds Univ. (BSc). FIMechE (Hon. FIMechE 1995); FIM, FIEE; FREng (FEng 1979); CIMgt. Graduate apprentice and Production Engr, Joseph Lucas Industries, 1951; Glacier Metal Company Ltd: Production Engr, 1953; Production Manager, 1956; Chief Production Engr, 1956; Factory Gen. Manager, 1959; Managing Director, 1969; Bearings Div. Man. Dir, Associated Engineering Ltd, 1972; Group Man. Dir, AE plc, 1975, Chm., 1981–86. Chairman: MK Electric Gp PLC, 1987–88; Fulmer Ltd, 1987–91; Dir, Hollis plc, 1987–88. Chm., Technology Requirements Bd, DTI, 1985–88. President: Motor Industry's Res. Assoc., 1987–97; Inst. of Materials, 1992–94. Hon. Bencher, Gray's Inn, 2000. FRSA 1987. *Publications:* Management Precepts, 1975; The Practice of First Level Management, 1976. *Recreations:* golf, bridge, piano music. *Address:* Walnut Tree House, Nether Westcote, Oxon OX7 6SD. *T:* (01993) 831247. *Club:* Athenæum.

COLMAN, Hon. Sir Anthony (David), Kt 1992; **Hon. Mr Justice Colman;** a Judge of the High Court of Justice, Queen's Bench Division, Commercial Court, since 1992; *b* 27 May 1938; *s* of late Solomon and Helen Colman, Manchester; *m* 1964, Angela Glynn; two *d.* *Educ:* Harrogate Grammar Sch.; Trinity Hall, Cambridge (Aldis Schol.; Double First in Law Tripos; MA). FCIArb 1978. Called to the Bar, Gray's Inn, 1962, Master of the Bench, 1986; QC 1977; a Recorder, 1986–92; Judge in charge of Commercial Court List, 1996–97. Mem., Bar Council, 1990–92 (Chm., Central and E European Sub-Cttee, 1991–92); Chairman: Commercial Bar Assoc., 1991–92 (Treasurer, 1989–91); Lloyd's Disciplinary Cttee for PCW and Minet, 1984; Mem., Cttee of Enquiry into Fidentia at Lloyd's, 1982–83; conducted Investigation into loss of MV Derbyshire, 1999–2000. Special Advr to Govt of Czech Republic on civil litigation procedure, 2000–01. *Publications:* Mathew's Practice of the Commercial Court (1902), 2nd edn, 1967; The Practice and Procedure of the Commercial Court, 1983, 5th edn 2000; (Gen. Editor and contrib.) Encylopedia of International Commercial Litigation, 1991. *Recreations:* tennis, music, gardening, the 17th Century, Sifnos, the River Chess. *Address:* Royal Courts of Justice, Strand, WC2A 2LL.

COLMAN, Anthony John; MP (Lab) Putney, since 1997; *b* 24 July 1943; *s* of late William Benjamin Colman and Beatrice (*née* Hudson); *m* Juliet Annabelle, *d* of Alec and June Owen; two *s,* and four *s* two *d* by prev. marriages. *Educ:* Paston Grammar Sch.; Magdalene Coll., Cambridge (MA); Univ. of E Africa, 1964–66; LSE, 1966. Unilever (United Africa Co.), 1964–69; Burton Group, 1969–90: Merchandise Manager, 1971–74, Buying and Merchandising Dir, 1974–76, Top Shop; Asst Man. Dir, Womenswear Sector, 1976–81; Director: Burton Menswear, 1976–81; Top Man, 1976–81; Dorothy Perkins, 1979–81; Dir, 1981–90. Director: GLE, 1990–97 (Chm., GLE Development Capital, 1990–); Aztec, 1990–98; London First Centre Ltd, 1994–. Mem. (Lab) Merton LBC, 1990–98 (Leader of Council, 1991–97). Vice-Chm., ALA, 1991–95. PPS to Minister of State, NI Office, 1998–2000. Member: Treasury Select Cttee, 1997–98; Internat. Develt Select Cttee, 2000–; Chairman: All Party Gp on Socially Responsible Investment, 1998–; All Party Gp on Mgt, 2001–; PLP Trade and Industry Cttee, 1997–99. Chairman: Low Pay Unit, 1990–98; London Res. Centre, 1994–97; Dir, Public Private Partnerships Prog. Ltd, 1998– (Chm., 1996–98); Member: Price Commn, 1977–79; Labour Finance & Industry Gp, 1973–; Labour Party Enquiry into Educn & Trng in Europe, 1991–93; Exec. Cttee, UNED Forum, 1995–. Chm., Wimbledon Theatre Trust, 1991–96; Dir, London Arts Bd,

1994–98. Contested (Lab), SW Herts, 1979. Industrial Fellow, Kingston Univ. (formerly Poly.), 1983–. FRSA 1983. *Address:* 14 Lambourne Avenue, Wimbledon Village, SW19 7DW. *T:* (020) 8879 0045. *Club:* Reform.

COLMAN, Sir Michael (Jeremiah), 3rd Bt *cr* 1907; Chairman, Reckitt and Colman plc, 1986–95; First Church Estates Commissioner, 1993–99; *b* 7 July 1928; *s* of Sir Jeremiah Colman, 2nd Bt, and Edith Gwendolyn Tritton; *S* father, 1961; *m* 1955, Judith Jean Wallop, JP, DL, *d* of Vice-Adm. Sir Peveril William-Powlett, KCB, KCMG, CBE, DSO; two *s* three *d*. *Educ:* Eton. Director: Reckitt & Colman plc, 1970–95; Foreign and Colonial Ventures Advisors Ltd, 1988–99; Foreign and Colonial Private Equity Trust, 1995–. Member: Council of Royal Warrant Holders, 1977–, Pres., 1984–85; Trinity House Lighthouse Bd, 1985–94 (Younger Brother, 1994). Member: Council, Chemical Industries Assoc., 1982–84; Bd, UK Centre for Econ. and Environmental Develt, 1985–99 (Chm., 1996–99). Mem., Council, Scout Assoc., 1985–2000. Mem. Gen. Council and Mem. Finance Cttee, King Edward's Hosp. Fund for London, 1978–; Special Trustee, St Mary's Hosp., 1988–99; Trustee: Royal Foundn of Grey Coat Hosp., 1989–; Allchurches Trust Ltd, 1994. Capt., Yorks Yeomanry, RARO, 1967. Mem. Ct, Skinners' Co., 1985– (Master, 1991–92). Hon. LLD Hull, 1993. Cross of St Augustine, 1999. *Recreations:* farming, shooting. *Heir: s* Jeremiah Michael Powlett Colman [*b* 23 Jan. 1958; *m* 1981, Susan Elizabeth, *yr d* of John Henry Britland, York; two *s* one *d*]. *Address:* Malshanger, Basingstoke, Hants RG23 7EY. *T:* (01256) 780241; 40 Chester Square, SW1W 9HT; Tarvie, Bridge of Cally, Blairgowrie, Perthshire PH10 7PJ. *Clubs:* Cavalry and Guards, Boodle's.

COLMAN, Dr Peter Malcolm, FAA, FTSE; Head, Structural Biology Division, Walter and Eliza Hall Institute of Medical Research, Melbourne, since 2001; *b* 3 April 1944; *s* of Clement Colman and Kathleen Colman (*née* Malcolm); *m* 1967, Anne Elizabeth Smith; two *s*. *Educ:* University of Adelaide (BSc 1st Cl. Hons 1966; PhD 1970). FAA 1989; FTSE 1997. Postdoctoral Fellow: Univ. of Oregon, 1969–72; Max Planck Inst., Munich, 1972–75; Queen Elizabeth II Fellow, 1975–77, Principal Investigator, NH&MRC, 1977–78, Univ. of Sydney; Scientist, 1978–89, Chief, Div. of Biomolecular Engrg, 1989–97, CSIRO; Dir, Biomolecular Res. Inst., Melbourne, 1991–2000. Involved in res. which determined the 3-dimensional structure of influenza virus neuraminidase and established and led the group which subsequently discovered Relenza, the first neuraminidase inhibitor to be approved for use in treatment of influenza. Professorial Associate, 1988–98, Professorial Fellow, 1998–, Univ. of Melbourne: Adjunct Prof., La Trobe Univ., 1998–. Mem., Asia-Pacific Internat. Molecular Biol. Network, 1998–. Hon. DSc Sydney, 2000. (Jtly) Australia Prize, 1996. *Publications:* contribs to scientific jls on structural biol., influenza virus and drug discovery. *Recreation:* music. *Address:* 74 Hotham Street, E Melbourne, Vic 3002, Australia. *T:* (3) 94161969.

COLMAN, Sir Timothy (James Alan), KG 1996; Lord-Lieutenant of Norfolk, since 1978; *b* 19 Sept. 1929; 2nd but *o* surv. *s* of late Captain Geoffrey Russell Rees Colman and Lettice Elizabeth Evelyn Colman, Norwich; *m* 1951, Lady Mary Cecelia (Extra Lady in Waiting to Princess Alexandra), twin *d* of late Lt-Col Hon. Michael Claude Hamilton Bowes Lyon and Elizabeth Margaret, Glamis; two *s* three *d*. *Educ:* RNC, Dartmouth and Greenwich. Lieut RN, 1950, retd 1953. Chm., Eastern Counties Newspapers Group Ltd, 1969–96; Director: Reckitt & Colman plc, 1978–89; Whitbread & Co. PLC, 1980–86; Anglia Television Group PLC, 1987–94; Trustee, Carnegie UK Trust (Chm., 1983–87). Pro-Chancellor, Univ. of E Anglia (Chm. Council, 1973–86); Chairman: Trustees, Norfolk and Norwich Festival, 1974–; Royal Norfolk Agricl Assoc., 1985–96 (Pres., 1982, 1997). Member: Countryside Commn, 1971–76; Water Space Amenity Commn, 1973–76; Adv. Cttee for England, Nature Conservancy Council, 1974–80; Eastern Regional Cttee, National Trust, 1967–71; Pres., Norfolk Naturalists Trust, 1962–78. Pres., E. Anglian TAVRA, 1989–95. FRSA 1995. JP 1958, DL 1968, High Sheriff 1970, Norfolk. Hon. DCL E Anglia, 1973. KStJ 1979. *Address:* Bixley Manor, Norwich, Norfolk NR14 8SJ. *T:* (01603) 625298. *Clubs:* Turf, Pratt's; Norfolk (Norwich); Royal Yacht Squadron.
See also P. J. C. Troughton.

COLMER, Ven. Malcolm John; Archdeacon of Middlesex, since 1996; *b* 15 Feb. 1945; *s* of Frederick and Gladys Colmer; *m* 1966, Kathleen Elizabeth Colmer (*née* Wade); one *s* three *d*. *Educ:* Sussex Univ. (BSc (Maths); MSc (Fluid Mechs)); Nottingham Univ. (BA (Theol.)). Scientific Officer, RAE, 1967–71; ordained deacon, 1973, priest, 1974; Assistant Curate: St John the Baptist, Egham, 1973–76; St Mary, Chadwell, 1976–79; Vicar: St Michael, S Malling, Lewes, 1979–85; St Mary, Hornsey Rise, 1985–87; Team Rector, Hornsey Rise, Whitehall Park Team, 1987–96. Area Dean of Islington, 1990–95. *Recreations:* music, painting, natural history, gardening. *Address:* 59 Sutton Lane South, W4 3JR. *T:* (020) 8994 8148, *Fax:* (020) 8995 5374; *e-mail:* archdeacon.middlesex@dlondon.org.uk.

COLOMBO, Metropolitan Archbishop of, (RC), since 1977; **Most Rev. Nicholas Marcus Fernando;** *b* 6 Dec. 1932. *Educ:* St Aloysius' Seminary, Colombo; Universitas Propaganda Fide, Rome. BA (London); PhL (Rome); STD (Rome). Pres., Catholic Bishops' Conf. of Sri Lanka, 1989–95. Mem., Sacred Congregation for Evangelization of Peoples. *Address:* Archbishop's House, Borella, Colombo 8, Sri Lanka. *T:* (1) 695471/2/3, *Fax:* (1) 692009.

COLOMBO, Emilio; Minister of Foreign Affairs, Italy, 1980–83 and 1992–93; *b* Potenza, Italy, 11 April 1920. *Educ:* Rome Univ. Deputy: Constituent Assembly, 1946–48; (Christian Democrat), Italian Parlt, 1948–94; Under-Secretary: of Agriculture, 1948–51; of Public Works, 1953–55; Minister: of Agriculture, 1955–58; of Foreign Trade, 1958–59; of Industry and Commerce, 1959–60, March-April 1960, July 1960–63; of the Treasury, 1963–70, Feb.-May 1972, 1974–76; Prime Minister, 1970–72; Minister of State for UN Affairs, 1972–73; Minister of Finance, 1973–74. European Parliament: Mem., 1976–80; Chm., Political Affairs Cttee, 1976–77; Pres., 1977–79. Formerly Vice-Pres., Italian Catholic Youth Assoc. Charlemagne Prize, 1979. *Address:* Via Aurelia 239, Rome, Italy.

COLQUHOUN, Prof. Alan Harold; architect; Professor, School of Architecture, Princeton University, 1981–91, now Emeritus; *b* 27 June 1927; *s* of John Sydney Plumptree Colquhoun and Clariss Thelma Colquhoun (*née* Soden). *Educ:* Edinburgh Coll. of Art; AA Dip 1949. Architects' Dept, LCC, 1949–55; Candilis and Woods, Paris, 1955–56; Lyons Israel and Ellis, London, 1956–61; own practice, Colquhoun & Miller, Architects, 1961–88. Lectr, PCL, 1974–78; many short-term or part-time teaching posts in UK, Switzerland, Ireland and USA, 1957–; lectures and seminars in UK, France, Germany, Spain, Holland, Switzerland, Portugal, USA, Canada, Brazil, Argentina, Chile, India and Singapore, 1960–. Guggenheim Fellowship, 1996; Centre for Advanced Study in the Visual Arts Fellowship, Nat. Gall. of Art, Washington, 1996. *Publications:* Modern Architecture and Historical Change, 1982 (trans. French, German, Italian and Spanish); Modernity and the Classical Tradition, 1987; contrib. learned jls in UK, USA and Europe. *Recreations:* music (as listener), painting (as occasional practitioner and enjoyer), literature. *Address:* 96 Regent's Park Road, NW1 8UG; c/o School of Architecture, Princeton University, Princeton, NJ 08544, USA.

COLQUHOUN, Andrew John, PhD; Director General, Royal Horticultural Society, since 1999; *b* 21 Sept. 1949; *s* of late Kenneth James Colquhoun, MC, and of Christine Mary Colquhoun (*née* Morris); *m* 1975, Patricia Beardall; one *s* one *d*. *Educ:* Tiffin Sch.; Nottingham Univ. (BSc 1st Cl. Hons 1971); Glasgow Univ. (PhD 1974); City Univ. Business Sch. (MBA Dist. 1987). Joined HM Diplomatic Service, 1974; Third Sec., FCO, 1974–75; Second Sec., MECAS, 1975–77; Second, later First, Sec., Damascus, 1977–79; First Sec., Tel Aviv, 1979–81; Principal, Cabinet Office, 1981–83; Planning Staff, FCO, 1983–84; Shandwick Consultants (on secondment to ICA), 1984–86; Dir of Educn and Trng, 1987–90; Sec. and Chief Exec., 1990–97, ICAEW. Sec., Consultative Cttee of Accountancy Bodies, 1990–97. Member: Audit Cttee, Edexcel Foundn, 1997–; BITC Headteacher Mentoring Prog., 1998–; Mid Sussex Literacy Project, 1998–; Rail Passengers (formerly Rail Users Consultative) Cttee for Southern England, 1999–. Mem. Council, Nottingham Univ., 1999–. *Publications:* various articles on accountancy, professions, educn and recruitment in nat., educnl and professional press. *Recreations:* bird watching, gardening, country life, reading. *Address:* Radford, Haywards Heath Road, Balcombe, Sussex RH17 6NJ. *Club:* Reform.

COLQUHOUN, Prof. David, FRS 1985; Professor of Pharmacology, since 1983, and Director, Wellcome Laboratory for Molecular Pharmacology, since 1993, University College London; *b* 19 July 1936; *s* of Gilbert Colquhoun and Kathleen Mary (*née* Chambers); *m* 1976, Margaret Ann Boultwood; one *s*. *Educ:* Birkenhead Sch.; Liverpool Technical Coll.; Leeds Univ. (BSc); Edinburgh Univ. (PhD). Lectr, Dept of Pharmacol., UCL, 1964–70; Vis. Asst, then Associate Prof., Dept of Pharmacol., Yale Univ. Med. Sch., 1970–72; Sen. Lectr, Dept of Pharmacol., Univ. of Southampton Med. Sch., 1972–75; Sen. Lectr, Dept of Pharmacol., St George's Hosp. Med. Sch., 1975–79; Reader, Dept of Pharmacol., UCL, 1979–83. Guest Prof., Max-Planck-Institut für Medizinische Forschung, Heidelberg, 1990–91. Krantz Lectr, Univ. of Maryland, 1987. Trustee, Sir Ronald Fisher Meml Cttee, 1975–. Alexander von Humboldt Prize, 1990. Member Editorial Board: Jl of Physiology, 1974–81; Jl Gen. Physiology, 1998–; Series B, Proceedings of Royal Soc. *Publications:* Lectures on Biostatistics, 1971; articles in Jl of Physiology, British Jl of Pharmacology, Proc. of Royal Soc., etc. *Recreations:* walking, running, sailing, linear algebra. *Address:* Chiddingstone, Common Lane, Kings Langley, Herts WD4 8BL. *T:* (01923) 266154.

COLQUHOUN OF LUSS, Captain Sir Ivar (Iain), 8th Bt *cr* 1786; JP; DL; Hon. Sheriff (formerly Hon. Sheriff Substitute); Chief of the Clan; Grenadier Guards; *b* 4 Jan. 1916; *s* of Sir Iain Colquhoun, 7th Bt, and Geraldine Bryde (Dinah) (*d* 1974), *d* of late F. J. Tennant; *S* father, 1948; *m* 1943, Kathleen, 2nd *d* of late W. A. Duncan and of Mrs Duncan, 53 Cadogan Square, SW1; one *s* one *d* (and one *s* decd). *Educ:* Eton. JP 1951, DL 1952, Dunbartonshire. *Heir: s* Malcolm Rory Colquhoun, Younger of Luss [*b* 20 Dec. 1947; *m* 1st, 1978, Susan Timmerman (marr. diss.); one *s*; 2nd, 1989, Katharine, *e d* of A. C. Mears; one *s* one *d*]. *Address:* Camstraddan, Luss, Argyllshire G83 8NX; 26A Thorney Crescent, SW11 3TT. *Clubs:* White's, Royal Ocean Racing.
See also Duke of Argyll.

COLQUHOUN, Ms Maureen Morfydd; political researcher and writer; Chief Executive, North West Government Relations, since 1994; *b* 12 Aug. 1928; *m* 1949, Keith Colquhoun (marr. diss. 1980); two *s* one *d*; partner, 1975–, Ms Barbara Todd; extended family, two *d*. Mem. Labour Party, 1945–; Member: Shoreham UDC, 1965–74; Adur District Council, 1973–74; West Sussex CC, 1971–74; Hackney BC, 1982–90; Lakes Parish Council, 1994–. MP (Lab) Northampton North, Feb. 1974–1979. Information Officer, Gingerbread, 1980–82. Hon. Sec., All-Party Parly Gp on AIDS, 1987–88; Chm., Secretaries and Assistants' Council, H of C, 1992–93. Founder and Chairman: Historic Ambleside Trust, 1992–; Pensions Lobbying, 1996–; Co-Founder, Lakes Vision Gp, 1997; Mem. Exec. Cttee, Ambleside Civic Trust, 1993–; Mem., Lake Dist Nat. Park Authy, 1998–. Co-Founder and Chairperson to Trustees, Harriet Martineau Foundn, 2000. *Publications:* A Woman In the House, 1980; Inside the Westminster Parliament, 1992; New Labour–New Lobbying, 1998. *Recreations:* fell-walking, jazz, opera, theatre. *Address:* South Knoll, Rydal Road, Ambleside, Cumbria LA22 9AY.

COLSTON, Colin Charles, QC 1980; **His Honour Judge Colston;** a Circuit Judge, since 1983; *b* 2 Oct. 1937; *yr s* of late Eric Colston, JP, and Catherine Colston; *m* 1963, Edith Helga, *d* of late Med. Rat Dr Wilhelm and Frau Gisela Hille, St Oswald/Freistadt, Austria; two *s* one *d*. *Educ:* Rugby Sch.; The Gunnery, Washington, Conn, USA; Trinity Hall, Cambridge (MA). National Service, RN, 1956–58; commissioned, RNR, 1958–64. Called to the Bar, Gray's Inn, 1962; Midland and Oxford Circuit (formerly Midland Circuit); Recorder of Midland Circuit, 1968–69; Member, Senate of Inns of Court and Bar, 1977–80; Recorder of the Crown Court, 1978–83; Resident Judge, St Albans, 1989–2000. Lay Judge, Court of Arches, Canterbury, 1992–. Mem., Criminal Cttee, Judicial Studies Bd, 1989–92. Chm., St Albans Diocesan Bd of Patronage, 1987–2000. *Address:* The Crown Court, Bricket Road, St Albans, Herts AL1 3JW.

COLSTON, Michael; Chairman: Ewelme Park Farm Ltd, since 1996; *b* 24 July 1932; *s* of Sir Charles Blampied Colston, CBE, MC, DCM, FCGI and Lady (Eliza Foster) Colston, MBE; *m* 1st, 1956, Jane Olivia Kilham Roberts (marr. diss.); three *d*; 2nd, 1977, Judith Angela Briggs. *Educ:* Ridley Coll., Canada; Stowe; Gonville and Caius Coll., Cambridge. Joined 17th/21st Lancers, 1952; later seconded to 1st Royal Tank Regt for service in Korea. Founder Dir, Charles Colston Group Ltd (formerly Colston Appliances Ltd) together with late Sir Charles Colston, 1955, Chm. and Man. Dir, 1969–89; Chm. and Man. Dir, Colston Domestic Appliances Ltd, 1969–79. Chairman: Colston Consultants Ltd, 1989–93; Tallent Engineering Ltd, 1969–89; Tallent Holdings plc, 1989–90; ITS Rubber Ltd, 1969–85; Quit Ltd, 1989–93; Dishwasher Council, 1970–75. Dir, Farming and Wildlife Adv. Gp, 1991–. Chm., Assoc. Manufrs of Domestic Electrical Appliances, 1976–79. Member Council: Inst. of Directors, 1977–93 (Pres., Thames Valley Br., 1983–93); CBI, 1984–90 (Chm., S Regl Council, 1986–88); British Electrotechnical Approvals Bd, 1976–79; SMMT, 1987–90. Trustee, Hawk and Owl Trust, 1991–96. *Recreations:* fishing, shooting, tennis; founder Cambridge Univ. Water Ski Club. *Address:* C6 Albany, Piccadilly, W1V 9RF. *T:* (020) 7734 2452.

COLT, Sir Edward (William Dutton), 10th Bt *cr* 1694; MB, FRCP, FACP; Attending Physician, St Luke's-Roosevelt Hospital, New York; Associate Professor of Clinical Medicine (part-time), Columbia University, New York; *b* 22 Sept. 1936; *s* of Major John Rochfort Colt, North Staffs Regt (*d* 1944), and of Angela Miriam Phyllis (*née* Kyan; she *m* 1946, Capt. Robert Leslie Cock); *S* uncle, 1951; *m* 1st, 1966, Jane Caroline (marr. diss. 1972), *d* of James Histed Lewis, Geneva and Washington, DC; 2nd, 1979, Suzanne Nelson (*née* Knickerbocker); one *d* (one *s* decd). *Educ:* Stoke House, Seaford; Douai Sch.; University Coll., London. Lately: Medical Registrar, UCH; House Physician, Brompton Hosp. *Publications:* contribs, especially on sports medicine, particularly running, to British and American med. jls. *Recreations:* squash, tennis. *Heir:* none. *Address:* 444 Central Park West, Apt 5F, New York, NY 10025, USA.

COLTART, Simon Stewart; His Honour Judge Coltart; a Circuit Judge, since 1991; *b* 3 Sept. 1946; *s* of Gilbert McCallum Coltart and Mary Louise (*née* Kemp); *m* 1973, Sarah Victoria Birts; three *s*. *Educ:* Epsom Coll.; Leeds Univ. (LLB). Called to the Bar, Lincoln's Inn, 1969; a Recorder, 1987–91. Mem., Parole Bd, 1997–. Mem., Court of Assts, Grocers' Co., 1991–. *Recreations:* sailing, golf. *Address:* The Law Courts, Lewes, East Sussex BN2 3JH. *Club:* Rye Golf.

COLTHURST, Sir Richard La Touche, 9th Bt *cr* 1744; *b* 14 Aug. 1928; *er s* of Sir Richard St John Jefferyes Colthurst, 8th Bt, and Denys Maida Hanmer West (*d* 1966), *e d* of Augustus William West; *S* father, 1955; *m* 1953, Janet Georgina, *d* of L. A. Wilson-Wright, Coolcarrigan, Co. Kildare; three *s* one *d*. *Educ:* Harrow; Peterhouse, Cambridge (MA). Host and Organiser, Blarney Castle International Horse Trials, 1992– (Competition Complet Internat.). Liveryman of Worshipful Company of Grocers. Member: Internat. Dendrology Soc; Cork Chamber of Commerce. *Recreations:* forestry, cricket, tennis, swimming. *Heir:* *s* Charles St John Colthurst [*b* 21 May 1955; *m* 1987, Nora Mary, *d* of Mortimer Kelleher, Dooniskey, Lissarda, Co. Cork; one *s* three *d*. *Educ:* Eton; Magdalene Coll., Cambridge (MA); University Coll., Dublin]. *Address:* Blarney Castle, Co. Cork, Eire; Ardrum, Inniscarra, Co. Cork, Eire. *Clubs:* MCC, I Zingari, Free Foresters; Hawks, Pitt (Cambridge).

COLTMAN, Anne Clare, (Mrs T. C. Coltman); *see* Riches, A. C.

COLTMAN, Sir (Arthur) Leycester (Scott), KBE 1997; CMG 1993; HM Diplomatic Service, retired; Ambassador to Colombia, 1994–98; *b* 24 May 1938; *s* of late Arthur Cranfield Coltman and Vera Vaid; *m* 1969, Maria Piedad Josefina Cantos Aberasturi; two *s* one *d*. *Educ:* Rugby School; Magdalene Coll., Cambridge. Foreign Office, 1961–62; Third Secretary, British Embassy, Copenhagen, 1963–64; Second Secretary, Cairo 1964–65, Madrid 1966–69; Manchester Business School, 1969–70; Foreign Office, 1970–74; Commercial Secretary, Brasilia, 1974–77; Foreign Office, 1977–79; Counsellor, Mexico City, 1979–83; Counsellor and Hd of Chancery, Brussels, 1983–87; Head: Mexico and Central America Dept, 1987–90; Latin America Dept, 1990; Ambassador to Cuba, 1991–94. *Recreations:* squash, chess, bridge, music. *Address:* Flat 4, 37 de Vere Gardens, W8 5AW.

COLTON, Rt Rev. (William) Paul; *see* Cork, Cloyne and Ross, Bishop of.

COLTRANE, Robbie; actor and director; *b* Glasgow, 31 March 1950; *m* 1999, Rhona Irene Gemmell; one *s* one *d*. *Educ:* Trinity Coll., Glenalmond; Glasgow Sch. of Art (DA Drawing and Painting). *Television* includes: Laugh? I nearly paid my licence fee!, 1985; Hooray for Hollyrood, 1986; Tutti Frutti, 1986; The Miners' Strike, 1987; Mistero Buffo, 1990; Coltrane in a Cadillac, 1992; Cracker (3 series), 1993, 1994, 1995, TV film (White Ghost), 1996; The Ebb Tide, 1997; Coltrane's Planes and Automobiles, 1997; *films* include: Absolute Beginners, 1985; Mona Lisa, 1985; Danny Champion of the World, 1988; Henry V, 1988; Nuns on the Run, 1989; The Pope Must Die, 1990; Oh, What a Night, 1991; Huck Finn, 1992; Goldeneye, 1995; Buddy, 1996; Montana, 1997; Frogs for Snakes, 1997; Message in a Bottle, 1999; The World Is Not Enough, 1999; Harry Potter and the Philosopher's Stone, 2001; *theatre:* has appeared and toured with Traverse Theatre Co. and Borderline Theatre Co., 1976–, incl. Mistero Buffo, 1990; Yr Obedient Servant, Lyric, 1987. Silver Rose Award, Montreux TV Fest., 1987; Evening Standard Peter Sellers Award, 1991; TV Best Actor Awards: BAFTA, 1994, 1995, 1996; Silver Nymph, Monte Carlo, 1994; BPG, 1994; RTS, 1994; FIPA (French Acad.), 1994; Cable Ace, 1994; Cannes TV Fest., 1994. *Publications:* Coltrane in a Cadillac, 1993; (with John Binias) Planes and Automobiles, 1997; newspaper and magazine articles. *Recreations:* politics, drawing, vintage cars, reading, sailing, piano, fishing, arguing and drinking (together, usually), film, ships. *Address:* c/o CDA, 19 Sydney Mews, SW3 6HL. *T:* (020) 7581 8111. *Clubs:* Groucho, Soho House, Chelsea Arts, Marzipan; Glasgow Arts.

COLVER, Hugh Bernard, CBE 1991; Corporate Communications Director, BAE SYSTEMS, since 2000; *b* 22 Aug. 1945; *s* of late Rev. Canon John Lawrence Colver and Diana Irene (*née* Bartlett); *m* 1970, Gillian Ogilvie (marr. diss. 2001), *y d* of late Morris and Dorothy Graham, Christchurch, NZ; one *s* one *d*. *Educ:* King Edward VI Grammar Sch., Louth, Lincs. Reporter: Market Rasen Mail, 1961–63; Hereford Times and Hereford Evening News, 1963–67; Asst Editor, Helicopter World and Hovercraft World, 1967–68; Journalist, FT Surveys, Financial Times, 1968–71; freelance journalist, writer and PR consultant, 1971–75; Press Officer, MoD, 1975–78; PRO, RAE, 1978–79; Staff PRO to Flag Officer, Scotland and NI, 1979–81; Press Officer, Prime Minister's Office, 1981–82; Chief Press Officer, Dept of Employment, 1982–84; Dep. Dir of Information, Metropolitan Police, 1984–85; Ministry of Defence: Dep. Chief of PR, 1985–87; Chief of PR, 1987–92; Public Affairs Dir, British Aerospace Defence Ltd, 1992–95; Dir of Communications, Cons. Central Office, 1995. Non-executive Chairman: Europac Gp Ltd, 2000– (Dir, 1997–); Defence Public Affairs Consultants, 2000– (Dir, 1997–). FRAeS 1998; FRSA. *Publication:* This is the Hovercraft, 1972. *Recreations:* driving rapid cars, motor racing, walking, messing about in boats. *Address:* 39 Tufton Court, Tufton Street, SW1P 3QH. *Club:* Reform.

COLVILLE, family name of **Viscount Colville of Culross** and of **Baron Clydesmuir**.

COLVILLE OF CULROSS, 4th Viscount *cr* 1902; **John Mark Alexander Colville;** QC; 14th Baron (Scot.) *cr* 1604; 4th Baron (UK) *cr* 1885; a Circuit Judge, 1993–99; *b* 19 July 1933; *e s* of 3rd Viscount and Kathleen Myrtle (*d* 1986), OBE 1961, *e d* of late Brig.-Gen. H. R. Gale, CMG, RE, Bardsey, Saanichton, Vancouver Island; *S* father, 1945; *m* 1st, 1958, Mary Elizabeth Webb-Bowen (marr. diss. 1973); four *s*; 2nd, 1974, Margaret Birgitta, Viscountess Davidson, LLB, JP, Barrister, *o d* of Maj.-Gen. C. H. Norton, CB, CBE, DSO; one *s*. *Educ:* Rugby (Scholar); New Coll., Oxford (Scholar) (MA; Hon. Fellow, 1997). Lieut Grenadier Guards Reserve. Barrister-at-law, Lincoln's Inn, 1960 (Buchanan prizeman), Bencher, 1986; QC 1978; a Recorder, 1990–93. Minister of State, Home Office, 1972–74; elected Mem., H of L, 1999. Dir, Securities and Futures Authy (formerly Securities Assoc.), 1987–93. Chm., Norwich Information and Technology Centre, 1983–85; Director: Rediffusion Television Ltd, 1961–68; British Electric Traction Co. Ltd, 1968–72, 1974–84 (Dep. Chm., 1980–81); Mem., CBI Council, 1982–84. Chairman: Mental Health Act Commn, 1983–88; Alcohol Educn and Res. Council, 1984–90; Parole Bd, 1988–92; UK rep., UN Human Rights Commn, 1980–83; Mem., UN Working Gp on Disappeared Persons, 1980–84 (Chm., 1981–84); Special Rapporteur on Human Rights in Guatemala, 1983–86; Mem., UN Human Rights Cttee, 1995–2000. Reports on Prevention of Terrorism Act and NI Emergency Powers Act, for HM Govt, 1986–93. Mem. Council, Univ. of E Anglia, 1968–72. Mem., Royal Company of Archers (Queen's Body Guard for Scotland). Governor, BUPA, 1990–93. Hon. DCL UEA, 1998. *Heir:* *s* Master of Colville, *qv*. *Address:* House of Lords, SW1A 0PW.

See also Baron Carrington.

COLVILLE, Master of; Hon. Charles Mark Townshend Colville; *b* 5 Sept. 1959; *s* and *heir* of 4th Viscount Colville of Culross, *qv*. *Educ:* Rugby; Univ. of Durham. *Address:* Harpers Farm, Wenhaston, Halesworth, Suffolk.

COLVILLE, Lady Margaret, CVO 1994; an Extra Woman of the Bedchamber to HM Queen Elizabeth the Queen Mother, since 1990; *b* 20 July 1918; *d* of 4th Earl of Ellesmere; *m* 1948, Sir John Rupert Colville, CB, CVO (*d* 1987); two *s* one *d*. Served War of 1939–45 in ATS (Junior Subaltern). Lady in Waiting to the Princess Elizabeth, Duchess of Edinburgh, 1946–49. *Address:* The Close, Broughton, near Stockbridge, Hants SO20 8AA. *T:* (01794) 301331.

COLVIN, Andrew James; Comptroller and City Solicitor, Corporation of London, since 1989; *b* 28 April 1947; *s* of Gilbert Russell Colvin, OBE, MA, and Dr Beatrice Colvin, MRCS, LRCP, DPH; *m* 1971, Helen Mary Ryan; one *s* three *d*. *Educ:* qualified Solicitor, 1975; LLM Leicester Univ., 1996. Articled to Borough Solicitor, subseq. Asst Town Clerk, London Borough of Ealing, 1971–82; Dep. Town Clerk and Borough Solicitor, Royal Borough of Kensington and Chelsea, 1982–89. Legal Advr, Assoc. of London Govt, 1996– (London Boroughs' Assoc., 1984–96); Advr, English Nat. Stadium Trust, 1997–. Governor: St Gregory's RC Sch., 1989–93; Cardinal Wiseman RC Sch., 1992–99 (Chm., 1994–99). Freeman: City of London, 1989; City of London Solicitors' Co., 1996. *Recreations:* sailing, music, cycling. *Address:* Guildhall, EC2P 2EJ.

COLVIN, David, CBE 1991; Chief Adviser in Social Work, The Scottish Office, 1980–91; Scottish Secretary, British Association of Social Workers, 1992–97; *b* 31 Jan. 1931; *s* of James Colvin and Mrs Crawford Colvin; *m* 1957, Elma Findlay, artist; two *s* three *d*. *Educ:* Whitehill Sch., Glasgow; Glasgow and Edinburgh Univs. Probation Officer, Glasgow City, 1955–60; Psychiatric Social Worker, Scottish Prison and Borstal Service, 1960–61; Sen. Psychiatric Social Worker, Crichton Royal Hosp., Child Psychiatric Unit, 1961–65; Director, Family Casework Unit, Paisley, 1965; Social Work Adviser, Scottish Office, 1966, and subseq.; Interim Dir of Social Work, Shetland Islands Council, 1991. At various times held office in Howard League for Penal Reform, Assoc. of Social Workers and Inst. for Study and Treatment of Delinquency. Sen. Associate Research Fellow, Brunel Univ., 1978. Chm., Dumfries Constituency Labour Party, 1963–65. Chairman: Scotland Cttee, Nat. Children's Homes, 1991–97; Marriage Council, Scotland, 1991–95; SACRO, 1997– (Mem., Exec. Cttee, 1992–94); Vice-Chm., Scottish Consortium on Criminal Justice, 1998–; Vice-Pres., Scottish Carers Assoc., 1998–. Governor, Nat. Inst. for Social Work, 1986–89; Hon. Adviser, British Red Cross, 1982–90. Gov., St Columba's Hospice, 1998–; Trustee, Scottish Disability Foundn, 1998–. Chm., Exhibiting Socs of Scotland Assoc., 1999. Mem., Labour Party. DUniv Stirling, 1998. *Recreations:* collector; swimming, climbing, social affairs. *Address:* The Studio, 53 Windsor Place, Edinburgh EH15 2AF.

COLVIN, David Hugh, CMG 1993; HM Diplomatic Service, retired; Ambassador to Belgium, 1996–2001; *b* 23 Jan. 1941; 3rd *s* of late Major Leslie Hubert Boyd Colvin, MC, and of Edna Mary (*née* Parrott); *m* 1971, (Diana) Caroline Carew, *y d* of Gordon MacPherson Lang Smith and Mildred (*née* Carew-Gibson); one *s* one *d*. *Educ:* Lincoln Sch.; Trinity Coll., Oxford (MA). Assistant Principal, Board of Trade, 1966. Joined HM Foreign (later Diplomatic) Service, 1967; Central Dept, FO, 1967; Second Secretary, Bangkok, 1968–71; European Integration Dept, FCO, 1971–75; First Sec., Paris, 1975–77; First Sec. (Press and Inf.), UK Permanent Representation to the European Community, 1977–82; Asst Sec., Cabinet Office, 1982–85; Counsellor and Hd of Chancery, Budapest, 1985–88; Hd, SE Asian Dept, FCO, 1988–91; Minister, Rome, 1992–96. Patron, Drones Club of Belgium (P. G. Wodehouse Soc.), 1997–2001. *Recreations:* military history, tennis, shooting, rallying old cars. *Address:* 15 Westmoreland Terrace, SW1V 4AG. *T:* (020) 7630 8349. *Club:* Travellers.

COLVIN, Sir Howard (Montagu), Kt 1995; CVO 1983; CBE 1964; MA; FBA 1963; FRHistS; FSA, 1980; Fellow of St John's College, Oxford, 1948–87, now Emeritus (Tutor in History, 1948–78; Librarian, 1950–84); Reader in Architectural History, Oxford University, 1965–87; Member: Historic Buildings Council for England, 1970–84; Historic Buildings and Monuments Commission, 1984–85; Historic Buildings Advisory Committee, since 1984; Royal Commission on Ancient and Historical Monuments of Scotland, 1977–89; Royal Commission on Historical Manuscripts, 1981–88; Reviewing Committee on the Export of Works of Art, 1982–83; Royal Fine Art Commission, 1962–72; Royal Commission on Historical Monuments, England, 1963–76; President, Society of Architectural Historians of Great Britain, 1979–81; *b* 15 Oct. 1919; *s* of late Montagu Colvin; *m* 1943, Christina Edgeworth, *d* of late H. E. Butler, Prof. of Latin at University Coll., London; two *s*. *Educ:* Trent Coll.; University Coll., London (Fellow, 1974). Served in RAF, 1940–46 (despatches). Asst Lecturer, Dept of History, University Coll., London, 1946–48. Hon. FRIBA; Hon. FSA (Scot.) 1986. DUniv York, 1978. Wolfson Literary Award, 1978. *Publications:* The White Canons in England, 1951; A Biographical Dictionary of English Architects 1660–1840, 1954, 2nd edn as A Biographical Dictionary of British Architects 1600–1840, 1978, 3rd edn 1995; (General Editor and part author) The History of the King's Works, 6 Vols, 1963–82; A History of Deddington, 1963; Catalogue of Architectural Drawings in Worcester College Library, 1964; Architectural Drawings in the Library of Elton Hall (with Maurice Craig), 1964; (ed with John Harris) The Country Seat, 1970; Building Accounts of King Henry III, 1971; (introduction) The Queen Anne Churches, 1980; (ed with John Newman) Roger North, Of Architecture, 1981; Unbuilt Oxford, 1983; Calke Abbey, Derbyshire, 1985; The Canterbury Quadrangle, St John's College, Oxford, 1988; (with J. S. G. Simmons) All Souls: an Oxford college and its buildings, 1989; Architecture and the After-Life, 1991; (ed with Susan Foister) Anthonis van den Wyngaerde, The Panorama of London, 1996; Essays in English Architectural History, 1999; articles on mediæval and architectural history in Archaeological Journal, Architectural Review, etc. *Recreation:* gardening. *Address:* 50 Plantation Road, Oxford OX2 6JE. *T:* (01865) 557460.

COLVIN, John Horace Ragnar, CMG 1968; HM Diplomatic Service, retired; *b* Tokyo, 18 June 1922; *s* of late Adm. Sir Ragnar Colvin, KBE, CB and Lady Colvin; *m* 1st, 1948, Elizabeth Anne Manifold (marr. diss., 1963); one *s* one *d*; 2nd, 1967, Moranna Sibyl de Lerisson Cazenove; one *s* one *d*. *Educ:* RNC Dartmouth; University of London. Royal Navy, 1935–51. Joined HM Diplomatic Service, 1951; HM Embassies, Oslo, 1951–53 and Vienna, 1953–55; British High Commn, Kuala Lumpur, 1958–61; HM Consul-General, Hanoi, 1965–67; Ambassador to People's Republic of Mongolia, 1971–74; HM Embassy, Washington, 1977–80. Dir for Internat. Relations, Chase Manhattan Bank, 1980–86. Hon. Vis. Fellow, Sch. of E European Studies, 1995–. *Publications:* Twice Around the World, 1991; Not Ordinary Men, 1994; Volcano Under Snow, 1996; Lions of Judah, 1997; Nomonhan, 1999; contribs to British and US jls. *Address:* 12A Evelyn Mansions, Carlisle Place, SW1P 1NH. *Clubs:* Brooks's, Beefsteak.

COLVIN, Kathryn Frances, FIL; HM Diplomatic Service; Vice-Marshal of the Diplomatic Corps, and Head, Protocol Division, Foreign and Commonwealth Office, since 1999; *b* 11 Sept. 1945; *d* of Ernest Osborne and Frances Joy Osborne (*née* Perman); *m* 1971, Brian Colvin. *Educ:* Walthamstow Hall, Sevenoaks; Bristol Univ. (BA Hons

1967); Bordeaux Univ. (Diplome d'Etudes Supérieures 1965). FIL 1968. Joined FO (later FCO), 1968; Res. Analyst, Western and Central Europe, 1968–94: Inf. Res. Dept, 1968–77; Res. Dept, 1977–94; Mem., UK Delegn to UN Commn on Human Rights, 1980–90; Temp. Duty as 1st Sec., Political, Rome, 1988 and 1991, and Paris, 1992; Deputy Head: OSCE Dept, 1994–95; Western Eur. Dept, 1995–98; Whitehall Liaison Dept, 1998–99. Officier, Légion d'Honneur (France), 1996. *Recreations:* art, design, opera, theatre, cinema, swimming. *Address:* c/o Foreign and Commonwealth Office, King Charles Street, SW1A 2AH. *T:* (020) 7008 0989.

COLWYN, 3rd Baron, *cr* 1917; **Ian Anthony Hamilton-Smith,** CBE 1989; Bt 1912; dental surgeon, since 1966; *b* 1 Jan. 1942; *s* of 2nd Baron Colwyn and Miriam Gwendoline (*d* 1996), *d* of Victor Ferguson; *S* father 1966; *m* 1st, 1964, Sonia Jane (marr. diss. 1977), *d* of P. H. G. Morgan; one *s* one *d*; 2nd, 1977, Nicola Jeanne, *d* of Arthur Tyers, The Avenue, Sunbury-on-Thames; two *d*. *Educ:* Cheltenham Coll.; Univ. of London. BDS London 1966; LDS, RCS 1966. Dir, Dental Protection Ltd, 1990–2001 (Chm., 1996–2001). Non-exec. Dir, Project Hope UK, 1998–. President: Natural Medicines Soc., 1989–; Huntington's Disease Assoc., 1991–98; Arterial Health Foundn, 1992–; Soc. for Advancement of Anaesthesia in Dentistry, 1994–97; Mem. Council, Med. Protection Soc., 1994–. Pres., All Party Parly Gp for Alternative and Complementary Medicine, 1989–; elected Mem., H of L, 1999. Patron: Res. Council for Complementary Medicine; Blackie Foundn; Eastman Res. Fund. *Recreations:* riparian activities, music, dance band and orchestra, golf. *Heir:* *s* Hon. Craig Peter Hamilton-Smith, *b* 13 Oct. 1968. *Address:* (practice) 53 Wimpole Street, W1M 7DF. *T:* (020) 7935 6809.

COLYER, His Honour John Stuart; QC 1976; a Circuit Judge, 1991–2000; *b* 25 April 1935; *s* of late Stanley Herbert Colyer, MBE, and Louisa (*née* Randle); *m* 1961, Emily Warner, *o d* of late Stanley Leland Dutrow and Mrs Dutrow, Blue Ridge Summit, Pa, USA; two *d*. *Educ:* Dudley Grammar Sch.; Shrewsbury; Worcester Coll., Oxford (Open History Scholarship; BA 1958, MA 1961). 2nd Lieut RA, 1954–55. Called to the Bar, Middle Temple, 1959 (Bencher, 1983); Instructor, Univ. of Pennsylvania, Philadelphia, 1959–60, Asst Prof., 1960–61; practised English Bar, Midland and Oxford Circuit (formerly Oxford Circuit), 1961–91; a Recorder, 1986–91. Hon. Reader, 1985–, and Mem. Council, 1985–91, Council of Legal Educn (Lectr (Law of Landlord and Tenant), 1970–89); Vice-Pres., Lawyers' Christian Fellowship, 1993– (Chm., 1981–89); Mem., Anglo-American Real Property Inst., 1980– (Treasurer, 1984). Blundell Meml Lectr, 1977, 1982, 1986. Trustee and Gov., Royal Sch. for Deaf Children, Margate, 2000–. *Publications:* (ed jtly) Encyclopaedia of Forms and Precedents (Landlord and Tenant), vol. XI, 1965, vol. XII, 1966; A Modern View of the Law of Torts, 1966; Landlord and Tenant, in Halsbury's Laws of England, 4th edn, 1981, new edn, 1994; Gen. Ed., Megarry's The Rent Acts, 11th edn, 1988; articles in Conveyancer and other professional jls. *Recreations:* entertaining my family, opera, cultivation of cacti and of succulents (esp. Lithops), gardening generally, travel, education and welfare of the profoundly deaf. *Address:* c/o Falcon Chambers, Falcon Court, EC4Y 1AA. *T:* (020) 7353 2484, *Fax:* (020) 7353 1261, (01732) 457534.

COLYER, Peter John; Executive Secretary, Academia Europaea, since 1995; *b* 24 March 1943; *s* of Sydney Colyer and Beryl Colyer; *m* 1968, Kay Holloway; three *s*. *Educ:* Hertford Coll., Oxford (MA 1969). Research Scientist, Hydraulics Res., Wallingford, Oxon, 1966–83; Scientific Advr, Laboratorio de Hidraulica Aplicada, Buenos Aires, 1972–74; Science Policy Unit, Dept of Transport, 1983–86 and 1990; Sen. Principal, Sci. and Technol. Secretariat, Cabinet Office, 1986–90; Co-ordinator of Scientific Networks, ESF, Strasbourg, 1991–95. *Publications:* numerous scientific reports and papers. *Recreations:* sport, marquetry, travel. *Address:* Academia Europaea, 31 Old Burlington Street, W1S 3AS. *T:* (020) 7734 5402, *Fax:* (020) 7287 5115; *e-mail:* acadeuro@compuserve.com.

COLYER-FERGUSSON, Sir James Herbert Hamilton, 4th Bt *cr* 1866; *b* 10 Jan. 1917; *s* of Max Christian Hamilton Colyer-Fergusson (*d* on active service, 1940) and Edith Jane (*d* 1936), singer, *d* of late William White Miller, Portage la Prairie, Manitoba; *S* grandfather, 1951. *Educ:* Harrow; Balliol Coll., Oxford. BA 1939; MA 1945. Formerly Capt., The Buffs; served War of 1939–45 (prisoner-of-war, 1940). Entered service of former Great Western Railway Traffic Dept, 1947, later Operating Dept of the Western Region of British Rlys. Personal Asst to Chm. of British Transport Commission, 1957; Passenger Officer in SE Division of Southern Region, BR, 1961; Parly and Public Correspondent, BRB, 1967; Deputy to Curator of Historical Relics, BRB, 1968. *Heir:* none. *Address:* 61 Onslow Square, SW7 3LS. *Club:* Naval and Military.

See also Sir Lingard Goulding, Bt, Viscount Monckton of Brenchley.

COLYTON, 2nd Baron *cr* 1956, of Farway, Devon and of Taunton, Somerset; **Alisdair John Munro Hopkinson;** *b* 7 May 1958; *s* of Hon. Nicholas Henry Eno Hopkinson (*d* 1991), *o s* of 1st Baron Colyton, PC, CMG and Fiona Margaret (*d* 1996), *o d* of Sir Thomas Torquil Alphonso Munro, 5th Bt; *S* grandfather, 1996; *m* 1980, Philippa, *d* of P. J. Bell; two *s* one *d*. *Heir:* *s* Hon. James Patrick Munro Hopkinson, *b* 8 May 1983. *Address:* Lindertis, by Kirriemuir, Angus DD8 5NT.

COMBER, Ven. Anthony James; Archdeacon of Leeds, 1982–92, now Archdeacon Emeritus; *b* 20 April 1927; *s* of late Norman Mederson Comber and Nellie Comber. *Educ:* Leeds Grammar School; Leeds Univ. (MSc Mining); St Chad's Coll., Durham (DipTh); Munich Univ. Colliery underground official, 1951–53. Vicar: Oulton, 1960–69; Hunslet, 1969–77; Rector of Farnley, 1977–82. *Publication:* (contrib.) Today's Church and Today's World, 1977. *Recreations:* politics; walking in Bavaria. *Address:* 10 Tavistock Park, Oldfield Lane, Leeds LS12 4DD.

COMBERMERE, 6th Viscount *cr* 1827; **Thomas Robert Wellington Stapleton-Cotton;** Bt 1677; Baron 1814; *b* 30 Aug. 1969; *o s* of 5th Viscount Combermere; *S* father, 2000. *Heir:* *uncle* Hon. David Peter Dudley Stapleton-Cotton [*b* 6 March 1932; *m* 1955, Susan Nomakepu, *d* of Sir George Werner Albu, 2nd Bt; two *s* two *d*].

COMFORT, Anthony Francis; HM Diplomatic Service, retired; *b* Plymouth, 12 Oct. 1920; *s* of Francis Harold Comfort and Elsie Grace (*née* Martin); *m* 1948, Joy Margaret Midson; two *s* one *d*. *Educ:* Bristol Grammar Sch.; Oriel Coll., Oxford. Entered Foreign Service, 1947; 2nd Sec. (Commercial), Athens, 1948–51; Consul, Alexandria, 1951–53; 1st Sec. (Commercial), Amman, 1953–54; Foreign Office, 1954–57; seconded to Colonial Office, 1957–59; 1st Sec. (Commercial), Belgrade, 1959–60; 1st Sec. and Consul, Reykjavik, 1961–65; Inspector of Diplomatic Establishments, 1965–68, retired 1969. *Recreations:* walking, gardening, looking at churches. *Address:* Nymet Cottage, Trowbridge Road, Bradford on Avon, Wilts BA15 1EE. *T:* (01225) 866046.

COMINS, David; Rector, Glasgow Academy, since 1994; *b* 1 March 1948; *s* of Jack Comins and Marjorie Mabel (*née* Rowbotham); *m* 1972, Christine Anne Speak; one *s* two *d*. *Educ:* Scarborough Boys' High Sch.; Downing Coll., Cambridge (BA, MA, PGCE). Assistant Mathematics Teacher: Mill Hill Sch., 1971–75; Strathallan Sch., Perthshire, 1975–76; Glenalmond College, Perthshire: Asst Maths Teacher, 1976–80; Head of Maths, 1980–85; Dir of Studies, 1985–89; Dep. Head, Queen's Coll., Taunton, 1989–94. Churchill Fellow, 1981. *Recreations:* mountaineering, ballet, music, crosswords. *Address:* 11 Kirklee Terrace, Glasgow G12 0TH. *T:* (0141) 357 1776. *Clubs:* East India, Alpine.

COMNINOS, Sophie Henrietta; *see* Turner Laing, S. H.

COMPSTON, Alastair; *see* Compston, D. A. S.

COMPSTON, Christopher Dean, MA; **His Honour Judge Compston;** a Circuit Judge, since 1986; *b* 5 May 1940; *s* of Vice Adm. Sir Peter Maxwell Compston, KCB and Valerie Bocquet; *m* 1st, 1968, Bronwen Henniker Gotley (marr. diss. 1982); one *d* (and two *s* decd); 2nd, 1983, Caroline Philippa, *d* of Paul Odgers, *qv*; two *s* one *d*. *Educ:* Epsom Coll. (Prae Sum.); Magdalen Coll., Oxford (MA). Called to the Bar, Middle Temple, 1965; a Recorder, 1982–86. Mem. Senate, Inns of Court, 1983–86. *Publications:* Recovery from Divorce: a practical guide, 1993; (contrib.) Relational Justice, 1994; Cracking up without Breaking up, 1998. *Recreations:* the arts, writing, family. *Address:* c/o Royal Courts of Justice, Strand, WC2A 2LL.

COMPSTON, Prof. (David) Alastair (Standish), FRCP, FMedSci; Professor of Neurology, University of Cambridge, since 1989; Fellow of Jesus College, Cambridge, since 1990; *b* 23 Jan. 1948; *s* of late Nigel Dean Compston and of Diana Mary Compston (*née* Standish); *m* 1973, Juliet Elizabeth, *d* of Sir Denys Lionel Page, FBA; one *d*. *Educ:* Rugby Sch.; Middlesex Hospital Med. Sch., London Univ. (MB BS (Hons); PhD). FRCP 1986. Jun. Hosp. appts, Nat. Hosp. for Nervous Diseases, 1972–82; Cons. Neurologist, University Hosp. of Wales, 1982–87; Prof. of Neurology, Univ. of Wales Coll. of Medicine, 1987–88. Founder FMedSci 1998. FRSA 1997. *Publications:* (ed) McAlpine's Multiple Sclerosis, 3rd edn 1998; contribs to human and experimental demyelinating diseases, in learned jls. *Recreation:* being outside. *Address:* Pembroke House, Mill Lane, Linton, Cambridge CB1 6JY. *T:* (01223) 893414. *Club:* Garrick.

COMPSTON, Prof. William, PhD; FRS 1987; FAA; FTSE; Australian National University: Professor in Isotope Geochemistry, 1987–96, now Emeritus; Visiting Fellow and Consultant, Research School of Earth Sciences, 1997–99 and since 2002; *b* 19 Feb. 1931; *s* of late J. A. Compston; *m* 1952, Elizabeth Blair; three *s* one *d*. *Educ:* Christian Brothers' Coll., Fremantle; Univ. of WA (BSc (Hons); PhD). Res. Fellow, CIT, 1956–58; Res. Fellow, Dept of Terrestrial Magnetism, Carnegie Inst. of Washington, 1958; Lectr, Univ. of WA, 1959–60; Australian National University: Fellow, then Sen. Fellow, 1961–74; Professorial Fellow, 1974–87; Univ. Fellow, 2000–2001. *Address:* Research School of Earth Sciences, Australian National University, Canberra, ACT 0200, Australia; 8 Wells Gardens, Manuka, ACT 2603, Australia.

COMPTON, family name of **Marquess of Northampton**.

COMPTON, Earl; Daniel Bingham Compton; *b* 16 Jan. 1973; *s* and *heir* of Marquess of Northampton, *qv*; *m* 2001, Lucy, 5th *d* of Lt-Col Benedict Cardozo. *Address:* Castle Ashby, Northants NN7 1LF.

COMPTON, Rt Hon. Sir John (George Melvin), KCMG 1997; PC 1983; Senior Minister, St Lucia, 1996–97; *b* 29 April 1926; *m*; five *c*. *Educ:* London School of Economics. Called to the Bar, Gray's Inn; practice in St Lucia, 1951. Indep. Mem., Legislative Council, 1954, joined Labour Party, 1954; Dep. Leader, 1957–61; resigned, and formed Nat. Labour Movement, 1961 (later United Workers' Party; Leader, 1964); Chief Minister of St Lucia, 1964–67, Premier, 1967–79, Prime Minister, Feb.-July 1979 and 1982–96; Minister for Finance, Planning and Develt, 1982–96. *Address:* PO Box 149, Castries, St Lucia.

COMPTON, Michael Graeme, CBE 1987; Keeper of Museum Services, Tate Gallery, 1970–87, retired; *b* 29 Sept. 1927; *s* of Joseph Nield Compton, OBE, and Dorothy Margaret Townsend Compton; *m* 1952, Susan Paschal Benn; two *d*. *Educ:* Courtauld Institute, London (BA Hons History of Art). Asst to Director, Leeds City Art Gallery and Templenewsam, 1954–57; Keeper of Foreign Schools, Walker Art Gallery, Liverpool, 1957–59; Dir, Ferens Art Gall., Hull, 1960–65; Asst Keeper, Modern Collection, Tate Gall., 1965–70. Frederick R. Weisman Art Foundn Award, 1991. *Publications:* Optical and Kinetic Art, 1967; Pop Art, 1970; (jtly) Catalogue of Foreign Schools, Walker Art Gallery, 1963; Marcel Broodthaers, 1989; articles in art jls, exhibn catalogues.

COMPTON, Robert Edward John; DL; Chairman: Time-Life International Ltd, 1979–90 (Chief Executive Officer, 1985–88); Time SARL, 1985–90; *b* 11 July 1922; *yr s* of late Major Edward Robert Francis Compton, JP, DL, and Sylvia Farquharson of Invercauld; *m* 1951, Ursula Jane Kenyon-Slaney; two *s*. *Educ:* Eton; Magdalen Coll., Oxford, 1940–41. Served War, Coldstream Guards, 1941–46 (wounded); Mil. Asst to British Ambassador, Vienna (temp. Major), 1946. Studied fruit growing and horticulture (Diploma), 1946–48; with W. S. Crawford Ltd, Advertising Agency, 1951–54; Sen. Acct Exec., Crawfords Internat., 1954; joined Time International, 1954; advertising sales, 1954–58, UK Advtsg Dir, 1958–62; also Dir, Time-Life Internat. Ltd, 1958–79. Chm., CXL UK Ltd, 1971–73; Pres., Highline Finances Services, SA, and Dir, Highline Leasing Ltd, 1985–94; Bd Dir, Extel Corp., Chicago, 1973–80; Dir, Transtel Communications Ltd, Slough, 1974–83. Vice-Chm., Yorks, Nat. Trust, 1970–85. President: Nat. Council for the Conservation of Plants and Gardens, 1994– (Chm., 1988–94); N of England Horticultural Soc., 1984–86; Northern Horticultural Soc., 1986–96; Yorks Agricl Soc., 1995–96; Life Vice Pres., RHS, 1996. High Sheriff, 1978–79, DL 1981, N Yorks. VMH 1994. *Recreations:* gardening, shooting, golf, music. *Address:* The Manor House, Marton Le Moor, Ripon, N Yorks HG4 5AT. *T:* (01423) 323315; Newby Hall Estate Office, Ripon, Yorkshire HG4 5AE. *T:* (01423) 322583. *Clubs:* White's; Swinley Forest (Ascot).

See also Captain A. A. C. Farquharson of Invercauld.

COMRIE, Rear-Adm. (Alexander) Peter, CB 1982; defence equipment consultant; Director, A. Comrie & Sons Ltd, since 1983; *b* 27 March 1924; *s* of Robert Duncan Comrie and Phyllis Dorothy Comrie; *m* 1945, Madeleine Irene (*née* Bullock) (*d* 1983); one *s* one *d*. *Educ:* Sutton Valence Sch., Kent; County Technical Coll., Wednesbury, Staffs, and in the Royal Navy. Joined Royal Navy, 1945; served in cruisers, frigates, minesweepers and RN air stations; RCDS 1973; Captain HMS Daedalus, 1974; Director of Weapons Coordination and Acceptance (Naval), 1975; Deputy Controller Aircraft, MoD, 1978–81; Dir-Gen. Aircraft (Navy), 1981–83, retired. Vice Pres., IEE, 1988–91 (Mem. Council, 1981–84); Member: IEE Electronics Divisional Bd, 1976–77; IEE Qualifications Bd, 1981–88; Chairman: IEE International (formerly Overseas) Bd, 1988–91; Executive Gp Cttee 3, Engrg Council, 1986–94. FIEE 1975; FRAeS 1978; Eur Ing 1987. *Recreations:* sailing, swimming, DIY. *Clubs:* Royal Commonwealth Society; Hayling Island Sailing.

COMYNS, Jacqueline Roberta; a District Judge (Magistrates' Courts) (formerly a Metropolitan Stipendiary Magistrate), since 1982; a Recorder, since 1991; *b* 27 April 1943; *d* of late Jack and Belle Fisher; *m* 1963, Malcolm John Comyns, medical practitioner; one *s*. *Educ:* Hendon County Grammar Sch.; London Sch. of Econs and Pol. Science (LLB Hons 1964). Called to the Bar, Inner Temple, 1969. Practised on South Eastern Circuit.

Recreations: theatre, travel, swimming, tennis. *Address:* Thames Magistrates' Court, 58 Bow Road, E3 4DJ. *T:* (020) 8980 1000.

CONANT, Sir John (Ernest Michael), 2nd Bt *cr* 1954; farmer and landowner, since 1949; *b* 24 April 1923; *s* of Sir Roger Conant, 1st Bt, CVO, and Daphne, Lady Conant, *d* of A. E. Learoyd; *S* father, 1973; *m* 1st, 1950, Periwinkle Elizabeth (*d* 1985), *d* of late Dudley Thorp, Kimbolton, Hunts; two *s* two *d* (and one *s* decd); 2nd, 1992, Mrs Clare Attwater, *yr d* of W. E. Madden. *Educ:* Eton; Corpus Christi Coll., Cambridge (BA Agric). Served in Grenadier Guards, 1942–45; at CCC Cambridge, 1946–49. Farming in Rutland, 1950–; High Sheriff of Rutland, 1960. *Recreations:* fishing, shooting, tennis. *Heir: s* Simon Edward Christopher Conant, *b* 13 Oct. 1958. *Address:* Periwinkle Cottage, Lyndon, Oakham, Rutland LE15 8TU. *T:* (01572) 737275.

CONCANNON, Dr Harcourt Martin Grant; President, Pensions Appeal Tribunals for England and Wales, since 1998; *s* of Edwin Martin Joseph Concannon and Caroline Elizabeth Margaret Concannon (*née* Grant); *m* 1978, Elaine Baldwin; one *s* one *d*. *Educ:* University Coll. Sch.; University College London (LLB, LLM, PhD). Solicitor. Articled to Town Clerk, London Borough of Bexley, 1960–64; Lectr in Law, Nottingham Poly., 1964–68; Senior Lecturer: Sheffield City Poly., 1968–71; Univ. of Salford, 1972–93; Full-time Chm., Independent Tribunal Service, 1993–98. *Recreations:* languages, garden design, walking. *Address:* Pensions Appeal Tribunals, 48–49 Chancery Lane, WC2A 1JR.

CONCANNON, Rt Hon. John Dennis, (Don); PC 1978; *b* 16 May 1930; *m* 1953, Iris May Wilson; two *s* two *d*. *Educ:* Rossington Sec. Sch. Coldstream Guards, 1947–53; Mem. Nat. Union of Mineworkers, 1953–66; Branch Official, 1960–65. Mem., Mansfield Town Council, 1962–66. MP (Lab) Mansfield, 1966–87. Asst Govt Whip, 1968–70; Opposition Whip, 1970–74; Vice-Chamberlain, HM Household, 1974; Parly Under-Sec. of State, NI Office, 1974–76; Minister of State, NI Office, 1976–79; Opposition Spokesman for Defence, 1979–80, for NI, 1980–83. Mem., Commonwealth War Graves Commn, 1986–94. *Recreations:* cricket, basket-ball. *Address:* 69 Skegby Lane, Mansfield, Notts NG19 6QS. *T:* (01623) 627235.

CONDON, family name of **Baron Condon**.

CONDON, Baron *cr* 2001 (Life Peer), of Langton Green in the County of Kent; **Paul Leslie Condon,** Kt 1994; QPM 1989; DL; Commissioner, Metropolitan Police, 1993–2000; Director, Anti-Corruption Unit, International Cricket Council, since 2000; *m*; two *s* one *d*. *Educ:* St Peter's Coll., Oxford (Bramshill Scholar; MA; Hon. Fellow). Joined Metropolitan Police, 1967; Inspector, 1975–78; Chief Inspector, 1978–81; Superintendent, Bethnal Green, 1981–82; Staff Officer to Comr as Superintendent, then as Chief Superintendent, 1982–84; Asst Chief Constable, Kent Constabulary, 1984–87; Dep. Asst Comr, 1987–88, Asst Comr, 1988–89, Metropolitan Police; Chief Constable, Kent Constabulary, 1989–92. CIMgt 1991; FRSA 1992. DL Kent, 2001. *Address:* c/o ICC, The Clock Tower, Lord's Cricket Ground, NW8 8QN.

CONGDON, David Leonard; Director of Public Affairs, MENCAP, since 1998; *b* 16 Oct. 1949; *s* of Archibald George Congdon and late Marjorie Congdon; *m* 1972, Teresa Winifred Hill; one *d*. *Educ:* Alleyn's Sch.; Thames Polytechnic (BSc Hons Econ.). Graduate Systems Analyst, ICL, 1970; Philips Electronics: Systems Analyst, 1973–85; Computer Consultant, 1985–92. London Borough of Croydon: Councillor, 1976–92; Vice-Chm., Educn Cttee, 1979–83; Chm., Social Services, 1983–86, 1990–91; Dep. Leader, 1986–92; Chm., Finance Sub-Cttee. Vice-Chm., local Cons. Assocs, 1979–82. MP (C) Croydon North East, 1992–97; contested (C) Croydon Central, 1997, 2001. PPS to Minister of State for Social Security, 1995–97. Mem., Select Cttee on Health, 1992–95. Governor, Croydon Coll., 1979–92. *Recreations:* tennis, badminton, reading political biographies, listening to music; lapsed Fulham fan. *Address:* MENCAP, 123 Golden Lane, EC1Y 0RT.

CONGDON, Timothy George, CBE 1997; Managing Director, Lombard Street Research Ltd, since 1989; *b* 28 April 1951; *s* of D. G. Congdon and Olive Emma Congdon (*née* Good); *m* 1988, Dorianne Preston-Lowe; one *d*. *Educ:* Univ. of Oxford (BA 1st cl. Hons Mod. Hist. and Econs). MSI. On economics staff, The Times, 1973–76; Chief Economist, L. Messel & Co., 1976–86 (Partner, 1980–86); Chief London Economist, Shearson Lehman, 1986–88. Non-exec. Chm., SBW Insurance Research, 1994–97. Mem., Treasury Panel of Independent Forecasters, 1993–97. Hon. Prof., Cardiff Business Sch., 1990–; Vis. Prof., City Univ. Business Sch., 1998–. Hon. Sec., Political Economy Club, 1999–. FRSA 1991; Fellow, Soc. of Business Economists, 2000. *Publications:* Monetary Control in Britain, 1982; The Debt Threat, 1988; Reflections on Monetarism, 1992. *Recreations:* reading, walking, chess, opera. *Address:* Lombard Street Research Ltd, 30 Watling Street, EC4M 9BR. *Club:* Royal Automobile.

CONGLETON, 8th Baron *cr* 1841; **Christopher Patrick Parnell;** Bt 1766; *b* 11 March 1930; 3rd *s* of 6th Baron Congleton (*d* 1932) and Hon. Edith Mary Palmer Howard (MBE 1941) (she *m* 2nd, 1946, Flight Lieut A. E. R. Aldridge, who died 1950), *d* of late R. J. B. Howard and late Lady Strathcona and Mount Royal; *S* brother, 1967; *m* 1955, Anna Hedvig, *d* of G. A. Sommerfelt, Oslo, Norway; two *s* three *d*. *Educ:* Eton; New Coll., Oxford (MA). Mem., Salisbury and Wilton RDC, 1964–74; Vice-President: RDCA, 1973–74; Assoc. of District Councils, 1974–79. Chm., Salisbury and S Wilts Museum, 1972–77; Mem., Adv. Bd for Redundant Churches, 1981–87. President: Nat. Ski Fedn of GB, 1976–81; Ski Club of GB, 1991–97; Mem., Eligibility Cttee, Internat. Ski Fedn, 1976–88. Trustee: Sandroyd Sch. Trust, 1975–92 (Chm., 1980–84); Wessex Med. Trust, 1984–90 (Chm., 1996–2000); Southampton Univ. Develt Trust, 1986–95. Hon. LLD Southampton, 1990. *Recreations:* music, ski-ing, fishing. *Heir: s* Hon. John Patrick Christian Parnell [*b* 17 March 1959; *m* 1985, Marjorie-Anne, *o d* of John Hobdell, Cobham, Surrey; two *s* one *d*]. *Address:* West End Lodge, Ebbesbourne Wake, Salisbury, Wilts SP5 5JR.

CONGO, Sonia, (Mrs C. W. Congo); *see* Lawson, S.

CONGREVE, Ambrose, CBE 1965; *b* London, 4 April 1907; *s* of Major John Congreve, DL, JP, and Helena Blanche Irene Ponsonby, *d* of 8th Earl of Bessborough; *m* 1935, Marjorie (*d* 1995), *d* of Dr Arthur Graham Glasgow, London, and Richmond, Virginia, and Margaret, *d* of John P. Branch, President of Virginia's Merchants National Bank. *Educ:* Eton; Trinity Coll., Cambridge. Employed by Unilever Ltd, in England and China, 1927–36; joined Humphreys & Glasgow Ltd, as Director, 1936; responsible for the company, 1939–83, in succession to Dr Glasgow who founded the firm in 1892. Served War of 1939–45: Air Intelligence for Plans and Bomber Command, then Min. of Supply. Vice-Pres., RHS. Patron, Tree Council of Southern Ireland. Hon. Fellow IChemE 1967. Veitch Meml Medal, RHS, 1987. *Recreation:* collection and large-scale outdoor cultivation in Ireland of plant species and hybrids from all over the world. *Address:* Mount Congreve, Waterford, Ireland. *T:* (51) 384103, *Fax:* (51) 384576; Warwick House, Stable Yard, St James's, SW1A 1BD. *T:* (020) 7839 3301. *Club:* Beefsteak.

CONINGSBY, Thomas Arthur Charles, QC 1986; **His Honour Judge Coningsby;** a Circuit Judge, since 1992; Designated Civil Judge, since 1999; Chancellor of the Diocese of York, since 1977, of the Diocese of Peterborough, since 1989; Vicar General of the Province of York, since 1980; *b* 21 April 1933; *s* of Francis Charles and Eilleen Rowena Coningsby; *m* 1959, Elaine Mary Coningsby; two *s* three *d*. *Educ:* Epsom; Queens' Coll., Cambridge (MA). Called to the Bar, Gray's Inn, 1957; Mem., Inner Temple, 1988. A Recorder, 1986–92; Head of Chambers, 3 Dr Johnson's Building, Temple, 1988–92; Dep. High Court Judge, 1992–; Liaison Judge, 1995–. Member: Lord Chancellor's Matrimonial Causes Rule Cttee, 1986–89; Gen. Council of the Bar, 1988–90; Supreme Court Procedure Cttee, 1988–92; Chm., Family Law Bar Assoc., 1988–90 (Sec., 1986–88); Pres., SE London Magistrates Assoc., 1996–. Member, General Synod, 1970– (Member: Legal Adv. Commn, 1975–; Fees Adv. Commn, 1979–92). Mem. Governing Body, SPCK, 1990–92. *Recreation:* lawn tennis. *Address:* Leyfields, Chipstead, Surrey CR5 3SG. *T:* (01737) 553304. *Club:* Athenæum.

CONLAN, Bernard; engineer; *b* 24 Oct. 1923; *m*; one *d*. *Educ:* Manchester Primary and Secondary Schs. Mem., AEU (now AEEU), 1940–, Officer, 1943–87. City Councillor, Manchester, 1954–66. Joined Labour Party, 1942; contested (Lab) High Peak, 1959. MP (Lab) Gateshead East, 1964–87. A Vice-Chm., Parly Lab. Party Trade Union Gp, 1974–. Member: House of Commons Expenditure Cttee (since inception), 1971–79; Trade and Industry Select Cttee, 1983–86; Select Cttee on Defence, 1979–83. *Address:* 33 Beccles Road, Sale, Cheshire M33 3RP. *T:* (0161) 973 3991.

CONN, Edward, CBE 1979; FRCVS; Technical Consultant, Norbrook Laboratories Ltd, Newry, Northern Ireland, 1983–90, retired; *b* 25 March 1918; *s* of late Edward and Elizabeth Conn; *m* 1st, 1943, Kathleen Victoria Sandford (*d* 1974); three *d*; 2nd, 1975, Lilian Frances Miley. *Educ:* Coleraine Academical Instn; Royal (Dick) Veterinary Sch., Edinburgh Univ. Qual. Vet. Surgeon, 1940; Diploma; MRCVS 1940; FRCVS 1984. Gen. practice, Coleraine, 1940–43; Chief Vet. Officer, Hampshire Cattle Breeders, 1943–47; Dept of Agriculture, NI, 1947–83, Chief Vet. Officer, 1958–83. Pres., Coleraine Old Boys Assoc., 1979–80 (Pres., Belfast Br., 1991–92). Governor, Coleraine Academical Instn, 1972–. *Recreations:* golf, walking; watching all sports, particularly Rugby and athletics. *Address:* Ardeena, 23 The Brae, Groomsport, Co. Down BT19 2JQ. *Clubs:* Clandeboye Golf; Bangor Rugby and Athletic (Pres., 1974–75).

CONNARTY, Michael; MP (Lab) Falkirk East, since 1992; *b* 3 Sept. 1947; *m* 1969, Margaret Doran; one *s* one *d*. *Educ:* St Patrick's High Sch., Coatbridge; Stirling and Glasgow Univs (Student Pres., Stirling Univ., 1970–71); Jordanhill Coll. of Educn (BA; DCE). Teacher of children with special needs, 1976–92. Exec. Mem., Central region, EIS, 1978–84 (Pres., 1982–83). Rector, Stirling Univ., 1983–84. Mem. (Lab) Stirling DC, 1977–90 (Leader of Council, 1980–90); Chm., Lab. Party Scottish Local Govt Cttee, 1988–90. Mem., Lab. Party Scottish Exec., 1981, 1983–92. Contested (Lab) Stirling, 1983, 1987. PPS to Minister of State for Film and Tourism, 1997–98. Secretary: All-Party Parly Gp on Chemical Industries, 2000– (Treas., 1994–97; Chm., 1997–2000); PLP Sci. and Technol. Cttee, 1992–97; Vice Chm., Scottish PLP Gp, 1996–98 (Chm., 1998–99); Co-ordinator, PLP Scottish Task Force, Skills and Trng, Youths and Students, 1994–97. Member: Information Select Cttee, 1997–; European Scrutiny Select Cttee, 1998–; Bd, POST, 1997–. JP 1977–90. *Address:* House of Commons, SW1A 0AA; Ashgrove, California Road, Maddiston, E Stirlingshire, FK2 0NH.

CONNELL, Charles Percy; Puisne Judge, Kenya Colony, 1951–64, retired; *b* 1 Oct. 1902; *s* of late C. R. Connell, Barrister-at-Law and late K. Adlard; *m* 1946, Mary O'Rourke. *Educ:* Charterhouse; New Coll., Oxford (Hons, Jurisprudence). Called to Bar, Lincoln's Inn, 1927. Joined Kenya Judicial Service, 1938 (Resident Magistrate). Served War of 1939–45 (8th Army Clasp and war medals); commissioned King's African Rifles, 1941; British Military Administration (Legal and Judicial), Eritrea and Tripolitania, 1942–46. Acting Puisne Judge, Kenya, 1950, retired 1964. *Recreations:* tennis, cricket and trout fishing. *Address:* c/o Isle of Man Bank, Bowring Road, Ramsey, Isle of Man.

CONNELL, His Eminence Cardinal Desmond; *see* Dublin, Archbishop of, and Primate of Ireland, (RC).

CONNELL, George Edward, OC 1987; PhD; FCIC; FRSC; President, University of Toronto, 1984–90; *b* 20 June 1930; *m* 1955, Sheila Horan; two *s* two *d*. *Educ:* Univ. of Toronto (BA, PhD Biochemistry). FCIC 1971; FRSC 1975. Post-doctoral Fellow, Div. of Applied Biol., National Res. Council, Ottawa, Ont, 1955–56; Fellow, National Science Foundn (US), Dept of Biochem., New York University Coll. of Medicine, 1956–57; University of Toronto: Asst Prof. of Biochem., 1957–62; Associate Prof. of Biochem., 1962–65; Prof. and Chm. Dept of Biochem., 1965–70; Associate Dean, Faculty of Med., 1972–74; Vice-Pres., Res. and Planning, 1974–77; Pres. and Vice-Chancellor, Univ. of Western Ontario, 1977–84. Prin. Advr, Commn of Enquiry on Blood System of Canada, 1993–95; Sen. Policy Advr, Canada Foundn for Innovation, 1997; Mem., Res. Adv. Panel, Walkerton Inquiry, 2000–01. Chairman: Exec. Cttee, Internat. Congress of Biochem., 1979; Nat. Round Table on the Envmt and the Economy, 1991–95; Technical Cttee 207 (Envmtl Management), ISO, 1993–96; Task Force on Funding and Delivery of Med. Care in Ontario, 1995–96; Canadian Prostate Cancer Res. Initiative, 2000–; Vice-Chairman: Envmtl Assessment Bd, Ontario, 1990–93; Sustainable Cities Foundn, 1993–98; Protein Engrg Nat. Centre of Excellence, 1995–97; Member: MRC of Canada, 1966–70; Ont Council of Health, 1978–84; Bd of Dirs and Nat. Exec. Cttee, Canadian Arthritis and Rheumatism Soc., 1965–75; Bd of Dirs, Nat. Inst. of Nutrition, 1984–91; Bd of Res. Inst., Toronto Hosp., 1994–96; Council, Ont Univs, 1977–90 (Chm., 1981–83); Bd of Governors, Upper Canada Coll., 1982–90; Bd of Trustees, Royal Ont Mus., 1984–90; Trustee, R. Samuel McLaughlin Foundn, 1996–. Mem., Ontario Press Council, 1996–. Member, Board of Directors: Southam Inc., 1985–93; Allelix Biopharmaceuticals Inc., 1995–99. Hon. LLD: Trent, 1984; Univ. of Western Ont, 1985; McGill, 1987; Hon. DSc Toronto, 1993. *Publications:* scientific papers in jls incl. Canadian Jl of Biochem., Biochemical Jl (UK), and Jl of Immunol. *Recreations:* ski-ing, tennis, wilderness canoe trips. *Address:* 240 Walmer Road, Toronto, ON M5R 3R7, Canada; *e-mail:* george.connell@synpatico.ca. *Clubs:* Queen's, Badminton and Racquet (Toronto).

CONNELL, Prof. John Jeffrey, CBE 1985; PhD; FRSE; FIFST; Director, Torry Research Station, Aberdeen (Ministry of Agriculture, Fisheries and Food), 1979–87 (Assistant Director, 1969–79); Emeritus Professor, Aberdeen University, 1987; *b* 2 July 1927; *s* of John Edward Connell and Margaret Connell; *m* 1950, Margaret Parsons; one *s* two *d* (and one *d* decd). *Educ:* Burnage High Sch.; Univ. of Manchester (BSc 1947); Univ. of Edinburgh (PhD 1950). FIFST 1970; FRSE 1984. Torry Research Station: Scientific Officer, 1950; Sen. Sci. Officer, 1955; Principal Sci. Officer, 1961; Dep. Chief Sci. Officer, 1979; Officer i/c Humber Lab., Hull (Sen. Principal Sci. Officer), 1968–69. Res. Associate, 1969–79 and Hon. Res. Lectr, 1979–83, Aberdeen Univ. Mem., Fisheries Res. and Develt Bd, 1979–84. *Publications:* Control of Fish Quality, 1975, 4th edn 1995 (Spanish edn 1978); Trends in Fish Utilisation, 1982; scientific and technical papers related to use of fish as food. *Recreations:* music, hill walking. *Address:* 61 Burnieboozle Crescent, Aberdeen AB15 8NR. *T:* (01224) 315852.

CONNELL, John MacFarlane; Chairman, The Distillers Company plc, 1983–86; *b* 29 Dec. 1924; *s* of late John Maclean Connell and late Mollie Isobel MacFarlane; *m* 1949, Jean Matheson Sutherland Mackay, *d* of late Major George Sutherland Mackay and late Christine Bourne; two *s*. *Educ:* Stowe; Christ Church, Oxford. Joined Tanqueray, Gordon & Co. Ltd, 1946, Export Dir 1954, Man. Dir 1962–70; Dir, Distillers Co. Ltd, 1965, Mem., Management Cttee, 1971–86; Chm., United Glass Holdings plc, 1979–83. Chm., Gin Rectifiers and Distillers Assoc., 1968–71. Pres., Royal Warrant Holders Assoc., 1975. *Recreations:* golf, shooting, fishing. *Club:* Royal and Ancient (St Andrews).

CONNELL, Margaret Mary, MA; Principal, Queen's College, London, since 1999; *b* 3 Jan. 1949; *d* of Leo Connell and Margaret Isobel Connell. *Educ:* Lady Margaret Hall, Oxford (MA). Physics teacher, Headington Sch., Oxford, 1970–76; maths teacher, North London Collegiate Sch., 1976–86; Dep. Headmistress, Bromley High Sch. (GPDST), 1986–91; Headmistress, More House Sch., 1991–99. *Recreations:* music, travel, reading. *Address:* Flat E, 4 Kingswood Road, Bromley, Kent BR2 0HQ. *T:* (020) 8460 1577. *Club:* University Women's.

CONNELL, Hon. Sir Michael (Bryan), Kt 1991; **Hon. Mr Justice Connell;** a Judge of the High Court of Justice, Family Division, since 1991; *b* 6 Aug. 1939; *s* of late Lorraine Connell and Joan Connell; *m* 1965, Anne Joan Pulham; three *s* one *d*. *Educ:* Harrow; Brasenose Coll., Oxford (MA Jurisprudence). Called to the Bar, Inner Temple, 1962, Bencher, 1988; QC 1981; a Recorder, 1980–91. Governor, Harrow Sch., 1983– (Chm., 1997–). Mem., Jockey Club, 1988–. *Recreations:* steeplechasing, cricket, foxhunting. *Address:* Royal Courts of Justice, Strand, WC2A 2LL. *Club:* Buck's.

See also S. A. O'Sullivan.

CONNELL-SMITH, Prof. Gordon Edward, PhD; FRHistS; Professor of Contemporary History, University of Hull, 1973–85; *b* 23 Nov. 1917; 2nd *s* of George Frederick Smith and Margaret Smith (*née* Woolerton); surname changed to Connell-Smith by deed-poll, 1942; *m* 1954, Wendy Ann (*d* 1987), *o d* of John Bertram and Kathleen Tomlinson; one *s* one *d*. *Educ:* Richmond County Sch., Surrey; University Coll. of SW of England, Exeter (BA); Birkbeck Coll., London (PhD). FRHistS 1959. Served War, RA and Staff, 1940–46 (Staff Major). Julian Corbett Prize, Inst. of Historical Res., 1949; University of Hull: Staff Tutor/Lectr in Adult Educn and History Depts, 1952–63; Sen. Lectr, 1963–69; Reader in Contemp. Internat. History, 1969–73. Mem., Cttee of Management, Univ. of London Inst. of Latin Amer. Studies, 1973–85. Chm., Latin American Newsletters, Ltd, London, 1969–72. *Publications:* Forerunners of Drake, 1954; Pattern of the Post-War World, 1957; The Inter-American System, 1966 (Spanish edn 1971); (co-author) The Relevance of History, 1972; The United States and Latin America, 1974 (Spanish edn 1977); The Future of History, 1975; Latin American Relations with the World 1826–1976, 1976; contrib. to Bull. Inst. of Historical Res., Contemp. Rev., Econ. History Rev., Eng. Historical Rev., History, Internat. Affairs, Jl of Latin Amer. Studies, World Today, etc. *Recreations:* travel, sport. *Address:* 7 Braids Walk, Kirk Ella, Hull HU10 7PA. *T:* (01482) 652624.

CONNELLY, Brian Norman; HM Diplomatic Service, retired; High Commissioner, Kingdom of Tonga, and Consul for Pacific Islands under American sovereignty South of the Equator, 1999–2001; *b* 25 Dec. 1941; *s* of late Bernard and Julia Murphy; *m* 1965, Theresa, (Terrie), Hughes; one *s* one *d*. *Educ:* Holycross Acad., Edinburgh. Joined FO, 1967; Budapest, 1969–71; Montevideo, 1971–74; FCO, 1974–76; Kuwait, 1976–80; Seoul, 1980–84; First Sec., FCO, 1984–86; First Sec. (Commercial), Dhaka, 1987–90; Adminr, Ascension Island, 1991–95; High Comr, Solomon Is, 1996–98. *Recreations:* golf, tennis, snorkelling. *Address:* Foreign and Commonwealth Office, King Charles Street, SW1A 2AH. *Club:* Nuku'alofa.

CONNER, Rt Rev. David John; Dean of Windsor, since 1998; Register, Order of the Garter, since 1998; Domestic Chaplain to the Queen, since 1998; Bishop to the Forces, since 2001; *b* 6 April 1947; *s* of late William Ernest Conner and Joan Millington Conner; *m* 1969, Jayne Maria Evans; two *s*. *Educ:* Erith Grammar School; Exeter College, Oxford (Symes Exhibnr; MA); St Stephen's House, Oxford. Asst Chaplain, St Edward's School, Oxford, 1971–73, Chaplain, 1973–80; Team Vicar, Wolvercote with Summertown, Oxford, 1976–80; Senior Chaplain, Winchester College, 1980–86; Vicar, St Mary the Great with St Michael, Cambridge, 1987–94; RD of Cambridge, 1989–94; Bishop Suffragan of Lynn, 1994–98. Hon. Fellow, Girton Coll., Cambridge, 1995. *Address:* The Deanery, Windsor Castle, Berks SL4 1NJ. *T:* (01753) 865561, *Fax:* (01753) 819002.

CONNERY, Sir Sean, Kt 2000; actor; *b* 25 Aug. 1930; *s* of Joseph and Euphamia Connery; named Thomas; adopted stage name of Sean, 1953; *m* 1st, 1962, Diane Cilento (marr. diss. 1974); one *s*; 2nd, 1975, Micheline Roquebrune; two step *s* one step *d*. Served Royal Navy. Has appeared in films: No Road Back, 1956; Action of the Tiger, 1957; Another Time, Another Place, 1957; Hell Drivers, 1958; Tarzan's Greatest Adventure, 1959; Darby O'Gill and the Little People, 1959; On the Fiddle, 1961; The Longest Day, 1962; The Frightened City, 1962; Woman of Straw, 1964; The Hill, 1965; A Fine Madness, 1966; Shalako, 1968; The Molly Maguires, 1968; The Red Tent (1st Russian co-production), 1969; The Anderson Tapes, 1970; The Offence, 1973; Zardoz, 1973; Ransom, 1974; Murder on the Orient Express, 1974; The Wind and the Lion, 1975; The Man Who Would Be King, 1975; Robin and Marian, 1976; The First Great Train Robbery, 1978; Cuba, 1978; Meteor, 1979; Outland, 1981; The Man with the Deadly Lens, 1982; Wrong is Right, 1982; Five Days One Summer, 1982; Highlander, 1986; The Name of the Rose, 1987 (BAFTA Award for Best Actor, 1988); The Untouchables, 1987 (Best Supporting Actor, Academy Awards, 1988; Golden Globe Award); The Presidio, 1989; Indiana Jones and the Last Crusade, 1989; Family Business, 1990; The Hunt for Red October, 1990; The Russia House, 1991; Highlander II–The Quickening, 1991; Medicine Man, 1992; Rising Sun, 1993; A Good Man in Africa, 1994; First Knight, 1995; Just Cause, 1995; The Rock, 1996; Dragonheart, 1996; The Avengers, 1998; Entrapment, 1999; Playing by Heart, 1999; Finding Forrester, 2001; as James Bond: Dr No, 1963; From Russia With Love, 1964; Goldfinger, 1965; Thunderball, 1965; You Only Live Twice, 1967; Diamonds are Forever, 1971; Never Say Never Again, 1983. Producer, Art, Wyndhams, 1996 (Tony Award, 1998). FRSAMD 1984. Fellow, BAFTA, 1998. Freedom of City of Edinburgh, 1991. Hon. DLitt: Heriot-Watt, 1981; St Andrews, 1988. BAFTA Life Time Achievement Award, 1990; Man of Culture Award, 1990; Scot of the Year Award, BBC Scotland, 1991; American Cinematique Award, 1992; Rudolph Valentino Award, 1992; Nat. Board of Review Award, 1994; Golden Globe Cecil B. De Mille Award, 1996. Commander, Order of Arts and Literature (France), 1987; Légion d'Honneur. *Recreations:* golf, tennis, reading.

CONNING, David Michael, OBE 1994; FRCPath; FIBiol; Director-General, British Nutrition Foundation, 1985–94; *b* 27 Aug. 1932; *s* of Walter Henry Conning and Phyllis Elsie Conning (*née* Lovell); *m* 1st, 1956, Betty Sleightholme (marr. diss. 1991); three *s* one *d*; 2nd, 1991, Lesley Myra Yeomans (*née* Beresford). *Educ:* Dame Allan's Boys' Sch., Newcastle upon Tyne; Med. Sch., King's Coll., Univ. of Durham (MB, BS). FRCPath 1982; FIBiol 1984; FIFST 1988. RAMC, 1956–59. SMO Pathology, Middlesborough Gen. Hosp., 1959–61; Lectr in Pathology, Royal Victoria Infirmary, 1961–65; Hon. Consultant Pathologist, Newcastle and Dist Hosps, 1963–65; Dep. Dir. Central Toxicol. Lab., ICI plc, 1966–78; Dir, BIBRA, 1978–85. Chm., Brit. Toxicol Soc., 1981. Hon. Mem., European Toxicol Soc. (Pres., 1983–86). Hon. Prof. of Toxicology, Surrey Univ., 1977–86. *Publications:* Toxic Hazards in Foods, 1983; Experimental Toxicology, 1988, 2nd edn 1993; contrib. book chapters and articles in jls of toxicol. and nutrition. *Recreation:* mending things. *Address:* Blacksmith's Cottage, Totnor, Brockhampton, Hereford HR1 4TJ. *T:* (01989) 740303.

CONNOLLY, Billy; stand-up comedian, actor; *b* 24 Nov. 1942; *m* 1st, Iris (marr. diss. 1985); one *s* one *d*; 2nd, 1990, Pamela Stephenson; three *d*. Welder, Clyde shipyards; (with Gerry Rafferty) formed folk duo, Humblebums; first solo concert, 1971; *theatre* includes: writer, The Red Runner, Edinburgh, 1979; performer: Die Fledermaus, Scottish Opera, 1978; The Pick of Billy Connolly, Cambridge, 1981; The Beastly Beatitudes of Balthazar B, Duke of York's, 1982; one-man show, London Palladium, 1985; Rebel Without a Clue, world tour, 1987; *films* include: Big Banana Feet; Absolution, 1979; Bullshot, 1984; Water, 1985; The Big Man, 1990; Muppet Treasure Island, 1996; Mrs Brown, 1997; Ship of Fools, 1997; Paws, 1997; Still Crazy, 1998; The Changeling, 1998; Boon Dock Saints, 1998; The Debt Collector, 1999; The Imposters, 1999; Beautiful Joe, 2000; An Everlasting Piece, 2001; Gabriel and Me, 2001; *television* includes: Head of the Class (series, USA), 1990–92; Billy (series, USA), 1992; Billy Connolly's World Tour of Scotland (series), 1994; A Scot in the Arctic, 1995; Billy Connolly's World Tour of Australia (series), 1996; Erect for 30 Years, 1998; Gentlemen's Relish, 2000; presenter, The Bigger Picture, 1994; *plays:* Androcles and the Lion, 1984; Down Among the Big Boys, 1993; Deacon Brodie, 1997. Numerous recordings. *Publications:* Gullible's Travels, 1982; Billy Connolly's World Tour of Australia, 1996. *Address:* c/o Tickety-boo Ltd, The Boathouse, Crabtree Lane, SW6 6TY. *T:* (020) 7610 0122.

CONNOLLY, Edward Thomas; Regional Chairman of Industrial Tribunals, Manchester, 1988–98; *b* 5 Sept. 1935; *s* of Edward Connolly and Alice Joyce; *m* 1962, Dr Pamela Marie Hagan; one *s* one *d*. *Educ:* St Mary's Coll., Crosby; Prior Park Coll.; Liverpool Univ. (LLB). Qualified as solicitor, 1960. Asst Solicitor, Lancs CC, 1960–63; Asst Prosecuting Solicitor, Liverpool City Council, 1963–65; Dep. Chief Legal Officer, Skelmersdale Develt Corp., 1965–68; Asst Clerk of the Peace, Lancs CC, 1968–71; Dep. Circuit Administrator, Northern Circuit, 1971–76; Chm. of Industrial Tribunals, 1976–88. *Club:* Royal Automobile.

CONNOLLY, John Patrick, FCA; Chief Executive and Senior Partner, Deloitte & Touche, since 1999; Global Managing Partner, Assurance, Accounting and Advisory Services, Deloitte Touche Tohmatsu; *b* 29 Aug. 1950; *s* of John Connolly and Mary Connolly (*née* Morrison); *m* 1992, Odile Lesley Griffith; one *s* one *d* (and one *s* decd) from former marriage. *Educ:* St Bede's Coll., Manchester. FCA 1971. Partner: Mann Judd, Chartered Accountants, 1976; Touche Ross, 1980: Regl Partner i/c North, 1983–87; Managing Partner: Regl Offices, 1987–90; London and South, 1990–95; Managing Partner, Deloitte & Touche, 1995–99. *Recreations:* opera, horseracing, shooting, country pursuits. *Address:* Deloitte & Touche, Stonecutter Court, 1 Stonecutter Street, EC1A 4TR. *T:* (020) 7936 3000.

CONNOR, Bishop of, since 1995, **Rt Rev. James Edward Moore;** *b* 1933; *m* 1962, Pamela Mary Fetherston; one *s* one *d*. *Educ:* Trinity Coll., Dublin (BA 1954; MA 1964). Ordained deacon, 1956, priest, 1957; Assistant Curate: Knock, 1956–60; St Comgall, Bangor, 1960–62; Priest-in-charge, Belvoir, 1962–68; Incumbent: Groomsport, 1968–75; Dundela, 1975–95; Archdeacon of Down, 1989–95. Canon, 1985–89, Treasurer, 1987–89, Down Cathedral. *Address:* Bishop's House, 113 Upper Road, Greenisland, Carrickfergus, Co. Antrim BT38 8RR. *T:* (028) 9086 3165.

CONNOR, Prof. James Michael, MD, DSc; FRCPGlas, FRCPE; Burton Professor of Medical Genetics, Glasgow University, since 1987; *b* 18 June 1951; *s* of James Connor and Mona Connor (*née* Hall); *m* 1979, Dr Rachel Alyson Clare Brooks; two *d*. *Educ:* Liverpool Univ. (BSc (Hons); MB ChB (Hons); MD; DSc). MRCP 1977; FRCPGlas 1988; FRCPE 1990. Gen. med. professional trng in various Liverpool hosps, 1975–77; Resident in Internal Medicine, Johns Hopkins Hosp., Baltimore, 1977–78; Univ. Res. Fellow, Dept of Medicine, Liverpool Univ., 1978–81; Instr in Med. Genetics, John Hopkins Hosp., 1981–82; Cons. in Med. Genetics, 1982–84, Wellcome Trust Sen. Lectr in Med. Genetics, 1984–87, Duncan Guthrie Inst. of Med. Genetics, Glasgow. *Publications:* Essential Medical Genetics, 1984, 6th edn 2001; Prenatal Diagnosis in Obstetric Practice, 1989, 2nd edn 1995; (ed jtly) Emery and Rimoin's Principles and Practice of Medical Genetics, 3rd edn 1996, 4th edn 2001; articles on pathophysiology and prevention of genetic disease. *Recreations:* windsurfing, fly-fishing, mountaineering. *Address:* East Collarie Farm, Waterside, by Fenwick, Ayrshire KA3 6JJ. *T:* (01560) 600790. *Club:* Arlington Baths.

CONNOR, Jeremy George; His Honour Judge Jeremy Connor; a Circuit Judge, since 1996; *b* 14 Dec. 1938; *s* of Joseph Connor and Mabel Emmeline (*née* Adams), ARCA. *Educ:* Beaumont; University Coll., London (LLB; DRS). Called to the Bar, Middle Temple, 1961; S Eastern Circuit. Apptd to Treasury List, Central Criminal Court, 1973; Metropolitan Stipendiary Magistrate, 1979–96; a Recorder, 1986–96; a Chm., Inner London Youth Cts (formerly Juvenile Cts), 1980–96; Chairman: Family Proceedings Court, 1991–94; Inner London and City Probation Cttee, 1989–96; Member: Exec. Cttee, Central Council of Probation for England and Wales, 1982–89; Parole Bd, 1998–; Lord Chancellor's Adv. Cttee on Legal Educn and Conduct, 1996–99. Referee, Mental Health Foundn, 1993–. Mem., Judicial Studies Bd, 1990–95. Pres., British Acad. of Forensic Scis, 1989–90 (Chm., Exec. Council, 1983–86; Mem. Council, 1982–93); Chm., Inst. for Study of Treatment of Delinquency, 1992–93. Trustee: Grubb Inst. of Social Studies, 1995–; Stapleford Trust for Drug Treatment and Res., 1995–98; London Action Trust, 1996–; Assoc. of Blind Catholics, 1996–; Rainer Foundn, 1997–98 (Mem. Council, 1996–97); New Lease Trust, 1997–99; Royal Philanthropic Soc., 1998–99. Vice-Patron, Blind in Business, 1999–. Fellow, Soc. of Advanced Legal Studies, 1999. Freeman, City of London, 1980; Liveryman, Fanmakers' Co., 1981 (Mem., Livery Cttee, 1987–90; Mem. Ct of Assts, 1995–). *Publications:* chapter in Archbold, Criminal Pleading, Evidence and Practice, 38th and 39th edns. *Recreations:* travel, theatre, occasional broadcasting. *Clubs:* Garrick, Royal Society of Medicine.

CONNOR, Michael Henry; HM Diplomatic Service, retired; Director of Trade Promotion, and Commercial Counsellor, Madrid, 1995–2000; *b* 5 Aug. 1942; *s* of late Henry Connor and Agnes Cecilia Connor (*née* Lindsey); *m* 1964, Valerie Jannita Cunningham; three *s*. *Educ:* St John's Coll., Portsmouth. Joined HM Diplomatic Service, 1964; FO, 1964–68; Attaché, Cairo, 1968–70; Commercial Officer, Vienna, 1970–73; Second Sec. (Commercial/Aid), Kathmandu, 1973–76; FCO, 1976–81; First Sec., 1979; Havana: First Sec. (Commercial) and Consul, 1981–82; First Sec. and Hd of Chancery, 1982–83; Hd of Chancery, Ottawa, 1983–88; First Sec., FCO, 1988–91; Ambassador, El Salvador, 1991–95. *Recreations:* swimming, photography, trekking, theatre.

CONNOR, Roger David; His Honour Judge Connor; a Circuit Judge, since 1991; *b* 8 June 1939; *s* of Thomas Bernard Connor and Susie Violet Connor (*née* Spittlehouse); *m* 1967, Sandra Home Holmes; two *s*. *Educ:* Merchant Taylors' School; Brunel College of Advanced Science and Technology; The College of Law. Solicitor; articled to J. R. Hodder, 1963–68; Asst Solicitor, 1968–70; Partner, Hodders, 1970–83; Metropolitan Stipendiary Magistrate, 1983–91; a Recorder, 1987–91. *Recreations:* music, golf, gardening. *Address:* Watford County Court, Cassiobury House, 11–19 Station Road, Watford, Herts WD1 1EZ. *Club:* Beaconsfield Golf.

CONNOR, William; General Secretary, Union of Shop Distribution and Allied Workers, since 1997; *b* 21 May 1941; *s* of William and Mary Connor; *m* 1962, Carol Ann Beattie; one *s* one *d*. Union of Shop Distributive and Allied Workers: Area Organiser, 1971–78; Nat. Officer, 1978–89; Dep. Gen. Sec., 1989–97. *Recreations:* music, reading, computers. *Address:* USDAW, 188 Wilmslow Road, Fallowfield, Manchester M14 6LJ. *T:* (0161) 249 2401.

CONNORS, James Scott, (Jimmy); tennis player; tennis commentator, CBS television; *b* 2 Sept. 1952; *s* of James Scott Connors and Gloria Thompson Connors; *m*; one *s*. *Educ:* Univ. of California at Los Angeles. Amateur tennis player, 1970–72, professional, 1972; major Championships won: Australia, 1974; Wimbledon, 1974, 1982; USA, 1974, 1976, 1978, 1982, 1983; South Africa, 1973, 1974; WCT, 1977, 1980; Grand Prix, 1978; played for USA, Davis Cup, 1976, 1981. BBC Overseas Sports Personality, 1982; Champions Tour, 1993–.

CONOLLY, Mrs Yvonne Cecile; consultant in primary education; Head of Inspection and Monitoring, London Borough of Islington, 1995–99 (Senior Inspector for Primary Education, 1989–95); *b* 12 June 1939; *d* of Hugh Augustus and Blanche Foster; *m* 1965, Michael Patrick Conolly (marr. diss. 1996); one *d*. *Educ:* Westwood High Sch., Jamaica; Shortwood Coll., Jamaica (Teachers' CertEd); Polytechnic, N London (BEd Hons Primary Educn). Primary school teacher: Jamaica, 1960–63; London, 1963–68; Head Teacher, London, 1969–78; ILEA Inspector, Multi-ethnic Education, 1978–81; Inspector of Primary Schools, 1981–90, Dist Primary Inspector, 1988–90, ILEA. Member: Home Secretary's Adv. Council on Race Relations, 1977–86; IBA, 1982–86; Consumer Protection Adv. Cttee, 1974–75. Governor, former Centre for Information and Advice on Educnl Disadvantage, 1975–80; (first) Chm., Caribbean Teachers' Assoc., 1974–76. Registered Inspector, OFSTED, 1993–2000. Governor: Stroud Green Primary Sch., 1992–; Park View Community Coll. (formerly Langham, Sch.), 1997–. *Publications:* (contrib.) Mango Spice, book of 44 Caribbean songs for schools, 1981; (contrib.) Against the Tide—Black Experience in the ILEA, 1990. *Recreations:* special interest in the activities of ethnic minority groups; travelling, conversing.

CONOLLY-CAREW, family name of **Baron Carew**.

CONQUEST, (George) Robert (Acworth), CMG 1996; OBE 1955; writer; *b* 15 July 1917; *s* of late Robert Folger Westcott Conquest and Rosamund, *d* of H. A. Acworth, CIE; *m* 1st, 1942, Joan Watkins (marr. diss. 1948); two *s*; 2nd, 1948, Tatiana Mihailova (marr. diss. 1962); 3rd, 1964, Caroleen Macfarlane (marr. diss. 1978); 4th, 1979, Elizabeth, *d* of late Col Richard D. Neece, USAF. *Educ:* Winchester; Magdalen Coll., Oxford. MA Oxon 1972; DLitt 1975. Oxf. and Bucks LI, 1939–46; Foreign Service, 1946–56; Fellow, LSE, 1956–58; Vis. Poet, Univ. of Buffalo, 1959–60; Literary Editor, The Spectator, 1962–63; Fellow: Columbia Univ., 1964–65; Woodrow Wilson International Center, 1976–77; Hoover Instn, 1977–79 and 1981–; Distinguished Vis. Scholar, Heritage Foundn, 1980–81; Research Associate, Harvard Univ., 1982–83; Adjunct Fellow, Center for Strategic and Internat. Studies, 1983–. Jefferson Lecture in Humanities, 1993. FRSL 1972; Corresp. FBA 1994. *Publications:* Poems, 1955; A World of Difference, 1955; (ed) New Lines, 1956; Common Sense About Russia, 1960; Power and Policy in the USSR, 1961; Courage of Genius, 1962; Between Mars and Venus, 1962; (ed) New Lines II, 1963; (with Kingsley Amis) The Egyptologists, 1965; Russia after Khrushchev, 1965; The Great Terror, 1968; Arias from a Love Opera, 1969; The Nation Killers, 1970; Lenin, 1972; Kolyma, 1978; The Abomination of Moab, 1979; Present Danger, 1979; Forays, 1979; We and They, 1980; (with Jon Manchip White) What to do when the Russians Come, 1984; Inside Stalin's Secret Police, 1985; The Harvest of Sorrow, 1986; New and Collected Poems, 1988; Tyrants and Typewriters, 1989; Stalin and the Kirov Murder, 1989; The Great Terror Reassessed, 1990; Stalin: breaker of nations, 1991; Demons Don't, 1998; Reflections on a Ravaged Century, 1999. *Address:* 52 Peter Coutts Circle, Stanford, CA 94305, USA. *Club:* Travellers.

CONRAD, Alan David; QC 1999; a Recorder, since 1997; *b* 10 Dec. 1953; *s* of Maurice and Peggy Conrad; *m* 1982, Andrea Williams (marr. diss. 1998); one *s* one *d*. *Educ:* Bury Grammar Sch.; Brasenose Coll., Oxford (BA Hons Jurisp.). Called to the Bar, Middle Temple, 1976; Asst Recorder, 1993–97. *Recreations:* travel, reading, music, motor cars, food and drink, cricket. *Address:* Lincoln House Chambers, 1 Brazennose Street, Manchester M2 5EL. *T:* (0161) 832 5701. *Club:* Lancashire County Cricket.

CONRAN, Elizabeth Margaret, OBE 1994; MA, FMA; Curator, The Bowes Museum, Barnard Castle, 1979–2001; *b* 5 May 1939; *d* of James Johnston and Elizabeth Russell Wilson; *m* 1970, George Loraine Conran (*d* 1986); one *d*. *Educ:* Falkirk High Sch.; Glasgow Univ. (MA). FMA 1969. Res. Asst, Dept of History of Fine Art, Glasgow Univ., 1959–60; Asst Curator, The Iveagh Bequest, Kenwood, 1960–63; Keeper of Paintings, City Art Galls, Manchester, 1963–74; Arts Adviser, Greater Manchester Council, 1974–79. FRSA 1987. *Publications:* exhibn catalogues; articles in art and museum jls. *Recreations:* gardens, ballet. *Address:* 31 Thorngate, Barnard Castle, Co. Durham DL12 8QB. *T:* (01833) 631055.

CONRAN, Jasper Alexander Thirlby; Designer (clothing and theatre) and Managing Director, Jasper Conran Ltd, since 1978; *b* 12 Dec. 1959; *s* of Sir Terence Conran, *qv* and Shirley Conran, *qv*. *Educ:* Bryanston School, Dorset; Parsons School of Art and Design, New York. Costumes for: Anouilh's The Rehearsal, 1990 (Laurence Olivier Award, 1991); My Fair Lady, 1992; (also sets), Bintley's Tombeaux, Royal Opera House, 1993; Sleeping Beauty, Scottish Ballet, 1994; The Nutcracker Sweeties, 1996, Edward II, 1997, Arthur, 2000, Birmingham Royal Ballet. Fil d'Or (Internat. Linen Award), 1982 and 1983; British Fashion Council Designer of the Year Award, 1986–87; Fashion Group of America Award, 1987; British Collections Award, 1991. *Address:* 2 Munden Street, W14 0RH. *T:* (020) 7603 6668.

CONRAN, Shirley Ida; writer; *b* 21 Sept. 1932; *d* of W. Thirlby Pearce and Ida Pearce; *m* 1955, Sir Terence Conran (marr. diss. 1962); two *s*. *Educ:* St Paul's Girls' Sch.; Southern College of Art, Portsmouth. Fabric Designer and Director of Conran Fabrics, 1956–62; Member, Selection Cttee, Design Centre, 1961–69. Journalist; (first) Woman's Editor, Observer Colour Magazine, 1964; Woman's Editor, Daily Mail, 1969; Life and Style Editor, Over 21, 1972–74. Founder: Mothers in Mgt, 1998; Work-Life Balance Trust, 2001. *Publications:* Superwoman, 1975, revd edn as Down with Superwoman, 1990; Superwoman Year Book, 1976; Superwoman in Action, 1977; (with E. Sidney) Futurewoman, 1979; The Magic Garden, 1983; The Amazing Umbrella Shop, 1990; *novels:* Lace, 1982; Lace 2, 1985; Savages, 1987; Crimson, 1991; Tiger Eyes, 1994; The Revenge, 1997. *Recreations:* reading, swimming, Yoga.

See also J. A. T. Conran.

CONRAN, Sir Terence (Orby), Kt 1983; Chairman: The Conran Shop Ltd, since 1976; Terence Conran Ltd, since 1990; Conran Holdings Ltd, since 1993; Conran & Partners (formerly C. D. Partnership), since 1993; Conran Restaurants Ltd, since 1994; *b* 4 Oct. 1931; *m*; two *s*; *m* 1963, Caroline Herbert (marr. diss. 1996); two *s* one *d*; *m* 2000, Vicki Davis. *Educ:* Bryanston, Dorset. Chm., Conran Holdings Ltd, 1965–68; Jt Chm., Ryman Conran Ltd, 1968–71; Chairman: Habitat Group Ltd, 1971–88; RSCG Conran Design (formerly Conran Design Group/Conran Associates), 1971–92; Habitat France SA, 1973–88; Conran Stores Inc., 1977–88; J. Hepworth & Son Ltd, 1981–83 (Dir, 1979–83); Habitat Mothercare Ltd, 1982–88; Jasper Conran Ltd, 1982–; Heal & Sons Ltd, 1983–87; Richard Shops, 1983–87; Storehouse plc, 1986–90 (Chief Exec., 1986–88; non-exec. Dir, 1990); Butlers Wharf Ltd, 1984–90; Bibendum Restaurant Ltd, 1986–; Benchmark Woodworking Ltd, 1989–; Blue Print Café Ltd, 1989–; Conran Shop Holdings Ltd, 1990–; Le Pont de La Tour Ltd, 1991–; Conran Shop SA, 1991–; Butlers Wharf Chop House Ltd, 1993–; Quaglino's Restaurant Ltd, 1991–; Bluebird Store Ltd, 1994–; Mezzo Ltd, 1995–; Conran Shop Marylebone, 1995–; Conran Shop Germany, 1996–; Gustavino's Inc., 1997–; Conran Collection Ltd, 1997–; Conran Shop Manhattan Inc., 1997–; Coq d'Argent Ltd, 1997–; Orrery Restaurant Ltd, 1997–; The Great Eastern Hotel Co. Ltd, 1997–; Sartoria Restaurant Ltd, 1997–; Zinc Bar & Grill Ltd, 1997–; Atlantic Blue SNC, 1998–; Conran Finance Ltd, 1998–; Director: Conran Ink Ltd, 1969–; The Neal Street Restaurant, 1972–89; Conran Octopus, 1983–; BhS plc, 1986–88; Savacentre Ltd, 1986–88; Michelin House Investment Co. Ltd, 1989–; Vice-Pres., FNAC, 1985–89. Estabd Conran Foundn for Design Educn and Research, 1981–. Mem., Royal Commn on Environmental Pollution, 1973–76. Member: Council, RCA, 1978–81, 1986–; Adv. Council, V&A Mus., 1979–83; Trustee: V&A Museum, 1984–90; Internat. Design (formerly Design) Museum, 1989– (Chm., 1992–). Gov., Bryanston Sch. RSA Presidential Medal for Design Management to Conran Group; RSA Presidential Award for Design Management to Habitat Designs Ltd, 1975; SIAD Medal, 1981; Assoc. for Business Sponsorship of the Arts and Daily Telegraph Award to Habitat Mothercare, 1982; RSA Bicentenary Medal, 1982; President's Award, D&AD, 1989. Hon. FRIBA 1984. Commandeur de l'Ordre des Arts et des Lettres (France), 1991. *Publications:* The House Book, 1974; The Kitchen Book, 1977; The Bedroom & Bathroom Book, 1978; (with Caroline Conran) The Cook Book, 1980, rev. edn as The Conran Cookbook, 1997; The New House Book, 1985; Conran Directory of Design, 1985; Plants at Home, 1986; The Soft Furnishings Book, 1986; Terence Conran's France, 1987; Terence Conran's DIY by Design, 1989; Terence Conran's Garden DIY, 1990; Toys and Children's Furniture, 1992; Terence Conran's Kitchen Book, 1993; Terence Conran's DIY Book, 1994; The Essential House Book, 1994; Terence Conran on Design, 1996; (with Dan Pearson) The Essential Garden Book, 1998; Easy Living, 1999; Chef's Garden, 1999; Terence Conran on Restaurants, 2000; Terence Conran on London, 2000; Terence Conran on Small Spaces, 2001; Q & A: a sort of autobiography, 2001. *Recreations:* gardening, cooking, cigar smoking. *Address:* 22 Shad Thames, SE1 2YU. *T:* (020) 7378 1161, *Fax:* (020) 7403 4309.

See also J. A. T. Conran.

CONROY, Harry; author, financial journalist; Proprietor, Conroy Associates, public relations consultants, since 1992; *b* Scotland, 6 April 1943; *s* of Michael Conroy and Sarah (*née* Mullan); *m* 1965, Margaret Craig (*née* Campbell); twin *s* one *d*. Trainee Lab. Technician, Southern Gen. Hosp., 1961–62; Night Messenger (copy boy), 1962–63, Jun. Features Sub-Editor, 1963–64, Scottish Daily Express; Daily Record: Reporter, 1964–66 and 1967–69; Financial Correspondent, 1969–85; Reporter, Scottish Daily Mail, 1966–67. Campaign Dir, Scottish Constitutional Convention, 1990–92. Mem., ASTMS, 1961–62. National Union of Journalists: Mem., 1963–; Mem., Nat. Exec. Council, 1976–85; Vice-Pres., 1980–81; Pres., 1981–82; Gen. Sec., 1985–90. Bureau Mem., Internat. Fedn of Journalists, 1986–90; Founding Mem., Inst. of Employment Rights, 1989. Associate Mem., GMBATU, 1984–85. Trustee, Share Charity, 1993–; Dir, Consumer Credit Counselling (Glasgow) Ltd, 1996–99. *Publications:* (with Jimmy Allison) Guilty By Suspicion, 1995; (with Allan Stewart) The Long March of the Market Men, 1996; Off The Record: a life in journalism, 1997; (ed) The People Say Yes: the making of Scotland's Parliament, 1997. *Recreations:* stamp and post-card collecting, supporting Glasgow Celtic FC. *Address:* 24 Eskdale Drive, Rutherglen, Glasgow G73 3JS. *T:* (0141) 647 3511; *e-mail:* harry@pronline.co.uk.

CONROY, Paul Martin; President, Virgin Records UK Ltd, since 1992; *b* Surbiton, 14 June 1949; *s* of D. and M. Conroy; *m* 1st, 1980, Maxine Felstead (marr. diss. 1989); one *s*; 2nd, 1994, Katie Rennie; one *d*. *Educ:* John Fisher Sch., Purley. Has worked in various areas of music business, 1971–: agent: Terry King Associates, 1971–73; Charisma Artistes, 1973–75; Manager, Kursaal Flyers, 1975–77; Gen. Manager, Stiff Records, 1977–83; Man. Dir, US Div., WEA Records, 1983–89; Pres., Chrysalis Records, 1989–92. President's Award, Country Music Assoc. of USA, 1987. *Recreations:* cycling, supporting Chelsea, cricket, antique collecting. *Address:* c/o Virgin Records, Kensal House, 553/579 Harrow Road, W10 4RH.

CONRY, Rt Rev. Kieran Thomas; *see* Arundel and Brighton, Bishop of, (RC).

CONS, Sir Derek, Kt 1990; Commissioner of the Supreme Court of Brunei, since 1974; Justice of Appeal, Bermuda, since 1984; Member, Court of Final Appeal, Hong Kong, since 1997; *b* 15 July 1928; *s* of Alfred Henry Cons and Elsie Margaret (*née* Neville); *m* 1952, Mary Roberta Upton Wilkes. *Educ:* Rutlish; Birmingham Univ. (LLB (Hons)). Called to Bar, Gray's Inn, 1953. RASC (2nd Lieut), 1946–48. Hong Kong: Magistrate, 1955–62, Principal Magistrate, 1962–66; District Judge, 1966–72; Judge of Supreme Court, 1972–80, Justice of Appeal, 1980–86, Vice Pres., Court of Appeal, 1986–93. *Recreations:* walking, ski-ing. *Address:* Mulberry Mews, Church Street, Fordingbridge, Hants SP6 1BE. *Club:* Bramshaw Golf (Hants).

CONSTABLE, (Charles) John, DBA; management educator and consultant; Director-General, British Institute of Management, 1985–86; *b* 20 Jan. 1936; *s* of late Charles and of Gladys Constable; *m* 1960, Elisabeth Mary Light; three *s* one *d*. *Educ:* Durham Sch.; St John's Coll., Cambridge (MA); Royal Sch. of Mines, Imperial Coll. London (BSc); Harvard Grad. Sch. of Bus. Admin. (DBA). NCB, 1959–60; Wallis & Linnel Ltd, 1960–63; Arthur Young & Co., 1963–64; Lectr and Sen. Lectr, Durham Univ. Business Sch., 1964–71; Prof. of Operations Management, Business Policy, 1971–82, Dir 1982–85, Cranfield Sch. of Management. Chm., Bright Tech Develts, 1989–98; non-executive Director: IMS Ltd, 1984–91; Lloyds Abbey Life (formerly Abbey Life), 1987–97; Sage Gp, 1996–; NMBZ Holdings Ltd, 1997–. Member: Heavy Electrical EDC, NEDO, 1977–87; N Beds HA, 1987–90; Res. Grants Bd, ESRC, 1989–90. Chm. of Govs, Harpur Trust, 1995– (Governor, 1979–); Trustee, Pensions Trust, 1996–. *Publications:* (jtly) Group Assessment Programmes, 1966; (jtly) Operations Management Text and Cases, 1976; (jtly) Cases in Strategic Management, 1980; The Making of British Managers (BIM/CBI report), 1987. *Recreations:* golf, family. *Address:* 20 Kimbolton Road, Bedford MK40 2NR. *T:* (01234) 212576.

CONSTABLE, Sir Frederic S.; *see* Strickland-Constable.

CONSTABLE, John Robert; Principal Pianist, London Sinfonietta, since 1968; Principal Harpsichordist, Academy of St Martin in the Fields, since 1984; Professor, Royal College of Music, since 1984; *b* 5 Oct. 1934; *s* of Ernest Charles William Constable and May Jane Constable (*née* Rippin); *m* 1956, Kate Ingham; two *d. Educ:* Leighton Park Sch., Reading; Royal Acad. of Music (pupil of Harold Craxton; LRAM and Recital Dip.; FRAM 1986). Pianist, piano accompanist and harpsichordist, music from medieval and baroque to modern; repetiteur, Royal Opera House, 1960–72; concerts at Wigmore Hall, Queen Elizabeth Hall, Royal Opera House and in major European, USA and Japanese cities; numerous TV and radio appearances; many records incl. lieder, chansons, Spanish songs, Victorian ballads, song cycles, chamber music, harpsichord concertos and harpsichord continuo in operas. *Recreations:* travel, looking at paintings, watching cricket. *Address:* 13 Denbigh Terrace, W11 2QJ. *T:* (020) 7229 4603.

CONSTANT, Charles Kenvyn ff.; *see* ffrench-Constant.

CONSTANTINE, family name of **Baron Constantine of Stanmore**.

CONSTANTINE OF STANMORE, Baron *cr* 1981 (Life Peer), of Stanmore in Greater London; **Theodore Constantine,** Kt 1964; CBE 1956; AE 1945; DL; *b* 15 March 1910; *er s* of Leonard and Fanny Louise Constantine; *m* 1935, Sylvia Mary (*d* 1990), *y d* of Wallace Henry Legge-Pointing; one *s* one *d. Educ:* Acton Coll. Personal Asst to Chm. of public company, 1926–28; Executive in industry, 1928–38; Managing Dir of public company subsidiary, 1938–39. Served War of 1939–45, AAF (AEA 1945). Dir of Industrial Holding Company, 1956–59; Chm. of Public Companies, 1959–86. Organisational work for Conservative Party as Constituency Chm., Area Chm., Mem. Nat. Exec. Cttee, Policy Cttee, Nat. Advisory Cttee on Publicity. Chm., Nat. Union Cons. and Unionist Assocs, 1967–68, Pres. 1980. Trustee, Sir John Wolstenholme Charity; Master, Worshipful Co. of Coachmakers, 1975; Freeman of City of London, 1949. High Sheriff of Greater London, 1967; DL Greater London, 1967–85. *Recreations:* watching motor racing, reading, walking. *Address:* House of Lords, SW1A 0PW. *Club:* Carlton.

CONSTANTINOU, Sir Georgkios, (Sir George), Kt 1997; OBE 1992; Chairman, Constantinou Group of Companies; *b* 11 May 1930; *s* of Costas Savva Constantinou and Eleni Lazarou; *m* 1955, Maria (separated); two *s* two *d*; Cecelia; three *s* three *d. Educ:* in Cyprus. Established companies which form Constantinou Group: Papuan Welders, 1954; Papuan Transport Contractors/Roadmakers, 1955; Rouna Quarries Pty Ltd, 1960; Hebou Constructions (PNG) Pty Ltd, 1973; Airways Hotel & Apartments Pty Ltd, 1986; Yodda Resources Pty Ltd, 1996; Kidu Kidu Pty Ltd, 1996. Hon. Consul of Cyprus in PNG, 1986–. *Recreations:* fishing, walking. *Address:* PO Box 120, Port Moresby, Papua New Guinea. *T:* 3253077. *Clubs:* Royal Papua Yacht (Port Moresby); Queensland Turf.

CONTE-HELM, Marie Theresa, (Mrs A. W. Purdue); Director General, Daiwa Anglo-Japanese Foundation, since 2000; *b* 13 Nov. 1949; *d* of Angelo and Santa Conte; *m* 1979, Arthur William Purdue; one *d. Educ:* CUNY (BA Art History 1971); East-West Center, Univ. of Hawaii (MA Asian Art 1973). Cultural Officer, Embassy of Japan, 1975–79; Lectr in Art History, Sunderland Poly., 1979–86; Head of Japanese Studies Div., and Reader in Japanese Studies, Sunderland Poly., subseq. Univ. of Sunderland, 1986–94; Reader in Japanese Studies and Dir, East Asian Affairs, Univ. of Northumbria at Newcastle, 1994–99. Vis. Prof., Univ. of Northumbria at Newcastle, 1999–. *Publications:* Japan and the North East of England: from 1862 to the present day, 1989 (trans. Japanese 1991); The Japanese and Europe: economic and cultural encounters, 1996; academic papers, articles and book reviews. *Recreations:* theatre, film, swimming. *Address:* Daiwa Anglo-Japanese Foundation, 13/14 Cornwall Terrace, NW1 4QP. *T:* (020) 7486 4348; The Old Rectory, Allendale, near Hexham, Northumberland NE47 9DA. *T:* (01434) 683350. *Club:* National Liberal.

CONTI, Rt Rev. Mario Joseph; *see* Aberdeen, Bishop of, (RC).

CONTI, Tom; actor, since 1960; director; *b* Scotland, 1942; *m* Kara Wilson; one *d.* London appearances include: Savages, Royal Court and Comedy, 1973; Other People, The Black and White Minstrels, Hampstead; The Devil's Disciple, RSC Aldwych, 1976; Whose Life is it Anyway?, Mermaid and Savoy, 1978, NY 1979 (SWET Award for Best Actor in a new play, Variety Club of GB Award for Best Stage Actor, 1978, Tony Award for Best Actor, 1979); They're Playing Our Song, Shaftesbury, 1980; Romantic Comedy, Apollo, 1983; An Italian Straw Hat, Shaftesbury, 1986; Otherwise Engaged (also directed), Theatre Royal, Windsor, 1990; The Ride Down Mount Morgan, Wyndham's, 1991; Present Laughter (also directed), Globe, 1993; Chapter Two, Gielgud, 1996; Jesus, My Boy, Apollo, 1998; *directed:* Last Licks, Broadway, 1979; Before the Party, Oxford Playhouse and Queen's, 1980; The Housekeeper, Apollo, 1982; Treats, Hampstead, 1989; *films include:* Galileo, Flame, 1974; Eclipse, 1975; Full Circle, The Duellists, 1977; The Wall, 1980; Merry Christmas, Mr Lawrence, 1983; Reuben, Reuben, 1983; American Dreamer, 1985; Miracles, 1985; Saving Grace, 1986; Heavenly Pursuits, 1987; Beyond Therapy, 1987; The Dumb Waiter (USA); White Roses; Shirley Valentine, 1989; Two Brothers Running; Someone Else's America, 1997; Sub Down, 1997; Out of Control, 1997; Something To Believe In, 1997; Don't Go Breaking My Heart, 1998; *television appearances include:* Madame Bovary, The Norman Conquests, Glittering Prizes, The Beate Klarsfeld Story, Fatal Dosage, The Quick and the Dead, Blade on the Feather, Wright Verdicts, Friends, The Cosby Show. *Address:* Chatto & Linnit, 123A King's Road, SW3 4PL.

CONTOGEORGIS, George; Member, Commission of the European Communities, 1981–85; *b* 21 Nov. 1912; *s* of Leonidas and Angeliki Contogeorgis; *m* 1949, Mary Lazopoulou. *Educ:* Athens Sch. (now University) of Economic and Commercial Sciences. Ministry of Trade, Greece: Administrator, 1937; Chief of Section, 1945; Dir, 1952; Dir Gen., 1964–67, resigned. Gen. Sec., Tourism, Govt of Nea Dimokratia, 1974; Dep. Minister of Co-ordination (Econs), 1974–77; Minister for EEC Affairs, 1977–81; Minister of Nat. Economy, 1989–90. MP, 1977–81. Grand Comdr, Order of the Phoenix (Greece), 1966; Grand Croix de l'Ordre de Leopold II (Belgium), 1984; Grand Comdr, Order of Lion (Finland), 1962; Comdr, OM (Germany, 1956, Italy, 1964 and France, 1977). *Publications:* Greece's Association Agreement with the EEC, 1962; Greece in Europe, 1985; Problems and issues in EEC–USA relations, 1989; European Union and the Balkan States, 1993; The European Idea, 1995; The European Union, 1995; Greece, 1995. *Address:* Rue Anagnostopoulou 26–28, Athens 10673, Greece. *T:* (1) 3616844.

CONTRERAS, Prof. (Carmen) Marcela, MD; FRCP, FRCPE, FRCPath; Professor of Transfusion Medicine, Royal Free and University College Medical School of University College London, since 1998; Director, Diagnostics, Development and Research, National Blood Service, since 1999; *b* 4 Jan. 1942; *d* of Dr Juan Eduardo Contreras and Elena Mireya (*née* Arriagada); *m* 1968, Dr Roberto Jaime Guiloff (marr. diss. 1997); one *s* one *d. Educ:* Dunalastair British Sch. for Girls, Santiago; Sch. of Medicine, Univ. of Chile (BSc 1963; LMed 1967; MD 1972). MRCPath 1988, FRCPath 1997; FRCPE 1992; FRCP 1998. British Council Schol., RPMS and MRC Blood Gp Unit, London, 1972–74; SSO, 1974–76, Med. Asst in Blood Transfusion, 1976–78, N London Blood Transfusion Centre, Edgware; Sen. Registrar in Haematology, St Mary's Hosp., London, 1978–80; Dep. Dir, 1980–84, Chief Exec. and Med. Dir, 1984–95, N London Blood Transfusion Centre; Exec. Dir, London and SE Zone, Nat. Blood Service, 1995–99. Home Office apptd Tester for Paternity Testing, 1980–89. Hon. Mem., MRC Blood Gp Unit, 1987–95. Ed.-in-Chief, Vox Sanguinis, 1996–. *Publications:* (jtly) Blood Transfusion in Clinical Medicine, 8th edn 1987, 10th edn 1997; ABC of Blood Transfusion, 1990, 3rd edn 1998; Blood Transfusion: the impact on new technologies, 1990; contrib. numerous papers in the field of blood transfusion. *Recreations:* theatre, travelling, opera, horse riding, walking, training in developing countries. *Address:* National Blood Service, Colindale Avenue, NW9 5BG. *T:* (020) 8258 2705.

CONVILLE, David Henry, OBE 1983; theatre director and producer; *b* 4 June 1929; *s* of Lt Col Leopold Henry George Conville, CBE and Katherine Mary Conville; *m* 1st, 1956, Jean Margaret Bury (*d* 1967); one *d*; 2nd, 1970, Philippa Falcke (*d* 1999); one *s. Educ:* Marlborough Coll.; St John's Coll., Oxford; RADA (Dip.). Commnd Royal W African Frontier Force, Royal Welch Fusiliers, 1948–49. *Actor:* Ipswich Rep. Co., 1952; Colchester Rep. Co., 1953; Dial M for Murder, Dundee Rep. Co. (tour), 1954; King Lear and Much Ado About Nothing (European, London and provincial tour), 1955, Titus Andronicus (European and London tour), 1957, Stratford Meml Theatre Co.; Folkestone and Richmond Rep. Cos, and TV, 1956; Dry Rot, Brian Rix Co. (London and tour), 1957; The Reluctant Débutante, 1957, Not in the Book, 1959, tours with Jack Hulbert; Surgical Spirit, Granada TV, 1988–95; *producer:* provincial tours, then several West End prodns, 1959–61; Toad of Toad Hall, London, Dec.–Jan., 1960–84; founded New Shakespeare Co., Open Air Theatre, Regent's Park, 1962 (Chm., 1987–); prod./dir of more than 100 classical prodns, 1962–87; *writer: plays:* Chetwode, Sandy and Co., Orange Tree Theatre, 1985; Wind in the Willows, London, 1986–87, Chichester, 1989; Look Here Old Son, BBC Radio, 1987; Obituaries, King's Head Theatre and BBC 1, 1989; Births, King's Head Theatre, 1990. Pres., SWET, 1975–76, 1982. Coronation Medal, 1953. *Recreations:* Real tennis, walking, travel. *Address:* The Old Farmhouse, Okeford Fitzpaine, Blandford, Dorset DT11 0RP. *T:* (01258) 860034. *Clubs:* Garrick; Royal Tennis Court, Canford Tennis.

CONWAY, Christopher John; Chief Executive, 1993, Chairman, 1994, Digital Equipment Co. Ltd; *b* 3 Nov. 1944; *s* of John Francis Conway and Monica Conway (*née* Hawksworth); *m* 1969, Gillian May Burrow; two *s* one *d. Educ:* Univ. of S Africa (BA Hons 1967). IBM (UK) Ltd, 1969–93: Dir, Southern Reg., 1989–92; Dir, Financial Services, 1992–93. Non-exec. Dir, Brammer plc. *Recreations:* sailing, tennis, classical music.

CONWAY, (David) Martin; President, Selly Oak Colleges, Birmingham, 1986–97; *b* 22 Aug. 1935; *s* of Geoffrey S. and Dr Elsie Conway; *m* 1962, Ruth, *d* of Rev. Richard Daniel; one *s* two *d. Educ:* Sedbergh Sch.; Gonville and Caius Coll., Cambridge (BA, MA); and by friends and fellow Christians in many different cultures. Internat. Sec., SCM of GB and Ire., 1958–61; Study Sec., World Student Christian Fedn, Geneva, 1961–67; Sec. for Chaplaincies in Higher Educn, Gen. Synod of C of E, 1967–70; Publications Sec., WCC, 1970–74; Asst Gen. Sec. for Ecumenical Affairs, BCC, 1974–83; Dir, Oxford Inst. for Church and Society, and Tutor, Ripon Coll., Cuddesdon, Oxford, 1983–86. Simultaneous interpreter at assemblies and major world confs of WCC, 1961–; Consultant, Faith and Order Commn, WCC, 1971–82; Consultant, 1974–83, and Mem., 1986–91, C of E Bd for Mission and Unity. DLitt Lambeth, 1994. Editor: The Ecumenical Review, 1972–74; Christians Together, 1983–91; Oxford Papers on Contemporary Society, 1984–86. *Publications:* The Undivided Vision, 1966; (ed) University Chaplain?, 1969; The Christian Enterprise in Higher Education, 1971; Seeing Education Whole, 1971; Look Listen Care, 1983; That's When the Body Works, 1991; Journeying Together Towards Jubilee, 1999; contribs to Student World, New Christian, Audenshaw Papers, Internat. Rev. of Mission, etc. *Recreations:* other people—family, friends, colleagues; travel, music. *Address:* 303 Cowley Road, Oxford OX4 2AQ. *T:* (01865) 723085.

CONWAY, Derek Leslie, TD 1990; MP (C) Old Bexley and Sidcup, since 2001; *b* 15 Feb. 1953; *s* of Leslie and Florence Conway; *m* 1980, Colette Elizabeth Mary (*née* Lamb); two *s* one *d. Educ:* Beacon Hill Boys' School. Principal Organiser, Action Research for the Crippled Child, 1974–83; Chief Exec., Cats Protection League, 1998–2001. Borough Councillor and Dep. Leader of the Opposition, Gateshead Metropolitan Borough Council, 1974–78; Mem., Tyne and Wear Metropolitan County Council, 1977–83 (Leader, 1979–82); Member Board: Washington Develt Corp., 1979–83; North of England Develt Council, 1979–83; Newcastle Airport, 1980–83; Northern Arts, 1980–83. Non-exec. Dir, Foreign & Colonial Gp Investment Fund, 1997–. MP (C) Shrewsbury and Atcham, 1983–97; contested (C) same seat, 1997. PPS to Minister of State: Welsh Office, 1988–91; Dept of Employment, 1992–93; an Asst Govt Whip, 1993–94; a Lord Comr of HM Treasury (Govt Whip), 1994–96; Vice Chamberlain of HM Household, 1996–97. Mem., Speaker's Panel of Chairmen, 2001–; Member, Select Committee: on Agric., 1987; on Transport, 1987–88; on Armed Forces Discipline, 1991; Liaison, 2001–; Chm., Select Cttee on Accommodation and Works, 2001–. Chairman: British–Morocco Parly Gp, 1988–97; British–Venezuelan Gp, 1987–93; Mem. Exec., British American Parly Gp, 2001–; Vice Chm., Cons. backbench Defence Cttee, 1991–97; Mem. Exec. Cttee, IPU, 1986–97 (Vice-Chm., British Gp, 1992–93). Member, Conservative Party Committees: Nat. Exec. Cttee, 1971–81; Nat. Gen. Purposes Cttee, 1972–74; Nat. Local Govt Cttee, 1979–83; Nat. Vice-Chm., Young Conservatives, 1972–74. Mem. Exec. Cttee, British Venezuela Soc., 1987–93. Commnd RMA Sandhurst into Royal Regt of Fusiliers; Major, 5th Bn (TA) Light Infantry. *Recreation:* historical fiction. *Address:* House of Commons, SW1A 0AA. *Club:* Institute of Directors.

CONWAY, Prof. Gordon Richard, FIBiol; President, Rockefeller Foundation, since 1998; *b* 6 July 1938; *s* of Cyril Conway and Thelma (*née* Goodwin); *m* 1965, Susan Mary Mumford; one *s* two *d. Educ:* Kingston Grammar Sch.; Kingston Polytechnic; University Coll. of North Wales, Bangor (BSc 1959). DipAgricSci, Cambridge, 1960; DTA University Coll. of West Indies, Trinidad, 1961; PhD Univ. of California, Davis, 1969; FIBiol 1978 (Hon. FIBiol 2001). Research Officer (Entomology), Agric. Res. Centre, State of Sabah, Malaysia, 1961–66; Statistician, Inst. Ecology, Univ. of California, Davis, 1966–69; Imperial College, London: Res. Fellow and Lectr, Dept of Zoology and Applied Entomology, 1970–76; Dir, 1977–80, Chm., 1980–86, Centre for Envtl Technol.; Reader in Environmental Management, Univ. of London, 1976–80; Prof. of Environmental Technol., 1980–88; Rep. for India, Nepal and Sri Lanka, Ford Foundn, 1989–92; Vice-Chancellor, Univ. of Sussex, 1992–98. Vis. Prof., Imperial Coll., 1989–. Director: Sustainable Agric. Prog., Internat. Inst. for Envmt and Develt, 1986–88; BOC Foundn, 1994–97; Sussex Enterprise, 1995–98. Mem., Royal Commn on Environmental Pollution, 1984–88. Chm. Bd, Inst. Develt Studies, 1992–98; Member: Internat. Inst. for

Envmt and Develt, 1993–97; Bd, Internat. Food Policy Res. Inst., Washington, 1994–97; UK Round Table on Sustainable Develt, 1995–97. Chairman:, Runnymede Trust Commn on Muslims in Britain, 1996–97; Nat. Community Develt Initiative, 2000–01. Fellow, Amer. Acad. of Arts and Scis, 2000. Hon. Fellow, Univ. of Wales, Bangor, 1997. Hon. LLD Sussex, 1998; Hon. DSc: W Indies, 1999; Brighton, 2001. *Publications:* Pest and Pathogen Control, 1984; (jtly) After the Green Revolution, 1990; (jtly) Unwelcome Harvest, 1991; Doubly Green Revolution: food for all in the 21st century, 1997; papers and reports on agricl ecology. *Recreations:* travel, movies, music. *Address:* Rockefeller Foundation, 420 Fifth Avenue, New York, NY 10018–2702, USA. *Club:* Reform.

CONWAY, Prof. John Horton, FRS 1981; John von Neumann Professor of Mathematics, Princeton University, USA, since 1986. *Educ:* Gonville and Caius Coll., Cambridge (BA 1959; MA 1963; PhD 1964). Cambridge University: Lectr in Pure Maths, to 1973; Reader in Pure Mathematics and Mathematical Statistics, 1973–83; Prof. of Maths, 1983–87; Fellow: Sidney Sussex Coll., 1964–70; Gonville and Caius Coll., 1970–87. Polya Prize, London Mathematical Soc., 1987; Frederic Esser Nemmers Prize, Northwestern Univ., 1999; Steele Prize, AMS, 1999. *Publications:* Regular Algebra and Finite Machines, 1971; On Numbers and Games, 1976; Atlas of Finite Groups, 1985; The Book of Numbers, 1996; The Sensual Quadratic Form, 1997. *Address:* Department of Mathematics, Princeton University, Fine Hall, Washington Road, Princeton, NJ 08540, USA.

CONWAY, Martin; *see* Conway, D. M.

CONWAY, Sari Elizabeth; Chief Executive, Eastbourne Borough Council, since 1995; *b* 3 March 1951; *d* of Gordon and Gladys Mary Wright; *m* 1973, Vincent Conway; three *s*. *Educ:* Leeds Polytechnic (Teaching Cert.); Leeds Univ. (Advanced Diploma in Guidance and Counselling; Postgrad. Cert. in Educn of Maladjusted Children); Nottingham Univ. (MPhil); Warwick Univ. (MEd). Teacher of Home Econs, Leeds LEA, 1973–75; Head of Home Economics, Nat. Children's Home, Leeds, 1975–77; Sen. Mistress, Disruptive Unit, and Head of Girls' Studies, Calderdale, 1977–79; part-time Adult Educn Tutor/Organiser, Youth Worker, and Lectr in Further Educn, Derbys, 1979–82; Educn Advr, Leics CC, 1982–88; Asst Dir of Community and Continuing Educn, South Tyneside MBC, 1988–91; Dir of Educn, City of Bradford MBC, 1991–95; Interim Chief Exec., London Borough of Lambeth, 1994–95. *Publications:* Educational Perceptions of Unemployed Adolescents in an LEA, 1984; Women Senior Officers in the Statutory Youth Service, 1992. *Recreations:* travel, dressmaking, theatre, voluntary youth work. *Address:* Chief Executive's Department, Town Hall, Grove Road, Eastbourne BN21 4UG. *T:* (01323) 415009, *Fax:* (01323) 430745.

CONWAY MORRIS, Prof. Simon, PhD; FRS 1990; Professor of Evolutionary Palaeobiology, since 1995, and Fellow of St John's College, since 1987, Cambridge University; *b* 6 Nov. 1951; *s* of Richard Conway Morris and Barbara Louise Maxwell; *m* 1975, Zoë Helen James; two *s*. *Educ:* Univ. of Bristol (BSc Hons); Univ. of Cambridge (PhD). Research Fellow, St John's Coll., Cambridge, 1975–79; Lectr, Open Univ., 1979–83; Lectr in Palaeontology, 1983–91, Reader in Evolutionary Palaeobiology, 1991–95, Cambridge Univ. Gallagher Vis. Scientist, Univ. of Calgary, 1981; Nuffield Sci. Res. Fellowship, 1987–88; Merrill W. Haas Vis. Dist. Prof., Univ. of Kansas, 1988; Selby Fellow, Aust. Acad. of Scis, 1992. Chm., Internat. Trust for Zool Nomenclature, 1991–. Member Council: Systematics Assoc., 1981–85; NERC, 1996–. Royal Instn Christmas Lectr, 1996. Hon. Fellow, Eur. Union of Geoscis, 1997. Hon. DPhil Uppsala, 1993. Walcott Medal, Nat. Acad. of Scis, 1987; Charles Schuchert Award, Paleontol. Soc., 1989; George Gaylord Simpson Prize, Yale Univ., 1992; Lyell Medal, Geol Soc. of London, 1998. *Publications:* The Crucible of Creation, 1998; contribs to professional jls. *Recreations:* travel, wine, punting. *Address:* Department of Earth Sciences, Downing Street, Cambridge CB2 3EQ. *T:* (01223) 333414.

CONYNGHAM, family name of **Marquess Conyngham.**

CONYNGHAM, 7th Marquess *cr* 1816; **Frederick William Henry Francis Conyngham;** Baron Conyngham, 1781; Viscount Conyngham, 1789; Earl Conyngham, Viscount Mount Charles, 1797; Earl of Mount Charles, Viscount Slane, 1816; Baron Minster (UK), 1821; late Captain Irish Guards; *b* 13 March 1924; *e s* of 6th Marquess Conyngham and Antoinette Winifred (*d* 1966), *er d* of late J. W. H. Thompson; *S* father, 1974; *m* 1st, 1950, Eileen Wren (marr. diss. 1970), *o d* of Capt. C. W. Newsam, Ashfield, Beauparc, Co. Meath; three *s*; 2nd, 1971, Mrs Elizabeth Anne Rudd; 3rd, 1980, Mrs D. G. A. Walker (*d* 1986); 4th, 1987, Annabelle Agnew. *Educ:* Eton. *Heir: s* Earl of Mount Charles, *qv*. *Address:* Myrtle Hill, Andreas Road, Ramsey, Isle of Man IM8 3UA. *T:* (01624) 815532. *Club:* Royal St George Yacht.

COOGAN, Ven. Robert Arthur William; Archdeacon of Hampstead, 1985–94, now Archdeacon Emeritus; *b* 11 July 1929; *s* of Ronald Dudley Coogan and Joyce Elizabeth Coogan (*née* Roberts). *Educ:* Univ. of Tasmania (BA); Univ. of Durham (DipTheol). Asst Curate, St Andrew, Plaistow, 1953–56; Rector of Bothwell, Tasmania, 1956–62; Vicar: North Woolwich, 1962–73; St Stephen, Hampstead, 1973–77; Priest in Charge, All Hallows, Gospel Oak, 1974–77; Vicar of St Stephen with All Hallows, Hampstead, 1977–85; Priest in Charge: Old St Pancras with St Matthew, 1976–80; St Martin with St Andrew, Gospel Oak, 1978–81; Area Dean, South Camden 1975–81, North Camden 1978–83; Prebendary of St Paul's Cathedral, 1982–85. Commissary for Bishop of Tasmania, 1968–88; Exam. Chaplain to Bishop of Edmonton, 1985–94. *Recreations:* reading, gardening, travel. *Address:* Glenmore, Cook Street, Hadspen, Tas 7290, Australia. *T:* (3) 63937772. *Club:* Oriental.

COOK, Sir Alan (Hugh), Kt 1988; FRS 1969; Master of Selwyn College, Cambridge University, 1983–93; *b* 2 Dec. 1922; *s* of late Reginald Thomas Cook, OBE, and of Ethel Cook; *m* 1948, Isabell Weir Adamson; one *s* one *d*. *Educ:* Westcliff High Sch. for Boys; Corpus Christi Coll. Cambridge. MA, PhD, ScD. Admty Signal Estabt, 1943–46; Research Student, then Res. Asst, Dept of Geodesy and Geophysics, Cambridge, 1946–51; Metrology Div., Nat. Physical Laboratory, Teddington, 1952; Vis. Fellow, Jt Inst. for Laboratory Astrophysics, Boulder, Colorado, 1965–66; Supt, Standards (subseq. Quantum Metrology) Div., Nat. Physical Laboratory, 1966–69; Prof. of Geophysics, Univ. of Edinburgh, 1969–72; Cambridge University: Jacksonian Prof. of Natural Philosophy, 1972–90; Fellow, King's Coll., 1972–83; Head of Dept of Physics, 1979–84. Vis. Prof. and Green Schol., Univ. of Calif. at Los Angeles, Berkeley and San Diego, 1981–82; Vis. Fellow, Center of Theol Inquiry, Princeton, 1993. Mem. SERC, 1984–88. Chm., Press Syndicate, Cambridge Univ. Press, 1988–93. FInstP; FRSE 1970; Foreign Fellow, Acad. Naz. dei Lincei, 1971. Pres., RAS, 1977–79. Fellow, Explorers' Club, NY, 1980. Humphry Davy Lectr, Royal Soc., 1994. C. V. Boys Prize, 1967, Charles Chree Medal and Prize, 1993, Inst. of Physics. *Publications:* Gravity and the Earth, 1969; Global Geophysics, 1970; Interference of Electromagnetic Waves, 1971; Physics of the Earth and Planets, 1973; Celestial Masers, 1977; Interiors of the Planets, 1980; The Motion of the Moon, 1988; Gravitational Experiments in the Laboratory, 1993; Observational Foundations of Physics, 1994; Edmond Halley: charting the heavens and the seas, 1998; many contribs learned jls on gravity, artificial satellites, precise measurement, fundamental constants of physics and astronomy, history of science. *Recreations:* amateur theatre, travel, painting, gardening. *Address:* 8 Wootton Way, Cambridge CB3 9LX. *T:* (01223) 356887.

COOK, Andrew John, CBE 1996; Chairman and Chief Executive, William Cook Ltd, since 1982; *b* 11 Oct. 1949; *s* of Andrew McTurk Cook and late Barbara Jean (*née* Gale); *m* 1987, Alison Jane Lincoln; one *s* three *d*. *Educ:* High Storrs Grammar Sch., Sheffield; University Coll. London (LLB). Called to the Bar, Gray's Inn, 1972. Dir, William Cook & Sons (Sheffield) Ltd, 1974–82. *Publication:* Thrice Through the Fire: the history of the William Cook company 1985–1998, 1999. *Recreations:* boats, mountains, my children, history, trains, planes, bikes. *Address:* The Manor House, Froggatt Edge, Hope Valley S32 3ZB. *T:* (01433) 631973. *Clubs:* Royal Thames Yacht; Sheffield Sports Cycling.

COOK, Ann; *see* Christopher, A.

COOK, Mrs Beryl Frances, OBE 1996; painter; *b* 10 Sept. 1926; *d* of Adrian Lansley and Ella Farmer-Francis; *m* 1948, John Victor Cook; one *s*. *Educ:* Kendrick Girls' Sch., Reading, Berks. *Exhibitions:* Plymouth Arts Centre, 1975, 1995; Whitechapel Art Gallery, London, 1976; The Craft of Art, Walker Art Gallery, 1979; Musée de Cahors, 1981; Chelmsford Museum, 1982; Portal Gall., 1985, 1991, 2000, 2001; travelling, Plymouth, Stoke-on-Trent, Preston, Nottingham and Edinburgh, 1988–89; Drumcroon Arts Centre, Wigan, 1993; travelling, Blackpool, Durham, Stockton-on-Tees, Hartlepool, 1998. *Publications:* The Works, 1978; Private View, 1980; Seven Years and a Day (illustrations), 1980; One Man Show, 1981; Bertie and the Big Red Ball (illustrations), 1982; My Granny (illustrations), 1983; Beryl Cook's New York, 1985; Beryl Cook's London, 1988; Mr Norris Changes Trains (illustrations), 1990; Bouncers, 1991; The Loved One (illustrations), 1993; Happy Days, 1995; The Prime of Miss Jean Brodie (illustrations), 1998; Cruising, 2000; The Bumper Edition, 2000. *Recreation:* reading. *Address:* The Coach House, 1a Camp Road, Clifton, Bristol BS8 3LW.

COOK, Brian Francis, FSA; classical archaeologist; Keeper of Greek and Roman Antiquities, British Museum, 1976–93; *b* 13 Feb. 1933; *yr s* of late Harry Cook and Renia Cook; *m* 1962, Veronica Dewhirst. *Educ:* St Bede's Grammar Sch., Bradford; Univ. of Manchester (BA); Downing Coll. and St Edmund's House, Cambridge (MA); British Sch. at Athens. FSA 1971. NCO 16/5 Lancers, 1956–58. Dept of Greek and Roman Art, Metropolitan Museum of Art, New York: Curatorial Asst, 1960; Asst Curator, 1961; Associate Curator, 1965–69; Asst Keeper, Dept of Greek and Roman Antiquities, BM, 1969–76. Corr. Mem., German Archaeol. Inst., 1977. Hon. Member: Anglo-Hellenic League, 1981; Caryatids, 1992. *Publications:* Inscribed Hadra Vases in the Metropolitan Museum of Art, 1966; Greek and Roman Art in the British Museum, 1976; The Elgin Marbles, 1984, 2nd edn 1997; The Townley Marbles, 1985; Greek Inscriptions, 1987 (Dutch edn 1990, French edn 1994, Japanese edn 1996); (ed) The Rogozen Treasure, 1989; articles and revs on Greek, Etruscan and Roman antiquities in Brit. and foreign periodicals. *Recreations:* reading, gardening. *Address:* 4 Belmont Avenue, Barnet, Herts EN4 9LJ. *T:* (020) 8440 6590.

COOK, Brian Hartley K.; *see* Kemball-Cook.

COOK, Charles Alfred George, MC 1945; GM 1945; FRCS; Consultant Ophthalmic Surgeon: Guy's Hospital, 1954–73; Moorfields Eye Hospital, 1956–73; Teacher of Ophthalmology, University of London (Guy's Hospital and Institute of Ophthalmology), 1955–73; *b* 20 Aug. 1913; *s* of late Charles F. Cook and Beatrice Grist; *m* 1939, Edna Constance Dobson; one *s* one *d*. *Educ:* St Edward's Sch., Oxford; Guy's Hospital. MRCS, LRCP 1939; DOMS (Eng.), 1946; FRCS 1950. Capt. and Major RAMC, 1939–45. Moorfields Eye Hospital: Clinical Asst, 1946–47; Ho. Surg., 1948–49; Sen. Resident Officer, 1950; Chief Clin. Asst, 1951–55. Sen. Registrar, Eye Dept, Guy's Hospital, 1951–55; Moorfields Research Fellow, Inst. of Ophthalmology, 1951–58; Ophthalmic Surg., West Middlesex Hospital, 1954–56. Mem., Court of Examrs, RCS; Examr for DOMS, RCP and RCS; Examr Brit. Orthoptic Board; Sec., Ophthalmological Soc. of UK, 1956–57. Member: Cttee of Management, Inst. of Ophthalmology, 1960–63 (Vice-Dean of Inst., 1959–62); Cttee of Management, London Refraction Hosp., 1983–88; Council, Coll. of Opth. Opticians, 1979–83 (Hon. Fellow 1982); Bd of Governors, Faculty of Dispensing Opticians, 1980–84. Governor: Royal Nat. Coll. for Blind, 1967–80; Moorfields Eye Hosp., 1962–65. Hon. DSc Aston, 1983. Renter Warden, Upper Warden, then Master, Worshipful Co. of Spectacle Makers, 1975–81. Freeman, City of London. *Publications:* (ed) S. Duke Elder, Embryology, vol. 3, 1963; (contrib.) Payling, Wright and Symers, Systematic Pathology, 1966; (jt) May and Worth, Diseases of the Eye, 1968; articles in Brit. Jl of Ophthalmology, Trans Ophthalmological Soc., Jl of Pathology and other Med. Jls. *Recreations:* swimming, reading; an interest in all outdoor recreations. *Address:* 13 Clarence Terrace, Regent's Park, NW1 4RD. *T:* (020) 7723 5111. *Clubs:* Athenæum, Garrick.

COOK, Sir Christopher Wymondham Rayner Herbert, 5th Bt *cr* 1886; company director since 1979; Director, Diamond Guarantees Ltd, 1980–91; *b* 24 March 1938; *s* of Sir Francis Ferdinand Maurice Cook, 4th Bt and Joan Loraine, *d* of John Aloysius Ashton-Case; *S* father, 1978; *m* 1st, 1958, Mrs Malina Gunasekera (from whom he obtained a divorce, 1975); one *s* one *d*; 2nd, 1975, Mrs Margaret Miller, *d* of late John Murray; one *s* one *d*. *Educ:* King's School, Canterbury. *Recreations:* reading, philately, painting. *Heir: s* Richard Herbert Aster Maurice Cook, *b* 30 June 1959. *Address:* La Fosse Equierre, Bouillon Road, St Andrew's, Guernsey GY6 8YN.

COOK, David Somerville; solicitor; Senior Partner, Messrs Sheldon & Stewart, Solicitors, Belfast; Chairman, Police Authority for Northern Ireland, 1994–96; Lord Mayor of Belfast, 1978–79; *b* 25 Jan. 1944; *s* of late Francis John Granville Cook and Jocelyn McKay (*née* Stewart); *m* 1972, Mary Fionnuala Ann Deeny; four *s* one *d*. *Educ:* Campbell Coll., Belfast; Pembroke Coll., Cambridge (MA). Alliance Party of Northern Ireland: Founder Member, 1970; Hon. Treasurer, 1972–75; Central Executive Cttee, 1970–78, 1980–85; Dep. Leader, 1980–84; Pres., 1992–. Chm., NI Voluntary Trust, 1979–99. Mem., Belfast City Council, 1973–85; Mem. (Alliance) for Belfast S, NI Assembly, 1982–86; contested (Alliance): Belfast South, Feb. 1974, by-elections March 1982 and Jan. 1986, gen. election, 1987; N Ireland, European Parly elecn, 1984. Trustee: Ulster Museum, 1974–85; The Buttle Trust, 1991–2001; Vice Pres., NI Council on Alcohol, 1978–83; Member: NI Council, European Movement, 1980–84; Cttee, Charity Know How Fund, 1991–94; Exec. Cttee, Assoc. of Community Trusts and Foundns, 1992–98 (Chm., 1994–95); Exec. Cttee, Clanmil Housing Assoc. (formerly RBL Housing Assoc. Ltd), 1994–99; Chm., Craigavon and Banbridge Community Health and Social Services Trust, 1994–. Director: Ulster Actors' Co. Ltd, 1981–85; Crescent Arts Centre, Belfast, 1994–96. Mem., Royal Naval Assoc. Gov., Brownlow Coll. (Integrated Secondary Sch.), 1994–98. Obtained Orders of Mandamus and fines for contempt of court against Belfast City Council, following its unlawful protest against the Anglo-Irish Agreement, 1986, 1987. *Publications:* Blocking the Slippery Slope, 1997; (contrib.) The Republican Ideal, ed Norman Porter, 1998. *Recreations:* pamphleteering, wine, marmalade making, observing politicians, hunting on foot. *Address:* 70 Donegall Pass, Belfast BT7 1BU. *Clubs:* Oxford and Cambridge; Ulster Reform (Belfast).

COOK, Derek Edward, TD 1967; Deputy Chairman, 1987–92, and Group Managing Director, 1990–92, Pilkington plc (Director, 1984–92); *b* 7 Dec. 1931; 2nd *s* of late Hubert Edward Cook and Doris Ann Cook (*née* Appleyard); *m* 1968, Prudence Carolyn Wilson; one *s* one *d.* *Educ:* Fyling Hall; Denstone Coll.; Corpus Christi Coll., Oxford (MA); Salford Univ.; Huddersfield Tech. Coll. FSS; CText, FTI. Commissioned Z Battery, BAOR, 1951; W Riding Artillery, 1952–68. Tootal Ltd, 1955–61; John Emsley Ltd, 1961–63; Man. Dir, A. & S. Henry & Co. Ltd (Bradford), 1963–70; Man. Dir, 1971–75, Chm., 1976–79, Fibreglass Pilkington Ltd, India; Chm. and Man. Dir, Hindusthan-Pilkington Glass Works Ltd, India, 1976–79; Director: R. H. Windsor Ltd, India, 1976–79; Killick Halco Ltd, India, 1977–79; Chm. and Man. Dir, Pilkington Cos, S Africa and Zimbabwe, 1979–84, incl. Pilkington Bros S Africa Pty, Armour Plate Safety Glass Pty, and Glass S Africa Pty; Director: Pilkington Glass Ltd, 1982–85 (Chm., 1984–85); Pilkington Holdings Inc., 1984–89; Triplex Safety Glass Co. Ltd, 1984–85 (Chm.); Pilkington Floatglas AB, 1985–87; Flachglas AG, 1985–89. Chm., Pilkington Superannuation Scheme, 1987–; Director: Rowntree plc, 1987–88; Libby-Owens-Ford Co., USA, 1987–92; Charter Consolidated plc, 1988–93; Charter plc, 1993–97; Powell Duffryn plc, 1989–98; Leeds Permanent Building Soc., 1991–95; MFI (Furniture Group) plc, 1992–99; Littlewoods Organisation plc, 1992–99; D. E. Cook (Consultants), 1992– (Sen. Consultant, 1992–); Kwik Save Gp plc, 1993–98; Halifax Bldg Soc., 1995–97; Halifax plc, 1996–98; Somerfield plc, 1998–99; Hobart Pension Trustee Ltd, 1993–97; Littlewoods Pension Trust Ltd, 1994–2001; Trustee: MFI Pension Plan, 1994–99; Halifax plc (formerly Bldg Soc.) Retirement Fund, 1995–98; Kwik Save Retirement Fund, 1997–2000 (Chm., 1998–2000). Member: Council of Industry and Parlt Trust, 1987–92; Council, CBI, 1988–92; Council, Textile Inst., 1994–99; Court, Univ. of Leeds, 1989–2001; Dir, Leeds Univ. Foundn Ltd, 1989–. Gov., Cathedral Sch., Bombay, 1974–79; Dir, Breach Candy Hosp. Trust, 1974–79. Mem., Cook Soc., 1985–. Holder of Royal Warrant of Appointment, 1984–85. FInstD; CIMgt; FRSA. Freeman, City of London; Liveryman, Glass Sellers' Co., 1991–. *Recreations:* sailing (British Admirals Cup team, 1967), general sporting and country life interests. *Address:* Windmill Farm, Wrigley Lane, Over Alderley, Macclesfield, Cheshire SK10 4SA. *T:* (01625) 827985. *Clubs:* Oriental, Army and Navy, Cavalry and Guards, East India, Royal Thames, Royal Ocean Racing; Royal Yorkshire Yacht (Bridlington); Leander (Henley); St James's, Racquets (Manchester); Rand, Country (Johannesburg); Royal Bombay Yacht (Cdre, 1977–78).

COOK, Francis; MP (Lab) Stockton North, since 1983; *b* 3 Nov. 1935; *s* of James Cook and Elizabeth May Cook; *m* 1959, Patricia (marr. diss. 1998), *d* of Thomas and Evelyn Lundrigan; one *s* three *d.* *Educ:* Corby School, Sunderland; De La Salle College, Manchester; Institute of Education, Leeds. Schoolmaster, 9½ years; Construction Project Manager with Capper-Neill International. Vice-Pres., NATO Parly Assembly, 1998–; a Dep. Speaker in Westminster Hall, 1999–. *Recreations:* climbing, fell walking, singing, swimming. *Address:* 84 Southwark Park Road, SE16 3RS.

COOK, Frank Patrick, (Pat); Member, Commission for Local Administration in England and first Local Ombudsman for the North and North Midlands, 1974–85; *b* 28 March 1920; *o c* of Frank Cook, FRCS, FRCOG and Edith Harriet (*née* Reid); *m* 1st, 1945, Rosemary Eason (marr. diss. 1975); two *s* one *d;* 2nd, 1975, Margaret Rodgers, 2nd *d* of Dr J. W. Rodgers, PhD; one *s.* *Educ:* Rugby; Trinity Hall, Cambridge (Open Schol.); LSE (Personnel Management); ASC (Session 16). Royal Marines, 1939–46 (Major; despatches). Courtaulds Ltd, 1946–56; Nat. Coal Board, 1956–61; Venesta Ltd, 1961–64 (Dir, 1963); Principal, British Transport Staff Coll., 1964–69; First Chief Exec., English Tourist Board, 1970–74. Chm., Microtest Research Ltd, 1982–87; Dir and Sec., Mellory Ltd, 1993–99. Indep. Mem., Council, FIMBRA, 1988–90; a Vice President: IPM, 1965–67; RCN, 1973–95; Member: Nat. Nursing Staff Cttee, 1967–72; Brighton and Lewes HMC, 1972–74; Ombudsman Adv. Bd, Internat. Bar Assoc., 1975–85; Exec. Cttee, Fawcett Soc., 1975–77; Council, Univ. of York, 1979–85; Merchant Taylors' Co. of York, 1981–; N Yorks FPC, 1985–87. Conducted inquiry into provision for health care in St Helens and Knowsley, 1990. Governor: Martin House Hospice for Children, 1984–86; Bootham and The Mount Quaker Schs, 1987–89. Hon. LLD Hull, 1986. *Publications:* Shift Work, 1954; Ombudsman (autobiog.), 1981; articles on personnel management. *Address:* Mellory, Old Cleeve, near Minehead, Somerset TA24 6HS. *T:* (01984) 640176.

COOK, George David, CEng, FIEE; Consultant, Quantel Ltd, 1985–93, retired; *b* 23 Sept. 1925; *s* of late John and Jean C. Cook; *m* 1954, Sylvia Ann Sampson; two *d.* *Educ:* Hendon College of Technology. BBC Planning and Installation Dept, 1947; Asst to Supt Engineer, Television Outside Broadcasts, 1955; Head of Engineering, Wales, 1963; Asst Chief Engr, Television, 1967; Chief Engr Transmitters, 1974; Asst Dir of Engrg, 1978; Dep. Dir of Engrg, 1984–85. *Recreations:* golf, theatre. *Address:* 26 Ridge Lane, Watford, Herts WD1 3TA. *T:* (01923) 229638.

COOK, Gordon Charles, DSc, MD; FRCP; physician with special interest in tropical and infectious diseases; Hon. Senior Lecturer in Medicine (Infectious Diseases), University College London, since 1981; Research Associate, Wellcome Trust Centre for the History of Medicine, at University College London, since 1997; *b* Wimbledon, 17 Feb. 1932; *e s* of late Charles Francis Cook and Kate Cook (*née* Kraninger, then Grainger); *m* 1963, Elizabeth Jane, *d* of late Rev. Stephen Noel Agg-Large; one *s* three *d.* *Educ:* Wellingborough, Kingston-upon-Thames and Raynes Park Grammar Schs; Royal Free Hosp. Sch. of Medicine, London Univ. (BSc Physiol 1955; MB BS 1957; MD 1965; Charlotte Brown Prize, 1965; Cunning Award, 1967; Legg Award, 1969; DSc 1976). MRCS; LRCP 1957, MRCP 1960, FRCP 1972; FRACP 1978; FLS 1989. Commissioned RAMC, seconded to Royal Nigerian Army, 1960–62. Hosp. appts, Royal Free, Hampstead Gen., Royal Northern, Brompton, St George's, 1958–63; Lectr, Royal Free Hosp Sch. of Medicine and Makerere Univ. Coll., Uganda, 1963–69; Prof. of Medicine and Cons. Physician, Univs of Zambia, 1969–74, Riyadh, 1974–75, Papua New Guinea, 1978–81; Sen. MO, MRC, 1975–76; Sen. Lectr in Clinical Scis, LSHTM, 1976–97. Hon. Consultant Physician: Hosp. for Trop. Diseases and UCL Hosps, 1976–97; St Luke's Hosp. for the Clergy, 1988–; Hon. Lectr in Clinical Parasitology, St Bart's Hosp. Med. Coll., 1992–. Vis. Prof., Univs of Basrah, Mosul, Doha. Consultant, advr and mem., professional and learned bodies; Mem., Jt Cttee on Higher Med. Trng, 1987–93. Member: Assoc. of Physicians of GB and Ireland, 1973–; Exec. Council, Med. Writers Gp, Soc. of Authors, 1994–99 (Chm., 1997–99); Mem. Exec. Cttee and Examiner, Faculty of Hist. and Philosophy of Medicine and Pharmacy, Soc. of Apothecaries, 1997–; Examiner for membership of RCP, 1977–84. Lectures: Ahmed Hafez Moussa Meml, 1994; Stanley Browne Meml, 1995; Monckton Copeman, Soc. of Apothecaries, 2000. President: RSTM&H, 1993–95; Osler Club, London, 1993–95; Baconian Club of St Albans, 1995–96; Fellowship of Postgrad. Medicine, 2000–; Vice-Pres., History of Medicine Sect., RSM, 1994–96; 1996–; Chm., Erasmus Darwin Foundn, Lichfield, 1994–; Trustee, Educnl Low-priced Sponsored Texts, 1996–. Mem. Council, Cathedral and Abbey Church of St Alban, 1983–88. Liveryman, Apothecaries' Co., 1981. Editor, Jl of Infection, 1995–97; mem., editl bds, med. jls. Frederick Murgatroyd Meml Prize, RCP, 1973; Hugh L'Etang Prize, RSM, 1999. *Publications:* (ed jtly) Acute Renal Failure, 1964; Tropical Gastroenterology, 1980; (jtly) 100 Clinical Problems in Tropical Medicine, 1987, 2nd edn 1998; Communicable and Tropical Diseases, 1988; Parasitic Disease in Clinical Practice, 1990; From the Greenwich Hulks to Old St Pancras: a history of tropical disease in London, 1992; (ed) Gastroenterological Problems from the Tropics, 1995; (ed) Travel-associated disease, 1995; (ed) Manson's Tropical Diseases, 20th edn, 1996; numerous research papers, chapters, reviews and editorials. *Recreations:* cricket, walking, listening to baroque and classical music, medical/scientific history. *Address:* 11 Old London Road, St Albans, Herts AL1 1QE. *T:* (01727) 869000; Wellcome Trust Centre for the History of Medicine at UCL, 183 Euston Road, NW1 2BE. *T:* (020) 7611 8615, *Fax:* (020) 7611 0678; Infectious Diseases Unit, Middlesex Hospital, 46 Cleveland Street, W1P 6DB. *T:* (020) 7679 9311, *Fax:* (020) 7679 9311. *Clubs:* Athenæum, MCC.

COOK, Cdre Henry Home; Vice-President, Chiltern Society, since 1994 (Chairman, 1988–93); Director of Public Relations, Scientific Exploration Society, 1984–88; *b* 24 Jan. 1918; *o s* of George Home Cook, Edinburgh; *m* 1943, Theffania, *yr d* of A. P. Saunders, Gerrards Cross; two *s* two *d.* *Educ:* St Lawrence Coll., Ramsgate; Pangbourne College. Entered RN as Paymaster Cadet, 1936; Comdr 1955; Captain 1963; Cdre 1970. Naval Sec. to Vice-Adm. Sir Guy Sayer, 1953–59; Sqdn Supply Officer, 1st S/m Sqdn, 1959; Comdr, RNC Greenwich, 1961; Naval Attaché, Ankara, 1964; Dir of Public Relations (RN), 1966; Defence Adviser to British High Comr, and Head of British Defence Liaison Staff, Ottawa, 1970–72; retired, 1973. ADC to HM the Queen, 1971–72. A Gen. Comr of Income Tax, 1983–92. Dir, Ellerman City Liners Ltd, 1973–80. Pres., Anchorites, 1978; Vice-Pres., Inst. of Admin. Management, 1983–. FInstAM 1973 (Chm., 1982). DipCAM 1975. *Recreations:* fencing, swimming, sailing. *Address:* Ramblers Cottage, Layters Green, Chalfont St Peter, Bucks SL9 8TH. *T:* (01753) 883724. *Club:* Army and Navy.

COOK, Rear-Adm. James William Dunbar, CB 1975; DL; Vice President, Surrey Branch of Soldiers', Sailors', and Airmen's Families Association; *b* 12 Dec. 1921; *s* of James Alexander Cook, Pluscarden, Morayshire; *m* 1st, 1949, Edith May Williams (*d* 1997); one *s* two *d;* 2nd, 2000, Elizabeth Provan (*née* Gooding). *Educ:* Bedford Sch.; HMS Worcester. CO, HM Ships Venus, Dido and Norfolk; Sen. British Naval Officer, S Africa, 1967–69 (as Cdre); Dir RN War College, 1969–71; Asst Chief of Naval Staff (Ops), 1973–75; retired from RN, 1975. Comdr 1957; Captain 1963; Rear-Adm. 1973; jssc 1958; sowc 1970. Pres., Age Concern (Haslemere), 1990–. DL Surrey, 1989. *Recreations:* golf, gardening. *Address:* Springways Cottage, Farnham Lane, Haslemere, Surrey GU27 1EY. *T:* (01428) 643615. *Club:* Army and Navy.

COOK, Jeremy Laurence C.; *see* Curnock Cook.

COOK, John, FRCSEd; FRSE 1970; Consultant Surgeon, Eastern General Hospital, Edinburgh, 1964–87; *b* 9 May 1926; *s* of George Cook and Katherine Ferncroft (*née* Gauss); *m* 1953, Patricia Mary Bligh; one *s* four *d.* *Educ:* Fettes Coll., Edinburgh; Edinburgh Univ. (MB 1949, ChM 1963). FRCSEd 1954. Served Med. Br., RAF, 1950–52 (Flt Lieut). House Surgeon, Royal Infirmary, Edinburgh, 1949; Res. Asst, Radcliffe Infirm., Oxford, 1954–55; First Asst, Dept of Surg., Makerere University Coll., Uganda, 1955–64 (Reader in Surg., 1962–64). Royal Coll. of Surgeons of Edinburgh: Hon. Sec., 1969–72; Mem. Council, 1974–84. Representative Mem., GMC, 1982–86; Hon. Sec., Internat. Fedn of Surgical Colls, 1974–84. *Publications:* contrib. surgical jls. *Recreation:* music. *Address:* Medwel, Pleasant Row, Clehonger, Hereford HR2 9RE.

COOK, Dr John Barry; Principal, King George VI & Queen Elizabeth Foundation of St Catharine's at Cumberland Lodge, 1995–2000; *b* 9 May 1940; *er s* of late Albert Edward and Beatrice Irene Cook, Gloucester; *m* 1964, Vivien Margaret Roxana Lamb, *o d* of late Victor and Marjorie Lamb, St Albans; two *s* one *d.* *Educ:* Sir Thomas Rich's Sch., Gloucester; King's Coll., Univ. of London (BSc 1961, AKC 1961); Guy's Hosp. Med. Sch. (PhD 1965). Guy's Hospital Medical School: Biophysics research, 1961–64; Lectr in Physics, 1964–65; Haileybury College: Asst Master, 1965–72; Senior Science Master and Head of Physics Dept, 1967–72; Headmaster: Christ Coll., Brecon, 1973–82; Epsom Coll., 1982–92; Dir, Inner Cities Young People's Project, 1992–95. Church in Wales: Mem. Governing Body, 1976–83; Coll. of Episcopal Electors, 1980–83. Chairman: S Wales ISIS, 1978–82; Academic Policy Cttee, HMC, 1985–88. Children's Hospice Association for South-East: Chm., 1995–97; Trustee, 1995–. Chm. Governors, Royal School, Great Park, Windsor, 1998–2000. *Publications:* (jtly) Solid State Biophysics, 1969; Multiple Choice Questions in A-level Physics, 1969; Multiple Choice Questions in O-level Physics, 1970; papers in Nature, Molecular Physics, Internat. Jl of Radiation Biology, Jl of Scientific Instruments, Educn in Science, Conference and Trends in Education. *Recreations:* sports, photography, philately. *Address:* 6 Chantry Road, Bagshot, Surrey GU19 5DB. *T:* (01276) 475843.

COOK, Joseph, CChem, FRSC; management consultant; *b* 7 April 1917; *y s* of Joseph Cook, MBE, JP, and Jane Cook (*née* Adams), Cumberland; *m* 1950, Betty, *d* of James and Elizabeth Barlow, Standish, Lancs; two *d.* *Educ:* Whitehaven Grammar Sch.; Univ. of Liverpool (BSc, DipEd). RAF, 1939–40. Posts in Ministries of Supply, Aviation, Technology and Defence 1941–59; Dir, ROF Burghfield, 1959–65; Gp Dir, Ammunition Factories, 1966; Dir Gen. (Prodn), ROF, 1966–74; Man. Dir, Millbank Tech. Services Ordnance Ltd, 1974–77 (on secondment from MoD). *Recreations:* gardening, golf. *Address:* Abbots-wood, Bramley Road, Pamber End, near Basingstoke, Hants RG26 5QP. *T:* (01256) 850304.

COOK, Leonard Warren; National Statistician and Registrar General for England and Wales, since 2000; *b* 13 April 1949; *s* of late Archie Cook and of Jean (*née* Paterson). *Educ:* Univ of Otago, New Zealand (BA Hons Maths and Stats). Department of Statistics, New Zealand: Res. Officer, 1971–79; Dir, Statistical Methods, 1979–82; Asst Govt Statistician, 1982–86; Dep. Govt Statistician, 1986–91; Govt Statistician, 1992–2000. Secretariat, Task Force on Tax Reform, NZ, 1981; Mem., Royal Commn on Social Policy, NZ, 1987–88. Vis. Fellow, Nuffield Coll., Oxford, 2001–. *Publications:* contribs to NZ Population Review, Proceedings of ISI. *Recreations:* fly fishing, travel. *Address:* Office for National Statistics, 1 Drummond Gate, SW1V 2QQ. *T:* (020) 7533 6200.

COOK, Prof. Malcolm Charles, PhD; Professor of French Eighteenth-Century Studies, since 1994, and Deputy Vice-Chancellor, since 2001, University of Exeter; *b* 19 May 1947; *s* of Francis H. Cook and Betty J. G. Cook; *m* 1974, Odile Jaffré; two *s* one *d.* *Educ:* Univ. of Warwick (BA 1969; PhD 1974). Assistant associé, Université de Paris X, Nanterre, 1972–76; Lectr in French, Westfield Coll., London, 1977–78; Exeter University: Lectr in French, 1978–88; Sen. Lectr, 1988–93; Reader, 1993–94. Chm., MHRA, 1999–. Gen. Editor, MLR, 1994–2001 (French Ed., 1987–93). Chevalier, Ordre des Palmes Académiques (France), 1998. *Publications:* Fictional France, 1993; (ed) French Culture since 1945, 1993; (ed) Journalisme et Fiction au 18e siècle, 1999; (ed) Modern France: society in transition, 1999. *Recreations:* golf, walking, watching soccer and cricket. *Address:* Harling, Pennsylvania Close, Exeter, Devon EX4 6DJ. *T:* (01392) 661235.

COOK, Michael Edgar, CMG 2000; HM Diplomatic Service, retired; High Commissioner, Kampala, 1997–2000; *b* 13 May 1941; *s* of FO Aubrey Edgar Cook, RAFVR (killed in action, 1944) and late Muriel Constance Molly Bateman (*née* Wemyss); *m* 1st, 1970, Astri Edel Wiborg (marr. diss. 1983); one *s* one *d*; 2nd, 1983, Annebritt Maria Aslund; two step *d*. *Educ:* Bishops Stortford Coll.; Fitzwilliam Coll., Cambridge (MA Hons); Regent St Poly. (Dip. Mgt Studies). Export Manager, Young's Sea Foods, 1964–66; joined FCO, 1966; 3rd Sec., Commercial, Oslo, 1967–70; FCO, 1970–73; 1st Sec. then Head of Chancery, Accra, 1973–77; 1st Sec., Commercial, Stockholm, 1977–81; Head of Chancery and Dep. High Comr, Port of Spain, 1981–84; Counsellor and Dep. High Comr, Dar es Salaam, 1984–87; FCO, 1987–92; Consul Gen., Istanbul, 1992–97. *Recreations:* squash, tennis, wine and cooking, jazz. *Address:* 17 Denmark Villas, Hove, E Sussex BN3 3TD.

COOK, Michael John; His Honour Judge Michael Cook; a Circuit Judge, since 1986; *b* 20 June 1930; *s* of George Henry Cook and Nora Wilson Cook (*née* Mackman); *m* 1st, 1958, Anne Margaret Vaughan; three *s* one *d*; 2nd, 1974, Patricia Anne Sturdy; one *d*. *Educ:* Leeds Grammar Sch.; Worksop Coll.; Univ. of Leeds (LLB 2(1) Cl. Hons). Admitted Solicitor, 1953. National Service, commnd Royal Artillery, 1954. Willey Hargrave & Co., Solicitors, to 1957; Ward Bowie, Solicitors, 1957–86 (Senior Partner, 1965–86); a Recorder, 1980–86; Designated Family Judge for Surrey, 1995–. Founder Mem., Holborn and City of Westminster Law Socs, 1962–; Past Hon. Sec. and Pres., London Solicitors' Litigation Assoc.; Hon. Pres., Assoc. of Law Costs Draftsmen, 1997–; Member: Solicitors Disciplinary Tribunal, 1975–86; Law Society sub-cttees and working parties. Chm., Royal Med. Foundn, 2000–. Gov., Epsom Coll., 1990–. Freeman, City of London, 1990. Gen. Editor, Butterworths Costs Service, 1991–; Gen. Editor, The Litigation Letter, 1981–. *Publications:* The Courts and You, 1976; The Taxation of Contentious Costs, 1979; The Taxation of Solicitors Costs, 1986; Cook on Costs, 1991, 4th edn 2000; (jtly) The New Civil Costs Regime, 1999; contributions to: Butterworths Personal Injury Litigation Service, 1994–; Cordery on Solicitors, 1995–. *Recreations:* tennis, gardening, theatre, sitting on moving horses.

COOK, Nicholas (John), PhD; FBA 2001; Research Professor of Music, University of Southampton, since 1999; *b* Athens, 5 June 1950; *s* of late Prof. John Manuel Cook, FBA and Enid May Cook (*née* Robertson); *m* 1975, Catherine Bridget Louise Elgie; one *s* one *d*. *Educ:* King's Coll., Cambridge (BA 1971, MA 1976; PhD 1983); Univ. of Southampton (BA 1977). Lectr in Music, Univ. of Hong Kong, 1982-90; Prof. of Music, 1990-99, Dean of Arts, 1996-98, Univ. of Southampton. Chair, Music Panel, HEFC RAE 2001. Ed., Jl Royal Musical Assoc., 1999-. *Publications:* A Guide to Musical Analysis, 1987; Music, Imagination and Culture, 1990; Beethoven: Symphony No 9, 1993; Analysis Through Composition: principles of the classical style, 1996; Analysing Musical Multimedia, 1998; Music: a very short introduction, 1998; contrib. articles in most major musicological jls. *Address:* 15 Wilberforce Road, Cambridge CB3 0EQ. *T:* (01223) 352863; Old School House, School Hill, Alderbury, Salisbury SP5 3DR. *T:* (01722) 710012.

COOK, Pat; *see* Cook, F. P.

COOK, Prof. Paul Derek, MBE 1985; PhD; CEng; Chairman and Managing Director, Scientifica-Cook Ltd, since 1962; Professor of Laser Science, Brunel University, 1986–97; *b* 12 March 1934; *s* of James Walter Cook and Florence Jefferay; *m* 1954, Frances Ann James; four *d*. *Educ:* Queen Mary Coll., London (BSc Hons; PhD 1963; Sir John Johnson Scholar, 1959). CEng, MIEE 1963. Res. Scientist: MRC, 1960–62; Middlesex Hosp. Med. Sch., 1962–65. Prof. of Laser Physics, Brunel Univ., 1986–91. Scientific Adviser to: Minister for the Envmt and Countryside, DoE, 1990–92; British Gas, 1990–92; Laser Consultant, BAe, 1986–; former Consultant, W Midlands Police, 1991–92; Scientific Advr to Lady Olga Maitland, 1992–96. Responsible for design and develt of numerous laser systems used in med. and mil. estabts throughout world, incl. ophthalmic LaserSpec; originator and inventor of Laser Guidance Systems for weapon alignment in each Tornado; major contrib. to Europe's first laser gyroscope in 1970s; invention of laser instrument that improves safety of motorists by detecting and correcting night myopia; estab. world's first Night Vision Clinic for treating night blindness disorders. Dep. Chm., Conserve, 1990–93; Founder/Pres., British Science and Technol. Trust, 1985–96; UK Pres., Japanese Zen Nippon Airinkai, 1978–81. *Recreations:* breeding and rearing exotic Japanese carp, cultivating Japanese bonzai, inventing, experimenting with ideas, especially those related to improving safety on the roads, passion for early automobile number plates. *Address:* Carlton House, 78 Bollo Bridge Road, W3 8AU.

COOK, Dr Peter John, CBE 1996; FTSE; Consulting Geologist and Director, Australian Petroleum Co-operative Research Centre, since 1998; *b* 15 Oct. 1938; *s* of John and Rose Cook; *m* 1961, Norma Irene Walker; two *s*. *Educ:* Durham Univ. (BSc Hons, DSc); ANU (MSc); Univ. of Colorado (PhD). FTSE 1998. Geologist to Sen. Geologist, BMR, Canberra, 1961–76; Sen. Res. Fellow, ANU Res. Sch. of Earth Sci., 1976–82 (Vis. Fellow, 1982–90); Chief of Div./Chief Res. Scientist, BMR, 1982–90 (Prof., Univ. Louis Pasteur, Strasbourg, 1989); Dir, British Geol Survey, 1990–98. Adrian Fellow, Univ. of Leicester, 1992–98. Chairman: Consortium for Ocean Geosci., 1980–82; Commonwealth/State Hydrogeol. Cttee, 1983–88; Intergovtl Oceanographic Commn, Prog. Ocean Sci. and Non-Living Resources, 1984–; Member: Adv. Cttee, Aust. Nuclear Sci. and Tech. Orgn, 1984–90; Geolog. Adv. Panel, BM (Nat. Hist.), 1990–98; Earth Scis Cttee, 1990–94, Earth Scis Tech. Bd, 1995–98, NERC; Chm., Forum of European Geol Surveys, 1996–97; Pres., EuroGeoSurveys, 1995–96; Vice-Pres., Global Sedimentary Geol. Prog., 1996–. Member: Council, MIRO, 1991–98; Adv. Cttee for Protection of the Seas, 1997–. Major John Coke Medal, Geol Soc., 1997. *Publications:* more than 130 contribs to books and learned jls, on phosphate deposits, marine mineral resources, coastal zone studies, palaeogeography, science management and science policy. *Recreations:* skiing, hiking, travel, history. *Address:* 21 Empire Circuit, Forrest, Canberra, ACT 2603, Australia. *T:* (2) 62396504, *Fax:* (2) 62396049; *e-mail:* pjcook@spirit.com.au. *Club:* Commonwealth (Canberra).

COOK, Rt Hon. Robert Finlayson, (Rt Hon. Robin); PC 1996; MP (Lab) Livingston, since 1983 (Edinburgh Central, Feb. 1974–1983); Leader of the House of Commons and President of the Council, since 2001; *b* 28 Feb. 1946; *s* of late Peter Cook, headmaster and of Christina Cook (*née* Lynch); *m* 1969, Margaret K. Whitmore (marr. diss. 1998), medical consultant; two *s*; *m* 1998, Gaynor Regan. *Educ:* Aberdeen Grammar Sch.; Univ. of Edinburgh. MA Hons English Lit. Tutor-Organiser with WEA, 1970–74. Chm., Scottish Assoc. of Labour Student Organisations, 1966–67; Sec., Edinburgh City Labour Party, 1970–72; Mem., Edinburgh Corporation, 1971–74, Chm. Housing Cttee, 1973–74. An Opposition Treasury spokesman, 1980–83; opposition front bench spokesman on: European and community affairs, 1983–84; trade, 1986–87; health, 1987–92; trade and industry, 1992–94; foreign and commonwealth affairs, 1994–97; Sec. of State for Foreign and Commonwealth Affairs, 1997–2001. Labour's Campaigns Co-ordinator, 1984–86; Chm., Labour Party, 1996–97. Mem., Tribune Group. *Recreations:* eating, reading, talking. *Address:* c/o House of Commons, SW1A 0AA. *T:* (020) 7219 4040.

COOK, Rt Hon. Robin; *see* Cook, Rt Hon. Robert F.

COOK, Roger James; investigative journalist; broadcaster: The Cook Report, ITV, 1985–97; Cook Report Specials, ITV, since 1998; *b* 6 April 1943; *s* of Alfred and Linda Cook; *m* 1st, 1966, Madeline Koh (marr. diss. 1974); 2nd, 1982, Frances Knox; one *d*. *Educ:* Hurlstone Agricl Coll.; Sydney Univ. TV and radio reporter, ABC (Australia), 1960–66; TV and radio dir, Warnock Sandford Advertising (Aust.), 1966–68; reporter, BBC Radio 4, World at One, World This Weekend, PM, 1968–76; freelance documentary dir, 1968–72; creator and presenter, Checkpoint, Radio 4, 1973–85; presenter and reporter, Radio 4 documentary series: Time for Action; Real Evidence; investigative reporter, BBC TV: Nationwide; Newsnight, 1972–84. Vis. Prof. of Investigative Journalism, now Vis. Prof., Centre for Broadcast Journalism, Nottingham Trent Univ., 1997–. BPG Award, for outstanding contrib. to radio, 1978; Pye (now Sony) Radio Personality of the Year, 1979; Ross McWhirter Foundn Award, for courageous reporting, 1980; Valiant for Truth Award, 1988; TV and Radio Industries Award, for best ITV prog., 1993, and Special Award, for outstanding contrib. to broadcasting, 1998; RTS (Midlands) Best On-Screen Personality, 1996; Houston Worldfest Silver Award, for best interview, 1997; Charleston Worldfest Gold Award, for best investigative prog., 1997; Brigitte Bardot Internat. Award (Genesis Awards), for best campaigning wildlife prog., 1997; British Acad. Special Award, for outstanding investigative reporting, 1998. *Publications:* (with Tim Tate) What's Wrong With Your Rights?, 1988; (with Howard Foster) Dangerous Ground, 1999. *Recreations:* walking, music, motor sport. *Address:* c/o The Roseman Organisation, Suite 9, The Power House, 70 Chiswick High Road, W4 1SY.

COOK, Prof. Stephen Arthur, PhD; FRS 1998; FRSC 1984; University Professor, Department of Computer Science, University of Toronto, since 1985; *b* 14 Dec. 1939; *s* of Gerhard A. Cook and Lura Lincoln Cook; *m* 1968, Linda Craddock; two *s*. *Educ:* Univ. of Michigan (BSc Math. 1961); Harvard Univ. (SM Math. 1962; PhD Math. 1966). Asst Prof., Math. and Computer Science, Univ. of Calif at Berkeley, 1966–70; University of Toronto: Associate Prof., 1970–75, Prof., 1975–85, Dept of Computer Science. Member: Nat. Acad. of Scis (US), 1985; Amer. Acad. of Arts and Scis, 1986. A. M. Turing Award, ACM, 1982. *Publications:* numerous papers in jls. *Recreation:* sailing. *Address:* Department of Computer Science, University of Toronto, Toronto, ON M5S 3G4, Canada. *T:* (416) 9785183. *Club:* Royal Canadian Yacht.

COOK, Timothy, OBE 1997; Clerk to the Trustees, City Parochial Foundation, 1986–98; *b* 25 April 1938; *s* of late Stephen Cook and of Kathleen (*née* Henwood); *m* 1967, Margaret Taylor; one *s* one *d*. *Educ:* Loughborough Grammar Sch.; Trinity Hall, Cambridge (BA); Brunel Univ. (MA). Called to the Bar, Middle Temple, 1961. Asst Lectr in Law, Sheffield Univ., 1960–61; Asst Warden, Norman House, 1962–64; Prison Welfare Officer, HM Prison, Blundeston, 1964–66; Dir, Alcoholics Recovery Project, 1966–74; Hd, Cambridge House and Talbot, 1975–77; Dir, Family Service Units, 1978–85. *Publications:* Vagrant Alcoholics, 1975; (ed jtly) The Drunkenness Offence, 1969; (ed) Vagrancy, 1979; Merfyn Turner: practical compassion, 1999; (jtly) A Management Companion for the Voluntary Sector, 2000; Reflections on Good Grant Making, 2000. *Recreations:* cinema, reading, theatre. *Address:* 26 Criffel Avenue, SW2 4AZ. *T:* (020) 8674 3141.

COOK, William Birkett, MA; Master of Magdalen College School, Oxford, 1972–91; *b* 30 Aug. 1931; *e s* of late William James and Mildred Elizabeth Cook, Headington, Oxford; *m* 1958, Marianne Ruth, *yr d* of late A. E. Taylor, The Schools, Shrewsbury; one *s* one *d* (and one *d* decd). *Educ:* Dragon Sch.; Eton (King's Schol.); Trinity Coll., Cambridge (Schol.). National Service, 1950–51 (commnd in RA). Porson Prizeman, 1953; 1st cl. Classical Tripos Pt I, 1953, Pt II, 1954; Henry Arthur Thomas Student, 1954; MA Oxon by incorporation, 1972. Asst Master, Shrewsbury Sch., 1955–67, and Head of Classical Faculty, 1960–67; Headmaster of Durham Sch., 1967–72. Governor: Oxford High Sch., 1979–2000; Bedford Modern Sch., 1992–2001. Administrator, Choir Schools' Assoc. Bursary Trust, 1987–92; Dir, Thomas Wall Trust, 1992–; Gov., Ewelme Exhibn Endowment, 1993–(Chm., 1999–). *Recreations:* music, gardening, Scottish country dancing. *Address:* 2 Cannon's Field, Old Marston, Oxford OX3 0QR. *T:* (01865) 250882.

COOKE, family name of **Barons Cooke of Islandreagh** and **Cooke of Thorndon**.

COOKE OF ISLANDREAGH, Baron *cr* 1992 (Life Peer), of Islandreagh in the County of Antrim; **Victor Alexander Cooke,** OBE 1981; DL; CEng, FIMechE; Chairman: Henry R. Ayton Ltd, Belfast, 1970–89; Springvale EPS (formerly Polyproducts) Ltd, 1964–2000; *b* 18 Oct. 1920; *s* of Norman Victor Cooke and Alice Harman Cooke (*née* Peavey); *m* 1951, Alison Sheila Casement; two *s* one *d*. *Educ:* Marlborough Coll., Wilts; Trinity Coll., Cambridge (MA). Engineer Officer, Royal Navy, 1940–46 (Lieut (E) RN). Henry R. Ayton Ltd, Belfast, 1946–89; Chairman: Belfast Savings Bank, 1963; Harland & Wolff Ltd, 1980–81 (Dir, 1970–87); Dir, NI Airports, 1970–85. Member: Senate, Parliament of N Ireland, 1960–68; N Ireland Economic Council, 1974–78; Commissioner, Belfast Harbour, 1968–79; Commissioner of Irish Lights, 1983–95 (Chm. of Comrs, 1990–92). DL Co. Antrim, 1970. *Recreations:* sailing, shooting. *Club:* Naval.

COOKE OF THORNDON, Baron *cr* 1996 (Life Peer), of Wellington in New Zealand and of Cambridge in the County of Cambridgeshire; **Robin Brunskill Cooke,** KBE 1986; Kt 1977; PC 1977; PhD; President, Court of Appeal of New Zealand, 1986–96 (Judge, 1976–86); *b* 9 May 1926; *s* of Hon. Philip Brunskill Cooke, MC (Judge of Supreme Court), and Valmai Digby Gore; *m* 1952, Phyllis Annette Miller; three *s*. *Educ:* Wanganui Collegiate Sch.; Victoria University Coll., Wellington (LLM); Clare Coll., Cambridge; Gonville and Caius Coll., Cambridge (MA, PhD). Trav. Scholarship in Law, NZ, 1950; Res. Fellow, Gonville and Caius Coll., Cambridge, 1952–56 (Yorke Prize, 1954), Hon. Fellow, 1982. Called to the Bar, Inner Temple, 1954, Hon. Bencher 1985; practised at NZ Bar, 1955–72; QC 1964; Judge of Supreme Court, 1972–76; Pres., Court of Appeal of Western Samoa, 1982 and 1994–, of Cook Is, 1981 and 1982, of Kiribati, 1999; Judge of Supreme Court of Fiji, 1995–; a Lord of Appeal, UK, 1996–2001; Non-Perm. Judge, Hong Kong Court of Appeal, 1997–. Chm., Commn of Inquiry into Housing, 1970–71; Commn Mem., Internat. Commn of Jurists, 1993–. Life Mem., Lawasia. Special Status Mem., Amer. Law Inst., 1993–. Vis. Fellow, All Souls Coll., Oxford, 1990; Hon. Fellow, Legal Res. Foundn, NZ, 1993; Distinguished Vis. Fellow, Victoria Univ. of Wellington, 1996–. Lectures: Sultan Azlan Shah Law, Malaysia, 1990; Peter Allan Meml, Hong Kong, 1994; Hamlyn (4), UK, 1996. Hon. LLD: Victoria Univ. of Wellington, 1989; Cambridge Univ., 1990; Hon. DCL Oxford, 1991. *Publications:* (ed) Portrait of a Profession (Centennial Book of NZ Law Society), 1969; (Editor in Chief) The Laws of New Zealand, 1990–; Turning Points of the Common Law (Hamlyn Lectures), 1997; articles in law reviews and papers at internat. law confs. *Recreations:* theatre, The Times crossword, watching cricket (Patron, Wellington Cricket Assoc., 1995–). *Address:* 4 Homewood Crescent, Karori, Wellington, New Zealand. *T:* (4) 4768059; House of Lords, SW1A 0PW; Brick Court Chambers, 7–8 Essex Street, WC2R 3LD. *Clubs:* Oxford and Cambridge; Wellington, Wellington Golf (NZ).

COOKE, (Alfred) Alistair, KBE (Hon.) 1973; journalist and broadcaster; *b* 20 Nov. 1908; *s* of Samuel Cooke and Mary Elizabeth Byrne; *m* 1st, 1934, Ruth Emerson; one *s*; 2nd, 1946, Jane White Hawkes; one *d*. *Educ:* Blackpool Grammar Sch.; Jesus Coll., Cambridge (Scholar; Hon. Fellow, 1986); Yale Univ.; Harvard. Founded Cambridge University Mummers, 1928; First Class, English Tripos, 1929; Second Class, 1930. Editor, The Granta, 1931; Commonwealth Fund Fellow, 1932–34. BBC Film Critic, 1934–37; London Correspondent for NBC, 1936–37; Commentator on American Affairs for BBC, 1938–; Special Correspondent on American Affairs, The London Times, 1938–40; American Feature Writer, The Daily Herald, 1941–43; UN Correspondent of the Manchester Guardian (which changed name to Guardian, 1959), 1945–48; Chief Correspondent in US of The Guardian, 1948–72. Master of ceremonies: Ford Foundation's television programme, Omnibus, 1952–61; UN television programme, International Zone, 1961–67; Masterpiece Theatre, 1971–92. Wrote and narrated, America: a personal history of the United States, BBC TV, 1972–73 (Peabody Award for meritorious services to broadcasting, 1972; Writers' Guild of GB award for best documentary of 1972; Dimbleby Award, Soc. of Film and TV Arts, 1973; four Emmy awards of (US) Nat. Acad. of TV Arts and Sciences, 1973). Hon. LLD: Edinburgh, 1969; Manchester, 1973; Hon. LittD: St Andrews, 1975; Cantab, 1988. Peabody Award for internat. reporting, 1952 and 1983; Benjamin Franklin Medal, RSA, 1973; Howland Medal, Yale Univ., 1977. *Publications:* (ed) Garbo and the Night Watchmen, 1937, repr. 1972; Douglas Fairbanks: The Making of a Screen Character, 1940; A Generation on Trial: USA v Alger Hiss, 1950; Letters from America, 1951; Christmas Eve, 1952; A Commencement Address, 1954; (ed) The Vintage Mencken, 1955; Around the World in Fifty Years, 1966; Talk about America, 1968; Alistair Cooke's America, 1973; Six Men, 1977, repr. 1995; The Americans: fifty letters from America on our life and times, 1979; (with Robert Cameron) Above London, 1980; Masterpieces, 1982; The Patient has the Floor, 1986; America Observed, 1988; Fun & Games with Alistair Cooke, 1994; Memories of the Great and the Good, 1999. *Recreations:* playing golf, watching tennis, music, biography. *Address:* 1150 Fifth Avenue, New York City, NY 10128, USA; Nassau Point, Cutchogue, Long Island, NY, USA. *Clubs:* Athenæum; Lotos, National Arts, Links (New York); San Francisco Golf.

COOKE, Alistair Basil, OBE 1988; PhD; General Secretary, Independent Schools Council, since 1997; *b* 20 April 1945; 2nd *s* of Dr Basil Cooke and Nancy Irene Cooke (*née* Neal). *Educ:* Framlingham Coll., Suffolk; Peterhouse, Cambridge (MA 1970); Queen's Univ., Belfast (PhD 1979). Lectr and Tutor in Modern History, Queen's Univ., Belfast, 1971–77; Conservative Research Department: Desk Officer, 1977–83; Political Advr to Shadow Minister for NI, 1977–79; Asst Dir, 1983–85; Dep. Dir, 1985–97. Dir, Conservative Political Centre, 1988–97. Chm. of Trustees, Friends of the Union, 1995–. Gov., John Lyon Sch., Harrow, 1999–. *Publications:* (ed jtly) Lord Carlingford's Journal, 1971; (jtly) The Governing Passion: cabinet government and party politics in Britain 1885–86, 1974; (ed) The Ashbourne Papers 1869 1913, 1974; (ed) The Conservative Party's Campaign Guides, 6 vols, 1987–97; (ed) The Conservative Party: seven historical studies, 1997; pamphlets on Northern Ireland and constitutional issues; articles in historical jls and educnl pubns. *Recreations:* writing letters to the press (and getting them published), collecting political memorabilia, music. *Address:* Flat 1, 68 St George's Square, SW1V 3QT. *T:* (020) 7821 9520. *Clubs:* Carlton, St Stephen's Constitutional.

COOKE, Rear-Adm. Anthony John, CB 1980; Private Secretary to Lord Mayor of London, 1981–92; *b* 21 Sept. 1927; *s* of Rear-Adm. John Ernest Cooke, CB and late Kathleen Mary Cooke; *m* 1st, 1951, Margaret Anne (marr. diss. 1994), *d* of late Frederick Charles Hynard; two *s* three *d*; 2nd, 1995, Patricia Sinclair Stewart, *d* of late William Sinclair Stewart and of Margaret Jane Stewart; one step *s* two step *d*. *Educ:* St Edward's Sch., Oxford. Entered RN 1945; specialised in navigation, 1953; Army Staff Coll., 1958; Sqdn Navigating Officer, HMS Daring, Second Destroyer Sqdn, 1959–61; Staff Navigating Officer to Flag Officer, Sea Trng, 1961; Comdr 1961; Directorate of Naval Ops and Trade, 1961–63; i/c HMS Brighton, 1964–66; Directorate of Navigation and Tactical Control, 1966; Captain 1966; Captain of Dockyard and Queen's Harbourmaster, Singapore, 1967–69; Captain 1st Destroyer Sqdn, Far East, later Divnl Comdr 3rd Div. Western Fleet, i/c HMS Galatea, 1969–71; Dir, Royal Naval Staff Coll., 1971–73; Cdre Clyde i/c Clyde Submarine Base, 1973–75; Rear-Adm. 1976; Senior Naval Mem., Directing Staff, RCDS, 1975–78; Adm. Pres., RNC Greenwich, 1978–80, retd. Police Foundn, 1980–81. A Younger Brother, Trinity House, 1974. Freeman: City of London, 1979; Shipwrights' Co., 1980. OStJ 1990. *Recreation:* keeping my wife in champagne and out of the red. *Address:* Sinclair House, 4 Amherst Road, Ealing, W13 8ND. *T:* (020) 8997 2620.

COOKE, Brian; Circuit Administrator, South Eastern Circuit, 1989–95; *b* 16 Jan. 1935; *s* of Norman and Edith Cooke; *m* 1958, Edith Mary Palmer; two *s* one *d*. *Educ:* Manchester Grammar Sch.; University Coll. London (LLB). Served Royal Air Force, 1956–59. Called to Bar, Lincoln's Inn, 1959; Dept of Director of Public Prosecutions, 1960–68; Deputy Clerk of the Peace, Inner London Quarter Sessions, 1968–71; Dep. Circuit Administrator, North Eastern Circuit, 1971–81, Circuit Administrator 1981–82; Sec. of Commissions, 1982–88, Hd of Judicial Appointments Gp, 1987–88, Lord Chancellor's Dept. Part-time Pres., Mental Health Rev. Tribunals, 1996–. JP Mddx, 1985–99. *Recreations:* golf, walking, theatre, music. *Address:* 12 The Pryors, East Heath Road, NW3 1BS. *Club:* Hampstead Golf.

COOKE, Prof. Brian Ernest Dudley; Professor Emeritus, University of Wales, 1983; Professor of Oral Medicine and Oral Pathology, University of Wales, Dean of Welsh National School of Medicine Dental School and Consultant Dental Surgeon to University Hospital of Wales, 1962–82; *b* 12 Jan. 1920; *e s* of Charles Ernest Cooke and Margaret Beatrice Wood; *m* 1948, Marion Neill Orkney Hope; one *s* one *d*. *Educ:* Merchant Taylors' Sch.; London Univ. LDSRCS 1942; LRCP, MRCS 1949; FDSRCS 1952; MDSU London 1959; MRCPath 1965, FRCPath 1974. Served RNVR (Dental Br.), 1943–46. Nuffield Dental Fellow, 1950–52; Trav. Nuffield Fellow, Australia, 1964. Lectr 1952–57, Reader in Dental Med. 1958–62, Guy's Hosp. Dental School. Rep. Univ. of Wales on Gen. Dental Council, 1964–82; Mem. Bd of Faculty of Dental Surgery, RCS England, 1964–72 (Vice-Dean 1971–72); Chm., Dental Educn Adv. Council, GB, 1975–78 (Mem. 1962–82); Sec.-Gen., Assoc. for Dental Educn in Europe, 1982–84. Adviser in Dental Surgery to Welsh Hosp. Bd, 1962–74; Civilian Consultant in Dental Surgery to RN, 1967–. Hon. Adviser, Editorial Bd, British Jl of Dermatology, 1967–76. Mem., S Glamorgan AHA, 1974–76. Mem. Bd of Governors: United Cardiff Hosps, 1965–71; HMC (Cardiff) Univ. Hosp. of Wales, 1971–74. Vice-Provost, Welsh Nat. Sch. of Medicine, 1974–76. Examr in Dental Surgery and Oral Pathology, Liverpool, Manchester and London Univs; Examr for Primary Fellowship in Dental Surgery, RCS, 1967–73. Hon. Mem., Pierre Fauchard Acad., 1967. Charles Tomes Lectr, RCS, 1963; Guest Lectr, Students' Vis. Lectrs Trust Fund, Witwatersrand Univ., 1967; Vis. Prof., Univ. of Sydney Dental Sch., 1986–87. Pres., Section of Odontology, RSocMed, 1975 (Hon. Mem., 1990); Founder Pres., British Soc. for Oral Medicine, 1981. Hon. Coll. Fellow, Univ. of Wales Coll. of Medicine, 1990. Cartwright Prize and Medal, RCS, 1955; Chesterfield Prize and Medal, St John's Hosp. for Diseases of Skin, 1955. *Publications:* (jtly) Oral Histopathology, 1959, 2nd edn 1970; scientific contribs to medical and dental jls. *Recreations:* various. *Address:* 21 Redwood Court, Station Road, Llanishen, Cardiff CF14 5UX. *T:* (029) 2074 7167.

COOKE, Colin Ivor; non-executive Chairman, Fenner PLC, since 1993; *b* 17 Dec. 1939; *m* 1983, Sheila Handley; four *s* one *d*. *Educ:* Cardiff High Sch.; Advanced Coll. of Technology, Newport (HND Metallurgy). GKN, 1956–63; Hepworth Ceramic, 1963–71; RTZ, 1971–72; Du-Port, 1972–80, Main Bd Dir, 1982–86; Dir, WDA, 1987–89; Dir, 1989–98, Chm., 1991–98, Triplex Lloyd. Non-exec. Chm., Transtec plc, 1998–; Chm., Dynacast Internat., 1999–; non-executive Director: Ash & Lacy, 1987–97; British Dredging, 1990–93; Yorkshire Water, 1995–97. Chm., Tipton City Challenge, 1993–98. FIM 1996. Freeman, City of London, 1996; Liveryman, Founders' Co., 1996–. *Recreations:* golf, swimming, military history. *Clubs:* Wig and Pen; Royal Porthcawl Golf; Cardiff County.

COOKE, Cynthia Felicity Joan, CBE 1975; RRC 1969; Matron-in-Chief, Queen Alexandra's Royal Naval Nursing Service, 1973–76; *b* 11 June 1919; *d* of late Frank Alexander Cooke, MBE, DCM, and of Ethel May (*née* Buckle). *Educ:* Rosa Bassett Sch. for Girls; Victoria Hosp. for Children, Tite Street, Chelsea; RSCN, 1940; University Coll. Hosp., London, SRN, 1942; Univ. of London, Sister Tutor Diploma, 1949. Joined QARNNS, 1943; served in: Australia, 1944–45; Hong Kong, 1956–58; Malta, 1964–66. HMS: Collingwood, Gosling, Goldcrest; RN Hospitals: Chatham, Plymouth, Haslar. Principal Tutor, Royal Naval School of Nursing, 1967–70; Principal Matron, RN Hosp., Haslar, 1970–73. QHNS 1973–76. CStJ 1975. *Address:* The Banquet House, Kings Head Mews, The Pightle, Needham Market, Suffolk IP6 8AQ.

COOKE, David Arthur Lawrence; Director, Criminal Policy Group, Home Office, since 2000; *b* 11 March 1956; *s* of James Robert Cooke and Verity Cooke (*née* Brandrick); *m* 1984, Kathleen Joyce Collins, *qv*. *Educ:* University Coll., Oxford (BA 1st Cl. Hons Mod Hist.; MA). Home Office: admin trainee, 1977–81; Private Sec. to Patrick Mayhew, MP (Minister of State), 1981–82; Principal, Prisons, Drugs and Broadcasting Depts, 1982–89; G5, Broadcasting Dept, 1990; on loan to other govt depts, 1990–93; Dir, Asylum, and Immigration Service Enforcement, Home Office, 1994–97; G3, Constitution Secretariat, Cabinet Office, 1997; Dir, Central Inf. Technol. Unit, Cabinet Office, 1997–2000. *Recreations:* reading, music, sport, cooking. *Address:* Home Office, 50 Queen Anne's Gate, SW1H 9AT.

COOKE, David Charles; Partner, Pinsent Curtis Biddle (formerly Pinsent & Co., then Pinsent Curtis), solicitors, since 1969 (Senior Partner, 1986–94); *b* 22 March 1938; *s* of F. J. E. Cooke and Hilda Cooke. *Educ:* Bolton Sch.; Accrington Grammar Sch.; Manchester Univ. (LLB). Hall Brydon & Co., Manchester, 1961–64; King & Partridge, Madras, 1964–67; Asst Solicitor, Pinsent & Co., Birmingham, 1967. *Recreations:* classical music, fell walking, theatre, reading. *Address:* Pinsent Curtis Biddle, 3 Colmore Circus, Birmingham B4 6BH. *T:* (0121) 200 1050. *Club:* Oriental.

COOKE, Col Sir David (William Perceval), 12th Bt *cr* 1661; freelance consultant/researcher; *b* 28 April 1935; *s* of Sir Charles Arthur John Cooke, 11th Bt, and Diana (*d* 1989), *o d* of late Maj.-Gen. Sir Edward Maxwell Perceval, KCB, DSO; *S* father, 1978; *m* 1959, Margaret Frances, *o d* of Herbert Skinner, Knutsford, Cheshire; three *d*. *Educ:* Wellington College; RMA Sandhurst; Open Univ. (BA). FCIT; FIMgt; Associate, Internat. Inst. of Risk and Safety Management. Commissioned 4/7 Royal Dragoon Guards, 1955; served BAOR, 1955–58; transferred to RASC, 1958; served: BAOR, 1958–60; France, 1960–62; Far East, 1962–65; UK. Transferred to RCT on formation, 1965, and served UK, 1965–76, and BAOR, 1976–80; AQMG, MoD, 1980–82; Comdr, Transport and Movements, HQ British Forces, Hong Kong, 1982–84; Comdr, Transport and Movts, NW Dist, Western Dist and Wales, 1984–87; Col, Movements 1 (Army), MoD, 1987–90. Operational service: Brunei, 1962; Malay Peninsula, 1964–65; N Ireland, 1971–72. Attended Staff Coll., Camberley, 1968 and Advanced Transport Course, 1973–74. Col 1984. Dir of Finance and Resources, Bradford City Technol. Coll., 1990–92. Silver Jubilee Medal, 1977. *Recreations:* fishing, ornithology, military history. *Heir: cousin* Edmund Harry Cooke-Yarborough [*b* 25 Dec. 1918; *m* 1952, Anthea Katharine, *er d* of J. A. Dixon; one *s* one *d*]. *Address:* c/o HSBC, Knutsford, Cheshire WA16 6BZ.

COOKE, George Venables, CBE 1978; *b* 8 Sept. 1918; *s* of William Geoffrey Cooke and Constance Eva (*née* Venables); *m* 1941, Doreen (*née* Cooke); one *s* two *d*. *Educ:* Sandbach Sch., Cheshire; Lincoln Coll., Oxford, 1936–39 and 1946. MA, DipEd (Oxon). Served Army, 1939–46 (Major). Teacher, Manchester Grammar Sch., 1947–51; Professional Asst (Educn), W Riding of Yorkshire CC, 1951–53; Asst Dir of Educn, Liverpool, 1953–58; Dep. Dir of Educn, Sheffield, 1958–64; Dir of Educn, Lindsey (Lincs) CC, 1965–74; County Educn Officer, Lincolnshire CC, 1974–78; Gen. Sec., Soc. of Education Officers, 1978–84. Chm., Secretary of State's Adv. Cttee on Handicapped Children, 1973–74; Vice-Chm., Nat. Cttee of Enquiry into Special Educn (Warnock Cttee), 1974–78; Member: Jt Adv. Cttee on Agricultural Educn (Hudson Cttee), 1971–74; Parole Bd, 1984–87. Pres., Soc. of Educn Officers, 1975–76; Chm., County Educn Officers' Soc., 1976–77. Chm., Lincs and Humberside Arts, 1987–92. Hon. LLD Hull, 1991. *Address:* 4 Cathedral View Court, Cabourne Avenue, Lincoln LN2 2GF. *T:* (01522) 522667. *Club:* Royal Over-Seas League.

COOKE, Gilbert Andrew, FCA; Chairman and Chief Executive, C. T. Bowring & Co. Ltd, 1982–88; Director, Marsh & McLennan Companies Inc., 1980–88; *b* 7 March 1923; *s* of Gilbert N. Cooke and Laurie Cooke; *m* 1949, Katherine Margaret Mary McGovern; one *s* one *d*. *Educ:* Bournemouth Sch. FCA 1950. Sen. Clerk, chartered accountants, 1950–54; Bowmaker Ltd: Chief Accountant, 1955; Dir, 1968; Man. Dir, 1968; Dep. Chm. and Chief Exec., 1972; C. T. Bowring & Co. Ltd: Dir, 1969; Gp Man. Dir, 1976–82. Chm., Bowring UK, 1984–88. Chm., Finance Houses Assoc., 1972–74. *Recreations:* music, reading. *Address:* Kilmarth, 66 Onslow Road, Burwood Park, Walton-on-Thames, Surrey KT12 5AY. *T:* (01932) 240451.

COOKE, Gregory Alan; Senior Partner, Weatherall Green & Smith, since 1998; *b* 28 April 1949; *m* Elizabeth; one *s* two *d*. *Educ:* Trent Coll. (BSc). ARICS. Henley Sch. of Business Studies. Capital & Counties Property Co. Ltd, 1972–73; with Weatherall Green & Smith, 1973–. *Recreations:* ski-ing, sailing, tennis. *Address:* Weatherall Green & Smith, Norfolk House, 31 St James's Square, SW1Y 4JR. *Club:* Royal Automobile.

COOKE, Helen Jane; Director of Therapy, Bristol Cancer Help Centre, since 2000; *b* 20 Sept. 1963; *d* of Dr Michael Cooke and Mary Cooke (now Brash). *Educ:* Orme Girls' Sch., Newcastle, Staffs; St Bartholomew's Hosp., London (RGN Cert.); Univ. of Exeter (MA Complementary Health Studies 2001). Staff Nurse, St Bartholomew's Hosp., London, 1987; Hd of Nursing, Promis Recovery Centre, 1988-90; Sister, Abbotsleigh Nursing Home, 1990-92; Therapy Manager, then Patient Services Manager, Bristol Cancer Help Centre, 1992-2000. *Publication:* contrib. Complementary Therapies in Nursing and Midwifery jl. *Recreations:* stained glass design, art, travel, walking, laughing. *Address:* Bristol

Cancer Help Centre, Grove House, Cornwallis Grove, Clifton, Bristol BS8 4PG. *T:* (0117) 980 9514.

COOKE, Sir Howard (Felix Hanlan), ON 1991; GCMG 1991; GCVO 1994; CD 1978; Governor-General of Jamaica, since 1991; *b* 13 Nov. 1915; *s* of David Brown Cooke and Mary Jane Minto; *m* 1939, Ivy Sylvia Lucille Tai; two *s* one *d.* Teacher, Mico Trng Coll., 1936–38; Headmaster, Belle Castle All-Age Sch., 1939–50; Teacher: Port Antonio Upper Sch., 1951; Montego Bay Boys' Sch., 1952–58; Br. Manager, Standard Life Insce Co., 1960–71; Unit Manager, Jamaica Mutual Life Assce Co., 1971–81; Br. Manager, Alico Jamaica, 1982–91. Member: WI Federal Parlt, 1958–62; Senate, 1962–67; House of Representatives, 1967–80; Govt Minister, 1972–80. Sen. Elder, United Church of Jamaica and Grand Cayman; lay pastor and former Chm., Cornwall Council of Churches. Mem., Ancient and Accepted Order of Masons. Special Plaque for Distinguished Service, CPA, 1980. *Recreations:* cricket, football, gardening, reading. *Address:* (office) King's House, Hope Road, Kingston 6, Jamaica, WI. *T:* 9276143, 9276426.

COOKE, Jean Esme Oregon, RA 1972 (ARA 1965); (professional name Jean E. Cooke); Lecturer in Painting, Royal College of Art, 1964–74; *b* 18 Feb. 1927; *d* of Arthur Oregon Cooke, Grocer, and of Dorothy Emily Cooke (*née* Cranefield); *m* 1953, John Randall Bratby, RA (marr. diss., he *d* 1992); three *s* one *d. Educ:* Blackheath High Sch.; Central Sch. of Arts and Crafts, Camberwell; City and Guilds; Goldsmiths' Coll. Sch. of Art; Royal Coll. of Art. NDD in Sculpture, 1949. Pottery Workshop, 1950–53; Tutor, Summer Sch., Swiss Alps, 1992–94. Member: Council, Royal Acad., 1983–85 and 1992–94 (Sen. Hanger, 1993, 1994); Academic Bd, Blackheath Sch. of Art, 1986–88; Governor: Central Sch. of Art and Design, 1984–86; Tertiary Educn Bd, Greenwich, 1984–86. Life Pres., Friends of Woodlands Art Gall., Blackheath, 1990. Purchase of self-portrait, 1969, and portrait of John Bratby (called Lilly, Lilly on the Brow), 1972, by Chantry Bequest; portraits: Dr Egon Wellesz and Dr Walter Oakshott for Lincoln Coll., Oxford; Mrs Bennett, Principal, for St Hilda's Coll., Oxford, 1976; Peter Carlisle, 1985–86; Clare Chalmers and Jane Lee, 1987–88; John Petty, 1989. Started Homage to Birling Gap (large painting), 1985. Television film: Portrait of John Bratby, BBC, 1978. *One-man shows:* Establishment Club, 1963; Leicester Gall., 1964; Bear Lane Gall., Oxford, 1965; Arun Art Centre, Arundel; Ashgate Gall., Farnham; Moyan Gall., Manchester; Bladon Gall., Hampshire, 1966; Lane Gall., Bradford, 1967; Gallery 66, Blackheath, 1967; Motley Gall., Lewisham, 1968; Phoenix, Suffolk, 1970; New Grafton Gall., 1971; Ansdell Gall., 1974; Woodlands Gall., Blackheath, 1976 and 1991; J. K. Taylor Gall., Cambridge, 1976; Garden Gall., Greenwich, 1983; Alpine Gall., 1986; Friends Room, RA, 1990; Bardolf Hall, Sussex, 1990, in aid of Birling Gap Safety Boat; Blackheath Concert Halls, 1990; Linton Court Gall., Settle, 1991; In the Looking Glass, touring, 1996–97; open studio for: Greenwich Festival, 1977–94; Blackheath High Sch. Art Fund, 1979; Bakehouse Gall., Blackheath, 1980; open studio in aid of: Royal Acad. Trust, 1982; Birling Gap Safety Boat, 1989. *Works exhibited:* annually, RA, 1956–; Furneaux Gall., 1968; Upper Grosvenor Gall., 1968; Ashgate Gall., 1973; Agnews, 1974; Gall. 10, Richmond Hill, 1974; Leonie Jonleigh Gall., 1976; Dulwich Coll. Picture Gall., 1976; British Painting 1952–77, Royal Acad., 1977; Business Art Galleries, 1978; New Ashgate Gall., 1979; Tate Gall., 1979; Grosvenor Street Gall., 1979, 1980; Norwich Gall., 1979, 1980; Imp. Coll. Gall., 1980; Patrick Seale Gall., Belgravia, 1981; WEA, 1987; Foss Gall. Gp, 1987, 1988, 1990; RCA, 1988; Hurlingham Gall., 1990; Patterson Gall., 1990, 1991, 1992, 1993, 1994; King Street Gall., 1992; Thompson's Gall., 1992; Sacker Galls, RA, 1993; Boston Coll., Lincoln, 1997; Woodlands Gall., 1997; Grimsby Art Centre, 1997; Highgate Fine Arts, 1997; Blackfriars Art Centre, 1997; A. T. Kearney, 1998. *Publications:* Contemporary British Artists; The Artist, 1980; The Artist's Garden, 1989; Seeing Ourselves: women's self-portraits, 1998. *Recreations:* ungardening, talking, shouting, walking along the beach. *Address:* 7 Hardy Road, Blackheath, SE3 7NS. *T:* (020) 8858 6288.

COOKE, Hon. Sir Jeremy Lionel, Kt 2001; **Hon. Mr Justice Cooke;** a Judge of the High Court, Queen's Bench Division, since 2001; *b* 28 April 1949; *s* of Eric Edwin Cooke and Margaret Lilian Cooke; *m* 1972, Barbara Helen Willey; one *s* two *d. Educ:* Whitgift Sch., Croydon; St Edmund Hall, Oxford (Open Exhibn, 1967; MA Jurisprudence, 1st cl. Hons 1970; Rugby blue, 1968, 1969). Admitted Solicitor, 1973; with Coward Chance, 1973–76; called to the Bar, Lincoln's Inn, 1976, Bencher, 2001; QC 1990; an Asst Recorder, 1994–98; a Recorder, 1998–2001. Chm., Christian Youth and Schs Charitable Co. Ltd, 1996–. Mem. Council, LICC Ltd (formerly London Inst. for Contemporary Christianity), 1997–. *Address:* Royal Courts of Justice, Strand, WC2A 2LL. *Club:* National.

COOKE, John Arthur; Head of International Relations, Association of British Insurers, since 1997; *b* 13 April 1943; *er s* of late Dr Arthur Hafford Cooke, MBE and Ilse Cooke (*née* Sachs); *m* 1970, Tania Frances, 2nd *d* of A. C. Crichton; one *s* two *d. Educ:* Dragon Sch.; Magdalen Coll. Sch., Oxford; Univ. of Heidelberg; King's Coll., Cambridge (Exhibnr, Sen. Scholar, BA History 1964, MA 1968); LSE. Mem., Cambridge Univ. expedition to Seistan, 1966. Asst Principal, Board of Trade, 1966; Second, later First, Sec., UK Delegn to European Communities, 1969–73; DTI, 1973–76; Office of UK Perm. Rep. to European Communities, 1976–77; Dept of Trade, 1977–80 (at Inst. Internat. d'Administration Publique, Paris, 1979); Asst Sec., Dept of Trade, 1980–84; seconded to Morgan Grenfell & Co. as Asst Dir, 1984–85; Department of Trade and Industry, 1985–97: Under Sec., Overseas Trade Div. 2, 1987–89; Head of Central Unit, 1989–92; Dir, Deregulation Unit, 1990–92; Head of Internat. Trade Policy Div., 1992–96; Dir and Advr on Trade Policy, 1996–97; Leader, UK delegn to 9th UN Conf. on Trade and Develt, 1996; Chm., OECD Trade Cttee, 1996–97. Non-executive Director: RTZ Pillar Ltd, 1990–93; W Middx Univ. Hosp. NHS Trust, 1996–98; Bd Sec., ENO, 1996–. Trustee, St Luke's Community Trust, 1983–93 and 1996–2000 (Vice-Chm., 1991–93; Patron, 2000–); Member: Council, Marie Curie Cancer Care (formerly Marie Curie Meml Foundn), 1992–; Bd, Marie Curie Trading Ltd, 1999–. Mem. Editl Bd, Internat. Trade Law Reports, 1997–. *Publications:* articles and contribs to seminars, mainly on internat. trade in financial services. *Recreations:* reading, travelling, looking at buildings. *Address:* 29 The Avenue, Kew, Richmond, Surrey TW9 2AL. *T:* (020) 8940 6712, *Fax:* (020) 8332 7447; *e-mail:* john.cooke@abi.org.uk. *Clubs:* Oxford and Cambridge; Cambridge Union.

COOKE, Air Vice-Marshal John Nigel Carlyle, CB 1984; OBE 1954; Consultant Physician: Civil Aviation Authority, since 1985; King Edward VII Hospital, Midhurst, 1988–93; *b* 16 Jan. 1922; *s* of Air Marshal Sir Cyril Bertram Cooke, KCB, CBE and Phyllis Amelia Elizabeth Cooke; *m* 1958, Elizabeth Helena Murray Johnstone; two *s* one *d. Educ:* Felsted Sch.; St Mary's Hosp., Paddington (MD, BS(London)). FRCP, FRCPEd, MRCS, MFOM. House Physician, St Mary's, Paddington, 1945; RAF medical Br., 1945–85; Sen. Registrar, St George's, London, 1956–58; Consultant Physician, RAF, 1958–85; overseas service in Germany, Singapore, Aden; Prof. of Aviation Medicine, 1974–79; Dean of Air Force Medicine, 1979–83; Senior Consultant, RAF, 1983–85. UK Mem., Medical Adv. Bd, European Space Agency, 1978–84; Consultant to CAA, UK, 1972–; Consultant Advr to Sultan of Oman's Air Force, 1985–91. Chairman: Defence Med. Services Postgrad. Council, 1980–82; Ethics Cttee, RAF Inst. of Aviation Medicine, 1987–89; Pres., Assoc. of Aviation Med. Examiners, 1986–94. QHP 1979–85. *Publications:* articles on metabolic and aviation medicine subjects in numerous medical jls. *Recreations:* gliding, fly fishing. *Address:* 4 Lincoln Close, Stoke Mandeville, Bucks HP22 5YS. *Club:* Royal Air Force.

COOKE, Joseph; *see* Cooke, P. J. D.

COOKE, Kathleen Joyce; *see* Collins, K. J.

COOKE, Nicholas Orton; QC 1998; a Recorder, since 1997; *b* 1 July 1955; 2nd and *o* surv. *s* of B. O. Cooke and V. Cooke; *m* 1979, Jean Ann Tucker; two *d. Educ:* King Edward's Sch., Birmingham; UC Wales, Aberystwyth (Sweet and Maxwell Prize; LLB 1st Cl. Hons 1976). Called to the Bar, Middle Temple, 1977 (Blackstone Entrance Exhibn 1976); in practice at the Bar, 1978–; an Asst Recorder, 1994–97; Wales and Chester Circuit. Dep. Pres., Mental Health Review Tribunal, Wales, 1999–. *Recreations:* hockey, theatre. *Address:* 9 Park Place, Cardiff CF1 3DP. *T:* (029) 2038 2731.

COOKE, (Patrick) Joseph (Dominic), FIMC; Vice-Chairman, Daily Telegraph, 1994–96 (Managing Director, 1987–94); *s* of Patrick Cooke and Mary (*née* Naughton); *m* 1960, Margaret Mary Brown; two *s* four *d. Educ:* St Joseph's Coll.; University Coll., Galway (BE). CEng, MICE, MIMechE; FIMC 1968; AIIRA. United Steel Cos, 1952–54; Workington Iron & Steel Co., 1954–61; Urwick, Orr and Partners Ltd, 1961–73: Sen. Partner, 1967; Principal Partner, 1970; founded Cooke Management Consultants Ltd, 1973; non-exec. Dir, EMAP plc, 1984–96; Consultant, Daily Telegraph, 1985–87; Non-Executive Director: IFRA, 1990–94 (Senator, 1994–); Hollinger, 1992–94. Sandford Smith Award, Inst. Management Consultants, 1967. *Recreations:* golf, gardening. *Address:* Apartment 305, Bâtiment les Terrasses, Parc Saint Roman, 7 Avenue de Saint Roman, MC 98000, Monaco.

COOKE, Peter; *see* Cooke, W. P.

COOKE, Randle Henry, LVO 1971; Chairman, Randle Cooke and Associates, Recruitment Consultants, since 1992 (Managing Director, 1987–92); *b* 26 April 1930; *o s* of late Col H. R. V. Cooke, Dalicote Hall, Bridgnorth, Salop and Mrs E. F. K. Cooke, Brodawel, Tremeirchion, N Wales; *m* 1961, Clare, *d* of late C. J. M. Bennett, CBE; one *s* one *d. Educ:* Heatherdown, Ascot; Eton College. 2nd Lieut, 8th King's Royal Irish Hussars, 1949; served Korea, 1950–53 with Regt and USAF (POW); ADC to GOC 7th Armoured Div., 1955; Regimental Adjt, 1957; Instructor, RMA Sandhurst, 1960; Sqdn Comdr, The Queen's Royal Irish Hussars, Malaya, Borneo and Germany, 1963; GSO3 (SD), HQ 1st Div., 1965. Equerry to the Duke of Edinburgh, 1968–71; Private Sec. to Lord Mayor of London, 1972–74. Dir, Personnel and Administration, Alginate Industries plc, 1974–78; Managing Director: ARA International Ltd, 1984–86; Mervyn Hughes International Ltd, 1986–87. Dep. Dir, Treasurers' Dept, Cons. Central Office, 1992–95; Fund-Raising Dir, Royal Botanic Gdns, Kew, 1995–97. Freeman of City of London, 1971. *Recreations:* most things to do with water. *Address:* Chess House, Green Lane, Prestwood, Great Missenden, Bucks HP16 0QA. *T:* (01494) 862147, *Fax:* (01494) 863632. *Clubs:* Cavalry and Guards; Caterpillar.

COOKE, Prof. Richard William Ingram, MD; FRCP, FRCPH, FMedSci; Professor of Neonatal Medicine, University of Liverpool, 1988–90 and since 1998; *b* 23 May 1947; *s* of Edward Ingram Cooke and Pauline Ellen Ross Cooke (*née* Foster); *m* 1977, Theresa Elizabeth Reardon Garside; one *s* three *d. Educ:* Colfe's Sch.; Charing Cross Hosp. Med. Sch. (qual. 1971; MD 1979). DCH 1973; FRCP 1986; FRCPCH 1997. Research Fellow, then Lectr, Oxford Univ., 1976–78; Staff Paediatrician, Sophia Kinderziekenhaus, Rotterdam, 1978–79; University of Liverpool: Sen. Lectr in Child Health, 1980–83; Reader, 1983–87; Prof. of Paediatric Medicine, 1991–98. President: British Assoc. Perinatal Paediatrics, 1990–92; Neonatal Soc., 1997–2000; Vice-Pres., RCPCH, 1997– (Actg Pres., 1999–2000). Founder FMedSci 1998. *Publications:* (ed jtly) Chemical Trade Names and Synonyms, 1978; (jtly) The Very Immature Infant, 1989; (ed jtly) The Baby under 1000 grams, 1989; (ed jtly) Practical Perinatal Care, 1999; numerous articles and papers on neonatal medicine. *Recreations:* jazz, contemporary painting. *Address:* Neonatal Unit, Liverpool Women's Hospital, Liverpool L8 7SS. *T:* (0151) 702 4093; 11 Western Drive, Liverpool L19 0LX. *Clubs:* Ronnie Scott's; Twenty (Liverpool).

COOKE, Roger Arnold; His Honour Judge Roger Cooke; a Circuit Judge, since 1989; *b* 30 Nov. 1939; *s* of late Stanley Gordon and Frances Mabel Cooke; *m* 1970, Hilary Robertson; two *s* two *d. Educ:* Repton; Magdalen Coll., Oxford (BA 1961; MA 1966). Astbury Scholar, Middle Temple, 1962; called to the Bar, Middle Temple, 1962, *ad eund* Lincoln's Inn, 1967 (Bencher, 1994); in practice, Chancery Bar, 1963–89; Asst Recorder, 1982–87; Recorder, 1987–89; authorised to sit as a Judge of the High Court, Chancery Div., 1993, QBD, 1995. Sec., Chancery Bar Assoc., 1979–89; Member: Bar Disciplinary Tribunal, 1988–89; Inns of Court Advocacy Trng Cttee, 1995–; Advocacy Studies Bd, 1996–. Mem., Inst. of Conveyancers, 1983–; MRI 1962. *Recreations:* gardening, photography, history, old buildings, travel. *Address:* Central London County Court, 13/14 Park Crescent, W1N 4HT. *T:* (020) 7917 5000. *Club:* Athenæum.

COOKE, Roger Malcolm; Partner in charge, Administration, Arthur Andersen, 1995–98; *b* 12 March 1945; *s* of Sidney and Elsie Cooke; *m* 1968, Antoinette; one *s* one *d.* FCA, FTII. Qualified Chartered Accountant, 1968; Arthur Andersen & Co.: joined 1968, Tax Div.; Partner, 1976; Head, London Tax Div., 1979; area co-ordinator, tax practice, Europe, Middle East, Africa and India, 1989–93; Dep. Man. Partner, UK, and Area Co-Ordinator, Tax Europe, 1989–93; Man. Partner-Chief Financial Officer, Chicago, 1993–95. Hon. Treas., Wooden Spoon Soc. *Publication:* Establishing a Business in the United Kingdom, 1978. *Recreations:* playing tennis, travel, ski-ing, cricket, football, good food. *Address:* c/o 1 Surrey Street, WC2R 2PS. *Club:* Royal Berkshire Fitness and Racquets.

COOKE, Prof. Ronald Urwick, MSc, PhD, DSc; Vice-Chancellor, University of York, since 1993; *b* 1 Sept. 1941; *y s* of Ernest Cooke and Lillian (*née* Mount), Maidstone, Kent; *m* 1968, Barbara Anne, *d* of A. Baldwin; one *s* one *d. Educ:* Ashford Grammar Sch.; University College London, Univ. of London (BSc 1st Cl. Hons, MSc, PhD, DSc; Fellow, 1994). Lectr, UCL, 1961–75; Prof. of Geography, 1975–81, Dean of Science, 1978–80, and Vice-Principal, 1979–80, Bedford Coll., Univ. of London; Prof. and Hd of Dept of Geography, 1981–93, Dean of Arts, 1991–92, and Vice-Provost, 1991–93, UCL. Dir, UCL Press, 1990–95. Amer. Council of Learned Societies Fellow, UCLA, 1964–65 and 1973; Visiting Professor: UCLA, 1968; Univ. of Arizona, Tucson, 1970; Arizona State Univ., Tempe, 1988. Desert research in N and S America, N Africa and ME. Chm., Geomorphological Services Ltd, 1986–90. Member: US-UK Fulbright Commn, 1995–2000; HEFCE, 1996–. Chm., British Geomorphological Res. Group, 1979; Pres., RGS, 2000– (Mem. Council, 1980–83; Back Grant, 1977; Founder's Medal, 1994); Mem. Council, Inst. of British Geographers, 1973–75 (Pres., 1991–92). Hon. Sec., York Archaeological Trust, 1994–96; Trustee, Laurence Sterne Trust, 1994–; Elvington Air

Mus., 1999–. Patron, York Early Music Fest., 1995–. Mem., Co. of Merchant Adventurers of City of York. Fellow, RHBNC, 1993. *Publications:* (ed with J. H. Johnson) Trends in Geography, 1969; (with A. Warren) Geomorphology in Deserts, 1973; (with J. C. Doornkamp) Geomorphology in Environmental Management, 1974, 2nd edn 1990; (with R. W. Reeves) Arroyos and Environmental Change in the American Southwest, 1976; (contrib.) Geology, Geomorphology and Pedology of Bahrain, 1980; (contrib.) Urban Geomorphology in Drylands, 1982; Geomorphological Hazards in Los Angeles, 1984; (with A. Warren and A. S. Goudie) Desert Geomorphology, 1993; (with G. B. Gibbs) Crumbling Heritage?, 1993; contribs mainly on desert and applied geomorphology in prof. jls. *Address:* University of York, Heslington, York YO10 5DD. *T:* (01904) 432001. *Club:* Athenæum.

COOKE, Roy, MA; JP; Director of Coventry School Foundation, 1977–92, retired; *b* Manchester, 6 May 1930; *s* of Reginald Herbert Cooke and Alice Cooke; *m* 1957, Claire Marion Medlicott Woodward, *d* of Lt-Col C. S. Woodward, CBE, JP, DL and Irene Anne Woodward, Glamorgan; three *s*. *Educ:* Manchester Grammar Sch. (schol.); Trinity Coll., Oxford (schol.; BA 1951; MA 1955; DipEd). Army service, 1951–54; commnd RAEC; Staff Officer in Germany (Captain, actg Major). Assistant Master: Gillingham Grammar Sch., Kent, 1955–56; Woking Grammar Sch., Surrey, 1956–58; Manchester Grammar Sch., 1958–64; Head of For. Langs, Stockport Sch., 1964–68; Headmaster: Gravesend Sch. for Boys, 1968–74; King Henry VIII Sch., Coventry, 1974–77. JP Kent, 1972, W Midlands, 1976. *Recreations:* photography, travel, reading, music. *Address:* 10 Stivichall Croft, Coventry CV3 6GN.

COOKE, (William) Peter, CBE 1997; Advisor, PricewaterhouseCoopers (formerly Price Waterhouse), since 1997; *b* 1 Feb. 1932; *s* of late Douglas Edgar Cooke, MC and Florence May (*née* Mills); *m* 1957, Maureen Elizabeth (*d* 1999), *er d* of late Dr E. A. Haslam-Fox; two *s* two *d*. *Educ:* Royal Grammar Sch., High Wycombe; Kingswood Sch., Bath; Merton Coll., Oxford (MA; Hon. Fellow 1997). Entered Bank of England, 1955; Bank for Internat. Settlements, Basle, 1958–59; Personal Asst to Man. Dir, IMF, Washington, DC, 1961–65; Sec., City Panel on Takeovers and Mergers, 1968–69; First Dep. Chief Cashier, Bank of England, 1970–73; Adviser to Governors, 1973–76; Hd of Banking Supervision, 1976–85; Associate Dir, 1982–88; Chm., Price Waterhouse Regulatory Adv. Practice, 1989–96. Housing Corporation: Mem. Bd, 1988–97; Dep. Chm., 1994–97; Chm., 1997. Chairman: City EEC Cttee, 1973–80; Group of Ten Cttee on Banking Regulations and Supervisory Practices at BIS, Basle, 1977–88. Director: Safra Republic Holdings SA, 1989–99; FSA (UK), 1994–; Alexander & Alexander Services Inc., 1994–96; Bank of China Internat. Hldgs Ltd, 1997–98; Bank of China Internat. UK Ltd, 1998–; State Street Bank (Europe) Ltd, 1998–; HSBC Republic Holdings SA, 2000–01. Member: Nat. Cttee, English Churches Housing Group, 1977–94; Council, RIIA, 1992– (Dep. Chm., 1998–). Governor: Pangbourne Coll., 1982–; Kingswood Sch., 1991–. Pres., Merton Soc., 1995–98. *Recreations:* music, golf, travel. *Address:* (office) Southwark Towers, 32 London Bridge Street, SE1 9SY; (home) Bow Wood Barn, Bottom House Farm Lane, Chalfont St Giles, Bucks HP8 4EE. *Clubs:* Reform; Denham Golf.

COOKE-PRIEST, Rear Adm. Colin Herbert Dickinson, CB 1993; Chief Executive, The Trident Trust, 1994–99; a Gentleman Usher to the Queen, since 1994; *b* 17 March 1939; *s* of Dr William Hereward Dickinson Priest and Harriet Lesley Josephine Priest (*née* Cooke); *m* 1965, Susan Mary Diana Hobler; two *s* two *d*. *Educ:* St Piran's, Maidenhead; Marlborough Coll.; BRNC, Dartmouth. Entered RN, 1957; Lieut, 1960; exchange service with RAN, 1968–70; commanded: HMS Plymouth, 1975–76; HMS Berwick, 1976; Airwarfare Directorate, Naval Staff, MoD, 1977–79; Naval Asst to C-in-C Fleet, 1979–81; Asst Dir, Naval Air Warfare, 1981–82; CO, HMS Boxer, 1983–85; Dir, Maritime Tactical Sch., 1985–87; CO, HMS Brilliant and Capt. Second Frigate Sqn, 1987–89; Dep. Asst Chief of Staff (Ops) to Supreme Allied Comdr Europe, 1989–90; Flag Officer, Naval Aviation, 1990–93. Chm., FAA Officers' Assoc., 1998–. FRAeS 1992. Freeman, City of London, 1985; Hon. Liveryman, Coachmakers' and Coachharness Makers' Co., 1985; Liveryman, GAPAN, 1999–. *Address:* Northwood Farmhouse, Northwood Lane, Hayling Island, Hants PO11 0LR. *Clubs:* Army and Navy, Naval and Military, Royal Navy of 1765 and 1785.

COOKSEY, Sir David (James Scott), Kt 1993; Managing Director, since 1981, and Chairman, since 1987, Advent Venture Partners; a Director, Bank of England, since 1994 (Senior Director, since 2001); *b* 14 May 1940; *s* of Dr Frank S. Cooksey, CBE, and Muriel M. Cooksey; *m* 1973, Janet Clouston Bewley Wardell-Yerburgh (*see* J. C. B. Cooksey); one *s* one *d*, and one step *d*. *Educ:* Westminster Sch.; St Edmund Hall, Oxford Univ. (MA; Hon. Fellow 1995). Dir of Manufacturing, Formica International, 1969–71; Man. Dir, Intercobra Ltd, 1971–80; Director: Advent International Corp., 1985–90; Electra Risk Capital, 1981–90; Bespak plc, 1993– (Chm., 1995–); William Baird plc, 1995– (Dep. Chm., 1997–98; Chm., 1999–); Advent VCT plc, 1996–; Advent 2 VCT plc, 1998–. Chairman: Audit Commn, 1986–95; Local Govt Commn for England, 1995–96. Member: Council, CBI, 1976–88; Scottish Economic Council, 1980–87; Council, British Venture Capital Assoc., 1983–89 (Chm., 1983–84); Innovation Adv. Bd, DTI, 1988–93. Mem. Council, Southampton Univ., 1993–. Trustee: CORDA, 1993–99; Mary Rose Trust, 1994–2001 (Chm., 1996–2001); Gov., Wellcome Trust, 1995–99. Hon. Fellow, Univ. of Wales, Cardiff, 1998. Hon. DBA Kingston, 1996. *Recreations:* sailing, music, theatre. *Address:* (office) 25 Buckingham Gate, SW1E 6LD. *T:* (020) 7630 9811. *Clubs:* Boodle's, Royal Thames Yacht; Royal Yacht Squadron.

COOKSEY, Janet Clouston Bewley, (Poppy), (Lady Cooksey); DL; PhD; art historian and picture restorer, since 1978; *b* 15 Feb. 1940; *d* of late Dr Ian Aysgarth Bewley Cathie and Dr Marian Josephine Cunning; *m* 1966, Hugh Arthur Wardell-Yerburgh (*d* 1970); one *d*; *m* 1973, Sir David Cooksey, *qv*; one *s* one *d*. *Educ:* Cheltenham Ladies' Coll.; Univ. of London (BSc ext.); Univ. of St Andrews (PhD Fine Arts). Amateur fencer, 1956–72, 1998–: Jun. Schs Champion, 1954 and 1955; Sen. Schs and under-20 Champion, 1956; British Ladies Foil Champion, 1965, 1967 and 1969–72; winner: De Beaumont International, 1967, 1971 and 1972; Desprez Cup, 1964–67, 1969 and 1972; Jubilee Bowl, 1964–67, 1970–72; double gold medallist, Commonwealth Games, 1966 and 1970; repr. GB in Olympic fencing teams, 1964, 1968, 1972 and in World Championships, 1963–72; veteran competitions include: British Veteran (over 50) foil champion, 1998; double gold medallist (foil individual and team) and double gold medallist (epée individual and team), Veteran Commonwealth Games, Johannesburg, 1999; double gold medallist (foil and epée), Veteran World Championships, Budapest, 2000. Lectr, extra-mural studies, Univ. of St Andrews, 1975–78, and Dir, Alexander Nasmyth exhibn, 1979; Dir, Special Projects, Univ. of Southampton, 1993–96. Mem., Bd of Trustees, Royal Armouries, 1993– (Mem., Design Cttee, 1994–). Chairman: RNLI Crew Training Appeal, 1996–; Countess Mountbatten Hospice Appeal, 1996–; Sir Arthur Hillier Gardens and Arboretum Appeal, 1997–99; Gift of Sight Appeal, Southampton Gen. Hosp., 1998–; Area Chm., Children's Hospice Appeal, 1994–96. Member: Corporate Develt Bd, NSPCC, 1997–; Bd Trustees, Mental Health Foundn, 1997–; Nat. Appeal Bd, Marie Curie Cancer Care, 1997–. FRSA 1986. DL Hants, 1998. *Publications:* The Pleasure of Antiques, 1973; Alexander Nasmyth 1758–1840 (exhibn catalogue), 1979; Alexander Nasmyth: a man of the Scottish Renaissance, 1991; (contrib.) The Dictionary of Art, 1996. *Recreations:* entertaining, reading, gardens, the arts, travel, tennis, sailing, fencing. *Address:* c/o Advent Ltd, 25 Buckingham Gate, SW1E 6LD. *T:* (020) 7630 9811, *Fax:* (020) 7828 1474. *Clubs:* Queen's; Royal Southern Yacht; Salle Paul, London Thames Fencing.

COOKSON, Lt-Col Michael John Blencowe, OBE 1986; TD 1969; Vice Lord-Lieutenant of Northumberland, since 1987; land owner, agriculturist; *b* 13 Oct. 1927; *s* of late Col John Charles Blencowe Cookson, DSO, TD, DL; *m* 1957, Rosemary Elizabeth, *d* of David Aubrey Haggie; one *s* three *d*. *Educ:* Eton; Cirencester Agricl Coll., 1951–52. Served with: E African Forces, Kenya, 1947–48; Northumberland Hussars (TA), 1952–69; Queen's Own Yeomanry, 1969–72; Chm., Northumberland Hussars (TA) Regtl Assoc., 1977–87. Hon. Col, Northumberland Hussars Sqn QOY, 1988–92. Chm., Co. Cttee, Northumberland Assoc. Boys' Clubs, 1974–86 (Mem., 1964–73). Chm., Northumberland Queen's Silver Jubilee Appeal, 1978. High Sheriff, 1976, DL 1983, Northumberland. *Recreations:* hunting (Joint Master: Haydon Foxhounds, 1955–57; Morpeth Foxhounds, 1960–64, 1971–95), gardening. *Address:* Meldon Park, Morpeth, Northumberland NE61 3SW. *T:* (01670) 772661. *Club:* Northern Counties (Newcastle upon Tyne).

COOKSON, Prof. Richard Clive, MA, PhD; FRS 1968, FRSC; Research Professor of Chemistry in the University of Southampton, 1983–85, Emeritus Professor, since 1985 (Professor of Chemistry, 1957–83); *b* 27 Aug. 1922; *s* of late Clive Cookson; *m* 1948, Ellen Fawaz; two *s*. *Educ:* Harrow Sch.; Trinity Coll., Cambridge. BA 1944; MA, PhD Cantab 1947. Research Fellow, Harvard Univ., 1948; Research Div. of Glaxo Laboratories Ltd, 1949–51; Lectr, Birkbeck Coll., London Univ., 1951–57. *Publications:* papers, mainly in Jl Chem. Soc. *Address:* Northfield House, Coombe Bissett, Salisbury, Wilts SP5 4JZ.

COOKSON, Thomas Richard, MA; Principal, British School in Colombo, since 2002; *b* 7 July 1942; *s* of Samuel Harold Cookson, MD, FRCP and Elizabeth Mary Cookson; *m* 1972, Carol Hayley; three *d*. *Educ:* Winchester Coll.; Balliol Coll., Oxford (MA Eng.Lit.). Assistant Master: Winchester, 1964–65; Hopkins Grammar Sch., New Haven, USA, 1965–67; Winchester, 1967–72; Manchester Grammar Sch., 1972–74; Head of English, Winchester, 1974–83, Housemaster, 1983–90; Headmaster: King Edward VI Sch., Southampton, 1990–96; Sevenoaks School, 1996–2002. *Publications:* John Keats, 1972; Bernard Shaw, 1972. *Recreation:* golf. *Address:* British School in Colombo, 883/18 Morris Rajapakse Mawatha, Etul Kotte, Kotte, Sri Lanka.

COOMBE, His Honour Gerald Hugh; a Circuit Judge, 1986–98; *b* 16 Dec. 1925; *s* of William Stafford Coombe and Mabel Florence Coombe; *m* 1957, Zoë Margaret Richards; one *s* one *d*. *Educ:* Alleyn's School, Dulwich; Hele's School, Exeter; Exeter College, Oxford. MA 1950. RAF (Navigator), 1944–48; Solicitor, 1953; Partner, Whitehead Monckton, Maidstone, 1956–86; HM Coroner, Maidstone, 1962–86; a Recorder, 1983–86. *Club:* Royal Air Force.

COOMBE, Michael Ambrose Rew; His Honour Judge Coombe; a Circuit Judge, since 1985, at Central Criminal Court, since 1986; *b* 17 June 1930; *s* of late John Rew Coombe and Phyllis Mary Coombe; *m* 1961, Elizabeth Anne Hull (*d* 1998); two *s* one *d* (and one *s* decd). *Educ:* Berkhamsted; New Coll., Oxford, MA (Eng. Lang. and Lit.). Called to Bar, Middle Temple, 1957 (Harmsworth Scholar), Bencher, 1984; Autumn Reader, 2001. 2nd Prosecuting Counsel to the Inland Revenue at Central Criminal Court and 5 Courts of London Sessions, 1971; 2nd Counsel to the Crown at Inner London Sessions, Sept. 1971; 1st Counsel to the Crown at Inner London Crown Court, 1974; 4th Junior Treasury Counsel at Central Criminal Court, 1974, 2nd Jun. Treasury Counsel, 1975, 1st Jun. Treasury Counsel, 1977; Recorder of the Crown Court, 1976–85; Sen. Prosecuting Counsel to the Crown, CCC, 1978–85. Freeman, City of London, 1986. *Recreations:* theatre, antiquity, art and architecture, printing. *Address:* Central Criminal Court, EC4M 7EH.

COOMBES, Charles; *see* Coombes, R. C. D. S.

COOMBES, Keva Christopher; formerly with R. M. Broudie & Co., solicitors; *b* 23 Dec. 1949; *s* of Arthur Edward Coombes and Beatrice Claire Coombes; *m* 1970, Kathy Gannon; two *s* one *d*. *Educ:* Chatham House Grammar Sch.; Univ. of East Anglia (BA). Admitted Solicitor, 1977; Consultant, David Phillips Harris & Whalley, 1986. Member: Liverpool CC, 1976–80, 1986–92 (Leader, 1987–90); Merseyside CC, 1981–86 (Leader, 1982–86). Contested (Lab) Hyndburn, 1987. *Address:* c/o R. M. Broudie & Co., 1–3 Sir Thomas Street, Liverpool L1 8BW. *T:* (0151) 227 1429.

COOMBES, Prof. (Raoul) Charles (Dalmedo Stuart), MD; PhD; FRCP; Professor of Medical Oncology and Head of Department of Cancer Medicine, Imperial College School of Medicine, Hammersmith Hospital, since 1997; Director of Cancer Services, Hammersmith Hospitals NHS Trust, since 1995; *b* 20 April 1949; *s* of Raoul Coombes and Doreen Coombes; *m* 1984, Caroline Sarah Oakes; two *s* two *d*. *Educ:* Douai Sch.; St George's Hosp. Med. Sch. (MB BS); Inst. of Cancer Res., London (PhD 1978; MD 1981). MRCP 1973, FRCP 1990. MRC Clinical Res. Fellow, 1974–77; Sen. Registrar, 1977–80, Hon. Consultant, 1980–83, Royal Marsden Hosp.; Sen. Clinical Scientist, Ludwig Inst. for Cancer Res., 1980–83; Consultant Physician, St George's Hosp., 1983–90; Prof. and Hd of Dept of Med. Oncology, 1990–97, Dean of Res., 1993–97, Charing Cross and Westminster Med. Sch. Civilian Consultant, RAF, 1993–. *Publications:* Breast Cancer Management, 1981; The New Endocrinology of Cancer, 1987; New Targets in Cancer Therapy, 1994; numerous papers and articles in professional jls. *Recreations:* painting, walking. *Address:* 13 Dorlcote Road, SW18 3RT.

COOMBS, Anthony Michael Vincent; Managing Director, S & U plc, since 1998; Director, Grevayne Properties Ltd, since 1972; Chairman, Businessesforsale.com plc, since 2000; *b* 18 Nov. 1952; *s* of Clifford Keith Coombs and Celia Mary Gostling (*née* Vincent); *m* 1984, Andrea Caroline (*née* Pritchard); one *s*. *Educ:* Bilton Grange Sch.; Charterhouse; Worcester Coll., Oxford (MA). Birmingham City Council: Mem., 1978–88: Deputy Chairman: Educn Cttee, 1982–84; Social Services Cttee, 1982–84; Cons. spokesman on educn, Birmingham MDC, 1984–86. MP (C) Wyre Forest, 1987–97; contested (C) same seat, 1997. PPS to Rt Hon. David Mellor, MP, 1989–92, to Rt Hon. Gillian Shephard, MP, 1995–96; an Asst Govt Whip, 1996–97. Vice-Chairman: Cons. Back-Bench Educn Cttee, 1993–97 (Sec., 1987–93); Cons Parly Educn Cttee, 1993–97; All Party Parly Sports Cttee, 1993–97; Parly Human Rights Gp, 1993–97 (Sec., 1987–93); Parly Social Scis Gp, 1994–97; Sec., Cons. Parly Finance Cttee, 1994–96. Mem., Exec. Cttee, Conservative Team 1000, 1997–. Dir, Company Sales Ltd, 1994–. Member: Bd, Develt Cttee, Worcester Coll., Oxford, 1996–98; Bd, Birmingham Royal Ballet Develt Trust, 1998–. Dir, Schools Outreach, 1997–. Pres., Wyre Forest "Solidarity" Campaign, 1987–97; Mem., One Nation Gp. Vice-Chm., Friends of Cyprus, 1992–97. Chm. of Governors, Perry Common Sch., Birmingham, 1978–93; Governor: King Edward Foundn, 1982–88; Birmingham Coll. of Tourism, 1982–88; Ind. Primary and Secondary Educn Trust, 1997–. Trustee, Nat. Inst. for Conductive Educn, 2001–. *Publications:* Bow Group papers, numerous articles in newspapers and jls. *Recreations:* golf, tennis, occasional football, music, theatre, ballet. *Address:* 18 Cheyne Walk, SW3 5RA. *Clubs:* Royal Automobile, Annabel's.

COOMBS, Derek Michael; *b* 12 Aug. 1937; *m* 1986, Jennifer Lonsdale; two *s*, and one *s* one *d* by previous marriage. *Educ:* Rydal Prep. Sch.; Bromsgrove. Chm., S & U plc, 1976–; Dir, Metalrax Group plc, 1975–; Chm., Prospect Publishing Ltd, 1995–. Political journalist. MP (C) Yardley, 1970–Feb. 1974. Successfully introduced unsupported Private Member's Bill for relaxation of Earnings Rule, 1972, establishing parly record for a measure of its kind; specialist on economic affairs. Lectured on foreign affairs at Cons. weekend confs. Active pro-European. Governor, Royal Hosp. and Home for Incurables. *Publications:* numerous articles on home, economic and European affairs. *Recreations:* friends, reading, tennis, skiing. *Address:* Cheyne Row, SW3. *T:* (020) 7352 6709.

COOMBS, Douglas Stafford, PhD; Controller, Books Division, British Council, 1980–83, retired; *b* 23 Aug. 1924; *s* of Alexander John Coombs and Rosina May (*née* Stafford); *m* 1950, Valerie Nyman; one *s* three *d*. *Educ:* Royal Liberty Sch., Romford; University College of Southampton; University College London (BA Hons, PhD). Served Royal Air Force, 1943–47. Lecturer in History, University College of the Gold Coast (subseq. Univ. of Ghana), 1952–60; British Council, 1960–: Nigeria, 1960–62; Overseas Student Centre, London, 1962–67; Bombay, 1967–73; Representative: Zambia, 1973–76; Yugoslavia, 1976–79; Visiting Fellow, Postgrad. School of Librarianship and Information Science, Univ. of Sheffield, 1979–80. Consultant, Byways and Bridleways Trust, 1984–; Chm., Wootton Rivers Village Soc., 1985–88. Election Agent, Devizes CLP, 1996–97. Jt Editor, Rights of Way Law Review, 1998–2001. *Publications:* The Conduct of the Dutch, 1958; The Gold Coast, Britain and The Netherlands, 1963; Spreading the Word: the library work of the British Council, 1988; articles in historical jls. *Recreations:* travel, walking, watching cricket. *Address:* 33 Whiteledges, Ealing, W13 8JB. *T:* (020) 8998 6311.

COOMBS, Kay; HM Diplomatic Service; *b* 8 July 1945; *d* of late William Tom Coombs and Beatrice Mabel Coombs (*née* Angel). *Educ:* Petersfield High Sch.; Aldershot High Sch.; Univ. of Newcastle upon Tyne (BA Hons). Joined FCO, 1967; Bonn, 1971–73; Latin American floater, 1974–75; Zagreb, 1976–79; FCO, 1979–82; La Paz, 1982–86; Rome, 1987–91; FCO, 1991–95; Beijing, 1995–98; Ambassador to Mongolia, 1999–2001. *Recreations:* listening to classical music, reading, flora, cooking, languages, enjoying the arts generally. *Address:* c/o Foreign and Commonwealth Office, King Charles Street, SW1A 2AH.

COOMBS, Ven. Peter Bertram; Archdeacon of Reigate, 1988–95, now Emeritus; *b* 30 Nov. 1928; *s* of Bertram Robert and Margaret Ann Coombs; *m* 1953, Catherine Ann (*née* Buckwell); one *s* one *d*. *Educ:* Reading Sch.; Bristol Univ. (MA 1960); Clifton Theological Coll. Curate, Christ Church, Beckenham, 1960–64; Rector, St Nicholas, Nottingham, 1964–68; Vicar, Christ Church, New Malden, 1968–75; Rural Dean of Kingston upon Thames, 1970–75; Archdeacon of Wandsworth, 1975–88. *Recreations:* walking, sketching. *Address:* 92 Locks Heath Park Road, Locks Heath, Southampton SO31 6LZ. *T:* (01489) 577288.

COOMBS, Prof. Robert Royston Amos, ScD; FRS 1965; FRCPath 1969; Quick Professor in Immunology, University of Cambridge, 1966–88, now Emeritus; Fellow of Corpus Christi College, since 1962; *b* 9 Jan. 1921; *s* of Charles Royston Amos and Edris Owen Amos (formerly Coombs); *m* 1952, Anne Marion Blomfield; one *s* one *d*. *Educ:* Diocesan Coll., Cape Town; Edinburgh and Cambridge Univs. BSc, MRCVS Edinburgh 1943; PhD Cambridge 1947. Stringer Fellow, King's Coll., Cambridge, 1947–56; Asst Director of Research, Dept of Pathology, University of Cambridge, 1948; Reader in Immunology, University of Cambridge, 1963–66. Foreign Hon. Mem., Royal Belgium Acad. of Medicine, 1991. Hon. FRCP 1973; Hon. Fellow, Amer. Coll. of Allergists, 1979; Hon. FRSocMed 1992; Hon. Member: Amer. Assoc. of Immunologists, 1973–; British Blood Transfusion Soc., 1984–; British Soc. for Immunology, 1988–; British Soc. Allergy and Clin. Immunology, 1988–; Pathol. Soc. of GB and Ire., 1990–; British Soc. Haematology, 1993–. Hon. MD Linköping Univ. 1973; Hon. dr med. vet. Copenhagen, 1979; Hon. DSc: Guelph, 1981; Edinburgh, 1984. Landsteiner Award, Amer. Assoc. of Blood Banks, 1961; Gairdner Foundn Award, 1965; Henry Steele Gold Medal, RCVS, 1966; James Calvert Spence Medal, British Paediatric Assoc., 1967; Philip Levine Medal, Amer. Soc. Clin. Pathol, 1969; Oliver Meml Award, 1979; Clemens von Pirquet Medal, Austrian Soc. of Allergy and Immunology, 1988; British Soc. Haematology Medal, 1993. *Publications:* (with Anne M. Coombs and D. G. Ingram) Serology of Conglutination and its relation to disease, 1960; (ed with P. G. H. Gell) Clinical Aspects of Immunology, 1963, 3rd edn (also with P. J. Lachmann), 1975; numerous scientific papers on immunology. *Recreation:* retreat to the country. *Address:* 6 Selwyn Gardens, Cambridge CB3 9AX. *T:* (01223) 352681.

COOMBS, Simon Christopher; Business Development Advisor, Institute of Customer Service, since 1997; *b* 21 Feb. 1947; *s* of late Ian Peter Coombs and of Rachel Robins Coombs; *m* 1983, Kathryn Lee Coe Royce. *Educ:* Reading University (BA, MPhil); Wycliffe College. Marketing Executive, British Telecom and Post Office, Data and Telex, 1970–82; Marketing Manager, Telex Networks, British Telecom, 1982–83. Mem., Southern Electricity Consultative Council, 1981–84. Reading Borough Council: Mem., 1969–84; Chm., Transportation Cttee, 1976–83; Vice-Chm., Policy Cttee, 1976–83; Dep. Leader, 1976–81; Chief Whip, 1983. MP (C) Swindon, 1983–97; contested (C) Swindon South, 1997, 2001. PPS to Minister of State for Industry and IT, 1984–85, to Parly Under-Sec. of State DoE, and Minister of State for the Environment, 1985, to Sec. of State for Scotland, 1993–95, to Pres. of BoT, 1995–97. Member: Select Cttee on Employment, 1987–92; British-American Parly Gp, 1983–; CPA, 1983–97; Chairman: Cable TV Gp, 1987–97 (Sec., 1986–87); British Malaŵi Parly Gp, 1985–93 (Sec., 1985–89); Pres., Parly Food and Health Forum, 1993–97 (Chm., 1989–93; Sec., 1985–89); Treasurer: Parly IT Cttee, 1987–97; Anglo-Malta Parly Gp, 1994–97; Sec., Anglo-Tunisia Parly Gp, 1994–97. Vice-Chairman: Cons. Tourism Cttee, 1988–93 (acting Chm., 1993–97); All Party Tourism Cttee, 1992–97; All Party Manuf. Gp, 1993–97; All Party Exports Gp, 1993–97; Sec., Cons. Employment Cttee, 1991; Chm., Cons. Party, Wessex Area, 1980–83; Chm., Wessex Area Young Conservatives, 1973–76; Pres., Wilts Young Conservatives, 1984–97. Gov., Wycliffe Coll., 1995–. *Recreations:* music, cricket, philately, reading. *Address:* 2 Okus Road, Swindon, Wilts. *Clubs:* Swindon Conservative; Hampshire Cricket.

COONEY, Lorna; *see* Fitzsimons, Lorna.

COONEY, Raymond George Alfred, (Ray); actor, author, director, theatrical producer; created Theatre of Comedy at Shaftesbury Theatre, and Little Theatre of Comedy at Ambassadors Theatre, 1983; purchased The Playhouse, London, 1992; *b* 30 May 1932; *s* of Gerard Cooney and Olive (*née* Clarke); *m* 1962, Linda Dixon; two *s*. *Educ:* Alleyn's Sch., Dulwich. First appeared in Song of Norway, Palace, 1946; toured in Wales, 1954–56; subseq. played in: Dry Rot and Simple Spymen, Whitehall; Mousetrap, Ambassador; Charlie Girl, Adelphi; Not Now Darling, Savoy (also film); Not Now Comrade (film); Run for your Wife, Guildford; Two into One, Leicester and Guildford; Caught in the Net, Windsor; (and dir) It Runs in the Family, Playhouse, 1992; (and dir) Funny Money, Playhouse, 1995; The Chiltern Hundreds, Vaudeville, 1999. Productions (some jointly) include: Thark (revival); Doctor at Sea; The Queen's Highland Servant; My Giddy Aunt; Move Over Mrs Markham; The Mating Game; Lloyd George Knew My Father; That's No Lady-That's My Husband; Say Goodnight to Grandma; Two and Two Make Sex; At the End of the Day; Why Not Stay for Breakfast?; A Ghost on Tiptoe; My Son's Father; The Sacking of Norman Banks; The Bedwinner; The Little Hut; Springtime for Henry; Saint Joan; The Trials of Oscar Wilde; The Dame of Sark; Jack the Ripper; There Goes the Bride (and played leading role, Ambassadors, 1974); Ipi Tombi; What's a Nice Country Like US Doing In a State Like This?; Some of My Best Friends Are Husbands; Banana Ridge; Fire Angel; Elvis; Whose Life is it Anyway? (London and NY); Clouds; Chicago; Bodies; Beatlemania; Not Now Darling (revival); Hello Dolly (revival); Duet for One (London and NY); They're Playing Our Song; Children of a Lesser God; Run for your Wife; Aladdin; See How They Run; Pygmalion; Two Into One; Passion Play; Loot (revival); Intimate Exchanges; Wife Begins at Forty; An Italian Straw Hat (revival); It Runs in the Family; Out of Order; Fools Rush In; Run for your Wife 2; Caught in the Net; Over the Moon. *Publications:* (with H. and M. Williams) Charlie Girl, 1965; *plays:* (with Tony Hilton) One for the Pot, 1961; Chase Me Comrade, 1964; (with Tony Hilton) Stand by your Bedouin, 1966; (with John Chapman) Not Now Darling, 1967; (with John Chapman) My Giddy Aunt, 1968; (with John Chapman) Move Over Mrs Markham, 1969; (with Gene Stone) Why Not Stay for Breakfast?, 1970; (with John Chapman) There Goes the Bride, 1973; Run for Your Wife, 1981; Two into One, 1983; Wife Begins at Forty, 1986; It Runs in the Family, 1989; Out of Order, 1990; Funny Money, 1996; Caught in the Net, 2000. *Recreations:* tennis, swimming, golf. *Address:* Ridge House, Forest Side, Epping, Essex CM16 4ED.

COOPER, family name of **Viscount Norwich**.

COOPER; *see* Ashley-Cooper, family name of Earl of Shaftesbury.

COOPER, Adam; dancer, choreographer and actor; *b* 1971; *m* Sarah Wildor, *qv*. *Educ:* Arts Educational Sch.; Royal Ballet Sch. Royal Ballet, 1989–97: Principal Dancer, 1994; main rôles include: Prince Rudolf, in Mayerling; Kings of the North and South, in Prince of the Pagodas; Romeo, and Tybalt, in Romeo and Juliet; Lescaut, in Manon; Espada, in Don Quixote; created rôles in Bloodlines, Ebony Concerto, Tombeaux, Firstext, Room of Cooks; with Adventures in Motion Pictures: The Swan, in Swan Lake, 1995; The Pilot, in Cinderella, 1998; *choreography* includes, for Scottish Ballet: Elegy for Two; Reflections for Images of Dance; *television:* Madame Bovary, 2000. Dir of Boys, London Studio Theatre. *Address:* c/o Adventures in Motion Pictures, 3rd Floor, Gloucester Mansions, 140A Shaftesbury Avenue, WC2H 8HD. *T:* (020) 7836 8716.

COOPER, Andrew Ramsden, CBE 1965; FREng, FIEE; Industrial Consultant, since 1966; Member for Operations and Personnel, Central Electricity Generating Board, 1957–66; *b* 1 Oct. 1902; *s* of Mary and William Cooper, Rotherham, Yorks; *m* 1922, Alice Robinson (marr. diss. 1982); one *s* two *d*; *m* 1982, Helen Louise Gordon (*d* 1997). *Educ:* Rotherham Grammar Sch.; Sheffield Univ. AssocEng; SFInstE; Hon. Life FIEEE. FREng (FEng 1977). Colliery Engineer, Yorks and Kent, 1918–28; Chief Electrical Engineer, Pearson & Dorman Long, 1928; Personal Asst to G. A. Mower, London, 1934; joined Central Electricity Board Operation Dept as Chief of Control, NW England and N Wales, 1935; transf. to HQ, 1937; during War, evacuated to Surrey (formed Surrey Social Council for helping troops; introd. self-educn and entertainment for isolated army units; granted uniform rank of Capt.); Operation Engineeer, SE and E England, 1942; Chief Operation Engineer to Central Electricity Board, 1944; Controller, Merseyside and N Wales Div. (Central Electricity Authority), 1948–52; NW Div., 1952–54; N West, Merseyside and N Wales Reg., 1954–57; Bd Mem., Ops, Grid Control and Personnel, CEGB, 1957–66. Inventor, ARCAID Deaf/Blind Conversation Machine; Pres. Electricity Industries Benevolent Assoc., 1964–66; Mem, GB-USSR Cttee, 1967–91. Faraday Lectr, 1952–53; Bernard Price Meml Lects, S African Inst. of Electr. Engrg, 1970. Internat. Pres., CIGRE, 1966–72. Mem., BBC Debating Soc., Manchester, 1952–55; Founder, Nasmyth Club, London and Manchester, 1936. Hon. Mem., Batti-Wallahs Assoc. Companion, EEIBA, 1994. Hon. MEng Liverpool Univ., 1954. Meritorious Service Award, Power Engrg Soc. of America, 1972; Willans Medal, IEE, 1952; Thornton Medal, AMEME, 1961; Donor, Power/Life Award, Power Engrg Soc., IEEE, 1970; Centennial Award and Plaque, IEEE, 1984. *Publications include:* Load Dispatching, with Special Reference to the British Grid System (a paper receiving John Hopkinson Award, 1948, and Willans Medal, 1952, IEE); The Human Approach to Management, 1989, 3rd edn 1994. *Recreations:* golf, art, music, writing, broadcasting, lecturing. *Address:* Victoria Nursing Home, 81 Dyke Road Avenue, Hove, Sussex BN3 6DA. *Clubs:* Savile, Energy Industries (Hon. Mem.), 25 (Hon. Mem.), Dynamicables (Hon. Mem.).

COOPER, Anthony; *see* Cooper, D. A.

COOPER, Beryl Phyllis; QC 1977; a Recorder of the Crown Court, 1977–98; Deputy High Court Judge, 1980–98; *b* 24 Nov. 1927; *o c* of late Charles Augustus Cooper and Phyllis Lillie Cooper (*née* Burrows). *Educ:* Surbiton High Sch. (Head Girl, 1945–46); Univ. of Birmingham (BCom 1950; Hon. Sec., Guild of Undergrads, 1949–50). Called to the Bar, Gray's Inn, 1960, Bencher, 1988; barrister, 1960–98; Dep. Circuit Judge, 1972–77. Hosp. Sec., Gray's Inn Rd and Liverpool Rd branches, Royal Free Hosp., 1951–57. Formerly: Councillor, St Pancras Metrop. Bor. Council; Mem., Homeopathic Hosp. Cttee; Mem., Bd of Visitors, Wandsworth Prison. Conservative Parly Candidate, Stepney, 1964; Founder Mem., Bow Gp (former Sec. and Council Mem.); Mem. Exec. Cttee, Soc. of Cons. Lawyers, 1981–87. Chm., Justice Report on Fraud Trials, 1985–86. Formerly Member: Cripps Cttee, Women and the Law; Home Office Cttee on Criminal Statistics (Perks Cttee); Member: Housing Corp., 1976–79; Lambeth, Southwark and Lewisham AHA (Teaching), 1980–82; Criminal Injuries Compensation Bd, 1978–98; Review Body for Nursing Staff, Midwives, Health Visitors, and Professions Allied to Medicine, 1983–90; Council of Justice, 1986–96; Family Law Bar Assoc. Cttee, 1986–88. FRHS 1951; FRSA 1992. *Publications:* pamphlets for CPC, Justice, etc.; articles on social, legal, criminal and local govt matters. *Recreations:* travel, swimming, golf. *Address:* 8d South Cliff Tower, Bolsover Road, Eastbourne, Sussex BN20 7JN. *T:* (01323) 32884. *Clubs:* English-Speaking Union; Devonshire (Eastbourne). *Address:* Royal Eastbourne Golf.

COOPER, Prof. Cary Lynn, CBE 2001; BUPA Professor of Organizational Psychology and Health (formerly Professor of Organizational Psychology), since 1975, Pro-Vice-Chancellor, since 1995, and Deputy Vice-Chancellor, since 2000, University of Manchester Institute of Science and Technology; *b* 28 April 1940; *s* of Harry and Caroline Cooper; *m* 1984, Rachel Faith Cooper; two *d*; one *s* one *d* from previous marr. *Educ:* Univ. of California (BS, MBA); Univ. of Leeds (PhD). FBPsS 1982. Lectr in Psychology, Univ. of Southampton, 1967–73. Advr to WHO and ILO, 1982–84. Founding Editor, Jl of Organizational Behavior, 1980–; Co-Editor: Stress Medicine, 1992– (Associate Ed., 1987–92); Internat. Jl Mgt Reviews, 1999–. Member: Bd of Trustees, Amer. Inst. of Stress, 1984–; Adv. Council, Nat. Inst. of Clin. Applications of Behavioral Medicine,

USA; ESRC Research Priorities Bd, 1998–2000; Pres., British Acad. of Management, 1987–90, 1997– (Fellow, 1995). President: Inst. of Welfare Officers, 1998–; Internat. Soc. for Stress Mgt (UK), 2000–; Vice Pres., British Assoc. of Counselling, 2000–. Ambassador, The Samaritans, 2000. Myers Lectr, BPsS, 1986. FRSA 1990; FRSocMed 1995; FRSH 1997; Fellow, Amer. Acad. of Mgt, 1997 (Mem. Bd of Govs, 2000–; Dist. Service Award, 1998); CIMgt 1997. Hon. Mem., Soc. of Psychosom. Res. Hon. MSc Manchester, 1979; Hon. DLitt Heriot-Watt, 1998; Hon. DBA Wolverhampton, 1999. *Publications:* (jtly) T-Groups, 1971; Group Training for Individual and Organizational Development, 1973; Theories of Group Processes, 1975; Developing Social Skills in Managers, 1976; OD in the US and UK, 1977; (jtly) Understanding Executive Stress, 1978; Advances in Experiential Social Processes, vol. 1, 1978, vol. 2, 1980; (jtly) Stress at Work, 1978; (jtly) Executives under Pressure, 1978; Behavioural Problems in Organizations, 1979; (jtly) The Quality of Working Life in Western and Eastern Europe, 1979; Learning from Others in Groups, 1979; The Executive Gypsy, 1979; Current Concerns in Occupational Stress, 1980; Developing Managers for the 1980's, 1980; (jtly) Combating Managerial Obsolescence, 1980; The Stress Check, 1980; White Collar and Professional Stress, 1981; Improving Interpersonal Relations, 1981; (jtly) Groups at Work, 1981; Executive Families Under Stress, 1981; (jtly) After Forty, 1981; Coping with Stress at Work, 1982; Psychology and Management, 1982; (jtly) Management Education, 1982; (jtly) Introducing Organization Behaviour, 1982; (jtly) High Pressure, 1982; Stress Research, 1983; (jtly) Human Behaviour in Organizations, 1983; (jtly) Stress and the Woman Manager, 1983; Public Faces, Private Lives, 1984; (jtly) Working Women, 1984; (jtly) Psychology for Managers, 1984; Psychosocial Stress and Cancer, 1984; (jtly) Women in Management, 1984; (jtly) The Change Makers, 1985; (jtly) Job Stress and Blue Collar Work, 1985; (jtly) International Review of Industrial and Organizational Psychology, annually 1986–; (jtly) Man and Accidents Offshore, 1986; (jtly) Stress and the Nurse Manager, 1986; (jtly) Pilots under Stress, 1986; (jtly) Psycho-social Factors at Work, 1987; (jtly) Retirement in Industrialized Societies, 1987; Living with Stress, 1988; Stress and Breast Cancer, 1988; (jtly) High Fliers, 1988; (jtly) Early Retirement, 1989; (jtly) Career Couples: contemporary lifestyles and how to manage them, 1989; (jtly) Understanding Stress: health care professionals, 1990; (jtly) Managing People at Work, 1990; Industrial and Organizational Psychology: critical writings, 1991; (jtly) Stress Survivors, 1991; (jtly) Cancer and Stress, 1991; (jtly) Work Psychology, 1991; (jtly) Stress and Accidents in the Offshore Oil and Gas Industry, 1991; Managing Organizations in 1992, 1991; (jtly) On the Move: the psychology of change and transitions, 1991; Personality and Stress, 1991; (jtly) Mergers and Acquisitions: the human factor, 1992; (jtly) Shattering the Glass Ceiling: the woman manager, 1992; (jtly) Relax: dealing with stress, 1992; (jtly) Women's Career Development, 1992; (jtly) Total Quality and Human Resources, 1992; (jtly) Successful Stress Management, 1993; (jtly) Stress in the Dealing Room, 1993; (jtly) The Workplace Revolution, 1993; (jtly) No Hassle: taking the stress out of work, 1994; (jtly) Business Elites, 1994; Handbook on Stress Medicine and Health, 1995; Trends in Organizational Behaviour, 1995; (jtly) Stress and Employer Liability, 1996; (jtly) Organizations and the Psychological Contract, 1996; (ed jtly) Blackwell Encyclopedia of Management, 1997; (jtly) Creating Tomorrow's Organizations, 1997; (jtly) Balancing Work, Life and Family, 1998; (ed jtly) Concise Encyclopedia of Management, 1998; (ed) Theories of Organizational Stress, 1998; (jtly) Stress and Strain, 1999; (ed) Who's Who in the Management Sciences, 2000; (ed jtly) Cancer and the Family, 2000; (jtly) Conquer your Stress, 2000; (ed) Classics in Management Thought, 2000; (jtly) Strategic Stress Management, 2000; (jtly) Organizational Stress, 2001; articles on social science and medicine, stress medicine. *Recreations:* reading 19th century Russian fiction, living in hope with Manchester City football, enjoying my four children. *Address:* 25 Lostock Hall Road, Poynton, Cheshire SK12 1DP. *T:* (01625) 871450. *Club:* St James's.

COOPER, David Antony; a District Judge (Magistrates' Courts) (formerly Metropolitan Stipendiary Magistrate), since 1991; *b* 12 June 1945; *s* of Rev. Stanley Francis Cooper and Jane Anne Cooper; *m* 1968, Françoise Armandine Henriette Fourré; three *s*. *Educ:* Sandown Grammar Sch., IoW; Exeter Univ. (LLB); College of Law. Articled to David Rule Pyott, Freshfields, London, 1966–69; admitted Solicitor, 1969; with Heppenstalls, Lymington, 1969–71; Solicitor and Partner in charge of criminal litigation, Ellison & Co., Colchester, 1971–91. *Recreation:* undisturbed reading. *Address:* Greenwich and Woolwich Courts, Blackheath Road, SE10 8PG.

COOPER, Prof. David Edward; Professor of Philosophy, University of Durham, since 1986; *b* 1 Oct. 1942; *s* of late Edward Cooper and Lilian Doris Cooper (*née* Turner); *m* 1st, 1971, Patricia Patterson; 2nd, 1980, Sheila Armstrong, *qv* (marr. diss. 1998); 3rd, 2000, Joy Palmer. *Educ:* Highgate Sch.; St Edmund Hall, Oxford; Nuffield Coll., Oxford (MA, BPhil). Lectr in Philosophy, Pembroke and Jesus Colls, Oxford, 1966–69; Asst Prof. of Philosophy, Univ. of Miami, 1969–72; Lectr in Phil. of Educn, Univ. of London Inst. of Educn, 1972–74; Reader in Phil., Univ. of Surrey, 1974–85. Visiting Professor, Universities of: Khartoum, 1975; Minnesota, 1977; Capetown, 1979; Heidelberg and Tübingen, 1985; Trinity (Texas), 1986; Alberta, 1987; Vanderbilt, 1990; Malta, 1994; Rivers Distinguished Vis. Prof. of the Humanities, E Carolina Univ., 1998; Vis. Sen. Res. Fellow, KCL, 1991–94; Leverhulme Res. Fellow, 1996–97; AHRB Res. Fellow, 1999–2000. Fellow, Internat. Soc. for Intercultural Studies and Res., India, 1993–. Chairman: Phil. of Educn Soc., 1987–90; Friedrich Nietzsche Soc., 1991–94; President: Mind Assoc., 1991; Aristotelian Soc., 1993–94; Member: Council, Royal Inst. of Philosophy, 1995–; Exec. Cttee, Royal Inst. of Phil., 1997–. Trustee, Philosophy in Britain, 1995–. Patron, Earthkind, 1991–. Hon. Diploma, Univ. Nacional de Educación a Distancia, Madrid, 1992. *Publications:* Philosophy and the Nature of Language, 1973; Presupposition, 1974; Knowledge of Language, 1975; (ed) The Manson Murders, 1975; Illusions of Equality, 1980; Authenticity and Learning, 1983; Metaphor, 1986; (ed) Education, Values and Mind, 1986; Existentialism: a reconstruction, 1990, 2nd rev. edn 1999; (ed jtly) The Environment in Question, 1992; (ed) Blackwell's Companion to Aesthetics, 1993; (ed jtly) Just Environments, 1995; World Philosophies: an historical introduction, 1995; Heidegger, 1996; (ed) Aesthetics: the classic readings, 1997; (ed) Ethics: the classic readings, 1998; (ed) Epistemology: the classic readings, 1998; (ed jtly) Spirit of the Environment, 1998; (ed) Metaphysics: the classic readings, 1999; Humanism, Humility and Mystery, 2002. *Recreations:* music, walking, wildlife. *Address:* Department of Philosophy, University of Durham, 50 Old Elvet, Durham DH1 3HN. *T:* (0191) 374 7641; *e-mail:* D.E.Cooper@durham.ac.uk.

COOPER, (Derek) Anthony; Joint General Secretary, Prospect, since 2001; *b* 11 Dec. 1943; *s* of Donald Cooper and Freda Cooper (*née* Sheridan); *m* 1967, June Iley; one *s* two *d*; one *s*. *Educ:* Whitehaven Grammar Sch.; Edinburgh Univ. (BSc Forestry and Wild Life Mgt). Forest Officer, Forestry Commn, 1967–76; Institution of Professionals, Managers and Specialists: Negotiations Officer, 1976–79; Asst Sec., 1979–82; Asst Gen. Sec., 1982–87; Dep. Gen. Sec., 1987–91; Gen. Sec., Engrs and Managers Assoc., 1991–2001. Chairman: Aid Tspt Ltd, 1993–98; 4U@work Ltd, 2000–; Dir, Way Ahead Training Ltd, 1999–. Commissioner: Postal Services Commn, 2000–; Forestry Commn, 2001–. Member: Govt Energy Adv. Panel, 1993–; EU Energy Consultative Cttee, 1998–. Gen. Council, TUC, 1997–. Trustee: Power Aid Logistics, 1993–98; Royal Hosp. for Neuro-disability, Putney, 1995–97. *Recreations:* reading, sailing, climbing. *Address:* 31 London Street, Chertsey, Surrey KT16 8AP.

See also Y. Cooper.

COOPER, Derek Macdonald, OBE 1997; author, broadcaster and journalist; *b* 25 May 1925; *s* of George Stephen Cooper and Jessie Margaret Macdonald; *m* 1953, Janet Marian Feaster; one *s* one *d*. *Educ:* Raynes Park Grammar Sch.; Portree High Sch.; University Coll., Cardiff; Wadham Coll., Oxford (MA Hons). Served RN, 1943–47. Joined Radio Malaya as producer, 1950, retired as Controller of Progs, 1960; Producer, Roving Report, ITN, 1960–61; has worked widely as presenter, interviewer and writer in both television and radio. Columnist: The Listener; Guardian; Observer magazine; Sunday Standard (House of Fraser Press Award, 1984); Homes & Gardens; Saga magazine; Woman's Journal; Scotland on Sunday. Founder Mem. and first Chm., 1985–88, Pres., 1988–95, Guild of Food Writers. Hon. DLitt Queen Margaret UC, Edinburgh, 1999. Glenfiddich Trophy as Wine and Food Writer, 1973, 1980; Broadcaster of the Year, 1984. *Publications:* The Bad Food Guide, 1967; Skye, 1970, 4th edn 1995; The Beverage Report, 1970; The Gullibility Gap, 1974; Hebridean Connection, 1977, 2nd edn 1991; Guide to the Whiskies of Scotland, 1978; Road to the Isles, 1979 (Scottish Arts Council Award, 1980), 2nd edn 1990; (with Dione Pattullo) Enjoying Scotch, 1980; Wine With Food, 1982, 2nd edn 1986; (with Fay Godwin) The Whisky Roads of Scotland, 1982; The Century Companion to Whiskies, 1983; Skye Remembered, 1983, 2nd edn 1993; The World Of Cooking, 1983; The Road to Mingulay, 1985, 2nd edn 1989; The Gunge File, 1986; A Taste of Scotch, 1989; The Little Book of Malt Whiskies, 1992; The Balvenie, 1993; Snail Eggs and Samphire, 2000. *Address:* 4 St Helena Terrace, Richmond, Surrey TW9 1NR. *T:* (020) 8940 7051.

COOPER, Wing Comdr Donald Arthur, CBE 1990; AFC 1961; Chief Inspector, Air Accidents Investigation Branch, Department of Transport, 1986–90; *b* 27 Sept. 1930; *s* of A. A. Cooper and E. B. Cooper (*née* Edmonds); *m* 1958, Belinda, 3rd *d* of Adm. Sir Charles Woodhouse, KCB and Lady Woodhouse; three *s*. *Educ:* Queen's Coll., British Guiana; RAF Coll., Cranwell. BA Open. ATPL (H) 1961, ATPL (A) 1972. FRAeS. Served on fighter and trng sqdns, 1952–56; Empire Test Pilot's Sch., 1957; RAE Farnborough, 1958–60; RAF sc 1961; Sqdn Comdr CFS Helicopter Wing, 1962–64; HQ FTC, 1964–66; Defence Operational Requirements Staff, MoD, 1966–70; joined Accidents Investigation Br., BoT, on retirement, 1970. *Recreations:* walking, ballroom dancing, amateur dramatics. *Address:* 7 Lynch Road, Farnham, Surrey GU9 8BZ.

COOPER, (Edward) John; Chief Executive, Hammersmith Hospitals NHS Trust, 1994–2001; *b* 21 April 1943; *s* of John and Rosalind Cooper; *m* 1977, Susan Hitchin. *Educ:* Malvern Coll.; Nottingham Univ. (BA); Manchester Business Sch. (MBA 1971). AHSM 1969. Nat. Admin. Trng Scheme, NHS, 1965–66; United Liverpool Hosps, 1966–67; Univ. Hosp., S Manchester, 1967–69; various posts, Llewelyn-Davies Internat., 1971–78; S Australian Health Commn, 1978–85 (Dep. Chm. and Comr, 1983–85); Dist Gen. Manager, Hampstead HA, 1985–91; Chief Exec., Royal Free Hampstead NHS Trust, 1991–94. *Recreations:* performing arts, travel. *Address:* c/o Hammersmith Hospital, Du Cane Road, W12 0HS. *T:* (020) 8383 4006.

COOPER, Rt Hon. Sir Frank, GCB 1979 (KCB 1974; CB 1970); CMG 1961; PC 1983; Chairman, High Integrity Systems Ltd, 1986–95; Director: Babcock International Group, 1983–90; Morgan Crucible, 1983–94; N. M. Rothschild & Sons, 1983–96; *b* 2 Dec. 1922; *s* of late V. H. Cooper, Fairfield, Manchester; *m* 1948, Peggie, *d* of F. J. Claxton; two *s* one *d* (and one *s* decd). *Educ:* Manchester Grammar Sch.; Pembroke Coll., Oxford (Hon. Fellow, 1976). War of 1939–45: Pilot, Royal Air Force, 1941–46. Asst Principal, Air Ministry, 1948; Private Secretary: to Parly Under-Sec. of State for Air, 1949–51; to Permanent Under-Sec. of State for Air, 1951–53; to Chief of Air Staff, 1953–55; Asst Sec., Head of the Air Staff, Secretariat, 1955–60; Dir of Accounts, Air Ministry, 1961–62; Asst Under-Sec. of State, Air Min., 1962–64, Min. of Defence, 1964–68; Dep. Under-Sec. of State, Min. of Defence, 1968–70; Dep. Sec., CSD, 1970–73; Permanent Under-Secretary of State: NI Office, 1973–76; MoD, 1976–82. Hon. Consultant, RUSI, 1982–. Chm., United Scientific Hldgs, 1985–89. Mem., Adv. Council on Public Records, 1989–92. Chm., Inst. of Contemp. British Hist., 1986–92. Member Council: KCL, 1981–89; Imperial Coll., 1983–96 (Chm., 1988–96); Chm. Delegacy, King's Coll. Med. and Dental Sch., 1983–89; Visitor, Univ. of Loughborough, 1988–; Chm., Liddell Hart Trustees, 1987–; Gov., Cranbrook Sch., 1982–92 (Chm., 1984–92). FKC 1987; FIC 1988. *Recreation:* walking. *Address:* Apartment 2, Oaklands, Kemnal Road, Chislehurst, Kent BR7 6LZ. *T:* (020) 8467 1263. *Clubs:* Athenæum, Royal Air Force.

COOPER, Sir (Frederick Howard) Michael C.; *see* Craig-Cooper.

COOPER, Gareth; *see* Cooper, W. G.

COOPER, George A.; marketing and business consultant; Chairman, Independent Television Publications Ltd, 1971–89; *b* 9 Oct. 1915; *s* of late Joseph Cooper; *m* 1944, Irene Burns; one *d*. Exec. with internat. publishing gp; served War of 1939–45, Royal Artillery (Captain); Exec., Hulton Press, 1949–55; Director: ABC Television Ltd, 1955–77; Thames Television Ltd, 1968 (Man. Dir, 1974–77); Independent Television News, 1976–77; Chm., Network Programme Cttee of Independent Television, 1975–77. FRTS 1987. *Address:* 43 Rivermill, 151 Grosvenor Road, SW1V 3JN. *T:* (020) 7821 9305. *Clubs:* Royal Automobile, Thirty.

COOPER, George Edward; Chairman, North Thames Gas Region (formerly North Thames Gas Board), 1970–78; Part-time Member, British Gas Corporation, 1973–78; *b* 25 Jan. 1915; *s* of H. E. Cooper and R. A. Jones, Wolverhampton; *m* 1941, Dorothy Anne Robinson (*d* 1993); one *s*. *Educ:* Wolverhampton Municipal Grammar Sch. Wolverhampton and Walsall Corp., 1933–40. Served War, 1940–45, with RA in Middle East (Bimbashi Sudan Defence Force), Captain. Qualified as Accountant, Inst. of Municipal Treasurers and Accountants (now Chartered Inst. of Public Accountants), 1947; Hemel Hempstead Development Corp., 1948–50; W Midlands Gas Bd (finally Dep. Chm.), 1950–70. IPFA (FIMTA 1965); CIGasE 1968. Officer OStJ 1976. *Recreations:* photography, geology, golf. *Club:* City Livery.

COOPER, Gen. Sir George (Leslie Conroy), GCB 1984 (KCB 1979); MC 1953; DL; Chief Royal Engineer, 1987–93; *b* 10 Aug. 1925; *s* of late Lt-Col G. C. Cooper and Mrs Y. V. Cooper, Bulmer Tye House, Sudbury; *m* 1957, Cynthia Mary Hume; one *s* one *d*. *Educ:* Downside Sch.; Trinity Coll., Cambridge. Commnd 1945; served with Bengal Sappers and Miners, 1945–48; Korea, 1952–53; psc 1956; jssc 1959; Instructor, RMA Sandhurst, 1959–62 and Staff Coll., Camberley, 1964; GSO1, 1st Div., 1964–66; CRE, 4th Div., 1966–68; MoD, 1968–69; Comdr, 19th Airportable Bde, 1969–71; Royal Coll. of Defence Studies, 1972; Dep. Dir Army Trng, 1973–74; GOC SW District, 1974–75; Dir, Army Staff Duties, 1976–79; GOC SE District, 1979–81; Adjt-Gen., 1981–84, retd. ADC General to the Queen, 1982–84. Mem., UK Bd of Management, and Dir of Management Devel, GEC, 1985–86. Colonel Commandant: RE, 1980–93; RPC,

1981–85; Col, Queen's Gurkha Engineers, 1981–91. Mem. Council, Nat. Army Mus., 1981–95. Chm., Knightstone Syndicate Management (formerly HGP Managing Agency), 1991–93 (Dir, 1990–91). Lay Rep., Senate and Bar Council Disciplinary Bodies, 1984–90. Chairman: Infantile Hypercalcæmia Foundn, later Williams Syndrome Foundation, 1980–95; Princess Alexandra's NHS Hosp. Trust, 1994–96; Mem. Council, Action Research (formerly Nat. Fund for Res. into Crippling Diseases), 1982–95. DL Essex, 1990. *Recreations:* shooting, gardening. *Address:* c/o Barclays Bank, 3–5 King Street, Reading, Berks RG1 2HD. *Clubs:* Army and Navy, MCC; Essex.

COOPER, Sir Henry, Kt 2000; OBE 1969; company director since 1972; *b* 3 May 1934; *s* of late Henry William Cooper and Lily Nutkins; *m* 1960, Albina Genepri; two *s*. *Educ:* Athelney Street Sch., Bellingham. Professional boxer, 1954–71. Presenter, Be Your Own Boss (series), Channel 4, 1983. KSG 1978. *Film:* Royal Flash, 1975. *Publications:* Henry Cooper: an autobiography, 1972; The Great Heavyweights, 1978; Henry Cooper's Book of Boxing, 1982; Henry Cooper's 100 Greatest Boxers, 1990. *Recreation:* golf. *Address:* 15 Barley House, Hildenbrook Farm, Riding Lane, Hildenborough, Kent TN11 9JN.

COOPER, Imogen; concert pianist; *b* 28 Aug. 1949; *d* of late Martin Du Pré Cooper, CBE; *m* 1982, John Alexander Batten. *Educ:* Paris Conservatoire, with Jacques Février and Yvonne Lefébure, 1961–67 (Premier Prix, 1967); Vienna, with Alfred Brendel, 1970. Plays regularly with all major British orchestras; regular appearances at Proms, 1975–; first British pianist, and woman, to have appeared in South Bank Piano Series, 1975; British festivals include Bath, Cheltenham, Harrogate, Brighton, Edinburgh and Aldeburgh. Overseas engagements incl. concerts with Berlin, Vienna, New York and Los Angeles Philharmonic Orchestras, and regular tours to Australasia, Holland, France, Scandinavia, USA and Japan. Recordings include: Schubert's late works; Schubert lieder (with Wolfgang Holzmair), Brahms and Schumann; Mozart's Concerti for Two and Three Pianos, with Alfred Brendel and Acad. of St Martin-in-the-Fields. Mozart Meml Prize, 1969. *Recreations:* architecture, hill-walking, cooking. *Address:* c/o Van Walsum Management, 3 Addison Bridge Place, W14 8XP. *T:* (020) 7371 4343, *Fax:* (020) 7371 4344.

COOPER, Jilly, (Mrs Leo Cooper); author; *b* 21 Feb. 1937; *d* of Brig. W. B. Sallitt, OBE, and Mary Elaine Whincup; *m* 1961, Leo Cooper; one *s* one *d*. *Educ:* Godolphin Sch., Salisbury. Reporter, Middlesex Independent, Brentford, 1957–59; followed by numerous short-lived jobs as account executive, copy writer, publisher's reader, receptionist, puppy fat model, switchboard wrecker, and very temporary typist. Columnist: Sunday Times, 1969–82; Mail on Sunday, 1982–87. *Publications:* How to Stay Married, 1969; How to Survive from Nine to Five, 1970 (new edn as Work and Wedlock, 1978); Jolly Super, 1971; Men and Super Men, 1972; Jolly Super Too, 1973; Women and Super Women, 1974 (new edn as Super Men and Super Women, 1977); Jolly Superlative, 1975; Super Jilly, 1977; Class, 1979; The British in Love, 1980; (with Tom Hartman) Violets and Vinegar, 1980; Supercooper, 1980; Intelligent and Loyal, 1981; Jolly Marsupial, 1982; (with Imperial War Museum) Animals in War, 1983; The Common Years, 1984; Leo and Jilly Cooper on Cricket, 1985; (with Patrick Lichfield) Hot Foot to Zabrieskie Point, the Unipart Calendar Book, 1985; How to Survive Christmas, 1986; Leo and Jilly Cooper on Horse Mania, 1986; Turn Right at the Spotted Dog, 1987; Angels Rush In, 1990; *novels:* Emily, 1975; Bella, 1976; Harriet, 1976; Octavia, 1977; Prudence, 1978; Imogen, 1978; Riders, 1985 (televised, 1993); Rivals, 1988; Polo, 1991; The Man who made Husbands Jealous, 1993; Araminta's Wedding, 1993; Appassionata, 1996; Score, 1999; *short stories:* Love and Other Heartaches, 1981; *for children:* Little Mabel, 1980; Little Mabel's Great Escape, 1981; Little Mabel Wins, 1982; Little Mabel Saves the Day, 1985. *Recreations:* merry-making, wild flowers, music, mongrels. *Address:* c/o Curtis Brown, Haymarket House, 28–29 Haymarket, SW1Y 4SP.

COOPER, John; *see* Cooper, E. J.

COOPER, Rev. Canon John Leslie; Archdeacon of Coleshill, 1990–93; *b* 16 Dec. 1933; *s* of Iris and Leslie Cooper; *m* 1959, Gillian Mary Dodds; two *s* one *d*. *Educ:* Tiffin School, Kingston, Surrey; Chichester Theological Coll. BD 1965, MPhil 1978, London Univ. (External Student). National Service, RA; commissioned, 1952–54. General Electric Co. management trainee, 1954–59; Chichester Theolog. Coll., 1959–62; Asst Curate, All Saints, Kings Heath, Birmingham, 1962–65; Asst Chaplain, HM Prison, Wandsworth, 1965–66; Chaplain: HM Borstal, Portland, Dorset, 1966–68; HM Prison, Bristol, 1968–72; Research Fellow, Queen's Coll., Birmingham, 1972–73; Priest-in-Charge 1973–81, Vicar 1981–82, St Paul's, Balsall Heath, Birmingham. Examining Chaplain to Bishop of Birmingham, 1981–82; Archdeacon of Aston, and Canon Residentiary, St Philip's Cathedral, Birmingham, 1982–90; Asst Curate, Holy Trinity, Sutton Coldfield, 1993–96. Hon. Canon, Birmingham Cathedral, 1993–97, now Canon Emeritus. *Recreations:* music, reading, walking, travel, carpentry, photography. *Address:* 4 Ireton Court, Kirk Ireton, Ashbourne, Derbys DE6 3JP. *T:* (01335) 370459.

COOPER, Prof. John Philip, CBE 1983; DSc; FRS 1977; FIBiol; Emeritus Professor of Agricultural Botany, University of Wales, 1984; *b* Buxton, Derbyshire, 16 Dec. 1923; *o s* of Frank Edward and Nora Goodwin Cooper; *m* 1951, Christine Mary Palmer; one *s* three *d*. *Educ:* Stockport Grammar Sch.; Univ. of Reading (BSc 1945, PhD 1953, DSc 1964); FitzWilliam House, Cambridge (DipAgrSc 1946). Scientific Officer, Welsh Plant Breeding Station, 1946–50; Lectr, Univ. of Reading, 1950–54; Welsh Plant Breeding Station, University College of Wales, Aberystwyth: Plant Geneticist, 1950–59; Head, Dept of Develtl Genetics, 1959–75; Dir, and Prof. of Agricl Botany, 1975–83. Consultant, FAO Headquarters, Rome, 1956; Nuffield Royal Society Bursary, CSIRO, Canberra, 1962; Visiting Professor: Univ. of Kentucky, 1965; Univ. of Khartoum, 1975; Univ. of Reading, 1984–89; Hon. Fellow, AFRC Inst. for Grassland and Envmtl Res., 1992–. Member: UK Seeds Exec., 1979–86; Internat. Bd for Plant Genetics Resources, 1981–86. *Publications:* (ed, with P. F. Wareing) Potential Crop Production, 1971; (ed) Photosynthesis and Productivity in Different Environments, 1975; various papers on crop physiology and genetics in sc. jls. *Recreations:* walking, field archaeology. *Address:* 31 West End, Minchinhampton, Glos GL6 9JA. *T:* (01453) 882533.

COOPER, Rear-Adm. John Spencer, OBE 1974; *b* 5 April 1933; *s* of Harold Spencer Cooper and Barbara (*née* Highet); *m* 1966, Jacqueline Street (*née* Taylor); two *d*. *Educ:* St Edward's Sch., Oxford; Clare Coll., Cambridge (MA 1959). Joined RN, 1951; served as Lieut on HM Ships Ceylon and Ark Royal; joined Submarines 1966, Polaris Systems Officer in HMS Renown; Comdr 1969; MoD, 1970–73; Flag Officer, Submarines Staff, 1974–76; Captain 1976; Director, Trials, Chevaline programme, 1976–78; Special Proj., RN, Washington, 1978–80; Cdre 1981; Dir, Weapons (Stragetic Systems), 1981–83; Dir Gen., Strategic Weapon Systems, 1983–85; Chief Strategic Systems Exec., MoD, 1985–88. Operations Manager: Naval Command and Control Div., Ferranti International, 1988–90; Ferranti Naval Systems, 1990–93. *Recreation:* cruising in the Mediterranean in Eleonora. *Address:* 2 Mulberry Close, Northampton NN5 7AW. *T:* (01604) 756823.

COOPER, Kenneth Reginald, CB 1991; Chief Executive, The British Library, 1984–91; *b* 28 June 1931; *s* of Reginald and Louisa May Cooper; *m* 1955, Olga Ruth (*née* Harvey); two *s* two *d*. *Educ:* Queen Elizabeth's Grammar Sch., Barnet; New Coll., Oxford (MA). FIPM; FITD (Pres., 1981–83); FIInfSc (Pres., 1988–89). Various appointments, Min. of Labour, 1954–62; Principal, HM Treasury, 1962–65; Principal Private Secretary to Minister of Labour, 1966–67; Asst Sec. for Industrial Training, Min. of Labour, 1967–70; Chief Executive: Employment Services Agency, 1971–75; Training Services Agency, 1975–79; Dir Gen., Nat. Fedn of Building Trades Employers, 1979–84. Vis. Prof., Strathclyde Univ., 1987–91. Dep. Chm., CICI, 1988–92; Dir, Book Trust, 1988–93. CIMgt (CBIM 1989); FRSA, 1987. Hon. Fellow, Brighton Poly., 1991. *Recreations:* music, Rugby football.

COOPER, Prof. Leon N., PhD; Thomas J. Watson, Sr, Professor of Science, Brown University, Providence, RI, since 1974; Director, Institute for Brain and Neural Systems, since 1991; Director, Brain Science Program, since 2000; *b* NYC, 28 Feb. 1930; *s* of Irving Cooper and Anna Cooper (*née* Zola); *m* 1969, Kay Anne Allard; two *d*. *Educ:* Columbia Univ. (AB 1951, AM 1953, PhD 1954). Nat. Sci. Foundn post-doctoral Fellow, and Mem., Inst. for Advanced Study, 1954–55; Res. Associate, Univ. of Illinois, 1955–57; Asst Prof., Ohio State Univ., 1957–58; Associate Prof., Brown Univ., 1958–62, Prof., 1962–66, Henry Ledyard Goddard Prof., 1966–74. Consultant, various governmental agencies, industrial and educational organizations. Lectr, Summer Sch., Varenna, Italy, 1955; Visiting Professor: Brandeis Summer Inst., 1959; Bergen Internat. Sch. Physics, Norway, 1961; Scuola Internazionale di Fisica, Erice, Italy, 1965; Ecole Normale Supérieure, Centre Universitaire Internat., Paris, 1966; Cargèse Summer Sch., 1966; Radiation Lab., Univ. of Calif at Berkeley, 1969; Faculty of Scis, Quai St Bernard, Paris, 1970, 1971; Brookhaven Nat. Lab., 1972; Chair of Math. Models of Nervous System, Fondation de France, 1977–83; Mem., Conseil Supérieur de la Recherche, l'Université René Descartes, Paris, 1981–87. Alfred P. Sloan Foundn Res. Fellow, 1959–66; John Simon Guggenheim Meml Foundn Fellow, 1965–66. Co-Chm., Bd of Dirs, Nestor Inc. Fellow: Amer. Physical Soc.; Amer. Acad. of Arts and Sciences. Member: Amer. Philosoph. Soc.; National Acad. of Sciences; Sponsor Fedn of Amer. Scientists; Soc. for Neuroscience, Amer. Assoc. for Advancement of Science; Defense Science Bd, 1989–93. Mem. Bd of Govs, Internat. Neural Network Soc., 1989–94. (Jtly) Comstock Prize, Nat. Acad. of Scis, 1968; (jtly) Nobel Prize for Physics, 1972; Award of Excellence, Grad. Fac. Alumni, Columbia Univ., 1974; Déscartes Medal, Acad. de Paris, Univ. René Déscartes, 1977; Yrjö Reenpää Medal, Finnish Cultural Foundn, 1982; John Jay Award, 1985, Award for Distinguished Achievement, 1989, Columbia Univ.; Alexander Hamilton Award, Columbia Coll., 1996. Hon. DSc: Columbia, 1973; Sussex, 1973; Illinois, 1974; Brown, 1974; Gustavus Adolphus Coll., 1975; Ohio State Univ., 1976; Univ. Pierre et Marie Curie, Paris, 1977. Public lectures, internat. confs, symposia. *Publications:* Introduction to the Meaning and Structure of Physics, 1968; (contrib.) The Physicist's Conception of Nature, 1973; How We Learn, How We Remember: toward an understanding of brain and neural systems, 1995; contrib. The Many Body Problem, 1963; contrib. to numerous jls incl. Physics Rev., Amer. Jl Physics, Biological Cybernetics, Jl of Neurosci., Jl of Neurophysiol., Procs of the US Nat. Acad. of Scis. *Recreations:* music, theatre, skiing. *Address:* Physics Department, Brown University, Providence, RI 02912, USA. *T:* (401) 8632172. *Clubs:* University, Faculty (Providence, RI).

COOPER, Sir Louis Jacques B.; *see* Blom-Cooper.

COOPER, Margaret Jean Drummond, OBE 1980; Chief Education Officer, General Nursing Council for England and Wales, 1974–82; *b* 24 March 1922; *d* of Canon Bernard R. Cooper and A. Jean Cooper (*née* Drackley). *Educ:* School of St Mary and St Anne, Abbots Bromley; Royal College of Nursing; Open Univ. (BA 1987). SRN, SCM, RNT. Nursing trng and early posts, Leicester Royal Infirmary, 1941–47; Midwifery trng, General Lying-in Hosp., SW1 and Coventry and Warwicks Hosp.; Nurse Tutor, Middlesex Hosp., 1953–55; Principal Tutor: General Hosp., Northampton, 1956–63; Addenbrooke's Hosp., Cambridge, 1963–68; Principal, Queen Elizabeth Sch. of Nursing, Birmingham, 1968–74. Chm., General Nursing Council for England and Wales, 1971–74 (Mem., 1965 and 1970). *Recreations:* birds, books, buildings. *Address:* Howard House, Vicarage Way, Gerrards Cross, Bucks SL9 8AT.

COOPER, Michael John; Director General, British Diabetic Association, 1991–98; *b* 24 July 1937; *s* of Frederick Walton Cooper and Ivy Kathleen (*née* Harris); *m* 1961, Kathy Cockett; two *s* one *d*. *Educ:* King's Sch., Rochester; Univ. of Exeter (BA 1960); Oberlin Coll., Ohio; Internat. Management Develt Inst., Switzerland (MBA 1970). RAF, 1955–57. Shell Internat. Petroleum Co. Ltd, 1961–69; Man. Dir, Panocean-Anco Ltd, 1970–82; Dir, Burmah Castrol PLC, 1982–91. Vice-Chm., E Sussex HA, 1996–2000 (Dir, 1992–). Vis. Prof., Univ. of Westminster, 1992–. Chm. Govs, High Hurstwood C of E Primary Sch., 1998–. *Recreations:* music, walking, cricket, tennis, travel. *Address:* Old Hall Cottage, High Hurstwood, Uckfield, E Sussex TN22 4AD. *T:* (01825) 733268; Flat 5, 130 Belgrave Road, SW1V 2BL; Le Goultat, 71520 Clermain, France. *T:* (3) 85508331. *Club:* Oriental.

COOPER, Michael John, OBE 1997; CBiol; Headmaster, Latymer School, since 1999; *b* 5 April 1949; *s* of Stanley and Evelyn Cooper; *m* 1975, Gillian Isted; two *s*. *Educ:* Sutton High Sch., Plymouth; York Univ. (BA). CBiol, MIBiol 1971. VSO, Chassa Secondary Sch., Zambia, 1972; Mill Hill Sch., London, 1973–78 (Dir of Biol., 1974–78); Dep. Head, Upper Sch., Moulsham High Sch., Chelmsford, 1978–81; Dep. Headteacher, Valley Sch., Worksop, 1982–85; Headmaster, Hillcrest Sch., Hastings, 1985–90; Principal, British Sch. in the Netherlands, 1990–99. Selector, VSO, 1975–90. FRSA 1991. *Recreations:* walking, gardening, swimming, reading. *Address:* Latymer School, Haselbury Road, N9 9TN. *T:* (020) 8807 4037. *Club:* East India.

COOPER, Nigel Cookson; Co-ordinator, Wimbledon Tennis Championships, 1988–95; *b* 7 May 1929; *s* of Richard and Violet Sarah Cooper; *m* 1972, Elizabeth Gillian Smith; two *s* one *d*. *Educ:* Leeds Training Coll., Leeds Univ. (LLB); State Univ. of Iowa, USA (MA). Teacher, primary and secondary schools, 1950–59; Lecturer: Trent Park Training Coll., 1959–61; Loughborough Training Coll., 1961–64; Provincial Supervisor (Schools and Community) for Nova Scotia, Canada, 1964–65; County Organiser of Schools for Norfolk, 1965–68; Asst Education Officer for Oldham, 1970–72; Asst Director of Educn for British Families Educn Service in Europe, 1972–78; Registrar, Kelvin Grove College of Advanced Education, Brisbane, Australia, 1978–82; Gen. Sec., BAAB, 1982–87. *Recreations:* playing the trumpet, squash, jogging. *Address:* 24 Southfields, East Molesey, Surrey KT8 0BP. *T:* and *Fax:* (020) 8224 0712.

COOPER, Sir Patrick Graham Astley, 6th Bt *cr* 1821; Director, Crendon Concrete Co. Ltd, Long Crendon, 1973–83; *b* 4 Aug. 1918; *s* of late Col C. G. A. Cooper, DSO, RA and I. M. M. A. Cooper, Abergeldie, Camberley, Surrey; *S* cousin, Sir Henry Lovick Cooper, 5th Bt, 1959; *m* 1942, Audrey Ann Jervoise, *d* of late Major D. P. J. Collas, Military Knight of Windsor; one *s* two *d*. *Educ:* Marlborough Coll. Qualified RICS, 1949; Sen. Asst Land Comr, Min. of Agric., Fisheries and Food, 1950–59. Joined Crendon Concrete Co. Ltd, 1959. Served 1939–40, Gunner, RA, 52 AA Bde TA (invalided out).

Recreations: golf, tennis. *Heir: s* Alexander Paston Astley Cooper [*b* 1 Feb. 1943; *m* 1974, Minnie Margaret, *d* of Charles Harrison]. *Address:* White Cottage, 3 Townside, Haddenham, Aylesbury, Bucks HP17 8BG. *T:* (01844) 292305.

COOPER, Philip John, CB 1989; Comptroller-General of Patents, Designs and Trade Marks, Department of Trade and Industry, 1986–89; *b* 15 Sept. 1929; *s* of Charles Cooper and Mildred Annie Marlow; *m* 1st, 1953, Dorothy Joan Chapman (*d* 1982); two *d*; 2nd, 1986, Pamela Mary Pysden (*d* 1988); 3rd, 1993, Antoinette Erasmus. *Educ:* Deacon's Sch., Peterborough; University Coll., Leicester. BSc (Chem. 1st Cl. Hons). CChem, FRSC. Joined Dept (later Laboratory) of Govt Chemist, 1952; Nat. Service, 2nd Lt, R Signals, 1953–55; Dept of Scientific and Ind. Res., 1956–67; Principal, Min. of Technology, 1967; Prin. Private Sec. to Minister for Industrial Develt, 1972–73; Asst Sec., 1973–79, Under Sec., 1979–89, DoI and DTI; Dir, Warren Spring Lab., DTI, 1984–85. *Publications:* various papers on analytical and chemical matters. *Address:* 12 The Lye, Tadworth, Surrey KT20 5RS.

COOPER, Sir Richard (Powell), 5th Bt *cr* 1905, of Shenstone Court, Co. Stafford; *b* 13 April 1934; *s* of Sir Francis Ashmole Cooper, 4th Bt and of Dorothy Frances Hendrika, *d* of late Emile Deen; *S* father, 1987; *m* 1957, Angela Marjorie, *e d* of Eric Wilson, Norton-on-Tees; one *s* two *d. Educ:* Marlborough. Chm., Rare Breeds Survival Trust, 1978–80, 1990–92. Chm., Royal Smithfield Club, 2000–. *Recreation:* foxhunting. *Heir: s* Richard Adrian Cooper, *b* 21 Aug. 1960. *Address:* Lower Farm, Chedington, Beaminster, Dorset DT8 3JA. *T:* (01935) 891463. *Club:* Carlton.

COOPER, Robert Francis, CMG 1997; MVO 1975; HM Diplomatic Service; Head of Defence and Overseas Secretariat, Cabinet Office, 1999–2001; *b* 28 Aug. 1947; *s* of late Norman and Frances Cooper. *Educ:* Delamere Sch., Nairobi; Worcester Coll., Oxford (BA); Univ. of Pennsylvania (MA). Joined FCO 1970; Tokyo 1972; London 1977; seconded to Bank of England, 1982; UK Rep. to EC, 1984; Head of Management Review Staff, FCO, 1987; Head of Far Eastern Dept, FCO, 1987; Hd of Policy Planning Staff, FCO, 1989; Counsellor, 1993, Minister and Dep. Hd of Mission, 1996–98, Bonn; Dir, Asia, FCO, 1998–99. *Publication:* The Postmodern State and the World Order, 1996. *Recreations:* Shakespeare, ballroom dancing, bicycling. *Address:* Foreign and Commonwealth Office, SW1A 2AH.

COOPER, Sir Robert (George), Kt 1998; CBE 1987; Chairman, Fair Employment Commission (formerly Agency) for Northern Ireland, 1976–99; Member, Northern Ireland Standing Advisory Commission on Human Rights, 1976–99; *b* 24 June 1936; *er s* of William Hugh Cooper and Annie (*née* Pollock); *m* 1974, Patricia, *yr d* of Gerald and Sheila Nichol, Belfast; one *s* one *d. Educ:* Foyle Coll., Londonderry; Queen's Univ., Belfast (LLB). Industrial Relations, International Computers Ltd, Belfast, 1958–63; Asst Sec., Engineering Employers' Fedn, NI, 1963–67, Sec. 1967–72; Gen. Sec., Alliance Party of Northern Ireland, 1972–73. Member (Alliance): West Belfast, NI Assembly, 1973–75; West Belfast, NI Constitutional Convention, 1975–76; Minister, Manpower Services, NI, 1974. Hon. LLD QUB, 1999. *Address:* Lynwood, 104 Bangor Road, Holywood, Co. Down, N Ireland BT18 0LR. *T:* (028) 9042 2071.

COOPER, Prof. Robin Hayes, PhD; FBA 1993; Professor of Computational Linguistics, Gothenburg University, since 1995; *b* 23 Dec. 1947; *s* of Dennis J. Cooper and Marjorie (*née* Wilding); *m* 1985, Elisabet B. Engdahl; two *d. Educ:* Corpus Christi Coll., Cambridge (MA); Univ. of Massachusetts at Amherst (PhD). Lektor, Universität Freiburg, 1969–71; Assistant Professor: Univ. of Texas at Austin, 1975–76; Univ. of Massachusetts at Amherst, 1976–77; Univ. of Wisconsin, Madison, 1977–81, Associate Prof., 1981–87; Docent, Lund Univ., 1984–87; University of Edinburgh: Lectr, 1986–89; Reader in Cognitive Sci., 1989–96. Mellon Fellow, Stanford Univ., 1980–81; Fellow, Center for Advanced Study in Behavioral Scis, Stanford, 1981–82; Guggenheim Fellow, Edinburgh and Stanford, 1986–87. *Publications:* Quantification and Syntactic Theory, 1983; (ed jtly) Situation Theory and its Applications, Vol 1, 1990; contribs to numerous books, contrib. Computational Intelligence, Ethnomusicology, Lang., Linguistics and Philosophy, Musique en Jeu, Nordic Jl Linguistics. *Recreations:* yoga, music. *Address:* Department of Linguistics, Gothenburg University, Box 200, 40530 Gothenburg, Sweden; Bigatan 1, 43139 Mölndal, Sweden.

COOPER, Ronald Cecil Macleod, CB 1981; Deputy Secretary, Department of Transport, 1986–90; *b* 8 May 1931; *s* of Cecil Redvers Cooper and Norah Agnes Louise Cooper (*née* Macleod); *m* 1st, 1953, June Bicknell (marr. diss. 1967); 2nd, 1967, Christine Savage; one *s* two *d. Educ:* Royal Grammar Sch., Newcastle upon Tyne; St Edmund Hall, Oxford (MA). Asst Principal, Min. of Supply, 1954–59; Principal, Min. of Aviation, 1959–62; on loan to European Launcher Develt Org., Paris, 1962–67; Asst Sec., Min. of Technology, 1968–70, DTI, 1970–73; Under Sec., Dept of Trade, 1973–78; Sec., Price Commn, 1979; Dep. Sec. and Principal Estabt and Finance Officer, DTI, 1979–85. *Recreations:* music, reading.

COOPER, Hon. Russell; *see* Cooper, Hon. T. R.

COOPER, Sidney Pool; Head of Public Services, British Museum, 1973–76; *b* 29 March 1919; *s* of late Sidney Charles Henry Cooper and Emily Lilian Baptie; *m* 1940, Denise Marjorie Peverett; two *s* one *d. Educ:* Finchley County Sch.; Northern Polytechnic (BSc); University Coll. London (MSc). Laboratory of the Government Chemist, 1947; Asst Keeper, National Reference Library of Science and Invention, British Museum, 1963; Dep. Keeper, NRLSI, 1969. *Address:* 11 Bridgewater Hill, Northchurch, Berkhamsted, Herts HP4 1LW. *T:* (01442) 864145.

COOPER, Maj.-Gen. Sir Simon (Christie), GCVO 2000 (KCVO 1991); Master of HM's Household, 1992–2000; *b* 5 Feb. 1936; *s* of Maj.-Gen. Kenneth Christie Cooper, CB, DSO, OBE and Barbara Harding-Newman; *m* 1967, Juliet Elizabeth Palmer; one *s* one *d. Educ:* Winchester College; rcds, psc. Commissioned Life Guards, 1956; served Aden, London, BAOR, 1957–63; Captain-Adjt, Household Cavalry Regt, 1963–65; ADC to CDS Earl Mountbatten of Burma, 1965–66; Borneo, Malaya, 1966–67; Staff Coll., 1968; BAOR, 1969–75; CO Life Guards, 1974–76; GSO1, Staff Coll., 1976–78; OC Household Cavalry and Silver Stick in Waiting, 1978–81; Commander, RAC Centre, 1981–82; RCDS, 1983; Dir, RAC, 1984–87; Comdt, RMA, Sandhurst, 1987–89; GOC London Dist and Maj.-Gen. Commanding Household Div., 1989–91. Hon. Colonel: Westminster Dragoons, 1987–97; Royal Yeomanry, 1987–97. *Recreations:* cricket, ski-ing, sailing, shooting. *Club:* MCC.

COOPER, Prof. Susan, PhD; Professor of Experimental Physics, and Fellow of St Catherine's College, University of Oxford, since 1995; *b* USA, 1949. *Educ:* Colby Coll., USA (BA); Univ. of California at Berkeley (PhD). Guest Physicist, Deutsches Electronen Synchrotron, Germany, 1980–83; Research Associate, Stanford Linear Accelerator Center, USA, 1984–86; Asst Prof., MIT, 1987–89; Group leader, Max Planck Inst. of Physics, Munich, 1989–96. *Publications:* numerous papers in sci. jls. *Address:* Nuclear and Astrophysics Laboratory, Oxford University, Keble Road, Oxford OX1 3RH.

COOPER, (Theo) Russell; MLA (National Party) Crows Nest, Queensland, since 1992 (Roma, Queensland, 1983–92); *b* 4 Feb. 1941; *s* of Theo Beverley Cooper and Muriel Frances Cooper; *m* 1965, Penelope Anne Parkinson; one *s* three *d. Educ:* Surfers Paradise State Sch.; Correspondence Sch.; Toowoomba Prep. Sch.; King's Sch., Parramatta. Councillor, 1976–88, Dep. Chm., 1982–86, Bendemere Shire Council; Dep. Chm., Roma Electorate NP Council, 1980–83; Chm., Wallumbilla-Yuleba Branch, NP, 1974–83. Minister for: Corrective Services and Admin. Services, 1987–89; Police and Emergency Services, 1989; Premier of Qld, Sept.–Dec. 1989; Leader of the Opposition, 1989–91; Opposition spokesman for police and corrective services, 1992–96; Minister for Police and Corrective Services and for Racing, 1996–98; Opposition spokesman on Primary Industries, 1998–2000. Vice-Pres., Maranoa Graziers Assoc., 1979–80 (Chm., Wallumbilla Br.); Pres., Roma and Dist Amateur Race Club, 1981–83. *Recreations:* golf, tennis (active), Rugby League, Rugby Union, cricket. *Address:* Donnabar, Wallumbilla, Qld 4428, Australia. *T:* (7) 46234341; 20 Nichols Road, Highfields, Qld 4352, Australia. *T:* (7) 46987226. *Clubs:* Brisbane. *Address:* Maranoa (Roma).

COOPER, Hon. Warren Ernest, CNZM 1997; MP (National Party) Otago, 1975–96; Minister of Defence and Minister responsible for War Pensions, New Zealand, 1990–96, also Minister of Civil Defence and of Internal Affairs, 1993–96; *b* Dunedin, 21 Feb. 1933; *s* of William Cooper; *m* 1959, Lorraine Margaret, *d* of Angus T. Rees; three *s* two *d. Educ:* Musselburgh Sch.; King's High Sch., Dunedin. Formerly Minister of Tourism, Minister of Regional Develt, Minister in charge of Publicity and in charge of Govt Printing Office; Postmaster Gen., 1980; Minister of Broadcasting and Assoc. Minister of Finance, 1981; Minister of Foreign Affairs and Overseas Trade, 1981–84; Minister of Local Govt and of Radio and Television, 1990–93. Mem., Cabinet Cttees on Expenditure Control and Revenue, State Sector, Appts and Honours, Social and Family Policy, Treaty of Waitangi Issues, 1990–96. Member Executive: S Island Publicity Assoc., 1971; NZ Municipal Assoc. Life Mem. and former Pres., Queenstown Jaycees. Mayor of Queenstown, 1968–71 and 1995–2001. JP Queenstown. Silver Jubilee Medal, 1977. *Address:* 8 Park Street, Queenstown, New Zealand.

COOPER, William, (Harry Summerfield Hoff), FRSL; novelist; *b* 4 Aug. 1910; *m* 1951, Joyce Barbara Harris (*d* 1988); two *d. Educ:* Christ's Coll., Cambridge. Assistant Commissioner, Civil Service Commission, 1945–58; Personnel Consultant to: UKAEA, 1958–72; CEGB, 1958–72; Commn of European Communities, 1972–73; Asst Dir, Civil Service Selection Bd, 1973–75; Mem. Bd of Crown Agents, 1975–77; Personnel Advr, Millbank Technical Services, 1975–77. Adjunct Prof. of English Lit., Syracuse Univ., 1977–90. *Publications:* (as H. S. Hoff) Trina, 1934; Rhéa, 1935; Lisa, 1937; Three Marriages, 1946; (as William Cooper) Scenes from Provincial Life, 1950; The Struggles of Albert Woods, 1952; The Ever-Interesting Topic, 1953; Disquiet and Peace, 1956; Young People, 1958; C. P. Snow (British Council Bibliographical Series, Writers and Their Work, No 115) 1959; Prince Genji (a play), 1960; Scenes from Married Life, 1961; Memoirs of a New Man, 1966; You Want The Right Frame of Reference, 1971; Shall We Ever Know?, 1971; Love on the Coast, 1973; You're Not Alone, 1976; Scenes from Metropolitan Life, 1982; Scenes from Later Life, 1983; From Early Life (autobiog.), 1990; Immortality at any Price, 1991; Scenes from Death & Life, 1999. *Address:* 22 Kenilworth Court, Lower Richmond Road, SW15 1EW. *T:* (020) 8788 8326. *Club:* Savile.

COOPER, Sir William (Daniel Charles), 6th Bt *cr* 1863, of Woollahra; Company Director of The Garden Maintenance Service and G.M.S. Vehicles; *b* 5 March 1955; *s* of Sir Charles Eric Daniel Cooper, 5th Bt, and Mary Elisabeth (*d* 1999), *e d* of Captain J. Graham Clarke; *S* father, 1984; *m* 1988, Julia Nicholson. *Educ:* Northease Manor, Lewes, Sussex. *Heir: b* George John Cooper, *b* 28 June 1956.

COOPER, Maj.-Gen. William Frank, CBE 1971; MC 1945; *b* 30 May 1921; *s* of Allan Cooper, Officer of Indian State Railways, and Margaret Cooper; *m* 1945, Elisabeth Mary Finch (*d* 1999); one *s* one *d. Educ:* Sherborne Sch.; RMA Woolwich. Commnd in RE, 1940; served N Africa and Italy (MC; despatches 1944); Malaya, 1956–58 (despatches); S Arabia, 1963–65 (OBE); Chief Engr FARELF, 1968–70; Dep. Dir Army Staff Duties, MoD, 1970–72; Dir, Mil. Assistance Office, 1972–73; DQMG, 1973–76, retd. Col Comdt, RE, 1978–83. Dir, Gin Rectifiers and Distillers Assoc. and Vodka Trade Assoc., 1976–90. *Recreations:* fishing, birdwatching, theatre, gardening. *Address:* c/o Lloyds TSB, 118 High Street, Hungerford, Berks RG17 0LY. *Club:* Army and Navy.

COOPER, (William) Gareth, FCIT; Chairman, Arriva plc, since 1999; *b* 19 Aug. 1943; *s* of William Alderson Cooper and Florence Morwen Cooper (*née* Matthews); *m* 1966, Carole Roberta Davies; one *s* one *d. Educ:* University Coll., Swansea (BScEng). Managing Director: Wallington Weston Co. Ltd, 1977–83; Weston Hyde Products Ltd, 1983–87; Crown Berger Ltd, 1987–91; Stena Line UK Ltd, 1991–97; Chairman: Stena Line, 1997–; White Young Green plc, 1997–. *Recreations:* opera, travel, photography. *Address:* Mount Charles House, Bridge, Canterbury, Kent CT4 5JS. *T:* (01227) 832142.

COOPER, William Robert W.; *see* White-Cooper.

COOPER, Yvette; MP (Lab) Pontefract and Castleford, since 1997; Parliamentary Under-Secretary of State for Public Health, Department of Health, since 1999; *b* 20 March 1969; *d* of (Derek) Anthony Cooper, *qv* and June Cooper (*née* Iley); *m* 1998, Edward Michael Balls, *qv*; one *s* one *d. Educ:* Eggars Comprehensive Sch., Hants; Balliol Coll., Oxford (BA 1st Cl. Hons PPE 1990); Harvard Univ.; London Sch. of Econs (MSc Econs 1995). Economic researcher for Rt Hon. John Smith, MP, 1991–92; Domestic Policy specialist, Clinton Presidential Campaign, Arkansas, 1992; Policy Advr to Labour's Treasury Team, 1992–95; leader writer and economic columnist, The Independent, 1995–97. Member: Select Cttee on Educn and Employment, 1997–99; Intelligence and Security Cttee, 1997–99. *Recreations:* swimming, painting portraits (badly), watching soap operas. *Address:* House of Commons, SW1A 0AA. *T:* (020) 7219 5080.

COORAY, His Honour (Bulathsinhalage) Anura (Siri); a Circuit Judge, 1991–97; *b* 20 Jan. 1936; *s* of (Bulathsinhalage) Vincent Cooray, accountant, and Dolly Perera Manchanayake, Etul Kotte, Sri Lanka; *m* 1957, Manel Therese, *d* of late George Perera, planter, and late Myrtle Perera, Kandy, Sri Lanka; two *s* three *d. Educ:* Christian Coll., Kotte, Sri Lanka; London Univ. Called to the Bar, Lincoln's Inn, 1968. Served RAF, Cranwell and Locking, 1952–55 (RAF Boxing Assoc. Sigrist Trophy, 1953–54); served Royal Ceylon Air Force, 1955–60. Practised in Common Law Chambers at Middle Temple; later, Dep. Head of Chambers at No 1 Gray's Inn Sq.; Mem., South Eastern Circuit; Prosecuting Counsel for DPP and Met. Police Solicitors, 1969–82; a Metropolitan Stipendiary Magistrate, 1982–91; a Recorder, 1989–91. Mem., Cttee of Magistrates, 1989. *Recreations:* wine making (and tasting too!), gardening. *Address:* 1 Gray's Inn Square, WC1R 5AA; Kingsland, Etul Kotte, Kotte, Sri Lanka.

COOTE, Sir Christopher (John), 15th Bt *cr* 1621; Senior Baronetcy of Ireland in use; *b* 22 Sept. 1928; *s* of Rear Adm. Sir John Ralph Coote, 14th Bt, CB, CBE, DSC, and Noreen Una (*d* 1996), *o d* of late Wilfred Tighe; *S* father, 1978; *m* 1952, Anne Georgiana, *d* of Lt-Col Donald Handford; one *s* one *d. Educ:* Winchester; Christ Church, Oxford

(MA 1957). Coffee and tea merchant. *Heir: s* Nicholas Patrick Coote [*b* 28 July 1953; *m* 1980, Mona, *d* of late Moushegh Bedelian; one *s* one *d*].

COOTE, Prof. John Haven; Bowman Professor, since 1987, and Head of Department of Physiology, since 1984, Birmingham University; *b* 5 Jan. 1937; *m* 1976, Susan Hylton; one *s* two *d*. *Educ:* Royal Free Hosp. Sch. of Medicine (BSc (Hons) Physiol.; PhD London); DSc Birmingham 1980. CBiol, FIBiol 1988. Birmingham University: Prof. of Physiology, 1984–; Hd of Sch. of Basic Med. Scis, 1988–91. Vis. Scientist, Inst. de Medicina Experimental, Univ. of Caracas, Venezuela, 1971; Visiting Professor, Department of Physiology: Inst. of Gerontology, Tokyo, 1974–75; Inst. of Physiological Scis, Warsaw, 1977–78. Chm., Human Scis Ethics Cttee, DERA, 2000–. Member: AAAS, 1989; NY Acad. of Scis, 1991. Chm. Editorial Bd, Experimental Physiology, 2000–. *Publications:* contribs to Jl of Physiol., Jl of the Autonomic Nervous System, Brain Res. *Recreation:* mountaineering. *Address:* Physiology Department, University of Birmingham, Birmingham B15 2TT.

COPE, family name of **Baron Cope of Berkeley**.

COPE OF BERKELEY, Baron *cr* 1997 (Life Peer), of Berkeley in the co. of Gloucestershire; **John Ambrose Cope,** Kt 1991; PC 1988; *b* 13 May 1937; *s* of George Cope, MC, FRIBA, Leicester; *m* 1969, Djemila Lovell Payne, *d* of Col P. V. L. Payne, Martinstown, Dorset and Mrs Tanetta Blackden, Jerusalem; two *d*. *Educ:* Oakham, Rutland. Chartered Accountant; Company Director. Commnd RA and RE, Nat Service and TA. Worked for Cons. party, Westminster, 1965–70; contested (C) Woolwich East, 1970; MP (C) South Gloucestershire, Feb. 1974–1983, Northavon, 1983–97; contested (C) Northavon, 1997. Special Asst to Sec. of State for Trade and Industry, 1972–74; a Govt Whip, 1979–87, and Lord Comr of HM Treasury, 1981–83; Treas. of HM Household and Dep. Chief Whip, 1983–87; Minister of State: Dept of Employment and Minister for Small Businesses, 1987–89; NI Office, 1989–90; Dep. Chm. and Jt Treas., Cons. Party, 1990–92; HM Paymaster Gen., 1992–94; Opposition spokesman on NI, 1997–98, on home affairs, 1998–2001, H of L; Opposition Chief Whip, H of L, 2001–. Sen. Comr, Royal Hospital Chelsea, 1992–94. Pres., Inst. of Business Counsellors, 1988–90; Dep. Chm., Small Business Bureau, 1995–2001; Pres., S Glos Chamber of Commerce, 1993–2001. Chm., Horse and Pony Taxation Cttee, 1994–2000. Vice Pres., Royal Soc. of St George, 1998–. Chm. Trustees, Friends of War Memls. Patron: Avon Riding for the Disabled; Vigilant Trust. *Publications:* (with Bernard Weatherill) Acorns to Oaks (Policy for Small Business), 1967; (ed) A Funny Thing Happened, 1991; I'm sorry you were in when I called, 1992. *Recreation:* woodwork. *Address:* House of Lords, SW1A 0PW. *Clubs:* Carlton, Beefsteak; Tudor House (Chipping Sodbury), Chipping Sodbury Yacht.

COPE, Alan, CPFA, FCCA; County Treasurer, Cheshire County Council, since 1997; *b* 8 Oct. 1946; *s* of John William Cope and Bertha Cope; *m* 1969, Gillian Mary Kirk; two *s*. *Educ:* Swanwick Hall Grammar Sch. CPFA 1968; FCCA 1981. Accountant, Derbyshire CC, 1963–69; Cheshire County Council: Sen. Auditor, 1969–72; Technical Accountant, 1972–74; Gp Accountant, 1974–78; Chief Accountant, 1978–85; Asst Dir, Policy Unit, 1985–87; Asst Co. Treas., 1987–89; Co. Finance Officer, 1989–97. Treasurer: Cheshire Fire Authy, 1997–; Cheshire Probation Service, 1997–; Cheshire Police Authy, 1998–. *Address:* The Meadows, 19 Dee Crescent, Farndon, Chester CH3 6QJ. *T:* (01829) 270602.

COPE, David Robert, MA; Director, Ashoka (UK) Trust, 1998–2001; *b* 24 Oct. 1944; *yr s* of late Dr Cuthbert Cope, FRCP and Eileen Cope (*née* Putt); *m* 1st, 1966, Gillian Margaret Peck (marr. diss. 1994); one *s* two *d*; 2nd, 1996, Juliet Caroline, *e d* of Prof. Richard Swinburne, *qv*; two *s*. *Educ:* Winchester Coll. (Scholar); Clare Coll., Cambridge (Scholar). 1st Cl. Hons Hist. Tripos Part II, 1965; BA 1965; MA 1972. Asst Master, Eton Coll., 1965–67; Asst British Council Rep. (Cultural Attaché), Mexico City, 1968–70; Asst Master, Bryanston Sch., 1970–73; Headmaster: Dover College, 1973–81; British Sch. of Paris, 1981–86; Master of Marlborough Coll., 1986–93; Field Dir, Zambia, VSO, 1994–97. FRSA. *Recreations:* music, running, books, travel. *Address:* Grove Cottage, 2 High Street, Shepreth, Royston, Herts SG8 6PP. *T:* (01763) 260657. *Club:* Athenæum.

COPE, David Robert; Director, Parliamentary Office of Science and Technology, since 1998; *b* 7 July 1946; *s* of Lawrence William and Ethel Anne Cope; *m* 1992, Reiko Takashina. *Educ:* Fitzwilliam Coll., Cambridge Univ. (MA); London School of Economics (MScEcon, with dist.). Res. Officer, University Coll. London, 1969–70; Lectr, Nottingham Univ., 1970–81; Environment Team Leader, Internat. Energy Agency Coal Unit, 1981–86; Exec. Dir, UK CEED, 1986–97; Prof. of Energy Econs, Doshisha Univ., Kyoto, Japan, 1997–98. Special Lectr in Energy and Environment Studies, Nottingham Univ., 1985–94; Vis. Lectr, Cambridge Univ., 1988–95; First Caltex Green Fund Fellow, 1992, and Ext. Examiner, 1992–, Centre of Urban Planning and Envmtl Mgt, Univ. of Hong Kong. Member: Council, Nat. Soc. for Clean Air, 1990–98; Standing Cttee on the Envmt, ACOST, 1990–92; Climate Change Wkg Gp, 1993; Packaging Standards Council (formerly Packaging Council), 1992–96; Envmtl Stats Adv. Cttee, DoE, later DETR, 1994–98. *Publications:* (with P. Hills and P. James) Energy Policy and Land Use Planning, 1984; (with S. Owens) Land Use Planning Policy and Climate Change, 1992; numerous papers on energy and environmental policy topics. *Recreations:* amateur volcanology, hill walking, woodworking. *Address:* Parliamentary Office of Science and Technology, Westminster House, 7 Millbank, SW1P 3JA. *T:* (020) 7219 2848, *Fax:* (020) 7219 2849; *e-mail:* coped@parliament.uk.

COPE, Hon. James Francis, CMG 1978; Speaker of the Australian House of Representatives, 1973–75; *b* 26 Nov. 1907; *s* of G. E. Cope; *m* 1931, Myrtle Irene, *d* of S. J. Hurst; one *d*. *Educ:* Crown Street Public Sch., NSW. Hon. Treaurer, NSW Br., Aust. Glass Workers' Union; Delegate to Federal Council, 1953–55. MHR (Lab) for divs of: Cook, 1955; Watson, 1955–69; Sydney, 1969–75. *Recreations:* billiards, horse racing, cricket, football. *Address:* 1/38–40 Fontainebleau Street, Sans Souci, NSW 2219, Australia.

COPE, Jeremy Ewart; Group Managing Director, Consignia (formerly Post Office), since 1999; *b* 30 Nov. 1951; *s* of Michael Ewart Cope and Maureen Ann Cope (*née* Casey); *m* 1985, Dianne Elizabeth Gilmour; one *s*. *Educ:* St Paul's Sch.; Jesus Coll., Cambridge (MA); Warwick Univ. (MSc). MIPM. Joined Post Office as management trainee, 1973; Asst Head Postmaster, Southend, 1980; Dir of Personnel, Royal Mail, 1986; Gen. Manager, London, 1988; Dir of Strategy, Royal Mail, 1989; Dir of Strategy and Commercial Develt, Post Office, 1992; Man. Dir, Strategy and Personnel, Post Office, 1995; Mem. for Strategy and Personnel, Post Office Bd, 1996–99. Chm., London Regl Cttee, FEFC, 2000–. Gov., Kingston Univ., 1999–. *Recreations:* bridge, supporting Fulham FC, cooking, theatre, avoiding the gardening. *Address:* Consignia, 148 Old Street, EC1V 9HQ. *T:* (020) 7250 2331. *Club:* Hurlingham.

COPE, Jonathan; Principal, Royal Ballet Company, 1987–90 and since 1992; *b* 1963; *m* Maria Almeida; one *s* one *d*. *Educ:* Royal Ballet Sch. Joined Royal Ballet Co., 1982; Soloist, 1985–86; property business, 1990–92. Leading rôles include: Cinderella, Pursuit, Giselle, Swan Lake, Prince of the Pagodas, Fearful Symmetries, The Sons of Horus, Romeo and Juliet, Sleeping Beauty, La Bayadère, Different Drummer, Frankenstein, Fleeting Figures, The Modern Prometheus, Words Apart, Manon, The Nutcracker, Ondine. *Address:* c/o Royal Ballet Company, Royal Opera House, Covent Garden, WC2E 9DD.

COPE, Wendy Mary, FRSL; writer, freelance since 1986; *b* 21 July 1945; *d* of Fred Stanley Cope and Alice Mary (*née* Hand). *Educ:* Farringtons Sch.; St Hilda's Coll., Oxford (MA); Westminster College of Education, Oxford (DipEd). Teacher in London primary schs, 1967–81 and 1984–86; Arts editor, ILEA Contact, 1982–84; Television columnist, The Spectator, 1986–90. FRSL 1992. Hon. DLitt Southampton, 1999. Cholmondeley Award for Poetry, 1987; Michael Braude Award, Amer. Acad. of Arts and Letters, 1995. *Publications:* Making Cocoa for Kingsley Amis (poems), 1986; Twiddling Your Thumbs (rhymes for children), 1988; (ed) Is That The New Moon?, 1989; The River Girl, 1991; Serious Concerns, 1992; (ed) The Orchard Book of Funny Poems, 1993; (ed) The Funny Side, 1998; (ed) The Faber Book of Bedtime Stories, 2000; If I Don't Know, 2001; (ed) Heaven on Earth: 101 happy poems, 2001. *Recreations:* music, gardening. *Address:* c/o Faber and Faber, 3 Queen Square, WC1N 3AU.

COPELAND, Dame Joyanne Winifred; *see* Bracewell, Hon. Dame J. W.

COPEMAN, Harold Arthur; Under-Secretary, HM Treasury, 1972–76; *b* 27 Jan. 1918; *s* of H. W. M. and G. E. Copeman; *m* 1948, Kathleen (Kay) Gadd (*d* 1992); one *s*. *Educ:* Manchester Grammar Sch.; The Queen's Coll., Oxford. BA, 1st Cl. Hons in PPE, 1939; MA. Served War, Army: Cheshire Regt, RA (Instructor in Gunnery) and Ordnance Board (Applied Ballistics Dept), 1940–45. HM Treasury, 1946–76. Consultant, Fiscal Affairs Dept, IMF, 1982. Vis. Fellow, Warwick Univ., 1976–84. *Publications:* (jtly) Health Care: priorities and management, 1980; The National Accounts: a short guide, 1981; Singing in Latin, 1990; The Pocket Singing in Latin, 1990; Singing the Meaning, 1996. *Recreations:* music, Latin pronunciation, photography. *Address:* 22 Tawney Street, Oxford OX4 1NJ. *T:* (01865) 243830.

COPISAROW, Sir Alcon (Charles), Kt 1988; FInstP; CEng; FIEE; Chairman, ARINSO International, since 2000; *b* 25 June 1920; *o s* of late Dr Maurice Copisarow, Manchester; *m* 1953, Diana, *y d* of Ellis James Castello, MC, Bucklebury, Berks; two *s* two *d*. *Educ:* Manchester Central Grammar Sch.; University of Manchester; Imperial Coll. of Science and Technology; Sorbonne, Paris (DUP 1960). Council of Europe Research Fellow. Served War, 1942–47; Lieut RN, 1943–47; British Admiralty Delegn, Washington, 1945. Home Civil Service, 1946–66; Office of Minister of Defence, 1947–54. Scientific Counsellor, British Embassy, Paris, 1954–60. Dir, Forest Products Research Laboratory, Dept of Scientific and Industrial Research, 1960–62; Chief Technical Officer, Nat. Economic Development Council, 1962–64; Chief Scientific Officer, Min. of Technology, 1964–66. Dir, McKinsey & Co. Inc., 1966–76; non-exec. Dir, British Leyland, 1976–77; Mem., BNOC, 1980–83; Chairman: APAX Venture Capital Funds, 1981–94; The Eden Trust, 1995–2000; Dir, Touche Remnant Holdings and portfolio cos, 1985–96. Special Advr, Ernst & Young, 1993–99. Chairman: Commonwealth Forest Products Pre-Conf., Nairobi, 1962; CENTO Conf. on Investment in Science, Teheran, 1963; Member: Scientific Manpower Cttee, Advisory Council on Scientific Policy, 1963–64; Econ. Develt Cttees for Electronics Industry and for Heavy Electrical Industry; Trop. Prod. Adv. Cttee, 1965–66; Press Council, 1975–81. A Chm., Gen. Comrs for Income Tax, 1975–95. External Mem., Council of Lloyd's, 1982–90; Dep. Chm., Lloyd's Tercentenary Trust, 1989– (Chm., 1988). Dep. Chm., Bd of Governors, English-Speaking Union, 1976–83; Chm., Youth Business Initiative, subseq. The Prince's Youth Business Trust, 1982–87. Dir, Windsor Fest., 1983–2000. Trustee: Duke of Edinburgh's Award, 1978–84; FMI, 1995–2001; Member Council: Royal Jubilee Trusts, 1981–87; Zoological Soc., 1990–91. Patron, Société des Ingénieurs et des Scientifiques de France, 1992–. Governor, Benenden Sch., 1976–86. Freeman, City of London, 1981. Hon. FTCL. *Address:* 25 Launceston Place, W8 5RN. *Clubs:* Athenæum (Trustee), Beefsteak.

COPLAND, Rev. Canon Charles McAlester; Provost of St John's Cathedral, Oban, 1959–79, and Dean of Diocese of Argyll and The Isles, 1977–79; *b* 5 April 1910; *s* of Canon Alexander Copland and of Violet Williamina Somerville McAlester; *m* 1946, Gwendoline Lorimer Williamson (*d* 2001); two *d*. *Educ:* Forfar Academy; Denstone Coll.; Corpus Christi Coll., Cambridge (MA); Cuddesdon College. Reserve of Officers, 1933–38. Curate, Peterborough Parish Church, 1934–38; Mission Priest, Chanda, CP, India, 1938–53 (Head of Mission, 1942–53); Canon of Nagpur, 1952; Rector, St Mary's, Arbroath, 1953–59; Canon of Dundee, 1953; Hon. Canon of Oban, 1979. *Publication:* Chanda: history of a mission, 1988. *Recreations:* formerly Rugby football, athletics; rifle shooting (shot for Cambridge, for Scotland 1932–84). *Address:* 3 West Hill Road, Kirriemuir, Angus DD8 4PR. *T:* (01575) 575415.

COPLAND, Geoffrey Malcolm, DPhil; CPhys; Rector and Vice-Chancellor, University of Westminster, since 1996; *b* 28 June 1942; *s* of late Cyril Charles Copland and Jessie Palmer Copland; *m* 1st, 1967, Janet Mary Todd (marr. diss. 1985); one *s* one *d*; 2nd, 1985, Dorothy Joy Harrison. *Educ:* Fitzmaurice Grammar Sch., Bradford-on-Avon; Merton Coll., Oxford (MA, DPhil 1967). MInstP 1973; CPhys 1973. Post-doctoral scientist, Yale Univ., 1967–69; University of London: Researcher and Lectr in Physics, QMC, 1969–71; Lectr in Physics, Queen Elizabeth Coll., 1971–80; Dean of Studies, Goldsmiths' Coll., 1981–87; Dep. Rector, Poly. of Central London, later Univ. of Westminster, 1987–95. Mem. Council, UUK (formerly CVCP), 1998–. Member Board: Edexcel Foundn, 1998–; PSI, 1998–; Central London Partnership, 2001–. Mem., Council for Industry and Higher Educn, 1999– (Trustee, 2001–); Chm., Thomas Wall Trust, 1999–; Trustee: Regent St Polytechnic Trust, 1996–; Quintin Hogg Trust, 1996–; Quintin Hogg Meml Fund, 1996–; Internat. Student House, 2000–; Learning from Experience Trust, 2000–. FRSA 1991. *Publications:* research papers in physics in various jls. *Recreations:* walking, cricket, gardening. *Address:* University of Westminster, 309 Regent Street, W1B 2UW. *T:* (020) 7911 5000. *Club:* Oxford and Cambridge.

COPLEY, John (Michael Harold); opera director; *b* 12 June 1933; *s* of Ernest Harold Copley and Lilian Forbes. *Educ:* King Edward's, Five Ways, Birmingham; Sadler's Wells Ballet Sch.; Central Sch. of Arts and Crafts, London (Dip. with Hons in Theatre Design). Appeared as the apprentice in Britten's Peter Grimes for Covent Garden Opera Co, 1950; stage managed: both opera and ballet companies at Sadler's Wells, in Rosebery Avenue, 1953–57; also various musicals, plays, etc, in London's West End, incl. The World of Paul Slickey and My Fair Lady. Joined Covent Garden Opera Co.: Dep. Stage Manager, 1960; Asst Resident Producer, 1963; Associate Resident Producer, 1966; Resident Producer, 1972; Prin. Resident Producer, 1975–88. *Productions include: at Covent Garden:* Suor Angelica, 1965; Così fan Tutte, 1968, 1981; Orpheo ed Euridice, 1969; Le Nozze di Figaro, 1971, 1985; Don Giovanni, 1973; La Bohème, 1974, 1985; Faust, 1974; L'elisir d'amore, 1975, 1981, 1985; Benvenuto Cellini, 1976; Ariadne auf Naxos, 1976; Maria Stuarda; Royal Silver Jubilee Gala, 1977; Werther, 1979; La Traviata, Lucrezia Borgia, 1980; Alceste, 1981; Semele, 1982, 1988, 1996; Norma, 1987; L'elisir d'amore, 1992; *at*

London Coliseum (for Sadler's Wells, subseq. ENO): Carmen, Il Seraglio, Il Trovatore, La Traviata, Mary Stuart; Rosenkavalier. La Belle Hélène, 1975; Werther, 1977; Manon, Aida, Julius Caesar, Les Mamelles de Tirésias, 1979; *Athens Festival:* Macbeth; *Netherlands Opera:* Lucia; *Opera National de Belge:* Lucia; *Wexford Festival:* La Clemenza di Tito; L'Infedelta delusa; *Dallas Civic Opera:* Lucia; Hansel and Gretel, 1991; Elektra, Il Trovatore, 1996; Ariodante, 1998; *Chicago Lyric Opera:* Lucia; La Bohème, 1983; Orlando, 1986; Tancredi, 1989; The Barber of Seville, 1989; Peter Grimes, Idomeneo, 1997; Gioconda, 1998; Die Fledermaus, 1999; *Canadian Opera, Toronto:* Lucia; Falstaff; La Bohème, 1984; Adriana Lecouvreur, La Forza del Destino, 1987; *Greek Nat. Opera:* Madame Butterfly; Otello; *Australian Opera:* Fidelio, Nozze di Figaro, Rigoletto, Magic Flute, Jenufa, Ariadne auf Naxos, Madame Butterfly, Fra Diavolo, Macbeth, La Traviata, Manon Lescaut, Lucia di Lammermoor, Tosca, Manon; Adriana Lecouvreur, 1984; Peter Grimes, 1986; Carmen, 1987; La Forza del Destino, 1988; *Victoria State Opera:* Don Carlos, 1984; La Bohème, 1985; *WNO:* La Traviata, Falstaff, Peter Grimes, Tosca; Peter Grimes, 1983; *Opera North:* Les Mamelles de Tirésias, Madama Butterfly; *Scottish Opera:* Lucia, Ballo in Maschera, Dido and Aeneas; Acis and Galatea for English Opera Group in Stockholm, Paris, Aldeburgh Fest.; *New York City Opera:* Le Nozze di Figaro; Der Freischutz; Don Quichotte; *Santa Fé Opera:* Ariodanie, 1987; Così fan tutte, 1988; Der Rosenkavalier, La Traviata, 1989; La Bohème, 1990; Tosca, 1994; Semele, 1997; Idomeneo, 1999; *Ottawa Festival:* Midsummer Night's Dream; Eugene Onegin, 1983; *Vancouver Opera:* Carmen; *San Francisco Opera:* Julius Caesar; The Midsummer Marriage, 1983; Don Giovanni, 1984; Orlando, 1985; Le Nozze di Figaro, Eugene Onegin, 1986; La Traviata, 1987; Idomeneo, 1989; Midsummer Night's Dream, 1992; Pique Dame, 1993; Peter Grimes, 1998; *San Diego Opera:* Eugene Onegin, 1985; Le Nozze di Figaro, 1986; Così fan tutte, 1991; *Staatsoper Munich:* Adriana Lecouvreur, 1984; *Teatro La Fenice, Venice:* Semele, 1991 and 1992; *Deutsche Oper, Berlin:* L'Elisir d'amore, 1988; *Metropolitan Opera, NY:* Julius Caesar, 1988; Semiramide, 1990; L'Elisir d'amore, 1991; *Opera Theatre of St Louis:* La Rondine, 1996. Sang as soloist in Bach's St John Passion, Bremen, Germany, 1965; appeared as Ferdy in John Osborne's play, A Patriot for Me, at Royal Court Theatre, 1965. Co-directed (with Patrick Garland): Fanfare for Europe Gala, Covent Garden, 3 Jan. 1973; Fanfare for Elizabeth gala, Covent Garden, 21 April 1986. Hon. RAM 1999. *Recreation:* cooking. *Address:* 9D Thistle Grove, SW10 9RR.

COPLEY, Peter Edward; His Honour Judge Copley; a Circuit Judge, since 1995; *b* 15 Feb. 1943; *s* of Edward Thomas Copley and Florence Hilda Copley; *m* 1st; one *s* one *d*; 2nd, 1986, Janice Patricia Webster; one *d*. *Educ:* College of Law. Qualified Solicitor, 1966. *Recreation:* sailing. *Address:* c/o Circuit Administrator, New Cavendish House, 18 Maltravers Street, WC2R 3EU.

COPP, Darrell John Barkwell, OBE 1981; General Secretary, Institute of Biology, 1951–82; *b* 25 April 1922; *s* of J. J. H. Copp and L. A. Hoad; *m* 1944, Margaret Henderson; two *s* one *d*. *Educ:* Taunton's Sch., Southampton; Southampton Univ. (BSc). Scientific Officer, Admty Signals Estabt, 1942–45; Asst Sec., British Assoc. for Advancement of Science, 1947–51. Sec., Council for Nature, 1958–63; originator and co-ordinator of first National Nature Week, 1963. Hon. Treas., Parly and Scientific Cttee, 1980–83; Sec., European Community Biologists' Assoc., 1975–85. Trustee, Rye Art Gall., 1985–90. Hon. MTech Bradford, 1975; Hon. FIBiol 1984. *Publications:* reports and reviews in scientific jls. *Recreations:* walking, renovating farm buildings. *Address:* Underhill Farmhouse, Wittersham, Tenterden, Kent TN30 7EU. *T:* (01797) 270633.

COPPEL, Andrew Maxwell, FCA; Group Chief Executive, Queens Moat Houses plc, since 1993; Chairman, Tourism Ireland Ltd, since 2001; *b* 22 Aug. 1950; *s* of Isaac Coppel and Marjorie Coppel; *m* 1974, June Vanessa Gillespie; one *s* one *d*. *Educ:* Belfast Royal Acad.; Queen's Univ., Belfast (LLB Hons). FCA 1982. With Coopers & Lybrand, 1973–77; Asst Dir, Morgan Grenfell & Co. Ltd, 1977–86; Finance Dir, Ratners Gp plc, 1986–90; Chief Exec., Sale Tilney plc, 1990–92. *Recreations:* tennis, golf, Rugby, cinema, reading. *Address:* (office) Queens Court, 9/17 Eastern Road, Romford, Essex RM1 3NG. *T:* (01708) 730522. *Clubs:* Claygate Tennis, St George's Hill Tennis, Burhill Golf, Esher Cricket (Surrey).

COPPEN, Dr Alec James, MD, DSc; FRCP, FRCPsych; Director, Medical Research Council Neuropsychiatry Laboratory, and Emeritus Consultant Psychiatrist, West Park Hospital, Epsom, Surrey, 1974–89, retired; *b* 29 Jan. 1923; *y s* of late Herbert John Wardle Coppen and Marguerite Mary Annie Coppen; *m* 1952, Gunhild Margareta, *y d* of late Albert and Sigrid Andersson, Båstad, Sweden; one *s*. *Educ:* Dulwich Coll.; Univ. of Bristol (MB, ChB 1953; MD 1958; DSc 1978); Maudsley Hosp.; Univ. of London (DPM 1957); MRCP 1975, FRCP 1980, FRCPsych 1971 (Hon. FRCPsych 1995). Registrar, then Sen. Registrar, Maudsley Hosp., 1954–59; MRC Neuropsychiatry Research Unit, 1959–74, MRC External Staff, 1974–89; Consultant Psychiatrist: St Ebba's Hosp., 1959–64; West Park Hosp., 1964–89; Hon. Cons. Psychiatrist, St George's Hosp., 1965–70. Head of WHO designated Centre for Biological Psychiatry in UK, 1974–89; Consultant, WHO, 1977–89; Examiner, Royal Coll. of Psychiatry, 1973–77; Andrew Woods Vis. Prof., Univ. of Iowa, 1981; Lectr to learned socs and univs in Europe, N and S America, Asia and Africa. Mem. Council, RMPA (Chm., Research and Clinical Section), 1965–70; Chairman, Biolog. Psychiatry Section, World Psychiatric Assoc., 1972; President, British Assoc. of Psychopharmacology, 1975; Member: Internat. Coll. Neuropsychopharm., 1960– (Mem. Council, 1979; Pres., 1988–90); RSM, 1960–; British Pharmacol. Soc., 1977–; Special Health Auth., Bethlem Royal and Maudsley Hosp., 1982–87; Hon. Member: Mexican Soc. for Biolog. Psychiatry, 1973–; Mexican Inst. of Culture, 1974–; Swedish Psychiatric Assoc., 1977–; European Collegium Neuro-Psychopharmacolgicum, 1987–; Corresponding Member: Amer. Coll. of Neuropsychopharm., 1977–; Deutsche Gesellschaft für Psychiatrie und Nervenheilkunde; Distinguished Fellow, APA, 1981. Freeman, City of London, 1980; Soc. of Apothecaries: Yeoman, 1980; Liveryman 1985. Anna Monika Prize, 1969; European Prize for Psychopharmacology, 1991; Lifetime Achievement Gold Medal, British Assoc. of Psychopharmacology, 1998. *Publications:* (jtly) Recent Developments in Schizophrenia, 1967; (jtly) Recent Developments in Affective Disorders, 1968; (jtly) Psychopharmacology of Affective Disorders, 1979; contribs to text books; papers in Nature, Lancet, BMJ, etc (Current Contents Citation Classic, 1978, Biochemistry of the Affective Disorders). *Recreations:* golf, opera. *Address:* 5 Walnut Close, Epsom, Surrey KT18 5JL. *T:* (01372) 720800. *Clubs:* Athenæum, Royal Automobile.

COPPIN, Alan Charles; Chief Executive, Historic Royal Palaces, since 1999; *b* 4 June 1950; *s* of Charles and Vera Coppin; *m* 1975, Gaynor Hilary Wareham; one *s*. *Educ:* Westlain Grammar Sch., Brighton; Brighton Poly. Mgt posts with cos incl. Strutt & Parker, THF Leisure, 1971–86; Sen. Mgt Consultant, KPMG, 1986–88; Chief Exec., Wembley plc, 1988–98. Exec. Dir, Compass Gp plc, 1998–99; non-exec. Dir, Carillion plc, 1999–; Dir, Expocentric plc, 2000–. Chairman: NW London TEC, 1990–92; Stadium and Arena Mgt Project, 1994–95. Chm., Include, nat. children's charity, 1997–2000. Hon. Vis. Prof., Business Sch., Univ. of N London, 1998–. CIMgt 1997. *Recreations:* family activities, fitness, sports-spectating, cinema, writing. *Address:* Briar Hedge, The Drive, Abbotsbrook, Bourne End, Bucks SL8 5RE. *T:* (01628) 850142.

COPPOCK, Surgeon Rear-Adm. (D) David Arthur, CB 1990; Director, Defence Dental Services, 1988–90; *b* 19 April 1931; *s* of Oswald John Coppock and Ada Katherine Beaven; *m* 1st, 1956, Maria Averil Ferreira (*d* 1985); two *d*; 2nd, 1990, Sally Annette Arnold. *Educ:* Bishop Wordsworth School; Guy's Hosp. (BDS); George Washington Univ. (MSc). Entered RN 1955; HM Ships Eagle, 1956, Tamar, Hong Kong, 1959, Hermes, 1963, Rooke, Gibraltar, 1965; US Navy exchange, 1972; Dep. Dir, Naval Dental Services, 1980; Comd Dental Surgeon to C-in-C Naval Home Command, 1983; Dir, Naval Dental Services, 1983–88. QHDS, 1983–90. Mem., Assoc. of Professional Game Angling Instructors, 1991–. OStJ 1983. *Recreation:* fishing. *Address:* Breamore Lodge, West Street, Hambledon, Hants PO7 4RW. *T:* (023) 9263 2566.

COPPOLA, Francis Ford; Artistic Director, Zoetrope Studios, since 1969; *b* 7 April 1939; *s* of late Carmine Coppola and of Italia Pennino; *m* 1963, Eleanor Neil; one *s* one *d* (and one *s* decd). *Educ:* Hofstra Univ. (BA); Univ. of Calif, LA (MFA). Films directed: Dementia 13, 1963; You're a Big Boy Now, 1967; Finian's Rainbow, 1968; The Rain People, 1969; The Godfather, 1972; The Conversation, 1974; The Godfather Part II, 1974; Apocalypse Now, 1979; One From the Heart, 1981; The Outsiders, 1983; Rumble Fish, 1983; The Cotton Club, 1984; Peggy Sue Got Married, 1987; Gardens of Stone, 1988; Tucker: The Man and his Dream, 1988; New York Stories (Life Without Zoe), 1989; The Godfather Part III, 1991; Bram Stoker's Dracula, 1993; Jack, 1996; John Grisham's The Rainmaker, 1998; executive producer: Black Stallion, 1979; Hammett, 1983; Lionhart, 1987; The Secret Garden, 1993; Mary Shelley's Frankenstein, 1994. Commandeur, Ordre des Arts et des Lettres, 1983. *Recreations:* reading, writing, scientific discovery. *Address:* Zoetrope Studios, 916 Kearny Street, San Francisco, CA 94133–5138, USA. *T:* (415) 7887500.

COPPS, Hon. Sheila Maureen; PC (Can.) 1993; MP (L) Hamilton East, Canada, since 1984; Minister of Canadian Heritage, since 1996; *b* 27 Nov. 1952; *d* of Vic Copps and Geraldine (*née* Guthro); one *d*. *Educ:* Univ. of Western Ontario (BA Hons English and French); Univ. of Rouen; McMaster Univ. Journalist, 1974–77; MPP (L) Ontario, 1981–84; Official Opposition Critic for: Housing and Labour, 1984–87; Health and Welfare and Fitness and Amateur Sport, 1987–89; Envmt and Co-Critic for Social Policy, 1989–90; Industry, 1990–91; Dep. Leader of Opposition, 1991–93; Minister of the Envmt, 1993–96; Dep. Prime Minister, 1993–97. *Publication:* Nobody's Baby, 1986. *Address:* House of Commons, Ottawa, ON K1A 0A6, Canada. *T:* (613) 9952772, *Fax:* (613) 9922727.

CORBEN, Albert Edward; Assistant Under Secretary of State, Radio Regulatory Department, Home Office (and subsequently with Department of Trade and Industry), 1980–83, retired; *b* 25 Nov. 1923; *s* of Ebenezer Joseph James Corben and Frances Flora (*née* Orchard); *m* 1953, Doris Dodd; two *s*. *Educ:* Portsmouth Grammar Sch.; Sir John Cass Technical Inst. Served Royal Artillery, 1943–47. Entered Home Office, as Executive Officer, 1947; Higher Executive Officer, 1955–62; Sen. Executive Officer, 1962–66; Principal, 1966–72; Secretary to Advisory Council on Penal System, 1966–68; Sen. Principal, 1972–73; Asst Sec., 1973–80. *Recreations:* swimming, golf, walking. *Address:* The Gables, 30 Kingswood Road, Bromley, Kent BR2 0NF. *T:* (020) 8460 4106.

CORBET, Dr Gordon Barclay; zoologist; *b* 4 March 1933; *s* of George and Mary Corbet; *m* 1959, Elizabeth Urquhart; one *s* one *d*. *Educ:* Morgan Acad., Dundee; Univ. of St Andrews (BSc, PhD). Asst Lectr in Biology, Sir John Cass Coll., London, 1958–59; British Museum (Natural History): Sen., later Principal, Scientific Officer, Dept of Zoology, 1960–71; Dep. Keeper of Zoology, 1971–76; Hd, Dept of Central Services, 1976–88. *Publications:* The Terrestrial Mammals of Western Europe, 1966; Finding and Identifying Mammals in Britain, 1975; The Handbook of British Mammals, 2nd edn (with H. N. Southern), 1977, 3rd edn (with S. Harris), 1991; The Mammals of the Palaearctic Region, 1978; The Mammals of Britain and Europe, 1980; A World List of Mammalian Species (with J. E. Hill), 1980, 3rd edn 1991; The Mammals of the Indomalayan Region (with J. E. Hill), 1992; The Nature of Fife, 1998. *Recreations:* natural history. *Address:* Little Dumbarnie, Newburn, Upper Largo, Fife KY8 6JG. *T:* (01333) 340634.

CORBETT, family name of **Barons Corbett of Castle Vale** and **Rowallan**.

CORBETT OF CASTLE VALE, Baron *cr* 2001 (Life Peer), of Erdington in the County of West Midlands; **Robin Corbett;** communication and public affairs consultant; *b* 22 Dec. 1933; *s* of Thomas Corbett and Marguerite Adele Mainwaring; *m* 1970, Val Hudson; one *s* two *d*. *Educ:* Holly Lodge Grammar Sch., Smethwick. Newspaper and magazine journalist, 1950–69; Editoral Staff Develt Exec., IPC Magazines, 1969–72; Sen. Lab. Adviser, IPC Magazines, 1972–74. Mem. Nat. Union of Journalists Nat. Exec. Council, 1965–69. MP (Lab): Hemel Hempstead, Oct. 1974–1979; Birmingham, Erdington, 1983–2001. Opposition front bench spokesman on home affairs, 1985–92, on broadcasting, the media and nat. heritage, 1992–94, on disabled people's rights, 1994–95. Member: Select Cttee on Agriculture, 1996–97; Select Cttee on Home Affairs, 1997–2001 (Chm., 1999–2001); Expenditure Cttee, 1976–79; Commons Home Affairs Cttee, 1984–86; Vice Chm., All Party Animal Welfare Gp, 1976–79; Jt Vice-Chm., All Party Motor Industry Gp, 1987–; Chairman: All Party Anzac Gp, 1997–2001 (Jt Sec., 1985); All Party MS Gp, 1997–2001; Vice-Chm., Indo-British Parly Gp, 1997–2001; Chairman: PLP Agric. Gp, 1977–78; PLP Home Affairs Cttee, 1984–86; Sec., PLP Civil Liberties Gp, 1974–79; Mem., PLP Campaign Unit, 1985–86. Jt Vice-Chm., Friends of Cyprus, 1987–. Mem., Food and Agriculture Sub-Cttee, Labour Party Nat. Exec. Cttee, 1974–79; Chm., farm animal welfare co-ordinating exec., 1977–92. Member, Council: RCVS, 1989–92; SCF, 1987–90; Mem. Bd, Rehab UK, 1996–; sponsor, Terrence Higgins Trust, 1987–99. Fellow, Industry and Parlt Trust, 1979. *Publications:* (jtly) Can I Count on your Support?, 1986; On the Campaign Trail, 1987. *Recreations:* visiting North Wales; pottering. *Address:* House of Lords, SW1A 0PW. *Clubs:* Castle Vale Residents Association; Forget-Me-Not (Erdington).

CORBETT, Dame Antoinette; *see* Sibley, Dame A.

CORBETT, Rev. Canon (Charles) Eric; *b* 6 Oct. 1917; *m* Sylvia Howe. *Educ:* Jesus College, Oxford (BA 1939; MA 1943); Wycliffe Hall, Oxford. Deacon 1940, priest 1941, St Asaph; Curate of Gresford, 1940–44; CF, 1944–47; Curate of Eglwys-Rhos, 1947–49; Rector of Harpurhey, 1949–54; Vicar of St Catherine's, Wigan, 1954–61; Vicar of St Luke, Farnworth, 1961–71; Rural Dean of Farnworth, 1964–71; Archdeacon of Liverpool, 1971–79; Canon-Treasurer of Liverpool Cathedral, 1979–83. *Address:* 80 Latham Avenue, Helsby, Cheshire WA6 0EB. *T:* (01928) 724184.

CORBETT, Gerald Michael Nolan; Chairman, Woolworths, 2001; *b* 7 Sept. 1951; *s* of late John Michael Nolan Corbett and of Pamela Muriel Corbett (*née* Gay); *m* 1976, Virginia Moore Newsum; one *s* three *d*. *Educ:* Tonbridge Sch.; Pembroke Coll., Cambridge (Foundn Schol.; MA); London Business Sch. (MSc with Dist.); Harvard Business Sch. (Exchange Schol.). Consultant and Case Leader, Boston Consulting Gp, 1976–82; Dixons Group plc: Gp Finance Controller, 1982–85; Corporate Finance Dir, 1985–87; Group Finance Director: Redland plc, 1987–94; Grand Metropolitan plc,

1994–97; Chief Exec., Railtrack plc, 1997–2000. Non-executive Director: MEPC Plc, 1995–98; Burmah Castrol Plc, 1998–. Chm. Govs, Abbot's Hill Sch., 1997–. *Recreations:* country pursuits, tennis, ski-ing, bridge. *Address:* Holtsmere End Farm, Redbourn, Herts AL3 7AW. *Club:* MCC.

CORBETT, Graham; *see* Corbett, P. G.

CORBETT, Prof. Greville George, PhD; FBA 1997; AcSS; Professor of Linguistics and of Russian Language, University of Surrey, since 1988; *b* 23 Dec. 1947; *s* of George Pilsbury Corbett and Elsie Mary Bates; *m* 1974, Judith Mary Baird; three *s*. *Educ:* Univ. of Birmingham (BA 1970; MA 1971; PhD 1976). Lectr, 1974–85, Reader, 1985–88, Univ. of Surrey. Pres., Linguistics Assoc. of GB, 1994–97. *Publications:* Predicate Agreement in Russian, 1979; Hierarchies, Targets and Controllers: agreement patterns in Slavic, 1983; (jtly) Computers, Language Learning and Language Teaching, 1985; Gender, 1991; (ed jtly) Heads in Grammatical Theory, 1993; (ed jtly) The Slavonic Languages, 1993; Number, 2000. *Recreation:* music. *Address:* Department of Linguistic and International Studies, University of Surrey, Guildford, Surrey GU2 5XH.

CORBETT, Captain Hugh Askew, CBE 1968; DSO 1945; DSC 1943; RN; (Retired); *b* 25 June 1916; *s* of late Rev. F. St John Corbett, MA, FRSL, FRHistS and late Elsie L. V. Askew; *m* 1945, Patricia Nancy, *d* of late Thomas Patrick Spens, OBE, MC, LLD; three *s*. *Educ:* St Edmund's Sch., Canterbury. Joined Royal Navy, 1933; HMS Cæsar as Capt. (D), 8th Destroyer Sqdn, 1961–63; HMS Fearless, 1965–67 (Capt.). *Address:* Holly Cottage, 3 Clare Road, Cambridge CB3 9HN. *T:* (01223) 357735.

CORBETT, James Patrick; QC 1999; FCIArb; a Recorder, since 2000; *b* 10 May 1952; *s* of late Patrick Francis Corbett and of Kathleen Mary Corbett (*née* O'Callaghan); *m* 1979, Barbara Janet Willett; one *s* four *d*. *Educ:* Sloane Sch., Chelsea; Univ. of Exeter (LLB 1973; LLM European Legal Studies 1975); Inns of Court Sch. of Law. FCIArb 1997. Called to the Bar, Inner Temple, 1975, Lincoln's Inn, *ad eundem*, 1998; Lectr in Law, Univ. of Leicester, 1975–77; in practice at the Bar, 1977–; joined Midland and Oxford Circuit, 1979; called to Irish Bar, 1981, Northern Irish Bar, 1994; Asst Recorder, 1996–2000. CEDR Accredited Mediator, 2000. Contested (SDP): Erewash, Derbys, 1983; Cheshire E, 1984; Staffs Moorlands, 1987. *Publications:* articles in legal and arbitration jls. *Recreations:* jazz, the cinema, Rugby League (London Broncos). *Address:* St Philips Chambers, 55 Temple Row, Birmingham B2 5LS; Serle Court, 6 New Square, Lincoln's Inn, WC2A 3QS.

CORBETT, Hon. Michael McGregor; Chief Justice of South Africa, 1989–96; *b* 14 Sept. 1923; *s* of Alan Frederick Corbett and Johanna Sibella McGregor; *m* 1949, Margaret Murray Corbett (*née* Luscombe); two *s* two *d*. *Educ:* Rondebosch Boys' High Sch.; Univ. of Cape Town (BA, LLB); Trinity Hall, Cambridge (Elsie Ballot Scholarship, 1946; Law Tripos 1st cl. 1947; LLB 1st cl. 1948; Hon Fellow, 1992). Enlisted S African Tank Corps, 1942, commissioned 1943; active service, Egypt and Italy with Royal Natal Carbineers, 1943–44. Admitted Advocate, Cape Bar, 1948; QC 1961; Judge, Cape Provincial Div., Supreme Court, 1963; Judge of Appeal, 1974. Hon. Bencher, Lincoln's Inn, 1991; Hon. Mem., Amer. Bar Assoc., 1997. Hon. LLD: Cape Town, 1982; Orange Free State, 1990; Rhodes, 1990; Pretoria, 1993; Witwatersrand, 1994; Stellenbosch, 1996. President of Convocation Medal, Univ. of Cape Town, 1998. Order for Meritorious Service (S Africa), 1996. *Publications:* (jtly) The Quantum of Damages in Bodily and Fatal Injury Cases, 1960, 3rd edn 1985; (jtly) The Law of Succession in South Africa, 1980. *Recreations:* tennis, walking. *Address:* 18 Ladies Mile Extension, Constantia, Cape 7800, South Africa. *Clubs:* City and Civil Service (Cape Town); Kelvin Grove (Newlands, Cape).

CORBETT, (Peter) Graham, CBE 1994; Chairman: Postal Services Commission, since 2000; Ricability (Research and Information for Consumers with Disabilities), since 1998; *b* 6 Nov. 1934; *s* of John and Greta Corbett; *m* 1964, Anne (*née* James), journalist; two *s*. *Educ:* Stowe Sch. ACA 1957, FCA 1962. Peat Marwick, London, 1959–75; Sen. Partner, Peat Marwick Continental Europe, 1975–87; Chief Financial Officer, Eurotunnel plc and Eurotunnel SA, 1987–96; Dep. Chm., Monopolies and Mergers, then Competition Commn, 1997–2000. Non-exec. Dir, Kier Gp plc, 1996–2000. Trustee, Franco-British Council, 1995–99. CIMgt 1994. FRSA 1999. DUniv Brunel 1995. *Address:* 95 Coleherne Court, Old Brompton Road, SW5 0ED. *T:* (020) 7373 9878.

CORBETT, Dr Richard Graham; Member (Lab) Yorkshire and the Humber Region, European Parliament, since 1999 (Merseyside West, Dec. 1996–99); *b* 6 Jan. 1955; *s* of Harry Graham Corbett and Kathleen Zita Corbett (*née* Bryant); *m* 1st, 1984, Inge van Gaal (marr. diss.); one *s*; 2nd, 1989, Anne de Malsche; two *d*. *Educ:* Farnborough Rd Sch., Southport; Internat. Sch., Geneva; Trinity Coll., Oxford (BA Hons PPE); Univ. of Hull (Extra Mural Doctorate 1995). Stagiare, Socialist Gp, European Parlt, 1976; UK Labour Delegn, 1977; Commn (Regl Policy), 1977; Sec. Gen., European Co-ordination Bureau, Internat. Youth Orgns, 1977–81; European civil servant, 1981–89; European Parliament: political advr, 1989–94, Dep. Gen. Sec., 1995–96, Socialist Gp; Vice Pres., Cttee on Instnl Affairs, 1997–99; Labour Party and Socialist Gp spokesman on constitutional affairs, 1999–; Bd, Britain in Europe, 2001–. Regl Bd, Yorks, Labour Party, 1999–2001. *Publications:* A Socialist Policy for Europe, 1985; The European Parliament, 1990, 4th edn 2000; The Treaty of Maastricht: from conception to ratification, 1993; The European Parliament's Role in closer EU integration, 1998; contrib. Annual Rev. on Instnl Develts in EU for Jl Common Mkt Studies. *Recreations:* cycling, squash, ski-ing, watching football, reading. *Address:* European Parliament, Rue Wiertz, 1047 Brussels, Belgium. *T:* (2) 2845504.

CORBETT, Maj.-Gen. Sir Robert (John Swan), KCVO 1994; CB 1991; Director, Dulverton Trust, since 1994; *b* 16 May 1940; *s* of Robert Hugh Swan Corbett and Patricia Elizabeth Cavan Corbett (*née* Lambart); *m* 1966, Susan Margaret Anne O'Cock; three *s*. *Educ:* Woodcote House; Shrewsbury School; Army Staff Coll., 1973; US Armed Forces Staff Coll., 1980. Commissioned Irish Guards, 1959; served UK, Cyprus, Hong Kong, Falkland Is, Belize, BAOR; Brigade Major, HQ Household Div., 1980–81; CO, 1st Bn Irish Guards (4 Armoured Brigade, BAOR), 1981–84; Chief of Staff, British Forces Falkland Is, 1984–85; Comdr, 5th Airborne Brigade, 1985–87; Mem., RCDS, 1987; Dir, Defence Programme, MoD, 1987–89; GOC Berlin (British Sector) and British Comdt, Berlin, 1989–3 Oct. 1990 (German re-unification); attached HQ BAOR, 1990–91; GOC London Dist, and Maj. Gen. Comdg Household Div., 1991–94. Mem. Adv. Bd, Deutsche Bank Berlin AG, 1991–2000. Chairman: Guards Chapel Adv. Cttee, 1993–; Berlin Infantry Bde Meml Trust Fund, 1992–99. Regtl Lt-Col, Irish Guards, 1988–91. Hon. Col, London Irish Rifles, 1993–2000. Liveryman, Vintners' Co., 1968. Hon. Citizen, 1993, Mem. Conseil Municipal, Pierrefeu, France, 1993. Order of Merit, Berlin, 1990; Hon. Grand Officier, Ordre de Mérite (Luxembourg), 1994; Hon. Grande Oficial, Ordem do Infante Dom Henrique (Portugal), 1994; Hon. Dato Paduka, Order of Crown of Brunei, 1993. *Publication:* Berlin and the British Ally 1945–1990, 1993. *Recreations:* travel, reading, walking, English church architecture. *Address:* c/o RHQ Irish Guards, Wellington Barracks, SW1E 6HQ. *Clubs:* Pratt's, Buck's.

CORBETT, Ronald Balfour, OBE 1978; comedian/character actor; *b* 4 Dec. 1930; *s* of William Balfour Corbett and Anne Elizabeth Corbett; *m* 1965, Anne Hart; two *d*. *Educ:* James Gillespie Sch., Edinburgh; Royal High Sch., Edinburgh. *Films:* Top of the Form; You're Only Young Once; Casino Royale, 1966; No Sex Please, We're British, 1974; Fierce Creatures, 1997; *television:* Frost Report, 1966–67; Frost on Sunday, 1968–69; The Two Ronnies (12 in series), 1971–85; The Two Ronnies Christmas Special, 1982, 1987; Variety Specials, 1977; Sorry! (8 in series), 1981–88; Small Talk (3 series), 1994–96; *theatre:* Twang (Lionel Bart musical), 1965; Cinderella, London Palladium, Christmas 1971–72; two seasons at London Palladium, 1978, 1983; The Dressmaker (Feydeau), 1990; Out of Order, UK and Australian tour, 1992–93. *Publications:* Small Man's Guide to Life; Armchair Golf, 1986; High Hopes (autobiog.), 2000. *Recreations:* golf, racing, soccer, cooking. *Clubs:* Annabel's, Saints and Sinners; Addington Golf (Surrey); Wisley Golf; Gullane Golf (East Lothian); Hon. Company of Edinburgh Golfers (Muirfield).

CORBETT, Lt-Col Uvedale, CBE 1984; DSO 1944; DL; *b* 12 Sept. 1909; *s* of Major C. U. Corbett, Stableford, Bridgnorth, Shropshire; *m* 1st, 1935, Veronica Marian Whitehead (marr. diss., 1952); two *s* one *d*; 2nd, 1953, Mrs Patricia Jane Walker (*d* 1985); 3rd, 1987, Mrs Peggy Roberts (*d* 1997). *Educ:* Wellington (Berks); RMA, Woolwich. Commissioned Royal Artillery, 1929; relinquished command 3rd Regt RHA 1945; retired. MP (C) Ludlow Div. of Shropshire, 1945–51. Chm., Sun Valley Poultry Ltd, 1961–83. DL Hereford and Worcester, 1983. *Address:* Easthampton House, Leominster, Herefordshire HR6 9NZ. *T:* (01568) 708260. *Club:* Army and Navy.

CORBIN, Christopher John; restaurateur; *b* 1 March 1952; *s* of Frederick Christopher Corbin and Vera Corbin (*née* Copperwaite); *m* 1982, Francine Checinski; one *s* one *d* (twins). *Educ:* St Christopher's, Bournemouth; Westminster Tech. Coll. Co-founder and Director (with Jeremy King): Caprice Hldgs Ltd, 1982–; Caprice Events Ltd, 1995–; co-proprietor (with Jeremy King), restaurants: Le Caprice, 1981–; The Ivy, 1990–; J. Sheekey, 1998–. Walnut Tree Inn, Abergavenny, 2000–. Restaurateur of Year, Caterer and Hotelkeeper, 1993. *Recreations:* eating, tennis, contemporary art, meditation. *Clubs:* Queen's, Royal Automobile, Groucho.

CORBIN, Maurice Haig Alleyne; Justice of Appeal, Supreme Court, Trinidad and Tobago, 1972–81; *b* 26 May 1916; *s* of L. A. Corbin; *m* 1943, Helen Jocelyn Child; one *s* two *d*; *m* 1968, Jean Barcant. *Educ:* Harrison Coll., Barbados; Queen's Royal Coll., Trinidad. Solicitor, 1941; appointed Magistrate, Trinidad, 1945; called to the Bar, Middle Temple, 1949; Crown Counsel, 1953; Registrar, Supreme Court, 1954; Puisne Judge, Supreme Court, 1957–72. *Recreation:* tennis. *Address:* 77 Brook Road, Goodwood Park, Pt Cumana, Trinidad. *Club:* Queen's Park Cricket (Port of Spain, Trinidad).

CORBITT, Air Vice Marshal Ian Stafford; Chief Executive, RAF Training Group Defence Agency, and Air Officer Commanding, RAF Training Group, since 1999; *b* 30 July 1947; *s* of John Kellock Corbitt and Hilda Mary Corbitt; *m* 1976, Anne Lucille Worthy; two *d*. *Educ:* Simon Langton Grammar Sch., Canterbury; Quaid-i-Azam Univ., Islamabad (MSc Defence and Strategic Studies 1993). ACCA; CDipAF 1999. No 48 Sqdn, RAF Changi, Singapore, 1970-72; qualified Flying Instructor, RAF Leeming, 1973; ADC to AOC 46 Gp, RAF Upavon, 1973-75; Flt Comdr, No 30 Sqdn, 1976-77, OC Hercules Conversion Sqdn, 1977-79, RAF Lyneham; Staff Coll., Bracknell, 1980; HQ British Forces, Hong Kong, 1981-83; OC 242 OCU, RAF Lyneham, 1983-86; Flt Examr, USAF, Scott AFB, Ill, 1986-88; OC RAF Lyneham, 1989-91; HCSC, 1992; Nat. Defence Coll., Rawalpindi, 1992-93; Contingency Plans, HQ STC, 1993-95; Air Cdre, Policy and Plans, HQ PTC, 1995-99. *Address:* RAF Innsworth, Gloucester, Glos GL3 1EZ. *T:* (01452) 712612. *Club:* Royal Air Force.

CORBY, Sir (Frederick) Brian, Kt 1989; FIA; Chairman, Prudential Corporation plc, 1990–95; *b* 10 May 1929; *s* of Charles Walter and Millicent Corby; *m* 1952, Elizabeth Mairi McInnes; one *s* two *d*. *Educ:* Kimbolton Sch.; St John's Coll., Cambridge (MA). Joined Prudential Assce Co. Ltd, 1952; Dep. Gen. Manager, 1974; Gen. Manager, 1976–79; Gp Gen. Manager, Prudential Corp. Ltd, 1979–82; Dir, 1981–89, Chief Gen. Manager, 1982–85, Chm., 1985–89, Prudential Assce Co. Ltd; Chief Exec., Prudential Corp., 1982–90. Dir, 1982–90, Chm., 1985–90, Mercantile & General Reinsce Co. Chm., South Bank Bd, 1990–98; a Dir, Bank of England, 1985–93. Vice-President, Inst. of Actuaries, 1979–82; Chm., Assoc. of British Insurers, 1985–87; President: CBI, 1990–92; NIESR, 1994–. Chancellor, Univ. of Hertfordshire, 1992–96. Hon. DSc: City, 1989; Hertfordshire, 1996; Hon. DLitt CNAA, 1991. *Publications:* contribs to Jl of Inst. of Actuaries. *Recreations:* reading, golf.

CORBY, George Arthur; international meteorological consultant, retired; *b* 14 Aug. 1917; *s* of Bertie John Corby and Agnes May (*née* Dale); *m* 1951, Gertrude Anne Nicoll; one *s* one *d*. *Educ:* St Marylebone Grammar Sch.; Univ. of London (BSc Special Maths 1st Cl.). Architect's Dept. LCC, 1936–42; entered Met. Office, 1942; Flt Lt, RAFVR, 1943; Sqdn Leader, Dep. Chief Met. Officer, ACSEA, 1945–46; Sen. Met. Off., Northolt Airport, 1947–53; research, 1953–73; Dep. Dir for Communications and Computing, 1973–76; Dir of Services and Dep. Dir Gen., 1976–78. Vice-Pres., Royal Meteorol Soc., 1975–77. *Publications:* official scientific pubns and res. papers on mountain airflow, dynamical meteorol., and numerical forecasting. *Recreations:* music, photography. *Address:* Kings Barn, High Street, Harwell, Oxon OX11 0EY. *T:* (01235) 832883.

CORBYN, Jeremy Bernard; MP (Lab) Islington North, since 1983; *b* 26 May 1949; *s* of David Benjamin Corbyn. *Educ:* Adams Grammar Sch., Newport, Shropshire. NUPE Official, 1975–83; sponsored NUPE, then UNISON, MP. Mem., Haringey Borough Council, 1974–84 (Chm., Community Develt Cttee 1975–78, Public Works 1978–79, Planning Cttee 1980–81, 1982–83). Mem., Select Cttee on Social Security, 1990–97; Chair, London Gp of Lab MPs, 1993–96 (Vice-Chair, 1985–93); Vice Chair, Parly Human Rights Gp. Chair of Liberation, Nat. Council CND. *Address:* House of Commons, SW1A 0AA. *T:* (020) 7219 3545, (home) (020) 7263 7538.

CORCORAN, Hon. (James) Desmond, AO 1982; Chairman, South Australia Greyhound Racing Board, 1983–95; Member, South Australia Totalisator Board, 1982–95; *b* 8 Nov. 1928; *s* of James and Catherine Corcoran; *m* 1957, Carmel Mary Campbell; four *s* four *d*. *Educ:* Tantanoola Public School. Enlisted Australian Regular Army, 1950; served Korea, Japan, Malaya and New Guinea (despatches twice); discharged, rank of Captain, 1962. Entered politics, contested and won House of Assembly seat of Millicen, SA Parliament, 1962, Member for Coles, 1975; MP (Lab) Hartley, 1977–82; held portfolios of Minister of Lands, Irrigation, Repatriation, Immigration and Tourism, in Labor Govt, 1965–68; Dep. Leader of Opposition, 1968–70; Dep. Premier, Minister of Works and Minister of Marine, 1970–77, additionally Minister of Environment, 1977–79; Premier, Treasurer, and Minister of Ethnic Affairs, of S Australia, Feb.-Sept. 1979. *Address:* 44/Stamford Grand Apts, Moseley Square, Glenelg, SA 5045, Australia.

CORDARA, Roderick Charles; QC 1994; *b* 26 March 1953; *s* of Carlo and Sylvia Cordara; *m* 1997, Tsambika Anastasas. *Educ:* City of London Sch.; Trinity Hall,

Cambridge. Called to the Bar, Middle Temple, 1975; SC (NSW) 2000. *Address:* Essex Court Chambers, 24 Lincoln's Inn Fields, WC2A 3ED. *Club:* Oxford and Cambridge.

CORDEROY, Rev. Graham Thomas; Minister, Hutton and Shenfield Union Church, 1987–96; *b* 15 April 1931; *s* of Thomas and Gladys Corderoy; *m* 1957, Edna Marian Barnes; six *d. Educ:* Emanuel Sch., London; Manchester Univ. (BA Theology 1957). Ordained 1957; King's Lynn, 1957–62; commissioned RAF Chaplain, 1962; Principal Chaplain, Church of Scotland and Free Churches, and Hon. Chaplain to the Queen, 1984–87. Inst. of Alcohol Studies Bd, 1986–. *Recreations:* Rugby referee 1964–87, Gilbert and Sullivan buff. *Address:* Longmead, 66 Hardwick Lane, Bury St Edmunds, Suffolk IP33 2RB. *Club:* Royal Air Force.

CORDINER, William Lawson, OBE 1995; HM Diplomatic Service, retired; High Commissioner, Kingdom of Tonga, and Consul for Pacific Islands under American sovereignty South of the Equator, 1990–94; *b* 9 March 1935; *s* of late Alexander Lamb Cordiner and Jessie Cordiner; *m* 1958, Anne Milton; one *s. Educ:* Peterhead Acad.; Boroughmuir, Edinburgh. Inland Revenue, 1952–60; E African Common Services Orgn, 1960–67; HM Diplomatic Service: London, 1967–68; Saigon, 1968–70; Addis Ababa, 1971–74; Kuwait, 1974–75; Baghdad, 1975–77; on secondment to Export Div., DHSS, 1977–79; Rhodesia Dept, FCO, 1979–80; Govt Rep., Antigua and Barbuda, and St Kitts Nevis, 1980–83; Consul for Pacific NW of USA, Seattle, 1983–87; Asst, Commonwealth Co-ordination Dept, FCO, 1988–90. British Delegn Sec., Commonwealth Heads of Govt Meeting, Kuala Lumpur, 1989. Hon. Citizen of Washington State, 1987; Hon. Ambassador of Goodwill, Washington State, 1987. *Recreations:* golf, gardening, oil painting, travel, music. *Address:* Les Mulots, 47120 Duras, France. *Clubs:* Royal Commonwealth Society; Château des Vigiers (Monestier, France).

CORDINGLEY, Maj-Gen. John Edward, OBE 1959; *b* 1 Sept. 1916; *s* of Air Vice-Marshal Sir John Cordingley, KCB, KCVO, CBE, and late Elizabeth Ruth Carpenter; *m* 1st, 1940, Ruth Pamela (marr. diss. 1961), *d* of late Major S. A. Boddam-Whetham; two *s*; 2nd, 1961, Audrey Helen Anne, *d* of late Maj-Gen. F. G. Beaumont-Nesbitt, CVO, CBE, MC; two step *d. Educ:* Sherborne; RMA, Woolwich. 2nd Lieut RA, 1936; served War of 1939–45, Europe and India. Brigade Comdr, 1961–62; Imperial Defence Coll., 1963; Dir of Work Study, Min. of Defence (Army), 1964–66; Dep. Dir, RA, 1967–68; Maj-Gen., RA, BAOR, 1968–71, retired. Controller, Royal Artillery Instn, 1975–82; Chm. Bd of Management, RA Charitable Fund, 1977–82. Col Comdt, RA, 1973–82. Bursar, Sherborne Sch., 1971–74; Chm., J. W. Carpenter Ltd, 1984–87. Fellow, Inst. of Work Study Practitioners, 1965; MIMgt (MBIM 1966); FInstD 1985. *Recreations:* golf and gardening. *Address:* 15 High Street, Ramsbury, Marlborough, Wilts SN8 2PA. *T:* (01672) 520056. *Clubs:* Army and Navy; Senior Golfers.

See also Maj.-Gen. P. A. J. Cordingley.

CORDINGLEY, Maj.-Gen. Patrick Anthony John, DSO 1991; Chairman, MMI Research, since 2001; *b* 6 Oct. 1944; *s* of Maj.-Gen. John Edward Cordingley, *qv* and Ruth Pamela St John Carpendale; *m* 1968, Melissa Crawley; two *d. Educ:* Sherborne School. Commissioned into 5th Royal Inniskilling Dragoon Guards, 1965; commanded, 1984–87; commanded 7th Armoured Brigade, 1988–91; served Libya, Cyprus, UK, BAOR, Gulf; Comdr, Combined Arms Trng Centre, 1991–92; GOC Eastern Dist, 1992–95; GOC 2nd Div., 1995–96; Sen. British Loan Service Officer, Sultanate of Oman, 1996–2000. FRGS 1986. OStJ 1993. USA Bronze Star, 1991; Order of Oman, 2000. *Publications:* Captain Oates: soldier and explorer, 1984, 3rd edn 1985; In the Eye of the Storm, 1996. *Recreations:* country pursuits, whale-watching. *Club:* Cavalry and Guards.

CORDINGLY, David Michael Bradley, DPhil; writer and exhibition organiser; *b* 5 Dec. 1938; *s* of late Rt Rev. Eric Cordingly, MBE, sometime Bishop of Thetford, and of Mary Mathews; *m* 1971, Shirley Elizabeth Robin; one *s* one *d. Educ:* Christ's Hosp., Horsham; Oriel Coll., Oxford; (MA); Univ. of Sussex (DPhil). Graphic designer, 1960–68; Exhibn designer at BM, 1968–71; Keeper of Art Gall., Royal Pavilion and Museums, Brighton, 1971–78; Asst Dir, Mus. of London, 1978–80; National Maritime Museum: Asst Keeper, 1980–82; Dep. Keeper, 1982–86; Keeper of Pictures, 1986–88; Head of Exhibns, 1988–93. Adjunct Curator, South Street Seaport Mus., NY, 1995–; Guest Curator, Mariners Mus., Va, 2000–01. Exhibns organised include: Looking at London, 1980; Sea Finland, 1986; Captain Cook, Brisbane Expo, 1988; Mutiny on the Bounty, 1989; Henry VIII at Greenwich, 1991; Pirates: Fact and Fiction, 1992. FRSA 1974. Order of the White Rose of Finland, 1986. *Publications:* Marine Painting in England, 1974; Painters of the Sea, 1979; (with W. Percival Prescott) The Art of the Van de Veldes, 1982; Nicholas Pocock, 1986; Captain James Cook, Navigator, 1988; Pirates: fact and fiction, 1992; Life Among the Pirates, 1995; Pirates: an illustrated history, 1996; Ships and Seascapes, 1997; Heroines & Harlots: women at sea in the great age of sail, 2001; articles in Apollo, Connoisseur and Burlington Magazine. *Recreations:* sailing, carpentry. *Address:* 2 Vine Place, Brighton, Sussex BN1 3HE.

CORDLE, John Howard; *b* 11 Oct. 1912; *s* of late Ernest William Cordle; *m* 1st, 1938 (marr. diss., 1956); three *s* (and one *s* one *d* decd); 2nd, 1957 (marr. diss. 1971), *e d* of Col A. Maynard, OBE; one *s* three *d*; 3rd, 1976, Terttu, *y d* of Mikko Heikura, Finland; two *s. Educ:* City of London Sch. Served RAF (commissioned), 1940–45. Owner, Church of England Newspaper, 1960–71. Member: Archbishops of Canterbury and York Commission on Evangelism, 1945–46; Church Assembly, 1946–53; Oxford Churches Patronage Trust, 1947– (Chm., 1955–); Ecclesiastical Cttee of H of C, 1975–77; Hon. Treas., The World's Evangelical Alliance, 1949–53. Lay-Reader, Rochester, 1941–. Mem. of Lloyd's, 1952. Freeman of City of London, 1956, and Mem., Founders' Livery Co. (Master, 1990–91); Mem., Consultative Livery Cttee, City of London, 1991–92. Prospective Parly Cand. (C) NE Wolverhampton, 1949; contested (C) Wrekin Div., 1951; MP (C) Bournemouth E and Christchurch, Oct. 1959–1974, Bournemouth E, 1974–77; Chairman: West Africa Cttee, Conservative Commonwealth Council, 1962–77; Church and Parliament All-Party Gp, 1975–77; Sec., All Party Anglo-Libyan Gp, H of C, 1964–67. Member UK Delegation to: Council of Europe, Strasbourg, 1974–77 (Vice-Chm., Parly and Public Relations Cttee, 1976–77); WEU, Paris, 1974–77; Rapporteur, 1976–77, to Cttee on Social and Health Questions, on the institution of Internat. Medical Card. Primrose League: Chm., Finance Cttee, 1964–67; Hon. Treas., 1964–67; Chm., Gen. Purposes Cttee, 1967–68. Chm., Wessex Aid to Addicts Gp, 1985–; Pres. Salisbury District Speech-impaired Children Trust, 1988–. Governor, London Coll. of Divinity, 1947–52; Life Governor: St Mary's and St Paul's Coll., Cheltenham; Epsom Coll.; Mem. Court of University of Southampton, 1960–77. Gold Staff Officer, Coronation, 1953. Grand Band, Order of the Star of Africa (Liberia), 1964. *Recreations:* shooting, golf, gardening. *Address:* Malmesbury House, The Close, Salisbury, Wilts SP1 2EB. *Clubs:* Carlton, National (Trustee, 1946–), English-Speaking Union.

See also Viscount Cowdray.

CORDY, Timothy Soames; Consultant, Global to Local Ltd, since 2000; *b* 17 May 1949; *s* of John Knutt Cordy and Margaret Winifred Cordy (*née* Sheward); *m* 1974, Dr Jill Margaret Tattersall; one *s* one *d. Educ:* Dragon Sch., Oxford; Sherborne Sch.; Durham Univ. (BA); Glasgow Univ. (MPhil). MRTPI 1976. Leicester City Council, 1974–85 (Asst City Planning Officer, 1980–85); Communauté Urbaine de Strasbourg, 1978–79; Asst Chief Exec., Bolton MBC, 1985–87; Chief Exec., RSNC, 1987–94. Director: UK 2000, 1987–95; Volunteer Centre UK, 1989–95; TCPA, 1995–97; Envmtl Trng Orgn, 1996–98. *Publications:* articles on housing renewal, local economic develt, biodiversity, sustainability. *Recreations:* music, France, food. *Address:* 20 Harrowby Lane, Grantham, NG31 9HX. *T:* (01476) 410902.

CORDY-SIMPSON, Lt-Gen. Sir Roderick (Alexander), KBE 1998 (OBE 1984); CB 1993; Lieutenant, HM Tower of London, since 2001; *b* 29 Feb. 1944; *s* of late Col John Roger Cordy-Simpson, CBE, MC and of Mrs Ursula Margaret Wadham; *m* 1974, Virginia Rosemary Lewis; one *s* one *d. Educ:* Radley College. Commissioned 1963, commanded, 1983–86, 13th/18th Royal Hussars (QMO); Comd 4th Armoured Brigade, 1988–90; COS, UN Bosnia Hercegovina, 1992–93; COS BAOR, 1993–94; GOC 1st (UK) Armd Div., 1994–96; Dep. Force Comdr, Bosnia Hercegovina, 1996–97; retd 1998. Hon. Col, Light Dragoons, 2000–. Chm., Regular Forces Employment Assoc., 1999–; Pres., RBL, 2000–. *Recreations:* ski-ing, shooting, reading. *Address:* c/o Coutts & Co., 440 Strand, WC2R 0QS. *Club:* Cavalry and Guards.

COREN, Alan; writer and broadcaster; *b* 27 June 1938; *s* of Samuel and Martha Coren; *m* 1963, Anne Kasriel; one *s* one *d. Educ:* East Barnet Grammar Sch.; Wadham Coll., Oxford (Open scholar; MA); Yale; Univ. of California, Berkeley. Asst Editor, Punch, 1963–66, Literary Editor 1966–69, Dep. Editor 1969–77, Editor, 1978–87; Editor, The Listener, 1988–89. TV Critic, The Times, 1971–78; Columnist: Daily Mail, 1972–76; Mail on Sunday, 1984–92; The Times, 1988–; Sunday Express, 1992–96; contributor to: Sunday Times, Atlantic Monthly, TLS, Spectator, Observer, Tatler, London Review of Books. Commonwealth Fellowship, 1961–63. Rector, St Andrews Univ., 1973–76. Hon. DLitt Nottingham, 1993. *Publications:* The Dog It Was That Died, 1965; All Except the Bastard, 1969; The Sanity Inspector, 1974; The Bulletins of Idi Amin, 1974; Golfing For Cats, 1975; The Further Bulletins of Idi Amin, 1975; The Lady From Stalingrad Mansions, 1977; The Peanut Papers, 1977; The Rhinestone as Big as the Ritz, 1979; Tissues for Men, 1980; The Best of Alan Coren, 1980; The Cricklewood Diet, 1982; Present Laughter, 1982; (ed) The Penguin Book of Modern Humour, 1983; Bumf, 1984; Something For The Weekend, 1986; Bin Ends, 1987; Seems Like Old Times, 1989; More Like Old Times, 1990; A Year in Cricklewood, 1991; Toujours Cricklewood?, 1993; Sunday Best, 1993; (ed) Animal Passions, 1994; A Bit on the Side, 1995; The Alan Coren Omnibus, 1996; The Cricklewood Dome, 1998; The Cricklewood Tapestry, 2000; (ed) The Pick of Punch (annual), 1979–87; (ed) The Punch Book of Short Stories, Bk 1, 1979, Bk 2, 1980, Bk 3, 1981; The Arthur Books (for children), 1976–83. *TV series:* The Losers, 1978; Call My Bluff, 1996–; *radio series:* The News Quiz, 1975–. *Recreations:* bridge, riding, broadcasting. *Address:* Robson Books, 10 Blenheim Court, Brewery Road, N7 9NY.

COREY, Prof. Elias James, PhD; Professor of Chemistry, Harvard University, since 1959; *b* 12 July 1928; *s* of Elias Corey and Tina Corey (*née* Hasham); *m* 1961, Claire Higham; two *s* one *d. Educ:* MIT (BS 1948; PhD 1951). University of Illinois, Urbana-Champaign: Instructor, 1951; Asst Prof., 1953–55; Prof. of Chemistry, 1955–59. Former Member: Bd of Dirs, physical sciences, Alfred P. Sloan Foundn; Sci. Adv. Bd, Robert A. Welch Foundn. Foreign Mem., Royal Soc., 1998. Hon. DSc: Chicago, 1968; Hofstra, 1974; Oxford, 1982; Liège, 1985; Illinois, 1985; Hon. ScD Cantab, 2000; Hon. AM Harvard, 1959. Numerous awards, medals and prizes from univs and learned bodies in USA, Europe and Asia, incl. US Nat. Medal of Science, 1988 and Nobel Prize for Chemistry, 1990. *Publications:* numerous papers in learned jls on pure and synthetic chemistry, esp. on development of methods of organic synthesis, making possible mass production of medicinal and other products, based on natural materials. *Address:* Department of Chemistry, Harvard University, 12 Oxford Street, Cambridge, MA 02138, USA. *T:* (617) 4954033.

CORFIELD, Rt Hon. Sir Frederick (Vernon), PC 1970; Kt 1972; QC 1972; a Recorder of the Crown Court, 1979–87; *b* 1 June 1915; *s* of late Brig. F. A. Corfield, DSO, OBE, IA, and M. G. Corfield (*née* Vernon); *m* 1945, Elizabeth Mary Ruth Taylor; no *c. Educ:* Cheltenham Coll. (Scholar); RMA, Woolwich. Royal Artillery, 1935; 8th Field Regt, RA, India, 1935–39; served War of 1939–45; Actg Captain and Adjutant, 23rd Field Regt, BEF, 3rd Div., 1939; 51st (Highland) Div., 1940 (despatches); prisoner of war, Germany, 1940–45. Called to Bar, Middle Temple, 1945; Bencher, 1980; JAG's Branch, WO, 1945–46; retired, 1946; farming, 1946–56. MP (C) South Glos, 1955–Feb. 1974; Jt Parly Sec., Min. of Housing and Local Govt, 1962–64; Minister of State, Board of Trade, June-Oct. 1970; Minister of Aviation Supply, 1970–71; Minister for Aerospace, DTI, 1971–72. Mem., British Waterways Bd, 1974–83 (Vice-Chm., 1980–83); Dir, Mid-Kent Water Co., 1975–91. Chm., London and Provincial Antique Dealers' Assoc., 1975–89. Pres., Council, Cheltenham Coll., 1985–88. *Publications:* Corfield on Compensation, 1959; A Guide to the Community Land Act, 1976; (with R. J. A. Carnworth) Compulsory Acquisition and Compensation, 1978.

CORFIELD, Sir Kenneth (George), Kt 1980; FREng; Chairman, 1979–85, and Managing Director, 1969–85, STC PLC (formerly Standard Telephones & Cables plc); Chairman, Tanks Consolidated Investments, 1990–; *b* 27 Jan. 1924; *s* of Stanley Corfield and Dorothy Elizabeth (*née* Mason); *m* 1960; one *d. Educ:* South Staffs Coll. of Advanced Technology. FREng (FEng 1979); FIMechE; CIMgt. Management Develt, ICI Metals Div., 1946–50; Man. Dir, K. G. Corfield Ltd, 1950–60; Exec. Dir, Parkinson Cowan, 1960–66; Dep. Chm., STC Ltd, 1969–79; Sen. Officer, ITT Corp. (UK), 1974–84. Chairman: Standard Telephones and Cables (NI), 1974–85; Distributed Information Processing Ltd, 1987–; Vice-Pres., ITT Europe Inc., 1967–85; Director: Midland Bank Ltd, 1979–91; Britoil PLC, 1982–88; Octagon Investment Management, 1987–95. Chairman: EDC for Ferrous Foundries Industry, 1975–78; British Engrg Council, 1981–85; Defence Spectrum Review, 1985–88; Radio Spectrum Review, 1990–93; Mem., ACARD, 1981–84. President: TEMA, 1974–80; BAIE, 1975–79; Vice-Pres., Engineering Employers' Fedn, 1979–85; Member Council: CBI, 1971–85; Inst. of Dirs, 1981– (Pres. 1984–85); BIM, 1978– (Vice-Pres. 1978–83). Trustee, Science Museum, 1984–92 (Mem. Adv. Council, 1975–83). CompIEE 1974, Hon. FIEE 1985. Hon. Fellow: Sheffield Polytechnic, 1983; Wolverhampton Polytechnic, 1986. DUniv: Surrey, 1976; Open, 1985; Hon. DSc: City, 1981; Bath, 1982; Aston in Birmingham, 1985; Hon. DScEng London, 1982; Hon. DSc (Engrg) QUB, 1982; Hon. LLD Strathclyde, 1982; Hon. DTech Loughborough, 1983; Hon. DEngrg Bradford, 1984. Bicentennial Medal for design, RSA, 1985. *Publications:* Product Design, Report for NEDO, 1979; No Man An Island, 1982 (SIAD Award). *Recreations:* photography, music. *Address:* 10 Chapel Place, Rivington Street, EC2A 3DQ. *Club:* Royal Anglo-Belgian.

CORK AND ORRERY, 14th Earl of, *cr* 1620; **John William Boyle,** DSC 1945; VRD 1952; Baron Boyle of Youghal 1616; Viscount Dungarvan 1620; Baron Boyle of Broghill 1621; Viscount Boyle of Kinalmeaky and Baron of Bandon Bridge 1621; Earl of Orrery 1660 (all Ire.); Baron Boyle of Marston (GB) 1711; *b* 12 May 1916; *yr s* of Hon. Reginald Courtenay Boyle, MBE, MC (*d* 1946), *ggs* of 8th Earl, and Violet (*d* 1974), *d* of Arthur Flower; *S* brother, 1995; *m* 1943, Mary Leslie, *o d* of Gen. Sir Robert Gordon-Finlayson,

KCB, CMG, DSO; three *s*. *Educ:* Harrow; King's Coll., London (BSc). FICE. Served War 1939–45; Lt-Comdr RNVR, 1939–54 (despatches twice). *Recreations:* home, family, country life, reading, making and mending. *Heir:* *s* Viscount Dungarvan, *qv*. *Address:* Nether Craigantaggart, Dunkeld, Perthshire PH8 0HQ. *T:* and *Fax:* (01738) 710239. *Club:* Lansdowne.

CORK, CLOYNE, AND ROSS, Bishop of, since 1999; **Rt Rev. (William) Paul Colton;** *b* 13 March 1960; *s* of George Henry Colton and Kathleen Mary Colton (*née* Jenkins); *m* 1986, Susan Margaret Good; two *s*. *Educ:* Lester B. Pearson Coll. of the Pacific, BC, Canada; University Coll., Cork (BCL Hons); Trinity Coll., Dublin (DipTh, MPhil). Curate, St Paul, Lisburn, dio. Connor, 1984–87; Domestic Chaplain to Bp of Connor, 1985–90; Vicar Choral, Belfast Cathedral, 1987–90, Minor Canon, 1989–90; Priest Vicar, Registrar and Chapter Clerk, Christ Church Cathedral, Dublin, 1990–95; Co-ordinator of Religious Programmes (Protestant), RTE, 1993–99; Incumbent of Castleknock and Mulhuddart with Clonsilla, dio. Dublin, 1990–99; Canon, Christ Church Cathedral, Dublin, 1997–99. *Recreations:* piano, organ, music, walking, gym, reading, computers, Manchester United Football Club. *Address:* The Palace, Bishop Street, Cork, Ireland. *T:* (21) 4316114. *Club:* Kildare Street and University (Dublin).

CORK, Richard Graham; Chief Art Critic, The Times, since 1991; *b* 25 March 1947; *s* of Hubert Henry Cork and Beatrice Hester Cork; *m* 1970, Vena Jackson; two *s* two *d*. *Educ:* Kingswood Sch., Bath; Trinity Hall, Cambridge (MA, PhD). Art critic, Evening Standard, 1969–77, 1980–83; Editor, Studio International, 1975–79; art critic, The Listener, 1984–90. Slade Prof. of Fine Art, Cambridge, 1989–90; Lethaby Lectr, RCA, 1974; Durning-Lawrence Lectr, UCL, 1987; Henry Moore Foundn Sen. Fellow, Courtauld Inst. of Art, 1992–95. Former Member: Hayward Gall. Advisory Panel; Fine Arts Advisory Cttee, British Council; Cttee, Contemp. Art Soc.; Mem., Arts Council of England, 1995–98 (Chm., Visual Art Panel, 1995–98). Selector: North Meadow Millennium Sculpture Project, 1998–; Sunderland Gateway Commn, 1999–; Elector, Slade Professorship of Fine Art, Univ. of Cambridge, 1999–; Member: Trafalgar Sq. Plinth Adv. Gp, 1999–2000; Selection Cttee, New St Paul's Cathedral Font, 1999–; Adv. Council, Paul Mellon Centre for British Art, 1999–; Design Cttee, Diana, Princess of Wales Meml Fountain, 2000–. Trustee, Public Art Develt Trust, 1988–95. Organiser of many exhibns, incl. shows in Milan, Paris, Berlin and at Hayward Gall., Tate Gall. and RA. Frequent broadcaster on radio and television. John Llewelyn Rhys Meml Prize, 1976; Sir Banister Fletcher Award, 1986; NACF Award, 1995. *Publications:* Vorticism and Abstract Art in the First Machine Age, vol. I: Origins and Development, 1975, vol. II: Synthesis and Decline, 1976; The Social Role of Art, 1979; Art Beyond the Gallery in Early Twentieth Century England, 1985; David Bomberg, 1987; Architect's Choice, 1992; A Bitter Truth: Avant-Garde Art and the Great War, 1994; Bottle of Notes, 1997; Breaking the Mould: British art of the 1980s and 1990s, 1997; Jacob Epstein, 1999; contribs to art magazines and exhibn catalogues. *Recreations:* enjoying family, looking at art. *Address:* 24 Milman Road, NW6 6EG. *T:* (020) 8960 2671.

CORK, Sir Roger (William), Kt 1997; FCA; Lord Mayor of London, 1996–97; Partner: Moore Stephens, 1994–99; Moore Stephens Booth White, 1995–99; *b* 31 March 1947; *s* of Sir Kenneth Cork, GBE and Nina (*née* Lippold); *m* 1970, Barbara Anita Pauline (*d* 1996), *d* of Reginald Harper; one *s* two *d*. *Educ:* St Martin's School, Northwood; Uppingham School. FICM, FIPA, FCIS. Partner, W. H. Cork Gully subseq. Cork Gully, 1970–93; associated with Coopers & Lybrand, 1980–93. Chm., Chester Boyd Ltd. Governor, St Dunstan's Coll. Educnl Foundn, 1983– (Chm. of Govs, 1991–99). City Fellow, Hughes Hall, Cambridge, 1998. Chm., London and SE Reg., CRC, 1998–; Patron and Vice Pres., Iain Rennie Hospice at Home, 1998–; Trustee and Vice Pres., Scannappeal, 1998–; Trustee and Mem. Council, Restoration of Appearence and Function Trust, 2000–; Pres., Wendover Arm Trust, 1992–. President: City of London Br., Inst. of Dirs, 1991– (Chm., 1987–91); Soc. of Young Freemen, 1994–97; Pres., Inst. of Credit Management, 1999– (Chm., 1985–87; Vice Pres., 1989–99); Mem., Assoc. of Business Recovery Professionals. City of London: Freeman, 1972; Alderman, Tower Ward, 1983–; Sheriff, 1992–93; Master, Bowyers' Co., 1990–92; Freeman, Co. of Watermen and Lightermen; Member Court: Chartered Accountants' Co.; World Traders' Co. (Master, 1999–2000); Butchers' Co.; Hon. Liveryman: Envmntl Cleaners' Co. (Mem. Court, 1998–); Chartered Secretaries' and Administrators' Co.; Hon. Mem., Co. (formerly Guild) of Tax Advrs. Hon. DSc City, 1996. OStJ. Bintang Darjah Seri Paduka Makkota Brunei Yang Amat Mulia (Brunei), 1993; Order of Infante D. Henrique 3rd cl. (Portugal), 1993. *Recreations:* sailing, photography, DIY. *Address:* Rabbs, The Lee, Great Missenden, Bucks HP16 9NX. *T:* (01494) 837296. *Clubs:* East India (Hon. Mem.), City Livery, Tower Ward (Pres., 1984–), Billingsgate Ward (Master, 1980–81), Royal Yachting Association, Little Ship; Hardway Sailing.

CORKERY, Michael; QC 1981; *b* 20 May 1926; *o s* of late Charles Timothy Corkery and of Nellie Marie Corkery; *m* 1967, Juliet Shore Foulkes, *o d* of late Harold Glyn Foulkes; one *s* one *d*. *Educ:* The King's Sch., Canterbury. Grenadier Guards, 1944; Commissioned in Welsh Guards, 1945; served until 1948. Called to Bar, Lincoln's Inn, 1949 (Bencher 1973, Master of the Library, 1991, Treasurer, 1992). Mem., South Eastern Circuit; 3rd Junior Prosecuting Counsel to the Crown at the Central Criminal Court, 1959; 1st Junior Prosecuting Counsel to the Crown, 1964; 5th Senior Prosecuting Counsel to the Crown, 1970; 3rd Sen. Prosecuting Counsel, 1971; 2nd Sen. Prosecuting Counsel, 1974; 1st Sen. Prosecuting Counsel, 1977–81. *Recreations:* shooting, sailing, gardening, music. *Address:* 5 Paper Buildings, Temple, EC4Y 7HB. *Clubs:* Cavalry and Guards, Hurlingham; Itchenor Sailing.

CORLETT, Clive William, CB 1995; Deputy Chairman, Board of Inland Revenue, 1994–98 (Under Secretary, 1985–92; Director General, 1992–94); *b* 14 June 1938; *s* of F. William and Hanna Corlett; *m* 1964, Margaret Catherine Jones; one *s*. *Educ:* Birkenhead Sch.; Brasenose Coll., Oxford (BA PPE). Merchant Navy, 1957. Joined Inland Revenue, 1960; seconded to: Civil Service Selection Bd, 1970; HM Treasury, 1972–74 (as Private Sec. to Chancellor of Exchequer) and 1979–81. Hon. Treas., Old Colfeians RFC, 2000–.

CORLETT, Rev. Ewan Christian Brew, OBE 1985; MA, PhD; FREng; Chairman and Managing Director, BCH Ltd (formerly Burness, Corlett & Partners Ltd), 1954–88, and since 1995; *b* 11 Feb. 1923; *s* of Malcolm James John and Catherine Ann Corlett; *m* 1946, Edna Lilian Büggs; three *s*. *Educ:* King William's Coll., IOM; Oxford Univ. (MA Engrg Sci.); Durham Univ. (PhD Naval Architecture); Diocesan Training Inst., IOM. Dept of Director of Naval Construction, Admiralty, Bath, 1944–46; Tipton Engrg Co., Tipton, 1946–47; Aluminium Develt Assoc. Research Scholar, Durham Univ., 1947–50; Naval Architect, British Aluminium Co., 1950–53; Design Dir, Burness, Corlett & Partners Ltd, 1953–54, Man. Dir, 1954–88. Ordained deacon, 1991, priest, 1992; Asst Curate, Maughold Parish, IOM, 1991–. Chm. Council, RINA, 1977–79, Vice-Pres., 1971–82, Hon. Vice-Pres., 1982. Home Office Assessor (Technical Inquiries), 1959–80; Assessor, Herald of Free Enterprise Inquiry, 1987. Originator and i/c salvage, SS Great Britain from Falkland Is, 1968–70; Hon. Naval Architect and Vice-Pres., SS Great Britain Project, 1970–. Mem. Board, Nat. Maritime Inst., 1978–82; Trustee, Nat. Maritime Museum, 1974–92. Mem. Court, Shipwrights' Co., 1976–, Prime Warden 1990. Pres., Ramsey Station, RNLI, 1994–. FIMarE 1954; FREng (FEng 1978); Hon. FRIN 1980; Hon. FNI 1992. *Publications:* The Iron Ship, 1976, revised edn 1990; The Revolution in Merchant Shipping 1950–1980, 1980; numerous papers to learned instns. *Recreations:* sailing, painting, astronomy. *Address:* Cottimans, Port-e-Vullen, Isle of Man IM7 1AP. *T:* (01624) 814009, *Fax:* (01624) 817248. *Club:* Manx Sailing and Cruising.

CORLETT, Gerald Lingham; Chairman, Higsons Brewery plc, 1980–88; *b* 8 May 1925; *s* of Alfred Lingham Corlett and Nancy Eileen Bremner; *m* 1957, Helen Bromfield Williamson; three *s* one *d*. *Educ:* Rossall School; Aberdeen University (short war-time course). RA, 1943–47 (Lieut, Royal Indian Artillery). Higsons Brewery, 1947–88. Director: Westminster (Liverpool) Trust Co., 1960–2001 (Chm., 1995–2001); Midshires Building Soc. (Northern Bd), 1977–87; Radio City (Sound of Merseyside), 1982–88 (Chm., 1985–88); Boddington Gp, 1985–88; Watson Prickard, 1991–96 (Chm., 1991–96). Member, Council: Brewers' Soc., 1964–88; Rossall Sch., 1956–95. Mem., Brewers' Co., 1983–. *Recreation:* family. *Address:* Kirk House, 4 Abbey Road, West Kirby, Wirral CH48 7EW. *T:* (0151) 625 5425. *Clubs:* Liverpool Racquet; West Kirby Sailing.

CORLETT, William John Howarth; QC (I of M) 1999; Attorney General, Isle of Man, since 1998; *b* 25 March 1950; *s* of William Thomas Kaneen Corlett and Jean Mary Corlett; *m* 1974, Janice Mary Crowe; one *s*. *Educ:* King William's Coll., Isle of Man; Univ. of Nottingham (LLB). Called to the Bar, Gray's Inn, 1972; admitted to Manx Bar, 1974; Partner, Dickinson Cruickshank & Co., Advocates, 1975–92; Sen. Partner, Corlett Bolton & Co., Advocates, 1992–98. *Recreations:* golf, salmon fishing. *Address:* Close Jairg, Old Church Road, Crosby, Isle of Man IM4 2HA. *T:* (01624) 852119. *Club:* Royal Over-Seas League.

CORLEY, Sir Kenneth (Sholl Ferrand), Kt 1972; Chairman and Chief Executive, Joseph Lucas (Industries) Ltd, 1969–73; *b* 3 Nov. 1908; *s* of late S. W. Corley and late Mrs A. L. Corley; *m* 1937, Olwen Mary Yeoman (*d* 1999); one *s* one *d*. *Educ:* St Bees, Cumberland. Joined Joseph Lucas Ltd, 1927; Director, 1948. Pres., Birmingham Chamber of Commerce, 1964. Governor, Royal Shakespeare Theatre; Life Governor, Birmingham Univ.; Pres., Soc. of Motor Mfrs and Traders, 1971. Chm. Governors, St Bees Sch., 1978–84. Chevalier, Légion d'Honneur, 1975. *Recreations:* fell-walking, bee-keeping, theatre. *Address:* Bradbury House, Gosforth, Cumbria CA20 IAU. *T:* (01946) 725987. *Club:* Royal Automobile.

CORLEY, Paul John; Managing Director, GMTV, since 2001; *b* 23 Dec. 1950; *s* of Robert Charles Corley and Margaret Dorothy Corley. *Educ:* Worcester Coll., Oxford (BA Hons Modern Hist.). Journalist, Westminster Press, 1972–76; News and Current Affairs, BBC TV, 1976–81; Producer, The Tube, Tyne Tees TV, 1982–84; Director of Programmes: Border TV, 1984–91; Granada Gp, NE TV, 1991–92; Controller: Factual Progs, Carlton TV, and Man. Dir, Carlton Broadcasting, 1992–96; Network Factual Progs, ITV Network Centre, 1996–98; Chief Exec., Border TV, 1998–2000. *Recreations:* television, music, ski-ing. *Address:* London Television Centre, Upper Ground, SE1 9TT. *Clubs:* Groucho, Soho House.

CORLEY, Peter Maurice Sinclair; Under Secretary, Department of Trade and Industry, 1981–93; *b* 15 June 1933; *s* of Rev. James Maurice Corley, MLitt and Mrs Barbara Shearer Corley; *m* 1961, Dr Marjorie Constance Doddridge; two *d*. *Educ:* Marlborough Coll.; King's Coll., Cambridge (MA). Min. of Power, 1957–61; Min. of Transport, 1961–65; BoT, 1965–69; Commercial Sec., Brussels, 1969–71; Asst Sec., DTI, 1972–75; Dir Gen., Econ. Co-operation Office, Riyadh, 1976–78; Dept of Industry, 1978–81. Consultant, Year of Engineering Success, 1993–96. *Recreation:* bookbinding. *Club:* Oxford and Cambridge.

CORLEY, Roger David, CBE 1993; Director, Clerical, Medical and General Life Assurance Society, 1975–97 (Managing Director, 1982–95); *b* 13 April 1933; *s* of Thomas Arthur and Erica Trent Corley; *m* 1964, Brigitte (*née* Roeder), PhD, FSA, FRSA; three *s*. *Educ:* Hymers College, Hull; Univ. of Manchester (BSc). FIA 1960. Joined Clerical Medical, 1956: Investment Manager, 1961–72; Actuary, 1972–80; Dep. Gen. Manager and Actuary, 1980–82. Chairman: Pharos SA, 1995–; St Andrew's Gp, 1995–; Director: Korea Asia Fund Ltd, 1990–2000; Nat. Westminster Life Assce Ltd, 1992–95; Lands Improvement Hldgs, 1994–99; City of Westminster Arts Council, 1994–; British Heart Foundn, 1995–; Medical Defence Union Ltd, 1996–; Fidelity Investments Life Insurance Ltd, 1997–; RGA Reinsurance UK Ltd, 1999–. Mem., Financial Services Commn of Gibraltar, 1995–2000. Pres., Inst. of Actuaries, 1988–90 (Mem. Council, 1976–94; Hon. Sec., 1980–82; Vice-Pres., 1985–88); Vice Pres., Internat. Actuarial Assoc., 1990–98 (Mem. Council, 1983–98; Nat. Correspondent for England, 1984–90); Mem., Deutsche Gesellschaft für Versicherungsmathematik, 1975–. Master, Actuaries' Co., 1992–93 (Mem. Court, 1985–). FRSA 1990. *Recreations:* theatre, travel, music. *Club:* Army and Navy.

CORMACK, Dr Douglas; independent consultant on environment and management; *b* 10 Jan. 1939; *s* of Douglas Cormack and Mary Hutton (*née* Bain); *m* 1966, Barbara Ann Jones; two *s*. *Educ:* Gourock High Sch.; Greenock High Sch.; Univ. of Glasgow (BSc 1961; PhD Physical Chemistry 1964). Res. Associate, Chemical Oceanography, Woods Hole Oceanographic Instn, Mass, USA, 1964–67; Warren Spring Laboratory, Department of Trade and Industry: SSO, 1967–72; PSO, 1972–74; Sen. Principal and Hd, Oil Pollution Div., 1974–79; Scientific Advr, Marine Pollution Control Unit, Depts of Trade and Industry and Transport, 1979–86; Warren Spring Laboratory, Department of Trade and Industry: Dep. Dir with responsibility for Envmtl Res. and Personnel, 1986–89; Dep. Dir and Business Manager, 1989–92; Chief Exec., 1992–94; Dir, Envmt, British Maritime Technology, 1994–96. Chairman: British Oil Spill Control Assoc., 2000–; British Marine Equipment Council, 2000–. Vice-Chm., Adv. Cttee on Protection of the Sea, 1992–95. Associate, Paragon Associates, Envmntl Consultants, 1994–97; Ind. Consultant, Cormack Associates, 1997–. FRSA 1988. Editor, Jl of Oil and Chem. Pollution, 1985–91. *Publications:* Response to Oil and Chemical Marine Pollution, Applied Science, 1983; Response to Marine Oil Pollution—Review and Assessment, 1999; numerous scientific papers and reports. *Recreations:* sailing, beagling, reading philosophy, history. *Address:* 1 Flint Copse, Redbourn, Herts AL3 7QE. *Club:* Civil Service.

CORMACK, John, CB 1982; Director, Parliamentary and Law, Institute of Chartered Accountants of Scotland, 1987–88 (Assistant Director, 1984–87); Fisheries Secretary, Department of Agriculture and Fisheries for Scotland, 1976–82; *b* 27 Aug. 1922; *yr s* of late Donald Cormack and Anne Hunter Cormack (*née* Gair); *m* 1947, Jessie Margaret Bain; one *s* one *d* (and one *d* decd). *Educ:* Royal High Sch., Edinburgh. Served RAPC, 1941–46; Captain and Command Cashier, CMF, 1946. Entered Department of Agriculture for Scotland, 1939: Principal, 1959; Private Sec. to Sec. of State for Scotland, 1967–69; Asst Sec., 1969; Under Sec., 1976. *Recreations:* golf, music. *Address:* 9/1 Murrayfield Road, Edinburgh EH12 6EW.

CORMACK, Sir Patrick (Thomas), Kt 1995; MP (C) Staffordshire South, since 1983 (Cannock, 1970–74; Staffordshire South West, 1974–83); *b* 18 May 1939; *s* of Thomas Charles and Kathleen Mary Cormack, Grimsby; *m* 1967, Kathleen Mary McDonald; two *s*. *Educ:* St James' Choir School and Havelock School, Grimsby; Univ. of Hull. Second Master, St James' Choir School, Grimsby, 1961–66; Company Education and Training Officer, Ross Group Ltd, Grimsby, 1966–67; Assistant Housemaster, Wrekin College, Shropshire, 1967–69; Head of History, Brewood Grammar School, Stafford, 1969–70. Vis. Lectr, Univ. of Texas, 1984. Dir, Historic House Hotels Ltd, 1981–89; Chm., Aitken Dott Ltd (The Scottish Gallery), 1983–89. Trustee: Historic Churches Preservation Trust, 1972–; Tradescant Trust, 1980–; President: Staffs Historic Buildings Trust, 1983–; Staffs Historic Churches Trust, 1997–; Vice-Pres., Lincs Old Churches Trust, 1997–; Member: Historic Buildings Council, 1979–84; Faculty Jurisdiction Commn, 1979–84; Heritage in Danger (Vice-Chm., 1974–); Council for British Archaeology, 1979–89; Royal Commn on Historical Manuscripts, 1981–; Council for Independent Educn (Chm., 1979–97); Lord Chancellor's Adv. Cttee on Public Records, 1979–84; Council, Georgian Gp, 1985–; Council, Winston Churchill Meml Trust, 1983–93; Chairman: William Morris Craft Fellowship, 1988–; Adv. Council, Nat. Fisheries Mus., 1997–2000. Dep. Shadow Leader of H of C, 1997–2000. Member: Select Cttee on Educn, Science and Arts, 1979–84; Chairman's Panel, H of C, 1983–97; Chm., H of C Works of Art Cttee, 1987–; Member: All Party Heritage Cttee (Chm. 1979–); Cons. Party Arts and Heritage Cttee, 1979–84 (Chm.); Chm., Cons. Party Adv. Cttee on Arts and Heritage, 1988–99. Chairman: British–Finnish Parly Gp, 1992–; British–Bosnian Parly Gp, 1992–97; British–Croatian Parly Gp, 1992–. Sen. Associate Mem., St Antony's Coll., Oxford, 1996– (Vis. Parly Fellow, 1994–95); Vis. Schol., Hull Univ., 1995–. Trustee, History of Parlt Trust, 1983–. Chm. Editorial Bd, Parliamentary Publications, 1983–; Ed., The House Magazine, 1983–; Internat. Pres., First mag., 1994–. FSA 1978 (Vice Pres., 1994–98). Rector's Warden, 1978–90, Parly Warden, 1990–92, St Margaret's Church, Westminster; Mem., Gen. Synod of C of E, 1995–. Governor, ESU, 1999–. Mem., Worshipful Co. of Glaziers, 1979–; Freeman, City of London, 1979. Hon. Citizen of Texas, 1985. Commander, Order of the Lion (Finland), 1998. *Publications:* Heritage in Danger, 1976; Right Turn, 1978; Westminster: Palace and Parliament, 1981; Castles of Britain, 1982; Wilberforce—the Nation's Conscience, 1983; Cathedrals of England, 1984. *Recreations:* fighting philistines, walking, visiting old churches, avoiding sitting on fences. *Address:* House of Commons, SW1A 0AA. *Club:* Athenæum.

CORMACK, Robert Linklater Burke, CMG 1988; DL; HM Diplomatic Service, retired; *b* 29 Aug. 1935; *s* of late Frederick Eunson Cormack, CIE, and Elspeth Mary (*née* Linklater), Dounby, Orkney; *m* 1962, Eivor Dorotea Kumlin; one *s* two *d*. *Educ:* Trinity Coll., Glenalmond; Trinity Hall, Cambridge (BA Agric.). National Service, 2nd Lieut, The Black Watch, 1954–56. Dist Officer, Kenya (HMOCS), 1960–64; entered CRO (subseq. Diplomatic Service), 1964: Private Sec. to Minister of State, 1964–66; 1st Secretary: Saigon, 1966–68; Bombay, 1969–70; Delhi, 1970–72; FCO, 1972–77; Counsellor and Consul-Gen., Kinshasa, 1977–79; RCDS, 1980; Counsellor (Economic and Commercial), Stockholm, 1981–85; Hd of Information Technology Dept, FCO, 1985–87; Ambassador, Zaire and (non-resident) Rwanda and Burundi, 1987–91; Ambassador, Sweden, 1991–95. Hon. Consul for Sweden in Orkney, 1997. Mem. (Ind.), Orkney Is Council, 1997–. DL Orkney, 1996. Comdr, Order of North Star (Sweden), 1983. *Address:* Westness, Rousay, Orkney KW17 2PT.

CORMACK, Prof. Robin Sinclair, PhD; FSA; Professor in the History of Art, since 1991, and Deputy Director, Courtauld Institute of Art, since 1999, London University; *b* 27 Sept. 1938; *s* of James Menzies Cormack and Meryl Joyce Cormack (*née* Pendred); *m* 1st, 1961, Annabel Shackleton (marr. diss. 1985); one *s* one *d*; 2nd, 1985, Mary Beard; one *s* one *d*. *Educ:* Bristol Grammar Sch.; Exeter Coll., Oxford (BA Lit.Hum. 1961; MA 1965); Courtauld Inst. of Art, London Univ. (AcDip 1964; PhD 1968). FSA 1975. Gall. Manager, ICA, 1961–62; Lectr in History of Slavonic and E European Art, SSEES and Courtauld Inst. of Art, London Univ., 1966–73; Vis. Fellow, Dumbarton Oaks, Center for Byzantine Studies, Harvard Univ., 1972–73; Lectr in History of Art, Courtauld Inst., London Univ., 1973–82; British Academy Reader, Warburg Inst., London Univ., 1982–85; Bye Fellow, Robinson Coll., Cambridge, 1984–85 (Sen. Mem., 1985–); Reader in History of Art, Courtauld Inst., London Univ., 1986–90. Geddes-Harrower Prof. of Greek Art and Archaeology, Aberdeen Univ., Sept. 2001–. *Publications:* Writing in Gold, 1985 (trans. French, Icones et Société à Byzance, 1993); The Church of S Demetrios of Thessaloniki, 1985; The Byzantine Eye, 1989; Painting the Soul, 1998 (Runciman Award, Anglo-Hellenic League and Onassis Foundn); Byzantine Art, 2000. *Address:* 120 Huntingdon Road, Cambridge CB3 0HL. *T:* (01223) 312734.

CORNBERG, Catherine, (Mrs Sol Cornberg); *see* Gaskin, C.

CORNELIUS, David Frederick, FIHT; transport and research consultant; *b* 7 May 1932; *s* of Frederick M. N. and Florence K. Cornelius; *m* 1956, Susan (*née* Austin); two *s* two *d*. *Educ:* Teignmouth Grammar Sch.; Exeter University Coll. (BSc (Hons) Physics). Royal Naval Scientific Service, 1953–58; UKAEA, 1958–64; Research Manager, Road Research Laboratory, 1964–72; Asst Director, Building Research Estabt, 1973–78; Head, Research, Transport and Special Programmes, 1978–80, Transport Science Policy Unit, 1980–82, Dept of Transport; Asst Dir, 1982–84, Dep. Dir, 1984–88, Actg Dir, 1988–89, Dir, 1989–91, Transport and Road Res. Lab. FRSA. *Publications:* Path of Duty (biog.), 2000; scientific papers to nat. and internat. confs and in jls of various professional instns on range of topics in tribology, world travel by container ships, highway transportation and internat. collaboration in res. *Recreations:* European caravanning, swimming, cycling, antiques. *Address:* White Poplars, 40 Webb Lane, Hayling Island, Hants PO11 9JE. *T:* (023) 9246 7212.

CORNELL, Jim Scott, FREng; FICE; FCIT; Executive Director, Railway Heritage Trust, since 1996; *b* 3 Aug. 1939; *s* of James William Cornell and Annie Cornell (*née* Scott); *m* 1962, Winifred Eileen Rayner; one *s* one *d*. *Educ:* Thirsk Grammar Sch.; Bradford Inst. of Technol. FICE 1983; FCIT 1986; FREng (FEng 1992). With British Rail, 1959–96: jun. and middle mgt civil engrg posts, 1959–76; Divisional Civil Engineer: King's Cross, 1976–78; Newcastle, 1978–81; Asst Regl Civil Engr, York, 1981–83; Regl Civil Engr, Scotland, 1983–84; Dep. Gen. Manager, 1984–86, Gen. Manager, 1986–87, ScotRail; Dir, Civil Engrg, 1987–92; Man. Dir, Regl Railways, 1992–93; Man. Dir, BR Infrastructure Services, 1993–96. FIMgt 1987. *Recreations:* tennis, golf, gardening. *Address:* 105 Camberton Road, Leighton Buzzard, Beds LU7 7UW. *T:* (01525) 851070.

CORNELL, Peter; Deputy Chief Executive, Clifford Chance, since 2001; *b* 5 Oct. 1952; *s* of Dr Sydney Page Cornell and Marjorie Joan Cornell; *m* 1981, Bernadette Conway; one *s* three *d*. *Educ:* Tonbidge Sch., Kent; Exeter Univ.; Chester Law Coll. SSC. Admitted solicitor, 1975; joined Clifford Chance, 1975: on secondment to Philip Morris, Lausanne, 1978–79; opened Singapore office, 1981; returned to London office, 1986; Man. Partner, Madrid office, 1989–2001; opened Barcelona office, 1993; Eur. Man. Partner, 1996–2001. *Recreations:* family, sport, tennis, golf, squash, ski-ing, snowboarding. *Clubs:* Roehampton; La Moraleja, de Campo (Madrid).

CORNER, Frank Henry, CMG 1980; retired New Zealand Civil Servant and Diplomat; *b* 17 May 1920; *y s* of Charles William Corner, Napier, NZ, and Sybil Corner (*née* Smith); *m* 1943, Lynette Robinson; two *d*. *Educ:* Napier Boys' High Sch.; Victoria Univ. of Wellington. MA, 1st cl. History; James Macintosh and Post-graduate Scholar. External Affairs Dept, NZ, and War Cabinet Secretariat, 1943; 1st Sec., NZ Embassy, Washington, 1948–51; Sen. Counsellor, NZ High Commn, London, 1952–58; Dep. Sec. NZ Dept of External Affairs, 1958–62; Perm. Rep. (Ambassador) to UN, 1962–67; Ambassador of NZ to USA, 1967–72; Permanent Head of Prime Minister's Dept, 1973–75; Secretary of Foreign Affairs, 1973–80; Administrator of Tokelau, 1976–85. Chm., NZ Defence Cttee of Enquiry, 1985–86. Mem., NZ Delegn to Commonwealth Prime Ministers' Meetings, 1944, 1946, 1951–57, 1973, 1975, 1977, 1979; Deleg. to UN Gen. Assembly, 1949–52, 1955, 1960–68, 1973, 1974; NZ Rep. to UN Trusteeship Council, 1962–66 (Pres., 1965–66; Chm., UN Vis. Mission to Micronesia, 1964); NZ Rep. on UN Security Coun., 1966; Adviser, NZ Delegn: Paris Peace Conf., 1946; Geneva Conf. on Korea, 1954; numerous other internat. confs as adviser or delegate. Mem., Bd of NZ-US Educnl Foundn, 1980–88; Patron, Assoc. of NZ Art Socs, 1973–88; Mem. Council, Victoria Univ. of Wellington, 1981–87. FRSA. *Publications:* contrib. to: New Zealand's External Relations, 1962; The Feel of Truth, 1969; An Eye, an Ear and a Voice, 1993; Unofficial Channels, 1999; Three Labour Leaders, 2001. *Recreations:* the arts, wine. *Address:* 26 Burnell Avenue, Wellington 1, New Zealand. *T:* (4) 4737022; 29 Kakariki Grove, Waikanae, New Zealand. *T:* (4) 2936235.

CORNER, Philip; Director General of Quality Assurance, Ministry of Defence Procurement Executive, 1975–84, retired; Chairman, Institute of Quality Assurance's Management Board (for qualification and registration scheme for lead assessors of quality assurance management system), 1984–92; *b* 7 Aug. 1924; *s* of late William Henry Corner and Dora (*née* Smailes); *m* 1948, Nora Pipes (*d* 1984); no *c*; *m* 1985, Paula Mason. *Educ:* Dame Allan's Boys' Sch., Newcastle upon Tyne; Bradford Technical Coll.; RNEC Manadon; Battersea Polytechnic. BScEng (London); CEng 1966; MIMechE 1952; MIEE 1957; Hon. FIQA 1985. Short Bros (Aeronautical Engrs), 1942–43; Air Br., RN, Sub-Lieut RNVR, 1944–46; LNER Co., 1946–47; Min. of Works, 1947–50; Min. of Supply, 1950; Ministry of Defence: Dir of Guided Weapons Prodn, 1968–72; Dir of Quality Assurance (Technical), 1972–75. Member: Metrology and Standards Requirements Bd, DoI, 1974–84; Adv. Council for Calibration and Measurement, DoI, 1975–84; BSI Quality Assurance Council, 1979–84; BSI Bd, 1980–84. *Recreations:* gardening, listening to music, building and flying radio controlled model aircraft. *Address:* 3 The Green, Dyke Road, Hove, E Sussex BN3 6TH.

CORNESS, Sir Colin (Ross), Kt 1986; Chairman, Glaxo Wellcome plc, 1995–97; *b* 9 Oct. 1931; *s* of late Thomas Corness and Mary Evlyne Corness. *Educ:* Uppingham Sch.; Magdalene Coll., Cambridge (BA 1954, MA 1958); Graduate Sch. of Business Admin, Harvard, USA (Advanced Management Program Dip. 1970). Called to the Bar, Inner Temple, 1956. Dir, Taylor Woodrow Construction Ltd, 1961–64; Man. Dir, Redland Tiles Ltd, 1965–70; Redland PLC: Man. Dir, 1967–82; Chief Exec., 1977–91; Chm., 1977–95. Chm., Nationwide Building Soc., 1991–96. Director: Chubb & Son PLC, 1974–84 (Dep. Chm., 1984); W. H. Smith & Son (Holdings) PLC, 1980–87; Gordon Russell PLC, 1985–89; Courtaulds PLC, 1986–91; S. G. Warburg Gp, 1987–95; Unitech, 1987–95; Union Camp Corp., 1991–99; Chubb Security, 1992–97; Taylor Woodrow plc, 1997–. A Dir, Bank of England, 1987–95. Chm., Building Centre, 1974–77; Pres., Nat. Council of Building Material Producers, 1985–87; Member: EDC for Building, 1980–84; Industrial Develt Adv. Bd, 1982–84. Trustee, Uppingham Sch., 1996–99. Hon. DBA Kingston, 1994. *Recreations:* tennis, travel, music.

CORNFORD, James Peters; Chairman, School for Social Entrepreneurs, since 2000; *b* 25 Jan. 1935; *s* of John Cornford and Rachel Peters; *m* 1960, Avery Amanda Goodfellow; one *s* three *d*. *Educ:* Winchester Coll.; Trinity Coll., Cambridge (MA). Fellow, Trinity Coll., Cambridge, 1960–64; Harkness Fellow, 1961–62; Univ. of Edinburgh: Lectr in Politics, 1964–68; Prof. of Politics, 1968–76; Dir, Outer Circle Policy Unit, 1976–80; Director: Nuffield Foundn, 1980–88; Inst. for Public Policy Res., 1989–94; Paul Hamlyn Foundn, 1994–97; Special Adviser to Chancellor of Duchy of Lancaster, 1997–98. Chm., Constitution Unit, UCL, 1995–97. Vis. Fellow, All Souls Coll., Oxford, 1975–76; Vis. Prof., Birkbeck Coll., Univ. of London, 1977–80. Mem., Cttee of Inquiry into Educn of Children from Ethnic Minority Gps (DES), 1981–85. Dir, 1979–97, Chm., 1999–, Job Ownership Ltd. Mem. Bd, Co-op. Develt Agency, 1987–90. Chairman of Council: RIPA, 1984–85; Campaign for Freedom of Information, 1984–97, 1998–. Chm. of Trustees, Southern African Advanced Educn Project, 1990–99; Trustee: Elm Farm Res. Centre, 1997–; Dartington Hall Trust, 1998–. Chm., The Political Quarterly, 1993–99 (Lit. Ed., 1976–93). *Publications:* contribs to books and jls. *Address:* Osborne House, High Street, Stoke Ferry, King's Lynn, Norfolk PE33 9SF. *T:* (01366) 500808.

CORNFORTH, Sir John (Warcup), AC 1991; Kt 1977; CBE 1972; FRS 1953; DPhil; Royal Society Research Professor, University of Sussex, 1975–82, now Emeritus; *b* 7 Sept. 1917; *er s* of J. W. Cornforth, Sydney, Aust.; *m* 1941, Rita, *d* of W. C. Harradence; one *s* two *d*. *Educ:* Sydney High Sch.; Universities of Sydney and Oxford. BSc Sydney 1937; MSc Sydney, 1938; 1851 Exhibition Overseas Scholarship, 1939–42; DPhil Oxford, 1941; scientific staff of Med. Research Coun., 1946–62; Dir, Shell Research, Milstead Lab. of Chem. Enzymology, 1962–75. Assoc. Prof. in Molecular Sciences, Univ. of Warwick, 1965–71; Vis. Prof., Univ. of Sussex, 1971–75; Hon. Prof., Beijing Med. Univ., 1986–. Lectures: Pedler, Chem. Soc., 1968–69; Max Tishler, Harvard Univ., 1970; Robert Robinson, Chem. Soc., 1971–72; Sandin, Univ. of Alberta, 1977. For. Hon. Mem., Amer. Acad., 1973; Corresp. Mem., Aust. Acad., 1977; For. Associate, US Nat. Acad. of Scis, 1978; For. Mem., Royal Netherlands Acad. of Scis, 1978. Hon. Fellow, St Catherine's Coll., Oxford, 1976; Hon. DSc: ETH Zürich, 1975; Oxford, Warwick, Dublin, Liverpool, 1976; Aberdeen, Hull, Sussex, Sydney, 1977; Kent, 1995. Corday-Morgan Medal and Prize, Chem. Soc., 1953; (with G. J. Popjak) CIBA Medal, Biochem. Soc., 1965; Flintoff Medal, Chem. Soc., 1966; Stouffer Prize, 1967; Ernest Guenther Award, Amer. Chem. Soc., 1969; (with G. J. Popjak) Davy Medal, Royal Soc., 1968; Prix Roussel, 1972; (jtly) Nobel Prize for Chemistry, 1975; Royal Medal, Royal Soc., 1976; Copley Medal, Royal Soc., 1982. Has been deaf since boyhood. *Publications:* numerous papers on organic chemical and biochemical subjects. *Recreations:* lawn tennis, chess, gardening. *Address:* Saxon Down, Cuilfail, Lewes, East Sussex BN7 2BE.

CORNICK, Rev. Dr David George; General Secretary, United Reformed Church, since 2001; Fellow of Robinson College, Cambridge, since 1997; *b* 12 Sept. 1954; *s* of Cecil George Cornick and Thelma (*née* Le Brun); *m* 1977, Mary Hammond; two *s*. *Educ:* Hertford and Mansfield Colls, Oxford (MA); King's Coll., London (BD; PhD 1982). United Reformed Church: Minister, Radlett and Borehamwood, 1981–84; Chaplain, Robinson Coll., Cambridge, 1984–87; Trng Officer, South-Western Province, 1987–92; Dir of Studies in Church Hist., 1992–2001, Principal, 1996–2001, Westminster Coll., Cambridge. *Publication:* Under God's Good Hand, 1998. *Recreations:* music, walking, embroidery. *Address:* Robinson College, Grange Road, Cambridge CB3 9AN; United Reformed Church House, 86 Tavistock Place, WC1H 9RT. *T:* (020) 7916 2020.

CORNISH, Prof. Alan Richard Henry, PhD; CEng, FIChemE; Ramsay Memorial Professor of Chemical Engineering and Head of Department of Chemical and Biochemical Engineering, University College London, 1990–96, now Professor Emeritus; *b* 14 March 1931; *s* of late Richard Heard Cornish and Evelyn Jennie Cornish (*née* Hatton); *m* 1957, Rita Ellen Wright; one *s* one *d. Educ:* Emanuel Sch.; Illinois Inst. of Technology (PhD). CEng, FIChemE, MIGasE, MInstE. Asst Lectr, Lectr, Sen. Lectr, Imperial Coll., London Univ., 1962–88; Prof. of Chemical Engineering, Univ. of Bradford, 1988–90. Vis. Prof., Univ. de Pau et des Pays de l'Adour, 1994, 1997, 1998. FRSA. Freeman, City of London, 1996; Liveryman, Engineers' Co., 1996–. Dr *hc* L'Institut Nat. Polytechnique de Toulouse, 1999. *Publications:* contribs to professional jls. *Address:* 3 Merlin Close, Croydon, Surrey CR0 5UQ. *T:* (020) 8681 5604. *Club:* Athenæum.

CORNISH, Francis; *see* Cornish, R. F.

CORNISH, Jack Bertram; HM Civil Service; Under-Secretary, Department of Health and Social Security, 1976–78; *b* 26 June 1918; *s* of Bertram George John Cornish and Nora Jarmy; *m* 1946, Mary Milton; three *d. Educ:* Price's Grammar Sch., Fareham; Cotham Grammar Sch., Bristol. Admiralty, 1937–61: London, Bath, Plymouth, Singapore; DHSS, 1961–78. Supply Ships in Singapore and Newfoundland, 1941 and 1942. *Recreations:* music, painting, gardening. *Address:* 13 Kingsley Road, Kingsbridge, South Devon TQ7 1EY. *T:* (01548) 852585.

CORNISH, James Easton; Director and European Market Strategist, BT Alex. Brown (formerly NatWest Securities), 1990–99; *b* 5 Aug. 1939; *s* of Eric Easton Cornish and Ivie Hedworth (*née* McCulloch); *m* 1968, Ursula Pink; one *s. Educ:* Eton Coll.; Wadham Coll., Oxford (BA); Harvard. Joined FO, 1961; Bonn, 1963; British Mil. Govt, Berlin, 1965; FCO, 1968; Washington, 1973; Dep. Head of Planning Staff, FCO, 1977; Central Policy Rev. Staff, 1980; seconded to Phillips & Drew, 1982; resigned HM Diplomatic Service, 1985; Manager, Internat. Dept, Phillips & Drew, 1982–87; Asst Dir, subseq. Associate Dir, County Securities Ltd, 1987–90.

CORNISH, (Robert) Francis, CMG 1994; LVO 1978; HM Diplomatic Service; Ambassador to Israel, 1998–2001; *b* 18 May 1942; *s* of Mr and Mrs C. D. Cornish; *m* 1964, Alison Jane Dundas; three *d. Educ:* Charterhouse; RMA Sandhurst. Commissioned 14th/20th King's Hussars, 1962–68; HM Diplomatic Service 1968; served Kuala Lumpur, Jakarta and FCO, 1969–76; First Sec., Bonn, 1976–80; Asst Private Sec. to HRH the Prince of Wales, 1980–83; High Comr, Brunei, 1983–86; Counsellor (Inf.), Washington, and Dir, British Inf. Service, NY, 1986–90; Head of News Dept, FCO, 1990–93; Sen. British Trade Comr, Hong Kong, 1993–97; Consul-Gen., HKSAR, 1997; Sen. Directing Staff, RCDS, 1998. *Address:* c/o Foreign and Commonwealth Office, SW1A 2AH. *Club:* Cavalry and Guards.

CORNISH, Prof. William Rodolph, FBA 1984; Herchel Smith Professor of Intellectual Property Law, Cambridge University, since 1995 (Professor of Law, 1990–95); Fellow, since 1990, and President, since 1998, Magdalene College, Cambridge; *b* 9 Aug. 1937; *s* of Jack R. and Elizabeth E. Cornish, Adelaide, S Australia; *m* 1964, Lovedy E. Moule; one *s* two *d. Educ:* Univs of Adelaide (LLB) and Oxford (BCL); LLD Cantab, 1996. Lectr in Law, LSE, 1962–68; Reader in Law, Queen Mary Coll., London, 1969–70; Prof. of English Law, LSE, 1970–90. Ext. Acad. Mem., Max-Planck-Inst. for Patent, Copyright and Competition Law, Munich, 1989–. Hon. QC 1997; Bencher, Gray's Inn, 1998. MAE 2001. *Publications:* The Jury, 1968; (Jt Editor) Sutton and Shannon on Contracts, 1970; (jtly) Encyclopedia of United Kingdom and European Patent Law, 1977; Intellectual Property, 1981, 4th edn 1999; Law and Society in England 1750–1950, 1989; articles etc in legal periodicals. *Address:* Magdalene College, Cambridge CB3 0AG.

CORNOCK, Maj.-Gen. Archibald Rae, CB 1975; OBE 1968; FIMgt; Chairman, London Electricity Consultative Council, 1980; *b* 4 May 1920; *s* of Matthew Cornock and Mrs Mary Munro MacRae; *m* 1951, Dorothy Margaret Cecilia; two *d. Educ:* Coatbridge. NW Frontier, 1940–42; Burma, 1942–43; transf. Royal Indian Navy, 1943; Burma (Arakan), 1944–46; Gordon Highlanders, 1947–50; transf. RAOC, 1950; psc 1954; GSO2 Intelligence, 1955–57; DAQMG Northern Army Gp, 1959–61; comd 16 Bn RAOC, 1961–64; SEATO Planning Staff, Bangkok, 1964; Defence Attaché, Budapest, 1965–67; Comdt 15 Base Ordnance Depot, 1967; DDOS Strategic Comd, 1968–70; Brig. Q (Maint.), MoD, 1970–72; Dir of Clothing Procurement, 1972; Dir of Army Quartering, 1973–75. Col Comdt, RAOC, 1976–80. Pres., Mahratta LI Regtl Assoc., 2000–. Chm., Army Athletic Assoc., 1968–75; Mem. Council, Back Pain Assoc., 1979–. FIMgt (MBIM 1965). *Recreations:* sailing, opera, golf. *Clubs:* Royal Thames Yacht, Roehampton; Royal Scots (Edinburgh); Highland Brigade.

CORNOCK, Maj-Gen. Charles Gordon, CB 1988; MBE 1974; Bursar, Cranleigh School, 1989–95; *b* 25 April 1935; *s* of Gordon Wallace Cornock and Edith Mary (née Keeley); *m* 1963, Kay Smith; two *s. Educ:* King Alfred Sch., Plön, Germany; RMA, Sandhurst. Commnd RA, 1956; served, 1957–71: 33 Para Lt Regt; 1 RHA; RMA, Sandhurst; Staff Coll., Camberley; BMRA; Armed Forces Staff Coll., Norfolk, Va; Second in Comd, 1972–74 and CO 1974–76, 7 Para RHA; GSO1 DS Staff Coll., Camberley, 1977–78; Col GS HQ UKLF, 1979; CRA 3rd Armoured Div., 1980–81; RCDS, 1982; Dep. Comdt, Staff Coll., Camberley, 1983; Dir, RA, 1984–86; C of S and Head of UK Delegn, Live Oak, SHAPE, 1986–89. Col Comdt RA, 1986–94; Rep. Col Comdt, RA, 1991–92. Chm., Confedn of British Service and Ex-Service Orgns, 1996–99. Comdr, St John Ambulance (Jersey), 1999–. Police Complaints Authy (Jersey), 2001–. Pres., RA Golfing Soc., 1989–98; Vice-Pres., Combined Services and Army Hockey Assoc. Mem., Sen. Golfers' Soc. FIMgt. *Recreations:* hockey, tennis, golf, ski-ing, water ski-ing. *Address:* Upton, Trinity, Jersey JE3 5DT. *Clubs:* Victoria (Jersey); La Moye Golf (Jersey).

CORNWALL, Archdeacon of; *see* Whiteman, Ven. R. D. C.

CORNWALL-LEGH, family name of **Baron Grey of Codnor**.

CORNWALLIS, family name of **Baron Cornwallis**.

CORNWALLIS, 3rd Baron *cr* 1927, of Linton, Kent; **Fiennes Neil Wykeham Cornwallis,** OBE 1963; DL; *b* 29 June 1921; *s* of 2nd Baron Cornwallis, KCVO, KBE, MC, and Cecily Etha Mary (*d* 1943), *d* of Sir James Walker, 3rd Bt; *S* father, 1982; *m* 1st, 1942, Judith Lacy Scott (marr. diss. 1948); one *s* (one *d* decd); 2nd, 1951, Agnes Jean Russell Landale (*d* 2001); one *s* three *d. Educ:* Eton. Served War, Coldstream Guards, 1940–44. Pres., British Agricultural Contractors Assoc., 1952–54; Pres., Nat. Assoc. of Agricultural Contractors, 1957–63 and 1986–98; Vice-Pres., Fedn of Agricl Co-operatives, 1984–86; Chm., Smaller Firms Council, CBI, 1978–81. Representative, Horticultural Co-operatives in the EEC, 1974–87. Chm., English Apples & Pears Ltd, 1990–94; Dir, Town & Country Building Soc.(formerly Planet, then Magnet & Planet, Bldg Soc.) 1967–92 (Chm., 1973–75; Dep. Chm., 1975–77; Chm., 1978–81 and 1991–92). Mem., Bd of Trustees, Chevening Estate, 1979–98. Fellow, Inst. of Horticulture, 1986; FRPSL 1998. Pro Grand Master, United Grand Lodge of England, 1982–91. DL Kent, 1976. *Recreations:* fishing, philately. *Heir: s* Hon. (Fiennes Wykeham) Jeremy Cornwallis [*b* 25 May 1946; *m* 1969, Sara Gray de Neufville, *d* of Lt-Col Nigel Stockwell, Benenden, Kent; one *s* two *d*]. *Address:* Ruck Farm, Horsmonden, Tonbridge, Kent TN12 8DT. *T:* (01892) 722267; 25B Queen's Gate Mews, SW7 5QL. *T:* (020) 7589 1167. *Clubs:* Brooks's, Pratt's, Flyfishers'.

CORNWELL, Bernard; *see* Wiggins, B.

CORNWELL, David John Moore, (John le Carré); writer; *b* 19 Oct. 1931; *s* of Ronald Thomas Archibald Cornwell and Olive (*née* Glassy); *m* 1954, Alison Ann Veronica Sharp (marr. diss. 1971); three *s*; *m* 1972, Valerie Jane Eustace; one *s. Educ:* Sherborne; Berne Univ.; Lincoln Coll., Oxford (1st cl. Modern Languages; Hon. Fellow 1984). Taught at Eton, 1956–58. Mem. of HM Foreign Service, 1960–64. Hon. DLitt: Exeter, 1990; St Andrews, 1996; Southampton, 1997; Bath, 1998. Cartier Diamond Dagger, CWA, 1988. *Publications:* Call for the Dead, 1961 (filmed as The Deadly Affair, 1967); A Murder of Quality, 1962; The Spy Who Came in from the Cold, 1963 (Somerset Maugham Award; Crime Writers' Assoc. Gold Dagger) (filmed); The Looking-Glass War, 1965 (filmed); A Small Town in Germany, 1968; The Naïve and Sentimental Lover, 1971; Tinker, Tailor, Soldier, Spy, 1974 (televised 1979); The Honourable Schoolboy, 1977 (James Tait Black Meml Prize; Crime Writers' Assoc. Gold Dagger); Smiley's People, 1980 (televised 1982); The Little Drummer Girl, 1983 (filmed 1985); A Perfect Spy, 1986 (televised 1987); The Russia House, 1989 (filmed 1991); The Secret Pilgrim, 1991; The Night Manager, 1993; Our Game, 1995; The Tailor of Panama, 1996 (filmed 2001); Single & Single, 1999; The Constant Gardener, 2001. *Address:* David Higham Associates, 5–8 Lower John Street, Golden Square, W1R 4HA.

CORNWELL, Patricia D(aniels); American crime novelist; *b* 9 June 1956; *d* of Sam and Marilyn Daniels; *m* 1980, Charles Cornwell (marr. diss. 1990). *Educ:* Davidson Coll., N Carolina (BA English 1979). Crime Reporter, Charlotte Observer, 1979–81 (N Carolina Press Assoc. Award, 1980); Technical Writer, then Computer Analyst, Office of Chief Med. Examr, Richmond, Va, 1984–90; Volunteer Police Officer. *Publications: non-fiction:* A Time For Remembering: the story of Ruth Bell Graham, 1983, re-issued as Ruth—a Portrait, 1997; *fiction:* Hornet's Nest, 1997; Southern Cross, 1999; Dr Kay Scarpetta novels: Postmortem, 1990 (John Creasey Meml Award, CWA; Edgar Award, MWA; Anthony Award, Boucheron Award, World Mystery Convention; MacAvity Award, Mystery Readers Internat.); Body of Evidence, 1991; All That Remains, 1992; Cruel and Unusual, 1993; The Body Farm, 1994; From Potter's Field, 1995; Cause of Death, 1996; Unnatural Exposure, 1997; Point of Origin, 1998; Black Notice, 1999; The Last Precinct, 2000. *Address:* c/o Little, Brown & Co., Brettenham House, Lancaster Place, WC2E 7EN; c/o Don Congdon Associates Inc., 156 5th Avenue, Suite 625, New York, NY 10010–7002, USA.

CORNWELL, Roger Eliot; Chairman, Louis Dreyfus & Co. Ltd, since 1982 (Director since 1978); *b* 5 Feb. 1922; *s* of Harold and Kathleen Cornwell. *Educ:* St Albans Sch.; Jesus Coll., Oxford (MA). *Address:* 42 Brompton Square, SW3 2AF.

COROB, Sidney, CBE 1993; Chairman: Corob Consolidated Ltd, since 1984; Corob Holdings Ltd, since 1959; Corob Construction Co. Ltd, since 1952; *b* 2 May 1928; *s* of Wolf and Rachel Corob; *m* 1949, Elizabeth Springer; three *d. Educ:* Tree of Life Coll. Chief Exec., W. Corob & Son, 1951–59; Chairman: Western & Northern Investments Ltd, 1964–68; Corob Intercity Ltd, 1968–77; Mayfair & City Properties plc, 1984–87. Lloyds Underwriter, 1978–85. Chairman: British Technion Soc., 1984 (now Hon. Pres.); Internat. Centre for Enhancement of Learning Potential, 1991–. Director: Eur. Jewish Publication Soc., 1995–; Jewish Assoc. for Business Ethics, 1994–. Vice President: CCJ, 1995– (Vice-Chm., 1978–95); British ORT, 1996–; Vice-Chm., Central Council for Jewish Social Services, 1989–. Hon. Treas., Westmount Housing Assoc., 1974–. Life Pres., Hope Charity, 1998. Hon. DSc Technion, Israel Inst. of Engrg and Technology, 1986. *Recreations:* foreign travel, hiking, Bible studies, opera, reading. *Address:* 62 Grosvenor Street, W1K 3JF. *T:* (020) 7499 4301. *Club:* Lansdowne.

CORP, Maj.-Gen. Philip James Gladstone, CB 1996; CEng, FIMechE; Chief Executive, Society of Operations of Engineers, since 2000 (Chief executive, Institute of Road Transport Engineers, 1998–2000); *b* 23 June 1942; *s* of Wilfred James Corp and Janet Maude Corp (*née* Gladstone); *m* 1st, 1965, Penelope Joan Smith (marr. diss. 1978); two *s*; 2nd, 1978, Dawn Phyllis Durrant (*née* Holder); one step *s* two step *d. Educ:* Warwick Sch.; Queen Elizabeth GS, Crediton; Pembroke Coll., Cambridge (MA Mech. Scis and Law). Commissioned REME from RMA Sandhurst, 1962; served ME, Germany, UK, to 1972; RMCS and Staff Coll., 1973–74; Op. Requirements, MoD, 1975–76; Comd 3 Field Workshop, 1977–78; REME Combat Develt, 1979–80; Dep. Project Manager, MoD (PE), 1981–83; Comd 7 Armd Workshop, BAOR, 1984–86; QMG Staff, MoD, 1987–89; Cmdt, REME Officers' Sch., 1990; Dir, Equipment Engrg, MoD, 1990–93; Dir-Gen. Equipment Support (Army), 1993–97. Col Comdt, REME, 1996–2000. MIRTE 1998. FRSA 1995. *Recreations:* music, furniture restoration, idleness. *Address:* c/o Society of Operations, Engineers, 22 Greencoat Place, SW1P 1PR.

CORP, Ronald Geoffrey; freelance conductor and composer; *b* 4 Jan. 1951; *s* of Geoffrey Charles Corp and Elsie Grace (*née* Kinchin). *Educ:* Blue Sch., Wells; Christ Church, Oxford (MA); Southern Theol Educn and Trng Scheme (DipTheol). Librarian, producer and presenter, BBC Radio 3, 1973–87; freelance, 1987–: Conductor: Highgate Choral Soc., 1984–; London Choral Soc., 1985–; New London Orch., 1988–; New London Children's Choir, 1991–; has conducted: BBC Singers, BBC Concert Orch., Leipzig Philharmonic Orch., Brussels Radio and TV Orch., Royal Scottish Nat. Orch. and at BBC Promenade concerts. Numerous recordings. Ed., Upper Voice series, 1994–. Ordained deacon, 1998, priest, 1999; NSM, St James, Hampstead and St Mary with All Souls, Kilburn, 1998–. *Compositions:* choral works including: And All The Trumpets Sounded (cantata), 1982; Laudamus, 1994; Four Elizabethan Lyrics, 1994; Cornucopia, 1997; Piano Concerto, 1997; A New Song (cantata), 1999; Mass: Christ our Future; Mary's Song, 2001; Adonai Echad, 2001. *Publication:* The Choral Singer's Companion, 1987, 2nd edn 2000. *Recreation:* reading. *Address:* 41 Aberdare Gardens, NW6 3AL. *T:* (020) 7625 4641.

CORREA, Charles Mark; Padma Shri, 1972; architect; *b* 1 Sept. 1930; *s* of Carlos M. Correa and Ana Florinda de Heredia; *m* 1961, Monika Sequeira; one *s* one *d. Educ:* Univ. of Michigan (BArch); MIT (MArch). Private practice, Bombay, 1958–; work includes: Mahatma Gandhi Memorial, Sabarmati Ashram; State Assembly for Madhya Pradesh; low cost housing projects in Delhi, Bombay, Ahmedabad and other cities in India; Jawahar Kala Kendra, Jaipur; Nat. Crafts Mus., and British Council HQ, Delhi; Chief Architect for planning of New Bombay. Jawaharlal Nehru Vis. Prof. and Fellow of Churchill Coll., Cambridge, 1985–86. Chm., Nat. Commn on Urbanisation, 1985–88. Founder Mem., Steering Cttee, Aga Khan Award for Architecture, 1977–86; Jury Mem., Pritzker Prize, 1993–98. Hon. Vis. Prof., Tonji Univ., Shanghai. Member: French Acad., 1985; Internat. Acad. of Architects, Bulgaria, 1987; Finnish Assoc. of Architects, 1992; Foreign Hon. Mem., Amer. Acad. of Arts and Scis, 1993; Hon. MRIAI, 1997; Amer. Acad. of Arts and

Letters, 1998. Hon. Fellow: United Architects of Philippines, 1990; RIBA 1993. Hon. FAIA 1979. Hon. Dr Univ. of Michigan, 1980. Royal Gold Medal for Architecture, RIBA, 1984; Gold Medal, Indian Inst. of Architects, 1987; Gold Medal, IUA, 1990; Praemium Imperiale Prize, Japan Art Assoc., 1994; Aga Khan Award for Architecture, 1998. *Publication:* The New Landscape, 1984; *relevant publications:* S. Cantacuzino, Charles Correa, 1984; Kenneth Frampton, Charles Correa, 1996. *Recreations:* tennis, model trains, chess. *Address:* 9 Mathew Road, Bombay 400004, India. *T:* (22) 3633307. *Clubs:* Bombay Gymkhana, Willingdon Sports, Bombay Sailing Association (Bombay).

CORRIE, John Alexander; Member (C) West Midlands Region, European Parliament, since 1999 (Worcestershire and South Warwickshire, 1994–99); *b* 29 July 1935; *s* of John Corrie and Helen Brown; *m* 1965, Sandra Hardie; one *s* two *d. Educ:* Kirkcudbright Acad.; George Watson's Coll.; Lincoln Agric. Coll., NZ. Farmed in NZ, 1955–59, in Selkirk, 1959–65 and in Kirkcudbright, 1965–. Lectr for British Wool Marketing Bd and Agric. Trng Bd, 1966–74; Mem. Cttee, National Farmers Union, 1964–74 (Vice-Chm. Apprenticeship Council, 1971–74); Nuffield Scholar in Agriculture, 1972. District Officer, Rotary International, 1973–74 (Community service). Nat. Chm., Scottish Young Conservatives, 1964. Contested (C): North Lanark, 1964; Central Ayr, 1966; Cunninghame N, 1987; Argyll and Bute, 1992. MP (C): Bute and N Ayr, Feb. 1974–1983; Cunninghame N, 1983–87. Opposition spokesman on educn in Scotland, Oct. 1974–75; an Opposition Scottish Whip, 1975–76 (resigned over Devolution); PPS to Sec. of State for Scotland, 1979–81; Mem., Council of Europe and WEU, 1982–87. Treas., Scottish Cons. Back Bench Cttee, 1980, Chm. 1981–82; Leader, Cons. Gp on Scottish Affairs, 1982–84; Sec., Cons. Backbench Fish-farming Cttee, 1982–86; brought in Pvte Mem.'s Bill, Diseases of Fish, 1983. Mem. European Parlt, 1975–76 and 1977–79 (Mem. Cttees of Agriculture, Reg. Develt and Transport, 1977–79). Vice-President: EEC-Turkey Cttee, 1975–76; EEC Fisheries Cttee, 1977–79; EEC Mediterranean Agricl Cttee, 1977–79; Rapporteur for EEC Fisheries Policy, 1977–78. European Parliament: Chief Whip of Cons. Gp, 1997–99; Member: Employment and Social Affairs, 1998–99; Agric. and Budgets Cttees, 1999; Chm., 1979 Back Bench Cttee; Dir, Human Rights Cttee, 1994–99; Dir, Animal Rights and Sustainable Develt Intergp, 1994–99. Chm., Pensions Cttee, 1999; Co-ordinator, Develt Cttee, 1999; Co-Pres., ACP/EU Jt Parly Assembly, 1999–. Chm., Transport Users' Consultative Cttee for Scotland, 1989–94; Mem., Central Transport Consultative Cttee, 1989–94 (Vice Chm., 1992–94; Mem., Railways Industry Adv. Cttee, 1993–94; Mem., Health Safety Cttee, 1993–94). Member: Council, Scottish Landowners Fedn, 1990–94 (Vice Chm., SW Reg., 1992–94); Judges Panel for Belted Galloway Soc., 1991–; Timber Growers UK (SW), 1991–94; Dir, Ayr Agricl Soc., 1990–95. Industry and Parlt Trust Fellowship with Conoco (UK) Ltd, 1986–87. *Publications:* (jtly) Towards a European Rural Policy, 1978; Towards a Community Forestry Policy, 1979; Fish Farming in Europe, 1979; The Importance of Forestry in the World Economy, 1980. *Recreations:* shooting, fishing. *Address:* Conservative Office, 10 Greenfield Crescent, Edgbaston, Birmingham B15 3AU.

CORRIE, Thomas Graham Edgar; His Honour Judge Corrie; a Circuit Judge, since 1994; *b* 18 Dec. 1946; *s* of John Alexander Galloway Corrie, OBE, MC and Barbara Phyllis Corrie (*née* Turner); *m* 1971, Anna Cathinca Logsdail; one *s* two *d. Educ:* Eton; Brasenose Coll., Oxford (MA). Called to the Bar, Gray's Inn, 1969; Midland and Oxford Circuit, 1971–94; a Recorder, 1988–94. *Recreations:* cycling, canal boating. *Address:* 2 Harcourt Buildings, Temple, EC4Y 9DB. *T:* (020) 7353 6961. *Club:* Frewen (Oxford).

CORRIGAN, Prof. (Francis) Edward, PhD; FRS 1995; Professor of Mathematics and Head of Department, University of York, since 1999; *b* 10 Aug. 1946; *s* of late Anthony Corrigan and of Eileen Corrigan (*née* Ryan); *m* 1970, Jane Mary Halton; two *s* two *d. Educ:* St Bede's Coll., Manchester; Christ's Coll., Cambridge (MA, PhD). A. J. Wheeler Fellow, Durham, 1972–74; CERN Fellow, Geneva, 1974–76; Durham University: Lectr, Sen. Lectr and Reader, 1976–92; Prof. of Maths, 1992–99; Hd, Dept of Math. Scis, 1996–98. Joliot-Curie Fellow, ENS Paris, 1977–78; Vis. Associate, CIT, 1978–79; Vis. Fellow, Dept of Applied Maths and Theoretical Physics, Cambridge, 1983; Derman Christopherson Fellow, Durham Univ., 1983–84; Vis. Prof., Centre for Particle Theory, Durham Univ., 1999–. Life Mem., Clare Hall, Cambridge. Hon. Ed., Jl of Physics A, 1999–. *Publications:* articles on elementary particle theory and mathematical physics in learned jls. *Recreations:* playing and listening to music, squash. *Address:* Department of Mathematics, University of York, Heslington, York YO10 5DD. *T:* (01904) 433774.

CORRIGAN, Margaret Mary; Marketing and Communications Officer, Falkirk College of Further and Higher Education, since 1999; *d* of Joseph Hamilton and Mary Anna (*née* Monaghan); *m* 1979, Gerard Michael Corrigan; one *s* two *d. Educ:* Univ. of Strathclyde (BA Hons English). Trainee journalist with newspaper/magazine publishers D. C. Thomson, Dundee, 1977–78; Advertising Copywriter and Acct Exec., Austin Knight Advertising, Glasgow, 1978–81; Depute Dir of Public Relns, Cumbernauld Develt Corp., 1981–83. Mem., Radio Authority, 1990–95. *Recreations:* swimming, music, theatre.

CORRIGAN, Thomas Stephen, OBE 1999; Adviser, 1994–2000, Member, Independent Panel of Judges, 2001, Charter Mark Awards, Modernising Public Services Group (formerly Citizen's Charter, then Service First, Unit), Cabinet Office; company director; *b* 2 July 1932; *s* of late Thomas Corrigan and Renée Victorine Chaborel; *m* 1963, Sally Margaret Everitt; two *d. Educ:* Beulah Hill; Chartered Accountant (Scottish Inst.). Nat. Service, Army (2nd Lieut), 1955–57. Chief Accountant, Lobitos Oilfields, 1957–62; Exec., Keyser Ullmann, 1962–64; Inveresk Group: Finance Dir, 1964; Man. Dir, 1971–74; Chm., 1974–83. Chairman: Havelock Europa, 1983–89; Rex Stewart Gp Ltd, 1987–90; Associate, cmb technologies, 2000–; dir of other cos. Pres., British Paper and Board Industry Fedn, 1975–77; Vice-Pres., European Confedn of Pulp, Paper and Board Industries, 1982–83; Mem., NEDC (Tripartite Sector Working Party on paper industry), 1976–77. Chairman: POUNC, 1984–94; Direct Mail Accreditation and Recognition Centre, 1995–97. Master: Makers of Playing Cards Co., 1978–79; Stationers and Newspaper Makers' Co., 1990–91; Marketors' Co., 1995. FRSA. *Recreations:* golf, bridge, tennis, travel. *Address:* Woodend, The Chase, Kingswood, Surrey KT20 6HZ. *T:* (01737) 832709; 57 Marsham Court, Marsham Street, SW1P 4JZ. *T:* (020) 7828 2078. *Clubs:* MCC, Royal Automobile, City Livery; Royal & Ancient Golf (St Andrews); Walton Heath Golf.

CORRIGAN-MAGUIRE, Mairead; Co-Founder and Hon. Life President, Community of the Peace People; *b* 27 Jan. 1944; *d* of Andrew and Margaret Corrigan; *m* 1981, Jackie Maguire; two *s* and three step *c. Educ:* St Vincent's Primary Sch., Falls Road, Belfast; Miss Gordon's Commercial Coll., Belfast. Secretarial qualification. Confidential Sec. to Managing Director, A. Guinness Son & Co. (Belfast) Ltd, Brewers, Belfast. Initiator of Peace Movement in Northern Ireland, Aug. 1976; Chm., Peace People Organisation, 1980–81. Hon. Dr of Law, Yale Univ., 1976; Nobel Prize for Peace (jtly), 1976; Carl-Von-Ossietzky Medaille for Courage, Berlin, 1976. *Address:* 224 Lisburn Road, Belfast, N Ireland BT9 6GE. *T:* (business) (028) 9066 3465, *Fax:* (028) 9068 3947; *e-mail:* info@peacepeople.com.

CORRIN, Prof. Bryan, MD; FRCPath; Professor of Thoracic Pathology, National Heart and Lung Institute, London University, 1979–98, now Emeritus; *b* 27 May 1933; *s* of George Henry and Eleanor Corrin; *m* 1957, Sheila Ann Carpenter; three *s* one *d. Educ:* King William's Coll., Isle of Man; St Mary's Hosp. Med. Sch., London Univ. (MB BS 1956; MD 1962). FRCPath 1977. Res. Pathologist, Birmingham Children's Hosp., 1957–58; Lectr in Pathology, Univ. of Manchester, 1958–64; Reader in Morbid Anatomy, St Thomas's Hosp. Med. Sch., London, 1964–79. Hon. Consultant Pathologist, Brompton Hosp., 1979–. Pres., London Manx Soc., 1999–2000. *Publications:* The Lungs, 1990; (ed jtly) Clinical Atlas of Respiratory Disorders, 1990; (ed) Pathology of Lung Tumors, 1997; Pathology of the Lungs, 2000. *Address:* 14 Foxgrove Road, Beckenham, Kent BR3 5AT.

CORRIN, His Honour John William, CBE 1995; Chairman, Merrill Lynch Investment Managers (Isle of Man) Ltd, since 1998; *b* 6 Jan. 1932; *s* of Evan Cain Corrin and Dorothy Mildred Corrin; *m* 1961, Dorothy Patricia, *d* of late J. S. Lace; one *d. Educ:* Murrays Road Primary Sch., Douglas; King William's Coll., IOM. Admitted to Manx Bar, 1954. Attorney Gen., IOM, 1974–80; Second Deemster, 1980–88; HM's First Deemster, Clerk of the Rolls, and Dep. Governor, IOM, 1988–98. Chairman (all IOM): Criminal Injuries Compensation Tribunal, 1980–88; Licensing Appeal Court, 1980–88; Prevention of Fraud (Unit Trust) Tribunal, 1980–88; Income Tax Appeal Comrs, 1988–98; Tynwald Ceremony Arrangements Cttee, 1988–98. Chairman: Manx Blind Welfare Soc.; Manx Workshop for the Disabled; Hon. Member: IOM Med. Soc.; IOM Law Soc.; President: IOM Br., Crossroads Care; Island Bridge Club; Lon Dhoo Male Voice Choir; IOM Br., SSAFA; Manx Asthma Assoc.; IOM Alcohol Adv. Council; Manx Housing Trust; Chm., Douglas Buxton Music Trust; Trustee: Manx Foundn for Physically Disabled; Manx Methodist Church. Freeman, Borough of Douglas, 1998. *Recreations:* music, gardening, bridge. *Address:* Carla Beck, 28 Devonshire Road, Douglas, Isle of Man IM2 3RB. *T:* (01624) 621806. *Club:* Ellan Vannin (Douglas) (Past Pres.).

CORRY; *see* Lowry-Corry, family name of Earl of Belmore.

CORRY, Viscount; John Armar Galbraith Lowry-Corry; *b* 2 Nov. 1985; *s* and *heir* of Earl of Belmore, *qv*.

CORRY, Sir James (Michael), 5th Bt *cr* 1885, of Dunraven, co. Antrim; Manager, LPG Operations, BP Nederland VOF, Netherlands, 1992–2001; *b* 3 Oct. 1946; *e s* of Sir William James Corry, 4th Bt and of Diana Pamela Mary Corry (*née* Lapsley); *S* father, 2000; *m* 1973, Sheridan Lorraine, *d* of A. P. Ashbourne; three *s. Educ:* Downside Sch. Joined Shell-Mex and BP Ltd, 1966; British Petroleum Co. Ltd, 1976; BP Nederland BV, 1992. *Recreations:* scuba diving, British Scouts. *Heir: s* William James Alexander Corry, *b* 7 Dec. 1981.

CORSAR, Col Charles Herbert Kenneth, LVO 1989; OBE 1981; TD 1960; retired; Vice Lord-Lieutenant, Lothian Region (District of Midlothian), 1993–97; *b* 13 May 1926; *s* of Kenneth Charles Corsar and Winifred Paton (*née* Herdman); *m* 1953, Mary Drummond Buchanan Smith (*see* Hon. Dame Mary Corsar); two *s* two *d* (and one *d* decd). *Educ:* Merchiston Castle Sch.; King's Coll., Cambridge (MA). Farmer, 1953–89. Commnd Royal Scots TA, 1948; comd 8/9 Royal Scots, 1964–67; Edinburgh and Heriot-Watt Univs OTC, 1967–72; TA Col, 1972–75; Hon. ADC to the Queen, 1977–81, Chm., Lowland TAVRA, 1984–87; Hon. Col., 1/52 Lowland Vols, 1975–87. Zone Comr, Home Defence, E of Scotland, 1972–74. County Cllr, Midlothian, 1958–67. Vice-Pres., Boys' Brigade, 1970–91; Chairman: Scottish Standing Conf. of Voluntary Youth Orgns, 1973–78; Earl Haig Fund (Scotland), 1984–90; Mem., Scottish Sports Council, 1972–75; Secretary: Prince's Trust (Lothian & Borders), 1982–93; (for Scotland) Duke of Edinburgh's Award, 1966–87. JP Midlothian, 1964; DL Midlothian, 1975. *Recreations:* gardening, bee-keeping, shooting. *Address:* Burg Torloisk, Ulva Ferry, Isle of Mull, Argyll PA74 6NH. *T:* (01688) 500289; 11 Ainslie Place, Edinburgh EH3 6AS. *T:* (0131) 225 6318. *Club:* New (Edinburgh).

CORSAR, Kenneth; Director of Education, Glasgow City Council, since 1995; *b* 16 July 1946; *s* of Peter and Ruby Corsar; *m* 1972, Mary Massie; two *s. Educ:* Alloa Acad.; St Andrews Univ. (MA Hons 1968); Aberdeen Univ. (DipEd 1970); Aberdeen Coll. of Education (PGCE 1970); Glasgow Univ. (MEd Hons 1976). Teacher of Classics, Dumbarton Acad., 1970–71; Principal Teacher: Kirkintilloch High Sch., 1971–72; Uddingston Grammar Sch., 1972–75; Strathclyde Regional Council: Educn Officer, 1975–86; Sen. Educn Officer, 1986–88; Divl Educn Officer, 1988–93; Depute Dir of Educn, 1993–95. Vice-Pres., 1992–93, Pres., 1993–94, Assoc. of Dirs of Educn in Scotland. FRSA 1996. *Publications:* Discovering the Greeks, 1975; Discovering Greek Mythology, 1977; articles in educn press on educn and local govt. *Recreations:* golf, calligraphy, gardening. *Address:* 9 Eaglesfield Crescent, Strathaven, S Lanarks ML10 6HY. *T:* (01357) 520817. *Club:* Strathaven Golf.

CORSAR, Hon. Dame Mary (Drummond), DBE 1993; FRSE; Chairman: TSB Foundation Scotland, 1994–97 (Trustee, 1992–97); Women's Royal Voluntary Service, 1988–93; *b* 8 July 1927; *o d* of Lord Balerno, CBE, TD, DL and Mary Kathleen Smith; *m* 1953, Col Charles Herbert Kenneth Corsar, *qv*; two *s* two *d* (and one *d* decd). *Educ:* Westbourne, Glasgow; St Denis, Edinburgh; Edinburgh Univ. (MA Hons). Dep. Chief Comr, Girl Guides, Scotland, 1972–77; Chm., Scotland WRVS, 1981–88. Member: Vis. Cttee, Glenochil Young Offenders Instn, 1976–94; Parole Bd for Scotland, 1982–89. Hon. Pres., Scottish Women's AAA, 1973–91. Member: Exec. Cttee, Trefoil Centre for Handicapped, 1975–; Convocation, Heriot Watt Univ., 1986–99; Royal Anniversary Trust, 1990–93. Gov., Fettes Coll., 1984–99. FRSE 1997. *Recreations:* hill walking, gardening, embroidery. *Address:* Burg, Torloisk, Isle of Mull, Argyll PA74 6NH. *T:* (01688) 500289; 11 Ainslie Place, Edinburgh EH3 6AS. *T:* (0131) 225 6318. *Club:* New (Edinburgh) (Associate Mem.).

CORSTON, Jean Ann; MP (Lab) Bristol East, since 1992; *b* 5 May 1942; *d* of late Charles Lawrence Parkin and Eileen Ada Parkin; *m* 1st, 1961, Christopher John Davy Corston; one *s* one *d*; 2nd, 1985, Peter Brereton Townsend, *qv*. *Educ:* LSE (LLB 1989). Labour Party posts: Asst Regl Organiser, 1976, Regl Organiser, 1981, South West; Asst National Agent, London, 1985–86; sponsored as MP by TGWU. Called to the Bar, Inner Temple, 1991; Bristol chambers. PPS to Sec. of State for Educn and Employment, 1997–2001. Mem., Select Cttee on Agric., 1992–95, on Home Affairs, 1995–97. Chm., Jt Cttee on Human Rights, 2001–; Co-Chm., PLP Women's Gp, 1992 97; Chairman: PLP Civil Liberties Gp, 1997–; PLP, 2001– (Dep. Chm., 1997–98 and 1999–2000; Mem., Parly Cttee, 1997–). Chm., Commonwealth Women Parliamentarians, 2000; Mem., Exec. Cttee, CPA, 1998–. *Recreations:* gardening, reading, walking, tap dancing. *Address:* House of Commons, SW1A 0AA. *T:* (020) 7219 4575.

CORTAZZI, Sir (Henry Arthur) Hugh, GCMG 1984 (KCMG 1980 CMG 1969); HM Diplomatic Service, retired; *b* 2 May 1924; *m* 1956, Elizabeth Esther Montagu; one *s* two *d. Educ:* Sedbergh Sch.; St Andrews and London Univs. Served in RAF, 1943–47; joined Foreign Office, 1949; Third Sec., Singapore, 1950–51; Third/Second Sec., Tokyo,

1951–54; FO, 1954–58; First Sec., Bonn, 1958–60; First Sec., later Head of Chancery, Tokyo, 1961–65; FO, 1965–66; Counsellor (Commercial), Tokyo, 1966–70; Royal Coll. of Defence Studies, 1971–72; Minister (Commercial), Washington, 1972–75; Dep. Under-Sec. of State, FCO, 1975–80; Ambassador to Japan, 1980–84. Director: Hill Samuel & Co., later Hill Samuel Bank, 1984–91; Foreign and Colonial Pacific Investment Trust, 1984–98; GT Japan Investment Trust plc, 1984–99. Senior Adviser: Mitsukoshi Ltd, 1984–; NEC Corp., Japan, 1992–98; Dai-ichi Kangyo Bank, Japan, 1992–99; Bank of Kyoto, 1992–99; Matsuura Machinery Corp., 1994–2000; Wilde Sapte, solicitors, 1992–99; PIFC, 1993–99. Mem., ESRC, 1984–89. Pres., Asiatic Soc. of Japan, 1982–83; Chm., Japan Soc., of London, 1985–95. Mem., Council and Court, Sussex Univ., 1985–92. Hon. Fellow, Robinson Coll., Cambridge, 1988. Hon. Dr Stirling, 1988. Grand Cordon, Order of the Sacred Treasure (Japan), 1995. *Publications:* trans. from Japanese, Genji Keita: The Ogre and other stories of the Japanese Salarymen, 1972; The Guardian God of Golf and other humorous stories, 1972, reprinted as The Lucky One, 1980; (ed) Mary Crawford Fraser, A Diplomat's Wife in Japan: sketches at the turn of the century, 1982; Isles of Gold: antique maps of Japan, 1983; Higashi No Shimaguni, Nishi No Shimaguni (collection of articles and speeches in Japanese), 1984; Dr Willis in Japan, 1985; (ed) Mitford's Japan, 1985; Victorians in Japan: in and around the Treaty Ports, 1987; for Japanese students of English: Thoughts from a Sussex Garden (essays), 1984; Second Thoughts (essays), 1986; Japanese Encounter, 1987; Zoku, Higashi no Shimaguni, Nishi no Shimaguni, 1987; (ed with George Webb) Kipling's Japan, 1988; The Japanese Achievement: a short history of Japan and Japanese culture, 1990; (ed) A British Artist in Meiji Japan, by Sir Alfred East, 1991; (ed) Building Japan 1868–1876, by Richard Henry Brunton, 1991; (ed with Gordon Daniels) Britain and Japan 1859–1991, 1991; Themes and Personalities, 1991; Modern Japan: a concise survey, 1993; (ed with Terry Bennett) Caught in Time: Japan, 1995; Japan and Back and Places Elsewhere, 1998; Collected Writings, 2000; (compiled and ed) Japan Experiences: Fifty Years, One Hundred Views: post-war Japan through British eyes, 2001; articles on Japanese themes in English and Japanese pubns. *Recreations:* Japanese studies, the arts including antiques, opera. *Address:* Ballsocks, Vines Cross, Heathfield, E Sussex TN21 9ET. *Club:* Royal Air Force.

CORVEDALE, Viscount; Benedict Alexander Stanley Baldwin; *b* 28 Dec. 1973; *s* and *heir* of 4th Earl Baldwin of Bewdley, *qv. Educ:* Newcastle Univ. (BMus 1996).

CORY, (Charles) Raymond, CBE 1982; Chairman: John Cory & Sons Ltd, 1965–91 (Director 1948–91); Milford Haven Port Authority (formerly Conservancy Board), 1982–94; *b* 20 Oct. 1922; *s* of Charles and Ethel Cory; *m* 1st, 1946, Vivienne Mary Roberts (*d* 1988), Kelowna, BC, Canada; three *d*; 2nd, 1989, Betty (*d* 2000), *widow* of Lt-Col Roy Horley. *Educ:* Harrow; Christ Church, Oxford. Served RNVR, Ord. Seaman to Lieut, 1942–46; Russian and N Atlantic convoys and Normandy landings (C-in-C's Commendation June 1944). Vice-Chm., A. B. Electronics Products Group PLC, 1979–92. Dir and Mem. Executive, Baltic and Internat. Maritime Conf., Copenhagen, 1957–67; Mem., Lloyd's Register of Shipping, 1963–67. Chairman: Barry Pilotage Authority, 1963–74 (Mem. 1953); Port Talbot Pilotage Authority, 1970–74; SE Wales Pilotage Authority, 1974–80; Welsh Council Mission to Seamen, 1984–95; Vice-Chm., BTDB, 1969–79 (Mem., 1966–79; Chm., S Wales Local Bd, 1966); Pres., Cardiff Chamber of Commerce, 1959–60. Chm., S Glamorgan HA, 1974–84. Church in Wales: Member: Governing Body, 1957–60; Rep. Body, 1960–97 (Dep. Chm., 1985–95; Treasurer, 1988–); Finance Cttee, 1960–88 (Vice-Chm. 1971, Chm. 1975–88); Dep. Chm., Finance and Resources Cttee, 1988–95. RNLI: Chm. Cardiff Br., 1950–73; Mem. Cttee of Management, 1954–97; Vice-Pres. 1969–97, Life Vice-Pres., 1997; Dep. Chm., 1985–93; Mem., Exec. Cttee, 1970–93. Chm., Council, Univ. of Wales Coll. of Medicine, 1988–97 (Mem., 1984–97). *Publication:* A Century of Family Shipowning, 1954. *Recreations:* formerly ski-ing, sailing and gardening. *Address:* The Coach House, Llanblethian, Cowbridge, Vale of Glamorgan CF71 7JF. *T:* (01446) 772251. *Club:* Cardiff and County.

CORY, Sir (Clinton Charles) Donald, 5th Bt *cr* 1919, of Coryton, Whitchurch, Glamorgan; *b* 13 Sept. 1937; *s* of Sir Clinton James Donald Cory, 4th Bt and of Mary, *o d* of Dr Arthur Douglas Hunt; *S* father, 1991. *Educ:* Brighton Coll.; abroad. *Recreations:* collecting Greek and Roman antiquities, student of classical studies. *Heir:* none. *Address:* 18 Cloisters Road, Letchworth, Herts SG6 3JS. *T:* (01462) 677206.

CORY, John; Vice Lord-Lieutenant of South Glamorgan, since 1990; Director, John Cory & Sons Ltd, 1949–91; *b* 30 June 1928; *s* of John and Cecil Cory; *m* 1965, Sarah Christine, *d* of John Meade, JP, DL; two *d. Educ:* Eton; Trinity College, Cambridge. Chm., Cardiff RDC, 1971–72. Member, Governing Body, 1957–74, Representative Body, 1960–99, Church in Wales. Pres., Nat. Light Horse Breeding Soc., 1977–78. Joint Master, Glamorgan Hounds, 1962–67. High Sheriff, 1959, JP 1961, DL 1968, Glamorgan. KStJ. *Address:* The Grange, St Brides-super-Ely, Cardiff CF5 6XA. *T:* (01446) 760211. *Clubs:* MCC; Cardiff and County (Cardiff).

CORY, Raymond; *see* Cory, C. R.

CORY, Prof. Suzanne, AC 1999; PhD; FRS 1992; FAA; Director, Walter and Eliza Hall Institute of Medical Research, since 1996; Professor of Medical Biology, University of Melbourne, since 1996; *b* 11 March 1942; *d* of Desmond and Joy Cory; *m* 1969, Prof. Jerry Adams; two *d. Educ:* Univ. of Melbourne (BSc, MSc); Wolfson Coll., Cambridge (PhD 1968; Hon. Fellow, 2000). Rothmans Fellow, Univ. of Geneva, 1969–71; Walter and Eliza Hall Institute of Medical Research, 1971–: Sen. Principal Res. Fellow, 1988–; Jt Head, Molecular Genetics of Cancer Div., 1988–. Internat. Res. Schol., Howard Hughes Med. Inst., 1992–97. FAA 1986. Foreign Mem., NAS, USA, 1997. Hon. DSc Sydney. Lemberg Medal, Australian Soc. Biochem. and Molecular Biol., 1995; Burnet Medal, Australian Acad. Sci., 1997; (jtly) Australia Prize, 1998; (jtly) Charles S. Mott Prize, General Motors Cancer Res. Foundn, 1998. *Publications:* numerous scientific papers and reviews. *Recreations:* camping, hiking, swimming, wilderness photography, ski-ing. *Address:* Walter and Eliza Hall Institute of Medical Research, Post Office, Royal Melbourne Hospital, Vic 3050, Australia. *T:* (3) 93452551.

CORY-WRIGHT, Sir Richard (Michael), 4th Bt *cr* 1903; *b* 17 Jan. 1944; *s* of Capt. A. J. J. Cory-Wright (killed in action, 1944), and Susan Esterel (*d* 1993; she *m* 2nd, 1949, Lt-Col J. E. Gurney, DSO, MC), *d* of Robert Elwes; *S* grandfather, 1969; *m* 1st, 1976, Veronica Bolton (marr. diss. 1994); three *s*; 2nd, 1998, Helga Wright, *e d* of George Godfrey. *Educ:* Eton; Birmingham Univ. *Heir:* *s* Roland Anthony Cory-Wright, *b* 11 March 1979.

COSGRAVE, Liam, SC; *b* April 1920; *s* of late William T. Cosgrave; *m* 1952, Vera Osborne; two *s* one *d. Educ:* Synge Street Christian Brothers; Castlenock College, Dublin; King's Inns. Served in Army during Emergency. Barrister-at-Law, 1943; Senior Counsel, 1958. Member, Dail Eireann, 1943–81; Chairman Public Accounts Committee, 1945; Parliamentary Secretary to Taoiseach and Minister for Industry and Commerce, 1948–51; Minister for External Affairs, 1954–57; Leader, Fine Gael Party, 1965–77; Taoiseach (Head of Govt of Ireland), 1973–77; Minister for Defence, 1976. Leader first delegation from Ireland to the UN Assembly, 1956. Hon. LLD: Duquesne Univ., Pittsburg, Pa, and St John's Univ., Brooklyn, 1956; de Paul Univ., Chicago, 1958; NUI, 1974; Dublin Univ., 1974. Knight Grand Cross of Pius IX, 1956. *Address:* Beechpark, Templeogue, Co. Dublin.

COSGROVE, Hon. Lady; Hazel Josephine Cosgrove; a Senator of the College of Justice in Scotland, since 1996; *b* 12 Jan. 1946; *d* of late Moses Aron Aronson and Julia Tobias; *m* 1967, John Allan Cosgrove, dental surgeon; one *s* one *d. Educ:* Glasgow High Sch. for Girls; Univ. of Glasgow (LLB). Advocate at the Scottish Bar. Admitted to Fac. of Advocates, 1968; QC (Scot.) 1991; Standing Junior Counsel to Dept of Trade, 1977–79; Sheriff of Glasgow and Strathkelvin, 1979–83; Sheriff of Lothian and Borders at Edinburgh, 1983–96. Temporary Judge, High Court and Court of Session, Scotland, 1992–96. Mem., Parole Bd for Scotland, 1988–91; Chairman: Mental Welfare Commn for Scotland, 1991–96; Expert Panel on Sex Offending, Scotland, 1997–2001; Dep. Chm., Boundary Commn for Scotland, 1997–. Hon. LLD Napier, 1997. *Recreations:* foreign travel, opera, swimming, walking, reading, langlauf. *Address:* Parliament House, Edinburgh EH1 1RQ.

COSGROVE, Brian Joseph; Joint Managing Director, Cosgrove Hall Films, since 1995; *b* 6 April 1934; *s* of Denis Cosgrove and Martha Cosgrove (*née* Hesketh); *m* 1963, Angela Helen Dyson; two *d. Educ:* Manchester Coll. of Art. Nat. Service, Army, 1952–54 (Malayan campaign). TV Graphic Designer, 1967–72; TV Programme Dir, 1972–76; Founder (with Mark Hall), Cosgrove Hall Productions, to produce animated films, 1976–95 (BAFTA Award, 1982, 1983, 1985, 1986, 1987; Prix Jeunesse, Munich Film Fest., 1982; Internat. Emmy, 1984, 1991; Prix Danube, Bratislava Film Fest., 1990; 2 Observer Children's Film Awards, 1990). Mem., MENSA. *Recreations:* writing, painting, sculpture, gardening. *Address:* Cosgrove Hall Films Ltd, 8 Albany Road, Chorlton-cum-Hardy, Manchester M21 0AW. *T:* (0161) 881 9211.

COSSERAT, Kay, RDI 1986; Director, Cosserat Design Ltd, since 1976; Part-time Lecturer, Royal College of Art, since 1990, and Chelsea School of Art, since 1985; *b* 24 Oct. 1947; *d* of Robert and Elizabeth Macklam; *m* 1972, Christopher Graham Peloquin Cosserat; two *s. Educ:* Cleveland Sch., Eaglescliffe; Goldsmiths' Sch. of Art (Dip AD 1st cl. Hons); Royal Coll. of Art (MA Textiles 1972); Sanderson Travel Scholarship, 1972. Formed Cosserat Design Partnership, 1974; Founder Mem., London Designer Collections, 1974; currently producing textile and garment designs on a consultancy basis. Mem., Fashion and Textile Bd, CNAA, 1978. Vis. Prof., London Inst., 1992–; Part-time Lecturer: St Martins Sch. of Art, 1972–80; RCA, 1976–79; External Assessor: Central Sch. of Art, 1982–85; Trent Poly., 1983–85; Liverpool Poly., 1985–87; Huddersfield Poly., 1985–88; QUB, 1990–92; Univ. of Ulster, 1990–93; Winchester Sch. of Art, 1991–93. *Recreations:* gardening, ski-ing, collecting '30s pottery. *Address:* The Manor, Sherington, Bucks MK16 9NB.

COSSHAM, Christopher Hugh, CB 1989; Senior Assistant Director of Public Prosecutions (Northern Ireland), 1973–89; *b* 12 April 1929; *s* of Lorimer and Gwendolin Cossham; *m* 1958, Joanna Howard Smith; one *s* one *d. Educ:* Monkton Combe Sch.; Bristol Univ. Called to Bar, Gray's Inn, 1958. Board of Trade, 1958–62; Director of Public Prosecutions Dept, 1962–73. Dep. Metropolitan Stipendiary Magistrate, 1978–86. Mem., Wkg Party on handling of complaints against police, 1974. *Recreations:* cycling, listening to music, writing humorous verse. *Address:* Valhalla, 1 The Grange, High Street, Portishead, Bristol BS20 6QL. *T:* (01275) 845237. *Clubs:* Civil Service, Northern Law.

COSSONS, Sir Neil, Kt 1994; OBE 1982; Chairman, English Heritage, since 2000; Collier Professor in the Public Understanding of Science, University of Bristol, 2001–Sept. 2002; *b* 15 Jan. 1939; *s* of Arthur Cossons and Evelyn (*née* Bettle); *m* 1965, Veronica Edwards; two *s* one *d. Educ:* Henry Mellish Grammar Sch., Nottingham; Univ. of Liverpool (MA). FSA 1968; FMA 1970. Curator of Technology, Bristol City Museum, 1964; Dep. Dir, City of Liverpool Museums, 1969; Dir, Ironbridge Gorge Museum Trust, 1971; Director: Nat. Maritime Museum, 1983–86; Science Museum, 1986–2000. Comr, Historic Buildings and Monuments Commn for England (English Heritage), 1989–95, and 1999–2000 (Mem., Ancient Monuments Adv. Cttee, 1984–98); Member: Curatorium Internat. Committee for the Conservation of the Industrial Heritage, 1973–78; BBC General Adv. Council, 1987–90; NEDO Tourism and Leisure Industries Sector Gp (formerly Leisure Industries EDC), 1987–90; Council, RCA, 1989–; Design Council, 1990–94; Comité Scientifique, Conservatoire Nat. des Arts et Métiers, 1991–2000. President: Assoc. for Industrial Archaeology, 1977–80; Assoc. of Independent Museums, 1983– (Chm., 1978–83); Museums Assoc., 1981–82; ASE, 1996; Member, Council: Newcomen Soc. for Study of Hist. of Engrg and Technol., 1992– (Mem., 1963–; Vice-Pres., 1997); FMI, 1993–98. Mem., British Waterways Bd, 1995–2001. Trustee, Civic Trust, 1987–93. Gov., Imperial Coll. of Sci., Technology and Medicine, 1989–93. Hon. Prof., Univ. of Birmingham, 1994–. FRSA 1988; Hon. Fellow, RCA, 1987; Comp IEE, 1991; CIMgt 1996; Hon. CRAeS 1996. Hon. DSocSc Birmingham, 1979; DUniv: Open, 1984; Sheffield Hallam, 1995; York, 1998; Hon. DLitt: Liverpool, 1989; Bradford, 1991; Nottingham Trent, 1994; UWE, 1995; Bath, 1997; Hon. DSc: Leicester, 1995; Nottingham, 2000; Hon. DArts De Montfort, 1997. Norton Medlicott Medal, Historical Assoc., 1991; President's Medal, Royal Acad. of Engrg, 1993. *Publications:* (with R. A. Buchanan) Industrial Archaeology of the Bristol Region, 1968; (with K. Hudson) Industrial Archaeologists' Guide, 1969, 2nd edn 1971; Industrial Archaeology, 1975, 3rd edn 1993; (ed) Transactions of the First International Congress on the Conservation of Industrial Monuments, 1975; (ed) Rees's Manufacturing Industry, 1975; (with H. Sowden) Ironbridge—Landscape of Industry, 1977; (with B. S. Trinder) The Iron Bridge—Symbol of the Industrial Revolution, 1979, 2nd edn (Japanese) 1989; (ed) Management of Change in Museums, 1985; (ed) Making of the Modern World, 1992; (ed) Perspectives on Industrial Archaeology, 2000; numerous papers, articles and reviews. *Recreations:* travel, industrial archaeology. *Address:* English Heritage, 23 Savile Row, W1S 2ET; The Old Rectory, Rushbury, Shropshire SY6 7EB. *T:* (01694) 771603. *Club:* Athenæum.

COSTA, António Maria, PhD; Secretary General, European Bank for Reconstruction and Development, since 1994; *b* 16 June 1941; *s* of Francesco Costa and Maria (*née* Contratto); *m* 1971, Patricia Wallace; two *s* one *d. Educ:* Turin Univ. (degree in political sci. 1964); Acad. of Scis, Moscow (Math. Econs 1967); Univ. of Calif at Berkeley (MA Econs 1969; PhD Econs 1971). Sen. Economic Advr, UN, NY, 1971–83; Dep. Sec. Gen. (Special Counsellor), OECD, 1983–87; Dir Gen. for Econs and Finance, Special Advr to Pres., and Mem., Monetary Cttee, EU, Brussels, 1987–92; Dir Gen. for Strategic Planning, Ferrero Gp, 1992–93. Member: Wkg Party for Co-ordination of Macroeconomic Policies of G10 Countries, OECD; Bd of Dirs, EIB; EU Rapporteur to EP. Vis. Prof. of Econs, Moscow Univ. and Acad. of Scis, Moscow, 1963–64; Adjunct Professor of Economics: Univ. of Calif at Berkeley, 1968–70; CU NY, 1970–76; New York Univ., 1976–87; Vis. Prof., Free Univ., Brussels, 1990–94. *Address:* European Bank for Reconstruction and Development, One Exchange Square, EC2A 2EH.

COSTA, Kenneth Johann; Vice-Chairman, UBS Warburg (formerly SBC Warburg, then Warburg Dillon Read), since 1996; *b* 31 Oct. 1949; *s* of late Joseph Costa and of Martha Costa; *m* 1982, Fiona Morgan-Williams; two *s* two *d. Educ:* Univ. of Witwatersrand (BA, LLB); Queens' Coll., Cambridge (LLM, Cert. in Theology). Joined S. G. Warburg, 1976; Dep. Chm., 1993; Chm., Investment Banking Bd, Hd of Global Mergers and Acquisitions, SBC Warburg, 1995. Church Warden, Holy Trinity, Brompton. *Recreations:* shooting, ski-ing, tennis, music, theology. *Address:* UBS Warburg, 2 Finsbury Avenue, EC2M 2PP.

COSTA-LOBO, António; Ambassador of Portugal to the Court of St James's, 1995–97; *b* 22 May 1932; *s* of Gumersindo da Costa Lobo and Maria Magdalena Teixeira Leal da Costa Lobo; *m* 1980, Maria Catarina de Locher Machado. *Educ:* Univ. of Coimbra, Portugal (Law degree). Joined Ministry of Foreign Affairs, Portugal, 1956: served Havana, 1961–63; The Hague, 1964–66; Consul-Gen., San Francisco, 1966–70; Perm. Mission to UN, NY, 1973–77; Council of Europe, 1980–82; Ambassador to China, 1982–85; Perm. Mission, Geneva, 1985–90; Ambassador to Russia, 1990–93; Sec. Gen., Ministry of Foreign Affairs, 1993–95. Grã-Cruz da Ordem do Infante Dom Henrique (Portugal), 1985; Grã-Cruz da Ordem Militar de Cristo (Portugal), 1997. *Publication:* As Operações de Paz das Nações Unidas, 1969. *Recreations:* reading, riding, ski-ing. *Address:* Av. D. Nuno Álvares Pereira 41, 2765 Estoril, Portugal. *Club:* Grémio Literário (Lisbon).

COSTAIN, Janice Elizabeth; *see* Hall, J. E.

COSTAIN, Noel Leslie, OBE 1964; Director of Works, University of Sheffield, 1964–78; *b* 11 Jan. 1914; *s* of George Wesley Costain and Minnie Grace Pinson; *m* 1945, Marie José Elizabeth (*née* Bishton); two *d. Educ:* King Edward's Sch., Five Ways, Birmingham; Univ. of Birmingham (BSc). CEng, MICE. Engineer with Sir R. MacAlpine & Sons, 1937–38; Epsom and Ewell BC, 1939; Air Min., Directorate-Gen. of Works; Section Officer, Orkneys and Shetlands, 1940–43; Prin. Works Officer, Sierra Leone, 1944–46; Superintending Engr, Air Ministry, 1946–51; RAF Airfield Construction Br.: Cmdg 5352 Wing, Germany, and OC, RAF Church Lawford, 1951–54; Superintending Engr, Works Area, Bristol, 1954–58; Chief Engr, MEAF, 1958–60; Chief Resident Engr, BMEWS, Fylingdales, 1960–63. Vice-Chm., Yorkshire Univs Air Squadron Cttee. FINucE 1959 (Mem. Council, 1965; Vice-Pres., 1969; Pres., 1972–76). *Recreations:* travel, gardening. *Address:* Villa Marie José, Avenida 3 no 59, Urbanisation Hacienda Las Chapas, Marbella, Málaga, Spain.
See also R. M. Bateman.

COSTAIN, Peter John, FCA; Deputy Chairman, Costain Group Plc, 1995–97 (Group Chief Executive, 1980–95); Director: Pearl Group, since 1989; London Life Ltd, since 1994; AMP UK plc, since 1994; *b* 2 April 1938; *s* of Sir Albert Costain; *m* 1963, Victoria M. Pope; three *s. Educ:* Charterhouse. Peat Marwick Mitchell & Co., 1956–63; Richard Costain Ltd, 1963–65; Costain Australia Ltd, 1965–92: Board Member, 1967; Managing Director, 1971; Chief Executive, 1973. Dir, Wessex Water Services Ltd, 1999–. Mem., London Adv. Bd, Westpac Banking Corp., 1981–86. Mem. Bd, CITB, 1989–93. FAIB. Prime Warden, Basketmakers' Co., 1998–99. *Recreations:* sailing, ski-ing, golf. *Clubs:* Royal Thames Yacht; Athenæum (Melbourne); Rye Golf, Royal St George's Golf.

COSTANZI, Edwin J. B.; *see* Borg-Costanzi.

COSTELLO, Declan; President, High Court of the Republic of Ireland, 1995–98; *b* 1 Aug. 1926; *s* of John A. Costello and Ida (*née* O'Malley); *m* 1953, Joan Fitzsimms; three *s* two *d. Educ:* Xavier Sch., Dublin; University Coll., Dublin. King's Inns, Dublin; Called to the Bar, 1948; Inner Bar, 1965. TD (FG): Dublin NW, 1951–69; Dublin SW, 1973–77; Attorney-Gen., 1973–77; Judge of the High Court, 1977–95. Mem., Consultative Assembly, Council of Europe, 1957–63. Chairman: Nat. Youth Policy Cttee, Ireland, 1983; Cttee on Fund-raising for Charitable Purposes, Ireland, 1989. *Recreations:* tennis, reading, film-going. *Address:* 8 Clonskeagh Road, Dublin 6, Republic of Ireland. *T:* (1) 2697963. *Clubs:* St Stephen's Green (Dublin); Fitzwilliam Lawn Tennis (Dublin).

COSTELLO, Elvis; *see* McManus, D. P.

COSTELLO, Gordon John; Chief Accountant of the Bank of England, 1975–78; *b* 29 March 1921; *s* of late Ernest James Costello and Hilda May Costello; *m* 1946, Joan Lilian Moore; two *s* one *d. Educ:* Varndean Sch. Served War, 1939–45 (RA). Bank of England, 1946; worked in various Departments; Asst Chief Accountant, 1964; Asst Sec., 1965; Dep. Sec., 1968; Dep. Chief Cashier, 1970. *Recreations:* music, travel, walking, tennis. *Address:* 26 Peacock Lane, Brighton, Sussex BN1 6WA. *T:* (01273) 552344.

COSTELLO, John Francis, MD; FRCP, FRCPI; Consultant Physician, King's College Hospital, since 1977; Director of Medicine, King's College Hospital (formerly King's Healthcare) NHS Trust, since 1997; *b* 22 Sept. 1944; *s* of late William and Sarah Costello; *m* 1972, Dr Christine Ellen McGregor White (marr. diss.); three *s*; *m* 1996, Susanna Clarke; two *s. Educ:* Belvedere Coll., Dublin; University Coll., Dublin (MB BCh, BAO Hons 1968; MD 1987). MRCP 1972, FRCP 1982; MRCPI 1995, FRCPI 1996. Hospital appts, Mater Hosp., Dublin, St Stephen's, and Royal Northern; RPMS, 1970–72; Registrar, Brompton Hosp., 1972–73; Lectr, Univ. of Edinburgh, Edinburgh Royal Infirmary, 1973–75; Asst Prof. of Medicine, and attending physician, Univ. of California, San Francisco, 1975–77; Dir, Respiratory Medicine, King's Coll. Sch. of Medicine and Dentistry, 1982–98; Med. Clinical Dir, Acute Services, KCH, 1989–93 (Chm. of Consultants, 1989–91); Med. Dir, King's Healthcare NHS Trust, 1991–94. Examr in Medicine, Conjoint Bd, 1979–83. Founder Pres., Respiratory Sect., RSocMed, 1991–93; Mem. Council, British Thoracic Soc., 1996. *Publications:* (ed jtly) Beta Agonists in the Treatment of Asthma, 1992; (ed) Methylxanthines and Phosphodiesterase Inhibitors, 1994; (jtly) A Colour Atlas of Lung Infections, 1996; (ed) Sympathomimetic Enantiomers in the Treatment of Asthma, 1997; papers, reviews and chapters on lung disease, esp. asthma. *Recreations:* opera, golf, running. *Address:* 12 Melville Avenue, Wimbledon, SW20 0NS. *T:* (020) 8879 1309; *e-mail:* johncostello@kcl.ac.uk. *Club:* Royal Wimbledon Golf.

COSTELLO, Hon. Peter Howard; MP (L) for Higgins, Victoria, since 1990; Treasurer of Australia, since 1996; *b* 14 Aug. 1957; *s* of Russell and Anne Costello; *m* 1982, Tanya Pamela Coleman; one *s* two *d. Educ:* Carey Baptist Grammar Sch.; Monash Univ. (LLB Hons, BA). Solicitor, 1981–84; Barrister, 1984–90. Shadow Minister for Corporate Law Reform and Consumer Affairs, 1990–92; Shadow Attorney Gen. and Shadow Minister for Justice, 1992–93; Shadow Minister for Finance, 1993–94; Shadow Treasurer, 1994–96; Dep. Leader of Opposition, 1994–96; Dep. Leader, Liberal Party, 1994–. *Recreations:* swimming, football, reading. *Address:* Parliament House, Canberra, ACT 2600, Australia. *T:* (2) 62777340. *Clubs:* Australian (Melbourne); Melbourne Cricket; Essendon Football.

COSTELOE, Prof. Michael Peter, PhD; FRHistS; Professor of Hispanic and Latin American Studies, University of Bristol, 1981–98, now Emeritus; *b* 12 March 1939; *s* of late John Myles Costeloe and of Etheleen Winifred Costeloe, Bishop Auckland; *m* 1962, Eleanor, *d* of late William and Margaret Bonney; one *d. Educ:* King James I Grammar Sch., Bishop Auckland; Univ. of Durham (BA 1961); Univ. of Newcastle (DipEd 1962; PhD 1965). FRHistS 1976. University of Bristol: Asst Lectr and Lectr in Latin American Studies, 1965–76; Reader, 1976–81; Dean of Arts, 1993–96. Vis. Prof., Univ. of Texas, 1967. Corresp. Fellow, Acad. Mexicana de la Historia, 1995. *Publications:* Church Wealth in Mexico, 1967; (ed and trans.) Alienation of Church Wealth in Mexico, by J. Bazant, 1971; (with C. Steele) Independent Mexico, 1973; La primera república federal de Mexico, 1975; Mexico State Papers, 1976; Response to Revolution: Imperial Spain and the Spanish American Revolutions, 1986; The Central Republic in Mexico 1835–1846, 1993. *Recreations:* Anthony Trollope, golf. *Address:* Department of Hispanic Studies, University of Bristol, 15 Woodland Road, Bristol BS8 1TE. *T:* (0117) 928 7496. *Club:* Henbury Golf.

COTILL, John Atrill T.; *see* Templeton-Cotill.

COTRAN, Eugene, LLD; **His Honour Judge Cotran;** a Circuit Judge, since 1992; *b* Jerusalem, Palestine, 6 Aug. 1938; *s* of Michael Cotran and Hassiba (*née* Khoury); *m* 1963, Christiane Avierino; three *s* one *d. Educ:* Victoria Coll., Alexandria, Egypt; Univ. of Leeds (LLB, LLM 1958); Trinity Hall, Univ. of Cambridge (Dip. Internat. Law 1959); LLD London, 1971. FCIArb. Called to the Bar, Lincoln's Inn, 1959. Res. Officer in African Law, SOAS, Univ. of London, 1960–63, Lectr, 1963–77; practised at the Bar, 1963–92; Law Comr, Kenya, 1967–68; High Court Judge, Kenya, 1977–82; a Recorder, 1989–92. Vis. Prof. of Law and Chm., Centre for Islamic and ME Law, SOAS, 1987–. Internat. Arbitrator, Internat. Court of Arbitration, Paris and London, 1985–92; Legal Mem., Immigration Appeal Tribunal, 1997–. Vice Pres., Med. Aid for Palestinians, 1996–; Mem. Bd, Palestinian Ind. Commn for Citizens Rights, 1994–. Gen. Editor, Yearbook of Islamic and Middle Eastern Law, 1994–; Jt Editor, CIMEL Book Series, 1994–. *Publications:* Restatement of African Law, Kenya: Vol. I, Marriage and Divorce, Vol. II, Succession, 1968; Casebook on Kenya Customary Law, 1987; Butterworth's Immigration Law Service, 1991; edited jointly: The Role of the Judiciary in the Protection of Human Rights, 1997; Democracy, the Rule of Law and Islam, 1999; The Palestinian Exodus 1948–1998, 1999; The Rule of Law in the Middle East and the Islamic World: human rights and the judicial process, 2000; articles in internat. law jls and African law jls. *Recreations:* horse-racing, swimming, bridge. *Address:* 16 Hart Grove, Ealing, W5 3NB. *T:* (020) 8992 0432, *Fax:* (020) 8992 7228.

COTRUBAS, Ileana, (Mme Manfred Ramin); opera singer, retired 1990; *b* Rumania; *d* of Vasile and Maria Cotrubas; *m* 1972, Manfred Ramin. *Educ:* Conservatorul Ciprian Porumbescu, Bucharest. Opera and concert engagements all over Europe, N America and Japan. Formerly permanent guest at Royal Opera House, Covent Garden; Member, Vienna State Opera (Hon. Mem., 1991); also frequently sang in Scala, Milan, Munich, Berlin, Paris, Chicago, NY Metropolitan Opera. Main operatic roles: Susanna, Pamina, Gilda, Traviata, Manon, Tatyana, Mimi, Melisande, Amina, Elisabetta, Nedda, Marguerite. Has made numerous recordings. Hon. Citizen, Bucharest, 1993. Kammersängerin, Austria, 1981; Grand Officer, Sant Iago da Espada (Portugal), 1990. *Publication:* Opernwahrheiten, 1998.

COTTAM, Harold; Chairman, Britannic plc, since 1996; *b* 12 Oct. 1938; *s* of Rev. Canon Frank and Elizabeth Cottam; *m* 1962, Lyn Minton; two *d. Educ:* Bedford School. FCA. Deloitte & Co., Tanganyika and Peru, 1960–64; Smith Kline UK, 1964–66; Simon Engineering Group, Spain, 1966–68; Ernst & Whinney, subseq. Ernst & Young, 1968–92; UK Man. Partner, 1987–92; Chairman: Ernst & Young Case Services (Internat.), 1992–93; Ernst & Young Pan-European Consulting Gp, 1992–93; Haden MacLellan Hldgs, 1992–97; Anglo United (Coalite Products, Charrington and Falkland Is Gp), 1993–96; Rebus Gp, 1996–99. Dir, Allied Colloids Gp, 1992–97. *Recreations:* piano, opera, tennis. *Address:* (office) Britannic plc, 1 Wythall Green Way, Wythall, Worcs B47 6WG.

COTTELL, Michael Norman Tizard, OBE 1988; FREng; FICE, FIHT; Chairman and Executive Director, Aspen Consultancy Group, since 1996; President, Institution of Civil Engineers, 1992–93; *b* 25 July 1931; *s* of late Norman James Cottell and Eileen Clare Cottell (*née* Tizard); *m* 1957, Joan Florence Dolton; two *s. Educ:* Peter Symonds Sch., Winchester; University Coll., Southampton. CEng, FREng (FEng 1990); FIHT 1954; MICE 1958, FICE 1976; MIM 1972; MASCE 1990. Trainee Civil Engr, Hants CC, 1949–51; Nat. Service, RE, Malaya and Suez, 1951–53, 1956; Engineering Assistant: Glos CC, 1954–57; Northants CC, 1957–58; Resident Engr, Oxford Western Bypass, 1958–61; Project Engr, M4 Motorway, Glos, 1961–67; Asst County Surveyor, Suffolk CC, 1967–73; Dep. County Surveyor, E Sussex CC, 1973–76; County Surveyor: Northants CC, 1976–84; Kent CC, 1984–91. Exec. Consultant, Travers Morgan, 1991–95. Lt-Col, RE & Logistics Staff Corps (TA), 1992–. *Recreations:* golf, swimming, walking, theatre, jazz, travel, viewing historic buildings, as a spectator keen on most sports. *Address:* Salcey Lawn, Harrow Court, Stockbury, Kent ME9 7UQ. *Clubs:* Athenæum, Royal Automobile.

COTTENHAM, 9th Earl of, *cr* 1850; **Mark John Henry Pepys;** Bt 1784 and 1801; Baron Cottenham 1836; Viscount Crowhurst 1850; *b* 11 Oct. 1983; *s* of 8th Earl of Cottenham; *S* father, 2000. *Educ:* Eton. *Heir: b* Hon. Sam Richard Pepys, *b* 26 April 1986.

COTTER, Brian Joseph; MP (Lib Dem) Weston-super-Mare, since 1997; *b* 24 Aug. 1938; *s* of Michael Joseph Cotter and Mary Cotter; *m* 1963, Eyleen Patricia Wade; two *s* one *d. Educ:* Downside Sch., Somerset. Sales Manager, then Man. Dir, Plasticable Ltd, 1989–. Lib Dem spokesman on small businesses, 1997–. *Recreations:* reading, gardening, films. *Address:* House of Commons, SW1A 0AA; Belmont House, Brinsea Road, Congresbury, Som BS49 5JF. *T:* (01934) 832755. *Club:* National Liberal.

COTTER, Sir Patrick Laurence Delaval, 7th Bt *cr* 1763, of Rockforest, Cork; *b* 21 Nov. 1941; *s* of Laurence Stopford Llewelyn Cotter; *S* uncle, 2001; *m* 1967, Janet, *d* of George Potter, Barnstaple; one *s* two *d. Educ:* Blundell's; RAC Cirencester. *Heir: s* Julius Laurence George Cotter, *b* 5 Jan. 1968.

COTTERELL, Geoffrey; author; *b* 24 Nov. 1919; *yr s* of late Graham Cotterell and Millicent (*née* Crews). *Educ:* Bishops Stortford College. Served War of 1939–45, Royal Artillery, 1940–46. *Publications:* Then a Soldier, 1944; This is the Way, 1947; Randle in Springtime, 1949; Strait and Narrow, 1950; Westward the Sun, 1952 (repr. 1973); The Strange Enchantment, 1956 (repr. 1973); Tea at Shadow Creek, 1958; Tiara Tahiti, 1960 (filmed 1962, screenplay with Ivan Foxwell); Go, said the bird, 1966; Bowers of Innocence, 1970; Amsterdam, the life of a city, 1972. *Recreation:* golf. *Address:* 2 Fulbourne House, Blackwater Road, Eastbourne, Sussex BN20 7DN. *Clubs:* Royal Automobile; Cooden Beach Golf.

COTTERELL, Sir John (Henry Geers), 6th Bt *cr* 1805; Vice Lord-Lieutenant, Herefordshire, since 1998; Chairman: Radio Wyvern, 1980–97; Herefordshire Community Health NHS Trust, 1991–97; *b* 8 May 1935; *s* of Sir Richard Charles Geers Cotterell, 5th Bt, CBE, and Lady Lettice Cotterell (*d* 1973), *d* of 7th Earl Beauchamp; *S* father, 1978; *m* 1959, Vanda Alexandra Clare (MBE 1997), *d* of Major Philip Alexander

Clement Bridgewater; three *s* one *d*. *Educ:* Eton; RMA Sandhurst. Officer, Royal Horse Guards, 1955–61. Vice-Chm. Hereford and Worcs CC, 1973–77, Chm., 1977–81. Pres., Nat. Fedn of Young Farmers Clubs, 1986–91 (Dep. Pres., 1979–86); Mem., Jockey Club, 1990–. Chairman: Hereford Mappa Mundi Trust, 1990–; Rural Voice, 1991–92. *Recreations:* cricket, shooting. *Heir:* *s* Henry Richard Geers Cotterell [*b* 22 Aug. 1961; *m* 1986, Carolyn (*d* 1999), *er d* of John Beckwith-Smith, Maybanks Manor, Rudgwick, Sussex; two *s* one *d*]. *Address:* Downshill House, Bishopstone, Herefordshire HR4 7JT. *T:* (01981) 590232. *Club:* Turf.

COTTERILL, Kenneth William, CMG 1976; Chairman, Commercial and Political Risk Consultants Ltd, 1986–98 (Deputy Chairman, 1981–86); *b* 5 June 1921; *s* of William and Ada May Cotterill; *m* 1948, Janet Hilda Cox; one *d*. *Educ:* Sutton County Sch.; London School of Economics, BSc (Econ). Served War in Royal Navy, 1941–46. After the war, joined ECGD; Principal, 1956; Asst Sec., 1966; Under Sec., 1970; Dep. Head of Dept, 1976–81. Dir, Tarmac Internat., 1981–86; Consultant: NEI International, 1981–87; Barclays Bank, 1981–87. *Recreations:* reading, walking, gardening. *Address:* 15 Minster Drive, Croydon CR0 5UP. *T:* (020) 8681 6700.

COTTESLOE, 5th Baron (UK) *cr* 1874; **Comdr John Tapling Fremantle;** Bt 1821; Baron of Austrian Empire 1816; RN (retired); JP; DL; Lord-Lieutenant of Buckinghamshire, 1984–97; *b* 22 Jan. 1927; *s* of 4th Baron Cottesloe, GBE and his 1st wife, Lady Elizabeth Harris (*d* 1983), *o d* of 5th Earl of Malmesbury; *S* father, 1994; *m* 1958, Elizabeth Ann, *e d* of late Lt-Col H. S. Barker, DSO; one *s* two *d*. *Educ:* Summer Fields, Hastings; Eton College. Joined RN, 1944; CO HMS Palliser, 1959–61; retired at own request, 1966. Governor, Stowe School, 1983–89. Chm., Radcliffe Trust, 1997– (Trustee, 1983–). Vice President: British Assoc. for Shooting and Conservation, 1975–; Hospital Saving Assoc., 1979–2001; Bucks County Agricl Assoc., 1988–; Bucks Guide Assoc., 1996–; Bucks Fedn of Young Farmers' Clubs, 1997–2000 (Trustee, 1985–96); Dep. Pres., RASE, 1995–96; President: Bucks Br., CLA, 1983–97; HMS Concord Assoc., 1984–; Bucks Assoc. for the Blind, 1997– (Trustee, 1984–96); Bucks Farming and Wildlife Adv. Gp, 1997–2000; Bucks County Rifle Assoc.; Chm., Oxon Bucks Div., Royal Forestry Soc., 1981–83. Councillor, Winslow RDC, 1971–74; Hon. Treas., Aylesbury Vale Assoc. of Local Councils, 1974–84. Patron: RN Assoc. Aylesbury (No 1) Br.; Ferris Foundn. High Sheriff, 1969–70, JP 1984, DL 1978–84, 1997, Bucks. KStJ 1984. DUniv Buckingham, 1993. *Recreations:* shooting, crosswords, steam railways, Sherlock Holmes. *Heir:* *s* Hon. Thomas Francis Henry Fremantle, *b* 17 March 1966. *Address:* Athawes Farm House, 15 Nearton End, Swanbourne, Milton Keynes, Bucks MK17 0SL. *T:* (home) (01296) 720263; *T:* and *Fax:* (office) (01296) 720256. *Clubs:* Travellers; Royal Naval and Royal Albert Yacht (Portsmouth).

COTTHAM, George William; Chairman, CentreWest London Buses Ltd, 1995–97; *b* 11 July 1944; *s* of George William and Elizabeth Cottham; *m* 1967, Joan Thomas; two *d*. *Educ:* Univ. of London; Polytechnic of Liverpool; Liverpool Coll. of Commerce. BSc 1st Cl. Hons, LLB 2nd Cl. Hons. FCIT. Various posts, Liverpool City Transport, 1960–74; District Transport Manager, St Helens, 1974–77; Transport General Manager, Newport, 1977–80; Gen. Manager, Cleveland Transit, 1980–83; Dir Gen., W Yorks PTE, 1983–86; Chairman and Managing Director: Yorkshire Rider, 1986–94; Rider Hldgs, 1988–94; Rider York, 1990–94. *Recreations:* family, home, garden, music, photography. *Address:* Hundhill Hall, Hundhill, East Hardwick, West Yorkshire WF8 3DZ. *T:* (01977) 602325.

COTTON; *see* Stapleton-Cotton, family name of Viscount Combermere.

COTTON, Bernard Edward, CBE 1976; Chairman, South Yorkshire Residuary Body, 1985–89; *b* 8 Oct. 1920; *s* of Hugh Harry Cotton and Alice Cotton; *m* 1944, Stephanie Anne, *d* of Rev. A. E. and Mrs Furnival; three *s*. *Educ:* Sheffield City Grammar Sch.; Sheffield Univ. Served Army, 1939–45, latterly as Lieut, Worcs Yeomanry (53rd Airlanding Light Regt RA). Joined Round Oak Steelworks, Brierley Hill, 1949, Sales Man., 1954–57; Gen. Man., Samuel Osborn (Canada) Ltd, Montreal, 1957–63; Samuel Osborn & Co. Ltd: Sales Dir, 1963–69; Man. Dir, 1969; Chm. and Chief Exec., 1969–78; Pres., 1978–80. Dir, Renold Ltd, 1979–84; Dep. Chm., Baker Perkins plc, 1983–86. Chairman: Yorks and Humberside Reg. Econ. Planning Council, 1970–79; Health Service Supply Council, 1980–85; Mem., BR Eastern Bd, 1977–85; Pres., Yorks and Humberside Develt Assoc., 1973–84. Chm., BIM Working Party on Employee Participation, 1975. Pro Chancellor, Sheffield Univ., 1982–87. Master, Cutlers' Co. in Hallamshire, 1979–80. Hon. Fellow, Sheffield Hallam Univ. (formerly Sheffield City Poly.), 1980. CIMgt (Hon. Life Mem.). Hon. LLD Sheffield, 1988. *Recreations:* gardening and other quiet pursuits. *Address:* 2 Hillcote Rise, Fulwood, Sheffield S10 3PW. *T:* (0114) 230 3082.

COTTON, Christopher P.; *see* Powell-Cotton.

COTTON, Diana Rosemary, (Mrs R. B. Allan); QC 1983; *b* 30 Nov. 1941; *d* of Arthur Frank Edward and Muriel Cotton; *m* 1966, Richard Bellerby Allan; two *s* one *d*. *Educ:* Berkhamsted School for Girls; Lady Margaret Hall, Oxford (MA). Joined Middle Temple, 1961; called to Bar, 1964; Bencher, 1990; Member, Midland and Oxford Circuit; a Recorder of the Crown Court, 1982–; Dep. High Ct Judge, 1993–. Member: Criminal Injuries Compensation Bd, 1989–2000; Criminal Injuries Compensation Appeal Panel, 1996–; Legal Mem., Mental Health Ind. Rev. Tribunal, 1997–; Asst Boundary Comr, 2000–. *Recreation:* her family and other animals. *Address:* Devereux Chambers, Devereux Court, Temple, WC2R 3JH. *T:* (020) 7353 7534. *Club:* Western (Glasgow).

COTTON, Jane Catherine; Human Resources Director, Oxfam, since 1999; *b* 10 Jan. 1959; *d* of Tony and Jean Alderson; *m* 1980, Stephen Paul Cotton. *Educ:* Girton Coll., Cambridge (MA). Department of Transport: graduate trainee posts, 1979–83; Aviation Policy, 1983–88; Personnel, 1989–92; Railways Policy/Finances, 1992–93; Hd of Resources, Charity Commn, 1993–96; Sec. to Board, Dept of Transport, 1996–97; Personnel Dir, DETR, 1997–99. *Recreations:* gardening, walking, football (spectator), theatre. *Address:* Oxfam, 274 Banbury Road, Oxford OX2 7DZ.

COTTON, His Honour John Anthony; a Circuit Judge, 1973–93; *b* 6 March 1926; *s* of Frederick Thomas Hooley Cotton and Catherine Mary Cotton; *m* 1960, Johanna Aritia van Lookeren Campagne; three *s* two *d*. *Educ:* Stonyhurst Coll.; Lincoln Coll., Oxford. Called to the Bar, Middle Temple, 1949; Dep. Chm., W Riding of Yorks QS, 1967–71; Recorder of Halifax, 1971; a Recorder and Hon. Recorder of Halifax, 1972–73. Mem., Parole Bd, 1995–. *Recreation:* golf. *Address:* Myrtle Garth, Rossett Beck Close, Harrogate HG2 9NU.

COTTON, Sir John Richard, KCMG 1969 (CMG 1959); OBE 1947 (MBE 1944); retired from HM Diplomatic Service, 1969; Adjudicator, Immigration Appeals, 1970–81; *b* 22 Jan. 1909; *s* of late J. J. Cotton, ICS, and late Gigia Ricciardi Arlotta; *m* 1937, Mary Bridget Connors (*d* 2000), Stradbally, County Waterford, Ireland; three *s*. *Educ:* Wellington Coll.; RMC, Sandhurst. Commissioned 1929; 8th King George's Own Light Cavalry (IA), 1930–34; transferred to Indian Political Service, 1934; served in: Aden, Abyssinia (Attaché HM Legation, 1935), Persian Gulf, Rajputana, Hyderabad, Kathiawar, Baroda, New Delhi (Dep. Sec. Political Dept). Transferred to HM Foreign Service, 1947; served in Karachi (First Sec.), 1947–48, Foreign Office, 1949–51, Madrid (Commercial Counsellor, HM Embassy), 1951–54; Consul-Gen., Brazzaville, 1954–55, Leopoldville, 1955–57; Counsellor (Commercial), HM Embassy, Brussels, 1957–62. Consul-Gen., São Paulo, Brazil, 1962–65; Ambassador to Kinshasa, Congo Republic (now Zaire), and to Burundi, 1965–69. *Address:* Lansing House, Hartley Wintney, Hants RG27 8RY. *T:* (01252) 842681.

COTTON, Hon. Sir Robert (Carrington), KCMG 1978; AO 1993; Chairman of Directors, Kleinwort Benson Australian Income Fund Inc., since 1986; *b* 29 Nov. 1915; *s* of H. L. Carrington Cotton; *m* 1937, Eve Elizabeth Macdougall; one *s* two *d*. *Educ:* St Peter's Coll., Adelaide, SA. FCPA 1977. State President of Liberal Party (NSW), 1956–59; Federal Vice-Pres., 1960–61; elected to Senate, 1965; Minister for Civil Aviation, 1969–72; Shadow Minister for Manufacturing Industry (in Opposition), 1972–75; Minister for Industry and Commerce, 1975–77; Australian Consul-Gen. in NY, 1978–81; Ambassador to USA, 1982–85. Chm. (acting), Allders International Pty Ltd, Australia, 1987. Sen. Advr, Hill & Knowlton Inc., 1988–93. Mem. Bd, Reserve Bank of Australia, 1982–83; Dir, Thomson–CSF Pacific Holdings Pty Ltd, 1996–. Chairman: Australian Nat. Gall. Foundn, 1991–94; Australian Photonics Co-operative Res. Centre, 1992–. Hon. DSc Sydney, 1995. *Recreations:* swimming, writing, photography. *Address:* Apartment 11, Southern Cross Gardens, 2 Spruson Street, Neutral Bay, NSW 2089, Australia. *T:* (2) 99545066. *Clubs:* The Brook (NY); Australian (Sydney). *Address:* Commonwealth (Canberra, ACT).

COTTON, Sir William Frederick, (Sir Bill Cotton), Kt 2001; CBE 1989 (OBE 1976); Chairman, Meridian Broadcasting, 1996–2001 (Deputy Chairman, 1992–96); Director, Alba plc, since 1988; *b* 23 April 1928; *s* of late William Edward (Billy) Cotton and Mabel Hope; *m* 1st, 1950, Bernadine Maud (*née* Sinclair) (*d* 1964); three *d*; 2nd, 1965, Ann Corfield (*née* Bucknall) (marr. diss. 1989); one step *d*; 3rd, 1990, Kathryn Mary (*née* Ralphes). *Educ:* Ardingly College. Jt Man. Dir, Michael Reine Music Co., 1952–56; BBC-TV: Producer, Light Entertainment Dept, 1956–62; Asst Head of Light Entertainment, 1962–67; Head of Variety, 1967–70; Head of Light Entertainment Gp, 1970–77; Controller, BBC 1, 1977–81; Dep. Man. Dir, 1981–82; Dir of Programmes, Television, and Dir of Develt, BBC, 1982; Chm., BBC Enterprises, 1982–86 and 1987–88 (Vice Chm., 1986–87); Man. Dir, Television, BBC, 1984–88. Chm., Noel Gay TV, 1988–97; Director: Noel Gay Orgn, 1988–97; Billy Marsh Associates, 1998–. Vice-Pres., Marie Curie Cancer Care (formerly Marie Curie Foundn), 1990–. FRTS 1983 (Vice-Pres., 1984–92; Pres., 1992–95); Fellow, BAFTA, 1998. Hon. DA Bournemouth Univ., 2001. *Publication:* Double Bill: 80 years of entertainment (autobiog.), 2000. *Recreations:* golf, boating. *Address:* Summer Hill, The Glebe, Studland, Dorset BH19 3AS. *Clubs:* Hurlingham; Royal & Ancient Golf (St Andrews); Royal Motor Yacht.

COTTRELL, Sir Alan (Howard), Kt 1971; FRS 1955; FREng; Master of Jesus College, Cambridge, 1974–86 (Hon. Fellow 1986); Vice-Chancellor, University of Cambridge, 1977–79; *b* 17 July 1919; *s* of Albert and Elizabeth Cottrell; *m* 1944, Jean Elizabeth Harber (*d* 1999); one *s*. *Educ:* Moseley Grammar Sch.; University of Birmingham. BSc 1939; PhD 1942; ScD(Cantab) 1976. Lectr in Metallurgy, University of Birmingham, 1943–49; Prof. of Physical Metallurgy, University of Birmingham, 1949–55; Deputy Head of Metallurgy Division, Atomic Energy Research Establishment, Harwell, Berks, 1955–58; Goldsmiths' Prof. of Metallurgy, Cambridge Univ., 1958–65; Fellow of Christ's Coll., Cambridge, 1958–70, Hon. Fellow, 1970; Dep. Chief Scientific Adviser (Studies), Min. of Defence, 1965–67, Chief Adviser, 1967; Dep. Chief Scientific Advr to HM Govt, 1968–71, Chief Scientific Advr, 1971–74. Part-time Mem., UKAEA, 1962–65, 1983–87; Member: Adv. Council on Scientific Policy, 1963–64; Central Adv. Council for Science and Technology, 1967–; Exec. Cttee, British Council, 1974–87; Adv. Council, Science Policy Foundn, 1976–; Security Commn, 1981–92. Dir, Fisons plc, 1979–90. A Vice-Pres., Royal Society, 1964, 1976, 1977. Foreign Hon. Mem., American Academy of Arts and Sciences, 1960; Foreign Associate: Nat. Acad. of Sciences, USA, 1972; Nat. Acad. of Engrg, USA, 1976; Mem., Academia Europaea, 1991–; Hon. Member: Amer. Soc. for Metals, 1972 (Fellow, 1974); Metals Soc., 1977 (Hon. FIM, 1989); Japan Inst. of Metals, 1981. FIC 1991; FREng (FEng 1979); Fellow, Royal Swedish Acad. of Scis; Hon. Fellow, Internat. Congress on Fracture, 1985–. Hon. DSc: Columbia Univ., 1965; Newcastle Univ., 1967; Liverpool Univ., 1969; Manchester, 1970; Warwick, 1971; Sussex, 1972; Bath, 1973; Strathclyde, 1975; Cranfield, 1975; Aston, 1975; Oxford, 1979; Birmingham, 1983; DUniv Essex, 1982; Hon. DEng Tech. Univ. of Nova Scotia, 1984; Hon. LLD Cantab, 1996. Rosenhain Medallist of the Inst. of Metals; Hughes Medal, 1961, Rumford Medal, 1974, Copley Medal, 1996, Royal Society; Inst. of Metals (Platinum) Medal, 1965; Réaumur Medal, Société Française de Métallurgie, 1964; James Alfred Ewing Medal, ICE, 1967; Holweck Medal, Société Française de Physique, 1969; Albert Sauveur Achievement Award, Amer. Soc. for Metals, 1969; James Douglas Gold Medal, Amer. Inst. of Mining, Metallurgy and Petroleum Engrs, 1974; Harvey Science Prize, Technion Israel Inst., 1974; Acta Metallurgica Gold Medal, 1976; Guthrie Medal and Prize, Inst. of Physics, 1977; Gold Medal, Amer. Soc. for Metals, 1980; Brinell Medal, Royal Swedish Acad. of Engrg Sciences, 1980; Kelvin Medal, ICE, 1986; Hollomon Award, Acta Metallurgica, 1991; Von Hippel Award, Materials Res. Soc., 1996. *Publications:* Theoretical Structural Metallurgy, 1948, 2nd edn 1955; Dislocations and Plastic Flow in Crystals, 1953; The Mechanical Properties of Matter, 1964; Theory of Crystal Dislocations, 1964; An Introduction to Metallurgy, 1967; Portrait of Nature, 1975; Environmental Economics, 1978; How Safe is Nuclear Energy?, 1981; Introduction to the Modern Theory of Metals, 1988; Chemical Bonding in Transition Metal Carbides, 1995; Concepts in the Electron Theory of Alloys, 1998; scientific papers to various learned journals. *Recreations:* music, fly-fishing. *Address:* 40 Maids Causeway, Cambridge CB5 8DD. *T:* (01223) 363806.

COTTRELL, Bryce Arthur Murray; Chairman, JWM Partners (UK) Ltd, since 1999; *b* 16 Sept. 1931; *s* of late Brig. A. F. B. Cottrell, DSO, OBE and Mrs M. B. Cottrell (*née* Nicoll); *m* 1955, Jeane Dolores Monk; two *s* two *d*. *Educ:* Charterhouse; Corpus Christi Coll., Oxford (MA). Joined Phillips & Drew, 1955; Partner, 1963; Sen. Partner, 1983; Chm., 1985–88. Dir, Long Term Capital Portfolio (GP) Ltd, 1994–99. Fellow and Funding Dir, Corpus Christi Coll., Oxford, 1990–92. *Recreations:* sport, railways. *Address:* Portreeves House, East Street, Tonbridge TN9 1HP. *T:* (01732) 773277.

COTTRELL, Peter John Waraker, AO 1987; OBE 1978; Chairman, Adsteam Marine Ltd, Sydney, since 1997; *b* 25 May 1928; *s* of Knowles Waraker Cottrell and Elmira Grenfell Cottrell; *m* 1952, Barbara Jean Wheeler; two *s* two *d*. *Educ:* Sydney Univ. (BEng, MEng); Birmingham Univ. (Postgrad. Dip. in Mgt). Cadet, Qld Irrigation Commn, 1945–46; cadet, then engr, Australian Dept of Munitions, 1947–60; Email Ltd: Manager, 1960–74; Man. Dir, 1974–92; Chm., 1993–98. Chairman: Export Finance & Insurance Corp., 1983–86; Pacifica Gp Ltd, 1989–95; Adelaide Steamship Co. Ltd, 1992–99; Boral Ltd, 1994–2000; Dep. Chm., Australian Telecommunications Commn, 1982–87; Dir, Nat. Australia Bank, 1985–98. Vice-Pres., Business Council of Australia, 1991–92. Hon. FIEAust 1994. Hon. DBus Charles Sturt Univ., 1996. Sir James Kirby Medal, IProdE,

1986; Sir Charles McGrath Award, Aust. Marketing Inst., 1989. *Recreations:* golf, family activities. *Address:* 14 Torokina Avenue, St Ives, NSW 2075, Australia. *T:* (2) 99839836, *Fax:* (2) 99830956. *Clubs:* Union (Sydney); Royal Sydney Yacht Squadron; Pymble Golf (Sydney).

COTTRELL, Richard John; Vice President: Rail Polska, Poland, since 1999; Cargo Central Europe, Poland, since 2000; *b* 11 July 1943; *s* of John Cottrell and Winifred (*née* Barter); *m* 1st, 1965, Dinah Louise (*née* David) (marr. diss. 1986); two *d*; 2nd, 1987, Tracy Katherine (*née* Wade) (marr. diss. 1996); one *d*; 3rd, 1997, Liliana (*née* Velitchkova) (marr. diss. 2001); *m* 2001, Diana (*née* Kiebdoj). *Educ:* Court Fields Sch., Wellington, Somerset. Journalist: Wellington Weekly News, 1958; South Devon Jl, 1960; Topic (internat. news weekly), 1962; Evening Argus, Brighton, 1963; Lincolnshire Standard, 1964; Evening Post, Bristol, 1965; TWW, subseq. HTV, 1967–79. Contested (C) Bristol, European Parly elecn, 1989. MEP (C) Bristol, 1979–89; Sec., backbench cttee, European Dem. Gp, 1979; Member: Transport Cttee, 1979–83; External Econ. Relns Cttee, 1979–82; Information Cttee, 1981–84; ACP-EEC Convention, 1981–84; Agriculture Cttee, 1982–86; Rules Cttee, 1982–89; Environment Cttee, 1983–89; Budget Cttee, 1983–86; Energy Cttee, 1986–88; deleg. to China, 1987. European Vice-Pres., Assoc. of District Councils; Vice-President: Nat. Council on Inland Transport; Railway Develt Soc. *Publications:* Energy, the Burning Question for Europe (jtly), 1981; (ed and contrib.) Transport for Europe, 1982; Blood on their Hands: the killing of Ann Chapman, 1987; The Sacred Cow, 1987; contribs to Encounter, Contemporary Review. *Recreations:* travel, reading, transport studies, appreciation of real ale, astronomy, ornithology. *Address:* (office) ul. Willowa 8/10 lok. 28, 00790 Warsaw, Poland.

COTTS, Sir Richard Crichton Mitchell, 4th Bt *cr* 1921, of Coldharbour Wood, Rogate, Sussex; *b* 26 July 1946; *er s* of Sir Robert Crichton Mitchell Cotts, 3rd Bt and Barbara Mary Winifrede (*d* 1982), *o d* of Captain H. J. A. Throckmorton, RN; *S* father, 1995. *Educ:* Oratory Sch. *Heir: b* Hamish William Anthony Mitchell Cotts, *b* 15 Sept. 1951.

COUCHMAN, James Randall; dealer in fine arts and antiques; *b* 11 Feb. 1942; *s* of Stanley Randall Couchman and Alison Margaret Couchman; *m* 1967, Barbara Jean (*née* Heilbrun); one *s* one *d*. *Educ:* Cranleigh School; King's College, Newcastle upon Tyne; Univ. of Durham. Oil industry, 1964–70; Public House Manager, family company, 1970–74; Gen. Manager, family licensed trade co., 1974–80, Director, 1980–95. Councillor, London Borough of Bexley, 1974–82 (Chm., Social Services, 1975–78, 1980–82). Chm., Bexley HA, 1981–83. Member: Assoc. of Metropolitan Authorities Social Services Cttee, 1975–80; Central Council for Educn and Training of Social Workers, 1976–80; Governor, Nat. Inst. for Social Workers, 1976–80. MP (C) Gillingham, 1983–97; contested (C) same seat, 1997. PPS to Minister of State for Social Security, 1984–86, to Minister of Health, 1986–88, to Chancellor of Duchy of Lancaster, 1988–89, to Sec. of State for Social Security, 1989–90, to Lord Pres. of the Council and Leader of the House, 1995–97. Member: Social Services Select Cttee, 1983–85; Select Cttee on Health, 1990–92; Public Accounts Cttee, 1992–95; Select Cttee on NI, 1995–97. Fellow, Industry and Parlt Trust, 1987. Mem., Vintners' Co. *Recreations:* travel, reading, listening to music, politics. *Address:* Dovecote House, Filkins Road, Langford, Lechlade, Glos GL7 3LW. *T:* (01367) 860289.

COUCHMAN, Martin; Deputy Chief Executive, British Hospitality Association, since 1993; *b* 28 Sept. 1947; *s* of late Frederick Alfred James Couchman and of Pamela Mary Couchman (*née* Argent); *m* 1983, Carolyn Mary Constance Roberts; three *s* one *d*. *Educ:* Sutton Valence Sch.; Exeter Coll., Oxford (BA Jurisprudence). Building Industry, 1970–77; National Economic Development Office, 1977–92: Industrial Advr, 1977–84; Hd of Administration, 1984–87; on secondment as UK Dir of European Year of the Environment, 1987–88; Sec., NEDC, 1988–92. Mem., Exec. Cttee, European Confedn of Nat. Assocs of Hotels, Restaurants, Cafés and Similar Estabts, 1997–2000; Chm., CBI Sectoral Employment Issues Cttee, 2000–. FRSA 1988. *Recreations:* Anglo-Saxon history, armchair archaeology, amateur dramatics. *Address:* The Old School, Halstead, Sevenoaks, Kent TN14 7HF. *T:* (01959) 532253. *Club:* St Julians (Sevenoaks).

COULL, Prof. Alexander, PhD; DSc; FRSE; FICE, FIStructE; Regius Professor of Civil Engineering, University of Glasgow, 1977–92; *b* 20 June 1931; *s* of William Coull and Jane Ritchie (*née* Reid); *m* 1962, Frances Bruce Moir; one *s* two *d*. *Educ:* Peterhead Acad.; Univ. of Aberdeen (BScEng, PhD; DSc 1983). FRSE 1971; FICE 1972, FIStructE 1973; Res. Asst, MIT, USA, 1955; Struct. Engr, English Electric Co. Ltd, 1955–57; Lectr in Engrg, Univ. of Aberdeen, 1957–62; Lectr in Civil Engrg, Univ. of Southampton, 1962–66; Prof. of Struct. Engrg, Univ. of Strathclyde, 1966–76. Chm., Clyde Estuary Amenity Council, 1981–86. *Publications:* Tall Buildings, 1967; Fundamentals of Structural Theory, 1972; (with B. Stafford Smith) Tall Building Structures: Planning Analysis and Design, 1991; author or co-author of 130 res. papers in scientific jls. *Recreations:* golf, hill walking, ski-ing. *Address:* 4 Monaltrie Way, Ballater, Aberdeenshire AB35 5PS. *T:* (01339) 755766.

COULL, Maj.-Gen. John Taylor, CB 1992; FRCS; FRCSE; Medico-Legal Adviser, Army Medical Directorate, Ministry of Defence, 1992–97; *b* 4 March 1934; *s* of late John Sandeman Coull and Ethel Marjory (*née* Taylor); *m* 1958, Mildred Macfarlane; three *s*. *Educ:* Robert Gordon's College; Aberdeen Univ. Med. Sch. MB ChB. House appts, Aberdeen Royal Infirmary, 1958–60; Commissioned RAMC, 1960; Surgeon: Colchester Mil. Hosp., 1960–63; Queen Alexandra Mil. Hosp., 1963; Sen. Registrar, Edinburgh East Gen. Hosp., 1963–65; Royal Herbert Hosp., 1965–67; Sen. Registrar, Birmingham Accident Hosp., 1967; Consultant Surgeon, BMH Singapore, 1967–70; Lectr, Dept of Orthopaedics, Univ. of Edinburgh, 1970–71; Consultant Orthopaedic Surgeon, BAOR, 1971–77; Consultant Adviser in Orthop. Surgery and Sen. Consultant, Queen Elizabeth Mil. Hosp., 1977–86; Consulting Surgeon, HQ BAOR, 1986–88; Dir of Army Surgery, 1988–92. Hon. Col 202 (Midland) Field Hosp. RAMC (V), 1992–97; Col Comdt, RAMC, 1994–99. QHS 1988–92. GSM N Ireland, 1976; Mitchiner Medal, RCS, 1980. OStJ. *Publications:* chapters in: Field Pocket Surgery, 1981; R. Smith's The Hand, 1985; Trauma, 1989; articles in learned jls. *Recreations:* home maintenance, carpentry, gardening, travel. *Address:* Monaltrie House, Ewshot, Farnham GU10 5TE. *Club:* Royal Society of Medicine.

COULSFIELD, Rt Hon. Lord; John Taylor Cameron, PC 2000; a Senator of the College of Justice in Scotland, since 1987; *b* 24 April 1934; *s* of late John Reid Cameron, MA, formerly Director of Education, Dundee; *m* 1964, Bridget Deirdre Sloan; no *c*. *Educ:* Fettes Coll.; Corpus Christi Coll., Oxford; Edinburgh Univ. BA (Oxon), LLB (Edinburgh). Admitted to Faculty of Advocates, 1960. Lecturer in Public Law, Edinburgh Univ., 1960–64. QC (Scot.) 1973; Keeper of the Advocates' Library, 1977–87; an Advocate-Depute, 1977–79. Judge, Courts of Appeal of Jersey and Guernsey, 1986–87; a Judge, Employment Appeal Tribunal, 1992–96; Mem., Scottish Court in the Netherlands, 2000–01. Chm., Medical Appeal Tribunals, 1985–87. Chm., Jt Standing Cttee on Legal Educn in Scotland, 1998–. Trustee, Nat. Liby of Scotland, 2000–. Editor, Scottish Law and Practice Qly, 1995–. *Publications:* articles in legal jls.

COULSON, Mrs Ann Margaret; Chairman, Leamington Hastings Consolidated Charity, since 1998; *b* 11 March 1935; *d* of Sidney Herbert Wood and Ada (*née* Mills); *m* 1958, Peter James Coulson; two *s* one *d*. *Educ:* The Grammar Sch., Chippenham, Wilts; UCL (BScEcon); Univ. of Manchester (DSA); Wolverhampton Technical Teachers' Coll. (CertEd). Hosp. Admin, 1956–62; Lectr in Econs and Management, Bromsgrove Coll. of Further Educn, 1968–76; Asst Dir, North Worcestershire Coll., 1976–80; Service Planning and Develt Co-ordinator, 1980–83, Regl Planning Administrator, 1983–88, Dir of Planning, 1988–91, W Midlands RHA; Gen. Manager, Age Concern, Solihull, 1991–94. City of Birmingham Dist Council, 1973–79; special interest in Social Services. Mem., IBA, 1976–81. Trustee, Age Concern, Warwicks, 1996–. *Recreations:* sailing, cooking, music, theatre. *Address:* Rowans, Leamington Hastings, near Rugby, Warwicks CV23 8DY. *T:* (01926) 633264.

COULSON, His Honour (James) Michael; a Circuit Judge, Midland and Oxford Circuit, 1983–90; a Deputy Circuit Judge, 1990–98; *b* 23 Nov. 1927; *s* of William Coulson, Wold Newton Hall, Driffield, E Yorks; *m* 1st, 1955, Dilys Adair Jones (marr. diss.; she *d* 1994); one *s*; 2nd, 1977, Barbara Elizabeth Islay, *d* of Dr Roland Moncrieff Chambers; one *s* one *d*. *Educ:* Fulneck Sch., Yorks; Merton Coll., Oxford; Royal Agricultural Coll., Cirencester. Served E Riding Yeomanry (Wenlocks Horse); Queen's Own Yorks Yeomanry (Major). Called to Bar, Middle Temple, 1951; Mem. North Eastern Circuit; Asst Recorder of Sheffield, 1965–71; Dep. Chm., NR of Yorks QS, 1968–71; a Chm. of Industrial Tribunals, 1968–83; a Recorder of the Crown Court, 1981–83. Dep. Chm., Northern Agricl Land Tribunal, 1967–73. Former Mem., Tadcaster RDC. MP (C) Kingston-upon-Hull North, 1959–64; PPS to Solicitor Gen., 1962–64; Mem., Executive Cttee, Conservative Commonwealth Council. Sometime Sec., Bramham Moor and York and Ainsty Point to Point Race Meetings. *Recreations:* hunting, reading, travel. *Address:* The Tithe Barn, Wymondham, Melton Mowbray, Leics LE14 2AS. *Club:* Cavalry and Guards.

COULSON, Michael; *see* Coulson, J. M.

COULSON, Peter David William; QC 2001; *b* 31 March 1958; *s* of David Coulson and Pamela Coulson (*née* Shorter); *m* 1985, Veronica Lachkovic; one *s* two *d*. *Educ:* Lord Wandsworth Coll.; Univ. of Keele (BA Hons 1980). ACIArb 1990. Called to the Bar, Gray's Inn, 1982 (Sir Malcolm Hilbery Award, 1982); in practice, 1984–. Contributor, Lloyd's Law Reports: Professional Negligence, 1999–2000. *Publication:* (jtly) Professional Negligence and Liability, 2000. *Recreations:* British art 1750-1950, comedy, music, cricket, Watford FC. *Address:* 10 Essex Street, WC2R 3AA. *T:* (020) 7544 2600. *Club:* Travellers.

COULTASS, (George Thomas) Clive; historian; Keeper of Audio-Visual Records, Imperial War Museum, 1983–91; *b* 5 July 1931; *m* 1962, Norma Morris. *Educ:* Tadcaster Grammar Sch.; Univ. of Sheffield (BA Hons). Teacher in various London schools, 1955–62; Lectr/Sen. Lectr in History, James Graham Coll., Leeds, 1962–69; Imperial War Museum: Keeper of Film Programming, 1969–70; Keeper, Dept of Film, 1970–83. Vice-Pres., Internat. Assoc. for Audio-Visual Media in Hist. Res. and Educn, 1978–85. Organiser: various film historical confs, 1973–90; exhibn on British film and World War II, 1982. *Publications:* Images for Battle, 1989; sections in: The Historian and Film, 1976; Britain and the Cinema in the Second World War, 1988; articles in various historical jls. *Recreations:* travel, music, including opera, reading. *Address:* 39 Fairfield Grove, SE7 8UA.

COULTER, Rev. Robert James; Member (UU) Antrim North, Northern Ireland Assembly, since 1998; *b* 23 Oct. 1929; *m* 1956, Elizabeth; one *s* one *d*. *Educ:* Trinity Coll., Dublin (BA, MA, BD); Univ. of Ulster (MA Educn). Ordained, 1963, Minister, 1963–76, Presbyterian Church in Ireland; Lectr in Further and Higher Educn, 1976–93. Mem. (UU), Ballymena BC, 1985–; Mayor of Ballymena, 1993–96. *Recreation:* vintage vehicles. *Address:* 18 Springmount Road, Clough, Ballymena, Co. Antrim BT44 9QQ. *T:* (028) 2568 5694.

COULTHARD, Air Vice-Marshal Colin Weal, CB 1975; AFC 1953 (Bar 1958); retired; *b* 27 Feb. 1921; *s* of late George Robert Coulthard and Cicely Eva Coulthard (*née* Minns); *m* 1st, 1941, Norah Ellen Creighton (marr. diss.); one *s* two *d*; 2nd, 1957, Eileen Pamela (*née* Barber); one *s*. *Educ:* Watford Grammar Sch.; De Havilland Aeronautical Tech. Sch. Commissioned RAF, 1941; Fighter Pilot, 1942–45 (despatches, 1945); HQ Fighter Comd, 1948–49; RAF Staff Coll., 1950; OC 266 Sqn, Wunstorf, 1952–54, DFLS, CFE, 1955; OC Flying, 233(F) OCU, 1956–57; OC AFDS, CFE, 1957–59; HQ Fighter Comd, 1959–60; Stn Cdr, Gutersloh, 1961–64; MoD, 1964–66; SOA, AHQ Malta, 1966–67; DOR 1(RAF), MoD, 1967–69; Air Attaché, Washington, DC, 1970–72; Mil. Dep. to Head of Defence Sales, MoD, 1973–75. Governor, Truro Sch., 1981–91. Hon. FRAeS 1975. *Recreations:* walking, shooting, motor sport. *Address:* Fiddlers, Old Truro Road, Goonhavern, Truro TR4 9NN. *T:* (01872) 540312. *Club:* Royal Air Force.

COULTON, Very Rev. Nicholas Guy; Dean (formerly Provost) of St Nicholas' Cathedral, Newcastle-upon-Tyne, since 1990; *b* 14 June 1940; *s* of Nicholas Guy Coulton and Audrey Florence Furneaux Coulton (*née* Luscombe); *m* 1978, Edith Mary Gainford; one *s* two *d*. *Educ:* Blundell's School, Tiverton; Cuddesdon Coll., Oxford. BD London (ext.) 1972. Admitted Solicitor, 1962; Asst Solicitor, Burges, Salmon & Co., Bristol, 1962–65. Ordination training, 1965–67; Curate of Pershore Abbey with Birlingham, Wick and Pinvin, 1967–71; Domestic Chaplain to Bishop of St Albans, 1971–75; Vicar of St Paul's, Bedford, 1975–90; part-time Industrial Chaplain, 1976–89. Proctor in Convocation, 1985–90; Hon. Canon of St Alban's Cathedral, 1989–90. Mem., Gen. Synod of C of E, 1998–. Chm., NE CCJ, 1991–. Dir, Ecclesiastical Insurance Gp, 1997–. Governor: Newcastle upon Tyne Church High Sch., 1990–; Dame Allan's Schs, 1990–. SBStJ 1994. *Publication:* Twelve Years of Prayer, 1989. *Recreations:* gardening, reading, listening to music, historical exploration, rearing children. *Address:* The Cathedral Vicarage, 26 Mitchell Avenue, West Jesmond, Newcastle upon Tyne NE2 3LA. *T:* (0191) 232 1939, *Fax:* (0191) 230 0735; *e-mail:* stnicholas@aol.com.

COUNSELL, Her Honour Hazel Rosemary; *see* Fallon, Her Honour H. R.

COUNT, Dr Brian Morrison; Chief Executive, Innogy Holdings plc, since 2001 (Chief Operating Officer, 2000–01); *b* 18 Feb. 1951; *s* of Douglas John Count and Ethel Sarah Count; *m* 1975, Jane Elizabeth Hudson; three *s*. *Educ:* King's College, Cambridge (MA Maths); Exeter Univ. (PhD Physics). Central Electricity Generating Board: Research Dept, 1974–84; Planning Dept, 1984–90; National Power: Project Develt Dir, 1990–95; Dir of Ops, 1995–96; Mem. Bd, 1996–2000; Man. Dir, UK, 1999–2000. *Recreations:* golf, Rugby, entertaining. *Address:* Innogy Holdings plc, Windmill Hill Business Park, Whitehill Way, Swindon, Wilts SN5 6PB. *Club:* Institute of Directors.

COUPER, Prof. Alastair Dougal, FNI; Research Professor, Seafarers International Research Centre for Safety and Occupational Health, University of Wales Cardiff, 1997–98 (Director, 1995–97); Emeritus Professor, University of Cardiff, since 1999; *b* 4 June 1931; *s* of Daniel Alexander Couper and Davina Couper (*née* Rilley); *m* 1958, Norma Milton; two *s* two *d*. *Educ:* Robert Gordon's School of Navigation (Master Mariner);

Univ. of Aberdeen (MA, DipEd); Australian National Univ. (PhD). FNI 1979. Cadet and Navigating Officer, Merchant Navy, 1947–57; student, Univ. of Aberdeen, 1958–62, postgraduate teaching course, 1962–63; Research Schol., Sch. of Pacific Studies, ANU, Canberra, 1963–66; Lectr, Univ. of Durham, 1967–70; Prof. of Maritime Studies, UWIST, then UWCC, 1970–97; Prof., World Maritime Univ. (UN), Malmö, Sweden, 1987–89 (on secondment). UN Consultant, 1972–98; Chm., Maritime Bd, CNAA, 1978–85; Assessor, Chartered Inst. of Transport, 1976–85; Founder Mem., Council, British Maritime League, 1982–85; Mem. Exec. Bd, Law of the Sea Inst., USA, 1989–95; Mem., British Commn, Internat. Commn for Maritime History, 1996–; Pres., Neptune Assoc. of Maritime Res. Insts, 1997–98. Trustee, Nat. Maritime Mus., 1992–2000. Editor (and Founder), Journal of Maritime Policy and Management, 1973–84. Hon. DSc Plymouth, 1995. *Publications:* Geography of Sea Transport, 1971; The Law of the Sea, 1978; (ed) Times Atlas of the Oceans, 1983; contrib. Pacific, in World Atlas of Agriculture, 1969; Pacific in Transition (ed Brookfield), 1973; New Cargo Handling Techniques: implications for port employment and skills, 1986; (ed) Development and Social Change in the Pacific, 1988; (ed) The Shipping Revolution, 1992; Voyages of Abuse: Seafarers, Human Rights and International Shipping, 1999; several UN Reports, UNCTAD, ILO, IMO; articles in jls; conf. papers. *Recreations:* hill walking, sailing, archaeology, Pacific history. *Address:* 112 Ely Road, Llandaff, Cardiff CF5 2DA. *T:* (029) 2056 5401.

COUPER, Heather Anita, FRAS; science broadcaster and author, since 1983; Director, Pioneer TV Productions, 1988–99; *b* 2 June 1949; *o d* of late George Couper Elder Couper and Anita Couper (*née* Taylor). *Educ:* St Mary's Grammar Sch., Northwood, Mddx; Univ. of Leicester (BSc Hons Astronomy and Physics); Univ. of Oxford. FRAS 1970; FInstP 1999. Management trainee, Peter Robinson Ltd, 1967–69; Res. Asst, Cambridge Observatories, 1969–70; Lectr, Greenwich Planetarium, Old Royal Observ., 1977–83. Gresham Prof. of Astronomy, 1993–96. Mem., Millennium Commn, 1994–. President: Brit. Astron. Assoc., 1984–86; Jun. Astron. Soc., 1987–89. Presenter on television: Heavens Above, 1981; Spacewatch, 1983; The Planets, 1985; The Stars, 1988; The Neptune Encounter, 1989; A Close Encounter of the Second Kind, 1992; producer/narrator: ET—Please Phone Earth, 1992; Space Shuttle Discovery, 1993; Electric Skies, 1994; Arthur C. Clarke: the Visionary, 1995; On Jupiter, 1996; Black Holes, 1997; narrator/presenter: Rendezvous in Space, and Avalanche, 1995; Raging Planet, 1997; The Sci-Fi Files, Killer Earth, and Stormforce, 1998; producer, Universe, 1999; presenter on radio: Science Now, 1983; Cosmic Pursuits, 1985; Seeing Stars, 1991–; ET on Trial, 1993; Starwatch, 1996; Sun Science, 1999; The Essential Guide to the 21st Century, 2000; also appearances and interviews on wide variety of television and radio progs. Astronomy columnist, The Independent. Hon. DLitt Loughborough, 1991; Hon. DSc: Hertfordshire, 1994; Leicester, 1997. *Publications:* Exploring Space, 1980; (jtly) Heavens Above, 1981; Journey into Space, 1984; (jtly) Starfinder, 1984; (jtly) The Halley's Comet Pop-Up Book, 1985; (jtly) The Universe: a 3-dimensional study, 1985; Space Scientist series, 1985–87: Comets and Meteors; The Planets; The Stars; jointly: The Sun; The Moon; Galaxies and Quasars; Satellites and Spaceprobes; Telescopes and Observatories; *with Nigel Henbest:* Space Frontiers, 1978; The Restless Universe, 1982; Physics, 1983; Astronomy, 1983; The Planets, 1985; The Stars, 1988; The Space Atlas, 1992; Guide to the Galaxy, 1994; How the Universe Works, 1994; Black Holes, 1996; Big Bang, 1997; Is Anybody Out There?, 1998; To the Ends of the Universe, 1998; Space Encyclopedia, 1999; Universe, 1999; Mars: the inside story of the red planet, 2001; numerous articles in nat. newspapers and magazines. *Recreations:* travel, the English countryside, classical music; wine, food and winemaking. *Address:* David Higham Associates, 5–8 Lower John Street, Golden Square, W1R 4HA. *Clubs:* Groucho, Rugby.

COUPER, Sir (Robert) Nicholas (Oliver), 6th Bt *cr* 1841; *b* 9 Oct. 1945; *s* of Sir George Robert Cecil Couper, 5th Bt, and Margaret Grace (*d* 1984), *d* of late Robert George Dashwood Thomas; *S* father, 1975; *m* 1972, Curzon MacKean (marr. diss. 1986); one *s* one *d*; *m* 1991, Katrina Frances, *d* of Sir Michael Walker, *qv*. *Educ:* Eton; RMA, Sandhurst. Major, Blues and Royals; retired, 1975. Now working as a property consultant. *Heir: s* James George Couper, *b* 27 Oct. 1977. *Address:* 79 Devonshire Road, W4 2HU.

COUPLAND, Prof. Rex Ernest; Professor of Human Morphology, 1967–89, and Dean of Medicine, 1981–87, University of Nottingham; Hon. Consultant, Trent Regional Hospital Board, 1970–89; *b* 30 Jan. 1924; *s* of late Ernest Coupland, company dir and Doris Coupland; *m* 1947, Lucy Eileen Sargent; one *s* one *d*. *Educ:* Mirfield Grammar Sch.; University of Leeds. MB, ChB with honours, 1947; MD with distinction, 1952; PhD 1954; DSc 1970. House appointments, Leeds General Infirmary, 1947; Demonstrator and Lecturer in Anatomy, University of Leeds, 1948, 1950–58; Asst Prof. of Anatomy, University of Minnesota, USA, 1955–56; Prof. of Anatomy, Queen's Coll., Dundee, University of St Andrews, 1958–67. Medical Officer, RAF, 1948–50. FRSE 1960. Member: Biological Research Board of MRC, 1964–70; Med. Adv. Bd, Crippling Diseases Foundn, 1971–75; CMO's Academic Forum, 1984–89; Chm., MRC Non-Ionizing Radiations Cttee, 1970–89; Derbyshire AHA, 1978–81; Trent RHA, 1981–88; Chm., Nottingham Div., BMA, 1978–79; GMC, 1982–88; Med. sub-cttee, UGC, 1984–89. President: Anat. Soc. GB and Ireland, 1976–78; British Assoc. of Clinical Anat., 1977–82. Wood Jones Medal for contrib. to clinical anatomy, RCS, 1984. *Publications:* The Natural History of the Chromaffin Cell, 1965; (ed jtly) Chromaffin, Enterochromaffin and Related Cells, 1976; (ed jtly) Peripheral Neuroendocrine Interaction, 1978; papers in jls of anatomy, physiology, endocrinology, pathology and pharmacology on endocrine and nervous systems and in jls of radiology on NMR imaging; *chapters on:* Anatomy of the Human Kidney, in Renal Disease (ed Black), 1962, 1968, 1973; The Chromaffin System, in Catecholamines (ed Blaschko and Muscholl), 1973; The Blood Supply of the Adrenal Gland, in Handbook of Physiology, 1974; The Adrenal Medulla, in The Cell in Medical Science (ed Beck and Lloyd), 1976; Endocrine System, in Textbook of Human Anatomy (ed W. J. Hamilton), 1976; *contribs to:* Hormones and Evolution, Vol. I, ed Barrington, 1979; Biogenic Amines in Development, ed Parvez and Parvez, 1980; Hormones in Human Tissues, Vol. I, ed Fotherby and Pal, 1981; Asst Editor, Gray's Anatomy (ed Davies), 1967. *Recreations:* shooting, gardening, watercolour painting. *Address:* Foxhollow, Quaker Lane, Farnsfield, Newark, Notts NG22 8EE. *T:* (01623) 882028.

COURAGE, Maj.-Gen. Walter James, CB 1994; MBE 1979; Director, Business Development, Risk Advisory Group Ltd, since 1997; Consultant: AMEC Project Investments Ltd, since 1997; DLA, since 2000; *b* 25 Sept. 1940; *s* of late Walter Henry Phipps and of Nancy Mary Courage (*née* Reeves, who *m* 3rd, John Frederick Gardner), and step *s* of late Lt-Col Nigel Anthony Courage, MC; *m* 1964, Lavinia Patricia, *d* of late John Emerson Crawhall Wood; one *s* one *d*. *Educ:* Abingdon Sch.; RMA, Sandhurst. Commnd 5th Royal Inniskilling Dragoon Guards, 1961; served BAOR, Libya and Canada, 1961–81; commanded Regt, 1982–84; Div. Col Staff Coll., 1985; Comdr 4th Armoured Bde, 1985–88; Chief of Staff, UN Force in Cyprus, 1988–90; Chief Joint Services Liaison Officer, BAOR, Bonn, 1990–94; Chief, Ext. Affairs Div., Germany, 1994–95; Dir-Gen., TA, 1995–96. FIMgt. *Recreations:* shooting, cricket, ski-ing, polo, fine art. *Address:* Brigmerston Farm House, Brigmerston, Salisbury, Wilts SP4 8HX. *Clubs:* Cavalry and Guards, MCC; I Zingari.

COURCY; *see* de Courcy, family name of Baron Kingsale.

COURT, Hon. Sir Charles (Walter Michael), AK 1982; KCMG 1979; Kt 1972; OBE 1946; MLA (Liberal Party) for Nedlands, 1953–82; Premier of Western Australia, 1974–82; also Treasurer, and Minister co-ordinating Economic and Regional Development, 1974–82; *b* Crawley, Sussex, 29 Sept. 1911; *s* of late W. J. Court, Perth; *m* 1st, 1936, Rita M. (*d* 1992), *d* of L. R. Steffanoni; five *s*; 2nd, 1997, Judith Butt. *Educ:* Leederville and Rosalie State Schs; Perth Boys' Sch. Chartered Accountant, 1933; Foundn Partner, Hendry, Rae & Court, 1938–70. Served AIF, 1940–46, Lt-Col. State Registrar, Inst. Chartered Accountants in Aust. (WA Br.), 1946–52, Mem. State Council, 1952–55. Dep. Leader, 1957–59, 1971–72, and Leader, 1972–74, of Opposition, WA; Minister, Western Australia: for Industrial Development and the NW, 1959–71; for Railways, 1959–67; for Transport, 1965–66. Chairman: Adv. Cttee under WA Prices Control Act, 1948–52; Taiwan Trade Assoc., 1984–87; President: WA Band Assoc., 1954–59; Order of Australia Assoc., 1987–89 (Hon. Life Mem., 1997). Warden, WA State War Meml, 1991–92. Chm. Adv. Council, Asia Res. Council, Murdoch Univ. Patron: WA Div., PGA; WA Youth Orch.; WA Opera Co. Hon. Colonel: WA Univ. Regt, 1969–75; SAS Regt, 1976–80. Paul Harris Fellow, 1982, Sapphire Pin, 1991, Rotary. FCA; FCIS; FASA. Hon. FAIM 1980. Freeman: City of Nedlands, 1982; Shire of West Kimberley, WA, 1983. Hon. LLD Univ. of WA, 1969; Hon. DTech WA Inst. of Technol., 1982; Hon. Dr Murdoch Univ., 1995; Hon. DLitt Edith Cowan Univ., 1999. Manufacturers' Export Council Award, 1969; James Kirby Award, Inst. of Production Engrs, 1971; Australian Chartered Accountant of the Year, 1983. Life Member: Musicians Union, 1953; ASA, 1979; Returned Services League, 1981; Inst. of Chartered Accountants in Australia, 1982. Order of the Sacred Treasure, 1st cl. (Japan), 1983; Kt Comdr, Order of Merit (Italian Republic), 1991; Order of Brilliant Star with Grand Cordon (Taiwan), 1991. *Publications:* many professional papers on accountancy, and papers on economic and resource development. *Recreations:* music and other cultural and sporting interests. *Address:* 18 Peel Parade, Coodanup, WA 6210, Australia. *Clubs:* Weld, Western Australian (Hon. Life Mem.), Commercial Travellers Association (Perth); Nedlands Rotary, Lions.

See also Hon. R. F. Court.

COURT, Hon. Richard Fairfax; Premier of Western Australia, Treasurer and Minister for Public Sector Management and for Federal Affairs, 1993–2001; *b* 27 Sept. 1947; *s* of Hon. Sir Charles Court, *qv*; *m* 1989, Joanne, *d* of B. Moffat; one *d*, and one *s* one *d* by previous marriage. *Educ:* Univ. of Western Australia (BCom). Man. Dir, Court Marine Pty, 1974–82. MLA (L) Nedlands, WA, 1982–2001; Shadow Minister for Small Business, 1986; Dep. Leader, Parly Lib. Party, 1987–90; Shadow Minister for: Resources, Develt, Mines, Fuel and Energy, NW and Goldfields, 1990–91; Resource and Industrial Develt, Mines and Aboriginal Affairs, 1991–92; Public Sector Management, also Leader of the Opposition and Shadow Treas., 1992–93; Minister for: Tourism, 1994–95; Youth, 1996–97.

COURTAULD, Rev. (Augustine) Christopher (Caradoc); Vicar of St Paul's, Knightsbridge, 1978–99; *b* 12 Sept. 1934; *s* of late Augustine Courtauld and of Lady Butler of Saffron Walden; *m* 1978, Dr Elizabeth Ann Molland, MD, FRCPath, *d* of late Rev. Preb. John W. G. Molland; two *d*. *Educ:* Trinity College, Cambridge (BA 1958, MA 1961); Westcott House, Cambridge. Deacon 1960, priest 1961, Manchester; Curate of Oldham, 1960–63; Chaplain: Trinity College, Cambridge, 1963–68; The London Hospital, 1968–78. Area Dean, Westminster (St Margaret), 1992–97. *Recreation:* sailing. *Address:* Broke House, The Drift, Levington, Ipswich, Suffolk IP10 0LF.

COURTENAY, family name of **Earl of Devon**.

COURTENAY, Lord; Charles Peregrine Courtenay; *b* 14 Aug. 1975; *o s* of Earl of Devon, *qv*. *Educ:* St John's Coll., Cambridge (BA Hons History of Art, 1997; MA 2001; Rugby half-Blue 1996). Called to the Bar, Inner Temple, 1999. London Scottish 1st XV Rugby.

COURTENAY, Sir Thomas Daniel, (Sir Tom), Kt 2001; actor; *b* 25 Feb. 1937; *s* of late Thomas Henry Courtenay and Annie Eliza Quest; *m* 1st, 1973, Cheryl Kennedy (marr. diss. 1982); 2nd, 1988, Isabel Crossley. *Educ:* Kingston High Sch., Hull; University Coll., London (Fellow 1994). RADA, 1958–60; started acting professionally, 1960; Old Vic, 1960–61: Konstantin Treplieff, Poins, Feste and Puck; Billy Liar, Cambridge Theatre, June 1961–Feb. 1962 and on tour; Andorra, National Theatre (guest), 1964; The Cherry Orchard, and Macbeth, Chichester, 1966; joined 69 Theatre Co., Manchester, 1966: Charley's Aunt, 1966; Romeo, Playboy of the Western World, 1967; Hamlet (Edinburgh Festival), 1968; She Stoops to Conquer, (transferred to Garrick), 1969; Peer Gynt, 1970; Charley's Aunt, Apollo, 1971; Time and Time Again, Comedy, 1972 (Variety Club of GB Stage Actor Award, 1972); The Norman Conquests, Globe, 1974; The Fool, Royal Court, 1975; Prince of Homburg, The Rivals, Manchester (opening prods of The Royal Exchange), 1976; Otherwise Engaged, NY, 1977; Clouds, Duke of York's, 1978; Crime and Punishment, Manchester, 1978; The Dresser, Manchester and Queen's, 1980 (Drama Critics Award and New Standard Award for best actor, 1980), NY 1981; The Misanthrope, Manchester and Round House, 1981; Andy Capp, Manchester and Aldwych, 1982; Jumpers, Manchester, 1984; Rookery Nook, Shaftesbury, 1986; The Hypochondriac, Lyric, Hammersmith, 1987; Dealing with Clair, Richmond, 1988; The Miser, Manchester, 1991; Moscow Stations (one-man show), Traverse Theatre, Edinburgh, 1993, 1994, Garrick, 1994 (Evening Standard and Critics Circle Award), NY, 1995; Poison Pen, Manchester, 1993; Uncle Vanya, NY, 1995, Manchester, 2001; Art, Wyndham's, 1996; King Lear, Manchester, 1999. Began acting in films, 1962. *Films:* The Loneliness of the Long Distance Runner; Private Potter; Billy Liar; King and Country (Volpi Cup, 1964); Operation Crossbow; King Rat; Dr Zhivago; The Night of the Generals; The Day the Fish Came Out; A Dandy in Aspic; Otley; One Day in the Life of Ivan Denisovitch; Catch Me a Spy; The Dresser (Golden Globe Award); The Last Butterfly; Let Him Have It; Redemption; The Boy from Mercury; Whatever Happened to Harold Smith?; Last Orders; *television* includes: Old Curiosity Shop (film), 1995; A Rather English Marriage, 1998. Best Actor Award, Prague Festival, 1968; TV Drama Award (for Oswald in Ghosts), 1968. *Publication:* Dear Tom: letters from home (memoirs), 2000. *Recreations:* listening to music (mainly classical, romantic and jazz); watching sport (and occasionally taking part in it, in a light-hearted manner), the countryside, playing the flute. *Address:* Putney. *Club:* Garrick.

COURTNEY, Prof. Edward, MA; Gildersleeve Professor of Classics, University of Virginia, since 1993; *b* 22 March 1932; *s* of George and Kathleen Courtney; *m* 1962, Brenda Virginia Meek; two *s*. *Educ:* Royal Belfast Academical Instn; Trinity Coll., Dublin (BA); BA (by incorporation) 1955, MA 1957, Oxford. University studentship, Dublin, 1954–55; Research Lectr, Christ Church, Oxford, 1955–59; Lectr in Classics, 1959, Reader in Classics, 1970, Prof. of Latin, 1977, King's Coll., London; Prof. of Classics, 1982–93, Leonard Ely Prof. of Humanistic Studies, 1986–93, Stanford Univ. *Publications:*

(ed) Valerius Flaccus, Argonautica (Leipzig), 1970; (ed jtly) Juvenal, Satires 1, 3, 10, 1977; (ed jtly) Ovid, Fasti (Leipzig), 1978, 4th edn 1997; A Commentary on the Satires of Juvenal, 1980; (ed) Juvenal, The Satires, a text, 1984; (ed) Statius, Silvae, 1990; The Poems of Petronius, 1991; The Fragmentary Roman Poets, 1993; Musa Lapidaria: a selection of Latin verse inscriptions, 1995; Archaic Latin Prose, 1999; many articles and reviews. *Recreation:* chess (schoolboy champion of Ireland, 1950). *Address:* 1500 West Pines Drive, Charlottesville, VA 22901, USA.

COURTNEY, Roger Graham, CPhys, FInstP; CEng, FCIBSE; consultant, construction research and innovation; *b* 11 July 1946; *s* of late Ronald Samuel Courtney and Marjorie Dixon Courtney; *m* 1973, Rosemary Madeleine Westlake; four *d. Educ:* Roan School for Boys, SE3; Trinity Coll., Cambridge (MA); Univ. of Bristol (MSc); Brunel Univ. (MTech(OR)). CPhys 1991, FInstP 1991; MCIOB 1993; FCIBSE 1993; CEng 1994. Building Research Station, later Building Research Establishment, 1969–77: res. on bldg and urban services and energy conservation; Sci. Officer, 1969–72; Sen. Sci. Officer, 1972–75; PSO, 1975–81; Inner Cities Directorate, DoE, 1977–78; Sci. and Technology Secretariat, Cabinet Office, 1978–84 (Sec. to ACARD and IT Adv. Panel); SPSO, 1981–83; DCSO, 1983–86; Technical Dir, Energy Efficiency Office, Dept of Energy, 1984–86; Dep. Dir, 1986–88, Dir, 1988–90, Chief Exec., 1990–97, BRE, DoE; Dep. Chm., BRE Ltd, 1997–99. *Publications:* papers in sci. and professional jls. *Address:* 89 Parkside Drive, Watford WD17 3AY. *T:* (01923) 446767.

COURTNEY, William Reid; Regional Chairman of Industrial Tribunals, Scotland, 1991–93; *b* 22 Nov. 1927; *s* of Samuel Courtney and Louisa Reid or Courtney; *m* 1951, Jean Ursula Page; one *s* two *d. Educ:* Allan Glens Sch., Glasgow; Glasgow Univ. (LLB). Solicitor, Supreme Courts. Failed professional cricketer, fell back on Law; Edinburgh solicitor, 1952–77; Chm., Industrial Tribunals, Scotland, 1978–91. *Recreations:* sea, hills. *Address:* 30 Millig Street, Helensburgh, Dunbartonshire G84 9PN. *T:* (01436) 676900. *Clubs:* Royal Northern & Clyde Yacht, Clyde Corinthian Yacht, Clyde Cruising, Old Gaffers.

COURTOWN, 9th Earl of, *cr* 1762; **James Patrick Montagu Burgoyne Winthrop Stopford;** Baron Courtown (Ire.), 1758; Viscount Stopford, 1762; Baron Saltersford (GB), 1796; *b* 19 March 1954; *s* of 8th Earl of Courtown, OBE, TD, DL, and Patricia, 3rd *d* of Harry S. Winthrop, Auckland, NZ; *S* father, 1975; *m* 1985, Elisabeth, *yr d* of I. R. Dunnett, Broad Campden, Glos; one *s* one *d. Educ:* Eton College; Berkshire Coll. of Agriculture; RAC, Cirencester. ARICS 1989. A Lord in Waiting (Govt Whip), 1995–97; an Opposition Whip, 1997–2000; elected Mem., H of L, 1999. *Heir: s* Viscount Stopford, *qv. Address:* House of Lords, SW1A 0PW.

COUSE, Philip Edward, FCA; Partner, Coopers & Lybrand, 1966–91; Director: Birmingham Heartlands and Solihull Hospital NHS Trust, 1991–2000; William King Ltd, 1993–99; *b* 24 March 1936; *s* of Oliver and Marion Couse; *m* 1st (marr. diss. 1973); two *s* one *d*; 2nd, Carol Ann Johannessen Pruitt; one step *d. Educ:* Uppingham Sch.; Hackley Sch., USA. Qualified as Chartered Accountant, 1961. Birmingham Chartered Accountants' Students Society: Sec., 1958–59; Chm., 1967–69; Pres., 1977–78; Birmingham and West Midlands Soc. of Chartered Accountants: Mem. Cttee, 1974–92, Pres., 1982–83; Institute of Chartered Accountants: Mem. Council, 1978–92; Chm. of various cttees; Pres., 1989–90; Chartered Accountants' Dining Club: Mem. Cttee, 1981–92; Treas., 1985–89; Pres., 1989–91. Part-time Comr, Friendly Socs Commn, 1992–97. Dir, Hillstone Sch. Trust, Malvern, 1971–86; Chairman: Edgbaston C of E Coll. for Girls, 1982–88; Birmingham Rep. Theatre Foundn, 1991–96; Dir, Birmingham Rep. Th., 1991–96; Chm., Birmingham Dio. Bd of Finance, 1992–2000, and Mem. of various cttees; Mem., C of E Pensions Bd, 1998–99. Mem., Council of Management, and Treas., Ironbridge Heritage Foundn, 1991–; Trustee, Birmingham Eye Foundn, 1981–91 (Treas., 1981–91). Liveryman, Co. of Chartered Accountants in England and Wales, 1977– (Mem., Court, 1987–90). *Recreations:* music, horse racing, woodwork, theatre going. *Address:* 23 Frederick Road, Edgbaston, Birmingham B15 1JN; 715 Greenwood Manor Circle, West Melbourne, FL 32904, USA. *Club:* Royal Automobile.

COUSINS, Brian Harry, CBE 1981; Principal Establishment and Finance Officer, Lord Chancellor's Department, 1989–93; *b* 18 July 1933; *s* of late William and Ethel Margaret Cousins; *m* 1957, Margaret (*née* Spark); two *s. Educ:* Devonport High School. Served RAF, pilot, 1952–54. Joined Ministry of Defence, 1954; Private Sec. to Permanent Secretary, 1962–65; Private Sec. Parliamentary Secretary, 1971–72; ndc 1972; Civil Sec., British Forces Germany, 1973–76; Asst Under Sec. of State, MoD, 1981–85, 1986–89; Chm., CSSB, 1985–86. *Recreations:* golf, local affairs, music, gardening. *Address:* c/o HSBC, Ewell, Surrey. *Club:* Royal Automobile.

COUSINS, Air Chief Marshal Sir David, KCB 1996 (CB 1991); AFC 1980; Controller, RAF Benevolent Fund, since 1998; *b* 20 Jan. 1942; *s* of late Peter and Irene Cousins; *m* 1966, Mary Edith McMurray, *e d* of late Rev. A. W. S. Holmes; two *s* one *d. Educ:* St Edward's Sch., Malta; Prince Rupert's Sch., Wilhelmshaven; RAF College; Open Univ. (BA 1992). 92 Sqn (Lightnings), 1965–68; ADC to CAS, 1968–70; 15 Sqn (Buccaneers), 1970–73; Air Plans, HQ RAF Germany, 1973; RAF Staff Coll., 1974; Staff Officer to ACAS (OR), 1975–77; OC 16 Sqn (Buccaneers), 1977–80; Central Trials and Tactics Orgn, 1980; PSO to CAS, 1981–83; OC RAF Laarbruch, 1983–85; RCDS 1986; Dir, Air Offensive, MoD, 1987–89; Dir Gen. Aircraft 2, MoD (PE), 1989–91; AOC and Comdt, RAF Coll., Cranwell, 1992–94; AOC No 38 Gp, and SASO Strike Comd, 1994–95; Air Mem. for Personnel, and AOC-in-C, Personnel and Trng Comd, 1995–98. ADC to the Queen, 1984–85. *Recreations:* dinghy sailing, walking, horology. *Club:* Royal Air Force.

COUSINS, James Mackay; MP (Lab) Newcastle upon Tyne Central, since 1987; *b* 23 Feb. 1944; *m*; two *s*, and one step *s* one step *d. Educ:* New Coll., Oxford (Schol.); London School of Economics. Contract Researcher, and Lectr in job markets, Commn on Industrial Relns and Depts of Employment and the Environment. Member: Wallsend Borough Council, 1969–73; Tyne and Wear County Council, 1973–86 (Dep. Leader, 1981–86). Mem., Treasury Select Cttee, 1997–. Founder, North Low Pay Unit. Member: CND; MSF. *Address:* (office) First Floor, 21 Portland Terrace, Newcastle upon Tyne NE2 1QQ; House of Commons, SW1A 0AA.

COUSINS, Jeremy Vincent; QC 1999; a Recorder, since 2000; *b* 25 Feb. 1955; *s* of Eric Cousins and Joyce Cousins; *m* 1993, Jane Owens; two *s* one *d. Educ:* Oxford Sch.; Warwick Univ. Called to the Bar, Middle Temple, 1977; in practice at the Bar, 1977–; an Asst Recorder, 1996–2000. *Recreations:* wine, travelling in France and Italy. *Address:* 4 Fountain Court, Steelhouse Lane, Birmingham B4 6DR. *T:* (0121) 236 3476.

COUSINS, John Peter; Chairman, Crown Asset Management Ltd, Hong Kong, since 1994; *b* 31 Oct. 1931; *s* of Rt Hon. Frank Cousins, PC; *m* 1976, Pauline Cousins (*née* Hubbard); three *d. Educ:* Doncaster Central Sch. Motor engineering apprentice, 1947–52; RAF Engineering, 1952–55; BOAC cabin crew and clerical work, 1955–63; Full Time Official, TGWU, 1963–75, Nat. Sec., 1966–75; Dir of Manpower and Industrial Relations, NEDO, 1975–79; Dir of Personnel, Plessey Telecommunications and Office Systems Ltd, 1979–81; Dir of Personnel and Industrial Relns, John Brown PLC, 1981–83; Gen. Sec., Clearing Bank Union, 1983–86; Head of Personnel, Scottish Daily Record & Sunday Mail (1986) Ltd, 1987; Personnel Dir, Maxwell Pergamon Publishing Corp., 1988–89; Sen. Consultant, Contract 2000, 1989–90; Man. Dir, Cousins Financial Services Ltd (Gibraltar), 1990–. Mem., Transport and Local Govt Cttees, TUC; UK Deleg., ILO; International Transport Workers Federation: Member: Aviation Sect.; Local Govt Cttee; Chemical Cttee; Civil Aviation Cttee; Mem. Industrial Training Bds. Member: Countryside Commn, 1972–84; New Towns Commn, 1975–79; Sandford Cttee to review National Parks in England and Wales, 1972–73; Council, RSPB, 1982; Bd of Trustees, Royal Botanic Gardens, Kew, 1983–88. Chm., British Council of Productivity Assocs, 1977–82. Travelling Fellow, Kingston Reg. Management Centre, 1977. FIMgt. *Recreations:* music, golf. *Address:* Room 1018, 10/F Star House, 3 Salisbury Road, Tsim Sha Tsui, Kowloon, Hong Kong.

COUSINS, Philip, CB 1982; Deputy Comptroller and Auditor General, National Audit Office (formerly Secretary, Exchequer and Audit Department), 1979–84; *b* 28 Feb. 1923; *s* of Herbert and Ella Cousins; *m* 1948, Ruby Laura Morris; two *d. Educ:* Royal Liberty School, Romford. Served in Royal Air Force, 1943–47. Joined Treasury, 1949; Under Secretary, 1974–79. *Address:* 102 Philbeach Gardens, SW5 9ET. *T:* (020) 7373 6164.

COUSINS, Richard John; Chief Executive, BPB plc, since 2000; *b* 29 March 1959; *s* of Philip Cousins and late Marian Cousins; *m* 1982, Caroline Thorpe; two *s. Educ:* Sheffield Univ. (BSc Maths and Stats); Lancaster Univ. (MA Operational Res.). OR Dept, Cadbury Schweppes plc, 1981–84; Corporate Planning Manager, Newey and Eyre Ltd, 1984–90; with BPB plc, 1990–: Corporate Planning, 1990–92; Gp Financial Controller, 1992–95; Gen. Manager, Packaging, 1995–96; Man. Dir, Abertay, 1996–98; Pres., BPB Westroc (Canada), 1998–2000. *Recreations:* cricket, walking, photography, history. *Address:* BPB plc, Park House, 15 Bath Road, Slough SL1 3UF. *T:* (01753) 898911.

COUTTS; *see* Money-Coutts.

COUTTS, Gordon; *see* Coutts, T. G.

COUTTS, Herbert, FSAScot; FMA; Director of Recreation, City of Edinburgh Council, since 1999; *b* 9 March 1944; *s* of late Herbert and Agnes Coutts, Dundee; *m* 1970, Angela Elizabeth Mason Smith; one *s* three *d. Educ:* Morgan Acad., Dundee. FSAScot 1965; AMA 1970, FMA 1976. Asst Keeper of Antiquities and Bygones, Dundee City Museums, 1965–68, Keeper, 1968–71; Supt, Edinburgh City Museums, 1971–73; City Curator, City of Edinburgh Museums and Art Galls, 1973–96; City of Edinburgh Council: Hd of Museums and Galls, 1996–97; Hd of Heritage and Arts, 1997–99. Vice Pres., Museums Assts Gp, 1967–70; Member: Bd, Scottish Museums Council, 1971–74, and 1986–88; Govt Cttee on Future of Scotland's National Museums and Galleries, 1979–80 (report publd 1981); Bd, Museums Trng Inst., 1995–; Council, Museums Assoc., 1977–78, 1987–88; Council, Soc. of Antiquaries of Scotland, 1981–82; Museums Advr, COSLA Arts and Recreation Cttee, 1985–90, 1995–99. Member: Paxton House Trust, 1988–; E Lothian Community Develt Trust, 1989–. External Examr, St Andrews Univ., 1993–97. Building Projects: City of Edinburgh Art Centre (opened 1980); Museum of Childhood Extension (opened 1986); People's Story Museum (opened 1989); City of Edinburgh Art Centre Extension (opened 1992); Scott Monument Restoration (completed 1999); Usher Hall Renovation (completed 2000). Exhibitions at City of Edinburgh Art Centre: The Emperor's Warriors, 1985; Gold of the Pharaohs, 1988; Gold of Peru, 1990; Golden Warriors of the Ukrainian Steppes, 1993; Star Trek—The Exhibition, 1995; Quest for a Pirate, 1996; Gateway to the Silk Road, 1996. Contested (Lab) Angus South, 1970. SBStJ 1977. *Publications:* Ancient Monuments of Tayside, 1970; Tayside Before History, 1971; Edinburgh: an illustrated history, 1975; Huntly House, 1980; Lady Stair's House, 1980; (ed) Gold of the Pharaohs, 1988; (ed) Dinosaurs Alive, 1990; (ed) Gold of Peru, 1990; (ed) Golden Warriors of the Ukrainian Steppes, 1993; (ed) Gateway to the Silk Road, 1996; exhibn catalogues; contrib. Museums Jl and archaeol jls. *Recreations:* relaxing with family, gardening, going to the opera, writing, reading, walking. *Address:* Kirkhill House, Queen's Road, Dunbar, East Lothian EH42 1LN. *T:* (01368) 863113.

COUTTS, Ian Dewar, CBE 1982; in practice as chartered accountant, 1950–95; Member, Forestry Commission, 1984–93; Director, Eastern Electricity plc, 1990–95 (Member, Eastern Electricity Board, 1982–90); *b* 15 May 1927; *s* of David Dewar Coutts and Dorothy Helen Coutts; *m* 1st, 1950, Sheila Margaret Cargill (marr. diss. 1983); one *s* two *d*; 2nd 1983, Hilary Ballard; one *s* one *d. Educ:* Ipswich Sch.; Culford Sch. BA 2000. Chartered Accountant, 1949. Served 1st Essex Regt, 1946–48. Norfolk County Councillor, 1970–89; Leader, Norfolk CC, 1973–79. Chm., ACC Finance Cttee, 1977–83; Mem., Consultative Council on Local Govt Finance, 1977–83. Mem., Local Govt Audit Commn, 1983–90. Chm., S Norfolk Conservative Assoc., 1970–73; Parly Cand., Norwich S, 1979. Mem., Council, Univ. of East Anglia, 1974–86. *Recreation:* sailing. *Address:* 3 Choseley Court, Wymondham, Norfolk NR18 0HR.

COUTTS, Prof. John Archibald; Professor of Jurisprudence in the University of Bristol, 1950–75, now Emeritus; Pro-Vice Chancellor, 1971–74; *b* 29 Dec. 1909; *e s* of Archibald and Katherine Jane Coutts; *m* 1940, Katherine Margaret Alldis (*d* 1998); two *s. Educ:* Merchant Taylors', Crosby; Downing Coll., Cambridge (MA, LLB). Barrister Gray's Inn, 1933; lectured in Law: University Coll., Hull, 1934–35; King's Coll., London, 1935–36; Queen's Univ., Belfast, 1936–37; Trinity Coll., Dublin, 1937–50; Prof. of Laws, University of Dublin, 1944–50. Fellow, Trinity College, Dublin, 1944–50. Visiting Professor: Osgoode Hall Law Sch., Toronto, 1962–63; Univ. of Toronto, 1970–71, 1975–76. *Publications:* The Accused (ed); contributions to legal journals. *Address:* 22 Hurle Crescent, Clifton, Bristol BS8 2SZ. *T:* (0117) 973 6984.

COUTTS, T(homas) Gordon; QC (Scotland) 1973; *b* 5 July 1933; *s* of Thomas Coutts and Evelyn Gordon Coutts; *m* 1959, Winifred Katherine Scott, PhD; one *s* one *d. Educ:* Aberdeen Grammar Sch.; Aberdeen Univ. (MA, LLB). Admitted Faculty of Advocates, 1959; Standing Junior Counsel to Dept Agric. (Scot.), 1965–73; called to the Bar, Lincoln's Inn, 1995. Temporary Judge, Court of Session, Scotland, 1991–; Vice Pres. (Scot.), VAT and Duties Tribunals, 1996–. Part-time Chairman: Industrial Tribunals, 1972–; Medical Appeal Tribunal, 1984–; VAT Tribunal, 1990–96; Mem., Panel of Arbitrators, 1995. FCIArb 1994. *Recreations:* travel, stamp collecting. *Address:* 6 Heriot Row, Edinburgh EH3 6HU. *Club:* New (Edinburgh).

COUTURE, Most Rev. Maurice; *see* Quebec, Archbishop of, (RC).

COUVE DE MURVILLE, Most Rev. Maurice Noël Léon; Archbishop of Birmingham, (RC), 1982–99; *b* 27 June 1929; *s* of Noël Couve de Murville and Marie, *d* of Sir Louis Souchon. *Educ:* Downside School; Trinity Coll., Cambridge (MA); STL (Institut Catholique, Paris); MPhil (Sch. of Oriental and African Studies, Univ. of London). Priest, 1957; Curate, St Anselm's, Dartford, 1957–60; Priest-in-Charge, St Francis, Moulsecoomb, 1961–64; Catholic Chaplain: Univ. of Sussex, 1961–77; Univ. of

Cambridge, 1977–82. DUniv Open, 1994; Hon. DD Birmingham, 1996. Grand Cross Conventual Chaplain, SMO Malta, 1982. *Publications:* (with Philip Jenkins) Catholic Cambridge, 1983; John Milner 1752–1826, 1986; Karl Leisner, 1988; Pierre Toussaint, 1995; Junípero Serra, 2000. *Recreations:* walking, gardening, local history. *Address:* 53 North Parade, Horsham, W Sussex RH12 2DE. *Club:* Lansdowne.

COUZENS, Brian William; classical recording producer; Chairman and Managing Director, Chandos Records Ltd, since 1979; Managing Director, Chandos Music, since 1961; *b* 17 Jan. 1933; *s* of William and Vera Couzens; *m* 1956, Ilse Elizabeth Hauguth; three *s* one *d*. Self educated. Musician, 1948–51; Nat. Service, 1951–53; composer and arranger for BBC and publishers, 1954–59; orchestration for films incl. Where Eagles Dare, Magnificent Men in their Flying Machines, 633 Squadron, and 34 films working for Ron Goodwin, John Williams, Dimitri Tiomkin, and others, 1959–69; formed Chandos Music Ltd, 1961; independent sound engr and record producer of classical music, 1969–78; formed Chandos Records Ltd, 1979. Numerous internat. awards incl. Grammy, and Gramophone. *Recreations:* photography, video, nature and wildlife. *Address:* Chandos Records Ltd, Chandos House, Commerce Way, Colchester CO2 8HQ. *T:* (01206) 225200; Tenpenny Hill, Thorrington, Essex CO7 8JB. *T:* (01206) 255381.

COUZENS, Air Vice-Marshal David Cyril, CEng, FIMechE, FRAeS; Director General Defence Logistics Capability, Ministry of Defence, since 2001; *b* 15 Oct. 1949; *s* of Cyril Couzens and Joyce Couzens (*née* Walker); *m* 1977, Deborah Cawse; one *s* one *d*. *Educ:* Ecclesbourne Sch.; Churchill Coll., Cambridge (MA); Open Univ. Business Sch. (MBA); Loughborough Univ. (Postgrad. Dip.). CEng 1979; FIMechE 1991; FRAeS 1995. Joined Royal Air Force, 1968: initial and professional trng, 1968–72; practical aircraft/weapon system appts, 1972–88; personnel mgt, 1988–89; Gp Captain 1990; Superintendent of Armament, 1990–91; Dep. Dir Support Policy (Op. Requirements) (RAF), MoD Policy, 1991–94; rcds 1994; Air Cdre 1995; Air Cdre, CIS, HQ Strike Comd, 1995–97; Dir, Logistic Inf. Strategy (RAF), MoD, 1997–98; AO, Logistic Inf. Strategy and Industrial Interface Study, MoD, 1998–99; Air Vice-Marshal 1999; Dir Gen. Defence Logistics (Communications and Inf. Systems), MoD, 1999–2001. *Recreations:* hill-walking, gardening, music. *Address:* HQ Defence Logistics Organisation, Ministry of Defence, Endsleigh, Bath BA1 5AB. *Club:* Royal Air Force.

COUZENS, Sir Kenneth (Edward), KCB 1979 (CB 1976); Chairman, Crédit Lyonnais Capital Markets, 1991–96 (Director, 1989–98; Vice-Chairman, 1996–98); *b* 29 May 1925; *s* of Albert Couzens and May Couzens (*née* Biddlecombe); *m* 1947, Muriel Eileen Fey; one *d* (one *s* decd). *Educ:* Portsmouth Grammar Sch.; Caius Coll., Cambridge. Inland Revenue, 1949–51; Treasury, 1951–68, and 1970–82; Civil Service Dept, 1968–70. Private Sec. to Financial Sec., Treasury, 1952–55, and to Chief Sec., 1962–63; Asst Sec., 1963–69; Under-Secretary: CSD, 1969–70; Treasury, 1970–73; Dep. Sec., Incomes Policy and Public Finance, 1973–77; Second Perm. Sec. (Overseas Finance), 1977–82; Perm. Under-Sec. of State, Dept of Energy, 1983–85. Dep. Chm., NCB, subseq. British Coal, 1985–88; Chm., Coal Products, 1988–92 (Dir, 1986–92). Vice-Chm., Monetary Cttee, European Community, 1982; Member: UK Adv. Bd, Nat. Econ. Res. Assocs, 1986–98; Local Govt Commn, 1993–95. *Address:* Coverts Edge, Woodsway, Oxshott, Surrey KT22 0ND. *T:* (01372) 843207. *Club:* Reform.

COVEN, Major Edwina Olwyn, CBE 1988; JP; DL; HM Lieutenant, City of London, since 1981; Director, Capital Corporation (formerly Crockfords) Plc, 1993–98; *b* 23 Oct. 1921; *d* of Sir Samuel Instone, DL, and Lady (Alice) Instone; *m* 1951, Frank Coven (*d* 2001). *Educ:* Queen's Coll., London; St Winifred's, Ramsgate; Lycée Victor Duruy, Paris; Marlborough Gate Secretarial Coll., London (1st Cl. Business Diploma). Volunteered for Mil. Service, Private ATS; commnd ATS (subseq. WRAC); Army Interpreter (French); served UK and overseas, incl. staff appts, Plans and Policy Div., Western Union Defence Org. and NATO, Directorate Manpower Planning, WO, 1942–56. 1959–: Children's Writer, Fleetway Publications; Gen. Features Writer, National Magazine Co.; Reporter, BBC Woman's Hour; performer and adviser, children's and teenage progs, ITV. Mem. Adv. Council, Radio London (BBC), 1978–81. Dir, 1985–93, Dep. Chm., 1990–93, TV-am. Chm., Davbro Chemists, 1967–71; stores consultant on promotion and fashion, 1960–77; Mem., Women's Adv. Cttee (Clothing and Footwear Sub-Cttee), BSI, 1971–73. Caseworker, Soldiers', Sailors' and Airmen's Assoc., 1995–99. JP Inner London, North Westminster, 1965–72 (Dep. Chm., 1971–72); JP City of London Commn, 1969–88 (Dep. Chm., 1971–88); Greater London: DL 1987, Rep. DL Hammersmith and Fulham, 1989–94; Mem., Central Council Probation and After-Care Cttee, 1971; Chm., City of London Probation and After-Care Cttee, 1971–77; Chm, City of London Police Cttee, 1984–87 (Dep. Chm., 1983–84); Mem., Police Cttee, AMA, 1985–97. Mem., Jt Cttee of Management, London Court of Internat. Arbitration 1983–89. Dowgate Ward, City of London: Court of Common Council, 1972–99; elected Alderman, 1973 and 1974; Deputy, 1975–. Chief Commoner, City of London, 1987–88. Freedom, City of London, 1967; Mem., Guild of Freemen, City of London, 1971; Freeman, Loriners' Co., 1967; Liveryman, Spectacle Makers' Co., 1972; Hon. Liveryman, Lightmongers' Co., 1990. Member: Council, WRAC Assoc., 1973–90 (Vice Pres., 1984–88; Vice-Chm., 1985–89; Chm., 1989–90); TAVRA, City of London, 1979–86; Associated Speakers, 1975–; London Home Safety Council, 1980–84; Vice Chm., Cities of London and Westminster Home Safety Council, 1984–89; Vice President: Nat. Org. for Women's Management Educn, 1983–90; FANY, 1989–; Operation Raleigh, 1989–95; Chm., Cttee for Celebration of 800th Year of Mayoralty, Corp. of London, 1988–90. Member: Court, Sussex Univ., 1994–; Bd of Governors, City of London Sch., 1972–77; Chm., Bd of Governors, City of London Sch. for Girls, 1978–81; Mem., Royal Soc. of St George, 1972–; Chm., Vintry and Dowgate Wards Club, 1977. FRSA 1988. Hon. Captain of Police, Salt Lake City, 1986; Order of Wissam Alouite (Morocco), 1987. OStJ 1987. *Publication:* Tales of Oaktree Kitchen, 1959 (2nd edn 1960; adapted for ITV children's educnl series). *Recreations:* looking after much-loved husband and homemaking generally; lawn tennis; watching a variety of spectator sports. *Address:* 23 Tavistock, Devonshire Place, Eastbourne, Sussex BN21 4AG. *Clubs:* Hurlingham; Devonshire (Eastbourne).

COVENEY, Prof. James; Professor of French, University of Bath, 1969–85, now Professor Emeritus; *b* 4 April 1920; *s* of James and Mary Coveney; *m* 1955, Patricia Yvonne Townsend; two *s*. *Educ:* St Ignatius Coll.; Univ. of Reading (BA 1st Cl. Hons French, 1950); Univ. of Strasbourg (Dr Univ. 1953). Served War of 1939–45: Welch Regt; Royal West Kent Regt; RAF (Flt-Lt (Pilot)). French Govt Res. Scholar, 1950–51, Lectr, 1951–53, Univ. of Strasbourg; Lectr in Medieval French, Univ. of Hull, 1953–58; Asst Dir, Civil Service Commn, 1958–59; UN Secretariat, New York, 1959–61; NATO Secretariat, 1961–64; University of Bath: Head of Mod. Langs Gp, 1964–68; Jt Dir, Centre for European Industrial Studies, 1969–75; Head of Sch. of Mod. Langs, 1969–77 and 1980–83. Visiting Professor: Ecole Nat. d'Administration, Paris, 1974–85; Univ. of Buckingham, 1974–86; Bethlehem Univ., 1985. Consultant: Univ. of Macau, 1988; Internat. Communications Inc., Toyko, 1991–94. Lang. Trng Advr, McKinsey & Co., 1967–73. Member: British-French Cultural Commn, 1973–79; Bd of Govs, British Inst. in Paris, 1975–79; European League for Econ. Co-operation, 1997–. Trustee, Friends of Birzeit Univ., 1991–. Corresp. Mem., Académie des Sciences, Agriculture, Arts et Belles-Lettres, Aix-en-Provence, 1975; Confrère de Saint-Etienne, Alsace, 1998. Chevalier de l'Ordre des Palmes Académiques (France), 1978; Officier de l'Ordre National du Mérite (France), 1986. *Publications:* La Légende de l'Empereur Constant, 1955; (with S. Moore) Glossary of French and English Management Terms, 1972; (with J. Grosjean) Le français pour l'ingénieur, 1974; (with S. Kempa) Guide to French Institutions, 1978; (with S. Moore) French Business Management Dictionary, 1993. *Address:* 40 Westfield Close, Bath BA2 2EB. *T:* (01225) 316670. *Club:* Travellers.

COVENEY, Michael William; theatre critic, Daily Mail, since 1997; *b* 24 July 1948; *s* of William Coveney and Violet Amy Coveney (*née* Perry); *m* 1977, Susan Monica Hyman; one *s*. *Educ:* St Ignatius College, London; Worcester College, Oxford. Editor, Plays and Players, 1975–78; theatre critic: Financial Times, 1981–89; The Observer, 1990–97. *Publications:* The Citz, 1990; Maggie Smith, 1992; The Aisle is Full of Noises, 1994; (with Robert Stephens) Knight Errant: memoirs of a vagabond actor, 1995; The World According to Mike Leigh, 1996; Cats on a Chandelier: the Andrew Lloyd Webber story, 1999. *Recreations:* music, running, travel. *Address:* c/o Daily Mail, Northcliffe House, 2 Derry Street, W8 5TT.

COVENTRY, family name of **Earl of Coventry**.

COVENTRY, 11th Earl of, *cr* 1697; **George William Coventry;** Viscount Deerhurst, 1697; *b* 25 Jan. 1934; *o s* of 10th Earl and Hon. Nesta Donne Philipps, *e d* of 1st Baron Kylsant; *S* father, 1940; *m* 1st, 1955, Marie Farquhar-Medart (marr. diss. 1963); (one *s* decd); 2nd, 1969, Ann (marr. diss. 1975), *d* of F. W. J. Cripps, Bickley, Kent; 3rd, 1980, Valerie Anne Birch (marr. diss. 1988); 4th, 1992, Rachel Wynne, *d* of J. Mason. *Educ:* Eton; RMA, Sandhurst. *Heir: cousin* Francis Henry Coventry [*b* 27 Sept. 1912; *m* 1945, Yolande Lucienne, *yr d* of Lucien P. di Benedetto; one *d*]. *Address:* Earls Croome Court, Earls Croome, Worcester WR8 9DE.

See also Earl of Harrowby.

COVENTRY, Bishop of, since 1998; **Rt Rev. Colin James Bennetts;** *b* 9 Sept. 1940; *s* of James Thomas Bennetts and Winifred Florence Bennetts (*née* Couldrey); *m* 1965, Veronica Jane Leat; two *s* two *d*. *Educ:* Battersea Grammar Sch.; Jesus Coll., Cambridge (Exhibnr); Ridley Hall, Cambridge. MA (Cantab); MA (Oxon) by incorporation. Assistant Curate: St Stephen, Tonbridge, 1965–69; St Aldate, Oxford, 1969–73; Chaplain to Oxford Pastorate, 1969–73; Chaplain, Jesus Coll., Oxford, 1973–80; Vicar, St Andrew, Oxford, 1980–90; RD of Oxford, 1984–90; Canon Residentiary of Chester Cathedral, 1990–94; Canon Librarian and Diocesan Director of Ordinands, Chester, 1990–94; Area Bishop of Buckingham, 1994–98. Co-Chm., Springboard, 1995–. Chm., Bible Reading Fellowship, 1999– (Vice-Chm., 1994–98). *Recreations:* mediaeval music, woodcutting. *Address:* Bishop's House, 23 Davenport Road, Coventry, W Midlands CV5 6PW. *T:* (024) 7667 2244, *Fax:* (024) 7671 3271; *e-mail:* bishcov@clara.net.

COVENTRY, Archdeacon of; *see* Bryant, Ven. M. W.

COVENTRY, Dean of; *see* Very Rev. J. D. Irvine.

COVILLE, Air Marshal Sir Christopher (Charles Cotton), KCB 2000 (CB 1995); Deputy Commander-in-Chief, Allied Forces North Europe, since 2000; *b* 2 June 1945; *s* of Henry and Anna Coville; *m* 1967, Irene Johnson; one *s* two *d*. *Educ:* De La Salle Grammar Sch., Liverpool; RAF Coll., Cranwell. BA Open. Lightning Pilot and Instructor, 1969–73; Phantom Pilot and Instructor, 1973–78; Central Tactics and Trials Orgn, 1978–80; Personal Staff Officer to UK Mil. Rep., Brussels, 1981–83; OC Ops Wing, RAF Stanley, 1983; OC 111 Fighter Sqn, 1983–85; Gp Capt. Air, HQ 11 Fighter Group, 1985–86; OC RAF Coningsby, 1986–88; RCDS 1989; Air Cdre Flying Training, HQ RAF Support Command, 1990–92; AO Trng and AOC Trng Gp, 1992–94; Chief Exec., Trng Gp Defence Agency, Apr.–Sept. 1994; ACDS, Op. Requirements (Air), 1994–98; Dep. C-in-C, AFCENT, 1998–2000. President: RAF Microlight Assoc., 1992–; RAF Football Assoc., 1996–. FIPD (FITD 1993); FRAeS 1994. *Recreations:* mountaineering, shooting. *Club:* Royal Air Force.

COVINGTON, Nicholas; Director, Office of Manpower Economics, 1986–89; *b* 9 June 1929; *s* of late Cyril Tim Covington and Margaret Joan (*née* Bray); *m* 1st, 1953, Pat Sillitoe; one *s* two *d*; 2nd, 1983, Kathy Hegarty. *Educ:* Cranleigh Sch.; Oriel Coll., Oxford. RAF, 1947–49; TA Commn, 1952. Metal Box Co. Ltd, South Africa, 1952–57; Gen. Manager and Dir, Garnier & Co. Ltd, 1957–66; entered Min. of Labour, 1966; Asst Sec., 1971; Industrial Relns Div., Dept of Employment, 1976–86. *Address:* Dovecote House, Lower Slaughter, near Cheltenham, Glos GL54 2HY.

COWAN, Annella Marie; Sheriff of Grampian, Highland and Islands at Aberdeen, since 1997; *b* 14 Nov. 1953; *m* 1979, James Temple Cowan (marr. diss. 1995). *Educ:* Elgin Acad.; Edinburgh Univ. (LLB 1976; MSc 1984). Admitted Solicitor, 1978; Procurator Fiscal Depute, 1978–86; seconded to Scottish Law Commn, 1984–86; admitted Faculty of Advocates, 1987; Temp. Sheriff, 1991; Sheriff of Tayside, Central and Fife at Stirling, 1993–97. *Recreation:* equestrianism. *Address:* Sheriff's Chambers, Sheriff Court, Aberdeen AB10 1WP. *T:* (01224) 648316.

COWAN, Prof. Charles Donald, (Jeremy), CBE 1988; MA Cantab, PhD London; FRAS; Chairman, External System, University of London, 1993–97; *b* London, 18 Nov. 1923; *s* of W. C. Cowan and Minnie Ethel (*née* Farrow); *m* 1st, 1945, Mary Evelyn (marr. diss. 1960), *d* of Otto Vetter, Perth, WA; two *d*; 2nd, 1962, Daphne Eleanor, *d* of Walter Rishworth Whittam, Rangoon. *Educ:* Kilburn Grammar Sch.; Peterhouse, Cambridge. Served Royal Navy, 1941–45. Lecturer in History, Raffles Coll., Singapore, 1947–48, and University of Malaya, 1948–50; School of Oriental and African Studies, University of London: Lectr in the History of South-East Asia, 1950–60; Prof., 1961–80, Prof. of Oriental History, 1980–89; Dir, 1976–89; London University: Pro-Vice-Chancellor, 1985–86; Dep. Vice-Chancellor, 1988–90; Chm. of Convocation, 1990–94. Visiting Prof. of Southeast Asian Hist., Cornell Univ., 1960–61. Chm., Cttee for SE Asian Studies, British Acad., 1990–97. Governor: James Allen's Girls School, 1977–89; Alleyn's Sch., 1980–98; Dulwich Coll., 1980–98; Richmond Coll., 1988–92. Trustee, Dulwich Estate, 1985–98. *Publications:* Nineteenth Century Malaya, 1961; (ed) The Economic Development of South-East Asia, 1964; (ed) The Economic Development of China and Japan, 1964; (with P. L. Burns) Sir Frank Swettenham's Malayan Journals, 1975; (with O. L. Wolters) Southeast Asian History and Historiography, 1976. *Address:* 34 Great Brownings, College Road, SE21 7HP.

COWAN, Brig. Colin Hunter, CBE 1984; Chief Executive, Cumbernauld Development Corporation, 1970–85; *b* 16 Oct. 1920; *s* of late Lt-Col S. Hunter Cowan, DSO and Mrs Jean Hunter Cowan; *m* 1st, 1949, Elizabeth Williamson, MD (*d* 1985); one *s* one *d* (and one *s* decd); 2nd, 1988, Mrs Jen Burnett, *widow* of A. H. Burnett. *Educ:* Wellington Coll.; RMA Woolwich; Trinity Coll., Cambridge (MA). MICE. Comd Engineer Regt, 1960–63; Defence Adviser, UK Mission to the UN, 1964–66; Brigadier Engineer Plans, MoD (Army), 1968–70. DL Dunbartonshire, 1973–88. *Recreations:* music, photography. *Address:* Flat 11, Varrich House, 7 Church Hill, Edinburgh EH10 4BG. *T:* (0131) 447 9768. *Club:* New (Edinburgh).

COWAN, Dr George Osborne, OBE 1986; FRCP, FRCPE; Medical Director, Joint Committee on Higher Medical Training, Royal Colleges of Physicians of UK, since 2001; *b* 5 Sept. 1939; *s* of late John Jardine Cowan and Marion Ramsay Cowan (*née* Corrie); *m* 1981, Beatrice Mary Hill, MA, MPhil, *d* of Leonard Charles Hill, OBE, DSC, FRGS and Joyce (*née* Snelus). *Educ:* Merchiston Castle Sch., Edinburgh; Univ. of St Andrews (MB ChB 1963). MRCPE 1967, FRCPE 1978; DTM&H 1968; MRCP 1967, FRCP 1983. Commissioned RAMC, 1962; served Australia, Hong Kong, Malaysia, Singapore, Nepal, The Gambia, Germany and NI; Consultant Physician in Army Hosps, 1973–96; Prof. of Mil. Medicine, RAMC, 1987–92; Dir of Army Medicine, 1992–93; Comdt and Post-Grad. Dean, Royal Army Med. Coll., 1993–96; QHP 1992–96; retired in rank of Maj.-Gen., 1996. Dean of Postgrad. Medicine, Univ. of London (N Thames) (formerly N Thames (E) Region), 1996–2001. Hon. Associate Physician, Hosp. for Tropical Diseases, 1986–. Cohen Lectr, Univ. of Liverpool, 1991. Examr in Trop. Med. to Univ. of Liverpool and RCP. Pres., RSTM&H, 1995–97 (Vice-Pres., 1993–95). Mitchiner Medal, RCS, 1992. OStJ 1994. *Publications:* (ed) Atlas of Medical Helminthology and Protozoology, 3rd edn, 1991; (with B. J. Heap) Clinical Tropical Medicine, 1993; (with N. R. H. Burgess) Atlas of Medical Entomology, 1993. *Recreations;* golf, music, medical history. *Address:* Joint Committee on Higher Medical Training, 5 St Andrews Place, NW1 4LB. *Clubs:* Army and Navy; Royal & Ancient Golf (St Andrews).

COWAN, James Robertson, CBE 1983 (OBE 1974); CEng, FIMinE; Chairman, NCB Coal Products, 1985–88; *b* 12 Sept. 1919; *s* of John and Jean Cowan; *m* 1945, Harriet Good Forrest; two *d. Educ:* Dalziel High Sch., Motherwell; Glasgow Univ. (BSc 1st Cl. Hons). CEng, FIMinE 1971. National Coal Board: Dir, Scottish Area, 1970–80; Bd Mem., 1977–85; Mem. for Industrial Relns, 1980–85; Dep. Chm., 1982–85. Chm., Scottish Brick Corp., 1980–88 (Dir, 1974–88); Dep. Chm., British Investment Trust (Dir, 1978–). Vis. Prof., Strathclyde Univ., 1978. CIMgt. *Recreation:* golf. *Address:* 11 The Paddock, Gullane, Scotland EH31 2BW. *T:* (01620) 843398. *Club:* Caledonian.

COWAN, Jeremy; *see* Cowan, C. D.

COWAN, Lionel David, (Nick Cowan); personnel management consultant; *b* 18 Dec. 1929; *m* 1953, Pamela Ida, *e d* of Hubert and Winifred Williams, Totton, Hants; one *s* two *d. Educ:* Surbiton County Grammar Sch.; King's Coll., London (BA Hons Spanish, 1995); Univ. of Salamanca (Dip. in Hispanic Studies, 1994). CIPD (CIPM 1979; AMIPM 1965). Served Royal Navy, 1945–61: Fleet Air Arm Aircrew (Lieut), 1953; Sen. Instr, RAN, 1958–60. Training Officer, Shoe and Allied Trades Res. Assoc., 1961–62; Perkins Engines Gp, 1962–72; Dir of Personnel, Philips Electronic and Associated Industries, 1972–78; Gp Personnel Dir, Unigate Ltd, 1978–79; Dir and Sec., Fedn of London Clearing Bank Employers, 1980–87; Personnel Dir, TSB England & Wales, 1987–89. Chm., W Lambeth HA, 1982–86; Member: Employment Appeal Tribunal, 1976–2000; Editorial Panel, Industrial Relns Law Reports, 1977–; Civil Service Arbitration Tribunal, 1979–; Central Arbitration Cttee, 1984–2000; Equal Opportunities Commn, 1988–91; NEDO Enquiry, Industrial Relns Trng for Managers, 1976, Supply and Demand for Skilled Manpower, 1977. Vice-Pres. (Employee Relations), IPM, 1977–79. Director, Oxford Univ. Business Summer Sch., 1980. *Publications:* Personnel Management and Banking, 1984; The Clearing Banks and the Trade Unions, 1984. *Recreations:* things Spanish, music and opera, bridge. *Address:* 15 Somerville Road, Cobham, Surrey KT11 2QT. *T:* (01372) 843441.

COWAN, Gen. Sir Samuel, KCB 1997 CBE 1988 (OBE 1983); Chief of Defence Logistics, Ministry of Defence, since 1998; Aide-de-camp to the Queen, since 2000; *b* 9 Oct. 1941; *s* of late Samuel Cowan and Rachel Cowan; *m* 1971, Anne Gretton; one *s* one *d. Educ:* Lisburn Technical Coll.; Open Univ. (BA 1980). Commissioned Royal Signals, 1963; CO 2 Armd Div. HQ and Signal Regt, 1980–82; Comdr Communications and Comdr 1 Signal Brigade, 1 (BR) Corps, 1985–87; Director of Public Relations (Army), 1987–88; Comdt, RMCS, 1989–91; ACDS OR (Land), 1991–94; Inspector Gen. Training, MoD, 1995–96; QMG, MoD, 1996–98. Col Comdt, Brigade of Gurkhas, 1994–. Hon. FCIPS 2000; Hon. FILT 2000. Hon. DSc Cranfield, 1999. *Recreations:* sport, trekking in Nepal. *Address:* c/o RHQ Royal Signals, Blandford Camp, Dorset DT11 8RH. *T:* (01258) 482082. *Club:* Army and Navy.

COWAN, Dr William Maxwell, FRS 1982; Vice President and Chief Scientific Officer, Howard Hughes Medical Insitute, 1988–2000; *b* 27 Sept. 1931; *s* of Adam Cowan and Jessie Sloan Cowan (*née* Maxwell); *m* 1956, Margaret Sherlock; two *s* one *d. Educ:* Univ. of the Witwatersrand, S Africa (BSc Hons); Hertford Coll., Oxford Univ. (MA, DPhil, BM, BCh; Hon. Fellow, 1997). University Lecturer in Anatomy, Oxford, 1958–66; Fellow of Pembroke Coll., Oxford, 1958–66 (Hon. Fellow, 1986); Associate Prof., Univ. of Wisconsin, 1966–68; Washington University, St Louis: Professor and Head of Dept of Anatomy, Sch. of Medicine, 1968–80; Director, Div. of Biological Sciences, 1975–80; Salk Institute for Biological Studies: non-resident Fellow, 1977–80; Professor, 1980–86; Vice Pres. and Dir, Develt Neurobiol., 1980–86; Provost and Exec. Vice-Chancellor, Washington Univ., St Louis, 1986–87. Mem., Amer. Philosophical Soc., 1987. Fellow, Amer. Acad. of Arts and Scis, 1975; For. Mem., Norwegian Acad. of Scis, 1980; Foreign Associate: US National Academy of Sciences, 1981; Royal Soc. of S Africa, 1986. Hon. DSc: Northwestern, 1994; Emory, 1994. *Publications:* The Use of Axonal Transport for Studies of Neuronal Connectivity, 1975; Aspects of Cellular Neurobiology, 1978; Studies in Developmental Neurobiology, 1981; Molecular and Cellular Approaches to Neural Development, 1998; Annual Reviews of Neuroscience, Vol. 1 1978, Vols 2–22, 1979–2000. *Recreations:* photography, reading, travel. *Address:* 6337 Windermere Circle, North Bethesda, MD 20852, USA. *T:* (301) 4939097.

COWARD, David John, CMG 1965; OBE 1962; Registrar General, Kenya, 1955–82; *b* 21 March 1917; *s* of late Robert J. Coward, Exmouth, Devon; *m* 1954, Joan, *d* of late Reginald Frank, Doncaster; three *d. Educ:* Exmouth Grammar Sch. and Law Society's Sch. of Law. FCIS 1961; ACIArb 1984. Admitted a solicitor, 1938. Joined RN as a rating at outbreak of war, 1939; commissioned, 1941; demobilized as Lieut-Comdr (S) RNVR, 1947. ADC to Governor of Trinidad, 1947. Joined Colonial Legal Service, 1948, Asst Registrar Gen., Kenya; Dep. Registrar Gen., 1952; Registrar Gen., Official Receiver and Public Trustee, 1955–82. Acted as Permanent Sec. for Justice and Constitutional Affairs, 1963–64. Served in Kenya Police Reserve, 1949–63, latterly as Senior Superintendent i/c Nairobi Area. Chm., Working Party on future of Company Secretarial Profession in Kenya; Mem. Accountants' Registration Bd, 1978–82; Trustee, Nat. Museums of Kenya, 1979–82. Chm., Storrington Br., Royal British Legion, 1993–97. Liveryman, 1985 and Hon. Archivist, 1995–, Chartered Secretaries' and Administrators' Co. Silver Medal, Internat. Olympic Cttee, 1981. *Recreations:* golf, genealogy. *Address:* North Perretts, Spinney Lane, West Chiltington, W Sussex RH20 2NX. *T:* (01903) 742521. *Clubs:* Naval; Nairobi and Limuru Country (Kenya).

COWARD, Vice Adm. Sir John (Francis), KCB 1990; DSO 1982; Lieutenant Governor and Commander-in-Chief of Guernsey, Channel Islands, 1994–2000; *b* 11 Oct. 1937; *s* of Reginald John Coward and Isabelle (*née* Foreman); *m* 1963, Diana (*née* Taylor); two *s. Educ:* Downside; RNC, Dartmouth. Served submarines, 1959–76, i/c HMS Oracle and HMS Valiant; Naval Asst to First Sea Lord, 1978–80; i/c HMS Brilliant, 1980–82; S Atlantic, 1982; Dir, Naval Operational Requirements, 1984; Flag Officer: Sea Trng, 1987–88; Flotilla One, 1988–89; Submarines, and Comdr Submarines Eastern Atlantic, 1989–91; Comdt, RCDS, 1992–94. Rear Adm. 1987; Vice Adm. 1989; retd 1994. Bd, N. M. Rothschild (CI) Ltd; Man. Cttee, RNLI. SAR and Younger Brother, Trinity Hse. *Recreations:* sailing, gardening, cricket, golf. *Address:* South Wilcove House, Torpoint, Cornwall PL11 2PE. *T:* (01752) 814331. *Clubs:* Royal Navy of 1919, Royal Navy of 1765 and 1785, Sloane; Royal Naval Sailing Association. *Address:* Royal Yacht Squadron.

COWARD, (John) Stephen; QC 1984; barrister-at-law; a Recorder of the Crown Court, since 1980; *b* 15 Nov. 1937; *s* of Frank and Kathleen Coward; *m* 1967, Ann Lesley Pye; four *d. Educ:* King James Grammar Sch., Almondbury, Huddersfield; University Coll. London (LLB). Lecturer in Law and Constitutional History, University Coll. London and Police Staff Coll., 1962–64; called to the Bar, Inner Temple, 1964; in practice on Midland and Oxford Circuit, 1964–. *Recreation:* trying to grow calceolarias and a decent row of peas. *Address:* The Grange, Scaldwell, Northampton NN6 9JP. *T:* (01604) 880255. *Club:* Scaldwell (Scaldwell, Northants).

COWARD, Richard Edgar; retired; Director for Library Planning, OCLC Inc., 1980–81; *b* 19 April 1927; *s* of Edgar Frank Coward and Jean (*née* McIntyre); *m* 1949, Audrey Scott Lintern; one *s* two *d. Educ:* Richmond Grammar Sch., Surrey. FLA. Dir Gen., Bibliographic Servs Div., British Library, 1975–79. Member: Adv. Cttee on BBC Archives, 1976–79; Library Adv. Council (England), 1976–. *Address:* Allfarthings, West Street, Mayfield, E Sussex TN20 6DT.

COWARD, Stephen; *see* Coward, J. S.

COWBURN, Norman; Chairman, Britannia Building Society, 1987–90 (Managing Director, 1970–84; Deputy Chairman, 1986–87); *b* 5 Jan. 1920; *s* of Harold and Edith Cowburn; *m* 1945, Edna Margaret Heatley; two *s* one *d. Educ:* Queen Elizabeth's Grammar Sch., Blackburn. FCIS, FCIB. Burnley Building Soc., 1936. Served War, 1940–46. Burnley Building Soc., 1946; Leek and Westbourne Building Soc., 1954 (renamed Britannia Building Soc., Dec. 1975). *Recreations:* golf, gardening. *Address:* Greywoods, Birchall, Leek, Staffs. *T:* (01538) 383214.

COWDEROY, Brenda; General Secretary, Girls' Friendly Society, 1978–85; *b* 27 June 1925; *o c* of Frederick and Evelyn Cowderoy (*née* Land). *Educ:* Surbiton High Sch.; St Hugh's Coll., Oxford (MA). Called to Bar, Gray's Inn, 1949. John Lewis Partnership: Asst Legal Adviser, 1954–56; Head of Legal Dept, 1956–70; Nat. Gen. Sec., YWCA, 1971–77. *Recreations:* gardens, golf. *Address:* 26 Rossetti Road, Birchington, Kent CT7 9ER. *Club:* Royal Commonwealth Society.

COWDRAY, 4th Viscount *cr* 1917; **Michael Orlando Weetman Pearson;** Bt 1894; Baron 1910; *b* 17 June 1944; *s* of 3rd Viscount Cowdray and of his 1st wife, Lady Anne Pamela Bridgeman, *d* of 5th Earl of Bradford; *S* father, 1995; one *s* by Barbara Page; *m* 1st, 1977, Ellen (marr. diss. 1984), *d* of Hermann Erhardt; 2nd, 1987, Marina Rose, *d* of John H. Cordle, *qv*, and of Mrs H. J. Ross Skinner; two *s* three *d. Educ:* Gordonstoun. *Recreation:* historic motor racing. *Heir: s* Hon. Peregrine John Dickinson Pearson, *b* 27 Oct. 1994. *Address:* Cowdray Park, Midhurst, West Sussex GU29 0AY. *Club:* White's.

COWDREY, Rev. Herbert Edward John, FBA 1991; Emeritus Fellow, St Edmund Hall, Oxford, since 1994 (Senior Research Fellow in Modern History, 1987–94); *b* 29 Nov. 1926; *s* of Herbert and Winifred Cowdrey; *m* 1959, Judith Watson Davis; one *s* two *d. Educ:* Queen Mary's Sch., Basingstoke; Trinity Coll., Oxford (BA Modern Hist. and Theology, 1951; MA); St Stephen's House, Oxford; DD Oxon 2000. Nat. service, RN, 1945–47. Deacon, 1952; priest, 1953; Tutor and Chaplain, St Stephen's House, Oxford, 1952–56; Fellow and Tutor in Modern History, St Edmund Hall, Oxford, 1956–87. Leverhulme Emeritus Fellow, 1996–98. *Publications:* The Cluniacs and the Gregorian Reform, 1970; The Epistolae vagantes of Pope Gregory VII, 1972; Two Studies in Cluniac History, 1978; The Age of Abbot Desiderius, 1983; Popes, Monks and Crusaders, 1984; Pope Gregory VII, 1998; The Crusades and Latin Monasticism, 1999; Popes and Church Reform in the 11th Century, 2000; articles and reviews in learned jls. *Recreations:* travel, listening to music, gardening. *Address:* 30 Oxford Road, Old Marston, Oxford OX3 0PQ. *T:* (01865) 243360.

COWE, Andrew Inglis, FRTPI; Chief Executive, North Lanarkshire Council, 1995–2000; *b* 21 April 1943; *s* of Andrew Mackay Cowe and Alice (*née* Urquhart); *m* 1964, Mary Geraldine McAleer; three *s* four *d. Educ:* Glasgow Sch. of Art (DipTP). MRTPI 1974, FRTPI 1986. Monklands District Council: Dir, Planning and Develt, 1974–84; Depute Chief Exec. (Computer Services and Strategic Issues), 1984–87; Renfrew District Council: Dir of Planning and Develt, 1987–89; Man. Dir, 1989–95. FIMgt (FBIM 1990). *e-mail:* aic@73ww.freeserve.co.uk.

COWELL, Peter Reginald; His Honour Judge Cowell; a Circuit Judge, since 1996; *b* 9 March 1942; *s* of Reginald Ernest Cowell and Philippa Eleanor Frances Anne Cowell (*née* Prettejohn); *m* 1975, Penelope Jane Bowring; two *s* one *d. Educ:* Bedford Sch.; Gonville and Caius Coll., Cambridge. Called to the Bar, Middle Temple, 1964, Bencher, 1997; Asst Recorder, 1985–92; Recorder, 1992–96. Mem. Senate, Inns of Court, 1975–78. *Recreations:* acting, running, genealogy. *Address:* 3 New Square, Lincoln's Inn, WC2A 3RS. *Club:* Garrick.

COWELL, Prof. Raymond; DL; Vice-Chancellor, The Nottingham Trent University, since 1992 (Director and Chief Executive, Nottingham Polytechnic (formerly Trent Polytechnic Nottingham), 1988–92); *b* 3 Sept. 1937; *s* of Cecil Cowell and Susan Cowell (*née* Green); *m* 1963, Sheila (*née* Bolton); one *s* one *d. Educ:* St Aidan's Grammar Sch., Sunderland; Bristol Univ. (BA, PhD); Cambridge Univ. (PGCE). Head of English, Nottingham Coll. of Educn, 1970–73; Dean of Humanities 1974–81, Dep. Rector 1981–87, Sunderland Polytechnic. Member: CNAA, 1974–77 and 1981–85; Unit for Develt of Adult and Continuing Educn, 1986–90; British Council Cttee for Internat. Co-op. in Higher Educn, 1990–; Bd, Greater Nottingham TEC, 1990–93; Directing Gp, Prog. on Instnl Management in Higher Educn, OECD, 1990–96; Council, NCVQ, 1991–97; Bd, Higher Educn Business Enterprise, 1993–95; Policy Liaison Gp, Open Learning Foundn, 1993–95; Adv. Panel, Nat. Reading Initiative, DNH, 1996–97. Chairman: Staff and Educnl Develt Assoc., 1993–98; CVCP working gp on vocational higher educn, 1993–95; Management Bd and Members Adv. Gp, Univs and Colls Staff Develt Agency (formerly Univs Staff Develt Unit), 1993–95; E Midlands Arts Bd Ltd, 1995– (Mem., Arts Council of England, 1996–98). Board Member:Nottingham City Challenge, 1992–93; Opera North, 2001. FRSA 1996. DL Notts, 1996. *Publications:* Twelve Modern Dramatists, 1967; W. B. Yeats, 1969; (ed) Richard II, 1969; Critics on Yeats, 1971; Critics on Wordsworth, 1973; The Critical Enterprise, 1975; articles and reviews on higher education. *Recreations:* books, music, theatre. *T:* (office) (0115) 941 8418. *Clubs:* Athenæum, Royal Automobile.

COWEN, Brian; Member (FF) of the Dáil (TD), since June 1984; Minister for Foreign Affairs, Republic of Ireland, since 2000; *b* Jan. 1960; *m* 1990, Mary Molloy; two *d. Educ:* Cistercian Coll., Roscrea; University Coll., Dublin. Solicitor. Minister: for Labour, 1991–92; for Transport, Energy and Communications, 1992–94; for Health and Children, 1997–2000. *Recreation:* all sports. *Address:* Department of Foreign Affairs, Iveagh House, 79-80 St Stephen's Green, Dublin 2, Republic of Ireland. *T:* (1) 4784438.

COWEN, Rt Hon. Sir Zelman, AK 1977; GCMG 1977 (CMG 1968); GCVO 1980; Kt 1976; PC 1981; QC; Provost of Oriel College, Oxford, 1982–90; Pro-Vice-Chancellor, University of Oxford, 1988–90; Director, John Fairfax Holdings Ltd, 1992–96 (Chairman, 1992–94); *b* 7 Oct. 1919; *s* of late Bernard and of Sara Cowen; *m* 1945, Anna Wittner; three *s* one *d. Educ:* Scotch Coll., Melbourne; Univ. of Melbourne; New and Oriel Colls, Oxford. BA 1939, LLB 1941, LLM 1942, Melbourne; BCL, MA 1947, DCL 1968, Oxford. Lieut, RANVR, 1941–45. Called to Bar, Gray's Inn, 1947; Hon. Bencher, 1978; called to Vic (Aust.) Bar, 1951, Queensland Bar, 1971; QC 1972. Victorian Rhodes Schol., 1941; Vinerian Schol., Oxford Univ., 1947. Fellow and Tutor, Oriel Coll., Oxford, 1947–50, Hon. Fellow 1977; Prof. of Public Law and Dean of Faculty of Law, Univ. of Melbourne, 1951–66; Dominion Liaison Officer to Colonial Office (UK), 1951–66; Prof. Emer., Univ. of Melbourne, 1967; Vice-Chancellor and Professor, Univ. of New England, Armidale, NSW, 1967–70; Vice-Chancellor, Qld Univ., 1970–77; Governor-General of Australia, 1977–82. Visiting Professor: Univ. of Chicago, 1949; Harvard Law Sch. and Fletcher Sch. of Law and Diplomacy, 1953–54 and 1963–64; Univ. of Utah, 1954; Univ. of Illinois, 1957–58; Washington Univ., St Louis, 1959; Tagore Law Prof., Univ. of Calcutta, 1975; Menzies Schol. in Res., Univ. of Va, 1983; Lee Kuan Yew Dist. Vis. Fellow, Singapore, 1986; Dist. Vis. Prof., Victoria Univ. of Technol., 1994–. Broadcaster on radio and TV on nat. and internat. affairs; Mem. and Chm., Victorian State Adv. Cttee of Australian Broadcasting Commn (at various times during 1950's and 1960's); Mem., Chief Justice's Law Reform Cttee, 1951–66; President: Asthma Foundn of Victoria, 1963–66; Adult Educn Assoc. of Australia, 1968–70; Aust. Inst. of Urban Studies, 1973–77; Mem., Law Reform Commn, Australia, 1976–77; Chairman: Aust. Vice-Chancellors' Cttee, 1977; Aust. Studies Centre Cttee, London, 1982–90; Nat Council, Australian Opera, 1983–95; Press Council, 1983–88; Trustees, Visnews Ltd, 1986–91; Victoria League for Commonwealth Friendship, 1987–89; Australian Nat. Acad. of Music, 1995–2000. Mem., Club of Rome, 1974–77. National President: Order of Australia Assoc. Ltd, 1992–95; Australia–Britain Soc., 1993–95. Academic Governor, Bd of Governors, Hebrew Univ. of Jerusalem, 1969–77, 1982–; Mem., Academic Bd of Govrs, Tel Aviv Univ., 1983–; Weizmann Inst., 1988–. Trustee: Van Leer Inst. of Jerusalem, 1985– (Chm. Trustees, 1988–95); Winston Churchill Meml Trust, 1987–89; Sir Robert Menzies Meml Trust, 1987–; Dir, Sir Robert Menzies Meml Foundn Ltd, 1990–97. For. Hon. Mem., Amer. Acad. of Arts and Scis, 1965. FRSA 1971; Fellow, Australian Nat. Acad. of Music, 2000; Hon. FASSA 1977; Hon. FACE 1978; Hon. FRAIA 1978; Hon. FTS 1979; Hon. FRACP 1979; Hon. FAHA 1980; Hon. FASA 1980; Hon. FRACMA 1981; Hon. FRACOG 1981; Hon. FCA 1981; Hon. FACRM 1982; Hon. Fellow: New Coll. Oxford 1978; University House, ANU, 1978; ANZAAS 1983; TCD, 1985; St John's Coll., Univ. of Qld, 1985; Australian Council of Educnl Admin, 1991. Hon. Law Prof., Griffith Univ., Qld, 1992. Hon. LLD: Hong Kong, 1967; Queensland, 1972; Melbourne, 1973; Western Australia, 1981; Turin, 1981; ANU, 1985; Tasmania, 1990; Victoria Univ. of Technol., 1998; Hon. DLitt: New England, 1979; Sydney, 1980; James Cook Univ. of N Qld, 1982; Oxford, 1983; Hon. DHL: Hebrew Union Coll., Cincinnati, 1980; Redlands Univ., Calif., 1986; DUniv: Newcastle, 1980; Griffith, 1981; Sunshine Coast, 1999; Hon. DPhil: Hebrew Univ. of Jerusalem, 1982; Tel Aviv, 1985. KStJ (A) 1977. Kt Grand Cross, Order of Merit (Italy), 1990. *Publications:* (ed jtly) Dicey's Conflict of Laws, 1949; Australia and the United States: Some Legal Comparisons, 1954; (with P. B. Carter) Essays on the Law of Evidence, 1956; American-Australian Private International Law, 1957; Federal Jurisdiction in Australia, 1959; (with D. M. da Costa) Matrimonial Causes Jurisdiction, 1961; Sir John Latham and other papers, 1965; British Commonwealth of Nations in a Changing World, 1964; Isaac Isaacs, 1967; The Private Man, 1969; Individual Liberty and the Law, 1977; The Virginia Lectures, 1984; Reflections on Medicine, Biotechnology, and the Law, 1986; A Touch of Healing, 1986; articles and chapters in legal works in UK, US, Canada, Germany, Australia. *Recreations:* swimming, music, performing and visual arts. *Address:* Commonwealth Offices, 4 Treasury Place, East Melbourne, Vic 3002, Australia. *Clubs:* Oxford and Cambridge; Queensland (Brisbane); Pioneer (Sydney).

COWEY, Prof. Alan, PhD; FMedSci; FRS 1988; Professor of Physiological Psychology, and Professorial Fellow of Lincoln College, University of Oxford, 1981–Sept. 2002; MRC Research Professor, 1997–Sept. 2002; *b* 28 April 1935; *s* of Harry and Mary Cowey; *m* 1959, Patricia Leckonby; three *d. Educ:* Bede Grammar Sch., Sunderland; Emmanuel Coll., Cambridge (MA, PhD). Rockefeller Foundn Fellow, Center for Brain Research, Univ. of Rochester, New York, 1961–62; Univ. Demonstrator in Experimental Psychology, Cambridge, 1962–67; Fellow and Coll. Tutor, Emmanuel Coll., Cambridge, 1964–67; Vis. Sen. Fulbright Fellow, Psychology Dept, Harvard Univ., 1967; Sen. Res. Officer, Inst. of Experimental Psychology, Univ. of Oxford, 1967–68; Nuffield Sen. Res. Fellow, Lincoln Coll., Oxford, 1968–81; Henry Head Res. Fellow of Royal Society, 1968–73; Reader in Physiolog. Psychology, Oxford Univ., 1973–81; Dir, Oxford Res. Centre in Brain and Behaviour, 1991–96. Member: MRC Neurosciences Grants Cttee, 1974–77 (Chm., 1979–81); MRC Neurosciences Board, 1979–83 (Chm., 1981–83); Mem. Council, MRC, 1981–85. President: European Brain and Behaviour Soc., 1986–88; Experimental Psychology Soc., 1990–92. Founder FMedSci 1998. Hon. DSc Durham, 2000. Spearman Medal, British Psychological Soc., 1967. *Publications:* numerous articles in psychological and physiological jls. *Recreations:* squash, swimming, reading. *Address:* Department of Experimental Psychology, South Parks Road, Oxford OX1 3UD. *T:* (01865) 271353.

COWGILL, Bryan; television producer; *b* 27 May 1927; *m* 1966, Jennifer E. Baker; two *s. Educ:* Clitheroe Grammar School. Marine, subseq. Lieut, 3rd Royal Marine Commando Bde, SE Asia, 1943–47. Copy boy, then reporter, then feature writer with Lancashire Evening Post and Preston Guardian Group, 1942–50; edited local newspaper, Clitheroe, 1950–55; joined BBC TV as Outside Broadcasts prodn asst, 1955; produced Sportsview and Grandstand, 1957–63; Head of BBC Sport, 1963; founder, Match of the Day, 1964, Sportsnight, 1968; coined phrase 'action replay' for slow motion video, first introd. in BBC World Cup coverage, 1966; Head of TV Outside Broadcasts Group, 1972; Controller, BBC1, 1974–77; Dir, News and Current Affairs, BBC, 1977; Man. Dir, Thames Television, 1977–85; Dep. Chm., Mirror Gp Newspapers, 1986–87; Man. Dir, Championship Television, 1989–90. Chairman: Euston Films, 1977–85; Cosgrove Hall Productions, 1977–85; Thames Television Internat., 1982–85; WTN (formerly UPITN), 1983–85; Thames Cable and Satellite Services, 1984–85. FRTS 1984. *Recreation:* golf. *Address:* Nethergill Barn, Bolton-by-Bowland, Clitheroe, Lancs BB7 4NW.

COWIE, Hon. Lord; William Lorn Kerr Cowie; a Senator of the College of Justice in Scotland, 1977–94; a Judge of the Court of Appeal, Botswana, 1995–98; *b* 1 June 1926; *s* of late Charles Rennie Cowie, MBE and Norah Slimmon Kerr; *m* 1958, Camilla Henrietta Grizel Hoyle; twin *s* two *d. Educ:* Fettes Coll.; Clare Coll., Cambridge; Glasgow Univ. Sub-Lieut RNVR, 1944–47; Cambridge, 1947–49; Glasgow Univ., 1949–51; Mem., Faculty of Advocates, 1952; QC (Scotland) 1967. *Address:* 20 Blacket Place, Edinburgh EH9 1RL. *T:* (0131) 667 8238. *Club:* New (Edinburgh).

COWIE, Ian McGregor; Personal Finance Editor, Daily Telegraph, since 1989; *b* 15 Sept. 1958; *s* of Joseph Cowie and Mary (*née* Proctor); *m* 1987, Susan Carole Fleming; one *s. Educ:* William Ellis Sch.; Univ. of York (BA Hons); City Univ. (Postgrad. Dip.). City Reporter, Daily Telegraph, 1986–89. Personal Finance Journalist of the Year: Golden Pen Awards, 1996; Assoc. of British Insurers Awards, 1996, 1997, 1998. *Publications:* Daily Telegraph Guides series on savings and investments, 1996–. *Recreations:* reading, gardening (especially dendrology), sailing. *Address:* 78 North Hill, Highgate, N6 4RL. *T:* (020) 7538 6919. *Clubs:* Little Ship, Wig and Pen.

COWIE, Sir Thomas, (Sir Tom), Kt 1992; OBE 1982; Life President, T. Cowie Ltd, subseq. T. Cowie PLC, now Arriva, motor vehicle distribution and finance, since 1993 (Chairman, 1948–93); *b* 9 Sept. 1922; *s* of late Thomas Stephenson Knowles Cowie and Florence Cowie; *m* 1st, 1948, Lillas Roberts Hunnam (marr. diss.; she *d* 1994); one *s* four *d*; 2nd, 1975, Diana Carole Wentworth Kenyon; three *d* and one step *s* one step *d. Educ:* Bede Grammar School, Sunderland. *Publication:* The Tom Cowie Story, 1988. *Recreations:* game shooting, walking, music. *Address:* Broadwood Hall, Lanchester, Co; Durham DH7 0TD. *T:* (01207) 520464.

COWIE, William Lorn Kerr; *see* Cowie, Hon. Lord.

COWLEY, 7th Earl *cr* 1857; **Garret Graham Wellesley;** Baron Cowley, 1828; Viscount Dangan, 1857; Senior Investment Partner, Thos R. Miller & Son (Bermuda), Isle of Man, 1990–2000; *b* 30 July 1934; 3rd *s* of 4th Earl Cowley (*d* 1962) and of Mary (Elsie May), Countess Cowley; *S* nephew, 1975; *m* Paige Deming, Reno, Nevada; one *s* five *d*, and one *s* one *d* of former marriage. *Educ:* Univ. of S California (BSc Finance 1957); Harvard Univ. (MBA 1962). Investment Research Analyst: Wells Fargo Bank, San Francisco, 1962–64; Dodge & Cox, San Francisco, 1964–66; Asst Head, Investment Research Dept, Wells Fargo Bank, 1966–67; Vice-Pres., Investment Counsel, Thorndike, Doran, Paine & Lewis, Los Angeles, 1967–69; Sen. Vice-Pres., Exec. Cttee Mem., Securities, Real Estate and Company Acquisition Advisor, Shareholders Capital Corp., Los Angeles, 1969–74; Vice-Pres., and Sen. Investment Manager, Trust Dept, Bank of America, San Francisco, 1974–78; Gp Vice-Pres. and Dir, Internat Investment Management Service, Bank of America NT & SA, 1980–85; Director: Bank of America Internat., London, 1978–85; BankAmerica Trust Co. (Hong Kong), 1980–85; Bank of America Banking & Trust Co. (Gibraltar), 1981–85; Bank of America Trust Co. (Jersey), 1982–85; Bank of America Banking & Trust Co. (Nassau), 1982–85; Bank of America Banking & Trust Co. (Cayman), 1982–85; indep. financial advr and co. dir, 1985–90; Director, Duncan Lawrie (IOM) Ltd, 1993–; Scottish Provident Internat. Ltd, 1998–. Served US Army Counter Intelligence Corps, primarily in France, 1957–60. Member: Assoc. of Conservative Peers, 1981–; Parly Arts and Heritage Gp, 1981–99, Defence Gp, 1982–99, and Anglo-Amer. Gp, 1987–99, H of L. *Heir: s* Viscount Dangan, *qv. Clubs:* Brooks's; Pilgrims, Philippics; Harvard (San Francisco).

COWLEY, Prof. Alan Herbert, FRS 1988; Robert A. Welch Professor of Chemistry, University of Texas at Austin, since 1991; *b* 29 Jan. 1934; *s* of late Herbert Cowley and Dora Cowley; *m* 1975, Deborah Elaine Cole; two *s* three *d. Educ:* Univ. of Manchester (BSc, MSc; Dalton Chem. Schol., 1956–58; PhD 1958). Technical Officer, ICI, 1960–61; University of Texas at Austin: Asst Prof. of Chemistry, 1962–67; Associate Prof., 1967–70; Prof., 1970–84; George W. Watt Centennial Prof., 1984–88; Richard J. V. Johnson Regents Prof. of Chemistry, 1989–91; Sir Edward Frankland Prof. of Inorganic Chem., Imperial Coll., London, 1988–89. Deutsche Akademische Austauschdienst Fellow, 1973; Guggenheim Fellow, 1976–77; von Humboldt Sen. Fellow, 1996; Lectures: Jeremy I. Musher Meml, Hebrew Univ., Jerusalem, 1979; Mobay, Univ. of New Hampshire, 1985; Karcher, Univ. of Oklahoma, 1985; Reilly, Univ. of Notre Dame, 1987; Fischel, Vanderbilt Univ., 1991; Baxter, Northern Illinois Univ., 1992; Etter Meml, Univ. of Minnesota, 1995; Vis. Prof., Univ. of Western Ont., 1987. Member: Chem. Soc., subseq. RSC, 1961 (Award for Main-Gp Element Chem., 1980; Centenary Medal and Lectureship, 1986); Amer. Chem. Soc., 1962 (Southwest Regl Award, 1986). Stiefvater Meml Award and Lectureship, Univ. of Nebraska, 1987; Chemical Pioneer Award, Amer. Inst. of Chemists, 1994. Mem. Bd of Trustees, Gordon Res. Confs, 1989–98 (Chm., 1994–95). Member, Editorial Board: Inorganic Chemistry, 1979–83; Chemical Reviews, 1984–88; Polyhedron, 1984–2000; Jl of Amer. Chem. Soc., 1986–91; Jl of Organometallic Chemistry, 1987–; Organometallics, 1988–91; Dalton Trans, 1997–2000; Mem. Bd, Inorganic Syntheses, 1983– (Ed.-in-Chief, vol. 31). *Publications:* over 400 pubns in learned jls. *Recreations:* squash, sailing, music. *Address:* Department of Chemistry and Biochemistry, University of Texas at Austin, Austin, TX 78712, USA. *Clubs:* Athenæum; Headliners (Austin).

COWLEY, Maj.-Gen. John Cain, CB 1971; DL; Paymaster-in-Chief and Inspector of Army Pay Services, Ministry of Defence, 1967–72, retired; with de Zoete and Bevan, Stockbrokers, 1972–79; *b* 17 July 1918; *er s* of late Philip Richard and Eleanor Cowley, Ballaquane, Peel, Isle of Man; *m* 1948, Eileen Rosemary, CBE 1982, *d* of late George Percival Stewart, Aigburth, Liverpool; three *s. Educ:* Douglas School, Isle of Man. War of 1939–45: commissioned, RAPC, 1940; served: Palestine, Western Desert, Italy, France, Belgium, Holland, Germany. Dep. Asst Adj.-Gen., Middle East, 1949–51; GSOI, with Permanent Under Sec., War Office, 1952–54; West African Frontier Force, 1956–59; Dep. Paymaster-in-Chief: War Office, 1960–63; BAOR, 1963–65; Chief Paymaster, Eastern Command, 1965–67. Capt. 1946, Maj. 1953, Lt-Col 1955, Col. 1960, Brig. 1963, Maj.-Gen. 1967; psc, 1948; jssc, 1955; Administrative Staff Coll., 1960. Col Comdt, RAPC, 1974–79. Chm., W Sussex, Duke of Edinburgh's Award Scheme, 1986–95; Vice-Pres., W Sussex Scouts, 1992–. Vice-Pres., St Catherine's Hospice, 1981–; Governor, St Michaels, Burton Park, 1982–88 (Chm. of Govs, 1986–88). High Sheriff, W Sussex, 1984–85; DL W Sussex, 1986. *Recreations:* shooting, fishing, ornithology. *Address:* The Old Post Office, Nuthurst, Horsham, West Sussex RH13 6LH. *T:* (01403) 891266. *Club:* Army and Navy.

COWLEY, Dr John Maxwell, FRS 1979; FAA; Galvin Professor of Physics, Arizona State University, USA, since 1970 (Regents' Professor, 1988–94, Emeritus, since 1994); *b* 18 Feb. 1923; *s* of Alfred E. and Doris R. Cowley; *m* 1951, Roberta J. (*née* Beckett); two *d. Educ:* Univ. of Adelaide (BSc 1942, MSc 1945, DSc 1957); MIT (PhD 1949). FAA 1961. Res. Officer, CSIRO, Australia, 1945–62; Prof. of Physics, Univ. of Melbourne, 1962–70. International Union of Crystallography: Mem. Exec. Cttee, 1963–69; Chm., Commn on Electron Diffraction, 1987–93; Ewald Prize, 1987. *Publications:* Diffraction Physics, 1975; approx. 400 articles in learned jls. *Recreations:* painting, music. *Address:* 2625 E Southern Avenue C-90, Tempe, AZ 85282, USA. *T:* (480) 8313123.

COWLEY, Kenneth Edward, AO 1988; Chief Executive, 1980–97, and Executive Chairman, 1996–97, News Ltd (Chairman, 1992–96); Chairman, Tasman Pacific Airways (trading as Qantas New Zealand, formerly Ansett New Zealand), since 1997; *b* 17 Nov. 1934; *s* of Edward Clegg Cowley and Patricia Bertha (*née* Curran); *m* 1958, Maureen Yvonne Manahan; one *s* one *d*. Sen. Exec., The Australian, 1964–97; Director: News Ltd, 1976–97; Internat. Bd, News Corp., 1980–; Chairman: PMP Communications (formerly Pacific Magazines and Printing) Ltd, 1991–; Ansett Transport Industries, then Ansett Australia Hldgs, 1992–98 (Dir, 1997–2000); R. M. Williams Holdings Ltd, 1994–; Ansett Internat., 1997–2000. Director: Qld Press Ltd, 1987–97; Independent Newspapers Ltd (NZ), 1990–; Commonwealth Bank of Australia, 1997–; Tower Lodge Pty, 1998–. Councillor, Royal Agricl Soc. of NSW, 1979–. Life Gov., Art Gall. of NSW, 1997 (Trustee, 1986–97); Chm., Australian Stockman's Hall of Fame & Outback Heritage Centre, 1976–. *Address:* The News Corporation Ltd, 2 Holt Street, Surry Hills, NSW 2010, Australia. *T:* (2) 2883209. *Clubs:* Union, Royal Sydney Yacht Squadron (Sydney).

COWLEY, Prof. Roger Arthur, FRS 1978; FRSE 1972; Dr Lee's Professor of Experimental Philosophy, and Fellow of Wadham College, University of Oxford, since 1988; *b* 24 Feb. 1939; *s* of Cecil A. Cowley and Mildred S. Cowley; *m* 1964, Sheila J. Wells; one *s* one *d*. *Educ:* Brentwood Sch., Essex; Cambridge Univ. (MA, PhD). Fellow, Trinity Hall, Cambridge, 1962–64; Research Officer, Atomic Energy of Canada Ltd, 1964–70; Prof. of Physics, Edinburgh Univ., 1970–88; Chm. of Physics, Univ. of Oxford, 1993–96, 1999–. Max Born Medal, 1973; Holweck Medal and Prize, 1990. *Publications:* Structural Phase Transitions, 1981; over 350 articles. *Address:* Oxford Physics Clarendon Laboratory, Parks Road, Oxford OX1 3PU. *T:* (01865) 272224; Tredinnock, Harcourt Hill, Oxford OX2 9AS. *T:* (01865) 247570.

COWLEY, Prof. Stanley William Herbert, PhD; CPhys; FRAS; FBIS; Professor of Solar–Planetary (formerly Space Plasma) Physics, and Head, Radio and Space Plasma Physics Group, Department of Physics and Astronomy, University of Leicester, since 1996; *b* 11 April 1947; *s* of late Herbert William Leslie Cowley and of Annie Jenny Cowley (*née* Clark); *m* 1970, Lynn Doreen Moore; two *s* one *d*. *Educ:* Imperial Coll., Univ. of London (BSc, ARCS, PhD, DIC). FBIS 1975; MInstP 1975; FRAS 1986; CPhys 1989. Imperial College, University of London: SERC Advanced Fellow, 1977–82; Lectr, 1982–85; Reader, 1985–88; Prof. of Physics, 1988–95; Head, Space and Atmospheric Physics Gp, Blackett Lab., 1990–95; PPARC Sen. Fellow, 2001–. Mem., PPARC, 1994–96. Fellow, Amer. Geophysical Union, 1995. Chapman Medal, RAS, 1991. *Publications:* contrib. numerous papers in solar system plasma physics in learned jls. *Recreation:* walking the dog. *Address:* Department of Physics and Astronomy, University of Leicester, University Road, Leicester LE1 7RH. *T:* (0116) 223 1331, (0116) 252 3563.

COWLING, Gareth; *see* Cowling, T. G.

COWLING, (James) Roy; HM Diplomatic Service, retired, Consul-General, Barcelona, 1996–99; *b* 9 Feb. 1940; *m* 1st, 1962, Monique Lassimonillas; 2nd, 1983, Janet Bell Barnshaw. Second Sec., Karachi, 1964; FCO, 1968; First Sec., Buenos Aires, 1972, Copenhagen, 1975; FCO, 1977; on loan to ODA, 1980; First Sec., Nairobi, 1983; First Sec., subseq. Counsellor, FCO, 1987; High Comr, Lesotho, 1992–96. *Address:* c/o Foreign and Commonwealth Office, SW1A 2AH.

COWLING, Maurice John; Fellow of Peterhouse, Cambridge, 1963–93, now Emeritus, *b* 6 Sept. 1926; *s* of Reginald Frederick Cowling and May (*née* Roberts). *Educ:* Battersea Grammar Sch.; Jesus Coll., Cambridge (Historical Tripos, Pt I 1948, Pt II 1949). Served British and Indian Armies (Captain Queen's Royal Regt), 1944–48. Fellow, Jesus Coll., Cambridge, 1950–53; Res. Fellow, Univ. of Reading, 1953–54; FO, 1954; Mem. Editorial Staff: The Times, 1955–56; Daily Express, 1957–58; Fellow, Jesus Coll., Cambridge, 1961–63; Lectr in History, then Reader in Modern English History, Univ. of Cambridge, 1961–88. Olin Vis. Prof. of Religion, Columbia Univ., 1989; Vis. Prof., Adelphi Univ., 1993–97. Literary Editor, The Spectator, 1970–71. Dir, Politeia, 1998–. Contested (C) Bassetlaw, 1959; Mem., Cambs and Isle of Ely CC, 1966–70. *Publications:* The Nature and Limits of Political Science, 1963; Mill and Liberalism, 1963, 2nd edn 1989; Disraeli, Gladstone and Revolution, 1967; The Impact of Labour, 1971; The Impact of Hitler, 1975; (ed) Conservative Essays, 1978; Religion and Public Doctrine in Modern England, Vol. i 1980, Vol. ii 1985, Vol. iii 2001; A Conservative Future, 1997. *Address:* Peterhouse, Cambridge CB2 1RD.

COWLING, Peter John; Director, National Maritime Museum, Cornwall, since 1998; *b* 11 Nov. 1944; *s* of Harold Cowling and Irene (*née* Phillips); *m* 1979, Sara Fox; two *d*. *Educ:* Bletchley Grammar Sch.; Britannia Royal Naval Coll. Joined RN 1963; commanded: HMS Naiad, 1979; HMS York and 3rd Destroyer Sqdn, 1988; Sen. Naval Officer, Middle East, 1991; Dir, Naval Ops, MoD, 1992; retired 1994. Dir, RSA, 1994–96; Head of Corporate Relns, Proshare, 1997–98. Younger Brother, Trinity House, 1981–. Queen's Gold Medal, 1967. *Recreations:* sailing, tennis, gardening. *Address:* King's Hayes House, Batcombe, Somerset BA4 6HF.

COWLING, Roy; *see* Cowling, J. R.

COWLING, (Thomas) Gareth; District Judge (Magistrates' Courts) (formerly Stipendiary Magistrate), Hampshire, since 1989; a Recorder, since 1998; *b* 12 Nov. 1944; *s* of late Clifford Cowling and of Beryl Elizabeth Cowling (*née* Thomas); *m* 1970, Jill Ann Stephens; one *s* one *d*. *Educ:* Eastbourne Coll.; College of Law. Articled to Clifford Cowling, of Clifford Cowling & Co., Hampshire, 1964; admitted Solicitor of Supreme Court, 1969; Solicitor, Solicitor's Dept, New Scotland Yard, 1969–72; called to Bar, Middle Temple, 1972; private practice at Bar, London and Winchester, Western Circuit, 1972–88; Metropolitan Stipendiary Magistrate, 1988–89. *Recreations:* family life, eating and drinking with friends, trying to play golf.

COWPER-COLES, Sherard Louis, CMG 1997; LVO 1991; HM Diplomatic Service; Ambassador to Israel, since 2001; *b* 8 Jan. 1955; *s* of Sherard Hamilton Cowper-Coles and Dorothy (*née* Short); *m* 1982, Bridget Mary Elliott; four *s* one *d*. *Educ:* Freston Lodge Sch.; New Beacon Sch.; Tonbridge Sch.; Hertford Coll., Oxford (MA). Joined HM Diplomatic Service, 1977: Third, later Second, Sec., Cairo, 1980–83; First Sec., Planning Staff, FCO, 1983–85; Private Sec. to Perm. Under-Sec. of State, 1985–87; First Sec., Washington, 1987–91; Asst, Security Policy Dept, FCO, 1991–93; Res. Associate, IISS, 1993–94; Head, Hong Kong Dept, FCO, 1994–97; Counsellor (Political) Paris, 1997–99; Prin. Private Sec. to Sec. of State for For. and Commonwealth Affairs, 1999–2001. *Publication:* contrib. Survival (IISS jl). *Address:* c/o Foreign and Commonwealth Office, King Charles Street, SW1A 2AH.

COWPERTHWAITE, David Jarvis; Under-Secretary, Scottish Home and Health Department, 1974–81, retired; *b* 14 Sept. 1921; *s* of J. J. Cowperthwaite and Mrs J. W. B. Cowperthwaite (*née* Jarvis); *m* 1944, Patricia Stockdale (*d* 1993); two *d*. *Educ:* Edinburgh Academy; Exeter Coll., Oxford (MA). Nigerian Admin. Service, 1942–48; joined Home Civil Service (Scottish Home Dept), 1948. *Address:* 69 Northumberland Street, Edinburgh EH3 6JG. *T:* (0131) 557 0215.

See also Sir J. J. Cowperthwaite.

COWPERTHWAITE, Sir John James, KBE 1968 (OBE 1960); CMG 1964; International Adviser to Jardine Fleming & Co. Ltd, Hong Kong, 1972–81; Financial Secretary, Hong Kong, 1961–71; *b* 25 April 1915; *s* of late John James Cowperthwaite and Jessie Wemyss Barron Jarvis Cowperthwaite; *m* 1941, Sheila Mary, *d* of Alexander Thomson, Aberdeen; one *s*. *Educ:* Merchiston Castle Sch.; St Andrews Univ; Christ's Coll., Cambridge. Entered Colonial Administrative Service, Hong Kong, 1941; seconded to Sierra Leone, 1942–45. *Address:* 25 South Street, St Andrews, Fife KY16 9QS. *T:* (01334) 474759. *Clubs:* Hong Kong Jockey, Hong Kong Golf; Royal and Ancient.

COWTAN, Maj.-Gen. Frank Willoughby John, CBE 1970 (MBE 1947); MC 1942 and Bar, 1945; *b* 10 Feb. 1920; *s* of late Air Vice-Marshal F. C. Cowtan, CB, CBE, KHS and late Mrs N. A. Cowtan (*née* Kennedy); *m* 1949, Rose Isabel Cope; one *s* one *d*. *Educ:* Wellington Coll.; RMA Woolwich. 2nd Lieut Royal Engineers, 1939; served War of 1939–45, BEF, N Africa, Italy, NW Europe (Captain); Palestine, Kenya, Middle East, 1945–50 (Major); psc 1951; Middle East, UK, BAOR, 1952–58; Liaison Officer to US Corps of Engrs, USA, 1958–60 (Bt Lt-Col); CO 131 Parachute Engr Regt, 1960–62; CO Victory Coll., RMA Sandhurst, 1962–65 (Lt-Col); Comd 11 Engr Bde, BAOR, 1965–67 (Brig.); ndc (Canada) 1967–68; Dir of Quartering (Army), 1968–70; Dep. QMG, MoD(AD), 1970–71; Comdt, RMCS, 1971–75, retired. Hon. Col, 131 Indep. Commando Sqn, RE, 1975–80; Col Comdt RE, 1977–82. Dep. Dir, CLA Game Fair, 1978–86. *Recreations:* shooting, travel, languages. *Address:* Rectory Cottage, Coleshill, Swindon, SN6 7PR.

COX, family name of **Baroness Cox**.

COX, Baroness *cr* 1982 (Life Peer), of Queensbury in Greater London; **Caroline Anne Cox;** a Deputy Speaker, House of Lords, since 1986; Co-Director, Education Research Trust, since 1980; *b* 6 July 1937; *d* of Robert John McNeill Love, MS, FRCS and Dorothy Ida Borland; *m* 1959, Dr Murray Cox, FRCPsych (*d* 1997); two *s* one *d*. *Educ:* Channing School. BSc (Sociology, 1st Cl. Hons) 1967, MSc (Economics) 1969, London Univ.; FRCN 1985. SRN, London Hosp., 1958; Staff Nurse, Edgware Gen. Hosp., 1960; Research Associate, Univ. of Newcastle upon Tyne, 1967–68; Department of Sociology, Polytechnic of North London: Lecturer, Senior Lectr, Principal Lectr, 1969–74; Head of Department, 1974–77; Dir, Nursing Educn Res. Unit, Chelsea Coll., London Univ., 1977–84. Dir, Centre for Policy Studies, 1983–85. A Baroness in Waiting, April–Aug. 1985. Chancellor, Bournemouth Univ., 1992–. Internat. Pres., Christian Solidarity Worldwide; Pres., Inst. of Admin. Mgt; Vice Pres., RCN, 1990–. Trustee: Medical Emergency Relief Internat.; Nuffield Prov. Hosps Trust; Hon. Prof. and Trustee, Siberian Med. Univ., Tomsk, Russia; Pres., Tushinskaya Children's Hosp. Trust; Patron, Medical Aid for Poland Fund. Hon. FRCS 1996. Hon. PhD Polish Univ. in London, 1988; Hon. LLD CNAA; DUniv: Surrey; UCE, 1998; Hon. DH Utah; Hon. Dr Yerevan; Hon. DSS QUB, 1996; Hon. DSc: City, 1999; Wolverhampton, 1999. Commander's Cross, Order of Merit (Poland), 1990. *Publications:* (ed jtly) A Sociology of Medical Practice, 1975; (jtly) Rape of Reason: The Corruption of the Polytechnic of North London, 1975; (jtly) The Right to Learn, 1982; Sociology: A Guide for Nurses, Midwives and Health Visitors, 1983; (jtly) The Insolence of Office, 1989; (jtly) Choosing a State School: how to find the best education for your child, 1989; Trajectories of Despair: misdiagnosis and maltreatment of Soviet orphans, 1991; (with John Eibner) Ethnic Cleansing in Progress: war in Nagorno Karabakh, 1993; (jtly) Made to Care: the case for residential and village communities for people with a mental handicap, 1995; (contrib.) Remorse and Reparation, ed Murray Cox, 1998. *Recreations:* campanology, squash, hill walking. *Address:* House of Lords, SW1A 0PW. *T:* (office) (020) 8204 7336, *Fax:* (020) 8204 5661. *Club:* Royal Over-Seas League.

COX, Sir Alan (George), Kt 1994; CBE 1988; FCA; FCMA; Chief Executive, ASW Holdings PLC, 1987–96; *b* 23 Aug. 1936; *s* of late George Henry Cox and Florence Ivy Cox; *m* 1994, Rosamund Shelley. *Educ:* Oldbury Grammar Sch. FCA 1959; ACMA 1961. Chm. and Chief Exec., GKN Rolled and Bright Steel Ltd, 1978–80; Corporate Management Dir, GKN, PLC, 1980–81; Chm. and Chief Exec., Allied Steel and Wire Ltd, 1981–87; Director: Morgan Crucible Co. plc, 1995–; Meggitt plc, 1996–; Chm., Wales Millennium Centre Ltd, 1996–2001. Member: Bd, Cardiff Bay Develt Corp., 1987–2000; School Teachers Review Body, 1991–95; Financial Reporting Council, 1996–99. *Recreations:* cookery, opera, walking. *Address:* PO Box 27, Chepstow, Monmouthshire NP16 6EY. *Club:* Cardiff and County.

COX, Alan Seaforth; Clerk to the Grocers' Company, 1965–81; Secretary, Grocers' Trust Company Ltd, 1968–81; *b* 15 Oct. 1915; *m* 1st, 1944, Jean Heriot-Maitland (marr. diss. 1952); one *s*; 2nd, 1954, Mary Thornton (*d* 1990); three *s* one *d*. Served War: London Scottish and Gold Coast Regt, 1939–45; Staff Officer, WO, 1945–46. Farming and banking, Argentine (Patagonia), 1947–52; joined Grocers' Co., 1954. Sec., Governing Body of Oundle Sch., 1965–81. Hon. Mem. Ct, Grocers' Co., 1981–. *Recreations:* bridge, cribbage, dining and wining. *Address:* The Mount, Winchelsea, East Sussex TN36 4EG. *T:* (01797) 226543.

COX, Alister Stransom, MA; Headmaster, Royal Grammar School, Newcastle upon Tyne, 1972–94; *b* 21 May 1934; *s* of Rev. Roland L. Cox and F. Ruth Cox; *m* 1960, Janet (*née* Williams); one *s* two *d*. *Educ:* Kingswood School, Bath; New College, Oxford (Scholar). Hon. Mods (1st Class); Lit. Hum. BA 1957, MA 1961. Sixth Form Master, Clifton Coll., 1957–63; Head of Classics, Wellington Coll., 1963–69; Dep. Head, Arnold Sch., Blackpool, 1969–72. Vis. Lectr in Greek, Bristol Univ., 1968. Founder Mem., Sinfonia Chorus, Northern Sinfonia of England, 1973–94 (Mem., Management Cttee, 1980–85). FRSA 1982. *Publications:* Lucretius on Matter and Man, 1967; Didactic Poetry, in Greek and Latin Literature (ed Higginbotham), 1969; articles in Greece and Rome, Times Educnl Supp. and educnl jls. *Recreations:* music, especially singing; French life and politics; touring lecturer Alliance Française. *Address:* 3 Lower Gale, Ambleside, Cumbria LA22 0BD. *T:* (015394) 32634; 36 rue Jeanne d'Arc, Montsoreau 49730, France.

COX, Anthony; *see* Cox, J. A.

COX, Anthony Robert, PhD, CEng; adviser on science and technology, since 1998; Director, Asia Pacific Technology Network; *b* 30 Nov. 1938; *s* of Robert George Cox and Gladys Cox; *m* 1963, Constance Jean Hammond; one *s* two *d*. *Educ:* Brockley County School; Imperial College, London. BScEng (Metallurgy). ARSM, MIM. RARDE, 1960–69; Exchange Scientist, US Naval Research Lab., Washington DC, 1969–71; Dep. Materials Supt, RARDE, 1971–75; Asst Dir, Armour and Materials, Military Vehicle Engineering Estab., 1975–80; MoD Central Staffs Defence Science, 1980–83; Counsellor, Science and Technol., Washington, 1983–87; Superintendent, Radiation Sci. and Acoustics, NPL, 1988–92; Counsellor, Sci. and Technol., Tokyo, 1993–98. *Publications:* papers on refractory metals, structure and strengthening mechanism on high strength steel, fractography, explosive effects, archaeological artefacts corrosion, composites, space, robotics, science policy, metrology. *Recreations:* sailing, foreign travel, gardening, industrial archaeology.

COX, Prof. Archibald; Carl M. Loeb University Professor, Harvard University, 1976–84, now Emeritus; *b* 17 May 1912; *s* of Archibald Cox and Frances Bruen (*née* Perkins); *m* 1937, Phyllis Ames; one *s* two *d. Educ:* St Paul's Sch., Concord; Harvard Univ. AB 1934, LLB 1937. Admitted to Mass Bar, 1937. Gen. practice with Ropes, Gray, Best, Coolidge & Rugg, 1938–41; Office of Solicitor-Gen., US Dept of Justice, 1941–43; Assoc. Solicitor, Dept of Labor, 1943–45; Lectr on Law, Harvard, 1945–46, Prof. of Law, 1946–61; Solicitor-Gen., US Dept of Justice, 1961–65; Williston Prof. of Law, Harvard Law Sch., 1965–76. Pitt Prof., Univ. of Cambridge, 1974–75; Vis. Prof. of Law, Boston Univ., 1984–97. Co-Chm., Constrn Industry Stablizn Commn, 1951–52; Chm., Wage Stablzn Bd, 1952; Mem. Bd Overseers, Harvard, 1962–65. Special Watergate Prosecutor, 1973. Hon. LLD: Loyola, 1964; Cincinnati, 1967; Rutgers, Amherst, Denver, 1974; Harvard, 1975; Michigan, 1976; Wheaton, 1977; Northeastern, 1978; Clark, 1980; Notre Dame, 1983; Hon. LHD: Hahnemann Med. Coll., 1980; Univ. of Mass, 1981; Illinois, 1985. *Publications:* Cases on Labor Law, 9th edn 1981; (jtly) Law and National Labor Policy, 1960; Civil Rights, the Constitution and the Courts, 1967; The Warren Court, 1968; The Role of the Supreme Court in American Government, 1976; Freedom of Expression, 1981; The Court and the Constitution, 1987; miscellaneous articles. *Address:* 78 Condon Point, Brooksville, MA 04617, USA; (office) Harvard Law School, Cambridge, MA 02138, USA. *T:* (617) 4953133. *Clubs:* Somerset (Boston, Mass); Century Association (New York).

See also A. Cox, Jr.

COX, Archibald, Jr; Chairman, Sextant Group Inc., since 1993; Vice-Chairman and President, Magnequench International Inc., since 1995; *b* 13 July 1940; *s* of Archibald Cox, *qv*; *m* 1977, Jean Inge; two *s* one *d. Educ:* Harvard Coll. (ABEcon 1962); Harvard Business Sch. (MBA 1964). Associate 1964–70, Vice Pres. 1971–72, Man. Dir, 1973–88, Morgan Stanley & Co. Incorp.; Man. Dir and Head of London Office, Morgan Stanley Internat., 1977–88; Pres. and Chief Exec. Officer, First Boston Corp., 1990–93. Director: Diamar Interactive Corp., 1995–; Hutchinson Technol. Inc., 1996–; Harris Chemical Gp, 1997–98. Member: Securities and Investments Board, 1986–88; Bd, Securities Industry Assoc., 1990–93. Mem., Adv. Council for Cell Biology and Pathology, Harvard Med. Sch. *Recreations:* cycling, sailing. *Address:* 630 Fifth Avenue, Suite 3240, New York, NY 10111, USA. *Clubs:* Royal Automobile; Links (New York); New York Yacht.

COX, Arthur George Ernest S.; *see* Stewart Cox.

COX, Brian; *see* Cox, Charles B.

COX, Brian Denis; actor, director, teacher and writer; *b* 1 June 1946; *s* of Charles Mcardle Campbell Cox and Mary Ann Gillerline (*née* Mccann); *m* 1968, Caroline Burt (marr. diss. 1987); one *s* one *d. Educ:* LAMDA. *Stage appearances:* début, Dundee Rep., 1961; Royal Lyceum, Edinburgh, 1965–66; Birmingham Rep., 1966–68; As You Like It, Birmingham and Vaudeville (London début), 1967; title rôle, Peer Gynt, Birmingham, 1967; When We Dead Awaken, Edinburgh Fest., 1968; In Celebration, Royal Court, 1969; The Wild Duck, Edinburgh Festival, 1969; The Big Romance, Royal Court, 1970; Don't Start Without Me, Garrick, 1971; Mirandolina, Brighton, 1971; Getting On, Queen's, 1971; The Creditors, Open Space, 1972; Hedda Gabler, Royal Court, 1972; Playhouse, Nottingham: Love's Labour's Lost, title rôle, Brand, What The Butler Saw, The Three Musketeers, 1972; Cromwell, Royal Court, 1973; Royal Exchange, Manchester: Arms and the Man, 1974; The Cocktail Party, 1975; Pilgrims Progress, Prospect Th., 1975; Emigres, Nat. Theatre Co., Young Vic, 1976; Olivier Theatre: Tamburlaine The Great, 1976; Julius Caesar, 1977; The Changeling, Riverside Studios, 1978; National Theatre: title rôle, Herod, The Putney Debates, 1978; On Top, Royal Court, 1979; Macbeth, Cambridge Th. and tour of India, 1980; Summer Party, Crucible, 1980; Have You Anything to Declare?, Manchester then Round House, 1981; title role, Danton's Death, Nat. Theatre Co., Olivier, 1982; Strange Interlude, Duke of York, 1984 (Drama Mag. Best Actor Award, 1985), Nederlander, NY, 1985; Rat in the Skull, Royal Court, 1984 (Drama Mag. and Olivier Best Actor Awards, 1985) and NY, 1985; Fashion, The Danton Affair, Misalliance, Penny for a Song, 1986, The Taming of the Shrew, Titus Andronicus (title rôle), 1987, The Three Sisters, 1989, RSC, and Titus Andronicus on tour, Madrid, Paris, Copenhagen, 1988 (Olivier Award, Best Actor in a Revival, and Drama Mag. Best Actor Award for RSC 1988 season); Frankie and Johnny in the Clare-de-Lune, Comedy, 1989; Richard III, and title rôle, King Lear, National and world tour, 1990–91; The Master Builder, Edinburgh, 1993, Riverside, 1994; St Nicholas, Bush, 1997, NY, 1998 (Lucille Lortel Award, 1998); Skylight, LA, 1997; Dublin Carol, Old Vic, and Royal Court, 2000; *films:* Nicholas and Alexandra, 1971; In Celebration, 1975; Manhunter, Shoot for the Sun, 1986; Hidden Agenda, 1990; Braveheart, The Cutter, 1994; Rob Roy, 1995; Chain Reaction, The Glimmer Man, Long Kiss Goodnight, 1996; Desperate Measures, Food for Ravens, Poodle Spring, 1997; The Boxer, The Corruptor, Mad About Mamba, The Minus Man, Rushmore, 1998; The Biographer, 2000; Saltwater, LIE, 2001; Morality Play; Affairs of the Necklace; *TV appearances:* Churchill's People: The Wallace, 1972; The Master of Ballantrae, 1975; Henry II, in The Devil's Crown, 1978; Thérèse Raquin, 1979; Dalhousie's Luck, Bothwell, 1980; Bach, 1981; Pope John Paul II, 1984; Florence Nightingale, 1985; Beryl Markham: a shadow in the sun, 1988; Secret Weapon, 1990; Acting in Tragedy (BBC Masterclass), 1990; The Lost Language of Cranes, The Cloning of Joanna May, 1992; The Big Battalions, 1992; The Negotiator, 1994; Witness for Hitler, 1995; Blow Your Mind See A Play, 1995; Nuremberg, 2001; *directed:* Edinburgh Festival: The Man with a Flower in his Mouth, The Stronger, 1973; Orange Tree, Richmond: I Love My Love, 1982; Mrs Warren's Profession, 1989; The Crucible, Moscow Art Theatre, London and Edinburgh, 1988–89; The Philanderer, Hampstead Th. Club, 1991 (world première of complete version). Internat. Theatre Inst. Award, 1990. *Publications:* Salem to Moscow: an actor's Odyssey, 1991; The Lear Diaries, 1992. *Recreations:* keeping fit, tango. *Address:* c/o Conway van Gelder, 18–21 Jermyn Street, SW1Y 6HP. *T:* (020) 7287 0077. *Clubs:* Savile, Garrick.

COX, Brian (Robert) Escott; QC 1974; a Recorder of the Crown Court, 1972–98; *b* 30 Sept. 1932; *yr s* of late George Robert Escott Cox, solicitor, and Doris Cox; *m* 1st, 1956; one *s* two *d*; 2nd, 1969, Noelle Gilormini; one *s* one *d. Educ:* Rugby Sch.; Oriel Coll., Oxford (BA Jurisprudence). Called to the Bar, Lincoln's Inn, 1954, Bencher, 1985; Midland and Oxford Circuit; a Dep. High Court Judge, 1980–98. *Recreations:* listening to and playing jazz. *Address:* 36 Bedford Row, WC1R 4JH. *T:* (020) 7421 8000.

COX, Prof. (Charles) Brian, CBE 1990; John Edward Taylor Professor of English Literature, University of Manchester, 1976–93, now Emeritus; *b* 5 Sept. 1928; *s* of late Hedley E. Cox and Rose Thompson; *m* 1954, Jean Willmer; one *s* two *d. Educ:* Wintringham Sec. Sch.; Pembroke Coll., Cambridge (MA, MLitt). Lectr, Univ. of Hull, 1954–66; Manchester University: Prof. of English Lit., 1966–76; Dean, Faculty of Arts, 1984–86; Pro-Vice-Chancellor, 1987–91. Vis. Associate Prof., Univ. of Calif, Berkeley, 1964–65; Brown Fellow, Univ. of the South, Sewanee, Tennessee, 1980; Lord Northcliffe Lectr, UCL, 1991; Visiting Professor: KCL, 1994–96; Sheffield Hallam Univ., 1994–98. Pres., Nat. Council for Educnl Standards, 1984–89 (Chm., 1979–84); Mem., Kingman Cttee, 1987–88; Chm., Nat. Curriculum English Working Gp, 1988–89. Chairman: NW Arts Bd, 1994–2000; Arvon Foundn, 1994–97; Mem., Arts Council of England, 1996–98. Co-editor: Critical Qly, 1959–; Black Papers on Education, 1969–77. FRSL 1993. Hon. Fellow, Westminster Coll., Oxford, 1994. Hon. DLitt De Montfort, 1999. *Publications:* The Free Spirit, 1963; (ed with A. E. Dyson) Modern Poetry, 1963; (ed with A. E. Dyson) Practical Criticism of Poetry, 1965; Joseph Conrad: the modern imagination, 1974; Every Common Sight (poems), 1981; Two-Headed Monster (poems), 1985; Cox on Cox: an English curriculum for the 1990s, 1991; The Great Betrayal (autobiog.), 1992; Collected Poems, 1993; The Battle for the English Curriculum, 1995; (ed) African Writers, 1996; (ed) Literacy is not Enough, 1998; Emeritus (poems), 2001. *Recreations:* Manchester United, walking. *Address:* 20 Park Gates Drive, Cheadle Hulme, Stockport SK8 7DF. *T:* (0161) 485 2162. *Club:* Lansdowne.

COX, Prof. Christopher Barry, PhD, DSc; Professor, Division of Life Sciences, and Assistant Principal, King's College London, 1989–96; *b* 29 July 1931; *s* of Herbert Ernest Cox and May Cox; *m* 1st, 1961, Sheila (*née* Morgan) (*d* 1996); two *s* one *d*; 2nd, 1998, Marie-Hélène (*née* Forges). *Educ:* St Paul's Sch., Kensington; Balliol Coll., Oxford (MA); St John's Coll., Cambridge (PhD); DSc London. Asst Lectr in Zoology, King's Coll. London, 1956–59; Harkness Fellow of Commonwealth Fund, at Mus. of Comparative Zoology, Harvard, 1959–60; King's College London: Lectr in Zoology, 1956–66; Sen. Lectr, 1966–69; Reader, 1970–76; Prof., 1976–96; Head: Dept of Zoology, 1982–85; Dept of Biology, 1985–88; Fulbright Schol., Stanford Univ., Calif, 1988–89. Mem. Council, Palaeontological Assoc., 1967–69, 1974; Vice-Pres., 1969–81. Editor, Palaeontology, 1975–79. Palaeontological collecting expedns to Central Africa, 1963; Argentina, 1967; N Brasil, 1972; Qld, Aust., 1978. *Publications:* Prehistoric Animals, 1969; (with P. D. Moore) Biogeography—an ecological and evolutionary approach, 1973, 6th edn 2000; (jtly) The Prehistoric World, 1975; (jtly) Illustrated Encyclopedia of Dinosaurs and Prehistoric Animals, 1988; (jtly) Atlas of The Living World, 1989; research papers on vertebrate palaeontology and historical biogeography, in Phil. Trans. Royal Soc., Proc. Zool. Soc., Nature, Bull. Brit. Mus. (Nat. Hist.), Jl Biogeog., etc. *Recreations:* theatre, tennis, local history (Chm., Domestic Bldgs Res. Gp). *Address:* Forge Cottage, Blacksmith Close, Ashtead, Surrey KT21 2BD. *T:* (01372) 273167.

COX, Prof. Sir David (Roxbee), Kt 1985; PhD; FRS 1973; Warden of Nuffield College, Oxford, 1988–94, Hon. Fellow, 1994; *b* 15 July 1924; *s* of S. R. Cox, Handsworth, Birmingham; *m* 1948, Joyce (*née* Drummond), Keighley, Yorks; three *s* one *d. Educ:* Handsworth Grammar Sch., Birmingham; St John's Coll., Cambridge (MA). PhD Leeds, 1949. Posts at Royal Aircraft Establishment, 1944–46; Wool Industries Research Assoc., 1946–50; Statistical Laboratory, Cambridge, 1950–55; Visiting Prof., University of N Carolina, 1955–56; Reader in Statistics, 1956–60, Professor of Statistics, 1961–66, Birkbeck Coll. (Fellow, 2001); Prof. of Statistics, 1966–88 and Head of Dept of Maths, 1970–74, Imperial Coll. of Sci. and Technology. SERC Sen. Res. Fellow, 1983–88. President: Bernoulli Soc., 1979–81; Royal Statistical Soc., 1980–82; Pres., ISI, 1995–97. Foreign Member: Royal Danish Acad. of Scis and Letters, 1983; Indian Acad. of Scis, 1997; For. Hon. Mem., Amer. Acad. of Arts and Sciences, 1974; For. Associate, Nat. Acad. of Scis, USA, 1988. FIC 1994. Hon. FIA 1991; Hon. FBA 1997. Hon. DSc: Reading, 1982; Bradford, 1982; Helsinki, 1986; Heriot-Watt, 1987; Limburg's Univ. Centrum, 1988; Queen's Univ., Kingston, Ont, 1989; Waterloo, 1991; Neuchâtel, 1992; Padua, 1994; Minnesota, 1994; Dundee, 1994; Toronto, 1994; Abertay Dundee, 1995; Tech. Univ. of Crete, 1996; Athens Univ. of Economics, 1998; Bordeaux II, 1999; Harvard, 1999; Elche, 1999; Rio de Janeiro, 2000. Weldon Meml Prize, Univ. of Oxford, 1984; Kettering Medal, General Motors Cancer Foundn, 1990; (jtly) Max Planck Forschungspreis, 1993. Editor of Biometrika, 1966–91. *Publications:* Statistical Methods in the Textile Industry, 1949 (jt author); Planning of Experiments, 1958; (jtly) Queues, 1961; Renewal Theory, 1962; (jtly) Theory of Stochastic Processes, 1965; (jtly) Statistical Analysis of Series of Events, 1966; Analysis of Binary Data, 1970, 2nd edn 1989; (jtly) Theoretical Statistics, 1974; (jtly) Problems and Solutions in Theoretical Statistics, 1978; (jtly) Point Processes, 1980; (jtly) Applied Statistics, 1981; (jtly) Analysis of Survival Data, 1984; (jtly) Asymptotic Methods, 1989; (jtly) Inference and Asymptotics, 1994; (jtly) Multivariate Dependencies, 1996; (jtly) Theory of Design of Experiments, 2000; papers in Jl of Royal Statistical Society, Biometrika, etc. *Address:* Nuffield College, Oxford OX1 1NF.

COX, Dennis George; Under-Secretary (Industrial Relations), Department of Employment, 1971–74; a Deputy Chairman, Central Arbitration Committee, 1977–84; *b* 23 Feb. 1914; *s* of George and Amelia Cox; *m* 1938, Victoria Barraclough (*d* 2000); one *s* (and one *s* decd). *Educ:* University College Sch.; Queens' Coll., Cambridge. Royal Navy, 1942–45; served with Netherlands and Norwegian navies, Lieut RNVR. Entered Min. of Labour, 1936; Asst Sec. 1966; Regional Controller, SW Region. *Recreations:* gardening, fishing. *Address:* 106 Court Road, Lewes, East Sussex BN7 2RZ. *T:* (01273) 472818. *Club:* Army and Navy.

COX, Sir Geoffrey (Sandford), CNZM 2000; Kt 1966; CBE 1959 (MBE 1945); *b* 7 April 1910; *s* of Sandford Cox, Wellington, NZ, and Mary Cox (*née* MacGregor); *m* 1935, Cecily Barbara Talbot Turner (*d* 1993); two *s* two *d. Educ:* Southland High Sch., New Zealand; Otago Univ., New Zealand (MA); Rhodes Scholar, 1932–35; Oriel Coll., Oxford (BA). Reporter, Foreign and War Corresp. News Chronicle, 1935–37, Daily Express, 1937–40. Enlisted New Zealand Army, 1940; commissioned, Dec. 1940; served in 2 New Zealand Div., Greece, Crete, Libya, Italy; Major, Chief Intelligence Officer, Gen. Freyberg's staff (despatches twice). First Sec. and Chargé d'Affaires, NZ Legation, Washington, 1943; NZ Rep., first UNRRA Conf., 1943; Political Corresp., News Chronicle, 1945; Asst Editor, News Chronicle 1954. Regular Contributor, BBC radio and TV, 1945–56; Editor and Chief Exec., Independent Television News, 1956–68; founded News at Ten, 1967; Dep. Chm., Yorkshire Television, 1968–71; Chm., Tyne Tees Television, 1971–74; Chm., LBC Radio, 1978–81; independent Dir, The Observer, 1981–89. FRTS (Silver Medal, 1963; Gold Medal, 1978); Fellow, British Kinematograph and TV Soc. TV Producers' Guild Award Winner, 1962. Hon. DLitt Otago, 1999. *Publications:* Defence of Madrid, 1937; The Red Army Moves, 1941; The Road to Trieste, 1946; The Race for Trieste, 1977; See It Happen, 1983; A Tale of Two Battles, 1987; Countdown to War, 1988; Pioneering Television News, 1995; Eyewitness, 1999. *Recreations:* fishing, tracing Roman roads. *Club:* Garrick.

COX, George Edwin; Director General, Institute of Directors, since 1999; *b* 28 May 1940; *s* of George Herbert Cox and Beatrice Mary Cox; *m* 1st, 1963, Gillian Mary Mannings (marr. diss. 1996); two *s*; 2nd, 1996, Lorna Janet Peach; two *d. Educ:* Quintin Sch.; Queen Mary Coll., Univ. of London (BScAeEng). FIMC. Engineer, BAC, 1962–64; Molins Machine Co.: Systems Designer, 1964–67; Manufacturing Manager, 1967–69; Management Consultant, Urwick Orr & Partners, 1969–73; UK Dir, Diebold Gp, 1973–77; Man. Dir, Butler Cox, 1977–92; Chm., 1992–94, Chief Exec., 1993–94, P-E International; Chief Exec., 1995–96, Chm., 1996–99, Unisys Ltd; Man. Dir, Unisys Inf. Services, Europe, 1996–99; Mem. Bd, Shorts, 2000–. Chm., Merlin (Med.

Emergency Relief Internat.), 2001–. Mem. Bd, LIFFE, 1995. Mem. Bd of Inland Revenue, 1996–99. Vis. Prof., Royal Holloway, Univ. of London, 1995–. Pres., Management Consultancies Assoc., 1991. Mem. Adv. Bd, Warwick Business Sch., 2001–. Mem., Information Technologists Co., 1992–; Master, Guild of Mgt Consultants, 1997–98. CIMgt. *Publications:* contribs to various jls. *Recreations:* theatre, rowing (Chief Coach, Univ. of London Boat Club, 1976–78, Chm. of Selectors, GB Men's Rowing, 1978–80), gliding, history of aviation. *Address:* Institute of Directors, 116 Pall Mall, SW1Y 5ED. *T:* (020) 7451 3116. *Club:* Leander.

COX, Gilbert Kirkwood, MBE; JP; Lord-Lieutenant of Lanarkshire, since 2000; *b* 24 Aug. 1935; *s* of William and Mary Bryce Cox; *m* 1959, Marjory Moir Ross Taylor; two *s* one *d*. *Educ:* Airdrie Acad.; Glasgow Royal Tech. Coll. NCB, 1953–63; David A. McPhail & Sons Ltd, 1963–71; Gen. Manager, Scotland, Associated Perforators & Weavers Ltd, 1971–97. Dir, Airdrie Savings Bank, 1985– (Chm., 1995–97). Chm. Bd of Mgt, Coatbridge Coll., 1996–2000. *Recreations:* golf, photography. *Address:* Bedford House, Commonhead Street, Airdrie, N Lanarkshire ML6 6NS. *T:* (01236) 763331.

COX, Graham Loudon; QC (Scot.) 1993; Sheriff Principal of South Strathclyde, Dumfries and Galloway, 1993–2000; *b* 22 Dec. 1933; *s* of Rev. Thomas Loudon Cox and Leonainie Violet Rose (*née* Watson); *m* 1st, 1959, June Mary Constance Gunner (marr. diss. 1975); three *d*; 2nd, 1977, Jean Nelson. *Educ:* Hamilton Acad.; Grove Acad.; Univ. of Edinburgh (MA 1954; LLB 1956). Commnd RASC, 1957; transferred to Directorate Army Legal Services, 1958–61 (Temp. Major). Called to Scottish Bar, 1962; Advocate Depute, 1967; Sheriff, Tayside Central and Fife, at Dundee, 1968–93. Mem., Scottish Criminal Justice Forum, 1996–2000; Hon. Vice Pres., Scottish Assoc. for Study of Delinquency, 1996–; Mem. Council, Commonwealth Magistrates and Judges Assoc., 1991–94, 1997–2000. Comr, Northern Lighthouses, 1993–2000 (Vice-Chm., 1997–2000). *Recreations:* golf, gardening, travelling. *Address:* Crail House, Crail, Fife KY10 3SJ. *T:* (01333) 450270, *Fax:* (01333) 450183. *Clubs:* Western (Glasgow); Royal & Ancient Golf (St Andrews).

COX, Major Horace Brimson T.; *see* Trevor Cox.

COX, His Honour (James) Anthony; a Circuit Judge, 1976–94; *b* 21 April 1924; *s* of Herbert Sidney Cox and Gwendoline Margaret Cox; *m* 1950, Doris Margaret Fretwell; three *s* one *d*. *Educ:* Cotham Sch., Bristol; Bristol Univ. LLB Hons 1948. War Service, Royal Marines, 1943–46. Called to Bar, Gray's Inn, 1949; a Recorder of the Crown Court, 1972–76. Pres., Anchor Soc., 1985–86. *Recreations:* watching cricket, the arts. *Address:* Haldonhay, Lower Court Road, Newton Ferrers, Plymouth, Devon PL8 1DE. *Clubs:* MCC; Royal Western Yacht (Plymouth); Yealm Yacht.

COX, John; freelance director of plays, opera, revue and musicals in Britain and abroad; *b* 12 March 1935; *s* of Leonard John Cox and Ethel M. (*née* McGill). *Educ:* Queen Elizabeth's Hosp., Bristol; St Edmund Hall, Oxford (MA; Hon. Fellow, 1991). Vis. Fellow, European Humanities Res. Centre, Oxford, 1995. Freelance dir, 1959–; Dir of Prodn, Glyndebourne Festival Opera, 1971–81; Gen. Adminr, 1981–85, Artistic Dir, 1985–86, Scottish Opera; Prodn Dir, Royal Opera House, Covent Gdn, 1988–94. Productions include: *Glyndebourne:* Richard Strauss cycle, Rake's Progress, The Magic Flute, La Cenerentola; *ENO:* Così Fan Tutte, Patience; *Scottish Opera:* L'Egisto, Manon Lescaut, Marriage of Figaro, Lulu, Don Giovanni; *Royal Opera:* Manon, Die Fledermaus, Guillaume Tell, Capriccio, Die Meistersinger, Il Viaggio a Reims, Die Frau ohne Schatten, Tosca, Eugene Onegin; *Australian Opera:* Barber of Seville, Albert Herring, Patience, Masked Ball, Capriccio (Olympic Arts Fest.); *Santa Fe Opera:* L'Egisto, La Calisto, Marriage of Figaro, Arabella; *Monte Carlo Opera:* Rake's Progress, Hamlet, Eugene Onegin, Picture of Dorian Gray (world première), Vanessa; *Salzburg Opera:* Il Re Pastore, Ariadne auf Naxos, Rake's Progress, Der Freischutz, La Traviata; *Madrid:* Eugene Onegin, La Cenerentola, Rake's Progress, Capriccio; *Drottingholm:* Zemire et Azor, Tom Jones; *San Francisco:* Arabella, Magic Flute, Rake's Progress, Capriccio, Don Carlos; *Metropolitan, NY:* Barber of Seville, Magic Flute, Capriccio, Werther; *La Scala, Milan:* Rake's Progress, Magic Flute; *Amsterdam:* Der Rosenkavalier, Tannhaüser, Intermezzo; *Chicago Lyric Opera:* Capriccio, Ariadne auf Naxos; *Copenhagen:* Hamlet, Falstaff; also opera in Brussels, Stockholm, Cologne, Frankfurt, Munich, Florence, Spoleto, Nice, Strasbourg, Toulouse, Lisbon, Vienna, Leeds, Dallas, San Diego, Los Angeles, Washington, Houston, Wexford, Melbourne, Vancouver, etc. *Address:* 7 West Grove, SE10 8QT. *T:* (020) 8692 2450.

COX, John Colin Leslie, CBE 1994; Chief Executive, Pensions, Protection and Investment Accreditation Board, since 2000; Chairman, London Europe Gateway Ltd, since 1996; *b* 23 Oct. 1933; *s* of late Dr Leslie Reginald Cox, OBE, FRS, and Hilda Cecilia Cox; *m* 1983, Avril Joyce Butt; one *s* one *d*. *Educ:* University College Sch., London; Queens' Coll., Cambridge (BA). National Service, 2nd Lieut, 2nd 10th Princess Mary's Own Gurkha Rifles, 1956–58 (GSM Malaya 1958). Joined Shell Group, 1958: Executive positions in Shell Ghana, 1962–65, and in Shell Gp in London, 1966–77; Shell Chemicals UK: Personnel Dir, 1978–81; Dir, Business Develt, and chm. of subsid. cos, 1981–86; Dir Gen., CIA, 1987–95; Chief Exec., London First Centre, 1995–96. Member: Armed Forces Pay Review Body, 1993–99; Steering Bd, Lab. of the Govt Chemist, 1992–96; Adv. Cttee, European Movement, 1994–; Bd, UK CEED, 1996– (Chm., 1999–); Bd, PHLS, 1997–; Standards Bd, Edexcel Foundn, 1997–; Envmt Cttee, Knightsbridge Assoc., 1997–; Vice Chm., Defence and Security Forum, 1996–. Mem. (C), Westminster CC, 1998– (Vice Chm., PFI Cttee, 1998–, Planning and Licensing Cttee, 2000–). Chm., Governing Body, Westminster Adult Educn Service, 1998–; Gov., City of Westminster Coll., 2000–. Mem., Caux Round Table, 1991–. FRSA 1989. *Recreations:* sailing, antiques, country pursuits, photography. *Address:* London Europe Gateway Ltd, 138 Brompton Road, SW3 1HY. *T:* (020) 7581 9510. *Clubs:* Army and Navy, Hurlingham; Leander (Henley on Thames); Royal Solent Yacht (IoW).

COX, Vice-Adm. Sir John (Michael Holland), KCB 1982; Director, Sound Alive, 1988–97; Flag Officer Naval Air Command, 1982–83; *b* Peking, China, 27 Oct. 1928; *s* of late Thomas Cox, MBE, and of Daisy Anne Cox; *m* 1962, Anne Garden Farquharson Seth-Smith; one *s* one *d*. *Educ:* Hilton Coll., Natal, SA. Joined BRNC, 1946; ADC to C-in-C Allied Forces, N Europe, 1952–53; ADC to Governor of Victoria, 1955; commanded HM Ships: Dilston, 1957 (despatches); Stubbington, 1958; sc Camberley, 1960; Cadet Trng Officer, BRNC Dartmouth, 1962; CSO, London Div., RNR, 1963; commanded HMS: Surprise, 1964; Naiad, 1965; Comdr, Sea Trng, Staff of Flag Officer Sea Trng, 1967; Naval Attaché, Bonn, 1969; comd HMS Norfolk, 1972; Dir, Naval Ops and Trade, 1973–75; Comdr, Standing Naval Force Atlantic, 1976–77; COS to C-in-C, Naval Home Command, 1977–79; Flag Officer Third Flotilla and Comdr Anti-Submarine Group Two, 1979–82. Dir, Spastics Soc., 1984–88. *Recreation:* gardening. *Club:* Lansdowne.

COX, Ven. John Stuart; Archdeacon of Sudbury, since 1995; *b* 13 Sept. 1940; *s* of Arthur F. W. Cox and Clarice M. Cox; *m* Mary Diane Williams; one *s* one *d*. *Educ:* Fitzwilliam House, Cambridge (MA); Linacre Coll., and Wycliffe Hall, Oxford (BA); Birmingham Univ. (DPS). Ordained deacon, 1968, priest, 1969; Assistant Curate: St Mary's, Prescot, 1968–71; St George, Newtown, Birmingham, 1971–73; Rector, St George, Newtown, Birmingham, 1973–78; Selection Sec., ACCM, 1978–83 (Sen. Selection Sec., 1979–83); Canon Residentiary, Southwark Cathedral, 1983–91; Diocesan Dir of Ordinands and Dir of Post-Ordination Training, Southwark, 1983–91; Vicar, Holy Trinity Church in the Ecumenical Parish of Roehampton, 1991–95. *Publications:* (contrib.) Religion and Medicine, Vol. 1, 1970; (contrib.) Say One for Me, 1992. *Recreations:* music, reading, theatre, golf, wine-making. *Address:* 84 Southgate Street, Bury St Edmunds, Suffolk IP33 2BJ.

COX, Jonson; Chief Operating Officer, Railtrack plc, since 2000; *b* 11 Oct. 1956; *s* of Peter Cox and Bobbie Cox (*née* Sutton); partner, Barbara Kennedy Wight; one *s* two *d*. *Educ:* King Edward VI Sch., Totnes; Clare Coll., Cambridge (BA Hons Econs). Various posts with companies of Royal Dutch/Shell Gp, 1979–92; Chm. and Man. Dir, Yorkshire Envmtl, 1993–96; Managing Director: and Mem. Bd, Kelda Gp plc, 1994–2000; Yorkshire Water, 1996–2000. *Recreations:* ski-ing, outdoor activities. *Address:* Railtrack plc, Railtrack House, Euston Square, NW1 2EE. *T:* (020) 7557 8000/8331.

COX, Josephine; writer; *b* 15 July 1940; *d* of Bernard and Mary Jane Brindle; *m* Kenneth George Cox; two *s*. Formerly: clerk, Milton Keynes Develt Council; secretarial and teaching posts, incl. Lectr in Sociol. and History, Bletchley Coll., Milton Keynes; Partner, family landscaping co. *Publications:* as Josephine Cox: Her Father's Sins, 1986; Let Loose the Tigers; Angels Cry Sometimes; Take This Woman, 1989; Whistledown Woman, 1990; Outcast, 1991; Alley Urchin, 1991; Vagabonds, Jessica's Girl, 1993; Nobody's Darling, 1993; More Than Riches, 1994; Living a Lie, 1995; Miss You Forever; Time For Us; Don't Cry Alone, 1992; Born to Serve, 1994; Little Badness, 1995; The Devil You Know, 1996; Cradle of Thorns, 1997; Love Me or Leave Me, 1998; Tomorrow the World, 1998; Gilded Cage, 1999; Somewhere, Someday, 1999; Rainbow Days, 2000; Looking Back; Let It Shine, 2001; as Jane Brindle: Scarlet: No Mercy; The Tallow Image, 1994; No Heaven, No Hell, 1995; The Seeker, 1997; Hiding Game, 1998. *Address:* c/o Sheil Land Associates, 43 Doughty Street, WC1N 2LF.

COX, Laura Mary, (Mrs David Cox); QC 1994; a Recorder, since 1995; a Judge, Employment Appeal Tribunal, since 2000; *b* 8 Nov. 1951; *d* of John Arthur Bryant and Mary Eileen Bryant (*née* Clarke); *m* 1970, David Cox; three *s*. *Educ:* Queen Mary Coll., Univ. of London (LLB 1973; LLM 1975). Called to the Bar, Inner Temple, 1975, Bencher, 1999; in practice at the Bar, 1976–; Head of Chambers, 1996–. Chm., Equal Opportunities Cttee, Bar Council, 2000–; Mem. Council, Justice, 1997–. UK Rep., ILO Cttee of Experts, 1998–. Hon. Life Pres., Univ. of Essex Law Soc. *Recreations:* music, theatre, cinema, watching football, cooking, novels, walking, arguing with sons! *Address:* Cloisters, 1 Pump Court, Temple, EC4Y 7AA. *T:* (020) 7827 4000.

COX, Nigel John; HM Diplomatic Service; Minister, Peking, since 2000; *b* 23 April 1954; *s* of late Basil Cox, DFC and of Anne (*née* Webber); *m* 1992, Olivia Jane, *d* of Lt-Col Sir Julian Paget, *qv*. *Educ:* The High Sch., Dublin; Trinity Coll., Dublin (BA, LLB); Ecole Nat. d'Administration, Paris. FCO 1975; Chinese lang trng, Cambridge and Hong Kong, 1976–78; Second Sec., Peking, 1978–81; Second, later First, Sec., FCO, 1981–84; Asst Political Advr, Hong Kong, 1984; First Sec., Paris, 1985–90; Assistant Head: Western European Dept, FCO, 1990–91; Hong Kong Dept, FCO, 1991–92; Counsellor, Peking, 1992–96; Hd of SE Asian Dept, FCO, 1996–99. *Recreations:* sinological claptrap, irony. *Address:* c/o Foreign and Commonwealth Office, SW1A 2AH. *Club:* Travellers.

COX, Norman Ernest, CMG 1973; MA; HM Diplomatic Service, retired; *b* 28 Aug. 1921; *s* of late Ernest William Cox and late Daisy Beatrice (*née* Edmonds); *m* 1945, Mary Margarita (*née* Cruz); one *s* one *d*. *Educ:* Lycée Français de Madrid; King's Coll., London (BA (Hons) 1956); Inst. of Latin Amer. Studies, London Univ. (MA 1973). Tax Officer, Inland Revenue, 1938–41; Army, Intell. Corps, 1941–45: Gibraltar, 1942–45; Attaché, Madrid, 1945–47; FO, 1947–50; 2nd Sec., Sofia, 1950–52; 2nd Sec., Montevideo, 1952–54; FO, 1954–57; Dep. Regional Information Officer for SE Asia, Singapore, 1957–60; FO, 1960–62: Laos Conf., Geneva, 1961; Sec. to UK Conf. Delegn to ECSC, Luxemburg, 1962–63; 1st Sec. (Commercial), Madrid, 1963–66; Counsellor (Information), Mexico, Regional Information Officer for Central American Republics, PRO to Duke of Edinburgh for 1968 Olympics, 1966–68; Counsellor (Commercial), Moscow, 1969–72; Diplomatic Service Inspector, 1973–74; Ambassador to: Ecuador, 1974–77; Mexico, 1977–81. Res. student, LSE, 1981–84. Vice-Pres., British Mexican Soc., 1985– (Chm., 1982–84). Hon. Mem. Bd, Anglo-Mexican Cultural Inst., Mexico, 1996. Order of Aztec Eagle (Mexico), 1994. *Publication:* (jtly) Politics in Mexico, 1985. *Recreations:* archaeology, history, genealogy, linguistics, comparative religion.

COX, Oliver Jasper, CBE 1982; RIBA; Partner, Jean & Oliver Cox, since 1989; *b* 20 April 1920; *s* of William Edward and Elsie Gertrude Cox; *m* 1953, Jean; one *s* two *d*. *Educ:* Mill Hill Sch.; Architectural Association School of Architecture (AADip Hons). DistTP. Architects Dept, Herts CC, New Schools Division, 1948–49; Architects Dept, LCC Housing Division, 1950–59; Dep. Chief Architect, and Leader, Research and Development Gp, Min. of Housing and Local Govt, 1960–64; Partner, Shankland/Cox Partnership, 1965–85. *Publications:* Upgrading and Renewing the Historic City of Port Royal, Jamaica, 1985; (jtly) Lauderdale Revealed, 1993; The Naval Hospitals of Port Royal, Jamaica, 1996; Oracabessa: the town, the people and the waterfront development, 1997. *Recreations:* painting, drawing and screen printing. *Address:* 22 Grove Terrace, NW5 1PL. *T:* (020) 7485 6929.

See also P. W. Cox.

COX, Patricia Ann, CB 1989; Under Secretary, Scottish Home and Health Department, 1985–88, retired; *b* 25 May 1931; *d* of Sir (Ernest) Gordon Cox, KBE, TD, FRS. *Educ:* Leeds Girls' High Sch.; Newnham Coll., Cambridge (MA). Asst Principal, Dept of Health for Scotland, 1953; Principal: SHHD, 1959–62; HM Treasury, 1962–65; SHHD, 1965–67; Asst Sec., 1967–76, Under Sec., 1976–85, Scottish Educn Dept. *Publication:* Sandal Ash (novel for children), 1950. *Recreations:* archaeology, needlework, botanical painting. *Address:* 2 Gloucester Place, Edinburgh EH3 6EF. *T:* (0131) 225 6370.

COX, Patricia Anne, (Mrs Roger Cox); *see* Edwards, P. A.

COX, Paul William; freelance artist and illustrator, since 1982; *b* 31 July 1957; *s* of Oliver Jasper Cox, *qv*; *m* 1987, Julia Claire Nichol; one *s* one *d*. *Educ:* Port Regis and Stanbridge Earls School; Camberwell Sch. of Art and Crafts (BA Hons); Royal Coll. of Art (MA). Contributor to: The Times, Daily Telegraph, Independent, Express, Spectator, Punch, Sunday Times, Observer, Guardian, New Yorker, Vanity Fair, Town and Country, Wall St Journal;Traditional Home, Chatelaine; founder contributor to Blueprint, 1984; designed PO stamps for 600th Lord Mayor's Show, 1989; exhibns of watercolour drawings: Workshop Gallery, 1984; Illustrators' Gallery, 1985; Chris Beetles Gallery, 1989, 1993, 2001. Vis Lectr in Illustration, Camberwell Sch. of Art and Crafts, 1982–90. *Publications:* illustrated books: Experiences of an Irish RM, 1984; The Common Years, 1984; A Varied Life, 1984; The Outing, 1985; The Character of Cricket, 1986; Romantic Gardens, 1988; Evacuee, 1988; Rebuilding the Globe, 1989; Dear Boy, 1989; Leave it to

Psmith, 1989; Three Men in a Boat, 1989; The Cricket Match, 1991; Honourable Estates, 1992; The Darling Buds of May, 1992; The Russian Tea Room, 1993; The Wind in the Willows, 1993; Rumpole, 1994; Look out London, 1995; Jeeves & Wooster, 1996; The Plumbs of P. G. Wodehouse, 1997; Three Men on the Bummel, 1998; Tinkerbill, 1999; Jeeves & Wooster II, 2000. *Address:* Twytten House, Wilmington, E Sussex BN26 5SN. *T:* (01323) 871264, *Fax:* (01323) 871265. *Club:* Chelsea Arts.

COX, Pauline Victoria, MA; Head Teacher, The Tiffin Girls' School, since 1994; *b* 9 Oct. 1948; *d* of Harold and Lily Greenwood; *m* 1970, Stephen James Cox, *qv*; one *s* one *d. Educ:* High Storrs Girls' Grammar Sch., Sheffield; Birmingham Univ. (BA Hons Geography 1970); Inst. of Education, London Univ. (PGCE 1973); W London Inst. of HE (RSA Dip. TEFL 1981); MA London 1983. Asst Editor, Polish News Bulletin of British and American Embassies, Warsaw, 1971–72; Teacher, subseq. also Head of Geography, Wandsworth Boys' Sch., 1973–75; Teacher of Geography, Lady Eleanor Holles Sch., Hampton, 1976–77; Lectr in ESL, Univ. of Legon, Accra, Ghana, 1978–80; Teacher of Geography: Tiffin Girls' Sch., 1981–83; Teddington Sch., 1983–84; Head of Geography, Waldegrave Sch. for Girls, Twickenham, 1984–87; Dep. Head, Cranford Community Sch., Hounslow, 1987–94. FRGS 1988. *Recreations:* reading crime fiction, listening to the Archers, watching sport, organising family! *Address:* The Tiffin Girls' School, Richmond Road, Kingston upon Thames KT2 5PL. *T:* (020) 8546 0773.

COX, Peter Arthur, BSc Eng; FREng, FICE; FCGI; FIC; consulting engineer; *b* 30 Oct. 1922; *m* 1944, Rosemary; one *s* two *d. Educ:* Westcliff High Sch., Essex; City and Guilds Coll., Imperial Coll., London (FIC 1991). Commissioned, Royal Engineers, 1942 (despatches). Lewis & Duvivier, 1947; Rendel Palmer & Tritton, 1952; Peter Lind & Co. Ltd, 1954; Sir Bruce White Wolfe Barry & Partners, 1955; Rendel Palmer & Tritton Ltd, Consulting Engineers, 1956, Partner, 1966, Sen. Partner, 1978–85, Chm., 1985–88. Chm., Ceemaid Ltd, 1984–85. Member: Dover Harbour Bd, 1983–89; Nat. Maritime Inst. Ltd, 1983–85; British Maritime Technology Ltd, 1986–93. Institution of Civil Engineers: Pres., 1980–81; Mem., Infrastructure Policy (formerly Planning) Gp, 1981–92 (Chm. 1981–84); Chm., Legal Affairs Cttee, 1988–92; Member: Smeatonian Soc. of Civil Engrs, 1980–; British Acad. of Experts, 1991–96. Mem., Commonwealth Scholarship Commn, 1982–88. Pres., Old Centralians, 1989–90. Governor, Westminster Coll., Wandsworth, 1990–92. *Publications:* papers to Instn of Civil Engrs on Leith Harbour and Belfast Dry Dock; many papers to conferences. *Recreations:* walking, gardening. *Address:* 18 Ranmore Avenue, Croydon, Surrey CR0 5QA. *Club:* East India.

COX, Peter Frederick; Head of Information & Archives (formerly of Libraries), BBC, 1993–98; *b* 1 Dec. 1945; *s* of George William and Edna May Cox; *m* 1968, Gillian Mary Stevens; two *d. Educ:* Bedford Sch.; University Coll. London (BA); Univ. of Herts (MSc 1999). ALA 1968; MIInfSc. Chartered Librarian, 1968; Sen. Asst County Librarian, Herts, 1979–88; City of Westminster: City Librarian, 1989–92; Asst Dir (Leisure and Libraries), 1992–93. Member: Library and Information Services Council for England and Wales, 1992–95; Cttee on Public Library Objectives, 1992; Adv. Cttee, Nat. Sound Archive, 1996–98. FRSA 1991. JP Stevenage, 1980–88. *Publications:* professional articles and symposia papers. *Recreations:* sailing, painting. *Address:* 94 Downlands, Stevenage, Herts SG2 7BJ. *T:* (01438) 237845.

COX, Philip (Joseph), DSC 1943; QC 1967; Honorary Recorder of Northampton, since 1972; *b* 28 Sept. 1922; *s* of Joseph Parriss Cox, Rugby; *m* 1951, Margaret Jocelyn Cox, *d* of R. C. H. Cox, Purley, Surrey; one *s* one *d. Educ:* Rugby Sch; Queens' Coll., Cambridge. RNVR, 1942–46 (Lieut). Called to Bar, Gray's Inn, 1949; Bencher, 1972 (Vice-Treas., 1990; Treas., 1991); practised at Bar, Birmingham, 1949–67. Dep. Chm., Northants QS, 1963–71; Dep. Chm., Warwicks QS, 1966–71; a Recorder, 1972–94; Leader, Midland and Oxford Circuit, 1975–79. Member: County Court Rules Cttee, 1962–68; Senate, Inns of Court and Bar, 1974–80. Legal Assessor to Disciplinary Cttee, RCVS, 1969–2000; Chm., Cttee of Enquiry into London Smallpox Outbreak, 1973; Chairman: Code of Practice Appeal Bd, Prescription Medicines Code of Practice Authy, 1993–2000; Code of Practice Cttee, Assoc. of British Pharmaceut. Industries, 1978–92; Code of Practice Cttee, Internat. Fedn of Pharmaceut. Manufacturers Assocs, 1985–2000; Gen. Optical Council, 1985–88; Code of Practice Cttee, Nat. Office of Animal Health, 1987–92. Pres., Mental Health Review Tribunals, 1984–95. Pres., Edgbaston Liberal Assoc., 1974–86. *Recreations:* sailing, golf, gardening, reading, woodwork. *Address:* 9 Sir Harry's Road, Edgbaston, Birmingham B15 2UY. *T:* (0121) 440 0278. *Clubs:* Naval; Royal Cruising, Bar Yacht.

COX, Richard Charles, MBE 1961; HM Diplomatic Service, retired; *b* 27 May 1920; *s* of Charles Victor Cox and Marjorie Eleanor Cox (*née* Fox); *m* 1941, Constance (*née* Goddard); one *s. Educ:* Gravesend Grammar Sch.; BA Open Univ., 1985. Served War of 1939–45, RAF; released with rank of Sqdn Leader, 1946. Entered Colonial Office, 1937; Dominions Office, 1946; High Commn, Colombo, 1949–52; Second Sec., Calcutta, 1953–54; CRO, 1954–56; First Sec., Bombay, 1956–59; CRO, 1960–63; First Sec., Valletta, 1964–68; FCO, 1968–72; NI Office, 1972–74; Dep. Sec. Gen., Cento, 1975–77. *Recreations:* swimming, gardening, watching Rugby football. *Address:* 31 Lotfield Street, Orwell, near Royston, Herts SG8 5QT. *T:* (01223) 207969.

COX, Roger Charles; His Honour Judge Roger Cox; a Circuit Judge, since 1988; *b* 18 April 1941; *s* of late Reginald William Cox and Hilda Cox; *m* 1970, Patricia Anne Edwards, *qv. Educ:* Cheltenham Grammar Sch.; Birmingham Univ. (LLB, LLM). Called to the Bar, Gray's Inn, 1965. Asst Lectr, Faculty of Law, Bristol Univ., 1964–66; Lord Justice Holker Sen. Schol., Gray's Inn, 1966; a Recorder, 1986. *Publication:* (contrib.) Guidelines for the Assessment of Damages in Personal Injury Cases. *Recreations:* travel, music, theatre, reading, Freemasonry. *Address:* Lambeth County Court, Cleaver Street, Kennington Road, SE11 4DZ. *T:* (020) 7735 4425.

COX, Roy Arthur, CBE 1987; JDipMA; FCA, FCMA, FCBSI, CIMgt; Chief General Manager, 1970–85, Director, 1976–89, Alliance and Leicester (formerly Alliance) Building Society; *b* 30 Nov. 1925; *s* of J. W. Arthur Cox; *m* 1st, 1951, Joy (*née* Dunsford); one *s* one *d*; 2nd, 1980, Audrey (*née* Brayham). *Educ:* Isleworth Grammar Sch. FCA 1953; FCMA 1957; FCBSI (FBS 1971); CIMgt (CBIM 1980). War Service, 1944–47. Wells & Partners, Chartered Accountants, 1942–49; Colombo Commercial Co. Ltd, 1950–61; Urwick, Orr & Partners, Management Consultants, 1961–65; Alliance Building Society: Sec., 1965; Gen. Man., 1967. Dir, Southern Bd, Legal & General Assce Soc. Ltd, 1972–86. Building Societies Association: Chm., S Eastern Assoc., 1972–74; Mem. Council, 1973–87; Chm., Gen. Purposes and Public Relations Cttee, 1975–77; Dep. Chm., Council, 1983–85; Chm., Council, 1985–87; Vice-Pres., 1987–. Mem., Royal Commn on Distribution of Income and Wealth, 1974–78; Dir, SE Electricity Bd, 1983–90; Dep. Chm., Seeboard plc, 1990–96; Chairman: PO Staff Superannuation Scheme, 1986–95; PO Pension Scheme, 1987–95; Siebe Pension Trustee Ltd, 1992–2000; Dir, Hermes Pensions Management Ltd, 1995–98. *Recreations:* golf, snooker, bridge. *Address:* C2 Marine Gate, Marine Drive, Brighton, East Sussex BN2 5TN.

COX, Sebert Leslie, OBE 1994; Partner, Kingston Reid Consulting, since 2001; Chairman, Places for People Group (formerly North British Housing Association), since 1997; *b* 27 Dec. 1950; *s* of Maunsell Newton Cox and Anna Louise Cox (*née* Reid); *m* 1974, Christine Lesley Hall; two *d. Educ:* Univ. of Lancaster (MSc). Granada Gp Ltd, 1967–70; Ford Motor Co. Ltd, 1970–72; Easton House Trust, 1972–73; Springboard Trust, 1973–76; Northumbria Probation Service, 1976–90; Develt Advr, Home Office, 1990–2001. MInstD 1996. *Recreations:* cooking and entertaining, gardening, walking, visiting historic buildings. *Address:* 126 Benfieldside Road, Shotley Bridge, Co. Durham DH8 0RT. *T:* (01207) 588303.

COX, Stephen James, CVO 1997; Executive Secretary, Royal Society, since 1997; *b* 5 Dec. 1946; *s* of late Harold James West Cox and of Norah Cox (*née* Wilkinson); *m* 1969, Pauline Victoria Greenwood (*see* P. V. Cox); one *s* one *d. Educ:* Queen Elizabeth Grammar Sch., Blackburn; Atlantic Coll.; Birmingham Univ. (BA Hons Geography 1969); Leeds Univ. (Postgrad. Dip. ESL 1970); Sussex Univ. (MA Educn 1977). VSO, Bolivia, 1965–66. British Council: Warsaw, 1970; Western Europe Dept, London, 1974; Accra, 1977; Staff Training Dept, 1981; Chm., British Council Whitley Council, Trade Union Side, 1981–84; Educn Attaché, Washington DC, 1984–85; Asst Sec., Royal Society, 1985–91; Dir Gen., Commonwealth Inst., 1991–97; Chief Exec., Westminster Foundn for Democracy, 1995–97. Member: Jt Commonwealth Socs Council, 1992–97; Court, RCA, 1993–; Council, Parly and Scientific Cttee, 1997–; Council, BAAS, 1997–. FRGS (Member: Sci. and Public Affairs Cttee, 1994–96; Educn Cttee, 1996–98; Expedn and Field Work Cttee, 1998–). Hon. Mem., ESU, 1994–. Mem., Editl Bd, Round Table, 1994–. *Recreations:* cricket, travel, visiting galleries, architecture. *Address:* Royal Society, 6 Carlton House Terrace, SW1Y 5AG. *T:* (020) 7839 5561, *Fax:* (020) 7930 2170. *Clubs:* Royal Over-Seas League, Geographical; Middlesex County Cricket.

COX, Thomas Michael; MP (Lab) Tooting, since 1983 (Wandsworth Central, 1970–74; Wandsworth Tooting, 1974–83); *b* London, 19 Jan. 1930. *Educ:* state schools; London Sch. of Economics. Electrical worker. Former Mem., Fulham Borough Council; contested (Lab) GLC elections, 1967; contested (Lab) Stroud, 1966. An Asst Govt Whip, 1974–77; a Lord Comr of the Treasury, 1977–79. Member: ETU; Co-operative Party. *Address:* House of Commons, SW1A 0AA.

COX, Prof. Timothy Martin, MD; FRCP, FMedSci; Professor of Medicine, since 1989 and Fellow of Sidney Sussex College, since 1990, University of Cambridge; *b* 10 May 1948; *s* of William Neville Cox and Joan Desirèe Cox (*née* Ward); *m* 1975, Susan Ruth Mason; three *s* one *d. Educ:* Oundle Sch.; London Hosp. Med. Coll., Univ. of London (Price Entrance Scholar; James Anderson Prize; MB 1971, MSc 1978, MD 1979); MA Cantab 1990, MD Cantab 1991. FRCP 1984. Junior posts, Med. Unit, Royal London Hosp., 1971; Dept of Morbid Anatomy, Bernard Baron Inst., Hammersmith and United Oxford Hosps, 1972–77; Royal Postgraduate Medical School, London University: MRC Training Fellow, Cell Biology Unit, 1977–79; Wellcome Sen. Clinical Fellow and Sen. Lectr, Dept of Medicine, 1979–87; Sen. Lectr, Depts of Haematology and Medicine, 1987–89. Hon. Consultant Physician, Addenbrooke's Hosp., 1989–. Vis. Scientist, Dept of Biology, MIT, 1983–84. Lectures: A. J. MacFazean, Univ. of Hong Kong, 1990; Schorstein Meml, London Hosp. Med Coll., 1994; Bradshaw, RCP, 1996; Flynn, RCPath, 2001. External examiner in Medicine: Univ. of Hong Kong, 1990; Univ. of London, 1993–97; RCSI, 1995–97; Chinese Univ. of HK, 2001; Univ. of Oxford, 2001–. Member: MRC Grants Cttee, 1990–94; MRC Clin. Trng Career Develt Panel, 2000–. Member: Vet. Panel, Wellcome Trust, 1996–98; Engelhorn Foundn, Rare Dis, Luxembourg, 2000–. Trustee, Croucher Foundn, HK, 2001–. Mem., Assoc. of Physicians of GB and Ire., 1984– (Mem., Exec. Cttee, 1995–97); Pres., Cambridge Philos. Soc., 2001–. Founder FMedSci 1998. FRSA 2000. Syndic, CUP, 1998–; Member, Editorial Board: Qly Jl of Medicine; Molecular Medicine Today; Bio Essays. *Publications:* Oxford Textbook of Medicine, (contrib.) 3rd edn, 1995, (ed) 4th edn, 2002; (ed jtly) Molecular Biology in Medicine, 1997 (trans. Spanish, 1998, Mandarin, 2001); contribs to sci. and med. jls on inborn errors metabolism. *Recreations:* natural history, piano, making cider. *Address:* Department of Medicine, University of Cambridge School of Clinical Medicine, Hills Road, Cambridge CB2 2QQ. *T:* (01223) 336864.

COX, Hon. William John Ellis, AC 1999; RFD 1985; ED 1968; **Hon. Mr Justice Cox;** Chief Justice, Tasmania, since 1995; Lieutenant Governor, Tasmania, since 1996; *b* 1 April 1936; *s* of Hon. William Ellis Cox, CBE, MC, and Alice Mary Cox; *m* 1970, Jocelyn Fay Wallace; two *s* one *d. Educ:* Xavier Coll., Melbourne; Univ. of Tasmania (BA, LLB). Called to the Bar, Tasmania, 1960; Partner, Dobson, Mitchell & Allport, 1961–76; Magistrate, Hobart, 1976–77; Crown Advocate, Tasmania, 1977–82; QC 1978; Judge, Supreme Court of Tasmania, 1982–95. Dep. Pres., Defence Force Discipline Appeal Tribunal, 1988–95. Pres., Bar Assoc. of Tasmania, 1973–75. Lt Col, Army Reserve; CO, 6 Field Regt, RAA, 1972–75; Hon. Col Comdt, RAA (Tas), 1993–97. Dir, Winston Churchill Meml Trust, 1988– (Nat. Chm., 2000–). *Recreations:* bush walking, gardening. *Address:* Judges' Chambers, Supreme Court of Tasmania, Salamanca Place, Hobart, Tas 7000, Australia. *Club:* Tasmanian.

COX, William Trevor; *see* Trevor, William.

COXETER, Harold Scott Macdonald, CC 1997; FRS 1950; PhD Cambridge, 1931; Professor of Mathematics, University of Toronto, 1948–80, now Emeritus Professor; *b* 9 Feb. 1907; *s* of Harold Samuel Coxeter and Lucy (*née* Gee); *m* 1936, Hendrina Johanna Brouwer, The Hague; one *s* one *d. Educ:* King Alfred Sch., London; St George's Sch., Harpenden; Trinity Coll., Cambridge (Hon. Fellow, 2001). Entrance Scholar, Trinity Coll., 1926; Smith's Prize, 1931. Fellow Trinity Coll., Cambridge, 1931–36; Rockefeller Foundation Fellow, Princeton, 1932–33; Procter Fellow, Princeton, 1934–35; Asst Prof., 1936–43, Associate Prof., 1943–48, University of Toronto. Visiting Professor: Notre Dame, 1947; Columbia Univ., 1949; Dartmouth Coll., 1964; Univ. of Amsterdam, 1966; Univ. of Edinburgh, 1967; Univ. of E Anglia, 1968; ANU, 1970; Univ. of Sussex, 1972; Univ. of Warwick and Univ. of Utrecht, 1976; Calif. Inst. of Technology, 1977; Univ. of Bologna, 1978. Editor Canadian Jl of Mathematics, 1948–57. President: Canadian Mathematical Congress, 1965–67; Internat. Mathematical Congress, 1974. Foreign Mem., Koninklijke Nederlandse Akademie van Wetenschappen, 1975; Hon. Member: Mathematische Gesellschaft, Hamburg, 1977; Wiskundig Genootschap, Amsterdam, 1978; London Mathematical Soc., 1978. Hon. LLD: Alberta, 1957; Trent, 1973; Toronto, 1979; Hon. DMath Waterloo, 1969; Hon. DSc: Acadia, 1971; Carleton, 1984; McMaster, 1988; York, 1994; Hon. Dr rer. nat. Giessen, 1984. Sylvester Medal, Royal Soc., 1997. *Publications:* Non-Euclidean Geometry, 1942, 6th edn 1998; Regular Polytopes, 1948, 3rd edn 1973; The Real Projective Plane, 1949, 3rd edn 1992; (with W. O. J. Moser) Generators and Relations, 1st edn, 1957, 4th edn, 1980; Introduction to Geometry, 1961 and 1969; Projective Geometry, 1964, 2nd edn, revd 1987; (with S. L. Greitzer) Geometry Revisited, 1967; Twelve Geometric Essays, 1968; Regular Complex Polytopes, 1974, 2nd edn 1990; (with W. W. Rouse Ball) Mathematical Recreations and Essays, 11th edn 1939, 13th edn 1987; (with R. W. Frucht and D. L. Powers) Zero-symmetric Graphs,

1981; Kaleidoscopes, 1995; various mathematical papers. *Recreation:* music. *Address:* 67 Roxborough Drive, Toronto, ON M4W 1X2, Canada.

COXWELL-ROGERS, Col Richard Annesley; Vice Lord-Lieutenant of Gloucestershire, since 1993; *b* 26 April 1932; *s* of Maj.-Gen. Norman Annesley Coxwell-Rogers, CB, CBE, DSO and Diana Coxwell-Rogers (*née* Coston); *m* 1965, Martha Felicity Hurrell (*d* 1998); two *s*. *Educ:* Eton Coll.; RMA Sandhurst. Commissioned 15th/19th Hussars, 1952; served Germany, UK, Malaya, Cyprus; Comd 15th/19th Hussars, 1973–75; Col, 15th/19th Hussars, 1988–92. Area Appeals Organiser, CRC, 1982–93. DL Glos 1990; High Sheriff of Glos, 1994. *Recreations:* country sports. *Address:* Close Farm House, Coberley, Cheltenham, Glos GL53 9QZ. *T:* (01242) 870519. *Club:* Cavalry and Guards.

COYLE, Eurfron Gwynne, (Mrs Michael Coyle); *see* Jones, E. G.

COYNE, James Elliott; Canadian banker and financial consultant; *b* Winnipeg, 17 July 1910; *s* of James Bowes Coyne and Edna Margaret Coyne (*née* Elliott); *m* 1957, Meribeth Stobie; one *s* one *d*. *Educ:* University of Manitoba (BA); University of Oxford (BCL). RCAF (Flying Officer), 1942–44. Admitted to the Bar, Manitoba, 1934; solicitor and barrister in Manitoba, 1934–38; Financial Attaché, Canadian Embassy, Washington, DC, 1941; Mem. War-time Prices and Trade Board, Ottawa, 1942 (Dep.-Chm.). Bank of Canada, Ottawa: Asst to the Governors, 1944–49; Deputy-Governor, 1950–54; Governor, 1955–61. *Address:* 16 Ruskin Row, Winnipeg, MB R3M 2R7, Canada.

COZENS, Andrew Geoffrey; Director of Social Services, Leicester City Council, since 2000; *b* 3 June 1955; *s* of late Geoffrey Cozens and Iris Cozens (*née* Hammett); *m* 1979, Prof. Gillian Parker. *Educ:* Peter Symonds Sch., Winchester; Magdalene Coll., Cambridge (BA 1977); Green Coll., Oxford (MSc, CQSW 1981). Social Worker, N Yorks CC, 1981–84; Develt Officer, N Yorks Forum for Vol. Orgns, 1984–88; North Yorkshire County Council: Principal Officer, 1988–90; Asst Dir, 1990–94; Sen. Asst Dir, 1994–96; Dir of Social Services, Glos CC, 1996–2000. Publishing Editor: Platform Mag., 1972–77; Green Horse Pubns, 1974–77; Avalon Editions, 1978–82. Hon. Fellow, Cheltenham and Gloucester Coll. of Higher Educn, 1998. *Recreations:* hill walking, the arts, reading, watching sport. *Address:* Leicester City Council, 1 Grey Friars, Leicester LE1 5PH. *T:* (0116) 256 8300.

COZENS, Robert William, CBE 1989; QPM 1981; Director, Police Requirements for Science and Technology, Home Office, 1985–88, retired; *b* 10 Nov. 1927; *s* of Sydney Robert and Rose Elizabeth Cozens; *m* 1952, Jean Dorothy Banfield; one *s* one *d*. *Educ:* Stoke C of E Sch., Guildford. Constable to Chief Superintendent, Surrey Constabulary, 1954–72; Asst Dir, Command Courses, Police Staff Coll., Bramshill, 1972–74; Asst Chief Constable, S Yorks Police, 1974–78; seconded to Federal Judicial Police in Mexico for advisory duties, 1975; Dep. Chief Constable, Lincs Police, 1978 81; Chief Constable, W Mercia Constabulary (Hereford, Worcester and Shropshire), 1981–85. *Recreations:* tennis, swimming, making friends.

CRABB, Most Rev. Frederick Hugh Wright; BD, DD; *b* Luppitt, Devon, 24 April 1915; *s* of William Samuel and Florence Mary Crabb; *m* 1946, Alice Margery Coombs; two *s* two *d*. *Educ.* Luppitt Parochial Sch.; Univ. of London (St John's Hall, Highbury, London). BD Lond. (1st Cl. Hons); ALCD (1st Cl. Hons). Asst Curate, St James', West Teignmouth, Devon, 1939–41; Asst Priest, St Andrew's, Plymouth, 1941–42; Missionary at Akot, S Sudan, 1942–44; Principal, Bishop Gwynne Divinity Sch., S Sudan, 1944–51; Vice Principal, London Coll. of Divinity, 1951–57; Principal, Coll. of Emmanuel and St Chad, Saskatoon, Sask., 1957–67; Assoc. Priest, Christ Church, Calgary, Alberta, 1967–69; Rector, St Stephen's Church, Calgary, 1969–75; Bishop of Athabasca, 1975–83; Metropolitan of Rupert's Land, 1977–82; Hon. Asst, St Cyprian, Calgary, and Dir, Anglican Sch. of Lay Ministry, 1983–87. Hon. Chaplain, Calgary Div., Royal Canadian Mounted Police Veterans' Assoc., 1985– (Hon. Life Mem. 1998). Mem. Governing Council, Athabasca Univ., 1982–85. Hon. DD: Wycliffe Coll., Toronto, 1960; St Andrew's Coll., Saskatoon, 1967; Coll. of Emmanuel and St Chad, Saskatoon, 1979. *Publication:* (jtly) Rupert's Land: A Cultural Tapestry, 1988. *Recreations:* gardening, mountain hiking. *Address:* 3483 Chippendale Drive NW, Calgary, AB T2L 0W7, Canada.

CRABB, Tony William; media consultant, since 1992; *b* 27 June 1933; *s* of William Harold Crabb and Ellen Emily Crabb; *m* 1957, Brenda Margaret (*née* Sullman); one *s* one *d*. *Educ:* Chiswick Grammar School; London School of Economics (BScEcon); Intelligence Corps Russian Interpreters Course, 1952–54. BBC, 1957–88; seconded as news adviser to Govt of Libya, 1968–69; Managing Editor: BBC TV News, 1979–82; BBC Breakfast Time, 1982–84; Controller, Corporate News Services, BBC, 1984–87; Special Asst, News and Current Affairs, BBC, 1987–88; Dep. Dir of Broadcasting, Radio TV Hong Kong, 1988–92. Gen. Manager, CCT Productions Ltd, 1995–97. Mem. (Lib Dem) Spelthorne BC, 1999–. *Address:* 38 The Avenue, Sunbury-on-Thames, Middx TW16 5ES; *e-mail:* tony.crabb@virgin.net.

CRABBE, Kenneth Herbert Martineau, TD; *b* 4 Nov. 1916; *m* 1st, 1940, Rowena Leete (*d* 1981); one *s*; 2nd, 1982, Belinda V. Fitzherbert (*née* Batt); three step *s* one step *d*. *Educ:* Stowe Sch. Commnd TA, 1937; psc; Major, RA. Member, Stock Exchange, London, 1937–; Mem. Council, The Stock Exchange, 1963–78 (Dep. Chm., 1970–73). *Recreations:* golf, fishing, shooting, painting. *Address:* Spandrels, Walliswood, Dorking, Surrey RH5 5RJ. *T:* (01306) 627275. *Clubs:* Boodle's; West Sussex Golf.

CRABBIE, Christopher Donald, CMG 1995; HM Diplomatic Service; UK Permanent Representative to OECD, Paris, (with rank of Ambassador), since 1999; *b* 17 Jan. 1946; *s* of late William George Crabbie and of Jane (*née* Coe). *Educ:* Rugby Sch.; Newcastle Univ.; Liverpool Univ.; Corpus Christi Coll., Oxford. Second Sec., FCO, 1973–75; First Secretary: Nairobi, 1975–79; Washington, 1979–83; FCO, 1983–85; Counsellor and Hd of European Communities Div., HM Treasury, 1985–87; Counsellor, FCO, 1987–90; Dep. UK Perm. Rep., OECD, Paris, 1990; Counsellor, British Embassy, Paris, 1990–94; Ambassador, Algeria, 1994–95; Ambassador to Romania, 1996–99. *Recreations:* ski-ing, flying, sailing, gardening. *Address:* c/o Foreign and Commonwealth Office, SW1A 2AH. *Club:* New (Edinburgh).

CRABTREE, Maj-Gen. Derek Thomas, CB 1983; *b* 21 Jan. 1930; *s* of late William Edward Crabtree and Winifred Hilda Burton; *m* 1960, Daphne Christine Mason; one *s* one *d*. *Educ:* St Brendan's Coll., Bristol. Commissioned, 1953; Regimental Service: 13th/18th Royal Hussars (QMO), 1953–56; Royal Berkshire Regt, 1956–59; Technical Staff Course, RMCS, 1960–62; sc Camberley, 1964; BM 11 Inf. Bde, BAOR, 1965–67; CO 1st Bn Duke of Edinburgh's Royal Regt, UK and Berlin, 1970–72; Col GS, MGO Secretariat, MoD, 1974–76; Dep. Comdr and Chief of Staff Headquarters British Forces Hong Kong, 1976–79; Dep. Comdt RMCS, 1979–80; Dir Gen. of Weapons (Army), MoD, 1980–84. Sen. Mil. Advr, Short Bros, 1984–86; Gen. Manager, Regular Forces Employment Assoc., 1987–94. Col, Duke of Edinburgh's Royal Regt, 1982–87, 1988–89. *Recreations:* golf, tennis, ski-ing, gardening, beekeeping. *Address:* 53 High Street, Shrivenham, Swindon SN6 8AW. *Club:* Army and Navy.

CRABTREE, Jonathan; His Honour Judge Crabtree; a Circuit Judge, since 1986; *b* 17 April 1934; *s* of Charles H. Crabtree and Elsie M. Crabtree; *m* 1st, 1957, Caroline Ruth Keigwin (*née* Oliver) (marr. diss. 1976); one *s* three *d* (and one *s* decd); 2nd, 1980, Wendy Elizabeth Hudson (*née* Ward). *Educ:* Bootham; St John's Coll., Cambridge (MA, LLM). Called to Bar, Gray's Inn, 1958. A Recorder, 1974–86. *Recreations:* cricket, cooking, history, archaeology. *Address:* c/o Crown Court, Sheffield S1 2EA. *T:* (0114) 275 5866.

CRABTREE, Prof. Lewis Frederick, PhD, FRAeS; FAIAA; Sir George White Professor of Aeronautical Engineering, University of Bristol, 1973–85, now Emeritus; *b* 16 Nov. 1924; *m* 1955, Averil Joan Escott; one *s* one *d*. *Educ:* Grange High Sch., Bradford; Univ. of Leeds; Imperial Coll. of Science and Technology; Cornell Univ., USA. BSc (Mech. Eng) Leeds, 1945; DIC (Aeronautics), 1947; PhD (Aero Eng), Cornell, 1952. Air Engr Officer, RNVR, 1945–46. Grad. apprentice, Saunders-Roe Ltd, E Cowes, IoW, 1947–50; ECA Fellowship, Grad. Sch. of Aero. Engrg, Cornell Univ., 1950–52; Aerodynamics Dept, RAE, Farnborough, 1953–73; Head of: Hypersonics and High temperature Gasdynamics Div., 1961–66; Low Speed Aerodynamics Div., 1966–70; Propulsion Aerodynamics and Noise Div., 1970–73. Visiting Prof., Cornell Univ., 1957. First Chm., Aerospace Technol. Bd, DSAC, 1980–83. Chairman: Brecknock Wildlife Trust, 1988–91; Welsh Wildlife Trusts Ltd, 1994–95. Lectures to RAeS: Lanchester Meml, 1977; Handley Page, 1979; Barnwell, 1981. Pres., RAeS, 1978–79 (Usborne Meml Prize, 1955). *Publications:* Elements of Hypersonic Aerodynamics, 1965; contributor to: Incompressible Aerodynamics, 1960; Laminar Boundary Layers, 1963; Engineering Structures, 1983; articles chiefly in Jl RAeS, Aeron. Quart., Jl Aeron. Sci., Jahrbuch der WGLR, and Reports and Memos of ARC. *Address:* Carlton House, 25 High Street, Crickhowell, Powys NP8 1BE. *T:* (01873) 810507.

CRABTREE, Simon; *see* Wharton, M. B.

CRACKNELL, Malcolm Thomas; His Honour Judge Cracknell; a Circuit Judge, since 1989; *b* 12 Dec. 1943; *s* of late Percy Thomas Cracknell and Doris Louise Cracknell; *m* 1st, 1968, Ann Carrington (*née* Gooding) (marr. diss. 1980); one *s* one *d*; 2nd, 1988, Felicity Anne Davies; two *s* one *d*. *Educ:* Royal Liberty Sch., Romford; Hull Univ. (LLB); King's Coll., London (LLM). Called to Bar, Middle Temple, 1969. Lectr in Law, Univ. of Hull, 1968–74; Barrister, NE Circuit, 1970–89; a Recorder, 1988; Designated Family Judge, Hull Combined Court Centre, 1994–. *Recreations:* golf, gardening, walking, cricket, reading. *Address:* Hull Combined Court Centre, Lowgate, Hull HU1 2EZ.

CRACKNELL, (William) Martin; Chief Executive, Glenrothes Development Corporation, 1976–93; *b* 24 June 1929; *s* of John Sidney Cracknell and Sybil Marian (*née* Wood); *m* 1962, Gillian Goatcher; two *s* two *d*. *Educ:* St Edward's School, Oxford; RMA Sandhurst. Regular Army Officer, Royal Green Jackets, 1949–69; British Printing Industries Fedn, 1969–76. Mem. Exec., Scottish Council (Develt and Industry), 1984–90; Chm., Scottish Cttee, German Chamber of Industry and Commerce in UK, 1987–92. Director: Glenrothes Enterprise Trust, 1983–89; New Enterprise Develt, 1987–90. FRSA 1993. Cross of Order of Merit (Germany), 1992. *Address:* West End Cottage, Freuchie, Fife KY15 7EZ. *T:* (01337) 857849. *Club:* Royal Green Jackets.

CRACROFT, Air Vice-Marshal Peter Dicken, CB 1954; AFC 1932; *b* 29 Nov. 1907; *s* of Lt-Col H. Cracroft, Bath; *m* 1932, Margaret Eliza Sugden Patchett; two *s*. *Educ:* Monkton Combe Sch., Bath. Commissioned RAF 1927; Fleet Air Arm, 1928–31; Central Flying Sch. Instructors' Course, 1931; Flying Instructor, Leuchars, 1931–35; Adjt HMS Courageous, 1936–37; Chief Flying Instructor, Oxford Univ. Air Sqdn, 1937–39; RAF Stn Mount Batten, 1939–40; Air Staff, Coastal Command, 1940–41; OC RAF Station, Chivenor, 1941–43; SASO 19 Gp (later 17 Gp), 1933–44; OC 111 Op. Trg Unit, Bahamas, 1944–45; SASO HQ Air Comd, SE Asia, Mil. Gov. Penang, 1945; AOC Bombay, 1945–46; SASO, HQ 19 Gp, 1946–48; RAF Dir and CO, Jt Anti-Submarine Sch., Londonderry, 1948–50; Sen. Air Liaison Officer, S Africa, 1950–52; AOC 66 Gp, Edinburgh, 1952–53; Senior Air Staff Officer, Headquarters Coastal Command, 1953–55; AOC Scotland and 18 Group, 1955–58; retired from RAF, Dec. 1958. *Address:* The Hyde, Walditch, Bridport, Dorset DT6 4LB. *T:* (01308) 427694.

CRACROFT-ELEY, Bridget Katharine; Lord-Lieutenant of Lincolnshire, since 1995; *b* 29 Oct. 1933; *d* of Weston Cracroft-Amcotts and Rhona (*née* Clifton-Brown); *m* 1959, Robert Peel Charles Cracroft-Eley (*d* 1996); one *s* one *d*. *Educ:* Lincoln Girls' High Sch.; Crofton Grange Sch., Buntingford, Herts. Voluntary and charity work, incl. WRVS, Girl Guides, Lincs Old Churches Trust and RNIB Looking Glass Appeal, 1970–. Parish Councillor, Hackthorn and Cold Hanworth, 1980–. Governor: Hackthorn C of E Primary Sch., 1988–; King's Sch., Grantham, 1995–. High Sheriff, Lincs, 1989–90. DStJ 1996. Hon. LLD De Montfort, 1999. *Recreations:* upholstery, gardening, the arts. *Address:* Hackthorn Hall, Lincoln LN2 3PQ. *T:* (01673) 860212.

CRADDOCK, Timothy James; HM Diplomatic Service; Head, Africa (Greater Horn) Department, Department for International Development, since 2000 (on secondment); *b* 27 June 1956; *s* of James Vincent Craddock and Kathleen Mary Craddock (*née* Twigg). *Educ:* King Edward's Sch., Birmingham; Gonville and Caius Coll., Cambridge (Exhibnr; MA); School of Oriental and African Studies, London Univ. Entered FCO, 1979; Third Sec. and Vice-Consul, Chad, 1979–80; Vice-Consul, Istanbul, 1981–82; Second Sec., Ankara, 1982–85; Hd of Section, South America Dept, FCO, 1985–87; Sec., FCO Bd of Mgt, 1988–90; First Sec., Paris, 1990–94; Dep. Hd, Aid Policy and Resources Dept, FCO, 1995–97; Ambassador to Estonia, 1997–2000. *Recreations:* hill walking, opera, London, gardening in France. *Address:* Room 451, Department for International Development, 94 Victoria Street, SW1E 5JL; 52 rue du Bourg Voisin, 21140 Semur-en-Auxois, France. *Club:* Royal Commonwealth Society.

CRADDOCK, (William) Aleck, LVO 1981; Director, Harrods Ltd, 1964–88 (Managing Director, 1980–84, Chairman, 1981–86, Deputy Chairman, 1987–88); Director, Cartier Ltd, 1986–97; *b* Nov. 1924; *m* 1947, Olive May Brown; one *s* one *d*. *Educ:* City of London School. Joined Druce and Craddock, Craddock and Tomkins Ltd (family firm), Meat and Provision Merchants, Marylebone, London, 1946; joined Harrods Ltd as Asst to Food Manager, 1954; Member of the Board, 1964; Director and General Manager, 1970; Asst Managing Director, 1975; a Director of House of Fraser, 1980–91. Vice Chm., Drapers' Cottage Homes, 1987–94 (Pres., Appeal, 1985–86); Pres., Twenty Club, 1988. Liveryman, Worshipful Company of Cooks, 1972 (Mem., Court of Assts, 1993–96). Cavaliere Ufficiale (Fourth Cl.), Order Al Merito Della Repubblica Italiana, 1980. *Recreation:* watercolour painting. *Address:* 17 Tretawn Park, Mill Hill, NW7 4PS. *Clubs:* Arts; Guards' Polo (Life Mem.).

CRADOCK, John Anthony, CB 1980; MBE 1952; Deputy Secretary, Ministry of Defence, 1981–82; *b* 19 Oct. 1921; *o s* of John Cradock and Nan Cradock (*née* Kelly); *m* 1948, Eileen (*née* Bell); one *s* one *d*. *Educ:* St Brendan's College, Bristol; Bristol Univ. (BA

1946). Military service, 1941–46 (Captain Royal Signals); Malayan Civil Service, 1946–57; War Office, 1957–67; MoD, 1967–75; Under Sec., N Ireland Office, 1975–77; MoD, 1977–82. *Address:* c/o Lloyds TSB, Morpeth, Northumberland NE61 1AN.

CRADOCK, Rt Hon. Sir Percy, GCMG 1983 (KCMG 1980; CMG 1968); PC 1993; the Prime Minister's Foreign Policy Adviser, 1984–92; *b* 26 Oct. 1923; *m* 1953, Birthe Marie Dyrlund. *Educ:* St John's Coll., Cambridge (Hon. Fellow, 1982). Served Foreign Office, 1954–57; First Sec., Kuala Lumpur, 1957–61, Hong Kong, 1961, Peking, 1962; Foreign Office, 1963–66; Counsellor and Head of Chancery, Peking, 1966–68; Chargé d'Affaires, Peking, 1968–69; Head of Planning Staff, FCO, 1969–71; Under-Sec., Cabinet Office, 1971–75; Ambassador to German Democratic Republic, 1976–78; Leader, UK Delegn to Comprehensive Test Ban Discussions at Geneva, 1977–78; Ambassador to People's Republic of China, 1978–83; Leader of UK team in negotiations over Hong Kong, 1983; Dep. Under Sec. of State, FCO, supervising Hong Kong negotiations, 1984. *Publications:* Experiences of China, 1994; In Pursuit of British Interests, 1997. *Club:* Reform.

CRAFT, Prof. Alan William, MD; FRCP, FRCPCH; Sir James Spence Professor of Child Health, University of Newcastle upon Tyne, since 1993 (Professor of Paediatric Oncology, 1991–93); *b* 6 July 1946; *s* of William and Yvonne Craft; *m* 1st, 1968, Dorothy Noble (decd); one *s*; 2nd, 1992, Anne Nicholson. *Educ:* Rutherford Grammar Sch., Newcastle upon Tyne; Univ. of Newcastle upon Tyne (MB, BS; MD). FRCP 1982; FRCPCH 1997. House Officer, Royal Victoria Infirmary, Newcastle upon Tyne, 1969–70; Sen. House Officer, then Registrar and Sen. Registrar, Newcastle Hosps, 1970–77; MRC Trng Fellow, Royal Marsden Hosp., 1976–77; Consultant Paediatrician: N Tyneside Hosp., 1977–86; Royal Victoria Infirmary, 1977–. Chm., European Osteosarcoma Intergroup, 1994–97; Sec. Gen., 1993–99, Pres., Sept. 2002–, Internat. Paediatric Oncology Soc.; Vice-Pres., RCPCH, 1998–. *Publications:* papers on childhood cancer and other childhood disorders in BMJ, Lancet, Archives of Disease in Childhood, etc. *Recreations:* marathon running, orienteering, crosswords. *Address:* 2 Ruthven Court, Adderstone Crescent, Newcastle upon Tyne NE2 2HH. *T:* (0191) 281 6718.

CRAFT, Prof. Ian Logan, FRCS; FRCOG; Director, London Gynaecology and Fertility Centre, since 1990; *b* 11 July 1937; *s* of Reginald Thomas Craft and Lois Mary (*née* Logan); *m* 1959, Jacqueline Rivers Symmons; two *s*. *Educ:* Owens Sch., London; Westminster Med. Sch., Univ. of London (MB, BS). FRCS 1966; MRCOG 1970, FRCOG 1986. Sen. Registrar, Westminster Hosp. Teaching Gp (Westminster Hosp. and Kingston Hosp.), 1970–72; Sen. Lectr and Consultant, Inst. of Obstetrics and Gynaecology, Queen Charlotte's Hosp., London, 1972–76; Prof. of Obstetrics and Gynaecology, Royal Free Hosp., London, 1976–82; Dir of Gynaecology, Cromwell Hosp., 1982–85; Dir of Fertility and Obstetric Studies, Humana Hosp. Wellington, 1985–90. FRSocMed. *Publications:* contrib. BMJ, Lancet and other medical jls. *Recreations:* art, music, ornithology, sports of most types. *Address:* 5 Devonshire Mews North, W1N 1FR; London Gynaecology and Fertility Centre, Cozens House, 112A Harley Street, W1N 1AF. *T:* (020) 7224 0707.

CRAFT, Prof. Maurice, PhD, DLitt; Professor of Education, Goldsmiths' College, University of London, since 1997; *b* 4 May 1932; *er s* of Jack and Polly Craft, London; *m* 1957, Alma, *y d* of Elio and Dinah Sampson, Dublin; two *d*. *Educ:* LCC Elem. Sch. and Colfe's Grammar Sch., SE13; LSE, Univ. of London (BSc Econ); Sch. of Education, Trinity Coll., Univ. of Dublin (HDipEd); Inst. of Education, Univ. of London (AcadDipEd); Dept of Sociology, Univ. of Liverpool (PhD 1972); Univ. of Nottingham (DLitt 1990). 2/Lt RAOC (Nat. Service), 1953–55. Asst Master, Catford Secondary Sch., SE6, 1956–60; Princ. Lectr and Head of Dept of Sociology, Edge Hill Coll. of Education, Ormskirk, Lancs, 1960–67; Sen. Lectr in Education, i/c Advanced Courses, Univ. of Exeter, 1967–73; Sub-Dean, Faculty of Educn, 1969–73; Prof. of Education, and Chairman, Centre for the Study of Urban Education, La Trobe Univ., Melbourne, 1973–75; Goldsmiths' Prof. of Education, Inst. of Educn, Univ. of London, and Head of Dept of Advanced Studies in Education, Goldsmiths' Coll., 1976–80; University of Nottingham: Prof. of Educn, and Hd, Div. of Advanced Studies, 1980–89; Dean, Faculty of Educn, 1981–83; Chm., Sch. of Educn, 1983–85, 1988–89; Pro-Vice-Chancellor, 1983–87; Foundn Dean of Humanities and Social Science, Hong Kong Univ. of Science and Technol., 1989–92; Sen. Consultant to Dir, Open Learning Inst. of Hong Kong, 1992–94; Res. Prof. in Educn, Univ. of Greenwich, 1994–97. Adviser: Devon CC, 1970–72; Aust. Federal Poverty Commn, 1974–75; ACU, 1976, 1979; CNAA, 1978–89; Centre for Advice and Inf. on Educn Disadvantage (Chm., Teacher Educn Working Gp, 1979–80); Schools Council, 1979; CRE (Chm., Teacher Educn Adv. Gp, 1980–84); H of C Home Affairs Cttee, 1981; Swann Cttee, 1982–84; Leverhulme Trust, 1982–; Macquarie Univ., Aust., 1982; Council for Educn and Trng in Youth and Community Work (Chm., In-service Wkg Gp, 1983); UNESCO, 1985; QUB, 1986; Univ. of Kuwait, 1988; Peshawar Univ., Pakistan, 1988; Hong Kong Council for Academic Accreditation, 1991; Hong Kong Educn Commn, 1991; Lagos Univ., Nigeria, 1991; City Polytechnic of Hong Kong, 1992; Hong Kong Baptist Univ., 1994; Griffith Univ., Aust., 1996; Hong Kong Govt Res. Grants Council, 1996–; Commonwealth of Learning, Vancouver, 1996; ESRC, 1997; Hong Kong Inst. of Educn, 1997; Southampton Univ., 1999; Chester UC, 2000; Surrey Univ., 2000–. Mem., UK Delegn to EEC Colloquium on Ethnic Min. Educn, Brussels, 1979, 1982; UK delegate to: Council of Europe Seminars on Intercultural Trng of Teachers, Lisbon, 1981, Rome, 1982, Strasbourg, 1983; UNESCO Colloquium on Educnl Disadvantage, Thessalonika, 1984. Member: Council of Validating Univs, 1982–89 (Vice-Chm., 1987–89); E Midlands Reg. Consultative Gp on Teacher Educn, 1980–84 (Chm., 1980–84); Exec. Cttee, Univs Council for Educn of Teachers, 1984–88 (Chm., Standing Cttee on Validation, 1984–87); Cttee on Validation, CVCP, 1986–88; Hong Kong Govt Bd of Inquiry in Educn, 1992; Hong Kong Govt Adv. Cttee on Teacher Educn and Qualifications, 1993; Froebel Council, 2000–. Member, Editorial Board: Sociology of Educn Abstracts, 1965–; Jl of Multilingual and Multicultural Develt, 1979–96; Multicultural Educn Abstracts, 1981–; Internat. Studies in Sociology of Educn, 1991–; British Jl of Educnl Studies, 1996–. FRSA 1989. *Publications:* (ed jtly) Linking Home and School, 1967 (3rd edn, 1980); (ed jtly) Guidance and Counselling in British Schools, 1969 (2nd edn, 1974); (ed) Family, Class and Education: a Reader, 1970; Urban Education—a Dublin case study, 1974; School Welfare Provision in Australia, 1977; (ed) Teaching in a Multicultural Society: the Task for Teacher Education, 1981; (jtly) Training Teachers of Ethnic Minority Community Languages, 1983; (ed jtly) Change in Teacher Education, 1984; (ed) Education and Cultural Pluralism, 1984; The Democratisation of Education, 1985; Teacher Education in a Multicultural Society, 1986; (ed jtly) Ethnic Relations and Schooling, 1995; (ed) Teacher Education in Plural Societies, 1996; contrib. to numerous books and to the following jls: Educnl Research, Internat. Review of Educn, Internat. Jl of Educnl Develt, Educnl Review, Social and Econ. Admin., Cambridge Jl of Educn, Educn for Teaching, British Jl of In-Service Educn, Internat. Social Work, Aust. Jl of Social Work, Aust. Educnl Researcher, THES, Higher Educn Jl, New Society, Education, Administration, New Era, Studies. *Recreations:* music, walking. *Address:* Department of Educational Studies, Goldsmiths' College, University of London, New Cross, SE14 6NW. *T:* and *Fax:* (020) 8852 7611. *Club:* Royal Over-Seas League.

CRAFTS, Prof. Nicholas Francis Robert, FBA 1992; Professor of Economic History, London School of Economics, since 1995; *b* 9 March 1949; *s* of Alfred Hedley Crafts and Flora Geraldine Mary Crafts; *m* 1969, Barbara Daynes; one *s* two *d*. *Educ:* Brunts Grammar Sch., Mansfield; Trinity Coll., Cambridge (BA Econs 1st cl., 1970). Lectr in Econ. Hist., Exeter Univ., 1971–72; Lectr in Econs, Warwick Univ., 1972–77; Fellow in Econs, University Coll., Oxford, 1977–86; Professor of Economic History: Leeds Univ., 1987–88; Univ. of Warwick, 1988–95 (Hon. Prof., 1995–). Vis. Asst Prof. of Econs, Univ. of Calif., Berkeley, 1974–76; Vis. Prof. of Econs, Stanford Univ., 1982–83. *Publications:* British Economic Growth during the Industrial Revolution, 1985; contrib. to Economic Jl, Jl of Economic Hist., Economic Policy, Population Studies, etc. *Recreations:* betting on horses, drinking beer. *Address:* Department of Economics, London School of Economics, Houghton Street, WC2A 2AE. *T:* (020) 7955 6399; *e-mail:* n.crafts@LSE.ac.UK.

CRAGG, Rt Rev. (Albert) Kenneth, DPhil; *b* 8 March 1913; *yr s* of Albert and Emily Cragg; *m* 1940, Theodora Melita (*d* 1989), *yr d* of John Wesley Arnold; three *s* (one *d* decd). *Educ:* Blackpool Grammar Sch.; Jesus Coll., Oxford (Hon. Fellow, 1999); Tyndale Hall, Bristol. BA Oxon 2nd Cl. Hons Mod. Hist., 1934; MA Oxon 1938; DPhil 1950. Ellerton Theol. Essay Prize, Oxford, 1937; Green Moral Philos. Prize, Oxford, 1947. Deacon, 1936; Priest, 1937; Curate, Higher Tranmere Parish Church, Birkenhead, 1936–39; Chaplain, All Saints', Beirut, Lebanon, 1939–47; Warden, St Justin's House, Beirut, 1942–47; Asst Prof. of Philos., Amer. University of Beirut, 1942–47; Rector of Longworth, Berks, 1947–51; Sheriff's Chap., Berks, 1948; Prof. of Arabic and Islamics, Hartford Seminary, Conn, USA, 1951–56; Rockefeller Travelling Schol., 1954; Res. Canon, St George's Collegiate Church, Jerusalem, 1956–61; Fellow, St Augustine's Coll., Canterbury, 1959–60, Sub-Warden, 1960–61, Warden, 1961–67; Examng Chaplain to Archbishop of Canterbury, 1961–67; Hon. Canon of Canterbury, 1961–80; Asst Bishop to Archbishop in Jerusalem, 1970–74; Reader in Religious Studies, Sussex Univ., and Asst Bishop, dio. of Chichester, 1973–78; Vicar of Helme, W Yorks, and Asst Bishop, dio. Wakefield, 1978–81; Asst Bishop, dio. Oxford, 1982–. Select Preacher: Cambridge, 1961; Dublin, 1962; Oxford, 1974. Proctor in Convocation, Canterbury, 1965–68; Visiting Prof., Union Theological Seminary, New York, 1965–66; Lectr, Faculty of Divinity, Cambridge, 1966; Jordan Lectr, Sch. of Oriental and African Studies, University of London, 1967; Vis. Prof., University of Ibadan, Nigeria, 1968; Bye-Fellow, Gonville and Caius Coll., Cambridge, 1968–74; Vis. Prof., Virginia Theol Seminary, 1984, 1985. Hon. DD Leeds, 1993. Editor, The Muslim World Quarterly, 1952–60. *Publications:* The Call of the Minaret, 1956, 2nd edn 1986; Sandals at the Mosque, 1959; The Dome and the Rock, 1964; Counsels in Contemporary Islam, 1965; Christianity in World Perspective, 1968; The Privilege of Man, 1968; The House of Islam, 1969; Alive to God, 1970; The Event of the Qur'ān, 1971; The Mind of the Qur'ān, 1973; The Wisdom of the Sufis, 1976; The Christian and Other Religion, 1977; Islam from Within, 1979; This Year in Jerusalem, 1982; Muhammad and the Christian, 1983; The Pen and the Faith, 1985; Jesus and the Muslim, 1985; The Christ and the Faiths, 1986; Readings in the Qur'ān, 1988; What Decided Christianity, 1989; The Arab Christian, 1991; Troubled by Truth, 1992; To Meet and to Greet, 1992; Faith and Life Negotiate (autobiog.), 1994; The Lively Credentials of God, 1996; Defending (the) Faith, 1997; Palestine: the prize and price of Zion, 1997; With God in Human Trust, 1999; The Weight in the Word, 1999; translated: City of Wrong, 1959; The Theology of Unity, 1965; A Passage to France, 1976; The Hallowed Valley, 1977; contributor: Journal of World History, 1957; Religion in the Middle East, 1969. *Address:* 3 Goring Lodge, White House Road, Oxford OX1 4QE.

CRAGG, Prof. Anthony Douglas, RA 1994; sculptor; Professor and Co-Director, Düsseldorf Kunstakademie, since 1988; *b* 9 April 1949; *m* 1990, Tatjana (*née* Verhasselt); one *s* one *d*, and two *s* by former *m*. *Educ:* Wimbledon Sch. of Art; Royal Coll. of Art. *One-man exhibitions include:* Lisson Gall., 1979, 1980, 1985, 1991, 1992, 1997, 1998; Whitechapel Art Gall., 1981, 1997; Kanrasha Gall., Tokyo, 1982, 1984, 1989, 1990; Konrad Fischer, Düsseldorf, 1982, 1986, 1989, 1990; Marian Goodman, NY, 1982, 1983, 1986, 1987, 1989; Palais des Beaux-Arts, Brussels, 1985; Brooklyn Mus. of Art, NY, 1986; Venice Biennale, 1986, 1988, 1997; Hayward Gall., 1987; Tate Gall., Liverpool, 1988, 2000; Tate Gall., 1989; Stedelijik Van Abbemus., Eindhoven, 1989, 1991; Corcoran Gall. of Art, Washington, 1991; Wiener Secession, 1991; IVAM, Valencia, 1992; *group exhibitions:* Documenta 7, Documenta 8, 1987, Kassel; Mus. van Hedendaagse Kunst, Ghent, 1980; Bienal de São Paulo, 1983; Tate Gall., 1983, 1985; Sydney Biennale, 1984, 1990; Hayward Gall., 1985, 1990; and many others throughout Europe, US, Japan and Australia. Turner Prize, 1988. Chevalier des Arts et des Lettres (France), 1992. *Address:* Adolf Vorwerk Strasse 24, 5600 Wüppertal 2, Germany.

CRAGG, Anthony John, CMG 2000; Assistant Under-Secretary of State, Ministry of Defence, since 1999; *b* 16 May 1943; *s* of late Leslie Cragg and Gwendolen Cragg (*née* Pevler); *m* 1971, Jeanette Ann Rix; two *d*. *Educ:* Hastings Grammar School; Lincoln College, Oxford (Open Schol.; BA). Ministry of Defence, 1966–: Asst Private Sec. to Sec. of State for Defence, 1974; UK Delegn to NATO, 1977; Asst Sec., 1979; Chief Officer, Sovereign Base Areas, Cyprus, 1983–85; RCDS 1988; Asst Under Sec. of State, 1990; Dir Gen. of Mgt Audit, MoD, 1991–93; Chm., Defence Organisation Planning Team, 1991–92; Asst Sec. Gen. for Defence Planning and Policy, then Ops, NATO, 1993–99. *Publications:* articles on internat. security issues in press and specialised jls. *Recreations:* the performing arts, reading. *Address:* Ministry of Defence, Whitehall, SW1A 2EU.

CRAGG, Rt Rev. Kenneth; *see* Cragg, Rt Rev. A. K.

CRAGG, Dr Martin Robert; Chief Executive and Secretary, Institution of Highways and Transportation, since 1990; *b* 8 June 1941; *s* of Robert Brooks Cragg and Hilda Cragg (*née* Bateman); *m* 1966, Pamela Watts; one *s* two *d*. *Educ:* Dixie Grammar Sch., Market Bosworth; Sheffield Univ. (BSc Hons Chem.; PhD Fuel Technol. 1966); London Business Sch. (Sloan Fellow). Industrial Advr, NEDO, 1979–88; Dir, then Dir-Gen. and Chief Exec., Business Equipt and Information Technol. Assoc., 1988–89, then Sen. Exec., Electronic and Business Equipt Assoc., 1989–90. *Recreations:* golf, fly fishing, ski-ing. *Address:* 10 Woodside Road, New Malden, Surrey KT3 3AH. *T:* (020) 8942 8008.

CRAGGS, Prof. James Wilkinson, BSc, PhD; Professor of Engineering Mathematics, University of Southampton, 1967–81; *b* 3 Feb. 1920; *s* of Thomas Gibson Craggs and Margaret (*née* Wilkinson); *m* 1946, Mary Baker; two *s* one *d*. *Educ:* Bede Collegiate Sch., Sunderland; University of Manchester. BSc 1941, PhD 1948, Manchester; PhD Cambridge, 1953. Junior Lectr, Royal Military Coll. of Science, 1941–45; Asst Lectr, University of Manchester, 1947–49; Lecturer, Queen's Coll., Dundee, 1951–52; King's Coll., Newcastle upon Tyne: Lectr, 1952–56; Senior Lecturer, 1956–60; Reader in Mathematics, 1960–61; Prof. of Mathematics, University of Leeds, 1961–63; Prof. of Applied Mathematics, Melbourne Univ., 1963–67. *Publications:* contrib. learned journals regarding the mechanics of solids and fluids. *Recreation:* Methodist lay preacher. *Address:* 23 Redhill, Bassett, Southampton SO16 7BR.

CRAGGS, Madeleine Jennifer; Chief Executive and Registrar, General Osteopathic Council, since 1997; *b* 28 Dec. 1945; *d* of René Beaumont-Craggs and Muriel (*née* Robinson). *Educ:* Couvent des Ursulines, Brussels; Alexandra Grammar Sch., Singapore;

WRAC Coll., Camberley. MIMgt. Commnd WRAC, 1965; served in UK and Germany, incl. staff appts, MoD and HQ BAOR; Maj., 1970; WRAC Advr, 16th Signal Regt, 1973–75; Battery Comdr, Royal Sch. Artillery, 1975–77; SO2(A), HQ York Dist, 1977–79; Chief Instructor, WRAC Trng Centre, 1979–81; Detachment Comdr, Manning and Records Office, Chester, 1981–82; SO2 (Manpower & Planning), WRAC Directorate, MoD, 1982–84; Develt Dir, St Bartholomew's Hosp. Med. Coll., 1984–90; Sec., ICRF, 1991–97. *Recreations:* good wine, good food, good company. *Address:* 7 Felstead Gardens, Felstead Wharf, Ferry Street, E14 3BS.

CRAIG, family name of **Viscount Craigavon** and of **Baron Craig of Radley**.

CRAIG OF RADLEY, Baron *cr* 1991 (Life Peer), of Helhoughton in the County of Norfolk; **Marshal of the Royal Air Force David Brownrigg Craig,** GCB 1984 (KCB 1981; CB 1978); OBE 1967; Chief of the Defence Staff, 1988–91; *b* 17 Sept. 1929; *s* of Major Francis Brownrigg Craig and Mrs Olive Craig; *m* 1955, Elisabeth June Derenburg; one *s* one *d*. *Educ:* Radley Coll.; Lincoln Coll., Oxford (MA; Hon. Fellow 1984). FRAeS 1986. Commnd in RAF, 1951; OC RAF Cranwell, 1968–70; ADC to the Queen, 1969–71; Dir, Plans and Ops, HQ Far East Comd, 1970–71; OC RAF Akrotiri, 1972–73; ACAS (Ops), MoD, 1975–78; AOC No 1 Group, RAF Strike Command, 1978–80; Vice-Chief of Air Staff, 1980–82; AOC-in-C, RAF Strike Command and C-in-C, UK Air Forces, 1982–85; CAS, 1985–88. Air ADC to the Queen, 1985–88. Dir, M. L. Holdings plc, 1991–92. Mem., H of L Select Cttee for Sci. and Technology, 1993–99; Convenor, Cross Bench Peers, 1999–. Chm. Council, King Edward VII's Hosp. (Sister Agnes) (formerly King Edward VII's Hosp. for Officers), 1998–. Dep. Chm. Council, RAF Benevolent Fund, 1996–. Pres., Not Forgotten Assoc., 1996–. Hon. DSc Cranfield, 1988. *Recreations:* fishing, shooting, golf. *Address:* House of Lords, SW1A 0PW. *Club:* Royal Air Force.

CRAIG, Rev. Canon Alan Stewart; Chaplain to the Bishop of Newcastle and Diocesan Director of Ordinands, since 1999; Chaplain to the Queen, since 1995; *b* 7 Feb. 1938; *s* of Dr John Gray Craig and Grace Craig (*née* Kay); *m* 1962, Marjorie (*née* Bell); one *s* two *d*. *Educ:* Uppingham Sch.; Leeds Univ. (BA (Hons)); Cranmer Hall, Durham Univ. (DipTh). Ordained deacon, Lichfield, 1961, priest, 1962; Assistant Curate: St Giles, Newcastle under Lyme, 1961–65; St Mary's, Scarborough, 1965–67; Vicar, Werrington, Stoke-on-Trent, 1967–72; Asst Chaplain, Manchester Prison, 1972–73; Chaplain: Hindley Borstal, 1973–78; Acklington Prison, 1978–84; Vicar, Longhirst and Hebron, Newcastle, 1984–90; Rector of Morpeth, 1990–99; Rural Dean of Morpeth, 1984–95. Hon. Canon, Newcastle Cathedral, 1990–. Chm., Newcastle Diocesan Pastoral Cttee, 1994–99. *Recreations:* music, theatre, fell-walking. *Address:* 83 Kenton Road, Gosforth, Newcastle upon Tyne NE3 4NL. *T:* (0191) 285 1502, *Fax:* (0191) 213 0728.

CRAIG, Sir (Albert) James (Macqueen), GCMG 1984 (KCMG 1981 CMG 1975); HM Diplomatic Service, retired; President, Middle East Association, since 1993 (Director General, 1985–93); *b* 13 July 1924; *s* of James Craig and Florence Morris; *m* 1952, Margaret Hutchinson (*d* 2001); three *s* one *d*. *Educ:* Liverpool Institute High Sch.; Univ. of Oxford. Queen's Coll., Oxford (Exhibr), 1942; 1st cl. Hon. Mods Classics, 1943 (Hon. Schol.); Army, 1943–44; 1st cl. Oriental Studies (Arabic and Persian), 1947; Sen. Demy, Magdalen Coll., 1947–48; student, Cairo Univ., 1950–51. Lectr in Arabic, Durham Univ., 1948–55; seconded to FO, 1955 as Principal Instructor at Middle East Centre for Arab Studies, Lebanon; joined Foreign Service substantively, 1956; served: FO, 1958–61; HM Political Agent, Trucial States, 1961–64; 1st Sec., Beirut, 1964–67; Counsellor and Head of Chancery, Jedda, 1967–70; Supernumerary Fellow, St Antony's Coll., Oxford, 1970–71; Head of Near East and N Africa Dept, FCO, 1971–75; Dep. High Comr, Kuala Lumpur, 1975–76; Ambassador to: Syria, 1976–79; Saudi Arabia, 1979–84. Vis. Prof. in Arabic, and Lectr, Pembroke Coll., Univ. of Oxford, 1985–91. Director: Saudi-British Bank, 1985–94; Hong Kong Egyptian Bank, 1987–94; Special Adviser, Hong Kong Bank Gp, 1985–92; Chm., Roxby Engineering Internat., 1988–97. Pres., British Soc. for ME Studies, 1987–94; Vice-Chm., Middle East Internat., 1990–. Sen. Associate Mem., St Antony's Coll., Oxford, 1989. Hon. Fellow, Middle East Centre, Durham Univ., 1987–. OStJ 1985; Mem. Council, Order of St John, 1985–90. *Publications:* Shemlan: a history of the Middle East Centre for Arab Studies, 1998; various articles on the Arab world. *Address:* c/o 33 Bury Street, SW1Y 6AX. *T:* (020) 7839 2137. *Club:* Travellers.

CRAIG, Surgeon Rear-Admiral Alexander; Member, Criminal Injuries Compensation Appeal Panel, since 1997; *b* 22 Nov. 1943; *s* of Rev. Dr Albert Craig and Agnes Nicol (*née* Wards); *m* 1968, Kate Margaret Elliott; one *s* two *d*. *Educ:* George Watson's Boys' Coll., Edinburgh; Edinburgh Univ. (MB ChB 1967). Royal Infirmary, Edinburgh, 1968; Regimental MO, 45 Commando, RM, 1969–72; Jt Services Families Clinic, Malta, 1972–74; OC Med. Sqn, CDO LOG Regt, 1974–78; MoD, 1978–80, NDC 1981; UK Support Unit, Naples, 1981–83; CSO to Surgeon Cdre (NMT), 1983–86; PMO, HMS Sultan, 1986–87; CSO to SRA (OMS), 1987–89; MO i/c, Inst. of Naval Medicine, 1989–90; Dir, Med. Organisation, MoD, 1990–93; Surg. Rear-Adm. Support Med. Services, 1993–94; Med. Dir Gen. (Naval), 1994–97. QHP, 1992–97. *Recreation:* travel. *Address:* 21 Barfield, Ryde, Isle of Wight PO33 2JP.

CRAIG, Mrs Barbara Denise, MA Oxon; Principal of Somerville College, Oxford, 1967–80, Honorary Fellow, 1980; *b* 22 Oct. 1915; *o d* of John Alexander Chapman and Janie Denize (*née* Callaway); *m* 1942, Wilson James Craig, CBE (*d* 1989); no *c*. *Educ:* Haberdashers' Aske's Girls' Sch., Acton; Somerville Coll., Oxford. Craven Fellow, 1938; Goldsmiths' Sen. Student, 1938; Woolley Fellow in Archæology of Somerville Coll., 1954–56. Temp. Asst Principal, Mins of Supply and Labour, 1939–40; Asst to Prof. of Greek, Aberdeen Univ., 1940–42; Temp. Asst Principal, Min. of Home Security, 1942; Temp. Principal, Min. of Production, 1943–45. Unofficial work as wife of British Council officer in Brazil, Iraq, Spain, Pakistan, 1946–65; from 1956, archæological work on finds from British excavations at Mycenae. *Recreation:* bird-watching (Mem. Brit. Ornithologists' Union). *Address:* The Wynd, Gayle, Hawes, North Yorkshire DL8 3SD. *T:* (01969) 667289.

CRAIG, Christopher John Sinclair, CB 1991; DSC 1982; RN retired; *b* 18 May 1941; *s* of Richard Michael Craig and Barbara Mary Craig; *m* 1973, Daphne Joan Underwood; two *s*. *Educ:* Portchester Sch., Bournemouth. Joined RN as officer cadet, 1959; qualified as Naval helicopter pilot, 1963; operational flying and sea service (Far East), 1963–70; in command: HMS Monkton, 1970–72; naval air sqdns 705 and 826, 1973–76; Asst Sec. to Chiefs of Staff, 1978–80; in command: HMS Alacrity, 1980–82 (incl. Falklands War); HMS Avenger and Fourth Frigate Sqdn, 1985–86; RNAS Portland/HMS Osprey, 1986–87; HMS Drake barracks, 1987–89; Comdr, RN Task Gp afloat, Gulf War, 1990–91; COS to FONA, 1991–93; retd 1994. United States Bronze Star, 1991. *Publication:* Call for Fire: sea combat in the Falklands and the Gulf War, 1995. *Recreations:* music, watercolour painting, reading, horse-racing. *Address:* National Westminster Bank, 48 Blue Boar Row, Salisbury, Wilts SP1 1DF.

CRAIG, Prof. David Parker, AO 1985; FRS 1968; FAA 1969; FRSC; University Fellow and Emeritus Professor, Australian National University, since 1985; *b* 23 Dec. 1919; *s* of Andrew Hunter Craig, Manchester and Sydney, and Mary Jane (*née* Parker); *m* 1948, Veronica, *d* of Cyril Bryden-Brown, Market Harborough and Sydney; three *s* one *d*. *Educ:* Sydney Church of England Grammar Sch.; University of Sydney; University Coll., London. MSc (Sydney) 1941, PhD (London) 1950, DSc (London) 1956. Commonwealth Science Scholar, 1940. War Service: Capt., Australian Imperial Force, 1941–44. Lectr in Chemistry, University of Sydney, 1944–46; Turner and Newall Research Fellow, 1946–49, and Lectr in Chemistry, University Coll., London, 1949–52; Prof. of Physical Chemistry, Univ. of Sydney, 1952–56; Prof. of Chemistry, University Coll., London, 1956–67; Prof. of Chemistry, 1967–85, Dean, Research Sch. of Chemistry, 1970–73 and 1977–81, ANU. Vis. Prof., UCL, 1968–; Firth Vis. Prof., Univ. of Sheffield, 1973; Vis. Prof., University Coll., Cardiff, 1975–89. Part-time Mem., CSIRO Exec., 1980–85. Chm., Adv. Cttee, Aust. Nat. Botanic Gdns, 1986–89. Pres., Australian Acad. of Sci., 1990–94. Fellow of University Coll., London, 1964–. Hon. FRSC 1987. Hon. Dr Chem Bologna, 1985; Hon. DSc Sydney, 1985. *Publications:* books and original papers on chemistry in scientific periodicals. *Address:* 199 Dryandra Street, O'Connor, ACT 2601, Australia. *Club:* Athenæum.

CRAIG, Douglas, OBE 1965; freelance opera producer, adjudicator and lecturer; *b* 26 May 1916; *m* 1955, Dorothy Dixon; two *d*. *Educ:* Latymer Upper Sch.; St Catharine's Coll., Cambridge (MA). FRCM, FRSA. Winchester Prize, Cambridge, 1938. Intell. Corps, 1940–46, Major 1944. Baritone, Sadler's Wells Opera and elsewhere, 1946–; Artistic Dir, Opera for All, 1949–65; Stage Dir, Glyndebourne, 1952–55; Asst Gen. Man., Glyndebourne, 1955–59; Producer, Royal Coll. of Music, 1958–; Freelance Opera Producer, 1959–; Dep. Dir, London Opera Centre, 1965–66; Administrator, Welsh Nat. Opera, 1966–70; Dir, Sadler's Wells Theatre, 1970–78; Dir, Opera and Drama Sch., RCM, 1976–80. Master Teacher in Residence, Adelaide Coll. of the Arts, 1981; taught in Adelaide, Canberra, Melbourne, Sydney and Hong Kong, 1984 (specialist tour award from British Council); prodns for S Australia Coll. of Advanced Educn and for NSW State Conservatorium of Music, master classes and lectures, Australia, 1985; Nat. Adjudicator, Australian Singing Competition, 1985. President: Council of Friends of Sadler's Wells, 1982–95; Sussex Opera and Ballet Soc., 1997–. Mem. Exec. and Editor, Music Jl of ISM, 1979–84. *Publication:* (ed) Delius: Koanga (opera), 1975. *Recreation:* travel. *Address:* 43 Park Road, Radlett, Herts WD7 8EG. *T:* (01923) 857240. *Club:* Garrick.

CRAIG, Prof. Edward John, FBA 1993; Knightbridge Professor of Philosophy, University of Cambridge, since 1998; Fellow, Churchill College, Cambridge, since 1966; *b* 26 March 1942; *s* of Charles William Craig and Annie (*née* Taylor); *m* 1st, 1973, Isabel Nina Barnard (marr. diss. 1986); two *d*; 2nd, 1987, Gillian Helen Elizabeth Edwards. *Educ:* Charterhouse; Trinity Coll., Cambridge (MA 1966; PhD 1970). Cricket for Cambridge Univ. and Lancs CCC, 1961–63; Cambridge University: Asst Lectr and Univ. Lectr in Philosophy, 1966–92; Reader in Modern Philosophy, 1992–98. Visiting University appointments: Melbourne, 1974; Hamburg, 1977–78; Heidelberg, 1981; Indian Inst. of Advanced Studies, 1996. Chief Ed., Routledge Encyclopedia of Philosophy, 1991–98; Editor, Ratio, 1988–92. *Publications:* David Hume: eine Einführung in seine Philosophie, 1979; The Mind of God and the Works of Man, 1987; Knowledge and the State of Nature, 1990; Pragmatische Untersuchungen zum Wissensbegriff, 1993; Hume on Religion, 1997. *Recreations:* music, golf. *Address:* Churchill College, Cambridge CB3 0DS. *T:* (01223) 336000.

CRAIG, George Charles Graham; Senior Director, Social Policy and Local Government Affairs, National Assembly for Wales, since 1999; *b* 8 May 1946; s of late George Craig and of E. S. Craig (*née* Milne); *m* 1968, (Ethne) Marian, *er d* of late H. H. A. Gallagher and of E. F. Gallagher; two *s* one *d*. *Educ:* Brockley County Grammar Sch.; Nottingham Univ. (BA). Asst Principal, Min. of Transport, 1967; Welsh Office: Private Sec. to Minister of State, 1970–72; Principal, 1972; PPS to Sec. of State for Wales, 1978–80; Asst Sec., 1980; Under Sec., 1986; Dep. Sec., 1999. *Address:* National Assembly for Wales, Cathays Park, Cardiff CF1 3NQ. *T:* (029) 2082 5111.

CRAIG, Gloria Linda; a Director General, Ministry of Defence, since 1999; *b* 23 Nov. 1948; *née* Kristler; adopted *d* of late George Edward Franklin and of Victoria Franklin; *m* 1987, Gordon Montgomery Craig. *Educ:* St Martin-in-the-Fields High Sch. for Girls; Lady Margaret Hall, Oxford (MA). GB–USSR Assoc., 1970–71; joined MoD, 1971; Private Sec. to Parly Under Sec. of State (Navy), 1975–76; Planning Staff, FCO, 1979–81; Asst Sec., 1984; RCDS 1988; Dep. Dir, Cabinet Office, 1989–92, 1995–99. Non-exec. Mem. Bd, Family Housing Assoc., 1999–. *Publications:* papers and lectures on defence and public service issues, white papers and best practice guides. *Recreations:* antiques, music, travel, animals, gardening. *Address:* c/o Ministry of Defence, Main Building, Whitehall, SW1A 2HB.

CRAIG, Sir James; *see* Craig, Sir A. J. M.

CRAIG, Dr (James) Oscar (Max Clark), FRCS, FRCP, FRCSI, FRCR; Consultant Radiologist since 1963, and Hon. Senior Clinical Lecturer, since 1987, St Mary's Hospital, London; President, Royal College of Radiologists, 1989–92; *b* 7 May 1927; *s* of James Oscar Max Clark Craig and Olivia Craig; *m* 1950, Louise Burleigh; four *d*. *Educ:* Royal College of Surgeons in Ireland. LRCP&SI 1950; FRCSI 1956; DMRD 1959; FRCR (FFR 1962); FRCS 1982; MRCP 1989, FRCP 1993; FRCGP 1991. Asst GP, 1950–51; Ho. Surg., St Helier Hosp., Carshalton, 1951–52; Gen. practice, Sutton, 1952–54. Surg., RAF, 1954–56. Sen. Ho. Officer, Surgery, Hammersmith Hosp., 1956–57; Registrar and Sen. Registrar, Dept of Radiology, St Mary's Hosp., London, 1957–63; Lectr in Radiology, London Univ., 1963–87; Dir of Clinical Studies, 1969–75, Dir of Post Grad. Studies, 1979–81, St Mary's Hosp. Med. Sch. Hon. Mem., Radiological Soc. of N America, 1993. Hon. FFR RCSI 1985; Hon. Fellow, Hong Kong Coll. of Radiologists, 1995. *Publications:* numerous papers and chapters in books on clinical radiology, phlebography, lymangiography, gastro-intestinal radiology, medico-legal medicine and the develt of digital radiology. *Recreation:* country-walking. *Address:* The White House, 18 Sandy Lane, Cheam, Surrey SM2 7NR. *T:* (020) 8642 2696. *Clubs:* Royal Society of Medicine, MCC.

CRAIG, John Egwin, CBE 1998 (OBE 1990); Director, European & General Investment Trust PLC, since 2000; *b* 16 Aug. 1932; *s* of late Thomas Joseph Alexander Craig, CIE, and Mabel Frances (*née* Quinnell); *m* 1959, Patricia Costa Lopes; three *s*. *Educ:* Charterhouse. FCA 1961–2000. Cooper Bros (later Coopers & Lybrands), 1958–61; Council of Stock Exchange, 1961–64; N. M. Rothschild & Sons, 1964–91, Dir, 1970–91; Man. Dir, N. M. Rothschild, 1981–89; Chm., Jupiter European Investment Trust, 1990–2000. Chairman: Powerscreen Internat. plc, 1989–99; Belfast Internat. Airport Hldgs, 1994–96; Director: Standard Chartered, 1989–94; Jupiter Tyndall Gp, then Jupiter Internat. Gp, 1991–2000 (Vice Chm., 1991–94). Govt Dir, Internat. Fund for Ireland, 1989–96. Member: Exec. Council, BBA, 1981–89 (Chm., 1987–89); Deposit Protection Bd, 1986–89. Mem. Council, LPO, 1983–87. Trustee, Restoration of Appearance and Function Trust, 2000–. FRSA 1988. *Address:* Saxonbury House, Frant, near Tunbridge Wells, Kent TN3 9HJ. *Club:* Brooks's.

CRAIG, John Frazer, CB 1994; Director, Economic Affairs (formerly Head of Economic and Industrial Affairs), Welsh Office, 1990–97; *b* 8 Nov. 1943; *s* of late John Frazer Craig and Margaret Jane Gibson Craig; *m* 1973, Janet Elizabeth. *Educ:* Robert Richardson Grammar Sch., Sunderland. Customs and Excise, 1961–69; Nat. Bd for Prices and Incomes, 1969–70; Welsh Office, 1970–97: Private Sec. to Perm. Sec., 1972–74; Private Sec. to Sec. of State for Wales, 1980–82; Asst Sec., 1982–85, Under Sec. (Dir), 1985–87, Industry Dept; Under Sec. (Principal Finance Officer), Welsh Office, 1987–90; Dep. Sec., 1990–97.

CRAIG, Rev. Maxwell Davidson; General Secretary, Action of Churches Together in Scotland, 1990–98; Chaplain to the Queen in Scotland, 1986–2001, now an Extra Chaplain; *b* 25 Dec. 1931; *s* of Dr William Craig and Alice M. Craig (*née* Semple); *m* 1957, Janet Margaret Macgregor; one *s* three *d. Educ:* Oriel Coll., Oxford (MA (Hons) Lit.Hum.); Edinburgh Univ. (BD); Princeton Theol Seminary, NJ (ThM). 2nd Lieut, 1st Bn Argyll and Sutherland Highlanders, 1954–56. Ministry of Labour: Asst Principal, 1957–61; Pvte Sec. to Parly Sec., 1959–61. Fulbright Schol., Princeton, 1964; ordained minister, Grahamston Parish Church, Falkirk, 1966; Minister: Wellington Church, Glasgow, 1973–89; St Columba's Parish Church, Aberdeen, 1989–90; St Andrew's Ch, Jerusalem, 1999–2000. Convener of the Church and Nation Cttee, Church of Scotland, 1984–88. Chairman: Falkirk Children's Panel, 1970–72; Hillhead Housing Assoc., 1977–89; Scottish Churches Housing Agency, 2000–. *Publications:* Stella: the story of Stella J. Reekie, 1984; For God's Sake Unity, 1998. *Recreations:* hill-walking, choral singing. *Address:* 9 Kilbryde Crescent, Dunblane, Perthshire FK15 9BA. *T:* (01786) 823147; *e-mail:* maxwellcraig@hotmail.com.

CRAIG, Norman; Assistant Under-Secretary of State, Ministry of Defence, 1972–79; *b* 15 May 1920; *s* of George Craig, OBE; *m* 1st, 1946, Judith Margaret Newling (marr. diss. 1957); one *s*; 2nd, 1960, Jane Hudson; two *s* one *d. Educ:* Penarth County Sch.; Cardiff Univ. Army Service, Royal Sussex Regt, 1940–47. Board of Trade, 1948; Min. of Supply (later Aviation), 1953; Private Sec. to Minister, 1959–60; Min. of Technology, 1964; Sec. to Cttee of Inquiry into Aircraft Industry, 1964–65; course at IDC, 1968; MoD, 1971. Lord Chancellor's Department: official, 1979–85; consultant, 1986–87; lay observer, 1990. *Publication:* The Broken Plume, 1982. *Address:* 51 Hayes Lane, Beckenham, Kent BR3 6RE. *T:* (020) 8650 7916.

CRAIG, Oscar; *see* Craig, J. O. M. C.

CRAIG, Pamela Tudor; *see* Wedgwood, Pamela, Lady.

CRAIG, Prof. Paul Philip, FBA 1998; Professor of English Law, since 1998 (Professor of Law, 1996–98), and Fellow of St John's College, since 1998, University of Oxford; *b* 27 Sept. 1951; *s* of Maurice and Beatrice Craig; *m* 1991, Dr Anita Cooper; one *s. Educ:* Worcester Coll., Oxford (MA, BCL). University of Oxford: Fellow, Worcester Coll., 1976–98, now Emeritus; Reader in Law, 1990–96. Vis. Prof. in Univs of Virginia, Cornell, Connecticut, York (Osgoode Hall) Canada, Indiana, Queensland. Hon. QC 2000. *Publications:* Administrative Law, 1983, 4th edn 1999; Public Law and Democracy in the United Kingdom and the United States of America, 1990; Text, Cases and Materials on Community Law, 1995, 2nd edn 1998; Law Making in the European Union, 1998; The Evolution of EU Law, 1999; articles in jls. *Recreations:* riding, ski-ing, theatre, acting, ballet. *Address:* St John's College, Oxford OX1 3JP. *T:* (01865) 277340.

CRAIG, Maj.-Gen. (Robert) Peter, MD; FRCS, FFAEM; Medical Member, since 1997, and Medical Chairman, since 2000, Pensions Appeals Tribunals; Medical Member, The Appeals Service, since 1998; *b* 24 June 1940; *s* of late Dr Robert Theodore Gilpin Craig, TD, MB BS, MRCGP and Jessie Craig (*née* McKinstry); *m* 1971, Jean Toft, MA; one *s* two *d. Educ:* George Watson's Boys' Coll.; Durham Univ. Med. Sch. (MB BS 1964); MD Newcastle upon Tyne 1987; FRCS 1972; FFAEM 1994. Commissioned RA (TA) 1958; RAMC 1963; Royal Victoria Infirmary, Newcastle, 1964–65; RMO 1/2 Gurkha Rifles, 1966–68; Queen Alexandra Mil. Hosp.; Birmingham Accident Hosp.; Dept of Surgery, Univ. of Newcastle upon Tyne; BMH Rinteln; Guy's Hosp., 1974–78; Consultant Surgeon: BMH Hong Kong, 1979–81; Queen Elizabeth Mil. Hosp., 1981–86; Sen. Lectr in Mil. Surgery, Royal Army Med. Coll., 1981–86; BMH Rinteln, 1986–89, CO, 1987–89; Comd Med., 4th Armoured Div., 1989–90; Comd Surgeon, HQ BAOR, 1990–92; Dir of Army Surgery, 1992–93; Comdr Medical, UKLF, 1993–94; Consultant in A & E Medicine, Wansbeck Gen. Hosp., 1994–96. QHS 1992–94. GSM Oman 1973, NI 1979. Montefiore Meml Medal, 1979; Leishman Meml Medal, 1987. OStJ 1993. *Publications:* contribs to surgical jls. *Recreations:* golf, bridge, military history. *Address:* c/o Drummonds Branch, Royal Bank of Scotland, 49 Charing Cross, SW1A 2DX. *Fax:* (020) 7252 5344; *e-mail:* rpcraig@trafalgar9774.freeserve.co.uk. *Clubs:* Athenæum, Army and Navy, Royal Society of Medicine; Northumberland Golf; Wildernesse (Sevenoaks).

CRAIG, Rt Hon. William; PC (N Ire.) 1963; solicitor and company director; *b* 2 Dec. 1924; *s* of late John Craig and Mary Kathleen Craig (*née* Lamont); *m* 1960, Doris Hilgendorff; two *s. Educ:* Dungannon Royal Sch.; Larne Grammar Sch.; Queen's Univ., Belfast. Served War of 1939–45, Royal Air Force, 1943–46. Qualified as solicitor, 1952. MP (U) Larne Div. of Antrim, NI Parliament, 1960–73; Mem. (Vanguard Unionist Progressive), N Antrim, NI Assembly, 1973–75; Mem. (UUC), E Belfast, NI Constitutional Convention, 1975–76; MP (UU) Belfast East, Feb. 1974–1979. Chief Whip, Parliament of Northern Ireland, 1962–63; Minister of Home Affairs, 1963–64, and 1966–68; Minister of Health and Local Government, 1964; Minister of Development, 1965–66. Founder: Ulster Vanguard, 1972 (Leader, 1972–77); Vanguard Unionist Party, 1973 (Leader, 1973–77). Member: Council of Europe, 1976–79; WEU, 1976–79. *Recreations:* travel, motoring, shooting.

CRAIG-COOPER, Sir (Frederick Howard) Michael, Kt 1991; CBE 1982; TD 1968 (3 bars); DL; Director: Craig-Lloyd, since 1968; National Bank of Kuwait (International) plc, since 1993; *b* 28 Jan. 1936; *s* of late Frederick William Valentine Craig-Cooper and of Elizabeth Oliver-Thompson Craig-Cooper (*née* Macdonald) (she *m* 1978, Col J. H. Carroll-Leahy, MC (decd)); *m* 1968, Elizabeth Snagge, MVO; one *s. Educ:* Horris Hill; Stowe; College of Law. Solicitor, 1961. National Service, RA, 1954–56; TA, 1956–88; Comdr, Naval Gunfire Liaison Unit, 29 Commando Regt, RA, 1972–75; Mem., Greater London TAVRA (Chm., Employers Support Cttee, 1987–90). Jaques & Co., 1956–61; Allen & Overy, 1962–64; Inco, 1964–85; Director: Paul Ray Internat., 1984–92 (merged with Carre Orban & Partners, 1989); Tichborne Enterprises Ltd, 1993–; Ely Place Holdings Ltd, 1994–; Craigmyle & Co. Ltd, 1995–; Westminster Forum (formerly WIB Publications) Ltd, 1996–; Advr, DBMI, 2000–. Royal Borough of Kensington & Chelsea: Councillor, 1968–74; Chief Whip, 1971–74; Chm. Finance Cttee, 1972–74; Alderman, 1974–78; Mem. Investment Panel, 1973–. Contested (C) Houghton-le-Spring, 1966, 1970; Chm., Cons. Nat. Property Adv. Cttee, 1986–93 (Mem., 1993–); Pres., Kensington and Chelsea (formerly Chelsea), Cons. Assoc., 1983– (Chm., 1974–77). Trustee: Copper Develt Trust Fund, 1974–85; Order of Malta Homes Trust, 1980–; Orders of St John Trust, 1988–. Mem. Council, Mining Assoc., 1977–82; Chm. Appeal Cttee, CIMA, 1994–. Comr, Royal Hosp. Chelsea, 1998–. Freeman, City of London, 1964; Liveryman, Drapers' Co., 1970– (Mem. Court of Assistants, 1987–; Master, 1997–98). DL Greater London, 1986–; Rep. DL Kensington & Chelsea, 1987–. FCIArb 1992. KStJ 1990 (Chm., Council for London, 1990–94; Mem., Chapter-Gen., 1993–99). Officer, SMO Malta, 1986. *Publications:* (with Philippe De Backer) Management Audit: how to create an effective management team, 1993; (jtly) Maw on Corporate Governance, 1994; (jtly) Maximum Leadership, 1995, revd edn as Maximum Leadership 2000, 1997. *Recreation:* admiring wife's gardening. *Clubs:* Beefsteak, Pratt's, White's.

CRAIG-McFEELY, Comdt Elizabeth Sarah Ann, (Mrs C. C. H. Dunlop), CB 1982; DL; Director, Women's Royal Naval Service, 1979–82; *b* 28 April 1927; *d* of late Lt-Col Cecil Michael Craig McFeely, DSO, OBE, MC, and Nancy Sarah (*née* Mann, later Roberts); *m* 1995, Rear-Adm. C. C. H. Dunlop, *qv. Educ:* St Rose's Convent, Stroud, Glos; Anstey College of Physical Educn, Birmingham. DipPhysEducn London. Taught PE at St Angela's Ursuline Convent Sch., 1948–52; joined WRNS, 1952; Third Officer, 1953; served in various Royal Naval, Royal Marines and Royal Naval Reserve Estabts, 1952–67; in charge, WRNS, Far Eastern Fleet, 1967–69; various appts, MoD (Navy), 1969–74; HMS Centurion, 1974–76; Supt WRNS, 1977. Naval member, NAAFI Bd of Management, 1977–79; Hon. ADC to the Queen, 1979–82; retired 1982. DL Kent, 1996. *Recreations:* gardening and country pursuits. *Address:* Moonrakers, Mockbeggar Lane, Biddenden, Kent TN27 8ES. *T:* (01580) 291325.

CRAIG-MARTIN, Prof. Michael, CBE 2001; artist; *b* 28 Aug. 1941; *s* of Paul and Rhona Craig-Martin; *m* 1963, Janice Lucia Hashey (separated); one *d. Educ:* Priory Sch., Washington; Yale Univ. Artist in Residence, King's Coll., Cambridge, 1970–72; Sen. Lectr, 1973–79, Prin. Lectr, 1979–85, Millard Prof. of Fine Art, 1994–2000, Goldsmiths' Coll., London (Hon. Fellow, 2001). Trustee, Tate Gall., 1989–99. *Exhibitions* include: Hayward Gall., 1972; Tate Gall., 1972; IX Biennale des Jeunes Artistes, Paris, 1975; Sydney Biennale, 1976, 1990; Whitechapel Art Gall., 1995; MOMA, NY, 1999; *one-man exhibitions:* Whitechapel Art Gall., 1989 (retrospective); MOMA, NY, 1991; Centre Pompidou, Paris, 1994; Hannover Kunstverein, 1998; São Paulo Bienal, 1998; Stuttgart Kunstverein, 1999; Peter Blum, NY, 1999; Waddington Galls, 2000; IVAM, Valencia, Spain, 2000.

CRAIGAVON, 3rd Viscount *cr* 1927, of Stormont, Co. Down; **Janric Fraser Craig;** Bt 1918; *b* 9 June 1944; *s* of 2nd Viscount Craigavon; *S* father, 1974. *Educ:* Eton; London Univ. (BA, BSc). FCA. Elected Mem., H of L, 1999. *Heir:* none.

CRAIGEN, Desmond Seaward; Director: Prudential Corporation plc, 1982–89; Pioneer Concrete (Holdings) Ltd, 1982–89; *b* 31 July 1916; *s* of late John Craigen and Ann Amelia Craigen (*née* Brebner); *m* 1961, Elena Ines (*née* Oldham Florez) (*d* 1995); one *s* one *d. Educ:* Holloway Sch.; King's Coll., London (BA Hons). Prudential Assurance Co. Ltd, 1934–81; India, 1950–57; attached O&M Div., Treasury, 1957–58; Dep. General Manager, 1968–69; General Manager, 1969–78; Chief General Manager, 1979–81; Chm., Vanbrugh Life Assurance Co. Ltd, 1982–87. Served War of 1939–45: 53rd Reconnaisance Regt RAC (Major; despatches). *Recreations:* music, reading. *Address:* 44 Crondace Road, SW6 4BT.

CRAIGEN, James Mark; JP; Director and Secretary, Scottish Federation of Housing Associations, 1988–90; freelance writer; *b* 2 Aug. 1938; *e s* of James Craigen, MA and Isabel Craigen; *m* 1971, Sheena Millar. *Educ:* Shawlands Academy, Glasgow; Strathclyde University. MLitt, Heriot-Watt, 1974. CIMgt. Compositor, 1954–61. Industrial Relations Asst, Scottish Gas Bd, 1963–64; Head of Organisation and Social Services at Scottish TUC, 1964–68; Asst Sec., and Industrial Liaison Officer, Scottish Business Educn Council, 1968–74. Glasgow City Councillor, 1965–68, Magistrate, 1966–68. Member: Scottish Ambulance Service Bd, 1966–71; Race Relations Bd, Scottish Conciliation Cttee, 1967–70; Police Adv. Bd for Scotland, 1970–74; ITC Viewer Consultative Council for Scotland, 1990–93; S Scotland Electricity Consumers' Cttee, 1994–97. Contested Ayr constituency, 1970. MP (Lab and Co-op) Glasgow Maryhill, Feb. 1974–1987 (retired on grounds of experience, not age); PPS to Rt Hon. William Ross, MBE, MP, Sec. of State for Scotland, 1974–76; Opposition Spokesman on Scottish Affairs, 1983–85. Member: Select Cttee on Employment, 1979–83 (Chm., 1982–83); Select Cttee on Scottish Affairs, 1987; Chairman: Co-op. Party Parly Group, 1978–79; Scottish Group, Labour MPs, 1978–79; PLP Employment Gp, 1981–83. Member: UK Delegn to Council of Europe Assembly, 1976–80; Extra Parly Panel, Private Legislation Procedure (Scotland) Act 1936, 1996–. Trustee, Industry and Parliament Trust, 1983–88 (Fellow, 1978–79). Mem., Bd of Trustees, Nat. Museums of Scotland, 1985–91. Hon. Vice-Pres., Building Societies Assoc., 1985–88. Hon. Lectr, Strathclyde Univ., 1980–85; Fellow, Inst. of Advanced Studies in Humanities, Edinburgh Univ., 1990–91. JP: Glasgow, 1966; Edinburgh, 1975. *Publications:* (contrib.) Forward! Labour Politics in Scotland 1888–1988, 1989; contribs to Co-operative News. *Address:* 38 Downie Grove, Edinburgh EH12 7AX.

CRAIGIE, Cathie; Member (Lab) Cumbernauld and Kilsyth, Scottish Parliament, since 1999; *b* Stirling, 14 April 1954; *d* of George Mitchell and Marion (*née* Mandelkau); *m* 1978, Arthur Craigie; one *s* one *d. Educ:* Kilsyth Acad. Mem., Ext. Audit Team for Chartered Accountants, 1970–80. Parly Asst to MP, 1992–97. Member (Lab): Cumbernauld and Kilsyth DC, 1984–96: Council Leader, 1994–96; Chm., Planning, Housing, Policy & Resources and Equal Opportunities Cttees, 1984–96; N Lanarks Council, 1995–99: Vice-Chm., Housing, 1995–98; Chairman: Envmtl Services, 1998–99; Kilsyth Local Area Cttee, 1998–99; Cumbernauld Housing Partnership, 1997–98. Scottish Parliament: Member: Audit Cttee, 1999–2000; Social Inclusion, Housing and Voluntary Sector Cttee, 1999–2000; Social Justice Cttee, 2001–. Labour Party: Mem., 1974–; Constituency Party Sec., 1992–99; Mem., Nat. Policy Forum, 1998–. *Recreations:* cycling, reading, family holidays. *Address:* Scottish Parliament, Edinburgh EH99 1SP.

CRAIGMYLE, 4th Baron *cr* 1929, of Craigmyle, co. Aberdeen; **Thomas Columba Shaw;** *b* 19 Oct. 1960; *s* of 3rd Baron Craigmyle and of Anthea Esther Christine (*née* Rich); *S* father, 1998; *m* 1987, (Katherine) Alice (*née* Floyd); four *s. Heir: e s* Alexander Francis Shaw; *b* 1 July 1988. *Address:* Scottas House, Knoydart, Inverness-shire PH41 4PL.

CRAIK, Roger George; QC (Scot.) 1981; Sheriff of Lothian and Borders, since 1984; *b* 22 Nov. 1940; *s* of George and Frances Craik; *m* 1964, Helen Sinclair Sutherland; one *s* one *d. Educ:* Lockerbie Academy; Breadalbane Academy, Aberfeldy; George Watson's Boys' Coll.; Edinburgh Univ. (MA 1960, LLB 1962). Qualified as solicitor, 1962; worked for Orr Dignam & Co., Solicitors, Pakistan, 1963–65; called to Scottish Bar, 1966. Standing junior counsel to Min. of Defence (Army), 1974–80; Advocate Depute, 1980–83. Mem., Sheriff Court Rules Council, 1990–95. *Publications:* The Advocates' Library 1689–1989, 1989; James Boswell: The Scottish Perspective, 1994; Parliament House Portraits: the art collection of the Faculty of Advocates, 2000. *Recreations:* Scottish antiquities, modern jazz. *Address:* Sheriff Court House, Chambers Street, Edinburgh EH1 1LB.

CRAMOND, Ronald Duncan, CBE 1987; Chairman, Greenbelt Foundation, since 1999; *b* 22 March 1927; *s* of Adam and Margaret Cramond; *m* 1st, 1954, Constance

MacGregor (*d* 1985); one *s* one *d*; 2nd, 1999, Ann Rayner. *Educ:* George Heriot's Sch.; Edinburgh Univ. (MA). Sen. Medallist History 1949. FIMgt; FSAScot 1978. Commnd Royal Scots, 1950. Entered War Office, 1951; Private Sec. to Parly Under-Sec. of State, Scottish Office, 1956; Principal, Dept of Health for Scotland, 1957; Mactaggart Fellow (Applied Econs), Glasgow Univ., 1962; Haldane Medallist in Public Admin, 1964; Asst Sec., Scottish Develt Dept, 1966, Under Sec., 1973; Under Sec., Dept of Agric. and Fisheries for Scotland, 1977; Dep. Chm., Highlands and Islands Develt Bd, 1983–88. Chm., Strathclyde Greenbelt Co., then Scottish Greenbelt Foundn, 1992–2000. Dir, Cairngorm Chairlift Co., 1988–90. Chairman: Scottish Museums Council, 1990–93; LandTrust, 1997–98; Member: Scottish Museums Adv. Bd, 1984–85; Scottish Tourist Board, 1985–88; CCS, 1988–92; Trustee: Nat. Museums of Scotland, 1985–96; Scottish Civic Trust, 1988–95; Sec., Intellectual Access Trust, 1995–; Vice-Pres., Architectural Heritage Soc. of Scotland, 1988–93. *Publication:* Housing Policy in Scotland, 1966. *Recreations:* hill walking, testing a plastic hip. *Address:* c/o Land Trust, 189 St Vincent Street, Glasgow G2 5QD.

CRAMOND, Dr William Alexander, AO 1994; OBE 1960; FRSE; Professor of Clinical Psychiatry, Flinders University, South Australia, 1983–92, Emeritus Professor of Psychiatry, 1993; *b* 2 Oct. 1920; *er s* of William James Cramond, MBE and of May Battisby, Aberdeen; *m* 1949, Bertine J. C. Mackintosh, MB, ChB, FRANZCP, Dornoch; one *s* one *d*. *Educ:* Robert Gordon's Coll., Aberdeen; Aberdeen Univ. MB, ChB, MD, FRCPsych, FRANZCP, FRACP, DPM. Physician Supt, Woodilee Mental Hosp., Glasgow, 1955–61; Dir of Mental Health, S Australia, 1961–65; Prof. of Mental Health, Univ. of Adelaide, 1963–71; Principal Medical Officer in Mental Health, Scottish Home and Health Dept, 1971–72; Dean of Faculty of Medicine and Prof. of Mental Health, Univ. of Leicester, 1972–75; Principal and Vice-Chancellor, Stirling Univ., 1975–80; Dir of Mental Health Services, NSW, 1980–83; Clinical Dir, Cleland House, Glenside Hosp., SA, 1983–85; Chm., Bd of Dirs, SA Mental Health Services, 1993–95. Hon. Prof., Clinical Psychiatry, Sydney, 1980–83. DUniv Stirling, 1984. *Publications:* papers on psychosomatic medicine and on care of dying in Brit. Jl Psychiat., Lancet, BMJ. *Recreations:* reading, theatre. *Address:* 28 Tynte Street, North Adelaide, SA 5006, Australia. *Club:* Adelaide (Adelaide).

CRAMP, Leslie Thomas; Deputy Inspector General and Senior Official Receiver, Insolvency Service, since 1998; *b* 25 Oct. 1949; *s* of Noel Clifford Cramp and Doris Nellie Irene Cramp; *m* 1974, Linda Ann Lipscomb; one *s* one *d*. *Educ:* Maidstone Grammar Sch. Local govt post, 1968–70; Insolvency Service, Department of Trade and Industry, 1970–: Companies Winding-up, London, 1970–82; Principal Examr, Policy Unit, 1982–88; Official Receiver, High Court, London, 1988–96; Manager, Anglia Reg., 1996–98. *Recreations:* music, football, reading, gardening. *Address:* Insolvency Service, 21 Bloomsbury Street, WC1B 3QW. *T:* (020) 7291 6728.

CRAMP, Prof. Rosemary Jean, CBE 1987; Professor of Archaeology, University of Durham, 1971–90, now Emeritus; *b* 6 May 1929; *er d* of Robert Kingston and Vera Cramp, Cranoe Grange, Leics. *Educ:* Market Harborough Grammar Sch.; St Anne's Coll., Oxford (MA, BLitt). Lectr, St Anne's Coll., Oxford, 1950–55; Lectr, Durham Univ., 1955, Sen. Lectr, 1966. Vis. Fellow, All Souls Coll., Oxford, 1992. Commissioner: Royal Commn on Ancient and Historical Monuments of Scotland, 1975–99; Historic Bldgs and Monuments Commn, 1984–89 (Mem., Adv. Cttee (Archaeology), 1984–89). Trustee, BM, 1978–98. Member: Adv. Bd for Redundant Churches, 1984–98; Validation Panel, Museums' Trng Inst., 1993–97; Reviewing Cttee on Export of Works of Art, 1994–. President: Council for British Archaeology, 1989–92 (Hon. Vice-Pres., 1992–); Cumberland and Westmorland Antiquarian and Archaeol Soc., 1984–87; Soc. for Church Archaeology, 1996–2001; Soc. of Antiquaries of London, 2001–; Vice-Pres., Royal Archaeol Inst., 1992–97; Chm., Archaeology Data Service, 1996–2001. Gen. Editor, Corpus of Anglo-Saxon Stone Sculpture, 1974–. Hon. DSc Durham, 1995. *Publications:* Corpus of Anglo-Saxon Stone Sculpture, vol. I, Durham and Northumberland, 1984, vol. 2, (with R. N. Bailey) Cumberland and Westmorland, 1986; contribs in the field of early monasticism, early medieval sculpture and glass, and northern archaeology. *Address:* 5 Leazes Place, Durham DH1 1RE.

CRAMPIN, Peter; QC 1993; a Recorder, since 1995; *b* 7 July 1946; *s* of John Hames Crampin and Gwendoline Edith (*née* Richardson); *m* 1975, Frida Yvonne Schoemann; one *s*. *Educ:* St Albans Sch.; University Coll., Oxford (Open Exhibnr; MA). Admitted Solicitor, 1973; called to the Bar, Middle Temple, 1976; in practice at Chancery Bar, 1978–; an Asst Recorder, 1990–95; 2nd Jun. Counsel to Attorney General in Charity Matters, 1988–93. *Address:* 11 New Square, Lincoln's Inn, WC2A 3QB. *T:* (020) 7831 0081.

CRAMPTON, Peter Duncan; *b* 10 June 1932; *s* of Edmund Crampton and Louisa Crampton (*née* Thurman); *m* 1955, Councillor Margaret Eva McMillan; two *s*. *Educ:* Blackpool Grammar School; Nottingham Univ. (BA Hons Geography); Birmingham Univ. (MA African Studies); Hull Univ. (Dip. W European Studies); London Univ. (PGCE). Casual work, mainly as farm worker, 1954–55; Statistician, Plessey Co., 1955–56; Geography Teacher, Coventry, 1957–61; Educn Officer, Uganda, 1961–64; Lectr i/c Geography, Technical Coll., Birmingham, 1964–70; Lectr in Geography, Hull Coll. of Educn, then Humberside Coll. of HE, 1970–85; part-time work as lectr, writer, parly assistant, 1985–89. Chairman: European Nuclear Disarmament Campaign, 1984–86; Internat. Cttee, CND, 1988–90. MEP (Lab) Humberside, 1989–99. European Parliament: First Vice-Pres., Political Affairs Cttee, 1989–94, For. Affairs Cttee, 1989–94; Member: Regl Policy Cttee, 1994–99; Fishing Cttee, 1994–99; Vice Pres., Delegn to Mongolia and Central Asia, 1994–96. *Publications:* (contrib.) Voices for One World, 1988; articles in jls on population geography in Africa, electoral behaviour and nuclear disarmament. *Recreations:* travel, hill-walking, music. *Address:* 135 Westbourne Avenue, Hull HU5 3HU. *T:* (01482) 494796, *Fax:* (01482) 449403.

CRAMPTON, Prof. Richard John, PhD; Professor of East European History, since 1996, and Fellow of St Edmund Hall, since 1990, University of Oxford; *b* 23 Nov. 1940; *s* of John Donald Crampton and Norah Crampton (*née* Haden); *m* 1965, Celia Harriss; two *s*. *Educ:* Univ. of Dublin (MA); MA Oxon; SSEES, Univ. of London (PhD). University of Kent at Canterbury: Lectr, 1967–78; Sen. Lectr, 1978–88; Prof. of East European History, 1988–90; Lectr in History, Univ. of Oxford, 1990–96. Dr *hc* Sofia. *Publications:* The Hollow Détente, 1981; Bulgaria 1878–1918: a history, 1984; Short History of Modern Bulgaria, 1987; Eastern Europe in the Twentieth Century, 1994; (with Ben Crampton) Atlas of Eastern Europe in the 20th Century, 1996; Concise History of Bulgaria, 1997. *Recreations:* cooking, bird-watching, trying to avoid pop music and mobile phones. *Address:* St Edmund Hall, Oxford OX1 4AR. *T:* (01865) 274151.

CRAMPTON SMITH, Alex; *see* Smith, A. C.

CRAN, James Douglas; MP (C) Beverley and Holderness, since 1997 (Beverley, 1987–97); *b* 28 Jan. 1944; *s* of James Cran and Jane McDonald Cran, Aberdeenshire; *m* 1973, Penelope Barbara Wilson; one *d*. *Educ:* Ruthrieston Sch., Aberdeen; Aberdeen Coll. of Commerce; King's Coll., Univ. of Aberdeen (MA Hons). Researcher, Cons. Res. Dept, 1970–71; Sec., 1971–73, Chief. Exec., 1973–79, Nat. Assoc. of Pension Funds; Northern Dir, 1979–84, West Midlands Dir, 1984–87, CBI. Councillor (C), London Borough of Sutton, 1974–79 (Chm., Health and Housing Cttee). PPS to Sec. of State for NI, 1995–96; an Opposition Whip, 1997–2001; Opposition Asst Chief Whip, 2001. Mem., Select Cttee on Trade and Industry, 1987–92, on NI, 1994–95, on Administration, 1997–98, on Selection, 1998–; Vice Chairman: Cons. Backbench NI Cttee, 1992–95; All-Party Anglo-Mongolian Gp, 1993–94; Order of St John All-Party Gp, 1994–95; Secretary: Cons. Backbench Cttee on Constitutional Affairs, 1989–91, on European Affairs, 1989–91; All-Party Anglo-Malta Gp, 1992–94; Co-Founder, Parly Gp on Occupational Pensions, 1992. Mem., NI Grand Cttee, 1996–. Fellow: Armed Forces Parly Scheme, attached to RM, 1992; Parlt and Industry Trust, 1994. Parly consultant, Lincoln Nat. (UK) plc, 1994–98. Treas., European Res. Gp, 1994–97. Vice-Pres., Beverley Combined Div., St John Ambulance. Council Mem., Pension Trustees Forum, 1992–95. Member of Court: Univ. of Birmingham, 1984–87; Univ. of Hull, 1987–. Dux Medallion, City of Aberdeen, 1959; Daily Mirror Nat. Speaking Trophy, 1969. OStJ. *Recreations:* travelling, reading biographies, autobiographies and military history. *Address:* House of Commons, SW1A 0AA. *T:* (020) 7219 3000.

CRAN, Mark Dyson Gordon; QC 1988; a Recorder, since 2000; *b* 18 May 1948; *s* of William Broadbent Gordon Cran and Diana Rosemary Cran (*née* Mallinson); *m* 1983, Prudence Elizabeth Binning (marr. diss.). *Educ:* Gordonstoun; Millfield; Bristol Univ. (LLB). Called to the Bar, Gray's Inn, 1973. *Recreations:* country sports, long walks, convivial disputation, wine and food, performing arts. *Address:* Brick Court Chambers, 7–8 Essex Street, WC2R 3LD. *T:* (020) 7379 3550. *Clubs:* Brooks's, MCC.

CRANBORNE, Viscount; Robert Michael James Gascoyne-Cecil; PC 1994; DL; Baron Gascoyne-Cecil (Life Peer), 1999; *b* 30 Sept. 1946; *s* and *heir* of 6th Marquess of Salisbury, *qv*; *m* 1970, Hannah Ann, *er d* of Lt-Col William Joseph Stirling of Keir; two *s* three *d*. *Educ:* Eton; Oxford. MP (C) Dorset South, 1979–87. Summoned to the Upper House of Parliament, 1992, as Baron Cecil, of Essendon in the County of Rutland; Parly Under-Sec. of State for Defence, MoD, 1992–94; Lord Privy Seal and Leader of H of L, 1994–97; Leader of the Opposition, H of L, 1997–98. DL Dorset, 1987. *Heir: s* Hon. Robert Edward William Gascoyne-Cecil, *b* 18 Dec. 1970. *Address:* Manor House, Cranborne, Wimborne, Dorset BH21 5PP.

CRANBROOK, 5th Earl of, *cr* 1892; **Gathorne Gathorne-Hardy;** Viscount Cranbrook, 1878; Baron Medway, 1892; DL; Chairman, ENTRUST, Environmental Trusts Regulatory Body Ltd, since 1996; *b* 20 June 1933; *er s* of 4th Earl of Cranbrook, CBE, and of the Dowager Countess of Cranbrook (Fidelity, OBE 1972, *o d* of late Hugh E. Seebohm); *S* father, 1978; *m* 1967, Caroline, *o d* of Col Ralph G. E. Jarvis, Doddington Hall, Lincoln; two *s* one *d*. *Educ:* Eton; Corpus Christi Coll., Cambridge (MA); University of Birmingham (PhD). Asst, Sarawak Museum, 1956–58; Fellow, Yayasan Siswa Lokantara (Indonesia), 1960–61; Sen. Lectr in Zoology, Univ. of Malaya, 1961–70. Editor of Ibis, 1973–80. Mem., H of L Select Cttee on EC, then EU, three terms, 1979–99 (Mem., Envmt Sub-Cttee, 1979–85, 1987–90 (Chm., 1980–83, 1987–90), Chm., Envmt, Public Health and Consumer Protection Sub-Cttee, 1998–99). Bd Mem., Anglian Water Authy, 1987–89; non-exec. Dir, Anglian Water, 1989–98. Chm., English Nature, 1990–98; Member: Royal Commn on Environmental Pollution, 1981–92; NERC, 1982–88; Foundn for Eur. Envmtl Policy, 1987–98 (Chm., 1990–98); UK Round Table on Sustainable Develt, 1994–98; Broads Authy, 1988–99; Harwich Haven Authy, 1989–97 (Vice Chm., 1995–97); NCC, 1990–91; Suffolk Coastal DC, 1974–83; Pres., Suffolk Wildlife Trust (formerly Suffolk Trust for Nature Conservation), 1979–; Chm. Adv. Cttee, NERC Centre for Ecology and Hydrology, 1998–. Trustee, BM (Natural History), 1982–86. Skinner and Freeman of the City of London. DL Suffolk, 1984. FLS; FZS; FRGS; FIBiol; MBOU. Hon. FCIWEM; Hon. FIWM. Hon. DSc: Aberdeen, 1989; Cranfield, 1996. Founder's Medal, RGS, 1995. OStJ. Hon. Johan Bintang Sarawak, 1997. *Publications:* Mammals of Borneo, 1965, 2nd edn 1977; Mammals of Malaya, 1969, 2nd edn 1978; (with D. R. Wells) Birds of the Malay Peninsula, 1976; Riches of the Wild: mammals of South East Asia, 1987, 2nd edn 1991; (ed) Key Environments: Malaysia, 1988; (with D. S. Edwards) Belalong: a tropical rain forest, 1994; Wonders of Nature in South-East Asia, 1997. *Heir: s* Lord Medway, *qv*. *Fax:* (home) (01728) 663339.

CRANE, Hon. Sir Peter (Francis), Kt 2000; **Hon. Mr Justice Crane;** a Judge of the High Court of Justice, Queen's Bench Division, since 2000; *b* 14 Jan. 1940; *s* of late Prof. Francis Roger Crane and Jean Berenice Crane (*née* Hadfield); *m* 1967, Elizabeth Mary Pittman; four *d*. *Educ:* Nottingham High Sch.; Highgate Sch.; Gonville and Caius Coll., Cambridge (MA, LLM); Tulane Univ., New Orleans (LLM). Called to the Bar, Gray's Inn, 1964 (Barstow Scholar, 1963); in practice on Midland and Oxford Circuit, 1965–87; Recorder, 1982–87; a Circuit Judge, 1987–2000; Resident Judge, Peterborough Crown and County Court, 1992–2000. Mem., Senate of Inns of Court and the Bar, 1983–86 (Member: Professional Conduct Cttee, 1984–86; Bar Cttee, 1985–86). Mem., Judicial Studies Bd, 1993–96 (Mem., Criminal Cttee, 1993–96). Chairman: Kettering Constituency Liberal Assoc., 1981–84; Pytchley Parish Council, 1985–86. *Publication:* (co-ed) Phipson on Evidence, 14th edn, 1990, 15th edn 2000. *Recreations:* walking, gardening, reading, wine. *Address:* Royal Courts of Justice, Strand, WC2A 2LL.

CRANE, Prof. Peter Robert, PhD; FRS 1998; CBiol, FIBiol; Director, Royal Botanic Gardens, Kew, since 1999; *b* 18 July 1954; *s* of Walter Robert Crane and Dorothy Mary Crane; *m* 1986, Elinor Margaret Hamer; one *s* one *d*. *Educ:* Univ. of Reading (BSc 1975; PhD 1981). CBiol, FIBiol 2000. Lectr, Dept of Botany, Univ. of Reading, 1978–81; Post-doctoral Res. Schol., Indiana Univ., 1981–82; Field Museum, Chicago: Curator, Dept of Geology, 1982–92; Vice Pres., Acad. Affairs, 1992–99; Dir, 1995–99. Pres., Paleontol Soc., 1998–2000. *Publications:* (ed jtly) The Origins of Angiosperms and their Biological Consequences, 1987; (ed jtly) The Evolution, Systematics and Fossil History of the Hamamelidae, vols 1 and 2, 1989; (jtly) The Origin and Diversification of Land Plants, 1997. *Address:* Royal Botanic Gardens, Kew, Richmond, Surrey TW9 3AB.

CRANFIELD, Rev. Prof. Charles Ernest Burland, FBA 1982; Emeritus Professor of Theology, University of Durham, since 1980; *b* 13 Sept. 1915; *s* of Charles Ernest Cranfield and Beatrice Mary Cranfield (*née* Tubbs); *m* 1953, Ruth Elizabeth Gertrude, *d* of Rev. T. Bole; two *d*. *Educ:* Mill Hill Sch.; Jesus Coll., Cambridge; Wesley House, Cambridge. MA Cantab. Research in Basel, cut short before it properly began by outbreak of war. Probationer in Methodist Church, 1939; ordained 1941; Minister, Shoeburyness; Chaplain to the Forces, 1942–46; from end of hostilities worked with German prisoners-of-war and was first staff chaplain to POW Directorate, War Office; Minister, Cleethorpes, 1946–50; admitted to Presbyterian Church of England (now United Reformed Church) as a minister, 1954. Lecturer in Theology, Durham Univ., 1950–62; Sen. Lectr, 1962–66; Reader, 1966–78; Prof. of Theology (personal), 1978–80. Joint general editor, new series of International Critical Commentary, 1966–. Hon. DD Aberdeen, 1980. Burkitt Medal for Biblical Studies, 1989. *Publications:* The First Epistle of Peter, 1950, 4th imp. 1958; The Gospel according to Saint Mark, 1959, supplemented and somewhat revised over the years, 12th imp. 1997; I and II Peter and Jude, 1960; A Ransom for Many, 1963; The Service of God, 1965; A Commentary on Romans 12–13, 1965; A Critical and Exegetical Commentary on the Epistle to the Romans, vol. 1 1975, 10th (corrected) imp. 2001, vol. 2 1979, 8th (corrected) imp. 2001; Romans: a shorter commentary, 1985, 5th imp. 1995; If God Be For Us: a collection of sermons, 1985; The Bible and Christian Life: a collection of essays, 1985; The Apostles' Creed: a faith to live by, 1993; On Romans and Other New Testament Essays, 1998; contribs to composite works and to various theological periodicals. *Address:* 30 Western Hill, Durham City DH1 4RL. *T:* (0191) 384 3096.

CRANLEY, Viscount; Rupert Charles William Bullard Onslow; *b* 16 June 1967; *s* and *heir* of 7th Earl of Onslow, *qv*; *m* 1999, Leigh, *d* of late E. Jones-Fenleigh. *Educ:* Eton; Western Kentucky Univ., USA. *Recreations:* photography, riding, shooting. *Address:* Temple Court, Clandon Park, Guildford, Surrey GU4 7RQ.

CRANMER, Philip; Secretary, Associated Board of the Royal Schools of Music, 1974–83; *b* 1 April 1918; *s* of Arthur Cranmer and Lilian Phillips; *m* 1939, Ruth Loasby (*d* 2000); one *s* three *d*. *Educ:* Wellington; Christ Church, Oxford (BMus, MA). Asst Music Master, Wellington Coll. 1938–40; served RA, 1940–46; Major, Education Officer, Guards Div., 1946; Dir of Music, King Edward's Sch., Birmingham, 1946; Staff Accompanist, Midland Region, BBC, 1948; Lectr in Music, Birmingham Univ., 1950; Hamilton Harty Prof. of Music, Queen's Univ., Belfast, 1954–70; Prof. of Music, Univ. of Manchester, 1970–74. Pres., Incorporated Soc. of Musicians, 1971; Chm., Musicians' Benevolent Fund, 1980–87. FRCO 1947; Hon. RAM 1967; FRNCM 1974; FRCM 1976. Hon. DMus QUB, 1985. Chevalier de l'Ordre de Léopold II, 1947; Croix de Guerre Belge, 1947. *Publications:* The Technique of Accompaniment, 1970; Sight-reading for Young Pianists, 1979; How to Follow a Score, 1982; Two Sonatinas for piano duet, 1981 and 1985. *Address:* Quince Cottage, Underhill Lane, Clayton, Hassocks, W Sussex BN6 9PJ.

CRANSTON, David Alan, CBE 1993; Director General, National Association of Pension Funds, since 2000; *b* 20 Oct. 1945; *s* of Stanley Cranston and Mary Cranston (*née* Fitzherbert); *m* 1968, Pippa Ann Reynolds; three *d*. *Educ:* Strathallan Sch., Perthshire; RMA, Sandhurst. Commnd RA, 1966; Army Staff Course, 1979–80; transf. to AAC, 1981; COS HQ, British Forces, Belize, 1983; DS, RMCS Shrivenham, 1984–86; Comd, 4th Regt, AAC, 1986–88; COS, 2nd Inf. Div., 1988–90; Higher Comd and Staff Course, 1990; Comd, British Army Aviation, Germany, 1990–92; Dep. Head of Mission, EC Monitor Mission to former Yugoslavia, 1992; rcds, 1993; Dep. Comdr, Multinational Airmobile Div., 1994–95. Head of Mem. Relns, PIA, 1995–97; Head of Gp Compliance, Royal Bank of Scotland, 1997–2000. Chm., British Biathlon Union, 1996–. *Recreations:* gardening, reading, tennis, ski-ing. *Address:* National Association of Pension Funds, NIOC House, 4 Victoria Street, SW1H 0NX. *T:* (020) 7808 1311. *Club:* Army and Navy.

CRANSTON, Ross Frederick; QC 1998; MP (Lab) Dudley North, since 1997; *b* 23 July 1948; *s* of late Frederick Hugh Cranston and of Edna Elizabeth Cranston (*née* Davies); *m* 1st, 1976, Prof. Jane Stapleton (marr. diss. 1985); 2nd, 1988, Anna Whyatt (marr. diss. 1998); one *d*. *Educ:* Univ. of Queensland (BA 1970; LLB 1971); Harvard Law Sch. (LLM 1973); Oxford (DPhil 1976; DCL 1998). Called to the Bar, Gray's Inn, 1976, Bencher, 1998; Asst Recorder, 1991–97; a Recorder, 1997–. Lectr, Univ. of Warwick, 1975–77; Res. Fellow, 1978–81, Sen. Lectr, then Reader, 1981–86, Assoc. Dean, 1984–86, Faculty of Law, ANU Canberra; W. G. Hart Sen. Fellow, QMC, 1983–84; Queen Mary and Westfield College, London University: Sir John Lubbock Prof. of Banking Law, 1986–92; Dean, Faculty of Laws, 1988–91; Dir, Centre for Commercial Law Studies, 1989–92; Cassel Prof. of Commercial Law, LSE, 1993–97. Vis. Prof., LSE, 1997–. Acad. Consultant, Woolf Inquiry into Access to Justice, 1994–96; Consultant to various international bodies including World Bank, IMF, UN Conf. on Trade and Develt, Commonwealth Secretariat, 1988–96. Contested (Lab) Richmond, Yorks, 1992. Solicitor-Gen., 1998–2001. Vice Pres., 1991–92, Pres., 1992–93, SPTL. Dep. Chm., 1993–96, Chm., 1996–97, Bd of Trustees, Public Concern at Work. Mem., American Law Inst., 1999. *Publications:* Consumers and the Law, 1978, 3rd edn, as Cranston's Consumers and the Law, 2000; Regulating Business, 1979; Legal Foundations of the Welfare State, 1985; Law, Government and Public Policy, 1987; (ed) Banks, Liability and Risk, 1990, 2nd edn 1995; (ed) The Single Market and the Law of Banking, 1991, 2nd edn 1995; (ed with R. M. Goode) Contemporary Issues in International Commercial Law, 1993; (ed) European Banking Law, 1993, 2nd edn 1999; (ed) Legal Ethics and Professional Responsibility, 1995; (ed with A. Zuckerman) Reform of the Administration of Civil Justice, 1995; (ed) Making Commercial Law, 1997; Principles of Banking Law, 1997. *Address:* House of Commons, SW1A 0AA.

CRANSTON, Prof. William Ian; Professor of Medicine, United Medical and Dental Schools of Guy's and St Thomas' Hospitals (formerly St Thomas's Hospital Medical School), 1964–93, now Emeritus; *b* 11 Sept. 1928; *s* of Thomas and Margaret Cranston; *m* Pamela Isabel Pearson (*d* 2000); four *s*. *Educ:* High Sch. for Boys, Glasgow; Aberdeen Grammar Sch.; Boys' High Sch., Oswestry; University of Aberdeen, FRCP London 1965 (MRCP 1952); MB, ChB (Hons), 1949; MD Aberdeen 1957; MA Oxon. 1962. Royal Infirmary, Aberdeen: House Physician, 1949–50; Medical Registrar, 1952–53; Asst in Medical Unit, St Mary's Hospital, Paddington, 1953–56; 1st Asst in Dept of Regius Prof. of Med., Radcliffe Inf., Oxford, 1961–64. Mem., Med. Res. Soc. *Recreation:* reading. *Address:* 31 Berrylands, Surbiton, Surrey KT5 8JT.

CRANWORTH, 3rd Baron *cr* 1899; **Philip Bertram Gurdon;** Lieutenant, Royal Wiltshire Yeomanry; *b* 24 May 1940; *s* of Hon. Robin Gurdon (killed in action, 1942) and Hon. Yoskyl Pearson (she *m* 2nd, 1944, as his 2nd wife, Lieut-Col. Alistair Gibb, and 3rd, 1962, as his 2nd wife, 1st Baron McCorquodale of Newton, PC, KCVO; she *d* 1979), *d* of 2nd Viscount Cowdray; *S* grandfather, 1964; *m* 1968, Frances Henrietta Montagu Douglas Scott (*d* 2000), *d* of late Lord William Scott and Lady William Scott; two *s* one *d*. *Educ:* Eton; Magdalene Coll., Cambridge. *Heir:* *s* Hon. Sacha William Robin Gurdon, *b* 12 Aug. 1970. *Address:* Grundisburgh Hall, Woodbridge, Suffolk IP13 6TW.

See also Marquess of Huntly.

CRASTON, Rev. Canon (Richard) Colin; Rector of St Paul with Emmanuel, Bolton, 1986–93, retired (Vicar, 1954); Hon. Canon, Manchester Cathedral, 1968–95, Canon Emeritus, since 1995; Area Dean of Bolton, 1972–92; Chaplain to the Queen, 1985–92; *b* 31 Dec. 1922; *s* of Albert Edward Craston and Ethel Craston; *m* 1st, 1948, Ruth Taggart (*d* 1992); one *s* one *d*; 2nd, 1993, Rev. Brenda H. Fullalove. *Educ:* Preston Grammar Sch.; Univ. of Bristol (BA Hons); Univ. of London (BD Hons); Tyndale Hall, Bristol. Served War, RN, 1941–46. Ordained 1951; Curate, St Nicholas, Durham, 1951–54. Chm., House of Clergy, Dio. of Manchester, 1982–94; Member: Gen. Synod, 1970–95 (Mem., Standing Cttee, 1975–95; Chm., Business Sub-Cttee, 1991–95); ACC, 1981–96 (Mem., Standing Cttee, 1981–96; Vice-Chm., 1986–90; Chm., 1990–96); Crown Appts Commn, 1982–92. DD Lambeth, 1992. *Publications:* Biblical Headship and the Ordination of Women, 1986; (ed) Open to the Spirit—Essays on Renewal, 1987; (contrib.) Authority in the Anglican Communion, 1987; (jtly) Anglicanism and the Universal Church, 1990; (ed) By Word and Deed, 1992; Debtor to Grace, 1998; contrib. Anvil. *Recreation:* football and cricket spectating. *Address:* 12 Lever Park Avenue, Horwich, Bolton BL6 7LE. *T:* (01204) 699972, *Fax:* (01204) 690813. *Club:* Union Jack.

CRATHORNE, 2nd Baron *cr* 1959; **(Charles) James Dugdale;** Bt 1945; JP; Lord-Lieutenant of North Yorkshire, since 1999; director of hotel cos; consultant and lecturer in Fine Art; *b* 12 Sept. 1939; *s* of 1st Baron Crathorne, PC, TD, and Nancy, OBE (*d* 1969), *d* of Sir Charles Tennant, 1st Bt; *S* father, 1977; *m* 1970, Sylvia Mary, *yr d* of Brig. Arthur Herbert Montgomery, OBE, TD; one *s* two *d*. *Educ:* Eton College; Trinity Coll., Cambridge. MA Cantab (Fine Arts). Impressionist and Modern Painting Dept, Sotheby & Co., 1963–66; Assistant to the President, Parke-Bernet, New York, 1966–69; James Dugdale & Associates, London, Independent Fine Art Consultancy Service, 1969–77; James Crathorne & Associates, 1977–; Director: Woodhouse Securities, 1989–99; Cliveden PLC, 1996–98; Hand Picked Hotels Ltd, 2001–. Member: Yorks Regl Cttee, NT, 1978–84 and 1988–94; Council, RSA, 1982–88; Exec. Cttee, Georgian Gp, 1985– (Chm., 1990–99); Cons. Adv. Gp on Arts and Heritage, 1988–98; Chm., Jt Cttee, Nat. Amenity Socs, 1996–99 (Dep. Chm., 1993–96); President: Cleveland Assoc., NT, 1982–96; Yarm Civic Soc., 1987–; Hambledon Dist, CPRE, 1988–; Cleveland Family History Soc., 1988–; Cleveland Sea Cadets, 1988–; Cleveland and N Yorks Br., Magistrates' Assoc., 1997–; Cleveland Search and Rescue Team, 1998–; Vice President: Cleveland Wildlife Trust, 1990–; Public Monuments and Sculpture Assoc., 1997–; N Yorks County Scouts, 1998–; Patron, Cleveland Community Foundn, 1990–. Member: Works of Art Sub-Cttee, H of L, 1983–; Editorial Bd, House Magazine, 1983–; Hon. Secretary: All-Party Parly Arts and Heritage Gp, 1981–; All Party Photography Gp, 1997–; elected Mem., H of L, 1999. Trustee: Captain Cook Trust, 1978– (Chm., 1993–); Georgian Theatre Royal, Richmond, Yorks, 1970–; Christian Inheritance, 1989–; Nat. Heritage Meml Fund, 1992–95; Patron, Attingham Trust for Study of the British Country House, 1991–; Hon. Patron, Friends of Yorks Sculpture Park, 1992–. Church Warden, All Saints, Crathorne, 1977–. Annual lecture tours to America, 1970–; lecture series, Metropolitan Mus., NY, 1981; Australian Bicentennial Lecture Tour, 1988. Member Court: Univ. of Leeds, 1985–97; Univ. of York, 1999–; Univ. of Hull, 1999–; Gov., Queen Margaret's Sch. York Ltd, 1986–99. FRSA 1972. DL Cleveland, 1983, N Yorks, 1996; JP N Yorks, 1999. KStJ 1999. *Exhibitions:* Photographs, Middlesbrough Art Gall., 1980; All Party Photography Gp annual exhibn, Westminster and touring, 1992–. *Publications:* Edouard Vuillard, 1967; (co-author) Tennant's Stalk, 1973; (co-author) A Present from Crathorne, 1989; Cliveden: the place and the people, 1995; The Royal Crescent Book of Bath, 1998; (co-photographer) Parliament in Pictures, 1999; contribs to Apollo and The Connoisseur. *Recreations:* photography, travel, collecting, shooting, fishing, music. *Heir:* *s* Hon. Thomas Arthur John Dugdale, *b* 30 Sept. 1977. *Address:* Crathorne House, Yarm, N Yorks TS15 0AT. *T:* (01642) 700431, *Fax:* (01642) 700632; House of Lords, SW1A 0PW. *T:* (020) 7219 5224, *Fax:* (020) 7219 5979.

CRAUFURD, Sir Robert (James), 9th Bt *cr* 1781; *b* 18 March 1937; *s* of Sir James Gregan Craufurd, 8th Bt and Ruth Marjorie (*d* 1998), *d* of Frederic Corder; *S* father, 1970; *m* 1st, 1964, Catherine Penelope (marr. diss.), *yr d* of late Captain Horatio Westmacott, Torquay; three *d*; 2nd, 1987, Georgina Anne, *d* of late John D. Russell, Lymington. *Educ:* Harrow; University College, Oxford. Elected Member of the London Stock Exchange, 1969. *Address:* East Grove, Grove Road, Lymington, Hants SO41 3RF.

CRAUSBY, David Anthony; MP (Lab) Bolton North East, since 1997; *b* 17 June 1946; *s* of Thomas Crausby and Kathleen Lavin; *m* 1965, Enid Anne Noon; two *s*. *Educ:* Derby Grammar Sch., Bury. Apprentice centre lathe turner, 1962, skilled turner, 1967; Works Convenor, AEEU (formerly AEU), 1978–97. Mem (Lab) Bury MDC, 1979–92. Contested (Lab): Bury N, 1987; Bolton NE, 1992. *Recreations:* football, walking, cinema. *Address:* 60 St Georges Road, Bolton BL1 2DD. *T:* (01204) 523574.

CRAVEN, family name of **Earl of Craven**.

CRAVEN, 9th Earl of, *cr* 1801; **Benjamin Robert Joseph Craven;** Baron Craven, 1665; Viscount Uffington, 1801; *b* 13 June 1989; *s* of 8th Earl and of Teresa Maria Bernadette Craven; *S* father, 1990. *Heir:* *cousin* Rupert José Evelyn Craven, Lt-Comdr RN [*b* 22 March 1926; *m* 1955, Margaret Campbell (*d* 1985), *d* of Alexander Smith, MBE].

CRAVEN, Archdeacon of; *see* Grundy, Ven. M. L.

CRAVEN, Sir John (Anthony), Kt 1996; Chairman, Deutsche Morgan Grenfell (formerly Morgan Grenfell) Group PLC, 1989–97 (Chief Executive, 1987–89); Member, Board of Managing Directors, Deutsche Bank AG, Frankfurt, 1990–96; *b* 23 Oct. 1940; *s* of William Herbert Craven and Hilda Lucy Craven; *m* 1st, 1961, Gillian Margaret (*née* Murray); one *s* one *d*; 2nd, 1970, Jane Frances (*née* Stiles-Allen); three *s*. *Educ:* Michaelhouse, S Africa; Jesus Coll., Cambridge (BA Hons Law); Queen's Univ., Kingston, Ont. Clarkson Gordon & Co., Toronto, Chartered Accountants, 1961–64; Wood Gundy, Investment Bankers, 1964–67; S. G. Warburg & Co., 1967–73, Dir 1969–73; Gp Chief Exec., White Weld & Co. Ltd, 1973–78; Vice Chm., S. G. Warburg & Co., 1979; Founder and Chm., Phoenix Securities Ltd, 1981–89; Dir, Mercury Securities Ltd, 1979. Non-executive Chairman: Tootal Group PLC, 1985–91; Lonmin plc (formerly Lonrho), 1997–; Director: Rothmans Internat. NV, 1993–95; Rothmans Internat. BV, 1995–99; non-executive Director: Reuters plc, 1997–; Robert Fleming Hldgs Ltd, 1999–2000; Ducati Motor Hldgs SpA, 1999–2000; Gleacher & Co. Ltd, 2000–; Fleming Family & Partners Ltd, 2000–. Mem., Conseil d'Administration, Société Générale de Surveillance, Switzerland, 1989–98; Dir, SIB, 1990–93. Member: Ontario Inst. of Chartered Accts; Canadian Inst. of Chartered Accountants. *Recreations:* hunting, shooting, ski-ing. *Clubs:* City, Mark's; Links (New York).

CRAVEN, Prof. John Anthony George; Vice-Chancellor, University of Portsmouth, since 1997; *b* 17 June 1949; *s* of late George Marriott Craven and of Dorothy Maude Craven (*née* Walford); *m* 1974, Laura Elizabeth Loftis; one *s* one *d*. *Educ:* Pinner GS; King's Coll., Cambridge (BA 1970; MA 1974). Kennedy Meml Schol., MIT, 1970–71; University of Kent at Canterbury: Lectr in Econs, 1971–76; Sen. Lectr, 1976–80; Reader, 1980–86; Prof., 1986–96; Dean of Faculty, Social Scis, 1987–91; Pro Vice-Chancellor, 1991–93; Dep. Vice-Chancellor, 1993–96. Vis. Associate Prof., Univ. of Guelph, 1982–83. Chair, St Martin's Trust for the Homeless, 1987–96. Governor: South Kent Coll., 1991–96; Highbury Coll., 1997–. Dir, New Th. Royal, Portsmouth, 1999–. *Publications:* The Distribution of the Product, 1979; Introduction to Economics, 1984, 2nd edn 1990; Social Choice, 1992; articles in learned jls. *Recreations:* cricket, choral singing, house restoration. *Address:* (home) Fyning Cross, Rogate, Petersfield GU31 5EF. *T:* (01730) 821392; (office) University House, Portsmouth PO1 2UP. *T:* (023) 9284 3190; *e-mail:* john.craven@port.ac.uk.

CRAVEN, Air Marshal Sir Robert Edward, KBE 1970 (OBE 1954); CB 1966; DFC 1940; *b* 16 Jan. 1916; *s* of Gerald Craven, Port Elizabeth, S Africa, and Edith Craven, York; *m* 1940, Joan Peters (*d* 1991); one *s* one *d*. *Educ:* Scarborough Coll. MN, 1932–37; Pilot Officer, RAF, 1937; 201, 210, 228 Sqdns, 1937–41; RAF Staff Coll., 1942; Staff Appts: Coastal Command, 1942 (despatches thrice); Directing Staff, RAF Staff Coll.,

1944; HQ, Mediterranean and Middle East, Cairo, 1945; CO Eastleigh, Kenya, 1946; RN Staff Coll., 1948; Directing Staff, Joint Services Staff Coll., 1949; Standing Group, NATO Washington, 1951; RAF St Eval, 1954; Directing Staff, RAF Staff Coll., 1957; Group Capt. 1957; CO RAF Lyneham, 1959; Director, Personal Services, RAF, 1961; Air Cdre 1961; Air Officer Admin., Transport Comd, 1964; Air Vice-Marshal, 1965; SASO, Flying Training Comd, 1967–68, Training Comd, 1968–69; Commander, Maritime Air Forces, NATO Air Comdr Eastern Atlantic, Channel and North Sea, 1969–72, retired. Order of Menelik (Ethiopia), 1955. *Recreations:* water fowl breeding, antique furniture restoration and reproduction. *Address:* Letcombe House, Letcombe Regis, Oxon OX12 9LD. *Club:* Royal Air Force.

CRAWFORD, 29th Earl of, *cr* 1398, **AND BALCARRES**, 12th Earl of, *cr* 1651; **Robert Alexander Lindsay,** KT 1996; PC 1972; Lord Lindsay of Crawford, before 1143; Lord Lindsay of Balcarres, 1633; Lord Balniel, 1651; Baron Wigan (UK), 1826; Baron Balniel (Life Peer), 1974; Premier Earl of Scotland; Head of House of Lindsay; DL; Lord Chamberlain to the Queen Mother, since 1992; *b* 5 March 1927; *er s* of 28th Earl of Crawford and 11th of Balcarres, KT, GBE, and Mary (*d* 1994), 3rd *d* of late Lord Richard Cavendish, PC, CB, CMG; *S* father, 1975; *m* 1949, Ruth Beatrice, *d* of Leo Meyer-Bechtler, Zürich; two *s* two *d.* *Educ:* Eton; Trinity College, Cambridge. Served with Grenadier Guards, 1945–49. MP (C) Hertford, 1955–74, Welwyn and Hatfield, Feb.-Sept. 1974; Parliamentary Private Secretary: to Financial Secretary of Treasury, 1955–57; to Minister of Housing and Local Government, 1957–60; Opposition front-bench spokesman on health and social security, 1967–70; Minister of State for Defence, 1970–72; Minister of State for Foreign and Commonwealth Affairs, 1972–74. First Crown Estate Comr, 1980–85. Chairman: Lombard North Central Bank, 1976–80; Abela Hldgs (UK), 1983–95; Director: Nat. Westminster Bank, 1975–88; Scottish American Investment Co., 1978–88; a Vice-Chm., Sun Alliance & London Insurance Gp, 1975–91. President, Rural District Councils Assoc., 1959–65; Chairman: National Association for Mental Health, 1963–70; Historic Buildings Council for Scotland, 1976–83; Royal Commn on Ancient and Historical Monuments of Scotland, 1985–95; Bd of Trustees, Nat. Library of Scotland, 1990–2000. DL Fife. *Heir:* *s* Lord Balniel, *qv.* *Address:* House of Lords, SW1A 0PW.

CRAWFORD, Prof. Andrew Charles, FRS 1990; Professor of Neurophysiology, Cambridge University, since 1992; Fellow of Trinity College, Cambridge, since 1974; *b* 12 Jan. 1949; *s* of Charles and Vera Crawford; *m* 1974, Catherine Jones; one *s* one *d.* *Educ:* King Edward VI Camp Hill Sch., Birmingham; Downing Coll., Cambridge (BA 1970); Emmanuel Coll., Cambridge (MA, PhD 1974). Cambridge University: Research Fellow, Emmanuel Coll., 1972; Univ. Demonstrator, 1974; Lectr, 1977; Reader in Sensory Physiology, 1987. *Publications:* contribs on physiology of hearing, in learned jls. *Address:* Physiological Laboratory, Downing Street, Cambridge CB2 3EG. *T:* (01223) 333879.

CRAWFORD, Bruce; *see* Crawford, R. H. B.

CRAWFORD, Charles Graham, CMG 1998; HM Diplomatic Service; Ambassador to Federal Republic of Yugoslavia, since 2001; *b* 22 May 1954; *s* of Graham Wellington James Crawford and Edith Ellen Crawford; *m* 1990, Helen Margaret Walsh; two *s* one *d.* *Educ:* St John's Coll., Oxford (BA Hons Jurisprudence 1976); Lincoln's Inn (part II Bar exams 1977); Fletcher Sch. of Law and Diplomacy, Boston, USA (MA 1979). Entered FCO, 1979; Second, later First Sec., Belgrade, 1981–84; FCO (speechwriter), 1985–87; First Sec., Pretoria/Cape Town, 1987–91; FCO, 1991–93; Political Counsellor, Moscow, 1993–96; Ambassador to Bosnia and Herzegovina, 1996–98; Weatherhead Center for Internat. Affairs, Harvard Univ., 1998–99; Dep. Political Dir, FCO, 1999–2000; Dir, SE Europe, FCO, 2000. *Recreations:* chess, music. *Address:* c/o Foreign and Commonwealth Office, SW1A 2AH.

CRAWFORD, Douglas; *see* Crawford, G. D.

CRAWFORD, Sir Frederick (William), Kt 1986; DL; FREng; Chairman, Criminal Cases Review Commission, since 1996; Vice-Chancellor, Aston University, 1980–96; *b* 28 July 1931; *s* of William and Victoria Maud Crawford; *m* 1963, Béatrice M. J. Hutter, LèsL, MA, PhD, Paris; one *d* (one *s* decd). *Educ:* George Dixon Grammar Sch., Birmingham; Univ. of London (BSc Eng (1st cl. hons), MSc, DSc); Univ. of Liverpool (DipEd, PhD, DEng). Pres., Guild of Undergraduates, 1955–56; Mem. Court, 1955–62 and 1981–; Treas., NUS, 1957–59; Winner, NUS-Observer Fifth Nat. Student Debating Tourn., 1958, followed by ESU debating tour of USA. FInstP 1964; FAPS 1965; FIEE 1965; FIEEE 1972; FIMA 1978; FREng (FEng 1985); CIMgt (CBIM 1986). Research Trainee, J. Lucas Ltd, 1948–52; Scientist, NCB Mining Res. Estabt, 1956–57; Sen. Lectr in Elec. Engrg, CAT Birmingham, 1958–59; Stanford University, California, 1959–82: Res. Associate, W. W. Hansen Labs of Physics, 1959–64; Institute for Plasma Research: Prof. (Research), 1964–67; Associate Prof., 1967–69; Prof., 1969–82; Consulting Prof., 1983–84; Chm., 1974–80; Dir, Centre for Interdisciplinary Res., 1973–77. Vis. Scientist, French Atomic Energy Commn, and Cons. to Comp. Française Thomson-Houston, 1961–62; Visiting Professor: Japan, 1969; Univ. of Paris, 1971; Australia, 1972; Mathematical Inst., Oxford Univ., 1977–78; Vis. Fellow, St Catherine's Coll., Oxford, 1977–78, 1996–97. Union Radio-Scientifique Internationale: Member: US Nat. Cttee, 1975–81; UK Nat. Cttee, 1980–84; Commn H (Waves in Plasmas); US Chm., 1975–78; Internat. Chm., 1978–81; UK Rep., 1982–84; Chm. Internat. Sci. Cttee, Internat. Conf. on Phenomena in Ionised Gases, 1979–81; Universities Space Research Association: Member: Council, 1973–81 (Chm. 1977–78); Bd of Trustees, 1975–81 (Chm. 1976–77). Dir, Sigma Xi, 1976–78; Mem. Council, Amer. Assoc. of Univ. Profs, 1980–82; Vice-Chm., CVCP, 1993–95; Dir, HEQC, 1994–96; Vice-Pres., Parly and Scientific Cttee, 1992–95 (Vice-Chm., 1989–92). Member: Council, IEE, 1985–88, 1989–92 and 1993–96; Smeatonian Soc. of Civil Engrs, 1995. Director: Birmingham Technology Ltd, 1982–96; West Midlands Technology Transfer Centre, 1985–93; Legal & General Gp plc, 1988–97; Rexam (formerly Bowater) plc, 1989–97; PowerGen plc, 1990–. Member: US-UK Educnl Commn, 1981–84; British-North American Cttee, 1987–; Franco-British Council, 1987–98; Vice-President: Birmingham Civic Soc., 1990– (Chm., 1983–88). Founder Mem., Lunar Soc., Birmingham, 1991. Freeman, City of London, 1986; Master: Co. of Engineers, 1996; Co. of Information Technologists, 2000. High Sheriff, W Midlands, 1995, DL W Midlands, 1995. Hon. Bencher, Inner Temple, 1996. Hon. FIL 1987. Hon. DSc Buckingham, 1996. *Publications:* numerous papers on plasma physics and higher educn. *Address:* Criminal Cases Review Commission, Alpha Tower, Suffolk Street Queensway, Birmingham B1 1TT. *T:* (0121) 633 1800. *Club:* Athenæum.

CRAWFORD, Geoffrey Douglas, CVO 2000 (LVO 1995); Consultant, Edelman Public Relations Worldwide (Sydney), since 2001; *b* 29 Sept. 1950; *s* of Rev. Canon Douglas Crawford and Edna Crawford; *m* 1st, 1980 (marr. diss.); one *s* two *d*; 2nd, 1998, Catherine Banks. *Educ:* King's Sch., Parramatta, NSW; Univ. of Sydney (BA Hons). Entered Australian Dept of Foreign Affairs, 1974: Third Sec., Port Moresby, 1974–75; Vice-Consul, Lae, 1975–76; lang. trng, Cairo, 1978–80; Second Sec., Jeddah, 1980–82; First Sec., Baghdad, 1983–84; seconded as Asst Press Sec. to the Queen, 1988–83; transferred to Civil List, 1991; Dep. Press Sec., 1993–97, Press Sec. to the Queen, 1997–2000. *Recreations:* swimming, classical music, reading. *Address:* Edelman Public Relations Worldwide, Level 7, 207 Kent Street, Sydney, NSW 2000, Australia. *T:* (2) 92413131, *Fax:* (2) 92212676. *Club:* Royal Over-Seas League.

CRAWFORD, (George) Douglas; author; *b* 1 Nov. 1939; *s* of Robert and Helen Crawford; *m* 1964, Joan Burnie (marr. diss.); one *s* one *d.* *Educ:* Glasgow Academy; St Catharine's Coll., Cambridge (MA). Features Editor, Business, 1961–63; Industrial Corresp., Glasgow Herald, 1963–66; Editor, Scotland Magazine, 1966–70; Dir, Polecon Gp of Cos, 1970–89; journalist, Glasgow Herald, subseq. The Herald, 1989–95; Editor, Business and Finance, 1993–95. MP (SNP) Perth and East Perthshire, Oct. 1974–1979; contested (SNP) Perth and Kinross, 1983. *Recreations:* hill-walking, swimming, playing piano and clavichord, watching cricket. *Address:* Flat 3/1, 8 Hall Street, Campbeltown PA28 6BU.

CRAWFORD, Iain; Director, Veterinary Field Service, Ministry of Agriculture, Fisheries and Food, 1988–98; *b* 8 April 1938; *s* of James and Agnes Crawford, Baillieston, Glasgow; *m* 1962, Janette Mary Allan; two *s* one *d.* *Educ:* Coatbridge High Sch., Lanarks; Glasgow Univ. (BVMS). MRCVS 1961. Entered private vet. practice, 1961; joined MAFF as a Vet. Officer, 1968; Dep. Regl Vet. Officer, Bristol, 1981; Vet. Head of Sect. (Regl Vet. Officer), 1983; Asst Chief Vet. Officer, 1986. *Recreations:* sailing, walking. *Address:* 14 Camilla Close, Great Bookham, Leatherhead, Surrey KT23 4BU.

CRAWFORD, Maj.-Gen. (Ian) Patrick, GM 1964; FFCM, FFOM; Commandant and Postgraduate Dean, Royal Army Medical College, Millbank, 1989–93; *b* 11 Oct. 1933; *s* of Donald Patrick and Florence Ireland Crawford; *m* 1956, Juliet Treharne James; two *s* one *d.* *Educ:* Chatham House, Ramsgate; St Thomas' Hosp., London. MRCS, LRCP; FFCM 1982; FFOM 1987; DPH, DIH, DTM&H. House Surgeon, Casualty and Orthopaedics and House Physician, Royal Sussex County Hosp., 1959–60; Nat. Service, RAMC, 1960–63; on active service, Borneo, 1962–64; commnd 1963; Regimental MO, 20 Regt RA and 1st/7th Gurkha Rifles, Malaya and Borneo, 1963–68; Staff Officer: Army Health Home Counties Dist, 1968; HQ Singapore Dist, 1968–70; Instructor, Sch. of Army Health, 1970–71; MoD, 1971–72; Exchange Officer, Australia, 1972–75; MoD, 1975–78; HQ 1 BR Corps, 1978–81; Parkes Prof. of Preventive Medicine, Royal Army Med. Coll., 1981–84; Defence Med. Services Directorate, 1984–86; Comdr, Saudi Arabian Nat. Guard Med. Team, 1986–88; Defence Med. Services Directorate, 1988–89. QHP 1991–93. Specialist in Preventive Medicine, Singapore, Australia, PNG, BAOR, Saudi Arabia and UK; Consultant Advr, Saudi Arabia Nat. Guard, Jeddah, 1986–88. Chm. Court of Govs, 1997–, and Mem. Bd, 1994–, LSHTM. Mem. Council, Shipwrecked Fishermen and Mariners' Royal Benevolent Soc., 1994–; Trustee, Florence Nightingale Mus., 1993–. Hon. Lectr, Dept of Occupational Med., Queensland Univ., 1973–75. FRSocMed 1981. OStJ 1992. *Publications:* papers and pubns on military preventive medicine. *Recreations:* golf, computing, travel, bridge. *Address:* Mill Cottage, Mill Lane, Cocking, near Midhurst, W Sussex GU29 0HJ. *T:* (01730) 817982. *Club:* Goodwood Golf.

CRAWFORD, Prof. James Richard, FBA 2000; DPhil; barrister; Whewell Professor of International Law, University of Cambridge, and Fellow of Jesus College, Cambridge, since 1992; *b* 14 Nov. 1948; *s* of James Allen and Josephine Margaret Crawford; *m* 1st, 1971, Marisa Luigina (marr. diss. 1991); two *d*; 2nd, 1992, Patricia Hyndman (marr. diss. 1998); two *d*; 3rd, 1998, Joanna Gomula. *Educ:* Adelaide Univ. (LLB Hons; BA 1971); Oxford Univ. (DPhil 1977). Called to the Bar, High Court of Australia, 1979; SC, NSW, 1997. University of Adelaide: Lectr, 1974; Sen. Lectr, 1977; Reader, 1982; Prof. of Law, 1983; Challis Prof. of Internat. Law, 1986–92, Dean, Faculty of Law, 1990–92, Univ. of Sydney. Comr, Australian Law Reform Commn, 1982–90; Mem., UN Internat. Law Commn, 1992–. *Publications:* The Creation of States in International Law, 1979; Australian Courts of Law, 1982, 2nd edn 1988; (ed) The Rights of Peoples, 1988. *Recreations:* cricket, reading. *Address:* Lauterpacht Research Centre for International Law, 5 Cranmer Road, Cambridge CB3 9LW.

CRAWFORD, John Michael; Director of Education (formerly Chief Education Officer), Birmingham, 1977–88; *b* 6 Dec. 1938; *s* of James and Emily Crawford; *m* 1962, Geraldine Kay Weaver; two *d.* *Educ:* Ipswich Sch.; University Coll., London (BA); Fitzwilliam House, Cambridge. Asst Master, Merchant Taylor's, Crosby, 1961–63; Admin. Asst, E Suffolk CC, 1963–66; Sen. Admin. Asst, Lancs CC, 1966–68; Asst Educn Officer, W Riding CC, 1968–73; Dep. Educn Officer, Birmingham, 1973–77. *Address:* July Green, Snuff Mill Walk, Bewdley, Worcs DY12 2HG. *T:* (01299) 400174.

CRAWFORD, Lionel Vivian, FRS 1988; Principal Scientist, Imperial Cancer Research Fund Tumour Virus Group, Department of Pathology, Cambridge University, 1988–95; *b* 30 April 1932; *s* of John Mitchell Crawford and Fanny May Crawford (*née* Barnett); *m* 1957, Elizabeth Minnie (*née* Green); one *d.* *Educ:* Rendcomb College, Cirencester; Emmanuel College, Cambridge (BA, MA, PhD). Virus Lab., Berkeley, Calif., 1958–59; Calif. Inst. of Technology, 1959–60; Inst. of Virology, Glasgow, 1960–68; Molecular Virology Lab., Imperial Cancer Res. Fund, 1968–88. Member: Soc. for Gen. Microbiology; EMBO. FRSE 1970. *Publications:* numerous scientific articles. *Recreation:* restoring old houses.

CRAWFORD, Michael, OBE 1987; actor since 1955; *b* 19 Jan. 1942. *Educ:* St Michael's Coll., Bexley; Oakfield Sch., Dulwich. In orig. prodn of Britten's Noyes Fludde and of Let's Make an Opera; *stage appearances include:* Come Blow Your Horn, Prince of Wales, 1961; Travelling Light, 1965; The Anniversary, 1966; No Sex Please, We're British, Strand, 1971; Billy, Drury Lane, 1974; Same Time, Next Year, Prince of Wales, 1976; Flowers for Algernon, Queen's, 1979; Barnum, Palladium, 1981, 1983, Victoria Palace, 1985–86 (Olivier Award; Show Business Personality of the Year, Variety Club of GB); The Phantom of the Opera, Her Majesty's, 1986 (Olivier Award, Best Actor in a Musical), NY, 1988 (Tony Award, Best Actor in a Musical), Los Angeles, 1989; The Music of Andrew Lloyd Webber (concert tour), USA, Australia and UK, 1991–92; EFX, Las Vegas, 1995–96. *Films include:* Soap Box Derby; Blow Your Own Trumpet; Two Left Feet; The War Lover; Two Living, One Dead; The Knack, 1964 (Variety Club Award for Most Promising Newcomer); A Funny Thing Happened on the Way to the Forum, 1965; The Jokers, How I Won the War, 1966; Hello Dolly, 1968; The Games, 1969; Hello and Goodbye, 1970; Alice in Wonderland, 1972; The Condorman, 1980. Numerous radio broadcasts and TV appearances; *TV series include:* Some Mothers Do 'Ave 'Em; Chalk and Cheese. *Publication:* Parcel Arrived Safely: Tied with String (autobiog.), 1999. *Address:* c/o ICM Ltd, Oxford House, 76 Oxford Street, W1R 1RB. *T:* (020) 7636 6565.

CRAWFORD, Prof. Michael Hewson, FBA 1980; Professor of Ancient History, University College London, since 1986; *b* 7 Dec. 1939; *s* of late Brian Hewson Crawford and Margarethe Bettina (*née* Nagel). *Educ:* St Paul's School; Oriel College, Oxford (BA, MA). Scholar, British School at Rome, 1962–64; Jane Eliza Procter Visiting Fellow, Princeton Univ., 1964–65; Cambridge University: Research Fellow, 1964–69, Fellow, 1969–86, Christ's Coll.; Lectr, 1969–86. Visiting Professor: Univ. of Pavia, 1983, 1992; Ecole Normale Supérieure, Paris, 1984; Univ. of Padua, 1986; Sorbonne, Paris, 1989; San Marino, 1989; Milan, 1990; L'Aquila, 1990; Ecole des Hautes Etudes, Paris, 1997; Ecole des Hautes Etudes en Sciences Sociales, Paris, 1999; Joseph Crabtree Orator, 2000. Joint Director: Excavations of Fregellae, 1980–86; Valpolcevera Project, 1987–93; Velleia Project, 1994–95; San Martino Project, 1996–. Chm., JACT, 1992–95 (Chm., Ancient History Cttee, 1978–84); Vice-Pres., Roman Soc., 1981–. Membro Straniero, Istituto Lombardo, 1990; Member: Academia Europaea, 1995; Reial Acadèmia de Bones Lletres, 1998. Editor: Papers of the British Sch. at Rome, 1975–79; Jl of Roman Studies, 1980–84. *Publications:* Roman Republican Coin Hoards, 1969; Roman Republican Coinage, 1974; The Roman Republic, 1978; La Moneta in Grecia e a Roma, 1981; (with D. Whitehead) Archaic and Classical Greece, 1982; Sources for Ancient History, 1983; Coinage and Money under the Roman Republic, 1985; (with M. Beard) Rome in the Late Republic, 1985; L'impero romano e la struttura economica e sociale delle province, 1986; (with A. M. Burnett) The Coinage of the Roman World in the Late Republic, 1987; (with C. Ligota and J. B. Trapp) Medals and Coins from Budé to Mommsen, 1990; (ed) Antonio Agustín between Renaissance and Counter-reform, 1993; (ed) Roman Statutes, 1995; contribs to Annales, Economic History Rev., Jl of Roman Studies, etc. *Address:* University College, Gower Street, WC1E 6BT.

CRAWFORD, Maj.-Gen. Patrick; *see* Crawford, I. P.

CRAWFORD, Peter John; QC 1976; **His Honour Judge Peter Crawford;** a Senior Circuit Judge, since 1992 (a Circuit Judge, 1988–92); *b* 23 June 1930; *s* of William Gordon Robertson and Doris Victoria Robertson (*née* Mann, subseq. Crawford); *m* 1st, 1955, Jocelyn Lavender; two *s* two *d*; 2nd, 1979, Ann Allen Travis. *Educ:* Berkhamsted Sch.; Brasenose Coll., Oxford (MA). Called to Bar, Lincoln's Inn, 1953; Bencher, 1984; a Recorder, 1974–88; Resident Judge, Oxford Crown Court, 1991–92; Recorder of Birmingham, 1992–2001; Recorder of Oxford, 2001–. Pres., Trent Region, Mental Health Review Tribunal, 1986–; Vice Chm., Appeal Cttee, ICA, 1987–88; Member: Council of Justice, 1986–88; Parole Bd, 1992–96. Mem., Paddington Borough Council, 1962–65; Chm., W London Family Service Unit, 1972–79; Mem., Family Service Units Nat. Council, 1975–81. Hon. Pres., English Nat. Sect., Internat. Assoc. of Penal Law, 1998–. *Recreation:* gardening. *Address:* The Law Courts, St Aldates, Oxford OX1 1TL. *Club:* Royal Over-Seas League.

CRAWFORD, Robert Gammie, CBE 1990; Chairman, Highlands and Islands Airports Ltd, 1986–93; *b* 20 March 1924; *s* of William and Janet Beveridge Crawford; *m* 1947, Rita Veiss; one *d*. *Educ:* Robert Gordon's Coll., Aberdeen. Solicitor of the Supreme Court, England. Navigator, RAF, 1942–47. Practised as Solicitor, 1950–73, Partner, Ince and Co. (Internat. Shipping Lawyers); Director: UK Freight Demurrage and Defence Assoc. Ltd, 1976– (Chm., 1987–90); UK Mutual Steamship Assurance Assoc. Ltd, 1980–94 (Chm., 1983–90); Sturge Aviation Syndicates Management Ltd, 1994–96; L. R. Integrity Management Ltd, 1994–96; Ockham Sturge Aviation Agency, 1996–97; Chairman: Silver Line Ltd, 1974–83; Silver Line Pension Fund, 1983–; UK Mutual War Risk Assoc. Ltd, 1982– (Dir, 1980–); Independent Claims Services Ltd, 1995–99. Mem., Lloyd's, 1975–95; Mem. Bd, 1982–94, Gen. Cttee, 1982–, Lloyd's Register of Shipping; Trustee, Lloyd's Register Superannuation Fund, 1982–. Member: Bd, CAA, 1984–93; Bd, PLA, 1985–92 (Vice Chm., 1986–92). Freeman: City of London, 1988; Co. of Watermen and Lightermen, 1985. *Recreations:* shooting, reading, conversation. *Address:* 9 London House, Avenue Road, NW8 7PX. *T:* and *Fax:* (020) 7483 2754. *Club:* Royal Northern and University (Aberdeen).

CRAWFORD, (Robert Hardie) Bruce; JP; Member (SNP) Scotland Mid and Fife, Scottish Parliament, since 1999; *b* 16 Feb. 1955; *s* of Robert and Wilma Crawford; *m* 1980, Jacqueline Hamilton Scott; three *s*. *Educ:* Kinross High Sch.; Perth High Sch. Personnel Officer, then Equal Opportunities Officer, later Develt Advr, Scottish Office, 1974–99. Member (SNP): Perth and Kinross DC, 1988–96; Perth and Kinross Council, 1995– (Leader, 1995–99). Scottish Parliament: Opposition Chief Whip, 1999; Opposition frontbench spokesman on transport and the envmt, 2000–. Member Board: Scottish Enterprise Tayside, 1996–99; Perthshire Tourist Bd, 1996–99; Perth Coll., 1996–99. Chairman: Perth and Kinross Recreational Facilities Ltd, 1996–99; Kinross-shire Partnership Ltd, 1998–99. JP Perth, Kinross, 1993. *Recreations:* politics, golf, football. *Address:* Scottish Parliament, Edinburgh EH99 1SP. *T:* (0131) 348 5686.

CRAWFORD, Prof. Robert James, FREng; Professor of Engineering Materials, since 1989, Director, Polymer Processing Research Centre, since 1996, and Pro-Vice-Chancellor, since 2001, Queen's University of Belfast; *b* 6 April 1949; *s* of Robert James Crawford and Teresa Harriet Crawford; *m* 1974, Isobel Catherine Allen; two *s* one *d*. *Educ:* Queen's Univ., Belfast (BSc 1st cl. Hons Mech. Engrg 1970; PhD 1973; DSc 1987). FIM 1985; FIMechE 1986; FREng 1997. Queen's University, Belfast: Asst Lectr in Engrg, 1972–74; Lectr, 1974–82; Sen. Lectr, 1982–84; Reader, 1984–89; Dir, Sch. of Mechanical and Process Engrg, 1989–97. Director: Rotosystems Ltd, 1991–; Hughes & McLeod Ltd, 1993–. *Publications:* Plastics Engineering, 1981, 3rd edn 1998; Mechanics of Engineering Materials, 1987, 2nd edn 1996; Rotational Moulding of Plastics, 1992, 2nd edn 1996. *Recreations:* reading, golf. *Address:* School of Mechanical and Process Engineering, Queen's University of Belfast, Ashby Building, Stranmillis Road, Belfast BT9 5AH. *T:* (028) 9027 4700.

CRAWFORD, Dr Robert McKay; Chief Executive, Scottish Enterprise, since 2000; *b* 14 June 1951; *s* of Robert and Catherine Crawford; *m* 1975, Linda Acheson; one *s* one *d*. *Educ:* Strathclyde Univ. (BA Hons Politics); Harvard Univ.(John F. Kennedy Schol.); Glasgow Univ. (PhD Govt 1982). Leverhulme Fellow, Fraser of Aberdeen Inst., Strathclyde Univ., 1983–85; SDA, 1985–87; Dir, N America, 1989–91, Dir, Glasgow, 1991–94, Locate in Scotland; Man. Dir, Scottish Enterprise Ops, 1994–96; Sen. Specialist, World Bank, 1996–98; Partner, Ernst & Young, 1998-2000. FRSA 1995. *Recreations:* running, reading, modern history, economics, biography. *Address:* Scottish Enterprise, 120 Bothwell Street, Glasgow G2 7JP. *T:* (0141) 228 2421.

CRAWFORD, Sir (Robert) Stewart, GCMG 1973 (KCMG 1966; CMG 1951); CVO 1955; HM Diplomatic Service, retired; *b* 27 Aug. 1913; *s* of late Sir William Crawford, KBE; *m* 1938, Mary Katharine (*d* 1992), *d* of late Eric Corbett, Gorse Hill, Witley, Surrey; three *s* one *d* (and one *s* decd). *Educ:* Gresham's Sch., Holt; Oriel Coll., Oxford. Home Civil Service (Air Ministry), 1936; Private Sec. to Chief of Air Staff, 1940–46; Asst Sec., Control Office for Germany and Austria, 1946; Foreign Office, 1947; Counsellor, British Embassy, Oslo, 1954–56; Counsellor, later Minister, British Embassy, Baghdad, 1957–59; Dep. UK Delegate to OEEC Paris, 1959–60; Asst Under Sec., Foreign Office, 1961–65; Political Resident, Persian Gulf, 1966–70; Dep. Under-Sec. of State, FCO, 1970–73. Chm., Cttee on Broadcasting Coverage, 1973–74; Mem., BBC Gen. Adv. Council, 1976–84; Chm., Broadcasters' Audience Res. Bd, 1980–88. *Address:* 19 Adam Court, Bell Street, Henley-on-Thames, Oxon RG9 2BJ. *T:* (01491) 574702. *Club:* Phyllis Court (Henley-on-Thames).

CRAWFORD, Robert William Kenneth; Director-General, Imperial War Museum, since 1995 (Deputy Director-General, 1982–95); *b* 3 July 1945; *s* of late Hugh Merrall Crawford, FCA, and Mary Crawford (*née* Percival); *m* 1975, Vivienne Sylvia Polakowski; one *d* one *s*. *Educ:* Culford Sch.; Pembroke Coll., Oxford (Cleobury Schol.; BA). Joined Imperial War Museum as Research Asst, 1968: Head of Research and Information Office, 1971–89; Keeper, Dept of Photographs, 1975–83; Asst Director, 1979–82. Chm., UK Nat. Inventory of War Memorials, 1995–; Nat. Mus. Dirs' Conf., 2001–; Member: British Nat. Cttee for History of Second World War, 1995–; Bd, Museum Documentation Assoc., 1998–. Trustee: Imperial War Mus. Trust, 1982–; Sir Winston Churchill Archives Trust, 1995–; Florence Nightingale Mus. Trust, 1999–; Royal Logistics Corps Mus. Trust, 2000–; Fleet Air Arm Mus., 2000; Nat. Historic Ships Cttee, 2000–. Freeman, City of London, 1998; Liveryman, Glovers' Co., 1998. *Address:* c/o Imperial War Museum, Lambeth Road, SE1 6HZ. *T:* (020) 7416 5206. *Club:* Special Forces.

CRAWFORD, Vice-Adm. Sir William (Godfrey), KBE 1961; CB 1958; DSC 1941; *b* 14 Sept. 1907; *s* of late H. E. V. Crawford, Wyld Court, Axminster, and late Mrs M. E. Crawford; *m* 1939, Mary Felicity Rosa (*d* 1995), *d* of late Sir Philip Williams, 2nd Bt; three *s* one *d*. *Educ:* RN Coll., Dartmouth. Lieut RN, 1929; specialised in gunnery, 1932; Lieut-Comdr, 1937; Gunnery Officer, HMS Rodney, 1940–42; Comdr, Dec. 1941; SO to 2nd i/c, Eastern Fleet, 1942–44; Exec. Officer, HMS Venerable, 1944–46; Capt. 1947; in comd HMS Pelican and 2nd Frigate Flotilla, Med., 1948–49; Dep.-Dir RN Staff Coll., 1950–52; in comd HMS Devonshire, 1952–53; in comd RN Coll., Dartmouth, 1953–56; Rear-Adm. 1956; Imperial Defence Coll., 1956–58; Flag Officer, Sea Training, 1958–60; Vice-Adm. 1959; Comdr British Navy Staff and Naval Attaché Washington, 1960–62; retired list, 1963. Dir, Overseas Offices, BTA, 1964–72. *Recreations:* sailing, fishing. *Address:* Broadlands, Whitchurch Canonicorum, Bridport, Dorset DT6 6RJ. *T:* (01297) 489591. *Club:* Cruising.

CRAWFORD, William Hamilton Raymund, QC 1980; **His Honour Judge Crawford;** a Circuit Judge, since 1986; *b* 10 Nov. 1936; *s* of late Col Mervyn Crawford, DSO, DL, JP, and Martha Hamilton Crawford; *m* 1965, Marilyn Jean Colville; one *s* two *d*. *Educ:* West Downs, Winchester; Winchester Coll.; Emmanuel Coll., Cambridge (BA). Commnd 2nd Lt, Royal Scots Greys, 1955–57. Called to the Bar, Inner Temple, 1964; Dep. Chm., Agricultural Land Tribunal, 1978; a Recorder, 1979–86. *Recreations:* hill farming, fishing, shooting (shot for GB in Kolapore Match, and for Scotland in Elcho and Twenty Matches on several occasions; mem., Scottish Rifle Team, Commonwealth Games, Jamaica, 1966). *Address:* c/o The Crown Court, Newcastle-upon-Tyne. *Club:* Northern Counties (Newcastle).

CRAWLEY, family name of **Baroness Crawley**.

CRAWLEY, Baroness *cr* 1998 (Life Peer), of Edgbaston in the co. of West Midlands; **Christine Mary Crawley;** Chair, Women's National Commission, since 1999; *b* 9 Jan. 1950; *m*; three *c* (incl. twins). *Educ:* Notre Dame Catholic Secondary Girls' School, Plymouth; Digby Stuart Training College, Roehampton. Formerly teacher; S Oxfordshire District Council; contested (Lab) Staffordshire SE, gen. election, 1983. Vice-Pres., AMA, 1987–98. MEP (Lab) Birmingham E, 1984–99; Dep. Leader, Eur. PLP, 1994–99. European Parliament: formerly: Mem., Civil Liberties and Internal Affairs Cttee; Sen. Mem., Women's Rights Cttee (Chair, 1989–94). Dir, Northfield Regeneration Forum; Chm., W Midlands Regl Cultural Consortium, 1999–. Patron: Orgn for Sickle Cell Anaemia Relief; Women's Returners Network. FRSA. *Address:* House of Lords, SW1A 0PW.

CRAWLEY, David Jonathan; Head of Food and Agriculture Group, Scottish Executive Rural Affairs Department, since 1999; *b* 6 May 1951; *s* of Frederick John Crawley and Olive Elizabeth Crawley (*née* Bunce); *m* 1983, Anne Anderson; one *s* two *d*. *Educ:* Chichester High Sch.; Christ Church, Oxford (BA Modern Hist. 1972; MA 1973). Scottish Office, 1972–81; Dept of Energy, 1981–84; Asst Sec., Scottish Educn Dept, 1984–87; Principal Private Sec. to Sec. of State for Scotland, 1987–89; Counsellor, UK Representation to EU, Brussels, 1990–94; Asst Dir, Finance, and Hd, Private Finance Unit, 1994–97, Hd, Powers and Functions, Constitution Gp, 1997–98, Scottish Office; Hd of Schs Gp, Scottish Office, then Scottish Exec., Educn Dept, 1998–99. Treas., St Fillan's Episcopal Ch, 1998–99. *Recreations:* gardening, music. *Address:* Scottish Executive, Pentland House, Edinburgh EH14 1TY. *T:* (0131) 244 6032.

CRAWLEY, Most Rev. David Perry; *see* Kootenay, Archbishop of.

CRAWLEY, Frederick William, CBE 1998; FCIB; Chairman: Alliance & Leicester Building Society, 1991–94 (Director, since 1988; Deputy Chairman, 1990–91); Girobank PLC, 1992–94 (Director, since 1990; Deputy Chairman, 1990–92); *b* 10 June 1926; *s* of William Clement Crawley and Elsie Florence Crawley; *m* 1951, Ruth Eva Jungman; two *d*. Joined Lloyds Bank, 1942; Chief Accountant, 1969–72; Asst Chief Gen. Man., 1977–78; Dep. Chief Gen. Man., 1978–82; Chief Exec., Lloyds Bank, Calif, 1982–83; Dep. Chief Gen. Man., 1983–84, Chief Gen. Man., 1984–85, Dep. Chief Exec., 1985–87, Lloyds Bank plc. Chairman: Black Horse Agencies Ltd, 1985–88; Betta Stores, 1990–92; Legal & General Recovery Investment Trust, 1994–98; Director: Black Horse Life Assce Co., 1977–82; Lloyds Bank Unit Trust Managers, 1977–82; Lloyds Leasing, 1977–82; Lloyds Development Capital, 1981–82; Lloyds Bank International, 1982–83; Internat. Commodities Clearing House Hldgs, 1984–87; Lloyds Bank, 1984–88; Lloyds Bank Export Finance, 1985–87; Lloyds Bowmaker Finance, 1985–87; FS Assurance, 1988–90; Barratt Developments, 1988–96; Lloyds Development Capital, 1988–92; Legal & General Bank Ltd, 1997–2001; Aeroclub Ltd, 1987–; Chm., The Property Jungle Ltd, 2000. RAF Benevolent Fund: Hon. Treas., 1988–, and Dep. Chm., 1988–, RAF Benevolent Fund Enterprises (formerly Internat. Air Tattoo); Dir, Air Shows Europe (formerly Battle of Britain Appeal,) 1988–. Develt Trustee, Mus. of Army Flying, 1993–. Fellow, St Andrews Strategic Management Ltd, 1995–96. FCIB (FIB 1971); CIMgt; ARAeS 1984. Freeman, GAPAN, 1992. *Recreations:* aviation, shooting, photography. *Address:* 4 The Hexagon, Fitzroy Park, N6 6HR. *T:* (020) 8341 2279. *Club:* Royal Air Force.

CRAWLEY, John Cecil, CBE 1972 (MBE 1944); Chairman of Trustees of Visnews, 1976–86; *b* 29 June 1909; *s* of John and Kathleen Crawley; *m* 1933, Constance Mary Griffiths (*d* 1998); two *d*. *Educ:* William Ellis Sch. War Service, Army, 1939–45. Journalism: Reynolds, 1927; Central News Agency, 1928; National Press Agency, 1929; Press Secretaries, 1933; BBC: Sub-Editor, 1945; Foreign Correspondent, New York, 1959–63; Foreign News Editor, 1963–67; Editor of News and Current Affairs, 1967–71; Chief Asst to Dir-Gen., BBC, 1971–75. *Recreations:* walking, bird-watching. *Address:* 157 Clarence Gate Gardens, NW1 6AP. *T:* (020) 7723 6876.

CRAWLEY, John Maurice, CB 1992; Under Secretary, Inland Revenue, 1979–93; *b* 27 Sept. 1933; *s* of late Charles William and Kathleen Elizabeth Crawley; *m* 1978, Jane Meadows Rendel; three *s*. *Educ:* Rugby Sch.; New Coll., Oxford (MA). Assistant Principal, Inland Revenue, 1959; Principal, 1963; Asst Secretary, 1969; Under Sec., 1979; seconded to Cabinet Office (Central Policy Review Staff), 1973–76 and 1979–81. *Recreations:* music, walking, book-binding.

CRAWLEY-BOEVEY, Sir Thomas (Michael Blake), 8th Bt *cr* 1784; *b* 29 Sept. 1928; *er s* of Sir Launcelot Valentine Hyde Crawley-Boevey, 7th Bt, and Elizabeth Goodeth (*d* 1976), *d* of Herbert d'Auvergne Innes, late Indian Police; *S* father, 1968; *m* 1957, Laura Coelingh (*d* 1979); two *s*. *Educ:* Wellington Coll.; St John's Coll., Cambridge (BA 1952, MA 1956). 2nd Lieut, Durham Light Infantry, 1948. With Shipping Agents, 1952–61; with Consumers' Association, 1961–82; Editor: Money Which?, 1968–76; Which?, 1976–82; Editor-in-Chief, Which? magazines, 1980–82. Master, Girdlers' Co., 1992–93. *Heir: er s* Thomas Hyde Crawley-Boevey, *b* 26 June 1958. *Address:* 47 Belvoir Road, Cambridge CB4 1JH. *T:* (01223) 368698.

CRAWSHAW, 5th Baron *cr* 1892, of Crawshaw, co. Lancaster and of Whatton, co. Leics; **David Gerald Brooks;** Bt 1891; *b* 14 Sept. 1934; *s* of 3rd Baron Crawshaw and Sheila (*d* 1964), *o d* of Lt-Col P. R. Clifton, CMG, DSO; *S* brother, 1997; *m* 1970, Belinda Mary, *d* of George Burgess; four *d*. *Educ:* Eton; RAC, Cirencester. *Heir: b* Hon. John Patrick Brooks [*b* 17 March 1938; *m* 1967, Rosemary Vans Agnew, *o d* of C. Vans Agnew Frank; one *s* one *d*].

CRAWSHAY, Elisabeth Mary Boyd, (Lady Crawshay), CBE 1986; DL; Chairman, Local Government Boundary Commission, Wales, 1981–94; Deputy Chief Commissioner, St John's Ambulance Brigade, Wales, 1979–84; *b* 2 July 1927; *d* of Lt-Col Guy Franklin Reynolds, late 9th Lancers, and Katherine Isobel (*née* Macdonell); *m* 1950, Col Sir William (Robert) Crawshay, DSO, ERD, TD. *Educ:* Convent of Sacred Heart, Roehampton; St Anne's Coll., Oxford (MA). Mem., Mental Health Act Commn, 1983–88. DL Gwent 1978; JP Abergavenny, 1972–96 (Chm., Juvenile Bench, 1980–95; Mem., Borstal Board of Visitors, 1975–84). DJStJ 1970. *Address:* Ty Carreg, Govilon, Abergavenny, Mon NP7 9PT. *T:* (01873) 832220.

CRAXTON, Christine Elizabeth; *see* Gamble, C. E.

CRAXTON, John Leith, RA 1993; artist; *b* 3 Oct. 1922; *s* of late Harold Craxton, OBE, LRAM and Essie Craxton. *Educ:* various private schs incl. Betteshanger, Kent; Westminster and Central Schs of Art; Goldsmiths' Coll. (with Lucian Freud). First solo exhibn, Leicester Galls, 1944; with Lucian Freud, worked in Scilly Is, then Greece, 1945–47, and held joint exhibn, London Gall., 1947; designed sets and costumes for Daphnis and Chloë, Royal Ballet, 1951, Apollo, 1966; Cotteral Meml Tapestry for Stirling Univ., 1971–74. Principal solo exhibitions include: St George's Gall., London, 1945; Galerie Gasser, Zürich, 1946; British Council, Athens, 1946, 1949, 1985; Mayor Gall., London, 1950; Leicester Galls, London, 1951, 1954, 1956, 1961, 1966; Crane Gall., Manchester, 1955; Whitechapel Art Gall., 1967; Hamet Gall., London, 1971; Christopher Hull Gall., London, 1982, 1985, 1987, 1993; Chrysostomos Gall., Hania, 1985; Pallant House Gall., Chichester, 1998. Work in public collections includes: Tate Gall.; V&A; BM; Gall. of Modern Art, Edinburgh; Nat. Mus. of Wales; Arts Council; British Council; Govt Picture Collection; Nat. Gall., Melbourne; Metropolitan Mus., NY; work in many private collections. HM Consular Correspondent, Hania, Crete, 1992–. *Relevant publication:* Illustrated Monograph 1941–1948, by Geoffrey Grigson, 1948. *Recreations:* music, museums, motorbikes, archaeology, seafood, cooking. *Address:* Moschon 1, Hania, Crete, Greece; 14 Kidderpore Avenue, NW3 7SU.

CRAY, Rt Rev. Graham Alan; *see* Maidstone, Bishop Suffragan of.

CREAGH, Maj.-Gen. Sir Kilner Rupert B.; *see* Brazier-Creagh.

CREAMER, Brian; Consulting Physician, St Thomas' Hospital, London, 1991 (Physician, 1959–91); Senior Lecturer in Medicine, United Medical and Dental Schools (St Thomas's), 1959–91; Hon. Consultant in Gastroenterology to the Army, 1970–90; *b* 12 April 1926; *s* of late L. G. Creamer and Mrs Creamer, Epsom; *m* 1953, Margaret Holden Rees; two *s* one *d*. *Educ:* Christ's Hosp.; St Thomas' Hosp. MB, BS Hons London, 1948; MD London, 1952; FRCP 1966 (MRCP 1950); Research Asst, Mayo Clinic, Rochester, USA, 1955–56; Dean: St Thomas's Hosp. Med. Sch., 1979–84; UMDS of Guy's and St Thomas's Hosps, 1984–86. Vis. Prof., Shiraz Univ., Iran, 1977–78. Sir Arthur Hurst Memorial Lectr, 1968; Watson Smith Lectr, RCP, 1971. Member: SE Thames RHA, 1982–85; Medway DHA, 1987–89; W Lambeth DHA, 1989–90. Member: British Soc. of Gastroenterology; Assoc. of Physicians of GB and NI; Exec. Subcttee, Univ. Hosps Assoc., 1981–86. Chm. Council, Trinity Hospice, 1987–92. Member: Collegiate Council, Univ. of London, 1980–86; Senate, Univ. of London, 1981–86; Council of Almoners, Christ's Hosp., 1986–98. *Publications:* (ed) Modern Trends in Gastroenterology, vol. 4, 1970; (ed) The Small Intestine, 1974; contributions to med. jls. *Recreations:* grappling with drawing and painting, listening to music. *Address:* Vine House, Highfields, East Horsley KT24 5AA. *T:* (01483) 283320.

CREAN, Hon. Frank; *b* Hamilton, Vic, 28 Feb. 1916; *s* of J. Crean; *m* 1946, Mary, *d* of late A. E. Findlay; three *s*. *Educ:* Hamilton High Sch.; Melbourne High Sch.; Melbourne Univ. BA Hons; BCom. DPA; FCPA. Income Tax Assessor, 1934–45. MLA: for Albert Park, Vic, 1945–47; for Prahran, 1949–51; MHR for Melbourne Ports, 1951–77; Mem. Exec., Federal Parly Labour Party, 1956–72, Dep. Leader, 1975–76; Mem., Jt Parly Cttee on Public Accounts, 1952–55; Treasurer, Commonwealth of Australia, 1972–74; Minister for Overseas Trade, 1974–75, also Deputy Prime Minister, 1975. Chm., Council of Adult Educn, 1947–74. Pres., Vict. Br., Aust. Inst. Internat. Affairs, 1983–86; Chm., Vict. Br., Freedom from Hunger Campaign, 1979. *Publication:* (with W. J. Byrt) Government and Politics in Australia, 1972, 2nd edn 1982. *Address:* 31/27 Queens Road, Melbourne, Vic 3004, Australia.

CREASY, Leonard Richard, CB 1972; OBE 1961; CEng, FICE, FIStructE; civil engineer in private practice with son, since 1974; *b* 20 Dec. 1912; *s* of William and Ellen Creasy; *m* 1937, Irene Howard; one *s* one *d*. *Educ:* Wimbledon Technical Coll. BSc(Eng) London. Served War, RE, E Africa, 1944–46. Service in Industry, 1928–34; HM Office of Works, Asst Engr, 1935; Min. of Works, Suptg Engr, 1959; MPBW: Dir, Civil Engrg, 1966; Dir, Central Services, 1968; Dir of Civil Engrg Develt, Dept of the Environment, 1970–73. Concerned with Inquiries into disasters at Aberfan, Ronan Point and Brent, and with design of Radio and Radar Towers, London Heathrow and Birmingham; Plant House, Royal Botanical Gardens, Edinburgh; Wind Tunnels, Bedford RAE; and other structures. Bronze Medal, Reinforced Concrete Assoc.; Manby and Telford Premiums, Instn Civil Engrs; Pres., Instn Struct. Engrs, 1973 (Bronze Medal and Certif. of Merit of the Instn). *Publications:* Pre-stressed Concrete Cylindrical Tanks, 1961; James Forrest Lecture, 1968; many other papers on civil and structural engrg projects and engrg economics. *Recreations:* music, opera, languages. *Address:* 5 The Oaks, Epsom, Surrey KT18 5HH. *T:* (01372) 722361.

CREDITON, Bishop Suffragan of, since 1996; **Rt Rev. Richard Stephen Hawkins;** *b* 2 April 1939; *s* of late Ven. Canon John Stanley Hawkins and Elsie Hawkins (*née* Briggs); *m* 1966, Valerie Ann Herneman; one *s* one *d* (and one *s* one *d* decd). *Educ:* Exeter School; Exeter Coll., Oxford; St Stephen's House, Oxford. MA (Oxon); BPhil (Exeter Univ.); CQSW. Asst Curate, St Thomas, Exeter, 1963–66; Team Vicar of Clyst St Mary, Clyst Valley Team Ministry, 1966–78; Bishop's Officer for Ministry and Joint Director, Exeter-Truro Ministry Training Scheme, 1978–81; Team Vicar, Central Exeter Team Ministry, 1978–81; Diocesan Director of Ordinands, Exeter, 1979–81; Priest-in-charge, Whitestone with Oldridge, 1981–87; Archdeacon of Totnes, 1981–88; Suffragan Bishop of Plymouth, 1988–96. *Address:* 10 Cathedral Close, Exeter EX1 1EZ. *T:* (01392) 273509.

CREECH, Hon. Wyatt (Beetham); MP (Nat.) Wairarapa, New Zealand, since 1988; *b* Oceanside, Calif, 13 Oct. 1946; arrived in NZ 1947; *s* of Jesse Wyatt Creech and Ellanora Sophia (*née* Beetham); *m* 1981, Diane Marie Rose; three *s*. *Educ:* Hadlow Prep. Sch., Masterton; Wanganui Collegiate Sch.; Massey Univ. (Dip. Sheep Farming); Victoria Univ. (BA Pol Sci. and Internat. Politics). Farmer, Wairarapa, 1974–79; horticulturalist (vineyard developer), 1979–88; Accountant, Masterton, 1983–87; Minister: of Revenue, of Customs, i/c Public Trust Office and responsible for Govt Superannuation Fund, 1990–91; for Sen. Citizens, and Associate Minister of Finance and of Social Welfare, 1991–93; for State Owned Enterprises, 1993; of Employment, 1993–96; of Revenue and Dep. Minister of Finance, 1993–96; Leader of the House, 1996–98; Minister of Educn, 1996–99; Minister of Courts and of Ministerial Services, 1997–98; Dep. Prime Minister, 1998–99. Dep. Leader, Nat. Party, 1997–2001. Mem., Parly Service Commn. *Recreations:* wine-tasting, gardening, outdoor pursuits. *Address:* Parliament Buildings, Wellington, New Zealand.

CREED, Prof. Francis Hunter, MD; FRCP, FRCPsych, FMedSci; Professor of Psychological Medicine and Research Dean, Faculty of Medicine, Dentistry, Nursing and Pharmacy, University of Manchester, since 1997; *b* 22 Feb. 1947; *s* of Albert Lowry Creed and Joyce Marian Creed; *m* 1972, Ruth Alison Kaye; two *s* two *d*. *Educ:* Kingswood Sch., Bath; Downing Coll., Cambridge (Pilley Schol.; MB BChir 1971; MA; MD 1985); St Thomas' Hosp. Med. Sch., London. FRCP 1991; FRCPsych 1991. Registrar, Maudsley Hosp., 1974–76; Sen. Registrar, Maudsley and London Hosps, 1976–78; Mental Health Leverhulme Res. Fellow, 1978–80; Sen. Lectr, Univ. of Manchester and Consultant Psychiatrist, Manchester Royal Infirmary, 1980–92; Prof. of Community Psychiatry, Univ. of Manchester, 1992–97; Hon. Consultant Psychiatrist, Central Manchester Healthcare Trust, 1981–. Churchill Travelling Fellow, 1993. FRSocMed 1980. *Publications:* Medicine and Psychiatry, 1981; Psychiatry in Medical Practice, 1989, 2nd edn 1994; over 100 articles in learned jls on psychological aspects of medicine and Community Psychiatry. *Recreations:* hill walking, swimming, travelling. *Address:* Department of Psychiatry, Manchester University, Rawnsley Building, Manchester Royal Infirmary, Oxford Road, Manchester M13 9WL. *T:* (0161) 276 5331.

CREEK, Malcolm Lars, LVO 1980; OBE 1985; HM Diplomatic Service, retired; Consul-General, Auckland, 1988–90; *b* 2 April 1931; *s* of Edgar Creek and Lily Creek (*née* Robertshaw); *m* 1st, 1953, Moira Pattison (marr. diss. 1970); one *d* (one *s* decd); 2nd, 1970, Gillian Bell; one *s* one *d* (and one *d* decd). *Educ:* Belle Vue School, Bradford. BA Hons London. National Service, 1950–52. Foreign Office, 1953; served Mogadishu, Harar, Mexico City, Abidjan, Chile; First Sec., San José, 1968; Havana, 1971; FCO, 1974; Head of Chancery, Tunis, 1978; Lima, 1981; High Comr, Vanuatu, 1985. *Recreations:* reading, family history, cricket. *Address:* 17 Bertram Drive North, Meols, Wirral, Merseyside L47 0LN. *T:* (0151) 632 5520.

CREELMAN, Graham Murray; Managing Director, Anglia Television, since 1996; Chairman, Anglia Multimedia, since 1999; *b* 20 May 1947; *s* of late Robert Kelly Creelman and of Jean Murray Creelman; *m* 1st, 1969, Eleanor McCullouch McAuslan (marr. diss. 1984); two *d*; 2nd, 1984, Sarah Katharine Bruce-Lockhart (marr. diss. 1996); two *d*; 3rd, 1997, Francesca Vivica Parsons; one step *s* one step *d*. *Educ:* Greenock Acad.; Univ. of Sussex (BA Hons). Journalist, Scotsman, 1969–70; journalist and producer, BBC Scotland, 1970–78; producer and dir documentaries, Anglia TV, 1978–89; Exec. Dir, Survival Anglia Ltd, 1989–94; Dir of Programmes, Anglia TV, 1994–96. Dir, Eastern Arts Bd, 1995–; Chairman: Eastern Screen Commn, 1997–; East of England Cultural Consortium, 1999–. Trustee/Dir, Wildscreen Trustees, 1993–; Dep. Chm., United Wildlife, 1997–. *Publications:* contribs to New Statesman, The Listener. *Recreations:* walking in Scotland, music of Schubert, the books of John Buchan, eating. *Address:* 22 Christchurch Road, Norwich NR2 2AE.

CREESE, Nigel Arthur Holloway, AM 1988; Executive Officer, Association of Heads of Independent Schools of Australia, 1989–95 (Chairman, 1985–87); *b* 4 June 1927; *s* of late H. R. Creese; *m* 1951, Valdai (*née* Walters); two *s* two *d*. *Educ:* Blundell's Sch.; Brasenose Coll., Oxford. Assistant Master: Bromsgrove Sch., 1952–55; Rugby Sch., 1955–63; Headmaster: Christ's Coll., Christchurch, NZ, 1963–70; Melbourne Grammar Sch., 1970–87. *Recreations:* Nordic ski-ing, tennis. *Address:* 75 Charles Street, Kew, Vic 3101, Australia. *Club:* Melbourne (Melbourne).

CREIGHTON, Alan Joseph, CEng, FRINA; RCNC; Chief Underwater Systems Executive, Ministry of Defence, 1989–91, retired; *b* 21 Nov. 1936; *s* of Joseph Kenneth and Iris Mary Creighton; *m* 1959, Judith Bayford; two *d*. *Educ:* Gillingham County Grammar School; Royal Naval College, Greenwich. Joined Admiralty, 1953; Cadetship to Royal Corps of Naval Constructors, 1957; pass out, RNC Greenwich, 1961; RCDS 1980; secondment to industry, 1981; resumed MoD (PE) career, 1984; Dir Gen., Surface Ships, 1986–89. *Recreations:* music, dinghy sailing, cabinet making. *Address:* Rose Cottage, West Littleton, Marshfield SN14 8JE. *T:* (01225) 891021.

CREIGHTON, Harold Digby Fitzgerald; *b* 11 Sept. 1927; *s* of late Rev. Digby Robert Creighton and Amy Frances Rohde; *m* 1964, Harriett Mary Falconer Wallace, *d* of late A. L. P. F. Wallace of Candacraig (Mem., Queen's Body Guard for Scotland); four *d*. *Educ:* Haileybury. Consolidated Tin Smelters, Penang, 1950–52; Dir, machine tool companies, London, 1952–63; Chm., Scottish Machine Tool Corp. Ltd, Glasgow, 1963–68. Chm., 1967–75, Editor, 1973–75, The Spectator. *Address:* 18 St James Chambers, Ryder Street, SW1Y 6QA. *Clubs:* Beefsteak, Brooks's.

See also Baron Fairhaven.

CREIGHTON, Robert Mandell; Chief Executive, Great Ormond Street Hospital for Children NHS Trust, since 1995; *b* 18 Feb. 1950; *s* of Hugh Creighton and Christian Creighton (*née* Barclay); *m* 1st, 1977, Sok-Chzeng Ong (marr. diss. 1983); 2nd, 1985, Rosanne Jelley; two *d*. *Educ:* Marlborough Coll.; King's Coll., Cambridge (MA Hist.); King's Coll. London (PGCE). Teacher, King's Coll. Sch., Wimbledon, 1974–78; Internat. Sec., United World Colls, 1978–88; Department of Health: Principal, 1988–91; Asst Sec., 1991–95; Principal Private Sec. to Sec. of State for Health, 1992–94. *Recreations:* tennis, squash, opera, theatre. *Address:* Great Ormond Street Hospital for Children NHS Trust, Great Ormond Street, WC1N 3JH. *T:* (020) 7813 8330. *Club:* Wimbledon Tennis and Squash.

CREMONA, Hon. John Joseph; Judge, 1965–92, Vice-President, 1986–92, European Court of Human Rights; Judge, 1985–92, Vice-President, 1987–92, European Tribunal in matters of State immunity; Emeritus Professor, University of Malta, since 1965; Chief Justice of Malta and President of the Constitutional Court, Court of Appeal and Court of

Criminal Appeal, 1971–81; *b* 6 Jan. 1918; *s* of late Dr Antonio Cremona, KM, MD and Anne (*née* Camilleri); *m* 1949, Marchioness Beatrice Barbaro of St George; one *s* two *d*. *Educ:* Malta Univ. (BA 1936, LLD *cum laude* 1942); Rome Univ. (DLitt 1939); London Univ. (BA 1st Cl. Hons 1946, PhD in Laws 1951). DrJur Trieste, 1972. Crown Counsel, 1947; Lectr in Constitutional Law, Malta Univ., 1947–65, Prof. of Criminal Law, 1959–65; Attorney-Gen., 1957–64; Vice-Pres., Constitutional Court and Court of Appeal, 1965–71; sometime Actg Governor General and Actg Pres., Republic of Malta. Chm., UN Cttee on Elimination of Racial Discrimination (CERD), 1986–88 (Mem., 1984–88). Chairman: Human Rights Section, World Assoc. of Lawyers; Planning Council, Foundn for Internat. Studies, Malta Univ.; Malta Human Rights Assoc.; Vice-Pres., Internat. Inst. of Studies, Documentation and Info. for the Protection of Envt, Italy; Member: Cttee of Experts on Human Rights and Cttee of Experts on State Immunity, Council of Europe, Strasbourg; Inst Internat. de Droits de l'Homme, Strasbourg; Scientific Council, Revue des Droits de l'Homme, Paris; Scientific Council, Centro Internazionale per la Protezione dei Diritti dell' Uomo, Pesaro, Italy; Scientific Council, Faculty of Law, Université de Saint Espirit, Lebanon; Editorial Adv. Board: Checklist of Human Rights Documents, NY; Rivista Internazionale dei diritti dell'Uomo, Milan; delegate and rapporteur, internat. confs. FRHistS; Fellow *ex titulo*, Internat. Acad. of Legal Medicine and Social Medicine; Hon. Fellow, LSE; Hon. Mem., Real Acad. de Jurisprudencia y Legislacion, Madrid. KStJ 1984 (Chm., St John Council, Malta, 1983–). KSG 1972. Kt, Sovereign Military Order of Malta, 1966; Companion, Order of Merit (Malta), 1994. Kt Comdr, 1968, Grand Officier, 1989, Kt Grand Cross, 1995, Order of Merit (Italy); Kt Comdr, 1971, Grand Cross of Merit, 1981, Constantinian Order of St George; Chevalier de la Légion d'Honneur (France), 1990. *Publications:* The Treatment of Young Offenders in Malta, 1956; The Malta Constitution of 1835, 1959; The Doctrine of Entrapment in Theft, 1959; The Legal Consequences of a Conviction, 1962; The Constitutional Development of Malta, 1963; From the Declaration of Rights to Independence, 1965; Human Rights Documentation in Malta, 1966; Selected Papers 1946–1989, 1990; The Maltese Constitution and Constitutional History, 1994; Malta and Britain: the early constitutions, 1996; articles in French, German, Italian, Portuguese and American law jls. *Recreation:* gardening. *Address:* Villa Barbaro, Main Street, Attard, Malta. *T:* 440818.

CRESPIN, Régine; Commandeur de la Légion d'Honneur, 1994 (Chevalier, 1969; Officier, 1981); Grand Officier de l'Ordre National du Mérite, 1997 (Chevalier, 1965; Commandeur, 1990); Commandeur des Arts et des Lettres, 1974; soprano singer; Professor of Singing, Conservatoire National Supérieur de Musique de Paris, since 1976; *b* Marseille, 23 Feb.; *d* of Henri Crespin and Marguerite (*née* Meirone); *m* 1962, Lou Bruder, French novelist, critic, poet, translator. *Educ:* Nîmes; Conservatoire National, Paris (Baccalauréat). Worked at the Opera, Paris, 1951–, in all the famous opera houses of Europe and all over the world, giving concerts, recitals, etc.; *Operas include:* Otello, Tosca, Il Trovatore, Le Nozze di Figaro, Ballo in Maschera, Der Rosenkavalier, Tannhäuser, Lohengrin, Die Walküre, Parsifal, Les Troyens, Dialogues of the Carmelites, Tales of Hoffmann, Iphigenie auf Tauris, Carmen, Le Medium. *Publications:* La vie et l'amour d'une femme (autobiog.), 1982; A la scène, à la ville, 1997 (trans. English as On stage, off stage, 1997). *Recreations:* sea, sun, sleep, books, theatre; and my dog! *Address:* 3 Avenue Frochot, 75009 Paris, France.

CRESSON, Edith; Commandeur du Mérite Agricole, 1983; Chevalier de la Légion d'Honneur; Grand Croix de l'Ordre National du Mérite, 1991; Member, European Commission, 1995–99; *b* 27 Jan. 1934; *née* Campion; *m* Jacques Cresson; two *d*. *Educ:* Diplômée de l'Ecole des Hautes Etudes Commerciales; Dr en démographie (doctoral thesis: the life of women in a rural district of Guéméné-Penfao, Loire-Atlantique). Mem., Convention des Institutions Républicaines (responsible for agricl problems), 1966; Dir of Studies, Bureau des Etudes Economiques privés (dealing especially with industrial investment); National Secretary, Parti Socialiste (in charge of youth organisation), 1974; Mem. Directing Cttee, Parti Socialiste; contested (for Parti Socialiste) Châtellerault, 1975; Mem., Eur. Parlt, 1979–81 (Mem., Cttee on Agriculture); elected Deputy, Vienne, 1981, 1986, 1988; Minister: of Agriculture, France, 1981–83; of For. Trade and Tourism, 1983–84; for Industrial Redeployment and Foreign Trade, 1984–86; for European Affairs, 1988–90; Pres.-Dir Gen., Schneider Industries Services Internat., 1990–91; Prime Minister of France, 1991–92; Pres. Dir Gen., Services Industries Strategies Internat. et Envmt, 1993–94. Pres., Assoc. Démocratique des Français à l'Etranger, 1986–91. Member, Conseil Général of Vienne, 1978–98; Mayor of Châtellerault, Vienne, 1983–97 (Dep. Mayor, 1997–). Dr *hc* Weizmann Inst., Israel, 1999; DUniv Open, 1999. *Publications:* Avec le soleil, 1976; Innover ou subir, 1998.

CRESSWELL, Rev. Amos Samuel; Chairman, Plymouth and Exeter District of the Methodist Church, 1976–91; President of the Methodist Conference, 1983–84; *b* Walsall Wood, 21 April 1926; *s* of Amos and Jane Cresswell; *m* 1956, Evelyn Rosemary Marchbanks; two *s* one *d*. *Educ:* Queen Mary's Grammar School, Walsall; University College, Durham Univ.; Wesley House, and Fitzwilliam Coll., Cambridge; Theological Seminary, Bethel bei Bielefeld, Westphalia. BA (Dunelm), Classics, 1947; BA (Cantab), Theology, 1952, MA (Cantab) 1956. Teacher of English and Latin, High School for Boys, Colchester, 1947–49; Methodist Minister, Clitheroe Circuit, 1949–50; Asst Tutor in New Testament, Richmond Coll., London, 1953–56; Minister in Darlaston (Slater St), 1956–61; Tutor in New Testament, Cliff Coll., Derbyshire, 1961–66; Minister in Bramhall Circuit (Cheadle Hulme), 1966–73; Superintendent Minister, Welwyn Garden City, 1973–76. Pres., Devonshire Assoc., 1985–86. Editor, Advance (religious weekly, formerly Joyful News), 1961–63; (with Evelyn Cresswell), Founder, Vigo Press, 1991. *Publications:* The Story of Cliff (a history of Cliff College), 1965, 2nd edn 1983; The Story They Told (a short study of the Passion Narratives in the Gospels), 1966, 2nd edn 1992; Life Power and Hope—a study of the Holy Spirit, 1972; Lord! I've had enough! (a collection of sermons), 1991; I've Told You Twice (sermons), 1995; (with Maxwell Tow) Franz Hildebrandt: Mr Valiant-for-Truth (biog.), 2000; (ed jtly) Methodist Hymns, Old and New, 2001. *Recreations:* compulsive watching of sport (especially West Bromwich Albion), collecting Roman Imperial coins, reading about American Civil War, listening to music and to Shakespeare, family and friends, research into German church struggle of 1930s and 1940s. *Address:* 2 Sage Park Road, Braunton, North Devon EX33 1HH. *T:* (01271) 813835.

CRESSWELL, Helen; freelance author and television scriptwriter; *b* July 1934; *d* of Annie Edna Clarke and Joseph Edward Cresswell; *m* 1962, Brian Rowe (marr. diss. 1995); two *d*. *Educ:* Nottingham Girls' High Sch.; King's College London (BA English Hons). Member: Soc. of Authors; BAFTA; RTS. Children's Writer's Award (jtly), BAFTA, 2000. *Television series:* Lizzie Dripping, 1973–75; Jumbo Spencer, 1976; The Bagthorpe Saga, 1980; The Secret World of Polly Flint, 1985; Moondial, 1988; The Return of the Psammead, 1993; The Watchers, 1994; The Famous Five, 1995; The Demon Headmaster, 1995; *adaptations:* Five Children and It, 1990; The Phoenix and the Carpet, 1997; Little Grey Rabbit, 2000; numerous TV plays. *Publications:* Sonya-by-the-Shire, 1961; Jumbo Spencer, 1963; The White Sea Horse, 1964; Pietro and the Mule, 1965; Jumbo Back to Nature, 1965; Where the Wind Blows, 1966; Jumbo Afloat, 1966; The Piemakers, 1967; A Tide for the Captain, 1967; The Signposters, 1968; The Sea Piper, 1968; The Barge Children, 1968; The Night-watchman, 1969; A Game of Catch, 1969; A Gift from Winklesea, 1969; The Outlanders, 1970; The Wilkses, 1970; The Bird Fancier, 1971; At the Stroke of Midnight, 1971; The Beachcombers, 1972; Lizzie Dripping, 1972; The Bongleweed, 1972; Lizzie Dripping Again, 1974; Butterfly Chase, 1975; The Winter of the Birds, 1975; My Aunt Polly, 1979; My Aunt Polly By the Sea, 1980; Dear Shrink, 1982; The Secret World of Polly Flint, 1982; Ellie and the Hagwitch, 1984; The Bagthorpe Saga: Pt 1, Ordinary Jack, 1977; Pt 2, Absolute Zero, 1978; Pt 3, Bagthorpes Unlimited, 1978; Pt 4, Bagthorpes *v* The World, 1979; Pt 5, Bagthorpes Abroad, 1984; Pt 6, Bagthorpes Haunted, 1985; Pt 7, Bagthorpes Liberated, 1988; Pt 8, The Bagthorpe Triangle, 1992; Moondial, 1987; Time Out, 1987; Rosie and the Boredom Eater, 1989; Whatever Happened in Winklesea?, 1989; Meet Posy Bates, 1990; Posy Bates Again, 1991; Lizzie Dripping and the Witch, 1991; The Return of the Psammead, 1992; Posy Bates and the Bag Lady, 1992; The Watchers, 1993; (ed) Puffin Book of Funny Stories, 1993; Classic Fairy Tales, 1993; Polly Thumb, 1994; Stonestruck, 1995; Bagthorpes Besieged, 1995; Mystery at Winklesea, 1995; Giant, 1995; Birdspell, 1995; (ed) Mystery Stories, 1996; Bag of Bones, 1997; Snatchers, 1998. *Recreations:* watercolour painting, collecting books, antiques and coincidences, sundial watching. *Address:* Old Church Farm, Eakring, Newark, Notts NG22 0DA. *T:* (01623) 870401.

CRESSWELL, Jeremy Michael, CVO 1996; HM Diplomatic Service; Minister and Deputy Head of Mission, Berlin, since 2001; *b* 1 Oct. 1949; *s* of late John Cresswell and of Jean Cresswell; *m* 1974, Petra Forwick; one *s* one *d*. *Educ:* Eton Coll. Choir Sch.; Sir William Borlase's Sch., Marlow; Exeter Coll., Oxford (BA Hons); Johannes-Gutenberg Univ., Mainz, Germany. Entered FCO, 1972: Brussels, 1973–77; Kuala Lumpur, 1977–78; FCO, 1978–82 (Private Sec. to Minister of State, 1980–82); Dep. Pol Advr, BMG, Berlin, 1982–86; Dep. Head, News Dept, 1986–88, Asst Head, S America Dept, 1988–90, FCO; Counsellor (Political), UK Delegn to NATO, 1990–94; Dep. Head of Mission, Prague, 1995–98; Sen. Directing Staff, RCDS, 1998; Hd of EU Dept (Bilateral), FCO, 1999–2001. *Recreations:* tennis, music. *Address:* c/o Foreign and Commonwealth Office, King Charles Street, SW1A 2AH.

CRESSWELL, Prof. Peter, PhD; FRS 2000; Professor of Immunobiology, and Investigator at Howard Hughes Medical Institute, Yale University, since 1991; *b* 6 March 1945; *s* of Maurice and Mary Cresswell; *m* 1969, Ann K. Cooney; two *s*. *Educ:* Univ. of Newcastle upon Tyne (BSc, MSc); Guy's Hosp. Med. Sch., Univ. of London (PhD 1971). Post-doctoral Fellow, Harvard Univ., 1971–73; Duke University: Asst Prof., 1973–78; Associate Prof., 1978–85; Prof., 1985–91. *Address:* Section of Immunobiology, Howard Hughes Medical Institute, Yale University School of Medicine, PO Box 208011, New Haven, CT 06520-8011, USA. *T:* (203) 7855176.

CRESSWELL, Hon. Sir Peter (John), Kt 1991; **Hon. Mr Justice Cresswell;** a Judge of the High Court of Justice, Queen's Bench Division, since 1991; *b* 24 April 1944; *s* of late Jack Joseph Cresswell and Madeleine Cresswell; *m* 1972, Caroline Ward; one *s* (and one *s* decd). *Educ:* St John's Sch., Leatherhead; Queens' Coll., Cambridge (MA, LLM). Called to the Bar, Gray's Inn, 1966 (Malcolm Hilbery Award), Bencher, 1989; QC 1983; a Recorder, 1986–91; Nominated Commercial List Judge, 1991– (Judge in Charge, 1993–94). Mem., Senate of Inns of Court and Bar, 1981–84, 1985–86; Chm., Common Law and Commercial Bar Assoc., 1985–87; Mem., 1987–88, Vice Chm., 1989, Chm., 1990, Gen. Council of the Bar. Mem., Civil Justice Council, 1999–. Mem., Council and Exec. Cttee, Cystic Fibrosis Res. Trust, 1983–. Hon. Mem., Canadian Bar Assoc., 1990. *Publication:* Encyclopaedia of Banking Law, 1982, and subseq. service issues. *Recreations:* fly-fishing, river management, the Outer Hebrides. *Address:* Royal Courts of Justice, Strand, WC2A 2LL. *Club:* Flyfishers'.

CRETNEY, Stephen Michael, DCL; FBA 1985; Fellow of All Souls College, Oxford, 1993–2001, now Emeritus; *b* 25 Feb. 1936; *yr s* of late Fred and Winifred M. V. Cretney; *m* 1973, Rev. Antonia Lois Vanrenen, *o d* of late Lt-Comdr A. G. G. Vanrenen, RN; two *s*. *Educ:* The Manchester Warehousemen & Clerks' Orphan Schs, Cheadle Hulme; Magdalen Coll., Oxford; DCL Oxon 1985. Nat. Service, 1954–56. Solicitor. Partner, Macfarlanes, London, 1964; Lecturer: Kenya Sch. of Law, Nairobi, 1966; Southampton Univ., 1968; Fellow and Tutor, Exeter Coll., Oxford, 1969–78; a Law Comr, 1978–83; Prof. of Law, 1984–93, and Dean, Faculty of Law, 1984–88, Univ. of Bristol. Pt-time Chm. of Social Security and other Appeal Tribunals, 1985–96. Member: Departmental Cttee on Prison Disciplinary System, 1984–85; Family and Civil Cttee, Judicial Studies Bd, 1985–90; Lord Chancellor's Adv. Cttee on Legal Educn, 1987–88; President's Ancillary Relief Adv. Gp, 2000–. Chm., Cttee of Heads of Univ. Law Schs, 1986–88. Hon. QC 1992. *Publications:* Theobald on Wills, (ed jtly) 13th edn 1970; Principles of Family Law, 1974, 6th edn (ed jtly) 1997; Family Law (Teach Yourself series), 1982; Enduring Powers of Attorney, 1986, 4th edn (ed jtly) 1996; Elements of Family Law, 1987, 4th edn 2000; (jtly) Simple Quarrels, 1994; (jtly) Divorce—the New Law, 1996; Law, Law Reform and the Family, 1998; (ed) Family Law at the Millennium, 2000; (contrib.) English Private Law, 2000; (contrib.) Halsbury's Laws of England, 4th edn; articles and notes in legal jls. *Recreations:* cooking, taking snapshots. *Address:* The Rectory, 3 Drake's Farm, Peasemore, Newbury, Berks RG20 7DF. *T:* (01635) 248925, *Fax:* (01635) 248191; *e-mail:* Smcretney@aol.com; All Souls College, Oxford OX1 4AL. *T:* (01865) 279379, *Fax:* (01865) 279299; *e-mail:* stephen.cretney@all-souls.ox.ac.uk. *Club:* Oxford and Cambridge.

CREW, Air Vice-Marshal Edward Dixon, CB 1973; DSO 1944 and Bar 1950; DFC 1941 and Bar 1942; FRAeS 1972; Planning Inspectorate, Department of the Environment, 1973–87; *b* 24 Dec. 1917; *er s* of F. D. Crew, MB, MRCS, LRCP; *m* 1945, Virginia Martin; one *s*. *Educ:* Felsted Sch.; Downing Coll., Cambridge (MA). Commissioned RAFVR, 1939; served War of 1939–45: night fighter sqdns; 604 sqdn, 85 Sqdn; Comd 96 Sqdn; permanent commission, 1945. Malayan Emergency, Comd No 45 Sqdn, 1948–50; on exchange, RCAF, 1952–54; CFE, 1954–56; Comd RAF Brüggen, Germany, 1959–62; Comdr, Air Forces Borneo, 1965–66; AOC Central Reconnaissance Estabt, 1968; Dep. Controller, Nat. Air Traffic Services, 1969–72; various Air Staff jobs at Air Min. and MoD; retd 1973. Mem., Cotswold DC, 1991–95. *Recreation:* golf. *Address:* National Westminster Bank, 10 Benet Street, Cambridge CB2 3PU. *Club:* Royal Air Force.

CREW, Sir Edward (Michael), Kt 2001; QPM 1991; DL; Chief Constable, West Midlands Police, since 1996; *b* 13 Jan. 1946; *s* of Joseph Edwin Crew and Cecilia May Crew (*née* Davis); *m* 1967, Gillian Glover; one *s* one *d*. *Educ:* Haberdashers' Aske's Hatcham Sch. for Boys; Police Staff Coll. Joined Metropolitan Police from Cadet Corps, 1965; Inspector, 1970; Mem., investigation team into breach of security at Buckingham Palace, 1982; Chief Supt, comdg SE London Traffic Div., 1982–84; Asst Chief Constable, 1984–89, Dep. Chief Constable, 1989–93, Kent County Constabulary; rcds, 1988; Chief Constable, Northants, 1993–96. DL West Midlands, 1999. OStJ 1989. *Recreations:* good food, walking, gardening, travel. *Address:* West Midlands Police Headquarters, PO Box 52, Lloyd House, Colmore Circus, Queensway, Birmingham B4 6NQ. *T:* (0121) 626 5000.

CREWE, Albert Victor, PhD; Professor, Department of Physics and the Enrico Fermi Institute, 1963–96, now Emeritus (Assistant Professor, 1956–59; Associate Professor, 1959–63; William E. Wrather Distinguished Service Professor, 1977–97), Dean of Physical Sciences Division, 1971–81, University of Chicago; *b* 18 Feb. 1927; US citizen, 1961; *m* 1949, Doreen Patricia Blunsdon; one *s* three *d*. *Educ:* Univ. of Liverpool (BS, PhD). Asst Lectr, 1950–52, Lectr, 1952–55, Univ. of Liverpool; Div. Dir, Particle Accelerator Division, Argonne National Laboratory, 1958–61; Dir, Argonne National Laboratory, 1961–67. Mem. Bd of Dirs, R. R. Donnelley & Sons, Co., 1974–93; Pres., Orchid One Corp., 1987–90. Member: Nat. Acad. of Sciences; Amer. Acad. of Arts and Sciences. Artist Mem., Palette and Chisel Acad., Chicago. Hon. FRMS 1984. Named Outstanding New Citizen by Citizenship Council of Chicago, 1962; received Immigrant's Service League's Annual Award for Outstanding Achievement in the Field of Science, 1962; Illinois Sesquicentennial Award, 1968; Industrial Research Award, 1970; Distinguished Service Award, Electron Microscope Soc. of America, 1976; Albert A. Michelson Award, Franklin Inst., 1977; Ernst Abbe Award, NY Microscope Soc., 1979; Duddell Medal, Inst. of Physics, 1980. *Publications:* Research USA (with J. J. Katz), 1964; contribs to: Proc. Royal Soc.; Proc. Phys. Soc.; Physical Review; Science; Physics Today; Jl of Applied Physics; Reviews of Scientific Instruments; Optik; Ultramicroscopy, etc. *Address:* 8 Summit Drive, Dune Acres, IN 46304, USA. *T:* (219) 7875018. *Clubs:* Quadrangle, Wayfarers' (Chicago).

CREWE, Prof. Ivor Martin; Vice-Chancellor, since 1995, and Professor of Government, since 1982, University of Essex (Pro-Vice-Chancellor (Academic), 1992–95); *b* 15 Dec. 1945; *s* of Francis and Lilly Crewe; *m* 1968, Jill Barbara (*née* Gadian); two *s* one *d*. *Educ:* Manchester Grammar Sch.; Exeter Coll., Oxford (MA; Hon. Fellow, 1998); London School of Economics (MScEcon). Assistant Lecturer, Univ. of Lancaster, 1967–69; Junior Research Fellow, Nuffield Coll., Oxford, 1969–71; Lectr, Dept of Govt, Univ. of Essex, 1971–74; Dir SSRC Data Archive, 1974–82. Mem., Exec. Cttee and UK Council, UUK. Co-Dir, Feb. 1974, Oct. 1974, 1979 British Election Studies; elections analyst for: BBC TV, 1982–89; The Times, 1990–92; BBC World TV, 1997; GMTV, 1997. Editor, 1977–82, Co-editor, 1984–92, British Journal of Political Science. Hon. DLitt Salford, 1999. *Publications:* (with A. H. Halsey) Social Survey of the Civil Service (HMSO), 1969; ed, British Political Sociology Yearbook, vol. 1 1974, vol. 2 1975; (with Bo Sarlvik) Decade of Dealignment, 1983; (with Anthony Fox) British Parliamentary Constituencies, 1984; (ed jtly) Electoral Change in Western Democracies, 1985; (ed jtly) Political Communications: the general election campaign of 1983, 1986, of 1987, 1989, of 1992, 1995, of 1997, 1998; (with Anthony Fox and Neil Day) The British Electorate 1963–87, 1991, 2nd edn as The British Electorate 1963–92, 1992; (with Anthony King) SDP: the birth, life and death of the Social Democratic Party, 1995; (jtly) The New British Politics, 1998; articles in various academic jls on public opinion and elections in Britain. *Recreations:* opera, organising walking holidays. *Address:* University of Essex, Colchester, Essex CO4 3SQ.

CREWE, Susan Anne; Editor, House and Garden, since 1994; *b* 31 Aug. 1949; *d* of late Richard Cavendish and Pamela Cavendish; *m* 1st, 1970, Quentin Crewe (marr. diss.; he *d* 1998); one *s* one *d*; 2nd, 1984, C. N. J. Ryan, *qv* (marr. diss.). *Educ:* St Mary's Sch., Wantage; Cheshire Coll. of Agriculture. Harpers & Queen magazine, 1986–92: shopping editor, 1987; consultant editor, 1990; social editor, 1991–92; subseq. freelance writer, broadcaster, journalist; contribs to The Times, Daily Telegraph, Daily Mail, Evening Standard and Literary Review. *Recreations:* gardening, sea-swimming, music. *Address:* Ladysyke House, Haverthwaite, Ulverston, Cumbria LA12 8PQ. *Club:* Academy.

See also Baron Cavendish of Furness.

CRIBB, Air Cdre Peter Henry, CBE 1957; DSO 1942, and Bar, 1944; DFC 1941; JP; retired 1983; *b* 28 Sept. 1918; *s* of late Charles B. Cribb and Mrs Ethel Cribb; *m* 1949, Vivienne Janet, *yr d* of late Col S. T. J. Perry, MC, TD, DL, Oxton, Birkenhead, Ches; three *s*. *Educ:* Bradford Grammar Sch.; Prince Henry's Sch., Otley. Flt Cadet, RAF Coll., 1936–38; Flying duties in Bomber Comd, 1938–45 (Comd No. 582 Sqdn, RAF Little Staughton); Comdg RAF Salbani, RAF Peshawar, India and Staff No. 1 Indian Gp, 1945–47; OC 203 Sqdn, 1947, and HQ Staff, 1950, Coastal Comd; RAF Staff Coll., Bracknell, 1951; Asst Dir Tech. Intell., Air Min., 1951–53; Gp Capt. Plans and Policy, HQ Bomber Comd, 1953–57; 2nd TAF, Germany (OC Oldenburg, Ahlhorn and Gutersloh), 1957–60; Air Min., Dep. Dir Air Staff Briefing, 1959–61, Dir, 1961–62; SASO, Air Forces, Middle East, 1962–63; IDC, 1964; Deputy to Asst Chief of Defence Staff (Joint Warfare), MoD 1965–66; retired, 1966. Administrative Manager, Goldsworthy Mining Ltd, 1966–68. Associate Fellow, Australian Inst. of Management, 1969; Past State Pres., Ryder-Cheshire Foundn of WA, Inc.; Past Pres., Pathfinder Assoc. of WA. Foundn Chm. Council, Univ. of Third Age (Univ. of Western Australia) Inc., 1986–88. Patron (RAF), UK Combined Services Fedn, WA, 1990–. JP Western Australia, 1968. *Recreations:* mainly cerebral. *Address:* Unit 183, RAAFA Estate, 250 Baltimore Parade, Merriwa, WA 6030, Australia.

CRICH, Michael Arthur, FCMA; Executive Director, Finance and Corporate Services, London Borough of Lambeth, since 1996; *b* 9 Jan. 1957; *s* of Arthur Crich and late Elizabeth Crich; *m* 1980, Gillian Anne Chamberlain; three *s* one *d*. *Educ:* Slough Grammar Sch.; Univ. of Hull; Emile Woolf Coll. FCMA 1991. Financial Controller, Wendy Restaurants (UK) Ltd, 1981–84; Sketchley Dry Cleaning: Finance Manager, 1984–86; Financial Controller, 1986–87; Financial Dir, 1987–91; London Borough of Brent: Gen. Manager, Contract Services, 1992–93; Dir, Brent Business Support, 1993–96. *Recreations:* food and wine, model motor racing. *Address:* London Borough of Lambeth, International House, Canterbury Crescent, SW9 7QE. *T:* (020) 7926 9337.

CRICHTON, family name of **Earl of Erne**.

CRICHTON, Viscount; John Henry Michael Ninian Crichton; *b* 19 June 1971; *s* and *heir* of Earl of Erne, *qv*. *Educ:* Sunningdale Prep. Sch.; Shiplake Coll.; L'Institut de Touraine, Tours. Associate Dir, Lane Fox Residential Ltd. *Address:* Flat 4, 40 Harcourt Terrace, SW10 9JR.

CRICHTON, Maj.-Gen. Edward Maitland-Makgill-, OBE 1948 (MBE 1945); GOC 51st Highland Division, 1966–68, retired; *b* 23 Nov. 1916; *s* of late Lt-Col D. E. Maitland-Makgill-Crichton, Queen's Own Cameron Highlanders and Phyllis (*née* Cuthbert); *m* 1951, Sheila Margaret Hibbins, Bexhill-on-Sea; three *s*. *Educ:* Bedford Sch.; RMC Sandhurst. 2nd Lieut Queen's Own Cameron Highlanders, 1937; Adjt 5th Bn Cameron Highlanders, 1939; served with 5th Cameron Highlanders and 51 (Highland) Div., N Africa, Sicily, Normandy, NW Europe, 1940–45; GSO 1, HQ British Commonwealth Occupation Force, Japan, 1946–47; Mobilisation Br., WO 1948–50; 1st Bn Cameron Highlanders, Tripoli and Canal Zone, 1950–52; Jt Services Staff Coll., 1953; GSO 1, 3rd Inf. Div. (UK Strategic Reserve), Canal Zone, Egypt, UK and Suez, 1953–57; with 1st Bn Cameron Highlanders, Aden, 1957; comd 1st Liverpool Scottish, 1958–61; Comdr 152 (Highland) Inf. Bde, 1962–64; Dep. Dir Army Staff Duties, MoD, 1965–66. *Recreations:* shooting, golf, gardening, fishing. *Address:* 211 Braid Road, Edinburgh EH10 6HT. *T:* (0131) 447 5662.

CRICHTON, (John) Michael, MD; author; film director; *b* Chicago, 23 Oct. 1942; *s* of John Henderson Crichton and Zula Crichton (*née* Miller); *m* 1987, Anne-Marie Martin; one *d*. *Educ:* Harvard Univ. (AB *summa cum laude* 1964); Harvard Med. Sch. (MD 1969). Henry Russell Shaw Travelling Fellow, 1964–65; Vis. Lectr in Anthropology, Univ. of Cambridge, 1965; Post-doctoral Fellow, Salk Inst. for Biol Scis, La Jolla, Calif, 1969–70. Vis. Writer, MIT, 1988. *Television:* creator and Co-Exec. Producer, ER, 1994–; *films:* writer/director: Westworld, 1973; Coma, 1977; The Great Train Robbery, 1978; Looker, 1981; Runaway, 1984; director: Pursuit, 1972; Physical Evidence, 1989; writer: Rising Sun, 1993; Jurassic Park, 1993; producer: Disclosure, 1995; Twister, 1996; Sphere, 1998. Member: Authors' Guild; Writers' Guild Amer.; Dirs' Guild Amer.; Producers' Guild; PEN Amer. *Publications: novels:* The Andromeda Strain, 1969; The Terminal Man, 1972; The Great Train Robbery, 1975; Eaters of the Dead, 1976; Congo, 1980; Sphere, 1987; Jurassic Park, 1990; Rising Sun, 1992; Disclosure, 1993; The Lost World, 1995; Airframe, 1996; Timeline, 1999; (as John Lange): Odds On, 1966; Scratch One, 1967; Easy Go, 1968; The Venom Business, 1969; Zero Cool, 1969; Grave Descend, 1970; Drug of Choice, 1970; Binary, 1972; (as Jeffery Hudson) A Case of Need, 1968; (as Michael Douglas) (with D. Crichton) Dealing, 1971; *non-fiction:* Five Patients, 1970; Jasper Johns, 1977; Electronic Life, 1983; Travels (autobiog.), 1988; *screenplays:* Westworld, 1975; (with A.-M. Martin) Twister, 1996. *Address:* 2118 Wilshire Boulevard #433, Santa Monica, CA 90403, USA; c/o Jenkins Financial Services, 433 N Camden Drive #500, Beverly Hills, CA 90210, USA.

CRICHTON, Nicholas; a District Judge (Magistrates' Courts) (formerly Metropolitan Stipendiary Magistrate), since 1987; a Recorder, since 1995; *b* 23 Oct. 1943; s of late Charles Ainslie Crichton and of Vera Pearl McCallum; *m* 1973, Ann Valerie (*née* Jackson); two *s*. *Educ:* Haileybury & ISC; Queen's Univ., Belfast (LLB, 2nd Cl. Hons). Schoolmaster, Pembroke House Sch., Gilgil, Kenya, 1963; cowhand, Montana, USA, 1966; articled to late T. J. Burrows, Currey & Co., SW1, 1968–70; Assistant Solicitor: Currey & Co., 1970–71; Nicholls Christie & Crocker, 1972–74; Partner, Nicholls Christie & Crocker, 1974–86. An Asst Recorder, 1991–95. *Recreations:* cricket (playing, coaching and watching), golf, watching rugby, gardening, walking, reading, bird watching, photography. *Address:* c/o Inner London Family Proceedings Court, 59–65 Wells Street, W1A 3AE. *Clubs:* Middlesex CC; Old Haileyburian RFC; Flackwell Heath Golf.

CRICHTON, Col Richard John Vesey, CVO 1986; MC 1940; *b* 2 Nov. 1916; *s* of late Col Hon. Sir George Crichton, GCVO, and Lady Mary Crichton; *m* 1948, Yvonne Avril Catherine, *d* of late Dr and Mrs H. E. Worthington; three *s*. *Educ:* Eton; RMC, Sandhurst. Commissioned 2/Lieut Coldstream Guards, 1936; served World War II: Belgium, 1940, Italy, 1943–44 (twice wounded, MC, despatches); Commanded: 1st Bn Coldstream Guards, 1954–57; Coldstream Guards, 1958–61, retired 1961. Comptroller, Union Jack Services Clubs, 1964–66; Member, HM Body Guard, Hon. Corps of Gentlemen at Arms, 1966–86; Clerk of the Cheque and Adjutant, 1979–81; Lieutenant, 1981–86. Mem., Hants CC and Police Authority, 1964–67. *Publication:* The Coldstream Guards 1946–1970, 1972. *Address:* Derwent House, Hartley Wintney, Hampshire RG27 8RE. *Club:* Cavalry and Guards.

CRICHTON-BROWN, Sir Robert, KCMG 1980; Kt 1972; CBE 1970; TD; Executive Chairman, Rothmans International plc, 1985–88; *b* Melbourne, 23 Aug. 1919; *s* of late L. Crichton-Brown, Sydney; *m* 1941, Norah Isabelle, *d* of late A. E. Turnbull; one *s* one *d*. *Educ:* Sydney Grammar Sch. Served War, 1939–45, BEF; Major, Royal Artillery and Gen. Staff, France, Iceland, India, Burma (despatches twice). Chairman: Lumley Corp. Ltd (formerly Edward Lumley Ltd), 1974–89 (Man. Dir, 1952–82); Lumley Life Ltd, 1961–87 (Dir, 1961–89); Lumley Gen. Insce Ltd, 1974–88 (Dir, 1952–88); NEI Pacific Ltd, 1961–85; Rothmans of Pall Mall (Australia) Ltd, 1981–85 (Dir, 1971–85 and 1987–88); Commercial Banking Co. of Sydney Ltd, 1976–82 (Dir, 1970–82); Commercial & General Acceptance Ltd, 1977–82; Westham Dredging Co. Pty Ltd, 1975–85; Vice Chairman: Nat. Australia Bank Ltd, 1982–85; Custom Credit Corp., 1982–85; Director: Daily Mail and General Trust Ltd (UK), 1979–95; Edward Lumley Hldgs, 1989–. Fed. Pres., Inst. of Dirs in Aust., 1967–80 (Chm., NSW Branch, 1965–80; Councillor, 1980–89; Hon. Life Mem.). Mem. Federal Exec. and Federal Hon. Treas., Liberal Party of Australia, 1973–85. Pres., Med. Foundn, Sydney Univ., 1962–87; Dir, Royal Prince Alfred Hosp., 1970–84; Hon. Life Governor, Aust. Postgraduate Fedn in Medicine; Member: Cttee, RACP, 1973–85; Adv. Bd, Girl Guides Assoc. of Australia, 1973–85; Adv. Bd, Salvation Army, 1973–85; Internat. Forum and Panel, Duke of Edinburgh's Award, 1979–84 (Nat. Co-ordinator, Duke of Edinburgh's Award Scheme in Aust., 1979–84); Council, Imperial Soc. of Knights Bachelor, 1983–97 (Vice-Chm., Pacific Reg.); Nat. Councillor, Scout Assoc. of Aust., 1980–85; Mem. Council, Maritime Trust (formerly Cutty Sark Maritime Trust), 1987–99; Gov., Cutty Sark Soc., 1987–89. Underwriting Mem. of Lloyd's, 1946–97. Hon. Fellow, Sydney Univ., 1987. Mem., Australia's winning Admiral's Cup Team (Balandra), UK, 1967; winner, Sydney-Hobart Yacht Race (Pacha), 1970. *Clubs:* White's, Royal Cruising; Royal Yacht Squadron; Australian, Union (Sydney); Cruising Yacht Club of Australia, Royal Sydney Yacht Squadron, Royal Prince Alfred Yacht.

CRICHTON-STUART, family name of **Marquess of Bute**.

CRICK, Prof. Bernard, BSc (Econ.), PhD (London); writer; Emeritus Professor, University of London; *b* 16 Dec. 1929; *s* of Harry Edgar and Florence Clara Crick. *Educ:* Whitgift Sch.; University Coll., London. Research student, LSE, 1950–52; Teaching Fellow, Harvard, 1952–54; Asst Prof., McGill, 1954–55; Vis. Fellow, Berkeley, 1955–56; Asst Lectr, later Lectr, later Sen. Lectr, LSE, 1957–65; Prof. of Political Theory and Institutions, Sheffield Univ., 1965–71; Prof. of Politics, Birkbeck Coll., Univ of London, 1971–84. Joint Editor, Political Quarterly, 1966–80; Chm., Political Qly Publishing Co., 1980–93; Literary Ed., Political Qly, 1993–2000. Joint Sec., Study of Parlt Gp, 1964–68; Jt Chm., British S African Conf., 1991–95. Chm., Cttee on Teaching Citizenship in English Schs, 1997–98. Advr on Citizenship to DfEE, 1998–2001. Hon. Pres., Politics Assoc., 1970–76; Vice Pres., Political Studies Assoc., 1995–; Hon. Mem., Hansard Soc., 1993 (Mem. Council, 1962–93). Fellow: Birkbeck Coll., 1999; UCL, 2001. Vis. Fellow, Woodrow Wilson Centre, 1995–96; Hon. Fellow in Politics, Univ. of Edinburgh, 1986. Hon. DSc Belfast, 1986; Hon. DLitt: Sheffield, 1990; E London Poly., 1990; Kingston, 1996. *Publications:* The American Science of Politics, 1958; In Defence of Politics, 1962, 5th edn 2000 (trans. German, Japanese, Spanish, Italian); The Reform of Parliament, 1964, 2nd edn 1968; (ed) Essays on Reform, 1967; (ed with W. A. Robson) Protest and Discontent, 1970; (ed) Machiavelli: The Discourses, 1971; Political Theory and Practice, 1972; (ed with W. A. Robson) Taxation Policy, 1973; Basic Forms of Government, 1973; Crime, Rape and Gin, 1975; (ed with Alex Porter) Political Education and Political Literacy, 1978; George Orwell: a Life, 1980, 3rd edn 1992; (ed) Unemployment, 1981; (ed) Clarendon edn, Orwell's Nineteen Eighty-Four, 1984; (ed with Audrey Coppard) Orwell Observed, 1984; Socialism, 1987; Essays on Politics and Literature, 1989; Political Thoughts and Polemics, 1990; (ed) National Identities, 1991; (with David Millar) To Make the Parliament of Scotland a Model for Democracy, 1995; Essays on Citizenship,

2000; Crossing Borders, 2001; (ed) Citizens: towards a citizenship culture, 2001. *Recreations:* polemicising, lecturing, theatre, hill-walking. *Address:* 8A Bellevue Terrace, Edinburgh EH7 4DT. *T:* (0131) 557 2517. *Club:* Savile.

CRICK, Francis Harry Compton, OM 1991; FRS 1959; BSc London, PhD Cantab; J. W. Kieckhefer Distinguished Professor, The Salk Institute for Biological Studies, since 1977 (President, 1994–95); Adjunct Professor of Psychology, University of California, San Diego; *b* 8 June 1916; *e s* of late Harry Crick and late Annie Elizabeth (*née* Wilkins); *m* 1st, 1940, Ruth Doreen Dodd (divorced, 1947); one *s*; 2nd, 1949, Odile Speed; two *d. Educ:* Mill Hill Sch.; University Coll., London (Fellow, 1962); Caius Coll., Cambridge (Hon. Fellow, 1976). Scientist in Admiralty, 1940–47; Strangeways Laboratory, Cambridge, 1947–49; MRC Lab. of Molecular Biology, Cambridge, 1949–77; Brooklyn Polytechnic, NY, USA, 1953–54. Vis. Lectr Rockefeller Inst., NY, USA, 1959; Vis. Prof., Chemistry Dept, Harvard, 1959; Fellow, Churchill Coll., Cambridge, 1960–61 (Hon. Fellow, 1965); Vis. Biophysics Prof., Harvard, 1962; Non-resident Fellow, Salk Inst. for Biological Studies, San Diego, 1962–73; Ferkhauf Foundn Visiting Prof., Salk Inst., 1976–77. For. Hon. Mem., Amer. Acad. of Arts and Sciences, 1962; Hon. Mem., Amer. Soc. Biological Chem., 1963; Hon. MRIA, 1964; FAAAS 1966; Fellow, INSA, 1982; Hon. FRSE, 1966; Hon. FIBiol, 1995; Hon. Fellow: Indian Acad. of Scis, 1985; Tata Inst. of Fundamental Res., Bombay, 1996; For. Associate, US Nat. Acad. of Sciences, 1969; Mem., German Acad. of Science, Leopoldina, 1969; MAE 1998; For. Mem., American Philos. Soc., Philadelphia, 1972; Hon. Mem., Hellenic Biochem. and Biophys. Soc., 1974. Associate For. Mem., French Acad. of Scis, 1978. 60 named lectures, 1959–94. Warren Triennial Prize, Boston, USA (with J. D. Watson), 1959; Lasker Award (jointly), 1960; Prix Charles Léopold Mayer, French Académies des Sciences, 1961; Research Corp. Award (with J. D. Watson), 1961; Gairdner Foundation Award, Toronto, 1962; Nobel Prize for Medicine (jointly), 1962; Royal Medal, Royal Soc., 1972; Copley Medal, Royal Soc., 1975; Michelson-Morley Award, Cleveland, 1981; Benjamin P. Cheney Medal, Spokane, Washington, 1986; Golden Plate Award, Phoenix, 1987; Albert Medal, RSA, 1987; Wright Prize VIII, Harvey Mudd Coll., Calif., 1988; Joseph Priestly Award, Dickinson Coll., Pennsylvania, 1988; Distinguished Achievement Award, Oregon State Univ., 1995. Friends of the Library. *Publications:* Of Molecules and Men, 1966; Life Itself, 1981; What Mad Pursuit: a personal view of scientific discovery, 1988; The Astonishing Hypothesis: The scientific search for the soul, 1994; papers and articles on molecular and cell biology and on neurobiology in scientific journals. *Address:* The Salk Institute for Biological Studies, PO Box 85800, San Diego, CA 92186–5800, USA; 1792 Colgate Circle, La Jolla, CA 92037, USA.

CRICK, R(onald) Pitts, FRCS, FRCOphth; Honorary Ophthalmic Surgeon, King's College Hospital, since 1982 (Ophthalmic Surgeon, 1950–82); Recognised Teacher in the Faculty of Medicine, University of London, 1960–82, Emeritus Lecturer, King's College Hospital Medical School, 1982; *b* 5 Feb. 1917; *yr s* of Owen J. Pitts Crick and Margaret Daw, Minehead, Som; *m* 1941, Jocelyn Mary Grenfell Robins, *yr d* of Leonard A. C. Robins and Geraldine Grenfell, Hendon; four *s* one *d. Educ:* Latymer Upper Sch., London; King's Coll. and (Science Schol.) King's Coll. Hosp. Med. Sch., Univ. of London. MRCS, LRCP 1939; DOMS 1946; FRCS 1950; FRCOphth 1988. Surgeon, MN, 1939–40; Surg. Lieut, RNVR, 1940–46. Ophthalmic Registrar, King's Coll. Hosp., 1946–48; Surgical First Asst, Royal Eye Hosp., 1947–50; Ophth. Surg., Epsom County Hosp., 1948–49; Ophth. Registrar, Belgrave Hosp. for Children, 1948–50; Ophth. Surg., Sevenoaks Hosp., 1948–50; Sen. Ophthalmic Surg., Royal Eye Hosp., 1950–69; Ophthalmic Surg., Belgrave Hosp. for Children, 1950–66. Vis. Res. Fellow, Univ. of Sussex, 1976–98. Chm., Ophthalmic Post-Grad. Trng, SE Thames RHA, 1972–82. Examr to RCS for Diploma in Ophthalmology, 1961–68. Hon. Ophth. Surg., Royal London Soc. for the Blind, 1954–57. FRSocMed, Vice-Pres. Ophthalmological Section, 1964, and Mem. Council Ophthalmolog. Section, 1953–54 and 1956–58. Member: Oxford Ophthalmolog. Congress; Southern Ophthalmolog. Soc. (Vice-Pres., 1969; Pres., 1970); Chm., Internat. Glaucoma Assoc., 1975–2000 (Pres., 2000–); Charter Member: Internat. Glaucoma Congress, USA, 1977–; Internat. Assoc. of Ocular Surgeons, 1981. Alim Meml Lectr, Ophthalmolog. Soc. of Bangladesh, Dhaka, 1991. Sir Stewart Duke-Elder Glaucoma Award, Internat. Glaucoma Congress, 1985; Lederle Medal for Ophthalmology, Amer. Soc. of Contemp. Ophthalmol., 1985. *Publications:* All About Glaucoma, 1981; A Textbook of Clinical Ophthalmology, 1986, 3rd edn (with Peng T. Khaw) 2001; Cardiovascular Affections, Arteriosclerosis and Hypertension (Section in Systemic Ophthalmology, ed A. Sorsby), 1950 and 1958; Computerised Monitoring of Glaucoma (Section in Glaucoma, ed J. G. Bellows), 1979; Diagnosis of Primary Open Angle Glaucoma (in Glaucoma, ed J. E. Cairns), 1986; medical and ophthalmic contribs to Brit. Jl Ophthalmology, BMJ, Lancet, Eye, Ophthalmic and Physiol Optics, etc. *Recreations:* walking, motoring, sailing. *Address:* International Glaucoma Association, 108c Warner Road, Camberwell, SE5 9HQ. *T:* (020) 7737 3265, *Fax:* (020) 7346 5929; 10 Golden Gates, Sandbanks, Poole, Dorset BH13 7QN. *T:* (01202) 707560, *Fax:* (01202) 701560. *Clubs:* Royal Automobile; Royal Motor Yacht.

CRICKHOWELL, Baron *cr* 1987 (Life Peer), of Pont Esgob in the Black Mountains and County of Powys; **Roger Nicholas Edwards;** PC 1979; Chairman: ITNET Plc, since 1995; HTV Ltd, since 1997 (Director, since 1987); *b* 25 Feb. 1934; *s* of late (H. C.) Ralph Edwards, CBE, FSA, and Marjorie Ingham Brooke; *m* 1963, Ankaret Healing; one *s* two *d. Educ:* Westminster Sch.; Trinity Coll., Cambridge, 1954–57; read History: BA 1957, MA 1968. Member of Lloyds, 1965–. Dir, Associated British Ports Hldgs, 1988–99; Vice-Chm., Anglesey Mining, 1988–2000. MP (C) Pembroke, 1970–87. Opposition spokesman on Welsh affairs, 1975–79; Sec. of State for Wales, 1979–87. Chm., NRA, 1989–96 (Chm., Adv. Cttee, 1988–89). Pres., Univ. of Wales, Cardiff (formerly Univ. of Wales Coll. of Cardiff), 1988–98 (Hon. Fellow, UC, Cardiff, 1985). Dir, WNO, 1988–92. President: Contemporary Art Society for Wales, 1988–93; SE Wales Arts Assoc., 1988–94; Mem., Cttee, AA, 1988–98. *Publications:* Opera House Lottery, 1997; Westminster, Wales and Water, 1999; articles and reviews in The Connoisseur and other jls. *Recreations:* fishing, gardening, collecting watercolours and drawings. *Address:* Pont Esgob Mill, Fforest Coal Pit, near Abergavenny, Monmouthshire NP7 7LS; 4 Henning Street, SW11 3DR. *Clubs:* Brooks's; Cardiff and County.

CRIGMAN, David Ian; QC 1989; *b* 16 Aug. 1945; *s* of late Jack Crigman and of Sylvia Crigman; *m* 1980, Judith Ann Penny; one *s. Educ:* King Edward's Sch., Birmingham; Univ. of Leeds (LLB Hons). Called to the Bar, Gray's Inn, 1969; a Recorder, 1985. *Recreations:* tennis, ski-ing, writing, travel. *Address:* 1 Fountain Court, Steelhouse Lane, Birmingham B4 6DR. *T:* (0121) 236 5721.

CRILL, Sir Peter (Leslie), KBE 1995 (CBE 1980); Kt 1987; Bailiff of Jersey, and President of the Court of Appeal of Jersey, 1986–95; Judge, Court of Appeal of Jersey and Guernsey, 1986–98; *b* 1 Feb. 1925; *s* of S. G. Crill, and Olive Le Gros; *m* 1953, A. F. R. Dodd, MB, *d* of E. A. Dodd, JP, Dromara, NI; three *d. Educ:* Victoria Coll., Jersey; Exeter Coll., Oxford (King Charles I Scholar; MA; Hon. Fellow, 1991). Called to the Bar, Middle Temple, 1949; called to the Jersey Bar, 1949. In private practice in Jersey, 1949–62. States of Jersey Deputy for St Clement, 1951–58; States of Jersey Senator, 1960–62; Solicitor General, Jersey, 1962–69; Attorney General, Jersey, 1969–75. Dep. Bailiff, 1975–86. Mem. Council, University of Buckingham, 1981–96. Pres., La Société Jersiaise, 1980–85; Chairman: Jersey Arts Trust, 1995–; Alliance Française (Jersey), 1996–; Mem., Conseil de la Fédération Britannique des Comités de l'Alliance Française, 1998–2000. Hon. LLD Buckingham, 1997. CStJ 1994. *Recreations:* books, coarse acting, pottering about. *Address:* Beechfield House, Trinity, Jersey, Channel Islands JE3 7JU. *T:* (01534) 20270. *Clubs:* Oxford and Cambridge; United (Jersey); Royal Yacht Squadron, St Helier Yacht.

CRIPPIN, Harry Trevor, FCIS; Chief Executive and Town Clerk, Cardiff City Council, 1979–88; *b* 14 May 1929; *s* of Harry and Mary Elizabeth Crippin; *m* 1959, Hilda Green, JP; one *s* one *d. Educ:* Leigh Grammar Sch., Lancs. DMA; FBIM; FCIS 1975. Asst Town Clerk, Manchester, 1970–74; City Sec., Cardiff CC, 1974–79. OStJ 1986. *Address:* 23 Greenwood Road, Llandaff, Cardiff CF5 2QD. *T:* (029) 2056 4103.

CRIPPS, family name of **Baron Parmoor**.

CRIPPS, Michael Leonard Seddon; His Honour Judge Cripps; a Circuit Judge, since 1998; President, Immigration Services Tribunal, since 2000; *b* 18 June 1942; *s* of (Matthew) Anthony Leonard Cripps, CBE, DSO, TD, QC and Dorothea Margaret Cripps; *heir-presumptive* to cousin, Baron Parmoor, *qv*; *m* 1971, Elizabeth Anne Millward Shennan; one *s* one *d* (and one *s* decd). *Educ:* Eton Coll. Called to the Bar, Middle Temple, 1965; Member *ad eundem*, Lincoln's Inn, 1969, Inner Temple, 1984; a Recorder, 1986–98; Standing Counsel to HM Customs and Excise, 1989–98. Chairman, Disciplinary Committee: Milk Mktg Bd, 1979–90; Potato Mktg Bd, 1979–90. Legal Mem., Immigration Appeal Tribunal, 1998–2000. Freeman, City of London, 1986; Hon. Lt Col, Alabama State Militia, 1975. *Recreations:* family, walking slowly. *Address:* St Albans Crown Court, Bricket Lane, St Albans, Herts AL1 3HY. *Club:* Wig and Pen.

CRISHAM, Catherine Ann; Head of Legal Group, Department for Environment, Food and Rural Affairs (formerly Ministry of Agriculture, Fisheries and Food), since 1994; *b* 29 April 1950; *d* of Air Vice-Marshal W. J. Crisham, CB, CBE and late Maureen Teresa Crisham (*née* Bergin). *Educ:* St Anne's Coll., Oxford (BA); Exeter Univ. (LLM). Lecturer in European Community Law: Leiden Univ., 1977–80; London Univ., 1980–82; called to the Bar, Gray's Inn, 1981; private practice, 1982–84; Lawyer, MAFF, now DEFRA, 1984–88 and 1991–; Legal Sec., European Court of Justice, 1988–90. *Recreations:* theatre, cinema, walking. *Address:* Legal Department, Department for Environment, Food and Rural Affairs, 55 Whitehall, SW1A 2EY.

CRISP, Prof. Arthur Hamilton, MD, DSc; FRCP, FRCPE, FRCPsych; Professor of Psychiatry, University of London at St George's Hospital Medical School, 1967–95, now Professor Emeritus of Psychological Medicine; *b* 17 June 1930; *s* of John and Elizabeth Crisp; *m* 1958, Irene Clare (*née* Reid); three *s. Educ:* Watford Grammar Sch.; Univ. of London (MD; DSc). FRCPsych 1971 (Hon. FRCPsych 1996); FRCPE 1972; FRCP 1973. Previously Lectr, then Sen. Lectr in Psych., Middlesex Hosp. Med. Sch., London; Hd, Dept of Psychiatry, later Dept of Mental Health Scis, St George's Hosp. Med. Sch., 1967–95; Dean, Faculty of Medicine, Univ. of London, 1976–80. Chairman: Educn Cttee, GMC, 1982–88; Adv. Cttee on Med. Educn, EEC, 1983–85. Chm., Changing Minds Campaign, RCPsych, 1998–. *Publications:* (jtly) Sleep, Nutrition and Mood, 1976; Anorexia Nervosa: Let Me Be, 1980; (jtly) Anorexia Nervosa and the Wish to Change, 1990; (jtly) Anorexia Nervosa: guidelines for assessment and treatment in primary and secondary care, 1994; approx. 330 articles in learned jls. *Recreations:* golf, study of the River Wandle and of poetic insights into relationship between sleep and depression. *Address:* 113 Copse Hill, Wimbledon, SW20 0NT. *T:* (020) 8946 0976. *Clubs:* Athenæum; Royal Wimbledon Golf, Thorpeness Golf and Country.

CRISP, Clement Andrew; contributor, since 1956, and Dance Critic, since 1970, Financial Times; *b* 21 Sept. 1931; *s* of Charles Evelyn Gifford Crisp and Bertha Dorothy (*née* Dean). *Educ:* Oxted Sch.; Bordeaux Univ.; Keble Coll., Oxford Univ. (BA). Critic and dance writer to various jls, 1956–; Ballet Critic, The Spectator, 1966–70. Lectr, Librarian and Archivist to Royal Acad. of Dancing, 1963–85, Archivist, 1985–. Associate Prof., Univ. of Notre Dame (London Faculty), 1987–. Queen Elizabeth II Coronation Award, Royal Acad. of Dancing, 1992; Vaslav Nijinsky Medal, Poland, 1995. Knight, Order of Dannebrog (Demark), 1992. *Publications include:* (with Peter Brinson) Ballet for All, 1971, rev. edn 1980; with Mary Clarke: Ballet: an illustrated history, 1973, rev. edn 1992; Making a Ballet, 1974; Ballet in Art, 1976; Design for Ballet, 1978; Introducing Ballet, 1978; Ballet-goer's Guide, 1981; History of Dance, 1981; How to Enjoy Ballet, 1983, 2nd edn 1987; Dancer, 1984; Ballerina, 1987; London Contemporary Dance, 1989. *Recreations:* avoiding noise, gardening, despair about dancing. *Address:* 82 Marsham Court, Marsham Street, SW1P 4LA.

CRISP, (Edmund) Nigel (Ramsay); Permanent Secretary, Department of Health, and National Health Service Chief Executive, since 2000; *b* 14 Jan. 1952; *s* of Edmund Theodore Crisp and Dorothy Shephard Crisp (*née* Ramsay); *m* 1976, Siân Elaine Jenkins; one *s* one *d. Educ:* Uppingham Sch.; St John's Coll., Cambridge (BA Hons 1973; MA 1976). Dep. Dir, Halewood Community Council, 1973; Production Manager, Trebor, 1978; Dir, Cambs Community Council, 1981; Unit Gen. Manager, E Berks HA, 1986; Chief Executive: Heatherwood and Wexham Park Hosps, 1988; Oxford Radcliffe Hosp. NHS Trust, 1993–96; Regl Dir, S Thames, 1977–98, London, 1999–2000, NHS Exec., DoH. *Recreation:* the countryside. *Address:* (office) Richmond House, 79 Whitehall, SW14 2NS. *Club:* Tutts Clump Tennis.

CRISP, Sir (John) Peter, 4th Bt *cr* 1913; *b* 19 May 1925; *o s* of Sir John Wilson Crisp, 3rd Bt, and Marjorie (*d* 1977), *d* of F. R. Shriver; *S* father, 1950; *m* 1954, Judith Mary (*d* 1998), *d* of late H. E. Gillett; three *s* one *d. Educ:* Westminster. *Heir: s* John Charles Crisp [*b* 10 Dec. 1955; *m* 1992, Mary Jo, *er d* of Dr and Mrs D. MacAuley]. *Address:* Crabtree Cottage, Drungewick Lane, Loxwood, Billingshurst, West Sussex RH14 0RP. *T:* (01403) 752374.

CRISP, June Frances; *see* de Moller, J. F.

CRISP, Nigel; *see* Crisp, E. N. R.

CRITCHETT, Sir Ian (George Lorraine), 3rd Bt *cr* 1908; BA Cantab; HM Diplomatic Service, retired; Counsellor, Foreign and Commonwealth Office, 1977–80; *b* 9 Dec. 1920; *s* of Sir Montague Critchett, 2nd Bt, and Innes (*d* 1982), 3rd *d* of late Col F. G. A. Wiehe, The Durham Light Infantry; *S* father, 1941; *m* 1st, 1948, Paulette Mary Lorraine (*d* 1962), *e d* of late Col H. B. Humfrey; 2nd, 1964, Jocelyn Daphne Margret, *e d* of late Comdr C. M. Hall; one *s* one *d. Educ:* Harrow; Clare Coll., Cambridge. RAFVR, 1942–46. Joined Foreign Office, 1948; 3rd Sec. (Commercial), at Vienna, 1950–51; 2nd Sec. (Commercial) at Bucharest, 1951–53; 2nd Sec. at Cairo, 1956; First Sec., FO, 1962. *Publication:* Selected Poems, 1998. *Heir: s* Charles George Montague Critchett, *b* 2 April 1965. *Address:* Uplands Lodge, Pains Hill, Limpsfield, Oxted, Surrey RH8 0RF. *Clubs:* Travellers, MCC.

CRITCHLEY, Philip, CB 1990; consultant, Martin Jack & Co., since 1991; *b* 31 Jan. 1931; *s* of Henry Stephen and Edith Adela Critchley; *m* 1962, Stella Ann Barnes; two *s* one *d*. *Educ:* Manchester Grammar Sch.; Balliol Coll., Oxford (MA, 2nd Classical Mods and Greats). National Service, Intelligence Corps, 1953–55. Joined Min. of Housing and Local Govt, later Dept of Environment, 1955: Principal, 1960; Asst Sec., 1969; Under Sec., 1980; Dir of Waste Disposal, 1983; Dir of Contracts, Highways Administration and Maintenance, 1985–90; Dir of Network Mgt and Maintenance, 1990–91, Dept of Transport. Volunteer, Ulverston Br., MIND, 1996–. FRSA 1990. *Recreations:* philosophy, writing poetry. *Address:* Infield House, Kendall Ground, Lowick, Ulverston, Cumbria LA12 8ER. *T:* (01229) 885254. *Clubs:* Blackheath Harriers; Oxford Union Society.

CRITCHLEY, Tom; international business adviser, since 1990; *b* 17 Aug. 1928; *s* of late Leonard and Jessie Critchley; *m* 1951, Margaret Bland; one *s*. *Educ:* Sheffield College of Technology (Freshgate Trust Award, 1958). Davy-Ashmore Group, 1951–66; Cammell Laird and Upper Clyde Groups, 1966–69; J. C. B. Group, 1969–70; EMI Group, 1970–80; Head, Investment Casting Mission to Canada; UN Adviser to Tanzanian Govt; Adviser to UN High Commn for Refugees; Chm., MATC Ltd; Senior Partner, internat. consultancy practice, 1980–85; Under Sec., DHSS, subseq. Dept of Health, and NHS Management Bd Mem., 1986–90; Head, healthcare missions to Japan, Philippines, Indonesia, USSR and Poland, 1989–90; UK Chm., Anglo-Soviet Health-care Gp, 1989–91; Managing Director: Bio-Flo Ltd, 1991–95; Eurosep, Poland, 1992–95. Chairman: UK Trade Assoc., 1990–92; European Timeshare Fedn, 1991–92; Mem. Board, Nat. Inst. of Govt Purchasing, USA, 1977–78; Sen. UK Deleg., Internat. Fedn of Purchasing & Materials Management, 1980–85; Dir, Internat. Management Inst., Paris, 1980–88; Faculty Mem., Management Centre Europe, Brussels, 1980–85; Mem., Business in the Community, 1989–92. Institute of Purchasing & Supply: FCIPS (Fellow, 1967); Chm. Council, 1974–75; Pres., 1977–78; Chm., Ext. Affairs, 1978–82; Mem., Internat. Council, 1979–82. Pres., Internat. Cttee of Friendship for Internat. Students, 1996–97. Millennium Adviser: The Children's Soc., 1996–98; Friends of the Elderly, 1998–2000; SE Regl Arts Centre, 2000–. Chm., Huntleigh Foundn, 1997–. *Recreations:* competitive sports, live theatre, North American history. *Address:* 3 Lincoln Close, Stoke Mandeville, Bucks HP22 5YS. *T:* (01296) 612511, *Fax:* (01296) 614203.

CRITCHLOW, Christopher Allan; His Honour Judge Critchlow; a Circuit Judge, since 2000; *b* 8 July 1951; *s* of late Charles Brandon Critchlow and of Eileen Margerie (*née* Bowers); *m* 1974, Wendy Anne Lucey; one *s* two *d*. *Educ:* Royal Grammar Sch., Lancaster; Exeter Univ. (LLB). FCIArb 1994. Called to the Bar, Inner Temple, 1973; Mem., Western Circuit; Asst Recorder, 1987–91; a Recorder, 1991–2000. *Recreations:* golf, bridge, listening to music, reading history. *Address:* Reading Crown Court, Old Shire Hall, Reading, Berks RG1 3EH. *Club:* Reform.

CROAN, Thomas Malcolm; Sheriff of North Strathclyde, since 1983; *b* 7 Aug. 1932; *s* of John Croan and Amelia Sydney; *m* 1959, Joan Kilpatrick Law; one *s* three *d*. *Educ:* St Joseph's Coll., Dumfries; Edinburgh University. MA 1953; LLB 1955. Admitted to Faculty of Advocates, 1956; Standing Junior Counsel, to Scottish Develt Dept, 1964–65 and (for highways work) 1967–69; Advocate Depute, 1965–66; Sheriff of Grampian, Highland and Islands (formerly Aberdeen, Kincardine and Banff), 1969–83. *Recreations:* sailing, reading. *Address:* Overdale, 113 Dundonald Drive, Troon KA10 6JB.

CROCKARD, (Hugh) Alan, DSc; FRCS, FRCSE; Director, Raven Department of Education, Royal College of Surgeons, since 1998; Consultant Neurosurgeon, National Hospital for Neurology and Neurosurgery, since 1978; *b* 24 Jan. 1943; *s* of Hugh and Mary Crockard; *m* 1977, Dr Caroline Orr; two *s*. *Educ:* Royal Belfast Academical Instn; Queen's Univ., Belfast (MB BCh, BAO 1966; DSc 2000). FRCSE 1970; FRCS 1971. Wellcome Surgical Fellow, 1973; Hunterian Prof., RCS, 1974; Fogarty Internat. Fellow, 1974, Asst Prof., 1975, Univ. of Chicago; Sen. Lectr, QUB, 1975–78. Vis. Prof. of Surgical Neurology, Univ. of WA, 2000. Co-Founder, Hill Surgical Workshops, 1990. President: British Cervical Spine Soc., 1997–99 (Co-Founder, 1986); Eur. Cervical Spine Res. Soc., 1999–2001; Member: British Soc. of Neurological Surgeons; Amer. Acad. of Neurological Surgeons. Sinclair Medal for Surgery, 1966; Olivecrona Lectr, Karolinska Inst., Stockholm, 1995; Harrington Medal, Scoliosis Res. Soc., USA, 1995; Arnott Demonstr., RCS, 1995. *Publications:* (jtly) Trauma Care, 1981; (jtly) Neurosurgery: scientific basis of clinical practice, 1985, 3rd edn 2000; more than 300 papers. *Recreations:* music, travel, sailing, ski-ing, photography. *Address:* Department of Education, Royal College of Surgeons, Lincoln's Inn Fields, WC2A 3PN. *Clubs:* Royal Ocean Racing, Royal Society of Medicine.

CROCKER, John Fraser; His Honour Judge Crocker; a Circuit Judge, since 1995; *b* 27 May 1943; *o s* of late Noel John Fraser Crocker and Marjorie Jean Crocker (*née* Heaton); *m* 1969, Janet Butteriss; one *s* twin *d*. *Educ:* The Leys, Cambridge; Christ's Coll., Cambridge (MA). Admitted Solicitor, 1969; called to the Bar, Inner Temple, 1973; a Recorder, 1991–95. *Recreations:* reading thrillers, avoiding gardening. *Address:* 3 Temple Gardens, Temple, EC4Y 9AU.

CROCKER, His Honour Peter Vernon; a Circuit Judge, 1974–91; *b* 29 June 1926; *s* of Walter Angus Crocker and Fanny Victoria Crocker (*née* Dempster); *m* 1950, Nancy Kathleen Sargent. *Educ:* Oundle; Corpus Christi Coll., Cambridge (BA). Called to Bar, Inner Temple, 1949. *Recreations:* gardening, tennis, swimming, horseracing.

CROCKER, Sir Walter (Russell), KBE 1978 (CBE 1955); Australian diplomat, retired 1970; Lieutenant-Governor of South Australia, 1973–82; *b* 25 March 1902; *e s* of late Robert Crocker and Alma Bray, Parnaroo, SA; *m* 1951, Claire (marr. diss. 1968), *y d* of F. J. Ward, Headmaster of Prince Alfred Coll., Adelaide, and *widow* of Dr John Gooden, Physicist; two *s*. *Educ:* University of Adelaide; Balliol Coll., Oxford; Stanford University, USA. Entered Colonial Administrative Service (Nigeria), 1930; transf. to League of Nations, 1934, and to ILO (Asst to Dir-Gen). Served War, 1940–45 (Lt-Col, Croix de Guerre avec palme, Ordre royal du Lion, Belgium). Farming at Parnaroo, 1946; UN Secretariat (Chief of Africa Sect.), 1946–50; Prof. of Internat. Relations, Aust. Nat. Univ., 1950–52; Actg Vice-Chancellor, 1951; High Commissioner for Australia to India, 1952–55; Ambassador of Australia to Indonesia, 1955–57; High Comr to Canada, 1957–58; High Comr for Australia to India and Ambassador to Nepal, 1958–62; Amb. of Australia to the Netherlands and Belgium, 1962–65; Ambassador to Ethiopia and High Commissioner to Kenya and Uganda, 1965–67; Ambassador to Italy, 1967–70. Hon. Colonel, Royal South Australia Regt, 1977–. L'Ordre royal du Lion (Belgium), 1945; Cavaliere di Gr. Croce dell'Ordine al Merito (Italy), 1970; Order of Malta (Grand' Ufficiale del Merito Melitense), 1975. *Publications:* The Japanese Population Problem, 1931; Nigeria, 1936; On Governing Colonies, 1946; Self-Government for the Colonies, 1949; Can the United Nations Succeed?, 1951; The Race Question as a factor in International Relations, 1955; Nehru, 1965; Australian Ambassador, 1971; Memoirs, 1981; Sir Thomas Playford, 1983. *Recreations:* gardening, walking, music; previously ski-ing, tennis. *Address:* 624 Seaview Road, Grange, SA 5022, Australia. *Club:* Adelaide.

CROCKETT, Andrew Duncan; General Manager, Bank for International Settlements, since 1994; *b* 23 March 1943; *s* of late Dr Andrew Stuart Crockett and of Sheilah Crockett (*née* Stewart); *m* 1966, Marjorie Frances Hlavacek; two *s* one *d*. *Educ:* Queens' College, Cambridge (MA Econ.); Yale Univ. (MA). Bank of England, 1966–72; International Monetary Fund, 1972–89; Exec. Dir, Bank of England, 1989–93. *Publications:* Money: theory, policy, institutions, 1973; International Money: issues and analysis, 1977; contribs to professional jls. *Recreations:* reading, golf, tennis. *Address:* Bank for International Settlements, Centralbahnplatz 2, 4002 Basle, Switzerland.

CROFT, family name of **Baron Croft**.

CROFT, 3rd Baron *cr* 1940, of Bournemouth, co. Southampton; **Bernard William Henry Page Croft;** Bt 1924; publisher; *b* 28 Aug. 1949; *s* of 2nd Baron Croft and Lady Antoinette Conyngham (*d* 1959), *o d* of 6th Marquess Conyngham; *S* father, 1997; *m* 1993, Elizabeth Mary Richardson, *o d* of late James Richardson, Co. Tyrone. *Educ:* Stowe; UCW, Cardiff (BScEcon). *Recreations:* shooting, fishing, ski-ing. *Address:* Croft Castle, Leominster, Herefordshire HR6 9PW; 5 Comeragh Mews, Comeragh Road, W14 9HW. *Clubs:* Naval and Military, Hurlingham.

CROFT, Charles Beresford, FRCS, FRCSE; Consultant Surgeon, Royal National Throat, Nose and Ear Hospital, and Royal Free Hospital, since 1979; *b* 14 Jan. 1943; *s* of Arthur James Croft and Margaret Bays Croft (later Conyers); *m* 1968, Hilary Louise Whitaker; one *d*. *Educ:* Worksop Coll., Notts; Leeds Univ. Med. Sch. (MB BCh Hons 1965). FRCS 1970; FRCSE 1972; Dip. Amer. Bd Otolaryngology, 1979. House Surg., then Physician, Leeds Gen. Infirmary, 1966–68; Demonstrator in Anatomy, Leeds Med. Sch., 1968–69; Surgical Registrar, 1969–73, Sen. Registrar, Otolaryngology, 1971–73, Leeds Gen. Infirmary; Fellow in Head and Neck Surgery, Albert Einstein Med. Sch., NY, 1973–76; Associate Prof. in Otolaryngology, Albert Einstein Med. Sch. and Montefiore Hosp., NY, 1976–79. Civil Consultant Laryngologist, RAF, 1984–. FRSocMed. Arnott Demonstrator and Medal, RCS, 1988. *Publications:* chapters and papers on mgt of head and neck tumours, surgery of sleep breathing disorders and sleep apnoea in textbooks on tumour mgt and otolaryngology. *Recreations:* golf, fly fishing, bridge. *Address:* 55 Harley Street, W1N 1DD. *T:* (020) 7580 2426. *Clubs:* MCC; Moor Park Golf.

CROFT, David Legh; QC 1982; **His Honour Judge Croft;** a Circuit Judge, since 1987; *b* 14 Aug. 1937; *s* of late Alan Croft and Doreen Mary Berry (*née* Mitchell); *m* 1963, Susan Mary (*née* Bagnall); two *s*. *Educ:* Haileybury and ISC; Nottingham Univ. (LLB). Called to the Bar, Middle Temple, 1960; called to the Hong Kong Bar, 1984; a Recorder, 1985–87. *Recreations:* patience and reflection at leisure.

CROFT, Frederick Lister; Divisional Manager, Legal Group, Department of the Environment, Transport and the Regions, since 2000; *b* 13 April 1951; *s* of Frederick Croft and Eirian Croft (*née* Spickett); *m* 1975, Elizabeth May Cohen; two *s* one *d*. *Educ:* Highgate Sch.; Jesus Coll., Oxford (MA). Called to the Bar, Middle Temple, 1975; Treasury Solicitor's Department: Litigation Div., 1977–84; Dept of Energy Div., 1984–86; HM Treasury Div., 1986–87, 1989–91; DES Div., 1987–89; Dep. Head of Litigation, 1991–97; Under Sec., 1997; Legal Adviser: DfEE, 1997–98; BBC, 1998–2000. *Recreations:* reading, theatre, running. *Address:* (office) Eland House, Bressenden Place, SW1E 5DU. *Club:* Thames Hare and Hounds.

CROFT, (Ivor) John, CBE 1982; painter; Head of Home Office Research and Planning Unit, 1981–83 (Head, Home Office Research Unit, 1972–81); *b* 6 Jan. 1923; *s* of Oswald Croft and Doris (*née* Phillips). *Educ:* Westminster Sch.; Christ Church, Oxford (Hinchcliffe Scholar in Mod. Hist.; MA); Inst. of Education, Univ. of London (MA); LSE. Temp. jun. admin. officer, FO, 1942–45; asst teacher, LCC, 1949–51; Inspector, Home Office Children's Dept, 1952–66; Sen. Research Officer, Home Office Research Unit, 1966–72. Member: Criminological Scientific Council, Council of Europe, 1978–83, Chm., 1981–83; Conservative Study Gp on Crime, 1983–87; Kensington Crime Prevention Panel, 1984–87; Tribunal under I of M Interception of Communications Act, 1989–94. Governor, ILEA Secondary Schs, 1959–68. Mem. Exec. Cttee, English Assoc., 1966–77 (Hon. Treas. 1972–75); Chairman: Pembridge Assoc., 1985–87; Peel Heritage Trust, 1991–93 (Mem. Cttee, 1989–93); Circus Area Residents' Assoc., 1997–99 (Mem. Cttee, 1996–99); Commn on Community Safety, Bath and NE Somerset Council, 1996–97. Group shows, 1958, 1963, 1967, 1968, 1969, 1973, 1992, 1993; one-man shows, 1970, 1971. *Publications:* booklets and pamphlets, and various studies of crime, criminological research and the administration of justice. *Address:* 15 Circus Mews, Bath BA1 2PW. *Club:* Reform.

CROFT, Sir Owen (Glendower), 14th Bt *cr* 1671; grazier; *b* 26 April 1932; *s* of Sir Bernard Hugh Denman Croft, 13th Bt, and of Helen Margaret (*née* Weaver); *S* father, 1984; *m* 1959, Sally Patricia, *d* of Dr T. M. Mansfield, Brisbane; one *s* two *d*. *Educ:* Armidale School, NSW. Mem., State Council of Advice to Rural Lands Protection Bds of NSW, 1983–96; Member: NSW Feral Animal Control Council, 1983–96; NSW Footrot Strategic Plan Steering Cttee, 1986–96; NSW Non-Indigenous Species Adv. Cttee; Armidale Rural Lands Protection Bd, 1978–2001; NSW National Parks and Wildlife Service: Chm., Armidale Dist Adv. Cttee, 1988–2000; Chm., Northern Tablelands Region Adv. Cttee, 2000–. *Recreations:* tennis; National Trust activities. *Heir: s* Thomas Jasper Croft [*b* 3 Nov. 1962; *m* 1989, Catherine Fiona, *d* of Graham William White; one *d*]. *Address:* Salisbury Court, Uralla, NSW 2358, Australia. *T:* (2) 67784624.

CROFT, Roy Henry Francis, CB 1983; Member, Competition (formerly Monopolies and Mergers) Commission, 1995–2001; *b* 4 March 1936; *s* of late William Henry Croft and Dorothy Croft; *m* 1961, Patricia Ainley; one *s* two *d*. *Educ:* Isleworth Grammar Sch.; Christ's Coll., Cambridge (MA). BoT, 1959; Treasury, 1961–62; DEA, 1964–67; Private Sec. to Pres. Bd of Trade, 1968–70; Cabinet Office, 1970–72; Civil Aviation Div., Dept of Trade, 1973–76; Finance and Economic Appraisal Div., DoI, 1976–79; Posts and Telecommunications Div., DoI, 1979–80; Dep. Sec. DTI, 1980–85; Exec. Dir and Chief Operating Officer, SIB, 1985–93. Dir (non-exec.), Morgan Stanley Dean Witter Bank Ltd, 1999–.

CROFT, Stanley Edward, TD 1951; life insurance consultant; formerly HM Diplomatic Service; *b* 18 Oct. 1917; *s* of Edward John and Alice Lucy Croft; *m* 1950, Joan Mary Kaye; four *s* two *d*. *Educ:* Portsmouth Grammar School. TA, 1939; served War of 1939–45, RA, Middle East, Aden, Italy, Germany. Min. of Labour, 1935; Admty, 1937–39 and 1946–47; transf. to Diplomatic Service, 1947; Vice-Consul, Barcelona, 1950; 2nd Sec., Lahore, 1951; Washington, 1955; Madrid, 1956; 1st Sec., FO, 1960; Consul, Geneva, 1961; FO and CRO, 1965–70; Consul-Gen., Madrid, 1970; Counsellor and Consul-Gen., Luanda, 1974–77. Sen. Associate, Abbey Life Assurance Co., 1977–90. *Recreations:* swimming, tennis, camping, fishing, carpentry.

CROFT, Rev. Dr Steven John Lindsey; Warden, Cranmer Hall, St John's College, Durham, since 1996; *b* 29 May 1957; *s* of James and Marian Croft; *m* 1978, Ann Christine Baker; two *s* two *d*. *Educ:* Worcester Coll., Oxford (BA Hons 1980, MA 1983); St John's

Coll., Durham (PhD 1984). Ordained deacon, 1983, priest, 1984; Curate, St Andrew's, Enfield, 1983–87; Vicar, St George's, Ovenden, Halifax, 1987–96; Mission Consultant, Dio. Wakefield, 1993–96; Priest-in-charge, St Augustine, Halifax, 1994–96. *Publications:* The Identity of the Individual in the Psalms, 1987; Growing New Christians, 1993; Making New Disciples, 1994; (jtly) Emmaus, The Way of Faith, vols 1–6, 1996, vols 7–8, 1998; Man to Man: friendship and faith, 1999; Ministry in Three Dimensions: ordination and leadership in the local church, 1999; (jtly) Travelling Well, 2000. *Recreations:* walking, cycling, films. *Address:* St John's College, 3 South Bailey, Durham DH1 3RJ. *T:* (0191) 374 3500, *Fax:* (0191) 374 3573; *e-mail:* Steven.Croft@durham.ac.uk.

CROFT, Sir Thomas (Stephen Hutton), 6th Bt *cr* 1818, of Cowling Hall, Yorkshire; Principal, Thomas Croft, Architect, since 1988; *b* 12 June 1959; *o s* of Major Sir John Croft, 5th Bt and of Lucy Elizabeth, *d* of late Major William Dallas Loney Jupp, OBE; *S* father, 1990. *Educ:* King's Sch., Canterbury; University Coll., London (BSc); Royal Coll. of Art, London (MA). Architect, Richard Meier & Partners, Architects, New York, 1985–86; Project Architect, Rick Mather, Architects, London, 1986–88. Completed buildings include Royal Yacht Squadron Pavilion, Cowes, 2000. *Heir: uncle* Cyril Bernard Croft, *b* 6 June 1918. *Address:* (office) 9 Evebury Court, 325 Latimer Road, W10 6RA. *T:* (020) 8962 0066, *Fax:* (020) 8962 0088; *e-mail:* email@thomascroft.com.

CROFT, Trevor Anthony; Director, National Trust for Scotland, 1997–2001; *b* 9 June 1948; *s* of late Kenneth Edward Croft and Gladys (*née* Bartle); *m* 1980, Janet Frances Halley; two *d. Educ:* Belle Vue Boys' GS, Bradford; Hull Univ. (BSc 1969); Sheffield Univ. (DipTRP 1971). MRTPI 1974. Sen. Asst Planning Officer, Min. of Develt, NI, 1971–72; Asst Planning Officer, Countryside Commn for Scotland, 1972–75; Physical Planning Officer, Office of the President, Malaŵi, 1976–78; Parks Planning Officer, Dept of Nat. Parks and Wildlife, Malaŵi, 1978–82; National Trust for Scotland: Planning Officer, 1982–84; Head of Policy Res., 1984–88; Regl Dir, 1988–95; Dep. Dir and Dir of Countryside, 1995–97. Mem., Regl Adv. Cttee, S Scotland, Forestry Commn, 1987–90. Member Council: RSGS, 1998– (Chm., Dunferline Br., 1993–96); Europa Nostra, 1999–. Associate, RSGS, 1995; FRSA 1997. *Recreations:* sailing, travel, equestrian vaulting, restoring Srs 1 Land Rover. *Address:* Glenside, Tillyrie, Kinross KY13 0RW. *T:* (01577) 864105. *Clubs:* New, Royal Scots (Edinburgh).

CROFTON, family name of **Baron Crofton.**

CROFTON, 7th Baron *cr* 1797 (Ire.); **Guy Patrick Gilbert Crofton;** Bt 1758; Lieutenant Colonel, 9/12 Royal Lancers (Prince of Wales's); Staff Officer, Defence Evaluation and Research Agency, since 1999; *b* 17 June 1951; *s* of 5th Baron Crofton and of Ann Pamela, *d* of Gp Capt. Charles Herbert Tighe, OBE, DFC; *S* brother, 1989; *m* 1985, Gillian, *o d* of Harry Godfrey Mitchell Bass, *qv;* twin *s. Educ:* Theresianistische Akademie, Vienna; Midhurst GS. Commissioned 9/12 Royal Lancers, 1971; Defence Attaché, Berne, 1995–98. *Recreations:* shooting, ski-ing. *Heir: er* twin *s* Hon. Edward Harry Piers Crofton, *b* 23 Jan. 1988. *Address:* Hamilton House, Bruton, Somerset BA10 0AH. *Club:* Cavalry and Guards.

CROFTON, (Sir) Hugh Dennis, (8th Bt *cr* 1801, of Mohill); *S* nephew, 1987, but does not use the title. *Heir: b* Major Edward Morgan Crofton.

CROFTON, Sir John (Wenman), Kt 1977; retired; Professor of Respiratory Diseases and Tuberculosis, University of Edinburgh, 1952–77; *b* 1912; *s* of Dr W. M. Crofton; *m* 1945, Eileen Chris Mercer, MBE 1984; two *s* three *d. Educ:* Tonbridge; Sidney Sussex Coll., Cambridge (BA 1933; MB BChir 1937; MD 1947); St Thomas's Hosp. FRCP 1951; FRCPE 1957. War of 1939–45, RAMC; France, Middle East, Germany. Lecturer in Medicine, Postgraduate Medical Sch. of London, 1947–51, Senior Lecturer, 1951; Part-time Tuberculosis Unit, Medical Research Council, Brompton Hosp., 1947–50; Dean of Faculty of Medicine, 1964–66, and Vice-Principal, 1969–70, Univ. of Edinburgh. Vice-Pres., 1972–73, Pres., 1973–76, RCPE. Hon. Mem., Acads of Medicine of Argentina, Catalonia and Singapore. Hon. FRCPI 1975; Hon. FRACP 1976; Hon. FACP 1976; Hon. FFCM 1978; Hon. FRCPE 1987; Hon. FRSE 1997. Dr *hc* Bordeaux, 1997; Hon. DSc London, 2001. Weber-Parkes Prize, RCP, 1966; City of Edinburgh Medal for Sci. and Soc., 1995; Galen Medal, Soc. of Apothecaries, 2001. *Publications:* (jtly) Respiratory Diseases, 1969, 3rd edn 1981; (jtly) Clinical Tuberculosis, 1992, 2nd edn 1999; Housing and Health in Scotland, 1993; (co-ed) Tobacco and Health, 1996; (jtly) Tobacco or Health: a global threat, 2001; contributor to BMJ, Lancet, Thorax, etc. *Recreations:* reading science and history, mountains. *Address:* 13 Spylaw Bank Road, Edinburgh EH13 0JW. *T:* (0131) 441 3730.

CROFTON, Sir Malby (Sturges), 5th Bt *cr* 1838 (orig. *cr* 1661); Partner, Messrs Fenn & Crosthwaite; Member of the London Stock Exchange, 1957–75; *b* 11 Jan. 1923; *s* of Sir Malby Richard Henry Crofton, 4th Bt, DSO and Bar, and Katharine Beatrix Pollard; *S* father, 1962; *m* 1998, Sally Eden; one step *s. Educ:* Eton (King's Scholar); Trinity Coll., Cambridge (scholar). Served with Life Guards, 1942–46, in Middle East and Italy. Member: Kensington Borough Council, 1962, Leader, 1968–77, Mayor, Kensington and Chelsea, 1978; GLC, 1970–73; ILEA, 1970–73; Ealing N, GLC, 1977–81; Leader, GLC Scrutiny Cttee, 1977–78. Vice-Chm., NW Thames RHA, 1980–85. Hon.Treasurer, Marie Curie Meml Foundn; Dir, St Edward's Housing Assoc.; Chm., Kensington and Chelsea, Age Concern, 1987–. Pres., Ealing N Cons. Assoc. Freeman, Royal Bor. of Kensington and Chelsea, 1983. Hon. Fellow, Chelsea Coll. *Recreations:* tennis, swimming, motoring, planting trees, farming. *Heir: kinsman* Henry Edward Melville Crofton [*b* 15 Aug. 1931; *m* 1955, Brigid, twin *d* of Gerald K. Riddle; two *s* one *d*]. *Address:* 12 Caithness Road, W14 0JB; Longford House, Beltra, Co. Sligo, Eire. *Clubs:* Cavalry and Guards, Hurlingham.

CROFTS, Roger Stanley, CBE 1999; FRSE; Chief Executive, Scottish Natural Heritage, since 1991; *b* 17 Jan. 1944; *s* of Stanley Crofts and Violet May Crofts (*née* Dawson); *m* 1996, Lindsay Manson; one *s* one *d* by previous marriage. *Educ:* Hinckley Grammar Sch.; Liverpool Univ. (BA); Leicester Univ. (PGCE); Aberdeen Univ. (MLitt). Res. Asst to Prof. K. Walton, Aberdeen Univ., 1966–72; British Geomorphological Res. Gp, UCL, 1972–74; Central Res. Unit, Scottish Office, 1974–84; Scottish Office: Head of Highlands and Tourism, 1984–88; Head of Rural Affairs, 1988–91. Vis. Prof. of Envmtl Mgt, Royal Holloway, Univ. of London, 1997– (Vis. Prof. of Geography, 1992–95); Hon. Prof. of Geography, Univ. of Aberdeen, 1997–. Chairman: UK Cttee, IUCN, 1999–; Europe Cttee, IUCN WCPA; Member: Council, NT for Scotland, 1992–; Council, Scottish Wildlife Trust, 1992–97; RSGS, 1994–; Scottish Assoc. for Marine Science, 1995–; Hon. Pres., Scottish Assoc. of Geography Teachers, 1994–95. FRSE 2001. *Publications:* contribs to books on marginal regions, geomorph. mapping, second homes, field studies, conservation; numerous articles. *Recreations:* designing gardens, choral singing, flower photography, cooking, hill walking. *Address:* 6 Old Church Lane, Duddington Village, Edinburgh EH15 3PX. *T:* (0131) 661 7858, *Fax:* (0131) 661 6430.

CROHAM, Baron *cr* 1978 (Life Peer), of the London Borough of Croydon; **Douglas Albert Vivian Allen,** GCB 1973 (KCB 1967; CB 1963); Chairman, Guinness Peat Group, 1983–87; Head of the Home Civil Service and Permanent Secretary, Civil Service Department, 1974–77; *b* 15 Dec. 1917; *s* of late Albert Allen; *m* 1941, Sybil Eileen Allegro (*d* 1994), *d* of late John Marco Allegro; two *s* one *d. Educ:* Wallington County Grammar Sch.; London School of Economics. BSc (Econ.) First Class Hons, 1938. Entered Board of Trade, 1939; Royal Artillery, 1940–45; Cabinet Office, 1947; Treasury, 1948–58; Under-Secretary, Ministry of Health, 1958–60; Under-Secretary, Treasury, 1960–62, Third Secretary, 1962–64; Dept of Economic Affairs: Dep. Under-Sec. of State, 1964–66; Second Permanent Under-Sec. of State, May-Oct. 1966; Permanent Under-Sec. of State, 1966–68; Permanent Sec., HM Treasury, 1968–74. Director: Pilkington plc (formerly Pilkington Bros), 1978–92; Guinness Mahon & Co., 1989–92; Dep. Chm., 1978–82, Chm., 1982–85, BNOC; Chm., Trinity Insurance, 1988–92. An Industrial Adviser to the Governor, Bank of England, 1978–83. President: Inst. for Fiscal Studies, 1979–92; British Inst. of Energy Economies, 1985–94. A Trustee, Anglo-German Foundn, 1977– (Chm., 1982–97). CIMgt; FRSA 1975. Hon. Fellow, LSE, 1969; Hon. DSc (Social Sciences) Southampton, 1977. *Recreations:* bridge, woodwork. *Address:* 9 Manor Way, South Croydon, Surrey CR2 7BT. *T:* (020) 8688 0496. *Club:* Reform.

CROLL, Prof. James George Arthur, FREng; Chadwick Professor of Civil Engineering, and Head of Department of Civil Engineering, University College London, since 1992; *b* 16 Oct. 1943; *s* of late Keith Waghorn Croll and Jean Croll; *m* 1966, Elisabeth Joan (*née* Sprackett) (marr. diss. 1997); one *s* one *d. Educ:* Palmerston North Boys' High Sch., NZ; Univ. of Canterbury, NZ (BE 1st cl. Hons, PhD). FIStructE, FICE, FIMA; CEng 1970, FREng (FEng 1990). Asst Engineer, Min. of Works, NZ, 1962–67; University College London: Res. Fellow, 1967–70; Lectr, 1970–81; Reader in Structural Engrg, 1981–85; Prof. of Structural Engrg, 1985–92. Vis. Fellow, Princeton, 1979; Visiting Professor: Fed. Univ. of Rio de Janeiro, 1973, 1981, 1984; Univ. of Hong Kong, 1985. *Publications:* Elements of Structural Stability, 1972; Force Systems and Equilibrium, 1974. *Recreations:* singing, piano, painting, drawing, sailing, ski-ing, travel. *Address:* 36 Bisham Gardens, Highgate, N6 6DD. *T:* (020) 8348 4753. *Club:* Natural Science (UCL).

CROLL, (Mary) Louise, CBE 1995; HM Diplomatic Service, retired; Ambassador to Costa Rica, 1992–95; *b* 10 Sept. 1935. Joined FO, subseq. FCO, 1953; Bahrain, 1957; Addis Ababa, 1959; UK Mission, NY, 1961; FO, 1964; S America floater, 1967; Bilbao, 1969; Lusaka, 1972; First Sec., Madrid, 1979, FCO, 1984; Consul, Florence, 1988.

CROMARTIE, 5th Earl of, *cr* 1861; **John Ruaridh Grant Mackenzie;** Viscount Tarbat, Baron Castlehaven, Baron MacLeod, 1861; Chief of the Clan Mackenzie; MIExpE; explosives engineer; *b* 12 June 1948; *s* of 4th Earl of Cromartie, MC, TD and Olga (*d* 1996), *d* of late Stuart Laurance; *S* father, 1989; *m* 1973, Helen, *d* of John Murray; (one *s* decd); *m* 1985, Janet Clare, *d* of Christopher J. Harley; two *s. Educ:* Rannoch School, Perthshire; Strathclyde University. Mem. Council, Mountaineering Council of Scotland, 1995–. *Publications:* Selected Climbs in Skye, 1982; articles in Classic Rock Climbs and Cold Climbs. *Recreations:* mountaineering, art, astronomy, geology. *Heir: s* Viscount Tarbat, *qv. Address:* Castle Leod, Strathpeffer, Ross-shire IV14 9AA. *Clubs:* Army and Navy; Scottish Mountaineering.

CROMER, 4th Earl of, *cr* 1901; **Evelyn Rowland Esmond Baring;** Baron Cromer, 1892; Viscount Cromer, 1899; Viscount Errington, 1901; Chief Executive, Cromer Associates Ltd, since 1994; *b* 3 June 1946; *e s* of 3rd Earl of Cromer, KG, GCMG, MBE, PC and of Hon. Esmé Harmsworth, CVO, *d* of 2nd Viscount Rothermere; *S* father, 1991; *m* 1971, Plern Isarangkun Na Ayudhya (marr. diss. 1993); 2nd, 1993, Shelly Hu Cheng-Yu, *e d* of Hu Guoquin, Shanghai; one *s* one *d. Educ:* Eton. Managing Director: Inchcape (China) Ltd, 1979–94; Inchcape Vietnam Ltd, 1987–94; Inchcape Special Markets Ltd, 1990–94; Dir, Inchcape Pacific Ltd, 1985–94. Chairman: Lloyd George Standard Chartered China Fund Ltd (Hong Kong), 1994–; Jardine Fleming China Region Fund Inc. (USA), 1994–; Korea Asia Fund Ltd, 1996–2000; Philippine Discovery Investment Co. Ltd, 1997–; Cambridge Asia Fund Ltd, 2001–; Director: Cluff Oil China Ltd (Hong Kong), 1990–99; China & Eastern Investments Ltd, 1991–96; Schroder AsiaPacific Fund Ltd, 1995–. Dir, Somerset TEC, 1999–2001; Chm., Business Link Somerset, 1999–. Mem. St John's Council (Hong Kong), 1980–85. *Recreations:* mountain climbing, deep sea diving. *Heir: s* Viscount Errington, *qv. Address:* 6 Sloane Terrace Mansions, SW1X 9DG. *Clubs:* White's, Oriental; Hong Kong (Hong Kong).

CROMPTON, Dan, CBE 1996; QPM 1990; HM Inspector of Constabulary, North of England, since 1995; *b* 15 Feb. 1941; *s* of Arthur and Elizabeth Crompton; *m* 1962, Olive Ramsden; one *s. Educ:* Didsbury Technical Sch., Manchester. Manchester City Police, 1960–68; Manchester and Salford Police, 1968–74; Greater Manchester Police, 1974–87; Nottinghamshire Constabulary, 1987–95 (Chief Constable, 1990–95). *Recreations:* reading, popular classics, gardening, cricket, Rugby. *Address:* HM Inspectorate, 4 South Parade, Wakefield, W Yorks WF1 1LR. *T:* (01924) 332822.

CROMPTON, Prof. Gareth, FRCP, FFPHM; Professor of Public Health Medicine, University of Wales College of Medicine, 1989–97, now Emeritus; Hon. Fellow, University of Wales Institute, Cardiff, since 1997; *b* 9 Jan. 1937; *s* of late Edward Crompton, Drefach-Felindre, Carmarthenshire; *m* 1965; one *d. Educ:* Llandysul Grammar Sch.; Welsh Nat. Sch. of Medicine. MB, BCh Wales, 1960; DObstRCOG 1962; DPH Wales, 1964; FFPHM (FFCM 1976); FRCP 1986 (MRCP 1980). County Med. Officer, County Welfare Officer and Principal Sch. Med. Officer, Anglesey CC, 1966–73; Area Med. Officer, Gwynedd Health Authority, 1974–77; CMO, Welsh Office, 1978–89; Chief Admin. MO and Dir of Public Health Medicine, S Glam HA, 1989–96. Specialty Advr, Health Service Comr for England and Wales, 1974–77; Advr in Wales, Faculty of Community Medicine, 1974–77. Chm., Anglesey Disablement Adv. Cttee, 1969–77; Sec., Fluoridation Study Gp, Soc. of Med. Officers of Health, 1969–73; Mem., Welsh Hosp. Bd, 1970–74. Member: GMC, 1981–83 and 1987–89; Bd, PHLS, 1990–97; Exec. Bd, FPHM, 1990–95. Med. Fellow, Council of Europe, 1971. QHP 1984–87. Hon. MD Wales, 1999. Alwyn Smith Prize Medal, RCP, 2000. *Publications:* papers on the effects of fluoridated water supplies on dental caries, and the epidemiology and management of chronic sickness and disablement. *Recreations:* bowls, watching Rugby football and cricket, reading contemporary Welsh verse. *Address:* 19 Kenilworth House, Castle Court, Westgate Street, Cardiff CF10 1DJ. *T:* (029) 2034 3192.

CROMPTON, Ian William; His Honour Judge Crompton; a Circuit Judge, since 1994; *b* 28 June 1936; *s* of Thomas and Hilda Crompton; *m* 1962, Audrey (*née* Hopewell); two *s. Educ:* Manchester Grammar School; Victoria University of Manchester. LLB. Asst Solicitor, County Magistrates' Court, Strangeways, Manchester, 1961–62; Asst Solicitor, O'Collier, Littler & Kilbeg, 1962–65, Partner, 1965–72; Clerk to the Justices: County Magistrates' Court, Strangeways, 1972–74; Eccles Magistrates' Court, 1974–83; Stipendiary Magistrate for S Yorks, 1983–94; a Recorder, 1989–94. *Recreations:* ballroom and Latin American dancing, golf. *Club:* Davyhulme Park Golf (Urmston).

CROMPTON, Kenneth Charles; Chief Executive and Director, Corporate Counsel Pty Ltd, since 1992; *b* 19 July 1948; *s* of late Charles Frederic Crompton and of Margaret Joan Crompton; *m* 1971, Elizabeth Anne Meek; one *s* two *d. Educ:* Melbourne Univ. (LLB).

Solicitor, Morris Komesaroff, Aarons & Co., 1971–75; Seton Williams & Smyth, 1975–79; Gen. Manager, Legal and Technical Services, Victorian Chamber of Manufactures, 1979–87; Dir, Industrial Relations, 1987–88, Chief Exec. (Vic.), 1988–92, Aust. Chamber of Manufactures; Agent-Gen. for Victoria in London, 1993–96. *Recreations:* wind surfing, tennis, photography, walking. *Address:* 104 Scenic Crescent, Eltham, Vic 3095, Australia. *Clubs:* Athenæum (Melbourne); Royal Automobile (Vic); Melbourne Cricket.

CROMWELL, 7th Baron *cr* 1375 (called out of abeyance, 1923); **Godfrey John Bewicke-Copley;** *b* 4 March 1960; *s* of 6th Baron Cromwell and of Vivian, *y d* of late Hugh de Lisle Penfold, Isle of Man; *S* father, 1982; *m* 1990, Elizabeth, *d* of John Hawksley; three *s* (incl. twins) one *d*. *Heir: s* Hon. David Godfrey Bewicke-Copley, *b* 21 Sept. 1997.

CRONIN, Vincent Archibald Patrick; author; *b* 24 May 1924; *s* of late Archibald Joseph Cronin, MD, MRCP, DPH and of Agnes Mary Gibson, MB, ChB; *m* 1949, Chantal, *d* of Comte Jean de Rolland; two *s* three *d*. *Educ:* Ampleforth; Harvard; Trinity Coll., Oxford. Rifle Bde, 1943–45. *Publications:* The Golden Honeycomb, 1954; The Wise Man from the West, 1955; The Last Migration, 1957; A Pearl to India, 1959; The Letter after Z, 1960; Louis XIV, 1964; Four Women in Pursuit of an Ideal, 1965; The Florentine Renaissance, 1967; The Flowering of the Renaissance, 1970; Napoleon, 1971; Louis and Antoinette, 1974; trans., Giscard d'Estaing, Towards a New Democracy, 1977; Catherine, Empress of all the Russias, 1978; The View from Planet Earth, 1981; Paris on the Eve, 1989; Paris: City of Light 1919–1939, 1995. *Address:* Manoir de Brion, Dragey 50530, France.

CROOK, family name of **Baron Crook**.

CROOK, 3rd Baron *cr* 1947, of Carshalton, Surrey; **Robert Douglas Edwin Crook;** *b* 19 May 1955; *S* father, 2001; *m* 1981, Suzanne Jane Robinson, BA, LLB; two *s*. *Educ:* Sir William Borlase's Sch., Marlow; Newcastle Univ. (BSc); MBA. *Heir: s* Hon. Matthew Robert Crook, *b* 28 May 1990.

CROOK, Arthur Charles William; Consultant to Times Newspapers, since 1974; Editor, The Times Literary Supplement, 1959–74; *b* 16 Feb. 1912; *m* 1948, Sarita Mary Vivien Bushell (marr. diss.); one *s* two *d*. Editorial staff of The Times; Asst Editor, The Times Literary Supplement, 1951–59. Pres. and Chm., Royal Literary Fund, 1984–90. *Recreation:* theatre. *Address:* 70 Regent's Park Road, NW1 7SX. *T:* (020) 7722 8446. *Club:* Garrick.

CROOK, Colin, FREng; Senior Technology Officer (formerly Chairman, Corporate Technology Committee), Citicorp, 1990–97; *b* 1 June 1942; *s* of Richard and Ruth Crook; *m* 1965, Dorothy Jean Taylor; two *d*. *Educ:* Harris Coll., Preston; Liverpool Polytechnic (ACT Hons; Dip. Elec. Engrg). CEng 1977, FREng (FEng 1981); MIEE 1976; MIERE 1976; MIEEE 1976; MACM 1977. Electronics Engr, Canadian Marconi, 1962–64; Computer Designer, The Plessey Co., 1964–68; Systems Engr, Eli Lilly Co., 1968–69; sen. appts, Motorola Semiconductor Div., Switzerland and USA, 1969–79; sen. appts, The Rank Organisation, 1979–83, including: Man. Dir, RPI, 1979–81; Man. Dir, Zynar, CEO Nestar Systems, USA, 1981–83; Mem. of Bd, British Telecom, and Man. Dir, BT Enterprises, 1983–84; Sen. Vice Pres., Data General Corp., 1984–89. Sen. Fellow, SEI Inst., Wharton Sch., 1997. Mem., various NAS adv. cttees, USA; advr to various global cos; Member Board: Center for Adaptive Systems Applications Inc., Los Alamos, 1998–; Onsett Internat., Boston, 1998–; Mem. Adv. Bd, Warburg Pincus, NY, 1998–. *Publications:* articles and learned papers on electronics and computers. *Recreations:* photography, walking, reading, wine, sailing. *Address:* Penberen House, Seifton, Shropshire SY7 9BY; 201 E 87 St 9D, New York, NY 10128, USA.

CROOK, Frances Rachel; Director, Howard League for Penal Reform, since 1986; *b* 18 Dec. 1952; *d* of Sheila Sibson-Turnbull and Maurice Crook; one *d*. *Educ:* Camden School; Liverpool University (BA Hons History). Historical Researcher, Liverpool, 1977–78; Teacher, 1978–79; Campaign Co-ordinator, Amnesty International, 1980–85. Councillor (Lab) Barnet, 1982–90. Mem. Court, Greenwich Univ., 1996– (Chm., Staffing and Gen. Cttee, 1997–). Chm., Old Barn Youth and Community Centre, Finchley, 1996–97. Freeman, City of London, 1997. *Recreation:* demonstrations. *Address:* The Howard League, 1 Ardleigh Road, N1 4HS. *T:* (020) 7249 7373.

CROOK, Maj.-Gen. James Cooper, MD, FRCPath; late RAMC, retired 1981; Civilian Medical Practitioner, Army Blood Supply Depot, Aldershot, 1982–88; *b* 19 March 1923; *s* of late Francis William Crook and late Mary Catherine Perry, *d* of late Sir Edwin Cooper Perry, GCVO, MD, Superintendent of Guy's Hospital and Vice-Chancellor of London Univ.; *m* 1950, Ruth, *d* of late W. A. Bellamy of Santa Cruz, Tenerife; one *s* two *d*. *Educ:* Worksop Coll.; Guy's Hosp. Med. Sch., Univ. of London. MB BS 1946, MD 1953; DTM&H 1952; FRCPath 1968. Guy's and Pembury Hosps, 1946; Commnd RAMC 1946; served Egypt and N Africa, 1946–49; Pathologist, Queen Alexandra's Mil. Hosp., 1950; David Bruce Laboratories, 1953; med. liaison officer to MRC Radiobiology Unit, AERE, Harwell, 1954; Asst Dir of Pathology, Middle East, 1957; Cons. in Pathology, 1958; RAMC Specialist, Chem. Defence Estab., Porton, 1960; Asst Dir of Pathology, Eastern Comd, 1963; ADGMS, 1966; Comd Cons. in Pathology, BAOR, 1969; Prof. of Pathology, Royal Army Med. Coll., 1974; Dir of Army Pathology and Consulting Pathologist to the Army, 1976–81; Hon. Physician to HM The Queen, 1978–81. Hon. Col, 380 Blood Supply Unit RAMC, TAVR, 1982–86. *Publications:* articles in Jl of Clinical Path., Nature, Med. Sci. and the Law, Jl of RAMC, British Jl of Radiology. *Recreations:* gardening, beekeeping. *Address:* Egloshayle, Fore Street, Kingsand, Torpoint, Cornwall PL10 1NB. *T:* (01752) 823666.

CROOK, Prof. John Anthony, MA; Professor of Ancient History, University of Cambridge, 1979–84; Fellow of St John's College, Cambridge, since 1951; *b* 5 Nov. 1921; *s* of Herbert Crook and Hilda Naomi (*née* Flower). *Educ:* St Mary's C of E Sch., Balham; Dulwich Coll.; St John's Coll., Cambridge 1939–41 and 1945–47 (John Stewart of Rannoch Scholar); BA 1947, Craven Student, 1947; Research Student of Balliol Coll., Oxford, 1947–48; MA (Cantab) 1949. Served War, Private and Corporal, 9th Royal Fusiliers, 1941–43 (PoW Stalag VIIIB, 1943–45); Sgt, RAEC, 1945. Univ. Asst Lectr in Classics, Reading Univ., 1948, Lectr, 1949–51; St John's Coll., Cambridge: Tutor, 1956–64; President, 1971–75; Univ. Asst Lectr in Classics, Cambridge Univ., 1953, Lectr, 1955–71, Reader in Roman History and Law, 1971–79, and Brereton Reader, 1974–79. FBA 1970–80. Dr jur *hc* Freiburg, 1995. *Publications:* Consilium Principis, 1955; Law and Life of Rome, 1967; Legal Advocacy in the Roman World, 1995; (contrib.) The Cambridge Ancient History, 2nd edn, vol. IX, 1994, vol. X, 1996. *Address:* St John's College, Cambridge CB2 1TP. *T:* (01223) 338621.

CROOK, Rt Rev. John Michael; *see* Moray, Ross and Caithness, Bishop of.

CROOK, Prof. Joseph Mordaunt, FBA 1988; Professor of Architectural History, University of London at Royal Holloway and Bedford New College (formerly at Bedford College), 1981–99, now Emeritus; *b* 27 Feb. 1937; *e s* of late Austin Mordaunt Crook and late Irene Woolfenden; *m* 1st, 1964, Margaret, *o d* of late James Mulholland; 2nd, 1975, Susan, *o d* of late F. H. Mayor. *Educ:* Wimbledon Coll.; Brasenose Coll., Oxford. BA (1st cl. Mod. Hist.) 1958; DPhil 1961, MA 1962, Oxon; FSA 1972. Research Fellow: Inst. of Historical Res., 1961–62; Bedford Coll., London, 1962–63; Warburg Inst., London, 1970–71; Asst Lectr, Univ. of Leicester, 1963–65; Lectr, Bedford Coll., London, 1965–75, Reader in Architectural Hist., 1975–81; Dir, Victorian Studies Centre, RHBNC, 1990–99. Slade Prof. of Fine Art, Oxford Univ., 1979–80; Vis. Fellow: Brasenose Coll., Oxford, 1979–80; Humanities Res. Centre, ANU, Canberra, 1985; Waynflete Lectr and Vis. Fellow, Magdalen Coll., Oxford, 1984–85; Vis. Fellow, Gonville and Caius Coll., Cambridge, 1986; Humanities Fellow, Princeton Univ., 1990. Public Orator, Univ. of London, 1988–90. Member: Exec. Cttee, Soc. Architect. Historians of Gt Britain, 1964–77 (Pres., 1980–84); RIBA Drawings Cttee, 1969–75; Exec. Cttee, Georgian Gp, 1970–77; Exec. Cttee, Victorian Soc., 1970–77, Council, 1978–88; Historic Buildings Council for England, 1974–80; Council, Soc. of Antiquaries, 1980–82; Adv. Council, Paul Mellon Centre for Studies in British Art, 1985–90; Gen. Cttee, Incorp. Church Building Soc., 1987–99; Council, British Acad., 1989–92; Adv. Bd for Redundant Churches, 1991–99; Westminster Abbey Architectural Adv. Panel, 1993–99 and Fabric Commn, 2000–. Freeman, 1979, Liveryman, 1984, Worshipful Co. of Goldsmiths. Editor, Architectural History, 1967–75. *Publications:* The Greek Revival, 1968; Victorian Architecture: A Visual Anthology, 1971; The British Museum, 1972, 2nd edn 1973; The Greek Revival: Neo-Classical Attitudes in British Architecture 1760–1870, 1972, 2nd edn 1995; The Reform Club, 1973; (jtly) The History of the King's Works, Vol. VI, 1782–1851, 1973 (Hitchcock Medallion, 1974), Vol. V, 1660–1782, 1976; William Burges and the High Victorian Dream, 1981; (jtly) Axel Haig and The Victorian Vision of the Middle Ages, 1984; The Dilemma of Style: architectural ideas from the picturesque to the post-modern, 1987, 2nd edn 1989; John Carter and the Mind of the Gothic Revival, 1995; The Rise of the Nouveaux Riches: style and status in Victorian and Edwardian architecture, 1999, 2nd edn 2000; *edited:* Eastlake, A History of the Gothic Revival, 1970, rev. edn, 1978; Emmet, Six Essays, 1972; Kerr, The Gentleman's House, 1972; The Strange Genius of William Burges, 1981; Clark, The Gothic Revival, 1995; Bedford College: memories of 150 years, 2001; *contrib. to:* Concerning Architecture, 1967; The Country Seat, 1970; The Age of Neo-Classicism, 1972; The Building of Early America, 1976; Seven Victorian Architects, 1976; The Ruskin Polygon, 1982; In Search of Modern Architecture, 1983; Rediscovering Hellenism, 1989; The University of London and the World of Learning 1836–1986, 1990; Brooks's: a social history, 1991; London: World City 1800–1840, 1992; Scottish Country Houses, 1995; The Question of Style in Philosophy and the Arts, 1995; Armchair Athenians, 2001; numerous articles in Architect. History, Architect. Review, Country Life, History Today, Jl Royal Soc. Arts, RIBA Jl, Antiquaries Jl, TLS, Architect Design, etc. *Recreation:* strolling. *Address:* 55 Gloucester Avenue, NW1 7BA. *T:* (020) 7485 8280; West Wing, Maristow, near Roborough, Devon PL6 7BZ. *T:* (01752) 696648. *Clubs:* Athenæum, Brooks's.

CROOK, Kenneth Roy, CMG 1978; HM Diplomatic Service, retired; Ambassador to Afghanistan, 1976–79; *b* 30 July 1920; *s* of Alexander Crook, Prescot, Lancs, and Margaret Kay Crook; *m* 1943, Freda Joan Vidler; two *d*. *Educ:* Prescot Grammar Sch., Lancs; Skerry's Coll., Liverpool. Appointed to: Board of Trade, 1937; Min. of War Transport, 1939. Royal Navy, 1941–46. Board of Trade, 1946–49; Commonwealth Relations Office, 1949; Second Sec., Canberra, 1951–54; First Sec., Madras, 1956–59; Deputy High Commissioner: Peshawar, W Pakistan, 1962–64; Dacca, E Pakistan, 1964–67; Counsellor, FCO, 1967; Head of Information Research Dept, FCO, 1969–71; Governor, Cayman Is, 1971–74; Canadian Nat. Defence Coll., 1974–75; Head of Science and Technology Dept, FCO, 1975–76. *Recreations:* walking, gardening, music appreciation. *Address:* 16 Burntwood Road, Sevenoaks, Kent TN13 1PT. *T:* (01732) 452774.

CROOK, Brig. Paul Edwin, CBE 1965 (OBE 1946); DSO 1957; *b* 19 April 1915; *s* of late Herbert Crook and Christine Crook, Lyme Regis; *m* 1st, 1944, Joan (marr. diss. 1967), *d* of late William Lewis; one *d*; 2nd, 1967, Betty, *d* of late John William Wyles. *Educ:* Uppingham Sch.; Emmanuel Coll., Cambridge. BA 1936, MA 1956. Commnd into QORWK Regt, 1935; served: India and Palestine, 1937–39; War of 1939–45, Africa, NW Europe, Burma; Chief Civil Affairs Officer (Col), Netherlands East Indies, 1946; comd 3rd Bn The Parachute Regt, 1954–57; Suez Ops, 1956; comd Army Airborne Trng and Develt Centre, 1959–62; Comdr and Chief of Staff, Jamaica Defence Force, 1962–65; Security Ops Advisor to High Comr for Aden and S Arabia, 1965–67; Comdr, Rhine Area, 1969–70. Col, 1959; Brig., 1963; retired 1971. ADC to The Queen, 1965. Hon. Col, 16 Lincoln Co. Parachute Regt (VR), 1974–79; Dep. Hon. Col, The Parachute Regt (TAVR): 15th (Scottish) Bn, 1979–83; 4th Bn, 1984–85. Chm., Lincs County Scouts, 1975–88. Bronze Star (US), 1945. *Publication:* Came the Dawn, 1989. *Recreations:* cricket, golf, jazz. *Address:* The Longhouse, Diptford, Totnes, Devon TQ9 7LY. *T:* (01548) 821609. *Clubs:* Naval and Military, MCC; Jamaica (W Indies).

CROOKALL, Ian; Chief Executive, Buckinghamshire County Council, 1995–2001; *b* 28 Dec. 1944; *s* of F. Harold Crookall and M. Ida Crookall (*née* Stubbs); *m* 1974, Georgina; one *s*. *Educ:* Arnold Sch., Blackpool; University Coll. London (LLB Hons). Admitted Solicitor, 1969; Asst Solicitor, N Yorks CC, 1974–82; Asst Clerk, Norfolk CC, 1982–85; Dep. County Solicitor, Dorset CC, 1985–89; Buckinghamshire County Council: County Secretary and Solicitor, 1989–95. *Recreations:* tennis, swimming, walking, theatre. *Address:* Flemings House, Old School, High Street, Wendover HP22 6DU. *T:* (01296) 696410.

CROOKENDEN, Maj.-Gen. George Wayet Derek; DL; Emeritus Fellow, Peterhouse, Cambridge, since 1989; *b* 11 Dec. 1920; *o s* of late Lt-Col John Crookenden and Iris Margherita Gay; *m* 1948, Elizabeth Mary Angela Bourke; one *s* one *d*. *Educ:* Winchester Coll.; Christ Church, Oxford. Commnd Royal Artillery, 1941. GSO1, SHAPE, 1961–62; CO, 19 Field Regt, RA, 1962–64; Comdr, 7 Artillery Bde, 1964–67; Exercise Controller, CICC (West), 1969–71; Chief, British Commanders-in-Chief Liaison Mission, 1971–72; C of S, Contingencies Planning, SHAPE, 1972–75. Col Comdt, RA, 1977–82. Fellow and Sen. Bursar, Peterhouse, Cambridge, 1975–88. DL Cambs, 1984. *Club:* Army and Navy.

CROOKENDEN, Lt-Gen. Sir Napier, KCB 1970 (CB 1966); DSO 1945; OBE 1954; DL; Lieutenant, HM Tower of London, 1975–81; *b* 31 Aug. 1915; 2nd *s* of late Col Arthur Crookenden, CBE, DSO; *m* 1948, Patricia Nassau, *d* of 2nd Baron Kindersley, CBE, MC, and of Nancy Farnsworth, *d* of Dr Geoffrey Boyd; two *s* two *d*. *Educ:* Wellington Coll.; RMC, Sandhurst. Commissioned, Cheshire Regt, 1935; Bde Major, 6th Airlanding Bde, 1943–44; CO, 9th Bn, The Parachute Regt, 1944–46; GSO1 (Plans) to Dir of Ops, Malaya, 1952–54; Comdr, 16th Parachute Bde, 1960–61; idc 1962; Dir, Land/Air Warfare MoD (Army Dept), 1964–66; Commandant, RMCS, Shrivenham, 1967–69; GOC-in-C, Western Comd, 1969–72. Col, The Cheshire Regt, 1969–71; Col Comdt, The Prince of Wales Div., 1971–74. Director: SE Regional Bd, Lloyds Bank Ltd, 1973–86; Flextech Ltd, 1978–86. A Trustee, Imperial War Museum, 1973–83. Chm., SSAFA, 1974–85; a Vice-Pres., RUSI, 1978–85. DL Kent, 1979. *Publications:* Dropzone Normandy, 1976; Airborne at War, 1978; Battle of the Bulge 1944, 1980. *Club:* Army and Navy.

CROOKENDEN, Simon Robert; QC 1996; a Recorder, since 1998; *b* 27 Sept. 1946; *s* of Spencer Crookenden and late Jean Phyllis (formerly Carter, *née* Dewing); *m* 1983, Sarah Anne Georgina Margaret Pragnell; one *s* two *d*. *Educ:* Winchester Coll.; Corpus Christi Coll., Cambridge (MA Mech. Scis). Management trainee, Westland Aircraft, 1968–69; various posts, incl. Brand Manager, Unilever, 1969–72; Brand Manager, Express Dairies, 1972–74; called to the Bar, Gray's Inn, 1975; in practice as barrister, 1975–; Asst Recorder, 1994–98. *Recreations:* ski-ing, rowing, sailing. *Address:* Essex Court Chambers, 24 Lincoln's Inn Fields, WC2A 3EG. *T:* (020) 7813 8000.

CROOKHAM, Ian; Chief Executive, Kingston upon Hull City Council, since 1995; *b* 7 Oct. 1952; *s* of George Edward Crookham and Jean Crookham; *m* 1977, Shirley Ann Green; four *s*. *Educ:* St Margaret's Sch., Liverpool (BA Hons). CPFA 1979. Graduate trainee, Liverpool CC, 1974–77; various finance posts, Gtr Manchester Council, 1977–86; Chief Accountant, Trafford MBC, 1986–88; Asst Dir of Finance, 1988, Sen. Asst Dir of Finance, 1988–94, Humberside CC; Dir of Finance, Hull CC, 1994–95. Clerk to: Hull and Goole Port HA, 1995–; Humber Bridge Bd, 1996–; Humberside Police Authy, 1997–. Co. Sec., Hull City Vision, 1995–. Chm. Governors, South Cave Sch., 1993–. *Recreations:* aviation, military history, reading. *Address:* Guildhall, Alfred Gelder Street, Hull HU1 2AA. *T:* (01482) 615000.

CROOKS, Air Marshal David Manson, CB 1985; OBE 1969; FRAeS; Chief of Defence Staff, New Zealand Armed Forces, 1986–87, retired; aviation and defence industry consultant, 1988–99; *b* 8 Dec. 1931; *s* of James and Gladys Meta Crooks; *m* 1954, Barbara Naismith McDougall; four *d*. *Educ:* Rangiora, NZ. Joined RNZAF, 1951; Head, NZ Defence Liaison Staff, Singapore, 1967–70; Commanding Officer: RNZAF Base: Ohakea, 1971–72; Wigram, 1973–74; RCDS, UK, 1974–75; AOC RNZAF Ops Gp, 1978–80; DCAS, 1980–83; CAS, RNZAF, 1983–86. *Recreations:* gardening, reading, sailing. *Address:* 13 Burrows Avenue, Karori, Wellington 5, New Zealand. *T:* (4) 4764588. *Club:* Wellington (Wellington, NZ).

CROOME, (John) Lewis, CMG 1957; *b* 10 June 1907; *s* of John and Caroline Croome; *m* 1st, 1931, Honoria Renée Minturn (*née* Scott; as Honor Croome, Editorial Staff of The Economist) (*d* 1960); four *s* one *d* (and one *s* decd); 2nd, 1961, Pamela Siola, *o d* of Lt-Col Tyrrel Hawker, Hurstbourne Priors, Hants; one *s*. *Educ:* Henry Thornton Sch., Clapham; London Sch. of Economics. Imperial Economic Cttee, 1931–39; Ministry of Food, 1939–48; Deputy (later Head), British Food Mission, Ottawa, 1942–46; HM Treasury (Central Economic Planning Staff), 1948–51; Min. of Food, 1951–54; UK Delegation to OEEC, Paris, 1954–57; Ministry of Agriculture, Fisheries and Food, 1957–58; Chief Overseas Relations Officer, UKAEA, 1958–72, retired. *Recreations:* painting, reading. *Address:* 8 The Holdens, Bosham, West Sussex PO18 8LN. *T:* (01243) 572292.

CROPPER, Hilary Mary, CBE 1999; Executive Chairman, FI Group, since 2000 (Chief Executive, 1985–2000); *b* 9 Jan. 1941; *d* of Arnold Trueman and Madeline Emily Trueman (*née* Sutton); *m* 1963, Peter John Cropper; one *s* two *d*. *Educ:* Univ. of Salford (BSc Hons Maths). Sen. management positions, ICL, 1970–85. Non-executive Director: TSB, 1987–90; London First, 1996–99; Barclays plc, 1998–; Barclays Bank plc, 1998–. Member: Financial Reporting Council, 1997–; New Deal Taskforce, 2000–. Non-exec. Member: POB, 1990–96; BOTB, 1992–96. External Advr, Civil Service Sen. Appts, 2000–. Gov., Univ. of Hertfordshire, 1995–2000. Freeman, City of London, 1987. CIMgt, FBCS, FRSA. *Address:* FI Group, Campus 300, Maylands Avenue, Hemel Hempstead, Herts HP2 7TQ. *T:* (01442) 233339.

CROPPER, James Anthony, FCA; Chairman, James Cropper PLC, since 1971; Lord-Lieutenant of Cumbria, since 1994 (Vice Lord-Lieutenant, 1991–94); *b* 22 Dec. 1938; *s* of Anthony Charles Cropper and Philippa Mary Gloria (*née* Clutterbuck); *m* 1967, Susan Rosemary, *y d* of Col F. J. N. Davis; one *s* one *d* (and one *s* decd). *Educ:* Eton; Magdalene Coll., Cambridge (BA). FCA 1966. James Cropper, 1966–, Dir, 1967–; Dir, East Lancashire Paper Group, 1982–84. Member: Lancs River Authority, 1968–74; NW Water Authority, 1973–80, 1983–89; Dir, NW Water Group, 1989–90. Dir, Cumbria Rural Enterprise Agency, 1986–; Mem., NW Business Leadership Team, 1991–98. Pres., British Paper and Bd Fedn, 1988–90. Chm., Frieda Scott Charitable Trust, 1981–94; Trustee, Abbot Hall Art Gall. and Mus., 1992– (Chm. Govs, 1983–88). Member (Indep.): S Westmorland RDC, 1967–74; S Lakeland DC, 1974–77. High Sheriff of Westmorland, 1971; DL Cumbria, 1985. KStJ 1997. *Recreations:* shooting, wind-surfing. *Address:* Tolson Hall, Kendal, Cumbria LA9 5SE. *T:* (01539) 722011. *Club:* Brooks's.

CROPPER, Peter John, CBE 1988; Special Adviser: to Chief Secretary to the Treasury, 1979–82; to Chancellor of the Exchequer, 1984–88; *b* 18 June 1927; *s* of late Walter Cecil Cropper and Kathleen Cropper; *m* 1965, Rosemary Winning; one *s*. *Educ:* Hitchin Grammar Sch.; Gonville and Caius Coll., Cambridge (MA). Served Royal Artillery, 1945–48. Conservative Research Dept, 1951–53, 1975–79, Dir, 1982–84. *Address:* 77 Hadlow Road, Tonbridge, Kent TN9 1QB. *Club:* Reform.

CROSBIE, Annette, OBE 1998; actress; *b* 12 Feb. 1934; *m* Michael Griffiths; one *s* one *d*. *Educ:* Bristol Old Vic Theatre Sch. *Stage* includes: Citizens' Theatre, Glasgow: A View from the Bridge; The Crucible; The Cherry Orchard; Bristol Old Vic: Romeo and Juliet; The Tempest; A Taste of Honey; Comedy Theatre: Tinker; A Singular Man; The Winslow Boy, New, 1970; Mr Bolfry, Aldwych; The Changeling, Royal Court; The Family Dance, Criterion, 1976; The Trojan War Will Not Take Place, NT, 1983; Curtains, Whitehall, 1988; I Thought I Heard a Rustling, Theatre Royal Stratford, 1991; A Delicate Balance, Haymarket, 1997; *television* includes: *series and serials:* The Six Wives of Henry VIII, 1970 (BAFTA Award for best actress); Edward VII, 1975 (BAFTA Award for best actress); Lillie, 1978; Paradise Postponed, 1986; Take Me Home, 1989; Summer's Lease, 1989; One Foot in the Grave, 1989–2000; Dr Finlay (Scottish TV Award for best actress), 1993; An Unsuitable Job for a Woman, 1997; *plays:* The Seagull; Waste, 1977; Richard III; Beyond the Pale, 1989; radio plays and serials; *films* include: The Slipper and the Rose (Eve. News British Film Award for best actress), 1975; Ordeal by Innocence; The Pope Must Die, 1990. Founding Mem., Greyhounds UK, 1998. *Address:* c/o ICM Ltd, Oxford House, 76 Oxford Street, W1N 0AX.

CROSBIE, Hon. John Carnell, PC (Canada) 1979; OC 1998; QC; Counsel, Patterson Palmer Hunt Murphy, Atlantic Canada lawyers; *b* 30 Jan. 1931; *s* of Chesley Arthur Crosbie and Jessie Carnell; *m* 1952, Jane Furneaux; two *s* one *d*. *Educ:* Bishop Field Coll., St John's, Nfld; St Andrew's Coll., Aurora, Ont.; Queen's Univ., Kingston, Ont. (Pol. Sc. and Econs); Dalhousie Univ., Halifax, NS (Law); LSE, London, Eng. Joined Newfoundland Law Soc. and Newfoundland Bar; entered law practice, St John's, 1957; Mem. City Council, St John's, 1965; Dep. Mayor, 1966; Minister of Municipal Affairs and Housing, Province of Newfoundland, (Lib. Admin), July 1966; MHA, Prov. of Newfoundland, Sept. 1966; Minister of Health, 1967; resigned from Govt, 1968; re-elected Member for St John's West (Progressive Conservative), Provincial election, 1971; Minister of Finance, Pres. of Treasury Bd and Minister of Econ. Devel, 1972–74; Minister of Fisheries, Min. for Intergovtl Affairs and Govt House Leader, 1974–75; Minister of Mines and Energy and Minister for Intergovtl Affairs, 1975–76; resigned from Newfoundland Govt, Sept. 1976; elected to House of Commons, Oct. 1976; MP (PC) St John's West, Newfoundland, 1976–93; Chm. of Progressive Conservative Caucus Cttee on Energy, 1977; PC parly critic for Industry, Trade and Commerce, 1977–79; Minister of Finance, 1979–80; Party Finance Critic, 1980; Party External Affairs Critic, 1981–83; Minister of Justice and Attorney General, 1984–86; Minister of Transport, 1986–88; Minister for International Trade, 1988–91; Minister for Fisheries and Oceans and for Atlantic Canada Opportunities Agency, 1991–93. Director: Atlantic Inst. of Market Studies; Bell Canada International Inc. and other Canadian cos. Hon. Consul of Mexico in Newfoundland and Labrador, 1996–. Chancellor, Meml Univ. of Newfoundland, 1994–. *Publication:* No Holds Barred (memoirs), 1997. *Address:* PO Box 23119, St John's, NF A1B 4J9, Canada; (office) 235 Water Street, St John's, NF A1C 5L3, Canada.

CROSBY, James Robert; Group Chief Executive, HBOS plc, since 2001; *b* 14 March 1956; *m*; four *c*. *Educ:* Lancaster Royal Grammar Sch.; Brasenose Coll., Oxford (BA 1977). FFA 1980. With Scottish Amicable, 1977–94: posts incl. Investment Dir, 1983, and Gen. Manager; Man. Dir, Halifax Life, Halifax Bldg Soc., 1994–96; Dir, Financial Services and Insurance, 1996–99, Chief Exec., 1999–2001, Halifax plc. *Address:* HBOS plc, PO Box 5, The Mound, Edinburgh EH1 1YZ.

CROSFIELD, Rev. Canon (George) Philip (Chorley), OBE 1990; Provost of St Mary's Cathedral, Edinburgh, 1970–90, retired, Hon. Canon, 1991; *b* 9 Sept. 1924; *s* of James Chorley Crosfield and Marjorie Louise Crosfield; *m* 1956, Susan Mary Jullion (*née* Martin); one *s* two *d*. *Educ:* George Watson's Coll., Edinburgh; Selwyn Coll., Cambridge (BA 1950; MA 1955). Royal Artillery, 1942–46 (Captain). Priest, 1952; Asst Curate: St David's, Pilton, Edinburgh, 1951–53; St Andrew's, St Andrews, 1953–55; Rector, St Cuthbert's, Hawick, 1955–60; Chaplain, Gordonstoun School, 1960–68; Canon and Vice Provost, St Mary's Cathedral, Edinburgh, 1968–70. *Recreations:* walking, reading, carpentry. *Address:* 21 Biggar Road, Silverburn, Penicuik EH26 9LQ. *T:* (01968) 676607.

CROSLAND, Susan Barnes; writer; *b* Baltimore, Maryland; *y c* of Susan Owens and Mark Skinner Watson; *m* 1st, Patrick Skene Catling (marr. diss.); two *d*; 2nd, Rt Hon. (Charles) Anthony (Raven) Crosland, PC, MP (*d* 1977). Journalism: Sunday Express, 1960–64; freelance, 1964–; profile-writer and columnist, Sunday Times and various jls. Trustee, Nat. Portrait Gallery, 1978–92. *Publications:* Behind the Image, 1974; Tony Crosland, 1982; Looking Out, Looking In, 1987; *novels:* Ruling Passions, 1989; Dangerous Games, 1991; The Magnates, 1994; The Prime Minister's Wife, 2001. *Recreation:* freedom. *Address:* 16 Stanford Court, 45 Cornwall Gardens, SW7 4AB. *Club:* Academy.

CROSS, family name of **Viscount Cross**.

CROSS, 3rd Viscount *cr* 1886; **Assheton Henry Cross;** late Lieut Scots Guards; *b* 7 May 1920; *e s* of 2nd Viscount and Maud Evelyn (who *m* 2nd, 1944, Guy Hope Coldwell (*d* 1948), Stoke Lodge, Ludlow, Salop; she *d* 1976), *d* of late Maj.-Gen. Inigo Jones, CVO, CB, Kelston Park, Bath; *S* father, 1932; *m* 1952, Patricia Mary (marr. diss., 1957; she *m* 1960, Comdr G. H. H. Culme-Seymour), *e d* of E. P. Hewetson, JP, The Craig, Windermere, Westmorland; two *d*; *m* 1972, Mrs Victoria Webb (marr. diss. 1977; she *d* 1997); *m* 1983, Mrs Patricia J. Rossiter (marr. diss. 1987). *Educ:* Shrewsbury; Magdalene Coll., Cambridge. *Heir:* none. *Club:* Cavalry and Guards.

CROSS, Alistair Robert Sinclair B.; *see* Bassett Cross.

CROSS, Prof. Anthony Glenn, FBA 1989; Professor of Slavonic Studies, since 1985, and Fellow of Fitzwilliam College, since 1986, Cambridge University; *b* 21 Oct. 1936; *s* of Walter Sidney Cross and Ada Cross; *m* 1960, Margaret (*née* Elson); two *d*. *Educ:* High Pavement Sch., Nottingham; Trinity Hall, Cambridge (BA 1960, MA 1964, PhD 1966); Harvard Univ. (AM 1961); LittD East Anglia 1981; LittD Cambridge 1997. Frank Knox Fellow, Harvard Univ., 1960–61; Univ. of East Anglia: Lectr in Russian, 1964–69; Sen. Lectr in Russian, 1969–72; Reader, 1972–81; Roberts Prof. of Russian, Univ. of Leeds, 1981–85. Vis. Fellow: Univ. of Illinois, 1969–70; All Souls Coll., Oxford, 1977–78. Pres., British Univs Assoc. of Slavists, 1982–84; Chm., British Academic Cttee for Liaison with Soviet Archives, 1983–95. Mem., Russian Acad. of Humanities, 1996. Reviews Editor, Jl of European Studies, 1971–; Editor, Study Group on Eighteenth-Century Russia Newsletter, 1973–. Nove Prize, 1997; Antsiferov Prize, St Petersburg, 1998. *Publications:* N. M. Karamzin, 1971; Russia Under Western Eyes 1517–1825, 1971; (ed) Russian Literature in the Age of Catherine the Great, 1976; Anglo-Russian Relations in the Eighteenth Century, 1977; (ed) Great Britain and Russia in the Eighteenth Century, 1979; By the Banks of the Thames, 1980; (ed) Russia and the West in the Eighteenth Century, 1981; The Tale of the Russian Daughter and her Suffocated Lover, 1982; (ed jtly) Eighteenth Century Russian Literature, Culture and Thought: a bibliography, 1984; The Russian Theme in English Literature, 1985; (ed jtly) Russia and the World of the Eighteenth Century, 1988; (ed) An English Lady at the Court of Catherine the Great, 1989; Anglophilia on the Throne: the British and the Russians in the age of Catherine II, 1992; (ed) Engraved in the Memory: James Walker, engraver to Catherine the Great and his Russian anecdotes, 1993; Anglo-Russica: aspects of Anglo-Russian cultural relations in the eighteenth and early nineteenth centuries, 1993; (ed jtly) Literature, Lives and Legality in Catherine's Russia, 1994; By the Banks of the Neva: chapters from the lives of the British in eighteenth-century Russia, 1996; (ed) Russia in the Reign of Peter the Great: old and new perspectives, 1998; (ed jtly) Britain and Russia in the Age of Peter the Great: historical documents, 1998; Peter the Great through British Eyes: perceptions and representations of the tsar since 1698, 2000; Catherine the Great and the British, 2001. *Recreations:* book collecting, cricket watching. *Address:* Department of Slavonic Studies, University of Cambridge, Sidgwick Avenue, Cambridge CB3 9DA. *T:* (01223) 335007; *e-mail:* agc@cam.ac.uk.

CROSS, Clifford Thomas, CB 1977; Commissioner, Customs and Excise, 1970–79; *b* 1 April 1920; *o s* of late Arthur and Helena Cross; *m* 1942, Ida Adelaide Barker; one *s* two *d*. *Educ:* Latymer Upper Sch., Hammersmith; Univ. of London (LLB). Joined Inland Revenue, 1939; Customs and Excise, 1946; Asst Sec. 1959; Comr 1970. *Recreations:* gardening, crosswords, watching television, etc. *Address:* Longacre, 101 Histon Road, Cottenham, Cambs CB4 8UQ. *T:* (01954) 250757.

CROSS, Dr Dolores Evelyn; President, Chicago State University, 1990–98; *b* 29 Aug. 1938; *d* of Ozie Johnson Tucker and Charles Tucker; *m* 1956, Thomas Edwin Cross; one *s* one *d*. *Educ:* Seton Hall Univ. (BS 1963); Hofstra Univ. (MS 1968); Univ. of Michigan (PhD 1971). Teaching posts, NY and Michigan, 1961–71; Asst Prof. in Educn, Northwestern Univ., 1971–74; Associate Prof. in Educn, Claremont Graduate Sch., 1974–78; Vice-Chancellor for student affairs and special programs, City Univ., NY, and Prof. in Educn, Brooklyn Coll., 1978–81; Pres., NY State Higher Educn Services Corp., 1981–88; Associate Provost and Associate Vice-Pres. for Academic Affairs, Univ. of Minnesota, 1988–90. Hon. LLD: Marymount Manhattan, 1984; Skidmore Coll., 1988. NAACP Muriel Silverberg Award, NY, 1987; John Jay Award, NYC Commn of Indep. Colls and Univs, 1989. *Publications:* Influence of Individual Difference on Theories of

Instruction, 1974; Teaching in a Multi-Cultural Society, 1977. *Recreations:* jogging, marathon running. *Address:* c/o Chicago State University, 95th Street at King Drive Avenue, Chicago, IL 60628, USA. *T:* (312) 9952400.

CROSS, Prof. George Alan Martin, FRS 1984; André and Bella Meyer Professor of Molecular Parasitology, since 1982, and Dean of Graduate and Postgraduate Studies, 1995–99, Rockefeller University, New York; *b* 27 Sept. 1942; *s* of George Bernard and Beatrice Mary Cross; *m*; one *d*. *Educ:* Cheadle Hulme Sch.; Downing Coll., Univ. of Cambridge (BA, PhD). ICI Postdoctoral Fellow, Biochemistry, Cambridge, 1967–69; Research Fellow, Fitzwilliam Coll., Cambridge, 1967–70; Scientist, MRC Biochemical Parasitology Unit, Molteno Inst., Cambridge, 1969–77; Head, Dept of Immunochemistry, Wellcome Research Laboratories, 1977–82. Fleming Lectr, Soc. for General Microbiology, 1978; Leeuwenhoek Lectr, Royal Soc., 1998. Chalmers Medal, Royal Soc. for Tropical Medicine and Hygiene, 1983; (jtly) Paul Ehrlich and Ludwig Darmstaedter Prize, 1984. *Publications:* in journals of parasitology, biochemistry, microbiology and molecular biology. *Recreations:* sailing, tennis, building projects, observing people. *Address:* Rockefeller University, 1230 York Avenue, New York, NY 10021, USA. *T:* (212) 3277571, *Fax:* (212) 3277845; *e-mail:* gamc@rockvax.rockefeller.edu.

CROSS, Gillian Clare, DPhil; author; *b* 1945; *d* of James Eric Arnold and Joan Emma (*née* Manton); *m* 1967, Martin Francis Cross; two *s* two *d*. *Educ:* North London Collegiate Sch. for Girls; Somerville Coll., Oxford (MA); Univ. of Sussex (DPhil). Mem., Adv. Council on Libraries, 1995–2000. Mem., Soc. of Authors. Mem., Octavian Droobers. *Publications:* The Runaway, 1979; The Iron Way, 1979; Revolt at Ratcliffe's Rags, 1980; Save Our School, 1981; A Whisper of Lace, 1981; The Dark Behind the Curtain, 1982; The Demon Headmaster, 1982; Born of the Sun, 1983; The Mintyglo Kid, 1983; On the Edge, 1984; The Prime Minister's Brain, 1985; Chartbreak, 1986 (USA as Chartbreaker, 1987); Swimathon, 1986; Roscoe's Leap, 1987; A Map of Nowhere, 1988; Rescuing Gloria, 1989; Wolf, 1990 (Carnegie Medal, LA, 1990); The Monster from Underground, 1990; Twin and Super-Twin, 1990; Gobbo The Great, 1991; Rent-A-Genius, 1991; The Great Elephant Chase, 1992 (Smarties Book Prize and Whitbread Children's Novel Award, 1992); Beware Olga!, 1993; Furry Maccaloo, 1993; The Tree House, 1993; Hunky Parker is Watching You, 1994; What will Emily Do?, 1994; New World, 1994; The Crazy Shoe Shuffle, 1995; Posh Watson, 1995; The Roman Beanfeast, 1996; Pictures in the Dark, 1996; The Demon Headmaster Strikes Again, 1996; The Demon Headmaster Takes Over, 1997; The Goose Girl, 1998; Tightrope, 1999; Calling a Dead Man, 2001. *Recreations:* playing the piano, orienteering. *Address:* c/o Oxford Children's Books, Oxford University Press, Great Clarendon Street, Oxford OX2 6DP.

CROSS, Hannah Margaret, (Mrs E. G. Wright); barrister-at-law; *b* 25 April 1908; *o d* of late F. J. K. Cross and Eleanor Mary Cross (*née* Phillimore); *m* 1936, Edmund Gordon Wright, Barrister-at-Law (*d* 1971); one *s* one *d*. *Educ:* Downe House Sch.; St Hilda's Coll., Oxford. BA 1929. Called to Bar, Lincoln's Inn, 1931; first woman Mem. of Gen. Council of Bar, 1938–45; Civil Defence, 1939–45. *Address:* The Quay House, Sidlesham, near Chichester, West Sussex PO20 7LX. *T:* (01243) 641258.

CROSS, James Richard, (Jasper), CMG 1971; Under-Secretary, Principal Establishment Officer, Department of Energy, 1970–80; *b* 29 Sept. 1921; *s* of J. P. Cross and Dinah Cross (*née* Hodgins); *m* 1945, Barbara Dagg; one *d*. *Educ:* King's Hosp., Dublin; Trin. Coll., Dublin. Scholar, First Cl. Moderatorship Economics and Polit. Science. RE (Lieut). Asst Principal, Bd of Trade, 1947; Private Sec. to Parly Sec., 1947–49; Principal, 1950; Trade Commissioner: New Delhi, 1953–56; Halifax, 1957–60; Winnipeg, 1960–62; Asst Sec., 1962; Sen. Trade Comr, Kuala Lumpur, 1962–66; Bd of Trade, 1966–67; Under Sec., 1968; Sen. British Trade Comr, Montreal, 1968–70 (kidnapped by terrorists and held for 59 days, Oct.–Dec. 1970); Under-Sec., Export Planning and Develt Div., DTI, 1971–73; Coal Div., DTI, later Dept of Energy, 1973–78. *Recreations:* theatre, bridge. *Address:* 61 Tudor Close, Seaford, East Sussex BN25 2LY.

CROSS, Air Chief Marshal Sir Kenneth (Brian Boyd), KCB 1959 (CB 1954); CBE 1945; DSO 1943; DFC 1940; *b* 4 Oct. 1911; *s* of Pembroke H. C. Cross and Mrs Jean Cross; *m* 1945, Brenda Megan (*d* 1991), *d* of Wing-Comdr F. J. B. Powell; two *s* one *d*. *Educ:* Kingswood Sch., Bath. Pilot Officer, RAF, 1930; Flying Badge, 1931; 25 Fighter Sqdn, 1931; Flying Officer, 1932; Flying Instructor, No 5 FTS Sealand and Cambridge Univ. Air Sqdn, 1934; Flt Lt 1935; Sqdn Ldr 1938; commanded No 46 Fighter Sqdn UK, Norway, 1939–40; Wing Comdr 1940; posted Middle East, 1941; Actg Group Capt. 1941; Actg Air Commodore, 1943; Director Overseas Operations, Air Ministry, 1944; Imperial Defence Coll., 1946; reverted Group Capt., 1946; Group Capt. Operations HQ BAFO Germany, 1947; OC Eastern Sector Fighter Command, 1949; Dir of Weapons, Air Ministry, 1952; subs. Air Cdre, 1953; Dir of Ops, Air Defence, 1954–Dec. 1955; Air Vice-Marshal, 1956; AOC No 3 (Bomber) Group, 1956–59; Air Marshal, 1961; AOC-in-C, Bomber Comd, 1959–63; AOC-in-C, Transport Comd, 1963–66; Air Chief Marshal, 1967; retd, 1967. Director: Suffolk Branch, 1968, London Branch, 1974, British Red Cross Soc. Norwegian War Cross, 1941; USA Legion of Merit, 1944; French Legion of Honour, 1944; French Croix de Guerre, 1944; Dutch Order of Orange Nassau, 1945. *Publication:* Straight and Level, 1993. *Recreations:* Rugby football and golf (colours RAF). *Address:* c/o Gorseway Retirement Community, 354 Seafront, Hayling Island, Hants PO11 0BA. *Club:* Royal Air Force.

CROSS, Dame Margaret Natalie; *see* Smith, Dame Maggie.

CROSS, Maj.-Gen. Timothy, CBE 2000; Director General, Defence Logistic Support, since 2000; *b* 19 April 1951; *s* of Sidney George and Patricia Mary Cross; *m* 1972, Christine Mary Pelly; two *s* one *d*. *Educ:* Welbeck; RMA, Sandhurst; RMCS Shrivenham (BSc Hons, MSc); ato. NI, 1978; Adjt 1 Ordnance Bn, 1979–80; UN, Cyprus, 1981; Army Staff Coll., 1982–83 (psc); British Liaison Bureaux, Milan, 1984–85; Co. Comdr, 1 Ordnance Bn, 1986–87; Directing Staff, Army Staff Coll., 1988–90; CO, 1 Ordnance Bn, 1990–92; Comdr, Logistic Support 3 (UK) Div., 1992–96; HCSC, 1995; Dir, Materiel Support (Army), 1996–97; Comdr, 101 Logistic Bde, 1998–2000; rcds 2000. Lay Reader, C of E. *Recreations:* golf, walking, reading. *Address:* Defence Logistic Organisation, Monxton Road, Andover, Hants SP11 8HT.

CROSSE, Gordon; composer; *b* 1 Dec. 1937; *s* of Percy and Marie Crosse; *m* 1965, Elizabeth Bunch. *Educ:* Cheadle Hulme Sch.; St Edmund Hall, Oxford; Accad. di S Cecilia, Rome. Music Fellow, Essex Univ., 1969–74; Composer in residence, King's Coll., Cambridge, 1974–76; Vis. Lectr, Univ. of Calif at Santa Barbara, 1977–78. Hon. RAM, 1980. *Operas:* Purgatory, 1966; The Grace of Todd, 1967; The Story of Vasco, 1970; Potter Thompson, 1973; *ballets:* Playground, 1979; Wildboy, 1981; *other compositions:* Concerto da Camera, 1962; Meet My Folks, 1963; "Symphonies", 1964; Second Violin Concerto, 1970; Memories of Morning: Night, 1972; Ariadne, 1973; Symphony 2, 1975; Wildboy (clarinet concerto), Play Ground, 1977; Dreamsongs, 1978; Cello Concerto, 1979; String Quartet, 1980; Dreamcanon (chorus), 1981; Trio for piano, violin and cello, 1986; Trumpet Concerto, 1986; Sea Psalms, 1990; much other orchestral, vocal and chamber music. *Address:* Brant's Cottage, Blackheath, Wenhaston, Halesworth, Suffolk IP19 9EX.

CROSSETT, Robert Nelson, (Tom), DPhil; Chairman, Southern Regional Environmental Protection Advisory Committee, Environment Agency, since 1996; *b* 27 May 1938; *s* of Robert Crossett and Mary Nelson; *m* 1966, Susan Marjorie Legg; two *s*. *Educ:* British School, Hamburg; Campbell College, Belfast; Queen's Univ., Belfast (BSc, BAgr); Lincoln College, Oxford (DPhil); Univ. of East Anglia. Group Leader Environmental Studies, Aust. Atomic Energy Commn, 1966; Sen. Sci. Officer, ARC Letcombe Lab., 1969; Develt Officer (Crops), Scottish Agricl. Develt Council, 1972; PSO, Dept of Agric. and Fisheries for Scotland, 1975; Ministry of Agriculture, Fisheries and Food: Sci. Liaison Officer (Horticulture and Soils), 1978; Head, Food Sci. Div., 1984; Chief Scientist (Fisheries and Food), 1985–89; Head of Envmtl Policy, 1989–90, Envmt Dir, 1990–91, National Power; Sec. Gen., Nat. Soc. for Clean Air and Envmtl Protection, 1992–96; Dir-Gen., Internat. Union of Air Pollution Prevention Assocs, 1996–98. Consultant, SE Inst. of Public Health, 1998–. Member: NERC, 1985–89; AFRC, 1985–89; UK Delgn, Tripartite Meetings on Food and Drugs, 1985–88; Cttee on Med. Aspects of Food Policy, 1985–89; Adv. Gp to Sec. of State for Envmt on Eco-Management and Audit, 1994–96; UK Round Table on Sustainable Develt, 1995–97. Vis. Fellow, Sci. Policy Res. Unit, Univ. of Sussex, 1997–; Sen. Vis. Fellow, Sch. of Health and Life Scis, KCL. *Publications:* papers in plant physiology, marine biology, food science and envmtl management. *Recreations:* walking, gardening, orienteering, boats. *Address:* Environment Agency, Guildborne House, Chatsworth Road, Worthing, W Sussex BN11 1LD.

CROSSLAND, Anthony, FRCO; Organist and Master of the Choristers, Wells Cathedral, 1971–96; *b* 4 Aug. 1931; *s* of Ernest Thomas and Frances Elizabeth Crossland; *m* 1960, Barbara Helen Pullar-Strecker; one *s* two *d*. *Educ:* Christ Church, Oxford. MA, BMus (Oxon), FRCO (CHM), ARCM. Asst Organist: Christ Church Cathedral, Oxford, 1957–61; Wells Cathedral, 1961–71. Conductor: Wells Cathedral Oratorio Soc., 1966–96; Wells Sinfonietta, 1985–96; Organs Advr to dio. of Bath and Wells, 1971–96. Pres., Cathedral Organists' Assoc., 1983–85. DMus Lambeth, 1994. *Recreations:* reading, photography, cooking. *Address:* Barton End, 10b Newtown, Bradford-on-Avon, Wilts BA15 1NE. *T:* (01225) 864496.

CROSSLAND, Sir Bernard, Kt 1990; CBE 1980; MSc (London); PhD (Bristol); DSc (Nottingham); FRS 1979; FREng; FIAE; MRIA; Emeritus Professor, The Queen's University, Belfast, since 1984 (Professor and Head of Department of Mechanical and Industrial Engineering, 1959–82, Research Professor, 1982–84; Dean, 1964–67; Pro-Vice-Chancellor, 1978–82); *b* 20 Oct. 1923; *s* of R. F. Crossland and K. M. Rudduck; *m* 1946, Audrey Elliott Birks; two *d*. *Educ:* Simon Langton's, Canterbury. Apprentice, Rolls Royce Ltd, 1940–41; Nottingham Univ., 1941–43; Technical Asst, Rolls Royce, 1943–45; Asst Lectr, Lectr and then Senior Lectr in Mechanical Engineering, Univ. of Bristol, 1946–59. Member: AFRC, 1981–87; Engrg Council, 1983–88; Chairman: Bd for Engineers' Registration, 1983–86; Youth Careers Guidance Cttee, NI, 1975–79, 1979–81; NI Manpower Council, 1981–86; Adv. Bd for Postgrad. Awards, NI Dept of Educn, 1982–95; Member: NI Training Council, 1964–76, 1977–81; NI Economic Council, 1981–85; NI Industrial Develt Bd, 1982–87. Dir, Gilbert Associates (Europe) Ltd, 1991–94. Assessor, King's Cross Fire Investigation, 1988; Chm., Public Hearing into Bilsthorpe Colliery Accident, 1994; Expert Witness for HSE in prosecution arising from Port of Ramsgate walkway disaster, 1997. Mem. Council and a Vice-Pres., Royal Soc., 1984–86; Mem. Council, Fellowship of Engrg, 1985–88; Pres., Section 6, British Assoc., 1987; Institution of Mechanical Engineers: Chm., Engineering Sciences Div., 1980–84; Vice-Pres., 1983–84; Dep. Pres., 1984–86; Pres., 1986–87; Past Pres., 1987–91; Leonardo da Vinci Lectr, 1970; George Stephenson Lectr, 1989; Thomas Lowe Gray Lectr, 1999; George Stephenson and Thomas Hawksley Medals; Hon. Fellow, 1997; James Watt Internat. Medal, 1999. Lectures: Richard Weck, Welding Inst., 1992; Seamus Timoney, NUI, 1993; McLaughlin, Instn of Engrs of Ireland, 1998. Trustee, Mackie Foundn, 1983–94. Freeman, City of London, 1987; Liveryman, Worshipful Co. of Engrs, 1988. FREng (FEng 1979); Founder FIAE 1998. Hon. MASME 1987; Hon. FWeldI 1990 (Pres., 1995–98); Hon. FIEI 1993; Hon. FIStructE 2001. Hon. Fellow, Univ. of Luton, 1994. Hon. DSc: NUI, 1984; Dublin, 1985; Edinburgh, 1987; QUB 1988; Aston, 1988; Cranfield Inst. of Technology, 1989; Hon. DEng: Bristol, 1992; Limerick, 1993; Liverpool, 1993. Kelvin Medal, ICE, 1992. *Publications:* An Introduction to the Mechanics of Machines, 1964; Explosive Welding and its Application, 1982; various papers on fatigue of metals and effect of very high fluid pressures on properties of materials; strength of thick-walled vessels, explosive welding, friction welding, design and history of engineering, engineering disasters. *Recreation:* walking. *Address:* The Queen's University, Belfast BT7 1NN. *T:* (028) 9038 0860; 16 Malone Court, Belfast BT9 6PA. *T:* (028) 9066 7495. *Club:* Athenæum.

CROSSLAND, Prof. Ronald Arthur, FSA 1982; Professor of Greek, University of Sheffield, 1958–82, now Emeritus (Dean, Faculty of Arts, 1973–75); *b* 31 Aug. 1920; *s* of late Ralph Crossland, BSc, and late Ethel Crossland (*née* Scattergood). *Educ:* Stanley Road Elementary Sch., Nottingham; Nottingham High Sch.; King's Coll., Cambridge. Major Scholar in Classics, King's Coll., Cambridge, 1939–41 and 1945–46. National Service in Royal Artillery, 1941–45. Henry Fellow, Berkeley Coll., Yale Univ., 1946–47; Instructor in Classics, Yale Univ., 1947–48; Senior Student of Treasury Cttee for Studentships in Foreign Languages and Cultures (for research in Hittite Philology and Linguistics), 1948–51; Hon. Lectr in Ancient History, University of Birmingham, 1950–51; Lecturer in Ancient History, King's Coll., University of Durham, Newcastle upon Tyne, 1951–58. Harris Fellow of King's Coll., Cambridge, 1952–56. Vis. Prof., Univ. Texas, 1962; Collitz Vis. Prof., Univ. Michigan, 1967; Vis. Fellow: Victoria Univ. of Wellington, NZ, 1979; German Democratic Republic Acad. of Scis, 1981. Pres., South Shields Archaeological and Historical Soc., 1976–77. *Publications:* Bronze Age Migrations in the Aegean (with A. Birchall), 1973; Teaching Classical Studies, 1976; chapters on: Immigrants from the North, in Cambridge Ancient History, rev. edn, 1967; Linguistic Problems of the Balkan Area, in Cambridge Ancient History, rev. edn, 1982; Early Greek Migrations, in Civilization of the Ancient Mediterranean (ed M. Grant), 1987; articles in Trans Philological Soc., Archivum Linguisticum, Studia Balcanica, Past and Present, Antiquity. *Recreations:* music, travel, pastime with good company. *Address:* 59 Sherlock Close, Cambridge CB3 0HP. *T:* (01223) 358085; (enquiries) (0114) 222 2555.

CROSSLEY, family name of **Baron Somerleyton**.

CROSSLEY, Geoffrey Allan, CMG 1974; HM Diplomatic Service, retired; Director, External Relations, Continuing Education, European Institute of Business Administration, INSEAD, Fontainebleau, 1980–84; *b* 11 Nov. 1920; *s* of Thomas Crossley and Winifred Mary Crossley (*née* Ellis); *m* 1945, Aline Louise Farcy; two *s* one *d*. *Educ:* Penistone; abroad; Gonville and Caius Coll., Cambridge (Scholar). Served War of 1939–45: Min. of Supply, 1941–; Foreign Office, 1942–; in Algeria and France. Foreign Service, 1945–: Second Sec., Paris, 1945–48; FO, 1948–49; Alternate UK Deleg. on UN Balkans

Commn, Greece, 1949–52; Dep. Regional Inf. Officer with Commissioner-Gen. for SE Asia, Singapore, 1952–55; FO, 1955–57; Consulate-Gen., Frankfurt, for Saar Transition from France to Germany, 1957–59; Political Office, NE Command, Cyprus (later in charge), 1959–61; Head of Chancery, Berne, 1961–65; on secondment to Min. of Overseas Development, as Head of W and N African Dept, 1965–67; Dep. High Comr, Lusaka, 1967–69; Counsellor, Oslo, 1969–73; Ambassador to Colombia, 1973–77; Envoy to the Holy See, 1978–80. Founder Mem., Cambridge Soc. Mem., French Inst. of Internat. Relations. *Recreations:* various. *Address:* 22 Rue Emeriau, 75015 Paris, France.

CROSSLEY, Sir Julian (Charles), 5th Bt *cr* 1909, of Glenfield, Dunham Massey, co. Chester; production manager, screen writer and consultant, film industry; *b* 11 Dec. 1964; *yr s* of Sir Christopher John Crossley, 3rd Bt and of his 1st wife, Carolyne Louise (*née* Sykes, now Murray); *S* brother, 2000. *Educ:* Marymount Palos Verdes Coll. (AA Pre-Business); Northern Arizona Univ. (BA Business Mgt). *Recreations:* golf, tennis, snow skiing, scuba diving. *Heir: cousin* Sloan Nicholas Crossley, *b* 20 March 1958. *Address:* 2829 Ocean Park Boulevard #4, Santa Monica, CA 90405, USA. *T:* (310) 392 8873.

CROSSLEY, Paul Christopher Richard, CBE 1993; concert pianist; Artistic Director, London Sinfonietta, 1988–94; *b* 17 May 1944; *s* of late Frank Crossley and Myra Crossley (*née* Barrowcliffe). *Educ:* Silcoates Sch., Wakefield; Mansfield Coll., Oxford (BA, MA; Hon. Fellow, 1992). International concert pianist; recitals and concerts with all major orchestras; numerous recordings and films for TV. *Recreations:* Mah-Jongg, reading. *Address:* c/o Connaught Artists Management Ltd, 2 Molasses Row, Plantation Wharf, SW11 3UX. *T:* (020) 7738 0017.

CROSSLEY, Maj.-Gen. Ralph John, CB 1987; CBE 1981; *b* 11 Oct. 1933; *s* of Edward Crossley and Eva Mary Crossley (*née* Farnworth); *m* 1957, Marion Hilary Crossley (*née* Bacon); one *s* one *d*. *Educ:* Quainton Sch., Harrow; Felsted School. Commnd 1952 (Nat. Service); Air Observation Post Pilots course, 1953; Regimental Duty: Canal Zone,1954–56; BAOR, 1956–59; Instructor in Gunnery, Larkhill, 1959–63; Technical Staff Course, 1963–65; Regtl Duty, BAOR, 1965–67, 1969–71; Weapons Staff, UK, 1967–69; Gen. Staff, UK, 1971–72; Instructor, RMCS, 1972–74; CO, 94 Locating Regt, 1974–77; Project Manager, 155 Systems, 1977–81; Dep. Comdt, RMCS, 1981–84; Dir Gen. of Weapons (Army), 1984–86; retired 1986. Defence Advr, Avon Rubber, 1987–91. Chairman: Salisbury HA, 1990–93; Salisbury Healthcare NHS Trust, 1994–97. Vice Pres., Hosp. Savings Assoc., 1995–. *Recreations:* golf, walking, gardening.

CROSSLEY-HOLLAND, Kevin John William, FRSL; author; *b* 7 Feb. 1941; *s* of late Prof. Peter Charles Crossley-Holland and of Joan Mary Crossley-Holland (*née* Cowper), MBE; *m* 1st, 1963, Caroline Fendall, *er d* of Prof. L. M. Thompson; two *s*; 2nd, 1972, Ruth, *er d* of John Marris; 3rd, 1982, Gillian Paula, *er d* of Peter Cook; two *d*; 4th, 1999, Linda Marie, *d* of Abner Jones. *Educ:* Bryanston Sch.; St Edmund Hall, Oxford (MA Hons; Hon. Fellow, 2001). FRSL 1998. Editor, Macmillan & Co., 1962–69; Gregory Fellow in Poetry, Univ. of Leeds, 1969–71; Talks Producer, BBC, 1972; Editl Dir, Victor Gollancz, 1972–77; Lectr in English: Tufts-in-London Program, 1967–78; Regensburg Univ., 1978–80; Arts Council Fellow in Writing, Winchester Sch. of Art, 1983 and 1984; Vis. Prof. of English and Fulbright Scholar, St Olaf Coll., Minnesota, 1987–90; Prof. and Endowed Chair in Humanities and Fine Arts, Univ. of St Thomas, Minnesota, 1991–95; Vis. Lectr for British Council in Germany, Iceland, India, Malawi, Yugoslavia, Slovakia. Editl Consultant, Boydell & Brewer, 1983–90. Chm., Literature Panel, Eastern Arts Assoc., 1986–89; Trustee, Wingfield Coll., 1989–99 (Chm., Friends, 1989–91). Dir, American Composers Forum, 1993–97. Chm., Poetry-next-the-Sea, 1999–. Contribs to radio (incl. drama), TV (incl. educl series), and musical works. *Publications: poetry:* The Rain-Giver, 1972; The Dream-House, 1976; Time's Oriel, 1983; Waterslain, 1986; The Painting-Room, 1988; New and Selected Poems, 1991; The Language of Yes, 1996; Poems from East Anglia, 1997; Selected Poems, 2001; *for children:* Havelok the Dane, 1964; King Horn, 1965; The Green Children, 1966 (Arts Council Award); The Callow Pit Coffer, 1968; (with Jill Paton Walsh) Wordhoard, 1969; Storm and Other Old English Riddles, 1970; The Pedlar of Swaffham, 1971; The Sea Stranger, 1973; The Fire-Brother, 1974; Green Blades Rising, 1975; The Earth-Father, 1976; The Wildman, 1976; The Dead Moon, 1982; Beowulf, 1982; (with Gwyn Thomas) The Mabinogion, 1984; Axe-Age, Wolf-Age, 1985; Storm, 1985 (Carnegie Medal); (with Susanne Lugert) The Fox and the Cat, 1985; British Folk Tales, 1987; Wulf, 1988; (with Gwyn Thomas) The Quest for Olwen, 1988; Piper and Pooka, 1988; Small Tooth Dog, 1988; Boo!, 1988; Dathera Dad, 1989; (with Ian Penney) Under the Sun and Over the Moon, 1989; Sleeping Nanna, 1989; Sea Tongue, 1991; Tales from Europe, 1991; Long Tom and The Dead Hand, 1992; (with Gwyn Thomas) Taliesin, 1992; The Labours of Herakles, 1993; Norse Myths, 1993; The Green Children, 1994; The Dark Horseman, 1995; The Old Stories, 1997; Short!, 1998; The King Who Was and Will Be, 1998; Enchantment, 2000; The Seeing Stone, 2000; At the Crossing-Places, 2001; The Magic Lands, 2001; *play:* (with Ivan Cutting) The Wuffings, 1999; *travel:* Pieces of Land, 1972; *mythology:* The Norse Myths, 1980; *history:* (with Andrew Rafferty) The Stones Remain, 1989; *translations from Old English:* (with Bruce Mitchell) The Battle of Maldon, 1965; (with Bruce Mitchell) Beowulf, 1968; The Exeter Book Riddles, 1978; The Illustrated Beowulf, 1987; The Anglo-Saxon Elegies, 1988; *edited:* Running to Paradise, 1967; Winter's Tales for Children 3, 1967; Winter's Tales 14, 1968; (with Patricia Beer) New Poetry 2, 1976; The Faber Book of Northern Legends, 1977; The Faber Book of Northern Folk-Tales, 1980; The Anglo-Saxon World, 1982; The Riddle Book, 1982; Folk-Tales of the British Isles, 1985; The Oxford Book of Travel Verse, 1986; Northern Lights, 1987; Medieval Lovers, 1988; Medieval Gardens, 1990; Peter Grimes by George Crabbe, 1990; The Young Oxford Book of Folk-Tales, 1998; (with Lawrence Sail) The New Exeter Book of Riddles, 1999; *operas:* (with Nicola LeFanu): The Green Children, 1990; The Wildman, 1995. *Recreations:* walks, wine, the company of friends, appreciating East Anglia. *Address:* Clare Cottage, Burnham Market, Norfolk PE31 8HE.

CROSTHWAIT, Timothy Leland, CMG 1964; MBE 1944; HM Diplomatic Service, retired; *b* 5 Aug. 1915; *s* of Lt-Col L. G. Crosthwait, Survey of India; *m* 1959, Anne Marjorie, *d* of Col T. M. M. Penney. *Educ:* Wellington Coll.; Peterhouse, Cambridge (MA). Appointed to Indian Civil Service, 1937; Asst Private Sec. to Viceroy, 1942–44; Air Min., 1948–55; Commonwealth Relations Office, 1955; British Deputy High Commissioner in Ceylon, 1957–61; Asst Sec., CRO, 1961–63; British High Commissioner, Zanzibar, 1963–64; British Deputy High Commissioner, Malta, 1965–66; British High Commissioner, Guyana, 1966–67; Ambassador, Malagasy Republic, 1970–75. *Address:* 39 Eaton Terrace, SW1W 8TP. *T:* (020) 7730 9553. *Club:* Oxford and Cambridge.

CROUCH, Prof. Colin John, DPhil; Professor of Comparative Social Institutions, European University Institute, Florence, since 1995; *b* 1 March 1944; *s* of Charles and Doris Crouch; *m* 1970, Joan Ann Freedman; two *s*. *Educ:* Latymer Upper Sch.; London School of Economics (BASoc; Pres., Students Union, 1968; Hobhouse Prize, 1969); Nuffield Coll., Oxford (MA, DPhil). Lecturer in Sociology: LSE, 1969–70; Univ. of Bath, 1972–73; Lectr, 1973–79, Sen. Lectr 1979–80, Reader 1980–85, in Sociology, LSE; Fellow and Tutor in Politics, Trinity College, Oxford, 1985–98; Prof. of Sociol., Univ. of Oxford, 1996–98. Curator, Bodleian Liby, 1991–95; Jun. Proctor, Oxford Univ., 1990–91; Deleg., OUP, 1992–98. External Scientific Mem., Max-Planck Institut für Gesellschaftsforschung, Cologne, 1997–. Mem., Exec. Cttee, Fabian Soc., 1969–78 (Chm., 1976); Dir, Andrew Shonfield Soc., 1989–95. Mem., Standing Cttee, Court of Govs, LSE, 1980–84. Chm. Editl Bd, The Political Qly, 1999– (Joint Editor, 1985–95). *Publications:* The Student Revolt, 1970; (ed jtly) Stress and Contradiction in Modern Capitalism, 1975; (ed) British Political Sociology Year Book, vol. III, 1977; Class Conflict and the Industrial Relations Crisis, 1977; (ed jtly) The Resurgence of Class Conflict in Western Europe since 1968, 2 vols, 1978; (ed) State and Economy in Contemporary Capitalism, 1979; The Politics of Industrial Relations, 1979, 2nd edn 1982; Trade Unions: the logic of collective action, 1982; (ed jtly) International Yearbook of Organizational Democracy, vol. I, 1983; (ed jtly) The New Centralism: Britain out of step in Europe?, 1989; (ed jtly) European Industrial Relations: the challenge of flexibility, 1990; (ed jtly) Corporatism and Accountability: organised interests in British public life, 1990; (ed jtly) The Politics of 1992: beyond the single European market, 1990; (ed jtly) Towards Greater Europe?, 1992; Industrial Relations and European State Traditions, 1993 (Political Studies Assoc. Book Prize, 1993); (ed jtly) Ethics and Markets: co-operation and competition in capitalist economies, 1993; (ed jtly) Reinventing Collective Action: the global and the local, 1995; (ed jtly) Organized Industrial Relations in Europe: what future?, 1995; (ed jtly) Les capitalismes en Europe, 1996; (ed jtly) Political Economy of Modern Capitalism, 1997; (jtly) Are Skills the Answer?, 1999; Social Change in Western Europe, 1999; (ed jtly) After the Euro, 2000; (ed jtly) Citizenship, Markets and the State, 2001; (ed) Coping with Post-Democracy, 2001; (jtly) Local Production Systems in Europe: rise or demise?, 2001; numerous articles on industrial relns, politics and social structure in Britain and Western Europe. *Recreations:* playing violin, music, gardening, watching and refereeing football matches. *Address:* European University Institute, Badia Fiesolana, via dei Roccettini, San Domenico da Fiesole (FI), Italy. *T:* (055) 4685441.

CROUCH, Sybil Edith; Director, Taliesin Arts Centre, University of Wales, Swansea (formerly University College of Swansea), since 1990; Chairman, Arts Council of Wales, since 1999; *b* 9 Aug. 1953; *d* of David George and Lilian Crouch. *Educ:* Birkenhead High Sch. for Girls; Swansea Coll. of Art. Specialist Art Teacher. Dep. Dir, W Wales Assoc. for the Arts, 1979–90. FRSA 1999. *Recreation:* the company of friends. *Address:* Arts Council of Wales, Museum Place, Cardiff CF1 3NX. *T:* (029) 2037 6500.

CROW, (Hilary) Stephen, CB 1995; FRTPI, FRICS; FRGS; Chief Planning Inspector and Chief Executive, Planning Inspectorate, executive agency in Department of the Environment and Welsh Office, 1992–94; Hon. Professor of Planning Practice and Policy, Cardiff University (formerly University of Wales College of Cardiff), since 1995; *b* 2 Sept. 1934; *s* of late Aubrey Everard Crow and Ivy Marion (*née* Warltier); *m* 1958, Margaret Anderson; two *s* one *d*. *Educ:* Leek High Sch.; William Ellis Sch.; St Catharine's Coll., Cambridge (MA). FRGS 1963; FRTPI 1986; FRICS 1992. Planning Asst, various grades, with Lancashire CC and Southport CBC, 1957–72; Divl Planning Officer, 1972–74, Prin. Asst County Planning Officer, 1974–76, Herts CC; joined Planning Inspectorate, 1976: Prin. Inspector for Wales, 1982–85; Asst Chief Inspector, 1985–88; Dep. Chief Inspector, then Chief Inspector, 1988–94. Chm., public examn of draft regl planning guidance for SE England, 1999. C of E Lay Reader, 1979–. *Recreations:* music, reading, garden. *Address:* The Pines, Lyncombe Vale Road, Bath BA2 4LS; *e-mail:* stephencrow@barclays.net.

CROW, Prof. Timothy John, PhD; FRCP, FRCPsych, FMedSci; MRC External Scientific Staff Member, University Department of Psychiatry, Warneford Hospital, Oxford, since 1994, and Scientific Director, Prince of Wales Centre for Research into Schizophrenia and Depression, since 1995; Titular Professor of Psychiatry, University of Oxford, since 1998; *b* 7 June 1938; *s* of late Percy Arthur Crow and of Barbara Bonner Davies; *m* 1966, Julie Carol Carter; one *s* one *d*. *Educ:* Shrewsbury Sch.; London Hosp. Med. Coll. MB BS, PhD, DPM. Maudsley Hosp., 1966; University of Aberdeen: Lectr in Physiology, 1966–70; Lectr in Mental Health, 1970–72; Sen. Lectr in Psychiatry, Univ. of Manchester, 1972–73; Head, Div. of Psychiatry, Clinical Res. Centre, Northwick Park Hosp., 1974–94. Part-time Mem., Sci. Staff, Div. Neurophysiology and Neuropharmacology, Nat. Inst. for Med. Res., 1974–83; Dep. Dir, Clinical Res. Centre, 1984–89. Member: MRC Neuroscis Projects Grants Cttee, 1978–80; Neuroscis Bd, 1986–90; Chm., Biol. Psych. Gp, RCPsych, 1983–88 (Sec., 1980–83). Andrew W. Woods Vis. Prof., Univ. of Iowa, 1980; Lectures: St George's Hosp., 1980; St Louis, 1981; Univ. of Minnesota, 1981; Univ. of Ohio, 1986; RSocMed, 1988; Roche, RCPsych, Dublin, 1988; Stockholm, 1988; Maudsley, RCPsych, 1989; APA Internat. Scholars, 1990; Univ. of Oregon, 1991. Founder FMedSci 1998. A. P. Noyes Award, 1988; US Nat. Alliance Lieber Award, 1989; Res. Prize, World Fedn of Socs of Biol Psychiatry, 1991; Alexander Gralnick Award, Amer. Psych. Foundn, 2000. Editor: Disorders of Neurohumoural Transmission, 1982; Recurrent and Chronic Psychoses, 1987. *Publications:* papers on brain reward mechanisms, learning, evolution of language, speciation of Homo Sapiens, and schizophrenia in sci. and med. jls. *Recreations:* sciolistic archaeology, anthropology. *Address:* 16 Northwick Circle, Kenton, Middx HA3 0EJ. *T:* (020) 8907 6124. *Club:* Royal Society of Medicine.

CROWDEN, James Gee Pascoe; JP; FRICS, FCIArb; Senior Partner, Grounds & Co., 1974–88; Lord-Lieutenant and Custos Rotulorum of Cambridgeshire, since 1992; *b* 14 Nov. 1927; *yr s* of late Lt-Col R. J. C. Crowden, MC, and Nina Mary (*née* Gee), Peterborough; *m* 1955, Kathleen Mary (*d* 1989), *widow* of Captain F. A. Grounds and *d* of late Mr and Mrs J. W. Loughlin, Upwell; (one *s* decd), and one step *s*. *Educ:* Bedford Sch.; Pembroke Coll., Cambridge (MA; Hon. Fellow, 1993). Chartered surveyor; FRICS 1959; FCIArb 1977. Commissioned Royal Lincs Regt, 1947. Rowed in Oxford and Cambridge Boat Race, 1951 and 1952 (Pres., 1952); Captain, Great Britain VIII, European Championships, Macon, 1951 (Gold Medallists); also rowed in 1950 European Championships (Bronze Medallists) and 1952 Olympics; coached 20 Cambridge crews, 1953–75; Steward, Henley Royal Regatta, 1959– (Mem., Cttee of Management, 1964–92); Mem. Council, Amateur Rowing Assoc., 1957–77; Hon. Mem. of Court and Freeman, Co. of Watermen and Lightermen of the River Thames (Master, 1991–92). Vice-Pres., British Olympic Assoc., 1988–; Chairman: Cambridgeshire Olympic Appeals, 1984, 1988, 1992, 1996 and 2000; Appeal Exec. Cttee, Peterborough Cathedral, 1979–80; Member: Ely Diocesan Pastoral Cttee, 1969–89; Ely Cathedral Fabric Cttee, 1986–90. Chm., Order of St Etheldreda, 1992–. Former Pres. Agricl Valuers' Assocs for Cambs, Herts, Beds and Bucks, Lincs, Norfolk, and Wisbech. President: Cambs Fedn of Young Farmers, 1971–73; Cambs Scouts, 1992–; Cambs TAVR and Cadet Cttee, 1992–; E Anglia TAVRA, 1996–2000 (Vice-Pres., 1992–96 and 2000–); Hon. Col, Cambs ACF, 1996–. Patron: Cambs RBL, 1992–; Cambs Red Cross, 1992–; Duke of Edinburgh's Award County Cttee, 1992–; Cambs Regt Old Comrades' Assoc., 1998–. Governor: March Grammar Sch., 1960–70 (Chm., 1967–70); King's Sch., Peterborough, 1980–90; St Hugh's Sch., Woodhall Spa, 1981–92. Church Warden, All Saints', Walsoken, 1964–76 and 1983–84. Pres., Old Bedfordians' Club, 1996–98. JP Wisbech, 1969; DL 1971, Vice Lord-Lieut, 1985–92, Cambridgeshire; High Sheriff, Cambridgeshire and Isle of Ely, 1970. FRSA 1990. KStJ 1992. *Recreations:* rowing, shooting. *Address:* 19 North Brink,

Wisbech, Cambridgeshire PE13 1JR. *T:* (01945) 583320. *Clubs:* East India, Devonshire, Sports and Public Schools, Sette of Odd Volumes; Hawks', University Pitt, Cambridge County (Cambridge); Leander (Henley-on-Thames).

CROWDER, Ven. Norman Harry; Archdeacon of Portsmouth, 1985–93, now Archdeacon Emeritus; *b* 20 Oct. 1926; *s* of Laurence Smethurst Crowder and Frances Annie (*née* Hicks); *m* 1971, Pauleen Florence Alison (*née* Styles); one *s*. *Educ:* Nottingham High School; St John's Coll., Cambridge (MA); Westcott House, Cambridge. Curate, St Mary's, Radcliffe-on-Trent, 1952–55; Residential Chaplain to Bishop of Portsmouth, 1955–59; Asst Chaplain, Canford School, 1959–64, Chaplain 1964–72; Vicar, St John's, Oakfield, Ryde, IoW, 1972–75; Dir of Religious Educn, Portsmouth Dio., and Res. Canon of Portsmouth Cathedral, 1975–85. *Recreations:* water colours of J. M. W. Turner, poetry of T. S. Eliot, conservation of elephants. *Address:* 37 Rectory Road, Salisbury SP2 7SD. *T:* (01722) 320052. *Club:* MCC.

CROWDY, Maj.-Gen. Joseph Porter, CB 1984; Commandant and Postgraduate Dean, Royal Army Medical College, 1981–84, retired; Hon. Consultant on nutrition to Army, 1985–88; *b* 19 Nov. 1923; *s* of late Lt-Col Charles R. Crowdy and Kate Crowdy (*née* Porter); *m* 1948, Beryl Elisabeth Sapsford (*d* 1997); four *d*. *Educ:* Gresham's Sch.; Edinburgh Univ. MB, ChB 1947, DTM&H 1956, DPH 1957, DIH 1957; FFPHM (FFCM 1974); MFOM 1981; FRIPHH 1982. House Surgeon, Norfolk and Norwich Hosp., 1947–48; joined RAMC, 1949; North Africa, 1952–55; Singapore, 1960–62; Head of Applied Physiology, Army Personnel Res. Estabt, 1963–73; Prof. of Army Health, Royal Army Med. Coll., 1973–76; SMO, Land Forces Cyprus, 1976–78; Dir, Army Preventive Medicine, 1978–81. Col Comdt, RAMC, 1985–88. QHP 1981–84. Editor, RAMC Jl, 1978–83. *Publications:* articles in medical jls, on smoking and health, nutrition, physical fitness and obesity. *Recreations:* antique furniture restoration, family genealogy, embroidery. *Address:* Pepperdon Mine, Lustleigh, Newton Abbot, Devon TQ13 9SN. *T:* and *Fax:* (01647) 277419; *e-mail:* crowdy@btinternet.com.

CROWE, Brian Lee, CMG 1985; Director General for External Relations, Council of the European Union, since 1994; *b* 5 Jan. 1938; *s* of Eric Crowe and Virginia Crowe; *m* 1969, Virginia Willis; two *s*. *Educ:* Sherborne; Magdalen Coll., Oxford (1st Cl. Hons PPE). Joined FO, 1961; served: Moscow, 1962–64; London, 1965–67; Aden, 1967; Washington, 1968–73; Bonn, 1973–76; Counsellor and Hd of Policy Planning Staff, FCO, 1976–78; Hd of Chancery, UK Perm. Representation to EEC, Brussels, 1979–81; Counsellor and Hd of EEC Dept (External), FCO, 1982–84; Minister, Commercial, Washington, 1985–89; Ambassador to Austria, 1989–92; Economic Dir (Dep. Under-Sec. of State), FCO, 1992–94. *Recreations:* winter sports, tennis, riding, swimming. *Address:* Secretariat of the Council, Rue de la Loi 175, 1048 Brussels, Belgium.

CROWE, His Honour Gerald Patrick; QC 1973; a Circuit Judge, 1980–95; *b* 3 April 1930; *y s* of Patrick Crowe and Ethel Maud Crowe (*née* Tooth); *m* 1954, Catherine Mary (*d* 2000), *d* of Joseph and Rose Murphy, Newry, N Ireland. *Educ:* St Francis Xavier's Coll.; Liverpool Univ. (LLB). Called to Bar, Gray's Inn, 1952; practised Northern Circuit. A Recorder of the Crown Court, 1976–80. Mem., Lord Chancellor's Adv. Cttee on Legal Aid, 1984–91. *Recreations:* golf, fishing. *Address:* The Spinney, Long Hey Road, Caldy, Cheshire L48 1LY. *T:* (0151) 625 8848.

CROWE, Dr Michael John, DM; FRCP, FRCPsych; Consultant Psychiatrist, Bethlem Royal and Maudsley Hospital, London, since 1978; *b* 16 Oct. 1937; *s* of Robert James Crowe and Olive (*née* Kingston-Jones); *m* 1968, Diane Jordan; one *s* one *d*. *Educ:* St Paul's Sch., London; Exeter Coll., Oxford (MA, BM 1963); London Hosp. Med. Coll. MPhil London, 1970; DM Oxon, 1977. MRCP 1967; MRCPsych 1973; FRCPsych 1984; FRCP 1992. House Officer: London Hosp., 1964; Chelmsford and Essex Hosp., 1964; Senior House Officer: Addenbrooke's Hosp., 1965–66; London Hosp., 1966–67; Maudsley Hospital: Registrar, 1967–69; Sen. Registrar, Res. Worker and Lectr, 1970–74; Sen. Lectr, Inst. of Psychiatry, 1974–77 (Course Leader, Couple Therapy Dip. Course, 1989–). Vis. Fellow, Univ. of Vermont, USA, 1969. Lectr on behavioural and couple therapy, USA, Trinidad, Denmark, Italy, etc. Founder Mem., Inst. of Family Therapy, London, 1976–. Chm., Assoc. of Sexual and Marital Therapists, 1986–88. Gaskell Gold Medal, RCPsych, 1972. *Publications:* (with J. Ridley) Therapy with Couples, 1990; papers in med. and psychol. jls on behaviour therapy, couple therapy and sexual dysfunctions. *Recreations:* music (performing and listening), poetry, literature, languages, walking. *Address:* 66 Palace View, Shirley, Croydon CR0 8QN. *T:* (020) 8777 4823; 21 Wimpole Street, W1M 7AD. *T:* (020) 7637 0146.

CROWE, Rev. Philip Anthony; Director, St Asaph Ministry Training Scheme, since 1996; *b* 16 Aug. 1936; *s* of late Frederick Francis Crowe and of Hilda Crowe; *m* 1963, Freda Maureen Gill; two *s* one *d*. *Educ:* Repton School; Selwyn Coll., Cambridge; Ridley Hall, Cambridge. National service, RA, 1955–57. Tutor in NT Greek and Mission, Oak Hill, 1962–67; Curate at Christchurch, Cockfosters, 1962–65; Editor, Church of England Newspaper, 1967–70; Sec., Bursary Scheme for Overseas Students, 1967–70; Senior Staff Member, St Martin-in-the Bull Ring, Birmingham, 1970–76; Rector of Breadsall, Derby, 1977–88; Derby Diocesan Missioner, 1977–83; Tutor in Ethics, St John's Coll., Nottingham, 1986–88; Principal, Salisbury and Wells Theol Coll., 1988–94; Rector, Overton, Penley and Erbistock, 1995–97; Hon. Canon, Salisbury Cathedral, 1991–97. Mem., Gen. Synod, C of E, 1992–95. *Publications:* (contrib.) Mission in the Modern World, Church and Sacraments, 1977; Pastoral Reorganisation, 1978; Christian Baptism, 1980; The Use and Abuse of Alcohol, 1980; A Whisper will be Heard, 1994; Strange Design, 1999. *Recreations:* gardening, music, squash, walking, caravanning. *Address:* Alderlea, Babbinswood, Whittington SY11 4PQ. *T:* and *Fax:* (01691) 671698.

CROWE, William James, Jr, DDSM, DSM; Ambassador of the United States of America to the Court of St James's, 1994–97; Professor, US Naval Academy, since 1999; *b* Kentucky, 2 Jan. 1925; *s* of William James Crowe and Eula (*née* Russell); *m* 1954, Shirley Mary Grenell; two *s* one *d*. *Educ:* US Naval Acad. (BS 1946); Stanford Univ. (MA 1956); Princeton (PhD 1965). Commnd Ensign, USN, 1946; Comdr, ME Force, Bahrain, 1976–77; Dep. Chief of Naval Ops, Navy Dept, Washington, 1977–80; C-in-C Allied Forces, S Europe, 1980–83; C-in-C Pacific, 1983–85; Chm., Jt Chiefs of Staff, 1985–89; retd 1989 in rank of Adm. Prof. of Geopolitics, Oklahoma Univ., 1989–94. Chm., Foreign Intelligence Adv. Bd, Washington, 1993–94. Director of several public cos. Numerous US and foreign decorations incl. Navy, Air Force, Army and Coastguard DSMs and Medal of Freedom. *Publications:* (jtly) The Line of Fire, 1993; Reducing Nuclear Danger: the road away from the brink, 1993; articles on military and foreign policy.

CROWFOOT, Maj.-Gen. Anthony Bernard, CB 1991; CBE 1982 (MBE 1974); General Officer Commanding North West District, 1989–91, retired; *b* 12 Aug. 1936; *s* of Thomas Bernard Crowfoot and Gladys Dorothy Crowfoot; *m* 1960, Bridget Sarah Bunting; three *s* one *d*. *Educ:* King Edward VII Sch., Norfolk; Royal Military Academy, Sandhurst, psc. Commissioned 1956; 1 E Yorks 1PWO: BAOR, UK, Aden, Gibraltar, 1956–60; Instructor, School of Infantry, 1960–62; 1PWO: BAOR, UK, Aden, 1962–66; Army Staff Coll. 1967; Brigade Major, HQ 5 Inf. Bde, 1968–69; Coy Comd 1PWO, Cyprus, 1970–71; DAAG, MoD, 1971–73; CO 1PWO: UK, BAOR, N Ireland, 1973–76; Instructor, Army Staff College, 1976–77; Col GS, MoD, 1977–80; Comd 39 Inf. Bde, N Ireland, 1980–82; Student, US Army War Coll., 1982–83; Dep. Comdr/COS, HQ British Forces Hong Kong, 1983–86; Dir Gen. Army Manning and Recruiting, MoD, 1986–89. Col, PWO Regt of York, 1986–96.

CROWLEY, Jane Elizabeth Rosser; QC 1998; a Recorder, since 1995; *b* 5 Aug. 1953; *d* of Robert Jenkyn Rosser and Marion Rosser (*née* Davies); *m* 1986, (Jonathan) Mark Crowley; one *s* one *d*. *Educ:* Howell's Sch., Llandaff, Cardiff; King's Coll. London (LLB 1975). Called to the Bar, Gray's Inn, 1976; in practice at the Bar, 1976–. Dep. High Ct Judge, Family Div., 1999–. Dir of Continuing Educn, Wales and Chester Circuit. Legal Mem., Mental Health Tribunal Restricted Order Panel, 2000–. *Recreations:* family, music, Pembrokeshire coast, Glamorgan County Cricket Club, good friends, good wine. *Address:* 30 Park Place, Cardiff CF1 3BA. *T:* (029) 2039 8421; 1 Garden Court, Temple, EC4Y 9BJ. *T:* (020) 7797 7900.

CROWLEY, Rt Rev. John; *see* Middlesbrough, Bishop of, (RC).

CROWLEY, John Desmond; QC 1982; a Recorder of the Crown Court, since 1980; *b* 25 June 1938; *s* of late John Joseph Crowley and Anne Marie (*née* Fallon); *m* 1977, Sarah Maria, *er d* of Christopher Gage Jacobs and late Joan Zara (*née* Atkinson); two *d*. *Educ:* St Edmund's College, Ware; Christ's College, Cambridge (BA 1961, LLB 1962). National Service, 2/Lieut 6th Royal Tank Regt, 1957–58. Called to the Bar, Inner Temple, 1962, Bencher, 1989. Member: Criminal Injuries Compensation Bd, 1985–; Criminal Injuries Compensation Appeal Panel, 2000–. Chm., Appeal Cttee, ICAEW, 2000–. *Recreations:* music, the turf, wine. *Address:* Crown Office Chambers, 1 Paper Buildings, Temple, EC4Y 7EP. *T:* (020) 7797 8100.

CROWLEY, Robert, RDI 1997; set designer for theatre, opera, ballet and film; *b* Cork, 1952. *Educ:* Crawford Municipal Sch. of Fine Art; Bristol Old Vic Theatre Sch. *Sets designed* include: *theatre:* Royal Shakespeare Company: Love's Labour's Lost, 1984; As You Like It, 1985; Les Liaisons Dangereuses, 1986, transf. Ambassadors, NY, LA, Tokyo; Macbeth, A Penny for a Song, Principia Scriptoriae, 1986; The Plantagenets, 1988; Othello, 1989; Hamlet, 1992; National Theatre, later Royal National Theatre: Ghetto, 1989 (Laurence Olivier Award for Designer of the Year, 1990); Hedda Gabler, 1989; White Chameleon, Murmuring Judges, 1991; Carousel, 1992, transf. Shaftesbury, 1993, NY (Tony Award, 1994); Ma Rainey's Black Bottom; Bristol Old Vic: Timon of Athens; A View from the Bridge; Destiny; Women All Over, King's, Edinburgh, 1985; Two Way Mirror, Young Vic, 1989; The Three Sisters, Gate, Dublin, 1990; The Cure at Troy, Guildhall, Derry, then Lyric, Belfast, 1990 (also Jt Dir); Saint Oscar, Field Day Theatre Co., Derry (Dir); Madame de Sade, Tokyo; No Man's Land, Almeida, 1992; When She Danced, Globe; Cunning Little Vixen, Châtelet, Paris; The Judas Kiss, Playhouse, then NY, 1998; The Capeman, NY, 1998; Twelfth Night, NY, 1998; Into the Woods, Donmar Warehouse, 1998; *opera:* Don Giovanni, Kent Opera; The Magic Flute, ENO, 1988, 1997; Royal Opera: costumes, The King Goes Forth to France, 1987; The Knot Garden, 1988; La Traviata; *ballet:* Anastasia, Pavane, Royal Ballet; *films:* Othello; Tales of Hollywood; The Crucible, 1997. *Address:* c/o Simpson Fox Associates Ltd, 52 Shaftesbury Avenue, W1V 7DE.

CROWLEY-MILLING, Michael Crowley, CMG 1982; CEng, FIEE; consultant on computer control systems; *b* 7 May 1917; *s* of Thomas William Crowley-Milling and Gillian May (*née* Chinnery); *m* 1958, Gee Dickson. *Educ:* Radley Coll.; St John's Coll., Cambridge (MA 1943). CEng, FIEE 1956. R&D on radar systems, Metropolitan-Vickers Electrical Co. Ltd, Manchester, 1938–46; design and develt of electron linear accelerators for physics, medical and irradiation purposes, 1946–63; contrib. to construction of electron synchrotron, Daresbury Nuclear Physics Lab., Warrington, 1963–71; CERN, Geneva: resp. for control system for Super Proton Synchrotron (SPS), 1971–75; SPS Div. Leader, 1977–78; Dir, Accelerator Prog., 1979–80; Consultant, 1982–83; Consultant to: SLAC, Stanford Univ., Calif., 1984–85; Los Alamos Nat. Lab., New Mexico, 1986–94; SSC Lab., Dallas, 1991–93; Dir, Crowley Consultants, 1984–. Crompton Premium, IEE, 1959; Glazebrook Medal, Inst. of Physics, 1980. Captain LMBC, 1938. Patents for improvements in radar systems and particle accelerators, 1940–60. *Publications:* (ed) Accelerator Control Systems, 1986; (ed) Accelerator and Large Experimental Control Systems, 1990, 1994; John Bertram Adams, Engineer Extraordinary, 1993; articles and chapters in books on particle accelerators and computer control systems. *Recreations:* vintage cars, sailing. *Address:* Apt 15, Les Ruches II, 1264–St Cergue, Switzerland. *Club:* Vintage Sports Car.

CROWN, Dr June Madge, CBE 1998; FRCP, FFPHM; President, Faculty of Public Health Medicine, Royal College of Physicians, 1995–98; *b* 5 June 1938; *d* of late Edward Downes and of Madge Edith Downes; *m* 1964, Sidney Crown; two *s* one *d*. *Educ:* Pate's Grammar Sch. for Girls, Cheltenham; Newnham Coll., Cambridge (MA); Middlesex Hosp. Med. Sch. (MB, BChir); London Sch. of Hygiene and Tropical Medicine (MSc). FFPHM 1986; FRCP 1991. Area MO, Brent and Harrow AHA, 1980–82; Dir of Public Health, Bloomsbury HA, 1982–91. Dir, SE Inst. of Public Health, UMDS, 1991–99. Chairman: DoH Adv. Gp on Nurse Prescribing, 1988–89; DoH Rev. of Prescribing, 1996–98; Member: Standing Med. Adv. Cttee, DoH, 1984–88 and 1995–98; Clinical Standards Adv. Gp, DoH, 1995–99. Advr to WHO, 1984–; Consultant on Health Sector Mgt Develt to Czech Republic and Slovakia, 1992–93; Advr to NZ Govt and Health Bds on Health Care Reforms, 1992. President: Sect. of Epidemiology and Public Health, RSocMed, 1994–96; Medical Action for Global Security (MEDACT), 1993–. Chm., Age Concern, England, 1998–. Member: Council, Queen's Nursing Inst., 1982–; Bd of Govs, Royal Nat. Orthopaedic Hosp., 1976–82 (Vice-Chm., 1980–82); Inst. of Orthopaedics, Univ. of London, 1978–88 (Chm., 1982–88); Bd of Mgt and Court of Govs, LSHTM, 1983–94; Vice-Pres., Chartered Inst. of Envmtl Health, 2001. Associate, Newnham Coll., Cambridge, 1992– (Associate Fellow, 1997–99; Chm., Associates, 1998–2000). Hon. Fellow: Soc. of Chiropodists, 1986; Australasian Faculty of Public Health Medicine, 1996; Faculty of Public Health Med., RCPI, 1997; RCPE, 1998. *Publications:* Health for All: revised targets, 1993; (with J. Connelly) Homelessness and Ill Health, 1995; Epidemiologically Based Needs Assessment: child and adolescent mental health, 1995. *Recreations:* family, opera, fine art, theatre, travel, jogging. *Address:* 118 Whitfield Street, W1P 5RZ. *T:* (020) 7387 6787.

CROWSON, Richard Borman, CMG 1986; HM Diplomatic Service, retired; Chairman, Uweso UK Trust Ltd, since 1996; *b* 23 July 1929; *s* of late Clarence Borman Crowson and Cecilia May Crowson (*née* Ramsden); *m* 1st, 1960, Sylvia Cavalier (marr. diss. 1974); one *s* one *d*; 2nd, 1983, Judith Elaine Turner. *Educ:* Downing Coll., Cambridge (MA). FCIS. HMOCS, Uganda, 1955–62; Foreign Office, 1962–63; First Sec. (Commercial), Tokyo, 1963–68; Dep. High Commissioner, Barbados, 1968–70; FCO, 1970–75; Counsellor (Commercial and Aid), Jakarta, 1975–77; Counsellor for Hong Kong Affairs, Washington, 1977–82; Counsellor and Head of Chancery, Berne, 1983–85; High Comr in Mauritius, 1985–89, and Ambassador (non-resident) to Federal Islamic Republic of the Comoros, 1986–89. *Recreations:* music, drama, travel. *Address:* 67 Crofton

Road, Orpington, Kent BR6 8HU. *T:* (01689) 891320. *Club:* Royal Commonwealth Society.

CROWTHER, Prof. Derek, PhD; FRCP, FRCR; Professor and Director, Cancer Research Campaign Department of Medical Oncology, Christie Hospital and Manchester University, 1974–97, now Professor Emeritus; *b* 1 July 1937; *s* of Robinson Westgarth Crowther and Gladys Hannah Crowther; *m* 1959, Margaret Frances Dickinson; two *d* (one *s* decd). *Educ:* City of London Sch.; Clare Coll., Cambridge (Foundn Scholar; MB, BChir, MA 1963); Baylor Univ., Texas (Fulbright Scholar, 1959–60); Royal Postgraduate Medical Sch., London (PhD 1968); Royal Marsden Hosp. MSc Manchester, 1977. FRCP 1976; FRCR 1993. Sen. Lectr and Dep. Dir of Med. Oncology, St Bartholomew's Hosp., 1972–74. CMO, Friends Provident, 1995–. Chairman: LRF Clinical Trials Adv. Panel, 2000–; London Cancer Res. Mapping Working Gp, 2000–01. Member: Statutory Gene Therapy Adv. Cttee, 1994–97; CRC Central Instl Review Bd, 2001–. Pres., Assoc. of Cancer Physicians, 1999–. Hon. MRSocMed. Prizes in medicine, paediatrics, and pathology, incl. Gold Medal in Obstetrics and Gynaeocology, St Bartholomew's Hosp.; Glyn Evans Gold Medal, RCR, 1980; Award of Distinction, CRC, 1997; Lifetime Achievement in Cancer award, Cancer BACUP, 1999. *Publications:* edited: Manual of Cancer Chemotherapy, 1978 (trans. several langs); Interferons, 1991; more than 250 publications in the field of anti-cancer therapy. *Recreations:* gardening, travel, camping, cosmology, oriental and modern art. *Address:* 52 Barlow Moor Road, Didsbury, Manchester M20 2TR. *T:* (0161) 434 6685.

CROWTHER, Eric (John Ronald), OBE 1977; Metropolitan Magistrate, 1968–89; a Recorder of the Crown Court, 1983–96; *b* 4 Aug. 1924; *s* of Stephen Charles Crowther, company secretary, and Olive Beatrix Crowther (*née* Selby); *m* 1959, Elke Auguste Ottilie Winkelmann; one *s* one *d*. *Educ:* University College Sch., Hampstead. Royal Navy, 1943–47 (Medit. Area of Ops). Awarded Tancred Studentship in Common Law, 1948; Called to Bar, Lincoln's Inn, 1951; winner of Inns of Court Contest in Advocacy, 1951; Lectr and Student Counsellor, British Council, 1951–81; Lecturer: on Elocution and Advocacy for Council of Legal Educn, 1955–91 (Dir of Studies, Post-Final Gps, 1975–77); on Evidence to RN, 1968–89. Joined Inner Temple *ad eundem*, 1960. Practised at Criminal Bar, 1951–68. Sen. Resident Magistrate, Montserrat, 1996. Chairman: Inner London Magistrates' Assoc. Trng Sub-Cttee, 1981–89; Prisoners' Wives Service, 1982–85. Mem. Council, British Council, 1985– (lectures world-wide); Mem., Bd of Academic Studies, St Catherine's, Cumberland Lodge, 1977–82; Director of Studies: Cromwell Sch. of English, 1973–91; Oxford Study Centre, 1992–94. Trustee: Professional and Academic Regional Visits Organisation, 1977–89; Fair Trials Abroad, 1997–2000; Outside Chance, 2000–. Vice-Patron, Missing Persons' Helpline, 1994–. Mem. Cttee, RADA, 1979–84. Hon. Officer, Internat. Students' Hse, 1981–. Volunteer dog-walker, Battersea Dogs' Home, 1999–. Editor, Commonwealth Judicial Jl, 1973–77. *Publications:* Advocacy for the Advocate, 1984; Last in the List, 1988; Look What's on the Bench!, 1992; Russian Roulette, 1997. *Recreations:* travel, transport, the theatre, debating, student welfare, Scottish dancing. *Club:* International Students' House.

CROWTHER, John Anthony; Chief Executive, Lawn Tennis Association, since 1997; *b* 16 Oct. 1951; *s* of Charles Alec Crowther and Joan Sylvia (*née* Boddam-Whetham); *m* 1975, Lorraine Ann Chadwick; three *s*. *Educ:* Malvern Coll.; Imperial Coll., London (BSc Eng). ACGI. British Aerospace PLC, 1970–77; Delta Neu Ltd, 1977–78; Panavia Aircraft GmbH, 1978–79; British Aerospace PLC, 1979–90; Vickers Defence Systems: Commercial Dir, 1990–92; Man. Dir, 1992–94; Chief Exec., 1994–96. Confederation of British Industry: Chm., Contracts Panel, 1990–92; Regl Council Mem., Yorks & Humberside, 1994–96. Chm., Leeds Career Guidance, 1995–96. Chm., Major Spectator Sports Div., CCPR, 2001– (Dep. Chm., 1999–2001). MInstD 1997. *Recreations:* piano, running, tennis, gardening. *Address:* c/o Lawn Tennis Association, Queen's Club, W Kensington, W14 9EG. *T:* (020) 7381 7002. *Club:* Queen's.

CROWTHER, (Joseph) Stanley; *b* 30 May 1925; *s* of Cyril Joseph Crowther and Florence Mildred (*née* Beckett); *m* 1948, Margaret Royston; two *s*. *Educ:* Rotherham Grammar Sch.; Rotherham Coll. of Technology. Royal Signals, 1943–47. Journalist: Rotherham Advertiser, 1941–43 and 1947–50; Yorkshire Evening Post, 1950–51; freelance, 1951–. Mem., Rotherham Borough Council, 1958–59, 1961–76; Mayor of Rotherham, 1971–72, 1975–76; Chm., Yorkshire and Humberside Develt Assoc., 1972–76. MP (Lab) Rotherham, June 1976–1992. Vice-Pres., Town and Country Planning Assoc. *Recreations:* walking, singing, listening to jazz. *Address:* 15 Clifton Crescent South, Rotherham S65 2AR. *T:* (01709) 364559. *Club:* Eastwood View Working Men's (Rotherham).

CROWTHER, Dr Richard Anthony, FRS 1993; Member of Scientific Staff, Medical Research Council Laboratory of Molecular Biology, Cambridge, since 1969; Fellow of Peterhouse, Cambridge, since 1981; *b* 26 July 1942; *s* of Albert Crowther and Joyce Edith Crowther (*née* Anthony); *m* 1964, Susan Elizabeth Hope; two *s*. *Educ:* Manchester Grammar Sch.; Jesus Coll., Cambridge (BA); PhD Cantab. Res. Fellow, Edinburgh Univ., 1968. *Publications:* research papers and reviews in sci. jls. *Recreations:* walking, bird watching. *Address:* MRC Laboratory of Molecular Biology, Hills Road, Cambridge CB2 2QH. *T:* (01223) 402410.

CROWTHER, Thomas Rowland; QC 1981; **His Honour Judge Crowther;** a Circuit Judge since 1985; *b* 11 Sept. 1937; *s* of late Kenneth Vincent Crowther, MB, BCh, and Winifred Anita Crowther, MPS; *m* 1969, Gillian Jane (*née* Prince); one *s* one *d*. *Educ:* Newport High Sch.: Keble Coll., Oxford (MA). President, Oxford Univ. Liberal Club, 1957; Editor, Oxford Guardian, 1957. Called to the Bar, Inner Temple, 1961; Junior and Wine Steward, Wales and Chester Circuit, 1974. A Recorder, 1980–85. Contested (L) General Elections: Oswestry, 1964 and 1966; Hereford, 1970. Founder Mem., Gwent Area Broadcasting, 1981. *Recreations:* garden, trout fishing. *Address:* Lansor, Llandegfedd, Caerleon NP6 1LS. *T:* (01633) 450224.

CROWTHER, William Ronald Hilton; QC 1980; a Recorder, 1984–96; *b* 7 May 1941; *s* of Ronald Crowther and Ann Bourne Crowther; *m* 1964, Valerie Meredith (*née* Richards); one *s*. *Educ:* Oundle Sch.; Univ. of Oxford (BA Jurisprudence). Called to the Bar, Inner Temple, 1963, Bencher, 1985–96. *Recreations:* bird-watching and all aspects of natural history.

CROXFORD, Ian Lionel; QC 1993; *b* 23 July 1953; *s* of Peter Patrick Croxford, BEM, and Mary Helen Croxford (*née* Richardson); *m* 1976, Sandra McCord; one *s* one *d*. *Educ:* Westcliff High Sch. for Boys; Univ. of Leicester (LLB 1st Cl. Hons). Called to the Bar, Gray's Inn, 1976 (Bacon Schol.); Lincoln's Inn, *ad eundem*, 1977. Gov., Westcliff High Sch. for Boys, 1990– (Chm. Govs, 1995–). *Recreation:* watching sport. *Address:* Wilberforce Chambers, 8 New Square, Lincoln's Inn, WC2A 3QP. *T:* (020) 7306 0102.

CROXON, Raymond Patrick Austen; QC 1983; *b* 31 July 1928; *s* of late Randolph Croxon, bandmaster, Salvation Army, and Rose Harvey, Home League Sec., Salvation Army; *m* 1952, Monica Howard (marr. diss. 1992); two *s* two *d*. *Educ:* Strand College; King's College London. LLB. Served in RAMC, 1946–49. Called to the Bar, Gray's Inn, 1960; Hd of Regency Chambers, 1995–. *Recreations:* travel, walking, swimming, reading, music, theatre, modern Greek language. *Address:* 8 King's Bench Walk, Temple, EC4Y 7DU. *T:* (020) 7797 8888, *Fax:* (020) 7797 8880; Regency Chambers, Cathedral Square, Peterborough, Cambs PE1 1XW. *Club:* Savage.

CROYDON, Area Bishop of, 1991–Sept. 2002; **Rt Rev. Wilfred Denniston Wood,** KA 2000; appointed Bishop Suffragan of Croydon, 1985; *b* Barbados, WI, 15 June 1936; *s* of Wilfred Coward and Elsie Elmira Wood; *m* 1966, Ina Eileen, *d* of L. E. Smith, CBE, Barbadian MP; three *s* two *d*. *Educ:* Combermere Sch. and Codrington Coll., Barbados. Lambeth Dip. in Theol., 1962. Ordained deacon, St Michael's Cath., Barbados, 1961; ordained priest, St Paul's Cath., London, 1962. Curate of St Stephen with St Thomas, Shepherd's Bush, 1962–66, Hon. Curate, 1966–74; Bishop of London's Officer in Race Relations, 1966–74; Vicar of St Laurence, Catford, 1974–82; RD of East Lewisham, 1977–82; Archdeacon of Southwark, 1982–85; Hon. Canon of Southwark Cathedral, 1977–85. Mem., General Synod, 1987–. Chairman: Martin Luther King Meml Trust; Cttee on Black Anglican Concerns, 1986–91. Member: Royal Commn on Criminal Procedure, 1978–80; Archbishop of Canterbury's Commn on Urban Priority Areas, 1983–85; Housing Corp. Bd, 1986–95. Non-exec. Dir, Mayday Healthcare NHS Trust, 1993– (Vice-Chm., 2000). JP Inner London, 1971–85. Hon. DD Gen. Theol Seminary, NY, 1986; DUniv Open, 2000. *Publications:* (contrib.) The Committed Church, 1966; (with John Downing) Vicious Circle, 1968; Keep the Faith, Baby!, 1994. *Recreations:* reading, cricket; armchair follower of most sports. *Address:* 53 Stanhope Road, Croydon CR0 5NS. *T:* (020) 8686 1822; (until Sept. 2002) (office) St Matthew's House, 100 George Street, Croydon CR0 1PJ. *T:* (020) 8681 5496, *Fax:* (020) 8686 2074.

CROYDON, Archdeacon of; *see* Davies, Ven. V. A.

CROYDON, Rear-Adm. John Edward Kenneth; JP; DL; CEng, FIEE; *b* 25 Feb. 1929; *s* of late Kenneth P. Croydon and Elizabeth V. Croydon; *m* 1953, Brenda Joyce Buss, MA; one *s* two *d*. *Educ:* King Edward's Sch., Birmingham; Selwyn Coll., Cambridge (MA). BA London; CEng, FIEE 1975; jssc 1969. RN Special Entry Cadet (L), 1947; HMS Verulam and HMS Undine, 1954–55; Royal Naval Coll., Dartmouth, 1959–61; HMS Devonshire, 1961–64; HMS London, 1970–72; MoD, 1972–74; Captain Weapon Trials, 1974–77; Dir, Underwater Weapon Projects (Naval), 1978–80; Dir Gen. Weapons (Naval), 1981–83; Dep. Controller, Warships Equipment, MoD (Navy), 1983–84, retd. Rear Cdre (Dinghies), Royal Naval Sailing Assoc., 1980. Gov., Milton Abbey Sch., 1985–. Chm. Bd of Visitors, HMP Weare, 1997–2000. County Comr for Scouts, Dorset, 1986–93. JP Weymouth, 1985; DL Dorset, 1993. *Recreations:* sailing, music, walking. *Clubs:* Royal Naval Sailing Association; Weymouth Sailing.

CROZIER, Adam Alexander; Chief Executive, Football Association, since 2000; *b* 26 Jan. 1964; *s* of Robert and Elinor Crozier; *m* 1994, Annette Edwards; two *d*. *Educ:* Heriot-Watt Univ. (BA Business Orgn). Pedigree Petfoods, Mars (UK) Ltd, 1984–86; Daily Telegraph, 1986–88; Saatchi & Saatchi, 1988–99: Dir, 1990; Media Dir, 1992; Vice Chm., 1994; Chief Exec., 1995. *Recreations:* football, golf, my children. *Address:* Football Association, 25 Soho Square, W1D 4FA.

CROZIER, Brian Rossiter; writer and consultant on international affairs; Distinguished Visiting Fellow, Hoover Institution on War, Revolution and Peace, Stanford University, California, 1996–2002; Contributing Editor, National Review, New York, since 1982; *b* 4 Aug. 1918; *s* of R. H. Crozier and Elsa (*née* McGillivray); *m* 1940, Mary Lillian Samuel (*d* 1993); one *s* three *d*; *m* 1999, Jacqueline Marie Mitchell. *Educ:* Lycée, Montpellier; Peterborough Coll., Harrow; Trinity Coll. of Music, London. Music and art critic, London, 1936–39; reporter-sub-editor, Stoke-on-Trent, Stockport, London, 1940–41; aeronautical inspection, 1941–43; sub-editor: Reuters, 1943–44; News Chronicle, 1944–48; and writer, Sydney Morning Herald, 1948–51; corresp., Reuters-AAP, 1951–52; features editor, Straits Times, 1952–53; leader writer, corresp. and editor, Foreign Report, Economist, 1954–64; commentator, BBC English, French and Spanish overseas services, 1954–66; Chm., Forum World Features, 1965–74; Columnist: Nat. Review, NY, 1978–95; Now!, 1979–81; The Times, 1982–83; Freedom Today (formerly The Free Nation), 1982–89. Co-founder, Inst. for the Study of Conflict, 1970 (Dir, 1970–79). Adjunct Scholar, Heritage Foundn, Washington, 1984–95. *Publications:* The Rebels, 1960; The Morning After, 1963; Neo-Colonialism, 1964; South-East Asia in Turmoil, 1965 (3rd edn 1968); The Struggle for the Third World, 1966; Franco, 1967; The Masters of Power, 1969; The Future of Communist Power (in USA: Since Stalin), 1970; De Gaulle, vol. 1 1973, vol. 2 1974; A Theory of Conflict, 1974; The Man Who Lost China (Chiang Kai-shek), 1976; Strategy of Survival, 1978; The Minimum State, 1979; Franco: crepúsculo de un hombre (Spanish orig.), 1980; The Price of Peace, 1980, new edn 1983; (jtly) Socialism Explained, 1984; (jtly) This War Called Peace, 1984; (as John Rossiter) The Andropov Deception (novel), 1984 (pubd under own name, NY, 1986); Socialism: dream and reality, 1987; (ed) The Grenada Documents, 1987; The Gorbachev Phenomenon, 1990; Communism: why prolong its death-throes?, 1990; Free Agent, 1993; The KGB Lawsuits, 1995; (jtly) Le Phénix rouge, 1995; The Rise and Fall of the Soviet Empire, 1999; contrib. to jls in many countries. *Recreations:* piano, taping stereo. *Address:* 18 Wickliffe Avenue, N3 3EJ. *T:* (020) 8346 8124. *Club:* Royal Automobile.

CROZIER, Julian Smyth, CB 1995; business consultant; Chief Executive, Training and Employment Agency, Northern Ireland, 1990–95; *b* 19 Sept. 1935; *m* 1961, Rose Mary Mauma; two *s* one *d*. *Educ:* Campbell Coll., Belfast; Queens' Coll., Cambridge (BA). HMOCS, N Rhodesia, 1958–64; N Ireland Civil Service, 1965–95: served in Dept of Agriculture, Office of Comr for Complaints (Ombudsman), Depts of Health and Social Services, Finance and Personnel, Economic Develt. Dep. Chm., Probation Bd for NI, 1998–. Director: Emerging Business Trust; Springside Trng. *Recreations:* hobby farming, country pursuits, golf, fishing, sailing, reading. *Clubs:* Royal Commonwealth Society; Royal Co. Down Golf.

CRUDDAS, Jon, PhD; MP (Lab) Dagenham, since 2001; *b* 7 April 1962; *s* of John and Pat Cruddas; *m* 1993, Anna Mary Healy; one *s*. *Educ:* Oaklands RC Comprehensive Sch., Waterlooville; Warwick Univ. (BSc, MA; PhD 1991). Labour Party: Policy Officer, 1989–94; Chief Asst to Gen. Sec., 1994–97; Dep. Political Sec., Prime Minister's Office, 1997-2001. Mem., White Heart Angling Soc., 2000–. Mem., Dagenham Royal Naval Assoc., 2000–. *Recreations:* golf, angling. *Address:* House of Commons, SW1A 0AA. *Club:* Dagenham Working Mens'.

CRUFT, John Herbert; Hon. Treasurer, Royal Society of Musicians, 1976–87; *b* 4 Jan. 1914; *er s* of late Eugene and Winifred Cruft; *m* 1938, Mary Margaret Miriam, *e d* of late Rev. Pat and Miriam McCormick; two *s*. *Educ:* Westminster Abbey Choir Sch.; Westminster Sch.; Royal College of Music (K. F. Boult Conducting Scholar). Oboist in BBC Television, London Philharmonic and Suisse Romande Orchestras, 1936–40. Served with Royal Corps of Signals, 1940–46. London Symphony Orchestra: Oboist, 1946–49; Sec., 1949–59. British Council: Dir of Music Dept, 1959–61; Dir of Drama and Music

Dept, 1961–65; Music Dir, Arts Council of GB, 1965–79; a Dir, National Jazz Centre, 1982–87. Member: Council, RCM, 1983–90, Life Gov., 1990; Council for Dance Educn and Trng, 1990–92. Trustee: Loan Fund for Musical Instruments, 1980–; Electro-Acoustic Music Trust, 1980–88; Governor: London Festival Ballet Trust Ltd, 1980–84; Contemporary Dance Trust Ltd, 1982–88. FRCM, Hon. RAM. *Publication:* The Royal College of Music: a Centenary Record 1883–1983 (with H. C. Colles), 1982. *Address:* 11 Broadhinton Road, Clapham, SW4 0LU. *T:* (020) 7720 2330.

CRUICKSHANK, Alistair Ronald; Chair, Sutton Future Network, since 2000; *b* 2 Oct. 1944; *s* of late Francis John Cruickshank and of Kate Cameron Cruickshank (*née* Brittain); *m* 1967, Sandra Mary Noble; three *d.* *Educ:* Aberdeen Grammar School; Aberdeen University (MA). Joined MAFF as Assistant Principal, 1966; Principal, 1970; Asst Secretary, 1978; Under Sec. (Animal Health), 1986; Principal Finance Officer, 1989–94; Under Sec. (Agricl Inputs), 1995–96. Chairman: Surrey Organic Gardening Gp, 1997–; Croydon, Merton and Sutton Dist, CPRE, 1998–. *Recreations:* gardening, looking at old buildings. *Address:* 3 Park Avenue, Carshalton, Surrey SM5 3ES.

CRUICKSHANK, Donald Gordon; Chairman: London Stock Exchange, since 2000; SMG plc (formerly Scottish Media Group), since 1999; *b* 17 Sept. 1942; *s* of Donald Campbell Cruickshank and Margaret Buchan Cruickshank (*née* Morrison); *m* 1964, Elizabeth Buchan Taylor; one *s* one *d.* *Educ:* Univ. of Aberdeen (MA); Inst. of Chartered Accountants of Scotland (CA); Manchester Business School (MBA). McKinsey & Co., 1972–77; Times Newspapers, 1977–80; Pearson, 1980–84; Man. Dir, Virgin Group, 1984–89; Chief Exec., NHS in Scotland, 1989–93; Dir Gen., Oftel, 1993–98. Non-exec. Dir, Christian Salvesen, 1994–95. Chairman: Wandsworth HA, 1986–89; Action 2000, 1997–2000; UK Banking Review, 1998–2000. *Recreations:* sport, golf, opera. *Address:* London Stock Exchange, Old Broad Street, EC2N 1HP.

CRUICKSHANK, Prof. Durward William John, PhD, ScD; FRS 1979; CChem, FRSC; Professor of Chemistry (Theoretical Chemistry), University of Manchester Institute of Science and Technology, 1967–83, now Emeritus; *b* 7 March 1924; *s* of William Durward Cruickshank, MB, ChB, and Margaret Ombler Meek, MA, MRCS, LRCP; *m* 1953, Marjorie Alice Travis (*d* 1983), MA, PhD; one *s* one *d.* *Educ:* St Lawrence Coll., Ramsgate; Loughborough Coll. (DLC 1944; BScEng 1st Cl. Hons London, 1944); Cambridge Univ. (Wrangler, Math. Tripos, 1949; Dist. Pt III Math. Tripos, 1950; BA 1949, MA 1954, ScD 1961). PhD Leeds, 1952; CChem, FRIC 1971. Engrg Asst, WO and Admiralty (Naval Opl Res.), 1944–46; Leeds University: Res. Asst, Chemistry Dept, 1946–47; Lectr, 1950–57; Reader in Math. Chemistry, 1957–62; Fellow, St John's Coll., Cambridge, 1953–56; Joseph Black Prof. of Chem. (Theor. Chem.), Glasgow Univ., 1962–67; Dep. Principal, UMIST, 1971–72. Hon. Vis. Prof. of Physics, York Univ., 1985–88; Bragg Lectr, British Crystallographic Assoc., 1997. Treasurer, 1966–72, and Gen. Sec., 1970–72, Internat. Union of Crystallography. Companion of UMIST, 1992. 1977 Chemical Soc. Award for Struct. Chem., 1978; (first) Dorothy Hodgkin Prize, British Crystallographic Assoc., 1991. *Publications:* (ed jtly) P. P. Ewald and his Dynamical Theory of X-ray Diffraction, 1992; (ed jtly) Time-resolved Macromolecular Crystallography, 1992; scientific papers on crystallography, molecular structure determination and theoretical chemistry in Acta Cryst., Proc. Royal Soc., and Jl Chem. Soc. *Recreations:* golf, genealogy. *Address:* 105 Moss Lane, Alderley Edge, Cheshire SK9 7HW. *T:* (01625) 582656.

CRUICKSHANK, Prof. Eric Kennedy, OBE 1961; MD; FRCP, FRCPGlas; Dean of Postgraduate Medicine, University of Glasgow, 1972–80; retired; *b* 29 Dec. 1914; *s* of John Cruickshank, CBE, and Jessie (*née* Allan); *m* 1st, 1951, Ann Burch; two *s* two *d*; 2nd, 1969, Josephine Williams. *Educ:* Aberdeen Grammar Sch.; Univ. of Aberdeen (MB, ChB Hons, 1937; MD Hons and gold medal, 1948). Fellow, Harvard and Massachusetts Gen. Hosp., USA, 1938–39; Lectr, then Sen. Lectr, Dept of Medicine, Univ. of Aberdeen, 1939–50; Hon. Consultant in Medicine, NHS, 1948–50; First Dean, Medical Faculty, and Prof. of Medicine, Univ. of West Indies, Kingston, Jamaica, 1950–72. Served War of 1939–45: Captain RAMC, Medical Specialist, Changi Prisoner of War Camp, Singapore (despatches twice). WHO Consultant in Medical Educn, 1959–, Nutrition, 1955–; Member: GMC, 1972–80; Inter-Univ. Council, 1972–84; Greater Glasgow Health Bd, 1972–80. Hon. FACP 1969. *Publications:* on nutrition, neurology, medical educn. *Recreations:* tennis, golf, gardening, ornithology. *Address:* Parsonage House, Oare, Wilts SN8 4JA.

CRUICKSHANK, Flight-Lieut John Alexander, VC 1944; ED 1947; late RAF; with Grindlay's Bank Ltd, London, 1952–76; retired; Administrator, Northern Division, North West Securities Ltd, 1977–85; *b* 20 May 1920; *s* of James C. Cruickshank, Aberdeen, and Alice Bow, Macduff, Banffshire; *m* 1955, Marion R. Beverley (*d* 1985), Toronto, Canada. *Educ:* Aberdeen Grammar Sch.; Daniel Stewart's Coll., Edinburgh. Entered Commercial Bank of Scotland, 1938; returned to banking, 1946. Mem. of Territorial Army and called for service, Aug. 1939, in RA; transferred to RAF 1941 and commissioned in 1942; all RAF service was with Coastal Command. ADC to Lord High Commissioner to the Gen. Assembly of the Church of Scotland, 1946–48. *Clubs:* Royal Northern and University (Aberdeen); Merchants of Edinburgh Golf.

CRUISE MAPOTHER, Thomas, IV, (Tom Cruise); actor and producer; *b* 3 July 1962; *s* of late Thomas Cruise Mapother, III and of Mary Lee Cruise Mapother (*née* Pfeiffer); *m* 1st, 1987, Mimi Rogers (marr. diss. 1990); 2nd, 1990, Nicole Kidman (marr. diss. 2001); one adopted *s* one adopted *d.* *Educ:* Glen Ridge High Sch., NJ. *Films:* actor: Endless Love, 1981; Taps, 1981; Losin' It, 1983; The Outsiders, 1983; Risky Business, 1983; All the Right Moves, 1983; Legend, 1985; Top Gun, 1986; The Color of Money, 1986; Rain Man, 1988; Cocktail, 1989; Born on the Fourth of July, 1989; Daytona, 1990; Rush, 1990; Days of Thunder, 1990; Sure as the Moon, 1991; Far and Away, 1992; A Few Good Men, 1992; The Firm, 1993; Interview with the Vampire, 1994; Jerry Maguire, 1996; Eyes Wide Shut, 1999; Magnolia, 2000; actor and producer: Mission Impossible, 1996; Mission Impossible 2, 2000; producer: Without Limits, 1998; The Hours, 2001; The Others, 2001. *Address:* c/o CAA, 9830 Wilshire Boulevard, Los Angeles, CA 90212, USA.

CRUM, Douglas Vernon E.; *see* Erskine Crum.

CRUMP, Rt Rev. William Henry Howes; *b* London, Ontario, Canada, 13 March 1903; *m* 1st, 1932, Betty Margaret Dean Thomas; one *s* one *d*; 2nd, 1964, Rose (*d* 1992). *Educ:* London, Ontario; University of Western Ontario; Huron College; Trinity College, Toronto. Ordained Deacon, 1926; Curate, Wawanesa, Manitoba, 1926; Priest, 1927. Rector: Glenboro, Manitoba, 1927; Holland, Manitoba, 1931; Boissevain, Manitoba, 1933; St Aidan's, Winnipeg, 1933–44; Christ Church, Calgary, 1944–60; Canon of St Paul, Diocese of Calgary, 1949; Bishop of Saskatchewan, 1960–71.

CRUMPTON, Michael Joseph, CBE 1992; PhD; FRS 1979; Director of Research (Laboratories), Imperial Cancer Research Fund Laboratories, London, 1991–93, retired (Deputy Director of Research, 1979–91); *b* 7 June 1929; *s* of Charles E. and Edith Crumpton; *m* 1960, Janet Elizabeth Dean; one *s* two *d.* *Educ:* Poole Grammar Sch., Poole; University Coll., Southampton; Lister Inst. of Preventive Medicine, London. BSc, PhD, London. National Service, RAMC, 1953–55. Member, scientific staff, Microbiological Research Estabt, Porton, Wilts, 1955–60; Visiting Scientist Fellowship, Nat. Insts of Health, Bethesda, Maryland, USA, 1959–60; Research Fellow, Dept of Immunology, St Mary's Hosp. Med. Sch., London, 1960–66; Mem., scientific staff, Nat. Inst. for Med. Research, Mill Hill, 1966–79, Head of Biochemistry Div., 1976–79. Visiting Fellow, John Curtin Sch. of Med. Research, ANU, Canberra, 1973–74. Non-exec. Dir, Imperial Cancer Research Technology Ltd, 1989–99 (Chief Operating Officer, 1993–94). Member: WHO Steering Cttee for Encapsulated Bacteria, 1984–91 (Chm., 1988–91); Cell Board, MRC, 1979–83; Scientific Adv. Cttee, Lister Inst., 1986–91; Sloan Cttee, General Motors Res. Foundn, 1986–88 (Chm., 1988); MRC AIDS Directed Prog. Steering Cttee, 1987–91; Scientific Cttee, Swiss Inst. for Experimental Cancer Res., 1989–96; DTI/SERC Biotech. Jt Adv. Bd, 1989–93. Member Council: Royal Instn, 1986–90 (Mem., Davy Faraday Lab. Cttee, 1985–90, Chm. of Cttee, 1988–90); MRC, 1986–90; Royal Soc., 1990–92; Mem. Sci. Council, Celltech Ltd, 1980–90; Chairman: Sci. Adv. Bd, Biomed. Res. Centre, Univ. of British Columbia, Vancouver, 1987–91; DoH/HSE Adv. Cttee on Dangerous Pathogens, 1991–98; Mem. Sci. Adv. Bd, Ciba Foundn, 1990–94. Chm., InferMed Ltd, 1998–2000; non-executive Director: Amersham Internat., 1990–97; Amersham Pharmacia Biotech Ltd, 1997–2001; Amersham Pharmacia Biotech Inc., 2001–. Mem. Council, Inst. of Cancer Res., 1994–; Member, Governing Body: Imperial Coll. of Sci., Technol. and Medicine, 1994–98; BPMF, 1987–95; Gov., Strangeways Res. Lab., 1993–2000. Mem., EMBO, 1982; MAE, 1996; Hon. Mem., Amer. Assoc. of Immunologists, 1995. Trustee: EMF Biol Res. Trust, 1996–; Breakthrough Breast Cancer, 1997–. Founder FMedSci 1998. Hon. FRCPath 2000. Mem. Editorial Board: Biochemical Jl, 1966–73 (Dep. Chm., 1969–72); Eur. Jl of Immunology, 1972–86; Immunochemistry, 1975–79; Immunogenetics, 1979–85; Biochemistry Internat., 1980–86; Molecular Biol. and Medicine, 1983–86; Human Immunology, 1985–96; Regional Editor, Molecular Immunology, 1982–86. Biochem. Soc. Vis. Lectr, Australia, 1983. Sen. Treas., Royal Soc. Club, 1988–89. *Publications:* contribs to learned scientific jls. *Recreations:* gardening, reading. *Address:* 33 Homefield Road, Radlett, Herts WD7 8PX. *T:* (01923) 854675.

CRUSH, His Honour Harvey Michael; a Circuit Judge, 1995–2001; *b* 12 April 1939; *s* of late George Stanley Crush, Chislehurst, and Alison Isabel Crush; *m* 1st, 1965, Diana Bassett (marr. diss. 1982); one *s* one *d*; 2nd, 1982, Maggie, *d* of Nicholas Dixson. *Educ:* Chigwell Sch. Admitted solicitor, 1963; Partner, Norton Rose, 1968–91; Asst Recorder, 1987–92; Recorder, 1992–95; Higher Courts Advocate, 1994; Dep. Circuit Judge, 2001–. Dir, TOSG Trust Fund Ltd, 1970–95. Mem., Supreme Court Rule Cttee, 1984–88. Mem., Law Soc., 1963–; Vice-Pres., City of London Law Soc., 1989–91. Hon. Solicitor, British Assoc. Aviation Consultants, 1990–95 (Mem. Council, 1991–95). MRAeS 1980. Hon. Life Member: Solicitors' Higher Courts Advocacy Assoc.; London Solicitors' Litigation Assoc. Liveryman: Co. of Solicitors, 1982 (Mem. Court, 1987–; Master, 1994–95); Co. of Farriers, 1984 (Mem. Court, 1997–); GAPAN, 2000 (Freeman, 1991). Hon. Life Mem., Sevenoaks & Dist Motor Club (Chm., 1968–71). *Recreations:* flying light aircraft, travel, Spain, walking.

CRUTCHLEY, Brooke, CBE 1954; Printer of the University of Cambridge, 1946–74; Fellow of Trinity Hall, 1951–73, Emeritus Fellow, 1977 (Vice-Master, 1966–70); Honorary Fellow of St Edmund's College (formerly St Edmund's House), Cambridge, since 1980; *b* 31 July 1907; *yr s* of late Ernest Tristram Crutchley, CB, CMG, CBE, and Anna, *d* of James Dunne; *m* 1936, Diana, *d* of late Lt-Col Arthur Egerton Cotton, DSO, and Beryl Marie (who *m* 2nd, John Lee Booker); two *s* one *d.* *Educ:* Shrewsbury; Trinity Hall, Cambridge. Editorial Staff of Yorkshire Post, 1929–30; Asst Univ. Printer at Cambridge, 1930–45; Secretary's Dept of the Admiralty, 1941–45. Pres., Inst. of Printing, 1972–74. Hon. Col, Commonwealth of Kentucky, 1974. Bicentenary Medal, RSA, 1977. *Publication:* To be a printer, (autobiog.), 1980. *Address:* 39 High Street, Great Shelford, Cambridge CB2 5EH. *T:* (01223) 845168. *Club:* Double Crown.

CRUTCHLOW, John Adrian; Director of Finance, Metropolitan Police, 1986–96, retired; *b* 30 March 1946; *s* of James William Crutchlow and Elsie Nellie Crutchlow (*née* King); *m* 1971, Valerie Elizabeth Farage. *Educ:* Finchley County Grammar Sch.; HNC (with dist.) in Business Studies; BA Open; postgraduate Dip. Management Studies. Paymaster General's Office, 1962–65; Metropolitan Police Civil Staff, 1965–96; Principal, 1974–81; Dep. Dir of Finance, 1981–84; Dep. Estabt Officer, 1984–86; Asst Sec., 1986–92; Asst Under-Sec. of State, 1992–96; Dep. to Receiver, Metropolitan Police Dist, 1994–96. President: New Scotland Yard Civil Staff Assoc., 1994–96; Metropolitan Police Former (formerly Metropolitan Police Retired) Civil Staff Assoc., 1996–. FIMgt (FBIM 1992); FInstAM 1995. *Recreations:* reading, gardening, renovating old houses. *Address:* Friars' Grange, Rushden, Herts SG9 0TF.

CRUTE, Prof. Ian Richard, PhD; Director, Institute of Arable Crops Research, since 1999; *b* 3 June 1949; *s* of Walter and Rose Crute; *m* 1973, J. Elizabeth Harden; two *d.* *Educ:* Univ. of Newcastle upon Tyne (BSc Hons Botany 1970; PhD 1973). Research Leader, Nat. Vegetable Res. Station, Wellesbourne, Warwick, 1973–86; Horticulture Research International: Head, Crop and Envmt Protection Dept, E Malling, Kent, 1987–93; Head, Plant Pathology Dept, 1993–95, Dir, 1995–99, Wellesbourne. Fulbright Fellow, Univ. of Wisconsin, 1986. *Publications:* numerous papers on plant pathol. and genetics in scientific jls. *Recreations:* gardening, golf, walking, theatre. *Address:* Institute of Arable Crops Research, Rothamsted, Harpenden, Herts AL5 2JQ. *T:* (01582) 763133.

CRUTHERS, Sir James (Winter), Kt 1980; company director; Vice-Chairman and Executive Vice-President, News America Publishing Inc., 1984–90 (Director, since 1983); Vice-Chairman, News America Holdings Inc., 1984–90 (Director, since 1984); *b* 20 Dec. 1924; *s* of James William and Kate Cruthers; *m* 1950, Alwyn Sheila Della; one *s* one *d.* *Educ:* Claremont Central State Sch.; Perth Technical College. Started as junior in Perth Daily News, 1939; war service, AIF and RAAF (Pilot), 1942; Journalist, Perth Daily News, 1946; Editor, Weekly Publications, West Australian Newspapers Ltd, 1953; TVW Enterprises Ltd: General Manager, 1958; Managing Director, 1969; Dep. Chm., 1974; Chm., 1976–81; Chm., Australian Film Commn, 1982–83. Director: News Corp. Ltd, 1981–92; Satellite Television plc, 1984–90 (Chm., 1985–88). Western Australian Citizen Of The Year, Industry and Commerce, 1980. *Recreations:* golf, jogging. *Address:* 8 Bird Street, Mosman Park, WA 6012, Australia. *Clubs:* Weld (Perth); Lake Karrinyup Country (Perth).

CRUTTWELL, Geraldine, (Mrs Hugh Cruttwell); *see* McEwan, G.

CRUTTWELL, Hugh (Percival); Principal of Royal Academy of Dramatic Art, 1966–84, retired; *b* 31 Oct. 1918; *s* of Clement Chadwick Cruttwell and Grace Fanny (*née* Robin); *m* 1953, Geraldine McEwan, *qv*; one *s* one *d.* *Educ:* King's Sch., Bruton; Hertford Coll., Oxford. *Address:* 8 Ranelagh Avenue, Barnes, SW13 0BY.

CRUTZEN, Prof. Dr Paul; Director, Atmospheric Chemistry Division, Max-Planck Institute for Chemistry, Germany, 1980–2000; *b* Amsterdam, 3 Dec. 1933; *m* 1958, Terttu Crutzen (*née* Soininen); two *d*. *Educ:* Stockholm Univ. (PhD 1968; DSc 1973). Member: Royal Swedish Acad. of Scis; Royal Swedish Acad. of Engrg Scis; Academia Europaea. (Jtly) Nobel Prize for Chemistry, 1995. *Address:* c/o Max-Planck Institute for Chemistry, PO Box 3060, 55020 Mainz, Germany.

CRWYS-WILLIAMS, Air Vice-Marshal David Owen, CB 1990; Managing Director, Services Sound and Vision Corporation (SSVC), since 1994 (Deputy Managing Director, 1993–94); *b* 24 Dec. 1940; *s* of Gareth Crwys-Williams and Frances Ellen Crwys-Williams (*née* Strange); *m* 1st, 1964, Jennifer Jean (*née* Pearce) (marr. diss. 1971); one *s* one *d*; 2nd, 1973, Irene Thompson (Suzie) (*née* Whan); one *s* two *d*. *Educ:* Oakham Sch.; RAF Coll., Cranwell. Commnd as pilot, RAF, 1961; served No 30 Sqn, Kenya, 1962–64, No 47 Sqn, Abingdon, 1964–66; ADC to C-in-C RAF Trng Comd, 1966–68; OC 46 Sqn, 1969; RAF Masirah, 1972; Army Staff Coll., 1973; Personal Staff Officer to C-in-C NEAF, 1974–75; OC No 230 Sqn, 1976–77; Air Sec. Dept, MoD, 1977–78; Dep. Dir Air Plans, MoD, 1979–82; OC RAF Shawbury, 1983–84; RCDS 1985; Dir of Air Support and Dir of Air Staff Duties, MoD, 1986–88; Comdr, British Forces Falkland Is, 1988–89; Dir Gen., RAF Personal Services, MoD, 1989–92. Gp Captain 1979; Air Cdre 1985; Air Vice-Marshal 1988. Executive Chairman: SSVC Services Ltd, 1994–99; Columbia Communications Europe, 1994–98; VISUA Ltd, 1996–99; Man. Dir, Teleport London Internat., 1994–98; Chm., Eur. Broadcasting Corp., 1995–98; Dir, Forces Events Ltd. Council Mem., Cinema and Television Benevolent Fund. Chm., New Island South Conservation Trust, 1995–. Trustee, British Forces Foundn. Chm. Governors, Amersham and Wycombe Coll., 2000– (Vice-Chm., 1998–2000). Mem., Inst. Dirs. FICPD (FIPM 1991); FIMgt 1993. *Recreations:* furniture restoration, walking, building, fishing. *Address:* c/o Barclays Bank, PO Box 354, Abingdon, Oxon OX14 1FL. *Club:* Royal Air Force.

CRYAN, Donald Michael; His Honour Judge Cryan; a Circuit Judge, since 1996; *b* 18 Jan. 1948; *s* of late Thomas Joseph Cryan and Helen McBeath Cryan (*née* Munro); *m* 1973, Pamela; two *s*. *Educ:* Salvatorian Coll.; UCL (LLB (Hons)). Called to the Bar, Inner Temple, 1970 (Bencher, 1992; Master of the House, 1993–98); a Recorder, 1993–96; SE Circuit. Designated Family Judge, Medway, 2001–. Freeman, City of London, 1978; Liveryman, Co. of Fruiterers, 1978 (Master, 1999–2000). Member, Committee: Marshall Hall Trust, 1991–; Centre for Child and Family Law Reform, City Univ., 1999–. *Recreation:* theatre. *Address:* 4 Paper Buildings, Temple, EC4Y 7EX. *T:* (020) 7583 0816. *Club:* Royal Automobile.

CRYER, (Constance) Ann; JP; MP (Lab) Keighley, since 1997; *b* 14 Dec. 1939; *d* of Allen Place and Margaret Ann Place; *m* 1963, George Robert, (Bob), Cryer, MP (*d* 1994); one *s* one *d*. *Educ:* St John's Primary Sch.; Spring Bank Secondary Mod. Sch., Darwen; Bolton Tech. Coll.; Keighley Tech. Coll. Clerk, ICI, 1955–60; telephonist, GPO, 1960–64; researcher, Social Hist. Dept, Essex Univ., 1969; PA to Bob Cryer, MP and MEP, 1974–94. Mem. (Lab), Darwen BC, 1962–65. JP Bradford, 1996. *Publication:* (contrib.) Boldness be My Friend: remembering Bob Cryer, 1997. *Recreations:* gardening, cinema, theatre, time with my 6 grandchildren. *Address:* House of Commons, SW1A 0AA; 32 Kendall Avenue, Shipley, W Yorks BD18 4DY. *T:* (01274) 584701.

See also J. R. Cryer.

CRYER, John Robert; MP (Lab) Hornchurch, since 1997; *b* 11 April 1964; *s* of late (George) Robert Cryer, MP and of Ann Cryer, *qv*; *m* 1994, Narinder Bains, *d* of Shiv Singh Bains and Bakhshish Bains; two *s* one *d*. *Educ:* Oakbank Sch., Keighley; Hatfield Poly. (BA). Underwriter, 1986–88; Journalist, Morning Star, 1989–92; Editor, Labour Briefing, 1992–93; Journalist: GPMU Jl, 1992–93; Tribune, 1993–96; Lloyd's of London Pubns, 1996–97. *Publication:* (jtly) Boldness be My Friend: remembering Bob Cryer, 1997. *Recreations:* most sports, reading, cinema, old cars. *Address:* House of Commons, SW1A 0AA.

CRYSTAL, Prof. David, OBE 1995; FBA 2000; author, lecturer, broadcaster on language and linguistics, and reference books editor; Hon. Professorial Fellow, University of Wales, Bangor (formerly University College of North Wales), since 1985; *b* 6 July 1941; *s* of late Samuel Cyril Crystal and Mary Agnes Morris; *m* 1st, 1964, Molly Irene Stack (*d* 1976); one *s* two *d* (and one *s* decd); 2nd, 1976, Hilary Frances Norman; one *s*. *Educ:* St Mary's Coll., Liverpool; University Coll. London (BA 1962); London Univ. (PhD 1966). Res. Asst, UCL, 1962–63; Asst Lectr, UCNW, 1963–65; University of Reading: Lectr, 1965–69; Reader, 1969–75; Prof., 1975–85. Vis. Prof., Bowling Green State Univ., 1969. Dir, Ucheldre Centre, Holyhead, 1991–. Mem. Bd, British Council, 1996–2001. Sec., Linguistics Assoc. of GB, 1965–70. Hon. Vice-Pres., Royal Coll. of Speech and Lang. Therapists, 1995– (Mem., Academic Bd, Coll. of Speech Therapists, 1972–79); FRCSLT (FCST 1983). Hon. President: Nat. Assoc. of Professionals concerned with Lang. Impaired Children, 1985–; Internat. Assoc. of Forensic Phonetics, 1991–; Soc. of Indexers, 1992–95; Patron, Internat. Assoc. of Teachers of English as a Foreign Lang., 1995–; Vice-Pres., Inst. of Linguists, 1998–; Chm., Nat. Literacy Assoc., 1995–. Editor: Language Res. in Progress, 1966–70; Jl of Child Language, 1973–85; The Language Library, 1978–; Applied Language Studies, 1980–84; Child Language Teaching and Therapy, 1985–96; Linguistics Abstracts, 1985–96; Blackwells Applied Language Studies, 1986–95; Consultant Editor, English Today, 1985–94; Adv. Editor, Penguin Linguistics, 1968–75; Associate Editor, Jl of Linguistics, 1970–73; Co-Editor, Studies in Language Disability, 1974–. Regular BBC broadcasts on English language and linguistics. FRSA 1983. Hon. DSc Queen Margaret UC, Edinburgh, 1997. *Publications:* Systems of prosodic and paralinguistic features in English (with R. Quirk), 1964; Linguistics, language and religion, 1965; (ed jtly) Proceedings, Modern approaches to language teaching at university level, 1967; What is linguistics?, 1968, 5th edn 1985; Prosodic systems and intonation in English, 1969; (with D. Davy) Investigating English style, 1969; (ed with W. Bolton) The English language, vol. 2, 1969; Linguistics, 1971, 2nd edn 1985; Basic linguistics, 1973; Language acquisition, 1973; The English tone of voice, 1975; (with D. Davy) Advanced conversational English, 1975; (with J. Bevington) Skylarks, 1975; (jtly) The grammatical analysis of language disability, 1976, 2nd edn 1989; Child language, learning and linguistics, 1976, 2nd edn 1987; Working with LARSP, 1979; Introduction to language pathology, 1980, 4th edn (with R. Varley) 1998; A first dictionary of linguistics and phonetics, 1980, 5th edn 2002; (ed) Eric Partridge: in his own words, 1980; Clinical linguistics, 1981; Directions in applied linguistics, 1981; Profiling linguistic disability, 1982, 2nd edn 1992; (ed) Linguistic controversies, 1982; Who cares about English usage?, 1984, 2nd edn 2000; Language handicap in children, 1984; Linguistic encounters with language handicap, 1984; Listen to your child, 1986; (ed with W. Bolton) The English language, 1987; Cambridge Encyclopedia of Language, 1987, 2nd edn 1997; Rediscover grammar, 1988, 2nd edn 1996; The English Language, 1988; Pilgrimage, 1988; (with J. C. Davies) Convent, 1989; (ed) Cambridge Encyclopedia, 1990, 4th edn 2000; Language A to Z, 1991; Making Sense of English Usage, 1991; Nineties Knowledge, 1992; Introducing Linguistics, 1992; An Encyclopedic Dictionary of Language and Languages, 1992, 2nd edn, as The Penguin Dictionary of Language, 1999; (ed) Cambridge Concise Encyclopedia, 1992, 2nd edn 1995; (ed) Cambridge Paperback Encyclopedia, 1993, 3rd edn 1999; (ed) Cambridge Factfinder, 1993, 4th edn 2000; (ed) Cambridge Biographical Encyclopedia, 1994, 2nd edn 1998; Cambridge Encyclopedia of the English Language, 1995; Discover Grammar, 1996; (ed) John Bradburne, Songs of the Vagabond, 1996; Cambridge Biographical Dictionary, 1996; English as a Global Language, 1997; Language Play, 1998; (with H. Crystal) Words on Words, 2000; Language Death, 2000; (with H. Crystal) John Bradburne's Mutemwa, 2000; Happenings, 2000; Language and the Internet, 2001; (with J. L. Foster) Databank series: Heat, Light, Sound, Roads, Railways, Canals, Manors, Castles, Money, Monasteries, Parliament, Newspapers, 1979; The Romans, The Greeks, The Ancient Egyptians, 1981; Air, Food, Volcanoes, 1982; Deserts, Dinosaurs and Electricity, 1983; Motorcycles, Computers, Horses and Ponies, Normans, Vikings, Anglo-Saxons, Celts, 1984; The Stone Age, Fishing, 1985; (with J. L. Foster) Datasearch series: Air and Breathing, Heating and Cooling, Light and Seeing, Sound and Hearing, 1991; contributions to: The Library of Modern Knowledge, 1978; A Dictionary of Modern Thought, 1978, 2nd edn 1987; Reader's Digest Great Illustrated Dictionary, 1984; Reader's Digest Book of Facts, 1985; A Comprehensive Grammar of the English Language, 1985; International Encyclopedia of Linguistics, 1992; and to numerous volumes on language, style, prosody, communication, religion, handicap, teaching and reading; symposia and proceedings of learned socs; articles and reviews in jls on linguistics, English language, speech pathology and education. *Recreations:* cinema, music, bibliophily, development of the arts. *Address:* Akaroa, Gors Avenue, Holyhead, Anglesey LL65 1PB. *T:* (01407) 762764, *Fax:* Holyhead (01407) 769728; *e-mail:* crystal@dial.pipex.com.

CRYSTAL, Michael; QC 1984; a Deputy High Court Judge, since 1995; Senior Visiting Fellow, Centre for Commercial Law Studies, Queen Mary and Westfield College (formerly Queen Mary College), University of London, since 1996 (Hon. Senior Visiting Fellow, 1987–96); *b* 5 March 1948; *s* of late Dr Samuel Cyril Crystal, OBE, and of Rachel Ettel Crystal; *m* 1972, Susan Felicia Sniderman; one *s* one *d*. *Educ:* Leeds Grammar Sch.; Queen Mary Coll., Univ. of London (LLB Hons; Hon. Fellow, QMW, 1996); Magdalen Coll., Oxford (BCL). Called to the Bar, Middle Temple, 1970, Bencher, 1993; called to the Bar *ad eundem*, Gray's Inn, 1989; Lecturer in Law, Pembroke Coll., Oxford, 1971–76. DTI Inspector into County NatWest Ltd and County NatWest Securities Ltd, 1988–89, and into National Westminster Bank plc, 1992. Member: Insolvency Rules Adv. Cttee, 1993–97; Financial Law Panel, 1996–. Member: Adv. Cttee, Pembroke Coll., Oxford, 1996–; Adv. Council, Centre for Commercial Law Studies, QMW, 1996–; Adv. Council, Univ. of Oxford Law Foundn, 1998–. Gov., RSC, 1988–. Hon. Fellow, Soc. for Advanced Legal Studies, 1997. *Publications:* various legal text books. *Recreations:* travel, music, theatre. *Clubs:* Royal Automobile, MCC.

CUBBON, Sir Brian (Crossland), GCB 1984 (KCB 1977; CB 1974); Permanent Under Secretary of State, Home Office, 1979–88; Member, Press Complaints Commission, since 1995; Vice-President, Hakluyt Foundation, since 1995; *b* 9 April 1928; *m* 1956, Elizabeth Lorin Richardson; three *s* one *d*. *Educ:* Bury Grammar Sch.; Trinity Coll., Cambridge. Entered Home Office, 1951; Cabinet Office, 1961–63, 1971–75; Private Sec. to Home Sec., 1968–69; Permanent Under-Sec. of State, Northern Ireland Office, 1976–79. *Address:* Brook Farm House, Capel, Tonbridge, Kent TN12 6TT. *T:* (01892) 832534. *Clubs:* Oxford and Cambridge, Beefsteak.

CUBIE, George; Clerk of Committees, House of Commons, since 2001; *b* 30 Aug. 1943; *s* of Dr Alexander Cubie and of late Elsie B. C. Thorburn; *m* 1966, Kathleen S. Mullan; one *s*. *Educ:* Dollar Acad.; Edinburgh Univ. (MA Hons). Clerk in H of C, 1966; Clerk of Financial Cttees, H of C, 1987–89; Sec. to Public Accounts Commn, 1987–89; Clerk of Select Cttees, H of C, 1989–91; Clerk of the Overseas Office, 1991–95; Principal Clerk, Table Office, 1995–97; Clerk Asst, H of C, 1998–2001. *Publications:* (contrib.) Erskine May's Parliamentary Practice, 22nd edn, 1997; (contrib.) Halsbury's Laws of England, 5th edn. *Recreation:* walking. *Address:* House of Commons, SW1A 0AA. *T:* (020) 7219 3000.

CUBITT, family name of **Baron Ashcombe**.

CUBITT, Sir Hugh (Guy), Kt 1983; CBE 1977; FRICS; JP; DL; Chairman, Peabody Trust, since 1998 (Governor, since 1991); Director, PSIT PLC (formerly Property Security Investment Trust PLC), 1962–97; *b* 2 July 1928; *s* of late Col Hon. (Charles) Guy Cubitt, CBE, DSO, TD, and Rosamond Mary Edith, *d* of Sir Montagu Cholmeley, 4th Bt; *m* 1958, Linda Ishbel, *d* of late Hon. Angus Campbell, CBE; one *s* two *d*. *Educ:* RNC Dartmouth and Greenwich. Lieut RN, 1949; served in Korea, 1949–51; Flag Lieut to Adm., BJSM Washington, 1952 and to C-in-C Nore, 1953; retd 1953. Qual. Chartered Auctioneer and Estate Agent, 1958; Chartered Surveyor (FRICS) 1970. Partner: Rogers Chapman & Thomas, 1958–67; Cubitt & West, 1962–79. Regl Dir, 1970–77, Dir, 1977–90, Mem., UK Adv. Bd, 1990–91, National Westminster Bank; Chairman: Lombard North Central PLC, 1980–91; The Housing Corp., 1980–90; Rea Brothers Group PLC, 1996–98. Comr, and Chm., London Adv. Cttee, English Heritage, 1988–94. Mem. Westminster City Council, 1963–78; Leader of Council, 1972–76; Alderman, 1974–78; Lord Mayor and Dep. High Steward of Westminster, 1977–78. Pres., London Chamber of Commerce, 1988–91. Chairman: Anchor Trust (formerly Anchor Gp of Housing Assocs), 1991–98; Housing Assocs' Charitable Trust, 1991–97; Chairman of Governors: West Heath Sch., 1978–91; Cranleigh Sch., 1981–95; Dir and Mem. Governing Body, RAM, 1978–98. Hon. Steward, Westminster Abbey, 1978 (Chief Steward, 1997–). Mem., Bd of Green Cloth Verge of Palaces, 1980–98. FRSA; Hon. FRAM 1985. JP Surrey, 1964; Chairman: Dorking PSD, 1991–93; SE Surrey PSD, 1993–95. High Sheriff of Surrey, 1983–84; DL Greater London, 1978. *Recreations:* country sports, travel, photography, painting. *Address:* Chapel House, Westhumble, Dorking, Surrey RH5 6AY. *T:* (01306) 882994. *Club:* Boodle's.

CUCKNEY, Baron *cr* 1995 (Life Peer), of Millbank in the City of Westminster; **John Graham Cuckney,** Kt 1978; *b* 12 July 1925; *s* of late Air Vice-Marshal E. J. Cuckney, CB, CBE, DSC and Lilian (*née* Williams); *m* 2nd, 1960, Muriel, *d* of late Walter Scott Boyd. *Educ:* Shrewsbury; St Andrews Univ. (MA). War Service, Royal Northumberland Fusiliers, King's African Rifles, followed by attachment to War Office (Civil Asst, Gen. Staff), until 1957; subseq. appts with various industrial and financial cos including: Chairman: Brooke Bond Gp, 1981–84 (Dir, 1979–84); Thomas Cook Gp, 1978–87; John Brown, 1983–86 (Dir, 1981–86; Dep. Chm., 1982–83); Westland Gp, 1985–89; Royal Insce Hldgs plc, 1985–94 (Dir, 1979–89; Dep. Chm., 1983–85); Investors in Industry Gp, subseq. 3i Gp, 1987–92 (Dir, 1986–92); Orion Publishing Gp Ltd, 1994–97; Dep. Chm., TI Gp, 1985–90; Vice Chm., Glaxo, 1993–95 (Dir, 1990–95); Director: Lazard Brothers, 1964–70 and 1988–90; Midland Bank, 1978–88; Brixton Estate, 1985–96. Public appointments include: Chm., Mersey Docks and Harbour Board, 1970–72; Chief Executive (Second Perm. Sec.), Property Services Agency, DoE, 1972–74; Chm., International Military Services Ltd (an MoD company), 1974–85; Sen. Crown Agent and Chm. of Crown Agents, for Oversea Governments and Administrations, 1974–78. Advr to Sec. of State for Social Security on Maxwell pensions affair, and Founder Chm., Maxwell Pensioners' Trust, 1992–95. Independent Mem., Railway Policy Review Cttee, 1966–67; special Mem., Hops Marketing Bd, 1971–72; Chairman: EDC for Building, 1976–80; Port of London Authority, 1977–79; Internat. Maritime Bureau, Internat.

Chamber of Commerce, 1981–85; NEDC Working Party on European Public Purchasing, 1990–92; Member: Docklands Joint Cttee, 1977–79; Council, British Exec. Service Overseas, 1981–84; Council, Foundn for Science and Technology, 1987–90; Dir, SBAC, 1986–89. Vice Pres., Liverpool Sch. of Tropical Med., 1985–93. Governor, Centre for Internat. Briefing, Farnham Castle, 1974–84; Chm., Understanding Industry Trust, 1988–91; Controller, ROH Develt Land Trust, 1993–96; Trustee, RAF Mus., 1987–99. Freeman, City of London, 1977. Elder Brother of Trinity House, 1980. Hon. DSc Bath, 1991; Hon. LLD St Andrews, 1993. *Address:* House of Lords, SW1A 0PW. *T:* (020) 7219 3000. *Club:* Athenæum.

CUDLIPP, Michael John; Secretary, The History of Advertising Trust, since 1994 (Governor, 1984–86; Hon. Secretary and Administrator, 1986–94); *b* 24 April 1934; *o s* of late Percy Cudlipp and Mrs Gwendoline May Cudlipp; *m* 1st, 1957, Margaret Susannah Rees (marr. diss. 1975); one *d*; 2nd, 1985, Jane Gale; two *d. Educ:* Tonbridge Sch., Kent. Trainee reporter, feature writer, gossip columnist, sub-editor, South Wales Echo, Cardiff, 1953–57; Sub-editor, Evening Chronicle, Manchester (various freelance jobs on daily and Sunday newspapers in Manchester), 1957–58; News Editor and Asst Editor (News), Sunday Times, 1958–67; Asst Editor (Night), Jt Man. Editor and sen. Dep. Editor, The Times, 1967–73; Chief Editor, London Broadcasting Co., 1973–74; Consultant on Public Relations to NI Office (temp. Civil Servant with rank of Under-Sec.), 1974–75; Dir of Information, Nat. Enterprise Bd, 1975–78; Director: External and Internal Communications, Internat. Thomson Orgn, 1979–85; The Georgian Gp, 1992–94. Mem., Consumer and Advertising Studies Course Adv. Cttee, Univ. of East London, 1992–. Exhibitions directed: The Image of Women in Advertising from Victorian Times to Today, Royal Instn and various mus, 1995–2001; Gilroy is good for you, Laing Gall., Newcastle upon Tyne, and RCA, 1998; From Ephesus to e-commerce: 2010 years of advertising, London Coll. of Printing and various mus, 2000–01. Mem., Soc. of Archivists, 1995–. US State Dept Leader Grant (to study race relations in the US), 1962. Ampleforth Sch. Headmaster's Lecture, on Prejudice, 1997. *Publication:* The Thirty Club of London: free speech within four walls, 1999. *Recreations:* wooden boats, conservation, Welsh rugby football. *Address:* Stepping Hill House, 25 Ballygate, Beccles, Suffolk NR34 9ND; *e-mail:* hatadvert@email.msn.com.

CUDLIPP, Reginald; writer specialising on Japan; Director, Anglo-Japanese Economic Institute, London, 1961–86, retired; *b* Cardiff, 11 Dec. 1910; *s* of William and Mrs B. A. Cudlipp, Cardiff; *m* 1945, Rachel Joyce Braham. *Educ:* Cardiff Technical Coll. Began journalistic career on Penarth News, Glamorgan; Sub-Ed., Western Mail, Cardiff; joined News of the World Sub-Editorial Staff, 1938; served War, 1940–46; rejoined News of the World and became Special Correspondent in USA, 1946–47; Features Ed., 1948–50, Dep. Ed., 1950–53, Ed., 1953–59; Dir, News of the World Ltd, 1955–60. Extensive industrial tours and on-the-spot economic study of Japan regularly, 1962–86. Completed 60 years in active journalism, 1926–86. Life Mem., NUJ, 1929. Editor, Japan (quarterly review and monthly survey), and special publications on the Japanese scene, 1961–86. Lecturer and writer on Japan's past, present and future; also first-hand research on developing nations and economic co-operation, especially in Africa and Asia; invited to Japan, 1989, to brief businessmen on the Japan/EEC partnership after 1992. Order of the Sacred Treasure, Japan, 1982. *Publications:* numerous contribs to newspapers and periodicals, on Japan and Anglo-Japanese affairs. *Recreations:* music, travel, and reading, writing and talking about Japan. *Address:* 42 Martlets Court, Queen Street, Arundel, West Sussex BN18 9NZ.

CUDMORE, Harold; yachtsman/consultant; *b* 21 April 1944; *s* of Harold Cudmore, LLD and late Sheila Coleman; *m* 1993, Lauren E. Dagge; two *d*. . Skipper, White Crusader, British challenger, America's Cup, 1986; Manager and sailor, British Admiral's Cup winning team, 1989; Adviser and Coach, America 3, America's Cup winning team, 1992; Chm., RYA Admiral's Cup Steering Gp, 1998–99; Captain, British Admiral's Cup team, 2001. Winner of many world championships, internat. match-racing regattas and major events. *Recreations:* other sports, walking, travelling, socialising. *Address:* 4 Queen's Road, Cowes, Isle of Wight PO31 8BQ. *T:* (01983) 280466, *Fax:* (01983) 291771; *e-mail:* haroldcudmore@cs.com. *Clubs:* Royal Thames Yacht, Royal Ocean Racing; Royal Cork Yacht, Island Sailing, Royal Corinthian Yacht, Irish Cruising, Fort Worth Boat.

CUENOD, Hugues; Swiss tenor, retired; *b* 26 June 1902; *s* of Frank Cuenod and Gabrielle de Meuron. *Educ:* Swiss schools and colleges; Conservatoire Basel; Vienna; with Mme Singer-Burian. First concert, Paris, 1928; gave many performances of classical and light music, incl. musical comedy, in Europe and USA; numerous concerts with Clara Haskil and Nadia Boulanger; taught at Conservatoire de Genève, 1940–46; after returning to Paris, concentrated on sacred and classical music; sang in all major opera houses, incl. Glyndebourne (début 1954) and NY Metropolitan (début 1987); latterly specialised in French songs; many master classes; still teaches vocal interpretation of French songs. 33 recordings, of Couperin, Fauré, Debussy, Schubert, Bach, etc, many now re-issued on CD; Grand Prix du Disque, 1980, for Socrate, by Erik Satie. Hon. Citizen of Boston, 1972. Händel and Haydn Soc. Medal, Boston, 1972; Fidelio Medal, Geneva, 1987. Commandeur de l'Ordre des Arts et des Lettres (France), 1976. *Relevant publications:* Hugues Cuenod: un diable de musicien, by Jerôme Spycket, 1978; Hugues Cuenod d'une voix légère: entretiens avec François Hudry, 1995. *Address:* 21 Place du Marché, 1800 Vevey, Switzerland; Château de Lully sur Morges, Vaud, Switzerland.

CUEVAS-CANCINO, Francisco, GCVO (Hon.) 1985; Mexican Ambassador to Austria, 1986–90; Permanent Mexican Representative to UNIDO and IAEA, since 1986; *b* 7 May 1921; *s* of José Luis Cuevas and Sofia Cancino; *m* 1946, Ana Hilditch; two *s* one *d*; *m* Cristina Flores de Cuevas. *Educ:* Free School of Law, Mexico (lawyer, 1943); McGill Univ., Montreal (MCL 1946). Entered Mexican Foreign Service, as Vice-Consul, 1946, reaching rank of Ambassador by own merit; Permanent Representative to UN, 1965–70; Mexican Rep. to UNESCO, 1971–75, and Mem. Exec. Council during first four years; Perm. Rep. to UN, 1978–79; Ambassador: to Brazil, 1979–80; to Belgium, 1980–83; to UK and to Republic of Ireland, 1983–85. Chm., Group of 77, Vienna, 1988. Order of the Liberator, 1970, Order Andrés Bello, 1971, (Venezuela); Medal of Mexican For. Service (25 years), 1972; Order Cruzeiro do Sur (Brazil), 1980; Great Cross of Order of the Crown (Belgium), 1983. *Publications:* La nullité des actes juridiques, 1947; La doctrina de Suárez en el derecho natural (award, Madrid), 1952; Roosevelt y la buena vecindad, 1955; Del Congreso de Panamá a la Conferencia de Caracas, 1955, re-ed 1979; Tratado sobre la organización internacional, 1962; (ed) Porvenir de México by Luis G. Cuevas, 1961; (ed) Pacto de Familia (vol. forms part of Hist. Archives of Mexican Diplomatic Service, 2nd series), 1963; (ed) Foro Internacional, 1961–62; contrib. to book of essays in homage to Hans Morgenthau, 1978; several works and articles on Bolivarian theatre, and on Simón Bolívar (The Liberator), incl.: Visión Surrealista del Libertador, (Bogotá) 1980; Homenaje a Bolívar en el Sesquicentenario de su Muerte, (Bogotá) 1980. *Address:* Secretariat for Foreign Affairs, Ricardo Flores Magón, 1 Tlatelolco, 06995 México DF, México.

CUI, Prof. Zhanfeng, PhD; CEng; Donald Pollock Professor of Chemical Engineering, and Fellow of Hertford College, Oxford University, since 2000; *b* 16 Nov. 1962; *s* of Chun-Ting Cui and Su-e Li; *m* 1985, Dr Jing Yu; one *s* one *d. Educ:* Inner Mongolia Poly. Univ., China (BSc 1982); Dalian Univ. of Technol., China (MSc 1984; PhD 1987); MA Oxon 1994. CEng 1997. Res. Fellow, Univ. of Strathclyde, 1988–91; Lectr in Chemical Engrg, Edinburgh Univ., 1991–94; Oxford University: Lectr in Engrg Sci., 1994–99; Reader, 1999–2000; Fellow, Keble Coll., 1994–2000. Vis. Prof., Georgia Inst. of Technol., Atlanta, 1999. *Publications:* contrib. numerous res. articles to professional jls, as sole or jt author. *Recreations:* bridge, basketball. *Address:* Department of Engineering Science, Oxford University, Parks Road, Oxford OX1 3PJ. *T:* (01865) 273118.

CULHAM, Michael John, CB 1992; Assistant Under Secretary of State (Civilian Management (Administrators)), Ministry of Defence, 1987–92, retired; *b* 24 June 1933; *s* of Cecil and Constance Culham; *m* 1963, Christine Mary Daish; one *s* two *d. Educ:* Reading Sch.; Lincoln Coll., Oxford (MA); Open Univ. (Dip. French, 1997). National Service, Queen's Own Royal West Kent Regt, RAEC, 1952–54. Exec. Officer, WO, 1957–61; Asst Principal, Air Min., 1962; Private Sec. to Under-Sec. of State for Air, 1962–64; Principal, MoD, 1964–72; Jt Services Staff Coll., 1969; 1st Sec. (Defence), UK Delegn to NATO, Brussels, 1972–74; Asst Sec., MoD, 1974–82; Asst Under-Sec. of State (Adjt-Gen.), MoD, 1982–87. Member: Royal Patriotic Fund Corp., 1983–87; Adv. Council, RMCS, Shrivenham, 1983–87. Commissioner: Duke of York's Royal Mil. Sch., 1982–87; Queen Victoria Sch., 1982–87; Welbeck Coll., 1985–87; Royal Hosp. Chelsea, 1985–88. Chm., Defence Sports and Recreation (formerly MoD Recreation) Assoc., 1985–92; Vice President: CS RFU, 1992–; Farnham Town Boys' FC, 1987– (Chm., 1983–85). Trustee, Nat. Army Mus., 1985–88. *Recreations:* music, sailing, walking, watching cricket. *Address:* 39 Waverley Lane, Farnham, Surrey GU9 8BH. *Clubs:* Civil Service; Surrey County Cricket; Hampshire County Cricket.

CULHANE, Prof. (John) Leonard, FRS 1985; Professor of Physics, since 1981, Director, Mullard Space Science Laboratory, since 1983, and Head of Department of Space and Climate Physics, since 1993, University College London; *b* 14 Oct. 1937; *s* of late John Thomas Culhane and Mary Agnes Culhane; *m* 1961, Mary Brigid, *d* of James Smith; two *s. Educ:* Clongowes Wood College, Co. Kildare; University College Dublin (BSc Phys 1959; MSc Phys 1960); UCL (PhD Phys 1966). FRAS 1970; FInstP 1991. Physics Department, University College London: Res. Asst, 1963; Lectr, 1967; Reader, 1976; Prof., 1981. Sen. Scientist, Lockheed Palo Alto Res. Lab., 1969–70; Vis. Prof., Inst. of Space and Astronautical Sci., Tokyo, 1997. Chairman: SERC/BNSC Space Sci. Prog. Bd, 1989–92 (Vice-Pres., and UK Deleg., ESA Sci. Prog. Cttee, 1990–94); Royal Soc. Space Res. Cttee, 1990–93; COSPAR Commn E, 1994–; Eur. Space Sci. Cttee, ESF, 1997–; Member: Council, RAS, 1975–78; Space Sci. Adv. Cttee, ESA, 1985–89 (Chm., Astrophysics Working Group, 1985–89); SERC/BNSC Earth Obs. Prog. Bd, 1986–88; SERC Astron. Plan. Sci. Bd, 1989–92; Adv. Panel, ESA Space Sci. Dept, 1995–; PPARC, 1996–2000. Mem. Council, Surrey Univ., 1985–90. Member: IAU; Amer. Astronomical Soc.; Amer. Geophys. Union; Internat. Acad. of Astronautics; For. Mem., Norwegian Acad. of Scis and Letters, 1966. Hon. DSc Wroclaw, 1993. *Publications:* X-ray Astronomy (with P. W. Sanford), 1981; over 250 papers on solar and cosmic X-ray astronomy, X-ray instrumentation and plasma spectroscopy. *Recreations:* music, racing cars. *Address:* 24 Warnham Road, Horsham, West Sussex RH12 2QU. *T:* (lab.) (01483) 274111; *e-mail:* jlc@mssl.ucl.ac.uk.

CULLEN, Rt Hon. Lord; (William) Douglas Cullen; PC 1997; a Senator of the College of Justice in Scotland, since 1986; Lord Justice-Clerk and President of the Second Division of the Court of Session, since 1997; *b* 18 Nov. 1935; *s* of late Sheriff K. D. Cullen and Mrs G. M. Cullen; *m* 1961, Rosamond Mary Downer; two *s* two *d. Educ:* Dundee High Sch.; St Andrews Univ. (MA); Edinburgh Univ. (LLB). FRSE 1993. Called to the Scottish Bar, 1960. Standing Jun. Counsel to HM Customs and Excise, 1970–73; QC (Scot.) 1973; Advocate-depute, 1978–81. Chairman: Medical Appeal Tribunal, 1977–86; Court of Inquiry into the Piper Alpha disaster, 1988–90; Review of Business of the Outer House of the Court of Session, 1995; Tribunal of Inquiry into the shootings at Dunblane Primary Sch., 1996; Ladbroke Grove Rail Inquiry, 1999–; Member: Scottish Valuation Adv. Council, 1980–86; Royal Commn on Ancient and Historical Monuments of Scotland, 1987–97. Pres., SACRO, 2000–. Chairman: Council, Cockburn Assoc. (Edinburgh Civic Trust), 1984–86; Govs, St Margaret's Sch., Edinburgh, 1994–; Mem. Court, Napier Univ., 1996–. Hon. FREng (Hon. FEng 1995). Hon. LLD: Aberdeen, 1992; St Andrews, 1997; Dundee, Edinburgh, Glasgow Caledonian, 2000; DUniv Heriot-Watt, 1995. *Publications:* The Faculty Digest Supplement 1951–60, 1965; non-legal booklets on buildings in Edinburgh. *Recreations:* gardening, natural history. *Address:* The Court of Session, Parliament House, Edinburgh EH1 1RQ. *T:* (0131) 240 6732. *Club:* New (Edinburgh).

CULLEN OF ASHBOURNE, 3rd Baron *cr* 1920, of Roehampton, co. Surrey; **Edmund Willoughby Marsham Cokayne;** *b* 18 May 1916; 2nd *s* of 1st Baron Cullen of Ashbourne, KBE and Grace Margaret (*née* Marsham); *S* brother, 2000; *m* 1943, Janet Muirhead Manson (*née* Watson); one adopted *d. Educ:* Eton; Royal Sch. of Mines. Mem., Assoc. of Professional Engrs of BC. Served War, Pilot (Flt-Lt) RAF, 1940-46. Jun. Engr, Sons of Gwalia Mine and Zinc Corp., Australia, 1937-40; Chief Engineer: Central Patricia Gold Mine, Ont, Canada, 1946-51; Algoma Ore Properties, Ont, 1951-65; Chief Engr, Mine Supt then Mine Mgr, Craigmont Mines, BC, 1965-76; Mine Mgr then Gen. Mgr, Lakeshore Mine, Casa Grande, Arizona, USA, 1976-84. *Publications:* technical papers. *Recreations:* music, gardening, volunteering. *Heir: b* John O'Brien Marsham Cokayne [*b* 11 Oct. 1920; *m* 1948, Anne Frances Clayton (*d* 1971); one *s*]. *Address:* 15-1901 Maxwell Avenue, Merritt, BC V1K 1L9, Canada. *T:* (250) 3789462.

CULLEN, Prof. Alexander Lamb, OBE 1960; DSc(Eng); FRS 1977; FREng, FIEE, FIEEE, FInstP, FCGI; Emeritus Professor, University of London; Hon. Research Fellow, Department of Electronic and Electrical Engineering, University College London, since 1984 (SERC Senior Research Fellow, 1980–84); *b* 30 April 1920; *s* of Richard and Jessie Cullen, Lincoln; *m* 1940, Margaret, *er d* of late Alexander Lamb, OBE; two *s* one *d. Educ:* Lincoln Sch.; City and Guilds Coll., London. Staff of Radio Dept, RAE Farnborough, working on development of radar, 1940–46; Lectr in Electrical Engineering, University Coll., London, 1946–55 (title of Reader conferred 1955); Prof. of Electrical Engineering, University of Sheffield, 1955–67; Pender Prof. of Electrical Engineering, University College London, 1967–80. Hon. Prof., Northwestern Polytechnical Univ., Xian, China, 1981. Mem., IBA, 1982–89. Institution of Electrical Engineers: Kelvin premium, 1952; Ambrose Fleming premium, 1956 (with J. C. Parr), 1975 (with Dr J. R. Forrest), 1988 (with S. P. Yeo); Duddell premium, 1957 (with Dr H. A. French); Faraday Medal, 1984; Electronics Letters premium, 1985; Maxwell premium, 1996 (jtly). Microwave Career Award, IEEE, 1989. Chm., Brit. Nat. Cttee, URSI, 1981–85; Vice-Pres., Internat. URSI, 1981–87, Pres., 1987–90; Mem. Council, Royal Soc., 1984–86. Clifford Paterson Lecture, Royal Soc., 1984; Clerk Maxwell Lecture, IERE, 1986. FREng (FEng 1977). Hon. FIERE 1987; Hon. Fellow, UCL, 1993. Hon. DSc: Chinese Univ. of Hong Kong, 1981; Kent, 1986. Hon. DEng Sheffield, 1985. Royal Medal, Royal Soc., 1984. *Publications:* Microwave Measurements (jointly with Prof. H. M. Barlow), 1950; a number of papers on electromagnetic waves and microwave measurement techniques in IEE proceedings and elsewhere. *Recreations:* music and reading. *Address:* Department of Electronic and Electrical Engineering, University College London, Torrington Place, WC1E 7JE.

CULLEN, Rt Hon. Douglas; *see* Cullen, Rt Hon. Lord.

CULLEN, Sir (Edward) John, Kt 1991; PhD; FREng; Chairman, Health and Safety Commission, 1983–93; *b* 19 Oct. 1926; *s* of William Henry Pearson Cullen and Ellen Emma Cullen; *m* 1954, Betty Davall Hopkins; two *s* two *d. Educ:* Cambridge Univ. (MA 1952, PhD 1956); Univ. of Texas (MS 1953). UKAEA, 1956–58; ICI, 1958–67; Rohm and Haas Co., 1967–83: Eur. Dir for Engrg and Regulatory Affairs, 1981–83; Dep. Chm., Rohm and Haas (UK) Ltd, 1981–83. Chm., British Nat. Cttee for Internat. Engrg Affairs, 1990–96; President: Pipeline Industries Guild, 1996–98; FEANI, 1996– (Vice-Pres., 1995–96); British Safety Industries Fedn, 1997–; Mem., Engrg Council, 1990–96. FREng (FEng 1987; Mem. Council, 1991–94); Pres., IChemE, 1988–89. Mem., McRobert Award Cttee, 1995–. MInstD 1978; FRSA 1988. Liveryman, Engineers' Co., 1989–. Hon. DSc Exeter, 1993. *Publications:* articles on gas absorption, in Trans Faraday Soc., Trans IChemE, Chem. Engrg Science; numerous articles on health and safety. *Recreations:* reading (detective stories), photography, swimming, gardening. *Address:* 14 Gloucester Walk, W8 4HZ. *T:* (020) 7937 0709. *Club:* Institute of Directors.

CULLEN, Sir John; *see* Cullen, Sir E. J.

CULLEN, Hon. Michael (John), PhD; MP (Lab) for Dunedin South, since 1996 (for St Kilda, 1981–96); Treasurer, Minister of Finance, Minister of Revenue and Leader of the House, New Zealand, since 1999; *b* London, 5 Feb. 1945; adopted NZ citizenship, 1975; *s* of John Joseph Thomas Cullen and Ivy Mary Cullen; *m* 1st, 1967, Rowena Joy Knight (marr. diss. 1987); two *d*; 2nd, 1989, Lowson Anne Collins. *Educ:* Christ's Coll., Christchurch; Canterbury Univ. (BA 1965; MA Hist. 1967); Edinburgh Univ. (PhD Social and Economic Hist.). Asst Lectr, Univ. of Canterbury; Tutor, Univ. of Stirling; Sen. Lectr, Univ. of Otago. Sen. Govt Whip, 1984–87; Minister of Social Welfare, and Associate Minister of Finance, 1987–90; Associate Minister of Health, 1988–90; of Labour, 1989–90; opposition spokesperson on social welfare, war pensions and Accident Compensation Corp., 1990–91, on finance, 1991. Dep. Leader, NZ Labour Party, 1996. Vis. Fellow, ANU. *Publications:* The Statistical Movement in Early Victorian Britain, 1974; Unlawfully Occupied, 1979; articles in jls. *Recreations:* music, reading, golf, house renovation. *Address:* Parliament Buildings, Wellington, New Zealand.

CULLEN, Paul Benedict; QC (Scot.) 1995; Solicitor General for Scotland, 1995–97; *b* 11 March 1957; *s* of James Finbarr Cullen and Ann Evaline Black or Cullen; *m* 1983, Joyce Nicol; two *s* one *d. Educ:* St Augustine's High Sch., Edinburgh; Edinburgh Univ. (LLB Hons). Admitted to Faculty of Advocates, 1982 (Clerk of Faculty, 1986–90); Standing Jun. Counsel to DoE in Scotland, 1988–91; Advocate Depute, 1992–95. Scottish Cons. spokesman on home and legal affairs, 1997–98; Chm. Disciplinary Panel, Scottish Cons. Party. Cons. rep. on Scottish Office consultative steering gp on Scottish Parlt, 1998–99. Vice Pres., Edinburgh S Cons. & Unionist Assoc. Contested (C) Eastwood, 1997. *Recreations:* tennis, bridge. *Address:* 25 Midmar Gardens, Edinburgh EH10 6DY. *T:* (0131) 447 4316. *Clubs:* New (Edinburgh); Braid Lawn Tennis (Edinburgh).

CULLEN, Raymond; Chairman, The Calico Printers' Association Ltd and subsidiaries, 1964–68; *b* 27 May 1913; *s* of late John Norman Cullen and Bertha (*née* Dearden); *m* 1940, Doris (*d* 1984), *d* of A. W. Paskin; two *d. Educ:* King's Sch., Macclesfield; St Catharine's Coll., Cambridge (Scholar, MA). Joined The Calico Printers' Assoc. Ltd Commn Printing, 1934; transf. overseas, 1938; service in India and China. Dir, W. A. Beardsell & Co. (Private) Ltd, Madras, 1946 (Chm. and Man. Dir, 1949–55); Chm. and Man. Dir, Mettur Industries Ltd, 1949–55; Chm. and Man. Dir, Marshall Fabrics Ltd, 1955–62; Director: Calico Printers' Assoc. Ltd, 1962–68; Barclays Bank Ltd Manchester Local Bd, 1965–69. Member: Textile Coun., 1967–69; Coun., Inst. of Directors, 1967–69; NW Economic Planning Coun., 1968–69; Governor, Manchester Grammar Sch., 1968–83. *Recreations:* fishing, golf (Pres., Cheshire Union of Golf Clubs, 1977–78). *Address:* Cranford, Ladybrook Road, Bramhall, Cheshire SK7 3NB. *T:* (0161) 485 3204.

CULLEN, Terence Lindsay Graham; QC 1978; *b* 29 Oct. 1930; *s* of late Eric Graham Cullen and Jean Morrison Hunter (*née* Bennett); *m* 1958, Muriel Elisabeth Rolfe; three *s. Educ:* RNC, Dartmouth. RN, 1948–55; Prestige Group Ltd, 1955–61. Called to the Bar: Lincoln's Inn, 1961 (Bencher, 1986); Singapore, 1978; Malaysia, 1980; Hong Kong, 1986; Bermuda, 1990; retired, 1998. *Recreation:* the Turf. *Address:* 24 High Street, Bridge, Canterbury, Kent CT4 5JY.

CULLIMORE, Charles Augustine Kaye, CMG 1993; HM Diplomatic Service, retired; Chief Executive, Southern Africa Business Association, since 1995; *b* 2 Oct. 1933; *s* of Charles Cullimore and Constance Alicia Kaye Cullimore (*née* Grimshaw); *m* 1956, Val Elizabeth Margot (*née* Willemsen); one *s* one *d. Educ:* Portora Royal Sch., Enniskillen; Trinity Coll., Oxford (MA). N Ireland Short Service Commn, 1955–57. HMOCS, Tanganyika, 1958–61; ICI Ltd, 1961–71; joined HM Diplomatic Service, 1971; FCO, 1971–73; Bonn, 1973–77; FCO, 1977–79; Counsellor, New Delhi, 1979–82; Dep. High Comr, Canberra, 1982–86; FCO, 1986–89; High Comr, Uganda, 1989–93. Dir, Transparency Internat. (UK), 1996–99. Council Mem., Royal African Soc., 2000–. *Publication:* contrib. Jl of Mod. African Studies. *Recreations:* theatre, walking, travel. *Address:* Deacon House, Bidborough, Kent TN3 0UP. *Clubs:* Royal Commonwealth Society, Royal Over-Seas League.

CULLIMORE, Colin Stuart, CBE 1978; DL; Director: Longhurst Housing Association, 1996–2001; Longhurst Group, 2000–02 (Chairman, Audit Committee, 2000–02); *b* 13 July 1931; *s* of Reginald Victor Cullimore and May Maria Cullimore; *m* 1952, Kathleen Anyta Lamming; one *s. Educ:* Westminster Sch.; Grenoble Univ.; National Coll. of Food Technol. Commnd Royal Scots Fusiliers, 1951; seconded Parachute Regt; transf. when perm. officer cadre formed; Major 1956; 10th Bn Parachute Regt TA, 1960. Gen. Man., Payne & Son (Butchers) Ltd, 1960; Asst Gen. Man., J. H. Dewhurst Ltd, 1965, Gen. Man. 1969, Man. Dir, 1976–90; Dir of External Affairs, Vestey Gp, 1990–92; Dir, Airborne Initiative Holdings Ltd, 1991–93; Chm., NAAFI, 1993–96 (non-exec. Dir, 1984–96). Trustee, Western United Gp Pension Scheme, 1986–. Chairman: Retail Consortium Food Cttee, 1973–74; Multiple Shops Fedn, 1977–78; Vice-Chairman: Multiple Food Retailers Assoc., 1972–74; Governors, Coll. for Distributive Trades, 1976–79, 1984–88; Retail Consortium, 1985–89; Pres., British Retailers Assoc., 1984–89 (Vice Pres., 1978–84); Dep. Chm., Meat Promotion Exec., 1975–78; Vice Pres., Bd of Admin, CECD (European Retailers), 1986–88 (Mem., 1981–85). Member: EDC for Distrib. Trades, 1972–80; Council and Management Cttee, Inst. of Meat (Vice-Chm., 1981–83); Cttee of Commerce and Distribn, EEC, 1984–93; Council, Industry & Parlt Trust, 1987–93. Chm. Council, Westminster Sch. Soc., 1999– (Mem., 1990–). Vice Pres., Royal Smithfield Club, 1991– (Mem. Council, 1993–95). Gov., Court of London Inst., 1984–87 and 1989–90; Exec. Trustee, Airborne Assault Normandy Trust, 1983–; Chm., Reserve Forces Ulysses Trust, 1992–96; Member: Regtl Council, Parachute Regt, 1991–97; Lincoln Diocese Trust and Bd of Finances, 1993–2001 (Chm. Resources Cttee, 1994–96); Chm. Council, Lincoln Cathedral, 2000– (Mem. Transitional Council, 1998–2000). FInstD 1979; CIMgt (CBIM 1984); FRSA 1987. Liveryman, Butchers' Co. (Mem. Court, 1992–; Warden, 1998–). DL Lincs, 1998. Gold Medal: Inst. of Meat, 1956; Butchers' Co., 1956. OStJ 1988. *Address:* The Old Rectory, Tydd St Mary, Wisbech PE13 5QL. *T:* (01945) 420627, *Fax:* (01945) 420778. *Clubs:* Naval and Military, Farmers'.

CULLINAN, Edward Horder, CBE 1987; RA 1991 (ARA 1989); Senior Partner, Edward Cullinan Architects, since 1965; *b* 17 July 1931; *s* of Dr Edward Cullinan and Joy (*née* Horder); *m* 1961, Rosalind Yeates; one *s* two *d. Educ:* Ampleforth Coll.; Cambridge Univ. (Anderson and Webb Schol., 1951; BA); Univ. of California at Berkeley (George VI Meml Fellow, 1956). AADip; RIBA. With Denys Lasdun, 1958–65. Bannister Fletcher Prof., UCL, 1978–79; Graham Willis Prof., Univ. of Sheffield, 1985–87; George Simpson Prof., Univ. of Edinburgh, 1987–90. Mem., Royal Fine Art Commn, 1996–99. Designed and built: Horder House, Hampshire, 1959–60; Minster Lovell Mill, 1969–72; Parish Ch. of St Mary, Barnes, 1978–84; Lambeth Community Care Centre, 1979–84; RMC Internat. HQ, 1985–90; Fountains Abbey visitor centre and landscape, 1987–92; Archeolink Visitor Centre, Oyne, Aberdeenshire, 1994–97; Faculty of Divinity, 1995–2000, Centre for Mathematical Scis, 1996–, Cambridge Univ., 1995–; Univ. of East London, 1997–99; Greenwich Millennium Sch. and Health Centre, 1998–2001; Singapore Mgt Univ., 2000–; Masterplans: Univ. of N Carolina, 1996; Bristol Harbourside, 2000–; all have received awards and been published internationally. FRSA 1984; Hon. FRIAS 1995. *Publications:* Edward Cullinan, Architects, 1984; (with K. Powell) Edward Cullinan, Architects, 1995; contribs to many architectural jls. *Recreations:* horticulture, surfing, travel, building, history, geography. *Address:* 1 Baldwin Terrace, N1 7RU. *T:* (020) 7704 1975.

CULLINGFORD, Eric Coome Maynard, CMG 1963; *b* 15 March 1910; *s* of Francis James and Lilian Mabel Cullingford; *m* 1938, Friedel Fuchs; two *s* one *d. Educ:* City of London Sch.; St Catharine's Coll., Cambridge (Exhibitioner). Entered Ministry of Labour as Third Class Officer, 1932; Principal, 1942. Served with Manpower Div. of CCG, 1946–50. Asst Sec., Min. of Labour, 1954. Labour Attaché, Bonn, 1961–65, 1968–72. Regional Controller, Eastern and Southern Region, Dept of Employment and Productivity, 1966–68; retired 1973. *Publications:* Trade Unions in West Germany, 1976; Pirates of Shearwater Island, 1983. *Address:* Combermere, Flat 1, 25 Avenue Road, Malvern, Worcs WR14 3AY.

CULLINGWORTH, Prof. (John) Barry; Emeritus Professor of Urban Affairs and Public Policy, University of Delaware, since 1994; *b* 11 Sept. 1929; *s* of Sidney C. and Winifred E. Cullingworth; *m* 1951, Betty Violet (*née* Turner); one *s* two *d. Educ:* High Pavement Sch., Nottingham; Trinity Coll. of Music, London; London Sch. of Economics. Research Asst, Asst Lectr and Lectr, Univ. of Manchester, 1955–60; Lectr, Univ. of Durham, 1960–63; Sen. Lectr and Reader, Univ. of Glasgow, 1963–66; Dir, Centre for Urban and Regional Studies, Univ. of Birmingham, 1966–72. Dir, Planning Exchange, Scotland, 1972–75; Official Historian, Cabinet Office, 1975–77. Prof. and Chm., Dept of Urban and Regional Planning, 1977–80, Res. Prof., Centre for Urban and Community Studies, 1980–82, Prof. of Planning, 1982–83, Univ. of Toronto; Unidel Prof. of Urban Affairs and Public Policy, Univ. of Delaware, 1983–94; Sen. Res. Fellow, Dept of Land Economy, Univ. of Cambridge, 1994–99. Vis. Prof., Univ. of Strathclyde, 1980–86. Vice-Chm., Scottish Housing Adv. Cttee; Chairman: Cttee on Community Facilities in Expanding Towns (Report, The Needs of New Communities, 1967); Cttee on Unfit Housing in Scotland (Report, Scotland's Older Houses, 1967); Cttee on Allocation of Council Houses (Report, Council Housing: Purposes, Procedures and Practices, 1968); Adv. Cttee on Rent Rebates and Rent Allowances, 1973–77. Mem., Ont. Council of Health, 1979–83; Vice-Pres., Housing Centre Trust, 1972–. FRSA 1974; Hon. MRTPI. *Publications:* Housing Needs and Planning Policy, 1960; Housing in Transition, 1963; Town and Country Planning in England and Wales, 1964; English Housing Trends, 1965; Housing and Local Government, 1966; Scottish Housing in 1965, 1967; A Profile of Glasgow Housing, 1968; (with V. Karn) Ownership and Management of Housing in New Towns, 1968; Housing and Labour Mobility, (Paris) 1969; Town and Country Planning in Britain, 1972, 13th edn (with V. Nadin) as Town and Country Planning in the UK, 2001; Problems of an Urban Society (3 vols), 1973; Environmental Planning—Reconstruction and Land Use Planning, 1975; Essays on Housing Policy, 1979; New Towns Policy, 1980; Canadian Housing Policy Research, 1980; Land Values, Compensation and Betterment, 1981; Rent Control, 1983; Canadian Planning and Public Participation, 1984; Urban and Regional Planning in Canada, 1987; Energy, Land and Public Policy, 1990; The Political Culture of Planning, 1993; Planning in the USA, 1997; British Planning: 50 years of urban and regional policy, 1999. *Address:* 102 Thornton Road, Girton, Cambridge CB3 0NN. *T:* (01223) 277170.

CULLIS, Prof. Charles Fowler; Professor of Physical Chemistry, City University, 1967–84, now Emeritus (Head, Chemistry Department, 1973–84; Pro-Vice-Chancellor, 1980–84; Saddlers' Research Professor, 1984–87; Leverhulme Emeritus Research Fellow, 1987–89); *b* 31 Aug. 1922; 2nd *s* of late Prof. C. G. Cullis, Prof. of Mining Geology, Univ. of London, and Mrs W. J. Cullis (*née* Fowler); *m* 1958, Marjorie Elizabeth, *er d* of late Sir Austin and Lady Anderson; two *s* two *d. Educ:* Stowe Sch. (Open Schol.); Trinity Coll., Oxford. BA 1944, BSc 1st Cl. Hons Chem. 1945, DPhil 1948, MA 1948, DSc 1960; FRSC (FRIC 1958); FRSA. ICI Research Fellow in Chem., Oxford, 1947–50; Lectr in Phys. Chem., Imperial Coll., London, 1950–59; Sen. Lectr in Chem. Engrg and Chem. Tech., Imperial Coll., 1959–64; Reader in Combustion Chemistry, Univ. of London, 1964–66. Vis. Prof., College of Chem., Univ. of California, Berkeley, 1966; Vis. Scientist, CSIRO, Sydney, 1970. Mem. Council, Chem. Soc., 1969–72, 1975–78; Hon. Sec., Brit. Sect. of Combustion Inst., 1969–74; Mem., Rockets Sub-cttee, 1968–73, and of Combustion Sub-cttee, 1969–72, Aeronautical Research Council; Member: Navy Dept Fuels and Lubricants Adv. Cttee (Fire and Explosion Hazards Working Gp), 1967–83; Safety in Mines Research Adv. Bd, 1973–88 (Chm., 1980–88); Chem. Cttee, Defence Sci. Adv. Council, 1979–82; Chem. Bd, 1982–87, Phys. Sci. Cttee, 1987–89, CNAA. Scientific Editor, Internat. Union of Pure and Applied Chem., 1976–78. Non-exec. Dir, City Technology Ltd, 1977–91. Mem., Mid Sussex DC, 1986–95. Mem. Council, Sussex Univ., 1993–95; Governor, City of London Polytechnic, 1982–84. Trustee, Sino-British Fellowship Trust, 1992–. Freeman, City of London, 1983; Liveryman, Bakers' Co., 1983. Joseph Priestley Award, 1974, Combustion Chem. Medal and Award, 1978, Chem. Soc. *Publications:* The Combustion of Organic Polymers (jtly with M. M. Hirschler), 1981; numerous sci. papers in Proc. Royal Soc., Trans Faraday Soc., Jl Chem. Soc., etc, mainly concerned with chemistry of combustion reactions. *Recreations:* music, travel. *Address:* Quinces, Courtmead Road, Cuckfield, W Sussex RH17 5LP. *T:* (01444) 453513. *Club:* Athenæum.

See also M. F. Cullis.

CULLIS, Michael Fowler, CVO 1955; HM Diplomatic Service, retired; Director, UK Committee, European Cultural Foundation, Amsterdam, 1983–92; *b* 22 Oct. 1914; *s* of Emeritus Prof. Charles Gilbert Cullis, Imperial Coll. of Science and Technology, London

Univ., and Winifred Jefford, *d* of Sir George Fowler; *m* Catherine Cameron (*d* 2001), *d* of Alexander Robertson, Arbroath, Scotland; no *c*. *Educ:* Wellington Coll. (scholar); Brasenose Coll., Oxford (Hulme Open Scholar). MA, classics. Law (Lincoln's Inn), and journalism, 1938–39. Military Intelligence, Gibraltar, 1939–40; served Min. of Economic Warfare (London, Spain and Portugal), 1940–44; joined FO as head of Austrian Section, 1945; Political Adviser on Austrian Treaty negotiations (London, Moscow, Vienna, Paris, New York), 1947–50; Special Asst, Schuman Plan, 1950; First Sec., British Embassy, Oslo, 1951–55; Regional (Information) Counsellor for the five Nordic countries, British Embassy, Copenhagen, 1955–58; Dep. Gov. of Malta, 1959–61; Sen. Research Associate, Atlantic Institute, Paris, 1962–65; writing, lecturing, etc, at various European centres, 1965–66; Dir, Arms Control and Disarmament Res., FO, then FCO, 1967–74; Advr on relations with non-govtl bodies, FCO, 1974–79; consultant for acad. and institutional fund-raising, and European affairs, 1980–82; Historical Advr to Royal Mint, 1986. Unsuccessful candidate (C), European Elections, 1979. Vice-Pres., Inst. of Linguists, 1984–89. Chevalier (1st cl.) Order of Dannebrog, 1957. *Publications:* (contrib.) The Price of Victory, 1983; (contrib.) Festschrift for Gerald Stourzh, 1990; articles and broadcasts, mainly on international affairs. *Recreations:* music, theatre. *Address:* Peel House, Buntingford, Herts SG9 9AE. *T:* (01763) 272209. *Club:* Athenæum.

See also C. F. Cullis.

CULME-SEYMOUR, Sir Michael Patrick; *see* Seymour.

CULPIN, Sir Robert (Paul), Kt 2001; Managing Director, Budget and Public Finances, HM Treasury, since 1998. *Educ:* Christ's Coll., Cambridge (BA 1968); Harvard Univ.; California Univ. HM Treasury, 1965–; Press Sec. and Hd of Information, 1984–87; Under-Sec., Fiscal Policy Div., 1987–93; Dep. Sec., Public Finance, 1993–94; Second Permanent Sec., 1994; Dir, Public Expenditure, then Public Spending, 1994–98. *Address:* HM Treasury, Parliament Street, SW1P 3AG.

CULSHAW, John Douglas; Assistant Chief Scientific Adviser (Capabilities), Ministry of Defence, 1985–87; *b* 22 Oct. 1927; *s* of Alfred Henry Douglas Culshaw and Dorothy Yeats Culshaw (*née* Hogarth); *m* 1951, Hazel Speirs Alexander (*d* 1998); one *s* one *d*. *Educ:* Washington Alderman Smith Grammar Sch., Co. Durham; University Coll., Nottingham. BSc London 1949; MSc Nottingham 1950. Joined Weapons Dept, Royal Aircraft Estabt, Min. of Supply, Farnborough, 1950; OC (Scientific) 6 Joint Services Trials Unit RAF (UK), 1956; OC (Sci.) 16 JSTU RA Weapons Research Estabt, Salisbury, S Australia, 1961; Co-ordinating Research and Development Authority Technical Project Officer, RAE, 1964; Supt Mine Warfare Br., Royal Armament R&D Estabt, MoD, Sevenoaks, 1967; Director, Scientific Adv. Br., Home Office, 1970; Dept of Chief Scientific Adviser (Army), 1972; Head of Mathematics and Assessment Dept, RARDE, MoD, Sevenoaks, 1974; Head of Defence Science II, MoD, 1975; RCDS 1976; Dep. Dir, Scientific and Technical Intelligence, 1977; Dir, Defence Operational Analysis Estabt and Asst Chief Scientific Advr (Studies), MoD, 1979–84. *Recreation:* historical research. *Club:* Civil Service.

CULSHAW, Robert Nicholas, MVO 1979; HM Diplomatic Service; Consul General, Chicago, since 1999; *b* 22 Dec. 1952; *s* of late Ivan Culshaw and of Edith Marjorie Jose Barnard; *m* 1977, Elaine Ritchie Clegg; one *s*. *Educ:* University Coll. Sch., Hampstead; King's Coll., Cambridge (BA 1st Cl. Hons Classics 1974; Major Univ. Scholarship for Classics, 1974; MA 1977). FCO, 1974–75; MECAS, Lebanon and Jordan, 1975–77; 3rd Sec., Muscat, 1977–79; 2nd Sec., Khartoum, 1979–80; 1st Sec., Rome, 1980–84; FCO, 1984–88; Head of Chancery, 1988–90, Dep. Hd of Mission and Consul-Gen., 1991–93, Athens; FCO Spokesman and Hd of News Dept, 1993–95; Minister-Counsellor (Trade and Transport), Washington, 1995–99. FRSA 1995. *Recreations:* ski-ing, singing, poetry. *Address:* c/o Foreign and Commonwealth Office, King Charles Street, SW1A 2AH.

CULVER, John Howard, LVO 2000; HM Diplomatic Service; Ambassador to Iceland, since 2001; *b* 17 July 1947; *s* of late Frank and of Peggy Culver; *m* 1973, Margaret Ann Davis; two *s* one *d*. Entered FO, 1968; Moscow, 1974–76; La Paz, 1977–80; FCO, 1980–83; Rome, 1983–87; Head of Chancery, Dhaka, 1987–90; FCO, 1990–92; Ambassador to Nicaragua, 1992–97; Consul-General, Naples, 1997–99; Rome, 2000. *Address:* c/o Foreign and Commonwealth Office, SW1A 2AH.

CULYER, Prof. Anthony John, CBE 1999; Professor of Economics, since 1979, and Director of Health Development, since 1997, University of York; status-only Professor, University of Toronto, since 1989; *b* 1 July 1942; *s* of late Thomas Reginald Culyer and Betty Ely (*née* Headland); *m* 1966, Sieglinde Birgit; one *s* one *d*. *Educ:* King's Sch., Worcester; Exeter Univ. (BA Hons); Univ. of California at Los Angeles. Tutor and Asst Lectr, Exeter Univ., 1965–69; York University: Lectr, Sen. Lectr and Reader, 1969–79; Dep. Dir, Inst. of Social and Economic Research, 1971–82; Hd, Dept of Econs and Related Studies, 1986–2001; Pro-Vice-Chancellor, 1991–94; Dep. Vice-Chancellor, 1994–97. Sen. Research Associate, Ontario Economic Council, 1976, Vis. Professorial Lectr, Queen's Univ., Kingston, 1976; William Evans Vis. Professor, Otago Univ., 1979; Vis. Fellow, Australian National Univ., 1979; Visiting Professor: Trent Univ., 1985–86; Inst. für Med. Informatik und Systemforschung, Munich, 1990–91; Toronto Univ., 1991; Central Inst. of Technology, NZ, 1996. Lectures: Woodward, Univ. of BC, 1986; Perey, McMaster Univ., and Champlain, Trent Univ., Canada, 1990; Francis Fraser, BPMF, 1994. Member: Standing Cttee, Conf. of Heads of Univ. Depts of Econs, 1988–; Coll. Cttee, King's Fund Coll., London, 1989–92; Res. Adv. Gp, Inst. for Work and Health, Toronto, 1990–; Adv. Cttee for Centre for Health and Society, UCL, 1992–; Rev. Adv. Cttee on London SHAs, 1992–93; Adv. Cttee, Canadian Inst. for Advanced Res., 1992–; Future Health Care Options Wkg Pty, IHSM, 1992–93; British Council Health Adv. Cttee, 1995–97; Academic Adv. Council, Univ. of Buckingham, 1996–; Dep. Chm., Nat. Inst. for Clinical Excellence, 1999–. Chm., York Dist, 1984–95, NE Yorks Area, 1995–, RSCM. Mem., 1982–90, non-exec. Mem., 1990–92, Northallerton HA; Dep. Chm., N Yorks HA, 1995–99 (non-exec. Mem., 1994–99); Member: Yorks RHA R&D Cttee, 1992–94; Northern and Yorks Regl R&D Adv. Cttee, 1995–; Central R&D Cttee, NHS, 1991–; NHS Standing Gp on Health Technol., 1992–97; R&D Cttee of High Security Psychiatric Hosps Commissioning Bd, 1995–99; Chair: Methodology Panel, NHS Standing Gp on Health Technol., 1993–97; NHS Task Force on Supporting R&D in NHS, 1994; Advr to NHS Dir of R&D, 1997–99. Chm., Office of Health Econs, 2001– (Chm., Edtl Bd, 1997–). Trustee, Canadian Health Services Res. Foundn, 2000–. Pres., Econs Section, BAAS, 1994. Founder FMedSci 1998. Co-Editor, Jl of Health Econs, 1982–; Member, Editorial Board: Econ. Rev., 1983–; Med. Law Internat., 1992–; BMJ, 1995–2000; Mem. Managing Cttee, Jl of Med. Ethics, 1994–. Hon. DEc Stockholm Sch. of Econs, 1999. *Publications:* The Economics of Social Policy, 1973; (ed with M. H. Cooper) Health Economics, 1973; (ed) Economic Policies and Social Goals, 1974; Need and the National Health Service, 1976; (with J. Wiseman and A. Walker) Annotated Bibliography of Health Economics, 1977; (ed with V. Halberstadt) Human Resources and Public Finance, 1977; Measuring Health: Lessons for Ontario, 1978; (ed with K. G. Wright) Economic Aspects of Health Services, 1978; The Political Economy of Social Policy, 1980; (ed) Health Indicators, 1983; (ed with B. Horisberger) Economic and Medical Evaluation of Health Care Technologies, 1983; Economics, 1985; (ed with G. Terny) Public Finance and Social Policy, 1985; (ed with B. Jonsson) Public and Private Health Services: complementarities and conflicts, 1986; (jtly) The International Bibliography of Health Economics: a comprehensive annotated guide to English language sources since 1914, 1986; Canadian Health Care Expenditures: myth and reality, past and future, 1988; (ed) Standards for the Socio-economic Evaluation of Health Care Products and Services, 1990; (ed jtly) Competition in Health Care: reforming the NHS, 1990; (ed) The Economics of Health, 1991; (ed jtly) Some Recent Developments in Health Economics, 1992; (ed jtly) Swedish Health Care: the best in the world?, 1993; (ed jtly) Reforming Health Care Systems: experiments with the NHS, 1996; (ed jtly) Being Reasonable about the Economics of Health: selected essays by Alan Williams, 1997; articles in Oxford Econ. Papers, Economica, Scottish Jl of Political Economy, Public Finance, Jl of Public Economics, Kyklos, Qly Jl of Economics, Jl Royal Statistical Soc., Jl of Health Economics, BMJ, Jl Med Ethics, and others. *Recreation:* church music (Organist and Choir Director, St Catherine's, Barmby Moor, 1971–). *Address:* The Laurels, Barmby Moor, York YO4 5EJ. *T:* (01759) 302639.

CUMANI, Luca Matteo; racehorse trainer; *b* 7 April 1949; *s* of Sergio Cumani and Elena Cardini Cumani; *m* 1979, Sara Doon Plunket; one *s* one *d*. *Educ:* Milan. Riding career: 85 winners in Italy, France and UK; champion amateur, Italy, 1972; won Moët and Chandon on Meissen, 1972; Prix Paul Noël de la Houtre on Harland, 1970, 1972, 1973; Asst to Sergio Cumani and to H. R. A. Cecil, 1974–75; first held licence, 1976; numerous major races won, incl. St Leger (Commanche Run), 1984; Derby and Irish Sweeps Derby, 1988 (Kahyasi); Breeders Cup Mile, 1994 (Barathea); Derby, 1998 (High Rise). *Address:* Bedford House Stables, Bury Road, Newmarket, Suffolk CB8 7BX. *T:* (01638) 665432.

CUMBERLEGE, family name of **Baroness Cumberlege**.

CUMBERLEGE, Baroness *cr* 1990 (Life Peer), of Newick in the County of East Sussex; **Julia Frances Cumberlege,** CBE 1985; Director: guideforlife.com, since 2001; Huntsworth plc, since 2001; Quo Health, since 2001; *b* 27 Jan. 1943; *d* of late Dr L. U. Camm and M. G. G. Camm; *m* 1961, Patrick Francis Howard Cumberlege; three *s*. *Educ:* Convent of the Sacred Heart, Tunbridge Wells. Mem., East Sussex AHA, 1977–81; Chairman: Brighton HA, 1981–88; SW Thames RHA, 1988–92; Mem. Council, NAHA, 1982–88 (Vice-Chm., 1984–87; Chm., 1987–88). Member (C): Lewes DC, 1966–79 (Leader, 1977–78); East Sussex CC, 1974–85 (Chm., Social Services Cttee, 1979–82). Chairman: Review of Community Nursing for England, 1985 (report, Neighbourhood Nursing—a focus for care, 1986); Expert Maternity Gp, 1993 (report, Changing Childbirth, 1993). Member: Social Security Adv. Cttee, 1980–82; DHSS Expert Adv. Gp on AIDS, 1987–89; Council, UK Central Council for Nursing, Midwifery and Health Visiting, 1989–92; NHS Policy Bd, 1989–97. Parly Under-Sec. of State, DoH, 1992–97. Exec. Dir, MJM Healthcare Solutions, 1997–2001. Lay Mem., 1977–83, Mem. Appts Commn, 1984–90, Press Council. Vice President: Age Concern, Brighton, 1984–96; RCN, 1989–; President: Age Concern, E Sussex, 1995–; E Sussex Care for the Carers, 1996–. Mem. Council, ICRF, 1998–; Trustee: Princess Royal Trust for Carers, 1992–93; Life Education Centres, 1997–99. Mem. Council, Brighton Poly, 1987–89; Chm. Trustees, Chailey Heritage Sch. and Hosp., 1997– (Governor, 1982–88); Chm Council, St George's Hosp. Med. Sch., 2000–; Governor: Chailey Comprehensive Sch., 1972–86; Ringmer Comprehensive Sch., 1979–85; Newick Primary Sch., 1977–85. Founder: Newick Playgp; Newick Youth Club. FRSA 1989. DL 1986, Vice Lord-Lieut, 1992, E Sussex; JP East Sussex, 1973–85. DUniv: Surrey, 1990; Brighton, 1994. *Recreations:* bicycling, other people's gardens. *Address:* Snells Cottage, The Green, Newick, Lewes, East Sussex BN8 4LA. *T:* (01825) 722154, *Fax:* (01825) 723873. *Club:* Royal Society of Medicine.

CUMING, Frederick George Rees, RA 1974 (ARA 1969); ARCA 1954; NDD 1948; NEAC 1960; painter; *b* 16 Feb. 1930; *m* Audrey Lee Cuming; one *s* one *d*. *Educ:* University School, Bexley Heath; Sidcup Art School; Royal College of Art; travelling schol., Italy. Exhibns in Redfern, Walker, New Grafton, Thackeray, Fieldborne Galleries; Group shows at NEAC, RA, Schools' Exhibn, John Moores London Group; One Man exhibns at Thackeray Gall., galls in Chichester, Lewes, Eastbourne, Guildford, Durham, Chester, Folkstone, Canterbury, New York; works in collections: DoE; Treasury; Chantrey Bequest; RA; Kendal Mus.; Scunthorpe Mus.; Bradford; Carlisle; Nat. Mus. of Wales; Brighton and Hove Mus.; Maidstone Mus.; Towner Gall., Eastbourne; Monte Carlo Mus.; St John's Coll., Oxford; Worcester Coll., Oxford; Faringdon Trust, Oxon; ITV collection; Southend Mus.; Preston Mus.; Nat. Trust collection; Baring's Bank; Lloyd's; Guinness collection; W. H. Smith; City private collections; works in galls in America, Argentina, Canada, Chile, France, Germany, Greece, Holland, Hong Kong and S Africa. Hon. ROI 1992. Grand Prix, Art Contemporaine, Monte Carlo. *Address:* The Gables, Wittersham Road, Iden, near Rye, E Sussex TN31 7UY. *T:* (01797) 280322.

CUMMING; *see* Gordon Cumming and Gordon-Cumming.

CUMMING, Alexander James; Chief Executive, Grampian University Hospitals (formerly Aberdeen Royal Hospitals) NHS Trust, since 1994; *b* 7 March 1947; *s* of Alexander George Cumming and Jean Campbell (*née* McWilliam); *m* 1973, Margaret Ada Callan; one *s* two *d*. *Educ:* Fordyce Acad., Banffshire; Robert Gordon's Coll., Aberdeen; Univ. of Aberdeen (MA). Mem., CIMA; IPFA. Volunteer teacher, VSO, India, 1968–70; Trainee Accountant, Wiggins Teape, Papermakers, 1970–72; Company Sec., Glen Gordon Ltd, Aberdeen, 1972–74; Chief Accountant, BOC Offshore, 1974–75; Accountant, then Dir of Finance, Grampian Health Bd., 1975–93; Actg Dir of Finance, Mgt Exec., Scottish Health Service, 1994. Chm., Langstane Housing Assoc., 1997– (Hon. Treas., 1984–97). *Recreations:* music, literature, history, the outdoors. *Address:* (office) Foresterhill House, Ashgrove Road West, Aberdeen AB9 8AQ.

CUMMING, Valerie Lynn, FMA; writer and lecturer; Deputy Director, Museum of London, 1988–97; *b* 11 Oct. 1946; *d* of late John Gunson Carter and Edna Ruth Carter (*née* Willis); *m* 1972, John Lawrence Cumming. *Educ:* Abbey Sch., Reading; Univ. of Leicester (BA); Courtauld Inst. of Art (Courtauld Cert. in History of Dress). Admin. trainee, Univ. of Surrey, 1968–69; Asst, Chertsey Mus., 1971–73; Res. Asst, 1973–75, Sen. Asst Keeper, 1975–78, Mus. of London; Curator, Court Dress Collection, Kensington Palace, 1978–81; Asst Dir, Mus. of London, 1981–88. Trustee, Olive Matthews Collection, Chertsey Mus., Surrey, 1983–. Curatorial advr, Chartered Insurance Inst., 1991–98. Vis. Lectr, Courtauld Inst. of Art, 1997. *Publications:* Exploring Costume History 1500–1900, 1981; Gloves, 1982; (contrib.) Tradescant's Rarities, 1983; A Visual History of Costume: the Seventeenth Century, 1984; (with Aileen Ribeiro) The Visual History of Costume, 1989; Royal Dress, 1989; (contrib.) The Late King's Goods, 1989; (contrib.) London – World City 1800–1840, 1992; The Visual History of Accessories, 1998. *Recreations:* gardening, watching cricket. *Address:* 36A Prince of Wales Drive, SW11 4SF. *T:* (020) 7223 1380.

CUMMINGS, Constance, CBE 1974; actress; *b* Seattle, USA; *d* of Kate Cummings and Dallas Vernon Halverstadt; *m* 1933, Benn Wolfe Levy, MBE (*d* 1973); one *s* one *d*. *Educ:*

St Nicholas Girls Sch., Seattle, Washington, USA. Began stage work, 1932; since then has appeared in radio, television, films and theatre; joined National Theatre Co., 1971. Member: Arts Council, 1965–71; Council, English Stage Co., 1978–; Chm., Young People's Theatre Panel, 1966–70. *Plays include:* Goodbye, Mr Chips, 1938; The Taming of the Shrew, 1938; The Good Natured Man, 1939; St Joan, 1939; Romeo and Juliet, 1939; The Petrified Forest, 1942; Return to Tyassi, 1952; Lysistrata, 1957; The Rape of the Belt, 1957; JB, 1961; Who's Afraid of Virginia Woolf?, 1964; Justice is a Woman, 1966; Fallen Angels, 1967; A Delicate Balance, 1969; Hamlet, 1969; Children, 1974; Stripwell, 1975; All Over, 1976; Wings, 1978 (televised, USA, 1982); Hay Fever, 1980; The Chalk Garden, NY, 1982; Mrs Warren's Profession, Vienna, 1982; Eve, 1984; The Glass Menagerie, USA, then London, 1985; Crown Matrimonial, 1988; Tête à Tête, USA, 1989; Uncle Vanya, Chichester, 1996; *National Theatre:* Coriolanus, Amphitryon 38, 1971; A Long Day's Journey into Night, 1972; The Cherry Orchard, The Bacchae, 1973; The Circle, 1974–75. Fanny Kemble at Home, one woman show, 1986; has appeared Albert Hall, performing with orchestra Peter and the Wolf and Honegger's Jeanne d'Arc au Bûcher. *Recreations:* anthropology and music. *Address:* 68 Old Church Street, SW3 6EP. *T:* (020) 7352 0437.

CUMMINGS, John Scott; MP (Lab) Easington, since 1987; *b* 6 July 1943; *s* of George Scott Cummings and Mary (*née* Cain); unmarried. *Educ:* Murton Council Infants, Jun. and Sen. Schs; Easington Technical Coll. Colliery apprentice electrician, 1958–63, colliery electrician, 1963–87. Vice-Chm., Coalfields Community Campaign, 1985–87; Member: Northumbrian Water Authority, 1977–83; Aycliffe and Peterlee Develt Corp., 1980–87; Easington RDC, 1970–73; Easington DC, 1973–87 (Chm., 1975–76; Leader, 1979–87). Mem., Envmt, Transport and Regions Select Cttee, 1997–; Chairman: All-Party Czech and Slovak Gp, 1997–; All-Party Aluminium Gp, 1998–. Mem., Council of Europe, 1992–97. Hon. Parliamentary Adviser: Nat. Assoc. of Councillors; Nat. Assoc. of Licenced House Managers. *Recreations:* Jack Russell terriers, walking, travel. *Address:* 18 Grasmere Terrace, Murton, Seaham, Co. Durham SR7 9NU. *T:* (0191) 526 1142; House of Commons, SW1A 0AA. *Clubs:* Murton Victoria, Democratic, Ex-Servicesman's (Murton); Peterlee Labour; Thornley Catholic.

CUMMINS, Frank; Examinations Liaison Officer, Sandwell Local Education Authority, 1987–89; Headmaster, Thomas Telford High School, Sandwell, West Midlands, 1973–87; *b* 20 Jan. 1924; *s* of Archibald Ernest and Ruth Elizabeth Cummins; *m* 1st, 1943, Joyce Swale (marr. diss.); three *s*; 2nd, 1973, Brenda Valerie Swift. *Educ:* Whitgift Middle Sch., Croydon; London School of Economics and Institute of Education, London Univ. Served Royal Signals, 1943–46. Assistant Teacher, Shireland Boys' Sch., Smethwick, 1949; Dep. Headmaster, 1956, Headmaster, 1961, Sandwell Boys' Sch., Smethwick. W Midlands Examinations Board: Chm., Exams Cttee, 1983–86 (Vice-Chm., 1980–83); Vice-Chm., Council, 1986–89; Chm., Bd, 1989–92; Mem. Jt Management Cttee, 1985–94, Governing Council, 1993–94, Midland Examining Gp for GCSE (Chm. Appeals Cttee, 1991–94). Chairman, Community Relations Councils: Warley, 1969, Sandwell, 1974; part-time Commissioner for Racial Equality, 1977–82; Chm., Schools Council Steering Group on Educn in a Multi-Cultural Soc., 1981–83. *Recreations:* cooking, camping, walking, theatre, City of Birmingham Symphony Orchestra. *Address:* 21 Green Street, Smethwick, Warley, West Midlands B67 7EB. *T:* (0121) 558 8484.

CUMMINS, Gus, RA 1992; artist; *b* 28 Jan. 1943; *s* of Harold George Cummins and Honor Cecilia (*née* Bird); *m* 1968, Angela Braven; two *s* one *d*. *Educ:* Sutton and Wimbledon Schs of Art; RCA (NDD, MA). Part-time teacher at nine art schs and colls, 1969–; currently at RA schs. Exhibns, mainly in UK, 1980–; 7 solo exhibns, 1991–. Henry Moore Prize, London Gp, 1982; Spirit of London 2nd Prize, 1983; Daler-Rowney Prize, RA, 1987; Hunting Gp 1st Prize, Mall Gall., 1990, RCA, 1999; House & Garden Prize and Blackstone Award, RA Summer Show, 1992. *Recreations:* music, poetry, literature, swimming, cycling, pubs, snooker. *Address:* Harpsichord House, Cobourg Place, Hastings, Sussex TN34 3HY. *T:* (01424) 426429.

CUMMINS, Michael John Austin; Serjeant at Arms, House of Commons, since 2000; *b* 26 Nov. 1939; *s* of Harold Leslie Cummins and Florence Gladys Cummins (*née* Austin); *m* 1st, 1964, Mary Isobel Farman (marr. diss. 1995); two *s*; 2nd, 1995, Catherine Ellen Lamb; one step *d*. *Educ:* Queen Mary Sch.; RMA Sandhurst; psc. Commnd 3rd Carabiniers (POW DG), 1959; Royal Scots Dragoon Guards, 1971–81. Serjeant at Arms Dept, H of C, 1981–; Dep. Serjeant at Arms, 1995–99. Trustee, Selwood Foundn, 1986–. *Publication:* (with Sir Peter Thorne) Serjeant for the Commons, 1994, 2nd edn 1999. *Recreations:* equitation, gardening, tennis, tapestry. *Address:* House of Commons, SW1A 0AA. *Club:* Cavalry and Guards.

CUMPSTY, Nicholas Alexander, PhD, FREng; Chief Technologist, Rolls-Royce plc, since 2000; *b* 13 Jan. 1943; *s* of Norman and Edith Cumpsty; *m* 1st, 1966, Annette Tischler (*d* 1982); one *s* one *d*; 2nd, 1983, Mary Cecily Hamer (*née* Turner); two step *d*. *Educ:* Haberdashers' Aske's Sch., Hampstead; Imperial Coll., London (BScEng 1964); Trinity Coll. and Peterhouse, Cambridge (PhD 1967; MA 1968). Post Office Student Apprentice, 1960–64; Peterhouse Research Fellow, 1966–69; Sen. Noise Engineer, Rolls Royce, 1969–71; Cambridge University: Sen. Asst in Research, Lectr, then Reader, Dept of Engineering, 1972–89; Prof. of Aerothermal Technology, 1989–99; Fellow of Peterhouse, 1972–99, now Emeritus. Hunsaker Vis. Prof., Dept of Aeronautics and Astronautics, MIT, 1991–92. FREng (FEng 1995). *Publications:* Compressor Aerodynamics, 1989; Jet Propulsion, 1997; numerous papers on aerodynamics, esp. relating to jet engines. *Recreations:* reading, music, walking, scuba diving. *Address:* 3 Fitzwilliam Road, Cambridge CB2 2BN. *T:* (01223) 350916.

CUNDY, Rt Rev. Ian Patrick Martyn; *see* Peterborough, Bishop of.

CUNINGHAME, Sir John Christopher Foggo M.; *see* Montgomery Cuninghame.

CUNLIFFE, family name of **Baron Cunliffe**.

CUNLIFFE, 3rd Baron *cr* 1914, of Headley; **Roger Cunliffe,** RIBA; MIMgt; consulting architect; *b* 12 Jan. 1932; *s* of 2nd Baron and Joan Catherine Lubbock (*d* 1980); *S* father, 1963; *m* 1957, Clemency Ann Hoare; two *s* one *d*. *Educ:* Eton; Trinity Coll., Cambridge (MA); Architectural Association (AA Dipl.); Open Univ. With various architectural firms in UK and USA, 1957–65; Associate, Robert Matthew, Johnson-Marshall & Partners, 1966–69; Dir, Architectural Assoc., 1969–71; Partner, SCP, 1973–78; own practice as architectural, planning and management consultant, 1977–; Dir, Exhibition Consultants Ltd, 1981–. Member: Urban Motorways Cttee, 1969–72; Council, British Consultants Bureau, 1986–90. Member: Council, Lancing Coll., 1967–85; Delegacy, Goldsmiths' Coll., 1972–78; Bd, Coll. of Estate Management, 1992– (Chm. Educn and Res. Cttee, 2000–). Chm., Suffolk Craft Soc., 1994–97. Mem. Ct, Goldsmiths' Co., 1986– (Prime Warden, 1997). *Publications:* (with Leonard Manasseh) Office Buildings, 1962; (with Santa Raymond) Tomorrow's Office, 1996; contrib. various professional jls. *Recreations:* photography, taxonomy, planting trees. *Heir: s* Hon. Henry Cunliffe, *b* 9 March 1962. *Address:* The Broadhurst, Brandeston, Woodbridge, Suffolk IP13 7AG.

CUNLIFFE, Prof. Barrington Windsor, CBE 1994; FBA 1979; FSA; Professor of European Archaeology, Oxford University, and Fellow of Keble College, since 1972; *b* 10 Dec. 1939. *Educ:* Portsmouth; St John's Coll., Cambridge (MA, PhD, LittD). Lecturer, Univ. of Bristol, 1963–66; Prof. of Archæology, Univ. of Southampton, 1966–72. O'Donnell Lectr in Celtic Studies, Oxford Univ., 1983–84. Member: Ancient Monuments Bd for England, 1976–84; Historic Bldgs and Monuments Commn for England, 1987–92 (Mem., Ancient Monuments Adv. Cttee, 1984–); President: Council for British Archaeology, 1976–79; Soc. of Antiquaries, 1991–95 (Vice-Pres., 1982–86). Gov., Mus. of London, 1995–99; Trustee, British Mus., 2000–. Hon. DLitt Sussex, 1983; Hon. DSc Bath, 1984; DUniv. Open, 1995. *Publications:* Fishbourne, a Roman Palace and its Garden, 1971; Roman Bath Discovered, 1971, rev. edn 1984; The Cradle of England, 1972; The Making of the English, 1973; The Regni, 1973; Iron Age Communities in Britain, 1974; Rome and the Barbarians, 1975; Hengistbury Head, 1978; Rome and her Empire, 1978; The Celtic World, 1979; Danebury: the anatomy of an Iron Age hillfort, 1984; The City of Bath, 1986; Greeks, Romans and Barbarians, 1988; Wessex before AD 1000, 1991; (ed) The Oxford Illustrated Prehistory of Europe, 1994; Iron Age Britain, 1995; The Ancient Celts, 1997; Facing the Ocean: the Atlantic and its peoples, 2001; The Extraordinary Voyage of Pytheas the Greek, 2001; contribs to several major excavation reports and articles to Soc. of Antiquaries, and in other learned jls. *Recreation:* mild self-indulgence. *Address:* Institute of Archaeology, 36 Beaumont Street, Oxford OX1 2PG.

CUNLIFFE, Sir David Ellis, 9th Bt *cr* 1759; business development manager; *b* 29 Oct. 1957; *s* of Sir Cyril Henley Cunliffe, 8th Bt and of Eileen Lady Cunliffe, *d* of Frederick William and Nora Anne Parkins; *S* father, 1969; *m* 1983, Linda Carol, *d* of John Sidney and Ella Mary Batchelor; three *d*. *Educ:* St Albans Grammar School. *Heir: b* Andrew Mark Cunliffe [*b* 17 April 1959; *m* 1980, Janice Elizabeth, *d* of Ronald William Kyle; one *s* three *d*]. *Address:* Sunnyside, Burnthouse Lane, Needham, near Harleston, Norfolk IP20 9LN.

CUNLIFFE, Jonathan Stephen, CB 2001; Managing Director, Financial Regulation and Industry, HM Treasury, since 2001; *b* 2 June 1953; *s* of Ralph and Cynthia Cunliffe; *m* 1984, Naomi Brandler; two *d*. *Educ:* St Marylebone GS, London; Manchester Univ. (BA Eng. 1975; MA 1976). Lectr in English and Drama, Univ of Western Ontario, 1976–79; res. student, 1979–80; joined Civil Service, 1980; DoE, 1980–85; Department of Transport: Principal, 1985; Pvte Sec. to Sec. of State, 1985–88; Transport Industry Finance, 1988–90; HM Treasury: Asst Sec., Pay Gp, 1990–93; Internat. Financial Instns, and UK Alternate Dir, EBRD (on secondment), 1993–95; Debt and Reserves Mgt, 1995–97; Dep. Dir, Macroeconomic Policy and Prospects, 1997–98; Dep. Dir, then Dir, Internat. Finance, later Macroeconomic Policy and Internat. Finance, 1998–2001. UK Alternate Mem., EU Monetary Cttee, 1996–98. *Recreations:* tennis, cooking, walking. *Address:* HM Treasury, Parliament Street, SW1P 3AG. *T:* (020) 7270 4399.

CUNLIFFE, Lawrence Francis; *b* 25 March 1929; *m* 1950, Winifred (marr. diss. 1985), *d* of William Haslem; three *s* two *d*. *Educ:* St Edmund's RC Sch., Worsley, Manchester. Engr, NCB, 1949–79. Member, Farnworth Borough Council, 1960–74, Bolton MDC, 1974–79. Contested (Lab) Rochdale, Oct. 1972 and Feb. 1974. MP (Lab) Leigh, 1979–2001. An Opposition Whip, 1985–87. JP 1967–79.

CUNLIFFE, Peter Whalley, CBE 1980; Chairman: Pharmaceuticals Division, Imperial Chemical Industries PLC, 1976–87; British Pharma Group, 1987–90; *b* 29 Oct. 1926; *s* of Fred Cunliffe and Lillie Whalley; *m* 1951, Alice Thérèse Emma Brunel; one *d*. *Educ:* Queen Elizabeth's Grammar Sch., Blackburn; Trinity Hall, Cambridge (Scholar; BA 1st Class Hons, 1948). Joined ICI Ltd, Pharmaceuticals Div., 1950; Services Dir, 1968; Overseas Dir, 1970; Dep. Chm., 1971. Pres., Assoc. of British Pharmaceutical Industry, 1981–83; Member: Council, Internat. Fedn of Pharmaceutical Manufrs Assoc., 1979–87 (Vice Pres., 1982–84, Pres. 1984–86); Exec. Cttee, European Fedn of Pharmaceutical Industries Assocs, 1982–85. *Address:* 11 St Edmund's Terrace, NW8 7QP.

CUNLIFFE, Stella Vivian, MBE 1993; consultant statistician; *b* 12 Jan. 1917; *d* of Percy Cunliffe and Edith Blanche Wellwood Cunliffe. *Educ:* privately, then Parsons Mead, Ashtead; London School of Economics (BScEcon). Danish Bacon Co, 1939–44; Voluntary Relief Work in Europe, 1945–47; Arthur Guinness Son and Co. Ltd, 1947–70; Head of Research Unit, Home Office, 1970–72; Dir of Statistics, Home Office, 1972–77. Statistical Adviser to Cttee of Enquiry into Engineering Profession, 1978–80. Pres., Royal Statistical Soc., 1975–77. *Recreations:* work with youth organisations; gardening; prison after-care. *Address:* 69 Harriotts Lane, Ashtead, Surrey KT21 2QE. *T:* (01372) 272343.

CUNLIFFE-LISTER, family name of **Baroness Masham of Ilton** and **Earl of Swinton**.

CUNLIFFE-OWEN, Sir Hugo Dudley, 3rd Bt *cr* 1920, of Bray; *b* 16 May 1966; *s* of Sir Dudley Herbert Cunliffe-Owen, 2nd Bt, and of Jean, *o d* of late Surg.-Comdr A. N. Forsyth, RN; *S* father, 1983. *Heir:* none.

CUNNANE, Most Rev. Joseph; Archbishop of Tuam, (RC), 1969–87, retired; *b* 5 Oct. 1913; *s* of William and Margaret Cunnane, Knock, Co. Mayo. *Educ:* St Jarlath's Coll., Tuam; St Patrick's Coll., Maynooth. BA 1st Hons, Ancient Classics, 1935; DD 1941; Higher Dip. Educn 1941. Priest, 1939. Prof. of Irish, St Jarlath's Coll., 1941–57; Curate, Balla, Co. Mayo, 1957–67; Curate, Clifden, Co. Galway, 1967–69. Cross of Chaplain Conventual, SMO Malta, 1970. *Publications:* Vatican II on Priests, 1967; contribs to Irish Ecclesiastical Record, Furrow, Doctrine and Life, Studies in Pastoral Liturgy, etc. *Address:* Bon Secours Hospital, Tuam, Co. Galway, Ireland.

CUNNINGHAM, Alexander Alan; Executive Vice President, General Motors, 1984–86, retired; *b* Bulgaria, 7 Jan. 1926; naturalised citizen, US; *m* 1976, Mary Helen; one *s* three *d* of former marr. *Educ:* General Motors Inst., Michigan. BSc (Industrial Engrg) 1951. Served War of 1939–45, navigation electronics radar specialist, RAF. General Motors: Jun. Process Engr, Frigidaire Div., 1951; Asst to Frigidaire Man., NY, Gen. Motors Overseas Ops, 1952; Prodn Planning Technician for Adam Opel AG, Germany, 1953; Exec. Asst to Man. Dir, GM Ltd, London, 1956; Master Mechanic, Gen. Motors do Brasil, 1957, Works Man. 1958; Works Man., Gen. Motors Argentina SA, 1962; Man. Dir, Gen. Motors do Brasil, 1963; Man., Adam Opel's Bochum plant, 1964; Asst Gen. Manufrg Man., Adam Opel AG, 1966, Gen. Manufrg Man. 1969; Man. Dir, Adam Opel AG, 1970; Gen. Dir, European Organisations, Gen. Motors Overseas Corp., 1974–76; Vice Pres., Group Exec. Overseas, 1978; Group Exec., Body Assembly, 1980. Exec. Vice-Pres., N American Cars, 1982. Trustee, Detroit SO, 1983–. *Address:* 70–671 Orville Circle, Rancho Mirage, CA 92270–3414, USA. *T:* (619) 3288671. *Clubs:* Thunderbird Country, Mission Hills Country (Rancho Mirage); Center (Orange County).

CUNNINGHAM, George; *b* June 1931; *s* of Harry Jackson Cunningham and Christina Cunningham, Dunfermline; *m* 1957, Mavis Walton; one *s* one *d*. *Educ:* Univ. of Manchester (BA 1952); Univ. of London (BSc(Econ) ext. 1969). Nat. Service in Royal Artillery (2nd Lieut), 1954–56; on staff of Commonwealth Relations Office, 1956–63; 2nd Sec., British High Commn, Ottawa, 1958–60; Commonwealth Officer of Labour

Party, 1963–66; Min. of Overseas Development, 1966–69; Chief Exec., Library Assoc., 1984–92. MP South West Islington, 1970–74, Islington South and Finsbury, 1974–83 (Lab, 1970–81, Ind, 1981–82, SDP, 1982–83). Opposition front bench spokesman (Lab) on home affairs, 1979–81. Contested: (Lab) Henley, 1966; (SDP) Islington South and Finsbury, 1983, 1987. Mem., Parlt of European Community, 1978–79. Pres., Study of Parlt Gp, 2000–. Hon. FLA. *Publications:* (Fabian pamphlet) Rhodesia, the Last Chance, 1966; (ed) Britain and the World in the Seventies, 1970; The Management of Aid Agencies, 1974; Careers in Politics, 1984. *Address:* 28 Manor Gardens, Hampton, Middlesex TW12 2TU. *T:* (020) 8979 6221.

CUNNINGHAM, Lt-Gen. Sir Hugh (Patrick), KBE 1975 (OBE 1966); *b* 4 Nov. 1921; *s* of late Sir Charles Banks Cunningham, CSI; *m* 1st, 1955, Jill (*d* 1992), *d* of J. S. Jeffrey, East Knoyle; two *s* two *d*; 2nd, 1995, Zoë Simpson (*née* Andrew), Constantia, Cape Town, S Africa. *Educ:* Charterhouse. 2nd Lieut, RE, 1942; served War of 1939–45, India, New Guinea, Burma; Greece, 1950–51; Egypt, 1951–53; Instructor, Sch. of Infantry, 1955–57, RMA Sandhurst, 1957–60; Cameroons, 1960–61; CRE 3 Div., Cyprus and Aden, 1963–66; comd 11 Engr Bde, BAOR, 1967–69; comd Mons OCS, 1969–70; Nat. Defence Coll., Canada, 1970–71; GOC SW District, 1971–74; ACGS (OR), 1974–75; DCDS (OR), 1976–78, retired. Lieutenant of Tower of London, 1983–86. Col, Queen's Gurkha Engineers (formerly Gurkha Engrs), 1976–81; Col Comdt, RE, 1976–81; Col, Bristol Univ. OTC, 1977–87. Director: Fairey Holdings Ltd, 1978–86; Fairey Engineering, 1981–86; MEL, 1982–89; TREND Communications Ltd, 1984–86, 1990–93; Chairman: LL Consultants Ltd, 1984–89; TREND Group, 1986–90. Pres., Old Carthusian Soc., 1982–87. Master, Glass Sellers' Co., 1981. Chm. of Governors, Port Regis School, 1982–94; Gov., Suttons Hosp. in Charterhouse, 1984–96. *Recreations:* bird-watching, opera, golf. *Address:* Granary Mill House, Fontmell Magna, Shaftesbury, Dorset SP7 0NY. *T:* (01747) 812025. *Clubs:* Army and Navy, MCC.

CUNNINGHAM, Rt Hon. Jack; *see* Cunningham, Rt Hon. John A.

CUNNINGHAM, James Dolan; MP (Lab) Coventry South, since 1997 (Coventry South East, 1992–97); *b* Coatbridge, 4 Feb. 1941; *s* of Adam and Elizabeth Cunningham; *m* 1985, Marion Douglas; one *s* one *d* and one step *s* one step *d*. *Educ:* St Columbia High Sch., Coatbridge. Trade Union Diplomas in Industrial Law and Social Sciences. Engineer, 1964–88. Mem. (Lab) Coventry CC, 1972–92 (Leader, 1988–92; formerly Dep. Leader, Chief Whip, Chm. and Vice Chm. of Cttees). Chm., W Midlands Jt Cttee of Local Authority, 1990–92; Sec., AMA, 1991–92. Mem., MSF. *Address:* House of Commons, SW1A 0AA.

CUNNINGHAM, Group Captain John, CBE 1963 (OBE 1951); DSO 1941; (Bars 1942, 1944); DFC 1941 (Bar); AE 1941; DL; Executive Director, British Aerospace, Hatfield, 1978–80; *b* 27 July 1917; *s* of late A. G. Cunningham and of E. M. Cunningham. *Educ:* Whitgift. Apprenticed to De Havilland Aircraft Co., Hatfield, 1935–38; employed, 1938–Aug. 1939, with De Havillands, Light Aircraft Development and Test Flying. Called up Aug. 1939; joined AAF, 1935; commanded 604 Sqdn, 1941–42; Staff job, 1942–43; commanded 85 Sqdn, 1943–44 (DSO and two bars, DFC and bar); Group Capt. Night Operations HQ 11 Group, 1944. Chief Test Pilot, de Havilland Aircraft Co., 1946–77; Exec. Dir, Hawker Siddeley Aviation, 1963–77. International Record Flight, 16 Oct. 1957: London to Khartoum direct; distance 3,064 statute miles in 5 hrs 51 mins, by Comet 3; average speed 523 statute mph. Derry and Richards Memorial Medal, GAPAN, 1965, Segrave Trophy, 1979; Air League Founders' Medal, 1979. DL: Middx, 1948; Greater London, 1965. Russian Order of Patriotic War 1st cl., 1944; USA Silver Star, 1945. *Address:* Canley, Kinsbourne Green, Harpenden, Herts AL5 3PE.

CUNNINGHAM, John, DM, FRCP; Physician to the Royal Household, since 1993; Consultant Physician, Royal London (formerly London) Hospital, since 1982; Physician, King Edward VII's Hospital for Officers, since 1993; *b* 27 June 1949; *s* of late Daniel John Chapman Cunningham and of Judith (*née* Hill); *m* 1970, Deborah Alison Yeates (marr. diss. 1996); three *s*. *Educ:* Magdalen Coll. Sch., Oxford; Trinity Hall, Cambridge (BA 1970); St John's Coll., Oxford (BM, BCh 1973; DM 1988). FRCP 1988. Junior appointments, 1973–77: Radcliffe Infirmary, Oxford; Whittington Hosp., London; Brompton Hosp., London; Central Middx Hosp., London; Lectr in Medicine, London Hosp. Med. Coll., 1977–80; Res. Fellow, Washington Univ. Sch. of Medicine, St Louis, USA, 1980–82; Sub-Dean for Med. Student Admissions, London Hosp. Med. Coll., 1990–97. Special Trustee, Royal London Hosp., 1985–. Jan Brod Meml Lecture, Prague, 1993, and other invited lectures. *Publications:* contrib. chapters in books, reviews and numerous articles in scientific jls. *Recreations:* music, sport, walking. *Address:* 31A King Henry's Road, NW3 3QR. *T:* (020) 7722 3883. *Club:* Addington Golf.

CUNNINGHAM, Rt Hon. John A., (Jack); PC 1993; DL; PhD; MP (Lab) Copeland, since 1983 (Whitehaven, Cumbria, 1970–83); *b* 4 Aug. 1939; *s* of Andrew Cunningham; *m* 1964, Maureen; one *s* two *d*. *Educ:* Jarrow Grammar Sch.; Bede Coll., Durham Univ. Hons Chemistry, 1962; PhD Chemistry, 1966. Formerly: Research Fellow in Chemistry, Durham Univ.; School Teacher; Trades Union Officer. PPS to Rt Hon. James Callaghan, 1972–76; Parly Under-Sec. of State, Dept of Energy, 1976–79; opposition spokesman on industry, 1979–83; Mem., Shadow Cabinet, 1983–95 and 1996–97; spokesman on the environment, 1983–89; Shadow Leader, H of C, 1989–92; opposition front bench spokesman on foreign and Commonwealth affairs, 1992–94; on trade and industry, 1994–95; on national heritage, 1995–97; Minister of Agriculture, Fisheries and Food, 1997–98; Minister for the Cabinet Office and Chancellor of the Duchy of Lancaster, 1998–99. DL Cumbria, 1991. *Recreations:* fell walking, fly-fishing, gardening, classical and folk music, reading, listening to other people's opinions. *Address:* House of Commons, SW1A 0AA.

CUNNINGHAM, Mark James; QC 2001; *b* 6 June 1956; *s* of James Arthur Cunningham and Carole Kathleen Cunningham; *m* 1980 (marr. diss. 1995); two *s* two *d*. *Educ:* Stonyhurst Coll.; Magdalen Coll., Oxford (BA Hons Modern Hist.); Poly. of Central London (Dip. Law). Called to the Bar, Inner Temple, 1980; Junior Counsel to the Crown: Chancery, 1991–99; A Panel, 1999–2001; DTI Inspector, 1998–99. *Recreations:* cricket, tennis, horses, food, travel. *Address:* Maitland Chambers, 7 Stone Buildings, Lincoln's Inn, WC2A 3SZ. *T:* (020) 7406 1200, *Fax:* (020) 7406 1300; *e-mail:* mcunningham@maitlandchambers.com. *Clubs:* Pegasus, Drayton Parslow Cricket, Stewkley Tennis.

CUNNINGHAM, Merce; Artistic Director, Merce Cunningham Dance Company, since 1953; *b* 16 April 1919; *s* of Clifford D. Cunningham. *Educ:* Cornish Coll., Seattle, Washington. Martha Graham Dance Co., 1939–45; 1st solo concert, NY, 1944; choreographed: The Seasons, for Ballet Society (later NY City Ballet), 1947; Un Jour ou deux, for Ballet of Paris Opéra, 1973; more than 200 works for own company; other works revived for NY City Ballet, American Ballet Theatre, Rambert Dance Co. (formerly Ballet Rambert), Théâtre du Silence, France, Ohio Ballet, Boston Ballet, Pacific Northwest Ballet, Zürich Ballet. Hon. Mem., Amer. Acad. and Inst. of Arts and Letters, 1984. DLitt Univ. of Illinois, 1972. Samuel H. Scripps American Dance Festival Award for lifetime contribs to dance, 1982; Award of Honor for Arts and Culture, NY, 1983; MacArthur Award, 1985; Kennedy Center Honors, 1985; Laurence Olivier Award, 1985; Meadows Award for excellence in the arts, Meadows Sch. of Arts, Southern Methodist Univ., Dallas, 1987; Nat. Medal of Arts, USA, 1990; Digital Dance Premier Award, 1990; Golden Lion, Venice Biennale, 1995; Premio Internazionale, Gino Tani, 1999; Dorothy and Lillian Gish Prize, 2000; Nijinsky Special Prize, Monaco, 2000. Comdr, Order of Arts and Letters, France, 1982; Chevalier de la Légion d'Honneur, 1989. *Publications:* Changes: notes on choreography (ed Frances Starr), 1968; Le Danseur et la danse: entretiens avec Jacqueline Lesschaeve, 1980, English edn The Dancer and the Dance, 1985; articles in 7 Arts, trans/formation, TriQuarterly. *Address:* 55 Bethune Street, New York, NY 10014, USA. *T:* (212) 2558240.

CUNNINGHAM, Phyllis Margaret, CBE 1997; Chief Executive, Royal Marsden NHS Trust, 1994–98 (Chief Executive, Royal Marsden Hospital Special Health Authority, 1980–94); *b* 15 Sept. 1937; *d* of late Andrew Cunningham and of Minnie Cunningham (*née* Rees). *Educ:* Chorlton Central Sch., Manchester; Loreburn Coll., Manchester (Dip. in Business Studies, 1956). Trainee Adminr, Withington Hosp., Manchester, 1956–59; PA/Res. Asst to Med. Dir, Geigy Pharmaceutical Co., 1959–62; Unit Adminr, Roosevelt Hosp., NY, 1962–64; Planning Officer, Royal Free Hosp., London, 1964–74; Dep. House Gov./Sec. to Board, Royal Marsden Hosp., 1974–80. Trustee and Mem. Council, St Christopher's Hospice, Sydenham, 1999–. Mem., Hospital Officers' Club. Gov., Christ's Sch., Richmond, 1996–99. FRSA 1992. *Recreations:* current affairs, travel, theatre, music, gardening. *Address:* 12 Augustus Close, Brentford Dock, Brentford, Middx TW8 8QE. *T:* (020) 8847 1067.

CUNNINGHAM, Roseanna; MP (SNP) Perth, since 1997 (Perth and Kinross, May 1995–1997); Member (SNP) Perth, Scottish Parliament, since 1999; Deputy Leader, Scottish National Party, since 2000; *b* 27 July 1951; *d* of Hugh and Catherine Cunningham. *Educ:* Univ. of Western Australia (BA Hons Politics 1975); Edinburgh Univ. (LLB 1982); Aberdeen Univ. (Dip. Legal Practice 1983). SNP Research Asst, 1977–79; Solicitor, 1983–90; admitted Faculty of Advocates, 1990; in practice, 1990–95. *Recreations:* music, reading, stirring up trouble. *Address:* 14/367 Argyle Street, Glasgow G2 8LT. *T:* (0141) 221 5651.

CUNNINGHAM, Thomas Anthony, (Tony); MP (Lab) Workington, since 2001; *b* 16 Sept. 1952; *s* of late Daniel Cunningham and of Bessie Cunningham; *m* 1985, Anne Gilmore; one *d*, and one step *s* one step *d*. *Educ:* Workington GS; Liverpool Univ. (BA Hons). Mem., Allerdale DC, then BC, 1987–95 (Leader, 1992–94); Mayor of Workington, 1990–91. MEP (Lab) Cumbria and Lancs N, 1994–99; contested (Lab) NW Reg., 1999. *Address:* 17 Carlton Road, Workington, Cumbria CA14 4BX. *T:* (01900) 605799.

CUNNINGHAM-JARDINE, Ronald Charles; Lord-Lieutenant, Dumfries and Galloway Region, districts of Nithsdale, Annandale and Eskdale, since 1991 (Vice Lord-Lieutenant, 1988–91); *b* 19 Sept. 1931; *s* of Charles Frederick Cunningham and Dorothy Agnes Jessie Jardine; *m* 1959, Constance Mary Teresa Inglis; one *s* one *d*. *Educ:* Ludgrove; Eton College; RMA Sandhurst. Royal Scots Greys, 1950–58; Edinburgh Agricultural College, 1959–60; farming, 1960–. *Recreations:* all country sports. *Address:* Fourmerkland, Lockerbie, Dumfriesshire DG11 1EH. *T:* (01387) 810226. *Clubs:* White's; Muthaiga (Kenya).

CUNY, Jean-Pierre; Chairman: Saint Eloi Finance, since 2000; Soloc Rabotage, since 2000; *b* 8 April 1940; *s* of Robert Cuny and Marie Louise Marchal; *m* 1968, Anne-Marie Fousse; two *d*. *Educ:* Ecole Centrale de Paris (Ingénieur); Massachusetts Inst. of Technol. (MSc). Ingénieur, Serete, 1965–68; Director: Firmin Didot, 1968–73; DAFSA, 1973–76; Project Manager, CGA, 1976–78; joined Placoplatre, France, 1978: Prodn Dir, 1978–82; Commercial Dir, 1982–86; Pres. Dir Gen., BPB France, 1986–92; Dir, 1988–99, Chief Exec., 1994–99, BPB plc. Chevalier de la Légion d'Honneur, 1994. *Recreations:* ski-ing, photography.

CUNYNGHAME, Sir Andrew (David Francis), 12th Bt *cr* 1702; FCA; *b* 25 Dec. 1942; *s* of Sir (Henry) David St Leger Brooke Selwyn Cunynghame, 11th Bt, and of Hon. Pamela Margaret Stanley (*d* 1991), *d* of 5th Lord Stanley of Alderley; *S* father, 1978; *m* 1st, 1972, Harriet Ann, *d* of late C. T. Dupont, Montreal; two *d*; 2nd, 1989, Isabella King, *d* of late Edward Everett Watts, Jr and of Isabella Hardy Watts. *Educ:* Eton. *Heir: b* John Philip Henry Michael Selwyn Cunynghame [*b* 9 Sept. 1944; *m* 1981, Marjatta, *d* of Martti Markus; one *s* one *d*]. *Address:* 12 Vicarage Gardens, W8 4AH. *Club:* Brooks's.

CUOMO, Mario Matthew; lawyer; Democrat; Partner, Willkie Farr & Gallagher, since 1995; *b* 15 June 1932; *s* of late Andrea and Immaculata Cuomo; *m* 1954, Matilda M. Raffa; two *s* three *d*. *Educ:* St John's Coll., NY (Latin Amer. Studies, English, Philosophy; BA 1953); St John's Univ. (LLB 1956). Admitted to NY Bar, 1956, US Supreme Court, 1960; Asst to Judge A. P. Burke, NY State Court of Appeals, 1956–58; joined Corner, Weisbrod, Froeb & Charles (later Corner, Finn, Cuomo & Charles), 1958, Partner, 1963–75; Prof., St John's Univ. Law Sch., 1963–73; Sec. of State for NY, 1975–78 (Chm., NY Urban & Rural Affairs, Adv. Council on Disabled; 1st NY Ombudsman); Lt-Governor, NY, 1979–82; Governor, NY State, 1983–95. *Publications:* The Forest Hills Controversy: a report and comment, 1972; Forest Hills Diary: the crisis of low income housing, 1974; Diaries of Mario M. Cuomo: the campaign for Governor, 1984; (ed jtly) Lincoln on Democracy, 1990; More than Words: the speeches of Mario Cuomo, 1993; New York Idea: an experiment in democracy, 1994; Reason to Believe, 1995; (for children) The Blue Spruce, 1999; articles in legal jls.

CUPITT, Rev. Don; Fellow of Emmanuel College, 1965–96, now Life Fellow (Dean, 1966–91) and University Lecturer in Divinity, 1973–96, Cambridge; *b* 22 May 1934; *s* of late Robert and Norah Cupitt; *m* 1963, Susan Marianne (*née* Day); one *s* two *d*. *Educ:* Charterhouse; Trinity Hall, Cambridge; Westcott House, Cambridge. Curate, St Philip's Church, Salford, 1959–62; Vice-Principal, Westcott House, Cambridge, 1962–65. Hon. DLitt Bristol, 1985. *Publications:* Christ and the Hiddenness of God, 1971; Crisis of Moral Authority, 1972; The Leap of Reason, 1976; The Worlds of Science and Religion, 1976; (with Peter Armstrong) Who Was Jesus?, 1977; Jesus and the Gospel of God, 1979; The Nature of Man, 1979; The Debate about Christ, 1979; Explorations in Theology, 1979; Taking Leave of God, 1980; The World to Come, 1982; The Sea of Faith, 1984 (TV series, 1984); Only Human, 1985; Life Lines, 1986; The Long-Legged Fly, 1987; The New Christian Ethics, 1988; Radicals and the Future of the Church, 1989; Creation Out of Nothing, 1990; What is a Story?, 1991; Rethinking Religion, 1992; The Time Being, 1992; After All, 1994; The Last Philosophy, 1995; Solar Ethics, 1995; After God, 1997; Mysticism After Modernity, 1998; The Religion of Being, 1998; The Revelation of Being, 1998; The New Religion of Life in Everyday Speech, 1999; The Meaning of It All in Everyday Speech, 1999; Kingdom Come in Everyday Speech, 2000; Philosophy's Own Religion, 2000; Reforming Christianity, 2001. *Address:* Emmanuel College, Cambridge CB2 3AP. *T:* (01223) 334200.

CURA, José; singer, composer and conductor; *b* Rosario, Argentina, 5 Dec. 1962; *m* 1985, Silvia Ibarra; two *s* one *d*. *Educ:* Nat. Univ. of Rosario; Sch. of Arts, Teatro Colon, Buenos Aires. Débuts: Father, in Pollicino, Verona, 1992; Stiffelio (title rôle), Royal Opera, Covent Garden, 1995; La Gioconda, La Scala, Milan, 1997; other rôles include: Cavaradossi, in Tosca; Samson, in Samson et Dalila; Don José, in Carmen; Rhadames, in Aida; Otello. Recordings include: all tenor arias from Puccini's operas; Annelo, Argentine songs; Verismo Arias; Samson et Dalila. *Address:* International José Cura Connexion, 3 Grove Court, Church End, Arlesey, Beds SG15 6UZ.

CURDS, Prof. Colin Robert, DSc, PhD; Keeper of Zoology, 1991–97, Research Associate, since 1997, Natural History Museum; *b* 16 Sept. 1937; *s* of Robert Redvers Curds and Daisy Violet Curds (*née* Howsam); *m* 1961, Pauline (Polly) Armitage; one *s* one *d*. *Educ:* East Ham Grammar Sch.; Univ. of London (BSc 1960; PhD 1963; DSc 1978). FIBiol 1979, CBiol 1982. Jun. Res. Fellow, Water Pollution Res. Lab., 1963–65; Min. of Technology, 1965–71; British Museum (Natural History), 1971–: Dep. Keeper of Zoology, 1976–89; Acting Keeper of Zoology, 1989–91. Visiting Lecturer: Chelsea Coll., 1965–73; Aston Univ., 1967–75; Surrey Univ., 1971–85; Vis. Prof., Mexico Univ., 1989–. Former mem., biol. and microbiol. cttees, 1972–; Member: Publications Policy Cttee, Inst. Biol., 1979–85; Council of Management, Project Urquhart, 1991–. Hon. Mem., Soc. of Protozoology, 1999–. Gov., Powell-Cotton Mus., 1992–97. *Publications:* (ed jtly) Ecological Aspects of Used-water Treatment Processes, vol. 1, 1979, vols 2 and 3, 1983; British and other freshwater ciliated protozoa, Pt 1, 1982, Pt 2 (jtly), 1983; Protozoa in the Water Industry, 1992; contribs to professional jls. *Recreations:* family life, furniture design, cabinet-making, France, cats, snorkelling, genealogy. *Address:* Department of Zoology, Natural History Museum, Cromwell Road, SW7 5BD. *T:* (020) 7942 5149; *e-mail:* curds@globalnet.co.uk.

CURE, (George) Nigel C.; *see* Capel Cure.

CURE, Kenneth Graham, OBE 1984; Executive Councilman, Amalgamated Engineering Union, 1979–89, retired; Member, Labour Party National Executive, 1981–89; *b* 22 Feb. 1924; *s* of Herbert and Doris Edith Cure; *m* 1949, Kathleen (*née* Taylor); two *s* one *d*. *Educ:* King Edward VI Grammar School, Birmingham. Apprentice, BSA; trained as Universal Miller and draughtsman; served War of 1939–45, RN (Atlantic convoys and combined ops). Joined AEU, 1952; Founder Sec., Castle Vale Birmingham Branch, 1970; held numerous offices in Branch and District; former Mem., W Midlands Regional Labour Party Exec.; former Chm., Disputes Cttee, Lab. Party NEC; former Mem., Gen. Purposes Cttee, TUC. Former Director: Co-operative Press Ltd; Prince's Trust Educn and Training. Member: Panel, Central Arbitration Cttee; ACAS. Chair, East Birmingham Coll. Corp. (formerly Govs), 1973–98; Chm., Birmingham Metropolitan Inst. of Technology, 1992–96; Governor, Fircroft Coll., 1981–94. Hon. Chancellor, City Coll., Birmingham, 1998–. FRSA. Hon. MSc CNAA, 1986. *Recreation:* reading.

CURIE, Eve, (Mrs Henry R. Labouisse); writer and journalist; *b* Paris, 6 Dec. 1904; *d* of late Marie and Pierre Curie; *m* 1954, Henry Richardson Labouisse (*d* 1987). *Educ:* Sévigné College; Bachelor of Science and Bachelor of Philosophy. Accompanied her mother in her tour of the US 1921; devoted several years to the study of the piano and gave her first concert in 1925 in Paris; later she took up musical criticism and under a pseudonym acted for several years as musical critic of the weekly journal Candide; after the death of her mother in 1934 she collected and classified all the papers, manuscripts, and personal documents left by Mme Curie and went to Poland in 1935 to obtain material as to Mme Curie's youth; wrote Mme Curie's biography; went to America again in 1939 and several times afterwards on lecture tours; was a co-ordinator of the women's war activities at the Ministry of Information in Paris at the beginning of the war; after the French capitulation went to live in London for six months, then to America for her third lecture tour; Vichy Govt deprived her of French citizenship in April 1941; in 1942, travelled, as a war correspondent to the battlefronts of Libya, Russia, Burma, China; enlisted in the Fighting French corps, Volontaires Françaises, 1943, as a private; received basic training in England; 2nd Lieut 1943; 1st Lieut 1944. Co-publisher of Paris-Presse, an evening paper in Paris, 1944–49. Special Adviser to the Sec. Gen. of NATO, Paris, Aug. 1952–Nov. 1954. *Publications:* Madame Curie (in US), 1937 (trans. into 32 langs); Journey Among Warriors, 1943. *Recreation:* swimming. *Address:* 1 Sutton Place South, New York, NY 10022, USA.

CURL, Philip; His Honour Judge Curl; a Circuit Judge, since 1996; *b* 31 Oct. 1947; *s* of Dr Oliver Curl and Joan Curl; *m* 1983, Nicola Ruth Gurney; two *d*. *Educ:* Radley Coll.; Southampton Univ. (LLB). Called to the Bar, Gray's Inn, 1970; Asst Recorder, 1991–95; Recorder, 1995–96. *Recreations:* playing and watching sport, art, travel. *Address:* c/o Norwich Combined Courts, Bishopgate, Norwich, Norfolk NR3 1UR. *Clubs:* MCC; Norfolk (Norwich).

CURL, Prof. Robert Floyd, PhD; Harry C. and Olga K. Wiess Professor of Natural Sciences, Rice University, Houston, since 1996; *b* 23 Aug. 1933; *s* of Robert Floyd Curl and Lessie Waldeen Curl; *m* 1955, Jonel Whipple; two *s*. *Educ:* Rice Inst. (BA 1954); Univ. of Calif, Berkeley (PhD 1957). Res. Fellow, Harvard, 1957–58; Rice Institute, then Rice University: Asst Prof., 1958–63; Associate Prof., 1963–67; Prof. of Chemistry, 1967–96; Chm., Chemistry Dept, 1992–96; Master, Lovett Coll., 1968–72. Dr (*hc*) Univ. of Buenos Aires, 1997. (Jtly) Clayton Prize, IMechE, 1958; (jtly) APS Prize for New Materials, 1992; (jtly) Nobel Prize for Chemistry, 1996; (jtly) Texas Distinguished Scientist, Texas Acad. of Sci., 1997; (jtly) Achievement in Carbon Science, Amer. Carbon Soc., 1997; Order of the Golden Plate, Amer. Acad. of Achievement, 1997. *Publications:* numerous contribs to scientific jls. *Recreations:* contract bridge, squash. *Address:* Chemistry Department, Rice University, Houston, TX 77005, USA. *T:* (713) 3484816; 1824 Bolsover, Houston, TX 77005, USA.

CURLE, James Leonard; Member and Managing Director, Civil Aviation Authority, 1984–87; *b* 14 Nov. 1925; *s* of Leonard and Mary Curle; *m* 1952, Gloria Madaleine Roch; one *s* one *d*. *Educ:* St Joseph's Academy, Blackheath; SE London Technical College; Borough Polytechnic. CEng, MIEE. Royal Signals, 1944–49; joined Telecommunications Div., MTCA, 1957; Dir Telecommunications, ATS, 1976–79; Dir Gen. Telecommunications, NATS, 1979–84. *Address:* 6 Nightingale Lane, Bickley, Kent BR1 2QH. *T:* (020) 8460 8023.

CURLEY, Carlo James; international concert organist; *b* 24 Aug. 1952; *s* of James Dennis Curley and Gladys Maynard Curley. *Educ:* N Carolina Sch. of Arts; privately with Virgil Fox, Robert Elmore and Sir George Thalben Ball. Organist/choirmaster, Druid Hills Baptist Ch, Atlanta, Ga, 1968–71; Artist-in-Residence, Fountain St Ch, Grand Rapids, Mich, 1970–71; Summer Organist-in-Residence, Alexandra Palace, London, 1977–78; numerous community and civic concerts, N America, 1979–88; played first solo classic organ recital at the White House, by invitation of the Pres., 1989; various Royal Comd performances; has performed world-wide, both solo and orchestral, 1989–; numerous radio, TV and media appearances world-wide, 1989–; has made numerous recordings. Hon. Fellow, Guild of Musicians and Singers, 1996. *Publication:* In the Pipeline (autobiog.), 1997. *Recreations:* reading, walking, swimming, fine food and wines. *Address:* c/o PVA Management Ltd, Hallow Park, Worcester WR2 6PG. *T:* (01905) 640663, *Fax:* (01905) 641842; *e-mail:* md@pva.co.uk.

CURNOCK COOK, Jeremy Laurence; consultant, biotechnology industry, since 2000; *b* 3 Sept. 1949; *s* of Colin Curnock Cook and Doris (*née* Wolsey); *m* 1st, 1975, Elizabeth Joanna Badgett (marr. diss. 1981); 2nd, 1987, Mary Elizabeth Thomasson (marr. diss. 1998); one *s* two *d*. *Educ:* Lycée Français de Londres; Westminster Sch.; Trinity Coll., Dublin (MA Natural Scis). Res. Scientist, Inst. Cancer Res., London, 1972–73; Managing Director: Badgett-Cook Biochems Ltd, London, 1973–75; Internat. Biochems Ltd, Dublin, London, 1975–87; Rothschild Asset Mgt (Biosci. Unit), 1988–2000. Chairman: Targeted Genetics Inc., 1995–; Bioscience Managers Ltd, 2001–; non-executive Director: Cantab Pharmaceuticals plc, 1990–; Biocompatibles Internat. plc, 1992–; Ribozyme Pharmaceuticals Inc., 1995–; Vernalis, 1995–2001; Angiotech Pharmaceuticals Inc., 1995–2001; Amrad Corp., 1995–; Inflazyme Pharmaceuticals Inc., 1996–; Delsys Pharmaceuticals Inc., 2000–; Valigen, 2000–; GlycoDesign Inc., 2001–. Mem., Soc. for Gen. Microbiol., 1971–. FInstD 1988; FRSA 1994. *Recreations:* keeping fit, music, ski-ing. *Address:* 2 Balfern Grove, Chiswick, W4 2JX. *Club:* Kildare Street and University (Dublin).

CURNOW, Rt Rev. Andrew William; Assistant Bishop, Diocese of Melbourne, since 1994; *b* 26 Feb. 1950; *s* of Thomas William Curnow and Esma Jean Curnow (*née* Cook); *m* 1978, Jan Christina Jenkins; two *s* one *d*. *Educ:* Univ. of Melbourne (BComm); Melbourne Coll. of Divinity (BD); Presbyterian Sch. of Christian Educn, Richmond, VA, USA, (MA). Asst Curate, St Alban's, West Coburg, 1973–75; Rector, Parish of Milloo, 1975–79; on leave, USA, dios New York and Virginia, 1979–80; Rector of Elmore, 1980–83; Dir, Council for Christian Educn in Schools, Prov. of Victoria, 1983–89; Vicar of St George's, Malvern, 1989–94; Archdeacon of Kew, 1991–94. Exec. Chm., Trinity Coll. Theol Sch., 1997- ; Chm., Anglicare Australia, 1997–. *Recreations:* reading, theatre, travel. *Address:* The Anglican Centre, 209 Flinders Lane, Melbourne, Vic 3000, Australia. *T:* (3) 96534220; 66 Baroda Street, Ascot Vale, Vic 3032, Australia. *T:* (3) 93704147. *Club:* Royal Automobile of Victoria (Melbourne).

CURNOW, (Elizabeth) Ann (Marguerite); QC 1985; a Recorder of the Crown Court, since 1980; *b* 5 June 1935; *d* of Cecil Curnow and Doris Curnow (*née* Behr); *m* 1981, (William) Neil Denison, *qv*. *Educ:* St Hilda's Sch., Whitby, Yorks; King's Coll., London (LLB). Called to the Bar, Gray's Inn, 1957, Bencher, 1985. Treasury Counsel, Mddx Crown Court, 1972–77; Central Criminal Court: Jun. Treasury Counsel, 1977–81; Sen. Prosecuting Counsel to the Crown, 1981–85. Member: Parole Bd, 1992–94; Criminal Injuries Compensation Bd, 1996–. *Recreations:* Burmese cats, listening to music, tapestry, gardening. *Address:* 6 King's Bench Walk, Temple, EC4Y 7DR. *T:* (020) 7583 0410, *Fax:* (020) 7353 8791.

CURRALL, Alexander, CB 1970; CMG 1965; Managing Director, Post Office, 1972–77; *b* 30 Jan. 1917; *s* of late R. T. Currall, Edinburgh; *m* 1940, Madeleine Crombie Saunders; one *s*. *Educ:* George Watson's Coll., Edinburgh; Edinburgh Univ. Min. of Supply, 1939–40; Royal Artillery and Indian Artillery, 1940–46. Successively in Min. of Supply, Min. of Materials and Board of Trade, concerned mainly with internat. economic negotiations, excepting the period 1950–54, when responsible for public trading in non-ferrous metals, and 1954–55, when holding a Commonwealth Fellowship for travel and study in USA. Seconded to Foreign Office as Dep. Consul-Gen., New York, 1960–62; Minister (Commercial), British High Commn, Ottawa, 1962–66; Under-Secretary: Board of Trade, 1966–67; DEA, 1967–68; Dir, Dept for Nat. Savings, 1968–72. Director: Renold, 1977–84; National Counties Building Soc., 1977–87 (Chm., 1984–86); Applied Photophysics Ltd, 1980–86 (Chm., 1981–86); Photophysics Research Ltd, 1980–86 (Chm., 1981–86); Grantham House Ltd, 1980–86 (Chm., 1981–86); The Pryors Ltd, 1983–87. Manager, Royal Instn, 1972–75, 1977–80, 1981–84. *Address:* Fairlawn, Buckden, Skipton, North Yorkshire BD23 5JA. *Club:* Caledonian.

CURRAN, Edmund Russell; Editor, Belfast Telegraph, since 1993; *b* 29 Sept. 1944; *s* of William John Curran and Elizabeth (*née* Russell); *m* 1st, 1968, Romaine Carmichael (marr. diss. 1991); two *s* two *d*; 2nd, 1994, Pauline Hall. *Educ:* Royal Sch., Dungannon; Queen's Univ., Belfast (BSc, DipEd). Dep. Editor, Belfast Telegraph, 1974–88; Editor, Sunday Life (NI), 1988–92; Actg Editor, Wales on Sunday, 1991. Pres., Soc. of Editors, 2001. Newspaper Focus UK Regl Newspaper Editor of Year, 1991. *Recreations:* tennis, golf, reading newspapers. *Address:* Belfast Telegraph, 124/144 Royal Avenue, Belfast BT1 1EB. *T:* (028) 9026 4400. *Clubs:* Belfast Boat, Belvoir Park Golf (Belfast); Royal County Down Golf (Newcastle).

CURRAN, John Terence; His Honour Judge Curran; a Circuit Judge, since 1996; Resident Judge, Merthyr Tydfil Combined Court Centre, since 1998; *b* 3 Oct. 1941; *s* of Eugene Curran, OBE and Joan Curran; *m* 1971, Elizabeth Ann Bowcott; one *s* one *d*. *Educ:* Ratcliffe; Jesus Coll., Cambridge (MA). Hallinans, solicitors, Cardiff: articled clerk, 1963–68; admitted solicitor, 1968; Partner, 1968–83; called to the Bar, Gray's Inn, 1983; Asst Recorder, 1989–93; Actg Stipendiary Magistrate, 1989; Provincial Stipendiary Magistrate (Mid-Glam), 1990–96; a Recorder, 1993–96. *Recreations:* walking, gardening, history, supporting Cardiff RFC, looking for my spectacles. *Address:* Law Courts, Glebeland Place, Merthyr Tydfil CF47 8BH. *Club:* Cardiff Athletic.

CURRAN, Leo Gabriel Columbanus, CEng, FIMechE; Chairman, Paleagle Ltd; *b* 23 Nov. 1930; *s* of B. L. Curran and R. Fanning; *m* 1957, Margaret Hickey; one *s* two *d*. *Educ:* St Malachy's Coll., Belfast; Dublin Coll. of Higher Technol. CEng 1974, FIMechE 1969; FIMarE 1974; MIProdE 1970. Managing Director: British Silverware Ltd, 1970–71; Delta Electrical (South African Delta Metal Electrical Pty) Ltd, 1971–73; Gen. Man. and Dir, Harland & Wolff Ltd, 1973–76; Man. Dir, Plessey Hydraulics International Ltd, 1976–79; Bd Mem. for Enginebuilding and Gen. Engrg, British Shipbuilders, 1979–80; Dir, Mica & Micanite (Ireland) Ltd, 1987. *Recreations:* music, walking.

CURRAN, Maj. Gen. Liam Diarmuid, CB 2001; CEng, FIEE; Engineer Adviser to Defence Procurement Agency and President of the Ordnance Board, 1998–2000; *b* 31 March 1946; *s* of late William James Curran and Genevieve Curran (*née* Lavery); *m* 1971, Evelyn Mary Elizabeth Strang; two *d*. *Educ:* Presentation Coll., Reading; Welbeck Coll.; Royal Military Acad., Sandhurst; Fitzwilliam Coll., Cambridge (MA 1970). CEng 1980; FIEE 1990. CO, 7 Armd Workshop, REME and Comdr, Fallingbostel Station, 1986–89; Equipt Support Manager on staff of QMG, 1989–91; Project Manager for Light Armd Vehicles, 1991–93; Equipt Support Dir on staff of QMG, 1993–96; Vice-Pres., Ordnance Bd, 1996–98. *Recreations:* walking, gardening, National Trust. *Address:* c/o Lloyds TSB, 38 Market Place, East Dereham, Norfolk NR19 2AT. *Club:* Army and Navy.

CURRAN, Margaret Patricia; Member (Lab) Glasgow Baillieston, Scottish Parliament, since 1999; *b* 24 Nov. 1958; *d* of James Curran and Rose McConnellogue; *m* (separated); two *s*. *Educ:* Glasgow Univ. (MA Hons Hist. and Econ. Hist.); Cert. Community Educn. Welfare rights officer, 1982–83; community worker, 1983–87, sen. community worker,

1987–89, Strathclyde Regl Council; Lectr, Dept of Community Educn, Univ. of Strathclyde, 1989–99. Dep. Minister for Social Justice, Scottish Exec., 2001–. *Recreations:* reading, cinema, being with children. *Address:* 112 Camphill Avenue, Langside, Glasgow G41 3DU. *T:* (0141) 649 7863.

CURRAN, Patrick David; QC 1995; a Recorder, since 1992; *s* of late David Curran and of Noreen Curran; *m* 1976; two *s* two *d*. *Educ:* Ratcliffe; Queen's Coll., Oxford (MA). Called to the Bar, Gray's Inn, 1972; Asst Recorder, 1988–92; admitted to Bar of Ireland, 1993. Asst Comr, Parly Boundary Commn for Wales, 1994–. Legal Mem., Mental Health Review Tribunal, 1995–. Governor, Westminster Cathedral Choir Sch., 2001–. Editor, Personal Injuries and Quantum Reports, 1992–. *Publications:* Personal Injury Pleadings, 1994, 2nd edn 2001; (contrib.) Criminal Law and Forensic Psychiatry, 1995; (ed and contrib.) Personal Injury Handbook, 1997; contrib. Criminal Law Rev., Personal Injuries and Quantum Reports. *Address:* 9-12 Bell Yard, WC2A 2JR. *T:* (020) 7400 1800.
See also Dame D. J. Hine.

CURRAN, Prof. Robert Crowe, MD; Leith Professor of Pathology, Birmingham University, 1966–86, now Emeritus; Hon. Consultant Pathologist, Birmingham Central Health District, 1966–86; *b* 28 July 1921; *s* of John Curran and Sarah Crowe, Netherton, Wishaw, Lanarkshire; *m* 1947, Margaret Marion Park; one *s* one *d*. *Educ:* Glasgow Univ. MB, ChB 1943, MD 1956; FRCPath 1967; FRCP 1969; Hon. FFPath, RCPI, 1983. RAMC, 1945–47. Lectr in Pathology, Glasgow Univ., 1950–55. Sen. Lectr and Cons. Pathologist, Sheffield Univ., 1955–58; Prof. of Pathology, St Thomas's Hospital Medical Sch., 1958–66. Registrar, Royal Coll. of Pathologists, 1968–73, Vice-Pres., 1977–80, Pres., 1981–84; Mem., GMC, 1979–86; Hon. Sec., Conf. of Med. Royal Colls and their Faculties in UK, 1982–86. *Publications:* Colour Atlas of Histopathology, 1966, 4th edn 2000; The Pathological Basis of Medicine, 1972; Gross Pathology—a Colour Atlas, 1974; Tumours: Structure and Diagnosis, 1991; scientific papers on lymphoid tissue, disorders of connective tissue, neoplasia. *Recreations:* golf, music. *Address:* 34A Carpenter Road, Edgbaston, Birmingham B15 2JH.

CURRAN, Terence Dominic; HM Diplomatic Service, retired; Consul-General, Toronto, and Director-General of Trade and Investment in Canada, 1996–2000; *b* 14 June 1940; *m* 1969, Penelope Anne Ford; two *s* one *d*. Joined HM Diplomatic Service, 1966; DSAO, 1966–68; Peking, 1968–69; Consul, Dakar, 1970–73; Asst Trade Comr, then Consul (Commercial), Edmonton, 1973–78; FCO, 1978–80; First Sec., Pretoria, 1980–84; FCO, 1984–87; Counsellor (Commercial and Economic), Singapore, 1987–90; Head of Training, FCO, 1990–93; Dep. High Comr, Bombay, 1993–96. *Address:* Rother House, Nyewood, Petersfield, Hants GU31 5HY.

CURRIE, family name of **Baron Currie of Marylebone**.

CURRIE OF MARYLEBONE, Baron *cr* 1996 (Life Peer), of Marylebone in the City of Westminster; **David Anthony Currie;** Dean, City University Business School, since 2001; *b* 9 Dec. 1946; *s* of Kennedy Moir Currie and Marjorie Currie (*née* Thompson); *m* 1st, 1975, Shaziye Gazioglu Currie (marr. diss. 1992); two *s*; 2nd, 1995, Angela Mary Piers Dumas. *Educ:* Battersea Grammar Sch.; Univ. of Manchester (BSc 1st cl. Maths); Univ. of Birmingham (MSocSci Econs); PhD Econs London. Economist: Hoare Govett, 1971–72; Economic Models, 1972; Lectr, Reader and Prof. of Economics, Queen Mary College, Univ. of London, 1972–88, London Business School: Prof. of Econs, 1988–2000; Res. Dean, 1989–92; Gov., 1989–95; Dep. Principal, 1992–95; Dep. Dean for External Relations, 1999–2000; Dir, Centre for Econ. Forecasting, 1988–95. Res. Fellow, Centre for Economic Policy Research, 1983–. Houblon-Norman Res. Fellow, Bank of England, 1985–86; Vis. Scholar, IMF, 1987. Member: ABRC, 1992–93; Retail Price Index Adv. Cttee, 1992–93; Treasury's Panel of Independent Forecasters, 1992–95; Gas and Electricity Mkts Authy, 2000–. Dir, 1994–, and Chm. Exec. Cttee, 1994–97, Charter 88; Director: Internat. Schs of Business Mgt, 1992–95; Joseph Rowntree Reform Trust (Investments) Ltd, 1989–; Joseph Rowntree Reform Trust (Properties) Ltd, 1991–; Abbey National plc, 2001–. Trustee, Joseph Rowntree Reform Trust, 1991–. Hon. Fellow, QMW, 1997. Hon. DLitt Glasgow, 1998. *Publications:* Advances in Monetary Economics, 1985; (with Charles Goodhart and David Llewellyn) The Operation and Regulation of Financial Markets, 1986; (with David Vines) Macroeconomic Interactions Between North and South, 1988; (with Paul Levine) Rules, Reputation and Macroeconomic Policy Co-ordination, 1993; (with David Vines) North-South Linkages and International Macroeconomic Policy, 1995; The Pros and Cons of EMU, 1997; Will the Euro Work?: the ins and outs of EMU, 1998; articles in jls. *Recreations:* music, literature, swimming. *Address:* City University Business School, Frobisher Crescent, Barbican Centre, EC2Y 8HB. *T:* (020) 7477 8601; *e-mail:* d.currie@city.ac.uk.

CURRIE, Maj. Gen. Archibald Peter Neil, CB 2001; Deputy Adjutant General, Ministry of Defence, since 2001; *b* Dar es Salaam, 30 June 1948; *s* of Donald and Ysobel Currie; *m* 1974, Angela Margaret Howell; two *s*. *Educ:* Sao Hill Sch., Tanzania; Monkton Combe Sch.; RMA, Sandhurst; Nottingham Univ. (BA Hons Hist. 1973). 2nd Regt, RA, 1970–75; 22 Regt, RA, 1975–79; RMCS, Shrivenham, 1980; psc, 1981; Operational Requirements, MoD, 1982–83; Batt. Comdr, 22 Regt, RA, 1984–86; Army Staff Duties, MoD, 1986–87; CO, 12 Regt, RA, 1987–90; Instr, Staff Coll., Camberley, 1990–91; Col, Mil. Ops 1, MoD, 1991–93; HCSC, 1993; Comdr Artillery, HQ ARRC, 1994; Dep. Comdr, Multinat. Div. Central (Airmobile), 1995; DPS (Army), MoD, 1996–98; Mil. Advr to High Rep. in Bosnia Herzegovina, 1998–99; COS to Adjt Gen., 1999–2001. Has served in NI and Falkland Is. *Recreations:* ski-ing, tennis, opera, walking. *Address:* c/o Army Personnel Centre, Kentigern House, 65 Brown Street, Glasgow G2 8EX.

CURRIE, Austin; *see* Currie, J. A.

CURRIE, Brian Murdoch; President, Institute of Chartered Accountants in England and Wales, 1996–97 (Vice-President, 1994–95; Deputy President, 1995–96); *b* 20 Dec. 1934; *s* of William Murdoch Currie and Dorothy (*née* Holloway); *m* 1961, Patricia Maria, *d* of Capt. Frederick Eaton-Farr; three *s* one *d*. *Educ:* Blundell's Sch. (Scholar); Oriel Coll., Oxford (Open Scholar; MA). ACA 1963, FCA 1973; MIMC 1968, FIMC 1990. Commnd RTR, 1957–59; Arthur Andersen Chartered Accountants, 1959–90: Partner, 1970–90; Dep. Man. Partner, 1975; Man. Partner, London, 1977–82; Chm., Partnership Council, 1983–85. Dist Auditor, 1982–87. Dept of Trade Inspector, Fourth City and other cos, 1978; Mem., Foster Cttee of Inquiry into Road Haulage Licensing, 1977. Member: Management Bd, HMSO, 1972–74; Restrictive Practices Court, 1979–; Takeover Panel, 1989–97; Lay Mem., GDC, 1994–99; Dep. Chm., Financial Reporting Council, 1996–98. Institute of Chartered Accountants in England and Wales: Mem. Council, 1988–99; Chm., Practice Regulation, 1993; Chm., Chartered Accountants Jt Ethics Cttee, 1994–95; Mem., IFAC Compliance Cttee. Trustee, Oriel Coll. Develt Trust, 1980–94. Chm., Peter Blundell Soc.; Member, Committee: Exmoor Soc., 1993–; Glass Assoc., 1998–; Founder Mem., Pluralists, 1992–. *Publications:* official public reports; papers and articles in professional and technical pubns. *Recreations:* natural history, Exmoor, church (lay assisting). *Address:* Westbrook House, Bampton, Tiverton, Devon EX16 9HU. *T:* (01398) 331418. *Club:* Athenæum.

CURRIE, Dr Christopher Richard John, FRHistS, FSA; Consultant Editor, Victoria History of the Counties of England, since 2000; *b* 3 March 1948; *s* of George Samson Currie, MC and Norah Currie (*née* Kennedy); *m* 1981, Katherine Ruth Gommon; one *s* one *d*. *Educ:* Winchester; Balliol Coll., Oxford (MA 1976, DPhil 1976). FRHistS 1979; FSA 1984. Victoria County History: Asst Editor, Staffs, 1972–78; Dep. Editor, 1978–94; Gen. Editor, 1994–2000. Mem. Council, RHistS, 1996–2000. Hon. Editor, Vernacular Architecture, 1980–82. *Publications:* (ed with C. P. Lewis) English County Histories: a guide, 1994; articles in Victoria County Hist. and learned jls. *Recreation:* sleep. *Address:* 14 Keston Road, N17 6PN. *T:* (020) 8801 2185.

CURRIE, Sir Donald Scott, 7th Bt *cr* 1847; Chief of Maintenance, National Park Service, Department of the Interior, 1976; *b* 16 Jan. 1930; *s* of George Donald Currie (*d* 1980) (*g g s* of 1st Bt) and Janet K. (*d* 1990), *d* of late James Scott; *S* cousin, 1987; *m* 1st, 1948, Charlotte (marr. diss. 1951), *d* of Charles Johnstone; twin *d* (and one *s* decd); 2nd, 1952, Barbara Lee (*d* 1993), *d* of A. P. Garnier; one *s* two *d*; 3rd, 1994, Barbara Lou Lebsack, *d* of Joshua Fenn. Rancher and farmer, 1949–75. *Heir: s* Gary Dwayne Currie [*b* 26 Sept. 1953; *m* 1970, Wilma Kathleen Wyatt; one *s* one *d*]. *Clubs:* American Legion (Colorado, USA); National Rifle Association (USA); North American Hunting.

CURRIE, Edwina; *b* 13 Oct. 1946; *m* 1st, 1972, Raymond F. Currie, BA, FCA (marr. diss. 2001); two *d*; 2nd, 2001, John Benjamin Paul Jones, former Det. Supt, Met. Police. *Educ:* Liverpool Inst. for Girls; St Anne's Coll., Oxford (scholar; MA 1972); London Sch. of Econs and Pol Science (MSc 1972). Teaching and lecturing posts in econs, econ. history and business studies, 1972–81. Birmingham City Council: Mem., 1975–86; Chm., Social Services Cttee, 1979–80; Chm., Housing Cttee, 1982–83. Chm., Central Birmingham HA, 1981–83; Mem., Birmingham AHA, 1975–82. MP (C) Derbyshire South, 1983–97; contested (C) same seat, 1997. PPS to Sec. of State for Educn and Science, 1985–86; Parly Under-Sec. of State (Health), DHSS, later Dept of Health, 1986–88. Member: European Movement, 1992– (Vice Chm., 1995–98); Cons. Gp for Europe, 1992– (Chm., 1995–97). Contested (C) Bedfordshire and Milton Keynes, Eur. Parly elecns, 1994. Regular contributor to nat. newspapers and magazines; presenter: Sunday Supplement, TV, 1993; Espresso, TV, 1997; various radio progs, incl. Late Night Currie, 1998–. Trustee, VOICE (UK) (Chm., 1994–97); Dir, Future of Europe Trust (Jt Chm., 1994–97). Speaker of the Year, Assoc. of Speakers' Clubs, 1990; Campaigner of the Year, Spectator Awards, 1994. *Publications:* Financing our Cities (Bow Group pamphlet), 1976; Life Lines, 1989; What Women Want, 1990; (jtly) Three-Line Quips, 1992; *novels:* A Parliamentary Affair, 1994; A Woman's Place, 1996; She's Leaving Home, 1997; The Ambassador, 1999; Chasing Men, 2000; This Honourable House, 2001. *Recreations:* earning a living, theatre, family, reading other people's books. *Address:* c/o Little, Brown, Brettenham House, Lancaster Place, WC2E 7EN. *T:* (020) 7911 8000. *Club:* Institute of Directors.

CURRIE, Dr Graham Alan, MD; FRCP, FRCPath; Research Director, Marie Curie, since 1982; *b* 17 Aug. 1939; *s* of Alan Currie and Dorothy Currie; *m* 1964, Dr Angela Wright; one *s* three *d*. *Educ:* Charing Cross Hosp. Med. Sch. (MB BS; Univ. of London Prize Medal, 1963; MD 1974). FRCPath 1982; FRCP 1984. Jun. appts, Charing Cross Hosp., 1963–69; staff mem., Chester Beatty Res. Inst., 1969–74; Sen. Lectr, Ludwig Inst. for Cancer Res., 1974–82; Hon. Consultant Physician, Royal Marsden Hosp., 1974–82. Saltwell Res. Scholar, RCP, 1966; Wellcome Res. Fellow, Charing Cross Hosp., 1968. Founding Ed., Oncogene, 1987. *Publications:* Cancer and the Immune Response, 1974, 2nd edn 1980; numerous papers and reviews in learned jls. *Recreations:* art, music, gardens, sleep. *Address:* Hunters, Forest Lodge, Epsom Road, Ashtead, Surrey KT21 1JX. *T:* (01372) 278707.

CURRIE, Heriot Whitson; QC (Scot.) 1992; *b* 23 June 1952; *s* of Heriot Clunas Currie and Evelyn Whitson; *m* 1975, Susan Carolyn Hodge; three *d*. *Educ:* Edinburgh Academy; Wadham Coll., Oxford (MA); Edinburgh Univ. (LLB). Admitted to Faculty of Advocates, 1979; practice as Advocate, 1979–; called to the Bar, Gray's Inn, 1991. *Recreations:* chamber music, cinema, golf, foreign languages. *Address:* 16 Greenhill Gardens, Edinburgh EH10 4BW. *T:* (0131) 447 4366. *Club:* New (Edinburgh).

CURRIE, James McGill; Director-General (Environment and Nuclear Safety), European Commission, 1997–2001; *b* 17 Nov. 1941; *s* of late David Currie and of Mary (*née* Smith); *m* 1968, Evelyn Barbara MacIntyre; one *s* one *d*. *Educ:* St Joseph's High Sch., Kilmarnock; Blairs Coll., Aberdeen; Royal Scots Coll., Valladolid; Univ. of Glasgow (MA). Asst Principal, Scottish Home and Health Dept, 1968–72; Principal, Scottish Educn Dept, 1972–75; Secretary, Management Gp, Scottish Office, 1975–77; Scottish Development Dept: Principal, 1977–79; Asst Sec., 1979–81; Asst Sec., Scottish Economic Planning Dept, 1981–82; Counsellor, UK Perm. Representation to EEC, 1982–87; Dir of Regional Policy, EEC, 1987–89; Chef de Cabinet to Leon Brittan, EEC, 1989–92; Dep. Head, EC Delegn to USA, 1993–96; Dir-Gen. (Customs and Indirect Taxation), EC, 1996–97. Vis. Prof. of Law, Georgetown Law Center, Washington, 1997–. Non-exec. Dir, Royal Bank of Scotland, 2001–. Hon. DLitt Glasgow, 2001. *Recreations:* tennis, guitar, good food. *Address:* Flat 7, 54 Queen's Gate Terrace, SW7 5PJ.

CURRIE, (Joseph) Austin; Teachta Dala (TD) (FG) for Dublin West, Dail Eireann (Irish Parliament), since 1989; *b* 11 Oct. 1939; *s* of John Currie and Mary (*née* O'Donnell); *m* 1968, Anne Ita Lynch; two *s* three *d*. *Educ:* Edendork Sch.; St Patrick's Academy, Dungannon; Queen's Univ., Belfast (BA). MP (Nat) Tyrone, Parlt of N Ireland, 1964–72; Founder Mem., SDLP, 1970; Mem. (SDLP), Fermanagh and S Tyrone, NI Assembly, 1973–75, NI Constitutional Convention, 1975–76, NI Assembly, 1982–86; Minister of Housing, Planning and Local Govt, 1974. Contested (FG) Presidency of Ireland, 1990. Mem., Anglo-Irish Parly tier; frontbench spokesperson: on communications, 1991–93; on equality and law reform, 1993–94; Minister of State, Depts of Health, Educn and Justice, 1994–97; spokesperson on energy, 1997–; dep. spokesperson on foreign affairs. Only person to have been elected to both Irish Parlts. Mem., Forum for Peace and Reconciliation, 1995–. Advr to Eur. Commn, 1984–. *Recreations:* Gaelic football, golf, snooker, reading. *Address:* Dungannon, Co. Tyrone, N Ireland; Ballyowen Lane, Lucan, Co. Dublin, Ireland.

CURRIMBHOY, Sir Mohamed; *see* Ebrahim, Sir M. C.

CURRY, Dr Alan Stewart; retired; Controller, Forensic Science Service, Home Office, 1976–82; *b* 31 Oct. 1925; *s* of late Richard C. Curry and of Margaret Curry; *m* 1973, J. Venise Hewitt; one *s* (by previous marriage). *Educ:* Arnold Sch., Blackpool; Trinity Coll., Cambridge (Scholar; MA; PhD 1952). CChem, FRSC, FRCPath. Served War of 1939–45 with RAF. Joined Home Office Forensic Science Service, 1952; served in NE Region, 1952–64; Dir, Nottingham Forensic Sci. Lab., 1964–66; Dir, Home Office Central Research Estabt, Aldermaston, 1966–76. Pres., Internat. Assoc. of Forensic Toxicologists, 1969–75; UN Consultant in Narcotics, 1972–91; Hon. Consultant in Forensic Toxicology to RAF, 1973–91; Consultant in Toxicology to British Airways, 1982–91. Fellow, Indian Acad. of Forensic Scis; Mem., Amer. Acad. of Forensic Scis; Hon. Mem., Belg. Pharmaceutical Soc. Hon. DSc Ghent, 1985. Stas Gold Medal, Gesellschaft für Toxicologische und Forensische Chemie, 1983. *Publications:* Poison

Detection in Human Organs, 1962, 4th edn 1988; (ed) Methods in Forensic Science, vols 3 and 4, 1964–65; Advances in Forensic and Clinical Toxicology, 1973; (ed) Analytical Methods in Human Toxicology, Part 1 1985, Part 2 1986; (ed, with wife) The Biochemistry of Women: Clinical Concepts; Methods for Clinical Investigation, 1974; over 100 papers in med. and sci. and police jls. *Recreations:* sailing, amateur radio. *T:* (0118) 958 1481. *Club:* Athenæum.

CURRY, Rt Hon. David (Maurice); PC 1996; MP (C) Skipton and Ripon, since 1987; *b* 13 June 1944; *s* of Thomas Harold Curry and Florence Joan (*née* Tyerman); *m* 1971, Anne Helene Maud Roullet; one *s* two *d*. *Educ:* Ripon Grammar Sch.; Corpus Christi Coll., Oxford (MA Hons); Kennedy Sch. of Govt, Harvard (Kennedy Scholar, 1966–67). Reporter, Newcastle Jl, 1967–70; Financial Times: Trade Editor, Internat. Cos Editor, Brussels Corresp., Paris Corresp., and European News Editor, 1970–79. Sec., Anglo-American Press Assoc. of Paris, 1978; Founder, Paris Conservative Assoc., 1977. MEP (C) Essex NE, 1979–89; Chm., Agriculture Cttee, 1982–84; Vice-Chm., Budgets Cttee, 1984–85; spokesman on budgetary matters for European Democratic Gp, 1985–89; Gen. Rapporteur for EEC's 1987 budget. Parly Sec., 1989–92, Minister of State, 1992–93, MAFF; Minister of State, DoE, 1993–97. Chairman, Select Committee: on agriculture, 1999–2001; on envmt, food and rural affairs, 2001–. *Publications:* The Food War: the EEC, the US and the battle for world food markets, 1982; (ed) The Conservative Tradition in Europe, 1998; Lobbying Government, 1999. *Recreations:* digging, windsurfing, bee-keeping. *Address:* Newland End, Arkesden, Essex CB11 4HF. *T:* (01799) 550368.

CURRY, Sir Donald Thomas Younger, Kt 2001; CBE 1997; farmer; Chairman, Meat and Livestock Commission, 1993–2001; *b* 4 April 1944; *s* of Robert Thomas Younger Curry and Barbara Ramsey Curry; *m* 1966, Rhoda Mary Murdie; two *s* one *d*. *Educ:* Northumberland Coll. of Agric. Estabd farming business, 1971; farms 650 acres in Northumberland (C&G Farm Mgt and Orgn). Comr, MLC, 1986– (Dep. Chm., 1992–93); Crown Estate Comr, 2000–. Founder/Chairman: N Country Primestock (livestock mktg co-op.), 1990–; At Home in the Community (provides residential homes for people with a learning disability), 1992–; Farm Assured British Beef and Lamb, 1992–94; Founder, Assured British Meat, 1997. Non-exec. Dir, NFU Mutual Insce Soc., 1997– (Vice-Chm., 2000–). *Recreations:* church responsibilities, photography, travel, gardening. *Address:* Middle Farm, Barrasford, Hexham, Northumberland NE48 4DA. *T:* (01434) 681080. *Club:* Farmers'.

CURRY, Dr Gordon Barrett; Reader, Division of Earth Sciences (formerly Department of Geology and Applied Geology), University of Glasgow, since 1992 (Royal Society University Research Fellow, 1984–92); *b* 27 June 1954; *s* of Robert and Violet Curry; *m* 1983, Gillian. *Educ:* Masonic Sch., Dublin; Trinity Coll., Dublin (BA Mod.); Imperial Coll. London (PhD, DIC). FGS. University of Glasgow: Research Asst to Sir Alwyn Williams, 1980–84; Dep. Dir, Human Identification Centre, 1995–98; Project Manager, Taxonomy Prog., 1996–99. Treas., Systematics Assoc., 1996–. President's Award, Geolog. Soc., 1985; Clough Award, Edinburgh Geolog. Soc., 1985–86; Wollaston Fund, Geolog. Soc., 1989. *Publications:* (jtly) British Brachiopods, 1979; (ed) Allochthonous Terranes, 1991; (jtly) Molecules through Time: fossil molecules and biochemical systematics, 1991; Biology of Living Brachiopods, 1992; numerous contribs to learned jls. *Recreations:* music, swimming, cricket, golf, travel. *Address:* Division of Earth Sciences, Gregory Building, University of Glasgow, Lilybank Gardens, Glasgow G12 8QQ. *T:* (0141) 330 5444; *e-mail:* g.curry@earthsci.gla.ac.uk.

CURRY, John Arthur Hugh, CBE 1997; Chairman, ACAL, since 1986; *b* 7 June 1938; *s* of Alfred Robert and Mercia Beatrice Curry; *m* 1962, Anne Rosemary Lewis; three *s* one *d*. *Educ:* King's College School, Wimbledon; St Edmund Hall, Oxford (MA); Harvard Univ. Graduate College (MBA). FCA. Arthur Andersen, 1962–64; Man. Dir, Unitech, 1966–86 (non-exec. Dir, 1986–96). Non-executive Director: Dixons, 1993–; Foreign & Colonial Smaller Cos PLC, 1996–; Terence Chapman Group plc, 1999–. *Publication:* Partners for Profit, 1966. *Recreations:* tennis, Rugby. *Clubs:* All England Lawn Tennis and Croquet (Chm., 1989–99, Mem. Cttee, 1979–99); International Lawn Tennis.

CURRY, (Thomas) Peter (Ellison); QC 1966, 1973; *s* of Maj. F. R. P. Curry; *m* 1950, Pamela Joyce, *d* of late Group Capt. A. J. Holmes, AFC, JP; two *s* two *d*. *Educ:* Tonbridge; Oriel Coll., Oxford (BA 1948; MA 1951). Served War of 1939–45; enlisted 1939; commnd, 1941; 17th Indian Div., India and Burma, 1941–45. War Office, 1946. Called to Bar, Middle Temple, 1953, Bencher, 1979. QC 1966. Solicitor, 1968; partner in Freshfields, Solicitors, 1968–70; returned to Bar; re-appointed QC 1973. Pres., Aircraft and Shipbuilding Industries Arbitration Tribunal, 1978–80. Chm., Chancery Bar Assoc., 1980–85; Dep. Chm., Barristers' Benevolent Assoc., 1989–91 (Hon. Treas., 1964–71, 1984–89). Rep. Army and Sussex at Squash Racquets (described as fastest mover in squash, 1947); triple blue, squash, cross country and athletics, Oxford (twice cross country winner; unbeaten, cross country, 1946–48); World Student Games (5000 m), 1947; British Steeplechase champion 1948, Olympic Games, 1948. Served on AAA Cttee of Inquiry, 1967. Holder of French certificate as capitaine-mécanicien for mechanically propelled boats. *Publications:* (ed jtly) Palmer's Company Law, 1959; (ed jtly) Crew on Meetings, 1966, 1975. *Recreations:* gardening, the Turf. *Address:* Hurlands, Dunsfold, Surrey GU8 4NT. *T:* (01483) 200356. *Club:* Army and Navy.

CURTEIS, Ian Bayley; television playwright; *b* 1 May 1935; *m* 1st, 1964, Mrs Joan Macdonald; two *s*; 2nd, 1985, Joanna Trollope, *qv* (marr. diss. 2001); two step *d*; 3rd, 2001, Lady Grantley, *widow* of 7th Baron Grantley, MC. *Educ:* Iver Council Sch.; Slough Grammar Sch.; Slough Trading Estate; London Univ. Director and actor in theatres all over Great Britain, and BBC-tv script reader, 1956–63; BBC and ATV staff director (drama), directing plays by John Betjeman, John Hopkins, William Trevor and others, 1963–67. Pres., Writers' Guild of GB, 1998–2001 (Mem. Exec. Council and Chm. various cttees, 1979–). Trustee, Joanna Trollope Charitable Trust, 1995–. *Television plays:* Beethoven, Sir Alexander Fleming (BBC's entry at 1973 Prague Fest.), Mr Rolls and Mr Royce, Long Voyage out of War (trilogy), The Folly, The Haunting, Second Time Round, A Distinct Chill, The Portland Millions, Philby, Burgess and Maclean (British entry 1978 Monte Carlo Fest., BAFTA nomination), Hess, The Atom Spies, Churchill and the Generals (BAFTA nomination; Grand Prize, Best Programme of 1980, NY Internat. Film and TV Fest.), Suez 1956 (BAFTA nomination), Miss Morison's Ghosts (British entry 1982 Monte Carlo Fest.), The Mitford Girls, BB and Joe (trilogy), Lost Empires (adapted from J. B. Priestley), The Trials of Lady Sackville, Eureka (1st Euroserial simultaneously shown in UK, West Germany, Austria, Switzerland, Italy and France), The Nightmare Years, The Zimmerman Telegram, The Choir (dramatisation of Joanna Trollope novel); also originated and wrote numerous popular television drama series; *film screenplays:* Andre Malraux's La Condition humaine, 1982; Graham Greene's The Man Within, 1983; Tom Paine (for Sir Richard Attenborough), 1983; *play:* A Personal Affair, Globe, 1982; *radio plays:* Eroica, 2000; Love, 2001. *Publications: plays:* Long Voyage out of War (trilogy), 1971; Churchill and the Generals, 1979; Suez 1956, 1980; The Falklands Play, 1987; numerous articles and speeches on the ethics and politics of broadcasting. *Recreation:* dissidence. *Address:* C1 Top, Albany, Piccadilly, W1J 0AW; West Cottage, Markenfield Hall, Ripon, N Yorks HG4 3AD. *Clubs:* Beefsteak, Garrick.

CURTIS, Prof. Adam Sebastian Genevieve, PhD; Professor of Cell Biology, University of Glasgow, since 1967; *b* 3 Jan. 1934; *s* of Herbert Lewis Curtis and Nora Patricia Curtis (*née* Stevens); *m* 1958, Ann Park; two *d*. *Educ:* Aldenham Sch.; King's Coll., Cambridge (BA 1955; MA); Univ. of Edinburgh (PhD 1957). University College London: Hon. Research Asst, 1957–62; Lectr in Zool., 1962–67; University of Glasgow: Head, Molecular and Cellular Biol. Planning Unit, 1991–94; Head, Molecular and Cellular Biol. Div., 1994–95; Jt Dir, Centre for Cell Engrg, 1996–. Pres., Tissue & Cell Engrg Soc., 2001–. Editor in Chief, Exptl Biology Online, 1996–99. Cuvier Medal, Zool Soc. of France, 1972. *Publications:* The Cell Surface, 1967; (with J. M. Lackie) Measuring Cell Adhesion, 1991; numerous articles in scientific jls; also articles on scuba diving. *Recreations:* scuba diving, underwater photography, gardening. *Address:* 2 Kirklee Circus, Glasgow G12 0TW. *T:* (0141) 339 2152. *Club:* Lansdowne.

CURTIS, Sir Barry (John), Kt 1992; Mayor of Manukau, New Zealand, since 1983; *b* 27 Feb. 1939; *s* of John Dixon Cory Curtis and Vera Gladys Curtis (*née* Johnson); *m* 1961, Miriam Ann Brooke (marr. diss. 1991); three *d*. *Educ:* Otahuhu College; Univ. of Auckland (Dip. TP). ARICS, MNZIS, MNZPI, MPMI. Town Planner, Chartered and Registered Surveyor. Manukau City Councillor, 1968–83; Member: Auckland Regl Authy, 1971–84 (Chm., Regl Planning Cttee, 1977–83); Prime Minister's Safer Communities Council, 1990–; Chairman: Hillary Commn Task Force on Recreation, 1988; Jean Batten Meml Trust, 1989; Manukau Healthy City Cttee, 1989–93; Manukau Safer Community Council, 1990–93; Auckland Mayors' Forum, 1990–96. Past Pres., NZ Sister Cities Cttee. A Dir, XIVth Commonwealth Games Ltd, 1989–92 (Mem. Exec. Bd, 1989–90). Patron, Auckland Hockey Assoc. Seiuli (High Chief Matai title) conferred by HE Malietoa Tanumafili II, Western Samoa, 1993. *Recreations:* jogging, surfing, gardening, follower of Rugby, hockey, cricket, tennis, yachting. *Address:* 40–42 The Parade, Bucklands Beach, City of Manukau, Auckland Region, New Zealand. *T:* (9) 5348153. *Clubs:* Pakuranga Combined Bowling (Foundn Chm.), Pakuranga Men's Bowling (Foundn Pres.).

CURTIS, Prof. Charles David, OBE 2001; Professor of Geochemistry, University of Manchester, since 1988 (Research Dean, Faculty of Science and Engineering, 1994–2000; Head of Department of Geology, 1989–92); *b* 11 Nov. 1939; *s* of Charles Frederick Curtis and Kate Margaret Curtis (*née* Jackson); *m* 1963, Dr Diana Joy Saxty; two *d*. *Educ:* Imperial College London; Univ. of Sheffield (BSc, PhD). University of Sheffield: Lectr, Sen. Lectr, Reader, 1965–83; Personal Chair in Geochem., 1983–88. Vis. Prof., Dept of Geology and Geophys., UCLA, 1970–71; Res. Associate, British Petroleum Res. Centre, 1987–88; Hon. Res. Fellow, Natural Hist. Mus., 1999–. Member: Council, NERC, 1990–93; Radioactive Waste Mgt Adv. Cttee, 1994– (Chm., 1999–); Radioactivity Res. and Envmtl Monitoring Cttee, 1995–. Pres., Geological Soc., 1992–94. Murchison Medal, Geological Soc., 1987. *Publications:* numerous articles in learned jls. *Recreations:* mountaineering, gardening, photography. *Address:* Department of Earth Sciences, The University, Oxford Road, Manchester M13 9PL. *T:* (0161) 275 3803.

CURTIS, Colin Hinton Thomson, CVO 1970; ISO 1970; retired; Chairman, Metropolitan Public Abattoir Board, 1971–81; Member, Queensland Meat Industry Authority, 1972–78; *b* 25 June 1920; *s* of A. Curtis, Brisbane; *m* 1943, Anne Catherline Drevesen; one *s*. *Educ:* Brisbane Grammar School. RANR Overseas Service, 1940–45. Sec. and Investigation Officer to Chm., Sugar Cane Prices Board, 1948–49; Asst Sec. to Central Sugar Cane Prices Board, 1949; Sec. to Premier of Queensland, 1950–64; Mem., Qld Trade Missions to SE Asia, 1963 and 1964; Asst Under-Sec., Premier's Dept, 1961–64; Assoc. Dir and Dir of Industrial Development, 1964–66; Under-Sec., Premier's Dept and Clerk of Exec. Council, 1966–70; State Dir, Royal Visit, 1970; Agent-General for Queensland in London, 1970–71. *Recreations:* squash, yachting, swimming. *Address:* 57 Daru Avenue, Runaway Bay, Gold Coast, Qld 4216, Australia. *Club:* RSL Memorial (Queensland).

CURTIS, Prof. David Roderick, AC 1992; FRACP 1987; FRS 1974; FAA 1965; Emeritus Professor, Australian National University, since 1993; *b* 3 June 1927; *s* of E. D. and E. V. Curtis; *m* 1951, Lauri Sewell; one *s* one *d*. *Educ:* Univ. of Melbourne; Australian National Univ. MB, BS Melbourne 1950, PhD ANU 1957. John Curtin School of Medical Research, Australian National University: Department of Physiology: Research Scholar, 1954–56; Research Fellow, 1956–57; Fellow, 1957–59; Sen. Fellow, 1959–62; Professorial Fellow, 1962–66; Prof. of Pharmacology, 1966–68; Prof. of Neuropharmacology, 1968–73; Prof. and Foundn Head, Dept of Pharmacology, 1973–88; Chm., Div. of Physiol Sciences, 1988–89; Howard Florey Prof. of Med. Res., and Dir of the Sch., 1989–92; University Fellow, 1993–95. President: Aust. Acad. of Sci, 1986–90 (Burnet Medal, 1983); Australian Physiol and Pharmacol Soc., 1992–95; Chairman: Res. Adv. Bd, Nat. Multiple Sclerosis Soc., Australia, 1978–83, 1993–96; Inaugural Australia Prize Cttee, 1989–90. *Publications:* papers in fields of neurophysiology, neuropharmacology in Jl Physiology, Jl Neurophysiol., Brain Research, Exper. Brain Research, etc. *Recreations:* woodwork, wombling. *Address:* 7 Patey Street, Campbell, Canberra, ACT 2612, Australia. *T:* and *Fax:* (2) 62485664.

CURTIS, Frank; *see* Curtis, R. F.

CURTIS, Very Rev. Frank; *see* Curtis, Very Rev. W. F.

CURTIS, James William Ockford; QC 1993; a Recorder, since 1991; *b* 2 Sept. 1946; *s* of Eric William Curtis, MC, TD and Margaret Joan Curtis (*née* Blunt); *m* 1985, Genevra Fiona Penelope Victoria Caws, QC (*d* 1997); one *d*. *Educ:* Bedford Sch.; Worcester Coll., Oxford (MA Jurisp). Called to the Bar, Inner Temple, 1970. *Recreations:* farming, field sports, ski-ing, classics. *Address:* 6 King's Bench Walk, Temple, EC4Y 7DR. *T:* (020) 7583 0410. *Clubs:* Reform, Flyfishers'.

CURTIS, Most Rev. John Barry; Archbishop of Calgary, 1994–99; Metropolitan of Rupert's Land, 1994–99; *b* 19 June 1933; *s* of Harold Boyd Curtis and Eva B. Curtis (*née* Saunders); *m* 1959, Patricia Emily (*née* Simpson); two *s* two *d*. *Educ:* Trinity Coll., Univ. of Toronto (BA 1955, LTh 1958); Theological Coll., Chichester, Sussex. Deacon 1958, priest 1959; Asst Curate, Holy Trinity, Pembroke, Ont, 1958–61; Rector: Parish of March, Kanata, Ont, 1961–65; St Stephen's Church, Buckingham, Que, 1965–69; Church School Consultant, Diocese of Ottawa, 1969; Rector, All Saints (Westboro), Ottawa, 1969–78; Director of Programme, Diocese of Ottawa, 1978–80; Rector, Christ Church, Elbow Park, Calgary, Alta, 1980–83; Bishop of Calgary, 1983–99. Member, Governing Board: Canadian Council of Churches, 1994– (Pres., 1999–); Habitat for Humanity Canada, 1994–. Hon. DD Trinity Coll., Toronto, 1985. Habitat for Humanity, Canada. *Recreations:* reading, hiking, skiing, cycling. *Address:* 12 Varanger Place NW, Calgary, AB T3A 0E9, Canada. *T:* (403) 2865127. *Club:* Ranchmen's (Calgary, Alta).

CURTIS, John Edward, PhD; FSA; Keeper, Department of Ancient Near East (formerly of Western Asiatic Antiquities), British Museum, since 1989; *b* 23 June 1946; *yr s* of late Arthur Norman Curtis and of Laura Letitia Ladd (*née* Thomas); *m* 1977, Vesta Sarkhosh; one *s* one *d*. *Educ:* Collyer's Grammar Sch., Horsham; Univ. of Bristol (BA); Inst. of Archaeology, Univ. of London (Postgrad. Diploma in Western Asiatic Archaeology; PhD 1979). FSA 1984. Fellow, British Sch. of Archaeology in Iraq, 1969–71; Res. Asst, Dept of Western Asiatic Antiquities, British Museum, 1971–74, Asst Keeper, 1974–89. Chm., British Assoc. for Near Eastern Archaeol., 1996–; Hon. Sec. and Trustee, Ancient Persia Fund, 1987–; Member, Governing Council: British Sch. of Archaeol. in Iraq, 1980–; British Inst. of Persian Studies, 1991–. *Publications:* (ed) Fifty Years of Mesopotamian Discovery, 1982; Nush-i Jan III: the Small Finds, 1984; (ed) Bronzeworking Centres of Western Asia *c* 1000–539 BC, 1988; Excavations at Qasrij Cliff and Khirbet Qasrij, 1989; Ancient Persia, 1989, 2nd edn 2000; (ed) Early Mesopotamia and Iran: Contact and Conflict 3500–1600 BC, 1993; (ed with J. E. Reade) Art and Empire: treasures from Assyria in the British Museum, 1995; (ed) Later Mesopotamia and Iran: tribes and empires 1600–539 BC, 1995; (ed) Mesopotamia and Iran in the Persian period: conquest and imperialism 539–331 BC, 1997; (with A. R. Green) Excavations at Khirbet Khatuniyeh, 1997; (ed) Mesopotamia and Iran in the Parthian and Sasanian periods: rejection and revival *c* 238 BC–AD 642, 2000; articles in learned jls. *Recreations:* local history, geneaology. *Address:* 4 Hillfield Road, NW6 1QE. *T:* (020) 7435 6153; 1 Francis Cottage, Sandy Hill Road, Saundersfoot, Dyfed SA69 9HW.

CURTIS, John Henry, CB 1981; FAIM, FTS; Chairman, Nortel Australia Pty Ltd, 1989–92, retired; *b* 20 March 1920; *s* of K. H. and E. M. Curtis; *m* 1943, Patricia Foote (*d* 1989); one *s* one *d*. *Educ:* Ipswich Grammar Sch.; Queensland Univ. (BE Hons 1950, BSc 1951, BA 1957). FIEAust 1981; FAIM 1970; FTS 1979. Dir of Posts and Telegraphs, Qld, 1971–73; Dep. Dir Gen., Postmaster-Gen.'s Dept, 1973–75; Man. Dir, Australian Telecommunications Commn, 1975–81; Chairman: D. Richardson & Sons, later Richardson Pacific, 1982–90; A. W. A. Nortel, 1986–89. Comr, Overseas Telecommunications Commn (Australia), 1974–87. Pres., Victorian Div., Aust. Inst. of Management, 1979–81; Dir, Cttee for Econ. Develt of Aust., 1981–93 (Hon. Life Mem., 1993). Mem., Bd of Management, Defence Aerospace, 1984–86. Gov., Internat. Council for Computer Communication, 1982–94. Hon. Life Mem., IREE, 1982. *Address:* 101 Kadumba Street, Yeronga, Qld 4104, Australia. *T:* (7) 38922743.

CURTIS, Michael Howard; Executive Aide to HH The Aga Khan, 1959–86; Director, Aga Khan Health and Education Services, Geneva, 1985–92; Chairman, Nation Printers and Publishers, Nairobi, Kenya, 1972–77; Director, Nation Newspapers, 1959–94 (Managing Director and Chief Executive, 1959, retired); *b* 28 Feb. 1920; *e s* of late Howard and Doris May Curtis; *m* 1st, 1947, Barbara Winifred Gough; two *s* two *d*; 2nd, 1961, Marian Joan Williams (*d* 1984); two step *s*. *Educ:* St Lawrence Coll.; Sidney Sussex Coll., Cambridge (MA). Eastern Daily Press, Norwich, 1945; News Chronicle: Leader Writer, 1946; Dep. Editor, 1952; Editor, 1954–57; Dir, News Chronicle Ltd, 1954–57; Personal Aide to HH The Aga Khan, 1957–59. *Clubs:* Garrick; Muthaiga (Nairobi).

CURTIS, Monica Anne; Head, Chelmsford County High School for Girls, since 1997; *b* 26 May 1946; *d* of H. L. Seale; *m* 1968, Timothy Chaytor Curtis (*d* 1986), former Dep. Dir, Lancashire Poly.; two *s*. *Educ:* Manchester Univ. (BA English and History of Art 1968). Teacher: Urmston Grammar Sch. for Girls, 1968–70; various schs in Newcastle upon Tyne, 1970–80; Lancaster Girls' Grammar Sch., 1980–89; Kesteven and Grantham Girls' Sch., 1989–97. *Address:* Chelmsford County High School for Girls, Broomfield Road, Chelmsford, Essex CM1 1RW. *T:* (01245) 352592.

CURTIS, Hon. Sir Richard Herbert, Kt 1992; **Hon. Mr Justice Curtis;** a Judge of the High Court of Justice, Queen's Bench Division, since 1992; Presiding Judge, Wales and Chester Circuit, 1994–97. *Educ:* Oxford Univ. (MA). Called to Bar, Inner Temple, 1958, Bencher, 1985; QC 1977; a Recorder, 1974–89; Recorder of Birmingham, 1989–92; Hon. Recorder, City of Hereford, 1981; Sen. Circuit Judge, Oxford and Midland Circuit, 1989–92. *Address:* c/o Royal Courts of Justice, Strand, WC2A 2LL.

CURTIS, Richard Whalley Anthony, CBE 2000 (MBE 1995); freelance writer; *b* 8 Nov. 1956; *s* of Anthony J. Curtis and Glynness S. Curtis; one *s* one *d* by Emma Vallencey Freud, *d* of Sir Clement Freud, *qv*. *Educ:* Papplewick Sch.; Harrow Sch.; Christ Church, Oxford (BA). Freelance writer: *television:* Not the Nine O'clock News (four series), 1979–83; Blackadder (four series), 1984–89; Mr Bean, 1989–95; Bernard and the Genie, 1993; The Vicar of Dibley, 1994–2000; *films:* The Tall Guy, 1988; Four Weddings and a Funeral, 1994; Bean, 1997; Notting Hill, 1999; (jtly) Bridget Jones's Diary, 2001; producer, Comic Relief, 1985–2000. *Recreations:* too much TV, too many films, too much pop music. *Address:* c/o Anthony Jones, Peters, Fraser & Dunlop, Drury House, 34–43 Russell Street, WC2B 5HA.

CURTIS, Prof. (Robert) Frank, CBE 1985; PhD, DSc; Chairman, Norfolk Mental Health Care NHS Trust, 1994–98; Professor, University of East Anglia, 1977–88, now Hon. Professor; *b* 8 Oct. 1926; *s* of late William John Curtis, Somerset, and Ethel Irene Curtis, Bath; *m* 1954, Sheila Rose, *y d* of Bruce Rose, Huddersfield; two *s* one *d*. *Educ:* City of Bath Sch.; Univ. of Bristol (BSc 1949, PhD 1952, DSc 1972). FRIC 1966; FIFST 1977. Johns Hopkins University: W. H. Grafflin Fellow, 1952; Instr in Chemistry, 1953; Technical Officer, ICI Ltd, Manchester, 1954–56; Res. Fellow, Univ. of WI, 1956–57; Lectr in Chem., University Coll., Swansea, 1957–62, Sen. Lectr, 1962–69; Reader, Univ. of Wales, 1969–70; Head, Chem. Div., 1970–77, Dir, 1977–85, ARC Food Res. Inst.; Dir, AFRC Inst. of Food Res., Reading, 1985–88. Chm., Food Adv. Cttee, MAFF, 1983–88 (Chm., Food Standards Cttee, 1979–83); Mem. Management Bd, AFRC, 1987–88. Mem., Norwich HA, 1989–94 (Vice-Chm., 1993–94); Mem. Council, RVC, 1991–2000. Hon. ScD UEA, 1988. *Publications:* res. papers on chemistry and food science in jls of learned socs. *Address:* Manor Barn, Colton, Norwich NR9 5BZ. *T:* (01603) 880379.

CURTIS, Stephen Russell; Managing Director, Professional Services Division, Jordans Ltd, since 1997; *b* 27 Feb. 1948; *s* of Barry Russell and Joyce Muriel (*née* Smith); *m* 1972, Gillian Mary Pitkin; three *s* one *d*. *Educ:* Forest Sch., E17; Exeter Univ. (BA Econs and Stats). Asst Statistician, Business Stats Office, 1970–72; DTI, 1972–78, Statistician, Export Stats, 1975–78; Statistician, 1978–83, Chief Statistician, 1983–85, Business Stats Office; Registrar of Companies, 1985–90, and Chief Exec., 1988–90, Companies House; Chief Exec., DVLA, 1990–95. *Recreations:* travel, photography, walking. *Club:* Civil Service.

CURTIS, Very Rev. (Wilfred) Frank; Provost of Sheffield, 1974–88, Provost Emeritus since 1988; *b* 24 Feb. 1923; *s* of W. A. Curtis, MC and Mrs M. Curtis (*née* Burbidge); *m* 1951, Muriel (*née* Dover); two *s* two *d*. *Educ:* Foster's Sch., Sherborne; Bishop Wordsworth's Sch., Salisbury; King's Coll., London (AKC). Served in RA, 1942–47; Major 1946. London Univ., 1947–52; Curate of High Wycombe, 1952–55; staff of Church Missionary Soc., 1955–74: Area Sec., Devon and Cornwall, 1955–65; Adviser in Rural Work, 1957–65; SW Regional Sec., 1962–65; Home Sec., 1965–74; Vice-Pres., 1977–. Rural Dean of Okehampton, 1989–92. Mem., General Synod, 1977–85. Chm., Community Action Panel (S Yorks Police), 1983–86; Mem., Sheffield Council Voluntary Service, 1978–88; Chm., Radio Sheffield Religious Adv. Panel, 1985–88. Chaplain to Master Cutler, 1976, 1978, 1982, 1984; Hon. Fellow, Sheffield City Polytechnic, subseq. Sheffield Hallam Univ., 1980. Hon. Canon, 1982–93, and Bishop's Commissary, 1983–93, Maseno North Diocese, Kenya; Bishop's Commissary, Nambale, Kenya, 1988–93. *Recreations:* walking, photography, nature study. *Address:* 17 Norwood Avenue, Exeter, Devon EX2 4RT. *T:* (01392) 432642.

CURTIS, Sir William (Peter), 7th Bt *cr* 1802; *b* 9 April 1935; *s* of Sir Peter Curtis, 6th Bt, and of Joan Margaret, *d* of late Reginald Nicholson; *S* father, 1976. *Educ:* Winchester College; Trinity College, Oxford (MA); Royal Agricultural College, Cirencester. *Heir: cousin* Major Edward Philip Curtis, 16th/5th The Queen's Royal Lancers (retd) [*b* 25 June 1940; *m* 1978, Catherine, *d* of H, J. Armstrong, Christchurch, NZ; two *s* two *d*. *Educ:* Bradfield; RMA Sandhurst]. *Address:* Oak Lodge, Bank Street, Bishop's Waltham, Hants SO3 1AN.

CURTIS-RALEIGH, Dr Jean Margaret Macdonald; Consultant Psychiatrist, Queen Mary's University Hospital, Roehampton, 1979–98; *b* 12 July 1933; *d* of late Dr Harry Hubert Steadman and Janet Gilchrist Steadman (*née* Macdonald); *m* 1964, His Honour Judge Nigel Hugh Curtis-Raleigh (*d* 1986); five *s*. *Educ:* Convent of the Sacred Heart, Epsom, Surrey; Sutton High Sch. for Girls; Guy's Hospital Med. Sch. (MB BS); FRCPsych; DPM. Psychiatric trng, Maudsley and Bethlem Royal Hosps, 1963–66. Med. Mem., Mental Health Review Tribunal. Mem., Broadcasting Standards Council, 1988–95. *Recreations:* opera, gardening, walking.

See also J. H. Steadman.

CURTIS-THOMAS, Claire; MP (Lab) Crosby, since 1997; *b* 30 April 1958; *d* of Joyce Curtis-Thomas; *m* Michael Lewis; one *s* two *d*. *Educ:* Mynyddbach Comp. Sch. for Girls, Swansea; UC Cardiff (BSc); Aston Univ. (MBA). CEng, FIMechE. Shell Chemicals, 1990–92; Hd, Strategic Planning, 1992–93, Hd R&D Lab., 1993–95, Birmingham CC; Dean, Faculty of Business and Engrg, Univ. of Wales Coll. Newport (formerly Gwent Coll. of Higher Educn), 1996–97. Senator, Engrg Council, 1996–. Hon. PhD Staffordshire Univ., 1999. *Address:* House of Commons, SW1A 0AA.

CURTISS, Air Marshal Sir John (Bagot), KCB 1981 (CB 1979); KBE 1982; FRAeS; *b* 6 Dec. 1924; *s* of Major E. F. B. Curtiss, RFC; *m* 1946, Peggy Drughorn Bowie; three *s* one *d*. *Educ:* Radley Coll.; Wanganui Collegiate Sch., NZ; Worcester Coll., Oxford. Served War: Oxford Univ. Air Sqdn, 1942–43; Bomber Comd, 578 and 158 sqdns, 1944–45; Transport Comd, 51 and 59 sqdn, 1945–49; Training Comd, 1950–53; Fighter Comd, 29 and 5 sqdns, 1953–64; Dir, RAF Staff Coll., 1967–69; Stn Comdr RAF Bruggen, RAFG, 1970–72; Gp Capt Ops, HQ Strike Comd, 1972–74; SASO, HQ 11 Gp, 1974–75; Dir-Gen. Organisation, RAF, 1975–77; Comdt, RAF Staff Coll., 1977–80; Air Comdr, Falklands Operations, 1982; AOC No 18 Gp, 1980–83, retd. Dir and Chief Exec., SBAC, 1984–89; Sec., Defence Inds Council, 1985–89. Mem. Exec. Cttee, Air League, 1982–; President: Aircrew Assoc., 1987–93; Berlin Airlift Assoc., 1998–; RAF Oxford and Cambridge Soc., 1998–. Chm., Pathfinders Disaster Relief, 1995–2000. Trustee, Buskaid, 1995– (Chm., 1999–). Chm., Governors, Canford Sch., 1990–95. FRAeS 1984. *Recreations:* sailing, reading, bicycling. *Address:* Normandy House, Barnes Lane, Milford-on-Sea, Hants SO41 0RQ. *Clubs:* MCC, Royal Air Force, Pilgrims; Colonels (Pres. and Founder Mem.); Keyhaven Yacht.

CURWEN, Sir Christopher (Keith), KCMG 1986 (CMG 1982); HM Diplomatic Service, retired; *b* 9 April 1929; *s* of late Rev. R. M. Curwen and Mrs M. E. Curwen; *m* 1st, 1956, Noom Tai (marr. diss. 1977); one *s* two *d*; 2nd, 1977, Helen Anne Stirling; one *s* one *d*. *Educ:* Sherborne Sch.; Sidney Sussex Coll., Cambridge (BA). Served HM Forces, 4th Queen's Own Hussars, 1948–49 (despatches). Joined FO, 1952; Bangkok, 1954; Vientiane, 1956; FO, 1958; Bangkok, 1961; Kuala Lumpur, 1963; FO, 1965; Washington, 1968; FCO, 1971; Geneva, 1977; FCO, 1980–88; Dep. Sec., Cabinet Office, 1989–91. Mem., Security Commn, 1991–98. Chm., Century Benevolent Fund, 1993–99. *Recreations:* books, gardening, motoring.

CURZON; *see* Roper-Curzon, family name of Baron Teynham.

CURZON, family name of **Earl Howe** and **Viscount Scarsdale**.

CURZON, Viscount; Thomas Edward Penn Curzon; *b* 22 Oct. 1994; *s* and *heir* of Earl Howe, *qv*.

CURZON, Leonard Henry, CB 1956; *b* 4 Jan. 1912; *s* of late Frederick Henry Curzon; *m* 1935, Greta, *e d* of late Willem and Anny van Praag; (one *s* decd). *Educ:* Sir Walter St John's Sch.; Jesus Coll., Cambridge (Scholar, BA, LLB). Civil Servant, 1934–72: Import Duties Adv. Cttee; Air Ministry, Ministries of Aircraft Production, Supply, Aviation and Defence. IDC 1947. *Address:* Southease, Derringstone Hill, Barham, Kent CT4 6QD. *T:* (01227) 831449.

CUSCHIERI, Prof. Sir Alfred, Kt 1998; MD; FRCS, FRCSE; FRSE; Professor, and Head of Department of Surgery, University of Dundee, since 1976; Director, Minimal Access Therapy Unit for Scotland, since 1992; *b* 30 Sept. 1938; *s* of Saviour and Angela Cuschieri; *m* 1966, Marguerite Holley; three *d*. *Educ:* Univ. of Malta (MD 1961); Univ. of Liverpool (ChM 1968). FRCSE 1965; FRCS 1967; FRSE 1998. University of Liverpool: Sen. Lectr in Surgery, 1970–74; Reader, 1974–76. Mem. Council, RCSE, 1980–; President: Internat. Hepatobiliary Pancreatic Assoc., 1992–93; European Assoc. Endoscopic Surgeons, 1995–97. Founder FMedSci 1998. Hon. FRCSGlas 1996; Hon. FRCSI 1996. Hon. MD Liverpool, 1997. Gold Medal, Scandinavian Soc. Gastroenterology, 1990; Society Prize for pioneering work in minimal access surgery, Internat. Soc. of Surgery, 1993. *Publications:* Essential Surgical Practice, 1986, 3rd edn 1995; contrib. to learned jls incl. Brit. Jl Surgery, Surgical Endoscopy, Lancet, Annals of Surgery, Archives of Surgery. *Recreations:* music, fly-fishing, carving. *Address:* Denbrae Mill, Strathkinness Low Road, St Andrews, Fife KY16 9TY. *T:* (01334) 475046. *Club:* Athanæum.

CUSDIN, Sidney Edward Thomas, OBE 1946; DSc (Hong Kong); FRIBA, AADip; *b* 28 July 1908; *s* of Sidney Herbert Cusdin, London; *m* 1936, Eva Eileen (Peggy) (*d* 1997), *d* of F. P. Dorizzi, London; no *c*. *Educ:* Municipal School of Arts and Crafts, Southend-on-Sea, Essex; Architectural Assoc., London. AA Holloway Scholarship, 1927; Fifth Year Travelling Studentship, 1929; joined staff of Stanley Hall & Easton and Robertson: British Pavilions at Brussels Internat. Exhibition and Johannesburg Exhibition; elected Member of AA Council, 1937, and worked on RIBA Cttees. Served War of 1939–45, RAF, on staff of HQ, No. 26 Group (despatches twice, OBE). Re-joined firm of Easton & Robertson, 1946; firm later known as Easton & Robertson, Cusdin, Preston and Smith, until 1965 when this partnership was dissolved; Sen. Partner, Cusdin, Burden and Howitt, until 1976. Pres. AA, 1950–51; Mem. Council RIBA, 1950–51. Awarded Henry Saxon Snell Prize and Theakston Bequest, 1950; Principal works: London: Development of the Hosp. for Sick Children, Great Ormond Street, British Postgraduate Medical Fedn, and

London Univ., Inst. of Child Health; Medical Coll. of St Bartholomew's Hosp., New Hostel and Labs; Middlesex Hosp. Medical Sch.; New Sch. Buildings and Astor Coll.; National Inst. for Medical Research Develt, Mill Hill; Cambridge: Dept of Engineering, New Workshops and Laboratories; Univ. Chemistry Laboratories; United Cambridge Hosps, Addenbrooke's Hosp., Hills Rd, New Develt; MRC, extension of Lab. of Molecular Biology; Harlow: Princess Alexandra Hosp.; Belfast: Queen's Univ. of Belfast, Inst. of Clin. Science; Royal Victoria Hosp. Develt; Royal Belfast Hosp. for Sick Children, alterations and additions; Malaya: plans for Develt of Univ. of Malaya; Hong Kong; plans for develt of Univ. of Hong Kong; Cons. Architect for: Queen Elizabeth Hosp., Hong Kong (awarded RIBA Bronze Medal); Faculty of Medicine, Univ. of Riyad, Saudi Arabia. Chm., British Consultants Bureau, 1972–74. Gov., Brendoncare Foundn, 1987–94 (Dir, 1992; Vice Patron, 1993). Hon. Freeman, Apothecaries' Soc., 1981. *Publications:* (with James Crooks) Suggestions and Demonstration Plans for Hospitals for Sick Children, 1947. *Recreations:* theatre, travel, fishing; spending time in believing that "WS" was Shakespeare. *Address:* 34 Ringshall, Little Gaddesden, near Berkhamsted, Herts HP4 1ND. *T:* (01442) 843364. *Clubs:* Savile, Royal Air Force, The Sette of Odd Volumes.

CUSENS, Prof. Anthony Ralph, OBE 1989; PhD; FRSE; FREng; FICE, FIStructE; Professor of Civil Engineering, University of Leeds, 1979–92, now Emeritus (Dean, Faculty of Engineering, 1989–91); *b* 24 Sept. 1927; *s* of James Cusens and May Edith (*née* Thomas); *m* 1953, Pauline Shirin German; three *d. Educ:* St John's Coll., Southsea; University Coll. London (BSc Eng; PhD 1955). FICE 1966; FIStructE 1972; FAmSCE 1972; FREng (FEng 1988). FRSE 1974. Res. Engr, British Cast Concrete Fedn, 1952–54; Sen. Lectr, RMCS, Shrivenham, 1954–56; Sen. Lectr, Univ. of Khartoum, Sudan, 1956–60; Prof. of Structl Engrg, Asian Inst. of Technol., Bangkok, 1960–65; Prof. of Civil Engineering: Univ. of St Andrews, 1965–67; Univ. of Dundee, 1967–78. Visitor, Transport and Road Res. Lab., 1982–88; President: Concrete Soc., 1983–84; IStructE, 1991–92; Chairman: Jt Bd of Moderators of ICE, IStructE and CIBSE, 1986–89; UK Certifying Authy for Reinforcing Steels, 1994–2001. Consultant, Brian Clancy Partnership, 1993–2000. Hon. DSc Aston, 1993. *Publications:* (jtly) Bridge Deck Analysis, 1975; Finite Strip Method in Bridge Engineering, 1978; res. papers on concrete technol. and structures. *Recreations:* golf, gardening. *Address:* Old Hall Cottage, Bramham, West Yorks LS23 6QR. *Clubs:* East India; Pannal Golf (Harrogate).

CUSHING, David Henry, DPhil; FRS 1977; Deputy Director, Fisheries Research, England and Wales, 1974–80; *b* 14 March 1920; *s* of W. E. W. Cushing and Isobel (*née* Batchelder); *m* 1943, Diana R. C. Antona-Traversi; one *d. Educ:* Duke's Sch., Alnwick; Newcastle upon Tyne Royal Grammar Sch.; Balliol Coll., Oxford (MA, DPhil). RA, 1940–45; 1st Bn, Royal Fusiliers, 1945–46. Fisheries Lab., 1946–80. Rosenstiel Gold Medal for Oceanographic Science, Rosenstiel Inst. for Marine and Atmospheric Scis, Miami, 1980; Albert Medal for Oceanography, Institut Océanographique, Paris, 1984; Award for Excellence, Amer. Fisheries Soc., 1986; Ecology Inst. Prize, 1993. *Publications:* The Arctic Cod, 1966; Fisheries Biology, 1968 (USA); Detection of Fish, 1973; Fisheries Resources and their Management, 1974; Marine Ecology and Fisheries, 1975; Science and the Fisheries, 1977; Climate and Fisheries, 1982; The Provident Sea, 1988; Population Production and Regulation in the Sea, 1995; Towards the Science of Recruitment, 1996. *Address:* 198 Yarmouth Road, Lowestoft, Suffolk NR32 4AB. *T:* (01502) 565569.

CUSHING, Penny; District Judge, Principal Registry, Family Division, since 1994; *b* 10 April 1950; *d* of George Norman Cushing and Doris Cushing; *m* 1995, Michael, (Mik), Norman. *Educ:* Birkenhead High Sch. (GPDST); University Coll., London (LLB Hons 1971). Admitted solicitor, 1974; Solicitor: London Bor. of Harrow, 1974–75; Camden Community Law Centre, 1975–80; Trng Officer, Law Centres Fedn, 1980–83; Partner, Cushing & Kelly, subseq. Clinton Davis Cushing & Kelly, solicitors, 1983–90. Mem., Mental Health Act Commn, 1991–94. *Recreations:* walking my dogs Jim and Jessie, South West Trains timetable. *Address:* Principal Registry, Family Division, First Avenue House, 42-49 High Holborn, WC1V 6NP.

CUSHING, Philip Edward; Chief Executive, Vitec, 2000–01; *b* 9 Sept. 1950; *s* of Cyril Edward Willis Cushing and Marguerite Ellen Cushing (*née* Whaite); *m* 1st, 1972, Margareta Barbro Westin (marr. diss.); one *s* one *d*; 2nd, 2000, Ruth Christine Clarke. *Educ:* Highgate Sch.; Christ's Coll., Cambridge (BA 1st Cl. Hons Econs). Marketing Manager, Norprint Ltd, 1972–78; Man. Dir, Modulex Systems, 1978–84; Norton Opax plc: Marketing Dir, 1984–86; Chief Exec., Internat. Ops, 1986–89; Inchcape plc: Chief Exec., Inchcape Berhad, 1990–92; Dir, Services, 1992–95; Gp Man. Dir, 1995–96; Gp Chief Exec., 1996–99. *Recreations:* golf, reading, bridge, cricket, travel, music. *Address:* Warren End, Warren Cutting, Kingston-upon-Thames KT2 7HS. *T:* (020) 8336 4544.

CUSHING, Sir Selwyn (John), KNZM 1999; CMG 1994; FCA; Chairman and Chief Executive, Brierley Investments Ltd, 1999–2001; *b* 1 Sept. 1936; *s* of Cyril John Cushing and Henrietta Marjory Belle Cushing; *m* 1964, Kaye Dorothy Anderson; two *s. Educ:* Hastings High Sch.; Univ. of NZ. FCA 1957; ACIS 1958; CMA 1959. Partner, Esam Cushing & Co., sharebrokers, Hastings, 1960–86; Exec. Dir, Brierley Investments Ltd, 1986–93; Chairman: Carter Holt Harvey Ltd, 1991–93; Electricity Corp. of NZ, 1993–99; Dir, Air New Zealand (Dep. Chm., 1988–98; Chm., 1998–2001). *Recreations:* cricket, music. *Address:* 1 Beatson Road, Hastings, New Zealand. *T:* (6) 8786160. *Clubs:* Wellington; Auckland; Dunedin.

CUSINE, Douglas James; Sheriff of Grampian, Highland and Islands at Peterhead, since 2000; *b* 2 Sept. 1946; *s* of James Fechnie Cusine and Catherine Cusine (*née* McLean); *m* 1973, Marilyn Calvert Ramsay; one *s* one *d. Educ:* Hutcheson's Boys' Grammar Sch.; Univ. of Glasgow (LLB (Hons)). Admitted Solicitor, 1971; in private practice, 1971–74; Lectr in Private Law, Univ. of Glasgow, 1974–76; University of Aberdeen: Lectr in Private Law, 1976–82; Sen. Lectr in Conveyancing and Professional Practice of Law, 1982–90; Prof. (personal), 1990–92; Hugh McLennan Prof. of Conveyancing, 1990–2001. Temp. Sheriff, 1998–1999; Hon. Sheriff: Aberdeen; Stonehaven. Member: Council, Law Soc. of Scotland, 1988–2000; Lord President's Adv. Council on Messengers-at-Arms and Sheriff Officers, 1989–2000; Legal Practice Course Bd, Law Soc. (England and Wales), 1993–97; Adv. Cttee on Feudal System, 1997–2000, Adv. Cttee on Real Burdens, 1998–2000, Scottish Law Commn; UK Mem., CCBE, 1997–2000; Rep., Internat. Union of Latin Notaries, 1989–1997. Examiner, Messengers-at-Arms and Sheriff Officers, 1989–92; Examiner in Conveyancing, Faculty of Advocates, 1992–. Mem., AID subcttee, RCOG, 1976–79. Mem., 1978, Fellow, 1981, Eugenics Soc.; FRSA 1998. Review Ed., Jl Law Soc. of Scotland, 1988–98. *Publications:* (ed jtly) The Impact of Marine Pollution: law and practice, 1980; (ed jtly) Scottish Cases and Materials in Commercial Law, 1987; (ed) A Scots Conveyancing Miscellany: essays in honour of Professor Halliday, 1988; New Reproductive Techniques: a legal perspective, 1988; (jtly) The Law and Practice of Diligence, 1990; (ed jtly) Reproductive Medicine and the Law, 1990; (ed) The Conveyancing Opinions of Professor Halliday, 1992; Standard Securities, 1991; (jtly) Missives, 1993, 2nd edn 1999; (jtly) The Requirements of Writing, 1995; (ed) Green's Practice Styles, vol. 1, 1996; (ed jtly) McDonald's Conveyancing Manual, 6th edn 1997; (jtly) Servitudes and Rights of Way, 1998; articles in legal journals. *Recreations:* golf, swimming, walking, bird watching. *Address:* Sheriff Court House, Queen Street, Peterhead AB42 6TP. *T:* (01779) 476676.

CUST, family name of **Baron Brownlow**.

CUSTIS, Patrick James, CBE 1981; FCA, FCMA, FCIS; director of companies; *b* 19 March 1921; *er s* of late Alfred and Amy Custis; *m* 1954, Rita, *yr d* of late Percy and Annie Rayner; one *s. Educ:* The High Sch., Dublin. JDipMA. FCA 1951; FCMA 1950; FCIS 1945. Served articles with Josolyne Miles & Co., Chartered Accountants, Cheapside, London, 1946–51; Asst to Gen. Man., Rio Tinto Co. Ltd, London, 1952–54; Gp Chief Accountant and Dir of subsid. cos, Glynwed Ltd, W Midlands, 1955–67; Guest Keen & Nettlefolds Ltd, W Midlands, 1967–81 (Dir of Finance, 1974–81); various sen. appts prior to 1974. Mem., Midlands and N Wales Reg. Bd (formerly Birmingham and W Midlands Reg. Bd), Lloyds Bank plc, 1979–91; Director: New Court Property Fund Managers Ltd, 1978–91; Associated Heat Services plc, 1981–90; Leigh Interests PLC, 1982–96 (Dep. Chm., 1990–93; Chm., 1993–96); Wolseley plc, 1982–90; Birmingham Technology Ltd, 1983–93; Wyko Group PLC, 1985–94; Benford Concrete Machinery plc, 1985–86; Chm., MCD Gp plc, 1983–86. Mem., Monopolies and Mergers Commn, 1981–82. Member: HM Prisons Bd, Home Office, 1980–85; Bi-Centenary Adv. Bd, Birmingham Gen. Hosp., 1978–90. Chm., Midlands Indust. Gp of Finance Dirs, 1977–80. Co-opted Mem. Council, Inst. of Chartered Accountants in England and Wales, 1979–85; Liveryman, Worshipful Co. of Chartered Accountants in England and Wales; Pres., Wolverhampton Soc. of Chartered Accountants, 1985–86. FRSA 1987. *Recreations:* walking, gardening, reading. *Address:* West Barn, Westmancote, Tewkesbury, Glos GL20 7ES. *T:* (01684) 772865.

See also R. A. Custis.

CUSTIS, Ronald Alfred; Director General, Energy Industries Council, 1981–92; *b* 28 Feb. 1931; *yr s* of late Alfred and Amy Custis, Dublin; *m* 1st, 1957, Enid Rowe (*d* 1984); one *s* one *d*; 2nd, 1986, Valerie Mackett (*née* Holbrook). *Educ:* The High Sch., Dublin. Joined HM Treasury, 1947; DES, 1964; Min. of Technology, 1964–70: Private Sec. to Permanent Under Sec., 1964–66; Principal, 1967; Sec. to Cttee of Inquiry into the Brain Drain, 1967–68; Min. of Aviation Supply, later MoD (Procurement Exec.), 1970–74: Private Sec. to Sec. of State for Defence, 1971–73; Asst Sec., 1973; Dept of Energy, 1974–81: Private Sec. to successive Secs of State for Energy, 1974–75; Under Sec., 1978; Dir Gen., Offshore Supplies Office, 1980–81. *Recreations:* reading, walking, listening to music, gardening. *Address:* 1 The Coaches, Fields Road, Chedworth, Glos GL54 4NQ. *T:* (01285) 720479.

See also P. J. Custis.

CUTHBERT, Prof. Alan William, ScD; FRS 1982; Sheild Professor of Pharmacology, 1979–99, and Deputy Vice-Chancellor, 1995–99, University of Cambridge; Master of Fitzwilliam College, Cambridge, 1990–99 (Hon. Fellow, 1999); *b* 7 May 1932; *s* of late Thomas William Cuthbert and Florence Mary (*née* Griffin); *m* 1957, Harriet Jane Webster; two *s. Educ:* Leicester Coll. of Technol.; St Andrews Univ. (BSc); London Univ. (BPharm, PhD); MA, ScD Cantab. Instructor Lieut, RN, 1956–59. Res. Fellow, then Asst Lectr, Dept of Pharmacology, Sch. of Pharmacy, Univ. of London, 1959–63; Demonstrator in Pharmacol., 1963–66, Lectr, 1966–73, and Reader, 1973–79, Dept of Pharmacol., Univ. of Cambridge; Fellow of Jesus Coll., Cambridge, 1968–90 (Hon. Fellow, 1991). Chm. Editorial Bd, British Jl of Pharmacology, 1974–82. For. Sec., British Pharmacol Soc., 1997–2000 (Hon. Mem., 2000); Member: AFRC, 1988–90; Council, Royal Soc., 1986–88; Council, Zool Soc. of London, 1988–91. Gov., De Montfort Univ., 1998–. Mem., Academie Royale de Médicine de Belgique, 1996–; MAE, 1996; Founder FMedSci 1998. Fellow, Sch. of Pharmacy, Univ. of London, 1996. Hon. DSc: De Montfort, 1993; Aston, 1995; Hon. LLD Dundee, 1995. Pereira Medal in Materia Medica, Pharmaceutical Soc. of GB, 1953; Sir James Irvine Medal in Chemistry, St Andrews Univ., 1955. *Publications:* scientific papers in pharmacol and physiol jls. *Recreations:* travel, painting, growing orchids, Duodecimos. *Address:* Department of Medicine, University of Cambridge, Addenbrooke's Hospital, Hills Road, Cambridge CB2 2QQ; 7 Longstanton Road, Oakington, Cambridge CB4 5BB. *T:* (01223) 233676.

CUTHBERT, Lady, (Betty Wake), CBE 1946 (OBE 1943); OStJ 1944; *b* 20 Jan. 1904; *d* of Guy Shorrock and Emma Wake; *m* 1928, Vice-Adm. Sir John Cuthbert, KBE, CB (*d* 1987); no *c.* Joined Auxiliary Fire Service, London, as driver, 1938; Fire Staff, Home Office, 1941; Chief Woman Fire Officer, National Fire Service, 1941–46. Nat. Chm., Girls' Venture Corps, 1946–67 (Pres. 1967). Mem., Hampshire CC, 1967–74. Chm. Govs, Cricklade Coll., Andover, 1973–81. *Address:* Ibthorpe Manor Farm, Hurstbourne Tarrant, Andover, Hants SP11 0BY.

CUTHBERT, Ceri Jayne; *see* Jones, C. J.

CUTHBERT, Sir Ian Holm; *see* Holm, Sir Ian.

CUTHBERT, Stephen Colin, FCA; Chief Executive, Port of London Authority, since 1999; *b* 27 Oct. 1942; *s* of Colin Samuel Cuthbert and Helen Mary Cuthbert (*née* Scott); *m* 1st, 1969, Jane Elizabeth Bluett (marr. diss. 1984); two *s* one *d*; 2nd, 1987, Susan Melanie Shepherd; one step *s* two step *d. Educ:* Trinity Sch. of John Whitgift; Bristol Univ. (BScEng). FCA 1968. Voluntary Service, UNRWA, Jordan, 1964–65; Price Waterhouse, London, 1965–76; Finance Dir, 1976–79, Chief Exec., 1980–93, Brent International plc; Dir Gen., Chartered Inst. of Marketing, 1994–99 (FCIM). Dir, London Chamber of Commerce and Industry, 2000. Mem. Council, 1989–99, Chm. Southern Reg., 1992–93, CBI. Freeman: City of London, 1998; Co. of Watermen and Lightermen, 2000; Liveryman, Co. of Marketors, 1998. *Recreations:* opera, sailing, family pursuits. *Address:* Port of London Authority, Bakers' Hall, 7 Harp Lane, EC3R 6LB. *T:* (020) 7743 7900.

CUTLER, Sir (Arthur) Roden, VC 1941; AK 1981; KCMG 1965; KCVO 1970; CBE 1957; Governor of New South Wales, 1966–81; company director; Chairman, State Bank of New South Wales, 1981–86; *b* 24 May 1916; *s* of Arthur William Cutler and Ruby Daphne (*née* Pope); *m* 1st, 1946, Helen Gray Annetta (*née* Morris), AC 1980 (*d* 1990); four *s*; 2nd, 1993, Joan Edith (*née* Goodwin). *Educ:* Sydney High Sch.; University of Sydney (BEc). Public Trust Office (NSW), 1935–42; War of 1939–45 (VC). State Secretary, RSS & AILA (NSW), 1942–43; Mem., Aliens Classification and Adv. Cttee to advise Commonwealth Govt, 1942–43; Asst Dep. Dir, Security Service, NSW, 1943; Asst Comr Repatriation, 1943–46; High Comr for Australia to New Zealand, 1946–52; High Comr for Australia to Ceylon, 1952–55; HM's Australian Minister to Egypt, 1955–56; Secretary General, SEATO Conference, 1957; Chief of Protocol, Dept of External Affairs, Canberra, 1957–58; State President of RSL, formerly RSSAILA (ACT), 1958; Australian High Comr to Pakistan, 1959–61; Australian Representative to Independence of Somali Republic, 1960; Australian Consul-General, New York, 1961–65; Ambassador to the Netherlands, 1965. Delegate to UN General Assembly, and Australian Rep., Fifth Cttee, 1962–63–64. Chairman: Occidental Life Assurance Co. of Australia, 1987–90; Ansett Express (formerly Air New South Wales), 1981–92; First Australia Fund, 1985–95; First

Australia Prime Income Fund, 1986–95; First Australia Prime Income Investment Co., 1986–95; Rothmans Foundn, 1987–93; First Commonwealth Fund, 1992–95; Director: Rothmans Hldgs Ltd (formerly Rothmans of Pall Mall), 1981–93; Permanent Trustee Co., 1981–92; Rothsay Property Investments Ltd, 1991–. Dep. Pres., VC and GC Assoc., 1991–. Hon. Col, Royal New South Wales Regt, 1966–85; Hon. Col, Sydney Univ. Regt, 1966–85; Hon. Air Cdre RAAF. Hon. LLD, Univ. of Sydney; Hon. DSc: Univ. of New South Wales; Univ. of Newcastle; Hon. DLitt: Univ. of New England; Univ. of Wollongong. KStJ 1965. *Address:* 12A Karoola, 442 Edgecliff Road, Edgecliff, NSW 2027, Australia. *T:* (2) 93261233, *Fax:* (2) 93273563. *Clubs:* Australian, Union (Sydney); Royal Sydney Yacht Squadron, Royal Prince Alfred Yacht (Sydney), Royal Sydney Golf.

CUTLER, Hon. Sir Charles (Benjamin), KBE 1973; ED 1960; Director, 1976–90, Chairman, 1978–90, Sun Alliance (Australia); *b* Forbes, NSW, 20 April 1918; *s* of George Hamilton Cutler and Elizabeth Cutler; *m* 1943, Dorothy Pascoe (OBE 1976); three *s* one *d*. *Educ:* rural and high schs, Orange, NSW. MLA for Orange, NSW, 1947; Leader of Country Party (NSW), 1959; Dep. Premier and Minister for Educn, 1965; Dep. Premier, 1972–76, Minister for Local Govt, 1972–76, and Minister for Tourism, 1975–76, NSW. Chm., United World Colls (Aust.) Trust, 1977. Hon. DLitt Newcastle Univ., NSW, 1968. *Recreation:* golf. *Address:* 52 Kite Street, Orange, NSW 2800, Australia. *T:* (2) 63626418. *Clubs:* Royal Automobile, Imperial Service, Union (Sydney); Orange Golf.

CUTLER, Ivor; humorist, poet, illustrator, playwright, singer and composer, since 1957; *b* 1923; *s* of Jack and Polly Cutler; two *s*. *Educ:* Shawlands Academy. *Radio and television:* Monday Night at Home, Radio 4, 1959–63; John Peel, Radio 1, 1969–; 14 radio plays, Radio 3, 1979–88; Prince Ivor (opera), Radio 3, 1983; King Cutler I to VI (with Phyllis King), Radio 3, 1990–; Magical Mystery Tour, TV, 1967; Ivor Cutler has 15, 1990, Cutler the Lax, 1991, Radio 4 (radio archive selections); A Stuggy Pren (series), Radio 3, 1994; A Jelly Mountain (series), Radio 3, 1996; A Wet Handle (series), Radio 3, 1997; *stage:* Establishment Club (cabaret), 1961–62; An Evening of British Rubbish, Comedy Th., 1963. Cartoonist, Private Eye and Observer, 1962–63. Pye Radio Award for humour, 1980. *Recordings:* Ivor Cutler of Y'hup, 1959; Get Away from the Wall, 1961; Who Tore Your Trousers?, 1961; Ludo, 1967, reissued 1997; Dandruff, 1974; Velvet Donkey, 1975; Jammy Smears, 1976; Life in a Scotch Sitting Room, vol. 2, 1978, reissued 1987 and 1995; Privilege, 1983; Women of the World (single), 1983; Prince Ivor, 1986; Gruts, 1986; A Wet Handle, 1997; A Flat Man, 1998; Cute, (H)ey?, 1999. Poetry cartoons, Scotland on Sunday mag., 1992–93. *Publications: stories:* Cockadoodledon't, 1967; (illustr. Martin Honeysett): Gruts, 1961, repr. 1986; Life in a Scotch Sitting Room, vol. 2, 1984, 2nd edn 1998; Fremsley, 1987; Glasgow Dreamer, 1990, 2nd edn 1998; *children's books:* (illustr. Helen Oxenbury): Meal One, 1971; Balooky Klujypop, 1974; The Animal House, 1977; (illustr. Alfreda Benge): Herbert the Chicken, 1984; Herbert the Elephant, 1984; (illustr. M. Honeysett) One and a Quarter, 1987; (illustr. Patrick Benson) Herbert: Five Stories, 1988; (illustr. Jill Barton) Grape Zoo, 1990; (illustr. Claudio Muñoz) Doris the Hen, 1992; (illustr. Claudio Muñoz) The New Dress, 1995; *poetry:* Many Flies Have Feathers, 1973; A Flat Man, 1977; Private Habits, 1981; Large et Puffy, 1984; Fresh Carpet, 1986; A Nice Wee Present from Scotland, 1988; (illustr. M. Honeysett) Fly Sandwich and other Menu, 1992; Is that your flap, Jack?, 1992; (photogr. Katrina Lithgow) A Stuggy Pren, 1994; A Wet Handle, 1997; A Flat Man, 1998; South American Bookworms, 1999; *philosophy:* (illustr. Martin Honeysett) Befriend a Bacterium, 1992. *Recreation:* 2000 catalyst and hypocrite. *Address:* c/o BBC, Broadcasting House, W1A 1AA.

CUTLER, Keith Charles; His Honour Judge Cutler; a Circuit Judge, since 1996; *b* 14 Aug. 1950; *s* of Henry Walter Cutler and Evelyn Constance Cutler; *m* 1975, Judith Mary Haddy; one *s* one *d*. *Educ:* Bristol Univ. (LLB Hons). Called to the Bar, Lincoln's Inn, 1972; Asst Recorder, 1989; Recorder, 1993–96. *Recreations:* church music, Italian travel, watching tennis. *Address:* 3 Pump Court, Temple, EC4Y 7AJ. *T:* (020) 7353 0711.

CUTLER, Robin; *see* Cutler, T. R.

CUTLER, Sir Roden; *see* Cutler, Sir A. R.

CUTLER, Timothy Robert, (Robin), CBE 1995; Director-General and Deputy Chairman, Forestry Commission, 1990–95; *b* 24 July 1934; *s* of Frank Raymond Cutler and Jeannie Evelyn Cutler (*née* Badenoch); *m* 1958, Ishbel Primrose; one *s* one *d*. *Educ:* Banff Academy; Aberdeen Univ. (BSc Forestry 1956). National Service, Royal Engineers, 1956–58. Colonial Forest Service, Kenya, 1958–64; New Zealand Forest Service: joined 1964; Dir of Forest Management, 1978; Dep. Dir-Gen., 1986; Chief Exec., Min. of Forestry, 1988–90. Hon. DSc Aberdeen, 1992. *Recreations:* tennis, golf, gardening, stamps. *Address:* 14 Swanston Road, Fairmilehead, Edinburgh EH10 7BB.

CUTT, Rev. Canon Samuel Robert; Canon Residentiary, 1979–93, and Treasurer, 1985–93, Wells Cathedral (Chancellor, 1979–85); *b* 28 Nov. 1925; *er s* of Robert Bush Cutt and Lilian Elizabeth Cutt (*née* Saint); *m* 1972, Margaret Eva (*d* 1975), *yr d* of Norman and Eva McIntyre. *Educ:* Skegness Grammar Sch.; Selwyn Coll., Cambridge; Cuddesdon Coll., Oxford. BA Cantab 1950, MA 1954. Deacon 1953, Priest 1954. Asst Curate, St Aidan, West Hartlepool, 1953–56; Tutor for King's Coll. London at St Boniface Coll., Warminster, 1956–59; Sub-Warden for KCL at St Boniface Coll., 1959–65; Lectr and Tutor of Chichester Theol Coll., 1965–71; Priest Vicar of Chichester Cath., 1966–71; Minor Canon, 1971–79, and Succentor, 1974–79, St Paul's Cathedral, and Warden, Coll. of Minor Canons, 1974–79; part-time Lectr, Theological Dept, KCL, 1973–79; Priest in Ordinary to the Queen, 1975–79; Dio. Dir of Ordinands, Bath and Wells, 1979–86; Examining Chaplain to Bishop of Bath and Wells, 1980–93; Warden, Community of St Denys, Warminster, 1987–91. OStJ 1981. *Recreations:* walking, music, biographical studies, heraldry, cooking.

CUTTER, Prof. Elizabeth Graham, PhD, DSc; FRSE; FLS; George Harrison Professor of Botany, University of Manchester, 1979–89, now Emeritus; *b* 9 Aug. 1929; *d* of Roy Carnegie Cutter and Alexandra (*née* Graham). *Educ:* Rothesay House Sch., Edinburgh; Univ. of St Andrews (BSc, DSc); Univ. of Manchester (PhD). Asst Lecturer in Botany, 1955–57, Lectr in Botany, 1957–64, Univ. of Manchester; Associate Professor of Botany, 1964–68, Professor of Botany, 1968–72, Univ. of California, Davis; Sen. Lectr in Cryptogamic Botany, 1972–74, Reader in Cryptogamic Botany, 1974–79, Univ. of Manchester. *Publications:* Trends in Plant Morphogenesis (principal editor), 1966; Plant Anatomy: Experiment and Interpretation, pt 1, Cells and Tissues, 1969, 2nd edn 1978; pt 2, Organs, 1971. *Recreations:* photography, fishing. *Address:* Barnyard Butts, Bakers Road, Gattonside, Melrose, Roxburghshire TD6 9NA. *T:* (01896) 822139.

CYPRUS AND THE GULF, Bishop in, since 1996; **Rt Rev. (George) Clive Handford;** *b* 17 April 1937; *s* of Cyril Percy Dawson Handford and Alice Ethel Handford; *m* 1962, Anne Elizabeth Jane Atherley; one *d*. *Educ:* Hatfield Coll., Durham (BA); Queen's Coll., Birmingham and Univ. of Birmingham (DipTh). Curate, Mansfield Parish Church, 1963–66; Chaplain: Baghdad, 1967; Beirut, 1967–73; Dean, St George's Cathedral, Jerusalem, 1974–78; Archdeacon in the Gulf and Chaplain in Abu Dhabi and Qatar, 1978–83; Vicar of Kneesall with Laxton, and Wellow and Rufford, 1983–84; RD of Tuxford and Norwell, 1983–84; Archdeacon of Nottingham, 1984–90; Suffragan Bishop of Warwick, 1990–96. ChStJ 1976. *Address:* 2 Grigori Afxentiou, PO Box 22075, Nicosia 1517, Cyprus. *T:* (2) 671220, *Fax:* (2) 674553.

D

d'ABO, Jennifer Mary Victoria; Chairman: Moyses Stevens Investments, 1990–99; Moyses Stevens Ltd, 1989–99; *b* 14 Aug. 1945; *d* of Michael Hammond-Maude and Rosamond Hammond-Maude (*née* Patrick); *m* 1st, David Morgan-Jones; one *d*; 2nd, Peter Cadbury, *qv*; one *s*; 3rd, Robin d'Abo (marr. diss. 1987). *Educ:* Hatherop Castle, Glos. Chairman: Ryman Ltd, 1981–87; Roffey Brothers Ltd, 1988; Director: Burlingtons Furnishing Co., 1977–80; Jean Sorelle, toiletry manufacturing co., 1980–83; Stormgard plc, 1985–87; London Docklands Develt Corp., 1985–88; Channel Four Television, 1986–87; (non.-exec.) Pentos plc, 1987–88; Mem., Industrial Develt Bd for NI, 1992–94. Mem., Doctors' and Dentists' Remuneration Review Body, 1989–92. Imperial Cancer Research Fund: Mem. Council, 1994–; Pres., Nat. Events Cttee, 1993–99. Trustee, BM (Natural History), 1988–99.

DACCA; *see* Dhaka.

DACIE, Prof. Sir John (Vivian), Kt 1976; FRS 1967; MD, FRCP; Professor of Haematology, Royal Post-graduate Medical School of London, University of London, 1957–77, now Emeritus; *b* 20 July 1912; British; *s* of John Charles and Lilian Maud Dacie, Putney; *m* 1938, Margaret Kathleen Victoria Thynne; three *s* two *d*. *Educ:* King's Coll. Sch., Wimbledon; King's Coll., London: King's Coll. Hospital, London. MB, BS London 1935; MD 1952; MRCP 1936, FRCP 1956; FRCPath (Pres., 1973–75). Various medical appointments, King's Coll. Hospital, Postgraduate Medical Sch. and Manchester Royal Infirmary, 1936–39. Pathologist, EMS, 1939–42; Major, then Lieut-Col, RAMC, 1943–46. Senior Lecturer in Clinical Pathology, then Reader in Haematology, Postgraduate Medical Sch., 1946–56. Chm., Med. and Scientific Adv. Panel, Leukaemia Research Fund, 1975–85. Hon. FRSocMed 1984 (Pres., 1977). Hon. MD: Uppsala, 1961; Marseille, 1977. *Publications:* Practical Haematology, 1950, 2nd edn, 1956, 8th edn (jointly), 1995; Haemolytic Anaemias, 1954: 2nd edn, Part I, 1960, Part II, 1962, Parts III and IV, 1967, 3rd edn, Part I, 1985, Part II, 1988, Part III, 1992, Part IV, 1995, Part V, 1999; various papers on anaemia in medical journals. *Recreations:* music, entomology, gardening. *Address:* 10 Alan Road, Wimbledon, SW19 7PT. *T:* (020) 8946 6086.

DACOMBE, William John Armstrong; Chairman, Postern Ltd, since 1996; *b* 21 Sept. 1934; *s* of late John Christian Dacombe and of Eileen Elizabeth Dacombe; *m* 1962, Margaretta Joanna (*née* Barrington); two *d*. *Educ:* Felsted School; Corpus Christi College, Oxford (MA). Kleinwort Benson, 1961–65; N. M. Rothschild & Sons, 1965–73 (Dir, 1970–73); Dir, 1973–84, Asst Chief Exec., 1979–82, Williams & Glyn's Bank; Group Exec. Dir, Royal Bank of Scotland Group, 1982–84; Chief Exec. Dir, Rea Brothers Group, 1984–88; Dir, W. A. Tyzack, 1987–89. Chairman: Brown Shipley Holdings, 1991–; Albert E. Sharp Hldgs, 1997–; Director: Capel Cure Sharp (Hldgs), 1998–; Capel Cure Sharp Ltd, 2000–; Albert E. Sharp Ltd, 2000–. Mem., Export Guarantees Adv. Council, 1982–86 (Dep. Chm., 1985–86). FRSA. *Recreations:* art, historic buildings, reading. *Address:* Mullion Cottage, Well Lane, SW14 7AJ. *T:* (020) 8876 4336. *Clubs:* Brooks's, Bankers, City of London.

da COSTA, Harvey Lloyd, CMG 1962; Judge of Appeal, Court of Appeal for Bermuda, 1982–96; *b* 8 Dec. 1914; *s* of John Charles and Martha da Costa. *Educ:* Calabar High Sch., Jamaica; St Edmund Hall, Oxford (Sen. Exhibnr; Rhodes Schol.; MA; BLitt 1952); BA (Hons) London. Practised at Chancery Bar, 1950–52; Crown Counsel, Jamaica, 1952–54; Sen. Crown Counsel, Jamaica, 1954–56; Asst Attorney-Gen., Jamaica, 1956–59; QC Jamaica 1959; Attorney-Gen. of West Indies, 1959–62; practised Private Bar, Jamaica, 1962–77; Puisne Judge, 1978–80, Chief Justice, 1980–81, Bahamas Supreme Court; Judge of Appeal, Court of Appeal for Bahamas, 1982–85. Mem., Anguilla, British Virgin Is and Seychelles Commns. Hon. LLD Univ. of W Indies, 1990. *Recreation:* swimming. *Address:* c/o Court of Appeal, Hamilton HM12, Bermuda.

da COSTA, Sergio Corrêa, Hon. GCVO 1968; Brazilian diplomat, retired; *b* 19 Feb. 1919; *s* of Dr I. A. da Costa and Lavinia Corrêa da Costa; *m* 1st, 1943, Zazi Aranha; one *s* two *d*; 2nd, 1992, Michèle Stemer-Sursock. *Educ:* Law Sch., Univ. of Brazil; post grad. UCLA; Brazilian War Coll. Career diplomat; Sec. of Embassy, Buenos Ayres, then Washington, 1944–48; Acting Deleg., Council of OAS, Wash., 1946–48; Inter-American Econ. and Social Council, Washington, 1946–48; Dep. Head, Economic Dept, Min. of Ext. Relations, 1952; Actg Pres., Braz. Nat. Techn. Assistance Commn, 1955–58; Minister-Counsellor, Rome, 1959–62; Permanent Rep. to FAO, Rome, 1960; Mem., Financial Cttee of FAO, 1962–63; Ambassador to Canada, 1962–65; Asst Sec.-Gen. for Internat. Organizations at Min. Ext. Relations, 1966; Sec.-Gen., Min. of Ext. Relations, 1967–68; Acting Minister for External Relations, 1967–68; Ambassador to UK, 1968–75; Permanent Rep. to UN in NY, 1975–83; Ambassador to USA, 1983–86. Member: Brazilian Acad. of Letters; Brazilian Hist. and Geographical Inst.; Brazilian Soc. of Internat. Law; American Soc. of Internat. Law. Grand Officer: Military Order of Aeronautical Merit, Brazil, 1967; Order of Naval Merit, Brazil, 1967; also numerous Grand Crosses, etc, of Orders, from other countries, 1957–. *Publications:* (mostly in Brazil): As 4 Coroas de Pedro I, 1941; Pedro I e Metternich, 1942; Diplomacia Brasileira na Questao de Leticia, 1943; A Diplomacia do Marechal, 1945; Every Inch a King—A biography of Pedro I, Emperor of Brazil, 1950 (NY 1964, London 1972); Mots sans frontières, Paris 1999. *Recreations:* reading, writing, boating. *Address:* 8/10 rue Guynemer, 75006 Paris, France. *Clubs:* White's, Travellers; Rideau, Country (Ottawa); Circolo della Caccia (Rome).

DACRE, Baroness (27th in line), *cr* 1321; **Rachel Leila Douglas-Home;** *b* 24 Oct. 1929;*er* surv. *d* of 4th Viscount Hampden, CMG (*d* 1965) (whose Barony of Dacre was called out of abeyance in her favour, 1970) and Leila Emily (*d* 1996), *o d* of late Lt-Col Frank Evelyn Seely; *m* 1951, Hon. William Douglas-Home (*d* 1992), author and playwright; one *s* three *d*. *Heir:* *s* Hon. James Thomas Archibald Douglas-Home; [*b* 16 May 1952; *m* 1979, Christine (*née* Stephenson); one *d*]. *Address:* Derry House, Kilmeston, near Alresford, Hants SO24 0NR.

DACRE OF GLANTON, Baron *cr* 1979 (Life Peer), of Glanton in the County of Northumberland; **Hugh Redwald Trevor-Roper;** Master of Peterhouse, Cambridge, 1980–87 (Hon. Fellow, 1987); *b* 15 January 1914; *er s* of late Dr B. W. E. Trevor-Roper, Glanton and Alnwick, Northumberland; *m* 1954, Lady Alexandra Howard-Johnston (*d* 1997), *e d* of late Field-Marshal Earl Haig, KT, GCB, OM. *Educ:* Charterhouse; Christ Church, Oxford. Research Fellow, Merton Coll., 1937–39 (Hon. Fellow, 1980). Student of Christ Church, Oxford, 1946–57; Censor, 1947–52; Hon. Student, 1979; Regius Prof. of Modern Hist., and Fellow of Oriel Coll., Oxford Univ., 1957–80 (Hon. Fellow, 1980). Dir, Times Newspapers Ltd, 1974–88. Chevalier, Legion of Honour, 1975. *Publications:* Archbishop Laud, 1940; The Last Days of Hitler, 1947; The Gentry, 1540–1640, 1953; (ed) Hitler's Table Talk, 1953; (ed with J. A. W. Bennett) The Poems of Richard Corbett, 1955; Historical Essays, 1957; (ed) Hitler's War Directives, 1939–45, 1964; (ed) Essays in British History Presented to Sir Keith Feiling, 1964; The Rise of Christian Europe, 1965; Religion, The Reformation and Social Change, 1967; (ed) The Age of Expansion, 1968; The Philby Affair, 1968; The European Witch-Craze of the 16th and 17th Centuries, 1970; The Plunder of the Arts in the Seventeenth Century, 1970; Princes and Artists, 1976; A Hidden Life, 1976; (ed) The Goebbels Diaries, 1978; Renaissance Essays, 1985; Catholics, Anglicans and Puritans, 1987; From Counter-Reformation to Glorious Revolution, 1992. *Address:* The Old Rectory, Didcot, Oxon OX11 7EB. *Clubs:* Beefsteak, Garrick.

See also Earl Haig, P. D. Trevor-Roper.

DACRE, Nigel; Editor, ITN News on ITV, since 1995; *b* 3 Sept. 1956; *s* of Peter and Joan Dacre; *m* 1979, Jane Verrill (Prof. Jane Dacre, MD, FRCP); one *s* two *d*. *Educ:* St John's Coll., Oxford (MA, PPE). BBC News Trainee, 1978; Regl Journalist, BBC Bristol, 1980; ITV, 1982–: ITN Scriptwriter, 1982; Programme Editor, Super Channel News, 1986; Editor, World News, 1987; Editor, News at One, 1989; Head of Programme Output and Exec. Producer, News at Ten, 1992; Dep. Editor, News Programmes, 1993–95. *Address:* Independent Television News, 200 Gray's Inn Road, WC1X 8X2.

See also P. M. Dacre.

DACRE, Paul Michael; Editor in Chief, Associated Newspapers, since 1998; Editor, Daily Mail, since 1992; *b* 14 Nov. 1948; *s* of Joan and Peter Dacre; *m* 1973, Kathleen Thomson; two *s*. *Educ:* University College Sch.; Leeds Univ. (Hons English). Reporter, feature writer, Associate Features Editor, Daily Express, 1970–76; Washington and NY corresp., Daily Express, 1976–79; Daily Mail: NY Bureau Chief, 1980; News Editor, 1981–85; Asst Editor (News and Foreign), 1986; Exec. Editor (Features), 1987; Associate Editor, 1989–91; Editor, Evening Standard, 1991–92. Director: Associated Newspaper Holdings, 1991–; Daily Mail & General Trust plc, 1998–; Teletext Hldgs Ltd, 2000–. Mem., Press Complaints Commn, 1998–. *Address:* Daily Mail, Northcliffe House, 2 Derry Street, W8 5TT. *T:* (020) 7938 6000.

See also N. Dacre.

da CUNHA, His Honour John Wilfrid, JP; a Circuit Judge (formerly Judge of County Courts), 1970–92; *b* 6 Sept. 1922; 2nd *s* of Frank C. da Cunha, MD, DPH, and Lucy (*née* Finnerty); *m* 1953, Janet, MB, ChB, *d* of Louis Savatard, (Hon.) MSc, LSA, and Judith Savatard, MB, BS; one *s* four *d*. *Educ:* Stonyhurst Coll., Lancs; St John's Coll., Cambridge. MA Cantab 1954. Served 1942–47: 23rd Hussars (RAC); wounded Normandy, 1944; Judge Advocate Gen. (War Crimes); Hon. Major. Called to Bar, Middle Temple, 1948; Northern Circuit. Chm., Local Appeal Tribunal, Min. of Social Security (Wigan), 1964–69. Asst Recorder, Oldham County Borough QS, 1966–70; Chm., Industrial Tribunals, 1966–70; Dep. Chm., Lancs County QS, 1968–71. Comr, NI (Emergency Provisions) Act, 1973; Member: Appeals Tribunal; Parole Bd, 1976–78; Criminal Injuries Compensation Bd, 1992–97. Pres., Bristol Medico-Legal Soc., 1989–91. Governor, Mount Carmel Sch., Alderley Edge, 1962–78. JP Lancs, 1968. *Recreations:* gardening, pottering.

DADSON, Prof. Trevor John, PhD; Professor of Hispanic Studies, University of Birmingham, since 1990 (Head, School of Modern Languages, 1993–97); *b* 7 Oct. 1947; *s* of Leonard John Dadson and Chrissie Vera (*née* Black); *m* 1975, Maria Angeles Gimeno; two *s*. *Educ:* Borden Grammar Sch., Sittingbourne; Univ. of Leeds (BA Hons); Univ. of Durham (PGCE); Emmanuel Coll., Cambridge (PhD 1974). Queen's University, Belfast: Lectr, 1978–86; Reader, 1986–88; Prof., 1988–90. *Publications:* The Genoese in Spain, 1983; Avisos a un Cortesano, 1985; (ed) G. Bocángel, La Lira de las Musas, 1985; (ed) D. Silva y Mendoza, Antología Poética, 1985; (ed) A. Barros, Filosofía Cortesana, 1987; Una Familia Hispano-Genovesa, 1991; Libros, lectores y lecturas: bibliotecas particulares españolas del Siglo de oro, 1998; (gen. ed) Actas del XII Congreso de la AIH, 1998; (ed) Ludismo e intertextualidad en la lírica española moderna, 1998; (ed) Voces subversivas: poesía bajo el Régimen, 2000; (ed) G. Bocángel, Obra Completa, 2000; numerous articles. *Recreations:* ski-ing, walking, tennis, reading. *Address:* 8 Over Mill Drive, Selly Park, Birmingham B29 7JL. *T:* (0121) 472 8250.

D'AETH, Prof. Richard, PhD; President, Hughes Hall, Cambridge, 1978–84; *b* 3 June 1912; *e s* of Walter D'Aeth and Marion Turnbull; *m* 1943, Pamela Straker; two *d*. *Educ:* Bedford Sch.; Emmanuel Coll., Cambridge (Scholar; 1st Cl. Hons Nat. Sci., PhD); Harvard Univ. (Commonwealth Fellow; AM). Served War, RAF, 1941–46 (Wing Comdr). Master, Gresham's Sch., 1938–40; HM Inspector of Schs, 1946–52; Prof. of Education: University Coll. of West Indies, 1952–58; Univ. of Exeter, 1958–77. Mem., Internat. Assoc. for Advancement of Educnl Res. (Pres., Warsaw, 1969); sometime mem. cttees of Schools Council, BBC, Schs Broadcasting Council, RCN and NSPCC.

Publications: Education and Development in the Third World, 1975; articles in jls. *Address:* Barton House, Rydon Acres, Stoke Gabriel, Totnes, Devon TQ9 6QJ.

DAFFERN, Paul George; Director, IMS, since 2000; *b* 5 May 1953; *s* of late George Thomas Daffern and Kathleen Esther Daffern; *m* 1984, Hilary Margaret Jenkins; one *s* one *d*. *Educ:* Foxford School, Coventry. Unbrako Ltd, 1969–73; Massey-Ferguson UK, 1973–75; Chrysler UK, 1975–77; Lucas Service UK, 1978–79; National Freight Co., 1980–88; Autoglass, 1988–91; Exec. Dir, Finance, AEA Technology, 1991–95; Chief Financial Officer, X/Open Co. Ltd, 1995–97; Finance Dir, Autoglass Ltd, 1998–2000. *Recreations:* golf, ski-ing. *T:* (01234) 273636.

DAFIS, Cynog Glyndwr; Member (Plaid Cymru) Mid and West Wales, National Assembly for Wales, since 1999; *b* 1 April 1938; *s* of Annie and George Davies; *m* 1963, Llinos Iorwerth Jones; two *s* one *d*. *Educ:* Aberaeron County Secondary Sch.; Neath Boys' Grammar Sch.; UCW Aberystwyth (BA Hons English, MEd). Teacher of English: Coll. of Further Educn, Pontardawe, 1960–62; Newcastle Emlyn Secondary Modern Sch., 1962–80; Aberaeron Comprehensive Sch., 1980–84; Dyffryn Teifi Comprehensive Sch., Llandysul, 1984–91; Research Officer, Dept of Adult Continuing Educn, UC Swansea, 1991–92. Contested (Plaid Cymru) Ceredigion and Pembroke North, 1983 and 1987. MP (Plaid Cymru) Ceredigion and Pembroke N, 1992–97, Ceredigion, 1997–Jan. 2000. Member: Select Cttee, Welsh Affairs, 1995–97; Envmtl Audit Cttee, 1997–2000. *Publications:* pamphlets and booklet (in Welsh) on bilingualism and Welsh politics. *Recreations:* walking, jogging, reading, listening to music. *Address:* Crugyreryr Uchaf, Talgarreg, Llandysul SA44 4HB. *T:* (01545) 590632.

DAHL, Mildred; *see* Gordon, M.

DAHRENDORF, Baron *cr* 1993 (Life Peer), of Clare Market in the City of Westminster; **Ralf Dahrendorf,** KBE 1982; PhD, DrPhil; FBA 1977; Warden of St Antony's College, Oxford, 1987–97; *b* Hamburg, 1 May 1929; adopted British nationality, 1988; *s* of Gustav Dahrendorf and Lina Dahrendorf (*née* Witt); *m* 1980, Ellen de Kadt (*née* Krug). *Educ:* several schools, including Heinrich-Hertz Oberschule, Hamburg; studies in philosophy and classical philology, Hamburg, 1947–52; DrPhil 1952; postgrad. studies at London Sch. of Economics, 1952–54; Leverhulme Research Schol., 1953–54; PhD 1956. Habilitation, and University Lecturer, Saarbrücken, 1957; Fellow at Center for Advanced Study in the Behavioral Sciences, Palo Alto, USA, 1957–58; Prof. of Sociology, Hamburg, 1958–60; Vis. Prof. Columbia Univ., 1960; Prof. of Sociology, Tübingen, 1960–66; Vice-Chm., Founding Cttee of Univ. of Konstanz, 1964–66; Prof. of Sociology, Konstanz, 1966–69; Parly Sec. of State, Foreign Office, W Germany, 1969–70; Mem., EEC, Brussels, 1970–74; Dir, 1974–84, Governor, 1986–, LSE; Prof. of Social Sci., Konstanz Univ., 1984–87. Member: Hansard Soc. Commn on Electoral Reform, 1975–76; Royal Commn on Legal Services, 1976–79; Cttee to Review Functioning of Financial Instns, 1977–80. Trustee, Ford Foundn, 1976–88. Chm. Bd, Friedrich Naumann Stiftung, 1982–88; Non-executive Director: Glaxo Holdings PLC, 1984–92; Bankges. Berlin (UK) plc, 1996–. Vis. Prof. at several Europ. and N American univs. Reith Lecturer, 1974; Jephcott Lectr, RSocMed, 1983. Hon. Fellow: LSE; Imperial Coll. Hon. MRIA 1974; Fellow, St Antony's Coll., Oxford, 1976. Foreign Hon. Member: Amer. Acad. of Arts and Sciences, 1975–; Nat. Acad. of Sciences, USA, 1977; Amer. Philosophical Soc., 1977; FRSA 1977; Hon. FRCS 1982. 24 hon. degrees from univs in 11 countries. Journal Fund Award for Learned Publication, 1966; Agnelli Prize, Giovanni Agnelli Foundation, 1992; Heuss Prize, Theodor-Heuss Stiftung, 1997. Grand Croix de l'Ordre du Mérite du Sénégal, 1971; Grosses Bundesverdienstkreuz mit Stern und Schulterband (Federal Republic of Germany), 1974; Grand Croix de l'Ordre du Mérite du Luxembourg, 1974; Grosses goldenes Ehrenzeichen am Bande für Verdienste um die Republik Österreich (Austria), 1975; Grand Croix de l'Ordre de Léopold II (Belgium), 1975; Comdr's Cross, Order of Civil Merit (Spain), 1990. *Publications include:* Marx in Perspective, 1953; Industrie- und Betriebssoziologie, 1956; Soziale Klassen und Klassenkonflikt, 1957 (Class and Class Conflict, 1959); Homo Sociologicus, 1959; Die angewandte Aufklärung, 1963; Gesellschaft und Demokratie in Deutschland, 1965 (Society and Democracy in Germany, 1966); Pfade aus Utopia, 1967 (Uscire dall'Utopia, 1971); Essays in the Theory of Society, 1968; Konflikt und Freiheit, 1972; Plädoyer für die Europäische Union, 1973; The New Liberty, 1975; Life Chances, 1979; On Britain, 1982; Die Chancen der Krise, 1983; Reisen nach innen und aussen, 1984; Law and Order, 1985; The Modern Social Conflict, 1988; Reflections on the Revolution in Europe, 1990; LSE: a history of the London School of Economics and Political Science 1895–1995, 1995; After 1989, 1997. *Address:* House of Lords, SW1A 0PW. *Clubs:* PEN, Reform, Garrick.

DAICHES, David, CBE 1991; MA Edinburgh; MA, DPhil Oxon; PhD Cantab; FRSL; FRSE; Director, Institute for Advanced Studies in the Humanities, Edinburgh University, 1980–86; Professor of English, University of Sussex, 1961–77, and Dean of the School of English Studies, 1961–68; now Emeritus Professor; *b* 2 Sept. 1912; *s* of late Rabbi Dr Salis Daiches and Flora Daiches (*née* Levin); *m* 1st, 1937, Isobel J. Mackay (*d* 1977); one *s* two *d*; 2nd, 1978, Hazel Neville (*née* Newman) (*d* 1986). *Educ:* George Watson's Coll., Edinburgh; Edinburgh Univ. (Vans Dunlop Schol., Elliot Prize); Balliol Coll., Oxford (Elton Exhibnr). Asst in English, Edinburgh Univ., 1935–36; Andrew Bradley Fellow, Balliol Coll., Oxford, 1936–37; Asst Prof. of English, Univ. of Chicago, 1939–43; Second Sec., British Embassy, Washington, 1944–46; Prof. of English, Cornell Univ., USA, 1946–51; University Lecturer in English at Cambridge, 1951–61; Fellow of Jesus Coll., Cambridge, 1957–62. Visiting Prof. of Criticism, Indiana Univ., USA, 1956–57; Hill Foundation Visiting Prof., Univ. of Minnesota, Spring 1966. Lectures: Elliston, Univ. of Cincinnati, 1960; Whidden, McMaster Univ., Canada, 1964; Ewing, Univ. of Calif, 1967; Carpenter Meml, Ohio Wesleyan Univ., 1969; Alexander, Univ. of Toronto, 1980; Gifford, Univ. of Edinburgh, 1983. Hon. Prof., Stirling Univ., 1980; Sen. Mellon Fellow, Nat. Humanities Center, USA, 1987–88. Fellow, Centre for the Humanities, Wesleyan Univ., Middletown, Conn, 1970. Hon. Fellow, Sunderland Polytechnic, 1977. Hon. LittD Brown Univ.; Docteur *hc* Sorbonne; Hon. DLitt: Edinburgh, 1976; Sussex, 1978; Glasgow, 1987; Guelph, 1990; DUniv Stirling, 1980; Dott. in *honorem* Bologna, 1989. Lifetime Achievement Award, 18th Century Scottish Studies Soc., 1988; Fletcher of Saltoun Award for Services to Scotland, 1988. *Publications:* The Place of Meaning in Poetry, 1935; New Literary Values, 1936; Literature and Society, 1938; The Novel and the Modern World, 1939 (new edn, 1960); Poetry and the Modern World, 1940; The King James Bible: A Study of its Sources and Development, 1941; Virginia Woolf, 1942; Robert Louis Stevenson, 1947; A Study of Literature, 1948; Robert Burns, 1950 (new edn 1966); Willa Cather: A Critical Introduction, 1951; Critical Approaches to Literature, 1956; Two Worlds (autobiog.), 1956; Literary Essays, 1956; John Milton, 1957; The Present Age, 1958; A Critical History of English Literature, 1960; George Eliot's Middlemarch, 1963; The Paradox of Scottish Culture, 1964; (ed) The Idea of a New University, 1964; English Literature (Princeton Studies in Humanistic Scholarship), 1965; More Literary Essays, 1968; Some Late Victorian Attitudes, 1969; Scotch Whisky, 1969; Sir Walter Scott and his World, 1971; A Third World (autobiog.), 1971; (ed) The Penguin Companion to Literature: Britain and the Commonwealth, 1971; Robert Burns and his World, 1971; (ed with A. Thorlby) Literature and Western Civilization, vol. I, 1972, vols II and V, 1973, vols III and IV, 1975, vol. VI, 1976; Charles Edward Stuart: the life and times of Bonnie Prince Charlie, 1973; Robert Louis Stevenson and his World, 1973; Was, 1975; Moses, 1975; James Boswell and his World, 1976; Scotland and the Union, 1977; Glasgow, 1977; Edinburgh, 1978; (with John Flower) Literary Landscapes of the British Isles: a narrative atlas, 1979; (ed) Selected Writings and Speeches of Fletcher of Saltoun, 1979; (ed) Selected Poems of Robert Burns, 1979; (ed) A Companion to Scottish Culture, 1981; Literature and Gentility in Scotland, 1982; Robert Fergusson, 1982; Milton's Paradise Lost, 1983; God and the Poets, 1984; Edinburgh, A Travellers' Companion, 1986; A Wee Dram, 1990; A Weekly Scotsman and Other Poems, 1994; Gen. Editor, Studies in English Literature, 1961–85. *Recreations:* talking, music. *Address:* 22 Belgrave Crescent, Edinburgh EH4 3AL.

DAIN, Rt Rev. Arthur John, OBE 1979; *b* 13 Oct. 1912; *s* of Herbert John Dain and Elizabeth Dain; *m* 1st, 1938, Edith Jane Stewart, MA, *d* of Dr Alexander Stewart, DD; four *d*; 2nd, 1986, Hester A. Quirk, BSc. *Educ:* Wolverhampton Grammar Sch.; Ridley Coll., Cambridge. Missionary in India, 1935–40; 10th Gurkha Rifles, 1940–41; Royal Indian Navy, 1941–47; Gen. Sec., Bible and Medical Missionary Fellowship, formerly Zenana Bible and Medical Mission, 1947–59; Overseas Sec., British Evangelical Alliance, 1950–59; Federal Sec., CMS of Australia, 1959–65; Hon. Canon of St Andrew's Cathedral, 1963; Asst Bishop, Diocese of Sydney, 1965–82; Sen. Asst Bishop and Chief Executive Officer, 1980–82. *Publications:* Mission Fields To-day, 1956; Missionary Candidates, 1959. *Recreation:* sport. *Address:* 1 Green Meadows, The Welkin, Lindfield, West Sussex RH16 2PE. *T:* (01444) 482736.

DAIN, Sir David (John Michael), KCVO 1997; CMG 1991; HM Diplomatic Service, retired; High Commissioner to Pakistan, 1997–2000; *b* 30 Oct. 1940; *s* of late John Gordon Dain and Joan (*née* Connop); *m* 1969, Susan Kathleen Moss; one *s* four *d*. *Educ:* Merchant Taylors' Sch.; St John's Coll., Oxford (MA Lit.Hum.). Entered HM Diplomatic Service, 1963; Third, later Second Sec., Tehran and Kabul, 1964–68; seconded to Cabinet Office, 1969–72; First Sec., Bonn, 1972–75; FCO, 1975–78; Head of Chancery, Athens, 1978–81; Counsellor and Dep. High Comr, Nicosia, 1981–85; Head of Western European Dept, FCO, 1985–89; on attachment to CSSB, 1989–90; High Comr, Cyprus, 1990–94; Asst Under-Sec. of State, then Dir, S Asian and SE Asian Depts, FCO, 1994–97. FIL 1986. Royal Order of Merit, Norway, 1988. *Recreations:* tennis, bridge, flying, golf, walking, natural history. *Address:* Manor Cottage, Frant, Tunbridge Wells, Kent TN3 9DR. *Clubs:* Oxford and Cambridge, Royal Over-Seas League; Oxford Union Society.

DAINTITH, Prof. Terence Charles; Professor of Law, University of London, since 1988; *b* 8 May 1942; *s* of Edward Terence and Irene May Daintith; *m* 1965, Christine Anne Bulport; one *s* one *d*. *Educ:* Wimbledon Coll.; St Edmund Hall, Oxford (BA Jurisp., MA); Univ. of Nancy (Leverhulme European Schol.). Called to the Bar, Lincoln's Inn, 1966; Additional Bencher, 2000. Associate in Law, Univ. of California, Berkeley, 1963–64; Lectr in Constitutional and Admin. Law, Univ. of Edinburgh, 1964–72; University of Dundee: Prof. and Head of Dept of Public Law, 1972–83 (leave of absence, 1981–83); Dir, Centre for Petroleum and Mineral Law Studies, 1977–83; Prof. of Law, European Univ. Inst., Florence, 1981–87; Dir, Inst. of Advanced Legal Studies, Univ. of London, 1988–95; Dean: Univ. of London Insts of Advanced Study, 1991–94; Univ. of London Sch. of Advanced Study, 1994–2001. MAE 1989 (Chm., Law Cttee, 1993–96; Chm., Social Scis Section, 1996–98). Editor, Jl Energy and Natural Resources Law, 1983–92. Hon. LLD De Montfort, 2001. *Publications:* The Economic Law of the United Kingdom, 1974; (with G. Willoughby) United Kingdom Oil and Gas Law, 1977, 2nd edn 1984; (with L. Hancher) European Energy Strategy: the legal framework, 1986, French edn 1987; (with S. Williams) The Legal Integration of Energy Markets, 1987; Law as an Instrument of Economic Policy, 1988; (with G. R. Baldwin) Harmonisation and Hazard, 1992; Implementing EC Law in the United Kingdom, 1995; (with A. C. Page) The Executive in the Constitution, 1999; contribs to UK and foreign law jls. *Recreations:* cycling, curling, carpentry. *Address:* Institute of Advanced Legal Studies, 17 Russell Square, WC1B 5DR. *T:* (020) 7862 5844. *Club:* Athenæum.

DAINTY, Prof. (John) Christopher, PhD; Pilkington Professor of Applied Optics, Imperial College, University of London, since 1984; Senior Research Fellow, Particle Physics and Astronomy Research Council, since 2001; *b* 22 Jan. 1947; *s* of Jack Dainty and Mary Elizabeth (*née* Elbeck); *m* 1978, Janice Hancock; one *s* one *d*. *Educ:* George Heriot's, Edinburgh; City of Norwich Sch.; Polytechnic of Central London (Diploma); Imperial Coll. of Science and Technol. (MSc; PhD 1972). Lectr, Queen Elizabeth Coll., Univ. of London, 1974–78; Associate Prof., Inst. of Optics, Univ. of Rochester, NY, USA, 1978–83. Sen. Res. Fellow, SERC, 1987–92. Pres., Internat. Commn for Optics, 1990–93. Internat. Commn of Optics Prize, 1984; Thomas Young Medal and Prize, Inst. of Physics, 1993. *Publications:* (with R. Shaw) Image Science, 1974; (ed) Laser Speckle and Related Phenomena, 1975, 2nd edn 1984; (ed with M. Nieto-Vesperinas) Scattering in Volumes and Surfaces, 1989; scientific papers. *Address:* Blackett Laboratory, Imperial College, SW7 2AZ. *T:* (020) 7594 7712.

DAISLEY, Paul; MP (Lab) Brent East, since 2001; *b* 20 July 1957; *m* 1984, Lesley Jordan. Accounting Officer, Texaco, 1976–84; Dir of Finance and Admin, Daisley Associates, 1984–96. Mem. (Lab), Brent BC, 1990– (Leader, 1996–2001). Mem., MSF, 1976–; Br. Sec., ASTMS, 1979–84. *Address:* (office) 102 Liddell Gardens, NW10 3QE; c/o House of Commons, SW1A 0AA.

DAKERS, Lionel Frederick, CBE 1983; DMus; FRCO; Director, Royal School of Church Music, 1972–89 (Special Commissioner, 1958–72); Examiner to the Associated Board of the Royal Schools of Music, 1958–94; Director: Hymns Ancient and Modern, since 1976; SCM Press, since 1998; *b* Rochester, Kent, 24 Feb. 1924; *o s* of late Lewis and Ethel Dakers; *m* 1951, Mary Elisabeth (*d* 1997), *d* of Rev. Claude Williams; four *d*. *Educ:* Rochester Cathedral Choir Sch. Studied with H. A. Bennett, Organist of Rochester Cathedral, 1933–40, with Sir Edward Bairstow, Organist of York Minster, 1943–45, and at Royal Academy of Music, 1947–51. Organist of All Saints', Frindsbury, Rochester, 1939–42. Served in Royal Army Educational Corps, 1943–47. Cairo Cathedral, 1945–47; Finchley Parish Church, 1948–50; Asst Organist, St George's Chapel, Windsor Castle, 1950–54; Asst Music Master, Eton Coll., 1952–54; Organist of Ripon Cathedral, 1954–57; Conductor, Ripon Choral Soc. and Harrogate String Orchestra, 1954–57; Hon. Conductor, Exeter Diocesan Choral Association, 1957–72; Lectr in Music, St Luke's Coll., Exeter, 1958–70; Organist and Master of the Choristers, Exeter Cathedral, 1957–72; Conductor: Exeter Musical Soc., 1957–72; Exeter Chamber Orchestra, 1959–65. President: Incorporated Assoc. of Organists, 1972–75; London Assoc. of Organists, 1976–78; ISM, 1990–91; Vice-President: Friends of Cathedral Music, 1977–; Fedn of Cathedral Old Choristers' Assocs, 1980–; Herbert Howells Soc., 1987–; Church Music Soc., 1990–; Mem. Council, Royal Coll. of Organists, 1967– (Pres., 1976–78; Dep. Pres., 1996–); Sec., Cathedral Organists' Assoc., 1972–88. Chairman: Organs Adv. Cttee of Council for Care of Churches of C of E, 1974–96; Nat. Learn the Organ Year, 1989–90; Friends of the Musicians' Chapel, 1988–; Salisbury DAC, 1990–98; Nat. Organ Teachers' Encouragement Scheme, 1990–92. Member: Archbishops' Commn in Church

Music, 1988–92; Salisbury Diocesan Liturgical Adv. Cttee, 1992–95; Editl Cttee, Common Praise, 2000. Lay Canon, Salisbury Cathedral, 1993–98. Gov., Godolphin Sch., 1990–94. Trustee, Ouseley Trust, 1990–. Hon. Mem., US Assoc. of Anglican Musicians, 1978; Hon. Life Mem., Methodist Church Music Soc., 1990. ARCO 1944; FRCO 1945; ADCM 1952; BMus Dunelm, 1951; ARAM 1955; FRAM 1962; FRSCM 1969; FRCM 1980. Fellow, St Michael's Coll., Tenbury, 1973. Hon. Fellow, Westminster Choir Coll., USA, 1975. Hon. DMus: Lambeth, 1979; Exeter, 1990. Compositions: church music, etc. *Publications:* Church Music at the Crossroads, 1970; A Handbook of Parish Music, 1976; Making Church Music Work, 1978; (ed) Music and the Alternative Service Book, 1980; (ed) The Choristers Companion, 1980; (ed) The Psalms—their use and performance today, 1980; The Church Musician as Conductor, 1982; Church Music in a Changing World, 1984; Choosing and Using Hymns, 1985; (ed) New Church Anthem Book, 1992; The Church Anthem Handbook, 1994; Places Where They Sing, 1995; (with E. Routley) A Short History of English Church Music, 1997; (ed) Ash Wednesday to Easter for Choirs, 1998; A Miscellany of Thoughts, 1999; Beauty beyond Words, 2000; (ed jtly) Beneath a Travelling Star, 2001. *Recreations:* book collecting, gardening, continental food, travel. *Address:* 6 Harcourt Terrace, Salisbury, Wilts SP2 7SA. *T:* (01722) 324880. *Clubs:* Athenæum; St Wilfrid's (NY) (Hon. mem.).

DAKIN, Dorothy Danvers, OBE 1982; JP; Assistant Chaplain, HM Prison and Remand Centre, Pucklechurch, 1984–87; *b* 22 Oct. 1919; *d* of Edwin Lionel Dakin, chartered civil engr and Mary Danvers Dakin (*née* Walker), artist. *Educ:* Sherborne Sch. for Girls; Newnham Coll., Cambridge. MA Geography. 2nd Officer WRNS (Educn), 1943–50; Housemistress, Wycombe Abbey Sch., 1950–60; Headmistress, The Red Maids' School, Bristol, 1961–81; Chm., ISIS Assoc., 1982–84. President: West of England Br., Assoc. of Headmistresses, 1969–71; Assoc. of Headmistresses of Girls' Boarding Schs, 1971–73; Girls' Schs Assoc. (Independent), 1973–75; Chm. Council, ISIS, 1975–81. Licensed Reader, C of E, 1982–86. FRSA 1988. JP Bristol, 1974. *Recreations:* fencing, painting, embroidery. *Address:* 41 Park Grove, Henleaze, Bristol BS9 4LF.

DALAI LAMA; *see* Tenzin Gyatso.

DALAL, Maneck Ardeshir Sohrab, OBE 1997; Director: Tata Ltd, SW1, since 1977 (Managing Director, 1977–88; Vice-Chairman, 1989–94); Tata Industries, Bombay, since 1979; *b* 24 Dec. 1918; *s* of Ardeshir Dalal, OBE and Amy Dalal; *m* 1947, Kathleen Gertrude Richardson; three *d. Educ:* Trinity Hall, Cambridge (MA). Cambridge Univ. Captain, tennis and squash rackets. Called to the Bar, Middle Temple, 1945. Manager: Air-India New Delhi, 1946–48; Air-India London, 1948–53; Regional Traffic Manager, 1953–59; Regional Director, 1959–77; Minister for Tourism and Civil Aviation, High Commn for India, 1973–77. President: Indian Chamber of Commerce in Great Britain, 1959–62; Indian Management Assoc. of UK, 1960–63; UK Pres., World Conf. on Religions and Peace, UK and Ireland Gp, 1985–; Vice-Pres., Friends of Vellore, 1979–; Chairman: Foreign Airlines Assoc. of UK, 1965–67; Indian YMCA, London, 1972–98; Bharatiya Vidhya Bhavan, London (Indian Cultural Inst. of Gt Britain), 1975–; Northbrook Soc., 1990– (Mem. Cttee, 1975–); Indian Women's Educn Assoc., 1985–95 (Mem. Cttee, 1975–95); Vice-Chm., Fest. of India in GB, 1980–81; Member: Sub-Cttee on Transport, Industrial Trng Bd of GB, 1975–77; Assembly, British Council of Churches, 1984–87; Internat. Bd, United World Colls, 1985–; Bd Govs, Nat. Inst. for Social Work, 1986–96; Chm. Central Council, Royal Over-Seas League, 1986–89 (Dep. Chm. Central Council, 1982–86; Mem., 1974–; Vice-Pres., 1989–). Patron: Internat. Centre for Child Studies, 1984–; Satyjit Ray Foundn, 1995–; Indian Professionals Assoc., UK, 1996–. FCIT 1975; FIMgt; FRSA 1997. *Recreations:* reading, walking. *Address:* Tall Trees, Marlborough Road, Hampton, Middx TW12 3RX. *T:* (020) 8979 2065. *Clubs:* Hurlingham, Royal Over-Seas League, MCC; Hawks (Cambridge).

DALBY, David; *see* Dalby, T. D. P.

DALBY, Ven. John Mark Meredith; Chaplain, The Beauchamp Community, Newland, since 2000; Archdeacon of Rochdale, 1991–2000, now Emeritus; *b* 3 Jan. 1938; *s* of William and Sheila Mary Dalby (*née* Arkell). *Educ:* King George V Sch., Southport; Exeter Coll., Oxford, (MA 1965); Ripon Hall, Oxford; Univ. of Nottingham (PhD 1977). Ordained deacon 1963, priest 1964; Curate: Hambleden, Bucks, 1963–68; Fawley, Fingest, Medmenham and Turville, Bucks, 1965–68; Vicar of St Peter, Spring Hill, Birmingham, 1968–75; Rural Dean of Birmingham City, 1973–75; Sec., Cttee for Theol Educn, and Selection Sec., ACCM, 1975–80; Hon. Curate of All Hallows, Tottenham, 1975–80; Vicar of St Mark, Worsley, 1980–84; Team Rector of Worsley, 1984–91; Rural Dean of Eccles, 1987–91. Examining Chaplain to the Bp of Manchester, 1980–2000. Member: Gen. Synod of C of E, 1985–95; Liturgical Commn, 1986–95. *Publications:* Open Communion in the Church of England, 1959; The Gospel and the Priest, 1975; Tottenham Church and Parish, 1979; The Cocker Connection, 1989; Open Baptism, 1989; Anglican Missals and their Canons, 1998. *Recreations:* travel, family history, philately, liturgy. *Address:* Chaplain's House, Beauchamp Community, Newland, Malvern, Worcestershire WR13 5AX. *T:* (01684) 899198. *Club:* Royal Over-Seas League.

DALBY, Dr (Terry) David (Pereira); Reader in West African Languages, School of Oriental and African Studies, University of London, 1967–83, now Emeritus; Director, Linguasphere Observatory (Observatoire linguistique), since 1987; *b* 7 Jan. 1933; *s* of Ernest Edwin Dalby and Rose Cecilia Dalby; *m* 1957, Winifred Brand; two *d*; *m* 1982, Catherine Jansens; one *s. Educ:* Cardiff High Sch.; Queen Mary Coll., London (BA 1954, PhD 1961; Hon. Life Mem., Queen Mary Coll. Union Soc., 1954). Served to Lieut, Intell. Corps, 1954–56. United Africa Co. Ltd, London and W Africa, 1957–60; Lectr in Mod. Languages, University Coll. of Sierra Leone, 1961–62; Lectr in W African Langs, SOAS, Univ. of London, 1962–67; Hon. Res. Fellow, Adran y Gymraeg, Univ. of Wales, Cardiff, 1996–. Hanns Wolff Vis. Prof., Indiana Univ., 1969. Chm., Centre for Afr. Studies, Univ. of London, 1971–74; Dir, Internat. African Inst., 1974–80; Chairman: Internat. Conf. on Manding Studies, 1972, and Drought in Africa Conf., 1973; UK Standing Cttee on Univ. Studies of Africa, 1978–82 (Dep. Chm., 1975–78). Vice-Pres., Unesco Meeting on Cultural Specificity in Africa, Accra, 1980. Member: Governing Body, SOAS, 1969–70; Council, African Studies Assoc. of UK, 1970–73; Cttee of Management, British Inst. in Paris, 1975–82; Conseil Internat. de Recherche et d'Etude en Linguistique Fondamentale et Appliquée, 1980–86 (Président, 1984); Centre Internat. de Recherche sur le Bilinguisme, Laval Univ., Que, 1981–89; Eur. Council on African Studies, 1985–87; Centre Internat. des Industries de la Langue, Univ. Paris X, 1993–95; Comité Français des Etudes Africaines, 1993–94. Hon. Mem., SOAS, 1983. Editor, African Language Review, 1962–72; Co-editor, Africa, 1976–80. *Publications:* Lexicon of the Mediaeval German Hunt, 1965; Black through White: patterns of communication in Africa and the New World, 1970; (ed) Language and History in Africa, 1970; (ed jtly) Drought in Africa, 1st vol. 1973, 2nd vol. 1978; Language Map of Africa and the adjacent islands, 1977; Clavier international de Niamey, 1984; (jtly) Les langues et l'espace du français, 1985; Afrique et la lettre, 1986; (jtly) Thesaurus of African Languages, 1987; Linguasphere Register of the World's Languages and Speech Communities, 2 vols, 2000; articles in linguistic and other jls. *Recreations:* cartography, local history. *Address:* Linguasphere Observatory, Hebron, Dyfed SA34 0XT; *e-mail:* dalby@linguasphere.org.

DALDRY, Stephen David; Director, Stephen Daldry Pictures, since 1998; Associate Director, Royal Court Theatre, since 1999; *b* 2 May 1961; *s* of late Patrick Daldry and of Cherry (*née* Thompson). *Educ:* Huish GS, Taunton; Univ. of Sheffield (BA). Trained with Il Circo di Nando Orfei, Italy; Artistic Dir, Metro Theatre, 1984–86; Associate Artist, Crucible Theatre, Sheffield, 1986–88; Artistic Director: Gate Theatre, Notting Hill, 1989–92; English Stage Co., Royal Court Theatre, 1992–99. Major productions include: Damned for Despair, Gate, 1991; An Inspector Calls, RNT, 1992, Aldwych, 1994, Garrick, 1995, NY, 1995, Playhouse, 2001; Machinal, RNT, 1993; Royal Court: The Kitchen, 1995; Via Dolorosa, 1998, NY, 1999, filmed 1999; Far Away, 2000, transf. Albery, 2001. *Films:* Eight (short), 1998; Billy Elliot (dir), 2000. *Address:* c/o Working Title, 77 Shaftesbury Avenue, W1V 8HQ.

DALE, Barry Gordon, FCA; Chairman, Creightons, 1997–99; Director: De Vere (formerly Greenalls) Group, since 1992; Marketfund Ltd, since 1995; *b* 31 July 1938; *s* of Francis and Catherine Dale; *m* 1963, Margaret (*née* Fairbrother); one *s* one *d. Educ:* Queen Elizabeth Grammar Sch., Blackburn. Coopers Lybrand, Montreal, 1960–62; Pilkington Brothers Glass, St Helens, 1962–65; ICI, 1965–85: Mond Div., Cheshire, 1966–68; Head Office, 1968–72; Dep. Chief Acct, Mond Div., 1972–78; Finance Dir, ICI Latin America (Wilmington, USA), 1978–80; Chief Acct, Organics Div., Manchester, 1980–84; Bd Mem. for Finance, LRT, 1985–88; Gp Finance Dir, 1988–92, Gp Chief Exec., 1993–95, Littlewoods Orgn. Director: Ellis & Everard, 1978–81; Magadi Soda Co. (Kenya), 1980–82; Triplex Lloyd, 1994–98; London Buses Ltd, 1985–88; London Underground Ltd, 1985–88; LRT Bus Engineering Ltd, 1985–88; Chairman: London Transport Trustee Co., 1985–88; London Transport Pension Fund Trustees, 1985–88; Datanetworks, 1987–88. *Recreations:* golf, fell walking, other sports. *Address:* Tanglewood, Spinney Lane, Knutsford WA10 0NQ. *Clubs:* Tatton (Knutsford); West Surrey Golf, Knutsford Golf.

DALE, David Kenneth Hay, CBE 1976; Governor, Montserrat, West Indies, 1980–85, retired 1988; *b* 27 Jan. 1927; *s* of Kenneth Hay Dale and Francesca Sussana Hoffman; *m* 1956, Hanna Szydlowska; one *s. Educ:* Dorchester Grammar Sch. Joined Queen's Royal Regt, 1944; 2/Lieut 8th Punjab Regt, 1945; Lieut 4 Bn (PWO) 8th Punjab Regt, 1946; Lieut Royal Regt of Artillery, 1948, Captain 1955: served Kenya and Malaya (despatches); Dist Officer, Kenya, 1960, Dist Comr, 1962; Admin Officer Cl. B, subseq. Cl. A, Anglo-French Condominium, New Hebrides, W Pacific, 1965–73; Perm. Sec., Min. of Aviation, Communications and Works, Seychelles, 1973–75; Dep. Governor, Seychelles, 1975; Sec. to Cabinet, Republic of Seychelles, 1976; FCO, 1977–80. Clerk, Shipwrights' Co., 1986–87. Pres., Somerton Frome Constit. Cons. Assoc., 1994–97 (Vice-Chm., Finance, 1990–94). *Recreations:* birdwatching, walking, colonial and military history. *Address:* Chatley Cottage, Batcombe, near Shepton Mallet, Somerset BA4 6AF. *T:* (01749) 850449. *Club:* East India.

DALE, Jim; actor, director, singer, composer, lyricist; *b* 15 Aug. 1935; *m*; three *s* one *d. Educ:* Kettering Grammar School. Music Hall comedian, 1951; singing, compèring, directing, 1951–61; films, 1965–, include: Lock Up Your Daughters, The Winter's Tale, The Biggest Dog in the World, National Health, Adolf Hitler—My Part in his Downfall, Joseph Andrews, Pete's Dragon, Hot Lead Cold Feet, Bloodshy, The Spaceman and King Arthur, Scandalous, Carry On films: Carry On Cabby, Carry On Cleo, Carry On Jack, Carry On Cowboy, Carry On Screaming, Carry On Spying, Carry On Constable, Carry On Doctor, Carry On Again Doctor, Carry On Don't Lose Your Head, Carry On Follow that Camel, Carry On Columbus. Joined Frank Dunlop's Pop Theatre for Edinburgh Festival, 1967–68; National Theatre, 1969–71: main roles in National Health, Love's Labour's Lost, Merchant of Venice, Good-natured Man, Captain of Kopenick, The Architect and the Emperor of Assyria; also appeared at Young Vic in Taming of the Shrew, Scapino (title rôle and wrote music); title rôle in musical The Card, 1973; Compère of Sunday Night at the London Palladium, 1973–74; Scapino (title rôle), Broadway, 1974–75 (Drama Critics' and Outer Circle Awards for best actor; Tony award nomination for best actor); Privates on Parade, Long Wharf Theatre, New Haven, Conn, 1979; Barnum (title rôle), Broadway, 1980 (Tony award for best actor in a musical, Drama Desk Award); A Day in the Death of Joe Egg, NY, 1985 (Tony nomination for best actor; Outer Circle Award for best actor); Me and My Girl, NY, 1987–88; Privates on Parade, NY, 1989; Oliver!, London Palladium, 1995; The Music Man, Travels With My Aunt, NY (Drama Desk Award, Outer Circle Award and Critics Award, 1995); television includes: host of Ringling Brothers Barnum and Bailey Circus (TV special), 1985; Adventures of Huckleberry Finn, 1985. Composed film music for: The Winter's Tale, Shaliko, Twinky, Georgy Girl (nominated for Academy Award), Joseph Andrews. *Address:* c/o Mark Sendroff, 139 W 82nd Street, New York, NY 10024, USA; c/o Janet Glass, 28 Berkeley Square, W1X 6HD.

DALE, Peter David; Head of Documentaries, Channel 4, since 2000 (Commissioning Editor, Documentaries, 1998–2000); b 25 July 1955; s of David Howard Dale and Betty Marguerite Dale (*née* Rosser); *m* 1988, Victoria Francesca Pennington; one *s* two *d. Educ:* King Henry VIII Grammar Sch., Coventry; Liverpool Univ. (BA Hons English Lit. and Lang.). BBC Television: research asst trainee, 1980–82; Dir and Producer, 1982–98. Journalism Prize, Anglo-German Foundn, 1992; Best Documentary Award, 1994, Best Documentary Series, 1996, RTS; Producer of Year Award, Broadcast Mag., 1997; Grierson Award for Best British Documentary, BFI, 1997. *Recreations:* family, sailing. *Address:* Channel 4, 124 Horseferry Road, SW1P 2TX. *T:* (020) 7306 8727.

DALE, Robert Alan; business consultant; Director, Business Development, Lucas Industries plc, 1992–93; *b* 31 Oct. 1938; *s* of Horace and Alice Dale; *m* 1963, Sheila Mary Dursley; one *s* one *d. Educ:* West Bromwich Grammar Sch.; Birmingham Univ. (BA Hons). Joined Lucas Industries as graduate apprentice, 1960; first management appt, 1965; first Bd appt, 1971; Dir, Lucas CAV, 1972–77; Dir and Gen. Man., Lucas Batteries, 1978–81; joined Exec. Cttee of Lucas (Joseph Lucas Ltd), 1980; Managing Director: Lucas World Service, 1981–85; Lucas Electrical, 1985–87; Lucas Automotive, 1987–92; Dir, Lucas Industries, 1987–93. *Recreations:* sport, photography, travel.

DALES, Sir Richard (Nigel), KCVO 2001; CMG 1993; HM Diplomatic Service; Ambassador to Norway, since 1998; *b* 26 Aug. 1942; *s* of late Kenneth Richard Frank Dales and of Olwen Mary (*née* Preedy); *m* 1966, Elizabeth Margaret Martin; one *s* one *d. Educ:* Chigwell Sch.; St Catharine's Coll., Cambridge (BA 1964). Entered FO, 1964; Third Sec., Yaoundé, Cameroon, 1965–67; FCO, 1968–70; Second Sec., later First Sec., Copenhagen, 1970–73; FCO, 1973; Asst Private Sec. to Foreign and Commonwealth Sec., 1974–77; First Sec., Head of Chancery and Consul, Sofia, Bulgaria, 1977–81; FCO, 1981; Counsellor and Head of Chancery, Copenhagen, 1982–86; Dep. High Comr, Harare, 1986–89; Head of Southern Africa, later Central and Southern Africa, Dept, FCO, 1989–91; Resident Chm. (FCO), CSSB, 1991–92; High Comr, Zimbabwe, 1992–95; Asst Under-Sec. of State, later Dir, Africa and Commonwealth, FCO, 1995–98. *Recreations:* music, walking. *Address:* c/o Foreign and Commonwealth Office, King

Charles Street, SW1A 2AH. *Clubs:* Oxford and Cambridge, Royal Commonwealth Society.

DALEY, Judith Mary Philomena; Her Honour Judge Daley; a Circuit Judge, since 1994; *b* 12 Aug. 1948; *d* of James Patrick Daley and Mary Elizabeth Daley (*née* Rawcliffe), BA. *Educ:* Seafield Convent Grammar Sch., Crosby; King's Coll. London (LLB Hons). Called to the Bar, Gray's Inn, 1970; Asst Recorder, 1984; Recorder, 1989–94 (Northern Circuit). *Recreations:* opera, music, theatre, travel, gardening. *Address:* Queen Elizabeth II Law Court, Derby Square, Liverpool L2 1XA. *Club:* Liverpool Racquet.

DALGARNO, Prof. Alexander, PhD; FRS 1972; Phillips Professor of Astronomy, since 1977, Chairman of Department of Astronomy, 1971–76, Associate Director of Centre for Astrophysics, 1973–80, Harvard University; Member of Smithsonian Astrophysical Observatory, since 1967; *b* 5 Jan. 1928; *s* of William Dalgarno; *m* 1st, 1957, Barbara Kane (marr. diss. 1972); two *s* two *d*; 2nd, 1972, Emily Izsák (marr. diss. 1987). *Educ:* Southgate Grammar Sch.; University Coll., London (Fellow 1976). BSc Maths, 1st Cl. Hons London, 1947; PhD Theoretical Physics London, 1951; AM Harvard, 1967. The Queen's University of Belfast: Lectr in Applied Maths, 1952; Reader in Maths, 1956; Dir of Computing Lab., 1960; Prof. of Quantum Mechanics, 1961; Prof. of Mathematical Physics, 1966–67; Prof. of Astronomy, Harvard Univ., 1967–; Acting Dir, Harvard Coll. Observatory, 1971–73. Chief Scientist, Geophysics Corp. of America, 1962–63. Spiers Meml Lectr, Faraday Div., RSC, 1992. Editor, Astrophysical Journal Letters, 1973–. Fellow: Amer. Acad. of Arts and Sciences, 1968; Amer. Geophysical Union, 1972; Amer. Physical Soc., 1980; Mem., Internat. Acad. Astronautics, 1972; MRIA 1989. FUMIST 1992. Hon. DSc QUB, 1980. Prize of Internat. Acad. of Quantum Molecular Sci., 1969; Hodgkins Medal, Smithsonian Instn, 1977; Davisson-Germer Prize, Amer. Physical Soc., 1980; Gold Medal, Royal Astronomical Soc., 1986; Meggers Prize, Optical Soc. of America, 1986; Fleming Medal, Amer. Geophys. Union, 1995. *Publications:* numerous papers in scientific journals. *Recreations:* squash, books. *Address:* c/o Harvard-Smithsonian Center for Astrophysics, 60 Garden Street, Cambridge, MA 02138, USA.

DALGETY, Ramsay Robertson; QC (Scot.) 1986; **Hon. Mr Justice Dalgety;** a Judge of the Supreme Court, Tonga, since 1991; *b* 2 July 1945; *s* of James Robertson Dalgety and Georgia Dalgety (*née* Whyte); *m* 1971, Mary Margaret Bernard; one *s* one *d*. *Educ:* High School of Dundee; Univ. of St Andrews (LLB Hons). Advocate, 1972; Temp. Sheriff, 1987–91. Dep. Traffic Comr for Scotland, 1988–93. Councillor, City of Edinburgh, 1974–80. Director/Chairman: Archer Transport Ltd and Archer Transport (London) Ltd, 1982–85; Venture Shipping Ltd, 1983–85. Director: Scottish Opera Ltd, 1980–90; Scottish Opera Theatre Trust Ltd, 1987–90; Chm., Opera Singers Pension Fund, 1990– (Dep. Chm., 1989–90; Trustee, 1983–); Dep. Chm., Edinburgh Hibernian Shareholders Assoc., 1990–92. *Recreations:* golf, boating, opera, travel, cricket, football. *Address:* Supreme Court, PO Box 869, Nuku'alofa, Kingdom of Tonga, South Pacific. *T:* 23400, *Fax:* 24538. *Clubs:* Surrey County Cricket; Nuku'alofa (Tonga).

DALHOUSIE, 17th Earl of *cr* 1633; **James Hubert Ramsay,** Baron Ramsay 1618; Lord Ramsay 1633; Baron Ramsay (UK) 1875; DL; Director, Jamestown Investments Ltd, since 1987; *b* 17 Jan. 1948; *er s* of 16th Earl of Dalhousie, KT, GCVO, GBE, MC; *m* 1973, Marilyn, *yr d* of Major Sir David Butter, *qv*; one *s* two *d*. *Educ:* Ampleforth. 2nd Bn Coldstream Guards, commnd 1968–71, RARO 1971. Director: Hambros Bank Ltd, 1981–82; (exec.) Enskilda Securities, 1982–87; Capel-Cure Myers Capital Management Ltd, 1988–91; Dunedin Smaller Cos Investment Trust, 1993– (Chm., 1998–); Scottish Woodlands Ltd, 1993– (Chm., 1998–). Chm., (Scotland) Mental Health Foundn, 2000. Brig., Royal Co. of Archers (The Queen's Body Guard for Scotland). Vice Chm., Game Conservancy Trust, 1994–; Pres., British Deer Soc., 1987–. DL Angus, 1993. OStJ. *Heir:* *s* Lord Ramsay, *qv*. *Address:* Brechin Castle, Brechin, Angus DD9 6SH. *Clubs:* White's, Pratt's, Caledonian (Pres., 1990–), Turf.

DALITZ, Prof. Richard Henry, FRS 1960; Professor Emeritus, Oxford University, and Emeritus Fellow of All Souls, since 1990; *b* 28 Feb. 1925; *s* of Frederick W. and Hazel B. Dalitz, Melbourne, Australia; *m* 1946, Valda (*née* Suiter), Melbourne, Australia; one *s* three *d*. *Educ:* Scotch Coll., Melbourne; Univ. of Melbourne; Trinity Coll., Univ. of Cambridge, PhD Cantab, 1950. Lecturer in Mathematical Physics, Univ. of Birmingham, 1949–55; research appointments in various Univs, USA, 1953–55; Reader in Mathematical Physics, Univ. of Birmingham, 1955–56; Prof. of Physics, Univ. of Chicago, 1956–66; Royal Soc. Res. Prof., Oxford Univ., 1963–90; Fellow of All Souls Coll., Oxford, 1964–90. Mem. Council, Royal Soc., 1979–81. Corresp. Mem., Australian Acad. of Science, 1978; Foreign Member: Polish Acad. of Sci., 1980; Nat. Acad. of India, 1990; For. Assoc., US Nat. Acad. Scis, 1991. Maxwell Medal and Prize, Institute of Physics and the Physical Soc., 1966; Bakerian Lectr and Jaffe Prize, 1969, Hughes Medal, 1975, Royal Medal, 1982, Royal Soc.; J. Robert Oppenheimer Meml Prize, Univ. of Miami, 1980; Harrie Massey Prize, Inst. of Physics and Aust. Inst. of Physics, 1990. *Publications:* Strange Particles and Strong Interactions, 1962; Nuclear Interactions of the Hyperons, 1965; (ed jtly) High Energy Physics, 1965; (jtly) Nuclear Energy Today and Tomorrow, 1971; (jtly) Paul A. M. Dirac 1902–1984, 1986; (jtly) A Breadth of Physics, 1988; (ed) Collected Works of P. A. M. Dirac 1924–48, 1995; (jtly) Selected Scientific Papers of Sir Rudolf Peierls, 1997; (ed jtly) The Foundations of Newtonian Scholarship, 2000; numerous papers on theoretical physics in various British and American scientific jls. *Recreations:* travelling, biographical research, study of the Sorbian (Wendish) people, especially their language and emigration. *Address:* 1 Keble Road, Oxford OX1 3NP. *T:* (01865) 273966; All Souls College, Oxford.

DALKEITH, Earl of; Richard Walter John Montagu Douglas Scott, KBE 2000; DL; *b* 14 Feb. 1954; *s* and *heir* of 9th Duke of Buccleuch, *qv*; *m* 1981, Lady Elizabeth Kerr, *d* of Marquess of Lothian, *qv*; two *s* two *d*. *Educ:* Eton; Christ Church, Oxford. Dir, Border Television, 1989–90, 2000. Member: Nature Conservancy Council, 1989–91; Nature Conservancy Council for Scotland, 1991–92; Scottish Natural Heritage, 1992–95 (Chm., SW Reg., 1992–95); IBA, 1990; ITC, 1991–98 (Dep. Chm., 1996–98); Millennium Commn, 1994–. Trustee: Nat. Heritage Meml Fund, 2000–; Heritage Lottery Fund, 2000–; Pres., RSGS, 1999–. Mem. Council, Winston Churchill Meml Trust, 1993–. Dist Councillor, Nithsdale, 1984–90. DL Nithsdale and Annandale and Eskdale, 1987. *Heir:* *s* Lord Eskdaill, *qv*. *Address:* Dabton, Thornhill, Dumfriesshire DG3 5AR. *T:* (01848) 330467; 24 Lansdowne Road, W11 3LL. *T:* (020) 7727 6573.

DALLAT, John James; Member (SDLP) Londonderry East, Northern Ireland Assembly, since 1998; *b* 24 March 1947; *s* of Daniel and Ellen Dallat; *m* 1975, Anne Philomena Long; two *s* one *d*. *Educ:* Coleraine Coll. of Further Educn (qual. teacher, commercial subjects, 1968); North West Inst., Derry (Business Studies Teacher's Dip., 1975); Univ. of Ulster (Dip. in Advanced Studies in Educn, 1979); UC, Galway (Dip. in Rural Studies, 1997). Teacher: Technical Coll., Carndonagh, 1968–74; St Paul's Coll., Kilrea, 1975–98. Mem. (SDLP) Coleraine BC, 1977–98. Contested (SDLP) Londonderry East, 2001. *Recreations:* attending meetings!, walking, reading. *Address:* Northern Ireland Assembly, Stormont Castle, Belfast BT4 3ST. *T:* (028) 2554 0798, *Fax:* (028) 2554 1798.

DALMENY, Lord; Harry Ronald Neil Primrose; *b* 20 Nov. 1967; *s* and *heir* of 7th Earl of Rosebery, *qv*; *m* 1994, Caroline, *e d* of Ronald Daglish and Mrs William Wyatt-Lowe. *Educ:* Dragon Sch., Oxford; Eton Coll.; Trinity Coll., Cambridge (BA Hons). *Address:* Dalmeny House, South Queensferry, West Lothian EH30 9TQ. *T:* (0131) 331 1784. *Clubs:* Beefsteak; University Pitt (Cambridge); St Moritz Tobogganing.

DALRYMPLE, family name of **Earl of Stair**.

DALRYMPLE, Sir Hew (Fleetwood) Hamilton-, 10th Bt, *cr* 1697; GCVO 2001 (KCVO 1985; CVO 1974); JP; late Major, Grenadier Guards; Lord-Lieutenant of East Lothian, 1987–2001 (Vice-Lieutenant, 1973–87); *b* 9 April 1926; *er s* of Sir Hew (Clifford) Hamilton-Dalrymple, 9th Bt, JP; *S* father, 1959; *m* 1954, Lady Anne-Louise Mary Keppel, *d* of 9th Earl of Albemarle, MC, and of (Diana Cicely) Countess of Albemarle, *qv*; four *s*. *Educ:* Ampleforth. Commnd, Grenadier Guards, 1944; Staff Coll., Camberley, 1957; DAAG HQ 3rd Div., 1958–60; Regimental Adjt, Grenadier Guards, 1960–62; retd 1962. Adjt, 1964–85, Pres. of Council, 1988–96, and Captain General and Gold Stick, 1996–, Queen's Body Guard for Scotland (Royal Company of Archers). Vice-Chm., Scottish & Newcastle Breweries, 1983–86 (Dir, 1967–86); Chm., Scottish American Investment Co., 1985–91 (Dir, 1967–93). DL 1964, JP 1987, East Lothian. *Heir:* *e s* Hew Richard Hamilton-Dalrymple [*b* 3 Sept. 1955; *m* 1987, Jane Elizabeth, *yr d* of Lt-Col John Morris; one *s* three *d*. *Educ:* Ampleforth; Corpus Christi Coll., Oxford (MA); Clare Hall, Cambridge (MPhil); Birkbeck Coll., London (MSc). ODI Fellow, Swaziland, 1982–84]. *Address:* Leuchie, North Berwick, East Lothian EH39 5NT. *T:* (01620) 892903. *Club:* Cavalry and Guards.

See also W. B. H. Dalrymple.

DALRYMPLE, William Benedict Hamilton; writer; *b* 20 March 1965; *s* of Sir Hew (Fleetwood) Hamilton-Dalrymple, *qv*; *m* 1991, Olivia Fraser; two *s* one *d*. *Educ:* Ampleforth Coll.; Trinity Coll., Cambridge (Exhibr; Sen. Hist. Schol., MA Hons 1992). Feature writer, Independent mag., 1988–89; India corresp., Sunday Corresp., 1989–90. Television series: Stones of the Raj, 1997; Indian Journeys, 2000. FRSL 1993; FRGS 1993; FRAS 1998. *Publications:* In Xanadu, 1989 (Yorks Post Best First Work Award, Scottish Arts Council Spring Book Award, 1990); City of Djinns, 1993 (Thomas Cook Travel Book Award, Sunday Times Young British Writer of Year Award, 1994); From the Holy Mountain (Scottish Arts Council Autumn Book Award), 1997; The Age of Kali (collected journalism), 1998; contribs to jls incl. TLS, Granta, Sunday Times and Guardian. *Address:* 1 & 2 Pages' Yard, Church Street, Old Chiswick, W4 2PA. *T:* (020) 8994 4500, *Fax:* (020) 8994 2660.

DALRYMPLE-HAMILTON of Bargany, Captain North Edward Frederick, CVO 1961; MBE 1953; DSC 1943; JP; Royal Navy; *b* 17 Feb. 1922; *s* of Admiral Sir Frederick Dalrymple-Hamilton of Bargany, KCB; *m* 1st, 1949, Hon. Mary Colville (*d* 1981), *d* of 1st Baron Clydesmuir, PC, GCIE, TD; two *s*; 2nd, 1983, Antoinette, *widow* of Major Rowland Beech, MC. *Educ:* Eton. Entered Royal Navy, 1940; Comdr 1954; Captain 1960. Comdg Officer HMS Scarborough, 1958; Executive Officer, HM Yacht Britannia, 1959; Captain (F) 17th Frigate Squadron, 1963; Dir of Naval Signals, 1965; Dir, Weapons Equipment Surface, 1967; retd, 1970. Lieut, Royal Company of Archers, Queen's Body Guard for Scotland. DL 1973, JP 1980, Ayrshire. *Address:* 3 New Court, Sutton Manor, Sutton Scotney, Winchester SO21 3JX. *T:* (01962) 761862. *Clubs:* Pratt's, Army and Navy, MCC.

DALRYMPLE HAMILTON, (North) John (Frederick), OBE 1992; TD 1989; farmer, since 1982; Vice Lord-Lieutenant, Ayrshire and Arran, since 1998; *b* 7 May 1950; *s* of Capt. North Edward Frederick Dalrymple-Hamilton, *qv*, and late Hon. Mary Colville; *m* 1980, Sally Anne How; two *s* one *d*. *Educ:* Eton Coll.; Aberdeen Univ. (MA Hons 1972); E of Scotland Coll. of Agriculture (Cert. Agric. 1983). Sales Manager, Scottish & Newcastle Breweries, 1973–82; Bargany estate, 1983–. Commnd TA, 1970; CO, QOY, 1989–92; Dep. Comdr (Col), 52 Bde, 1993–94. DL Ayrshire and Arran, 1995–98. *Address:* Lovestone House, Bargany, Girvan, Ayrshire KA26 9RF. *T:* (01465) 871227. *Club:* New (Edinburgh).

DALRYMPLE-HAY, Sir James Brian, 6th Bt *cr* 1798; estate agent, retired; *b* 19 Jan. 1928; *e s* of Lt-Col Brian George Rowland Dalrymple-Hay (*d* on active service, 1943) and Beatrice (*d* 1935), *d* of A. W. Inglis; *S* cousin, 1952; *m* 1958, Helen Sylvia, *d* of late Stephen Herbert Card and of Molly M. Card; three *d*. *Educ:* Hillsbrow Preparatory Sch., Redhill; Blundell's Sch., Tiverton, Devon. Royal Marine, 1946–47; Lieut Royal Marine Commando, 1947–49. Estate Agent and Surveyor's Pupil, 1949; Principal, 1955–67; Partner, Whiteheads PLC, Estate Agents, 1967, Dir, 1983–85; Principal, Dalrymple-Hay Overseas, 1985–87. *Heir:* *b* John Hugh Dalrymple-Hay [*b* 16 Dec. 1929; *m* 1962, Jennifer, *d* of late Brig. Robert Johnson, CBE; one *s*]. *Address:* The Red House, Church Street, Warnham, near Horsham, W Sussex RH12 3QW.

DALRYMPLE-WHITE, Sir Henry Arthur Dalrymple, 2nd Bt *cr* 1926; DFC 1941 and Bar 1942; *b* 5 Nov. 1917; *o s* of Lt-Col Sir Godfrey Dalrymple-White, 1st Bt, and late Hon. Catherine Mary Cary, *d* of 12th Viscount Falkland; *S* father, 1954; *m* 1948, Mary (marr. diss. 1956), *o d* of Capt. Robert H. C. Thomas; one *s*. *Educ:* Eton; Magdalene Coll., Cambridge; London Univ. Formerly Wing Commander RAFVR. Served War of 1939–45. *Heir:* *s* Jan Hew Dalrymple-White, *b* 26 Nov. 1950. *Address:* Fairseat Foundation, PO Box 670, Village Market, Nairobi, Kenya.

DALSAGER, Poul Christian; Member, Commission of the European Communities, 1981–84; *b* 5 March 1929; *m* 1951, Betty Jørgensen; two *s*. *Educ:* grammar sch. Bank employee, 1945–64; Mem. (Social Democrat), Danish Parliament, 1964–81; Chm., Market Cttee of Parlt, 1971–73; Chm., Social-Democratic Gp in Parlt, 1978–79; Minister for: Agriculture and Fisheries, 1975–77 and 1979–81; Agriculture, 1977–78. Mem. and Vice Pres., European Parlt, 1973 and 1974. Delegate to UN Gen. Assembly, 1969–71. Mayor, Hjørring, 1990–95 (Dep. Mayor, 1986–90). *Address:* Nørregade 4-3, 9800 Hjørring, Denmark.

DALTON, Sir Alan (Nugent Goring), Kt 1977; CBE 1969; DL; Chairman: Devon and Cornwall Development Company, 1988–91; British Railways (Western) Board, 1978–92; *b* 26 Nov. 1923; *s* of Harold Goring Dalton and Phyllis Marguerite (*née* Ash). *Educ:* Shendish Prep. Sch., King's Langley; King Edward VI Sch., Southampton. Man. Dir, English Clays, Lovering Pochin & Co. Ltd, 1961–84; Dep. Chm., 1968–84, Chm., 1984–89, English China Clays PLC. Member: Sun Alliance & London Assurance Group Bd, 1976–89; Western (formerly SW) Adv. Bd, Nat. Westminster Bank PLC, 1977–91; Director, Westland plc (formerly Westland Aircraft), 1980–85. DL Cornwall, 1982. *Recreations:* sailing, painting, reading.

DALTON, Alfred Hyam, CB 1976; Deputy Chairman, Board of Inland Revenue, 1973–82 (Commissioner of Inland Revenue, 1970–82); *b* 29 March 1922; *m* 1946, Elizabeth Stalker (*d* 1992); three *d*; *m* 1995, Sylvia Winifred West (*née* Boyce). *Educ:* Merchant Taylors' Sch., Northwood; Aberdeen Univ. Served War, REME, 1942–45 (despatches). Entered Inland Revenue, 1947; Asst Sec., 1958; Sec. to Board, 1969. *Address:* 22 Clifton Avenue, Eaglescliffe TS16 9BA. *T:* (01642) 648850.

DALTON, Duncan Edward S.; *see* Shipley Dalton.

DALTON, Vice-Adm. Sir Geoffrey (Thomas James Oliver), KCB 1986; Secretary-General of Mencap, 1987–90; *b* 14 April 1931; *s* of late Jack Rowland Thomas Dalton and Margaret Kathleen Dalton; *m* 1957, Jane Hamilton (*née* Baynes); four *s*. *Educ:* Parkfield, Sussex; Reigate Grammar Sch.; RNC Dartmouth. Midshipman 1950; served in HM Ships Illustrious, Loch Alvie, Cockade, Virago, Flag Lieut to C-in-C The Nore, and HMS Maryton (in comd), 1950–61; served HMS Murray, RN Staff Course and HMS Dido, 1961–66; served HMS Relentless (in Comd), RN Sch. of PT, HMS Nubian (in Comd), Staff of Flag Officers Second in Comd Far East Fleet and Second Flotilla, 1966–72; Asst Dir of Naval Plans, 1972–74; RCDS, 1975; Captain RN Presentation Team, 1976–77; in Comd HMS Jupiter, 1977–79 and HMS Dryad, 1979–81; Asst Chief of Naval Staff (Policy), 1981–84; Dep. SACLANT, 1984–87. Commander, 1966; Captain, 1972; Rear-Adm. 1981; Vice-Adm. 1984. President: RBL, 1993–97; Regular Forces Employment Assoc., 1999–; Chm., Ex-Services Fellowship Centres, 1991–. Hon. Col 71st (Yeomanry) Signal Regt (Volunteers), 1998–2001. Gov., QMW, 1992–. Mem. Ct of Assts, Drapers' Co., 1989– (Master, 1996). FIMgt (FBIM 1987). *Recreations:* tennis, ski-ing, fishing, gardening, motor cycling, walking. *Address:* Farm Cottage, Catherington, Waterlooville, Hants PO8 0TD. *Club:* Royal Over-Seas League.

DALTON, Prof. Howard, FRS 1993; Professor since 1983, and Chairman since 1999, Department of Biological Sciences, Warwick University; *b* 8 Feb. 1944; *s* of Leslie Alfred and Florence Dalton; *m* 1971, Kira Rozdestvensky; three *s* one *d*. *Educ:* Queen Elizabeth Coll., London Univ. (BSc); Univ. of Sussex (DPhil). Univs of London, 1962–65, and Sussex, 1965–68; Postdoctoral Fellow: Purdue Univ., Indiana, 1968–70; Sussex Univ., 1970–73; posts at Warwick Univ., 1973–. Pres., Soc. for Gen. Microbiology, 1997–2000. Leeuwenhoek Lectr, Royal Soc., 2000. *Publications:* contribs to learned scientific jls. *Recreations:* Real tennis, Japanese gardening. *Address:* Groves Mill, Shakers Lane, Long Itchington, Warwickshire CV47 9QB. *T:* (01926) 632746. *Club:* Leamington Tennis Court.

DALTON, Irwin, CBE 1986; Executive Vice-Chairman, 1985–88, and Chief Executive (Operations), 1986–88, National Bus Company; *b* 25 July 1932; *s* of Harry Farr Dalton and Bessie Dalton; *m* 1954, Marie Davies; two *d*. *Educ:* Cockburn High Sch., Leeds. FCA 1973; FCIT 1978. Accountancy profession, 1947–62; Asst Company Sec., 1962–67, Company Sec., 1968–70, West Riding Automobile, Wakefield; Company Sec., Crosville Motor Services, 1971–74; Dir and Gen. Manager, Ribble Motor Services, 1974–76; National Bus Company: Regional Dir, 1977–81; Mem. for Personnel Services, 1981–83; Exec. Bd Mem., 1983–84. Dir, Leyland Bus Gp, 1987–88. A Vice-Pres., Bus and Coach Council, 1983–87, Pres., 1987–88. *Recreations:* golf, other sporting activities. *Address:* Westview, 1 Birling Park Avenue, Birling Road, Tunbridge Wells, Kent TN2 5LQ. *T:* (01892) 533459. *Club:* Tunbridge Wells Golf.

DALTON, Maurice Leonard, LVO 1986 (MVO 1981); OBE 1996; HM Diplomatic Service, retired; Counsellor, Foreign and Commonwealth Office, and HM First Assistant Marshal of the Diplomatic Corps, 1998–2000; *b* 18 May 1944; *s* of late Albert William Dalton and Mildred Eliza (*née* Wraight); *m* 1982, Cathy Lee Parker. Joined FO, 1965; Enugu and Lagos, 1967–68; FCO, 1968–70; Attaché, Ankara, 1970–72; Third Secretary: E Berlin, 1973–74; Abu Dhabi, 1974–76; Second Sec., FCO, 1977–79; Second, later First Sec., Oslo, 1979–83; First Secretary: Kuala Lumpur, 1983–86; Peking, 1986; FCO, 1987–92; Asst Head of Protocol Dept, FCO, and Asst Marshal of Diplomatic Corps, 1992–96; Counsellor and Head of Conference Dept, FCO, 1996–98; Head of Protocol Dept, FCO, 1998–99. Royal Norwegian Order: of St Olav, 1981; of Merit, 1994. *Recreations:* genealogy, cross-country ski-ing, sailing. *Address:* 2 Loggetts, Alleyn Park, SE21 8AS.

DALTON, Peter Gerald Fox, CMG 1958; *b* 12 Dec. 1914; *s* of late Sir Robert (William) Dalton, CMG; *m* 1944, Josephine Anne Helyar; one *s* one *d*. *Educ:* Uppingham Sch.; Oriel Coll., Oxford. HM Embassy, Peking 1937–39; HM Consulate-Gen., Hankow, 1939–41; HM Embassy, Chungking, 1941–42; Foreign Office, 1942–46; HM Legation, Bangkok, 1946; HM Embassy, Montevideo, 1947–50; Foreign Office, 1950–53; Political Adviser, Hong Kong, 1953–56; Foreign Office, 1957–60; HM Embassy, Warsaw, 1960–63; HM Consul-General: Los Angeles, 1964–65; San Francisco, 1965–67; Minister, HM Embassy, Moscow, 1967–69; retd from HM Diplomatic Service, 1969. *Address:* North Lodge, North Street, Mayfield, Sussex TN20 6AN. *T:* (01435) 873421.

DALTON, Richard John, CMG 1996; HM Diplomatic Service; Ambassador to Libya, since 1999; *b* 10 Oct. 1948; *s* of Maj.-Gen. John Cecil D'Arcy Dalton, CB, CBE and Pamela Frances (*née* Segrave); *m* 1972, Elisabeth Mary Keays; two *s* two *d* (and one *s* decd). *Educ:* Winchester Coll.; Magdalene Coll., Cambridge (BA). Joined HM Diplomatic Service, 1970: FCO, 1971; MECAS, 1971–73; 3rd Sec., Amman, 1973–75; 2nd, later 1st, Sec., Mission to UN, NY, 1975–79; FCO, 1979–83; Dep. Head of Mission, Muscat, 1983–87; Dep. Head, Southern African Dept, FCO, 1987–88; Head, Tropical Foods Div. and Ext. Relns and Trade Div., MAFF, 1988–91; Vis. Fellow, RIIA, 1991–92; Head, CSCE Unit, FCO, 1992–93; Consul Gen., Jerusalem, 1993–97; Dir (Personnel), FCO, 1998–99. *Publication:* Peace in the Gulf: a long term view, 1992. *Recreation:* land and woodland management. *Address:* c/o Foreign and Commonwealth Office, King Charles Street, SW1A 2AH; Hauxwell Hall, Leyburn, N Yorks DL8 5LR.

DALTON, William, FCIB, FICB; Chief Executive, HSBC (formerly Midland) Bank plc, since 1998; *b* 8 Dec. 1943; *s* of Albert and Emily Dalton; *m* 1994, Starr Underhill; one *s* one *d*. *Educ:* Univ. of British Colombia (BComm 1971). FICB 1971; FCIB 1998. Joined Bank of Montreal, 1961; Wardley Canada Ltd, later HSBC Bank, Canada, 1980, Pres. and CEO, 1992–97; Dep. Chm., Merrill Lynch HSBC Ltd, 2000–; Director: HSBC Holdings, 1998–; HSBC Investment Bank Holdings, 1998–; HSBC Private Banking Hldgs (Suisse) SA, 2001–; Crédit Commercial de France, 2000–. Non-exec. Dir, Mastercard Internat., 1998–. Chm., Young Enterprise UK, 1998–; Trustee, Crimestoppers Trust, 2000–. *Address:* HSBC Bank plc, 27–32 Poultry, EC2P 2BX. *T:* (020) 7260 8000.

DALY, His Eminence Cardinal Cahal Brendan; Roman Catholic Archbishop Emeritus of Armagh and Primate Emeritus of All Ireland; *b* 1 Oct. 1917. *Educ:* St Malachy's Coll., Belfast; Queen's Univ., Belfast (BA Hons, Classics, MA); St Patrick's Coll., Maynooth (LTh 1942, DTh 1944; DD); Institut Catholique, Paris (LPh 1953); DHL Sacred Heart Univ., Conn, USA. Ordained priest, 1941. Classics Master, St Malachy's Coll., Belfast, 1945–46; Lecturer in Scholastic Philosophy, 1946–63; Reader, 1963–67, Queen's Univ., Belfast; consecrated Bishop, 1967; Bishop of Ardagh and Clonmacnois, 1967–82; Bishop of Down and Connor, 1982–90; Archbishop of Armagh and Primate of All Ireland, 1990–96. Cardinal, 1991. Hon. DD: QUB; Exeter; Hon. DLitt TCD; Hon. LLD: NUI; Notre Dame, Indiana; St John's, NY; Sacred Heart, Fairfield, Conn. *Publications:* Morals, Law and Life, 1962; Natural Law Morality Today, 1965; Violence in Ireland and Christian Conscience, 1973; Theologians and the Magisterium, 1977; Peace the Work of Justice, 1979; The Price of Peace, 1991; Tertullian: the Puritan and his influence, 1993; Morals and Law, 1993; Northern Ireland—Peace—Now is the Time, 1994; Love begins at Home, 1995; Moral Philosophy in Britain from Bradley to Wittgenstein, 1996; Steps on my Pilgrim Journey, 1998; The Minding of Planet Earth, 2000; chapters in: Prospect for Metaphysics, 1961; Intellect and Hope, 1968; New Essays in Religious Language, 1969; Understanding the Eucharist, 1969. *Address:* Ard Mhacha, 23 Rosetta Avenue, Belfast BT7 3HG.

DALY, Carol Yvonne; Headmistress, St Albans High School for Girls, since 1994; *b* 3 April 1950; *d* of Ronald D. Meeks and Irene M. A. Meeks (*née* Wright); *m* 1972, Nicholas John Peter Daly; one *d*. *Educ:* Nottingham Univ. (BSc Hons Geol. and Chem.; PGCE). Housemistress and Hd of Chemistry, King's Sch., Ely, 1973–85; Sen. Mistress, Netherhall Sch., Cambridge, 1985–90; Headmistress, Forest Girls' Sch., Snaresbrook, 1990–94. FRSA 1992. *Recreations:* gardening, travel, reading. *Address:* St Albans High School for Girls, Townsend Avenue, St Albans, Herts AL1 3SJ. *T:* (01727) 853800.

DALY, Hon. Francis Lenton; Judge of District Courts, Queensland, Australia, 1989–99; Judge of Planning and Environment Court, Queensland, 1994–99; *b* 23 June 1938; *s* of late Sydney Richard Daly and Lilian May Daly (*née* Lindholm); *m* 1964, Joyce Brenda (*née* Nicholls). *Educ:* Forest School; London School of Economics (LLB). Called to Bar, Gray's Inn, 1961 (Lord Justice Holker Exhibn). English Bar, 1961–66; Legal Secretary, Lord Chancellor's Office, 1966; Bermudian Bar, 1966–72; Asst Judge Advocate General to the Forces, UK, 1972–78; Principal Magistrate, Malaita, Solomon Islands, 1978; Attorney General, 1979, Chief Justice, 1980–84, Solomon Islands; Chief Justice, Nauru, 1983; admitted, Qld Bar, 1984. *Publications:* contribs to International and Comparative Law Qly, Commonwealth Judicial Jl. *Recreations:* yachting, rowing, reading. *Address:* 97 Florence Terrace, Scotland Island, Sydney, NSW 2105, Australia. *T:* (2) 99974631.

See also O. L. Aikin.

DALY, James, CVO 1994; HM Diplomatic Service, retired; High Commissioner, Mauritius, 1997–2000; *b* 8 Sept. 1940; *s* of late Maurice Daly and Christina Daly; *m* 1970, Dorothy Lillian Powell; two *s*. *Educ:* St Thomas More, Chelsea; University College London (BSc Hons Econ). Served RM, 1958–67. Joined Foreign Office, 1968: Third Secretary: Accra, 1971–73; Moscow, 1973–76; Second Sec., Karachi, 1976–78; First Secretary: FCO, 1978–79; Sofia, 1979–86; Consul-Gen., Paris, 1986–92; Counsellor and Consul-Gen., Moscow, 1992–95; High Comr, Vanuatu, 1995–97. *Recreations:* reading, music, walking. *Address:* Thwaite House, Ampleforth, York YO62 4DX. *T:* (01439) 788649, *Fax:* (01439) 788814; *e-mail:* jim.daly@btinternet.com. *Club:* Naval and Military.

DALY, Lawrence; General Secretary, National Union of Mineworkers, 1968–84, retired; *b* 20 Oct. 1924; *s* of James Daly and late Janet Taylor; *m* 1948, Renée M. Baxter; four *s* one *d*. *Educ:* primary and secondary schools. Glencraig Colliery (underground), 1939; Workmen's Safety Inspector, there, 1954–64. Part-time NUM lodge official, Glencraig, 1946; Chm., Scottish NUM Youth Committee, 1949; elected to Scottish Area NUM Exec. Cttee, 1962; Gen. Sec., Scottish NUM, 1964; National Exec., NUM, 1965. Mem., TUC General Council, 1971–81. TUC Gold Badge, 1981. *Publications:* (pamphlets): A Young Miner Sees Russia, 1946; The Miners and the Nation, 1968. *Recreations:* literature, politics, folk-song.

DALY, Margaret Elizabeth; *b* 26 Jan. 1938; *d* of Robert and Elizabeth Bell; *m* 1964, Kenneth Anthony Edward Daly; one *d*. *Educ:* Methodist Coll., Belfast. Departmental Head, Phoenix Assurance Co., 1956–60; Trade Union Official, Guild of Insurance Officials, later Union of Insurance Staffs, and subseq. merged with ASTMS, 1960–71; Consultant, Cons. Party, 1976–79; Nat. Dir of Cons. Trade Unionists, 1979–84. MEP (C) Somerset and Dorset W, 1984–94; contested (C) Somerset and N Devon, Eur. Parly elecns, 1994; Mem., Develt Cttee, Eur. Parlt, 1984–94 (Vice Chm., 1987–89; Cons. spokesman, 1989–94); Vice-Pres., Jt EEC/African Caribbean Pacific Lomé Assembly, 1988–94. Contested (C), Weston-super-Mare, 1997. Mem. Bd, Traidcraft PLC, 1995–98. Mgt Bd, European Movt, 1999–; Chair, Somerset European Movt; Mem. Bd, South West in Europe, 2000–. *Recreations:* swimming, music, travel. *Address:* The Old School House, Aisholt, Bridgwater, Somerset TA5 1AR.

DALY, Michael de Burgh, MA, MD, ScD Cambridge; FRCP; Emeritus Professor of Physiology in the University of London, since 1984; Distinguished Visitor (formerly Visiting Scientist), Department of Physiology, Royal Free and University College Medical School, Royal Free Campus (formerly Royal Free Hospital School of Medicine), London, since 1984; *b* 7 May 1922; *s* of late Dr Ivan de Burgh Daly, CBE, FRS; *m* 1948, Beryl Esmé, *y d* of late Wing Commander A. J. Nightingale; two *s*. *Educ:* Loretto Sch., Edinburgh; Gonville and Caius Coll., Cambridge; St Bartholomew's Hospital. Nat. Science Tripos Part I, 1943, Part II, 1944, Physiology with Pharmacology. House-physician, St Bartholomew's Hospital, 1947; Asst Lecturer, 1948–50, and Lecturer, 1950–54, in Physiology, University Coll., London. Rockefeller Foundation Travelling Fellowship in Medicine, 1952–53; Locke Research Fellow of Royal Soc., 1955–58; St Bartholomew's Hospital Medical College: Prof. and Hd of Dept of Physiology, 1958–84; Governor, 1975–95; Treas., 1983–84. Vis. Prof. of Physiology, Univ. of NSW, 1966; Vis. Lectr, Swedish Univs, 1959–60; G. L. Brown Lectr, Physiological Soc., 1985–86. Member: Personnel Res. Ethics Cttee, MoD (Navy) (formerly Adv. Panel for Underwater Personnel Res., MoD), 1975– (Chm., 1990–); MRC/RN Personnel Res. Cttee, Underwater Physiology Sub-Cttee, 1975–94; Res. Funds Cttee, British Heart Foundn, 1982–85; Armed Services Consultant Approval Bd in Applied Physiology/Aviation Medicine, MoD, 1989–. Mem., 1981–84, Chm., 1984–, Editorial Bd of Monographs of Physiological Soc.; Co-Editor of Journal of Physiology, 1956–63, 1984–89. FRSocMed 1959. Member: Soc. of Experimental Biol., 1965–; Physiological Soc., 1951–86 (Hon. Mem., 1986); Osler Med. Club, 1974–87; European Underwater Biomed. Soc., 1971–; Undersea Med. Soc. Inc., 1971–88. Schafer Prize in Physiology, University Coll., London, 1953; Thruston Medal, Gonville and Caius Coll., 1957; Sir Lionel Whitby Medal, Cambridge Univ., 1963; Gold Medal (jtly), BMA, 1972. *Publications:* Peripheral Arterial Chemoreceptors and Respiratory-Cardiovascular Integration, 1997; contributor to: Lippold and Winton, Human Physiology; Starling, Principles of Human Physiology; Emslie-Smith, Paterson, Scratcherd and Read, Textbook of Physiology; papers on the integrative control of respiration and the cardiovascular system in Journal of Physiology; contrib. to film on William Harvey and the Circulation of the Blood. *Recreation:* model engineering. *Address:* 7 Hall Drive, Sydenham, SE26 6XL. *T:* (020) 8778 8773.

DALY, Michael Francis, CMG 1989; HM Diplomatic Service, retired; *b* 7 April 1931; *s* of late William Thomas Daly and Hilda Frances Daly; *m* 1st, 1963, Sally Malcolm Angwin (*d* 1966); one *d*; 2nd, 1971, Juliet Mary Siragusa (*née* Arning); one step-*d*. *Educ:* Downside; Gonville and Caius Coll., Cambridge (Scholar; MA). Mil. Service, 1952–54: 2nd Lieut, Intell. Corps. E. D. Sassoon Banking Co., London, 1954; Transreef Industrial & Investment Co., Johannesburg, 1955–66; General Electric Co., London, 1966; HM Diplomatic Service: 1st Sec., FCO, 1967; 1st Sec. (Commercial), Rio de Janeiro, 1969; 1st Sec. (Inf.) and Head of Chancery, Dublin, 1973; Asst, Cultural Relations Dept, FCO,

1976; Counsellor, Consul-Gen. and Head of Chancery, Brasilia, 1977–78; Ambassador to Ivory Coast, Upper Volta and Niger, 1978–83; Head of West African Dept, FCO, and Ambassador (non-resident) to Chad, 1983–86; Ambassador: to Costa Rica and (non-resident) to Nicaragua, 1986–89; to Bolivia, 1989–91. Treas., Anglo-Central American Soc., 1996– (Chm., 1991–96); Sec., Margaret Mee Fellowship Programme, 1993–. *Recreations:* sailing, theatre, golf. *Address:* 45 Priory Road, Kew, Surrey TW9 3DQ. *T:* (020) 8940 1272. *Club:* Canning.

DALY, Lt-Gen. Sir Thomas (Joseph), KBE 1967 (CBE 1953; OBE 1944); CB 1965; DSO 1945; Chief of the General Staff, Australia, 1966–71; *b* 19 March 1913; *s* of late Lt-Col T. J. Daly, DSO, VD, Melbourne; *m* 1946, Heather, *d* of late James Fitzgerald, Melbourne; three *d. Educ:* St Patrick's Coll., Sale; Xavier Coll., Kew, Vic; RMC, Duntroon (Sword of Honour). 3rd LH, 1934; attached for training 16/5 Lancers, India, 1938; 3rd Carabiniers, 1939; Adjt, 2/10 Aust. Inf. Bn, 1939; Bde Major, 18 Inf. Bde, 1940 (despatches); GSO2 6 Aust. Div., 1941; GSO1 5 Aust. Div., 1942 (despatches); Instructor, Staff Sch. (Aust.), 1944; CO 2/10 Inf. Bn, AIF, 1944; Instr, Staff Coll., Camberley, UK, 1946; Joint Services Staff Coll., Latimer, 1948; Dir of Mil. Art, RMC Duntroon, 1949; Dir of Infantry, AHQ, 1951; Comd 28 Brit. Commonwealth Inf. Bde, Korea, 1952; Dir, Ops and Plans, AHQ, 1953; IDC, London, 1956; GOC Northern Command, Australia, 1957–60; Adjt Gen., 1961–63; GOC, Eastern Command, Australia, 1963–66. Col Comdt, Royal Australian Regt, and Pacific Is Regt, 1971–75. Director: Jennings Industries Ltd, 1974–85; Fruehauf Australia Ltd, 1974–88; Associated Merchant Bank (Singapore), 1975–77. Mem., Nat. Council, Australian Red Cross, 1972–75; Chm., Council, Australian Nat. War Memorial, 1974–82 (Mem., 1966–74); Councillor, Royal Agricl Soc. of NSW, 1972–85. Legion of Merit (US), 1953. *Recreations:* golf, watching football, cricket. *Address:* 16 Victoria Road, Bellevue Hill, NSW 2023, Australia. *Clubs:* Australian (Sydney); Ski Club of Australia (Thredbo, NSW); Royal Sydney Golf.

DALYELL, Kathleen Mary Agnes; DL; National Trust for Scotland Administrator at The Binns, since 1972; Chairman, Royal Commission on Ancient and Historical Monuments of Scotland, since 2000; Member, Royal Fine Art Commission for Scotland, since 1992; *b* 17 Nov. 1937; *o d* of Rt Hon. Lord Wheatley and Agnes (Nancy) Lady Wheatley (*née* Nichol); *m* 1963, Tam Dalyell, *qv*; one *s* one *d. Educ:* Convent of the Sacred Heart, Aberdeen; Edinburgh Univ. (MA Hons History 1960); Craiglochart Teacher Trng Coll., Edinburgh. Teacher of History: St Augustine's Secondary Sch., Glasgow, 1961–62; James Gillespie's High Sch. for Girls, Edinburgh, 1962–63. Member: Historic Buildings Council for Scotland, 1975–87; Lady Provost of Edinburgh's Delegn to China, 1987; Nat. Cttee of Architectural Heritage Soc. for Scotland, 1983–89 (Vice-Chm., 1986–89); Ancient Monuments Bd for Scotland, 1989–99. Chm., Bo'ness Heritage Trust, 1988–93; Director: Heritage Educn Trust, 1987–; Weslo Housing Assoc., 1994–; Trustee: Paxton Trust, 1988–92; Carmont Settlement Trust, 1997–. DL W Lothian, 2001. *Publication:* House of The Binns, 1973. *Recreations:* reading, travel, chess, hill walking. *Address:* The Binns, Blackness, Linlithgow, Scotland EH49 7NA. *T:* (01506) 834255.

DALYELL, Tam; MP (Lab) Linlithgow, since 1983 (West Lothian, 1962–83); *b* 9 Aug. 1932; *s* of late Gordon and Eleanor Dalyell; *m* 1963, Kathleen Dalyell, *qv*; one *s* one *d. Educ:* Eton; King's Coll., Cambridge; Moray House Teachers' Training Coll., Edinburgh. Trooper, Royal Scots Greys, 1950–52; Teacher, Bo'ness High Sch., 1956–60. Contested (Lab) Roxburgh, Selkirk, and Peebles, 1959. Dep.-Director of Studies on British India ship-school, Dunera, 1961–62. Member Public Accounts Cttee, House of Commons, 1962–66; Secretary, Labour Party Standing Conference on the Sciences, 1962–64; PPS to Rt Hon. Richard Crossman, Minister of Housing, Leader of H of C, Sec. of State for the Social Services, 1964–70; Opposition spokesman on science, 1980–82; Chairman: PLP Education Cttee, 1964–65; PLP Sports Group, 1964–74; PLP Foreign Affairs Gp, 1974–75; Vice-Chairman: PLP Defence and Foreign Affairs Gps, 1972–74; Scottish Labour Group of MPs, 1973–75; Parly Lab. Party, 1974–76; Sub-Cttee on Public Accounts; Mem., Labour Party NEC, 1986–87. Member: European Parlt, 1975–79; European Parlt Budget Cttee, 1976–79; European Parlt Energy Cttee, 1979; Member: House of Commons Select Cttee on Science and Technology, 1967–69; Liaison Cttee between Cabinet and Parly Labour Party, 1974–76; Chm., All-Pty Latin-America Gp, 1997–. Ldr, IPU Delegn to Peru, 1999. Chm., *ad hoc* Cttee against war in Iraq, 1998. Trustee, History of Parlt Trust, 1999–; Mem., Council, National Trust for Scotland. Mem. Scottish Council for Devlt and Industry Trade Delegn to China, Nov. 1971. Political columnist, New Scientist, 1967–. Hon. DSc Edinburgh, 1994; Hon. DLitt City Univ., 1998. *Publications:* The Case of Ship-Schools, 1960; Ship-School Dunera, 1963; Devolution: the end of Britain?, 1977; One Man's Falklands, 1982; A Science Policy for Britain, 1983; Thatcher's Torpedo, 1983; Misrule, 1987; Dick Crossman: a portrait, 1989. *Recreations:* tennis, swimming. *Address:* The Binns, Linlithgow, Scotland EH49 7NA. *T:* (01506) 834255.

DALZELL PAYNE, Henry Salusbury Legh, (Harry), CBE 1973 (OBE 1970; MBE 1961); *b* 1929; *m* 1963, Serena Helen (marr. diss. 1980), *d* of Col Clifford White Gourlay, MC, TD; two *d. Educ:* Cheltenham; RMA Sandhurst; Staff Coll.; RCDS. Commissioned, 7th Hussars, 1949; served Queen's Own Hussars, 1957–66; seconded to Sultan of Muscat's Armed Forces, 1959–60; commanded: 3rd Carabiniers, 1967–69; 6th Armoured Bde, 1974–75; 3rd Armoured Div., 1979– 80 ; resigned, 1981. *Recreations:* travel, the turf, fine wines. *Clubs:* Cavalry and Guards, Turf, White's.

DALZIEL, Geoffrey Albert; British Commissioner, Leader of Salvation Army activities in Great Britain, 1974–80; *b* 10 Dec. 1912; *s* of Alexander William and Olive Mary Dalziel; *m* 1937, Ruth Edith Fairbank; two *s* one *d. Educ:* Harrow Elementary Sch. Commissioned Salvation Army Officer, 1934; Corps Officer in Gt Britain, to 1946; on Internat. Trng Coll. Staff, 1946–51; Divisional Youth Sec., 1951–59; Trng Coll. Principal, Melbourne, Aust., 1959–64; Chief Side Officer, Internat. Trng Coll., London, 1964–66; Chief Secretary: Sydney, Aust., 1966–68; Toronto, Canada, 1968–70; Territorial Comdr, Kenya, Uganda and Tanzania, E Africa, 1970–74. *Recreations:* walking, gardening, reading.

DALZIEL, Ian Martin; chairman and director of companies; *b* 21 June 1947; *s* of late John Calvin Dalziel and of Elizabeth Roy Dalziel, *e d* of Rev. Ian Bain, FRSE and Mrs Christian Stuart Fisher Bain, Gairloch; *m* 1972, Nadia Maria Iacovazzi; four *s. Educ:* Daniel Stewart's Coll., Edinburgh; St John's Coll., Cambridge (BA Hons 1968; LLB Hons 1969; MA 1972); Université Libre de Bruxelles (Weiner Anspach Foundation Scholarship, 1970); London Business Sch. Mullens & Co., 1970–72; Manufacturers Hanover Ltd, 1972–83. Mem., Richmond upon Thames Council, 1978–79. Mem. (C) Lothian, European Parlt, 1979–84. Chairman: Continental Assets Trust plc, 1989–98; Cymbolic Sciences International Inc., 1992–2000; Precision Systems Inc., 1996–99; Invesco Smaller Continental Cos Trust plc, 1998–; Director: Adam & Co. plc, 1983–92; Lepercq-Amcur Fund NV, 1989–; Gen. Man., Devin SA, 1992–; Consultant, Primwest Hldg NV, 1992–. Mem., Queen's Body Guard for Scotland (Royal Company of Archers). *Recreations:* golf, shooting, tennis, ski-ing. *Address:* 45 route des Eaux-Belles, 1243 Presinge/Geneva, Switzerland. *T:* (22) 7591935; (business) 210 route de Jussy, 1243 Presinge/Geneva, Switzerland. *T:* (22) 7599050, *Fax:* (22) 7599055; *e-mail:* imd@primwest.com. *Clubs:* Brooks's; New (Edinburgh); Royal and Ancient Golf (St Andrews); Hon. Company of Edinburgh Golfers; Racquet and Tennis (New York).

DALZIEL, Malcolm Stuart, CBE 1984; international funding consultant, since 1991; *b* 18 Sept. 1936; *s* of late Robert Henderson Dalziel and Susan Aileen (*née* Robertson); *m* 1961, Elizabeth Anne Harvey; one *s* two *d. Educ:* Banbury Grammar Sch.; St Catherine's Coll., Oxford (BA 1960, MA 1965). National Service, 2nd Lieut Northamptonshire Regt, 1955–57. The British Council, 1960–87: student, SOAS, 1960; Asst Educn Officer, Lahore, Pakistan, 1961–63; Regional Dir, Penang, Malaya, 1963–67; Regional Rep., Lahore, 1967–70; Rep., Sudan, 1970–74; Dir, Management Services Dept, and Dep. Controller, Estabs Div., 1975–79; Rep., Egypt, and Counsellor (Cultural), British Embassy, Cairo, 1979–83; Controller, Higher Educn Div., British Council and Sec., IUPC, 1983–87; Associate Consultant, 1988–96, Dir, 1990–96, Consultants in Economic Regeneration in Europe Services; Associate Consultant, Eur. Econ. Develt Services, 1996–2001. Affiliate, Internat., Develt Centre, Queen Elizabeth House, Oxford Univ., 1988–. Dep. Chm., Council for Educn in the Commonwealth, 1990–2000 (Mem. Exec. Cttee, 1986–); Mem. Court, Univ. of Essex, 1986–88. Vice-Pres., Northants CCC, 1990–. *Recreations:* theatre, ballet, walking, Rugby. *Address:* 368 Woodstock Road, Oxford OX2 8AE. *T:* (01865) 558969. *Club:* Oxford and Cambridge.

DALZIEL, Dr Maureen, FFPHM; Chief Executive, Human Fertilisation and Embryology Authority, since 2001; *b* 7 April 1952; *d* of late Peter and of Eileen Farrell; *m* 1974, Ian Dalziel. *Educ:* Notre Dame High Sch., Glasgow; Univ. of Glasgow (MB ChB). MFCM 1985, FFPHM 1990. Jun. hosp. posts, Glasgow and Lanarkshire Hosps, 1976–79; GP, E Kilbride, 1979–81; Registrar, then Sen. Registrar in Public Health Medicine: SW Herts HA, 1981–83; Brent HA, 1983–85; Consultant in Public Health Medicine, 1985–89, Associate Dir, 1989, NW Thames RHA; Chief Executive: SW Herts DHA, 1990–93 (Dir, Public Health, 1989–90); Hillingdon Health Agency, 1993–95; Regl Dir of Public Health and Med. Dir, N Thames Regl HA, then N Thames Regl Office, NHS Exec., DoH, 1995–99; Dir, Nat. Co-ordinating Centre for NHS Service Delivery and Orgn, LSHTM, 1999–2001; Med. Dir, NHS Litigation Authy, 1999–2000. Lectr in Public Health Medicine, 1981–85, Sen. Lectr, 1989–90, LSHTM. Mem., European Steering Gp, Mégapoles, 1997–; Chm., Sub-network on Social Disadvantage, Mégapoles, 1997–. Member Board: Housing 21, 1995–; Intensive Care Nat. Audit and Res. Centre, 1997–. *Publications:* numerous articles in learned jls and papers presented at nat. confs. *Recreations:* ski-ing, reading novels and biographies, golf (par 3), watching old films. *Address:* Human Fertilisation and Embryology Authority, Paxton House, 30 Artillery Lane, E1 7LS.

DAMAZER, Mark David; Assistant Chief Executive (Director of Journalism), BBC News, since 2000; *b* 15 April 1955; *s* of Stanislaw and Suzanne Damazer; *m* 1981, Rosemary Jane Morgan; one *s* one *d. Educ:* Gonville & Caius Coll., Cambridge (BA History); Harvard Univ. Harkness Fellow, 1977–79; American Political Sci. Fellow, 1978–79. Trainee, ITN, 1979–81; Producer: BBC World Service, 1981–83; TV-AM, 1983–84; BBC: Six O'Clock News, 1984–86; Output Editor, Newsnight, 1986–88; Dep. Editor, 1988–89, Editor, 1989–94, Nine O'Clock News; Editor, TV News, 1994–96; Head: Current Affairs, 1996–98; Political Progs, 1998–2000. *Publications:* articles in Economist and various newspapers. *Recreations:* opera, Tottenham Hotspur, gardening, coarse tennis, Italian painting. *Address:* 29 Killieser Avenue, SW2 4NX. T: (020) 8674 9611.

DAMER; *see* Dawson-Damer, family name of Earl of Portarlington.

DAMERELL, Derek Vivian; Governor, 1974–88, and Deputy Chairman, 1984–88, BUPA (Chief Executive, 1974–84); *b* 4 Aug. 1921; *s* of William James Damerell (Lt-Col), MBE and Zoe Damerell; *m* 1942, Margaret Isabel Porritt, *d* of Prof. B. D. Porritt; three *s* three *d. Educ:* ISC; Edinburgh Univ.; Harvard Business Sch. Parent Bd, BPB Industries, 1953–64; Regional Dir, Internat. Wool Secretariat, 1965–73. Dir, Murrayfield plc, 1982–87. Governor, Nuffield Nursing Homes Trust, 1974–80; Founder, Ind. Hosp. Gp (Chm., 1975–80); Internat. Fedn of Voluntary Health Service Funds: Mem. Council, 1976–; Dep. Pres., 1980–81, Pres., 1981–84; Mem. Bd of Governors, Assoc. Internat. de la Mutualité, 1974–83. *Recreations:* sailing (jt founder, BCYC, 1947), travel. *Address:* Chevry-sous-le-Bignon, 45210 Ferrières, France. *T:* (2) 38909363. *Clubs:* various yacht.

DAMMERS, Very Rev. Alfred Hounsell, (Horace); Dean of Bristol, 1973–87; *b* 10 July 1921; *s* of late B. F. H. Dammers, MA, JP; *m* 1947, Brenda Muriel, *d* of late Clifford Stead; two *s* two *d. Educ:* Malvern Coll. (Schol.); Pembroke Coll., Cambridge (Schol., MA); Westcott House, Cambridge. Served RA (Surrey and Sussex Yeo.), 1941–44. Asst Curate, Adlington, Lancs, 1948; Asst Curate, S Bartholomew's, Edgbaston, Birmingham, and Lectr at Queen's Coll., Birmingham, 1950; Chaplain and Lectr at S John's Coll., Palayamkottai, S India, 1953; Vicar of Holy Trinity, Millhouses, Sheffield, and Examining Chaplain to Bishop of Sheffield, 1957; Select Preacher at Univ. of Cambridge, 1963; Select Preacher at Univ. of Oxford, 1975, 1989; Chairman, Friends of Reunion, 1965; Canon Residentiary and Director of Studies, Coventry Cathedral, 1965. Founder, The Life Style Movement, 1972. Companion, Community of the Cross of Nails, 1975. *Publications:* Great Venture, 1958; Ye Shall Receive Power, 1958; All in Each Place, 1962; God is Light, God is Love, 1963; AD 1980, 1966; Lifestyle: a parable of sharing, 1982, 2nd edn 2001; A Christian Life-style, 1986; Lord Make Us One, 1988; (ed) Preaching from the Cathedrals, 1998; St John's Gospel: a study guide, 1999. *Recreations:* campaigning on peace and justice issues, visiting friends and relations. *Address:* 4 Bradley Avenue, Shirehampton, Bristol BS11 9SL.

DANCE, Brian David, MA; Headmaster, St Dunstan's College, Catford, 1973–93; *b* 22 Nov. 1929; *s* of late L. H. Dance and late Mrs M. G. Swain (*née* Shrivelle); *m* 1955, Chloe Elizabeth, *o d* of late J. F. A. Baker, CB, FEng; two *s* two *d. Educ:* Kingston Grammar Sch.; Wadham Coll., Oxford. BA 1952, MA 1956. Asst Master, Kingston Grammar Sch., 1953–59; Sen. History Master: Faversham Grammar Sch., 1959–62; Westminster City Sch., 1962–65; Headmaster: Cirencester Grammar Sch., 1965–66; Luton Sixth Form Coll., 1966–73. Member: Cambridge Local Examination Syndicate, 1968–73; Headmasters' Assoc. Council, 1968–76 (Exec. Cttee, 1972–76, Hon. Legal Sec. 1975–76); Chm., London Area, SHA, 1984–85. Chm., Lewisham Environment Trust, 1987–88. Gov., Bromley High Sch., 1985–. Vice-Pres., Rugby Fives Assoc., 1993–. *Publications:* articles in: Times Educnl Supp.; Headmasters' Assoc. 'Review'. *Recreations:* watching most ball games (especially cricket and Rugby football), music, philately, theatre. *Address:* 59 Albyfield, Bickley, Bromley, Kent BR1 2HY. *T:* (020) 8467 9458.

DANCE, Charles Walter; actor; *b* 10 Oct. 1946; *s* of late Walter Dance and Eleanor Dance (*née* Perks); *m* 1970, Joanna Haythorn; one *s* one *d. Educ:* Widey Tech. Sch.; Plymouth Sch. of Art; Leicester Poly. Rep. theatre at Nottingham, Leeds, Greenwich and Chichester Fest.; joined RSC, 1975; appeared in Henry IV, Hamlet, Richard III, Perkin Warbeck, As You Like It, The Changeling, Henry VI, title rôles in Henry V and Coriolanus; other *theatre* includes: Irma La Douce, 1978; The Heiress, 1980; Turning Over, 1982; Good, Donmar Warehouse, 1999; Long Day's Journey Into Night, Lyric,

2000; *television:* Edward VII, 1973; The Fatal Spring, 1978; Little Eyolf, 1980; Frost in May, Nancy Astor, 1981; Saigon, the Last Day, The Jewel in the Crown, 1982; Rainy Day Women, The Secret Servant, 1984; Thunder Rock, The McGuffin, 1985; Out on a Limb, 1986; Out of the Shadows, First Born, 1988; Goldeneye, The Phantom of the Opera, 1989; Undertow, 1993; In the Presence of Mine Enemies, 1995; Rebecca, 1996; Randall & Hopkirk Deceased, Bloodlines, 1999; Justice in Wonderland, 2000; Nicholas Nickleby, 2001; *films:* For Your Eyes Only, 1979; Plenty, 1984; The Golden Child, Good Morning Babylon, 1985; White Mischief, Hidden City, 1986; Pascali's Island, Kalkstein, 1989; China Moon, 1990; Alien 3, 1991; Century, Last Action Hero, Exquisite Tenderness, 1992; Kabloonak (Best Actor, Paris Film Fest., 1994), Shortcut to Paradise, 1993; Michael Collins, Space Truckers, 1995; The Blood Oranges, Don't Go Breaking My Heart, What Rats Won't Do, 1997; Hilary and Jackie, 1998; Jurij, 1999; Dark Blue World, 2000. *Recreations:* tennis, swimming. *Address:* c/o ICM, Oxford House, 76 Oxford Street, W1N 0AX. *T:* (020) 7636 6565. *Club:* Groucho.

DANCER, Eric, CBE 1991; JP; Lord-Lieutenant of Devon, since 1998; Managing Director, Dartington Crystal Ltd, since 1986; *b* 17 April 1940; *s* of Joseph Cyril Dancer and Mabel Dancer; *m* 1980, Carole Anne Moxon. *Educ:* King Edward VII Sch., Sheffield; Sheffield Poly. Buyer: Moorwood-Vulcan Ltd, 1959–63; Balfour-Darwins Ltd, 1963–67; Purchasing Officer, Brightside Foundry and Engineering Co. Ltd, 1965–67; Dep. Chief Buyer, Metro-Cammell Ltd, 1967–68; Chief Buyer, Chrysler Parts Div., 1968–69; Supplies Manager, Jensen Motors Ltd, 1969–72; Dir, Anglo Nordic Hldgs plc, 1972–80; Man. Dir, Dartington Hall Corp., 1980–87; Chm., English Country Crystal, 1983–87. Trustee, Dartington Hall Trust, 1984–87; Member: SW Regl IDB, 1984–91; Council, CBI, 1997–; Chairman: Devon Cttee, Rural Develt Commn, 1981–86; Devon and Cornwall TEC, 1989–93; Gp of 10, 1990–92; West Country Develt Corp., 1993–; Nat. Assessor, TEC, 1993–98. Gov., Univ. of Plymouth, 1992–96. CIMgt 1987; FCIPS 1990 (President's Prize, 1964); FInstD 1981 (Dip. 1989); FRSA 1984 (Mem. Council, 1994–98). Freeman, City of London, 1992; Liveryman, Co. of Glass Sellers, 1992–. DL Devon, 1998; JP Devon and Cornwall, 1998 (Chm., Adv Cttee of Magistrates). Hon. Captain RNR, 2001. DUniv Sheffield Hallam, 1999. KStJ 1998. *Recreations:* motor boats, reading, music, private flying and gliding 1956–90. *Address:* The Roundhouse, Moreleigh, Totnes, Devon TQ9 7JN. *T:* (01548) 821465. *Clubs:* Army and Navy; Royal Western Yacht.

DANCEY, Roger Michael, MA; Chief Master, King Edward's School, Birmingham, and Educational Adviser, King Edward VI Foundation, since 1998; *b* 24 Nov. 1945; *s* of Michael and Rosalind Dancey; *m* 1988, Elizabeth Jane Shadbolt; one step *s* one step *d. Educ:* Lancing Coll.; Exeter Univ. (MA). Careers Master, Whitgift Sch., 1972–76; Head of Sixth Form, Greenshaw High Sch., 1976–81; Sen. Master, Royal Grammar Sch., Worcester, 1982–86; Headmaster: King Edward VI Camp Hill Sch. for Boys, 1986–95; City of London Sch., 1995–98. Mem. Council, Birmingham Univ., 1999–. *Recreations:* cricket, golf, theatre, cinema. *Address:* King Edward's School, Edgbaston Park Road, Birmingham B15 2UA. *Club:* Edgbaston Golf.

d'ANCONA, John Edward William, CB 1994; consultant; Director General, Offshore Supplies Office, Department of Trade and Industry (formerly of Energy), 1981–94; *b* 28 May 1935; *o s* of late Adolph and late Margaret d'Ancona; *m* 1958, Mary Helen, *o d* of late Sqdn-Ldr R. T. Hunter and late Mrs Hunter; three *s. Educ:* St Edward's Coll., Malta; St Cuthbert's Grammar Sch., Newcastle upon Tyne. BA (Hons) Mod. History, DipEd (Durham). Teacher, 1959–61; Civil Service, 1961–94: Asst Principal, Dept of Educn and Science, 1961; Private Sec. to Minister of State, DES, 1964–65; Principal: DES, 1965–67; Min. of Technology and DTI, 1967–74; Asst Sec., 1974, Under Sec., 1981, DoE. Chm., UK Maritime Forum, 2000–. Pres., Soc. for Underwater Technol., 1997–99. *Recreations:* cricket, philately, wine-bibbing. *Address:* 33 Culverley Road, Catford, SE6 2LD. *Club:* Travellers.

DANCY, Prof. John Christopher, MA; Professor of Education, University of Exeter, 1978–84, now Emeritus; *b* 13 Nov. 1920; *e s* of late Dr J. H. Dancy and Dr N. Dancy; *m* 1944, Angela Bryant; two *s* one *d. Educ:* Winchester (Scholar); New Coll., Oxford (Scholar, MA). 1st Class, Classical Hon. Mods, 1940; Craven Scholar, 1946; Gaisford Greek Prose Prize, 1947; Hertford Scholar, 1947; Arnold Historical Essay Prize, 1949. Served in Rifle Brigade, 1941–46; Capt. GSO(3)I, 30 Corps, 1945; Major, GSO(2)I, 1 Airborne Corps, 1945–46. Lecturer in Classics, Wadham Coll., 1946–48; Asst Master, Winchester Coll., 1948–53; Headmaster of Lancing Coll., 1953–61; Master, Marlborough Coll., 1961–72; Principal, St Luke's Coll. of Educn, Exeter, 1972–78. Dir, St Luke's Coll. Foundn, 1978–86. Member, Public Schools' Commission, 1966–68. Chm., Higher Educn Foundn, 1981–86. Chm., British Accreditation Council for Independent Further and Higher Educn, 1984–93. *Publications:* Commentary on 1 Maccabees, 1954; The Public Schools and the Future, 1963; Commentary on Shorter Books of Apocrypha, 1972; Walter Oakeshott: a diversity of gifts, 1995; The Divine Drama: the Old Testament as literature, 2001. *Address:* Wharf House, Mousehole, Penzance, Cornwall TR19 6RX. *T:* (01736) 731137.

DANDY, David James, MD; FRCS; Consultant Orthopaedic Surgeon, Addenbrooke's Hospital, Cambridge and Newmarket General Hospital, since 1975; *b* 30 May 1940; *s* of James Dandy, Great Shelford, Cambs, and late Margaret Dandy (*née* Coe); *m* 1966, (Stephanie) Jane Essex; one *s* one *d. Educ:* Forest Sch.; Emmanuel Coll., Cambridge (Windsor Student, 1965; BA 1961, MA 1963; BChir 1964; MB 1965; MD 1990; MChir 1994); London Hosp. Med. Coll. (Robert Milne Prize for Surgery, 1995). LRCP, MRCS 1964, FRCS 1969. Surg. Registrar, St Andrew's Hosp., Bow, 1966–67; Surg., then Orthopaedic Registrar, London Hosp., 1967–69; Orthopaedic Registrar: Royal Nat. Orthopaedic Hosp., 1969–71; St Bartholomew's Hosp., 1971; Princess Alexandra Hosp., Harlow, 1971–72; Norfolk and Norwich Hosp., 1972–73; Sen. Registrar: St Bartholomew's Hosp., 1973–75; Hosp. for Sick Children, Gt Ormond St, 1974; Sen. Fellow, Toronto Gen. Hosp., 1973–74; Associate Lectr, Univ. of Cambridge, 1975–; Civilian Advr in Knee Surgery, RN and RAF, 1980–. Lectures: Mackenzie Crooks, RAF Hosp., Ely, 1980; Munsif Meml Orator, Bombay, 1987; Sir Ernest Finch Meml, Sheffield, 1990; William Gissane, Inst. of Accident Surgery, 1998. Director: Internat. Soc. of the Knee, 1989–93; European Soc. for Sports Traumatology, Knee Surgery, Sports Medicine and Arthroscopy, 1992–96; President: Internat. Arthroscopy Assoc., 1989–91; British Orthopaedic Sports Trauma Assoc., 1993–95; British Orthopaedic Assoc., 1998–99 (Robert Jones Prize and Assoc. Medal, 1991; Naughton Dunn Lectr, 1991; Mem. Council, 1992–95); Mem. Council, RCS, 1994– (James Berry Prize, 1985; Hunterian Prof., 1994). Hon. FRCSE 1998. *Publications:* Arthroscopy of the Knee, 1973; Arthroscopic Surgery of the Knee, 1981, rev. edn 1987; Arthroscopy of the Knee: a diagnostic atlas, 1984; Essentials of Orthopaedics and Trauma, 1989, rev. edn 1998; articles on surgery of the knee and arthroscopic surgery. *Recreations:* travel, ablative horticulture. *Address:* The Old Vicarage, Great Wilbraham, Cambridge CB1 5JF. *Club:* East India.

DANGAN, Viscount; Garret Graham Wellesley, (Jr); Group Chief Executive, Zetters plc, since 2000; *b* 30 March 1965; *s* and *heir* of 7th Earl Cowley, *qv*; *m* 1990, Claire Lorraine, *d* of P. W. Brighton, Stow Bridge, Norfolk; two *s* one *d. Educ:* Franklin Coll., Switzerland (Associate of Arts degree). Traded Options, Hoare Govett, 1985–88; Manager, Ing (London) Derivatives Ltd, 1991–94; CEO, IFX Ltd, 1995–2000; Sen. Vice Pres., Index Futures Gp, 1995–98. *Heir: s* Hon. Henry Arthur Peter Wellesley, *b* 3 Dec. 1991. *Address:* Ashbourne Manor, High Street, Widford, Herts SG12 8SZ.

DANIEL, Brother; *see* Matthews, Brother D. F.

DANIEL, Gareth John; Chief Executive, London Borough of Brent, since 1998; *b* 30 March 1954; *s* of late Evan John Daniel and of Eileen Marie Daniel; partner, Margaret Wilson; three *s. Educ:* St Edward's Coll., Liverpool; Jesus Coll., Oxford (BA Hons); South Bank Poly. (DASS, CQSW). Pres., Oxford Univ. Students' Union, 1974–75. Social worker, London Borough of Ealing, 1976–83; London Borough of Brent, 1986–98: Principal Develt Officer; Divl Manager, Strategy; Head, Central Policy Unit; Dir, Partnership and Res. Member (Lab): Ealing LBC (Chm., Planning and Econ. Develt, 1986–90); Ealing North, GLC, 1981–86. Contested (Lab): Worcs S, 1979; Ealing, Acton, 1983. *Recreations:* family, hill-walking, foreign travel. *Address:* Brent Town Hall, Forty Lane, Wembley, Middx HA9 9HD. *T:* (020) 8937 1007.

DANIEL, Gerald Ernest, CPFA, FCA; County Treasurer, Nottinghamshire County Council, 1974–84; *b* 7 Dec. 1919; *s* of Ernest and Beata May Daniel; *m* 1942, Ecila Roslyn Dillow; one *s* one *d. Educ:* Huish's Grammar Sch., Taunton. Served War, 1939–46, Somerset LI. Various appts in Borough Treasurers' Depts at Taunton, Scunthorpe and Bexhill, 1935–50; Cost and machine accountant, subseq. Chief Accountant, City Treasury, Bristol, 1950–60; Dep. Borough Treasurer, Reading, 1960–64; Borough Treasurer, West Bromwich, 1965–68; City Treasurer, Nottingham, 1968–74. Public Sector Advr, Pannell Kerr Forster, Chartered Accountants, 1984–93; Financial Advr, British Assoc. of Med. Managers, 1995–97. Sec., 1971–76, Chm., 1976–81, Officers Side, Jt Negotiating Cttee for Chief Officers in Local Govt. Dir, Horizon Travel, 1975–85. Treasurer: E Midlands Airport, 1968–84; E Midlands Arts Assoc., 1969–84. President: Nottingham Soc. of Chartered Accountants, 1976; Assoc. of Public Service Finance Officers, 1978; Soc. of County Treasurers, 1979; Chartered Inst. of Public Finance and Accountancy, 1983–84 (Mem. Council, 1971–85; Vice-Pres., 1982). FMAAT (Mem. Council, 1981–83). FRSA. Organist, St Bartholomew's Church, Cross-in-Hand, E Sussex, 1986–99. *Recreations:* gardening, music. *Address:* Brookvale, Star Lane, Blackboys, Uckfield, East Sussex TN22 5LD. *T:* (01825) 890712.

DANIEL, Sir Goronwy Hopkin, KCVO 1969; CB 1962; DPhil Oxon; HM Lieutenant for Dyfed, 1978–89; *b* Ystradgynlais, 21 March 1914; *s* of David Daniel; *m* 1940, Lady Valerie, (*d* 2000), *d* of 2nd Earl Lloyd George; one *s* two *d. Educ:* Pontardawe Secondary Sch.; Amman Valley County Sch.; University College of Wales, Aberystwyth; Jesus Coll., Oxford (Hon. Fellow, 1979). Fellow of University of Wales; Meyricke Scholar, Jesus Coll.; Oxford Institute of Statistics, 1937–40; Lecturer, Dept of Economics, Bristol Univ., 1940–41; Clerk, House of Commons, 1941–43; Ministry of Town and Country Planning, 1943–47; Chief Statistician, Ministry of Fuel and Power, 1947–55; Under-Sec., Coal Div., 1955–62, Gen. Div., 1962–64; Permanent Under-Sec. of State, Welsh Office, 1964–69; Principal, Aberystwyth UC, 1969–79; Vice-Chancellor, Univ. of Wales, 1977–79; Chm., Welsh Fourth Channel Authority, 1981–86. Pres., West Wales Assoc. for the Arts, 1971–85; Member: Welsh Language Council, 1974–78; Gen. Adv. Council, BBC, 1974–79; Adv. Council on Energy Conservation, 1977–79; SSRC, 1980–83; Dep. Chm., Prince of Wales' Cttee, 1980–86. Dir, Bank of Wales, 1972–90 (Dep. Chm., 1985–90). Chairman: Home-Grown Timber Adv. Cttee, 1974–81; Cttee on Water Charges in Wales, 1974–75; Welsh Congregational Meml Coll., 1985–90; Working Gp on Powers and Functions of Univ. of Wales, 1988–89. Hon Mem., Gorsedd of Bards, 1966. Hon. LLD, Univ. of Wales, 1980. Hon. Freeman, City of London, 1982. *Publications:* papers in statistical, fuel and power, and other journals. *Recreations:* country pursuits, sailing. *Address:* Cae Ffynnon, 67 St Michaels Road, Cardiff CF5 2AN. *T:* (029) 2055 3150.

DANIEL, Gruffydd Huw Morgan; DL; **His Honour Judge Daniel;** a Circuit Judge, since 1986; Deputy Senior Judge, Sovereign Base Area, Cyprus, since 1995; *b* 16 April 1939; *s* of Prof. John Edward Daniel, MA, and Catherine Megan Daniel; *m* 1968, Phyllis Margaret (*née* Bermingham); one *d. Educ:* Ampleforth; University College of Wales (LLB); Inns of Court School of Law. Commissioned 2nd Lieut First Bn Royal Welch Fusiliers, 1959; Captain 6/7 Bn Royal Welch Fusiliers (TA), 1965; served MELF, Cyprus. Called to the Bar, Gray's Inn, 1967; Wales and Chester Circuit (Circuit Junior, 1975); Recorder, 1980–86; Asst Liaison Judge, 1983–87, Liaison Judge, 1988–, Gwynedd; Liaison Judge for N Wales, 1998–. Asst Parly Boundary Comr for Wales, 1981–82, 1985–86. Pres., Caerns Br., SSAFA, 1995–. Hon. Col, 6th Cadet Bn, Royal Welch Fusiliers, 1997–. DL Gwynedd, 1993. *Recreations:* gardening, shooting, fishing, sailing. *Address:* (residence) Rhiwgoch, Halfway Bridge, Bangor, Gwynedd LL57 3AX. *Clubs:* Reform; Royal Anglesey Yacht, Bristol Channel Yacht.

DANIEL, Jack; *see* Daniel R. J.

DANIEL, Joan; *see* Rodgers, J.

DANIEL, John, MA; Headmaster, Royal Grammar School, Guildford, 1977–92; *b* 7 March 1932; *s* of John Daniel and Mary (*née* Young); *m* 1956, Heather Joy Retey; two *d. Educ:* Truro Sch.; New Coll., Oxford (Hons Modern Langs 1955). Thomas Hedley & Son, 1955–57; Linton Lodge Hotel, Oxford, 1957–59; Hartford Motors, Oxford, 1959–62; Royal Grammar Sch., Worcester, 1963–65; Malvern Coll., 1965–72; Royal Grammar School, Guildford: Dep. Headmaster, 1972–75; Acting Headmaster, 1975–77. Chm. of Govs, Tormead Sch., Guildford, 1981–97. Asst Dir, Gap Activity Projects Ltd, 1994–. Chm., Guildford Symphony Orch., 1995–. *Recreations:* watching Rugby football, playing the piano and double bass. *Address:* 1 Orchard Road, Shalford, Guildford, Surrey GU4 8ER. *T:* (01483) 536033.

DANIEL, Sir John (Sagar), Kt 1994; DSc; Assistant Director-General for Education, UNESCO, since 2001; President, US Open University, since 1998; *b* 31 May 1942; *s* of John Edward Daniel and Winifred (*née* Sagar); *m* 1966, Kristin Anne Swanson; one *s* two *d. Educ:* Christ's Hosp.; St Edmund Hall, Oxford (BA Metallurgy, MA); Univ. of Paris (DSc Metallurgy); Thorneloe Univ., Ont (Associate 1992); Concordia Univ., Quebec (MA Educnl Technol. 1995). Asst Prof., then Associate Prof., Ecole Polytechnique, Montreal, 1969–73; Dir, Etudes Télé-Univ., Univ. of Quebec, 1973–77; Vice Pres., Learning Services, Athabasca Univ., Alberta, 1979–80; Vice-Rector, Academic Affairs, Concordia Univ., Montreal, 1980–84; Pres., Laurentian Univ., Sudbury, Ont, 1984–90; Vice-Chancellor, Open Univ., 1990–2001. Chairman: UNESCO-CEPES Adv. Council, 1990–92; Adv. Council for Develt of RN Personnel, 1996–; Member: HEQC, 1992–94; Council of Foundn, Internat. Baccalaureate, 1992–99; Council for Industry and Higher Educn, 1994–; British N American Cttee, 1995–; Council, CBI, 1996–98; Steering Cttee, Defence Trng Rev., 1999–. Member: Bd of Govs, Commonwealth of Learning, 1988–90; Council, Univ. of Buckingham, 1994–; Council, Open Univ. of Hong Kong, 1996–; Bd, Univ. for Industry, 1999– (Mem. Transition Bd, 1998–99); Trustee, Carnegie Foundn for

Advancement of Teaching, 1993–. Adv. Bd, Xerox, Canada, 1998–; Dir, Blackwells Publishing, 1998–. Forum Fellow, World Econ. Forum, 1998. CIMgt 1997 (Pres., Milton Keynes Br., 1998–). Hon. Fellow, St Edmund Hall, Oxford, 1990; Hon. FCP 1997. Hon. DLitt: Deakin, Aust., 1985; Athabasca, Canada, 1998; Hon. DHumLitt: Thomas Edison State Coll., USA, 1997; Richmond Coll., London, 1997; Hon. DSc: Royal Mil. Coll., St Jean, Canada, 1988; Open Univ., Sri Lanka, 1994; Paris VI, 2001; Hon. DEd: CNAA, 1992; Sukhothai Thammathirat Open Univ., Thailand, 1999; Hon. LLD Univ. of Waterloo, Canada, 1993; DUniv: Humberside, 1996; Aberta, Portugal, 1996; Anadolu, Turkey, 1998; Québec, Derby, and New Bulgarian, 2000. Individual Excellence Award, Commonwealth of Learning, 1995; Morris T. Keeton Award, Council for Adult and Experiential Learning, USA, 1999. Officier, Ordre des Palmes Académiques (France), 1991 (Chevalier, 1987). *Publications:* Learning at a Distance: a world perspective, 1982; Mega-universities and Knowledge Media, 1996; numerous articles to professional pubns. *Address:* UNESCO, 7 place de Fontenoy, 75352 Paris, France.

DANIEL, Nicholas; oboe soloist; conductor; *b* 9 Jan. 1962; *s* of Jeremy Daniel and late Margaret Louise Daniel; *m* 1986, Joy Farrall, clarinettist; two *s*. *Educ:* Salisbury Cathedral Sch.; Purcell Sch.; Royal Acad. of Music. ARAM 1986, FRAM 1987; FGSM 1996. Prof., GSMD, 1986–97; Oboe Prof., Indiana Univ., 1997–99; Prince Consort Lectr, RCM, 1999–. Dedicatee and first performer of many new works. Internat. appearances in USA, Japan, Europe, Australasia. Competition winner: BBC Young Musician of Year, 1980; Munich, 1983; Graz, 1984; Duino, Italy, 1986. Member: Assoc. for Improvement of Maternity Services; Assoc. of Radical Midwives; Good Practice; JABS; The Informed Parent. *Recreations:* childbirth studies (home birth), music, literature, Star Trek, travel, cinema. *Address:* Hedgerow House, 48 Station Road, Warboys, Huntingdon, Cambs PE28 2TH. *T:* (01487) 822723; *e-mail:* solooboe@aol.com.

DANIEL, Paul Wilson, CBE 2000; Music Director, English National Opera, since 1997; *b* 5 July 1958; *s* of Alfred Daniel and Margaret Daniel (*née* Poole); *m* 1988, Joan Rodgers, *qv*; two *d*. *Educ:* King Henry VIII Sch., Coventry; King's Coll., Cambridge; Guildhall Sch. of Music and Drama. Music Dir, Opera Factory, London, 1987–90; Artistic Dir, Opera North, 1990–97; Principal Conductor, English Northern Philharmonia, 1990–97. Has worked with ENO, Royal Opera House, Bayerische Staatsoper, Munich, La Monnaie, Brussels and Geneva Opera; has conducted many orchestras incl. LSO, LPO, RPO, BBC SO, London Sinfonietta, CBSO, Scottish Chamber Orch., and ABC orchestras, Australia; has also conducted in Germany, Holland, France and USA. Co-presenter, Harry Enfield's Guide to Opera, TV series, 1993. Has made numerous recordings. *Address:* c/o English National Opera, London Coliseum, St Martin's Lane, WC2N 4ES; c/o Ingpen & Williams, 26 Wadham Road, SW15 2LR. *T:* (020) 8874 3222.

DANIEL, (Reginald) Jack, OBE 1958; FREng, CEng, FRINA, FIMarE; RCNC; *b* 27 Feb. 1920; *o s* of Reginald Daniel and Florence Emily (*née* Woods); *m* 1st, Joyce Earnshaw (marr. diss.); two *s*; 2nd, 1977, Elizabeth, *o d* of George Mitchell, Long Ashton, Som. *Educ:* Royal Naval Engineering Coll., Keyham; Royal Naval Coll., Greenwich. Grad., 1942; subseq. engaged in submarine design. Served War of 1939–45; Staff of C-in-C's Far East Fleet and Pacific Fleet, 1943–45. Atomic Bomb Tests, Bikini, 1946; Admty, Whitehall, 1947–49; Admty, Bath, Aircraft Carrier Design, 1949–52; Guided Missile Cruiser design, 1952–56; Nuclear and Polaris Submarine design, 1956–65; IDC, 1966; Materials, R&D, 1967–68; Head of Forward Design, 1968–70; Director, Submarine Design and Production, 1970–74; Dir-Gen. Ships and Head of RCNC, MoD, 1974–79; British Shipbuilders: Bd Mem., 1979; Man. Dir, for Warshipbuilding, 1980–83; Dir (Training, Educn, Safety), 1981–85; Dir of Technology (Warships), British Shipbuilders, 1983–84; Dir, British Shipbuilders Australia Pty, 1983–86. Dep. Chm., Internationale Schiff Studien GmbH Hamburg, 1984–88; Man. Dir, Warship Design Services Ltd, 1984–87; VSEL Canadian Project Dir, 1987–91; Director: VSEL Australia Pty, 1986–91; VSEL Defence Systems Canada Inc., 1987–91; Chm., VSEL-CAP, 1987–91. Vice Pres., RINA, 1982. Liveryman, Worshipful Co. of Shipwrights, 1980. Hon. Res. Fellow, UCL, 1974. FREng (Founder Fellow, Fellowship of Engineering, 1976). *Publications:* Warship Design, New Concepts and New Technology, Parsons Meml Lecture, 1976; papers for RINA, etc. *Recreations:* gardening, motoring, music. *Address:* Meadowland, Cleveland Walk, Bath BA2 6JU.

DANIEL, William Wentworth, CBE 1997; independent social scientist; Director, Policy Studies Institute, 1986–93; *b* 19 Nov. 1938; *s* of late George Taylor Daniel and Margaret Elizabeth Daniel; *m* 1st, 1961, Lynda Mary Coles Garrett (marr. diss.); one *s* two *d*; 2nd, 1990, Eileen Mary Reid (*née* Loudfoot) (*d* 1996). *Educ:* Shebbear Coll., Devon; Victoria Univ. of Manchester (BA Hons); Univ. of Manchester Inst. of Science and Technology (MSc Tech). Directing Staff, Ashorne Hill Management Coll., 1963–65; Sen. Res. Officer, Research Services Ltd, 1965–67; Senior Research Fellow: Bath Univ., 1967–69; PSI (formerly PEP), 1969–81; Dep. Dir, PSI, 1981–86. Member: ESRC, 1992–96; Eur. Foundn for Improvement of Living and Wkg Conditions, Dublin, 1992–96. Dir, Holsworthy Biogas Ltd. Bd of Govs, Plymouth Univ. *Publications:* Racial Discrimination in England, 1968; Whatever Happened to the Workers in Woolwich?, 1972; The Right to Manage?, 1972; A National Survey of the Unemployed, 1974; Sandwich Courses in Higher Education, 1975; Pay Determination in Manufacturing Industry, 1976; Where Are They Now?: a follow-up survey of the unemployed, 1977; The Impact of Employment Protection Laws, 1978; Maternity Rights: the experience of women, 1980; Maternity Rights: the experience of employers, 1981; Workplace Industrial Relations in Britain, 1983; Workplace Industrial Relations and Technical Change, 1987; The Unemployed Flow, 1989; (with Terence Hogarth) Britain's New Industrial Gypsies, 1989. *Recreations:* golf, lawn tennis. *Address:* Bryn-Mor, 7 Maer Down Road, Bude, Cornwall EX23 8NG. *T:* (01288) 356678; Flat 2, 64 Queensway, W2 3RL. *Clubs:* National Liberal; Bude & N Cornwall Golf; David Lloyd Slazenger Racquet (Heston).

DANIELL, Brig. Averell John, CBE 1955 (MBE 1939); DSO 1945; *b* 19 June 1903; *s* of late Lt-Col Oswald James Daniell, QO Royal West Kent Regt, and late May Frances Drummond Daniell (*née* Adams); *m* 1934, Phyllis Kathleen Rhona Grove-Annesley; two *s* one *d*. *Educ:* Wellington Coll.; RM Acad., Woolwich. Commissioned, Royal Field Artillery, 1923; Captain, RA, 1936; Major, 1940; Lt-Col, 1943. Served War of 1939–45; Middle East, Iraq, Burma. Col, 1948; Brig., 1952; retired, 1955. Administrative Officer, Staff Coll., Camberley, 1955–61. Colonel Commandant, Royal Artillery, 1956–66. *Address:* c/o 46 Carson Road, West Dulwich SE21 8HU.

DANIELL, Prof. David John, PhD; Professor of English, University College London, 1992–94, now Emeritus Professor; *b* 17 Feb. 1929; *s* of late Rev. Eric Herbert Daniell, MA, and Betty (*née* Heap); *m* 1956, Dorothy Mary Wells; two *s*. *Educ:* Queen Elizabeth GS, Darlington; St Catherine's Coll., Oxford (BA English Lang. and Lit., MA; BA Theol.; Hon. Fellow, 2000); Univ. of Tübingen; UCL (PhD 1972). Radar fitter, RAF, 1947–49. Sixth Form Master, Apsley GS, 1958–69; Lectr, 1969–86, Sen. Lectr, 1986–92, English Dept, UCL. Vis. Prof., KCL, 1995; Vis. Fellow, Magdalen Coll., Oxford, 1996 (Hon. Mem., Sen. Common Room, 1996–); Leverhulme Emeritus Fellow, 1997–99; Mayers Fellow, Henry E. Huntington Liby, Calif, 1998; Special Lectr, Magdalen Coll., Oxford, 1999; Oxford Univ. Sermon, 2000. Lectures: Beatrice Warde Meml, 1994; Lambeth Tyndale, 1994; A. G. Dickens, Univ. of Cambridge, 1994; Hertford Tyndale, 1994; Hilda Hulme Meml, 1994; Waynflete, Univ. of Oxford, 1996; Staley, Michigan, 1998. Asst Ed., The Year's Work in English Studies, 1976–84; Gen. Ed., John Buchan series, OUP World's Classics, 1993–; Founder and Ed., Reformation, 1995–97. Mem., Acad. Adv. Cttee, Internat. Shakespeare Globe Centre, 1981–91; Founder and organiser, biennial Oxford Internat. Tyndale Confs, 1994–; Founder and Chm., Tyndale Soc., 1995–. Curator, Let There Be Light Exhibn, British Liby, 1994–97 (London, Calif, NY and Washington). Frequent broadcaster, incl. Tyndale, New Testament, Radio 3, 1993. Lectures widely in UK, Europe and USA. Hon. Fellow, Hertford Coll., Oxford, 1998. *Publications:* The Interpreter's House, 1975; Coriolanus in Europe, 1980; The Best Short Stories of John Buchan, vol. 1, 1980, vol. 2, 1982; The Critics Debate: The Tempest, 1989; (ed) Tyndale's 1534 New Testament, 1989; (ed) Tyndale's Old Testament, 1992; William Tyndale: a biography, 1994; The Arden Shakespeare: Julius Caesar, 1998; (ed) Tyndale, the Obedience of a Christian Man, 2000; numerous contribs to learned jls incl. Shakespeare Survey, TLS, The Year's Work in English Studies, MLR, Jl of Ecclesiastical Hist., Jl of Amer. Studies. *Recreations:* music, reading, hill-walking in Scotland. *Address:* 17 Crossfell Road, Leverstock Green, Hemel Hempstead, Herts HP3 8RF. *T:* (01442) 254766.

DANIELL, Sir Peter (Averell), Kt 1971; TD 1950; DL; Senior Government Broker, 1963–73; *b* 8 Dec. 1909; *s* of R. H. A. Daniell and Kathleen Daniell (*née* Monsell); *m* 1935, Leonie M. Harrison (*d* 1997); two *s* one *d*. *Educ:* Eton Coll.; Trinity Coll., Oxford (MA). Joined Mullens & Co., 1932, Partner, 1945; retd 1973. Served KRRC, 1939–45, Middle East and Italy. Master, Drapers' Co., 1980–81. DL Surrey 1976. *Recreations:* shooting, fishing, golf. *Address:* Glebe House, Buckland, Betchworth, Surrey RH3 7BL. *T:* (01737) 842320. *Clubs:* Brooks's, Alpine.

DANIELL, Ralph Allen, CBE 1965 (OBE 1958); HM Diplomatic Service, retired; *b* 26 Jan. 1915; 2nd *s* of late Reginald Allen Daniell; *m* 1943, Diana Lesley (*née* Tyndale); one *s* three *d*. *Educ:* Lancing Coll.; University Coll., Oxford. Appointed to Board of Trade, 1937. Joined HM Forces, 1942; served with Royal Tank Regt in North Africa and Italian campaigns, 1943–45. Appointed to HM Foreign Service as First Sec., 1946; Mexico City, 1946; Rome, 1949; Foreign Office, 1951; Helsinki, 1953; Counsellor, 1958; Washington, 1958; New York, 1959; Cairo, 1962; Wellington, 1967; Consul-Gen., Chicago, 1972–74. *Address:* 1A Collins Lane, Ringwood, Hants BH24 1LD. *T:* (01425) 473662.

DANIELS, David; countertenor; *b* S Carolina, 12 March 1966. *Educ:* Cincinnati Conservatoire; Univ. of Michigan. Singing début, 1992; début with Metropolitan Opera, as Sesto in Giulio Cesare, 1999; *rôles* include: Rinaldo, Nerone in L'Incoronazione di Poppea, Didymus in Theodora, Hamor in Jeptha, Arsamenes in Xerxes, Oberon in A Midsummer Night's Dream; title rôles in Tamerlano, Giulio Cesare, Orfeo ed Euridice; has performed with San Francisco SO, St Louis SO, New World SO , Philharmonia Baroque, San Francisco Opera, Florida Grand Opera, Bavarian State Opera, Glimmerglass Opera Fest., Brooklyn Acad. of Music, Royal Opera, Covent Gdn, Glyndebourne Fest., Salzburg Fest., NY City Opera, Canadian Opera Co., Lyric Opera of Chicago, Netherlands Opera, and Paris Opera; extensive recital and concert repertoire performed in US and Europe, incl. Promenade Concerts. Has made numerous recordings. Richard Tucker Award, 1997, Vocalist of Year Award, Musical America, 1999. *Recreations:* theatre, sports, especially baseball. *Address:* c/o Askonas Holt Ltd, Lonsdale Chambers, 27 Chancery Lane, WC2A 1PF. *T:* (020) 7400 1731.

DANIELS, George, MBE 1982; FSA, FBHI; author, watch maker; horological consultant to Sothebys, since 1970; *b* 19 Aug. 1926; *s* of George Daniels and Beatrice (*née* Cadou); *m* 1964, Juliet Anne (*née* Marryat); one *d*. *Educ:* elementary. 2nd Bn E Yorks Regt, 1944–47. Started professional horology, 1947; restoration of historical watches, 1956–; hand watch making to own designs, 1969–; invented co-Axial escapement, 1975, developed and patented, 1980, industrialised by Swiss makers, 1997; designed IOM Millennium postage stamps, commemorating English chronometer inventors, 1999. Horological lectures, both antiquarian and modern technical, to RSA, Royal Instn, Antiquarian Horol Soc., Harvard Univ., Cambridge Phil Soc., British Horol Inst., Amer. Watchmakers' Inst., Swedish Watchmakers' Inst., RAS, RCA. President: British Horological Inst., 1980 (Fellow, 1951); British Clock and Watchmakers' Benevolent Soc., 1980; Founding Chm., Horological Industries Cttee, 1985–; Chm. and Founder, BHI Educn Trust, 1998. One man exhibition, Goldsmiths' Hall, 1992. Worshipful Co. of Clockmakers: Liveryman, 1968; Warden, 1977; Master, 1980; Tompion Gold Medal, 1981; Asst Hon. Surveyor, 1972–81. Freeman, Goldsmiths' Co., 1979; FSA 1976. Hon. DSc City, 1994. Arts, Sciences and Learning Award, City Corporation, London, 1974; Victor Kullberg Medal, Stockholm Watch Guild, 1977; Gold Medal, British Horol Inst., 1981; Gold Badge and Hon. Fellow, Amer. Watchmakers Inst., 1985; Hon. FCGI 1986; City and Guilds Gold Medal for Craftsmanship, 1991. *Publications:* Watches (jtly), 1965, 3rd edn 1978 (trans. German, 1982); English and American Watches, 1967; The Art of Breguet, 1975, 3rd edn 1985 (trans. French, 1985, Italian, 1990); (jtly) Clocks and Watches of the Worshipful Company of Clockmakers, 1975; Sir David Salomons Collection, 1978; Watchmaking, 1981, 2nd edn 1985 (trans. French, 1993); The Practical Watch Escapement, 1995, 2nd edn 1997; All in Good Time (autobiog.), 2000, rev. edn 2001. *Recreations:* vintage cars, fast motorcycles, opera, Scotch whisky. *Address:* 34 New Bond Street, W1A 2AA.

DANIELS, Harold Albert; *b* 8 June 1915; *s* of Albert Pollikett Daniels and Eleanor Sarah Maud Daniels (*née* Flahey); *m* 1946, Frances Victoria Jerdan; one *s* decd. *Educ:* Mercers' Sch.; Christ's Coll., Cambridge. BA 1937; Wren Prize 1938; MA 1940. Asst Principal, Post Office, 1938; Admiralty, 1942; Post Office, 1945; Principal, 1946; Asst Sec., 1950; Under-Sec., 1961; Min. of Posts and Telecommunications, 1969; Asst Under Sec. of State, Home Office, 1974–76. *Address:* Lyle Court Cottage, Bradbourne Road, Sevenoaks, Kent TN13 3PZ. *T:* (01732) 454039.

DANIELS, Ruth; *see* Gledhill, R.

DANINOS, Pierre; French author; *b* Paris, 26 May 1913; *m* 1st, 1942, Jane Marrain; one *s* two *d*; 2nd, 1968, Marie-Pierre Dourneau. *Educ:* Lycée Janson de Sailly, Paris. Began to write for newspapers, 1931; reporter for French press in England, USA, etc. Liaison agent with British Army, Dunkirk, 1940. Published first book in Rio de Janeiro, 1940; returned to France, 1941, from South America, Chronicler for Le Figaro. *Publications:* Les Carnets du Bon Dieu (Prix Interallié 1947); L'Eternel Second, 1949; Sonia, les autres et moi (Prix Courteline, 1952) (English trans., Life with Sonia, 1958); Les Carnets du Major Thompson, 1954 (English trans., Major Thompson Lives in France, 1955); Le Secret du Major Thompson, 1956 (English trans., Major Thompson and I, 1957); Vacances à Tous Prix, 1958; Un certain Monsieur Blot, 1960 (English trans., 1961); Le Jacassin, 1962; Snobissimo, 1964; Le 36ème dessous, 1966; Le Major Tricolore, 1968; Ludovic Morateur, 1970; Le Pyjama, 1972; Les Touristocrates, 1974; Made in France, 1977; La Composition d'Histoire, 1979; Le Veuf Joyeux, 1981; La Galerie des Glaces, 1983; La France dans tous ses états, 1985; Profession: écrivain (autobiog.), 1988; Candidement Vôtre, 1992; Les

Derniers Carnets de Major Thompson, 2001. *Recreations:* tennis, ski-ing, collecting British hobbies. *Address:* 15 rue Chauveau, 92200 Neuilly, France.

DANKERT, Pieter, Kt of Order of Netherlands Lion; Commander, Order of Orange Nassau; *b* Jan. 1934; *m* 1962, Paulette Puig; one *s* two *d*. *Educ:* Amsterdam Free Univ. Member (Partij van de Arbeid) Tweede Kamer, Netherlands; Dutch Parlt, 1968–81; Sec. of State for Foreign Affairs, 1989–94. MEP, 1977–87 and 1994–99 (Pres., 1982–84). Mem., Adv. Cttee Internat. Questions, Min. of Foreign Affairs, Netherlands. Formerly InternatSec., Partij van de Arbeid. Member: NATO Assembly, WEU Assembly and Assembly of Council of Europe, 1971–77; Expert Cttee on Charter Regl and Minority Langs, Council of Europe. *Address:* Hoogstraat 1, 1135 BZ Edam, Netherlands.

DANKWORTH, Dame Clementine Dinah; *see* Laine, Dame Cleo.

DANKWORTH, John Philip William, CBE 1974; FRAM 1973; musician; *b* 20 Sept. 1927; British; *m* 1958, Dame Cleo Laine, *qv*; one *s* one *d*. *Educ:* Monoux Grammar Sch. Studied Royal Academy of Music, 1944–46. ARAM 1969. Closely involved with post-war development of British jazz, 1947–60; formed large jazz orchestra, 1953; with Cleo Laine founded Stables Theatre, Wavendon, 1969. Pops Music Dir, LSO, 1985–90; Principal Guest Pops Conductor, San Francisco Orch., 1987–89. Composed works for combined jazz and symphonic musicians including: Improvisations (with Matyas Seiber, 1959); Escapade (commissioned by Northern Sinfonia Orch., 1967); Tom Sawyer's Saturday, for narrator and orchestra (commissioned by Farnham Festival), 1967; String Quartet, 1971; Piano Concerto (commissioned by Westminster Festival, 1972); Grace Abounding (for RPO), 1980; The Diamond and the Goose (for City of Birmingham Choir and Orch.), 1981; Reconciliation (commnd for Silver Jubilee of Coventry Cathedral), 1987; Woolwich Clarinet Concerto (for Emma Johnson), 1995; Double Vision (for BBC Big Band, world première, BBC Proms), 1997; Objective 2000 (for combined orchs of Harpur Trust Schs), 2000. Many important film scores (1964–) including: Saturday Night and Sunday Morning, Darling, The Servant, Morgan, Accident, Gangster No 1; other works include: Palabras, 1970; dialogue and songs for Colette, Comedy, 1980. Numerous record albums, incl. Echoes of Harlem, Misty, Symphonic Fusions. Variety Club of GB Show Business Personality Award (with Cleo Laine), 1977. Hon. Fellow, Leeds Coll. of Music, 1999. Hon. MA Open Univ., 1975; Hon. DMus: Berklee Sch. of Music, 1982; York, 1993. Distinguished Artists Award, Internat. Soc. for the Performance Arts, 1999. *Publications:* Sax from the Start, 1996; Jazz in Revolution (autobiog.), 1998. *Recreations:* driving, household maintenance. *Address:* The Old Rectory, Wavendon, Milton Keynes MK17 8LT. *Fax:* (01908) 584414.

DANN, Mrs Jill; *b* 10 Sept. 1929; *d* of Harold Norman Cartwright and Marjorie Alice Thornton; *m* 1952, Anthony John Dann (*d* 2000); two *s* two *d* (and one *s* decd). *Educ:* Solihull High Sch. for Girls, Malvern Hall; Birmingham Univ. (LLB); St Hilda's Coll., Oxford (BCL). Called to the Bar, Inner Temple, 1952. Mayoress of Chippenham, 1964–65. Church Commissioner, 1968–93; Member: General Synod of Church of England, 1965–95, and of its Standing Cttee, 1971–90 (Vice-Chm. House of Laity, 1985–90); Crown Appointments Commn, 1977–87; Chairman: House of Laity, Bristol Diocesan Synod, 1982–88; C of E Evangelical Council, 1985–89; Trustee, Church Urban Fund, 1987–95. Vice Chm., Trinity Coll., Bristol; Pres. of Fellows, Cheltenham and Gloucester Coll. of Higher Educn. Director: Wiltshire Radio, 1981–88; ARK 2 TV Ltd, 1995–97. Pres., Inner Wheel, 1978–79. *Recreations:* reading, enjoying being a grandmother. *Address:* The Riverbank, Reybridge, Lacock, Wilts SN15 2PF. *T:* (01249) 730205.

DANN, Most Rev. Robert William; *b* 28 Sept. 1914; *s* of James and Ruth Dann; *m* 1949, Yvonne (*née* Newnham); one *s* two *d*. *Educ:* Trinity Coll., Univ. of Melbourne. BA Hons Melbourne 1946. Deacon, 1945; Priest, 1946. Dir of Youth and Religious Education, Dio. Melbourne, 1946; Incumbent: St Matthew's, Cheltenham, 1951; St George's, Malvern, 1956; St John's, Footscray, 1961; Archdeacon of Essendon, 1961; Dir of Evangelism and Extension, Dio. Melbourne, 1963; Bishop Coadjutor, Dio. Melbourne, 1969–77; Archbishop of Melbourne and Metropolitan of Province of Victoria, 1977–83. *Address:* 1 Myrtle Road, Canterbury, Vic 3126, Australia.

DANNATT, Maj.-Gen. Francis Richard, CBE 1996; MC 1973; Assistant Chief of the General Staff, since 2001; *b* 23 Dec. 1950; *s* of late Anthony Richard Dannatt and of Mary Juliet Dannatt (*née* Chilvers); *m* 1977, Philippa Margaret Gurney; three *s* one *d*. *Educ:* Felsted Jun. Sch.; St Lawrence Coll.; RMA, Sandhurst; Univ. of Durham (BA Hons Econ. Hist. 1976). Commnd Green Howards, 1971; Army Comd and Staff Coll., Camberley, 1982; COS, 20th Armd Bde, 1983–84; MA to Minister of State for Armed Forces, 1986–89; CO, 1 Green Howards, 1989–91; Col Higher Comd and Staff Course, Staff Coll., Camberley, 1992–94; Comdr, 4th Armd Bde, 1994–96; Dir, Defence Progs, MoD, 1996–98; GOC 3rd UK Div., 1999–2000; D Comdr Ops, HQ SFOR, 2000–01. Col, Green Howards, 1994–; Dep. Col Comdt, AGC (RMP), 1999–; Col Comdt, King's Div., 2001–. Vice Pres., Officers Christian Union, 1998–; President: Soldiers' and Airmen's Scripture Readers Assoc., 1999–; Army Rifle Assoc., 2000–. *Recreations:* cricket, tennis, fishing, shooting. *Address:* Regimental Headquarters, The Green Howards, Holy Trinity Church, Richmond, N Yorks DL10 4QN. *T:* (01748) 822133. *Club:* Army and Navy.

DANNATT, Prof. (James) Trevor, MA; RA 1983 (ARA 1977); FRIBA; Partner, Dannatt, Johnson Architects (formerly Trevor Dannatt & Partners), since 1975; Professor of Architecture: Manchester University, 1975–86; Royal Academy, 1988; *b* 15 Jan. 1920; *s* of George Herbert and Jane Ellen Dannatt; *m* 1st, 1953, Joan Howell Davies (marr. diss. 1991); one *s* one *d*; 2nd, 1994, Dr Ann Crawshaw (*née* Critchley). *Educ:* Colfes Sch.; Sch. of Architecture, Regent Street Polytechnic (Dip. Arch.). Professional experience in office of Jane B. Drew and E. Maxwell Fry, 1943–48; Architects Dept, LCC (Royal Festival Hall Gp), 1948–52; commenced private practice, 1952. Vis. Prof., Washington Univ., St Louis, 1976 and 1987. Assessor for national and international architectural competitions. Member: Cathedrals Adv. Commn, 1986–91; Historic Bldgs Adv. Cttee, English Heritage, 1988–91 (Mem., Post War Listing Adv. Cttee, 1986–); Fabric Cttees of Cathedrals: Lichfield, 1985–; Portsmouth, 1990–; St Paul's, 1991–. Founder Mem., and Chm., South Bank Gp, 1993–. Trustee, DOCOMOMO (Documents of the Modern Movement), 1991–. Editor, Architects' Year Book, 1945–62. Architectural work includes: private houses, housing, school buildings (for LCC, Bootham, St Paul's, Colfe's); university buildings (residences, Leicester, Hull; Trinity Hall Combination Room, Cambridge; Vaughan Coll. and Jewry Wall Mus., Leicester; develt plan and extensive works for Univ. of Greenwich, formerly Thames Polytechnic, inc. studies for occupation of several buildings of RNC at Greenwich, incl. conversion and refurbishment of Queen Anne Quarters and Dreadnought Seamen's Hosp., 1999, Queen Mary's Quarters, 2000 and King William's Quarters, 2001); welfare buildings (for London boroughs, Lambeth, Southwark, Greenwich); conservation and restoration, interiors for private, corporate and public clients; Architects for British Embassy and Diplomatic Staff housing, Riyadh, 1985; Consultant Architects, Royal Botanic Gardens, Kew, 1989; Victoria Gate visitors' reception and facilities building, 1992; various restorations and new buildings, Kew, 1988–. Won internat. competition for conference complex in Riyadh, Saudi Arabia, completed 1974. Hon. FAIA 1988. *Publications:* Modern Architecture in Britain, 1959; Trevor Dannatt: Buildings and Interiors 1951–72, 1972; (Editorial Adviser, and foreword) Buildings and Ideas 1933–83 from the Studio of Leslie Martin, 1983; (with P. Carolin) Sir Leslie Martin: architecture, education, research, 1996; contribs to Architectural Rev., Architects' Jl, and various foreign journals. *Recreations:* the arts, including architecture. *Address:* (office) 52c Borough High Street, SE1 1XN. *T:* (020) 7357 7100. *Clubs:* Travellers, Arts.

DANSON, Hon. Barnett Jerome; PC (Canada) 1974; OC 1996; consultant, since 1984; company director; *s* of Joseph B. Danson and Saidie W. Danson, Toronto; *m* 1943, Isobel, *d* of Robert John Bull, London, England; four *s*. *Educ:* Toronto public and high schs. Served War: enlisted Queen's Own Rifles as Rifleman, 1939; commnd, 1943; wounded in France, 1944; retd 1945, Lieut. Manager, Jos. B. Danson & Sons Ltd, Toronto, 1945–50; Sales Man., Maple Leaf Plastics Ltd, 1950–53; Principal (Pres.), Danson Corp. Ltd, Scarborough, 1953–74; Chairman: CSPG Consultants, 1980–84; de Havilland Aircraft of Canada Ltd, 1981–84; Canadian Consul General, Boston, Mass, 1984–86. Active in Liberal Party, 1946–: MP (L) for York North, 1968–79; Parly Sec. to Prime Minister Trudeau, 1970–72; Minister of State for Urban Affairs, 1974–76; Minister of Nat. Defence, Canada, 1976–79; former Mem., Standing Cttee on Finance, Trade and Econ. Affairs, and Ext. Affairs and National Defence. Chm., GSW Thermoplastics Co.; Dir, Algoma Central Railway Ltd. Dir Emeritus, Canadian Council of Native Business; Director: Atlantic Council of Canada; Canadian Inst. of Strategic Studies; Canadian Centre for Global Security; Canadian Exec. Services Orgn, Toronto; Royal Conservatory of Music, Canada; Sir Arthur Pearson Assoc. of War Blinded. Chm. Bd, No Price Too High Foundn; former Pres. and first Chm. Bd, Soc. of Plastics Engineers Inc. Dir, Canadian Council of Christians and Jews. Hon. Dir, Empire Club, Canada. Chm., Adv. Cttee, Canadian War Mus., 1998–. Trustee, Canadian Mus. of Civilisation, 1998–. Former Hon. Lt-Col, Queen's Own Rifles of Canada. Dr of Laws (*hc*) Royal Military Coll. of Canada, 1993. Award for Excellence in the cause of parly democracy, Churchill Soc., 1995; Vimy Award, Conf. of Defence Assocs, 2000. Officer, Order of Merit (France), 1994. *Recreations:* fishing, reading, music. *Address:* 1132 Bay Street, Apt 1501, Toronto, ON M5S 2Z4, Canada.

DANTZIC, Roy Matthew, CA; Managing Director, Lattice Property Holdings (formerly British Gas Properties, then BG Property Holdings), since 1996; *b* 4 July 1944; *s* of David and Renee Dantzic; *m* 1969, Diane Clapham; one *s* one *d*. *Educ:* Brighton Coll., Sussex. CA 1968. Coopers & Lybrand, 1962–69; Kleinwort, Benson Ltd, 1970–72; Drayton Corporation Ltd, 1972–74; Samuel Montagu & Co. Ltd, 1974–80 (Exec. Dir, 1975); Mem. for Finance, BNOC, subseq. Finance Dir, Britoil plc, 1980–84; Dir, Pallas SA, 1984–85; Dir, Wood Mackenzie & Co., 1985–89; Finance Dir, Stanhope Properties, 1989–95. Dir, Merrill Lynch Internat., 1995–96; Chairman: Premier Portfolio Ltd, 1985–95; Associated British Cinemas Ltd, 1998–2000; non-executive Director: Moor Park (1958) Ltd, 1980–90; Saxon Oil plc, 1984–85; Total Oil Holdings, 1995–96; Airplanes Ltd, 1996–. Pt-time Mem., CEGB, 1984–87; Pt-time Dir, BNFL, 1987–91. Mem., Council of Mgt, Architectural Heritage Trust, 2001–. Governor, Brighton Coll., 1990–98. *Recreations:* cinema, theatre, playing golf, watching cricket. *Clubs:* MCC; Moor Park Golf.

DARBY, John Oliver Robertson; Chairman, Arthur Young, Chartered Accountants, 1974–87; *b* 5 Jan. 1930; *s* of Ralph Darby and Margaret Darby (*née* Robertson); *m* 1955, Valerie Leyland Cole; three *s*. *Educ:* Charterhouse. FCA 1953. Pilot Officer, RAF, 1953–55; Arthur Young, Chartered Accts, 1955–87, Partner, 1959–87. Chairman: Nat. Home Loans Hldgs PLC, 1985–92; Property Lending Trust, later Property Lending Bank, PLC, 1987–92; Ultramar, 1988–91; BREL Gp, later ABB Transportation (Hldgs) Ltd, 1989–94; Director: British Rail Engineering Ltd, 1986–89; Lightgraphix Ltd, 1996–. *Recreations:* racing, golf. *Address:* The Tithe Barn, Headley, Bordon, Hants GU35 8PW. *Clubs:* Garrick, Royal Thames Yacht; Royal & Ancient Golf (St Andrews); Liphook Golf.

DARBY, Dr Michael Douglas, FRES; Coleoptera recorder for Wiltshire, since 1995; Editor, Recording Wiltshire's Biodiversity, since 1996; *b* 2 Sept. 1944; *s* of Arthur Douglas Darby and Ilene Doris Darby (*née* Eatwell); *m* 1977, Elisabeth Susan Done; two *s*. *Educ:* Rugby School; Reading Univ. (PhD). FRES 1977; FRGS 1984; AMA 1990. Asst to Barbara Jones, 1963; Victoria and Albert Museum: Textiles Dept, 1964–72; Prints and Drawings Dept, 1973–76; Exhibitions Officer, 1977–83; Dep. Dir, 1983–87; Hd of Publications, Exhibitions and Design, 1988–89; Surveyor Gen., Carroll Art Collection, 1990–94. Member: Crafts Council, 1984–88; IoW Adv. Cttee, English Heritage, 1986–; Council, Royal Entomol Soc., 1988–90; Council, National Trust, 1989–93; Council, Wilts Archaeol and Natural Hist. Soc., 1996–. FRSA 1989. *Publications:* Marble Halls, 1973; Early Railway Prints, 1974, 2nd edn 1979; British Art in the Victoria and Albert Museum, 1983; John Pollard Seddon, 1983; The Islamic Perspective, 1983; articles in art, architectural and entomological periodicals. *Recreations:* beetles, books. *Address:* The Old Malthouse, Sutton Mandeville, near Salisbury, Wilts SP3 5ND. *T:* (01722) 714295.

DARBY, Sir Peter (Howard), Kt 1985; CBE 1973; QFSM 1970; HM Chief Inspector of Fire Services, 1981–86; *b* 8 July 1924; *s* of William Cyril Darby and Beatrice Colin; *m* 1948, Ellen Josephine Glynn; one *s* one *d*. *Educ:* City of Birmingham Coll. of Advanced Technology. Fire Brigades: Dep. Ch. Officer, Suffolk and Ipswich FB, 1963; Chief Officer, Nottingham FB, 1966; Chief Officer, Lancashire FB, 1967; County Fire Officer, Greater Manchester FB, 1974; Regional Fire Comdr (No 10) NW Region, 1974–76; Regional Fire Adviser (No 5) Greater London Region, 1977; Chief Officer of the London Fire Brigade, 1977–80. Pres., Chief and Asst Chief Fire Officers' Assoc., 1975–76; Mem. Adv. Council, Central Fire Brigades, 1977; Principal Adviser to Sec. of State on Fire Service matters, 1981–86; Chm., Fire Services Central Examinations Bd, 1985. Chm., Certifire Ltd, 1987–. Foundation Gov., St James's Catholic High (formerly Secondary Modern) Sch., Barnet, 1985– (Chm. Governors, 1987–). Freeman, City of London; Liveryman, Worshipful Co. of Basketmakers. CStJ 1983. *Recreations:* fell-walking, golf, fishing, sailing. *Address:* Darby, York House, 7 Twatling Road, Barnt Green, Birmingham B45 8HX. *Clubs:* City Livery, KSC.

DARBYSHIRE, Jane Helen, (Mrs Jane Darbyshire-Walker), OBE 1994; Consultant, Jane Darbyshire and David Kendall Ltd (Director, 1995–2000); *b* 5 June 1948; *d* of Gordon Desmond Wroe and Patricia Keough; *m* 1st, 1973, David Darbyshire (marr. diss. 1987); one *d*; 2nd, 1993, Michael Walker. *Educ:* Univ. of Newcastle upon Tyne (BA Hons, BArch Hons). RIBA. Architect: Ryder and Yates, Newcastle upon Tyne, 1972–75; Barnett Winskell, 1975–79; Partner: Jane and David Darbyshire, 1979–87; Jane Darbyshire Associates, 1987–95. Ext. Examr, Newcastle upon Tyne Univ., 1993–95. Mem., RIBA Nat. Council, 1998–2001; Board Member: Tyne and Wear Develt Corp., 1992–98; NE Regl Cultural Consortium, 1999–2001. *Recreations:* classical music, horse riding, art. *Address:* Jane Darbyshire and David Kendall Ltd, Millmount, Ponteland Road, Newcastle upon Tyne NE5 3AL.

D'ARCY, Most Rev. Eric; Archbishop (RC) of Hobart (Australia), 1988–99, now Emeritus; *b* 25 April 1924; *s* of late Joseph D'Arcy, MM and Eileen (*née* McCoy). *Educ:*

De La Salle Coll. and Corpus Christi Coll., Melbourne; Univs of Melbourne (BA Hons; MA), Oxford (DPhil), and Gregoriana (PhD). Asst priest, Melbourne, 1949–55; Chaplain, Nat. Civic Council, 1955–59; Lectr, 1962, Sen. Lectr, 1966, Reader in Philosophy, 1975–81, Univ. of Melbourne; Bishop of Sale, 1981–88. Danforth Prof of Philosophy, Univ. of Minnesota, 1968. Member: Vatican Pontifical Congregation for Bishops, 1993–98; Pontifical Congregation for Catholic Educn, 1989–94; Pontifical Commn for Cultural Heritage of the Church, 1994–99. *Publications:* Conscience, Right to Freedom, 1961 (trans. Spanish 1964, French 1965); Human Acts, 1963; (ed and trans.) St Thomas Aquinas, Pleasure, 1967, The Emotions, 1975. *Recreations:* walking, reading. *Address:* Mount St Canice, GPO Box 62A, Hobart, Tas 7001, Australia. *T:* (3) 62251920. *Clubs:* Oxford and Cambridge; University House (Melbourne).

DARCY DE KNAYTH, Baroness (18th in line), *cr* 1332; **Davina Marcia Ingrams,** DBE 1996; *b* 10 July 1938; *née* Herbert; *d* of late Squadron Leader Viscount Clive (*d* on active service, 1943) (17th Baron Darcy de Knayth, and *s* of 4th Earl of Powis), and of Vida, *o d* of late Captain James Harold Cuthbert, DSO, Scots Guards (she *m* 2nd, 1945, Brig. Derek Schreiber, MVO (*d* 1972)); *S* to father's Barony, 1943; *m* 1960, Rupert George Ingrams (*d* 1964), *s* of late Leonard Ingrams and of Mrs Ingrams; one *s* two *d*. Elected Mem., H of L, 1999. *Heir: s* Hon. Caspar David Ingrams [*b* 5 Jan. 1962; *m* 1996, Catherine, *er d* of Bryan Baker and of Mrs Bryan Barnes]. *Address:* Camley Corner, Stubbings, Maidenhead, Berks SL6 6QW.

D'ARCY HART, Philip Montagu; *see* Hart.

DARELL, Brig. Sir Jeffrey (Lionel), 8th Bt *cr* 1795; MC 1945; *b* 2 Oct. 1919; *s* of late Lt-Col Guy Marsland Darell, MC (3rd *s* of 5th Bt); *S* cousin, 1959; *m* 1953, Bridget Mary, *e d* of Maj.-Gen. Sir Allan Adair, 6th Bt, GCVO, CB, DSO, MC; one *s* two *d*. *Educ:* Eton; RMC, Sandhurst. Commissioned Coldstream Guards, July 1939; served War of 1939–45: Coats Mission, 1940–41 (to guard Royal Family in case of invasion); ADC to GOC-in-C, Southern Comd, 1942; Bde Major, Guards Bde, 1953–55; Officer Comdg 1st Bn Coldstream Guards, 1957–59; GSO1, PS12, War Office, 1959; College Comdr RMA Sandhurst, 1961–64; Comdg Coldstream Guards, 1964–65; Comdr, 56 Inf. Brigade (TA), 1965–67; Vice-Pres., Regular Commns Bd, 1968–70; Comdt, Mons OCS, 1970–72; MoD, 1972–74; retd 1974. ADC to HM the Queen, 1973–74. Trustee and Mem., London Law Trust, 1981–99. High Sheriff, Norfolk, 1985. *Recreations:* normal. *Heir: s* Guy Jeffrey Adair Darell [*b* 8 June 1961; *m* 1988, Justine Samantha, *d* of Mr Justice T. Reynolds, Quambi Place, Sydney, Australia; one *s* two *d*]. *Address:* Denton Lodge, Harleston, Norfolk IP20 0AD. *T:* (01986) 788206. *Clubs:* Army and Navy, MCC.

DARESBURY, 4th Baron, *cr* 1927, of Walton, co. Chester; **Peter Gilbert Greenall;** Bt 1876; DL; Chairman, The De Vere (formerly Greenalls) Group plc, since 2000 (Director, since 1982); *b* 18 July 1953; *e s* of 3rd Baron Daresbury and of his 1st wife, Margaret Ada, *y d* of C. J. Crawford; *S* father, 1996; *m* 1982, Clare Alison, *d* of Christopher Weatherby; four *s*. *Educ:* Eton; Magdalene Coll., Cambridge (MA); London Business Sch. (Sloan Fellowship). Man. Dir, 1992–97, Chief Exec., 1997–2000, Greenalls Gp; Chm., Aintree Racecourse Co. Ltd, 1988–. DL Cheshire, 1993. *Heir: s* Hon. Thomas Edward Greenall, *b* 6 Nov. 1984. *Address:* Hall Lane Farm, Daresbury, Warrington, Cheshire WA4 4AF. *T:* (01925) 740212, *Fax:* (01925) 740884; The De Vere Group plc, PO Box 333, The Malt Building, Greenalls Avenue, Warrington, Cheshire WA4 6HL. *T:* (01925) 651234; *e-mail:* peter@daresburyltd.co.uk. *Clubs:* Jockey, MCC; Royal & Ancient Golf (St Andrews).

DARGIE, Sir William Alexander, Kt 1970; CBE 1969 (OBE 1960); FRSA 1951; artist; portrait, figure and landscape painter; Chairman, Commonwealth Art Advisory Board, Prime Minister's Department, 1969–73 (Member, 1953–73); *b* 4 June 1912; *s* of Andrew and Adelaide Dargie; *m* 1937, Kathleen, *d* of late G. H. Howitt; one *s* one *d*. Official War Artist (Capt.) with AIF in Middle East, Burma, New Guinea, India, 1941–46. Dir, National Gallery of Victoria Art Schs, 1946–53. Member: Interim Council of Nat. Gallery Canberra, 1968–72; Nat. Capital Planning Cttee, Canberra, 1970–73; Aboriginal Arts Adv. Cttee, 1970–72; Trustee: Native Cultural Reserve, Port Moresby, Papua-New Guinea, 1970–73; Museum of Papua-New Guinea, 1970–73; Mem. Council, Nat. Museum, Victoria, 1978–83; Chm., Bd of Trustees, McClelland Gall., 1981–87. MA *hc* Footscray Inst. of Technol., 1986. Archibald Prize for portraiture, 1941, 1942, 1945, 1946, 1947, 1950, 1952, 1956; Woodward Award, 1940; McPhillimy Award, 1940; McKay Prize, 1941. Painted portrait of The Queen for Commonwealth of Aust., 1954; the Duke of Gloucester, 1947; the Duke of Edinburgh for City of Melbourne, 1956. Portraits of Sir Macfarlane Burnet, Sir William Ashton, Sir Lionel Lindsay, acquired for Commonwealth Nat. Collection. Rep. in public and private collections in Aust., NZ, England and USA. One-man exhibition, Leger Galls, London, 1958. Exhibits with RA and Royal Soc. of Portrait Painters. *Publication:* On Painting a Portrait, 1956. *Recreations:* books, chess, tennis. *Address:* 19 Irilbarra Road, Canterbury, Victoria 3126, Australia. *T:* (3) 98363396. *Clubs:* Melbourne, Melbourne Savage (Melbourne).

DARK, Sir Anthony Michael B.; *see* Beaumont-Dark.

DARKE, Christopher; General Secretary, British Air Line Pilots Association, since 1992; *b* 5 Aug. 1949; *s* of late Derek Herbert Darke and Helen Navina Darke (*née* Davies); *m* 1st, 1976, Marian Dyson (marr. diss. 1982); one *s* one *d*; 2nd, 1992, Lorraine Julie Hinchliffe; two *d*. *Educ:* Handsworth Secondary Sch., Birmingham. Engrg apprentice, GEC, 1967–70; Engrg Draughtsman, Lucas Industries, 1970–77; TU Officer, AUEW-TASS, 1977–82; Nat. Officer, AUEW-TASS, later MSF, 1982–92. Mem., Competition (formerly Monopolies and Mergers) Commn, 1998–. *Recreations:* flying, travel, reading, gardening. *Address:* (office) 81 New Road, Harlington, Hayes, Middx UB3 5BG. *T:* (020) 8476 4000, *Fax:* (020) 8476 4077.

DARKE, Geoffrey James, RIBA; Principal, Geoffrey Darke Associates, Architects and Planners, since 1987; *b* 1 Sept. 1929; *s* of late Harry James Darke and Edith Anne (*née* Rose); *m* 1959, Jean Yvonne Rose, ARCM; one *s* two *d*. *Educ:* Prince Henry's Grammar Sch., Evesham, Worcs; Birmingham School of Architecture (DipArch); ARIBA 1956. National Service, Malaya, commnd RE, 1954–56. Asst Architect, Stevenage Development Corp., 1952–58; private practice, 1958–61; Partner, Darbourne and Darke, Architects and Landscape Planners, 1961–87. Work has included many large commissions, particularly public buildings. Success in national and internat. competitions, in Stuttgart, 1977, Hanover, 1979 and 1980, and in Bolzano, Italy, 1980; numerous medals and awards for architectural work; co-recipient of Fritz Schumacher Award, Hamburg, 1978, for services to architecture and townplanning. Mem. Council, RIBA, 1977–83; Chm., RIBA Competitions Cttee, 1979–84; has served on many professional committees; Mem., Access Cttee for England, 1992–. Mem., Aldeburgh Foundn, 1979–98. FRSA 1981. *Recreation:* music. *Address:* (office) Neptune House, 43 King Street, Aldeburgh, Suffolk IP15 5BY.

DARKE, Marjorie Sheila; writer, since 1962; *b* 25 Jan. 1929; *d* of Christopher Darke and Sarah Ann (*née* Palin); *m* 1952; two *s* one *d*. *Educ:* Worcester Grammar Sch. for Girls; Leicester Coll. of Art and Technol.; Central Sch. of Art, London. Worked in textile studio of John Lewis Partnership, 1950–54. *Publications:* Ride the Iron Horse, 1973; The Star Trap, 1974; A Question of Courage, 1975; The First of Midnight, 1977; A Long Way to Go, 1978; Comeback, 1981; Tom Post's Private Eye, 1982; Messages and Other Shivery Tales, 1984; A Rose from Blighty, 1990; *for young children:* Mike's Bike, 1974; What Can I Do, 1975; Kipper's Turn, 1976; The Big Brass Band, 1976; My Uncle Charlie, 1977; Carnival Day, 1979; Kipper Skips, 1979; Imp, 1985; The Rainbow Sandwich, 1989; Night Windows, 1990; Emma's Monster, 1992; Just Bear and Friends, 1996. *Recreations:* reading, music, sewing, country walks. *Address:* c/o Rogers, Coleridge & White Ltd, Literary Agency, 20 Powis Mews, W11 1JN. *Clubs:* Society of Authors; International PEN.

DARLEY, Gillian Mary, (Mrs Michael Horowitz); architectural writer, lecturer and photographer; Director, Landscape Foundation, 1994–98; *b* 28 Nov. 1947; *d* of Lt Col Robert Darley, MC and Caroline (*née* Swanston Ward); *m* 1986, Michael Horowitz, *qv*; one *d* (one *s* decd). *Educ:* Courtauld Inst. of Art, London Univ. (BA Hons 1969); Birkbeck Coll., London (MSc Politics and Admin 1986). Journalist and radio and TV broadcaster; contributor to daily and Sunday newspapers, magazines and professional press, 1975–; Architectural correspondent, Observer, 1991–93. Joint Partner, Edifice, architectural photographic liby, 1987–. Chm., SPAB, 1997–2000; Mem., Lottery Architecture Adv. Cttee, Arts Council of England, 1996–. External Assessor, Sch. of Three Dimensional Design, Kingston Univ., 1992–95. FRSA 1995. *Publications:* Villages of Vision, 1975; The National Trust Book of the Farm, 1981; Built in Britain, 1984; (with P. Lewis) Dictionary of Ornament, 1986; Octavia Hill: a life, 1990; (with A. Saint) The Chronicles of London, 1994; John Soane: an accidental romantic, 1999. *Recreations:* gardening in a small space, Jack Russell.

DARLEY, Kevin Paul; freelance flat race jockey; *b* 5 Aug. 1960; *s* of Clifford Darley and Dorothy Thelma Darley (*née* Newby); *m* 1983, Debby Ford; two *d*. *Educ:* Colton Hills Comprehensive Sch., Wolverhampton. Apprentice Jockey to Reg Hollinshead, 1976–78 (Champion apprentice, 1978, with 70 winners); has ridden 1800 winners, incl. 153 in one season, 1995; won French Derby, 1995, on Celtic Swing; Champion Jockey, 2000. *Recreations:* shooting, golf, hunting, ski-ing. *Address:* Castle Garth, York Road, Sheriff Hutton, York YO6 1RG. *T:* (01347) 878383.

DARLING; *see* Stormonth Darling.

DARLING, family name of **Baron Darling**.

DARLING, 2nd Baron *cr* 1924, of Langham; **Robert Charles Henry Darling;** DL; Major retired, Somerset Light Infantry; *b* 15 May 1919; *s* of late Major Hon. John Clive Darling, DSO; *S* grandfather, 1936; *m* 1942, Bridget Rosemary Whishaw (*d* 1997), *d* of Rev. F. C. Dickson; one *s* two *d*. *Educ:* Wellington Coll.; RMC Sandhurst. Retired, 1955. Sec., later Chief Executive, Royal Bath and West and Southern Counties Soc., 1961–79, Pres., 1989. DL Somerset 1972, Avon 1974, Somerset 1996. *Recreations:* fishing, gardening. *Heir: s* Hon. Robert Julian Henry Darling, FRICS [*b* 29 April 1944; *m* 1970, Janet, *yr d* of Mrs D. M. E. Mallinson, Richmond, Yorks; two *s* one *d*]. *Address:* Puckpits, Limpley Stoke, Bath, Somerset BA2 7JH. *T:* (01225) 722146.

DARLING, Rt Hon. Alistair (Maclean); PC 1997; MP (Lab) Edinburgh Central, since 1987; Secretary of State for Work and Pensions, since 2001; advocate; *b* 28 Nov. 1953; *m* 1986, Margaret McQueen Vaughan; one *s* one *d*. *Educ:* Aberdeen Univ. Admitted to Faculty of Advocates, 1984. Member: Lothian Regl Council, 1982–87; Lothian and Borders Police Bd, 1982–86. Shadow Chief Sec. to HM Treasury, 1996–97; Chief Sec. to HM Treasury, 1997–98; Sec. of State for Social Security, 1998–2001. Gov., Napier Coll., Edinburgh, 1982–87. *Address:* House of Commons, SW1A 0AA.

DARLING, Sir Clifford, GCVO 1994; Kt 1977; Governor-General, Bahamas, 1992–94; *b* Acklins Island, 6 Feb. 1922; *s* of Charles and Aremelia Darling; *m* Igrid Smith. *Educ:* Acklins Public Sch.; several public schs in Nassau. Became taxi-driver (Gen. Sec. Bahamas Taxicab Union for 8 yrs, Pres. for 10 yrs). An early Mem., Progressive Liberal Party; MHA for Englerston; Senator, 1964–67; Dep. Speaker, House of Assembly, 1967–69; Minister of State, Oct. 1969; Minister of Labour and Welfare, Dec. 1971; Minister of Labour and Nat. Insurance, 1974–77; Speaker, House of Assembly, 1977–92. Past Chm., Tourist Advisory Bd; instrumental in introd. of a comprehensive Nat. Insce Scheme in the Bahamas, Oct. 1974. Member: Masonic Lodge; Elks Lodge; Acklins, Crooked Is and Long Cays Assoc. *Address:* PO Box N-1050, Nassau, Bahamas.

DARLING, Rt Rev. Edward Flewett; Bishop of Limerick and Killaloe, 1985–2000; *b* 24 July 1933; *s* of late Ven. Vivian W. Darling and Honor F. G. Darling; *m* 1958, E. E. Patricia Mann; three *s* two *d*. *Educ:* Cork Grammar School; Midleton Coll., Co Cork. St John's School, Leatherhead, Surrey; Trinity Coll., Dublin (MA). Curate: St Luke's, Belfast, 1956–59; St John's, Orangefield, Belfast, 1959–62; Incumbent, St Gall's, Carnalea, Co. Down, 1962–72; Chaplain, Bangor Hosp., Co. Down, 1963–72; Rector, St John's, Malone, Belfast, 1972–85; Chaplain, Ulster Independent Clinic, Belfast, 1981–85. *Publications:* Choosing the Hymns, 1984; (ed) Irish Church Praise, 1990; Sing to the Word, 2000; (ed) Church Hymnal, 5th edn 2000. *Recreations:* music, gardening. *Address:* 15 Beechwood Park, Moira, Craigavon, Co. Armagh BT67 0LL. *T:* (028) 9261 2982; *e-mail:* darling.moira@churchofireland.net.

DARLING, Paul Antony; QC 1999; *b* 15 March 1960; *s* of William Martindale Darling, *qv*, and Ann Edith Darling; *m* 1st, 1983 (marr. diss.); 2nd, 1994 (marr. diss.). *Educ:* Tonstall Sch., Sunderland; Winchester Coll. (Schol.); St Edmund Hall, Oxford (BA Jurisp. 1981; BCL 1982). Treas., Oxford Union, 1980. Called to the Bar, Middle Temple, 1983; in practice, 1985–. Vice Chm., Technol. and Construction Bar Assoc., 2000–. Dir, J. M. & W. Darling Ltd (pharmaceutical chemists), 1978–. Ed., Construction Industry Law Letter, 1990–94; Mem., editl team, Keating on Building Contracts, 5th edn 1991 to 7th edn 2001. *Recreations:* horse racing, Newcastle United. *Address:* Keating Chambers, 10 Essex Street, WC2A 3AA. *T:* (020) 7544 2600. *Clubs:* Royal Ascot Racing; South Shields and Westoe (South Shields).

DARLING, Susan; Development advisor; *b* 5 May 1942; *d* of Eric Francis Justice Darling and Monica Darling (*née* Grant). *Educ:* Nonsuch County Grammar Sch. for Girls, Cheam; King's Coll., London (BA Hons). Joined BoT as Asst Principal, 1963; transf. to FCO, 1965; Nairobi, 1967–69; Second, later First Sec., Econ. and Social Affairs, UK Mission to UN, 1969–73; FCO, 1973–74; resigned, 1974; reinstated, 1975; FCO, 1975–78; Dep. High Comr and Head of Chancery, Suva, 1981–84; FCO, 1984–87; Consul-Gen., Perth, WA, 1987–88; resigned FCO, 1988; Dept of Chief Minister, NT, Australia, 1989–90; Quaker Service Australia, 1991–93; Aboriginal and Torres Strait Islander Commn, 1994–96; internat. policy, Law Soc. of England and Wales, 2000–. Trustee, Anti Slavery Internat., 1999–. *Recreations:* travel, draught horses. *Address:* Mayor House Farm Cottages, Farley Heath, Surrey GU5 9EW.

DARLING, William Martindale, CBE 1988 (OBE 1972); DL; FRPharmS; Managing Director, J. M. & W. Darling Ltd, since 1957; Chairman, Gateshead and South Tyneside (formerly South Tyneside, then South of Tyne) Health Authority, since 1974; *b* 7 May

1934; *s* of William Darling, MPS and Muriel Darling; *m* 1958, Ann Edith Allen; two *s*. *Educ:* Mortimer Road Primary Sch.; Newcastle Royal Grammar Sch.; Sunderland Polytechnic Sch. of Pharmacy. MPS 1956. Member: Medicines Commn, 1971–79; Health Educn Council, 1972–80; Pharmacy Bd, CNAA, 1972–78; Cttee on Safety of Medicines, 1979–86; Cttee on Review of Medicines, 1987–90; Health Service Supply Council, 1975–84 (Chm. and Vice-Chm.); Adv. Bd, NHS Purchasing and Supply Agency, 2000–; Lay Mem., GMC, 1995–99; Chairman: Standing Pharmaceutical Adv. Cttee, 1974–2001; Nat. Pharmaceutical Supplies Gp, 1984–; Head, UK Pharm. Delegn to EEC, 1972–; Pres., Pharm. Gp, EEC, 1985–86; Mem., Comité Consultatif pour formation des pharmaciens, 1988–. Pharmaceutical, later Royal Pharmaceutical, Society of Great Britain: Mem. Council, 1962–2001; Vice-Pres., 1969–71; Pres., 1971–73; Treas., 1992–95; Chm., Code of Ethics and Health Wkg Pty, 1970–. Vice Chm., S Tyneside Health Partnership and Gateshead Health Partnership; Mem., Tyne and Wear Health Action Zone Alliance. Member: Exec., Internat. Hosp. Fedn, 1994–; Council, NAHA, 1974–90 (Chm., 1980–82; Hon. Treasurer, 1988–89); first Chm., Nat. Assoc. of Health Authorities and Trusts, 1990–93; Pres., Internat. Hosp. Fedn, 1997–. Chm. Bd of Govs, Univ. of Sunderland (formerly Sunderland Poly.), 1994– (Gov., 1989–; Hon. Fellow, 1990). Hon. Life Mem., South Shields and Westoe Club, 1990. DL Tyne and Wear, 2000. Pharm. Soc. Gold Medal, 1985. *Recreations:* horse racing, sunbathing, eating good food, growing prize flowers and vegetables. *Address:* Hartside, 6 Whitburn Road, Cleadon, near Sunderland SR6 7QL. *T:* (0191) 536 2089.

See also P. A. Darling.

DARLINGTON, Joyce, (Mrs Anthony Darlington); *see* Blow, J.

DARLINGTON, Stephen Mark, FRCO; Organist and Official Student in Music, Christ Church, Oxford, since 1985; *b* 21 Sept. 1952; *s* of John Oliver Darlington and Bernice Constance Elizabeth (*née* Murphy); *m* 1975, Moira Ellen (*née* Hill); three *d*. *Educ:* King's Sch., Worcester; Christ Church, Oxford (Organ Schol.; MA). Asst Organist, Canterbury Cathedral, 1974–78; Master of the Music, St Albans Abbey, 1978–85. Artistic Dir, Internat. Organ Fest., 1979–85. Pres., RCO, 1998–2000. *Recreations:* travel, walking, punting, Italian food. *Address:* Christ Church, Oxford OX1 1DP. *T:* (01865) 276195.

DARLOW, Paul Manning; His Honour Judge Darlow; a Circuit Judge, since 1997; *b* 7 Feb. 1951; *s* of late Brig. Eric William Townsend Darlow, OBE and of Elsie Joan Darlow (*née* Ring); *m* 1985, Barbara Joan Speirs; one *d*. *Educ:* Audley House Prep. Sch, St Edward's Sch., Oxford; Mount Hermon Sch., Massachusetts; King's Coll., London (LLB). Called to the Bar, Middle Temple, 1973; in practice as barrister, London, 1974–78, Bristol, 1978–97; Asst Recorder, 1991–94; a Recorder, 1994–97. *Recreations:* sailing, tennis, bridge, walking. *Address:* Southampton Combined Court Centre, London Road, Southampton SO9 5AF.

DARNLEY, 11th Earl of, *cr* 1725; **Adam Ivo Stuart Bligh;** Baron Clifton of Leighton Bromswold, 1608; Baron Clifton of Rathmore, 1721; Viscount Darnley, 1723; *b* 8 Nov. 1941; *s* of 9th Earl of Darnley and of Rosemary, *d* of late Edmund Basil Potter; *S* half-brother, 1980; *m* 1965, Susan Elaine, JP, DL, *y d* of late Sir Donald Anderson; one *s* one *d*. *Educ:* Harrow; Christ Church, Oxford. Dir, City of Birmingham Touring Opera, 1990–2000. Governor, Cobham Hall Sch., 1981–. *Heir:* *s* Lord Clifton, *qv*. *Address:* Netherwood Manor, Tenbury Wells, Worcs WR15 8RT. *Clubs:* Brooks's, MCC.

DARROCH, Alasdair Malcolm; His Honour Judge Darroch; a Circuit Judge, since 2000; *b* 18 Feb. 1947; *s* of Ronald George Darroch and Diana Graburn Darroch; *m* 1972, Elizabeth Lesley Humphrey; one *s*. *Educ:* Harrow Sch.; Trinity Coll., Cambridge. Articled Mills & Reeve, Solicitors, Norwich, 1969; admitted as solicitor, 1971; Partner, Mills & Reeve, 1974-2000; a Recorder, 1996-2000. Pres., Norfolk and Norwich Incorporated Law Soc., 1996-97. *Publications:* contrib. articles to legal press. *Recreations:* gardening, European travel, real ale. *Address:* The Crown Court, New Street, Chelmsford, Essex.

DARROCH, (Nigel) Kim, CMG 1998; HM Diplomatic Service; Director, European Union Command, Foreign and Commonwealth Office, since 2000; *b* 30 April 1954; *s* of Alastair Macphee Darroch and Enid Darroch (*née* Thompson); *m* 1978, Vanessa Claire Jackson; one *s* one *d*. *Educ:* Abingdon Sch.; Durham Univ. (BSc Zool 1975). Joined FCO, 1976; First Secretary: Tokyo, 1980–84; FCO, 1985–86; Private Sec. to Minister of State, FCO, 1987–89; First Sec., Rome, 1989–92; Dep. Head, European Integration Dept, FCO, 1993–95; Head, Eastern Adriatic Dept, FCO, 1995–97; Counsellor (External Affairs), UK Perm. Rep. to EU, Brussels, 1997–98; Head, News Dept, FCO, 1998–2000. *Recreations:* squash, ski-ing, sailing, cinema. *Address:* c/o Foreign and Commonwealth Office, King Charles Street, Whitehall, SW1A 2AH.

DART, Dr Edward Charles, CBE 1997; Chairman, Plant Bioscience Ltd (formerly John Innes Centre Innovations), since 1999 (non-executive Director, 1997–99); *b* 8 March 1941; *s* of late Arthur and Alice Dart; *m* 1964, Jean Ellen Long; one *s* two *d*. *Educ:* Univ. of Manchester Inst. of Science and Technol. (BSc 1962; PhD 1965); Univ. of Calif, LA; Univ. of Calif, Berkeley. Imperial Chemical Industries: Sen. Res. Scientist, Petrochemical and Polymer Lab. (and Lectr in Org. Chem., Univ. of Liverpool), 1968–71; Sen. Res. Scientist, Corporate Lab., 1971–73; Jt Gp Head, Bioscience Gp, 1973–75; Gp Head, Bioscience, 1975–78; Jt Lab. Manager, Corporate Lab. Policy Gp, 1981–83; Head, Corporate Bioscience and Colloids Lab., 1983–85; Associate Res. Dir, Plant Protection Div., 1985–86; Res. Dir, ZENECA (formerly ICI) Seeds, 1986–97; Chief Executive Officer: Norwich Res. Park, 1997–98; AdProTech plc, 1997–99. Science and Engineering Research Council: Mem., Biotechnol. Directorate, 1981–84, Chm., 1984–89; Member: Molecular Biology Sub Cttee, 1980–82; Science Bd, 1985–88. Member: BBSRC, 1994–98 (Chm., Technol. Interaction Bd, 1994–97; Mem., Appointments Cttee, 1998–); BBSRC/Science Mus. Consensus Conf. Steering Cttee, 1994. Chairman: Biotechnol. Jt Adv. Bd, 1992–94; Agric., Horticulture and Forestry Foresight Panel, 1997–99; Member: Adv. Cttee on Genetic Manipulation, 1984–96; DTI/MAFF Agro Food Quality Link Cttee, 1991–98; John Innes Council, 1986–94; MAFF/AFRC Arable Crops Sectoral Gp, 1991–93; Agric. and Envmt Biotechnology Commn, 2000–. Pres., Berks and Oxfordshire Assoc. for Science Educn, 1989–92. *Publications:* review articles in scientific books; papers in chemical and bioscience jls. *Recreations:* travel, books, music, golf, gardening.

DART, Geoffrey Stanley; Director, Oil and Gas, Department of Trade and Industry, since 1998; *b* 2 Oct. 1952; *s* of Wilfred Stanley Dart and Irene Jean Dart; *m* 1974, Rosemary Penelope Hinton; one *s* one *d*. *Educ:* Torquay Boys' Grammar Sch.; St Peter's Coll., Oxford (BA and MA Mod. Hist.). Researcher, Electricity Council, 1974–77; Department of Energy: Energy Policy, Offshore Supplies, Oil Policy, Gas, Asst Private Sec. to Sec. of State, to 1984; Cabinet Secretariat, 1984–85; Principal Private Sec. to Sec. of State for Energy, 1985–87; Asst Sec., Electricity Div., 1987–89; Offshore Safety Div., 1989–91; Estabt and Finance Div., 1991–92; Department of Trade and Industry: Competitiveness Div., 1992–94; Under Sec., 1994–; Dir, Deregulation Unit, 1994; Hd, Regl Develt Div., 1995–96; Shell UK (on secondment), 1996; Dir, Insurance, 1997–98. Director: Laing Engineering, 1991–96; European Investment Bank, 1994–96. Gov., Gwyn Jones Sch., 1996–. *Recreations:* gardening, reading, music, films. *Address:* Department of Trade and Industry, 1 Victoria Street, SW1H 0ET. *T:* (020) 7215 5126.

DARTMOUTH, 10th Earl of, *cr* 1711; **William Legge;** Baron Dartmouth 1682; Viscount Lewisham 1711; Chartered Accountant; *b* 23 Sept. 1949; *e s* of 9th Earl of Dartmouth and of Raine, Countess Spencer, *qv*; *S* father, 1997. *Educ:* Eton; Christ Church, Oxford; Harvard Business Sch. Secretary, Oxford Union Soc., 1969. Contested (C): Leigh, Lancs, Feb. 1974; Stockport South, Oct. 1974; contested (C) Yorkshire and the Humber Region, Eur. Parly elecns, 1999. Founder, Kirklees Cable. *Recreations:* tennis, supporting American football. *Heir:* *b* Hon. Rupert Legge [*b* 1 Jan. 1951; *m* 1984, Victoria, *d* of L. E. B. Ottley; one *s* one *d*]. *Address:* Blakelea House, Marsden, near Huddersfield, W Yorks HD7 5AU. *Clubs:* Buck's; Harvard (New York); Travellers (Paris).

DARVALL, Sir (Charles) Roger, Kt 1971; CBE 1965; former company director; *b* 11 Aug. 1906; *s* of late C. S. Darvall; *m* 1931, Dorothea May (*d* 1997), *d* of late A. C. Vautier; two *d*. *Educ:* Burnie, Tasmania. FASA. Gen. Manager, Australia & New Zealand Bank Ltd, Melbourne, 1961–67; former Director: Broken Hill Pty; Rothmans of Pall Mall Aust.; H. C. Sleigh Ltd; Australia New Guinea Corp.; Electrolux Pty; L. M. Ericsson Pty; Munich Re-Insurance Co. of Aust.; Australian Eagle Insurance Co. Comr, State Electricity Commn of Vic, 1969–79. *Recreations:* motoring, gardening, outdoors. *Address:* c/o 33 Albion Street, South Yarra, Vic 3141, Australia. *Club:* Athenæum (Melbourne).

DARVALL, Sir Roger; *see* Darvall, Sir C. R.

DARVILL, Keith Ernest; *b* 28 May 1948; *s* of Ernest Arthur James Darvill and Ellen May (*née* Clarke); *m* 1971, Julia Betina de Saran; two *s* one *d*. *Educ:* Coll. of Law, Chester. Admitted solicitor, 1981. Port of London Authority: clerical posts, 1967–73; Asst Solicitor, 1973–84; Partner, Duthie Hart and Duthie, Solicitors, 1984–93; sole practitioner, 1993–97. MP (Lab) Upminster, 1997–2001; contested (Lab) same seat, 2001. *Recreations:* tennis, badminton, gardening. *Club:* Cranston Park Lawn Tennis (Upminster).

DARWALL SMITH, Simon Crompton; His Honour Judge Simon Darwall Smith; a Circuit Judge, since 1992; *b* 13 April 1946; *s* of late Randle Darwall Smith and Barbara Darwall Smith (*née* Crompton); *m* 1968, Susan Patricia Moss (*see* Susan Darwall Smith); two *d*. *Educ:* Charterhouse. Called to the Bar, Gray's Inn, 1968; in practice on Western Circuit, 1968–92; a Recorder, 1986–92. *Recreations:* opera, travel, ballet, theatre, concerts. *Address:* The Law Courts, Small Street, Bristol BS1 2HL. *Club:* Army and Navy.

DARWALL SMITH, Susan Patricia; Her Honour Judge Darwall Smith; a Circuit Judge, since 1992; *b* 27 Oct. 1946; *d* of late George Kenneth Moss, JP and of Jean Margaret Moss (*née* Johnston); *m* 1968, Simon Crompton Darwall Smith, *qv*; two *d*. *Educ:* Howell's Sch., Denbigh. Called to the Bar, Gray's Inn, 1968; in practice on Western Circuit, 1968–92; a Recorder, 1986–92. Gov., Red Maids' Sch., Bristol, 1990–. *Recreations:* travel, opera, ballet, theatre, gardening. *Address:* The Law Courts, Small Street, Bristol BS1 2HL. *Club:* Army and Navy.

DARWEN, 3rd Baron *cr* 1946, of Heys-in-Bowland; **Roger Michael Davies;** *b* 28 June 1938; *s* of 2nd Baron Darwen and of Kathleen Dora, *d* of George Sharples Walker; *S* father, 1988; *m* 1961, Gillian Irene, *d* of Eric G. Hardy, Bristol; two *s* three *d*. *Educ:* Bootham School, York. *Heir:* *s* Hon. Paul Davies, *b* 1962. *Address:* Labourer's Rest, Green Street, Pleshey, Chelmsford CM3 1HT.

DARWENT, Rt Rev. Frederick Charles; JP; Bishop of Aberdeen and Orkney, 1978–92; *b* Liverpool, 20 April 1927; *y s* of Samuel Darwent and Edith Emily Darwent (*née* Malcolm); *m* 1st, 1949, Edna Lilian (*d* 1981), *o c* of David Waugh and Lily Elizabeth Waugh (*née* McIndoe); twin *d* 2nd, 1983, Roma Evelyn, *er d* of John Michie and Evelyn Michie (*née* Stephen); 2nd, 1983, Roma Evelyn, *er d* of John Michie and Evelyn Michie (*née* Stephen). *Educ:* Warbreck Sch., Liverpool; Ormskirk Grammar Sch., Lancs; Wells Theological Coll., Somerset. Followed a banking career, 1943–61; War service in Far East with Royal Inniskilling Fusiliers, 1945–48. Deacon 1963; priest 1964, Diocese of Liverpool; Curate of Pemberton, Wigan, 1963–65 (in charge of St Francis, Kitt Green, 1964–65); Rector of: Strichen, 1965–71; New Pitsligo, 1965–78; Fraserburgh, 1971–78; Canon of St Andrew's Cathedral, Aberdeen, 1971; Dean of Aberdeen and Orkney, 1973–78. JP Aberdeen City, 1988. Hon. LTh St Mark's Inst. of Theology, 1974. *Recreations:* amateur stage (acting and production), music (especially jazz), calligraphy. *Address:* 107 Osborne Place, Aberdeen AB25 2DD. *T:* (01224) 646497. *Clubs:* Rotary International; Club of Deir (Aberdeens).

DARWIN, Kenneth; retired civil servant; *b* 24 Sept. 1921; *s* of late Robert Lawrence and Elizabeth Darwin (*née* Swain), Ripon, Yorks; unmarried. *Educ:* Elementary Sch.; Ripon Grammar Sch.; University Coll., Durham; Oflag VIIB (1943–45). BA 1947, MA 1948. Served 2nd Bn Lancs Fus., N Africa, (Captain) POW, 1942–46; TA Captain (Intelligence Corps), 1949–54. Asst Keeper, Public Record Office (NI), 1948; Dep. Keeper of Records of N Ireland, 1955–70; Vis. Lectr in Archives, UC Dublin, 1967–71; Fellow Commoner, Churchill Coll., Cambridge, 1970; Asst Sec., Min. of Commerce (NI), 1970–74; Sen. Asst Sec., Dept of Finance (NI) and Dept of Civil Service (NI), 1974–77; Dep. Sec., Dept of Finance (NI), 1977–81. Dir, Fountain Publishing, Belfast, 1995–. Member: Irish MSS Commn, Dublin, 1955–70; Adv. Bd for New History of Ireland, Royal Irish Acad., 1968–; Trustee: Ulster Historical Foundn, 1956–87; Ulster Museum, 1982–88 (Vice-Chm., 1984–86); Lyric Th., Belfast, 1966–69. Ed., Familia: Ulster Genealogical Rev., 1985–93. *Publications:* (ed jtly) Passion and Prejudice: Nationalist-Unionist conflict in Ulster in the 1930s and the founding of the Irish Association, 1993; articles on archives, history and genealogy, in jls and Nat. Trust guides. *Recreations:* travel, piano playing, walking, gardening. *Address:* 18 Seymour Road, Bangor, Co. Down BT19 1BL. *T:* (028) 9146 0718. *Clubs:* Royal Commonwealth Society; Royal British Legion, Bangor Drama (Bangor, Co. Down).

DASGUPTA, Prof. Partha Sarathi, PhD; FBA 1989; Frank Ramsey Professor of Economics, Cambridge University, since 1994 (Professor of Economics, 1985–94), and Fellow of St John's College, Cambridge, since 1985; *b* 17 Nov. 1942; *s* of late Prof. Amiya Dasgupta and of Shanti Dasgupta, Santiniketan, India; *m* 1968, Carol Margaret, *d* of Prof. James Meade, CB, FBA; one *s* two *d*. *Educ:* Univ. of Delhi (BSc Hons 1962); Univ. of Cambridge (BA 1965, PhD 1968; Stevenson Prize, 1967). Res. Fellow, Trinity Hall, Cambridge, 1968–71, Supernumerary Fellow, 1971–74; Lectr, 1971–75, Reader, 1975–78, Prof. of Econs, 1978–84, LSE (Hon. Fellow, 1994); Prof. of Econs and Philosophy, Stanford Univ., 1989–92. Sen. Res. Fellow, Inst. for Policy Reform, 1992–94. Visiting Professor: Stanford Univ., 1974–75 and 1983–84; Delhi Univ., 1978; Harvard Univ., 1987; Princeton Univ., 1988. Res. Advr, WIDER (UN Univ., 1989–94). Mem., Expert Panel on Environmtl Health, WHO, 1975–85. Chm., Beijer Internat. Inst. of Ecological Econs, Stockholm, 1991–97; Mem. Science Cttee, Santa Fe Inst., 1992–96; President: European Econ. Assoc., 1999; REconS, 1998–2001. For. Hon. Mem., Amer. Acad. of Arts and Scis, 1991; For. Mem., Royal Swedish Acad. of Scis, 1991; Hon. Mem., Amer. Econ. Assoc., 1997; Mem., Pontifical Acad. of Social Scis, 1998. Fellow,

Econometric Soc., 1975. Dr *hc* Wageningen, 2000. *Publications:* (with S. Marglin and A. K. Sen) Guidelines for Project Evaluation, 1972; (with G. Heal) Economic Theory and Exhaustible Resources, 1979; The Control of Resources, 1982; (with K. Binmore) Economic Organizations as Games, 1986; (with K. Binmore) The Economics of Bargaining, 1987; (with P. Stoneman) Economic Policy and Technological Performance, 1987; An Inquiry into Well-Being and Destitution, 1993; (with K. G. Mäler) The Environment and Emerging Development Issues, vols 1 and 2, 1997; (with I. Serageldin) Social Capital: a multifaceted perspective, 1999; articles on develt planning, optimum population, taxation and trade, welfare and justice, nat. resources, game theory, indust. org. and technical progress, poverty and unemployment, in Econ. Jl, Econometrica, Rev. of Econ. Stud., etc. *Address:* 1 Dean Drive, Holbrook Road, Cambridge CB1 7SW. *T:* (01223) 212179. *Club:* MCC.

DASH, Penelope Jane; Head of Strategy and Planning, Department of Health, since 2000; *b* 27 Jan. 1963; *d* of Hugo and Margaret Dash; *m* 1998, Guy Palmer; two *s*. *Educ:* Robinson Coll., Cambridge (BA Hons 1984); Middlesex Hosp. Med. Sch., London Univ. (MB BS 1987); LSHTM (MSc 1992); Stanford Univ. (MBA 1994). MRCP 1992. Jun. hosp. posts, UCH and Middlesex Hosps, 1987–88; Barnet Gen Hosp., 1988; Northwich P Hosp., 1988–90; Registrar in Public Health Medicine, NW Thames RHA, 1990-92; Mgt Consultant, Boston Consulting Gp, 1994-99. *Address:* Department of Health, Richmond House, 79 Whitehall, SW1A 2NL. *T:* (020) 7210 4987.

DASHWOOD, Prof. (Arthur) Alan; Professor of European Law, University of Cambridge, since 1995; Fellow, Sidney Sussex College, Cambridge, since 1995 (Vice-Master, 1997–2000); *b* 18 Oct. 1941; *s* of late Alan Stanley Dashwood and of Dorothy Mary Dashwood (*née* Childe); *m* 1971, Julie Rosalind Pashley. *Educ:* Michaelhouse, Natal, SA; Rhodes Univ., Grahamstown, SA (BA Hons 1962); Oriel Coll., Oxford (MA). Called to the Bar, Inner Temple, 1969. Asst Lectr, Dept of Civil Law, Univ. of Glasgow, 1966–67; Lecturer: Dept of Law, UCW, Aberystwyth, 1968–73; Centre of European Governmental Studies, Univ. of Edinburgh, 1973–75; Reader, Univ. of Sussex, 1975–78; Legal Sec. to Advocate General, Court of Justice of ECs, 1978–80; Prof. of Law, Univ. of Leicester, 1980–87; Dir, Legal Service, Council of EU, 1987–94. Editor: European Law Rev., 1975–91; Common Market Law Rev., 1995–. *Publications:* The Substantive Law of the EEC, 1980, 4th edn (with D. Wyatt) as Wyatt and Dashwood's European Community Law, 2000; contrib. to legal jls. *Recreation:* salmon and trout fishing. *Address:* Sidney Sussex College, Cambridge CB2 3HU. *T:* (01223) 338874; 2 Harcourt Buildings, Temple, EC4Y 9DB. *T:* (020) 7583 9020. *Club:* Athenæum; Porcupines.

DASHWOOD, Sir Edward (John Francis), 12th Bt *cr* 1707, of West Wycombe, Buckinghamshire; Premier Baronet of Great Britain; *b* 25 Sept. 1964; *o s* of Sir Francis Dashwood, 11th Bt and Victoria Ann Elizabeth Gwynne (*née* de Rutzen); *S* father, 2000; *m* 1989, Lucinda Nell (*née* Miesegaes); two *s* one *d*. *Educ:* Eton; Reading Univ. (BSc Estate Mgt). ARICS. Land Agent. *Recreations:* shooting, fishing, tennis, bridge. *Heir: s* George Francis Dashwood, *b* 17 June 1992. *Address:* West Wycombe Park, High Wycombe, Bucks HP14 3AJ. *T:* (01494) 524411/2. *Clubs:* White's, Pitt, Daniel's; Shikar; Eton Ramblers.

DASHWOOD, Sir Richard (James), 9th Bt *cr* 1684, of Kirtlington Park; TD 1987; Partner, Harris Allday (formerly Harris Allday Lea & Brooks), stockbrokers; *b* 14 Feb. 1950; *s* of Sir Henry George Massy Dashwood, 8th Bt, and Susan Mary (*d* 1985), *er d* of late Major V. R. Montgomerie-Charrington, Hunsdon House, Herts; *S* father, 1972; *m* 1984, Kathryn Ann (marr. diss. 1993), *er d* of Frank Mahon, Eastbury, Berks; one *s*. *Educ:* Maidwell Hall Preparatory Sch.; Eton College. Commissioned 14th/20th King's Hussars, 1969, later King's Royal Hussars; T&AVR, 1973– (Major 1992). *Heir: s* Frederick George Mahon Dashwood, *b* 29 Jan. 1988. *Address:* Ledwell Cottage, Sandford St Martin, Oxfordshire OX7 7AN. *T:* (01608) 683267.

da SILVA, John Burke, CMG 1969; HM Diplomatic Service, retired; Adviser, Commercial Union Assurance Co., 1973–84; *b* 30 Aug. 1918; *o s* of late John Christian da Silva and Gabrielle Guittard; *m* 1st, 1940, Janice (decd), *d* of Roy Mayor, Shrewsbury, Bermuda; one *d*; 2nd, 1963, Jennifer, *yr d* of late Capt. the Hon. T. T. Parker, DSC, RN, Greatham Moor, Hants; one *s* two *d*. *Educ:* Stowe Sch.; Trinity Coll., Cambridge (MA). Commnd Intell. Corps 1940, served with 1st Airborne Div., N Africa and Italy, GS02 SHAEF, France and Germany (despatches); Control Commn Germany and Austria. Joined Foreign Service, 1948; served Rome, Hamburg, Bahrain, Aden, Washington, FCO; retired 1973. Chm., Governors, Virginia Water Junior Sch., 1973–83; a Vice-Pres., Royal Soc. for Asian Affairs, 1983–86. Hon. Life Mem., Oriental Ceramic Soc., 1994. *Publications:* contributor: Oriental Art, Trans OCS, Asian Affairs, etc. *Recreation:* Oriental Art. *Address:* Copse Close, Virginia Water, Surrey GU25 4PH. *T:* (01344) 842342. *Club:* Travellers.

DATE, William Adrian, CBE 1973; Puisne Judge, Supreme Court of British Guiana, 1956–64; *b* 1 July 1908; *er s* of James C. Date; *m* 1st, 1933, Dorothy MacGregor Grant (*d* 1979); two *d*; 2nd, 1981, Rhoda Elaine Minors (*d* 1989). *Educ:* Queen's Royal Coll., Trinidad; Grenada Boys' Secondary Sch.; Lodge Sch., Barbados; Middle Temple, London. Magistrate and District Govt Officer, St Lucia, 1933–39; Crown Attorney, St Vincent, 1939–44; Legal Draughtsman, Jamaica, 1944–47; Chief Secretary, Windward Islands, 1947–50; Puisne Judge of the Supreme Court of the Windward and Leeward Islands, 1950–56. *Recreation:* bridge. *Address:* PO Box 133, St George's, Grenada, West Indies.

DATTA, Dr Naomi, FRS 1985; Professor Emeritus, London University; *b* 17 Sept. 1922; *d* of Alexander and Ellen Henrietta Goddard; *m* 1943, S. P. Datta; two *d* one *s*. *Educ:* St Mary's Sch., Wantage; University Coll. London; W London Hosp. Med Sch. MB BS (external); MD London. Junior medical posts, 1946–47; Bacteriologist in PHLS, 1947–57; Lectr, later Prof. of Microbiol Genetics, RPMS, London Univ., 1957–84; retired 1984. *Publications:* papers on the genetics and epidemiology of antibiotic resistance in bacteria. *Recreations:* gardening, cooking, travelling. *Address:* 9 Duke's Avenue, W4 2AA. *T:* (020) 8995 7562.

DAUBENY DE MOLEYNS, family name of **Baron Ventry**.

DAUNCEY, Brig. Michael Donald Keen, DSO 1945; DL; *b* 11 May 1920; *o s* of late Thomas Gough Dauncey and Alice Dauncey (*née* Keen); *m* 1945, Marjorie Kathleen, *d* of H. W. Neep, FCA; one *s* two *d*. *Educ:* King Edward's School, Birmingham; Inter. Exam., Inst. of Chartered Accountants. Commissioned, 22nd (Cheshire) Regt, 1941; seconded to Glider Pilot Regt, 1943; Arnhem, 1944 (wounded three times; taken prisoner, later escaped); MA to GOC-in-C, Greece, 1946–47; seconded to Para. Regt, 1948–49; Staff Coll., 1950; Instructor, RMA, 1957–58; CO, 1st Bn 22nd (Cheshire) Regt, 1963–66, BAOR and UN peace keeping force, Cyprus; DS plans, JSSC, 1966–68; Comdt, Jungle Warfare Sch., 1968–69; Comdt, Support Weapons Wing, Sch. of Infantry, 1969–72; Defence and Military Attaché, Madrid, 1973–75; retired 1976. Col, 22nd (Cheshire) Regt, 1978–85; Hon. Col, 1st Cadet Bn, Glos Regt (ACF), 1981–90. Pres., Glider Pilot Regtl Assoc., 1994–98; Leader, Airborne Pilgrimage to Arnhem, 2000. DL Glos 1983. *Recreations:* rough shooting, travelling, tennis; also under-gardener. *Address:* Uley Lodge, Uley, near Dursley, Glos GL11 5SN. *T:* (01453) 860216. *Club:* Army and Navy.

DAUNT, Patrick Eldon; Head of Bureau for Action in favour of Disabled People, EEC, 1982–87; retired; international consultant on education and disability; *b* 19 Feb. 1925; *s* of Dr Francis Eldon Daunt and Winifred Doggett Daunt (*née* Wells); *m* 1958, Jean Patricia, *d* of Lt-Col Percy Wentworth Hargreaves and of Joan (*née* Holford); three *s* one *d*. *Educ:* Rugby Sch.; Wadham Coll., Oxford. BA, 1st Cl. Hons Lit. Hum., 1949, MA 1954, Oxon. Housemaster, Christ's Hosp., 1959; Headmaster, Thomas Bennett Comprehensive Sch., Crawley, 1965. Chm., Campaign for Comprehensive Educn, 1971–73; Principal Administrator, EEC, 1974–82. Vis. Fellow, London Inst. of Educn, 1988–94. Chm., ASBAH, 1990–95. UNESCO consultant, special educn in Romania, 1992–97; ILO consultant, 1998–99. Ravenswood Foundn Internat. Award, 1992. *Publications:* Comprehensive Values, 1975; Meeting Disability, a European Response, 1991; (ed) Teacher Education for Special Needs in Europe, 1995. *Recreations:* books, botany. *Address:* 4 Bourn Bridge Road, Little Abington, Cambridge CB1 6BJ. *T:* (01223) 891485. *Club:* Oxford and Cambridge.

DAUNT, Sir Timothy Lewis Achilles, KCMG 1989 (CMG 1982); HM Diplomatic Service, retired; Lieutenant-Governor of the Isle of Man, 1995–2000; *b* 11 Oct. 1935; *s* of L. H. G. Daunt and Margery (*née* Lewis Jones); *m* 1962, Patricia Susan Knight; one *s* two *d*. *Educ:* Sherborne; St Catharine's Coll., Cambridge. 8th KRI Hussars, 1954–56. Entered Foreign Office, 1959; Ankara, 1960; FO, 1964; Nicosia, 1967; Private Sec. to Permanent Under-Sec. of State, FCO, 1970; Bank of England, 1972; UK Mission, NY, 1973; Counsellor, OECD, Paris, 1975; Head of South European Dept, FCO, 1978–81; Associate at Centre d'études et de recherches internationales, Paris, 1982; Minister and Dep. UK Perm. Rep. to NATO, Brussels, 1982–85; Asst Under-Sec. of State (Defence), FCO, 1985–86; Ambassador to Turkey, 1986–92; Dep. Under-Sec. of State (Defence), FCO, 1992–95. *Address:* 20 Ripplevale Grove, N1 1HU.

DAUNTON, Prof. Martin James, PhD; FBA 1997; Professor of Economic History, since 1997, and Chairman, Faculty of History, since 2001, University of Cambridge; Fellow of Churchill College, Cambridge, since 1997; *b* 7 Feb. 1949; *s* of Ronald James Daunton and Dorothy May Daunton (*née* Bellett); *m* 1984, Claire Hilda Gabriel Gobbi. *Educ:* Barry Grammar Sch.; Univ. of Nottingham (BA 1970); Univ. of Kent (PhD 1974). Lectr in Economic History, Univ. of Durham, 1973–79; University College London: Lectr in Economic History, 1979–85; Reader, 1985–89; Prof. of Modern History, 1989–92; Astor Prof. of British History, 1992–97. Vis. Fellow, ANU, 1985, 1994; Vis. Prof., Nihon Univ., Tokyo, 2000. Vice Pres., RHistS, 1996–2000 (Hon. Treas., 1986–91; Convener, Studies in History, 1994–2000); Chair, Inst. of Historical Research, 1994–98. Consultant Ed., New DNB, 1993–98; Member Editorial Board: Historical Jl, 2000–; English Historical Rev., 2001–. *Publications:* Coal Metropolis: Cardiff 1870–1914, 1977; House and Home in the Victorian City, 1983; Royal Mail: the Post Office since 1840, 1985; A Property Owning Democracy?, 1987; Progress and Poverty: an economic and social history of Britain 1700–1850, 1995; Cambridge Urban History of Britain, 2000; Trusting Leviathan: taxation and British society 1799–1914, 2001; Just Taxes: Britain 1914–79, 2002; articles in learned jls. *Recreations:* collecting modern ceramics, architectural tourism. *Address:* Churchill College, Cambridge CB3 0DS. *T:* (01223) 336216. *Club:* Reform.

DAUSSET, Prof. Jean Baptiste Gabriel Joachim; Grand Croix de la Légion d'Honneur; Professeur de Médecine Expérimentale au Collège de France, 1977–87; *b* 19 Oct. 1916; *s* of Henri Dausset and Elizabeth Brullard; *m* 1962, Rose Mayoral; one *s* one *d*. *Educ:* Lycée Michelet, Paris; Faculty of Medicine, University of Paris. Associate Professor, 1958–68, Professor of Immunohaematology, 1968–77, University of Paris. Institut Nationale de la Santé et de la Recherche Médicale: Director of Research Unit on Immunogenetics of Human Transplantation, 1968–84; Centre National de la Recherche Scientifique: Co-Director, Oncology and Immuno-haematology Laboratory, 1968–84. Gairdner Foundn Prize, 1977; Koch Foundn Prize, 1978; Wolf Foundn Prize, 1978; Nobel Prize for Physiology or Medicine, 1980. *Publications:* Immuno-hématologie biologique et clinique, 1956; (with F. T. Rapaport) Human Transplantation, 1968; (with G. Snell and S. Nathanson) Histocompatibility, 1976; (with M. Fougereau) Immunology 1980, 1980; (with M. Pla) HLA, 1985; Clin d'oeil à la vie, 1998. *Recreation:* plastic art. *Address:* 44 rue des Ecoles, 75005 Paris, France.

DAVAN WETTON, Hilary John; Director of Music, Tonbridge School, since 1993; conductor; *b* 23 Dec. 1943; *s* of late Eric Davan Wetton, CBE and (Kathleen) Valerie Davan Wetton (*née* Edwards); *m* 1st, 1964, Elizabeth Jane Tayler; three *d*; 2nd, 1989, Alison Mary Moncrieff Kelly; one *s* one *d*. *Educ:* Westminster Sch.; Royal Coll. of Music (ARCM); Brasenose Coll., Oxford (BA, MA, DipEd). Director of Music: St Alban's Sch., 1965–67; Cranleigh Sch., 1967–74; Stantonbury Music Centre, 1974–78; St Paul's Girls' Sch., 1978–93. Conductor: Guildford Choral Soc., 1968–; Milton Keynes City Orch., 1974–; Holst Singers, 1978–91; City of London Choir, 1989–; Wren Orch., 1990–; Scottish Schools Orch., 1984–95; Edinburgh Youth Orch., 1994–97; guest conducting and recording with Philharmonia, LPO, Royal Phil. Orch., BBC Concert Orch., Ulster Orch., orchestras in Bulgaria, Iceland, USA, Australia. Presenter, Classic FM Masterclass. Member: RSA; Pepys Soc. Hon. MA Open, 1984; Hon. DMus De Montfort, 1994. Diapason d'Or for Holst recording, 1994. *Publications:* contrib. musical jls and Guardian. *Recreation:* tennis. *Address:* Hartlake Roundels, Hartlake Road, Golden Green, Kent TN11 0BL. *Club:* Garrick.

See also P. H. D. Wetton.

DAVENPORT, (Arthur) Nigel; President, British Actors' Equity Association, 1986–92; *b* 23 May 1928; *s* of Arthur Henry Davenport and Katherine Lucy (*née* Meiklejohn); *m* 1st, 1951, Helena White (*d* 1978); one *s* one *d*; 2nd, 1972, Maria Aitken, *qv* (marr. diss.); one *s*. *Educ:* Cheltenham Coll.; Trinity Coll., Oxford (MA). Entered acting profession, 1951; for first ten years worked almost exclusively in theatre; original mem. English Stage Co. at Royal Court Th., 1956; A Taste of Honey, on Broadway, 1960; television and films, 1961–; Murder is Easy, Duke of York's, 1993; Our Betters, Chichester, 1997; toured England: King Lear (title rôle), 1986; The Old Country, 1989; Sleuth, 1990; The Constant Wife, 1994–95; Brideshead Revisited, 1995; On That Day, 1996; *films:* Look Back in Anger, 1958; Peeping Tom, 1960; In the Cool of the Day, 1963; The Third Secret, 1964; A High Wind in Jamaica, Life at the Top, Sands of the Kalahari, Where the Spies Are, 1965; A Man for All Seasons, 1966; Play Dirty, Sebastian/Mr Sebastian, The Strange Affair, 1968; Royal Hunt of the Sun, Sinful Davey, The Virgin Soldiers, 1969; The Last Valley, The Mind of Mr Soames, No Blade of Grass, 1970; Mary, Queen of Scots, Villain, 1971; Living Free, 1972; Charlie One-Eye, 1973; La Regenta, Phase IV, 1974; The Island of Dr Moreau, Stand Up Virgin Soldiers, 1977; The Omega Connection, Zulu Dawn, 1979; Chariots of Fire, Den Tuchtigen gehört Die Welt, Nighthawks, 1981; Strata, 1982; Greystoke, 1984; Caravaggio, 1986; Without a Clue, 1988; The Cutter, 1992; Hotel Shanghai, 1995; La Revuelta de El Coyote, 1997; David Copperfield, 1999; *television:* South Riding; George III in The Prince Regent; Howard's Way, 1987–88, 1990; Trainer,

1991; The Treasure Seekers, The Opium Wars, 1996; Longitude, 1999. Mem. Council, British Actors' Equity, 1976; Vice Pres., 1978–82, 1985–86. *Recreations:* gardening, travel. *See also H. B. Davenport.*

DAVENPORT, Major (retd) David John Cecil, CBE 1989; DL; Member, Rural Development Commission, 1982–90 (Deputy Chairman, April–Oct. 1988); *b* 28 Oct. 1934; *s* of late Major John Lewes Davenport, DL, JP, and Louise Aline Davenport; *m* 1st, 1959, Jennifer Burness (marr. diss. 1969); two *d*; 2nd, 1971, Lindy Jane Baker; one *s*. *Educ:* Eton College; Royal Military Academy, Sandhurst. Commnd into Grenadier Guards, 1954, retired 1967. RAC, Cirencester, 1968–69. Chairman, Leominster District Council, 1975–76. Chm., CoSIRA, 1982–88. Chm., Regional Adv. Cttee of the Forestry Commn (SW), 1974–87; Pres., Royal Forestry Soc., 1991–93. DL, 1974, High Sheriff, 1989–90, Hereford and Worcester. *Address:* Mansel Lacy House, Hereford HR4 7HQ. *T:* (01981) 590224. *Clubs:* Boodle's, MCC.

DAVENPORT, Hugo Benedick; freelance writer and broadcaster; *b* 6 June 1953; *s* of Arthur Nigel Davenport, *qv*; *m* 1988, Sarah Mollison; one *s* one *d*. *Educ:* Westminster Sch.; Univ. of Sussex (BA 1st Cl. Hons). With Visnews Ltd, 1976–77; trainee journalist, Liverpool Daily Post & Echo, 1977–80; reporter/diarist, Observer, 1981–84; feature writer, Mail on Sunday, 1985–87; news feature writer, then film critic, Daily Telegraph, 1987–96; contributor, BBC World Service, 1992–96; editor: FT New Media Markets, 1997–2000; Broad-band Media, 2000–01. Envmtl Reporting Award, Population Inst., Washington, 1988. *Recreations:* walking, reading, music. *Address:* 6 Ann's Close, Kinnerton Street, SW1X 8EG. *T:* and *Fax:* (020) 7235 0559.

DAVENPORT, Maurice Hopwood, FCIB; Director, First National Finance Corporation plc, 1985–95; *b* 19 March 1925; *s* of Richard and Elizabeth Davenport; *m* 1954, Sheila Timms; one *s* two *d*. *Educ:* Rivington and Blackrod Grammar Sch. FIB 1982. Served RN, 1943–46. Joined Williams Deacon's Bank, 1940; Sec., 1960; Asst Gen. Man., 1969; Dir, 1978–85, Man. Dir, 1982–85, Williams & Glyn's Bank; Dir, Royal Bank of Scotland Gp and Royal Bank of Scotland, 1982–85. *Recreations:* walking, gardening, reading. *Address:* Pines, Dormans Park, East Grinstead, West Sussex RH19 2LX. *T:* (01342) 870439.

DAVENPORT, Michael Hayward, MBE 1994; HM Diplomatic Service; Director of Trade Promotion, and Consul-General, Warsaw, since 2001; *b* 25 Sept. 1961; *s* of Montague Davenport and Olive Margaret Davenport (*née* Brabner); *m* 1992, Lavinia Sophia Elisabeth Braun; one *s* one *d*. *Educ:* Gonville and Caius Coll., Cambridge (BA 1983, MA 1985); Coll. of Law, London. Lectr, Graz Univ., Austria, 1983–84; with Macfarlanes, Solicitors, 1986–88; admitted solicitor, 1988; joined FCO, 1988: est. British Know-How Fund for Poland, Warsaw, 1990–93; Hd, Peacekeeping Section, FCO, 1993–95; First Sec. (Political), Moscow, 1996–99. *Recreations:* tennis, German literature, cooking. *Address:* c/o Foreign and Commonwealth Office, King Charles Street, SW1A 2AH. *Club:* Wig and Pen.

DAVENPORT, Nigel; *see* Davenport, A. N.

DAVENPORT, Walter Arthur B.; *see* Bromley-Davenport.

DAVENPORT-HANDLEY, Sir David (John), Kt 1980; OBE 1962; JP; DL; Chairman, Clipsham Quarry Co., since 1947; *b* 2 Sept. 1919; *s* of John Davenport-Handley, JP; *m* 1943, Leslie Mary Goldsmith; one *d* (one *s* decd). *Educ:* RNC Dartmouth. RN retd 1947. Chm., Rutland and Stamford Conservative Assoc., 1952–65; Treasurer, East Midlands Area Conservative Assoc., 1965–71, Chm. 1971–77; Vice-Chm., Nat. Union of Conservative & Unionist Assocs, 1977–79, Chm., 1979–80. Member: Consumers' Cttees for GB and for England and Wales, 1956–65; Parole Bd, 1981–84. Chm., Rutland Historic Churches Preservation Trust, 1987–. President: E Midlands Area Cons. Assoc., 1987–94; Nat. Union of Cons. and Unionist Assocs, 1990–91. Governor, Swinton Conservative Coll., 1973–77; Chairman: Board of Visitors, Ashwell Prison, 1955–73; Governors, Casterton Community Coll., 1960–78; Trustee, Oakham Sch., 1970–86. JP 1948, High Sheriff 1954, DL 1962, Vice-Lieutenant 1972, Rutland; Chm., Rutland Petty Sessional Div., 1957–84; DL Leicestershire 1974. *Recreations:* gardening, music, travel. *Address:* Clipsham Hall, Oakham, Rutland, Leics LE15 7SE. *T:* (01780) 410204.

DAVENTRY, 4th Viscount *cr* 1943; **James Edward FitzRoy Newdegate;** Director, R. K. Harrison Insurance Brokers Ltd; *b* 27 July 1960; *s* of 3rd Viscount Daventry and Hon. Rosemary, *e d* of 1st Baron Norrie, GCMG, GCVO, CB, DSO, MC; *S* father, 2000; *m* 1994, Georgia, *yr d* of John Stuart Lodge; one *s* two *d*. *Educ:* Milton Abbey; RAC Cirencester (MRAC). *Recreations:* shooting, fishing, racing, golf, farming, occasional gardening. *Heir: s* Hon. Humphrey John FitzRoy Newdegate, *b* 23 Nov. 1995. *Address:* Arbury, Nuneaton, Warwickshire CV10 7PT. *Clubs:* White's, Turf, Royal Automobile.

DAVEY, Hon. Sir David Herbert P.; *see* Penry-Davey.

DAVEY, Edward Jonathan; MP (Lib Dem) Kingston and Surbiton, since 1997; *b* 25 Dec. 1965; *s* of late John George Davey and Nina Joan (*née* Stanbrook). *Educ:* Nottingham High Sch.; Jesus Coll., Oxford (BA 1st Cl. Hons PPE); Birkbeck Coll., London (MSc Econs). Sen. Econs Advr to Lib Dem MPs, 1989–93; Mgt Consultant, Omega Partners, 1993–97. Lib Dem spokesman: on econ. affairs, 1997–2001; for London, 2000–01; on Treasury affairs, 2001–. Mem., Treasury Select Cttee, 1999–2001. Hon. Testimonial, RHS, and Cert. of Commendation from Chief Constable of Brit. Transport Police (for rescuing a woman who had fallen on the track at Clapham Junction), 1995. *Recreations:* walking, music. *Address:* House of Commons, SW1A 0AA. *T:* (020) 7219 3512; *e-mail:* daveye@parliament.uk. *Clubs:* National Liberal; Surbiton (Surbiton).

DAVEY, Eric; Chairman, Sea Fish Industry Authority, since 1996 (Deputy Chairman, 1990–96); *b* 16 Jan. 1933; *s* of William James Davey and Doris Evelynne Davey; *m* 1955, Janet Nicholson; two *d*. *Educ:* Woodbridge Sch.; Ilminster Sch. With Bank of England, 1953–88, Agent, Newcastle Br., 1980–88; Newcastle Building Society: Dir, 1988; Dep. Chm., 1992–98; Chm., 1998–2001. *Recreations:* foreign travel, motoring, reading, theatre. *Address:* (office) 18 Logie Mill, Logie Green Road, Edinburgh EH7 4HG.

DAVEY, Francis, MA; Headmaster of Merchant Taylors' School, 1974–82; *b* 23 March 1932; *er s* of Wilfred Henry Davey, BSc and Olive (*née* Geeson); *m* 1960, Margaret Filby Lake, MA Oxon, AMA, *o d* of Harold Lake, DMus Oxon, FRCO; one *s* one *d*. *Educ:* Plymouth Coll.; New Coll., Oxford (Hon. Exhibr); Corpus Christi Coll., Cambridge (Schoolmaster Fellow Commoner). 1st cl. Class. Hon. Mods 1953, 2nd cl. Lit. Hum. 1955, BA 1955, MA 1958. RAF, 1950–51; Classical Upper Sixth Form Master, Dulwich Coll., 1955–60; Head of Classics Dept, Warwick Sch., 1960–66; Headmaster, Dr Morgan's Grammar Sch., Bridgwater, 1966–73. *Publications:* (with R. Pascoe) The Camino Portugués, 1997; William Wey, 2000; (with P. Quaife) The Camino Inglés, 2000; articles in Enciclopedia dello Spettacolo, Classical Review, Jl of Royal Instn of Cornwall, Devon and Cornwall Notes and Queries. *Recreations:* Rugby, swimming, gardening, travel. *Address:* 1 North Street, Topsham, Exeter, Devon EX3 0AP. *T:* and *Fax:* (01392) 873251. *Clubs:* East India, Devonshire, Sports and Public Schools; Union (Oxford).

DAVEY, Geoffrey Wallace; a Recorder of the Crown Court, 1974–97; *b* 16 Oct. 1924; *s* of late Hector F. T. Davey and Alice M. Davey; *m* 1st, 1950, Barbara Jean Fairbairn (marr. diss. 1963); one *s* one *d*; 2nd, 1964, Joyce Irving Steel (*d* 1995); one step *s*; 3rd, 1995, June Mary Wheldon; two step *s*. *Educ:* Queen Elizabeth Grammar Sch., Faversham; Wadham Coll., Oxford (MA). Called to Bar, Lincoln's Inn, 1954; admitted Ghana Bar, 1957; resumed practice NE Circuit, 1970; retired, 1998. Chm., Med. Appeal Tribunal, 1982–96; Dep. Chm., Agricl Land Tribunal, 1982–96. FCIArb 1993 (ACIArb 1992). *Recreations:* golf, cooking, carpentry. *Address:* 22 Mill Hill Lane, Northallerton, N Yorkshire DL6 1DN. *T:* (01609) 780418; 19 Baker Street, Middlesbrough, Cleveland TS1 2LF. *T:* (01642) 217037–8.

DAVEY, Grenville; artist; Senior Research Fellow in Drawing, University of East London; *b* 28 April 1961; *s* of Clifford Henry and Lillian Joyce Davey. *Educ:* Goldsmiths' Coll., London. Vis. Prof., London Inst., 1997–. Exhibitions: Lisson Gall., London, 1987; Stichtung De Appel Foundn, Amsterdam, 1990; Kunsthalle, Berne, 1991; Kunstverein für die Rheinlandeund, Westfalen, Dusseldorf, 1992; Le Crypte Jules-Noriac, Limoges, 1993; Württembergisher, Kunstverein, Stuttgart, 1994; Henry Moore Foundn, Dean Clough Foundn, 1994; Mus. of Modern Art, Vienna, Kunstverein Hanover, 1996; Odense, Denmark, and Yorks Sculpture Park, 1999. Turner Prize, 1992. *Recreation:* work. *Address:* University of East London, Greengate House, Greengate Street, E13 0BG.

DAVEY, Jon Colin; Chairman, Media Matrix Partnership, since 1996; *b* 16 June 1938; *s* of late Frederick John Davey and Dorothy Mary Davey; *m* 1962, Ann Patricia Streames; two *s* one *d*. *Educ:* Raynes Park Grammar Sch. Joined Home Office, 1957; served in Civil Defence, Immigration, Criminal Policy, Prison and Criminal Justice Depts; Asst Sec., Broadcasting Dept, 1981–85; Dir-Gen., Cable Authy, 1985–90; Dir of Cable and Satellite, ITC, 1991–96; Dir, Communications Equity Associates Internat., 1996–98. Asst Sec., Franks Cttee on Sect. 2 of Official Secrets Act, 1971–72; Secretary: Williams Cttee on Obscenity and Film Censorship, 1977–79; Hunt Inquiry into Cable Expansion and Broadcasting Policy, 1982. Vice-Chm., Media Policy Cttee, Council of Europe, 1983–84; Member: British Screen Adv. Council, 1990–96; Adv. Panel on Public Appointments, DCMS, 1999–. Ed., Insight, 1997–. Hon. Fellow, Soc. of Cable Television Engrs, 1994. Silver Medal, RTS, 1999. *Recreations:* lawnmaking, Bach, English countryside. *Address:* 71 Hare Lane, Claygate, Esher, Surrey KT10 0QX. *T:* (01372) 810106, *Fax:* (01372) 815879; *e-mail:* joncdavey@cs.com.

DAVEY, Julian; mountaineer and mountain leader, since 1998; *b* 24 July 1946; *s* of Frederick Victor Davey and Dorothy Davey (*née* Stokes); *m* 1971, Prof. Katherine O'Donovan; one *d*. *Educ:* Kingston Grammar Sch.; Selwyn Coll., Cambridge; Inst. of Education, London Univ. (MA 1973). British Council: Ethiopia, 1969–72; E Africa Dept, 1973–75; Mgt Accountant, 1975–78; Malaysia, 1978–81; Dep. Controller, Finance, 1981–85; Dir, Hong Kong, 1985–90; Regl Dir, Asia-Pacific, 1992–94; Internat. Advr, Anglia Polytechnic Univ., 1994–97. Dir, Hesket Newmarket Brewery, 1999–. *Recreations:* ski-mountaineering, caving, performing arts, landscape gardening. *Address:* Potts Gill, Caldbeck, Cumbria CA7 8LB. *T:* (016974) 78499. *Clubs:* Royal Commonwealth Society; Eagle Ski; Eden Vale Mountaineering; Hong Kong (Hong Kong).

DAVEY, Keith Alfred Thomas, CB 1973; Solicitor and Legal Adviser, Department of the Environment, 1970–82; *b* 1920; *s* of W. D. F. Davey; *m* 1949, Kathleen Elsie, *d* of Rev. F. J. Brabyn; one *s* one *d*. *Educ:* Cambridge and County High Sch.; Fitzwilliam House, Cambridge (MA). Served War of 1939–45, Middle East (Captain). Called to the Bar, Middle Temple, 1947. Principal Asst Solicitor, DHSS, 1968–70. *Recreations:* looking at churches, reading history, keeping cats and dogs. *Address:* 172 Duxford Road, Whittlesford, Cambridge CB2 4NH. *Clubs:* Athenæum, Sette of Odd Volumes.

DAVEY, Peter Gordon, CBE 1986; Partner, Crossfell Consultants, since 1998; *b* 6 Aug. 1935; *s* of late Lt-Col Frank Davey, Royal Signals and H. Jean Davey (*née* Robley); *m* 1961; two *s* two *d*. *Educ:* Winchester Coll.; Gonville and Caius Coll., Cambridge (Mech. Scis Tripos, pt 2 Electrical; MA 1961). MIEE; MBCS 1967. Engineer: GEC Applied Electronics Labs, Stanmore, 1958–61; Lawrence Radiation Lab., Berkeley, Calif, 1961–64; Guest Researcher, Heidelberg Univ., 1964–65; Oxford University: Project Engr, Nuclear Physics Lab., 1966–79; Co-ordinator, Indust. Robotics Research Prog., SERC, 1979–84; Head of Inter-active Computing Facility, Rutherford Lab., SRC, 1978–80; of Robot Welding Project, Engrg Sci. Lab., 1979–84; Sen. Res. Fellow, St Cross Coll., 1981–89. Tech. Dir, Electro Pneumatic Equipment Ltd, Letchworth, 1968–87; Man. Dir, Meta Machines Ltd, 1984–87 (Dir, 1984–91); Man. Dir, Oxford Intelligent Machines Ltd, 1990–98; Dep. Chm., Oxim Ltd, 1999–2000. Ed., Open University Press Industrial Robotics Series, 1982–92. Hon. Prof., UCW, Aberystwyth, 1988–93. Hon. DSc Hull, 1987. *Publications:* (with W. F. Clocksin) A Tutorial Introduction to Industrial Robotics: artificial intelligence skills, 1982; (contrib.) Robot Vision, 1982; contribs to learned jls on robotics and image analysis systems. *Recreations:* buildings restoration, squash, sailing. *Address:* 22 Park Town, Oxford OX2 6SH.

DAVEY, Peter John, OBE 1998; Editor, The Architectural Review, since 1981; *b* 28 Feb. 1940; *s* of John Davey and Mary (*née* Roberts); *m* 1968, Carolyn Pulford; two *s*. *Educ:* Oundle Sch.; Edinburgh University (BArch). RIBA. News and Features Editor, 1974, Man. Editor, 1978, Architects' Journal; Managing Editor, Architectural Review, 1980. Mem. Council, RIBA, 1990–93 (Vice Pres. and Hon. Librarian, 1991–93). Editl Dir, EMAP Construct, 1995–. Member Jury, including: RIBA Royal Gold Medal, 1990–95; Carlsberg Architecture Prize, 1992, 1995, 1998; Brunel Prize, 1996; Constitutional Court Competition, S Africa, 1997–98; Jury Chairman: Prague Castle Phesantry (pleasure grounds) Competition, 1997; Hellenic Inst. of Arch. Nat. Prize, 2000; Commonwealth Assoc. of Architects Student Comp., Wellington, NZ, 2000. FRSA. Kt 1st Cl., Order of White Rose (Finland), 1991. *Publications:* Architects' Journal Legal Handbook (ed), 1973; Arts and Crafts Architecture, 1980, 2nd edn 1995; Heikkinen & Komonen, 1998; Peter Zumthor, 1998; numerous articles in architectural jls and books. *Recreations:* pursuit of edible fungi, fishing, cooking, classical music, gardening (badly). *Address:* 44 Hungerford Road, N7 9LP. *Club:* Athenæum.

DAVEY, Dr Ronald William, LVO 2001; Physician to the Queen, 1986–2001; *b* 25 Oct. 1943; *s* of Frederick George Davey and Cissy Beatrice Davey (*née* Lawday); *m* 1st, 1966; one *s* one *d*; 2nd, 1991, Priscilla Anne Kennedy. *Educ:* Trinity School of John Whitgift; King's College London; King's College Hosp. (MB BS; FFHom; AKC); MD Imperial Coll., London, 1998. Gen. med. practice, 1970–77; private homoeopathic medical practice, 1978–; research into: electro-stimulation and drug addiction, 1978–79; pain relief in spinally injured, 1983–94; antibiotic properties of propolis, 1984–94. Hon. Med. Res. Dir, Blackie Foundn Trust, 1980–98; Hon. Res. Fellow, Nat. Heart and Lung Inst., Univ. of London, 1990– (Blackie Res. Fellow, 1988–90); Vis. Schol., Green Coll., Oxford, 1998. Former Consultant to Res. Council for Complementary Medicine (Vice-

Chm., 1986–87). Freeman: City of London, 1997; Barbers' Co., 1997. MInstD 2001. *Publications:* medical papers. *Recreations:* Scottish reeling, opera, financial derivative trading, writing. *Address:* 1 Upper Wimpole Street, W1M 7TD. *T:* (020) 7580 5489. *Club:* Royal Society of Medicine.

DAVEY, Roy Charles; Headmaster, King's School, Bruton, 1957–72; *b* 25 June 1915; *s* of William Arthur Davey and Georgina (*née* Allison); *m* 1940, Kathleen Joyce Sumner; two *d. Educ:* Christ's Hospital; Brasenose Coll., Oxford (Open Scholar). Asst Master, Weymouth Coll., 1937–40. War Service, Royal Artillery, 1940–46. Senior Master, 1946–49, Warden, 1949–57, The Village Coll., Impington. FRSA. *Recreations:* poetry, botany, gardening, games. *Address:* Marley House Nursing Home, Winfrith Newburgh, Dorchester, Dorset DT2 8JR. *Club:* East India, Devonshire, Sports and Public Schools.

DAVEY, Valerie; MP (Lab) Bristol West, since 1997; *b* 16 April 1940; *m* 1966, Graham Davey; twin *d* one *s. Educ:* Birmingham Univ. (MA); London Univ. Inst. of Educn (PGCE). Teacher: Wolverhampton; Tanzania; FE Coll. Mem. (Lab) Avon CC, 1981–96. Mem., Educn and Employment Select Cttee, 1997–. Mem., Amnesty International. *Recreations:* gardens, cooking esp. marmalade. *Address:* PO Box 1947, Bristol BS99 2UG.

DAVEY, Prof. William, CBE 1978; PhD; FRSC; President, Portsmouth Polytechnic, 1969–82; Honorary Professor, University of Westminster (formerly Polytechnic of Central London), since 1979; *b* Chesterfield, Derbyshire, 15 June 1917; *m* 1941, Eunice Battye; two *s. Educ:* University Coll., Nottingham; Technical Coll., Huddersfield. BSc, PhD (London, external). Chemist: ICI Scottish Dyes, 1940; Boots, 1941; Shell, 1942–44. Lectr and Sen. Lectr in Organic Chemistry, Acton Techn. Coll., 1944–53; Head of Dept of Chemistry and Biology, The Polytechnic, Regent Street, London, W1, 1953–59; Principal, Coll. of Technology, Portsmouth, 1960–69. FRSA, FRSC, CIMgt. DUniv Portsmouth, 1993. *Publications:* Industrial Chemistry, 1961; numerous original papers in: Jl Chem. Soc., Inst. Petroleum, Jl Applied Chem. *Recreations:* motoring, foreign travel. *Address:* 67 Ferndale, Waterlooville, Portsmouth PO7 7PH. *T:* (023) 9226 3014.

DAVID, family name of **Baroness David**.

DAVID, Baroness *cr* 1978 (Life Peer), of Romsey in the City of Cambridge; **Nora Ratcliff David;** JP; *b* 23 Sept. 1913; *d* of George Blockley Blakesley, JP, and Annie Edith Blakesley; *m* 1935, Richard William David, CBE (*d* 1993); two *s* two *d. Educ:* Ashby-de-la-Zouch Girls' Grammar School; St Felix, Southwold; Newnham Coll., Cambridge (MA; Hon. Fellow 1986). Mem. Bd, Peterborough Develt Corp., 1976–78. A Baroness-in-Waiting (Government Whip), 1978–79; Opposition Whip, 1979–82; Dep. Chief Opposition Whip, 1982–87; opposition spokesman on education, 1987–97. Member: Cambridge City Council, 1964–67, 1968–74; Cambs County Council, 1974–78. Fellow, Anglia Poly. Univ (formerly Higher Educn Coll.), 1989. JP Cambridge City, 1965. *Recreations:* swimming, theatre, travel. *Address:* 50 Highsett, Cambridge CB2 1NZ. *T:* (01223) 350376; Cove, New Polzeath, Cornwall PL27 6UF. *T:* (01208) 863310. *Address:* House of Lords, SW1A 0PW. *T:* (020) 7219 3159.

DAVID, Sir (Jean) Marc, Kt 1986; CBE 1982; QC (Mauritius) 1969; Barrister, in private practice since 1964; Hon. Professor of Law, University of Mauritius, since 1990; *b* 22 Sept. 1925; *s* of late Joseph Claudius David and Marie Lucresia David (*née* Henrisson); *m* 1948, Mary Doreen Mahoney; three *s* three *d. Educ:* Royal Coll., Port Louis; Royal Coll., Curepipe, Mauritius (Laureate (classical side) of English Scholarship, 1945); LSE (LLB Hons). Called to the Bar, Middle Temple, 1949. Barrister in private practice, 1950–54; Dist Magistrate, then Crown Law Officer (Crown Counsel, Sen. Crown Counsel and Actg AAG), 1954–64. Chm., Mauritius Bar Assoc., 1968, 1979. Chairman: various arbitration tribunals, commns of enquiry and cttees apptd by govt, 1958–; Electoral Supervisory and Boundaries Commns, 1973–82 (Mem., 1968–73); Mem., Panel of Conciliators and Arbitrators, Internat. Centre for Settlement of Investment Disputes, 1969–. Visitor, Univ. of Mauritius, 1980–81. *Recreations:* reading, listening to music, horse racing. *Address:* (home) Villa da Mar, Trou-aux-Biches, Triolet, Mauritius. *T:* 2655070; (chambers) 11 Jules Koenig Street, Port-Louis, Mauritius. *T:* 2088938. *Clubs:* City (Port Louis); Turf, Racing (Mauritius).

DAVID, Prof. Paul Allan, PhD; FBA 1995; Senior Research Fellow, All Souls College, since 1994, and Professor of Economics and Economic History, since 1998, University of Oxford; Professor of Economics, Stanford University, California, since 1969; *b* 24 May 1935; *s* of Henry David and Evelyn (*née* Levinson); *m* 1st, 1958, Janet Williamson (marr. diss. 1982); one *s* one *d*; 2nd, 1982, Sheila Ryan Johansson; one step *s* one step *d. Educ:* High Sch. of Music and Art, NYC; Harvard Coll. (AB *summa cum laude* 1956); Pembroke Coll., Cambridge (Fulbright Schol.); Harvard Univ. (PhD 1973). Stanford University, California: Asst Prof. of Econs, 1961–66; Associate Prof., 1966–69; William Robertson Coe Prof. of American Econ. Hist., 1978–94. Vis. Fellow, All Souls Coll., Oxford, 1967–68 and 1992–93; Vis. Prof. of Econs, Harvard Univ., 1972–73; Pitt Prof. of American Hist. and Institutions, Univ. of Cambridge, 1977–78; Vis. Res. Prof. in Econs of Sci. and Technol., Rijksuniversiteit Limburg, 1993–; Marshall Lectr, Univ. of Cambridge, 1992. Guggenheim Fellow, 1975–76; Fellow, Center for Advanced Study in the Behavioral Scis, 1978–79. Pres.-Elect and Pres., Econ. Hist. Assoc., 1987–89. Mem. Council, REconS, 1996–. Fellow, Internat. Econometrics Soc., 1975; Amer. Acad. Arts and Scis, 1979. Phi Beta Kappa, Harvard, 1956. *Publications:* (ed) Households and Nations in Economic Growth, 1974; Technical Choice, Innovation and Economic Growth, 1975, 2nd edn 2001; Reckoning with Slavery, 1976; From the Economics of QWERTY to the Millennium Bug, 2001; Networks, Standards and Markets, 2001; Behind the Diffusion Curve, 2002; numerous articles and contribs to books. *Recreations:* photography, drawing, Chinese cooking, tennis, walking. *Address:* All Souls College, Oxford OX1 4AL. *Fax:* (01865) 279299; *e-mail:* paul.david@all-souls.ox.ac.uk; (Aug.–Dec.) Department of Economics, Stanford University, Stanford, CA 94305–6072, USA. *Fax:* (650) 7255702; *e-mail:* pad@leland.Stanford.Edu.

DAVID, Robert Allan; Head of International and Tourism Division, Department of Employment, 1989–91; *b* 27 April 1937; *s* of George David and Mabel Edith David; *m* 1961, Brenda Marshall; three *d. Educ:* Cathays High Sch., Cardiff. BoT, 1955–71; Dept of Employment, 1971–91. *Recreations:* badminton, tennis, gardening. *Address:* The Briars, Ninehams Road, Tatsfield, Westerham, Kent TN16 2AN. *T:* (01959) 577357.

DAVID, His Honour Sir Robert Daniel George, (Sir Robin), Kt 1995; QC 1968; DL; a Circuit Judge (formerly Chairman, Cheshire Quarter Sessions), 1968–97; *b* 30 April 1922; *s* of late Alexander Charles Robert David and late Edrica Doris Pole David (*née* Evans); *m* 1st, 1944, Edith Mary Marsh (*d* 1999); two *d*; 2nd, 2000, Zena (*née* Cooke). *Educ:* Christ Coll., Brecon; Ellesmere Coll., Salop. War Service, 1943–47, Captain, Royal Artillery. Called to Bar, Gray's Inn, 1949; joined Wales and Chester Circuit, 1949. Dep. Chairman, Cheshire QS, 1961; Dep. Chairman, Agricultural Land Tribunal (Wales), 1965–68; Commissioner of Assize, 1970; Dep. Presiding Judge, Judicial Trng, 1970–74; Mem., Parole Bd for England and Wales, 1971–74. DL Cheshire 1972. *Publication:* The Magistrate in the Crown Court, 1982. *Address:* Fieldgate, Willington Lane, Kelsall, Tarporley CW6 0PR. *T:* (01829) 751453.

DAVID, Timothy James; HM Diplomatic Service; *b* 3 June 1947; *s* of late Herman Francis David and Mavis Jean David (*née* Evans); *m* 1996, Rosemary (*née* Kunzel); one *s* one *d. Educ:* Stonyhurst Coll.; New Coll., Oxford (BA Hons 1969; MA Hons 1978); Univ. of Rhodesia (Grad. Cert. in Educn 1972); Univ. of London. Volunteer Teacher, Southern Rhodesia, 1965–66; Headmaster, St Peter's Community Secondary Sch., Salisbury (now Harare, Zimbabwe), 1970–71; British Council, 1973; Educn Dir, Help the Aged, 1974; FCO by open competition, 1974; 2nd, later 1st, Sec., Dar es Salaam, 1977–80; Commonwealth Co-ordination Dept, 1980–82; Sec. to UK Delegn to Commonwealth Heads of Govt Meeting, Melbourne, 1981; UKMIS to UN, NY, 1982; Central and Southern Africa Dept, ODA, 1983–84; UKMIS to UN, Geneva, 1985–88; Head of Internat. and Planning Section and Dep. Head, Aid Policy Dept, ODA/FCO, 1988–89; Counsellor and Head, Narcotics Control and Aids Dept, FCO, 1989–91; Ambassador to Fiji and High Comr to Nauru and Tuvalu, 1992–95, and to Kiribati, 1994–95; Counsellor, Middle East Dept, FCO, 1995; Dep. High Comr, Harare, 1996–98; High Comr, Belize, 1998–2001; Dean, Diplomatic Corps in Belize, 2001. UK Dir, Tuvalu Trust Fund, 1992–95. Mem. Council, Univ. of S Pacific, 1993–95. Patron, SCF (Fiji), 1993–95. *Recreations:* friends, reading, music, tennis, squash, walking. *Address:* c/o Foreign and Commonwealth Office, SW1A 2AH. *Clubs:* Royal Commonwealth Society; All England Lawn Tennis and Croquet.

DAVID, Wayne; MP (Lab) Caerphilly, since 2001; *b* 1 July 1957; *s* of D. Haydn David and Edna A. David; *m* 1991, Catherine Thomas. *Educ:* Cynffig Comprehensive Sch.; University Coll., Cardiff (BA Hons History; PGCE); University Coll., Swansea. History teacher, Brynteg Comprehensive Sch., Bridgend, 1983–85; Mid Glam Tutor Organiser, S Wales Dist, WEA, 1985–89. Policy Advr, Wales Youth Agency, 1999–2001. MEP (Lab) S Wales, 1989–94, S Wales Central, 1994–99. Treas., 1989–91, Leader, 1994–98, European Parly Labour Party (formerly British Labour Gp); 1st Vice-Pres., Regl Policy and Planning Cttee, Eur. Parlt, 1992–94; Sec., Tribune Gp of MEPs, 1992–94. Mem., Labour Party NEC, 1994–98. Mem., European Scrutiny Select Cttee, 2001–. Vice-President: City of Cardiff Br., UNA, 1989–; Council for Wales of Voluntary Youth Services, 2001; Mem., Cefn Cribwr Community Council, 1985–91. Fellow, Univ. of Wales Coll. of Cardiff, 1995. *Publications:* (contrib.) Oxford Companion to the Literature of Wales, 1986; three pamphlets; contrib. Llafur—Jl of Welsh Labour History. *Recreations:* music, reading. *Address:* c/o House of Commons, SW1A 0AA. *T:* (020) 7219 8152.

DAVID-WEILL, Michel Alexandre; Chairman, Lazard Frères & Co., LLC, New York, since 1977; Deputy Chairman, Lazard Brothers & Co., London, since 1991 (Chairman, 1990–91); Partner, Lazard Frères et Cie, Paris, since 1965; *b* 23 Nov. 1932; *s* of Berthe Haardt and Pierre David-Weill; *m* 1956, Hélène Lehideux; four *d. Educ:* Institut de Sciences Politiques, Paris; Lycée Français de New York. Brown Brothers Harriman, 1954–55; Lehman Brothers, NY, 1955–56; Lazard Frères & Co., NY, 1956–, Partner, 1961, Sen. Partner, 1977; Lazard Brothers & Co., London, Dir, 1965–; Chm., Lazard Partners, 1984–. Dir, French Amer. Foundn, NY; Member Council: Musée de la Légion d'Honneur, Paris, 1975; Cité Internat. des Arts, Paris, 1976; Mem., Acad. des Beaux-Arts, 1983; Trustee: MMA, NY; Pierpont Morgan Liby, NY; Pres., Conseil Artistique de la Réunion des Musées Nationaux, Paris. Gov., NY Hosp. Officier, Legion of Honour (France), 1990. *Address:* Lazard Frères & Co., 30 Rockefeller Plaza, New York, NY 10020, USA. *T:* (212) 6326000. *Clubs:* Knickerbocker, Brook (NY); Creek (Locust Valley).

DAVIDSON, family name of **Viscount Davidson**.

DAVIDSON, 2nd Viscount *cr* 1937, of Little Gaddesden; **John Andrew Davidson;** Captain of the Yeomen of the Guard (Deputy Government Chief Whip), 1986–91; *b* 22 Dec. 1928; *er s* of 1st Viscount Davidson, PC, GCVO, CH, CB, and Frances Joan, Viscountess Davidson (Baroness Northchurch), DBE (*d* 1985), *y d* of 1st Baron Dickinson, PC, KBE; *S* father, 1970; *m* 1st, 1956, Margaret Birgitta Norton (marr. diss. 1974); four *d* (including twin *d*); 2nd, 1975, Mrs Pamela Dobb (*née* Vergette). *Educ:* Westminster School; Pembroke College, Cambridge (BA). Served in The Black Watch and 5th Bn KAR, 1947–49. Pres., CU Footlights Club, 1951. A Lord in Waiting (Govt Whip), 1985–86. Director: Strutt & Parker (Farms) Ltd, 1960–75; Lord Rayleigh's Farms Inc., 1960–75; Member of Council: CLA, 1965–75; RASE, 1973; Chm., Management Committee, Royal Eastern Counties Hospital, 1966–72; Mem., East Anglia Economic Planning Council, 1971–75. *Recreation:* music. *Heir:* *b* Hon. Malcolm William Mackenzie Davidson [*b* 28 Aug. 1934; *m* 1970, Mrs Evelyn Ann Carew Perfect, *yr d* of William Blackmore Storey; one *s* one *d*]. *Address:* 19 Lochmore House, Cundy Street, SW1W 9JX.
See also Baron Rayleigh.

DAVIDSON, Hon. Lord; Charles Kemp Davidson, FRSE 1985; a Senator of the College of Justice in Scotland, 1983–96; Chairman, Scottish Law Commission, 1988–96; *b* Edinburgh, 13 April 1929; *s* of Rev. Donald Davidson, DD, Edinburgh; *m* 1960, Mary (OBE 1994), *d* of Charles Mactaggart, Campbeltown, Argyll; one *s* two *d. Educ:* Fettes Coll., Edinburgh; Brasenose Coll., Oxford; Edinburgh Univ. Admitted to Faculty of Advocates, 1956; QC (Scot.) 1969; Vice-Dean, 1977–79; Dean, 1979–83; Keeper, Advocates' Library, 1972–76. Procurator to Gen. Assembly of Church of Scotland, 1972–83. Dep. Chm., Boundary Commn for Scotland, 1985–96. *Address:* 22 Dublin Street, Edinburgh EH1 3PP. *T:* (0131) 556 2168.

DAVIDSON, Alan Eaton; author; HM Diplomatic Service, retired; Managing Director, Prospect Books Ltd, since 1982; *b* 30 March 1924; *s* of William John Davidson and Constance (*née* Eaton); *m* 1951, Jane Macatee; three *d. Educ:* Leeds Grammar Sch.; Queen's Coll., Oxford. 1st class hons Class. Mods and Greats. Served in RNVR (Ordinary Seaman, later Lieut) in Mediterranean, N Atlantic and Pacific, 1943–46. Member of HM Foreign Service, 1948; served at: Washington, 1950–53; The Hague, 1953–55; FO, 1955–59; First Secretary, British Property Commission, and later Head of Chancery, British Embassy, Cairo, 1959–61; Head of Chancery and Consul, Tunis, 1962–64; FO, 1964; Counsellor, 1965; Head, Central Dept, FO, 1966–68; Head of Chancery, UK Delegn to NATO, Brussels, 1968–71; seconded, as Vis. Fellow, Centre for Contemporary European Studies, Univ. of Sussex, 1971–72; Head of Defence Dept, FCO, 1972–73; Ambassador to Vientiane, 1973–75. *Publications:* Seafish of Tunisia and the Central Mediterranean, 1963; Snakes and Scorpions Found in the Land of Tunisia, 1964; Mediterranean Seafood, 1972; The Role of the Uncommitted European Countries in East-West Relations, 1972; Fish and Fish Dishes of Laos, 1975; Seafood of South East Asia, 1976; (with Jane Davidson) Dumas on Food, 1978; North Atlantic Seafood, 1979; (with Jennifer Davidson) Traditional Recipes of Laos, 1981; On Fasting and Feasting (annotated anthology), 1988; A Kipper with My Tea, 1988; (with Charlotte Knox) Seafood, 1989; (with Charlotte Knox) Fruit, 1991; The Oxford Companion to Food, 1999. *Address:* 45 Lamont Road, World's End, SW10 0HU. *T:* (020) 7352 4209.

DAVIDSON, Alfred Edward; international lawyer; Vice-President and General Counsel, Technical Studies, 1957–70, and 1973–91; *b* New York, 11 Nov. 1911; *s* of Maurice Philip Davidson and Blanche Reinheimer; *m* 1934, Claire H. Dreyfuss (*d* 1981); two *s*. *Educ:* Harvard Univ. (AB); Columbia Law Sch. (LLB). Advocate, Bar of New York, 1936; of Dist of Columbia, 1972; Asst to Gen. Counsel, US Dept of Labor, Wash., 1938–40; review section, Solicitor's Office, 1940–41; Legis. Counsel, Office of Emergency Management, in Exec. Office of President, 1941–43; Asst Gen. Counsel, Lend-Lease Admin (later Foreign Economic Admin), 1943–45; Gen. Counsel, 1945–; Gen. Counsel, UNRRA, Nov. 1945; Counsel, Preparatory Commn for Internat. Refugee Org., 1947; Dir, European Headqrs of UNICEF, 1947–51; Advisor, Office of Sec.-Gen. of UN, 1951–52; Gen. Counsel, UN Korean Reconstr. Agency, 1952–54; Exec. Asst to Chm., Bd of Rio Tinto of Canada, 1955–58; European Representative, Internat. Finance Corp., 1970–72; Counsel to Wilmer, Cutler & Pickering, Attorneys at Law, 1972–75. Dir, Channel Tunnel Study Gp, 1960–70; Hon. Chm., Democratic Party Abroad, 1989. Co-Founder, Assoc. for Promotion of Humor in Internat. Affairs; Hon. Chm., Common Cause Overseas. *Publications:* contribs various periodicals and newspapers. *Recreations:* tennis, bridge, chess, reading. *Address:* 5900 Wilson Blvd, Arlington, VA 22205, USA. *Clubs:* Lansdowne; Standard Athletic (France).

DAVIDSON, Arthur; QC 1978; *b* 7 Nov. 1928. *Educ:* Liverpool Coll.; King George V Sch., Southport; Trinity Coll., Cambridge. Served in Merchant Navy. Barrister, Middle Temple, 1953. Trinity Coll., Cambridge, 1959–62; Editor of the Granta. Legal Director: Associated Newspapers Hldgs, 1987–90; Mirror Gp, 1991–93. MP (Lab) Accrington, 1966–83; PPS to Solicitor-General, 1968–70; Chm., Home Affairs Gp, Parly Labour Party, 1971–74; Parly Sec., Law Officers' Dept, 1974–79; Opposition spokesman on Defence (Army), 1980–81, on legal affairs, 1981–83, Shadow Attorney-General, 1982–83; Member: Home Affairs Select Cttee, 1980–83; Armed Forces Bill Select Cttee, 1981–83. Contested (Lab): Blackpool S, 1955; Preston N, 1959; Hyndburn, 1983. Member: Council, Consumers' Association, 1970–74; Exec. Cttee, Soc. of Labour Lawyers, 1981; Nat. Exec., Fabian Soc.; Council, Nat. Youth Jazz Orchestra; Chm., House of Commons Jazz Club, 1973–83. *Recreations:* lawn tennis, ski-ing, theatre, listening to good jazz and playing bad jazz; formerly Member Cambridge Univ. athletics team. *Address:* Cloisters, 1st Floor, 1 Pump Court, Temple, EC4Y 7AA. *Clubs:* James Street Men's Working (Oswaldtwistle); Free Gardeners (Rishton); King Street, Marlborough Working Men's (Accrington).

DAVIDSON, Basil Risbridger, MC 1945; author and historian; *b* 9 Nov. 1914; *s* of Thomas and Jessie Davidson; *m* 1943, Marion Ruth Young; three *s*. Served War of 1939–45 (despatches twice, MC, US Bronze Star, Jugoslav Zasluge za Narod); British Army, 1940–45 (Balkans, N Africa, Italy); Temp. Lt-Col demobilised as Hon. Major. Editorial staff of The Economist, 1938–39; The Star (diplomatic correspondent, 1939); The Times (Paris correspondent, 1945–47; chief foreign leader-writer, 1947–49); New Statesman (special correspondent, 1950–54); Daily Herald (special correspondent, 1954–57); Daily Mirror (leader-writer, 1959–62). Vis. Prof., Univ. of Ghana, 1964; Vis. Prof., 1965, Regents' Lectr, 1971, Univ. of California; Montagu Burton Vis. Prof. of Internat. Relations, Edinburgh Univ., 1972; Sen. Simon Res. Fellow, Univ. of Manchester, 1975–76; Hon. Res. Fellow, Univ. of Birmingham, 1978–; Agnelli Vis. Prof., Univ. of Turin, 1990. A Vice-Pres., Anti-Apartheid Movement, 1969–85. Author/presenter, Africa (8-part TV documentary series), 1984. Associate Mem., Acad. des Scis d'Outre-Mer, Paris, 1973. Freeman of City of Genoa, 1945. Hon. Fellow, SOAS, London Univ., 1998. DLitt *hc*: Ibadan, 1975; Dar es Salaam, 1985; Edinburgh, 1981; Western Cape, S Africa, 1997; Bristol, 1999; DUniv Open, 1980. Haile Selassie African Research Award, 1970; Medalha Amílcar Cabral, 1976. *Publications: novels:* Highway Forty, 1949; Golden Horn, 1952; The Rapids, 1955; Lindy, 1958; The Andrassy Affair, 1966; *non-fiction:* Partisan Picture, 1946; Germany: From Potsdam to Partition, 1950; Report on Southern Africa, 1952; Daybreak in China, 1953; (ed) The New West Africa, 1953; The African Awakening, 1955; Turkestan Alive, 1957; Old Africa Rediscovered, 1959; Black Mother, 1961, rev. edn 1980; The African Past, 1964; Which Way Africa?, 1964; The Growth of African Civilisation: West Africa AD 1000–1800, 1965; Africa: History of a Continent, 1966; A History of East and Central Africa to the late 19th Century, 1967; Africa in History: Themes and Outlines, 1968; The Liberation of Guiné, 1969; The Africans, An Entry to Cultural History, 1969; Discovering our African Heritage, 1971; In the Eye of the Storm: Angola's People, 1972; Black Star, 1974; Can Africa Survive?, 1975; Discovering Africa's Past, 1978 (Children's Rights Workshop Award, 1978); Africa in Modern History, 1978; Crossroads in Africa, 1980; Special Operations Europe, 1980; The People's Cause, 1980; No Fist is Big Enough, 1981; Modern Africa, 1982, 3rd edn 1994; The Story of Africa, 1984; The Fortunate Isles, 1989; African Civilisation Revisited, 1991; The Black Man's Burden: Africa and the curse of the nation-state, 1992; The Search for Africa (essays), 1994; West Africa before the Colonial Era: a history to 1850, 1998. *Address:* Old Cider Mill, North Wootton, Somerset BA4 4HA.

DAVIDSON, Charles Kemp; *see* Davidson, Hon. Lord.

DAVIDSON, Charles Peter Morton; a District Judge (Magistrates' Courts) (formerly Metropolitan Stipendiary Magistrate), since 1984; a Recorder, 1991–99; *b* 29 July 1938; *s* of late William Philip Morton Davidson, MD, and Muriel Maud Davidson (*née* Alderson); *m* 1966, Pamela Louise Campbell-Rose. *Educ:* Harrow; Trinity Coll., Dublin (MA, LLB). Called to the Bar, Inner Temple, 1963; employed by Legal and General Assurance Soc., 1963–65; in practice at Bar, 1966–84. Chairman, London Rent Assessment Panel, 1973–84; part-time Immigration Appeals Adjudicator, 1976–84; a Chairman: Inner London Juvenile Courts, 1985–88; Family Court, 1991–. Contested (C) North Battersea, 1966 General Election; Councillor, London Boroughs: of Wandsworth, 1964–68, of Merton, 1968–71. *Recreations:* music, gardening. *Address:* c/o Camberwell Green Magistrates' Court, 15 D'Eynsford Road, SE5 7UP. *Club:* Hurlingham.

DAVIDSON, David; Member (C) Scotland North East, Scottish Parliament, since 1999; *b* 25 Jan. 1943; *s* of John and Marjory Davidson; *m* 1968, Christine Hunter; three *s* two *d*. *Educ:* Heriot-Watt Univ. (Pharmacy); Manchester Business Sch. (DipBA). MRPharmS. Manager, 1966–69, Proprietor, 1969–74, community pharmacy, Kent; developed gp of community pharmacies in Northern England, 1974–93; Dir, Unichem Ltd, 1977–90; Regl Chm., Unichem plc, 1990–93; Managing Director: Earlston Ltd, 1984–; Carse Ltd, 1996–. Mem. (C) Stirling Council, 1995–99. Founder Chm., Assoc. Scottish Community Councils, 1993–95. *Recreations:* country pursuits, pedigree stock breeding, Rugby football, travel. *Address:* Scottish Parliament, Edinburgh EH99 1SP; North Hilton, Netherley, by Stonehaven, Kincardine, Aberdeenshire AB39 3QL. *T:* (01569) 730449.

DAVIDSON, Duncan Henry; Chairman, Persimmon plc, since 1972; *b* 29 March 1941; *s* of late Col Colin Keppel Davidson, CIE, OBE, RA (killed in action 1943) and late Lady (Mary) Rachel Davidson (later Lady (Mary) Rachel Pepys, DCVO); *m* 1965, Sarah Wilson; four *d*. *Educ:* Ampleforth Coll. Lieut, Royal Scots Greys, 1959–63; Manager, George Wimpey plc, 1963–65; Founder and Chm., Ryedale Homes Ltd, 1965–72. *Recreation:* country pursuits. *Address:* Lilburn Tower, Alnwick, Northumberland NE66 4PQ. *T:* (01668) 217291. *Clubs:* White's, Turf.

DAVIDSON, Edward Alan; QC 1994; *b* 12 July 1943; *o s* of late Alan T. Davidson and H. Muriel Davidson, Sheffield; *m* 1973, Hilary Jill, *er d* of late Major N. S. Fairman, MBE; two *s*. *Educ:* King's Sch., Canterbury; Gonville and Caius Coll., Cambridge (schol., Tapp Postgrad Schol.; MA, LLB). Called to the Bar, Gray's Inn, 1966 (Atkin and Birkenhead Schol.). *Recreations:* tennis, bridge, gardening. *Address:* 11 Old Square, Lincoln's Inn, WC2A 3TS. *T:* (020) 7430 0341, *Fax:* (020) 7831 2469.

DAVIDSON, Ian Graham; MP (Lab and Co-op) Glasgow, Pollok, since 1997 (Glasgow, Govan, 1992–97); *b* 8 Sept. 1950; *s* of Graham Davidson and Elizabeth Crowe; *m* 1978, Morag Mackinnon; one *s* one *d*. *Educ:* Jedburgh Grammar Sch.; Galashiels Acad.; Edinburgh Univ. (MA Hons); Jordanhill Coll. (Teacher Cert.). Chm., Nat. Orgn of Labour Students, 1973–74; Pres., Jordanhill Coll. Students' Assoc., 1975–76; PA/Researcher, Janey Buchan, MEP, 1978–85; Community Service Volunteers, 1985–92. Councillor, Strathclyde Region, 1978–92 (Chm., Educn Cttees, 1986–92). Mem., Public Accounts Select Cttee, 1997–; Chairman: MSF Parly Gp, 1996–97; Co-op Gp, 1998–99; Bermuda Gp, 1998–; Secretary: Tribune Gp of MPs, 1997–; Trade Union Gp of Lab MPs, 1998–; British/German Gp, 1998–; British/Japanese Gp, 1998–; Aerospace Gp, 1998–; Parly Rugby Union team, 1996–. *Recreations:* running, swimming, family. *Address:* House of Commons, SW1A 0AA.

DAVIDSON, Ian Robert, RIBA; Director, Lifschutz Davidson Ltd, since 1986; *b* 3 June 1954; *s* of Sir Robert (James) Davidson, *qv*; *m* 1977, Lenaura Mary Nelmes; one *s* one *d*. *Educ:* Leamington Coll. for Boys; Leicester Poly. (DipArch with Commendation 1978). Registered Architect 1979; RIBA 1979. With Richard Rogers Partnership, 1978–81, Foster Associates, 1981–86; with Alex Lifschutz, founded Lifschutz Davidson Ltd, 1986. *Projects* include: Richard Rogers & Partners' office ext., Thames Wharf Studios, 1991 (RIBA Award, 1992); Broadwall Community Housing, London, 1994 (Royal Fine Arts Commn/Sunday Times Bldg of Year, RIBA Award, 1995; DoE Nat. Housing Design Award, Civic Trust Housing Award, 1996); develt at Oxo Tower Wharf, 1996 (Royal Fine Art Commn Urban Regeneration Award, RIBA Award, 1997; Civic Trust Award, 1998; Waterfront Center Honor Award, 2000); Royal Victoria Dock Bridge, 1999 (Royal Acad./A. J. Bovis Award, 1997; ICE Award of Merit, RIBA Arch. Award, Design Council Millennium Product, 1999). Chm., RIBA Awards Gp, 2000–; Mem. Bd, Architects' Registration Bd, 2000–. FRSA 1993. *Recreations:* my children, sailing, travel. *Address:* Lifschutz Davidson Ltd, Thames Wharf Studios, Rainville Road, W6 9HA.

DAVIDSON, His Honour Ian Thomas Rollo; QC 1977; a Circuit Judge, 1984–97; *b* 3 Aug. 1925; *s* of late Robert Davidson and Margaret Davidson; *m* 1954, Gyöngyi (marr. diss. 1982), *d* of Prof. Cs. Anghi; one *s* one *d*; *m* 1984, Barbara Ann Watts; one *s*. *Educ:* Fettes Coll.; Corpus Christi Coll., Oxford (Schol.). MA, Lit. Hum. Royal Armoured Corps, 1943–47, Lieut Derbs Yeomanry. Called to Bar, Gray's Inn, 1955. Asst Lectr, University Coll., London, 1959–60; Deputy Recorder, Nottingham, 1971; a Recorder of the Crown Court, 1974. *Recreations:* music, golf, photography. *Address:* c/o Crown Court, Canal Street, Nottingham NG1 7EJ.

DAVIDSON, Ivor Macaulay; Chairman, D. O. Sanbiet Ltd, since 1980; *b* 27 Jan. 1924; *s* of late James Macaulay and Violet Alice Davidson; *m* 1948, Winifred Lowes; four *s* one *d*. *Educ:* Bellahouston Sch.; Univ. of Glasgow. Royal Aircraft Establishment, 1943; Power Jets (R&D) Ltd, 1944; attached RAF, 1945; National Gas Turbine Establishment, 1946: Dep. Dir, 1964; Dir, 1970–74; Dir-Gen. Engines, Procurement Exec., MoD, 1974–79. *Publications:* numerous, scientific and technical. *Recreations:* music, gardening.

DAVIDSON, James Alfred, OBE 1971; retired RN and Diplomatic Service; *b* 22 March 1922; *s* of Lt-Comdr A. D. Davidson and Mrs (Elizabeth) Davidson; *m* 1955, Daphne (*née* While); two *d*, and two step *s*. *Educ:* Christ's Hospital; RN Coll., Dartmouth. Royal Navy, 1939–60 (war service Atlantic, Mediterranean and Far East); commanded HM Ships Calder and Welfare; Comdr 1955; retd 1960. Holds Master Mariner's Cert. of Service. Called to the Bar, Middle Temple, 1960. Joined CRO (later FCO) 1960; served Port of Spain, Phnom Penh (periods as Chargé d'Affaires 1970 and 1971); Dacca (Chargé d'Affaires, later Dep. High Comr, 1972–73); Vis. Scholar, Univ. of Kent, 1973–74; British High Comr, Brunei, 1974–78; participated, Sept. 1978, in finalisation of Brunei Independence Treaty; Governor, British Virgin Islands, 1978–81. Vis. Fellow, LSE Centre for Internat. Studies, 1982–84. Legal Mem. and Pres., Mental Health Review Tribunal, 1982–95; a Chm., Pensions Appeals Tribunals, 1984–95. *Publications:* Brunei Coinage, 1977; Indo-China: Signposts in the Storm, 1979. *Address:* Little Frankfield, Seal Chart, near Sevenoaks, Kent TN15 0HA. *T:* (01732) 761600. *Club:* Army and Navy.

DAVIDSON, James Duncan Gordon, OBE 1984; MVO 1947; Chief Executive, Royal Highland and Agricultural Society of Scotland, 1970–91; *b* 10 Jan. 1927; *s* of Alastair Gordon Davidson and M. Valentine B. Davidson (*née* Osborne); *m* 1st, 1955, Catherine Ann Jamieson; one *s* two *d*; 2nd, 1973, Janet Stafford; one *s*. *Educ:* RN Coll., Dartmouth; Downing Coll., Cambridge. Active List, RN, 1944–55. Subseq. farming, and political work; contested (L) West Aberdeenshire, 1964; MP (L) West Aberdeenshire, 1966–70. FRAgS; MIEx. *Recreations:* family, walking, ski-ing, music, forestry. *Address:* Coire Cas, Newtonmore, Inverness-shire PH20 1AR. *T:* (01540) 673322.

DAVIDSON, James Patton, CBE 1980; *b* 23 March 1928; *s* of Richard Davidson and Elizabeth Ferguson Carnichan; *m* 1st, 1953, Jean Stevenson Ferguson Anderson (marr. diss. 1981); two *s*; 2nd, 1981, Esmé Evelyn Ancill. *Educ:* Rutherglen Acad.; Glasgow Univ. (BL). Mil. service, commissioned RASC, 1948–50. Clyde Navigation Trust, 1950; Asst Gen. Manager, 1958. Clyde Port Authority: Gen. Manager, 1966; Managing Dir, 1974; Dep. Chm. and Man. Dir, 1976; Chm., 1980–83. Chairman: Ardrossan Harbour Co. Ltd, 1976–83; Clydeport Stevedoring Services Ltd, 1977–83; Clyde Container Services Ltd, 1968–83; S. & H. McCall Transport (Glasgow) Ltd, 1972–83; Rhu Marina Ltd, 1976–80; Scotway Haulage Ltd, 1976–81; R. & J. Strang Ltd, 1976–81; Nat. Assoc. of Port Employers, 1974–79; British Ports Assoc., 1980–83 (Dep. Chm., 1978–80); Port Employers' & Registered Dock Workers' Pension Fund Trustee Ltd, 1978–83; Pilotage Commn, 1983–91 (Mem., 1979–83); UK Dir, 1976–83 and Mem., Exec. Cttee, 1977–83, Hon. Mem., 1983, Internat. Assoc. of Ports and Harbours. Dir, Iron Trades Insurance Gp, 1981–94; Chm., Foods & Feeds (UK), 1982–83. FCIT, CIMgt; FRSA. *Recreations:* golf, bridge, travel, reading, sailing. *Club:* Nautico (Altea).

DAVIDSON, Jane Elizabeth; Member (Lab) Pontypridd, National Assembly for Wales, since 1999; Minister (formerly Secretary) for Education and Life-long Learning, since 2000; *b* 19 March 1957; *d* of Dr Lindsay Alexander Gordon Davidson and Dr Joyce Mary Davidson; *m* 1994, Guy Roger George Stoate; one *d*, and two step *s*. *Educ:* Malvern Girls' Coll.; Birmingham Univ. (BA 2nd Cl. Hons English); UCW, Aberystwyth (PGCE). Teacher, Cardigan and Pontypridd, 1981–83; youth and community worker, Dinas Powys Youth Centre, 1983–86; Develt Officer, YHA, 1986–89; researcher to Rhodri Morgan, MP, 1989–94; Welsh Co-ordinator, Nat. Local Govt Forum Against Poverty,

1994–96; Hd, Social Affairs, Welsh Local Govt Assoc., 1996–99. Dep. Presiding Officer, Nat. Assembly for Wales, 1999–2000. *Publications:* The Anti Poverty Implications of Local Government Reorganisation, 1990; contrib. to social policy jls. *Recreations:* theatre, walking, swimming. *Address:* National Assembly for Wales, Crickhowell House, Cardiff Bay, Cardiff CF99 1NA. *T:* (029) 2089 8174, (constituency office) (01443) 406400.

DAVIDSON, Prof. John Frank, FRS 1974; FREng; Shell Professor of Chemical Engineering, University of Cambridge, 1978–93 (Professor of Chemical Engineering, 1975–78); Vice-Master, Trinity College, Cambridge, 1992–96; Adjunct Professor, Monash University, Australia, 1996–99; *b* 7 Feb. 1926; *s* of John and Katie Davidson; *m* 1948, Susanne Hedwig Ostberg; one *s* one *d*. *Educ:* Heaton Grammar Sch., Newcastle upon Tyne; Trinity Coll., Cambridge. MA, PhD, ScD; FIChemE, MIMechE. 1st cl. Mech. Scis Tripos, Cantab, 1946, BA 1947. Engrg work at Rolls Royce, Derby, 1947–50; Cambridge Univ.: Research Fellow, Trinity Coll., 1949; research, 1950–52; Univ. Demonstrator, 1952; Univ. Lectr, 1954; Steward of Trinity Coll., 1957–64; Reader in Chem. Engrg, Univ. of Cambridge, 1964–75. Visiting Professor: Univ. of Delaware, 1960; Univ. of Sydney, 1967. Member: Flixborough Ct of Inquiry, 1974–75; Adv. Cttee on Safety of Nuclear Installations, HSC, 1977–87. Pres., IChemE, 1970–71; Vice Pres. and Mem. Council, Royal Soc., 1988. FREng (Founder FEng, 1976). For. Associate, Nat. Acad. of Engrg, US, 1976; For. Fellow, Indian National Science Acad., 1990; For. Mem., Russian Engrg Acad., 1998. Dr *hc* Institut Nat. Polytech. de Toulouse, 1979; Hon. DSc Aston, 1989. Leverhulme Medal, Royal Soc., 1984; Messel Medal, Soc. of Chemical Industry, 1986; Royal Medal, Royal Soc., 1999. *Publications:* (with D. Harrison): Fluidised Particles, 1963; Fluidization, 1971, 2nd edn (with R. Clift and D. Harrison), 1985; (with D. L. Keairns) Fluidization (Conference Procs), 1978. *Recreations:* hill walking, gardening, mending bicycles and other domestic artefacts. *Address:* 5 Luard Close, Cambridge CB2 2PL. *T:* (01223) 246104.

DAVIDSON, John Roderick; Director of Administration, since 1991, Clerk of the Council, since 1994, University of London; *b* 29 Jan. 1937; *yr s* of late Alexander Ross Davidson and Jessie Maud (*née* Oakley). *Educ:* Portsmouth Northern Grammar Sch.; Univ. of Manchester (BA). Advr to students, Chelsea Sch. of Art, 1966–68; Asst Sch. Sec., RPMS, 1968–74; Imperial College of Science, Technology and Medicine: Asst Sec., 1974–77; Personnel Sec., 1977–85; Admin. Sec., 1985–89; London University: Clerk of Senate, 1989–94; Member: Exams and Assessment Council, 1991–2000; Bd, British Inst. in Paris, 1993–. Director: London E Anglian Gp, 1990–96; Superannuation Arrangements of Univ. of London Trustee Co., 1993–98; London and S Eastern Library Region, 1995–2001; Senate House Services Ltd, 1996–. Chm., Lansdowne (Putney) Ltd, 1999–. Trustee, Univ. of London Convocation Trust, 1997–. Governor: Charterhouse Sch., 1994–; More House Sch., 2000–. *Recreations:* theatre, opera, genealogy. *Address:* Senate House, University of London, Malet Street, WC1E 7HU. *T:* (020) 7862 8010, *Fax:* (020) 7862 8012; *e-mail:* j.davidson@admin.lon.ac.uk; (home) 10 Lansdowne, Carlton Drive, SW15 2BY. *T:* (020) 8789 0021. *Club:* Athenæum.

DAVIDSON, Keith; *see* Davidson, W. K.

DAVIDSON, Martin Stuart; Director, East Asia and Americas, British Council, since 2000; *b* 14 Oct. 1955; *s* of Westland Davidson and Freda (*née* Hill); *m* 1980, Elizabeth Fanning; two *s* one *d*. *Educ:* Royal Grammar Sch., Guildford; St Andrews Univ. (MA). Admin. Officer, Hong Kong Govt, 1979–83; British Council: Peking, 1984–87; Regl Officer, China, 1987–89; Dir, S China, 1989–93; Asst Regl Dir, E and S Europe, 1993–95; Cultural Counsellor and Dir, British Council, Peking, 1995–2000. *Recreations:* hill walking, reading. *Address:* c/o British Council, 10 Spring Gardens, SW1A 2BN. *Clubs:* Royal Commonwealth Society; Foreign Correspondents (Hong Kong).

DAVIDSON, Neil Forbes; QC (Scot.) 1993; Solicitor General for Scotland, since 2000; *b* 13 Sept. 1950; *s* of John and Flora Davidson; *m* 1980, Regina Anne Sprissler, Philadelphia. *Educ:* Univs of Stirling (BA), Bradford (MSc), Edinburgh (LLB, LLM). Admitted Faculty of Advocates, 1979; Standing Jun. Counsel to Registrar Gen., 1982, to Depts of Health and Social Security, 1988; called to the Bar, Inner Temple, 1990. Dir, City Disputes Panel, 1993–. ICJ missions to Egypt, 1997, 1998. *Publications:* (jtly) Judicial Review in Scotland, 1986; (contrib.) ADR in Scotland, 1995. *Address:* Crown Office, 25 Chambers Street, Edinburgh EH1 1LA. *T:* (0131) 226 2626.

DAVIDSON, Nicholas Ranking; QC 1993; a Deputy High Court Judge, since 2000; *b* 2 March 1951; *s* of late Brian Davidson, CBE and Priscilla Margaret (*née* Chilver); *m* 1978, Gillian Frances Watts; two *d*. *Educ:* Winchester (Schol.); Trinity Coll., Cambridge (Exhibnr; BA). Called to the Bar, Inner Temple, 1974 (Treas.'s Prize, Hughes Parry Prize and Inner Temple Scholarship, 1974; Bencher, 1998). Chm., Professional Negligence Bar Assoc., 1997–99. Governor, St Mary's Sch., Ascot, 1996–. *Publications:* (contrib.) Now and Then, 1999; (contrib.) Professional Negligence and Liability, 2000. *Recreations:* bridge, music, ski-ing. *Address:* 4 New Square, Lincoln's Inn, WC2A 3RJ. *T:* (020) 7822 2000.

DAVIDSON, Prof. Peter Robert Keith Andrew, PhD; Chalmers Regius Professor of English, University of Aberdeen, since 2000; *b* 14 May 1957; *s* of Robert Ritchie Davidson and Daphne Davidson (*née* Sanderson); *m* 1989, Jane Barbara Stevenson. *Educ:* Clare Coll., Cambridge (BA 1979; PhD 1986); Univ. of York (MA 1980). FSAScot 1984. Lectr, Univ. of St Andrews, 1989–90; Docent in Lit. and Book Studies, Rijksuniversiteit Leiden, Netherlands, 1990–92; University of Warwick: Lectr in English, 1992–97; Sen. Lectr, 1997–99; Reader, 1999–2000. *Publications:* (with A. H. van der Weel) Poems of Sir Constantijn Huygens, 1996; The Vocall Forest, 1996; The Poems and Translations of Sir Richard Fanshawe, vol. I, 1998, vol. II, 1999; Poetry and Revolution, 1998; (with Jane Stevenson) Early Modern Women's Verse, 2000. *Recreations:* casuistry, obelisks. *Address:* King's College, Aberdeen AB24 2UB.

DAVIDSON, Very Rev. Prof. Robert, FRSE; Professor of Old Testament Language and Literature, University of Glasgow, 1972–91; Principal, Trinity College, Glasgow, 1982–91; *b* 30 March 1927; *s* of George Braid Davidson and Gertrude May Ward; *m* 1952, Elizabeth May Robertson; four *s* four *d*. *Educ:* Univ. of St Andrews (MA 1st Cl Hons Classics, 1949; BD, Distinction in Old Testament, 1952). FRSE 1989. Asst Lectr, then Lectr in Biblical Studies, Univ. of Aberdeen, 1953–60; Lectr in Hebrew and Old Testament, Univ. of St Andrews, 1960–66; Lectr in Old Testament Studies, Univ. of Edinburgh, 1966–69, Sen. Lectr, 1969–72. Edward Cadbury Lectr, Birmingham Univ., 1988–89. Moderator, Gen. Assembly, Church of Scotland, 1990–91. Hon. DD: Aberdeen, 1985; Glasgow, 1993. *Publications:* The Bible Speaks, 1959; The Old Testament, 1964; (with A. R. C. Leaney) Biblical Criticism (Vol. 3 of Pelican Guide to Modern Theology), 1970; Genesis 1–11 (Cambridge Bible Commentary), 1973; Genesis 12–50 (Cambridge Bible Commentary), 1979; The Bible in Religious Education, 1979; The Courage to Doubt, 1983; Jeremiah 1–20 (Daily Study Bible), 1983; Jeremiah II, Lamentations (Daily Study Bible), 1986; Ecclesiastes and Song of Songs (Daily Study Bible), 1986; Wisdom and Worship, 1990; A Beginner's Guide to the Old Testament, 1992; Go By the Book, 1996; The Vitality of Worship, 1998; articles in Vetus Testamentum, Annual Swedish Theol Inst., Expository Times, Scottish Jl of Theol., Epworth Review and The Furrow. *Recreations:* music, gardening. *Address:* 30 Dumgoyne Drive, Bearsden, Glasgow G61 3AP. *T:* (0141) 942 1810.

DAVIDSON, Sir Robert (James), Kt 1989; Chairman, Devonport Management Ltd, 1994–96; Director, BICC plc, 1991–96; *b* 21 July 1928; *m* 1953, Barbara Elsie Eagles; two *s* two *d*. *Educ:* Royal Tech Coll., Glasgow (DRC 1949); Imperial Coll., London (DIC 1953). FREng (FEng 1984); FIMechE. Joined English Electric Co. as grad. apprentice, 1949; Develt Engr, 1951–52; Design Engr, Hydro Electric Project, 1953–55; Project Manager, Priest Rapids Hydro-Electric Power Stn, USA, 1956–61; Manufg Manager, then Gen. Manager, Netherton Works, 1962–69; English Electric taken over by GEC, 1969; Manager, Outside Construction Dept, 1969–72, Manufg Dir, 1972–74, Man. Dir, 1974–88, GEC Turbine Generators Ltd; Dir, GEC plc, 1985–91; Man. Dir, GEC Power Systems Ltd, 1988–89; Vice-Chm. and Chief Exec. Officer, GEC Alsthom NV, 1989–91; Chm. and Man. Dir, GEC ALSTHOM Ltd, 1989–91; Dir, GEC ALSTHOM SA, 1989–91; Chairman: NNC, 1988–91; Balfour Beatty Ltd, 1991–94. Mem., British Coal Corp., 1993–. Hon. DSc Strathclyde, 1991. *Recreations:* walking, gardening, listening to music.

See also I. R. Davidson.

DAVIDSON, Air Vice-Marshal Rev. Sinclair Melville, CBE 1968; Priest-in-charge, Holy Trinity, High Hurstwood, 1982–88; *b* 1 Nov. 1922; *s* of late James Stewart Davidson and Ann Sinclair Davidson (*née* Cowan); *m* 1944, Jean Irene, *d* of late Edward Albert Flay; one *s* (and one *s* decd). *Educ:* Bousfield Sch., Kensington; RAF Cranwell; RAF Techn College; Chichester Theol College. CEng, FRAeS, FIEE. War service with 209, 220 and 53 Sqdns RAF, 1941–45 (despatches); Staff RAF Coastal and Fighter Comds, 1946–53; Air Staff, Egypt, Iraq and Cyprus, 1954–55; psa 1956; Air Staff, Air Min., 1957–60; jssc 1960; Dirg Staff, RAF Staff Coll., Bracknell, 1961–63; Asst Comdt, RAF Locking, 1963–64; Chm. Jt Signal Bd (Middle East), 1965; Chief Signal Officer and Comd Electrical Engr, Near East Air Force, 1966–67; idc 1968; Dir of Signals (Air), MoD, 1969–71; AO Wales and Stn Comdr, RAF St Athan, 1972–74; Asst Chief of Defence Staff (Signals), 1974–77. Sec., IERE, 1977–82. Deacon 1981, priest 1982. *Address:* Trinity Cottage, High Hurstwood, E Sussex TN22 4AA. *T:* (01825) 732151. *Club:* Royal Air Force.

DAVIDSON, Stephen Robert; DL; Headmaster, Bradford Grammar School, since 1996; *b* 20 Oct. 1950; *er s* of Robert Davidson and Joan Davidson, Tynemouth; *m* 1983, Carol, *d* of Ralston and Dorothy Smith, St Bees; one *s*. *Educ:* Univ. of Manchester Inst. of Sci. and Technol. (BSc Hons Engrg 1972); Univ. of Newcastle (PGCE 1974). Teacher, Lord Wandsworth Coll., 1974–83; Middle Sch. Master, Manchester Grammar Sch., 1983–96. DL W Yorks, 2001. *Recreations:* travel (especially USA), sport, civil aviation. *Address:* Bradford Grammar School, Keighley Road, Bradford BD9 4JP. *T:* (01274) 553702; *e-mail:* hm@bgs.bradford.sch.uk.

DAVIDSON, Dr (William) Keith, CBE 1982; FRCGP; JP; Chairman, Scottish Health Service Planning Council, 1984–90; *b* 20 Nov. 1926; *s* of James Fisher Keith Davidson and Martha Anderson Davidson (*née* Milloy); *m* 1952, Dr Mary Waddell Aitken Davidson (*née* Jamieson); one *s* one *d*. *Educ:* Coatbridge Secondary Sch.; Glasgow Univ. DPA 1967; FRCGP 1980. MO 1st Bn Royal Scots Fusiliers, 1950; 2nd Command (Major) 14 Field Ambulance, 1950–51; MO i/c Holland, 1952. Gen. Medical Practitioner, 1953–90. Chairman: Glasgow Local Medical Cttee, 1971–75, Glasgow Area Medical Cttee, 1975–79; Scottish Gen. Medical Services Cttee, 1972–75; Dep. Chm., Gen. Medical Services Cttee (UK), 1975–79; Member: Scottish Medical Practices Cttee, 1968–80; Scottish Council on Crime, 1972–75; GMC, 1983–94; Scottish Health Service Policy Bd, 1985–88; Greater Glasgow Health Bd, 1989–93. British Medical Association: Mem. Council, 1972–81; Fellow, 1975; Chm., Scottish Council, 1978–81; Vice-Pres., 1983–. Hon. Pres., Glasgow Eastern Med. Soc., 1984–85; Pres., Scottish Midland and Western Med. Soc., 1985–86; FRSocMed 1986. Chm., Chryston High Sch. Bd, 1995–98 (Vice-Chm., 1990–95). Mem., Bonnetmaker Craft. Elder, Church of Scotland, 1956–; Session Clerk, Stepps Parish Church, 1983–98. JP Glasgow, 1962. SBStJ 1976. *Recreation:* gardening. *Address:* Dunvegan, Stepps, Glasgow G33 6DE. *T:* (0141) 779 2103.

DAVIE, Alan, CBE 1972; RWA 1991; HRSA 1977; painter, poet, musician, silversmith and jeweller; *b* 28 Sept. 1920. *Educ:* Edinburgh Coll. of Art. DA. Gregory Fellowship, Leeds Univ., 1956–59. Teaching, Central Sch. of Arts and Crafts, London, 1953–56 and 1959–60, and Emily Carr Coll. of Art, Vancouver, 1982. *One-man exhibitions:* Gimpel Fils Galleries in London, Zürich and New York, 1946–; Edinburgh Fest., 1972; Brussels, Paris, Athens and London, 1977; London, Florida, Stuttgart, Zürich, Amsterdam, St Andrews and Edinburgh, 1978; Florida, Edinburgh Fest., Belgium, Sydney and Perth, Australia, 1979; New York, Australia, Colchester and Philadelphia, 1980; London, Frankfurt, NY and Toronto, 1981; Toronto, Edinburgh, Basle, Harrogate, Hong Kong, Paris (Foire Internat. d'Art Contemporain) and Vancouver, 1982; Amsterdam, FIAC Paris, Basel, Madrid, Glasgow and London, 1983; New York, Frankfurt, Cologne, Edinburgh, Windsor, Hertford and Bath, 1984; London (Art Fair, Olympia), Edinburgh and Bonn, 1985; London, Arizona and NY, 1986; Gal. Carre and FIAC, Paris, London, Edinburgh, 1987; Paintings 1956–88, touring Scotland, Helsingborg, 1988; Edinburgh (Scottish Art Gall., and Nat. Gall. of Modern Art), and galleries and museums in Scotland and Sweden, 1989; Madrid, Paris, Helsingford, New York, 1990; Bath, Cracow, Penzance, Copenhagen, 1991; Edinburgh, Vienna, and British Council Travelling Exhibn, 1992; Brighton, Hastings, Ramsgate, Newcastle upon Tyne, Nottingham, Stirling, 1993; Porto, Lisbon, 1994; Brighton, Chichester, 1996; Edinburgh, Brighton, London, Chichester, NY, Inverness, 1997; Pier Arts Centre, Stromness, 1998; Milan, 2001; *retrospective exhibitions:* Sheffield and Lincoln, 1965; Texas, Montreal and Oakland, 1970; Edinburgh, 1972; Germany, 1973; Edinburgh, and Glasgow, 1992; S America, 1993; Barbican, NY and Ireland, 1993; Chicago, 1994; Edinburgh (Scottish Nat. Gall. of Modern Art), 2000; (small paintings) Brighton and Edinburgh Univs, 2001. Work represented in exhibitions: 4th Internat. Art Exhibn, Japan; Pittsburgh Internat.; Documenta II & III, Kassel, Germany; British Painting 1700–1960, Moscow; Salon de Mai, Paris; Peggy Guggenheim Collection; ROSC Dublin; Peter Styvesant Collection; British Painting and Sculpture 1960–1970, Washington; III Bienal de Arte Coltejer, Colombia; Hannover, 1973; British Paintings, 1974; Hayward Gall., 1974; Paris, 1975; Lausanne, 1975; 25 years of British Art, RA, 1977; South America, 1977; Kassell, 1977; Sydney, 1979; Works on paper, Gimpel Fils, 1989; SW Arts Touring Exhibn, 1989; Glasgow and Edinburgh, and Royal W of England Acad., 1992. Works in Public Collections: Tate Gall., Gulbenkian Foundn London, Belfast, Bristol, Durham, Edinburgh, Hull, Leeds, Manchester, Newcastle, Wakefield; Boston, Buffalo, Dallas, Detroit, Yale New Haven, Phoenix, Pittsburgh, Rhode Island, San Francisco, NY (MOMA); Ottawa, Adelaide, Sydney, Auckland, São Paulo, Tel Aviv, Venice, Vienna, Baden-Baden, Bochum, Munich, Amsterdam, Eindhoven, The Hague, Rotterdam, Oslo, Basle, Stockholm, Gothenburg, St Paul de Vence and Paris. Created mural, Tarot Sculpture Gdn, Garavicchio, Tuscany, 1987. First public recital of music, Gimpel Fils Gall., 1971; music and lecture tour, Sydney, Melbourne, Canberra, 1979. Vis. Prof., Brighton Univ., 1993–. Hon. DLitt: Heriot-Watt, 1994; Hertfordshire, 1995. Prize for Best Foreign Painter, VII Bienal de São Paulo, 1963;

Saltire Award, 1977. *Publications:* Magic Reader: eighteen original lithographs, 1992; Alan Davie Drawings, 1997; *relevant publications:* Alan Davie (ed Alan Bowness), 1967; Alan Davie, by D. Hall and M. Tucker, 1992; Alan Davie: the quest for the miraculous (ed Michael Tucker), 1993. *Address:* Gamels Studio, Rush Green, Hertford SG13 7SB.

DAVIE, Sir Michael F.; *see* Ferguson Davie.

DAVIE, Rex; *see* Davie, S. R.

DAVIE, Prof. Ronald, PhD; FBPsS; CPsychol; consulting psychologist; Visiting Professor, Cheltenham and Gloucester College of Higher Education, since 1997; *b* 25 Nov. 1929; *s* of late Thomas Edgar Davie and Gladys (*née* Powell); *m* 1957, Kathleen, *d* of William Wilkinson, Westhoughton, Lancs; one *s* one *d. Educ:* King Edward VI Grammar Sch., Aston, Birmingham; Univ. of Reading (BA 1954); Univ. of Manchester (PGCE and Dip. Deaf Educn 1955); Univ. of Birmingham (Dip. Educnl Psych. 1961); Univ. of London (PhD 1970). FBPsS 1973. Teacher, schs for normal and handicapped children, 1955–60; Co. Educnl Psychologist, IoW, 1961–64; Nat. Children's Bureau, London: Sen. Res. Officer, 1964; Dep. Dir, 1968; Dir of Res., 1972; Prof. of Educnl Psychology, Dept of Educn, UC Cardiff, 1974–81; Dir, Nat. Children's Bureau, 1982–90. Mem., Special Educnl Needs Tribunal, 1994–. Vis. Prof., Oxford Poly., later Oxford Brookes Univ., 1991–97; Vis. Fellow, Inst. of Educn, Univ. of London, 1985–93; Hon. Res. Fellow, UCL, 1991–; Vis. Fellow, Univ. of Newcastle, 1995–. Co-Dir, Nat. Child Develt Study, 1968–77; Scientific Adviser: Local Authority Social Services Res. Liaison Gp, DHSS, 1975–77; Mental Handicap in Wales Res. Unit, 1977–79; Mental Handicap Res. Liaison Gp, DHSS, 1977–81; Prof. Advr, All Party Parly Gp for Children, 1983–91; Consultant, Whitefield Sch., 1994–98 (Chm., Academic Bd, 1991–94); Hon. Consultant: Play Board, 1984–87; 1981 Educn Act Res. Dissemination Project, 1986–89. President: Links Assoc., 1977–90; Child Develt Soc., 1990–91; Nat. Assoc. for Special Educnl Needs, 1992–94; Vice-Pres., British Assoc. for Early Childhood Educn, 1984–, Young Minds, 1991–; Chairman: Trng and Educn Cttee, Nat. Assoc. Mental Health, 1969–72; Assoc. for Child Psychol. and Psychiatry, 1972–73 (Hon. Sec. 1965–70); Standing Conf. of Professional Assocs in S Wales Concerned with Children, 1974–84; Working Party, Children Appearing Before Juvenile Courts, Children's Reg. Planning Cttee for Wales, 1975–77; Develt Psychol. Section, Brit. Psychol. Soc., 1975–77 (Treas. 1973–75); Wales Standing Conf. for Internat. Year of the Child, 1978–79; Steering Cttee, Child Health and Educn Study, 1979–84; Adv. Bd, Whitefield Library, 1983–98; Task Gp on Special Educnl Needs, 1989, Steering Gp on Severe Learning Difficulties, 1991, Nat. Curriculum Council; Policy Sub-Cttee, Nat. Assoc. for Special Educnl Needs, 1994–97 (Mem., 1998–); Vice Chm., Bd of Trustees, Eden Valley Hospice, 2001– (Trustee, 1998–99; Chm., 2000). Member: Council of Management, Nat. Assoc. Mental Health, 1969–77; Working Party, Children at Risk, DHSS, 1970–72; Educn and Employment Cttee, Nat. Deaf Children's Soc., 1972–78; Management Cttee, Craig y Parc Sch., 1974–76; Cttee, Welsh Br., Assoc. for Child Psychol. and Psychiatry, 1975–80; Bd of Assessors, Therapeutic Educn, 1975–82; Council, British Psychol Soc., 1977–80; Experimental Panel on Children in Care, SSRC, 1978–79; NCSE Internat. Conf. Prog. Cttee, 1982–85; Council, Child Accident Prevention Trust, 1982–88; Evaluation Panel, Royal Jubilee Trusts, 1982–94; Steering Cttee on Special Educn Needs Res., DES, 1983–86; Bd of Trustees, Stress Syndrome Foundn, 1983–85; Adv. Bd, Ravenswood Village, 1984–91; Bd of Governors, Elizabeth Garrett Anderson Sch., 1985–88; Council, Caldecott Community, 1985–; Research Cttee, Froebel Inst., 1987–88; Nat. Curriculum Council, 1988–90; BBC/IBA Central Appeals Adv. Cttee, 1989–93. Chm. Govs, Fellview Sch., 1998–. Patron, Action for Special Educnl Needs, 1994–97. FRSA 1991. Hon. FRCPCH 1996. Hon. DEd: CNAA, 1991; UWE, 1998; Hon. DLitt Birmingham, 1999. Member Editorial Board: Internat. Jl of Adolescence and Youth, 1986–; Children and Society, 1987–90. *Publications:* (co-author) 11,000 Seven-Year Olds, 1966; Directory of Voluntary Organisations concerned with Children, 1969; Living with Handicap, 1970; From Birth to Seven, 1972; Child Sexual Abuse: the way forward after Cleveland, 1989; Listening to Children in Education, 1996; The Voice of the Child, 1996; chapters in books and papers in sci. and other jls on special educn, psychol., child care health, and effects of TV on children. *Recreations:* photography, antiques, good music of all kinds. *Address:* Bridge House, Upton, Caldbeck, Cumbria CA7 8EU.

DAVIE, (Stephen) Rex, CB 1993; Member: Council on Tribunals, since 1995; Civil Service Appeal Board, since 1995; Principal Establishment and Finance Officer (Under Secretary), Cabinet Office, 1989–93; *b* 11 June 1933; *s* of late Sydney and Dorothy Davie; *m* 1955, Christine Stockwell; one *s* one *d. Educ:* Ilfracombe Grammar Sch. Executive Officer, Inland Revenue, 1951. National Service, RAF, 1952–54. Office of Minister for Science, 1962; NEDO, 1967; CSD, 1970; Asst Sec. 1979; Cabinet Office, 1983; Sen. Sec., Security Commn, 1979–89. Mem. Council, Inst. of Cancer Res., 1993– (Vice Chm., 1995–). *Recreations:* reading, travel. *Address:* 2 Linnet Close, Basingstoke, Hants RG22 5PD. *Clubs:* Athenæum, Civil Service.

DAVIES; *see* Prys-Davies.

DAVIES, family name of **Barons Darwen, Davies, Davies of Coity** and **Davies of Oldham.**

DAVIES, 3rd Baron *cr* 1932, of Llandinam; **David Davies;** DL; MA; CEng, MICE, MBA; Chairman, Welsh National Opera Company, 1975–2000; *b* 2 Oct. 1940; *s* of 2nd Baron and Ruth Eldrydd (*d* 1966), 3rd *d* of Major W. M. Dugdale, CB, DSO; *S* father (killed in action), 1944; *m* 1972, Beryl, *d* of W. J. Oliver; two *s* two *d. Educ:* Eton; King's Coll., Cambridge. DL Powys, 1997. *Heir: s* Hon. David Daniel Davies, *b* 23 Oct. 1975. *Address:* Plas Dinam, Llandinam, Powys SY17 5DQ.

DAVIES OF COITY, Baron *cr* 1997 (Life Peer), of Penybont, in the co. of Mid Glamorgan; **David Garfield Davies,** CBE 1996; General Secretary, Union of Shop, Distributive and Allied Workers, 1986–97; *b* 24 June 1935; *s* of David John Davies and Lizzie Ann Davies; *m* 1960, Marian (*née* Jones); four *d. Educ:* Heolgam Secondary Modern School; Bridgend Tech Coll. (part time). Served RAF, 1956–58. Junior operative, Electrical Apprentice and Electrician, British Steel Corp., Port Talbot, 1950–69; Area Organiser, USDAW, Ipswich, 1969–73; Dep. Divl Officer, USDAW, London/Ipswich, 1973–78; Nat. Officer, USDAW, Manchester, 1978–85. Mem., TUC Gen. Council, 1986–97; Chm., TUC Internat. Cttee, 1992–94; TUC spokesperson on internat. affairs, 1994–97. Member: Exec. Bd, ICFTU, 1992–97; Exec. Cttee, ETUC, 1992–97. Mem., Employment Appeal Tribunal, 1991–. Governor, Birmingham Coll. of Food, Tourism and Creative Studies, 1995–99. JP 1972–79. *Recreations:* swimming, reading, spectator sports (supporter, Stockport County FC); formerly soccer, cricket, Rugby. *Address:* 64 Dairyground Road, Bramhall, Stockport, Cheshire SK7 2QW. *T:* (0161) 439 9548. *Clubs:* Reform; Lancashire CC.

DAVIES OF OLDHAM, Baron *cr* 1997 (Life Peer), of Broxbourne in the co. of Hertfordshire; **Bryan Davies;** a Lord in Waiting (Government Whip), since 2000; *b* 9 Nov. 1939; *s* of George William and Beryl Davies; *m* 1963, Monica Rosemary Mildred Shearing; two *s* one *d. Educ:* Redditch High Sch.; University Coll. London (BA Hons History); Inst. of Education (CertEd); London Sch. of Economics (BScEcons). Teacher, Latymer Sch., 1962–65; Lectr, Middlesex Polytechnic at Enfield, 1965–74. Sec., Parly Labour Party, 1979–92. Contested (Lab): Norfolk Central, 1966; Newport W, 1983. MP (Lab): Enfield North, Feb. 1974–1979; Oldham Central and Royton, 1992–97. An Asst Govt Whip, 1979; front bench spokesman on Further and Higher Educn, 1993–97. Member: Select Cttee on Public Expenditure, 1975–79; Select Cttee on Overseas Develt, 1975–79; Select Cttee on Nat. Heritage, 1992–93. Chm., FEFCE, 1998–2000. Mem., MRC, 1977–79. *Recreations:* sport, literature. *Address:* 28 Churchfields, Broxbourne, Herts EN10 7JS. *T:* (01992) 410418.

DAVIES, Adele, (Mrs R. O. Davies); *see* Biss, A.

DAVIES, Sir Alan (Seymour), Kt 2000; Headmaster, Copland Community School and Technology Centre Foundation, since 1988; *b* 21 Feb. 1947; *s* of Seymour George Davies and Sarah Louise Davies; *m* 1972, Frances Patricia Williamson; one *s* two *d. Educ:* Inst. of Educn, London Univ. (BEd, CertEd); NE London Poly. (MEd). Teacher, E Barnet Sch., 1972–75; Teacher, 1975–80, Dep. Head, 1980–86, McEntee Sen. High Sch.; Headteacher, Sidney Chaplin Sch., 1986–88. JP Barnet, 1984. *Recreation:* sport. *Address:* 39 Grants Close, Mill Hill, NW7 1DD. *T:* (020) 8349 9731.

DAVIES, (Albert) Meredith, CBE 1982; Principal, Trinity College of Music, 1979–88; Guest Conductor, Royal Opera House, Covent Garden, and Sadler's Wells, 1960–72; also BBC; *b* 30 July 1922; 2nd *s* of Reverend E. A. Davies; *m* 1949, Betty Hazel, *d* of late Dr Kenneth Bates; three *s* one *d. Educ:* Royal College of Music; Stationers' Company's Sch.; Keble Coll., Oxford; Accademia di S. Cecilia, Rome. Junior Exhibitioner, RCM, 1930; Organist to Hurstpierpoint Coll., Sussex, 1939; elected Organ Scholar, Keble Coll., 1940. Served War of 1939–45, RA, 1942–45. Conductor, St Albans Bach Choir, 1947; Organist and Master of the Choristers, Cathedral Church of St Alban, 1947–49; Musical Dir, St Albans Sch., 1948–49; Organist and Choirmaster, Hereford Cathedral, and Conductor, Three Choirs' Festival (Hereford), 1949–56; Organist and Supernumerary Fellow of New Coll., Oxford, 1956; Associate Conductor, City of Birmingham Symphony Orchestra, 1957–59; Dep. Musical Dir, 1959–60; Conductor, City of Birmingham Choir, 1957–64; Musical Dir, English Opera Group, 1963–65; Musical Dir, Vancouver Symphony Orchestra, 1964–71; Chief Conductor, BBC Trng Orchestra, 1969–72; Music Dir, Royal Choral Soc., 1972–85; Conductor, Leeds Phil. Soc., 1975–84. Pres., ISM, 1985–86. Chm., Delius Trust, 1991–97. *Address:* 10 Mallard Close, New Alresford, Hants SO24 9BX.

DAVIES, Sir (Alfred William) Michael, Kt 1973; a Judge of the High Court of Justice, 1973–91, Acting High Court Judge, 1991–97, Queen's Bench Division; *er s* of Alfred Edward Davies, Stourbridge; *m* 1947, Margaret, *y d* of Robert Ernest Jackson, Sheffield; one *s* three *d. Educ:* King Edward's Sch., Birmingham; University of Birmingham (LLB). Called to Bar, Lincoln's Inn, 1948, Bencher 1972, Treasurer 1991; QC 1964; Dep. Chm. Northants QS, 1962–71; Recorder of: Grantham, 1963–65; Derby, 1965–71; Crown Court, 1972–73; Leader of Midland Circuit, 1968–71, Jt Leader of Midland and Oxford Circuit, 1971–73; Barrister, NSW, 1996. Chm. Mental Health Review Tribunal, for Birmingham Area, 1965–71; Comr of Assize (Birmingham), 1970; Chancellor, Dio. of Derby, 1971–73; Mem., Gen. Council of the Bar, 1968–72. Chm., Hospital Complaints Procedure Cttee, 1971–73. Conducted Visitor's Inquiry, UC, Swansea, 1992–93. Founding Chm., Expert Witness Inst., 1996–98. Over 100 TV and radio broadcasts, 1991–. *Publications:* articles and stories. *Recreations:* golf, the theatre. *Address:* Elliot House, Wolverley, Kidderminster, Worcs DY11 5XE. *T:* (01562) 851111. *Club:* Garrick.

DAVIES, Very Rev. Alun Radcliffe; Dean of Llandaff, 1977–93; *b* 6 May 1923; *s* of Rev. Rhys Davies and Jane Davies; *m* 1952, Winifred Margaret Pullen; two *s* one *d. Educ:* Cowbridge Grammar Sch.; University Coll., Cardiff (BA 1945; Fellow, 1983); Keble Coll., Oxford (BA 1947, MA 1951); St Michael's Coll., Llandaff. Curate of Roath, 1948–49; Lecturer, St Michael's Coll., Llandaff, 1949–53; Domestic Chaplain to Archbishop of Wales, 1952–57, to Bishop of Llandaff, 1957–59; Chaplain RNR, 1953–60; Vicar of Ystrad Mynach, 1959–75; Chancellor of Llandaff Cathedral, 1969–71; Archdeacon of Llandaff, 1971–77; Residentiary Canon of Llandaff Cathedral, 1975–77. Chaplain, Lieutenancy of S Glam, 1994–. *Address:* 15 Sinclair Drive, Penylan, Cardiff CF23 9AH. *T:* (029) 2045 6149.

DAVIES, Prof. Alwyn George, FRS 1989; Professor of Chemistry, University College London, 1969–91, now Emeritus; *b* 13 May 1926; *s* of John Lewis and Victoria May Davies; *m* 1956, Margaret Drake; one *s* one *d. Educ:* Hamond's Grammar Sch., Swaffham; University College London (BSc, PhD, DSc; Fellow 1991). CChem, FRSC. Lectr, Battersea Polytechnic, 1949; Lectr, 1953, Reader, 1964, UCL. Ingold Lectr, RSC, 1992–93. Medal for Organic Reaction Mechanism, RSC, 1989; Humboldt Prize, Freiburg Univ., 1994. *Publications:* Organic Peroxides, 1959; Organotin Chemistry, 1997; scientific papers on physical organic chemistry and organometallic chemistry in learned jls. *Address:* Chemistry Department, University College London, 20 Gordon Street, WC1H 0AJ. *T:* (020) 7679 4701; *e-mail:* a.g.davies@ucl.ac.uk.

DAVIES, Andrew; *see* Davies, D. A.

DAVIES, Andrew L.; *see* Lloyd-Davies.

DAVIES, Andrew Owen Evan; Partner, Lee Bolton & Lee (Senior Partner, 1987–2000); Legal Adviser of Dean and Chapter of Canterbury Cathedral, since 1984 (Registrar and Legal Adviser of the Diocese of Canterbury, 1982–96); *b* 1936; *s* of late Ninian Rhys Davies and Gweneth Elizabeth Davies; *m* 1963, G. Margaret Stephens; one *s* two *d. Educ:* Shrewsbury Sch. Solicitor, Notary Public. National Service, Royal Fusiliers, 1954–56. Law studies and articles, 1956–62; admitted Solicitor, 1962; Partner, Evan Davies & Co., 1964–80; Evan Davies & Co. amalgamated with Lee Bolton & Lee, 1980; Partner, Lee Bolton & Lee, 1980–83, Dep. Sen. Partner, 1983–87. *Recreations:* country pursuits, golf, reading, family. *Address:* 1 The Sanctuary, Westminster, SW1P 3JT. *T:* (020) 7222 5381. *Club:* Boodle's.

DAVIES, Andrew Wynford; writer; *b* Rhiwbina, Cardiff, 20 Sept 1936; *e s* of Wynford and Hilda Davies; *m* 1960, Diana Lennox Huntley; one *s* one *d. Educ:* Whitchurch Grammar Sch., Cardiff; University College London. Teacher: St Clement Danes Grammar Sch., 1958–61; Woodberry Down Comprehensive Sch., 1961–63; Lecturer: Coventry Coll. of Educn, 1963–71; Univ. of Warwick, 1971–87. Hon. Fellow, Univ. of Wales, Cardiff, 1997. Hon. DLitt Coventry, 1994. Guardian Children's Fiction Award, 1979; Boston Globe Horn Award, 1979; BPG Award, 1980, 1990; Pye Colour TV Award, best children's writer, 1981; writer's awards: RTS, 1986–87; BAFTA, 1989, 1993, 1998; Writers' Guild, 1991, 1992, 1996; Primetime Emmy, 1991. *Television includes:* To Serve Them All My Days, 1979; A Very Peculiar Practice, 1986–87; Mother Love, 1989; House of Cards, 1990; Filipina Dreamers, 1991; The Old Devils, Anglo-Saxon Attitudes, A Very Polish Practice, 1992; Anna Lee, Harnessing Peacocks, To Play the King, 1993;

Middlemarch, A Few Short Journeys of the Heart, 1994; Game On, Pride and Prejudice, The Final Cut, 1995; Emma, Moll Flanders, Wilderness, 1996; Bill's New Frock, 1997; Getting Hurt, Vanity Fair, A Rather English Marriage, 1998; Wives and Daughters, 1999; Take a Girl Like You, 2000; Othello, The Way We Live Now, 2001; *stage plays:* Rose, 1981; Prin, 1990; *film screenplays:* Circle of Friends, 1995; B. Monkey, 1996; Bridget Jones's Diary, The Tailor of Panama, 2001. *Publications: for children:* The Fantastic Feats of Dr Boox, 1972; Conrad's War, 1978; Marmalade and Rufus, 1980; Marmalade Atkins in Space, 1981; Educating Marmalade, 1982; Danger Marmalade at Work, 1983; Marmalade Hits the Big Time, 1984; Alfonso Bonzo, 1987; Marmalade on the Ball, 1995; (with Diana Davies): Poonam's Pets, 1990; Raj in Charge, 1994; *fiction:* A Very Peculiar Practice, 1986; The New Frontier, 1987; Getting Hurt, 1989; Dirty Faxes, 1990; B. Monkey, 1992. *Recreations:* tennis, food, alcohol. *Address:* c/o The Agency, 24 Pottery Lane, W11 4LZ.

DAVIES, (Angie) Michael; Chairman: National Express Group, since 1992; Simon Group (formerly Simon Engineering), since 1993; Corporate Services Group, since 1999; *b* 23 June 1934; *s* of Angelo Henry and Clarice Mildred Davies; *m* 1962, Jane Priscilla, *d* of Oliver Martin and Kathleen White; one *d* (one *s* decd). *Educ:* Shrewsbury Schools; Queens' College, Cambridge. Director: Ross Group, 1964–82; Fenchurch Insurance Holdings, 1969–76; Brown Brothers Corp., 1976–81; Imperial Group, 1972–82; Chairman: Imperial Foods, 1979–82; Tozer Kemsley & Millbourn (Holdings) plc, 1982–86; Bredero Properties, 1986–94; John Perkins Meats, then Perkins Foods, 1987–2001; Worth Investment Trust, 1987–95; Wiltshier, 1988–95; Calor Group, 1989–97 (Dir, 1987–97); Shearings Gp plc, 1997–2000; Deputy Chairman: TI Gp, 1990–93 (Dir, 1984–93); AerFi (formerly GPA) Gp plc, 1993–2000; Director: Littlewoods Organisation, 1982–88; Avdel (formerly Newman Industries), 1983–95; British Airways, 1983–; TV-am, 1983–89; Broadwell Land, 1984–90; James Wilkes, 1987–88; Blue Arrow, later Manpower, 1987–92; Worcester Gp, 1991–92; Falcon Agencies, 1994–99. *Address:* Little Woolpit, Ewhurst, Cranleigh, Surrey GU6 7NP. *T:* (01483) 277344.

DAVIES, Prof. Anna Elbina, (A. Morpurgo Davies), Hon. DBE 2000; FBA 1985; Professor of Comparative Philology, Oxford University, since 1971; Fellow of Somerville College, Oxford, since 1971; *b* Milan, 21 June 1937; *d* of Augusto Morpurgo and Maria (*née* Castelnuovo); *m* 1962, J. K. Davies, *qv* (marr. diss. 1978). *Educ:* Liceo-Ginnasio Giulio Cesare, Rome; Univ. of Rome. Dott.lett. Rome, 1959; Libera docente, Rome, 1963; MA Oxford, 1964. Asst in Classical Philology, Univ. of Rome, 1959–61; Junior Research Fellow, Center for Hellenic Studies, Harvard Univ., 1961–62; Univ. Lectr in Classical Philology, Oxford, 1964–71; Fellow of St Hilda's Coll., Oxford, 1966–71, Hon. Fellow, 1972–. Visiting Professor: Univ. of Pennsylvania, 1971; Yale Univ., 1977; Collitz Prof. of Ling. Soc. of America, Univ. of South Florida, 1975; Webster Vis. Prof., Stanford Univ., 1988; Sather Prof. of Classics, Univ. of Calif at Berkeley, 2000 (Sather Lectr, 2000). Lectures: Semple, Univ. of Cincinnati, 1983; Jackson, Harvard Univ., 1990. Pres., Philological Soc., 1976–80, Hon. Vice-Pres., 1980–. Delegate, Oxford University Press, 1992–. FSA 1974; Foreign Mem., Amer. Philosophical Soc., 1991; Foreign Hon. Mem., Amer. Acad. of Arts and Sciences, 1986; Corresponding Member: Österreichische Akademie der Wissenschaften, Vienna, 1988; Inst. de France (Acad. des inscriptions et belles-lettres), 1992; Bayerische Akademie der Wissenschaften, 1998; Mem., Academia Europaea, 1989; Hon. Mem., Linguistic Soc. of America, 1993. Hon. DLitt St Andrews, 1981. Premio linceo per la linguistica, Accad. dei Lincei, 1996. *Publications:* (as A. Morpurgo) Mycenaeae Graecitatis Lexicon, 1963; (ed with W. Meid) Studies in Greek, Italic and Indo-European Linguistics, festschrift for L. R. Palmer, 1976; (ed with Y. Duhoux) Linear B: a 1984 survey, 1985; La linguistica dell'Ottocento, 1996; Nineteenth-Century Linguistics, 1998; articles and reviews on comparative and classical philology in learned jls. *Address:* Somerville College, Oxford OX2 6HD. *T:* (01865) 270600.

DAVIES, Ven. Anthony; *see* Davies, Ven. V. A.

DAVIES, Rear-Adm. Anthony, CB 1964; CVO 1972; Royal Navy, retired; *b* 13 June 1912; *s* of late James Arthur and Margaret Davies; *m* 1940, Lilian Hilda Margaret (*d* 1980), *d* of late Admiral Sir Harold Martin Burrough, GCB, KBE, DSO, and Lady (Nellie Wills) Burrough; two *s* two *d*. *Educ:* Royal Naval College, Dartmouth; Open Univ. (BA 1983). Midshipman, HMS Danae, 1930–32; Sub-Lieut, HMS Despatch, 1934; Lieut, HMS Duncan, 1935–37; Gunnery course, 1938; HMS Repulse, 1939; HMS Cossack, 1940–41; Lieut-Comdr, HMS Indefatigable, 1943–45; Comdr, HMS Triumph, 1950; HMS Excellent, 1951–54; Capt., HMS Pelican, 1954–55; Dep. Dir, RN Staff Coll., 1956–57; Far East Fleet Staff, 1957–59; Dep. Dir, Naval Intelligence, 1959–62; Rear-Adm., 1963; Head of British Defence Liaison Staff, Canberra, Australia, 1963–65. Warden, St George's House, Windsor Castle, 1966–72. *Address:* Witts Piece, 11A South Street, Aldbourne, Marlborough, Wilts SN8 2DW. *T:* (01672) 540418.

DAVIES, (Anthony) Roger; a District Judge (Magistrates' Courts) (formerly Metropolitan Stipendiary Magistrate), since 1985; Chairman, Family Courts, since 1989; a Recorder, since 1993; *b* 1 Sept. 1940; *er s* of late R. George Davies and Megan Davies, Penarth, Glam; *m* 1967, Clare, *e d* of Comdr W. A. Walters, RN; twin *s* one *d*. *Educ:* Bridgend; King's Coll., London. LLB (Hons); AKC. Called to the Bar, Gray's Inn, 1965 (Lord Justice Holker Sen. Schol.). Practised at Bar, London and SE Circuit, 1965–85. *Recreations:* reading (history, biography), music (especially opera), travel, family life. *Address:* c/o Horseferry Road Magistrates' Court, SW1P 2AX. *Club:* Travellers.

DAVIES, Dr Arthur Gordon; Managing Director, Medical & Electrical Instrumentation Co. Ltd, 1965–90; *b* 6 Nov. 1917; *s* of Louis Bernard Davies and Elizabeth Davies; *m* 1945, Joan (*née* Thompson); two *d*. *Educ:* Westminster Hosp. (MB, BS 1943). LRCP, MRCS 1943. Called to the Bar, Lincoln's Inn, 1955. Served War, RAMC (Captain). Coroner to the Royal Household, 1959–83; Coroner, Inner South London, 1959–87. *Recreations:* chess, bridge, photography, electronics.

DAVIES, Barry George; broadcaster, BBC Television sport and events; *b* 24 Oct. 1939; *s* of Roy Charles Davies and Dorothy Davies; *m* 1968, Edna (Penny) Pegna; one *s* one *d*. *Educ:* Cranbrook Sch., Kent; London Univ. (King's Coll. Royal Dental Hosp.). Commnd RASC, 1960. Sub-editor/reporter, The Times, 1963–66; Independent Television, 1966–69; commentator, World Cup 1966, Olympic Games 1968; joined BBC Television, 1969; commentator and presenter covering variety of sports, including: World Cup, 1970–; Olympic Games, 1972–; Winter Olympics, 1984–; Commonwealth Games, 1978–; Wimbledon, 1983–; University Boat Race, 1993–. Commentator, Lord Mayor's Show, 1996–; (last) Royal Tournament, 1999. Presenter, Maestro Series, 1985–87. *Recreations:* family, theatre, political biographies, all sports (enthusiasm way ahead of talent). *Address:* Ensor Byfield, Equity Court, 73–75 Millbrook Road East, Southampton SO15 1RJ. *T:* (01703) 483240. *Clubs:* Lord's Taverners; Hawks (Cambridge); Wentworth.

DAVIES, Brian; *see* Davies, E. B.

DAVIES, Brian Meredith; *see* Davies, J. B. M.

DAVIES, Brigid Catherine Brennan; *see* Gardner, B. C. B.

DAVIES, Bryn, CBE 1987 (MBE 1978); DL; Member, General Council, Wales Trades Union Congress, 1974–91 (Vice-Chairman, 1983–84, Chairman, 1984–85); *b* 22 Jan. 1932; *s* of Gomer and Ann Davies; *m* 1st, 1956, Esme Irene Gould (*d* 1988); two *s*; 2nd, 1991, Katherine Lewis. *Educ:* Cwmlai School, Tonyrefail. Served HM Forces (RAMC), 1949–51; Forestry Commn, 1951–56; South Wales and Hereford Organiser, Nat. Union of Agricultural and Allied Workers, subseq. TGWU (following merger), 1956–91. Chm., Mid Glamorgan AHA, 1978–94; Member: Welsh Council, 1965–81; Development Commn, 1975–81; Nat. Cttee (Wales), Forestry Commn, 1978–; Nat. Water Council, 1982–85; Council, British Heart Foundn, 1986–. Trustee, Sir Geraint Evans Wales Heart Res. Inst. Patron, Mencap Jubilee Festival. DL Mid Glamorgan, 1992. *Recreations:* cricket, Rugby football. *Address:* 3 Lias Cottages, Porthcawl, Mid Glamorgan CF36 3AD. *T:* (01656) 785851. *Clubs:* Tonyrefail Rugby (Pres., 1985–88); Pyle and Kenfig Golf; Pyle Rugby; Pirates (Porthcawl).

DAVIES, Byron, CEng, FICE; Chief Executive, Cardiff County Council, since 1996; *b* 23 April 1947; *s* of Cecil and Elizabeth Gwendoline Davies; *m* 1972, Sarah Kay Lott; one *s* one *d*. *Educ:* Swansea Univ. (BSc Hons); Univ. of Glamorgan (MPhil). CEng 1976; FICE 1992. Work in private sector orgns, 1968–72; with Swansea CC and Devon CC, 1972–77; South Glamorgan County Council, 1977–96: various sen. civil engrg, property develt and gen. mgt posts; Dir, Property Services, 1990–92, Chief Exec., 1992–96. Director: Cardiff-Wales Airport, 1992–; Millennium Stadium plc, 1996–; Cardiff Chamber of Trade and Commerce, 1999–; Cardiff Marketing, 1999–; Cardiff Initiative, 1999–. Clerk to Lieutenancy of S Glam, 1992–; Sec. to Lord Chancellor's Adv. Cttee for S Glam, 1992–. Ex-Officio Mem., Council and Court, Univ. of Wales, Cardiff, 1992–. FIMgt 1992; Pres., Cardiff Inst. of Mgt, 1999–. *Publications:* contrib. on engrg and mgt to professional jls. *Recreations:* walking, sport, cinema, photography. *Address:* 11 Heol Denys, Lisvane, Cardiff, S Glam CF4 5RU. *T:* (029) 2075 0530.

DAVIES, Caleb William, CMG 1962; FFPHM; MRCS; LRCP; DPH; retired; Regional Specialist in Community Medicine, 1974–82 (Acting Regional Medical Officer, 1977–78, 1979–80), South Western Regional Health Authority; *b* 27 Aug. 1916; *s* of Caleb Davies, KIH, MB, ChB, and Emily (*née* Platt); *m* 1939, Joan Heath; three *s* one *d*. *Educ:* Kingswood Sch., Bath; University Coll. and University Coll. Hosp. Med. Sch., London; Edinburgh Univ.; London Sch. of Hygiene and Tropical Med. Kenya: MO, 1941; MOH, Mombasa, 1946; Tanganyika: Sen. MO, 1950; Asst Dir of Med. Services, 1952; Uganda: Dep. Dir of Medical Services, 1958; Permanent Sec. and Chief Medical Officer, Ministry of Health, 1960; retired 1963; South-Western Regional Hosp. Bd: Asst SMO, 1963–66; Principal Asst SMO, 1966–74. *Recreations:* swimming, photography. *Address:* 76 Westwood Green, Cookham, Maidenhead, Berks SL6 9DE. *T:* (01628) 527980.

DAVIES, Sir (Charles) Noel, Kt 1996; CEng, FIMechE; Chairman, Ricardo PLC, since 1997; *b* 2 Dec. 1933; *s* of Henry Norman Davies and Vena Mary Bebb; *m* 1958, Sheila Rigby; two *s* one *d*. *Educ:* Ellesmere Coll., Shropshire; Imperial Coll., London (BSc). CEng 1956; FIMechE 1980; FCGI 1980. Dir, Vickers PLC, 1980–84; Chief Executive: 600 Gp, 1984–89; VSEL PLC, 1989–95; Dep. Chm., British Energy PLC, 1995–99; Chairman: Nuclear Electric Ltd, 1995–98; Powell Duffryn PLC, 1996–2000. Mem., Sec. of State's Industrial Develt Adv. Bd, 1987–94. Pres., EEF, 1994–96. *Recreations:* vintage cars, motor-cycles, gardening.

DAVIES, Christopher Evelyn K.; *see* Kevill-Davies.

DAVIES, Christopher Graham, (Chris); Member (Lib Dem) North West Region, England, European Parliament, since 1999; *b* 7 July 1954; *s* of Caryl St John Davies and Margaret (*née* McLeod); *m* 1979, Carol Hancox; one *d*. *Educ:* Cheadle Hulme Sch.; Gonville and Caius Coll., Cambridge (BA 1975, MA 1978); Univ. of Kent. Member: Liverpool City Council, 1980–84 (Chm., Housing Cttee, 1982–83); Oldham MBC, 1994–98. Manager: Public Affairs Div., Extel, 1983–85; Northern PR, Liverpool, 1985–87; Dir, Abercromby Consultancy Ltd, 1988–91; marketing and communications consultant, 1991–95; Sen. Consultant, Concept Communications, 1997–99. Contested (Lib Dem) Littleborough and Saddleworth, 1987, 1992. MP (Lib Dem) Littleborough and Saddleworth, July 1995–1997; contested (Lib Dem) Oldham East and Saddleworth, 1997. *Recreation:* fell running. *Address:* 4 Higher Kinders, Greenfield, Oldham OL3 7BH; European Parliament, Rue Wiertz, 1047 Brussels, Belgium. *T:* (2) 2847353.

DAVIES, (Claude) Nigel (Byam); *b* 2 Sept. 1920; unmarried. *Educ:* Eton. Studied at Aix en Provence University, 1937, and at Potsdam, 1938. PhD London (archaeology). Entered Sandhurst, 1939, and later commissioned Grenadier Guards. Served Middle East, Italy and Balkans, 1942–46. Formerly Managing Dir of Windolite Ltd. MP (C) Epping Div. of Essex, 1950–51. *Publications:* Los Señorios Independientes del Imperio Azteca, 1968; Los Mexicas: Primeras Pasos Hacia el Imperio, 1973; The Aztecs, 1973; The Toltecs, 1977; Voyagers to the New World: fact and fantasy, 1979; The Toltec Heritage, 1980; Human Sacrifice, 1981; The Ancient Kingdoms of Mexico, 1983; The Rampant God, 1984; The Aztec Empire, 1987; The Incas, 1995; The Ancient Kingdoms of Peru, 1997. *Recreation:* travel. *Address:* Sonora 75, Colonia Chapultepec, Tijuana, Baja California, Mexico. *T:* (66) 861036. *Club:* Carlton.

DAVIES, Prof. Colin; architectural journalist; Professor of Architecture, University of North London, since 2000 (Lecturer, 1992–2000); *b* 24 March 1948; *s* of John and Hazel Davies; *m* 1st, 1973, Diana Lamont (marr. diss.); one *s*; 2nd, 1992, Susan Wallington. *Educ:* King Henry VIII Sch., Coventry; Oxford Polytechnic; Architectural Assoc.; University College London (MSc). AADip, RIBA. Asst Editor, Building Magazine, 1975–77; Associate Partner, Derek Stow and Partners, 1977–81; freelance journalist, 1981–88; Editor, Architects' Jl, 1989–90. Lectr, Bartlett, Canterbury and Brighton Schs of Architecture, 1983–91. *Publications:* High Tech Architecture, 1988; Century Tower, 1992; Hopkins, 1993; Commerzbank, Frankfurt, 1997; contribs to arch. jls. *Recreation:* choral singing. *Address:* 3 The Copse, Fortis Green, N2 9HL.

DAVIES, Colin Godfrey, CEng, FIEE; FRAeS; Director (formerly Director General, Projects and Engineering), National Air Traffic Services, 1991–97; *b* 9 Nov. 1934; *s* of Thomas William Godfrey Davies and Kathleen Mabel Davies; *m* 1966, Enid Beryl Packham; two *s*. *Educ:* King's Sch., Bruton; Loughborough Univ. (BSc Hons). FIEE 1986; FRAeS 1995. RAF Flying Officer (Aircrew), 1952–54. Cable and Wireless, 1955–90: Radio Technician, 1955–59; student, 1960–64; Special Projects Engr, Engr-in-Chief's Dept, 1964–68; Project Manager, 1968–75; Manager Transmission, Omantel, 1975–76; Manager Engrg, Fintel, 1976–77; Chief Engr Long Distance Services, Emirtel, 1978–79; Manager Internat. Services, 1980–82, Gen. Manager, 1983–87, Qatar; Dir of Corporate Technology and of two associated cos, 1987–90; Dep. Dir, Communications, NATS, 1990–91. Sen. Advr, Frequentis, Vienna, 1998–. *Recreations:* sport (badminton, sailing, skiing), gardening, photography. *Address:* Ibex House, Church Lane, Worplesdon, Guildford, Surrey GU3 3RU. *T:* (01483) 233214.

DAVIES, Cynog Glyndwr; *see* Dafis, C. G.

DAVIES, Cyril James, CBE 1987; DL; Chief Executive, City of Newcastle upon Tyne, 1980–86; *b* 24 Aug. 1923; *s* of James and Frances Davies; *m* 1948, Elizabeth Leggett; two *s* two *d.* *Educ:* Heaton Grammar Sch. CIPFA. Served RN, Fleet Air Arm, 1942–46. Entered City Treasurer's Dept, Newcastle upon Tyne, 1940: Dep. City Treas., 1964; City Treas., 1969; Treas., Tyne and Wear Co., 1973–80. Mem. Court, Univ. of Newcastle upon Tyne, 1999. DL Tyne and Wear, 1989. Hon. DCL Newcastle, 1998. *Recreations:* theatre, walking, music. *Address:* 4 Montagu Court, Gosforth, Newcastle upon Tyne NE3 4JL. *T:* (0191) 285 9685.

DAVIES, Dr David; Director: Elmhirst Trust, since 1987; Open College of the Arts, 1989–99 (Administrative Director, 1988–89); *b* 11 Aug. 1939; *s* of late Trefor Alun and Kathleen Elsie Davies; *m* 1968, Joanna Rachel, *d* of David Brian Peace, *qv*; one *s* three *d.* *Educ:* Nottingham High Sch.; Peterhouse, Cambridge. MA, PhD. Res. Scientist, Dept of Geophysics, Cambridge, 1961–69; Leader, Seismic Discrimination Gp, MIT Lincoln Laboratory, 1970–73; Editor of Nature, 1973–79; Dir, Dartington N Devon Trust, 1980–87. Rapporteur, Seismic Study Gp of Stockholm Internat. Peace Res. Inst. (SIPRI), 1968–73; Chm., British Seismic Verification Res. Project, 1987–91. Member: Warnock Cttee on artificial human fertilisation, 1982–84; BMA Working Party on Surrogacy, 1988–89. Chm., Ivanhoe Trust, 1986–2001. Member Council: Internat. Disaster Inst., 1979; Beaford Arts Centre, 1980–87; Voluntary Arts Network, 1992–95; Trustee: Bristol Exploratory, 1983–90; Cooper Art Gall., Barnsley, 1994–2001; Yorks Organiser, Open Coll. of the Arts, 1987–89. Musical Dir, Blackheath Opera Workshop, 1977–79; Conductor, Exmoor Chamber Orchestra, 1980–87. Hon. Lectr, Bretton Hall Coll., 1987–2001. Hon. Fellow: Univ. of Leicester, 1988; Univ. of Leeds, 1989. *Publications:* Seismic Methods for Monitoring Underground Explosions, 1968; numerous scientific papers. *Recreations:* orchestral and choral conducting. *Address:* Cross Keys House, Fovant, Wilts SP3 5JH.

DAVIES, (David) Andrew; Member (Lab) Swansea West, National Assembly for Wales, since 1999; Minister for Assembly Business (formerly Business Manager), since 1999; *b* 5 May 1952; *s* of Wallace Morton Davies and Elizabeth Muriel Jane Davies (*née* Baldwin); *m* 1978, Deborah Frost (marr. diss. 1991). *Educ:* UC, Swansea (BSc Econ 1979; PGCE 1981); Gwent Coll. of Higher Educn (Dip. Counselling). Lectr in Adult and Further Educn, Swansea Univ., WEA and Swansea Coll., 1980–84; Regl Official, Wales Labour Party, 1984–91; Head of Employee Develt and Assistance Prog., Ford Motor Co., 1991–96; Lectr, Swansea Coll., 1994–97; Special Projects Officer (Referendum), Wales Labour Party, 1997–98; Associate Dir, Welsh Context, 1998–99. Chief Whip, Labour Gp, Nat. Assembly for Wales, 1999. *Recreations:* bird watching, cooking, gardening, the arts (especially contemporary dance and film). *Address:* National Assembly for Wales, Cardiff Bay, Cardiff CF99 1NA. *T:* (029) 2089 8249.

DAVIES, Air Vice-Marshal David Brian Arthur Llewellyn, FRCGP; Principal Medical Officer, Headquarters RAF Support Command, 1989–91; *b* 4 Feb. 1932; *s* of Graham and Iris Davies; *m* 1958, Jean Mary Goate; two *s.* *Educ:* University Coll. London (BSc); University Coll. Hosp. (MB BS). MFCM, MFOM; DAvMed. Sen. MO, various RAF units, incl. Brize Norton, Scampton, Gütersloh and HQ AFCENT, 1958–80; Dep. Dir, Medical Personnel, MoD, 1980–82; OC RAF Hosp., Wegberg, 1982–85; Comdt, Central Med. Estabt, 1985–87; Dep. PMO, Strike Command, 1987–88. QHP, 1989–91. *Recreations:* travel, music, theatre, gardening. *Address:* c/o Royal Bank of Scotland, 127–128 High Holborn, WC1V 2PQ. *Club:* Royal Air Force.

DAVIES, David Cyril, BA, LLB; Headmaster, Crown Woods School, 1971–84; *b* 7 Oct. 1925; *s* of D. T. E. Davies and Mrs G. V. Davies, JP; *m* 1952, Joan Rogers, BSc; one *s* one *d.* *Educ:* Lewis Sch., Pengam; UCW Aberystwyth. Asst Master, Ebbw Vale Gram. Sch., 1951–55; Head, Lower Sch., Netteswell Bilateral Sch., 1955–58; Sen. Master and Dep. Headmaster, Peckham Manor Sch., 1958–64; Headmaster: Greenway Comprehensive Sch., 1964–67; Woodberry Down Sch., 1967–71. Pres., Inverliever Lodge Trust, 1971–84. *Recreations:* reading, Rugby and roughing it. *Address:* 9 Plaxtol Close, Bromley, Kent BR1 3AU. *T:* (020) 8464 4187.

DAVIES, Sir David (Evan Naunton), Kt 1994; CBE 1986; PhD, DSc; FRS 1984; FREng; Chairman, Railway Safety, since 2001; President, Royal Academy of Engineering, 1996–2001; *b* 28 Oct. 1935; *s* of David Evan Davies and Sarah (*née* Samuel); *m* 1st, 1962, Enid Patilla (*d* 1990); two *s*; 2nd, 1992, Jennifer E., (Jenna), Rayner. *Educ:* Univ. of Birmingham (MSc 1958; PhD 1960; DSc 1968). FIEE 1969; FIERE 1975; FREng (FEng 1979). Lectr and Sen. Lectr in Elec. Engrg, Univ. of Birmingham, 1961–67 (also Hon. SPSO, RRE, Malvern, 1966–67); Asst Dir of Elec. Res., BR Bd, Derby, 1967–71; Vis. Industrial Prof. of Elec. Engrg, Loughborough Univ. of Technol., 1969–71; University College London: Prof. of Elec. Engrg, 1971–88; Pender Prof. and Hd of Dept of Electronic and Electrical Engrg, 1985–88; Vice-Provost, 1986–88; Vice-Chancellor, Loughborough Univ. of Technology, 1988–93; Chief Scientific Advr, MoD, 1993–99. Director: Gaydon Technology (Rover Group), 1986–88; Loughborough Consultants, 1988–93; Inst. Consumer Ergonomics, 1988–93; ERA Technology, 1997–; Lattice plc, 2000–. Member: SERC, 1985–89; IT Adv. Bd, DTI, 1988–91; EPSRC, 1994–99; Chm., Defence Scientific Adv. Council, 1992–93. Pres., IEE, 1994–95; Vice Pres., Royal Acad. of Engrg, 1995–96. Pro Chancellor, Univ. of Sussex, 1998–2001. Hon. FIChemE 1997; Hon. FIMechE 1998; Hon. FIStructE 2001. Hon DSc: Birmingham, Loughborough, South Bank, 1994; Bradford, 1995; Surrey, 1996; Bath, Warwick, 1997; Heriot-Watt, 1999; Hon. DEng UMIST 2000. Rank Prize for Optoelectronics, 1984; Callendar Medal, Inst. of Measurement & Control, 1984; Faraday Medal, IEE, 1987. *Publications:* technical papers and articles on radar, antennae and aspects of fibre optics. *Address:* Railway Safety, Evergreen House, 160 Euston Road, NW1 2DX. *T:* (020) 7904 7701.

DAVIES, Sir (David Herbert) Mervyn, Kt 1982; MC 1944; TD 1946; a Judge of the High Court of Justice, Chancery Division, 1982–93; *b* 17 Jan. 1918; *s* of Herbert Bowen Davies and Esther Davies, Llangunnor, Carms; *m* 1951, Zita Yollanne Angelique Blanche Antoinette, 2nd *d* of Rev. E. A. Phillips, Bale, Norfolk. *Educ:* Swansea Gram. Sch. Solicitor, 1939 (Travers Smith Scholar and Daniel Reardon Prize, Law Soc., 1939). 18th Bn Welch Regt and 2nd London Irish Rifles, Africa, Italy and Austria, 1939–45. Called to Bar, Lincoln's Inn, 1947; Bencher, 1974; QC 1967; a Circuit Judge, 1978–82. Mem., Bar Council, 1972; Mem., Senate of Inns of Court, 1975. *Address:* The White House, Great Snoring, Norfolk NR21 0AH. *T:* (01328) 820575. *Club:* Army and Navy.

DAVIES, (David) Hywel, MA, PhD; FREng; FIEE; consultant; Deputy Director-General for Science, Research and Development, EEC, Brussels, 1982–86; *b* 28 March 1929; *s* of John and Maggie Davies; *m* 1961, Valerie Elizabeth Nott; one *s* two *d.* *Educ:* Cardiff High Sch.; Christ's Coll., Cambridge. Radar Research Estabt, 1956; Head of Airborne Radar Group, RRE, 1970; Head of Weapons Dept, Admty Surface Weapons Estabt, 1972; Asst Chief Scientific Advr (Projects), MoD, 1976–79; Dir, RARDE, MoD, 1979–80; Dep. Controller, Res. Programmes, MoD, 1980–82. Man. Dir, Topexpress Ltd, 1988–89. FREng (FEng 1988). *Publications:* papers on electronics, radar and remote sensing, in Proc. IEE, etc. *Recreations:* Europe, computing, knots. *Address:* 52 Brittains Lane, Sevenoaks, Kent TN13 2JP. *T:* (01732) 456359.

DAVIES, Sir David (John), Kt 1999; Chairman, EFG Private Bank Ltd, since 1999; *b* 1 April 1940; *s* of late Stanley Kenneth Davies, CBE and Stephanie Davies; *m* 1st, 1967, Deborah Frances Loeb (marr. diss.); one *s*; 2nd, 1985, Linda Wong Lin-Tye; one *s* two *d.* *Educ:* Winchester Coll., Winchester; New Coll., Oxford (MA); Harvard Business Sch. (Advanced Management Program). Chase Manhattan Bank, 1963–67; Hill Samuel Group, 1967–73: Dir, Hill Samuel Inc., New York, 1970–73; Dir, Hill Samuel Ltd, London, 1973; Finance Dir, 1973–83, and Vice-Chm., 1977–83, MEPC Ltd; Man. Dir, The Hongkong Land Co. Ltd, 1983–86; Chm., Hong Kong Land Property Co. Ltd, 1983–86; Dir, 1986–88, Chief Exec. and Exec. Vice Chm., 1987–88, Hill Samuel Gp; Jt Chm., Hill Samuel & Co., 1987–88. Chm., 1990–98, Chief Exec., 1994–98, Johnson Matthey plc. Chairman: Wire Ropes Ltd, Wicklow, 1979–; Mandarin Oriental Hotel Group, 1983–86; Dairy Farm Ltd, 1983–86; Imry Merchant Developers (formerly Imry Internat.), 1987–89; Imry Holdings, 1992–98; MBO Partners Ltd, HK, 1992–2000; Semara (formerly Sketchley) PLC, 1990–2000; Dep. Chm., Charter Consolidated, 1988–89; Director: Jardine Matheson Group, 1983–86; Hong Kong Electric Co., 1983–85; American Barrick Resources Corp., Toronto, 1986–94; Delaware North Cos Inc., Buffalo, NY, 1986–; Singapore Land Ltd, 1986–90; Fitzwilton PLC, Dublin, 1987–90; Asia Securities, Hong Kong, 1987–89; Hardwicke Ltd, Dublin, 1987–; TSB Group, 1987–89; First Pacific Co., Hong Kong, 1988–91; Irish Life Assce, 1991–97; The Wharf (Holdings) Ltd, Hong Kong, 1992–99; Wheelock NatWest, 1994–97; Glyndebourne Productions Ltd, 1990–2000; Hilton Gp (formerly Ladbroke Gp) plc, 1997–2001; General Enterprise Mgt Services Ltd, 1998–2001. Mem. Council and Chm., UK Finance Cttee, Wexford Opera Festival, 1995– (Chm., Wexford Festival UK Trust, 1996–); Chm., Grange Park Opera, 1998–. Chm., Adv. Cttee on Business and the Envmt, 1995–98 (Mem., 1993–98); Dep. Chm., Prince of Wales' Business Leaders Forum, 1997–98 (Dir, 1991–96); Mem., Prince of Wales Business and the Envmt Prog., 1993–99. Mem. Council, Ireland Fund of GB, 1988–; Trustee, Anglo-Hong Kong Trust, 1989–. Mem. Adv. Cttee for Fund Raising, Ashmolean Mus., 1991–96; Trustee: Monteverdi Trust, 1991–97; New Coll. Develt Fund, 1995– (Mem., New Coll. Endowment Cttee, 1994–); Royal Opera House Trust, 1997–2001 (Mem., Appeal Cttee, 1997–); St Catherine Foundn. *Recreations:* farming, skiing, tennis, travel, opera. *Address:* 23 Robinson Road, Apartment 25D, Hong Kong. *Clubs:* Beefsteak, Garrick; All England Lawn Tennis; Kildare Street and University (Dublin); Hong Kong, China (Hong Kong).

DAVIES, Rt Hon. (David John) Denzil; PC 1978; MP (Lab) Llanelli, since 1970; *b* 9 Oct. 1938; *s* of G. Davies, Conwil Elfed, Carmarthen; *m* 1963, Mary Ann Finlay (marr. diss. 1988), Illinois; one *s* one *d.* *Educ:* Queen Elizabeth Grammar Sch., Carmarthen; Pembroke Coll., Oxford. Bacon Scholar, Gray's Inn, 1961; BA (1st cl. Law) 1962; Martin Wronker Prize (Law), 1962. Teaching Fellow, Univ. of Chicago, 1963; Lectr in Law, Leeds Univ., 1964; called to Bar, Gray's Inn, 1964. Member: Select Cttee on Corporation Tax, 1971; Jt Select Cttee (Commons and Lords) on Delegated Legislation, 1972; Public Accounts Cttee, 1974; PPS to the Secretary of State for Wales, 1974–76; Minister of State, HM Treasury, 1975–79; Opposition spokesman on Treasury matters, 1979–81, on foreign affairs, 1981–82, on defence, 1982–83; chief opposition spokesman: on Welsh affairs, 1983; on defence and disarmament, 1983–88. *Address:* House of Commons, SW1A 0AA.

DAVIES, David Levric, CB 1982; OBE 1962; Under Secretary (Legal), Treasury Solicitor's Office, 1977–82; *b* 11 May 1925; *s* of Benjamin and Elizabeth Davies; *m* 1955, Beryl Justine Hammond. *Educ:* Llanrwst Grammar Sch.; University Coll. of Wales, Aberystwyth (LLB Hons). Called to the Bar, Middle Temple, 1949. Served War, 1943–46: Sub-Lt RNVR. Crown Counsel, Aden, 1950–55; Tanganyika: Asst to Law Officers, 1956–58; Parly Draftsman, 1958–61; Solicitor-Gen., 1961–64; Home Civil Service, 1964–82: seconded to Jamaica as Sen. Parly Draftsman, 1965–69, and to Seychelles as Attorney-Gen., 1970–72; Sen. Legal Asst, Treasury Solicitor's Office, 1972–73; Asst Treasury Solicitor, 1973–77. *Recreations:* gardening, loafing, reading. *Address:* Greystones, Breach Lane, Shaftesbury, Dorset SP7 8LF. *T:* (01747) 851224.

DAVIES, Prof. David Roy, OBE 1995; PhD; Professor of Applied Genetics, University of East Anglia, 1968–94, now Professor Emeritus (Dean of School of Biological Sciences, 1985–91); Deputy Director, John Innes Institute, 1978–94; *b* 10 June 1932; *s* of late J. O. Davies and A. E. Davies; *m* 1957, Winifred Frances Davies, JP, BA (*née* Wills); two *s* two *d.* *Educ:* Llandyssul and Grove Park, Wrexham Grammar Schs; Univ. of Wales. BSc, PhD. UK Atomic Energy Authority, 1956–62 and 1963–68; US Atomic Energy Commn, 1962–63. Editor, Heredity, 1975–82. *Publications:* edited: The Plant Genome, 1980; Temperate Legumes, 1983; Peas: genetics, molecular biology and biotechnology, 1993; papers on radiobiology and plant genetics in scientific jls. *Address:* 57 Church Lane, Eaton, Norwich NR4 6NY. *T:* (01603) 451049.

DAVIES, David Theodore Alban; His Honour Judge David Davies; a Circuit Judge, since 1994; *b* 8 June 1940; *s* of late John Rhys Davies, Archdeacon of Merioneth, and Mabel Aeronwy Davies; *m* 1966, Janet Mary, *er d* of late Frank and Barbara Welburn, Cheadle Hulme, Cheshire; one *s* one *d.* *Educ:* Rossall School (Scholar); Magdalen College, Oxford (Exhibnr, 2nd cl. Mods 1960, 1st cl. Lit Hum, 1962, BA 1962; Eldon Law Schol., 1963; MA 1967). Called to the Bar, Gray's Inn, 1964 (Entrance Schol., Arden Atkin and Mould Prize, Lord Justice Holker Sen. Schol.). Practised SE Circuit, 1965–83; Registrar, then a Dist Judge, Family Div., High Court, 1983–94; a Recorder, 1989–94. Chancellor, dio. of Bangor, 1995–. Sec., Family Law Bar Assoc., 1976–80, Treasurer, 1980–83; Member: Senate Law Reform Cttee, 1979–83; Civil and Family Cttee, 1988–93, Main Bd, 1991–93, Judicial Studies Bd. *Publication:* (ed jtly) Jackson's Matrimonial Finance and Taxation, 2nd edn 1975, 5th edn 1992. *Recreations:* reading, walking, history. *Address:* Chester County Court, Centurion House, 77 Northgate Street, Chester CH1 2HQ.

DAVIES, David Thomas Charles; Member (C) Monmouth, National Assembly for Wales, since 1999; *b* 27 July 1970; *s* of Peter Hugh Charles Davies and Kathleen Diane Davies (*née* Elton). *Educ:* Clytha Sch., Newport; Bassaleg Sch., Newport. MInstTA; MILog; MIFF. BSC, 1988–89; grape picking, working on roads, rickshaw driver in tourist resort, Australia, 1989–91; Gen. Manager, Tea Importing and Shipping Co. (family business), 1991–99. Contested (C) Bridgend, 1997. *Recreations:* surfing, long distance running, keeping fit. *Address:* National Assembly for Wales, Cardiff Bay, Cardiff CF99 1NA. *T:* (029) 2089 8325; The Grange, 16 Maryport Street, Usk, Monmouthshire NP15 1AB. *Clubs:* Oriental; Abergavenny Constitutional; Chepstow Conservative; Monmouth Conservative; Usk Conservative.

DAVIES, Rt Hon. Denzil; *see* Davies, Rt Hon. David J. D.

DAVIES, Dickie; television sports presenter, since 1964; *s* of Owen John Davies and Ellen Davies; *m* 1962, Elisabeth Ann Hastings Mann; twin *s.* *Educ:* William Ellis Sch., Highgate; Oldershaw Grammar Sch., Wallasey, Cheshire. Purser, Cunard Line, 1953–60; Television Announcer, Southern TV, 1960–63; World of Sport Presenter, 1964–85, Presenter: ITV Sport, 1985–89; Sportsmasters, 1988–92; The World of Golf, 1990; Classic FM, 1995–;

Bobby Charlton's Football Scrapbook, Sky Sports TV, 1995–; Dickie Davies's Sporting Heroes, 1998–; World Cup Classics, 1999. *Recreations:* golf, walking our dogs.

DAVIES, Donald, CBE 1978 (OBE 1973); consultant; *b* 13 Feb. 1924; *s* of late Wilfred Lawson Davies and Alwyne Davies; *m* 1948, Mabel (*née* Hellyar); two *d. Educ:* Ebbw Vale Grammar Sch.; UC Cardiff (BSc). CEng, FIMinE. Nationl Coal Board: Colliery Man., 1951–55; Gp Man., 1955–58; Dep. Prodn Man., 1958–60; Prodn Man., 1960–61; Area Gen. Man., 1961–67; Area Dir, 1967–73; Bd Mem., 1973–84; Chairman: Nat. Fuel Distributors, 1973–89; Southern Depot Co., 1973–89; NCB (Ancillaries), 1979–89; Horizon Exploration, 1981–89. *Recreations:* golf, walking. *Address:* Wendy Cottage, Dukes Wood Avenue, Gerrards Cross, Bucks SL9 7LA. *T:* (01753) 885083.

DAVIES, Douglas; *see* Davies, Percy D.

DAVIES, Rev. Prof. Douglas James, PhD; Professor in the Study of Religion, University of Durham, since 2000; *b* 11 Feb. 1947; *s* of Llewelyn James Davies and Gladys Evelyn Davies (*née* Morgan). *Educ:* Lewis Sch., Pengam; St John's Coll., Durham (BA 1969); St Peter's Coll., Oxford (MLitt 1972); Univ. of Nottingham (PhD 1980). Ordained deacon 1975; priest 1976; University of Nottingham: Lectr in Theology, 1974–90; Sen. Lectr, 1990–93; Prof. of Religious Studies, 1993–97; Principal, Coll. of St Hild and St Bede, and Prof. of Theol., Univ. of Durham, 1997–2000. Hon. DTheol Uppsala, 1998. *Publications:* Meaning and Salvation in Religious Studies, 1984; Mormon Spirituality, 1987; (jtly) Church and Religion in Rural England, 1991; Frank Byron Jevons: an evolutionary realist, 1991; (jtly) Reusing Old Graves, 1995; (ed) Mormon Identities in Transition, 1996; Death, Ritual and Belief, 1997; The Mormon Culture of Salvation, 2000. *Recreations:* squash, cacti. *Address:* Abbey House, Palace Green, Durham DH1 3RS. *Club:* Royal Over-Seas League.

DAVIES, Ednyfed Hudson, BA (Wales); MA (Oxon); barrister; *b* 4 Dec. 1929; *s* of Rev. E. Curig Davies and Enid Curig (*née* Hughes); *m* 1972, Amanda Barker-Mill, *d* of Peter Barker-Mill and Elsa Barker-Mill; two *d. Educ:* Friars Sch., Bangor; Dynevor Grammar Sch., Swansea; University College of Swansea; Balliol Coll., Oxford. Called to the Bar, Gray's Inn, 1975. Lecturer in Dept of Extra-Mural Studies, University of Wales, Aberystwyth, 1957–61; Lecturer in Political Thought, Welsh Coll. of Advanced Technology, Cardiff, 1961–66. MP: (Lab) Conway, 1966–70; Caerphilly, 1979–83 (Lab, 1979–81, SDP, 1981–83); Mem., H of C Select Cttee on Energy, 1980–83; Sec., H of C All-Party Tourism Cttee, 1979–83. Contested (SDP) Basingstoke, 1983. Part-time TV and Radio Commentator and Interviewer on Current Affairs, 1962–66; on full-time contract to BBC presenting Welsh-language feature programmes on overseas countries, 1970–76; Chm., Wales Tourist Board, 1976–78. Chm., Lincs FM plc, 1991–; Dep. Chm., Ocean Sound Radio, 1989–94 (Dir, 1986–94); Dir, Southern Radio, 1989–94. Director: New Forest Butterfly Farm, 1984–94; New Forest Industrial Assoc. Ltd, 1989–. Trustee, 1986–, Chm., 1994–, New Forest Ninth Centenary Trust. Captain, Southern Sqdn, Royal Welsh YC, 1995–. *Address:* 2 King's Bench Walk, Temple, EC4Y 7DE. *Clubs:* Cardiff and County (Cardiff); Royal Welsh Yacht (Caernarfon); Royal Lymington Yacht; Royal Southampton Yacht.

DAVIES, Prof. (Edward) Brian, DPhil; FRS 1995; Professor of Mathematics, King's College London, since 1981; *b* 13 June 1944; *s* of Arthur Granville Davies and Mary Davies (*née* Scudamore); *m* 1968, Jane Christine Phillips; one *s* one *d. Educ:* Jesus Coll., Oxford (BA 1965; MA); Brasenose Coll., Oxford (DPhil Maths 1968). Tutorial Fellow, St John's Coll., Oxford, 1970–81; Univ. Lectr, Oxford Univ., 1973–81; Head, Dept of Maths, KCL, 1990–93; FKC 1996. Editor, Qly Jl of Mathematics, 1973–81; Founding Editor, London Mathematical Soc. Student Text Series, 1983–90. *Publications:* Quantum Theory of Open Systems, 1976; One-Parameter Semigroups, 1980; Heat Kernels and Spectral Theory, 1989; Spectral Theory and Differential Operators, 1995. *Recreations:* family, scientific reading. *Address:* Department of Mathematics, King's College, Strand, WC2R 2LS.

DAVIES, (Edward) Hunter; author, broadcaster, publisher; *b* Renfrew, Scotland, 7 Jan. 1936; *s* of late John Hunter Davies and Marion (*née* Brechin); *m* 1960, Margaret Forster, *qv*; one *s* two *d. Educ:* Creighton Sch., Carlisle; Carlisle Grammar Sch.; University Coll., Durham. BA 1957, DipEd 1958; Editor of Palatinate. Reporter: Manchester Evening Chronicle, 1958–59; Sunday Graphic, London, 1959–60; Sunday Times, 1960–84: Atticus, 1965–67; Chief Feature Writer, 1967; Editor, Sunday Times Magazine, 1975–77; Columnist: Punch, 1979–89; Stamp News, 1981–86; London Evening Standard, 1987; The Independent, 1989–93; New Statesman & Society, 1996–; Presenter, Bookshelf, Radio 4, 1983–86. Mem., British Library Consultative Gp on Newspapers, 1987–89; Dir, Edinburgh Book Festival Bd, 1990–95; Chm., Cumbria Wildlife Trust, 1995–. Dep. Pro-Chancellor, Lancaster Univ., 1996–97. *Television:* The Playground (play), 1967; The Living Wall, 1974; George Stephenson, 1975; A Walk in the Lakes, 1979. *Publications: fiction:* Here We Go, Round the Mulberry Bush, 1965 (filmed, 1968); The Rise and Fall of Jake Sullivan, 1970; (ed) I Knew Daisy Smuten, 1970; A Very Loving Couple, 1971; Body Charge, 1972; Flossie Teacake's Fur Coat, 1982; Flossie Teacake—Again!, 1983; Flossie Teacake Strikes Back, 1984; Come on Ossie!, 1985; Ossie Goes Supersonic, 1986; Ossie the Millionaire, 1987; Saturday Night, 1989; S.T.A.R.S (12 books in Penguin series), 1989–90; Snotty Bumstead, 1991; Striker, 1992; Snotty Bumstead and the Rent-a-Mum, 1993; Snotty the Hostage, 1995; Flossie Wins the Lottery, 1996; Flossie Teacake's Holiday, 2000; *non-fiction:* The Other Half, 1966; (ed) The New London Spy, 1966; The Beatles, 1968, 2nd edn 1985; The Glory Game, 1972, 4th edn 2000; A Walk Along the Wall, 1974, 2nd edn 1984; George Stephenson, 1975; The Creighton Report, 1976; (ed) Sunday Times Book of Jubilee Year, 1977; A Walk Around the Lakes, 1979; William Wordsworth, 1980; The British Book of Lists, 1980; The Grades, 1981; Father's Day, 1981 (television series, 1983); Beaver Book of Lists, 1981; A Walk Along the Tracks, 1982; England!, 1982; (with Frank Herrmann) Great Britain: a celebration, 1982; A Walk Round London Parks, 1983; The Joy of Stamps, 1983; London at its Best, 1984; (also publisher) The Good Guide to the Lakes, 1984, 5th edn 1997; The Grand Tour, 1986; The Good Quiz Book to the Lakes, 1987; Back in the USSR, 1987; Beatrix Potter's Lakeland, 1988; My Life in Football, 1990; In Search of Columbus, 1991; Teller of Tales: in search of Robert Louis Stevenson, 1994; Hunting People: thirty years of interviews with the famous, 1994; Wainwright: the biography, 1995; Living on the Lottery, 1996; Born 1900, 1998; London to Loweswater, 1999; Dwight Yorke, 1999; A Walk Around the West Indies, 2000; Joe Kinnear: still crazy, 2000; The Quarrymen, 2001; The Eddie Stobart Story, 2001. *Recreations:* walking, Lakeland books, Beatles memorabilia, swimming, football. *Address:* 11 Boscastle Road, NW5 1EE. *T:* (020) 7485 3785; Grasmoor House, Loweswater, Cumbria CA13 0RU.

DAVIES, Emrys Thomas, CMG 1988; HM Diplomatic Service, retired; Appointments Adviser to Welsh Office, since 1997; *b* 8 Oct. 1934; *s* of Evan William Davies and Dinah Davies (*née* Jones); *m* 1960, Angela Audrey, *er d* of late Paul Robert Buchan May, ICS and of Esme May; one *s* two *d. Educ:* Parmiters Foundation Sch. RAF, 1953–55; commnd RAFVR, 1955. Sch. of Slavonic Studies, Cambridge Univ., 1954; Sch. of Oriental and African Studies, London Univ., 1955–56. Served Peking, 1956–59; FO, 1959–60; Bahrain, 1960–62; FO, 1962–63; Asst Political Adviser to Hong Kong Govt, 1963–68; First Sec., British High Commn, Ottawa, 1968–71; FCO, 1972–76; Commercial Counsellor, Peking, 1976–78 (Chargé, 1976 and 1978); Oxford Univ. Business Summer Sch., 1977; NATO Defense Coll., Rome, 1979; Dep. High Comr, Ottawa, 1979–82; Overseas Inspector, FCO, 1982–84; Dep. UK Perm. Rep. to OECD, and Counsellor (Econ. and Financial) to UK Delegn, Paris, 1984–87; Ambassador to Hanoi, 1987–90; High Comr, Barbados, Grenada, St Lucia, Dominica, Antigua and Barbuda, St Vincent and the Grenadines, and St Kitts and Nevis, 1990–94; Hd, UK Delegn to EC Monitoring Mission to former Yugoslavia, 1995 and 1998–99. Sec. Gen., Tripartite Commn for Restitution of Monetary Gold, Brussels, 1995–98. Mem., Cambridge Soc. *Address:* 8 Alison Way, St Paul's Hill, Winchester, Hants S022 5BT. *Clubs:* Royal Air Force; Glamorgan CC.

DAVIES, Dr Ernest Arthur; JP; management consultant and lecturer, retired 1987; *b* 25 Oct. 1926; *s* of Dan Davies and Ada (*née* Smith), Nuneaton; *m* 1st, 1956, Margaret Stephen Tait Gatt (marr. diss. 1967), *d* of H. Gatt, Gamesley, near Glossop; no *c*; 2nd, 1972, Patricia (marr. diss. 1980), *d* of S. Bates, Radford, Coventry; no *c. Educ:* Coventry Jun. Techn. Coll.; Westminster Trng Coll., London; St Salvator's Coll., University of St Andrews; St John's Coll., Cambridge. PhD Cantab 1959; MInstP 1959, CPhys 1986. Techn. Coll.; Westminster Trng Coll., London; St Salvator's Coll., University of St Andrews; St John's Coll., Cambridge. PhD Cantab 1959; MInstP 1959, CPhys 1986. RAF Aircraft Apprentice, 1942–43 (discharged on med. grounds). Westminster Trng Coll., 1946–48; Teacher, Foxford Sch., Coventry, 1948–50; University of St Andrews, 1950–54 (1st cl. hons Physics, Neil Arnott Prize, Carnegie Schol.); subseq. research in superconductivity, Royal Society Mond Lab., Cambridge; AEI Research Scientist, 1957–63; Lectr in Physics, Faculty of Technology, University of Manchester, 1963–66; Management Selection Consultant, MSL, 1970–81; Lectr in Business Studies, Hammersmith and West London Coll., 1981–87. MP (Lab) Stretford, 1966–70; Parliamentary Private Secretary to: PMG (Mr Edward Short), Nov.-Dec. 1967; Foreign Secretary (Mr George Brown), Jan.-Mar. 1968; Foreign and Commonwealth Sec. (Mr Michael Stewart), 1968–69; Jt Parly Sec., Min. of Technology, 1969–70. Co-Vice-Chm., Parly Labour Party's Defence and Services Group; Mem., Select Cttee on Science and Technology, 1966–67, 1967–68, 1968–69; Parly Deleg. to 24th Gen. Assembly of UN (UK Rep. on 4th Cttee). Councillor: Borough of Stretford, 1961–67; Borough of Southwark, 1974–82. JP Lancs, 1962, Inner London, 1972. *Publications:* contribs to Proc. Royal Society, Jl of Physics and Chem. of Solids. *Recreations:* reading, walking, art and design practice, computer studies. *Address:* 43 Frensham Drive, Nuneaton, Warwickshire CV10 9QH.

DAVIES, Prof. Eurfil Rhys, CBE 1990; FRCR, FRCPE; FFR (RCSI); FDSRCS; Professor of Clinical Radiology (formerly Radiodiagnosis), University of Bristol, 1981–93; *b* 18 April 1929; *s* of late Daniel Haydn Davies and Mary Davies; *m* 1962, Zoë Doreen Chamberlain; three *s. Educ:* Rhondda Grammar Sch.; Llandovery Coll.; Clare Coll., Cambridge (MB, BChir 1953; MA); St Mary's Hosp., London. FRCR (FFR 1964); FRCPE 1971; FFR (RCSI) 1978; FDSRCS 1989. Served RAMC, 1954–56 (Regtl MO 24 Regt). Sen. Registrar, St Mary's Hosp., 1963–66; Consultant Radiologist, United Bristol Hosps, 1966–81; Clinical Lectr, 1972–81, Hd, Clinical Sch., 1992–93, Univ. of Bristol. Vis. Sen. Lectr, Lagos Univ., 1971; Mayne Vis. Prof., Queensland Univ., 1982. Civilian Cons. Advr to RN, 1989–94. Mem., Bristol and Weston DHA, 1983–86. Member: Admin of Radio Active Substances Adv. Cttee, DHSS, 1970–83; Clin. Standards Adv. Cttee, 1991–93; GMC, 1989–93; Ionising Radiation Adv. Cttee, HSC, 1995–97 (Mem., Working Gp, 1987–95). Royal Coll. of Radiologists: Sen. Examr, 1973–74; Mem., Fellowship Bd, 1974–76; Registrar, 1976–81; Chm., Examining Bd, 1981–84; Warden of the Fellowship, 1984–86; Pres., 1986–89; Chairman: Nuclear Medicine Cttee, 1972–78; Examng Bd, 1982–84; Knox Lectr, 1990. Pres., Nuclear Medicine Soc., 1974–76 (Sec., 1972–74); Chm., Inter Collegiate Standing Cttee for Nuclear Medicine, 1982–84 (Sec., 1980–82). Hon. Fellow, Faculty of Radiologists, RCSI, 1978. *Publications:* (contrib.) Textbook of Radiology, ed Sutton, 1969, Associate Editor, 6th edn 1998; (contrib.) Textbook of Urology, ed J. P. Blandy, 1974; (jtly) Radioisotopes in Radiodiagnosis, 1976; (contrib.) Radiological Atlas of Biliary and Pancreatic Disease, 1978; Textbook of Radiology by British Authors, 1984; (ed with W. E. G. Thomas) Nuclear Medicine for Surgeons, 1988; papers in Clin. Radiology, British Jl of Radiology, Lancet. *Recreations:* theatre, cooking, wine, travel. *Address:* 19 Hyland Grove, Bristol BS9 3NR.

DAVIES, Rt Rev. (Francis James) Saunders; *see* Bangor, Bishop of.

DAVIES, Sir Frank (John), Kt 1999; CBE 1993; Deputy Chairman, Railway Safety, since 2001; Chairman, Health and Safety Commission, 1993–99; *b* 24 Sept. 1931; *s* of late Lt-Col F. H. Davies and Veronica Josephine Davies; *m* 1956, Sheila Margaret Bailey; three *s. Educ:* Monmouth Sch.; UMIST. BPB Industries plc, 1953–63; RTZ Piller Ltd, 1964–67; Alcan Aluminium (UK) Ltd, 1967–83: Div. Man. Dir, 1971–83; Dir, 1977–83; Dir, Alcan Booth, 1972–82; Gp Chief Exec., Rockware Gp, 1983–93. Chairman: Dartington Crystal, 1989–94; ACI Europe Ltd, 1991–93; Bardon Gp plc, 1994–97; Director: Ian Proctor M. Masts, 1974–83; Ardagh plc, 1985–; BTR Nylex, 1991–94; Saltire (formerly Cannon St Investments), 1993–99; Aggregate Industries plc, 1997–; Investor Champions plc, 2000–. Mem., Oxfordshire HA, 1981–90; Chm., Nuffield Orthopaedic Centre NHS Trust, 1990–98. President: Glass Manufrs Fedn, 1985, 1986; Fédn Européene du Verre d'Emballage, 1987–88; Member: Council, Cttee Permanent Industrie du Verre, Brussels, 1984–86; Council, Aluminium Fedn, 1980–82; Council, CBI, 1985–93; Council, Industry Council for Packaging and the Envmt, 1986–93; Packaging Standards Council, 1992–93; Vice-President: Inst. of Packaging, 1992; Inst. of Occupational Safety & Health, 1995. Trustee, British Occupnl Health Res. Foundn, 1993–99; Chm. and Trustee, Back Care. Governor: Inst. of Occupl Medicine, 2000–; British Safety Council, 2000–. CIMgt (CBIM 1986); FRSA 1986. Freeman, City of London, 1986; Liveryman: Basketmakers' Co., 1987; Glass-Sellers' Co., 1990. OStJ 1977 (Mem., Council of St John, Oxfordshire, 1973–2000); Vice-Pres., Oxfordshire St John Ambulance, 1973–2000. *Recreations:* NHS, gardening, theatre, travel. *Address:* Stonewalls, Castle Street, Deddington, Banbury, Oxon OX15 0TE. *Clubs:* Carlton, Royal Automobile.

DAVIES, Col (Frederic) Nicolas (John); JP; DL; Secretary for Appointments and Chief Clerk, Duchy of Lancaster, since 1992; *b* 11 May 1939; *s* of late Rev. William John Davies and Winifred Mary Davies (*née* Lewis); *m* 1970, Caroline Tweedie; one step *s* one step *d*; one *s* one *d* by previous *m. Educ:* King's Coll., Taunton; RMA Sandhurst. FIMgt. Nat. Service, Queen's Royal Regt, 1957; commnd Royal Regt of Artillery, 1959; served in UK, Cyprus, Hong Kong and Germany; COS, Catterick Garrison, N Yorks, 1982–85; Defence and Military Attaché, Hungary, 1986–91; retd 1992. Member: St John Council for Surrey, 1995–; Court, Univ. of Surrey, 1997–. Gov., Corp. of Sons of the Clergy, 1997– (Mem., Court of Assts, 1999–). JP Inner London 1997; DL Surrey, 1997. Hon. Mem., Order of Vitéz (Hungary), 1994. *Recreations:* walking, gardening, reading. *Address:* Duchy of Lancaster Office, Lancaster Place, Strand, WC2E 7ED. *T:* (020) 7836 8277. *Club:* Army and Navy.

DAVIES, Gareth, CBE 1992; FCA; Group Chief Executive, 1984–93, Chairman, 1986–98, Glynwed International plc; *b* 13 Feb. 1930; *s* of Lewis and Margaret Ann Davies; *m* 1953, Joan Patricia Prosser; one *s*. *Educ:* King Edward's Grammar School, Aston, Birmingham. Joined Glynwed Group, 1957; Computer Manager, 1964; Financial Dir, 1969; Man. Dir, 1981. Non-executive Director: Midlands Electricity Plc, 1989–96; Midlands Indep. Newspapers plc, 1994–97; Lloyds Chemists plc, 1995–97. *Recreations:* music, gardening. *Address:* 4 Beechgate, Roman Road, Little Aston Park, Sutton Coldfield, West Midlands B74 3AR. *T:* (0121) 353 4780.

DAVIES, Gareth; *see* Davies, W. G.

DAVIES, Gareth Lewis; His Honour Judge Gareth Davies; a Circuit Judge, since 1990; *b* 8 Sept. 1936; *s* of David Edward Davies and Glynwen Davies; *m* 1962; two *s* two *d*. *Educ:* Brecon County Grammar Sch.; Univ. of Wales (LLB). National Service, RAF, 1954–56. Articled 1959, qualified Solicitor, 1962; Partner, Ottaways', Solicitors, St Albans, 1965–90; a Recorder, 1987. *Recreations:* sailing instructor, ski guide, classic cars, cycling. *Address:* Bronllys Castle, Bronllys, Brecon, Powys LD3 0HL. *T:* (01874) 711930.

DAVIES, Gavyn, OBE 1979; Chairman, Board of Governors, BBC, since 2001 (Vice-Chairman, 2001); *b* 27 Nov. 1950; *s* of W. J. F. Davies and M. G. Davies; *m* 1989, Susan Jane Nye; two *s* one *d*. *Educ:* St John's Coll., Cambridge (BA); Balliol Coll., Oxford. Economic Advr, Policy Unit, 10 Downing Street, 1974–79; Economist, Phillips and Drew, 1979–81; Chief UK Economist, Simon & Coates, 1981–86; Goldman Sachs: Chief UK Economist, 1986–93; Partner, 1988–2001; Hd of Investment Res. (London), 1991–93; Head, later Co-Head, Eur. Investment Res., 1993–99; Chief Internat. Economist, 1993–2001; Chm., Investment Res. Dept, 1999–2001. Vis. Prof. of Economics, LSE, 1988–98. Principal Econs Commentator, The Independent, 1991–99. Mem., HM Treasury's Indep. Forecasting Panel, 1993–97. Chm., Future Funding of the BBC (govt inquiry), 1999. Hon. DSc (Social Sci.) Southampton, 1998. *Recreation:* Southampton FC. *Address:* BBC, Broadcasting House, W1A 1AA.

DAVIES, George Raymond, (Gerry), OBE 1977; FLA; Director, The Booksellers Association of Great Britain and Ireland, 1964–66 and 1970–81 (Hon. Life Member, 1981); *b* 3 Oct. 1916; *s* of George John Davies and Eva Florence Davies; *m* 1945, Sylvia Newling (*d* 1998); one *s* one *d*. *Educ:* East Ham Grammar Sch. FLA 1948. Local govt service, 1934–40; land reclamation, 1940–45; estate under-bailiff, 1945–46; W Suffolk and Cambridge Public Libraries, 1947–54 (Dep. City Librarian, 1953); Gen. Sec., Booksellers Assoc., 1955–64; Man. Dir, Bowker Publishing Co. Ltd, 1966–67; Editor, Publishers Inf. Card Services Ltd, 1968–69; Jt Dep. Editor, The Bookseller, 1969–70. Founder-Mem., Internat. Community of Booksellers Assocs, 1956 (Mem. Council, 1972–78); Mem. Council, Internat. Booksellers Fedn, 1978–85 (Pres. 1978–81; Editor, Booksellers International, 1982–88; Hon. Life Mem., 1989); Chm., BA Service House Ltd, 1977–82; Patron, Book Trade Benevolent Soc., 1989– (Chm., 1974–86; Pres., 1986–89). *Publications:* (ed jtly) Books are Different, 1966; A Mortal Craft, 1980; One Hundred Years: the history of the Booksellers Association, 1995; (contrib.) The Book of Westminster, 1964; (contrib.) Books and Their Prices, 1967; The End Game (poems), 1999; Out and Roundabout (poems), 2001; contrib. to Logos, Library Rev., Library World, Year's Work in Librarianship, DNB, Canadian Bookseller, American Bookseller, Australian Bookseller and Publisher, Publishers Weekly, and The Bookseller. *Recreations:* estate management, writing words and music. *Address:* Crotchets, Rotherfield Lane, Mayfield, East Sussex TN20 6AS. *T:* (01435) 872356. *Club:* Savile.

DAVIES, George William; Chairman, Per Una clothing for Marks and Spencer plc, since 2001; *b* 29 Oct. 1941; *s* of George and Mary Davies; *m* 1st, 1964, Anne; three *d*; 2nd, 1985, Liz; two *d*; 3rd, 1992, Fiona; two *s*. *Educ:* Netherton Moss Primary Sch.; Bootle Grammar Sch.; Birmingham Univ. Littlewoods, 1967–72; School Care (own business), 1972–75; Pippa Dee (subsid. of Rosgill Hldgs)—Party Plan/Lingerie, 1975–81; J. Hepworth & Son plc (responsible for launch of Next), 1981; Jt Gp Man. Dir, J. Hepworth & Son, 1984; Chief Exec., 1985–88, Chm., 1987–88, Next (name changed from J. Hepworth & Son); Managing Director: George Davies Partnership plc, 1989–2000; George Clothing, 1995–2000; Pres., Asda Gp, 1995–2000. Sen. Fellow, RCA, 1988. FRSA. Hon. DBA Liverpool Polytechnic, 1989. Guardian Young Businessman of the Year, 1985; Wood Mackenzie Retailer of the Year, 1987; Marketing Personality of the Year, 1988. *Publication:* What Next? (autobiog.), 1989. *Recreations:* tennis, golf, cycling. *Clubs:* Formby Golf; Liverpool Ramblers; Blackwell Golf.

DAVIES, Geraint Rhys; Member (Plaid Cymru) Rhondda, National Assembly for Wales, since 1999; *b* 1 Dec. 1948; *s* of John Davies and Sarah Olwen Davies; *m* 1973, Merril Margaret Williams; three *s* one *d*. *Educ:* Pentre Grammar Sch.; Chelsea Coll., London (BPharm). MRPharmS. Community pharmacist: Boots, Treorci, Rhondda, 1972–75; self-employed, 1975–. Member (Plaid Cymru): Rhondda CBC, 1983–95; Rhondda Cynon Taff, 1995–. *Recreations:* playing tennis, listening to music, reading. *Address:* National Assembly for Wales, Cardiff Bay, Cardiff CF99 1NA. *T:* (029) 2089 8280; (constituency) 45 Gelligaled Road, Ystrad, Rhondda CF41 7RQ. *T:* (01443) 421691.

DAVIES, Geraint Richard; MP (Lab) Croydon Central, since 1997; *b* 3 May 1960; *s* of David Thomas Morgan Davies and Betty Ferrer Davies; *m* 1991, Dr Vanessa Catherine Fry; three *d*. *Educ:* Llanishen Comp. Sch., Cardiff; Jesus Coll., Oxford (JCR Pres.; BA Hons PPE). Joined Brooke Bond Oxo as sales and mkting trainee, 1982; subseq. Gp Product Manager, Unilever; Marketing Manager, Colgate Palmolive Ltd; Founder, and Partner, Pure Crete, 1989–; Dir, Equity Creative Ltd, 1989–; Founder, and Dir, Pure Aviation Ltd, 1996–. Mem., Croydon BC, 1986–97 (Chm. of Housing, 1994–96; Leader of Council, 1996–97); Chm., London Boroughs Housing Cttee, 1994–96. Contested (Lab): Croydon S, 1987; Croydon Central, 1992. Chairman: Lab. Finance and Industry Gp, 1998– (Mem. Exec., 1994–); Envmt, Transport and Regions Deptl Cttee, 1997–2001; Mem., Public Accounts Select Cttee, 1997–. *Recreation:* spending time with the family. *Address:* House of Commons, SW1A 0AA. *T:* (020) 7219 4599, *Fax:* (020) 7219 5962. *Club:* Ruskin House (Croydon).

DAVIES, Geraint Talfan; Chairman, Institute of Welsh Affairs, since 1992; Controller, BBC Wales, 1990–99; *b* 30 Dec. 1943; *s* of late Aneirin Talfan Davies, OBE and Mary Anne (*née* Evans); *m* 1967, Elizabeth Shân Vaughan (*née* Yorath); three *s*. *Educ:* Cardiff High Sch.; Jesus Coll., Oxford (MA). Western Mail, Cardiff, 1966–71; The Journal, Newcastle upon Tyne, 1971–73; The Times, 1973; Asst Editor, Western Mail, Cardiff, 1974–78; HTV Wales: Head, News and Current Affairs, 1978–82; Asst Controller of Progs, 1982–87; Dir of Progs, Tyne Tees TV, 1987–90. Non-exec. Dir, Glas Cymru Ltd. Chairman: Newydd Housing Assoc., 1975–78; Cardiff Bay Arts Trust, 1997–; Wales Internat. Film Festival, 1998–2001. Mem., Prince of Wales' Cttee, 1993–95; Trustee: Tenovus Cancer Appeal, 1984–87; British Bone Marrow Donor Appeal, 1987–95. Member: Management Cttee, Northern Sinfonia, 1989–90; Radio Authy, 2001–; Chm., WNO, 2000–. Governor: Welsh Coll. of Music and Drama, 1993–97; UWIC, 2000–. *Recreations:* theatre, music, architecture. *Address:* 15 The Parade, Whitchurch, Cardiff CF14 2EF. *T:* (029) 2062 6571; *e-mail:* gtalfandavies@aol.com.

DAVIES, Dr Gillian; DL; Chairman, Technical Board of Appeal, European Patent Office, Munich, since 1997; *b* 5 April 1940; *d* of late Ninian Rhys Davies and Gweneth Elizabeth Davies (*née* Griffith). *Educ:* Cheltenham Ladies' Coll.; Grenoble Univ.; Univ. of Wales, Aberystwyth (PhD 1997). Called to the Bar, Lincoln's Inn, 1961; in practice at the Bar, 1961–63; Legal Assistant: De La Rue Co., 1963–65; United Internat. Bureaux for Protection of Intellectual Property, Geneva, 1965–70; Legal Advr, 1970–73, Asst Dir Gen., 1973–80, Associate Dir Gen. and Chief Legal Advr, 1980–91, IFPI. Res. Fellow, Max Planck Inst. for Foreign and Internat. Patent, Copyright, and Competition Law, Munich, 1990; Hon. Prof., Univ. of Wales, Aberystwyth, 1994–. Mem., Wkg Gp on the Rôle of the State vis-à-vis the Cultural Industries, Council of Europe, 1980–86; Legal Mem., Bds of Appeal, 1991, Mem., Enlarged Bd of Appeal, 1996, European Patent Office. DL Gwynedd, 2001. *Publications:* Piracy of Phonograms, 1981, 2nd edn 1986; Private Copying of Sound and Audiovisual Recordings, 1984; (jtly) Challenges to Copyright and Related Rights in the European Community, 1983; (jtly) Music and Video Private Copying, 1993; Copyright and the Public Interest, 1994, 2nd edn 2001; Copinger and Skone James on Copyright, suppl. (jtly) 1994, 14th edn (ed jtly) 1999; many articles in intellectual property law jls. *Recreations:* golf, tennis, art, travel. *Address:* Arthur-Kutscher-Platz 2/II, 80802 Munich, Germany. *T:* (89) 347184; Trefaes, Abersoch, Gwynedd LL53 7AD. *T:* (01758) 712426. *Clubs:* Royal Anglo-Belgian, Hurlingham.

DAVIES, Glyn; *see* Davies, R. H. G.

DAVIES, Glyn; Member (C) Mid & West Wales, National Assembly for Wales, since 1999; *b* 16 Feb. 1944; *m* 1969, Bobbie; three *s* one *d*. *Educ:* Caereinion High Sch.; UCW, Aberystwyth. Mem. (C) Montgomeryshire DC, 1985–88 (Chm.). Chm., Develt Bd for Rural Wales, 1989–94. *Recreations:* countryside, sport. *Address:* National Assembly for Wales, Cardiff Bay, Cardiff CF99 1NA. *T:* (029) 2089 8337; Cil Farm, Berriew, Welshpool, Montgomeryshire, Mid Wales SY21 8AZ. *T:* (01686) 640698.

DAVIES, Prof. Glyn Arthur Owen, FRAeS; Professor of Aeronautical Structures, since 1985, and Senior Research Fellow, since 1999, Imperial College of Science, Technology and Medicine, London (Head of Department of Aeronautics, 1982–89; Pro-Rector (Resources), 1997–99); *b* 11 Feb. 1933; *s* of Arthur and Florence Davies; *m* 1959, Helen Rosemary (*née* Boot); two *d*. *Educ:* Liverpool Inst., Univ. of Liverpool (BEng); Cranfield Inst. of Technology (DCAe); PhD Sydney, 1966. Res. Asst, MIT, 1956; Advanced Project Engr, Brit. Aerospace, 1957–59; Lectr, Sen. Lectr, Dept of Aeronautics, Univ. of Sydney, 1959–66; Lectr, Sen. Lectr, Dept of Aeronautics, Imperial Coll. of Sci. and Technol., 1966–72. Consultant to: ARC, 1975–81; MoD, 1980–; Nat. Agency for Finite Element Methods and Standards, 1983–95; SERC, 1986–90 (Supercomputing, 1991–93); The Computer Bd, 1989–91; ABRC (Supercomputing), 1991–94; UFC (IT), 1991–93; DTI (Aviation), 1991–; EPSRC, 1994–; OST (Foresight) Defence & Aerospace, 1994–. FRAeS 1987; FCGI 2000. *Publications:* Virtual Work in Structural Analysis, 1982; Mathematical Methods in Engineering, 1984; Finite Element Primer, 1986; Background to Benchmarks, 1993. *Recreations:* photography, archaeology, painting, theatre, music. *Address:* Hedsor School House, Bourne End, Bucks SL8 5JJ.

DAVIES, Sir Graeme (John), Kt 1996; FREng; FRSE; Principal and Vice-Chancellor, University of Glasgow, since 1995; *b* 7 April 1937; *s* of Harry John Davies and Gladys Edna Davies (*née* Pratt); *m* 1959, Florence Isabelle Martin; one *s* two *d*. *Educ:* Mount Albert Grammar School, Auckland, NZ; Univ. of Auckland (BE, PhD); St Catharine's College, Cambridge (MA, ScD). Junior Lectr, Univ. of Auckland, 1960–62; University of Cambridge: TI Research Fellow, 1962–64; Univ. Demonstrator in Metallurgy, 1964–66; Lectr, 1966–76; Fellow of St Catharine's Coll., 1967–76 (Hon. Fellow 1989); Prof. of Metallurgy, Univ. of Sheffield, 1977–86; Vice Chancellor, Univ. of Liverpool, 1986–91; Chief Executive: UFC, 1991–93; PCFC, 1992–93; HEFCE, 1992–95. Visiting Professor: Brazil, 1976–77; Israel, 1978; Argentina, 1980; China, 1981; Hon. Professor: Zhejiang Univ., China, 1985; Yantai Univ., China, 1996. Mem., ACOST, 1991–93. Mem., Merseyside Enterprise Forum, 1986–90; Chm., Scottish Educn and Trng, 1996–. Guardian, Sheffield Assay Office, 1983–86; Member Council: Inst. Metals, 1981–86; Sheffield Metallurgical and Engineering Assoc., 1977–86 (Pres., 1984–85); ACU, 1987–91, 1998–; CVCP, 1996–. Trustee: Bluecoat Soc. of Arts, 1986–91; Museums and Galls on Merseyside, 1987–92; Iona Trust, 1995–; Carnegie Trust for the Univs of Scotland, 1995–; Scottish Science Trust, 1996–. Gov., Shrewsbury Sch., 1989–95. FRSA 1989; CIMgt (CBIM 1991). Freeman, City of London, 1987; Liveryman, Co. of Ironmongers, 1989 (Mem., Court, 1992–); Freeman and Burgess Holder, City of Glasgow, 1996. DL Merseyside, 1989–92. Hon. FTCL 1995; FRCPSGlas 1999. Hon. LLD: Liverpool, 1991; Strathclyde, 2000; Hon. DSc Nottingham, 1995; Hon. DMet Sheffield, 1995; Hon. DEng Manchester Metropolitan, 1996. Rosenhain Medal, Inst. of Metals, 1982. *Publications:* Solidification and Casting, 1973; Texture and Properties of Materials, 1976; Solidificacao e Fundicao das Metais e Suas Ligas, 1978; Hot Working and Forming Processes, 1980; Superplasticity, 1981; Essential Metallurgy for Engineers, 1985; papers to learned jls. *Recreations:* cricket, birdwatching, golf, The Times crossword. *Address:* The Principal's Lodging, The University, Glasgow G12 8QQ. *Club:* Athenæum.

DAVIES, Prof. Graham Arthur, PhD, DSc; FREng; Professor and Head of Chemical Engineering Department, University of Manchester Institute of Science and Technology, since 1989; *b* 2 July 1938; *s* of Evan Henry Davies and Esther Davies; *m* 1963, Christine; one *s* one *d*. *Educ:* Wolverhampton Grammar Sch.; Univ. of Birmingham (BSc 1st Cl. Hons; PhD 1963; DSc 1987). FREng (FEng 1995). R&D Div., Procter & Gamble Ltd, 1961–65; Lectr, 1965–69, Sen. Lectr, 1969–74, Reader, 1974–89, Chemical Engrg Dept, UMIST. *Publications:* Recent Advances in Liquid-Liquid Extraction, 1971; Hydrometallurgy, 1985; Science and Practice of Liquid Liquid Extraction, 1993. *Recreations:* golf, music. *Address:* Department of Chemical Engineering, University of Manchester Institute of Science and Technology, PO Box 88, Sackville Street, Manchester M60 1QD. *T:* (0161) 200 4342.

DAVIES, Prof. Graham Michael; Professor of Psychology, University of Leicester, since 1989; *b* 19 Feb. 1943; *s* of Harold Cecil Davies and Mona Florence Daisy Wisbey; *m* 1st, 1966, Heather Jane Neale; one *s* one *d*; 2nd, 1987, Noelle Robertson; two *d*. *Educ:* Bodmin Grammar Sch.; Univ. of Hull (BA, PhD, DSc). CPsychol, FBPsS. Lectr in Psychology, 1967–77, Sen. Lectr, 1977–87, Univ. of Aberdeen; Prof. of Psychology, NE London Poly., 1987–89. Chm., Soc. for Applied Res. in Memory and Cognition, 1998–99; Pres. elect, Eur. Assoc. for Psychology and Law. Founding Editor, Applied Cognitive Psychology, 1987. *Publications:* Perceiving and Remembering Faces, 1981; Identification Evidence: a psychological evaluation, 1982; Memory in Context, 1988; An evaluation of the live link for child witnesses (Home Office report), 1991; Memory in Everyday life, 1993; Psychology, Law and Criminal Justice: international developments in research and practice, 1995; Videotaping of children's evidence: an evaluation (Home Office report), 1995; Recovered Memories: seeking the middle ground, 2001. *Recreations:* reading, walking. *Address:* Department of Psychology, University of Leicester, University Road, Leicester LE1 7RH. *T:* (0116) 252 2178.

DAVIES, (Gwilym) E(dnyfed) Hudson; *see* Davies, Ednyfed H.

DAVIES, Handel, CB 1962; MSc; FREng; Hon. FRAeS; FAIAA; aeronautical engineering consultant; *b* 2 June 1912; *m* 1942, Mary Graham Harris. *Educ:* Aberdare Grammar Sch.; University of Wales. Royal Aircraft Establishment and Ministry of Aircraft Production, 1936–47; Head of Aerodynamics Flight Division, RAE, 1948–52. Chief Superintendent, Aeroplane and Armament Experimental Establishment, Boscombe Down, 1952–55; Scientific Adviser to Air Ministry, 1955–56; Director-General, Scientific Research (Air), Ministry of Supply, 1957–59; Dep. Director, RAE, Farnborough, 1959–63. Dep. Controller of Aircraft, (R&D), Ministry of Aviation, 1963–67, Ministry of Technology, 1967–69. Tech. Dir, British Aircraft Corp., 1969–77. Chm., Standing Conf. on Schools Sci. and Technology, 1978–82. Fellow, University Coll., Cardiff, 1981. Wilbur and Orville Wright Meml Lectr, 1979. Hon. FRAeS 1982 (FRAeS 1948; Pres., 1977–78; Gold Medal, 1974). *Publications:* papers in Reports and Memoranda of Aeronautical Research Council and in Journal of Royal Aeronautical Society. *Recreation:* sailing. *Address:* Keel Cottage, Woodham Road, Horsell, Woking, Surrey GU21 4DL. *T:* (01483) 714192. *Club:* Royal Air Force Yacht (Hamble).

DAVIES, Howard; *see* Davies, S. H.

DAVIES, (Sir) Howard (John), Kt 2000; Chairman, Financial Services Authority, since 1997; a Director, Bank of England, since 1998; *b* 12 Feb. 1951; *s* of late Leslie Powell Davies and of Marjorie Davies; *m* 1984, Prudence Mary Keely; two *s*. *Educ:* Manchester Grammar Sch.; Memorial Univ., Newfoundland; Merton Coll., Oxford (MA History and Mod. Langs); Stanford Graduate Sch. of Business, USA (MS Management Science). Foreign Office, 1973–74; Private Sec. to HM Ambassador, Paris, 1974–76; HM Treasury, 1976–82; McKinsey & Co. Inc., 1982–87 (Special Adviser to Chancellor of the Exchequer, 1985–86); Controller, Audit Commn, 1987–92; Dir Gen., CBI, 1992–95; Dep. Gov., Bank of England, 1995–97. Dir, GKN plc, 1990–95; Mem., NatWest Internat. Adv. Bd, 1992–95. Director: BOTB, 1992–95; BITC, 1992–95. Pres., Age Concern England, 1994–98. Governor, De Montfort Univ. (formerly Leicester Polytechnic), 1988–95. *Recreations:* cricket, children. *Address:* c/o Financial Services Authority, 25 The North Colonnade, Canary Wharf, E14 5HS. *Clubs:* Barnes Common Cricket; Manchester City Supporters.

DAVIES, Rt Rev. Howell Haydn; Bishop of Karamoja, Uganda, 1981–87; Vicar of St Jude's Parish, Wolverhampton, 1987–93, now retired; *b* 18 Sept. 1927; *s* of Ivor Thomas Davies and Sarah Gladys Davies (*née* Thomas); *m* 1958, Jean Wylam (*née* King); three *s* three *d*. *Educ:* Birmingham. DipArch (Birm.) 1954; ARIBA 1955. DipArch (Birm.) 1954; ARIBA 1955. Corporal Clerk (Gen. Duties) RAF, Mediterranean and Middle East, 1945–48. Assistant Architect, 1952–56. Deacon 1959, priest 1960; Curate, St Peter's Parish, Hereford, 1959–61; Missionary of Bible Churchmen's Missionary Soc., Kenya, 1961–79, Uganda, 1981–87; Archdeacon of Maseno North, 1971–74; Provost of Nairobi, 1974–79; Vicar of Woking, 1979–81. Buildings designed and completed in Kenya: Church Trng Centre, Kapsabet; Teachers' Coll. Chapel, Mosoriot; St Andrew's Parish Centre, Kapenguria; Cathedral Church of the Good Shepherd, Nakuru; three-storey admin block, bookshop and staff housing for Maseno N Dio., Kakamega; various church and mission staff housing in Kenya and Uganda. *Recreations:* walking, reading, d-i-y, building design. *Address:* 3 Gilberts Wood, Ewyas Harold, Hereford HR2 0JL. *T:* (01981) 240984.

DAVIES, Hugh Llewelyn, CMG 1994; HM Diplomatic Service, retired; Executive Director, Prudential Corporation Asia, since 1999; *b* 8 Nov. 1941; *s* of Vincent Davies (formerly ICS), OBE, and late Rose (*née* Temple); *m* 1968, Virginia Ann Lucius; one *d* one *s*. *Educ:* Rugby School; Churchill College, Cambridge (Hons History degree). HM Diplomatic Service, 1965–99: Chinese Language Studies, Hong Kong, 1966–68; Second Sec., Office of British Chargé d'Affaires, Peking, 1969–71; Far Eastern Dept, FCO, 1971–74; First Sec. (Econ.), Bonn, 1974–77; Head of Chancery, Singapore, 1977–79; Asst Head, Far Eastern Dept, FCO, 1979–82; on secondment, Barclays Bank International, 1982–83; Commercial Counsellor, Peking, 1984–87; Dep. British Permanent Rep., OECD, Paris, 1987–90; Hd, Far Eastern Dept, FCO, 1990–93; Sen. British Trade Comr, Hong Kong, June–Sept. 1993; British Sen. Rep., (Ambassador), Sino-British Jt Liaison Gp, Hong Kong, 1993–97; Special Enquiry on China Trade and Special Co-ordinator, China, Taiwan and Hong Kong, FCO, 1997–98. *Recreations:* watersports, sketching, tennis, gardens, walking. *Address:* Bentley Lodge, Dormans Park, East Grinstead, West Sussex RH19 2NB.
See also J. M. Davies.

DAVIES, Humphrey; *see* Davies, Morgan Wynn Humphrey.

DAVIES, Hunter; *see* Davies, E. H.

DAVIES, Huw; QC 2001; a Recorder, since 1998; *b* 25 Oct. 1955; *s* of Walter Stephen Davies and May Davies. *Educ:* UCW, Aberystwyth (LLB); Sidney Sussex Coll., Cambridge (MPhil). Called to the Bar, Gray's Inn, 1978; Asst Recorder, 1994–98; Standing Counsel to HM Customs and Excise, Wales and Chester Circuit, 1996-2001. *Recreations:* flying, motor-racing. *Address:* 30 Park Place, Cardiff CF10 3BS. *T:* (029) 2039 8421. *Club:* Goodwood Road Racing.

DAVIES, Huw Humphreys; Chief Executive Channel Television, since 2000; Chairman, Square Circle Productions Ltd, since 1996; *b* 4 Aug. 1940; *s* of William Davies and Harriet Jane Davies (*née* Humphreys); *m* 1966, Elizabeth Shân Harries; two *d*. *Educ:* Llangynog Primary School; Llandovery College; Pembroke College, Oxford. MA (Lit.Hum) 1964. Director/Producer: Television Wales and West, 1964; HTV, 1968; HTV Cymru/Wales: Asst Controller of Programmes, 1978; Controller of Programmes, 1979–81; Dir of Programmes, 1981–87; Chief Exec., 1987–91; Gp Dir of Television, HTV, 1989–94; Pres,, HTV Internat., 1994–96. Produced and directed many programmes and series in English and Welsh; latterly numerous plays and drama-documentaries. Chm., Regional Controllers, ITV, 1987–88. Dir, Winchester Entertainment (formerly Winchester Multimedia), 1996–. Mem., Gorsedd of Bards. *Recreations:* reading, swimming. *Address:* 27 Victoria Road, Penarth, S Glamorgan CF64 3HY. *T:* (029) 2071 2293.

DAVIES, Hywel; *see* Davies, D. H.

DAVIES, Lt-Col Hywel William; Chairman, Pentland Goup, since 2000; *b* 28 June 1945; *s* of late William Lewis Davies, JP and Barbara Beatrice Eleanor Davies, JP, MFH, Pantyderi, Boncath, Pembs; *m* 1969, Patricia, *d* of late Lt-Col E. B. Thornhill, MC; one *s* one *d*. *Educ:* Harrow; Magdalene Coll., Cambridge (MA). Commnd RHG (The Blues, later Blues & Royals), 1965; Staff Coll., 1977; Operational Requirements, MoD, 1978–80; Defence Intelligence, MoD, 1982–84; CO, Blues & Royals, 1985–87; with Pilkington Optronics, 1988–89; Chief Executive: RHASS, 1991–98; BHS, 1998–2000. Director: G. D. Golding & Son Ltd, 1988–; Challenger Consultancy Ltd, 1987–91; Ingliston Hotels Ltd, 1997–98; Scottish Farming and Educnl Trust, 1991–98; Scottish Agricl & Rural Develt Centre Ltd, 1992–98; The Countryside Movt, 1995–97; Ingliston Develt Trust, 1996–98; British Horse Soc. Trading Co. Ltd, 1998–2000. Mem., Countryside Cttee, Countryside Alliance, 1997–. Chairman: Assoc. of Show and Agricl Orgns, 1998–99 (Hon. Life Mem., 2000); Draught Horse Trng Cttee, 1998–2000; Central Region, Assoc. of Order of St John, 1998. ARAgS 1996. OStJ 1997. *Recreations:* equestrian pursuits (Mem., Coaching Club; represented UK at Four-in-Hand Carriage Driving, 1984–87), shooting, fishing, gardening. *Address:* Peatland, Gatehead, Ayrshire KA2 9AN. *T:* (01563) 851020. *Club:* Farmers'.

DAVIES, Ian; HM Diplomatic Service; Deputy Head of Mission, Peru, since May 2002; *b* 1 Aug. 1956; *s* of late John Davies and of Freda Mary Davies; *m* 1979, Purificación Bautista Hervias; two *d*. *Educ:* Queen Mary Coll., London (BSc Econs 1983); Birkbeck Coll., London (MSc Econs 1985). Joined FCO, 1976; Moscow, 1978–80; Protocol Dept, FCO, 1983–85; Paris, 1985–88; Moscow, 1988–90; Far Eastern Dept, FCO, 1990–93; Dep. Head of Mission, Bolivia, 1993–96; Consul Gen., Marseilles, 1997–2001. *Recreations:* walking, classical music, cinema, theatre. *Address:* c/o Foriegn and Commonwealth Office, King Charles Street, SW1A 2AH.

DAVIES, His Honour Ian Hewitt, TD; a Circuit Judge, 1986–2000; *b* 13 May 1931; *s* of late Rev. J. R. Davies; *m* 1962, Molly Cecilia Vaughan Vaughan. *Educ:* Kingswood Sch.; St John's Coll., Cambridge (MA). Nat. Service, commnd KOYLI; served with 3rd Bn Parachute Regt, 1950–51; TA, 1952–71 (Lt-Col). Called to the Bar, Inner Temple, 1958. *Clubs:* Boodle's, Royal Automobile, MCC, Hurlingham.

DAVIES, Ian Leonard, CB 1983; MA; CEng, FIEE; Director, Admiralty Underwater Weapons Establishment, 1975–84; *b* 2 June 1924; *s* of late H. Leonard Davies and Mrs J. D. Davies; *m* 1951, Hilary Dawson, *d* of late Rear-Adm. Sir Oswald Henry Dawson, KBE; two *s* two *d*. *Educ:* Barry County Sch.; St John's Coll., Cambridge. Mechanical Sciences Tripos, 1944, and Mathematical Tripos Pt 2, 1949. Telecommunications Research Estabt, 1944; Blind Landing Experimental Unit, 1946. TRE (later the Royal Radar Establishment), 1949–69; Imperial Defence Coll., 1970; Asst Chief Scientific Adviser (Projects), MoD, 1971–72; Dep. Controller Electronics, 1973, Dep. Controller Air Systems (D), 1973–75, MoD(PE). Tech. Advr, Monopolies and Mergers Commn, 1986. Mem. Council, IEE, 1974–77 (Chm., Electronics Div. Bd, 1975–76). *Publications:* papers on information theory, radar, and lasers. *Recreations:* music, walking. *Address:* 37 Bowleaze Coveway, Preston, Weymouth, Dorset DT3 6PL. *T:* (01305) 832206. *Club:* Athenæum.

DAVIES, Isobel Mary M.; *see* Macdonald-Davies.

DAVIES, Prof. (Ivor) Norman (Richard), CMG 2001; PhD; FBA 1997; Professor of Polish History, School of Slavonic and East European Studies, University of London, 1985–96, now Emeritus; Senior Research Associate, Oxford University, since 1997; Supernumerary Fellow, Wolfson College, Oxford, since 1998; *b* Bolton, 8 June 1939; *s* of Richard Davies and Elizabeth Bolton; *m* 1st, 1966, Maria Zielińska; one *s*; 2nd, 1984, Maria Korzeniewicz; one *s*. *Educ:* Bolton Sch.; Grenoble Univ.; Magdalen Coll., Oxford (MA); Sussex Univ. (MA); Jagiellonian Univ., Cracow (PhD). Asst Master, St Paul's Sch., London, 1963–65; Alistair Horne Res. Fellow, St Antony's Coll., Oxford, 1969–71; Lectr, 1971–84, Reader, 1984–85, SSEES, London Univ. Visiting Professor: Columbia Univ., 1974; McGill Univ., 1977–78; Hokkaido Univ., 1982–83; Stanford Univ., 1985–86; Harvard Univ., 1991. FRHistS 1974. Dr *hc* Marie Curie-Skłodowska Univ., Lublin, 1993; Univ. of Gdańsk, 2000. Hon. Citizen: Cracow, 1999; Lublin, 2000. Kt Cross, Order of Polonia Restituta (Poland), 1984; Commander Cross, 1992, Grand Cross, 1998, Order of Merit (Poland). *Publications:* White Eagle, Red Star: the Polish-Soviet war of 1919–20, 1972; Poland Past and Present: a bibliography of works in English on Polish history, 1976; God's Playground: a history of Poland, 2 vols, 1981; Heart of Europe: a short history of Poland, 1984; (ed with A. Polonsky) The Jews in Eastern Poland and the Soviet Union 1939–45, 1991; Europe: a history, 1996; The Isles: a history, 1999. *Recreation:* not writing. *Address:* Wolfson College, Oxford OX2 6UD.

DAVIES, Jacqueline, (Mrs P. N. R. Clark); Her Honour Judge Jacqueline Davies; a Circuit Judge, since 1993; *b* 21 May 1948; one *d*; *m* 1997, Paul Nicholas Rowntree Clark, *qv*. *Educ:* Manchester High Sch. for Girls; Univ. of Leeds (LLB Hons). Called to the Bar, Middle Temple, 1975; a Recorder, 1991–93. *Address:* Doncaster Crown Court, College Way, Doncaster DN1 3HS.

DAVIES, (James) Brian Meredith, MD, DPH, FFPHM; Director of Social Services, City of Liverpool, 1971–81; *b* 27 Jan. 1920; *s* of late Dr G. Meredith Davies and Caroline Meredith Davies; *m* 1944, Charlotte (*née* Pillar); three *s*. *Educ:* Bedford Sch.; Medical Sch., St Mary's Hosp., London Univ. MB, BS (London) 1943, MD (London) 1948; DPH 1948; FFPHM (MFCM 1972, FFCM 1974). Various hosp. appts. Served War, RAMC, Captain, 1944–47. Asst MOH, Lancashire CC, 1948–50; Dep. MOH, City of Oxford, 1950–53; Clin. Asst (infectious Diseases), United Oxford Hosps, 1950–53; Dep. MOH, 1953–69, Dir of Personal Health and Social Services, 1969–71, City of Liverpool; pt-time Lectr in Public Health, 1953–71, and Hon. Lectr in Preventive Paediatrics, 1964–85, Liverpool Univ. Chm., Liverpool div., BMA, 1958–59; Council of Europe Fellowship, to study Elderly: in Finland, Sweden, Norway and Denmark, 1964 (report awarded special prize); Mem. Public Health Laboratory Service Bd, 1966–71. Teaching Gp of Soc. of Community Med. (Sec. of Gp, 1958–72, Pres. Gp, 1972–73). Member: Personal Social Services Council, 1978–80; Mental Health Review Tribunal, Mersey Area, 1982–. Governor, Occupational Therapy Coll., Huyton, Liverpool, 1969–85; Dir of MERIT (Merseyside Industrial Therapy Services Ltd), 1970–75; Mem. Council, Queen's Inst. of District Nursing, 1971–78; Assoc. of Dirs of Social Services: Chm., NW Br., 1971–73; Mem. Exec. Council, 1973–78; Pres. 1976–77; Mem. Exec. Cttee of Central Council for the Disabled, 1972–76; Adviser to Social Services Cttee of Assoc. of Metropolitan Authorities, 1974–81; Member: RCP Cttee on Rheumatism and Rehabilitation, 1974–83; DES Cttee of Enquiry into Special Educn for Disabled Children, 1975–78; Exec. Cttee, Liverpool Personal Services Soc., 1973–81; Adv. Panel Inf. Service, Disabled Living Foundn, 1979–81; UK Steering Cttee, Internat. Year for the Disabled, 1979–80; Jt Cttee on Mobility of Blind and Partially Sighted People, 1980–81; Exec. Cttee, N Regional Assoc. for the Blind, 1980–81. Vice Pres., MIND Appeal, 1978–79. Christopher Kershaw Meml Lectr, London, 1984. Pres., Merseyside Ski Club, 1970–77. Mem. Council, Prospect Hall Coll., 1973–77; Chm., Bd of Governors, William Rathbone Staff Coll., Liverpool, 1961–75. Duncan Medal, 1998 (for services to public health in Liverpool, 1953–71). *Publications:* Community Health and Social Services, 1965, 6th edn as Public Health, Preventive Medicine and Social Services, 1995; Community Health, Preventive Medicine and Social Services, 1966, 6th edn 1993; (contrib.) Going Home (a Guide for helping the patient on leaving hospital), 1981; The Disabled Child and Adult, 1982; (contrib.) Rehabilitation: a practical guide to the management of physical disability in adults, 1988; numerous papers on Public Health, Physically and Mentally Handicapped and various social services, in scientific and other jls. *Recreations:* skiing, golf, fishing, gardening, music. *Address:* Tree Tops, Church Road, Thornton Hough, Wirral, Merseyside L63 1JN. *T:* (0151) 336 3435. *Club:* Bromborough Golf.

DAVIES, Janet; Member (Plaid Cymru) South West Wales, National Assembly for Wales, since 1999; *b* 29 May 1938; *d* of late David Rees and Jean Wardlaw Rees; *m* 1965, Basil Peter Ridley Davies (*d* 2000); one *s* one *d*. *Educ:* Howell's Sch., Llandaff; Trinity Coll., Carmarthen (BA); Open Univ. (BA Hons Social Scis). Mem. (Plaid Cymru) Taff Ely BC, 1983–96 (Leader, 1991–96); Mayor, Taff Ely, 1995–96. Plaid Cymru Local Govt spokesperson, 1993–99, Housing spokesperson, 1999–. Dir of Elections, Plaid Cymru, 1996–. *Address:* National Assembly for Wales, Cardiff Bay, Cardiff CF99 1NA. *T:* (029) 2089 8289.

DAVIES, Janet Mary H.; *see* Hewlett-Davies.

DAVIES, Jocelyn Ann; Member (Plaid Cymru) SE Wales, National Assembly for Wales, since 1999; *b* 18 June 1959; *d* of Edward and Marjorie Davies; one *s* two *d* by Michael Davies. *Educ:* Harris Manchester Coll., Oxford. Work in local govt, Islwyn BC and Newport BC, 1976–80. Mem. (Plaid Cymru) Islwyn BC, 1987–91. *Recreations:* gym workout, people watching. *Address:* 3 Meredith Terrace, Newbridge, Gwent NP11 4FN. *T:* (01495) 240324; (constituency) *T:* (01633) 220022, *Fax:* (01633) 220603.

DAVIES, John; *see* Davies, L. J.

DAVIES, Prof. John Brian, FREng; Professor of Electrical Engineering, University College London, 1985–97, now Emeritus Professor; *b* 2 May 1932; *s* of John Kendrick Davies and Agnes Ada Davies; *m* 1956, Shirley June (*née* Abrahart); one *s* two *d*. *Educ:* Jesus Coll., Cambridge (MA); Univ. of London (MSc, PhD, DSc Eng). Research Engineer, Mullard Res. Labs, Redhill, 1955–63; Lectr, Dept of Electrical Engineering, Univ. of Sheffield, 1963; Sen. Lectr 1967, Reader 1970–85, Dean of Engrg, 1989–91, University College London. Vis. Scientist, Nat. Bureau of Standards, Boulder, Colo, 1971–72; Visitor, Univ. of Oxford, 1983; Vis. Prof., Univ. of Colorado, 1988–89. FREng (FEng 1988). *Publications:* Electromagnetic Theory, vol. 2, 1972; (contrib.) Numerical Techniques for Microwave and Millimeter Wave Passive Structures, 1989. *Recreations:* fell walking, music, ski-ing. *Address:* 14 Gaveston Drive, Berkhamsted, Herts HP4 1JE. *T:* (01442) 864954.

DAVIES, Very Rev. John David Edward; Dean of Brecon, since 2000; *b* 6 Feb. 1953; *s* of William Howell Davies and Doiran Rallison Davies; *m* 1986, Joanna Lucy Davies (*née* Aulton); one *s* one *d*. *Educ:* Southampton Univ. (LLB 1974); Coll. of Law; St Michael's Coll., Llandaff (DipTh Wales 1984); Univ. of Wales (LLM Canon Law 1995). Admitted Solicitor, 1977; private practice, 1975–82. Ordained deacon, 1984, priest, 1985; Asst Curate, Chepstow, 1984–86; Curate-in-charge, Michaelston-y-Fedw and Rudry, 1986–89; Rector, Bedwas and Rudry, 1989–95; Vicar, St John Evangelist, Newport, 1995–2000. *Recreations:* music (mainly classical), playing the organ, theatre, reading, current affairs, sport (especially Test Match Special and Peter Alliss), planning walks for the family (and accompanying them when feeling energetic), entertaining my family by trying to convince them of the inestimable benefits of knowing Latin and of appreciating other lost glories of the past. *Address:* The Deanery, The Cathedral Close, Brecon, Powys LD3 9DP. *T:* (01874) 623344, (office) (01874) 623857.

DAVIES, Rt Rev. John Dudley; Assistant Bishop, diocese of Lichfield, since 1995; Bishop Suffragan of Shrewsbury, 1987–94; *b* 12 Aug. 1927; *s* of Charles Edward Steedman Davies and Minnie Paton Davies; *m* 1956, Shirley Dorothy Gough; one *s* two *d*. *Educ:* Trinity Coll., Cambridge (BA 1951, MA 1963); Lincoln Theol Coll. Deacon 1953, priest 1954, dio. Ripon; Curate: Halton, Leeds, 1953–56; Yeoville, Johannesburg, 1957; Priest-in-Charge, Evander, dio. Johannesburg, 1957–61; Rector and Dir of Missions, Empangeni, dio. Zululand and Swaziland, 1961–63; Anglican Chaplain, Univ. of Witwatersrand and Johannesburg Coll. of Educn, 1963–70; Chm., Div. of Christian Educn, S African Council of Churches, 1964–70; Mem. Exec., Univ. Christian Movement of Southern Africa, 1966–69; Sec. for Chaplaincies of Higher Educn, C of E Bd of Educn, 1970–74; Vicar of Keele and Chaplain, Univ. of Keele, 1974–76; Principal, Coll. of Ascension, Selly Oak, 1976–81; Preb. of Sandiacre, Lichfield Cathedral, 1976–87; Diocesan Missioner, St Asaph, 1982–87; Canon Res. and Hellins Lectr, St Asaph, 1982–85; Vicar/Rector, Llanrhaeadr-ym-Mochnant, Llanarmon-Mynydd-Mawr, Pennant, Hirnant and Llangynog, 1985–87. *Publications:* Free to Be, 1970; Beginning Now, 1971; Good News in Galatians, 1975; Creed and Conflict, 1979; The Faith Abroad, 1983; (with John J. Vincent) Mark at Work, 1986; World on Loan, 1992; The Crisis of the Cross, 1997; Be Born in us Today, 1999; God at Work, 2001; contribs to jls. *Address:* Nyddfa, By Pass Road, Gobowen, Oswestry SY11 3NG. *T:* (01691) 653434.

DAVIES, John Duncan, OBE 1984; DSc, PhD; Director, Polytechnic of Wales, 1978–92, then University of Glamorgan, Jan.–Oct. 1992, now Emeritus Professor; *b* 19 March 1929; *s* of Ioan and Gertrude Davies; *m* 1949, Barbara, *d* of Ivor and Alice Morgan; three *d*. *Educ:* Pontardawe School; Treforest School of Mines. BSc, MSc, PhD, DSc, Univ. of London. Junior Engineer, Consulting Engineers, 1949; Site Engineer, Cleveland Bridge Co., 1950–54; Royal Engineers, 1952–53; Design Engineer, Local Authority, 1955–56; Asst Lectr, Manchester Univ., 1957–58; University College, Swansea: Lecturer, 1959; Senior Lecturer, 1965; Reader, 1968; Professor of Civil Engineering, 1971–76; Dean, 1974–76; Principal, West Glamorgan Inst. of Higher Education, 1976–77. Member: Open University Delegacy, 1978–83; OU Cttee, 1987–90; Manpower Services Cttee (Wales), 1980–83; Wales Adv. Bd for Public Sector Higher Educn, 1982–83, 1986–89; Council, CNAA, 1985–93; Chm., Coleg Powys Corp., 1994–98. Hon. Fellow, Univ. of Wales, 1996. Hon. DTech Glamorgan, 1995. *Publications:* contribs to Structural Mechanics. *Address:* Beech House, Dehewydd Lane, Llantwit Fardre, Mid Glam CF38 2EN.

DAVIES, John Hamilton; Chairman, Civil Service Appeal Board, since 1998; Member, Armed Forces Pay Review Body, since 1998; *b* 24 Nov. 1943; *s* of Albert Victor Davies and Betty Davies; *m* 1971, Helen Ruth Thomas; three *s*. *Educ:* Lewis Sch., Pengam, S Wales; Selwyn Coll., Cambridge (MA). ACIB 1970, FCIB 1991; FCIPD (FIPD 1991). With Barclays Bank, 1966–98: Local Dir, Chelmsford Reg., 1983–86; Hd, Career Planning, Gp Personnel, 1986–90; Dep. Dir, Gp Personnel, 1991–95; Dir, Personnel, Barclays UK Banking Services, 1995–98. Non-executive Director: Birchin Internat. plc, 1999–2000; Time2Learn plc, 2000–. Vis. Fellow, Cranfield Univ. Sch. of Mgt, 1998–. Board Member: Employers' Forum on Disability, 1991–96; BESO, 1991–98; Mem., CBI Employment Policy Cttee, 1996–98. Treas. and Mem., Exec. Bd, CIB, 1998–99. Gov., Felsted Sch., 1990–95 and 1998–. Trustee, Farleigh Hospice, Chelmsford, 2000–. *Recreations:* walking, Church of England, music, travel. *Address:* Denbies, Bardfield Saling, Essex CM7 5EG. *T:* (01371) 850735. *Clubs:* Oxford and Cambridge; Essex.

DAVIES, Rev. Canon John Howard; Director of Theological and Religious Studies, University of Southampton, 1981–94; *b* 19 Feb. 1929; *s* of Jabez Howard and Sarah Violet Davies; *m* 1956, Ina Mary (*d* 1985), *d* of Stanley William and Olive Mary Bubb; two *s* (and two *s* decd). *Educ:* Southall Grammar Sch.; St John's Coll., Cambridge (MA); Westcott House, Cambridge; Univ. of Nottingham (BD); FRCO 1952. Ordained deacon, 1955, priest 1956. Succentor of Derby Cathedral, 1955; Chaplain of Westcott House, 1958; Lectr in Theology, Univ. of Southampton, 1963, Sen. Lectr 1974. Canon Theologian of Winchester, 1981–91. *Publication:* A Letter to Hebrews, 1967. *Recreations:* music, architecture, the countryside. *Address:* 13 Glen Eyre Road, Southampton SO16 3GA. *T:* (023) 8067 9359.

DAVIES, John Irfon, CBE 1998 (MBE (mil.) 1963); Under Secretary, Welsh Office, 1985–90, retired; Chairman, Health Promotion Authority for Wales, 1992–99; *b* 8 June 1930; *s* of late Thomas M. Davies and Mary M. Davies (*née* Harris); *m* 1950, Jean Marion Anderson (*d* 2000); one *d*. *Educ:* Stanley School; Croydon Polytechnic. psc, awc; Specialist Navigator course. Joined RAF, 1948, commissioned 1950; MoD, 1964–66; Chief Navigation Instructor, Cranwell, 1967; OC Flying, Muharraq, 1967–69; MoD, 1970–72; Cabinet Office, 1972–74; retd from RAF, 1974; Principal, Welsh Office, 1974, Asst Sec., 1978. Mem., GMC, 1990–99. *Recreations:* golf, piano, fishing, books. *Address:* Friston, 15 Windsor Road, Radyr, Cardiff CF4 8BQ. *Clubs:* Royal Air Force; Cardiff and County; Radyr Golf.

DAVIES, Prof. John Kenyon, MA, DPhil; FSA; FBA 1985; Rathbone Professor of Ancient History and Classical Archaeology, University of Liverpool, since 1977; *b* 19 Sept. 1937; *s* of Harold Edward Davies and Clarice Theresa (*née* Woodburn); *m* 1st, 1962, Anna Elbina Morpurgo (*see* Anna Elbina Davies) (marr. diss. 1978); 2nd, 1978, Nicola Jane, *d* of Dr and Mrs R. M. S. Perrin; one *s* one *d*. *Educ:* Manchester Grammar Sch.; Wadham Coll., Oxford (BA 1959; MA 1962; DPhil 1966). FSA 1986. Harmsworth Sen. Scholar, Merton Coll., Oxford, 1960–61 and 1962–63; Jun. Fellow, Center for Hellenic Studies, Washington, DC, 1961–62; Dyson Jun. Res. Fellow, Balliol Coll., Oxford, 1963–65; Lectr in Ancient History, Univ. of St Andrews, 1965–68; Fellow and Tutor in Ancient History, Oriel Coll., Oxford, 1968–77; Pro-Vice-Chancellor, Univ. of Liverpool, 1986–90. Leverhulme Res. Prof., 1995–2000. Vis. Lectr, Univ. of Pennsylvania, 1971. Chairman: St Patrick's Isle (IOM) Archaeological Trust Ltd, 1982–86; NW Archaeol Trust, 1982–91. FRSA. Editor: Jl of Hellenic Studies, 1972–77; Archaeol Reports, 1972–74. *Publications:* Athenian Propertied Families 600–300 BC, 1971; Democracy and Classical Greece, 1978, 2nd edn 1993 (Spanish trans. 1981, German and Italian trans. 1983); Wealth and the Power of Wealth in Classical Athens, 1981; (ed with L. Foxhall) The Trojan War: its historicity and context, 1984; articles and reviews in learned jls. *Recreation:* choral singing. *Address:* 20 North Road, Grassendale Park, Liverpool L19 0LR. *T:* (0151) 427 2126.

DAVIES, John Michael; Clerk of the Parliaments, House of Lords, since 1997; *b* 2 Aug. 1940; *s* of Vincent Ellis Davies and late Rose Trench (*née* Temple); *m* 1971, Amanda Mary Atkinson; two *s* one *d*. *Educ:* The King's Sch., Canterbury; Peterhouse, Cambridge. Joined Parliament Office, House of Lords, 1964; seconded to Civil Service Dept as Private Sec. to Leader of House of Lords and Govt Chief Whip, 1971–74; Establishment Officer and Sec. to Chm. of Cttees, 1974–83; Principal Clerk, Overseas and European Office, 1983–85; Principal Clerk, Private Bill and Overseas Offices and Examiner of Petitions for Private Bills, 1985–88; Reading Clerk, 1988–90, and Clerk of Public Bills, 1988–94; Clerk Asst, 1991–97, and Principal Finance Officer, 1994–97. Secretary: Soc. of Clerks-at-the-Table in Commonwealth Parlts, and Jt Editor, The Table, 1967–83; Statute Law Cttee, 1974–83. Pres., Assoc. of Secs-General of Parlts, 1997–2000 (Mem. Exec. Cttee, 1995–). *Address:* 26 Northchurch Terrace, N1 4EG.

See also H. L. Davies.

DAVIES, (John) Quentin; MP (C) Grantham and Stamford, since 1997 (Stamford and Spalding, 1987–97); *b* 29 May 1944; *e s* of Dr Michael Ivor Davies and Thelma Davies (*née* Butler), Oxford; *m* 1983, Chantal, *e d* of Lt-Col R. L. C. Tamplin, 17/21 Lancers, Military Kt of Windsor, and Claudine Tamplin (*née* Pleis); two *s*. *Educ:* Dragon Sch.; Leighton Park (exhibnr); Gonville and Caius Coll., Cambridge (Open Scholar; BA Hist. Tripos 1st cl. Hons 1966); Harvard Univ. (Frank Know Fellow, 1966–67). HM Diplomatic Service, 1967; 3rd Sec., FCO, 1967–69; 2nd Sec., Moscow, 1969–72; 1st Sec., FCO, 1973–74. Morgan Grenfell & Co.: Manager, later Asst Dir, 1974–78; Rep. in France, later Dir-Gen. and Pres., Morgan Grenfell France SA, 1978–81; Director, and Hd of Eur. Corporate Finance, 1981–87; Consultant, 1987–93. Director: Dewe Rogerson International, 1987–95; SGE, 1999–; Adviser: NatWest Securities, then NatWest Markets, 1993–99; Bank of Scotland, 1999–. Parly Advr, Chartered Inst. of Taxation, 1993–. Contested (C) Birmingham, Ladywood, Aug. 1977. Parliamentary Private Secretary: to Minister of State for Educn, 1988–90; to Minister of State, Home Office, 1990–91; Opposition spokesman on social security and pensions, 1998–99; Shadow Paymaster-Gen., 1999–2000; Opposition spokesman on defence, 2000–01; Shadow NI Sec., 2001–. Member: Treasury Select Cttee, 1992–98; Cttee on Standards and Privileges, 1995–98; Eur. Standing Cttee, 1991–97; Eur. Legislation Cttee, 1997–98; Jt Chm., Anglo-German Parly Gp, 1997–; Vice Chairman: Anglo-French Parly Gp, 1997–; British-Netherlands Parly Gp, 1999–. Chm., City in Europe Cttee, 1975. Liveryman, Goldsmiths' Co. Freeman, City of London. Freedom of Information Award, 1996; Guardian Backbencher of the Year Award, 1996; Spectator Parliamentarian of the Year Award, 1997. *Publication:* Britain and Europe: a Conservative view, 1996. *Recreations:* reading, walking, riding, ski-ing, travel, playing bad tennis, looking at art and architecture. *Address:* House of Commons, SW1A 0AA. *Clubs:* Brooks's, Beefsteak, Travellers; Grantham Conservative (Grantham).

DAVIES, Rt Rev. John Stewart; *see* St Asaph, Bishop of.

DAVIES, John Thomas, FCIB; Director, 1990–98, a Deputy Chairman, 1995–98, Lloyds Bank plc; a Deputy Chairman, Lloyds TSB Group plc, 1995–98; *b* 9 Feb. 1933; *s* of Joseph Robert and Dorothy Mary Davies; *m* 1957, Margaret Ann Johnson; two *s* three *d*. *Educ:* King Edward's Grammar Sch., Camp Hill, Birmingham. FCIB. Joined Lloyds Bank, 1949; served RAF, 1951–53; Lloyds Bank: Manager of branches, 1963–78; Gen. Management, 1978–89; Dir, Internat. Banking Div., 1989–91; Asst Chief Exec., 1991–92; Dep. Chief Exec., 1992–94. Director: Nat. Bank of NZ, 1989–90 and 1995–98; Cheltenham & Gloucester Building Society, 1995–98; Dir, 1995–98, Chm., 1997–98, Lloyds Abbey Life, later Lloyds TSB Financial Hldgs plc. Chm. Bd, Office of the Banking Ombudsman, 1995–. *Recreations:* opera, gardening, walking, reading. *Address:* c/o Lloyds TSB Group plc, 71 Lombard Street, EC3P 3BS.

DAVIES, Jonathan, MBE 1995; writer and commentator on Rugby Union and League football; *b* 24 Oct. 1962; *s* of Len and Diana Davies; *m* 1984, Karen Hopkins (*d* 1997); two *s* one *d*. *Educ:* Gwendraeth Grammar Sch. Rugby Union footballer to 1989; played for Neath and Llanelli; 28 Wales caps, 4 as Captain; transferred to Rugby League, 1989; with Widnes, 1989–93, Warrington, 1993–95; returned to Rugby Union, 1995; with Cardiff, 1995–97, retired. Player of the Year Award, 1991, 1994; Stones Bitter Man of Steel, 1994. *Publication:* Jonathan (autobiog.), 1989. *Recreations:* golf, football. *Address:* c/o Cardiff RUFC, Cardiff Arms Park, Cardiff CF1 1JL.

DAVIES, His Honour Joseph Marie, QC 1962; a Circuit Judge (formerly Judge of County Courts), 1971–91; *b* 13 Jan. 1916; *s* of Joseph and Mary Davies, St Helen's; *m* 1948, Eileen Mary (*née* Dromgoole); two *s* two *d*. *Educ:* Stonyhurst Coll.; Liverpool Univ. Called to Bar, Gray's Inn, Nov. 1938; practice in Liverpool. Recorder of Birmingham, 1970–71; Cumberland Co. QS: Dep. Chm., 1956–63, 1970–71; Chm., 1963–70. Served

War of 1939–45; The King's Regt, Nov. 1939–Dec. 1941; RIASC and Staff Allied Land Forces, SE Asia, 1942–46. *Address:* 4 Elm Grove, Eccleston Park, Prescot, Lancs L34 2RX. *T:* (0151) 426 5415.

DAVIES, Prof. Julian Edmund, PhD; FRS 1994; FRSC 1996; Executive Vice-President for Technology Development, Cubist Pharmaceuticals (Vancouver), since 2000; *b* 9 Jan. 1932; *s* of Norman Alfred Davies and Lilian Constance (*née* Clarke); *m* 1957, Dorothy Jean Olney; two *s* one *d. Educ:* Univ. of Nottingham (BSc Hons Chem., Maths and Phys.; PhD 1956). Lectr in Chem., Univ. of Manchester, 1959–62; Associate in Bacteriol., Harvard Univ., 1962–67; University of Wisconsin: Associate Prof. of Biochem., 1967–70; Prof., 1970–80; Biogen: Res. Dir, 1980–83; Pres., 1983–85; Prof., Inst. Pasteur, Paris, 1986–91; University of British Columbia: apptd Prof. and Hd of Dept of Microbiol. and Immunol., 1992, Prof. Emeritus, 1997; Dir, West-East Center, 1993–96; Chief Scientific Officer, and Vice-Pres. of Res., TerraGen Diversity Inc., 1996. Pres., Amer. Soc. for Microbiol., 1999–2000. Hoechst-Roussel Award, Amer. Soc. for Microbiol., 1986; Thom Award, Soc. for Industrial Microbiol., 1993; Scheele Prize, Swedish Acad. of Pharmaceutical Scis, 1997; Bristol Myers Squibb Award, 1999. *Publications:* Elementary Biochemistry, 1980; Milestones in Biotechnology, 1992. *Recreations:* cycling, ski-ing, squash, wine. *Address:* 4428 West 6th Avenue, Vancouver, BC V6R 1Z3, Canada. *T:* (604) 2228235.

DAVIES, Karl; *see* Davies, R. K.

DAVIES, Prof. Kay Elizabeth, CBE 1995; DPhil; FMedSci; Dr Lee's Professor of Anatomy, and Fellow of Hertford College, Oxford University, since 1998; *b* 1 April 1951; *d* of Harry Partridge and Florence Partridge (*née* Farmer); *m* 1973, Stephen Graham Davies (marr. diss. 2000); one *s. Educ:* Stourbridge Girl's High Sch.; Somerville Coll., Oxford (BA, MA; DPhil; Hon. Fellow, 1995). MRCPath 1990, FRCPath 1997. Guy Newton Jun. Res. Fellow, Wolfson Coll., Oxford, 1976–78; Royal Soc. European Post-doctoral Fellow, Service de Biochimie, Centre d'Etudes, Gif-sur-Yvette, France, 1978–80; St Mary's Hospital Medical School: Cystic Fibrosis Res. Fellow, 1980–82; MRC Sen. Res. Fellow, 1982–84; Nuffield Department of Clinical Medicine, John Radcliffe Hospital, Oxford: MRC Sen. Res. Fellow, 1984–86; MRC Ext. Staff, 1986–92; Univ. Res. Lectr, 1990; MRC Ext. Staff, Inst. of Molecular Medicine, Oxford, 1989–95; Fellow of Green Coll., Oxford, 1990–95; MRC Res. Dir, MRC Clin. Scis Centre, Hammersmith Hosp., 1992–94; Prof. of Genetics, and Fellow, Keble Coll., Oxford Univ., 1995–98. Editor (with S. Tilghman), Genome Analysis Reviews, 1990–. Bristol-Myers Prof., USA, 1986; 7th Annual Colleen Giblin Dist. Lectr, Columbia Univ., 1992; Dist. Lectr, Mayo Clinic, USA, 1994. Founder FMedSci 1998. Hon. FRCP 1994. Hon. DSc Victoria, Canada, 1990; DUniv Open, 1999. Wellcome Trust Award, 1996; SCI Medal, 1999. *Publications:* (with A. P. Read) Molecular Analysis of Inherited Diseases, 1988, rev. edn 1992; (ed) Human Genetics Diseases: a practical approach, 1988, rev. edn 1993; (ed) Genome Analysis: a practical approach, 1988; (ed) The Fragile X Syndrome, 1989; (ed) Application of Molecular Genetics to the Diagnosis of Inherited Diseases, 1989; numerous reviews and 250 peer-reviewed pubns. *Recreations:* sport, music, gardening. *Address:* Department of Human Anatomy and Genetics, University of Oxford, South Parks Road, Oxford OX1 3QX.

DAVIES, Keith Laurence M.; *see* Maitland Davies.

DAVIES, Sir Lancelot Richard B.; *see* Bell Davies.

DAVIES, Laura Jane, CBE 2000 (MBE 1988); professional golfer; *b* 5 Oct. 1963; *d* of David Thomas Davies and Rita Ann Davies (*née* Foskett). *Educ:* Fullbrook County Secondary Sch. Mem., Curtis Cup team, 1984; professional début, 1985; Mem., Solheim Cup team, 1990, 1992; Winner: Belgian Ladies' Open, 1985; Ladies' British Open, 1986; US Ladies' Open, 1987; Italian Open, 1987, 1988, 1996; Ford Classic, Woburn, 1988; Biarritz Ladies' Open, 1988; Itoki Classic, Japan, 1988; European Open, 1992; Thailand Ladies' Open, 1993, 1994; English Open, 1993, 1995; Australian Ladies' Masters, 1993, 1994; LPGA Championship, 1994, 1996; Irish Open, 1994, 1995; Scottish Open, 1994; French Masters, 1995; Danish Open, 1997; Championship of Europe, 1999. Mem., Golf Foundn. *Publication:* Carefree Golf, 1991. *Address:* c/o Women's Professional Golf European Tour, The Tytherington Club, Dorchester Way, Tytherington, Macclesfield SK10 2JP.

DAVIES, Leighton; *see* Davies, R. L.

DAVIES, His Honour (Lewis) John; QC 1967; a Circuit Judge (Official Referee), 1984–93; *b* 15 April 1921; *s* of William Davies, JP, and Esther Davies; *m* 1956, Janet Mary Morris; one *s* two *d. Educ:* Pontardawe Grammar Sch.; University College of Wales, Aberystwyth; Trinity Hall (Common Law Prizeman, 1943; Scholar, 1943–44), Cambridge. LLB Wales 1942 (1st cl.); BA Cantab (1st cl.); LLB Cantab (1st cl.). Asst Principal, HM Treasury, 1945–46; Senior Law Lecturer, Leeds Univ., 1946–48; Administrative Asst, British Petroleum, 1949–52. Called to the Bar, Middle Temple, 1948, Bencher, 1973 (Emeritus, 1993); a Recorder, 1974–84. Mem., Bar Council, 1969–71; Mem., Senate, 1976–78. Mem., Council of Legal Educn, 1976–79. Inspector, DoT, 1977. Mem., Gorsedd, 1986–. *Recreations:* gardening, golf. *Address:* Old Manor Cottage, 24 Park Road, Teddington, Mddx TW11 0AQ. *T:* (020) 8977 3975. *Club:* Travellers.
See also W. R. Davies.

DAVIES, Lewis Mervyn, CMG 1966; CBE 1984 (OBE 1962); HM Overseas Civil Service, retired; *b* 5 Dec. 1922; *s* of late Rev. Canon L. C. Davies; *m* 1st, 1950, Ione Podger (*d* 1973); one *s*; 2nd, 1975, Mona A. Birley; two step *s. Educ:* St Edward's Sch., Oxford. Served with Fleet Air Arm, 1941–46: Lieut A, RNVR. District Commissioner, Gold Coast, 1948; Western Pacific: Senior Asst Secretary, 1956–62; Financial Secretary, 1962–65; Chief Secretary, 1965–70; Deputy Governor, Bahamas, 1970–73; Secretary for Security, Hong Kong, 1973–82; Secretary (Gen. Duties), Hong Kong, 1983–85. Lay Canon, Cathedral Church of St Barnabas, Honiara, Solomon Islands, 1965–70. Commandeur de l'Ordre National du Mérite, 1966. *Address:* Carrer Cals Julians 16, 07141 Sa Cabineta-Marratxi, Mallorca, Spain. *T:* and *Fax:* (971) 602519. *Club:* Oriental.

DAVIES, Linda Hillary; Her Honour Judge Linda Davies; a Circuit Judge, since 1992; *b* 31 May 1945; *d* of Lt-Col Robert Blowers and Doris Rhoda (*née* Hillary); *m* 1966, Michael Llewelyn Lifton Davies; two *d. Educ:* Folkestone Grammar Sch. for Girls; King's Coll., London (LLB Hons). Called to the Bar, Gray's Inn, 1969; Barrister, 1972–92, a Recorder, 1990–92, Western Circuit. Part-time Chm., Industrial Tribunals, 1986–92.

DAVIES, Dr Lindsey Margaret, FFPHM; Regional Director of Public Health and Regional Medical Director, Trent Regional Office, NHS Executive, since 1996 (Director of Public Health, Trent Regional Health Authority, 1994–96); *b* 21 May 1953; *d* of Dr Frank Newby and Margaret Newby; *m* 1974, Peter Davies (marr. diss. 1994); two *s. Educ:* Univ. of Nottingham (BM, BS). MHSM 1987; FFPHM 1991. Community paediatrics, 1976–82; trainee in public health medicine, 1982–85; Director of Public Health: Southern Derbys HA, 1985–89; Nottingham HA, 1989–92; Hd, Public Health Div., NHS Exec., DoH, 1992–94. Special Lectr, Nottingham Univ. Med. Sch., 1991–. British Medical Association: Mem. Council, 1989–92; Chm., Cttee for Public Health Medicine and Community Health, 1990–92. *Publications:* contribs to learned jls. *Recreations:* family life, enjoying modern architecture. *Address:* NHS Executive—Trent, Fulwood House, Old Fulwood Road, Sheffield S10 3TH. *T:* (0114) 282 0303.

DAVIES, Ven. Lorys Martin; Archdeacon of Bolton, 1992–2001; *b* 14 June 1936; *s* of Evan Tudor Davies and Eigen Morfydd Davies; *m* 1960, Barbara Ethel (*née* Walkley); two *s. Educ:* Whitland Grammar Sch.; St David's Coll., Lampeter, Univ. of Wales (BA Hons); Philips Hist. Schol.; Organ Exhibnr. Wells Theol Coll. ALCM 1952. Ordained: deacon, 1959; priest, 1960; Curate, St Mary's, Tenby, 1959–61; Asst Chaplain, Brentwood Sch., 1962–66; Chaplain and Head of Dept, Solihull Sch., 1966–68; Vicar, St Mary's, Moseley, 1968–81; Residentiary Canon, Birmingham Cathedral, 1981–92; Diocesan Dir of Ordinands, Birmingham, 1982–90; Advr to Bishop of Manchester on Hosp. Chaplaincies, 1992–2001, Warden of Readers, 1994–2001, dio. of Manchester. Chm., House of Clergy, Birmingham Diocesan Synod, 1990–91; Proctor in Convocation, 1998–2001. JP Birmingham, 1978–92. *Recreations:* sport, theatre, music, reading. *Address:* Heolcerrig, 28 Penshurst Road, Bromsgrove, Worcestershire B60 2SN.

DAVIES, Marcus John A.; *see* Anwyl-Davies.

DAVIES, Mark Edward Trehearne; Chairman, Thornhill Holdings Ltd, since 2001; *b* 20 May 1948; *s* of Denis Norman Davies and Patricia Helen (*née* Trehearne); *m* 1987, Antonia Catharine Chittenden; two *s* two *d. Educ:* Stowe. Chief Exec., Gerrard Gp plc, 1995–2001 (Dir, 1986-2001); Director: Rank Foundn Ltd, 1991–; Jockey Club Charitable Trust, 1996–; Foundn for Christian Communication Ltd, 2000–; Old Mutual Financial Services (UK) plc, 2000–; Hillside Studios Ltd, 2000–; Racing Welfare, 2001–; Thornhill Investment Mgt Ltd, 2001–; Chairman: Townhouse Hotel Investments Ltd, 1994–; Admington Hall Farms Ltd, 1995–. *Publication:* (jtly) Trading in Commodities, 1974. *Recreations:* hunting, racing. *Address:* 26 Chester Street, SW1X 7BL; Thornhill Hldgs Ltd, 77 South Audley Street, W1K 1DX. *Club:* White's.

DAVIES, Meredith; *see* Davies, Albert Meredith.

DAVIES, Hon. Sir Mervyn; *see* Davies, Hon. Sir D. H. M.

DAVIES, Sir Michael; *see* Davies, Sir A. W. M.

DAVIES, Michael; *see* Davies, A. M.

DAVIES, Michael Jeremy Pugh, CBE 2000; RIBA; FICPD; Founder Director, Richard Rogers Partnership, Architects, since 1977; *b* 23 Jan. 1942; *er s* of late Leonard Gwerfyl Davies and of Nancy Hannah Davies; *m* 1977, Elizabeth Renee Yvonne Escalmel; one *s* one *d. Educ:* Highgate Sch.; Architectural Assoc. (AA Dip.); UCLA (Charles Scott Fellow; MArch Urban Design). Dir, Airstructures Design, 1966–68; Partner, Chrysalis USA, 1969–72; Project architect, Piano and Rogers, 1972–77; Partner, Chrysalis Architects (London), 1978–83. Richard Rogers Partnership projects incl. Project Dir, Millennium Dome, London, 1996–. Has lectured at univs, confs and schools of architecture worldwide. FRGS; FICPD 1998. *Publications:* contrib. articles and papers to professional jls. *Recreations:* astronomy, sailing, rock-climbing. *Address:* Richard Rogers Partnership, Thames Wharf, Rainville Road, W6 9HA. *T:* (020) 7385 1235.

DAVIES, Prof. (Morgan Wynn) Humphrey, DSc; CEng, FIEE; FCGI; Professor of Electrical Engineering, Queen Mary College, University of London, 1956–79, now Emeritus (Fellow of the College, 1984); *b* 26 Dec. 1911; *s* of late Richard Humphrey Davies, CB; *m* 1944, Gwendolen Enid, *d* of late Canon Douglas Edward Morton, Camborne, Cornwall; one *s. Educ:* Westminster Sch.; University College of N Wales, Bangor (BSc 1931); Charlottenburg Technische Hochschule, Berlin; Commonwealth Fellow, MIT, 1938–39 (MSc 1940). Grad. Apprentice with Metropolitan-Vickers, 1933; Lecturer in Electrical Engineering, University of Wales, 1935–42; Education Officer to Instn of Electrical Engineers, 1944–47; Lecturer, 1947, and University Reader, 1952, in Electrical Engineering, Imperial Coll., University of London, 1947–56; Dean of Engrg, Univ. of London, 1976–79. Member: Council, IEE, 1948–51, 1958–61 (Chm., Science and Gen. Div. 1964–65). Council, City & Guilds of London Inst., 1952–62; Engineering Adv. Cttee, BBC, 1965–71; Computer Bd for Univs and Res. Councils, 1968–71; Council, Univ. of Wales, Bangor (formerly UCNW, Bangor), 1976– (Chm., Finance and GP Cttee, 1981–); Chm., Bd of Univ. of London Computer Centre, 1968–79. Gov., Howell's Sch., Denbigh, 1987–96; Chm., Educn Cttee, 1991–96. Freeman: Drapers' Co., 1995; City of London, 1996. Hon. LLM London, 1977; Hon. DSc Wales, 1985. *Publications:* Power System Analysis (with J. R. Mortlock), 1952; papers in Proc. of Instn of Electrical Engineers. *Recreation:* travel. *Address:* Church Bank, Beaumaris, Anglesey LL58 8AB. *Club:* Athenæum.

DAVIES, Prof. Nicholas Barry, DPhil; FRS 1994; Professor of Behavioural Ecology, University of Cambridge, since 1995, and Fellow of Pembroke College, Cambridge, since 1979; *b* 23 May 1952; *s* of Anthony Barry Davies and Joyce Margaret Davies (*née* Parrington); *m* 1979, Jan Parr; two *d. Educ:* Merchant Taylors' Sch., Crosby; Pembroke Coll., Cambridge (BA 1973, MA 1977); Edward Grey Inst., Oxford Univ. (DPhil 1976). Demonstrator, Dept of Zoology (Edward Grey Inst. of Field Ornithology), Oxford Univ., 1976–79, and Jun. Res. Fellow, Wolfson Coll., Oxford, 1977–79; Demonstrator and Lectr in Zoology, 1979–92, Reader in Behavioural Ecology, 1992–95, Univ. of Cambridge. Pres., Internat. Soc. for Behavioural Ecology, 2000–Aug. 2002. Scientific Medal, Zool Soc., 1987; Cambridge Foundn Teaching Prize, 1995; William Bate Hardy Prize, Cambridge Phil Soc., 1995; Medal, Assoc. Study Animal Behaviour, 1996. *Publications:* (ed with J. R. Krebs) Behavioural Ecology, 1978, 4th edn 1997; (with J. R. Krebs) An Introduction to Behavioural Ecology, 1981, 3rd edn 1993; Dunnock Behaviour and Social Evolution, 1992; Cuckoos, Cowbirds and other Cheats, 2000; contribs to learned jls. *Recreations:* bird watching, cricket. *Address:* Department of Zoology, Downing Street, Cambridge CB2 3EJ. *T:* (01223) 336600.

DAVIES, Nicola Velfor; QC 1992; a Recorder, since 1998; *b* 13 March 1953. *Educ:* Bridgend Girls' Grammar School; Birmingham Univ. (LLB). Called to the Bar, Gray's Inn, 1976, Bencher, 2001. *Address:* 3 Serjeants Inn, EC4Y 1BQ. *T:* (020) 7353 5537.

DAVIES, Col Nicolas; *see* Davies, F. N. J.

DAVIES, Nigel; *see* Davies, Claude N. B.

DAVIES, Sir Noel; *see* Davies, Sir C. N.

DAVIES, Rev. Noel Anthony; Minister, Ebeneser Newydd Congregational Church, Swansea, since 1996; Swansea and Clydach Ecumenical Pastorate, since 2000; Hon. Research Fellow, University of Wales, Cardiff, since 1999; *b* 26 Dec. 1942; *s* of late Rev. Ronald Anthony Davies and of Anne Davies; *m* 1968, Patricia Barter. *Educ:* UCNW, Bangor (BSc Chem. and Biochem.); Mansfield College, Oxford (BA Theol.); PhD Wales

1998. Ordained, 1968; Minister, Bryn Seion Welsh Congregational Church, Glanaman, 1968–77; General Secretary: Council of Churches for Wales and Commn of Covenanted Churches in Wales, 1977–90; Cytûn: Churches Together in Wales, 1990–98. Pres., Union of Welsh Independents (Congregational), 1998–99 (Chm. Council, 1990–93); Moderator, Churches' Commn on Mission, CCBI, 1991–95. Part-time Lectr, Trinity Coll., Carmarthen, 1998–. *Publications:* Wales: language, nation, faith and witness, 1996; (ed jtly) Wales: a moral society?, 1996; Un er mwyn y byd (A History of Welsh Ecumenism), 1998; God in the Centre, 1999; articles in ecumenical jls and Welsh language items. *Recreations:* classical music and hi-fi, gardening, West Highland White terriers, oriental cookery. *Address:* 16 Maple Crescent, Uplands, Swansea SA2 0QD.

DAVIES, (Norah) Olwen, MA; Headmistress, St Swithun's School, Winchester, 1973–86; *b* 21 March 1926; *d* of late Rev. and Mrs E. A. Davies. *Educ:* Tregaron County Sch.; Walthamstow Hall, Sevenoaks; Edinburgh Univ. (MA). DipEd Oxon. Staff of Girls' Remand Home, Essex, 1948–50; Russell Hill Sch., Purley, 1950–53; Woodford House, NZ, 1953–57 (Dep. Headmistress); Westonbirt Sch., 1957–65; Headmistress, St Mary's Hall, Brighton, 1965–73. Pres., Girls' Schools Association, 1981–82. Governor, Lord Mayor Treloar Coll., Alton. *Address:* 28 Arle Gardens, Alresford, Hants SO24 9BA.

DAVIES, Norman; *see* Davies, I. N. R.

DAVIES, Col Norman Thomas, OBE 1996 (MBE (mil.) 1970); JP; Registrar, General Dental Council, 1981–96; *b* 2 May 1933; *s* of late Edward Ernest Davies and of Elsie Davies (*née* Scott); *m* 1961, Penelope Mary, *e d* of Peter Graeme Agnew, *qv*; one *s* one *d*. *Educ:* Holywell; RMA, Sandhurst; Open Univ. (BA 1979). Commnd RA, 1954; Regtl and Staff Appts, Malaya, Germany and UK, 1954–64; ptsc 1966; psc 1967; Mil. Asst to C of S Northern Army Gp, 1968–69; Commanded C Bty RHA and 2IC 3RHA, 1970–72; GSOI (DS), Staff Coll., Camberley, and Canadian Land Forces Comd and Staff Coll., 1972–74; Commanded 4 Field Regt, RA, 1975–77; Mil. Dir of Studies, RMCS, Shrivenham, 1977–80. Mem., EEC Adv. Cttee on the Training of Dental Practitioners, 1983–96. Vice Pres., British Dental Hygienists Assoc., 1996–99. Hon. Mem., BDA, 1990; Hon. FDSRCS 1997. JP Hants, 1984. *Recreations:* Rugby football (Treas., RARFC, 1984–), the renaissance of Welsh Rugby football, fly fishing, gardening, wine. *Address:* 6 Weatherby Gardens, Hartley Wintney, Hook, Hants RG27 8PA. *T:* (01252) 843303. *Club:* Royal Society of Medicine.

DAVIES, Olwen; *see* Davies, N. O.

DAVIES, Owen Handel; QC 1999; a Recorder, since 2000; *b* 22 Sept. 1949; *s* of Trevor Davies and Mary Davies (*née* Jacobs); *m* 1971, Dr Caroline Jane Smith; one *s* one *d*. *Educ:* Hazelwick Sch.; Magdalene Coll., Cambridge (MA). Called to the Bar, Inner Temple, 1973; in practice at the Bar, 1974–; Jt Head of Chambers, 1980–. Sec., Admin. Law Bar Assoc., 1998–; Mem., Bar Council, 1998–; Chm., Bar IT Panel, 1999–. *Publications:* numerous contribs on humanitarian laws of conflict, extradition, information technol. and legal practice. *Recreations:* silversmithing, stained glass windows, narrowboating. *Address:* 2 Garden Court, Middle Temple, EC4Y 9BL. *T:* (020) 7353 1633; *e-mail:* brief@dial.pipex.com. *Club:* India.

DAVIES, Patrick Taylor, CMG 1978; OBE 1967; HM Overseas Civil Service, retired; *b* 10 Aug. 1927; *s* of Andrew Taylor Davies and Olive Kathleen Mary Davies; *m* 1959, Marjorie Eileen (*née* Wilkinson); two *d*. *Educ:* Shrewsbury Sch.; St John's Coll., Cambridge (MA); Trinity Coll., Oxford. Lieut, RA, Nigeria, 1945–48. Colonial Admin. Service, Nigeria, 1952; Permanent Sec., Kano State, 1970; Chief Inspector, Area Courts, Kano State, 1972–79. *Address:* 1 Millfield Drive, Market Drayton, Shropshire TF9 1HS. *T:* (01630) 653408.

DAVIES, Paul; General Manager, St John's, Smith Square, since 1985; *b* 28 Dec. 1955; *s* of Thomas Rees Davies and Eirlys Davies. *Educ:* Gowerton Boys' Grammar Sch.; University Coll. London (BA Hons English). Asst, Camden Fest. and Shaw Theatre, 1978–79; Wigmore Hall: Concert Asst, 1979–84; Dep. Manager, 1984–85. *Recreations:* music, opera, theatre, reading, swimming. *Address:* St John's, Smith Square, SW1P 3HA.

DAVIES, Prof. Paul Lyndon, FBA 2000; Cassel Professor of Commercial Law, London School of Economics and Political Science, since 1998; *b* 24 Sept. 1944; *s* of John Clifford Davies and Kathleen Gertrude Davies (*née* Webber); *m* 1973, Saphié Ashtiany; two *d*. *Educ:* Cardiff High Sch.; Balliol Coll., Oxford (BA, MA); London Sch. of Econs and Pol Sci. (LLM); Yale Univ. (LLM). Lectr, Univ. of Warwick, 1969-73; University of Oxford: CUF Lectr, 1973-91; Reader in Law of Enterprise, 1991-96, Prof., 1996-98; Chm. Bd, Faculty of Law, 1992-95; Balliol College: Fellow and Tutor in Law, 1973–98, Emeritus Fellow, 1998; Estates Bursar, 1983–86. Mem., Steering Gp, Co. Law Rev., 1999-2001. *Publications:* (with K. W. Wedderburn) Employment Grievances and Disputes Procedures in Britain, 1969; Takeovers and Mergers, 1976; (with M. R. Freedland) Labour Law: text and materials, 1979, 2nd edn 1984; (with M. R. Freedland) Labour Legislation and Public Policy, 1993; (ed) Gower's Principles of Modern Company Law, 6th edn 1997; (ed) Palmer's Company Law, 23rd to 25th edns. *Recreation:* walking. *Address:* Law Department, London School of Economics and Political Science, Houghton Street, WC2A 2AE.

DAVIES, Pauline Elizabeth, MEd; Headmistress, Wycombe Abbey School, since 1998; *b* 8 April 1950; *d* of Gordon White and Petrula White (*née* Theohari); *m* 1970, Alan Henry Davies; two *s*. *Educ:* Univ. of Manchester (BSc (Jt Hons) 1971; PGCE 1972; MEd 1978). Teacher of Biology, 1972–77, Head of Dept, 1974–77, Urmston Girls' Grammar Sch.; various posts, incl. Dep. Head and Head of Middle Sch., King Edward VI Grammar Sch. for Boys, Chelmsford, 1979–90; Headmistress, Croydon High Sch., 1990–98. *Recreations:* reading, theatre, music, travel. *Address:* Wycombe Abbey School, High Wycombe, Bucks HP11 1PE. *T:* (01494) 520381. *Clubs:* Lansdowne, University Women's.

DAVIES, (Percy) Douglas, CB 1981; *b* 17 Sept. 1921; *m* 1947, Renée Margaret Billings; one *s* one *d*. *Educ:* Liverpool Collegiate School; Open Univ. (BA 1989). Clerical Officer, Ministry of Transport, 1938; served Royal Armoured Corps, 1941–46; Chief Executive Officer, Min. of Transport, 1963; Asst Secretary, 1966; Principal Establishment Officer, Under Secretary, Property Services Agency, Dept of the Environment, 1972–81. Chm., Council of Management, London Hostels Assoc., 1983–2000. *Recreations:* gardening, making things work. *Address:* 3 Court Avenue, Old Coulsdon, Surrey CR5 1HG. *T:* (01737) 553391.

DAVIES, Peter Douglas Royston, CMG 1994; HM Diplomatic Service, retired; international business consultant, Lewis Companies Inc., and MEC International; *b* 29 Nov. 1936; *e s* of Douglas and Edna Davies; *m* 1967, Elizabeth Mary Lovett Williams; one *s* two *d*. *Educ:* Brockenhurst County High Sch.; LSE (BSc(Econ)). Joined HM Diplomatic Service, 1964; FO, 1964–66; Second Sec., Nicosia, 1966–67; FO, 1967–68; First Sec., Budapest, 1968–71; FCO, 1971–74; Consul (Commercial), Rio de Janeiro, 1974–78; Counsellor (Commercial): The Hague, 1978–82; Kuala Lumpur, 1982–83; Dep. High Comr, Kuala Lumpur, 1983–85; RCDS 1986; Head of Arms Control and Disarmament Dept, FCO, 1987–91; Consul-Gen., Toronto, and Dir-Gen. of Trade and Investment in Canada, 1991–96. *Recreations:* tennis, ski-ing, biography, travel. *Address:* South Wing, The Manor, Moreton Pinkney, Northants NN11 3SJ.

DAVIES, Maj.-Gen. Peter Ronald, CB 1992; Director General, Royal Society for the Prevention of Cruelty to Animals, since 1991; *b* 10 May 1938; *e s* of Lt-Col Charles Henry Davies and Joyce Davies (*née* Moore); *m* 1960, Rosemary Julia, *er d* of late David Felice of Douglas, IoM; one *s* one *d*. *Educ:* Llandovery College; Welbeck College; RMA Sandhurst; student: RMCS 1969; Staff Coll., 1970; RCDS, 1985. Commissioned Royal Corps of Signals, 1958; service in BAOR, Berlin, Borneo, Cyprus and UK, 1958–68; OC Artillery Bde Sig. Sqn, 1971–72; Bde Maj., 20 Armd Bde, 1973–75; Directing Staff, Staff Coll., Camberley, 1975–76; CO 1 Armd Div. Signal Regt, 1976–79; Col GS SD, HQ UKLF, 1979–82; Brigade Comdr, 12 Armd Brigade, 1982–84; Dep. Comdt and Dir of Studies, Staff College, Camberley, 1985–86; Comdr Communications, BAOR, 1987–90; GOC Wales, 1990–91. Mem., Internat. Strategic Planning and Adv. Bd, Andrew Corp., USA, 1991–92. Executive Director: WSPA, 1992– (Vice Pres., 1998–2000; Pres., 2000–); Eurogroup for Animal Welfare, 1992–; Chairman: Freedom Food Ltd, 1994–; Animals at War Meml Fund, 1996–; Trustee, Flora for Fauna Soc., 2000–. Colonel, King's Regt, 1986–94; Chm., Regtl Council and King's and Manchester Regts' Assoc., 1986–94; Col Comdt, RCS, 1990–96. Member, Executive Committee: Lord Roberts Workshops and Forces Help Soc., 1994–96; Addaction (Drug and Alcohol Abuse), 1997–2000. Gov., Welbeck Coll., 1980–81; Trustee, Llandovery Coll., 1992–. CIMgt 1994; FIPD 1991; FZS 1994. *Recreations:* music, wine, Welsh nostalgia, constant motion. *Address:* c/o RSPCA Headquarters, Causeway, Horsham, Sussex RH12 1HG; *e-mail:* pdavies@rspca.org.uk. *Clubs:* Buck's, Army and Navy, Royal Over-Seas League; Fadeaways.

See also T. D. H. Davies.

DAVIES, Peter Wilton; Chief Executive, Cornwall County Council, since 1999; *b* 7 March 1945; *s* of late John Finden Davies and Mary (*née* Harrison); *m* 1971, Ann Mary Dawn Jones; two *d*. *Educ:* Blundell's Sch.; Southampton Inst. FIPD 1979. Grad. trainee, Devon CC, 1964–67; Personnel Officer, Berkshire CC, 1967–69; Sen. Personnel Officer, Camden LBC, 1969–70; Industrial Relns Officer, Hampshire CC, 1970–74; Dep. County Personnel Officer, 1974–81, Dir of Personnel, 1981–99, Cornwall CC. FIMgt 1988; FRSA 1994. *Recreations:* bee-keeping, walking, shooting, the arts. *Address:* Trehane Mill, Tresillian, Truro, Cornwall TR2 4AS. *T:* (01872) 520427.

DAVIES, Ven. Philip Bertram; Archdeacon of St Albans, 1987–98, now Emeritus; *b* 13 July 1933; *s* of Rev. Bertram Davies and Nancy Jonsson Davies (*née* Nicol); *m* 1963, (Elizabeth) Jane, *d* of late Ven. John Farquhar Richardson; two *s* one *d* (and one *d* decd). *Educ:* Lancing College. Travancore Tea Estates Ltd, 1954–58; Lewis's Ltd, 1959–61. Cuddesdon Theological College, 1961–63. Curate, St John the Baptist, Atherton, 1963–66; Vicar, St Mary Magdalene, Winton, Eccles, 1966–71; Rector, St Philip with St Stephen, Salford, 1971–76; Vicar, Christ Church, Radlett, 1976–87; RD of Aldenham, 1979–87. *Recreations:* gardening, fishing. *Address:* Stone Cottage, 34 School Road, Finstock, Oxon OX7 3DJ. *T:* (01993) 868207.

DAVIES, Philip John, CB 2001; Parliamentary Counsel, since 1994; *b* 19 Sept. 1954; *s* of late Glynn Davies and of Mary (*née* Adams); *m* 1981, Jacqueline Sara Boutcher; one *d*. *Educ:* St Julian's High Sch., Newport, S Wales; Hertford Coll., Oxford (MA, BCL). Called to the Bar, Middle Temple, 1981; Lectr in Law, Univ. of Manchester, 1977–82; Asst and Sen. Asst Parly Counsel, 1982–90; Dep. Parly Counsel, 1990–94 (seconded to Law Commn, 1992–94). *Publications:* articles and notes in Law Qly Rev., Modern Law Rev. and other legal jls. *Recreations:* family, Welsh terrier, the garden. *Address:* Pinecroft, The Downs, Givons Grove, Leatherhead, Surrey KT22 8JY. *T:* (01372) 373915; Office of the Parliamentary Counsel, 36 Whitehall, SW1A 2AY. *T:* (020) 7210 6630.

DAVIES, Maj.-Gen. Philip Middleton, OBE 1975; *b* 27 Oct. 1932; *s* of late Hugh Davies and Miriam Allen (*née* Tickler); *m* 1956, Mona Wallace; two *d*. *Educ:* Charterhouse; RMA, Sandhurst. Commnd Royal Scots, 1953; served Korea, Canal Zone, Cyprus, Suez, Berlin, Libya 1st Bn Royal Scots, 1953–63; Staff Coll., 1963; National Defence Coll., 1971; commanded 1st Bn Royal Scots, Norway, Cyprus, N Ireland (despatches), 1973–76; DS, Staff Coll., 1976–77; comd 19 Bde/7 Fd Force, 1977–79; RCDS, 1980; Comd Land Forces, Cyprus, 1981–83; GOC NW Dist, 1983–86; retired. *Recreations:* fishing, gardening.

DAVIES, Quentin; *see* Davies, J. Q.

DAVIES, Rees; *see* Davies, Robert R.

DAVIES, Rhodri; *see* Davies, W. R.

DAVIES, Sir Rhys (Everson), Kt 2000; QC 1981; **His Honour Judge Rhys Davies;** a Senior Circuit Judge, since 1990; Hon. Recorder of Manchester, since 1990; *b* 13 Jan. 1941; *s* of late Evan Davies and Nancy Caroline Davies; *m* 1963, Katharine Anne Yeates; one *s* one *d*. *Educ:* Cowbridge Grammar School; Neath Grammar School; Victoria University of Manchester. LLB (Hons). Called to the Bar, Gray's Inn, 1964, Bencher, 1993. Northern Circuit, 1964–90; a Recorder, 1980–90. Mem. Court and Council, Univ. of Manchester, 1993– (Dep. Chm. Council, 2000–). *Recreations:* music, conversation. *Address:* Crown Court, Crown Square, Manchester M3 3FL. *T:* (0161) 954 1800.

DAVIES, Richard John; Group Director, Training and Education Department, National Assembly for Wales (formerly Education Department, Welsh Office), since 1997; *b* 12 Aug. 1949; *s* of Sydney John Davies and Valerie Reynolds Davies; *m* 1971, Margaret Mary Goddard; one *s* one *d*. *Educ:* King's Coll., Taunton; Univ. of Liverpool (BA Hons 1971; MA 1976). Teaching Asst, Dept of Political Theory and Instns, Liverpool Univ., 1972–73; entered Civil Service, 1973; MoD, FCO, MPO, etc, 1973–84; Welsh Office: Asst Sec., 1985; Head of Division: Health Mgt, Systems and Personnel, 1985–87; Health and Social Services Policy, 1987–89; Housing, 1989–94; School Performance, 1994–97. Nuffield-Leverhulme Fellow, 1990. *Recreations:* family, walking, swimming, music. *Address:* Training and Education Department, National Assembly for Wales, Cathays Park, Cardiff CF1 3NQ. *T:* (029) 2082 3207.

DAVIES, Richard Llewellyn; QC 1994; *b* 7 April 1948; *s* of Richard Henry Davies and Margaret Davies; *m* 1979, Elizabeth Ann Johnston; one *s* one *d*. *Educ:* St Julian's High Sch., Newport, Gwent; Univ. of Liverpool (LLB Hons). Called to the Bar, Inner Temple, 1973. *Recreations:* music, wine, reading, cycling. *Address:* 39 Essex Street, WC2R 3AT.

DAVIES, Robert, CMG 2000; Chief Executive, The Prince of Wales International Business Leaders Forum, since 1990; *b* 21 April 1951; *s* of Bob Davies and late Betty Davies. *Educ:* Brierly Hill GS; Univ. of Durham (BA Hons 1972); LSE (post-grad. res., 1975–79). Manager, various charities and regl arts initiatives, 1971–74; NCVO, 1974–80; Dir and Jt Founder, Neighbourhood Energy Action, 1979–83; Chm. and Founder, Rainbow Educational TV Productions, 1982–90; Dir of Develt, 1983–86, Dep. Chief Exec., 1986–90, BITC; Founder and Chief Exec., Digital Partnership, 2000–. Chairman: Marylebone & Soho CHC, 1979–80; Kensington & Chelsea and Westminster FHSA,

1984–96; Coll. of Health, 1989–94; Vice Chm., Westminster Assoc. for Mental Health, 1980–86; Jt Chair, Kensington & Chelsea and Westminster NHS Health Commning Jt Authy, 1994–96. Member: Crown Agents Foundn, 1997–; Performance and Innovation Unit Trade Adv. Gp, Cabinet Office, 1999–2000; External Mem., Comprehensive Spending Review, DFID, 1997–98; Bd Mem., UK Know-How Fund, DFID, 1998–99. Founder and Council Mem., Urban Villages Forum, 1992–2001; Bd Mem., British Hungarian Small Business Foundn, 2001–. Trustee: Sch. for the Performing Arts Trust, 1985–; New Acad. of Business, 1998–; Central Sch. of Ballet, 2001–; Advr, Abu Dhabi Higher Colls of Technol., 2000–. Comr, St Petersburg Action Commn, Centre for Internat. Strategic Studies, 1994–96; Dir, Pushkin Cultural Trust, 1995–. *Recreations:* skiing, opera, urban life, technology. *Address:* Prince of Wales International Business Leaders Forum, 15–16 Cornwall Terrace, Regent's Park, NW1 4QP. *T:* (020) 7467 3666, *Fax:* (020) 7467 3610; *e-mail:* robert.davies@iblf.org.

DAVIES, Robert David, CB 1982; CVO 1977; RD 1963; JP; Director, Office of the Premier, Department of the Premier and Cabinet, Western Australia, 1983 and Clerk of Executive Council, 1975–83, retired; *b* 17 Aug. 1927; *s* of late William Harold Davies and of Elsie Davies; *m* 1948, Muriel Patricia Cuff; one *s* one *d.* *Educ:* Fremantle Boys High Sch.; Perth Technical Coll. Senior AASA. Defence Service, 1945–47; Asst Commissioner, State Taxation Dept, 1973; Under Sec., Premier's Dept, WA, 1975. Comdr, RANR, 1972. JP 1970. *Recreations:* fishing, sailing. *Address:* 68 Beazley Road, Leeming, WA 6149, Australia. *T:* (9) 3324041.

DAVIES, Rt Rev. Robert Edward, CBE 1981; MA, ThD; *b* Birkenhead, England, 30 July 1913; *s* of late R. A. Davies, Canberra; *m* 1953, Helen M., *d* of H. M. Boucher; two *d.* *Educ:* Cessnock High School; Queensland University; St John's Theological College, Morpeth, NSW. Assistant Priest, Christ Church Cathedral, Newcastle, NSW, 1937–41. War of 1939–45: Toc H Army Chaplain, 1941–42; Chaplain, Royal Australian Air Force, Middle East and Mediterranean, 1942–46. Vice-Warden, St John's College, University of Queensland, Brisbane, 1946–48; Archdeacon of Canberra and Rector of Canberra, 1949–53; Archdeacon of Wagga Wagga, NSW, 1953–60; Assistant Bishop of Newcastle and Warden of St John's Theological College, Morpeth, NSW, 1960–63; Bishop of Tasmania, 1963–81. *Recreations:* golf, tennis. *Address:* 12 Elboden Street, Hobart, Tasmania 7000, Australia. *Clubs:* Tasmanian, Naval Military and Air Force of Tas. (Tas.).

DAVIES, (Robert Harold) Glyn; HM Diplomatic Service; Ambassador to Panama, since 1999; *b* 23 March 1942; *s* of late Robert Leach Davies and Edith Greenwood Davies (*née* Burgoyne); *m* 1968, Maria Del Carmen Diaz; one *s.* *Educ:* Hulme Grammar Sch., Oldham; St John's Coll., Cambridge. Joined FO, 1963; Havana, 1964; FO, 1964; Third, later Second Sec., Mexico, 1968; FCO, 1972; Consul (Commercial), Zagreb, 1980; First Sec., on loan to Cabinet Office, 1983; First Sec., Consul and Head of Chancery, Luanda, 1986; FCO, 1989; High Commissioner to Namibia, 1996–98. *Address:* c/o Foreign and Commonwealth Office, SW1A 2AH.

DAVIES, Dr Robert James; President, British Allergy Foundation, since 1997 (Founder and Chairman, 1991–97); Scientific Director, Allergy Research Ltd, since 2000; *b* 24 Feb. 1943; *s* of late Rev. Canon Dilwyn Morgan Davies and Kate Davies (*née* Maltby); *m* 1st, 1969 (marr. diss. 1980); two *s*; 2nd, 1981, Karen, *d* of Dennis Henley. *Educ:* St Catharine's Coll., Cambridge (BA 1964); St Thomas's Hosp. Med. Sch. (BChir 1967; MB BS, MA 1968); Univ. of Cambridge (MD 1977). FRCP 1982. Res. Fellow, Brompton Hosp., 1971–73; Lectr in Medicine, St Thomas's Hosp., 1973–76; MRC Res. Fellow, Univ. of Tulane, New Orleans, 1976–77; St Bartholomew's Hospital: Consultant Physician, 1977–82; Dir, Asthma & Allergy Res. Dept, 1981–99; Reader in Respiratory Medicine, 1982–90; Dir, General and Emergency Medicine, 1994–96; Prof. of Respiratory Medicine, St Bartholomew's and Royal London Sch. of Medicine and Dentistry, QMW, London Univ., 1991–99; Cons. Physician, 1994–99, Dir of R&D, 1995–97, Royal Hosps NHS Trust. Ed., Respiratory Medicine, 1988–95. Pres., Brit. Soc. for Allergy and Clin. Immunology, 1987–90; 2nd Vice Pres., Internat. Assoc. of Allergology and Clin. Immunology, 1997–99 (Treas., 1985–94); Chm., World Allergy Forum, 1996–99; Mem., Collegium Internationale Allergologicum, 1998–. Hon. Mem., Argentinian Assoc. of Allergy and Immunology, 1997. Fellow, Amer. Acad. Allergy, Asthma and Immunology, 1984. Medal, Faculty of Medicine, Univ. of Montpellier, 1981. *Publications:* Allergy The Facts, 1989; (ed) Formoterol: clinical profile of a new long acting inhaled B2-Agonist, 1990; Hay Fever and Other Allergies, 1995; contrib. Allergy. *Recreations:* hill-walking, mountain and moorland ponies. *Address:* 96 Vanbrugh Park, Blackheath, SE3 7AL.

DAVIES, Robert John; Chief Executive, Arriva plc, since 1999; *b* 12 Oct. 1948; *s* of William Davies and Janet Davies (*née* Robinson); *m* 1971, Eileen Susan Littlefield; one *s.* *Educ:* Univ. of Edinburgh (LLB Law and Econs). FCMA 1976. With Ford Motor Co., in UK, USA and latterly as Finance Dir, Ford Spain, 1970–85; Coopers & Lybrand, 1985–87; Finance Director: Waterford Wedgwood plc, 1987–91; Ferranti Internat. plc, 1991–93; Finance Dir, 1994–97, Chief Exec., 1997–98, E Midlands Electricity plc. Non-executive Director: T & S Stores plc, 1998–; Geest plc, 1998–. *Recreations:* golf, vintage cars. *Address:* Arriva plc, Admiral Way, Doxford International Business Park, Sunderland, Tyne and Wear SR3 3XP.

DAVIES, (Robert) Karl; Chief Executive, Plaid Cymru, since 1993; *b* 26 July 1963; *s* of R. Keith Davies and Dilys Catherine Davies (*née* Hughes). *Educ:* Ysgol Glan Clywd, St Asaph; University Coll. of Wales, Aberystwyth (BA). Editor, Tafod Y Ddraig, 1983–84; Chm., Welsh Lang. Soc., 1984–85; Res. Dir, Plaid Cymru, 1985–89; BBC Wales: Producer, Radio, 1989–90; Parly Editor, 1990–93. Mem. Council, UCW, Aberystwyth, 1988–91. Fellow, British American Proj., 1996–. *Publication:* Beth am Gynnau Tân?, 1985. *Recreations:* travel, cinema, gossip, Italy. *Address:* Plaid Cymru, 18 Park Grove, Cardiff CF10 3BN. *T:* (029) 2064 6000; *e-mail:* karl.davies@plaidcymru.org. *Clubs:* London Welsh; Cameo, Ifor Bach (Cardiff).

DAVIES, (Robert) Leighton; QC 1994; a Recorder, since 1994; *b* 7 Sept. 1949; *s* of Robert Brinley Davies and Elizabeth Nesta Davies (*née* Jones); *m* 1979, Linda Fox; two *s* one *d.* *Educ:* Rhondda Co. Grammar Sch., Porth, Rhondda; Corpus Christi Coll., Oxford (MA, BCL; boxing blue, 1971–72); Inns of Court Sch. of Law. Called to the Bar, Gray's Inn, 1975; practising on Wales and Chester Circuit, 1975–; Asst Recorder, 1990–94. *Recreations:* fly-fishing, gardening, military history. *Address:* Farrar's Building, Temple, EC4Y 7BD. *T:* (020) 7583 9241; Bryn Corun, Glyncoli Road, Treorchy, Rhondda CF42 6SB. *T:* (01443) 774559. *Club:* Vincent's (Oxford).

DAVIES, Prof. (Robert) Rees, CBE 1995; DPhil; FBA 1987; Chichele Professor of Medieval History, and Fellow of All Souls College, University of Oxford, since 1995; *b* 6 Aug. 1938; *s* of William Edward Davies and Sarah Margaret Williams; *m* 1966, Carys Lloyd Wynne; one *s* one *d.* *Educ:* University College London (BA; Hon. Fellow, 1998); Merton Coll., Oxford (DPhil). FRHistS 1968. Asst Lectr, UC, Swansea, 1961–63; Lectr, UCL, 1963–76; Prof. of History, 1976–95, British Academy Wolfson Res. Prof. in Humanities, 1993–95, and Vice-Principal, 1988–91, Univ. (formerly Univ. Coll.) of Wales, Aberystwyth. Wiles Lectr, QUB, 1988; James Ford Special Lectr, Univ. of Oxford, 1988; Vis. Fellow, Magdalen Coll., Oxford, 1992; Special History Lectr, Univ. of Newcastle upon Tyne, 1994; Ford Lectures, Univ. of Oxford, 1998. Chm., Nat. Curriculum History Cttee for Wales, 1989–91; Mem., Res. Gp, HEFCW, 1993–94. Convenor, History at Univs Defence Gp, 1991–92. Chm., Ancient Monuments Bd for Wales, 1995– (Mem., 1977–; Dep. Chm., 1993–95); Member: Council, Nat. Museum of Wales, 1987–90; Council, Historical Assoc., 1991–93; President: RHistS, 1992–96 (Mem. Council, 1979–82; Vice Pres., 1987–91); Assoc. of History Teachers of Wales, 1994–; Chm., Cttee on Acad. Res. Projects, British Acad., 1997–. Mem., Welsh Acad., 1990. Hon. Fellow: UC of Swansea, 1993; Univ. of Wales, Aberystwyth, 1996. Hon. DLitt Wales, 2000. Wolfson Literary Award for History, 1987; Norton Medlicott Medal, Historical Assoc., 1994. Asst Editor and Review Editor, History, 1963–73. *Publications:* Lordship and Society in the March of Wales 1282–1400, 1978; (ed) Welsh Society and Nationhood, 1984; Conquest, Co-existence and Change: Wales 1063–1415, 1987; (ed) The British Isles 1100–1500, 1988; Domination and Conquest: the experience of Ireland, Scotland and Wales 1100–1300, 1990; The Revolt of Owain Glyn Dwr, 1995; The First English Empire: power and identities in the British Isles 1093–1343, 2000; numerous contribs to learned jls. *Recreations:* walking, music. *Address:* All Souls College, Oxford OX1 1TU. *T:* (01865) 279288.

DAVIES, (Robert) Russell; freelance writer and broadcaster, since 1970; *b* 5 April 1946; *s* of John Gwilym Davies and Gladys Davies (*née* Davies); *m* 1972, Judith Anne Slater (separated); one *s.* *Educ:* Manchester Grammar Sch.; St John's Coll., Cambridge (Scholar; BA Mod. Langs). Comedy actor and TV presenter, 1970–71; literary reviewer and caricaturist, 1972–; football reporter, 1973–76, film critic, 1973–78, Observer; TV critic, Sunday Times, 1979–83; Dep. Editor and acting Editor, Punch, 1988; sports columnist, Sunday Telegraph, 1989–94. Presenter and feature-maker, 1979–: radio includes: When Housewives had the Choice; Turns of the Century; Word of Mouth (Premio Ondas, 1997); Jazz Century; television includes: What the Papers Say (also Annual Awards, 1989–97); jazz weeks and weekends; Saturday Review. *Publications:* Vicky (with Liz Ottaway), 1987; Ronald Searle, 1990; (ed) The Kenneth Williams Diaries, 1993; (ed) The Kenneth Williams Letters, 1994. *Recreations:* playing trombone, tuba and piano, comic art, cartooning, American cookery, following baseball. *Address:* c/o Peters, Fraser & Dunlop, 5th Floor, The Chambers, Chelsea Harbour, Lots Road, SW10 0XF. *T:* (020) 7340 1000.

DAVIES, Prof. Rodney Deane, CBE 1995; DSc, PhD; FRS 1992; CPhys, FInstP; FRAS; Professor of Radio Astronomy, University of Manchester, 1976–97, now Professor Emeritus; Director, Nuffield Radio Astronomy Laboratories, Jodrell Bank, 1988–97; *b* 8 Jan. 1930; *s* of Holbin James Davies and Rena Irene (*née* March), Mallala, S Australia; *m* 1953, Valda Beth Treasure; one *s* two *d* (and one *s* decd). *Educ:* Adelaide High Sch.; Univ. of Adelaide (BSc Hons, MSc); Univ. of Manchester (PhD, DSc). Research Officer, Radiophysics Div., CSIRO, Sydney, 1951–53; Univ. of Manchester: Asst Lectr, 1953–56; Lectr, 1956–67; Reader, 1967–76. Visiting Astronomer, Radiophysics Div., CSIRO, Australia, 1963. Member: Internat. Astronomical Union, 1958; Org. Cttee and Working Gps of various Commns; Bd and various panels and cttees of Astronomy Space and Radio Bd and Science Bd of Science Research Council; British Nat. Cttee for Astronomy, 1974–77. Royal Astronomical Society: Mem. Council, 1972–75 and 1978–89; Sec., 1978–86; Vice-Pres., 1973–75 and 1986–87; Pres., 1987–89. *Publications:* Radio Studies of the Universe (with H. P. Palmer), 1959; Radio Astronomy Today (with H. P. Palmer and M. I. Large), 1965; The Crab Nebula (co-ed with F. G. Smith), 1971; numerous contribs to Monthly Notices of RAS and internat. jls on the galactic and extragalactic magnetic fields, structure and dynamics of the Galaxy and nearby external galaxies, use of radio spectral lines, the early Universe and studies of the Cosmic Microwave Background. *Recreations:* gardening, fell-walking. *Address:* University of Manchester, Jodrell Bank Observatory, Macclesfield, Cheshire SK11 9DL. *T:* (01477) 571321.

DAVIES, Roger; *see* Davies, A. R.

DAVIES, Prof. Roger Llewelyn, PhD; FRAS; Professor of Astronomy, Department of Physics, University of Durham, since 1994; *b* 13 Jan. 1954; *s* of Albert Edward Davies and Gwendoline Mary Davies; *m* 1982, Ioana Christina Westwater; one *s* one *d.* *Educ:* John Leggott Grammar Sch., Scunthorpe; University Coll. London (BSc Physics 1975); Inst. of Astronomy and Churchill Coll., Cambridge (PhD 1979). FRAS 1979. Lindemann Fellow, Lick Observatory, Calif, 1979–80; Res. Fellow, Christ's Coll., Cambridge, 1979–82; Staff Mem., US Nat. Optical Astronomy Observatories, Tucson, Arizona, 1982–88; Scientist, UK Gemini Project, 1988–96; Lectr in Physics, Oxford Univ. and Fellow, St Peter's Coll., Oxford, 1992–94. PPARC Sen. Res. Fellow, 2001–. Mem., PPARC, 1999–2001. Chairman: Anglo-Australian Telescope Bd, 1997–99 (Mem., 1996–99); Eur. Space Telescope Co-ordinating Facility Users Cttee, 2001–; Gemini Telescopes Bd, 2002– (Mem., 2001–; Chm., UK Gemini Telescopes Steering Cttee, 1996–99). Mem., VISTA Telescope Bd, 1999–2001. Member: IAU, 1980; AAS, 1980; AAAS, 1997. *Publications:* contrib. papers to Astrophysical Jl, Monthly Notices of RAS, Astronomical Jl and conf. procs. *Recreations:* hiking, gardening, photography, films, listening to music. *Address:* Department of Physics, Rochester Building, University of Durham, South Road, Durham DH1 3LE. *T:* (0191) 374 2163.

DAVIES, Roger Oliver; *b* 4 Jan. 1945; *s* of Griffith William Davies and Dorothy Anne Davies; *m* 1973, Adele Biss, *qv*; one *s.* *Educ:* Reading Sch.; Devonport High Sch.; London School of Economics (BScEcon). Marketing Dir, 1972, Man. Dir, 1977, Thomson Holidays; Man. Dir, 1982, Chm., 1984–90, Thomson Travel Gp; Chairman: Going Places, 1994–97; Sunway Travel, 1997–2000; Travel Chest.com, 2000; Dir, Airtours PLC, 1994–2000. Mem., Monopolies and Mergers Commn, 1989–98. Governor, LSE, 1995–. Commandeur de la République (Tunisia), 1987. *Recreations:* walking, ski-ing, reading. *Address:* 7 Elsworthy Road, NW3 3DS.

DAVIES, Rt Hon. Ronald; PC 1997; Member (Lab) Caerphilly, National Assembly for Wales, since 1999; *b* 6 Aug. 1946; *s* of late Ronald Davies; *m* 1981, Christina Elizabeth Rees (marr. diss. 2000); one *d.* *Educ:* Bassaleg Grammar Sch.; Portsmouth Polytechnic; Univ. Coll. of Wales, Cardiff. Schoolteacher, 1968–70; WEA Tutor/Organiser, 1970–74; Further Educn Adviser, Mid-Glamorgan LEA, 1974–83. Councillor, Rhymney Valley DC (formerly Bedwas and Machen UDC), 1969–84 (Vice-Chm.). MP (Lab) Caerphilly, 1983–2001. Opposition Whip, 1985–87; Opposition spokesman on agriculture and rural affairs, 1987–92, front bench spokesman on Wales, 1992–97; Sec. of State for Wales, May 1997–Oct. 1998. Mem., Econ. Develt Cttee, Nat. Assembly for Wales, 1999– (Chm., 1999). Highest Order, Gorsedd of the Bards, 1998. *Publication:* paper on devolution. *Address:* Bedwas Community Council Offices, Newport Road, Bedwas CF83 8YB. *T:* (029) 2085 2477, *Fax:* (029) 2086 6022.

DAVIES, Rt Rev. Roy Thomas; Bishop of Llandaff, 1985–99; *b* 31 Jan. 1934; *s* of Hubert and Dilys Davies; unmarried. *Educ:* St David's Coll., Lampeter (BA); Jesus Coll., Oxford (BLitt); St Stephen's House, Oxford. Asst Curate, St Paul's, Llanelli, 1959–64; Vicar of Llanafan, 1964–67; Chaplain to Anglican Students, University Coll. of Wales, Aberystwyth, 1967–73; Sec., Provincial Council for Mission and Unity of Church in Wales, 1973–79; Vicar of St David's, Carmarthen, 1979–83; Vicar of Llanegwad,

1983–85; Archdeacon of Carmarthen, 1982–85; Clerical Sec., Governing Body of Church in Wales, 1983–85. ChStJ 1986–2000. *Recreations:* walking, reading. *Address:* 25 Awel Tywi, Llangunnor, Carmarthen SA31 2NL.

DAVIES, Russell; *see* Davies, Robert R.

DAVIES, Ryland; opera singer; tenor; *b* 9 Feb. 1943; *s* of Gethin and Joan Davies; *m* 1st, 1966, Anne Elizabeth Howells (marr. diss. 1981), *qv*; 2nd, 1983, Deborah Rees; one *d*. *Educ:* Royal Manchester College of Music (Fellow, 1971) (studied with Frederic R. Cox, OBE). Voice teacher, RNCM, 1987–94; teaches privately and gives masterclasses at home and abroad. Début as Almaviva in The Barber of Seville, WNO, 1964; Glyndebourne Fest. Chorus, 1964–66; has since sung with Royal Opera, Sadler's Wells Opera, WNO, Scottish Opera, at Glyndebourne, and in Brussels, Chicago, NY, San Francisco, Paris, Salzburg, Buenos Aires, Hong Kong, Berlin, Hamburg and Stuttgart; solo rôles include: Belmonte in Il Seraglio; Fenton, and Dr Caius, in Falstaff; Ferrando in Così Fan Tutte; Flamand in Capriccio; Tamino in The Magic Flute; Essex in Britten's Gloriana; Hylas in The Trojans; Don Ottavio in Don Giovanni; Cassio in Otello; Ernesto in Don Pasquale; Lysander in A Midsummer Night's Dream; title rôle in Werther; Prince in L'Amour des Trois Oranges; Nemorino in L'Elisir d'amore; Don Basilio in Le Nozze di Figaro; Rector in Peter Grimes; Triquet in Eugene Onegin; Alfredo in La Traviata, Pelléas in Pelléas et Melisande; Eneas in Esclarmonde; Jack in The Midsummer Marriage; Chaplin in Dialogues des Carmelites; Remendado in Carmen; Sellem in The Rake's Progress; Albazar in The Turk in Italy; Gaudenzio in Leoncavallo's La Bohème. Many concerts at home with all major British orchestras, and abroad with such orchestras as: Boston Symphony, Cleveland Symphony, Chicago Symphony, Philadelphia, San Francisco, Los Angeles, Bavarian Radio and Vienna Symphony. Principal oratorio rôles include: Bach, B minor Mass; Beethoven: Mass in C; Berlioz, narrator in L'Enfance du Christ; Elgar, St John, in The Kingdom; Handel: Acis, in Acis and Galatea; title rôle, Judas Macoabeus; Messiah; Jonathan, in Saul; Haydn: Nelson Mass; The Seasons; Mendelssohn: Obidiah, in Elijah; Hymn of Praise; Rossini, Messe Solenelle; Schubert, Lazarus; Tippett, Child of Our Time. Has sung in all major religious works including: Missa Solemnis, Verdi's Requiem, Dream of Gerontius, St Matthew Passion, The Creation. Many recordings incl. Il Seraglio, The Trojans, Saul, Così Fan Tutte, Thérèse, Monteverdi Madrigals, Idomeneo, Haydn's The Seasons, Messiah, L'Oracolo (Leone), Judas Maccabaeus, Il Matrimonio Segreto (Cimarosa), L'Amore dei Tre Re (Montemezzi), La Navarraise (Massenet), Lucia di Lammermoor (Donizetti). FWCMD 1996. John Christie Award, 1965. *Recreations:* antiques, art, cinema, sport. *Address:* c/o IMG Artists, 616 Chiswick High Road, W4 5RX.

DAVIES, Prof. Sally Claire; Director of Research and Development, London Region, NHS Executive, Department of Health, since 1997; Consultant Haematologist, Central Middlesex Hospital, since 1985; *b* 24 Nov. 1949; *d* of John Gordon Davies and Emily Mary Davies (*née* Tordoff); *m* 1st, 1974, R. F. W. Skilbeck (marr. diss. 1982); 2nd, 1982, P. R. A. Vulliamy (*d* 1982); 3rd, 1999, W. H. Ouwehand; two *d*. *Educ:* Manchester Univ. (MB ChB); London Univ. (MSc). FRCP 1992; FRCPath 1997; FRCPCH 1997; FFPHM 1999. House Phys. and Surg., and SHO, Manchester, 1972–74; clin. assistant in cardiology, Clínica la Concepción, Fundación Jimenez Díaz, Madrid, 1974–77; SHO in Paediatrics, Middlesex Hosp., 1978–79; Lectr, 1979–83, MRC Fellow in Recombinant DNA Technology, 1983–85, Middlesex Hosp. Med. Sch. Wkg Gp on Haemoglobinopathies, European Haematology Assoc., 1999–. Ed. for haemoglobinopathies, Internat. Cochrane Collaboration. *Publications:* contribs to med. jls, mainly relating to sickle cell disease and the haemoglobinopathies. *Recreations:* travel, opera, music, cooking, art, architecture. *Address:* 147 Hemingford Road, N1 1BZ. *T:* (020) 7607 3163.

DAVIES, Sam; *see* Davies, Stanley Mason.

DAVIES, Rt Rev. Saunders; *see* Bangor, Bishop of.

DAVIES, Siobhan; *see* Davies, Susan.

DAVIES, Stanley Mason, (Sam Davies), CMG 1971; Director, ACM (formerly Alliance) International Health Care Fund (formerly Trust), since 1986 (Consultant, 1984–86); *b* 7 Feb. 1919; *s* of late Charles Davies, MBE and Constance Evelyn Davies; *m* 1943, Diana Joan (*née* Lowe); three *d*. *Educ:* Bootle Grammar School. War Service, UK and W Europe, 1939–46; Royal Army Dental Corps, 1939–41 (Sgt); Corps of Royal Engineers, 1941–46 (Staff Captain). Clerical Officer, Min. of Labour, 1936; Exec. Officer, Inland Revenue, 1938; Higher Exec. Officer, Min. of Pensions, 1946–53; Min. of Health, 1953–68; Asst Sec., DHSS, 1968–75; Under Sec., Industries and Exports Div., DHSS, 1975–76. Consultant: Monsanto Health Care, 1977–85; Sterling Winthrop Drug, 1977–86. FSAScot. Croix de Guerre (France), 1944. *Recreations:* reading, archæology, philately. *Address:* 31 Leverstock Green Road, Hemel Hempstead, Herts HP2 4HH. *T:* (01442) 217142. *Club:* Royal Over-Seas League.

DAVIES, (Stephen) Howard; Associate Director, Royal National Theatre, since 1989; *b* 26 April 1940; *s* of Thomas Emrys Davies and late (Eileen) Hilda Davies; *m* Susan Wall; two *d*. *Educ:* Christ's Hosp.; Univ. of Durham; Univ. of Bristol. Associate Dir, Bristol Old Vic, 1971–73; Asst Dir, 1974, Associate Dir, 1976–86, RSC; freelance dir, 1974–76; Jt Founder, The Warehouse, RSC, 1977, Co. Dir, 1977–82; Vis. Dir, Nat. Theatre, 1987–88. *Productions* include: Bristol Old Vic: Troilus and Cressida; Candida; Spring Awakening; The Caucasian Chalk Circle, Birmingham Rep.; The Threepenny Opera, York Rep.; The Iceman Cometh, RSC; The Warehouse: Bandits, 1977; Bingo, 1977; The Jail Diary of Albie Sachs, 1979; Much Ado About Nothing, 1980; No Limits to Love, 1980; Outskirts, 1981; Piaf; Henry VIII, RSC, 1983; Verdi's Messiah, Municipal Hall, Pontypridd, 1985; Les Liaisons Dangereuses, 1986; After Aida, Old Vic, 1986; Royal National Theatre: The Shaughraun; Cat on a Hot Tin Roof, 1988; The Secret Rapture; Hedda Gabler, 1989; The Crucible, 1990; A Long Day's Journey into Night; Mary Stuart, 1996; Chips with Everything, 1997; Flight, 1998; Battle Royal, 1999; All My Sons, 2000 (Best Dir, Laurence Olivier Awards, 2001); I Due Foscari, King's Theatre, Edinburgh Fest., 1993; Who's Afraid of Virginia Woolf?, Almeida, transf. Aldwych, 1996; The Iceman Cometh, Almeida, transf. Old Vic, 1998; Vassa, Alberg, 1999; Collected Stories, Haymarket, 1999; Conversations After a Burial, Almeida, 2000; Private Lives, Albery, 2001. *Address:* c/o Royal National Theatre, South Bank, SE1 9PX.

DAVIES, Stephen Rees; QC 2000; *b* 2 May 1960; *s* of John Stephen Davies and Auriol (*née* Huber, now Barriball); partner, Romola Anne Pocock; one *s* one *d*. *Educ:* Stanwell Comprehensive Sch.; Cowbridge Comprehensive Sch.; London Sch. of Economics (LLB 1981); Trinity Hall, Cambridge (LLB 1982). Called to the Bar, Gray's Inn, 1983; in practice at the Bar, 1983–. Mem., Woodside Saturday Club (for children with special needs), Bristol. *Recreations:* music, poetry, Welsh Rugby. *Address:* 23 Broad Street, Bristol BS1 2HG; *e-mail:* stephen.davies@guildhallchambers.co.uk.

DAVIES, Susan, (Siobhan Davies), MBE 1995; freelance choreographer; Director, Siobhan Davies Dance Company, since 1988; *b* 18 Sept. 1950; *d* of Grahame Henry Wyatt Davies and Tempé Mary Davies (*née* Wallich); lives with David John Buckland; one *s* one *d*. *Educ:* several schools, ending with Queensgate School for Girls; Hammersmith College of Art and Building. With London Contemporary Dance Theatre, 1967–87: first choreography, 1972; Associate Choreographer, 1971; Associate Dir, 1983. Formed Siobhan Davies and Dancers, 1980; Jt Dir, with Ian Spink and Richard Alston, Second Stride, 1981–86; Associate Choreographer, Rambert Dance Co., 1988–93. Choreographed works include: White Man Sleeps, 1988; Art of Touch, 1995; Eighty-Eight, 1998. Hon. FTCL 1996. DUniv Surrey, 1999. Arts Award, Fulbright Commn, 1987, to travel and study in America; Digital Dance Award, 1988, 1989, 1990, 1992; Laurence Olivier Award for Outstanding Achievement in Dance, 1993, 1996; Prudential Award for Dance, Evening Standard Dance Award, 1996; Time Out Award, 1997; South Bank Show Award for Dance, Prudential Creative Britons Award, 2000.

DAVIES, Susan Elizabeth, (Mrs John Davies), OBE 1988; Founder and Director, Photographers' Gallery, 1971–91; freelance consultant; *b* 14 April 1933; *d* of Stanworth Wills Adey and Joan Mary Margaret Adey (*née* Charlesworth); *m* 1954, John Ross Twiston Davies; two *d* (and one *d* decd). *Educ:* Nightingale Bamford Sch., NY; Eothen Sch., Caterham. Municipal Journal, 1952–54; local and voluntary work, 1960–67; Artists Placement Group, 1967–68; ICA, 1968–71. Curator, Istanbul Photo-Biennial, 1995–96. Mem. (Ind) S Bucks DC, 1995–99; Parish Councillor, Burnham, Bucks, 1995–. Hon. FRPS (President's Medal, 1982). Photokina Award, 1986; National Artist Karel Plicka Medal, Czechoslovakia, 1989. *Recreations:* jazz live and recorded, reading, gardening. *Address:* Walnut Tree Cottage, 53 Britwell Road, Burnham, Bucks SL1 8DH. *T:* (01628) 604811. *Club:* Chelsea Arts.

DAVIES, Dr Susan Jane; Lecturer in Palaeography, University of Wales, Aberystwyth, since 1979; Member, Royal Commission on Historical Manuscripts, since 1995; *b* 4 April 1941; *d* of Iorwerth Howells and Megan Howells; *m* 1966, Brian Harold Davies; one *s* one *d*. *Educ:* Queen Elizabeth Grammar Sch. for Girls, Carmarthen; University Coll. of Wales, Aberystwyth (BA Hist., Dip. in Palaeography and Archive Admin, PhD). Mem., Council and Court of Govs, Nat. Museums and Galls of Wales, 1994–. *Address:* Department of History and Welsh History, University of Wales, Aberystwyth SY23 3DY.

DAVIES, Tristan David Henry; Editor, Independent on Sunday, since 2001; *b* 26 Oct. 1961; *s* of Maj.-Gen. Peter Ronald Davies, *qv*; *m* 1986, Julia Brook; two *s* one *d*. *Educ:* Douai; Bristol Univ. (English and Hist. (failed)). Editor: Covent Gdn Courier, 1983–86; Piazza Mag., 1986–87; joined The Independent, 1987: Listings Ed., 1988–90; Arts and Weekend Ed., 1990–93; Dep. Features Ed., 1993–96; Asst Ed., Mail on Sunday, Night and Day Mag., 1996–98; Exec. Ed., The Independent, 1998–2001. *Recreations:* football, golf, singing, rowing. *Address:* Independent on Sunday, Independent House, 191 Marsh Wall, E14 9RS. *T:* (020) 7005 2000.

DAVIES, Ven. (Vincent) Anthony; Archdeacon of Croydon, since 1994; *b* 15 Sept. 1946; *s* of Vincent Davies and Maud Mary Cecilia Davies (*née* Hackett); unmarried. *Educ:* Brasted Place Theol Coll.; St Michael and All Angels Theol Coll., Llandaff. Curate: St James, Owton Manor, dio. Durham, 1973–76; St Faith, Wandsworth, dio. Southwark, 1976–78; Parish Priest: St Faith, Wandsworth, 1978–81; St John, Walworth, 1981–94; RD of Southwark and Newington, 1988–93. *Recreations:* walking, swimming, country pubs, all things Italian. *Address:* 246 Pampisford Road, South Croydon, Surrey CR2 6DD. *T:* (020) 8688 2943; (office) St Matthew's House, 100 George Street, Croydon CR0 1PE. *T:* (020) 8681 5496.

DAVIES, Vivian; *see* Davies, W. V.

DAVIES, Walter, OBE 1966; Secretary-General and Chief Executive of The British Chamber of Commerce for Italy 1961–86, retired; *b* 7 Dec. 1920; *s* of late William Davies and late Frances Poole; *m* 1947, Alda, *d* of Tiso Lucchetta, Padua; two *d*. *Educ:* St Margaret's Higher Grade Sch., Liverpool; Liverpool Coll. of Commerce. Served War: RA, 1940–41; Scots Guards, 1942–47. Commendatore dell'Ordine al Merito della Repubblica Italiana, 1967. *Recreations:* good food, good company, fishing, motoring. *Address:* Via G. Dezza 27, 20144 Milan, Italy. *T:* (2) 4694391.

DAVIES, Prof. Wendy Elizabeth, FSA; FRHistS; FBA 1992; Professor of History, since 1985, and Pro-Provost, since 1995, University College London; *b* 28 Aug. 1942; *d* of Douglas Charles Davies and Lucy (*née* Evans). *Educ:* University Coll. London (BA, PhD). Temporary Lectr 1970, Res. Fellow 1971, Lectr 1972, Univ. of Birmingham; University College, London: Lectr 1977; Reader 1981; Hd, Dept of Hist., 1987–92; Dean of Arts, 1991–94; Dean of Social and Historical Scis, 1994–95; Fellow, 1997. Member: Ancient Monuments Bd for Wales, 1993–; Humanities Res. Bd, 1996–98. Gov., Mus. of London, 1995–2001. *Publications:* An Early Welsh Microcosm, 1978; The Llandaff Charters, 1979; Wales in the Early Middle Ages, 1982; (ed with P. Fouracre) Settlement of Disputes in Early Medieval Europe, 1986; Small Worlds: the village community in early medieval Brittany, 1988; Patterns of Power, 1990; (with G. Astill) The East Brittany Survey, Field Work and Field Data, 1994; (ed with P. Fouracre) Property and Power, 1995; (with G. Astill) A Breton Landscape, 1997; Inscriptions of Early Medieval Brittany, 2000; papers in Eng. Historical Rev., Past and Present, Francia, Bull. of Bd of Celtic Studies, Etudes Celtiques, Hist. and Anthropology, etc. *Recreations:* walking, gardening, friends, early music. *Address:* Department of History, University College London, Gower Street, WC1E 6BT. *T:* (020) 7391 1348.

DAVIES, Dame Wendy (Patricia), DBE 2001; Head Teacher, Selly Park Technology College (formerly Selly Park School), since 1986; *b* 19 Dec. 1942; *d* of Cecil and Mary Trotter; *m* 1967, Mansel John Davies; one *s* (one *d* decd). *Educ:* Portsmouth High Sch., GPDST; UCNW (BSc Hons); DipEd Oxford Univ. Teacher, Birmingham LEA, 1966; Dep. Hd, 1969–74, Hd, 1974–80, Dept of Maths; Dep. Head Teacher, 1980–86. *Recreations:* maths, travelling, reading, ICT. *Address:* 82 Lugtrout Lane, Solihull, W Midlands B91 2SN. *T:* (0121) 624 2693. *Club:* Selly Park Technol. Coll. Saturday.

DAVIES, (William) Gareth; Chairman, Sports Council for Wales, since 1999; *b* 29 Sept. 1955; *s* of late David Elvet Davies and Sarah Davies; *m* 1979, Helen; two *d*. *Educ:* UWIST, Cardiff (BSc). Oxford Univ. Manager, Burnley Bldg Soc. (Nat. and Provincial Bldg Soc.), 1979–87; Asst Dir, CBI, Wales, 1987–89; Hd of Sport, BBC Wales, 1989–94; Chief Exec., Cardiff Rugby Club, 1994–99. Sports Advr, S4C, 1999–; Rugby journalist, Independent on Sunday, 1999–. Hon. Fellow, Cardiff Univ., 1995. *Publication:* Standing Off, 1985. *Recreations:* golf, wine (Burgundy and Bordeaux). *Address:* Greenacre, 43 Llantrisant Road, Llandaff, Cardiff CF5 2PU. *Club:* Royal Porthcawl Golf.

DAVIES, William Llewellyn M.; *see* Monro Davies.

DAVIES, (William) Rhodri; QC 1999; *b* 29 Jan. 1957; *s* of His Honour John Davies, *qv*; *m* 1984, Vicky Platt; three *d*. *Educ:* Winchester Coll.; Downing Coll., Cambridge (BA Hons Law). Called to the Bar, Middle Temple, 1979; practising barrister, 1980–.

Recreations: running, sailing, swimming. *Address:* 1 Essex Court, Temple, EC4Y 9AR. *T:* (020) 7583 2000. *Club:* Thames Hare and Hounds.

DAVIES, Rev. Dr William Rhys; Principal of Cliff College, Sheffield, 1983–94; Moderator of the Free Church Federal Council, 1991–92; *b* Blackpool, 31 May 1932; *m* 1955, Barbara; one *s* one *d.* *Educ:* Junior, Central Selective and Grammar schools, Blackpool; Hartley Victoria Methodist Coll., Manchester; Univ. of Manchester. BD London 1955; MA 1959, PhD 1965, Manchester. Junior Rating and Valuation Officer (Clerical), Blackpool Corp., 1950–51. Methodist Circuit Minister: Middleton, Manchester, 1955–60; Fleetwood, 1960–65; Stockton-on-Tees, 1965–66; Sen. Lectr in Religious Studies, Padgate Coll. of Higher Education, and Methodist Minister without pastoral charge on Warrington Circuit, 1966–79; Superintendent Minister, Bradford Methodist Mission, 1979–83. Pres., Methodist Conf., 1987–88. Methodist Committees: Chairman: Cttee for Relations with People of Other Faiths, 1988–98; Ministerial Candidates Appeals Cttee, 1994–; Member: Cliff Coll. Gen. Cttee, 1974–77 and 1981–94; Faith and Order Cttee, 1975–82; Doctrinal Cttee, 1979–82; Divl Bd for Social Responsibility, 1982–85; Home Mission Bd, 1983–94. Mem. Council, Garden Tomb (Jerusalem) Assoc., 1992–95. Co-Editor, Dunamis (renewal magazine for Methodists), 1972–94. *Publications:* (with Ross Peart) The Charismatic Movement and Methodism, 1973; Spirit Baptism and Spiritual Gifts in Early Methodism, (USA) 1974; Gathered into One (Archbishop of Canterbury's Lent Book), 1975; (with Ross Peart) What about the Charismatic Movement?, 1980; Rocking the Boat, 1986; (contrib.) A Dictionary of Christian Spirituality, 1983; Spirit without Measure, 1996; contribs to jls. *Recreations:* reading, sport (soccer). *Address:* 25 Grange Avenue, Thornton Cleveleys, Lancs FY5 4PA. *T:* (01253) 864678.

DAVIES, (William) Vivian, FSA 1980; Keeper of Egyptian Antiquities, British Museum, since 1988; *b* 14 Oct. 1947; *s* of late Walter Percival Davies and of Gwenllian Davies (*née* Evans); *m* 1970, Janet Olwen May Foat (marr. diss. 1994); one *s* one *d*; *m* 1996, Renée Frances Friedman. *Educ:* Llanelli Grammar Sch.; Jesus Coll., Oxford (BA, MA). Randall-MacIver Student in Archaeology, Queen's Coll., Oxford, 1973–74; Asst Keeper, 1974–81, Dep. Keeper, 1981–88, Dept of Egyptian Antiquities, BM. Vis. Prof. of Egyptology, Univ. of Heidelberg, 1984–85. Hon. Librarian, 1975–85, Gen. Ed. of Pubns, 1990–99, Egypt Exploration Soc.; Chm., Sudan Archaeol Res. Soc., 1991–; Member: Governing Council, British Inst. in Eastern Africa, 1989–; German Archaeol Inst., 1992–. Reviews Editor, Jl of Egyptian Archaeology, 1975–85. *Publications:* A Royal Statue Reattributed, 1981; (with T. G. H. James) Egyptian Sculpture, 1983; The statuette of Queen Tetisheri: a reconsideration, 1984; (with A. el-Khouli, A. B. Lloyd, A. J. Spencer) Saqqara Tombs, I: The Mastabas of Mereri and Wernu, 1984; (ed with J. Assmann and G. Burkard) Problems and Priorities in Egyptian Archaeology, 1987; Egyptian Hieroglyphs, 1987; Catalogue of Egyptian Antiquities in the British Museum, VII: Tools and Weapons—1: Axes, 1987; (ed) Egypt and Africa: Nubia from prehistory to Islam, 1991; (ed with R. Walker) Biological Anthropology and the Study of Ancient Egypt, 1993; (ed with J. Putnam) Time Machine: Ancient Egypt and contemporary art, 1994; (ed with L. Schofield) Egypt, the Aegean and the Levant: interconnections in the second millennium BC, 1995; (with R. Friedman) Egypt, 1998; (ed) Studies in Egyptian Antiquities: a tribute to T. G. H. James, 1999; contribs to : Egypt's Golden Age: the art of living in the New Kingdom, 1982; Excavating in Egypt: The Egypt Exploration Society 1882–1982, 1982; Tanis: l'or des pharaons, 1987; Africa: the art of a continent, 1996; reviews and articles in learned jls. *Address:* Department of Ancient Egypt and Sudan, British Museum, WC1B 3DG. *T:* (020) 7323 8306.

DAVIES-SCOURFIELD, Brig. Edward Grismond Beaumont, CBE 1966 (MBE 1951); MC 1945; DL; General Secretary, National Association of Boys Clubs, 1973–82; *b* 2 Aug. 1918; 4th *s* of H. G. Davies-Scourfield and Helen (*née* Newton); *m* 1945, Diana Lilias (*née* Davidson); one *s* one *d.* *Educ:* Winchester Coll.; RMC Sandhurst. Commnd into KRRC, 1938; served War of 1939–45 (despatches 1945); psc; commanded: 1st Bn The Rifle Bde, 1960–62; Green Jackets Bde, 1962–64; British Jt Services Trng Team (Ghana), 1964–66; British Troops Cyprus and Dhekelia Area, 1966–69; Salisbury Plain Area, 1970–73; retd 1973. DL Hants, 1984. *Publications:* In presence of my foes: travels and travails of a POW, 1991. *Recreations:* country pursuits. *Address:* c/o Lloyds Bank plc, Cox's and Kings Branch, PO Box 1190, 7 Pall Mall, SW1Y 5NA. *Clubs:* Army and Navy, Mounted Infantry.

DAVIGNON, Viscount Etienne; Ambassador of HM the King of the Belgians; Chairman: Société Générale de Belgique, since 1989 (Executive Director, 1984–89); Sibeka, since 1985; Union Minière, since 1992 (Director, 1989); Royal Institute for International Relations, since 1987; Foundation P. H. Spaak, since 1983; *b* Budapest, 4 Oct. 1932; *m* 1959, Françoise de Cumont; one *s* two *d.* *Educ:* University of Louvain (LLD). Diplomat; Head of Office of Minister for Foreign Affairs, Belgium, 1963; Political Director, Ministry for Foreign Affairs, Belgium, 1969; Chm., Gov. Board, Internat. Energy Agency, 1974. Mem., 1977–84 (with responsibility for internal mkt, customs, union and industl affairs), and Vice-Pres., 1981–84 (with responsibility for industry, energy and research policies), EEC. Vice-Chairman: Fortis, 1989–; Arbed, 1992–; Tractebel, 1998–; ACCOR, 2000–; Petrofina (Dir, 1990–); Director: Solvay SA, 1985–; ICL, 1991–; Suez Lyonnaise des Eaux, 1989–; Pechiney, 1994–; Anglo American, 1999–; Mem. Adv. Bd, BASF, 1998– (Dir, 1993–). *Recreations:* tennis, golf. *Address:* 12 Avenue des Fleurs, 1150 Brussels, Belgium.

DAVIS; *see* Clinton-Davis.

DAVIS; *see* Hart-Davis.

DAVIS, Alan Henry; Director, Integrated and Local Transport, Department for Transport, Local Government and the Regions (formerly Department of the Environment, Transport and the Regions), since 2001; *b* 1 May 1948; *s* of Arthur Wallace Davis and Phyllis Marjorie Davis (*née* Grudgings); *m* 1972, Angela Joy Wells (separated 1999); two *s* one *d.* *Educ:* Wyggeston Boys' Sch., Leicester; University Coll., Oxford (MA Chem. 1973). Joined DoE, 1973; on secondment to GLC, 1979–80; Private Sec. to successive Secs of State, 1983–85; Asst Sec., 1986; Head of Divs in Local Govt, Housing, Global Atmosphere; Principal Private Sec. to Sec. of State, 1994–97; Under-Sec., 1997; Dir, Water and Land, DETR, 1997–2001. *Recreations:* gardening, walking, watching sport. *Address:* Department for Transport, Local Government and the Regions, Great Minster House, 76 Marsham Street, SW1P 4DR. *T:* (020) 7944 3000.

DAVIS, Ven. Alan Norman; Archdeacon of West Cumberland, since 1996; *b* 27 July 1938; *s* of Arthur William and Bertha Eileen Davis; *m* 1966, Francoise Marguerite; one *s* two *d.* *Educ:* King Edward's Sch., Birmingham; Durham Univ.; Lichfield Theol Coll.; Open Univ. (BA). Ordained deacon, 1965, priest, 1966; Asst Curate, St Luke's Birmingham, 1965–68; Priest-in-charge, 1968–73, Vicar, 1973–75, St Paul, Wordsworth Avenue, Sheffield; Vicar, St James and St Christopher, Shiregreen, Sheffield, 1975–80; Team Rector, Maltby, Sheffield, 1980–89; Archbishop's Officer for Urban Priority Areas, 1990–92; Priest-in-charge, St Cuthbert, Carlisle, and Diocesan Communications Officer, 1992–96. *Recreations:* French holidays, supporting Aston Villa FC. *Address:* 50 Stainburn Road, Workington, Cumbria CA14 1SN. *T:* (01900) 66190.

DAVIS, Alan Roger M.; *see* Maryon Davis.

DAVIS, Sir Andrew (Frank), Kt 1999; CBE 1992; conductor; Musical Director, Chicago Lyric Opera, since 2000; Principal Guest Conductor, Royal Stockholm Philharmonic, since 1995; *b* 2 Feb. 1944; *m* 1989, Gianna Rolandi; one *s.* *Educ:* Watford Grammar Sch.; King's Coll., Cambridge (MA, BMus); Accademia di S Cecilia, Rome. Assistant Conductor, BBC Scottish Symphony Orchestra, 1970–72; Asst Conductor, New Philharmonia Orchestra, 1973–77; Artistic Dir and Chief Conductor, Toronto Symphony, 1975–88, now Conductor Laureate; Musical Dir, Glyndebourne Fest. Opera, 1988–2000; Chief Conductor, BBC SO, 1989–2000, now Conductor Laureate. Principal Guest Conductor, Royal Liverpool Philharmonic Orchestra, 1974–77. Has conducted major US orchestras: New York, Boston, Chicago, Cleveland, Philadelphia and LA. Particularly noted for interpretations of Strauss operas; conducts at: La Scala, Milan; Metropolitan Opera, NY; Chicago Lyric; San Francisco; Glyndebourne; Royal Opera House, Covent Gdn. Toronto Symphony Orchestra tours: US Centres, China, Japan, 1978; Europe, 1983, 1986, incl. London, Helsinki, Bonn, Paris and Edinburgh Fest.; BBC SO tours: Far East, 1990; Europe, 1992 and 1996; Japan, 1993; N America, 1995 and 1998; Korea and Japan, 1997; Salzburg Fest., 1997. Many commercial recordings include: complete Dvorak Symphonies, Philharmonia Orch.; Mendelssohn Symphonies, Bavarian Radio Symphony; Borodin Cycle, Holst's The Planets and Handel's Messiah, Toronto Symphony; Tippett's The Mask of Time, BBC SO and Chorus (Record of the Year, Gramophone Awards, 1987); The British Line (British Orchestral Series), BBC SO; world première of Elgar/Payne Symphony No 3. *Recreation:* the study of mediaeval stained glass. *Address:* c/o Askonas Holt Ltd, Lonsdale Chambers, 27 Chancery Lane, WC2A 1PF.

DAVIS, Anthony Ronald William James; media consultant, since 1990; *b* 26 July 1931; *e s* of Donald William Davis, Barnes and Mary Josephine Davis (*née* Nolan-Byrne), Templeogue Mill, Co. Dublin; *m* 1960, Yolande Mary June, *o d* of Patrick Leonard, retd civil engr; one *s* two *d* (and one *d* decd). *Educ:* Hamlet of Ratcliffe and Oratory; Regent Street Polytechnic. Joint Services School for Linguists on Russian course as National Serviceman (Army), 1953–55; Architectural Asst, Housing Dept, Mddx County Architect's Dept, 1956–58; Sub-Editor, The Builder, 1959; Editor: Official Architecture and Planning, 1964–70; Building, 1970–74; Director, Building, 1972–77; Editor-in-Chief, New World Publishers Ltd, 1978–83; Editl Dir, New World Publishers Ltd, Middle East Construction and Saudi Arabian Construction, 1983–86; Editor, World Property, 1986–90. Member Board: Architecture and Planning Publications Ltd, 1966; Building (Publishers) Ltd, 1972. Mem. Council, Modular Soc., 1970–71. JP Berkshire, 1973–81. *Publications:* contribs to various, architectural and technical. *Recreations:* collecting porcelain, music and dreaming. *Address:* 5 Stukeley Park, Chestnut Grove, Great Stukeley, Huntingdon, Cambs PE28 4AD. *T:* (01480) 458175. *Club:* Architecture.

DAVIS, (Arthur) John, RD 1967; FCIB; Vice-Chairman, Lloyds Bank, 1984–91 (Chief General Manager, 1978–84); *b* 28 July 1924; *s* of Alan Wilfrid Davis and Emily Davis; *m* 1950, Jean Elizabeth Edna Hobbs; one *s* one *d* (and one *d* decd). *Educ:* grammar schs. FCIB (FIB 1969). Served War, RN, 1942–46. Entered Lloyds Bank, 1941; Jt Gen. Manager, 1973; Asst Chief Gen. Man., 1973; Dep. Chief Gen. Man., 1976. Pres., Chartered Inst. of Bankers, 1985–87. *Recreations:* gardening, music, country pursuits. *Address:* Little Dailey End, Aldbury, Tring, Herts HP23 5RZ. *T:* (01442) 851321. *Club:* Naval.

DAVIS, Barbara Ann; *see* Cassani, B. A.

DAVIS, Dr Brian Elliott, CBE 2000; Chief Executive, Nationwide Building Society, since 1994; *b* 22 Sept. 1944; *s* of William and Bessie Davis; *m* 1972, Elizabeth Rose; one *s* two *d.* *Educ:* St John's Coll., Southsea; Sussex Univ. (BSc); Sheffield Univ. (PhD). FCIB 2000. With Esso Petroleum Co., 1969–86; joined Nationwide Building Soc., 1986; Gen. Manager (Technology), 1987; Resource Dir, 1989; Ops Dir, 1992. Chm., BSA, 1996–98. FRSA 1990; CIMgt 1994. *Recreations:* squash, golf, amateur dramatics, computing. *Address:* Nationwide Building Society, Nationwide House, Pipers Way, Swindon SN38 4SN. *T:* (01793) 655002.

DAVIS, Maj-Gen. Brian William, CB 1985; CBE 1980 (OBE 1974); Head of Public Affairs, Royal Ordnance plc, 1987–94 (Director, Product Support Group, 1985–87); *b* 28 Aug. 1930; *s* of late Edward William Davis, MBE, and Louise Jane Davis (*née* Webber); *m* 1954, Margaret Isobel Jenkins; one *s* one *d.* *Educ:* Weston-super-Mare Grammar Sch.; Mons OCS, Aldershot. Commissioned Royal Artillery, 1949; Regtl Duty, 1949–56 and 1960–61, UK/BAOR; Instr-in-Gunnery, 1956–59; Staff Coll. Camberley, 1962; DAA and QMG HQ 7 Armd Bde BAOR, 1963–66; GSO2 SD UN Force, Cyprus, 1966; Regtl Duty, 1967–69; Lt-Col 1969, Directing Staff, Staff Coll. Camberley, 1969–71; CO 32 Lt Regt RA BAOR/England/N Ireland, 1971–74; Col AQ Ops HQ BAOR, 1975; Brig. 1975; CRA 3 Div., 1976–77; RCDS 1978; Chief of Staff N Ireland, 1979–80; Chief of Comdrs-in-Chief Mission to Soviet Forces in Germany, 1981–82; Maj. Gen., 1982; C of S, Logistic Exec. (Army), 1982–83; DGLP (A) (formerly VQMG), MoD, 1983–85, retired. Col Comdt RA, 1987–93. Mem., HAC, 1987–95. *Recreations:* Rugby (President, RARFC, 1975–78; Dep. Pres., Army Rugby Union, 1984–89), cricket, fishing, ornithology. *Clubs:* Special Forces, MCC; Llanelli Rugby Football; Fadeaways; Leicestershire County Cricket; Piscatorial Society.

DAVIS, Carl; composer; Principal Guest Conductor, Munich Symphony Orchestra, since 1990; *b* 28 Oct. 1936; *s* of Isadore and Sara Davis; *m* 1971, Jean Boht; two *d.* *Educ:* New England Conservatory of Music; Bard Coll. (BA). Associate Conductor, London Philharmonic Orchestra, 1987–88; Principal Conductor, Bournemouth Pops, 1984–87; *major TV credits:* The Snow Goose, 1971; World at War (Emmy Award), 1972; The Naked Civil Servant, 1975; Marie Curie, 1977; Our Mutual Friend, 1978; Prince Regent, The Old Curiosity Shop, 1979; Hollywood, Oppenheimer, The Sailor's Return, Fair Stood the Wind for France, 1980; The Commanding Sea, Private Schulz, 1981; The Last Night of the Poms, Home Sweet Home, La Ronde, 1982; The Unknown Chaplin, The Tale of Beatrix Potter, The Far Pavilions, 1983; The Day the Universe Changed, 1985; Hotel du Lac, 1986; The Accountant (BAFTA Award), The Pied Piper, 1989; Flight Terminal, Secret Life of Ian Fleming, 1990; The Black Velvet Gown, Buried Mirror, Yellow Wallpaper, The Last of the Romantics, Ashenden, Separate But Equal, 1991; The Royal Collection, A Very Polish Practice, A Sense of History, Fame in the 20th Century, 1992; A Year in Provence, Genghis Cohen, Thatcher: the Downing Street Years, 1993; Red Eagle, Hope in the Year 2, 1994; Pride and Prejudice, 1995; A Dance to the Music of Time, 1997; Cold War, Good Night Mr Tom, Seesaw, Coming Home, 1998; The Great Gatsby, 2000; *radio:* presenter, Carl Davis Classics, R2, 1997–2000; *scores:* for RSC and National Theatre; *musicals:* The Projector, 1971; Pilgrim, 1975; Cranford, 1976; Alice in Wonderland, 1978; The Wind in the Willows, 1985; Kip's War, 1987; *opera:* Peace, 1978; *TV operas:* The Arrangement, 1967; Orpheus in the Underground, 1976; *West End:* Forty Years On, 1969; Habeas Corpus, 1973; *films:* The French Lieutenant's Woman (BAFTA Original Film Score Award), 1981; Champions, 1984; King David, 1985; Girl in a Swing,

Scandal, The Rainbow, 1988; Frankenstein Unbound, Fragments of Isabella, 1989; Crucifer of Blood, Raft of the Medusa, 1991; The Voyage, 1992; The Trial, 1993; Widows Peak, 1994; Topsy-Turvy, 1999; *silent films:* Napoleon, 1980, newly adapted, 2000; The Crowd, 1981; Flesh and the Devil, Show People, How to Make Movies, 1982; Broken Blossoms, The Wind, The Musketeers of Pig Alley, An Unseen Enemy, 1983; Thief of Bagdad, 1984; The Big Parade, Greed, 1985; The General, Ben Hur, 1987; Mysterious Lady, Intolerance, City Lights (re-creation of Chaplin score), 1988; Safety Last, Kid Brother, 1989; The Immigrant, 1991; IT, The Four Horsemen of the Apocalypse, 1992; Wings; The Gold Rush (re-creation of Chaplin score), 1993; The Wedding March, 1998; Old Heidelberg, 1999; The Iron Mask, 1999; The Adventurer, 2000; *ballets:* Dances of Love and Death, 1981; Fire and Ice (ice ballet for Torvill and Dean), 1986; The Portrait of Dorian Gray (for SWRB), 1987; A Simple Man (based on L. S. Lowry, for Northern Ballet Theatre), 1987; Liaisons Amoureuses, 1988; Lipizzaner (Northern Ballet Theatre), 1988; A Christmas Carol (Northern Ballet Theatre), 1992; Savoy Suite (English Nat. Ballet), 1993; Alice in Wonderland (English Nat. Ballet), 1995; Aladdin (Scottish Ballet), 2000; *orchestral compositions:* Lines on London (symphony), 1984 (commnd by Capital Radio); Clarinet Concerto, 1984; Fantasy for flute, 1985 (commnd by Acad. of St Martin's-in-the-Fields); Glenlivit Firework Music, 1987; Beginners Please!, 1987; (with Paul McCartney) Paul McCartney's Liverpool Oratorio, 1991; On the Beach at Night Alone, 1999. Has made numerous recordings. Mem. BAFTA, 1979–. First winner, BAFTA Award for Original TV Music, 1981. Chevalier de L'Ordre des Arts et des Lettres, 1983. *Publications:* sheet music of television themes. *Recreations:* reading, gardening, playing chamber music, cooking. *Address:* c/o Paul Wing, 16 Highland Road, Amersham, Bucks HP7 9AU. *T:* (01494) 431667, *Fax:* (01494) 431714; *e-mail:* paulwing@englandmail.com.

DAVIS, Christine Agnes Murison, CBE 1997; Chairman, Scottish Legal Aid Board, 1991–98 (Member, 1986–89, 1990–91); *b* 5 March 1944; *d* of William Russell Aitken and Betsy Mary Murison or Aitken; *m* 1968, Robin John Davis; twin *d. Educ:* Perth Acad.; Ayr Acad.; St Andrews Univ. (MA Hons Modern History 1966); Aberdeen Univ. (DipEd 1967). Teacher of History and Modern Studies: Cumbernauld High Sch., 1967–68; High Sch. of Stirling, 1968–69; HM Instn, Cornton Vale, 1979–87. Member: Dunblane Town Council (non-political), 1972–75; (ex-officio) Perth and Kinross Jt County Council, 1972–75. Mem., 1974–77, Vice Chm., 1978–79, Chm., 1980–90, Electricity Consultative Council for N of Scotland Dist; Member: N Scotland Hydro Electric Bd, 1980–90; Legal Aid Central Cttee, 1980–87; Scottish Econ. Council, 1987–95; Scottish Cttee, Council on Tribunals, 1989–95; Rail Users' Consultative Cttee for Scotland, 1997–; Vice Chm., IT82 Scottish Cttee, 1981–83; Chm., Scottish Agricl Wages Bd, 1995– (Mem., 1991–95); Ind. Advr on Public Appts, 1998–. Trustee: Nat. Energy Foundn, 1991–; Energy Action Scotland, 1991–; Joseph Rowntree Charitable Trust, 1996–. Is a Quaker; a Pres., CCBI, 1990–92. *Recreations:* gardening, walking, sewing. *Address:* 24 Newton Crescent, Dunblane, Perthshire FK15 0DZ. *T:* (01786) 823226, *Fax:* (01786) 825633; *e-mail:* camdavis@gn.apc.org. *Clubs:* Penn; Scottish Arts (Edinburgh).

DAVIS, Sir Colin (Rex), CH 2001; Kt 1980; CBE 1965; Principal Conductor, London Symphony Orchestra, since 1995; *b* 25 Sept. 1927; *s* of Reginald George and Lillian Davis; *m* 1949, April Cantelo (marr. diss. 1964); one *s* one *d*; *m* 1964, Ashraf Naini; three *s* two *d. Educ:* Christ's Hospital; Royal College of Music. Orchestral Conductor, Freelance wilderness, 1949–57; Asst Conductor, BBC Scottish Orchestra, 1957–59. Conductor, Sadler's Wells, 1959, Principal Conductor, 1960–65, Musical Director, 1961–65; Chief Conductor, BBC Symphony Orchestra, 1967–71, Chief Guest Conductor, 1971–75; Musical Dir, Royal Opera House, Covent Garden, 1971–86; Chief Conductor, Bavarian Radio Symphony Orch., 1983–92; Principal Guest Conductor: Boston SO, 1972–84; LSO, 1975–95; NY Philharmonic, 1998–; Hon. Conductor, Dresden Staatskapelle, 1990. Conducted at: Metropolitan Opera House, New York, 1969, 1970, 1972; Bayreuth Fest., 1977; Vienna State Opera, 1986; Bavarian State Opera, 1994. Sibelius Medal, Finland Sibelius Soc., 1977; Grosse Schallplattenpreis, 1978; Gold Medal, Royal Philharmonic Soc., 1995; Distinguished Musician Award, ISM, 1996; Sibelius Birthplace Medal, 1998. Commendatore of Republic of Italy, 1976; Commander's Cross, Order of Merit (FRG), 1987; Commandeur, l'Ordre des Arts et des Lettres (France), 1990; Commander, Order of Lion (Finland), 1992; Order of Merit (Bavaria), 1993; Officier, Légion d'Honneur (France), 1999 (Chevalier, 1982); Order of Maximilian (Bavaria), 2000. *Recreations:* reading, cooking, gardening, knitting. *Address:* c/o Alison Glaister, 39 Huntingdon Street, N1 1BP. *Club:* Athenæum.

DAVIS, Crispin Henry Lamert; Chief Executive Officer, Reed Elsevier, since 1999; *b* 19 March 1949; *s* of late Walter Patrick Carless Davis and Jane (*née* Lamert); *m* 1970, Anne Richardson; three *d. Educ:* Charterhouse; Oriel Coll., Oxford (MA Mod. Hist.). Joined Procter & Gamble, 1970: Man. Dir, Procter & Gamble Germany, 1981–84; Vice-Pres., Food Div., Procter & Gamble USA, 1984–90; European Man. Dir, 1990–92, Gp Man. Dir, 1992–94, United Distillers; CEO, Aegis plc, 1994–99. Mem., Finance Cttee, NT. *Recreations:* sport: tennis, squash, golf, ski-ing; gardening, collecting antique furniture. *Address:* Hills End, Titlarks Hill, Sunningdale, Berks SL5 0JD. *T:* (01344) 291233. *Clubs:* Royal Automobile, MCC.

See also I. E. L. Davis, Hon. Sir N. A. L. Davis.

DAVIS, Rt Hon. David (Michael); PC 1997; MP (C) Haltemprice and Howden, since 1997 (Boothferry, 1987–97); Chairman, Conservative Party, since 2001; *b* 23 Dec. 1948; *s* of Ronald and Elizabeth Davis; *m* 1973, Doreen Margery Cook; one *s* two *d. Educ:* Warwick Univ. (BSc); London Business Sch. (MSc); Harvard (AMP). Joined Tate & Lyle, 1974: Strategic Planning Dir, 1984–87; Dir, 1987–89. PPS to Parly Under-Sec. of State, DTI, 1989–90; an Asst Govt Whip, 1990–93; Parly Sec., Office of Public Service and Science, Cabinet Office, 1993–94; Minister of State, FCO, 1994–97. Chm., H of C Public Accounts Cttee, 1997–. Mem., Financial Policy Cttee, CBI, 1977–79; Exec. Mem., Industrial Soc., 1985–87. Chm., Fedn of Cons. Students, 1973–74. *Recreations:* writing, flying, mountaineering. *Address:* House of Commons, SW1A 0AA.

DAVIS, Dennis Tyrone, OBE 1996; QFSM 1991; CEng, FIFireE; HM Chief Inspector of Fire Services for Scotland, since 1999; *b* 10 Feb. 1947; *s* of Dennis and Winifred Davis; *m* 1968, Maureen; two *s. Educ:* Queen Mary's Grammar Sch., Walsall. Joined Fire Bde, 1965; Walsall, 1965–71; Cheshire, 1971–99, Chief Fire Officer, 1986–99. FIFireE 1981 (Life Fellow, 1999); CEng 1998, MInstE 1998, CIMgt 1995. OStJ 1996. *Recreation:* sailing. *Address:* (office) Saughton House, Broomhouse Drive, Edinburgh EH11 3XD. *T:* (0131) 244 2342.

DAVIS, Derek Alan, CEng; Director, World Energy Council Commission, 1990–93; *b* 5 Oct. 1929; *s* of Irene Davis (*née* Longstaff) and Sydney George Davis; *m* 1954, Ann Margery Willett; three *s. Educ:* private schools; Battersea Polytechnic; London University. BScEng (First Hons) 1950; MIMechE; CBIM. De Havilland Engine Co Ltd: post-graduate apprentice, 1950–52; develt engineer, Gas Turbine Div., 1952–53, Rocket Div., 1953–56; Central Electricity Generating Board: Research Labs, 1956–60; Manager, Mech. and Civil Engineering, 1960–65; Group Head Fuel, 1965, System Econ. Engineer, 1970, System Planning Engineer, 1973–75, Planning Dept; Dir, Resource Planning, later Dir Production, NE Region, 1975–81; Dir Corporate Strategy Dept, 1981–84; Mem., 1984–90. Member: SERC, 1989–94; Meteorology Cttee, MoD, 1986–99; ACORD, Dept of Energy, 1990–92. *Publications:* articles in tech. and engineering jls. *Recreations:* playing, now watching, sport; gardening, DIY, reading.

DAVIS, Derek Richard; Director, Chemicals, Biotechnology, Consumer Goods and Posts, Department of Trade and Industry, since 1999; *b* 3 May 1945; *s* of Stanley Lewis Davis, OBE and Rita Beatrice Rachel Davis (*née* Rosenheim), MBE; *m* 1987, Diana Levinson; one *s* one *d. Educ:* Clifton Coll., Bristol; Balliol Coll., Oxford (BA 1967). Asst Principal, BoT, 1967; Pvte Sec. to Perm. Sec., DTI, 1971–72; Principal, 1972; Asst Sec., Dept of Energy, 1977; Secretary: Energy Commn, 1977–79; NEDC Energy Task Force, 1981; seconded to NCB, 1982–83; Under Sec., Gas Div., 1985–87, Oil and Gas Div., 1987–93, Dept of Energy, subseq. DTI; Dir Gen., BNSC, 1993–99. Mem., BBSRC, 2000–. Trustee, Nat. Space Sci. Centre, 1998–99. *Address:* Department of Trade and Industry, 151 Buckingham Palace Road, SW1W 9SS. *T:* (020) 7215 4184.

DAVIS, Sir (Ernest) Howard, Kt 1978; CMG 1969; OBE 1960; Deputy Governor, Gibraltar, 1971–78; *b* 22 April 1918; *m* 1948, Marie Davis (*née* Bellotti); two *s. Educ:* Christian Brothers Schs, Gibraltar and Blackpool; London Univ. (BA 1st cl. hons). Gen. Clerical Staff, Gibraltar, 1936–46; Asst Sec. and Clerk of Councils, 1946–54; seconded Colonial Office, 1954–55; Chief Asst Sec., Estabt Officer and Public Relations Officer (responsible for opening Radio Gibraltar), Gibraltar, 1955–62; Director of Labour and Social Security, 1962–65; Financial and Development Secretary, 1965–71; Acting Governor, various periods, 1971–77. Chairman, Committee of Enquiry: PWD, 1980–81; Electricity Dept, 1982; Chm., Gibraltar Broadcasting Corp., 1982–83. Pres., Calpe Rowing Club, 1985–92. *Recreations:* cricket, gardening, bridge. *Address:* Flat 7/6, Jumpers Building, Witham's Road, Gibraltar. *T:* 70358.

DAVIS, Gareth; Chief Executive Officer, Imperial Tobacco Group plc, since 1996; *b* 13 May 1950; *m* 1973, Andrea Allan; one *d* (and one *d* decd). *Educ:* Beal Grammar Sch., Ilford; Univ. of Sheffield (BA Hons Econ.). Mgt trainee, Imperial Tobacco, 1972; W. D. & H. O. Wills: Prodn Manager, Newcastle, 1973–79; Prodn Control Manager, Bristol, 1979–83; Factory Manager, Players, Nottingham, 1983–89; Mfg Dir, Imperial, 1987–95, and Man. Dir, Imperial Internat., 1988–95. *Recreations:* most sports, especially cricket, golf, soccer. *Address:* (office) PO Box 244, Southville, Bristol BS99 7UJ. *T:* (0117) 963 6636.

DAVIS, Rear-Adm. Graham Noel, CB 1993; software development consultant, since 1993; *b* 24 Dec. 1937; *s* of Edward Davis and Ruth (*née* Bullen); *m* 1964, Mary Jenkins; one *s* one *d. Educ:* Eltham Coll.; London Univ. (BSc Hons Physics). FIMgt 1984. Joined RN 1963: Comdr, 1973; Capt., 1981; Dean, RNC, Greenwich, 1981–83; rcds 1983; Dir, various depts, MoD, 1984–90; Rear-Adm., 1991; Dir-Gen., Fleet Support for Ops and Plans, 1991–93. *Recreations:* Net surfing, cooking, pottery, exploring UK and European canals by boat, gardening by choice, D-I-Y by necessity. *Address:* Lynchetts, Lewes Road, Ringmer, Lewes, E Sussex BN8 5ET. *T:* (01273) 812907.

DAVIS, Gray; *see* Davis, J. G.

DAVIS, Rt Hon. Helen Elizabeth; *see* Clark, Rt Hon. H. E.

DAVIS, Sir Howard; *see* Davis, Sir E. H.

DAVIS, Ian Edward Lamert; Managing Director, McKinsey & Company Inc. UK, since 1996; *b* 10 March 1951; *s* of late Walter Patrick Carless Davis and Jane Davis (*née* Lamert); *m* 1st, 1977, Sally J. Fuller; one *s* one *d*; 2nd, 1994, Penny A. Thring. *Educ:* Charterhouse; Balliol Coll., Oxford (MA). Bowater, 1972–79; McKinsey & Company: Associate, 1979–85; Principal, 1985–90; Dir, 1990–. *Recreations:* sports, opera. *Clubs:* Hurlingham, Queen's.

See also C. H. L. Davis, Hon. Sir N. A. L. Davis.

DAVIS, Ian Paul, CEng; Director General, Federation of Master Builders, since 1997; *b* 26 Dec. 1954; *s* of George Davis and Margaret Davis (*née* Proctor); *m* 1978, Jane Fidell; two *d. Educ:* Grove Sch., Newark; Univ. of Liverpool (BEng 1976); Open Univ. (MBA 1999). CEng, MICE 1982. Site Engr, Head Wrightson Process Engrg, 1976–78; Design Engr, Simpson Coulson & Partners, 1978–80; Project Engr, Davy International, 1980–83; Regl Engr, 1983–90, Dir of Standards, 1990–94, Dep. Chief Exec., 1994–97, NHBC. Chm., S Oxfordshire Housing Assoc. (Dir, 1996–). *Address:* Federation of Master Builders, 14/15 Great James Street, WC1N 3DP.

DAVIS, Ivan; Member (UU) Lagan Valley, Northern Ireland Assembly, since 1998; *b* 16 April 1937; *s* of late James and Susan Davis; *m* 1960, Hannah Elizabeth, (Betty), Murphy; three *s* one *d. Educ:* Lisburn Public Elementary Sch. Lisburn Borough Council: Mem., 1973–; Chairman: Police Liaison Cttee, 1977–81; Recreation and Allied Services, 1977–79, 1993–95; Housing Liaison Cttee, 1984–; Planning Cttee, 1987–89; Leisure Services Cttee, 1997–; Capital Develt Cttee, 1997–99; Member: Health Cttee, 1994–; Strategic Policy Cttee, 1997–99; Mayor of Lisburn, 1991–93. Member: NI Assembly, 1982–86; NI Forum (Dep. Chm.), 1996–98. Northern Ireland Assembly: Dep. Whip, 1998–; Member: Culture, Arts and Leisure Business Cttee, 1998–; Cttee on Procedures, 2001–. Member: UUP, 1987– (Mem. Exec. Cttee, 1993–99, 2000–); UU Council, 1993– (Mem., Exec. Cttee, 1993–99). Member: Lisburn Sports Adv. Council, 1989–; SE Educn and Liby Bd, 1993–95; Lisburn CAB, 1997–; Cttee, Lisburn Partnership of Peace and Reconciliation, 1997–. Pres., Kirkpatrick Charity Cttee, 1988–; Vice Pres., Lisburn Swimming Club, 1989–. *Address:* 29 Roseville Park, Lisburn BT27 4XT. *T:* (028) 9267 8164. *Club:* Lambeg Golf (Pres., 1998–2000).

DAVIS, Ivor John Guest, CB 1983; Director, Common Law Institute of Intellectual Property, 1986–91; *b* 11 Dec. 1925; *s* of Thomas Henry Davis and Dorothy Annie Davis; *m* 1954, Mary Eleanor Thompson; one *s* one *d. Educ:* Devonport High Sch.; HM Dockyard Sch., Devonport. BSc London (ext.). Apprentice, HM Dockyard, Devonport, 1941–45, Draughtsman, 1946–47; Patent Office, Dept of Trade: Asst Examr, 1947; Asst Comptroller, 1973; Comptroller Gen., Patents, Designs and Trade Marks, 1978. Pres., Administrative Council, European Patent Office, 1981–85. Mem. Adv. Panel, Centre d'études de la propriété industrielle, Strasbourg, 1979–85. Mem. Council, Inst. of Intellectual Property, 1991–99. Mem., Editorial Adv. Bd, World Patent Information Journal, 1979–85. *Recreations:* crosswords, music, gardening. *Address:* 5 Birch Close, Eynsford, Dartford DA4 0EX.

DAVIS, James Gresham, CBE 1988; FCIT, FILT; FICS; Chairman: International Maritime Industries Forum, since 1981; Global Ocean Carriers Ltd, since 1996 (Director, since 1988); Trinitas Services Ltd, since 1993; Liberia Maritime Advisory Board, since 1998; *b* 20 July 1928; *s* of Col Robert Davis, OBE, JP and Josephine Davis (*née* Edwards); *m* 1973, Adriana Johanna Verhoef, Utrecht, Holland; three *d. Educ:* Bradfield Coll.; Clare Coll., Cambridge (MA). FCIT 1969, FILT; FIEx. Served RN, 1946–49. P&OSN Co., 1952–72: Calcutta, 1953; Kobe, Japan, 1954–56; Hong Kong, 1956–57; Director: P&O Lines, 1967–72; Kleinwort Benson Ltd, 1973–88; DFDS Ltd, 1975–97 (Chm., 1984–95;

Advr, 1995–97); Pearl Cruises of Scandinavia Inc., 1982–86; Rodskog Shipbrokers (Hong Kong) Ltd, 1983–88; Associated British Ports Holdings plc, 1983–97; Transport Develt Gp plc, 1984–91; TIP Europe Plc, 1987–93 (Chm., 1990–93); Sedgwick Energy & Marine Ltd, 1988–99; Sedgwick Gp Develt Ltd, 1991–99; Hempel Paints Ltd, 1992–2000; Tsavliris Salvage (International) Ltd, 1994–2000; 2M Invest AS (Copenhagen), 1996–2000; Chairman: Bromley Shipping, 1989–94; Marine Risk Mgt Services, 1995–99; Member Advisory Board: J. Lauritzen A/S, Copenhagen, 1981–85; DFDS A/S, Copenhagen, 1981–85; Adviser, Tjaerborg (UK) Ltd, 1985–87. Mem. (part-time), British Transport Docks Bd, 1981–83; Chm., SITPRO, 1987–98; Dir, British Internat. Freight Assoc., 1989–; Chm., Danish-UK Chamber of Commerce, 1992–. Chairman: Friends of the World Maritime Univ., 1985–; Marine Soc., 1987–93; Anglian Bd, BR, 1988–92; Mem. Council, Missions to Seamen, 1981–. President: World Ship Soc., 1969, 1971, 1984–86; CIT, 1981–82; Inst. of Freight Forwarders, 1984–86; National Waterways Transport Assoc., 1986–91; Inst. of Supervisory Management, 1989–92; Inst. of Chartered Shipbrokers, 1990–92 (Vice-Pres., 1988–90); Inst. of Export, 1995– (Vice Pres., 1991–95); Harwich Lifeboat, RNLI, 1984–; Vice-President: British Maritime League, 1984–88; British Maritime Charitable Foundn, 1992–; Member: Baltic Exchange, 1973; Greenwich Forum, 1982–; Internat. and UK Cttees, Bureau Veritas, 1989–; Gen. Cttee, Lloyds Register, 1998–. Trustee, Nat. Maritime Mus., 1993–98. FRSA 1986. Hon. FNI 1985; Hon. FIFF 1986. Freeman, City of London, 1972; Liveryman and Mem., Court of Assts, Shipwrights' Co.; Master, World Traders' Co., 1996–97; Associate Mem., Master Mariners' Co., 1998. Younger Brother, Trinity House, 1989. Knight Commander, Order of Dannebrog (Denmark), 1996. *Recreations:* golf, family, ships. *Address:* 115 Woodsford Square, W14 8DT. *T:* (020) 7602 0675; Summer Lawn, Dovercourt, Essex CO12 4EF. *T:* (01255) 502981. *Clubs:* Brooks's, Hurlingham, Golfers; Fanlingerers (Hong Kong); Harwich & Dovercourt Golf, Royal Calcutta Golf; Holland Park Lawn Tennis.

DAVIS, John; *see* Davis, A. J.

DAVIS, Prof. John Allen, MD, FRCP, FRCPCH; Professor of Paediatrics, and Fellow of Peterhouse, University of Cambridge, 1979–88, now Professor Emeritus and Fellow Emeritus; *b* 6 Aug. 1923; *s* of Major H. E. Davis, MC, and Mrs M. W. Davis; *m* 1957, Madeleine Elizabeth Vinicombe Ashlin (author with D. Wallbridge of Boundary and Space: introduction to the work of D. W. Winnicott, 1981) (*d* 1991); three *s* two *d*. *Educ:* Blundells Sch., Tiverton (Scholar); St Mary's Hosp. Med. Sch. (Scholar; MB, BS 1946; London Univ. Gold Medal); MSc Manchester 1967; MA Cantab 1979, MD 1988. FRCP 1967. Army Service, BAOR, 1947–49. House Physician: St Mary's Hosp., 1947; Gt Ormond St Hosp. for Sick Children, 1950; Registrar/Sen. Registrar, St Mary's Paediatric Unit and Home Care Scheme, 1951–57; Sen. Asst Resident, Children's Med. Centre, Boston, Mass, and Harvard Teaching Fellow, 1953; Nuffield Res. Fellowship, Oxford, 1958–59; Sen. Lectr, Inst. of Child Health, and Reader, Hammersmith Hosp., 1960–67; Prof. of Paediatrics and Child Health, Victoria Univ. of Manchester, 1967–79. Second Vice Pres., RCP, 1986; Member: Assoc. of Physicians; Société française de pédiatrie; Hon. Member: BPA (former Chm., Academic Bd); Hungarian Acad. Paediatrics; Neonatal Soc.; Pres., Eur. Soc. for Pediatric Research, 1984–85; Patron: Soc. for Reproductive and Infant Psychology, 1981–; Child Psychotherapy Trust, 1987–; Arts for Health, 1989–; Squiggle Foundn, 1993–. Greenwood Lectr, Univ. of Exeter, 1981; Teale Lectr, RCP, 1990. Dawson Williams Prize, BMA, 1986; James Spence Medal, BPA, 1991; Hunterian Medal, Hunterian Soc., 1995. *Publications:* Scientific Foundations of Paediatrics (ed and contrib.), 1974 (2nd edn 1981); Place of Birth, 1978; (ed jtly) Parent-Baby Attachment in Premature Infants, 1984; papers in various medical and scientific jls. *Recreations:* collecting and painting watercolours, gardening, reading, music. *Address:* Four Mile House, 1 Cambridge Road, Great Shelford, Cambridge CB2 5JE.

DAVIS, Brig. John Anthony; Chief Executive, Commonwealth Society for the Deaf, since 1994; *b* 2 Dec. 1936; *s* of late Horace Albert Davis and Jean Isobel Davis (*née* Marshall); *m* 1960, Deirdre Telford; two *d*. *Educ:* Hurstpierpoint Coll.; RMA, Sandhurst. FCIS 1979. Commnd York and Lancaster Regt, 1958; served BAOR, Cyprus, Swaziland, Aden, Kenya; Green Howards, 1968, tranf. RAPC, 1970; HQ 1 Armd Div., 1966–68; Staff Paymaster, HQ 2 Armd Div., 1978–80; Chief Instructor, RAPC Trng Centre, 1980–83; Comd Finance HQ 1 (BR) Corps, 1983–86; Regtl Paymaster, Regtl Pay Office, Glasgow, 1986–88; Dep. Paymaster-in-Chief, 1988–89; Comd Finance HQ BAOR, 1989–92. Dep. Controller, SSAFA, 1992–94. *Recreations:* photography, travel. *Address:* Little Foxes, 8 Dinorben Beeches, Fleet, Hants GU52 7SR.

DAVIS, John Darelan R.; *see* Russell-Davis, J. D.

DAVIS, Sir John (Gilbert), 3rd Bt *cr* 1946; *b* 17 Aug. 1936; *s* of Sir Gilbert Davis, 2nd Bt, and of Kathleen, *d* of Sidney Deacon Ford; *S* father, 1973; *m* 1960, Elizabeth Margaret, *d* of Robert Smith Turnbull; one *s* two *d*. *Educ:* Oundle School; Britannia RNC, Dartmouth. RN, 1955–56. Joined Spicers Ltd, 1956; emigrated to Montreal, Canada, 1957; joined Inter City Papers and progressed through the company until becoming Pres., 1967; transf. to parent co., Abitibi-Price Inc., 1976 and held several exec. positions before retiring as Exec. Vice-Pres., 1989; co-developer, Greenfield de-inked pulp business, Château Thierry, France. Director: Greenfield NV, 1996–; Productos Recidados de Balaguer, 1999–; Cellstructures Internat., 1999–. *Recreations:* golf, tennis, music, reading. *Heir:* *s* Richard Charles Davis, *b* 11 April 1970. *Address:* 5 York Ridge Road, Willowdale, ON M2P 1R8, Canada. *T:* (416) 2224916. *Clubs:* East India; Donalda, Rosedale Golf (Toronto).

DAVIS, John Horsley Russell, PhD; FBA 1988; Warden of All Souls College, Oxford, since 1995; *b* 9 Sept. 1938; *s* of William Russell Davis and Jean (*née* Horsley); *m* 1981, Dymphna Gerarda Hermans; three *s*. *Educ:* University Coll., Oxford (BA); Univ. of London (PhD). University of Kent, 1966–90: progressively, Lectr, Sen. Lectr, Reader, Social Anthropology; Prof., 1982–90; Prof. of Social Anthropology, and Fellow of All Souls College, Univ. of Oxford, 1990–95. Chm., European Assoc. of Social Anthropologists, 1993–94; Pres., Royal Anthropological Inst., 1997–2001. *Publications:* Land and Family in Pisticci, 1973; People of the Mediterranean, 1977; Libyan Politics: tribe and revolution, 1987; Exchange, 1992. *Recreations:* gardens, music. *Address:* All Souls College, Oxford OX1 4AL.

DAVIS, John Michael N.; *see* Newsom Davis.

DAVIS, Jonathan James A.; *see* Acton Davis.

DAVIS, Joseph Graham, (Gray), Jr; Governor of California, since 1999; *b* New York City, 26 Dec. 1942; *s* of Joseph G. and Doris Davis; *m* 1983, Sharon Ryer. *Educ:* Stanford Univ. (BA Hist. *cum laude*); Columbia Univ. Law Sch. (JD). Served US Army, 1967–69 (Bronze Star for Meritorious Service, Vietnam War). Chief of Staff to Gov. of Calif., Edmund G. Brown Jr, 1975–81; Mem. for Los Angeles, Calif. State Assembly, 1983–87; Controller, State of Calif., 1987–95; Lt Gov., Calif., 1995–99. Mem., Calif. State Bar, 1969–. *Recreations:* golf, reading. *Address:* State Capitol, Sacramento, CA 95814, USA. *T:* (916) 4452841.

DAVIS, Dame Karlene (Cecile), DBE 2001; General Secretary, Royal College of Midwives, since 1997; *b* 10 Oct. 1946; *d* of late Herman Leiba and of Inez Leiba; *m* 1975, Victor Davis; one *s*. *Educ:* Titchfield Secondary Sch., Port Antonio, Jamaica; BEd Hons South Bank Poly. 1986; MA Inst. of Educn, London Univ. 1989. RN 1970; RM 1974; MTD 1980. SRN, 1967–70; SCM, 1973–74; Midwife Clinician, 1974–80; Midwife Tutor, Pembury Hosp., 1980–84; Sen. Midwife Teacher, Mayday Hosp., Croydon, 1984–87; Dir, Midwifery Educn, Olive Hayden Sch. of Midwifery, Guy's, St Thomas' and Lewisham Hosps, 1987–91; Regl Nurse, Midwifery Practice and Educn, SE Thames RHA, 1991–94; Dep. Gen. Sec., Royal Coll. of Midwives, 1994–97. Mem., Modernisation Bd overseeing implementation of NHS plan, 2000–. Dir, WHO Collaborating Centre for Midwifery; Vice Chairperson, Eur. Forum of Nursing and Midwifery Assocs and WHO; Eur. Rep., Internat. Confedn of Midwives. FRSocMed; FRSA. Hon. DSc Brighton, 2001. *Recreations:* theatre, reading, travel. *Address:* (office) 15 Mansfield Street, W1M 0BE. *T:* (020) 7312 3443.

DAVIS, Kenneth Joseph; Director of Education, London Borough of Bromley, since 1996; *b* 19 March 1948; *s* of late Kenneth Sydney Joseph Davis and of Dorothy May Davis (now Addison); *m* 1970, Susan Mary Thomson; one *s*. *Educ:* Mark Hall Sch., Harlow; City of Portsmouth Coll. of Education (BEd Hons); Wolverhampton Poly. (DMS 1978); Inst. of Education, London Univ. (MA 1981). Computer operator, London & Manchester Assce Co., 1966–67; Asst Teacher, Brune Pk Comp. Sch., Gosport, 1971–73; Head of Physics, Darlaston Comp. Sch., Walsall, 1973–78; Professional Asst, E Sussex CC, 1978–80; Kent County Council: Asst Educn Officer, 1980–83; Divl Educn Officer, 1983–86; Area Educn Officer, 1986–89; Area Dir of Educn Services, 1989–96. FIMgt. *Recreations:* sailing, ski-ing. *Address:* Cobham Cottage, 246 Maidstone Road, Chatham, Kent ME4 6JN. *Club:* Medway Yacht.

DAVIS, Leonard Andrew, (Leon); Deputy Chairman, Rio Tinto, since 2000 (Chief Executive, 1997–2000); *b* 3 April 1939; *s* of Leonard Harold Davis and Gladys Davis; *m* 1963, Annette Brakenridge; two *d*. *Educ:* S Australian Inst. of Technol. (Dip. in Primary Metallurgy). Man. Dir, Pacific Coal, 1984–89; Gp Exec., CRA Ltd, 1989–91; Mining Dir, RTZ Corp., 1991–94; Man. Dir and Chief Exec., CRA Ltd, 1994–95; Chief Operating Officer, RTZ-CRA, 1996. Hon. DSc Curtin Univ., 1998. *Address:* (office) 35th Floor, 55 Collins Street, Melbourne, Vic 3000, Australia. *T:* (3) 92833333. *Clubs:* Melbourne; Brisbane.

DAVIS, Leslie Harold Newsom, CMG 1957; *b* 6 April 1909; *s* of Harold Newsom Davis and Aileen Newsom Davis (*née* Gush); *m* 1950, Judith Anne, *d* of L. G. Corney, CMG; one *s* two *d*. *Educ:* Marlborough; Trinity Coll., Cambridge. Apptd to Malayan Civil Service, 1932; Private Sec. to Governor and High Comr, 1938–40; attached to 22nd Ind. Inf. Bde as Liaison Officer, Dec. 1941; interned by Japanese in Singapore, 1942–45; District Officer, Seremban, 1946–47; British Resident, Brunei, 1948; Asst Adviser, Muar, 1948–50; Sec. to Mem. for Education, Fed. of Malaya, 1951–52. Mem. for Industrial and Social Relations, 1952–53; Sec. for Defence and Internal Security, Singapore, 1953–55; Permanent Sec., Min. of Communications and Works, Singapore, 1955–57; Special Rep., Rubber Growers' Assoc. in Malaya, 1958–62. *Recreation:* golf. *Address:* Berrywood Heyshott, near Midhurst, West Sussex GU29 0DH. *Club:* Oxford and Cambridge.

DAVIS, Madeline; *see* Gibson, M.

DAVIS, Prof. Mark Herbert Ainsworth; Professor of Mathematics, Imperial College of Science, Technology and Medicine, since 2000; *b* 1 May 1945; *s* of Christopher A. Davis and Frances E. Davis (*née* Marsden); *m* 1988, Jessica I. C. Smith. *Educ:* Oundle Sch.; Clare College, Cambridge (BA 1966, MA 1970, ScD 1983); Univ. of California (PhD 1971). FSS 1985; FIMS 1994. Research Asst, Electronics Res. Lab., Univ. of California, Berkeley, 1969–71; Lectr, 1971–79, Reader, 1979–84, Prof. of System Theory, 1984–94, Imperial College, London; Hd of Res. and Product Develt, Tokyo-Mitsubishi Internat., 1995–99. Visiting appointments: Polish Acad. of Sciences, 1973; Harvard, 1974; MIT, 1978; Washington Univ., St Louis, 1979; ETH Zurich, 1984; Oslo Univ., 1991; Technical Univ., Vienna, 2000. Editor, Stochastics and Stochastics Reports, 1979–94; Founding Co-Editor, Mathematical Finance, 1991–93. *Publications:* Linear Estimation and Stochastic Control, 1977, Russian edn 1984; (with R. B. Vinter) Stochastic Modelling and Control, 1985; Markov Models and Optimization, 1993; jl articles on stochastic analysis, control theory, maths of finance. *Recreation:* classical music (violin and viola). *Address:* 11 Chartfield Avenue, SW15 6DT. *T:* (020) 8789 7677; Department of Mathematics, Imperial College, SW7 2BZ. *T:* (020) 7594 8486.

DAVIS, Dr Michael; Hon. Director General, European Commission, Brussels, since 1989; *b* 9 June 1923; *s* of William James Davis and Rosaline Sarah (*née* May); *m* 1951, Helena Hobbs Campbell, *e d* of Roland and Catherine Campbell, Toronto. *Educ:* Exeter Univ. (BSc); Bristol Univ. (PhD). CEng, FIMM; CPhys, FInstP. Radar Officer, Flagship, 4th Cruiser Sqdn, British Pacific Fleet, Lieut (Sp. Br.) RNVR, 1943–46 (despatches). Res. Fellow, Canadian Atomic Energy Project, Toronto Univ., 1949–51; Sen. Sci. Officer, Services Electronics Res. Lab., 1951–55; UKAEA: Commercial Dir and Techn. Adviser, 1956–73; Dir of Nuclear Energy, Other Primary Sources and Electricity, EEC, 1973–81; Dir for Energy Saving, Alternative Sources of Energy, Electricity and Heat, EEC, 1981–88. Chm., OECD Cttee on World Uranium Resources, 1969–73; Dir, NATO Advanced Study Inst., 1971; advised NZ Govt on Atomic Energy, 1967. McLaughlin Meml Lectr, Instn of Engineers of Ireland, 1977. *Publications:* (ed jtly) Uranium Prospecting Handbook, 1972; papers in various sci. jls. *Recreation:* sculpture. *Club:* Oxford and Cambridge.

DAVIS, Michael McFarland; Director for Wales, Property Services Agency, Department of the Environment, 1972–77; *b* 1 Feb. 1919; 2nd *s* of Harold McFarland and Gladys Mary Davis; *m* 1942, Aline Seton Butler; three *d*. *Educ:* Haberdashers' Aske's, Hampstead. Entered Air Ministry, 1936. Served War, RAF, 1940–45 (PoW, 1942–45). Private Sec. to Chiefs and Vice-Chiefs of Air Staff, 1945–49, and to Under-Secretary of State for Air, 1952–54; Harvard Univ. Internat. Seminar, 1956; Student, IDC, 1965; Command Sec., FEAF, 1966–69; on loan to Cabinet Office (Central Unit on Environmental Pollution), 1970; transf. to Dept of Environment, 1971. Delegate to UN Conf. on Human Environment, Stockholm, 1972. *Recreations:* doing up old things, music, croquet, bonsai, wine. *Address:* Avalon, 1 Foxborough Road, Radley OX14 3AB. *T:* (01235) 535541.

DAVIS, Miles Garth H.; *see* Hunt-Davis.

DAVIS, Nathanael Vining; Chairman, 1947–86, and Chief Executive Officer, 1947–79, Alcan Aluminium Limited; *b* 26 June 1915; *s* of Rhea Reineman Davis and Edward Kirk Davis; *m* 1941, Lois Howard Thompson; one *s* one *d*. *Educ:* Harvard Coll.; London Sch. of Economics. With Alcan group since 1939 with exception of 3 years on active duty with

US Navy. Director: Bank of Montreal, 1961–86; Canada Life Assurance Co., Toronto, 1961–86. *Address:* Box 309, Osterville, MA 02655, USA. *Club:* University (New York).

DAVIS, Hon. Sir Nigel Anthony Lamert, Kt 2001; **Hon. Mr Justice Davis;** a Judge of the High Court, Queen's Bench Division, since 2001; *b* 10 March 1951; *s* of late Walter Patrick Carless Davis and Jane (*née* Lamert); *m* 1977, Sheila Ann Gillies Nickel (marr. diss. 1992); three *d. Educ:* Charterhouse; University Coll., Oxford (BA 1975; MA 1983). Called to the Bar, Lincoln's Inn, 1975 (Hardwicke Schol., Kennedy Schol.; Bencher, 2000). Jun. Counsel to Crown (Chancery), 1985–92; QC 1992; a Recorder, 1998–2001. *Address:* Royal Courts of Justice, Strand, WC2A 2LL. *Clubs:* Riverside, MCC; Vincent's (Oxford).
See also C. H. L. Davis, I. E. L. Davis.

DAVIS, Peter Anthony; Director General, National Lottery, 1993–98; *b* 10 Oct. 1941; *s* of Stanley H. S. Davis and late Betty H. Davis (*née* Back); *m* 1971, Vanessa C. E. Beale; two *s. Educ:* Winchester Coll.; Lincoln Coll., Oxford (MA Law). CA 1967. With Price Waterhouse, 1963–80, Gen. Audit Partner, 1974–80; Exec. Dep. Chm., Harris Queensway PLC, 1980–87; Sturge Holdings PLC: Gp Finance Dir, 1988–93; Dep. Chm., 1991–93; Abbey National PLC: non-exec. Dir, 1982–94; Dep. Chm., 1988–94; Chm., Audit Cttee, 1988–93, and Scottish Adv. Bd, 1989–92. Non-executive Director: Horne Bros, 1984–87; Symphony Gp, 1984–87; Avis Europe, 1987–89; Provident Financial, 1994–2000; Proned Holdings, 1992–94; Equitable Life Assurance Soc., 1995–2001; Boosey & Hawkes, 1998–. Institute of Chartered Accountants in England and Wales: Council Mem., 1989–95; Chm., Bd for Chartered Accountants in Business, 1991–94; Mem., Senate, 1989–. MInstD 1993. *Recreations:* fishing, tennis, football, theatre. *Address:* 29 Arthur Road, SW19 7DN. *Club:* Hurlingham.

DAVIS, Sir Peter (John), Kt 1997; Chief Executive, J. Sainsbury plc, since 2000; *b* 23 Dec. 1941; *s* of John Stephen Davis and Adriaantje de Baat; *m* 1968, Susan Hillman; two *s* one *d. Educ:* Shrewsbury Sch.; Grad. Inst. of Marketing (Drexler Travelling Schol., 1961). Management trainee and sales, Ditchburn Orgn, 1959–65; marketing and sales posts, General Foods Ltd, Banbury, 1965–72; Fitch Lovell Ltd, 1973–76: Marketing Dir, Key Markets; Man. Dir, Key Markets and David Greig; J. Sainsbury, 1976–86: Marketing Dir, 1977; Asst Man. Dir, 1979; Dep. Chief Exec., 1986, Chief Exec., 1986–92, Chm., 1990–94, Reed Internat.; Chief Exec., 1993, Chm., 1993–94, Reed Elsevier; Gp Chief Exec., Prudential Corp., 1995–2000. Director: Boots Co. PLC, 1991–2000; UBS AG, 2001–. Chairman: Basic Skills Agency (formerly Adult Literacy and Basic Skills Unit), 1989–97; Nat. Adv. Council for Educn and Training Targets, 1993–97; BITC, 1997– (Dep. Chm., 1991–97); Welfare to Work New Deal Task Force, 1997–2000. Vice Pres., Chartered Inst. of Marketing, 1991–. Dir, Royal Opera House, 1999– (Trustee, 1994–, and Dep. Chm., Royal Opera House Trust); Trustee, V&A Mus., 1994–97. Governor: Duncombe Sch., Hertford, 1976–; Queenswood Sch., 1993–95. FRSA. Hon. LLD Exon, 2000. *Recreations:* sailing, reading, opera, wine. *Address:* J. Sainsbury plc, Stamford House, Stamford Street, SE1 9LL. *Club:* Trearddur Bay Sailing (Cdre, 1982–84).

DAVIS, Philip Michael; Member (Lab), since 1997, Leader, since 2000, Telford and Wrekin Council; Commissioner, English Heritage, since 1999; *b* 15 May 1954; *o s* of late Ronald Davis and of Joan Davis; *m* 1977, Susan Jean Wolton; one *s* two *d. Educ:* Holly Lodge High Sch.; Southampton Univ. (BA Jt Hons Mod. Hist./Politics); Warwick Univ. (Master Ind. Relns). Full-time Officer, GMB, 1979-2000. Mem. (Lab) Wrekin DC, 1979-97 (Chm., Planning and Envmt Cttee, 1991-97). Chairman: W Midlands Constitnl Convention, 1999–; W Midlands Regl Chamber, 2001–; Vice-Chm., W Midlands LGA, 2000–01. Chairman: W Midlands Low Pay Unit, 1989-2000; W Midlands Regl Mus Council, 1995-2000; Midlands Rail Passengers' Council, 1999-; Mem., Nat. Rail Passengers' Council, 1999-. Founder Chm., UK World Heritage Forum, 1995–; Bd Mem., Ironbridge Mus. Trust, 1982–. Contested (Lab): Ludlow, 1983; W Midlands, EP, 1999. *Address:* Leader's Office, Telford and Wrekin Council, Civic Office, Telford TF3 4LD. *T:* (01952) 202451.

DAVIS, Air Vice-Marshal Robert Leslie, CB 1984; RAF, retired 1983; *b* 22 March 1930; *s* of Sidney and Florence Davis; *m* 1956, Diana, *d* of Edward William Bryant; one *s* one *d. Educ:* Wolsingham Grammar Sch., Co. Durham; Bede Sch. Collegiate, Sunderland, Co. Durham; RAF Coll., Cranwell. Commnd, 1952; served fighter units, exchange posting, USAF, Staff Coll., OR and Ops appts, MoD, DS Staff Coll., 1953–69; comd No 19 Sqdn, 1970–72; Dep. Dir Ops Air Defence, MoD, 1972–75; comd RAF Leuchars, 1975–77; Comdr RAF Staff, and Air Attaché, British Defence Staff, Washington, DC, 1977–80; Comdr, British Forces Cyprus, and Administrator, Sovereign Base Areas, Cyprus, 1980–83, retired. Man. Dir, Bodenseewerk Geratetechnik/British Aerospace GmbH, 1983–86, retd. Chm. Durham Br., SSAFA Forces Help, 1993–; Hon. County Rep., RAF Benevolent Fund. *Recreations:* golf, antiques, music. *Address:* High Garth Farm, Witton-le-Wear, Bishop Auckland, Co. Durham DL14 0BL.

DAVIS, Prof. Stanley Stewart, CChem, FRSC; Lord Trent Professor of Pharmacy, Nottingham University, since 1975; *b* 17 Dec. 1942; *s* of William Stanley and Joan Davis; *m* 1984, Lisbeth Illum; three *s. Educ:* Warwick Sch.; London Univ. (BPharm, PhD, DSc). FRPharmS. Lecturer, London Univ., 1976–80; Sen. Lectr, Aston Univ., 1970–75. Fulbright Scholar, Univ. of Kansas, 1978–79; various periods as visiting scientist to pharmaceutical industry. Chairman: Danbiosyst (UK) Ltd; Pharmaceutical Profiles Ltd. Mem., Medicines Commn, 1994–97. *Publications:* (co-ed) Radionuclide Imaging in Drug Research, 1982; (co-ed) Microspheres and Drug Therapy, 1984; (co-ed) Site Specific Drug Delivery, 1986; (co-ed) Polymers in Controlled Drug Delivery, 1988; (co-ed) Drug Delivery to the Gastrointestinal Tract, 1989; (co-ed) Pharmaceutical Application of Cell and Tissue Culture to Drug Transport, 1991; ed jtly over 700 research pubns in various scientific jls. *Recreations:* tennis, ski-ing. *Address:* 19 Cavendish Crescent North, The Park, Nottingham NG7 1BA. *T:* (0115) 948 1866; University of Nottingham, University Park, Nottingham NG7 2RD. *T:* (0115) 951 5121.

DAVIS, Steve, OBE 2000 (MBE 1988); snooker player; *b* 22 Aug. 1957; *s* of Harry George Davis and Jean Catherine Davis; *m* 1990, Judy Greig; two *s. Educ:* Alexander McLeod Primary School and Abbey Wood School, London. Became professional snooker player, 1978; has won numerous championships in UK and abroad; major titles include: UK Professional Champion, 1980, 1981, 1984, 1985, 1986, 1987; Masters Champion, 1981, 1982, 1988, 1997; International Champion, 1981, 1983, 1984, 1987, 1988, 1989; World Professional Champion, 1981, 1983, 1984, 1987, 1988, 1989. BBC Sports Personality of the Year, 1988. Mem. Bd, World Professional Billiards and Snooker Assoc., 1993–. *Publications:* Steve Davis, World Champion, 1981; Frame and Fortune, 1982; Successful Snooker, 1982; How to be Really Interesting, 1988. *Recreations:* chess, keep fit, listening to records (jazz/soul), Tom Sharpe books. *Address:* 10 Western Road, Romford, Essex RM1 3JT. *T:* (01708) 782200. *Club:* Matchroom (Romford).

DAVIS, Rt Hon. Terence Anthony Gordon, (Terry); PC 1999; MP (Lab) Birmingham, Hodge Hill, since 1983 (Birmingham, Stechford, 1979–83); *b* 5 Jan. 1938; *s* of Gordon Davis and Gladys (*née* Avery), Stourbridge, West Midlands; *m* 1963, Anne, *d* of F. B. Cooper, Newton-le-Willows, Lancs; one *s* one *d. Educ:* King Edward VI Grammar Sch., Stourbridge, Worcestershire; University Coll. London (LLB); Univ. of Michigan, USA (MBA). Company Executive, 1962–71. Motor Industry Manager, 1974–79. Joined Labour Party, 1965; contested (Lab): Bromsgrove, 1970, Feb. and Oct. 1974; Birmingham, Stechford, March 1977. MP (Lab) Bromsgrove, May 1971–Feb. 1974; Opposition Whip, 1979–80; opposition spokesman: on the health service and social services, 1980–83; on Treasury and economic affairs, 1983–86; on industry, 1986–87. Member: Public Accounts Cttee, 1987–94; Adv. Council on Public Records, 1989–94. Chm., Birmingham Lab. MPs, 1992–97. Leader: British delegn to WEU Assembly, 1997– (Mem., 1992–; Leader, Lab. delegn, 1995–97; Pres., Socialist Gp, 1996–; Vice Pres. Assembly, 1997–); British delegn to Council of Europe Assembly, 1997– (Mem., 1992–; Chairman: Econ. Affairs and Develt Cttee, 1995–98; Pol Affairs Cttee, 2000–; Vice Pres. Assembly, 1997–). Mem., MSF. Member, Yeovil Rural District Council, 1967–68. *Address:* House of Commons, SW1A 0AA.

DAVIS, Hon. Sir Thomas (Robert Alexander Harries), KBE 1981; Pa Tu Te Rangi Ariki 1979; Prime Minister, Cook Islands, 1978–87; *b* 11 June 1917; *s* of Sidney Thomes Davis and Mary Anne Harries; *m* 1940, Myra Lydia Henderson; three *s*; *m* 1979, Pa Tepaeru Ariki. *Educ:* King's Coll., Auckland, NZ; Otago Univ. Med. Sch. (MB, ChB 1945); Sch. of Tropical Medicine, Sydney Univ., Australia (DTM&H 1950); Harvard Sch. of Public Health (Master of Public Health 1952). FRSTM&H 1949. MO and Surg. Specialist, Cook Islands Med. Service, 1945–48; Chief MO, Cook Is Med. Service, 1948–52; Res. Staff, Dept of Nutrition, Harvard Sch. of Public Health, 1952–55; Chief, Dept of Environmental Medicine, Arctic Aero-medical Lab., Fairbanks, Alaska, 1955–56; Res. Physician and Dir, Div. of Environmtl Med., Army Medical Res. Lab., Fort Knox, Ky, 1956–61; Dir of Res., US Army Res. Inst. of Environmtl Med., Natick, 1961–63; Res. Exec., Arthur D. Little, Inc., 1963–71. Involved in biol aspects of space prog., first for Army, later for NASA, 1957–71. Formed Democratic Party, Cook Islands, 1971; private med. practice, Cook Islands, 1974–78 and 1987–. Mem., RSocMed, 1960; twice Pres., Med. and Dental Assoc., Cook Islands; President: Liby and Mus. Soc., 1991–92; Cook Islands Voyaging Soc., 1992–; Cook Islands Yachting Fedn, 1995–; Pacific Islands Voyaging Soc. (Internat.), 1995–. Designed, built and sailed Polynesian voyaging canoes, Takitumu, 1991–92, Te Au o Tonga, 1994–95. Cook Islander Man of the Year, 1996. Silver Jubilee Medal, 1977; Order of Merit, Fed. Republic of Germany, 1978; Papua New Guinea Independence Medal, 1985. *Publications:* Doctor to the Islands, 1954; Makutu, 1956; Island Boy, 1992; Vaka, 1992; over 150 scientific and other pubns. *Recreations:* deep sea fishing, yacht racing, agriculture/planting, amateur radio. *Address:* PO Box 116, Avarua, Rarotonga, Cook Islands; *e-mail:* davis@gatepoly.co.ck. *Clubs:* Harvard (Boston, Mass); Wellington (NZ); Avatiu Sports (patron), Ivans (Pres. 1990), Rarotonga Yacht (patron); Avatiu Cricket (patron).

DAVIS, William; author, publisher, and columnist; Chairman, Headway Publishing, since 1999; Editor and Publisher, Private Patient, since 2000; *b* 6 March 1933; *m* 1967, Sylvette Jouclas. *Educ:* City of London Coll. On staff of Financial Times, 1954–59; Editor, Investor's Guide, 1959–60; City Editor, Evening Standard, 1960–65 (with one year's break as City Editor, Sunday Express); Financial Editor, The Guardian, 1965–68; Editor, Punch, 1968–77; Editor-in-Chief: High Life, 1973–97; Financial Weekly, 1977–80. Presenter: Money Programme, BBC TV, 1967–69; World at One, BBC Radio, 1972–79. Chairman: BTA, 1990–93; English Tourist Bd, 1990–93; Allied Leisure, 1993–94; Premier Magazines, 1992–99; Director: Fleet Publishing International, Morgan-Grampian, and Fleet Holdings, 1977–80; Thomas Cook, 1988–98; British Invisibles, 1990–93. Mem., Develt Council, Royal Nat. Theatre, 1990–92. Knight, Order of Merit of Italian Republic. *Publications:* Three Years Hard Labour: the road to devaluation, 1968; Merger Mania, 1970; Money Talks, 1972; Have Expenses, Will Travel, 1975; It's No Sin to be Rich, 1976; (ed) The Best of Everything, 1980; Money in the 1980s, 1981; The Rich: a study of the species, 1982; Fantasy: a practical guide to escapism, 1984; The Corporate Infighter's Handbook, 1984; (ed) The World's Best Business Hotels, 1985; The Supersalesman's Handbook, 1986; The Innovators, 1987; Children of the Rich, 1989; The Lucky Generation: a positive view of the 21st century, 1995; Great Myths of Business, 1997; Business Life Wit and Wisdom: a treasury of international quotations, 1998. *Recreations:* travel, tennis, lunch. *Address:* Headway Publishing, 1 Morley House, 314–322 Regent Street, W1R 5AD. *Club:* Garrick.

DAVIS, William Easthope; QC 1998; a Recorder, since 1995; *b* 20 June 1954; *s* of Prof. Ralph Davis, FBA and Dorothy Davis (*née* Easthope); *m* 1990, Susan Virginia Smith; one *s* one *d. Educ:* Wyggeston Boys' Sch., Leicester; Queen Mary Coll., London (LLB 1974). Called to the Bar, Inner Temple, 1975. Asst Treas., Midland and Oxford Circuit, 1992–99. *Recreations:* Rosie and Ralph, writing and performing in sketches, wine. *Address:* St Philip's Chambers, 55 Colmore Row, Birmingham B2 5LS. *T:* (0121) 246 7000.

DAVIS, Hon. William Grenville; PC (Can.) 1982; CC (Canada) 1986; QC (Can.); barrister and solicitor; Counsel to Torys, Toronto; Member of the Provincial Parliament, Ontario, 1959–85; Premier of Ontario, Canada, and President of the Council, Ontario, 1971–85; Leader, Progressive Conservative Party, 1971–85; *b* Brampton, Ont., 30 July 1929; *s* of Albert Grenville Davis and Vera M. Davis (*née* Hewetson); *m* 1st, 1953, Helen MacPhee (*d* 1962), *d* of Neil MacPhee, Windsor, Ontario; 2nd, 1963, Kathleen Louise, *d* of Dr R. P. Mackay, California; two *s* three *d. Educ:* Brampton High Sch.; University Coll., Univ. of Toronto (BA); Osgoode Hall Law Sch. (grad. 1955). Called to Bar of Ontario, 1955; practised gen. law, Brampton, 1955–59. Elected Mem. (C) Provincial Parlt (MPP) for Peel Riding, 1959, 1963, Peel North Riding, 1967, 1971, Brampton Riding, 1975, 1977, 1981. Minister of Educn, 1962–71; also Minister of Univ. Affairs, 1964–71; Special Envoy on Acid Rain, apptd by Prime Minister of Canada, 1985–86. Director: Magna Internat. Inc.; NIKE Canada; Power Corp. of Canada; St Lawrence Cement; Algoma Steel Inc.; First American Title Insurance Co.; Magellan Aerospace Corp.; Dylex Ltd. Holds hon. doctorates in Law from eight Ontario Univs: Waterloo Lutheran, W Ontario, Toronto, McMaster, Queen's, Windsor; Hon. Graduate: Albert Einstein Coll. of Med.; Yeshiva Univ. of NY; NUI; Ottawa; Tel Aviv. Amer. Transit Assoc. Man of the Year, 1973. A Freemason. *Publications:* Education in Ontario, 1965; The Government of Ontario and the Universities of the Province (Frank Gerstein Lectures, York Univ.), 1966; Building an Educated Society 1816–1966, 1966; Education for New Times, 1967. *Address:* 61 Main Street South, Brampton, ON L6Y 1M9, Canada; Torys, Suite 3000, Maritime Life Tower, PO Box 270, Toronto-Dominion Centre, Toronto, ON M5K IN2, Canada. *Clubs:* Kiwanis, Shriners, Masons, Albany (Ont.).

DAVIS, William Herbert, BSc; CEng, FIMechE; former executive with BL and Land Rover Ltd, retired 1983; *b* 27 July 1919; *s* of William and Dora Davis; *m* 1945, Barbara Mary Joan (*née* Sommerfield); one *d. Educ:* Waverley Grammar Sch.; Univ. of Aston in Birmingham (BSc). Army Service, 1939–46. Austin Motor Co.: Engr Apprentice, 1935–39; Mech. Engr and Section Leader, Works Engrs, 1946–51; Supt Engr, 1951; Asst Production Manager, 1954; Production Manager, 1956; Dir and Gen. Works Manager, 1958. British Motor Corp. Ltd: Dir of Production, 1960; Dep. Managing Dir (Manufacture and Supply), 1961; Dep. Managing Dir, British Leyland (Austin-Morris Ltd), 1968; Chairman and Chief Executive, Triumph Motor Co. Ltd, 1969; Managing

Dir, Rover Triumph BLUK Ltd, 1972; Dir (Manufacture), British Leyland Motor Corporation, 1973; Dir, Military Contracts and Govt Affairs, Leyland Cars, 1976–81; Consultant, BL and Land Rover Ltd, 1981–83; Dir, Land Rover Santana (Spain), 1976–83. Member: Engrg ITB, 1976–81; CBI Regl Council, 1978–83. Gov., Solihull Coll. of Technol., 1978–87. FIIM, SME(USA). Silver Jubilee Medal, 1977. *Recreations:* motoring, photography; interests in amateur boxing. *Address:* The Courtyard House, Marley, South Brent, Devon TQ10 9JX.

DAVIS-GOFF, Sir Robert William; *see* Goff.

DAVIS-RICE, Peter; Director of Nursing and Personnel, North Western Regional Health Authority, 1990–94; *b* 1 Feb. 1930; *s* of Alfred Davis-Rice and Doris Eva (*née* Bates); *m* 1993, Joan Margaret Walton; one *s* two *d* by previous marriage. *Educ:* Riley High Sch., Hull; Royal Coll. of Nursing, Edinburgh; Harefield Hosp., Mddx; City Hosp., York. SRN; British Tuberculosis Assoc. Cert.; MIMgt; NAdmin(Hosp)Cert. Staff Nurse, Charge Nurse, St Luke's Hosp., Huddersfield, 1954–57; Theatre Supt, Hull Royal Infirmary, 1957–62; Asst Matron (Theatres), Walton Hosp., Liverpool, 1962–66; Matron, Billinge Hosp., Wigan, 1966–69; Chief Nursing Officer, Oldham and District HMC, 1969–73; Regl Nursing Officer, 1973–90, Asst Gen. Manager (Personnel Services), 1985–90, N Western RHA. Chm., Management Cttee, Manchester CAB, 1995–2001. Sec., High Peak Div., SSAFA, Forces Help, 1996–2001. *Publications:* contrib. Nursing Times. *Recreations:* walking, music. *Address:* 17 Storthbank, Simmondley, Glossop, Derbys SK13 6UX. *T:* (01457) 856224.

DAVISON, family name of **Baron Broughshane**.

DAVISON, Air Vice Marshal Christopher, MBE 1978; Director, RAF Sports Board, since 2001; *b* 26 Sept. 1947; *s* of Dixon and Kathleen Lillian Davison; *m* 1971, Rosemary Stamper; one *s* one *d*. *Educ:* Tynemouth Grammar Technical Sch.; Borough Road Coll., London. Joined RAF Phys. Educn Br., 1970; RAF Halton, Inst. of Aviation Medicine, Farnborough and RAF Hereford, 1970–76; Comd, RAF Outdoor Activity Centre, Scotland, 1976–78; Sqn Leader, 1978; HQ Strike Comd, 1979–80; Chief Instr, RAF Sch. of Physical Trng, RAF Cosford, 1981–82; RAF Staff Coll., Bracknell, 1983; PSO to Controller Aircraft, MoD, 1984–85; Wing Comdr, 1985; OC Admin Wing, RAF Wattisham, 1985–87; Dep. Comdr, Support Gp, HQ AFCENT, 1987–89; Gp Capt., 1989; Admin Trng, HQ Support Comd, 1989–91; OC RAF Swinderby, 1991–93; Head of Physical Educn Specialisation, RAF, 1994; Air Cdre, 1994; AOA and AOC Directly Administered Units, RAF HQ PTC, 1994–96 and 2000–01; Dir Personnel (Airmen) and Controller Reserve Forces, RAF, 1997–99; retd 2001. FIMgt. *Recreations:* golf, ski-ing, Rugby. *Address:* c/o National Westminster Bank plc, 225 High Street, Lincoln LN2 1AZ. *Club:* Royal Air Force.

DAVISON, Ian Frederic Hay, FCA; Managing Partner, Arthur Andersen & Co., Chartered Accountants, 1966–82; Deputy Chairman and Chief Executive, Lloyd's of London, 1983–86; *b* 30 June 1931; *s* of late Eric Hay Davison, FCA, and Inez Davison; *m* 1955, Maureen Patricia Blacker; one *s* two *d*. *Educ:* Dulwich Coll.; LSE (BScEcon); Univ. of Mich. ACA 1956, FCA 1966. Chairman: Crédit Lyonnais Capital Markets, 1988–91; Storehouse plc, 1990–96; NMB Group plc, 1992–2000; McDonnell Information Systems, later MDIS, Group plc, 1993–99; Director: Midland Bank, 1986–88; Newspaper Publishing, 1986–94 (Chm., 1993–94); Chloride plc, 1988–98; Cadbury-Schweppes plc, 1990–2000; CIBA plc, 1991–96. Mem. Council, ICA, 1975–99; Chm., Accounting Standards Cttee, 1982–84. Mem., NEDC for Bldg Industry, 1971–77; Member: Price Commn, 1977–79; Audit Commn, 1983–85; Chairman: EDC for Food and Drink Manufg Industry, 1981–83; Securities Review Cttee, Hong Kong, 1987–88. Dept of Trade Inspector, London Capital Securities, 1975–77; Inspector, Grays Building Soc., 1978–79. Trustee, V&A Museum, 1984–93 (Chm., V&A Enterprises Ltd, 1993–); Dir, Royal Opera House, 1984–86; Chairman: Monteverdi Trust, 1979–84; Sadler's Wells Foundation, 1995–. Pres., Nat. Council for One-Parent Families, 1991–; Chairman: SANE, 2000–; Railway Heritage Cttee, 2000–. Council Mem., Nat. Trust, 1992–94. Governor, LSE, 1982– (Chm., Library Panel); Pro-Provost and Chm. Council, RCA, 1996–. Councillor and Alderman, London Bor. of Greenwich, 1961–73. Hon. DSc Aston, 1985; Hon. LLD Bath, 1998. *Publication:* A View of the Room: Lloyd's change and disclosure, 1987. *Recreations:* opera, theatre, music, ski-ing, gardening under supervision, bell-ringing. *Address:* 40 Earlham Street, WC2H 9LA. *Clubs:* Athenæum, MCC.

DAVISON, (John) Stanley, OBE 1981; Secretary General, World Federation of Scientific Workers, 1987–99; *b* 26 Sept. 1922; *s* of George Davison and Rosie Davison (*née* Segger); *m* 1959, Margaret Smith; two *s* one *d*. *Educ:* Timothy Hackworth Sch., Shildon, Co. Durham; Shildon Senior Boys' Sch.; St Helens Tech. Coll. RAF, 1941–46. Civil Servant (Technical), 1946–52; Regional Organiser, 1953–60, Dep. Gen. Sec., 1960–68, Assoc. of Scientific Workers; Dep. Gen. Sec., ASTMS, 1968–87. Member: Engineering Council, 1986–94; Heavy Electrical NEDO, 1976–87; Exec. Council, CSEU, 1981–88; Exec. Council, Internat. Metalworkers' Fedn, 1986–87; All Party Energy Cttee, 1982–88; Chm., Trade Union Side, GEC NJC, 1965–87; Governor, Aston CAT, 1955–60; Mem. Council, Brunel Univ., 1989–2000. MUniv Brunel, 2001. *Recreations:* science policy, amateur dramatics, bridge, caravanning. *Address:* 1 Hazel Grove, Shefford, Beds SG17 5BB. *Clubs:* Players' Theatre; Addington Theatre Group (Hon. Mem.); Caravan.

DAVISON, Rt Hon. Sir Ronald (Keith), GBE 1978; CMG 1975; PC 1978; Chief Justice of New Zealand, 1978–89; *b* 16 Nov. 1920; *s* of Joseph James Davison and Florence May Davison; *m* 1948, Jacqueline May Carr; one *s* one *d* (and one *s* decd). *Educ:* Auckland Univ. (LLB). Admitted as barrister and solicitor, 1948; QC (NZ) 1963. Chairman: Environmental Council, 1969–74; Legal Aid Bd, 1969–78; Member: Council, Auckland Dist Law Soc., 1960–65 (Pres., 1965–66); Council, NZ Law Soc., 1963–66; Auckland Electric Power Bd (13 yrs); Aircrew Indust. Tribunal, 1970–78. Chm., Montana Wines Ltd, 1971–78; Dir, NZ Insurance Co. Ltd, 1975–78. *Recreations:* golf, fishing, bowls. *Address:* 1 Lichfield Road, Parnell, Auckland, New Zealand. *T:* (9) 3020493. *Clubs:* Wellington; Northern (Auckland, NZ).

DAVISON, Stanley; *see* Davison, J. S.

DAVISON, Timothy Paul; Chief Executive, Greater Glasgow Primary Care NHS Trust, since 1999; *b* 4 June 1961; *s* of late John Paul Davison and of Patricia Davison; *m* 1984, Hilary Williamson Gillick; one *s*. *Educ:* Univ. of Stirling (BA Hons Hist.); Univ. of Glasgow (MBA, MPH); Dip. Healthcare Mgt. NHS nat. mgt trainee, 1983–84; Gen. Services Manager, Stirling Royal Infirmary, 1984–86; Asst Unit Administrator, Royal Edinburgh Hosp., 1986–87; Patient Services Manager, Lothian Mental Health Unit, 1987–88; Hosp. Administrator, Glasgow Royal Infirmary, 1988–90; Sector Gen. Manager, Gartnavel Royal Hosp., 1990–91; Unit Gen. Manager, Gtr Glasgow Community and Mental Health Unit (formerly Gtr Glasgow Mental Health Unit), 1991–94; Chief Exec., Gtr Glasgow Community and Mental Health Services NHS Trust, 1994–99. Non-exec. Dir, Clinical Standards Bd for Scotland, 1999–. *Recreation:* tennis, military and political history, motor-cycling. *Address:* Greater Glasgow Primary Care NHS Trust, Gartnavel Royal Hospital, 1055 Great Western Road, Glasgow G12 0XH.

DAVSON, Sir Christopher (Michael Edward), 3rd Bt *cr* 1927, of Berbice, British Guiana; *b* 26 May 1927; *yr s* of Sir Edward Rae Davson, 1st Bt, KCMG (*d* 1937) and Margot Elinor (*née* Glyn; *d* 1966), OBE; *S* brother, Sir Anthony Glyn, 2nd Bt, 1998; *m* 1st, 1962, Evelyn Mary (marr. diss. 1971), *o d* of James Wardrop; one *s*; 2nd, 1975, Kate, *d* of Ludovic Foster. *Educ:* Eton Coll. FCA. Articled Price Waterhouse & Co., London, 1948–51; sugar planter, British Guiana, 1951–55; (last) Chm., S. Davson & Co. Ltd (founded 1816), 1955; Dir, Bookers Sugar Co. Ltd, 1956–65; Finance Director: Bookers Engineering Holdings Ltd, 1957–65; Bookers Agricultural Holdings Ltd, 1958–65; Founder Dir, The Nigerian Sugar Co. Ltd, 1962–65. Captain, late Welsh Guards, 1945–48, RARO, 1949–77. Liveryman, Musicians' Co., 1969–. *Publication:* I Merlin—an Historical Recreation, 2000. *Recreations:* archaeology, history, opera. *Heir: s* George Trenchard Simon Davson [*b* 5 June 1964; *m* 1985, Joanna (marr. diss. 1996), *e d* of Rev. Dr James Bentley; one *s* one *d*]. *Address:* 4 Mermaid Street, Rye, East Sussex TN31 7ET. *T:* (01797) 222661, *Fax:* (01797) 224424. *Club:* Lansdowne.

DAVY, Margaret Ruth; *see* Bowron, M. R.

DAWANINCURA, Sir John (Norbert), Kt 1999; OBE 1992; Secretary General, Papua New Guinea Sports Federation, since 1994 (Vice President, 1983); *b* 25 May 1945; *s* of Stephen Joe Frank Dawanincura and Giro Paulo; *m* Lenah; one *s* two *d*. *Educ:* Chevalier Coll., NSW. Dist Valuer, W Highlands Province, Valuer Gen.'s Office; Manager, E Highlands Province, Bureau of Mgt Services; Graemme Dunnage Real Estate, 1977–78; Partner, Property Mgt and Maintenance, 1979–85. Rugby Football Union Player, Papua New Guinea team, 1965–70; Gen. Team Manager, PNG Contingents, 1981–86; Chief of PNG Delegation: Olympic Games, 1984–; Commonwealth Games, 1982–97, 1999–; S Pacific Games, 1983–98 (Chm. of Sports, Organising Cttee, Port Moresby, 1991); Mini S Pacific Games, 1981–; Mem., 1984–97, Vice Pres., 1993–97, Oceania Nat. Olympic Cttee (Chm., Develt Commn, 1993–97); Alternate Mem., PNG Sports Commn, 1992–; Schol. Mem., Mgt Cttee, Oceania Olympic Trng Coll., 1993–97; Mem. Mgt Cttee, Australia S Pacific 2000 Prog., 1995–97; Mem., Assoc. of Nat. Olympic Cttees, 1993–97; Deleg., 1981–86, Bd Mem., 1987–91, Pres. and Chm., 1995–99, S Pacific Games Council; Mem., Nat. Coaching Council, 1988–. Sir Buri Kidu Heart Inst., 1996–. *Recreations:* golf, circuit training, fishing. *Address:* PO Box 467, Boroko, NCD, Papua New Guinea. *T:* 3251411, 3251449. *Clubs:* Carbine, Golf, Yacht (Papua New Guinea).

DAWBARN, Sir Simon (Yelverton), KCVO 1980; CMG 1976; HM Diplomatic Service, retired; *b* 16 Sept. 1923; *s* of Frederic Dawbarn and Maud Louise Mansell; *m* 1948, Shelby Montgomery Parker; one *s* two *d*. *Educ:* Oundle Sch.; Corpus Christi Coll., Cambridge. Served in HM Forces (Reconnaissance Corps), 1942–45. Reckitt & Colman (Overseas), 1948–49. Joined Foreign Service, 1949. Foreign Office, 1949–53; Brussels, 1953; Prague, 1955; Tehran, 1957; seconded to HM Treasury, 1959; Foreign Office, 1961; Algiers, 1965; Athens, 1968; FCO, 1971–75. Head of W African Dept and concurrently non-resident Ambassador to Chad, 1973–75; Consul-General, Montreal, 1975–78; Ambassador to Morocco, 1978–82. *Address:* 44 Canonbury Park North, N1 2JT. *T:* (020) 7226 0659.

DAWE, Roger James, CB 1988; OBE 1970; educational consultant, KPMG, since 2001; *b* 26 Feb. 1941; *s* of late Harry James and Edith Mary Dawe; *m* 1965, Ruth Day Jolliffe; one *s* one *d*. *Educ:* Hardyes Sch., Dorchester; Fitzwilliam House, Cambridge (MA; Hon. Fellow, Fitzwilliam Coll., 1996). Entered Min. of Labour, 1962; Dept of Economic Affairs, 1964–65; Private Sec. to Prime Minister, 1966–70; Principal, Dept of Employment, 1970; Private Sec. to Secretary of State for Employment, 1972–74; Asst Sec., Dept of Employment, 1974–81; Under Sec., MSC, 1981; Chief Exec., Trng Div., MSC, 1982–84; Dep Sec., Dept of Employment, 1985–87; Dir Gen., MSC, then Training Commn, subseq. Training Agency, 1988–90; Department of Employment, then for Education and Employment: Dir Gen., Training Enterprise and Educn Directorate, 1990–92; Dep. Sec., Further and Higher Educn, 1992–95; Dir Gen. for Further and Higher Educn and Youth Trng, 1995–2000. Chm. Exec., Methodist Church Council, 2000–. FRSA. Hon. DEduc UWE, 2000. *Recreations:* tennis, Plymouth Argyle supporter, music, theatre, cinema. *Address:* 35 Cromwell Avenue, Bromley, Kent BR2 9AG.

DAWES, Prof. Edwin Alfred, CBiol, FIBiol; CChem, FRSC; Reckitt Professor of Biochemistry, University of Hull, 1963–90, now Emeritus; *b* 6 July 1925; *s* of late Harold Dawes and Maude Dawes (*née* Barker); *m* 1950, Amy Rogerson; two *s*. *Educ:* Goole Grammar Sch.; Univ. of Leeds. (BSc, PhD, DSc). Asst Lectr, later Lectr, in Biochemistry, Univ. of Leeds, 1947–50; Lectr, later Sen. Lectr, Univ. of Glasgow, 1951–63; Hull University: Head of Biochemistry Dept, 1963–86; Dean of Science, 1968–70; Pro-Vice-Chancellor, 1977–80; Dir, Biomed. Res. Unit, 1981–92. Visiting Lecturer: Meml Univ., Newfoundland, Dalhousie Univ., 1959; Univ. of Brazil, 1960, 1972; Univ. of S California, 1962; Univ. of Rabat, 1967; Univ. of Göttingen, 1972; Osmania Univ., Hyderabad, 1986; Univ. of Massachusetts, Amherst, 1989; Univ. of Padua, 1991; Lectures: Biochemical Soc., Australia and NZ, 1975; Amer. Medical Alumni, Univ. of St Andrews, 1980–81; Biodegradable Plastics Soc., Japan, 1991. Editor, Biochemical Jl, 1958–65; Editor-in-Chief, Jl of Gen. Microbiol., 1976–81; Man. Editor, Fedn of European Microbiol Socs, and Editor-in-Chief, FEMS Microbiology Letters, 1982–90. Dep. Chm., 1987–, Chm., Scientific Adv. Cttee, 1978–, Yorks Cancer Res. Campaign; Member: Scientific Adv. Cttee, Whyte-Watson-Turner Cancer Res. Trust, 1984–91; Adv. Gp for Cancer Res., Sheffield Univ., 1991–96. President: Hull Lit. Philosophical Soc., 1976–77; British Ring of Internat. Brotherhood of Magicians, 1972–73; Hon. President: Scottish Conjurers' Assoc.; Scottish Assoc. Magical Socs, 1996–; Hon. Vice-Pres., Magic Circle (Official Historian, 1987–; Mem., 1959–; Maskelyne Trophy, 1998). Chm., Philip Larkin Soc., 1995–. Governor, Pocklington Sch., 1965–74; Member, Court: Leeds Univ., 1974–; Bradford Univ., 1985–. Mem., Hall of Fame and H. A. Smith Literary Award, Soc. Amer. Magicians, 1984, 1997; Literary Fellowship and Hon. Life Mem., Acad. Magical Arts, USA, 1985; Hon. Mem. Bd, Houdini Historical Center, Wisconsin, 1990–. Consultant, The Mysteries of Magic, Learning Channel, 1998. Hon DSc Hull, 1992. Maskelyne Literary Award, 1988; Literary Award, Milbourne Christopher Foundn, USA, 1999. *Publications:* Quantitative Problems in Biochemistry, 1956, 6th edn 1980; (jtly) Biochemistry of Bacterial Growth, 1968, 3rd edn 1982; The Great Illusionists, 1979; Isaac Fawkes: fame and fable, 1979; The Biochemist in a Microbial Wonderland, 1982; Vonetta, 1982; The Barrister in the Circle, 1983; (ed) Environmental Regulation of Microbial Metabolism, 1985; (ed) Enterobacterial Surface Antigens, 1985; Microbial Energetics, 1985; (jtly) The Book of Magic, 1986, re-issued as Making Magic, 1992; The Wizard Exposed, 1987; (ed) Continuous Culture in Biotechnology and Environment Conservation, 1988; (contrib.) Philip Larkin: the man and his work, 1989; Henri Robin: expositor of science and magic, 1990; (ed) Molecular Biology of Membrane-Bound Complexes in Photosynthetic Bacteria, 1990; (ed) Novel Biodegradable Microbial Polymers, 1990; The Magic of Britain, 1994; Charles Bertram: the court conjurer, 1997; Stodare: the Enigma variations, 1998; Stanley Collins: conjuror and iconoclast, 2001; (ed jtly) The Annals of Conjuring, 2001; numerous papers in scientific jls. *Recreations:* conjuring, book-collecting. *Address:* Dane Hill, 393 Beverley Road, Anlaby, E Yorkshire HU10 7BQ. *T:* (01482) 657998, *Fax:* (01482) 655941.

DAWES, Rt Rev. Peter Spencer; Bishop of Derby, 1988–95; *b* 5 Feb. 1928; *s* of Jason Spencer Dawes and Janet Dawes; *m* 1954, Ethel Marrin; two *s* two *d. Educ:* Bickley Hall School; Aldenham School; Hatfield Coll., Durham (BA); Tyndale Hall, Bristol. Assistant Curate: St Andrew's, Whitehall Park, 1954–57; St Ebbe's, Oxford, 1957–60; Tutor, Clifton Theological Coll., 1960–65; Vicar, Good Shepherd, Romford, 1965–80; Archdeacon of West Ham, 1980–88. Examining Chaplain to Bishop of Chelmsford, 1970–95. Member, General Synod, 1970–95. *Address:* 45 Arundell, Ely, Cambs CB6 1BQ. *T:* (01353) 661241.

DAWES, Prof. William Nicholas, PhD; FREng, FRAeS; Francis Mond Professor of Aeronautical Engineering, Cambridge University, since 1996; Fellow of Churchill College, Cambridge, since 1984; *b* 5 Sept. 1955; *s* of Kenneth Frederick Dawes and Doris Jacyntha Hulm; *m* 1980, Luigia Cuomo; two *d. Educ:* Churchill Coll., Cambridge (BA; MA; PhD). CEng; FRAeS 1997; FREng 2000. Res. Officer, CEGB, 1980–84; Sen. Res. Asst, 1984–86, Lectr, 1986–96, Engrg Dept, Cambridge Univ. Mem., Amer. Inst. Aeronautics and Astronautics, 1990. *Publications:* articles in professional jls. *Recreations:* Italy, good food and good wine. *Address:* Church Farm, Church Lane, Little Eversden CB3 7HQ. *T:* (01223) 263318.

DAWICK, Viscount; Alexander Douglas Derrick Haig; farmer; *b* 30 June 1961; *s* and *heir* of 2nd Earl Haig, *qv. Educ:* Stowe School; Royal Agricl Coll., Cirencester. *Address:* Third Farm, Melrose, Roxburgh TD6 9DR. *Club:* New (Edinburgh).

DAWKINS, Prof. (Clinton) Richard, FRS 2001; Charles Simonyi Professor of the Public Understanding of Science, University of Oxford, since 1996; Fellow, New College, Oxford, since 1970; *b* 26 March 1941; *s* of Clinton John Dawkins and Jean Mary Vyvyan (*née* Ladner); *m*; one *d. Educ:* Oundle Sch.; Balliol Coll., Oxford (MA, DPhil, DSc). Asst Prof. of Zoology, Univ. of California, Berkeley, 1967–69; Oxford University: Lectr, 1970–89; Reader in Zoology, 1989–95; Charles Simonyi Reader in the Public Understanding of Science, 1995–96. Gifford Lectr, Glasgow Univ., 1988; Sidgwick Meml Lectr, Newnham Coll., Cambridge, 1988; Kovler Vis. Fellow, Univ. of Chicago, 1990; Nelson Lectr, Univ. of California, Davis, 1990; Royal Instn Christmas Lects for Young People, 1991. Presenter, BBC TV Horizon progs, 1985, 1986. Editor: Animal Behaviour, 1974–78; Oxford Surveys in Evolutionary Biology, 1983–86. FRSL 1997. Hon. Fellow, Regent's Coll., London, 1988. Hon. DLitt: St Andrews, 1995; ANU, 1996; Hon. DSc Westminster, 1997. Silver Medal, Zool Soc., 1989; Michael Faraday Award, Royal Soc., 1990; Nakayama Prize, Nakayama Foundn for Human Scis, 1994; Internat. Cosmos Prize, 1997. *Publications:* The Selfish Gene, 1976, 2nd edn 1989; The Extended Phenotype, 1982; The Blind Watchmaker, 1986 (RSL Prize 1987; LA Times Lit. Prize 1987); River Out of Eden, 1995; Climbing Mount Improbable, 1996; Unweaving the Rainbow: science, delusion and the appetite for wonder, 1998. *Recreation:* the Apple Macintosh. *Address:* Oxford University Museum, Parks Road, Oxford OX1 3PW. *T:* (01865) 514103.

DAWKINS, Douglas Alfred; Associate Director, Bank of England, 1985–87; *b* 17 Sept. 1927; *s* of Arthur Dawkins and Edith Annie Dawkins; *m* 1953, Diana Pauline (*née* Ormes); one *s* one *d. Educ:* Edmonton County Secondary Sch.; University Coll. London (Rosa Morison Scholar; BA Hons). Entered Bank of England, 1950; Bank for Internat. Settlements, 1953–54; Adviser to Governors, Bank of Libya, 1964–65; Asst Chief of Overseas Dept, 1970; First Dep. Chief of Exchange Control, 1972; Chief of Exchange Control, 1979; Asst Dir, 1980. *Address:* c/o Bank of England, Threadneedle Street, EC2R 8AH.

DAWKINS, Hon. John Sydney, AO 2000; economist, consultant, company director; Chairman: John Dawkins & Co., since 1994; M & C Saatchi (Australia), since 1996; Medical Corporation of Australasia, since 1997; Elders Rural Services, since 1998; *b* 2 March 1947; *s* of Dr A. L. Dawkins and M. Dawkins (*née* Lee Steere); *m* 1987, Maggie Maruff; one *d*, one step *s*, and one *s* one *d* by previous marr. *Educ:* Roseworthy Agricl Coll., SA (RDA); Univ. of WA (BEc). MHR, Tangney, 1974–75; Press Officer, WA Trades and Labor Council, 1976–77; MP (ALP) Fremantle, WA, 1977–94; Shadow Minister for Educn, 1980–83; Minister: for Finance and assisting Prime Minister for Public Service Matters, 1983–84; for Trade and assisting Prime Minister for Youth Affairs, 1984–87; for Employment, Educn and Trng, 1987–91; Treasurer of Australia, 1991–93. Special investment rep., 1994–95; Dir, Sealcorp Hldgs, 1994–. Bd Mem., Fred Hollows Foundn, 1995–. Hon. Dr: Univ. of S Australia, 1996; Queensland Univ. of Technol., 1997. *Address:* Level 25, 91 King William Street, Adelaide, SA 5081, Australia.

DAWKINS, Richard; *see* Dawkins, C. R.

DAWKINS, Simon John Robert, MA; Headmaster, Merchant Taylors' School, Crosby, since 1986; *b* 9 July 1945; *s* of Col William John Dawkins, TD and Mary Doreen Dawkins (*née* King); *m* 1968, Janet Mary Stevens; one *s* one *d. Educ:* Solihull Sch.; Univ. of Nottingham (BA); Queens' Coll., Cambridge (PGCE); Birkbeck Coll. London (MA distn). Head of Economics: Eltham Coll., 1968–71; Dulwich Coll., 1971–86 (Housemaster, 1979–86). Headmasters' Conference: Chm. NW Div., 1996 (Sec., 1995); Member: Memship Cttee, 1996–99; Academic Policy Cttee, 2000–. *Recreations:* physical exercise, tennis, golf, reading. *Address:* Brackenwood, St George's Road, Hightown, Liverpool L38 3RT. *T:* (0151) 929 3546. *Clubs:* East India; Hightown (Lancs); Formby Golf, St Enodoc Golf.

DAWNAY, family name of **Viscount Downe**.

DAWNAY, Lady Jane Meriel; Member of Board, Historic Buildings Council for Scotland, 1996–99; *b* 8 Feb. 1953; *yr d* of 5th Duke of Westminster, TD and Hon. Viola Maud Lyttelton (*d* 1987); *m* 1st, 1977, Duke of Roxburghe, *qv* (marr. diss. 1990); two *s* one *d*; 2nd, 1996, Edward William Dawnay. *Educ:* Collegiate Sch., Enniskillen; Sherborne Hill; Switzerland; Bedgebury Park; Paris. Vice Pres., Arthritis and Rheumatism Council for Res., 1998– (Regl Chm., 1983–98); Macmillan Cancer Relief (formerly Cancer Relief Macmillan Fund): Vice Pres., Scotland, 1994– (Dir and Bd Mem., 1990–94); Chm., Scotland and NI, 1989–94. Mem. Bd, Ancient Monuments Scotland, 1993–96; Member: Adv. Cttee, Royal Parks, 1994–99; Royal Highland & Agricultural Soc. of Scotland, 1998 (Pres., 1998–). Trustee, Atlantic Salmon Trust Scotland, 1995–. Director: Beltane Partners Ltd, 1994–98; Radio Borders, 1992–98. Mem., Racehorse Owners' Assoc. Pres., NW Norfolk Cons. Assoc., 1999–. Patron, British Lymphology Soc., 1998–; Life Patron, George Thomas Soc. MInstD 1997. Freeman, City of Chester, 1997. Queen Elizabeth the Queen Mother's Award for Envmt, Scotland, 1996. *Recreations:* fishing, gardening, reading. *Address:* Hillington Hall, Hillington, King's Lynn, Norfolk PE31 6BW; 48 Eaton Square, SW1W 9BD.

See also Marquis of Bowmont and Cessford.

DAWOOD, Nessim Joseph; Arabist and Middle East Consultant; Managing Director, The Arabic Advertising and Publishing Co. (Aradco) Ltd, London, since 1958; Director, Contemporary Translations Ltd, London, since 1962; *b* Baghdad, 27 Aug. 1927; 4th *s* of late Yousef Dawood, merchant, and Muzli (*née* Tweg); *m* 1949, Juliet, 2nd *d* of late M. and N. Abraham, Baghdad and New York; three *s. Educ:* The American Sch. and Shamash Sch., Baghdad; Iraq State Scholar in England, UC Exeter, 1945–49; Univ. of London, BA (Hons). FIL 1959. Dir, Bradbury Wilkinson (Graphics) Ltd, 1975–86. Has written and spoken radio and film commentaries. *Publications:* The Muqaddimah of Ibn Khaldun, 1967 (US, 1969); Penguin Classics: The Thousand and One Nights, 1954; The Koran, 1956, 46th edn 2001, parallel Arabic/English edn, 1990; Aladdin and Other Tales, 1957; Tales from The Thousand and One Nights, 1973, 26th edn 2001; Arabian Nights (illus. children's edn), 1978; Puffin Classics: Aladdin & Other Tales, 1989; Sindbad the Sailor & other Tales, 1989; contribs to specialised and technical English-Arabic dictionaries; translated numerous technical publications into Arabic; occasional book reviews. *Recreation:* going to the theatre. *Address:* Aradco House, 132 Cleveland Street, W1P 6AB. *T:* (020) 7692 7700. *Club:* Hurlingham.

DAWS, Dame Joyce (Margaretta), DBE 1975; FRCS, FRACS; Surgeon, Queen Victoria Memorial Hospital, Melbourne, Victoria, Australia, 1958–85; Thoracic Surgeon, Prince Henry's Hospital, Melbourne, 1975, now retired; President, Victorian Branch Council, Australian Medical Association, 1976; *b* 21 July 1925; *d* of Frederick William Daws and Daisy Ethel Daws. *Educ:* Royal School for Naval and Marine Officers' Daughters, St Margaret's, Mddx; St Paul's Girls' Sch., Hammersmith; Royal Free Hosp., London. MB, BS (London) 1949; FRCS 1952, FRACS. Ho. Surg., Royal Free Hosp.; SHMO, Manchester Royal Infirmary; Hon. Surg., Queen Victoria Meml Hosp., Melb., 1958; Asst Thoracic Surg., Prince Henry's Hosp., Melb., 1967–75. Pres., Bd of Management, After-Care Hosp., Melbourne, 1980–85; Chairman: Victorian Nursing Council, 1983–89; Academic and Professional Panel, Victoria, for Churchill Fellowship Awards, 1984; Jt Adv. Cttee on Pets in Society, 1984; Internat. Protea Assoc., 1987–96. Hon. Sec., Victorian Br., AMA, 1974. *Recreations:* opera, ballet, theatre, desert travel, protea grower. *Address:* 26 Edwin Street, Heidelberg Heights, Vic 3081, Australia. *T:* (3) 4572579. *Clubs:* Lyceum, Soroptimist International (Melbourne).

DAWSON, Hon. Lord; Thomas Cordner Dawson; a Senator of the College of Justice in Scotland, since 1995; *b* 14 Nov. 1948; *s* of Thomas Dawson and Flora Chisholm (*née* Dunwoodie); *m* 1975, Jennifer Richmond Crombie; two *s. Educ:* Royal High Sch. of Edinburgh; Edinburgh Univ. (LLB Hons). Advocate, 1973; QC (Scot.) 1986. Lectr, Univ. of Dundee, 1971–74; Advocate Depute, 1983–87; Solicitor-Gen. for Scotland, 1992–95. Member: Supreme Court Legal Aid Cttee, 1980–83; Criminal Injuries Compensation Bd, 1988–92. *Recreations:* golf, cricket, reading, crosswords. *Address:* 19 Craiglea Drive, Edinburgh EH10 5PB. *T:* (0131) 447 4427. *Club:* Caledonian (Edinburgh).

DAWSON, (Archibald) Keith; Headmaster, Haberdashers' Aske's School, Elstree, 1987–96; *b* 12 Jan. 1937; *s* of Wilfred Joseph and Alice Marjorie Dawson; *m* 1961, Marjorie Blakeson; two *d. Educ:* Nunthorpe Grammar School for Boys, York; The Queen's College, Oxford. MA, Dip Ed distinction. Ilford County High School for Boys, 1961–63; Haberdasher's Aske's Sch., 1963–71 (Head of History, 1965–71); Headmaster, John Mason Sch., Abingdon, 1971–79; Principal, Scarborough Sixth Form Coll., 1979–84; Principal, King James's College of Henley, 1984–87. FRSA 1994. Liveryman, Haberdashers' Co., 1996–. *Publications:* Society and Industry in 19th Century England (with Peter Wall), 1968; The Industrial Revolution, 1971. *Recreations:* theatre, music, cricket, hill walking. *Address:* Puffins, 77 Chapel Street, Sidbury, Sidmouth EX10 0RQ.

DAWSON, Hon. Sir Daryl (Michael), AC 1988; KBE 1982; CB 1980; Justice of the High Court of Australia, 1982–97; Non permanent Member, Hong Kong Court of Final Appeal, since 1998; Adjunct Professor of Law, Monash University, since 1997; Professorial Fellow, University of Melbourne, since 1998; *b* 12 Dec. 1933; *s* of Claude Charles Dawson and Elizabeth May Dawson; *m* 1971, Mary Louise Thomas. *Educ:* Canberra High Sch.; Ormond Coll., Univ. of Melbourne (LLB Hons); LLM Yale. Sterling Fellow, Yale Univ., 1955–56. QC 1971; Solicitor-General for Victoria, 1974–82. Mem. Council, Univ. of Melbourne, 1976–86; Chm. Council, Ormond Coll., Univ. of Melbourne, 1991–92. Chm., Australian Motor Sport Appeal Court, 1986–88 (Mem., 1970–86). Chm., Menzies Foundn, 1988–; Gov., Ian Potter Foundn, 1988–. *Recreation:* gardening. *Address:* PO Box 147, East Melbourne, Vic 3002, Australia. *Clubs:* Melbourne, Savage, RACV, Beefsteaks (Melbourne).

DAWSON, Dee; *see* Dawson, J. D.

DAWSON, (Edward) John; Assistant Chief Executive, 1989–90, and Director, 1989–91, Lloyds Bank; *b* 14 Oct. 1935; *s* of late Edward Dawson and Kathleen Dawson (*née* Naughton); *m* 1st, 1963, Ann Prudence (*née* Hicks) (marr. diss. 1997); two *s* one *d*; 2nd, 1998, Jill Solveig (*née* Linton). *Educ:* St Joseph's Coll., Blackpool; London Graduate Sch. of Business Studies (Sloan Fellow, 1969–70); Manchester Coll., Univ. of Oxford (BA Hons PPE 1994; MA 1998). FCIB. Entered Lloyds Bank, 1952; served RAF, 1954–56; General Manager, Lloyds Bank and Exec. Dir, Lloyds Bank International, 1982–84; Asst Chief Gen. Manager, 1985, Dir, UK Retail Banking, 1985–88, Lloyds Bank; Chairman: Lloyds Bowmaker Finance, 1988–90 (Dir, 1985–90); Black Horse Agencies, 1988–89 (Dir, 1985–89). Chm., Walsingham Community Homes Ltd, 1991–96. *Recreations:* life in South Africa during Northern winter, golf, cricket, tennis, choral singing, hiking, climbing, T'ai chi ch'uan. *Address:* c/o Lloyds TSB, Westminster House, 4 Dean Stanley Street, SW1P 3HU. *Clubs:* MCC; Wareham Golf.

DAWSON, Hilton; *see* Dawson, T. H.

DAWSON, Sir (Hugh) Michael (Trevor), 4th Bt *cr* 1920, of Edgewarebury; *b* 28 March 1956; *s* of Sir (Hugh Halliday) Trevor Dawson, 3rd Bt; *S* father, 1983. *Heir: b* Nicholas Antony Trevor Dawson, *b* 17 Aug. 1957.

DAWSON, Ian David; Assistant Under-Secretary of State (Policy), Ministry of Defence, 1991–93; *b* 24 Nov. 1934; *s* of Harry Newton Dawson and Margaret (*née* Aspinall); *m* 1955, Barbara (*née* Mather); two *s* one *d. Educ:* Hutton Grammar Sch.; Fitzwilliam House, Cambridge (MA). Directorate of Military Survey, 1958–71; Principal, MoD, 1971; Private Sec. to CAS, 1975–77; Asst Sec., Naval Staff, 1977–80; Sec., AWRE, 1980–83; RCDS, 1984; Dir, Defence and Security Agency, WEU, Paris, 1986–88; Asst Under-Sec. of State (Resources), MoD, 1988–90; Fellow, Center for Internat. Affairs, Harvard, 1990–91. *Recreations:* music, mountaineering, travel. *Address:* 7 Claremont Falls, Killigarth, Polperro, Cornwall PL13 2HT.

DAWSON, James Gordon, CBE 1981; FREng, FIMechE, FSAE; Consultant; *b* 3 Feb. 1916; *s* of James Dawson and Helen Mitchell (*née* Tawse); *m* 1941, Doris Irene (*née* Rowe) (*d* 1982); one *s* one *d. Educ:* Aberdeen Grammar Sch.; Aberdeen Univ. (BScEng Hons Mech. Eng, BScEng Hons Elect. Eng). Develt Test Engr, Rolls Royce Ltd, Derby, 1942; Chief Engr, Shell Research Ltd, 1946; Technical Dir, Perkins Engines Ltd, 1955; Dir,

Dowty Group Ltd, 1966; Man. Dir, Zenith Carburetter Co. Ltd, 1969, Chm., 1977–81. Pres., IMechE, 1979–80; FIMechE 1957; Hon. FIMechE 1986. *Publications:* technical papers publd in UK and abroad. *Recreation:* golf. *Address:* Mildmay House, Apethorpe, Peterborough PE8 5DP. *T:* (01780) 470348. *Club:* Caledonian.

DAWSON, James Grant Forbes, CEng, FICE; Chairman, GIBB Ltd, since 1995; *b* 6 Sept. 1940; *s* of William Maxwell Hume Dawson and Caroline Margaret Storey Dawson; *m* 2nd, 1993, Joan Margaret Davison. *Educ:* Edinburgh Univ. (BSc). FIPENZ (FNZIE); Eur Ing. GIBB Ltd: Chief Engr, 1975–78; Associate, 1978–80; Head of Transport, 1980–82; Partner, 1982–; Director, 1989–. Member: DTI Cttee for S Africa Trade, 1998–; E Europe Trade Council, 1999–. Chm., ACE, 1999–2000. *Recreations:* sport, gardening, ornithology. *Address:* (office) GIBB House, London Road, Reading, Berks RG6 1BL. *T:* (0118) 963 5000. *Club:* East India.

DAWSON, Joan Denise, (Dee); Medical Director, Rhodes Farm Clinic, since 1991; *b* 17 Jan. 1947; *d* of Horace and Joan Webb; *m* 1st, 1969, Stephen Dawson (marr diss.); 2nd, 1979, Ian Dear; one *s* four *d*. *Educ:* Chelsea Coll., London Univ. (BSc); London Business Sch.; Royal Free Hosp. Sch. of Medicine (MB BS 1989). Voluntary Teacher, VSO, Madagascar, 1969–71; Mkt Res. Manager, Parker Ltd, 1974–75; Man. Dir, Dee Dawson Fashion Ltd, 1977–84; House Physician, 1989–90, House Surgeon, 1990–91, North Middx Hosp.; set up Rhodes Farm Clinic, first residential unit, incl. full-time school, dedicated solely to treatment of anorexic children, 1991. *Publication:* A Quick Guide to Eating Disorders, 1995. *Recreations:* tennis, water ski-ing. *Address:* The Old House, Totteridge Green, N20 8PA.

DAWSON, John; *see* Dawson, E. J.

DAWSON, Prof. John Alan; Professor of Marketing, University of Edinburgh, since 1990; *b* 19 Aug. 1944; *s* of Alan and Gladys Dawson; *m* 1967, Jocelyn M. P. Barker; one *s* one *d*. *Educ:* University College London (BSc, MPhil); University of Nottingham (PhD). Lectr, Univ. of Nottingham, 1967–71; Lectr, 1971, Sen. Lectr, 1974, Reader, 1981–83, Univ. of Wales, Lampeter; Fraser of Allander Prof. of Distributive Studies, and Dir, Inst. for Retail Studies, Univ. of Stirling, 1983–90. Vis. Lectr, Univ. of Western Australia, 1973; Vis. Res. Fellow, ANU, 1978; Visiting Professor: Florida State Univ., 1982; Chuo Univ., 1986; Univ. of S Africa, 1999; Sch. for Higher Mgt and Business Strategy, Barcelona, 2000; Univ. of Mktg and Distbn Sci., Kobe, 2000; Boconni Univ., Milan, 2000. Chm., Nat. Museums of Scotland Retailing Co., 1992–. Member: Distributive Trades EDC, 1984–87; Board, Cumbernauld Develt Corp., 1987–96. Hon. Sec., Inst. of British Geographers, 1985–88. *Publications:* Evaluating the Human Environment, 1973; Man and His World, 1975; Computing for Geographers, 1976; Small Scale Retailing in UK, 1979; Marketing Environment, 1979; Retail Geography, 1980; Commercial Distribution in Europe, 1982; Teach Yourself Geography, 1983; Shopping Centre Development, 1983; Computer Programming for Geographers, 1985; Shopping Centres Policies and Prospects, 1985; Evolution of European Retailing, 1989; Competition and Markets, 1991; Retail Environments in Developing Countries, 1991; Distribution Statistics, 1992; articles in geographical, management and marketing jls. *Recreations:* sport, travel. *Address:* Department of Business Studies, University of Edinburgh, Edinburgh EH8 9JY. *T:* (0131) 650 3830.

DAWSON, John Anthony Lawrence, FICE, FIHT; Policy Director (formerly Director, Group Public Affairs), Automobile Association, since 1995 (Member Committee, 1996–99); *b* 6 Feb. 1950; *m* 1980, Frances Anne Elizabeth Whelan; two *d*. *Educ:* Mill Hill Sch.; Southampton Univ. British Rail Engineering Scholar, 1968–72; Depts of Envt and Transport, 1972–81; Overseas Transport Consultant, 1981–85; Dir (Transport), London Regl Office, Dept of Transport, 1985–88; Chief Road Engineer, Scottish Develt Dept, 1988; Dir of Roads and Chief Road Engr, Scottish Office, 1989–95. Mem. Bd, Ertico, 1995–97, 1999–; Man. Dir, AA Foundn for Road Safety Research, 1995–. *Recreations:* touring, music. *Address:* Automobile Association, Norfolk House, Priestley Road, Basingstoke, Hants RG24 9NY. *T:* (01256) 492966. *Club:* Royal Scottish Automobile (Glasgow).

DAWSON, John Kelvin; Agent-General for Queensland in London, and Commissioner, Europe, since 2001; *b* Melbourne, 15 Sept. 1943; *s* of John Inglis Dawson and Marie Victoria Dawson; one *s* one *d*. *Educ:* Ivanhoe Grammar Sch.; Univ. of Melbourne (BA). National Australia Bank Ltd: Gen. Manager, Strategic Develt, 1991-93; Man. Dir, UK and Europe, 1993-95; Gp Gen. Manager, Asian and Internat. Banking, 1995; CEO, Bank of Queensland Ltd, 1996-2001. Director: Clydesdale Bank, 1993-95; Nat. Irish Bank, 1993-95; Northern Bank, Belfast, 1993-95; Yorkshire Bank, 1993-95; Bank of Hawaii Internat., 1999–2001. Chm., Exec. Cttee, Aust. Bankers' Assoc., 1992-93. *Recreations:* all sports, wine, reading. *Address:* Queensland Government Office Europe, 392 Strand, WC2R 0LZ. *Clubs:* East India; Australian, Melbourne Cricket (Melbourne); Brisbane, Tattersalls (Qld); Hong Kong Foreign Correspondents.

DAWSON, (Joseph) Peter; Consultant, Education International, since 1998 (Co-ordinator for Europe, 1993–98); *b* 18 March 1940; *s* of Joseph Glyn and Winifred Olwen Dawson; *m* 1964, Yvonne Anne Charlton Smith; one *s* one *d*. *Educ:* Bishop Gore Grammar Sch., Swansea; University College of Swansea (BSc, DipEd). Assistant Master, Chiswick Grammar Sch., 1962; Field Officer, 1965, Sen. Field Officer, 1966, NUT; Asst Sec., 1969, Negotiating Sec., 1974, ATTI; Negotiating Sec., 1976, Gen. Sec., 1979–89, Asst Sec. (Pensions and Memship Services) and Internat. Rep., 1989–93, NATFHE. Gen. Sec., ETUCE, 1991–93 (Mem. Exec. Bd, 1984–93; Chm., Higher Educn Working Gp, 1989–93). Vice-Pres., 1962–64, Sen. Treasurer, 1965–68, National Union of Students. Member: Teachers' Panel, Teachers' Superannuation Working Party, 1969–93 (Chm., 1979–93); Eur. Cttee, World Confedn of Organisations of Teaching Profession, 1983–93; Cttee on Workers' Capital, ICFTU, 2000–. Sec., Horniman Br., W Lewisham Lab. Party, 1999–. Gov., Holy Trinity Sch., Forest Hill, 1989–93, 1998–. Hon. FCP 1984. *Recreations:* football, cricket, theatre. *Address:* 3 Westwood Park, Forest Hill SE23 3QB. *T:* and *Fax:* (020) 8291 6200. *Club:* Surrey County Cricket.

DAWSON, Keith; *see* Dawson, A. K.

DAWSON, Sir Michael; *see* Dawson, Sir H. M. T.

DAWSON, Peter; *see* Dawson, J. P.

DAWSON, Ven. Peter; Archdeacon of Norfolk, 1977–93, now Emeritus; *b* 31 March 1929; *s* of late Leonard Smith and Cicely Alice Dawson; *m* 1955, Kathleen Mary Sansome; one *s* three *d*. *Educ:* Manchester Grammar School; Keble Coll., Oxford (MA); Ridley Hall, Cambridge. Nat. service, Army, 1947–49; University, 1949–52; Theological College, 1952–54. Asst Curate, St Lawrence, Morden, Dio. Southwark, 1954–59; Vicar of Barston, Warwicks, Dio. Birmingham, 1959–63; Rector of St Clement, Higher Openshaw, Dio. Manchester, 1963–68; Rector of Morden, Dio. Southwark, 1968–77, and Rural Dean of Merton, 1975–77. *Recreations:* gardening, politics, the rural community, historical studies. *Address:* The Coach House, Harmony Hill, Milnthorpe LA7 7QA. *T:* (015395) 62020.

DAWSON, Rev. Peter, OBE 1986; Member, Employment Appeal Tribunal, since 1992; *b* 19 May 1933; *s* of Richard Dawson and Henrietta Kate Dawson (*née* Trueman); *m* 1957, Shirley Margaret Pentland Johnson; two *d*. *Educ:* Beckenham Technical Sch.; Beckenham Grammar Sch.; London School of Economics (BScEcon); Westminster Coll. (Postgrad. CertEd). Schoolmaster Fellow Commoner, Keble Coll., Oxford, 1969, and Corpus Christi Coll., Cambridge, 1979. Asst Master, Roan Grammar School for Boys, London, 1957–62; Head of Upper School, Sedgehill Sch., London, 1962–67; Second Master, Gateacre Comprehensive Sch., Liverpool, 1967–70; Headmaster, Eltham Green Sch., London, 1970–80; Gen. Sec., Professional Assoc. of Teachers, 1980–92; OFSTED Registered Inspector of Schs, 1993–2000. Methodist Minister, ordained 1985; Asst Minister, Queen's Hall Methodist Mission, Derby, 1984–87; Minister, Spondon Methodist Ch., Derby, 1989–90; Free Church Minister, Church on Oakwood, Derby, 1990–94; Minister, Mayfield Rd Methodist Church, Derby, 1994–98. Member: Burnham Cttee, 1981–87; Council of Managerial and Professional Staffs, 1989–92 (Pres.); Econ. and Social Cttee, EC, 1990–94. *Publications:* Making a Comprehensive Work, 1981; Teachers and Teaching, 1984; Why Preach?, 2000. *Recreations:* reading, theatre, cinema, golf, grandparenthood. *Address:* 72 The Ridings, Ockbrook, Derby DE72 3SF. *T:* (01332) 672669. *Club:* Horsley Lodge (Derby).

DAWSON, Peter; Secretary, Royal and Ancient Golf Club of St Andrews, since 1999; *b* 28 May 1948; *s* of George Dawson and Violet Dawson (*née* Smith); *m* 1969, Juliet Ann Bartlett; one *s* one *d*. *Educ:* Westcliff High Sch.; Corpus Christi Coll., Cambridge (MA). Managing Director: Grove Cranes, 1977–83; Blackwood Hodge (UK), 1983–89; Grove Europe, 1989–93; Thos Storey, 1994–97. *Address:* Royal and Ancient Golf Club of St Andrews, Fife KY16 9JD. *T:* (01334) 472112. *Clubs:* Northumberland Golf; Royal Worlington and Newmarket Golf; Golf House (Elie).

DAWSON, Air Vice-Marshal Reginald Thomas, CBE 1987; Director of Legal Services, Royal Air Force, 1989–92, retired; *b* 6 Aug. 1930; *s* of Herbert James and Lilian Ethel Dawson; *m* 1963, Geraldine Sandra Peters; one *s* one *d*. *Educ:* Hastings Grammar Sch.; Skinners' Sch., Tunbridge Wells. Qualified as solicitor, 1953. Nat. service, RAF, as pilot, 1953–55; in private practice as solicitor, 1955–57; RAF Reserve, 1955–57; rejoined RAF, 1957; Flt Lt, later Sqn Ldr, RAF Legal Branch, 1957–68; Wing Comdr, 1968; Dep. Dir of Legal Services, NEAF, 1968–71; UK Legal Officer, Australian, NZ and UK Force, Singapore, 1971–74; Gp Captain, 1974; Dep. Dir of Legal Services, RAF Germany, 1974–78; Legal Services 1, RAF, 1978–82, Dep. Dir, 1982–89; Air Cdre, 1982; Air Vice-Marshal, 1989. *Recreations:* game shooting, golf, sailing, walking, gardening, reading. *Address:* The Minstrels, Netherfield Hill, Battle, E Sussex TN33 0LH. *T:* (01424) 772186. *Club:* Royal Air Force.

DAWSON, Rex Malcolm Chaplin, FRS 1981; PhD, DSc; Deputy Director and Head of Biochemistry Department, Institute of Animal Physiology, Babraham, Cambridge, 1969–84, retired (Deputy Chief Scientific Officer, 1969–84); *b* 3 June 1924; *s* of late James Dawson and Ethel Mary Dawson (*née* Chaplin); *m* 1946, Emily Elizabeth Hodder; one *s* one *d*. *Educ:* Hinckley Grammar Sch.; University Coll., London (BSc 1946, DSc 1960); Univ. of Wales (PhD 1951). MRC Fellowship followed by Beit Meml Fellowship, Neuropsychiatric Res. Centre, Whitchurch Hosp., Cardiff, 1947–52; Betty Brookes Fellow, Dept of Biochemistry, Univ. of Oxford, 1952–55. Vis. Res. Fellow, Harvard Univ., 1950; Vis. Prof., Northwestern Univ., Chicago, 1974. International Lipid Prize Amer. Oil Chemists' Assoc., 1981. *Publications:* Metabolism and Physiological Significance of Lipids, 1964; Data for Biochemical Research, 1959, 3rd edn 1986; Form and Function of Phospholipids, 1973; numerous papers on structure, turnover and role of phospholipids in cell membranes in various scientific jls. *Recreations:* mercantile marine history, sailing, gardening. *Address:* Kirn House, Holt Road, Langham, Norfolk NR25 7BX. *T:* (01328) 830396.

DAWSON, Prof. Sandra June Noble; KPMG Peat Marwick Professor of Management Studies, Director, Judge Institute of Management Studies, since 1995, and Master of Sidney Sussex College, since 1999, University of Cambridge; *b* 4 June 1946; *d* of Wilfred Denyer and Joy (*née* Noble); *m* 1969, Henry R. C. Dawson; one *s* two *d*. *Educ:* Dr Challoner's Grammar Sch., Amersham; Univ. of Keele (BA 1st Cl. Hons Hist. and Sociol. 1968). Research Officer, Govt Social Survey, 1968–69; Imperial College of Science, Technology and Medicine: Res. Officer, Lectr, then Sen. Lectr, Industrial Sociol. Unit, Dept of Social and Econ. Studies, 1969–90; Prof. of Organisational Behaviour, Mgt Sch., 1990–95; Fellow, Jesus Coll. Cambridge, 1995–99. Non-exec. Dir, Riverside HA, 1990–92; Chm., Riverside Mental Health Trust, 1992–95. Member: Res. Strategy Bd, Offshore Safety Div., HSE, 1991–95; Strategic Review Gp, PHLS, 1994; Sen. Salaries Review Body, 1997–; Futures and Innovation Bd, DTI, 1998–; Res. Priorities Bd, ESRC. Non-executive Director: Cambridge Econometrics, 1996–; Fleming Claverhouse Investment Trust, 1996–; PHLS, 1997–99; Soc. for Advancement of Mgt Studies, 1999–. Mem. Adv. Bd, Alchemy Partners. Trustee, RAND Europe (UK). *Publications:* Analysing Organisations, 1986, 3rd edn 1996; Safety at Work: the limits of self regulation, 1988; Managing in the NHS, 1995; contribs to mgt learned jls. *Recreations:* music, walking, family. *Address:* Judge Institute of Management Studies, Trumpington Street, Cambridge CB2 1AG. *T:* (01223) 339700.

DAWSON, Stephen Eric; a District Judge (Magistrates' Courts) (formerly Metropolitan Stipendiary Magistrate), since 1994; a Recorder, since 2000; *b* 16 Feb. 1952; *s* of late Leslie Eric Dawson and of Margaret Kathleen Dawson; *m* 1977, Sandra Mary Bate; two *d*. *Educ:* St Joseph's Acad., Blackheath; Coll. of Law. Admitted Solicitor, 1977. Articled and subseq. Partner, Victor Lissack, solicitors, 1978–82; Partner, Reynolds Dawson, 1982–94; an Asst Recorder, 1998–2000. Treas. and Mem. Council, British Acad. of Forensic Scis, 1985–; Treas. and Mem. Cttee, London Criminal Courts Solicitors' Assoc., 1987–94; Member: Criminal Law Cttee, Law Soc., 1993–; Inner London Magistrates' Courts Cttee, 1997–2000; Gtr London Magistrates' Cts Authy, 2000–. *Publication:* Profitable Legal Aid, 1991. *Recreations:* occasional gardening, gentle jogging. *Address:* c/o Principal Chief Clerk's Office, Secretariat Department, 65 Romney Street, SW1P 3RD.

DAWSON, Thomas Cordner; *see* Dawson, Hon. Lord.

DAWSON, (Thomas) Hilton; MP (Lab) Lancaster and Wyre, since 1997; *b* 30 Sept. 1953; *s* of late Harry Dawson and of Sally Dawson; *m* 1973, Susan, *d* of Ellis and Alice Williams; two *d*. *Educ:* Warwick Univ. (BA Hons Philos. and Pols 1975); Lancaster Univ. (Dip. in Social Work 1982). Brickworks labourer, 1975; clerk, 1976; kibbutz volunteer, 1976; community worker, 1977; social worker, 1979; Lancs Social Services, 1982–97; youth justice worker, 1983; social work manager, 1989. Mem. (Lab) Lancaster CC, 1987–97. *Recreations:* family, the arts, walking, keeping fit. *Address:* 1 Malham Close, Lancaster LA1 2SJ. *T:* (01524) 66075.

DAWSON-DAMER, family name of **Earl of Portarlington**.

DAWTRY, Sir Alan, Kt 1974; CBE 1968 (MBE (mil.) 1945); TD 1948; Chief Executive (formerly Town Clerk), Westminster City Council, 1956–77; Chairman: Sperry Rand

Ltd, 1977–86; Sperry Rand (Ireland) Ltd, 1977–86; President, London Rent Assessment Panel, 1979–86; *b* 8 April 1915; *s* of Melancthon and Kate Nicholas Dawtry, Sheffield; *m* 1997, Sally Ann, *d* of Mr and Mrs D. P. Chalklin. *Educ:* King Edward VII Sch., Sheffield; Sheffield Univ. (LLB). Served War of 1939–45: commissioned RA; campaigns France, N Africa, Italy (MBE, despatches twice); released with rank of Lt-Col. Admitted Solicitor, 1938; Asst Solicitor, Sheffield, 1938–48; Deputy Town Clerk, Bolton, 1948–52; Deputy Town Clerk, Leicester, 1952–54; Town Clerk, Wolverhampton, 1954–56; Hon. Sec., London Boroughs Assoc., 1965–78. Member: Metrication Bd, 1969–74; Clean Air Council, 1960–75; Council of Management, Architectural Heritage Fund, 1977–89; CBI Council, 1982–86. Pres., Soc. of Local Authority Chief Execs, 1975–76. Vice-Chm., Dolphin Square Trust, 1985–99. FIMgt (FBIM 1975); FRSA 1978. Foreign Orders: The Star (Afghanistan); Golden Honour (Austria); Leopold II (Belgium); Rio Branco (Brazil); Merit (Chile); Legion of Honour (France); Merit (W Germany); the Phœnix (Greece); Merit (Italy); Homayoun (Iran); The Rising Sun (Japan); the Star (Jordan); African Redemption (Liberia); Oaken Crown (Luxembourg); Loyalty (Malaysia); the Right Hand (Nepal); Orange-Nassau (Netherlands); the Two Niles (Sudan); the Crown (Thailand); Zaire (Zaire). *Address:* 901 Grenville House, Dolphin Square, SW1V 3LR. *T:* (020) 7798 8100.

DAY, Prof. Alan Charles Lynn; Professor of Economics, London School of Economics, University of London, 1964–83, now Professor Emeritus; *b* 25 Oct. 1924; *s* of late Henry Charles Day, MBE, and Ruth Day; *m* 1962, Diana Hope Bocking (*d* 1980); no *c*; *m* 1982, Dr Shirley E. Jones. *Educ:* Chesterfield Grammar Sch.; Queens' Coll., Cambridge. Asst Lecturer, then Lecturer, LSE, 1949–54; Economic Adviser, HM Treas., 1954–56; Reader in Economics, London Univ., 1956–64. Ed., National Inst. Econ. Review, 1960–62; Econ. Correspondent, The Observer, intermittently, 1957–81. Economic Adviser on Civil Aviation, BoT, later Dept of Trade and Industry, 1968–72; Economic Adviser, Civil Aviation Authority, 1972–78. Member: Council, Consumers' Assoc., 1963–82; Board, British Airports Authority, 1965–68; SE Region Econ. Planning Council, 1966–69; Home Office Cttee on the London Taxicab Trade, 1967–70; Layfield Cttee on Local Govt Finance, 1974–76; Air Transport Users' Cttee, CAA, 1978–79; Home Office Adv. Panel on Satellite Broadcasting Standards, 1982. British Acad. Leverhulme Vis. Prof., Graduate Inst. for International Studies, Geneva, 1971. Governor, LSE, 1971–76, 1977–79, Pro-Director, 1979–83; Hon. Fellow, 1988. *Publications:* The Future of Sterling, 1954; Outline of Monetary Economics, 1956; The Economics of Money, 1959; (with S. T. Beza) Wealth and Income, 1960. *Address:* Chart Place, Chart Sutton, Maidstone, Kent ME17 3RE. *T:* (01622) 842236; 13 Gower Mews Mansions, WC1E 6HP. *T:* (020) 7631 3928.

DAY, Andrew Christopher King; Deputy Bailiff of Guernsey, since 1999; *b* 30 Oct. 1941; *m* José Guillemette; one *s* two *d*. *Educ:* Gresham's Sch., Holt; Magdalen Coll., Oxford (BA 1964); Inst. of Educn, London Univ. (Cert. Ed. 1965). Teacher, Kenya, 1965–69; called to the Bar, Gray's Inn, 1970; Advocate, Royal Court of Guernsey, 1971; in private practice, 1971–82; QC (Guernsey) 1989; Solicitor General, HM Comptroller, 1982–92, Attorney General, HM Procureur and Receiver General, 1992–99, Guernsey. *Address:* c/o Royal Court of Guernsey, Guernsey, Channel Islands.

DAY, Bernard Maurice, CB 1987; Director, The Riverside (East Molesey) Management Co., since 1999 (Chairman, 1996–99); *b* 7 May 1928; *s* of M. J. Day and Mrs M. H. Day; *m* 1956, Ruth Elizabeth Stansfield; two *s* one *d*. *Educ:* Bancroft's Sch.; London School of Economics (BScEcon). Army service, commnd RA, 1946–48. British Electric Traction Fedn, 1950–51; Asst Principal, Air Ministry, 1951; Private Sec. to Air Mem. for Supply and Organisation, 1954–56; Principal, 1956; Cabinet Secretariat, 1959–61; Asst Sec., 1965; Sec., Meteorological Office, 1965–69; Estabt Officer, Cabinet Office, 1969–72; Head of Air Staff Secretariat, MoD, 1972–74; Asst Under Sec. of State, MoD, 1974; Civilian Staff Management, 1974–76; Operational Requirements, 1976–80; Programmes and Budget, 1980–82; Supply and Orgn, Air, 1982–84; Resident Chm., CSSB, 1984–85; Asst Under-Sec. of State (Fleet Support), MoD, 1985–88. Panel Chm., CSSB, 1988–96. Chairman: MoD Branch, First Div. Assoc., 1983–84; MoD Liaison Cttee with CS Benevolent Fund, 1975–84. *Recreations:* local church, arts and environment. *Address:* 26 The Riverside, Graburn Way, East Molesey, Surrey KT8 9BF. *T:* (020) 8941 4520. *Club:* Royal Commonwealth Society.

DAY, Prof. Christopher, DPhil; Professor, School of Education, University of Nottingham, since 1993; *b* 3 May 1943; *s* of Walter Day and Patricia Jane Day; *m* 1984, Alison Jane Stewart; two *s*. *Educ:* St Luke's Coll., Exeter (Cert Ed 1964); Univ. of Sussex (MA 1976; DPhil 1979). LRAM 1966. School teacher, 1964–68; Lectr, 1968–71; LEA Advr, London Borough of Barking and Dagenham, 1972–76; Associate Prof., Univ. of Calgary, Alberta, 1979–81; Lectr, Sen. Lectr and Reader, Univ. of Nottingham, 1981–93. Editor, Developing Teachers and Schools series, 1991–94; Founding Editor, Teachers and Teaching, 1995–; Co-Editor: Jl of In-Service Teacher Educn, 1975–; Educational Action Res. Jl, 1993–. FRSA 1972. Hon. PhD Linköping, Sweden, 1993. *Publications:* Developing Teachers: the challenges of lifelong learning, 1999; *jointly:* Managing Primary Schools, 1985; Appraisal and Professional Development in Primary Schools, 1987; Reconceptualising School-Based Curriculum Development, 1990; Managing Primary Schools in the 1990s, 1990; Leadership and Curriculum in Primary Schools, 1993; Developing Leadership in Primary Schools, 1998; Leading Schools in Time of Change, 2000; *edited jointly:* Staff Development in Secondary Schools, 1986; Partnership in Educational Management, 1988; Insights into Teachers' Thinking and Practice, 1990; Managing the Professional Development of Teachers, 1991; Research on Teacher Thinking, 1993; Childen and Youth at Risk and Urban Education, 1997; Teachers and Teaching: international perspectives on school reform and teacher education, 1997; The Life and Work of Teachers in Changing Times: international perspectives, 1999. *Recreations:* hockey, tennis, reading. *Address:* School of Education, University of Nottingham, Jubilee Campus, Wollaton Road, Nottingham NG8 1BB. *T:* (0115) 951 4423.

DAY, Rev. David Vivian; Principal, St John's College, University of Durham, 1993–99; non-stipendiary Curate, St Nicholas, Durham, since 1999; *b* 11 Aug. 1936; *s* of Frederick Vivian Day and Enid Blodwen (*née* Evans); *m* 1959, Lorna Rosemary Taylor; two *s* one *d*. *Educ:* The Grammar Sch., Tottenham; QMC, Univ. of London (BA Classics); Univ. of Nottingham (MEd, MTheol). Classics Master, Southgate County Sch., 1958–64; Head of Religious Education: Southgate Sch., 1964–66; Bilborough Sch., 1966–73; Sen. Lectr in Theol., Bishop Lonsdale Coll., Derby, 1973–79; Sen. Lectr in Educn, Univ. of Durham, 1979–97. Ordained deacon, 1999, priest, 2000. *Publications:* This Jesus, 1980, 2nd edn 1981; Jeremiah: speaking for God in a time of crisis, 1987; Teenage Beliefs, 1991; (ed jtly) The Contours of Christian Education, 1992; Beyond the Here and Now, 1996; A Preaching Workbook, 1998, 3rd edn 2002; A Pearl beyond Price, 2002. *Recreations:* keeping fit, watching Rugby and soccer. *Address:* 35 Orchard Drive, The Sands, Durham DH1 1LA. *T:* (0191) 386 6909.

DAY, Sir Derek (Malcolm), KCMG 1984 (CMG 1973); HM Diplomatic Service, retired; High Commissioner to Canada, 1984–87; *b* 29 Nov. 1927; *s* of late Mr and Mrs Alan W. Day; *m* 1955, Sheila Nott; three *s* one *d*. *Educ:* Hurstpierpoint Coll.; St Catharine's Coll., Cambridge. Royal Artillery, 1946–48. Entered HM Foreign Service, Sept. 1951; Third Sec., British Embassy, Tel Aviv, 1953–56; Private Sec. to HM Ambassador, Rome, 1956–59; Second, then First Sec., FO, 1959–62; First Sec., British Embassy, Washington, 1962–66; First Sec., FO, 1966–67; Asst Private Sec. to Sec. of State for Foreign Affairs, 1967–68; Head of Personnel Operations Dept, FCO, 1969–72; Counsellor, British High Commn, Nicosia, 1972–75; Ambassador to Ethiopia, 1975–78; Asst Under-Sec. of State, 1979, Dep. Under-Sec. of State, 1980, and Chief Clerk, 1982–84, FCO. Dir, Monenco Ltd (Canada), 1988–92; Chm., Crystal Palace Sports and Leisure Ltd, 1992–97. Mem., Commonwealth War Graves Commn, 1987–92; Vice-Chm. of Council, British Red Cross, 1988–94. Chm. Governors, Hurstpierpoint Coll., 1987–97; Gov., Bethany Sch., 1987–2000. GB Hockey XI, Olympic Games, 1952. *Address:* Etchinghill, Goudhurst, Kent TN17 1JP. *Club:* Hawks.
See also W. M. Day.

DAY, Douglas Henry; QC 1989; a Recorder, since 1987; *b* 11 Oct. 1943; *s* of James Henry Day and Nancy Day; *m* 1970, Elizabeth Margaret (*née* Jarman); two *s* one *d*. *Educ:* Bec Sch.; Selwyn Coll., Cambridge (MA). Called to the Bar, Lincoln's Inn, 1967, Bencher, 1996. Asst Parly Boundary Comr, 1994–. Treas., Gen. Council of the Bar, 1999–. *Address:* Farrar's Building, Temple, EC4Y 7BD. *T:* (020) 7583 9241. *Club:* Bec Old Boys Rugby.

DAY, Sir Graham; *see* Day, Sir J. G.

DAY, Air Chief Marshal Sir John (Romney), KCB 1999; OBE 1985; Commander-in-Chief, Strike Command, since 2001; Air Aide-de-Camp to the Queen, since 2001; *b* 15 July 1947; *er s* of John George Day and Daphne Myrtle Kelly; *m* 1969, Jane Richards; two *s*. *Educ:* King's Sch., Canterbury; Imperial Coll., Univ. of London (BSc Aer. Eng.). No 72 Sqn, 1970–73; Flying Instructor, RAF Linton-on-Ouse, 1973–76; OC Oxford Univ. Air Sqn, 1976–79; RAF Staff Coll., 1981; PSO to Air Mem. for Personnel, 1982–83; OC No 72 Sqn, 1983–85; OC RAF Odiham, 1987–89; RCDS, 1990; Dir, Air Force Plans and Progs, MoD, 1991–94; AOC No 1 Gp, 1994–97; DCDS (Commitments), MoD, 1997–2000; AMP and C-in-C, RAF PTC, 2000–01. *Address:* c/o Lloyds TSB, Ashford, Kent TN24 8SS. *Club:* Royal Air Force.

DAY, Sir (Judson) Graham, Kt 1989; Chairman, PowerGen, 1990–93 (Director, 1990–93); *b* 3 May 1933; *s* of Frank Charles Day and Edythe Grace (*née* Baker); *m* 1958, Leda Ann (*née* Creighton); one *s* two *d*. *Educ:* Queen Elizabeth High Sch., Halifax, NS; Dalhousie Univ., Halifax, NS (LLB). Private practice of Law, Windsor, Nova Scotia, 1956–64; Canadian Pacific Ltd, Montreal and Toronto, 1964–71; Chief Exec., Cammell Laird Shipbuilders Ltd, Birkenhead, Eng., 1971–75; Dep. Chm., Organising Cttee for British Shipbuilders and Dep. Chm. and Chief Exec. designate, British Shipbuilders, 1975–76; Prof. of Business Admin and Dir, Canadian Marine Transportation Centre, Dalhousie Univ., NS, 1977–81; Vice-Pres., Shipyards & Marine Develt, Dome Petroleum Ltd, 1981–83; Chm. and Chief Exec., British Shipbuilders, 1983–86; Chief Exec., 1986–88, Chm., 1986–91, BL, subseq. The Rover Gp Hldgs. Chm., Cadbury Schweppes, 1989–93 (Dir, 1988–93); Deputy Chairman: MAI plc, 1989–93 (Dir, 1988–93); Ugland Internat. Hldgs plc, 1997–; Director: The Laird Gp plc, 1985–; British Aerospace, 1986–92 (Chairman, 1991–92); Extendicare (formerly Crownx) Inc. (Canada), 1989–; Bank of Nova Scotia (Canada), 1989–; NOVA Corp. of Alberta, 1990–; EMI Gp, 1991–. Counsel, Stewart McKelvey Stirling Scales, 1991–. Pres., ISBA, 1991–93. Member: Nova Scotia Barristers' Soc.; Law Soc. of Upper Canada; Canadian Bar Assoc. Freeman, City of London. ARINA. Hon. Fellow, Univ. of Wales Coll. of Cardiff, 1990. Hon. doctorates: Dalhousie; City; CNAA; Cranfield; Aston; Warwick; Humberside; South Bank. *Recreation:* reading. *Address:* 18 Avon Street, PO Box 423, Hantsport, NS B0P 1P0, Canada.

DAY, Lance Reginald; Keeper, Science Museum Library, 1976–87; *b* 2 Nov. 1927; *s* of late Reginald and Eileen Day; *m* 1959, Mary Ann Sheahan; one *s* two *d*. *Educ:* Sherrardswood Sch., Welwyn Garden City; Alleyne's Grammar Sch., Stevenage; Northern Polytechnic (BSc London); University Coll., London (MSc Hist. and Philos. of Sci.). Res. Asst, Science Museum Library, 1951–64, Asst Keeper 1964–70; Asst Keeper, Science Museum, Dept of Chemistry, 1970–74; Keeper, Science Museum, Dept of Communications and Electrical Engrg, 1974–76. Sec., Nat. Railway Museum Cttee, 1973–75; Newcomen Society: Hon. Sec., 1973–82; Hon. Mem., 1996; Hon. Ed., Trans of Newcomen Soc., 1990–2000. *Publications:* Broad Gauge, 1985; (contrib.) Encyclopaedia of the History of Technology, 1990; (ed jtly and contrib.) Biographical Dictionary of the History of Technology, 1996; reviews and articles. *Recreation:* music. *Address:* 12 Rhinefield Close, Brockenhurst, Hants SO42 7SU. *T:* (01590) 622079.

DAY, Lucienne, RDI 1962; in freelance practice, since 1948; Consultant, with Robin Day, to John Lewis Partnership, 1962–87; *b* 1917; *d* of Felix Conradi and Dulcie Lilian Duncan-Smith; *m* 1942, Robin Day, *qv*; one *d*. *Educ:* Convent Notre Dame de Sion, Worthing; Croydon School of Art; Royal Coll. of Art. ARCA 1940; FSIAD 1955. Teacher, Beckenham Sch. of Art, 1942–47; began designing full-time, dress fabrics and later furnishing fabrics, carpets, wallpapers, table-linen, 1947 for Edinburgh Weavers, Heal's Fabrics, Cavendish Textiles, Tomkinsons, Wilton Royal, Thos Somerset etc, and firms in Scandinavia, USA and Germany; also china decoration for Rosenthal China, Selb, Bavaria, 1956–68; work for Barbican Art Centre, 1979; currently designing and making silk wall-hangings (silk mosaics). Retrospective exhibitions: Whitworth Art Gall., Manchester, and RCA, 1993; Aberdeen, 1994. Work in permanent collections: V&A; Whitworth Art Gall. Museum; Trondheim Museum, Norway; Cranbrook Museum, Michigan, USA; Art Inst. of Chicago; Röhsska Mus., Gothenberg, Sweden; Musée des Arts Décoratifs, Montreal. Member: Rosenthal Studio-line Jury, 1960–68; Cttee, Duke of Edinburgh's Prize for Elegant Design, 1960–63; Council, RCA, 1962–67; RSA Design Bursaries Juries. Master, Faculty of Royal Designers for Industry, 1987–89. Hon. FRIBA 1997. Sen. Fellow, RCA, 1999. Hon. DDes Southampton, 1995. First Award, Amer. Inst. of Decorators, 1950; Gold Medal, 9th Triennale di Milano, 1951; Gran Premio, 10th Triennale di Milano, 1954; Design Council Awards, 1957, 1960, 1968. *Recreations:* plant collecting in Mediterranean regions, gardening. *Address:* 21 West Street, Chichester, W Sussex PO19 1QW. *T:* (01243) 781429.

DAY, Sir Michael (John), Kt 1992; OBE 1981; Chairman, Commission for Racial Equality, 1988–93; *b* 4 Sept. 1933; *s* of Albert Day and Ellen Florence (*née* Itter); *m* 1960, June Marjorie, *d* of late Dr John William and Edith Mackay; one *s* one *d*. *Educ:* University College Sch., Hampstead; Selwyn Coll., Cambridge (MA); London School of Economics (Cert. Social Work and Social Admin). Probation Officer, Surrey, 1960–64; Sen. Probation Officer, W Sussex, 1964–67; Asst Prin. Probation Officer, 1967–68, Chief Probation Officer, 1968–76, Surrey; Chief Probation Officer, W Midlands, 1976–88. Chm., Chief Probation Officers' Conf., 1974–77; First Chm., Assoc. Chief Officers of Probation, 1982–84. Member: Probation Adv. and Trng Bd, Home Office, 1970–73;

Adv. Council for Probation and Aftercare, 1973–78. Pres., Telford and Shropshire Race Equality Council, 1994–. Member Council: Howard League for Penal Reform, 1966–73; Volunteer Centre, 1977–81; Grubb Inst., 1980–93. Dir, Shropshire and Mid Wales Hospice, 1998–. FRSA 1989. *Publications:* contribs to professional jls and others. *Recreations:* family, books, music, woodturning, gardening, the countryside. *Address:* Thornhill, Oldbury, Bridgnorth, Shropshire WV16 5EQ.

DAY, Prof. Nicholas Edward, CBE 2001; PhD; FRCPath; MRC Research Professor in Epidemiology, since 1999, and Fellow of Hughes Hall, since 1992, University of Cambridge; *b* 24 Sept. 1939; *s* of late John King Day, TD and Mary Elizabeth (*née* Stinton); *m* 1961, Jocelyn Deanne Broughton; one *s* one *d. Educ:* Magdalen Coll., Oxford (BA Maths); Aberdeen Univ. (PhD Med. Stats). FRCPath 1997. Res. Fellow, Aberdeen Univ., 1962–66; Fellow, ANU, 1966–69; Statistician, 1969–78, Head, Unit of Biostats and Field Studies, 1979–86, Internat. Agency for Res. on Cancer, Lyon; Cancer Expert, Nat. Cancer Inst., USA, 1978–79; Dir, 1986–89, Hon. Dir, 1989–99, MRC Biostats Unit; Prof. of Public Health, Cambridge Univ., 1989–99; Fellow, Churchill Coll., Cambridge, 1986–92. Founder FMedSci 1998. *Publications:* Statistical Methods in Cancer Research, vol. 1 1980, vol. 2 1988; Screening for Cancer of the Uterine Cervix, 1986; Screening for Breast Cancer, 1988; over 300 articles in scientific jls. *Recreations:* sea fishing, fruit growing. *Address:* 39 Tower Court, Ely, Cambs CB7 4XS. *T:* (01353) 661172.

DAY, Prof. Peter, DPhil; FRS 1986; Fullerian Professor of Chemistry, Royal Institution, since 1994; Royal Institution Professorial Research Fellow, University College London, since 1995; *b* 20 Aug. 1938; *s* of Edgar Day and Ethel Hilda Day (*née* Russell); *m* 1964, Frances Mary Elizabeth Anderson; one *s* one *d. Educ:* Maidstone Grammar School; Wadham College, Oxford (BA 1961; MA, DPhil 1965; Hon. Fellow, 1991). Cyanamid European Research Institute, Geneva, 1962; Jun. Res. Fellow, 1963–65, Official Fellow, 1965–91, Hon. Fellow, 1994, St John's College, Oxford; Departmental Demonstrator, 1965–67, Lectr in Inorganic Chemistry, 1967–89, *ad hominem* Prof. of Solid State Chemistry, 1989–91, Oxford Univ. Dir, Inst. Laue-Langevin, Grenoble, 1988–91 (on secondment); Royal Institution: Dir, 1991–98; Resident Prof. of Chemistry, 1991–94; Dir, Davy Faraday Res. Lab., 1991–98. Prof. Associé, Univ. de Paris-Sud, 1975; Guest Prof., Univ. of Copenhagen, 1978; Vis. Fellow, ANU, 1980; Senior Research Fellow, SRC, 1977–82. Lectures: Du Pont, Indiana Univ., 1988; Royal Soc. Blackett Meml, 1994; Bakerian, 1999; ACL, Chinese Univ. Hong Kong, 1997; Birch, ANU, 1997. Science and Engineering Research Council: Member: Neutron Beam Res. Cttee, 1983–88; Chemistry Cttee, 1985–88; Molecular Electronics Cttee, 1987—88; Nat. Cttee on Superconductivity, 1987–88; Materials Commn, 1988–90; COPUS, 1991–98. Member: Sci. and Engrg Cttee, British Council, 1991–98; Phys. and Engrg Sci. Cttee, ESF, 1994–; Medicines Commn, 1998–; Council Member: Inst. for Molecular Scis, Okazaki, Japan, 1991–95; Parly and Scientific Cttee, 1992–98. Royal Society of Chemistry: Vice-Pres., Dalton Div., 1986–88; Corday-Morgan Medal, 1971; Solid State Chem. Award, 1986; Daiwa Adrian Prize, Daiwa Foundn, 1998. Gov., Birkbeck Coll., London, 1993–. Mem., Academia Europaea, 1992 (Mem. Council, 2000–; Treas., 2000–). Hon. Foreign Mem., Indian Soc. of Materials Res., 1994. Hon. Fellow, Indian Acad. of Sci., 1995. Hon. DSc: Newcastle, 1994; Kent, 1999. *Publications:* Physical Methods in Advanced Inorganic Chemistry (ed with H. A. O. Hill), 1968; Electronic States of Inorganic Compounds, 1974; Emission and Scattering Techniques, 1980; Electronic Structure and Magnetism of Inorganic Compounds, vols 1–7, 1972–82; (ed with A. K. Cheetham) Solid State Chemistry, vol. 1 1987, vol. 2 1992; The Philosopher's Tree, 1999; papers in Jl Chem. Soc.; Inorg. Chem. *Recreation:* pruning shrubbery (horticultural and intellectual). *Address:* 21 Albemarle Street, W1X 4BS. *T:* (020) 7670 2928.

DAY, Peter Rodney, PhD; Director, Biotechnology Center for Agriculture and the Environment (formerly Center for Agricultural Molecular Biology), Rutgers University, New Jersey, since 1987; *b* 27 Dec. 1928; *s* of Roland Percy Day and Florence Kate (*née* Dixon); *m* 1950, Lois Elizabeth Rhodes; two *s* one *d. Educ:* Birkbeck Coll., Univ. of London (BSc, PhD). John Innes Institute, 1946–63; Associate Prof. of Botany, Ohio State Univ., 1963–64; Chief, Dept of Genetics, Connecticut Agricl Experiment Station, 1964–79; Dir, Plant Breeding Inst., Cambridge, 1979–87. Sec., Internat. Genetics Fedn, 1984–93. Special Prof. of Botany, Nottingham Univ., 1982–88. Commonwealth Fund Fellow, 1954; John Simon Guggenheim Meml Fellow, 1973. *Publications:* Fungal Genetics (with J. R. S. Fincham), 1963, 4th edn 1979; Genetics of Host-Parasite Interaction, 1974; contrib. Genetical Research, Genetics, Heredity, Nature, Proc. Nat. Acad. Sci., Phytopathology, etc. *Recreation:* Scottish country dancing. *Address:* Biotechnology Center for Agriculture and the Environment, Rutgers, State University of New Jersey, NJ 08901–8520, USA. *T:* (732) 9328165.

DAY, Robin, OBE 1983; RDI 1959; FCSD (FSIAD 1948); design consultant and freelance designer; *b* 25 May 1915; *s* of Arthur Day and Mary Shersby; *m* 1942, Lucienne Conradi (*see* Lucienne Day); one *d. Educ:* Royal Coll. of Art (ARCA). National scholarship to RCA, 1935–39; teacher and lectr for several yrs; Design Consultant: Hille International, 1948–; John Lewis Partnership, 1962–87. Commissions include: seating for many major concert halls, theatres, stadia, etc.; interior design of Super VC10 and other aircraft. Mem., juries for many national and internat. indust. design competitions. Many awards for design work, including: 6 Design Centre awards; Gold Medal, Triennale di Milano, 1951, and Silver Medal, 1954; Designs Medal, SIAD, 1957. *Recreations:* mountaineering, ski touring, hill-walking. *Address:* 21 West Street, Chichester, W Sussex PO19 1QW. *T:* (01243) 781429. *Clubs:* Alpine, Alpine Ski.

DAY, Rosemary; non-executive Director: National Air Traffic Services, since 1997; UK Atomic Energy Authority, since 1999; *b* 20 Sept. 1942; *d* of Albert Rich and Alice Rich (*née* Wren); *m* (marr. diss.). *Educ:* Bedford Coll., Univ. of London (BA Hons 1964). ATII 1978. Asst Dir Gen., GLC, 1964–83; Admin. Dir, London Transport, 1983–88; Ops Dir, Allied Dunbar, 1988–94; Chm., London Ambulance Service, 1995–99. Non-executive Director: Nationwide Building Soc., 1984–88; Milk Mktg Bd, 1993–95; London Transport, 1994–; Govt Offices Mgt Bd, 1996–98. Member: Legal Aid Adv. Bd, 1992–94; Member, Sen. Salaries Review Body, 1994–2000. Chm., Joyful Company of Singers, 1988–. CIMgt (CBIM 1984); FRSA. *Recreations:* singing, the arts, gardening, books. *Address:* 63a Barrowgate Road, W4 4QT.

DAY, Sir Simon (James), Kt 1997; farmer; *b* 22 Jan. 1935; *s* of late John Adam Day and Kathleen Day (*née* Hebditch); *m* 1959, Hilary Maureen Greenslade Gomm; two *s* (and one *s* decd). *Educ:* Bedales Sch.; S Devon Tech. Coll.; Emmanuel Coll., Cambridge (MA Hist.). Nat. Service, RN, 1954–56. Devon County Council: Councillor, Modbury Div., 1964–74, Salcombe Div., 1974–; Whip, 1981–89; Dep. Leader, 1989, Leader, 1991–93. Non-exec. Dir, SW Water, 1989–98; Regl Dir, Portman Building Soc., 1989–91; Director: Plymouth Sound Radio, 1966–80; Plymouth Develt Corp., 1993–96; Exeter Internat. Airport, 1997–; Chm., West of England Newspapers Gp, 1981–86. Mem., Exec. Council, ACC, 1981–85, 1990– (Chm., Police Cttee, 1991; Dep. Leader, 1992; Vice Chm., 1993–95; Leader Cons. Gp, 1993–95); Chm., Devon and Cornwall Police Authy, 1990–93; Member: Police Adv. Bd, Home Office, 1989–; Police Negotiating Bd, 1989–; Chairman: Devon Sea Fisheries Cttee, 1986–95; Assoc. of Sea Fisheries Cttees, England and Wales, 1993– (Vice-Chm., 1991–93); Mem., Govt Salmon Adv. Cttee, 1987–90; Chm., Devon and Cornwall Develt Bureau, 1989–91; Vice Chairman: Nat. Parks Cttee for England and Wales, 1981–83; Local Govt Finance Cttee, 1983–85; Member: Consultative Council, Local Govt Finance, 1983–85 and 1993–; Standing Conf. of Local and Regl Authies, Council of Europe, 1990–97; Cttee of Regions, EU, 1994–97, 1998–; Chm., Cons. Nat. Local Govt Adv. Cttee, 1994–95. Pres., S Devon Herd Book Soc., 1986. Chm. Govs, Bicton Coll. of Agric., 1983–2000. Mem. Court, Exeter Univ., 1964–. Contested (C): Carmarthen, 1966, by-election 1966; N Cornwall, 1970. High Sheriff, Devon, 1999–2000. Hereditary Freeman, City of Norwich. *Recreations:* shooting, sailing, fishing. *Address:* Keaton House, near Ivybridge, Devon PL21 0LB. *T:* (01752) 691212. *Clubs:* Buck's, Royal Thames Yacht; Royal Yacht Squadron; Hawks (Hon.).

DAY, Stephen Charles; Regional Director, West Midlands, NHS Executive, Department of Health, since 1996; *b* 17 Feb. 1954; *s* of Peter Charles Day and June Lillian Day; *m* 1975 (marr. diss.); one *s* one *d*; *m* 2000, Dr V. A. Chishty. *Educ:* Queen Elizabeth's GS for Boys, Barnet. CPFA 1978. Various NHS posts, 1972–84; Dep. Treas., Canterbury and Thanet HA, 1984–86; Dep. Regl Treas., South Western RHA, 1986–89; Dir of Finance and Computing, Southmead HA, 1989–92; Dir of Finance, Southmead Health Services NHS Trust, 1992–93; Regl Dir of Finance, W Midlands RHA, 1993–96. *Recreations:* classical music, gardening. *Address:* (office) Bartholomew House, 142 Hagley Road, Edgbaston, Birmingham B16 9PA.

DAY, Stephen Nicholas; a District Judge (Magistrates' Courts) (formerly Stipendiary Magistrate), Middlesex, since 1991; *b* 17 Aug. 1947; *s* of late Robert Weatherston Day and of Margaret Diana (*née* McKenzie); *m* 1973, Shama (*née* Tak); one *s* one *d. Educ:* St Mary's Coll., Southampton; King Edward VI Sch., Southampton; Brasenose Coll., Oxford (MA). Called to the Bar, Middle Temple, 1972. Sen. Court Clerk, Nottingham, 1973–77; Justices Clerk, Abingdon, Didcot and Wantage, 1977–91. *Address:* c/o Feltham Magistrates' Court, Hanworth Road, Feltham, Middlesex TW13 5AG. *T:* (020) 8917 3400.

DAY, Stephen Peter, CMG 1989; HM Diplomatic Service, retired; consultant, Middle East affairs; *b* 19 Jan. 1938; *s* of Frank William and Mary Elizabeth Day; *m* 1965, Angela Doreen (*née* Waudby); one *s* two *d. Educ:* Bancroft's School; Corpus Christi Coll., Cambridge. MA. Entered HMOCS as Political Officer, Western Aden Protectorate, 1961, transf. to FO, 1965; Senior Political Officer, South Arabian Federation, 1964–67; FO, 1967–70; First Sec., Office of C-in-C, Far East, Singapore, 1970–71; First Sec. (Press), UK Mission to UN, NY, 1971–75; FCO, 1976–77; Counsellor, Beirut, 1977–78; Consul-Gen., Edmonton, 1979–81; Ambassador to Qatar, 1981–84; Head of ME Dept, FCO, 1984–87; attached to Household of the Prince of Wales, 1986; Ambassador to Tunisia, 1987–92; Sen. British Trade Comr, Hong Kong, 1992–93; Dir, Council for Advancement of Arab-British Understanding, 1993–94. Dir, Claremont Associates, 1995–. Member: Maghreb Adv. Gp, BOTB, 1995–; Exec. Cttee, Soc. for Arabian Studies, 1995–. Chairman: British-Tunisian Soc., 1993–; Palestine Exploration Fund, 1995–; British-Yemeni Soc., 1998–99; MBI Trust, SOAS, 2000–. Governor, Qatar Academy, 1996–. *Publication:* At Home in Carthage, 1991. *Recreations:* walking, family. *Address:* Oakfield Cottage, 92 West End Lane, Esher, Surrey KT10 8LF. *T:* and *Fax:* (01372) 464138. *Clubs:* Athenæum; Hong Kong.

DAY, Stephen Richard; *b* 30 Oct. 1948; *s* of late Francis and of Anne Day; *m* 1982, Frances (*née* Booth); one *s* by former marriage. *Educ:* Otley Secondary Modern Sch.; Park Lane Coll., Leeds; Leeds Polytechnic. MIEx 1972. Sales Clerk, William Sinclair & Sons, stationary manufrs, Otley, W Yorks, 1965–70, Asst Sales Manager (working in Home and Export Depts), 1970–77; Sales Representative: Larkfield Printing Co. Ltd (part of Hunting Group), Brighouse, W Yorks, 1977–80; A. H. Leach & Co. (part of Hunting Gp), photographic processing lab., Brighouse, 1980–84; Sales Executive: PPL Chromacopy, photographic labs, Leeds and Manchester, 1984–86; Chromogene, photographic lab., Leeds, 1986–87. Vice-President: Stockport Chamber of Commerce, 1987–; Stockport and Dist Heart Foundn, 1985–. Chm., Yorks Area Cons. Political Centre, 1983–86; Vice-Chm., NW Leeds Constituency, 1983–86. Town Councillor, Otley, 1975–76 and 1979–83; City Councillor, Leeds, 1975–80. Contested (C): Bradford West, 1983; Cheadle, 2001. MP (C) Cheadle, 1987–2001. An Opposition Whip, 1997–2001. Member: Select Cttee on Social Security, 1990–97; Select Cttee on Envmt, Transport and Regions, 1997; Co-Chm., Parly Adv. Council for Transport Safety, 1989–97; Vice-Chm., All-Party Non-Profit-Making Clubs Gp, 1995–2001; Co-Chm., All-Party West Coast Main Line Gp, 1993–2001. Sponsor, Private Member's Bill to introduce compulsory wearing of rear car seat belts by children, 1988. Vice-Chairman: CPA (UK), 1996–97; Assoc. of Cons. Clubs, 1995–. Hon. Mem., Bramhall and Woodford Rotary Club; Mem., RBL Club, Cheadle Hulme. *Publications:* pamphlets on Otley and on rate reform. *Recreations:* movies, music, history (particularly Roman). *Club:* Cheadle Hulme Conservative (Cheadle Hulme); Royal Wharfedale (Otley).

DAY, Prof. William, PhD; CPhys; Director, Silsoe Research Institute, BBSRC, since 1999; *b* 11 June 1949 *s* of late Arthur Thomas Day and Barbara Nan Day; *m* 1973, Virginia Lesley Elisabeth Playford; two *s* one *d. Educ:* Norwich Sch.; Gonville and Caius Coll., Cambridge (MA Natural Scis (Physics)); PhD Physics Cantab 1974. Cphys 1980. Higher Scientific Officer, SSO, then PSO, Physics Dept, Rothamsted Exptl Stn, 1974–81 Head: Envmtl Physiol. Gp, Long Ashton Res. Stn, 1982–83; Physiology and Envmtl Physics Dept, Rothamsted Exptl Stn, 1983–88; Process Engrg Div., Silsoe Res. Inst., 1988-89. Special Prof. of Agricl Engrg, Univ. of Nottingham, 1993–. *Publications:* contribs relating to interaction between biological systems and envmt in numerous jls, include. Jl Agricl Sci., Agricl and Forest Meteorol. and Phytopathol. *Recreations:* bird watching, choral singing, running. *Address:* Silsoe Research Institute, Wrest Park, Silsoe, Beds MK45 4HS.

DAY, William Michael; Chief Executive, CARE International UK, since 1996; *b* 26 June 1956; *s* of Sir Derek (Malcolm) Day, *qv*; *m* 1986, Kate Gardener; one *s* two *d. Educ:* Univ. of Exeter (BA). Save the Children Fund: Uganda, 1983; Ethiopia, 1983–84; Sudan, 1984–86; BBC World Service for Africa, 1986–87; Oxfam, Ethiopia, 1987–88; Grants Dir for Africa, Charity Projects/Comic Relief, 1988–94; Dir, Opportunity Trust, 1994–96. Non-exec. Dir, S Kent Hosps NHS Trust, 1994–96. Public Appts Ind. Advr, DCMS, 1999–; Mem. Council, ODI, 2000–. Member: BBC Central Appeals Cttee, 1992– (Chm., 1997–); Grants Council, Charities Aid Foundn, 1990–94; Trustee: BBC Children in Need, 1998–; Disasters Emergency Cttee, 1998–. *Address:* CARE International UK, 1–7 Crawford Place, W1H 4LB. *T:* (020) 7723 9777; *e-mail:* day@uk.care.org.

DAY-LEWIS, Daniel; actor; *s* of Cecil Day-Lewis, CBE and Jill Angela Henriette Balcon; *m* 1996, Rebecca, *d* of Arthur Miller, *qv*; one *s. Educ:* Bedales; Bristol Old Vic Theatre Sch. *Stage:* The Recruiting Officer, Troilus and Cressida, Funny Peculiar, Old King Cole, A Midsummer Night's Dream, Class Enemy, Edward II, Oh! What a Lovely War, Look Back in Anger, Dracula, Another Country, Romeo and Juliet, The Futurists, Hamlet; *films:* Gandhi, 1981; The Saga of HMS Bounty, 1983; My Beautiful Laundrette, 1985; A Room With a View, 1985; Nanou, 1985; The Unbearable Lightness of Being, 1986; Stars and Bars, 1987; My Left Foot, 1988 (Oscar best actor and numerous other awards); Ever Smile New Jersey, 1988; Last of the Mohicans, 1991 (Variety Club best actor); Age of Innocence, 1992; In the Name of the Father, 1993; The Crucible, 1997; The Boxer, 1998; Gangs of New York, 2001; principal roles in TV. *Address:* c/o Julian Belfrage Associates, 46 Albemarle Street, W1S 4DF.

DAY-LEWIS, Séan; journalist and author; *b* 3 Aug. 1931; *s* of Cecil Day-Lewis, CBE, CLit and Mary Day-Lewis; *m* 1960, Anna Mott; one *s* one *d*. *Educ:* Allhallows Sch., Rousdon, Devon. National Service, RAF, 1949–51. Bridport News, 1952–53; Southern Times, Weymouth, 1953–54; Herts Advertiser, St Albans, 1954–56; Express and Star, Wolverhampton, 1956–60; The Daily Telegraph, 1960–86 (first nat. newspaper Arts Reporter, 1965–70; TV and Radio Editor, 1970–86); TV Editor, London Daily News, 1987. Arts Editor, Socialist Commentary, 1966–71; Founder-Chm., 1975, Chm., 1990–92, BPG; Vice Pres., Bulleid Soc., 1970; Member, BAFTA, 1976. *Publications:* Bulleid: last giant of steam, 1964; C. Day-Lewis: an English literary life, 1980; (ed) One Day in the Life of Television, 1989; TV Heaven: a review of British television from the 1930s to the 1990s, 1992; Talk of Drama: views of the television dramatist now and then, 1998. *Recreations:* music (J. S. Bach preferred), tennis, walking, giving in to temptation. *Address:* Restorick Row, Rosemary Lane, Colyton, Devon EX24 6LW. *T:* (01297) 553039.

DAYKIN, Christopher David, CB 1993; FIA; Government Actuary, since 1989; *b* 18 July 1948; *s* of John Francis Daykin and Mona Daykin; *m* 1977, Kathryn Ruth (*née* Tingey); two *s* one *d*. *Educ:* Merchant Taylors' Sch., Northwood; Pembroke Coll., Cambridge (BA 1970, MA 1973). FIA 1973. Government Actuary's Department, 1970; VSO, Brunei, 1971; Govt Actuary's Dept, 1972–78; Principal (Health and Social Services), HM Treasury, 1978–80; Govt Actuary's Dept, 1980–, Principal Actuary, 1982–84, Directing Actuary (Social Security), 1985–89. Mem., Council, Inst. of Actuaries, 1985–99 (Hon. Sec., 1988–90; Vice Pres., 1993–94; Pres., 1994–96); Chm., Internat. Forum of Actuarial Assocs, 1996–97; Chairman: Perm. Cttee for Statistical, Actuarial and Financial Studies, ISSA, 1992–; Educn Cttee, Groupe Consultatif des Assocs d'Actuaires des Pays des Communautés Européennes, 1992–. Mem. Pensions Observatory, EC Commn, 1992–96. Visiting Professor: City Univ., 1997–; Shanghai Univ. of Finance and Econs, 1998–. Treasurer, Emmanuel Church, Northwood, 1982–87 and 1998–; Chm., VSO Harrow and Hillingdon, 1976–91. Hon. DSc City, 1995. *Publications:* Practical Risk Theory, 1993; articles and papers on pensions, demography, consumer credit, social security and insurance. *Recreations:* travel, photography, languages. *Address:* Government Actuary's Department, New King's Beam House, 22 Upper Ground, SE1 9RJ. *T:* (020) 7211 2620.

DEACON, Keith Vivian; consultant, since 1996; Under Secretary, 1988–95, and Director of Quality Development, 1993–95, Inland Revenue; *b* 19 Nov. 1935; *s* of Vivian and Louisa Deacon; *m* 1960, Brenda Chater; one *s* one *d*. *Educ:* Sutton County Grammar School; Bristol Univ. (BA Hons English Lang. and Litt.). Entered Inland Revenue as Inspector of Taxes, 1962; Regional Controller, 1985; Dir, Technical Div. I until Head Office reorganisation, 1988; Dir, Insce and Specialist Div., 1988–91; Dir of Operations, 1991–93. Part time work for Civil Service Selection Board: Observer, 1969–72; Chairman, 1985–87. FRSA 1992. *Recreations:* living for part of the year in France, keeping up with four grandchildren, photography, music, reading.

DEACON, Richard, CBE 1999; RA 1998; sculptor; *b* Bangor, 15 Aug. 1949; *s* of Gp Capt. Edward William Deacon, RAF (retd) and late Dr Joan Bullivant Winstanley; *m* 1977, Jacqueline Poncelet (marr. diss. 2000); one *s* one *d*. *Educ:* Somerset Coll. of Art; St Martin's Sch. of Art; RCA; Chelsea Sch. of Art. *Solo exhibitions* include: Orchard Gall., Londonderry, 1983; Lisson Gall., 1983, 1985, 1987, 1992, 1995; Riverside Studios, Chapter Arts Centre, Cardiff, and Fruitmarket Gall., Edinburgh, 1984; Tate Gall., 1985; tour of UK, 1986; Marian Goodmen Gall., NY, 1986, 1988, 1990, 1992, 1997; tour of US, 1988; Musée Nat. d'Art Moderne, Paris, 1989; Kunstnernes Hus, Oslo, and Mala Galerija, Slovenia, 1990; Kunstverein Hanover, 1993; LA Louver, 1995; tour of South America, 1996–97; Musée de Rochechouart, 1997; Tate Gall., Liverpool, 1999; DCA, Dundee, 2001; represented in collections in: Tate Gall.; Mus. of Modern Art, NY; Art Gall. of NSW, Sydney; Musée Beaubourg, Paris; Bonnefanten Mus., Maastricht. Vis. Prof., Chelsea Sch. of Art, 1992–; Prof., Ecole Nat. Superieure des Beaux-Arts, Paris, 1998–. Member: Grants to Artists Sub Cttee, 1986–92, Visual Arts Adv. Gp, 1990–93, British Council; Architecture Adv. Gp, Arts Council of England, 1996–; Trustee, Tate Gall., 1991–96; Vice Chm. Trustees, Baltic Flour Mills Centre for Contemporary Art, 1999–. Turner Prize, 1987; Robert Jakobsen Prize, Mus. Wurth, Germany, 1995. Chevalier des Arts et des Lettres (France), 1997. *Publications:* Stuff Box Object, 1972, 1984; For Those Who Have Ears #2, 1985; Atlas: Gondwanaland & Laurasia, 1990. *Address:* c/o Lisson Gallery, 67 Lisson Street, NW1 5DA.

DEACON, Susan Catherine; Member (Lab) Edinburgh East and Musselburgh, Scottish Parliament, since 1999; Minister for Health and Community Care, since 1999; *b* 2 Feb. 1964; *d* of James Deacon and Barbara Deacon (*née* Timmins); partner, John Boothman; one *d*. *Educ:* Edinburgh Univ. (MA Hons 1987; MBA 1992). Local Govt officer, 1987–94; Open Univ. Tutor (part-time), 1992–94; sen. mgt consultant, 1994; Dir of MBA Programmes, Edinburgh Business Sch., Heriot-Watt Univ., 1994–98; business consultant, 1998–99. *Address:* Scottish Parliament, Edinburgh EH99 1SP.

DEAKIN, Sir (Frederick) William (Dampier); *see* Deakin, Sir William.

DEAKIN, George Anthony Hartley, CBE 1996; Chairman, Addenbrooke's NHS Trust, since 1996; *b* 4 June 1937; *s* of Capt. George Deakin, MC and Bar, and Winsome Deakin, MBE (*née* Combe); *m* 1962, Daphne Caroline Gill; two *s* two *d*. *Educ:* Dragon Sch., Oxford; Sherborne Sch., Dorset; Trinity Coll., Oxford (MA Hons); MBA INSEAD. Called to the Bar, Gray's Inn, 1963. 2nd Lieut, 13/18 Royal Hussars, 1956–57; Exercise Whiteshod, Norway, 1957; Lieut and Capt., AER, 1957–66. Joined British Petroleum Co. Ltd, 1961; posts include: Pres., BP N America Trading, 1979–82; Man. Dir, BP Africa, 1982–86; Pres., BP Belgium, 1987–88; Head, IT Gp Centre, 1989–90; Chm. and Chief Exec., BP Southern Africa, 1990–95; Head, Africa Reg., BP Oil Internat., 1993–95. Mem. Cttee, Assoc. of MBAs (East), 1997–. Trustee, Fund for Addenbrooke's, 1997–. Mem., HAC, 1983–. Haute route Chamonix to Zermatt (skis), 2000. *Recreations:* Laser sailing, ski-ing, bridge, reading Trollope. *Address:* Manting House, Meldreth, Royston, Herts SG8 6NU. *T:* (01763) 260276. *Clubs:* Farmers', Ski of GB; Overy Staithe Sailing (Norfolk); Zeekoevlei Yacht (Cape Town).

DEAKIN, Prof. (John Francis) William, PhD; FRCPsych; Professor of Psychiatry, Manchester University, since 1990; *b* 5 July 1949; *s* of John Deakin and Kathleen Brown; *m* 1973, Hildur Jakobsdottir; three *d*. *Educ:* ltham Coll., Kent; Leeds Univ. (BSc 1st Cl. Physiol. 1970; MB Hons, ChB dist. and prize 1973); PhD London 1982. MRCPsych 1984, FRCPsych 1990. MRC Trng Fellow, NIMR, Mill Hill, and Clin. Res. Centre, Harrow, 1974-83; Sen. Lectr, Manchester Univ., 1983-90. FMedSci 2000. *Publications:* contrib. numerous articles to learned jls on neuroscientific basis of mental illness, especially the role of serotonin in neuroses. *Recreations:* listening to jazz, playing the game of Go, speculation of all kinds. *Address:* 3 Chesham Place, Bowdon, Cheshire WA14 2JL. *T:* (0161) 941 6385.

DEAKIN, Michael; writer, documentary and film maker; Director, Gryphon Productions Ltd, since 1985; *b* 21 Feb. 1939; *s* of Sir William Deakin, *qv*, and Margaret Hodson (*née* Beatson-Bell). *Educ:* Bryanston; Univ. d'Aix-Marseille; Emmanuel Coll., Cambridge (MA Hons). Founding Partner, Editions Alecto, Fine Art Publishers, 1960–64; Producer, BBC Radio Current Affairs Dept, 1964–68; Producer, then Editor, Yorkshire Television Documentary Unit, 1968–81; Sen. Vice-Pres., Paramount/Revcom, 1987–93. Documentary film productions include: Out of the Shadow into the Sun—The Eiger; Struggle for China; The Children on the Hill; Whicker's World—Way Out West; The Japanese Experience; The Good, the Bad and the Indifferent; Johnny Go Home (British Academy Award, 1976); David Frost's Global Village; The Frost Interview—The Shah; Rampton—The Secret Hospital; Painting With Light (co-prodn with BBC); other films: Act of Betrayal, 1987; Not a Penny More, Not a Penny Less, 1990 (TV mini series); Secret Weapon, 1990; The Supergun, 1994; Good King Wenceslas, 1994; The Human Bomb, 1996; The Place of Lions, 1997; Varian's War, 2001; also many others. Founding Mem., TV-am Breakfast Television Consortium, 1980; Consultant, TV-am, 1984–87 (Dir of Programmes, 1982–84; Bd Mem., 1984–85). *Publications:* Restif de la Bretonne—Les Nuits de Paris (critical edn and trans. with Nicholas Deakin), 1968; Gaetano Donizetti—a biography, 1968; (for children) Tom Grattan's War, 1970, 2nd edn 1971; The Children on the Hill, 1972, 9th edn 1982; (with John Willis) Johnny Go Home, 1976; (with Antony Thomas) The Arab Experience, 1975, 2nd edn 1976; Flame in the Desert, 1976; (with David Frost) I Could Have Kicked Myself, 1982, 2nd US edn 1983; (with David Frost) Who Wants to be a Millionaire, 1983; (with David Frost) If You'll Believe That You'll Believe Anything …, 1986. *Recreations:* travel, music, books, pictures, motorcycling. *Address:* 6 Glenhurst Avenue, NW5 1PS; La Marsaulaie, Saint Mathurin, 49250 Beaufort-en-Vallée, France. *Club:* Hat.

See also N. D. Deakin.

DEAKIN, Prof. Nicholas Dampier, CBE 1997; Professor of Social Policy and Administration, University of Birmingham, 1980–98, now Hon. Professor (Dean, Faculty of Commerce and Social Science, 1986–89); Visiting Professor: London School of Economics, since 1998; Warwick Business School, since 1998; *b* 5 June 1936; *s* of Sir (Frederick) William Deakin, *qv* and Margaret Ogilvy Hodson; *m* 1st, 1961, Rose Albinia Donaldson (marr. diss. 1988), *d* of Baron Donaldson of Kingsbridge, OBE and Frances Donaldson; one *s* two *d*; 2nd, 1988, Lucy Moira, *d* of Jack and Moira Gaster. *Educ:* Westminster Sch.; Christ Church Coll., Oxford (BA (1st cl. Hons) 1959, MA 1963); DPhil Sussex 1972. Asst Principal, Home Office, 1959–63, Private Sec. to Minister of State, 1962–63; Asst Dir, Nuffield Foundn Survey of Race Relations in Britain, 1963–68; Res. Fellow, subseq. Lectr, Univ. of Sussex, 1968–72; Head of Social Studies, subseq. Head of Central Policy Unit, GLC, 1972–80. Scientific Advr, DHSS, later Dept of Health, 1986–91. Chm., Indep. Commn on Future of Voluntary Sector in England, 1995–96. Vice-Chm., Social Affairs Cttee, ESRC, 1984–86. Chair, Social Policy Assoc., 1989–92; Member: Exec. Cttee, NCVO, 1988–90; Council, RIPA, 1984–88; Governing Council, Family Policy Studies Centre, 1987–. Trustee, Nationwide Foundn, 1999–. Chair, Birmingham City Pride, 1998–2001. FRSA 1996. *Publications:* (ed and trans.) Memoirs of the Comte de Gramont, 1965; Colour and the British Electorate 1964, 1965; Colour, Citizenship and British Society, 1969; (with Clare Ungerson) Leaving London, 1977; (jtly) Government and Urban Poverty, 1983; (ed) Policy Change in Government, 1986; The Politics of Welfare, 1987, 2nd edn 1994; (ed jtly) Consuming Public Services, 1990; (jtly) The Enterprise Culture and the Inner Cities, 1992; (ed jtly) The Costs of Welfare, 1993; (jtly) Public Welfare Services and Social Exclusion, 1995; (jtly) Contracting for Change, 1997; (with Richard Parry) The Treasury and Social Policy, 2000; In Search of Civil Society, 2001; contribs to other vols and learned jls. *Recreations:* reading fiction, music. *Address:* Chedington, Lynmouth Road, N2 9LR.

See also M. Deakin.

DEAKIN, Sir William, Kt 1975; DSO 1943; MA; Warden of St Antony's College, Oxford, 1950–68, retired; Hon. Fellow, 1969; *b* 3 July 1913; *e s* of Albert Witney Deakin, Aldbury, Tring, Herts; *m* 1st, 1935, Margaret Ogilvy (marr. diss. 1940), *d* of late Sir Nicholas Beatson Bell, KCSI, KCIE; two *s*; 2nd, 1943, Livia Stela (*d* 2001), *d* of Liviu Nasta, Bucharest. *Educ:* Westminster Sch.; Christ Church, Oxford (Hon. Student, 1979). 1st Class, Modern History, 1934; Amy Mary Preston Read Scholar, 1935. Fellow and Tutor, Wadham Coll., Oxford, 1936–49; Research Fellow, 1949; Hon. Fellow, 1961. Served War of 1939–45; with Queen's Own Oxfordshire Hussars, 1939–41; seconded to Special Operations, War Office, 1941; led first British Military Mission to Tito, May 1943. First Secretary, HM Embassy, Belgrade, 1945–46. Hon. FBA, 1980. Russian Order of Valour, 1944; Chevalier de la Légion d'Honneur, 1953; Grosse Verdienstkreuz, 1958; Yugoslav Partisan Star (1st Class), 1969. *Publications:* The Brutal Friendship, 1962; (with G. R. Storry) The Case of Richard Sorge, 1964; The Embattled Mountain, 1971. *Address:* 83330 Le Castellet Village, Var, France. *Clubs:* White's, Brooks's.

See also M. Deakin, N. D. Deakin.

DEAKIN, William; *see* Deakin, J. F. W.

DEAKINS, Eric Petro; international public affairs consultant; *b* 7 Oct. 1932; *er s* of late Edward Deakins and Gladys Deakins; *m* 1990, Sandra Weaver; one *s* two *d*. *Educ:* Tottenham Grammar Sch.; London Sch. of Economics. BA (Hons) in History, 1953. Executive with FMC (Meat) Ltd, 1956; General Manager, Pigs Div., FMC (Meat) Ltd, 1969. Contested (Lab): Finchley, 1959; Chigwell, 1966; Walthamstow, 1967. MP (Lab): Walthamstow W, 1970–74; Walthamstow, 1974–87. Parly Under-Sec. of State, Dept of Trade, 1974–76, DHSS, 1976–79. *Publications:* A Faith to Fight For, 1964; You and your MP, 1987; What Future for Labour?, 1988. *Recreations:* writing, cinema, squash, football. *Address:* 36 Murray Mews, NW1 9RJ.

DEAL, Hon. Timothy Edward; Senior Vice President, United States Council for International Business, Washington, since 1996; *b* 17 Sept. 1940; *s* of Edward Deal and Loretta (*née* Fuemuller); *m* 1964, Jill Brady; two *s*. *Educ:* Univ. of California at Berkeley (AB Pol Sci.). First Lieut, US Army, 1963–65. Joined Foreign Service, US Dept of State, 1965; served Tegucigalpa, Honduras, Warsaw, Poland, and Washington, 1965–76; Sen. Staff Mem., Nat. Security Council, 1976–79 and 1980–81; Special Asst to Asst Sec. of State for European Affairs, 1979–80; Counsellor for Econ. Affairs, London, 1981–85; Dep. US Rep., OECD, Paris, 1985–88; Dir, Office of Eastern European Affairs, Washington, 1988–89; Special Asst to President and Sen. Dir for Internat. Econ. Affairs, Nat. Security Council, 1989–92; Minister and Dep. Chief of Mission, US Embassy, London, 1992–96. Presidential Awards for: Meritorious Service, 1991; Distinguished Service, 1993. *Recreations:* theatre, cinema, horse racing. *Address:* 5721 MacArthur Boulevard NW, Washington, DC 20016, USA.

DEALTRY, Prof. (Thomas) Richard; Managing Director, Intellectual Partnerships Consultancy Ltd, since 1999; Programmes Director: BAA plc, since 1997; University of

Surrey Management Learning Partnership, since 1997; *b* 24 Nov. 1936; *s* of George Raymond Dealtry and Edith (*née* Gardner); *m* 1962, Pauline (*née* Sedgwick) (marr. diss. 1982); one *s* one *d*. *Educ:* Cranfield Inst. of Advanced Technol.; MBA. CEng, MIMechE; MInstM; FIMCB. National Service Commn, 1959–61: Temp. Captain 1960. Divl Exec., Tube Investments Ltd, 1967–71; Sen. Exec., Guest, Keen & Nettlefold Gp Corporate Staff, 1971–74; Dir, Simpson-Lawrence Ltd, and Man. Dir, BUKO BV, Holland, 1974–77; Under Sec./Industrial Adviser, Scottish Econ. Planning Dept, 1977–78; Director, Gulf Regional Planning, Gulf Org. for Industrial Consulting, 1978–82; Man. Dir, RBA Management Services Ltd, London and Kuwait, 1982–85; Regl Dir, Diverco Ltd, 1985–; Prof. of Strategic Mgt, Internat. Mgt Centres, Buckingham, 1989–97. *Recreations:* golf, squash. *Address:* 43 Hunstanton Avenue, Harborne, Birmingham B17 8SX.

DEAN OF HARPTREE, Baron *cr* 1993 (Life Peer), of Wedmore in the County of Somerset; **Arthur Paul Dean,** Kt 1985; PC 1991; company director; *b* 14 Sept. 1924; *s* of Arthur Percival Dean and Jessie Margaret Dean (*née* Gaunt); *m* 1st, 1957, Doris Ellen Webb (*d* 1979); 2nd, 1980, Peggy Parker. *Educ:* Ellesmere Coll., Shropshire; Exeter Coll., Oxford (MA, BLitt). Former President Oxford Univ. Conservative Assoc. and Oxford Carlton Club. Served War of 1939–45, Capt. Welsh Guards; ADC to Comdr 1 Corps BAOR. Farmer, 1950–56. Resident Tutor, Swinton Conservative Coll., 1957; Conservative Research Dept, 1957–64, Assistant Director from 1962. MP (C) Somerset North, 1964–83, Woodspring, Avon, 1983–92. A Front Bench Spokesman on Health and Social Security, 1969–70; Parly Under-Sec. of State, DHSS, 1970–74; Dep. Chm. of Ways and Means and Dep. Speaker, 1982–92. Member: Exec. Cttee, CPA, UK Branch, 1975–92; House of Commons Services Select Cttee, 1979–82; House of Commons Chairman's Panel, 1979–82; Chm., Conservative Health and Social Security Cttee, 1979–82. A Dep. Speaker, H of L, 1995–. Mem., Exec. Cttee, Assoc. of Conservative Peers, 1995–. Formerly, Member Governing Body of Church in Wales. *Publications:* contributions to political pamphlets. *Recreation:* fishing. *Address:* Archer's Wyck, Knightcott, Banwell, Weston-super-Mare, Avon BS24 6HS. *Club:* Oxford and Cambridge.

DEAN OF THORNTON-LE-FYLDE, Baroness *cr* 1993 (Life Peer), of Eccles in the Metropolitan County of Greater Manchester; **Brenda Dean;** PC 1998; Chairman, Housing Corporation, since 1998; *b* 29 April 1943; *d* of Hugh Dean and Lillian Dean; *m* 1988, Keith Desmond McDowall, *qv*. *Educ:* St Andrews Junior Sch., Eccles; Stretford High Sch. for Girls. Admin. Sec., SOGAT, 1959–72; SOGAT Manchester Branch: Asst Sec., 1972–76; Sec., 1976–83; Mem., Nat. Exec. Council, 1977–83; Pres., 1983–85, Gen.-Sec., 1985–91, SOGAT '82; Dep. Gen. Sec., Graphical, Paper and Media Union, 1991–92; Chm., ICSTIS, 1993–99 (Mem., 1991–93). Non-executive Director: Inveresk plc, 1993–97; Chamberlain Phipps Gp plc, 1994–96; Takare plc, 1995–98; Assured British Meat, 1997–. Co-Chm., Women's Nat. Commn, 1985–87; Dep. Chm., UCL Hosps NHS Trust, 1993–98; Chm., Armed Forces Pay Review Body, 1999– (Mem., 1993–94); Member: Printing and Publishing Trng Bd, 1974–82; Supplementary Benefits Commn, 1976–80; Price Commn, 1977–79; Occupational Pensions Bd, 1983–87; Gen. Adv. Council, BBC, 1984–88; TUC Gen. Council, 1985–92; NEDC, 1989–92; Employment Appeal Tribunal, 1991–93; Broadcasting Complaints Commn, 1993–94; Press Complaints Commn, 1993–98; Nat. Cttee of Inquiry into Future of Higher Educn, 1996–97; Royal Commn on H of L reform, 1999; H of L Appts Commn, 2000–; Bd, Gen. Ins. Standards Council, 1999–; Sen. Salaries Review Body, 1999–. Mem. Council, ABSA, 1990–95. Member: Council, City Univ., 1991–96; Bar Council of Legal Educn, 1992–95; Council, Open Univ., 1996–98; Court of Governors, LSE, 1996–98; Gov., Ditchley Foundn, 1992–. Pres., Coll. of Occupational Therapy, 1995–. Mem. Adv. Bd of Mgt, PYBT, 1999– (Trustee, 1996–99); Trustee, Prince's Foundn, 1999–. FRSA 1992. Hon. Fellow, Lancs Poly., 1991. Hon. MA: Salford, 1986; South Bank, 1995; Hon. DCL City, 1993; Hon. LLD: North London, 1996; Exeter, 1999; Hon. LLB De Montfort, 1998. *Recreations:* sailing, reading, relaxing, thinking! *Address:* House of Lords, SW1P 0PW. *Clubs:* Reform; Royal Cornwall Yacht.

DEAN, (Catherine) Margaret; HM Lord Lieutenant of Fife, since 1999; *b* 16 Nov. 1939; *d* of Thomas Day McNeil Scrimgeour and Catherine Forbes Scrimgeour (*née* Sunderland); *m* 1962, Brian Dean; three *d*. *Educ:* George Watson's Ladies' Coll., Edinburgh; Univ. of Edinburgh (MA). *Address:* (home) Viewforth, 121 Rose Street, Dunfermline, Fife KY12 0QT. *T:* (01383) 722488, *Fax:* (01383) 738027; (office) Clerk to the Lieutenancy, Fife House, North Street, Glenrothes, Fife KY7 5LT, *T:* (01592) 416303, *Fax:* (01592) 414200.

DEAN, (Cecil) Roy; HM Diplomatic Service, retired; writer and broadcaster; *b* 18 Feb. 1927; *s* of Arthur Dean and Flora Dean (*née* Clare); *m* 1954, Heather Sturtridge; three *s*. *Educ:* Watford Grammar Sch.; London Coll. of Printing and Graphic Arts (diploma); Coll. for Distributive Trades (MIPR). Served RAF, 1945–48, SEAC; Central Office of Information, 1948–58; Second, later First Sec., Colombo, 1958–62; Vancouver, 1962–64; Lagos, 1964–68; FCO, 1968–71; Consul, Houston, 1971, Acting Consul-Gen., 1972–73; FCO, 1973–76; Dir, Arms Control and Disarmament Res. Unit, 1976–83; Dep. High Comr, Accra, 1983–86, Acting High Comr, 1984 and 1986. Mem., UN Sec.-General's expert group on disarmament instns, 1980–81. Trustee, Urbanaid, 1987–96. Mem., RSL. Editor: Insight, 1964–68; Arms Control and Disarmament, 1979–83; author and presenter, The Poetry of Popular Song (BBC Radio Four series), 1989–91. Vice-Pres., Bromley Arts Council; Press Officer: Bromley Music Soc.; Drawing Room Singers. *Compositions:* A Century of Song, 1996; A Shropshire Lass, 2000. *Publications:* Peace and Disarmament, 1982; chapter in Ethics and Nuclear Deterrence, 1982; Mainly in Fun, 1998; numerous research papers; contribs to learned jls. *Recreations:* crosswords (Times national champion, 1970 and 1979, world record for fastest solution, 1970), humour, light verse, song-writing, book collecting. *Address:* 14 Blyth Road, Bromley, Kent BR1 3RX. *T:* (020) 8402 0743. *Club:* Bromley Labour.

DEAN, His Honour (Charles) Raymond; QC 1963; a Circuit Judge (formerly Judge of County Courts), 1971–88; Senior Circuit Judge, 1985–88; *b* 28 March 1923; *s* of late Joseph Irvin Gledhill Dean and late Lilian Dean (*née* Waddington); *m* 1948, Pearl Doreen (*née* Buncall); one *s* one *d*. *Educ:* Hipperholme Grammar Sch.; The Queen's Coll., Oxford (1941–42 and 1945–47). RAF Flying Duties, 1942–45 (Flt Lieut). BA (Jurisprudence) 1947, MA 1948; called to Bar, Lincoln's Inn, 1948; Deputy Chairman, West Riding QS, 1961–65; Recorder: of Rotherham, 1962–65; of Newcastle upon Tyne, 1965–70; of Kingston-upon-Hull, 1970–71. *Recreations:* fishing, motoring, reading, Rugby Union (now non-playing), golf. *Address:* Inner Court, 3 Hudson Mews, Boston Spa, West Yorks LS23 6AD. *T:* (01937) 844155. *Club:* Leeds.

DEAN, Christopher Colin, OBE 2000 (MBE 1981); professional ice skater; *b* 27 July 1958; *s* of Colin Gordon Dean and Mavis (*née* Pearson) and step *s* of Mary Betty (*née* Chambers); *m* 1st, 1991, Isabelle Duchesnay (marr. diss. 1993); 2nd, 1994, Jill Trenary; one *s*. *Educ:* Calverton Manor Sch., Nottingham; Sir John Sherbrooke Sch., Nottingham; Col Frank Seely Sch., Nottingham. Police constable, 1974–80. Ice dancer, with Jayne Torvill, *qv*: British Champions, 1978, 1979, 1980, 1981, 1982, 1983, 1994; European Champions, 1981, 1982, 1984, 1994; World Champions, 1981, 1982, 1983, 1984; World Professional Champions, 1984, 1985, 1990, 1995 and 1996; Olympic Champions, 1984; Olympic Bronze Medallists, 1994. Choreographed Encounters, English Nat. Ballet, 1996. Hon. MA Nottingham Trent, 1993. With Jayne Torvill: BBC Sportsview Personality of the Year, 1983–84; Figure Skating Hall of Fame, 1989. *Publication:* (with Jayne Torvill) Facing the Music, 1995. *Recreations:* motor racing, films, dance. *Address:* PO Box 32, Heathfield, E Sussex TN21 0BW. *T:* (01435) 867825. *Club:* Groucho.

DEAN, Janet Elizabeth Ann; MP (Lab) Burton, since 1997; *b* 28 Jan. 1949; *d* of late Harry Gibson and Mary Gibson (*née* Walley); *m* 1968, Alan Dean (*d* 1994); two *d*. *Educ:* Winsford Verdin County Grammar Sch., Cheshire. Clerk: Barclays Bank, 1965–69; Bass Charrington, 1969–70. Member (Lab): Staffordshire County Council, 1981–97; E Staffordshire BC, 1991–97; Uttoxeter Town Council, 1995–97. Mem., Red-Rose Club, Burton upon Trent. *Recreations:* dressmaking, reading. *Address:* 53 Carter Street, Uttoxeter ST14 8EY.

DEAN, His Honour Joseph (Jolyon); a Circuit Judge, South Eastern Circuit, 1975–87; *b* 26 April 1921; *s* of late Basil Dean, CBE; *m* 1962, Hon. Jenefer Mills, *yr d* of late 5th Baron Hillingdon, MC, TD; one *s* two *d*. *Educ:* Elstree Sch.; Harrow Sch.; Merton Coll., Oxford (MA Classics and Law). 51st (Highland) Div., RA, 1942–45. Called to the Bar, Middle Temple, 1947; Bencher 1972. Member (C): Westminster City Council, 1961–65; Ashford BC, 1991–95. Chm., E Ashford Rural Trust, 1988–91. *Publication:* Hatred, Ridicule or Contempt, 1953 (paperback edns 1955 and 1964). *Address:* The Hall, West Brabourne, Ashford, Kent TN25 5LZ.

See also Winton Dean.

DEAN, Katharine Mary Hope, (Mrs Robert Dean); *see* Mortimer, K. M. H.

DEAN, Margaret; *see* Dean, C. M.

DEAN, Michael; QC 1981; **His Honour Judge Dean;** a Circuit Judge, since 1991; *b* 2 Feb. 1938; *s* of late Henry Ross Dean and Dorothea Alicia Dean; *m* 1st, 1967, Diane Ruth Griffiths; 2nd, 1992, Jane Isabel Glaister; one *s*. *Educ:* Altrincham Co. Grammar Sch.; Univ. of Nottingham (LLB 1st Cl. Hons 1959). Lectr in Law, Univ. of Manchester, 1959–62; called to the Bar, Gray's Inn, 1962 (Arden Scholar and Holker Sen. Scholarship, 1962); Northern Circuit, Manchester, 1962–65; Lectr in Law, LSE, 1965–67; practice at the Bar, London, 1968–91; an Asst Recorder, 1986–89; a Recorder, 1989–91. *Publications:* articles in various legal periodicals. *Recreations:* conversation, music, theatre, sailing, family life.

DEAN, Dr Paul, CB 1981; Director, National Physical Laboratory, 1977–90 (Deputy Director, 1974–76); *b* 23 Jan. 1933; *s* of late Sydney and Rachel Dean; *m* 1961, Sheila Valerie Gamse; one *s* one *d*. *Educ:* Hackney Downs Grammar Sch.; Queen Mary Coll., Univ. of London (Fellow, 1984). BSc (1st cl. Hons Physics), PhD; CPhys; FInstP, FIMA, CMath. National Physical Laboratory: Sen. Sci. Officer, Math. Div., 1957; Principal Sci. Officer, 1963; Sen. Principal Sci. Officer (Individual Merit), 1967; Head of Central Computer Unit, 1967; Supt, Div. of Quantum Metrology, 1969; Under-Sec., DoI (Head of Space and Air Res. and R&D Contractors Divs), 1976–77; initiated testing lab. accreditation in UK, leading to NAMAS, 1985. Part-time Head, Res. Estabts Management Div., DoI, 1979–82; Exec. Dep. Chm., Council of Res. Estabts, 1979–82. Mem., Internat. Cttee of Weights and Measures, 1985–90; Pres., Comité Consultatif pour les Etalons de Mesure des Rayonnements Ionisants, 1987–90; Founder Pres., British Measurement and Testing Assoc., 1990–95; First Chm., EUROMET, 1988–90. *Publications:* papers and articles in learned, professional and popular jls. *Recreations:* mathematics, computing, astronomy, chess, music, bridge. *Address:* Dorset.

DEAN, Peter Henry, CBE 1993; Chairman, Gaming Board for Great Britain, since 1998; *b* 24 July 1939; *s* of late Alan Walduck Dean and Gertrude (*née* Bürger); *m* 1965, Linda Louise Keating; one *d*. *Educ:* Rugby Sch.; London Univ. (LLB). Admitted Solicitor, 1962. Joined Rio Tinto-Zinc Corp., 1966; Sec., 1972–74; Dir, 1974–85; freelance business consultant, 1985–96. Director: Associated British Ports Holdings, 1982–2001 (Mem., British Transport Docks Bd, 1980–82); Liberty Life Assce Co., 1986–95; Seeboard, 1993–96; G. H. Dean & Co., 1999–. Dep. Chm., Monopolies and Mergers Commn, 1990–97 (Mem., 1982–97); Investment Ombudsman, 1996–2001. Chm., Council of Management, Highgate Counselling Centre, 1991– (Mem., 1985–); Chm., English Baroque Choir, 1985–89, 1999–2000. *Recreations:* choral singing, ski-ing. *Address:* 52 Lanchester Road, Highgate, N6 4TA. *T:* (020) 8883 5417, *Fax:* (020) 8365 2398.

DEAN, Raymond; *see* Dean, C. R.

DEAN, Roy; *see* Dean, C. R.

DEAN, Winton (Basil), FBA 1975; author and musical scholar; *b* Birkenhead, 18 March 1916; *e s* of late Basil Dean, CBE, and Esther, *d* of A. H. Van Gruisen; *m* 1939, Hon. Thalia Mary Shaw (*d* 2000), 2nd *d* of 2nd Baron Craigmyle; one *s* one adopted *d* (and two *d* decd). *Educ:* Harrow; King's Coll., Cambridge (MA). Translated libretto of Weber's opera Abu Hassan (Arts Theatre, Cambridge) 1938. Served War of 1939–45: in Admiralty (Naval Intelligence Div.), 1944–45. Member: Music Panel, Arts Council, 1957–60, Cttee of Handel Opera Society (London), 1955–60; Council, Royal Musical Assoc., 1965–98 (Vice-Pres., 1970–98; Hon. Mem., 1998–). Ernest Bloch Prof. of Music, 1965–66, Regent's Lectr, 1977, Universiy of California (Berkeley); Matthew Vassar Lectr, Vassar Coll., Poughkeepsie, NY, 1979. Member: Management Cttee, Halle Handel Soc., 1979– (Vice-Pres., 1991–99; Hon. Mem., 1999); Kuratorium, Göttingen Handel Fest., 1981–97 (Hon. Mem., 1997–); Corresp. Mem., Amer. Musicological Soc., 1989–. Ed, with Sarah Fuller, Handel's opera Julius Caesar (Barber Inst. of Fine Arts, Birmingham), performed 1977. Hon. RAM 1971. Hon. MusD Cambridge, 1996. *Publications:* The Frogs of Aristophanes (trans. of choruses to music by Walter Leigh), 1937; Bizet (Master Musicians), 1948 (3rd rev. edn, 1975); Carmen, 1949; Introduction to the Music of Bizet, 1950; Franck, 1950; Hambledon *v* Feathercombe, the Story of a Village Cricket Match, 1951; Handel's Dramatic Oratorios and Masques, 1959; Shakespeare and Opera (Shakespeare in Music), 1964; Georges Bizet, His Life and Work, 1965; Handel and the Opera Seria, 1969; Beethoven and Opera (in The Beethoven Companion), 1971; ed, Handel, Three Ornamented Arias, 1976; (ed) E. J. Dent, The Rise of Romantic Opera, 1976; The New Grove Handel, 1982; (with J. M. Knapp) Handel's Operas 1704–1726, 1987, 2nd edn 1995; Essays on Opera, 1990; (ed jtly) Handel, Julius Caesar, 1999; contributed to Grove's Dictionary of Music and Musicians (5th and 6th edns), New Oxford History of Music and to musical periodicals and learned journals. *Recreations:* cricket, shooting, salmon fishing, naval history. *Address:* Hambledon Hurst, Godalming, Surrey GU8 4HF. *T:* (01428) 682644.

See also J. J. Dean.

DEANE, family name of **Baron Muskerry**.

DEANE, Prof. Basil; Professor of Music, University of Birmingham, 1987–92, now Emeritus; *b* 27 May 1928; *s* of Canon Richard A. Deane and Lorna Deane; *m* 1955, Norma Greig (*d* 1991); two *s*. *Educ:* Armagh Royal School; The Queen's Univ., Belfast (BA, BMus). PhD Glasgow. FRNCM 1978. Lecturer in Music, Glasgow Univ., 1953–59; Senior Lectr, Melbourne Univ., 1959–65; Lectr, Nottingham Univ., 1966–68; Prof., Sheffield Univ., 1968–74; Prof., Manchester Univ., 1975–80; Music Dir, Arts Council, 1980–83; Dir, Hongkong Acad. for Performing Arts, 1983–87. Member of Arts Council, 1977–79 (Chairman, Music Advisory Panel, 1977–79); Chairman of Music Board, Council for Nat. Academic Awards, 1978–80. *Publications:* Albert Roussel, 1962; Cherubini, 1965; Hoddinott, 1979; contribs to periodicals. *Address:* 21 Lough Shore Road, Portaferry, Co. Down, N Ireland BT22 1PD.

DEANE, Derek, OBE 2000; Artistic Director, English National Ballet, 1993–2001; *b* 18 June 1953; *s* of William Gordon Shepherd and Margaret Shepherd; adopted Deane as stage name. *Educ:* Royal Ballet School. With Royal Ballet Co., 1972–89; Asst Dir, Rome Opera, 1990–92. *Recreations:* theatre, all performing arts, travelling, tennis.

DEANE, Prof. Phyllis Mary, FBA 1980; Professor of Economic History, University of Cambridge, 1981–83; Fellow of Newnham College, 1961–83, Hon. Fellow, 1983; *b* 13 Oct. 1918; *d* of John Edward Deane and Elizabeth Jane Brooks; single. *Educ:* Chatham County Sch.; Hutcheson's Girls' Grammar Sch., Glasgow; Univ. of Glasgow (MA Hons Econ. Science 1940); MA Cantab. Carnegie Research Scholar, 1940–41; Research Officer, Nat. Inst. of Econ. and Social Research, 1941–45; Colonial Research Officer, 1946–48; Research Officer: HM Colonial Office, 1948–49; Cambridge University: Dept of Applied Econs, 1950–61; Lectr, Faculty of Econs and Politics, 1961–71; Reader in Economic History, 1971–81. Vis. Prof., Univ. of Pittsburgh, 1969. Editor, Economic Jl, 1968–75. Pres., Royal Economic Soc., 1980–82. Hon. DLitt Glasgow, 1989. *Publications:* (with Julian Huxley) The Future of the Colonies, 1945; The Measurement of Colonial National Incomes, 1948; Colonial Social Accounting, 1953; (with W. A. Cole) British Economic Growth 1688–1959, 1962; The First Industrial Revolution, 1965; The Evolution of Economic Ideas, 1978; The State and the Economic System, 1989; The Life and Times of Neville Keynes, 2001; papers and reviews in econ. jls. *Recreations:* walking, gardening. *Address:* 4 Stukeley Close, Cambridge CB3 9LT.

DEANE, Hon. Sir William (Patrick), AC 1988; KBE 1982; Governor General of the Commonwealth of Australia, 1996–2001; *b* 4 Jan. 1931; *s* of C. A. Deane, MC and Lillian Hussey; *m* 1965, Helen, *d* of Dr Gerald and Kathleen Russell; one *s* one *d*. *Educ:* St Christopher's Convent, Canberra; St Joseph's College, Sydney; Univ. of Sydney (BA, LLB); Trinity Coll., Dublin; Dip. Internat. Law, The Hague. Called to the Bar of NSW, 1957. Teaching Fellow in Equity, Univ. of Sydney, 1956–61 (Actg Lectr in Public Internat. Law, 1956–57); QC 1966; Judge, Supreme Court of NSW, 1977; Judge, Fed. Court of Australia, 1977–82; Pres., Trade Practices Tribunal, 1977–82; Justice of the High Court of Australia, 1982–95. Hon. LLD: Sydney, Griffith, Notre Dame, TCD; DUniv: Southern Cross, Aust. Cath., Western Sydney, Qld Univ. of Technol.; Hon. Dr Sac. Theol. Melbourne Coll. of Divinity. KStJ 1996.

DEANE-DRUMMOND, Maj.-Gen. Anthony John, CB 1970; DSO 1960; MC 1942 and Bar, 1945; *b* 23 June 1917; *s* of late Col J. D. Deane-Drummond, DSO, OBE, MC; *m* 1944, Mary Evangeline Boyd; four *d*. *Educ:* Marlborough Coll.; RMA, Woolwich. Commissioned Royal Signals, 1937. War Service in Europe and N Africa; POW, Italy, 1941 (escaped, 1942); Staff Coll., 1945; Bde Major, 3rd Parachute Bde, 1946–47; Instructor, Sandhurst, 1949–51 and Staff Coll., 1952–55; CO, 22 Special Air Service Regt, 1957–60; Bde Comdr, 44 Parachute Bde, 1961–63; Asst Comdt, RMA, Sandhurst, 1963–66; GOC 3rd Division, 1966–68; ACDS (Operations), 1968–70, retired 1971. Col Comdt, Royal Corps of Signals, 1966–71. Director: Paper and Paper Products Industry Trng Bd, 1971–79; Wood Burning Centre, 1980–83. British Gliding Champion, 1957; Pilot, British Gliding Team, 1958, 1960, 1963, 1965. *Publications:* Return Ticket, 1951; Riot Control, 1975; Arrows of Fortune (autobiog.), 1991; (contrib.) The Imperial War Museum Book of Wars since 1945—the British Experience, 2002. *Recreations:* carpentry and carving, antique furniture restoration, shooting. *Address:* c/o Royal Bank of Scotland, PO Box 412, 62–63 Threadneedle Street, EC2R 8LA.

DEAR, Sir Geoffrey (James), Kt 1997; QPM 1982; Vice Lord-Lieutenant, Worcestershire, since 1998; HM Inspector of Constabulary, 1990–97; *b* 20 Sept. 1937; *er s* of Cecil William Dear and Violet Mildred (*née* Mackney); *m* 1st, 1958, Judith Ann Stocker (*d* 1996); one *s* two *d*; 2nd, 1998, Alison Jean Martin Jones. *Educ:* Fletton Grammar Sch., Hunts; University Coll., London (LLB). Joined Peterborough Combined Police after cadet service, 1956; Mid-Anglia (now Cambridgeshire) Constab., 1965; Bramshill Scholarship, UCL, 1965–68 (Fellow, 1990); Asst Chief Constable (Ops), Notts (City and County), 1972–80; seconded as Dir of Comd Training, Bramshill, 1975–77; Metropolitan Police: Dep. Asst Comr, 1980–81; Asst Comr, 1981–85 (Personnel and Trng, 1981–84; Ops, 1984–85); Chief Constable, W Midlands Police, 1985–90. Member: Govt Adv. Cttee on Alcoholism, 1975–78; Glidewell Rev. into CPS, 1997–98; Council, RUSI, 1982–89 (Mem. Cttee, 1976–94). Lecture tour of Eastern USA univs, 1978; visited Memphis, Tenn, USA to advise on reorganisation of Police Dept, 1979. Non-exec. Chm., Image Metrics plc, 2001–; non-executive Director: Reliance Security Services Ltd, 1997–; Reliance Custodial Services, 1999–. Vice Chm., London and SE Reg., Sports Council, 1984–85. Vice President: Warwickshire CCC, 1985–; W Midlands and Hereford & Worcester Grenadier Guards Assocs, 1992–. Hon. Fellow, Univ. of Central England in Birmingham, 1991. FRSA 1990. DL W Midlands, 1985, Hereford and Worcester, 1995. CStJ 1996. Queen's Commendation for Bravery, 1979. *Publications:* (contrib.) The Police and the Community, 1975; articles in Police Jl and other pubns. *Recreations:* field sports, Rugby football (Pres., Met. Police RFC, 1983–85), fell-walking, literature, gardening, music, fine arts. *Address:* The Old Rectory, Willersey, Broadway, Worcs WR12 7PN. *Clubs:* East India, Special Forces.

DEARING, family name of **Baron Dearing**.

DEARING, Baron *cr* 1998 (Life Peer), of Kingston upon Hull in the co. of the East Riding of Yorkshire; **Ronald Ernest Dearing,** Kt 1984; CB 1979; Chairman, Committee of Inquiry into Future of Church of England Schools, 2000–01; *b* 27 July 1930; *s* of late E. H. A. Dearing and of M. T. Dearing (*née* Hoyle); *m* 1954, Margaret Patricia Riley; two *d*. *Educ:* Doncaster Grammar Sch.; Hull Univ. (BScEcon); London Business Sch. (Sloan Fellow). Min. of Labour and Nat. Service, 1946–49; Min. of Power, 1949–62; HM Treasury, 1962–64; Min. of Power, Min. of Technology, DTI, 1965–72; Regional Dir, N Region, DTI, 1972–74, and Under-Sec., DTI later Dept of Industry, 1972–76; Dep. Sec. on nationalised industry matters, Dept of Industry, 1976–80; Dep. Chm., 1980–81, Chm., 1981–87, Post Office Corp.; Chairman: Co. Durham Develt Co., 1987–90; Northern Develt Co., 1990–94; Camelot Gp, 1993–95; Write Away, 1997–. Director (non-executive): Whitbread Co. plc, 1987–90; Prudential plc, 1987–91; IMI plc, 1988–95; British Coal, 1988–91; Ericsson Ltd, 1988–93; English Estates, 1988–90; SDX Business Systems, 1996–. Chairman: NICG, 1983–84; Accounting Standards Review Cttee, CCAB, 1987–88; Financial Reporting Council, 1990–93. Mem. Council, Industrial Soc., 1985–99. CIMgt (CBIM 1981; Mem. Council, 1985–88; Vice-Chm., 1986; Gold Medal, 1994). Chairman: CNAA, 1987–88; PCFC, 1988–93; UFC, 1991–93; HEFCE, 1992–93; SCAA, 1993–96; Nat. Cttee of Inquiry into Higher Educn, 1996–97. Vice Pres., LGA, 2000–. McKechnie Lectr, Liverpool Univ., 1995. Mem. Governing Council, London Business Sch., 1985–89, Fellow, 1988; Member: Council, Durham Univ., 1988–91; Governing Body, Univ. of Melbourne, 1997–2000; Chm., London Educn Business Partnership, 1989–92. Chm., Northern Sinfonia Appeals Cttee, 1993–94. Pres., Inst. of Direct Mkting, 1994–97. Chancellor, Nottingham Univ., 1993–2001. Patron: Sascha Lasserson Meml Trust, 1995; Music in Allendale, 1995; Univ. for Industry, 2000– (Chm., 1999–2000). Trustee, TRAC, 1995–97. Freeman, City of London, 1982. Hon. FREng (Hon. FEng 1992); Hon. FTCL 1993; Hon. Fellow, Inst. of Educn, 1995. Hon. Fellow, Sunderland Poly., 1991. Hon. DSc Hull, 1986; Hon. DTech: CNAA, 1991; Staffordshire, 1995; Hon. DCL: Durham, 1992; Northumbia, 1993; Hon. LLD Nottingham, 1993; Dr *hc* Humberside, 1993; DUniv Open, 1995; Hon. DLitt: Brighton, 1998; Exeter, 1998. *Recreations:* car boot sales, DIY, gardening. *Address:* House of Lords, SW1A 2PW.

DEARLOVE, Sir Richard Billing, KCMG 2001; OBE 1984; HM Diplomatic Service; Chief, Secret Intelligence Service, since 1999; *b* 23 Jan. 1945; *m* 1968, Rosalind McKenzie; two *s* one *d*. *Educ:* Monkton Combe Sch.; Kent Sch., Conn, USA; Queens' Coll., Cambridge (BA 1966). Entered FO, 1966; Nairobi, 1968–71; Prague, 1973–76; FCO, 1976–80; First Secretary: Paris, 1980–84; FCO, 1984–87; Counsellor: UKMIS Geneva, 1987–91; Washington, 1991–93; Dir, Personnel and Admin, 1993–94, Dir, Ops, 1994–99, Asst Chief, 1998–99, SIS. *Address:* c/o Foreign and Commonwealth Office, King Charles Street, SW1A 2AH.

DEARNALEY, Dr Geoffrey, FRS 1993; President, Cambritec Consulting, since 1999; Vice-President, Materials and Structures Division, Southwest Research Institute, 1994–99; *b* 22 June 1930; *s* of Eric and Dora Dearnaley; *m* 1957, Jean Rosalind Beer; two *s*. *Educ:* Univ. of Cambridge (MA 1955; PhD 1956). Research Fellow, Pembroke Coll., Cambridge, 1955–58; joined AERE, Harwell, Nuclear Physics Division, 1958: Individual Merit Promotion, 1975; Chief Scientist, Surface Technologies, 1991–93; joined Southwest Res. Inst., Texas, 1993, Inst. Scientist, 1993–94. Vis. Prof. in Physics, Sussex Univ., 1972–. *Publications:* Semiconductor Counters for Nuclear Radiations, 1963; Ion Implantation, 1973; numerous articles on interaction of energetic ion beams with materials. *Recreations:* travel, walking, the life and work of William Blake. *Address:* Southwest Research Institute, 6220 Culebra Road, PO Drawer 28510, San Antonio, TX 78228–0510, USA. *T:* (210) 5225579.

DEAVE, John James; former barrister-at-law; *b* 1 April 1928; *s* of Charles John Deave and Gertrude Debrit Deave; *m* 1958, Gillian Mary, *d* of Adm. Sir Manley Power, KCB, CBE, DSO; one *s* one *d*. *Educ:* Charterhouse; Pembroke Coll., Oxford (MA). Served RA, 2nd Lieut, 1946–48; Pembroke Coll., 1948–51; called to the Bar, Gray's Inn, 1952; in practice at Nottingham, 1957–98; a Recorder, 1980–98. *Recreations:* history, gardening. *Club:* Nottinghamshire United Services.

DEAYTON, (Gordon) Angus; writer and presenter; *b* 6 Jan. 1956; *s* of Roger Davall Deayton and Susan Agnes Deayton (*née* Weir). *Educ:* Caterham Sch.; New Coll., Oxford (BA Modern Langs (French and German)). Dir, Oxford Revue, 1979. Writer and performer: *radio:* Radio Active, 1980–87 (Mem., Hee Bee Gee Bees pop parody band); *stage:* Rowan Atkinson's Stage Show, 1986–90; *television:* Alexei Sayle's Stuff, 1987–90; KYTV, 1990–93; One Foot in the Grave, 1990–2000; Have I Got News For You?, 1990–; TV Hell, 1992; End of the Year Show, 1995–2000; Before They Were Famous, 1997–2000; Not Another Awards Show, 1999; *documentaries:* In Search of Happiness, 1995; The Lying Game, 1997; The Temptation Game, 1998; The History of Alternative Comedy, 1999. *Publications:* Radio Active Times, 1986; The Uncyclopaedia of Rock, 1987; Have I Got News For You?, 1994; In Search of Happiness, 1995; Have I Got 1997 For You?, 1997. *Recreations:* soccer, tennis, ski-ing. *Address:* c/o TalkBack, 36 Percy Street, W1P 9FG. *T:* (020) 7631 3940. *Clubs:* Groucho, Soho House, Home House.

De BAKEY, Prof. Michael Ellis, MD, MS; Chancellor, Baylor College of Medicine, 1978–96, now Emeritus (Professor and Chairman, Department of Surgery, 1948–93, President, 1969–79, Chief Executive Officer, and Vice-President for Medical Affairs, 1968–69, Distinguished Service Professor, since 1968, and Olga Keith Wiess Professor of Surgery, since 1981); Surgeon-in-Chief, Ben Taub General Hospital, Houston, Texas, 1963–93; Senior Attending Surgeon, Methodist Hospital, Houston; Director: National Heart and Blood Vessel Research and Demonstration Center, 1976–84; DeBakey Heart Center, Baylor College of Medicine, since 1985; President, DeBakey Medical Foundation, since 1961; Consultant in Surgery to various Hospitals etc., in Texas, and to Walter Reed Army Hospital, Washington, DC; *b* 7 Sept. 1908; *s* of Shaker Morris and Raheeja Zorba DeBakey; *m* 1st, 1936, Diana Cooper (*d* 1972); four *s*; 2nd, 1975, Katrin Fehlhaber; one *d*. *Educ:* Tulane Univ., New Orleans, La, USA (BS 1930; MD 1932; MS 1935; Alumni Assoc. Distinguished Alumnus of Year, 1974; Sesquicentennial Medal for Most Distinguished Alumni, 1997). Residency in New Orleans, Strasbourg, and Heidelberg, 1933–36; Instructor, Dept of Surgery, Tulane Univ., 1937–40; Asst Prof. of Surgery, 1940–46; Associate Prof. of Surgery, 1946–48. Colonel Army of US (Reserve). In Office of Surgeon-General, 1942–46, latterly Director Surgical Consultant Div. (US Army Legion of Merit, 1945). Chairman, President's Commission on Heart Disease, Cancer and Stroke, 1964 (Report to the President published in 2 vols, 1964, 1965); US Chm., Task Force for Mechanical Circulatory Assistance, Jt US-USSR Cttee, 1974; Dir, Cardiovascular Res. and Trng Center, Methodist Hosp. (Houston), 1964–75; Adv. Council, Nat. Heart, Lung, Blood Inst., 1982–86; Member: VTEL Med. Adv. Panel, 1996; Med. Res. Panel, Health Speakers, Research America, 1996; has served on governmental and university cttees, etc., concerned with public health, research and medical education. Member, Advisory Editorial Boards, including: Ann. Surg., 1970–; Coeur, 1969–; Biomaterials, Med. Develt & Artificial Organs (formerly Biomedical Materials and Artificial Organs), 1971–; Editor, Jl of Vascular Surgery, 1984–88. Member and Hon. Member of medical societies, including: Inst. of Medicine, Nat. Acad. of Sciences (Sen. Mem., 1981); American Assoc. for Thoracic Surgery (Pres. 1959); International Cardiovascular Society (Pres. 1957–59); BMA (Hon. Foreign Corresp. Member 1966); Royal Society Med., London; Acad. of Medical Sciences, USSR; US—China Physicians Friendship Assoc., 1974; Assoc. Internat. Vasc. Surgeons (Pres., 1983, 1990); Southern Surgical Assoc. (Pres., 1989–90); Assoc. Française de Chirurgie, 1991; Acad. of Athens, 1992; Royal Coll. of Physicians and Surgeons of USA (Hon. Dist. Fellow, 1992); Amer. Inst. Med. and Biol Engrg (Founding Fellow, 1993); Soc. for Biomaterials (Fellow, Biomaterials Sci. and Engrg, 1994). Hon. FRCS 1974. Has received numerous awards from American and foreign medical institutions, and over 50 honorary doctorates; Hektoen Gold Medal, Amer. Med. Assoc., 1954, 1970; Albert Lasker Award for Clin. Res., 1963; Presidential Medal of Freedom with Distinction, 1969; Meritorious Civilian Service Medal, 1970; USSR Acad. of Science 50th Anniversary Jubilee Medal, 1973; Nat. Medal of Science, 1987; Markowitz Award, Acad. of Surgical Res., 1988; Assoc. of Amer. Med. Colls. Award, 1988; Crile Award, Internat. Platform Assoc., 1988;

Thomas Alva Edison Foundn Award, 1988; Scripps Clinic and Res. Foundn Inaugural Award, 1989; Centennial Award, 1980, and first Michael DeBakey Medal, 1989, ASME; Jacobs Award, Amer. Task Force for Lebanon, 1991; Gibbon Award, Amer. Soc. for Extracorporeal Tech., 1993; Maxwell Finland Award, Nat. Foundn for Infectious Diseases, 1992; Ellis Island Medal of Honor, Nat. Ethics Coalition of Orgns, 1993; Lifetime Achievement Award, Amer. Heart Assoc., 1994; Boris Petrovsky Internat. Surgeons Award and first Gold Medal, Russian Mil. Med. Acad., 1997; Global Peace and Tolerance Lifetime Achievement Award, Children Uniting Nations, 1999; Jonathan Rhoads Medal, Amer. Philosophical Soc., 2000; Bicentennial Living Legend Award, Liby of Congress, 2000. Merit Order of the Republic, 1st class (Egypt), 1980; The Independence of Jordan Medal, 1st class, 1980; Commander Cross of Merit, Sovereign Order of the Knights of the Hospital of St John (Denmark), 1980; Commander's Cross, Order of Merit (Germany), 1992; Order of Independence 1st cl. medal (UAE), 1992; Nat. Order of Vasco Nuñez de Balboa (Panama), 1995. *Publications:* The Blood Bank and the Technique and Therapeutics of Transfusions, 1942; (jtly) Battle Casualties: incidence, mortality, and logistic considerations, 1952; (jtly) Cold Injury, Ground Type, in World War II, 1958; (with B. M. Cohen) Buerger's Disease, 1963; A Surgeon's Diary of a Visit to China, 1974; The Living Heart, 1977; The Living Heart Diet, 1984; The Living Heart Brand Name Shopper's Guide, 1992; The Living Heart Guide to Eating Out, 1993; The New Living Heart Diet, 1996; The New Living Heart, 1997; contributions to standard textbooks of medicine and surgery, and many symposia; Editor, Year Book of General Surgery, etc; over 1,500 articles in medical journals. *Recreations:* literature, music. *Address:* Baylor College of Medicine, One Baylor Plaza, Houston, TX 77030, USA. *T:* (713) 7903185. *Clubs:* Cosmos, University, Federal City (Washington, DC); River Oaks Country (Houston, Texas).

de BASTO, Gerald Arthur; Judge of the High Court of Hong Kong, 1982–89; *b* London, 31 Dec. 1924; *s* of Bernard de Basto and Lucie Marie, *d* of Raoul Melchior Pattard, Paris; *m* 1961, Diana, *d* of Dr Frederick Osborne Busby Wilkinson; two *s*. *Educ:* Riverview Coll., Sydney, Australia; Univ. of Sydney (LLB). Called to the Bar: Supreme Court of New South Wales and High Court of Australia, 1952; Lincoln's Inn, 1955; admitted to the Hong Kong Bar, 1957; Chairman, Hong Kong Bar, 1968–70, 1973; QC 1968; Judge of the District Court of Hong Kong, 1973–82; Pres., Deportation Tribunal, 1986–89. *Recreations:* antiques, travel, reading. *Address:* Canterbury Lodge, 21 Canterbury Drive, Bishopscourt, 7708, South Africa. *T:* (21) 7625626. *Clubs:* Boodle's; Hong Kong, Hong Kong Jockey (Hong Kong); Kelvin Grove (Cape Town).

de BELLAIGUE, Sir Geoffrey, GCVO 1996 (KCVO 1986; CVO 1976; LVO 1968); FSA; FBA 1992; Director of the Royal Collection, 1988–96; Surveyor of the Queen's Works of Art, 1972–96, now Surveyor Emeritus; *b* 12 March 1931; *s* of Vicomte Pierre de Bellaigue and late Marie-Antoinette Ladd; *m* 1971, Sheila, (LVO 2000), 2nd *d* of late Rt Rev. J. K. Russell; two *d*. *Educ:* Wellington Coll.; Trinity Coll., Cambridge (BA 1951, MA 1959); Ecole du Louvre. With J. Henry Schroeder & Co., 1954–59; with the National Trust, Waddesdon Manor, 1960–63 (Keeper of the Collection, 1962–63); Dep. Surveyor, the Queen's Work's of Art, 1963–72. Mem., Exec. Cttee, NACF, 1977–. Trustee, Wallace Collection, 1998. Hon. Pres., French Porcelain Soc., 1985–. Officier de l'Ordre des Arts et des Lettres (France), 1987; Officier, Légion d'Honneur, 1999. *Publications:* The James A. de Rothschild Collection at Waddesdon Manor: furniture, clocks and gilt bronzes, 1974; (jtly) Buckingham Palace, 1986; Sèvres Porcelain in the Collection of HM the Queen, Vol. I, 1986; (with S. Eriksen) Sèvres Porcelain, 1987; articles in art historical jls and exhibn catalogues, principally for The Queen's Gallery. *Address:* Store Tower, Windsor Castle, Windsor, Berks SL4 1NJ.

DE BENEDETTI, Carlo; Cavaliere del Lavoro, Italy, 1983; Chairman: Compagnie Industriali Riunite, since 1995 (Vice-Chairman and Chief Executive, 1976–95); Compagnia Finanziaria De Benedetti, since 1995 (Chief Executive, 1991–95); Cerus, since 1986; Sogefi, since 1981; *b* 14 Nov. 1934; *m*; three *s*. *Educ:* Turin Polytechnic (degree in electrotech. engrg). Chm./Chief Exec., Gilardini, 1972–76; Chief Exec., Fiat, 1976; Olivetti SpA: Chief Exec., 1978–96; Chm., 1983–96; Hon. Chm., 1996. Director: Pirelli SpA; Valeo Editoriale; l'Espresso SpA; Mem., European Adv. Cttee, NY Stock Exchange, 1985. Dir, Center for Strategic and Internat. Studies, Washington, 1978; Member: Bd of Trustees, Solomon R. Guggenheim Foundn, NY, 1984; Roundtable of European Industrialists, Brussels. Foreign Mem., Royal Swedish Acad. of Engrg Scis, Stockholm, 1987. *Publications:* lectures and articles in business jls. *Address:* CIR SpA, Via Ciovassino 1, 20121 Milano, Italy. *T:* (2) 722701.

DEBENHAM, Sir Thomas Adam, 4th Bt *cr* 1931, of Bladen, co. Dorset; *b* 28 Feb. 1971; *s* of George Andrew Debenham and of Penelope Jane (*née* Carter); *S* grandfather, 2001. *Heir: uncle* William Michael Debenham [*b* 30 June 1940; *m* 1974, Gunnel Birgitta Holmgren; two *s*].

DEBENHAM TAYLOR, John, CMG 1967; OBE 1959; TD 1967; HM Diplomatic Service, retired; *b* 25 April 1920; *s* of John Francis Taylor and Harriett Beatrice (*née* Williams); *m* 1966, Gillian May James; one *d*. *Educ:* Aldenham School. Eastern Counties Farmers Assoc. Ltd, Ipswich and Great Yarmouth, 1936–39. Commd in RA (TA), Feb. 1939; served War of 1939–46 in Finland, Middle East, UK and SE Asia (despatches, 1946). Foreign Office, 1946; Control Commn for Germany, 1947–49; 2nd Sec., Bangkok, 1950; Actg Consul, Songkhla, 1951–52; Vice-Consul, Hanoi, 1952–53; FO, 1953–54; 1st Sec., Bangkok, 1954–56; FO, 1956–58; Singapore, 1958–59; FO, 1960–64; Counsellor, 1964; Counsellor: Kuala Lumpur, 1964–66; FCO (formerly FO), 1966–69; Washington, 1969–72; Paris, 1972–73; FCO, 1973–77. *Recreations:* walking, reading, history. *Address:* The East Wing, Gunton Hall, Norfolk NR11 7HJ. *T:* (01263) 768301. *Club:* Naval and Military.

de BERNIÈRE-SMART, Louis Henry Piers; author, as Louis de Bernières; *b* 8 Dec. 1954; *s* of Major Reginald Piers Alexander de Bernière-Smart, *qv*. *Educ:* Grenham House; Bradfield Coll.; Manchester Univ. (BA Hons Philosophy 1977); Leicester Poly. (PGCE 1981); Inst. of Educn, London Univ. (MA 1985). Landscape gardener, 1972–73; teacher and rancher, Colombia, 1974; philosophy tutor, 1977–79; car mechanic, 1980; English teacher, 1981–84; bookshop asst, 1985–86; supply teacher, 1986–93. FTCL 1999. *Publications:* The War of Don Emmanuel's Nether Parts, 1990; Señor Vivo and the Coca Lord, 1991; The Troublesome Offspring of Cardinal Guzman, 1992; Captain Corelli's Mandolin, 1994 (filmed, 2001); Red Dog, 2001. *Recreations:* music, literature, golf, fishing, carpentry, gardening, cats. *Address:* c/o Lavinia Trevor Agency, 7 The Glasshouse, 49a Goldhawk Road, W12 8QP. *T:* (020) 8749 8481.

de BERNIÈRE-SMART, Major Reginald Piers Alexander; Director, The Shaftesbury Homes and Arethusa, 1988–89, retired (General Secretary, 1971–88); general duties, Chichester Division, SSAFA/FHS, 1995–2000 (caseworker, 1990–94); *b* 3 March 1924; *s* of Kenneth de Bernière-Smart and Audrey (*née* Brown); *m* 1951, Jean Ashton Smithells; one *s* two *d*. *Educ:* Bowden House, Seaford; Bradfield Coll. Commnd The Queen's Bays (2nd Dragoon Guards), 1943; Italian Campaign, 1944–45 (despatches); Staff, RAC OCTU and Mons OCS, 1948–49; GSO 3 7th Armd Bde, 1951; Adjt, The Queen's Bays, 1952–54; Adjt, RAC Centre, Bovington, 1956–58; retired from 1st The Queen's Dragoon Guards, 1959. Exec. Sec., British Diabetic Assoc., 1960–65; joined Shaftesbury Homes and Arethusa exec. staff, 1966. Dir, Wad (West Wittering) Management Co., 1992–94. Chm., Management Cttee, Bradfield Club, Peckham, 1990–92 (Mem. Council, 1992–2000). Member: IAM, 1959–; NCVCCO, 1971–89. West Wittering PCC, 1991–97; Foundn Gov., W Wittering Parochial C of E Sch., 1997– (Chm. of Govs, 1998–2000). Life Governor, ICRF, 1990. *Recreations:* open air activities, photography, steam and model railways, theatre, poetry, militaria. *Address:* 9 The Wad, West Wittering, Chichester, W Sussex PO20 8AH. *T:* (01243) 511072. *Clubs:* Victoria League for Commonwealth Friendship; West Wittering Sailing.

See also L. H. P. de Bernière-Smart.

de BERNIÈRES, Louis; *see* de Bernière-Smart, L. H. P.

de BLANK, Justin Robert; Vice Chairman, The Justin de Blank Co. Ltd, since 1996; *b* 25 Feb. 1927; *s* of William de Blank and Agnes Frances de Blank (*née* Crossley); *m* 1st, 1972, Mary Jacqueline Christina du Bois Godet (Molly); 2nd, 1977, Melanie Alexandra Margaret Irwin; three *d*. *Educ:* Grenham House School, Birchington-on-Sea; Marlborough College; Corpus Christi College, Cambridge (BA); Royal Acad. Sch. of Architecture. Unilever, 1953–58; J. Walter Thompson, London and Paris, 1958–66; Conran Design Group, 1967; formed own company, 1968; Chm. and Man. Dir, Justin de Blank Provisions Ltd, 1968–93; Chm., de Blank Restaurants, 1986–95; Pres., Justin de Blank Foods Ltd, 1993–95. Director: Kitchen Range Foods Ltd, 1976–96; Millers Damsels Ltd, 1989–96; The Original Porter's Provisions Co. Ltd, 1993–96; Chm., Chantdene, 1999–. *Recreations:* gardening, golf, food and wine. *Address:* 12 Trigon Road, SW8 1NH. *T:* (020) 7582 2996. *Clubs:* Annabel's; Royal West Norfolk Golf.

de BLOCQ van KUFFELER, John Philip; Chairman, Provident Financial plc, since 1997; *b* 9 Jan. 1949; *s* of Captain Frans de Blocq van Kuffeler and Stella de Blocq van Kuffeler (*née* Hall); *m* 1971, Lesley Callander; two *s* one *d*. *Educ:* Atlantic Coll.; Clare Coll., Cambridge (MA). FCA 1975. Peat Marwick & Mitchell, 1970–77; Grindlays Bank: Manager, 1977–80; Head of Corporate Finance, 1980–82; Brown Shipley & Co.: Head: Corporate Finance, 1983–88; Investment Banking, UK and USA, 1986–88; Gp Chief Exec., 1988–91; Chief Exec., Provident Financial plc, 1991–97. Chm., Finsbury Smaller Quoted Cos Trust; Dir, Fleming Technol. Trust. *Recreations:* field sports, opera. *Address:* Provident Financial plc, Colonnade, Sunbridge Road, Bradford BD1 2LQ. *T:* (01274) 731111. *Club:* City of London.

de BONO, Dr Edward Francis Charles Publius; Lecturer in Medicine, Department of Medicine, University of Cambridge, 1976–83; Director of The Cognitive Research Trust, Cambridge, since 1971; Secretary-General, Supranational Independent Thinking Organisation (SITO), since 1983; *b* 19 May 1933; *s* of late Prof. Joseph de Bono, CBE and of Josephine de Bono (*née* O'Byrne); *m* 1971, Josephine, *d* of Maj. Francis Hall-White, MBE; two *s*. *Educ:* St Edward's Coll., Malta; Royal Univ. of Malta; Christ Church, Oxford (Rhodes Scholar). BSc, MD Malta; DPhil Oxon; PhD Cantab. Research Asst, Dept of Regius Prof. of Medicine, Univ. of Oxford, 1958–60; Jun. Lectr in Med., Oxford, 1960–61; Asst Dir of Res., Dept of Investigative Medicine, Cambridge Univ., 1963–76. Research Associate, also Hon. Registrar, St Thomas' Hosp. Med. Sch., Univ. of London; Harvard Med. Sch., and Hon. Consultant, Boston City Hosp., 1965–66. Chm. Council, Young Enterprise Europe, 2000–. TV series: The Greatest Thinkers, 1981; de Bono's Thinking Course, 1982. *Publications:* The Use of Lateral Thinking, 1967; The Five-Day Course in Thinking, 1968; The Mechanism of Mind, 1969; Lateral Thinking: a textbook of creativity, 1970; The Dog Exercising Machine, 1970; Technology Today, 1971; Practical Thinking, 1971; Lateral Thinking for Management, 1971; Beyond Yes and No, 1972; Children Solve Problems, 1972; Eureka!: an illustrated history of inventions from the wheel to the computer, 1974; Teaching Thinking, 1976; The Greatest Thinkers, 1976; Wordpower, 1977; The Happiness Purpose, 1977; The Case of the Disappearing Elephant, 1977; Opportunities: a handbook of business opportunity search, 1978; Future Positive, 1979; Atlas of Management Thinking, 1981; de Bono's Thinking Course, 1982; Tactics: the art and science of success, 1984; Conflicts: a better way to resolve them, 1985; Six Thinking Hats, 1985; Masterthinker's Handbook, 1985; Letters to Thinkers, 1987; I am Right, You are Wrong, 1990; Positive Revolution for Brazil, 1990; Handbook for a Positive Revolution, 1990; Six Action Shoes, 1992; Sur/Petition, 1992; Serious Creativity, 1992; Teach your child to think, 1992; Water Logic, 1993; Parallel Thinking, 1994; Teach Yourself to Think, 1995; Mind Pack, 1995; Edward de Bono's Textbook of Wisdom, 1996; How To Be More Interesting, 1997; Simplicity, 1998; New Thinking for the New Millennium, 1999; Why I want to be King of Australia, 1999; The de Bono Code Book, 2000; contribs to Nature, Lancet, Clinical Science, Amer. Jl of Physiology, etc. *Recreations:* travel, toys, thinking. *Address:* L2 Albany, Piccadilly, W1V 9RR. *Club:* Athenæum.

de BOTTON, Alain; author, since 1993; *b* 20 Dec. 1969; *s* of late Gilbert de Botton and of Jacqueline (*née* Burgauer). *Educ:* Gonville and Caius Coll., Cambridge (BA Hist. 1st Cl. Hons). *Publications:* Essays in Love, 1993; The Romantic Movement, 1994; Kiss and Tell, 1995; How Proust Can Change Your Life, 1997; The Consolations of Philosophy, 2000; The Art of Travel, 2002. *Recreations:* French Cinema 1960–1970, nature, art. *Address:* 73 Sterndale Road, W14 0HU.

de BOTTON, Hon. Janet Frances Wolfson; Trustee: Tate Gallery, since 1992; Wolfson Foundation, since 1987; *b* 31 March 1952; *d* of Baron Wolfson, *qv* and Ruth, Lady Wolfson; *m* 1st, 1972, Michael Philip Green, *qv* (marr. diss. 1989); two *d*; 2nd, 1990, Gilbert de Botton (*d* 2000). *Educ:* St Paul's Girls' Sch. Dir. Christie's International, 1994–98. Chm. Council, Tate Modern (formerly Tate Gall. of Modern Art), 1999–. *Address:* c/o Tate Gallery, Millbank, SW1P 4RG. *T:* (020) 7887 8000.

DEBRÉ, Jean Louis; Deputy (RPR) for Eure, National Assembly, France, 1986–95 and since 1997; *b* Toulouse, 30 Sept. 1944; *s* of late Michel Jean-Pierre Debré; *m* 1971, Anne-Marie Engel; two *s* one *d*. *Educ:* Lycée Janson-de-Sailly; Institut d'Etudes Politiques, Paris; Faculté de Droit, Paris (DenD); Ecole Nationale de la Magistrature. Asst, Faculté de Droit, Paris, 1972–75; Technical Counsellor, then Chargé de Mission, office of Jacques Chirac, as Minister of Agric., 1973 74, Minister of the Interior, 1974, and Prime Minister, 1974–76; Dep. Public Prosecutor, High Court of Evry, 1976–78; Magistrate, Central Admin, Ministry of Justice, 1978; Chef de Cabinet to Minister of the Budget, 1978; Examng Magistrate, High Court of Paris, 1979. Minister of the Interior, France, 1995–97. Vice-Pres., 1990–95, Pres., 1997–, RPR Gp in Nat. Assembly. Councillor: Evreux, 1989–95; Paris, 1995–97; Conseiller Général, Canton de Nonancourt, 1992–. *Publications:* Les Idées constitutionnelles du Général de Gaulle, 1974; La Constitution de la Ve République, 1974; Le Pouvoir politique, 1977; Le Gaulisme, 1978; La Justice au XIXe, 1981; Les Républiques des Avocats, 1984; Le Curieux, 1986; En mon for intérieur, 1997; Pièges, 1998. *Recreations:* horse-riding, tennis. *Address:* c/o Assemblée Nationale, 126 rue de l'Université, 75355 Paris, France.

DEBREU, Prof. Gerard; Professor of Economics, 1962–91, Professor of Mathematics, 1975–91, and University Professor, 1985–91, now Emeritus, University of California, Berkeley; *b* 4 July 1921; *s* of Camille Debreu and Fernande (*née* Decharne); *m* 1945, Françoise Bled; two *d*. *Educ:* Ecole Normale Supérieure, Paris; Agrégé de l'Université, Paris, 1946. DSc Univ. de Paris, 1956. Research Associate: Centre National de la Recherche Scientifique, Paris, 1946–48; Cowles Commn for Research in Economics, Univ. of Chicago, 1950–55; Associate Prof. of Economics, Cowles Foundn for Research in Economics, Yale Univ., 1955–61. Fellow, Amer. Acad. of Arts and Sciences, 1970; President: Econometric Soc., 1971; American-Economic Assoc., 1990. Member: Nat. Acad. of Sciences, USA, 1977; Amer. Philos. Soc., 1984; Dist. Fellow, Amer. Economic Assoc., 1982; For. Associate, French Acad. of Scis, 1984. Hon. degrees: Bonn, 1977; Lausanne, 1980; Northwestern, 1981; Toulouse, 1983; Yale, 1987; Université de Bordeaux I, 1988. Nobel Prize in Economic Sciences, 1983. Officier de la Légion d'Honneur, 1993 (Chevalier, 1976); Comdr de l'Ordre National du Mérite, 1984. *Publications:* Theory of Value: an axiomatic analysis of economic equilibrium, 1959, 2nd edn 1971 (trans. into French, Spanish, German and Japanese); Mathematical Economics: twenty papers, 1983; contribs to Econometrica, Procs of Nat. Acad. of Sciences, Review of Economic Studies, Economie Appliquée, Procs of Amer. Math. Soc., Internat. Economic Review, Review of Economic Studies, La Décision, Jl of Mathematical Economics, Amer. Economic Review. *Address:* Department of Economics, 549 Evans Hall, University of California, Berkeley, CA 94720–3880, USA. *T:* (510) 6427284.

de BROKE; *see* Willoughby de Broke.

de BRÚN, Bairbre; Member (SF) West Belfast, since 1998, and Minister of Health, Social Services and Public Safety, since 1999, Northern Ireland Assembly. *Educ:* University Coll., Dublin (BA Hons); Queen's Univ., Belfast (PGCE). Teacher, specialised in Irish Medium Educn, 1991–97. *Recreations:* hill-walking, theatre, cinema. *Address:* Sinn Féin Offices, Stormont, Belfast BT4 3XX. *T:* (028) 9052 1675.

DE BUTTS, Brig. Frederick Manus, CMG 1967; OBE 1961 (MBE 1943); DL; *b* 17 April 1916; *s* of late Brig. F. C. De Butts, CB, DSO, MC, and K. P. M. O'Donnell; *m* 1944, Evelyn Cecilia, *d* of Sir Walter Halsey, 2nd Bt; one *s* one *d*. *Educ:* Wellington Coll.; Oriel Coll., Oxford. Commissioned into Somerset LI, 1937. Served War of 1939–45, in Middle East, Italy, France and Germany (despatches, 1941, 1944). Staff Coll., 1944; Malaya (despatches, 1950); Joint Services Staff Coll., 1954; Bt Lieut-Colonel, 1957; Commanded 3rd Bn Aden Protectorate Levies, 1958–60; Bde Colonel, Light Infantry, 1961–64; Comdr, Trucial Oman Scouts, 1964–67; HQ Home Counties District, Shorncliffe, Kent, 1967–68; Defence Attaché, Cairo, 1968–71; retired 1971; employed on contract as COS (Brig.), MoD, United Arab Emirates, 1971–73; Hon. Brig. 1973. Mem., Dacorum DC, 1976–83. Hon. Dir, Herts Soc., 1981–91. County Chm., 1973–76, County Comr, 1976–81, Vice-Pres., 1981–89, Pres., 1989–97, Herts Scouts; Vice-Pres., Herts Girl Guides, 1981–; Governor, Abbot's Hill School, 1971–92 (Chm., 1975–84). DL Herts 1975. *Publication:* Now the Dust has Settled: memories of war and peace 1939–1994, 1995. *Recreations:* tennis, hill-walking, ski-ing. *Address:* Church Cottage, Hoggeston, Buckingham, Bucks MK18 3LL. *T:* (01296) 713811.

DEBY, John Bedford; QC 1980; a Recorder of the Crown Court, 1977–96; *b* 19 Dec. 1931; *s* of Reginald Bedford Deby and Irene (*née* Slater). *Educ:* Winchester Coll.; Trinity Coll., Cambridge (MA). Called to the Bar, Inner Temple, 1954, Bencher, 1986. *Address:* 11 Britannia Road, Fulham, SW6 2HJ. *T:* (020) 7736 4976. *Club:* Athenæum.

de CARDI, Beatrice Eileen, OBE 1973; archaeologist; *b* 5 June 1914; *d* of Edwin Count de Cardi and Christine Berbette Wurrflein. *Educ:* St Paul's Girls' Sch.; University Coll. London (BA; Fellow, 1995). Secretary (later Asst), London Museum, 1936–44; Personal Asst to Representative of Allied Supplies Exec. of War Cabinet in China, 1944–45; Asst UK Trade Comr: Delhi, 1946; Karachi, 1947; Lahore, 1948–49; Asst Sec. (title changed to Sec.), Council for British Archæology, 1949–73. Archæological research: in Kalat, Pakistan Baluchistan, 1948; in Afghanistan, 1949; directed excavations: in Kalat, 1957; at Bampur, Persian Baluchistan, 1966; survey in Ras al-Khaimah (then Trucial States), 1968; Middle East lecture tour for British Council, 1970; survey with RGS's Musandam Expedn (Northern Oman), 1971–72; directed archæological research projects: in Qatar, 1973–74; in Central Oman, 1974–76, 1978; survey in Ras al-Khaimah, 1977, 1982, 1992. Winston Churchill Meml Trust Fellowship for work in Oman, 1973; Hon. Vis. Prof., UCL, 1998–. FSA 1950 (Vice-Pres., 1976–80; Dir, 1980–83). Al-Qasimi Medal (UAE), 1989 (for services to Ras al-Khaimah); Burton Meml Medal, RAS, 1993. *Publications:* Excavations at Bampur, a third millennium settlement in Persian Baluchistan, 1966 (Vol. 51, Pt 3, Anthropological Papers of the American Museum of Natural History), 1970; Archaeological Surveys in Baluchistan 1948 and 1957 (Inst. of Archaeology, Occasional Paper No 8), 1983; contribs to Antiquity, Iran, Pakistan Archæology, East and West, Jl of Oman Studies, Oriens Antiquus, Proc. Seminar for Arabian Studies. *Recreations:* archæological fieldwork, travel, cooking. *Address:* 1a Douro Place, Victoria Road, W8 5PH. *T:* (020) 7937 9740.

de CARMOY, Hervé Pierre; Comte de Carmoy; Managing Director, Rhône Group LLC, New York, since 1999; *b* 4 Jan. 1937; *s* of Guy de Carmoy and Marie de Gourcuff; *m* Roseline de Rohan Chabot; two *c*. *Educ:* Institut d'Etudes Politiques, Paris; Cornell Univ. Gen. Man., Western Europe, Chase Manhattan Bank, 1963–78; Chm., Exec. Bd, Midland Bank, Paris, 1978–79; Gen. Man., Europe, Midland Bank, London, 1979–84; Chief Exec., Internat. Midland Bank, London, 1984–86; Dir and Chief Exec., Global Banking Sector, Midland Bank, 1986–88; Chief Exec. Officer, Société Générale de Belgique, 1988–91; Chairman and Chief Executive: Union Minière, 1989–91; Banque Industrielle et Mobilière Privée, 1992–98. Chairman: Cimenteries Belges Réunies, 1989–; Gechem, 1989–; Parvalind Gérance, 1991–; Vice Chm., Générale de Banque, 1989–. Prof., Institut d'Etudes Politiques, Paris, 1995. Commandeur de la Légion d'Honneur (Côte d'Ivoire), 1978; Chevalier de l'Ordre du Mérite (France), 1987; Chevalier de la Légion d'Honneur (France), 1992. *Publications:* Third World Debt, 1987; Stratégie Bancaire: le refus de la dérive, 1988; La Banque du XXIe Siècle, 1996; L'entreprise, l'individu, l'Etat: conduire le changement, 1999. *Recreations:* tennis, music. *Address:* 10 rue Guynemer, 75006 Paris, France; Rhône Group LLC, 630 Fifth Avenue, New York, NY 10111, USA; Rhône Group, 9–11 rue Montalivet, 75008 Paris.

de CHARETTE, Hervé; Deputy (UDF) for Maine-et-Loire, 1988–93, and since 1997; Deputy President, Union pour la Démocratie Française, since 1999; *b* 30 July 1938; *s* of Hélion de Charette; *m* 1980, Michelle Delor; one *d*, and one *s* three *d* by former marriage. *Educ:* Institut des Etudes Politiques; HEC; Ecole Nationale de l'Administration. Conseil d'Etat: Mem., 1966–; Auditor, 1966–73; Dep. Sec. Gen., 1969–73; Maître des Requêtes, 1973–; tech. advr to Minister of Social Affairs, 1973–74; Cabinet Director for: Sec. of State for Immigration, 1974–76; Minister of Employment, 1976–78; Chargé de Mission for Minister of Commerce, 1978–81; Conseil d'Etat, 1982–86; Asst to Prime Minister and Minister of Public Service, Planning and Social Econs, 1986–88; Minister of Housing, 1988–95; Minister for Foreign Affairs, 1995–97. Vice-Pres., UDF, 1989; Delegate-Gen., 1995–97, Pres., 1997–, PPDF. Vice-Pres., Pays-de-Loire Regl Council, 1992–; Mayor, St Florent-le-Vieil, 1989–. Pres., St Florent-le-Vieil Music and Dance Fest., 1989–. *Publications:* Whirlwind over the Republic, 1995; Lyautey, 1997. *Address:* 250 boulevard Saint Germain, 75007 Paris, France.

de CHASSIRON, Charles Richard Lucien, CVO 2000; HM Diplomatic Service; Foreign and Commonwealth Office, since 2001; *b* 27 April 1948; *s* of Hugo and Deane de Chassiron; *m* 1974, Britt-Marie Medhammar; one *s* one *d*. *Educ:* Jesus Coll., Univ. of Cambridge (BA Hons 1969, MA 1973); Univ. of Harvard (MPA 1971). Joined Diplomatic Service, 1971; service in: Stockholm, 1972–75; Maputo, 1975–78; Mem., UK Delegn at Lancaster House Conf. on Rhodesia, 1979; FCO, 1980–82; service in Brasilia, 1982–85; Asst Hd, later Hd, S America Dept, FCO, 1985–89; Counsellor (Comm./Econ.), Rome, 1989–94; Ambassador to Estonia, 1994–97; Dir-Gen. for British Trade Develt in Italy, and Consul-Gen., Milan, 1997–2001. *Recreations:* art history, walking, tennis. *Address:* c/o Foreign and Commonwealth Office, SW1A 2AH.

de CHASTELAIN, Gen. (Alfred) John (Gardyne Drummond), CMM 1984; OC 1993; CH 1999; Chairman, Independent International Commission on Decommissioning, Northern Ireland, since 1997; *b* Bucharest, 30 July 1937; *s* of late Alfred George Gardyne de Chastelain, DSO, OBE, and Marion Elizabeth de Chastelain (*née* Walsh); *m* 1961, MaryAnn Laverty; one *s* one *d*. *Educ:* Fettes Coll., Edinburgh; Mount Royal Coll., Calgary, Alberta; Royal Mil. Coll. of Canada (BA Hons Hist. 1960); Army Staff Coll., Camberley. Commnd 2nd Lieut, 2nd Bn, PPCLI, 1960; Capt. 1962; Maj. 1967; Lt-Col 1970; CO, 2nd Bn, PPCLI 1970–72; Col 1974; Commander: Canadian Forces Base, Montreal, 1974–76; Canadian Contingent, UN Forces, Cyprus, 1976–77; Brig. Gen. 1977; Comdt, RMC of Canada, 1977–80; Comdr, 4th Canadian Mechanized Bde Gp, Germany, 1980–82; Maj.-Gen. 1983; Dep. Comdr, Mobile Comd, Quebec, 1983–86; Lt-Gen. 1986; Asst Dep. Minister (Personnel), NDHQ, 1986–88; Vice Chief, Defence Staff, 1988–89; Gen. 1989; Chief of Defence Staff, 1989–92; Ambassador for Canada to USA, 1993; Chief of Defence Staff, 1994–95; Mem., Internat. Body on Decommissioning of Arms in NI, 1995–96; Chm., Business Cttee and Strand Two Talks, NI Peace Process, 1996–98. Col of Regt, PPCLI, 2000–. Hon. DScMil RMC, Canada, 1996. CStJ 1991. CD (Canada), 1968; Medal of Merit and Honour (Greece), 1992; Comdr, Legion of Merit (USA), 1995. *Publications:* (contrib.) Canada on the Threshold of the 21st Century, 1992; contrib. to Canadian Defence Qly. *Recreations:* painting, fishing, bagpipes. *Address:* 170 Acacia Avenue, Ottawa, Ont K1M 0R3, Canada. *T:* (613) 7447300.

DECIES, 7th Baron *cr* 1812 (Ire.); **Marcus Hugh Tristram de la Poer Beresford;** *b* 5 Aug. 1948; *o s* of 6th Baron Decies and of his 2nd wife, Diana, *d* of Wing Comdr George Turner-Cain and *widow* of Major David Galsworthy; *S* father, 1992; *m* 1st, 1970, Sarah Jane Gunnell (marr. diss. 1974); 2nd, 1981, Edel Jeannette, *d* of late Vincent Hendron; two *s* two *d*. *Educ:* St Columba's Coll.; Dublin Univ. (MLitt). *Heir:* *s* Hon. Robert Marcus Duncan de la Poer Beresford, *b* 14 July 1988.

DE CLERCQ, Willy; Member (L) European Parliament, 1979–81, and since 1989; Minister of State, Belgium, since 1985; *b* 8 July 1927; *s* of Frans De Clercq; *m* 1953, Fernande Fazzi; two *s* one *d*. *Educ:* Ghent Univ. (Dr in Law 1950); Univ. of Syracuse, USA (MA SocSci 1951). Called to Belgian Bar, 1951; Municipal Councillor, Ghent, 1952–79; Dep. Sec.-Gen., Belgian Liberal Party, 1957; MP Ghent-Eeklo, 1958–85; Dep. State Sec., Min. of Budget, 1960; Leader, Parly Gp of Belgian Liberal Party, 1965; Dep. Prime Minister, 1966–68; created Flemish Liberal Party (PVV) (Chm., 1972–73 and 1977–81); Dep. Prime Minister, 1973; Minister of Finance, 1974–77 (Chm., Interim Cttee, IMF; Mem., Bd of Governors, EIB; Governor, World Bank); Dep. Prime Minister and Minister of Finance and Foreign Trade, 1981–85; Mem., Commn of European Communities, 1985–88. European Parliament: Chairman: External Econ. Relations Cttee, 1989–97; Cttee on Legal Affairs and Citizens' Rights, 1997–. Pres., European Liberal Democrat and Reform Party (formerly Fedn of Europ. Liberal Democratic and Reform Parties), 1981–85 and 1991–95 (Hon. Pres., 1995). President: Eur. Movt, Belgium, 1992–; Eur. Federalist Movt, Belgium, 1992–. Comdr, Order of Leopold; Grand Cross, Order of Leopold II; holds numerous foreign decorations. *Address:* (office) Belliardstraat 97–113, 1047 Brussels, Belgium. *T:* (2) 2845149; (home) Cyriel Buyssestraat 12, 9000 Ghent, Belgium. *T:* (9) 2211813.

de CLIFFORD, 27th Baron *cr* 1299; **John Edward Southwell Russell;** *b* 8 June 1928; *s* of 26th Baron de Clifford, OBE, TD, and Dorothy Evelyn (*d* 1987), *d* of late Ferdinand Richard Holmes Meyrick, MD; *S* father, 1982; *m* 1959, Bridget Jennifer, *yr d* of Duncan Robertson, Llangollen, Denbighshire. *Educ:* Eton. *Heir:* *b* Hon. William Southwell Russell [*b* 26 Feb. 1930; *m* 1961, Jean Brodie, *d* of Neil Brodie Henderson; one *s* two *d*]. *Address:* Riggledown, Pennymoor, Tiverton, Devon EX16 8LR. *Club:* Naval and Military.

de COURCY, family name of **Baron Kingsale**.

de COURCY-IRELAND, Patrick Gault, CVO 1980; HM Diplomatic Service, retired; Director of Marketing, Alireza Group of Companies, since 1987; Director, Rezayat Europe Ltd, since 1988; *b* 19 Aug. 1933; *e s* of late Lawrence Kilmaine de Courcy-Ireland and Elizabeth Pentland Gault; *m* 1957, Margaret Gallop; one *s* three *d*. *Educ:* St Paul's Sch.; Jesus Coll., Cambridge (MA). HM Forces (2nd Lieut), 1952–54. Joined Foreign Service, 1957; Student, ME Centre for Arab Studies, 1957–59; Third, later Second Sec., Baghdad, 1959–62; Private Sec. to HM Ambassador, Washington, 1963; Consul (Commercial), New York, 1963–67; UN (Polit.) Dept, 1967–69; Asst Head of Amer. Dept, 1969–71; First Sec. and Hd of Chancery, Kuwait, 1971–73; Asst Hd of SW Pacific Dept, 1973–76; Hd of Trng Dept and Dir, Diplomatic Serv. Language Centre, FCO, 1976–80; Consul-Gen., Casablanca, 1980–84; Consul-Gen., Jerusalem, 1984–87. Chm., British Sch. of Archaeology in Jerusalem, 1990–99; Member: Exec. Cttee, Palestine Exploration Fund, 1991–95; Council, Soc. for Moroccan Studies, 1992–. MInstPet 1992. Great Comdr, Order of KHS, 1985. *Recreations:* book collecting, opera. *Address:* 49 Napier Court, Ranelagh Gardens, SW6 3UU. *T:* (020) 7736 0622; Crellow House, Stithians, Truro, Cornwall TR3 7RN. *T:* (01209) 860030.

de COURCY LING, John, CBE 1990; HM Diplomatic Service, 1959–78; politician, publisher and writer, since 1978; *b* 14 Oct. 1933; *s* of Arthur Norman Ling, Warwick, and Veronica de Courcy, Painestown, Co. Kildare; *m* 1959, Jennifer Rosemary Haynes, 2nd *d* of Stanley Haynes, Denham and Margaret McLurg, Vancouver; one *s* three *d*. *Educ:* King Edward's Sch., Edgbaston; Clare Coll., Cambridge (BA 1955; MA 1981). 2nd Lieut, Royal Ulster Rifles, 1956; Lieut on active service, Cyprus, 1957–58. Res. Dept, FO, 1959; a private sec. to Ministers of State for Foreign Affairs, Lord Harlech, 1960–61, to Joseph Godber, 1961–63; 2nd Sec., Santiago, 1963–66; 1st Sec., Nairobi, 1966–69; Chargé d'Affaires, Chad, 1973; Counsellor, HM Embassy, Paris, 1974–77; resigned, 1978, to enter politics. MEP (C) Midlands Central, 1979–89. Mem., Council of Lloyds, 1986–88. Mem., Catholic Bishops' Cttee on Europe, 1983–2001. Mem. Council, RIIA, 1990–93. *Publications:* (with T. R. McK. Sewell) Famine and Surplus, 1985; Tales of Imperial Decline, 1993; Empires Rise and Sink, 1996; contribs to the Tablet and various political papers. *Recreations:* racing, ski-ing, yachting, sociable golf. *Address:* Coutts & Co.,

440 Strand, WC2 0QS. *Clubs:* Beefsteak; Leander (Henley-on-Thames); Chipping Norton Golf.

See also Sir M. I. Wigan, Bt.

DeCRANE, Alfred Charles, Jr; Chairman of the Board, 1987–96, and Chief Executive Officer, 1993–96, Texaco Inc.; *b* 11 June 1931; *s* of Alfred Charles DeCrane and Verona (Marquard) DeCrane; *m* 1954, Joan Hoffman; one *s* five *d.* *Educ:* Notre Dame Univ. (BA); Georgetown Univ. (LLB). Texaco Inc.: Attorney, Houston and NY, 1959–65; Asst to Vice-Chm., 1965–67; Asst to Chm., 1967–68; Gen. Manager, 1968–70, Vice-Pres., 1970–76, Producing Dept, E Hemisphere; Sen. Vice-Pres., General Counsel, 1976–78; Board Dir, 1977–96; Exec. Vice-Pres., 1978–83; Pres., 1983. *Address:* Two Greenwich Plaza, PO Box 1247, Greenwich, CT 06836, USA.

de DENEY, Sir Geoffrey Ivor, KCVO 1992 (CVO 1986); Clerk of the Privy Council, 1984–92; Chief Executive, Royal College of Anaesthetists, 1993–97; *b* 8 Oct. 1931; *s* of late Thomas Douglas and Violet Ivy de Deney; *m* 1959, Diana Elizabeth Winrow; two *s.* *Educ:* William Ellis Sch.; St Edmund Hall, Oxford (MA, BCL); Univ. of Michigan. Home Office: joined, 1956; Asst Principal, 1956–61 (Private Sec. to Parly Under Sec. of State, 1959–61); Principal, 1961–69; Sec. to Graham Hall Cttee on maintenance limits in magistrates' courts; Sec. to Brodrick Cttee on Death Certification and Coroners; Private Sec. to Sec. of State, 1968; Asst Sec., 1969–1978; seconded to Cabinet Office, 1975; Asst Under Sec. of State, 1978–84; Community Programmes and Equal Opportunities Dept, 1978–80; General Dept (and Registrar of the Baronetage), 1980–84. Hon. FRCA. *Recreations:* books, walking. *Address:* 17 Ladbroke Terrace, W11 3PG.

DEDMAN, Peter George; His Honour Judge Dedman; a Circuit Judge, since 2000; *b* 22 May 1940; *s* of late George Stephen Henry Dedman and of Jessie Maud Dedman (*née* Hanson); *m* 1965, Patricia Mary Gordon, JP, RGN, RHV; one *d.* *Educ:* Tottenham Grammar Sch. Magistrates' Courts Service, Brentford, Tottenham and Newham; Principal Asst to Clerk to the Justices, Newham, 1965–69; called to the Bar, Gray's Inn, 1968 (amongst first to qualify following removal of embargo on Justices' Clerks and their assts from reading for the Bar); in practice at the Bar, specialising in personal injury litigation; a Recorder, 1992–2000; South Eastern Circuit. *Recreations:* music – playing the piano and trombone, theatre, film, attending concerts. *Address:* Chelmsford Crown Court, New Street, Chelmsford, Essex CM1 1EL. *T:* (01245) 603000.

de DUVE, Prof. Christian René Marie Joseph, Grand Cross Order of Leopold II 1975; Professor of Biochemistry, Catholic University of Louvain, 1951–85, now Emeritus; Founding Member, and President 1974–91, International Institute of Cellular and Molecular Pathology, Brussels; Andrew W. Mellon Professor at Rockefeller University, New York, 1962–88, now Emeritus; *b* England, 2 Oct. 1917; *s* of Alphonse de Duve and Madeleine Pungs; *m* 1943, Janine Herman; two *s* two *d.* *Educ:* Jesuit Coll., Antwerp; Catholic Univ. of Louvain; Med. Nobel Inst., Stockholm; Washington Univ., St Louis. MD 1941, MSc 1946, Agrégé de l'Enseignement Supérieur 1945, Louvain. Lectr, Med. Faculty, Catholic Univ. of Louvain, 1947–51. Vis. Prof. at various univs. Mem. editorial and other bds and cttees; mem. or hon. mem. various learned socs, incl. For. Assoc. Nat. Acad. of Scis (US) 1975, and For. Mem of Royal Soc., 1988. Holds hon. degrees. Awards incl. Nobel Prize in Physiol. or Med., 1974. *Publications:* A Guided Tour of the Living Cell, 1985; Blueprint for a Cell, 1991; Vital Dust, 1995; numerous scientific. *Recreations:* tennis, ski-ing, bridge. *Address:* Le Pré St Jean, 239 rue de Weert, 1390 Nethen (Grez-Doiceau), Belgium. *T:* (10) 866628; 80 Central Park West, New York, NY 10023, USA. *T:* (212) 7248048.

DEECH, Ruth Lynn; Principal, St Anne's College, Oxford, since 1991; Chairman, Human Fertilisation and Embryology Authority, since 1994; *b* 29 April 1943; *d* of Josef Fraenkel and Dora (*née* Rosenfeld); *m* 1967, Dr John Stewart Deech; one *d.* *Educ:* Christ's Hosp., Hertford; St Anne's Coll., Oxford (BA 1st Cl. 1965; MA 1969); Brandeis Univ., USA (MA 1966). Called to the Bar, Inner Temple, 1967, Hon. Bencher, 1996. Legal Asst, Law Commn, 1966–67; Asst Prof., Faculty of Law, Univ. of Windsor, Canada, 1968–70; Oxford University: Fellow and Tutor in Law, 1970–91, Vice-Principal, 1988–91, St Anne's Coll.; CUF Lectr in Law, 1971–91; Sen. Proctor, 1985–86; Mem., Hebdomadal Council, 1986–2000; Chm., Jt Undergrad. Admissions Cttee, 1993–97, Admissions Exec., 2000–. Member: Cttee of Inquiry into Equal Opportunities on Bar Vocational Course, 1993–94; Human Genetics Commn, 2000–. Non-exec. Dir, Oxon HA, 1993–94. Mem., Exec. Council, Internat. Soc. on Family Law, 1988–. Vis. Prof., Osgoode Hall Law Sch., York Univ., Canada, 1978. Governor: Carmel Coll., 1980–90; Oxford Centre for Hebrew and Jewish Studies, 1994–2000; UCS, 1997–. Rhodes Trustee, 1997–. Gov., United Jewish Israel Appeal, 1997–99. FRSocMed 2001. Hon. Fellow, Soc. for Advanced Legal Studies, 1997. *Publications:* articles on family law and property law. *Recreations:* after-dinner speaking, music, entertaining. *Address:* St Anne's College, Oxford OX2 6HS. *T:* (01865) 274800. *Club:* Oxford and Cambridge.

DEEDES, family name of **Baron Deedes**.

DEEDES, Baron *cr* 1986 (Life Peer), of Aldington in the County of Kent; **William Francis Deedes,** KBE 1999; MC 1944; PC 1962; DL; Editor, The Daily Telegraph, 1974–86; *b* 1 June 1913; *s* of (Herbert) William Deedes; *m* 1942, Evelyn Hilary Branfoot; one *s* three *d* (and one *s* decd). *Educ:* Harrow. Journalist with Morning Post, 1931–37; war correspondent on Abyssinia, 1935. Served war of 1939–45, Queen's Westminsters (12 KRRC). MP (C) Ashford Div. of Kent, 1950–Sept. 1974; Parliamentary Sec., Ministry of Housing and Local Government, Oct. 1954–Dec. 1955; Parliamentary Under-Sec., Home Dept., 1955–57; Minister without Portfolio, 1962–64. DL, Kent, 1962. Hon. DCL Kent, 1988. *Publication:* Dear Bill: W. F. Deedes Reports (autobiog.), 1997. *Address:* New Hayters, Aldington, Kent TN25 7DT. *T:* (01233) 720269. *Club:* Carlton.

See also Hon. J. W. Deedes, Baron Latymer.

DEEDES, Maj.-Gen. Charles Julius, CB 1968; OBE 1953; MC 1944; *b* 18 Oct. 1913; *s* of General Sir Charles Deedes, KCB, CMG, DSO; *m* 1939, Beatrice Murgatroyd, Brockfield Hall, York; three *s.* *Educ:* Oratory Sch.; Royal Military Coll., Sandhurst. Served War of 1939–45 (despatches); Asst Military Secretary, GHQ Middle East, 1945; Officer Comdg Glider Pilot Regt, 1948; GSO1 War Office, 1950; Officer Comdg 1st Bn KOYLI, 1954 (despatches); Colonel General Staff, War Office, 1956; Comd 146 Infantry Brigade (TA), 1958; Deputy Director, MoD, 1962; C of S, HQ Eastern Comd, 1965; C of S, HQ Southern Comd, 1968. Colonel of the KOYLI, 1966–68. Dep. Colonel, The Light Infantry (Yorks), 1968–72. Military Cross (Norway), 1940. *Recreations:* riding, tennis. *Address:* Lea Close, Brandsby, York YO61 4RW. *T:* (01347) 888239.

DEEDES, Hon. Jeremy (Wyndham); Managing Director, Telegraph Group Ltd, since 1996; *b* 24 Nov. 1943; *s* of Baron Deedes, *qv*; *m* 1973, Anna Gray, *d* of late Maj. Elwin Gray; two *s.* *Educ:* Eton Coll. Reporter: Kent and Sussex Courier, 1963–66; Daily Sketch, 1966–69; Londoner's Diary, Evening Standard, 1969–76; Dep. Editor, Daily Express, 1976–79; Managing Editor: Evening Standard, 1979–85; Today, 1985–86; Editorial Dir, Daily Telegraph and Sunday Telegraph, 1986–96. Chm., Trafford Park Printers, 1998–; Dep. Chm., West Ferry Printers, 1998–; Director: Millbourne Productions (Watermill Theatre), 1985–; Horserace Totalisator Bd, 1992–98. Chm., Nat. Publishers Assoc., 1998–99. *Recreations:* racing, cricket, golf, cabinet making. *Address:* Hamilton House, Compton, Newbury, Berks RG20 6QJ. *T:* (01635) 578695. *Clubs:* Boodle's; Frilford Heath Golf; Royal Cape (Cape Town).

DEELEY, Michael; film producer; *b* 6 Aug. 1932; *s* of John Hamilton-Deeley and Anne Deeley; *m* 1955, Teresa Harrison; one *s* two *d*; *m* 1970, Ruth Stone-Spencer. *Educ:* Stowe. Entered film industry as film editor, 1952; Distributor, MCA TV, 1958–60; independent producer, 1961–63; Gen. Man., Woodfall Films, 1964–67; indep. prod., 1967–72; Man. Director: British Lion Films Ltd, 1973–76; EMI Films Ltd, 1976–77; Pres., EMI Films Inc., 1977–79; Chief Exec. Officer, Consolidated Television Inc., 1984–90. Dep. Chm., British Screen Adv. Council, 1985–. Member: Prime Minister's Film Industry Working Party, 1975–76; Film Industry Interim Action Cttee, 1977–84. *Films* include: Robbery; The Italian Job; The Knack; Murphy's War; Conduct Unbecoming; The Man who fell to Earth; The Deer Hunter (Academy Award, Best Picture Producer, 1978); Convoy; Blade Runner; many TV films and series. *Address:* 14 Cadogan Square, SW1X 0JU; PO Box 397, Osterville, MA 02655–0397, USA. *Clubs:* Garrick; Wianno (Osterville); New York Yacht.

DEENY, Michael Eunan McLarnon, FCA; Chairman: MultiMedia Television plc, since 1999; Association of Lloyd's Members, since 1998 (Director, since 1995); *b* 12 Nov. 1944; *s* of late Dr Donnell Mclarnon Deeny and Annie Deeny (*née* McGinley); *m* 1975, Dr Margaret Irene Vereker; one *s* two *d.* *Educ:* Clongowes Wood Coll., Ireland; Magdalen Coll., Oxford (MA). FCA 1974. Articled Clerk, Chalmers Impey, 1966–70; Chief Accountant, Peter Kennedy Ltd, 1970–71; Manager (Murray Head, Horslips, Barry McGuigan, etc), 1971–91; Concert Promoter (U2, Bruce Springsteen, Nirvana, Wet, Wet, Wet, Aerosmith, Pavarotti, etc), 1984–. Chairman: Gooda Walker Action Gp, 1993–; Litigating Names' Cttee, 1994–. Dir, GW Run-Off, 1995–97; Dep. Chm., Equitas Trust, 1966–; Dir, Equitas Ltd, 1996–. Mem. Council, Lloyd's 1996–97. *Recreations:* history, anecdotes, occasional revelry. *Address:* c/o Association of Lloyd's Members, 100 Fenchurch Street, EC3M 5LG.

DEER, Prof. William Alexander, MSc Manchester, PhD Cantab; FRS 1962; FGS; Emeritus Professor of Mineralogy and Petrology, Cambridge University; Hon. Fellow of Trinity Hall, Cambridge, 1978; *b* 26 Oct. 1910; *s* of William Deer; *m* 1939, Margaret Marjorie (*d* 1971), *d* of William Kidd; two *s* one *d*; *m* 1973, Rita Tagg. *Educ:* Manchester Central High Sch.; Manchester Univ.; St John's Coll., Cambridge. Graduate Research Scholar, 1932, Beyer Fellow, 1933, Manchester Univ.; Strathcona Studentship, St John's Coll., Cambridge, 1934; Petrologist on British East Greenland Expedition, 1935–36; 1851 Exhibition Senior Studentship, 1938; Fellow, St John's Coll., Cambridge, 1939; served War of 1939–45, RE, 1940–45. Murchison Fund Geological Soc. of London, 1945 (Murchison Medal, 1974); Junior Bursar, St John's Coll., 1946; Leader NE Baffin Land Expedition, 1948; Bruce Medal, Royal Society of Edinburgh, 1948; Tutor, St John's Coll., 1949; Prof. of Geology, Manchester Univ., 1950–61; Fellow of St John's Coll., Cambridge, 1961–66, Hon. Fellow, 1969; Prof. of Mineralogy and Petrology, 1961–78, Vice-Chancellor, 1971–73, Cambridge Univ.; Master of Trinity Hall, Cambridge, 1966–75. Percival Lecturer, Univ. of Manchester, 1953; Joint Leader East Greenland Geological Expedition, 1953; Leader British East Greenland Expedition, 1966. Trustee, British Museum (Natural History), 1967–75. President: Mineralogical Soc., 1967–70; Geological Soc., 1970–72; Member: NERC, 1968–71; Marshall Aid Commemoration Commn, 1973–79. Hon. DSc Aberdeen, 1983. *Publications:* (jtly) Rock-forming Minerals, 5 vols, 1962–63, 2nd edn 1978– (vol. IIA 1978, vol. IA 1982, vol. IB 1986, vol. IIB 1997, Introduction 1992); Introduction to Rock-forming Minerals, 1966, 2nd edn 1992; papers in Petrology and Mineralogy. *Recreation:* bassoon playing. *Address:* 12 Barrington House, Southacre Drive, Cambridge CB2 2TY.

de FARIA, Antonio Leite, Hon. GCVO 1973; Grand Cross of Christ (Portugal), 1949; Portuguese Ambassador to the Court of St James's, 1968–73; retired; *b* 23 March 1904; *s* of Dr Antonio B. Leite de Faria and Dona Lucia P. de Sequeira Braga Leite de Faria; *m* 1926, Dona Herminia Cantilo de Faria; two *s.* *Educ:* Lisbon University (Faculty of Law). Attaché to Min. of Foreign Affairs, 1926; Sec. to Portuguese Delegn, League of Nations, 1929–30; 2nd Sec., Rio de Janeiro, 1931, Paris, 1933, Brussels, 1934; 1st Sec., London, 1936; Counsellor, London, 1939; Minister to Exiled Allied Govts, London, 1944; Minister to The Hague, 1945; Dir Gen., Political Affairs, and Acting Sec. Gen., Min. of Foreign Affairs, 1947; Ambassador: Rio de Janeiro, 1950; NATO, 1958; Paris, 1959; Rome (Holy See), 1961; London, 1968. Holds many foreign decorations. *Address:* Rua da Horta Seca 11, 1200 Lisboa, Portugal. *T:* (1) 3422538.

de FERRANTI, Sebastian Basil Joseph Ziani; DL; Chairman, Ferranti plc, 1963–82 (Managing Director, 1958–75; Director 1954); Director, GEC plc, 1982–97; *b* 5 Oct. 1927; *er s* of Sir Vincent de Ferranti, MC, and late Dorothy H. C. Wilson; *m* 1st, 1953, Mona Helen, *d* of T. E. Cunningham; one *s* two *d*; 2nd, 1983, Naomi Angela Rae, DL. *Educ:* Ampleforth. 4th/7th Dragoon Guards, 1947–49; Cheshire Yeo. Brown Boveri, Switzerland, and Alsthom, France, 1949–50. Director: British Airways Helicopters, 1982–84; Nat. Nuclear Corp., 1984–88. President: Electrical Research Assoc., 1968–69; BEAMA, 1969–70; Centre for Educn in Science, Educn and Technology, Manchester and region, 1972–82. Chm., Internat. Electrical Assoc., 1970–72. Member: Nat. Defence Industries Council, 1969–77; Council, IEE, 1970–73. Trustee, Tate Gallery, 1971–78; Chm., Civic Trust for the North-West, 1978–83; Comr, Royal Commn for Exhibn of 1851, 1984–97. Vice-Pres., RSA, 1980–84. Pres., Hallé Concerts Soc., 1997– (Chm., 1988–96). Mem. Bd of Govs, RNCM, 1988–2000 (Hon. RNCM 1997). Chm. assessors, architect for Manchester City Art Gall extn, 1995–. Lectures: Granada, Guildhall, 1966; Royal Instn, 1969; Louis Blériot, Paris, 1970; Faraday, 1970–71. High Sheriff of Cheshire, 1988–89; DL Cheshire, 1995. Hon. Fellow, UMIST. Hon. DSc: Salford Univ., 1967; Cranfield Inst. of Technology, 1973; Hon. LLD Manchester, 1998. *Address:* Henbury Hall, Macclesfield, Cheshire SK11 9PJ. *Clubs:* Cavalry and Guards, Pratt's.

de FONBLANQUE, John Robert, CMG 1993; HM Diplomatic Service; Head, UK Delegation to the Organisation for Security and Co-operation in Europe, Vienna, (with rank of Ambassador), since 1999; *b* 20 Dec. 1943; *s* of late Maj.-Gen. E. B. de Fonblanque, CB, CBE, DSO and of Elizabeth de Fonblanque; *m* 1984, Margaret Prest; one *s.* *Educ:* Ampleforth; King's College, Cambridge (MA); London School of Economics (MSc). FCO, 1968; Second Sec., Jakarta, 1969; Second, later First Sec., UK Representation to European Community, Brussels, 1972; Principal, HM Treasury, 1977; FCO, 1980; Asst Sec., Cabinet Office, 1983; Head of Chancery, New Delhi, 1986; Counsellor (Pol and Instnl), UK Repn to EC, Brussels, 1988; Vis. Fellow, RIIA, 1993; Asst Under-Sec. of State, Internat. Orgns, then Dir, Global Issues, FCO, 1994–98; Dir (Europe), FCO, 1998–99. Mem., PPARC, 1994–98. *Recreation:* mountain walking. *Address:* c/o Foreign and Commonwealth Office, SW1A 2AH.

de FRANCIA, Prof. Peter Laurent; Professor, School of Painting, Royal College of Art, London, 1973–86; *b* 25 Jan. 1921; *s* of Fernand de Francia and Alice Groom. *Educ:*

Academy of Brussels; Slade Sch., Univ. of London. Canadian Exhibition Commn, Ottawa, 1951; American Museum, Central Park West, NY, 1952–53; BBC, Television, 1953–55; Teacher, St Martin's Sch., London, 1955–63; Tutor, Royal College of Art, 1963–69; Principal, Dept of Fine Art, Goldsmiths Coll., 1969–72. Work represented in public collections: Tate Gall.; Nat. Portrait Gall.; V&A Mus.; Mus. of Modern Art, NY; Arts Council of GB; British Mus.; Graves Art Gall., Sheffield; Mus. of Modern Art, Prague. *Publications:* Fernand Léger, 1969; Léger, 1983; Untitled, 1990. *Address:* 44 Surrey Square, SE17 2JX. *T:* (020) 7703 8361.

DE FREYNE, 7th Baron *cr* 1851; Feudal Baron of Coolavin; **Francis Arthur John French;** Knight of Malta; *b* 3 Sept. 1927; *s* of 6th Baron and Victoria (*d* 1974), *d* of Sir J. Arnott, 2nd Bt; *S* father 1935; *m* 1st, 1954 (marr. diss. 1978); two *s* one *d*; 2nd, 1978, Sheelin Deirdre, *widow* of William Walker Stevenson and *y d* of late Lt-Col H. K. O'Kelly, DSO. *Educ:* Ladycross, Glenstal. *Heir: s* Hon. Fulke Charles Arthur John French [*b* 21 April 1957; *m* 1986, Julia Mary, *o d* of Dr James H. Wellard; two *s*].

DEFRIEZ, Alistair Norman Campbell, FCA; Managing Director, UBS Warburg (formerly Warburg Dillon Read), since 1999; *b* 2 Nov. 1951; *s* of Norman William Defriez and late Helen Catherine Defriez (*née* Maclean); *m* 1978, Linda Mavis Phillips, BSc, PGCE, ACA; two *s* one *d*. *Educ:* Dulwich Coll.; University Coll., Oxford (Open Gladstone Schol., MA). FCA 1981. With Coopers & Lybrand, 1973–78; joined S. G. Warburg & Co. Ltd, 1978, Dir, 1987; Dir-Gen., Panel on Takeovers and Mergers, 1996–99 (on secondment). *Recreations:* golf, Rugby, music, reading. *Address:* UBS Warburg, 1 Finsbury Avenue, EC2M 2PP. *T:* (020) 7568 6657. *Clubs:* Bankers', London Scottish; Royal Mid-Surrey Golf; St George's Hill Golf.

de GENNES, Prof. Pierre-Gilles, PhD; Professor of Condensed Matter Physics, Collège de France, since 1971; *b* 24 Oct. 1932; *s* of Robert de Gennes and Yvonne de Gennes (*née* Morin-Pons). *Educ:* Ecole Normale Supérieure, Paris. Prof., Univ. Orsay, 1961–71; Dir, Ecole de Physique et Chimie, 1976–. Nobel Prize in Physics, 1991. *Publications:* Superconductivity of Metals and Alloys, 1966; The Physics of Liquid Crystals, 1974; Scaling Concepts in Polymer Physics, 1979; Les objets fragiles, 1994. *Recreations:* ski, kayak, windsurfing. *Address:* (office) 10 rue Vauquelin, Paris 75005, France. *T:* 140794500.

de GIER, Johannes Antonie, (Hans); Vice Chairman, UBS AG, since 2001 (Member, Group Executive Board, 1998–99; Adviser, 1999–2001); *b* 24 Dec. 1944; *s* of W. G. de Gier and A. M. de Gier (*née* van Heijningen); *m* 1969, Anne-Marie Wintermans; one *s* one *d*. *Educ:* Amsterdam Univ. (LLM). Legal counsel, ABN, 1970–73; Divl Man., Capital Markets, 1975, Dep. Gen. Man., Internat. Finance, 1978, AMRO; Dir, Corporate Finance, Orion Bank, 1979–80; Swiss Bank Corporation: Exec. Dir, Corporate Finance, 1980; Man. Dir and Chief Exec. Officer, 1987; Mem., Exec. Bd, and Hd, Global Corporate Finance, 1991; Mem., Gp Exec. Cttee, 1996; Chm. and Chief Exec., SBC Warburg, then Warburg Dillon Read, 1996–99. Member: Supervisory Bd, SHV Hldgs; Bd, Groupe Lhoist. Vice-Chm., Centre for Econ. Policy Res. Trustee, Fitzwilliam Mus. *Recreations:* wildlife, music, art. *Club:* Turf.

de GREY, family name of **Baron Walsingham.**

de GREY, Flavia, (Lady de Grey), (Flavia Irwin), RA 1996; RWEA; painter; *b* 15 Dec. 1916; *d* of Clinton and Everilda Irwin; *m* 1942, Sir Roger de Grey, KCVO, PPRA (*d* 1995); two *s* one *d*. *Educ:* Hawnes Sch., Ampthill; Chelsea Sch. of Art. Teacher, 1960–97: Bexley Girls' Sch.; Sheppey Comprehensive Sch.; Medway Coll. of Art; City and Guilds of London Art Sch. (Head of Decorative Arts). Exhibitions include: Andsdell Gall. (solo); Curwen and Phoenix Galls; London Gp; Friend's Room, Royal Acad. (solo), 2001. Pictures in various public and private collections, incl. Carlisle City Art Gall. and Walker Art Gall. *Recreations:* swimming, walking. *Address:* Camer Street, Meopham, Kent DA13 0XR.

See also S. T. de Grey.

de GREY, Spencer Thomas, CBE 1997; RIBA; Design Partner, Foster & Partners, since 1991; *b* 7 June 1944; *s* of Sir Roger de Grey, KCVO, PPRA, and of Flavia de Grey, *qv*; *m* 1977, Hon. (Amanda) Lucy, *d* of Baron Annan, *qv*; one *s* one *d*. *Educ:* Eton Coll.; Churchill Coll., Cambridge (BA 1966; MA 1970; DipArch 1969). ARCUK 1969; RIBA 1993. Architect, Merton LBC, 1969–73; joined Foster Associates, later Foster & Partners, 1973–: estabd Hong Kong office, 1979; Dir, 1981– (responsible for Third London Airport, Stansted, 1991, and Sackler Galls, Royal Acad., 1991); *projects* include: Lycée Albert Camus, Fréjus, 1995; Law Faculty, Univ. of Cambridge, 1995; EDF Regl operational centre, Bordeaux, 1996; Commerzbank HQ, Frankfurt, 1997; Music Centre, Gateshead, 1997–; World Squares for All, London, 1997–; Sir Alexander Fleming Med. Bldg, Imperial Coll., London, 1998; Great Court, BM, 1998–2000; Nat. Botanical Gdns for Wales, 1999; Mus. of Fine Art, Boston, USA. Lectures incl. Le Louvre, Paris, 1996, and RIBA, London, 1996, 1998. Trustee, Royal Botanical Gardens, Kew, 1995–; Gov., Bldg Centre Trust, 1998–; Mem., Bd, London First Centre, 1999–. *Recreations:* music, theatre, travel. *Address:* (office) Riverside 3, 22 Hester Road, SW11 4AN. *T:* (020) 7738 0455, *Fax:* (020) 7738 1107.

de GRUCHY, Nigel Ronald Anthony; General Secretary, National Association of Schoolmasters Union of Women Teachers, 1990–March 2002; *b* 28 Jan. 1943; *s* of Robert Philip de Gruchy and Dorothy Louise de Gruchy (*née* Cullinane); *m* 1970, Judith Ann Berglund, USA; one *s*. *Educ:* De La Salle Coll., Jersey; Univ. of Reading (BA Hons (Econs and Philosophy) 1965); PGCE London Univ. 1969; Cert. Pratique de Langue Française, Paris Univ., 1968; Cert. de Française Parlé et du Diplôme de Langue Française, L'Alliance Française, 1968. TEFL, Berlitz Schs, Santander, 1965–66, Versailles, 1966–67; student of French/Tutor in English, Paris, 1967–68; Head of Econs Dept, St Joseph's Acad., ILEA, 1968–78; Asst Sec., 1978–82, Dep. Gen. Sec., 1982–89, NAS UWT. Sec., London Assoc., 1975–78, Mem., Nat. Exec., 1975–78, NAS UWT. Member: Gen. Council, TUC, 1989–2002; Exec., The Educn Internat., 1993–. *Publications:* contribs to Career Teacher. *Recreations:* golf, cricket, football, literature, music, opera, France, Spain. *Address:* (until March 2002) (office) 5 King Street, Covent Garden, WC2E 8SD. *T:* (020) 7420 9760.

de HAAN, Kevin Charles; QC 2000; *b* 30 Oct. 1952; *s* of Michael James de Haan and Barbara Ada de Haan; *m* 1983, Katy Monica Foster. *Educ:* Davenant Foundn Grammar Sch.; Queen Mary Coll., Univ. of London (LLB); Vrije Univ., Brussels (LLM Internat. and Comparative Law). Called to the Bar, Inner Temple, 1976, Bencher, 1997. *Publications:* Food Safety Law and Practice, 1994; Pollution in the United Kingdom, 1994; (contrib.) Smith & Monckom, The Law of Betting, Gaming and Lotteries, 2nd edn 2000. *Recreations:* ski-ing, flying light aircraft, mountain bicycling, cooking. *Address:* 3 Raymond Buildings, Gray's Inn, WC1R 5BH. *T:* (020) 7400 6400. *Club:* Ski of GB.

de HAAS, Margaret Ruth, (Mrs I. S. Goldrein); QC 1998; a Recorder, since 1999; *b* 21 May 1954; *d* of Josef and Lilo de Haas; *m* 1980, Iain Saville Goldrein, *qv*; one *s* one *d*. *Educ:* Townsend Sch., Zimbabwe; Bristol Univ. (LLB Hons 1976). Called to the Bar, Middle Temple, 1977; in practice at the Bar, 1977–. Mem., Criminal Injuries Compensation Bd, 1999–. *Publications:* (jtly) Butterworths Personal Injury Litigation Service, 1988–; (jtly) Property Distribution on Divorce, 1989; (jtly) Domestic Injunctions, 1997; (jtly) Medical Negligence: cost effective case management, 1997; (jtly) Structured Settlements, 1997. *Recreations:* family, swimming, reading, theatre. *Address:* (chambers) 7 Harrington Street, Liverpool L2 9QA. *T:* (0151) 242 0707; 12 King's Bench Walk, Temple, EC4Y 7EL. *T:* (020) 7583 0811.

DEHAENE, Jean-Luc; Senator; Prime Minister of Belgium, 1992–99; *b* Montpellier, 7 Aug. 1940; *s* of late Albert Dehaene and of Andrée Verstraete; *m* 1965, Celie Verbeke; four *c*. *Educ:* Univ. of Namur; Univ. of Kul. Comr, Flemish Assoc. of Catholic Scouts, 1963–67; Christian Social Party (CVP): Nat. Vice Pres., CVP Youth, 1967–71; Mem., Nat. Cttee; Councillor: for Public Works, 1972–73; for Public Health, 1973–74; then Leader of Cabinet for Econ. Affairs, 1974–77; Leader of Cabinet for Flemish Affairs, 1977–78; Pres., CVP, Bruxelles-Hal-Vivorde, 1977–81; Leader of Cabinet, 1979–81; Leader of Cabinet for Instnl Reforms, 1981; co-opted Senator, 1982–87; Deputy, 1987–99; Minister of Social Affairs and Instnl Reforms, 1981–88; Dep. Prime Minister and Minister of Communications and Instnl Reforms, 1988–92. *Address:* Berkendallaan 52, 1800 Vilvoorde, Belgium.

de HALPERT, Rear Adm. Jeremy Michael, CB 2001; Naval Secretary, and Chief Executive, Naval Manning Agency, since 1998; *b* 9 July 1947; *s* of Lt Comdr Michael Frances de Halpert and Eleanor Anne Love de Halpert; *m* 1972, Jane Fattorini, *d* of late Joseph Fattorini; two *s* one *d*. *Educ:* Canford Sch., Wimborne. Joined Royal Navy, 1966. BRNC, Dartmouth; served HM Ships Aurora, Chilcompton, London, Phoebe, Lowestoft, 1967–75; CO, HMS Sheraton, 1975–76; Specialised Principal Warfare Officer (Navigation): HMS Dryad and HMS Mercury, 1977–78; HMS Ajax and HMS Ariadne, 1978–80; HMS Bristol and Falklands Campaign, 1982–84; Comdr, 1984; CO, HMS Apollo, 1985–86; jsdc 1987; Directorate of Naval Staff Duties, MoD, 1987–89; USN War Coll., Newport, RI, 1989–90; Capt., 1990; CO, HMS Campbeltown, 1990–92; CoS, Flag Officer Surface Flotilla, 1992–94; Dep. UK Mil. Rep., SHAPE, 1994–96; Cdre, 1996; Dir, Overseas Mil. Activity, MoD, 1996–98; Rear-Adm., 1998. Younger Brother, Trinity House. Pres., RN Winter Sports Assoc.; Mem., Tennis & Racquets Assoc. MRIN 1980. *Recreations:* Royal tennis, ski-ing, squash, cricket, military history. *Address:* Victory Building, HM Naval Base, Portsmouth PO1 3LS. *Clubs:* Boodle's, Royal Navy of 1765 and 1785, MCC.

de HAMEL, Christopher Francis Rivers, DPhil; FSA; FRHistS; Donnelley Librarian, and Fellow, Corpus Christi College, Cambridge, since 2000; *b* 20 Nov. 1950; *s* of Dr Francis Alexander de Hamel and Joan Littledale de Hamel (*née* Pollock); *m* 1st, 1978 (marr. diss. 1989); two *s*; 2nd, 1993, Mette Tang Simpson (*née* Svendsen) (*see* M. T. de Hamel). *Educ:* Otago Univ., NZ (BA Hons); Oxford Univ. (DPhil). FSA 1981; FRHistS 1986. Sotheby's: cataloguer of medieval manuscripts, 1975; Asst Dir, 1977; Dir, Western and Oriental, later Western, Manuscripts, 1982–2000. Vis. Fellow, All Souls Coll., Oxford, 1999–2000. Chm., Assoc. for Manuscripts and Archives in Res. Collections, 2000–. Hon. LittD St John's, Minn, 1994. *Publications* include: Glossed Books of the Bible and the Origins of the Paris Booktrade, 1984; A History of Illuminated Manuscripts, 1986, 2nd edn 1994; (with M. Manion and V. Vines) Medieval and Renaissance Manuscripts in New Zealand Collections, 1989; Syon Abbey, The Library of the Bridgettine Nuns and their Peregrinations after the Reformation, 1991; Scribes and Illuminators, 1992; The British Library Guide to Manuscript Illumination, 2001; The Book: a history of the Bible, 2001. *Address:* Corpus Christi College, Trumpington Street, Cambridge CB2 1RH. *Clubs:* Grolier (New York); Association Internationale de Bibliophilie (Paris).

de HAMEL, Mette Tang, FIIC; art conservator; *b* 15 May 1945; *d* of late Axel Tang Svendsen and of Grethe (*née* Selchau); *m* 1st, 1965, David Melville Bromby Simpson (marr. diss.); two *s*; 2nd, 1993, Dr Christopher Francis Rivers de Hamel, *qv*. *Educ:* Newcastle upon Tyne Poly. (BA Hons History of Art 1979; Dip. in Conservation 1982). Conservator, Bowes Mus., 1979–80; Lectr, Newcastle upon Tyne Poly., 1982–86; Dir, Textile Conservation Centre, Hampton Court Palace, 1986–88; Sen. Conservator, Sotheby's, 1988–99. *Recreations:* painting, gardening. *Address:* 40 Lansdowne Gardens, SW8 2EF. *Club:* Lansdowne.

de HAVILLAND, Olivia Mary; actress; *b* Tokyo, Japan, 1 July 1916; *d* of Walter Augustus de Havilland and Lilian Augusta (*née* Ruse) (parents British subjects); *m* 1st, 1946, Marcus Aurelius Goodrich (marr. diss., 1953); one *s*; 2nd, 1955, Pierre Paul Galante (marr. diss. 1979); one *d*. *Educ:* in California; won scholarship to Mills Coll., but career prevented acceptance. Played Hermia in Max Reinhardt's stage production of Midsummer Night's Dream, 1934. *Legitimate theatre* (USA): Juliet in Romeo and Juliet, 1951; Candida, 1951 and 1952; A Gift of Time, 1962. Began film career 1935, Midsummer Night's Dream. Nominated for Academy Award, 1939, 1941, 1946, 1948, 1949; Acad. Award, 1946, 1949; New York Critics' Award, 1948, 1949; San Francisco Critics' Award, 1948, 1949; Hollywood Foreign Press Assoc. Golden Globe Award, 1949, 1986; Women's National Press Club Award for 1950; Belgian Prix Femina, 1957; British Films and Filming Award, 1967; Filmex Tribute, 1978; Amer. Acad. of Achievement Award, 1978. *Important films:* The Adventures of Robin Hood, 1938; Gone With the Wind, 1939; Hold Back the Dawn, 1941; Princess O'Rourke, 1943; To Each His Own, 1946; The Dark Mirror, 1946; The Snake Pit, 1948; The Heiress, 1949; My Cousin Rachel, 1952; Not as a Stranger, 1955; The Ambassador's Daughter, 1956; Proud Rebel, 1957; The Light in the Piazza, 1961; Lady in a Cage, 1963; Hush . . . Hush, Sweet Charlotte, 1965; The Adventurers, 1969; Pope Joan, 1971; Airport '77, 1976; The Swarm, 1978. *Television includes:* Noon Wine, 1966; The Screaming Woman, 1971; Roots, The Next Generations, 1979; 3 ABC Cable-TV Cultural Documentaries, 1981; Murder is Easy, 1982; Charles & Diana, a Royal Romance, 1982; North and South, Book II, 1986; Anastasia, 1986; The Woman He Loved, 1988. US Lecture tours, 1971, 1972, 1973, 1974, 1975, 1976, 1978, 1979, 1980. Pres. of Jury, Cannes Film Festival, 1965. Took part in narration of France's BiCentennial Gift to US, Son et Lumière, A Salute to George Washington, Mount Vernon, 19 May 1976; read excerpts from Thomas Jefferson at BiCentennial Service, American Cathedral in Paris, 4 July 1976. Hon. DHL Amer. Univ. of Paris, 1994; Hon. Dr Letters Univ. of Hertfordshire, 1998. Amer. Legion Humanitarian Medal, 1967; Freedoms Foundn Exemplar American Award, 1981. *Publications:* Every Frenchman Has One, 1962; (contrib.) Mother and Child, 1975. *Address:* BP 156–16, 75764 Paris, Cedex 16, France.

DEHENNIN, Baron Herman; Hon. Grand Marshal of Belgian Royal Court; Hon. Belgian Ambassador; *b* 20 July 1929; created Baron, 1990; *s* of Alexander Dehennin and Flora Brehmen; *m* 1954, Margareta-Maria Donvil; two *s*. *Educ:* Catholic Univ. of Leuven. Dr in Law 1951. Lieut, Royal Belgian Artillery, 1951–53; entered Belgian Diplomatic Service, 1954; served The Hague, New Delhi, Madrid, the Congo; Ambassador to Rwanda, 1966–70; Economic Minister, Washington, 1970–74; Dir-Gen., Foreign Econ. Relations, Brussels, 1974–77; Ambassador to Japan, 1978–81; Grand Marshal, Belgian Royal Court, 1981–85; Ambassador: to USA, 1985–91; to UK, 1991–94. President:

Special Olympics, Belgium, 1995–; Club Ste Anne, Brussels, 1997–. Grand Cross, Order of Leopold, 1985; Grand Cross, Order of the Crown, 1983; foreign Orders: France, Greece, Japan, Luxembourg, Mexico, Portugal, Rwanda, Zaire. *Recreations:* hiking, tennis, fishing, hunting, reading (history, philosophy). *Clubs:* Travellers, Royal Anglo-Belgian; Prince Albert, University Foundation, Cercle Gaulois (Brussels); Royal Golf of Belgium.

DEHMELT, Prof. Hans Georg; Professor of Physics, University of Washington, Seattle, since 1961; *b* 9 Sept. 1922; *s* of Georg Karl Dehmelt and Asta Ella Dehmelt (*née* Klemmt); US Citizen, 1961; *m* 1st; one *s*; 2nd, 1989, Diana Elaine Dundore. *Educ:* Graues Kloster, Berlin; Technische Hochschule, Breslau; Univ. of Göttingen (Dr rer. nat. 1950). Res. Fellow, Inst. Kopfermann, Göttingen, 1950–52; Res. Associate, Duke Univ., USA, 1952–55; Vis. Asst Prof., 1955, Associate Prof., 1957, Univ. of Washington. Consultant, Varian Associates, Palo Alto, Calif, 1956–70. Member: Amer. Acad. of Arts and Scis; Nat. Acad. of Scis; Fellow, Amer. Phys Soc.; FAAAS. Numerous awards and hon. degrees; Nobel Prize for Physics (jtly), 1989; Nat. Medal of Science, US, 1995. Leader of group which first saw with own eyes individual atom at rest in free space, 1979, reported 1980; isolated individual electron/positron at rest in empty space, 1973, 1981, and precisely measured its magnetism and size, 1976–87. *Publications:* papers on electron and atomic physics, charged atoms, proposed cosmonium world-atom hypothesis of big bang. *Address:* 1600 43rd Avenue East, Seattle, Washington, DC 98112, USA.

DEHN, Conrad Francis; QC 1968; Barrister; a Recorder of the Crown Court, 1974–98; a Deputy High Court Judge, 1988–96; *b* London, 24 Nov. 1926; *o s* of late C. G. Dehn, Solicitor and Cynthia Dehn (*née* Fuller) painter, as Francyn; *m* 1st, 1954, Sheila (*née* Magan) (marr. diss.); two *s* one *d*; 2nd, 1978, Marilyn, *d* of late Peter and Constance Collyer. *Educ:* Charterhouse (Sen. Exhibr); Christ Church, Oxford (Holford Schol.). Served RA, Best Cadet Mons Basic OCTU, 1946, 2nd Lieut 1947. 1st cl. hons PPE Oxon. 1950, MA 1952; Holt Schol., Gray's Inn, 1951; Pres., Inns of Court Students Union, 1951–52. WEA Tutor, 1951–55. Called to Bar, Gray's Inn, 1952; Bencher, 1977; Chm., Management Cttee, 1987; Vice-Treas., 1995; Treas., 1996. Head, Fountain Court Chambers, 1984–89. Chairman: Bar Council Working Party on Liability for Defective Products, 1975–77; Planning Cttee, Senate of Inns of Court and Bar, 1980–83; London Univ. Disciplinary Appeals Cttee, 1986–; Adv. Cttee, Gen. Comrs of Income Tax, Gray's Inn, 1994–. Dir, Bar Mutual Indemnity Fund Ltd, 1988–. Mem., Foster Cttee of Inquiry into Operators' Licensing, Dept of Transport, 1978. Member: Council of Legal Educn, 1981–86; London Legal Aid Cttee, 1965–92 (Vice-Chm., 1987–92); Hon. Advr, S London Psychotherapy Centre, 1982–; Hon. Legal Advr, Age Concern London, 1987– (Vice-Pres., 2001–). Pres., Camberwell Soc., 1996–. Mem. Governing Body, United Westminster Schs, 1953–57; Gov., Inns of Court Sch. of Law, 1996–. *Publications:* (contrib.) Ideas, 1954; (contrib.) Reform of Civil Procedure, 1996; (ed) Commercial Court Practice, 1999, 2000. *Recreations:* theatre, living in France, walking. *Address:* Fountain Court, Temple, EC4Y 9DH. *T:* (020) 7583 3335. *Club:* Reform.

De HOCHEPIED LARPENT, Lt Col Andrew Lionel Dudley, OBE 1992; Chief Executive, Cancer and Leukaemia in Childhood, since 1997; *b* 10 Feb. 1951; *s* of Douglas De Hochepied Larpent and Patience (*née* Johnson); *m* 1974, Anne Marion Knights; two *s* one *d*. *Educ:* Bradfield Coll.; RMA Sandhurst; Reading Univ. (BSc Hons Estate Mgt 1976). Royal Regt of Fusiliers, 1969–94, CO, 3rd Bn, 1990–92; Dir, Rehau Ltd, 1994–96; construction industry consultant, 1996–97. *Recreations:* country pursuits, ski-ing. *Address:* CLIC, Abbey Wood, Bristol BS34 7JU.

de HOGHTON, Sir (Richard) Bernard (Cuthbert), 14th Bt *cr* 1611; KM; DL; *b* 26 Jan. 1945; 3rd *s* of Sir Cuthbert de Hoghton, 12th Bt, and of Philomena, *d* of late Herbert Simmons; *S* half-brother, 1978; *m* 1974, Rosanna Stella Virginia (*née* Buratti); one *s* one *d*. *Educ:* Ampleforth College, York; McGill Univ., Montreal (BA Hons); Birmingham Univ. (MA); PhD (USA). Turner & Newall Ltd, 1967–70; international fund management, Vickers Da Costa & Co. Ltd, 1970–77; international institutional brokerage, de Zoete & Bevan & Co., 1977–86 (Partner, 1984–86); Dir, BZW Ltd (Europe), 1986–89; Asst Dir, Brown Shipley, 1989–94; Associate Dir, Teather & Greenwood, 1994–98; Dir, Tutton & Saunders Ltd, 1998–99. Pres., Royal Lancs Agricl Soc., 1995; Nat. Vice-Pres., Internat. Tree Foundn, 1983–. Patron: ACU (NW), 1980–; Internat. Spinal Res. Trust, 1984–. Historic house and estate management, 1978–. DL Lancs, 1988. Constantinian Order of S George (Naples), 1984; Kt SMO, Malta, 1980. *Recreations:* tennis, shooting, travelling, local historical research. *Heir: s* Thomas James Daniel Adam de Hoghton, *b* 11 April 1980. *Address:* Hoghton Tower, Hoghton, Preston, Lancs PR5 0SH.

DEHQANI-TAFTI, Rt Rev. Hassan Barnaba; Hon. Assistant Bishop of Winchester, since 1990 (Assistant Bishop, 1982–90); *b* 14 May 1920; *s* of Muhammad Dehqani-Tafti and Sakinneh; *m* 1952, Margaret Isabel Thompson; three *d* (one *s* decd). *Educ:* Stuart Memorial Coll., Isfahan, Iran; Tehran Univ.; Ridley Hall, Cambridge. Iran Imperial Army, 1943–45; layman in Diocese of Iran, 1945–47; theological coll., 1947–49; Deacon, Isfahan, 1949; Priest, Shiraz, 1950; Pastor: St Luke's Church, Isfahan, 1950–60; St Paul's Church, Tehran, 1960–61; Bishop in Iran, 1961–90, Vicar-Gen., 1990–91; Pres.-Bishop, Episcopal Church in Jerusalem and Middle East, 1976–86; Episcopal Canon, St George's Cathedral, Jerusalem, 1976–90; Commissary to Bishop in Iran, 1991–. Hon. DD Virginia Theol Seminary, USA, 1981. *Publications:* many books in Persian; in English: Design of my World, 1959; The Hard Awakening, 1981; Christ and Christianity in Persian Poetry, 1986; The Unfolding Design of My World, 2000. *Recreations:* Persian poetry (primarily mystical); painting in water colours; walking.

DEISENHOFER, Prof. Johann, PhD; Regental Professor and Professor in Biochemistry, University of Texas Southwestern Medical Center at Dallas, since 1988; Investigator, Howard Hughes Medical Institute, since 1988; *b* 30 Sept. 1943; *s* of Johann and Thekla Deisenhofer; *m* 1989, Kirsten Fischer-Lindahl, PhD. *Educ:* Technische Universität München (Physics Diploma 1971; PhD 1974). Max-Planck-Institut für Biochemie: graduate student, 1971–74; Postdoctoral Fellow, 1974–76; Staff Scientist, 1976–88. (Jtly) Biological Physics Prize, Amer. Physical Soc., 1986; (jtly) Otto Bayer Preis, 1988; (jtly) Nobel Prize in Chemistry, 1988. *Publications:* contribs to Acta Crystallographica, Biochemistry, Jl of Molecular Biology, Nature, Methods in Enzymology, etc. *Recreations:* ski-ing, swimming, classical music. *Address:* University of Texas Southwestern Medical Center, 5323 Harry Hines Boulevard, Dallas, TX 75390–9050, USA. *T:* (214) 6485089.

de JERSEY, Hon. Paul, AC 2000; Chief Justice of Queensland, since 1998; a Judge of the Supreme Court, Queensland, since 1985; *b* 21 Sept. 1948; *s* of Ronald Claude and Moya Clarice de Jersey; *m* 1971, Kaye Brown; one *s* two *d*. *Educ:* C of E Grammar Sch., Brisbane; Univ. of Qld (BA, LLB Hons). Admitted to Qld Bar, 1971; QC (Qld) 1981; Chm., Qld Law Reform Commn, 1996–98; Pres., Industrial Court of Qld, 1996–98. Chancellor, Anglican Dio. Brisbane, 1991–. Chm., Qld Cancer Fund, 1994–2001; Pres., Australian Cancer Soc., 1998–2001. Hon. LLD Qld, 2000. *Recreations:* reading, music. *Address:* Chief Justice's Chambers, Supreme Court, George Street, Brisbane, Qld 4000, Australia. *T:* (7) 32474279. *Clubs:* Queensland, United Service (Brisbane).

de JONGH, Nicholas Raymond; Theatre Critic, Evening Standard, since 1991; *b* London; *s* of Louis de Jongh and late Vivian (*née* Creditor). *Educ:* Hall Sch., Hampstead; St Paul's Sch.; University Coll. London (BA Hons, MPhil). Secker & Warburg, 1967; Scriptwriter, BBC External Services, 1968; The Guardian: Reporter, 1968; Theatre Reviewer, 1969; Dep. Theatre Critic, 1970–91; Arts Reporter, 1973–78; Arts Corresp., 1978–90; Theatre Critic, Mail on Sunday, 1983. Chm., Drama Section, Critics' Circle, 1984–86. Theatre Book Prize, Soc. of Theatre Res., 2000. *Publications:* (ed) Bedside Guardian, 1989, 1990; Not in Front of the Audience, 1992; (contrib.) Approaching the Millennium: essays on Angels in America, 2000; Politics, Prudery and Perversions, 2000. *Recreations:* fantasising, riding hobby-horses. *Address:* Evening Standard, Northcliffe House, 2 Derry Street, W8 5EE. *Club:* Groucho.

DEJOUANY, Guy Georges André; Commandeur, Légion d'Honneur; Hon. Chairman, Vivendi (Chairman and Managing Director, Compagnie Générale des Eaux, 1976–96); Managing Director, Société Monégasque des Eaux, since 1970; *b* 15 Dec. 1920; *s* of André Dejouany and Jeanne (*née* Imbard); *m* (wife decd); two *s* one *d*; *m* 1996, Renée Marnet. *Educ:* Ecole Polytechnique, Paris; Ponts et Chaussées, Paris. Civil Engineer: Metz, 1945–49; Paris, 1949–50; joined Compagnie Générale des Eaux, 1950: Manager, 1961–65; Dep. Man. Dir, 1965–72; Man. Dir, 1972–73; Dir, 1973–, co. name now Vivendi. Chm. and Man. Dir, Cie des Eaux et de l'Ozone, 1970–96. Director: Alcatel Alsthom; Soc. Générale; Canal Plus; Havas; Electrafina; Pétrofina; Mem., Supervisory Bd, AXA-UAP. *Address:* (office) 52 rue d'Anjou, 75008 Paris, France; 26 rue de Franqueville, 75116 Paris, France.

de KLERK, Frederik Willem; Leader of the Opposition, National Assembly of South Africa, 1996–97; *b* 18 March 1936; *s* of J. de Klerk; *m* 1st, 1959, Marike Willemse (marr. diss. 1998); two *s* one *d*; 2nd, 1998, Elita Georgiades. *Educ:* Monument High School, Krugersdorp; Potchefstroom Univ. Law practice, 1961–72; MP (Nat. Party) Vereeniging, 1972–89; Information Officer, Transvaal, Nat. Party, 1975; Minister: of Posts and Telecommunications and Social Welfare and Pensions, 1978; of Posts and Telecommunications and of Sport and Recreation, 1978–79; of Mines, Energy and Environmental Planning, 1979–80; of Mineral and Energy Affairs, 1980–82; of Internal Affairs, 1982–85; of Nat. Educn and Planning, 1984–89; Leader, Nat. Party, 1989–97 (Transvaal Leader, 1982–89); Chm., Council of Ministers, 1985–89; State President, 1989–94, Dep. President, 1994–96, S Africa. Hon. LLD: Potchefstroom Univ., 1990; Bar-Ilan Univ., Tel Aviv; Hon. DPhil: Stellenbosch Univ., 1990; Nat. Chengchi Univ., Taipei, Taiwan. Nobel Peace Prize (with N. R. Mandela), 1993. *Publication:* The Last Trek: a new beginning, 1999. *Address:* Private Bag X 999, Cape Town 8000, South Africa.

de LA BARRE de NANTEUIL, Luc; Commandeur de l'Ordre National du Mérite; Officier de la Légion d'Honneur; Ambassadeur de France; Chairman, Les Echos Group, since 1991; *b* 21 Sept. 1925; *m* 1st, Philippa MacDonald; one *s*; 2nd, 1973, Hedwige Frerejean de Chavagneux; one *s* one *d*. *Educ:* school in Poitiers; BA, LLB Lyon and Paris; Dip. d'Etudes Supérieures (Econ); Graduate, Ecole Nat. d'Admin, 1949. French Ministry of Foreign Affairs: Economic Affairs Dept, 1950–51; Secrétariat Général, 1951–52; Pacts Service, 1952–53; Econ. Affairs Dept, 1954–59; First Sec., London, 1959–64; Asst Dir, Afr. and ME Affairs Dept, 1964–70; Hd of Econ. Co-operation Service, Directorate of Econ. Affairs, 1970–76; Ambassador to the Netherlands, 1976–77, French Permanent Representative: to EEC, Brussels, 1977–82 and 1985–86; to Security Council and to UN, New York, 1981–84; Diplomatic Adviser, 1986; Ambassador to UK, 1986–91. *Publication:* David (Jacques Louis), 1985. *Address:* Les Echos, 46 rue la Boetie, Paris 75008, France. *T:* 49536565.

De la BÈRE, Sir Cameron, 2nd Bt *cr* 1953; jeweller, Geneva; *b* 12 Feb. 1933; *s* of Sir Rupert De la Bère, 1st Bt, KCVO, and Marguerite (*d* 1969), *e d* of late Sir John Humphery; *S* father, 1978; *m* 1964, Clairemonde, *o d* of late Casimir Kaufmann, Geneva; one *d*. *Educ:* Tonbridge, and on the Continent. Translator's cert. in Russian. British Army Intelligence Corps, 1951–53. Company director of Continental Express Ltd (subsid. of Hay's Wharf), 1958–64. Engaged in promotion of luxury retail jewellery stores, Switzerland and France, 1965–. Liveryman, Skinners' Co. *Recreations:* riding, swimming, history. *Heir: b* Adrian De la Bère, *b* 17 Sept. 1939. *Address:* 1 Avenue Theodore Flournoy, 1207 Geneva, Switzerland. *T:* (22) 7860015. *Clubs:* Hurlingham, Société Litéraire (Geneva).

de la BILLIÈRE, Gen. Sir Peter (Edgar de la Cour), KCB 1988; KBE 1991 (CBE 1983); DSO 1976; MC 1959 and Bar 1966; DL; Chairman, Meadowland Meats Ltd, since 1994; *b* 29 April 1934; *s* of Surgeon Lieut Comdr Claude Dennis Delacour de Labillière (killed in action, HMS Fiji, 1941) and of Frances Christine Wright Lawley; *m* 1965, Bridget Constance Muriel Goode; one *s* two *d*. *Educ:* Harrow School; Staff College; RCDS. Joined KSLI 1952; commissioned DLI; served Japan, Korea, Malaya (despatches 1958), Jordan, Borneo, Egypt, Aden, Gulf States, Sudan, Oman, Falkland Is; CO 22 SAS Regt, 1972–74; GSO1 (DS) Staff Coll., 1974–77; Comd British Army Training Team, Sudan, 1977–78; Dir SAS and Comd, SAS Group, 1978–83; Comd, British Forces Falkland Is and Mil. Comr, 1984–85; GOC Wales, 1985–87; GOC SE Dist, and Perm. Peace Time Comdr, Jt Forces Operations Staff, 1987–90; Comdr British Forces, ME, 1990–91; ME Advr to MOD, 1991–92, retd. Col Comdt, Light Div., 1986–89. Chm., ME Div., Robert Fleming Hldgs, 1998–99 (non-exec. Dir, 1992–98). Mem. Council, RUSI, 1975–77. Chm., FARM Africa, 1998– (Mem. Bd, 1992–; Vice-Chm., 1995–98). Chm., Jt Services Hang Gliding, 1986–89; Cdre, Army Sailing Assoc., 1989–91. President: SAS Assoc., 1991–96; ACF, 1992–99. Vice-Pres., UK Falkland Is Assoc., 1993–. Comr, Duke of York's Mil. Sch., 1988–90. Trustee, Imperial War Mus., 1992–99. Freeman, City of London, 1991; Hon. Freeman, Fishmongers' Co., 1991. Stowaway Mem., Southampton Master Mariners Assoc., 1992. DL Hereford and Worcester, 1993. Hon. DSc Cranfield Inst. of Technol., 1992; Hon. DCL Durham, 1993. Order of Bahrain, 1st Cl., 1991; Chief Comdr, Legion of Merit (USA), 1992; Meritorious Service Cross, (Canada), 1992; Order of Abdul Aziz, 2nd Cl. (Saudi Arabia), 1992; Kuwait Decoration, 1st Cl., 1992; Qatar Sash of Merit, 1992. *Publications:* Storm Command: a personal story, 1992; (autobiog.) Looking for Trouble, 1994. *Recreations:* family, squash, down market apiculture, tennis, farming, sailing. *Clubs:* Farmers', Naval and Military (Trustee, 1999–), Special Forces.

DELACOUR, Jean-Paul; Officer of Legion of Honour; Knight of National Order of Merit; Inspector General of Finance; Vice-Chairman, Société Générale, Paris, since 1992 (Chief Operating Officer, 1986–95); *b* 7 Nov. 1930; *s* of Henri Delacour and Denise Brochet; *m* 1958, Claude Laurence; four *s* one *d*. *Educ:* Inst. of Political Studies, Paris (Dipl.); ENA (Nat. Sch. of Administration). Inspector of Finance, 1955–61; Dep. Dir, Crédit National, 1961–68; Dir, 1969, Dep. Gen. Manager, 1974, Bd Mem. and Man. Dir, 1986, Société Générale; Chm. and Chief Exec. Officer, Soc. Gén. Alsacienne de Banque, 1978–82; Chm., Sogebail, 1985–; senior functions in internat. banking and financial insts. Chm., Bd of Catholic Inst. Paris, 1984–. *Address:* Société Générale, 29 boulevard Haussmann, 75009 Paris, France. *T:* 42142336.

DELACOURT-SMITH OF ALTERYN, Baroness *cr* 1974 (Life Peer), of Alteryn, Gwent; **Margaret Delacourt-Smith;** *b* 1916; *d* of Frederick James Hando; *m* 1st, 1939, Charles Smith (subsequently Lord Delacourt-Smith, PC) (*d* 1972); one *s* two *d*; 2nd, 1978, Professor Charles Blackton. *Educ:* Newport High School for Girls; St Anne's College, Oxford (MA). *Address:* House of Lords, SW1A 0PW.

de LACY, Richard Michael; QC 2000; *b* 4 Dec. 1954; *e s* of Michael de Lacy, MN, and Barbara de Lacy (*née* Greene), Hobart, Tasmania; *m* 1980, Sybil del Strother; one *s* two *d*. *Educ:* Hymers Coll., Kingston upon Hull; Clare Coll., Cambridge (BA 1975; MA 1979). Called to the Bar, Middle Temple, 1976 (Harmsworth Schol.), Bencher, 2001; in practice at the Bar, 1976–, specialising in commercial law, 1986–. Mem., Practice Regulation Review Cttee, ICAEW, 1998–. Jt Hon. Treas., Barristers' Benevolent Assoc., 1989–99. FCIArb 1991 (Chartered Arbitrator 2000); accredited Mediator, CEDR, 1998. *Recreations:* music, equestrianism, wine. *Address:* 3 Verulam Buildings, Gray's Inn, WC1R 5NT. *T:* (020) 7831 8441. *Club:* Academy.

DELAFONS, John, CB 1982; Visiting Professor, Department of Land Management and Development, University of Reading, since 1993; *b* 14 Sept. 1930; *m* 1957, Sheila Egerton; four *d*. *Educ:* Ardingly; St Peter's College, Oxford. 1st cl. Hons English. Asst Principal, Min. of Housing and Local Govt, 1953; Harkness Fellowship, Harvard, 1959–60; Principal, 1959–66; Principal Private Sec. to Minister, 1965–66; Department of the Environment: Assistant Sec., 1966–72; Under Sec., 1972–77; Under Sec., Cabinet Office, 1977–79; Dep. Sec., DoE, 1979–90, retd. Leverhulme and Nuffield Fellowship, 1989–90; Res. Associate, Inst. of Urban and Regl Develt, Univ. of California, 1990; Associate, Dept of Land Economy, Univ. of Cambridge, 1990–93. Chm., 1981–83, Vice Pres., 1985–92, RIPA; Mem. Council, 1992–95, 1997–99, Vice-Pres., 2000–, TCPA. *Publications:* Land-Use Controls in the United States, 1962, revd edn 1969; Development Impact Fees, 1990; Aesthetic Control, 1991; Politics and Preservation, 1997. *Recreations:* woodturning, travel. *Address:* 34 Castlebar Road, W5 2DD.

de la LANNE-MIRRLEES, Robin Ian Evelyn Stuart; *see* Mirrlees.

de la MADRID HURTADO, Miguel; President of Mexico, 1982–88; Director General, Fondo de Cultura Económica, 1990–2000; *b* 12 Dec. 1934; *m* 1959, Paloma Cordero de la Madrid; four *s* one *d*. *Educ:* Nat. Autonomous Univ., Mexico (Law degree with hon. mention for thesis; with master); Harvard Univ. (MPA). Legal Dept, Nat. Bank of Foreign Trade, 1953–57; Asst Gen. Man., Bank of Mexico, 1960–64; Asst Dir Gen., Credit Mexican, Min. of Treasury, 1965–70; Dir of Finance, Pemex, 1970–72; Gen. Dir, Credit, 1972–75, Under Sec., 1975–79, Min. of Treasury; Minister, Nat. Planning and Budget, Govt of Mexico, 1979–81. Pres., Nat. Assoc. of Lawyers, 1989–. Pres., Mexican Inst. of Culture, 1989–. Mem., InterAction Council, 1989–. *Publications:* economic and legal essays. *Address:* (office) Parras #46, Barrio Sta Catarina, Deleg. Coyoacán, 04010, México DF. *T:* (525) 6584459.

de la MARE, Prof. Albinia Catherine, OBE 1993; FBA 1987; Professor of Palaeography, King's College, London, 1989–97; *b* 2 June 1932; *d* of Richard Herbert Ingpen de la Mare and Amy Catherine Donaldson. *Educ:* Queen's Coll., Harley St., W1; Lady Margaret Hall, Oxford (MA); Warburg Inst., London (PhD). FRHistS; FSA. Dept of Western MSS, Bodleian Liby, 1962–88, Asst Librarian, 1964–88. Susette Taylor Fellow, 1964, Hon. Res. Fellow, 1979, Hon. Fellow, 1989, Lady Margaret Hall, Oxford; Guest Scholar, J. Paul Getty Museum, Malibu, 1992; Sen. Res. Fellow, Center for Advanced Study in the Visual Arts, Nat. Gall. of Art, Washington, 1998. Mem., Comité Internat. de Paléographie Latine, 1986–. *Publications:* Catalogue of the Italian manuscripts of Major J. R. Abbey (with J. J. G. Alexander), 1969; Catalogue of the Lyell Manuscripts, Bodleian Library, Oxford, 1971; The Handwriting of Italian Humanists, 1973; New Research on Humanistic Scribes in Florence, in Miniatura Fiorentina del Rinascimento, ed A. Garzelli, 1985; articles in learned periodicals, etc. *Recreations:* music, gardening, travel. *Address:* Tithe Barn House, 11 High Street, Cumnor, Oxford OX2 9PE. *T:* (01865) 863916.

de la MARTINEZ, Odaline, (Odaline de la Caridad Martinez); Cuban conductor and composer; *b* 31 Oct. 1949; *d* of Julian J. Martinez and Odaline M. Martinez. *Educ:* schs and univ. in USA; Royal Acad. of Music, London; Surrey Univ. Jt Founder, Lontano (chamber ensemble), 1976; first woman to conduct an entire Promenade Concert programme, Royal Albert Hall, 1984; Dir, European Women's Orchestra, 1990–. Founder, 1992, and Man. Dir, Lorelt recording co. Founder Mem., Women in Music, 1985. *Compositions include:* First String Quartet; *opera:* Sister Aimée: an American Legend, 1984. *Publication:* Mendelssohn's Sister. *Address:* c/o Kantor Concert Management, 67 Teignmouth Road, NW2 4EA.

DELAMERE, 5th Baron *cr* 1821; **Hugh George Cholmondeley;** *b* 18 Jan. 1934; *s* of 4th Baron Delamere, and Phyllis Anne (*d* 1978), *e d* of late Lord George Scott, OBE; *S* father, 1979; *m* 1964, Mrs Ann Willoughby Tinne, *o d* of late Sir Patrick Renison, GCMG and Lady Renison, Mayfield, Sussex; one *s*. *Educ:* Eton; Magdalene Coll., Cambridge. MA Agric. *Heir:* *s* Hon. Thomas Patrick Gilbert Cholmondeley [*b* 19 June 1968; *m* 1998, Dr Sally Brewerton, *d* of Prof. and Mrs Derrick Brewerton; two *s*]. *Address:* Soysambu, Elmenteita, Kenya.

de la MORENA, Felipe; Ambassador of Spain; Chairman, British Hispanic Foundation, Madrid, since 1993; *b* 22 Oct. 1927; *s* of Felipe de la Morena and Luisa Calvet; *m* 1958, María Teresa Casado Bach; two *s* two *d*. *Educ:* Univ. Complutense de Madrid; Univs of Grenoble and Oxford; Diplomatic Sch., Madrid. Entered diplomatic service 1957; served Beirut, Berne, Washington and Min. of Foreign Affairs, Madrid; Dir, Technical Office, later Dir-Gen., Territorial Planning, Min. of Develt Planning, 1974–76; Minister Counsellor, Lisbon, 1976; Ambassador to People's Republic of China, 1978; Dir-Gen., Foreign Policy for Latin America, 1982; Ambassador to Syria and Cyprus (residence Damascus), 1983; Ambassador to Tunisia, 1987, to UK, 1990–93. Orders: Alfonso X el Sabio, 1965; Mérito Civil, 1973; Isabel la Católica, 1970; Carlos III, 1980; Gran Cruz del Mérito Naval, 1992; holds foreign decorations. *Recreation:* golf. *Address:* Fundación Hispano-Británica, Maestro Lasalle 46, 28016 Madrid, Spain. *Clubs:* Travellers; Puerta de Hierro, Real Automóvil de España, Gran Peña (Madrid).

DELANEY, Francis James Joseph, (Frank); writer and broadcaster, since 1972; *b* 24 Oct. 1942; 5th *s* of Edward Delaney and Elizabeth Josephine O'Sullivan; *m* 1st, 1966, Eilish (*née* Kelliher) (marr. diss. 1978); three *s*; 2nd, 1988, Susan Jane Collier (marr. diss. 1997); 3rd, 1998, Salley Vickers. *Educ:* Abbey Schools, Tipperary, Ireland; Rosse Coll., Dublin. Bank of Ireland, 1961–72; journalism, 1972–: includes: broadcasting news with RTE, Dublin; current affairs with BBC Northern Ireland, BBC Radio Four, London, and BBC Television. Chm., NBL, 1984–86. *Publications:* James Joyce's Odyssey, 1981; Betjeman Country, 1983; The Celts, 1986; A Walk in the Dark Ages, 1988; *fiction:* A Walk to the Western Isles, 1993; My Dark Rosaleen, 1989; The Sins of the Mothers, 1992; Telling the Pictures, 1993; A Stranger in their Midst, 1995; The Amethysts, 1997; Desire and Pursuit, 1998; Pearl, 1999; At Ruby's, 2001; (as Francis Bryan) Jim Hawkins and the Curse of Treasure Island, 2001; sundry criticisms and introductions. *Recreations:* reading, conversation, walking. *Address:* *e-mail:* frankdelaney@frankdelaney.com. *Clubs:* Athenæum, Chelsea Arts.

DELANEY, Ven. Peter Anthony, MBE 2001; Archdeacon of London, since 1999; Vicar, All Hallows by the Tower, since 1977; *b* 20 June 1939; *s* of Anthony Mario Delaney and Ena Margaret Delaney. *Educ:* King's Coll., London (AKC); St Boniface Coll., Warminster. Ordained deacon, 1966, priest, 1967; Curate, St Marylebone Parish Church, 1966–70; Chaplain, London University Church of Christ the King, 1970–74; Canon Residentiary and Precentor, Southwark Cathedral, 1974–77. Canon, St Paul's Cathedral, Nicosia, Dio. Cyprus and the Gulf, 1984–; Prebendary, St Paul's Cathedral, London, 1995–; Guild Vicar, St Katharine Cree, 1997–; Dir, City Churches Develt Gp, 1997–. Gov., St Dunstan's Coll., Catford, 1977–; Master: Co. of World Traders of City of London, 1994–95; Gardeners' Co., 1999–2000. Kt Comdr, SMO of Knights Templars. *Publications:* The Artist and his Exploration into God, 1981; (contrib.) The Canon Law of the Church of England, 1975. *Recreations:* painting, theatre, gardening. *Address:* Archdeacon's Office, 43 Trinity Square, EC3N 4DJ. *T:* (020) 7488 2335; *e-mail:* archdeacon.london@london.anglican.org.

DELANEY, Shelagh; playwright; *b* Salford, Lancs, 1939; one *d*. *Educ:* Broughton Secondary Sch. *Plays:* A Taste of Honey, Theatre Royal, Stratford, 1958 and 1959, Wyndhams, 1959, New York, 1960 and 1961, off-Broadway revival, trans. to Broadway, 1981 (Charles Henry Foyle New Play Award, Arts Council Bursary, New York Drama Critics' Award); The Lion in Love, Royal Court 1960, New York 1962. *Films:* A Taste of Honey, 1961 (British Film Academy Award, Robert Flaherty Award); The White Bus, 1966; Charlie Bubbles, 1968 (Writers Guild Award for best original film writing); Dance with a Stranger, 1985 (Prix Film Jeunesse-Etranger, Cannes, 1985). *TV plays:* St Martin's Summer, LWT, 1974; Find Me First, BBC TV, 1979; *TV series:* The House that Jack Built, BBC TV, 1977 (stage adaptation, NY, 1979). *Radio plays:* So Does the Nightingale, BBC, 1980; Don't Worry About Matilda, 1983. FRSL 1985. *Publications:* A Taste of Honey, 1959 (London and New York); The Lion in Love, 1961 (London and New York); Sweetly Sings the Donkey, 1963 (New York), 1964 (London). *Address:* c/o Tessa Sayle, 11 Jubilee Place, SW3 3TE.

DELANO, Juan Carlos; Director, Universidad Adolfo Ibañez, since 1998; *b* Santiago, 14 June 1941; *m* Maria Paz Valenzuela; three *s* one *d*. *Educ:* St George's Coll., Catholic Univ., Chile; OCD, Belgium. Private enterprise: Distribuidora Audicol SA, Commercial Magara Ltd; Pres., Trading Assoc. of Chile, Dir, Chamber of Commerce of Santiago, 1979–83; Pres., Chilean Nat. Chamber of Commerce and Advr to Confedn of Trade and Industry, 1983–85; Minister of Economy, Promotion and Reconstruction, 1985–87; Ambassador to UK, 1987–90. Chief Exec. Officer, Equs SA, 1990–; Dir, Icare, 1990–. *Address:* Evaristo Lillo 178, Of. 12, Las Condes, Santiago, Chile. *Clubs:* Union, Polo.

De-la-NOY, Michael; author; *b* 3 April 1934; *yr s* of late Eric De-la-Noy Walker and Kathleen Harvard (*née* Johnson). *Educ:* Bedford Sch. Commnd RAC; served in Egypt, 1952–54. Member, editorial staff: Bedfordshire Times, 1954–57; Brighton & Hove Herald, 1958–60; Editor, Richard Thomas & Baldwin, 1961–62; Religious Editor, Prism Pubns, 1962–65; Editor, Pergamon Press, 1966–67; Press Officer to Archbp of Canterbury and Asst Information Officer, Church Inf. Office, 1967–70; Dir, Albany Trust and Sec., Sexual Law Reform Soc., 1970–71; Editor, Open Univ., 1975–77. Member: House of Laity, Church Assembly, 1965–67; Steering Cttee on Liturgical Revision, 1965–67. *Publications:* Before the Storm (poems), 1958; A Child's Life of Christ, 1964; Young Once Only: a study of boys on probation, 1965; The Fields of Praise: an anthology of religious poetry, 1968; A Day in the Life of God, 1971; Elgar: the man, 1983; (ed) The Journals of Denton Welch, 1984; Denton Welch: the making of a writer, 1984; The Honours System, 1985, rev. edn 1992; Acting as Friends: the story of the Samaritans, 1987; (ed) Fragments of a Life Story: the collected short writings of Denton Welch, 1987; Eddy: the life of Edward Sackville-West, 1988; Michael Ramsey: a portrait, 1990; Windsor Castle: past and present, 1990; Exploring Oxford, 1991; The Church of England: a portrait, 1993; The Queen Behind the Throne, 1994; The King who never was: the story of Frederick, Prince of Wales, 1996; Mervyn Stockwood: a lonely life, 1996; Scott of the Antarctic, 1997; George IV, 1998; Bedford School: a history, 1999; The House of Hervey: a history of tainted talent, 2001; contrib. DNB. *Recreation:* going for very short walks. *Address:* c/o Hodson-Margetts, 65 Brook Street, Raunds, Wellingborough, Northants NN9 6LL. *Club:* Wig and Pen.

de LAROSIÈRE de CHAMPFEU, Jacques (Martin Henri Marie), Hon. KBE 1998; Commander, Legion of Honour, 1996; Chevalier, National Order of Merit, 1970; Inspector General of Finance, since 1981; President, European Bank for Reconstruction and Development, 1993–98; *b* 12 Nov. 1929; *s* of Robert de Larosière and Hugayte de Champfeu; *m* 1960, France du Bos; one *s* one *d*. *Educ:* Institut d'Etudes Politiques, Paris (L ès L, licencié en droit); Nat. Sch. of Administration, Paris. Inspecteur des Finances, 1958; appointments at: Inspectorate-General of Finance, 1961; External Finance Office, 1963; Treasury 1965; Asst Dir, Treasury, 1967; Dep. Dir then Head of Dept, Min. of Economics and Finance, 1971; Principal Private Sec. to Minister of Economics and Finance, 1974; Dir, Treasury, 1974–78; Man. Dir, IMF, 1978–87; Gov., Bank of France, 1987–93. Director: Renault, 1971–74; Banque Nat. de Paris, 1973–78; Air France and French Railways, 1974–78; Société nat. industrielle aérospatiale, 1976–78; Power Corp., 1998–; Alstom, 1998–2000; France Telecom, 1998–; Advr, Paribas, 1998–; Trustee, Reuters, 1999–. Director appointed by Treasury, General Council, Bank of France, 1974–78; Auditor: Crédit national, 1974–78; Comptoir des entrepreneurs, 1973–75; Crédit foncier de France, 1975–78. Vice Pres., Caisse nat. des télécommunications, 1974–78. Chairman: OECD Econ. and Develt Review Cttee, 1967–71; Deputies Gp of Ten, 1976–78; Cttee of Gp of Ten, 1990–93. Mem., Acad. of Moral and Pol Scis, 1993; Hon. Mem., Société des Cincinnati de France. Grand Cordon, Order of Sacred Treasure (Japan), 1993; Grand Cross, Order of Merit: Argentina, 1992; Italy, 1993; Order of Aztec Eagle (Mexico), 1994; Cross, Order of Merit (Germany), 1996; Comdr, Order of Merit (Poland), 1997; Order of Friendship (Russia), 1997; Order of Merit (Hungary); Comdr, Order of Southern Cross (Brazil), 1999. *Address:* 5 rue de Beaujolais, 75001 Paris, France.

de la RÚA, Fernando; President of Argentina, since 1999; *b* 15 Sept. 1937; *m* Inés Pertiné; three *c*. *Educ:* Liceo Militar General Paz, Córdoba Univ. (Dr of Laws). Mem., Unión Cívica Radical. Advr, Min. of the Interior, Argentina, 1963–66; Senator (UCR) for Buenos Aires, 1973–76 and 1989; Nat. Senator (UCR), 1983–89, 1992–99; Nat. Deputy (UCR), 1991; (Pres., UCR Gp); Mayor, City Buenos Aires, 1996. *Address:* General Secretariat to the Presidency, Balcarce 50, 1064 Buenos Aires, Argentina.

de la RUE, Sir Andrew (George Ilay), 4th Bt *cr* 1898, of Cadogan Square; company director; farmer; *b* 3 Feb. 1946; *s* of Sir Eric Vincent de la Rue, 3rd Bt and Cecilia (*d* 1963), *d* of late Maj. Walter Waring; *S* father, 1989; *m* 1984, Tessa Ann, *er d* of David Dobson; two *s*. *Educ:* Millfield. With Lloyd's (Insurance), 1966; Dir, Private Company, 1976–. *Recreations:* shooting, coursing, tennis. *Heir:* *s* Edward Walter de la Rue, *b* 25 Nov. 1986. *Address:* Stragglethorpe Grange, Brant Broughton, Lincolnshire LN5 0QZ. *T:* (01636) 626505; 21 Atherton Street, SW11 2JE.

de la TOUR, Frances; actress; *b* 30 July 1944; *d* of Charles de la Tour and Moyra (*née* Fessas); one *s* one *d*. *Educ:* Lycée français de Londres; Drama Centre, London. Royal Shakespeare Company, 1965–71: rôles include Audrey in As You Like It, 1967; Hoyden in The Relapse, 1969; Helena in A Midsummer Night's Dream (Peter Brooks's production), 1971 (also USA tour); Belinda in The Man of Mode, 1971; Violet in Small Craft Warnings, Comedy, 1973 (Best Supporting Actress, Plays and Players Award); Ruth Jones in The Banana Box, Apollo, 1973; Isabella in The White Devil, Old Vic, 1976; appearances at Hampstead Theatre, and Half Moon Theatre incl. title rôle in Hamlet, 1979; Stephanie in Duet for One (written by Tom Kempinski), Bush Theatre and Duke of York's, 1980 (Best New Play, and Best Perf. by Actress, Drama Awards, Best Perf. by Actress in New Play, SWET Award, Best Actress, New Standard Award); Jean in Skirmishes, Hampstead, 1982 (also television, 1982); Sonya in Uncle Vanya, Haymarket, 1982; Josie in A Moon for the Misbegotten, Riverside, 1983 (SWET Best Actress award); title rôle in St Joan, NT, 1984; Dance of Death, Riverside, 1985; Sonya and Masha in Chekhov's Women, Lyric, 1985; Brighton Beach Memoirs, NT, 1986; Lillian, Lyric, 1986, Fortune, 1987; Façades, Lyric, Hammersmith, 1988; Regan in King Lear, Old Vic, 1989; Arkadina, Ranyevskaya and Olga Knipper in Chekhov's Women, Moscow Art Theatre, 1990; Miss Belzer in When She Danced, Globe, 1991 (Olivier Award); Witch in The Pope and the Witch, Comedy, 1992; Yoko Sitsuki in Greasepaint, Lyric, Hammersmith, 1993; Leonie in Les Parents Terribles, RNT, 1994; Three Tall Women, Wyndham's, 1994; Elinor in Blinded by the Sun, RNT, 1996; the woman in The Play about the Baby, Almeida, 1998; Raisa in The Forest, RNT, 1999; Cleopatra in Antony and Cleopatra, RSC, 1999; Jane in Fallen Angels, Apollo, 2000. *Films* include: Rising Damp, 1979 (Best Actress, New Standard British Film Award, 1980); The Cherry Orchard, 1998. *Television* includes: Play for Today (twice), 1973–75; Rising Damp (series), 1974, 1976; Flickers, 1980; Duet for One, 1985; Cold Lazarus, 1995; Tom Jones, 1997. *Address:* c/o Kate Feast, 10 Primrose Hill Studios, Fitzroy Road, NW1 8TR. *T:* (020) 7586 5502.

DE LA WARR, 11th Earl *cr* 1761; **William Herbrand Sackville;** Baron De La Warr, 1299 and 1572; Viscount Cantelupe 1761; Baron Buckhurst 1864; Stockbroker, Credit Lyonnais Securities (formerly Laing and Cruickshank), since 1980; dairy farmer; *b* 10 April 1948; *s* of 10th Earl De La Warr and of Anne Rachel, *d* of Geoffrey Devas, MC; *S* father, 1988; *m* 1978, Anne, Countess of Hopetoun, *e d* of Arthur Leveson; two *s* and two step *s*. *Educ:* Eton. *Heir: s* Lord Buckhurst, *qv*. *Address:* Buckhurst Park, Withyham, Sussex TN7 4BL; 14 Bourne Street, SW1W 8JU. *Clubs:* White's, Turf.
See also Hon. T. G. Sackville.

DELBRIDGE, Richard; Director: Egg plc, since 2000; Innogy plc, since 2000; Tate & Lyle plc, since 2000; *b* 21 May 1942; *s* of late Tom Delbridge and of Vera Kate Delbridge (*née* Lancashire); *m* 1966, Diana Genevra Rose Bowers-Broadbent; one *s* two *d*. *Educ:* Copleston Sch., Ipswich; LSE (BSc Econ); Univ. of California at Berkeley (MBA). FCA. Arthur Andersen & Co., 1963–66 and 1968–76, Partner 1974–76; Morgan Guaranty Trust Co., NY: Vice-Pres., 1976–79; Sen. Vice-Pres. and Comptroller of Morgan Guaranty Trust Co. and J. P. Morgan Inc., 1979–85; Sen. Vice-Pres. and Asst Gen. Manager, 1985–87, Man. Dir and Gen. Manager, 1987–89, London offices, J. P. Morgan Inc.; Dir, Group Finance, Midland Bank, 1990–92; Gp Finance Dir, HSBC Hldgs, 1993–95; Dir and Chief Financial Officer, NatWest Gp, 1996–2000. Member: Bd, Securities Assoc., 1988–89; UK Council, INSEAD, 1993–99; Financial Reporting Review Panel, 1998–. Dir, City Arts Trust, 1998–. Trustee, Wordsworth Trust, 2000–. CIMgt; FRSA. *Recreations:* hill walking, books. *Address:* 48 Downshire Hill, NW3 1NX.

DELIGHT, Ven. John David; Archdeacon of Stoke, 1982–90, Archdeacon Emeritus, 1990; *b* 24 Aug. 1925; *s* of Rev. Sidney John Delight and Elizabeth Ethel Tuckett; *m* 1952 Eileen Elsie Braden; four *s* two *d*. *Educ:* Christ's Hospital, Horsham; Liverpool Univ.; Oak Hill Theol Coll.; Open Univ. RNVR (Fleet Air Arm), 1942–46. Curate: Tooting Graveney, 1952–55; Wallington, 1955–58; Travelling Sec., Inter-Varsity Fellowship, 1958–61; Vicar, St Christopher's, Leicester, 1961–69; Chaplain, Leicester Prison, 1965–67; Rector of Aldridge, 1969–82; RD, Walsall, 1981–82; Prebendary of Lichfield Cathedral, 1980–82; volunteer associate of Crosslinks (formerly BCMS) and CMS, to develop theol educn by extension in dio. of Machakos, Kenya, 1990–94; retired 1994 and licensed to officiate, dio. of Lichfield and dio. of Chester. Hon. Canon, All Souls Cathedral, Machakos. *Publication:* (contrib.) Families, Facts and Frictions, 1976. *Recreations:* travel, music, gardening, reading. *Club:* Christ's Hospital.

DE L'ISLE, 2nd Viscount *cr* 1956; **Philip John Algernon Sidney,** MBE 1977; Baron De L'Isle and Dudley 1835; Bt 1806; Bt 1818; DL; *b* 21 April 1945; *s* of 1st Viscount De L'Isle, VC, KG, GCMG, GCVO, PC and Hon. Jacqueline Vereker (*d* 1962), *o d* of Field-Marshal 6th Viscount Gort, VC, GCB, CBE, DSO, MVO, MC; *S* father, 1991; *m* 1980, Isobel Tresyllian, *y d* of Sir Edmund Compton, GCB, KBE; one *s* one *d*. *Educ:* Tabley House; Mons OCS; RMA Sandhurst. Commnd Grenadier Guards, 1966. Served BAOR, UKLF, NI, Belize and Sudan at Regtl Duty; GSO3 Ops/SD HQ 3 Inf. Bde, 1974–76; retired 1979. Landowner, 1979–. Mem., H of L Adv. Panel on Works of Art, 1994–97. Chm., Kent County Cttee, CLA, 1983–85. Hon. Col, 5th (V) Bn, Princess of Wales's Royal Regt, 1992–99. Freeman, City of London; Liveryman, Goldsmiths' Co. DL Kent, 1996. *Heir: s* Hon. Philip William Edmund Sidney, *b* 2 April 1985. *Address:* Penshurst Place, Penshurst, Tonbridge, Kent TN11 8DG. *T:* (01892) 870307, *Fax:* (01892) 870866; *e-mail:* delisle@penshurstplace.com. *Clubs:* White's, Pratt's.

de LISLE, Everard John Robert March Phillipps; stockbroker; Vice Lord-Lieutenant of Leicestershire, since 1990; *b* 8 June 1930; *s* of late Maj. J. A. F. M. P. de Lisle, DL and Elizabeth Muriel de Lisle; *m* 1959, Hon. Mary Rose Peake, *d* of 1st Viscount Ingleby, PC; two *s* one *d*. *Educ:* Eton; RMA Sandhurst. Commnd RHG, 1950; Captain, 1954; Major, 1960; retired 1962. Mem., London Stock Exchange, 1965–. High Sheriff, 1974–75, DL 1980, Leics. *Recreations:* shooting, country pursuits. *Address:* Stockerston Hall, Oakham, Leics LE15 9JD; 11 Buckingham Court, Kensington Park Road, W11 3BP. *Clubs:* Pratt's, MCC; Leicestershire Far and Near.

DELL, David Michael, CB 1986; Deputy Secretary, Department of Trade and Industry, 1983–91; *b* 30 April 1931; *s* of late Montague Roger Dell and Aimée Gabrielle Dell; unmarried. *Educ:* Rugby Sch.; Balliol Coll., Oxford (MA). 2nd Lieut Royal Signals, Egypt and Cyprus, 1954–55. Admiralty, 1955; MoD, 1960; Min. of Technol., 1965; DTI, 1970; DoI, 1974, Under Sec., 1976; Regl Dir, Yorks and Humberside, DTI, 1976–78; Dir, EIB, 1984–87; Chief Exec., BOTB, 1987–91. Dir, Nesbit Evans Gp, 1991–93. Mem. Council, Oxford Soc., 1995–2001; Mem., British–Peruvian Trade & Investment Gp, 1997–2001. Chm., Christ Church Bentinck Sch., 1979–92. Companion, BITC, 1992. *Recreations:* committees, dining out. *Clubs:* Royal Automobile, St Stephen's Constitutional; Leeds (Leeds).

DELL, Michael S.; Chairman and Chief Executive Officer, Dell Computer Corporation (formerly PCs Ltd), since 1984; *b* Houston, Texas, 23 Feb. 1965; *s* of Alexander and Lorraine Dell; *m* 1989, Susan Lieberman; four *c* (incl. twins). *Educ:* Univ. of Texas. Founder, PCs Ltd, 1984; co. renamed Dell Computer Corp., 1987. Member: Computer Systems Policy Proj.; The Business Council; Member Board: US Chamber of Commerce; World Econ. Forum. *Publication:* Direct From Dell: strategies that revolutionized an industry, 1999. *Address:* Dell Computer Corporation, 1 Dell Way, Round Rock, TX 78682, USA.

DELL, Dame Miriam (Patricia), ONZ 1993; DBE 1980 (CBE 1975); JP (NZ); Hon. President, International Council of Women, 1986–88 (President, 1979–86; Vice-President, 1976–79); *b* 14 June 1924; *d* of Gerald Wilfred Matthews and Ruby Miriam Crawford; *m* 1946, Richard Kenneth Dell; four *d*. *Educ:* Epsom Girls Grammar Sch.; Univ. of Auckland (BA); Auckland Teachers' Coll. (Teachers' Cert. (Secondary Sch.)). Teaching, 1945–47, 1957–58 and 1961–71. Nat. Pres., Nat. Council of Women, 1970–74 (Vice-Pres., 1967–70); Chm., Cttee on Women, NZ, 1974–81; Chm., Envmt and Conservation Orgns of NZ, 1989–94; Chm., 1993 Suffrage Centennial Year Trust, 1991–94. Member: Nat. Develt Council, 1969–74; Cttee of Inquiry into Equal Pay, 1971–72; Nat. Commn for UNESCO, 1974–83; Social Security Appeal Authority, 1974–99; Anglican Provincial Commn on Ordination of Women, 1974; Project Develt Bd, Mus. of NZ, 1988–92; Dep. Chm., Wellington Conservation Bd, 1990–98; Nat. Convener, Internat. Women's Year, 1975; Co-ordinator, Internat. Council of Women Develt Prog., 1988–91; Sec., Inter-Church Council on Public Affairs, 1986–89 (Chm., 1982–86); Convener, Public Affairs Unit, Anglican Church of NZ, 1988–92. JP NZ 1975. Jubilee Medal, 1977; NZ Commemoration Medal, 1990; NZ Suffrage Centennial Medal, 1993. *Publications:* Role of Women in National Development, 1970; numerous articles in popular and house magazines, on role and status of women. *Recreations:* gardening, reading, handcrafts, beachcombing. *Address:* 2 Bowline Place, Whitby, Porirua 6006, New Zealand. *T:* (4) 2341406, *Fax:* (4) 2341407.

DELL, Ven. Robert Sydney; Archdeacon of Derby, 1973–92, now Archdeacon Emeritus; Canon Residentiary of Derby Cathedral, 1981–92, now Canon Emeritus; *b* 20 May 1922; *s* of Sydney Edward Dell and Lilian Constance Palmer; *m* 1953, Doreen Molly Layton; one *s* one *d*. *Educ:* Harrow County Sch.; Emmanuel Coll., Cambridge (MA); Ridley Hall. Curate of: Islington, 1948; Holy Trinity, Cambridge, 1950; Asst Chaplain, Wrekin Coll., 1953; Vicar of Mildenhall, Suffolk, 1955; Vice-Principal of Ridley Hall, Cambridge, 1957; Vicar of Chesterton, Cambridge, 1966 (Dir, Cambridge Samaritans, 1966–69). Mem., Archbishops' Commn on Intercommunion, 1965–67; Proctor in Convocation and Mem. Gen. Synod of C of E, 1970–85. Vis. Fellow, St George's House, Windsor Castle, 1981. Hon. Fellow, Univ. of Derby, 1994. *Publications:* Atlas of Christian History, 1960; Honest Thinker—John Rawlinson 1884–1960: theologian, bishop, ecumenist, 1998; contributor to: Charles Simeon, 1759–1836: essays written in commemoration of his bi-centenary, 1959; Jl of Ecclesiastical History. *Recreations:* reading, walking, travelling. *Address:* Pinehurst Lodge, 35 Grange Road, Cambridge CB3 9AU. *T:* (01223) 365466.

DELLAL, Jack; Chairman, Allied Commercial Holdings Ltd; *b* 2 Oct. 1923; *s* of Sulman and Charlotte Dellal; *m* 1st, 1952, Zehava Helmer (marr. diss. 1975); one *s* five *d* (and one *d* decd); 2nd, 1997, Ruanne Louw; one *s*. *Educ:* Heaton Moor Coll., Manchester. Chm., Dalton, Barton & Co. Ltd, 1962–72; Dep. Chm., Keyser Ullman Ltd, 1972–74; Chm., Highland Electronics Group Ltd, 1971–76; Director: Anglo African Finance PLC, 1983–; General Tire & Rubber (SA) Ltd, 1983–87; Williams, Hunt South Africa Ltd, 1983–87. Vice-Pres., Anglo-Polish Conservative Society, 1970–. Officer, Order of Polonia Restituta, 1970. Freeman Citizen of Glasgow, 1971. *Recreations:* lawn tennis, squash, music, art. *Clubs:* Royal Thames Yacht, Queen's, Hurlingham.

DELLOW, Sir John (Albert), Kt 1990; CBE 1985 (OBE 1979); DL; Deputy Commissioner, Metropolitan Police, 1987–91; *b* 5 June 1931; *s* of Albert Reginald and Lily Dellow; *m* 1952, Heather Josephine Rowe; one *s* one *d*. *Educ:* William Ellis Sch., Highgate; Royal Grammar Sch., High Wycombe. Joined City of London Police, 1951; seconded Manchester City Police, 1966; Superintendent, Kent County Constabulary, 1966, Chief Supt, 1968; jssc 1969; Asst Chief Constable, Kent Co. Constabulary, 1969; Metropolitan Police: Deputy Assistant Commissioner: Traffic Planning, 1973; Personnel, 1975; No 2 Area, 1978; 'A' Dept Operations, 1979; Inspectorate, 1980; Assistant Commissioner: 'B' Dept, 1982; Crime, 1984; Asst Comr (Specialist Ops), 1985–87. Pres., ACPO, 1989–90 (Vice-Pres., 1988–89). Trustee, Metropolitan Museum Trust; Former Chairman: Metropolitan Police History Soc.; Metropolitan Police Climbing, Canoe, Rowing and Heavy Boat Sections; Cdre, Metropolitan Police Sailing Club. Member Council: London Dist, Order of St John of Jerusalem, 1988–96; RUSI, 1991–95. DL Greater London, 1991. *Publications:* contrib. RUSI Defence Studies series and other jls. *Recreations:* walking, history, listening to wireless, water colour painting.

DELORS, Jacques Lucien Jean; President, International Commission on Education for the Twenty First Century, UNESCO, since 1994; President, Commission of the European Economic Community, 1985–95; *b* Paris, 20 July 1925; *s* of Louis Delors and Jeanne (*née* Rigal); *m* 1948, Marie Lephaille; one *d* (one *s* decd). *Educ:* Paris Univ.; Dip., Centre for Higher Studies of Banking. Joined Banque de France, 1945; in office of Chief of Securities Dept, 1950–62, and in Sect. for the Plan and Investments, Conseil Economique et Social, 1959–61; Chief of Social Affairs, Gen. Commissariat of Plan Monnet, 1962–68; Gen. Sec. for Perm. Trng and Social Promotion, 1968; Gen. Sec., Interministerial Cttee for Professional Educn, 1969–73; Mem., Gen. Council, Banque de France, 1973–79, and Dir, on leave of absence, 1973. Special Advr on Social and Cultural Affairs to Prime Minister, 1969–72. Socialist Party Spokesman on internat. econ. matters, 1976–81; Minister of the Economy and Finance, 1981–83; Minister of Economy, Finance and Budget, 1983–84. Mem., European Parlt, 1979–81 (Pres., Econ. and Financial Cttee, 1979–81). Mayor of Clichy, 1983–84. Associate Prof., Univ. of Paris-Dauphine, 1973–79. Dir, Work and Society Res. Centre, 1975–79; President: Bd of Admin, College of Europe, Bruges, 1996–; Notre Europe, 1996–. Founder, Club Echange et Projets, 1974–79. Hon. doctorates from 24 univs. Awards and honours from 15 countries. *Publications:* Les indicateurs sociaux, 1971; Changer, 1975; (jtly) En sortir ou pas, 1985; La France par L'Europe, 1988 (Our Europe: the community and national development, 1992); Le Nouveau Concert Européen, 1992; L'unité d'un homme, 1994; Combats pour l'Europe, 1996; essays, articles and UN reports on French Plan. *Address:* Association Notre Europe, 44 rue Notre Dame des Victoires, 75002 Paris, France.

de los ANGELES, Victoria; Cross of Lazo de Dama of Order of Isabel the Catholic, Spain; Condecoracíon Banda de la Orden Civil de Alfonso X (El Sabio), Spain; Opera and Concert-Artiste (singing in original languages), Lyric-Soprano, since 1944; *b* Barcelona, Spain, 1 Nov. 1923; *m* 1948, Enrique Magriñá (decd); two *s*. *Educ:* Escoles Milà i Fontanals de la Generalitat de Catalunya, Barcelona; Conservatorium of Barcelona; University of Barcelona. Studied until 1944 at Conservatorium, Barcelona; first public concert, in Barcelona, 1944; début at Gran Teatro del Liceo de Barcelona, in Marriage of Figaro, 1945; concert and opera tours in Spain and Portugal, 1945–49; winner of first prize at Concours International of Geneva, 1947; first appearances at Paris Opéra, Stockholm Royal Opera, Copenhagen Royal Opera, and début at the Scala, Milan, also South-American and Scandinavian concert tours, 1949; first appearance at Covent Garden, and

Carnegie Hall Début, 1950; first United States concert tour, and Metropolitan Opera of New York season, first appearances at La Monnaie, Brussels, Holland and Edinburgh Festivals, 1951; first appearances at Teatro Colón, Buenos Aires, and Teatro Municipal, Rio de Janeiro, 1952. Since 1952 has appeared at the most important opera theatres and concert halls of Europe, North, South and Central America and Canada; first tour in S Africa, 1953; first tour in Australia and New Zealand, 1956; first appearance, Vienna State Opera, 1957; opening Festival, Bayreuth, with Tannhäuser, 1961; first tour in Japan and Far East, 1964. Gold Medal, Barcelona, 1958; Silver Medal, province of Barcelona, 1959; Premio Nacional de Música, Spain; Medal Premio Roma, 1969, and various French, Italian, Dutch and American awards; Gold Disc for 5 million copies sold, UK; Hon. Dr Univ. of Barcelona. *Address:* Avenida de Pedralbes 57, 08034 Barcelona, Spain.

DELPY, Prof. David Thomas, DSc; FRS 1999; Hamamatsu Professor of Medical Photonics, since 1991, and Vice Provost, since 1999, University College London; *b* 11 Aug. 1948; *s* of R. M. Delpy and M. H. Delpy; *m* 1972, Margaret E. Kimber; two *s*. *Educ:* Heaton Grammar Sch., Newcastle upon Tyne; Brunel Univ. (BSc 1st Cl. Hons Applied Phys); UCL (DSc Med. Phys London). Technical Mgt Services, Darchem Ltd, Darlington, 1970–71; Non-clinical Lectr, UCL Med. Sch., 1971–76; University College Hospital, London: Sen. Physicist, 1976–82; Principal Physicist, 1982–86; Sen. Lectr, Dept of Med. Phys and Bioengrg, UCL, 1986–91, Head of Dept, 1992–99. *Publications:* numerous scientific papers. *Recreations:* work, classical music, gardening. *Address:* Department of Medical Physics and Bioengineering, University College London, Shropshire House, Capper Street, WC1E 6JA. *T:* (020) 7209 6262.

DELVIN, Lord; title borne by eldest son of Earl of Westmeath, *qv*; not at present used.

DELVIN, Dr David George; television and radio broadcaster, writer and doctor; Director, The Medical Information Service, since 1995; *b* 28 Jan. 1939; *s* of William Delvin, Ayrshire and Elizabeth Falvey, Kerry; *m* 1st, Kathleen Sears, SRN, SCM; two *s* one *d*; 2nd, Christine Webber. *Educ:* St Dunstan's Coll.; King's Coll., Univ. of London; King's Coll. Hosp. (MB, BS 1962; psychol medicine, forensic medicine and public health prizes, 1962). LRCP, MRCS 1962; MRCGP 1974; DObstRCOG 1965; DCH 1966; DipVen, Soc. of Apothecaries, 1977; FPA Cert. 1972; FPA Instructing Cert. 1974. Dir, Hosp. Medicine Film Unit, 1968–69. Vice-Chm., Med. Journalists' Assoc., 1982–87; General Medical Council: Elected Mem., 1979–94; Member: Health Cttee 1980–86; Professional Conduct Cttee, 1987–94; Standards & Ethics Cttee, 1992–94. Member: Educn Cttee, Back Pain Assoc., 1983–87; Faculty of Family Planning, RCOG, 1993–. Medical Consultant: FPA, 1981–90; Nat. Assoc. of Family Planning Doctors, 1990–93; Medical Advisor to: various BBC and ITV progs, 1974–; NetDoctor website, 1999–. Med. Editor, General Practitioner, 1972–90; Sen. Editor, The Lancet, 1996–98; Chm., Editorial Boards of Medeconomics, Monthly Index of Med. Specialities, and MIMS Magazine, 1988–91; Mem. Editorial Adv. Bd, British Jl of Family Planning, 1994–; Dr Jekyll Columnist in World Medicine, 1973–82; Columnist, BMA News Review, 1992–98; Med. Columnist, Glasgow Herald, 1995–97. Cert. of Special Merit, Med. Journalists' Assoc., 1974 and (jtly) 1975. American Medical Writers' Assoc. Best Book Award, 1976; Consumer Columnist of the Year Award, 1986. Médaille de la Ville de Paris (échelon argent), 1983. *Publications:* The Good Sex Guide, 1994, and other books, articles, TV and radio scripts, short stories, humorous pieces, medical films and videos; papers on hypertension and contraception in BMJ etc. *Recreations:* athletics, opera, orienteering, scuba-diving, hang-gliding (retired hurt). *Address:* c/o Coutts, 2 Harley Street, W1A 1EE. *Club:* Royal Society of Medicine.

de MARCO, Prof. Guido, KUOM 1999; LLD; President of Malta, since 1999; *b* 22 July 1931; *s* of Emanuele de Marco and Giovanna (*née* Raniolo); *m* 1956, Violet Saliba; one *s* two *d*. *Educ:* St Joseph High Sch.; St Aloysius Coll.; Royal Univ. of Malta (BA Philosophy, Econs and Italian 1952; LLD 1955). Warrant of Advocate, Superior Courts of Malta, 1956; Crown Counsel, 1964–66. Lectr and Prof. of Criminal Law, Univ. of Malta, 1967–. MP (Nat.) Malta, 1966–99; Dep. Prime Minister and Minister of Interior and Justice, 1987–90; Dep. Prime Minister and Minister of Foreign Affairs, 1990–96; Shadow Minister and Opposition Spokesman on Foreign Affairs, 1996–98; Dep. Prime Minister and Minister of Foreign Affairs, 1998–99. Nationalist Party: Sec. Gen., 1972–77; Dep. Leader, 1977–99. Rep. of Maltese Parlt, Council of Europe, 1967–87 and 1996–98 (Chm., Monitoring Cttee, 1997–98); Pres., UN Gen. Assembly (45th Session), 1990. Hon. LLD Seconda Università degli Studi di Napoli, 1999. *Publications:* A Presidency with a Purpose: United Nations General Assembly 45th Session, 1991; Malta's Foreign Policy in the Nineties: its evolution and progression, 1996; (with M. Bartolo) A Second Generation United Nations: for peace in freedom in the 21st century, 1997. *Recreations:* reading, travelling. *Address:* Office of the President, The Palace, Valletta, Malta. *T:* 221221, *Fax:* 241241.

DEMARCO, Prof. Richard, OBE 1985; RSW, SSA; Professor of European Cultural Studies, Kingston University, since 1993; *b* 9 July 1930; *s* of Carmine Demarco and Elizabeth (*née* Fusco); *m* 1957, Anne Muckle. *Educ:* Holy Cross Academy, Edinburgh; Edinburgh College of Art. National Service, KOSB and RAEC, 1954–56. Art Master, Duns Scotus Academy, Edinburgh, 1956–67; Co-Founder, Traverse Theatre Club; Vice-Chm. and Director, Traverse Art Gall., 1963–67; Dir, Richard Demarco Gall., Melville Crescent, Edinburgh, 1966–92, appointed by co-founders John Martin, Andrew Elliott and James Walker; introduced contemporary visual arts into official Edinburgh Festival programme with Edinburgh Open 100 Exhibn, 1967; introduced work of 330 internat. artists to UK, mainly through Edinburgh Fest. exhibns, from Canada, 1968, W Germany, 1970, Romania, 1971, Poland, 1972 and 1979, France, 1973, Austria, 1973, Yugoslavia, 1975, Aust. and NZ, 1984, Netherlands, 1990; incl. Joseph Beuys, 1970, Gunther Uecker, 1991, and Tadeusz Kantor's Cricot Theatre, with prodns of The Water Hen, 1972, Lovelies and Dowdies, 1973, The Dead Class, 1976. Has presented, 1969–, annual programmes of theatre, music and dance prodns, incl. the Freehold Company's Antigone, 1970; Dublin Project Company's On Baille Strand, 1977; Mladen Materio's Obala Theatre from Sarajevo, 1988 and 1989; Teatro Settimo from Turin, and Grupa Chwilowa from Lublin, 1991; Yvette Bozsik Theatre from Budapest, 1993. Prod Macbeth for Edinburgh Fest., on Inchcolm Is, 1988 and 1989. Director: Sean Connery's Scottish Internat. Educn Trust, 1972–74; Edinburgh Arts annual summer sch. and expedns, 1972–92; Artistic Advr, Eur. Youth Parlt, 1992–. Has directed annual exhib. prog. with Special Unit, HM Prison, Barlinnie, with partic. reference to sculpture of James Boyle, 1974–80; directed Edinburgh Fest. Internat. Confs, Towards the Housing of Art in the 21st Century, 1983, Art and the Human Environment, 1984 (also at Dublin Fest.). Was subject of film, Walkabout Edinburgh, dir. by Edward McConnell, 1970; acted in feature films: Long Shot, 1978; That Sinking Feeling, 1980; subject of TV film, The Demarco Dimension, 1987. Has broadcast regularly on television and radio, 1966–; has lectured in over 150 univs, art colls, schools, art galls; as water-colour painter and printmaker is represented in over 1600 public and private collections, incl. Nat. Gall. of Modern Art of Scotland, V&A Museum, Scottish Arts Council. Trustee: Kingston Demarco European Cultural Foundn, 1993–; Green Cross (UK), 1999–. Contributing Editor, Studio International, 1982–. SSA 1964; RWSScot 1966. Mem., AICA, 1992; FRSA 1998. Hon. FRIAS 1991. Hon. DFA Atlanta Coll. of Art, 1993. Gold Order of Merit, Polish People's Republic, 1976; Order of the Cavaliere della Repùbblica d'Italia, 1987; Chevalier de l'Ordre des Arts et des Lettres, France, 1991. *Publications:* The Artist as Explorer, 1978; The Road to Meikle Seggie, 1978; A Life in Pictures, 1994. *Recreations:* exploring: the small and secret spaces in townscape; cathedrals, abbeys, parish churches; coastlines and islands and The Road to Meikle Seggie. *Address:* Kingston University, River House, 51–52 High Street, Kingston-upon-Thames, Surrey KT1 1LQ; 23A Lennox Street, Edinburgh EH4 1PY. *T:* (0131) 343 2124, *Fax:* (0131) 343 3124. *Club:* Scottish Arts (Hon. Mem.) (Edinburgh).

de MARÉ, Eric, RDI 1997; RIBA; writer and photographer; *b* 10 Sept. 1910; *s* of Bror and Ingrid de Maré; *m* 1st, 1936, Vanessa Burrage (*d* 1972); 2nd, 1974, Enid Verity. *Educ:* St Paul's Sch., London; Architectural Assoc., London (Dip.). RIBA 1934. Asst in several arch. practices, 1933–36; in private practice, 1936–40. War Service, survived, with spell in Home Guard designing frondy camouflage. Editor, Architects' Jl, 1942–46; freelance writer and photographer, mostly on architectural, topographical and photographic subjects, 1946–. Has travelled extensively in British Isles, Europe and USA in search of freelance fodder; much lecturing. Hon. Treasurer, Social Credit Party, 1938–46. Hon. Mem., Glos Architectural Assoc., 1986. Photography exhibitions: Architectural Assoc., 1990; Glasgow Sch. of Architecture, 1991. *Publications:* Britain Rebuilt, 1942; The Canals of England, 1950, 2nd edn 1952, repr. 1987; Scandinavia, 1952; Time on the Thames, 1952; The Bridges of Britain, 1954, 3rd edn 1989; Gunnar Asplund, 1955; Penguin Photography, 1957, 7th edn 1980; London's Riverside: past, present and future, 1958; (with Sir James Richards) The Functional Tradition in Early Industrial Buildings, 1958; Photography and Architecture, 1961; Swedish Cross Cut: the story of the Göta Canal, 1964; London's River: the story of a city, 1964, 2nd edn 1975 (Runner-up for 1964 Carnegie Award); The City of Westminster: heart of London, 1968; London 1851: the year of the Great Exhibition, 1972; The Nautical Style, 1973; The London Doré Saw: a Victorian evocation, 1973, repr. as Victorian London Observed, 2001; Wren's London, 1975; Architectural Photography, 1975; The Victorian Wood Block Illustrators, 1980 (Yorkshire Post Award for best book on art, 1980); A Matter of Life or Debt, 1983, 4th edn 1986; contrib. Arch. Rev., TLS, Illustrated London News, etc; *relevant publication:* Eric de Maré, Builder with Light, 1990 (Architectural Association monograph of selected photographs, with text by Andrew Higgott and bibliography). *Recreations:* talking to friends, reading history, philosophizing, looking at trees, preaching Douglas Social Credit and the Age of Leisure. *Address:* Dynevor House, New Street, Painswick, Glos GL6 6UN. *T:* (01452) 812543.

de MAULEY, 6th Baron *cr* 1838; **Gerald John Ponsonby;** *b* 19 Dec. 1921; *er s* of 5th Baron de Mauley and Elgiva Margaret (*d* 1987), *d* of late Hon. Cospatrick Dundas and Lady Cordeaux; *S* father, 1962; *m* 1954, Helen Alice, *d* of late Hon. Charles W. S. Douglas and *widow* of Lieut-Col B. L. L. Abdy Collins, OBE, MC, RE. *Educ:* Eton; Christ Church, Oxford (MA). Served War of 1939–45, France; Lieut Leics Yeo., Captain RA. Called to Bar, Middle Temple, 1949. *Heir:* *b* Col Hon. Thomas Maurice Ponsonby, TD, late Royal Glos Hussars [*b* 2 Aug. 1930; *m* 1956, Maxine Henrietta, *d* of W. D. K. Thellusson; two *s*]. *Address:* Langford House, Little Faringdon, Lechlade, Glos GL7 3QN.

DEMERITTE, Richard Clifford; Managing Partner, MGI Richard C. Demeritte & Co., Chartered Accountants, since 1997; Auditor-General, Commonwealth of the Bahamas, 1980–84 and 1988–96; *b* 27 Feb. 1939; *s* of R. H. Demeritte and late Miriam Demeritte (*née* Whitfield); *m* 1966, Ruth Smith; one *s* two *d*. *Educ:* Bahamas Sch. of Commerce; Metropolitan Coll., London; Century Univ., USA. Treasury Department, Bahamas: Asst Accountant, 1967; Accountant, 1969–71; Asst Treasurer, Jan.–Dec. 1972; Dep. Treasurer, 1973–79; High Comr, London, 1984–88; Amb. to EEC, 1986–88, and to Belgium, France, FRG, 1987–88. Exec. Partner, Caribo Partners, 1996–. Mem., Midsnell Gp Internat. (Mem. Nominating Cttee, N America, 1999–); Pres., Universal Financial and Business Consultants, 1996–. Fellow: Inst. of Admin. Accountants, London, 1969; Corp. of Accountants and Auditors, Bahamas, 1971 (Pres., 1973–84; Hon. Fellow, 1983); Assoc. of Internat. Accountants, 1976 (Pres./Chm. Council, 1985–); FCGA 1996 (Certified Gen. Accountant, 1982); Mem., Bahamas Inst. of Chartered Accountants, 1991; Certified Fraud Examr, 2001. President: Certified Gen. Accts Assoc., Bahamas, 1996–; Certified Gen. Accts Assoc., Caribbean, 1996–; Mem., Nat. Assoc. of Fraud Investigators. FIMgt (FBIM 1985); FRSA 1988. Hon. Life Pres.: YMCA (Grand Bahama); Toastmasters Internat. (Grand Bahama). *Recreations:* chess, golf, billiards, weightlifting. *Address:* (office) PO Box CB 11001, Nassau, Bahamas; (home) Rurick, Cable Beach, PO Box CB 11001, Nassau, Bahamas; *e-mail:* demeritte@bahamas.net.bs.

DEMEURE de LESPAUL, Edouard Henri; Officer, Order of Leopold II; General Manager, Marketing, Petrofina SA, 1993; *b* 6 Jan. 1928; *s* of Charles Demeure de Lespaul and Adrienne Demeure de Lespaul (*née* Escoyez); *m* 1953, Myriam van Cutsem; two *d*. *Educ:* Univ. of Louvain (Mining Engineering); ENSP 1952 (Petroleum Engineering). Petrofina: Exploration and Production Dept, Brussels, 1952–53; Manager, Drilling Activities, Congo, 1955–56; Man. Dir, Egypt, 1956–61; Manager, Exploration and Production, Brussels, 1961–63; Chm. and Man. Dir, Finaneste NV, Belgium, 1963–89; Man. Dir and Chief Exec., Petrofina UK, later Fina plc, 1989–92. Military Medal, war voluntary. *Recreations:* swimming, history reading, mountain walking. *Address:* Petrofina SA, Rue de l'Industrie 52, 1040 Brussels, Belgium.

DEMIDENKO, Nikolai Anatolyevich; concert pianist; *b* 1 July 1955; *s* of Anatoli Antonovich Demidenko and Olga Mikhailovna Demidenko; *m* 1994, Julia B. Dovgiallo; one *s* by a previous marriage. *Educ:* Gnessin Music Sch., Moscow; Moscow State Conservatoire. Professional début, 1975; Teacher: Moscow State Conservatoire, 1979–84; Yehudi Menuhin Sch. of Music, 1990–95. 2nd prize, Montreal Piano Competition, 1976; 3rd prize, Moscow Tchaikovsky Competition, 1978. Has made numerous recordings. Gramophone Award, 1992; Classic CD Award, 1995. *Recreations:* photography, computing. *Address:* Georgina Ivor Associates, 28 Old Devonshire Road, SW12 9RB.

de MILLE, Peter Noël; His Honour Judge de Mille; a Circuit Judge, Midland and Oxford Circuit, since 1992; *b* 11 Nov. 1944; *s* of late Noël James de Mille and of Ailsa Christine (*née* Ogilvie); *m* 1977, Angela Mary Cooper; one *d*. *Educ:* Fettes Coll.; Trinity Coll., Dublin (BA, LLB). Called to the Bar, Inner Temple, 1968; a Recorder, 1987–92. *Recreations:* sailing, music, theatre. *Address:* Judges Chambers, Crown and County Court, Crown Buildings, Rivergate, Peterborough PE1 1EJ. *Club:* Aldeburgh Yacht.

DE MOLEYNS; *see* Daubeny de Moleyns, family name of Baron Ventry.

de MOLLER, June Frances; Managing Director, Carlton Communications plc, 1993–99; *b* 25 June 1947; *m* 1st, 1967 (marr. diss. 1980); 2nd, 1996, John Robert Giles Crisp. *Educ:* Roedean; Hastings Coll.; Sorbonne Univ., Paris. Exec. Dir, Carlton Communications, 1983–99. Non-executive Director: Anglian Water plc, 1992–2000; Riverside Mental Health NHS Trust, 1992–96; Lynx Gp plc, 1999–; Cookson Gp plc, 1999–; British Telecommunications plc, 1999–; J. Sainsbury plc, 1999–; Eastern Counties Newspapers Gp Ltd, 1999–. Mem., Listed Cos Adv. Cttee, Stock Exchange, 1998–99. Mem., Adv. Bd, Judge Inst. for Management Studies, Cambridge, 1996–. Mem. Council, Aldeburgh

Productions, 2000–. Mem. Cttee, Home of Rest for Horses, 1999–. *Recreations:* reading, riding, tennis, Rare Breed Society.

de MONTEBELLO, (Guy) Philippe (Lannes); Director, since 1978, and Chief Executive Officer, Metropolitan Museum of Art; *b* 16 May 1936; *s* of Roger Lannes de Montebello and Germaine (*née* Croisset); *m* 1961, Edith Bradford Myles; two *s* one *d*. *Educ:* Harvard Coll. (BA *magna cum laude*); New York Univ., Inst. of Fine Arts (MA). Curatorial Asst, European Paintings, Metropolitan Mus. of Art, 1963; Asst Curator, Associate Curator, MMA, until 1969; Director, Museum of Fine Arts, Houston, Texas, 1969–74; Vice-Director: for Curatorial Affairs, MMA, Jan. 1974–June 1974; for Curatorial and Educnl Affairs, 1974–77; Actg Dir, MMA, 1977–78. Gallatin Fellow, New York Univ., 1981; Hon. LLD: Lafayette Coll., East Pa, 1979; Bard Coll., Annandale-on-Hudson, NY, 1981; Hon. DFA Iona Coll., New Rochelle, NY, 1982. Alumni Achievement Award, New York Univ., 1978. *Publication:* Peter Paul Rubens, 1968. *Address:* 1150 Fifth Avenue, New York, New York 10028, USA. *T:* (212) 2894475. *Club:* Knickerbocker (New York).

de MONTMORENCY, Sir Arnold (Geoffroy), 19th Bt *cr* 1631; President, Contemporary Review Co. Ltd, since 1995 (Literary Editor 1960–90; Chairman, 1962–95); *b* 27 July 1908; *s* of Prof. James Edward Geoffrey de Montmorency (*d* 1934) and Caroline Maud Saumarez (*d* 1973), *d* of Maj.-Gen. James de Havilland; *S* cousin, 1979; *m* 1949, Nettie Hay Anderson (marr. annulled 1953, remarried 1972), *d* of late William Anderson and Janet Hay, Morayshire; no *c*. *Educ:* Westminster School (Triplett Exhibn); Peterhouse, Cambridge. BA 1930, LLM 1931, MA 1934. Harmsworth Law Scholar. Called to the Bar, 1932. Served War, RASC and staff in ME, Italy and Yugoslavia, 1940–45. Contested (L) Cambridge, 1959, Cirencester and Tewkesbury, 1964. Chm. (pt-time), Industrial Tribunals, 1975–81. Member, RIIA; Pres., Friends of Peterhouse. *Publication:* Integration of Employment Legislation, 1984. *Heir:* none. *Club:* National Liberal.

DEMPSEY, Andrew; *see* Dempsey, J. A.

DEMPSEY, Dr Anthony Michael; Headmaster, Tiffin School, since 1988; *b* 12 June 1944; *s* of Michael and Bertha Laura Dempsey; *m* 1970, Sandra Lynn Atkins; one *s*. *Educ:* Tiffin Sch.; Bristol Univ. (BSc, PhD). Chemistry Teacher, King's College Sch., 1969–73; Heathland School, Hounslow: Head of Sci., 1973–75; Head, Maths and Sci. Faculty, 1975–79; Feltham Community School: Dep. Head, 1979–82; Sen. Dep. Head, 1982–88. *Publications:* Visual Chemistry, 1983; Science Master Pack, 1985; contrib. to Nuffield Chemistry books; papers in carbohydrate res. *Recreations:* walking, travel, sport, church, industrial archaeology. *Address:* Tiffin School, Queen Elizabeth Road, Kingston, Surrey KT2 6RL. *T:* (020) 8546 4638; 63 Gilpin Crescent, Twickenham TW2 7BP. *T:* (020) 8898 2860.

DEMPSEY, (James) Andrew; independent exhibition curator and organiser, since 1996; *b* 17 Nov. 1942; *s* of James Dempsey, Glasgow; *m* 1966, Grace (marr. diss. 1998), *d* of Dr Ian MacPhail, Dumbarton; one *s* one *d*. *Educ:* Ampleforth Coll.; Glasgow Univ. Whistler Research Asst, Fine Art Dept, Univ. of Glasgow, 1963–65; exhibn work for art dept of Arts Council, 1966–71; Keeper, Dept of Public Relations, V&A, 1971–75; Asst Dir of Exhibitions, Arts Council of GB, 1975–87; Asst Dir, 1987–94, Associate Curator, 1994–96, Hayward Gall., S Bank Centre. *Address:* 92 Lenthall Road, E8 3JN. *T:* and *Fax:* (020) 7241 2065.

DEMPSEY, Michael Bernard, RDI 1994; FCSD; Chairman and Creative Director, CDT Design Ltd, since 1993; *b* 25 July 1944; *s* of John Patrick Dempsey and Britannia May (*née* Thompson); *m* 1st, 1967, Sonja Green (marr. diss. 1988); two *s* one *d*; 2nd, 1989, Charlotte Antonia Richardson; three *d*. *Educ:* St Vincent RC Primary Sch., Dagenham; Bishop Ward RC Secondary Mod. Sch., Dagenham. Asst designer, Cheveron Studio, 1963–64; in-house designer, Bryan Colmer Artist Agent, 1964–65; freelance designer, 1965–66; Designer, Cato Peters O'Brien, 1966–68; Art Director: William Heinemann Publishers, 1968–74; William Collins Publishers, 1974–79; Founder Partner, Carroll & Dempsey Ltd, 1979–85; Partner, Carroll, Dempsey Thirkell Ltd, later CDT Design Ltd, 1985–. Consultant Art Dir to Royal Mail for 1999 Millennium stamps, 1997–99, designer, Mind and Matter stamps, 2000; identity and communications consultant, DCMS, 1997–99; Art Dir and Mem., Editl Bd, RSA Jl, 1997–. Pres., British Design and Art Dirs Assoc., 1997–98. Mem., Alliance Graphique Internationale, 1998–2000. *Publications:* Bubbles: early advertising art from A. & F. Pears, 1978; The Magical Paintings of Justin Todd, 1978; Pipe Dreams: early advertising art from the Imperial Tobacco Company, 1982. *Recreations:* art history, photography, film, painting, architecture, theatre, opera. *Address:* Osmington House, West Wing, Osmington, Dorset DT3 6ES. *T:* (01305) 832520.

DEMPSTER, John William Scott, CB 1994; Director, United Kingdom Major Ports Group Ltd, since 1999; *b* 10 May 1938; *m* 1965, Ailsa Newman (marr. diss. 1972). *Educ:* Plymouth Coll.; Oriel Coll., Oxford (MA(PPE)). HM Inspector of Taxes, Inland Revenue, 1961–65; Ministry of Transport: Asst Principal, 1965–67; Principal, 1967–73; Asst Sec., Property Services Agency, 1973–76; Principal Private Sec. to Sec. of State for the Environment, 1976–77; Asst Sec., Dept of Transport, 1977–80; Principal Estabt and Finance Officer, Lord Chancellor's Dept, 1980–84; Department of Transport: Head of Marine Directorate, 1984–89; Principal Establishment Officer, 1989–90; Principal Establishment and Finance Officer, 1990–91; Dir Gen. of Highways, 1991–94; Dep. Sec., Aviation and Shipping, 1994–96; Dir, Bahamas Maritime Authy, 1996–99. *Recreations:* mountaineering, sailing, bridge, Munro collecting. *Address:* 16 Hill View, Primrose Hill Road, NW3 3AX. *T:* (020) 7722 1364. *Clubs:* Alpine, Fell and Rock; Royal Southampton Yacht.

DEMPSTER, Prof. Michael Alan Howarth, PhD; Professor of Management, Judge Institute of Management Studies, since 1996, Director of Research and Director, Centre for Financial Research, since 1997, University of Cambridge; *b* 10 April 1938; *s* of Cedric William Dempster and Honor Fitz Simmons Dempster (*née* Gowan); *m* 1st, 1963, Ann Laura Lazier (marr. diss. 1980); one *d*; 2nd, 1981, Elena Anatolievna Medova; one *d*. *Educ:* Univ. of Toronto (BA 1961); Carnegie-Mellon Univ. (MS 1963; PhD 1965); Oxford Univ. (MA 1967). IBM Res. Fellow, Math. Inst., Oxford, 1965–66; Jun. Res. Fellow, Nuffield Coll., Oxford, 1966; Fellow, Tutor and Univ. Lectr in Maths, 1967–81, Lectr in Maths, 1982–87, Balliol Coll., Oxford; R. A. Jodrey Res. Prof. of Mgt and Inf. Scis, Sch. of Business Admin, and Prof. of Maths, Stats and Computing Science, Dalhousie Univ., 1981–93; Prof. of Maths, 1990–95, and Dir, Inst. for Studies in Finance, 1993–95, Univ. of Essex. Fellow, Center for Advanced Study in Behavioral Scis, Stanford, 1974–75; Sen. Res. Scholar, Internat. Inst. for Applied Systems Analysis, Laxenberg, Austria, 1979–81; Vis. Prof., Univ. of Rome, La Sapienza, 1988–89. Chm., Oxford Systems Associates Ltd, 1974–79; Man. Dir, Cambridge Systems Associates Ltd, 1996–. Cons. to numerous cos and govts, 1965–. Mem., Res. Adv. Bd, Canadian Inst. for Advanced Res., 1986–. FIMA 1974. Hon. Ed., Quantitative Finance, 2000–. *Publications:* (jtly) Introduction to Optimization Methods, 1974; (ed) Stochastic Programming, 1980; (ed jtly) Analysis and Optimization of Stochastic Systems, 1980; (ed jtly) Large-Scale Linear Programming, 1981; (ed jtly) Deterministic and Stochastic Scheduling, 1982; (ed jtly) Mathematical Models in Economics, 1994; (ed jtly) Mathematics of Derivative Securities, 1997; *translations* from Russian: (jtly) Stochastic Models of Control and Economic Dynamics, 1987; (jtly) Sequential Control and Incomplete Information, 1990. *Recreations:* reading, gardening, tennis, sailing, ski-ing. *Address:* 1 Earl Street, Cambridge CB1 1JR; Judge Institute of Management, University of Cambridge, Trumpington Street, Cambridge CB2 1AG.

DEMPSTER, Nigel Richard Patton; Editorial Executive, Mail Newspapers Plc (formerly Associated Newspapers), since 1973; Editor: Mail Diary, since 1973; Mail on Sunday Diary, since 1986; *b* 1 Nov. 1941; *s* of Eric R. P. Dempster and Angela Grace Dempster (*née* Stephens); *m* 1st, 1971, Emma de Bendern (marr. diss. 1974), *d* of Count John de Bendern and late Lady Patricia Douglas, *d* of 11th Marquess of Queensberry; 2nd, 1977, Lady Camilla Godolphin Osborne, *o c* of 11th Duke of Leeds and Audrey (who *m* 1955, Sir David Lawrence, Bt, *qv*); one *d*. *Educ:* Sherborne. Broker, Lloyd's of London, 1958–59; Stock Exchange, 1959–60; PR account exec., Earl of Kimberley Associates, 1960–63; journalist, Daily Express, 1963–71; columnist, Daily Mail, 1971–. London correspondent, Status magazine, USA, 1965–66; contributor to Queen magazine, 1966–70; columnist ('Grovel'), Private Eye magazine, 1969–85. Broadcaster with ABC (USA) and CBC (Canada), 1976–, and with TV-am, 1983–92; resident panellist, Headliners, Thames TV, 1987–89. *Publications:* HRH The Princess Margaret—A Life Unfulfilled (biog.), 1981; Heiress: the story of Christina Onassis, 1989; Nigel Dempster's Address Book, 1990; (with Peter Evans) Behind Palace Doors, 1993; Dempster's People, 1998. *Recreations:* photography, squash, running marathons, bicycling. *Address:* c/o Daily Mail, Northcliffe House, Derry Street, W8 5TT. *Clubs:* Royal Automobile; Chappaquiddick Beach (Mass, USA).

DENARO, Maj.-Gen. Arthur George, CBE 1996 (OBE 1991); General Officer Commanding 5th Division, since 2000; Extra Equerry to the Prince of Wales, since 2000; *b* 23 March 1948; *s* of late Brig. George Tancred Denaro, CBE, DSO and of Francesca Violet Denaro (*née* Garnett); *m* 1980, Margaret Roney Acworth, *widow* of Major Michael Kealy, DSO; one *s* one *d*, and one step *s* two step *d*. *Educ:* Downside Sch.; RMA Sandhurst. Commissioned Queen's Royal Irish Hussars, 1968; Staff Coll., 1979–80; CO QRIH, 1989–91; Comdr 33 (later 20) Armd Bde, 1992–94; RCDS 1994; COS HQ UNPROFOR, former Yugoslavia, 1994–95; COS HQ British Forces, Cyprus, 1995–96; Chief, Combat Support, HQ ARRC, 1996–97; Comdt, RMA Sandhurst, 1997–2000. Chm., Prince's Trust Volunteers, 2000–. Pres., Army Rugby Union. *Recreations:* hunting, shooting, polo, ski-ing. *Club:* Cavalry and Guards.

de NAVARRO, Michael Antony; QC 1990; a Recorder, since 1990; *b* 1 May 1944; *s* of A. J. M. (Toty) de Navarro and Dorothy M. de Navarro; *m* 1975, Jill Margaret Walker; one *s* two *d*. *Educ:* Downside School; Trinity College, Cambridge (BA Hons). Called to the Bar, Inner Temple, 1968, Bencher, 2000; pupil of Hon. Mr Justice Cazalet and Hon. Mr Justice Turner; Mem., Western Circuit. Chm., Personal Injuries Bar Assoc., 1997–99. *Recreations:* opera, cricket, gardening, cooking. *Address:* 2 Temple Gardens, Temple, EC4Y 9AY. *T:* (020) 7822 1200.

DENBIGH, 12th Earl of, *cr* 1622, **AND DESMOND,** 11th Earl of, *cr* 1622; **Alexander Stephen Rudolph Feilding;** Baron Feilding 1620; Viscount Feilding 1620; Viscount Callan 1622; Baron St Liz 1663; *b* 4 Nov. 1970; *o s* of 11th Earl of Denbigh and of Caroline Judith Vivienne, *o d* of Lt-Col Geoffrey Cooke; *S* father, 1995; *m* 1996, Suzanne Jane, *d* of Gregory R. Allen. *Heir: cousin* William David Feilding [*b* 12 Aug. 1939; *m* 1980, Lydia Sarah Harding]. *Address:* Newnham Paddox, Monks Kirby, Rugby CV23 0RX; 34 Keildon Road, Battersea, SW11 1XH.

DENBIGH, Prof. Kenneth George, FRS 1965; MA Cantab, DSc Leeds; Principal of Queen Elizabeth College, University of London, 1966–77; Professor Emeritus in the University of London, 1977; Visiting Research Fellow, King's College, London, since 1985; *b* 30 May 1911; *s* of late G. J. Denbigh, MSc, Harrogate; *m* 1935, Kathleen Enoch; two *s*. *Educ:* Queen Elizabeth Grammar Sch., Wakefield; Leeds University. Imperial Chemical Industries, 1934–38, 1945–48; Lecturer, Southampton Univ., 1938–41; Ministry of Supply (Explosives), 1941–45; Lecturer, Cambridge Univ., Chemical Engineering Dept, 1948–55; Professor: of Chemical Technology, Edinburgh, 1955–60, of Chemical Engineering Science, London Univ., 1960–61; Courtauld's Prof., Imperial Coll., 1961–66. Dir, Council for Science and Society, 1977–83. Fellow, Imperial Coll., 1976; FKC, 1985. Hon. DèsSc Toulouse, 1960; Hon. DUniv. Essex, 1967. *Publications:* The Thermodynamics of the Steady State, 1951; The Principles of Chemical Equilibrium, 1955; Science, Industry and Social Policy, 1963; Chemical Reactor Theory, 1965; An Inventive Universe, 1975; Three Concepts of Time, 1981; (with J. S. Denbigh) Entropy in Relation to Incomplete Knowledge, 1985; various scientific papers. *Address:* 19 Sheridan Road, Merton Park, SW19 3HW.

DENCH, Dame Judith Olivia, (Dame Judi Dench), DBE 1988 (OBE 1970); actress (theatre, films and television); *b* 9 Dec. 1934; *d* of Reginald Arthur Dench and Eleanora Olave Dench (*née* Jones); *m* 1971, Michael Leonard Williams, actor (*d* 2001); one *d*. *Educ:* The Mount Sch., York; Central Sch. of Speech and Drama. *Theatre:* Old Vic seasons, 1957–61: parts incl.: Ophelia in Hamlet; Katherine in Henry V; Cecily in The Importance of Being Earnest; Juliet in Romeo and Juliet; also 1957–61: two Edinburgh Festivals; Paris-Belgium-Yugoslavia tour; America-Canada tour; Venice (all with Old Vic Co.). Subseq. appearances incl.: Royal Shakespeare Co., 1961–62: Anya in The Cherry Orchard; Titania in A Midsummer Night's Dream; Dorcas Bellboys in A Penny for a Song; Isabella in Measure for Measure; Nottingham Playhouse tour of W Africa, 1963; Oxford Playhouse, 1964–65: Irina in The Three Sisters; Doll Common in The Alchemist; Nottingham Playhouse, 1965: Saint Joan; The Astrakhan Coat (world première); Amanda in Private Lives; Variety London Critics' Best Actress of the Year Award for perf. as Lika in The Promise, Fortune, 1967; Sally Bowles in Cabaret, Palace, 1968; Associate Mem., RSC, 1969–; London Assurance, Aldwych, 1970, and New, 1972; Major Barbara, Aldwych, 1970; Bianca in Women Beware Women, Viola in Twelfth Night, doubling Hermione and Perdita in The Winter's Tale, Portia in The Merchant of Venice, the Duchess in The Duchess of Malfi, Beatrice in Much Ado About Nothing, Lady Macbeth in Macbeth, Adriana in The Comedy of Errors, Regan in King Lear, Imogen in Cymbeline; The Wolf, Oxford and London, 1973; The Good Companions, Her Majesty's, 1974; The Gay Lord Quex, Albery, 1975; Too True to be Good, Aldwych, 1975, Globe, 1976; Pillars of the Community, The Comedy of Errors, Aldwych, 1977; The Way of the World, 1978; Juno and the Paycock, Aldwych, 1980 (Best Actress award, SWET, Evening Standard, Variety Club, and Plays and Players); The Importance of Being Earnest, A Kind of Alaska, Nat. Theatre, 1982; Pack of Lies, Lyric, 1983 (SWET award); Mother Courage, Barbican, 1984; Waste, Barbican and Lyric, 1985; Mr and Mrs Nobody, Garrick, 1986; Antony and Cleopatra (Best Actress award, SWET, Evening Standard), Entertaining Strangers, Nat. Theatre, 1987; Hamlet, Royal Nat. Theatre, and Dubrovnik Theatre Fest., 1989; The Cherry Orchard, Aldwych, 1989; The Plough and the Stars, Young Vic, 1991; The Sea,

Nat. Theatre, 1991; Coriolanus, Chichester, 1992; The Gift of the Gorgon, Barbican, 1992, transf. Wyndham's, 1993; The Seagull, RNT, 1994; Absolute Hell, RNT, 1995 (Best Actress, Olivier award, 1996); A Little Night Music, RNT, 1995 (Best Actress in a Musical, Olivier award, 1996); Amy's View, RNT, 1997, transf. Aldwych (Critics' Circle Drama Award), 1998, NY (Tony Award), 1999; Filumena, Piccadilly, 1998; The Royal Family, Theatre Royal, Haymarket, 2001; Director, for Renaissance Theatre Co.: Much Ado About Nothing, 1988; Look Back in Anger, 1989; Director: The Boys from Syracuse, Regent's Park, 1991; Romeo and Juliet, Regent's Park, 1993. Recital tour of W Africa, 1969; RSC tours: Japan and Australia, 1970; Japan, 1972. *Films:* He Who Rides a Tiger; A Study in Terror; Four in the Morning (Brit. Film Acad. Award for Most Promising Newcomer, 1965); A Midsummer Night's Dream, 1968; The Third Secret; Dead Cert; Saigon: Year of the Cat; Wetherby, 1984; A Room with a View, 1985 (Best Supporting Actress, BAFTA award, 1987); 84 Charing Cross Road, 1986; A Handful of Dust (Best Supporting Actress, BAFTA award), 1988; Henry V, 1990; Goldeneye, 1995; Mrs Brown, 1997 (Best Actress awards: BAFTA Scotland, 1997; Golden Globe, London Film Critics, BAFTA, and Screen Actors' Guild, NY, 1998); Tomorrow Never Dies, 1997; Shakespeare in Love (Oscar and BAFTA Award for Best Supporting Actress), Tea with Mussolini, The World is Not Enough, 1999; Chocolat, 2001. *Television* appearances include, 1957–: Talking to a Stranger (Best Actress of Year award, Guild of Television Dirs, 1967); Major Barbara; Hilda Lessways; Langrishe, Go Down; Macbeth; Comedy of Errors; On Giant's Shoulders; A Village Wooing; Love in a Cold Climate; Saigon; A Fine Romance (BAFTA Award, 1985); The Cherry Orchard; Going Gently; Mr and Mrs Edgehill (Best Actress, Amer. Cable Award, 1988); The Browning Version; Make or Break; Ghosts; Behaving Badly; Absolute Hell; Can You Hear Me Thinking?; As Time Goes By (8 series); Last of the Blonde Bombshells, 2000 (Best Actress, BAFTA TV Award, 2001). Mem. Bd, Royal Nat. Theatre, 1988–. Awards incl. British and foreign, for theatre, films and TV, incl. BAFTA award for best television actress, 1981, Rothermere Award for Lifetime Achievement, 1997, and Critics' Circle Award for Outstanding Achievement, 1998. Hon. DLitt: Warwick, 1978; Birmingham, 1989; Loughborough, 1991; London, 1994; Oxford, 2000; DUniv: York, 1983; Open, 1992; RSAMD, 1995; Surrey, 1996. *Recreations:* sewing, drawing, catching up with letters.

DENEUVE, Catherine; French film actress; *b* 22 Oct. 1943; *d* of Maurice Dorléac and Renée (*née* Deneuve); one *s* by Roger Vadim (*d* 2000); *m* 1967, David Bailey, *qv* (marr. diss.); one *d* by Marcello Mastroianni (*d* 1996). *Educ:* Lycée La Fontaine, Paris. Pres.-Dir Gen., Films de la Citrouille, 1971–79. Chm. Jury, Cannes Film Fest., 1994. *Films include:* Les petits chats, 1959; Les portes claquent, 1960; Le vice et la vertu, 1962; Les parapluies de Cherbourg, 1963; La Constanza della Ragione, 1964; Repulsion, 1964; Liebes Karusell, 1965; Belle de jour, 1967; Folies d'avril, 1969; Un flic, 1972; Le sauvage, 1975; Âmes perdues, 1976; Hustle, 1976; A nous deux, 1978; Le dernier métro, 1980 (César for best actress, 1981); Le choc, 1982; The Hunger, 1982; Le bon plaisir, 1984; Let's Hope It's A Girl, 1987; Drôle d'Endroit pour une Rencontre (Strange Place to Meet), 1989; Indochine, 1992; Ma Saison préférée, 1994; The Convent, 1995; Les voleurs, 1996; Genealogie d'un Crime, 1997; Place Vendôme, 1998; Pola X, 2000; Time Regained, 2000; Dancer in the Dark, 2000; East-West, 2000. *Address:* c/o Artmedia, 10 avenue George-V, 75008 Paris, France.

DENHAM, 2nd Baron *cr* 1937, of Weston Underwood; **Bertram Stanley Mitford Bowyer,** KBE 1991; PC 1981; Bt 1660, of Denham; Bt 1933, of Weston Underwood; Captain of the Gentlemen at Arms (Government Chief Whip in the House of Lords), 1979–91; an Extra Lord-in-Waiting to the Queen, since 1998; *b* 3 Oct. 1927; *s* of 1st Baron and Hon. Daphne Freeman-Mitford (*d* 1996), 4th *d* of 1st Baron Redesdale; *S* father, 1948; *m* 1956, Jean, *o d* of Kenneth McCorquodale, Fambridge Hall, White Notley, Essex; three *s* one *d*. *Educ:* Eton; King's Coll., Cambridge. Mem. Westminster CC, 1959–61. A Lord-in-Waiting to the Queen, 1961–64 and 1970–71; Opposition Jun. Whip, 1964–70; Captain of the Yeomen of the Guard, 1971–74; Opposition Dep. Chief Whip, 1974–78; Opposition Chief Whip, 1978–79; elected Mem., H of L, 1999–. Countryside Comr, 1993–99. Dep. Pres., British Field Sports Soc., 1992–98. *Publications:* The Man who Lost his Shadow, 1979; Two Thyrdes, 1983; Foxhunt, 1988; Black Rod, 1997. *Recreations:* field sports. *Heir: s* Hon. Richard Grenville George Bowyer [*b* 8 Feb. 1959; *m* 1st, 1988, Eleanor (marr. diss. 1993), *o d* of A. Sharpe; 2nd, 1996, Dagmar, *o d* of Karel and Jaroslava Božek, Břeslaw, Czech Republic]. *Address:* The Laundry Cottage, Weston Underwood, Olney, Bucks MK46 5JZ. *T:* (020) 7219 6056. *Clubs:* White's, Pratt's, Garrick.

DENHAM, Ernest William; Deputy Keeper of Public Records, Public Record Office, 1978–82; *b* 16 Sept. 1922; *s* of William and Beatrice Denham; *m* 1957, Penelope Agatha Gregory; one *s* one *d*. *Educ:* City of London Sch.; Merton Coll., Oxford (Postmaster). MA 1948. Naval Intell., UK and SEAC, 1942–45. Asst Sec., Plant Protection Ltd, 1947–49; Asst Keeper 1949, Principal Asst Keeper 1967, Records Admin. Officer 1973, Public Record Office; Lectr in Palaeography and Diplomatic, UCL, 1957–73. *Recreation:* armchair criticism. *Address:* 4 The Ridge, 89 Green Lane, Northwood, Mddx HA6 1AE. *T:* (01923) 827382.

DENHAM, Rt Hon. John (Yorke); PC 2000; MP (Lab) Southampton, Itchen, since 1992; Minister of State, Home Office, since 2001; *b* 15 July 1953; *s* of Albert Edward Denham and Beryl Frances Ada Denham; *m* 1979, Ruth Eleanore Dixon (separated); one *s* one *d*. *Educ:* Woodroffe Comprehensive Sch., Lyme Regis; Univ. of Southampton (BSc Hons Chemistry; Pres., Students' Union, 1976–77). Advr, Energy Advice Service, Durham, 1977; Transport Campaigner, Friends of the Earth, 1977–79; Head, Youth Affairs, British Youth Council, 1979–82; Publications Sec., Clause IV Publications, 1982–84; Campaigns Officer, War on Want, 1984–88; Consultant to develt NGOs, 1988–92. Member (Lab): Hants CC, 1981–89; Southampton CC, 1989–93 (Chm., Housing Cttee, 1990–92). Contested (Lab) Southampton, Itchen, 1983, 1987. Parly Under-Sec. of State, DSS, 1997–98; Minister of State: DSS, 1998; Dept of Health, 1998–2001. *Address:* House of Commons, SW1A 0AA.

DENHAM, Maurice, OBE 1992; actor since 1934; *b* 23 Dec. 1909; *s* of Norman Denham and Winifred Lillico; *m* 1936, Margaret Dunn (*d* 1971); two *s* one *d*. *Educ:* Tonbridge Sch. Hull Repertory Theatre, 1934–36; theatre, radio and television, 1936–39. Served War of 1939–45: Buffs, 1939–43; Royal Artillery, 1943–45; despatches, 1946. Theatre, films, radio and television, 1946–. *Radio includes:* ITMA, 1939–40; Much Binding in the Marsh, 1946; Winston, 6 series, 1986–93; Tale of Two Cities, 1988; The Sitter, 1990; Forsyte Chronicles, 1990; Six P. G. Wodehouse stories, 1995; The Oldest Member, 1998. *Theatre includes:* The Andersonville Trial, Mermaid, 1960; Macbeth, King John, Old Vic, 1961; The Apple Cart, Mermaid, 1970; Uncle Vanya, Hampstead, 1979; Incident at Tulse Hill, Hampstead, 1981. *Films include:* The Purple Plain, 1954; Doctor at Sea, 1955; Day of the Jackal, 1972; 84 Charing Cross Road, 1986. *Television includes:* Talking to a Stranger, 1968; All Passion Spent, 1986; Klaus Barbie, 1987; Behaving Badly, 1988; Inspector Morse, 1991; La Nonna, 1991; You Rang M'Lord, 1992; Lovejoy, 1992; Memento Mori, 1992; Sherlock Holmes, 1992; Peak Practice, 1993; Bed, 1994; Pie in the Sky, The Last Journey of Robert Rylands, 1995; Casualty, The Beggar Bride, 1997. *Recreations:* conducting gramophone records, golf. *Clubs:* Garrick, Green Room; Stage Golfing.

DENHAM, Pamela Anne, CB 1997; DL; PhD; management consultant, since 1998; Regional Director, Government Office for the North East, 1994–98; *b* 1 May 1943; *d* of late Matthew Gray Dobson and Jane (*née* Carter); *m* 1965, Paul Denham (marr. diss. 1980); partner, Brian Murray (*d* 1993). *Educ:* Central Newcastle High Sch.; King's Coll., Univ. of London (BSc 1964; PhD 1969). Asst Principal, Ministry of Technol., 1967–72; Department of Trade and Industry: Principal, 1972–79; Asst Sec., 1979–85; Under Sec., 1985–89; Under Sec., Cabinet Office (Office of Minister for CS), 1989–90; Regl Dir, DTI NE, 1990–94. Non-exec. Dir, Mono Pumps and Saunders Valve, 1982–85. Member: Governing Body, Sunderland Univ., 1993, 1998–; Local Governing Body, Central Newcastle High Sch., 1992– (Vice-Chair); Trustee, Univ. of Sunderland Develt Trust, 1999–. Chair: Project North East, 1998–; Women's Fund Panel, Community Foundn serving Tyne & Wear and Northumberland, 1999–. Trustee, Age Concern, Newcastle, 2000–. FRSA. DL Tyne and Wear, 2000. Hon. LLD Sunderland, 1994. *Publications:* papers in scientific jls. *Recreations:* travel, reading, cooking. *Address:* 43 Lindisfarne Close, Jesmond, Newcastle upon Tyne NE2 2HT. *T:* (0191) 212 0390.

DENHAM, Lt-Col Seymour Vivian G.; *see* Gilbart-Denham.

DENHAM, Susan Gageby; Hon. Mrs Justice Gageby Denham; Judge, Supreme Court of Ireland, since 1992; *b* 22 Aug. 1945; *d* of Douglas Gageby and Dorothy Mary Gageby (*née* Lester); *m* 1970, Brian Denham; three *s* one *d* (and one *s* decd). *Educ:* Trinity Coll. Dublin (BA (Mod.), LLB); Columbia Univ., NY (LLM). Called to the Irish Bar, 1971; in practice on Midland Circuit, 1971–87; SC, called to Inner Bar, 1987; Judge of High Court, 1991–92. Chair: Working Gp on Courts Commn, 1995–98; Cttee on Court Practice and Procedure, 2000–; Mem., Courts Service Bd, 1999–. Hon. Sec., Cttee on Judicial Conduct and Ethics, 1999–. Pro-Chancellor, Dublin Univ., 1996–. *Recreations:* gardens, horses, reading. *Address:* The Supreme Court, Four Courts, Dublin, Ireland. *T:* (1) 8886533.

DENHOLM, Allan; *see* Denholm, J. A.

DENHOLM, Sir Ian; *see* Denholm, Sir J. F.

DENHOLM, (James) Allan, CBE 1992; Chairman, East Kilbride Development Corporation, 1983–94 (Member, 1979–94); Director, William Grant & Sons Ltd, 1975–96 (Secretary, 1966–96); President, Institute of Chartered Accountants of Scotland, 1992–93; *b* 27 Sept. 1936; *s* of James Denholm and Florence Lily Keith (*née* Kennedy); *m* 1964, Elizabeth Avril McLachlan, CA; one *s* one *d*. *Educ:* Hutchesons' Boys' Sch., Glasgow. CA. Apprentice with McFarlane Hutton & Patrick, 1954–60; Chief Accountant, A. & W. Smith & Co. Ltd, 1960–66. Councillor, Eastwood DC, 1962–64. Mem., Council, Inst. of Chartered Accountants, Scotland, 1978–83 (Sen. Vice-Pres., 1991–92). Chm., Glasgow Jun. Chamber of Commerce, 1972–73. Director: Scottish Cremation Soc. Ltd, 1980–; Scottish Mutual Assurance PLC, 1987– (Dep. Chm., 1992–); Abbey National PLC, 1992–97; Dep. Chm., Abbey National Life PLC, 1997–. Visitor, Incorporation of Maltmen, Glasgow, 1980–81. Trustee, Scottish Cot Death Trust, 1985–96; Dir, Assoc. for the Relief of Incurables in Glasgow and W of Scotland, 1999–. Mem., W of Scotland Adv. Bd, Salvation Army, 1996–. Elder, New Kilpatrick Parish Church, Bearsden, 1971–. Preses, Weavers' Soc., Anderston, 1994–95; Pres., Assoc. of Deacons of the Fourteen Incorporated Trades, Glasgow, 1994–95; Deacon Convener, The Trades House, Glasgow, 1998–99; Deacon, Soc. of Deacons and Free Preseses, Glasgow, 1999–2000. FSAScot 1987. FRSA 1992. *Recreations:* golf, shooting. *Address:* Greencroft, 19 Colquhoun Drive, Bearsden, Glasgow G61 4NQ. *T:* and *Fax:* (0141) 942 1773. *Club:* Western (Glasgow).

DENHOLM, Sir John Ferguson, (Sir Ian), Kt 1989; CBE 1974; JP; DL; Chairman, J. & J. Denholm Ltd, 1974–98; *b* 8 May 1927; *s* of Sir William Lang Denholm, TD; *m* 1952, Elizabeth Murray Stephen; two *s* two *d*. *Educ:* St Mary's Sch., Melrose; Loretto Sch., Musselburgh. Joined J. & J. Denholm Ltd, 1944. Chm., Murray Investment Trusts, 1985–93; Dep. Chm., P&O, 1980–85 (Dir, 1974–85); Director: Fleming Mercantile Investment Trust, 1985–94; Murray Trusts, 1973–93; Murray Johnstone, 1985–93; Member: London Bd, Bank of Scotland, 1988–91; West of Scotland Bd, Bank of Scotland, 1991–95. Member: Nat. Ports Council, 1974–77; Scottish Transport Gp, 1975–82. President: Chamber of Shipping of the UK, 1973–74; Gen. Council of British Shipping, 1988–89; British Internat. Freight Assoc., 1990–91; Baltic and Internat. Maritime Council, 1991–93. Hon. Norwegian Consul in Glasgow, 1975–97. DL 1980, JP 1984, Renfrewshire. *Recreation:* fishing. *Clubs:* Western (Glasgow); Royal Thames Yacht, Royal Northern and Clyde Yacht.

DENISON, family name of **Baron Londesborough**.

DENISON, Ann, (Mrs W. N. Denison); *see* Curnow, E. A. M.

DENISON, Dulcie Winifred Catherine, (Dulcie Gray), CBE 1983; actress, playwright, authoress; *b* 20 Nov. 1920; *d* of late Arnold Savage Bailey, CBE, and of Kate Edith (*née* Clulow Gray); *m* 1939, Michael Denison, CBE (*d* 1998). *Educ:* England and Malaya. In Repertory in Aberdeen, 1st part Sorrel in Hay Fever, 1939; Repertory in Edinburgh, Glasgow and Harrogate, 1940; BBC Serial, Front Line Family, 1941; Shakespeare, Regents Park; Alexandra in The Little Foxes, Piccadilly; Midsummer Night's Dream, Westminster, 1942; Brighton Rock, Garrick; Landslide, Westminster, 1943; Lady from Edinburgh, Playhouse, 1945; Dear Ruth, St James's; Wind is 90, Apollo, 1946; on tour in Fools Rush In, 1946; Rain on the Just, Aldwych, 1948; Queen Elizabeth Slept Here, Strand, 1949; The Four-poster, Ambassadors, 1950 (tour of S Africa, 1954–55); See You Later (Revue), Watergate, 1951; Dragon's Mouth, Winter Garden, 1952; Sweet Peril, St James's, 1952; We Must Kill Toni, Westminster; The Diary of a Nobody, Arts, 1954; Alice Through the Looking Glass, Chelsea Palace, 1955, Ashcroft Theatre, Croydon, 1972; appeared in own play, Love Affair, Lyric Hammersmith, 1956; South Sea Bubble, Cape Town, 1956; Tea and Sympathy, Melbourne and Sydney, 1956; South Sea Bubble, Johannesburg, 1957; Double Cross, Duchess, 1958; Let Them Eat Cake, Cambridge, 1959; Candida, Piccadilly and Wyndham's, 1960; Heartbreak House, Wyndham's, 1961; A Marriage Has Been Arranged, and A Village Wooing (Hong Kong); Shakespeare Recital (Berlin Festival); Royal Gambit for opening of Ashcroft Theatre, Croydon, 1962; Where Angels Fear to Tread, Arts and St Martin's, 1963; An Ideal Husband, Strand, 1965; On Approval, St Martin's, 1966; Happy Family, St Martin's, 1967; Number 10, Strand, 1967; Out of the Question, St Martin's, 1968; Three, Fortune, 1970; The Wild Duck, Criterion, 1970; Clandestine Marriage (tour), 1971; Ghosts, York; Hay Fever (tour), 1972; Dragon Variation (tour), 1973; At the End of the Day, Savoy, 1973; The Sack Race, Ambassadors, 1974; The Pay Off, Comedy, 1974, Westminster, 1975; Time and the Conways (tour), 1976; Ladies in Retirement (tour), 1976; Façade, QEH, 1976; The Cabinet Minister (tour), 1977; A Murder is Announced, Vaudeville, 1977; Bedroom Farce, Prince of Wales, 1979; The Cherry Orchard, Exeter, 1980; Lloyd George

Knew my Father (tour), 1980; The Kingfisher, Windsor, 1980, Worthing and on tour, 1981; Relatively Speaking (Dinner Theatre Tour, Near and Far East), 1981; A Coat of Varnish, Haymarket, 1982; Cavell, Chichester Fest., 1982; School for Scandal, Haymarket, transf. to Duke of York's, and British Council 50th Anniversary European Tour, 1983; There Goes the Bride (Dinner Theatre tour, Near and Far East), 1985; The Living Room, Royalty, 1987; The Chalk Garden, Windsor and tour, 1989; The Best of Friends (tour) 1990, 1991; The Importance of Being Earnest (tour), 1991; Tartuffe, Playhouse, 1991–92; Bedroom Farce (tour), 1992; An Ideal Husband, Globe, 1992, tour, 1993, Haymarket and NY, 1996, Haymarket, transf. Gielgud, 1997; Pygmalion, and The Schoolmistress, Chichester Fest., 1994; Two of a Kind (tour), 1995; The Importance of Being Earnest, Leatherhead, 1995; The Ladykillers (tour), 1999; Les Liaisons Dangereuses (tour), 2000; The Lady Vanishes (tour), 2000. *Films indude:* They were Sisters, 1944; Wanted for Murder, 1945; A Man about the House, 1946; Mine Own Executioner, 1947; My Brother Jonathan, 1947; The Glass Mountain, 1948; The Franchise Affair, 1951; Angels One Five, 1952; There was a Young Lady, 1953; A Man Could Get Killed, 1965; The Black Crow, 1994. Has appeared in television plays and radio serials; *television series:* Howard's Way, 1985–90. Fellow, Linnean Soc., 1984. FRSA. Queen's Silver Jubilee Medal, 1977. *Publications: play:* Love Affair; *books:* Murder on the Stairs; Murder in Melbourne; Baby Face; Epitaph for a Dead Actor; Murder on a Saturday; Murder in Mind; The Devil Wore Scarlet; No Quarter for a Star; The Murder of Love; Died in the Red; The Actor and His World (with Michael Denison); Murder on Honeymoon; For Richer, For Richer; Deadly Lampshade; Understudy to Murder; Dead Give Away; Ride on a Tiger; Stage-Door Fright; Death in Denims; Butterflies on my Mind (TES Senior Information Book Prize, 1978); Dark Calypso; The Glanville Women; Anna Starr; Mirror Image; Looking Forward, Looking Back (autobiog.); J. B. Priestley. *Recreations:* swimming, butterflies. *Address:* Shardeloes, Amersham, Bucks HP7 0RL; c/o Barry Burnett plc, Prince of Wales Theatre, Coventry Street, W1V 8AS. *T:* (020) 7839 0202.

DENISON, John Law, CBE 1960 (MBE (mil.) 1945); FRCM; Hon. RAM; Hon. GSM; Director, South Bank Concert Halls (formerly General Manager, Royal Festival Hall), 1965–76; Chairman, Arts Educational Schools, 1977–91; *b* 21 Jan. 1911; *s* of late Rev. H. B. W. and Alice Dorothy Denison; *m* 1st, 1936, Annie Claudia Russell Brown (marriage dissolved, 1946); 2nd, 1947, Evelyn Mary Donald (*née* Moir) (*d* 1958), *d* of John and Mary Scott Moir, Edinburgh; one *d*; 3rd, 1960, Audrey Grace Burnaby (*née* Bowles) (*d* 1970); 4th, 1972, Françoise Charlotte Henriette Mitchell (*née* Garrigues) (*d* 1985). *Educ:* St George's Sch., Windsor; Brighton Coll.; Royal Coll. of Music. Played horn in BBC Symphony, London Philharmonic, City of Birmingham, and other orchestras, 1934–39. Served War of 1939–45; gazetted Somerset Light Inf., 1940; DAA and QMG 214 Inf. Bde and various staff appts, 1941–45 (despatches). Asst Dir, Music Dept, British Council, 1946–48; Music Dir, Arts Council of Great Britain, 1948–65. Chairman: Cultural Programme, London Celebrations Cttee, Queen's Silver Jubilee, 1976–78; Royal Concert Cttee, St Cecilia Fest., 1976–88; Hon. Treasurer, Royal Philharmonic Soc., 1977–89 (Hon. Mem., 1989); Member: Council, RCM, 1975–90; Council, Musicians Benevolent Fund, 1992– (Exec. Cttee, 1984–92); Trustee, Prince Consort Foundn, 1990–96. FRSA. Comdr, Order of Lion (Finland), 1976; Chevalier de l'Ordre des Arts et des Lettres (France), 1988. *Publications:* articles for various musical publications. *Address:* 9 Hays Park, near Shaftesbury, Dorset SP7 9JR. *Clubs:* Garrick, Army and Navy.

DENISON, His Honour (William) Neil; QC 1980; a Circuit Judge, 1985–2001; Common Serjeant in the City of London, 1993–2001; *b* 10 March 1929; *s* of William George Denison and Jean Brodie; *m*; three *s*; *m* 1981, Elizabeth Ann Marguerite Curnow, *qv. Educ:* Queen Mary's Sch., Walsall; Univ. of Birmingham (LLB); Hertford Coll., Univ. of Oxford (BCL). Called to the Bar, Lincoln's Inn, 1952, Bencher, 1993. A Recorder of the Crown Court, 1979–85. Liveryman, Wax Chandlers' Co., 1988 (Master, 2001–Aug. 2002). *Recreations:* walking, reading rubbish. *Club:* Garrick.

DENISON-PENDER, family name of **Baron Pender**.

DENISON-SMITH, Lt-Gen. Sir Anthony (Arthur), KBE 1995 (MBE 1973); DL; Lieutenant, HM Tower of London, 1998–2001; *b* 24 Jan. 1942; *s* of late George Denison-Smith and Dorothy Gwendolin Phillips; *m* 1966, Julia Henrietta Scott; three *s. Educ:* Harrow; RMA, Sandhurst. Commissioned Grenadier Guards, 1962; Staff Coll., 1974; Brigade Major, 7th Armoured Brigade, 1977–79; Directing Staff, Staff Coll., 1979–81; CO 2nd Bn Grenadier Guards, 1981–83; Chief of Staff, 4th Armoured Div., 1983–85; Comdr, 22nd Armoured Brigade, 1985–87; Chief of Staff, 1 (BR) Corps, 1987–89; Dir Gen. Trng and Doctrine (Army), 1990–91; Comdr, 4th Armoured Div., 1991–93; Comdr, 1st (UK) Armoured Div., 1993–94; GOC Southern Dist, 1994–95; GOC 4th Div., 1995–96. Col, Princess of Wales's Royal Regt (Queen's and Royal Hampshires), 1992–99. Chm., ACFA, 1996–2001; Pres., Essex Br., Grenadier Guards Assoc., 1998–. Consultant, Rave Technologies Ltd (formerly Karnataka Gp Ltd), 1996–. DL Essex, 2001. Comdr (1st cl.), Order of the Dannebrog (Denmark), 1996. *Recreations:* cricket, golf, fishing, Hawkwoods. *Address:* Hawkwoods, Gosfield, Halstead, Essex CO9 1SB. *Club:* MCC.

DENMAN, family name of **Baron Denman**.

DENMAN, 5th Baron *cr* 1834; **Charles Spencer Denman,** CBE 1976; MC 1942; TD; Bt 1945; *b* 7 July 1916; *e s* of Hon. Sir Richard Douglas Denman, 1st Bt; *S* father, 1957 and to barony of cousin, 1971; *m* 1943, Sheila Anne (*d* 1987), *d* of late Lt-Col Algernon Bingham Anstruther Stewart, DSO, Seaforth Highlanders, of Ornockenoch, Gatehouse of Fleet; three *s* one *d. Educ:* Shrewsbury. Served War of 1939–45 with Duke of Cornwall's Light Infantry (TA), India, Middle East, Western Desert and Dodecanese Islands; Major, 1943. Contested (C) Leeds Central, 1945. Director: Close Brothers Group Plc; British Water & Wastewater Ltd; Albaraka Internat. Bank Ltd; Arab-British Centre Ltd; New Zealand Holdings (UK) Ltd; formerly Chairman: Marine and General Mutual Life Assurance Soc.; Tennant Guaranty Ltd; Gold Fields Mahd adh Dhahab Ltd; Arundell House Plc; formerly Director: C. Tennant Sons & Co. Ltd; Consolidated Gold Fields Plc; British Bank of the Middle East; Saudi British Bank; British Arabian Corp.; Fletcher Challenge Corp.; MGM Life Assurance Soc. Member: Cttee for ME Trade, 1963 (Chm., 1971–75); Advisory Council of Export Credits Guarantee Department, 1963–68; British National Export Council, 1965; Cttee on Invisible Exports, 1965–67; British Invisible Exports Council; Guild of World Traders in London; Res. Inst. for Study of Conflict and Terrorism; UK/Saudi Jt Cultural Cttee; Lord Kitchener Nat. Meml Fund. President: RSAA, 1984–; NZ–UK Chamber of Commerce and Industry; Vice Pres., ME Assoc.; Chairman: Arab British Chamber Charitable Foundn; Saudi-British Soc.; formerly Chm., Governors of Windlesham House Sch. *Heir: s* Hon. Richard Thomas Stewart Denman [*b* 4 Oct. 1946; *m* 1984, (Lesley) Jane, *d* of John Stevens; one *s* three *d*]. *Club:* Brooks's.

DENMAN, Sir George Roy; *see* Denman, Sir Roy.

DENMAN, Sir Roy, KCB 1977 (CB 1972); CMG 1968; Ambassador and Head of European Communities Delegation in Washington, 1982–89; *b* 12 June 1924; *s* of Albert Edward and Gertrude Ann Denman; *m* 1966, Moya Lade; one *s* one *d. Educ:* Harrow Gram. Sch.; St John's Coll., Cambridge. War Service 1943–46; Major, Royal Signals. Joined BoT, 1948; Asst Private Sec. to successive Presidents, 1950–52; 1st Sec., British Embassy, Bonn, 1957–60; UK Delegn, Geneva, 1960–61; Counsellor, Geneva, 1965–67; Under-Sec., 1967–70, BoT; Deputy Secretary: DTI, 1970–74; Dept of Trade, 1974–75; Second Permanent Sec., Cabinet Office, 1975–77; Dir-Gen. for External Affairs, EEC Commn, 1977–82. Business Fellow, John F. Kennedy Sch. of Govt, Harvard, 1989–90. Mem. negotiating delegn with European Communities, 1970–72. Mem., British Overseas Trade Bd, 1972–75. *Publication:* Missed Chances: Britain and Europe in the twentieth century, 1996. *Address:* c/o Coutts & Co., 2 Lower Sloane Street, SW1W 8BJ. *Club:* Oxford and Cambridge.

DENMAN, Sylvia Elaine, CBE 1994; Member, Housing Corporation, since 1996; Member, 1992–2000, Chairman, 1996–2000, Camden and Islington (formerly Bloomsbury and Islington) Health Authority; *b* Barbados; *d* of late Alexander Yarde and Euleen Yarde (*née* Alleyne), Barbados; *m* Hugh Frederick Denman (marr. diss.); one *d. Educ:* Queen's College, Barbados; LSE (LLM); called to the Bar, Lincoln's Inn, 1962. Lectr then Sen. Lectr, Oxford Polytechnic, 1965–76; Sen. Lectr and Tutor, Norman Manley Law Sch., Univ. of West Indies, Jamaica, 1977–82; Fulbright Fellow, New York Univ. Sch. of Law, 1982–83; Prin. Equal Opportunities Officer, ILEA, 1983–86; Pro Asst Dir, Polytechnic of South Bank, 1986–89; Dep. Dir of Educn, ILEA, 1989–90. Ind. Internal Inquiry, CPS, 2000–01. Member: Oxford Cttee for Racial Integration, 1965–76; Oxford, Bucks and Berks Conciliation Cttee, Race Relations Bd, 1965–70; London Rent Assessment Panel, 1968–76 and 1984–; Race Relations Bd, 1970–76; Equal Opportunities Commission, 1975–76; Lord Chancellor's Adv. Cttee on Legal Aid, 1975–76; Criminal Justice Consultative Council, 1991–97; Council, NACRO, 1994–99; SSAC, 1998–. Trustee: Runnymede Trust, 1985–91; Windsor Fellowship, 1994–98; CAF, 1997–. Governor: Haverstock Sch., 1989–94; Oxford Brookes Univ., 1996–2000. FRSA. *Recreations:* music, theatre, wandering about in the Caribbean.

DENNAY, Charles William, CEng, FIEE; FIIE; Consultant, Quantel Ltd, since 1993; *b* 13 May 1935; *s* of Charles Dennay and Elsie May Smith; *m* 1955, Shirley Patricia Johnston; one *s. Educ:* Humberston Foundation Sch.; Borough Polytechnic. DiPEE, MIERE. Scientific Asst (Govt), 1953; Technician, BBC, 1956; Transmitter Engineer, 1958; Asst Lectr/Lectr, 1961; Head of Ops Transmitters, 1973; Head of Engrg Transmitter Ops, 1976; Asst Chief Engineer, Transmitters, 1978; Chief Engineer, External Broadcasting, 1979; Controller, Ops and Engineering Radio, 1984; Asst Dir of Engineering, 1985; Dir of Engineering, 1987; Man. Dir, Resources Engrg and Services, 1993, retd. Director: Brighton Fest. Soc. Ltd, 1996–; Brighton Dome & Museum Develt Co. Ltd, 1999–. Mem., Steering Bd, Radio Communication Agency, 1996–. Pres., IEIE, 1994–98 (Vice-Pres., 1990–94); FRTS 1997 (a Vice-Pres., 1989–94). FRSA 1993. Hon. FBKS 1990. *Recreations:* photography, music, civil aviation. *Address:* Junipers, 111 Winchester Street, Overton, Basingstoke, Hants RG25 3HZ. *T:* (01256) 770183.

DENNE, Christopher James Alured, CMG 1991; HM Diplomatic Service, 1967–78 and 1983–98; *b* 20 Aug. 1945; *s* of late Lt Comdr John Richard Alured Denne, DSC, RN and Alison Patricia Denne; *m* 1968, Sarah Longman; two *s* one *d. Educ:* Wellington Coll.; Southampton Univ. (BSc Soc. Sci. 1967). Entered Diplomatic Service, 1967; New Delhi, 1969–72; Second Sec., FCO, 1972–74; First Sec. (Information), Lagos, 1974–77; FCO, 1977; resigned, 1978; BBC External Services, 1979–80; reinstated FCO, 1983; First Sec. and Dep. Permanent Rep., UK Mission to UN, Vienna, 1985–89; Head of Consular Dept, FCO, 1989–92; Dep. Hd of Mission, Athens, 1993–97. *Address:* Churchtown Farm, Sydenham Damerel, Tavistock, Devon PL19 8PU.

DENNEN, Ven. Lyle; Archdeacon of Hackney, and Vicar, St Andrew, Holborn, since 1999; *b* 8 Jan. 1942; *s* of Ernest and Rose Dennen; *m* 1977, Xenia Howard-Johnston, *d* of Rear Adm. C. D. Howard-Johnston, CB, DSO, DSC, and Lady Alexandra Haig (who *m* 1954, Hugh Trevor-Roper (*see* Lord Dacre of Glanton)); two *s. Educ:* Trinity Coll., Cambridge (BA 1970, MA 1975); Harvard Law Sch. (DJur); Harvard Univ. (PhD); Cuddesdon Coll., Oxford. Ordained deacon, 1972, priest, 1973; Curate, St Anne, S Lambeth, Southwark, 1972–75; Curate in charge, St Matthias, Richmond, 1975–78; Vicar, St John the Divine, Kennington, 1978–99; RD of Brixton, 1988–99. Hon. Canon, Southwark Cathedral, 1999. Chairman of Governors: St John the Divine Primary Sch., 1978–99; Charles Edward Brooke Secondary Sch., 1978–99; Chm., Lambeth WelCare, 1978–99. Trustee, St Gabriel's Coll. Trust, 1978–99. *Recreation:* sailing. *Address:* 5 St Andrew Street, EC4 3AB. *T:* (020) 7353 3544, *Fax:* (020) 7583 2750; *e-mail:* archdeacon.hackney@dlondon.org.uk. *Club:* Athenæum.

DENNER, Dr William Howard Butler; freelance photographer, especially of pop, blues and jazz musicians, since 1996; *b* 14 May 1944; *s* of late William Ormonde Ralph Denner and Violet Evelyn Arscott; *m* 1966, Gwenda Williams; two *d. Educ:* Cyfarthfa Castle Grammar School, Merthyr Tydfil; UCW Cardiff (BSc, PhD Biochem.). Research Associate: Miami Univ., 1968; Cardiff Univ., 1969; Ministry of Agriculture, Fisheries and Food, 1972–96: Secretary: Food Additives and Contaminants Cttee, 1974–84; Cttee on Toxicity of Chemicals in Food, Consumer Products and the Environment, 1978–84; Mem., Jt FAO/WHO Expert Cttee on Food Additives, 1978–85; Head of Food Composition and Information Unit, 1984; Chm., Codex Cttee on Fats and Oils, 1987–92; Assessor, Adv. Cttees on Novel Foods and Processes and on Genetic Modification, 1985–92; Head of Food Sci. Div. II, 1989; Chief Scientist (Food), 1992–96. Lectr and Judge, E Anglia Fedn of Photographic Alliance of GB, 1978–88; Judge, Essex Internat. Salon of Photography, 1987–88. One-man exhibn of photographs, Half Moon Gallery, 1974; individual photographs in internat. exhibns, newspapers, jls and books. AFIAP 1972. *Publications:* papers on food safety in learned jls. *Recreations:* photography, golf. *Address:* 33 Waldegrave Gardens, Upminster, Essex RM14 1UT. *T:* (01708) 223742; *e-mail:* hdenner@compuserve.com.

DENNINGTON, Dudley, FREng; FICE; FIStructE; Partner, 1972–92, Senior Partner, 1989–92, Bullen & Partners; *b* 21 April 1927; *s* of John Dennington and Beryl Dennington (*née* Hagon); *m* 1951, Margaret Patricia Stewart; two *d. Educ:* Clifton Coll., Bristol; Imperial Coll., London Univ. (BSc). National Service, 2nd Lieut, RE, 1947–49; Sandford Fawcett and Partners, Consulting Engineers, 1949–51; D. & C. Wm Press, Contractors, 1951–52; AMICE 1953; Manager, Design Office, George Wimpey & Co., 1952–65; GLC 1965–72: Asst Chief Engineer, Construction, 1965–67; Chief Engineer, Construction, 1967–70; Traffic Comr and Dir of Development, 1970–72. Mem., Bd for Engineers' Registration, Engrg Council, 1983–85. Pres., British Sect., Conseil Nat. des Ingénieurs et des Scientifiques de France, 1992. Vis. Prof., King's Coll., London Univ., 1978–81. Chm., Blythe Sappers, 1997. FICE 1966 (Mem. Council, 1975–78 and 1981–84; Vice-Pres., 1990–92); FCGI 1984; FREng (FEng 1985). *Recreations:* mathematics, painting. *Address:* 25 Corkran Road, Surbiton, Surrey KT6 6PL.

DENNIS, Maj.-Gen. Alastair Wesley, CB 1985; OBE 1973; *b* 30 Aug. 1931; *s* of late Ralph Dennis and of Helen (*née* Henderson); *m* 1957, Susan Lindy Elgar (*d* 1998); one *s* two *d. Educ:* Malvern Coll.; RMA, Sandhurst. Commanded 16th/5th The Queen's Royal Lancers, 1971–74; Col GS, Cabinet Office, 1974–75; Comd 20 Armoured Bde, 1976–77;

Dep. Comdt, Staff Coll., 1978–80; Director of Defence Policy (B), MoD, Whitehall, 1980–82; Dir, Military Assistance Overseas, MoD, 1982–85. Sec., Imperial Cancer Res. Fund, 1985–91; Chm., Assoc. of Med. Res. Charities, 1987–91. Mem., Malvern Coll. Council, 1988–92. Col, 16th/5th The Queen's Royal Lancers, 1990–93, The Queen's Royal Lancers, 1993–95. *Recreations:* fishing, golf, gardening. *Address:* c/o Barclays Bank, Wallingford Branch, PO Box 42, Abingdon, Oxon OX14 1GU.

DENNIS, Rt Rev. John; Bishop of St Edmundsbury and Ipswich, 1986–96; an Assistant Bishop, Diocese of Winchester, since 2000; *b* 19 June 1931; *s* of late Hubert Ronald and Evelyn Dennis; *m* 1956, Dorothy Mary (*née* Hinnels); two *s*. *Educ:* Rutlish School, Merton; St Catharine's Coll., Cambridge (BA 1954; MA 1959); Cuddesdon Coll., Oxford (1954–56). RAF, 1950–51. Curate, St Bartholomew's, Armley, Leeds, 1956–60; Curate of Kettering, 1960–62; Vicar of the Isle of Dogs, 1962–71; Vicar of John Keble, Mill Hill, 1971–79; Area Dean of West Barnet, 1973–79; Prebendary of St Paul's Cathedral, 1977–79; Bishop Suffragan of Knaresborough, 1979–86; Diocesan Dir of Ordinands, Dio. Ripon, 1980–86; Asst Bp, Ely, 1996–99. Episcopal Guardian of Anglican Focolarini, 1981–96; Chaplain to Franciscan Third Order, 1988–94. Co-Chairman: English ARC, 1988–92; Anglican-Oriental Orthodox Dialogue, 1989–95. *Recreations:* walking, toy making, wood working. *Address:* 7 Conifer Close, Winchester, Hants SO22 6SH.

DENNIS, Mark Jonathan; Senior Treasury Counsel, Central Criminal Court, since 1998; a Recorder, since 2000; *b* 15 March 1955; *s* of Edward John Dennis and Patricia Edna Dennis; *m* 1985, Christabel Birbeck; one *s* one *d*. *Educ:* Battersea Grammar Sch.; Peterhouse, Cambridge (MA Law). Called to the Bar, Middle Temple, 1977; Jun. Treasury Counsel, Central Criminal Court, 1993–98. *Address:* (chambers) 6 King's Bench Walk, Temple, EC4Y 7DR. *T:* (020) 7583 0410.

DENNIS, Ronald, CBE 2000; Chairman and Chief Executive, TAG McLaren Group, since 2000; *b* 1 June 1947; *s* of late Norman Stanley Dennis and of Evelyn (*née* Reader); *m* 1985, Lisa Ann Shelton; one *s* two *d*. *Educ:* Guildford Technical Coll. (vehicle technology course). Apprentice, Thomson & Taylor; Owner/Manager, Project Four Team, 1976–80 (winners: Procar Championship, 1979; Formula 3 Championship, 1979–80); merged with McLaren Team, 1980; McLaren Formula 1 Racing Team (winners: Constructors' Championship 1984, 1985, 1988, 1989, 1990, 1991, 1998; 9 Drivers' Championships). Trustee, Tommy's Campaign. Hon. DTech De Montfort, 1996; Hon. Dsc City, 1997; DUniv Surrey, 2000. *Recreations:* golf, snow and water ski-ing, diving, shooting. *Address:* McLaren International Ltd, Woking Business Park, Albert Drive, Woking, Surrey GU21 5JY. *T:* (01483) 711002, *Fax:* (01483) 750852. *Club:* British Racing Drivers'.

DENNISON, Stanley Richard, CBE 1990; PhD; FRSC; Group Chief Executive, ECC Group (formerly English China Clays) plc, 1988–90; *b* 28 May 1930; *s* of Arthur and Ellen Dennison; *m* 1955, Margaret Janet Morrison; two *s* two *d*. *Educ:* Latymer's Sch., Edmonton; University Coll. London (BSc, PhD). CBIM 1988. Chemist, Min. of Supply, 1954; English China Clays: Res. Chemist, 1956; Res. Man., 1970; Res. Dir, Clay Div., 1980; Man. Dir, Clay Div., 1984; Dir, English China Clays PLC, 1984. Dir, Devon and Cornwall TEC, 1990–91. Chm., Cornwall and Is of Scilly HA, 1994–98. *Publications:* on industrial minerals, their technology and application in paper, in a number of pubns. *Recreations:* music, walking. *Address:* Lower Colvreath Farm, Roche, St Austell, Cornwall PL26 8LR.

DENNISS, Gordon Kenneth, CBE 1979; Consultant Chartered Surveyor, Eastman & Denniss, Surveyors, 1983–88 (Senior Partner, 1945–83); Senior Partner, G. K. Denniss Farms, since 1990; *b* 29 April 1915; *e s* of late Harold W. Denniss; *m* 1939, Violet Fiedler, Montreal; one *s* two *d*. *Educ:* Dulwich Coll.; Coll. of Estate Management. FRICS. Articled to uncle, Hugh F. Thoburn, Chartered Surveyor, Kent, developing building estates, 1935, professional asst 1938; Eastman & Denniss: Junior Partner, 1943; sole principal, 1945. Crown Estate Comr, 1965–71. Farming 2500 acres in E Sussex and Kent. Pres., Ashurst CC, Kent, 1989–97. *Recreations:* farming, cricket, political economy, golf. *Address:* Evans Leap, Withyham, Hartfield, E Sussex TN7 4DA. *T:* (01892) 770720; 4 Winterhaldenweg, 79856 Hinterzarten, Black Forest, Germany. *Clubs:* Farmers', MCC; Surrey County Cricket.

DENNISTON, Rev. Robin Alastair, PhD; Oxford Publisher and Senior Deputy Secretary to the Delegates, Oxford University Press, 1984–88 (Academic and General Publisher, 1980–84); Priest-in-charge of Great with Little Tew and Over Worton with Nether Worton, since 1995; *b* 25 Dec. 1926; *s* of late Alexander Guthrie Denniston, CMG, CBE, head of Govt code and cipher school, and late Dorothy Mary Gilliat; *m* 1st, 1950, Anne Alice Kyffin Evans (*d* 1985), *y d* of late Dr Geoffrey Evans, MD, FRCP, consulting Physician at St Bartholomew's Hosp., and late Hon. E. M. K. Evans; one *s* two *d*; 2nd, 1987, Dr Rosa Susan Penelope Beddington, FRS (*d* 2001). *Educ:* Westminster Sch. (King's Schol.; Captain of School, 1945); Christ Church, Oxford (Classical Schol.; 2nd cl. Hons Lit. Hum.); MSc Edinburgh 1992; PhD London 1997. National Service: commnd into Airborne Artillery, 1948. Editor at Collins, 1950–59; Man. Dir, Faith Press, 1959–60; Editor, Prism, 1959–61; Promotion Man., Hodder & Stoughton Ltd, 1960–64, Editorial Dir, 1966, Man. Dir, 1968–72; Dir, Mathew Hodder Ltd (and subsid. cos), 1968–72; Dep. Chm., George Weidenfeld & Nicolson (and subsid. cos), 1973–75; Non-exec. Chm., A. R. Mowbray & Co., 1974–88; Dir, Thomson Publications Ltd, 1975–77; also Chm. of Michael Joseph Ltd, Thomas Nelson & Sons (and subsid. cos), George Rainbird Ltd, 1975–77 and Sphere Books, 1975–76; Academic Publisher, OUP, 1978; non-exec. Dir, W. W. Norton, 1989–. Student of Christ Church, 1978–88. Ordained Deacon, 1978, Priest, 1979; Hon. Curate: Clifton-on-Teme, 1978; New with South Hinksey, 1985; Non-Stipendiary Minister: Great with Little Tew, 1987–90; West Fife Team Ministry, 1990–93. A Church Comr, 1989–90. *Publications:* The Young Musicians, 1956; Partly Living, 1967; (ed) Part Time Priests?, 1960; (co-ed) Anatomy of Scotland, 1992; Churchill's Secret War, 1997; Trevor Huddleston: a life, 1999; articles in Intelligence and Nat. Security and Diplomacy and Statecraft. *Recreations:* walking, music. *Address:* The Vicarage, Great Tew, Oxon OX7 4AG; 112 Randolph Avenue, W9 1PQ.

DENNY, Sir Anthony Coningham de Waltham, 8th Bt *cr* 1782, of Tralee Castle, Co. Kerry, Ireland; designer; Partner in Verity and Beverley, Architects and Designers (offices in Tetbury, Lisbon and New York), since 1959; *b* 22 April 1925; *s* of Rev. Sir Henry Lyttleton Lyster Denny, 7th Bt, and Joan Lucy Dorothy, *er d* of Major William A. C. Denny, OBE; *S* father, 1953; *m* 1949, Anne Catherine, *e d* of S. Beverley, FRIBA; two *s* one adopted *d*. *Educ:* Clayesmore Sch. Served War of 1939–45: Middle East, RAF (Aircrew), 1943–47. Anglo-French Art Centre, 1947–50; Mural Painter and Theatrical Designer, 1950–54. Trustee, Waltham Abbey. Hereditary Freeman of City of Cork. FRSA; MCSD. *Recreations:* architecture, painting. *Heir:* *s* Piers Anthony de Waltham Denny [*b* 14 March 1954; *m* 1987, Ella Jane, *o d* of Peter P. Huhne; two *d*]. *Address:* The Priest's House, Muchelney, Langport, Somerset TA10 0DQ. *T:* (01458) 252621. *Clubs:* Arts, Chelsea Arts.

See also B. L. Denny.

DENNY, Barry Lyttelton, LVO 1979; HM Diplomatic Service, retired; *b* 6 June 1928; *s* of Rev. Sir Henry Lyttelton Lyster Denny, 7th Bt, and Joan Lucy Dorothy, *er d* of Major William A. C. Denny, OBE; *m* 1st, 1951 (marr. diss. 1968); one *s* one *d*; 2nd, 1969, Anne Rosemary Jordon, *o d* of late Col James F. White, MC; one *d*. *Educ:* Clayesmore Sch.; RMA, Sandhurst. Indian Army Cadet, 1946–47; commnd RA, 1949; retd from HM Forces as Captain (Temp. Major), 1960. Joined Foreign Office, 1962; First Sec., Nicosia, 1964; FO, later FCO, 1966; Kaduna, 1969; FCO, 1972; Vientiane, 1973; FCO, 1975; Kuwait, 1977; Counsellor, Oslo, 1980; seconded to MoD, 1984–89. Comdr, Order of St Olav (Norway), 1981. *Recreations:* collecting, photography, my family.

See also Sir A. C. de W. Denny.

DENNY, Sir Charles Alistair Maurice, 4th Bt *cr* 1913, of Dumbarton, co. Dunbarton; *b* 7 Oct. 1950; *e s* of Sir Alistair Maurice Archibald Denny, 3rd Bt and of Elizabeth Hunt, *y d* of Major Sir Guy Lloyd, 1st Bt, DSO; *S* father, 1995; *m* 1981, Belinda, *yr d* of J. P. McDonald; one *s* one *d*. *Educ:* Wellington Coll.; Edinburgh Univ. *Heir:* *s* Patrick Charles Alistair Denny, *b* 2 Jan. 1985. *Address:* East Winchet, Winchet Hill, Goudhurst, Cranbrook, Kent TN17 1JX.

DENNY, John Ingram, CMG 1997; RIBA; Managing Director, Cecil Denny Highton Partnership, since 1995; Joint Managing Director, HOK International, since 1995; Senior Vice President, Hellmuth, Obata + Kassabaum Inc., since 1995; *b* 28 May 1941; *s* of Thomas Ingram Denny, Macclesfield and Claire Dorothy Denny (*née* Lewis); *m* 1967, Carol Ann Frances, *d* of Walter James Hughes, St Leonards, Bournemouth; one *s* two *d*. *Educ:* Normain Coll., Chester; Northern Poly. (Dip. Arch. (Hons)); Univ. of Reading (MSc). RIBA 1967. Partner, 1970–90, Sen. Partner, 1990–95, Cecil Denny Highton, architects and project managers. Involved in architecture, conservation and mgt; Consultant to FCO, Home Office, MoD, Parly Works Office, Royal Household, HM Treasury, Cabinet Office, PACE and Natural Hist. Mus. Mem., Assoc. of Consultant Architects, 1987. Mem., Victorian Soc. FRSA. *Recreations:* golf, photography. *Address:* Cecil Denny Highton/HOK, 216 Oxford Street, W1R 1AH. *T:* (020) 7636 2006, *Fax:* (020) 7636 1987; *e-mail:* john.denny@hok.com. *Club:* Reform.

DENNY, Rev. Norwyn Ephraim; retired Methodist minister; President of the Methodist Conference, 1982–83; *b* 23 Oct. 1924; *s* of Percy Edward James Denny and Dorothy Ann Denny (*née* Stringer); *m* 1950, Ellen Amelia Shaw; three *d*. *Educ:* City of Norwich School; Wesley College, Bristol. BD (Hons), London Univ. Ordained Methodist Minister, 1951; Methodist Minister in Jamaica, 1950–54; Minister in Peterborough, 1955–61; Member of Notting Hill Group (Ecumenical) Ministry, 1961–75; Chm., Liverpool Dist Methodist Church, 1975–86; Supt, Lowestoft and E Suffolk Methodist Circuit, 1986–91. Mem., Fellowship of Reconciliation. *Publications:* (with D. Mason and G. Ainger) News from Notting Hill, 1967; Caring, 1976; Worship, 1995. *Recreations:* gardening, astronomy, association football, World Development movement. *Address:* 5 Red Hill, Lodge Park, Redditch, Worcs B98 7JE. *T:* (01527) 522426.

DENNY, Ronald Maurice; Director, The Catalogue Co. Ltd (Malta), since 1991; *b* 11 Jan. 1927; *s* of Maurice Denny and Ada (*née* Bradley); *m* 1952, Dorothy Hamilton; one *s* two *d*. *Educ:* Gosport County Sch. CEng, FIEE. BBC Engineering, 1943; served Royal Navy, 1946–49; BBC Engr (TV), 1949–55; ATV Ltd, 1955, Gen. Man., ATV, 1967; Rediffusion Ltd, 1970; Chief Exec., 1979–85, Chm., 1985–89, Rediffusion PLC; Director: (non-exec.) Thames Television, 1981–89; BET, 1983–89; Electrocomponents, 1984–95. Mem. of Trust, Philharmonia Orch., 1983–93. Hon. Mem., RCM, 1984–. FRSA 1985. *Recreations:* music, sport. *Address:* 19 Nichols Green, W5 2QU. *T:* (020) 8998 3765. *Clubs:* Athenæum, Arts.

DENNY, William Eric, CBE 1984; QC 1975; a Recorder of the Crown Court, 1974–93; *b* 2 Nov. 1927; *s* of William John Denny and Elsie Denny; *m* 1960, Daphne Rose Southern-Reddin; one *s* two *d*. *Educ:* Ormskirk Grammar Sch.; Liverpool Univ. (Pres., Guild of Undergraduates, 1952–53; LLB). Served RAF, 1946–48. Called to the Bar, Gray's Inn, 1953, Bencher, 1985. Lectured at LSE, 1953–58. Chm., Home Secretary's Adv. Bd on Restricted Patients, 1980–85 (Mem., 1979). *Recreations:* music, sailing, gardening. *Address:* 1 Hare Court, Temple, EC4Y 7BE.

DENNYS, Nicholas Charles Jonathan; QC 1991; a Recorder, since 2000; *b* 14 July 1951; *m* 1977, Frances Winifred Markham; four *d*. *Educ:* Eton; Brasenose Coll., Oxford (BA 1973). Admitted Middle Temple, 1973; called to the Bar, 1975; Asst Recorder, 1996–2000. *Recreations:* windsurfing, golf, music. *Address:* The Old Rectory, Arborfield, Berks RG2 9HZ. *T:* (0118) 9761003.

DENT, Sir John, Kt 1986; CBE 1976 (OBE 1968); Chairman, Civil Aviation Authority, 1982–86; *b* 5 Oct. 1923; *s* of Harry F. Dent; *m* 1954, Pamela Ann, *d* of Frederick G. Bailey; one *s*. *Educ:* King's Coll., London Univ. BSc(Eng), FEng, FRAeS, FIMechE, FIEE, CBIM. Admty Gunnery Estabs at Teddington and Portland, 1944–45; Chief Engr, Guided Weapons, Short Bros & Harland Ltd, Belfast, 1955–60; Chief Engr, Armaments Div., Armstrong Whitworth Aircraft, Coventry, 1961–63; Dir and Chief Engr, Hawker Siddeley Dynamics Ltd, Coventry, 1963–67; Director: Engrg Gp, Dunlop Ltd, Coventry, 1968–76; Dunlop Holdings Ltd, 1970–82; Industrie Pirelli SpA, 1978–81; Dunlop AG, 1979–82; Pirelli Gen. plc, 1980–92; Pirelli Ltd, 1985–92; Man. Dir, Dunlop Ltd, 1978–82. President: Coventry and District Engrg Employers' Assoc., 1971 and 1972; Engrg Employers' Fedn, 1974–76 (1st Dep. Pres., 1972–74); Inst. of Travel Managers, 1986–94; Internat. Fedn of Airworthiness, 1987–89; Chm., Nationalized Industries' Chairman's Group, 1984–85. Member: Engineering Industries Council, 1975–76; Review Bd for Government Contracts, 1976–82; Royal Dockyards Policy Bd, 1976–82; NCB, 1980–82. *Recreations:* gardening, fishing, cabinet-making. *Address:* Helidon Grange, Helidon, near Daventry, Northants NN11 6LG.

DENT, Maj.-Gen. Jonathan Hugh Baillie, CB 1984; OBE 1974; Director General, Fighting Vehicles and Engineer Equipment, Ministry of Defence, 1981–85; *b* 19 July 1930; *s* of Joseph Alan Guthrie Dent and Hilda Ina Dent; *m* 1957, Anne Veronica Inglis; one *s* three *d*. *Educ:* Winchester College. Commissioned, Queen's Bays, 1949; regtl and instructional employment in BAOR, UK, Jordan, Libya, 1949–61; Adjt 1958; Adjt Shropshire Yeomanry, 1959–60; Staff trng, RMCS, 1962–63; Staff Coll. Camberley, 1964; Sqdn Comd, Queen's Dragoon Guards, N Ireland and Borneo, 1965–66; MoD (Operational Requirements), 1967–69; Second in Comd, Queen's Dragoon Guards, 1970; Ministry of Defence: MGO Secretariat, 1971–74; Project Manager Chieftain, 1974–76; RCDS 1977; Defence R&D Attaché, British Embassy, Washington, 1978–80. *Recreations:* fishing, bird watching, walking, shooting, classical music.

DENTON, Dame Catherine Margaret Mary; *see* Scott, Dame M.

DENTON, Charles; Head of Drama, BBC Television, 1993–96; *b* 20 Dec. 1937; *s* of Alan Charles Denton and Mary Frances Royle; *m* 1961, Eleanor Mary Player; one *s* two *d*. *Educ:* Reading Sch.; Bristol Univ. BA History (Hons). Deckhand, 1960; advertising trainee,

1961–63; BBC TV, 1963–68; freelance television producer with Granada, ATV and Yorkshire TV, 1969–72; Dir, Tempest Films Ltd, 1969–71; Man. Dir, Black Lion Films, 1979–81; ATV: Head of Documentaries, 1974–77; Controller of Programmes, 1977–81; Dir of Progs, Central Indep. TV, 1981–84; Dir, Central Indep. Television plc, 1981–87; Chief Exec., Zenith Prodns, 1984–93; Chairman: Zenith North Ltd, 1988–93; Action Time Ltd, 1988–93; Producers Alliance for Cinema and TV, 1991–93. Mem., Arts Council of England, 1996–98. Governor, BFI, 1992–99; Mem. Bd, Film Council, 1999–. FRSA 1988; FRTS 1988. *Recreations:* walking, music.

DENTON, Prof. Derek Ashworth, (Dick), FRS 1999; FRACP, FRCP; Founding Director, Howard Florey Institute of Experimental Physiology and Medicine, Melbourne, 1971–89, Emeritus Director and Consultant Scientist, since 1990; *b* 27 May 1924; *s* of Arthur A. and Catherine Denton; *m* 1953, Catherine Margaret Mary Scott (*see* Dame Margaret Scott); two *s*. *Educ:* Launceston Grammar Sch.; Univ. of Melbourne (MB BS). FAA 1979; FRACP 1986; FRCP 1988. Haley Res. Fellow, Walter & Eliza Hall Inst., Melbourne, 1948; Med. Res. Fellow, then Sen. Med. Res. Fellow, 1948–62, Principal Res. Fellow, 1962–70, NH&MRC. Adjunct Scientist, SW Foundn for Biomed. Res., San Antonio, Texas, 1991–; Pres., Howard Florey Biomed. Foundn, Melbourne, 1997–. Dir, David Syme Ltd, 1984–93. First Vice-Pres., Internat. Union of Physiol. Sci., 1983–89 (Chm., Nominating Cttee, and Cttee on Commns, 1986–93). Mem. Jury, Albert and Mary Lasker Foundn Awards in Med. Sci., 1979–90. For. Med. Mem., Royal Swedish Acad. of Sci., 1974; Mem., Amer. Acad. Arts & Sci., 1986; Foreign Associate: NAS, 1995; French Acad. of Scis, 2000. *Publications:* The Hunger for Salt, 1982; The Pinnacle of Life, 1994 (trans. French, 1997, Japanese, 1998). *Recreations:* wine, tennis, fly-fishing. *Address:* Howard Florey Institute, University of Melbourne, Parkville, Vic 3052, Australia; 816 Orrong Road, Toorak, Vic 3142, Australia. *Club:* Melbourne (Melbourne).

DENTON, Sir Eric (James), Kt 1987; CBE 1974; FRS 1964; ScD; Director, Laboratory of Marine Biological Association, Plymouth, 1974–87; Member, Royal Commission on Environmental Pollution, 1973–76; *b* 30 Sept. 1923; *s* of George Denton and Mary Anne (*née* Ogden); *m* 1946, Nancy Emily, *d* of Charles and Emily Jane Wright; two *s* one *d*. *Educ:* Doncaster Grammar Sch.; St John's Coll., Cambridge. Biophysics Research Unit, University Coll., London, 1946–48; Lectr in Physiology, University of Aberdeen, 1948–56; Physiologist, Marine Biological Assoc. Laboratory, Plymouth, 1956–74; Royal Soc. Res. Professor, Univ. of Bristol, 1964–74, Hon. Professor, 1975. Fellow, University Coll., London, 1965. Hon. Sec., Physiological Soc., 1963–69. Hon. DSc: Exeter, 1976; Göteborg, 1978. Royal Medal, Royal Soc., 1987; Frink Medal, Zool Soc. of London, 1987; International Prize for Biology, Japan Soc. for the Promotion of Science, 1989. *Publications:* Scientific papers in Jl of Marine Biological Assoc., etc. *Recreation:* gardening. *Address:* Fairfield House, St Germans, Saltash, Cornwall PL12 5LS. *T:* (01503) 230204; The Laboratory, Citadel Hill, Plymouth PL1 2PB. *T:* (01752) 6333348.

DENTON, Jane; Director, Multiple Births Foundation, since 1999; *b* 30 June 1953; *d* of Ronald and Joan Gulliver; *m* 1987, Nigel Denton. *Educ:* Nottingham Bluecoat Sch.; St Bartholomew's Hosp., London (RGN 1974); Mill Rd Maternity Hosp., Cambridge (RM 1976). Staff Nurse, St Bartholomew's Hosp., 1974–76; Midwife, Mill Road Maternity Hosp., 1977–78; Nursing Director: Hallam Med. Centre, 1978–91; Multiple Births Foundn, 1991–99. Mem., HFEA, 1992– (Dep. Chm., 1997–2000). *Publications:* (ed jtly) Infertility: nursing and caring, 1995; contrib. articles on multiple births. *Recreations:* music, walking. *Address:* Multiple Births Foundation, Queen Charlotte's and Chelsea Hospital, W12 0HS. *T:* (020) 8383 3519.

DENTON, Prof. John Douglas, PhD; FRS 2000; FREng; Professor of Turbomachinery Aerodynamics, Cambridge University, since 1991; Fellow of Trinity Hall, Cambridge, since 1977; *b* 1 Dec. 1939; *s* of Donald and Mary Denton; *m* 1966, Maureen Hunt; three *d*. *Educ:* Trinity Hall, Cambridge (BA, PhD); Univ. of British Columbia (MASc). MIMechE, CEng, FREng (FEng 1993). Lectr, Univ. of East Africa, 1967–69; Res. Officer, later Section Head, CEGB, 1969–77; Lectr, Dept of Engrg, Cambridge, 1977–91. *Recreations:* travel, mountain walking. *Address:* 16 Green End, Comberton, Cambridge CB3 7DY.

DENTON, John Grant, OBE 1977; General Secretary, Anglican Church of Australia, 1969–94 (part time until 1977); *b* 16 July 1929; *s* of Ernest Bengrey Denton and Gladys Leonard Stevenson; *m* 1956, Shirley Joan Wise; two *s* two *d*. *Educ:* Camberwell C of E Grammar School, Melbourne. Personnel and Industrial Relations Dept, Mobil Oil (Aust.), 1950–54; Administrative Sec., Dio. of Central Tanganyika, as CMS missionary, 1954–64; Dir of Information, Dio. of Sydney, 1964–69; Registrar, Dio. of Sydney, 1969–77 (part time). Mem., ACC, 1976–84 (Chm., 1980–84); Chm., Aust. Churches' Cttee for Seventh Assembly of WCC, Canberra, 1991. *Recreation:* model railway. *Address:* 1/50 Scenic Circle, Budgewoi, NSW 2262, Australia.

DENTON, Dame Margaret; *see* Scott, Dame M.

DENTON, Prof. Richard Michael, PhD, DSc; FRS 1998; FMedSci; Professor of Biochemistry, since 1987, and Chairman of Medical Sciences, since 2000, University of Bristol; *b* 16 Oct. 1941; *s* of Arthur Benjamin Denton and Eileen Mary Denton (*née* Evans); *m* 1965, Janet Mary Jones; one *s* two *d*. *Educ:* Wycliffe Coll.; Christ's Coll., Cambridge (MA, PhD 1967); Univ. of Bristol (DSc 1976). University of Bristol: Lectr in Biochemistry, 1967–78; Reader in Biochemistry, 1978–87. MRC Sen. Res. Leave Fellow, 1984–88. Mem., MRC, 1999–. Founder FMedSci 1998. *Publications:* more than 240 res. papers, mainly on molecular basis of effects of insulin on metabolism, and role of calcium ions in mitochondria, in internat. res. jls. *Recreations:* family, walking, keeping fit, cooking. *Address:* Department of Biochemistry, University of Bristol School of Medical Sciences, University Walk, Bristol BS8 1TD. *T:* (0117) 928 8097.

DENTON-THOMPSON, Aubrey Gordon, OBE 1958; MC 1942; *b* 6 June 1920; *s* of late M. A. B. Denton-Thompson; *m* 1944, Ruth Cecily Isaac (*d* 1959); two *s* (one *d* decd); *m* 1961, Barbara Mary Wells. *Educ:* Malvern Coll. Served in RA 1940–44; seconded to Basutoland Administration, 1944; apptd to HM Colonial Service, 1945; transferred to Tanganyika as Asst District Officer, 1947; seconded to Colonial Office, 1948–50, District Officer; seconded to Secretariat, Dar es Salaam, as Asst Sec., 1950; Colonial Sec., Falkland Islands, 1955–60; Dep. Permanent Sec., Ministry of Agriculture, Tanganyika, 1960–62; retired from Tanganyika Civil Service, 1963. Man. Dir, Tanganyika Sisal Marketing Assoc. Ltd, 1966–68 (Sec. 1963); Sen. Agricl Advr, UNDP, 1968–78, and FAO Country Rep.: Korea, 1970–73, Indonesia, 1973–76, Turkey, 1976–78; Sen. Advr to Director General, FAO, Rome, July–Dec. 1978; retd Jan. 1979. Chm., New Forest Conservative Assoc., 1985–88 (Dep. Chm., 1983–85). *Address:* Octave Cottage, 43 Ramley Road, Pennington, Lymington, Hants SO41 8GZ. *T:* (01590) 676626.

DENYER, Roderick Lawrence; QC 1990; a Recorder, since 1990; *b* 1 March 1948; *s* of Oliver James Denyer and Olive Mabel Jones; *m* 1973, Pauline (*née* Vann); two *d*. *Educ:* Grove Park Grammar School for Boys, Wrexham; London School of Economics (LLM). Called to the Bar, Inner Temple, 1970, Bencher, 1996; Lectr in Law, Bristol Univ., 1971–73; in practice at Bar, 1973–. Vis. Fellow, UWE, 1994–. Mem., Bar Council, 1992–95. *Publications:* Children and Personal Injury Litigation, 1993; various, in legal jls. *Recreations:* cricket, 19th Century history, theatre, restaurants. *Address:* St John's Chambers, Small Street, Bristol BS1 1DW.

DENZA, Mrs Eileen, CMG 1984; Visiting Professor, University College London, since 1997 (Senior Research Fellow, 1996–97); Second Counsel to Chairman of Committees and Counsel to European Communities Committee, House of Lords, 1987–95; *b* 23 July 1937; *d* of Alexander L. Young and Mrs Young; *m* 1966, John Denza; two *s* one *d*. *Educ:* Aberdeen Univ. (MA); Somerville Coll., Oxford (MA); Harvard Univ. (LLM). Called to the Bar, Lincoln's Inn, 1963. Asst Lectr in Law, Bristol Univ., 1961–63; Asst Legal Adviser, FCO (formerly FO), 1963–74; Legal Counsellor, FCO, 1974–80; Counsellor (Legal Adviser), Office of UK Perm. Rep. to European Communities, 1980–83; Legal Counsellor, FCO, 1983–86. Pupillage and practice at the Bar, 1986–87. Member: EC Law Section of Adv. Bd, British Inst. of Internat. and Comparative Law, 1988–; Adv. Bd, Inst. of European Public Law, 1992–96; Justice Expert Panel on Human Rights in the EU, 1997–. FRSA 1995. *Publications:* Diplomatic Law, 1976, 2nd edn 1998; contribs to: Satow's Guide to Diplomatic Practice, 5th edn; Essays in Air Law; Lee's Consular Law and Practice, 2nd edn; Institutional Dynamics of European Integration; The European Union and World Trade Law; articles in British Yearbook of Internat. Law, Revue du Marché Commun, International and Comparative Law Quarterly, Statute Law Review.

de OSUNA, Sheelagh Marilyn; High Commissioner for Trinidad and Tobago in London, since 1996; also Ambassador (non-resident) to Germany, Norway, Sweden and Denmark; *b* 25 March 1948; *d* of Henry Wells Macnaughton-Jones and Cynthia Maud Macnaughton-Jones; *m* 1971, Alfredo Osuna (marr. diss. 1980); one *d*. *Educ:* Univ. of Sussex (BA Hons Internat. Relns); Universidad Javeriana, Bogotá (Dip. in Spanish); Internat. Law Inst., Georgetown Univ., Washington (Dip. in Loan Negotiation and Renegotiation). Entered Foreign Service of Trinidad and Tobago, 1970: Second Sec., Perm. Mission to UN, Geneva, 1970–72; First Sec., Caracas, 1972–77; Foreign Service Officer III, Political Bureau, Min. of Foreign Affairs, 1977–79; Econ. Counsellor, Washington, 1979–88; Dir, Internat. Econ. Relns Div., Min. of Foreign Affairs, 1988–92; Dep. High Comr, London, 1992–95; Ambassador for Trade, Min. of Trade and Industry, Port-of-Spain, 1995–96. *Recreations:* swimming, scuba diving, theatre and opera, foreign travel, cooking. *Address:* High Commission of Trinidad and Tobago, 42 Belgrave Square, SW1X 8NT. *T:* (020) 7245 9351. *Clubs:* Royal Over-Seas League; Country, Union (Port-of-Spain, Trinidad).

de PALACIO del VALLE LERSUNDI, Loyola; a Vice President, European Commission, since 1999; *b* Madrid, 16 Sept. 1950; *d* of Luis de Palacio and Luisa del Valle-Lersundi. *Educ:* Univ. Complutense de Madrid (Law Degree). First Gen. Pres., Nuevas Generaciones, 1977–78; Tech. Sec. Gen., Fedn of Press Assocs, 1979–82. Mem. Senate, Spain, 1986–89 (Vice Pres., Popular Party Gp); Deputy (Popular Party) for Segovia, 1989–96 (Vice Pres., Popular Party Gp); Minister for Agric., Fisheries and Food, 1996–99. Mem., NEC, Popular Party, 1988–99. *Address:* European Commission, Rue Demot 28, 8/101, 1040 Brussels, Belgium.

DEPARDIEU, Gérard; actor; *b* 27 Dec. 1948; *m* 1970, Elisabeth Guignot (marr. diss. 1996); one *s* one *d*. *Educ:* Ecole d'art dramatique de Jean Laurent Cochet. Pres., Cannes Film Fest. Jury, 1992. Fellow BFI, 1989. Chevalier, Ordre Nat. du Mérite (France), 1985; Chevalier, Légion d'Honneur (France), 1996. *Stage:* Les Garçons de la Bande, Th. Edouard VII, 1968; Une fille dans ma soupe, 1970, Galapagos, 1971, Th. de la Madeleine; Saved, Th. Nat. de Chaillot, 1972; Home, 1972, Isme, Isaac, 1973, La Chevauchée sur le Lac de Constance, 1974, Espace Pierre Cardin; Les Gens deraisonnables sont en voie de disparition, Nanterre, 1977; Tartuffe, Strasbourg, 1983; Lily Passion (musical), Zénith, 1986. *Films:* Le Tueur, 1971; L'affaire Dominici, Un peu de soleil dans l'eau froide, Au rendez-vous de la mort joyeuse, La Scoumoune, Deux hommes dans la ville, Le viager, 1972; Rude journée pour la reine, Stavisky, Les Gaspards, Les Valseuses, 1973; Vincent, François, Paul et les autres, Pas si méchant que ça, 1974; 1900, La dernière femme, Sept morts sur ordonnance, Maîtresse, 1975; Barocco, René la Canne, Baxter, Vera Baxter, 1976; Dites-lui que je l'aime, Le Camion, La nuit tous les chats sont gris, Préparez vos mouchoirs, Rêve de singe, 1977; Le Sucre, Les chiens, Le Grand embouteillage, 1978; Buffet froid, Rosy la bourrasque, Loulou, Mon oncle d'Amérique, 1979; Le dernier métro (Caesar best actor award, 1980), Inspecteur la Bavure, Je vous aime, 1980; Le Choix des armes, La Femme d'à côté, La Chèvre, Le Retour de Martin Guerre, Danton, 1981; Le Grand frère, La Lune dans le caniveau, 1982; Les Compères, Fort Saganne, 1983; Tartuffe (also dir), Rive droite, rive gauche, Police, 1984; Une femme ou deux, Tenue de soirée, Jean de Florette, 1985; Les Fugitifs, Sous le soleil de Satan, 1986; Camille Claudel, 1987; Drôle d'endroit pour une rencontre, Deux, Trop belle pour toi, I Want to go Home, 1988; Cyrano de Bergerac, 1989 (Best Actor, Cannes, 1990; Caesar and de Donatello best actor awards, 1991); Green Card (Golden Globe award, 1991), Uranus, Merci la vie, 1990; Mon Père ce héros, 1492: Colombus, Tous les matins du monde, 1991; Hélas pour moi, Germinal, 1992; Une pure formalité, Le Colonel Chabert, 1993; La Machine, Elisa, Les Cents et une nuits, Les anges gardiens, 1994; Unhook the Stars, 1995; Hamlet, 1997; The Man in the Iron Mask, 1998; Asterix et Obelix contre César, Un pont entre deux rives (dir), 1999; 102 Dalmatians, 2000; has also appeared on TV. *Publication:* Lettres volées, 1988. *Address:* c/o Artmédia, 10 avenue George V, 75008 Paris, France.

de PAULA, (Frederic) Clive, CBE 1970; TD 1950 and Clasp 1951; FCA, JDipMA; Chairman, Dennys Sanders & Greene Ltd, since 1987; *b* 17 Nov. 1916; 2nd *s* of late F. R. M. de Paula, CBE, FCA, and Agnes Smithson de Paula (*née* Clark) (American Medal of Freedom, 1947). *Educ:* Rugby Sch.; Spain and France. ACA 1940, FCA 1951; JDipMA 1966. Articled to de Paula, Turner, Lake & Co., chartered accountants, London, 1934–39. 2nd Lieut, TA, 1939; Liaison Officer, Free French Forces in London and French Equatorial Africa, 1940; Specially employed Middle East and E Africa, 1941; SOE Madagascar, 1942; comd special forces unit with 11th E African Div., Ceylon and Burma, 1943; Finance Div., Control Commn, Germany, 1945; demobilised as Major, 1946; Captain 21st Special Air Service Regt (Artists) TA, 1947–56. Joined Robson, Morrow & Co., management consultants, 1946; Partner, 1951; seconded to DEA then to Min. of Technology as an Industrial Adviser, 1967; Co-ordinator of Industrial Advisers to Govt, 1969; returned as Sen. Partner, Robson, Morrow & Co., 1970–71; Man. Dir, Agricultural Mortgage Corp. Ltd, 1971–81; Dir, 1972–83, Dep. Chm., 1978–80, Chm., 1980–83, Tecalemit plc; Non-Exec. Dir, Green's Economiser Group plc, 1972–83; Dep. Chm., C. & J. Clark Ltd, 1985–86. Mem., EDC for Agric., 1972–81. Member: ICAEW, 1940–; Inst. of Cost & Works Accountants, 1947–72; British Computer Soc., 1964–74 (Mem. Council, 1965–68); Management Consultants Assoc., 1964–72 (Mem. Council, 1970–71); BIM, 1970–84 (Mem. Council, 1971–76; CIMgt 1970). Gen. Comr of Income Tax, Winslow Div., Bucks, 1965–82. Vice Pres., Schoolmistresses and Governesses Benevolent Instn, 1982– (Hon. Treas., 1947–81); Chm., Internat. Wine and Food Soc., 1980–83 (Silver Medal, 1996). *Publications:* first paper on future of electronic computers on accountancy, 1952; Accounts for Management, 1954; (ed) P. Tovey, Balance Sheets: how to read and understand them, 4th edn, 1954; (ed) F.R.M. de Paula, The Principles of Auditing, 12th edn 1957 (trans. Sinhalese, 1967), (with F.A. Attwood) 15th edn as Auditing: Principles and Practice, 1976, (with F. A. Attwood and N. D. Stein) 17th edn as de Paula's Auditing, 1986; Management Accounting in Practice, 1959 (trans. Japanese, 1960); (ed with A. G Russell) A.C. Smith, Internal Control and Audit, 2nd edn, 1968; (with A. W. Willsmore) The Techniques of Business Control, 1973; (with F. A. Attwood) Auditing Standards, 1978. *Address:* c/o National Westminster Bank, 60 High Street, Esher, Surrey KT10 9QY.

de PEYER, David Charles; Director General, Cancer Research Campaign, 1984–96; *b* 25 April 1934; *s* of late Charles de Peyer, CMG and Flora (*née* Collins); *m* 1959, Ann Harbord. *Educ:* Rendcomb Coll., Cirencester; Magdalen Coll., Oxford (BA PPE). Asst Principal, Min. of Health, 1960; Sec., Royal Commn on NHS, 1976–79; Under Sec., DHSS, 1979–84. Vice-Chm., Suffolk HA, 1996–98. Mem., Criminal Injuries Compensation Appeals Panel, 1997–. Trustee: Disabled Living Foundn, 1988–; Res. into Ageing, 1996–. *Address:* 21 Southwood Park, N6 5SG.

de PEYER, Gervase; solo clarinettist; conductor; Founder and Conductor, Melos Sinfonia of Washington, 1992; Director, London Symphony Wind Ensemble; solo clarinettist, Chamber Music Society of Lincoln Center, New York, since 1969; Co-founder and Artistic Director, Innisfree Music Festival, Pa, USA; *b* London, 11 April 1926; *m* 1980, Katia Perret Aubry; one *s* two *d* by a previous marriage. *Educ:* King Alfred's, London; Bedales; Royal College of Music. Served HM Forces, 1945 and 1946. Founder Mem., Melos Ensemble of London, 1950–72; Principal Clarinet, London Symphony Orchestra, 1955–72; formerly: Associate Conductor, Haydn Orch. of London; Resident Conductor, Victoria Internat. Fest., BC, Canada. ARCM; FRCM 1992; Hon. ARAM. Gold Medallist, Worshipful Co. of Musicians, 1948; Charles Gros Grand Prix du Disque, 1961, 1962; Plaque of Honour for recording, Acad. of Arts and Sciences of America, 1962. Most recorded solo clarinettist in world. *Recreations:* travel, cooking, kite-flying, sport, theatre. *Address:* Porto Vecchio #109, 1250 S Washington Street, Alexandria, VA 22314, USA. *T:* (703) 7390824, *Fax:* (703) 7390572; 42 Tower Bridge Wharf, St Katherine's Way, E1 9UR. *T:* and *Fax:* (020) 7265 1110.

de PIRO, His Honour Alan C. H.; QC 1965; FCIArb 1978; a Circuit Judge, 1983–91; *b* Singapore, 31 Aug. 1919; *e s* of late J. W. de Piro and Louise Bell Irvine; *m* 1947, Mary Elliot (deceased); two *s*; *m* 1964, Mona Addington (*d* 1998) (Baroness and Bohemian); one step *s* one step *d*. *Educ:* Repton; Trinity Hall, Cambridge (Sen. Scholar; BA 1945 (1st cl. Hons Nat. Sci. and Law), MA 1947). Royal Artillery, 1940–45 (Capt.); West Africa. Called to Bar, Middle Temple, 1947; Inner Temple, 1962; Bencher, Middle Temple, 1971, Reader, 1988; in practice at the Bar, London and Midlands, 1947–83; Deputy Chairman: Beds QS, 1966–71; Warwicks QS, 1967–71; a Recorder of the Crown Court, 1972–83. Inspector, Canvey Island (Liquid Natural Gas) Public Local Inquiry, 1981–82. Member: Gen. Council of the Bar, 1961–65, 1966–70, 1971–73; Senate of the Inns of Court and the Bar, 1976–81; Council Internat. Bar Assoc., 1967–86 (Chm., Human Rights Cttee, 1979–82); Editorial Advisory Cttee, Law Guardian, 1965–73; Law Panel British Council, 1967–74. Vice-Pres., L'Union Internat. des Avocats, 1968–73, Co-Pres., 1969. Legal Assessor, Disciplinary Cttee, RCVS, 1970–83. *Publications:* Mona, a life, 1999; Mona and Alan, 2000. *Address:* 206 Mountjoy House, Barbican, EC2Y 8BP. *Clubs:* Hawks, Avla (Cambridge).

DERAMORE, 6th Baron *cr* 1885; **Richard Arthur de Yarburgh-Bateson;** Bt 1818; Chartered Architect, retired; *b* 9 April 1911; *s* of 4th Baron Deramore and of Muriel Katherine (*née* Duncombe); *S* brother, 1964; *m* 1948, Janet Mary, *d* of John Ware, BA Cantab, MD Edin., Askham-in-Furness, Lancs; one *d*. *Educ:* Harrow; St John's Coll., Cambridge. AA Diploma, 1935; MA Cantab 1936; ARIBA 1936. Associate, A. W. Kenyon, FRIBA, 1936–39. Served as Navigator, RAFVR, 1940–45: 14 Sqdn, RAF, 1942–44 and 1945. County Architect's Dept, Herts, 1949–52; in private practice, London, Buckinghamshire and Yorkshire, 1952–81. Member: Council, Queen Mary Sch., Duncombe Park, Helmsley, 1977–85; Management Cttee, Purey Cust Nursing Home, York, 1976–84; Governor: Heslington Sch., York, 1965–88; Tudor Hall Sch., Banbury, 1966–75. Fellow, Woodard Schs (Northern Div.) Ltd, 1978–84. *Publications:* (jtly) Winged Promises, 1996; freelance articles and short stories. *Recreation:* water-colour painting. *Heir:* none. *Address:* Heslington House, Aislaby, Pickering, North Yorks YO18 8PE. *Clubs:* Royal Air Force, Royal Automobile.

DE RAMSEY, 4th Baron *cr* 1887, of Ramsey Abbey, Huntingdon; **John Ailwyn Fellowes;** DL; Chairman, Environment Agency, 1995–2000; *b* 27 Feb. 1942; *s* of 3rd Baron De Ramsey, KBE and Lilah Helen Suzanne (*d* 1987), *d* of Frank Labouchere; *S* father, 1993; m 1st, 1973, Phyllida Mary Forsyth; one *s*; 2nd, 1984, Alison Mary Birkmyre; one *s* two *d*. *Educ:* Winchester Coll.; Writtle Inst. of Agriculture. Dir, Cambridge Water Co., 1974–94 (Chm., 1983–89). Crown Estate Comr, 1994–2001. President: CLA, 1991–93; Assoc. of Drainage Authorities, 1993–94. FRAgS 1993. DL Cambs, 1993. Hon. DSc Cranfield, 1997. *Recreations:* golf, fishing, fine arts. *Heir: s* Freddie John Fellowes, *b* 31 May 1978. *Address:* Abbots Ripton Hall, Huntingdon PE28 2PQ. *T:* (01487) 773555. *Club:* Boodle's.

DERBY, 19th Earl of, *cr* 1485; **Edward Richard William Stanley;** Bt 1627; Baron Stanley 1832; Baron Stanley of Preston 1886; DL; merchant banker with Robert Fleming Holdings Ltd, since 1987; *b* 10 Oct. 1962; *er s* of Hon. Hugh Henry Montagu Stanley (*d* 1971), *g s* of 17th Earl, and of Mary Rose Stanley (*née* Birch); *S* uncle, 1994; *m* 1995, Hon. Caroline Emma Neville, *d* of 10th Baron Braybrooke, *qv*; one *s* one *d*. *Educ:* Ludgrove; Eton Coll.; RAC Cirencester. Commnd Grenadier Guards, 1982, resigned 1985. Director: Fleming Private Fund Management Ltd, 1991–96; Fleming Private Asset Management Ltd, 1992–; The Haydock Park Racecourse Co. Ltd, 1994–; Robert Fleming & Co. Ltd, 1996–98; Robert Fleming Internat. Ltd, 1998–. Trustee, Nat. Mus and Galls Commn, 1995–. President: Liverpool Chamber of Commerce and Industry, 1995–; Knowsley Chamber of Commerce and Industry, 1995–; Sefton Chamber of Commerce and Industry, 1998; Liverpool Council of Social Service, 1996–. Aintree Trustee, 1995–. President: Royal Liverpool Philharmonic Soc., 1995–; Rugby Football League Assoc., 1997–. Mem. Council, Univ. of Liverpool, 1998–. DL Merseyside, 1999. *Recreations:* shooting, ski-ing, food and wine. *Heir: s* Lord Stanley, *qv*. *Address:* Knowsley, Prescot, Merseyside L34 4AF. *T:* (0151) 489 6148, *Fax:* (0151) 482 1988; *e-mail:* private.office@knowsley.com. *Clubs:* White's, Jockey Club Rooms.

DERBY, Bishop of, since 1995; **Rt Rev. Jonathan Sansbury Bailey;** Clerk of the Closet to the Queen, since 1996; *b* 24 Feb. 1940; *s* of late Walter Eric and of Audrey Sansbury Bailey; *m* 1965, Rev. Susan Mary Bennett-Jones; three *s*. *Educ:* Quarry Bank High School, Liverpool; Trinity College, Cambridge (MA). Assistant Curate: Sutton, St Helens, Lancs, 1965–68; St Paul, Warrington, 1968–71; Warden, Marrick Priory, 1971–76; Vicar of Wetherby, Yorks, 1976–82; Archdeacon of Southend and Bishop's Officer for Industry and Commerce, dio. of Chelmsford, 1982–92; Suffragan Bishop of Dunwich, 1992–95. *Recreations:* theatre, music, beekeeping, carpentry. *Address:* (home) The Bishop's House, 6 King Street, Duffield, Belper, Derbyshire DE56 4EU; (office) Derby Church House, Full Street, Derby DE1 3DR. *T:* (01332) 346744, *Fax:* (01332) 295810; *e-mail:* bishopderby@clara.net.

DERBY, Dean of; *see* Perham, Very Rev. M. F.

DERBY, Archdeacon of; *see* Gatford, Ven. I.

DERBYSHIRE, Sir Andrew (George), Kt 1986; FRIBA; Chairman, Robert Matthew, Johnson-Marshall & Partners & RMJM Ltd, 1983–89; President, RMJM Group, 1989–98; *b* 7 Oct. 1923; *s* of late Samuel Reginald Derbyshire and late Helen Louise Puleston Derbyshire (*née* Clarke); *m*, Lily Rhodes (*née* Binns), *widow* of late Norman Rhodes; three *s* one *d*. *Educ:* Chesterfield Grammar Sch.; Queens' Coll., Cambridge; Architectural Assoc. MA (Cantab), AA Dip. (Hons). Admty Signals Estabt and Bldg Research Station, 1943–46. Farmer & Dark, 1951–53 (Marchwood and Belvedere power stations); West Riding County Architect's Dept, 1953–55 (bldgs for educn and social welfare). Asst City Architect, Sheffield, 1955–61; responsible for central area redevelt. Mem. Research Team, RIBA Survey of Architects' Offices, 1960–62. Since 1961, as Mem. RM, J-M & Partners, later RMJM Ltd, responsible for: develt of Univ. of York, 1961–98, Central Lancs New Town, NE Lancs Impact Study, Univ. of Cambridge, West Cambridge Develt and New Cavendish Laboratory, Preston Market and Guildhall, London Docklands Study, Hillingdon Civic Centre, Cabtrack and Minitram feasibility studies, Suez Master Plan Study; Castle Peak Power Stations, and Harbour Reclamation and Urban Growth Study, Hong Kong. Member: RIBA Council, 1950–72, 1975–81 (Senior Vice-Pres., 1980); NJCC, 1961–65; Bldg Industry Communications Res. Cttee, 1964–66 (Chm. Steering Cttee); DoE Planning and Transport Res. Adv. Council, 1971–76; Commn on Energy and the Environment, 1978–81. Pt-time Mem., CEGB, 1973–84; Board Member: Property Services Agency, 1975–79; London Docklands Develt Corp., 1984–88 (Chm., Planning Cttee, 1984–88); Construction Industry Sector Group, NEDC, 1988–92; Mem., Construction Industry Council, 1990–94. Hoffman Wood Prof. of Architecture, Univ. of Leeds, 1978–80; External Prof., Dept of Civil Engineering, Univ. of Leeds, 1981–85; Gresham Prof. of Rhetoric, Gresham Coll., 1990–92; Hon. Fellow, Inst. of Advanced Architectural Studies, Univ. of York, 1994; Hon. FIStructE 1992. FRSA 1981 (Chm., Art for Architecture Project, 1994–98). DUniv York, 1972. *Publications:* The Architect and his Office, 1962; on professional consultancy, town planning, public transport, and energy conservation in construction. *Recreations:* his family, the garden. *Address:* 4 Sunnyfield, Hatfield, Herts AL9 5DX. *T:* (01707) 265903.

DERHAM, Patrick Sibley Jan, MA; Head Master, Rugby School, since 2001; *b* 23 Aug. 1959; *s* of John Joseph Sibley Derham and Helena Petronella Trimby (*née* Verhagen); *m* 1982, Alison Jane Sheardown; one *s* one *d*. *Educ:* Training Ship Arethusa; Pangbourne Coll. (Hd of Sch.); Pembroke Coll., Cambridge (Foundn Schol., 1st Cl. Hons Hist. 1982, MA 1985). Assistant Master: Cheam, 1982–84; Radley Coll., 1984–96 (Hd of Hist. and Tutor, 1990–96); Headmaster, Solihull Sch., 1996–2001. *Publications:* The Irish Question 1868–1886: a collection of documents, 1988; contrib. articles and reviews. *Recreations:* quizzes, collecting Tom Merry political cartoons, reading contemporary fiction, running, family. *Address:* Rugby School, Rugby, Warwickshire CV22 5EH. *T:* (01788) 543465. *Club:* East India.

DERHAM, Sir Peter (John), AC 2001; Kt 1980; FAIM; FPIA; FInstD; Chairman: Circadian Technologies Ltd (formerly Circadian Pharmaceuticals Ltd), since 1984; Vos Industries Ltd, since 1997; See Australia (formerly Partnership Australia Domestic Ltd), since 1999; *b* 21 Aug. 1925; *s* of John and Mary Derham; *m* 1950, Averil C. Wigan; two *s* one *d*. *Educ:* Melbourne Church of England Grammar School; Univ. of Melbourne (BSc 1958); Harvard Univ. (Advanced Management Programme, 1965). Served RAAF and RAN, 1944–46. Joined Moulded Products (Australasia) Ltd (later Nylex Corp.), 1943; Dir, 1953–82, Sales Dir, 1960, Gen. Manager, 1967, Man. Dir, 1972–80. Chairman: Internat. Pacific Corp. Ltd, later Rothschild Australia Ltd, 1981–85; Australia New Zealand Foundn, 1978–83; Australian Canned Fruits Corp., 1981–89; Robert Bryce & Co. Ltd, 1982–91; Davy McKee Pacific Pty, 1984–90; Leasing Corp. Ltd, 1987–93; Multistack, 1993–99; Greenchip Develt Capital Ltd, 1993–99; Greenchip Investments Ltd, 1997–99; Bays and Peninsulas, 1999; Deputy Chairman: Prime Computer of Australia Ltd, 1986–92; Australian Mutual Provident Society State Board of Advice, 1990–91 (Dir, Victoria Br. Bd, 1974–90); Director: Lucas Industries Aust., 1981–84; Station 3XY Pty, 1980–87; Radio 3XY Pty, 1980–87; Perpetual Trustees Victoria Ltd, 1992–93; Perpetual Trustees Australia Ltd, 1993–97; Advance Australia Foundn, 1983–96; Jt Chm., Advance Australia America Cup Challenge Ltd, 1981–83; Councillor Enterprise Australia, 1975–82 (Dep. Chm., 1975–78). Chairman: Nat. Training Council, 1971–80; Adv. Bd, CSIRO, 1981–86; Australian Tourist Commn, 1981–85; Member: Manufg Industries Adv. Council, 1971–74; Victorian Econ. Develt Corp., 1981–82. Federal Pres., Inst. of Directors in Australia, 1980–82 (Mem., 1975–89, Chm., 1975–82, Victorian Council; Life Mem., 1986); Councillor: Yooralla Soc. of Victoria, 1972–79 (Chm. Workshops Cttee, 1972–81); Aust. Industries Develt Assoc., 1975–80; State Councillor, Industrial Design Council, 1967–73, Federal Councillor, 1970–73; Mem. Council, Inst. of Public Affairs, 1971–; Life Mem., Plastics Inst. of Australia Inc. (Victorian Pres., 1964–66; Nat. Pres., 1971–72); Mem. Board of Advisors, Inst. of Cultural Affairs, 1971–81. Victorian State Treas., Liberal Party of Australia, 1981–83. Member: Rotary Club of Melbourne (Mem., Bd of Dirs, 1974–75, 1975–76); Victorian State Cttee, Child Accident Prevention Foundn of Australia; Appeal Cttee, Royal Victorian Eye and Ear Hosp.; Bd of Management, Alfred Hosp., 1980–93 (Pres., 1990–92), Amalgamated Alfred, Caulfield and Royal Southern Meml Hosp., 1987–93; Alfred Foundn Bd, 1993–; St John Ambulance, 1988– (Chm., State Council, 1991–96; Pres., Victoria, 1996–99); Chm., Caulfield Hosp. Cttee, 1984–87 (Dir, 1981–87; Vice Pres., 1989). President: Alcohol and Drug Foundn (formerly Victorian Foundn on Alcoholism and Drug Dependence), 1986–91 (Appeal Chm., 1981–86); Victorian Soc. for Prevention of Child Abuse and Neglect, 1987–96; Dep Chm., Australian Assoc. for Support of Educn, 1983–87; Mem., Melbourne C of E Grammar Sch. Council, 1974–75, 1977–80; Pres., Old Melburnians, 1974–75; Governor, Ian Clunies Ross Meml Foundn, 1981–99; Chairman: Trade & Industry Cttee, Victoria's 150th Anniv. Celebration; Police Toy Fund for Underprivileged Children; Pres., Somers Area, Boy Scout Assoc. of Australia, 1985–90; Vict. Trustee, Australian Koala Foundn Inc., 1986–92; Trustee, H & L Hecht Trust, 1990–; Life Governor, Assoc. for the Blind. Rotary Paul Harris Fellowship, 1997. CStJ 1995. *Recreations:* golf, sailing, tennis, gardening, viticulture. *Address:* Suite 329, 23 Milton Parade, Malvern, Vic 3144, Australia. *T:* (3) 98220770; *e-mail:* pjderham@bigpond.com.au. *Clubs:* Australian, Melbourne (Melbourne); Royal Melbourne Golf, Flinders Golf, Royal South Yarra Lawn Tennis, Melbourne Cricket.

DERMODY, Paul Bernard; Director, since 1997, Chief Executive, since 2000, De Vere Group plc (formerly Greenalls Group plc); *b*1 Oct. 1945; *s* of Bernard and Jessie Dermody; *m* 1967, Margaret Eileen Horsfield; one *s* one *d*. *Educ:* De La Salle Coll., Salford; Salford Tech. Coll. ACMA 1971. Mgt accounting trainee, 1963–68, Asst Accountant, 1968–72, Groves & Whitnall; Mgt Accountant, Grenalls Brewery, 1972–77; Financial Controller, Greenalls Retail Div., 1977–84; Finance Dir and Dep. Man. Dir, 1984–89, Dep. Chm.,

1989–95, De Vere Hotels; Chief Exec., Premier House & Village Leisure Hotels, 1995–97; Man. Dir, Greenalls Hotels & Leisure Ltd, 1997–2000. School Governor. FHCIMA 1997; FBAHA 1985; FRSA 2000. *Recreations:* singing, swimming, reading. *Address:* 6 Row Green, Worsley, Manchester M28 2RF.

DERMOTT, William, CB 1984; Under Secretary, Head of Agricultural Science Service, Agricultural Development and Advisory Service, Ministry of Agriculture, Fisheries and Food, 1976–84, retired; *b* 27 March 1924; *s* of William and Mary Dermott; *m* 1946, Winifred Joan Tinney; one *s* one *d*. *Educ:* Univ. of Durham. BSc, MSc. Agricl Chemist, Univ. of Durham and Wye Coll., Univ. of London, 1943–46; Soil Scientist, Min. of Agriculture, at Wye, Bangor and Wolverhampton, 1947–70; Sen. Sci. Specialist, and Dep. Chief Sci. Specialist, MAFF, 1971–76; Actg Dir Gen., ADAS, 1983–84. Pres., British Soc. of Soil Science, 1981–82. *Publications:* papers on various aspects of agricultural chemistry in scientific journals. *Recreations:* gardening, the countryside. *Address:* 22 Chequers Park, Wye, Ashford, Kent TN25 5BB. *T:* (01233) 812694.

de ROHAN, Maurice John, OBE 1992; Agent General for South Australia, since 1998; *b* 13 May 1936; *s* of late Louis Maurice Virgil de Rohan and Joann Stewart de Rohan (*née* Roger); *m* 1958, Margaret Jennifer Roads; one *s* one *d* (and one *d* decd). *Educ:* Univ. of Adelaide; South Australian Inst. of Technology (BTech Civil Engrg 1958). Partner, Kinnaird Hill de Rohan & Young, 1959–73; Man. Dir, Kinhill Engrs Pty Ltd, Adelaide, 1973–76; Dep. Chm. and Man. Dir, Llewelyn-Davies International, London, 1976–78; Chairman: Tibbalds Monro Ltd, 1978–96; Transcon Ltd, 1979–94; Davis Brody & Associates, NY, 1988–95; Facilities Management Pty Ltd, 1988–95. Dir, Australian Business in Europe, London, 1976–. Dir, Gracechurch Bellyard Ltd, 1997–. Mem. Council, 1996–2000, Chm., Exec. Cttee, 1998–2000, Maritime Trust; Chm., Cutty Sark Trust, 2000–. Liveryman, Engineers' Co., 2000–. *Recreations:* narrow boating, following cricket, theatre. *Address:* 114 Clifton Hill, St John's Wood, NW8 0JS. *T:* (020) 7887 5124. *Clubs:* East India, MCC (Mem. Cttee, Exec. Bd, 2000–; Chm., Estates Cttee, 1999–); Adelaide (Adelaide).

de ROS, 28th Baron *cr* 1264 (Premier Barony of England); **Peter Trevor Maxwell;** *b* 23 Dec. 1958; *s* of Comdr John David Maxwell, RN, and late Georgiana Angela Maxwell, 27th Baroness de Ros; *S* mother, 1983; *m* 1987, Siân Ross; one *s* one *d*. *Educ:* Headfort School, Kells, Co. Meath; Stowe School, Bucks; Down High School, Co. Down. Upholstered furniture maker. *Recreations:* gardening, travel and sailing. *Heir:* *s* Hon. Finbar James Maxwell, *b* 14 Nov. 1988.

de ROTHSCHILD; *see* Rothschild.

DERRETT, Prof. (John) Duncan (Martin), MA, PhD, DCL, LLD, DD; Professor of Oriental Laws in the University of London, 1965–82, now Emeritus; *b* 30 Aug. 1922; *s* of John West Derrett and Fay Frances Ethel Kate (*née* Martin); *m* 1950, Margaret Esmé Griffiths; four *s* one *d*. *Educ:* Emanuel Sch., London; Jesus Coll., Oxford; Sch. of Oriental and Afr. Studies, London; Inns of Court School of Law. MA 1947, DCL 1966 (Oxon); PhD 1949, LLD 1971, DD 1983 (London). Called to the Bar, Gray's Inn, 1953. Lectr in Hindu Law, SOAS, 1949; Reader in Oriental Laws, 1956, Prof. of Oriental Laws, 1965, Univ. of London; Tagore Prof. of Law, Univ. of Calcutta, 1953 (lectures delivered, 1955); Vis. Professor: Univ. of Chicago, 1963; Univ. of Michigan, 1970; Wilde Lectr in Natural and Compar. Religion, Univ. of Oxford, 1978–81; Japan Soc. Prom. Sci. Fellow and Vis. Prof., Oriental Inst., Univ. of Tokyo, 1982. Fellow, Indian Law Inst., Delhi, 1988. Mem., Editorial Bd, Zeitschrift für vergleichende Rechtswissenschaft, 1954–85, subseq. of Kannada Studies, Bharata Manisha, Kerala Law Times. Mem., Stud. Novi Test. Soc., 1971. Barcelona Prize in Comparative Law, 1954; N. C. Sen-Gupta Gold Medal, Asiatic Soc. (Calcutta), 1977. *Publications:* The Hoysalas, 1957; Hindu Law Past and Present, 1957; Introduction to Modern Hindu Law, 1963; Religion, Law and the State in India, 1968, repr. 1999; Critique of Modern Hindu Law, 1970; Law in the New Testament, 1970; Jesus's Audience, 1973; Dharmaśāstra and Juridical Literature, 1973; History of Indian Law (Dharmaśāstra), 1973; Henry Swinburne (?1551–1624) Civil Lawyer of York, 1973; trans. R. Lingat, Classical Law of India, 1973, repr. 1998; Bhāruci's Commentary on the Manusmrti, 1975; Essays in Classical and Modern Hindu Law, vols I-IV, 1976–79; Studies in the New Testament, vols I-VI, 1977–96; The Death of a Marriage Law, 1978; Beiträge zu Indischen Rechtsdenken, 1979; The Anastasis: the Resurrection of Jesus as an Historical Event, 1982; A Textbook for Novices: Jayarakshita's Perspicuous Commentary on the 'Compendium of Conduct', 1983; The Making of Mark, 1985; New Resolutions of Old Conundrums: a fresh insight into Luke's Gospel, 1986; The Ascetic Discourse: an explanation of the Sermon on the Mount, 1989; The Victim: the Johannine passion narrative reexamined, 1993; The Sermon on the Mount, 1994; Prophecy in the Cotswolds 1804–1947, 1994; Studies in Hindu Law, 1994; Two Masters: the Buddha and Jesus, 1995; Some Telltale Words in the New Testament, 1997; Law and Morality, 1998; The Bible and the Buddhists, 2000; *edited:* Studies in the Laws of Succession in Nigeria, 1965; Introduction to Legal Systems, 1968; (with W. D. O'Flaherty) The Concept of Duty in South Asia, 1978; A Second Blockley Miscellany, 1994; collab. with Yale Edn, Works of St Thomas More, Société Jean Bodin, Brussels, Max Planck Inst., Hamburg, Fritz Thyssen Stiftung, Cologne, Institut für Soziologie, Heidelberg, Aufstieg und Niedergang der Römischen Welt, Tübingen, and Sekai Kyusei Kyo, Atami; *Festschriften:* Indology and Law, 1982; Novum Testamentum, 24, 1982, fasc. 3 and foll. *Address:* Half Way House, High Street, Blockley, Moreton-in-Marsh, Glos GL56 9EX. *T:* (01386) 700828.

DERRICK, Patricia, (Mrs Donald Derrick); *see* Lamburn, P.

DERRICK, Peter; Chamberlain, Corporation of London, since 1999; *b* 2 April 1948; *s* of John Moorhead Derrick and Lucy (*née* Norman); *m* 1972, Joyce Bainbridge; two *d*. *Educ:* Univ. of Lancaster (BA Hons Politics 1974). CPFA 1971. Gateshead CBC, 1965–71; Principal Accountant, Carlisle CC, 1974–77; Chief Tech. Asst, Knowsley MBC, 1977–79; Principal Accountant, Lothian Regl Council, 1979–81; Under Sec. (Finance), ADC, 1981–85; Director of Finance: London Bor. of Hounslow, 1985–88; London Bor. of Camden, 1988–91; Chief Exec., London Bor. of Hammersmith and Fulham, 1991–93; Dir, Finance and Corporate Services, Surrey CC, 1993–98. Chm., London Financial Adv. Cttee, 2000–; Advr, Local Govt Pension Cttee, 1997–; Council Mem., Nat. Assoc. of Pension Funds, 1997–. Order of the Dannebrog (Denmark), 2000. *Recreations:* football, golf, squash, film, opera. *Address:* Corporation of London, PO Box 270, Guildhall, EC2P 2EJ. *T:* (020) 7332 1300. *Clubs:* Wimbledon Racquets and Fitness; Malden Golf; Sunderland AFC Supporters.

DERRIDA, Jacques; writer; *b* 15 July 1930; *s* of Aimé Derrida and Georgette Safar; *m* 1957, Marguerite Aucouturier; two *s*. *Educ:* Ecole Normale Supérieure, Paris. Taught at Sorbonne, 1960–64; at Ecole Normale Supérieure, 1965–84. Hon. DLitt Cambridge, 1992. *Publications:* La voix et le phénomène, 1967; De la grammatologie, 1967; L'écriture et la différence, 1967; Marges, 1972; La dissémination, 1972; Glas, 1974; La vérité en peinture, 1979; La carte postale, 1980; Positions, 1981; Spurs: Nietzsche's styles, 1981; Archaeology of the Frivolous, 1987; Psyché, 1987; De l'esprit, 1987; Mémoires: pour Paul De Man, 1988; Du droit à la philosophie, 1990; Mémoires d'aveugle, 1990; Le problème de la genèse dans la philosophie de Husserl, 1990; L'autre cap, 1991; Donner le temps, 1991; Qu'est-ce que la poésie?, 1991; Reader, 1991; Acts of Literature, 1992; Cinders, 1992; Spectres de Marx, 1993; Aporias, 1994; De l'hospitalité, 1997; Politiques de l'amitié, 1997. *Address:* Ecole des Hautes Etudes en Sciences Sociales, 54 boulevard Raspail, 75006 Paris, France.

DERRY, Bishop of, (RC), since 1994; **Most Rev. Séamus Hegarty;** *b* 26 Jan. 1940; *s* of James Hegarty and Mary O'Donnell. *Educ:* Kilcar National School; St Eunan's Coll., Letterkenny; St Patrick's Coll., Maynooth; University Coll., Dublin. Priest, 1966; post-grad. studies, University Coll., Dublin, 1966–67; Dean of Studies 1967–71, President 1971–82, Holy Cross College, Falcarragh; Bishop of Raphoe, 1982–94. *Publication:* contribs to works on school administration and student assessment. *Recreations:* bridge, angling. *Address:* St Eugene's Cathedral, Derry BT48 9AP. *T:* (028) 7126 2302, *Fax:* (028) 7137 1960; *e-mail:* derrydio@aol.com.

DERRY AND RAPHOE, Bishop of, since 1980; **Rt Rev. James Mehaffey;** *b* 29 March 1931; *s* of John and Sarah Mehaffey; *m* 1956, Thelma P. L. Jackson; two *s* one *d*. *Educ:* Trinity College, Dublin (MA, BD); Queen's University, Belfast (PhD). Curate Assistant: St Patrick's, Belfast, 1954–56; St John's, Deptford, London, 1956–58; Minor Canon, Down Cathedral, 1958–60; Bishop's Curate, St Christopher's, Belfast, 1960–62; Incumbent: Kilkeel, Diocese of Dromore, 1962–66; Cregagh, Diocese of Down, 1966–80. Hon. DLitt Ulster, 1999. *Address:* The See House, 112 Culmore Road, Londonderry BT48 8JF. *T:* (028) 7135 1206.

DERVAIRD, Hon Lord; John Murray; Dickson Minto Professor of Company Law, Edinburgh University, 1990–99, now Professor Emeritus; a Senator of the College of Justice in Scotland, 1988–89; *b* 8 July 1935; *o s* of J. H. Murray, farmer, Stranraer; *m* 1960, Bridget Jane, *d* of Sir William Godfrey, 7th Bt, and of Lady Godfrey; three *s*. *Educ:* Stranraer schs; Edinburgh Academy; Corpus Christi Coll., Oxford (BA 1st cl. Lit. Hum., 1959); Edinburgh Univ. (LLB 1962). FCIArb 1991. Advocate, 1962; QC (Scot.) 1974. Dean, Faculty of Law, Edinburgh Univ., 1994–96. Mem., Scottish Law Commn, 1979–88. Chairman: Scottish Lawyers' European Gp, 1975–78; Scottish Council of Law Reporting, 1978–88; Scottish Cttee on Law of Arbitration, 1986–96; Scottish Council for Internat. Arbitration, 1989–; Member: City Disputes Panel, 1994–; Panel of Arbitrators, Internat. Centre for Investment Disputes, 1998–; Adv. Bd, Internat. Arbitration Inst., Paris, 2000–; Vice-Pres., Centre of Conciliation and Arbitration for Advanced Techniques, Paris, 2000–. Vice-President: Agricultural Law Assoc., 1985–91 (Chm., 1979–85); Comité Européen de Droit Rural, 1989–91, 1995–96. Hon. Pres., Advocates' Business Law Group, 1988–. Dir and Chm., BT Scottish Ensemble, 1988–2000. Corresp. Mem., ICC Cttee on Business Law, Paris, 1994–. Trustee, David Hume Inst, 1994–. Grand Chaplain, Von Poser Soc. of Scotland, 1995; Knight, Order of Von Poser, 1996. *Publications:* contributed to: Festschrift für Dr Pikalo, 1979; Mélanges offert à Jean Megret, 1985; Stair Encyclopedia of Scots Law, 1987, 1992, 1998, 2001; Scottish Legal Tradition, 1991; Corporate Law – the European Dimension, 1991; European Company Law, 1992; International Handbook on Commercial Arbitration, 1995; Essays in Honour of Lord Mackenzie-Stuart of Dean, 1996; Science and Law, 2000; articles in legal and ornithological jls. *Recreations:* farming, gardening, birdwatching, music, curling, field sports. *Address:* Auchenmalg House, Auchenmalg, Glenluce, Wigtownshire DG8 0JJ. *T:* (01581) 500205; Wood of Dervaird Farm, Glenluce DG8 9JT. *T:* (01581) 300222, *Fax:* (0131) 220 0644. *Clubs:* New, Puffins (Edinburgh); Aberlady Curlers.

DERWENT, 5th Baron *cr* 1881; **Robin Evelyn Leo Vanden-Bempde-Johnstone,** LVO 1957; Bt 1795; DL; Deputy Chairman, Hutchison Whampoa (Europe) Ltd, since 1998 (Managing Director, 1985–97); *b* 30 Oct. 1930; *s* of 4th Baron Derwent, CBE and Marie-Louise (*d* 1985), *d* of Albert Picard, Paris; *S* father, 1986; *m* 1957, Sybille, *d* of late Vicomte de Simard de Pitray and Madame Jeanine Hennessy; one *s* three *d*. *Educ:* Winchester College; Clare Coll., Cambridge (Scholar, MA 1953). 2nd Lieut 1949, 60th Rifles; Lieut 1950, Queen Victoria's Rifles (TA). HM Diplomatic Service, 1954–69; served FO, Paris, Mexico City, Washington. Director, NM Rothschild & Sons, Merchant Bankers, 1969–85. Director: F&C (Pacific) Investment Trust Ltd, 1989–2001; Scarborough Building Soc., 1991–2001. Chm., London & Provincial Antique Dealers' Assoc., 1989–95. Mem., N York Moors Nat. Park Authy, 1997–99. DL N Yorks, 1991. Chevalier de la Légion d'Honneur (France), 1957; Officier de l'Ordre National du Mérite (France), 1978. *Recreations:* shooting, fishing. *Heir:* *s* Hon. Francis Patrick Harcourt Vanden-Bempde-Johnstone [*b* 23 Sept. 1965; *m* 1990, Cressida, *o d* of Christopher John Bourke, *qv*]. *Address:* Hackness Hall, Hackness, Scarborough YO13 0BL; Flat 6, Sovereign Court, 29 Wrights Lane, W8 5SH. *Club:* Boodle's.

DERWENT, Henry Clifford Sydney; Director, Environment: Risks and Atmosphere, Department for Environment, Food and Rural Affairs (formerly Department of the Environment, Transport and the Regions), since 1999; *b* 19 Nov. 1951; *s* of late Clifford Sydney Derwent and of Joan Kathleen (*née* Craft); *m* 1988, Rosemary Patricia Jesse Meaker; three *d*. *Educ:* Berkhamsted Sch.; Worcester Coll., Oxford. Department of the Environment, 1974–86; planning policy; PSA; London housing; commercial property; Rayner scrutiny; seconded to Midland Bank; inner cities; Department of Transport, subseq. DETR, now DEFRA, 1986–: private office; local finance; vehicle licensing; central finance; highways; Under Sec., then Dir, Nat. Roads Policy, 1992–97; (on secondment) Corporate Finance Div., SBC Warburg, later Warburg Dillon Read, 1997–99. *Recreations:* flute, trombone, riding, watercolours. *Address:* c/o Department for Environment, Food and Rural Affairs, Ashdown House, 123 Victoria Street, SW1E 6DE.

DERX, Donald John, CB 1975; non-executive Director, Glaxo Holdings, later Glaxo Wellcome plc, 1991–97; *b* 25 June 1928; *s* of John Derx and Violet Ivy Stroud; *m* 1956, Luisa Donzelli; two *s* two *d*. *Educ:* Tiffin Boys' Sch., Kingston-on-Thames; St Edmund Hall, Oxford (BA). Asst Principal, BoT, 1951; seconded to Cabinet Office, 1954–55; Principal, Colonial Office, 1957; Asst Sec., Industrial Policy Gp, DEA, 1965; Dir, Treasury Centre for Admin. Studies, 1968; Head of London Centre, Civil Service Coll., 1970; Under Sec., 1971–72, Dep. Sec., 1972–84, Dept of Employment; Dir, Policy Studies Inst., 1985–86; with Glaxo Holdings plc, 1986–90.

DERYCKE, Erik; MP (Flemish Socialist) Kortrijk, since 1984; Minister of Foreign Affairs, Belgium, 1995–99; *b* Waregem, Flanders, 28 Oct. 1949. *Educ:* State Univ. of Ghent (degree in Law 1972). Lawyer, 1972–. Flemish Socialist Party: Mem. Council, W Flanders, 1975–84; Mem., Public Commn for Social Assistance, Waregem, 1976–88; Municipal Councillor, Waregem, 1989–; Mem., Exec. Cttee; National Parliament: Dep. Minister, Sci. Policy, 1990–92, and Minister of Develt Co-operation, 1991–92; Dep. Minister of Develt Co-operation, 1992–95; Minister of Foreign Affairs and Develt Co-operation, March–June 1995; formerly Belgian Rep. at Council of Europe and WEU. *Address:* Chambre des Représentants, Rue de Louvain, 1008 Brussels, Belgium.

DESAI, family name of **Baron Desai**.

DESAI, Baron *cr* 1991 (Life Peer), of St Clement Danes in the City of Westminster; **Meghnad Jagdishchandra Desai,** PhD; Professor of Economics, since 1983, and Director, Centre for the Study of Global Governance, since 1992, London School of Economics and Political Science; *b* 10 July 1940; *s* of late Jagdishchandra and of Mandakini Desai; *m* 1970, Gail Graham Wilson (separated 1995); one *s* two *d*. *Educ:* Univ. of Bombay (BA Hons, MA); Univ. of Pennsylvania (PhD 1964). Associate Specialist, Dept of Agricultural Econs, Univ. of Calif, Berkeley, 1963–65; London School of Economics: Lectr, 1965–77, Sen. Lectr, 1977–80, Reader, 1980–83, Dept. of Econs; Head, Develt Studies Inst., 1990–95. Pres., Assoc. of Univ. Teachers in Econs, 1987–90; Mem. Council, REconS, 1988. Life Pres., Islington South and Finsbury Constituency Labour Pty, 1993– (Chm., 1986–92). Hon. DSc Kingston, 1992; Hon. DSc (Econ) E London, 1994; DUniv Middlesex, 1993; Hon. DPhil London Guildhall, 1996. *Publications:* Marxian Economic Theory, 1974; Applied Econometrics, 1976; Marxian Economics, 1979; Testing Monetarism, 1981; (Asst Editor to Prof. Dharma Kumar) The Cambridge Economic History of India 1757–1970, 1983; (ed jtly) Agrarian Power and Agricultural Productivity in South Asia, 1984; (ed) Lenin on Economics, 1987; Macroeconomics and Monetary Theory: selected essays, vol. 1, 1995; Poverty, Famine and Economic Development: selected essays, vol. 2, 1995; (ed jtly) Global Governance, 1995; (ed) On Inequality, 1995; contrib. Econometrica, Econ. Jl, Rev. of Econ. Studies, Economica, Econ. Hist. Rev. *Address:* London School of Economics and Political Science, Houghton Street, Aldwych, WC2A 2AE.

DESAI, Anita, FRSL; novelist; *b* 24 June 1937; *d* of Toni Nimé and D. N. Mazumbar; *m* 1958, Ashvin Desai; two *s* two *d*. *Educ:* Queen Mary's Sch., Delhi; Miranda House, Univ. of Delhi (BA Hons). FRSL 1963. First story published 1946; novelist and book reviewer (freelance), 1963–. Helen Cam Vis. Fellow, 1986–87, Hon. Fellow, 1988, Girton Coll., Univ. of Cambridge; Elizabeth Drew Prof., Smith Coll., USA, 1987–88; Purington Prof. of English, Mount Holyoke Coll., USA, 1988–92; Prof. of Writing, MIT, 1993–; Ashby Fellow, 1989, Hon. Fellow, 1991, Clare Hall, Univ. of Cambridge. Hon. Mem., Amer. Acad. of Arts and Letters, 1993. Neil Gunn Prize for Internat. Writers, Scotland, 1993; Alberto Moravia Prize for Internat. Writers, Italy, 1999. Padma Sri, 1990. *Publications:* Cry, The Peacock, 1963; Voices in the City, 1965; Bye-Bye Blackbird, 1971; Where Shall We Go This Summer?, 1973; Fire on the Mountain, 1978 (Winifred Holtby Award, RSL, 1978); Games at Twilight, 1979; Clear Light of Day, 1980; The Village by the Sea, 1983 (Guardian Prize for Children's Fiction, 1983; filmed, 1992); In Custody, 1984 (screenplay, filmed 1994); Baumgartner's Bombay, 1988 (Hadassah Prize, Hadassah Magazine, NY, 1989); Journey to Ithaca, 1995; Fasting, Feasting, 1999; Diamond Dust and Other Stories, 2000. *Address:* c/o Deborah Rogers Ltd, 20 Powis Mews, W11 1JN.

de SAUMAREZ, 7th Baron *cr* 1831; **Eric Douglas Saumarez;** Bt 1801; farmer; *b* 13 Aug. 1956; *s* of 6th Baron de Saumarez and Joan Beryl, (Julia), *d* of late Douglas Raymond Charlton; *S* father, 1991; *m* 1st, 1982, Christine Elizabeth (marr. diss. 1990), *yr d* of B. N. Halliday; two *d*; 2nd, 1991, Susan M. Hearn. *Educ:* Milton Abbey; Nottingham Univ.; RAC, Cirencester. *Recreations:* flying, shooting, ski-ing, fishing. *Heir: twin b* Hon. Victor Thomas Saumarez, *b* 13 Aug. 1956. *Address:* Shrubland Park, Coddenham, Ipswich, Suffolk IP6 9QQ.

de SAVARY, Peter John; international entrepreneur; *b* 11 July 1944; *m* 1986, (Lucille) Lana Paton; three *d* (and two *d* by a former marriage). *Educ:* Charterhouse. Activities in the energy, property, finance, maritime and leisure fields. Chm., Victory Syndicate, 1983 British Challenge for America's Cup. Chm., Carnegie Club, 1994–. Contested (Referendum) Falmouth and Camborne, 1997. Tourism Personality of the Year, English Tourist Bd, 1988. *Recreations:* sailing, riding, carriage driving. *Address:* Skibo Castle, Dornoch, Sutherland IV25 3RQ. *Clubs:* St James's, Royal Automobile, Royal Thames Yacht; Royal Burnham Yacht, Royal Torbay Yacht, Royal Corinthian Yacht, Port Pendennis Yacht (Cdre).

de SILGUY, Count Yves-Thibault Christian Marie; Senior Executive Vice-President, SUEZ, since 2000; *b* Rennes, 22 July 1948; *s* of Raymond de Silguy and Claude de Pompery; *m* 1976, Jacqueline de Montillet de Grenaud; one *s* one *d*. *Educ:* Collège Saint-Martin; Univ. of Rennes (Law and Econ Scis); Sch. of Public Service, Institut d'Etudes Politiques, Paris (Dip.); Ecole Nationale d'Administration. Sec. for Foreign Affairs to Dir for Econ. and Financial Affairs, 1976–80; Advr, then Dep. Staff Dir for Vice-Pres. Ortoli, Comr for Econ. and Monetary Affairs, 1981–84; Advr i/c Econ. Affairs, French Embassy in Washington, 1985–86; Tech. Advr to Prime Minister i/c European Affairs and Internat. Econ. and Financial Affairs, 1986–88; Manager, Internat. Business Div. and Gp Internat. Business Dir, Usinor Sacilor, 1988–93; Sec. Gen., Interministerial Cttee for European Econ. Co-operation and Advr for European Affairs to Prime Minister, 1993–95. Mem., European Commn, 1995–99. Gen. Deleg. of French Steel Fedn, 1990–93; Chm. Bd, Professional Center for Steel Stats, 1990–93; Chm., Finance Cttee, Eurofer, 1990–93. Officier des Arts et des Lettres (France), 1994; Officier du Mérite Agricole (France), 1995; Chevalier de la Légion d'Honneur (France), 1996. *Recreations:* tennis, yachting, hunting. *Address:* SUEZ, 16 rue de la Ville l'Evèque, 75008 Paris, France. *Clubs:* Polo, Cercle de l'Union Interallié (Paris).

de SILVA, Desmond (George Lorenz); QC 1984; *b* 13 Dec. 1939; *s* of Edmund Frederick Lorenz de Silva, MBE, retired Ambassador, and late Esme Gregg de Silva; *m* 1987, HRH Princess Katarina of Yugoslavia, *d* of TRH late Prince Tomislav of Yugoslavia and Princess Margarita of Baden; one *d*. *Educ:* Dulwich College Prep Sch.; Trinity College, Ceylon. Served with 3rd Carabiniers (3rd Dragoon Guards). Called to the Bar: Middle Temple, 1964; Sierra Leone, 1968; The Gambia, 1981; Gibraltar, 1992; a Dep. Circuit Judge, 1976–80. Vice-Chm., Westminster Community Relations Council, 1980–82; Councilman, City of London, 1980–95; Main Session Chm., First Internat. Conf. on Human Value, 1981. Member: Home Affairs Standing Cttee, Bow Gp, 1982; Editl Adv. Bd, Crossbow, 1984; Crime and Juvenile Delinquency Study Gp, Centre for Policy Studies, 1983–87. Member: Governing Council, Manorial Soc. of GB, 1982–; Nat. Cttee for 900th anniv. of Domesday. Patron: Meml Gates Trust, 1999–; PRESET, 2000–. Liveryman, Gunmakers' Co. Vice-Pres., St John Ambulance London (Prince of Wales's) Dist, 1984–; Mem., St John Council for London, 1986–; KStJ 1994. *Publication:* (ed) English Law and Ethnic Minority Customs, 1986. *Recreations:* politics, shooting, travel. *Address:* 2 Paper Buildings, Temple, EC4Y 7ET; 28 Sydney Street, SW3 6PP; Taprobane Island, off Weligama, Sri Lanka. *Clubs:* Brooks's, Naval and Military, Carlton; Orient (Colombo).

de SILVA, Harendra (Aneurin Domingo); QC 1995; a Recorder, since 1991; *b* 29 Sept. 1945; *s* of Annesley de Silva and Maharani of Porbandar; *m* 1972, Indira Raj; one *s* one *d*. *Educ:* Doon Sch., Dehra Dun, India; Millfield Sch.; Queens' Coll., Cambridge (MA, LLM). Called to the Bar, Middle Temple, 1970. *Recreations:* golf, bridge. *Address:* 2 Paper Buildings, Temple, EC4Y 7ET. *T:* (020) 7936 2611. *Clubs:* Oxford and Cambridge; Roehampton; Ooty (Ootacamund, S India).

DESIO, Prof. Ardito, Dr nat. sci.; FRGS; Professor of Geology (and Past Director of Institute of Geology), at the University of Milan, and of Applied Geology, at the Engineering School of Milan, 1931–72, now Emeritus; *b* Palmanova, Frioul, 18 April 1897; *s* of Antonio Desio and Caterina Zorzella; *m* 1932, Aurelia Bevilacqua; one *s* one *d*. *Educ:* Udine and Florence. Grad. Univ. of Florence in Nat. Sciences, 1920. Asst, University of Florence, 1922, and of Pavia, 1923, also Univ. and Engineering Sch., Milan, 1924–25 to 1930–31; Lectr in Geology, Phys. Geography, University of Milan, 1929–30 and in Palaeontology there until 1935. Volunteer, 1st World War, 1915, Lieut, Alpine Troops, 1916–17, POW, 1917–18; Captain, 1924–53; Major, 1954. Geol Consultant, Edison Co. and Public Power Corp. of Greece, 1948–79. Pres., Italian Geological Cttee, 1966–73. Dir, Rivista Italiana di Paleontologia e Stratigrafia, 1942–95; Past Dir, Geologia Tecnica. Past Pres., Ital. Geolog. Soc.; Mem. (Hon. Pres.) Ital. Assoc. of Geologists; Past Pres., Ital. Order of Geologists; Mem., Ital. Order of Journalists; Hon. Member: Ital. Paleont. Soc.; Gesellschaft für Erdkunde zu Berlin, 1941; Italian Geog. Soc., 1955; Faculty of Sciences University of Chile, 1964; Geological Soc. of London, 1964; Indian Paleont. Soc.; Soc. Ital. Progresso delle Scienze, 1978; Ist. per il Medio ed Estremo Oriente, 1979; Assoc. Mineraria Subalpina, 1985; Corresp. Member: Soc. Géol. Belgique, 1952; Explorer Club, USA, 1987; Life Mem., Geog. Soc., USA, 1955; Member: Institut d'Egypte, 1936; Accademia Naz. Lincei, 1948; Inst. Lombardo Accad. Scienze Lettere, 1949. In 1938 discovered first deposits of natural oil and gas in subsoil of Libya and Mg-K salt deposit in Marada Oasis; led expedition to K2 (8611 m, 2nd highest peak in the World; reached for 1st time on 31 July 1954), and 18 expeditions in Africa (Libya, Ethiopia) and Asia (Iran, Afghanistan, Pakistan, Nepal, Burma, Philippines, Tibet); in summer 1987 organised expedition which re-measured height of two highest mts in the world, Mt Everest and K2; in summer 1988 expedition visited the northern slope of Karakorum as far as the Kun Lun mountain range; in summers 1989 and 1990 organised a permanent scientific lab. (a glass and aluminium pyramid) in Nepal below the top of Everest at 5050m; also organised every year until 1993 a dozen ambient expeditions in the Himalaya and Karakorum, concerning geodesy, geophysics, geology, ethnography, physiology, and medicine of high altitude. Santoro Prize, 1931; Royal Prize, 1934, Royal Acad. Lincei; Gold Medal of the Republic of Pakistan, 1954; Gold Medal of the Sciences, Letters and Arts, of Italy, 1956; Patrons medal of Royal Geog. Soc. of London, 1957; USA Antarctic Service Medal, 1974; Gold Lion of Lion's Club, Udine, 1976; Paul Harris Award, Internat. Rotary Club, 1986; Gold Medal of Ital. Geol. Soc., 1988; Gold Medal of Rotary Club, 1988. Kt Grand Cross, Order of Merit, Italy, 1955. *Publications:* about 440, among them: Le Isole Italiane dell'Egeo, 1931; La spedizione geografica Italiana al Karakoram 1929, 1936; scientific reports of his expedns to Libyan Sahara, 7 vols, 1938–42; Le vie della sete, 1950; Geologia applicata all'ingegneria, 1949, 3rd edn 1973–89; Ascent of K2, 1956 (11 languages, 15 editions); Geology of the Baltoro Basin (Karakorum), 1970; Results of half-a-century investigation on the glaciers of the Ortler-Cevedale, 1973; La Geologia dell'Italia, 1973; Geology of Central Badakhshan (NE Afghanistan), 1975; Geology of the Upper Shaksgam Valley, Sinkiang, China, 1980; L'Antartide, 1985; Sulle Vie della Sete, dei Ghiacci e dell'Oro, 1987; Which is the highest mountain in the world?, 1988; Geographic features of the Karakorum, 1991; some 250 articles in newspapers and magazines of different countries. *Recreation:* alpinist. *Address:* Via S. Andrea delle Fratte 38/A, 00186 Roma, Italy. *Clubs:* Italian Alpine; Touring (Italy); Hon. Member: Alpine; Andino Venezolano (Caracas); Internat. Rotary; Panatlon; Himalayan; Excursionista Carioca (Brazil); Alpin Français.

DESLANDES, Ian Anthony; Chief Executive, Construction Confederation, 1997–99; *b* 17 July 1941; *s* of Albert Deslandes and Christine Veronica Deslandes (*née* Hale); *m* 1965, Mary Catherine Bowler; two *s*. *Educ:* Stonyhurst Coll.; St Catherine's Coll., Oxford. Conservative Res. Dept., 1965–70; PA to Conservative Party Chm., 1970–72; Dir, Housebuilders' Fedn, 1973–78; Dir, Manpower Services, 1978–86, Dep. Dir Gen., 1985–92, Dir Gen., 1992–97, Building Employers' Confedn. CBI: Chm., Trade Assoc. Council, 1999; Mem., Council and President's Cttee, 1999. *Recreations:* reading, jazz, gardening, walking. *Address:* Greystones, Downhouse Lane, Higher Eype, Bridport, Dorset DT6 6AH. *T:* (01308) 424498.

DESLONGCHAMPS, Prof. Pierre, OC 1989; OQ 1997; PhD; FRS 1983; FRSC 1974; FCIC; Professor of Organic Chemistry, Université de Sherbrooke, Canada, since 1972; *b* 8 May 1938; *s* of Rodolphe Deslongchamps and Madeleine Magnan; *m* 1st, 1960, Micheline Renaud (marr. diss. 1975); two *c*; 2nd, 1976, Shirley E. Thomas (marr. diss. 1983); 3rd, 1987, Marie-Marthe Leroux. *Educ:* Univ. de Montréal (BSc Chem., 1959); Univ. of New Brunswick (PhD Chem., 1964). FCIC 1980; FAAAS 1988. Post-doctoral Student with Dr R.B. Woodward, Harvard Univ., USA, 1965; Asst Prof., Univ. de Montréal, 1966; Asst Prof. 1967, Associate Prof. 1968, Univ. de Sherbrooke. A.P. Sloan Fellow, 1970–72; E. W. R. Steacie Fellow, 1971–74. Member: New Swiss Chemical Soc.; Amer. Chem. Soc.; Assoc. of Harvard Chemists; Ordre des Chemistes du Québec; Assoc. Canadienne-Française pour l'Avancement des Sciences; Assoc. for Advancement of Science in Canada; Canadian Cttee of Scientists and Scholars; Soc. Française de Chimie; Associate Mem., World Innovation Foundn (UK), 1999; For. Asst Mem., Acad. des Scis de Paris, 1995. Dr *hc:* Univ. Pierre et Marie Curie, Paris, 1983; Bishop's Univ., Univ. de Montréal, and Univ. Laval, 1984; New Brunswick Univ., 1985; Univ. of Moncton, 1995. Scientific Prize of Québec, 1971; E. W. R. Steacie Prize (Nat. Scis), NRCC, 1974; Médaille Vincent, ACFAS, 1975; Merck, Sharp and Dohme Lectures Award, CIC, 1976; Canada Council Izaak Walton Killam Meml Scholarship, 1976–77; John Simon Guggenheim Meml Foundn Fellow, 1979; Medáille Pariseau, ACFAS, 1979; Marie-Victorin Médaille, Province of Que., 1987; Alfred Bader Award in Organic Chemistry, Canadian Soc. of Chemistry, 1991; Canada Gold Medal for Science and Engrng, NSERCC, 1993; Lemieux Award, Canadian Soc. for Chemistry, 1994. Holder of 9 patents. *Publications:* Stereoelectronic Effects in Organic Chemistry, 1983; over 200 contribs on organic chemistry in Tetrahedron, Jl Amer. Chem. Soc., Canadian Jl of Chem., Pure Applied Chem., Synth. Commun., Nouv. Jl Chim., Heterocycles, Jl Molecular Struct., Interface, Aldrichimica Acta, and Bull. Soc. Chim., France. *Recreations:* fishing, reading. *Address:* Department of Chemistry, Faculty of Sciences, Université de Sherbrooke, Sherbrooke, QC J1K 2R1, Canada. *T:* (819) 8217002, *Fax:* (819) 8217910; RR 1, 11 McFarland Road, North Hatley, QC J0B 2C0, *T:* (819) 8424238.

DESMOND, Denis Fitzgerald, CBE 1989; Lord-Lieutenant of Co. Londonderry, since 2000; Chairman, Desmond & Sons Ltd, since 1970; *b* 11 May 1943; *s* of late Major James Fitzgerald Desmond, DL, JP and Harriet Ivy Desmond (*née* Evans); *m* 1965, Anick Marie Françoise Marguerite Faussemagne; one *d*. *Educ:* Trinity Coll., Glenalmond. 2nd Lieut, then Lieut RCT (TA), 1964–69. ADC to Governor of NI, 1967–69. Dir, Ulster Bank, 1990–97. Chm., Altnagelvin Hosps Health Trust, 1996–. High Sheriff 1973, DL 1992, Co. Londonderry. Hon. DSc: QUB, 1987; Ulster, 1991. *Address:* Bellarena, Limavady, Co. Londonderry BT49 0HZ. *Club:* Queen's.

DESMOND, Richard Clive; Chairman, Northern & Shell Network, since 1974; Proprietor, Express Newspapers, since 2000; *b* 8 Dec. 1951; *s* of Cyril and Millie Desmond; *m* 1983, Janet Robertson; one *s*. *Educ:* Christ's Coll., Finchley. Musician, 1967; Advertisement Exec., Thomson Gp, 1967–68; Group Advertisement Manager, Beat Pubns Ltd, 1968–74; launched International Musician, 1974 (separate editions in US, Europe, Australia and Japan); publr of numerous magazines in areas incl. leisure, music, hi tech, fitness, cooking, envmt, business, automative, and men's and women's lifestyle; De

Monde Advertising Ltd, 1976–89; OK! magazine, 1993–; Fantasy Channel, 1995–; OK! TV, 1999–. *Recreations:* music, fitness. *Address:* Express Newspapers, Ludgate House, 245 Blackfriars Road, SE1 9UX. *T:* (020) 7928 8000.

de SOUZA, Christopher Edward; freelance composer; broadcaster; Artistic Director, Southern Sinfonia, since 1998; *b* 6 June 1943; *s* of Denis Walter de Souza and Dorothy Edna (*née* Woodman); *m* 1971, Robyn Ann Williams (marr. diss. 1981); partner, Elinor Anne Kelly; two *s*. *Educ:* Prior Park Coll., Bath; Univ. of Bristol (BA Music 1966); Old Vic Theatre Sch. Head of Music, St Bernadette's RC Comp. Sch., Bristol, 1966–70; Producer, Sadlers Wells/ENO, 1971–75; Arts Producer, BBC Radio London, 1975–79; Producer, BBC Radio 3, 1980–95. Founder Dir, Liszt Fest. of London, 1977; (with J. Piper) music organiser, HM Silver Jubilee Fireworks, 1977. Director: UK stage premières: Don Sanche (Liszt), 1977; The Mother of Us All (Virgil Thompson), 1979; The Duenna (Prokofiev), 1980; Palestrina (Pfitzner), 1981; William Tell (Gretry), 1984; USA première: Don Sanche (Liszt), 1986. *Compositions include:* music for TV, incl. Maharajahs, 1987; orch., chamber and choral works including The Ides of March, 1993. *Publications:* A Child's Guide to Looking at Music, 1979; (ed jtly) Liszt: Don Sanche, 1985; Kingfisher Book of Music, 1996; contrib. to The Listener, Music and Musicians, Musical Times, Radio Times, Strad, The Times, British Music Year Book. *Recreations:* reading, travel, swimming, drawing. *Address:* Westbrook Farm Cottage, Boxford, Berks RG20 8DL. *Club:* Royal Over-Seas League.

DESPRÉS, Robert; President, DRM Holdings Inc., since 1987; *b* 27 Sept. 1924; *s* of Adrien Després and Augustine Marmen; *m* 1949; two *s* two *d*. *Educ:* Académie de Québec (BA 1943); Laval Univ. (MCom 1947); (postgrad. studies) Western Univ. Comptroller, Québec Power Co., 1947–63; Reg. Manager, Administration & Trust Co., 1963–65; Dep. Minister, Québec Dept of Revenue, 1965–69; Pres. and Gen. Man., Québec Health Insurance Bd, 1969–73; Pres., Université du Québec, 1973–78; Pres. and Chief Exec. Officer, National Cablevision Ltd, 1978–80, and Netcom Inc., 1978–89; Chm. of the Bd, Atomic Energy of Canada Ltd, 1978–86. Chairman: Domosys Corp.; Alliance Forest Products; Director: Sidbec Corp.; UniMedia; South Shore Industries Ltd; Greyvest Inc.; PMG Financial Inc.; Greyvest Capital Inc.; Cominar-Reit; McWatters Mines; Printera; Amisco Industries Ltd; HRS Holdings Ltd; Infectio Diagnostic Inc.; Nat. Optics Inst.; Canadian Certified General Accountants' Res. Foundn; Council for Canadian Unity; la Soc. du Musée du Séminaire de Québec; Inst de cardiologie de Québec. *Publications:* contrib. Commerce, and Soc. of Management Accountants Revue. *Recreations:* golf, reading. *Address:* 890 rue Dessane, Québec, QC G1S 3J8, Canada. *T:* (418) 6872100. *Clubs:* Rideau, Cercle Universitaire; Lorette Golf.

de SWIET, Eleanor Jane, (Mrs Michael de Swiet), MA; Headteacher, The Henrietta Barnett School, 1989–99, retired; *b* 18 Aug. 1942; *d* of Richard and Joan Hawkins; *m* 1964, Prof. Michael de Swiet; two *s* one *d*. *Educ:* Girton Coll., Cambridge (MA Classics); Inst. of Education (PGCE). Francis Holland Sch., 1965–67; St Paul's Girls' Sch., 1967–70; break from teaching to have children and to travel to US for a year; Head of Careers, Queen's Coll., London, 1975–84; Head of Classics, Head of 4th and 5th years, City of London Sch., 1984–89. President: JACT, 1995–97; Assoc. of Maintained Girls' Schs, 1997–98 (Treas., 1995–97). Ext. Advr to Governing Bodies on Assessment of Headteachers, 2000–. Dir, Smallpeice Enterprises, 1995–2000. Mem. of Council, Cheltenham Ladies' Coll., 1999–. Trustee: Open Door, 2000–; Toynbee Hall, 2001–. Member: The Ramblers; National Trust. *Recreations:* walking, reading, Yorkshire, travelling. *Address:* 60 Hornsey Lane, N6 5LU. *T:* (020) 7272 3195; *e-mail:* jdeswiet@freenetname.co.uk.

DETMER, Prof. Don Eugene, MD; Dennis Gillings Professor of Health Management, Judge Institute of Management, and Fellow of Clare Hall, University of Cambridge, since 1999; *b* 3 Feb. 1939; *s* of Lawrence D. Detmer and Esther B. Detmer (*née* McCormick); *m* 1961, Mary Helen McFerson; two *d*. *Educ:* Univ. of Kansas (MD 1965). Asst Prof., 1973–77, Associate Prof., 1977–80, Prof., 1980–84, of Surgery and Preventive Medicine, Univ. of Wisconsin-Madison; Vice Pres. for Health Sci., and Prof. of Surgery and Med. Informatics, Univ. of Utah, 1984–88; University of Virginia: Vice Pres. for Health Sci., and Prof. of Surgery and Business Admin, 1988–92; Co-Dir, Virginia Health Policy Center, 1992–99; Vice Pres. and Provost for Health Sci., and Prof. of Health Policy and Surgery, 1993–96; Louis Nerancy Prof. of Health Scis Policy, Univ. Prof. and Sen. Vice Pres., 1996–99. *Publications:* (ed jtly and contrib.) The Computer-Based Patient Record: an essential technology for health care, 1991, rev. edn 1997; articles in jls and contribs to books. *Recreations:* fly-fishing, reading biographies, wilderness canoeing, handcrafts. *Address:* Judge Institute of Management, Trumpington Street, Cambridge CB2 1AG. *T:* (01223) 339700. *Club:* Cosmos (Washington DC).

de TRAFFORD, Sir Dermot Humphrey, 6th Bt *cr* 1841; VRD 1963; Director, 1977–90, Chairman, 1982–90, Low & Bonar plc (Deputy Chairman, 1980–82); Chairman: GHP Group Ltd, 1965–77 (Managing Director, 1961); Calor Gas Holding, 1974–88; *b* 19 Jan. 1925; *s* of Sir Rudolph de Trafford, 5th Bt, OBE and June Lady Audley (*née* Chaplin), MBE (*d* 1977); *S* father, 1983; *m* 1st, 1946, Patricia Mary Beeley (marr. diss. 1973); three *s* six *d*; 2nd, 1973, Mrs Xandra Caradini Walter. *Educ:* Harrow Sch.; Christ Church, Oxford (MA). Trained as Management Consultant, Orr & Boss and Partners Ltd, 1949–52; Director: Monks Investment Trust; Imperial Continental Gas Assoc., 1963–87 (Dep. Chm., 1972–87); Petrofina SA, 1971–87. Chm. Council, Inst. of Dirs, 1990–93. *Recreations:* theatre, travel. *Heir:* *s* John Humphrey de Trafford [*b* 12 Sept. 1950; *m* 1975, Anne, *d* of J. Faure de Pebeyre; one *s* one *d*]. *Address:* The Old Vicarage, Appleshaw, Andover, Hants SP11 9BH. *T:* (01264) 772357. *Clubs:* White's, Royal Ocean Racing; Island Sailing.

DETTORI, Lanfranco, (Frankie), Hon. MBE 2000; flat race jockey; *b* Italy, 15 Dec. 1970; *s* of Gianfranco Dettori and Maria Dettori (*née* Nieman); *m* 1997, Catherine, *d* of W. R. Allen, *qv*; one *s*. Winner: World Young Jockey Championship, Japan, 1992, 1993; Ascot Gold Cup, on Drum Taps, 1992, 1993; French Derby; German Derby; Nonthorpe; Abbeye The Longchamp; Sussex Stakes; Fillies Mile; Irish Derby, on Balanchine, 1994; Oaks, on Balanchine, 1994, on Moonshell, 1995; Queen Elizabeth II, on Lammtarra, 1995; Epsom Derby, 1995; St Leger, on Classic Cliché, 1995, on Shantou, 1996; Prix de l'Arc de Triomphe, on Lammtarra, 1995; Two Thousand Guineas, on Mark of Esteem, 1996, on Island Sands, 1999; One Thousand Guineas, on Cape Verdi, 1998; French Two Thousand Guineas, on Bachir, 2000, on Noverre, 2001; Irish Champion Stakes, and Breeders' Cup Turf, NY, on Fantastic Light, 2001; Prix de l'Arc de Triomphe, on Sakhee, 2001; all seven winners, Ascot, 28 Sept. 1996. Champion Jockey, 1994, 1995. *Publication:* A Year in the Life of Frankie Dettori, 1996. *Address:* c/o Peter Burrell, 53 Stewarts Grove, SW3 6PH. *T:* (020) 7352 4448, *Fax:* (020) 7352 9697.

DEUCHAR, Rev. Andrew Gilchrist; Rector of St Peter with St James, Nottingham, since 2000; *b* 3 June 1955; *s* of late David and of (Lucretia) Marian Deuchar; *m* 1977, Francesca Fowler; three *s* two *d*. *Educ:* Royal Hospital Sch., Ipswich; Southampton Univ. (BTh); Salisbury and Wells Theol Coll. HM Diplomatic Service, 1974–81; ordained deacon, 1984, priest, 1985; Asst Curate, Alnwick, Northumberland, 1984–88; Team Vicar, S Wye Team Ministry, Hereford, 1988–90; Social Responsibility Advr, Canterbury and Rochester dios, 1990–94; Archbp of Canterbury's Sec. for Anglican Communion Affairs, 1994–2000. Hon. Canon, Canterbury Cathedral, 1995–2000. *Publications:* (contrib.) Anglicanism: a global communion, 1998; (contrib.) An Introduction to the Anglican Communion, 1998. *Recreations:* music, travel, walking, football, the Isle of Skye. *Address:* St Peter's Rectory, 3 King Charles Street, Nottingham NG1 6GB. *T:* (0115) 947 4891. *Club:* Nikaean.

See also P. L. Deuchar.

DEUCHAR, Patrick Lindsay; *b* 27 March 1949; *s* of late David and of Marian Deuchar; *m* Gwyneth Miles (marr. diss.); one *s* one *d*; *m* 1997, Liz Robertson; one *d*. *Educ:* Christ's Hospital; Lackham Coll. of Agriculture. Farming, 1967–72; IPC Business Press, 1972–74; PR Manager, RASE, 1974–77; PR Manager, Earls Court and Olympia, 1977–80; European Dir, World Championship Tennis, 1981–89; Chief Exec., Royal Albert Hall, 1989–98; Chm., London Centre Mgt Co., 1998–99; Chief Exec., Rugby Hospitality for Rugby World Cup, 1998–99; Events Consultant: Somerset House Trust Ltd, 1998–99; 7th Regt Armory Conservancy, NY, 1998–99. Director: London First, 1996–99; TS2K (Trng and Skills 2000) (formerly Trafalgar Square 2000), 1996– (Dep. Chm.); Covent Gdn Fest., 1998–; (non-exec.) Cavendish Consultancy, 2000–. Chm., Sparks Charity, 1992–96; Member: Nat. Fundraising Cttee, Muscular Dystrophy Group, 1989–92; Nat. Music Day Cttee, 1993–97; London Visitor Council, 1994–97; Royal Concert Cttee, 1994–97; Mem. Council, 1995–, Chm. Develt Cttee, 2000–, RCM. Trustee: Albert Meml Trust, 1994–99; Cardiff Bay Opera House, 1994–96. Barker, Variety Club of GB, 1992; Mem., Inst. of Dirs. FRSA 1992. *Recreations:* music, theatre, art, cooking, wines, family life. *Address:* 19 Parsons Green Lane, SW6 4HL.

See also Rev. A. G. Deuchar.

DEUCHAR, Dr Stephen John; Director, Tate Britain, since 1998; *b* 11 March 1957; *s* of Rev. John Deuchar and Nancy Dorothea Deuchar (*née* Jenkyns); *m* 1982, Dr Katie Scott; one *s* three *d*. *Educ:* Dulwich Coll. (Schol.); Univ. of Southampton (BA 1st Cl. Hons Hist.); Westfield Coll., London (PhD Hist. of Art 1986). National Maritime Museum: Curator of Paintings, 1985–87; Curator, Armada exhibn, 1987–88; Corporate Planning Manager, 1988–89; organizer of various exhibns and display projects, 1990–95; Dir, Neptune Court Project, 1995–97. Andrew W. Mellon Fellow in British Art, Yale Univ., 1981–82. Mem., Visual Arts Adv. Cttee, British Council, 1999–. *Publications:* Noble Exercise: the sporting ideal in 18th century British art, 1982; Paintings, Politics and Porter: Samuel Whitbread and British art, 1984; (jtly) Concise Catalogue of Oil Paintings in the National Maritime Museum, 1988; Sporting Art in 18th Century England: a social and political history, 1988; (jtly) Nelson: an illustrated history, 1995; contrib. articles on British art. *Recreation:* living on the North Downs. *Address:* Tate, Millbank, SW1P 4RG. *T:* (020) 7887 8048; Dunn Street Farmhouse, Pilgrims' Way, Westwell, Kent TN25 4NJ. *T:* (01233) 714203.

DEUKMEJIAN, George; lawyer; Partner, Sidley & Austin, 1991–2000; Republican; *b* 6 June 1928; *s* of C. George Deukmejian and Alice (*née* Gairdan); *m* 1957, Gloria M. Saatjian; one *s* two *d*. *Educ:* Watervliet Sch., NY; Siena College (BA 1949); St John's Univ., NY (JD 1952). Admitted to NY State Bar, 1952, Californian Bar, 1956, US Supreme Court Bar, 1970. US Army, 1953–55. Law practice, Calif., 1955; Partner, Riedman, Dalessi, Deukmejian & Woods; Mem., Calif. Assembly, 1963–67; Mem., Calif. Senate (minority leader), 1967–79; Attorney Gen., Calif., 1979–83; Governor, California, 1983–91. *Address:* 5366 E Broadway, Long Beach, CA 90803, USA.

DEUTCH, John Mark, PhD; Institute Professor, Department of Chemistry, Massachusetts Institute of Technology, since 1990; Director of Central Intelligence, USA, 1995–96; *b* 27 July 1938; *s* of Michael Joseph Deutch and Rachel Felicia Deutch (*née* Fischer); *m* Pat Lyon; three *s* by previous marr. *Educ:* Amherst Coll. (BA 1961); MIT (BChemEng 1961; PhD PhysChem 1965). Sec. of Defence Office, 1961; Nat. Bureau of Standards, 1966; Asst Prof., Princeton, 1967–70; Prof., Chemistry Dept, MIT, 1971– (Mem. Faculty, 1976–; Dean of Science, 1982–85; Provost, 1985–90); Dept of Energy, 1977–80; Department of Defence: Under-Sec., 1993–94, Dep. Sec., 1994–95. Member: Army Sci. Adv. Panel, 1975–78; President's Commn on Strategic Forces, 1983; White House Sci. Council, 1985–89; President's Foreign Intell. Adv. Bd, 1990–93. Mem., Amer. Acad. of Arts and Scis. Hon. DSc Amherst, 1978; Hon. DPhil: Lowell, 1986; Northeastern, 1995. *Publications:* numerous research articles. *Recreations:* tennis, squash, reading. *Address:* Department of Chemistry, Room 6-208, Massachusetts Institute of Technology, Cambridge, MA 02139, USA.

DEUTSCH, James Chobot, PhD; Chief Executive, Crusaid, since 1997; *b* 28 Nov. 1963; *s* of Harold Kauffman Deutsch and late Barbara Hope Deutsch (*née* Chobot). *Educ:* St George's Sch., Newport, RI; Harvard Coll. (AB 1987); King's Coll., Cambridge (MPhil 1988, PhD 1992). Temp. Lectr, UEA, 1992-93; Res. Fellow, Churchill Coll., Cambridge, 1993-95; Lectr, Imperial Coll., London, 1995-97. Director: AIDS Treatment Project, 1996-2000; Crusaid (Enterprises) Ltd, 1997-. Mem. Exec. Cttee, British HIV Assoc., 1999-2001. *Publications:* contrib. articles to Nature, Proc. Royal Soc., Evolution, HIV Medicine, Animal Behaviour, Conservation Biol., African Jl Ecol., and other jls. *Address:* 97 Belgrave Road, SW1V 2BH. *T:* (020) 7821 0580.

DEVA, Niranjan Joseph Aditya, (Nirj); DL; Member (C) South East Region, England, European Parliament, since 1999; Director-General, Policy Research Centre for Business, since 1997; *b* Colombo, 11 May 1948; *s* of late Thakur Dr Kingsley de Silva Deva Aditya and of Zita Virginia Deva; *m* Indra Lavinia, *d* of Romy Govindia; one step *s*. *Educ:* St Joseph's Coll., Colombo; Loughborough Univ. of Technol. (BTech Hons Aero. Eng.). Company dir and adviser; Dep. Chm., Symphony Environmental Plastics Ltd; Director: Orient Garments (Sri Lanka) Ltd; Ceylon and Foreign Trades (Sri Lanka) Ltd; Travel Ties.com (Europe) Ltd. Pol. Officer, 1979, Chm., 1981, Bow Gp. Organiser, Conf. on Overseas Develt and Brandt Report, 1979. Member: Governing Council, Royal Commonwealth Soc., 1979–83; Nat. Consumer Council, 1982–88; Dept of Employment Adv. Cttee, 1988–91; Chairman: DTI/NCC Cttee on De-regulation of European Air Transport, 1985–86; One Nation Forum Political Cttee, 1986–91. Pres., Bow Group Trade and Industry Cttee, 1996. Contested (C) Hammersmith, 1987; MP (C) Brentford and Isleworth, 1992–97; contested (C) same seat, 1997. PPS to Minister of State, Scottish Office, 1996–97. Mem., Select Cttee on Parly Admin (Ombudsman), 1992–96, on Educn, 1995–96; Vice-Chm., Cons. back bench Aviation Cttee, 1994–97 (Jt Sec., 1992); Member: Asylum Bill Cttee, 1992; Deregulation Bill Cttee, 1994–97; Caravans Rating Bill Cttee, 1996–97; Asylum and Immigration Bill Cttee, 1996–97; European Standing Cttee B, 1992–97; All-Party Manufacturing Gp, 1993–97; Hon. Sec., All-Party Uganda Gp, 1994–97. European Parliament: spokesman, overseas develt and co-operation, 1999–; Member: Envmt Cttee, 1999–; EU-ACP Delegn, 1999–; Rapporteur: WTO and Develt Issues of World Trade, 2000–; Aid to Uprooted People in Asia and Latin America, 2000–. Editor, Crossbow, 1983–85. Presenter, Deva's Hour, Sunrise Radio, 1995, 1998–99. FRSA 1997. DL Greater London, 1986. *Publications:* Wealth of Nations Part II: Adam Smith revisited, 1998; various pamphlets and memoranda for Bow Group, 1980–85.

Recreations: riding, reading, tennis. *Address:* Policy Research Centre for Business, 169 Kennington Road, SE11 6SF. *T:* (020) 7642 8880; European Parliament, 43–60 rue Wiertz, 1047 Brussels, Belgium; *e-mail:* nirjdevamep@hotmail.com. *Clubs:* Carlton; Hounslow Conservative.

DEVANEY, John Francis, CEng, FIEE, FIMechE; Chairman, Exel (formerly NFC) plc, since 2000 (Director, since 1996); *b* 25 June 1946; *s* of late George Devaney and Alice Ann Devaney; two *s* one *d*. *Educ:* St Mary's Coll., Blackburn; Sheffield Univ. (BEng). FIMechE. Perkins Engines, 1968–89: manufacturing positions, Peterborough, 1968–76; Project Manager, Ohio, 1976–77; Director posts, UK, 1977–82; President, 1983–88; Group Vice-Pres., European Components Group, Peterborough, 1988 and Enterprises Group, Toronto, 1988–89; Chm. and Chief Exec. Officer and Group Vice-Pres., Kelsey-Hayes Corp., Michigan, 1989–92; Man. Dir, 1992, Chief Exec., 1993, Exec. Chm., 1995–98, Eastern Electricity plc, later Eastern Gp plc. Non-exec. Director: HSBC (formerly Midland Bank), 1994–; British Steel, 1998–. President: Electricity Assoc., 1994–95; Inst. for Customer Services, 1998–. *Recreations:* ski-ing, golf, tennis, sailing. *Address:* Exel plc, Ocean House, The Ring, Bracknell RG12 1AN. *Club:* Reform.

DEVAUX, John Edward; His Honour Judge Devaux; a Circuit Judge, since 1993; Resident Judge, Ipswich, since 1998; *b* 25 March 1947; *s* of Henry Edward Devaux and Anne Elizabeth Devaux; *m* 1979, Fiona O'Conor; two *d*. *Educ:* Beaumont Coll.; Bristol Univ. (LLB). Called to the Bar, Lincoln's Inn, 1970; a Recorder, 1989–93. Hon. Recorder of Ipswich, 2000. *Address:* Ipswich Crown Court, The Courthouse, Civic Drive, Ipswich, Suffolk IP1 2DX. *T:* (01473) 213841.

DEVENPORT, Rt Rev. Eric Nash; Auxiliary Bishop in the diocese of Europe, since 1992; Hon. Assistant Bishop, Diocese of Norwich, since 2000; *b* 3 May 1926; *s* of Joseph and Emma Devenport; *m* 1954, Jean Margaret Richardson; two *d*. *Educ:* Kelham Theological Coll. BA (Open Univ.). Curate, St Mark, Leicester, 1951–54; St Matthew, Barrow-in-Furness, 1954–56; Succentor, Leicester Cathedral, 1956–59; Vicar of Shepshed, 1959–64; Oadby, 1964–73; Proctor in Convocation, 1964–80; Hon. Canon of Leicester Cathedral, 1973–80; Leader of Mission, Diocese of Leicester, 1973–80; Bishop Suffragan of Dunwich, 1980–92, retd; Archdeacon of Italy and Chaplain of St Mark's, Florence, 1992–97. Chairman: Diocesan Communication Officers Cttee, 1986–92; C of E Hospital Chaplaincies Council, 1986–91; Jt Hosp. Chaplaincies Cttee, 1988–91; E Anglian Ministerial Trng Course, 1990–92. Chaplain, Worshipful Company of Framework Knitters, 1964–80; Area Chaplain, Actors' Church Union, 1980–92. Chm., Local Radio Adv. Council for Radio Suffolk, 1990–92. *Publication:* Preaching at the Parish Communion: ASB Gospels-Sundays: Year One, Vol. 2, 1989. *Recreation:* theatre. *Address:* 32 Bishopgate, Norwich NR1 4AA. *T:* (01603) 664121.

de VERE, Anthony Charles Mayle, CMG 1986; HM Diplomatic Service, retired; Foreign and Commonwealth Office, 1986–93; *b* 23 Jan. 1930; *m* 1st, 1959, Geraldine Gertrude Bolton (*d* 1980); 2nd, 1986, Rosemary Edith Austin. *Educ:* St John's College, Cambridge. Served Army, Malaya, 1950–52; joined Colonial Service (later HMOCS), 1953, Provincial Admin, Tanganyika; Kibondo, 1953–56; in charge Kondoa-Irangi Develt Scheme, 1957–59; Res. Magistrate, Singida, 1959; Dist Comr, Tunduru, 1960–61, Kigoma, 1961–62; Head of local govt, Western Region, 1962–63, retired 1963; joined FO, later FCO, 1963; First Sec., Lusaka, 1967–70, NY, 1972–74; Counsellor, Washington, 1982–86. *Recreations:* riding, most things rural, sculpture, music, books. *Address:* Haddiscoe Hall, Norfolk NR14 6PE.

DEVEREAU, (George) Michael, CB 1997; Head of Government Information Service, 1990–97; Chief Executive (formerly Director General), Central Office of Information, 1989–96; *b* 10 Nov. 1937; *s* of George Alfred Devereau and Elspeth Mary Duff Devereau; *m* 1961, Sarah Poupart; four *s*. *Educ:* King William's Coll., Isle of Man; University Coll. London. Asst Ed., Architects' Jl, 1962; Information Officer, MPBW, BRE and DoE, 1967–75; Chief Information Officer: Price Commn, 1975; DoE, 1978; Dept of Transport, 1982; Gp Dir, 1985, Dep. Dir Gen., 1987, COI. *Publication:* Architects Working Details, 1964. *Recreations:* house restoration, travel. *Address:* Mill View, 5 Guildhall Cottages, Laxfield, Suffolk IP13 8DU.

DEVERELL, Gen. Sir John Freegard, (Sir Jack), KCB 1999; OBE 1986; Commander-in-Chief, Allied Forces North, since 2001; *b* 27 April 1945; *s* of Harold James Frank Deverell and Joan Beatrice Deverell (*née* Carter); *m* 1973, Jane Ellen Solomon; one *s* one *d*. *Educ:* King Edward's Sch., Bath; RMA Sandhurst. Commnd Somerset and Cornwall LI, 1965; RN Staff Coll., Greenwich, 1977; Comd 3rd Bn LI, 1984–86; Mil. Dir of Studies, RMCS, Shrivenham, 1988; Higher Command and Staff Course, Camberley, 1988; Comdr 1st Infantry Bde (UK Mobile Force), 1988–90; NDC, India, 1991; Dir, Army Recruiting, 1992–93; Dir Gen., Army Manning and Recruiting, 1993–95; Comdt, RMA Sandhurst, 1995–97; Dep. C-in-C, HQ Land Comd and Inspr Gen. TA, 1997–98 and 1999–2001; Dep. Comdr (Ops), HQ SFOR, Bosnia, 1998–99. FICPD; FRSA. *Recreations:* golf, cricket, horses. *Address:* HQ Allied Forces North, Brunssum, BFPO 28. *Clubs:* Cavalry and Guards; Free Foresters, I Zingari.

DEVEREUX, family name of **Viscount Hereford**.

DEVEREUX, Alan Robert, CBE 1980; DL; Founder Director, Quality Scotland Foundation, since 1991; Director: Scottish Mutual Assurance Society, since 1975; Gleneagles Group, since 1990; Abbey National Life, since 1999; *b* 18 April 1933; *s* of Donald Charles and Doris Devereux; *m* 1st, 1959, Gloria Alma Hair (*d* 1985); one *s*; 2nd, 1987, Elizabeth Tormey Docherty. *Educ:* Colchester School; Clacton County High School; Mid-Essex Technical Coll. CEng, MIEE, CIMgt. Marconi's Wireless Telegraph Co., 1950–56; Halex Div. of British Xylonite Co., 1956–58; Spa Div., Sanitas Trust, 1958–65; Gen. Man., Dobar Engineering, 1965–67; Norcros Ltd, 1967–69; Gp Man. Dir 1969–78, Dep. Chm. 1978–80, Scotcros Ltd; Dir-Gen., Scotcros Europe SA, 1976–79. Director: Walter Alexander PLC, 1980–90; Hambros Scotland Ltd, 1984–; Scottish Advisor, Hambros Bank, 1984–90. Dep. Chm. 1975–77, Chm. 1977–79, CBI Scotland; CBI: Council Mem., 1972–; Mem. President's Adv. Cttee, 1979; UK Regional Chm., 1979; Mem., F and GP Cttee, 1982–84. Chairman: Small Industries Council for Rural Areas of Scotland, 1975–77; Scottish Tourist Bd, 1980–90; Scottish Ambulance Service NHS Trust, 1994–97; Member: Scottish Development Agency, 1977–82; BTA, 1980–90. Chm., Police Dependants' Trust, Scotland. Scottish Free Enterprise Award, 1978. DL Renfrewshire, 1985. *Recreations:* reading, work, Glasgow City Mission. *Address:* South Fell, 24 Kirkhouse Road, Blanefield, Stirlingshire G63 9BX. *T:* (01360) 770464. *Club:* East India, Devonshire, Sports and Public Schools.

de VERE WHITE, Hon. Mrs; *see* Glendinning, Hon. Victoria.

de VESCI, 7th Viscount *cr* 1766; **Thomas Eustace Vesey;** Bt 1698; Baron Knapton, 1750; *b* 8 Oct. 1955; *s* of 6th Viscount de Vesci and Susan Anne (*d* 1986), *d* of late Ronald (Owen Lloyd) Armstrong-Jones, MBE, QC, DL, and of the Countess of Rosse; *S* father, 1983; *m* 1987, Sita-Maria, *o c* of late Brian de Breffny; two *s* one *d*. *Educ:* Eton; Oxford. *Address:* 14 Rumbold Road, SW6 2JA.

See also Earl of Snowdon.

DEVESI, Sir Baddeley, GCMG 1980; GCVO 1982; Deputy Prime Minister and Minister for Transport, Works, Communication and Aviation, Solomon Islands, 1996–2000; *b* 16 Oct. 1941; *s* of late Mostyn Tagabasoe Norua and Laisa Otu; *m* 1969, June Marie Barley; six *s* three *d* (and one *d* decd). *Educ:* St Stephen's Sch., Auckland, NZ; Ardmore Teachers' Coll., Auckland, NZ; Univ. of Western Aust.; Univ. of S Pacific. MLC and Mem. Exec. Council, 1967–69. Headmaster, St Nicholas Sch., Honiara, 1968; Educn Officer and Lectr, Solomon Is Teachers' Coll., 1970–71; Sen. Assst Sec., Solomon Is, 1972; Dist. Officer, 1973; District Comr, District Magistrate and Clerk to Malaita Council, 1974–75; Permanent Sec., Ministry of Transport and Communications, 1976; Governor-Gen. of the Solomon Islands, 1978–88; Minister for Home Affairs and Dep. Prime Minister, 1989; Minister for For. Affairs and Trade Relations and Dep. Prime Minister, 1990–92; Minister for Health and Med. Services and Dep. Prime Minister, 1993; Leader of the Opposition, 1994. Dep. Chm., Solomon Islands Broadcasting Corp., 1976; Chm., AcP, 1990–91. Chancellor, Univ. of S Pacific, 1980–83. Captain, Solomon Islands team, 2nd South Pacific Games, 1966. Comr, Boy Scouts Assoc., 1968; Chief Scout, 1980–88. Hon. DU Univ. of the South Pacific, 1981. KStJ 1984. *Recreations:* reading, snooker, golf. *Address:* PO Box 227, Honiara, Solomon Islands.

DE VILLE, Sir Harold Godfrey, (Sir Oscar), Kt 1990; CBE 1979; PhD; Chairman, Meyer International plc, 1987–91 (Deputy Chairman, 1985–87; Director, 1984–91); *b* Derbyshire, 11 April 1925; *s* of Harold De Ville and Anne De Ville (*née* Godfrey); *m* 1947, Pamela Fay Ellis; one *s*. *Educ:* Burton-on-Trent Grammar Sch.; Trinity Coll., Cambridge (MA); PhD London 1995. Served RNVR, 1943–46. Ford Motor Co. Ltd, 1949–65; BICC, 1965–84: Dir, 1971–84; Exec. Dep. Chm., 1978–84. Director: Balfour Beatty Ltd, 1971–78; Phillips Cables Ltd, Canada, 1982–84; Metal Manufacturers Ltd, Australia, 1983–84; Scottish Cables Ltd, S Africa, 1983–84. Mem., BRB, 1985–91. Chairman: Iron and Steel EDC, 1984–86; Govt Review of vocational qualifications, 1985–86; NCVQ, 1986–90; Nat. Jt Council for Engrg Construction Industry, 1985–87. Member: Commn on Industrial Relations, 1971–74; Central Arbitration Cttee, 1976–77; Council: ACAS, 1976–91; BIM, 1982–86; Confederation of British Industry, 1977–85 (Chm., Working Party on Employee Participation, 1975–78). Mem. Council, Reading Univ., 1985–91. *Recreation:* genealogy.

de VILLIERS, 3rd Baron *cr* 1910; **Arthur Percy de Villiers;** retired; *b* 17 Dec. 1911; *s* of 2nd Baron and Adelheid, *d* of H. C. Koch, Pietermaritzburg, Natal; *S* father, 1934; *m* 1939, Lovett (marr. diss. 1958), *d* of Dr A. D. MacKinnon, Williams Lake, BC; one *s* two *d*. *Educ:* Magdalen Coll., Oxford. Barrister, Inner Temple, 1938. Farming in New Zealand. Admitted as a barrister to the Auckland Supreme Court, 1949. *Recreations:* gardening, golf. *Heir:* s Hon. Alexander Charles de Villiers, *b* 29 Dec. 1940. *Address:* PO Box 66, Kumeu, Auckland 1250, NZ. *T:* (9) 4118173. *Club:* Royal Commonwealth Society (Auckland).

de VILLIERS, Dawid Jacobus, DPhil; Minister for the Environment and Tourism, South Africa, 1994–96; *b* 10 July 1940; *m* 1964, Suzaan Mangold; one *s* three *d*. *Educ:* Univ. of Stellenbosch (BA Hons Philosophy; BTh, DPhil); Rand Afrikaans Univ. (MA Phil., 1972). Abe Bailey Scholar, 1963–64; Markotter Scholar, 1964. Part-time Lectr in Philosophy, Univ. of Western Cape, 1963–64; Minister of Dutch Reformed Church, Wellington, Cape, 1967–69; Lectr in Philosophy, 1969–72, and Pres. Convocation, 1973–, Rand Afrikaans Univ.; MP for Johannesburg W, 1972–79, for Piketberg, 1981–94, party list, 1992–99; Chm., Nat. Party's Foreign Affairs Cttee in Parlt; Ambassador of S Africa to London, 1979–80; Minister: of Trade and Industry (formerly Industries, Commerce and Tourism), SA, 1980–86; of Budget and Welfare, 1986–88; for Admin and Privatisation, 1988–90; for Public Enterprises, 1989–91; for Mineral and Energy Affairs, 1990–91; for Economic Co-ordination, 1991–92; for Public Enterprises, 1992–94; Leader, Houses of Parliament, 1989–92. Leader, Nat. Party, Cape Province, 1990–96. National Party Delegn Leader, Constitutional Conf., Convention for a Democratic S Africa, 1992. Visited: USA on US Leaders Exchange Prog., 1974; UK as guest of Brit. Govt, 1975; Israel as guest of Israeli Govt, 1977. Represented S Africa in internat. Rugby in S Africa, UK, Ireland, Australia, NZ, France and the Argentine, 1962–70 (Captain, 1965–70). State President's Award for Sport, 1968 and 1970; S African Sportsman of the Year, 1968; Jaycee's Outstanding Young Man of the Year Award, 1971; State President's Decoration for Meritorious Service, Gold, 1988. *Recreations:* sports, reading. *Address:* PO Box 15, Cape Town, 8000, South Africa.

DEVINE, Hon. (Donald) Grant; founded Grant Devine Management Inc., 1992; President, Grant Devine Farms & Consulting Services Ltd; Premier of Saskatchewan, 1982–91; *b* Regina, 5 July 1944; *m* 1966, (Adeline) Chantal Guillaume; two *s* three *d*. *Educ:* Saskatchewan Univ. (BScA 1967); Alberta Univ. (MSc 1969; MBA 1970); Ohio State Univ. (PhD 1976). Farming, 1962–; marketing specialist, Fed. Govt, Ottawa, 1970–72; Graduate Assistant, Ohio State Univ., 1972–76; Prof. of Agricl Econs, Saskatchewan Univ., 1976–79. Leader, Progressive Cons. Party of Saskatchewan, 1979–92; MLA for Estevan, 1982–95; Leader, Official Opposition, Saskatchewan, 1991–92; Minister of Agriculture, 1985–91. Advisor: Food Prices Rev. Bd and Provincial Govts; Sask. Consumers' Assoc. Member: Amer. Econ. Assoc.; Amer. Marketing Assoc.; Amer. Assoc. for Consumer Res.; Canadian Agricl Econs Soc.; Consumers' Assoc. of Canada. *Publications:* contribs to professional jls on retail food pricing and market performance. *Recreations:* golf, ski-ing, baseball, horses. *Address:* (office) 177 Victoria Avenue, Regina, SK S4P 4K5, Canada.

DEVINE, Rt Rev. Joseph; *see* Motherwell, Bishop of, (RC).

DEVINE, Prof. Thomas Martin, PhD, DLitt; FBA 1994; FRSE; FRHistS; University Research Professor in Scottish History and Director, Research Institute of Irish and Scottish Studies, University of Aberdeen, since 1998; Director, AHRB Centre for Irish-Scottish Studies, since 2001; *b* 30 July 1945; *s* of Michael Gerard Devine and Norah Martin; *m* 1971; Catherine Mary Lynas; two *s* three *d*. *Educ:* Strathclyde Univ. (BA; PhD 1972; DLitt 1992). FRHistS 1980; FRSE 1992. University of Strathclyde: Lectr in History, 1969–78; Sen. Lectr in History, 1978–83; Reader in Scottish History, 1983–88; Prof. of Scottish History, 1988–98; Dir, Res. Centre in Scottish History, 1993–98; Dean, Faculty of Arts and Social Studies, 1993–94; Dep. Principal, 1994–97. Adjunct Professor in History: Univ. of Guelph, Canada, 1989–; Univ. of N Carolina, 1997–. Chm., Econ. and Social History Soc. of Scotland, 1984–88; Convenor of Council, Scottish Catholic Historical Assoc., 1990–95; Convener, Irish-Scottish Academic Initiative, 1998–. Mem. Council, British Acad., 1998–2001. Trustee, 1995–, Chair, European Ethnol Res. Centre, Nat. Museums of Scotland. Gov., St Andrews Coll. of Educn, 1990–94. Sen. Hume Brown Prize in Scottish Hist., 1976; Saltire Prize, 1992; Henry Duncan Prize, RSE, 1994. Hon. DLitt QUB. *Publications:* The Tobacco Lords, 1975, 2nd edn 1990; (ed) Ireland and Scotland 1600–1850, 1983; (ed) Farm Servants and Labour in Lowland Scotland, 1984; A Scottish Firm in Virginia 1767–77, 1984; (ed) People and Society in Scotland, 1988; The Great Highland Famine, 1988; (ed) Improvement and Enlightment, 1989; (ed) Conflict and Stability in Scottish Society 1700–1850, 1990; (ed) Irish Immigrants and Scottish Society in 18th and 19th Centuries, 1991; Scottish Emigration and Scottish Society, 1992; The Transformation of Rural Scotland 1660–1815, 1994; Clanship to Crofters' War, 1994; (ed) Scottish Elites, 1994; Glasgow, vol. I, 1995; Exploring The Scottish Past, 1995; (ed) Scotland in the Twentieth Century, 1996; (ed) Eighteenth Century Scotland: new perspectives, 1999; (ed) Celebrating Columba: Irish-Scottish connections 1597–1997, 1999; The Scottish Nation 1700–2000, 1999; (ed) Scotland's Shame?: bigotry and sectarianism in modern Scotland, 2000. *Recreations:* walking in the Hebrides, foreign travel, music, watching skilful soccer. *Address:* Research Institute of Irish and Scottish Studies, University of Aberdeen, Humanity Manse, 19 College Bounds, Old Aberdeen AB24 3UG. *T:* (01224) 273683; *e-mail:* riiss@abdn.ac.uk.

de VIRION, Tadeusz; Cross of Valour, Cross of the Home Army, Warsaw Uprising Cross, 1944; Polish Ambassador to the Court of St James's, 1990–93; *b* 28 March 1926; *s* of Jerzy de Virion (killed in Auschwitz, 1941); *m* 1985, Jayanti Hazra; two *d. Educ:* Univ. of Warsaw (LLM). Barrister, 1950–, specialising in criminal law; Judge of Tribunal of State, elected by Polish Parlt, 1989, 1990, 1993–. Cross of Knights of Malta, 1980; Golden Insignia of Barrister's Merit, 1988; Comdr's Cross, Order of Polonia Restituta; Grand Officier, Order of Pro Merito Melitensi. *Recreations:* Jayanti, books. *Address:* ul. Zakopiańska 17, 03 934 Warsaw, Poland. *T:* (2) 6178880. *Clubs:* Polish Hearth, Travellers, Special Forces.

DEVITT, Sir James (Hugh Thomas), 3rd Bt *cr* 1916, of Chelsea, Co. London; hotel and leisure consultant; Director, PKF, since 1998; *b* 18 Sept. 1956; *o s* of Sir Thomas Gordon Devitt, 2nd Bt and of Janet Lilian, *o d* of Col H. S. Ellis, CBE, MC; *S* father, 1995; *m* 1985, Susan Carol (*née* Duffus); two *s* one *d. Educ:* Corpus Christi Coll., Cambridge (MA). ARICS. *Recreations:* family, football. *Heir: s* Jack Thomas Michael Devitt, *b* 29 July 1988. *Address:* The Old Rectory, Ford Lane, Alresford, Colchester, Essex CO7 8AX. *T:* (01206) 827315.

DEVLIN, Alexander, OBE 1977; JP; Member, Glenrothes New Town Development Corporation, 1958–78; *b* 22 Dec. 1927; *s* of Thomas Devlin and Jean Gibson; *m* 1949, Annie Scott Gordon. *Educ:* Cowdenbeath St Columba's High Sch.; National Council of Labour Colls (Local Govt and Public Speaking). Member: Fife CC, 1956–74; Fife Regional Council, 1974–78; Chm., Fife Educn Cttee, 1963–78; Vice-Chm., Educn Cttee of Convention of Scottish Local Authorities, 1974–78. Member: Dunning Cttee on Scottish System for Assessment of Pupils after 4 years Secondary Educn, 1974–77; Scottish Sports Council, 1964–74; Manpower Services Commn, 1978–79. Mem. Bd, 1992–, Fellow, 1996–, Glenrothes Coll. Pres., Glenrothes & Dist Burns Club, 1995–97. JP Fife, 1963. *Address:* 40 Falcon Drive, Glenrothes, Fife KY7 5HP. *T:* (01592) 759883.

DEVLIN, Rt Rev. Mgr Bernard Patrick, CMG 1996; RC Bishop of Gibraltar, 1985–98, now Emeritus; *b* Youghal, Co. Cork, 10 March 1921. *Educ:* Mount Melleray Cistercian Coll.; Holy Cross Seminary, Dublin; Nat. Univ. of Ireland (BA 1942); Pontifical Beda Coll. Ordained, 1945; Curate, Cathedral of St Mary the Crowned, Gibraltar, 1946–60; Parish Priest, St Theresa's Church, Gibraltar, 1961–85; Vicar General, 1976–85. Freeman, City of Gibraltar, 1999. *Recreations:* golf, painting. *Address:* Cathedral of St Mary the Crowned, Gibraltar. *T:* 76688, 45454.

DEVLIN, (Josephine) Bernadette; *see* McAliskey, J. B.

DEVLIN, His Honour Keith Michael, PhD; a Circuit Judge, 1984–95; a Deputy Circuit Judge, 1995–99; *b* 21 Oct. 1933; *e s* of late Francis Michael Devlin and of Norah Devlin (*née* Gregory); *m* 1958, Pamela Gwendoline Phillips; two *s* one *d. Educ:* Price's Sch., Fareham; Eaton Hall OCS; King's Coll., London Univ. (LLB 1960, MPhil 1968, PhD 1976). Commnd RAOC, 1953. Called to the Bar, Gray's Inn, 1964; Dep. Chief Clerk, Metropolitan Magistrates' Courts Service, 1964–66; various appts as Dep. Metropolitan Stipendiary Magistrate, 1975–79; Asst Recorder, 1980–83; a Recorder, 1983–84; Liaison Judge, Bedfordshire, 1990–93; Resident Judge, Luton Crown Court, 1991–93. Brunel University: Lectr in Law, 1966–71; Reader in Law, 1971–84; Associate Prof. of Law, 1984–96; Professorial Res. Fellow, 1996–; Mem., Court, 1985–88. Fellow, Netherlands Inst. for Advanced Study in the Humanities and Social Sciences, Wassenaar, 1975–76. Chm., Mental Health Review Tribunals, 1991–93, 1995–98. Mem., Consumer Protection Adv. Cttee, 1976–81. MRI (Member: Finance Cttee, 1988–97; Council, 1994–97). Magistrates' Association: Mem., 1974–89, Vice-Chm., 1984–89, Legal Cttee; co-opted Mem. Council, 1980–88; a Vice-Pres., Bucks Br., 1993–. Mem. Court, Luton Univ., 1994–98. Mem. Council, Inst. of Cancer Res., 1999–2001. JP Inner London (Juvenile Court Panel), 1968–84 (Chm., 1973–84). Liveryman, Feltmakers' Co. (Mem., Ct of Assts, 1991–; Master, 1998–99). FRSA 1989. Jt Founder and Editor, Anglo-Amer. Law Rev., 1972–84. *Publications:* Sentencing Offenders in Magistrates' Courts, 1970; (with Eric Stockdale) Sentencing, 1987; articles in legal jls. *Recreations:* watching cricket, fly-fishing, Roman Britain. *Clubs:* Athenæum, MCC; Hampshire County Cricket.

DEVLIN, Stuart Leslie, AO 1988; CMG 1980; goldsmith, silversmith and designer in London since 1965; Goldsmith and Jeweller by appointment to HM The Queen, 1982; *b* 9 Oct. 1931; *m* 1986, Carole Hedley-Saunders. *Educ:* Gordon Inst. of Technology, Geelong; Royal Melbourne Inst. of Technology; Royal Coll. of Art. DesRCA (Silversmith), DesRCA (Industrial Design/Engrg). Art Teacher, Vic. Educn Dept, 1950–58; Royal Coll. of Art, 1958–60; Harkness Fellow, NY, 1960–62; Lectr, Prahran Techn. Coll., Melbourne, 1962; one-man shows of sculpture, NY and Sydney, 1961–64; Inspr Art in Techn. Schs, Vic. Educn Dept, 1964–65; exhibns of silver and gold in numerous cities USA, Australia, Bermuda, Middle East and UK, 1965–. Executed many commissions in gold and silver: designed coins for Australia, Singapore, Cayman Is, Gibraltar, IoM, Burundi, Botswana, Ethiopia and Bhutan; designed and made: cutlery for State Visit to Paris, 1972; Duke of Edinburgh trophy for World Driving Championship, 1973; silver to commemorate opening of Sydney Opera House, 1973; Grand National Trophy, 1975, 1976; Australian Bravery Awards, 1975; Regalia for the Order of Australia, 1975–76; Queen's Silver Jubilee Medal, 1977; Centrepiece for RE to commemorate their work in NI, 1984; Bas-relief portrait of Princess of Wales for Wedgwood, 1986; full set of Defence Awards for Australia, 1989; portraits of HM the Queen Mother, HRH the Princess of Wales, HRH the Princess Royal, HRH the Princess Margaret, 1991; British Athletics Fedn Badge and Chain of Office, 1992; 24 Sydney 2000 Olympic coins, 1997; Millennium commemorative dishes for Goldsmiths' Co. and Inf. Technologists' Co., 2000. Developed strategy for use of champagne diamonds in jewellery for Argyle Diamond Mines, 1987. Computer presentations in USA and UK; Inaugural Chm., Engrg Modelling Systems Special Interest Gp, 1993; Vice Chm., Intergraph Graphics Users' Gp UK, 1996. Freeman, City of London, 1966; Liveryman, 1972, Mem. Ct of Assts, 1986, Prime Warden, May 1996–97, Goldsmiths' Co. Hon. DocArts RMIT, 2000. *Recreations:* work, computer graphics, tennis, windsurfing. *Address:* Highwater House, Kingston Gorse, W Sussex BN16 1SQ. *T:* (01903) 858939.

DEVLIN, Tim; Founder, Tim Devlin Enterprises, public relations consultancy, 1989; *b* 28 July 1944; 3rd *s* of Rt Hon. Lord Devlin, PC, FBA, and of Madeleine, *yr d* of Sir Bernard Oppenheimer, 1st Bt; *m* 1967, Angela Denise, *d* of late A. J. G. and Mrs Laramy; two *s* two *d. Educ:* Winchester Coll.; University Coll., Oxford (Hons degree, History). Feature Writer, Aberdeen Press & Journal, 1966; Reporter, Scotsman, 1967; Educn Reporter, Evening Echo, Watford, 1968–69; Reporter, later News Editor, The Times Educnl Supplement, 1969–71; Reporter, The Times, 1971–73, Educn Corresp., 1973–77; Nat. Dir, ISIS, 1977–84; Public Relations Dir, Inst. of Dirs, 1984–86; Assoc. Dir, Charles Barker Traverse-Healy, 1986–89. *Publications:* (with Mary Warnock) What Must We Teach?, 1977; Good Communications Guide, 1980; Independent Schools—The Facts, 1981; Choosing Your Independent School, 1984; (with Brian Knight) Public Relations and Marketing for Schools, 1990; (with Hywel Williams) Old School Ties, 1992; (with Angela Devlin) Anybody's Nightmare, 1998; Public Relations Manual for Schools, 1998. *Recreations:* writing, art, tennis. *T:* Staplehurst (01580) 893176.

DEVLIN, Timothy Robert; barrister; *b* 13 June 1959; *e s* of late H. Brendan Devlin, CBE, FRCS and of Anne Elizabeth Devlin, MB BCh; *m* 1st, 1986 (marr. diss. 1989); 2nd, 1991, Carol-Anne Aitken. *Educ:* Dulwich Coll.; LSE; City Univ. Called to the Bar, Lincoln's Inn, 1985 (Hardwick and Thomas More Scholar). Sen. Expert, Technical Assistance to CIS, EU, 1998–99; Consultant, Stanbrook & Hooper, Brussels, 1999–2000. Dep. Chm., NHS Tribunal, 2001–. Mem., Cons. Research Dept, 1981; former Chm., LSE Conservatives; Chm., Islington North Cons. Assoc., 1986. MP (C) Stockton South, 1987–97; contested (C) same seat, 1997, 2001. PPS to Attorney Gen., 1992–94; PPS to Ministers of Trade and Industry, 1995–97. Mem., Select Cttee on Scottish Affairs, 1995–97; formerly Chm., Parly Panel on Charity Law; Chm., Northern Gp of Cons. MPs, 1992–97. Dep. Chm., Foreign Affairs Forum, 1990–92; Member: Islington South Cons. Assoc.; Stockton on Tees Cons. Assoc.; Soc. of Cons. Lawyers; European Bar Assoc.; Friends of the RA; Rare Breeds Survival Trust; Scotch Malt Whisky Soc. Trustee, NSPCC, 1993–95; Gov., Yarm Sch., 1988–98. *Recreations:* hill-walking, opera, travel. *Address:* 2 Pump Court, Temple, EC4Y 7AH.

DEVON, 18th Earl of, *cr* 1553; **Hugh Rupert Courtenay,** Bt 1644; DL; landowner, farmer; *b* 5 May 1942; *o s* of 17th Earl of Devon, and of Venetia, former wife of 6th Earl of Cottenham and *d* of Captain J. V. Taylor; *S* father, 1998; *m* 1967, Dianna Frances, *er d* of J. G. Watherston, Jedburgh, Roxburghshire; one *s* three *d. Educ:* Winchester; Magdalene Coll., Cambridge (BA). ARICS. Captain, Wessex Yeomanry, retd. Chm., Devon Br., CLA, 1987–89. DL Devon, 1991. *Recreations:* riding, hunting, shooting. *Heir: s* Lord Courtenay, *qv. Address:* Powderham Castle, near Exeter, Devon EX6 8JQ. *T:* (01626) 890370.

DEVONPORT, 3rd Viscount *cr* 1917, of Wittington, Bucks; **Terence Kearley;** Bt 1908; Baron 1910; architect and landowner; Chairman, Millhouse Developments Ltd, since 1989; *b* 29 Aug. 1944; *s* of 2nd Viscount Devonport and of Sheila Isabel, *e d* of Lt-Col C. Hope Murray; *S* father, 1973; *m* 1968, Elizabeth Rosemary (marr. diss. 1979), *d* of late John G. Hopton; two *d. Educ:* Aiglon Coll., Switzerland; Selwyn Coll., Cambridge (BA, DipArch, MA); Newcastle Univ. (MPhil). Architect: Davis Brody, New York City, 1967–68; London Borough of Lambeth, 1971–72; Barnett Winskell, Newcastle-upon-Tyne, 1972–75; landscape architect, Ralph Erskine, Newcastle, 1977–78; in private practice, 1979–84 (RIBA, ALI); Forestry Manager, 1973–; farmer, 1978–. Member: Lloyds, 1976–90; Internat. Dendrology Soc., 1978 (Council, 1995–); N Adv. Cttee, TGEW, 1978–94; N Adv. Cttee, CLA, 1980–85; Nat. Land Use and Envmt Cttee, TGUK, 1984–87. Pres., Arboricultural Assoc., 1995–; Vice Pres., Forestry Commn Reference Panel, 1987–94. Man. Dir, Tweedswood Enterprises, 1979–, and dir various other cos, 1984–. MInstD. Order of Mark Twain (USA), 1977. *Recreations:* nature, travel and good food; interests: trees, the arts, country sports. *Heir: cousin* Chester Dagley Hugh Kearley [*b* 29 April 1932; *m* 1974, Josefa Mesquida]. *Address:* Ray Demesne, Kirkwhelpington, Newcastle upon Tyne NE19 2RG. *Clubs:* Royal Automobile, Beefsteak, Farmers', MCC; Northern Counties (Newcastle upon Tyne).

DEVONS, Prof. Samuel, FRS 1955; Professor of Physics, Columbia University, New York, 1960–85, now Emeritus, and Special Research Scientist (Chairman, Dept of Physics, 1963–67); Director, History of Physics Laboratory, Barnard College, Columbia University, 1970–85; *b* 1914; *s* of Rev. David I. Devons and E. Edleston; *m* 1938, Celia Ruth Toubkin; four *d. Educ:* Trinity Coll., Cambridge. BA 1935; MA, PhD 1939. Exhibition of 1851 Senior Student, 1939. Scientific Officer, Senior Scientific Officer, Air Ministry, MAP, and Ministry of Supply, 1939–45. Lecturer in Physics, Cambridge Univ., Fellow and Dir of Studies, Trinity Coll., Cambridge, 1946–49; Prof. of Physics, Imperial Coll. of Science, 1950–55; Langworthy Prof. of Physics and Dir of Physical Laboratories, Univ. of Manchester, 1955–60. Royal Soc. Leverhulme Vis. Prof., Andhra Univ., India, 1967–68; Balfour Vis. Prof., History of Science, Weizmann Inst., Rehovot, Israel, 1973; Racah Vis. Prof. of Physics, Hebrew Univ., Jerusalem, 1973–74. Rutherford Meml Lectr, Royal Soc., Australia, 1989. Rutherford Medal and Prize, Inst. of Physics, 1970. *Publications:* Excited States of Nuclei, 1949; (ed) Biology and Physical Sciences, 1969; (ed) High Energy Physics and Nuclear Structure, 1970; contributions to Proc. Royal Society, Proc. Phys. Soc., etc. *Recreations:* plastic arts, travel. *Address:* Nevis Laboratory, Columbia University, PO Box 137, Irvington-on-Hudson, NY 10533, USA. *T:* (914) 5912860, *Fax:* (914) 5917080.

DEVONSHIRE, 11th Duke of, *cr* 1694; **Andrew Robert Buxton Cavendish,** KG 1996; PC 1964; MC; Baron Cavendish, 1605; Earl of Devonshire, 1618; Marquess of Hartington, 1694; Earl of Burlington, 1831; Baron Cavendish (UK) 1831; Vice-Lord-Lieutenant of the County of Derby, 1957–87; Chancellor of Manchester University, 1965–86; *b* 2 Jan. 1920; *o surv. s* of 10th Duke of Devonshire, KG, and Lady Mary Cecil, GCVO, CBE (*d* 1988), *d* of 4th Marquess of Salisbury, KG, GCVO; *S* father, 1950; *m* 1941, Hon. Deborah Vivian Freeman-Mitford (*see* Duchess of Devonshire); one *s* two *d. Educ:* Eton; Trinity Coll., Cambridge. Served War of 1939–45, Coldstream Guards (MC). Contested (C) Chesterfield Div. of Derbyshire, 1945 and 1950. Parliamentary Under-Sec. of State for Commonwealth Relations, Oct. 1960–Sept. 1962; Minister of State, Commonwealth Relations Office, Sept. 1962–Oct. 1964 and for Colonial Affairs, 1963–Oct. 1964. Steward of the Jockey Club, 1966–69. Mem., Horserace Totalisator Board, 1977–86; a Trustee, Nat. Gallery, 1960–68; President: The Royal Hosp. and Home, Putney, 1954–91; Lawn Tennis Assoc., 1955–61; RNIB, 1979–85; Nat Assoc. for Deaf Children, 1978–95; Building Societies Assoc., 1954–61; Vice-Pres., London Library, 1993–; Chairman: Grand Council, British Empire Cancer Campaign, 1956–81; Throughbred Breeders' Assoc., 1978–81. Mayor of Buxton, 1952–54. Hon. Col, Manchester and Salford Univs OTC, 1981–85. Hon. LLD: Manchester; Sheffield; Liverpool; Hon. Dr Law, Memorial Univ. of Newfoundland. *Publication:* Park Top: a romance of the Turf, 1976. *Heir: s* Marquess of Hartington, *qv. Address:* Chatsworth, Bakewell, Derbyshire DE45 1PP. *T:* (01246) 582204; 4 Chesterfield Street, W1X 7HG. *T:* (020) 7499 5803. *Clubs:* Brooks's, Jockey, White's.

See also Lady E. G. A. Cavendish, Baron Margadale, Lady E. Tennant.

DEVONSHIRE, Duchess of; Deborah Vivien Cavendish, DCVO 1999; housewife; Trustee, Royal Collections Trust, 1993–99; *b* 31 March 1920; 6th *d* of 2nd Baron

Redesdale and Sydney (*née* Bowles); *m* 1941, Lord Andrew Cavendish (*see* Duke of Devonshire); one *s* two *d*. *Educ:* private. Director: Peacock Hotel (Baslow) Ltd, 1975–; Elm Tree Farm Ltd, 1975–; Chatsworth House Trust, 1981–; Devonshire Arms Hotel (Bolton Abbey) Ltd, 1981–; Partner, Chatsworth Carpenters, 1981–; non-executive Director: Tarmac plc, 1984–92; W. & F. C. Bonhams & Sons Ltd, 1988–95. President: Royal Smithfield Show, 1972–74 and 1985; Royal Smithfield Club, 1975 (Vice-Pres., 1974–); RASE, 1995; Vice-Pres., Derbys Br., BRCS; Pres. or Patron, local charitable orgns, Derbys. Hon. Fellow, Sheffield City Poly., 1990. DUniv Middlesex, 1996; Hon. LittD Sheffield, 1998. *Publications:* The House: a portrait of Chatsworth, 1982; The Estate: a view from Chatsworth, 1990; Farm Animals, 1991; Treasures of Chatsworth: a private view, 1991; The Garden at Chatsworth, 1999; contribs to Spectator, Daily Telegraph. *Recreations:* field sports, shop-keeping. *Address:* Chatsworth, Bakewell, Derbyshire DE45 1PP. *T:* (01246) 582204.

See also Marquess of Hartington, Baron Margadale, Lady E. Tennant.

DEVONSHIRE, His Honour Michael Norman, TD 1969; a Circuit Judge, 1991–2000; *b* 23 May 1930; *s* of late Norman George Devonshire and late Edith Devonshire (*née* Skinner); *m* 1962, Jessie Margaret Roberts. *Educ:* King's Sch., Canterbury. Military Service, 2nd Lt, RA, served Korea, 1953–55; 4/5 Bn Queen's Own Royal West Kent Regt TA and 8 Bn Queen's Regt TA, 1955–69; retired in rank of Major, 1969. Admitted Solicitor, 1953; Partner, Doyle Devonshire Co., 1957–79; Master of the Supreme Court, Taxing Office, 1979–91; a Recorder, 1987–91. Chm., SE London Area Adv. Cttee on Magistracy, 1995–99. Pres., London Solicitors' Litigation Assoc., 1974–76; Mem., Law Soc. Family Law and Contentious Remuneration Cttees, 1969–79. Mem., Recreation and Conservation Cttee, Southern Water Authy, 1984–89. Mem., Council, Royal Yachting Assoc., 1978–92 and 1993–96 (Trustee, Seamanship Foundn, 1981–85; Chairman: Gen. Purposes Cttee, 1982–87; Regl Cttee, 1987–92; Internat. Affairs Cttee, 1990–; SE Region, 1993–98; Life Mem., 2000); Chm., Internat. Regs Cttee, ISAF (formerly IYRU), 1994– (Mem., 1986–90; Vice Chm., 1991–94); Mem., Pleasure Navigation Commn, Union Internat. de Motorautique, 1986–2000. *Recreation:* sailing. *Club:* Royal Thames Yacht.

DEVOY, Dame Susan (Elizabeth Anne), DNZM 1998; CBE 1993 (MBE 1986); professional squash rackets player, 1982–92, retired; *b* 4 Jan. 1964; *d* of John and Tui Devoy; *m* 1986, John Brandon Oakley; four *s*. *Educ:* McKillop Coll., Rotorua. Ranked no 1 internat. women's squash rackets player, 1984–92; winner: World Championships: Dublin, 1985; Auckland, 1987; Sydney, 1990; Vancouver, 1992; British Open Championships, 1984–90, 1992; 86 other internat. titles. Walked length of NZ in 53 days, raising NZ$500,000 for Muscular Dystrophy, 1988. Chm., Halberg Trust for Crippled Children, 1996–. NZ Sportsperson of Year, Halberg Trust, 1985–87, 1990, 1992. *Publications:* Susan Devoy on Squash, 1988; Out on Top, 1993. *Recreation:* yoga. *Address:* c/o PO Box 62083, Mount Wellington, Auckland, New Zealand. *T:* (9) 5222184.

DEW, John Anthony; HM Diplomatic Service; Head of Latin America and Caribbean Department, Foreign and Commonwealth Office, since 2000; *b* 3 May 1952; *s* of Roderick Dew and Katharina (*née* Kohlmeyer); *m* 1975, Marion, *d* of late Prof. Kenneth Kirkwood; three *d*. *Educ:* Hastings Grammar Sch.; Lincoln Coll., Oxford (Schol.); Ruskin Sch. of Drawing, Oxford. Joined HM Diplomatic Service, 1973; Third Sec., Caracas, 1975–79; FCO, 1979–83; First Sec., UK Delegn to OECD, Paris, 1983–87; Asst Hd, Falkland Is and Resource Mgt Depts, FCO, 1987–92; Counsellor, Dublin, 1992–96; Minister, Madrid, 1996–2000. *Recreations:* books, pictures. *Address:* c/o Foreign and Commonwealth Office, King Charles Street, SW1A 2AH. *Clubs:* Kildare Street and University (Dublin); Gran Pena (Madrid).

DEW, Prof. Ronald Beresford; Professor Emeritus, University of Manchester Institute of Science and Technology, since 1980; *b* 19 May 1916; *s* of Edwyn Dew-Jones, FCA, and Jean Robertson Dew-Jones, BA, (*née* McInnes); *m* 1940, Sheila Mary Smith, BA; one *s* one *d*. *Educ:* Sedbergh; Manchester Univ. (LLB); Cambridge Univ. (MA). FCA 1947. Barrister-at-Law, Middle Temple, 1965. Lieut, RNVR, 1940–45. Asst Managing Dir, P-E Consulting Gp, 1952–62. Visiting Prof. of Industrial Administration, Manchester Univ., 1960–63; Head of Dept of Management Sciences, Univ. of Manchester Inst. of Science and Technology, 1963–70 and 1974–77; Prof. of Industrial Administration, Manchester Univ., 1963–67; Prof. of Management Sciences, 1967–80. Mem. Council, Internat. Univ. Contact for Management Educn, 1966–71; Dir, Centre for Business Research, 1965–69; Dir, European Assoc. of Management Training Centres, 1966–71; Dep. Chm., Manchester Polytechnic, 1970–72; Co-Chm., Conf. of Univ. Management Schools (CUMS), 1970–73. Member: Council of BIM, 1971–76 (Bd of NW Region, 1966–80); Council of Manchester Business School, 1967–76; Court of Manchester Univ., 1978–80; Trustee, European Foundation for Management Develt, 1975–77. *Recreations:* archaeology, ornithology, travel. *Address:* University of Manchester Institute of Science and Technology, School of Management, Sackville Street, Manchester M60 1QD. *T:* (0161) 236 3311.

de WAAL, Sir Constant Hendrik, (Sir Henry), KCB 1989 (CB 1977); QC 1988; First Parliamentary Counsel, 1987–91; *b* 1 May 1931; *s* of late Hendrik de Waal and Elizabeth von Ephrussi; *m* 1964, Julia Jessel; two *s*. *Educ:* Tonbridge Sch. (scholar); Pembroke Coll., Cambridge (scholar; Hon. Fellow, 1992). 1st cl. Law Tripos, 1st cl. LLM. Called to the Bar, Lincoln's Inn, 1953, Bencher 1989; Buchanan Prize, Cassel Scholar. Fellow of Pembroke Coll., Cambridge, and Univ. Asst Lectr in Law, 1958–60. Entered Parliamentary Counsel Office, 1960; with Law Commission, 1969–71; Parly Counsel, 1971–81; Second Parly Counsel, 1981–86; Parly Counsel to Law Commn, 1991–96. *Recreation:* remaining (so far as possible) unaware of current events. *Address:* 62 Sussex Street, SW1V 4RG.

See also Rev. V. A. de Waal.

de WAAL, Rt Rev. Hugo Ferdinand; Bishop Suffragan of Thetford, 1992–2000; *b* 16 March 1935; *s* of Bernard Hendrik and Albertine Felice de Waal; *m* 1960, Brigit Elizabeth Townsend Massingberd-Mundy; one *s* three *d*. *Educ:* Tonbridge School; Pembroke Coll., Cambridge (MA); Münster Univ., Germany; Ridley Hall, Cambridge. Curate, St Martin's-in-the Bull Ring, Birmingham, 1960; Chaplain, Pembroke Coll., Cambridge, 1964–68; Rector of Dry Drayton, Cambs, 1964–73; with Bar Hill Ecumenical Area, 1967–73; Vicar of St John's, Blackpool Parish Church, 1974–78; Principal, Ridley Hall Theol Coll., Cambridge, 1978–91. Hon. Canon, Ely Cathedral, 1986–91. *Recreations:* music, tennis, fly-fishing. *Address:* Folly House, The Folly, Haughley, Stowmarket, Ipswich IP14 3NS. *T:* (01449) 774915.

de WAAL, Rev. Victor Alexander; Chaplain, Society of the Sacred Cross, Tymawr, 1990–2000; *b* 2 Feb. 1929; *s* of late Hendrik de Waal and Elizabeth von Ephrussi; *m* 1960, Esther Aline Lowndes Moir, PhD; four *s*. *Educ:* Tonbridge School; Pembroke Coll., Cambridge (MA); Ely Theological College. With Phs van Ommeren (London) Ltd, 1949–50; Asst Curate, St Mary the Virgin, Isleworth, 1952–56; Chaplain, Ely Theological Coll., 1956–59; Chaplain and Succentor, King's Coll., Cambridge, 1959–63; Chaplain, Univ. of Nottingham, 1963–69; Chancellor of Lincoln Cathedral, 1969–76; Dean of Canterbury, 1976–86. Hon. DD Nottingham, 1983. *Publications:* What is the Church?, 1969; The Politics of Reconciliation: Zimbabwe's first decade, 1990; contrib.: Theology and Modern Education, 1965; Stages of Experience, 1965; The Committed Church, 1966; Liturgy Reshaped, 1982; Liturgie et Espace Liturgique, 1987; Vie Ecclesiale—communauté et communautés, 1989; Beyond Death, 1995; La Confession et les Confessions, 1995; Les Artisans de Paix, 1996; Travail et Repos, 2000. *Address:* The Skreen, Erwood, Builth Wells, Powys LD2 3SJ. *T:* (01982) 560744.

See also Sir C. H. de Waal.

DEWAR, family name of **Baron Forteviot**.

DEWAR, David Alexander; an Assistant Auditor General, National Audit Office, 1984–94; *b* 28 Oct. 1934; *s* of James and Isabella Dewar; *m* 1959, Rosalind Mary Ellen Greenwood; one *s* one *d*. *Educ:* Leith Academy, Edinburgh. Entered Exchequer and Audit Dept, 1953; Chief Auditor, 1966; Deputy Director of Audit, 1973; Director of Audit, 1977; Dep. Sec. of Dept, 1981. *Recreations:* gardening, golf. *Address:* 15 Whitwell Hatch, Scotland Lane, Haslemere, Surrey GU27 3AW. *T:* (01428) 658095.

DEWAR, Ian Stewart; JP; Member: South Glamorgan County Council, 1985–93 (Vice-Chairman, 1990–91; Finance Chairman, 1992–93); South Wales Valuation Tribunal, since 1995; *b* 29 Jan. 1929; *er s* of late William Stewart Dewar and of Eileen Dewar (*née* Godfrey); *m* 1968, Nora Stephanie House; one *s* one *d*. *Educ:* Penarth County Sch.; UC Cardiff; Jesus Coll., Oxford (MA). RAF, 1947–49. Asst Archivist, Glamorgan County Council, 1952–53. Entered Min. of Labour, 1953; Asst Private Sec. to Minister, 1956–58; Principal, Min. of Labour and Civil Service Commn, 1958–65; Asst Sec., Min. of Labour, Dept of Employment and Commn on Industrial Relations, 1965–70; Asst Sec., 1970–73, and Under-Sec., 1973–83, Welsh Office. Member, Governing Body: Univ. of Wales, 1985–93; Nat. Mus. of Wales, 1985–93; Chm., Museum Schs Service Cttee, 1989–93. Mayor of Penarth, 1998–99. JP S Glam, 1985. *Address:* 59 Stanwell Road, Penarth, South Glamorgan CF64 3LR. *T:* (029) 2070 3255.

DEWAR, Robert James, CMG 1969; CBE 1964; World Bank, retired 1984; *b* 13 Jan. 1923; *s* of late Dr Robert Scott Dewar, MA, MB, ChB, and Mrs Roubaix Dewar, Dumbreck, Glasgow; *m* 1947, Christina Marianne, *d* of late Olof August Ljungberger, Stockholm, Sweden; two *s* one *d*. *Educ:* High Sch. of Glasgow; Edinburgh Univ. (BSc, Forestry); Wadham Coll., Oxford. Asst Conservator of Forests, Colonial Forest Service, Nigeria and Nyasaland, 1944–55; Dep. Chief Conservator of Forests, Nyasaland, 1955–61; Chief Conservator of Forests, Dir of Forestry and Game, Nyasaland (now Malawi), 1961–64; Mem. Nyasaland Legislative Council, 1960. Permanent Secretary, Malawi: Min. of Natural Resources, 1964–67 and 1968–69; Min. of Economic Affairs, 1967–68; retd from Malawi CS, 1969; World Bank: Sen. Agriculturalist, 1969–74; Chief of Agricl Div., Regl Mission for Eastern Africa, 1974–84. Mem. Nat. Development Council, Malawi, 1966–69. Vice-Chm. of Trustees, Zimbabwe Trust, 1993–. Chm., Friends of Malawi Assoc., 1996–. *Recreations:* gardening, golf, angling. *Address:* Hawkshaw, Comrie Road, Crieff, Perthshire PH7 4BJ. *T:* (01764) 654830. *Clubs:* Royal Commonwealth Society, New Cavendish.

See also R. S. Dewar.

DEWAR, Robert Scott; HM Diplomatic Service; High Commissioner to Mozambique, since 2000; *b* 10 June 1949; *s* of Robert James Dewar and Christina Marianne Dewar (*née* Ljungberger); *m* 1979, Jennifer Mary Ward; one *s* one *d*. *Educ:* Springvale, Southern Rhodesia; Loretto; Brasenose Coll., Oxford. VSO, Port Sudan, 1971–72; Scottish Office, 1972–73; FCO, 1973; served Colombo and FCO, to 1981, Asst Sec. Gen. to Lancaster House Conf. on Southern Rhodesia, 1979; Head of Chancery, Luanda, 1981–84; FCO, 1984–88; Dep. Head of Mission, Dakar, 1988–92; Dep. High Comr, Harare, 1992–96; Ambassador to Republic of Madagascar and concurrently (non-res.) to Federal Islamic Republic of the Comoros, 1996–99; FCO, 1999–2000. *Recreations:* sport, esp. fly fishing. *Address:* c/o Foreign and Commonwealth Office, SW1A 2AH.

DEWAR, His Honour Thomas; a Circuit Judge (formerly Judge of the County Court), 1962–84; Joint President, Council of Circuit Judges, 1980 (Vice-President, 1979); *b* 5 Jan. 1909; *s* of James Stewart Dewar and Katherine Rose Dewar; *m* 1950, Katherine Muriel Johnson; one *s* decd. *Educ:* Penarth Intermediate School; Cardiff Technical Coll.; Sch. of Pharmacy, University of London; Birkbeck Coll., University of London. Pharmaceutical Chemist, 1931; BPharm 1931, PhD 1934, BSc (Botany, 1st cl. hons) 1936, London. Called to Bar, Middle Temple, 1939; Blackstone Pupillage Prize, 1939. Admin. staff of Pharmaceutical Soc., 1936–40; Sec., Middx Pharmaceutical Cttee, 1940–41; Asst Dir, Min. of Supply, 1943; Sec., Wellcome Foundation, 1943–45. Mem. of Western Circuit, 1945–62; Judge of the County Court (circuit 59, Cornwall and Plymouth), 1962–65, (circuit 38, Edmonton, etc), 1965–66 (circuit 41, Clerkenwell), 1966–71; Circuit Judge, SE circuit, 1972–84. Presided over inquiry into X-ray accident at Plymouth Hosp., 1962. Mem. Executive Council, Internat. Law Assoc., 1974–89. Governor, Birkbeck Coll., 1944–46 and 1971–82 (Fellow, 1981). *Publications:* Textbook of Forensic Pharmacy, 1946 and four subsequent editions; scientific papers in Quarterly Jl of Pharmacy and Pharmacology. *Recreations:* horticulture, travel. *Address:* 1 Garden Court, Temple, EC4Y 9BJ. *T:* (020) 7353 3326. *Club:* Royal Over-Seas League.

de WARDENER, Prof. Hugh Edward, CBE 1982 (MBE (mil.) 1946); MD, FRCP; Professor of Medicine, University of London, Charing Cross Hospital, 1960–81, now Emeritus; Honorary Consultant Physician to the Army, 1975–80; *b* 8 Oct. 1915; *s* of Edouard de Wardener and Becky (*née* Pearce); *m* 1st, 1939, Janet Lavinia Bellis Simon (marr. diss. 1947); one *s*; 2nd, 1947, Diana Rosamund Crawshay (marr. diss. 1954); 3rd, 1954, Jill Mary Foxworthy (marr. diss. 1969); one *d*; 4th, 1969, Josephine Margaret Storey, MBE; two *s*. *Educ:* Malvern Coll. St Thomas's Hosp., 1933–39; RAMC, 1939–45; St Thomas's Hosp., 1945–60, Registrar, Senior Lecturer, Reader. MRCP 1946, MD 1949, FRCP 1958. Hon. MD: Univ. Pierre et Marie Curie, Paris, 1980; Univ. Paul Sabatier, Toulouse, 1996. President: Internat. Soc. of Nephrology, 1969–72; Renal Assoc., 1973–76; Mem. Council, Imp. Cancer Res. Fund, 1981–88. *Publications:* The Kidney: An Outline of Normal and Abnormal Structure and Function, 1958, 5th edn 1986; (with G. A. MacGregor) Salt, Diet and Health, 1998; papers in various scientific journals. *Recreations:* writing, walking. *Address:* 9 Dungarvan Avenue, Putney, SW15 5QU. *T:* (020) 8878 3130.

DEWBERRY, David Albert; HM Diplomatic Service; Deputy Head of Mission, the Holy See, Rome, since 1996; *b* 27 Sept. 1941; *s* of Albert Dewberry and Grace Dewberry (*née* Tarsey); *m* 1974, Catherine Mary (*née* Stabback); three *s* one *d*. *Educ:* Cray Valley Sch., Foots Cray, Kent. Joined CRO, 1958; Karachi, 1963; Kingston, 1966; Warsaw, 1970; Brussels, 1971; Second Sec. (Aid), Dhaka, 1972; FCO, 1974; Consul: Mexico City, 1977; Buenos Aires, 1980; FCO, 1982; Dep. High Comr, Dar es Salaam, 1987; FCO, 1991–96. *Recreations:* reading, walking. *Address:* Foreign and Commonwealth Office, SW1A 2AH.

DEWE, Roderick Gorrie; Chairman, Dewe Rogerson Group Ltd, 1969–99; *b* 17 Oct. 1935; *s* of Douglas Percy Dewe and Rosanna Clements Gorrie; *m* 1964, Carol Anne Beach

Thomas; one *s* one *d*. *Educ:* abroad and University Coll., Oxford (BA Hons). FIPR. Treasury, Fedn of Rhodesia and Nyasaland Govt, 1957–58; Angel Court Consultants, 1960–68; founded Dewe Rogerson, 1969, Chm., 1969–95. *Recreations:* golf, travel. *Address:* 55 Duncan Terrace, N1 8AG; Old Southhill Station House, near Biggleswade, Beds SG18 9LP. *T:* (01462) 811274. *Clubs:* City of London, Beefsteak, Savile.

DEWE MATHEWS, Marina Sarah, (Mrs John Dewe Mathews); *see* Warner, M. S.

de WET, Dr Carel; South African Ambassador to the Court of St James's, 1964–67 and 1972–77; Director of companies; farmer; *b* Memel, OFS, S Africa, 25 May 1924; *g s* of Gen. Christian de Wet; *m* 1949, Catharina Elizabeth (Rina) Maas, BA; one *s* three *d*. *Educ:* Vrede High Sch., OFS; Pretoria Univ. (BSc); University of Witwatersrand (MB, BCh). Served at Nat. Hosp., Bloemfontein; subseq. practised medicine at Boksburg, Transvaal, at Winburg, OFS, and, from 1948, at Vanderbijlpark, Transvaal. Mayor of Vanderbijlpark, 1950–53; MP (Nat. Party) for Vanderbijlpark, 1953–64, for Johannesburg West, 1967–72; Mem. various Parly and Nat. Party Cttees, 1953–64; Minister of Mines and Health, Govt of S Africa, 1967–72. *Recreations:* game farming, golf, rugby, cricket, hunting, deep sea fishing. *Address:* PO Box 70292, Bryanston, 2021, South Africa. *T:* (office) 8051948, *Fax:* 8053902; (home) 7066202. *Clubs:* Royal Automobile, East India, Institute of Directors, MCC, Les Ambassadeurs, Eccentric, Wentworth; Here XVII (Cape Town); Constantia (Pretoria); New, Rand Park Golf, Country (Johannesburg); Maccauvlei Country (Vereeniging), Emfuleni Golf (Vanderbijlpark).

DEWEY, Sir Anthony Hugh, 3rd Bt *cr* 1917; JP; *b* 31 July 1921; *s* of late Major Hugh Grahame Dewey, MC (*e s* of 2nd Bt), and Marjorie Florence Isobel (who *m* 2nd, 1940, Sir Robert Bell, KCSI; she *d* 1988), *d* of Lieut-Col Alexander Hugh Dobbs; *S* grandfather, 1948; *m* 1949, Sylvia, *d* of late Dr J. R. MacMahon, Branksome Manor, Bournemouth; two *s* three *d*. JP Somerset, 1961. *Heir: s* Rupert Grahame Dewey [*b* 29 March 1953; *m* 1978, Suzanne Rosemary, *d* of late Andrew Lusk, Perthshire; two *s* one *d*]. *Address:* Rag, Galhampton, Yeovil, Som BA22 7AJ. *T:* (01963) 440213. *Club:* Army and Navy.

DEWEY, Prof. John Frederick, FRS 1985; FGS; Professor of Geology, University of Oxford, since 1986; Fellow, since 1986 and Senior Research Fellow, since 2001, University College, Oxford; Professor of Geology, University of California, Davis, since 2001; *b* 22 May 1937; *s* of John Edward and Florence Nellie Mary Dewey; *m* 1961, Frances Mary Blackhurst, MA, DSc; one *s* one *d*. *Educ:* Bancroft's School; Queen Mary Coll. and Imperial Coll., Univ. of London (BSc, PhD, DIC); MA 1965, ScD 1988, Cantab; DSc Oxon 1989. CGeol 1990. Lecturer: Univ. of Manchester, 1960–64; Univ. of Cambridge, 1964–70; Prof., State Univ. of New York at Albany, 1970–82; Prof. of Geology, Durham Univ., 1982–86. Vis. Res. Fellow, British Geol Survey, 2001–; Vis. Res. Prof., Imperial Coll., Univ. of London, 2001–. MAE, 1990. Hon. DSc Meml Univ. of Newfoundland, 1996; Hon. LLD NUI, 1998. Numerous honours and awards, UK and overseas, incl. Penrose Medal, Geol Soc. of America, 1992; Arthur Holmes Medal, Europ. Union of Geoscis, 1993; Wollaston Medal, Geol Soc. of London, 1999. *Publications:* contribs to Geol Soc. of America Bulletin, Geol Soc. London Jl, Jl Geophysical Res. and other learned jls. *Recreations:* skiing, cricket, water colour painting, English music 1850–1950, model railways. *Address:* University College, Oxford OX1 4BH.

DEWHURST, Prof. Sir (Christopher) John, Kt 1977; FRCOG, FRCSE; Professor of Obstetrics and Gynaecology, University of London, at Queen Charlotte's Hospital for Women, 1967–85, now Professor Emeritus; *b* 2 July 1920; *s* of John and Agnes Dewhurst; *m* 1952, Hazel Mary Atkin; two *s* one *d*. *Educ:* St Joseph's Coll., Dumfries; Manchester Univ. MB, ChB. Surg. Lieut, RNVR, 1943–46. Sen. Registrar, St Mary's Hosp., Manchester, 1948–51; Lectr, Sen. Lectr and Reader, Sheffield Univ., 1951–67. Pres., RCOG, 1975–78. Hon. FACOG 1976; Hon. FRCSI 1977; Hon. FCOG (SA) 1978; Hon. FRACOG 1985. Hon. DSc Sheffield, 1977; Hon. MD Uruguay, 1980. *Publications:* A Student's Guide to Obstetrics and Gynaecology, 1960, 2nd edn 1965; The Gynaecological Disorders of Infants and Children, 1963; (jtly) The Intersexual Disorders, 1969; (ed) Integrated Obstetrics and Gynaecology for Postgraduates, 1972, 3rd edn 1981; (jtly) A General Practice of Obstetrics and Gynaecology, 1977, 2nd edn 1984; Practical Paediatric and Adolescent Gynaecology, 1980; Royal Confinements, 1980; Female Puberty and its Abnormalities, 1984. *Recreations:* cricket, gardening, music. *Address:* 21 Jack's Lane, Harefield, Middlesex UB9 6HE. *T:* (01895) 825403.

de WILDE, (Alan) Robin; QC 1993; a Recorder, since 2000; *b* 12 July 1945; *s* of late Capt. Ronald Cedric de Wilde and of Dorothea Elizabeth Mary (*née* Fenningworth); *m* 1977, Patricia Teresa Bearcroft; three *s*. *Educ:* Dean Close Sch.; RAF Coll., Cranwell; Inns of Court Sch. of Law. Called to the Bar, Inner Temple, 1971, Bencher, 1996. Mem., Bar Council, 1985–90, 1998–99; Chm., Professional Negligence Bar Assoc., 1995–97 (Hon. Vice Pres., 1998–; Gen. Editor, Facts & Figures–Tables for the Calculation of Damages, annually 1996–. FRSocMed 1997. *Address:* 199 Strand, WC2R 1DR. *T:* (020) 7520 4000, *Fax:* (020) 7379 9481.

de WINTER, Carl; Secretary General, Federation of British Artists, 1978–84; *b* 18 June 1934; *s* of Alfred de Winter; *m* 1958, Lyndall Bradshaw; one *s* one *d*. *Educ:* Pangbourne. Purser, Orient Line, 1951–60. Art Exhibitions Bureau: PA to Man. Dir, 1961–66; Director, 1967–84; Royal Soc. of Portrait Painters: Asst Sec., 1962–78; Sec., 1978–84; Royal Soc. of Miniature Painters, Sculptors and Gravers: Asst Sec., 1964–67; Sec., 1968–84; Hon. Mem., 1984; Royal Soc. of Marine Artists: Asst Sec., 1964–70; Sec., 1971–78; Royal Soc. of British Artists: Asst Keeper, 1969–73; Keeper, 1974–84; Royal Inst. of Oil Painters: Sec., 1973–84; Royal Inst. of Painters in Watercolours: Sec., 1979–84; National Soc. of Painters, Sculptors and Printmakers: Sec., 1973–84; New English Art Club: Sec., 1973–84; United Soc. of Artists: Sec., 1975–81. *Address:* Holbrook Park House, Old Holbrook, near Horsham, W Sussex RH12 4TW.

DEWS, Vivienne Margaret, (Mrs Alan Cogbill); Chief Executive, Police Information Technology Organisation, since 1999; *b* 29 Dec. 1952; *d* of Albert Dews and Eva Margaret Dews (*née* Hayman); *m* 1st, 1972, Stephen Ladner (marr. diss. 1977); 2nd, 1979, Alan Cogbill; one *s* one *d* (and two *d* decd). *Educ:* Northampton High Sch. for Girls; Newnham Coll., Cambridge (BA 1974). Joined Home Office, 1974; Private Sec. to Minister for Police and Prisons, 1980–82; Dep. Dir, Top Mgt Prog., Cabinet Office, 1982–89; Home Office: Head: Immigration Policy, 1989–91; After Entry Casework and Appeals, 1991–93; Consulting Efficiency and Market Testing, 1994–95; Dir, Finance and Services, Immigration and Nationality Directorate, 1995–99. *Recreations:* family, home, garden. *Address:* Police Information Technology Organisation, New Kings Beam House, 22 Upper Ground, SE1 9QY.

DEXTER, Colin; *see* Dexter, N. C.

DEXTER, Edward Ralph, CBE 2001; Managing Director, Ted Dexter & Associates, since 1978; *b* 15 May 1935; *m* 1959, Susan Georgina Longfield; one *s* one *d*. *Educ:* Radley College; Jesus College, Cambridge (Captain of cricket and of golf). Served 11th Hussars, 1956–57 (Malaya Campaign Medal 1955). Cricketer, 1958–68; Captain of Sussex, 1960–65; Captain of England, 1962–65; freelance journalist, 1965–88; sports promotion consultant, 1978–. Chm., England (Cricket) Cttee, TCCB, 1989–93. Contested (C) Cardiff, 1965. *Publications:* Ted Dexter's Cricket Book, 1963; Ted Dexter Declares, 1966; (jtly) Test Kill, 1976; Deadly Putter, 1979; From Bradman to Boycott, 1981; My Golf, 1982; Ted Dexter's Little Cricket Book, 1996. *Recreations:* golf, reading, motor cycling. *Address:* Ivanhoe Cottage, Watersplash Lane, Ascot SL5 7QP. *T:* (01344) 638587. *Clubs:* MCC (Chm., Cricket Cttee, 1998–; Pres., 2001–02); Sunningdale Golf, Royal and Ancient Golf.

DEXTER, (Norman) Colin, OBE 2000; author of crime novels; *b* 29 Sept. 1930; *s* of Alfred Dexter and Dorothy Dexter (*née* Towns); *m* 1956, Dorothy Cooper; one *s* one *d*. *Educ:* Stamford Sch.; Christ's Coll., Cambridge (MA). Assistant Classics Master: Wyggeston Boys' Sch., Leicester, 1954–57; Loughborough GS, 1957–59; Sen. Classics Master, Corby GS, 1959–66; Sen. Asst Sec., Oxford Delegacy of Local Exams, 1966–88. Member: CWA, 1978; Detection Club, 1980. Freedom, City of Oxford, 2001. Hon. MA Leicester, 1996; Hon. DLitt Oxford Brookes, 1998. Cartier Diamond Dagger, CWA, 1998. *Publications:* Last Bus to Woodstock, 1975; Last Seen Wearing, 1976; The Silent World of Nicholas Quinn, 1977; Service of All the Dead (Silver Dagger, CWA), 1979; The Dead of Jericho (Silver Dagger, CWA), 1981; The Riddle of the Third Mile, 1983; The Secret of Annexe 3, 1986; The Wench is Dead (Gold Dagger, CWA), 1989; The Jewel that was Ours, 1991; The Way Through the Woods (Gold Dagger, CWA), 1992; Morse's Greatest Mystery, 1993; The Daughters of Cain, 1994; Death is Now My Neighbour, 1996; The Remorseful Day, 1999. *Recreations:* poetry, crosswords, Wagner. *Address:* 456 Banbury Road, Oxford OX2 7RG.

DEXTER, Dr (Thomas) Michael, FRS 1991; Director, Wellcome Trust, since 1998; *b* 15 May 1945; *s* of Thomas Richard Dexter and Agnes Gertrude Deplege; *m* 1966, Frances Ann Sutton (marr. diss. 1978); one *s* one *d* (twins); one *s* one *d* by Dr Elaine Spooncer. *Educ:* Salford Univ. (BSc 1st class Hons 1970; DSc 1982); Manchester Univ. (PhD 1973). MRCPath 1987, FRCPath 1997; CBiol, FIBiol 1997. Lady Tata Meml Scholar, 1970–73; Paterson Institute for Cancer Research: Res. Scientist, 1973; Prof. of Haematology and Hd of Dept of Exptl Haematol., 1982–98; Dep. Dir, 1994–97; Dir, 1997–98. Life Fellow, Cancer Res. Campaign, Manchester, 1978; Personal Chair, Univ. of Manchester, 1985; Gibb Res. Fellow, CRC, 1992–97. Visiting Fellow: Sloan Kettering Inst., NY, 1976–77; Weizmann Inst., Israel, 1980. Lectures: Annual, Leukaemia Res. Fund, 1987; Michael Williams, RSM, 1990; Maximov, Leningrad, 1990; Almoth-Wright, St Mary's, London, 1992; Medawar, RPMS, 1994; Henry Hallett Dale, Nat. Inst. of Biol Standards of Control, 1997; Annual, British Soc. of Haematology, 1998; Inst. Distinguished, Inst. of Cancer Res., 1999; 5th Chamlong-Harinasuta, Bangkok, 1999; Lloyd Roberts, RCP, 2000. Member: MRC, 1993–96 (Chairman: Molecular and Cellular Medicine Bd, 1994–96; Human Genome Mapping Project Co-ordinating Cttee, 1996–98); Scientific Cttee, Leukaemia Res. Fund, 1983–86; Scientific Grants Cttee, CRC, 1987–93; Scientific Adv. Bd, Biomedical Res. Center, BC, 1987–91; Scientific Adv. Bd, Wellcome/CRC Inst., Cambridge, 1992–98; AFRC Grants Cttee, 1992–94; Cttee on Med. Aspects of Radiation in Envmt, 1994–98; Adv. Bd, EMF Trust, 1995–. Pres., Internat. Soc. for Exptl Hematology, 1988. Founder FMedSci 1998. Hon. MRCP 1995, Hon. FRCP 1998. Hon. DSc Salford, 1998; UMIST, 1999. *Publications:* author of 300 articles in scientific jls; editor of four books. *Recreations:* folk singing, gardening, poetry, dominoes. *Address:* Wellcome Trust, 183 Euston Road, NW1 2BE. *T:* (020) 7611 8422.

de YARBURGH-BATESON, family name of **Baron Deramore**.

DEYERMOND, Prof. Alan David, DLitt; FSA; FBA 1988; Professor of Spanish, Queen Mary and Westfield College, London (formerly Westfield College), 1969–97, now Research Professor; *b* 24 Feb. 1932; *s* of late Henry Deyermond and Margaret Deyermond (*née* Lawson); *m* 1957, Ann Marie Bracken; one *d*. *Educ:* Quarry Bank High Sch., Liverpool; Victoria Coll., Jersey; Pembroke Coll., Oxford (MA; BLitt 1957; DLitt 1985). FSA 1987. Westfield, subseq. Queen Mary and Westfield, College, London: Asst Lectr, 1955; Lectr, 1958; Reader, 1966; Senior Tutor, 1967–72; Dir, Medieval Hispanic Res. Seminar, 1967–97; Dean, Faculty of Arts, 1972–74, 1981–84; Head of Dept of Spanish, 1983–89; Vice-Principal, 1986–89; Dir of Grad. Studies, Sch. of Modern Langs, 1995–97; Hon. Fellow, 2000. Visiting Professor, Universities of: Wisconsin, 1972; California LA, 1977; Princeton, 1978–81; Victoria, 1983; N Arizona, 1986; Johns Hopkins, 1987; Nacional Autónoma de México, 1992; A Coruña, 1996; California Irvine, 1998–99; Scholar in Residence, Indiana Univ., 1998. Lectures: Sir Henry Thomas, Univ. of Birmingham, 1985; Taylorian, Univ. of Oxford, 1999. Chm. Trustees, Kentish's Educnl Foundn, 1992–98. President: Internat. Courtly Literature Soc., 1977–83, Hon. Life Pres., 1983; Asociación Internacional de Hispanistas, 1992–95 (Vice-Pres., 1983–89; Hon. Life Pres., 1995). Corresponding Fellow: Medieval Acad. of America; Real Acad. de Buenas Letras de Barcelona; Mem., Hispanic Soc. of America; Hon. Fellow, Asociación Hispánica de Literatura Medieval. Hon. LHD Georgetown, 1995. Premio Internacional Elio Antonio de Nebrija, 1994. Gen. Ed., papers of Medieval Hispanic Res. Seminar, 1995–. *Publications:* The Petrarchan Sources of La Celestina, 1961, 2nd edn 1975; Epic Poetry and the Clergy, 1969; A Literary History of Spain: The Middle Ages, 1971; Apollonius of Tyre, 1973; Lazarillo de Tormes: a critical guide, 1975; Historia y crítica de la literatura española: Edad Media, 1980, supplement, 1991; El Cantar de Mio Cid y la épica medieval española, 1987; Tradiciones y puntos de vista en la ficción sentimental, 1993; La literatura perdida de la Edad Media castellana: catálogo y estudio, vol. 1, 1995; Point of View in the Ballad, 1996; contribs to Hispanic Res. Jl etc. *Recreations:* dog-walking, psephology, vegetarian cookery. *Address:* 20 Lancaster Road, St Albans, Herts AL1 4ET. *T:* (01727) 855383; *e-mail:* a.d.deyermond@qmw.ac.uk.

d'EYNCOURT, Sir Mark Gervais T.; *see* Tennyson-d'Eyncourt.

DHAKA, Archbishop of, (RC), since 1978; **Most Rev. Michael Rozario,** STL; *b* Solepore, Dhaka, Bangladesh, 18 Jan. 1926; *s* of Urban Rozario. *Educ:* Little Flower Seminary, Dhaka, Bangladesh; St Albert's Seminary, Ranchi, India. Jagannath Coll., Dhaka, Bangladesh, 1948–50; Univ. of Notre Dame, USA, 1951–53; Urbano Univ., Rome, 1953–57. Ordained priest, 1956; Bishop of Dinajpur, 1968. Pres., Catholic Bishops' Conf. of Bangladesh. *Address:* Archbishop's House, PO Box 3, Dhaka 1000, Bangladesh.

DHANDA, Parmjit Singh; MP (Lab) Gloucester, since 2001; *b* 17 Sept. 1971; *s* of Balbir Singh Dhanda and Mrs Balbir Singh Dhanda. *Educ:* Mellow Lane Comprehensive, Hayes, Middx; Univ. of Nottingham (BEng (Hons) Elec Eng; MSc IT 1995). Labour Party Organiser, W London, 1996–98; Asst Nat. Organiser, Connect, 1998–2001. Mem. (Lab), Hillingdon BC, 1998–. Contested (Lab) SE Reg., England, EP elecn, 1999. Member: Fabian Society; Co-operative Society; USDAW. *Recreations:* football, cricket, writing. *Address:* House of Commons, SW1A 0AA.

DHENIN, Air Marshal Sir Geoffrey (Howard), KBE 1975; AFC 1953 and Bar, 1957; GM 1943; MA, MD, DPH; FFCM 1975; FRAeS 1971; Director-General, Medical Services (RAF), 1974–78; *b* 2 April 1918; *s* of Louis Richard Dhenin and Lucy Ellen Dagg;

m 1946, Claude Andree Evelyn Rabut (*d* 1996); one *s* two *d* (and one *s* decd). *Educ:* Hereford Cathedral Sch.; St John's Coll., Cambridge; Guy's Hosp., London. Joined RAF; various sqdn and other med. appts, Bomber Comd, 2nd TAF, 1943–45 (despatches 1945); pilot trng, 1945–46; various med. officer pilot appts, 1946–58; Staff Coll., Bracknell, 1958–59; comd Princess Mary's RAF Hosp. Akrotiri, Cyprus, 1960–63; comd RAF Hosp. Ely, 1963–66; PMO Air Support Comd, 1966–68; Dir of Health and Research, RAF, 1968–70; Dep. DGMS, RAF, 1970–71; PMO Strike Comd, 1971–73. Fellow, Internat. Acad. of Aerospace Medicine, 1972. CStJ 1974. QHP 1970–78. Adviser to Saudi Arabian Nat. Guard, 1978–79. *Publication:* (ed) Textbook of Aviation Medicine, 1978. *Recreations:* golf, ski-ing, sub-aqua. *Address:* Ruxbury Lodge, St Ann's Hill, Chertsey, Surrey KT16 9NL. *T:* (01932) 563624. *Clubs:* Royal Air Force; Wentworth; Royal Porthcawl Golf.

DHOLAKIA, family name of **Baron Dholakia**.

DHOLAKIA, Baron *cr* 1997 (Life Peer), of Waltham Brooks in the co. of West Sussex; **Navnit Dholakia,** OBE 1994; JP, DL; *b* 4 March 1937; *s* of Permananddas Mulji Dholakia and Shantabai Permananddas Dholakia; *m* 1967, Ann McLuskie; two *d*. *Educ:* Home Sch. and Inst. of Science, Bhavnagar, Gujarat; Brighton Tech. Coll. Medical Lab. Technician, Southlands Hosp., Shoreham-by-Sea, 1960–66; Develt Officer, Nat. Cttee for Commonwealth Immigrants, 1966–68; Sen. Develt Officer, 1968–74, Principal Officer and Sec., 1974–76, Community Relns Commn; Commission for Racial Equality: Principal Fieldwork, Admin. and Liaison Officer, 1976–78; Principal Officer, Management, 1978–81; Head of Admin., Justice Section, 1984–94. Lib Dem spokesman on home affairs, 1997–; an Asst Lib Dem Whip, H of L, 1997–. Member: Hunt Cttee on Immigration and Youth Service, 1967–69; Bd of Visitors, HM Prison, Lewes, 1978–95; Home Office Inter-Deptl Cttee on Racial Attacks and Harassment, 1987–92; Carlisle Cttee on Parole Systems Review, 1987–88; Sussex Police Authority, 1991–94; Ethnic Minority Adv. Cttee, Judicial Studies Bd, 1992–96; Howard League for Penal Reform, 1992– (Mem. Editl Bd, Howard Jl of Criminology, 1993–); Police Complaints Authy, 1994–97. Mem., H of L Appts Commn, 1999–. Chm., NACRO, 1998– (Mem. Council, 1984–; Chm., Race Issues Adv. Cttee, 1989–; Vice-Chm., 1995–98); Vice-Chm., Policy Res. Inst. on Ageing and Ethnicity, 1999–. Trustee, Mental Health Foundn, 1997–. Gov., Commonwealth Inst., 1998–. Chairman: Brighton Young Liberals, 1959–62; Brighton Liberal Assoc., 1962–64; Sec., Race and Community Relns Panel, Liberal Party, 1969–74; Mem., Federal Policy and Federal Exec. Cttee, Liberal Democrats, 1996–97; Pres., Lib Dem Party, 1999–. Mem. (L) Brighton CBC, 1961–64. Mem. Council, SCF, 1992– (Chm., Programme Adv. Cttee, 1992–). JP Mid Sussex, 1978; DL West Sussex, 1999. *Publications:* articles on criminal justice. *Recreations:* photography, travel, gardening, cooking exotic dishes. *Address:* 76 Penland Road, Haywards Heath, West Sussex RH16 1PH. *T:* and *Fax:* (01444) 450065.

DHRANGADHARA, Maharaja Sriraj of Halvad-, His Highness Jhaladhip Maharana Sriraj Meghrajji III, KCIE 1947; 45th Ruler and Head of Jhalla–Makhvan Clan; MP for Jhalavad (Gujarat), 1967–70; *b* 3 March 1923; *s* of HH Ghanashyamsinhji Bava, GCIE, KCSI; *S* father 1942, assumed powers 1943 on termination of political minority; *m* 1943, Princess Brijrajkunvarba of Jodhpur; three *s*. *Educ:* Dhrangadhara Rajmahal Shala (Palace Sch.) which was moved to UK to become Millfield Sch., Som., 1935; Heath Mount Sch.; Haileybury Coll.; St Joseph's Acad., Dehra Dun; Sivaji Military Sch., Poona; later, Christ Church, Oxford, 1952–58 (Mem. High Table and Sen. Common Room); Philosophy course; Ruskin Sch. of Drawing; Associate Vice Pres., Amateur Fencing Assoc. of GB; Postgrad. Diploma in Social Anthropology (with distinction), 1955; research in Hindu sacraments, 1956–58; BLitt (Oxon). FRAS, FRAI; Associate, RHistS. Darbar-in-Council proclaimed fundamental rights; estab. public adv. body; accepted attachment of Lakhtar, Sayla, Chuda and Muli States and the transfer of British suzerainty over them to the Dhrangadhara Darbar, 1943, and promulgated rigorous reforms; local self-govt, removal of untouchability, compulsory free primary educn, women's property rights, Hindu widows' remarriage, child marriage restraint, labour laws. Mem., Standing Cttee, Chamber of Princes, 1945–47; proposed Confedn of Saurashtra, 1945, and carried it in States-General meeting (as Chm.), 1946; first state in W India to accept participation in India's Constituent Assembly. Reserving sovereignty acceded to India, 1947; instituted Dhrangadhara Coronation Medal, 1942 and Accession to India Medal, 1947; under Covenant ceded admin and army to United State of Saurashtra, 1948; nominated to India's Constituent Assembly, instead became Uparajpramukh, Actg Rajpramukh and C-in-C of State Forces of United State of Saurashtra, 1948–52; First Pres., State Bank of Saurashtra; proclaimed India's constitution for United State of Saurashtra, 1949; resigned and went to Oxford Univ., 1952. Mem., Gujarat Legislative Assembly, Feb.-March 1967; main Oppn speaker against Parlt's power to abridge fundamental rights; introd own Referendum Bill for plebiscite; lead opposition to abrogation of Rulers' covenanted rights and constitutional guarantees, 1967–71; Intendant General, Consultation of Rulers of Indian States in Concord for India, 1967. Life Member: Indian Council of World Affairs and Inst. of Const. and Parly Studies, 1967; Indian Parly Gp and CPA, 1967; Linguistic Soc. of India; Internat. Phonetic Assoc. and Simplified Spelling Soc., London; Numismatic Soc. of India; Heraldry Soc.; WWF; Wildlife Preservation Soc. of India; Cricket Club of India; Delhi Golf Club; India Internat. Centre. Freemason, Bombay Lodge. Perm. Pres., Srirajman (Educ.) Foundn; Pres., Rajkumar Coll., Rajkot, 1966–; Mem., Ind. Cttee, United World Colls. Patron, Bhandarkar Oriental Res. Inst. *Heir: s* Maharajkumar Shri Sodhsalji, *b* 22 March 1944. *Address:* Ajitnivas Palace, Dhrangadhara, Jhalavad, Gujarat 363310, India; Dhrangadhara Bhavan, 1065 Chatuhsrungi Road, Pune 411016, India.

DIAMANTOPOULOU, Anna; Member, European Commission, since 1999; *b* 1959; *m*; one *c*. *Educ:* Aristotle Univ. of Thessaloniki (Civil Engrg); Panteion Univ. of Athens (Postgrad. Studies in Regl Develt). Civil engr, 1981–85; Lectr, Insts of Higher Technol Educn, 1983–85; Prefect of Kastoria, 1985–86; Sec. Gen. for Adult Educn, 1987–88, for Youth, 1988–89; Man. Dir, regl develt co., 1989–93; Sec. Gen. for Industry, 1994–96; MP for Kozani, 1996–99; Dep. Minister for Develt, Greece, 1996–99. Mem. Central Cttee, Panhellenic Socialist Movt, 1991–99. *Address:* European Commission, Rue de la Loi 200, 1049 Brussels, Belgium.

DIAMOND, family name of **Baron Diamond**.

DIAMOND, Baron *cr* 1970 (Life Peer), of the City of Gloucester; **John Diamond;** PC 1965; FCA; Chairman: Royal Commission on Distribution of Income and Wealth, 1974–79; Industry and Parliament Trust, 1976–82; Trustee, Social Democratic Party, 1981–82, Leader of SDP in House of Lords, 1982–88; *b* Leeds, 30 April 1907; *s* of Henrietta and Rev. S. Diamond, Leeds; *m*; two *s* two *d*. *Educ:* Leeds Grammar Sch. Qualified as Chartered Accountant, 1931, and commenced practice as John Diamond & Co. MP (Lab) Blackley Div. of Manchester, 1945–51, Gloucester, 1957–70; Chief Secretary to the Treasury, 1964–70 (in the Cabinet, 1968–70); formerly PPS to Minister of Works; Deputy Chm. of Cttees, House of Lords, 1974. Chm., Prime Minister's Adv. Cttee on Business Appts of Crown Servants, 1975–88. Chm. of Finance Cttee, Gen. Nursing Council, 1947–53; Dir of Sadler's Wells Trust Ltd, 1957–64; Hon. Treas., Fabian Soc., 1950–64. Hon. LLD Leeds, 1978. *Publications:* Socialism the British Way (jtly), 1948; Public Expenditure in Practice, 1975. *Recreations:* music, gardening, reading the classics. *Address:* Aynhoe, Doggetts Wood Lane, Chalfont St Giles, Bucks HP8 4TH.

DIAMOND, His Honour Anthony Edward John; QC 1974; a Circuit Judge, 1990–98; international and maritime arbitrator; *b* 4 Sept. 1929; *s* of late Arthur Sigismund Diamond, former Master of the Supreme Court, and of Gladys Elkah Diamond (*née* Mocatta); m 1965, Joan Margaret Gee; two *d*. *Educ:* Rugby; Corpus Christi Coll., Cambridge (MA). Served RA, 1947–49. Called to the Bar, Gray's Inn, 1953 (Bencher, 1985); practised at Bar as a specialist in commercial law, 1958–90; Head of Chambers at 4 Essex Court, EC4, 1984–90; Dep. High Court Judge, 1982–90; a Recorder, 1985–90; Judge i/c of Central London County Court Business List, 1994–98. Chm., Banking Act Appeals, 1980; Mem., indep. review body under colliery review procedure, 1985. *Publications:* papers on maritime law and arbitration. *Recreation:* the visual arts. *Address:* 1 Cannon Place, NW3 1EH. *T:* (020) 7435 6154. *Club:* Athenæum.

DIAMOND, Prof. Aubrey Lionel; Professor of Law, University of Notre Dame, and Co-Director, London Law Centre, since 1987; Emeritus Professor of Law, University of London; solicitor; *b* 28 Dec. 1923; *s* of Alfred and Millie Diamond, London; *m* 1955, Dr Eva M. Bobasch; one *s* one *d*. *Educ:* elementary schs; Central Foundation Sch., London; London Sch. of Economics (LLB, LLM; Hon. Fellow, 1984). Clerical Officer, LCC, 1941–48. Served RAF, 1943–47. Admitted a solicitor, 1951. Sen. Lectr, Law Society's Sch. of Law, 1955–57; Asst Lectr, Lectr and Reader, Law Dept, LSE, 1957–66; Prof. of Law, Queen Mary Coll., Univ. of London, 1966–71; Law Comr, 1971–76; Prof. of Law and Dir, Inst. of Advanced Legal Studies, Univ. of London, 1976–86, now Emeritus; Hon. Fellow, QMW, 1989 (Fellow, QMC, 1984). Partner in Lawford & Co., Solicitors, 1959–71 (consultant, 1986–). Part-time Chm. of Industrial Tribunals, 1984–90; Dep. Chm., Data Protection Tribunal, 1985–96; Consultant, DTI, 1986–88. Member: Central London Valuation Court, 1956–73; Consumer Advisory Council, BSI, 1961–63; Council, Consumers' Assoc., 1963–71 (Vice-Pres., 1981–84); Consumer Council, 1963–66, 1967–71; Cttee on the Age of Majority, 1965–67; Council, Law Society, 1976–92. Chairman: Social Sciences and the Law Cttee, SSRC, 1977–80; Hamlyn Trust, 1977–88; Advertising Adv. Cttee, IBA, 1980–88. President: Nat. Fedn of Consumer Groups, 1977–81 (Chm., 1963–67); British Insurance Law Assoc., 1988–90; Vice-Pres., Inst. of Trading Standards Administration, 1975–. Visiting Professor: University Coll. Dar es Salaam, Univ. of E Africa, 1966–67; Law Sch., Stanford Univ., 1971; Melbourne Univ., 1977; Univ. of Virginia, 1982; Tulane Univ., 1984; Vis. teacher, LSE, 1984–93. Hon. QC 1992. Hon. MRCP 1990. Hon. DCL City, 1992. *Publications:* The Consumer, Society and the Law (with Sir Gordon Borrie), 1963 (4th edn, 1981); Introduction to Hire-Purchase Law, 1967 (2nd edn. 1971); (ed) Instalment Credit, 1970; (co-ed) Sutton and Shannon on Contracts (7th edn) 1970; Commercial and Consumer Credit: an introduction, 1982; A Review of Security Interests in Property, 1989; articles and notes in legal and medical jls and symposia. *Address:* University of Notre Dame, London Law Centre, 1 Suffolk Street, SW1Y 4HG. *T:* (020) 7484 7821. *Club:* Reform.

DIAMOND, Prof. Derek Robin; Professor of Geography with special reference to Urban and Regional Planning, London School of Economics and Political Science, 1982–95, now Emeritus Professor; *b* 18 May 1933; *s* of John Diamond (Baron Diamond, *qv*) and Sadie Diamond; *m* 1957, Esme Grace Passmore; one *s* one *d*. *Educ:* Oxford Univ. (MA); Northwestern Univ., Illinois (MSc). Lecturer: in Geography, 1957–65, in Town and Regional Planning, 1965–68, Glasgow Univ.; Reader in Geography, London School of Economics, 1968–82. Pres., IBG, 1994–95. Hon. MRTPI, 1989. Hon. Prof. of Human Geography, Inst. of Geography, Beijing, 1990. Editor: Progress in Planning, 1973–; Geoforum, 1974–93. *Publications:* Regional Policy Evaluation, 1983; Infrastructure and Industrial Costs in British Industry, 1989; Evaluating the Effectiveness of Land Use Planning, 1992; Metropolitan Governance: its contemporary transition, 1997. *Recreation:* philately. *Address:* 9 Ashley Drive, Walton-on-Thames, Surrey KT12 1JL. *T:* (01932) 223280. *Club:* Geographical.

DIAMOND, (Peter) Michael, OBE 1996; MA, FMA; Director, Birmingham City Museums and Art Gallery, 1980–95; *b* 5 Aug. 1942; *s* of late William Howard and Dorothy Gladys Diamond; *m* 1968, Anne Marie; one *s* one *d*. *Educ:* Bristol Grammar Sch.; Queens' Coll., Cambridge (BA Fine Art 1964, MA 1966). Dip. of Museums Assoc. 1968, FMA 1980. Sheffield City Art Galleries: Art Asst, 1965; Keeper, Mappin Art Gall., 1967; Dep. Dir, 1969; City Arts and Museums Officer, Bradford, 1976. Chairman: Gp of Dirs of Museums, 1985–89; Public Art Commns Agency, 1987–88. Member, Executive Committee: Yorks Arts Assoc., 1977–80; Yorks Sculpture Park, 1978–82 (Chm., 1978–82); Pres., Yorks Fedn of Museums, 1978–80; Member: Crafts Council, 1980–84; Council, Museums Assoc., 1987–90; Board, Museums Training Inst., 1990–93; Fabric Adv. Cttee, Lichfield Cathedral, 2001–. Mem. Council, Aston Univ., 1983–92. FRSA 1990. Hon. DSc Aston, 1993. *Publications:* numerous exhibition catalogues incl. Victorian Paintings, 1968; Art and Industry in Sheffield 1850–75, 1975; Bike Art, 1994; (contrib.) Manual of Curatorship, 1984 and 1992; articles in Museums Jl. *Address:* 5 Anchorage Road, Sutton Coldfield, W Midlands B74 2PJ.

DIAS, Most Rev. Ivan Cornelius; *see* Bombay, Archbishop of, (RC).

DIBBEN, Michael Alan Charles; HM Diplomatic Service, retired; High Commissioner, Fiji, also accredited to Tuvalu, Kiribati and Nauru, 1997–2000; *b* 19 Sept. 1943; *s* of Lt-Col Alan Frank Dibben and Eileen Beatrice Dibben (*née* Donoghue). *Educ:* Dulwich College. With Ottoman Bank, London, 1961–64; CRO 1964; Min. of Overseas Develt, 1965; Protocol Dept, FCO, 1966; served Montreal, Nassau, Stuttgart, Port of Spain, Douala; First Sec., 1981; Nuclear Energy Dept, FCO, 1981–83; Munich and Hamburg, 1983–87; Inf. Dept, FCO, 1987–90; Ambassador to Paraguay, 1991–95; Head of Contracts, Travel and Related Services Gp, FCO, 1995–96. Mem., Horners' Co. *Recreations:* reading, walking, golf, classical music. *Address:* 154 Banstead Road, Banstead, Surrey SM7 1QG.

DIBBLE, Roy Edwin, CEng, FBCS; HM Diplomatic Service, retired; Director, General Services, Foreign and Commonwealth Office, 1996–2000; *b* 16 Dec. 1940; *s* of Edwin Dibble and Gwendoline Vera Dibble (*née* Nicholls); *m* 1967, Valerie Jean Denham Smith. *Educ:* Maidstone Tech. High Sch. DipEE; MIEE. Central Computer Telecommunications Agency: Head of Div., HM Treasury, 1985–91, Cabinet Office, 1991–94; Dir, OPS, Cabinet Office, 1994–96. *Recreation:* sailing.

DIBDIN, Michael; author; *b* 21 March 1947; *s* of Frederick John Dibdin and Peigi (*née* Taylor); *m* 1st, 1971, Benita Mitbrodt (marr. diss. 1986); one *d*; 2nd, 1987, Sybil Sheringham (marr. diss. 1995); one *d*; 3rd, 1997, Kathrine Beck. *Educ:* Univ of Sussex (BA English Lit.); Univ. of Alberta (MA). Gold Dagger, CWA, 1988; Grand Prix de Littérature Policière (France), 1994. *Publications:* The Last Sherlock Holmes Story, 1978; A Rich Full Death, 1986; Ratking, 1988; The Tryst, 1989; Vendetta, 1990; Dirty Tricks, 1991; Cabal, 1992; The Dying of the Light, 1993; (ed) The Picador Book of Crime Writing, 1993;

Dead Lagoon, 1994; Dark Spectre, 1995; Così Fan Tutti, 1996; A Long Finish, 1998; Blood Rain, 1999; Thanksgiving, 2000; And Then You Die, 2002. *Recreations:* music, travel. *Address:* c/o Pat Kavanagh, Peters Fraser & Dunlop, Drury House, 34–43 Russell Street, WC2B 5HA. *T:* (020) 7344 1000. *Club:* Groucho.

DIBELA, Sir Kingsford, GCMG 1983 (CMG 1978); Governor-General of Papua New Guinea, 1983–89; *b* 16 March 1932; *s* of Norman Dibela and Edna Dalauna; *m* 1952, Winifred Tomolarina; two *s* four *d. Educ:* St Paul's Primary Sch., Dogura. Qualified as primary school teacher; teacher, 1949–63. Pres., Weraura Local Govt Council, 1963–77; MP, PNG, 1975–82; Speaker of Nat. Parlt, 1977–80. *Recreations:* golf, cricket. *Address:* PO Box 113, Port Moresby, Papua New Guinea. *Club:* Port Moresby Golf.

DICE, Brian Charles, OBE 1997; Chief Executive, British Waterways Board, 1986–96; *b* 2 Sept. 1936; *s* of late Frederic Charles Dice; *m* 1965, Gwendoline Tazeena Harrison; two *d. Educ:* Clare College, Cambridge; Middle Temple. Cadbury Schweppes, 1960–86, Director, 1979; Managing Director, Schweppes, 1983. *Address:* Stratton Wood, Beaconsfield, Bucks HP9 1HS.

DICK, Gavin Colquhoun; Vice-Chairman, Mobile Radio Training Trust, since 1990; *b* 6 Sept. 1928; *s* of late John Dick and Catherine MacAuslan Henderson; *m* 1952, Elizabeth Frances, *e d* of late Jonathan Hutchinson; two *d. Educ:* Hamilton Academy; Glasgow Univ. (MA 1950); Balliol Coll., Oxford (Snell Exhibnr, 1949, MA 1957); SOAS (Cert. in Turkish, 1986). National Service, 3rd RTR (Lieut), 1952–54. Asst Principal, BoT, 1954, Principal, 1958; UK Trade Comr, Wellington, NZ, 1961–64; Asst Sec., 1967; Jt Sec., Review Cttee on Overseas Representation, 1968–69; Under-Sec., 1975–84, Dept of Industry, 1981–84. Consultant: Office of Telecommunications, 1984–87; DTI Radiocommunications Div., 1987–89. Bd Mem., English Industrial Estates Corp., 1982–84. Governor, Coll. of Air Training (Hamble), 1975–80. Hon. Pres., Anglo–Turkish Assoc. of Academics and Professionals, 1995–. *Recreation:* words. *Address:* Fell Cottage, Bayley's Hill, Sevenoaks, Kent TN14 6HS. *T:* (01732) 453704. *Club:* Oxford and Cambridge.

DICK, Iain Charles M.; *see* Mackay-Dick.

DICK, James Brownlee, CB 1977; MA, BSc, FInstP, FCIBS, FIOB; consultant; *b* 19 July 1919; *s* of James Brownlee Dick and Matilda Forrest; *m* 1944, Audrey Moira Shinn; two *s. Educ:* Wishaw High Sch.; Glasgow Univ. Royal Naval Scientific Service, 1940. Building Research Station, later Building Research Establishment: Physics Div., 1947; Head of User Requirements Div., 1960; Head of Production Div., 1963; Asst Dir, 1964; Dep. Dir, 1969; Dir, 1969–79. Pres., Internat. Council for Building Res., 1974–77. *Publications:* papers in professional and scientific journals. *Address:* 10 Stanier Rise, Berkhamsted, Herts HP4 1SD. *T:* (01442) 862580.

DICK, Kay; writer; *b* 29 July 1915; *o d* of Mrs Kate Frances Dick. *Educ:* Geneva, Switzerland; Lycée Français de Londres, S Kensington. Worked in publishing and bookselling; edited (as Edward Lane) 13 issues of magazine, The Windmill. *Publications: fiction:* By the Lake, 1949; Young Man, 1951; An Affair of Love, 1953; Solitaire, 1958; Sunday, 1962; They, 1977 (South-East Arts Literature Prize, 1977); The Shelf, 1984; *non-fiction:* Pierrot, 1960; Ivy and Stevie, 1971; Friends and Friendship, 1974; *edited:* London's Hour: as seen through the eyes of the fire-fighters, 1942; Late Joys at the Players Theatre, 1943; The Mandrake Root, 1946, At Close of Eve, 1947, The Uncertain Element, 1950 (three vols of strange stories); Bizarre and Arabesque (anthology from Edgar Allan Poe), 1967; Writers at Work, 1972. *Recreations:* friends, gardening, walking the dog. *Address:* Flat 5, 9 Arundel Terrace, Brighton, East Sussex BN2 1GA. *T:* (01273) 697243.

DICK, Air Vice-Marshal Ronald, CB 1988; writer and lecturer in air power history; Head of British Defence Staff, Washington, and Defence Attaché, 1984–88, retired; *b* Newcastle upon Tyne, 18 Oct. 1931; *s* of Arthur John Craig Dick and Lilian Dick; *m* 1955, Pauline Lomax; one *s* one *d. Educ:* Beckenham and Penge County Grammar Sch.; RAF Coll., Cranwell. Commnd 1952; served, 1953–69: No 64 Fighter Sqdn; Flying Instr, No 5 FTS; Central Flying Sch. Examg Wing and Type Sqdn; Flt Comdr, 3615th Pilot Trng Sqdn, USAF, and No IX Bomber Sqdn; Trng (Operational) 2a (RAF), MoD; RAF Staff Coll., Bracknell; Ops B2 (RAF), MoD; Jt Services Staff Coll.; OC No IX Bomber Sqdn, RAF Akrotiri, 1970–72; Staff, RCDS, 1972–74; PSO to Dep. SACEUR, SHAPE, 1974–77; OC RAF Honington, 1978–80; Air Attaché, Washington, DC, 1980–83; Dir of Organization and Estabts, 1983–84, of Organization and Quartering, 1984, RAF. Internat. Fellow, Nat. Air and Space Mus., Smithsonian Instn, 1988–91; Vis. Prof. in Air Power History, USAF Air Univ., Ala, 1992–94. Mem., Bd of Trustees, Amer. Airpower Heritage Foundn, 1987–94. Consulting Editor, Air & Space Smithsonian Magazine, 1990–. FRAeS 1987. Wright Jubilee Aerobatic Trophy Winner, 1956. *Publications:* (jtly) The Means of Victory, 1992; (jtly) Classic RAF Battles, 1995; Lancaster, 1996; American Eagles: a history of the United States Air Force, 1997; Messerschmitt Bf109, 1997; Spitfire, 1997; Reach and Power: the heritage of the United States Air Force, 1997; Hurricane, 2000; The Aviation Century, 2001; articles for Air and Space Smithsonian, Air Power History, Flight, and other aviation jls and magazines. *Recreations:* wild life conservation, bird watching, private flying, military history, opera. *Address:* Cherrywood, 3011 Jenny Lane, Woodbridge, VA 22192, USA. *Club:* Royal Air Force.

DICK-LAUDER, Sir Piers Robert; *see* Lauder.

DICKEN, Air Vice-Marshal Michael John Charles Worwood, CB 1990; Private Secretary to Lord Mayor of London, 1992–99; Air Officer Administration and Air Officer Commanding Support Group, RAF Support Command, 1989–92; *b* 13 July 1935; *s* of late Air Cdre Charles Worwood Dicken, CBE and Olive Eva Dicken (*née* Eustice); *m* 1962, Jennifer Ann Dore; two *d* (one *s* decd). *Educ:* Sherborne; St Peter's Hall, Oxford; RAF College, Cranwell. Commissioned 1958; served Cyprus, Borneo and UK to 1970; RAF Staff College, 1971; Asst Defence Advr, Canberra, 1972–74; RAF Uxbridge, 1975–76; NDC, 1976; RAF Coningsby, 1977–79; Staff Coll. Directing Staff and Dir, Comd and Staff Training, 1980–82; OC RAF Hereford, 1982–83; HQ 1 Gp, 1984–85; Dir of Personnel Management (Airmen), 1986–88. Hon. Freeman, Chartered Secretaries' and Administrators' Co., 1989; Liveryman, Scriveners' Co., 1991–. *Recreations:* golf, light aircraft, field sports. *Club:* Royal Air Force.

DICKENS, James McCulloch York, OBE 1991; Chief Personnel Officer, Agricultural and Food Research Council, 1983–91; *b* 4 April 1931; *e s* of A. Y. Dickens and I. Dickens (*née* McCulloch); *m* 1st, 1955, M. J. Grieve (marr. diss. 1965); 2nd, 1969, Mrs Carolyn Casey. *Educ:* Shawlands Academy, Glasgow; Newbattle Abbey Coll., Dalkeith, Midlothian; Ruskin Coll. and St Catherine's Coll., Oxford. Administrative Asst, National Coal Board, 1956–58; Industrial Relations Officer, National Coal Board, 1958–65; Management Consultant, 1965–66; MP (Lab) West Lewisham, 1966–70; Asst Dir of Manpower, Nat. Freight Corp., 1970–76; National Water Council: Asst Dir (Ind. Rel.), Manpower Services Div., 1976–80; Dir of Manpower, 1980–82; Dir of Manpower and Trng, 1982–83. Trustee, Citizens Income Trust, 1995–. Dep. Chm., Anerley Primary Sch., 1996–. *Recreations:* music, theatre, the countryside. *Address:* 64 Woodbastwick Road, Sydenham, SE26 5LH.

DICKENSON, Prof. Anthony Henry, PhD; Professor of Neuropharmacology, University College London, since 1995; *b* 5 Oct. 1952; *s* of Henry and Kathleen Dickenson; *m* 1975, Joanna Schepp; two *d. Educ:* St Mary's Coll., Southampton; Univ. of Reading (BSc 1974); PhD London 1977. MRC French Exchange Fellow, 1978–79; Scientific Staff, MRC, 1979–83; University College London: Lectr, 1983–90; Sen. Lectr, 1990–92; Reader, 1992–95. Mem. Council, Internat. Assoc. for Study of Pain, 1996–. Vis. Prof., Univ. of Calif, 1986; RSocMed Vis. Prof., USA, 1995; Medal and Lecture in Neuroscience, Univ. of Pavia, Italy, 1993. *Publications:* (with M. M. Dale and D. G. Haylett) Companion to Pharmacology, 1993, 2nd edn 1995; (with J.-M. Besson) Pharmacology of Pain, 1997; contrib. chapters in books; numerous contribs to learned jls. *Recreations:* drum and bass, friends, family, travel, tennis. *Address:* Department of Pharmacology, University College, Gower Street, WC1E 6BT. *T:* (020) 7419 3742.

DICKENSON, Sir Aubrey Fiennes T.; *see* Trotman-Dickenson.

DICKENSON, Lt-Col Charles Royal, CMG 1965; Postmaster-General of Rhodesia, 1964–68, retired; *b* 17 June 1907; *e s* of Charles Roland and Gertrude Dickenson; *m* 1950, Hendrika Jacoba Margaretha Schippers; two *d. Educ:* Shaftesbury Grammar Sch., Dorset. Entered British Post Office as Engineering Apprentice, 1923; British Post Office HQ, 1932–39. Served War in Royal Signals, 1939–45, attaining rank of Lieut-Col. BPO NW Regional HQ as Asst Controller of Telecommunications, 1945–47; BPO HQ, London, 1947–50; loaned to S Rhodesia Govt, 1950–54; Controller of Telecommunications. Ministry of Posts, Federation of Rhodesia and Nyasaland, 1954–57; Regional Controller for N Rhodesia, Fedn of Rhodesia and Nyasaland, 1957–61; Dep. Postmaster-Gen., Rhodesia and Nyasaland, 1961–62; Postmaster-Gen., Rhodesia and Nyasaland, 1962–63. Hon. Mem., S Africa Inst. of Electronic and Radio Engineers (Hon. M(SA) IERE), 1966. ICD, OLM, Rhodesia, 1979. *Recreations:* growing orchids, photography. *Address:* 4600 Gatlin Oaks Lane, Orlando, FL 32806, USA.

DICKENSON, Joseph Frank, PhD, CEng, FIMechE; Director, North Staffordshire Polytechnic, 1969–86, retired; *b* 26 Nov. 1924; *s* of late Frank Brand Dickenson and late Maud Dickenson (*née* Beharrell); *m* 1948, Sheila May Kingston; two *s* one *d. Educ:* College of Technology, Hull. BSc (1st Cl. Hons) Engrg, PhD (both London). Engrg apprenticeship and Jun. Engr's posts, 1939–52; Lectr and Sen. Lectr, Hull Coll. of Technology, 1952–59; Head of Dept of Mechanical Engrg and later Vice-Principal, Lanchester Coll. of Technology, 1960–64; Principal, Leeds Coll. of Technology, 1964–69. *Recreations:* motor cars, computers. *Address:* 5 Byron Walk Mews, Harrogate HG2 0LQ. *T:* (01423) 525899.

DICKIE, Brian James; General Director, Chicago Opera Theater, since 1999; *b* 23 July 1941; *s* of late Robert Kelso Dickie, OBE and Harriet Elizabeth (*née* Riddell); *m* 1st, 1968, Victoria Teresa Sheldon (*née* Price); two *s* one *d*; 2nd, 1989, Nancy Gustafson. *Educ:* Haileybury; Trinity Coll., Dublin. Admin. Asst, Glyndebourne Opera, 1962–66; Administrator, Glyndebourne Touring Opera, 1967–81; Glyndebourne Festival Opera: Opera Manager, 1970–81; Gen. Administrator, 1981–89. Artistic Dir, Wexford Fest., 1967–73; Artistic Advr, Théâtre Musical de Paris, 1981–87; Gen. Dir, Canadian Opera Co., 1989–93; Artistic Counsellor, Opéra de Nice, 1994–97; Gen. Dir, EU Opera, 1997–99. Mem. Bd, Opera America, 1991–93. Chm., London Choral Soc., 1978–85; Vice-Chm., TNC, 1980–85 (Chm., TNC Opera Cttee, 1976–85); Vice-Pres., Theatrical Management Assoc., 1983–85. *Address:* Chicago Opera Theater, 70 East Lake Street, Suite 540, Chicago, IL 60601, USA. *T:* (312) 7048420, *Fax:* (312) 7048421. *Club:* Garrick.

DICKINS, Mark Frederick Hakon S.; *see* Scrase-Dickins.

DICKINSON, family name of **Baron Dickinson.**

DICKINSON, 2nd Baron *cr* 1930, of Painswick; **Richard Clavering Hyett Dickinson;** *b* 2 March 1926; *s* of late Hon. Richard Sebastian Willoughby Dickinson, DSO (*o s* of 1st Baron) and May Southey, *d* of late Charles Lovemore, Melsetter, Cape Province, S Africa; *S* grandfather, 1943; *m* 1st, 1957, Margaret Ann (marr. diss. 1980), *e d* of late Brig. G. R. McMeekan, CB, DSO, OBE; two *s*; 2nd, 1980, Rita Doreen Moir. *Heir: s* Hon. Martin Hyett Dickinson, *b* 30 Jan. 1961. *Address:* The Stables, Gloucester Road, Painswick, Glos GL6 6TH. *T:* (01452) 813646.

See also Very Rev. H. G. Dickinson, Hon. P. M. de B. Dickinson.

DICKINSON, Anne; *see* Dickinson, V. A.

DICKINSON, Basil Philip Harriman; Under Secretary, Department of the Environment (formerly Ministry of Transport), 1959–74; *b* 10 Sept. 1916; *yr s* of F. H. and I. F. Dickinson; *m* 1941, Beryl Farrow; three *s* one *d. Educ:* Cheltenham Coll.; Oriel Coll., Oxford. *Address:* c/o Child & Co., 1 Fleet Street, EC4Y 1BD.

DICKINSON, Sir Ben; *see* Dickinson, Sir S. B.

DICKINSON, Brian Henry Baron; Under Secretary, Animal Health Group, Ministry of Agriculture, Fisheries and Food, 1996–2000; *b* 2 May 1940; *s* of Alan Edgar Frederic Dickinson and Ethel Mary Dickinson (*née* McWilliam); *m* 1971, Sheila Minto Lloyd. *Educ:* Leighton Park School, Reading; Balliol College, Oxford (BA). Ministry of Agriculture, Fisheries and Food, 1964; Dept of Prices and Consumer Protection, 1975; MAFF, 1978; Under Sec., 1984; Principal Finance Officer, 1986; Under Sec. (Food Safety), 1989. FRSA 1995. *Recreation:* bird-watching.

DICKINSON, Prof. Christopher John, DM, FRCP; ARCO; Professor of Medicine and Chairman, Department of Medicine, St Bartholomew's Hospital Medical College, 1975–92, now Professor Emeritus; *b* 1 Feb. 1927; *s* of Reginald Ernest Dickinson and Margaret Dickinson (*née* Petty); *m* 1953, Elizabeth Patricia Farrell; two *s* two *d. Educ:* Berkhamsted School; Oxford University (MA, MSc, DM); University College Hospital Medical College. FRCP 1968. Junior med. posts, UCH, 1953–54; RAMC (Junior Med. Specialist), 1955–56; Registrar and Research Fellow, Middlesex Hosp., 1957–60; Rockefeller Travelling Fellow, Cleveland Clinic, USA, 1960–61; Lectr, then Sen. Lectr and Consultant, UCH and Med. Sch., 1961–75. R. Samuel McLoughlin Vis. Prof., McMaster Univ., Canada, 1970; King Edward Fund Vis. Fellow, NZ, 1972. Examr in Medicine, UC Dublin and Univs of Oxford, Cambridge, London, Sheffield, Leeds, Southampton, Hong Kong, Singapore, Kuwait. Sec., European Soc. for Clinical Investigation, 1969–72; Censor, 1978–80, Senior Censor and Vice-Pres., 1982–83, Croonian Lectr, 1986, RCP; Pres., Sect. of Medicine, RSM, 1975–76. Chairman: Med. Research Soc., 1983–87; Assoc. of Professors of Medicine, 1983–87; Vice Chm. Council, BHF, 1995–2000; Mem., MRC, 1986–90. Medical Adviser: Jules Thorn Charitable Trust, 1994–98; St Thomas'/Guy's Hosps' Special Trustees, 1996–98; Trustee: St Bartholomew's Hosp. Foundn for Res., 1983–; BHF, 1995–2000; Chronic Disease Res. Foundn, 1996–. ARCO 1987. FRSA 1995. *Publications:* Electrophysiological Technique,

1950; Clinical Pathology Data, 1951, 2nd edn 1957; (jtly) Clinical Physiology, 1959, 5th edn 1984; Neurogenic Hypertension, 1965; A Computer Model of Human Respiration, 1977; (jtly) Software for Educational Computing, 1980; Neurogenic Hypertension, 1991; 21 Medical Mysteries, 2000; papers on hypertension, respiratory physiology, and general medicine. *Recreations:* theatre, opera, playing the organ. *Address:* Wolfson Institute of Preventive Medicine, Charterhouse Square, EC1M 6BQ. *T:* (020) 7882 6219; Griffin Cottage, 57 Belsize Lane, NW3 5AU. *T:* (020) 7431 1845. *Club:* Garrick.

DICKINSON, Sir Harold (Herbert), Kt 1975; *b* 27 Feb. 1917; *s* of late William James Dickinson and Barwon Venus Clarke; *m* 1946, Elsie May Smith; two *d. Educ:* Singleton Public Sch.; Tamworth High Sch.; Univ. of Sydney (LLB, 1st Cl. Hons). Barrister-at-Law. Served War, 2nd AIF HQ 22 Inf. Bde, 1940–45 (despatches); Japanese POW (Sgt). Dept of Lands, NSW, 1933–40; NSW Public Service Bd, 1946–60: Sec. and Sen. Inspector, 1949–60; Chief Exec. Officer, Prince Henry Hosp., 1960–63; NSW Public Service Bd: Mem., 1963–70; Dep. Chm., 1970–71; Chm., 1971–79. Formerly: Chm., AFT Property Co.; Director: Development Finance Corp.; Australian Fixed Trusts Ltd. Hon. Mem., NSW Univs Bd, 1967–71; Hon. Dir, Prince Henry, Prince of Wales, Eastern Suburbs Teaching Hosps, 1965–75, Chm. of Dirs, 1975–82; Governor, NSW Coll. of Law, 1972–77. *Publications:* contribs to administration jls. *Recreation:* sailing. *Address:* 649 Old South Head Road, Vaucluse, NSW 2030, Australia. *T:* (2) 93717475. *Club:* Probus (Sydney).

DICKINSON, Prof. Harry Thomas, DLitt; FRHistS; FRSE; Richard Lodge Professor of British History, University of Edinburgh, since 1980; *b* 9 March 1939; *s* of Joseph Dickinson and Elizabeth Stearman Dickinson (*née* Warriner); *m* 1961, Jennifer Elizabeth Galtry; one *s* one *d. Educ:* Gateshead Grammar Sch.; Durham Univ. (BA 1960, DipEd 1961, MA 1963); Newcastle Univ. (PhD 1968); DLitt Edinburgh 1986. FRSE 1998. History Master, Washington Grammar Sch., 1961–64; Earl Grey Fellow, Newcastle Univ., 1964–66; Edinburgh University: Asst Lectr, Lectr and Reader, 1966–80; Associate Dean of Arts (Postgrad. Studies), 1992–95; Convener (Senatus, Postgrad. Studies), 1998–. Fulbright Award, 1973; Huntington Library Fellowship, 1973; Folger Shakespeare Library Sen. Fellowship, 1973; Winston Churchill Meml Trust Travelling Fellowship, 1980; Leverhulme Award, 1986–87; William Andrews Clark Library Fellow, 1987. Vis. Prof., Nanjing Univ., 1980, 1983, 1994, Concurrent Prof. of Hist., 1987–; Douglas Southall Freeman Prof., Univ. of Richmond, Va, 1997. Anstey Meml Lectr, Kent Univ., 1989; Vis. Lectr to USA, Japan, Canada, France, Czech Republic, Italy and Germany; Dean, Scottish Universities Summer School, 1979–85. Acad. Sponsor, Scotland's Cultural Heritage, 1984–91; Mem., Marshall Aid Commemoration Commn, 1986–98; Specialist Advr, CNAA, 1987–93 (Mem., Cttee on Humanities, 1990–93); Auditor, Quality Assurance Gp, Higher Educn Quality Council, 1992–; Mem., Hist. Panel, UFC Res. Assessment Exercise, 1992; Team Assessor (Hist.), Teaching Quality Assessment, SHEFC, 1995–96; Hist. Benchmarking Panel, 1998–, Academic Reviewer, 1999–, QAA. Vice-Pres., RHistS, 1991–95 (Mem., Council, 1986–90); Historical Association: Mem. Council, 1982–; Vice-Pres., 1995–96; Dep. Pres., 1996–98; Chm. of Publications, 1991–95. Editor, History, 1993–2000; Mem. Editl Bds, Nineteenth Century Short Title Catalogue and Nineteenth Century Microfiche Series. *Publications:* (ed) The Correspondence of Sir James Clavering, 1967; Bolingbroke, 1970; Walpole and the Whig Supremacy, 1973; (ed) Politics and Literature in the Eighteenth Century, 1974; Liberty and Property, 1977; (ed) The Political Works of Thomas Spence, 1982; British Radicalism and the French Revolution 1789–1815, 1985; Caricatures and the Constitution 1760–1832, 1986; (ed) Britain and the French Revolution 1789–1815, 1989; The Politics of the People in Eighteenth Century Britain, 1995; (ed) Britain and the American Revolution, 1998; (ed jtly) The Challenge to Westminster, 2000; pamphlets, essays, articles and reviews. *Recreations:* films, watching sports. *Address:* 44 Viewforth Terrace, Edinburgh EH10 4LJ. *T:* (0131) 229 1379.

DICKINSON, Very Rev. Hugh Geoffrey; Dean of Salisbury, 1986–96, now Emeritus; *b* 17 Nov. 1929; *s* of late Hon. Richard Sebastian Willoughby Dickinson, DSO (*o s* of 1st Baron Dickinson) and of May Southey, *d* of late Charles Lovemore; *m* 1963, Jean Marjorie Storey; one *s* one *d. Educ:* Westminster School (KS); Trinity Coll., Oxford (MA, DipTh); Cuddesdon Theol Coll. Deacon 1956, priest 1957; Curate of Melksham, Wilts, 1956–58; Chaplain: Trinity Coll., Cambridge, 1958–63; Winchester College, 1963–67; Bishop's Adviser for Adult Education, Diocese of Coventry, 1969–77; Vicar of St Michael's, St Albans, 1977–86. *Recreations:* woodturning, fishing, gardening. *Address:* 22 St Peter's Road, Cirencester, Glos GL7 1RG. *T:* (01285) 657710.
See also Hon. P. M. de B. Dickinson.

DICKINSON, Prof. Hugh Gordon; Sherardian Professor of Botany, Oxford, since 1991; *b* 5 Aug. 1944; *s* of Reginald Gordon Dickinson and Jean Hartley Dickinson; *m* 1980, Alana Gillian Fairbrother; one *s* one *d. Educ:* St Lawrence Coll., Ramsgate; Univ. of Birmingham (BSc, PhD, DSc). Postdoctoral Fellow, UCL, 1969–72; University of Reading: Lectr, 1972–79; Reader, 1979–85; Prof. of Plant Cell Genetics, 1985–91. Trustee, Royal Botanic Gardens, Kew, 1996–. *Publications:* (ed with C. W. Evans) Controlling Events in Meiosis, 1984; (ed with P. Goodhew) Proceedings of IXth European Congress for Electron Microscopy, 1988; (ed jtly) Post-Translational Modification in Plants, 1992; contribs to internat. sci. jls and magazines. *Recreations:* owning and restoring Lancia cars of the '50s and '60s, rock music 1955–75, Mozart operas. *Address:* Magdalen College, Oxford OX1 4AU.

DICKINSON, Mark; *see* Dickinson, S. M. and Dickinson, W. M. L.

DICKINSON, Matthew John, (Matt); Football Correspondent, The Times, since 2000; *b* 16 Nov. 1968; *s* of Jimmy Gordon and Celia Dickinson; *m* 2000, Helen Willis. *Educ:* Perse Sch., Cambridge; Robinson Coll., Cambridge (BA); NCTJ Postgrad. Dip in Journalism, Cardiff. Staff News Reporter, Cambridge Evening News, 1992–94; Sports Reporter: Daily Express, 1994–97; The Times, 1997–. Young Sports Writer of the Year, Sports Council, 1992; Sports Journalist of the Year, British Press Awards, 2000. *Publication:* (assisted with) David Beckham: My World, 2000. *Recreations:* playing football (Mem. Fleet Street Football Boys), golf, film, travel. *Address:* c/o The Times, 1 Pennington Street, E98 1XY. *Club:* Cambridge University Lightweight Rowing.

DICKINSON, Patric Laurence; Richmond Herald of Arms, since 1989; Earl Marshal's Secretary, since 1996; *b* 24 Nov. 1950; *s* of John Laurence Dickinson and late April Katherine, *d* of Robert Forgan, MC, MD, sometime MP. *Educ:* Marling Sch.; Exeter Coll., Oxford (Stapeldon Schol.; MA). Pres., Oxford Union Soc., 1972. Called to the Bar, Middle Temple, 1979. Res. Asst, College of Arms, 1968–78; Rouge Dragon Pursuivant, 1978–89. Hon. Treasurer: English Genealogical Congress, 1975–91; Bar Theatrical Soc., 1978–; Treas., Coll. of Arms, 1995–. Hon. Sec. and Registrar, British Record Soc., 1979–; Vice-President: Assoc. of Genealogists and Record Agents, 1988–; Soc. of Genealogists, 1997–; Pres., Bristol and Glos Archaeol Soc., 1998–99. FSG 2000. *Recreation:* beating about the bush. *Address:* College of Arms, Queen Victoria Street, EC4V 4BT. *T:* (020) 7236 9612. *Club:* Brooks's.

DICKINSON, Prof. Peter, DMus; composer, pianist; Professor of Music, Goldsmiths College, London University, 1991–97, now Emeritus; *b* 15 Nov. 1934; *s* of late Frank Dickinson, FBOA(Hons), FAAO, DOS, FRSH, contact lens specialist, and of Muriel Porter; *m* 1964, Bridget Jane Tomkinson, *d* of late Lt-Comdr E. P. Tomkinson, DSO, RN; two *s. Educ:* The Leys Sch.; Queens' Coll., Cambridge (organ schol., Stewart of Rannoch schol.; MA); Juilliard Sch. of Music, New York (Rotary Foundn Fellow). DMus London 1992; LRAM, ARCM; FRCO. Teaching and freelance work in New York, 1958–61, London and Birmingham, 1962–74; first Prof. of Music, Keele Univ., 1974–84, subseq. Prof. Emeritus; founded Centre for American Music, broadcasts and records as pianist, mostly with sister Meriel Dickinson, mezzo soprano, 1960–. Member: Bd, Trinity Coll. of Music, 1984–98; Royal Soc. of Musicians, 1985–; Bd, Inst. of US Studies, London Univ., 1994–. FRSA 1981. Hon. FTCL 1992. Hon. DMus Keele, 1999. *Publications: compositions include: orchestral:* Monologue for Strings, 1959; Five Diversions, 1969; Transformations, 1970; Organ Concerto, 1971; Piano Concerto, 1984; Violin Concerto, 1986; Jigsaws, 1988; Merseyside Echoes, 1988; *chamber:* String Quartet No 1, 1958; Juilliard Dances, 1959; Fanfares and Elegies, 1967; Translations, 1971; String Quartet No 2, 1975; American Trio, 1985; London Rags, 1986; Sonatas for piano and tape playback, 1987; Auden Studies, 1988; Swansongs, 1992; works for solo organ, piano, clavichord, recorder, flute, violin, guitar and baryton; *vocal:* Four Auden Songs, 1956; A Dylan Thomas Cycle, 1959; Elegy, 1966; Five Poems of Alan Porter, 1968; Extravaganzas, 1969; An E. E. Cummings Cycle, 1970; Winter Afternoons (Emily Dickinson), 1970; Three Comic Songs (Auden), 1972; Surrealist Landscape (Lord Berners), 1973; Lust (St Augustine), 1974; A Memory of David Munrow, 1977; Reminiscences (Byron), 1979; The Unicorns (John Heath Stubbs), 1982; Stevie's Tunes (Stevie Smith), 1984; Larkin's Jazz (Philip Larkin), 1989; Summoned by Mother (Betjeman), 1991; *choral:* Martin of Tours (Thomas Blackburn), 1966; The Dry Heart (Alan Porter), 1967; Outcry, 1969; Late Afternoon in November, 1975; A Mass of the Apocalypse, 1984; Tiananmen 1989 (Dickinson), 1990; *ballet:* Vitalitas, 1959; *musical drama:* The Judas Tree (Thomas Blackburn), 1965; various church music, music for children and for films; (ed) Twenty British Composers, 1975; (ed) Songs and Piano Music by Lord Berners, 1982, 2nd edn 2000; The Music of Lennox Berkeley, 1989; Marigold: the music of Billy Mayerl, 1999; contrib. to The New Grove, and various books and periodicals. *Recreation:* book collecting. *Address:* c/o Novello & Co., 8–9 Frith Street, W1V 5TZ. *Club:* Garrick.

DICKINSON, Hon. Peter Malcolm de Brissac, FRSL; author; *b* 16 Dec. 1927; *s* of late Hon. Richard Sebastian Willoughby Dickinson and of May Southey (Nancy) Lovemore; *m* 1st, 1953, Mary Rose Barnard (*d* 1988); two *d* two *s*; 2nd, 1992, Robin McKinley. *Educ:* Eton; King's Coll., Cambridge (BA). Asst Editor, Punch, 1952–69. Chm., Management Cttee, Soc. of Authors, 1978–80. FRSL 1999. *Publications: children's books:* The Weathermonger, 1968; Heartsease, 1969; The Devil's Children, 1970 (trilogy republished 1975 as The Changes); Emma Tupper's Diary, 1970; The Dancing Bear, 1972; The Gift, 1973; The Iron Lion, 1973; Chance, Luck and Destiny, 1975; The Blue Hawk, 1976 (Guardian Award); Annerton Pit, 1977; Hepzibah, 1978; Tulku, 1979 (Whitbread Prize; Carnegie Medal); The Flight of Dragons, 1979; City of Gold, 1980 (Carnegie Medal); The Seventh Raven, 1981; Healer, 1983; Giant Cold, 1984; (ed) Hundreds and Hundreds, 1984; A Box of Nothing, 1985; Mole Hole, 1987; Merlin Dreams, 1988; Eva, 1988; AK, 1990 (Whitbread Children's Award); A Bone from a Dry Sea, 1992; Time and the Clockmice etcetera, 1993; Shadow of a Hero, 1994; Chuck and Danielle, 1996; The Kin, 1998; Touch and Go, 1999; The Lion Tamer's Daughter, 1999; The Ropemaker, 2001; *TV series,* Mandog (Mandog, by Lois Lamplugh, 1972, is based on this series); *novels:* Skin Deep, 1968; A Pride of Heroes, 1969; The Seals, 1970; Sleep and His Brother, 1971; The Lizard in the Cup, 1972; The Green Gene, 1973; The Poison Oracle, 1974; The Lively Dead, 1975; King and Joker, 1976; Walking Dead, 1977; One Foot in the Grave, 1979; A Summer in the Twenties, 1981; The Last House-party, 1982; Hindsight, 1983; Death of a Unicorn, 1984; Tefuga, 1986; Perfect Gallows, 1988; Skeleton-in-Waiting, 1989; Play Dead, 1991; The Yellow Room Conspiracy, 1994; Some Deaths Before Dying, 2000. *Recreation:* manual labour. *Address:* Bramdean Lodge, near Alresford, Hants SO24 0JN.
See also Baron Dickinson, Very Rev. H. G. Dickinson.

DICKINSON, Robert Henry, CBE 1998; DL; Senior Partner, Dickinson Dees, 1987–97; Chairman, Northern Rock PLC (formerly Northern Rock Building Society), 1992–99; *b* 12 May 1934; *s* of Robert Joicey Dickinson and Alice Penelope Dickinson (*née* Barnett); *m* 1963, Kyra Irina Boissevain; one *s* two *d. Educ:* Harrow; Christ Church, Oxford (MA). Admitted solicitor (Hons), 1960; Partner, Dickinson Dees, 1963–97. Chairman: Northern Investors PLC, 1984–; Grainger Trust PLC, 1992–; Director: Reg Vardy PLC, 1988–; Yorkshire Tyne Tees TV PLC, 1992–97; Univ. of Newcastle upon Tyne Develt Trust. DL Northumberland, 1992. *Recreations:* shooting, fishing. *Address:* Styford Hall, Stocksfield, Northumberland NE43 7TX. *T:* (01434) 682467, *Fax:* (01434) 634634. *Clubs:* Beefsteak, Boodle's, Pratt's; Northern Counties (Newcastle).

DICKINSON, Sally Jane; Secretary, Magistrates' Association, since 1994; *b* 12 Sept. 1955; *d* of Colin James Rayner Godden and Margaret Godden (*née* Cowin); *m* 1987, James Anthony Dickinson. *Educ:* Chatham Grammar Sch. for Girls; Bristol Univ. (BA Theol); Bristol Poly. (BA Law). Clerical Officer, Inland Revenue Collection, 1978–81; Exec. Officer, Law Soc. (Legal Aid), 1981–85; Regl Dir, Apex Charitable Trust, 1985–92; Cttee Sec., Magistrates' Assoc., 1992–93. *Recreations:* walking, cycling, sleeping, dogs. *Address:* 65 Cranmore Road, Chislehurst BR7 6ER. *T:* (020) 7733 2524.

DICKINSON, Sir Samuel Benson, (Sir Ben), Kt 1980; Chairman, Burmine Pty Ltd, 1985–88; Mining Advisor to South Australian Government, 1975–84; Chairman, South Australian Government Uranium Enrichment Committee, 1979–84; *b* 1 Feb. 1912; *s* of Sydney Rushbrook Dickinson and Margaret Dickinson (*née* Clemes); *m* 1960, Dorothy Joan Weidenhofer; three *s* one *d. Educ:* Haileybury College, Melbourne; Univ. of Melbourne. MSc. N Australia Aerial Geological and Geophysical Survey, 1935–36; geologist: Electrolytic Zinc, Mt Lyell, Mt Isa, mining cos, 1937–41; S Australian Geological Survey, 1941–42. Dir of Mines, Govt Geologist, Sec. to Minister of Mines, Dep. Controller, Mineral Production, Chm. Radium Hill Mines, 1943–56; Director: Rio Tinto Mining Co. of Australia, 1956–60; Sir Frank Duval's Gp of Cos, 1960–62; Chief Technical Adviser, Pechiney Australia, 1962–65; Project Manager, Clutha Development Ltd and Daniel K. Ludwig Cos Australia, 1965–75. *Publications:* technical reports for Australian Dept of Mines, Inst. of Mining and Metallurgy and mining jls and bulletins. *Recreations:* correspondence, media writing. *Address:* 21 Tiers Road, PO Box 321, Woodside, SA 5244, Australia. *T:* (8) 83899069. *Clubs:* Athenæum (Melbourne); American National (Sydney).

DICKINSON, (Stephen) Mark; Editor, Liverpool Echo, since 2000; *b* 20 Jan. 1951; *s* of Stanley Park Dickinson and Beatrice Joan Dickinson; *m* Pauline Patricia Mills; two *s* two *d. Educ:* Dame Alice Owen's Sch.; Univ. of Manchester (BA 2nd Cl. Hons Psychol). Publicity asst, Macmillan Jls, 1975–76; sub-editor, Daily Telegraph, Manchester, 1976–87; author, 1988–89; Chief Sub Editor: Tonight, Chester, 1990–91; Aberdeen Evening Express, 1991–92; Asst Ed., The Journal, Newcastle, 1992–93; Dep. Ed. in Chief,

Chronicle Newspapers, Chester, 1993–96; Ed., The Journal, Newcastle, 1996–2000. *Publications:* The Manchester Book, 1984; To Break a Union, 1986; Goodbye Piccadilly: the history of abolition of Greater Manchester Council, 1990. *Recreations:* reading, gardening, football, entertaining, my family. *Address:* c/o Liverpool Echo, PO Box 48, Old Hall Street, Liverpool L69 3EB. *T:* (0151) 472 2507.

DICKINSON, (Vivienne) Anne, (Mrs Basil Phillips); Chairman, Forexia UK, 1997–98; Director, Leedex Public Relations, 1993–96; *b* 27 Sept. 1931; *d* of F. Oswald Edward Dickinson and M. Ida Ismay Dickinson; *m* 1st, 1951, John Kerr Large (marr. diss.); one *s* decd; 2nd, 1979, David Hermas Phillips (*d* 1989); 3rd, 1993, Basil B. Phillips, OBE. *Educ:* Nottingham Girls' High School. Account Executive, W. S. Crawford, 1960–64; Promotions Editor: Good Housekeeping, 1964–65; Harpers Bazaar, 1965–67; Dir in charge of Promotions, Nat. Magazine Co., 1967–68; Dir, Benson PR (later Kingsway), 1968–69; Chm. and Chief Exec., Kingsway Rowland, 1969–89; Chairman: The Rowland Co., 1989–90; Graduate Appointments Ltd, 1993–94; Dir, Birkdale Group plc, 1991–96. Chm., PR Consultants' Assoc., 1989 (Chm., Professional Practices Cttee, 1989). Chm., Family Welfare Assoc., 1990–94. Member: Rye Town Council, 1995–99; Bd, Rye Health Care, 1996–. FIPR 1985; CIMgt (CBIM 1986). PR Professional of the Year, PR Week, 1988–89. *Recreations:* friends, food, dogs. *Address:* St Mary's House, 62 Church Square, Rye TN31 7HF.

DICKINSON, William Michael, MBE 1960; Managing Director, Africa Research Ltd, 1966–90; *b* 13 Jan. 1930; *s* of late Comdr W. H. Dickinson, RN, and Ruth Sandeman Betts; *m* 1971, Enid Joy Bowers (*d* 1997); one *s* two *d*. *Educ:* St Edward's Sch., Oxford. Army Service, 1948–51; 2/Lieut, Oxford and Bucks LI, Sept. 1948; seconded Somaliland Scouts; Lieut 1950; Colonial Service Devonshire Course, 1951–52; Somaliland Protectorate: Admin. Officer, 1952; Dist Officer, 1953–54; Asst Sec. (Political), 1955–56; seconded to British Liaison Orgn, Ethiopia, as Sen. Asst Liaison Officer, 1957–59; Brit. Liaison Officer in charge, 1959; transf. N Rhodesia as Dist Officer, 1960; Dist Comr, 1961; seconded to FO as HM Consul-Gen., Hargeisa, 1961–63; Principal, External Affairs Section, Office of Prime Minister, N Rhodesia, during 1964; Sen. Principal, Min. of Foreign Affairs, Govt of Zambia, 1964–65. *Address:* Wooladon, Waterloo, Blisland, Bodmin, Cornwall PL30 4JX. *T:* (01208) 850110.

DICKINSON, (Woodman) Mark (Lowes), OBE 2000; HM Diplomatic Service; Ambassador to Macedonia, 1997–2001; *b* 16 Jan. 1955; *s* of Woodman Gilbert Dickinson and Dorothy Priscilla Dickinson (*née* Cashmore); *m* 1st, 1986, Francesca Infanti (marr. diss. 1995); 2nd, 1995, Christina Houlder (*née* Bass); one *s*. *Educ:* Christ's Hosp.; Sidney Sussex Coll., Cambridge (MA). Joined HM Diplomatic Service, 1976; Second Sec., Ankara, 1979–82; FCO, 1982–87; First Sec., Dublin, 1987–90; FCO, 1990–94; Bank of England, 1994–97. Actg Chief Exec., Westminster Foundn for Democracy, 1992. *Address:* c/o Foreign and Commonwealth Office, King Charles Street, SW1A 2AH.

DICKS, Prof. Anthony Richard; QC (Hong Kong) 1994; Professor of Chinese Law, School of Oriental and African Studies, University of London, since 1995; *b* 6 Jan. 1936; *s* of Henry Victor Dicks and Pretoria Maud Dicks (*née* Jeffery); *m* 1969, Victoria Frances Mayne. *Educ:* Westminster Sch.; Trinity Coll., Cambridge (Open and Westminster Exhibnr; BA Hist. and Law, LLB 1st Cl., MA). Called to the Bar, Inner Temple, 1961; admitted Hong Kong Bar, 1965, Brunei Bar, 1971. Nat. Service, 2nd Lieut, 3rd King's Own Hussars, 1954–56. Teaching Fellow, Univ. of Chicago Law Sch., 1960–61; Res. Fellow, Brit. Inst. Internat. and Comparative Law and Inst. Current World Affairs, London, Hong Kong and Japan, 1962–68; Fellow, Trinity Hall, and Univ. Asst Lectr in Law, Cambridge, 1968–70; Lectr in Oriental Laws, SOAS, 1970–74; in practice as barrister and arbitrator, Hong Kong, 1974–94. Vis. Prof., SOAS, 1987–94. Mem., various acad., professional and public cttees in Hong Kong, 1974–94. Advr, Foreign Compensation Commn on China Claims, 1987–88; Arbitrator in various Internat. Chambers of Commerce, London Court of Internat. Arbitration, Hong Kong Internat. Arbitration Centre and China Internat. Econ. and Trade Arbitration Commn and other arbitrations. *Publications:* articles in China Qly and other jls. *Address:* Department of Law, School of Oriental and African Studies, Thornhaugh Street, Russell Square, WC1H 0XG. *T:* (020) 7323 6359. *Clubs:* Athenæum; Hong Kong (Hong Kong).

DICKS, Terence Patrick, (Terry); *b* 17 March 1937; *s* of Frank and Winifred Dicks; *m*; one *s* two *d*. *Educ:* London Sch. of Econs and Pol Science (BScEcon); Oxford Univ. (DipEcon). Clerk: Imperial Tobacco Co. Ltd, 1952–59; Min. of Labour, 1959–66; Admin. Officer, GLC, 1971–86. Contested (C) Bristol South, 1979. MP (C) Hayes and Harlington, 1983–97. Mem., Select Cttee on Transport, 1986–92. Member: Council of Europe, 1993–97; WEU, 1993–97.

DICKSON, Arthur Richard Franklin, CBE 1974; QC (Belize), 1979; Commissioner for Law Revision, Belize, 1978; *b* 13 Jan. 1913; *m* 1949, Joanna Maria Margaretha van Baardwyk (decd); four *s*. *Educ:* Rusea's Secondary Sch. and Cornwall Coll., Jamaica. Called to the Bar, Lincoln's Inn, 1938. Judicial Service. HM Overseas Judiciary: Jamaica, 1941; Magistrate, Turks and Caicos Islands, 1944–47; Asst to Attorney-Gen., and Legal Draftsman, Barbados, 1947–49; Magistrate, British Guiana, 1949–52; Nigeria, 1952–62: Magistrate, 1952–54; Chief Magistrate, 1954–56; Chief Registrar, High Court, Lagos, 1956–58; Judge of the High Court, Lagos, 1958–62; retired. Temp. appointment, Solicitors Dept, GPO London, 1962–63; served Northern Rhodesia (latterly Zambia), 1964–67; Judge of the High Court, Uganda, 1967–71; Deputy Chm., Middlesex QS, July–Aug., 1971; Chief Justice, Belize, 1973–74; Judge of the Supreme Court, Anguilla (part-time), 1972–76; part-time Chm., Industrial Tribunals, 1972–85. *Publications:* Revised Ordinances (1909–1941) Turks and Caicos Islands, 1944; (ed) Revised Laws of Belize, 1980. *Recreations:* gardening, walking, swimming. *Address:* 14 Meadow Lane, Lindfield, Haywards Heath, West Sussex RH16 2RJ. *T:* (01444) 484450.

DICKSON, Brice; *see* Dickson, S. B.

DICKSON, David John Scott; News Editor, Nature; *b* 30 Aug. 1947; *s* of David and Rachel Mary Dickson; *m* 1973, Prudence Mary (marr. diss. 1999); one *s* one *d*. *Educ:* Westminster Sch.; Trinity Coll., Cambridge. Medical News, 1968–70; Sec., Brit. Soc. for Social Responsibility in Science, 1970–72; science corresp., 1973–75, features editor, 1975–77, THES; Washington corresp., Nature, 1977–82; European corresp., Science, 1982–89; news editor, 1989–90, Editor, 1990–92, New Scientist. Lectures organiser, ICA, 1976–77. Visiting Research Fellow: Univ. of Linköping, Sweden, 1981; Open Univ., 1989. *Publications:* Alternative Technology, 1974; The New Politics of Science, 1984; Het verval van de Geest (The Death of the Spirit), 1990; contribs to various jls on science, technology and society. *Recreations:* music, photography, gardening. *Address:* Nature, 4 Crinan Street, N1 9XW.

DICKSON, George, CBE 1991 (OBE 1974); HM Diplomatic Service, retired; Consul General, Amsterdam, 1987–91; *b* 23 May 1931; *s* of late George James Stark Dickson and of Isobel (*née* Brown). *Educ:* Aberdeen Acad. DSIR, 1952; CRO, 1952–54; Karachi, 1954–56; Penang, 1957–59; Nicosia, 1960–62; Kampala, 1962–66; FCO, 1966–68; Manila, 1968–71; Jakarta, 1971–75; Stuttgart, 1975–76; Beirut, 1976–79; Baghdad, 1979–81; Asst Dir, Internat. Affairs, Commonwealth Secretariat, 1981–85; Dep. High Comr, Kingston, Jamaica, 1985–87. *Recreations:* friends, travel. *Address:* Milton of Braichlie, by Ballater, Aberdeenshire AB35 5SQ. *T:* (01339) 755708.

DICKSON, Prof. Gordon Ross; Professor of Agriculture, University of Newcastle upon Tyne, 1973–97; Chairman, North England Regional Advisory Committee, Forestry Commission, 1987–97; *b* 12 Feb. 1932; *s* of T. W. Dickson, Tynemouth; *m* 1st, 1956, Dorothy Stobbs (*d* 1989); two *s* one *d*; 2nd, 1991, Violet Adams. *Educ:* Tynemouth High Sch.; Durham Univ. BSc (Agric) 1st cl. hons 1953, PhD (Agric) 1958, Dunelm. Tutorial Research Student, Univ. Sch. of Agric., King's Coll., Newcastle upon Tyne, 1953–56; Asst Farm Dir, Council of King's Coll., Nafferton, Stocksfield-on-Tyne, 1956–58; Farms Director for the Duke of Norfolk, 1958–71; Principal, Royal Agric. Coll., Cirencester, 1971–73. Chm., Agricl Wages Bd for England and Wales, 1981–84; Dep. Chm., Home-Grown Cereals Authy, 1982–94. FRAgS; FIAgrM 1992. *Address:* The West Wing, Bolam Hall, Morpeth, Northumberland NE61 3UA.

DICKSON, Jennifer (Joan), (Mrs R. A. Sweetman), CM 1995; RA 1976 (ARA 1970); RE 1965; graphic artist, photographer and painter; *b* 17 Sept. 1936; 2nd *d* of late John Liston Dickson and Margaret Joan Turner, S Africa; *m* 1962, Ronald Andrew Sweetman; one *s*. *Educ:* Goldsmith's College Sch. of Art, Univ. of London; Atelier 17, Paris. Taught at Eastbourne Sch. of Art, 1959–62 (French Govt Schol., to work in Paris under S. W. Hayter). Directed and developed Printmaking Dept, Brighton Coll. of Art, 1962–68; developed and directed Graphics Atelier, Saidye Bronfman Centre, Montreal, 1970–72. Exhibn, L'Ultimo Silenzio, Palazzo Te, Mantua, Italy, 1993. Has held appointments of Vis. Artist at following Universities: Ball State Univ., Muncie, Indiana, 1967; Univ. of the West Indies, Kingston, Jamaica, 1968; Univ. of Wisconsin, Madison, 1972; Ohio State Univ., 1973; Western Illinois Univ., 1973; Haystack Mountain Sch. of Crafts, Maine, 1973; Vis. Artist, Queen's Univ., Kingston, Ont., 1977; part-time Instructor of Drawing, 1980–81, 1983, Sessional Instructor, 1980–85, Ottawa Univ.; Vis. Prof., 1987, Hon. LLD 1988, Univ. of Alberta. Founder Mem., Brit. Printmakers' Council. Prix des Jeunes Artistes (Gravure), Biennale de Paris, 1963; Major Prize, World Print Competition, San Francisco, 1974; Norwegian Print Biennale Prize, 1981. *Publications:* suites of original prints and photographs: Genesis, 1965; Alchemic Images, 1966; Aids to Meditation, 1967; Eclipse, 1968; Song of Songs, 1969; Out of Time, 1970; Fragments, 1971; Sweet Death and Other Pleasures, 1972; Homage to Don Juan, 1975; Body Perceptions, 1975; The Secret Garden, 1976; Openings, 1977; Three Mirrors to Narcissus, 1978; Il Paradiso Terrestre, 1980; Il Tempo Classico, 1981; Grecian Odes, 1983; Aphrodite Anadyomene, 1984; The Gardens of Paradise, part 1, 1984, part 2, 1985; Reflected Palaces, 1985; The Gilded Cage, 1986; Water Gardens, 1987; The Hospital for Wounded Angels, 1987; The Gardens of Desire, 1988; Pavane to Spring, 1989; Sonnet to Persephone, 1990; The Gardener's Journal, 1990; Cadence and Echo: the song of the garden, 1991; The Spirit of the Garden, 1992; The Haunted Heart, 1993; Sanctuaries and Paradeisos, 1994; Old and New Worlds, 1995; Quietude and Grace, 1996; Water Song, 1997; Sanctuary: a landscape of the mind, 2000. *Address:* 20 Osborne Street, Ottawa, ON K1S 4Z9, Canada. *T:* (613) 7302083, *Fax:* (613) 7301818.

DICKSON, Leonard Elliot, CBE 1972; MC 1945; TD 1951; Solicitor, Dickson, Haddow & Co., 1947–84; *b* 17 March 1915; *s* of Rev. Robert Marcus Dickson, DD, Lanark, and Cordelia Elliot; *m* 1950, Mary Elisabeth Cuthbertson; one *s* one *d*. *Educ:* Uppingham, Rutland; Univ. of Cambridge (BA 1936); Univ. of Glasgow (LLB 1947). Served War, with 1st Bn Glasgow Highlanders, HLI, 1939–46. Clerk to Clyde Lighthouses Trust, 1953–65. Chm., Lowland TAVR, 1968–70; Vice-Chm. Glasgow Exec. Council, NHS, 1970–74. DL Glasgow, 1963–98. *Publication:* Historical Sketch of Glasgow Society of Sons of the Clergy, 1990. *Recreations:* travel, gardening. *Address:* Bridge End, Gartmore, by Stirling FK8 3RR. *T:* (01877) 382220. *Club:* Royal Scottish Automobile (Glasgow).

DICKSON, Niall Forbes Ross; Social Affairs Editor, BBC, since 1995; *b* 5 Nov. 1953; *s* of late Sheriff Ian Anderson Dickson, WS and Margaret Forbes Ross or Dickson; *m* 1979, Elizabeth Selina Taggart, *d* of James Mercer Taggart, Lisburn, Co. Antrim; one *s* two *d*. *Educ:* Glasgow Acad.; Edinburgh Acad.; Edinburgh Univ. (MA Hons; DipEd); Moray House Coll. of Educn (Cert Ed). Teacher, Broughton High Sch., Edinburgh, 1976–78; Publicity Officer, Nat. Corp. for Care of Old People, 1978; Press Officer, 1978–79, Hd of Publication, 1979–81, Age Concern England; Editor: Therapy Weekly, 1981–83; Nursing Times, 1983–88; BBC News: Health Corresp., 1988–90; Chief Social Affairs Corresp., 1990–95. Charles Fletcher Med. Broadcaster of Year, BMA, 1997. *Publications:* contribs to newspapers, jls and specialist pubns on health and social issues. *Recreations:* golf, tennis, history, current affairs. *Address:* BBC Television Centre, Wood Lane, W12 7RJ. *T:* (020) 8624 9051; *e-mail:* niall.dickson@bbc.co.uk. *Clubs:* Reform; Westerham Golf (Kent).

See also R. H. Dickson.

DICKSON, Prof. Peter George Muir, DPhil, DLitt; FBA 1988; Professor of Early Modern History, University of Oxford, 1989–96; Fellow, St Catherine's College, Oxford, since 1960; *b* 26 April 1929; *s* of William Muir Dickson, and Regina Dowdall-Nicolls; *m* 1964, Ariane Faye; one *d*. *Educ:* St Paul's Sch.; Worcester Coll., Oxford (Schol.; BA (1st Cl. Hons), MA, DPhil); DLitt Oxon 1992. FRHistS. Research Fellow, Nuffield Coll., Oxford, 1954–56; Tutor, St Catherine's Soc., Oxford, 1956–60; Vice-Master, St Catherine's Coll., 1975–77; Reader in Modern Hist., Oxford Univ., 1978–89. *Publications:* The Sun Insurance Office 1710–1960, 1960; The Financial Revolution in England 1688–1756, 1967, rev. edn 1993; Finance and Government under Maria Theresia 1740–1780, 2 vols, 1987. *Recreations:* tennis, swimming, cinema. *Address:* Field House, Iffley, Oxford OX4 4EG. *T:* (01865) 779599.

DICKSON, Prof. Robert Andrew, DSc; FRCS, FRCSE; Professor and Head of Department of Orthopaedic Surgery, University of Leeds, since 1981; Consultant Surgeon, St James's University Hospital, Leeds, and Leeds General Infirmary, since 1981; *b* 13 April 1943; *s* of Robert Campbell Miller Dickson and late Maude Evelyn Dickson; *m* 1980, Ingrid Irene Sandberg; one *s*. *Educ:* Edinburgh Academy; Edinburgh Univ. (MB, ChB 1967, ChM 1973); MA 1979, DSc 1992, Oxon. FRCSE 1972; Moynihan Medal (Assoc. of Surgeons of GB and Ire.), 1977; FRCS *ad eund.* 1982. Lecturer, Nuffield Dept of Orthopaedic Surgery, Univ. of Oxford, 1972–75; Fellow in Spinal Surgery, Univ. of Louisville, Kentucky, 1975–76; Reader, Nuffield Dept of Orthopaedic Surgery, Univ. of Oxford, 1976–81. Arris and Gale Lectr, and Hunterian Prof., RCS. Fellow, Brit. Orthopaedic Assoc.; Member: Brit. Soc. for Surgery of the Hand; Brit. Orthopaedic Research Soc.; Brit. Scoliosis Soc. *Publications:* Surgery of the Rheumatoid Hand, 1979; Musculo-skeletal disease, 1984; Management of spinal deformities, 1984; Management of spinal deformities, 1988; papers on scoliosis, spinal surgery, hand surgery, and microsurgery. *Recreations:* squash, music. *Address:* 14A Park Avenue, Leeds LS8 2JH.

DICKSON, Robert Hamish, WS; Sheriff of South Strathclyde, Dumfries and Galloway, at Airdrie, since 1988; *b* 19 Oct. 1945; *s* of late Sheriff Ian Anderson Dickson, WS, and

Mrs Margaret Forbes Ross or Dickson; *m* 1976, Janet Laird, *d* of late Alexander Campbell, Port of Menteith; one *s*. *Educ:* Glasgow Acad.; Drumtochty Castle; Glenalmond; Glasgow Univ. (LLB). WS 1969. Solicitor: Edinburgh, 1969–71; Glasgow, 1971–86 (Partner, Brown Mair Mackintosh, 1973–86); Sheriff of South Strathclyde, Dumfries and Galloway, at Hamilton, 1986–88 (floating). *Publications:* (jtly) Powers & Harris' Medical Negligence, 2nd edn 1994, 3rd edn 1999; Medical and Dental Negligence, 1997; articles in medical legal jls. *Recreations:* golf, music, reading. *Address:* Airdrie Sheriff Court, Airdrie ML6 6EE. *T:* (01236) 751121. *Club:* Elie Golf House (Capt., 1997–99).

DICKSON, (Sidney) Brice; Chief Commissioner, Northern Ireland Human Rights Commission, since 1999; *b* 5 Dec. 1953; *s* of Sidney Dickson and Mary Dickson (*née* Murray); *m* 1993, Patricia Mary Josephine Mallon; one step *d* (one step *s* decd). *Educ:* Wadham Coll., Oxford (BA, BCL); Univ. of Ulster (MPhil). Called to the Bar, NI, 1976; Lectr in Law, Univ. of Leicester, 1977–79; Lectr, 1979–89, Sen. Lectr, 1989–91, QUB; Prof. of Law, Univ. of Ulster, 1991–99. Leverhulme Eur. Student, 1976–77; Salzburg Fellow, 1985; Churchill Fellow, 1994; Leverhulme Res. Fellow, 1999. *Publications:* The Legal System of Northern Ireland, 1984, 4th edn 2001; Introduction to French Law, 1994; (ed) Human Rights and the European Convention, 1997; (ed) Civil Liberties in Northern Ireland: the CAJ handbook, 1990, 4th edn 2001; (ed with P. Carmichael) The House of Lords: its parliamentary and judicial roles, 1999. *Recreations:* modern fiction, travel, philately. *Address:* 42 Rugby Road, Belfast BT7 1PS. *T:* (028) 9032 1327.

DICKSON MABON, Rt Hon. Jesse; *see* Mabon.

DIEHL, John Bertram Stuart; QC 1987; **His Honour Judge Diehl;** a Circuit Judge, since 1990; *b* 18 April 1944; *s* of late E. H. S. Diehl and of C. P. Diehl; *m* 1967, Patricia L. Charman; two *s*. *Educ:* Bishop Gore Grammar Sch., Swansea; University Coll. of Wales, Aberystwyth (LLB 1965). Called to the Bar, Lincoln's Inn, 1968. Asst Lectr and Lectr in Law, Univ. of Sheffield, 1965–69; barrister, in practice on Wales and Chester Circuit, 1969–90; a Recorder, 1984–90. *Address:* c/o Crown Court, St Helen's Road, Swansea SA1 4PF. *T:* (01792) 510200.

DIEPPE, Prof. Paul Adrian, MD; FRCP; Director, MRC National Collaboration on Health Services Research, since 1997; *b* 20 May 1946; *s* of Richard Willan Dieppe and Muriel Grace Dieppe (*née* Gascoigne); *m* 1970, Elizabeth Anne Stadward; two *d*. *Educ:* Caterham Sch.; St Bartholomew's Hosp. Med. Coll. (BSc 1967; MB BS 1970; MD 1985). FRCP 1985. General medical trng posts in London and Southend, 1970–74; Rheumatology Registrar, Guy's Hosp., London, 1974–75; Res. Fellow and Sen. Registrar in Medicine and Rheumatology, St Bartholomew's Hosp., London, 1975–78; University of Bristol: Consultant Sen. Lectr, 1978–87; ARC Prof. of Rheumatology, 1987–97; Res. Dir, Clinical Medicine and Dentistry, 1993–95; Dean, Faculty of Medicine, 1995–97; Hon. Prof. of Health Services Res., 1997–; Hon. Consultant Rheumatologist: to Bristol and Bath hosps, 1978–; United Bristol Healthcare NHS Trust, 1992–; N Avon Hosp. Trust, 1997–. *Publications:* Crystals and Joint Disease, 1983; Rheumatological Medicine, 1985; Atlas of Clinical Rheumatology, 1986; Arthritis: BMA Family Doctor Guide, 1988; Rheumatology, 1993, 2nd edn 1997; contrib. chapters in books and numerous papers in jls. *Recreations:* sailing, running, reading, writing, resting. *Address:* 4 Post Office Lane, Flax Bourton, Bristol BS49 3PL.

DIESKAU, Dietrich F.; *see* Fischer-Dieskau.

DIGBY, family name of **Baron Digby**.

DIGBY, 12th Baron (Ire.) *cr* 1620, and 5th Baron (GB) *cr* 1765; **Edward Henry Kenelm Digby,** KCVO 1999; JP; DL; Lord-Lieutenant, Dorset, 1984–99 (Vice Lord-Lieutenant, 1965–84); Captain, late Coldstream Guards; *b* 24 July 1924; *o s* of 11th and 4th Baron Digby, KG, DSO, MC, and Hon. Pamela Bruce, OBE (*d* 1978), *y d* of 2nd Baron Aberdare; *S* father, 1964; *m* 1952, Dione Marian Sherbrooke (*see* Lady Digby); two *s* one *d*. *Educ:* Eton; Trinity Coll., Oxford; RMC. Served War of 1939–45. Capt., 1947; Malaya, 1948–50; ADC to C-in-C: FARELF, 1950–51; BAOR, 1951–52. Director: Brooklyns Westbrick Ltd, 1970–83; Beazer plc, 1983–91; Kier Internat., 1986–91; Gifford-Hill Inc., 1986–91; PACCAR (UK) Ltd, 1990–97. Dep. Chm., SW Economic Planning Council, 1972–77. Mem. Council, Royal Agricultural Soc. of England, 1954; Chm., Royal Agricultural Soc. of Commonwealth, 1966–77, Hon. Fellow 1977. Pres., 1976, Vice Pres., 1977, Royal Bath and West Soc. Dorchester Rural District Councillor, 1962–68; Dorset County Councillor, 1966–81 (Vice Chm. CC, 1977–81). President: Wessex Br., Inst. of Dirs, 1980–97; Council, St John, Dorset, 1984–99; Patron, Dorset Br., British Red Cross Soc. Hon. Col, 4th Bn, Devonshire and Dorset Regt, 1992–96. DL 1957, JP 1959, Dorset. KStJ 1985. *Recreations:* ski-ing, shooting, tennis. *Heir:* *s* Hon. Henry Noel Kenelm Digby, ACA [*b* 6 Jan. 1954; *m* 1980, Susan, *er d* of Peter Watts; one *s* one *d*]. *Address:* Minterne, Dorchester, Dorset DT2 7AU. *T:* (01300) 341370. *Clubs:* Pratt's, Farmers'.

DIGBY, Lady; Dione Marian Digby, DBE 1991; DL; Founder Chairman and Hon. Secretary, Summer Music Society of Dorset, since 1964; Chairman, South and West Concerts Board, since 1989; *b* 23 Feb. 1934; *d* of Rear-Adm. Robert St Vincent Sherbrooke, VC, CB, DSO, and of Rosemary Neville Sherbrooke (*née* Buckley), Oxton, Notts; *m* 1952, Baron Digby, *qv*; two *s* one *d*. *Educ:* Talindert State Sch., Victoria, Australia; Southover Manor Sch., Lewes, Sussex. Chairman: Dorset Assoc. of Youth Clubs, 1966–73; Dorset Community Council, 1977–79; Standing Conf. of Rural Community Councils and Councils of Voluntary Service SW Region, 1977–79. Councillor (Ind.) W Dorset DC, 1976–86; Mem. Dorset Small Industries Cttee, CoSIRA, 1977 (Chm. 1982–85); Mem., Wessex Water Authority, 1983–89; National Rivers Authority: Mem., 1989–96; Chm., Wessex Regl Adv. Bd, 1989–93; Co-Chm., S Western Adv. Bd, 1993–95; Chm., Southern Regl Adv. Bd, 1995–96. Dir, SW Regl Bd, then Western Adv. Bd, Nat. Westminster Bank, 1986–92. Member: BBC/IBA Central Appeals Adv. Cttee, 1975–80; Ethical Trust Adv. Bd, Abbey Life Investment Services, 1996–; Cttee of Reference, Credit Suisse Fellowship Trust, 1997–. Governor: Dorset Coll. of Agriculture, 1978–83; Sherborne Sch., 1986–2000; Chm. Adv. Bd, Jt Univ. Centre at Yeovil Coll., Bournemouth and Exeter Univs; Mem. Council, Exeter Univ., 1981–96. Mem. Bath Festival Soc. Council of Management, 1971–81 (Chm. of the Society, 1976–81); Chm. Bath Fest. Friends Trust, 1982–87; Foundation Trustee, RAM, 1985–2000; Trustee, Tallis Scholars Trust, 1984–. Member: SW Arts Management Cttee, 1981–86; Arts Council of GB, 1982–86 (Chm., Trng Cttee; Vice-Chm., Dance Panel; Mem., Music Panel); South Bank Bd, 1985–88 (Gov., 1988–90); Bd of Mgt, Bournemouth Orchs, 1989–2000 (Mem. Bd of Mgt, Western Orchestral Soc., 1989–91); President: Dorset Opera, 1975–; Dorset Youth Assoc., 1994–. Mem., Council of Management, The Joseph Weld (formerly Dorset Respite) Hospice Trust, 1990– (Pres., 1993–). DL Dorset, 1983. Hon. DArt Bournemouth, 1997. *Recreations:* music and the arts, skiing, sailing; interest in local government, politics, history, people. *Address:* Minterne, Dorchester, Dorset DT2 7AU. *T:* (01300) 341370.

DIGBY, Adrian, CBE 1964; MA Oxon; FSA; Keeper, Department of Ethnography, British Museum, 1953–69; excavated Maya site of Las Cuevas, British Honduras, 1957; *b* 13 June 1909; *s* of late William Pollard Digby, FInstP, MIME, MIEE; *m* 1939, Sylvia Mary, *d* of late Arnold Inman, OBE, KC; two *d*. *Educ:* Lancing; Brasenose Coll., Oxford. Entered British Museum as Asst Keeper, 1932. Hon. Asst Sec. of International Congress of Anthropological and Ethnological Sciences, London, 1934; Hon. Sec. of International Congress of Americanists, Cambridge, 1952. Served in Intelligence Division Naval Staff, Admiralty, 1942–44; Hydrographic Dept, Admiralty, 1944–45. Vis. Prof. in Archaeology, Univ. de Los Andes, Bogota, 1970. Pres. Sect. H of The British Association for the Advancement of Science, 1962; Vice-Pres. Royal Anthropological Inst., 1962–66. Granted patent for a walking stick with pick-up device, 2000. *Publications:* Ancient American Pottery (with G. H. S. Bushnell), 1955; Maya Jades, 1964; articles on anthropological subjects in Man and in Chambers's Encyclopædia. *Recreation:* sundials. *Address:* Greentrees, Eastcombe, Stroud, Glos GL6 7DR. *T:* (01452) 770409.

DIGBY, Very Rev. Richard Shuttleworth W.; *see* Wingfield Digby.

DIGGLE, Prof. James, LittD; FBA 1985; Professor of Greek and Latin, University of Cambridge, since 1995; Fellow of Queens' College, since 1966; *b* 29 March 1944; *m* 1973, Sedwell Mary Chapman; three *s*. *Educ:* Rochdale Grammar School; St John's College, Cambridge (Major Scholar; Classical Tripos Pt I, first cl., 1964, Pt II, first cl. with dist., 1965; Pitt Scholar, Browne Scholar, Hallam Prize, Members' Latin Essay Prize, 1963; Montagu Butler Prize, Browne Medals for Greek Elegy and Latin Epigram, 1964; Porson Prize, Chancellor's Classical Medal, Craven Student, Allen Scholar, 1965; BA 1965; MA 1969; PhD 1969; LittD 1985). Queens' College, Cambridge: Research Fellow, 1966–67; Official Fellow, 1967–95; Professorial Fellow, 1995–; Director of Studies in Classics, 1967–; Librarian, 1969–77; Praelector, 1971–73, 1978–; Cambridge University: Asst Lectr in Classics, 1970–75; Lectr, 1975–89; Reader in Greek and Latin, 1989–95; Chm., Faculty Bd of Classics, 1989–90; Orator, 1982–93. Chm., Classical Jls Bd, 1991–97 (Hon. Treas., 1979–91); Jt Editor, Cambridge Classical Texts and Commentaries, 1977–. Corresponding Mem., Acad. of Athens, 2001. *Publications:* The Phaethon of Euripides, 1970; (jtly) Flavii Cresconii Corippi Iohannidos, Libri VIII, 1970; (ed jtly) The Classical Papers of A. E. Housman, 1972; (ed jtly) Dionysiaca: nine studies in Greek poetry, presented to Sir Denys Page, 1978; Studies on the Text of Euripides, 1981; Euripidis Fabulae (Oxford Classical Texts), vol. ii 1981, vol. i 1984, vol. iii 1994; (ed jtly) Studies in Latin Literature and its Tradition, in honour of C. O. Brink, 1989; The textual tradition of Euripides' Orestes, 1991; (ed jtly) F. R. D. Goodyear, Papers on Latin Literature, 1992; Euripidea: collected essays, 1994; Cambridge Orations 1982–1993: a selection, 1994; Tragicorum Graecorum Fragmenta Selecta, 1998. *Address:* Queens' College, Cambridge CB3 9ET. *T:* (01223) 335527.

DIGGLE, Judith Margaret, (Mrs P. J. Diggle); *see* Brown, J. M.

DIGGORY, Colin; Headmaster: Latymer Upper School, 1991–Sept. 2002; Alleyn's School, from Sept. 2002; *b* 22 July 1954; *s* of John Harold Diggory and late Olga Diggory; *m* 1976, Susan Janet Robinson; one *s* two *d*. *Educ:* Sir William Turner's Sch., Redcar; Univ. of Durham (BSc 1st cl. Hons Maths, PGCE); MA Open Univ. 1999. CMath, FIMA 1994. Assistant Master: Manchester Grammar Sch., 1976–83; St Paul's Sch., Barnes, 1983–87; Head of Maths, Merchant Taylors' Sch., 1987–90; Second Master, Latymer Upper Sch., 1990–91. Chief Examr, A Level Maths, Univ. of London, 1989–91. Chm., London Div., 1999, Jun. Schs Sub-Cttee, 1999–, HMC. Governor: Durston House Prep. Sch., Ealing, 1995–; John Betts' Primary Sch., Hammersmith, 1996–. FRSA 1994. *Recreations:* walking, theatre. *Address:* (until Sept. 2002) Latymer Upper School, King Street, W6 9LR; (from Sept. 2002) Alleyn's School, Dulwich, SE22 8SU. *Club:* East India, Devonshire, Sports and Public Schools.

DIGGORY, Elizabeth Mary; High Mistress, St Paul's Girls' School, since 1998; *b* 22 Dec. 1945; *d* of Clarence Howard Diggory and Beatrice Mary Diggory. *Educ:* Shrewsbury High Sch. for Girls; Westfield Coll., Univ. of London (BA Hons Hist.); Hughes Hall, Univ. of Cambridge (PGCE). King Edward VI High School for Girls, Birmingham: Asst Teacher, 1968–73; Hd of History Dept, 1973–82; Head Mistress: St Albans High Sch. for Girls, 1983–94; Manchester High Sch. for Girls, 1994–98. Pres., GSA, 1991–92. FRSA 1993. *Recreations:* theatre, the arts in general, travel, walking. *Address:* St Paul's Girls' School, Brook Green, W6 7BS. *T:* (020) 7603 2288.

DIGNAN, Maj.-Gen. Albert Patrick, CB 1978; MBE 1952; FRCS, FRCSI; Director of Army Surgery and Consulting Surgeon to the Army, 1973–78; Hon. Consultant Surgeon, Royal Hospital, Chelsea, 1973–78; Hon. Consultant in Radiotherapy and Oncology, Westminster Hospital, 1974–78; *b* 25 July 1920; *s* of Joseph Dignan; *m* 1952, Eileen White (*d* 2001); two *s* one *d*. *Educ:* Trinity Coll., Dublin (Med. Schol.). MB, BCh, BAO, BA 1943, MA, MD 1968, FRCSI 1947, FRCS 1976. Prof. of Physiol. Prize, TCD. Posts in Dublin, Belfast and Wigan; subseq. NS Sen. Specialist in Surgery, Major RAMC Malaya; Sen. Registrar in Surgery, Bristol Royal Infirmary and Wanstead Hosp.; Sen. Specialist in Surgery, BAOR Mil. Hosps and Consultant Surg., Brit. Mil. Hosps Singapore and Tidworth, 1953–68; Brig., and Consulting Surg., Farelf, 1969–70; Consultant Surg., Mil. Hosp. Tidworth, 1971–72; Consultant Surgeon, Queen Alexandra Mil. Hosp. Millbank, 1972–73; Consultant in Accident and Emergency, Ealing Dist, DHSS, 1978–79. Pres., Army Med. Bds, 1980–90. Fellow, Association of Surgeons of GB and Ireland; FRSocMed. Mem., Acad. of Medicine, Singapore, 1969–71. QHS, 1974–78. *Publications:* A Doctor's Experiences of Life (autobiog.), 1994; papers in Brit. Jl Surgery, BMJ, Jl of RAMC, Postgrad. Med. Jl, Univ. Singapore Med. Soc. Med. Gazette. *Recreations:* gardening, golf. *Address:* Ramridge Dene, 182 Beckenham Hill Road, Beckenham, Kent BR3 1SZ.

DILHORNE, 2nd Viscount *cr* 1964, of Green's Norton; **John Mervyn Manningham-Buller;** Bt 1866; Baron 1962; Barrister-at-Law; *b* 28 Feb. 1932; *s* of 1st Viscount Dilhorne, PC, and of Lady Mary Lilian Lindsay, 4th *d* of 27th Earl of Crawford, KT, PC; *S* father, 1980; *m* 1st, 1955, Gillian Evelyn (marr. diss. 1973), *d* of Colonel George Stockwell; two *s* one *d*; 2nd, 1981, Prof. Susannah Jane Eykyn, MB BS, FRCS, FRCP, FRCPath. *Educ:* Eton; RMA Sandhurst. Called to the Bar, Inner Temple, 1979. Formerly Lieut, Coldstream Guards. Managing Director, Stewart Smith (LP&M) Ltd, 1970–74. Mem., Wilts County Council, 1967–70. Chm., VAT Tribunal, 1988–95; Member, Joint Parliamentary Committee: on Statutory Instruments, 1981–88; on Consolidation Bills, 1994–99; Mem., EC Select Cttee (Law and Instns), 1989–92. FTII (Mem. Council, 1967–74). *Heir:* *s* Hon. James Edward Manningham-Buller, formerly Captain Welsh Guards [*b* 20 Aug. 1956; *m* 1985, Nicola Marion, *e d* of Sven Mackie; one *s* one *d*. *Educ:* Harrow; Sandhurst]. *Address:* 4 Breams Buildings, EC4A 1AQ. *T:* (020) 7353 5835; 382 Imperial Court, 225 Kennington Lane, SE11 5QN. *T:* (020) 7820 1660, *Fax:* (020) 7820 1418; The Dower House, Minterne Parva, Dorchester, Dorset DT2 7AP. *T:* (01300) 341392. *Clubs:* Pratt's, Buck's, Beefsteak; Swinley Forest Golf.

DILKE; *see* Fetherston-Dilke.

DILKE, Rev. Sir Charles (John Wentworth), 6th Bt *cr* 1862, of Sloane Street; priest of the London Oratory, since 1966; *b* 21 Feb. 1937; *er s* of Sir John Dilke, 5th Bt and of Sheila (*née* Seeds, now Knapp); *S* father, 1998. *Educ:* Ashdown House, Sussex; Winchester Coll.; King's Coll., Cambridge (BA). Joined the London Oratory, 1961; ordained priest, 1966; elected Provost (Superior), 1981–87. *Recreations:* painting, study of architecture, astronomy. *Heir: b* Dr Timothy Fisher Wentworth Dilke [*b* 1 Aug. 1938; *m* 1965, Caroline Sophia Dilke; one *s* one *d*]. *Address:* The Oratory, SW7 2RP. *T:* (020) 7589 4811. *Club:* Athenæum.

DILKS, Prof. David Neville, FRHistS; FRSL; Vice-Chancellor, University of Hull, 1991–99; *b* Coventry, 17 March 1938; *s* of Neville Ernest Dilks and Phyllis Dilks; *m* 1963, Jill Medlicott; one *s*. *Educ:* Royal Grammar Sch., Worcester; Hertford Coll., Oxford (BA Modern Hist., Class II, 1959); St Antony's Coll., Oxford (Curzon Prizeman, 1960). Research Assistant to: Rt Hon. Sir Anthony Eden (later Earl of Avon), 1960–62; Marshal of the RAF Lord Tedder, 1963–65; Rt Hon. Harold Macmillan, 1964–67; Asst Lectr, then Lectr, in International History, LSE, 1962–70; University of Leeds: Prof. of Internat. History, 1970–91; Chm., Sch. of History, 1974–79; Dean, Faculty of Arts, 1975–77. Vis. Fellow, All Souls' Coll., Oxford, 1973. Consultant, Sec.-Gen. of the Commonwealth, 1967–75; Chm., Commonwealth Youth Exchange Council, 1968–73. Member: Adv. Council on Public Records, 1977–85; Central Council, 1982–85, Library Cttee, 1982–91, Royal Commonwealth Soc.; British Nat. Cttee for History of Second World War, 1983– (Pres., Internat. Cttee, 1992–2000); UFC, 1989–91; Adv. Council, Politeia, 1995–. Trustee: Edward Boyle Meml Trust, 1982–96 (Hon. Sec., 1981–82); Imperial War Museum, 1983–90; Lennox-Boyd Meml Trust, 1984–91; Nathaniel Trust, 1986–90. Pres., Worcester Old Elizabethans' Assoc., 1986–87. FRSL 1986; FCGI 1999. Liveryman, Goldsmiths' Co., 1984– (Freeman, 1979). Wrote and presented BBC TV series, The Loneliest Job, 1977; interviewer in BBC TV series, The Twentieth Century Remembered, 1982. Hon. Dr of History, Russian Acad. of Scis, 1996. Médaille de Vermeil, Acad. Française, 1994. *Publications:* Curzon in India, Vol. I, 1969, Vol. II, 1970; (ed) The Diaries of Sir Alexander Cadogan, 1971; (contrib.) The Conservatives (ed Lord Butler of Saffron Walden), 1977; (ed and contrib.) Retreat from Power, vol. 1, 1906–1939, Vol. 2, after 1939, 1981; (ed and contrib.) Britain and Canada (Commonwealth Foundn Paper), 1980; (ed and contrib.) The Missing Dimension: governments and intelligence communities in the twentieth century, 1984; Neville Chamberlain, Vol. I: Pioneering and Reform 1869–1929, 1984; (ed jtly and contrib.) Grossbritannien und der deutsche Widerstand, 1994; (ed jtly) Barbarossa: the axis and the allies, 1994; reviews and articles in English Historical Rev., Survey, History, Scandinavian Jl of History, etc. *Recreations:* ornithology, painting, railways, Bentley cars. *Address:* Wits End, Long Causeway, Leeds LS16 8EX. *T:* (0113) 267 3466. *Clubs:* Brooks's, Royal Over-Seas League.

DILKS, John Morris Whitworth; Managing Director, Peribase Ltd, since 1999; *b* 10 Feb. 1950; *s* of John Amos Whitworth Dilks and Margaret (*née* Thraves); *m*; one *s* one *d*. *Educ:* Oakham Sch.; Sheffield Univ. (BA Hons). ACMA; CIGasE. Audit Manager, British Gas E Midlands, 1980–85; Asst Dir of Finance, British Gas, 1985–86; Regl Dir of Finance, British Gas NE, 1986–91; Regl Chm., British Gas Eastern, 1991–93; Dir, Transco, 1994–98. *Recreations:* sailing, walking, gardening. *Address:* 6 Hatherley Road, Cheltenham, Gloucestershire GL51 6DZ.

DILLAMORE, Ian Leslie, PhD, DSc; FREng; FIM; Chairman and Chief Executive, Doncasters plc, 1996–2000; *b* 22 Nov. 1938; *s* of Arthur Leslie Dillamore and Louise Mary Dillamore; *m* 1962, Maureen Birch; two *s*. *Educ:* Birmingham Univ. (BSc, MSc, PhD, DSc). ICI Research Fellow, Birmingham Univ., 1962–63, Lectr in Physical Metallurgy, 1963–69; Head of Phys. Metallurgy, BISRA, 1969–72; Head of Metals Technology Unit, British Steel Corp., 1972–76; Head of Metallurgy Dept, Aston Univ., 1976–81, Dean of Engineering, 1980–81; Director of Research and Development, INCO Europe, 1981–82; Dir of Technology, 1982–87, Gp Man. Dir, 1987–96, INCO Engineered Products Ltd. Hon. Professor of Metallurgy, Birmingham Univ., 1981–. Mem. Council: Metals Soc., 1980–84; Instn of Metallurgists, 1981–84; Vice-Pres., Inst. of Metals, 1985–88; Mem. SRC Metallurgy Cttee, 1972–75, Materials Cttee, 1977–82; Chm., Processing Sub-Cttee, SRC, later SERC, 1979–82; Mem., DTI Non Ferrous Metals Exec. Cttee, 1982–85; Pres. Birmingham Metallurgical Assoc., 1980–81. FREng (FEng 1985). Hon. DEng Birmingham, 1999. Sir Robert Hadfield Medal and Prize, Metals Soc., 1976; Platinum Medal, Inst. of Materials, 1999. *Publications:* numerous contribs to metallurgical and engrg jls. *Recreation:* industrial archaeology. *Address:* 4 Heather Court Gardens, Sutton Coldfield, W Midlands B74 2ST. *T:* (0121) 308 1363.

DILLON, family name of **Viscount Dillon**.

DILLON, 22nd Viscount *cr* 1622, of Castello Gallen, Co. Mayo, Ireland; **Henry Benedict Charles Dillon;** Count in France, 1711; *b* 6 Jan. 1973; *s* of 21st Viscount Dillon and of Mary Jane, *d* of late John Young, Castle Hill House, Birtle, Lancs; *S* father, 1982. *Heir: uncle* Hon. Richard Arthur Louis Dillon [*b* 23 Oct. 1948; *m* 1975, Hon. Priscilla Frances Hazlerigg, *d* of 2nd Baron Hazlerigg, *qv*; one *s* one *d*].

DILLON, Andrew Patrick; Chief Executive, National Institute for Clinical Excellence, since 1999; *b* 9 May 1954; *s* of Patrick Joseph Dillon and Kathleen Mary Dillon; *m* 1991, Alison Goodbrand; two *d*. *Educ:* St Ambrose Coll., Hale Barns, Cheshire; North Cheshire Coll. of Further Educn; Univ. of Manchester (BSc Hons Geog.). Dip. IHSM 1978. Asst Sector Adminr, Bolton Royal Infirmary, 1978–81; Unit Adminr, Queen Elizabeth Hosp. for Children, London, 1981–83; Dep., then Actg Unit Adminr, Royal London Hosp., 1983–86; Unit Gen. Manager, Royal Free Hosp., 1986–91; Chief Exec., St George's Gp, then St George's Healthcare NHS Trust, 1991–99. Mem. Council, NHS Trust Fedn, 1995–97. FRSA 1998. *Recreation:* family. *Address:* National Institute for Clinical Excellence, 11 Strand, WC2N 5HR. *T:* (020) 7766 9191.

DILLON, Hon. Sir Brian; *see* Dillon, Hon. Sir G. B. H.

DILLON, C(larence) Douglas; Chairman, US & Foreign Securities Corporation, 1967–84; Managing Director, Dillon, Read & Co. Inc., 1971–83; retired; *b* Geneva, Switzerland, 21 Aug. 1909; *s* of Clarence Dillon; *m* 1st, 1931, Phyllis Ellsworth (*d* 1982); two *d*; 2nd, 1983, Susan Sage. *Educ:* Groton Sch.; Harvard Univ. (AB). Mem., NY Stock Exchange, 1931–36; US and Foreign Securities Corporation and US and International Securities Corporation, 1937–53 (Dir, 1938–53; Pres., 1946–53); Dir, Dillon, Read & Co. Inc., 1938–53 (Chm. of Bd, 1946–53); American Ambassador to France, 1953–57; Under-Sec. of State for Economic Affairs, USA, 1957–59, Under-Sec. of State, USA, 1959–61; Sec. of the Treasury, USA, 1961–65. Served US Naval Reserve, 1941–45 (Lieut-Comdr; Air Medal, Legion of Merit). Dir, Council on Foreign Relations, 1965–78 (Vice-Chm. 1977–78); Pres., Board of Overseers, Harvard Coll., 1968–72; Chm., Rockefeller Foundn, 1971–75; Chm., Brookings Instn, 1971–75. Trustee Emeritus, Metropolitan Museum of Art (President, 1970–77; Chm., 1977–83). Hon. Dr of Laws: New York Univ., 1956; Lafayette Coll., 1957; Univ. of Hartford, Conn, 1958; Columbia Univ., 1959; Harvard Univ., 1959; Williams Coll., 1960; Rutgers Univ., 1961; Princeton Univ., 1961; University of Pennsylvania, 1962; Bradley Univ., 1964; Middlebury Coll., 1965; Tufts Univ., 1982; Marymount Manhattan Coll., 1984. US Presidential Medal of Freedom, 1989.

DILLON, Rt Hon. Sir (George) Brian (Hugh), Kt 1979; PC 1982; a Lord Justice of Appeal, 1982–94; *b* 2 Oct. 1925; *s* of late Captain George Crozier Dillon, RN; *m* 1954, Alison, *d* of late Hubert Samuel Lane, MC and Dr Isabella Lane, MB, ChB Edin.; two *s* two *d*. *Educ:* Winchester College; New College, Oxford. Called to the Bar, Lincoln's Inn, 1948; QC 1965; a Judge of the High Court of Justice, Chancery Division, 1979–82. *Address:* Tanyard House, 17 Station Road, Woodbridge, Suffolk IP12 4AU.

DILLON, His Honour Thomas Michael; QC 1973; a Circuit Judge, 1985–2000; *b* 29 Nov. 1927; *yr s* of Thomas Bernard Joseph Dillon, Birmingham, and Ada Gladys Dillon (*née* Noyes); *m* 1956, Wendy Elizabeth Marshall Hurrell; two *s* one *d*. *Educ:* King Edward's Sch., Aston, Birmingham; Birmingham Univ. (LLB); Lincoln Coll., Oxford (BCL). Called to Bar, Middle Temple, 1952, Master of the Bench 1981. 2nd Lieut, RASC, 1953–54. In practice as barrister, 1954–85; a Recorder, 1972–85; Part-time Chm. of Industrial Tribunals, 1968–74. *Recreations:* reading, listening to music. *Address:* 1 Fountain Court, Birmingham B4 6DR. *T:* (0121) 236 5721.

DILLWYN-VENABLES-LLEWELYN, Sir John Michael; *see* Venables-Llewelyn.

DILNOT, Andrew William, CBE 2000; Director, Institute for Fiscal Studies, since 1991; *b* 19 June 1960; *s* of Anthony William John Dilnot and Patricia Josephine Dilnot; *m* 1984, Catherine Elizabeth Morrish; two *d*. *Educ:* Olchfa Comprehensive Sch.; St John's Coll., Oxford (BA Hons PPE). Institute for Fiscal Studies: Res. Asst, 1981–83; Res. Officer, 1983–84; Sen. Res. Officer, 1984–86; Prog. Dir, 1986–90; Dep. Dir, 1990–91. Lectr (part-time) in Econs, Exeter Coll., Oxford, 1988–89. Vis. Fellow, ANU, 1986; Downing Meml Fellow, Melbourne Univ., 1989. Presenter, Analysis, Radio 4, 1994–. Member: Social Security Adv. Cttee, 1992–; Retirement Income Inquiry, 1994–95; Foresight Panel on Aging Population, 1999–. Member: Council, REconS, 1993–98; Acad. Social Scis, 1999–. Mem. Council, Westfield Coll., then QMW, Univ. of London, 1987–95. Mem. Bd, World Vision UK, 1991–97. Trustee, Relate, Oxon, 1999–. *Publications:* The Reform of Social Security, 1984; The Economics of Social Security, 1989; Pensions Policy in the UK: an economic analysis, 1994; contrib. articles on taxation, public spending and economics of public policy. *Address:* Institute for Fiscal Studies, 7 Ridgmount Street, WC1E 7AE. *T:* (020) 7291 4800.

DILNOT, Mary, (Mrs Thomas Ruffle), OBE 1982; Director, IPC Women's Magazines Group, 1976–81; Editor, Woman's Weekly, 1971–81; *b* 23 Jan. 1921; 2nd *d* of George Dilnot, author, and Ethel Dilnot; *m* 1974, Thomas Ruffle. *Educ:* St Mary's Coll., Hampton. Joined Woman's Weekly, 1939. *Recreations:* home interests, reading, travel, golf. *Address:* 28 Manor Road South, Hinchley Wood, Esher, Surrey KT10 0QL.

DILWORTH, Prof. Jonathan Robin, DPhil, DSc; FRSC; Professor of Chemistry, University of Oxford, since 1998; Fellow of St Anne's College, Oxford, since 1997; *b* 20 Aug. 1944; *s* of Robert Arnold Dilworth and Jean Marion Dilworth; *m* 1971, Nicola Jane Still; two *d*. *Educ:* Jesus Coll., Oxford (BA 1967, MA 1972); Univ. of Sussex (DPhil 1970; DSc 1983). FRSC 1984. AFRC Unit of Nitrogen Fixation, 1967–85; Prof. of Chemistry, Univ. of Essex, 1985–97. *Publications:* some 230 papers and review articles in internat. chemistry jls. *Recreations:* tennis, badminton, golf. *Address:* The Croft, Newland Close, Eynsham, Oxon OX8 1LE. *T:* (01865) 884102.

DIMBLEBY, Bel, (Mrs Jonathan Dimbleby); *see* Mooney, Bel.

DIMBLEBY, David; broadcaster and newspaper proprietor; Chairman, Dimbleby & Sons Ltd, since 1986 (Managing Director, 1966–86); *b* 28 Oct. 1938; *e s* of (Frederick) Richard and Dilys Dimbleby; *m* 1967, Josceline Rose Gaskell (*see* J. R. Dimbleby) (marr. diss. 2000); one *s* two *d*; *m* 2000, Belinda Giles; one *s*. *Educ:* Glengorse Sch.; Charterhouse; Christ Church, Oxford (MA); Univs of Paris and Perugia. News Reporter, BBC Bristol, 1960–61; Presenter and Interviewer on network programmes on: religion (Quest), science for children (What's New?), politics (In My Opinion), Top of the Form, etc, 1961–63; Reporter, BBC2 (Enquiry), and Dir films, incl.: Ku-Klux-Klan, The Forgotten Million, Cyprus: Thin Blue Line, 1964–65; Special Correspondent CBS News, New York; documentary film (Texas-England) and film reports for '60 minutes', 1966–68; Reporter, BBC1 (Panorama), 1967–69; Presenter, BBC1 (24 Hours), 1969–72; Yesterday's Men, 1971; Chm., The Dimbleby Talk-In, 1971–74; films for Reporter at Large, 1973; Presenter: BBC 1 (Panorama), 1974–77, 1980–82, 1989–; (People and Power), 1982–83; (This Week, Next Week), 1984–86; Chm., BBC Question Time, 1994–; Election Campaign Report, 1974; BBC Election and Results programmes, 1979, 1983, 1987, 1992, 1997; film series: The White Tribe of Africa, 1979 (Royal TV Soc. Supreme Documentary Award); An Ocean Apart, 1988; The Struggle for South Africa, 1990 (Emmy Award, 1991; Golden Nymph Award, 1991); David Dimbleby's India, 1997; live commentary, Funeral of Diana, Princess of Wales, 1997. Richard Dimbleby Award, BAFTA, 1998. *Publication:* An Ocean Apart (with David Reynolds), 1988. *Address:* (office) 14 King Street, Richmond, Surrey TW9 1NF. *T:* (020) 8940 6668.
See also J. Dimbleby.

DIMBLEBY, Jonathan; freelance broadcaster, journalist, and author; *b* 31 July 1944; *s* of Richard and Dilys Dimbleby; *m* 1968, Bel Mooney, *qv*; one *s* one *d*. *Educ:* University Coll. London (BA Hons Philosophy). TV and Radio Reporter, BBC Bristol, 1969–70; BBC Radio, World at One, 1970–71; for Thames TV: This Week, 1972–78, 1986–88; TV Eye, 1979; Jonathan Dimbleby in South America, 1979; documentary series, Witness (Editor), 1986–88; for Yorkshire TV: series, Jonathan Dimbleby in Evidence: The Police, 1980; The Bomb, 1980; The Eagle and the Bear, 1981; The Cold War Game, 1982; The American Dream, 1984; Four Years On—The Bomb, 1984; First Tuesday (Associate Editor/Presenter), 1982–86; for TV-am: Jonathan Dimbleby on Sunday (Presenter/ Editor), 1985–86; for BBC TV: On the Record, 1988–93; Election Call, 1992; documentary series, The Last Governor (presenter/producer), 1997; for Central TV: Charles: the private man, the public role (documentary), 1994; for LWT: Jonathan Dimbleby, 1995–; for ITV: chief presenter, Gen. Election coverage, 1997; An Ethiopian Journey (writer/producer/dir), 1998; A Kosovo Journey (writer/presenter), 2000; Heseltine—A Life in the Political Jungle (writer/presenter), 2000; Presenter, BBC Radio 4: Any Questions?, 1987–; Any Answers, 1989–; The Candidate, 1998. Pres., Soil Assoc., 1997–; Vice-Pres., CPRE, 1997– (Pres., 1992–97); Chm., Bath Fests Trust, 1998–; Pres., VSO, 1999–; Trustee: Richard Dimbleby Cancer Fund, 1966–; Forum for the Future, 1995–. SFTA Richard Dimbleby Award, for most outstanding contribution to factual TV, 1974. *Publications:* Richard Dimbleby, 1975; The Palestinians, 1979; The Prince of Wales: a biography, 1994; The Last Governor, 1997. *Recreations:* music, sailing, tennis. *Address:* c/o David Higham Associates Ltd, 5 Lower John Street, W1R 4HA.

DIMBLEBY, Josceline Rose; cookery and travel writer; *b* 1 Feb. 1943; *d* of late Thomas Josceline Gaskell and of Barbara Montagu-Pollock; *m* 1967, David Dimbleby, *qv* (marr.

diss. 2000); one *s* two *d*. *Educ:* Cranborne Chase Sch., Dorset; Guildhall School of Music. Contributor, Daily Mail, 1976–78; cookery writer for Sainsbury's, 1978–; Cookery Editor, Sunday Telegraph, 1982–97. André Simon Award, 1979. *Publications:* A Taste of Dreams, 1976, 3rd edn 1984; Party Pieces, 1977; Josceline Dimbleby's Book of Puddings, Desserts and Savouries, 1979, 2nd edn 1983; Favourite Food, 1983, 2nd edn 1984; Josceline Dimbleby's Complete Cookbook, 1997; Josceline Dimbleby's Cooking Course, 1999; Josceline Dimbleby's Almost Vegetarian Cookbook, 1999; (for Sainsbury's): Cooking for Christmas, 1978; Family Meat and Fish Cookery, 1979; Cooking with Herbs and Spices, 1979; Curries and Oriental Cookery, 1980; Salads for all Seasons, 1981; Marvellous Meals with Mince, 1982; Festive Food, 1982; Sweet Dreams, 1983; First Impressions, 1984; The Josceline Dimbleby Collection, 1984; Main Attractions, 1985; A Traveller's Tastes, 1986; The Josceline Dimbleby Christmas Book, 1987; The Josceline Dimbleby Book of Entertaining, 1988; The Essential Josceline Dimbleby, 1989; The Cook's Companion, 1991; The Almost Vegetarian Cookbook, 1994; The Christmas Book, 1994. *Recreations:* singing, travel. *Address:* 14 King Street, Richmond, Surrey TW9 1NF. *T:* (020) 8940 6668.

DIMMOCK, Peter, CVO 1968; OBE 1961; Chairman, Zenith Entertainment (formerly Television Enterprise and Asset Management) plc, 1991–2000; *e s* of late Frederick Dimmock, OBE, and Paula Dimmock (*née* Hudd); *m* 1st, 1960, Mary Freya, (Polly) (*d* 1987), *e d* of late Hon. Mr Justice Elwes, OBE, TD; three *d*; 2nd, 1990, Christabel Rosamund, *e d* of Sir John Bagge, 6th Bt, ED, DL and *widow* of James Hinton Scott. *Educ:* Dulwich Coll.; France. TA; RAF pilot, instr, and Air Ministry Staff Officer, 1939–45. After demobilisation became Press Association correspondent; joined BBC as Television Outside Broadcasts Producer and commentator, 1946; produced both studio and outside broadcasts, ranging from documentaries to sporting, theatrical and public events; has produced or commentated on more than 500 television relays, including Olympic Games 1948, Boat Race 1949, first international television relay, from Calais, 1950, King George VI's Funeral, Windsor, 1952. Produced and directed television outside broadcast of the Coronation Service from Westminster Abbey, 1953; first TV State Opening of Parliament, 1958; first TV Grand National, 1960; TV for Princess Margaret's Wedding, 1960. Created BBC Sportsview Unit and introduced new television programme Sportsview, 1954, regular presenter of this live weekly network programme, 1954–64; Gen. Manager and Head of Outside Broadcasts, BBC TV, 1954–72; responsible for Liaison between BBC and Royal Family, 1963–77; Gen. Manager, BBC Enterprises, 1972–77; Vice-Pres., ABC Worldwide Sales and Marketing TV Sports, 1978–86; Vice-Pres. and Consultant, ABC Video Enterprises Div., Capital Cities/ABC Inc., NY, 1984–91; Dir, Entertainment and Sports Cable Network, 1984–90. Chm. Sports Cttee and Adviser, European Broadcasting Union, 1959–72. Mem., Greater London and SE Sports Council, 1972–77; Chm., Sports Develt Panel, 1976–77. FRTS 1978 (Hall of Fame, 1996). Freeman, City of London, 1977. *Publications:* Sportsview Annuals, 1954–65; Sports in View, 1964; (contrib.) The BBC Book of Royal Memories, 1990. *Recreations:* flying, winter sports, golf. *Address:* c/o Coutts & Co., 440 Strand, WC2R 0QS. *Fax:* (01276) 452202. *Clubs:* Garrick, Turf, Boodle's; Berkshire Golf; St Enedoc Golf; New York Athletic.

DIMMOCK, Rear-Adm. Roger Charles, CB 1988; Chairman, Archer Mullins Ltd, since 1989; *b* 27 May 1935; *s* of late Frank Dimmock and Ivy Dimmock (*née* Archer); *m* 1958, Lesley Patricia Reid; two *d* (and one *d* decd). *Educ:* Price's School. Entered Royal Navy, 1953; pilot's wings FAA, 1954, USN, 1955; qualified Flying Instructor, 1959; Master Mariner Foreign Going Cert. of Service, 1979. Served RN Air Sqdns and HM Ships Bulwark, Albion, Ark Royal, Eagle, Hermes, Anzio, Messina, Murray, Berwick (i/c), Naiad (i/c), to 1978; CSO to FO Carriers and Amphibious Ships, 1978–80; Comd RNAS Culdrose, 1980–82; Comd HMS Hermes, 1982–83; Dir, Naval Air Warfare, MoD, 1983–84; Naval Sec., 1985–87; FONAC, 1987–88. Dir, Charnauds (formerly Manufg and Marketing Services) Ltd, 1993–98. Mem. Cttee of Management, RNLI, 1987– (Pres., Denmead and Hambledon Br., 1981–). Chm. Trustees, Fleet Air Arm Museum, 1987–88. President: RN Hockey Assoc., 1985–89; CS Hockey Assoc., 1987–93; Vice Pres., Hockey Assoc., 1997–. Mem., Royal Aero Club, 1988–. *Recreations:* hockey (player and umpire), cricket, squash, golf, family, home and garden, RNLI. *Address:* Beverley House, Beverley Grove, Farlington, Portsmouth PO6 1BP. *T:* (023) 9261 7224. *Club:* Royal Navy of 1765 and 1785.

DIMOND, Paul Stephen; HM Diplomatic Service; Ambassador to the Philippines, from Feb. 2002; *b* 30 Dec. 1944; *yr s* of late Cyril James Dimond and of Dorothy Mabel Louisa Hobbs (*née* Knight); *m* 1965, Carolyn Susan Davis-Mees, *er d* of late Dennis Charles Mees and of Eileen Lilian (*née* Barratt); two *s*. *Educ:* St Olave's and St Saviour's Grammar Sch. for Boys, Bermondsey. FCIM 1989; FIL 1988. British Bakeries Ltd, 1962–63; FO, 1963–65; Diplomatic Service Admin, 1965–66; Japanese lang. student, Tokyo, 1966–68; Vice-Consul (Commercial), 1968–70, Consul (Commercial), 1970–72, Osaka; Second Sec. (Commercial), Tokyo, 1972–73; seconded to Dept of Trade as assistant to Special Advr on Japanese Mkt, BOTB, 1973–75; FCO, 1975–76; First Secretary: (Economic), Stockholm, 1977–80; FCO, 1980–81; (Commercial), Tokyo, 1981–86; FCO, 1986–88; seconded to Smiths Industries plc as Strategic Marketing Advr, Smiths Industries Med. Systems, 1988–89; Commercial Counsellor, Tokyo, 1989–93; Dep. Hd of Mission, The Hague, 1994–97; Consul-Gen., Los Angeles, 1997–2001. Sec., First Anglo–Mongolian Round Table, Ulaan Baatar, 1987. Governor: British Sch. in the Netherlands, 1994–97; British Film Office, LA, 1998–2000. FRSA 1980. *Recreations:* the arts, manufactures and commerce, vintage Batsfords, walking. *Address:* c/o Foreign and Commonwealth Office, King Charles Street, SW1A 2AH. *Club:* Travellers.

DINES, Very Rev. Griff; *see* Dines, Very Rev. P. J.

DINES, Peter Munn, CBE 1991; Secretary, School Examinations and Assessment Council, 1988–91; *b* 29 Aug. 1929; *e s* of Victor Edward Dines and Muriel Eleanor Dines (*née* Turner); *m* 1952, Kathleen Elisabeth Jones; two *s* one *d*. *Educ:* Palmer's Sch., Grays, Essex; Imperial Coll. London (ARCS; BSc 1st cl. 1949); Inst. of Education, London (PGCE 1950); Bristol Univ. (MEd 1968). RAF, 1950–53. Teaching maths, 1953–69; Headmaster, Cramlington High Sch., 1969–76; Jt Sec., Schools Council, 1976–78; Headmaster, Sir John Leman High Sch., Beccles, 1978–80; Examinations Officer, Schools Council, 1980–83; Dep. Chief Exec., 1983–87, Chief Exec., 1988, Secondary Examinations Council. Educn Consultant, British Council, Swaziland, 1993 and Pakistan, 1994. Mem., Schools Broadcasting Council, later Educn Broadcasting Council, 1982–91; occasional broadcaster on radio and TV. *Recreations:* sailing, esp. on W coast of Scotland; walking. *Address:* Applegarth, Middleton, Pickering, N Yorks YO18 8NU.

See also Very Rev. P. J. Dines.

DINES, Very Rev. Philip Joseph, (Griff), PhD; Provost and Rector of St Mary's Cathedral, Glasgow, since 1998; *b* 22 June 1959; *s* of Peter Munn Dines, *qv* and Kathleen Elisabeth Dines; *m* 1987, Dr Margaret Owen; two *d*. *Educ:* Royal Grammar Sch., Newcastle upon Tyne; University Coll. London (BScEng 1980); Clare Coll., Cambridge (PhD 1984); Westcott House, Cambridge; MA (Theol) Manchester 1993. Ordained deacon, 1986, priest, 1987; Curate: St Mary, Northolt, 1986–89; St Paul, Withington, 1989–91; Vicar, St Martin, Wythenshawe, 1991–98, and Priest-in-charge, St Francis, Newall Green, 1995–98. Mem., Iona Community, 1999–. Founder Mem., Unicorn Grocery Co-op, Manchester, 1996–. *Recreations:* travelling hopefully, exploring the boundaries, art of navigation, sailing. *Address:* Provost's Office, St Mary's Cathedral, 300 Great Western Road, Glasgow G4 9JB. *T:* (0141) 339 6691, *Fax:* (0141) 334 5669; *e-mail:* provost@glasgow.anglican.org.

DINEVOR; *see* Dynevor.

DINGEMANS, Rear-Adm. Peter George Valentin, CB 1990; DSO 1982; Head of Benefits Payroll and Insurances, Slaughter and May, since 1992; *b* 31 July 1935; *s* of Dr George Albert and Marjorie Dingemans; *m* 1961, Faith Vivien Bristow; three *s*. *Educ:* Brighton College. Entered RN 1953; served HM Ships Vanguard, Superb, Ark Royal, 1953–57; qualified Torpedo Anti Submarine specialist, 1961; Comd, HMS Maxton, 1967; RAF Staff Course, 1968; Directorate of Naval Plans, 1971–73; Comd, HMS Berwick, HMS Lowestoft, 1973–74; Staff Asst, Chief of Defence Staff, 1974–76; Captain, Fishery Protection, 1977–78; RCDS, 1979; Comd HMS Intrepid, 1980–83 (incl. service South Atlantic, 1982); Commodore, Amphibious Warfare, 1983–85; Flag Officer Gibraltar, 1985–87; COS to C-in-C Fleet, 1987–90, retd. Director: Administration, Argosy Asset Management PLC, 1990–91; Ivory and Sime, 1991–92. President: Royal Naval Assoc., Horsham, 1994–; British Legion, Cowfold, 1994–; Assoc. of Old Brightonians, 1995–97. Member Council: Brighton Coll., 1998–; Sussex Univ., 1999–. FIMgt (FBIM 1990). Freeman, City of London, 1984; Liveryman, Coach Makers and Coach Harness Makers Co., 1984. *Recreations:* family and friends, tennis, shooting. *Address:* c/o Lloyds TSB, Steyning, Sussex BN44 3ZA. *Clubs:* City Livery, Royal Naval of 1765 and 1785 (Trustee, 1995–, Chm. Trustees, 1996–).

DINGLE, John Thomas, PhD, DSc; President, Hughes Hall, Cambridge, 1993–98 (Hon. Fellow, 1998); *b* 27 Oct. 1927; *s* of Thomas Henry and Violet Nora Dingle; *m* 1953, Dorothy Vernon Parsons; two *s*. *Educ:* King Edward Sch., Bath; London Univ. (BSc, DSc); Clare Coll., Cambridge (PhD). Royal National Hosp. for Rheumatic Diseases, Bath, 1951–59; Research Fellowship, Strangeways Research Laboratory, Cambridge, 1959–61; MRC External Staff, 1961–79; Strangeways Research Laboratory: Head of Tissue Physiology Dept, 1966; Dep. Dir, 1970–79; Dir, 1979–93; Fellow, Corpus Christi Coll., Cambridge, 1968–93 (Life Fellow, 1998); Bursar of Leckhampton, 1972–80, Warden, 1980–86. Co-Dir, Rheumatism Res. Unit, Addenbrooke's Hosp., 1997–. Visiting Professor: of Biochemistry, Royal Free Hosp. Med. Sch., 1975–78; of Rheumatology, New York Univ., 1977. Chm., British Connective Tissue Soc., 1980–87. Chm. Editorial Bd, Biochemical Jl, 1975–82. Pres., Cambridge Univ. RFC, 1990– (Treas., 1982–90). Heberden Orator and Medalist, 1978; American Orthopaedic Assoc. Steindler Award, 1980. *Publications:* communications to learned jls. *Recreations:* Rugby football (playing member, Bath, Bristol, Somerset RFCs, 1943–57), sailing. *Address:* Hughes Hall, Cambridge CB1 2EW; Corpus Christi College, Cambridge CB2 1RH; Rheumatology Department, Addenbrooke's Hospital, Cambridge CB2 2QQ; Middle Watch, Mount Boone Hill, Dartmouth, Devon TQ6 9NZ. *Clubs:* Hawks (Cambridge); Royal Dart (Dartmouth).

See also T. T. Dingle.

DINGLE, Prof. Robert Balson, PhD; FRSE; Professor of Theoretical Physics, University of St Andrews, 1960–87, now Emeritus; *b* 26 March 1926; *s* of late Edward Douglas Dingle and Nora Gertrude Balson; *m* 1958, Helen Glenronnie Munro; two *d*. *Educ:* Bournemouth Secondary Sch.; Cambridge University. PhD 1951. Fellow of St John's Coll., Cambridge, 1948–52; Theoretician to Royal Society Mond Lab., 1949–52; Chief Asst in Theoretical Physics, Technical Univ. of Delft, Holland, 1952–53; Fellow, Nat. Research Council, Ottawa, 1953–54; Reader in Theoretical Physics, Univ. of WA, 1954–60. *Publications:* Asymptotic Expansions: their derivation and interpretation, 1973; contribs to learned journals. *Recreations:* music, local history, gastronomy. *Address:* 6 Lawhead Road East, St Andrews, Fife, Scotland KY16 9ND. *T:* (01334) 474287.

DINGLE, Timothy Thomas; Headmaster, Royal Grammar School, High Wycombe, since 1999; *b* 9 June 1959; *s* of Dr John Thomas Dingle, *qv*; *m* 1984, Laura Sack; one *d*. *Educ:* Perse Sch., Cambridge; UEA (BSc 1980; PGCE 1981); Univ. of Westminster (MBA 1998). Mill Hill School: Head of Biology Dept, 1985–90; Housemaster, 1990–95; Dep. Head, 1995–99. Member: Cttee, Nat. Grammar Schs Assoc., 1999–; Conservative Party Task Force on Grammar Schs, 2000–. Nat. Selector (Rugby), 1998–; Member: Cttee, England Schs RFU (16 Gp), 1997–; Middlesex RFU, 1985–2001; London and SE RFU, 1990–. *Publications:* Cartilage Disc Degeneration, 1981; European Dimension in Schools, 1994. *Recreations:* Rugby, cricket, painting, sailing, travel, poetry. *Address:* Royal Grammar School, High Wycombe, Amersham Road, High Wycombe, Bucks HP13 6QT. *T:* (01494) 551422. *Clubs:* MCC; Cambridge University RUFC.

DINGWALL, Baron; *see* Lucas of Crudwell and Dingwall.

DINGWALL-SMITH, Ronald Alfred, CB 1977; *b* 24 Feb. 1917; 2nd *s* of Robert Frederick Sydney Smith (*d* in action 1917) and Alice Olive Brookman; *m* 1946, Margaret Eileen Dingwall; adopted surname Dingwall-Smith; one *s* one *d*. *Educ:* Alleyn's Sch., Dulwich; London School of Economics (evening classes). Entered Civil Service as Clerical Officer, Ministry of Transport, 1934; Exchequer and Audit Dept, 1935–47; Scottish Educn Dept, 1947–65; Scottish Development Dept, 1965–70; Under-Sec. (Principal Finance Officer), Scottish Office, 1970–78. Sen. Res. Fellow, Glasgow Univ., 1979–81. Director: St Vincent Drilling Ltd, 1979–80; Hanover (Scotland) Housing Assoc. Ltd, 1979–92 (Chm., 1988–92); Heritage Housing Ltd, 1982–92 (Chm., 1988–92); Hanover (Caol) Housing Assoc. Ltd, 1986–92 (Chm., 1988–92). Mem., Commn for Local Auth. Accts in Scotland, 1980–85. Governor, Moray Hse Coll. of Educn, Edinburgh, 1980–87. *Recreations:* golf, bowls (Pres., Braid Bowling Club, Edinburgh, 1990 (Hon. Sec., 1980–89)), gardening. *Address:* 14 Mains Grove, Davidson's Mains, Edinburgh EH4.

DINHAM, Martin John, CBE 1997; Director, Asia and the Pacific, Department for International Development, since 2000; *b* 9 July 1950; *s* of late John A. Dinham and of Gwenyth Dinham; *m* 1980, Jannie Sanderson; one *s* one *d*. *Educ:* Haberdashers' Aske's Sch., Elstree; Christ's Coll., Cambridge (BA Mod. Langs 1971). Joined ODM, later ODA, as exec. officer, 1974; Asst Private Sec. to successive Ministers for Overseas Develt, 1978–79; Desk Officer for Zambia and Malawi, ODA, 1979–81; on secondment to World Bank, Washington, as Asst to UK Exec. Dir, 1981–83; Hd, Personnel Br., ODA, 1983–85; Private Sec. to successive Ministers for Overseas Develt, 1985–87; Hd, SE Asia Develt Div., ODA, Bangkok, 1988–92; on secondment to Hong Kong Govt as Advr to Governor, 1992–97; Hd of Personnel and Principal Estabt Officer, DFID, 1997–2000. *Recreations:* tennis, cinema, planning holidays. *Address:* Department for International Development, 1 Palace Street, SW1E 5HE. *T:* (020) 7023 0352.

DINKIN, Anthony David; QC 1991; barrister; a Recorder of the Crown Court, since 1989; *b* 2 Aug. 1944; *s* of Hyman Dinkin and late Mary (*née* Hine); *m* 1968, Derina Tanya (*née* Green), MBE. *Educ:* Henry Thornton Grammar Sch., Clapham; Coll. of Estate

Management, London (BSc (Est. Man.)). Called to the Bar, Lincoln's Inn, 1968. Legal Mem., Lands Tribunal, 1998–; Mem., Mental Health Review Tribunal, 2000–. Examr in Law, Reading Univ., 1985–93. Pres., Estate Mgt Club, 1998–99. *Recreations:* gardening, theatre, music, travel. *Address:* 2–3 Gray's Inn Square, WC1R 5JH. *T:* (020) 7242 4986. *Club:* Players.

DINWIDDY, Bruce Harry; HM Diplomatic Service; Foreign and Commonwealth Office, since 2001; *b* 1 Feb. 1946; *s* of late Thomas Lutwyche Dinwiddy and Ruth Dinwiddy (*née* Abbott); *m* 1974, Emma Victoria Llewellyn; one *s* one *d*. *Educ:* Winchester Coll.; New Coll., Oxford (MA). Economist, Govt of Swaziland (ODI Nuffield Fellow), 1967–70; Res. Officer, ODI, 1970–73; HM Diplomatic Service, 1973; First Sec., UK Deleg. to MBFR talks, Vienna, 1975–77; FCO, 1977–81; Head of Chancery, Cairo, 1981–83; FCO, 1983–86; Asst Sec., Cabinet Office, 1986–88; Counsellor, Bonn, 1989–91; Dep. High Comr, Ottawa, 1992–95; Head of African Dept (Southern), FCO, 1995–98; Comr (non-resident), British Indian Ocean Territory, 1996–98; High Comr, Tanzania, 1998–2001. *Publication:* Promoting African Enterprise, 1974. *Recreations:* golf (captained Oxford *v* Cambridge, 1967), lawn tennis, music, travel. *Address:* c/o Foreign and Commonwealth Office, SW1A 2AH. *Clubs:* Vincent's (Oxford); Aldeburgh Golf, Royal Wimbledon Golf.

DIOUF, Jacques, PhD; Director-General, United Nations Food and Agriculture Organization, since 1994; *b* 1 Aug. 1938; *m* 1963, Aïssatou Seye; one *s* four *d*. *Educ:* Ecole nationale d'agriculture, Grignon-Paris (BSc Agric.); Ecole nationale d'application d'agronomie tropicale, Nogent-Paris, (MSc Trop. Agronomy); Panthéon-Sorbonne, Paris (PhD Agricl Econs). Dir, European Office and Agricl Prog. of Mkting Bd, Dakar/Paris, 1963–64; Executive Secretary: African Groundnut Council, Lagos, 1965–71; W Africa Rice Develt Assoc., Liberia, 1971–77; Sec. of State for Sci. and Technol., Senegal, 1978–83; MP Senegambian Confedn, 1983–84: Chm. and Elected Sec., Foreign Relns Cttee, 1983–84; Chm., Friendship Parly Gp, Senegal–UK, 1983–84; Advr to Pres. and Regl Dir, Internat. Develt Res. Centre, Ottawa, 1984–85; Central Bank for W African States, Dakar: Sec.-Gen., 1985–90; Special Advr to Governor, 1990–91; Ambassador, Senegal Perm. Mission to UN, 1991–93. Comdr Legion of Honour (France), 1998; Grand Comdr, Order of Star of Africa (Liberia), 1977. Comdr, Order of Agricl Merit (Canada), 1995; Grand Cross, Order of Merit in Agric., Fisheries and Food (Spain), 1996; Grand Cross, Order of May for Merit (Argentina), 1998; Order of Solidarity (Cuba), 1998. *Publications:* contrib. to learned jls. *Address:* United Nations Food and Agriculture Organization, Viale delle Terme di Caracalla, 00100 Rome, Italy.

DI PALMA, Vera June, (Mrs Ernest Jones), OBE 1986; FCCA, FTII; Chairman, Mobile Training Ltd (formerly Mobile Training & Exhibitions Ltd), since 1978; *b* 14 July 1931; *d* of late William Di Palma and Violet Di Palma; *m* 1972, Ernest Jones (*d* 1995). *Educ:* Haverstock Central Sch., London. Accountant in public practice, 1947–64; Taxation Accountant, Dunlop Co., 1964–67; Sen. Lectr in Taxation, City of London Polytechnic, 1967–71; taxation consultant, 1971–80. Pres., Assoc. of Certified Accountants, 1980–81 (Dep. Pres., 1979–80); Public Works Loan Comr, 1978– (Dep. Chm., 1997–); Dep. Chm., Air Travel Trust Cttee, 1986–2000; Mem., VAT Tribunals, 1977–2000; Non-exec. Mem., S Warwicks HA, 1991–93. *Publications:* Capital Gains Tax, 1972, 5th edn 1981; Your Fringe Benefits, 1978. *Recreations:* dog walking, golf, tennis, dancing, gardening. *Address:* Temple Close, Sibford Gower, Banbury, Oxon OX15 5RX. *T:* (01295) 780222.

DISLEY, John Ivor, CBE 1979; Director, London Marathon Ltd, since 1980; *b* Gwynedd, 20 Nov. 1928; *s* of Harold Disley and Marie Hughes; *m* 1957, Sylvia Cheeseman; two *d*. *Educ:* Oswestry High Sch.; Loughborough Coll. (Hon. DCL). Schoolmaster, Isleworth, 1951; Chief Instructor, CCPR Nat. Mountaineering Centre, 1955; Gen. Inspector of Educn, Surrey, 1958–71. Director: Ski Plan, 1971–75; Reebok, 1985–95. Member: Adv. Sports Council, 1964–71; Mountain Leadership Trng Bd, 1965–; Canal Adv. Bd, 1965–66; Internat. Orienteering Fedn, 1972–78; Countryside Commn, 1974–77; Water Space Adv. Council, 1976–81; Royal Commn on Gambling, 1976–78. Vice-Chm., Sports Council, 1974–82; Chairman: Nat. Jogging Assoc., 1978–80; The Olympians, 1996–. Mem., British athletics team, 1950–59; Brit. record holder steeplechase, 1950–56; Welsh mile record holder, 1952–57; bronze medal, Olympics, Helsinki, 1952; Sportsman of the Year, 1955; Athlete of the Year, 1955. *Publications:* Tackle Climbing, 1959; Young Athletes Companion, 1961; Orienteering, 1966; Expedition Guide for Duke of Edinburgh's Award Scheme, 1965; Your Way with Map and Compass, 1971. *Recreations:* running games, mountain activities. *Address:* Hampton House, Upper Sunbury Road, Hampton, Middx TW12 2DW. *T:* (020) 8979 1707. *Clubs:* Alpine, Climbers'; Southern Navigators; London Athletic.

See also Rev. Canon B. L. Hebblethwaite.

DISMORE, Andrew; MP (Lab) Hendon, since 1997; *b* 2 Sept. 1954; *s* of late Ian and of Brenda Dismore. *Educ:* Warwick Univ. (LLB 1972); LSE, London Univ. (LLM 1976). Educn Asst, GMWU, 1976–78; Partner: Robin Thompson & Partners, Solicitors, 1978–95; Russell Jones & Walker, Solicitors, 1995–. Mem. (Lab), Westminster CC, 1982–97 (Leader, Labour Gp, 1990–97). *Recreations:* gardening, travel, Greece, Greek culture. *Address:* House of Commons, SW1A 0AA. *T:* (020) 7219 3000.

DISS, Eileen, (Mrs Raymond Everett), RDI 1978; freelance designer for theatre, film and television, since 1959; *b* 13 May 1931; *d* of Thomas and Winifred Diss; *m* 1953, Raymond Everett; two *s* one *d*. *Educ:* Ilford County High Sch. for Girls; Central Sch. of Art and Design. FRSA. BBC Television design, 1952–59. *Television* series and plays: Maigret, 1962–63; The Tea Party, 1964; Up the Junction, 1965; Somerset Maugham, 1969; Uncle Vanya, 1970; The Duchess of Malfi, and Candide, 1972; The Importance of Being Earnest, and Pygmalion, 1973; Caesar and Cleopatra, 1974; Moll Flanders, 1975; Ghosts, and The Winslow Boy, 1976; You Never Can Tell, 1977; The Rear Column, Hedda Gabler, 1980; The Potting Shed, 1981; Porterhouse Blue, 1987; Behaving Badly, 1989; Jeeves & Wooster, 1989, 1990, and 1992; Best of Friends, 1991; Head Over Heels, 1993; Love on a Branch Line, 1993; A Dance to the Music of Time, 1997; television opera: The Merry Widow, 1968; Tales of Hoffmann, 1969; Die Fledermaus, 1971; Falstaff, 1972; The Yeomen of the Guard, 1974; television films: Cider with Rosie, 1971; Robinson Crusoe, 1974; Longitude, 1999. *Theatre:* Exiles, 1969; Butley, 1971; The Caretaker, 1972 and 1991; Otherwise Engaged, 1975; The Apple-cart, 1977; The Rear Column, The Homecoming, 1978; The Hothouse, 1980; Translations, Quartermaine's Terms, Incident at Tulse Hill, 1981; Rocket to the Moon, 1982; The Communication Cord, 1983; The Common Pursuit, 1984; Other Places, The Seagull, Sweet Bird of Youth, 1985; Circe and Bravo, 1986; The Deep Blue Sea, 1988; Veterans Day, The Mikado, Steel Magnolias, 1989; Burn This, 1990; The Philanthropist, 1991; Private Lives, A Month in the Country, 1992; Oleanna, 1993; Pinter Fest., Dublin, 1994; Cell Mates, 1995; Taking Sides, The Hothouse, 1995; Twelve Angry Men, 1996; Ashes to Ashes, 1996; Life Support, 1997; A Letter of Resignation, 1997; The Heiress, 1997; Arcadia, 1999; The Late Middle Classes, 1999; The Room, and Celebration, 2000; Port Authority, and The Homecoming, 2001; National Theatre: Blithe Spirit, 1976; The Philanderer, 1978; Close of Play, When We Are Married, 1979; Watch on the Rhine, 1980; The Caretaker, 1980; Measure for Measure, 1981; The Trojan War Will Not Take Place, 1983; Landscape, 1994. *Films:* Joseph Losey's A Doll's House, 1972; Sweet William, 1978; Harold Pinter's Betrayal, 1982; Secret Places, 1984; 84 Charing Cross Road, 1986; A Handful of Dust, 1988; August, 1994. BAFTA Television Design Award, 1962, 1965, 1974 and 1992. *Recreations:* music, cinema. *Address:* 4 Gloucester Walk, W8 4HZ. *T:* (020) 7937 8794.

DITLHABI OLIPHANT, Tuelonyana Rosemary; Permanent Secretary for Political Affairs, Botswana, since 1999 (Deputy Permanent Secretary, 1998–99); *b* 13 Sept. 1954; *d* of late Matlhape Ditlhabi and of Tsetsele Ditlhabi; *m* 1986, Clement S. Oliphant; one *s*. *Educ:* Univ. of Botswana (BA Admin 1977); Pennsylvania State Univ. (MPA 1981). Joined Public Service, Botswana, 1977: Asst, Sen. and Principal Admin Officer, Min. of Mineral Resources and Water Affairs, 1977–85; transferred to Dept of Foreign Affairs, 1985: Counsellor: Washington, 1985–88; NY, 1988–90; High Comr, Namibia and Ambassador, Angola, 1990–96; Doyenne of Diplomatic Corps and African Gp, 1992–96; High Comr, UK, 1996–98. *Recreations:* music, reading, swimming, squash. *Address:* c/o Office of the President, Private Bag 001, Gaborone, Botswana; *e-mail:* toliphant@gov.bw.

DITTNER, Patricia Ann; *see* Troop, P. A.

DIX, Alan Michael, OBE 1985; Director General, Motor Agents' Association Ltd, 1976–85; *b* 29 June 1922; *s* of late Comdr Charles Cabry Dix, CMG, DSO, RN, and Ebba Sievers; *m* 1955, Helen Catherine McLaren; one *s* one *d*. *Educ:* Stenhus Kostskole, Denmark. Escaped Nazi occupied Denmark to Scotland, 1943; joined RAF, commissioned 1944. President, Capitol Car Distributors Inc., USA, 1958–67; Gp Vice-Pres., Volkswagen of America, USA, 1967–68; Man. Dir, Volkswagen (GB) Ltd, London, 1968–72; Pres., Mid Atlantic Toyota Inc., USA, 1972–73; Dir Marketing, British Leyland International, 1973–74; Proprietor, Alan M. Dix Associates, 1974–76. Chm., Motor Agents Pensions Administrators Ltd, 1976–85; Dir, Hire Purchase Information Ltd, 1977–85. Freedom and Livery, Coachmakers' and Coach Harness Makers' Co., 1980. FIMI, FInstM, FIMH, FIMgt. King Christian X war medal, 1947. *Publications:* contribs to automotive trade jls. *Recreations:* yachting, photography; the study of professional management (internat. speaker on management and organisation). *Address:* Hillside, Peebles, Letham Grange, Arbroath, Angus DD11 4QA. *T:* (01241) 890421. *Clubs:* Danish, Royal Air Force, Burkes; Royal Air Force Yacht (Hamble).

DIX, Geoffrey Herbert, OBE 1979; Secretary-General, The Institute of Bankers, 1971–82; *b* 1 March 1922; *o s* of late Herbert Walter and Winifred Ada Dix; *m* 1945, Margaret Sybil Outhwaite, MA (Cantab) (*d* 1981); one *s*. *Educ:* Watford Grammar Sch.; Gonville and Caius Coll., Cambridge. MA (Mod. langs). Served War, 1942–45: commissioned into Royal Devon Yeomanry; later served with HQ 1st Airborne Corps. Inst. of Export, 1946–51; with Inst. of Bankers, 1951–: Asst Sec., 1956; Under-Sec. 1962; Dep. Sec. 1968. Mem., Jt Cttee for National Awards in Business Studies, 1960–76. *Recreations:* Mozart, theatre. *Address:* 2 Kirklands, Old Costessey, Norwich NR8 5BW. *T:* (01603) 745181. *Club:* Caterham Players.

DIX, Prof. Gerald Bennett, RIBA; Lever Professor of Civic Design, University of Liverpool, 1975–88; Professor Emeritus and Hon. Senior Fellow, Liverpool University, since 1988; Hon. Senior Research Fellow, Chinese Research Academy of Environmental Sciences, since 1989; *b* 12 Jan. 1926; *s* of late Cyril Dix and Mabel Winifred (*née* Bennett); *m* 1st, 1956 (marr. diss.); two *s*; 2nd, 1963, Lois Nichols; one *d*. *Educ:* Altrincham Grammar Sch.; Univ. of Manchester (BA (Hons Arch.), DipTP (dist.)); Harvard Univ. (MLA). Studio Asst, 1950–51, Asst Lectr in Town and Country Planning, 1951–53, Manchester Univ.; Asst Architect, 1954; Chief Architect-Planner, Addis Ababa, and chief asst to Sir Patrick Abercrombie, 1954–56; Planning Officer, Singapore, 1957–59; Acting Planning Adviser, 1959; Sen. Research Fellow, Univ. of Science and Technol., Ghana, 1959–63; UN Planning Mission to Ghana, 1962; Planner, later Sen. Planner, BRS/ODM, 1963–65 (adv. missions to W Indies, W Africa, Aden, Bechuanaland, Swaziland, Cyprus); Nottingham University: Lectr, 1966–68; Sen. Lectr, 1968–70; Prof. of Planning, and Dir, Inst. of Planning Studies, 1970–75; Liverpool University: Chm., Fac. of Social and Environmental Studies, 1983–84; Pro Vice-Chancellor, 1984–87. Dir, Cyprus Planning Project, 1967–71; adv. visits on planning educn, to Uganda 1971, Nigeria 1972, Sudan 1975, Mexico 1978, Egypt 1980; UK Mem., Adv. Panel on planning Canal towns, Egypt, 1974, and Western Desert, 1975; Jt Dir, Alexandria Comprehensive Master Plan Project, 1980–86. Member: Professional Literature Cttee, RIBA, 1966–80, 1981–88 (Chm. 1975–80); Library Management Cttee, 1969–72, 1975–80; Historic Areas Adv. Cttee, English Heritage, 1986–88. Vice-Pres., World Soc. for Ekistics, 1975–79, Pres., 1987–90. Editorial adviser, Ekistics (journal), 1972–; Chm., Bd of Management, Town Planning Rev., 1976–88; (Founder) Editor, Third World Planning Rev., 1978–90. FRTPI (resigned 2001); FRSA. Hon. DEng Dong-A Univ., Korea, 1995. *Publications:* ed, C. A. Doxiadis, Ecology and Ekistics, 1977, Boulder, Colo, 1978, Brisbane, 1978; numerous planning reports to govts in various parts of world; articles and reviews in Town Planning Rev., Third World Planning Rev., Ekistics, RIBA Jl, Arch. Rev. *Recreations:* photography, listening to music, travel, cooking. *Address:* 13 Friar's Quay, Norwich, Norfolk NR3 1ES. *T:* (01603) 632433. *Club:* Athenæum.

DIXEY, John, OBE 1976; Newspaper Consultant, since 1991; Development Co-ordinator, Evening Standard Company, since 1987; *b* 29 March 1926; *s* of John Dixey and Muriel Doris Dixey; *m* 1948, Pauline Seaden; one *s* one *d*. *Educ:* Battersea Grammar Sch. Served Royal Marines and Royal Fusiliers, 1944–47. Press Telegraphist, Yorkshire Post and Glasgow Herald, 1948–59; Asst to Gen. Sec., Nat. Union of Press Telegraphists, 1959; Labour Officer, Newspaper Soc., 1959–63; Labour Adviser, Thomson Organisation Ltd, 1963–64; Asst Gen. Man., Liverpool Daily Post & Echo, 1964–67; Executive Dir, Times Newspapers, 1967–74; Special Adviser to Man. Dir, Thomson Org., 1974; Dir, Newspaper Publishers Assoc. Ltd, 1975–76; Employment Affairs Advr, IPA, 1977–79; Sec., Assoc. of Midland Advertising Agencies, 1977–79; Production Dir and Bd Mem., The Guardian, 1979–84; Asst Man. Dir, Mirror Gp Newspapers, 1985; Newspaper Consultant, 1986. Chm., Advertising Assoc. Trade Union Liaison Group, 1975–84; Mem., TUC New Daily Newspaper Advisory Group, 1982–83. Ward-Perkins Vis. Fellow, Pembroke Coll., Oxford, 1978. Mem., Printing and Publishing Industry Trng Bd, 1975–76; Governor, London Coll. of Printing, 1975–76. *Recreations:* cooking, photography. *Address:* 23 West Hill, Sanderstead, Surrey CR2 0SB. *T:* (020) 8657 7940.

DIXIT, Prof. Avinash Kamalakar; John J. F. Sherrerd '52 Professor of Economics, Princeton University, USA, since 1989 (Professor of Economics, 1981–89); *b* 8 June 1944; *s* of Kamalakar Ramchandra Dixit and Kusum Dixit (*née* Phadke). *Educ:* Bombay Univ. (BSc); Cambridge Univ. (BA, MA); Massachusetts Inst. of Technology (PhD). Acting Asst Professor, Univ. of California, Berkeley, 1968–69; Lord Thomson of Fleet Fellow and Tutor in Economics, Balliol Coll., Oxford, 1970–74; Professor of Economics, Univ. of Warwick, 1974–80. Guggenheim Fellowship, 1991–92. Fellow: Econometric Society, 1977 (Pres., 2001); Amer. Acad. of Arts and Scis, 1992. Co-Editor, Bell Journal of Economics, 1981–83. *Publications:* Optimization in Economic Theory, 1976; The Theory of Equilibrium Growth, 1976; (with Victor Norman) Theory of International Trade, 1980; (with Barry Nalebuff) Thinking Strategically, 1991; (with Robert S. Pindyck) Investment Under Uncertainty, 1994; The Making of Economic Policy: a transaction-cost politics perspective, 1996; (with Susan Skeath) Games of Strategy, 1999; several articles in professional jls. *Recreations:* listening to music (pre-Schubert only), watching cricket (when possible). *Address:* Department of Economics, Princeton University, Princeton, NJ 08544, USA. *T:* (609) 2584013; *e-mail:* dixitak@princeton.edu.

DIXON; *see* Graham-Dixon.

DIXON, family name of **Barons Dixon** and **Glentoran**.

DIXON, Baron *cr* 1997 (Life Peer), of Jarrow in the co. of Tyne and Wear; **Donald Dixon;** PC 1996; DL; *b* 6 March 1929; *s* of late Christopher Albert Dixon and Jane Dixon; *m* Doreen Morad; one *s* one *d*. *Educ:* Ellison Street Elementary School, Jarrow. Shipyard Worker, 1947–74; Branch Sec., GMWU, 1974–79. Councillor, South Tyneside MDC, 1963–81. MP (Lab) Jarrow, 1979–97. An Opposition Whip, 1984–96, Dep. Chief Opposition Whip, 1987–96. Mem. Select Cttee on H of C Services; Chm., PLP Shipbuilding Gp. Freeman of: Jarrow, 1972; S Tyneside, 1998. DL Tyne and Wear, 1997. *Recreations:* football, reading. *Address:* 1 Hillcrest, Jarrow NE32 4DP. *T:* (0191) 897635. *Clubs:* Jarrow Labour, Ex Servicemen's (Jarrow); Hastings (Hebburn).

DIXON, Prof. Adrian Kendal, MD; FRCP, FRCR, FMedSci; Professor of Radiology, University of Cambridge, since 1994; Fellow of Peterhouse, Cambridge, since 1986; *b* 5 Feb. 1948; *s* of Kendal Cartwright Dixon and Anne Sybil (*née* Darley); *m* 1979, Anne Hazel Lucas; two *s* one *d*. *Educ:* Uppingham; King's Coll., Cambridge; St Bartholomew's Hosp. Med. Coll., London; MDCantab 1988. FRCR 1978; FRCP 1991. Medical posts in: St Bartholomew's Hosp., 1972–79; Gen. Hosp., Nottingham, 1973–75; Hosp. for Sick Children, Gt Ormond St, 1978; Lectr, Dept of Radiology, Univ. of Cambridge, 1979–94; Hon. Cons. Radiologist, Addenbrooke's Hosp., Cambridge, 1979–. Visiting Professor: Md and Washington, 1988; Dublin, 1991; Univ. of Otago, NZ, 1992. Arnott Demonstrator, RCS, 1995; Skinner Lectr, RCR, 1996. FMedSci 1998. Hon. Fellow, Faculty of Radiology, RCSI, 1999 (Houghton Medal, 1999). Editor, Clinical Radiology, 1998–. *Publications:* Body CT, 1983; CT and MRI, Radiological Anatomy, 1991; Human Cross Sectional Anatomy, 1991, 2nd edn as Human Sectional Anatomy, 1999; papers on computed tomography, magnetic resonance imaging and radiological strategies. *Recreations:* family, golf. *Address:* Peterhouse, Cambridge CB2 1RD. *T:* (01223) 336890.

DIXON, Dr Bernard, OBE 2000; science writer and consultant; *b* Darlington, 17 July 1938; *s* of late Ronald Dixon and Grace Peirson; *m* 1963, Margaret Helena Charlton (marr. diss. 1988); two *s* one *d*. *Educ:* Queen Elizabeth Grammar Sch., Darlington; King's Coll., Univ. of Durham; Univ. of Newcastle upon Tyne. BSc, PhD. Luccock Res. Fellow, 1961–64, Frank Schon Fellow, 1964–65, Univ. of Newcastle; Asst Editor, 1965–66, Dep. Editor, 1966–68, World Medicine; Editor, New Scientist, 1969–79; European Editor: The Scientist, 1986–89; Bio Technology, 1989–97; Amer. Soc. for Microbiol., 1997–; Mem. Editorial Board: Biologist, 1988–; World Jl of Microbiology and Biotechnology, 1988–; Columnist, Current Biol., Lancet, Infectious Diseases. Chm., Cttee, Assoc. of British Science Writers, 1971–72; Member: Soc. for General Microbiology, 1962–; Amer. Inst. of Biol Sci., 1986–; European Assoc. of Sci. Eds, 1980–; Amer. Assoc. for Advancement of Sci., 1980–; CSS, 1982–91 (Vice-Chm., 1989–91); Soc. for Applied Microbiol. (formerly Applied Bacteriol.), 1989–; Amer. Soc. for Microbiology, 1995–; Council: BAAS, 1977–83 (Pres., Section X, 1979; Vice-Pres., 1986–); European Envtl Res. Orgn; Bd, Edinburgh Internat. Science Fest., 1990–. Convenor, Eur. Fedn of Biotechnology Task Gp on Public Perceptions of Biotechnol., 1996–. FIBiol 1982; CBiol 1984. Hon. DSc Edinburgh, 1996. Charter Award, Inst. of Biol., 1999. *Publications:* (ed) Journeys in Belief, 1968; What is Science For?, 1973; Magnificent Microbes, 1976; Invisible Allies, 1976; Beyond the Magic Bullet, 1978; (with G. Holister) Ideas of Science, 1984; Health and the Human Body, 1986; Engineered Organisms in the Environment, 1986; Recombinant DNA: what's it all about, 1987; The Science of Science: changing the way we think, 1989; The Science of Science: changing the way we live, 1989; (ed) From Creation to Chaos: classic writings in science, 1989; (with A. L. W. F. Eddleston) Interferons in the Treatment of Chronic Virus Infections of the Liver, 1989; (with E. Millstone) Our Genetic Future: the science and ethics of genetic technology, 1992; Genetics and the Understanding of Life, 1993; Power Unseen: how microbes rule the world, 1994; Enzymes Make the World Go Round, 1994; *contributor to:* Animal Rights—A Symposium, 1979; The Book of Predictions, 1980; Development of Science Publishing in Europe, 1980; Medicine and Care, 1981; From Biology to Biotechnology, 1982; Encyclopædia Britannica, 15th edn, 1984; Encyclopædia Britannica Yearbook, 1986–; Inquiry into Life, 1986; The Domesday Project, 1986; Industrial Biotechnology in Europe: issues for public policy, 1986; Biotechnology Information, 1987; Future Earth, 1989; Harrap's Illustrated Dictionary of Science, 1989; Biotechnology—A Brave New World?, 1989; Soundings from BMJ columnists, 1993; Taking Sides: clashing views on controversial issues in health and society, 1993; Wider Application and Diffusion of Bioremediation Technologies, 1996; Biotechnology for Clean Industrial Products and Processes, 1998; numerous articles in scientific and general press on microbiology, and other scientific topics. *Recreation:* listening to Elgar, Mahler and Scottish traditional music, collecting old books. *Address:* 130 Cornwall Road, Ruislip Manor, Middlesex HA4 6AW. *T:* (01895) 632390, *Fax:* (01895) 678645.

DIXON, Bernard Tunbridge; legal consultant; *b* 14 July 1928; *s* of Archibald Tunbridge Dixon and Dorothy Dixon (*née* Cardinal); *m* 1962, Jessie Netta Watson Hastie; one *s* three *d*. *Educ:* Owen's Sch.; University Coll. London (LLB). Admitted Solicitor, 1952 (Edmund Thomas Child Prize); Partner in Dixon & Co., Solicitors, 1952–59; Legal Asst/Sen. Legal Asst with Treasury Solicitor, 1959–67; Sen. Legal Asst with Land Commission, 1967–70; Sen. Legal Asst with Charity Comrs, 1970–74; Dep. Charity Comr, 1975–81; Charity Comr, 1981–84. *Recreations:* photography, exploring Lancashire. *Address:* c/o Maxwell Entwistle & Byrne, 14 Castle Street, Liverpool L2 0SG.

DIXON, Sir (David) Jeremy, Kt 2000; RIBA; architect in private practice; Principal, Jeremy Dixon·Edward Jones, since 1991; *b* 31 May 1939; *s* of late Joseph Lawrence Dixon and Beryl Margaret Dixon (*née* Braund); *m* 1964, Fenella Mary Anne Clemens (separated 1990); one *s* two *d*; partner, Julia Somerville, *qv*. *Educ:* Merchant Taylors' School; Architectural Assoc. Sch. of Architecture (AA Dip. (Hons)). Principal: Jeremy Dixon, 1975–90 (with Fenella Dixon); Jeremy Dixon BDP, 1983–90. Work includes: international competitions, first prize: Northampton County Offices, 1973; (with William Jack) Royal Opera House, 1983; Piazzale Roma, Venice, 1990; other competitions won: housing, Lanark Road, London, 1982; Tate Gallery Coffee Shop and Restaurant, 1984; Study Centre, Darwin Coll., Cambridge, 1988; Robert Gordon Univ. Residence, Aberdeen, 1991; Portsmouth Univ. Science Bldg, 1993; Nat. Portrait Gallery extension, 1994; Saïd Business Sch., Oxford, 1996; other works: reconstruction of Tatlin Tower, 1971; London housing, St Mark's Road, 1975, Ashmill Street, 1984; Compass Point, Docklands, 1989; Henry Moore Sculpture Inst., Leeds, 1988; Sainsbury's superstore, Plymouth, 1991. Tutor: Architectural Assoc., 1974–83; RCA, 1979–81. Chm., RIBA Regl Awards Gp, 1991–. Exhibitions: Venice Biennale, 1980; Paris, 1981; Bordeaux Chateau, Paris, 1988. *Recreations:* walking in English landscape, contemporary sculpture and painting, music. *Address:* (office) Unit 6c, 44 Gloucester Avenue, NW1 8JD. *Club:* Peg's.

DIXON, Prof. Gordon Henry, OC 1993; PhD; FRS 1978; FRSC; Professor of Medical Biochemistry, 1974–94, now Emeritus, and Head of the Department, 1983–88, Faculty of Medicine, University of Calgary; *b* 25 March 1930; *s* of Walter James Dixon and Ruth Nightingale; *m* 1954, Sylvia Weir Gillen; three *s* one *d*. *Educ:* Cambs High Sch. for Boys; Trinity Coll., Cambridge (Open Schol. 1948; BA Hons, MA); Univ. of Toronto (PhD). FRSC 1970. Res. Asst Prof., Dept of Biochem., Univ. of Washington, Seattle, USA, 1954–58; Mem. staff, MRC Unit for res. in cell metabolism, Univ. of Oxford, 1958–59; Univ. of Toronto: Res. Associate, Connaught Med. Res. Lab., 1959–60; Associate Prof., Dept of Biochem., 1960–63; Prof., Dept of Biochem., Univ. of BC, Vancouver, 1963–72; Prof., Biochem. Group, Univ. of Sussex, 1972–74. Vis. Fellow Commoner, Trinity Coll., Cambridge, 1979–80. Mem. Exec., IUBMB (formerly IUB), 1988–94; President: Canadian Biochemical Soc., 1982–83; Pan-American Assoc. of Biochemical Socs, 1987–90 (Vice-Pres., 1984–87; Past Pres., 1990–93). Ayerst Award, Canadian Biochemistry Soc., 1966; Steacie Prize, 1966; Flavelle Medal, RSC, 1980; Izaak Walton Killam Meml Prize, 1991. *Publications:* over 200 pubns in learned jls, incl. Jl Biol Chem., Proc. Nat. Acad. Sci. (US), Nature, and Biochemistry. *Recreations:* music, reading, gardening. *Address:* 4402 Shore Way, Victoria, BC V8N 3T9, Canada.

DIXON, (Henry) Joly; Deputy Special Representative in charge of economic reconstruction and development, UN Mission, Kosovo, since 1999 (on secondment); *b* 13 Jan. 1945; *s* of late Gervais Joly Dixon and Kay Dixon; *m* 1976, Mary Minch; three *s* two *d*. *Educ:* Shrewsbury Sch.; York Univ. Lecturer in: Econs and Stats, York Univ., 1970–72; Econs, Exeter Univ., 1972–74; European Commission, 1975–: Econ. Advr to Jacques Delors, 1987–92; Dir for Internat. Econ. and Financial Affairs, 1992–99. Guest Scholar, Brookings Instn, Washington, 1980. *Recreations:* gardening, photography. *Address:* 70 rue Notre Dame, 1200 Brussels, Belgium. *T:* (2) 7706977; *e-mail:* JDX@pophost.ennet.be.

DIXON, Sir Jeremy; *see* Dixon, Sir D. J.

DIXON, Joly; *see* Dixon, H. J.

DIXON, Jon Edmund, CMG 1975; Under Secretary, Ministry of Agriculture, Fisheries and Food, 1971–85; *b* 19 Nov. 1928; *e s* of Edmund Joseph Claude and Gwendoline Alice Dixon; *m* 1953, Betty Edith Stone; two *s* one *d* (and one *d* decd). *Educ:* St Paul's Sch., West Kensington; Peterhouse, Cambridge (Natural Sciences Tripos Part I and Part II (Physiology); MA). Asst Principal, Min. of Agric. and Fisheries, 1952; Private Sec. to successive Parliamentary Secretaries, 1955–58; Principal, 1958; Asst Sec., 1966; Under-Sec., 1971; Minister in UK Delegn, subseq. Office of Permanent Rep., to EEC, 1972–75. Founder, Music Publisher and Gen. Editor, JOED Music, 1988– (editing and publishing Renaissance polyphonic choral music). Recordings: Choral, Organ and String Music: a selection of works by Jon Dixon, 1970–85 (two LPs), 1986. *Publications:* Calico Pie (suite for vocal sextet), 1988; The Leuven Carols, 1988; The Pobble Who Has No Toes (4 part-songs), 1989; Missa pro defunctis super Regina coeli (for double choir), 1999; editions of Renaissance choral music by Animuccia, Arcadelt, Byrd, Clemens, Croce, Dering, Ferrabosco, Festa, A. Gabrieli, G. Gabrieli, Gombert, Guerrero, Hassler, Josquin, Lassus, de Monte, Morales, Mouton, Mundy, Palestrina, Philips, Schütz, Senfl, Sheppard, Taverner, Tallis, de Silva, Victoria (complete works), Walther, White and Willaert; contribs to Early Music News, Early Music Review, Musical Times. *Recreations:* musical composition, oil painting, building harpsichords, gardening, walking.

DIXON, Sir Jonathan (Mark), 4th Bt *cr* 1919, of Astle, Chelford, Co. Chester; Technical and Development Director, Lawson Mardon Flexible, since 1989; *b* 1 Sept. 1949; *s* of Captain Nigel Dixon, OBE, RN (*d* 1978), and of Margaret Josephine Dixon; *S* uncle, 1990; *m* 1978, Patricia Margaret, *d* of James Baird Smith; two *s* one *d*. *Educ:* Winchester Coll.; University Coll., Oxford (MA). *Recreation:* fishing. *Heir: s* Mark Edward Dixon, *b* 29 June 1982. *Address:* 19 Clyde Road, Redland, Bristol BS6 6RJ.

DIXON, Kenneth Herbert Morley, CBE 1996; DL; Chairman: Joseph Rowntree Foundation, since 2001; Rowntree (formerly Rowntree Mackintosh) plc, 1981–89, retired; Vice-Chairman, Legal & General Group, 1986–94 (Director, 1984–94); Deputy Chairman, Bass, 1990–96 (Director, 1988–96); *b* 19 Aug. 1929; *yr s* of Arnold Morley Dixon and Mary Jolly; *m* 1955, Patricia Oldbury Whalley; two *s*. *Educ:* Cathedral Sch., Shanghai; Cranbrook Sch., Sydney, Australia; Manchester Univ. (BA(Econ) 1952); Harvard Business Sch. AMP, 1969. Lieut Royal Signals, 1947–49. Calico Printers Assoc., 1952–56; joined Rowntree & Co. Ltd, 1956; Dir, 1970; Chm., UK Confectionery Div., 1973–78; Dep. Chm., 1978–81. Dir, Yorkshire–Tyne Tees (formerly Yorks) TV Hldgs, 1989–97; Mem., British Railways Bd, 1990–97. Member: Council, Incorporated Soc. of British Advertisers, 1971–79; Council, Cocoa, Chocolate and Confectionery Alliance, 1972–79; Council, Advertising Assoc., 1976–79; BIM Econ. and Social Affairs Cttee, 1980–84; Council, CBI, 1981–90 (Mem., Companies Cttee, 1979–84; Mem., Employment Policy Cttee, 1983–90); Governing Council, Business in the Community, 1983–90; Council, Food from Britain, 1986–89; Exec. Cttee, Food and Drink Fedn, 1986–89 (Mem. Council, 1986–87); Council for Industry and Higher Educn, 1986–97; Council, Nat. Forum for Management Educn & Develt, 1987–96; HEQC (Chm., Quality Audit Steering Council, 1993–97); Chm., Cttee of Univ. Chairmen, 1998–2000. Chm., Food Assoc., 1986. Mem. Exec. Cttee and Council, York Civic Trust, 1996–. Trustee, Joseph Rowntree Foundn, 1996 (Dep. Chm., 1998). Treas., York Archaeol Trust, 1993–97. Mem. Council, York Univ., 1983–2001 (Chm., 1990–2001), Pro-Chancellor, 1987–2001; Chm., Vis. Cttee, Open Univ., 1990–92. FRSA; CIMgt. Member: Co. of Merchant Adventurers, 1981–; Co. of Merchant Taylors, 1981–. DL N Yorks, 1991. DUniv: York, 1993; Open, 1997. *Recreations:* reading, music, fell walking. *Address:* Joseph Rowntree Foundation, The Homestead, Water End, York YO30 6WP. *T:* (01904) 615901. *Club:* Reform.

DIXON, Dr Michael; Director General, Zoological Society of London, since 2000; *b* 16 March 1956; *s* of Walter Dixon and late Sonia Ivy Dixon (*née* Doidge); *m* 1988, Richenda Milton-Thompson (marr. diss. 1999); two *s* one *d*. *Educ:* Tiffin Boys' Sch., Kingston-upon-Thames; Imperial Coll., London (BSc; ARCS); Univ. of York (DPhil 1984). Sponsoring Ed., Pitman Publishing Ltd, 1980–83; Publisher, then Publishing Dir, John Wiley & Sons Ltd, 1983–96; Man. Dir, Thomson Sci. Europe, 1996–98; Gp Man. Dir, Sweet & Maxwell Ltd, 1998–99. *Recreations:* natural history, photography, music. *Address:* Zoological Society of London, Regent's Park, NW1 4RY. *T:* (020) 7449 6207. *Club:* Royal Society of Medicine.

DIXON, Dr Philip Willis, FSA, FRHistS; Reader in Archaeology, University of Nottingham, since 1996; *b* 2 Jan. 1945; *s* of Dr C. Willis Dixon and Marjorie Dixon (*née* Harbron); *m* 1st, 1968, Doris Janet Davenport Sisson (marr. diss. 1973); 2nd, 1979, Patricia Borne (*d* 1987); 3rd, 2001, Jan White (*née* Greenwood). *Educ:* Tiffin Sch.; New Coll.,

Oxford (MA 1971; DPhil 1976). FSA 1977; FRHistS 1995. Lectr, 1972–81, Sen. Lectr, 1981–96, Nottingham Univ. Vis. Prof., Univ. of Aarhus, Denmark, 1997. Comr, Cathedrals Fabric Commn, 1996–. Sec., 1981–95, Pres., 1995–98, Council for British Archaeol. Director of excavations: Crickley Hill, Glos, 1969–96; Greenwich Palace, 1970–71; Richmond Palace, 1972, and other sites. *Publications:* Excavations at Greenwich Palace, 1972; Barbarian Europe, 1976; Crickley Hill: the Defences, 1994, the Hillfort Settlement, 2001, the Long Mound, 2002; contrib. numerous articles to learned jls. *Recreation:* visiting places, photographing them and consuming their food and drink. *Address:* Castle End, Dunstanburgh Road, Craster, Alnwick, Northumberland NE66 3TT. *T:* (01665) 576064.

DIXON, Piers; *b* 29 Dec. 1928; *s* of late Sir Pierson Dixon (British Ambassador in New York and Paris) and Lady (Ismene) Dixon; *m* 1st, 1960, Edwina (marr. diss. 1973), *d* of Rt Hon. Lord Duncan-Sandys, CH, PC; two *s*; 2nd, 1976, Janet (marr. diss. 1981), *d* of R. D. Aiyar, FRCS, and *widow* of 5th Earl Cowley; 3rd, 1984, Anne (marr. diss. 1985), *d* of John Cronin; one *s*; 4th, 1994, Ann Mavroleon, *d* of John Davenport. *Educ:* Eton (schol.); Magdalene Coll., Cambridge (exhibnr); Harvard Business Sch. Grenadier Guards, 1948. Merchant banking, London and New York, 1954–64; Sheppards and Chase, stockbrokers, 1964–81. Centre for Policy Studies, 1976–78. Contested (C) Brixton, 1966; MP (C) Truro, 1970–Sept. 1974; Sec., Cons. Backbenchers' Finance Cttee, 1970–71, Vice-Chm., 1972–74; sponsor of Rehabilitation of Offenders Act, 1974. *Publications:* Double Diploma, 1968; Cornish Names, 1973. *Recreations:* tennis, modern history. *Address:* 22 Ponsonby Terrace, SW1P 4QA. *T:* (020) 7828 6226. *Clubs:* Beefsteak, Brooks's, Pratt's.

DIXON, Prof. Raymond Alan, DPhil; FRS 1999; Research Group Leader, Nitrogen Fixation Laboratory and Department of Molecular Microbiology, John Innes Centre, since 1995; *b* 1 Dec. 1947; *s* of late Henry George Dixon and of Emily Dixon (*née* Emmins); *m* 1st, 1971, Ing-Britt Maj Wennerhag (marr. diss. 1980); one *d*; 2nd, 1985, Greta Margaret Dunne (marr. diss. 1995). *Educ:* Univ. of Reading (BSc 1st cl. Hons Microbiology 1969); Univ. of Sussex (DPhil Microbial Genetics 1972). University of Sussex: Postdoctoral Res. Fellow, 1973–75; Higher Scientific Officer, 1975–76, SSO, 1976–78, PSO, 1978–87, SPSO, 1987–95, Unit of Nitrogen Fixation. Hon. Prof., UEA, 1998–. Mem., EMBO, 1987. Fleming Medal, Soc. for Gen. Microbiology, 1984. *Publications:* numerous articles in learned jls. *Recreations:* music, various outdoor pursuits. *Address:* Department of Molecular Microbiology, John Innes Centre, Norwich NR4 7UH. *T:* (01603) 450747.

DIXON, Prof. Richard Newland, PhD, ScD; FRS 1986; CChem, FRSC; Senior Research Fellow, since 1996, and Alfred Capper Pass Professor of Chemistry, 1990–96, now Emeritus Professor, University of Bristol; *b* 25 Dec. 1930; *s* of late Robert Thomas Dixon and Lilian Dixon; *m* 1954, Alison Mary Birks; one *s* two *d*. *Educ:* The Judd Sch., Tonbridge; King's Coll., Univ. of London (BSc 1951); St Catharine's Coll., Univ. of Cambridge (PhD 1955; ScD 1976). FRSC 1976. Scientific Officer, UKAEA, 1954–56; Res. Associate, Univ. of Western Ontario, 1956–57; Postdoctoral Fellow, NRCC, Ottawa, 1957–59; ICI Fellow, Univ. of Sheffield, 1959–60, Lectr in Chem., 1960–69; Bristol University: Prof. and Hd of Dept of Theoretical Chemistry, 1969–90; Dean, Faculty of Science, 1979–82; Pro-Vice-Chancellor, 1989–92. Sorby Res. Fellow, Royal Soc., 1964–69; Vis. Schol., Stanford Univ., 1982–83. Leverhulme Emeritus Fellow, 1996–98. Hallam Lectr, Univ. of Wales, 1988; Harkins Lectr, Univ. of Chicago, 1994. Mem. Council, Faraday Div., RSC, 1985–98, Vice-Pres., 1989–98; Mem., and Chm. sub-cttee, Laser Facility Cttee, SERC, 1987–90. Non-exec. Dir, United Bristol Healthcare NHS Trust, 1994– (Vice-Chm., 1995–). Corday-Morgan Medal, Chemical Soc., 1966; RSC Award for Spectroscopy, 1984; Liversidge Lectr and Medal, RSC, 1993–94. *Publications:* Spectroscopy and Structure, 1965; Theoretical Chemistry: Vol. 1, 1974, Vol. 2, 1975, Vol. 3, 1978; numerous articles in res. jls of chemistry and physics. *Recreations:* mountain walking, travel, theatre, concerts. *Address:* 22 Westbury Lane, Bristol BS9 2PE. *T:* (0117) 968 1691; School of Chemistry, The University, Bristol BS8 1TS. *T:* (0117) 928 7661; *e-mail:* r.n.dixon@bris.ac.uk.

DIXON, Maj.-Gen. Roy Laurence Cayley, CB 1977; CVO 1991; MC 1944; Chapter Clerk, College of St George, Windsor Castle, 1981–90; *b* 19 Sept. 1924; *s* of Lt-Col Sidney Frank Dixon, MC and Edith Mary (Sheena) (*née* Clark); *m* 1986, Anne Maureen Aspeslåen (marr. diss. 1988). *Educ:* Haileybury; Edinburgh Univ. Commnd Royal Tank Regt, 1944; served in armd units and on staff; psc 1956; Instructor, Staff Coll., 1961–64; comd 5th Royal Tank Regt, 1966–67; Royal Coll. of Defence Studies, 1971; Comdr Royal Armd Corps, Germany, 1968–70; qual. helicopter pilot, 1973; Dir, Army Air Corps, 1974–76; Chief of Staff, Allied Forces Northern Europe, 1977–80. Col Comdt, RTR, 1978–83. Vice-Pres., Salisbury Civic Soc., 1998– (Chm., 1991–97). Freeman, City of London, 1990. *Address:* c/o Lloyds TSB, Cox's & Kings Branch, PO Box 1190, 7 Pall Mall, SW1Y 5NA. *Club:* Army and Navy.

DIXON-LEWIS, Prof. Graham, DPhil; FRS 1995; Professor of Combustion Science, University of Leeds, 1978–87, now Emeritus; *b* Newport, Gwent, 1 July 1922; *s* of Daniel Watson Dixon-Lewis and Eleanor Jane Dixon-Lewis; *m* 1950, Patricia Mary Best; one *s* two *d*. *Educ:* Newport High Sch.; Jesus Coll., Oxford (MA; DPhil 1948). Research Chemist, Courtaulds, 1946–49; Sen. Scientific Officer, Gas Res. Bd, Beckenham, 1949–53; University of Leeds: Gas Council Sen. Res. Fellow, 1953–70; Reader, 1970–78. Vis. Prof., Applied Physics Lab., Johns Hopkins Univ., 1965; Vis. Scientist, Sandia Nat. Labs, Calif, 1987. Alfred Egerton Gold Medal 1990, Silver Medal 1990, Combustion Inst.; Award for Combustion and Hydrocarbon Oxidation Chemistry, RSC, 1993; Dionizy Smoleński Medal, Thermodynamics and Combustion Cttee, Polish Acad. of Scis, 1995. *Publications:* numerous scientific papers on combustion topics, chemically reacting flows, and molecular transport processes. *Recreations:* walking, gardening. *Address:* 16 West Park Grove, Leeds LS8 2HQ. *T:* (0113) 266 2269.

DIXON-SMITH, family name of **Baron Dixon-Smith**.

DIXON-SMITH, Baron *cr* 1993 (Life Peer), of Bocking in Essex; **Robert William Dixon-Smith;** DL; farmer, since 1958; *b* 30 Sept. 1934; 2nd *s* of Dixon Smith, Braintree, Essex and Winifred Smith (*née* Stratton); Dixon Smith adopted by Deed Poll as surname, 1961; *m* 1960, Georgina Janet, *d* of George Cook, Halstead, Essex and Kathleen Cook; one *s* one *d*. *Educ:* Oundle; Writtle Coll. Nat. Service, 2nd Lt, King's Dragoon Guards, 1955–57. Member: Essex CC, 1965–93 (Chm., 1986–89); Association of County Councils, 1983–93 (Chm., 1992–93). Member: H of L EC Cttee sub-cttee C (Envmt), 1994–96; H of L Select Cttee on Sci. and Technol., 1994–98. Opposition spokesman on local govt, H of L, 1998–. Member: Local Govt Management Bd, 1991–93; Council, Essex Univ., 1991–94; Chm., Anglia Polytechnic Univ., 1992–93. Governor, Writtle Coll., 1967–94 (Chm., 1973–85; Fellow, 1993). Hon. Dr Anglia Poly. Univ., 1995. Freeman, City of London, 1988; Liveryman, Farmers' Co., 1991. DL Essex, 1986. *Recreations:* shooting, fishing, golf. *Address:* Lyons Hall, Braintree, Essex CM7 6SH. *T:* (01376) 326834.

DIXON-WARD, Frank, CBE 1979; Member, Board of Overseers, Massachusetts SPCA, since 1988; *b* 28 June 1922; *s* of late Cecil Ward, LRAM, and Helen Cecilia Ward (*née* Woodward), Eastbourne; *m* 1960, Claire Collasius (*d* 1985); one *s* one *d*. *Educ:* Eastbourne Grammar School. Solicitor (Hons), 1948. Articled to Town Clerk, Eastbourne, 1940. Served War, Royal Air Force, 1941–46. Solicitor posts, Peterborough, 1948–51, West Ham, 1952–54; Deputy Town Clerk, Hove, 1954–62; Chairman: Local Govt Legal Soc., 1957; Hove Round Table, 1961–62; Mem. Council, Sussex LTA, 1957–62; Town Clerk: Camberwell, 1963–65; Southwark, 1964–70; Chief Exec., Lambeth, 1970–81; Consultant, 1982. Exec. Dir, RSPCA, 1982–87. Lawyer/Chm., London Rent Assessment Cttees, 1982, 1986–93. Hon. Clerk: South London Housing Consortium, 1965–70; Social Service Cttee, London Boroughs Assoc., 1966–82; Hon. Legal Adviser: Age Concern (Gtr London), 1965–82; Eurogroup for Animal Welfare, 1986–92; Hon. Vice-Pres., WSPA, 1998 (Mem., Bd of Dirs, 1986–98). Member official committees: London Welfare Services, 1963–65; NHS Reorganisation, 1969–74; Homelessness, 1970–72; Citizens Advice Bureaux, 1973–74; Jt Approach to Social Policies, 1975–76; Exec. Cttee, SOLACE, 1975–81. Chm., St Dunstan's College Soc., 1975–78. Eurogroup Medal, 1992. *Recreations:* music, lawn tennis. *T:* (020) 8650 8312. *Club:* Royal Over-Seas League.

DIXSON, Maurice Christopher Scott, DPhil; FRAeS; Chief Executive, Simon Group (formerly Simon Engineering), since 1993; Director, Swan Hill (formerly Higgs & Hill) plc, since 1994; *b* 5 Nov. 1941; *s* of late Herbert George Muns Dixson and Elizabeth Eileen Dixson; *m* 1965, Anne Beverley Morris. *Educ:* Palmers Grammar Sch.; University Coll., Swansea (BA Jt Hons); Carleton Univ., Ottawa (MA); Pembroke Coll., Oxford (DPhil). Commercial Exec., Hawker Siddeley Aviation, 1969–74; Contracts Man., Export, later Commercial Man., Export, Mil. Aircraft Div., BAC, 1974–80; British Aerospace: Warton Division: Div. Commercial Man., 1980–81; Exec. Dir, Contracts, 1981–83; Divl Commercial Dir, 1983–86; Military Aircraft Division: Dir-in-Charge, Saudi Arabian Ops, March–Aug. 1986; Commercial Dir and Dir-in-Charge, Saudi Arabian Ops, 1986–87; Chief Exec., Royal Ordnance PLC, 1987–88; Man. Dir, British Aerospace (Commercial Aircraft), 1988–90; Supervisory Man. Dir, Electronic Metrology and Components Groups, and Main Bd Dir, GEC, 1990–93. *Recreations:* played representative soccer at school and university, supporter of Tottenham Hotspur Football Club, fishing, shooting, sport, politics and current affairs. *Address:* (office) Simon House, 2 Eaton Gate, SW1W 9BJ. *T:* (020) 7730 0777. *Club:* Royal Automobile.

DJANOGLY, Sir Harry Ari Simon, Kt 1993; CBE 1983; Chairman, Nottingham Manufacturing Co. Ltd; *b* 1 Aug. 1938. Former Man. Dir and Dep. Chm., Vantona Viyella; Chm., Coats Viyella, 1999–; Dep. Chm., Singer & Friedlander, 1999–. *Address:* Serck House, 60 Trafalgar Square, WC2N 5DS.

DJANOGLY, Jonathan Simon; MP (C) Huntingdon, since 2001; *b* 3 June 1965; *m* 1991, Rebecca Silk; one *s* one *d*. *Educ:* University Coll. Sch.; Oxford Poly. (BA Hons); Guildford Law Sch. Admitted solicitor, 1988; Partner, S J Berwin, 1998–. Mem. (C) Westminster LBC, 1994-2001 (Chairman: Traffic and Works Cttee, 1995; Planning Applications Cttee, 1995; Contracts Cttee, 1996; Social Services Cttee, 1998; Envmt Cttee, 1999). Contested (C) Oxford East, 1997. Mem., Trade and Industry Select Cttee, 2001–. Officer, Westminster N Cons. Assoc., 1993–94. *Recreations:* sport, [illegible]. *Address:* House of Commons, SW1A 0AA. *T:* (020) 7219 2367.

DLHOPOLČEK, František, PhD; Ambassador of Slovak Republic to the Court of St James's, since 2000; *b* 13 Sept. 1953; *s* of Jozek Dlhopolček and Anna Pončková; *m* 1977, Dagmar Jztaelova; one *s* one *d*. *Educ:* Sch. of Econs, Banská Bystrica, Czechoslovakia; Diplomatic Acad., Moscow (PhD History and Politology 1989). Univ. Asst Lectr, Sch. of Econs, Banská Bystrica, 1977–79; joined Federal Ministry of Foreign Affairs, Czechoslovakia, 1979: Diplomatic Officer: Nairobi, 1979–83; African Dept, 1983–84; Office of Minister of Foreign Affairs, 1984–87; Dept of Arab and Africa Countries, 1989–90; Dir, African Dept, 1990–91; Consul-Gen., Pretoria, 1991–92; Ambassador of Czech and Slovak Fed. Republic (subseq. of Slovak Republic) to RSA, 1992–93; *Dir-Gen., Political Affairs,* Min. of Foreign Affairs 1993–94; Ambassador to Israel, 1994–98; Political Dir Gen., Min. of Foreign Affairs, 1998–2000. *Address:* Embassy of the Slovak Republic, 25 Kensington Palace Gardens, W8 4QY. *Club:* Rotary.

DOBBIE, Dr Robert Charles, CB 1996; Regional Director, Government Office for the North East, since 1998; *b* 16 Jan. 1942; *s* of Scott U. Dobbie and Isobel M. Dobbie (*née* Jamieson); *m* 1964, Elizabeth Barbour; three *s*. *Educ:* Univ. of Edinburgh (BSc); Univ. of Cambridge (PhD). Res. Fellow, Univ. of Alberta, 1966–67; ICI Res. Fellow, Univ. of Bristol, 1967–68; Lectr in Inorganic Chemistry, Univ. of Newcastle upon Tyne, 1968–76; sabbatical, California State Univ., LA, 1974; Tutor, Open Univ., 1975–85; Principal, DTI, 1976–83; Asst Sec., Dept. of Industry, 1983–90; Under Sec., DTI, 1990–97; Dir, Merseyside Task Force, 1990–92 (seconded to DoE); Head, Competitiveness Unit (formerly Industrial Competitiveness Div.), DTI, 1992–97. *Publications:* on inorganic and organometallic chemistry. *Recreations:* theatre, hill walking, malt whisky. *Address:* Government Office for the North East, Wellbar House, Gallowgate, Newcastle upon Tyne NE1 4TD.

See also S. J. Dobbie.

DOBBIE, Scott Jamieson, CBE 1998; Adviser, Global Equities, Deutsche Bank AG, London, since 1999; Chairman, Securities Institute, since 2000; *b* 24 July 1939; *s* of Scott U. Dobbie and Isobel M. Dobbie (*née* Jamieson); *m* 1962, Brenda M. Condie; two *d*. *Educ:* Dollar Acad.; Univ. of Edinburgh (BSc). Industrial mktg, Unilever, 1961–66, and ICI, 1966–72; Wood Mackenzie & Co., stockbrokers, 1972–88: Partner, 1975–82; Man. Partner, 1982–88; acquired by NatWest Securities, 1988: Man. Dir, 1988–93; Chm., 1993–98; acquired by Bankers Trust Internat., 1998–99 (Vice-Chm.). Non-executive Director: CRESTCo Ltd, 1996– (Chm., 1996–2001); Edinburgh Investment Trust PLC, 1998–; Murray VCT4 plc, 2000–; Premier Oil plc, 2000–; Standard Life European Private Equity Trust, 2001– (Chm., 2001–). Director: SFA, 1993–2001; Financial Services NTO, 2001–; Comr, Jersey Financial Services Commn, 1999–. *Recreations:* mechanical objects, buildings, books. *Address:* Securities Institute, Centurion House, 24 Monument Street, EC3R 8AQ. *T:* (020) 7645 0600.

See also R. C. Dobbie.

DOBBIN, James; MP (Lab and Co-op) Heywood and Middleton, since 1997; *b* 26 May 1941; *s* of William Dobbin and Catherine McCabe; *m* 1964, Pat Russell; two *s* two *d*. *Educ:* St Columba's High Sch., Cowdenbeath; St Andrew's High Sch., Kirkcaldy; Napier Coll., Edinburgh. Microbiologist, NHS, 1966–94. Mem., Rochdale MBC, 1983–97 (Leader, 1996–97). Contested (Lab) Bury N, 1992. *Address:* House of Commons, SW1A 0AA; 43 Stonehill Drive, Rochdale, Lancs OL12 7JN.

DOBBIN, Rev. Dr Victor, CB 2000; MBE 1980; QHC 1993; Chaplain General to the Forces, 1995–2000; *b* 12 March 1943; *s* of late Vincent Dobbin and Annie Dobbin (*née* Doherty); *m* 1967, Rosemary Gault; one *s* one *d*. *Educ:* Trinity Coll., Dublin (MA 1967); Queen's Univ., Belfast (MTh 1979; PhD 1984). Asst Minister, Rosemary Presbyterian Ch, Belfast, 1970–72; joined RAChD, 1972; Dep. Warden, RAChD Centre, 1982–86;

Sen. Chaplain, 3rd Armd Div., 1986–89; Staff Chaplain, HQ BAOR, 1989–91; Sen. Chaplain, SE Dist, 1991–93; Asst Chaplain Gen., Southern Dist, 1993–94. Chm. Cttee, Naval, Military and Air Force Bible Soc., 2000–; Vice-Pres., Assoc. for Christian Confs, Teaching and Service, Central and Southern Europe, 2001–; Member: Council of Reference, Barnabas Fund, 1998–; Internat. Council, Scripture Gift Mission, 2000–. Hon. DD Presbyterian Theol Faculty, Ireland, 1995. *Recreations:* golf, walking, cycling, reading. *Address:* Glenview, 20 Cushendall Road, Bonamargy, Ballycastle, Co. Antrim, N Ireland BT54 6QR.

DOBBS, Bernard; *see* Dobbs, W. B. J.

DOBBS, Prof. (Edwin) Roland, PhD, DSc; Hildred Carlile Professor of Physics, University of London, 1973–90, and Head of Department of Physics, Royal Holloway and Bedford New College, 1985–90; Emeritus Professor of Physics, University of London, 1990; *b* 2 Dec. 1924; *s* of late A. Edwin Dobbs, AMIMechE, and Harriet Dobbs (*née* Wright); *m* 1947, Dorothy Helena, *o d* of late Alderman A. F. T. Jeeves, Stamford, Lincs; two *s* one *d*. *Educ:* Ilford County High Sch.; Queen Elizabeth's Sch., Barnet; University College London. BSc (1st cl. Physics) 1943, PhD 1949; DSc London 1977; FInstP 1964; FIOA 1977. Radar research, Admiralty, 1943–46; DSIR Res. Student, UCL, 1946–49; Lectr in Physics, QMC, Univ. of London, 1949–58; Fulbright Scholar, Applied Maths, 1958–59, Associate Prof. of Physics, 1959–60, Brown Univ., USA; AEI Fellow, Cavendish Lab., Univ. of Cambridge, 1960–64; Prof. and Head of Dept of Physics, Univ. of Lancaster, 1964–73; Bedford College, London University: Head of Dept of Physics, 1973–85; Vice-Principal, 1981–82; Dean, Faculty of Science, 1980–82; Chm., Bd of Studies in Physics, Univ. of London, 1982–85; Vice-Dean, 1986–88, Dean, 1988–90, Faculty of Science, Univ. of London. Member: Physics Cttee, SRC, 1970–73, SERC, 1983–86; Nuclear Physics Bd, SRC, 1974–77; Paul Instrument Fund Cttee, 1984–Sept. 2002. Visiting Professor: Brown Univ., 1966; Wayne State Univ., 1969; Univ. of Tokyo, 1977; Univ. of Delhi, 1983; Cornell Univ., 1984; Univ. of Florida, 1989; Univ. of Sussex, 1989–2001. Pres., Inst. of Acoustics, 1976–78; Hon. Sec., Inst. of Physics, 1976–84. Convenor, Standing Conf. of Profs of Physics of GB, 1985–88. Member: Caius Coll. Club; Physical Soc. Club. Hon. Fellow, Indian Cryogenics Council, 1977. *Publications:* Electricity and Magnetism, 1984 (trans. Chinese 1990); Electromagnetic Waves, 1985 (trans. Chinese 1992); Basic Electromagnetism, 1993; Solid Helium Three, 1994; Helium Three, 2001; research papers on metals and superconductors in Procs of Royal Soc., on solid state physics and acoustics in Jl of Physics, Physical Rev. Letters, Physical Acoustics, and on superfluid helium 3 in Jl Low Temperature Physics, etc. *Recreations:* travel, opera, gardening. *Address:* Merryfield, Best Beech Hill, Wadhurst, E Sussex TN5 6JT. *T:* (01892) 784864. *Club:* Athenæum.

See also M. A. Jeeves.

DOBBS, Joseph Alfred, CMG 1972; OBE 1957 (MBE 1945); TD 1945; HM Diplomatic Service, retired; *b* Abbeyleix, Ireland, 22 Dec. 1914; *s* of John L. Dobbs and Ruby (*née* Gillespie); *m* 1949, Marie, *d* of Reginald Francis Catton, Sydney; four *s*. *Educ:* Worksop Coll.; Trinity Hall, Cambridge (Schol.). Pres., Cambridge Union Soc., 1936. Served War of 1939–45, Major, Royal Artillery (despatches). Joined Foreign Office, 1946; served Moscow, 1947–51, 1954–57 and 1965–68; FO, 1951–54; Delhi, 1957–61; Warsaw, 1961–64; Rome, 1964–65; Consul-Gen., Zagreb, 1969–70; Minister, Moscow, 1971–74. *Recreations:* reading, gardening. *Address:* The Coach House, Charlton Musgrove, Wincanton, Somerset BA9 8ES. *T:* (01963) 33356.

DOBBS, Linda Penelope, PhD; QC 1998; *b* 3 Jan. 1951; *m* (marr. diss.). *Educ:* Univ. of Surrey (BSc 1976); London School of Economics and Political Science (LLM 1977; PhD 1980). Called to the Bar, Gray's Inn, 1981; in practice at the Bar, 1982–. *Publications:* (with M. Lucraft) Road Traffic Law and Practice, 1993, 3rd edn 1995; (Contributing Ed.) Archbold, Road Traffic Bulletin, 1998–. *Recreations:* reading, music, theatre, travel, food and wine. *Address:* 18 Red Lion Court, EC4A 3EB. *T:* (020) 7520 6000.

DOBBS, Mattiwilda; Order of North Star (Sweden), 1954; opera singer (coloratura soprano); *b* 11 July 1925, Atlanta, Ga, USA; *d* of John Wesley and Irene Dobbs; *m* 1957, Bengt Janzon, retired Dir. of Information, Nat. Ministry of Health and Welfare, Sweden; no *c*. *Educ:* Spelman Coll., USA (BA 1946); Columbia Univ., USA (MA 1948). Studied voice in NY with Lotte Leonard, 1946–50; special coaching Paris with Pierre Bernac, 1950–52. Marian Anderson Schol., 1948; John Hay Whitney Schol., 1950; 1st prize in singing, Internat. Comp., Geneva Conservatory of Music, 1951. Appeared Royal Dutch Opera, Holland Festival, 1952. Recitals, Sweden, Paris, Holland, 1952; appeared in opera at La Scala, Milan, 1953; Concerts, England and Continent, 1953; Glyndebourne Opera, 1953–54, 1956, 1961; Covent Garden Opera, 1953, 1954, 1956, 1958; command performance, Covent Garden, 1954. Annual concert tours: US, 1954–; Australia, New Zealand, 1955, 1959, 1968; Australia, 1972, 1977; Israel, 1957 and 1959; USSR concerts and opera (Bolshoi Theater), 1959; San Francisco Opera, 1955; début Metropolitan Opera, 1956; there annually, 1956–64. Appearances Hamburg State Opera, 1961–63; Royal Swedish Opera, 1957 and there annually, 1957–73; Norwegian and Finnish Operas, 1957–64. Vis. Prof., Univ. of Texas at Austin, 1973–74; Professor: Univ. of Illinois, 1975–76; Univ. of Georgia, 1976–77; Howard Univ., Washington, 1977–91. Hon. Dr of Music: Spelman Coll., Atlanta, 1979; Emory Univ., Atlanta, 1980. *Address:* 1101 South Arlington Ridge Road, Apt 301, Arlington, VA 22202, USA.

DOBBS, Michael John; novelist and broadcaster; *b* 14 Nov. 1948; *s* of Eric William Dobbs and Eileen Dobbs (*née* Saunders); *m*; two *s*. *Educ:* Christ Church, Oxford (MA); Fletcher School of Law and Diplomacy, USA (PhD, MALD, MA). Govt Special Adviser, 1981–87; Chief of Staff, Conservative Party, 1986–87; Dep. Chm., Saatchi & Saatchi, 1983–86, 1988–91; Jt Dep. Chm., Cons. Party, 1994–95. Presenter, Despatch Box, BBC, 1999–. *Publications:* House of Cards, 1989 (televised, 1990); Wall Games, 1990; Last Man to Die, 1991; To Play the King, 1992 (televised, 1993); The Touch of Innocents, 1994; The Final Cut, 1995 (televised, 1995); Goodfellowe MP, 1996; The Buddha of Brewer Street, 1998; Whispers of Betrayal, 2000. *Recreations:* genealogy, losing weight. *Address:* 18 Bruton Place, W1J 6LY. *Club:* Royal Automobile.

DOBBS, Captain Sir Richard (Arthur Frederick), KCVO 1991; Lord-Lieutenant of County Antrim, 1975–94 (HM Lieutenant for County Antrim, 1959–75); *b* 2 April 1919; *s* of Senator Major Arthur F. Dobbs, DL, of Castle Dobbs, and Hylda Louisa Dobbs; *m* 1953, Carola Day, *d* of Christopher Clarkson, Old Lyme, Conn, USA; four *s* one *d*. *Educ:* Eton; Magdalene Coll., Cambridge (MA). Served War: 2nd Lieut Irish Guards (Supp. Reserve), 1939; Captain 1943. Called to Bar, Lincoln's Inn, 1947; Member, Midland Circuit, 1951–55. *Address:* Castle Dobbs, Carrickfergus, County Antrim, N Ireland BT38 9BX. *T:* (028) 9337 2238. *Club:* Cavalry and Guards.

DOBBS, Roland; *see* Dobbs, E. R.

DOBBS, (William) Bernard (Joseph); HM Diplomatic Service, retired; Ambassador to Laos (Lao People's Democratic Republic), 1982–85; *b* 3 Sept. 1925; *s* of late William Evelyn Joseph Dobbs and Maud Clifford Dobbs (*née* Bernard); *m* 1952, Brigid Mary Bilitch; one *s* one *d*. *Educ:* Shrewsbury Sch.; Trinity Coll., Dublin (BA Hons Mod. History 1951; MA 1977). Served Rifle Bde/7th Gurkha Rifles, 1943–47 (Captain). Forbes Forbes Campbell and Co. Ltd, 1952–56; Examiner, Patent Office, 1957–61; British Trade Commission, 1961–65: Lagos, 1961–64; Freetown, 1964–66; HM Diplomatic Service: Freetown, London, Rangoon, Milan, Kinshasa, Vientiane, 1965–85. *Recreations:* reading, walking, writing. *Club:* Royal Automobile.

DOBKIN, Ian James; His Honour Judge Dobkin; a Circuit Judge, since 1995; *b* 8 June 1948; *s* of Morris Dobkin, dental surgeon, Leeds, and Rhoda Dobkin; *m* 1980, Andrea, *d* of Jack and Rose Dante; two *s*. *Educ:* Leeds Grammar Sch.; Queen's Coll., Oxford (Hastings Exhibnr in Classics; BA Jurisp. 1970; MA 1974). Called to the Bar, Gray's Inn, 1971; barrister, North Eastern Circuit, 1971–95; Asst Recorder, 1986–90; Recorder, 1990–95. Mem., Adv. Cttee, Centre for Criminal Justice Studies, Univ. of Leeds, 1987–. United Hebrew Congregation, Leeds: Vice-Pres., 1981–84 and 1992–96; Pres., 1984–88 and 1996–99; Vice-Chm., Leeds Hillel Foundn, 1989–. Contested (C) Penistone, July 1978, gen. election, 1979. *Recreations:* crosswords, reading, music. *Address:* Leeds Combined Court Centre, Leeds LS1 3BE. *Clubs:* Moor Allerton Golf (Leeds); Yorkshire County Cricket.

DOBLE, Denis Henry; HM Diplomatic Service, retired; Consul-General, Amsterdam, 1991–96; *b* 2 Oct. 1936; *s* of Percy Claud Doble and Dorothy Grace (*née* Petley); *m* 1975, Patricia Ann Robinson; one *d* one *s*. *Educ:* Dover Grammar School; New College, Oxford (MA Modern Hist.). RAF, 1955–57. Colonial Office, 1960–64; Asst Private Sec. to Commonwealth and Colonial Sec., 1963–64; HM Diplomatic Service, 1965; First Sec., Brussels, 1966–68, Lagos, 1968–72; S Asian and Defence Depts, FCO, 1972–75; First Sec. (Economic), Islamabad, 1975–78; Head of Chancery, Lima, 1978–82; E African Dept, FCO, 1982–84; Actg Dep. High Comr, Bombay, 1985; Deputy High Commissioner: Calcutta, 1985–87; Kingston, 1987–91. FRGS 1997; Mem, Royal Soc. for Asian Affairs, 1997–. Member, Council: Anglo-Netherlands Soc., 1996; USPG, 2000–. Pres.-elect, Battersea Pk Rotary Club. SBStJ. *Recreations:* international cricket and tennis, Real tennis, Indian cinema, long rail and road journeys, 19th century British colonial history. *Address:* 4 Paveley Drive, Morgan's Walk, Battersea, SW11 3TP. *Club:* MCC (Life Mem.).

DOBLE, John Frederick, OBE 1981; HM Diplomatic Service, retired; High Commissioner to Swaziland, 1996–99; *b* 30 June 1941; *s* of Comdr Douglas Doble, RN and Marcella (*née* Cowan); *m* 1975, Isabella Margaret Ruth (marr. diss. 1992), *d* of late Col W. H. Whitbread, TD; one *d*. *Educ:* Sunningdale; Eton (Scholar); RMA Sandhurst; Hertford College, Oxford. 17th/21st Lancers, 1959–69 (Captain); attached Lord Strathcona's Horse (Royal Canadians), 1967–69; joined HM Diplomatic Service, 1969; Arabian Dept, FCO, 1969–72; Beirut, 1972–73; Brussels, 1973–77; Commonwealth Dept, FCO, 1977–78. Maputo, 1978–81; Inf. Dept, FCO, 1981–83; attached Barclays Bank International, 1983–85; Consul General, Edmonton, Canada, 1985–89; Consul General, Johannesburg, 1990–94. *Recreations:* horse and water sports, history, manual labour. *Address:* Hole Farm, Hockworthy, Devon TA21 0NQ; 48 Narrow Street, Limehouse, E14 8BP.

DOBREV, Valentin; Ambassador of Bulgaria to the Court of St James's, since 1998; *b* Varna, 21 Nov. 1955. Joined Bulgarian Foreign Service, 1982; Trainee Attaché, Budapest, 1982–83; Third Sec., Legal and Treaty Dept, 1984–90, and Head, Law of the Sea and Implementation of Internat. Treaties Sect., 1987–90, Min. of Foreign Affairs; Second Sec., Helsinki, 1990–91; Dep. Foreign Minister, 1991–93; Govt Co-ordinator for Bulgaria's accession to Council of Europe and EU, 1992; Ambassador and Perm. Rep. to UN, Geneva, 1993–96; First Dep. Foreign Minister, 1997; Foreign Policy Sec. to Pres. of Bulgaria, 1997–98. *Address:* Bulgarian Embassy, 186–188 Queen's Gate, SW7 5HL.

DOBROSIELSKI, Marian, PhD Zürich; Banner of Labour, 1st Class 1975 (2nd Class 1973); Knight Cross of the Order of Polonia Restituta, 1964; Professor of Philosophy, Warsaw University, 1974–88; Ambassador *ad personam*, since 1973; *b* 25 March 1923; *s* of Stanislaw and Stefania Dobrosielski; *m* 1950; one *d*. *Educ:* Univ. of Zürich; Univ. of Warsaw. Served in Polish Army in France, War of 1939–45. With Min. of Foreign Affairs, 1948–81; Polish Legation, Bern, 1948–50; Head of Section, Min. of Foreign Affairs, 1950–54; Asst Prof., Warsaw Univ. and Polish Acad. of Sciences, 1954–57; Mem. Polish delegn to UN Gen. Assembly, 1952, 1953, 1958, 1966, 1972, 1976. First Sec., Counsellor, Polish Embassy in Washington, 1958–64; Min. of Foreign Affairs: Counsellor to Minister, 1964–69; Acting Dir, Research Office, 1968–69; Polish Ambassador to London, 1969–71; Dir, Polish Inst. of Internat. Affairs, 1971–80; Dep. Minister of Foreign Affairs, 1978–81. Univ. of Warsaw: Associate Prof., 1966; Vice-Dean of Faculty of Philosophy, 1966–68; Dir, Inst. of Philosophy, 1971–73 (Chm. Scientific Council, 1969). Chair of Diplomacy, Private Coll. of Business and Admin, Warsaw, 1999–. Chm., Editorial Bd of Studia Filozoficzne, 1968–69; Sec., Polish Philos. Soc., 1955–57 and 1965–69. Chm., Polish Cttee for European Security and Co-operation, 1973–79 (Vice-Chm., 1971–73); Vice-Chm., Cttee on Peace Research, Polish Acad. of Scis, 1984–91; Chm., Scientific Council, Inst. of Peace Res. and Security Policy, Univ. of Hamburg, 1987–97. Hon. Vice-Pres., Scottish-Polish Cultural Assoc., Glasgow, 1969–71; Chm., Polish delegn to: 2nd stage Conf. on Security and Co-operation in Europe, 1973–75; CSCE Belgrade Meeting, 1977–78; CSCE Meeting, Madrid, 1980–81. Chm., Polish Nat. Interest Club, 1991–98. Hon. Mem., World Innovation Foundn, 1999. *Publications:* A Basic Epistemological Principle of Logical Positivism, 1947; The Philosophical Pragmatism of C. S. Peirce, 1967; On some contemporary problems: Philosophy, Ideology, Politics, 1970; (trans. and introd) Selection of Aphorisms of G. C. Lichtenberg, Oscar Wilde, Karl Kraus, M. von Ebner-Eschenbach, Mark Twain, C. Norwid, 1970–85; On the Theory and Practice of Peaceful Coexistence, 1976; Belgrad 77, 1978; Chances and Dilemmas, 1980; The Crisis in Poland, 1984; On Politics and Philosophy, 1988; Philosophy of Reason, 1988; Karl R. Popper's Philosophy of History and Politics, 1991; (jtly) Next Europe, 1993; (jtly) Prominent Diplomats of the XX Century, 1996; Rationalism and Irrationalism, 1999; numerous articles on philosophy and internat. problems in professional jls, 1999. *Recreation:* tennis. *Address:* Kozia Street 9–14, 00–070 Warszawa, Poland.

DOBRY, His Honour George Leon Severyn, CBE 1977; QC 1969; international arbitrator, since 1998; a Circuit Judge, 1980–92; *b* 1 Nov. 1918; *m* 1948, Margaret Headley Smith (*d* 1978), *e d* of late Joseph Quartus Smith, JP, Bardfield Saling, Essex; two *d*; *m* 1982, Rosemary Anne Alexander, *qv*. *Educ:* Warsaw Univ.; Edinburgh Univ. (MA). ACIArb. Served War of 1939–45: Army, France and Norway, 1939–42 (despatches); Air Force, 1942–46. Called to Bar, Inner Temple, 1946; Bencher 1977. A Recorder of the Crown Court, 1977–80. Legal Sec., Internat. Commn of Jurists at The Hague, 1955–57. Member Council: Justice, 1956–68; on Law Reporting, 1984–94. Adviser to Sec. of State for Environment and Sec. of State for Wales on Develt Control, 1973–75; Mem., Docklands Jt Cttee, 1974–76; Inspector, Inquiry into M25, 1978–79; Review of Internat. Legal Relns for Lord Chancellor, 2000. Pres., British Centre for English Legal Studies, Warsaw Univ., 1991–. Associate Prof., Danish Sch. of Public Admin, 1997–. Founder, and Chm. Trustees, Lord Slynn of Hadley European Law Foundn, 1997–. Chm., Panel, Avon Structure Plan, 1992–93; Mem., Panel, Polish Arbitration Court. Jt Pres., British-

Polish Legal Assoc., 1989–. Hon. Dr Juris Warsaw, 1994. Comdr, Starred Cross of Merit (Poland), 1999 (Order of Merit, 1993). Gold Medal, Polish Bar, 1999. *Publications:* Woodfall's Law of Landlord and Tenant, 25th edition (one of the Editors), 1952; Blundell and Dobry, Town and Country Planning, 1962; Blundell and Dobry, Planning Appeals and Inquiries, 1962, 5th edn, as Planning, 1996; Review of the Development Control System (Interim Report), 1972 (Final Report), 1975; (ed jtly) Development Gains Tax, 1975; Hill and Redman, Landlord and Tenant (Cons. Editor), 16th edn, 1976; (Gen. Editor) Encyclopedia of Development Law, 1976. *Address:* 105 Whitelands House, Cheltenham Terrace, SW3 4RA. *T:* (020) 7730 7335, *Fax:* (020) 7259 0157. *Clubs:* Garrick, Beefsteak, Travellers.

DOBRY, Rosemary Anne; *see* Alexander, R. A.

DOBRYNIN, Anatoly Fedorovich; Hero of Socialist Labour; Order of Lenin (five awards); Order of Red Banner of Labour; Secretary, Central Committee, Communist Party of the Soviet Union, 1986–91; Deputy, Supreme Soviet of the USSR, 1986–91; *b* 16 Nov. 1919; *m* Irina Nikolaevna Dobrynina; one *d. Educ:* Moscow Inst. of Aviation, 1942; Higher Sch. of Diplomacy, 1946 (doctorate in History). Asst to Dean of Faculty, Moscow Inst. of Aviation, engr-designer, 1942–44; Official, Min. of For. Affairs, 1946–52; Counsellor, Counsellor-Minister, Embassy to USA, 1952–54; Asst to Minister for For. Affairs, 1955–57; Dep. Sec. Gen., UN, 1957–60; Chief, Dept of Amer. Countries, Min. of For. Affairs, 1960–62; Amb. to USA, 1962–86. Mem., CPSU Central Cttee, 1971–91 (Candidate Mem., 1966–71); Chief, Internat. Dept, CPSU Central Cttee, 1986–91.

DOBSON, Prof. Christopher Martin, DPhil; FRS 1996; John Humphrey Plummer Professor of Chemical and Structural Biology, University of Cambridge, and Fellow of St John's College, Cambridge, since 2001; *b* 8 Oct. 1949; *s* of Arthur Dobson and Mabel Dobson (*née* Pollard); *m* 1977, Dr Mary Janet Schove (*see* M. J. Dobson); two *s. Educ:* Abingdon Sch.; Keble and Merton Colls, Oxford (BSc, MA, DPhil). Jun. Res. Fellow, Merton Coll., Oxford, 1974–76; IBM Res. Fellow, Linacre Coll., Oxford, 1976–77; Asst Prof. of Chemistry, Harvard Univ., 1977–80; Vis. Scientist, MIT, 1977–80; University of Oxford: Lectr in Chemistry, 1980–95; Reader in Chemistry, 1995–96; Aldrichian Praelector, 1995–2001; Prof. of Chemistry, 1996–2001; Dir, Oxford Centre for Molecular Scis, 1998–2001; Fellow, LMH, 1980–2001; Lectr, Brasenose Coll., Oxford, 1980–2001. Howard Hughes Med. Inst. Internat. Res. Scholar, 1992–97; Royal Soc. Leverhulme Trust Sen. Res. Fellow, 1993–94. Fellow, Eton Coll., 2001–. Lectures: Nat., Biophysical Soc., USA, 1998; John S. Colter, Univ. of Alberta, 1998; Frederic M. Richards, Yale Univ., 1999; Cynthia Ann Chan Meml, Univ. of Calif, Berkeley; A. D. Little Lectr, MIT, 2001. Pres., Protein Soc., 1999–2001. Corday Morgan Medal and Prize, 1983, Interdisciplinary Award, 1999, RSocChem; Dewey and Kelly Award, Univ. of Nebraska, 1997. *Publications:* numerous contribs to learned jls. *Recreations:* gardening, family, friends. *Address:* Department of Chemistry, University of Cambridge, Lensfield Road, Cambridge CB2 1EW. *T:* (01223) 763070, *Fax:* (01223) 763418; *e-mail:* cmd44@cam.ac.uk.

DOBSON, Christopher Selby Austin, CBE 1976; FSA; Librarian, House of Lords, 1956–77; *b* 25 Aug. 1916; *s* of late Alban Tabor Austin Dobson, CB, CVO, CBE; *m* 1941, Helen Broughton (*d* 1984), *d* of late Capt. E. B. Turner, Holyhead; one *d* (one *s* decd). *Educ:* Clifton Coll.; Emmanuel Coll., Cambridge (BA). With National Council of Social Service, 1938–39. Served War of 1939–45, Lieut Middx Regt (despatches). Asst Principal (Temp.), Ministry of Education, 1946–47; Asst Librarian, House of Lords, 1947–56. *Publication:* (ed) Oxfordshire Protestation Returns 1641–42, 1955. *Recreations:* collecting books, stamps, etc. *Address:* Swan House, Symonds Lane, Linton, Cambridge CB1 6HY. *T:* (01223) 893796. *Clubs:* Roxburghe; (Hon.) Rowfant (Cleveland).

DOBSON, Vice-Adm. Sir David (Stuart), KBE 1992; Secretary-General, Institute of Investment Management and Research, since 1995; *b* 4 Dec. 1938; *s* of Walter and Ethel Dobson; *m* 1962, Joanna Mary Counter; two *s* one *d. Educ:* English School, Nicosia, Cyprus; RN College, Dartmouth. Joined RN 1956; qualified Observer, 1961; served HM Ships Ark Royal, Protector, Eagle; BRNC Dartmouth, 1968–70; Flight Comdr, HMS Norfolk, 1970–72; Staff of FO Naval Air Comd, 1972–74; CO HMS Amazon, 1975–76; Naval Sec's Dept, MoD, 1976–78; Naval and Air Attaché, Athens, 1980–82; Senior Naval Officer, Falklands, 1982–83; Captain 5th Destroyer Sqdn (HMS Southampton), 1983–85; Captain of the Fleet, 1985–88; Naval Sec., 1988–90; Chief of Staff to Comdr Allied Naval Forces Southern Europe, 1991–94. Chm. of Trustees, Hands Around the World, charity, 1995–. Gov., Royal Star and Garter Home, Richmond, 1995– (Chm. Govs, 1999–). Mem. Council, Union Jack Club, 1996–. CIMgt 1996; FIPD (FIPM 1991). *Recreations:* tennis, hill walking, bird watching, choral singing. *Address:* (office) 21 Ironmonger Lane, EC2V 8EY. *Clubs:* Army and Navy, Royal Navy of 1765 and 1785 (Chm., 1995–98).

DOBSON, Rt Hon. Frank (Gordon); PC 1997; MP (Lab) Holborn and St Pancras, since 1983 (Holborn and St Pancras South, 1979–83); *b* 15 March 1940; *s* of late James William and Irene Shortland Dobson, York; *m* 1967, Janet Mary, *d* of Henry and Edith Alker; three *c. Educ:* Dunnington County Primary Sch., York; Archbishop Holgate's Grammar Sch., York; London School of Economics (BScEcon). Administrative jobs with Central Electricity Generating Bd, 1962–70, and Electricity Council, 1970–75; Asst Sec., Commn for Local Administration (local Ombudsman's office), 1975–79. Member, Camden Borough Council, 1971–76 (Leader of Council, 1973–75); Chm., Coram's Fields and Harmsworth Meml Playground, 1977–. Front bench spokesman on educn, 1981–83, on health, 1983–87; Shadow Leader of the Commons and Party Campaign Co-ordinator, 1987–89; opposition front bench spokesman on energy, 1989–92, on employment, 1992–93, on transport, 1993–94, on London, 1993–97, and on the envmt, 1994–97; Sec. of State for Health, 1997–99. Chm., NHS Unlimited, 1981–89. Governor: LSE, 1986–; Inst. of Child Health, 1987–92. *Address:* House of Commons, SW1A 0AA; 22 Great Russell Mansions, Great Russell Street, WC1B 3BE. *T:* (020) 7242 5760. *Club:* Covent Garden Community Centre.

DOBSON, Keith; *see* Dobson, W. K.

DOBSON, Dr Mary Janet; Director, Wellcome Unit for the History of Medicine and Reader in the History of Medicine, University of Oxford, since 1999; Fellow, Green College, Oxford, since 1997; *b* 27 Dec. 1954; *d* of late Derek Justin Schove and of Vera Florence Schove; *m* 1977, Christopher Martin Dobson, *qv*; two *s. Educ:* Sydenham High Sch. (GPDST); St Hugh's Coll., Oxford (BA 1st Cl. Hons Geog. 1976); Harvard Univ. (AM 1980); Nuffield Coll., Oxford (DPhil 1982). Harkness Fellow, Harvard Univ., 1978–80; University of Oxford: E. P. Abraham and Prize Res. Fellow, Nuffield Coll., 1981–84; Deptl Demonstrator, Sch. of Geog., 1983-89; Lectr in Human Geog., Keble Coll., 1985-88; Res. Fellow, Wolfson Coll., 1987-94; Wellcome Fellow in Health Services Res., Dept of Community Medicine and Gen. Practice, 1989-90; Wellcome Unit for History of Medicine: Wellcome Res. Fellow in Historical Epidemiol., 1990-93; Sen. Res. Officer, 1993-98; Asst Dir, 1995-98; Actg Dir and Wellcome Trust Unit Fellow, 1998-99. Member: Historical Geog. Res. Gp, IBG, 1980-; Local Population Studies Gp, 1980-; IUSSP, 1990-97; British Soc. of Population, 1992-. FRSTM&H 1997. Mem., Nat. Meningitis Trust, 1989-. Member: Soc. of Authors, 1996-; Historical Novel Soc., 1997-. *Publication:* Contours of Death and Disease in Early Modern England, 1997. *Address:* Cripps Barn, Otmoor Lane, Beckley, Oxon OX3 9UX. *T:* (01865) 351548.

DOBSON, Captain Michael F.; *see* Fulford-Dobson.

DOBSON, Michael William Romsey; Chief Executive, Schroders, since 2001; *b* 13 May 1952; *s* of Sir Denis (William) Dobson, KCB, OBE, QC; *m* 1998, Frances, *d* of Count Charles de Salis; one *d. Educ:* Eton; Trinity Coll., Cambridge. Joined Morgan Grenfell, 1973: Morgan Grenfell NY, 1978–80, Man. Dir, 1984–85; Hd, Investment Div., 1987–88; Dep. Chief Exec., 1988–89; Gp Chief Exec., Morgan Grenfell, then Deutsche Morgan Grenfell, 1989–97; Mem., Bd of Man. Dirs, Deutsche Bank AG, 1996–2000; Chm., Beaumont Capital Mgt, 2001. *Address:* Schroders, 31 Gresham Street, EC2V 7QA.

DOBSON, Sir Patrick John H.; *see* Howard-Dobson.

DOBSON, Prof. Richard Barrie, FSA; FRHistS; FBA 1988; Professor of Medieval History, and Fellow of Christ's College, University of Cambridge, 1988–99; Hon. Professor of History, University of York, since 1999; *b* 3 Nov. 1931; *s* of Richard Henry Dobson and Mary Victoria Dobson (*née* Kidd); *m* 1959, Narda Leon; one *s* one *d. Educ:* Barnard Castle Sch.; Wadham Coll., Oxford (BA 1st cl. Modern Hist.; MA 1958; DPhil 1963). Senior demy, Magdalen Coll., Oxford, 1957–58; Lectr in Medieval History, Univ. of St Andrews, 1958–64; University of York: Lectr, Sen. Lectr, Reader, Prof. of History, 1964–88; Dep. Vice-Chancellor, 1984–87. British Acad. Fellow, Folger Shakespeare Liby, Washington, 1974; Cornell Vis. Prof., Swarthmore Coll., USA, 1987; Vis. Fellow, Trinity Coll., Toronto, 1994. FRHistS 1972 (Vice-Pres., 1985–89); FSA 1979; President: Surtees Soc., 1987; Jewish Historical Soc. of England, 1990–91; Ecclesiastical History Soc., 1991–92; Chairman: York Archeol Trust, 1990–96; Friends of the PRO, 1994–98. Life Mem., Merchant Taylors' Co., York. Gen. Editor, Yorks Archaeol. Soc., Record Series, 1981–86. *Publications:* The Peasants' Revolt of 1381, 1971, 2nd edn 1983; Durham Priory 1400–1450, 1973; The Jews of Medieval York and the Massacre of March 1190, 1974; (with J. Taylor) Rymes of Robyn Hood, 1977; (ed) York City Chamberlains' Accounts 1396–1500, 1980; (ed) The Church, Politics and Patronage in the Fifteenth Century, 1984; (contrib.) A History of York Minster, 1977; (contrib.) History of the University of Oxford, Vol. II, 1993; Church and Society in the Medieval North of England, 1996; articles in learned jls. *Recreations:* hill walking, cinema, chess, modern jazz. *Address:* Centre for Medieval Studies, University of York, The King's Manor, York YO1 2EP. *T:* (01904) 433910.

DOBSON, Roger Swinburne, OBE 1987; FREng, FICE; Managing Director, Hill Farm Orchards Ltd, since 2000; *b* 24 June 1936; *s* of Sir Denis William Dobson, KCB, OBE, QC and Thelma Swinburne; *m* 2nd, Deborah Elizabeth Sancroft Burrough; one *s* one *d. Educ:* Bryanston Sch.; Trinity Coll., Cambridge (MA); Stanford Univ., Calif (DofEng). MBCS 1981; FICE 1990; FREng 1993. Qualified pilot, RN, 1955. Binnie & Partners, 1959–69; Bechtel Ltd, 1969–90: Gen. Manager, PMB Systems Engrg, 1984–86; Man. Dir, Laing-Bechtel Petroleum Develt, 1986–90; Dir-Gen. and Sec., ICE, 1990–99. Deputy Chairman: Thomas Telford (Holdings) Ltd, 1990–99; Thomas Telford Ltd (formerly Thomas Telford Services Ltd), 1991–99; Director: Yearco Ltd, 1996–98; Quinco: campaign to promote engineering, 1997– (Hon. Treas.). Chairman: Computer Aided Design Computer Aided Manufacturing Gp, NEDC, 1981–85; Energy Industries Council, 1987–90; Mem., Construction Industry Sector Gp, NEDC, 1988–92. Dir, Pathfinder Fund Internat, 1997–. *Publications:* Applications of Digital Computers to Hydraulic Engineering, 1967; contrib. Procs of ICE and IMechE. *Recreations:* sailing, tennis, squash, gardening. *Address:* Etchilhampton House, Etchilhampton, Devizes, Wilts SN10 3JH. *Clubs:* Royal Ocean Racing, Royal Thames Yacht.

See also M. W. R. Dobson.

DOBSON, Sue; Editor-in-Chief, Choice, since 1994; *b* 31 Jan. 1946; *d* of Arthur and Nellie Henshaw; *m* 1966, Michael Dobson (marr. diss. 1974). *Educ:* convent schs; BA Hons CNAA. From 1964, worked for a collection of women's magazines, including Femina and Fair Lady in S Africa, variously as fashion, cookery, beauty, home and contributing editor, editor at SA Institute of Race Relations and editor of Wedding Day and Successful Slimming in London, with breaks somewhere in between in PR and doing research into the language and learning of children; Editor, Woman and Home, 1982–94. Mem. Bd, Plan Internat., 1993–. *Publication:* The Wedding Day Book, 1981, 2nd edn 1989. *Recreations:* travelling, photography, reading, exploring. *Address:* Kings Chambers, 39–41 Priestgate, Peterborough PE1 1FR.

DOBSON, (William) Keith, OBE 1988; Secretary-General, Anglo-German Foundation, since 2000; *b* 20 Sept. 1945; *s* of Raymond Griffin Dobson and Margaret (*née* Wylie); *m* 1972, Valerie Guest; two *d. Educ:* King Edward's Grammar School, Camp Hill, Birmingham; Univ. of Keele (BA Internat. Relns 1968); Univ. of Essex (DipSoc 1972). With Clarks Ltd, Shoemakers, 1968–71; British Council, 1972–2000: Lagos, 1972–75; London, 1975–77; Ankara, 1977–80; Caracas, 1980–84; Budapest, 1984–87; London, 1987–90; Europe Div., 1990–93; Dir, Germany, 1993–2000. *Recreations:* music, cinema, bridge, woodworking. *Address:* Anglo-German Foundation, 17 Bloomsbury Square, WC1A 2LP. *T:* (020) 7404 3137, *Fax:* (020) 7405 2071.

DOCHERTY, Dr Daniel Joseph; JP; General Medical Practitioner, 1949–87, retired; Examining Medical Officer, Department of Health and Social Security, 1982–86; *b* 24 Oct. 1924; *s* of Michael Joseph Docherty and Ellen Stewart; *m* 1952, Dr Rosemary Catherine Kennedy; eight *s* two *d. Educ:* St Aloysius' Coll.; Anderson Coll. of Medicine; Glasgow Univ. LRCP, LRCS, LRFPS. MO, King's Flight, RAF Benson, 1950. Glasgow Town Councillor, 1959–75; Sen. Magistrate, City of Glasgow, 1964–65; Chm. of Police Cttee, 1967–68; Chm. of Educn Cttee, 1971–74. Mem., MSC, 1974–77; Chm. in Scotland, Job Creation Programme, 1975–78. Member: Strathclyde Univ. Ct, 1971–72; Glasgow Univ. Ct, 1972–74; Council, Open Univ., 1972–75. JP Glasgow, 1961. *Recreation:* travel. *Address:* 1a Briar Gardens, Briar Road, Glasgow G43 2TF. *T:* (0141) 637 5005.

DOCHERTY, Michael, FCCA, CPFA; Chief Executive, South Lanarkshire Council, since 1999; *b* 12 Jan 1952; *s* of Michael and Susan Docherty; *m* 1972, Linda Thorpe; two *s* one *d. Educ:* St Mungo's Acad., Glasgow. FCCA 1978; CPFA 1986. Accountancy trainee, S of Scotland Electricity Bd, 1970–74; Accounts Asst, Coatbridge Burgh Council, 1974–75; Accountant: Monklands DC, 1975–77; Stirling DC, 1977–79; Sen. Accountant, 1979–80, Principal Accountant, 1980–82, Monklands DC; Principal Accountant, Renfrew DC, 1982–84; Depute Dir of Finance, Motherwell DC, 1984–92; Dir of Finance, 1992–94, Chief Exec., 1994–95, Hamilton DC; Depute Chief Exec. and Exec. Dir, Corporate Resources, 1995–97, Depute Chief Exec. and Exec. Dir, Enterprise Resources, 1997–99, S Lanarkshire Council. *Recreations:* music, reading, running, golf. *Address:* South Lanarkshire Council, Council Offices, Almada Street, Hamilton ML3 0AA. *T:* (01698) 454208.

DOCHERTY, Paul Francis; Director, Czech Republic, British Council, and Cultural Counsellor, Prague, since 2000; *b* 17 Sept. 1951; *s* of Joseph Docherty and Elizabeth Eileen Docherty (*née* Waters); *m* 1987, Karen Leithead; three *s*. *Educ:* Queen Victoria Sch., Dunblane; Univ. of Strathclyde (BA Hons 1977; MLitt 1985). English teacher, Spain, 1977–83; Lectr in English, Moscow State Univ., 1983–84; joined British Council, 1985: Helsinki, 1986–89; English Language Div., 1989–93; Moscow, 1993–96; Corporate Affairs, 1996–97; Sec., 1997–2000. *Recreations:* listening to opera, playing blues/rock guitar, film and television. *Address:* c/o British Council, 10 Spring Gardens, SW1A 2BN. *T:* (020) 7930 8466.

DOCKER, Rt Rev. Ivor Colin; Bishop Suffragan of Horsham, 1975–91; an Assistant Bishop, diocese of Exeter, since 1991; *b* 3 Dec. 1925; *s* of Colonel Philip Docker, OBE, TD, DL, and Doris Gwendoline Docker (*née* Whitehill); *m* 1950, Thelma Mary, *d* of John William and Gladys Upton; one *s* one *d*. *Educ:* King Edward's High Sch., Birmingham; Univ. of Birmingham (BA); St Catherine's Coll., Oxford (MA). Curate of Normanton, Yorks, 1949–52; Lecturer of Halifax Parish Church, 1952–54; CMS Area Sec., 1954–59; Vicar of Midhurst, Sussex, 1959–64; RD of Midhurst, 1961–64; Vicar and RD of Seaford, 1964–71; Canon and Prebendary of Colworth in Chichester Cathedral, 1966–81; Vicar and RD of Eastbourne, 1971–75; Proctor in Convocation, 1970–75. Chairman: Nat. Council for Social Concern (formerly C of E Nat. Council for Social Aid), 1987–; Caring and Resource for People with HIV/AIDS, 1995–97. Patron, Cara, 2001–. *Recreations:* photography, travel, reading. *Address:* Braemar, Bradley Road, Bovey Tracey, Newton Abbot, Devon TQ13 9EU. *T:* (01626) 832468.

DOCTOR, Brian Ernest; QC 1999; *b* 8 Dec. 1949; *s* of Hans and Daphne Doctor; *m* 1973, Estelle Ann Lewin; three *s*. *Educ:* Balliol Coll., Oxford (BCL); Univ. of Witwatersrand (BA, LLB). Solicitor, 1978–80; Advocate, S Africa, 1980–92; SC S Africa 1990; called to the Bar, Lincoln's Inn, 1991; in practice at the Bar, 1992–. *Recreations:* reading, theatre, opera, tennis, cycling. *Address:* Fountain Court Chambers, Temple, EC4Y 9DH. *T:* (020) 7583 3335.

DOCTOROW, Edgar Lawrence; Glucksman Professor of American and English Letters, New York University, since 1987; *b* 6 Jan. 1931; *s* of David R. Doctorow and Rose Doctorow Buck; *m* 1954, Helen Setzer; one *s* two *d*. *Educ:* Kenyon College (AB 1952); Columbia Univ. (graduate study). Script-reader, Columbia Pictures, NY, 1956–59; sen. editor, New American Library, 1959–64; editor-in-chief, 1964–69, publisher, 1968–69, Dial Press; writer-in-residence, Univ. of California, Irvine, 1969–70; Mem., Faculty, Sarah Lawrence Coll., NY, 1971–78; Creative Writing Fellow, Yale Sch. of Drama, 1974–75; Vis. Sen. Fellow, Council on Humanities, Princeton, 1980–81. Hon. degrees from Brandeis Univ., Kenyon, Hobart and William Smith Colls. Guggenheim Fellowship, 1972; Creative Arts Service Fellow, 1973–74. *Publications:* Welcome to Hard Times, 1960; Big as Life, 1966; The Book of Daniel, 1971; Ragtime, 1975 (Amer. Acad. Award, Nat. Book Critics Circle Award); Drinks Before Dinner, 1979 (play, 1978); Loon Lake, 1980; Lives of the Poets, 1984; World's Fair, 1985 (American Book Award); Billy Bathgate, 1989 (Howells Medal, Amer. Acad.; PEN/Faulkner and Nat. Books Critics Awards; Premio Letterario Internationale, 1991); The Waterworks, 1994; City of God, 2000. *Address:* c/o Random House Publishers, 299 Park Avenue, New York, NY 10171, USA. *Club:* Century Association (NY).

DODD, Kenneth Arthur, (Ken Dodd), OBE 1982; entertainer, comedian, singer and actor; *b* 8 Nov. 1931; *s* of late Arthur and Sarah Dodd; unmarried. *Educ:* Holt High School, Liverpool. Made professional début at Empire Theatre, Nottingham, 1954; created record on London Palladium début, 1965, by starring in his own 42 week season; has also starred in more than 20 pantomimes. Now travels widely in quest to play every theatrical venue in British Isles. Shakespearean début as Malvolio, Twelfth Night, Liverpool, 1971. Record, Tears, topped British charts for six weeks; awarded two Gold, one Platinum, many Silver Discs (Love Is Like A Violin, Happiness, etc). *Relevant publication:* How Tickled I Am: Ken Dodd, by Michael Billington, 1977. *Recreations:* racing, soccer, reading, people. *Address:* c/o Inspirational Artiste Booking, PO Box 1AS, W1A 1AS; 76 Thomas Lane, Knotty Ash, Liverpool L14 5NX.

DODD, Philip; Director, Institute of Contemporary Arts, since 1997; *b* 25 Oct. 1949; *s* of Ernest and Mavis Dodd; *m* 1976, Kathryn; two *s*. *Educ:* UC, Swansea (BA Hons); Univ. of Leicester (MA). Lectr in English Literature, Univ. of Leicester, 1976–89; Dep. Editor, New Statesman and Society, 1989–90; Editor, Sight and Sound, BFI, 1990–97. Consultant, Music and Arts: BBC, 1986–91; Wall to Wall TV, 1991–97. *Publications:* (ed jtly) Englishness: politics and culture 1880–1920, 1986; (jtly) Relative Values: what's art worth, 1991; The Battle over Britain, 1995; (ed jtly) Spellbound, Art and Film, 1996. *Address:* Institute of Contemporary Arts, 12 Carlton House Terrace, SW1Y 5AH. *T:* (020) 7930 0493.

DODD, Philip Kevin, OBE 1987; a District Judge (Magistrates' Courts) (formerly Stipendiary Magistrate), Cheshire, since 1991; *b* 2 April 1938; *s* of Thomas and Mary Dodd; *m* 1962, Kathleen Scott; one *s* one *d*. *Educ:* St Joseph's Coll., Dumfries; Leeds Univ. (BA, LLB). Admitted Solicitor, 1966. Articled Clerk, Ashton-under-Lyne Magistrates' Court, 1961–63; Dep. Justices' Clerk, 1963–67; Justices' Clerk: Houghton-le-Spring and Seaham, 1967–70; Wolverhampton, 1970–76; Manchester, 1976–91. Council Member: Justices' Clerks' Soc., 1974–89 (Pres., 1985–86); Manchester Law Soc., 1978–91 (Pres., 1987–88). Sec., Standing Conf., Clerks to Magistrates' Courts Cttees, 1974–82 (Chm., 1983–84). *Recreations:* growing mimosa, planning holidays. *Address:* Warrington Magistrates' Court, Winmarleigh Street, Warrington WA1 1PB. *T:* (01925) 653136.

DODD, William Atherton, CMG 1983; *b* 5 Feb. 1923; *s* of Frederick Dodd and Sarah Atherton; *m* 1949, Marjorie Penfold; two *d*. *Educ:* Chester City Grammar Sch.; Christ's Coll., Cambridge (MA, CertEd). Served War, 1942–45: Captain, 8 Gurkha Rifles. Sen. History Master, Ipswich Sch., 1947–52; Educn Officer, Dept of Educn, Tanganyika, 1952–61; Sen. Educn Officer, Min. of Educn, Tanzania, 1961–65; Lectr, Dept of Educn in Developing Countries, Univ. of London Inst. of Educn, 1965–70; Educn Adviser, ODM, 1970–77; Chief Educn Advr, 1978–83, and Under Sec. (Educn Div.), 1980–83, ODA. Consultant: UC Cardiff, 1983–87; Inst. of Educn, Univ. of London, 1983–91; Child-to-Child Trust, 1988–91. UK Mem., Unesco Exec. Bd, 1983–85. Chm., Christopher Cox Meml Fund, 1983–96. Trustee, Internat. Extension Coll., 1987–96. *Publications:* A Mapbook of Exploration, 1965; Primary School Inspection in New Countries, 1968; Education for Self-Reliance in Tanzania, 1969; (with J. Cameron) Society, Schools and Progress in Tanzania, 1970; (ed) Teacher at Work, 1970; (with C. Criper) Report on the Teaching of the English Language in Tanzania, 1985. *Recreations:* music, cricket. *Address:* 20 Bayham Road, Sevenoaks, Kent TN13 3XD. *T:* (01732) 454238. *Clubs:* MCC; Sevenoaks Vine, Sevenoaks Probus.

DODDERIDGE, Morris, CBE 1974 (OBE 1962); British Council Representative, Rome, 1970–75, retired; *b* 17 Oct. 1915; *s* of Reginald William Dodderidge and Amy Andrew; *m* 1941, Esme Williams (*d* 1997); one *s* one *d* (and one *s* decd). *Educ:* Hertford Grammar Sch.; King's Coll., London; Inst. Educn, London. BA 1st cl. hons English 1937; Brewer Prize for Lit.; Teachers Dip. 1938; DipEd 1952. Asst Master, Hele's Sch., Exeter, 1938–40. War of 1939–45, Royal Signals; served N Africa, Italy, Austria (Captain, despatches). Joined British Council, 1946: Dir of Studies, Milan, 1947–53; Rep., Norway, 1953–57; Teaching of English Liaison Officer, 1957–59; Dir, Recruitment Dept, 1959–64; Controller: Recruitment Div., 1964–66; Overseas Div. A, 1966–67; Home Div. I, 1967–68; Appts Div., 1968–70. *Publications:* Man on the Matterhorn, 1940; (with W. R. Lee) Time for a Song, 1965.

DODDS, Denis George, CBE 1977; LLB (London); CompIEE; Solicitor; Chairman, British Approval Service for Electricity Cables Ltd, 1982–93; *b* 25 May 1913; *s* of Herbert Yeaman Dodds and Violet Katharine Dodds; *m* 1st, 1937, Muriel Reynolds Smith (*d* 1989); two *s* three *d*; 2nd, 1995, Penelope Jane Tuohy. *Educ:* Rutherford Coll., Newcastle upon Tyne; King's Coll., Durham Univ. Asst Solicitor and Asst Town Clerk, Gateshead, 1936–41. Served Royal Navy (Lieut RNVR), 1941–46. Dep. Town Clerk and Dep. Clerk of the Peace, City of Cardiff, 1946–48; Sec., S Wales Electricity Board, 1948–56; Chief Industrial Relations Officer, CEA and Industrial Relations Adviser, Electricity Council, 1957–59; Dep. Chm., 1960–62, Chm., 1962–77, Merseyside and N Wales Electricity Bd. Chairman: Merseyside Chamber of Commerce and Industry, 1976–78; Port of Preston Adv. Bd, 1978; Assoc. of Members of State Industry Boards, 1976–89. Member: CBI Council for Wales, 1960–78; NW Economic Planning Council, 1971; Dir, Development Corporation for Wales, 1970–83. Mem., Nat. Adv. Council for Employment of the Disabled, 1978–91. *Recreations:* music and gardening. *Address:* Corners, 28 Grange Park, Westbury on Trym, Bristol BS9 4BP. *T:* (0117) 962 1440.

DODDS, Nigel Alexander, OBE 1997; MP (DemU) Belfast North, since 2001; Member (DemU) Belfast North, Northern Ireland Assembly, since 1998; barrister; *b* 20 Aug. 1958; *s* of Joseph Alexander and Doreen Elizabeth Dodds; *m* 1985, Diana Jean Harris; two *s* one *d*. *Educ:* Portora Royal Sch., Enniskillen; St John's Coll., Cambridge (MA); Inst. of Professional Legal Studies, Belfast (Cert. of Professional Legal Studies). Called to the Bar, NI, 1981. Mem., Belfast City Council, 1985– (Chairman: F and GP Cttee, 1985–87; Develt Cttee, 1997–); Lord Mayor of Belfast, 1988–89 and 1991–92; Alderman, Castle Area, 1989–97. Minister of Social Develt, NI Assembly, 1999–2000. Vice Pres., Assoc. of Local Authorities of NI, 1988–89. Mem., NI Forum, 1996–98. Mem., Senate, QUB, 1987–93. *Address:* City Hall, Belfast BT1 5GS.

DODDS, Sir Ralph (Jordan), 2nd Bt *cr* 1964; *b* 25 March 1928; *o s* of Sir (Edward) Charles Dodds, 1st Bt, MVO, FRS, and Constance Elizabeth (*d* 1969), *o d* of late J. T. Jordan, Darlington; *S* father, 1973; *m* 1954, Marion, *er d* of late Sir Daniel Thomas Davies, KCVO; two *d*. *Educ:* Winchester; RMA, Sandhurst. Regular commission, 13/18th Royal Hussars, 1948; served UK and abroad; Malaya, 1953 (despatches); resigned, 1958. Underwriting Member of Lloyd's, 1964–97. *Address:* 49 Sussex Square, W2 2SP. *Clubs:* Cavalry and Guards, Hurlingham.

DODDS-PARKER, Sir (Arthur) Douglas, Kt 1973; MA (Oxford); company director since 1946; *b* 5 July 1909; *o s* of A. P. Dodds-Parker, FRCS, Oxford; *m* 1946, Aileen, *d* of late Norman B. Coster and late Mrs Alvin Dodd, Grand Detour, Ill., USA; one *s*. *Educ:* Winchester; Magdalen Coll., Oxford. BA in Modern History, 1930; MA 1934. Entered Sudan Political Service, 1930; Kordofan Province, 1931–34; Asst Private Sec. to Governor-General, Khartoum, 1934–35; Blue Nile Province, 1935–38; Public Security Dept, Khartoum, 1938–39; resigned 1938; joined Grenadier Guards, 1939; employed on special duties, March 1940; served in London, Cairo, East African campaign, North Africa, Italy and France, 1940–45; Mission Comdr, SOE, Western and Central Mediterranean, 1943–44; Col, 1944 (despatches, French Legion of Honour, Croix de Guerre). MP (C): Banbury Div. of Oxon, 1945–Sept. 1959; Cheltenham, 1964–Sept. 1974; Jt Parly Under-Sec. of State for Foreign Affairs, Nov. 1953–Oct. 1954, Dec. 1955–Jan. 1957; Parly Under-Sec. for Commonwealth Relations, Oct. 1954–Dec. 1955. Chairman: British Empire Producers Organisation; Joint East and Central Africa Board, 1947–50; Conservative Commonwealth Council, 1960–64; Cons. Parly Foreign and Commonwealth Cttee, 1970–73; Europe Atlantic Gp, 1976–79; Delegate to Council of Europe, North Atlantic and W European Assemblies, 1965–72; led Parly Delegn to China, 1972; Mem., British Parly Delegn to European Parlt, Strasbourg, 1973–75. Mem., Adv. Bd, 1947–99, Vice-Pres., 1999–, FANY (Princess Royal's Volunteer Corps)–. Freeman, City of London, 1983. *Publications:* Setting Europe Ablaze, 1983; Political Eunuch, 1986. *Address:* 9 North Court, Great Peter Street, SW1P 3LL. *Clubs:* Special Forces (Pres., 1977–81); Vincent's (Oxford); Leander.

DODGSON, Clare; Chief Operating Officer (formerly Director of Jobcentre Services), Employment Services Agency, 1999–March 2002; Chief Operating Officer, Jobcentre Plus, from April 2002; *b* 10 Sept. 1962; *d* of William Baxter and Ann Baxter (*née* Mattimoe); *m* 1988, Gerard Dodgson. *Educ:* St Robert of Newminster Sch., Washington; Newcastle Business Sch. (MBA). Dir of Planning and Service Develt, S Tyneside FHSA, 1990–92; Chief Executive: Newcastle FHSA, 1992–93; Sunderland HA, 1993–99. *Recreations:* travel, fast cars, good food and wine. *Address:* (office) Level 3, Steel City House, Sheffield S1 2GQ. *T:* (0114) 259 5005.

DODGSON, Paul; His Honour Judge Dodgson; a Circuit Judge, since 2001; *b* 14 Aug. 1951; *s* of late Reginald Dodgson and of Kathleen Dodgson; *m* 1982, Jan Hemingway; one *s* two *d*. *Educ:* Tiffin Sch.; Univ. of Birmingham (LLB Hons). Called to the Bar, Inner Temple, 1975; Asst Recorder, 1992–96; a Recorder, 1996–2001. Treas., Criminal Bar Assoc., 1992–94. *Recreations:* ski-ing, sailing, golf, socialising. *Address:* The Crown Court, 1 English Grounds, Southwark, SE1 2HU. *Clubs:* Hardway Sailing (Gosport); Drift Golf (E Horsley).

DODSON, family name of **Baron Monk Bretton**.

DODSON, Sir Derek (Sherborne Lindsell), KCMG 1975 (CMG 1963); MC 1945; DL; HM Diplomatic Service, retired; Special Representative of Secretary of State for Foreign and Commonwealth Affairs, 1981–95; *b* 20 Jan. 1920; *e* and *o* surv. *s* of late Charles Sherborne Dodson, MD, and Irene Frances Lindsell; *m* 1st, 1952, Julie Maynard Barnes (*d* 1992); one *s* one *d*; 2nd, 1997, Urania Massouridis (*née* Papadam); two step *s*. *Educ:* Stowe; RMC Sandhurst. Commissioned as 2nd Lieut in Royal Scots Fusiliers, 1939, and served in Army until Feb. 1948. Served War of 1939–45 (MC): India, UK, Middle East, and with Partisans in Greece and N Italy. Mil. Asst to Brit. Comr, Allied Control Commn for Bulgaria, July 1945–Sept. 1946; GSO 3, War Office, Oct. 1946–Nov. 1947; apptd a Mem. HM Foreign Service, 1948; 2nd Sec., 1948; Acting Vice-Consul at Salonika, Sept. 1948; Acting Consul Gen. there in 1949 and 1950; Second Sec., Madrid, 1951; promoted First Sec., Oct. 1951; transferred to Foreign Office, Sept. 1953; apptd Private Sec. to Minister of State for Foreign Affairs, 1955; First Sec. and Head of Chancery, Prague, Nov. 1958; Chargé d'Affaires there in 1959, 1960, 1961, 1962; promoted and apptd Consul at Elisabethville, 1962; Transf. FO and apptd Head of the Central Dept, 1963; Counsellor, British Embassy, Athens, 1966–69; Ambassador: to Hungary, 1970–73; to Brazil, 1973–77; to Turkey, 1977–80. Chm., Beaver Guarantee Ltd, 1984–86; Consultant, Benguela Rly Co. (Director, 1984–92). Chm., Anglo-Turkish

Soc., 1982–95. Mem., Bd of Governors, United World College of the Atlantic, 1982–95. DL Lincoln, 1987. Order of the Southern Cross, Brazil. *Recreations:* reading, walking. *Address:* 47 Ovington Street, SW3 2JA. *T:* (020) 7589 5055; Gable House, Leadenham, Lincoln LN5 0PN. *T:* (01400) 272212. *Clubs:* Boodle's, Travellers.

DODSON, Prof. (George) Guy, PhD; FRS 1994; Professor of Biochemistry, University of York, since 1985; Head, Division of Protein Structure, MRC National Institute for Medical Research, London, since 1993; *b* 13 Jan. 1937; *m* 1965, Eleanor McPherson; three *s* one *d.* *Educ:* New Zealand Univ. (MSc, PhD). Rockefeller res. award, Oxford Univ., 1962; Res. Fellow, Wolfson Coll., Oxford, 1973; Lectr, 1976, Reader, 1983, York Univ. *Publications:* (ed jtly) Structural Studies on Molecules of Biological Interest, 1981; articles in learned jls on protein structure and function, particularly insulin and proteins of medical interest. *Recreations:* music, wife's gardening, cricket. *Address:* Department of Chemistry, University of York, York YO1 5DD. *T:* (01904) 432520, *Fax:* (01904) 410519; MRC National Institute for Medical Research, Mill Hill, NW7 1AA. *T:* (020) 8959 3666, *Fax:* (020) 8906 4477.

DODSON, Joanna; QC 1993; *b* 5 Sept. 1945; *d* of Jack Herbert Dodson and Joan Muriel (*née* Webb); *m* 1974 (marr. diss. 1981). *Educ:* James Allen's Girls' Sch.; Newnham Coll., Cambridge (BA 1967; MA 1971). Called to the Bar, Middle Temple, 1971, Bencher, 2000. *Address:* 14 Gray's Inn Square, Gray's Inn, WC1R 5JP. *T:* (020) 7242 0858.

DODSON, Robert North; *see* North, R.

DODSWORTH, Geoffrey Hugh; JP; FCA; Chairman: Dodsworth & Co. Ltd, since 1988; Jorvik Finance Corporation Ltd, since 1986; *b* 7 June 1928; *s* of late Walter J. J. Dodsworth and Doris M. Baxter; *m* 1st, 1949, Isabel Neale (decd); one *d*; 2nd, 1971, Elizabeth Ann Beeston; one *s* one *d.* *Educ:* St Peter's Sch., York. MP (C) Herts SW, Feb. 1974–Oct. 1979, resigned. Mem. York City Council, 1959–65; JP York 1961, later JP Herts. Dir, Grindlays Bank Ltd, 1976–80; Chief Exec., Grindlay Brandts Ltd, 1977–80; Pres. and Chief Exec., Oceanic Finance Corp., 1980–85, Dep. Chm., 1985–86; Chm., Oceanic Financial Services, 1985–86; Director: County Properties Group, 1987–88; First Internat. Leasing Corp., 1990–94. *Recreation:* riding. *Address:* Mill Hill House, Constable Burton, Leyburn, N Yorks DL8 5RQ. *T:* (01677) 450448, *Fax:* (01677) 450335; *e-mail:* dodsworth@jorvikf.demon.6.uk. *Clubs:* Carlton; Royal Bermuda Yacht.

DODSWORTH, Prof. (James) Martin; Professor of English, Royal Holloway (formerly Royal Holloway and Bedford New College), University of London, since 1987; *b* 10 Nov. 1935; *s* of Walter Edward and Kathleen Ida Dodsworth; *m* 1967, Joanna Rybicka; one *s.* *Educ:* St George's Coll., Weybridge; Univ. of Fribourg, Switzerland; Wadham Coll., Oxford (MA). Asst Lectr and Lectr in English, Birkbeck Coll., London, 1961–67; Lectr and Sen. Lectr, Royal Holloway Coll., later Royal Holloway and Bedford New Coll., London, 1967–87. Vis. Lectr, Swarthmore Coll., Pa, 1966. Chairman: English Assoc., 1987–92; Cttee for University English, 1988–90. Editor, English, 1976–87. *Publications:* (ed) The Survival of Poetry, 1970; Hamlet Closely Observed, 1985; (ed) English Economis'd, 1989; (ed) The Penguin History of Literature, vol. 7: The Twentieth Century, 1994; (with J. B. Bamborough) Commentary to Robert Burton, the Anatomy of Melancholy, 1998–2000; contribs to The Guardian, Essays in Criticism, The Review, etc. *Recreations:* reading, eating and drinking, short walks. *Address:* 59 Temple Street, Brill, Bucks HP18 9SU. *T:* (01844) 237106.

DODSWORTH, Sir John Christopher S.; *see* Smith-Dodsworth.

DODSWORTH, Martin; *see* Dodsworth, J. M.

DODWORTH, Air Vice-Marshal Peter, CB 1994; OBE 1982; AFC 1971; FRAeS; Royal Air Force, retired; Military Adviser to Bombardier Aerospace Defence Services, 1996–2000; *b* 12 Sept. 1940; *e s* of Eric and Edna Dodworth; *m* 1963, Kay Parry; three *s.* *Educ:* Southport Grammar Sch.; Leeds Univ. (BSc Physics, 1961). FRAeS 1997. Served: 54 Sqn Hunters, 1963–65; 4 FTS Gnats, 1965–67; Central Flying Sch., 1967–68; Harrier Conversion Team, 1969–72; Air Staff RAF Germany, 1972–76; OC Ops, RAF Wittering, 1976–79; ndc 1980; Air Comdr, Belize, 1980–82; staff, RAF Staff Coll., 1982–83; Stn comdr, RAF Wittering, 1983–85; Command Group Exec., HQ AAFCE, Ramstein, 1985–87; RCDS, 1987; Dir of Personnel, MoD, 1988–91; Defence Attaché and Hd, British Defence Staff (Washington), 1991–94; Sen. DS (A), RCDS, 1995–96. *Recreations:* golf, DIY, reading. *Club:* Royal Air Force.

DOE, Rt Rev. Michael David; *see* Swindon, Bishop Suffragan of.

DOE, Prof. William Fairbank, FRCP, FRACP, FMedSci; Professor, Dean of Medicine, Dentistry and Health Sciences and Head of Medical School, University of Birmingham, since 1998; *b* 6 May 1941; *s* of Asa Garfield Doe and Hazel Thelma Doe; *m* 1982, Dallas Elizabeth Edith Ariotti; two *s.* *Educ:* Newington Coll., Sydney; Univ. of Sydney (MB BS); Chelsea Coll., Univ. of London (MSc). FRACP 1978; FRCP 1982. MRC Fellow, 1970–71, Lectr, 1973–74, RPMS; Consultant, Hammersmith Hosp., 1973–74; Lilly Internat. Fellow, 1974–75, NIH Fellow, 1975–77, Scripps Clinic and Res. Foundn, Calif; Associate Prof., Univ. of Sydney, and Hon. Physician, Royal N Shore Hosp., 1978–81; Prof. of Medicine and Clin. Scis, 1982–88, Head of Div. of Molecular Medicine, 1988–98, John Curtin Sch. of Med. Res., ANU; Dir of Gastroenterology, Canberra Hosp., 1991–97; Prof. of Medicine, Univ. of Sydney, 1995–98. WHO Cons., Beijing, 1987; Dist. Vis. Fellow, Christ's Coll., Cambridge, 1988–89. Non-exec. Dir, 1998–, Dep. Chm., 2000–, Birmingham HA. Pres., Gastroenterological Soc. of Australia, 1989–91 (Dist. Res. Medal, 1997); Member: NH&MRC Social Psychiatry Adv. Cttee, 1982–92; Council, Nat. Centre for Epidemiology Population Health, 1987–98; Aust. Drug Evaluation Cttee, 1988–95; Council, RACP, 1993–98 (Censor, 1980–87); NH&MRC Res. Strategy Cttee, 1997–98. Lunar Soc., 1999–. FMedSci 1999. Sen. Editor, Jl Gastroenterology and Hepatology, 1993–. *Publications:* numerous scientific papers on molecular cell biology of mucosal inflammation and colon cancer. *Recreations:* opera, reading, wine, tennis. *Address:* Medical School, University of Birmingham, Edgbaston, Birmingham B15 2TT. *T:* (0121) 414 4044; *e-mail:* w.f.doe@bham.ac.uk. *Club:* Commonwealth (Canberra).

DOERR, Michael Frank, FIA; Group Chief Executive, Friends Provident Life Office, 1992–97; *b* 25 May 1935; *s* of Frank and May Doerr; *m* 1958, Jill Garrett; one *s* one *d.* *Educ:* Rutlish Sch. FIA 1959. Friends Provident Life Office, 1954–97: Pensions Actuary, 1960–66; Life Manager, 1966–73; Gen. Manager, Marketing, 1973–80; Gen. Manager, Ops, and Dir, 1980–87; Dep. Man. Dir, 1987–92. Director: Endsleigh Insce Services Ltd, 1980–94; Seaboard Life Insce Co. (Canada), 1987–92; Friends Provident Life Assce Co. (Australia), 1990–92; Friends Provident Life Assce Co. (Ireland), 1990–92; Friends Vilas-Fischer Trust Co. (US), 1996–98. Chairman: Preferred Direct Insce, 1992–97; FP Asset Mgt, 1996–97. *Recreations:* golf, tennis, chess, theatre, sailing. *Clubs:* Royal Automobile; Royal Southern Yacht; Meon Valley Country.

DOGGART, George Hubert Graham, OBE 1993; Headmaster, King's School, Bruton, 1972–85; *b* 18 July 1925; *e s* of late Alexander Graham Doggart and Grace Carlisle Hannan; *m* 1960, Susan Mary, *d* of R. I. Beattie, Eastbourne; one *s* two *d.* *Educ:* Winchester; King's Coll., Cambridge. BA History, 1950; MA 1955. Army, 1943–47 (Sword of Honour, 161 OCTU, Mons, 1944); Coldstream Guards. On staff at Winchester, 1950–72 (exchange at Melbourne C of E Grammar Sch., 1963); Housemaster, 1964–72. HMC Schools rep. on Nat. Cricket Assoc., 1964–75; President: English Schools Cricket Assoc., 1965–2000; Quidnuncs, 1983–88; Cricket Soc., 1983–98; Member: Cricket Council, 1968–71, 1972, 1983–92; MCC Cttee, 1975–78, 1979–81, 1982–92 (Pres., 1981–82; Treas., 1987–92). Captain, Butterflies CC, 1986–97. Chm., Friends of Arundel Castle CC, 1992–. *Publications:* (ed) The Heart of Cricket: memoir of H. S. Altham, 1967; (jtly) Lord Be Praised: the story of MCC's bicentenary celebrations, 1988; (jtly) Oxford and Cambridge Cricket, 1989. *Recreations:* literary and sporting (captained Cambridge v Oxford at cricket, Association football, rackets and squash, 1949–50; played in Rugby fives, 1950; played for England v W Indies, two tests, 1950; captained Sussex, 1954). *Address:* 19 Westgate, Chichester, West Sussex PO19 3ET. *Clubs:* MCC, Lord's Taverners; Hawks (Cambridge).

DOGGETT, (Thomas) Stephen; Executive Director, Cottage and Rural Enterprises Ltd, 1990–98 (Director of Development, 1984–90); *b* 7 Jan. 1935; *s* of Arthur Francis Doggett and Mary Elizabeth Doggett (*née* Horder); *m* 1960, Susan Gillian Tyndale; two *s* one *d.* *Educ:* St Faith's, Cambridge; Gresham's Sch., Holt; Queens' Coll., Cambridge (BA Nat. Scis 1958; MA 1963). Nat. Service, Royal Signals, 1953–55. Sketchley PLC, 1958–84; Technical Dir, Sketchley Cleaners, 1978–84. Pres., Assoc. of British Launderers and Cleaners, 1981–83. *Recreations:* ski-ing, golf, vintage and classic cars, family. *Address:* Bay Tree Cottage, 47 Lutterworth Road, Burbage, Hinckley, Leics LE10 2DJ. *T:* (01455) 239410.

DOHA, Aminur Rahman S.; *see* Shams-ud Doha, A. R.

DOHERTY, Arthur; Member (SDLP) Londonderry East, Northern Ireland Assembly, since 1998; *b* 19 Jan. 1932; *s* of Michael Doherty and Mary Doherty (*née* Devlin); *m* 1956, Mary Farrell; one *s* two *d.* *Educ:* Barrack Street Primary Sch., Strabane; St Columb's Coll., Derry; St Joseph's Coll. of Education, Belfast (Teacher's Cert. 1956; ATC 1956); Univ. of Ulster (BEd Hons Education and Art 1981). Teacher, St Columba's Primary Sch., Derry, 1953–57; Principal, Duncrun Primary Sch., Derry, 1957–69; Head of Art and Design, St Mary's High Sch., Limavady, Co. Derry, 1969–89. Mem., NI Forum for Political Dialogue, 1996. Mem. (SDLP), Limavady BC, 1977–; Mayor, Limavady, 1993–94. Member: NW Reg. Cross-Border Gp, 1989– (former Chair); Western Educn and Liby Bd, 1993–; Council for Nature Conservation and the Countryside, 1995–; Chair, Forum for Local Govt and the Arts, 1995–. Contested (SDLP) Londonderry E, UK parly elecns, 1983, 1987, 1992, 1997. *Recreations:* wife and family, reading, crosswords, galleries and museums, physical recreation no longer possible except for gentle walking, gardening, swimming. *Address:* Gartan, 30 Tircreven Road, Magilligan, Limavady BT49 0LN.

DOHERTY, (Joseph) Raymond; QC (Scot.) 1997; *b* 30 Jan. 1958; *s* of James Doherty and Mary Doherty (*née* Woods); *m* 1994, Arlene Donaghy; one *s* two *d.* *Educ:* St Mungo's Primary Sch., Alloa; St Joseph's Coll., Dumfries; Univ. of Edinburgh (LLB 1st Cl. Hons 1980); Hertford Coll., Oxford (BCL 1982); Harvard Law Sch. (LLM 1983). Lord Reid Schol., 1983–85; admitted Faculty of Advocates, 1984; Standing Junior Counsel: MoD (Army), Scotland, 1990–91; Scottish Office Industry Dept, 1992–97; Advocate Depute, 1998–2001. Clerk of the Faculty of Advocates, 1990–95. *Publications:* (ed jtly) Armour on Valuation for Rating, 1990–; (contrib.) Stair Memorial Encyclopaedia of the Laws of Scotland. *Address:* Advocates' Library, Parliament House, Parliament Square, Edinburgh EH1 1RF. *T:* (0131) 226 5071.

DOHERTY, Michael Eunan; Chairman, King's College Hospital (formerly King's Healthcare) NHS Trust, since 1996; *b* 21 Sept. 1939; *s* of Michael Joseph Doherty and Grace Doherty (*née* Gallagher); *m* 1965, Judy Battams; two *s* two *d.* *Educ:* St Bernard's RC Sch., London. FCA 1977. Partner, Turquands Barton Mayhew, 1960–72; Man. Dir, Anglo-Thai Gp, 1973–82; Chief Exec., Cope Allman Internat. plc, 1982–88; Chairman: Henlys plc, 1985–88, 1991–97; Norcros plc, 1988–97. Trustee, KCH Charitable Trust, 1999–. Chm. Govs, St John's Sch., Leatherhead, 1997–. CIMgt 1985. *Recreations:* golf, music, reading, politics. *Address:* 43 Crown Road, Twickenham TW1 3EJ. *T:* (020) 8892 7727. *Club:* Royal Automobile.

DOHERTY, Pat; MP (SF) Tyrone West, since 2001; Member (SF) Tyrone West, Northern Ireland Assembly, since 1998; *b* Glasgow, 18 July 1945; *m*; two *s* three *d.* Sinn Féin: Dir of Elections, 1984–85; Nat. Organiser, 1985–88; Vice-Pres., 1988–; Leader of delegn to Forum for Peace and Reconciliation, Dublin, 1994–96. Chm., Enterprise, Trade and Investment Cttee, NI Assembly, 1999–. Contested (SF) Tyrone West, 1997. *Address:* (office) 12 Bridge Street, Strabane, Co. Tyrone BT82 9AE; Northern Ireland Assembly, Stormont Castle, Belfast BT4 3ST; c/o House of Commons, SW1A 0AA.

DOHERTY, Prof. Peter Charles, AC 1997; FRS 1987; FAA 1983; Chairman, Department of Immunology, St Jude Children's Research Hospital, since 1988; *b* 15 Oct. 1940; *s* of Eric C. and Linda M. Doherty; *m* 1965, Penelope Stephens; two *s.* *Educ:* Univ. of Queensland (BVSc, MVSc); Univ. of Edinburgh (PhD). Veterinary Officer, Queensland Dept of Primary Industries, 1962–67; Scientific Officer, Moredun Research Inst., Edinburgh, 1967–71; Research Fellow, Dept of Microbiology, John Curtin Sch. of Med. Research, Canberra, 1972–75; Associate Prof., later Prof., Wistar Inst., Philadelphia, 1975–82; Prof. of Experimental Pathology, John Curtin Sch. of Medical Res., ANU, 1982–88. Bd Mem., Internat. Lab. for Res. on Animal Disease, Nairobi, 1987–92. Mem., US Nat. Acad. of Sci., 1998. Hon. DVSc Queensland, 1995; Hon. DSc: ANU, 1996; Tufts, 1997; Edinburgh, Warsaw Agricl Univ., 1998. Paul Ehrlich Prize and Medal for Immunology, 1983; Gairdner Internat. Award for Med. Research, 1987; Alumnus of Year, Univ. of Queensland, 1993; Lasker Award for Basic Med. Res., 1995; (jtly) Nobel Prize in Physiology or Medicine, 1996. *Publications:* papers in scientific jls. *Recreations:* walking, reading. *Address:* c/o St Jude Children's Research Hospital, 332 North Lauderdale Street, Memphis, TN 38105–2794, USA. *T:* (901) 4953470, *Fax:* (901) 4953107.

DOHERTY, Raymond; *see* Doherty, J. R.

DOHMANN, Barbara; QC 1987; a Recorder, since 1990; a Deputy High Court Judge, since 1994; *b* Berlin; *d* of Paul Dohmann and Dora Dohmann (*née* Thiele). *Educ:* schools in Germany and USA; Univs of Erlangen, Mainz and Paris. Called to the Bar, Gray's Inn, 1971. Mem., Learned Soc. for Internat. Civil Procedure Law, 1991–; Chm., Commercial Bar Assoc., 1999– (Treas., 1997–99); Member: Gen. Council of the Bar, 1999–; Legal Services Cttee, 2000–. Mem. Bd of Govs, London Inst. Higher Educn Corp., 1993–2000. *Recreations:* gardening, opera, fiction, art. *Address:* Blackstone Chambers, Blackstone House, Temple, EC4Y 9BW. *T:* (020) 7583 1770. *Club:* CWIL.

DOHNÁNYI, Christoph v.; *see* von Dohnányi.

DOIG, Ralph Herbert, CMG 1974; CVO 1954; *b* 24 Feb. 1909; *s* of late William and Rose Doig; *m* 1937, Barbara Crock; two *s* four *d.* *Educ:* Guildford Grammar Sch.; University of Western Australia (BA, DipCom). Entered Public Service of WA, 1926; Private Sec. to various Premiers, 1929–41; Asst Under-Sec., Premier's Dept, 1941; Under-Sec., Premier's Dept, and Clerk of Executive Council, Perth, Western Australia, 1945–65; Public Service Comr, W Australia, 1965–71; Chm., Public Service Board, WA, 1971–74. State Director: visit to Western Australia of the Queen and the Duke of Edinburgh, 1954; visit of the Duke of Edinburgh for British Empire and Commonwealth Games, 1962; visit of the Queen and the Duke of Edinburgh, 1963. *Recreation:* bowls. *Address:* Chrystal Halliday Homes, Unit 17, 61 Jeanes Road, Karrinyup, WA 6018, Australia. *T:* (8) 92456452.

DOLBY, Elizabeth Grace; *see* Cassidy, E. G.

DOLBY, Ray Milton, Hon. OBE 1986; PhD; engineering company executive; electrical engineer; Owner and Chairman, Dolby Laboratories Inc., San Francisco and London, since 1965; *b* Portland, Ore, 18 Jan. 1933; *s* of Earl Milton Dolby and Esther Eufemia (*née* Strand); *m* 1966, Dagmar Baumert; two *s.* *Educ:* San Jose State Coll.; Washington Univ.; Stanford Univ. (Beach Thompson award, BS Elec. Engrg); Pembroke Coll., Cambridge (Marshall schol., 1957–60, Draper's studentship, 1959–61, NSF Fellow, 1960–61; PhD Physics 1961; Fellow, 1961–63; research in long-wave length x-rays, 1957–63; Hon. Fellow 1983). Electronic technician/jun. engr, Ampex Corp., Redwood City, Calif, 1949–53. Served US Army 1953–54. Engr, 1955–57; Sen. Engr, 1957; UNESCO Advr, Central Sci. Instruments Org., Punjab, 1963–65; Cons., UKAEA, 1962–63. Inventions, research, pubns in video tape rec., x-ray microanalysis, noise reduction and quality improvements in audio and video systems; 50 UK patents. Trustee, Univ. High Sch., San Francisco, 1978–84; Mem., Marshall Scholarships Selection Cttee, 1979–85; Dir, San Francisco Opera; Governor, San Francisco Symphony. Fellow: Audio Engrg Soc. (Silver Medal, 1971; Gold Medal, 1992; Governor, 1972–74, 1979–84; Pres., 1980–81); Brit. Kinematograph, Sound and Television Soc. (Outstanding Technical and Scientific Award, 1995); Soc. Motion Picture, TV Engrs (S. L. Warner award, 1978; Alexander M. Poniatoff Gold Medal, 1982; Progress Medal, 1983; Hon. Mem., 1992); Inst. of Broadcast Sound, 1987; Hon. Fellow, Assoc. of Motion Picture Sound, 1999. MIEEE (Ibuka Award, 1997); Tau Beta Pi. Hon. ScD Cambridge, 1997; DUniv York, 1999. Other Awards: Emmy, for contrib. to Ampex video recorder, 1957, and for noise reduction systems on video recorder sound tracks, 1989; Trendsetter, Billboard, 1971; Lyre, Inst. High Fidelity, 1972; Emile Berliner Assoc. Maker of Microphone award, 1972; Top 200 Execs Bi-Centennial, 1976; Sci. and Engrg, 1979, Oscar, 1989, Acad. of Motion Picture Arts and Scis; Man of the Yr, Internat. Tape Assoc., 1987; Pioneer Award, Internat. Teleproduction Soc., 1988; Eduard Rhein Ring, Eduard Rhein Foundn, 1988; Life Achievement Award, Cinema Audio Soc., 1989; Grammy, Nat. Acad. of Recording Arts and Scis, 1995; Medal of Achievement, Amer. Electronics Assoc., 1997; Nat. Medal of Technol., US Dept of Commerce, 1997; inductee, Hall of Fame, Consumer Electronics Assoc., 2000; Internat. Honour for Excellence (John Tucker Award), Internat. Broadcasting Convention, 2000. *Recreations:* yachting, ski-ing, flying. *Address:* (home) 3340 Jackson Street, San Francisco, CA 94118, USA. *T:* (415) 563–6947; (office) 100 Potrero Avenue, San Francisco, CA 94103. *T:* (415) 5580200.

DOLE, Bob; *see* Dole, R. J.

DOLE, John Anthony; Controller and Chief Executive of HM Stationery Office, and the Queen's Printer of Acts of Parliament, 1987–89, retired; *b* 14 Oct. 1929; *s* of Thomas Stephen Dole and Winifred Muriel (*née* Henderson); *m* 1952, Patricia Ivy Clements; two *s.* *Educ:* Bideford Grammar Sch.; Berkhamsted Sch. Air Ministry: Exec. Officer, 1950; Higher Exec. Officer, 1959; Principal, 1964; Ministry of Transport: Principal, 1965; Asst Sec. (Roads Programme), 1968; Administrator of Sports Council, 1972–75; Under Sec., Freight Directorate, 1976–78; Dir, Senior Staff Management, Depts of the Environment and Transport, 1978–82; Controller of Supplies, PSA, DoE, 1982–84; Controller of the Crown Suppliers, 1984–86. *Publications: plays:* Cat on the Fiddle, 1964; Shock Tactics, 1966; Lucky for Some, 1968; Once in a Blue Moon, 1972; Top Gear, 1976; *verse:* Odd Bodikins, 1992. *Recreations:* writing, philately.

DOLE, Robert Joseph, (Bob); Purple Heart; United States Senator, 1968–96; Leader, United States Senate, 1995–96 (Senate Republican Leader, 1985–96); Leader, Republican Party, United States, 1992–96; *b* Russell, Kansas, 22 July 1923; *s* of Doran and Bina Dole; *m* 1975, Elizabeth Hanford; one *d.* *Educ:* Univ. of Kansas (AB); Washburn Municipal Univ. (LLB). Served US Army, 1943–48; Platoon Ldr, 10th Mountain Div., Italy; wounded and decorated twice for heroic achievement; Captain. Kansas Legislature, 1951–53; Russell County Attorney, Kansas, 1953–61; US House of Representatives, 1960–68. Republican Nominee for President, 1996. US Presidential Medal of Freedom, 1997. *Address:* (office) Suite 410, 901 15th Street NW, Washington, DC 20005, USA.

DOLL, Prof. Sir (William) Richard (Shaboe), CH 1996; Kt 1971; OBE 1956; DM, MD, DSc; FRCP, FMedSci; FRS 1966; Hon. Consultant, Imperial Cancer Research Fund Cancer Studies Unit, Radcliffe Infirmary, Oxford, since 1983; first Warden, Green College, Oxford, 1979–83; *b* Hampton, 28 Oct. 1912; *s* of Henry William Doll and Amy Kathleen Shaboe; *m* 1949, Joan Mary Faulkner, MB, BS, MRCP, DPH (*d* 2001); one *s* one *d.* *Educ:* Westminster Sch. (Hon. Fellow, 1991); St Thomas's Hosp. Med. Sch., London. MB, BS 1937; MD 1945; FRCP 1957; DSc London 1958. RAMC, 1939–45. Appts with Med. Research Council, 1946–69; Mem. Statistical Research Unit, 1948; Dep. Dir, 1959; Dir, 1961–69; Hon. Associate Physician, Central Middlesex Hosp., 1949–69; Teacher in Medical Statistics and Epidemiology, University Coll. Hosp. Med. Sch., 1963–69; Regius Prof. of Medicine, Oxford Univ., 1969–79. Member: MRC, 1970–74; Royal Commn on Environmental Pollution, 1973–79; Standing Commn on Energy and the Environment, 1978–81; Scientific Council of Internat. Cancer Research Agency, 1966–70 and 1975–78; Council, Royal Society, 1970–71, 1996–98 (a Vice-Pres., 1970–71); Chairman: Adverse Reaction Sub-Cttee, Cttee on Safety of Medicines, 1970–77; UK Co-ordinating Cttee on Cancer Research, 1972–77. William Julius Mickle Fellow, Univ. of London, 1955. Hon. Lectr London Sch. of Hygiene and Tropical Med., 1956–62 (Hon. Fellow 1982); Milroy Lectr, RCP, 1953; Marc Daniels Lectr, RCP, 1969; Harveian Orator, RCP, 1982. Founder FMedSci 1998. Emeritus Fellow, Academia Europaea, 1990; Hon. Fellow: FPHM, 1974; RCGP, 1978; FOM, 1987; RCOG, 1992; UMDS, 1992; RCR, 1993; RCS, 1997; Hon. FIA 1999. Hon. Foreign Member: Norwegian Acad. of Scis, Amer. Acad. of Arts and Scis. Hon DSc: Newcastle, 1969; Belfast, 1972; Reading, 1973; Newfoundland, 1973; Stony Brook, 1988; Harvard, 1988; London, 1988; Oxon, 1989; Oxford Brookes, 1994; Kingston, 1996; Hon. DM Tasmania, 1976; Hon. MD: Birmingham, 1994; Bergen, 1996. David Anderson Berry Prize (jt), RSE 1958; Bisset Hawkins Medal, RCP, 1962; UN award for cancer research, 1962; Gairdner Award, Toronto, 1970; Buchanan Medal, Royal Soc., 1972; Presidential award, NY Acad. Sci., 1974; Prix Griffuel, Paris, 1976; Gold Medal, RIPH&H, 1977; Mott Award, Gen. Motors' Cancer Res. Foundn, 1979; Bruce Medal, Amer. Coll. of Physicians, 1981; National Award, Amer. Cancer Soc., 1981; Gold Medal, BMA, 1983; Conrad Röntgen prize, Accademia dei Lincei, 1984; Johann-Georg-Zimmermann Prize, Hanover, 1985; Royal Medal, Royal Soc., 1986; Ettore Majorana Erice Science for Peace Prize, 1990; first Helmut Horten Award, Lugano, 1991; first Prince Mahidol Award, Bangkok, 1992; Gold Medal, RSocMed, 1997; British Thoracic Soc. Medal, 1998; Hewitt Award, RSocMed, 1999. *Publications:* Prevention of Cancer: pointers from epidemiology, 1967; (jtly) Causes of Cancer, 1982; (jtly) Cancer Incidence and Mortality in England and Wales, 2001; articles in scientific journals on aetiology of lung cancer, leukaemia and other cancers, also aetiology and treatment of peptic ulcer, effects of smoking, ionizing radiations, oral contraceptives; author (jt) Med. Research Council's Special Report Series, 1951, 1957, 1964. *Recreations:* food and conversation. *Address:* 12 Rawlinson Road, Oxford OX2 6UE.

DOLLERY, Sir Colin (Terence), Kt 1987; FRCP, FMedSci; Senior Consultant, Research and Development, Smithkline Beecham plc, since 1996; Dean, Royal Postgraduate Medical School, 1991–96, Pro-Vice-Chancellor for Medicine (formerly Medicine and Dentistry), 1992–96, University of London; *b* 14 March 1931; *s* of Cyril Robert and Thelma Mary Dollery; *m* 1958, Diana Myra (*née* Stedman); one *s* one *d.* *Educ:* Lincoln Sch.; Birmingham Univ. (BSc, MB,ChB); FRCP 1968. House officer: Queen Elizabeth Hosp., Birmingham; Hammersmith Hosp., and Brompton Hosp., 1956–58; Hammersmith Hospital: Med. Registrar, 1958–60; Sen. Registrar and Tutor in Medicine, 1960–62; Consultant Physician, 1962–; Lectr in Medicine, 1962–65, Prof. of Clinical Pharmacology, 1965–87, Prof. of Medicine, 1987–91, Royal Postgrad. Med. Sch. Member: MRC, 1982–84; UGC, subseq. UFC, 1984–91. Founder FMedSci 1998. Hon. Mem., Assoc. of Amer. Physicians, 1982. Chevalier de l'Ordre National du Mérite (France), 1976. *Publications:* The Retinal Circulation, 1971 (New York); Therapeutic Drugs, 1991, 2nd edn 1998; numerous papers in scientific jls concerned with high blood pressure and drug action. *Recreations:* travel, amateur radio, work. *Address:* 101 Corringham Road, NW11 7DL. *T:* (020) 8458 2616. *Club:* Athenæum.

DOLLEY, Christopher; Chairman, Damis Agencies Ltd, since 1983; *b* 11 Oct. 1931; *yr s* of late Dr Leslie George Francis Dolley and of Jessie, Otford, Kent; *m* 1966, Christine Elizabeth Cooper; three *s.* *Educ:* Bancroft's Sch.; Corpus Christi Coll., Cambridge. Joined Unilever, 1954; with Unilever subsidiaries, 1954–62: G. B. Ollivant Ltd, 1954–59; United Africa Co., 1959–62. Joined Penguin Books Ltd as Export Manager, 1962; became Dir, 1964, Man. Dir, 1970–73, Chm., 1971–73; Dir for Book Develt, IPC, 1973–77. Exec. Vice-Pres., Penguin Books Inc., Baltimore, 1966; Director: Penguin Publishing Co., 1969–73 (Jt Man. Dir, 1969); Pearson Longman Ltd, 1970–73; The Hamlyn Group, 1971–81; Globalscan Ltd, 1997–. Mem., Nat. Film Finance Corp., 1971–81; Dir, Nat. Film Trustee Corp., 1971–81. *Publication:* (ed) The Penguin Book of English Short Stories, 1967. *Recreations:* golf, gardening, collecting. *Clubs:* Savile; 14 West Hamilton Street (Baltimore, Md).

DOLMAN, Edward James; Chief Executive Officer, Christie's International plc, since 1999; *b* 24 Feb. 1960; *s* of James William Dolman and Jean Dolman; *m* 1987, Clare Callaghan; one *s* one *d.* *Educ:* Dulwich Coll.; Southampton Univ. (BA Hons History). Joined Christie's, 1984; Dir and Head of Furniture Dept, Christie's S Kensington, 1990–95; Man. Dir, Christie's Amsterdam, 1995–97; Commercial Dir, 1997, Man. Dir, 1998–99, Christie's Europe; Dir, Christie, Manson & Woods Ltd, 1997; Man. Dir, Christie's America, 1999–. *Recreations:* art history, Rugby, cricket, sailing. *Address:* Christie's, 8 King Street, St James's, SW1Y 6QT. *T:* (020) 7389 2881. *Clubs:* Royal Automobile, Old Alleynian (Vice Pres., 1998–).

DOLMAN, Dr William Frederick Gerrit; JP; HM Coroner, North London, since 1993; *b* 14 Nov. 1942; *s* of Dr Gerrit Arnold Dolman and Madeline Joan Dolman. *Educ:* Whitgift Sch., Croydon; KCH Med. Sch., Univ. of London (MB BS 1965); LLB Hons London (ext.) 1987. MRCS 1965; LRCP 1965. Principal in Gen. Practice, 1967–74; Asst Dep. Coroner, 1974–86, Dep. Coroner, 1986–93, S London; Medical Referee, Croydon Crematorium, 1986–; Asst Dep. Coroner, 1988–89, Dep. Coroner, 1989–93, Inner W London. Associate Dermatology Specialist, St Helier Hosp., Carshalton, 1992–. BBC Radio Doctor, Jimmy Young Show, Radio 2, 1977–96. FRSocMed 1967 (Mem. Council, Forensic and Legal Medicine Section, 1996–2000). Pres., Croydon Medical Soc., 2002. Med. Editor, Modern Medicine, 1976–80. JP Croydon, 1975. *Publications:* Can I Speak to the Doctor?, 1981; Doctor on Call, 1987. *Recreations:* classical music, good food, fine wine, real ale, sitting in the garden looking at work that ought to be done. *Address:* Coroner's Court, Myddelton Road, Hornsey, N8 7PY. *T:* (020) 8348 4411. *Club:* Authors' (Chm., 2000–).

DOLTON, David John William; management consultant, since 1989; *b* 15 Sept. 1928; *e s* of late Walter William and Marie Frances Duval Dolton; *m* 1959, Patricia Helen Crowe (marr. diss. 1985); one *s* one *d*; *m* 1986, Rosalind Jennifer Chivers. *Educ:* St Lawrence Coll., Ramsgate. FCIS, FCIPD, FIMgt. 2nd Lt RA, 1946–48. Various appointments in Delta Metal Co. Ltd, 1950–76, incl. Commercial Director, Extrusion Division, and Director of Administration and Personnel, Rod Division, 1967–76; Chief Exec., Equal Opportunities Commn, 1976–78; Asst Gen. Manager, Nat. Employers Mutual Gen. Insce Assoc. Ltd, 1979–89. Governor, The Queen's Coll., Birmingham, 1974–88. Reader Emeritus, Dio. Gloucester. Liveryman, Worshipful Co. of Gold and Silver Wyre Drawers. *Recreations:* music, reading, walking, crewing on Tall Ships, travel, photography. *Address:* Arrabon, Cirencester Road, South Cerney, Cirencester, Glos GL7 6HT. *T:* (01285) 862600.

DOMB, Prof. Cyril, PhD; FRS 1977; Professor of Physics, Bar-Ilan University, 1981–89, now Emeritus; *m* Shirley Galinsky; three *s* three *d.* *Educ:* Hackney Downs Sch.; Pembroke Coll., Cambridge. Major Open Schol., Pembroke Coll., 1938–41; Radar Research, Admiralty, 1941–46; MA Cambridge, 1945; Nahum Schol., Pembroke Coll., 1946; PhD Cambridge, 1949; ICI Fellowship, Clarendon Laboratory, Oxford, 1949–52; MA Oxon, 1952; University Lecturer in Mathematics, Cambridge, 1952–54; Prof. of Theoretical Physics, KCL, 1954–81; FKC 1978. Max Born Prize, Inst. of Physics and German Physical Soc., 1981. *Publications:* (ed) Clerk Maxwell and Modern Science, 1963; (ed) Memories of Kopul Rosen, 1970; Phase Transitions and Critical Phenomena, (ed with M.S. Green) vols 1 and 2, 1972, vol. 3, 1974, vols 5a, 5b, 6, 1976, (ed with J. L. Lebowitz) vols 7 and 8, 1983, vol. 9, 1984, vol. 10, 1986, vol. 11, 1987, vol. 12, 1988, vol. 13, 1989, vol. 14, 1991, vol. 15, 1992, vol. 16, 1994, vol. 17, 1995, vols 18–20, 2001; (ed with A. Carmell) Challenge, 1976; The Critical Point, 1996; articles in scientific journals. *Recreations:* walking, swimming. *Address:* Department of Physics, Bar-Ilan University, 52900 Ramat-Gan, Israel; 28 St Peter's Court, Queens Road, NW4 2HG.

DOMINGO, Placido; tenor singer, conductor; Artistic Director, Washington Opera, since 1994; Artistic Director, since 2000, and Artistic Adviser and Principal Guest Conductor, Los Angeles Opera; *b* Madrid, 21 Jan. 1941; *s* of Placido Domingo and Pepita (*née* Embil), professional singers; *m* 1962, Marta Ornelas, lyric soprano; two *s* (and one *s* by former marriage). *Educ:* Instituto, Mexico City; Nat. Conservatory of Music, Mexico City. Operatic début, Monterrey, as Alfredo in La Traviata, 1961; with opera houses at

Dallas, Fort Worth, Israel, to 1965; NY City Opera, 1965–; débuts: at NY Metropolitan Opera, as Maurizio in Adriana Lecouvreur, 1968; at La Scala, title role in Ernani, 1969; at Covent Garden, Cavaradossi in Tosca, 1971. Has conducted in Vienna, Barcelona, NY and Frankfurt; début as conductor in UK, Covent Garden, 1983. *Films:* La Traviata, 1983; Carmen, 1984; Otello, 1986; appears on TV, makes recordings, throughout USA and Europe. FRCM; FRNCM. Officer, Legion of Honour, 1983; Medal of City of Madrid. *Publication:* My First Forty Years (autobiog.), 1983. *Recreations:* piano, swimming.

DOMINGO SOLANS, Dr Eugenio; Member, Executive Board, European Central Bank, since 1998; *b* Barcelona, 26 Nov. 1945. *Educ:* French Lycée, Barcelona; Univ. of Barcelona (BEc 1968); Autonomous Univ. of Madrid (DEc 1975). Professor of Public Finance: Univ. of Barcelona, 1968-70; Autonomous Univ. of Madrid, 1970-; economist: Banco Atlántico, 1970, 1973-77, 1978-79; Res. Gp, Spanish Govt's Econ. and Social Develt Plan Dept, 1970-73; Econ. Advr, Min. of Economy, 1977-78; Manager, Res. Dept, Inst. of Econ. Studies, 1979-86; Asst Pres., 1986-94, Mem. Bd and Exec. Commn, 1988-94, Banco Zaragozano; Mem. Governing Council and Exec. Commn, Bank of Spain, 1994-98. Prof. of Monetary Policy and Spanish Tax System, UC of Financial Studies, Complutense Univ. of Madrid, 1996-. Member Board: BZ Gestión, 1987-91; Banco de Toledo, 1988-94 (Sec. Bd, 1990-94). *Address:* European Central Bank, Kaiserstrasse 29, 60311 Frankfurt-am-Main, Germany.

DOMINIAN, Dr Jacobus, (Jack), MBE 1994; FRCPEd, FRCPsych; DPM; Hon. Consultant, Central Middlesex Hospital, since 1988 (Senior Consultant Psychiatrist, 1965–88); *b* 25 Aug. 1929; *s* of late Charles Joseph Dominian and Mary Dominian (*née* Scarlatou); *m* 1955, Edith Mary Smith; four *d. Educ:* Lycée Leonin, Athens; St Mary's High Sch., Bombay; Stamford Grammar Sch., Lincs; Cambridge Univ.; Oxford Univ. MA, MB BChir (Cantab). Postgraduate work in medicine, various Oxford hosps, 1955–58, Maudsley Hosp. (Inst. of Psychiatry), 1958–64; training as psychiatrist at Maudsley Hosp.; Dir, One Plus One: Marriage and Partnership Research, 1971–. Hon. DSc Lancaster, 1976. *Publications:* Psychiatry and the Christian, 1961; Christian Marriage, 1967; Marital Breakdown, 1968; The Church and the Sexual Revolution, 1971; Cycles of Affirmation, 1975; Depression, 1976; Authority, 1976; (with A. R. Peacocke) From Cosmos to Love, 1976; Proposals for a New Sexual Ethic, 1977; Marriage, Faith and Love, 1981; Make or Break, 1984; The Capacity to Love, 1985; Sexual Integrity: the answer to AIDS, 1987; Passionate and Compassionate Love, 1991; (with Edmund Flood) The Everyday God, 1993; Marriage, 1995; One Like Us, 1998; Let's Make Love, 2001; contribs to Lancet, BMJ, the Tablet, TLS. *Recreations:* enjoyment of the theatre, music, reading and writing. *Address:* Pefka, The Green, Croxley Green, Rickmansworth, Herts WD3 3JA. *T:* (01923) 720972.

DOMINIC, Zoë Denise, FBIPP, FRPS; professional photographer; *b* 4 July 1920; *d* of Lionel J. Levi and Dora Jane Macdonald; name changed to Dominic by Deed Poll, 1960. *Educ:* Francis Holland Sch., Regent's Park. FRPS 1972 (Hood Medal, 1986); FBIPP 1993. Photographer, stage, opera and ballet: English Stage Co. at Royal Court Theatre, 1957–67; National Theatre, 1963–70; Royal Shakespeare Co., 1958; Royal Ballet; Royal Opera Co.; ENO; English Music Theatre; WNO; Stratford, Ontario, 1975. Chm., Avenue Productions, 1987– (Dir, 1986); produced: A Private Treason, Watford, 1986; Blithe Spirit, Vaudeville, 1987; Noël and Gertie, Donmar Warehouse 1987, Comedy, 1989; specialist photographer on films: Dr Zhivago, Nijinsky, Reds, Travels With My Aunt, Victor Victoria; exhibns of ballet photographs, Photographers' Gallery, 1971, Riverside Studios, 1979. Mem. Council, LAMDA, 1989– (Mem., Finance Cttee (Chm., 1991–94)). Trustee, Theatre Projects Trust, 1970 (Chm., 1983–92). *Publications:* Frederick Ashton, 1971; (jtly) John Cranko and the Stuttgart Ballet, 1973; Theatre at Work (text Jim Hiley), 1981; Full Circle (text Dame Janet Baker), 1982; The Best of Plays and Players 1953–68, 1987. *Recreation:* gardening. *Address:* 3 Lexham Walk, W8 5JD. *T:* (020) 7373 6461.

DOMOKOS, Dr Mátyás; Ambassador, retired; General Director, CD Hungary (formerly Diplomatic Service Directorate, Ministry of Foreign Affairs, Hungary), 1989–95; *b* 28 Oct. 1930; *m* 1956, Irén Beretyán; one *d. Educ:* Karl Marx Univ. of Econs, Budapest. Foreign trading enterprises, 1954–57; Commercial Sec., Damascus and Trade Comr, Khartoum, 1958–61; various posts in Ministry for Foreign Trade, Hungary, 1961–74; Ambassador to UN, Geneva, 1974–79; Head of Dept of Internat. Organisations, Ministry of Foreign Affairs, 1979–84; Ambassador to UK, 1984–89. *Recreations:* gardening, chess. *Address:* 32 Str. Árnyas, 1121 Budapest, Hungary.

DON, Montagu Denis Wyatt, (Monty); writer and broadcaster; *b* 8 July 1955; *s* of Denis Don and Janet Wyatt; *m* 1983, Sarah; two *s* one *d. Educ:* Magdalene Coll., Cambridge (MA Eng. 1979). Jt Founder, Monty Don Ltd (costume jewellery co.), 1981–91; freelance gardening journalist, 1988–; TV broadcaster, 1989–. Gardening Editor, The Observer, 1994–. *Publications:* The Prickotty Bush, 1990; The Weekend Gardener, 1995; The Sensuous Garden, 1997; Gardening Mad, 1997; Urban Jungle, 1998; Fork to Fork, 1999. *Recreations:* gardening, running, blues guitar, reading, cooking; *e-mail:* montydon@btclick.com.

DON-WAUCHOPE, Sir Roger Hamilton; *see* Wauchope.

DONAGHY, Rita Margaret, OBE 1998; Chair, Advisory, Conciliation and Arbitration Service, since 2000; *b* 9 Oct. 1944; *d* of late William Scott Willis and of Margaret Brenda (*née* Howard, now Bryan); *m* 1968, James Columba Donaghy (*d* 1986); *m* 2000, Ted Easen-Thomas. *Educ:* Leamington Coll. for Girls; Durham Univ. (BA 1967). Tech. asst, NUT, 1967–68; Asst Registrar, 1968–84, Perm. Sec., Students' Union, 1984-2000, Inst. of Educn, Univ. of London. Member: Low Pay Commn, 1997-2000; Cttee on Standards in Public Life (Wicks Cttee), 2001–. Member: Nat. Exec. Council, NALGO/UNISON, 1973-2000; TUC Gen. Council, 1987-2000; President: NALGO, 1989-90; TUC, 2000; Mem. Exec., Eur. TUC, 1992-2000. *Recreations:* theatre, gardening, photography, watching cricket, eating out, reading. *Address:* Advisory, Conciliation and Arbitration Service, Brandon House, 180 Borough High Street, SE1 1LW. *T:* (020) 7210 3670. *Club:* Surrey County Cricket.

DONAHOE, Arthur Richard; QC (Can.) 1982; Secretary-General, Commonwealth Parliamentary Association, 1993–2001; *b* 7 April 1940; *s* of Richard A. Donahoe and Eileen (*née* Boyd); *m* 1972, Carolyn Elizabeth MacCormack. *Educ:* public schools in Halifax, NS; St Mary's Univ. (BComm 1959); Dalhousie Univ. (LLB 1965). Admitted to Bar of Nova Scotia, 1966; Exec. Asst to Leader of Opposition, Senate of Canada, 1967; barrister and solicitor, 1968–81; Lectr in Commercial Law, St Mary's Univ., 1972–75; MLA (PC), Nova Scotia, 1978–92, Speaker, 1981–91. Canadian Regl Rep., CPA Exec. Cttee, 1983–86. *Publications:* contrib. articles to Parliamentarian, Canadian Parly Rev., and Round Table. *Recreations:* golf, reading. *Address:* 128 Kenilworth Court, Lower Richmond Road, Putney, SW15 1HB. *T:* (020) 8788 2208. *Clubs:* Royal Mid-Surrey Golf; Ashburn Golf (Pres., 1982–83), Halifax (Halifax, NS).

DONALD, Sir Alan (Ewen), KCMG 1988 (CMG 1979); *b* 5 May 1931; 2nd *s* of Robert Thomson Donald and Louise Turner; *m* 1958, Janet Hilary Therese Blood; four *s. Educ:* Aberdeen Grammar Sch.; Fettes Coll., Edinburgh; Trinity Hall, Cambridge. BA, LLM. HM Forces, RA (L Battery, 2nd Regt RHA), 1949–50. Joined HM Foreign Service, 1954: Third Sec., Peking, 1955–57; FO, 1958–61: Private Sec. to Parly Under-Sec., FO, 1959–61; Second, later First Sec., UK Delegn to NATO, Paris, 1961–64; First Sec., Peking, 1964–66; Personnel Dept, Diplomatic Service Admin. Office, later FCO, 1967–71; Counsellor (Commercial), Athens, 1971–73; Political Advr to Governor of Hong Kong, 1974–77; Ambassador to: Republics of Zaire, Burundi and Rwanda, 1977–80; People's Republic of the Congo, 1978–80; Asst Under-Sec. of State (Asia and the Pacific), FCO, 1980–84; Ambassador to: Republic of Indonesia, 1984–88; People's Republic of China, 1988–91. Director: China Fund Inc. (NY), 1992–; HSBC China Fund Ltd, 1994–; J. P. Morgan Fleming Asian Investment Trust Ltd (formerly Fleming Asian Investment Trust), 1997–2001 (Fleming Far Eastern Investment Trust, 1991–97). Hon. LLD Aberdeen, 1991. *Recreations:* music, military history, water colour sketching, films. *Address:* Applebys, Chiddingstone Causeway, Kent TN11 8JH. *Clubs:* Oxford and Cambridge, Caledonian, Noblemen and Gentlemen's Catch; Aula (London/Cambridge).

DONALD, Dr Alastair Geoffrey, CBE 1993 (OBE 1982); FRCGP, FRCPE, FRCPSGlas; General Medical Practitioner, 1952–92; Assistant Director, Edinburgh Postgraduate Board for Medicine, 1970–91; Regional Adviser in General Practice, SE Scotland, 1972–91; President, Royal College of General Practitioners, 1992–94; *b* 24 Nov. 1926; *s* of Dr Pollok Donald and Henrietta Mary (*née* Laidlaw); *m* 1952, Patricia Ireland (marr. diss. 1996); two *s* one *d*; partner, Gladys Leslie. *Educ:* Edinburgh Academy; Corpus Christi Coll., Cambridge (MA); Edinburgh Univ. (MB, ChB); Member: Cambridge and Edinburgh Univs Athletic Teams, RAF Medical Branch, 1952–54; general medical practice, Leith and Cramond (Edin.), 1954–92; Lectr, Dept of General Practice, Univ. of Edinburgh, 1960–70. Royal College of General Practitioners: Vice-Chm. of Council, 1976–77, Chm., 1979–82; Chm., Bd of Censors, 1978–79; past Chm. and Provost, SE Scotland Faculty. Chairman: UK Conf. of Postgrad. Advisers in Gen. Practice, 1978–80; Jt Cttee on Postgrad. Trng for Gen. Practice, 1982–85; Armed Services Gen. Practice Approval Bd, 1987–98. Vice-Chm., Medical and Dental Defence Union of Scotland, 1992–97 (Hon. Fellow, 1998). Specialist Advr, H of C Social Services Select Cttee, 1986–87. Radio Doctor, BBC (Scotland), 1976–78. Chm., Scottish Cttee, ASH, 1985–92. Chm. Court of Directors, Edinburgh Acad., 1978–85 (Dir, 1955–85); President: Edinburgh Academical Club, 1978–81; Rotary Club of Leith, 1957–58. Lectures: James Mackenzie, RCGP, 1985; David Bruce, RAMC, 1987; Robert Campbell, Ulster Med. Soc., 1989; Ian Murray Scott, 1991, Pinsent, 1993, Fulton, 1994, RCGP; Richard Scott, Edinburgh Univ., 1996. James Mackenzie Medal, RCPE, 1983; Defence Med. Services Medal, 1993; Hippocrates Medal, SIMG, 1994; Foundn Council Award, RCGP, 1997; Paul Harris Fellow, Rotary Internat., 1996. *Publications:* contribs to medical jls. *Recreations:* golf, family life, reading The Times. *Address:* 2 Northlawn Terrace, Easter Park Drive, Edinburgh EH4 6SD. *T:* (0131) 336 3824. *Clubs:* Royal Air Force; Hawks (Cambridge).

DONALD, Prof. Athene Margaret, PhD; FRS 1999; Professor of Experimental Physics, University of Cambridge, since 1998; Fellow of Robinson College, Cambridge, since 1981; *b* 15 May 1953; *d* of Walter Griffith and Annette Marian (*née* Tylor); *m* 1976, Matthew J. Donald; one *s* one *d. Educ:* Camden Sch. for Girls; Girton Coll., Cambridge (BA, MA; PhD 1977). Postdoctoral researcher, Cornell Univ., 1977–81; University of Cambridge: SERC Res. Fellow, 1981–83; Royal Soc. Res. Fellow, 1983–85; Lectr, 1985–95; Reader, 1995–98. Mem., Governing Council, Inst. Food Res., 1999–. Samuel Locker Award in Physics, Birmingham Univ., 1989; Charles Vernon Boys Prize, Inst. Physics, 1989; Rosenhain Medal and Prize, Inst. Materials, 1995. *Publications:* (with A. H. Windle) Liquid Crystalline Polymers, 1992; (ed jtly) Starch: structure and function, 1997; articles on polymer, colloid and food physics in learned jls. *Address:* Cavendish Laboratory, University of Cambridge, Madingley Road, Cambridge CB3 0HE.

DONALD, Brian George; Sheriff of Tayside, Central and Fife at Kirkcaldy, since 1999; *b* 11 July 1944; *s* of George J. Donald and Anna Auchterlonie Donald. *Educ:* Lawside Acad., Dundee; Univ. of St Andrews (LLB 1965). Postgrad. legal trng, Edinburgh, 1965-67; admitted as solicitor, 1967; Asst Solicitor, Ayr, 1967–69; admin, London Univ., 1969; teacher of English, Shenker Inst., Rome, 1970-72; resumed legal practice, with J. & A. Hastie, SSC, Edinburgh, Glasgow and Galashiels, 1972, Partner, 1973–96; Lectr in Civil Advocacy, Law Faculty, Edinburgh Univ., 1981-91; Temp. Sheriff, 1984-99; Consultant, Gillam Mackie, SSC and Fyfe Ireland, WS, 1997–99. Member: Stewart Cttee on Alternatives to Prosecution, 1978–83; (Founder) Scottish Legal Aid Bd, 1986-91. *Recreations:* theatre, music, choral singing, good food and wine, foreign travel, maintaining fluent French and Italian and improving German. *Address:* Sheriff's Chambers, Kirkcaldy Sheriff Court, Kirkcaldy, Fife KY1 1XQ; *e-mail:* sheriff.bgdonald@scotcourts.gov.uk; (home) 20 Howe Street, Edinburgh EH3 6TG. *T:* (0131) 225 8755.

DONALD, Craig Reid Cantlie, CMG 1963; OBE 1959; *b* 8 Sept. 1914; *s* of Rev. Francis Cantlie and Mary Donald, Lumphanan, Aberdeenshire; *m* 1945, Mary Isabel Speid (*d* 1989); one *d. Educ:* Fettes; Emmanuel Coll., Cambridge (Scholar; BA 1937, MA 1947). Administrative Officer, Cyprus, 1937; Military Service, 1940–46, Lieut-Col. Commissioner, Famagusta, 1948; Registrar, Cooperative Societies, 1951; Deputy Financial Sec., Uganda, 1951; MLC, 1954–62; Sec. to the Treasury, 1956–63. Fellow, Econ. Develt Inst., World Bank, 1956. Bursar, Malvern Coll., 1964–79. Governor: Hillstone Sch., 1979–86; Ellerslie, 1979–93; Downs Sch., Colwall, 1979–92. *Recreation:* country pursuits. *Address:* 55 Geraldine Road, Malvern WR14 3NU. *T:* (01684) 561446. *Club:* Travellers.

See also I. G. Gilbert.

DONALD, George Malcolm, RSA 1992 (ARSA 1975); RSW 1976; SSA 1976; Lecturer, School of Drawing and Painting, Edinburgh College of Art, since 1972; *b* 12 Sept. 1943; *s* of George Donald and Margaret (*née* Tait); *m* 1966 (marr. diss.); one *s* one *d. Educ:* Edinburgh Coll. of Art (DA 1966; Post Grad. Dip. 1967); Hornsey Coll. of Art, London Univ. (ATC 1969); Edinburgh Univ. (MEd 1980). Edinburgh College of Art: Tutor and Asst to Vice Principal (Art and Design), 1984–87; Director: Summer Sch., 1991–; Centre for Continuing Studies, 1996–. Printmaker in Residence, Soulisquoy Print Workshop, Orkney Is, 1988; Visiting Artist: Szechuan Fine Art Inst., China, 1989; Silpakorn Univ., Thailand, 1989; Chulalongkorn Univ., Thailand, 1989; Vis. Prof., Zhejiang Acad. Fine Art, China, 1994–; British Council Vis. Prof., Kyoto, 1999, Korea, 2000. Solo exhibitions include: Art Dept Gall., Univ. of Central Florida, 1985; Dept of Fine Art, Univ. of Georgia, 1987; Open Eye Gall., Edinburgh, 1987, 1990, 1993, 1995, 1998; Galerija Fakulteta Likovnih Umetnosti, Belgrade, 1987; touring exhibn, UK and France, 1990; Christopher Hull Gall., London, 1992; World Trade Centre, Dubai, 1994; commissions: portrait, Glasgow Univ. and Scottish Arts Council, 1985; window design, New Scottish Nat. Lib., Edinburgh, 1986; portrait: Edinburgh Chamber of Commerce, 1986; St John's Hosp., Livingston, 1994; public collections include: Scottish Arts Council; Edinburgh, Aberdeen and Leeds CCs; Hunterian Mus., Glasgow Univ.; Heriot Watt Univ.; Victoria and Albert Mus.; IBM; BBC; Nat. Library of Scotland; private collections in UK, Europe, Canada and USA, Asia and Australia. Latimer Award 1970, Guthrie Award 1973, Royal Scottish Acad.; Scottish Arts Council Bursary, 1973; Gillies Bequest Travel Award to India, Royal Scottish Acad., 1978. *Publications:* The New Maths, 1969; An Account of Travels in Turkey, Iran, Afghanistan, Pakistan, India, Kashmir and Nepal, 1969; An Indian Diary, 1980; Aims and Objectives in Teaching Drawing and Painting, 1980; The Day Book, 1987. *Recreations:* pottering, fiddling, travelling. *Address:* Edinburgh College of Art, Lauriston Place, Edinburgh EH3 9DF.

DONALD, James Graham, FRICS; Chairman, Strutt & Parker, since 1996; *b* 4 April 1944; *s* of William Graham Donald and Jean (Bubbles) Donald; *m* 1976, Jennifer Seaman; one *s* two *d*. *Educ:* Cranleigh Sch.; Coll. of Estate Mgt (BSc Estate Mgt). FRICS 1981. Savills, 1966–72; Strutt & Parker, 1972– (Partner, 1978). *Recreations:* sport, running around after the children, travel, reading. *Address:* Strutt & Parker, 13 Hill Street, W1X 8DL. *T:* (020) 7318 5020. *Clubs:* Boodle's; Wisley; Richmond FC; Old Cranleighans.

DONALD, Air Marshal Sir John (George), KBE 1985 (OBE 1972); Medical Adviser, AMI Middle East Services Ltd, 1989–95; *b* 7 Nov. 1927; *s* of John Shirran Donald and Janet Knox (*née* Napier); *m* 1954, Margaret Jean Walton; one *s* two *d*. *Educ:* Inverurie Acad.; Aberdeen Univ. (MB, ChB 1951); DTM&H Edin 1964; MRCGP 1971, FRCGP 1977; MFCM 1972, FFCM 1985; MFOM 1982 (AFOM 1980); FRCPE 1986. Commnd RAF, 1953; Senior Medical Officer: Colombo, Ceylon, 1954–57; RAF Stafford, 1957–60; RAF Waddington, 1960–63; student, RAF Staff Coll., 1965; SMO, HQ AFCENT, France and Holland, 1966–68; Dep. Dir, Medical Personnel (RAF), 1969–72; OC, The Princess Mary's RAF Hosp., Akrotiri, Cyprus, 1972–76; OC, RAF Hosp., Ely, 1976–78; PMO, RAF Germany, 1978–81; PMO, RAF Strike Comd, 1981–84; Dir-Gen., RAF Med. Services, 1984–85; Dep. Surg. Gen. (Ops), MoD, and Dir Gen., RAF Med. Services, 1985–86; Med. Dir, Security Forces Hosp., 1986–89. QHS, 1983–86. CStJ 1984. *Recreations:* golf, skiing, camping, ornithology. *Address:* 8 Oratory Gardens, Canford Cliffs, Poole, Dorset BH13 7HJ. *Club:* Royal Society of Medicine.

DONALD, Rob, CEng, FCIT; Director General, Centro (West Midlands Passenger Transport Executive), since 1995; *b* 25 March 1949; *s* of John Donald and Mary Donald (*née* Gardiner); *m* 1st, 1972, Yvonne Dyer (marr. diss.); two *d*; 2nd, 1991, Marilyn Downie. *Educ:* George Heriot's Sch., Edinburgh; Univ. of Edinburgh (BSc Hons); Imperial Coll., Univ. of London (MSc). MICE 1976; CEng 1976; FCIT 1996. Graduate Asst, Brian Colquhoun and Partners, Consultants, London, 1971–73; Sen. Asst Officer, SIA Transport Consultants, London, 1973–75; Project Leader, County Surveyor's Dept, Kent CC, 1975–79; Chief Transportation Officer, Jt Transportation Unit, Merseyside CC, 1979–86; Merseytravel: Section Leader, then Manager, 1986–91; Passenger Services Dir, 1991–95. *Recreations:* travelling, computing, hill-walking. *Address:* Centro House, 16 Summer Lane, Birmingham B19 3SD. *T:* (0121) 214 7001.

DONALDSON, family name of **Baron Donaldson of Lymington**.

DONALDSON OF LYMINGTON, Baron *cr* 1988 (Life Peer), of Lymington in the County of Hampshire; **John Francis Donaldson,** Kt 1966; PC 1979; Master of the Rolls, 1982–92; *b* 6 Oct. 1920; *er s* of late Malcolm Donaldson, FRCS, FRCOG, and late Evelyn Helen Marguerite Maunsell; *m* 1945, Dorothy Mary (*see* Dame Mary Donaldson); one *s* two *d*. *Educ:* Charterhouse; Trinity Coll., Cambridge (Hon. Fellow, 1983); MA Oxon 1982. Sec. of Debates, Cambridge Union Soc., 1940; Chm. Federation of University Conservative and Unionist Assocs, 1940; BA (Hons) 1941; MA 1959. Commissioned Royal Signals, 1941; served with Guards Armoured Divisional Signals, in UK and NW Europe, 1942–45; and with Military Government, Schleswig-Holstein, 1945–46; Hon. Lieut-Col, 1946. Called to Bar, Middle Temple, 1946; Harmsworth Law Scholar, 1946; Bencher 1966; Treas. 1986; Mem. Gen. Council of the Bar, 1956–61, 1962–66, Junior Counsel to Registrar of Restrictive Trading Agreements, 1959–61; QC 1961; Dep. Chm., Hants QS, 1961–66; Mem. Council on Tribunals, 1965–66; Judge of the High Court, Queen's Bench Div., 1966–79; Pres., Nat. Industrial Relations Court, 1971–74; a Lord Justice of Appeal, 1979–82. Chairman: inquiry into prevention of pollution from merchant shipping, 1993–94; MV Derbyshire Assessment, 1995; Review of Salvage and Intervention and their Command and Control, 1999; Review of Five Year Strategy for HM Coastguard, 1999. Pres. Council, Inns of Court, 1987–90. Mem. Croydon County Borough Council, 1949–53. President: Carthusian Soc., 1978–82; British Maritime Law Assoc., 1979–95 (Vice-Pres., 1969–78); British Insurance Law Assoc., 1979–81 (Dep. Pres., 1978–79); British Records Assoc., 1982–92; Chairman: Adv. Council on Public Records, 1982–92; Magna Carta Trust, 1982–92; Financial Law Panel, 1992–. FCIArb 1980 (Pres., 1980–83). Hon. Member: Assoc. of Average Adjusters, 1966 (Chm., 1981); Grain and Feed Trade Assoc., 1979; Liverpool Cotton Assoc., 1979; Law Soc., 1994. Governor, Sutton's Hosp. in Charterhouse, 1981–84. Visitor: UCL, 1982–92; Nuffield Coll., Oxford, 1982–92; London Business Sch., 1986–92. Hon. Freeman, 1984, Hon. Liveryman, 2000, Worshipful Co. of Drapers. DU Essex, 1983; Hon. LLD: Sheffield, 1984; Nottingham Trent, 1992; Southampton, 1998. Silver Medal, Thomas Gray Meml Trust, 1995. *Publications:* Jt Ed., Lowndes and Rudolf on General Average and the York-Antwerp Rules (8th edn), 1955, (9th edn), 1964 and (10th edn), 1975; contributor to title Insurance, in Halsbury's Laws of England (3rd edn), 1958. *Recreations:* sailing, do-it-yourself. *Address:* House of Lords, SW1A 0PW. *T:* (home) (01590) 675716. *Clubs:* Royal Cruising, Royal Lymington Yacht.
See also J. M. Williams.

DONALDSON OF LYMINGTON, Lady; *see* Donaldson, Dame D. M.

DONALDSON, Dr Alexander Ivan; Head, Pirbright Laboratory, Institute for Animal Health, since 1989; *b* 1 July 1942; *s* of Basil Ivan Donaldson and Dorothy Cunningham Donaldson; *m* 1966, Margaret Ruth Elizabeth Swan; one *d* one *s*. *Educ:* High Sch., Dublin; Trinity Coll., Univ. of Dublin (BA, MA, ScD); Ontario Veterinary Coll., Univ. of Guelph (PhD). MRCVS. Post-doctoral research, 1969–71, Vet. Res. Officer, 1973–76, Principal Vet. Res. Officer, 1976–89, Animal Virus Res. Inst., subseq. AFRC. Inst. for Animal Health, Pirbright Lab.; Head, World Ref. Lab. for Foot-and-Mouth Disease, 1985–89. Vis. Prof., Ontario Vet. Coll., Univ. of Guelph, 1972–73. Research Medal, RASE, 1988. *Publications:* numerous articles on animal virology in learned jls. *Recreations:* reading, jogging, windsurfing, photography. *Address:* Institute for Animal Health, Pirbright Laboratory, Ash Road, Pirbright, Woking, Surrey GU24 0NF. *T:* (01483) 232441, *Fax:* (01483) 232448; *e-mail:* alex.donaldson@bbsrc.ac.uk.

DONALDSON, Brian; HM Diplomatic Service; High Commissioner to Republic of Namibia, 1999–April 2002; *b* 6 April 1946; *s* of William Donaldson and Elsie Josephine Donaldson; *m* 1969, Elizabeth Claire Sumner; three *s*. Assistant, Establishments Office, Min. of Civil Aviation, 1963–65; joined HM Diplomatic Service, 1965: Mgt Officer, Algiers, 1968–71; Archivist, La Paz, 1971–73; Communications Ops Dept, FCO, 1974–75; Entry Clearance Officer, Lagos, 1975–79; Vice Consul, Luxembourg, 1979–82; Second Sec., Trade Relns and Exports Dept, FCO, 1982–83; Asst Private Sec. to Minister of State, FCO, 1983–85; Second, later First Sec., Port Louis, Mauritius, 1985–89; Dep. Hd of Mission, Yaoundé, Cameroon, 1989–92; First Sec., Dhaka, 1992–96; Personnel Mgt Dept, FCO, 1996–97; Dep. Hd, Information Dept, FCO, 1997–99. *Recreations:* amateur dramatics, family, people watching. *Address:* c/o Foreign and Commonwealth Office, King Charles Street, SW1A 2AH; 116 Robert Mugabe Avenue, Windhoek, Namibia.

DONALDSON, Prof. (Charles) Ian (Edward), FBA 1993; Grace I Professor of English, and Fellow, King's College, since 1995 and Director, Centre for Research in the Arts, Social Sciences and Humanities, since 2001, University of Cambridge; *b* 6 May 1935; *s* of Dr William Edward Donaldson and Elizabeth Donaldson (*née* Weigall); *m* 1st, 1962, Tamsin Jane Procter (marr. diss. 1990); one *s* one *d*; 2nd, 1991, Grazia Maria Therese Gunn. *Educ:* Melbourne Grammar Sch.; Melbourne Univ. (BA 1957); Magdalen Coll., Oxford (BA 1960; MA 1964). Sen. Tutor in English, Univ. of Melbourne, 1958; Oxford University: Harmsworth Sen. Scholar, Merton Coll., 1960–62; Fellow and Lectr in English, Wadham Coll., 1962–69; CUF Lectr in English, 1963–69; Prof. of English, ANU Canberra, 1969–91; Foundn Dir, Humanities Res. Centre, ANU, 1974–90; Regius Prof. of Rhetoric and English Lit., Univ. of Edinburgh, 1991–95; Chm., English Faculty, Univ. of Cambridge, 1999–2001. Vis. appts, Univ. of California Santa Barbara, Gonville and Caius Coll., Cambridge, Cornell Univ., Melbourne Univ. Syndic, CUP, 1997–. FAHA 1975; corresp. FBA 1987; FRSE 1993. *Publications:* The World Upside-Down: comedy from Jonson to Fielding, 1970; (ed) Ben Jonson Poems, 1975; The Rapes of Lucretia, 1982; (ed) Jonson and Shakespeare, 1983; (ed) Transformations in Modern European Drama, 1983; (ed with Tamsin Donaldson) Seeing the First Australians, 1985; (ed) Ben Jonson, 1985; (ed jtly) Shaping Lives: reflections on biography, 1992; (ed) Ben Jonson: Selected Poems, 1995; Jonson's Magic Houses, 1997. *Address:* King's College, Cambridge CB2 1ST. *T:* (01223) 331100.

DONALDSON, David Torrance; QC 1984; a Recorder, since 1994; *b* 30 Sept. 1943; *s* of Alexander Walls Donaldson and Margaret Merry Bryce. *Educ:* Glasgow Academy; Gonville and Caius College, Cambridge (Maj. Schol.; MA); University of Freiburg i. Br., West Germany (Dr jur). Fellow, Gonville and Caius College, Cambridge, 1965–69. Called to the Bar, Gray's Inn, 1968, Bencher, 1995. *Address:* Blackstone Chambers, Blackstone House, Temple, EC4Y 9BW. *T:* (020) 7583 1770.

DONALDSON, Dame (Dorothy) Mary, GBE 1983; JP; Lord Mayor of London for 1983–84; Alderman, City of London Ward of Coleman Street, 1975–91; *b* 29 Aug. 1921; *d* of late Reginald George Gale Warwick and Dorothy Alice Warwick; *m* 1945, John Francis Donaldson (*see* Baron Donaldson of Lymington); one *s* two *d*. *Educ:* Portsmouth High Sch. for Girls (GPDST); Wingfield Morris Orthopædic Hosp.; Middlesex Hosp., London. SRN 1946. Chairman: Women's Nat. Cancer Control Campaign, 1967–69; Interim Licensing Authy for Human In Vitro Fertilisation and Embryol., 1985–91; Vice-Pres., British Cancer Council, 1970; Member: NE Met. Regional Hosp. Bd, 1970–74; NE Thames RHA, 1976–81. Governor: London Hosp., 1971–74; Gt Ormond Street Hosp. for Sick Children, 1978–80; Member: Cities of London and Westminster Disablement Adv. Cttee, 1974–79; Inner London Educn Authority, 1968–71; City Parochial Foundn, 1969–75; Cttee, Royal Humane Soc., 1968–83; Cttee, AA, 1985–89; Press Complaints Commn, 1991–; Chm. Council, Banking Ombudsman, 1985–94; Vice-Pres., Counsel and Care for the Elderly, 1980–; Pres., BACUP, 1985–93. Governor: City of London Sch. for Girls, 1971–83; Berkhamsted Schools, 1976–80; Mem., Governing Body, Charterhouse Sch., 1980–85; Mem., Court of Common Council, 1966–75, Sheriff, 1981–82, HM Lieutenant, 1983, City of London; Mem. Guild of Freemen, City of London, 1970 (Mem. Court, 1983–86); Liveryman, Gardeners' Co., 1975; Hon. Freeman, Shipwrights' Co., 1985. JP Inner London, 1960; Mem., Inner London Juvenile Court Panel, 1960–65. Hon. Mem., CIArb, 1981; Hon. Fellow: Girton Coll., Cambridge, 1983; Portsmouth Univ. (formerly Poly.), 1984. FRSH 1984; Hon. FRCOG 1991. Hon. DSc City, 1983. DStJ 1984. Freedom, City of Winnipeg, 1968. Order of Oman, 1982; Order of Bahrain, 1984. Grand Officier, Ordre Nat. du Mérite, 1984. *Recreations:* gardening, sailing, geriatric ski-ing. *T:* (home) (01590) 675292. *Clubs:* Reform; Royal Cruising, Royal Lymington Yacht.
See also J. M. Williams.

DONALDSON, Hamish; corporate adviser and company director; *b* 13 June 1936; *s* of late James Donaldson and Marie Christine Cormack; *m* 1965, Linda, *d* of late Dr Leslie Challis Bousfield; three *d*. *Educ:* Oundle School; Christ's College, Cambridge (MA). De La Rue Bull, 1960–66; Urwick, Orr & Partners, 1966–73; Hill Samuel & Co., 1973–91; Man. Dir, Hill Samuel Merchant Bank (SA), 1985–86; Chief Exec., Hill Samuel Bank, 1987–91. Chairman: London Bridge Finance, 1993–95 (Dir, 1992–95); Gresham Telecomputing, 1993–97; Director: TSB Bank, 1988–91; TSB Group, 1990–91; Macquarie Bank, 1989–91; South African Business News, 1991–94; RSH Trading Ltd, 1994–; Sanlic (UK) Ltd, 1994–; UCC Gp, 1998–2000; London Dir, Mid-Med Bank Ltd of Malta, 1997–99. Mem., Co. Affairs Cttee, Inst. of Dirs, 1991–95. Chm., Guildford DAC for the Care of Churches and Churchyards, 1992–; Founder Chm., Surrey Churches Preservation Trust, 1997–. Gov., Royal Sch., Haslemere, 1994–. Freeman, City of London, 1988; Liveryman, Information Technologists' Co., 1992–. *Publication:* a Guide to the Successful Management of Computer Projects, 1978. *Recreation:* amateur operatics. *Address:* Edgecombe, Hill Road, Haslemere, Surrey GU27 2JN. *T:* (01428) 644473.

DONALDSON, Ian; *see* Donaldson, C. I. E.

DONALDSON, Jeffrey Mark; MP (UU) Lagan Valley, since 1997; *b* 7 Dec. 1962; *s* of James Alexander Donaldson and Sarah Anne Donaldson; *m* 1987, Eleanor Mary Elizabeth Cousins; two *d*. *Educ:* Castlereagh Coll. (DipEE); Chartered Insurance Inst. (Financial Planning Cert.). Agent to Rt Hon. J. Enoch Powell, MP, 1983–85; Mem., NI Assembly, 1985–86; Partner in financial services/estate agency practice, 1986–97. Mem., NI Forum, 1996–98. Hon. Sec., 1988–2000, Vice-Pres., 2000–, UU Council. *Recreations:* travelling, walking, reading, music. *Address:* House of Commons, SW1A 0AA. *T:* (020) 7219 3407; 2 Sackville Street, Wallace Avenue, Lisburn, Co. Antrim BT27 4AB. *T:* (028) 9266 8001.

DONALDSON, Liam Joseph, MD; FRCP, FRCPE, FRCSE, FFPHM, FRCGP; Chief Medical Officer, Department of Health, since 1998. *Educ:* Univ. of Bristol (MB, ChB 1972); Univ. of Birmingham (MSc 1976); Univ. of Leicester (MD 1982). FRCSE 1977; FFPHM 1990 (FFCM 1987); FRCP 1997; FRCGP 1999; FRCPE 1999. House Officer, United Bristol Hosps, 1972; Surgical Registrar, United Birmingham Hosps, 1975–77; Lectr in Anatomy, then Sen. Lectr in Epidemiol., Univ. of Leicester; Regl Med. Officer and Head of Clinical Policy, then Director of Public Health, Northern RHA; Regl Gen. Manager and Dir of Public Health, Northern and Yorks RHA, later Regl Dir and Dir of Public Health, Northern and Yorks NHS Exec., 1994–98. Hon. Prof. of Applied Epidemiol., Univ. of Newcastle upon Tyne. QHP 1996. *Publications:* (with R. J. Donaldson) Essential Community Medicine, 1983, 2nd edn as Essential Public Health, 2000; (ed with B. R. McAvoy) Health Care for Asians, 1990; over 100 papers on various aspects of health services research. *Address:* Department of Health, Richmond House, 79 Whitehall, SW1A 2NS.

DONALDSON, Dame Mary; *see* Donaldson, Dame D. M.

DONALDSON, Air Vice-Marshal Michael Phillips, MBE 1973; Chief Executive and Principal, Yorkshire Coast College, since 1996; *b* 22 July 1943; *s* of George Millar Donaldson and Mabel Donaldson (*née* Phillips); *m* 1970, Mavis Cornish; one *s* one *d*. *Educ:* Chislehurst and Sidcup Grammar Sch. for Boys. RAF Gen. Duties; Pilot and Weapons Instructor; No 23 Sqn (Lightning), 1965–68; No 226 OCU, 1969; USAF Florida (F106), 1970–73; No 29 Sqn (Phantom), 1974–76; No 228 OCU, 1977; Army Staff Coll., 1978; PSO to Dep. Comdr in Chief AFCENT, Brunssum, 1979–80; MoD, 1980–83; OC 19 Sqn, 1983–85; OC 23 Sqn (Falkland Is), 1985; Dep. PSO to CDS, 1986–87; OC RAF Wattisham, 1987–89; RCDS 1990; SASO, 11 Group, 1990–93; Comdt, RAF Staff Coll., 1993–96. Life Vice-Pres., RAF Squash Rackets Assoc., 1996. MInstD; FRAeS 1997; FRSA 1999. *Recreations:* music, history, squash, tennis, golf. *Address:* Brook Farmhouse, Brook Lane, Thornton Dale, Pickering, N Yorks YO18 7RZ. *T:* (01751) 477046. *Club:* Royal Air Force.

DONALDSON, Patricia Anne; *see* Hodgson, P. A.

DONALDSON, Prof. Simon Kirwan, DPhil; FRS 1986; Professor of Pure Mathematics, Imperial College, London University, since 1998; *b* 20 Aug. 1957; *m* 1986, Ana Nora Hurtado; two *s* one *d*. *Educ:* Sevenoaks Sch., Kent; Pembroke Coll., Cambridge (BA 1979; Hon. Fellow, 1992); Worcester Coll., Oxford (DPhil 1983). Jun. Res. Fellow, All Souls Coll., Oxford, 1983–85; Wallis Prof. of Maths, and Fellow, St Anne's Coll., Univ. of Oxford, 1985–98, Hon. Fellow, 1998. Fields Medal, IMU, 1986. *Publications:* (with P. B. Kronheimer) The Geometry of Four-manifolds, 1990; papers in mathematical jls. *Recreation:* sailing. *Address:* Department of Mathematics, Imperial College, 180 Queen's Gate, SW7 2BZ.

DONCASTER, Bishop Suffragan of, since 2000; **Rt Rev. Cyril Guy Ashton;** *b* 6 April 1942; *s* of William Joseph Ashton and Margaret Anne Ashton (*née* Todd); *m* 1965, Muriel Ramshaw; three *s* one *d*. *Educ:* Oak Hill Theol Coll.; Lancaster Univ (MA 1986). Ordained deacon, 1967, priest, 1968; Curate, St Thomas', Blackpool, 1967–70; Vocations Sec., CPAS, 1970–74; Vicar, St Thomas', Lancaster, 1974–91; Dir of Training, Dio. Blackburn, 1991–2000. Hon. Canon, Blackburn Cathedral, 1991–2000. *Publications:* Church on the Threshold, 1988, 2nd edn 1991; Threshold God, 1992; (with Jack Nicolls) A Faith Worth Sharing?: a Church Worth Joining?, 1995. *Recreations:* motorcycling, swimming, cycling, vintage cars. *Address:* Bishop's House, 3 Farrington Court, Goose Lane, Wickersley, Rotherham S66 1JG.

DONCASTER, Archdeacon of; *see* Fitzharris, Ven. R. A.

DONDELINGER, Jean; Ambassador of Luxembourg to Greece, 1993–95; *b* Luxembourg, 4 July 1930; *m*; one *s*. *Educ:* Nancy Univ.; Paris Univ.; St Antony's Coll., Oxford. Barrister, Luxembourg, 1954–58; Asst to Head, Internat. Economic Relations Service, Dept of Foreign Affairs, 1958–61; Dep. Permanent Rep. of Luxembourg to EEC, 1961–70, Ambassador and Permanent Rep., 1970–84; Sec.-Gen., Min. of Foreign Affairs, 1984; Mem., EEC, 1989–92. Rep. of Pres. of Govt, Cttee on Institutional Affairs (Dooge Cttee), 1984–85; Chm., Negotiating Gp on Single Act, 1986; Vice-Pres., ITU World Conf. on Fixing of Orbital Frequencies of Satellites, 1988.

DONEGALL, 7th Marquess of, *cr* 1791, **Dermot Richard Claud Chichester,** LVO 1986; Viscount Chichester and Baron of Belfast, 1625; Earl of Donegall, 1647; Earl of Belfast, 1791; Baron Fisherwick (GB), 1790; Baron Templemore, 1831; Hereditary Lord High Admiral of Lough Neagh; late 7th Queen's Own Hussars; Standard Bearer, Honourable Corps of Gentlemen at Arms, 1984–86 (one of HM Bodyguard, since 1966); *b* 18 April 1916; 2nd *s* of 4th Baron Templemore, PC, KCVO, DSO, and Hon. Clare Meriel Wingfield, 2nd *d* of 7th Viscount Powerscourt, PC Ireland (she *d* 1969); *S* father 1953, and to Marquessate of Donegall, 1975; *m* 1946, Lady Josceline Gabrielle Legge (*d* 1995), *y d* of 7th Earl of Dartmouth, GCVO, TD; one *s* two *d*. *Educ:* Harrow; RMC, Sandhurst. 2nd Lt 7th Hussars, 1936; Lt 1939; served War of 1939–45 in Middle East and Italy (prisoner); Major, 1944; retired, 1949. *Recreations:* hunting, shooting, fishing. *Heir: s* Earl of Belfast, *qv*. *Address:* Dunbrody Park, Arthurstown, Co; Wexford, Eire. *T:* (51) 389104. *Clubs:* Cavalry and Guards; Kildare Street and University (Dublin).

DONERAILE, 10th Viscount *cr* 1785 (Ire.); **Richard Allen St Leger;** Baron Doneraile, 1776; *b* 17 Aug. 1946; *s* of 9th Viscount Doneraile and of Melva, Viscountess Doneraile; *S* father, 1983; *m* 1970, Kathleen Mary Simcox, Churchtown, Mallow, Co. Cork; one *s* one *d*. *Educ:* Orange Coast College, California; Mississippi Univ. Served US Army. Air Traffic Control specialist; antiquarian book appraiser, 1970–73; food marketing analyst, 1974. *Recreations:* outdoor sports, skiing, golf, sailing. *Heir: s* Hon. Nathaniel Warham Robert St John St Leger, *b* 13 Sept. 1971. *Club:* Yorba Linda Country (California).

DONKIN, Dr Robin Arthur, FBA 1985; Reader in Historical Geography, 1990–96, now Emeritus, and Fellow of Jesus College, 1972–96, now Emeritus, University of Cambridge; *b* Morpeth, 28 Oct. 1928; *s* of Arthur Donkin and Elizabeth Jane Kirkup; *m* 1970, Jennifer Gay Kennedy; one *d*. *Educ:* Univ. of Durham (BA 1950; PhD 1953); MA Cantab 1971; LittD Cantab 1993. Lieut, Royal Artillery, 1953–55 (Egypt). King George VI Meml Fellow, Univ. of California, Berkeley, 1955–56; Asst Lectr, Dept of Geography, Univ. of Edinburgh, 1956–58; Lectr, Dept of Geography, Univ. of Birmingham, 1958–70; Lectr in the Geography of Latin America, Univ. of Cambridge, 1971–90; Tutor, Jesus Coll., Cambridge, 1975–96. Leverhulme Research Fellow, 1966; Vis. Associate Prof. of Geography, Univ. of Toronto, 1969. Carl O. Sauer Meml Lectr, Univ. of Calif, Berkeley, 1995. Field work in Middle and S America, NW Africa, India, China, Turkestan. *Publications:* The Cistercian Order in Europe: a bibliography of printed sources, 1969; Spanish Red: cochineal and the Opuntia cactus, 1977; The Cistercians: studies in the geography of medieval England and Wales, 1978; Agricultural Terracing in the Aboriginal New World, 1979; Manna: an historical geography, 1980; The Peccary, 1985; The Muscovy Duck, 1986; Meleagrides: an historical and ethnogeographical study of the Guinea fowl, 1991; Beyond Price: pearls and pearl-fishing, origins to the Age of Discoveries, 1998; Dragon's Brain Perfume: an historical geography of camphor, 1999; articles in geographical, historical and anthropological jls. *Address:* Jesus College, Cambridge CB5 8BL; 13 Roman Hill, Barton, Cambridge. *T:* (01223) 262572.

DONLEAVY, James Patrick; author and artist; *b* 23 April 1926; *m* Valerie Heron (marr. diss.); one *s* one *d*; *m* Mary Wilson Price (marr. diss.); one *s* one *d*. *Educ:* schs in USA; Trinity Coll., Dublin. Evening Standard Drama Critics' Award, 1961; Brandeis Univ. Creative Arts Award, 1962; AAAL Grantee, 1975; Worldfest Houston Gold Award, 1992. *Art exhibitions:* Painter's Gall., Dublin, 1950, 1951; Bronxville, NY, 1959; Langton Galls, London, 1975; Caldwell Galls, Belfast, 1987; Anna Mei Chadwick Gall., London, 1989, 1991; Alba Fine Art Gall., London, 1991; The Front Lounge, Dublin, 1995. *Publications:* The Ginger Man (novel), 1955; Fairy Tales of New York (play), 1960; What They Did In Dublin With The Ginger Man (introd. and play), 1961; A Singular Man (novel), 1963 (play, 1964); Meet My Maker The Mad Molecule (short stories), 1964; The Saddest Summer of Samuel S (novella), 1966 (play, 1967); The Beastly Beatitudes of Balthazar B (novel), 1968 (play, 1981); The Onion Eaters (novel), 1971; The Plays of J. P. Donleavy, 1972; A Fairy Tale of New York (novel), 1973; The Unexpurgated Code: a complete manual of survival and manners, 1975; The Destinies of Darcy Dancer, Gentleman (novel), 1977; Schultz (novel), 1980; Leila (novel), 1983; De Alfonce Tennis: the superlative game of eccentric champions, its history, accoutrements, rules, conduct and regimen (sports manual), 1984; J. P. Donleavy's Ireland, in all her Sins and in some of her Graces, 1986 (Cine Golden Eagle Award, 1993, for television prodn (writer and narrator)); Are You Listening Rabbi Low (novel), 1987; A Singular Country, 1989; That Darcy, That Dancer, That Gentleman (novel), 1990; The History of the Ginger Man (autobiog.), 1994; The Lady Who Liked Clean Rest Rooms (novella), 1996; An Author and His Image: the collected short pieces, 1997; Wrong Information Is Being Given Out at Princeton (novel), 1998; contribs to jls etc, incl. The Observer, The Times (London), New York Times, Washington Post, Daily Telegraph, Daily Mail, Irish Ind., Esquire, Envoy, Punch, Guardian, Saturday Evening Post, Holiday, Atlantic Monthly, Saturday Review, The New Yorker, Queen, Vogue, Penthouse, Playboy, Architectural Digest, Vanity Fair, Rolling Stone, Liberation (Paris). *Address:* Levington Park, Mullingar, Co. Westmeath, Ireland.

DONN, Mary Cecilia; *see* Spinks, M. C.

DONNACHIE, Prof. Alexander, FInstP; Professor of Physics, University of Manchester, since 1969; *b* 25 May 1936; *s* of John Donnachie and Mary Ramsey Donnachie (*née* Adams); *m* 1960, Dorothy Paterson; two *d*. *Educ:* Kilmarnock Acad.; Glasgow Univ. (BSc, PhD). DSIR Res. Fellow 1961–63, Lectr 1963–65, UCL; Res. Associate, CERN, Geneva, 1965–67; Sen. Lectr, Univ. of Glasgow, 1967–69; University of Manchester: Hd of Theoretical Physics 1975–85; Dean of Faculty of Science, 1985–87; Chm., Dept of Physics, 1988–94; Dir of Physical Labs, 1989–94; Dean, Faculty of Science and Engrg, 1994–97. Mem., SERC, 1989–94 (Chm., Nuclear Phys Bd, 1989–93); CERN: Chairman: Super Proton Synchrotron Cttee, 1988–90; Super Proton Synchrotron and LEAR Cttee, 1991–93; Member: Res. Bd, 1988–95; Sci. Policy Cttee, 1988–93; Council, 1989–94; Particle, Space and Astronomy Bd, 1993–94; Sec., C11 Commn, IUPAP, 1989–91. *Publications:* Electromagnetic Interactions of Hadrons, vols I and II, 1978; over 100 articles in learned jls of Particle Physics. *Recreations:* sailing, walking. *Address:* Department of Physics and Astronomy, University of Manchester, Manchester M13 9PL. *T:* (0161) 275 4200.

DONNE, David Lucas; Director: Marathon Asset Management, since 1989; Guinness Flight Extra Income Trust, since 1995; *b* 17 Aug. 1925; *s* of late Dr Cecil Lucas Donne, Wellington, NZ, and of Marjorie Nicholls Donne; *m* 1st, 1957, Jennifer Margaret Duncan (*d* 1975); two *s* one *d*; 2nd, 1978, Clare, *d* of Maj. F. J. Yates. *Educ:* Stowe; Christ Church, Oxford (MA Nat. Science). Called to the Bar, Middle Temple, 1949. Studied Business Admin, Syracuse Univ., 1952–53; Charterhouse Group, 1953–64; William Baird, 1964–67. Chairman: Crest Nicholson, 1973–92; Dalgety, 1977–86 (Dep. Chm., 1975–77); Steetley, 1983–92 (Dep. Chm., 1979–83); ASDA-MFI, 1986–87; Argos, 1990–95; Director: Royal Trust Bank, 1972–93 (Dep. Chm., 1989–93); Sphere Investment Trust, 1982–95 (Chm., 1989–95); Brodie & Knight, 1998–. Member: Nat. Water Council, 1980–83; Bd, British Coal (formerly NCB), 1984–87; Stock Exchange Listed Cos Adv. Cttee, 1987–91. Trustee, BACUP, 1993–; Chm., Calibre Cassette Library for the Blind, 1997–. Fellow, Game Conservancy, 1987. *Recreations:* shooting, opera, sailing. *Address:* 8 Montagu Mews North, W1H 2JU. *Club:* Royal Thames Yacht.

DONNE, Hon. Sir Gaven (John), KBE 1979; Chief Justice: of Nauru, since 1985; of Tuvalu, since 1986; Member, Kiribati Court of Appeal, since 1987; *b* 8 May 1914; *s* of Jack Alfred Donne and Mary Elizabeth Donne; *m* 1946, Isabel Fenwick, *d* of John Edwin Hall; two *s* two *d*. *Educ:* Palmerston North Boys' High Sch.; Hastings High Sch.; Victoria Univ., Wellington; Auckland Univ. (LLB New Zealand). Called to the Bar and admitted solicitor, 1938. Military Service, 2nd NZEF, Middle East and Italy, 1941–45. Stipendiary Magistrate, NZ, 1958–75; Puisne Judge, Supreme Court of Western Samoa, 1970–71; Chief Justice, Western Samoa, 1972–75, Mem. Court of Appeal of Western Samoa, 1975–82; Judge, High Court of Niue, 1973; Chief Justice of the Cook Islands, 1975–82, and of Niue, 1974–82; Queen's Rep. in the Cook Islands, 1982–84. Hon. Counsellor, Internat. Assoc. of Youth Magistrates, 1974–. Member: Takapuna Bor. Council, 1957–58; Auckland Town Planning Authority, 1958; Bd of Governors, Westlake High Sch., 1957–58. Grand Cross 2nd Cl., Order of Merit of Fed. Republic of Germany, 1978. *Recreations:* golf, fishing, walking. *Address:* Meneng Drive, Nauru, Central Pacific. *T:* 4443713; RD4, Otaramarae, Lake Rotoiti, Rotorua, New Zealand. *T:* (73) 624861. *Club:* University (Auckland).

DONNE, Sir John (Christopher), Kt 1976; Chairman, National Health Service Training Authority, 1983–86; *b* 19 Aug. 1921; *s* of late Leslie Victor Donne, solicitor, Hove, and Mabel Laetitia Richards (*née* Pike); *m* 1945, Mary Stuart (*née* Seaton); three *d*. *Educ:* Charterhouse. Royal Artillery, 1940–46 (Captain); served Europe and India. Solicitor, 1949; Notary Public; Consultant, Donne Mileham & Haddock, 1985–92; Pres., Sussex Law Soc., 1969–70. Chairman: SE (Metropolitan) Regional Hosp. Bd, 1971–74; SE Thames RHA, 1973–83. Governor, Guy's Hosp., 1971–74, Guy's Hosp. Med. Sch., 1974–82; Dep. Chm., RHA Chairmen, 1976–78 (Chm., 1974–76); Mem., Gen. Council, King Edward's Hosp. Fund for London, 1972–91 (Mem., Management Cttee, 1978–84); a Governing Trustee, Nuffield Provincial Hosp. Trust, 1975–98; Dir, Nuffield Health and Soc. Services Fund, 1976–98. Member: Council, Internat. Hosp. Fedn, 1979–85; Council, Inst. for Med. Ethics (formerly Soc. for Study of Medical Ethics), 1980–86; Court of Univ. of Sussex, 1979–87. FRSA 1985–92; FRSocMed 1985. Mem. Ct of Assts, Hon. Company of Broderers, 1979– (Master, 1983–84). Mem., Editorial Bd, Jl Medical Ethics, 1977–79. *Recreations:* genealogy, gardening, photography, listening to music. *Address:* The Old School House, Acton Burnell, Shrewsbury SY5 7PG. *T:* and *Fax:* (01694) 731647. *Clubs:* Army and Navy, Pilgrims, MCC; Butterflies, Sussex Martlets.

DONNELLAN, Declan Michael Martin; Artistic Director, Cheek By Jowl, since 1981; Associate Director, Royal National Theatre, 1989–97; *b* 4 Aug. 1953; *s* of Thomas Patrick John Donnellan and Margaret Josephine Donnellan. *Educ:* Queens' Coll., Cambridge (MA). Called to the Bar, Middle Temple, 1978. Productions include: Cheek By Jowl: Andromache, 1985; Twelfth Night, 1987; Lady Betty, 1989; As You Like It, 1992, 1995; Measure for Measure, 1994; Much Ado About Nothing, 1998; Royal National Theatre: Fuente Ovejuna, 1989; Angels in America: part 1, Millennium, 1991, part 2, Perestroika, 1993; Sweeney Todd, 1992; The Winter's Tale, Maly Drama Theatre, St Petersburg, 1997; The School for Scandal, RSC, 1998; Le Cid (Corneille), Avignon Fest., 1998; The Home Body, NY, 2001; Falstaff, Salzburg Spring Fest., 2001; Boris Godunov, UK tour 2001. Several internat. awards incl. Observer Award for Outstanding Achievement. *Address:* c/o Michelle Braidman Associates, 10–11 Lower John Street, W1R 3PE. *Fax:* (020) 7439 3600.

DONNELLY, Alan John; Managing Director, Sovereign Strategy, since 2000; Secretary, Co-operative Commission, since 2000; *b* 16 July 1957; *s* of John and Josephine Donnelly; *m* 1979 (marr. diss. 1982); one *s*. *Educ:* Valley View Primary School and Springfield Comprehensive School, Jarrow; Sunderland Poly. (Hon. Fellow, Sunderland Univ.,

1993). GMBATU Northern Region: Health and Safety Officer, 1978–80; Education Officer, 1980–84; Finance and Admin Officer, 1984–87; GMB Central Finance Manager, 1987–89. European Parliament: Member (Lab): Tyne and Wear, 1989–99; NE Reg., England, 1999–Jan. 2000; Pres., Delegn, Relations with USA, 1992–98; Leader, Lab. Party, 1998–2000; a Vice Pres., Socialist Gp. Mem., S Tyneside MBC, 1979–82. B Director, Unity Trust Bank, 1987–89. Kt Comdr, Order of Merit (Germany), 1991. *Recreations:* tennis, swimming, reading. *Address:* 1 St George's Avenue, South Shields, Tyne and Wear NE34 6EU. *T:* (0191) 425 3825.

DONNELLY, Brendan Patrick; *b* 25 Aug. 1950; *s* of Patrick Aloysius Donnelly and late Mary Josephine Donnelly (*née* Barrett). *Educ:* Christ Church, Oxford (BA Classics 1972; MA 1976). Theodor Heuss Travelling Scholar, Munich, 1974–76; FCO, 1976–82; Private Sec. to Sir Henry Plumb, 1983–86; on staff of Lord Cockfield, a Vice-Pres. of CEC, 1986–87; Political Consultant on EC, 1987–90; Special Advr to Leader of Conservatives in EP, 1990–94. MEP (C) Sussex S and Crawley, 1994–99. *Recreations:* watching cricket, modern languages, modern history. *Address:* 61 Leopold Road, N2 8BG. *T:* (020) 8444 0154. *Clubs:* Carlton; Middlesex County Cricket, Sussex County Cricket.

DONNELLY, (Joseph) Brian, CMG 1998; HM Diplomatic Service; High Commissioner to Zimbabwe, since 2001; *b* 24 April 1945; *s* of Joseph Donnelly and Ada Agnes (*née* Bowness); *m* 1st, 1966, Susanne Gibb (marr. diss. 1994); one *d*; 2nd, 1997, Julia Mary Newsome; one step *s* one step *d*. *Educ:* Workington Grammar Sch.; Queen's Coll., Oxford (Wyndham Scholar, MA); Univ. of Wisconsin (MA). Joined HM Diplomatic Service, 1973; 2nd Sec., FCO, 1973; 1st Sec., UK Mission to UN, NY, 1975–79; Head of Chancery, Singapore, 1979–82; Asst Head, Personnel Policy Dept, FCO, 1982–84; Dep. to Chief Scientific Adviser, Cabinet Office, 1984–87; Counsellor and Consul General, Athens, 1988–91; RCDS, 1991; Head of Non-Proliferation Dept, FCO, 1992–95; Minister and Dep. Perm. Rep., UK Delegn to NATO and WEU, Brussels, 1995–97; Ambassador to Yugoslavia, 1997–99; Dir and Special Rep. for SE Europe, FCO, 1999–2001, on secondment to BP Amoco, 2000–01. *Recreations:* MG cars, flying kites, reading, running, golf. *Address:* c/o Foreign and Commonwealth Office, King Charles Street, SW1A 2AH. *Clubs:* MG Owners'; Maryport Golf.

DONNELLY, Martin Eugene; Deputy Head, European Secretariat, Cabinet Office, since 1997; *b* 4 June 1958; *s* of Eugene Lawrence Donnelly and Mary Jane Ormsby; *m* 1st, 1985, Carol Jean Heald (*d* 1996); three *d*; 2nd, 1998, Susan Jane Catchpole. *Educ:* Campion Hall, Oxford (MA); Coll. of Europe (Dip. European Studies 1980). Joined HM Treasury, 1980; Private Sec. to Financial Sec., 1982–83; Ecole Nationale d'Admin, Paris, 1983–84; Principal, HM Treasury, 1984–87; Private Sec. to Sec. of State for NI, 1988; Mem., cabinet of Sir Leon Brittan, EC, 1989–92; Asst Sec., Defence Team, HM Treasury, 1993–95; chargé de mission, Direction du Trésor, Finance Min., France, 1995–96; Team Leader, Economic and Monetary Union, HM Treasury, 1996–97. *Publications:* articles on European Commission and cabinet system. *Recreations:* reading, music, walking. *Address:* European Secretariat, Cabinet Office, 70 Whitehall, SW1A 1AS. *T:* (020) 7270 0177.

DONNELLY, Prof. Peter James, DPhil; Professor of Statistical Science, and Fellow of St Anne's College, University of Oxford, since 1996; *b* 15 May 1959; *s* of Augustine Stanislaus Donnelly and Sheila Bernadette Donnelly (*née* O'Hagan); *m* 1986, Dr Sarah Helen Harper; one *s* two *d*. *Educ:* St Joseph's Coll., Brisbane; Univ. of Queensland (BSc 1979; Univ. Medal 1980); Balliol Coll., Oxford (Rhodes Schol., DPhil 1983). Vis. Asst Prof., Michigan Univ., 1983–84; Res. Fellow, UC Swansea, 1984–85; Lectr, UCL, 1985–88; Prof. of Math. Stats and Operational Res., QMW, 1988–94; Prof. of Stats and Ecology and Evolution, Chicago Univ., 1994–96 Hon. FIA. *Publications:* (ed jtly) Progress in Population Genetics and Human Evolution, 1997; contrib. to learned jls. *Recreations:* sport, music, children. *Address:* Department of Statistics, University of Oxford, 1 South Parks Road, Oxford OX1 3TG. *T:* (01865) 272860.

DONNISON, David Vernon; Research Fellow, Glasgow University, since 1991; *b* 19 Jan. 1926; *s* of late Frank Siegfried Vernon Donnison, CBE and Ruth Seruya Singer, MBE, JP; *m* 1st, Jean Kidger; two *s* two *d*; 2nd, 1987, Catherine McIntosh, (Kay), Carmichael, *qv*. *Educ:* Marlborough Coll., Wiltshire; Magdalen Coll., Oxford. Asst Lectr and Lectr, Manchester Univ., 1950–53; Lectr, Toronto Univ., 1953–55; Reader, 1956–61, Prof. of Social Administration, 1961–69, LSE (Hon. Fellow, 1981); Dir, Centre for Environmental Studies, 1969–75; Chm., Supplementary Benefits Commn, 1975–80; Prof. of Town and Regl Planning, Glasgow Univ., 1980–91, now Emeritus. Vis. Prof., Warwick Univ., 1993–. Chm., Public Schs Commn, 1968–70. Hon. doctorates: Bradford, 1973; Hull, 1980; Leeds, Southampton, 1981. *Publications:* The Neglected Child and the Social Services, 1954; Welfare Services in a Canadian Community, 1958; Housing since the Rent Act, 1961; The Government of Housing, 1967; An Approach to Social Policy, 1975; Social Policy and Administration Revisited, 1975; (with Paul Soto) The Good City, 1980; The Politics of Poverty, 1982; (with Clare Ungerson) Housing Policy, 1982; (ed with Alan Middleton) Regenerating the Inner City: Glasgow's Experience, 1987; (ed with D. Maclennan) The Housing Service of the Future, 1991; A Radical Agenda, 1991; Long-term Unemployment in Northern Ireland, 1996; Policies for a Just Society, 1998. *Address:* 23 Bank Street, Glasgow G12 8JQ. *T:* (0141) 334 5817.

DONNISON, Kay; *see* Carmichael, C. M.

DONOGHUE, Barbara Joan, (Mrs S. Vavalidis); Member, Independent Television Commission, since 2000; Teaching Fellow, London Business School, since 2000; *b* 16 July 1951; *d* of Hubert Graham Donoghue and Marjorie Larlham Donoghue; *m* 1976, Stefanos Vavalidis; two *s*. *Educ:* McGill Univ., Montreal (BCom 1972; Schol.; Transportation Develt Agency Fellow, 1974; MBA 1974). Canadian Pacific Ltd, 1973–77; Bank of Nova Scotia, 1977–79; Vice Pres., Bankers Trust Co., 1979–93; Man. Dir, NatWest Markets/Hawkpoint Partners, 1994–98. *Address:* Independent Television Commission, 33 Foley Street, W1P 7LB; *e-mail:* barbara.donoghue@btinternet.com. *Club:* Hurlingham.

DONOGHUE, Prof. Denis, MA, PhD, LittD; literary critic; Henry James Professor of Letters, New York University, since 1979; *b* 1 Dec. 1928. *Educ:* University College, Dublin. BA 1949, MA 1952, PhD 1957; MA Cantab 1965. Admin. Office, Dept of Finance, Irish Civil Service, 1951–54. Asst Lectr, Univ. Coll., Dublin, 1954–57; Coll. Lectr, 1957–62; Visiting Schol., Univ. of Pennsylvania, 1962–63; Coll. Lectr, Univ. Coll., Dublin, 1963–64; University Lectr, Cambridge Univ., 1964–65; Fellow, King's Coll., Cambridge, 1964–65; Prof. of Modern English and American Literature, University Coll., Dublin, 1965–79. Mem. Internat. Cttee of Assoc. of University Profs of English. Mem. BBC Commn to monitor the quality of spoken English on BBC Radio, 1979. Reith Lectr, BBC, 1982. *Publications:* The Third Voice, 1959; Connoisseurs of Chaos, 1965; (ed jtly) An Honoured Guest, 1965; The Ordinary Universe, 1968; Emily Dickinson, 1968; Jonathan Swift, 1969; (ed) Swift, 1970; Yeats, 1971; Thieves of Fire, 1974; (ed) W. B. Yeats, Memoirs, 1973; Sovereign Ghost: studies in Imagination, 1978; Ferocious Alphabets, 1981; The Arts without Mystery, 1983; We Irish (selected essays), 1987; Pure Good of Theory, 1992; Walter Pater: lover of strange souls, 1995; The Practice of Reading, 1998; Words Alone: the poet T. S. Eliot, 2001; contribs to reviews and journals. *Address:* New York University, English Department, 726 Broadway (7th Floor), New York, NY 10003, USA; Gaybrook, North Avenue, Mount Merrion, Dublin, Ireland.

DONOHOE, Brian Harold; MP (Lab) Cunninghame South, since 1992; *b* 10 Sept. 1948; *s* of late George Joseph Donohoe and Catherine Sillars Donohoe (*née* Ashworth); *m* 1973, Christine Pawson; two *s*. *Educ:* Irvine Royal Academy; Kilmarnock Technical Coll. Apprentice fitter-turner, 1965–69; draughtsman, 1969–81; Trade Union Official, NALGO, 1981–92. Mem., Select Cttee on transport, 1993–97, on environment, transport and the regions, 1997–2001, on transport, local govt and the regions, 2001–. *Recreation:* gardening. *Address:* 5 Greenfield Drive, Irvine KA12 0ED. *T:* (01294) 274419. *Club:* NALGO Staff Social.

DONOHOE, Peter Howard; pianist; *b* 18 June 1953; *s* of Harold Donohoe and Marjorie Donohoe (*née* Travis); *m* 1980, Elaine Margaret Burns; one *d*. *Educ:* Chetham's School of Music, Manchester; Leeds Univ.; Royal Northern Coll. of Music; Paris Conservatoire. BMus; GRNCM, ARCM; Hon. FRNCM 1983. Professional solo pianist, 1974–; London début, 1978; concert tours in Europe, USA, Canada, Australia, Asia, USSR; regular appearances at Royal Festival Hall, Barbican Hall, Queen Elizabeth Hall, Henry Wood Promenade concerts, 1979–; numerous TV and radio broadcasts, UK and overseas; recordings include music by Rachmaninov, Stravinsky, Prokofiev, Britten, Messiaen, Muldowney, Tchaikovsky. Competition finalist: British Liszt, London, 1976; Liszt-Bartok, Budapest, 1976; Leeds International Piano, 1981; winner, Internat. Tschaikovsky competition, Moscow, 1982. Concerto Recording Award, Gramophone, 1988. *Recreations:* jazz, golf, helping young musicians, clock collecting. *Address:* c/o Askonas Holt Ltd, Lonsdale Chambers, 27 Chancery Lane, WC2A 1PF. *T:* (020) 7400 1700.

DONOUGHMORE, 8th Earl of, *cr* 1800; **Richard Michael John Hely-Hutchinson;** Baron Donoughmore, 1783; Viscount Hutchinson (UK), 1821; Chairman, Hodder Headline (formerly Headline Book Publishing) PLC, 1986–97; *b* 8 Aug. 1927; *er s* of 7th Earl of Donoughmore and Dorothy Jean (MBE 1947) (*d* 1995), *d* of late J. B. Hotham; *S* father, 1981; *m* 1951, Sheila (*d* 1999), *o c* of late Frank Frederick Parsons and Mrs Learmond Perkins; four *s*. *Educ:* Winchester; New College, Oxford (MA; BM, BCh). *Heir: s* Viscount Suirdale, *qv*. *Address:* The Manor House, Bampton, Oxon OX18 2LQ.

See also Hon. T. M. Hely Hutchinson.

DONOUGHUE, family name of **Baron Donoughue**.

DONOUGHUE, Baron *cr* 1985 (Life Peer), of Ashton in the County of Northamptonshire; **Bernard Donoughue;** *b* 8 Sept. 1934; *s* of late Thomas Joseph Donoughue and of Maud Violet Andrews; *m* 1959, Carol Ruth Goodman (marr. diss. 1989); two *s* two *d*. *Educ:* Secondary Modern Sch. and Grammar Sch., Northampton; Lincoln Coll. and Nuffield Coll., Oxford. BA (1st class hons), MA, DPhil (Oxon). FRHistS. Henry Fellow, Harvard, USA. Mem., Editorial Staff: The Economist, Sunday Times, Sunday Telegraph. Sen. Res. Officer, PEP, 1960–63; Lectr, Sen. Lectr, Reader, LSE, 1963–74; Sen. Policy Advr to the Prime Minister, 1974–79; Development Dir, Economist Intelligence Unit, 1979–81; Asst Editor, The Times, 1981–82; Partner, 1983–86, Head of Res. and Investment Policy, 1984–86, Grieveson, Grant & Co; Dir, 1986–88, Head of Res., 1986–87, of Internat. Res. and Investment Policy, 1987–88, Kleinwort Grieveson Securities; Exec. Vice-Chm., London and Bishopsgate Internat. Investment Holdings, 1988–91. Opposition spokesman on Treasury, 1991–92, on Energy, 1991–93, on Nat. Heritage, 1992–97; Parly Under-Sec. of State, MAFF, 1997–99. Treas., All Party Parly Gp on Integrated Educn in NI; Sec., All Party Racing and Bloodstock Cttee, 2001–. Dir, Towcester Racecourse Ltd, 1992–97. Vis. Prof., LSE, 2000–. Member: Sports Council, 1965–71; Commn of Enquiry into Association Football, 1966–68; Ct of Governors, LSE, 1968–74, 1982–97; Civil Service Coll. Adv. Council, 1976–79; Adv. Bd, Wissenschaftzentrum, Berlin, 1978–91; Bd, Centre for European Policy Studies, Brussels, 1982–87; London Arts Bd, 1991–97. Trustee, Inst. for Policy Res., 1990–. Consultant, British House Industry Confedn, 1999–. Chm. Exec. Cttee, London Symphony Orch., 1978–93 (Patron, 1989–96); Vice-Pres., Newbury Music Fest., 1995–. Associate Mem., Nuffield Coll., Oxford, 1982–87; Mem., Sen. Common Room, Lincoln Coll., Oxford, 1985– (Hon. Fellow, 1986); Patron, Inst. of Contemporary British History, 1988–; Vice Pres., Assoc. of Comprehensive Schs, 2000–. Pres., Gambling Care, 1997. FRSA. Hon. Fellow, LSE, 1989. Hon. LLD Leicester, 1990. *Publications:* (ed jtly) Oxford Poetry, 1956; Wage Policies in the Public Sector, 1962; Trade Unions in a Changing Society, 1963; British Politics and the American Revolution, 1964; (with W. T. Rodgers) The People into Parliament, 1966; (with G. W. Jones) Herbert Morrison: portrait of a politician, 1973; Prime Minister, 1987. *Recreations:* politics, sport, economics, music. *Address:* 71 Ebury Mews East, SW1W 9QA. *Club:* Pratt's.

DONOVAN, Charles Edward; Board Member, 1981–92, and Senior Managing Director, Corporate Activities, 1991–92, British Gas plc; *b* 28 Jan. 1934; *s* of Charles and Sarah Donovan; *m* 1963, Robina Evelyn (*née* Anderson); three *s*. *Educ:* Camphill Sch., Paisley; Royal Technical Coll., Glasgow. FIPM 1990; CIGasE 1985; CIMgt (CBIM 1991). Personnel Officer: HQ, BEA, 1962; London and SE, Richard Costain Ltd, Constr. and Civil Engrs, 1963; Sen. Personnel Officer, Engrg, W Midlands Gas Bd, 1966; Southern Gas, 1970–77: Personnel Manager, 1973; Personnel Dir, 1975; British Gas: Dir, Indust. Relations, 1977–81; Man. Dir, Personnel, 1981–91, also Group Services, 1989–91. Dir, Inst. of Citizenship Studies, 1992–97. FRSA 1992. *Recreations:* sailing, hill walking. *Address:* 65 Moss Lane, Pinner, Middx HA5 3AZ.

DONOVAN, Prof. Desmond Thomas; Yates-Goldsmid Professor of Geology and Head of Department of Geology, University College, London, 1966–82; Hon. Curator, Wells Museum, Somerset, 1982–85; *b* 16 June 1921; *s* of T. B. Donovan and M. A. Donovan (*née* Benker); *m* 1959, Shirley Louise Saward; two *s* one *d*. *Educ:* Epsom Coll.; University of Bristol. BSc 1942; PhD 1951; DSc 1960. FGS 1942, CGeol 1991; FLS 1960. Asst Lectr in Geology, University of Bristol, 1947; Lectr in Geology, Bristol, 1950; Prof. of Geology, University of Hull, 1962. Pres., Palaeontographical Soc., 1979–84. *Publications:* Stratigraphy: An Introduction to Principles, 1966; (ed) Geology of Shelf Seas, 1968; papers on fossil cephalopods, Jurassic stratigraphy, Pleistocene deposits, marine geology. *Recreation:* opera. *Address:* 52 Willow Road, NW3 1TP. *T:* (020) 7794 8626.

DONOVAN, Ian Edward, FRAeS; FCMA; Director, English Symphony Orchestra, since 2000; *b* 2 March 1940; *s* of late John Walter Donovan and Ethel Molyneux; *m* 1969, Susan Betty Harris; two *s*. *Educ:* Leighton Park, Reading. FCMA 1985. Gen. Factory Manager, Lucas CAV, 1969–72; Finance Man., Lucas Girling, 1972–78; Finance Director: Lucas Girling, Koblenz, 1978–81; Lucas Electrical Ltd, 1982–84; Mem., 1985–88, Gp Dir, Finance and Central Services, 1986–88, CAA; Dir and Gp Controller, 1988–98, Gp Dir, Aerospace, 1998–2000, Smiths Industries Aerospace & Defence Ltd; Chm., Chart Co. Ltd, 1998–2000; Pres., Lambda Advanced Analog Inc., 2000. Mem. Council, SBAC, 1994–97; Hon. Treasurer: Air League, 1995–2000; Homeless Network, 1999–; Trustee, Air League Educnl Trust, 1995–2000. FRAeS 2001. *Recreations:* fly fishing, sailing, gardening, music, golf. *Address:* Lawn Farm, Church Lane, Tibberton, Droitwich, Worcs WR9 7NW. *Club:* Royal Air Force.

DONOVAN, Judith, CBE 1997; Chairman, JDA, 1982–2000; *b* 5 July 1951; *d* of late Ernest and Joyce Nicholson; *m* 1977, John Patrick Donovan. *Educ:* Univ. of Hull (BA Hons English 1973); DipCAM 1979. Mktg Asst, Ford Motor Co., 1973–75; Account Handler, J. Walter Thomson, 1975–77; Advertising Manager, Grattan, 1977–82. Dir, British Direct Marketing Assoc., 1987–91; Chm., Direct Marketing Assoc., 1999–2001 (Dir, 1991–2001); Pres., Bradford Chamber of Commerce, 1999–2001 (Dir, 1988–); Director: Bradford City Challenge, 1988–89; BusinessLink West Yorks, 2001–; Dep. Chm., Bradford Breakthrough, 1988–90; Chairman: Bradford & Dist TEC, 1989–98; Northern Region CCPS (Postwatch), 2001–. Mem., Millennium Commn, 2000–. Dir, Northern Ballet Theatre, 1991–. Gov., Margaret McMillan Sch., 1985–87. FRSA 1996; FCAM 1996; FCIM 1998; FInstD 2000; CIMgt 2000. Freeman, City of London, 1999; Liveryman, Co. of Marketors, 1999. *Recreations:* after dinner speaking, the Western Front, dogs and cats. *Address:* DIY Direct Marketing Ltd, Biggin Barns, Ringbeck, Kirkby Malzeard, Ripon, N Yorks HG4 3TT. *T:* (01765) 650000, *Fax:* (01765) 650153; *e-mail:* judith@diydirectmarketing.co.uk.

DONOVAN, Katharine Mary; *see* Barker, K. M.

DONOVAN, Stephen Kenneth, PhD, DSc; Keeper of Palaeontology, Natural History Museum, since 1998; *b* 3 June 1954; *s* of Alfred Haig Donovan and Beatrice Georgina Donovan (*née* Nichols); *m* 1997, Catriona Margaret Isobel MacGillivray; one *s* one *d*. *Educ:* Univ. of Manchester (BSc 1980); Univ. of Liverpool (PhD 1983; DSc 1994). Royal Soc. Res. Fellow, TCD, 1983–84; Higher Scientific Officer, NERC, 1985–86; University of West Indies, Jamaica: Lectr, 1986–89; Sen. Lectr, 1989–92; Reader in Palaeozoology, 1992–96; Prof. of Palaeozoology, 1996–98. Sen. Res. Fellow, Nat. Mus. of Natural History, Smithsonian Instn, Washington, 1994–95; Visiting Professor: Univ. of Portsmouth, 1996–; UCL, 2000–; Adjunct Prof., Univ. of New Brunswick, 2000–. FGS 1998. *Publications:* (ed) Mass Extinctions: processes and evidence, 1989; (ed) The Processes of Fossilization, 1991; (ed) The Palaeobiology of Trace Fossils, 1994; (ed jtly) Caribbean Geology: an introduction, 1994; (ed jtly) The Adequacy of the Fossil Record, 1998; numerous res. papers and reviews, particularly on palaeontology and Caribbean geology. *Recreations:* reading, writing, walking, cricket, tramway and railway history. *Address:* Department of Palaeontology, Natural History Museum, Cromwell Road, SW7 5BD. *T:* (020) 7942 5204.

DOOGE, Prof. James Clement Ignatius; Professor of Civil Engineering, University College, Dublin, 1970–84, now Professor Emeritus; research consultant; Consultant: United Nations specialised agencies; European Commission; President, Royal Irish Academy, 1987–90; *b* 30 July 1922; *s* of Denis Patrick Dooge and Veronica Catherine Carroll; *m* 1946, Veronica O'Doherty; two *s* three *d*. *Educ:* Christian Brothers' Sch., Dun Laoghaire; University Coll., Dublin (BE, BSc 1942, ME 1952); Univ. of Iowa (MSc 1956). FICE; FASCE. Jun. Civil Engr, Irish Office of Public Works, 1943–46; Design Engr, Electricity Supply Bd, Ireland, 1946–58; Prof. of Civil Engrg, UC Cork, 1958–70. Irish Senate: Mem., 1965–77 and 1981–87; Chm., 1973–77; Leader, 1983–87; Minister for Foreign Affairs, Ireland, 1981–82. President: ICEI, 1968–69 (Hon. FICEI; Kettle Premium and Plaque, 1948, 1985; Mullins Medal, 1951, 1962); Internat. Assoc. for Hydrologic Scis, 1975–79; Member: Exec. Bureau, Internat. Union for Geodesy and Geophysics, 1979–87; Gen. Cttee, ICSU, 1980–86, 1988– (Sec. Gen., 1980–82; Pres., 1993–96). Fellow, Amer. Geophysical Union (Horton Award, 1959; Bowie Medal, 1986); Hon. Mem., Eur. Geophysical Soc., 1993 (John Dalton Medal, 1998). Foreign Member: Polish Acad. of Scis, 1985; Russian Acad. of Scis, 1994; Spanish Acad. of Sci., 1998; Royal Acad. of Engrg, 2000. Hon. DrAgrSc Wageningen, 1978; Hon. DrTech. Lund, 1980; Hon. DSc Birmingham, 1986; Hon. ScD Dublin, 1988. Internat. Prize for Hydrology, 1983; Internat. Prize for Meteorology, 1999. *Address:* Centre for Water Resources Research, University College, Earlsfort Terrace, Dublin 2, Ireland.

DOOKUN, Sir Dewoonarain, Kt 1984; Chairman and Managing Director, Mauritius Cosmetics Ltd, since 1966; *b* 7 Dec. 1929; *s* of Jadoonath Dookun; *m* 1959, Henriette Keupp; two *s*. *Educ:* St Joseph College; Univ. of Edinburgh. Manufacturing, marketing, business administration and accounts, Mainz, West Germany; founder of: Mauritius Cosmetics, 1966; Paper Converting Co., 1967; Jet Industries, 1967; FDG Garments Industries, 1968; Agri-Pac, 1979; Deramann, 1979; Gumboots Manufacturers, 1976; DG Rubber, 1979; Elite Textiles, 1982; Deodan Textile, 1984. *Recreations:* reading, walking, golf. *Address:* Queen Mary Avenue, Floreal, Mauritius. *T:* 6862361; *telex:* 4239 Dookun IW. *Clubs:* Institute of Directors; Mauritius Gymkhana; Swastika.

DORAN, Frank; MP (Lab) Aberdeen Central, since 1997; *b* 13 April 1949; *s* of Francis Anthony Doran and Betty Hedges or Doran; *m* 1967, Patricia Ann Govan or Doran (separated 1990); two *s*. *Educ:* Ainslie Park Secondary Sch.; Leith Acad.; Dundee Univ. (LLB Hons). Admitted Solicitor, 1977. Eur. Parly Cand. (Lab) NE Scotland, 1984. MP (Lab) Aberdeen South, 1987–92; contested (Lab) same seat, 1992. Asst Editor, Scottish Legal Action Group Bulletin, 1975–78. *Recreations:* cinema, art, sports. *Address:* House of Commons, SW1A 0AA. *Club:* Aberdeen Trades Council.

DORAN, Gregory; Associate Director, Royal Shakespeare Company, since 1996; *b* 24 Nov. 1958; *s* of John Doran and Margaret Freeman; partner, Sir Antony Sher, *qv*. *Educ:* Bristol Univ. (BA Hons); Bristol Old Vic Theatre Sch. Joined RSC 1987; *RSC productions include:* The Odyssey, 1992; Henry VIII, 1996; Cyrano de Bergerac, 1997; The Merchant of Venice, The Winter's Tale, 1998; Oroonoko, Timon of Athens, Macbeth, 1999; As You Like It, 2000; King John, Jubilee, 2001; *other productions include:* Long Day's Journey into Night, Waiting for Godot, Nottingham Playhouse, 1982–83; Titus Andronicus, Market Th., Johannesburg, and RNT, 1995 (TMA Award for Best Production); Black Comedy, and The Real Inspector Hound, Comedy Th., 1998; York Millennium Mystery Plays, York Minster, 2000; Mahler's Conversion, Aldwych, 2001; *film:* Macbeth, 1999. *Publication:* (with Sir Antony Sher) Woza Shakespeare!, 1996. *Address:* c/o Royal Shakespeare Theatre, Stratford-upon-Avon, Warwicks CV37 6BB.

DORCHESTER, Area Bishop of, since 2000; **Rt Rev. Colin William Fletcher,** OBE 2000; *b* 17 Nov. 1950; *s* of Alan Philip Fletcher, *qv*; *m* 1980, Sarah Elizabeth Webster; one *s* two *d*. *Educ:* Marlborough Coll.; Trinity Coll., Oxford (MA 1976). Ordained deacon, 1975, priest, 1976; Asst Curate, St Peter, Shipley, 1975–79; Tutor, Wycliffe Hall, Oxford and Asst Curate, St Andrew, N Oxford, 1979–84; Vicar, Holy Trinity, Margate, 1984–93, Rural Dean of Thanet, 1988–93; Chaplain to the Archbishop of Canterbury, 1993–2000. *Recreations:* ornithology, walking, sport. *Address:* Arran House, Sandy Lane, Yarnton, Oxford OX5 1PB. *T:* (01865) 375541.

See also P. J. Fletcher.

DORE, Prof. Ronald Philip, CBE 1989; FBA 1975; Senior Research Fellow, Centre for Economic Performance, London School of Economics and Political Science, since 1991; *b* 1 Feb. 1925; *s* of Philip Brine Dore and Elsie Constance Dore; *m* 1957, Nancy Macdonald; one *s* one *d*; one *s* with Maria Paisley. *Educ:* Poole Grammar Sch.; SOAS, Univ. of London (BA). Lectr in Japanese Instns, SOAS, London, 1951; Prof. of Asian Studies, Univ. of BC, 1956; Reader, later Prof. of Sociol., LSE, 1961–69 (Hon. Fellow, 1980); Fellow, IDS, Univ. of Sussex, 1969–82; Asst Dir, Technical Change Centre, 1982–86; Dir, Japan–Europe Industry Res. Centre, ICSTM, 1986–91. Adjunct Prof., MIT, 1989–94. Mem., Academia Europaea, 1989. Hon. Foreign Mem., Amer. Acad. of Arts and Scis, 1978; Hon. Foreign Fellow, Japan Acad., 1986–. Order of the Rising Sun (Third Class), Japan, 1988. *Publications:* City Life in Japan, 1958; Land Reform in Japan, 1959, 2nd edn 1984; Education in Tokugawa Japan, 1963, 2nd edn 1983; (ed) Aspects of Social Change in Modern Japan, 1967; British Factory, Japanese Factory, 1973, 2nd edn 1990; The Diploma Disease, 1976, 2nd edn 1997; Shinohata: portrait of a Japanese village, 1978, 2nd edn 1992; (ed with Zoe Mars) Community Development, Comparative Case Studies in India, The Republic of Korea, Mexico and Tanzania, 1981; Energy Conservation in Japanese Industry, 1982; Flexible Rigidities: structural adjustment in Japan, 1986; Taking Japan Seriously: a Confucian perspective on leading economic issues, 1987; (ed jtly) Japan and World Depression, Then and Now: essays in memory of E. F. Penrose, 1987; (with Mari Sako) How the Japanese Learn to Work, 1988, rev. edn 1998; (ed jtly) Corporatism and Accountability: organized interests in British public life, 1990; Will the 21st Century be the Age of Individualism?, 1991; (ed with Masahiko Aoki) The Japanese Firm: the source of competitive strength, 1994; Japan, Internationalism and the UN, 1997; Stockmarket Capitalism, Welfare Capitalism: Japan and Germany *vs* the Anglo Saxons, 2000; Social Evolution, Economic Development and Culture, 2001. *Address:* 157 Surrenden Road, Brighton, East Sussex BN1 6ZA. *T:* (01273) 501370.

DOREY, Sir Graham (Martyn), Kt 1993; Bailiff of Guernsey, 1992–99 (Deputy Bailiff, 1982–92); a Judge of the Court of Appeal of Jersey, 1992–99; President, Guernsey Court of Appeal, 1992–99; *b* 15 Dec. 1932; *s* of late Martyn Dorey and Muriel (*née* Pickard); *m* 1962, Penelope Cecile (*d* 1996), *d* of Maj. E. A. Wheadon, ED; two *s* two *d*; *m* 1998, Mrs Cicely Ruth Lummis. *Educ:* Kingswood Sch., Bath; Ecole des Roches, Verneuil; Univs of Bristol and Caen. Admitted Solicitor, 1959; Advocate, Royal Court of Guernsey, 1960; called to the Bar, Gray's Inn, 1992; People's Deputy, States of Guernsey, 1970; Solicitor Gen., 1973, Attorney Gen., 1977, Guernsey. KStJ 1996 (CStJ 1992). *Recreations:* sailing, maritime history, music. *Address:* La Hougue ès Pies, Vale, Guernsey. *T:* (01481) 44868, *Fax:* (01481) 43833. *Clubs:* Royal Ocean Racing; Royal Yacht Squadron.

DOREY, Gregory John, CVO 1997; HM Diplomatic Service; Deputy Head of Mission and Director, Trade and Investment, Hong Kong, since 2000; *b* 1 May 1956; *s* of Michael John Dorey and Avril Dorey (*née* Gregory); *m* 1981, Alison Patricia Taylor; two *s* one *d*. *Educ:* Painswick Co. Primary Sch.; Rendcomb Coll., Cirencester; Exeter Coll., Oxford (MA Modern Hist.). Nat. Westminster Bank, 1973–74; Supply and Transport Service, RN, 1977–78; Army Dept, 1978–79, Defence Secretariat, 1979–81, MoD; UK Delegn to NATO, 1982–84; MoD PE, 1984–86; Soviet Dept, FCO, 1986–89; First Sec., Budapest, 1989–92; Private Sec., Minister of State, FCO, 1992–94; Asst Hd, ME Dept, FCO, 1994–96; Counsellor, then Dep. Head of Mission, Islamabad, 1996–99; on secondment to HSBC plc, 2000. *Recreations:* literature, theatre, cinema, tennis, gardening, travel. *Address:* c/o Foreign and Commonwealth Office, King Charles Street, SW1A 2AH. *T:* (Hong Kong) 29013031. *Clubs:* Hong Kong Cricket, Oxford & Cambridge Society (Hong Kong).

DORGAN, John Christopher, FRCS; Consultant Orthopaedic Surgeon, Royal Liverpool Children's Hospital, since 1984; *b* 26 Nov. 1948; *s* of William Leonard Dorgan and Mary Ellen Dorgan (*née* Gorringe); *m* 1978, Ann Mary Gargan; three *d*. *Educ:* Thornleigh Salesian Coll., Bolton; Liverpool Univ. (MB ChB 1973; MChOrth 1979). FRCS 1977. House Officer, Walton Hosp., Liverpool, 1973–74; Sen. House Officer, Royal Southern Hosp., Liverpool, 1974–75; Registrar, Whiston and St Helens Hosps, 1975–77; Research Fellow, Univ. of Liverpool, 1977–78; Registrar, Broadgreen Hosp. and Royal Liverpool Children's Hosp., 1978–80; Lectr, Dept of Orthopaedic Surgery, Univ. of Liverpool, 1981–84; Consultant Orthopaedic Surgeon, Royal Liverpool Univ. Hosp., 1984–96. Hon. Sec. and Treas., British Scoliosis Soc., 1999–. *Publications:* articles on orthopaedic and spinal surgery in med. jls. *Recreations:* member of trad jazz band, watching Bolton Wanderers FC. *Address:* 72 Rodney Street, Liverpool L1 9AF. *T:* (0151) 709 2177.

DORIN, Bernard Jean Robert, Hon. GCVO; Officier de la Légion d'Honneur; Officier de l'Ordre National du Mérite; Ambassadeur de France; Conseiller d'Etat, 1993–97, now honorary; *b* 25 Aug. 1929; *s* of Robert Dorin and Jacqueline Dorin (*née* Goumard); *m* 1971, Christine du Bois de Meyrignac; two *s* two *d*. *Educ:* Inst. d'Etudes Politiques, Paris; Ecole Nat. d'Administration. Attaché, French Embassy, Ottawa, 1957–59; Min. of Foreign Affairs, 1959–64; technical adviser: for sci. research, nuclear and space, 1966–67; to Minister of Nat. Educn, 1967–68; to Minister for sci. research, 1968–69; Harvard Univ., 1969–70; Min. of Foreign Affairs, 1970–71; Ambassador in Port-au-Prince, 1972–75; Head of Francophone Affairs Dept, 1975–78; Ambassador in Pretoria, 1978–81; Dir for America, Min. of Foreign Affairs, 1981–84; Ambassador, Brazil, 1984–87, Japan, 1987–90, UK, 1990–93. President: Avenir de la langue française, 1998–; Les Amitiés francophones, 1998–; Les Amitiés Acadiennes, 1998–. *Recreation:* collections of naïve paintings. *Address:* 96 rue de Grenelle, 75007 Paris, France; 39 Avenue de Saxe, 75007 Paris, France. *Club:* Richelieu (Paris).

DORKEN, (Anthony) John; Director, British Rubber Manufacturers' Association, since 1997 (Deputy Director, 1996–97); *b* 24 April 1944; *s* of late Oscar Roy Dorken, OBE and of Margaret Dorken (*née* Barker); *m* 1972, Satanay Mufti; one *s* one *d*. *Educ:* Mill Hill Sch.; King's Coll., Cambridge (BA Classics 1965; MA 1969). VSO, Libya, 1965–66; Asst Principal, BoT, 1967–71; Private Sec. to Parly Under Sec. of State for Industry, 1971–72; Principal, DTI, later Dept of Energy, 1972–77; seconded to Cabinet Office, 1977–79; Asst Sec., Dept of Energy, 1980–86; seconded to Shell UK Exploration and Prodn, 1986–89; Dir of Resource Management, Dept of Energy, 1989–92; Dep. Dir Gen., Office of Gas Supply, 1992–93; Head of Consumer Affairs Div., DTI, 1993–96. *Publications:* articles on gas regulation in specialist jls. *Recreations:* reading, walking, music, squash, tennis. *Address:* 10 Connaught Gardens, N10 3LB. *T:* (020) 8372 6213. *Club:* Stormont Lawn Tennis and Squash Rackets (Highgate) (Hon. Treas.).

DORKING, Suffragan Bishop of, since 1996; **Rt Rev. Ian James Brackley;** *b* 13 Dec. 1947; *s* of Frederick Arthur James Brackley and Ivy Sarah Catherine (*née* Bush); *m* 1971, Penny Saunders; two *s*. *Educ:* Westcliff High Sch.; Keble Coll., Oxford (MA); Cuddesdon Coll., Oxford. Ordained deacon, 1971, priest, 1972; Asst Curate, Lockleaze, Bristol, 1971–74; Asst Chaplain, 1974–76, Chaplain, 1976–80, Bryanston Sch., Dorset; Vicar, East Preston with Kingston, 1980–88; Team Rector, St Wilfrid, Haywards Heath, 1988–96. Rural Dean: Arundel and Bognor, 1982–87; Cuckfield, 1989–95. *Recreations:* cricket, classical music, pipe organs. *Address:* 13 Pilgrims Way, Guildford, Surrey GU4 8AD. *T:* (01483) 570829, *Fax:* (01483) 567268; *e-mail:* bishop.ian@cofeguildford.org.uk.

DORKING, Archdeacon of; *see* Wilson, Ven. M. J. C.

DORMAN, Sir Philip (Henry Keppel), 4th Bt *cr* 1923, of Nunthorpe, co. York; tax accountant; *b* 19 May 1954; *s* of Richard Dorman (*d* 1976) and of Diana Keppel (*née* Barrett); *S* cousin, 1996; *m* 1982 (marr. diss. 1992); one *d*; *m* 1996, Sheena Alexandra Faro.

Educ: Marlborough; Univ. of St Andrews. Life Protector, Dorman Mus., Middlesbrough, 1996–. *Recreation:* golf. *Address:* Belmont House, St Georges Lane, Hurstpierpoint, West Sussex BN6 9QX. *T:* (01273) 835757, *Fax:* (01273) 835746; *e-mail:* philipdorman@compuserve.com. *Club:* MCC.

DORMAN, Richard Bostock, CBE 1984; HM Diplomatic Service, retired; High Commissioner to Vanuatu, 1982–85; Chairman, British Friends of Vanuatu, 1990–99 (Co-ordinator, 1986–90); *b* 8 Aug. 1925; *s* of late John Ehrenfried and Madeleine Louise Dorman; *m* 1950, Anna Illingworth; one *s* two *d*. *Educ:* Sedbergh Sch.; St John's Coll., Cambridge. Army Service (Lieut, S Staffs Regt), 1944–48; Asst Principal, War Office, 1951; Principal, 1955; transferred to Commonwealth Relations Office, 1958; First Sec., British High Commission, Nicosia, 1960–64; Dep. High Commissioner, Freetown, 1964–66; SE Asia Dept, FO, 1967–69; Counsellor, Addis Ababa, 1969–73; Commercial Counsellor, Bucharest, 1974–77; Counsellor, Pretoria, 1977–82. Order of Merit (Vanuatu), 1999. *Address:* 67 Beresford Road, Cheam, Surrey SM2 6ER. *T:* (020) 8642 9627. *Club:* Royal Commonwealth Society.

DORMAND, family name of **Baron Dormand of Easington**.

DORMAND OF EASINGTON, Baron, *cr* 1987 (Life Peer), of Easington in the county of Durham; **John Donkin Dormand;** *b* 27 Aug. 1919; *s* of Bernard and Mary Dormand; *m* 1963, Doris Robinson; one step *s* one step *d*. *Educ:* Bede Coll., Durham; Loughborough Coll.; St Peter's Hall, Oxford (Hon. Fellow, St Peter's Coll., 1993); Univ. of Harvard. Teacher, 1940–48; Education Adviser, 1948–52 and 1957–63; District Education Officer, Easington RDC, 1963–70. MP (Lab) Easington, 1970–87. An Asst Govt Whip, 1974; a Lord Comr of HM Treasury, 1974–79; Chm., PLP, 1981–87. *Recreations:* music, sport, films.

DORMANN, Jürgen; Chairman, Board of Management, Aventis, since 1999; *b* Heidelberg, 12 Jan. 1940. Joined Hoechst AG as mgt trainee, 1963; Fiber Sales Dept, 1965–72; Corporate Staff Dept, 1973–84 (Head of Dept, 1980–84); Dep. Mem., Bd of Mgt, 1984–87; Chief Financial Officer, 1987–94; Chm., 1994–99; Hoechst merged with Rhône-Poulenc to form Aventis, 1999. Director: IBM; ABB; Allianz AG. *Address:* Aventis, 6c place Austerlitz, Strasbourg 67000, France.

DORMENT, Richard, PhD; Art Critic, Daily Telegraph, since 1986; *b* 15 Nov. 1946; *s* of James Dorment and Marguerite Dorment (*née* O'Callaghan); *m* 1st, 1970, Kate S. Ganz (marr. diss. 1981); one *s* one *d*; 2nd, 1985, Harriet Mary Waugh. *Educ:* Georgetown Prep. Sch.; Princeton Univ. (BA 1968); Columbia Univ. (MA 1969, MPhil, PhD 1975). Faculty Fellow, Columbia Univ., 1968–72; Asst Curator, European Painting, Philadelphia Mus. of Art, 1973–76; Curator, Alfred Gilbert: Sculptor and Goldsmith, RA, 1985–86; Art Critic, Country Life, 1986; Co-curator, James McNeill Whistler, Tate Gall., 1994–95. Member: Judging Panel, Turner Prize, 1989; Adv. Cttee, Govt Art Collection, 1996–; Reviewing Cttee on the Export of Works of Art, 1996–; British Council Visual Arts Adv. Cttee, 1997–. Trustee, Watts Gallery, 1996–. Hawthornden Prize for art criticism in Britain, 1992; Critic of the Year, British Press Awards, 2000. *Publications:* (contrib.) Victorian High Renaissance (exhibn catalogue), 1978; Alfred Gilbert, 1985; British Painting 1750–1900: A Catalogue of the British Paintings in the Philadelphia Museum of Art, 1986; Alfred Gilbert Sculptor and Goldsmith, 1986; (with Margaret McDonald) James McNeill Whistler, 1994; reviews for NY Rev. of Books, TLS, Literary Rev.; has contrib. to Burlington Magazine. *Address:* 10 Clifton Villas, W9 2PH. *T:* (020) 7266 2057. *Club:* Brooks's.

DORMER, family name of **Baron Dormer**.

DORMER, 17th Baron *cr* 1615, of Wenge, co. Buckingham; **Geoffrey Henry Dormer;** Bt 1615; *b* 13 May 1920; *s* of Captain Edward Henry Dormer (*d* 1943) and Hon. Vanessa Margaret Dormer (*d* 1962), *d* of 1st Baron Borwick; *S* cousin, 1995, but does not use the title; *m* 1st, 1947, Janet Readman (marr. diss. 1957); two *d*; 2nd, 1958, Pamela Simpson; two *s*. *Educ:* Eton; Trinity Coll., Cambridge. RNVR Officer, 1939–46; RNR Officer, 1960–70 (Lt-Comdr 1968); RNVR Officer, 1970–81. Farmer until 1958; small-holder; gardener. *Recreations:* sailing, gardening. *Heir:* *s* Hon. William Robert Dormer [*b* 8 Nov. 1960; *m* 1985, Paula, *d* of Peter Robinson; one *s* one *d*]. *Address:* Dittisham, Devon.

DORNHORST, Antony Clifford, CBE 1977; MD, FRCP; Professor of Medicine, St George's Hospital Medical School, 1959–80; Civilian Consultant in Aviation Medicine to RAF, 1973–85; *b* 2 April 1915; *s* of Ernst Dornhorst and Florence, *née* Partridge; *m* 1946, Helen Mary Innes; three *d*. *Educ:* St Clement Danes Sch.; St Thomas's Hosp. Medical Sch. MB BS London 1937; MD London 1939; FRCP 1955. Junior Appointments, St Thomas' Hosp., 1937–39. Served with RAMC, mostly in Mediterranean theatre, 1940–46. Reader in Medicine, St Thomas's Hosp. Medical Sch., 1949–59. Member: MRC, 1973–77; SW Thames RHA, 1974–82. *Publications:* papers in various journals on normal and abnormal physiology. *Recreation:* music. *Address:* 8 Albert Place, W8 5PD. *T:* (020) 7937 8782.

DORR, Noel; Personal Representative of Irish Minister for Foreign Affairs, European Union Intergovernmental Conference, since 1996; *b* Limerick, 1933; *m* 1983, Caitríona Doran. *Educ:* St Nathy's Coll., Ballaghaderreen; University Coll., Galway (BA, BComm, HDipEd); Georgetown Univ., Washington, DC (MA). Entered Dept of Foreign Affairs, 1960; Third Sec., 1960–62; Third Sec., Brussels, 1962–64; First Sec., Washington, 1964–70; First Sec., Dept of For. Affairs, 1970–72; Counsellor (Press and Inf.), Dept of For. Affairs, 1972–74; Asst Sec., Political Div., and Political Dir, 1974–77, Dep. Sec. and Political Dir, 1977–80; Perm. Rep. of Ireland to UN, New York, 1980–83; Rep of Ireland, Security Council, 1981–82; Ambassador of Ireland to UK, 1983–87; Sec., Dept of Foreign Affairs, Ireland, 1987–95. *Address:* Department of Foreign Affairs, 76–78 Harcourt Street, Dublin 2, Ireland.

DORRANCE, Dr Richard Christopher; Chief Executive: Council for Awards in Children's Care and Education, since 1994; Early Years National Training Organisation, since 1998; Partner, since 1996, Company Secretary, since 2000, Brilliant Publications Ltd; *b* 25 Feb. 1948; *s* of Eric and Joan Dorrance; *m* 1996, Priscilla Hannaford; one *d*. *Educ:* Wolverhampton GS; Aylesbury GS; Univ. of East Anglia (BSc Chem. 1969; PhD 1973). FRSC. Res. into properties of detergents, Unilever and UEA, 1969–72; taught chemistry and geology, Royal GS, High Wycombe (and i/c stage lighting), 1972–80; Head of Science, Monks Walk Sch., Welwyn Garden City, 1980–83; Gen. Advr, Berks CC, 1983–88; Asst Chief Exec., Nat. Curriculum Council, 1989–91; Dep. Chief Exec., Sch. Exams and Assessment Council, 1991–93 (acting Chief Exec., 1991–92). Mem. UK Cttee, Organisation Mondiale pour l'Education Prescolaire, 1996–99 (Treas., 1998–99). Gov., West Herts Coll., 1997–2001. Advr, Nursery World magazine, 1997–. *Publications:* Eye (computer prog.), 1983; GAS 81, 1982; papers in professional jls. *Recreations:* walking, foreign travel, natural history, bowling, gardening, model making, photography. *Address:* The Old School Yard, Leighton Road, Northall, Dunstable, Beds LU6 2HA. *T:* (01525) 221273.

DORRELL, Ernest John; Secretary, Headmasters' Conference, 1975–79; General Secretary, Secondary Heads Association, 1978–79 (Secretary, Incorporated Association of Headmasters, 1975–77); *b* 31 March 1915; *s* of John Henry Whiting Dorrell and Amy Dorrell (*née* Roberts); *m* 1940, Alwen Irvona Jones; one *s* one *d*. *Educ:* Taunton Sch.; Exeter Coll., Oxford (Exhibr). Hon. Mods and Lit. Hum., MA. Served with 71 Field Regt and HQ 46 Div. RA, 1940–46. Asst Master, Dauntsey's Sch., 1937–40 and 1946–47; Admin. Asst, WR Educn Dept, 1947; Dep. Dir of Educn, Oxfordshire CC, 1950; Dir of Educn, Oxfordshire CC, 1970; Report on Educn in St Helena, 1974. Member: BBC Schs Broadcasting Council, 1975–79; Thames TV Educn Adv. Council, 1976–79. *Recreations:* walking, travel, golf. *Address:* Lynfield, 2 Gravel Lane, Warborough, Wallingford, Oxon OX10 7SD. *T:* (01865) 858342.

DORRELL, Rt Hon. Stephen James; PC 1994; MP (C) Charnwood, since 1997 (Loughborough, 1979–97); *b* 25 March 1952; *s* of Philip Dorrell; *m* 1980, Penelope Anne Wears, *y d* of Mr and Mrs James Taylor, Windsor; three *s* one *d*. *Educ:* Uppingham; Brasenose Coll., Oxford. BA 1973. RAFVR, 1971–73. Personal asst to Rt Hon. Peter Walker, MBE, MP, Feb. 1974; contested (C) Kingston-upon-Hull East, Oct. 1974. PPS to the Secretary of State for Energy, 1983–87; Asst Govt Whip, 1987–88; a Lord Comr of HM Treasury (Govt Whip), 1988–90; Parly Under-Sec. of State, DoH, 1990–92; Financial Sec. to HM Treasury, 1992–94; Secretary of State: for Nat. Heritage, 1994–95; for Health, 1995–97. Sec., Cons. Backbench Trade Cttee, 1980–81. Bd Mem., Christian Aid, 1985–87. *Recreations:* aviation, reading. *Address:* House of Commons, SW1A 0AA.

DORRIAN, Leeona June; QC (Scot.) 1994; *b* 16 June 1957; *d* of Thomas and June Dorrian. *Educ:* Cranley Sch.; Univ. of Aberdeen (LLB 1977). Admitted to Faculty of Advocates, 1981; Standing Jun. Counsel, Health and Safety Exec. and Commn, 1987–94; Advocate Depute, 1988–91; Standing Jun. Counsel, Dept of Energy, 1991–94. Mem., English Bar, Inner Temple, 1991–. Mem., CICB, 1998–. *Address:* Advocates' Library, Parliament House, Parliament Square, Edinburgh EH1 1RF. *T:* (0131) 226 5071. *Clubs:* Scottish Arts (Edinburgh); Royal Scottish Automobile (Glasgow); Royal Forth Yacht.

DORSET, Archdeacon of; *see* Magowan, Ven. A. J.

DORWARD, David Keay; Director of Finance, Dundee City Council, since 1995; *b* 24 May 1954; *s* of David Dorward and Christina Dorward (*née* Keay); *m* 1977, Gail Elizabeth Bruce; three *d*. *Educ:* Kinross High Sch.; Perth High Sch.; Glasgow Coll. of Technology. CPFA 1982. Trainee Accountant, Perth and Kinross Jt CC, 1971–75; Tayside Regional Council: Trainee Accountant, 1975–82; Sen. Accountant, 1982–83; Principal Accountant, 1983–84; Financial Planning Officer, 1984–86; Chief Financial Planning Officer, 1986–93; Depute Dir of Finance, 1993–95. *Recreations:* golf, supporting Dundee United, bowls, going to the theatre. *Address:* 4 Norrie Street, Broughty Ferry, Dundee DD5 2SD. *T:* (01382) 739006. *Clubs:* Dundee United Businessmen's (Dundee); Broughty Bowling; Abertay Golf.

DORWARD, William, OBE 1977; Commissioner for Hong Kong Economic Affairs, United States, 1983–87, retired; *b* 25 Sept. 1929; *s* of Alexander and Jessie Dorward; *m* 1960, Rosemary Ann Smith; one *s*. *Educ:* Morgan Academy, Dundee. Colonial Office, 1951–53; Commerce and Industry Dept, Hong Kong Govt, 1954–74; Counsellor (Hong Kong Affairs) UK Mission, Geneva, 1974–76; Hong Kong Government: Dep. Dir of Commerce and Industry, 1974–77; Comr of Industry and Customs, 1977–79; Dir of Trade, Industry and Customs, 1979–82; Sec. for Trade and Industry, 1982–83; MLC, 1979–83. Mem., GATT Dispute Settlement Panel, 1991–96. *Address:* Waulkmill House, Skirling, by Biggar ML12 6HB. *Clubs:* Carlton, Royal Over-Seas League; Hong Kong.

DOSANJH, Hon. Ujjal, MLA; (NDP) Vancouver-Kensington, since 1991; Premier of British Columbia, since 2000; *b* India, 9 Sept. 1947; *s* of Giani Pritam Singh and Surjit Kaur; *m* Raminder; three *s*. *Educ:* Simon Fraser Univ. (BA); Univ. of BC (LLB). Called to Canadian Bar, 1977; opened law practice, Dosanjh & Pirani, 1979. Attorney Gen., BC, 1995–2000. Leader, NDP, 2000–. Hon. LLD Gura Nanak Dev Univ., Amritsar, 2000. *Recreations:* jogging, reading. *Address:* Office of the Premier, PO Box 9041 Stn Prov Govt, Victoria, BC V8W 9E1, Canada. *T:* (250) 3871715.

DOSSER, Prof. Douglas George Maurice; Professor of Economics, University of York, 1965–81; retired, 1981; *b* 3 Oct. 1927; *s* of George William Dosser; *m* 1954, Valerie Alwyne Elizabeth, *d* of Leslie Jack Lindsey; three *d*. *Educ:* Latymer Upper School; London School of Economics. Lecturer in Economics, Univ. of Edinburgh, 1958–62; Vis. Prof. of Economics, Univ. of Washington, Seattle, 1960; Vis. Res. Prof. of Economics, Columbia Univ., NY, 1962; Reader in Economics, Univ. of York, 1963–65. *Publications:* Economic Analysis of Tax Harmonisation, 1967; (with S. Han) Taxes in the EEC and Britain, 1968; (with F. Andic) Theory of Economic Integration for Developing Countries, 1971; European Economic Integration and Monetary Unification, 1973; (with K. Hartley) The Collaboration of Nations, 1981; articles in Economic Jl, Economica, Rev. of Economic Studies. *Recreations:* art and antiques.

DOTRICE, Roy; actor (stage, films and television); *b* 26 May 1925; *m* 1946, Kay Newman, actress; three *d*. *Educ:* Dayton and Intermediate Schs, Guernsey, CI. Served War of 1939–45: Air Gunner, RAF, 1940; PoW, 1942–45. Acted in Repertory, 1945–55; formed and directed Guernsey Theatre Co., 1955; Royal Shakespeare Co., 1957–65 (Caliban, Julius Caesar, Hotspur, Firs, Puntila, Edward IV, etc); World War 2½, New Theatre, London, 1966; Brief Lives, Golden Theatre, New York, 1967; Latent Heterosexual and God Bless, Royal Shakespeare Co., Aldwych, 1968; Brief Lives (one-man play), Criterion, 1969 (over 400 perfs, world record for longest-running solo perf.), toured England, Canada, USA, 1973, Mayfair, 1974 (over 150 perfs), Broadway season, and world tour (over 1,700 perfs), 1974, Australian tour, 1975; Peer Gynt, Chichester Festival, 1970; One At Night, Royal Court, 1971; The Hero, Edinburgh, 1970; Mother Adam, Arts, 1971; Tom Brown's Schooldays, Cambridge, 1972; The Hollow Crown, seasons in USA 1973 and 1975, Sweden 1975; Gomes, Queen's, 1973; The Dragon Variation, Duke of York's, 1977; Australian tour with Chichester Festival, 1978; Passion of Dracula, Queen's, 1978; Oliver, Albery, 1979; Mister Lincoln (one-man play on Abraham Lincoln), Washington, NY and TV special, 1980, Fortune, 1981; A Life, NY, 1980–81; Henry V, and Falstaff in Henry IV, American Shakespeare Theatre, Stratford, Conn, 1981; Murder in Mind, Strand, 1982; Winston Churchill (one-man play), USA 1982 (also CBS TV); Kingdoms, NY, 1982; The Genius, Los Angeles, 1984 (Dramalogue Best Perf. Award); Down an Alley, Dallas, 1984; Great Expectations, Old Vic, 1985; Enemy of the People, NY, 1985; Hay Fever, NY and Washington, 1986; The Homecoming, NY, 1991; The Best of Friends, NY, 1993; The Woman in Black, USA, 1995, A Moon for the Misbegotten, NY, 2000; *films include:* Heroes of Telemark, Twist of Sand, Lock up Your Daughters, Buttercup Chain, Tomorrow, One of Those Things, Nicholas and Alexandra, Amadeus, Corsican Brothers, The Eliminators, Camilla, L-Dopa, The Lady Forgets, Lounge People, The Cutting Edge, The Scarlet Letter, Swimming with Sharks. *Television:* appearances in: Dear Liar, Brief Lives, The Caretaker (Emmy award), Imperial Palace, Misleading Cases, Clochemerle, Dickens of London, Stargazy on Zummerdown, Strange Luck, Babylon 5, Earth 2, Mr and Mrs Smith (series), Murder She

Wrote, Picket Fences (series), Children of the Dark, Family Reunion (USA), Tales of the Gold Monkey (USA), The Wizard (USA), A Team (USA), Tales from the Dark-Side (USA), Beauty and the Beast (USA), series, Going to Extremes (USA), The Good Policeman (USA). TV Actor of the Year Award, 1968; Tony Nomination for A Life, 1981. *Recreations:* fishing, riding. *Club:* Garrick.

DOUBLEDAY, John Vincent; sculptor since 1968; *b* 9 Oct. 1947; *s* of late Gordon V. and Margaret E. V. Doubleday; *m* 1969, Isobel J. C. Durie; two *s* (and one *s* decd). *Educ:* Stowe; Goldsmiths' College School of Art. *Exhibitions include:* Waterhouse Gallery, 1968, 1969, 1970, 1971; Galerie Sothmann, Amsterdam, 1969, 1971, 1979; Richard Demarco Gallery, Edinburgh, 1973; Laing Art Gallery, Newcastle, Bowes Museum, Barnard Castle, 1974; Pandion Gallery, NY, Aldeburgh Festival, 1983; *works include:* Baron Ramsey of Canterbury, 1974; King Olav of Norway, 1975; Prince Philip, Duke of Edinburgh, Earl Mountbatten of Burma, Golda Meir, 1976; Charlie Chaplin (Leicester Square), 1981; Caduceus (Harvard, Mass), Lord Feather (TUC Congress House), Isambard Kingdom Brunel (two works), 1982; Beatles (Liverpool), Dylan Thomas, 1984; Royal Marines Commando Meml, Lympstone, Devon, 1986; Sherlock Holmes (Meiringen), 1991; Graham Gooch (Chelmsford), 1992; Dorothy L. Sayers (Witham), J. B. Pflug (Biberach), 1994; Nelson Mandela (Mbabane and London), 1997; Gerald Durrell (Jersey Zoo), 1999; The Dorset Shepherd (Dorchester), 2000; *works in public collections:* Ashmolean Mus., British Mus., Herbert F. Johnson Mus., USA, Tate Gall., V & A, Nat. Mus. of Wales. *Recreation:* enthusiasm for the unnecessary. *Address:* Goat Lodge, Goat Lodge Road, Great Totham, Maldon, Essex CM9 8BX. *T:* (01621) 891329.

DOUCE, Prof. John Leonard, FREng; FIEE; Professor of Electrical Science, Warwick University, 1965–94 (part-time 1989–94), now Emeritus; *b* 15 Aug. 1932; *s* of John William and Florrie Douce; *m* 1959, Jean Shanks; one *s* one *d. Educ:* Manchester Grammar Sch.; Manchester Univ. (BSc, MSc, PhD, DSc). SMIEEE. Lectr, Sen. Lectr, Reader, Queen's Univ., Belfast, 1958–65. Member: Technology Sub-Cttee, UGC, 1980–89; Engrg Bd, 1987–91, Science Bd, 1989–91, SERC; Contract Assessor, HEFCE, 1993–94. FREng 1991. Sir Harold Hartley Silver Medal, Inst. of Measurement and Control, 1989. *Publications:* Introduction to Mathematics of Servomechanisms, 1963, 2nd edn 1972; papers on control engineering. *Recreations:* bridge, boating, home-brewing. *Address:* 259 Station Road, Balsall Common, Coventry CV7 7EG. *T:* (01676) 532070.

DOUEK, Ellis Elliot, FRCS; Consultant Otologist since 1970, and Chairman, Hearing Research Group, since 1974, Guy's Hospital; *b* 25 April 1934; *s* of Cesar Douek and Nelly Sassoon; *m* 1993, Gill Green; two *s* by former marriage. *Educ:* English School, Cairo; Westminster Medical School. MRCS, LRCP 1958; FRCS 1967. House appts, St Helier Hosp., 1959, and Whittington Hosp., 1963; nat. service, RAMC, 1960–62; ENT Registrar, Royal Free Hosp., 1966; Sen. Registrar, King's College Hosp., 1968. Mem., MRC working party on Hearing Research, 1975; MRC Rep. to Europ. Communities on Hearing Res., 1980; UK Rep. to Europ. Communities on Indust. Deafness, 1983; Mem., Scientific Cttee, Inst. de Recherche sur la surdité, Paris, 1989–. Dalby Prize for hearing research, RSM, 1978. *Publications:* Sense of Smell—Its Abnormalities, 1974; Eighth Nerve, in Peripheral Neuropathy, 1975; Olfaction, in Scientific Basis of Otolaryngology, 1976; Cochlear Implant, in Textbook of ENT, 1980; papers on hearing and smell. *Recreations:* drawing and painting; studying history. *Address:* (home) 24 Reynolds Close, NW11 7EA. *T:* (020) 8455 6427; 97 Harley Street, W1N 1DF. *T:* (020) 7935 7828. *Club:* Athenæum.

DOUGAL, Andrew James Harrower; Chief Executive, Hanson plc, since 1997; *b* 2 Sept. 1951; *s* of Andrew James Harrower Dougal and Muriel Mary Dougal (*née* MacDonald); *m* 1978, Margaret Mairi MacDonald; two *s* one *d. Educ:* Greenock Acad.; Paisley GS; Glasgow Univ. (BAcc 1972). CA 1975. Articled Clerk, then Asst Manager, Arthur Young Glasgow, 1972–77; Gp Chief Accountant, Scottish & Universal Investments Ltd, 1977–86; Hanson plc: Finance Comptroller, 1986–89; Finance Dir, ARC Ltd, 1989–92; Man. Dir, ARC Southern, 1992–93; Dep. Finance Dir, 1993–95; Finance Dir, 1995–97. *Recreations:* family, sports, reading. *Address:* (office) 1 Grosvenor Place, SW1X 7JH. *T:* (020) 7245 1245.

DOUGAL, Malcolm Gordon; HM Diplomatic Service, retired; Warden, John Spedan Lewis Trust for the Advancement of the Natural Sciences, since 1998; *b* 20 Jan. 1938; *s* of late Eric Gordon Dougal and Marie (*née* Wildermuth); *m* 1st, 1964, Elke (marr. diss.); one *s*; 2nd, 1995, Brigid Pritchard (*née* Turner) (*d* 2000); two step *s. Educ:* Ampleforth Coll., Yorkshire; The Queen's Coll., Oxford (MA Mod. History). National Service in Korea and Gibraltar with Royal Sussex Regt, 1956–58; Oxford, 1958–61; Contracts Asst, De Havilland Aircraft, Hatfield, 1961–64; Asst to Export Manager, Ticket Equipment Ltd (Plessey), 1964–66; Export Manager, Harris Lebus Ltd, 1967–69; entered HM Diplomatic Service, 1969; Foreign Office, 1969–72; 1st Secretary (Commercial): Paris, 1972–76; Cairo, 1976–79; Foreign Office, 1979–81; Consul Gen., Lille, 1981–85; Dep. High Comr and Head of Chancery, Canberra, 1986–89; RCDS, 1990; Dir, Jt FCO/DTI Directorate of Overseas Trade Services, FCO, 1991–94; Consul Gen., San Francisco, 1994–98. *Publication:* (contrib.) The Third Battle of Ypres (Seaford House Papers), 1990. *Recreations:* natural history, history, walking, books, sport, wine. *Address:* John Spedan Lewis Trust, c/o Leckford Estate Office, Leckford, Stockbridge, Hants SO20 6JF.

DOUGAN, (Alexander) Derek; company director and marketing consultant; *b* 20 Jan. 1938; *s* of John and Josephine Dougan; *m* 1963, Jutta Maria; two *s. Educ:* Mersey Street primary sch., Belfast; Belfast Technical High School. Professional footballer with: Distillery, NI, 1953–57; Portsmouth, 1957–59; Blackburn Rovers, 1959–61; Aston Villa, 1961–63; Peterborough, 1963–65; Leicester, 1965–67; Wolverhampton Wanderers, 1967–75. Represented N Ireland at all levels, from schoolboy to full international, more than 50 times. Chm., PFA, 1970–78. Chief Exec., Kettering Town FC, 1975–77; Chm. and Chief Exec., Wolverhampton Wanderers' FC, 1982–85. Sports Presenter, Yorkshire Television. Mem. Council, Co-Operation North, 1987–. *Publications:* Attack! (autobiog.), 1969; The Sash He Never Wore (autobiog.), 1972, rev. edn, The Sash He Never Wore: 25 years on, 1997; The Footballer (novel), 1974; On the Spot (football as a profession), 1974; Doog (autobiog.), 1980; How Not to Run Football, 1981; (with Patrick Murphy) Matches of the Day 1958–83, 1984. *Recreations:* watching football, playing squash. *Address:* 25 Campbell Park Avenue, Belfast, N Ireland BT4 3FL.

DOUGAN, Dr David John; County Arts Officer, Essex County Council, 1989–97; *b* 26 Sept. 1936; *s* of William John Dougan and Blanche May; *m* 1st, 1959, Eileen Ludbrook (marr. diss. 1985); one *s*; 2nd, 1986, Barbara Taylor; one *s* one *d. Educ:* Durham Univ. (BA, MA); City Univ. (PhD). Reporter, Tyne Tees Television, 1963; presenter, BBC, 1966; Director, Northern Arts, 1970; Dir, Crafts Council, 1984–88. Chairman: Nat. Youth Dance Trust, 1985–91; Dance East, 1999–. Special Advr, H of C Educn, Sci. and Arts Cttee, 1981–82; Mem., Calouste Gulbenkian Foundn Enquiry into the Arts in Schs, 1982. *Publications:* History of North East Shipbuilding, 1966; Great Gunmaker, 1968; Shipwrights Trade Union, 1971; The Jarrow March, 1976. *Recreations:* theatre, music, tennis. *Address:* Grovelands, 1 Grove Road, Bury St Edmunds, Suffolk IP33 3BE. *T:* (01284) 752588.

DOUGHTY, Sir (Graham) Martin, Kt 2001; Chair, English Nature, since 2001; *b* 11 Oct. 1949; *s* of Harold Doughty and Eva Mary (*née* Swift); *m* 1st, 1974, Eleanor Lamont (*d* 1988); two *d*; 2nd, 1996, Gillian Gostick. *Educ:* New Mills Grammar Sch.; Imperial Coll., London (BSc Eng, MSc). Res. Chem. Engr, Booth (Internat.), 1971-72; Lectr, 1973-90, Sen. Lectr, 1990-95, Sheffield Poly., later Sheffield Hallam Univ. Mem. (Lab), Derbys CC, 1981- (Chairman: Highways and Transport, 1983-86; Planning and Countryside, 1986-92; Council Leader, 1992-2001). Board Member: E Midlands Develt Agency, 1998-2001; Countryside Agency, 1999-. Mem., Peak Dist Nat. Park Authy, 1987- (Chm., 1993-); Chm., Assoc. of Nat. Park Authorities, 1997-2001. Non-executive Director: Entrust, 1996-; Derbys Ambulance Services NHS Trust, 1996-98. *Publication:* The Park under the Town, 2001. *Recreations:* hill-walking, gardening, cooking fish well, natural history. *Address:* English Nature, Northminster House, Peterborough PE1 1UA. *T:* (01733) 455345; *e-mail:* martin.doughty@englishnature.org.uk.

DOUGHTY, Susan Kathleen, (Mrs D. Orchard); MP (Lib Dem) Guildford, since 2001; *b* 13 April 1948; *d* of Ronald and Olive Powell; *m* 1st, 1974, John Doughty (marr. diss.); two *s*; 2nd, 1995, David Orchard; two step *d. Educ:* Northumberland Coll. of Educn (CertEd); holds various business qualifications. Primary sch. teacher, 1969–70; Northern Gas Mgt Services, 1970–73; CEBG Mgt Services, 1974–75; Wilkinson Match Mgt Services, 1976–77; career break (charity work), 1977–83; Indep. Mgt Consultant, 1984–89, 1999–2001; Project Manager, Thames Water, 1989–98. *Recreations:* gardening, cricket, walking, theatre, opera. *Address:* House of Commons, SW1A 0AA. *Club:* National Liberal.

DOUGHTY, Sir William (Roland), Kt 1990; Chairman, North West Thames Regional Health Authority, 1984–94; Deputy Chairman, Britannia Refined Metals Ltd, since 1982 (Director, since 1978); *b* 18 July 1925; *s* of Roland Gill Doughty and Gladys Maud Doughty (*née* Peto); *m* 1952, Patricia Lorna Cooke; three *s. Educ:* Headstone Sch.; Acton Technical Coll.; Trinity Coll., Dublin (MA); Harvard Business Sch. (AMP). Metal Box Co. Ltd, 1953–66; Molins Ltd, 1966–69, Dir, 1967; Cape Industries, 1969–84, Dir, 1972, Man. Dir, 1980–84. Member: SE Economic Planning Council, 1966–79 (Chm., Industry and Employment Cttee, 1972–79); CBI Council, 1975–86 (Chm., London Region, 1981–83). Founder and Chm., Assoc. for Conservation of Energy, 1981–85, Pres., 1985–. Governor: SE Tech. Coll., 1967–69; Gt Ormond St Hosp. for Sick Children, 1978–90; Mem., Gen. Council, King Edward VII's Hosp. Fund for London, 1984– (Mem., Management Cttee, 1987–95); Chairman: King's Fund Centre Cttee, 1991–95; Adv. Cttee on Distinction Awards, 1994–97. LHSM 1986. CIMgt; FRSA. *Recreations:* cricket, theatre, golf, horse racing. *Clubs:* Savile, MCC, Middlesex County Cricket; Kildare Street and University (Dublin).

DOUGILL, John Wilson, FREng, FICE, FIStructE, FASCE; Chief Executive and Secretary, Institution of Structural Engineers, 1994–99 (Director of Engineering, 1987–94); *b* 18 Nov. 1934; *s* of William John Dougill and Emily Firmstone Wilson; *m* 1959, Daphne Maude Weeks; one *s* one *d. Educ:* Trinity Sch. of John Whitgift, Croydon; King's Coll., London; Imperial Coll. of Science and Technology. MScEng, DIC, PhD; FREng 1990. Engineer with George Wimpey, 1956–58 and 1960–61; Research Asst to Prof. A. L. L. Baker, Imperial Coll., 1961–64; King's College London: Lectr in Civil Engrg, 1964–73; Reader in Engrg Science, 1973–76; Prof. of Engrg Science, 1976–81; Prof. of Concrete Structures and Technology, Imperial Coll., 1981–87. Vis. Res. Engineer, Univ. of California, Berkeley, 1967–68; Visiting Professor: Dept of Civil Engrg, Imperial Coll., 1991–97; Sch. of Engrg, Univ. of Surrey, 2000–. Chm., SERC Civil Engrg Sub-Cttee, 1982–83; Mem., NEDO Res. Strategy Cttee, 1983–85. Sec. Gen., Fedn Internat. de la Precontrainte, 1992–98. Mem. Court of Governors, Whitgift Foundn, 1981–. FCGI. *Publications:* papers in jls of engrg mech., materials and struct. engrg. *Recreations:* coarse gardening, travel, good food, walking. *Address:* Ashcroft, Larch Close, The Glade, Kingswood, Surrey KT20 6JF. *T:* (01737) 833283.

DOUGLAS, family name of **Viscount Chilston, Earl of Morton,** and **Marquess of Queensberry**.

DOUGLAS AND CLYDESDALE, Marquess of; Alexander Douglas-Hamilton; *b* 31 March 1978; *s* and *heir* of Duke of Hamilton, *qv*.

DOUGLAS, Anthony Jude; Chairman, FCB Europe, since 1998; *b* 14 Dec. 1944; *s* of Arthur Sidney Douglas and Margaret Mary Douglas; *m* 1968, Jacqueline English; two *d. Educ:* Cardinal Vaughan Grammar Sch., London; Southampton Univ. (BA Hons English). Head of Client Services, Lintas Advertising, 1967–81; Jt Chm. and Chief Exec., DMB&B Advertising, 1981–95; Chief Exec., COI, 1996–98. *Recreations:* cooking, walking, reading, anthropology. *Address:* FCB Europe, 110 St Martin's Lane, WC2N 4DY; 20 Malbrook Road, Putney, SW15 6UE. *T:* (020) 8788 3209.

DOUGLAS, Barry; concert pianist; *b* 23 April 1960; *m* Deirdre O'Hara; one *s* one *d. Educ:* Royal College of Music; private study with Maria Curcio. Gold Medal, Tchaikovsky International Piano Competition, Moscow, 1986; Berlin Philharmonic début, 1987; engagements incl. regular appearances in major European, US and Far East cities. Artistic Founder Dir, Camerata Ireland, 1999– (first all-Ireland orch.; concerts in Ireland and abroad; début USA tour, 2001). Prince Consort Prof. of Piano, Royal Coll. of Music, 1998–. Recordings incl. Tchaikovsky Concerto No 1 and Sonata in G, Mussorgsky Pictures at an Exhibition, Brahms Piano Quintet in F minor and Piano Concerto No 1, Liszt Concertos Nos 1 and 2, Beethoven Sonata Op 106, Prokofiev Sonatas 2 and 7, Rachmaninov Concerto No 2, Reger Concerto, Strauss Burleske, Britten Concerto, Debussy Fantaisie. Vis. Fellow, Oriel Coll., Oxford, 1992–93. Hon. DMus QUB, 1986. *Recreations:* driving, reading, food and wine. *Address:* c/o IMG Artists, Lovell House, 616 Chiswick High Road, W4 5RX.

DOUGLAS, Boyd; Member (U) East Londonderry, Northern Ireland Assembly, since 1998; *b* 13 July 1950; *s* of William Douglas and late May Douglas; *m* 1972, Kathleen Semple; two *s* two *d. Educ:* Burnfoot Primary Sch.; Dungiven Secondary Sch.; Strabane Agriculture Coll. Farmer, 1970–. Mem. (U) Limavady Council, 1997–. *Address:* 279 Drumrane Road, Dungiven, Co. Londonderry BT47 4NL.

DOUGLAS, Prof. Charles Primrose, FRCOG; Professor of Obstetrics and Gynæcology, University of Cambridge, 1976–88, now Emeritus; Fellow, Emmanuel College, Cambridge, 1979–88; *b* 17 Feb. 1921; *s* of Dr C. Douglas, Ayr, Scotland; *m* 1948, Angela Francis; three *s* one *d. Educ:* Loretto Sch.; Peterhouse; Edinburgh Univ. Surg. Lieut RNVR, 1944–47. Registrar and Sen. Registrar, Victoria Infirmary, Glasgow, 1950–59; William Waldorf Astor Foundn Fellow, 1957; Visiting Fellow, Duke Univ., NC, 1957; Sen. Lectr, Univ. of the West Indies, 1959–65; Prof. of Obst. and Gyn., Royal Free Hosp. Sch. of Medicine, 1965–76. Member: Bd of Governors, Royal Free Hosp., 1972–74; Camden and Islington AHA, 1974–76, Cambridge AHA, 1981–82; Cambridge DHA, 1983–88. Mem., Council, RCOG, 1980–86. Hon. FACOG 1983. *Publications:* contribs to BMJ, Amer. Heart Jl, Jl of Obst. and Gynæc. of Brit. Commonwealth, etc. *Recreations:* golf, travel, art. *Address:* 32 Lorimer Street, Bathurst, NSW 2795, Australia.

DOUGLAS, Gavin Stuart, RD 1970; QC (Scot.) 1971; *b* 12 June 1932; *y s* of late Gilbert Georgeson Douglas and Rosena Campbell Douglas. *Educ:* South Morningside Sch.; George Heriot's Sch.; Edinburgh Univ. MA 1953, LLB 1955. Qual. as Solicitor, 1955; nat. service with RN, 1955–57. Admitted to Faculty of Advocates, 1958; Sub-editor (part-time), The Scotsman, 1957–61; Mem. Lord Advocate's Dept in London (as Parly Draftsman), 1961–64; returned to practice at Scots Bar, 1964; Junior Counsel to BoT, 1965–71; Counsel to Scottish Law Commn, 1965–96; Hon. Sheriff in various sheriffdoms, 1965–71; a Chm. of Industrial Tribunals, 1966–78; Counsel to Sec. of State for Scotland under Private Legislation Procedure (Scotland) Act 1936, 1969–75, Sen. Counsel under that Act, 1975–; Temporary Sheriff, 1990–99. Mem., Lothian Health Bd, 1981–85. Pres., Temporary Sheriffs' Assoc., 1998–99. Mem. Bd, Leith Nautical Coll., 1981–84. Editor, Session Cases, 7 vols, 1976–82. *Recreations:* golf, ski-ing. *Address:* Parliament House, Parliament Square, Edinburgh EH1 1RF. *Clubs:* Army and Navy; Royal Scots (Edinburgh); Rolls-Royce Enthusiasts'; Hon. Company of Edinburgh Golfers (Muirfield).

DOUGLAS, Henry Russell, FCIJ; Media law consultant; Legal Manager, News Group Newspapers, 1976–89; *b* Bishopbriggs, Lanarkshire, 11 Feb. 1925; 2nd *s* of late Russell Douglas and Jeanie Douglas Douglas (*née* Drysdale); *m* 1951, Elizabeth Mary, *d* of late Ralph Nowell, CB; two *s* three *d*. *Educ:* various Scottish and English Grammar Schools; Lincoln Coll., Oxford (MA Hons). Served RNVR, 1943–46 (Sub-Lt, submarines). Merchant Navy, 1946–47; Oxford Univ., 1947–50; Liverpool Daily Post, 1950–69; The Sun, 1969–76. Inst of Journalists, 1956: Fellow, 1969; Pres., 1972–73; Chm. of Executive, 1973–76; Member: Press Council, 1972–80; Council, Newspaper Press Fund, 1972–76, 1986– (Chm., 1990–91); Founder Mem., Media Society, 1973 (Treas., 1973–86, Vice-Pres., 1987–89); Founder, Soc. of Fleet Street Lawyers, 1989. *Recreations:* chess, travel, history. *Address:* Austen Croft, 31 Austen Road, Guildford, Surrey GU1 3NP. *T:* (01483) 576960.

DOUGLAS, Hilary Kay; Managing Director, Corporate Services and Development, HM Treasury, since 2000; *b* 27 July 1950; *d* of late James Robert Keith Black and of Joan Margaret Black (*née* Boxall); *m* 1972, Robert Harold Douglas; two *s*. *Educ:* Wimbledon High Sch.; New Hall, Cambridge (BA Hons History 1971). Press Librarian, RIIA, 1971–73; joined DES, 1973: Sec. of State's Private Office, 1975–76; appts in teacher trng, educnl disadvantage and local authy finance, 1977–84; Head: Teacher Supply Div., 1985–87; School Govt Div., 1987–89; freelance consultancy and teaching, Netherlands, 1989–91; Sec., FEFC, 1991–92; set up SCAA, 1992–93; Hd of Personnel, DFE, 1993–94; Dir of Admin, Office for Standards in Educn, 1994–96; Dir, Civil Service Employer Gp, Cabinet Office, 1996–97; Dir, Personnel and Support Services, DfEE, 1997–2000. *Recreations:* travel, European languages, singing. *Address:* HM Treasury, Allington Towers, 19 Allington Street, SW1E 5EB. *T:* (020) 7270 1690.

DOUGLAS, James Murray, CBE 1985; Director-General, Country Landowners' Association, 1970–90; *b* 26 Sept. 1925; *s* of Herbert and Amy Douglas, Brechin; *m* 1950, Julie Kemmner; one *s* one *d*. *Educ:* Morrison's Acad., Crieff; Aberdeen Univ.; Balliol Coll., Oxford. Entered Civil Service, 1950; Treasury, 1960–63; Asst Sec., Min. of Housing and Local Govt, 1964; Sec. to Royal Commn on Local Govt, 1966–69. Dir, Booker Countryside, 1990–93; Public Affairs Consultant, John Kendall Associates, 1990–93. Vice-Pres., Confedn of European Agriculture, 1971–88 (Chm., Environment Cttee, 1988–90); Mem., Econ. Develt Cttee for Agriculture, 1972–90; Sec., European Landowning Orgns Gp, 1972–87. Mem., Council, CBI, 1986–89. *Publications:* various articles on local govt planning, agriculture and landowning. *Address:* 1 Oldfield Close, Bickley, Kent BR1 2LL. *T:* (020) 8467 3213. *Club:* Oxford and Cambridge.
See also M. J. Douglas.

DOUGLAS, Kenneth, CBE 1991; CEng; Managing Director, Austin and Pickersgill Ltd, 1958–69, and 1979–83; Chairman, Kenton Shipping Services, Darlington, 1968–83; *b* 28 Oct. 1920; British; *m* 1942, Doris Lewer; one *s* two *d*. *Educ:* Sunderland Technical Coll. (Dip. Naval Architecture). CEng. Dep. Shipyard Manager, Vickers Armstrong Naval Yard, Newcastle-upon-Tyne, 1946–53; Dir and Gen. Manager, Wm Gray & Co. Ltd, West Hartlepool, 1954–58; Man. Dir, Upper Clyde Shipbuilders Ltd, Chm., Simons Lobnitz Ltd and Chm., UCS Trng Co., 1969–73; Dep. Chm., Govan Shipbuilders, 1971–73; Chm., Douglas (Kilbride) Ltd, 1972–77; Chm. and Man. Dir, Steel Structures Ltd, 1974–76; Shiprepair Marketing Dir, British Shipbuilders, 1978–79; Mem. Bd, PCEF, 1988–91. Mem., Tyne and Wear Residuary Body, DoE, 1985–89. Hon. Fellow, Sunderland Univ., 1993 (Fellow, 1980 and 1992–93, Chm. of Govs, 1982–93, Sunderland Poly., subseq. Univ.). Formerly: FRINA, MBIM, MInstD. *Recreations:* fishing, golf. *Address:* 2 Abbots Lea, Dalton Piercy, Hartlepool, Cleveland TS27 3JS. *Club:* Ashbrooke Cricket and Rugby Football (Sunderland).

DOUGLAS, Kenneth George, ONZ 1999; President, New Zealand Council of Trade Unions, since 1987; *b* 15 Nov. 1935; *s* of John Atholwood Douglas and Marjorie Alice (*née* Farrow); *m* 1956, Lesley Barbara Winter (marr. diss. 1986); two *s* two *d*; partner, Marilyn Gay Tucker. *Educ:* Wellington Coll. President: Wellington Section, Drivers Union, 1958–79; NZ Drivers Fedn, 1972–79; Treas., Nat. Section, NZ Fedn of Labour, 1979–87. Mem., Exec. Bd, ICFTU, 1987–; Pres., ICFTU—Asia Pacific Regl Orgn, 1990–. Mem., Prime Minister's Enterprise Council, 1990–. Mem. (Ind.), Porirua CC, 1998–. JP Porirua, 1999. Hon. LLD Victoria Univ. of Wellington, 1999. *Publications:* contrib. articles on industrial relns and Labour movement to jls. *Recreation:* golf. *Address:* 8 View Road, Titahi Bay, Porirua, New Zealand. *T:* (4) 2368857. *Clubs:* Porirua, Titahi Golf (NZ).

DOUGLAS, Margaret Elizabeth, (Mrs T. Lancaster), OBE 1994; Supervisor of Parliamentary Broadcasting, 1993–99; *b* 22 Aug. 1934; *d* of Thomas Mincher Douglas and Dorothy Jones; *m* 2000, Terence Lancaster. *Educ:* Parliament Hill Grammar Sch., London. Joined BBC as sec., 1951; subseq. researcher, dir and producer in Current Affairs television, working on Panorama, Gallery, 24 Hours and on special progs with Lord Avon and Lord Stockton; Editor, Party Conf. coverage, 1972–83; Chief Asst to Dir-Gen., 1983–87; Chief Political Advr, BBC, 1987–93. *Recreations:* watching politics and football. *Address:* Flat 49, The Anchor Brewhouse, 50 Shad Thames, SE1 2LY.

DOUGLAS, Prof. (Margaret) Mary, CBE 1992; FBA 1989; Avalon Foundation Professor in the Humanities, Northwestern University, 1981–85, Professor Emeritus, since 1985; *b* 25 March 1921; *d* of late Gilbert Charles Tew and Phyllis Twomey; *m* 1951, James A. T. Douglas, OBE; two *s* one *d*. *Educ:* Sacred Heart Convent, Roehampton; St Anne's Coll., Oxford (MA, BSc, DPhil; Hon. Fellow, 1992). Returned to Oxford, 1946, to train as anthropologist; fieldwork in Belgian Congo, 1949–50, 1953 and 1987; Lectr in Anthropology, Univ. of Oxford, 1950; Univ. of London, 1951–78, Prof. of Social Anthropology, UCL, 1970–78. Res. Scholar, Russell Sage Foundn, NY, 1977–81; Vis. Prof., Princeton Univ., 1986–88. Gifford Lectr, Univ. of Edinburgh, 1989. Mem., Academia Europaea, 1988. Hon. Fellow, UCL, 1994. Hon. Dr of Philosophy, Univ. of Uppsala, 1986; Hon. LLD Univ. of Notre Dame, 1988; Hon. DLitt: UEA, Jewish Theol Soc. of America, 1992; Warwick, 1993; Exeter, 1995; DU Essex, 1992; Hon. DPhil Oslo, 1997; Pennsylvania, 1999; DUniv Surrey, 1999. *Publications:* The Lele of the Kasai, 1963; Purity and Danger, 1966; Natural Symbols, 1970; Implicit Meanings, 1975; (with Baron Isherwood) The World of Goods: towards an anthropology of consumption, 1979; Evans-Pritchard, 1980; (with Aaron Wildavsky) Risk and Culture, 1982; In the Active Voice, 1982; Risk Acceptability, 1986; How Institutions Think, 1986; Risk and Blame, 1992; In the Wilderness, 1993; Thought Styles, 1996; (with Steven Ney) Missing Persons, 1998; Leviticus as Literature, 1999. *Address:* 22 Hillway, Highgate, N6 6QA.

DOUGLAS, Michael John; QC 1997; a Recorder, since 2000; *b* 7 Aug. 1952; *s* of James Murray Douglas, *qv*. *Educ:* Westminster Sch.; Balliol Coll., Oxford (BA Hons Jurisprudence). Called to the Bar, Gray's Inn, 1974. *Recreations:* theatre, cinema, eating out, football, travel. *Address:* 4 Pump Court, Temple, EC4Y 7AN. *T:* (020) 7353 2656.

DOUGLAS, Michael Kirk; actor and producer; *b* 25 Sept. 1944; *s* of Kirk Douglas, actor and Diana Douglas; *m* 1977, Diandra Morrell Luker (marr. diss.); one *s*; *m* 2000, Catherine Zeta-Jones; one *s*. *Educ:* Univ. of Calif at Santa Barbara (BA 1967). *Films* include: *actor:* Hail Hero, 1969; Napoleon and Samantha, 1972; Star Chamber, 1983; A Chorus Line, 1985; Black Rain, 1990; The War of the Roses, 1990; Shining Through, 1992; Basic Instinct, 1992; Falling Down, 1993; Disclosure, 1994; The American President, 1995; The Game, 1997; Traffic, 2001; One Night at McCool's, 2001; *producer:* One Flew Over the Cuckoo's Nest, 1975; Flatliners, 1990; (jtly) Made in America, 1993; The Rainmaker, 1997; A Song for David, 2000; *actor and producer:* The China Syndrome, 1979; Romancing the Stone, 1984; The Jewel of the Nile, 1985; Fatal Attraction, 1987; Wall Street, 1988 (Academy Award for best actor); A Perfect Murder, 1998; Wonder Boys, 1999; Still Life, 1999; narrator, One Day in September (documentary), 2000; *television* includes: Streets of San Francisco, 1972–76. UN Messenger of Peace, 1998; UN Ambassador for Nuclear Disarmament, 2000. *Address:* c/o Creative Artists Agency, 9830 Wilshire Boulevard, Beverly Hills, CA 90212, USA.

DOUGLAS, Neil; Sheriff of North Strathclyde at Paisley, since 1996; *b* 15 Oct. 1945; *s* of Dr Neil Douglas and Doreen Douglas; *m* 1971, Morag Isles; two *d*. *Educ:* Glasgow Acad.; Glasgow Univ. (LLB). Solicitor, 1968; Notary Public, 1972. Trainee solicitor, Brechin Welsh & Risk, Glasgow, 1968–70; Asst Solicitor, Ross Harper & Murphy, Glasgow, 1970–72; Partner, Brechin Robb, Glasgow, 1972–95; Floating Sheriff, All Scotland, 1995–96. *Recreations:* hill-walking, ski-ing, Scottish country dancing. *Address:* Paisley Sheriff Court, St James Street, Paisley PA3 2HW. *T:* (0141) 887 5291.

DOUGLAS, Richard Giles; *b* 4 Jan. 1932; *m* 1954, Jean Gray, *d* of Andrew Arnott; two *d*. *Educ:* Co-operative College, Stanford Hall, Loughborough; Univ. of Strathclyde; LSE. Engineer (Marine). Tutor organiser in Adult Educn, Co-operative movement, 1957; Sectional Educn Officer, Scotland, 1958–61; Lectr in Economics, Dundee Coll. of Technol., 1964–70. Contested (Lab): South Angus, 1964, Edinburgh West, 1966, Glasgow Pollok, March 1967; (Lab and Co-op) Clackmannan and E Stirlingshire, Oct. 1974; MP (Lab and Co-op) Clackmannan and E Stirlingshire, 1970–Feb. 1974; MP Dunfermline, 1979–83, Dunfermline West, 1983–92 (Lab and Co-op, 1979–90, SNP, 1990–92); contested (SNP) Glasgow, Garscadden, 1992. Contested (SNP) Scotland Mid and Fife, Euro. Parly elecns, 1994. Chm., Scottish Water and Sewerage Customers' Council, 1995–98. *Address:* Braehead House, High Street, Auchtermuchty, Fife KY14 7AR.

DOUGLAS, Richard Philip; Director of Finance, Department of Health, since 2001; *b* 20 Nov. 1956; *s* of William Ronald Douglas and Margery Alice Douglas; *m* 1978, Carole Elizabeth Hodgson; two *s* one *d*. *Educ:* Archbishop Holgate's Grammar Sch., York; Hull Univ. (BA Hons). HM Customs and Excise, 1978–80; Exchequer and Audit Dept, later Nat. Audit Office, 1980–96 (Dir, 1994–96); Dep. Dir of Finance, NHS Exec., 1996–99; Dir of Finance, Nat. Savings, 1999–2001. Mem., CIPFA, 1983. *Recreations:* reading, gardening, walking. *Address:* Department of Health, Richmond House, 79 Whitehall, SW1A 2NS.

DOUGLAS, Hon. Sir Roger (Owen), Kt 1991; Director, Brierley Investments Ltd, 1990–99 (Chairman, 1998); *b* 5 Dec. 1937; *s* of Norman and Jennie Douglas; *m* 1961, Glennis June Anderson; one *s* one *d*. *Educ:* Auckland Grammar Sch.; Auckland Univ. (Accountancy Degree). Company Sec. and Acct. MP (Lab) Manurewa, 1969–90; Cabinet Minister, NZ, 1972–75; Minister in Charge of Inland Revenue Dept and Minister in Charge of Friendly Societies, 1984; Minister of Finance, 1984–88; Minister of Immigration and Minister of Police, 1989–90. *Publications:* There's Got to be a Better Way, 1981; papers on NZ economy: An Alternative Budget, 1980; Proposal for Taxation, 1981; Toward Prosperity, 1987; Unfinished Business, 1993; Completing the Circle, 1996. *Recreations:* cricket, Rugby League, reading. *Address:* 411 Redoubt Road, Papatoetoe RD1, Auckland, New Zealand. *T:* (9) 2639596.

DOUGLAS, Susan; *see* Douglas Ferguson, S. M.

DOUGLAS, Prof. Thomas Alexander; Professor of Veterinary Biochemistry and Head of Department of Veterinary Biochemistry (Clinical), University of Glasgow, 1977–90; *b* 9 Aug. 1926; *s* of Alexander and Mary Douglas; *m* 1957, Rachel Ishbel McDonald; two *s*. *Educ:* Battlefield Public Sch.; High Sch. of Glasgow; Glasgow Vet. Coll., Univ. of Glasgow (BSc; Animal Health Schol., 1950–54; PhD). MRCVS. General Veterinary Practice: Ulverston, 1948–49; Lanark, 1949–50; University of Glasgow: Faculty of Sci., 1950–54; Asst Lectr, Biochemistry, 1954–57; Lectr 1957–71, Sen. Lectr 1971–77, in Vet. Biochem., Vet. Sch.; Dean of Faculty of Vet. Medicine, 1982–85. Mem. Council, RCVS, 1982–85. Mem., UGC, 1986–89 (Chm., Agriculture and Veterinary Studies Sub-Cttee, 1986–89). *Publications:* sci. articles in vet. and biochem. jls. *Recreations:* golf, hill walking. *Address:* 77 South Mains Road, Milngavie, Glasgow G62 6DE. *T:* (0141) 956 2751.

DOUGLAS, Rt Hon. Sir William (Randolph), KCMG 1983; Kt 1969; PC 1977; High Commissioner for Barbados in London, 1991–93; *b* Barbados, 24 Sept. 1921; *e s* of William P. Douglas and Emily Frances Douglas (*née* Nurse); *m* 1st, 1951, Thelma Ruth (*née* Gilkes) (*d* 1992); one *s* one *d*; 2nd, 1997, Denise Alva (*née* Hope). *Educ:* Bannatyne Sch. and Verdun High Sch., Verdun, Que., Canada; McGill Univ. (BA, Hons); London Sch. of Economics (LLB). Private Practice at Barbados Bar, 1948–50; Dep. Registrar, Barbados, 1950; Resident Magistrate, Jamaica, 1955; Asst Attorney-Gen., Jamaica, 1959; Solicitor-Gen., Jamaica, 1962; Puisne Judge, Jamaica, 1962; Chief Justice of Barbados, 1965–86; Ambassador to USA, 1987–91. Chairman: Commonwealth Caribbean Council of Legal Education, 1971–77; ILO Cttee of Experts on the Application of Conventions and Recommendations, 1995– (Mem., 1975–); ILO Fact-Finding and Conciliation Commn to S Africa, 1993; Commn of Inquiry into three Crown Corps, Bahamas, 1993–96; ILO Commn of Enquiry on Forced Labour in Myanmar, 1997–98; Pres., ILO Administrative Tribunal, 1994–98 (Judge, 1982–98). *Clubs:* Barbados Yacht; Pau Golf (France).

DOUGLAS FERGUSON, Prof. Niall Campbell, DPhil; Professor of Political and Financial History, University of Oxford, since 2000; *b* 18 April 1964; *s* of Dr James Campbell Ferguson and Molly Archibald Ferguson (*née* Hamilton); *m* 1994, Susan

Margaret Douglas (*see* S. M. Douglas Ferguson); two *s* one *d. Educ:* Glasgow Acad.; Magdalen Coll., Oxford (BA 1st Cl. Hons; DPhil 1989). Hanseatic Schol., Hamburg, 1986–88; Research Fellow, Christ's Coll., Cambridge, 1989–90; Official Fellow and Lectr, Peterhouse, Cambridge, 1990–92; Lectr in Mod. Hist., Oxford Univ., 1992–2000. Houblon-Norman Fellow, Bank of England, 1998–99. *Publications:* Paper and Iron: Hamburg business and German politics in the era of inflation 1897–1927, 1995; (ed) Virtual History: alternatives and counterfactuals, 1997; The World's Banker: the history of the house of Rothschild, 1998; The Pity of War, 1998; The Cash Nexus, 2001; contrib. English Historical Rev., Past & Present, Econ. Hist. Rev., Jl of Econ. Hist. *Recreations:* double bass, journalism. *Address:* Jesus College, Oxford OX1 3DW. *T:* (01865) 279758. *Clubs:* Beefsteak, Savile, Royal Automobile.

DOUGLAS FERGUSON, Susan Margaret; President, New Business, Condé Nast, since 2001 (Director, New Business, 1999–2001); *b* 29 Jan. 1957; *d* of Kenneth Frank Douglas and Vivienne Mary Douglas; *m* 1994, Prof. Niall Douglas Ferguson, *qv*; two *s* one *d. Educ:* Tiffin Girls' Sch., Kingston; Southampton Univ. (BSc Hons Biochem.). Management consultant, Arthur Andersen & Co., 1978–79; Haymarket Publishing, 1979; reporter, writer, Sunday Express, Johannesburg, 1979–80; Mail on Sunday: medical corresp., 1980–81; Features Editor and Associate Editor, 1981–86; Asst Editor, Daily Mail, 1986–91; Sunday Times: Associate Editor, 1991–94; Dep. Editor, 1995; Editor, Sunday Express, 1996; Consultant Editor, Scotsman, Scotland on Sunday, Edinburgh Evening News, Sunday Business, and Gear magazine (NY), 1997–2001; Exec. Consultant, Sunday Business, 1998–2001. *Recreations:* riding, hunting. *Address:* Middle Park Farm, Beckley, Oxford OX3 9SX. *Clubs:* Chelsea Arts, Royal Automobile.

DOUGLAS-HAMILTON, family name of **Duke of Hamilton and Brandon, Earldom of Selkirk** and **Baron Selkirk of Douglas**.

DOUGLAS-HOME, family name of **Earl of Home** and **Baroness Dacre**.

DOUGLAS HOME, Mark; Editor, The Herald, since 2000; *b* 31 Aug. 1951; *s* of Edward Charles Douglas Home and Nancy Rose Douglas Home; *m* 1976, Colette O'Reilly; one *s* one *d. Educ:* Eton Coll.; Univ. of Witwatersrand. Scottish corresp., The Independent, 1986–90; News Ed., 1990–93, Asst Ed., 1993–94, The Scotsman; Deputy Editor: Scotland on Sunday, 1994–98; Sunday Times Scotland, 1998–99; Scotland Editor, Sunday Times, 1999–2000. *Recreation:* gardening. *Address:* (office) 200 Renfield Street, Glasgow G2 3PR. *T:* (0141) 302 7000.

DOUGLAS MILLER, Robert Alexander Gavin; Chairman, Jenners (Princes St Edinburgh) Ltd; Director: Kennington Leasing Ltd; Dunedin Income Growth Trust; Edinburgh Worldwide Investment Trust; *b* 11 Feb. 1937; *s* of F. G. Douglas Miller and Mora Kennedy; *m* 1963, Judith Madeleine Smith; three *s* one *d. Educ:* Harrow; Oxford Univ. (MA). 9th Lancers, 1955–57; Oxford, 1958–61. Treasurer, Queen's Body Guard for Scotland (Royal Company of Archers). Pres., Edinburgh Chamber of Commerce & Manufactures, 1985–87. Member, Council: Assoc. of Scottish Salmon Fishery Bds, 1984–90; Atlantic Salmon Trust, 1989–90; Chm., Game Conservancy (Scotland), 1990–94. Chm., Outreach Trust, 1976–94. *Recreations:* shooting, fishing. *Address:* Bavelaw Castle, Balerno, Midlothian EH14 7JS. *T:* (0131) 449 3972. *Club:* New (Edinburgh).

See also Ian MacArthur.

DOUGLAS-PENNANT, family name of **Baron Penrhyn**.

DOUGLAS-SCOTT, Douglas Andrew Montagu; *see* Scott.

DOUGLAS-SCOTT-MONTAGU, family name of **Baron Montagu of Beaulieu**.

DOUGLAS-WILSON, Ian, MD; FRCPE; Editor of the Lancet, 1965–76; *b* 12 May 1912; *o s* of late Dr H. Douglas-Wilson; *m* 1939, Beatrice May, *e d* of late R. P. Bevan; one *s* two *d. Educ:* Marlborough Coll.; Edinburgh Univ. MB ChB 1936; MD (commended) Edinburgh 1938; FRCP Edinburgh 1945. Served with RAMC, 1940–45 (temp. Major). House-physician, Royal Infirmary, Edinburgh, 1937; joined the Lancet staff, 1946; Asst Ed., 1952–62; Dep. Ed., 1962–64. Corresp. Mem., Danish Soc. of Int. Med., 1965. Dr (*hc*) Edinburgh, 1974. *Address:* 10 Homan Court, Friern Watch Avenue, N12 9HW. *T:* (020) 8446 9047.

DOULTON, John Hubert Farre; Principal, Elizabeth College, Guernsey, 1988–98; *b* 2 Jan. 1942; *s* of late Alfred John Farre, CBE, TD; *m* 1986, Margaret Anne (*née* Ball); two step *d. Educ:* Rugby School; Keble College, Oxford (1st Mods, 2nd Greats). Teacher: Rugby, 1965–66; Radley, 1966–88. *Recreations:* music, walking, boats, foreign travel, carpentry. *Address:* Boucher's House, Boucher's Hill, North Tawton, Devon EX20 2DG.

DOUNE, Lord; John Douglas Stuart; *b* 29 Aug. 1966; *s* and *heir* of 20th Earl of Moray, *qv. Educ:* Loretto School, Musselburgh; University Coll. London (BA Hist. of Art). *Address:* Doune Park, Doune, Perthshire; Darnaway Castle, Forres, Moray.

DOURO, Marquess of; Arthur Charles Valerian Wellesley, OBE 1999; DL; Chairman: Framlington Group plc, since 1994; Richemont Holdings UK Ltd (formerly Vendôme Luxury Group Ltd), since 1993; Director: Global Asset Management Worldwide Inc., since 1984; Compagnie Financière Richemont, since 1999; *b* 19 Aug. 1945; *s* and *heir* of 8th Duke of Wellington, *qv*; *m* 1977, Antonia von Preussen (*see* Marchioness of Douro); two *s* three *d. Educ:* Eton; Christ Church, Oxford. Deputy Chairman: Thames Valley Broadcasting, 1975–84; Deltec Panamerica SA, 1985–89; Guinness Mahon Hldgs, 1988–91; Director: Antofagasta and Bolivia Railway Co., 1977–80; Eucalyptus Pulp Mills, 1979–88; Transatlantic Hldgs, 1983–95; Continental and Industrial Trust plc, 1987–90; Rothmans International, 1990–93; Chairman: Deltec Securities (UK) Ltd, 1985–89; Dunhill Holdings, 1991–93; Sun Life Corp., subseq. Sun Life and Provincial Hldgs plc, 1995–2000. MEP (C): Surrey, 1979–84, Surrey West, 1984–89; contested (C) Islington N, Oct. 1974; Mem., Basingstoke Borough Council, 1978–79. DL Hants, 1999. Kt Comdr, Order of Isabel the Catholic (Spain), 1986; Grand Officer, Order of Merit (Portugal), 1987. *Heir: s* Earl of Mornington, *qv. Address:* Apsley House, Piccadilly, W1V 9FA; The Old Rectory, Stratfield Saye, Reading RG7 2DA.

DOURO, Marchioness of; Antonia Elisabeth Brigid Luise Wellesley; Trustee, since 1976, and Chairman, since 1984, Guinness Trust; President, Royal Hospital for Neurodisability, since 1991; *b* 28 April 1955; *d* of late Prince Friedrich of Prussia and Lady Brigid (*née* Guinness; she; *m* 2nd, Maj. A. P. Ness); *m* 1977, Marquess of Douro, *qv*; two *s* three *d. Educ:* Cobham Hall, Kent; King's Coll., London (BA). Director: Thames Valley Broadcasting, 1984–87; English Nat. Ballet, 1987–90; Scenarist, Frankenstein (ballet), Covent Garden, 1987. Mem. Cttee, London Library, 1981–86; Trustee: Getty Endowment Fund for Nat. Gall., 1985–92; Hermitage Develt Trust, Somerset House, 2000–. Patron, Loddon Sch., 1996–. *Address:* The Old Rectory, Stratfield Saye, Reading RG7 2DA; Apsley House, Piccadilly, W1V 9FA.

DOVE, Arthur Allan, CBE 1998; CEng, CStat; Chairman, Council for Registered Gas Installers, 1994–2000; *b* 20 May 1933; *s* of William Joseph Dove and Lucy Frances Dove; *m* 1958, Nancy Iris Powell; two *s* one *d. Educ:* Taunton's Sch., Southampton; King's Coll. and London Sch. of Econs and Pol. Science, Univ. of London (BSc; AKC 1954). CEng, FIGasE 1974; MIS 1962. Asst Statistician, 1958, Marketing Officer, 1961, Southern Gas; Controller of Sales and Marketing, Scottish Gas, 1965; Commercial Sales Manager, Gas Council, 1969; Dep. Chm., South Eastern Gas, 1973; Regl Chm., British Gas plc, S Eastern, 1982–87, N Thames, 1988–91; Managing Director: Regions, 1991–92; Regl Services, 1992–93. Chm., Parkside Housing Gp, 1998–. *Recreation:* sailing. *Address:* 19 Sunning Avenue, Sunningdale, Berks SL5 9PN.

DOVE, Jonathan; composer; Music Adviser, Almeida Theatre, since 1990; Artistic Director, Spitalfields Festival, since 2001; *b* 18 July 1959; *s* of Myles Harrison Dove and Deirdre Cecily Dove. *Educ:* St Joseph's Acad., Blackheath; ILEA Centre for Young Musicians; Trinity Coll., Cambridge (MA); Goldsmiths' Coll., London (MMus). Asst Chorus Master, Glyndebourne, 1987–88. Trustee: Stephen Oliver Trust, 1997–; Michael Tippett Foundn, 1999–. *Compositions* include: Figures in the Garden, 1991; Pig, 1992; L'Augellino Belverde, 1994; Siren Song (opera), 1994; Seaside Postcards, 1995; Tuning In, 1995; The Ringing Isle, 1997; Flight (opera), 1998; The Magic Flute Dances, 1999; Tobias and the Angel (opera), 1999; The Passing of the Year, 2000; The Palace in the Sky (opera), 2000; L'Altra Euridice, 2001; Stargazer, 2001. *Recreation:* visiting Greek islands. *Address:* c/o Peters Edition Ltd, 10-12 Baches Street, N1 6DN. *T:* (020) 7553 4000.

DOVER, Suffragan Bishop of, and Bishop in Canterbury, since 1999; **Rt Rev. Stephen Squires Venner;** *b* 19 June 1944; *s* of Thomas Edward Venner and Hilda Lester Venner; *m* 1972, Judith Sivewright Johnstone; two *s* one *d. Educ:* Hardyes Sch., Dorchester; Birmingham Univ. (BA); Linacre Coll., Oxford (MA); London Univ. (PGCE). Curate, St Peter, Streatham, 1968–71; Hon. Curate: St Margaret, Streatham Hill, 1971–72; Ascension, Balham, 1972–74; Head of RE, St Paul's Girls' Sch., Hammersmith, 1972–74; Vicar, St Peter, Clapham and Bishop's Chaplain to Overseas Students, 1974–76; Vicar: St John, Trowbridge, 1976–82; Holy Trinity, Weymouth, 1982–94; RD of Weymouth, 1988–94; Canon and Prebendary of Salisbury Cathedral, 1989–94; Bishop Suffragan of Middleton, 1994–99. Vice Pres., Woodard Corp., 1995–98 (Pres., 1999–); Co-Chm., Church of England/Moravian Contact Gp, 1996–99; Mem. Council, Greater Manchester, 1996–99, Kent, 2000–, Order of St John. *Recreations:* playing organ and piano, watersports, computing, reading adventure novels. *Address:* Upway, 52 St Martin's Hill, Canterbury, Kent CT1 1PR. *T:* (home) (01227) 464537, (office) (01227) 459382, *Fax:* (01227) 784987; *e-mail:* bishdover@diocant.clara.co.uk.

DOVER, Den; Member (C) North West Region, England, European Parliament, since 1999; *b* 4 April 1938; *s* of Albert and Emmie Dover; *m* 1st, 1959, Anne Marina Wright (marr. diss. 1986); one *s* one *d*; 2nd, 1989, Kathleen Edna Fisher. *Educ:* Manchester Grammar Sch.; Manchester Univ. BSc Hons. CEng, MICE. John Laing & Son Ltd, 1959–68; National Building Agency: Dep. Chief Executive, 1969–70; Chief Exec., 1971–72; Projects Dir, Capital and Counties Property Co. Ltd, 1972–75; Contracts Manager, Wimpey Laing Iran, 1975–77. Director of Housing Construction, GLC, 1977–79. Member, London Borough of Barnet Council, 1968–71. MP (C) Chorley, 1979–97; contested (C) same seat, 1997. Mem., Commons Select Cttee on Transport, 1979–87, on Envmt, 1995–97. *Recreations:* cricket, hockey, golf; Methodist. *Address:* 30 Countess Way, Euxton, Chorley, Lancs PR7 6PT; 166 Furzehill Road, Boreham Wood, Herts WD6 2DS. *T:* (020) 8953 5945.

DOVER, Sir Kenneth James, Kt 1977; DLitt; FRSE 1975; FBA 1966; Chancellor, University of St Andrews, since 1981; *b* 11 March 1920; *o s* of P. H. J. Dover, London, Civil Servant; *m* 1947, Audrey Ruth Latimer; one *s* one *d. Educ:* St Paul's Sch. (Scholar); Balliol Coll., Oxford (Domus Scholar); Gaisford Prize, 1939; 1st in Classical Hon. Mods., 1940; Ireland Scholar, 1946; Cromer Prize (British Academy), 1946; 1st in Lit. Hum., Derby Scholar, Amy Mary Preston Read Scholar, 1947; Harmsworth Sen. Scholar, Merton Coll., 1947 (Hon. Fellow, 1980); DLitt Oxon 1974. Served War of 1939–45: Army (RA), 1940–45; Western Desert, 1941–43, Italy, 1943–45 (despatches). Fellow and Tutor, Balliol Coll., 1948–55 (Hon. Fellow, 1977); Prof. of Greek, 1955–76, Dean of Fac. of Arts, 1960–63, 1973–75, Univ. of St Andrews; Pres., Corpus Christi Coll., Oxford, 1976–86 (Hon. Fellow, 1986); Prof. of Classics (Winter Quarter), Stanford Univ., 1988–92. Vis. Lectr, Harvard, 1960; Sather Prof. of Classical Literature, Univ. of California, 1967; Prof.-at-large, Cornell Univ., 1984–89. President: Soc. for Promotion of Hellenic Studies, 1971–74; Classical Assoc., 1975; Jt Assoc. of Classical Teachers, 1985. Pres., British Acad., 1978–81. For. Hon. Mem., Amer. Acad. of Arts and Sciences, 1979; For. Mem., Royal Netherlands Acad. of Arts and Sciences, 1979. Hon. LLD: Birmingham, 1979; St Andrews, 1981; Hon. DLitt: Bristol, 1980; London, 1980; St Andrews, 1981; Durham, 1984; Hon. LittD Liverpool, 1983; Hon. DHL Oglethorpe, 1984. Kenyon Medal, British Acad., 1993. *Publications:* Greek Word Order, 1960; Commentaries on Thucydides, Books VI and VII, 1965; (ed) Aristophanes' Clouds, 1968; Lysias and the Corpus Lysiacum, 1968; (with A. W. Gomme and A. Andrewes) Historical Commentary on Thucydides, vol. IV, 1970, vol. V, 1981; (ed) Theocritus, select poems, 1971; Aristophanic Comedy, 1972; Greek Popular Morality in the Time of Plato and Aristotle, 1974; Greek Homosexuality, 1978; (ed) Plato, Symposium, 1980; (ed and co-author) Ancient Greek Literature, 1980; The Greeks, 1980 (contrib., The Greeks, BBC TV series, 1980); Greek and the Greeks, 1987; The Greeks and their Legacy, 1989; (ed) Perceptions of the Ancient Greeks, 1992; (ed) Aristophanes, Frogs, 1993; Marginal Comment (memoirs), 1994; The Evolution of Greek Prose Style, 1997; articles in learned journals; Co-editor, Classical Quarterly, 1962–68. *Recreations:* historical linguistics, gardening. *Address:* 49 Hepburn Gardens, St Andrews, Fife KY16 9LS.

DOW, Andrew Richard George; railway historian and writer; *b* 1 Dec. 1943; *s* of late George Dow and Doris Mary Dow (*née* Soundy); *m* 1973, Stephanie Brenda Murphy; one *s* one *d. Educ:* The Hall, Hampstead; Brighton Coll. Chartered Secretary; ACIS. Commercial Apprentice, Bristol Siddeley Engines, 1962–67; appts in Bristol Siddeley and Rolls-Royce Commercial Depts, Bristol, Coventry and New Jersey, 1967–89; Commercial Exec., 1989; Head of Business (Mil.), 1990; Head, Nat. Railway Mus., 1992–94; Contracts Manager, BR Special Trains Unit, and Commercial Man., BR Infrastructure Services, 1994–95; Dir, 1995–97, and Commercial Dir, 1996–97, Fastline Track Renewals Ltd. Director: Fastline Group Ltd, 1996–97; Fastline Hldgs Ltd, 1996–97; Lynton and Barnstaple Light Railway Co., 1995– (Chm., 2000–); Locomotive Construction Co., 1997–99; Tornado Steam Traction Ltd, 1998–. Director: York Visitor and Conf. Bureau, 1992–94; FNRM Enterprises Ltd, 1992–94, 1999–; A1 Steam Locomotive Trust, 1994–; Gresley Soc. Trust Ltd, 1999–. President: Leighton Buzzard Narrow Gauge Rly Soc., 1994–99; Lynton and Barnstaple Rly Assoc., 1994–. Pres., Stephenson Locomotive Soc., 2000– (Vice-Pres., 1992–2000); Vice-President: Great Central Rly Soc., 1994–; British Overseas Rly Historical Trust, 1994–; Vice-Chm., Gresley Soc., 1997–. Fellow, Permanent Way Instn, 1994. FRSA. *Publications:* Norfolk and Western Coal Cars, 1998 (US); book reviews, monthly column, and articles in British and American railway jls. *Recreations:* family life, railways, travel, photography, collecting. *Address:* Wyverns, Newton-on-Ouse, York YO30 2BR. *T:* and *Fax:* (01347) 848808.

DOW, Rear-Adm. Douglas Morrison, CB 1991; DL; Director, National Trust for Scotland, 1992–97; *b* 1 July 1935; *s* of George Torrance Dow and Grace Morrison MacFarlane; *m* 1959, Felicity Margaret Mona Napier, *d* of John Watson Napier and Beatrix Mary Carson; two *s*. *Educ:* George Heriot's School; BRNC Dartmouth. Joined RN, 1952; served Staff of C-in-C Plymouth, 1959–61; HMS Plymouth, 1961–63; RN Supply Sch., 1963–65; Staff of Comdr FEF, 1965–67; HMS Endurance, 1968–70; BRNC Dartmouth, 1970–72; Asst Dir, Officer Appointments (S), 1972–74; Sec. to Comdr British Navy Staff, Washington, 1974–76; HMS Tiger, 1977–78; NDC Latimer, 1978–79; CSO(A) to Flag Officer Portsmouth, 1979; Sec. to Controller of the Navy, 1981; Captain, HMS Cochrane, 1983; Commodore, HMS Centurion, 1985; RCDS 1988; Dir Gen., Naval Personal Services, 1989–92. Hon. ADC to the Queen, 1986–89. President: South Queensferry Sea Cadets, 1994–; Royal Naval Assoc., Edin., 1996–. Gov., George Heriot's Sch., 1993– (Vice Chm., 1997–). DL Edinburgh, 1996. *Recreations:* Royal Navy Rugby Union (Chairman, 1985–91), fly fishing, shooting, golf, gardening.

DOW, Rt Rev. Geoffrey Graham; *see* Carlisle, Bishop of.

DOW, Harold Peter Bourner; QC 1971; *b* 28 April 1921; *s* of late Col H. P. Dow and P. I. Dow; *m* 1943, Rosemary Merewether, *d* of late Dr E. R. A. Merewether, CB, CBE, FRCP; two *s* one *d*. *Educ:* Charterhouse; Trinity Hall, Cambridge (MA). Served RAF (Air Crew), 1941–42. Min. of Supply, 1943–45. Barrister, Middle Temple, 1946. *Publications:* Restatement of Town and Country Planning, 1947; National Assistance, 1948; (with Q. Edwards) Rights of Way, 1951; (ed) Hobsons Local Government, 1951 and 1957 edns. *Recreations:* music, painting. *Address:* Mustow House, Mustow Street, Bury St Edmunds, Suffolk IP33 1XL. *T:* (01284) 725093.

DOWD, James Patrick; MP (Lab) Lewisham West, since 1992; *b* Germany, 5 March 1951; *s* of late James Patrick Dowd and Elfriede Anna Dowd (*née* Janocha). *Educ:* Dalmain JM&I Sch., London; Sedgehill Comprehensive, London; London Nautical School. Apprentice telephone engineer, GPO, 1967–72; Station Manager, Heron petrol stations, 1972–73; Telecomms Engineer, Plessey Co., later GPT, 1973–92. Group Rep. and Br. Cttee, PO Engrg Union, 1967–72; Sen. Negotiator, ASTMS, then MSF. Lewisham Council: Councillor, 1974–94: Chief Whip; Chm. of Cttees; Dep. Leader; Dep. Mayor, 1987, 1991; Mayor, 1992. Former Mem., Lewisham and Southwark DHA. Contested (Lab): Beckenham, 1983; Lewisham W, 1987. An Opposition Whip, 1993–95; opposition front-bench spokesman on Northern Ireland, 1995–97; a Lord Comr of HM Treasury (Govt Whip), 1997–2001. Mem., Select Cttee on Health, 2001–. Former school governor. *Recreations:* music, reading, theatre, Cornwall, being with friends. *Address:* House of Commons, SW1A 0AA. *T:* (020) 7219 4617. *Club:* Bromley Labour.

DOWDALL, John Michael; Comptroller and Auditor-General for Northern Ireland, since 1994; *b* 6 Sept. 1944; *s* of W. Dowdall, MBE, and late E. Dowdall; *m* 1964, Aylerie (*née* Houston); three *s* one *d*. *Educ:* King Edward's Sch., Witley, Surrey; Queen's Univ., Belfast (BScEcon). Lectr in Economics, Royal Univ. of Malta, 1966–69; Lectr in Political Econ., King's Coll., Univ. of Aberdeen, 1969–72; Economic Advr, Dept of Commerce, N Ireland, 1972–78, Principal, Dept of Commerce, 1978–82; Asst Sec., Dept of Finance and Personnel, N Ireland, 1982–85; Dep. Chief Exec., Industrial Develt Bd, NI, 1986–89; Under Sec., Dept of Finance and Personnel, NI, 1989–94.

DOWDEN, Richard George; journalist, The Economist, since 1995; *b* 20 March 1949; *s* of Peter Dowden and Eleanor Dowden; *m* 1976, Penny Mansfield; two *d*. *Educ:* St George's Coll., Weybridge, Surrey; London Univ. (BA History). Volunteer Teacher, Uganda, 1971–72; Asst Sec., Justice and Peace Commn, 1973–76; Editor, Catholic Herald, 1976–79; journalist, The Times, 1980–86; Africa Editor, 1986–94, Diplomatic Editor, 1994–95, Independent. *Address:* 7 Highbury Grange, N5 2QB.

DOWDESWELL, Lt-Col (John) Windsor, MC 1943; TD 1947; Chairman, Gateshead Health Authority, 1984–93; Vice Lord-Lieutenant of Tyne and Wear, 1987–93; *b* 11 June 1920; *s* of Thomas Reginald Dowdeswell and Nancy Olivia Pitt Dowdeswell; *m* 1948, Phyllis Audrey Horsfield; one *s* one *d*. *Educ:* Malvern Coll. Commnd RA (TA), 1938; served War, RA 50 (N) Division: France, 1940; Western Desert, 1941–43; Sicily, 1943; NW Europe, 1944–46; Lt-Col Comdg 272 (N) Field Regt, RA (TA), 1963–66; Hon. Col, 101 (N) Field Regt, RA (TA), 1981–86. Emerson Walker Ltd, 1946–68 (Man. Dir, 1961–68); Clarke Chapman Ltd, 1968–77; NEI plc, 1977–83. JP Gateshead, 1955–90 (Chm., 1979–86); DL Tyne and Wear, 1976. *Address:* 40 Oakfield Road, Gosforth, Newcastle upon Tyne NE3 4HS. *T:* (0191) 285 2196. *Club:* Northern Counties (Newcastle upon Tyne).

DOWDESWELL, Prof. Julian Andrew, PhD; Professor of Physical Geography, and Director, Bristol Glaciology Centre, University of Bristol, since 1998; *b* 18 Nov. 1957; *s* of Robert Dowdeswell and Joan Marion Dowdeswell (*née* Longshaw); *m* 1983, Evelyn Kae Lind; one *s* one *d*. *Educ:* Magdalen Coll. Sch., Oxford; Jesus Coll., Cambridge (BA 1980; schol., 1980; PhD 1985); Univ. of Colorado (MA 1982). Research Associate, Scott Polar Res. Inst., Univ. of Cambridge, 1985; Lectr, Univ. of Wales, Aberystwyth, 1986–89; University of Cambridge: Sen. Asst in Research, 1989–92; Asst Dir of Res., Scott Polar Res. Inst., 1992–94; Dir, Centre for Glaciology, 1994–98, and Dir, Inst. of Geog. and Earth Scis, 1997–98, Univ. of Wales, Aberystwyth. Natural Environment Research Council: Member: Polar Science and Technol. Bd, 1995–97; Earth Scis Res. Grants and Training Awards Cttee, 1996–2000; Polar Scis Expert Gp, 1997–99; Earth Scis Bd, 1997–2000. Hd of Glaciers and Ice Sheets Div., Internat. Commn for Snow and Ice, 1999–. Mem. Council, Internat. Glaciol Soc., 1993–96. Gov., Plascrug Sch., Aberystwyth, 1996–98. FRGS 1985. Polar Medal, 1995; Gill Meml Award, RGS, 1998. *Publications:* (ed jtly) Glacimarine Environments: processes and sediments, 1990; (ed jtly) The Arctic and Environmental Change, 1996; (ed jtly) Glacial and Oceanic History of the Polar North Atlantic Margins, 1998; papers in learned jls on glaciology, glacier-marine interactions, cryosphere and climate change, and satellite remote sensing of ice. *Recreations:* hill-walking, ski-ing. *Address:* Bristol Glaciology Centre, School of Geographical Sciences, University of Bristol, University Road, Bristol BS8 1SS.

DOWDING, family name of **Baron Dowding.**

DOWDING, 3rd Baron *cr* 1943, of Bentley Priory, Middlesex; **Piers Hugh Tremenheere Dowding;** Professor of English, Okayama Shoka University, Japan, since 1999 (Associate Professor, 1977–99); *b* 18 Feb. 1948; *s* of 2nd Baron Dowding and of his 2nd wife, Alison Margaret, *d* of Dr James Bannerman and *widow* of Major R. W. H. Peebles; *S* father, 1992; *m* Noriko Shiho; two *d*. *Educ:* Fettes. *Heir:* *b* Hon. Mark Denis James Dowding, *b* 11 July 1949.

DOWDING, Nicholas Alan Tatham; QC 1997; *b* 24 Feb. 1956; *s* of Alan Lorimer Dowding and Jennifer Mary Dowding (*née* Hughes); *m*; three *d*. *Educ:* Radley Coll.; St Catharine's Coll., Cambridge (BA 1978; MA 1982). Called to the Bar, Inner Temple, 1979. *Publications:* (ed jtly) Handbook of Rent Review, 1980–85; (ed jtly) Woodfall on Landlord and Tenant, 1994–; (jtly) Dilapidations: the modern law and practice, 1995, 2001. *Recreations:* sailing, music, juggling. *Address:* Falcon Chambers, Falcon Court, EC4Y 1AA. *T:* (020) 7353 2484, *Fax:* (020) 7353 1261; *e-mail:* dowding@falcon-chambers.com.

DOWDING, Hon. Peter M'Callum; barrister; *b* 6 Oct. 1943; *m*; five *c*. *Educ:* Hale School, Perth; Univ. of Western Australia (LLB 1964). Churchill Fellowship, 1974, UK and Canada. In practice as solicitor and barrister until 1983 and as barrister, 1990–; Partner, Briggs Paul Dowding, 1992–94; Man. Partner, DCH Legal Gp, 1994–96. Dir, Biotech Internat. Ltd, 1998–. MLC North Province, WA, 1980–86; MLA (ALP) Maylands, 1986–90; Cabinet Member, 1983–90; Minister for: Mines, Fuel and Energy, 1983; Planning, and Employment and Training, 1983–84; Consumer Affairs, 1983–86; Minister assisting the Minister for Public Sector Management, 1984–88; Minister for Works and Services, Labour, Productivity and Employment, and assisting the Treasurer, 1987–88; Treasurer, and Minister for Productivity, 1988–89; Leader, WA Parly Lab. Party, 1987–90; Premier, WA, 1988–90; Minister, Public Sector Management, and Women's Interests, 1989–90. *Recreations:* sailing, bushwalking, reading. *Address:* PO Box 1099, Subiaco, WA 6904, Australia. *T:* (8) 93809252, *Fax:* (8) 93809253; *e-mail:* pdowding@attglobal.net.

DOWELL, Sir Anthony (James), Kt 1995; CBE 1973; Senior Principal, 1967–2001, Director, 1986–2001, Royal Ballet, Covent Garden (Assistant to Director, 1984–85; Associate Director, 1985–86); *b* 16 Feb. 1943; *s* of late Catherine Ethel and Arthur Henry Dowell; unmarried. *Educ:* Hampshire Sch., St Saviour's Hall, Knightsbridge; Royal Ballet Sch., White Lodge, Richmond, Surrey; Royal Ballet Sch., Barons Court. Joined Opera Ballet, 1960, Royal Ballet, for Russian Tour, 1961; promoted Principal Dancer, 1966. *Principal roles with Royal Ballet include:* La Fête Etrange, 1963; Napoli, 1965; Romeo and Juliet, 1965; Song of the Earth, 1966; Card Game, Giselle, Swan Lake, 1967; The Nutcracker, Cinderella, Monotones, Symphonic Variations, new version of Sleeping Beauty, Enigma Variations, Lilac Garden, 1968; Raymonda Act III, Daphnis and Chloe, La Fille Mal Gardée, 1969; Dances at a Gathering, 1970; La Bayadère, Meditation from Thaïs, Afternoon of a Faun, Anastasia, 1971; Triad, Le Spectre de la Rose, Giselle, 1972; Agon, Firebird, 1973; Manon, 1974; Four Schumann Pieces, Les Sylphides, 1975; Four Seasons, 1975; Scarlet Pastorale, 1976; Rhapsody, 1981; A Month in the Country, The Tempest, Varii Capricci, 1983; Sons of Horus, Frankenstein: the modern Prometheus, 1986; Ondine, 1988. Guest Artist with Amer. Ballet Theater, 1977–79; *performed in:* The Nutcracker; Don Quixote; Other Dances; *created:* The Dream, 1964; Shadow Play, 1967; Pavane, 1973; Manon, 1974; Contredanses; Solor in Makarova's La Bayadère; Fisherman in Le Rossignol (Ashton's choreography), NY Metropolitan Opera, 1981; Winter Dreams, 1991. Narrator in A Wedding Bouquet (first speaking role), Joffrey Ballet, 1977; guest appearances with Nat. Ballet of Canada (The Dream, Four Schumann Pieces), 1979 and 1981; Anthony Dowell Ballet Gala, Palladium, 1980 (for charity); narrated Oedipus Rex, NY Metropolitan Opera, 1981. *Television performances:* La Bayadère (USA); Swan Lake, Cinderella, Sleeping Beauty, A Month in the Country, The Dream, Les Noces (all BBC); Winter Dreams; All the Superlatives (personal profile), Omnibus, BBC. Dance Magazine award, NY, 1972. *Recreations:* painting, paper sculpture, theatrical costume design. *Address:* c/o Royal Opera House, Covent Garden, WC2E 9DD.

DOWELL, Ian Malcolm, MBE 1999; Editor, Birmingham Evening Mail, 1987–2001; *b* 15 Nov. 1940; *s* of late James Mardlin and Lilian Dowell; *m* 1st, 1967, Maureen Kane; two *d*; 2nd, 1980, Pauline Bridget Haughian. *Educ:* Exmouth Grammar Sch., Devon. Reporter, Exmouth and East Devon Journal, 1958; Sub-Editor, Woodrow Wyatt Newspapers, 1960; Editor, Wallingford News, Berks, 1962; Dep. Editor, Birmingham Planet, 1964–66; Birmingham Evening Mail: Sub-Editor, 1966; Dep. Features Editor, 1972; Chief Sub-Editor, 1976; Asst Editor, 1981; Dep. Editor, 1985. Bd Mem., Birmingham Post & Mail Ltd, 1992–2001. Chm., W Midlands Reg. Guild of Editors, 1994; Mem., Code of Practice Cttee, Newspaper and Magazine Publishing in the UK, 1996–. Pres., Black Country Olympics Cttee, 1985–94; Mem. Foundn Bd, Solihull Coll., 1994–98. Chm., Birmingham Mail Christmas Tree Fund, 1992–2001; Member: Bd, Birmingham Jazz Festival, 1996–; Birmingham Town Hall Adv. Panel, 1999–. Fellow, RSPB, 1987. *Recreations:* the countryside, gardening. *Address:* c/o The Birmingham Post & Mail Ltd, 28 Colmore Circus, Birmingham B4 6AX. *T:* (0121) 236 3366.

DOWELL, Prof. John Derek, FRS 1986; CPhys, FInstP; Poynting Professor of Physics, University of Birmingham, since 1997; *b* 6 Jan. 1935; *s* of William Ernest Dowell and Elsie Dorothy Dowell (*née* Jarvis); *m* 1959, Patricia Clarkson; one *s* one *d*. *Educ:* Coalville Grammar Sch., Leics; Univ. of Birmingham (BSc, PhD) CPhys, FInstP 1987. Research Fellow, Univ. of Birmingham, 1958–60; Res. Associate, CERN, Geneva, 1960–62; University of Birmingham: Lectr, 1962–70; Sen. Lectr, 1970–75; Reader, 1975–80; Prof. of Elementary Particle Physics, 1980–97. Vis. Scientist, Argonne Nat. Lab., USA, 1968–69. CERN, Geneva: Scientific Associate, 1973–74, 1985–87; Mem., Scientific Policy Cttee, 1982–90, 1993–96; Mem., Res. Bd, 1993–96; Chairman: Large Electron Positron Collider Cttee, 1993–96; ATLAS Collaboration Bd, 1996–97. Mem., Nuclear Physics Bd, 1974–77, 1981–85, Chm., Particle Physics Cttee, 1981–85, SERC; Member: Europ. Cttee for Future Accelerators, 1989–93; BBC Science Consultative Gp, 1992–94; Deutsches Elektronen Synchrotron Extended Scientific Council, 1992–98; PPARC, 1994–97. Mem., Panel for Physics, 2001 RAE, HEFCE. Vice Pres. and Mem. Council, Royal Soc., 1997–98. Mem. Court, Univ. of Warwick, 1992–. Rutherford Prize and Medal, InstP, 1988. *Publications:* numerous, in Phys. Letters, Nuovo Cimento, Nuclear Phys., Phys. Rev., Proc. Royal Soc., and related literature. *Recreations:* piano, amateur theatre, squash, ski-ing. *Address:* 57 Oxford Road, Moseley, Birmingham B13 9ES; School of Physics and Space Research, University of Birmingham, Birmingham B15 2TT.

DOWER, Michael Shillito Trevelyan, CBE 1996; Director-General, Countryside Commission, 1992–96; Visiting Professor, Cheltenham and Gloucester College of Higher Education, since 1996; *b* 15 Nov. 1933; *s* of late John Gordon Dower and Pauline Dower; *m* 1960, Agnes Done; three *s*. *Educ:* Leys Sch., Cambridge; St John's Coll., Cambridge (MA); University Coll. London (DipTP). MRTPI, ARICS. Town Planner: LCC, 1957–59; Civic Trust, 1960–65; Amenity and Tourism Planner, UN Develt Prog., Ireland, 1965–67; Dir, Dartington Amenity Res. Trust and Dartington Inst., Devon, 1967–85; Nat. Park Officer, Peak Park Jt Planning Bd, 1985–92. Member: Sports Council, 1965–72; English Tourist Bd, 1969–76; Founder Chm., Rural Voice, 1980; Pres., 1986–90, Vice-Pres., 2000–, European Council for Village and Small Town; Vice-President: YHA, 1996–; BTCV, 1996–; Hon. Councillor, Rural Buildings Preservation Trust, 1996–; Patron, Landscape Design Trust, 1997. Hon. FLI 1995. Hon. DSc Plymouth, 1994. *Publications:* Fourth Wave, 1965; Hadrian's Wall, 1976; (jtly) Leisure Provision and People's Needs, 1981; research and consultancy reports. *Recreations:* walking, landscape painting, dry-stone walling, travel. *Address:* 56 Painswick Road, Cheltenham, Glos GL50 2ER. *T:* (01242) 226511.

DOWLING, Prof. Ann Patricia, (Mrs T. P. Hynes), PhD; FREng; FIMechE; FRAeS; Professor of Mechanical Engineering, University of Cambridge, since 1993; Fellow, Sidney Sussex College, Cambridge, since 1979; *b* 15 July 1952; *d* of Mortimer Joseph Patrick Dowling and Joyce Dowling (*née* Barnes); *m* 1974, Dr Thomas Paul Hynes. *Educ:*

Ursuline Convent Sch., Westgate, Kent; Girton Coll., Cambridge (BA 1973; MA 1977; PhD 1978). CEng, FIMechE 1990; FREng (FEng 1996); FRAeS 1997; Fellow, Inst. Acoustics, 1989. Cambridge University: Res. Fellow, 1977–78, Dir of Studies in Engrg, 1979–90, Sidney Sussex Coll.; Asst Lectr in Engrg, 1979–82; Lectr, 1982–86; Reader in Acoustics, 1986–93; Dep. Hd, Engrg Dept, 1990–93, 1996–99. Jerome C. Hunsaker Vis. Prof., MIT, 1999–2000. Member: AIAA, 1990; Defence and Aerospace Technology Foresight Panel, 1994–97; Defence Sci. Adv. Council, 1998–; EPSRC, 2001– (Mem., Technical Opportunities Panel, 1998–). Non-exec. Dir, DRA, 1995–97; Mem. Scientific Adv. Bd, DERA, 1997–. Mem. Council, Royal Acad. of Engrg, 1998– (Vice-Pres., 1999–). Trustee: Ford of Britain Trust, 1993–; Cambridge European Trust, 1994–; Nat. Mus. of Sci. and Industry, 1999–. Gov., Felsted Sch., 1994–99. A. B. Wood Medal, Inst. of Acoustics, 1990. *Publications:* (with J. E. Ffowcs Williams) Sound and Sources of Sound, 1983; (with D. G. Crighton *et al.*) Modern Methods in Analytical Acoustics, 1992; contribs to scientific and engrg jls, mainly on fluid mechanics, combustion, vibration and acoustics. *Recreations:* opera, flying light aircraft. *Address:* Engineering Department, Cambridge University, Trumpington Street, Cambridge CB2 1PZ. *T:* (01223) 332739.

DOWLING, Dame Jean (Elizabeth), DCVO 1978 (CVO 1976; MVO 4th Cl. 1971, 5th Cl. 1964); retired; *b* 7 Nov. 1916; *d* of Captain William Taylor (killed in action, 1917) and late Margery Hooper Alchin; *m* 1993, Ambrose Francis Dowling, MVO, MBE, TD. *Educ:* Tunbridge Wells High School (GPDST). Entered Office of Private Secretary to the Queen, 1958; Chief Clerk, 1961–78. *Recreations:* music, walking, looking at old buildings. *Address:* Church Cottage, Frittenden, Cranbrook, Kent TN17 2DD.

DOWLING, Kenneth, CB 1985; Deputy Director of Public Prosecutions, 1982–85; *b* 30 Dec. 1933; *s* of Alfred and Maria Dowling; *m* 1957, Margaret Frances Bingham; two *d.* *Educ:* King George V Grammar Sch., Southport. Called to the Bar, Gray's Inn, 1960. RAF, 1952–54. Immigration Branch, Home Office, 1954–61; joined DPP Dept: Legal Asst, 1961; Sen. Legal Asst, 1966; Asst Solicitor, 1972; Asst Dir, 1976; Princ. Asst Dir, 1977. *Recreations:* reading, golf.

DOWLING, Rt Rev. Owen Douglas; Bishop of Canberra and Goulburn, 1983–92; *b* 11 Oct. 1934; *s* of Cecil Gair Mackenzie Dowling and Winifred Hunter; *m* 1st, 1958, Beverly Anne Johnston (*d* 1985); two *s* one *d*; 2nd, 1993, Gloria Helen Goodwin. *Educ:* Melbourne High School; Trinity Coll., Melbourne Univ. (BA, DipEd, ThL). Victorian Education Dept, Secondary Teacher, 1956–60; ordained to ministry of Anglican Church, 1960; Asst Curate, Sunshine/Deer Park, Dio. Melbourne, 1960–62; Vicar of St. Philip's, W Heidelberg, 1962–65; Precentor and Organist, St Saviour's Cathedral, Goulburn, 1965–67; Rector of South Wagga Wagga, 1968–72; Rector of St John's, Canberra, 1972–81; Archdeacon of Canberra, 1974–81; Asst Bishop, Dio. Canberra and Goulburn, 1981–83; Rector: St James's, New Town, Hobart, 1993–96; Christ Church, Longford, Tas, 1996–99. Comr, Australian Heritage Commn, 1993–95. *Recreation:* pipe organ and piano playing. *Address:* 9 Borrowdale Street, Red Hill, ACT 2603, Australia. *Club:* Southern Cross (Canberra).

DOWLING, Prof. Patrick Joseph, CBE 2001; DL; PhD; FRS 1996; FREng; Vice Chancellor and Chief Executive, University of Surrey, since 1994; Partner, Chapman and Dowling, Consulting Engineers, 1981–94; *b* 23 March 1939; *s* of John Dowling and Margaret McKittrick, Dublin; *m* 1966, Grace Carmine Victoria Lobo, *d* of Palladius Lobo and Marcilia Moniz, Zanzibar; one *s* one *d.* *Educ:* Christian Brothers Sch., Dublin; University Coll., Dublin (BE NUI 1960); Imperial Coll. of Science and Technol., London (DIC 1961; PhD 1968; FIC 1997). FRINA 1985; FIStructE 1978; FICE 1979; FREng (FEng 1981); FCGI 1989; FIAE 2000. Demonstr in Civil Engrg, UC Dublin, 1960–61; Post-grad. studies, Imperial Coll., London, 1961–65; Bridge Engr, British Constructional Steelwork Assoc., 1965–68; Imperial Coll., London: Res. Fellow, 1968–74; Reader in Structural Steelwork, 1974–79; British Steel Prof. of Steel Structures, 1979–94; Hd of Civil Engrg Dept, 1985–94. Chm., Eurocode 3 (Steel Structures) Drafting Cttee, 1981–94. Mem. Council, RHBNC, 1990–95. Senator, Engrg Council, 1996–. Institution of Structural Engineers: Pres., 1994–95; Oscar Faber Award, 1971; Henry Adams Medal, 1976; Guthrie Brown Medal, 1979; Oscar Faber Medal, 1985, 1996; Telford Premium, ICE, 1976; Gustave Trasenster Medal, Assoc. des Ingénieurs sortis de l'Univ. de Liège, 1984; Silver Medal, RINA, 1993; Curtin Medal, ICE, 1993. For. Mem., Nat. Acad. of Engrg, Korea, 1997. Editor, Jl of Constructional Steel Research, 1980–. DL Surrey, 1999. Hon. LLD NUI, 1995; Hon. DSc: Vilnius Tech. Univ., 1996; Ulster, 1998. *Publications:* Steel Plated Structures, 1977; Buckling of Shells in Offshore Structures, 1982; Structural Steel Design, 1988; Constructional Steel Design, 1992; technical papers on elastic and inelastic behaviour and design of steel and composite land-based and offshore structures. *Recreations:* travelling, sailing, reading, the enjoyment of good company. *Address:* University of Surrey, Guildford GU2 7XH. *Clubs:* Athenæum, Chelsea Arts; National Yacht of Ireland.

DOWN AND CONNOR, Bishop of, (RC), since 1991; **Most Rev. Patrick Joseph Walsh;** *b* 9 April 1931; *s* of Michael and Nora Walsh. *Educ:* Queen's Univ. Belfast (MA); Christ's Coll., Cambridge (MA); Pontifical Lateran Univ., Rome (STL). Ordained 1956; Teacher, St MacNissi's Coll., Garron Tower, 1958–64; Chaplain, Queen's Univ., Belfast, 1964–70; Pres., St Malachy's Coll., Belfast, 1970–83; Auxiliary Bishop of Down and Connor, 1983–91. *Recreations:* walking, music, theatre. *Address:* 73 Somerton Road, Belfast BT15 4DE. *T:* (028) 9077 6185.

DOWN AND DROMORE, Bishop of, since 1997; **Rt Rev. Harold Creeth Miller;** *b* 23 Feb. 1950; *s* of Harold Miller and Violet (*née* McGinley); *m* 1978, Elizabeth Adelaide Harper; two *s* two *d.* *Educ:* Trinity Coll., Dublin (MA); Nottingham Univ. (BA Hons Theol.); St John's Theol Coll., Nottingham (DPS). Ordained deacon, 1976, priest, 1977; Asst Curate, St Nicholas, Carrickfergus, 1976–79; Dir of Extension Studies and Chaplain, St John's Coll., Nottingham, 1979–84; Chaplain, QUB, 1984–89; Rector of Carrigrohane Union of Parishes, Cork, 1989–97. *Publications:* Anglican Worship Today, 1980; Whose Office? daily prayer for the people of God, 1982; Finding a Personal Rule of Life, 1984, 2nd edn 1987; New Ways in Worship, 1986; Making an Occasion of It, 1994; Outreach in the Local Church, 2000; articles in Search. *Recreations:* caravanning, music, swimming. *Address:* The See House, 32 Knockdene Park South, Belfast BT5 7AB. *T:* (028) 9047 1973, *Fax:* (028) 9065 0584; *e-mail:* bishop@down.anglican.org.

DOWN, Sir Alastair (Frederick), Kt 1978; OBE 1944 (MBE 1942); MC 1940; TD 1951; Chairman, The Burmah Oil Co. PLC, 1975–83 (Chief Executive, 1975–80); *b* 23 July 1914; *e s* of Frederick Edward Down and Margaret Isobel Down (*née* Hutchison); *m* 1947, Bunny Mellon; two *s* two *d.* *Educ:* Edinburgh Acad.; Marlborough Coll. Commissioned in 7th/9th Bn, The Royal Scots (TA), 1935. CA 1938. Joined British Petroleum Co. Ltd in Palestine, 1938. Served War of 1939–45 (despatches twice, MC, MBE, OBE, Kt Comdr, Order of Orange Nassau, with swords, 1946): Middle East, N Africa, Italy and Holland, with Eighth Army and 1st Canadian Army as Lt-Col and full Col. Rejoined BP, in Iran, 1945–47; Head Office, 1947–54; Canada, 1954–62 (Chief Rep. of BP in Canada, 1954–57; Pres., BP Group in Canada, 1957–62); Pres. BP Oil Corp., 1969–70; Man. Dir, 1962–75 and Dep. Chm., 1969–75, British Petroleum Co. Ltd; Director: TRW Inc., USA, 1977–86; Scottish American Investment Co. Ltd, 1980–85; Royal Bank of Canada, 1981–85; Chairman: British-North American Res. Assoc., 1980–84; London American Energy NV, 1981–85. Member: Review Body for pay of doctors and dentists, 1971–74; Television Adv. Cttee, 1971–72; Council, Marlborough Coll., 1979–87 (Chm. Council, 1982–87); Hon. Treasurer, Field Studies Council, 1977–81. FRSA 1970; FIMgt (FBIM 1972); JDipMA (Hon.), 1966. Hambro British Businessman of the Year Award, 1980; Cadman Meml Medal, Inst. of Petroleum, 1981. *Recreations:* shooting, golf, fishing. *Address:* Greystones, Newland, Sherborne, Dorset DT9 3AG. *Club:* New (Edinburgh).

DOWN, Antony Turnbull L.; *see* Langdon-Down.

DOWN, Rt Rev. William John Denbigh; Assistant Bishop of Leicester and Priest-in-charge, St Mary, Humberstone, 1995–2001; *b* 15 July 1934; *s* of late William Leonard Frederick Down and Beryl Mary Down (*née* Collett); *m* 1960, Sylvia Mary Aves; two *s* two *d.* *Educ:* Farnham Grammar School; St John's Coll., Cambridge (BA 1957; MA 1961); Ridley Hall, Cambridge. Deacon 1959, priest 1960, Salisbury; Asst Curate, St Paul's Church, Salisbury, 1959–63; Chaplain, Missions to Seamen, 1963–74: South Shields, 1963–65; Hull, 1965–71; Fremantle, WA, 1971–74; Dep. Gen. Secretary, Missions to Seamen, 1975, Gen. Sec. 1976–90; Chaplain, St Michael Paternoster Royal, 1976–90; Hon. Asst Curate, St John's, Stanmore, 1975–90; Bishop of Bermuda, 1990–95. Hon. Canon of Gibraltar, 1985–90, of Kobe, 1987–. Chaplain RANR, 1972–74. Hon. Chaplain, Worshipful Co. of Carmen, 1977–90 (Hon. Chaplain Emeritus, 1990), of Farriers, 1983–90 (Hon. Chaplain Emeritus, 1990), of Innholders, 1983–90. Freeman, City of London, 1981. Hon. FNI 1991. *Publications:* On Course Together, 1989; (contrib.) Chaplaincy, 1999; contrib. to Internat. Christian Maritime Assoc. Bulletin. *Recreations:* sport (keen follower of soccer, cricket, golf), ships and the sea, travel, walking. *Address:* 54 Dark Lane, Witney, Oxfordshire OX28 6LX. *T:* (01993) 706615. *Clubs:* Royal Commonwealth Society, MCC (Associate).

DOWNE, 11th Viscount, *cr* 1680; **John Christian George Dawnay;** Bt 1642; Baron Dawnay of Danby (UK) *cr* 1897; DL; technology manager; *b* Wykeham, 18 Jan. 1935; *s* of 10th Viscount Downe, OBE and Margaret Christine (*d* 1967), *d* of Christian Bahnsen, NJ; *S* father, 1965; *m* 1965, Alison Diana, *d* of I. F. H. Sconce, OBE; one *s* one *d.* *Educ:* Eton Coll.; Christ Church, Oxford. 2nd Lieut, Grenadier Guards, 1954–55. Non-marine broker at Lloyd's, 1958–65. Part-time Mem., Electronics Res. Gp, J. J. Thomson Physical Lab., Univ. of Reading, 1964–78; Brookdeal Electronics Ltd: Man. Dir. 1965–68; Vice-Chm., 1968–71; Chm., 1971–84; Director: Dawnay Faulkner Associated Ltd (Consultants), 1968–; Allen Bradley Electronics Ltd, 1970–81; George Rowney & Co. Ltd, 1978–83; York Ltd, 1980–99 (Chm., 1980–93; Pres., 1993–); Yorkshire Bank PLC, 1990–96; SensorDynamics Ltd, 1990–; Aaston Ltd, 1992–; Aaston Inc., 1992–; Dir, Scarborough Theatre Trust, 1981– (Vice-Chm., 1986–). Member: CLA Yorks Br. Cttee, 1966– (Chm., 1988–90); CLA Exec. Cttee, 1990–94; N Yorks Moors Nat. Park Cttee, 1969–97 (Vice-Chm., 1982–85); N Riding/N Yorks County Council, 1969–85; Nat. Railway Mus. Cttee, 1974– (Chm., 1985–97); N Yorks and ER Rural Develt Cttee (formerly N Yorks Rural Develt Commn County Cttee), 1978– (Chm., 1986–99); President: N York Moors Hist. Railway Trust, 1970–; Yorks Rural Community Council, 1977–; Aston Martin Owners Club, 1980–; Friends of the Nat. Railway Mus., 1988–; Trustee: Nat. Mus. of Science and Industry, 1985–97; Burton Constable Foundn, 1992–2000. Hon. Col, 150 (Yorkshire) Regt RLC(V) (formerly 150 (Northumbrian) Regt RCT(V)), 1984–95. Freeman, Co. of the Staple of England, 1979; Liveryman, Co. of Scientific Instrument Makers, 1991–. DL N Yorks, 1981. *Publications:* contributions to various journals. *Recreations:* linear circuit design, railways (selectively). *Heir:* *s* Hon. Richard Henry Dawnay, *b* 9 April 1967. *Address:* Wykeham Abbey, Scarborough, North Yorks YO13 9QS. *T:* (01723) 862404; 5 Douro Place, W8 5PH. *T:* (020) 7937 9449. *Club:* Pratt's.

DOWNER, Hon. Alexander John Gosse; MP (L) Mayo, South Australia, since 1984; Minister for Foreign Affairs, Australia, since 1996; *b* 9 Sept. 1951; *s* of Hon. Sir Alexander Downer, KBE and of Mary Downer (*née* Gosse); *m* 1978, Nicola Robinson; one *s* three *d.* *Educ:* Geelong GS, Vic; Radley Coll., Oxford; Univ. of Newcastle upon Tyne (BA Hons Pol. and Econs). Economist, Bank of NSW, Sydney, 1975–76; Australian Diplomatic Service, 1976–82: Mission to EEC, Representation to NATO, and Belgium and Luxembourg, 1977–80; Sen. Foreign Affairs Rep., S Australia, 1981; political advr to Prime Minister and Federal Leader of Opposition, 1982–83; Exec. Dir, Australian Chamber of Commerce, 1983–84; Shadow Minister: for Arts, Heritage and Envmt, 1987; for Housing, Small Business and Customs, 1988–89; for Trade and Trade Negotiations, 1990–92; for Defence, 1992–93; Shadow Treas., 1993–94; Leader of Opposition, 1994–95; Shadow Minister for Foreign Affairs, 1995–96. *Recreations:* reading, music, tennis. *Address:* Parliament House, Canberra, ACT 2600, Australia. *T:* (2) 62777500, *Fax:* (2) 62734112. *Club:* Adelaide.

DOWNER, Dame Jocelyn Anita; *see* Barrow, Dame J. A.

DOWNER, Prof. Martin Craig; Hon. Professor, Universities of London and Manchester, since 1996; Director, Oral Health Consultancy Services, since 1996; *b* 9 March 1931; *s* of Dr Reginald Lionel Ernest Downer and Mrs Eileen Maud Downer (*née* Craig); *m* 1961, Anne Catherine (*née* Evans); four *d.* *Educ:* Shrewsbury Sch.; Univ. of Liverpool; Univ. of Manchester (PhD 1974; DDS 1989); Univ. of London. LDSRCS 1958; DDPH RCS 1969. Dental Officer, St Helens Local Authority, 1958–59; gen. dental practice, 1959–64; Dental Officer, Bor. of Haringey, 1964–67; Principal Dental Officer, Royal Bor. of Kensington and Chelsea, 1967–70; Res. Fellow in Dental Health, Univ. of Manchester, 1970–74; Area Dental Officer, Salford HA (also Hon. Lectr, Univ. of Manchester), 1974–79; Chief Dental Officer, SHHD (also Hon. Sen. Lectr, Univs of Edinburgh and Dundee), 1979–83; Chief Dental Officer (Under Sec.), Dept of Health (formerly DHSS), 1983–90; Prof. and Head of Dept, Dental Health Policy, and Hon. Consultant in Dental Public Health, Eastman Dental Inst., London Univ., 1990–96. *Publications:* contribs to books and papers in learned jls in gen. field of dental public health, incl. epidemiology and biostatistics, clin. trials and trial methodology, inf. systems, health services res., and econs of dental care. *Recreations:* music, reading, cookery, natural history, vintage aviation, walking. *Address:* 5 Ashlyns Court, Berkhamsted, Herts HP4 3BU. *T:* (01442) 872088.

DOWNES, Prof. David Malcolm; Professor of Social Administration, London School of Economics, since 1987; *b* 26 Aug. 1938; *s* of Bernice Marion Downes and Herman Leslie Downes; *m* 1961, Susan Onaway Correa-Hunt; one *s* two *d.* *Educ:* King Edward VII Grammar Sch., Sheffield; Keble Coll., Oxford (BA Hons Mod. Hist. 1959); LSE (PhD Criminology 1964). London School of Economics: Asst Lectr, Lectr, Sen. Lectr in Social Admin, 1963–82; Reader, 1982–87; Dir, Mannheim Centre for Criminology and Criminal Justice, 1998–; Vice-Chm., Academic Bd, 1996–99. Sen. Res. Fellow, Nuffield Coll., Oxford, 1970–72. Visiting Professor/Academic Visitor: Univ. of California at Berkeley, 1975; Univ. of Toronto, 1977; Free Univ. of Amsterdam, 1981; Univ. of Bologna, 1991. British Mem., Harvard Internat. Seminar, 1966. Mem., BFI. Editor,

British Jl of Criminology, 1985–90. *Publications:* The Delinquent Solution, 1966, 3rd edn 1973; Gambling, Work and Leisure, 1976; (ed with Paul Rock) Deviant Interpretations, 1979; (with Paul Rock) Understanding Deviance, 1982, 3rd edn 1998; Contrasts in Tolerance: postwar penal policy in the Netherlands and England and Wales, 1988; (ed) Crime and the City: essays in memory of John Mays, 1989; (ed) Unravelling Criminal Justice, 1992. *Recreations:* modern literature, cinema, theatre. *Address:* 25 Rosehill Road, Wandsworth, SW18 2NY. *T:* (020) 8870 3410.

DOWNES, Sir Edward (Thomas), Kt 1991; CBE 1986; Associate Music Director and Principal Conductor, Royal Opera House, Covent Garden, since 1991; *b* 17 June 1924. FRCM. Royal Opera House, Covent Garden, 1952–69; Music Dir, Australian Opera, 1972–76; Prin. Conductor, BBC Northern Symphony Orch., subseq. BBC Philharmonic Orch., 1980–91. *Address:* c/o Royal Opera House, Covent Garden, WC2E 7QA.

DOWNES, George Robert, CB 1967; Director of Studies, Royal Institute of Public Administration, 1972–94; *b* 25 May 1911; *o s* of late Philip George Downes; *m* Edna Katherine Millar; two *d. Educ:* King Edward's Grammar School, Birmingham; Grocers', London. Entered GPO, 1928; Assistant Surveyor, 1937; Asst Principal, 1939. Served War of 1939–45: RNVR, in destroyers, 1942–45. Principal, GPO, 1946; Principal Private Sec. to: Lord President of the Council, 1948–50, Lord Privy Seal, 1951; Assistant Secretary, 1951; Imperial Defence College, 1952; Deputy Regional Director, GPO London, 1955; Dir, London Postal Region, 1960–65; Dir of Postal Services, 1965–67; Dir, Operations and Overseas, PO, 1967–71. *Recreations:* music, gardening. *Address:* Orchard Cottage, Frithsden, Berkhamsted, Herts HP4 1NW.

DOWNES, George Stretton, CBE 1976; Deputy Receiver for the Metropolitan Police District, 1973–76; retired; *b* London, 2 March 1914; *e s* of late George and Rosalind S. Downes; *m* 1st, 1939, Sheilah Gavigan (*d* 1986); two *s* two *d*; 2nd, 1991, Barbara (*née* Haydon). *Educ:* Cardinal Vaughan Sch., Kensington. Joined Metropolitan Police Office, 1934; Secretary, 1969. *Recreations:* golf, gardening. *Address:* 13 Ember Gardens, Thames Ditton, Surrey KT7 0LL.

See also G. P. S. Downes, Dame J. S. Higgins.

DOWNES, Giles Patrick Stretton, CVO 1998; RIBA; Partner, Sidell Gibson Partnership, since 1988; *b* 11 Nov. 1947; *s* of George Stretton Downes, *qv*; *m* 1989, Jessica Jane Harness; one *d. Educ:* Wimbledon Coll.; Kingston Coll. of Art (DipArch 1972). ARCUK 1973; RIBA 1989. Foster Associates, 1969–73; Farrell Grimshaw Partnership, 1973–74; joined Sidell Gibson Partnership, 1974: Associate in charge of Housing Projects, 1980; Equity Partner, 1988. *Projects* include: Sheltered Housing Schemes for English Courtyard Assoc., 1978– (Housing Design Awards, 1983 (2), 1987 (3), 1989, 1991, 1993 (2)); Redevelt of Winchester Peninsula Barracks, 1988; Prince of Wales Sch., Dorchester, 1992; Thomas Hardye Sch., Dorchester, 1993; New Design Areas for Fire Restoration of Windsor Castle, 1994 (Bldg of the Year award, Royal Fine Art Commn, for Lantern Lobby, RIBA Award, RICS Conservation Award, 1998; Carpenters Special Award, 1999; Europa Nostra Conservation Award, 2000). *Recreations:* sculpture, ceramics, building craft skills, sketching. *Address:* Sidell Gibson Partnership, Fitzroy Yard, Fitzroy Road, NW1 8TP. *T:* (020) 7722 5009.

See also Dame J. S. Higgins.

DOWNES, Prof. Kerry John, OBE 1994; FSA; Professor of History of Art, University of Reading, 1978–91, now Emeritus; *b* 8 Dec. 1930; *s* of late Ralph William Downes, CBE and Agnes Mary Downes (*née* Rix); *m* 1962, Margaret Walton. *Educ:* St Benedict's, Ealing; Courtauld Institute of Art. BA, PhD London. Library, Courtauld Inst. of Art, 1954–58; Librarian, Barber Inst. of Fine Arts, Univ. of Birmingham, 1958–66; Lectr in Fine Art, Univ. of Reading, 1966–71, Reader, 1971–78. Vis. Lectr, Yale Univ., 1968; Hon. Vis. Prof., Univ. of York, 1994–. Mem., Royal Commission on Historical Monuments of England, 1981–93; Pres., Soc. of Architectural Historians of GB, 1984–88. Consultant for Trophy Room, St Paul's Cathedral, 1995–97. Hon. DLitt Birmingham, 1995. *Publications:* Hawksmoor, 1959, 2nd edn 1979; English Baroque Architecture, 1966; Hawksmoor, 1969; Christopher Wren, 1971; Whitehall Palace, in Colvin and others, History of the King's Works, V, 1660–1782, 1976; Vanbrugh, 1977; The Georgian Cities of Britain, 1979; Rubens, 1980; The Architecture of Wren, 1982, 2nd edn 1988; Sir John Vanbrugh, a Biography, 1987; Sir Christopher Wren: Design for St Paul's Cathedral, 1988; St Paul's and its Architecture, 1998; contribs to Burlington Magazine, Architectural History, Architectural Rev., TLS, etc. *Recreations:* drawing, making music, learning electronics, procrastination. *Address:* c/o Department of History of Art, University of Reading, Blandford Lodge, Whiteknights, PO Box 217, Reading RG6 2AN. *T:* (0118) 931 8890.

DOWNES, Paul Henry; His Honour Judge Downes; a Circuit Judge, since 1995; *b* 23 Nov. 1941; *s* of Eric and Lavinia Downes; *m* 1st, 1965, Joyce Tarrant (marr. diss.); two *s* one *d*; 2nd, 1986, Beverley Jill Rogers; one *s. Educ:* Ducie High Sch., Manchester; Coll. of Commerce, UMIST; Coll. of Law, London (Bar degree 1967). Deputy Magistrates' Clerk: Manchester Co. Magistrates' Court, 1960–63; Sheffield City Magistrates' Court, 1963–67; Nottingham City Magistrates' Court, 1967; County Prosecuting Service, Suffolk, 1967–71; in private practice at Norwich Bar, 1971–95; Asst Recorder, 1991–94; Recorder, 1994–95. Vice Chancellor, Dio. St Edmundsbury and Ipswich, 2001–. *Recreations:* music, singing, chamber choir, instrumental playing, reading, walking, solo baritone singing. *Address:* c/o Norwich Combined Court, Bishopgate, Norwich NR3 1UR.

DOWNEY, Anne Elisabeth; Her Honour Judge Downey; a Circuit Judge, since 1986; *b* 22 Aug. 1936; *d* of John James Downey and Ida May Downey. *Educ:* Notre Dame Convent, Liverpool; Liverpool Univ. LLB (Hons.). Called to the Bar, Gray's Inn, 1958. A Recorder, 1980–86. *Recreations:* antiques, reading. *Address:* Copperfield, 4 Pine Walk, Prenton, Merseyside. *T:* (0151) 608 2404.

DOWNEY, Sir Gordon (Stanley), KCB 1984 (CB 1980); Parliamentary Commissioner for Standards, 1995–98; Comptroller and Auditor General, 1981–87; *b* 26 April 1928; *s* of Stanley William and Winifred Downey; *m* 1952, Jacqueline Goldsmith; two *d. Educ:* Tiffin's Sch.; London Sch. of Economics (BSc(Econ)). Served RA, 1946–48. Ministry of Works, 1951; entered Treasury, 1952; Asst Private Sec. to successive Chancellors of the Exchequer, 1955–57; on loan to Ministry of Health, 1961–62; Asst Sec., 1965, Under-Sec., 1972, Head of Central Unit, 1975; Dep. Sec., Treasury, 1976–81; on loan as Dep. Head, Central Policy Review Staff, Cabinet Office, 1978–81. Special Advr, Ernst & Young (formerly Ernst & Whinney), 1988–90; Complaints Comr, The Securities Assoc., 1989–90; Chairman: FIMBRA, 1990–93; PIA, 1993. Readers' Rep., The Independent, 1990–95. Chm., Delegacy, King's College Med. and Dental Sch., 1989–91. *Recreations:* reading, visual arts, tennis. *Address:* 137 Whitehall Court, SW1A 2EP. *T:* (020) 7321 0914.

DOWNEY, Air Vice-Marshal John Chegwyn Thomas, CB 1975; DFC 1945, AFC; Deputy Controller of Aircraft (C), Ministry of Defence, 1974–75, retired; *b* 26 Nov. 1920; *s* of Thomas Cecil Downey and Mary Evelyn Downey; *m* Diana, (*née* White); one *s* two *d. Educ:* Whitgift Sch. Entered RAF 1939; served War of 1939–45 in Coastal Command (DFC 1945 for his part in anti-U-boat ops). Captained Lincoln Aries III on global flight of 29,000 miles, during which London-Khartoum record was broken. RAF Farnborough 1956–58; commanded Bomber Comd Develt Unit 1959–60; head of NE Defence Secretariat, Cyprus, 1960–62; Comd RAF Farnborough, 1962–64; a Dir, Op. Requirements (RAF) MoD, 1965–67; IDC, 1968; Comdt, RAF Coll. of Air Warfare, Manby, Jan./Oct. 1969; Comdr Southern Maritime Air Region, 1969–71; Senior RAF Mem., RCDS, 1972–74. *Publications:* Management in the Armed Forces: an anatomy of the military profession, 1977; (contrib.) Yearbook of World Affairs, 1983. *Recreations:* sailing, ski-ing. *Address:* c/o Lloyds TSB, 7 Pall Mall, SW1Y 5NA. *Club:* Royal Air Force.

DOWNEY, William George, CB 1967; *b* 3 Jan. 1912; *s* of late William Percy Downey; *m* 1936, Iris (*d* 2000), *e d* of late Ernest Frederick Pickering; three *d. Educ:* Southend Grammar Sch. ACWA 1935, ACA 1937, FCA 1960. Ministry of Aircraft Production, 1940; Ministry of Supply, 1946 (Director of Finance and Administration, Royal Ordnance Factories, 1952–57); Ministry of Aviation, 1959; Under-Secretary, 1961; Chm., Steering Gp, Develt Cost Estimation, 1964–66; Min. of Technology, 1967, Min. of Aviation Supply, 1970; DTI, 1971; Management Consultant to Procurement Exec., MoD, 1972–74; Under Sec., NI Office, 1974–75; Dir, Harland and Wolff, 1975–81; Consultant to CAA, 1976–79, to Dept of Energy, 1980. *Address:* Starvelarks, 168 Dawes Heath Road, Rayleigh, Essex SS6 7NL. *T:* (01268) 774138.

DOWNIE, Prof. Robert Silcock, FRSE 1986; Professor of Moral Philosophy, Glasgow University, since 1969; *b* 19 April 1933; *s* of late Robert Mackie Downie and late Margaret Barlas Downie; *m* 1958, Eileen Dorothea Flynn; three *d. Educ:* The High Sch. of Glasgow; Glasgow Univ.; The Queen's Coll., Oxford. MA, first cl. hons, Philosophy and Eng. Lit., Glasgow, 1955; Russian linguist, Intelligence Corps, 1955–57; Ferguson Schol., 1958; BPhil Oxford Univ., 1959. Glasgow University: Lectr in Moral Philosophy, 1959; Sen. Lectr in Moral Philosophy, 1968; Stevenson Lectr in Med. Ethics, 1985–88. Vis. Prof. of Philosophy, Syracuse Univ., NY, USA, 1963–64. FRSA 1997. *Publications:* Government Action and Morality, 1964; (jtly) Respect for Persons, 1969; Roles and Values, 1971; (jtly) Education and Personal Relationships, 1974; (jtly) Values in Social Work, 1976; (jtly) Caring and Curing, 1980; Healthy Respect, 1987; (jtly) Health Promotion: models and values, 1990; (jtly) The Making of a Doctor, 1992; (ed) Francis Hutcheson: selected writings, 1994; (ed) The Healing Arts: an Oxford anthology, 1994; Palliative Care Ethics, 1996; (ed) Medical Ethics, 1996; Clinical Judgement: evidence in practice, 2000; contribs to: Mind, Philosophy, Analysis, Aristotelian Society, Political Studies. *Recreation:* music. *Address:* Department of Moral Philosophy, University of Glasgow G12 8QQ. *T:* (0141) 330 4273.

DOWNING, Dr Anthony Leighton, FREng; Consultant, Binnie & Partners, Consulting Engineers, 1986–96 (Partner, 1974–86); *b* 27 March 1926; *s* of Sydney Arthur Downing and Frances Dorothy Downing; *m* 1952, Kathleen Margaret Frost; one *d. Educ:* Arnold Sch., Blackpool; Cambridge and London Universities. BA Cantab. 1946; BSc Special Degree 2 (1) Hons. London, 1950; DSc London 1967. Joined Water Pollution Research Lab., 1946; seconded to Fisheries Research Lab., Lowestoft, 1947–48; granted transfer to Govt Chemist's Lab., 1948; returned to WPRL as Scientific Officer, 1950; subsequently worked mainly in field of biochemical engrg; Dir, Water Pollution Res. Lab., 1966–73. Vis. Prof., Imperial Coll. of Science and Technology, 1978–82. FIChemE 1975; FIWPC 1965 (Pres., 1979); FIBiol 1965; Hon. FIPHE 1965; FIWES 1975; Hon. FCIWEM 1987; FREng (FEng 1991). Freeman, City of London, 1988. Member: Probus Club, Stevenage; CGA. *Publications:* 120 papers in scientific and technical journals. *Recreations:* golf, snooker, gardening. *Address:* 2 Tewin Close, Tewin Wood, Welwyn, Herts AL6 0HF. *T:* (01438) 798474. *Club:* Knebworth Golf.

DOWNING, David Francis, PhD; Head of Land Systems Group, British Defence Staff, British Embassy, Washington, 1983–87; *b* 4 Aug. 1926; *e s* of late Alfred William and Violet Winifred Downing; *m* 1948, Margaret Joan Llewellyn; one *s* one *d. Educ:* Bristol Grammar Sch.; Univ. of Bristol (BSc 1952, PhD 1955); BA Open, 1996. Served Coldstream Gds and Royal Welch Fusiliers, 1944–48 (Lieut RWF, 1947). Student Mem. of delegn from Brit. univs to Soviet univs, 1954; Eli Lilley Res. Fellow, Univ. of Calif, LA, and Fulbright Travel Scholarship, 1955–56; Long Ashton Res. Stn, Univ. of Bristol, 1957–58; Chem. Def. Estab., 1958–63; Def. Res. Staff, Washington, 1963–66; Chem. Def. Estab., 1966–68; Counsellor (Scientific), British High Commn, Ottawa, 1968–73; Head, Management Services, RARDE, 1973–75, and Head, Pyrotechnics Br., 1975–78; Counsellor (Scientific), British Embassy, Moscow, 1978–81; Asst Dir, Resources and Programmes B, MoD, 1981–83. Pt-time Chm., CS Sci. Recruitment Bds, 1988–95. Reader, Salisbury Cathedral, 1990– (Archbishops' Diploma for Readers, 1995). Governor: Salisbury and Wells Theological Coll., 1987–94 (Chm., 1990–94); Sarum Coll., 1994–. FRSA 1969. *Publications:* scientific papers, mainly in Jl of Chem. Soc., and Qly Revs of Chem. Soc. *Recreations:* cathedral music, Arctic and Antarctic travel, bird watching, skiing. *Address:* 13 The Close, Salisbury, Wilts SP1 2EB. *T:* (01722) 323910. *Club:* Army and Navy.

DOWNPATRICK, Lord; Edward Edmund Maximilian George Windsor; *b* 2 Dec. 1988; *s* and *heir* of Earl of St Andrews, *qv*.

DOWNS, Sir Diarmuid, Kt 1985; CBE 1979; FRS 1985; FREng, FIMechE; Managing Director, 1967–84, Chairman, 1976–87, Ricardo Consulting Engineers plc; *b* 23 April 1922; *s* of John Downs and Ellen McMahon; *m* 1951, Mary Carmel Chillman; one *s* three *d. Educ:* Gunnersbury Catholic Grammar Sch.; Northampton Poly. (BScEng London Univ., 1942). CEng, FIMechE 1961. Ricardo Consulting Engineers Ltd, 1942–87: Head, Petrol Engine Dept, 1947; Dir, 1957. Mem., Adv. Council for Applied R&D, 1976–80; Member: SERC, 1981–85 (Chm., Engineering Bd); Design Council, 1981–89; Bd of Dirs, Soc. of Automotive Engineers Inc., 1983–86; Bd of British Council, 1987–93; Council, Motor Industry Res. Assoc., 1987–89. President: Assoc. of Indep. Contract Res. Organisations, 1975–77; Fédération Internationale des Sociétés d'Ingénieurs des Techniques de L'Automobile, 1978 (Vice-Pres., 1975); IMechE, 1978–79 (Vice-Pres., 1971–78); Section G, British Assoc. for Advancement of Science, 1984; Royal Commn for Exhibn of 1851, 1985–96. Chm., Technology Activities Cttee, Royal Soc., 1989–95; Mem., Adv. Bd, Parly Office of Science and Technology, 1988–93. Dir, Gabriel Communications (formerly Universe Publications) Ltd, 1986–93. Vis. Fellow, Lincoln Coll. Oxford, 1987–88. Hinton Lecture, Fellowship of Engrg, 1987. Foreign Associate, Nat. Acad. of Engrg, USA, 1987; Hon. Mem., Hungarian Acad. of Scis, 1988. Liveryman, Co. of Engineers, 1984–. Pro Chancellor, Surrey Univ., 1992–94 (Mem. Council, 1983–94, Chm., 1989–92); Mem. Council, City Univ., 1980–82. Hon. Fellow, St Mary's UC, Strawberry Hill, 1995. Hon. DSc: City, 1978; Cranfield Inst. of Technol., 1981; DUniv Surrey, 1995. George Stephenson Research Prize, 1951, Crompton Lanchester Medal, 1951 and Dugald Clerk Prize, 1952, IMechE; James Alfred Ewing Medal, ICE, 1985; Medal, Internat. Fedn of Automobile Engrs' and Technicians' Assocs, 1986. KSG 1993. *Publications:* papers on internal combustion engines in British and internat. engrg jls and conf. proc. *Recreation:* theatre. *Address:* The Downs, 143 New Church Road, Hove, East Sussex BN3 4DB. *T:* (01273) 419357. *Club:* Hove (Hove).

DOWNS, Rosalyn, (Mrs George Wallingford Downs); *see* Tureck, R.

DOWNSHIRE, 8th Marquess of, *cr* 1789 (Ire.); **Arthur Robin Ian Hill;** Viscount Hillsborough, Baron Hill 1717; Earl of Hillsborough, Viscount Kilwarlin 1751; Baron Harwich (GB) 1756; Earl of Hillsborough, Viscount Fairford (GB) 1772; Hereditary Constable of Hillsborough Fort; farmer, since 1963; *b* 10 May 1929; *s* of Lord Arthur Francis Henry Hill (*d* 1953) (*yr s* of 6th Marquess) and Sheila (*d* 1961), *d* of Col Stewart MacDougall of Lunga; *S* uncle, 1989; *m* 1st, 1957, Hon. Juliet Mary (*d* 1986), *d* of 7th Baron Forester; two *s* one *d*; 2nd, 1989, Mrs Diana Hibbert (*née* Cross; *d* 1998). *Educ:* Eton. 2nd Lieut Royal Scots Greys, 1948–50. Articled clerk, 1950–55; Chartered Accountant (ACA 1959). *Recreations:* shooting, travel. *Heir: s* Earl of Hillsborough, *qv*. *Address:* High Burton House, Masham, Ripon, North Yorks HG4 4BS. *T:* (01765) 689326. *Clubs:* White's, Pratt's.

DOWNSIDE, Abbot of; *see* Yeo, Rt Rev. C. R.

DOWNWARD, Maj.-Gen. Sir Peter (Aldcroft), KCVO 1999; CB 1979; DSO 1967; DFC 1952; Governor, Military Knights of Windsor, 1989–2000; *b* 10 April 1924; *s* of late Aldcroft Leonard and Mary Downward; *m* 1st, 1953, Hilda Hinckley Wood (*d* 1976); two *s*; 2nd, 1980, Mrs Mary Boykett Procter (*née* Allwork). *Educ:* King William's Coll., Isle of Man. Enlisted 1942; 2nd Lieut, The South Lancashire Regt (Prince of Wales's Volunteers), 1943; served with 13th Bn (Lancs) Parachute Regt, NW Europe, India, Far East, 1944–46, Greece and Palestine, 1947; transf. to Glider Pilot Regt, 1948; Berlin Airlift, 1949, Korea, 1951–53; 1st Bn The South Lancs Regt (PWV) in Egypt and UK, 1953–54; instructor at Light Aircraft Sch., 1955–56; RAF Staff Coll., 1958; War Office, 1959–60; BAOR, 1961–63; Brigade Major 127 Bde, 1964; Comd 4th Bn The East Lancs Regt, 1965–66; Comd 1st Bn The Lancs Regt (PWV), Aden, 1966–67; Allied Forces N Europe, Oslo, 1968–69; instructor, Sch. of Infantry, 1970–71; Comd Berlin Inf. Bde. 1971–74; Comdt, Sch. of Infantry, 1974–76; GOC West Midland District, 1976–78; Lt-Governor and Sec., The Royal Hosp., Chelsea, 1979–84. Col, The Queen's Lancashire Regt, 1978–83; Col Comdt, The King's Division, 1979–83; Hon. Col, Liverpool Univ. OTC, 1980–89. Dir, Oxley Develts Co. Ltd, 1984–89. Chm., Museum of Army Flying, 1984–88; President: British Korean Veterans Assoc., 1986–97; Assoc. of Service Newspapers, 1986–; Trustee, Princess Christian Hosp., Windsor, 1989–94. *Recreations:* sailing, skiing, shooting. *Address:* 71 Kings Road, Windsor, Berks SL4 2AD.

DOWNWARD, Sir William (Atkinson), Kt 1977; JP; Lord-Lieutenant of Greater Manchester, 1974–87; Councillor, Manchester City Council, 1946–75; Alderman, Manchester, 1971–74; *b* 5 Dec. 1912; *s* of late George Thomas Downward; *m* 1946, Enid, *d* of late Ald. Charles Wood. *Educ:* Manchester Central High Sch.; Manchester Coll. of Technology. Dir, Royal Exchange Theatre Co., 1976–89; Chairman: Manchester Overseas Students Welfare Conf., 1972–87; Peterloo Gall., 1974–76. Chm., Pat Seed Appeal Fund, 1977–98; President: Manchester Opera Soc., 1977–; Gtr Manchester Fedn of Boys' Clubs, 1978–; Broughton House Home for Disabled Ex-Servicemen, 1978–98. Mem. Court of Governors: Manchester Univ., 1969–96; Salford Univ., 1974–87. Hon. LLD Manchester, 1977. Hon. RNCM 1982. FRSA 1978. Lord Mayor of Manchester, 1970–71; DL Lancs, 1971; JP Manchester, 1973. KStJ 1974. *Address:* 23 Kenmore Road, Northenden, Manchester M22 4AE. *T:* (0161) 998 4742.

DOWSON, Prof. Duncan, CBE 1989; FRS 1987; FREng; Professor of Engineering Fluid Mechanics and Tribology, 1966–93, now Professor Emeritus, Hon. Fellow, since 1993, and Research Professor, since 1995, Leeds University; *b* 31 Aug. 1928; *o s* of Wilfrid and Hannah Dowson, Kirkbymoorside, York; *m* 1951, Mabel, *d* of Mary Jane and Herbert Strickland; one *s* (and one *s* decd). *Educ:* Lady Lumley's Grammar Sch., Pickering, Yorks; Leeds Univ. (BSc Mech Eng. 1950; PhD 1952; DSc 1971) FIMechE; Fellow ASME 1973 (Life Fellow); FREng (FEng 1982); Fellow ASLE 1983. Research Engineer, Sir W. G. Armstrong Whitworth Aircraft Co., 1953–54; Univ. of Leeds: Lecturer in Mechanical Engineering, 1954; Sen. Lecturer, 1963; Reader, 1965; Dir, Inst. of Tribology, Dept of Mech. Engrg, 1967–87; Pro-Vice-Chancellor, 1983–85; Head of Dept of Mech. Engrg, 1987–92; Dean for Internat. Relns, 1987–93. Hon. Professor: Hong Kong Univ., 1992–; Bradford Univ., 1996–; External Prof., Loughborough Univ., 2001–. Hinton Lectr, Royal Acad. of Engrg, 1990. Pres., IMechE, 1992–93 (Chm., Tribology Group Cttee, 1967–69). Chm., Yorks Region, RSA, 1992–97. Editor: Pt H (Engrg in Medicine), IMechE Proceedings, 1981–90; Pt C, Jl Mech. Engrg Sci., 1990–; WEAR, 1983–98, now Emeritus; Engrg Res. Bk Series, 1999–. Foreign Mem., Royal Swedish Acad. of Engrg Sciences, 1986. FCGI, 1997. Hon. FIPEM 1998; Hon. Fellow STLE; Hon. FIMechE 2001. Hon. DTech Chalmers Univ. of Technology, Göteborg, 1979; Hon. DSc Institut Nat. des Sciences Appliquées de Lyon, 1991; Dr *hc* Liège, 1996; DEng *hc* Waterloo, Canada, 2001. James Clayton Fund Prize (jtly), IMechE, 1963; Thomas Hawksley Gold Medal, IMechE, 1966; Gold Medal, British Soc. of Rheology, 1969; Nat. Award, ASLE, 1974; ASME Lubrication Div. Best Paper Awards (jt), 1975, 1976, 1999; ASME Melville Medal (jt), 1976; James Clayton Prize, IMechE, 1978; ASME Mayo D. Hersey Award, 1979; Tribology Gold Medal, IMechE, 1979; ASME Engr Historian Award, 1995; Kelvin Medal, ICE, 1998. *Publications:* Elastohydrodynamic Lubrication—the fundamentals of roller and gear lubrication (jtly), 1966, 2nd edn 1977; History of Tribology, 1979, 2nd edn 1998; (jtly) An Introduction to the Biomechanics of Joints and Joint Replacement, 1981; (jtly) Ball Bearing Lubrication: The Elastohydrodynamics of Elliptical Contacts, 1981; papers on tribology and bio-medical engrg, published by: Royal Society; Instn of Mech. Engineers; Amer. Soc. of Mech. Engineers; Amer. Soc. of Lubrication Engineers. *Recreations:* genealogy, calligraphy. *Address:* Ryedale, 23 Church Lane, Adel, Leeds LS16 8DQ. *T:* (0113) 267 8933.

DOWSON, Graham Randall; Partner, Graham Dowson and Associates, since 1975; Chairman, Dowson Shurman (formerly Dowson-Salisbury) Associates Ltd, since 1987; *b* 13 Jan. 1923; *o s* of late Cyril James Dowson and late Dorothy Celia (*née* Foster); *m* 1954, Fay Weston (marr. diss. 1974); two *d*; *m* 1975, Denise Shurman. *Educ:* Alleyn Court Sch.; City of London Sch.; Ecole Alpina, Switzerland. Served War of 1939–45 (1939–43 and Africa Stars, Atlantic, Defence and Russian Arctic Medals, etc); RAF, 1941–46 (Pilot, Sqdn-Ldr). US Steel Corporation (Columbia Steel), Los Angeles, 1946–49; Sales Senior Commentator, Mid South Network (MBS), radio, US, 1949–52; Dir, Rank Organization Ltd, 1960–75, Chief Exec., 1974–75; Chairman: Erskine House Investments, 1975–83; Mooloya Investments, 1975–78; Pincus Vidler Arthur Fitzgerald Ltd, 1979–83; Marinex Petroleum, 1981–83; Nash Industries, 1988–90; Premier Speakers, 1987–91; Chm. and Chief Exec., Teltech Ltd, 1984–87; Deputy Chairman: Nimslo European Hldgs, 1978–87; Nimslo International Ltd, 1981–87; Nimslo Ltd, 1978–87 (Dir, 1978); Paravision (UK) Ltd, 1988–91; Director: A. C. Nielsen Co., Oxford, 1953–58; Carron Co. (Holdings) Ltd, 1976–; Carron Investments Ltd, 1976–; RCO Holdings PLC (formerly Barrowmill Ltd), 1979–; Nimslo Corp., 1978–87; Filmbond plc, 1985–88; Fairhaven Internat. Ltd, 1988–95; Grovewood Securities, 1990–91. Chm., European League for Econ. Co-operation (British Section), 1974–87 (Pres., 1987–); Vice Pres., NPFA, 1972–; Chm., Migraine Trust, 1985–88; Patron, Internat. Centre for Child Studies. Liveryman, Distillers' Co.; Mem., Court of Common Council, City of London, 1992–95. FInstD 1957; CIMgt (CBIM 1969); FInstM 1971. Officier de l'Ordre des Coteaux de Champagne, 1998. *Recreations:* sailing, shooting. *Address:* 193 Cromwell Tower, Barbican, EC2Y 8DD. *Clubs:* Carlton, City Livery, Royal Air Force, Saints and Sinners, Thirty; Royal London Yacht (Ex-Commodore).

DOWSON, Sir Philip (Manning), Kt 1980; CBE 1969; MA; PPRA (RA 1986; ARA 1979); RIBA, FCSD; a Senior Partner, Ove Arup Partnership, 1969–90, Consultant, since 1990; Architectural Founder Partner, Arup Associates, architects and engineers; President, Royal Academy of Arts, 1993–99; *b* 16 Aug. 1924; *m* 1950, Sarah Crewdson (MBE 1998); one *s* two *d*. *Educ:* Gresham's Sch.; University Coll., Oxford; Clare Coll., Cambridge (Hon. Fellow, 1991); Architectural Association. AA Dip. Lieut, RNVR, 1943–47. Award-winning work includes: university and college buildings in Oxford, Cambridge, Birmingham and Leicester; headquarter buildings; buildings for music and the arts; urban and landscape projects. Member: Royal Fine Art Commn, 1971–97; Craft Adv. Cttee, 1972–75. Governor, St Martin's Sch. of Art, 1975–82. Trustee: The Thomas Cubitt Trust, 1978–98; Royal Botanic Gdns, Kew, 1983–95; Royal Armouries, 1984–89; Nat. Portrait Gall., 1993–99; Coram Foundn, 1993–99. Hon. Fellow, Duncan of Jordanstone Coll. of Arts, 1985; Hon. FAIA; Hon. FRCA, 1989; Hon. FRIAS. Hon. DArt De Montfort, 2000. Royal Gold Medal for Architecture, RIBA, 1981. *Recreation:* sailing. *Clubs:* Garrick, MCC.

DOYLE, Most Rev. Adrian Leo; *see* Hobart (Australia), Archbishop of, (RC).

DOYLE, Dr Anthony Ian, FBA 1992; Hon. Reader in Bibliography, Durham University, since 1985; *b* 24 Oct. 1925; *s* of Edward Doyle and Norah Keating. *Educ:* St Mary's Coll., Great Crosby, Liverpool; Downing Coll., Cambridge (BA 1945; MA 1949; PhD 1953). Durham University: Asst Librarian, 1950–59; Keeper of Rare Books, 1959–82; Reader in Bibliography, 1972–85. Pres., Assoc. for Manuscripts and Archives in Res. Collections, 2000. Corresp. Fellow, Mediaeval Academy of America, 1991. Israel Gollancz Prize, British Academy, 1983. *Publications:* Palaeographical introductions to facsimiles of the Hengwrt Manuscript, 1979, Vernon Manuscript, 1987, and Ellesmere Manuscript, 1995, of Chaucer's Canterbury Tales; articles on medieval MSS, early printed books and collectors. *Address:* University Library, Palace Green, Durham DH1 3RN. *T:* (0191) 374 3001, 3029.

DOYLE, Bernard; *see* Doyle, F. B.

DOYLE, Brian André; Judge, Botswana Court of Appeal, 1973–79 and 1988–91; *b* 10 May 1911; *s* of John Patrick Doyle, ICS and Louise Doyle (*née* Renard); *m* 1937, Nora (*née* Slattery) (*d* 1992); one *s* one *d*. *Educ:* Douai Sch.; Trinity Coll., Dublin. BA, LLB. British Univs and Hosps Boxing Champion, 1929, 1930, 1931 (Flyweight), 1932 (Bantamweight); Irish Free State Army Boxing Champion, 1930 (Flyweight). Called to Irish Bar, 1932; Magistrate, Trinidad and Tobago, 1937; Resident Magistrate, Uganda, 1942; Solicitor-Gen., Fiji, 1948; Attorney-Gen., Fiji, 1949; KC (Fiji), 1950, later QC; Attorney-Gen., N Rhodesia, 1956; Minister of Legal Affairs and Attorney-Gen., Northern Rhodesia (Zambia, 1964), 1959–65, retired as minister, 1965; Chm., Local Govt Service Commn, Zambia, 1964; Justice of Appeal, 1965; Chief Justice and Pres., Supreme Court of Zambia, 1969–75. Dir, Law Develt Commn, Zambia, 1976–79; Chm., Delimitation Commn, Botswana, 1981–82. *Recreations:* fishing, golf. *Address:* 26 Choumert Square, Peckham Rye, SE15 4RE.

DOYLE, (Frederick) Bernard; Head of Public Sector Practice, Hoggett Bowers Executive Search and Selection, 1999–2000; *b* 17 July 1940; *s* of James Hopkinson Doyle and Hilda Mary Doyle (*née* Spotsworth); *m* 1963, Ann Weston; two *s* one *d*. *Educ:* St Bede's Coll.; Univ. of Manchester (BSc Hons); Harvard Business Sch., 1965–67 (MBA). CEng 1965; FICE 1980; FIWEM (FIWES 1986); CIMgt (CBIM 1987). Resident Civil Engineer with British Rail, 1961–65; Management Consultant with Arthur D. Little Inc., 1967–72; Booker McConnell Ltd: Secretary to Executive Cttee, 1973; Director, Engineering Div., 1973–76; Chairman, General Engineering Div., 1976–78; Chm. and Chief Exec., Booker McConnell Engineering, and Director, Booker McConnell, 1978–81; Chief Executive: SDP, 1981–83; Welsh Water Authy, 1983–87; MSL International, then MSL Search and Selection: Dir, Public Sector Ops, 1988–90; Dir, 1994–97; Man. Dir, 1997–99; Man. Dir, Hamptons, 1990–92; Gen. Manager, Bristol & West Building Soc., 1992–94; Dir, MSL Gp, 1996–99. FRSA 1987. *Recreations:* sailing, theatre, reading, walking, bird watching. *Address:* 38A West Road, Bromsgrove, Worcs B60 2NQ. *T:* (01527) 873565.

DOYLE, John Howard, MBE 1995; RWS 1968; landscape painter; President, Royal Watercolour Society, 1996–2000; *b* 15 Feb. 1928; *s* of Eric Howard Doyle and Frances Doyle (*née* Maclean); *m* 1st, 1956, Caroline Knapp-Fisher (marr. diss.); one *s* one *d*; 2nd, 1968, Elizabeth Rickatson-Hatt; one *s* one *d*. *Educ:* Sherborne Sch. Dir, C. F. Doyle Ltd, 1961–96; Chm., Thomas Seager Ltd, 1968–86. Mem., Canterbury DAC, 1975–85 (Advr, 1985–). Founder Mem. and Chm., Romney Marsh Historic Churches Trust, 1980–90 (Pres., 1986–). Exhibitions: Chapter House, Canterbury Cathedral, 1973–76 and 1997; Spink & Sons, 1981–84, 1991, 1997; Catto Gall., 1988; Sanders of Oxford, 1999; exhibitor, RA, 1982–90. Hon. RE 1996; Hon. RI 1996. *Publications:* An Artist's Journey down the Thames, 1993. *Recreations:* golf, gardening. *Address:* Church Farm, Warehorne, Ashford, Kent TN26 2LP. *Clubs:* Garrick; Rye Golf.

DOYLE, Hon. John Jeremy; Chief Justice, Supreme Court of South Australia, since 1995; *b* 4 Jan. 1945; *s* of John Malcolm Doyle and Mary Margaret Doyle; *m* 1969, Marie McLoughlin; two *s* three *d*. *Educ:* St Ignatius' Coll., Norwood; Univ. of Adelaide (LLB); Magdalen Coll., Oxford (BCL). Partner, Kelly & Co., 1970–77; called to the Bar, SA, 1970; Barrister, Hanson Chambers, 1977–86; QC (SA) 1981; Solicitor-General for S Australia, 1986–95. Pro-Chancellor, Flinders Univ. of S Australia, 1988–. *Address:* c/o Chief Justice's Chambers, Supreme Court, 1 Gouger Street, Adelaide, SA 5000, Australia. *T:* (8) 82040390, *Fax:* (8) 82040442.

DOYLE, Dr Peter, CBE 1992; FRSE; Chairman, Biotechnology and Biological Sciences Research Council, since 1998; *b* 6 Sept. 1938; *s* of late Peter and Joan Penman Doyle; *m* 1962, Anita McCulloch; one *s* one *d*. *Educ:* Univ. of Glasgow (BSc Hons 1st class 1960; PhD 1963). FRSE 1993. Research Chemist, ICI Pharmaceuticals, 1963; Manager, Quality Control Dept, 1973–75; Manager, Chemistry Dept, 1975–77; Research Dir, ICI Plant Protection, 1977–86; Business Dir, ICI Seeds, 1985–86; Dep. Chm. and Technical Dir, ICI Pharmaceuticals, 1986–88; Res. and Technol. Dir, ICI Gp, 1989–93; Dir, Zeneca Gp, 1993–99. Dir, AFRC Rothamsted Experimental Station, 1991–98; non-exec. Dir, Oxford Molecular Group PLC, 1997–. Member: ACOST, 1989–93; MRC, 1990–94; Royal Commn on Envmtl Pollution, 1994–98; Central R&D Cttee for NHS, 1995–98; UK Round Table on Sustainable Develt, 1998–. Trustee, Nuffield Foundn, 1998–. Foreign Mem., Royal Swedish Acad. of Engineering Scis, 1990. Liveryman, Salters' Co., 1983. Hon. DSc: Glasgow, 1992; Nottingham, 1993; Dundee, 1995; Sussex, 1996.

Publications: contribs to Chemical Communications and Jl Chem. Soc. *Recreation:* golf. *Address:* Biotechnology and Biological Sciences Research Council, Polaris House, North Star Avenue, Swindon SN2 1UH. *T:* (01793) 413200.

DOYLE, Sir Reginald (Derek Henry), Kt 1989; CBE 1980; HM Chief Inspector of Fire Services, 1987–94; *b* 13 June 1929; *s* of John Henry and Elsie Doyle; *m* 1953, June Margretta (*née* Stringer); two *d. Educ:* Aston Commercial College. RN 1947–54. Fire Brigades, 1954–84; Chief Fire Officer: Worcester City and County, 1973; Hereford and Worcester County, 1974; Kent County, 1977; Home Office Fire Service Inspector, 1984–87. Warden, Guild of Fire Fighters. OStJ 1990. *Recreations:* shooting, swimming, badminton, horses. *Address:* Glebecroft, Marley Road, Harrietsham, Kent ME17 1BS. *T:* (01622) 859259. *Club:* Rotary (Weald of Kent).

DOYLE, Prof. William, DPhil; FBA 1998; FRHistS; Professor of History, University of Bristol, since 1986; *b* 4 March 1942; *s* of Stanley Joseph Doyle and Mary Alice Bielby; *m* 1968, Christine Thomas. *Educ:* Bridlington Sch.; Oriel Coll., Oxford (BA 1964; MA, DPhil 1968). FRHistS 1976. University of York: Asst Lectr, 1967; Lectr, 1969; Sen. Lectr, 1978; Prof. of Modern History, Univ. of Nottingham, 1981–85. Visiting Professor: Univ. of S Carolina, 1969–70; Univ. de Bordeaux III, 1976; Ecole des Hautes Etudes en Sciences Sociales, Paris, 1988; Vis. Fellow, All Souls Coll., Oxford, 1991–92. Dr *hc* Bordeaux, 1987. *Publications:* The Parlement of Bordeaux, 1974; The Old European Order 1660–1800, 1978; Origins of the French Revolution, 1980; The Ancien Régime, 1986; (ed jtly) The Blackwell Dictionary of Historians, 1988; The Oxford History of the French Revolution, 1989; Officers, Nobles and Revolutionaries, 1995; Venality: the sale of offices in eighteenth century France, 1996; (ed jtly) Robespierre, 1999; Jansenism, 1999; La Vénalité, 2000; (ed) Old Regime France, 2001; contribs to Past and Present, Historical Jl, French Historical Studies, Studies on Voltaire, Trans RHistS. *Recreations:* books, decorating, travelling about. *Address:* Department of Historical Studies, University of Bristol, 13 Woodland Road, Bristol BS8 1TB. *T:* (0117) 928 7932; (home) Linden House, College Road, Lansdown, Bath BA1 5RR. *T:* (01225) 314341. *Clubs:* Athenæum, Oxford and Cambridge.

DOYLE, William Patrick, PhD; CIMgt; President/Proprietor, Middle East-Asia Consultants, since 1997; President, Texaco Middle East/Far East, 1991–96; *b* 15 Feb. 1932; *s* of James W. Doyle and Lillian I. Doyle (*née* Kime); *m* 1957, Judith A. Gosha; two *s* one *d* (and one *s* decd). *Educ:* Seattle Univ. (BS 1955); Oregon State Univ. (PhD 1959). CIMgt (FBIM 1980); MInstD 1982. Texaco, USA: Chemist, 1959; Res. Supervisor, 1966; Asst to Vice Pres. of Petrochemicals, 1968; Asst to Sen. Vice Pres. of Supply and Distribn, 1971; Asst Manager, Producing, 1972; Asst Regional Man., Marketing, 1974; Texaco Ltd: Dep. Man. Dir, 1977; Man. Dir, Exploration and Production, 1981; Vice President: Texaco Europe, 1987; Texaco Latin America and Africa, 1989. Pres., UK Offshore Operators Assoc., 1985 (Vice Pres., 1984). Mem. Council, Amer. Geographic Soc., 1994–; Vice Chm., Forum of World Affairs, 1998. *Publications:* contrib. Jl of Amer. Chem. Soc. *Recreations:* tennis, music, theatre. *Address:* 24 Running Brook Lane, New Canaan, CT 06840, USA.

D'OYLY, Sir Hadley Gregory, 15th Bt *cr* 1663, of Shottisham, Norfolk; *b* 29 May 1956; *o s* of Sir Nigel D'Oyly, 14th Bt and Dolores, *d* of R. H. Gregory; *S* father, 2000; *m* 1st, 1978, Margaret May Dent (marr. diss. 1982); 2nd, 1991, Annette Frances Elizabeth (*née* White); one *d. Educ:* Milton Abbey. *Address:* Flat B, 37 New North Road, Islington, N1 6JB.

DRABBLE, Jane; *see* Drabble, M. J.

DRABBLE, Margaret, (Mrs Michael Holroyd), CBE 1980; author; *b* 5 June 1939; 2nd *d* of His Honour J.F. Drabble, QC and late Kathleen Marie Bloor; *m* 1st, 1960, Clive Walter Swift, *qv* (marr. diss. 1975); two *s* one *d*; 2nd, 1982, Michael Holroyd, *qv*. *Educ:* The Mount Sch., York; Newnham Coll., Cambridge. Lives in London and W Somerset. Chm., Nat. Book League, 1980–82 (Dep. Chm., 1978–80). E. M. Forster Award, Amer. Acad. of Arts and Letters, 1973; Hon. Fellow, Sheffield City Polytechnic, 1989. Hon. DLitt: Sheffield, 1976; Manchester, 1987; Keele, 1988; Bradford, 1988; Hull, 1992; UEA, 1994; York, 1995. *Publications:* A Summer Birdcage, 1962; The Garrick Year, 1964; The Millstone, 1966 (filmed, as A Touch of Love, 1969); Wordsworth, 1966; Jerusalem the Golden, 1967; The Waterfall, 1969; The Needle's Eye, 1972; (ed with B. S. Johnson) London Consequences, 1972; Arnold Bennett, a biography, 1974; The Realms of Gold, 1975; (ed) The Genius of Thomas Hardy, 1976; (ed jtly) New Stories 1, 1976; The Ice Age, 1977; For Queen and Country, 1978; A Writer's Britain, 1979; The Middle Ground, 1980; (ed) The Oxford Companion to English Literature, 5th edn, 1985, 6th edn 2000; The Radiant Way, 1987; (ed with Jenny Stringer) The Concise Oxford Companion to English Literature, 1987; A Natural Curiosity, 1989; Safe as Houses, 1989; The Gates of Ivory, 1991; Angus Wilson: a biography, 1995; The Witch of Exmoor, 1996; The Peppered Moth, 2001. *Recreations:* walking, dreaming. *Address:* c/o Peters, Fraser & Dunlop, Drury House, 34–43 Russell Street, WC2B 5HA.

See also R. J. B. Drabble.

DRABBLE, (Mary) Jane, OBE 2000; Director of Education, BBC, 1994–99; *b* 15 Jan. 1947; *d* of Walter Drabble and Molly (*née* Boreham). *Educ:* Bristol Univ. (BA Hons 1968). BBC: Studio Manager, 1968–72; Producer, Radio Current Affairs, 1972–75; Asst Producer, then Producer, TV Current Affairs, 1975–87; Editor, Everyman, 1987–91; Head of Factual Progs, 1993–94, Asst Man. Dir, 1991–94, Network TV. *Recreations:* music, theatre, walking. *Address:* 2 Greenend Road, W4 1AJ.

DRABBLE, Richard John Bloor; QC 1995; *b* 23 May 1950; *s* of His Honour John Frederick Drabble, QC and late Kathleen Marie Drabble; *m* 1980, Sarah Madeleine Hope Lewis; two *s* (and one *s* decd). *Educ:* Leighton Park Sch., Reading; Downing Coll., Cambridge (BA Hons). Called to the Bar, Inner Temple, 1975; Junior Counsel to the Crown, Common Law, 1992. Chm., Administrative Law Bar Assoc., 1999–. *Publications:* contrib. on Social Security to Halsbury's Laws of England, 4th edn; (contrib.) Judicial Review, ed Supperstone and Goudie, 1992, 2nd edn 1997; various articles. *Recreations:* reading, walking. *Address:* 4 Bream's Buildings, EC4A 1AQ. *T:* (020) 7353 5835.

See also Dame A. S. Byatt, M. Drabble.

DRABU, Khurshid Hassan; a Vice President, Immigration Appeal Tribunal, since 2001; *b* Srinagar, Kashmir, 8 March 1946; *o s* of Ghulam Nabi and late Zarifa Nabi Drabu; *m* 1972, Reefat Khurshid Drabu, GP; one *s* three *d. Educ:* Univ. of Jammu and Kashmir (BA Hons 1967); Aligarh Muslim Univ., India (LLB 1st Cl., Gold Medal, 1969). Called to the Bar, Inner Temple, 1977; Counsellor, 1977–84, Dep. Dir, 1984–89, UKIAS; Dep. Legal Dir and Hd of Litigation, CRE, 1990–97; Special Adjudicator, Immigration Appeals, 1997–2000. Part-time Legal Mem., Mental Health Rev. Tribunal, 1987–2000. Advr on Constitutional Affairs, Muslim Council of Britain, 1996–. Founder Trustee, Kashmir Med. Relief Trust UK, 1982–; Chm., Kashmiri Assoc. of GB, 1997–; Chm., Art Asia Trust Ltd, 1996–. Mem., Edtl Bd, Immigration and Nationality, Law and Practice, 1985–89. JP Eastleigh, 1985–98. *Publication:* Mandatory Visas, 1991. *Recreations:* cricket, gardening, photography, travel. *Address:* Hillside, Main Road, Otterbourne, Hants SO21 2HH. *T:* (023) 8026 2471.

DRACE-FRANCIS, Charles David Stephen, CMG 1987; HM Diplomatic Service; High Commissioner to Papua New Guinea, 1997–2000; *b* 15 March 1943; *m* 1967, Griselda Hyacinthe Waldegrave; two *s* one *d. Educ:* Magdalen Coll., Oxford. Third Sec., FO, 1965; Tehran, 1967; Second, later First Sec., FCO, 1971; Asst Political Advr, Hong Kong, 1974; First Sec., Office of UK Rep. to EEC, Brussels, 1978; FCO, 1980; All Souls Coll., Oxford, 1983; Chargé d'affaires, Kabul, 1984; Counsellor, Lisbon, 1987; Govt Affairs Dir, BAe, 1991 (on secondment); Head, West Indian and Atlantic Dept, FCO, 1994–97. *Address:* c/o Foreign and Commonwealth Office, SW1A 2AH.

DRAKE, Sir (Frederick) Maurice, Kt 1978; DFC 1944; a Judge of the High Court of Justice, Queen's Bench Division, 1978–95; *b* 15 Feb. 1923; *o s* of late Walter Charles Drake and Elizabeth Drake; *m* 1954, (Alison) May, *d* of late W. D. Waterfall, CB; two *s* three *d. Educ:* St George's Sch., Harpenden; Exeter Coll., Oxford. MA Hons 1948. Served War of 1939–45 as Navigator, RAF 96 and 255 Nightfighter Squadrons. Called to Bar, Lincoln's Inn, 1950, QC 1968, Bencher, 1976. Dep. Chm., Beds QS, 1966–71; a Recorder of the Crown Court, 1972–78; Dep. Leader, Midland and Oxford Circuit, 1975–78, Presiding Judge, 1979–83. Standing Senior Counsel to RCP, 1972–78. Nominated Judge for appeals from Pensions Appeal Tribunal, 1985–95. Vice-Chm., Parole Bd, England and Wales, 1985–86 (Mem., 1984–86). Treas., Lincoln's Inn, 1997. Chm. Governors, Aldwickbury Prep. Sch. (Trust), 1969–80; Governor, St George's Sch., Harpenden, 1975–79. Hon. Alderman, St Albans DC, 1976–. *Recreations:* music, opera, gardening. *Address:* The White House, West Common Way, Harpenden, Herts AL5 2LH. *T:* (01582) 712329.

DRAKE, Howard Ronald; HM Diplomatic Service; Director, Invest UK-USA (formerly Invest in Britain Bureau USA), and Deputy Consul-General, New York, since 1997; *b* 13 Aug. 1956; *s* of Ronald Henry Drake and late Marie Kathleen Drake; *m* 1988, Gillian Summerfield; one *s* one *d. Educ:* Churcher's Coll., Petersfield. Joined Foreign and Commonwealth Office, 1975; Vice-Consul (Commercial), Los Angeles, 1981–83; Second Sec. (Political), Chile, 1985–88; First Sec., FCO, 1988–92; First Sec. and Head of Chancery, Singapore, 1992–95; Dep. Head, Non-Proliferation Dept, FCO, 1995–97. *Recreations:* cricket, tennis, golf, squash, ski-ing, music. *Address:* c/o Foreign and Commonwealth Office, King Charles Street, SW1A 2AH.

DRAKE, Jack Thomas Arthur H.; *see* Howard-Drake.

DRAKE, John Gair; Chief Registrar and Chief Accountant, Bank of England, 1983–90; *b* 11 July 1930; *s* of John Nutter Drake and Anne Drake; *m* 1957, Jean Pamela Bishop; one *s* one *d. Educ:* University College School; The Queen's College, Oxford. MA. Joined Bank of England, 1953; editor, Quarterly Bulletin, 1971; Asst Chief Cashier, 1973; Management Development Manager, 1974; Dep. Chief, Economic Intell. Dept, 1977; Dep. Chief Cashier and Dep. Chief, Banking Dept, 1980. Governor, South Bank Univ. (formerly Poly.), 1987–96 (Hon. Fellow, 1997). *Address:* 114 Stanstead Road, Caterham, Surrey CR3 6AE. *T:* (01883) 346130. *Clubs:* MCC; Chaldon Cricket; Bletchingly Golf.

DRAKE, Julius Michael; pianist and accompanist; Director, Perth International Chamber Music Festival, Australia, since 2001; *b* 5 April 1959; *s* of Michael and Jean Drake; *m* 1987, Belinda Gow; two *d. Educ:* Purcell Sch.; Royal Coll. of Music (ARCM). Débuts: Wigmore Hall, with Nicholas Daniel, 1983; Paris, with Sally Burgess, 1990; New York, with Derek Lee Ragin, 1991; Tokyo, with Emma Johnson, 1993; since 1983 has appeared regularly at all major concert halls and music fests in Britain and abroad, with Victoria de los Angeles, Thomas Allen, Olaf Bär, Barbara Bonney, Ian Bostridge, Wolfgang Holzmair (incl. Schubert recital tour, USA, 1997), Philip Langridge, Felicity Lott, Benjamin Luxon, etc; has also performed in vocal and instrumental recitals in Amsterdam, Cologne, Edinburgh, Frankfurt, London, NY, Paris, San Francisco, Vienna and Zurich. Devised song recital series: Schumann, S Bank, 1990; Britten, 1995–96, Nineties, 1997–98, Wigmore Hall. Broadcasts include: presenting and performing Complete Songs of Gabriel Fauré (radio), 1994; with Ian Bostridge, Schubert's Winterreise (TV film and documentary), 1997. Recordings incl. Britten Songs, Schumann Myrten op. 25, Howells Complete Songs, French Sonatas, Schubert Lieder, Schumann Lieder, The English Songbook, Sibelius Songs, Gurney Songs, Britten Canticles. Hon. FRAM. Gramophone Award, 1998. *Recreations:* theatre, novels, walking, tennis. *Address:* c/o IMG Artists, 616 Chiswick High Road, W4 5RX. *T:* (020) 8233 5800, *Fax:* (020) 8742 8758.

DRAKE, Madeline Mary; consultant and writer; Chief Executive, Richmond Fellowship, 1995–2001; *b* 5 Oct. 1945; *d* of Ernest and Olive Drake; *m* 1st, 1971, Anthony Gerald Biebuyck (marr. diss.); 2nd, 1983, Prof. Stephen Bernard Torrance; one *s* one *d. Educ:* Birmingham Univ. (BA Hons Russian/French; DipSocSc). Home Office researcher, 1972–73; researcher, Centre for Envmtl Studies, 1973–80; Founder and Dir, Housing and Social Policy Res., 1980–95. Member, Board: Circle Thirty Three Gp, 1976– (Vice-Chm., 1987–94); Shelter, 1987–; Mem. Council, Internat. Year for Shelter for Homeless, 1987. Lectures, broadcasts. FRSA; IPSM. *Publications:* Single and Homeless, 1981; Homelessness: a capital problem, 1984; Managing Hostels, 1986; Housing Associations and 1992, 1992; Europe and 1992, 1992; numerous articles on housing, Europe and the Soviet Union in nat. and internat. jls. *Recreations:* violin, walking, riding, gardening. *Address:* 13 Quernmore Road, N4 4QT.

DRAKE, Sir Maurice; *see* Drake, Sir F. M.

DRAPER, Alan Gregory; Director, Defence Procurement Management Group, Royal Military College of Science, 1988–91; *b* 11 June 1926; *e s* of late William Gregory Draper and Ada Gertrude (*née* Davies); *m* 1st, 1953, Muriel Sylvia Cuss, FRSA (marr. diss.); three *s*; 2nd, 1977, Jacqueline Gubel; one step *d. Educ:* Leeds Grammar Sch.; The Queen's Coll., Oxford (Scholar 1944; MA 1951). RNVR, 1945; Sub-Lt, 1946–47. Admiralty: Asst Principal, 1950; Private Sec. to Civil Lord of the Admiralty, 1953–55; MoD, 1957–60; Head of Polit. Sect., Admiralty 1960–64; First Sec., UK Delegn to NATO, 1964–66; Asst Sec., MoD, 1966; Counsellor, UK Delegn to NATO, 1974–77; Chm., NATO Budget Cttees, 1977–81; Royal Ordnance Factories: Personnel Dir, 1982–84; Dir Gen., Personnel, 1984; Dir, Management/Career Develt, Royal Ordnance plc, 1985; Sen. Lectr, Defence Procurement, RMCS, 1986–91. MIPM 1985. *Publication:* British Involvement in Major European Collaborative Defence Projects: 1957–1987, 1990. *Recreations:* reading, music, walking the dog. *Address:* 75 rue Fernand Piette, 4520 Bas-Oha, Belgium.

DRAPER, Gerald Carter, OBE 1974; Chairman: G. Draper Consultancy, since 1988; Draper Associates Ltd, 1982–88; *b* 24 Nov. 1926; *s* of Alfred Henderson Draper and Mona Violanta (*née* Johnson); *m* 1951, Winifred Lilian Howe; one *s* three *d. Educ:* Univ. of Dublin, Trinity Coll. (MA). FInstM, FCIT. Joined Aer Lingus, 1947; Advertising and PR Manager, 1950; Commercial Man., Central Afr. Airways, 1959; British European Airways: Advertising Man., 1964; Asst Gen. Man. (Market Develt), 1966; Gen. Man. and

Dir, Travel Sales Div., 1970; British Airways: Dir, Travel Div., 1973; Marketing Dir, 1977; Dir, Commercial Ops, 1978; Mem. Bd, 1978–82; Man. Dir, Intercontinental Services Div., 1982. Chairman: British Air Tours Ltd, 1978–82; Silver Wing Surface Arrangements Ltd, 1971–82; Deputy Chairman: Trust Houses Forte Travel Ltd, 1974–82; ALTA Ltd, 1977–82; Hoverspeed, 1984–87; Member Board: Internat. Aeradio Ltd, 1971–82; British Airways Associated Cos Ltd, 1972–82; British Intercontinental Hotels Ltd, 1976–82; Communications Strategy Ltd, 1984–86; AGB Travel Research Internat. Ltd, 1984–86; Centre for Airline and Travel Marketing Ltd, 1986–; BR (Southern Region), 1990–92; British Travel Educnl Trust, 1990–. Chm., Outdoor Advertising Assoc., 1985–92. Mem., Samuel Pepys Club. Master, Co. of Marketors, 1990; Mem., Guild of Freemen, 1991. FRSA 1979. Chevalier de l'Ordre du Tastevin, 1980; Chambellan de l'Ordre des Coteaux de Champagne, 1982. *Recreations:* shooting, golf. *Address:* Old Chestnut, Onslow Road, Burwood Park, Walton-on-Thames, Surrey KT12 5AY; 13B La Frenaie, Cogolin, Var, France. *Clubs:* British Sporting Rifle; Burhill Golf (Weybridge); Clandon Regis Golf.

DRAPER, (John Haydn) Paul; Senior Planning Inspector, Department of Environment, 1977–86, retired; *b* 14 Dec. 1916; *o c* of late Haydn Draper, clarinet player, and Nan Draper; *m* 1941, Nancy Allum (*d* 1998), author and journalist; one *s* one *d* (and one *d* decd). *Educ:* LCC primary sch.; Bancroft's Sch.; University Coll. London. Engr in Post Office, 1939–48; Royal Signals, Signalman to Major, Middle East, N Africa, Sicily, NW Europe (despatches), 1940–46; MoT, 1948–64 and 1968–70; Jt Principal Private Sec. to Minister, 1956–58; Asst Sec., 1959; Counsellor (Shipping), British Embassy, Washington, 1964–67; BoT, 1967–68; Under-Sec., 1968; DoE, 1970–74; Senior Planning Inspector, 1973–74; Resident Chm., Civil Service Selection Bd, 1975–76. *Address:* 24 Gordon Mansions, Huntley Street, WC1E 7HF.

DRAPER, Michael William; Under Secretary, Department of Health and Social Security, 1976–78, retired; *b* 26 Sept. 1928; *s* of late John Godfrey Beresford Draper and Aileen Frances Agatha Draper (*née* Masefield); *m* 1952, Theodora Mary Frampton, *o d* of late Henry James Frampton, CSI, CIE; one *s* two *d*. *Educ:* St Edward's Sch., Oxford. FCA. Chartered Accountant, 1953; various posts in England, Ireland, Burma, Nigeria, Unilever Ltd, 1953–64; joined Civil Service, 1964; Principal, Min. of Power, 1964; Asst Sec., DHSS, 1972–76. Sec., Diocese of Bath and Wells, 1978–88; mem. of staff team, Lamplugh House, Christian Renewal Conf. Centre, 1988–89; working with Anglican Church in Zambia, 1991; associated with Sharing of Ministries Abroad, 1992–2000. *Recreations:* mountain walking, church affairs. *Address:* 21 Kent Park Avenue, Kendal, Cumbria LA9 5JT.

DRAPER, Paul; *see* Draper, J. H. P.

DRAPER, Peter Sydney, CB 1994; Member, Civil Service Appeal Board, since 1996; Principal Establishment and Finance Officer, Property Services Agency, Department of the Environment, 1993–95; *b* 18 May 1935; *s* of late Sydney George Draper and Norah Draper; *m* 1959, Elizabeth Ann (*née* French); three *s*. *Educ:* Haberdashers' Aske's; Regent Polytechnic Sch. of Management (Dip. in Management Studies). AMBIM 1966. Joined GCHQ, Cheltenham, 1953; Min. of Transport, 1956–70; Principal, 1969; Department of the Environment, 1970–95: Directorate of Estate Management Overseas, PSA, 1970; Asst Sec., 1975; Head of Staff Resources Div., 1975–78, Asst Dir, Home Regional Services, 1978–80; RCDS, 1981; Dir, Eastern Reg., 1982–84, Under Sec., Dir of Defence Services II, 1985–87, Principal Establishment Officer, 1987–93, PSA. *Recreations:* gardening, golf, walking. *Address:* Langdale, 22 Brewery Road, Pampisford, Cambs CB2 4EN. *Club:* Saffron Walden Golf.

DRAPER, Prof. Ronald Philip, PhD; Regius Chalmers Professor of English, University of Aberdeen, 1986–94, now Professor Emeritus; *b* 3 Oct. 1928; *s* of Albert William and Elsie Draper; *m* 1950, Irene Margaret Aldridge; three *d*. *Educ:* Univ. of Nottingham (BA, PhD). Educn Officer, RAF, 1953–55. Lectr in English, Univ. of Adelaide, 1955–56; Lectr, Univ. of Leicester, 1957–68, Sen. Lectr, 1968–73; Prof., Univ. of Aberdeen, 1973–86. *Dramatic scripts:* (with P. A. W. Collins) The Canker and the Rose, Mermaid Theatre, 1964; (with Richard Hoggart) D. H. L., A Portrait of D. H. Lawrence, Nottingham Playhouse, 1967 (televised 1980). *Publications:* D. H. Lawrence, 1964, 3rd edn 1984; (ed) D. H. Lawrence, The Critical Heritage, 1970, 3rd edn 1986; (ed) Hardy, The Tragic Novels, 1975, rev. edn 1991; (ed) George Eliot, The Mill on the Floss and Silas Marner, 1977, 3rd edn 1984; (ed) Tragedy, Developments in Criticism, 1980; Lyric Tragedy, 1985; The Winter's Tale, Text and Performance, 1985; (ed) Hardy, Three Pastoral Novels, 1987; (ed) The Literature of Region and Nation, 1989; (with Martin Ray) An Annotated Critical Bibliography of Thomas Hardy, 1989; (ed) The Epic: developments in criticism, 1990; (ed with P. Mallett) A Spacious Vision: essays on Hardy, 1994; An Introduction to Twentieth-Century Poetry in English, 1999; Shakespeare: the comedies, 2000; articles and reviews in Archiv für das Studium der Neueren Sprachen und Literaturen, Critical Qly, Essays in Criticism, Etudes Anglaises, English Studies, Jl of D. H. Lawrence Soc., Lit. of Region and Nation, Longman Critical Essays, MLR, New Lit. Hist., Notes and Queries, Revue des Langues Vivantes, Rev. of English Studies, Shakespeare Qly, Studies in Short Fiction, THES, Thomas Hardy Annual, Thomas Hardy Jl. *Recreations:* reading, listening to music. *Address:* Maynestay, Chipping Campden, Glos GL55 6DJ. *T:* (01386) 840796.

DRAYCOTT, Gerald Arthur; a Recorder of the Crown Court, 1972–86; *b* 25 Oct. 1911; *s* of Arthur Henry Seely Draycott and Maud Mary Draycott; *m* 1939, Phyllis Moyra Evans; two *s* one *d*. *Educ:* King Edward's Sch., Stratford-on-Avon. FCII. Called to Bar, Middle Temple, 1938. Served in RAF, 1939–46 (Sqdn Ldr; despatches). Practised at Bar, SE Circuit, 1946–90; Dep. Recorder, Bury St Edmunds and Great Yarmouth, 1966–72. Chairman: Eastern Rent Assessment Panel, 1965–77; Nat. Insurance Tribunal, Norwich, 1970–84; E Anglia Med. Appeal Tribunal, 1978–84. *Address:* Nethergate House, Saxlingham Nethergate, Norwich NR15 1PB. *T:* (01508) 498306.

DRAYSON, Robert Quested, DSC 1943; MA; *b* 5 June 1919; *s* of late Frederick Louis Drayson and late Elsie Mabel Drayson; *m* 1943, Rachel, 2nd *d* of Stephen Spencer Jenkyns; one *s* two *d*. *Educ:* St Lawrence Coll., Ramsgate; Downing Coll., Cambridge. Univ. of Cambridge: 1938–39, 1946–47; History Tripos, BA 1947, MA 1950. Served RNVR, 1939–46; Lieut in command HM Motor Torpedo Boats. Asst Master and Housemaster, St Lawrence Coll., 1947–50; Asst Master, Felsted Sch., 1950–55; Headmaster, Reed's Sch., Cobham, 1955–63; Headmaster of Stowe, 1964–79; Resident Lay Chaplain to Bishop of Norwich, 1979–84; Lay Reader, 1979. Member: HMC Cttee, 1973–75 (Chm., Midland Div., 1974–75); Council, McAlpine Educnl Endowments Ltd, 1979–97; Allied Schools Council, 1980–94; Gen. Council, S Amer. Missionary Soc., 1980–96 (Chm. Selection Cttee, 1980–95); Scholarship Cttee, Indep. Schs Travel Assoc., 1982–; Martyrs' Meml and C of E Trust, 1983–94. Treas., Swifts Sports Trust, 1988–. Chm. of Govs, Riddlesworth Hall, 1980–84; Governor: Parkside, 1958–63; Beachborough, 1965–79; Bilton Grange, 1966–79; Beechwood Park, 1967–79; Monkton Combe, 1976–85; Felixstowe Coll., 1981–84; Vice President: Reed's Sch., 1991–; St Lawrence Coll., 1993– (Gov., 1977–93). Chm., E Sussex Coastal Forces Veterans Assoc., 2000. FRSA 1968. *Recreations:* formerly hockey (Cambridge Blue, 1946, 1947; Kent XI (Captain), 1947–56; England Final Trial, 1950); now golf, walking, watching cricket. *Address:* Three Gables, Linkhill, Sandhurst, Cranbrook, Kent TN18 5PQ. *T:* (01580) 850447. *Clubs:* Hawks (Cambridge); Acrostics; Rye Golf; Band of Brothers.

See also G. M. Pugh.

DREHER, Derek; Consultant, Northern Ireland Office, since 1997; *b* 12 Jan. 1938; *s* of Frederick Charles Dreher and Mary Emily Dreher (*née* Rutherford); *m* 1961, Patricia Audrey Dowsett; one *s* one *d*. *Educ:* Roan Grammar Sch., Greenwich. Joined War Office as Exec. Officer, 1956; Nat. Service, RAF, 1956–58 (trained as Russian linguist); with War Office, 1958–64, then MoD: postings include: Cyprus, 1962–65; NI, 1969–71; on secondment to Treasury, 1976–79; Asst Sec., 1980; Asst Under Sec. of State, 1992–97. *Recreations:* all forms of sport, but particularly tennis, theatre, foreign travel, reading, particularly political works. *Address:* Kantara, Church Road, Hartley, Kent DA3 8DL. *Club:* Hartley Country.

DREW, David Elliott; MP (Lab and Co-op) Stroud, since 1997; *b* 13 April 1952; *s* of Ronald Montague Drew and late Maisie Joan Drew; *m* 1990, Anne Baker, *d* of Brian and Sheila Baker; two *s* two *d*. *Educ:* Kingsfield Sch., Glos; Nottingham Univ. (BA Hons 1974); Birmingham Univ. (PGCE 1976); Bristol Poly., later UWE (MA 1988; MEd 1994). Teacher: Princethorpe Coll., Warwicks, 1976–78; St Michael's Sch., Stevenage, 1978–82; Maidenhill Sch., Glos, 1982–85; Dene Magna Sch., Glos, 1985–86; Sen. Lectr, Bristol Poly., later UWE, 1986–97. Member: Stevenage BC, 1981–82; Stroud DC, 1987–95; Stonehouse Town Council, 1987–; Glos CC, 1993–97. Contested (Lab) Stroud, 1992. *Address:* House of Commons, SW1A 0AA.

DREW, David Ernest; Character Principal Dancer, Royal Ballet, since 1974; choreographer; *b* London, 12 March 1938; *s* of Thomas Ernest Drew and Phyllis Adelaide (*née* Talbot-Tindale); *m* 1st, 1962, Avril Bergen (marr. diss. 1973); one *s*; 2nd, 1985, June Ritchie; one step *d*. *Educ:* Bristol Grammar Sch.; Westbury Sch. of Dancing, Bristol; Royal Ballet Upper Sch. Nat. Service, commnd RCS, 1958–60. Joined Royal Ballet at Royal Opera House, Covent Gdn, 1955: Soloist, 1961; Prin. Dancer, 1974; *created rôles* with Royal Ballet include: Bay Middleton, Mayerling; Demetrius, The Dream; Max Merx, Isadora; Celestial, Shadow-Play; Gaoler, Manon; The Master, Rituals; The Captain, Different Drummer; Leading Baboon, Prince of the Pagodas; G. B. Shaw, Grand Tour; Giles, The Crucible; *major rôles* include: Von Rothbart, Swan Lake; Monsieur G. M., Manon; Hilarion and Duke of Courtland, Giselle; Thomas, La Fille Mal Gardée; Catalabutte and King, Sleeping Beauty; Mercutio, Lord Capulet and Tybalt, Romeo and Juliet; Ugly Sister, Cinderella; Ivan and Kostchei, The Firebird; Mrs Pettitoes, Tales of Beatrix Potter; Armand's Father, Marguerite and Armand; Rajah and Brahmin, La Bayadère; *choreographic work* includes: five ballets for Sadlers Wells Royal Ballet: Intrusion, 1969; From Waking Sleep, 1970; St Thomas' Wake, 1971; Sacred Circles, 1972; Sword of Alsace, 1973; *musicals* include: Canterbury Tales, 1968; His Monkey Wife, 1970; *operas* include: Dido and Aeneas; Macbeth; Die Fledermaus; also contribs to theatre and TV. Teacher, Royal Ballet Upper Sch., Pas de Deux at all levels, incl. Grad. Class, 1976–99; assisted in Direction of Choreographic Composition Course, 1986–99. Gold Medal, Royal Acad. of Dancing, 1954. *Recreations:* writing, gardening, theatre, art, photography, playing and inventing games. *Address:* c/o Royal Opera House, Covent Garden, WC2 9DD.

DREW, Dorothy Joan; a Vice President, Immigration Appeal Tribunal, since 2000; *b* 31 March 1938; *d* of late Francis Marshall Gant and Wilhelmina Frederica Gant (*née* Dunster); *m* 1959, Patrick K. Drew; two *s* one *d*. *Educ:* Sch. of St Helen and St Katharine; Univ. of London (LLB ext.). Called to the Bar, Gray's Inn, 1981; Chm. (pt-time), Social Security Appeal Tribunal, 1986–92; Adjudicator, Immigration Appeal Tribunal, 1989–93 (Special Adjudicator, 1993–2000); Regl Adjudicator, Hatton Cross, 1998–2000; Chm., Child Support Appeal Tribunal, 1993–94. JP Reading, 1975–95. *Recreations:* music, theatre, family and friends, walking in Cornwall. *Address:* Handpost, Swallowfield, Berks RG7 1PU.

DREW, Joanna Marie, CBE 1985; Director, Hayward and Regional Exhibitions, South Bank Centre, 1987–92; *b* Naini Tal, India, 28 Sept. 1929; *d* of Brig. Francis Greville Drew, CBE, and Sannie Frances Sands. *Educ:* Dartington Hall; Edinburgh Univ. (MA Hons Fine Art); Edinburgh Coll. of Art (DA). Arts Council of GB, 1952–88: Asst Dir of Exhibns, 1970; Dir of Exhibns, 1975; Dir of Art, 1978–86. Mem. Council, RCA, 1979–82. Officier: l'Ordre des Arts et Lettres, 1988 (Chevalier, 1979); l'Ordre Nat. du Mérite, 1994 (Chevalier, 1990).

DREW, John Sydney Neville; Chairman, Durham Research Institute (formerly Director, Research Institute for the Study of Change), and Visiting Professor of European Business, University of Durham, since 1995; Director, Change Group International, since 1996; *b* 7 Oct. 1936; *s* of late John William Henry Drew and Kathleen Marjorie (*née* Wright); *m* 1962, Rebecca Margaret Amanda (*née* Usher); two *s* one *d*. *Educ:* King Edward's Sch., Birmingham; St John's Coll., Oxford (MA); Fletcher School of Law and Diplomacy, Tufts Univ. (AM). Sloan Fellow of London Business Sch., 1971. 2nd Lieut, Somerset LI, 1955–57. HM Diplomatic Service, 1960–73: Third Sec., Paris, 1962; MECAS, 1964; Second Sec., Kuwait, 1965; First Sec., Budapest, 1968; FCO, 1970; Dir of Marketing and Exec. Programmes, London Business Sch., 1973–79; Dir of Internat. Corporate Affairs, Rank Xerox, 1979–84; Dir of European Affairs, Touche Ross Internat., 1984–86; Head of UK Offices, EEC, 1987–93; Dir, Europa Times, 1993–94; Dep. Chm., ESG, 1993–95. Associate Fellow, Templeton Coll., Oxford, 1982–86; Visiting Professor of European Management: Imperial Coll. of Science and Technology, 1987–91; Open Univ., 1993–96. Special Advr, Howlands Trust, Durham Univ., 1994–95. Chm., DSL Ltd, 1995–97. President: Inst. of Linguists, 1993–99 (Hon. FIL 1993); European Transpersonal Assoc., 1998–. Trustee, Thomson Foundn, 1996–. Hon. Editor, European Business Jl, 1987–. Hon. MBA Univ. of Northumbria, 1991. *Publications:* Doing Business in the European Community, 1979, 3rd edn 1991 (trans. Spanish and Portuguese 1987); Networking in Organisations, 1986; (ed) Readings in International Enterprise, 1995, 2nd edn 1999; articles on European integration and management development. *Recreations:* travel, personal development, golf. *Address:* 49 The Ridgeway, NW11 8QP. *Club:* Oxford and Cambridge.

DREW, Peter Robert Lionel, OBE 1979; Hon. Director, World Trade Centers Association, New York, since 1992; Chairman, Taylor Woodrow Group of Companies, 1989–92; *b* 4 Sept. 1927; *s* of Edith Mary Drew (*née* Ball) and Sydney Herbert Drew; *m* 1st, 1952, June Durham; one *s* one *d*; 2nd, 1966, Monica Margaret Mary Allman (marr. diss. 1993); one *d*; 3rd, 1993, Wendy Ferris. *Educ:* Kingston College (Dip. Eng., later Architecture). Helicopter research, Don Juan de la Cierva enterprise, 1949; archit. studies and practice, London, 1951; started housing co., Lytham St Anne's, for Sir Lindsay Parkinson & Co., 1954; Willetts and Bernard Sunley Investment Trust, 1962–90; Taylor Woodrow Property Co., 1965, Dir, 1979–92; Founder Chm., St Katharine by the Tower Ltd (pioneer, London Docks redevelt), 1970–92; founded World Trade Centre, London, 1973. Chm. and Vice-Pres., internat. WTCA movement, 1974–89; Pres., London World

Trade Centre Assoc., 1985–89. Dir, Develt Bd, 1990–, Gov., 1992–2000, Museum of London; Trustee, Silver Jubilee Walkway Trust, 1977–. Gov., Sadler's Wells, 1990–95. CIMgt (CBIM 1990). FRSA. Church Warden, All Hallows by the Tower, 1972–94; Quaker, Bury Meeting House, 1997–. Founder Liveryman, Worshipful Co. of World Traders, 2000– (first Master; Guild of World Traders, 1982; Co. of World Traders, 1993); Liveryman, Painter-Stainers' Co., 1984–; Freeman, Co. of Watermen and Lightermen, 1975. *Publications:* Buy Your Own Home!, 1957; papers on world trade and urban renewal. *Recreations:* water colour painting, sailing, public speaking. *Address:* 18 Westgate Street, Bury St Edmunds, Suffolk IP33 1QG. *T:* (01284) 725990; 43 Trinity Square, EC3N 4DJ.

DREW, Philippa Catherine, CB 2001; Director for Education, Training, Arts and Sport, Department for Culture, Media and Sport, since 1999; *b* 11 May 1946; *d* of Sir Arthur Charles Walter Drew, KCB and Rachel Anna Drew (*née* Lambert). *Educ:* St Paul's Girls' Sch.; St Anne's Coll., Oxford (MA Hons 1968 PPE); Univ. of Pennsylvania (MA Hons 1969 Internat. Relations). Foreign and Commonwealth Office: Central and Southern Africa Dept, 1969; New Delhi, 1970–74; First Sec., S Asia Dept, 1974–75; Home Office: EEC Referendum Count Unit, 1975; Criminal Dept, 1975–78; Police Dept, 1978–81; Gen. Dept, 1981–84; Prison Dept, 1984–85; Field Dir, SCF, Nepal, 1985–87; Head, Probation Service Div., 1987–91; Dir of Custody, HM Prison Service, 1992–95; Dir, Personnel and Office Services, then Corporate Resources, Home Office, 1995–99. *Recreations:* opera, travel, talk. *Address:* Department for Culture, Media and Sport, 2–4 Cockspur Street, SW1Y 5DH.

See also J. R. Bretherton.

DREWIENKIEWICZ, Maj.-Gen. Karol John, CB 1998; CMG 2000; consultant, peace support operations; Senior Army Member, Royal College of Defence Studies, 1999–2000, retired 2001; *b* 2 Jan. 1946; *s* of late Wojciech Drewienkiewicz and of Barbara Drewienkiewicz; *m* 1970, Christine Elizabeth Bailey; two *s*. *Educ:* Stamford Sch.; RMA, Sandhurst; Sidney Sussex Coll., Cambridge (BA 1970; MA 1974). Commnd RE, 1966; Staff Coll., Camberley, 1978 and 1985; CO, 22 Engr Regt, 1985–88; Sec. to UK Chiefs of Staff, MoD, 1988–90; Comdr, RE Trng Bde, 1990–91; RCDS 1992; Dir of Manning, Army, 1993–94; Engr-in-Chief, Army, 1994–95; Dir of Support, HQ Allied Land Forces, Central Europe, 1995–96; COS HQ IFOR/SFOR (Sarajevo), 1996–97; Comdg Gen., SFOR Support Comd (Zagreb), May–Aug. 1997; Dir of Support, HQ Allied Land Forces, Central Europe, Sept.–Dec. 1997; Mil. Advr to High Representative, Sarajevo, 1998; Dep. Hd of Mission, OSCE Kosovo Verification Mission, 1998–99. *Publication:* Training the Territorial Army in 1939 and 1940, 1992. *Recreations:* military history, wargaming, gardening. *Address:* c/o Cox's & Kings, 7 Pall Mall, SW1Y 5NA. *Club:* Army and Navy.

DREWITT, (Lionel) Frank; Managing Director, Harrods Ltd, 1984–87; *b* 24 Sept. 1932; *s* of William and Jeanne Drewitt; *m* 1959, Doris Else Heybrok; three *d*. *Educ:* London Univ. (BSc Econ). FCA. National Service, 1951–53. Wells & Partners, later Thornton Baker, 1956–64; Chartered Accountant, 1961; joined Harrods Store group, 1964; positions incl. Asst Internal Auditor, Chief Accountant, Company Sec., Asst Man. Dir. *Recreation:* cottages. *Address:* 23 Hertford Avenue, East Sheen, SW14 8EF. *T:* (020) 8876 9348.

DREWRY, Dr David John; Vice-Chancellor, University of Hull, since 1999; *b* 22 Sept. 1947; *s* of late Norman Tidman Drewry and Mary Edwina Drewry (*née* Wray); *m* 1971, Gillian Elizabeth (*née* Holbrook). *Educ:* Havelock School, Grimsby; Queen Mary Coll., Univ. of London (BSc 1st cl. hons 1969; Hon. Fellow, QMW, 1992); Emmanuel College, Cambridge (PhD 1973). FRGS 1972. UK-US Antarctic Expdns, 1969–70 and 1971–72; Sir Henry Strakosh Fellow, 1974; UK-US Antarctic Expdns, 1974–75, 1977–78 (leader), 1978–79 (leader); Sen. Asst in Research, Univ. of Cambridge, 1978–83; leader, UK-Norwegian Svalbard Expdns, 1980, 1983, 1985, 1986; Asst Dir of Research, Univ. of Cambridge, 1983; Director: Scott Polar Res. Inst., Univ. of Cambridge, 1984–87; British Antarctic Survey, 1987–94; Sci. and Technol., NERC, 1994–98; Dir Gen., British Council, 1998. Vis. Fellow, Green Coll., Oxford, 1995; Vis. Prof., QMW, 1996–98; Vis. Scholar, Univ. of Cambridge, 1999. Vice-President: Council, RGS, 1990–93 (Mem., 1986–93 and 1995–96); Council, Internat. Glaciological Soc., 1990–96 (Mem., 1980–82); Member: Council of Managers, Nat. Antarctic Programmes, 1988–95 (Chm., 1988–91); Royal Soc. Interdisciplinary Scientific Cttee on Antarctic Res., 1990–98; Internat. Arctic Sci. Cttee, 1994– (Pres., 1997–); Exec. Council, ESF, 1996–98 (Mem., Eur. Polar Bd); Trustee, Antarctic Heritage Trust, 1993–. UK alternate deleg., Sci. Cttee on Antarctic Res., 1985–97. FRSA 1998. Hon. DSc: Robert Gordon, 1993; Humberside, 1994; Anglia Poly. Univ., 1998. US Antarctic Service Medal, 1979; Cuthbert Peek Award, 1979, Patron's Medal, 1998, RGS; Polar Medal, 1986; Prix de la Belgica Gold Medal, Royal Acad. of Belgium, 1995. *Publications:* Antarctica: glaciological and geophysical folio, 1983; Glacial Geologic Processes, 1986; papers on polar glaciology, geophysics, remote sensing science policy in learned jls. *Recreations:* music, skiing, walking, gastronomy. *Address:* University of Hull, Hull HU6 7RX. *Club:* Geographical.

DREYER, Adm. Sir Desmond (Parry), GCB 1967 (KCB 1963; CB 1960); CBE 1957; DSC; JP; DL; *b* 6 April 1910; *yr s* of late Adm. Sir Frederic Dreyer, GBE, KCB; *m* 1st, 1934, Elisabeth (*d* 1958), *d* of late Sir Henry Chilton, GCMG; one *s* one *d* (and one *s* decd); 2nd, 1959, Marjorie Gordon (*d* 1997), *widow* of Hon. R. G. Whiteley. Served War of 1939–45 (DSC). Cdre First Class, 1955. Chief of Staff, Mediterranean, 1955–57; Asst Chief of Naval Staff, 1958–59; Flag Officer (Flotillas) Mediterranean, 1960–61; Flag Officer Air (Home), 1961–62; Comdr, Far East Fleet, 1962–65; Second Sea Lord, 1965–67; Chief Adviser (Personnel and Logistics) to Sec. of State for Defence, 1967–68. Principal Naval ADC to the Queen, 1965–68. Gentleman Usher to the Sword of State, 1973–80. Member: Nat. Bd for Prices and Incomes, 1968–71; Armed Forces Pay Review Body, 1971–79. President: RN Benevolent Trust, 1970–78; Officers' Pension Soc., 1978–84; Regular Forces Employment Assoc., 1978–82; Not Forgotten Assoc., 1973–91. JP 1968, High Sheriff, 1977–78, DL 1985, Hants. *Recreations:* fishing, golf. *Address:* Brook Cottage, Cheriton, near Alresford, Hants SO24 0QA. *T:* (01962) 771215. *Club:* Army and Navy.

DREYFUS, John Gustave, FIOP; typographical consultant and historian; *b* 15 April 1918; *s* of late Edmond and Marguerite Dreyfus; *m* 1948, Irène Thurnauer; two *d* (one *s* decd). *Educ:* Oundle Sch.; Trinity Coll., Cambridge (MA). FIOP 1977. Served War, Army, 1939–45. Joined Cambridge University Press as graduate trainee, 1939; Asst Univ. Printer, 1949–56; Typographical Adviser, 1956–82; Typographical Adviser to Monotype Corp., 1955–82; European Consultant to Limited Editions Club, USA, 1956–77; Dir, Curwen Press, 1970–82; Sandars Reader in Bibliography, Univ. of Cambridge, 1979–80. Helped plan exhibn, Printing and the Mind of Man, 1963 (also designed catalogues). President: Assoc. Typographique Internationale, 1968–73 (organised internat. congresses for Assoc.); Printing Historical Soc., 1991 (org. Caxton Internat. Congress, 1976). FRSA. Sir Thomas More Award, Univ. of San Francisco, 1979; Laureate, Amer. Printing Historical Soc., 1984; Frederic W. Goudy Award, Rochester Inst. of Technology, NY, 1984; Gutenberg Prize, Mainz, 1996. *Publications:* The Survival of Baskerville's Punches, 1949; The Work of Jan van Krimpen, 1952; (ed series) Type Specimen Facsimiles, 1963–71; Italic Quartet, 1966; (ed with François Richaudeau) La Chose Imprimée (French encyc. on printing), 1977; A History of the Nonesuch Press, 1981; French Eighteenth Century Typography, 1982; A Typographical Masterpiece, 1990; Into Print, 1994; contrib. The Library. *Recreations:* travel, theatre-going. *Address:* 38 Lennox Gardens, SW1X 0DH. *T:* (020) 7584 3510. *Club:* Garrick.

DREYFUS, Prof. Laurence, PhD; Professor of Performance Studies in Music, since 1992 and Thurston Dart Professor of Performance Studies in Music, since 1996, King's College, London; *b* Boston, Mass, 28 July 1952. *Educ:* studied 'cello with Leonard Rose, Juilliard Sch.; Yeshiva Univ. (BA Pol Sci. 1973); Columbia Univ. (MA 1975, MPhil 1976, PhD 1980, in Musicology); studied viola da gamba with Wieland Kuijken, Royal Conservatory, Brussels, 1979–81 (Premier Prix, 1980; Diplôme supérieur, 1981). Lectr, Univ. of Wisconsin-Madison, 1979; Mellon Fellow in Humanities, Columbia Univ., 1979–81; Asst Prof., Washington Univ. in St Louis, 1981–82; Asst Prof., 1982–88, Associate Prof. of History of Music and Sen. Faculty Fellow, 1988–89, Yale Univ.; Associate Professor of Music: Univ. of Chicago, 1989–90; Stanford Univ., 1990–93; King's College, London: Prof., Centre for Advanced Performance Studies, 1992–95; Hd, Dept of Music, 1995–99. *Appearances* include: Berkeley Early Music Fest., 1990, 1992; Bergen Fest., Norway, 1990; Early Music Network tour of GB, 1990; Utrecht Early Music Fest., 1991; San Francisco SO, 1992; Skálholt Music Fest., Iceland, 1992–95; London Bach Fest., 1993, 1994. Dir-at-Large, Amer. Musicol Soc., 1989–91 (Otto Kinkeldey Prize, 1997); Vice-Pres., Amer. Bach Soc., 1992–94; Mem. Council, RMA, 1994–98. Hon. RAM 1995. First Prize, Bodky Competition in Early Music, Boston, 1978. Several solo and chamber recordings; Gramophone award for best baroque instrumental recording, 1997. Jt Gen. Ed., Musical Performance and Reception, 1994–. *Publications:* Bach's Continuo Group: players and practices in his vocal works, 1987; Bach and the Patterns of Invention, 1996; (contrib.) The Cambridge Companion to Bach, 1997; papers, and articles in jls. *Address:* Department of Music, King's College London, Strand, WC2R 2LS. *T:* (020) 7873 2392, *Fax:* (020) 7873 2326.

DRIELSMA, Claude Dunbar H.; *see* Hankes Drielsma.

DRIFE, Prof. James Owen, MD; FRCOG, FRCSE, FRCPE; Professor of Obstetrics and Gynaecology, University of Leeds, since 1990; *b* 8 Sept. 1947; *s* of late Thomas Drife and Rachel Drife (*née* Jones); *m* 1973, Diana Elizabeth, *d* of Ronald Haxton Girdwood, *qv*; one *s* one *d*. *Educ:* Cumnock Acad.; Univ. of Edinburgh (BSc Hons; MB ChB 1971; MD 1982). FRCPE 1998. Hosp. appts, Edinburgh, 1971–79; MRC Res. Fellow in Reproductive Biology, Edinburgh, 1974–76; Lectr in Obst. and Gyn., Univ. of Bristol, 1979–82; Dept of Surgery, Frenchay Hosp., Bristol, 1980–81; Sen. Lectr, Obst. and Gyn., Univ. of Leicester, 1982–90. Non-Exec. Dir, United Leeds Teaching Hosps NHS Trust, 1991–98. Mem., Cases Cttee, Medical Protection Soc., 1985–94; Assessor for England, Enquiries into Maternal Deaths, 1992–; Mem., Midwifery Cttee, UKCC, 1993–99; Mem. Council, RCOG, 1993– (Convenor of Study Gp, 1989–92; Chm., Liby Cttee, 1994–97; Jun. Vice-Pres., 1998–2001); Mem., GMC, 1994–. FRSA 1997. Hon. FASPOG, 1988; Hon. Fellow, Amer. Gynecol and Obstetrical Soc., 1998; Hon. Mem., Jordanian Soc. of Obstetricians and Gynaecologists, 2000. Editor or co-editor, obst. and gyn. jls, 1985–. *Publications:* Dysfunctional Uterine Bleeding and Menorrhagia, 1989; (jtly) Micturition, 1990;(with J. Studd) HRT and Osteoporosis, 1990; (with D. Donnai) Antenatal Diagnosis of Fetal Abnormalities, 1991; (with A. Calder) Prostaglandins and the Uterus, 1992; (with A. Templeton) Infertility, 1992; (with D. Baird) Contraception, 1993; The Benefits and Risks of Oral Contraceptives, 1994; (with J. J. Walker) Caesarean Section, 2001; contribs to BMJ. *Recreations:* songwriting, theatregoing, visiting the pub with wife. *Address:* School of Medicine, Clarendon Wing, Belmont Grove, Leeds LS2 9NS. *T:* (0113) 292 3888. *Clubs:* Athenæum, National Liberal, Royal Society of Medicine.

DRING, Richard Paddison; Editor of Official Report (Hansard), House of Commons, 1972–79; *b* 6 Nov. 1913; *s* of late Fred Dring and late Florence Hasleham Dring, East Sheen; *m* 1939, Joan Wilson (*d* 1999); one *s*; *m* 2000, Margaret Forde. *Educ:* St Paul's School. Captain, RAOC during the War, serving in Europe and later in India with IA. Herts Advertiser, 1932; Press Association, 1936; Official Report (Hansard), House of Commons, 1940: Asst Editor, 1954; Dep. Editor, 1970. *Recreation:* golf. *Address:* 24 Vicarage Drive, SW14 8RX. *T:* (020) 8876 2162. *Club:* Richmond Golf.

DRINKALL, John Kenneth, CMG 1973; HM Diplomatic Service, retired; High Commissioner to Jamaica, and Ambassador (non-resident) to Haiti, 1976–81; *b* 1 Jan. 1922; *m* 1961, Patricia Ellis; two *s* two *d*. *Educ:* Haileybury Coll.; Brasenose Coll., Oxford. Indian Army, 1942–45. Entered HM Foreign Service, 1947; 3rd Sec., Nanking, 1948; Vice-Consul, Tamsui, Formosa, 1949–51; Acting Consul, 1951; Foreign Office, 1951–53; 1st Sec., Cairo, 1953–56; Foreign Office, 1957–60; 1st Sec., Brasilia, 1960–62; Foreign Office, 1962–65. Appointed Counsellor, 1964; Counsellor: Nicosia, Cyprus, 1965–67; British Embassy, Brussels, 1967–70; FCO, 1970–71; Canadian Nat. Defence Coll., 1971–72; Ambassador to Afghanistan, 1972–76. *Recreations:* lawn tennis, golf, racquets and squash. *Address:* 68 Rivermead Court, Ranelagh Gardens, SW6 3RZ. *Clubs:* Hurlingham, All England Lawn Tennis.

DRINKWATER, Surgeon Rear-Adm. John Brian, FRCS; Clinical Medical Officer, Community Child Health, Mid Argyll, Kintyre, Islay and Jura, 1989–97; *b* 5 June 1931; *s* of Ellis Drinkwater and Hilda May Drinkwater; *m* 1958, Rosalind Joy Taylor; two *d*; *m* 1986, Carole Anne Coutts; two *d*. *Educ:* Henry Mellish Grammar Sch., Nottingham; Sheffield Univ. Med. Sch. (MB, ChB). FRCS 1961. House appts, 1954–55; joined RN 1955: SMO, 6th FS (Cyprus, Suez), 1955–57; RN Hosp., Haslar, 1957; Hammersmith Hosp., 1961; HMS Ganges, 1962; RN Hosps, Malta, Gibraltar, Plymouth, Haslar, 1962–67; Gt Ormond St Hosp., 1967; Consultant Surgeon, RN Hosps, 1968–82; Advr in Surgery, 1981–82; Dir of Medical Orgn, 1982–83; MO i/c RN Hosp., Haslar, 1983–84; QHS 1983–87; Dep. Med. Dir Gen. (Naval), 1984; Surgeon Rear-Adm. (Operational Med. Services), 1985–87; Dir of Support Services, Muscular Dystrophy Gp, 1987–88. Member: British Soc. for Digestive Endoscopy, 1972; British Soc. of Gastroenterology, 1980–83. FRSM 1961; Fellow, Assoc. of Surgeons, 1974. OStJ 1983. *Recreations:* music, bridge. *Address:* c/o HSBC, 567 Fulham Road, SW6 1EX.

DRINKWATER, Sir John (Muir), Kt 1988; QC 1972; a Commissioner of Income Tax, since 1983; *b* 16 March 1925; *s* of late Comdr John Drinkwater, OBE, RN (retd); *m* 1st, 1952, Jennifer Marion (*d* 1990), *d* of Edward Fitzwalter Wright, Morley Manor, Derbs; one *s* three *d* (and one *d* decd); 2nd, 1998, Deirdre, *d* of Derek Curtis-Bennett, QC and *widow* of James Boscawen. *Educ:* RNC Dartmouth. HM Submarines, 1943–47; Flag Lieut to C-in-C Portsmouth and First Sea Lord, 1947–50; Lt-Comdr 1952; invalided 1953. Called to Bar, Inner Temple, 1957, Bencher, 1979; a Recorder, 1972–90. Mem., Parly Boundary Commn for England, 1977–80. Mem. Bd, British Airports Authy, 1985–87, Dir, BAA plc, 1987–94. Life Mem. Council, SPAB, 1982. Pres., Cotswold Cons. Assoc., 1999– (Chm., 1995–99). Governor, St Mary's Hosp., 1960–64. *Recreations:* gardening, reading, travel. *Address:* Meysey Hampton Manor, Cirencester, Glos GL7 5JS. *T:* (01285) 851366; Lohitzun, 64120 St Palais, France. *Clubs:* Garrick, Pratt's.

DRISCOLL, Daphne Jane; *see* Todd, D. J.

DRISCOLL, James; Senior Partner, Woodcote Consultancy Services, 1990–96; *b* 24 April 1925; *s* of Henry James Driscoll and Honorah Driscoll; *m* 1955, Jeanne Lawrence Williams, BA, CertEd; one *s* one *d*. *Educ:* Coleg Sant Illtyd, Cardiff; University Coll., Cardiff. BA (1st Cl. Hons). Chm., Welsh Young Conservatives, 1948–49; Nat. Dep. Chm., Young Conservatives, 1950; Dep. Chm., Univ. Cons. Fedn, 1949–50; Dep. Chm., NUS, 1951–53. Vice-Chm., European Youth Campaign, 1951–53. Contested (C) Rhondda West, 1950. Asst Lectr, UC Cardiff, 1950–53; Council of Europe Res. Fellowship, 1953. Joined British Iron and Steel Fedn, 1953; various econ. and internat. posts; Econ. Dir and Dep. Dir-Gen., 1963–67; various posts, British Steel Corporation, 1967–80; Man. Dir, Corporate Strategy, 1971–76, Board Adviser, 1976–80; Dir, 1976–90, Policy Advr, 1990–96, NICG; Chm. and Man. Dir, Woodcote Consultants Ltd, 1980–90. Chm., Lifecare NHS Trust, 1990–94. Member: Grand Council, FBI, 1957–65; CBI Council, 1970–93; Observer, NEDC, 1977–91; Lay Mem., Investigation Cttee, ICA, 1991–96. Chm., Econ. Studies Cttee, Internat. Iron and Steel Inst., 1972–74. Vice-Chm., Croydon Mencap, 1997–. Mem., Court of Governors, Cardiff Univ. (formerly UC, Cardiff, then Univ. of Wales Coll. of Cardiff), 1970– (Fellow, 1986). FREconS; FRSA. *Publications:* various articles and pamphlets on econ. and internat. affairs, esp. steel affairs, European integration, wages policy and financing of world steel investment. *Recreations:* travel, bridge, reading. *Address:* Foxley Hatch, Birch Lane, Purley, Surrey CR8 3LH.

DRISCOLL, Dr James Philip, CEng; Partner, PricewaterhouseCoopers (formerly Coopers & Lybrand, then Coopers & Lybrand Deloitte), 1990–99, retired; *b* 29 March 1943; *s* of Reginald Driscoll and Janetta Bridget Driscoll; *m* 1969, Josephine Klapper, BA; two *s* two *d*. *Educ:* St Illtyd's Coll., Cardiff; Birmingham Univ. (BSc 1964; PhD 1972); Manchester Business Sch. MIChemE 1975; MIGasE 1975; MInstF 1975. Taught at St Illtyd's Coll., Cardiff, 1964; res. posts with Joseph Lucas, Solihull, 1968–69; British Steel Corporation: res. posts, 1969–70; commercial posts, 1971–79, incl. Manager, Divl Supplies, 1973; Reg. Manager, BSC (Industry), 1979–82; Dir, S Wales Workshops, 1980–82; Industrial Dir, Welsh Office, 1982–85; Associate Dir, 1985–87, Dir, 1987–90, Coopers & Lybrand Associates. *Publications:* various technical papers. *Recreations:* family, sport. *Address:* 6 Cory Crescent, Wyndham Park, Peterston-super-Ely, Cardiff CF5 6LS. *T:* (01446) 760372. *Club:* Peterston Football (Cardiff).

DRISCOLL, Lindsay Jane; Consultant, Sinclair Taylor & Martin (Partner, 1995); *b* 17 April 1947; *d* of Clement Milligan Woodburn and Evelyn Miriam Woodburn; *m* 1978, Rev. Canon David Driscoll; two *s*. *Educ:* Queen's Sch., Chester; St Hugh's Coll., Oxford (MA Hons Jurisp.). Admitted Solicitor, 1971; Asst Solicitor, Biddle & Co., 1971–73; Asst Public Trustee of Kenya, 1973–78; Lectr, Kenya Sch. of Law, 1973–78; charity law consultant, 1982–87; Consultant, Bowling & Co., 1985, Asst Legal Advr, 1987–90, Legal Advr, 1990–95, NCVO. Non exec. Dir, Internat. Center for Not for Profit Law, US, 1996–. Mem., Exec. Cttee, Charity Law Assoc., 1997–. Trustee: Newham Community Renewal Prog., 1981–87; Friends of Internat. Centre of Insect Physiology and Ecology Trust, 1997–; Assoc. of Church Accountants and Treasurers, 1998–2000; Womankind Worldwide, 1998–; ICNL Charitable Trust, 1998–; Empowering Widows in Develt, 2000–. Gov., Davenant Foundn Sch., 1990–97. *Publications:* (with Bridget Phelps) The Charities Act 1992: a guide for charities and other voluntary organisations, 1992, 2nd edn as The Charities Acts 1992 and 1993, 1993, 4th edn 1995; articles on charity law in charity and legal press. *Recreations:* travel, walking, theatre. *Address:* The Vicarage, 2 Piercing Hill, Theydon Bois, Essex CM16 7JN. *T:* (01992) 814725.

DRISCOLL, Michael John; QC 1992; *b* 22 Feb. 1947; *s* of John and Gladys Mary Driscoll; *m* 1970, Heather Edyvean Nichols (marr. diss. 1986); one *s* two *d* (and one *s* decd). *Educ:* Rugby Sch.; St John's Coll., Cambridge (BA, LLB). Asst Lectr, Manchester Univ., 1969–70; called to the Bar, Middle Temple, 1970. *Recreation:* family. *Address:* 9 Old Square, Lincoln's Inn, WC2A 3SR. *T:* (020) 7405 4682.

DRISCOLL, Prof. Michael John; Professor of Economics, since 1989, and Vice-Chancellor, since 1996, Middlesex University (formerly Middlesex Polytechnic); *b* 27 Oct. 1950; *s* of late Michael Driscoll and of Catherine Driscoll; one *s* one *d*. *Educ:* Boteler GS, Warrington; Trent Poly. (BA 1973). Res. Asst, Sheffield Univ., 1973–77; Lectr, Birmingham Univ., 1977–89; Economist, OECD, Paris, 1986–89; Middlesex Polytechnic, later University: Hd of Sch. of Econs, 1989–91; Dean of Business Sch., 1991–95; Pro Vice-Chancellor, 1993–95; Dep. Vice-Chancellor, 1995–96. Visiting Professor: Indian Statistics Inst., 1978; Centre for Econs and Maths Inst., Moscow, 1981; Limoges Univ. (annually), 1981–89; Univ. of the S Pacific, 1984. Chair, Lee Valley Business and Innovation Centre, 1996; Member: Ealing Tertiary Coll. Corp., 1995–96; Weald Coll. Corp., 1996–98; Coll. of NE London Corp., 1997. Member: Council, London Playing Fields Soc., 1998–; N London Learning and Skills Council; Steering Cttee, London Higher Educn Consortium. MInstD 1997; FIMgt 1995; FRSA 1995. *Publications:* (jtly) Risk and Uncertainty in Economics, 1994; (jtly) The Effects of Monetary Policy on the Real Sector, 1994; numerous articles in academic jls. *Recreations:* following Aston Villa FC, music, theatre, cinema, water sports, walking, mountain biking, food and wine. *Address:* Middlesex University, Trent Park, Bramley Road, N14 4YZ. *T:* (020) 8362 5000, *Fax:* (020) 8449 0798; *e-mail:* m.driscoll@mdx.ac.uk.

DRIVER, Sir Antony (Victor), Kt 1986; Chairman, South West Thames Regional Health Authority, 1982–88; *b* London, 20 July 1920; *s* of late Arthur William Driver and Violet Clementina Driver (*née* Browne); *m* 1948, Patricia (née Tinkler); three *s*. *Educ:* King's Coll., Univ. of London (BScEng Hons); Dip., Graduate Sch. of Industrial Admin., Carnegie-Mellon Univ., Pittsburgh. CEng; FIMechE, FInstPet; FIMgt. In oil industry with Shell-Mex and BP Ltd, until 1975, and BP Oil Ltd, 1976–80: seconded to British Petroleum Co., as Marketing Manager, N Europe, 1969–71; General Manager, Sales, 1971–78; Director, Personnel and Admin, 1979–80. Non-executive Director: Candles Ltd, 1976–80; Rockwool Ltd, 1978–80; Baxter Fell & Co. Ltd, 1980–85; Chm., Hoogovens (UK) Ltd, 1985–88. Director: Inst. of Cancer Research, 1981–95; Breakthrough Breast Cancer, 1995–; Oil Industries Club Ltd, 1981–; Surrey Assoc. of Youth Clubs and Surrey PHAB Ltd, 1991–. Liveryman, Tallow Chandlers' Co., 1977–; Freeman, City of London. *Recreations:* travel, gardening, wine, pyrotechnics. *Address:* Winterdown, Holmbury St Mary, Dorking, Surrey RH5 6NL. *T:* (01306) 730238.

DRIVER, Bryan; part-time Chairman, Rail Access Disputes Resolution Committee, since 1996; *b* 26 August 1932; *s* of Fred and Edith Driver; *m* 1955, Pamela Anne (*née* Nelson); two *d*. *Educ:* Wath-upon-Dearne Grammar School. Joined British Railways (Junior Clerk), 1948; Royal Air Force, 1950–52; management training with BR, 1958–59; posts in London, Doncaster, Newcastle, 1959–69; Divisional Operating Manager, Norwich, 1969–71, Liverpool Street, 1971–72; Divisional Manager, West of England, 1972–75, South Wales, 1975–77; Dep. Gen. Manager, Eastern Region, 1977–82; Man. Dir, 1982–87, Chm., 1985–87, Freightliners Ltd; Bryan Driver Associates, 1987–96; Consultant Advr, 1987–88, Ops Dir, then Dir, Ops and Rolling Stock, 1988–93, Transmanche-Link (Channel Tunnel Contractors). *Recreations:* cricket, Rugby football, golf. *Address:* Riverds Lea, 4 Shilton Garth Close, Earswick, York YO32 9SQ. *T:* (01904) 762848. *Clubs:* Savile, MCC; Yorkshire CC, York Golf.

DRIVER, Charles Jonathan, MPhil; writer and school consultant; Master of Wellington College, 1989–2000; *b* 19 Aug. 1939; *s* of Rev. Kingsley Ernest Driver and Phyllis Edith Mary (*née* Gould); *m* 1967, Ann Elizabeth Hoogewerf; two *s* one *d*. *Educ:* St Andrews Coll., Grahamstown; Univ. of Cape Town (BA Hons, BEd, STD); Trinity Coll., Oxford (MPhil). Pres., National Union of S African Students, 1963–64; Asst Teacher, Sevenoaks Sch., 1964–65 and 1967–68; Housemaster, Internat. Sixth Form Centre, Sevenoaks Sch., 1968–73; Dir of Sixth Form Studies, Matthew Humberstone Sch., 1973–78; Res. Fellow, Univ. of York, 1976; Principal, Island Sch., Hong Kong, 1978–83; Headmaster, Berkhamsted Sch., 1983–89. FRSA. Trustee: Lomans Trust, 1986–; Beit Trust, 1998–; Governor: Benenden Sch., 1987–; Eagle House Prep. Sch., 1989–2000; Milton Abbey Sch., 1998–; Farlington Sch., 1999– (Chm. Governors, 2000–); Millfield, 2001–. Editor, Conference and Common Room, 1993–2000. *Publications: novels:* Elegy for a Revolutionary, 1968; Send War in Our Time, O Lord, 1969; Death of Fathers, 1972; A Messiah of the Last Days, 1974; *poetry:* I Live Here Now, 1979; (with Jack Cope) Occasional Light, 1979; Hong Kong Portraits, 1986; In the Water-Margins, 1994; Holiday Haiku, 1997; Requiem, 1998; *biography:* Patrick Duncan, 1980, 2nd edn 2000. *Recreations:* keeping fit, playing the violin, reading, writing, Rugby. *Address:* Apple Yard Cottage, Mill Lane, Mill Corner, Northiam, Rye, E Sussex TN31 6JU; *e-mail:* jontydriver@hotmail.com.

DRIVER, Sir Eric (William), Kt 1979; retired; Chairman, Mersey Regional Health Authority, 1973–82; Chairman, National Staff Committee, (Works), 1979–82; *b* 19 Jan. 1911; *s* of William Weale Driver and Sarah Ann Driver; *m* 1st, 1938, Winifred Bane; two *d*; 2nd, 1972, Sheila Mary Johnson. *Educ:* Strand Sch., London; King's Coll., London Univ. (BSc). FICE. Civil Engr with ICI Ltd, 1938–73, retd as Chief Civil Engr Mond Div. *Recreations:* walking, gardening, travel. *Address:* Conker Tree Cottage, South Bank, Great Budworth, Cheshire CW9 6HG. *Club:* Budworth Sailing.

DRIVER, Olga Lindholm; *see* Aikin, O. L.

DRIVER, Paul William; freelance writer and critic; *b* 14 Aug. 1954; *s* of Thomas Driver and Thelma Driver (*née* Tavernor). *Educ:* Salford Grammar Sch.; St Edmund Hall, Oxford (MA Hons English Lit.). Contrib. music reviews, later book and theatre reviews to FT, 1979–95; Music Critic: Daily Telegraph, 1982–83; Boston Globe, 1983–84; Sunday Times, 1984–; contributor to: The Listener, Tempo, Musical Times, TLS, London Rev. of Books, Guardian, NY Times and numerous other pubns; frequent broadcasts on Radio 3, BBC 2, Channel 4, etc; has lectured on music in Britain and USA. Mem. Bd, Contemporary Music Rev., 1981–. Patron, Manchester Musical Heritage Trust, 2000. *Publications:* (ed) A Diversity of Creatures, by Rudyard Kipling, 1987; (ed jtly) Music and Text, 1989; (ed) Penguin English Verse, 1995; (ed) Penguin Popular Poetry, 6 vols, 1996; Manchester Pieces, 1996. *Recreations:* walking, swimming, travel. *Address:* 15 Victoria Road, NW6 6SX. *T:* (020) 7624 4501. *Club:* Critics' Circle.

DRIVER, Sheila Elizabeth; a District Judge (Magistrates' Courts) (formerly Stipendiary Magistrate), South Yorkshire, since 1995; *b* 7 Oct. 1950; *d* of Alfred Derek Robinson and Joan Elizabeth Robinson; *m* 1974, John Graham Driver; one *s* two *d*. *Educ:* Bradford Girls' GS; Leeds Univ. (BA Hons Hist.); London School of Economics (MA Internat. Hist.). Admitted Solicitor, 1978; Solicitor: City of Bradford MDC, 1978–79; County Prosecuting Office, W Yorks, 1979–80; in private practice, 1981–95. *Recreations:* amateur dramatics, reading.

DROGHEDA, 12th Earl of, *cr* 1661 (Ireland); **Henry Dermot Ponsonby Moore;** Baron Moore of Mellifont, 1616; Viscount Moore, 1621; Baron Moore of Cobham (UK), 1954; photographer; *b* 14 Jan. 1937; *o s* of 11th Earl of Drogheda, KG, KBE and of Joan *o d* of late William Henry Carr; *S* father, 1989; *m* 1st, 1968, Eliza Lloyd (marr. diss. 1972), *d* of Stacy Barcroft Lloyd, Jr, and Mrs Paul Mellon; 2nd, 1978, Alexandra, *d* of Sir Nicholas Henderson, *qv*; two *s* one *d*. *Educ:* Eton; Trinity College, Cambridge. *Publications:* (as Derry Moore): (with Brendan Gill) The Dream Come True, Great Houses of Los Angeles, 1980; (with George Plumptre) Royal Gardens, 1981; (with Sybila Jane Flower) Stately Homes of Britain, 1982; (with Henry Mitchell) Washington, Houses of the Capital, 1982; (with Michael Pick) The English Room, 1984; (with Alvilde Lees-Milne) The Englishwoman's House, 1984; (with Alvilde Lees-Milne) The Englishman's Room, 1986; (with the Marchioness of Salisbury) The Gardens of Queen Elizabeth the Queen Mother, 1988; (with Sarah Hollis) The Shell Guide to the Gardens of England and Wales, 1989; Evening Ragas, 1997; (with Clive Aslet) The House of Lords, 1998. *Heir: s* Viscount Moore, *qv*. *Address:* 40 Ledbury Road, W11 2AB. *Club:* Brooks's.

DROMGOOLE, Jolyon, MA Oxon; Director (Council Secretariat), Institution of Civil Engineers, 1985–91; Deputy Under-Secretary of State (Army), Ministry of Defence, 1984–85; *b* 27 March 1926; 2nd *s* of late Nicholas and Violet Dromgoole; *m* 1956, Anthea, *e d* of Sir Anthony Bowlby, 2nd Bt; five *d* (incl. triplets). *Educ:* Christ's Hospital; Dulwich Coll.; University Coll., Oxford, 1944. 2nd Cl. Hons (History), MA. Entered HM Forces, 1944; commissioned 14/20 King's Hussars, 1946. University Coll., 1948–50. Entered Administrative Cl., Civil Service; assigned to War Office, 1950; Private Sec. to Permanent Under-Sec., 1953; Principal, 1955; Private Sec. to Sec. of State, 1964–65; Asst Sec., 1965; Command Sec., HQ FARELF, Singapore, 1968–71; Royal Coll. of Defence Studies, 1972; Under-Sec., Broadcasting Dept, Home Office, 1973–76; Asst Under-Sec. of State, Gen. Staff, 1976–79, Personnel and Logistics, 1979–84, MoD. FRSA. Trustee and Gov., Royal Sch., Hampstead, 1985–99. Mem., Samuel Pepys Club. *Recreations:* polo, literature, publisher. *Address:* 13 Gladstone Street, SE1 6EY. *T:* (020) 7928 2162; Montreal House, Barnsley, Glos GL7 5EL. *T:* (01285) 740331. *Club:* Athenæum.

See also P. S. B. F. Dromgoole.

DROMGOOLE, Patrick Shirley Brookes Fleming; Chairman, PDP Ltd, since 1992; Director, Isle of Arran Distillers Ltd, since 1996; *b* 30 Aug. 1930; *s* of late Nicholas and Violet Dromgoole; *m* 1st, 1960, Jennifer Veronica Jill Davis (marr. diss. 1991); two *s* one *d*; 2nd, 1991, June Kell Morrow. *Educ:* Dulwich Coll.; University Coll., Oxford (MA). Actor and various employments in London and Paris, 1947–51; BBC Drama Producer/Dir, 1954–63; freelance theatre, film and television dir (directed first plays in West End of Orton, Wood, Welland, Halliwell and others), 1963–69; directed regularly Armchair Theatre for ABC TV and Thames TV; made number of films for cinema; joined HTV Ltd as Programme Controller, 1969; Asst Man. Dir, 1981; Man. Dir, HTV, 1987; Chief Exec., HTV Gp, 1988–91. Various awards incl. Pye Oscar, RTS, for Thick as Thieves, 1971; Best Play of the Year, for Machinegunner, 1973; Amer. Emmy, for D.P., 1985. FRTS 1978; FRSA 1989. *Recreations:* travel, œnophilia, pre-Raphaelite art, reading. *Address:* Penkill Castle, Girvan, Ayrshire KA26 9TQ. *Clubs:* Savile, Groucho; Castel's (Paris).

See also J. Dromgoole.

DRONFIELD, Ronald; Chief Insurance Officer for National Insurance, Department of Health and Social Security, 1976–84, retired; *b* 21 Dec. 1924; *m* 1966, Marie Renie (*née*

Price). *Educ:* King Edward VII Sch., Sheffield; Oriel Coll., Oxford. RN, 1943–46. Entered Min. of National Insurance, 1949; Principal Private Sec. to Minister of Pensions and Nat. Insurance, 1964–66; Cabinet Office, 1970–71. *Recreation:* reading, biography. *Address:* 8 Beechrow, Ham Common, Richmond, Surrey TW10 5HE.

DRONKE, Prof. (Ernst) Peter (Michael), FBA 1984; Fellow of Clare Hall, since 1964, and Professor of Medieval Latin Literature, since 1989, University of Cambridge; *b* 30 May 1934; *s* of Senatspräsident A. H. R. Dronke and M. M. Dronke (*née* Kronfeld); *m* 1960, Ursula Miriam (*née* Brown); one *d*. *Educ:* Victoria University, NZ (MA 1st Cl. Hons 1954); Magdalen College, Oxford (BA 1st Cl. Hons 1957; MA 1961); MA Cantab 1961. Research Fellow, Merton Coll., Oxford, 1958–61; Lectr in Medieval Latin, 1961–79, Reader, 1979–89, Univ. of Cambridge. Guest Lectr, Univ. of Munich, 1960; Guest Prof., Centre d'Etudes Médiévales, Poitiers, 1969; Leverhulme Fellow, 1973; Guest Prof., Univ. Autónoma, Barcelona, 1977; Vis. Fellow, Humanities Res. Centre, Canberra, 1978; Vis. Prof. of Medieval Studies, Westfield Coll., 1981–86. Lectures: W. P. Ker, Univ. of Glasgow, 1976; Matthews, Birkbeck Coll., 1983; Jackson, Harvard Univ., 1992; O'Donnell, Univ. of Toronto, 1993; Barlow, UCL, 1995. Corresp. Fellow: Real Academia de Buenas Letras, 1976; Royal Dutch Acad., 1997; Medieval Acad. of America, 1999. Hon. Pres., Internat. Courtly Literature Soc., 1974. Co-Editor, Mittellateinisches Jahrbuch, 1977–. Premio Internazionale Ascoli Piceno, 1988. *Publications:* Medieval Latin and the Rise of European Love-Lyric, 2 vols, 1965–66; The Medieval Lyric, 1968; Poetic Individuality in the Middle Ages, 1970; Fabula, 1974; Abelard and Heloise in Medieval Testimonies, 1976; (with Ursula Dronke) Barbara et antiquissima carmina, 1977; (ed) Bernardus Silvestris, Cosmographia, 1978; Introduction to Francesco Colonna, Hypnerotomachia, 1981; Women Writers of the Middle Ages, 1984; The Medieval Poet and his World, 1984; Dante and Medieval Latin Traditions, 1986; Introduction to Rosvita, Dialoghi drammatici, 1986; (ed) A History of Twelfth-Century Western Philosophy, 1988; Hermes and the Sibyls, 1990; Latin and Vernacular Poets of the Middle Ages, 1991; Intellectuals and Poets in Medieval Europe, 1992; Verse with Prose: from Petronius to Dante, 1994; Nine Medieval Latin Plays, 1994; (ed with A. Derolez) Hildegard of Bingen, *Liber divinorum operum*, 1996; Sources of Inspiration, 1997; Dante's Second Love, 1997; Introduction to Alessandro nel medioevo occidentale, 1997; (with Ursula Dronke) Growth of Literature: the sea and the God of the sea, 1998; (ed) Etienne Gilson's Letters to Bruno Nardi, 1998; (ed with Charles Burnett) Hildegard of Bingen: the context of her thought and art, 1998; essays in learned jls and symposia. *Recreations:* music, film, Brittany. *Address:* 6 Parker Street, Cambridge CB1 1JL.

DROWN, Julia Kate; MP (Lab) Swindon South, since 1997; *b* 23 Aug. 1962; *d* of David Christopher Robert Drown and Audrey Marion Harris; partner, Bill Child; one *s* (one *d* decd). *Educ:* Hampstead Comprehensive Sch.; University Coll., Oxford (BA); Educn and Trng Coll., CIPFA. Unit Accountant, Oxfordshire Unit for People with Learning Difficulties, 1988–90; Dir of Finance, Radcliffe Infirmary, Oxford, 1990–96. Mem. (Lab) Oxfordshire CC, 1989–96. Chair, All Pty Gp on Maternity, 2000–; Vice Chair, All Party Group: on Further Educn, 1998–99; on Rwanda, the Great Lakes Region and the Prevention of Genocide, 1998–; Voice, 1998–; Jubilee 2000, 1999–; Hon. Sec., All Pty Gp on Osteoporosis. *Recreations:* family, walking, cinema, music. *Address:* House of Commons, SW1A 0AA; 13 Bath Road, Swindon SN1 4AS.

DRU DRURY, Martin; *see* Drury.

DRUCKER, Henry Matthew, PhD; Chairman, Oxford Philanthropic, since 1999 (Managing Director, 1994–99); *b* 29 April 1942; *s* of Arthur and Frances Drucker; *m* 1975, Nancy Livia Newman. *Educ:* Allegheny Coll., Meadville, Penn (BA Philosophy); London School of Economics (PhD PolPhil). Lectr in Politics 1964–76, Sen. Lectr in Politics 1976–86, Univ. of Edinburgh; Dir, Univ. Develt Office, Oxford Univ., 1987–93; Dir, Campaign for Oxford, 1988–93. Mem., British Museum Develt Trust, 2000–. Vis. Prof. of Govt, LSE, 1994–99. *Publications:* Political Uses of Ideology, 1974; (ed with M. G. Clarke) Our Changing Scotland, 1977; Breakaway—The Scottish Labour Party, 1978; (ed with Nancy Drucker) Scottish Government Yearbook, 1978–82; Doctrine and Ethos in the Labour Party, 1979; (ed) Multi-Party Britain, 1979; (with Gordon Brown) The Politics of Nationalism and Devolution, 1980; (ed) John P. Mackintosh on Scotland, 1982; (general ed.) Developments in British Politics, 1983; (general ed.) Developments in British Politics 2, 1986, revd edn 1988. *Recreations:* reading aloud to wife, walking. *Address:* Oxford Philanthropic Ltd, 36 Windmill Road, Headington, Oxford OX3 7BX. *T:* (01865) 744300; *e-mail:* consult@oxphil.com.

DRUCKER, Prof. Peter (Ferdinand); writer and consultant; Clarke Professor of Social Science and Management, Claremont Graduate School, Claremont, Calif, since 1971; *b* 19 Nov. 1909; *s* of Adolph B. Drucker and Caroline (*née* Bond); *m* 1937, Doris Schmitz; one *s* three *d*. *Educ:* Austria, Germany, England. Investment banker, London, 1933–36; newspapers, 1937–41; Professor of Philosophy and Politics, Bennington Coll., Bennington, Vt, USA, 1942–49; Prof. of Management, NY Univ., 1950–71; Professorial Lectr in Oriental Art, Claremont Colls, 1980–86. Management Consultant (internat. practice among businesses and govts) (as well as Professorships), 1943–. Has recorded audio-cassettes and video cassettes on management practice. Holds hon. doctorates from univs in Belgium, Czech Republic, GB, Japan, Spain, Switzerland, USA. Hon. FIMgt; FAAAS; Fellow: Amer. Acad. of Management; Internat. Acad. of Management. Godkin Lectr, Harvard Univ., 1994. Order of Sacred Treasure, Japan; Grand Cross, Austria. *Publications:* End of Economic Man, 1939, new edn 1995; Future of Industrial Man, 1942, new edn 1994; Concept of the Corporation, 1946, new edn 1992; The New Society, 1950, new edn 1992; Practice of Management, 1954, new edn 1992; America's Next Twenty Years, 1959; Landmarks of Tomorrow, 1960, new edn 1996; Managing for Results, 1964, new edn 1992; The Effective Executive, 1966, new edn 1992; The Age of Discontinuity, 1969, new edn 1992; Technology, Management and Society, 1970; Men, Ideas and Politics, 1971; The New Markets . . . and other essays, 1971; Management: tasks, responsibilities, practices, 1974, new edn 1992; The Unseen Revolution: how pension fund socialism came to America, 1976, 2nd edn 1995; Adventures of a Bystander, 1979, new edn 1998; Managing in Turbulent Times, 1980, new edn 1992; Toward the New Economics, 1981; The Changing World of the Executive (essays), 1982; Innovation and Entrepreneurship, 1985, new edn 1992; The Frontiers of Management, 1986; The New Realities, 1989; Managing the Non-Profit Organisation, 1990; Managing for the Future, 1992; The Ecological Vision, 1993; Post Capitalist Society, 1993; Managing at a Time of Great Change, 1995; Drucker on Asia: a dialogue with Isao Nakauchi, 1997; Peter Drucker on the Profession of Management, 1998; Management Challenges for the 21st Century, 1999; The Essential Drucker (anthol.), 2001; *novels:* The Last of All Possible Worlds, 1982; The Temptation to Do Good, 1984. *Recreations:* mountaineering; Japanese history and paintings.

DRUMLANRIG, Viscount; Sholto Francis Guy Douglas; *b* 1 June 1967; *s* and *heir* of 12th Marquess of Queensberry, *qv*.

DRUMM, Rt Rev. Mgr Walter Gregory; Rector, Pontifical Beda College, Rome, 1987–91; *b* 2 March 1940; *s* of Owen and Kathleen Drumm. *Educ:* St Joseph's Sch. and St Aloysius' Coll., Highgate; Balliol Coll., Oxford (MA). Tutor, The Grange, Warlingham, 1962–66; studied at Beda Coll., 1966–70; ordained, Westminster Dio., 1970; Asst Priest, Wood Green, 1970–73; Chaplain, Oxford Univ., 1973–83; Parish Priest, Our Lady of Victories, Kensington, 1983–87. Prelate of Honour to the Pope, 1988. *Address:* Westminster Cathedral Clergy House, Francis Street, SW1P 1QW. *Club:* Oxford and Cambridge.

DRUMMOND, family name of **Earl of Perth** and **Baroness Strange**.

DRUMMOND, Maj.-Gen. Anthony John D.; *see* Deane-Drummond.

DRUMMOND, Colin Irwin John Hamilton; Chief Executive, Viridor Ltd, since 1998; Director, Pennon Group plc, since 1992; *b* 22 Feb. 1951; *s* of Rev. William Balfour Drummond, MA and Annie Rebecca Drummond (*née* Roy); *m* 1975, Georgina Lloyd; two *s*. *Educ:* Wadham Coll., Oxford (BA (double 1st Cl. Hons Classics), MA 1978); Harvard Graduate Sch. of Business Admin (Harkness Fellow; MBA 1977). LTCL 1969 (Colman Prize). Asst Superintendent, Economic Intelligence Dept, Bank of England, 1973–78; Consultant, Boston Consulting Gp, 1978–84; Dir for Corporate Develt, Renold plc, 1984–86; Chief Exec., Yarns Div., Coats Viyella plc, 1986–92. Non-exec. Dir, Vymura plc, 1998–99. Freeman, City of London, 1999; Liveryman and Bailiff, Co. of Water Conservators. *Recreations:* organist and choirmaster, parish church of St John the Baptist, Wellington, Somerset; sport, gardening. *Address:* Pennon Group plc, Peninsula House, Rydon Lane, Exeter EX2 7HR. *T:* (01392) 443011.

DRUMMOND, David Classon, FIBiol; Deputy Director, Research and Development Service, Agricultural Development Advisory Service, Ministry of Agriculture, Fisheries and Food, 1987–88, retired; *b* 25 July 1928; *s* of Roger Hamilton Drummond and Marjorie Holt Drummond; *m* 1952, Barbara Anne, *d* of late Prof. Alfred Cobban; three *d*. *Educ:* St Peter's Sch., York; University Coll., London (BSc 1952); Pennsylvania State Univ., USA (Kellogg Fellow; MS 1962). FIBiol 1975. Project Manager, FAO, UN, Karachi, 1971–72; Agricultural Science Service, MAFF: Head of Rodent Res. Dept, and Officer i/c Tolworth Lab., 1974–82; Head of Biol. Div., and Officer i/c Slough Lab., 1982–85; Sen. Agricl Scientist with special responsibilities for R&D, 1985–87. Mem., WHO Expert Adv. Panel on Vector Biology and Control, 1980–97. *Publications:* scientific papers and reviews mainly concerned with rodent biology and control and develt of agricl and urban rat control programmes. *Recreations:* travel, gardening, history of rat catching. *Address:* 22 Knoll Road, Dorking, Surrey RH4 3EP.

DRUMMOND, Sir John (Richard Gray), Kt 1995; CBE 1990; writer and broadcaster; *b* 25 Nov. 1934; *s* of late Captain A. R. G. Drummond and Esther (*née* Pickering), Perth, WA. *Educ:* Canford; Trinity Coll., Cambridge (MA History). RNVR, 1953–55. BBC Radio and Television, 1958–78, latterly as Asst Head, Music and Arts; programmes produced incl.: Tortelier Master Classes, 1964; Leeds Piano Comp., 1966 (1st Prize, Prague Fest., 1967); Diaghilev, 1967; Kathleen Ferrier, 1968; Music Now, 1969; Spirit of the Age, 1975; The Lively Arts, 1976–78; Dir, Edinburgh Internat. Fest., 1978–83; Controller of Music, 1985–92, and of Radio 3, 1987–92, BBC; Dir, BBC Prom. Concerts, 1986–95. Dir, European Arts Fest., 1992. Pres., Kensington Soc., 1985–2001; Vice Pres., British Arts Festivals Assoc., 1993– (Vice-Chm., 1981–83); Chm., Nat. Dance Co-ordinating Cttee, 1986–94; Mem. various adv. councils and cttees concerning music, theatre and dance; Governor, Royal Ballet, 1986–2000; Mem., Theatres Trust, 1989– (Chm., 1998–). FRCM 1995; Hon. GSM 1988; Hon. RAM 1994; Hon. FRNCM 1994; Hon. FTCL 1994. FRSA. DUniv UCE, 1997; Hon. DMus Keele, 1998; Hon. DArts De Montfort, 1998. Chevalier, Légion d'Honneur (France), 1996. *Publications:* (with Joan Bakewell) A Fine and Private Place, 1977; (with N. Thompson) The Turn of Dance?, 1984; Speaking of Diaghilev, 1997; Tainted by Experience (autobiog.), 2000. *Recreations:* conversation, looking at architecture, browsing in bookshops. *Address:* 61c Campden Hill Court, W8 7HL. *T:* (020) 7937 2257. *Club:* New (Edinburgh).

DRUMMOND, Kevin; *see* Drummond, T. A. K.

DRUMMOND, Maldwin Andrew Cyril, OBE 1990; DL; farmer and author; *b* 30 April 1932; *s* of late Maj. Cyril Drummond, JP, DL, and Mildred Joan Quinnell; *m* 1st, 1955, Susan Dorothy Cayley (marr. diss. 1977); two *d*; 2nd, 1978, Gillian Turner Laing, DL; one *s*. *Educ:* Eton Coll.; Royal Agricl Coll., Cirencester; Univ. of Southampton (Cert. in Environmental Sci., 1972). 2nd Lieut, Rifle Bde, 1950–52; Captain, Queen Victoria's, later Queen's, Royal Rifles (TA), retd 1967. Official Verderer of the New Forest, 1999– (Verderer of New Forest, 1961–90); Chairman: Heritage Coast Forum, 1989–95; New Forest Cttee, 1990–98 (Chm., Consultative Panel, 1982–98); Mem., Countryside Commn, 1980–86. Member: Southampton Harbour Bd, 1967; British Transport Docks Bd, Southampton, 1968–74; Southern Water Authority, 1984–87. Chairman: Sail Training Assoc., 1967–72; Maritime Trust, 1979–89; Cutty Sark Soc., 1979–89; Warrior (formerly Ships) Preservation Trust, 1979–91; Vice-Pres., 1983–, and Chm. Boat Cttee, 1983–92, RNLI; Trustee, World Ship Trust, 1980–91; Chm., Hampshire Bldgs Preservation Trust, 1986–92. Younger Brother of Trinity House, 1991–. Prime Warden, Fishmongers' Co., 1996–97. Mem., New Forest RDC, 1957–66; Hampshire: County Councillor, 1967–75; JP 1964–98 (Chm., New Forest Bench, 1992–97); DL 1975; High Sheriff, 1980–81. FRGS 1978; FRSA 1987. Hon. DSc: Bournemouth, 1994; Southampton Inst., 1996. *Publications:* Conflicts in an Estuary, 1973; Tall Ships, 1976; Salt-Water Places, 1979; (with Paul Rodhouse) Yachtsman's Naturalist, 1980; (with Philip Allison) The New Forest, 1980; The Riddle, 1985; West Highland Shores, 1990. *Recreations:* cruising under sail and wondering about the sea. *Address:* Cadland House, Fawley, Southampton SO45 1AA. *T:* (office) (023) 8089 2039, (home) (023) 8089 1543; Wester Kames Castle, Port Bannatyne, Isle of Bute PA20 0QW. *T:* (01700) 503983. *Clubs:* White's, Pratt's, Royal Cruising; Royal Yacht Squadron (Cdre, 1991–96) (Cowes); Leander (Henley).

DRUMMOND, Rev. Norman Walker, MA; BD; Chairman: Drummond International, since 1999; Columba 1400, Community and International Leadership Centre, Isle of Skye, since 1997; Community Action Network, Scotland, since 2001; *b* 1 April 1952; *s* of late Edwin Payne Drummond and Jean (*née* Walker); *m* 1976, Lady Elizabeth Helen Kennedy, *d* of 7th Marquess of Ailsa, OBE; three *s* two *d*. *Educ:* Merchiston Castle Sch.; Fitzwilliam Coll., Cambridge (MA Law); New Coll., Univ. of Edinburgh (BD). Ordained as Minister of the Church of Scotland, and commnd to serve as Chaplain to HM Forces in the Army, 1976; Chaplain: Depot, Parachute Regt and Airborne Forces, 1977–78; 1st Bn The Black Watch (Royal Highland Regt), 1978–82; to the Moderator of the Gen. Assembly of the Church of Scotland, 1980; Fettes Coll., 1982–84; Headmaster, Loretto Sch., 1984–95; Minister of Kilmuir and Stenscholl, Isle of Skye, 1996–98. Chaplain to Gov. of Edinburgh Castle, 1991–93; Chaplain to the Queen in Scotland, 1993–99. Scottish Gov., BBC, and Chm., Broadcasting Council for Scotland, 1994–99. Chm., Musselburgh and Dist Council of Social Service, 1984–94; Dir, The Change Partnership, 1999–. Mem., Queen's Bodyguard for Scotland (Royal Co. of Archers). Mem. Court, Heriot-Watt Univ., 1986–92; Gov., Gordonstoun Sch., 1995–2000; Chm. Govs, Aiglon Coll., Switzerland, 1999–. Mem., Scottish Cttee, ICRF; Trustee: Arthur Smith Meml Trust; Foundn for Skin

Res. President: Edinburgh Bn, Boys' Bde, 1993–98; Victoria League in Scotland, 1995–98. Cambridge Univ. Rugby Blue, 1971; Captain: Scottish Univs XV, 1974; Army XV and Combined Services XV, 1976–77. *Publications:* The First Twenty-five Years: official history of The Black Watch Kirk Session, 1979; Mother's Hands (collection of short stories for children, parents and teachers), 1992. *Recreations:* Rugby football, cricket, golf, curling, traditional jazz, Isle of Skye. *Address:* 10A Drummond Place, Edinburgh EH3 6PH. *Clubs:* MCC, Free Foresters; New (Edinburgh); Hawks (Cambridge).

DRUMMOND, (Thomas Anthony) Kevin; QC (Scot.) 1987; Sheriff of Lothian and Borders at Jedburgh, Selkirk and Duns, since 2000; *b* 3 Nov. 1943; *s* of Thomas Drummond, BSc, and Mary (*née* Hughes); *m* 1966, Margaret Evelyn Broadley; one *d* (and one *d* decd). *Educ:* Blair's Coll., Aberdeen; St Mirin's Acad., Paisley; Edinburgh Univ. (LLB). Estate Duty Office, CS, 1963–70; Solicitor, 1970; admitted Faculty of Advocates, 1974; Advocate-Depute, 1985–90, Home Advocate-Depute, 1996–97, Crown Office, Edinburgh; Sheriff of Glasgow and Stathkelvin, 1997–2000. Member: Criminal Injuries Compensation Bd, 1990–96; Firearms Consultative Cttee, 1990–97; Criminal Injuries Compensation Authy, 1996. Chm., Discipline Tribunal, Inst. of Chartered Accts of Scotland, 1994–. Cartoonist, Scots Law Times, 1981–. *Publications:* legal cartoons under name of TAK: The Law at Work, 1982; The Law at Play, 1983; Great Defences of Our Time, 1995. *Recreations:* shooting, hill-walking, fishing, under water hang-gliding. *Address:* Pomathorn House, Howgate, Midlothian EH26 8PJ. *T:* (01968) 74046.

DRUMMOND YOUNG, James Edward; QC (Scot.) 1988; *b* 17 Feb. 1950; *s* of Duncan Drummond Young, MBE, DL, Edinburgh, and Annette (*née* Mackay); *m* 1991, Elizabeth Mary, *d* of John Campbell-Kease, Connel, Argyll; one *d*. *Educ:* John Watson's Sch.; Sidney Sussex Coll., Cambridge (BA 1971); Harvard Univ. (Joseph Hodges Choate Meml Fellow, 1971–72; LLM 1972); Edinburgh Univ. (LLB 1974). Admitted to Faculty of Advocates, 1976. Standing Jun. Counsel in Scotland to Bd of Inland Revenue, 1986–88; Advocate-Depute, 1999–. *Publications:* (with J. B. St Clair) The Law of Corporate Insolvency in Scotland, 1988, 2nd edn 1992; (contrib.) Stair Memorial Encyclopaedia of Scots Law, 1989. *Recreations:* music, travel. *Address:* 14 Ainslie Place, Edinburgh EH3 6AS. *T:* (0131) 225 6393. *Club:* New (Edinburgh).

DRUON, Maurice Samuel Roger Charles, Hon. CBE 1988; Grand Officier de la Légion d'Honneur; Commandeur des Arts et Lettres; author; Member of the French Academy since 1966 (Permanent Secretary, 1986–2000); Member: French Parliament (Paris), 1978–81; Assembly of Council of Europe, 1978–81; European Parliament, 1979–80; Franco-British Council, since 1972; *b* Paris, 23 April 1918; *s* of René Druon de Reyniac and Léonilla Jenny Samuel-Cros; *m* 1968, Madeleine Marignac. *Educ:* Lycée Michelet and Ecole des Sciences Politiques, Paris. Ecole de Cavalerie de Saumur, aspirant, 1940; joined Free French Forces, London, 1942; Attaché Commissariat à l'Intérieur et Direction de l'Information, 1943; War Correspondent, 1944–45; Lieut de réserve de cavalerie. Journalist, 1946–47; Minister for Cultural Affairs, France, 1973–74. Member: Acad. of Morocco, 1980; Athènes' Acad., 1981; Acad. de Lisbonne, 1994; Acad. Bresilienne de Lettres, 1995; Acad. Roumaine, 1996; Pres., Franco-Italian Assoc., 1985–91. Dr *hc* York Univ., Ontario, 1987. Prix de Monaco, 1966. Commandeur du Phénix de Grèce; Grand Officer of l'Ordre de l'Honneur de Grèce; Grand Officier du Mérite de l'Ordre de Malte; Commandeur de l'Ordre de la République de Tunisie; Grand Officier du Lion du Sénégal; Grand Croix du Mérite de la République Italienne; Grand Croix de l'Aigle Aztèque du Mexique; Grand Officier Ouissam Alaouite (Morocco); Commandeur du Mérite de Monaco; Commandeur du Cruseiro del Sul (Brazil); Commandeur de l'ordre du Cèdre (Lebanon); Comdr, Ordre de Léopold (Belgium); Grand Croix, l'ordre du Christ (Portugal), 1994. *Publications:* Lettres d'un Européen, 1944; La Dernière Brigade (The Last Detachment), 1946 (publ. in England 1957); Les Grandes Familles (Prix Goncourt, 1948), La Chute des Corps, Rendez-Vous aux Enfers, 1948–51 (trilogy publ. in England under title The Curtain falls, 1959); La Volupté d'Etre (Film of Memory), 1954 (publ. in England 1955); Les Rois Maudits (The Accursed Kings), 1955–60 (six vols: The Iron King, The Strangled Queen, The Poisoned Crown, The Royal Succession, The She-Wolf of France, The Lily and the Lion, publ. in England 1956–61); Tistou les pouces verts (Tistou of the green fingers), 1957 (publ. in England 1958); Alexandre le Grand (Alexander the God), 1958 (publ. in Eng. 1960); Des Seigneurs de la Plaine- (The Black Prince and other stories), 1962 (publ. in Eng. 1962); Les Mémoires de Zeus I (The Memoirs of Zeus), 1963 (in Eng. 1964); Bernard Buffet, 1964; Paris, de César à Saint Louis (The History of Paris from Caesar to St Louis), 1964 (in Eng. 1969); Le Pouvoir, 1965; Les Tambours de la Mémoire, 1965; Le Bonheur des Uns, 1967; Les Mémoires de Zeus II (The Memoirs of Zeus II), 1967; L'Avenir en désarroi, 1968; Vézelay, colline éternelle, 1968; Nouvelles lettres d'un Européen, 1970; Une Eglise qui se trompe de siècle, 1972; La Parole et le Pouvoir, 1974; Oeuvres complètes, 25 vols, 1973–79; Quand un roi perd la France (Les Rois Maudits 7), 1977; Attention la France!, 1981; Réformer la Démocratie, 1982; Lettre aux Français sur leur langue et leur âme, 1994; Circonstances, 1997; Circonstances politiques, 1998 (Prix Saint Simon, 1998); Circonstances politiques II, 1999; *plays:* Mégarée, 1942; Un Voyageur, 1953; La Contessa, 1962; *song:* Le Chant des Partisans (with Joseph Kessel and Anna Marly), 1943 (London). *Recreations:* riding, travel. *Address:* Palais Mazarin, 1 rue de Seine, 75006 Paris, France; Abbaye de Faise, Les Artigues de Lussac, 33570 Lussac, France. *Clubs:* Savile, Garrick; Travellers (Paris).

DRURY, Very Rev. John Henry; Dean of Christ Church, Oxford, since 1991; *b* 23 May 1936; *s* of Henry and Barbara Drury; *m* 1972, (Frances) Clare Nineham, *d* of Rev. Prof. D. E. Nineham, *qv*; two *d*. *Educ:* Bradfield; Trinity Hall, Cambridge (MA (Hist. Pt 1, Cl. 1; Theol. Pt 2, Cl. 2/1); Hon. Fellow, 1997); Westcott House, Cambridge. Curate, St John's Wood Church, 1963; Chaplain of Downing Coll., Cambridge, 1966; Chaplain and Fellow of Exeter Coll., Oxford, 1969 (Hon. Fellow, 1991); Res. Canon of Norwich Cathedral and Examining Chaplain to Bp of Norwich, 1973–79; Vice-Dean of Norwich, 1978; Fleck Resident in Religion, Bryn Mawr Coll., USA, 1978; Lectr in Religious Studies, Sussex Univ., 1979–81; Dean, 1981–91, Fellow, 1982–91, King's College, Cambridge. Syndic, Fitzwilliam Museum, Cambridge, 1988–91. Examining Chaplain to Bp of Chichester, 1980–82. Mem., Doctrine Commn for C of E, 1978–82. Hussey Lectr, Univ. of Oxford, 1997. Hon. Fellow, Exeter Coll., Oxford, 1992. Jt Editor, Theology, 1976–86. *Publications:* Angels and Dirt, 1972; Luke, 1973; Tradition and Design in Luke's Gospel, 1976; The Pot and The Knife, 1979; The Parables in the Gospels, 1985; Critics of the Bible 1724–1873, 1989; The Burning Bush, 1990; Painting the Word, 1999; articles and reviews in Jl of Theol. Studies, Theology, Expository Times, TLS. *Recreations:* drawing, carpentry, reading. *Address:* Christ Church, Oxford OX1 1DP.

DRURY, Martin Dru, CBE 2001; FSA; Director-General, National Trust, 1996–2001 (Deputy Director-General, 1992–95); *b* 22 April 1938; *s* of late Walter Neville Dru Drury, TD; *m* 1971, Elizabeth Caroline, *d* of Hon. Sir Maurice Bridgeman, KBE; two *s* one *d*. *Educ:* Rugby. Commissioned, 3rd The King's Own Hussars, 1957. Insurance Broker at Lloyd's, 1959–65; Mallett & Son (Antiques) Ltd, 1965–73 (Associate Dir, 1970–73); joined National Trust as Historic Buildings Rep., SE, and Furniture Advr, 1973; Historic Buildings Sec., 1981–95. Trustee: Landmark Trust, 1989– (Chm., 1992–95, 2001–); Heritage of London Trust, 1996–; Wallace Collection, 2001–; Vice-Chm., Attingham Trust, 1982–. Member: Council, Georgian Group, 1994– (Mem. Exec. Cttee, 1976–94); Fabric Adv. Cttee, St Paul's Cathedral, 1991–; Exec. Cttee, UK Overseas Territories Conservation Forum, 2000–. FSA 1992. Mem., Court of Assts, Goldsmiths' Co., 1994–. Mem., Assembly, Greenwich Univ., 2000. Hon. DArt Greenwich, 2000. *Publications:* contribs on buildings and furniture to books and periodicals; National Trust guides. *Address:* 3 Victoria Rise, SW4 0PB; 18 The Street, Stedham, West Sussex GU29 0NR. *Clubs:* Brooks's, Pratt's; Seaview Yacht.

DRURY, Sir Michael; *see* Drury, Sir V. W. M.

DRURY, Raymond Michael; Under Secretary and Executive Director (Personnel), NHS Executive, Department of Health, 1993–95; *b* 28 Sept. 1935; *s* of late James Joseph Drury and Annie Drury (*née* Greenwood); *m* 1959, Joyce Mary (*née* Clare); two *s* two *d*. *Educ:* Manchester Grammar Sch.; University Coll. London (BA Hons Classics (Latin and Greek)). Exec. Officer, Nat. Assistance Bd, 1958–64; HEO and Manager, Legal Aid Assessment Office, N Western Reg., 1964–70; Principal, DHSS, 1970–77; Asst Sec. and Dir (Exports), DHSS, 1977–79; Sec. of State's Rep. on Mgt Sides of Whitley Councils for Health Services (GB) responsible for NHS pay and conditions of service, 1979–88; Hd, Industrial Relns and Negotiations, DoH, 1988–93. *Recreations:* family, gardening, walking, DIY. *Address:* Moorview Cottage, Cracoe, Skipton, Yorks BD23 6LA. *T:* (01756) 730270.

DRURY, Sir (Victor William) Michael, Kt 1989; OBE 1978; FRCP; FRCGP; FRACGP; Professor of General Practice, University of Birmingham, 1980–91, now Emeritus; Vice President, Age Concern England, since 1995 (Chairman, 1992–95); *b* 5 Aug. 1926; *s* of Leslie and Beatrice Drury; *m* 1950, Joan (*née* Williamson); three *s* one *d*. *Educ:* Bromsgrove Sch.; Univ. of Birmingham (MB ChB Hons); MRCS LRCP 1949; FRCGP 1970 (MRCGP 1963); FRCP 1988; FRACGP 1988. Ho. Surg., Birmingham Gen., 1949–50; RSO, Kidderminster, 1950–51; Major, RAMC, 1951–53; Principal in Gen. Practice, Bromsgrove, 1953–91; Nuffield Trav. Fellow, 1965; Clarkson Sen. Clin. Tutor, Univ. of Birmingham, 1973–80. Lectures: James MacKenzie, 1983, Eli Lilley, 1984; Sir David Bruce, 1985; Gale, 1986; Fulton, 1996. Royal College of General Practitioners: Mem. Council, 1971–85 (Vice-Chm., 1980); Chm., Practice Org., 1966–71, Cttee and Res. Div., 1983–85; Pres., 1985–88. Member: Cttee on Safety of Medicines (Adverse Drug Reaction), 1975–79; Prescription Pricing Authy, 1981–86; DHA, 1981–85; Res. Cttee, RHA, 1982–86; GMC, 1984–94; Standing Cttee, Post Grad. Med. Educn, 1988–93. Chairman: Med. and Social Services Cttee, Muscular Dystrophy Gp, 1992–99; UK Centre for Advancement of Interprofessional Educn, 1994–97; Trustee, Nat. Asthma Trng Centre, 1991–. Civilian Advr in Gen. Practice to Army, 1984–91. Vice-Pres., Age Concern, England, 1995– (Chm., 1992–95). Mem. Ct, Liverpool Univ., 1980–87; Gov. and Trustee, Bromsgrove Sch., 1990–. Mem., Lunar Soc., 1993–. Hon. FRCPCH 1996. *Publications:* Introduction to General Practice, 1974; (ed) Treatment, 1978–; Medical Secretaries Handbook, 6th edn 1992; Treatment and Prognosis, 1990; The New Practice Manager, 1990, 3rd edn 1994; Teaching and Training Techniques for Hospital Doctors, 1998; General Practice and Clinical Negligence, 2000; various chapters in books on Drug Safety, Gen. Practice, etc; res. articles in Lancet, BMJ, Brit. Jl of Surgery, Jl RCGP. *Recreations:* gardening, reading, bridge, talking and listening. *Address:* Rossall Cottage, Church Hill, Belbroughton, near Stourbridge DY9 0DT. *T:* (01562) 730229.

DRY, Philip John Seaton; Partner, Biggart Baillie, since 1971; President, Law Society of Scotland, 1998–99 (Vice-President, 1997–98); *b* 21 April 1945; *s* of William Good Dry and Georgina Wilson Macpherson or Dry; *m* 1970, Joyce Christine Hall; one *s* one *d*. *Educ:* George Watson's Coll.; Greenock Acad.; Glasgow Univ. (LLB). Apprenticeship, 1966–68, Asst Solicitor, 1968–70, with Biggart Lumsden & Co. Dir, Fyfe Chambers (Glasgow) Ltd, 1990–98. Mem., Disciplinary Appeal Bd, Faculty of Actuaries, 1999–. Dir, Westcot Homes plc and Westcot Homes II plc, 1989–2000. Mem., PO Users' Council for Scotland, 1994–98. Director: Scots Law Trust, 1998–99; Scottish Council of Law Reporting, 1998–99. Dir, Glasgow Renfrewshire Soc. *Recreations:* sailing, the garden, opera, swimming, travel. *Address:* (office) Dalmore House, 310 St Vincent Street, Glasgow G2 5QR. *T:* (0141) 228 8000. *Club:* Royal Scottish Automobile.

DRYDEN, Sir John (Stephen Gyles), 8th and 11th Bt *cr* 1795 and 1733; *b* 26 Sept. 1943; *s* of Sir Noel Percy Hugh Dryden, 7th and 10th Bt, and Rosamund Mary (*d* 1994), *e d* of late Stephen Scrope; *S* father, 1970; *m* 1970, Diana Constance, *o d* of Cyril Tomlinson, Highland Park, Wellington, NZ; one *s* one *d*. *Educ:* Oratory School. *Heir:* *s* John Frederick Simon Dryden, *b* 26 May 1976. *Address:* Spinners, Fairwarp, Uckfield, East Sussex TN22 3BE.

DRYSDALE, Laura, (Mrs John Tipler); Head of Advisory Services, Museums and Galleries Commission, since 1999; *b* 28 April 1958; *d* of Andrew and Merida Drysdale; *m* 1989, John Tipler; one *s* one *d*, and one step *s* one step *d*. *Educ:* Charterhouse; St Andrews Univ. (MA 1979); City Univ. (C&G MA 1987). Textile Conservator: Dalmeny House, 1979–81; V&A Mus., 1981–83; Textile Conservation Studio, 1983–86; Conservation Projects, 1986–92; Partner, Drysdale and Halahan, 1992–96; Head of Collections Conservation, English Heritage, 1996–99. FIIC 1996. *Publications:* articles in learned jls, conf. proceedings. *Recreation:* treading grapes. *Address:* 49 The Close, Norwich NR1 4EG.

DRYSDALE, Thomas Henry, WS; Partner, Olivers WS since 1999; *b* 23 Nov. 1942; *s* of late Ian Drysdale and Rosalind Marion Drysdale (*née* Gallie); *m* 1967, Caroline, *d* of Dr Gavin B. Shaw and late Margaret Mabon Shaw (*née* Henderson); one *s* two *d*. *Educ:* Cargilfield; Glenalmond; Edinburgh Univ. (LLB). Partner, Shepherd & Wedderburn WS, 1967–99 (Man. Partner, 1988–94); Dep. Keeper of HM Signet, 1991–98. Dir, Edinburgh Solicitors' Property Centre, 1976–89 (Chm., 1981–88). Hon. Consul in Scotland, Republic of Hungary, 2001–. Mem., Audit Registration Cttee, ICAS, 2000–. Trustee, Clark Foundn for Legal Educn, 1999–. *Recreations:* ski-ing, walking, reading, amateur photography. *Address:* Olivers WS, 25 Manor Place, Edinburgh EH3 7DX. *T:* (0131) 225 2089. *Club:* New (Edinburgh).

DRYSDALE WILSON, John Veitch, CEng, FIMechE, FCIArb; Deputy Secretary, Institution of Mechanical Engineers, 1979–90; *b* 8 April 1929; *s* of Alexander Drysdale Wilson and Winifred Rose (*née* Frazier); *m* 1954, Joan Lily, *e d* of Mr and Mrs John Cooke, Guildford; one *s* one *d*. *Educ:* Solihull School; Guildford Technical Coll. Dennis Bros Ltd, Guildford: Engineer Apprentice, 1946–50; MIRA Research Trainee, 1949–50; Jun. Designer, 1950–51. National Service Officer, REME, 1951–53, Captain on Staff of CREME, 6th Armd Div. Management Trainee, BET Fedn, 1953–55; Technical Sales Engr, subseq. Head of Mechanical Laboratories, Esso Petroleum Co. Ltd, 1955–66; Chief Engr, R&D, Castrol Ltd, subseq. Burmah Oil Trading Ltd and Edwin Cooper Ltd, 1966–77; Projects and Res. Officer, Instn of Mechanical Engineers, 1977–79. Director: Mechanical Engineering Publications Ltd, 1979–90; Professional Engineers Insurance Bureau Ltd, 1989–90. Freeman, City of London, 1986; Liveryman: Co. of Engineers, 1987; Co. of Arbitrators, 1987. *Publications:* numerous papers to learned societies in USA and Europe on subjects related to engine lubrication. *Recreations:* travel, genealogy, horology. *Club:* Caravan.

D'SOUZA, Frances Gertrude Claire, CMG 1999; DPhil; Fellow, Open Society Institute (Soros Institute), 1998–99; *b* 18 April 1944; *d* of Robert Anthony Gilbert Russell and Pauline Mary Russell (*née* Parmet); *m* 1st, 1959, Stanislaus D'Souza (marr. diss. 1974); two *d*; 2nd, 1985, Martin Griffiths (marr. diss. 1994). *Educ:* St Mary's, Princethorpe; UCL (BSc 1970); Lady Margaret Hall, Oxford (DPhil 1976). Ford Foundn Res. Fellow in Comparative Physiology, Nuffield Inst. of Comparative Medicine, 1973–77; pt-time adult educn lectr, Morley Coll. and City Lit., 1973–78; pt-time Lectr on Race and Culture, LSE, 1974–80; Sen. Lectr, Dept of Humanities, Oxford Poly., 1977–80; Founder Dir and Res. Dir, Internat. Relief and Develt Inst., 1977–85; Indep. Res. Cons. for UN, SCF, Ford Foundn, carrying out field work in Africa, Asia, S Europe, Pacific Region, 1985–88; ODA Res. Fellow, 1988–89; Exec. Dir, Article 19, Internat. Centre against Censorship, 1989–98. Mem., RGS expedn to the Karakorums, 1980. Regular broadcasts, 1989–98. Editor, Internat. Jl of Disaster Studies and Practice, 1978–82. *Publications:* (ed) Striking a Balance: hate speech, freedom of expression and non-discrimination, 1992; (jtly) The Right to Know: human rights and access to reproductive health information, 1995; numerous reports, scientific papers, contribs to books and articles in jls, incl. Nature, Scientific American, Third World Qly. *Recreations:* music (opera and string quartets), serious walking. *Address:* Long Barn, Idbury, Chipping Norton, Oxon OX7 6RU.

D'SOUZA, Most Rev. Henry Sebastian; *see* Calcutta, Archbishop of, (RC).

DUBE, Alfred Uyapo Majaye; Ambassador of Botswana to People's Republic of China, since 1996; concurrently High Commissioner to Malaysia and Singapore; *b* 8 June 1949; *s* of Mbangwa Edison Majaye and Phakela Majaye; *m* 1977, Elvyn Jones; three *s*. *Educ:* Poly. of North London; Univ. of Essex (BA Hons Govt). Librarian, Nat. Liby Service, 1971–74; Foreign Service Officer, Dept of Ext. Affairs, Botswana, 1977–79; First Sec., Botswana Embassy and Mission to EC, Brussels, 1979–80; Counsellor, London, 1980–81; Under-Sec., Min. of Mineral Resources and Water Affairs, 1981–83; Minister Counsellor, Brussels, 1983–87; Under-Sec., Dept of Ext. Affairs, 1987–89; Ambassador to Sweden, all Nordic countries and USSR/Russia, 1989–93; High Comr, UK, 1993–96. *Recreations:* reading, jazz, wine, golf. *Address:* Embassy of Botswana, Unit 811, IBM Tower, Pacific Century Place, 2A Gong Ti Bei Lu Chaoyang District, Beijing 100027, China. *T:* (10) 65391616, *Fax:* (10) 65391199.

DUBLIN, Archbishop of, and Primate of Ireland, since 1996; **Most Rev. Walton Newcombe Francis Empey;** *b* 26 Oct. 1934; *m* 1960, Louise E. Hall; three *s* one *d*. *Educ:* Portora Royal School and Trinity College, Dublin. Curate Assistant, Glenageary, Dublin, 1958–60; Priest-in-charge, Grand Falls, NB, Canada, 1960–63; Parish Priest, Edmundston, NB, 1963–66; Incumbent, Stradbally, Co. Laois, Ireland, 1966–71; Dean of St Mary's Cathedral and Rector, Limerick City Parish, 1971–81; Bishop of Limerick and Killaloe, 1981–85; Bishop of Meath and Kildare, 1985–96. *Recreations:* reading, fishing, walking. *Address:* The See House, 17 Temple Road, Milltown, Dublin 6.

DUBLIN, Archbishop of, and Primate of Ireland, (RC), since 1988; **His Eminence Cardinal Desmond Connell,** DD; *b* 24 March 1926; *s* of John Connell and Maisie Connell (*née* Lacy). *Educ:* St Peter's National School, Phibsborough; Belvedere College; Clonliffe College; University Coll., Dublin (MA); St Patrick's Coll., Maynooth; Louvain Univ., Belgium (DPhil); DLitt NUI, 1981. University College, Dublin: Dept of Metaphysics, 1953–72; Prof. of General Metaphysics, 1972–88; Dean, Faculty of Philosophy and Sociology, 1983–88. Chaplain: Poor Clares, Donnybrook, 1953–55; Carmelites, Drumcondra, 1955–66; Carmelites, Blackrock, 1966–88. Prelate of Honour, 1984; Cardinal, 2001. *Publications:* The Vision in God, 1967; articles in reviews. *Address:* Archbishop's House, Drumcondra, Dublin 9. *T:* (1) 373732.

DUBLIN, Auxiliary Bishop of, (RC); *see* Dunne, Most Rev. Patrick.

DUBLIN, (Christ Church), Dean of; *see* Paterson, Very Rev. J. T. F.

DUBLIN, (St Patrick's), Dean of; *see* MacCarthy, Very Rev. R. B.

du BOULAY; *see* Houssemayne du Boulay.

DU BOULAY, Prof. (Francis) Robin (Houssemayne), FBA 1980; Emeritus Professor of Mediæval History in the University of London, 1982; *b* 19 Dec. 1920; *er s* of late Philip Houssemayne Du Boulay and Mercy Tyrrell (*née* Friend); *m* 1948, Cecilia Burnell Matthews (*d* 2000); two *s* one *d*. *Educ:* Christ's Hospital; Phillip's Academy, Andover, Mass., USA; Balliol Coll., Oxford. Williams Exhibitioner at Balliol Coll., 1939; Friends' Ambulance Unit and subsequently Royal Artillery, 1940–45; MA 1947; Asst Lecturer at Bedford Coll., 1947, Lecturer, 1949; Reader in Mediæval History, in University of London, 1955, Prof., 1960–82. Hon. Sec., RHistS, 1961–65. Mem. Court, Univ. of Hull, 1992–95. *Publications:* The Register of Archbishop Bourgchier, 2 vols, 1953–55; Medieval Bexley, 1961, 2nd edn 1994; Documents Illustrative of Medieval Kentish Society, 1964; The Lordship of Canterbury, 1966; An Age of Ambition, 1970; (ed jtly) The Reign of Richard II, 1972; Germany in the later Middle Ages, 1983; Legion, and other poems, 1983; The England of Piers Plowman, 1991; various essays and papers on late medieval subjects, English and German, in specialist journals and general symposia. *Address:* 23 Molescroft Road, Beverley, E Yorks HU17 7DX.

DUBOWITZ, Prof. Victor, MD, PhD; FRCP; Professor of Paediatrics, University of London, at the Royal Postgraduate Medical School, 1972–96, now Emeritus; Consultant Paediatrician, Hammersmith Hospital, 1972–96; Director, Muscle Research Centre, Royal Postgraduate Medical School, 1975–96; Director of Therapeutic Studies, European Neuro Muscular Centre, since 1999; *b* 6 Aug. 1931; *s* of late Charley and Olga Dubowitz (*née* Schattel); *m* 1960, Dr Lilly Magdalena Suzanne Sebok; four *s*. *Educ:* Beaufort West Central High Sch., S Africa; Univ. of Cape Town (BSc, MB, ChB, 1954; MD 1960). PhD Sheffield, 1965; DCH 1958; FRCP 1972. Intern, Groote Schuur Hosp., Cape Town, 1955; Sen. House Officer, Queen Mary's Hosp. for Children, Carshalton, 1957–59; Res. Associate in Histochem., Royal Postgrad. Med. Sch., 1958–59; Lectr in Clin. Path., National Hosp. for Nervous Diseases, Queen Square, London, 1960; Lectr in Child Health, 1961–65, Sen. Lectr, 1965–67, and Reader, 1967–72, Univ. of Sheffield; Res. Associate, Inst. for Muscle Diseases, and Asst Paediatrician, Cornell Med. Coll., New York, 1965–66. Several lectureships and overseas vis. professorships. President: British Paediatric Neurol. Assoc., 1992–94; European Paediatric Neurology Soc., 1994–97; World Muscle Soc., 1995–; Medical Art Soc., 1996–2000. Curator of Art, RCPCH, 1997–. Founding Editor: Neuromuscular Disorders, 1990–; European Jl of Paediatric Neurology, 1996–. Hon. FRCPCH 1997. Arvo Ylppö Gold Medal, Finland, 1982; Baron ver Heyden de Lancey Prize, Med. Art Soc., 1980 and 1982; Jean Hunter Prize, RCP, 1987; Gaetano Conte Medal, Italy, 1991; Cornelia de Lange Medal, Netherlands, 1997; Duchenne Erb Prize, German Speaking Muscular Dystrophy Assocs, 1999. Comdr, Order of Constantine the Great, 1980. *Publications:* Developing and Diseased Muscle: a histochemical study, 1968; The Floppy Infant, 1969, 2nd edn 1980; (with M. H. Brooke) Muscle Biopsy: a modern approach, 1973, 2nd edn 1985; (with L. M. S. Dubowitz) Gestational Age of the Newborn: a clinical manual, 1977; Muscle Disorders in Childhood, 1978, 2nd edn 1995; (with L. M. S. Dubowitz) The Neurological Assessment of the Preterm and Full-term Newborn Infant, 1981, 2nd edn 2000; Colour Atlas of Muscle Disorders in Childhood, 1989; (jtly) A Colour Atlas of Brain Lesions in the Newborn, 1990; chapters in books and articles in learned jls on paediatric topics, partic. muscle disorders and newborn neurology. *Recreations:* sculpting, photography. *Address:* 25 Middleton Road, Golders Green, NW11 7NR. *T:* (020) 8455 9352.

DUBS, family name of **Baron Dubs**.

DUBS, Baron *cr* 1994 (Life Peer), of Battersea in the London Borough of Wandsworth; **Alfred Dubs;** Chairman, Broadcasting Standards Commission, since 2001 (Joint Deputy Chairman, 1997); *b* Prague, Czechoslovakia, Dec. 1932; *m*; one *s* one *d*. *Educ:* LSE. BSc (Econs). Local govt officer. Mem., Westminster CC, 1971–78; Chm., Westminster Community Relns Council, 1972–77; Mem., Kensington, Chelsea and Westminster AHA, 1975–78. Dir, British Refugee Council, 1988–95. Member: TGWU; Co-operative Party. Contested (Lab): Cities of London and Westminster, 1970; Hertfordshire South, Feb. and Oct. 1974; Battersea, 1987 and 1992. MP (Lab): Wandsworth, Battersea S, 1979–83; Battersea, 1983–87. Mem., Home Affairs Select Cttee, 1981–83 (Mem., Race Relations and Immigration Sub-Cttee, 1981–83); opposition front bench spokesman on home affairs, 1983–87. House of Lords: Mem., Select Cttee on European Communities, 1995–97; an Opposition Whip, 1994–97; opposition front bench spokesman on energy, 1995–97, on health and safety, 1996–97; Parly Under-Sec. of State, NI Office, 1997–99. Mem., 1988–94, Dep. Chm., 1995–97, Broadcasting Standards Council. *Recreation:* walking in the Lake District. *Address:* c/o House of Lords, SW1P 0PW.

DU CANE, John Peter, OBE 1964; Director, Amax Inc., 1966–91; *b* 16 April 1921; *s* of Charles and Mathilde Du Cane; *m* 1945, Patricia Wallace (*née* Desmond); two *s*. *Educ:* Canford Sch., Wimborne. Pilot, Fleet Air Arm, RN, 1941–46. De Beers Consolidated Mines, 1946–54; Sierra Leone Selection Trust, 1955–63; Director: Consolidated African Selection Trust, 1963–81; Selection Trust Ltd, 1966–81 (Man. Dir, 1975–80; Chm., 1978–81); BP International Ltd, 1981; Chief Exec., BP Minerals Internat. Ltd, 1980–81; Director: Australian Consolidated Minerals Pty, 1981–86 (Dep. Chm., 1983–86); Ultramar Plc, 1983–87; Austamax Resources Ltd, 1984–86 (Dep. Chm., 1984–86). Mem., RNSA. *Recreations:* sailing, fishing, photography. *Address:* 21 Framers Court, Ellis Way, Lane End, High Wycombe, Bucks HP14 3LL. *Club:* Naval and Military.

du CANN, Col Rt Hon. Sir Edward (Dillon Lott), KBE 1985; PC 1964; Chairman, Lonrho Plc, 1984–91 (Director, 1972–92; Joint Deputy Chairman, 1983–84); *b* 28 May 1924; *er s* of late C. G. L. du Cann, Barrister-at-Law, and Janet (*née* Murchie); *m* 1st, 1962, Sallie Innes (marr. diss. 1990), *e d* of late James Henry Murchie, Caldy, Cheshire; one *s* two *d*; 2nd, 1990, Jenifer Patricia Evelyn (*d* 1995), *yr d* of late Evelyn Mansfield King, and *widow* of Sir Robert Cooke. *Educ:* Colet Court; Woodbridge Sch.; St John's Coll., Oxford (MA, Law). Served with RNVR, 1943–46 (CO, HMMTB 5010). Vice-Pres., Somerset and Wilts Trustee Savings Bank, 1956–75; Founder, Unicorn Group of Unit Trusts, 1957 (pioneered modern British unit trust industry and equity linked life assurance); Chairman: Barclays Unicorn Ltd and associated cos, 1957–72; Keyser Ullman Holdings Ltd, 1970–75; Cannon Assurance Ltd, 1972–80. Chm., Association of Unit Trust Managers, 1961. Contested: West Walthamstow Div., 1951; Barrow-in-Furness Div., 1955. MP (C) Taunton Div. of Somerset, Feb. 1956–1987. Economic Sec. to the Treasury, 1962–63; Minister of State, Board of Trade, 1963–64. Mem., Lord Chancellor's Adv. Cttee on Public Records, 1960–62; Joint Hon. Sec.: UN Parly Group, 1961–62; Conservative Parly Finance Group, 1961–62; Mem., Select Cttee on House of Lords Reform, 1962; Founder Chairman: Select Cttee on Public Expenditure, 1971–73; All-Party Maritime Affairs Parly Gp, 1984–87; Mem., Select Cttee on Privilege, 1972–87; Chairman: Select Cttee on Public Accounts, 1974–79; 1922 Cttee, 1972–84; Liaison Cttee of Select Cttee Chairmen, 1974–83; (founder) Select Cttee on Treasury and Civil Service Affairs, 1979–83; (first) Public Accounts Commn, 1984–87; Cons. Party Organisation, 1965–67; Burke Club, 1968–79. President: (founder) Anglo-Polish Cons. Soc., 1972–74; Nat. Union of Conservative and Unionist Assocs, 1981–82; Cons. Parly European Community Reform Gp, 1985–87; Vice-Chm., British American Parly Gp, 1978–81. Jt Leader, British-American Parly Gp delegns to USA, 1978, 1980; Leader, British Parly Gp delegn to China, IPU, 1982. Dir, James Beattie Ltd, 1965–79. Pres., Inst. of Freight Forwarders Ltd, 1988–89; Vice-Pres., British Insurance Brokers Assoc., 1978–; Patron, Assoc. of Insurance Brokers, 1974–77. Visiting Fellow, Univ. of Lancaster Business School, 1970–82. Member: Panel of Judges, Templeton Foundn, 1984; Management Council, GB-Sasakawa Foundn, 1984–91. Patron, Human Ecology Foundn, 1987–. Mem. Governing Council, Taunton Sch., 1972–93; Governor, Hatfield Coll., Durham Univ., 1988–92. Commodore, 1962, Admiral, 1974–87, House of Commons Yacht Club. Hon. Col, 155 (Wessex) Regt, RCT (Volunteers), 1972–82; Hon. Life Member: Instn of RCT, 1983; Taunton Racecourse, 1991. Lecturer, broadcaster. Mem. Court of Assts, Fruiterers' Co. (Master, 1990); elected first Freeman of Taunton Deane Borough, 1977. FRSA 1986. *Publications:* Investing Simplified, 1959; Two Lives: the political and business careers of Edward du Cann, 1995; Wellington Caricatures, 2000; pamphlets, and articles on financial and international affairs (incl. The Case for a Bill of Rights, How to Bring Government Expenditure within Parliamentary Control, A New Competition Policy, Hoist the Red Ensign). *Recreations:* travel, gardening, sailing. *Address:* Lemona, 8545 Pafos, Cyprus; Grosnez Lodge, Victoria Street, Alderney, Channel Islands GY9 3TA. *Clubs:* Carlton (Hon. Mem.); Royal Western Yacht.

DUCAT, Dawn, (Mrs Thomas Ducat); *see* Primarolo, D.

DUCAT-AMOS, Air Comdt Barbara Mary, CB 1974; RRC 1971; Director of Royal Air Force Nursing Services and Matron-in-Chief, Princess Mary's Royal Air Force Nursing Service, 1972–78; Nursing Sister, Medical Department, Cable and Wireless plc, 1978–85; *b* 9 Feb. 1921; *d* of late Captain G. W. Ducat-Amos, Master Mariner, and late Mrs M. Ducat-Amos. *Educ:* The Abbey Sch., Reading; St Thomas's Hosp., London (The Nightingale Trng Sch.). SRN 1943; CMB Pt 1 1948. PMRAFNS, 1944–47: served in RAF Hosps, UK and Aden; further training; nursing in S Africa and SW Africa, 1948–52; rejoined PMRAFNS, 1952: served in RAF Hosps as General Ward and Theatre Sister, UK, Germany, Cyprus, Aden and Changi (Singapore); Matron 1967; Sen. Matron 1968; Principal Matron 1970. QHNS 1972–78. Vice-Pres., Girls' Venture Corps Air Cadets, 1991– (Nat. Chm., 1982–91). CStJ 1975. *Recreations:* music, theatre, travel. *Address:* c/o Barclays Bank, PO Box 850, Barclays House, Alexandra Road, SW19 7LA. *Club:* Royal Air Force.

duCHARME, Gillian Drusilla Brown; educational consultant, since 2000; Headmistress, Benenden School, 1985–2000; *b* 23 Jan. 1938; *d* of Alfred Henry Brown and Alice Drusilla Grant; *m* 1969, Jean Louis duCharme (marr. diss.). *Educ:* Girton College, Cambridge. BA 1960, MA 1964. British Council, 1964–66; Chm., French Dept and Head of Upper Sch., Park Sch., Brookline, Mass, 1969–77; Registrar, Concord Acad., Concord, Mass, 1977–80; Headmistress, The Town Sch., New York City, 1980–85.

Governor: Univ. of Greenwich; Wellington Coll., Crowthorne; Marlborough House Sch. Mem. Council, Friends of Nat. Maritime Mus. *Recreations:* tennis, hill-walking, art, design and architecture, film, birdwatching, travel, books. *Address:* 3 Saint Alfege Passage, Greenwich, SE10 9JS. *T:* (020) 8858 8186; *e-mail:* gillianducharme@hotmail.com.

DUCHÊNE, Louis-François; author; *b* 17 Feb. 1927; *s* of Louis Adrien Duchêne and Marguerite Lucienne Duchêne (*née* Lainé); *m* 1952, Anne Margaret Purves (*d* 1997); one *d. Educ:* St Paul's Sch.; London Sch. of Economics. Leader writer, Manchester Guardian, 1949–52; Press attaché, High Authority, European Coal and Steel Community, Luxembourg, 1952–55; Correspondent of The Economist, Paris, 1956–58; Dir, Documentation Centre of Action Cttee for United States of Europe (Chm. Jean Monnet), Paris, 1958–63; Editorial writer, The Economist, London, 1963–67. Director: Internat. Inst. for Strategic Studies, 1969–74; European Res. Centre, Sussex Univ., 1974–82. *Publications:* (ed) The Endless Crisis, 1970; The Case of the Helmeted Airman, a study of W. H. Auden, 1972; New Limits on European Agriculture, 1985; (ed with G. Shepherd) Managing Industrial Change in Western Europe, 1987; Jean Monnet: first statesman of interdependence, 1994. *Address:* 3 Powis Villas, Brighton, East Sussex BN1 3HD. *T:* (01273) 329258.

DUCIE, 7th Earl of, *cr* 1837; **David Leslie Moreton;** Baron Ducie, 1763; Baron Moreton, 1837; *b* 20 Sept. 1951; *e s* of 6th Earl of Ducie and Alison May, *d* of L. A. Bates; *S* father, 1991; *m* 1975, Helen, *er d* of M. L. Duchesne; one *s* one *d. Educ:* Cheltenham College; Wye Coll., London Univ. (BSc 1973). *Heir: s* Lord Moreton, *qv. Address:* Talbots End Farm, Cromhall, Glos GL12 8AJ.

DUCK, Hywel Ivor, CMG 1998; Hon. Director-General, Council of the European Union, since 1998; Director of Fisheries, Secretariat General, Council of Ministers of European Communities, 1987–98; *b* 12 June 1933; *s* of Dr Ernest Frank Duck and Minnie Isabel Duck (*née* Peake); *m* 1980, Dr Barbara Elisabeth Huwe (*d* 1994); one *s* one *d. Educ:* King's School, Canterbury; Trinity College, Cambridge (MA); Diplôme d'Etudes Supérieures Européennes, Nancy. Called to the Bar, Gray's Inn, 1956. Foreign Office, 1956; served Warsaw, FO, Cairo, Khartoum, Damascus; Second later First Sec., Bonn, 1964; DSAO, later FCO, 1968; Consul (Commercial), Zürich and Dep. Dir, British Export Promotion in Switzerland, 1970–73; Head of Div., Secretariat Gen., Council of Ministers, EC, 1973–75; Dir of Ops and Translation, 1975–84; Dir, Directorate-Gen. for Agriculture and Fisheries, 1984–87. *Recreation:* classical music. *Clubs:* Oxford and Cambridge; American and Common Market (Brussels).

DUCKWORTH, Brian Roy; His Honour Judge Duckworth; DL; a Circuit Judge, since 1983; Deputy Senior Judge, Cyprus Sovereign Base Areas Court, since 1998; *b* 26 July 1934; *s* of late Roy and Kathleen Duckworth; *m* 1964, Nancy Carolyn Duckworth, JP, *d* of late Chris and Annie Holden; three *s* one *d. Educ:* Sedbergh Sch.; Worcester Coll., Oxford (MA). Called to Bar, Lincoln's Inn, 1958; a Recorder of the Crown Court, 1972–83; Member: Northern Circuit; Bar Council, 1979–82. Councillor, Blackburn RDC, 1960–74 (Chm. 1970–72); Mem., Blackburn HMC, 1966–74. Liaison Judge and Hon. Pres., South Cumbria Magistracy, 1987–92; Liaison Judge, SW Lancs Magistracy, 1993–. Member: Lord-Lieut's Magistracy Adv. Cttee, 1993–; Lancs Probation Cttee, 1991–; Cttee, Council of Circuit Judges, 1995–. Chm., Samlesbury Hall Charitable Trust, 1993–; Pres., Old Sedberghian Club, 1996–99. DL Lancs 1995. *Recreations:* golf, gardening, motor sport. *Address:* c/o The Crown Court, Ringway, Preston PR1 2LL. *T:* (01772) 832443. *Club:* Pleasington Golf.

DUCKWORTH, Sir Edward Richard Dyce, 4th Bt *cr* 1909, of Grosvenor Place, City of Westminster; *b* 13 July 1943; *er s* of Sir Richard Dyce Duckworth, 3rd Bt and Violet Alison (*d* 1996), *d* of Lt-Col G. B. Wauchope, DSO; *S* father, 1997; *m* 1976, Patricia, *o d* of Thomas Cahill; one *s* one *d. Educ:* Marlborough; Cranfield. *Heir: s* James Dyce Duckworth, *b* 1984.

DUCKWORTH, Eric; *see* Duckworth, W. E.

DUCKWORTH, John Clifford, FREng; FIEE, FInstP; Managing Director, National Research Development Corporation, 1959–70; *b* 27 Dec. 1916; *s* of late H. Duckworth, Wimbledon, and of Mrs A. H. Duckworth (*née* Woods); *m* 1942, Dorothy Nancy Wills; three *s. Educ:* KCS, Wimbledon; Wadham Coll., Oxford (MA). FIEE 1957; FInstP 1957; SFInstE 1957; FREng (FEng 1976). Radar Research and Development, Telecommunications Research Establishment, Malvern, 1939–46; National Research Council, Chalk River, Ont, 1946–47; Atomic Energy Research Establishment, Harwell, 1947–50; Chief Engineer, Wythenshawe Laboratories, Ferranti Ltd, 1950–54; Nuclear Power Engineer, Brit. Electricity Authority, 1954–58; Central Electricity Authority, 1957–58; Chief Research and Development Officer, Central Electricity Generating Board, 1958–59. Mem. Bd, AEA, 1963–68. Mem., Defence Res. Adv. Council, 1955–65. Chm., IDT Investment Services Ltd, 1970–82; Chm. or non-exec. dir of various public cos, 1970–83. Pres., Institute of Fuel, 1963–64; Vice-Pres., Parliamentary and Scientific Cttee, 1964–67. Chairman: MacRobert Award Cttee, 1970–76; Science Mus. Adv. Council, 1972–84; Trustee, Science Mus., 1984–90. Vice-Pres., IEE, 1974–77. *Address:* Huefield, Helford Passage, Falmouth TR11 5LD. *Club:* Athenæum.

DUCKWORTH, Prof. Roy, CBE 1987; MD; FRCS, FDSRCS, FRCPath; Emeritus Professor of Oral Medicine, University of London; Dean, The London Hospital Medical College, 1986–94; *b* Bolton, 19 July 1929; *s* of Stanley Duckworth and Hilda Evelyn Moores; *m* 1953, Marjorie Jean Bowness, Flimby; two *s* one *d. Educ:* King George V Sch., Southport; Univ. of Liverpool (BDS; MD 1964). FDSRCS 1957; FRCPath 1973; FRCS 1986. Served RAF Dental Br., 1953–55. Nuffield Fellow, RPMS and Guy's Hosp. Dental Sch., 1959–61; The London Hospital Medical College: Sen. Lectr in Oral Medicine, 1961; Reader in Oral Medicine, 1965; Dean of Dental Studies, 1969–75; Prof. and Head, Dept of Oral Medicine, 1968–90. Consultant in Oral Medicine, The London Hosp., 1965–90. Dean, Faculty of Dental Surgery, RCS, 1983–86. Civil Consultant: in Dental Surg., to Army, 1977–90; in Oral Medicine and Oral Path., to RN, 1982–90; Temp. Consultant, WHO, 1973; British Council Visitor, 1977. Vis. Prof. in many countries. President: British Soc. of Periodontology, 1972–73; British Soc. for Oral Medicine, 1986–87; BDA, 1990–91. Chm., Standing Dental Adv. Cttee, Dept of Health, 1988–92 (Mem., 1984–88); Member: Adv. Council on Misuse of Drugs, 1977–85; Medicines Commn, 1980–83; Council, Fédération Dentaire Internationale, 1981–90 (Mem., List of Honour, 1993); GDC, 1984–89. Hon. Fellow, QMW, 1997. Scientific Adviser, British Dental Jl, 1975–82; Editor, Internat. Dental Jl, 1981–90. *Publications:* contrib. professional jls. *Recreation:* sailing.

DUCKWORTH, (Walter) Eric, OBE 1991; PhD; FREng; FIM, FInstP; Managing Director, Fulmer Ltd (formerly Fulmer Research Institute), 1969–90; Chairman, Bournville Consultants Ltd, since 1994; *b* 2 Aug. 1925; *s* of Albert Duckworth and Rosamund (*née* Biddle); *m* 1949, Emma Evans; one *s. Educ:* Cambridge Univ. (MA, PhD). Research Manager, Glacier Metal Co., 1955; Asst Director, BISRA, 1966; Chm., Yarsley Technical Centre, 1973–89; Director: Ricardo Consulting Engineers plc, 1978–85; H. Darnell Ltd, 1982–94; Fleming Technol. Investment Trust plc, 1984–90. Chm., Council of Science and Technology Insts, 1977–78; first Charter Pres., Instn of Metallurgists, 1974–75; Pres., Assoc. of Independent Res. and Technol. Organisations (formerly Assoc. of Indep. Contract Res. Organs), 1978–79, 1988–89; Hon. Treas., Metals Soc., 1981–84; Chm., Professional Affairs Bd, Inst. of Metals, 1985–88. Member: Parly and Scientific Cttee, 1968–; Res. and Technol. Cttee, 1979–88, and Indust. Policy Cttee, 1983–88, Council, 1988–89, CBI; Nominations Cttee, 1983–88, Standing Cttee on Industry, 1988–94, Engrg Council; Engrg Bd, SERC, 1985–87; Council, Assoc. for Schools' Sci., Engrg and Technol. (formerly Standing Conf. on Schools' Sci. and Technol.), 1994–99. Chm., Christian Nationals Evangelism Commn, 1974–93; Trustee: Comino Foundn, 1981–; FMI, 1995–99 (Mem. Council, 1995–99); Vice-Pres., St Mary's Hosp. Med. Sch., 1976–97; Mem. Court, Brunel Univ., 1978–85, and 1991–. Liveryman: Worshipful Co. of Scientific Instrument Makers; Co. of Engineers; Freeman, City of London. First Edwin Liddiard Meml Lectr, London Metallurgical Soc. of Inst. of Metals, 1982. FREng (FEng 1980). Hon. DTech Brunel, 1976; DUniv Surrey, 1980. Editor, 1978–85, Chm., Editorial Bd, 1985–92, Materials and Design. *Publications:* A Guide to Operational Research, 1962, 3rd edn 1977; Statistical Techniques in Technological Research, 1968; Electroslag Refining, 1969; Manganese in Ferrous Metallurgy, 1976; Contract Research, 1991; *circa* 100 contribs to learned and other jls on many topics. *Recreations:* gardening, photography, changing other people's attitudes. *Address:* Orinda, Church Lane, Stoke Poges, Bucks SL2 4PB. *T:* (01753) 645778. *Club:* Stoke Park Golf.

du CROS, Sir Claude Philip Arthur Mallet, 3rd Bt *cr* 1916; *b* 22 Dec. 1922; *s* of Sir (Harvey) Philip du Cros, 2nd Bt, and of Dita, *d* of late Sir Claude Coventry Mallet, CMG; *S* father, 1975; *m* 1st, 1953, Mrs Christine Nancy Tordoff (marr. diss. 1974; she *d* 1988), *d* of late F. R. Bennett, Spilsby, Lincs; one *s*; 2nd, 1974, Mrs Margaret Roy Cutler (marr. diss. 1982), *d* of late R. J. Frater, Gosforth, Northumberland. *Heir: s* Julian Claude Arthur Mallet du Cros [*b* 23 April 1955; *m* 1984, Patricia, *o d* of Gerald Wyatt, Littlefield School, Liphook; one *s* one *d*]. *Address:* Long Meadow, Ballaugh Glen, IoM.

DUDA, Dr Karel; Ambassador of the Czech and Slovak Federal Republic to the Court of St James's, 1990–92; *b* 31 May 1926; *s* of Karel Duda and Marie Dudová; *m* 1952, Danuše Barešová; one *s* two *d. Educ:* Charles Univ., Prague (LLD). Ministry of Finance, 1950–54; Min. of Foreign Affairs, 1954–92; Ambassador to USA, 1963–69. *Address:* Oravská 3, 10000 Prague 10, Czech Republic.

DUDBRIDGE, Prof. Glen, PhD; FBA 1984; Shaw Professor of Chinese and Fellow of University College, Oxford, since 1989; *b* 2 July 1938; *s* of George Victor Dudbridge and Edna Kathleen Dudbridge (*née* Cockle); *m* 1965, Sylvia Lo (Lo Fung-young); one *s* one *d. Educ:* Bristol Grammar School; Magdalene College, Cambridge (MA, PhD); New Asia Institute of Advanced Chinese Studies, Hong Kong. MA Oxon. Nat. Service, RAF, 1957–59. Research Fellow, Magdalene College, Cambridge, 1965; Lectr in Modern Chinese, 1965–85 and Fellow, Wolfson Coll., 1966–85, Univ. of Oxford; Prof. of Chinese and Fellow, Magdalene Coll., Univ. of Cambridge, 1985–89. Visiting Professor: Yale Univ., 1972–73; Univ. of California, Berkeley, 1980, 1998. Hon. Mem., Chinese Acad. of Social Scis, 1996. *Publications:* The Hsi-yu chi: a study of antecedents to the sixteenth century Chinese novel, 1970; The Legend of Miao-shan, 1978 (Chinese edn, 1990); The Tale of Li Wa: study and critical edition of a Chinese story from the ninth century, 1983; Religious experience and lay society in T'ang China, 1995; Lost Books of Medieval China, 2000. *Address:* Institute for Chinese Studies, Walton Street, Oxford OX1 2HG.

DUDDING, Richard Scarbrough; Director General, Strategy and Corporate Services, Department for Transport, Local Government and the Regions (formerly Department of the Environment, Transport and the Regions), since 1997; *b* 29 Nov. 1950; *s* of Sir John Scarbrough Dudding and of Lady (Enid Grace) Dudding; *m* 1987, Priscilla Diana Russell; two *s. Educ:* Cheltenham Coll.; Jesus Coll., Cambridge (MA 1st Cl. Hons History). Joined DoE, 1972; Private Sec. to John Smith, MP, 1976–78; Principal, 1977; Asst Sec., 1984; Sec., Cttee of Inquiry into Conduct of Local Govt Business, 1985–86; Under Sec., 1990; Finance Dir, 1990–93; Director: Pollution Control and Wastes, 1993–96; Personnel and Central Support Services, 1996–97. *Recreations:* gardening, walking, golf. *Address:* Department for Transport, Local Government and the Regions, Great Minster House, 76 Marsham Street, SW1P 4DE.

DUDGEON, Air Vice-Marshal Antony Greville, CBE 1955; DFC 1941; *b* 6 Feb. 1916; *s* of late Prof. Herbert William Dudgeon, Guy's Hosp. and Egyptian Government Service; *m* 1942, Phyllis Margaret (*d* 1994), *d* of late Group Capt. John McFarlane, OBE, MC, AFC, Lowestoft, Suffolk; one *s* one *d. Educ:* Eton; RAF Cranwell. RAF Service, 1933–68, in UK, Europe, Near, Middle and Far East, USA; personnel work, training, operations, flight safety, organisation of new formations, liaison with civilian firms and youth organisations; courses at Staff Coll., Flying Coll., and London Polytechnic (Dip.); NATO Staff; 6 command appointments; over 100 operational sorties; 3,500 hours on over 70 types of aircraft as pilot. Manager, Professional Staff Services, McKinsey & Co., Paris, 1968–78; representative, France, Grangersol Ltd, 1978–81. *Publications: autobiographical works:* A Flying Command (under pen-name Tom Dagger), 1962; The Luck of the Devil (1929–41), 1985; Wings Over North Africa (1941–43), 1987; The War That Never Was (1941), 1991; Hidden Victory (1941), 2000; stories and articles contributed to Blackwood's Magazine and to other jls. *Recreations:* writing, lecturing, photography, swimming; languages (French, Egyptian). *Address:* 155 Rivermead Court, Ranelagh Gardens, SW6 3SF. *Clubs:* Royal Air Force, Hurlingham.

DUDLEY, 4th Earl of, *cr* 1860; **William Humble David Ward;** Baron Ward, 1644; Viscount Ednam, 1860; *b* 5 Jan. 1920; *e s* of 3rd Earl of Dudley, MC, TD, and Rosemary Millicent, RRC (*d* 1930), *o d* of 4th Duke of Sutherland; *S* father, 1969; *m* 1st, 1946, Stella (marr. diss., 1961), *d* of M. A. Carcano, KCMG, KBE; one *s* twin *d*; 2nd, 1961, Maureen Swanson; one *s* five *d. Educ:* Eton; Christ Church, Oxford. Joined 10th Hussars, 1941, Adjt, 1944–45; ADC to Viceroy of India, 1942–43. Served War of 1939–45 (wounded). Pres., Baggeridge Brick Co. Ltd. *Heir: s* Viscount Ednam, *qv. Address:* 6 Cottesmore Gardens, W8 5PR; The Mansard, Putsborough, Braunton, N Devon EX33 1LD. *Clubs:* White's, Pratt's.

DUDLEY, Baroness (14th in line), *cr* 1439–1440 (called out of abeyance, 1916); **Barbara Amy Felicity Hamilton;** *b* 23 April 1907; *o d* of 12th Baron Dudley and Sybil Augusta (*d* 1958), *d* of late Rev. Canon Henry William Coventry; *S* brother, 1972; *m* 1929, Guy Raymond Hill Wallace (*d* 1967), *s* of late Gen. Hill Wallace, CB, RHA; three *s* one *d*; *m* 1980, Charles Anthony Crosse Hamilton. *Recreations:* floral water-colours (has exhibited Royal Watercolour Society); gardening. *Heir: e s* Hon. Jim Anthony Hill Wallace [*b* 9 Nov. 1930; *m* 1962, Nicola Jane, *d* of Lt-Col Philip William Edward Leslie Dunsterville; two *s*]. *Address:* Hill House, Kempsey, Worcestershire WR5 3PY. *T:* (01905) 820253.

DUDLEY, Area Bishop of, since 2000; **Rt Rev. David Stuart Walker;** *b* 30 May 1957; *s* of late Fred Walker and of Joyce Walker; *m* 1980, Susan Ann (*née* Pearce); one *s* one *d. Educ:* King's Coll., Cambridge (MA 1981); Queen's Coll., Birmingham (DipTh 1982).

Ordained deacon, 1983, priest, 1984; Curate, Handsworth, Sheffield, 1983–86; Team Vicar, Maltby, 1986–91; Industrial Chaplain, 1986–91; Vicar, Bramley and Ravenfield, 1991–95; Team Rector, Bramley and Ravenfield with Hooton Roberts and Braithwell, 1995–2000. Member: Council, Nat. Housing Fedn, 1996–; Govt Policy Action Team on Housing Mgt, 1998–. *Publications:* various articles in housing jls. *Recreations:* cricket, hill walking, embroidery, reading. *Address:* Bishop's House, Bishop's Walk, Cradley Heath, W Midlands B64 7RH. *T:* (0121) 550 3407, *Fax:* (0121) 550 7340; *e-mail:* bishop.david@CofE-worcester.org.uk.

DUDLEY, Archdeacon of; *see* Trethewey, Ven. F. M.

DUDLEY, Prof. Hugh Arnold Freeman, CBE 1988; FRCSE, FRCS, FRACS; Professor of Surgery, St Mary's Hospital, London University, 1973–88, now Emeritus; *b* 1 July 1925; *s* of W. L. and Ethel Dudley; *m* 1947, Jean Bruce Lindsay Johnston; two *s* one *d*. *Educ:* Heath Grammar Sch., Halifax; Edinburgh and Harvard Univs. MB, ChB Edin. 1947; ChM (Gold Medal and Chiene Medal) Edin. 1958; FRCSE 1951; FRACS 1965; FRCS 1974. Research Fell., Harvard Univ., 1953–54; Lecturer in Surgery, Edinburgh Univ., 1954–58; Sen. Lectr, Aberdeen Univ., 1958–63; Foundation Prof. of Surgery, Monash Univ., Melbourne, 1963–72. President: Surgical Res. Soc. of Australasia, 1968; Biol. Engrg Soc. of GB, 1978–80; Surgical Res. Soc. of GB, 1981. Regl Research Co-ordinator, NW Thames RHA, 1989–92. Chairman, Independent Ethics Committee: Army Personnel Res. Estabt, Farnborough, 1989–94; Chemical and Biological Defence Estabt, Porton Down, 1988–96 (Mem. Council, 1992–94). Chm., Med. Writers Gp, 1980–83, Mem. Cttee, 1984–87, Soc. of Authors. Corresponding Member: Surgical Res. Soc., Australia; Surgical Res. Soc. of SA; Vascular Soc. of SA; Hon. Member: Hellenic Soc. of Experimental Medicine; Aberdeen Medico-Chirurgical Soc.; Hon. Fellow: Amer. Surgical Assoc.; Amer. Assoc. for the Surgery of Trauma; S African Coll. of Surgeons. Chm. Editorial Board of Br. Jl of Surgery and of Br. Jl Surgery Soc. Ltd, 1980–88; Associate Editor, BMJ, 1988–91. *Publications:* Principles of General Surgical Management, 1958; (jtly); Access and Exposure in Abdominal Surgery, 1963; (jtly) Guide for House Surgeons in the Surgical Unit, 5th edn 1974, to 8th edn 1988; (ed) Rob and Smith's Operative Surgery, 3rd edn 1976, 4th edn 1988; Hamilton Bailey's Emergency Surgery, 10th edn 1977, 11th edn 1986; Communication in Medicine and Biology, 1977; (ed) Aid to Clinical Surgery, 2nd edn 1978 to 4th edn 1988; (jtly) Practical Procedures for House Officers, 1988; (jtly) The People's Hospital of North East Scotland, 1992; (ed jtly) Scientific Foundations of Trauma, 1996; papers in med. and sci. jls. *Recreations:* missing pheasants; annoying others; surgical history. *Address:* House of Broombrae, Glenbuchat, Strathdon, Aberdeenshire AB36 8UA. *T:* (01975) 641341, *Fax:* (01975) 641201; *e-mail:* hugh.dudley@btinternet.com.

DUDLEY, Rev. Martin Raymond, PhD; Rector, Priory Church of St Bartholomew the Great, London, since 1995; *b* 31 May 1953; *s* of Ronald Frank Dudley and Joyce Mary (*née* Gardiner); *m* 1976, Paula Jones; two *s*. *Educ:* King Edward's Sch., Birmingham; RMA Sandhurst; KCL (BD, AKC 1977, MTh 1978); St Michael's Coll., Llandaff; PhD London 1994. Ordained deacon, 1979, priest, 1980; Curate, Whitchurch, 1979–83; Vicar, Weston, 1983–88; Priest i/c, Ardeley, 1986–88; Vicar, Owlsmoor, 1988–95. Chaplain: Imperial Soc. of Kts Bach., 1995–; Butchers' Co., 1995–; Co. of Chartered Secretaries and Administrators, 1995–2000; Master, Farmers' Co., 1999–2000; Co. of Inf. Technologists, 2001–; Master, Fletchers' Co., 2001–April 2002. Mem., Professional Conduct and Complaints Cttee, Bar Council, 2000–. Trustee, Butchers' and Drovers' Charitable Instn, 1996–. FRHistS 1995; FSA 1997. SBStJ 1998. *Publications:* The Collect in Anglican Liturgy, 1994; (ed) Like a Two-edged Sword, 1995; A Manual of Ministry to the Sick, 1997; Humanity and Healing, 1998; Ashes to Glory, 1999; A Herald Voice, 2000; Risen, Ascended, Glorified, 2001. *Recreations:* visiting French cathedrals, reading modern fiction. *Address:* Church House, Cloth Fair, EC1A 7JQ. *T:* (020) 7606 5171.

DUDLEY, Prof. Norman Alfred, CBE 1977; FREng; Lucas Professor of Engineering Production, 1959–80, Emeritus Professor 1981, University of Birmingham; Head of Department of Engineering Production and Director of Lucas Institute of Engineering Production, 1955–80; *b* 29 Feb. 1916; *s* of Alfred Dudley; *m* 1940, Hilda Florence, *d* of John Miles; one *s* two *d*. *Educ:* Kings Norton Grammar Sch.; Birmingham Coll. of Technology. BSc London, PhD Birmingham. FREng (FEng 1981). Industrial training and appts: H. W. Ward & Co. Ltd, 1932–39; Imperial Typewriter Co. Ltd, 1940–45; Technical Coll. Lectr, 1945–52; Sen. Lectr, Wolverhampton and Staffs, 1948–52; Lectr in Eng. Prod., 1952, Reader, 1956, University of Birmingham. Chm., Manufacturing Processes Div., Birmingham Univ. Inst. for Advanced Studies in Engineering Sciences, 1965–68. Director: Birmingham Productivity Services Ltd; West Midlands Low Cost Automation Centre. Member: SRC Manufacturing Technol. Cttee; SRC and DoI Teaching Company Cttee, 1977–80. Chm., Cttee of Hds of Univ. Depts of Production Studies, 1970–80. Governor: Dudley and Staffs Tech. Coll., and Walsall and Staffs Tech. Coll., 1955–60; Letchworth Coll. of Technol., 1964–66. Member: Council, West Midlands Productivity Assoc.; Council, Internat. Univ. Contact for Management Education, 1957; UK Delegn to UNCSAT Geneva, 1963; W Midlands Economic Planning Council, 1970–78; British Council Mission to Bulgaria, 1971; Adv. Panel on Economic Develt, West Midlands Metropolitan CC, 1976–77; Council, Nat. Materials Handling Centre. Institution of Production Engineers: Mem. Council, 1959–61; Chm., Res. Cttee, 1965–66; J. D. Scaife Silver Medal, 1958; Viscount Nuffield Meml Lectr, 1969. Pres., Midlands Operational Research Soc., 1966–80. Mem., Ergonomics Res. Soc.; Emeritus Mem., Internat. Inst. of Production Engrg Research. Fellow, World Acad. of Productivity Sci., 2000; FIMgt; Hon. FIMfgE; Hon. FIEE. Hon. Member: Japanese Industrial Management Assoc.; Internat. Foundn of Prodn Research. Hon. DTech Loughborough, 1981. Editor, International Journal of Production Research, 1961–80. Norman Dudley Lect. inaugurated at 11th Internat. Conf. on Prodn Res., China, 1991; Norman Dudley award estab. by Internat. Jl of Production Res., 1996. Granted armorial bearings, 1994. *Publications:* Work Measurement: Some Research Studies, 1968; (co-ed) Production and Industrial Systems, 1978; The Bulstrodes alias Bolstridges of Bedworth, 1991; The Dudleys of Northwich Hundred, 1994; various papers on Engineering Production. *Address:* 37 Abbots Close, Knowle, Solihull, West Midlands B93 9PP. *T:* (01564) 775976.

DUDLEY, William Stuart, RDI 1989; Associate Designer, Royal National Theatre, since 1981; *b* 4 March 1947; *s* of William Dudley and Dorothy Stacey. *Educ:* Highbury Sch., London; St Martin's School of Art; Slade School of Art. DipAD, BA Fine Art; UCL Postgrad. Dip. Fine Art. First production, Hamlet, Nottingham Playhouse, 1970; subseq. prodns include: The Duchess of Malfi and Man is Man, Royal Court, 1971; *National Theatre*, 1971–: Tyger, 1974; The Good-Natured Man, 1974; The Passion, 1977; Lavender Blue, 1977; The World Turned Upside Down, Has Washington Legs?, 1978; Dispatches, Lost Worlds, Lark Rise, Candleford, Undiscovered Country (SWET award, Designer of the Year, 1980), 1979; Good Soldier Schweyk, 1982; Cinderella, 1983; The Mysteries, Real Inspector Hound/The Critic, 1985 (Laurence Olivier (formerly SWET) Award, Designer of the Year, 1985); Futurists, 1986; Waiting for Godot, 1987; Cat on a Hot Tin Roof, The Shaugraun, and The Changeling, 1988; Bartholemew Fair, 1988; The Crucible, 1990; The Coup, 1991; Pygmalion, 1992; On the Ledge, 1993; Under Milk Wood, 1995; Mary Stuart, 1996; The Homecoming, 1997; The London Cuckolds, 1998; All My Sons, 2000 (Laurence Olivier Awards, Best Set Designer, 2001); *Royal Court:* Live Like Pigs, 1972; Merry-Go-Round, 1973; Magnificence, 1975; The Fool, 1975; Small Change, 1976; Hamlet, 1980; Kafka's Dick, 1986; Etta Jenks, 1990; I Licked a Slag's Deodorant, 1996; *RSC:* Twelfth Night, 1974; Ivanov, 1976; That Good Between Us, 1977; Richard III, The Party, Today, 1984; Merry Wives of Windsor, 1985, 1992; A Midsummer Night's Dream, Richard II, 1986; Kiss Me Kate, 1987; *West End:* Mutiny, Piccadilly, 1985; Heartbreak House, Haymarket, 1992; The Deep Blue Sea, Almeida, 1993; A Streetcar Named Desire, Haymarket, 1996; *opera:* WNO: Il barbiere di Siviglia, 1976; Idomeneo, 1991; Metropolitan, NY: Billy Budd, 1978; Glyndebourne: Die Entführung aus dem Serail, 1980; Il barbiere di Siviglia, 1981; Royal Opera: Les Contes d'Hoffman (sets), 1980, 1986; Don Giovanni, 1981; The Cunning Little Vixen, 1990; Bayreuth: Der Ring des Nibelungen, 1983; Der Rosenkavalier, 1984; Salzburg Festival: Un ballo in maschera, 1989; *other productions:* The Ship, Glasgow, 1990; The Big Picnic, Glasgow, 1994; Some Sunny Day, Hampstead, 1996; The Alchemist, Birmingham, 1996; *television film:* Persuasion, 1994 (BAFTA and RTS Awards for set design). Designer of the Year, Laurence Olivier Awards, 1980, 1985, 1986, 1993. *Recreation:* playing the concertina. *Address:* 11 Halstow Road, SE10 0LD.

DUDLEY-SMITH, Rt Rev. Timothy; Bishop Suffragan of Thetford, 1981–92; *b* 26 Dec. 1926; *o s* of Arthur and Phyllis Dudley Smith, Buxton, Derbyshire; *m* 1959, June Arlette MacDonald; one *s* two *d*. *Educ:* Tonbridge Sch.; Pembroke Coll., and Ridley Hall, Cambridge. BA 1947, MA 1951; Certif. in Educn 1948. Deacon, 1950; priest, 1951; Asst Curate, St Paul, Northumberland Heath, 1950–53; Head of Cambridge Univ. Mission in Bermondsey, 1953–55; Hon. Chaplain to Bp of Rochester, 1953–60; Editor, Crusade, and Editorial Sec. of Evangelical Alliance, 1955–59; Asst Sec. of Church Pastoral-Aid Soc., 1959–65, Sec., 1965–73; Archdeacon of Norwich, 1973–81; Commissary to Archbp of Sydney, 1971–92; Exam. Chap. to Bp of Norwich, 1971–85. President: Evangelical Alliance, 1987–91; C of E Evangelical Council, 1990–93; Vice-Pres., UCCF, 1992–. Chm. of Govs, 1992–96, Patron, 1996–, Monkton Combe Sch. Fellow, Hymn Soc. in the US and Canada, 1997. MLitt Lambeth, 1991. *Publications:* Christian Literature and the Church Bookstall, 1963; What Makes a Man a Christian?, 1966; A Man Named Jesus, 1971; Someone who Beckons, 1978; Lift Every Heart, 1984; A Flame of Love, 1987; Songs of Deliverance, 1988; Praying with the English Hymn Writers, 1989; A Voice of Singing, 1992; John Stott: a comprehensive bibliography, 1995; (compiled) Authentic Christianity, 1995; Great is the Glory, 1997; John Stott: the making of a leader, 1999; John Stott: a global ministry, 2001; (ed jtly) Beneath a Travelling Star, 2001; contributor to various hymn books. *Recreations:* reading, verse, woodwork, family and friends. *Address:* 9 Ashlands, Ford, Salisbury, Wilts SP4 6DY. *T:* (01722) 326417.

DUDLEY-WILLIAMS, Sir Alastair (Edgcumbe James), 2nd Bt *cr* 1964, of Exeter; Director, Wildcat Consultants, since 1986; *b* 26 Nov. 1943; *s* of Sir Rolf Dudley Dudley-Williams, 1st Bt and of Margaret Helen, *er d* of F. E. Robinson, OBE; *S* father, 1987; *m* 1972, Diana Elizabeth Jane, twin *d* of R. H. C. Duncan; three *d*. *Educ:* Pangbourne College. Hughes Tool Co. (Texas), 1962–64; Bay Drilling Corp. (Louisiana), 1964–65; Bristol Siddeley Whittle Tools Ltd, 1965–67; Santa Fe Drilling Co., 1967–72; Inchcape plc, 1972–86. *Recreations:* shooting, fishing. *Heir: b* Malcolm Philip Edgcumbe Dudley-Williams [*b* 10 Aug. 1947; *m* 1973, Caroline Anne Colina, twin *d* of R. H. C. Duncan; two *s* one *d*]. *Address:* c/o The Old Manse, South Petherton, Somerset TA13 5DB. *Club:* Royal Cornwall Yacht.

DUE, Ole; Grand Cross, Order of Dannebrog 1994 (Kt 1970); President, Court of Justice of European Communities, 1988–94; *b* 10 Feb. 1931; *s* of Stationmaster H. P. Due and Jenny Due (*née* Jensen); *m* 1954, Alice Maud Halkier Nielsen; three *s* one *d*. *Educ:* Copenhagen Univ. (Law degree, 1955). Ministry of Justice, Copenhagen: civil servant, 1955; Head of Div., 1970; Head of Dept, 1975; Appeal Court Judge *ai*, 1978; Judge, Court of Justice of EC, 1979–88. Legal Counsellor to Danish Delegn, negotiations of adhesion to EC, 1970–72; Mem., Danish Delegn to Hague Conf. on private internat. law, 1964–76. Chm., Danish Inst. of Internat. Affairs, 1995–. Joint Ed., series, EF-Karnov, 1973–98. Hon. Member: Gray's Inn; King's Inn, Dublin. Hon. Prof., Copenhagen, 1994. Dr *hc* Stockholm, 1991. *Publications:* (ed) EF-lovregister, 1973–75; (jtly) Juridisk Grundbog, 1975; (jtly) Kommenteret færdselslov, 1979; articles on community law, private internat. law and legal technique. *Recreation:* hiking. *Address:* Mördrupvej 116, 3060 Espergärde, Denmark.

DUFF, Andrew Nicholas, OBE 1997; Member (Lib Dem) Eastern England, European Parliament, since 1999; *b* 25 Dec. 1950; *s* of Norman Bruce Duff and Diana (*née* Wilcoxson). *Educ:* Sherborne Sch.; St John's Coll., Cambridge (MA; MLitt 1978); Université Libre de Bruxelles. Res. Officer, Harvard. Soc. for Parly Govt, 1974–76; consultant and researcher on EC affairs, 1977–88 (clients incl. BBC, Cambridge Univ., EC, Federal Trust for Educn and Res., PSI); Res. Fellow, Joseph Rowntree Reform Trust, 1989–92; Dir, Federal Trust, 1993–99. Mem. (L), 1982–87, (Lib Dem), 1987–90, Cambridge CC. Contested: (L) Cambridge and N Beds, 1984, (Lib Dem) Cambridgeshire, 1989, 1994, EP elecns; (Lib Dem) Huntingdon, Parly elecns, 1992. Vice Pres., Liberal Democrats, 1994–97. Constitutional Affairs spokesman, Eur. Lib Dem Gp, 1999–. *Publications:* include: (ed jtly) Maastricht and Beyond: building the European Union, 1994; Reforming the European Union, 1997; (ed) The Treaty of Amsterdam, 1997; (ed) Understanding the Euro, 1998. *Recreation:* music. *Address:* Orwell House, Cowley Road, Cambridge CB4 0PP; *e-mail:* mep@andrewduffmep.org. *Club:* National Liberal.

DUFF, Anthony Michael; communications strategist and life coach, since 1999; *b* 7 Aug. 1946; *s* of Anthony Duff and Alice Mary Duff (*née* Conway); *m* 1997, Marisol de Lafuente. *Educ:* St Conleth's Coll., Dublin; University Coll., Dublin (BA Hons). LGSM (Drama) 1968; LRAM (Drama) 1970; RSA Dip. TEFLA 1972. Dir, Teacher Trng and Foundn Dir, Câfé Théatre Anglais, Internat. House, Paris, 1971–74; Vis. Lectr in Drama, Thomond Coll., Co. Limerick, 1975–76; Pedagogic Advr to Longman Italia, 1977–79; International House, London: Dir of Educn, 1979–83; Dir, 1984–89; Dir-Gen., 1990–99. FRSA 1993. *Publications:* English For You, 2 vols, 1979, 1981; (ed) Explorations in Teacher Training, 1989. *Recreations:* music, reading, the theatre, walking, being solitary. *Address:* 39 St Dunstan's Road, W6 8RE.

DUFF, Graham, CB 1999; barrister; *b* 7 Jan. 1947; *s* of Norman Alexander Duff and Doris Duff; *m* 1987, Jacqueline Tremble; one *s* one *d*. *Educ:* Newcastle Royal Grammar Sch.; Univ. of Durham (BA (Hons) Law); Univ. of Newcastle upon Tyne (Grad. Cert Ed). Called to the Bar, Lincoln's Inn, 1976. Asst Dir of Public Prosecutions, 1986; Br. Crown Prosecutor, Inner London, 1986; Chief Crown Prosecutor, Northumbria and Durham, 1987; a Dir, CPS, 1990–98. *Recreations:* breeding foreign birds, old Riley motor cars, riding, Northumbrian countryside. *Address:* Trinity Chambers, 9–12 Trinity Chare, Quayside, Newcastle upon Tyne NE1 3DF. *T:* (0191) 232 1927.

DUFF GORDON, Sir Andrew (Cosmo Lewis), 8th Bt *cr* 1813; *b* 17 Oct. 1933; *o s* of Sir Douglas Duff Gordon, 7th Bt and Gladys Rosemary (*d* 1933), *e d* of late Col Vivien Henry, CB; *S* father, 1964; *m* 1st, 1967, Grania Mary (marr. diss. 1975), *d* of Fitzgerald Villiers-Stuart, Ireland; one *s*; 2nd, 1975, Eveline Virginia, BA, *d* of S. Soames, Newbury; three *s*. *Educ:* Repton. Served with Worcs Regiment and 1st Bn Ches Regt, 1952–54. Mem. of Lloyd's, 1962–91. *Recreations:* golf, shooting, skiing. *Heir: s* Cosmo Henry Villiers Duff Gordon, *b* 18 June 1968. *Address:* Downton House, Walton, Presteigne, Powys LD8 2RD. *T:* (01544) 350223; 27 Cathcart Road, SW10 9JG. *T:* (020) 7351 1170. *Clubs:* City University; Kingston Golf; Sunningdale Golf.

DUFFELL, Lt-Gen. Sir Peter Royson, KCB 1992; CBE 1988 (OBE 1981); MC 1966; Chief Executive, Dechert (formerly Titmuss Sainer Dechert), since 1995; *b* 19 June 1939; *s* of late Roy John Duffell, Lenham, Kent, and Ruth Doris (*née* Gustaffson); *m* 1982, Ann Murray, *d* of late Col Basil Bethune Neville Woodd, Rolvenden, Kent; one *s* one *d*. *Educ:* Dulwich Coll. psc, rcds. FRGS 1975; FRAS 1992. Commnd 2nd KEO Gurkha Rifles, 1960; Staff Coll., Camberley, 1971; Bde Major 5 Bde, 1972–74; MA to C-in-C UKLF, 1976–78; Comdt 1st Bn 2nd KEO Gurkha Rifles, 1978–81; Col GS, MoD, 1981–83; Comdr Gurkha Field Force, 1984–85; COS 1 (BR) Corps, 1986–87; RCDS, 1988; Cabinet Office Efficiency Unit, 1989; Comdr, British Forces Hong Kong, and Maj.-Gen. Brigade of Gurkhas, 1989–92; Inspector Gen. Doctrine and Trng, MoD, 1992–95. Col, Royal Gurkha Rifles, 1994–99. Hon. Vice-Pres., FA, and Pres., Army Football Assoc., 1992–95; Pres., Army Rifle Assoc., 1993–95. Gov., Sandroyd Sch., 1995–. Pres., Lighthouse Club (construction industry charity), 1999–. Liveryman, Paviours' Co., 2001–. *Recreations:* family, collecting pictures, drinking wine, taking photographs, playing elephant polo. *Clubs:* Travellers, Pratt's, MCC.

DUFFERIN AND CLANDEBOYE, 11th Baron *cr* 1800 (Ire.); **John Francis Blackwood;** Bt (Ire.) 1763; Bt (UK) 1814; architect; *b* 18 Oct. 1944; *s* of 10th Baron and of Margaret Alice, *d* of Hector Kirkpatrick; *S* father, 1991 (claim to peerage not yet established); *m* 1971, Annette Kay, *d* of Harold Greenhill; one *s* one *d*. *Educ:* Barker Coll., Hornsby; Univ. of NSW (BArch). ARAIA. *Recreations:* antiques, building conservation, fishing. *Heir: s* Hon. Francis Senden Blackwood, *b* 6 Jan. 1979. *Address:* PO Box 1815, Orange, NSW 2800, Australia. *T:* (2) 63625399.

DUFFETT, Roger Hugh Edward; Secretary, Royal College of Surgeons of England, 1988–97; *b* 20 Jan. 1936; *s* of Dr Edward Cecil Duffett and Cicely Duffett (*née* Haw); *m* 1959, Angela Julie Olden; one *d* (one *s* decd). *Educ:* Sherborne Sch. (Scholar); Peterhouse, Cambridge (Scholar; MA). Commissioned RA (Nat. Service), 1954–56; British Petroleum Co.: joined 1956; refinery process foreman, 1959–60; research, molecular sieve properties of synthetic zeolites and reactions of frozen free radicals, 1960–64; creation of computerised manpower planning models, 1964–68; creation and operation of computerised linear programming models for integrated oil ops, 1968–71; application of mathematical models to corporate planning, 1971–73; planning, internat. ops for lubricants, 1973–78; negotiation and op., crude oil contracts, 1978–79; consultancy for analysis and resolution of orgnl problems: in shipping, research, engrg, marketing and personnel; for management of secondary schools, Cambs; Unicef (UK); employment of secondees to Enterprise Bds, 1979–87; orgn and systems consultant for BP Oil Internat., for Riding for Disabled, 1987–88. Member: Management Cttee, Clare Park, 1979–83; Riding for Disabled, 1990– (Trustee, 1999–2002); Dir, Quinta Nursing Home, Farnham, 1983–88. Freeman, Barbers' Co., 1998. Hon. FRCS 1997; Hon. DGDP 1998. *Publications:* contribs to learned jls. *Recreations:* golf, coarse gardening, creating brain teasers, writing, reading. *Address:* Marelands Cottage, Bentley, Farnham, Surrey GU10 5JA. *T:* and *Fax:* (01420) 520283; *e-mail:* scatsa@aol.com. *Club:* Liphook Golf.

DUFFIELD, Linda Joy; HM Diplomatic Service; High Commissioner, Sri Lanka, since 1999; *b* 18 April 1953; *d* of Bryan Charles Duffield and Joyce Eileen Duffield (*née* Barr). *Educ:* St Mary's Sch., Northwood, Middx; Exeter Univ. (BA Hons 1975). DHSS, 1976–85; Ecole Nat. d'Admin, Paris, 1985–86; joined FCO, 1987; First Sec., Moscow, 1989–92; First Sec., later Counsellor, FCO, 1993–95; Dep. High Comr, Ottawa, 1995–99. *Recreations:* music, ski-ing. *Address:* c/o Foreign and Commonwealth Office, King Charles Street, SW1A 2AH.

DUFFIELD, Dame Vivien (Louise), DBE 2000 (CBE 1989); *b* 26 March 1946; *d* of Sir Charles Clore and Mrs Francine Clore (née Halphen); *m* 1969, John Duffield (marr. diss. 1976); one *s* one *d*. *Educ:* Cours Victor Hugo, Paris; Lycée Français de Londres; Heathfield Sch.; Lady Margaret Hall, Oxford (MA). Member: NSPCC Centenary Appeal Cttee, 1983; NSPCC Financial Develt Cttee, 1985; Vice-Chairman: Great Ormond Street Hosp. Wishing Well Appeal, 1987; Royal Marsden Hosp. Cancer Appeal, 1990; Director: Royal Opera House Trust, 1985–2001 (Dep. Chm., 1988–2001); Royal Opera House, 1990–2001; Mem., Royal Ballet Bd, 1990–; Trustee, Dulwich Coll. Picture Gall., 1993–. Hon. DLitt Buckingham, 1990; Hon. DPhil Weizmann Inst., 1985; Hon. RCM, 1987. *Recreations:* ski-ing, opera, ballet, shooting. *Address:* c/o Clore Foundation, 3 Chelsea Manor Studies, Flood Street, SW3 5SR; 39 Quai Wilson, Geneva 1201, Switzerland.

DUFFUS, Sir Herbert (George Holwell), Kt 1966; *b* 30 Aug. 1908; *e s* of William Alexander Duffus, JP, and Emily Henrietta Mary (*née* Holwell); *m* 1939, Elsie Mary (*née* Hollinsed); no *c*. *Educ:* Cornwall Coll., Jamaica. Admitted as Solicitor: Jamaica, 1930, England, 1948. Resident Magistrate, Jamaica, 1946–58; Called to the Bar, Lincoln's Inn, 1956; acted as Puisne Judge, Jamaica, 1956–58; Puisne Judge, Jamaica, 1958–62; Judge of Appeal, Jamaica, 1962–64; Pres. Court of Appeal, 1964–67; Chief Justice of Jamaica, 1968–73; Acting Governor General of Jamaica, 1968, 1973. Chairman: Commn of Enquiry into Prisons of Jamaica, 1954; Commn of Enquiry into the administration of justice and police brutality in Grenada, WI, 1974; Police Service Commission (Jamaica), 1958–68. Sole Commissioner, Enquiries into: Maffesanti Affair, 1968; Operations of Private Land Developers in Jamaica, 1975–76; Barbados Govt's Private Enterprises, 1977–78; Electoral Malpractices (Jamaican Local Govt Elecns), 1986. Pres., Boy Scouts Assoc., Jamaica, 1967–70. Chm., Western Regl Council, Cheshire Homes, 1975–89. Chancellor of the Church (Anglican) in Jamaica, 1973–76. *Address:* 6 Braywick Road, PO Box 243, Liguanea PO, Kingston 6, Jamaica. *T:* 9279980; 119 Main Street, Witchford, Ely, Cambs CB6 2HQ. *T:* (01353) 663281.

DUFFY, Sir (Albert Edward) Patrick, Kt 1991; PhD; *b* 17 June 1920. *Educ:* London Sch. of Economics (BSc(Econ.), PhD); Columbia Univ., Morningside Heights, New York, USA. Served War of 1939–45, Royal Navy, incl. flying duties with FAA. Lecturer, University of Leeds, 1950–63, 1967–70. Visiting Professor: Drew Univ., Madison, NJ, 1966–70; Amer. Grad. Sch. of Internat. Business, 1982–. Contested (Lab) Tiverton Division of Devon, 1950, 1951, 1955. MP (Lab): Colne Valley Division of Yorks, 1963–66; Sheffield, Attercliffe, 1970–92. PPS to Sec. of State for Defence, 1974–76; Parly Under-Sec. of State for Defence (Navy), MoD, 1976–79; opposition spokesman on defence, 1979–80, 1983–84. Chairman: PLP Economic and Finance Gp, 1965–66, 1974–76; Trade and Industry Sub-Cttee of Select Cttee on Expenditure, 1972–74; PLP Defence Cttee, 1984; Vice-Chairman: PLP Defence Gp, 1979–84; Anglo-Irish Gp, 1979–92. Pres., N Atlantic Assembly, 1988–90 (Mem. 1979–92; Chm., Defence Co-op. sub-cttee, 1983–87); Dep. Chm., Atlantic Council of UK, 1994–97. Pres., Lower Don Valley Community Devlt Trust, 1997–. Member: Catholic Club, Doncaster; Irish Soc., Doncaster. Hon. DHL Dominican Univ., Illinois, 1993. *Publications:* contrib. to Economic History Review, Victorian Studies, Manchester School, Annals of Amer. Acad. of Pol. and Soc. Sci., etc. *Recreation:* annual pilgrimages on foot, incl. Walsingham and Santiago de Compostela. *Address:* 153 Bennetthorpe, Doncaster, South Yorks DN2 6AH. *Clubs:* Naval; Trades and Labour (Doncaster).

DUFFY, Dame Antonia Susan; *see* Byatt, Dame A. S.

DUFFY, Carol Ann, OBE 1995; FRSL; poet and freelance writer; *b* 23 Dec. 1955; *d* of Frank Duffy and May Black; one *d*. *Educ:* St Joseph's Convent, Stafford; Stafford Girls' High Sch.; Univ. of Liverpool (BA Hons Philosophy 1977). FRSL 1999. *Awards:* Eric Gregory, 1983; Somerset Maugham, 1987; Dylan Thomas, 1990; Cholmondeley, 1992; Whitbread Poetry, 1993; Forward Poetry, 1993; Lannan, USA, 1995; Signal Poetry, 1997. *Plays:* Take My Husband, 1982; Cavern of Dreams, 1984; Little Women, Big Boys, 1986; Loss (radio), 1986; Grimm Tales, 1994, More Grimm Tales, 1996, Young Vic. *Publications:* Standing Female Nude, 1985; Selling Manhattan, 1987, 4th edn 1994; (ed) Home and Away, 1988; The Other Country, 1990; (ed) I Wouldn't Thank You for a Valentine, 1992; Mean Time, 1993; Selected Poems, 1994; (ed) Anvil New Poets, 1995; (ed) Stopping for Death, 1996; The Pamphlet, 1998; The World's Wife (poetry), 1999; Meeting Midnight (for children), 1999; Rumpelstiltskin and other Grimm Tales (for children), 1999; (ed) Time's Tidings (poetry), 1999; The Oldest Girl in the World (for children), 2000; (ed) Hand in Hand, 2001. *Recreations:* poker, holidays. *Address:* c/o Anvil Press, 69 King George Street, SE10 8PX. *T:* (020) 8858 2946.

DUFFY, Daniel; Chairman, Transport and General Workers' Union, 1988–96; *b* 3 Oct. 1929; *s* of late William and Mary Duffy; *m* Susan (*née* Salton). *Educ:* St Mungo's Academy. Transport Driver, 1947; joined S. H. & M. Assoc., 1947. Member: Exec. Council, Scottish Commercial Motormen's Union, 1960–71 (Pres., 1969–71); TGWU Exec. Council, 1971–96; TUC General Council, 1988–96. *Recreation:* bowls. *Address:* c/o TGWU, 16 Palace Street, SW1E 5JD. *T:* (020) 7828 7788.

DUFFY, Dr Francis Cuthbert, CBE 1997; PPRIBA; Founder, DEGW plc, 1974; with DEGW North America, since 2001; *b* 3 Sept. 1940; *s* of late John Austin Duffy and of Annie Margaret Duffy (*née* Reed); *m* 1965, Jessica Bear; three *d*. *Educ:* Architectural Assoc. Sch. (AA Dip Hons); Univ. of California at Berkeley (MArch); Princeton Univ. (MA, PhD). Asst Architect, Nat. Building Agency, 1964–67; Commonwealth Fund Harkness Fellow, Berkeley and Princeton, 1967–70; established London office, JFN Associates (of NY), 1971. Member: Council, RIBA, 1989– (Pres., 1993–95); Architects Registration Bd, 1997–; Pres., Architects' Council of Europe, 1994. Vis. Prof., MIT, 2001–. Editor, AA Jl, 1965–67; founder Editor, Facilities, 1985–90. *Publications:* Office Landscaping, 1966; (jtly) Planning Office Space, 1976; (jtly) The Changing City, 1989; The Changing Workplace, 1992; (jtly) The Responsible Workplace, 1993; The New Office, 1997; Architectural Knowledge, 1998; (jtly) New Environments for Working, 1998. *Recreations:* walking, talking, reading. *Address:* c/o DEGW plc, 8 Crinan Street, N1 9SQ. *T:* (020) 7239 7777; DEGW NA LLC, 589 8th Avenue, 12th Floor, New York 10018, USA. *T:* (212) 2901601; Threeways, The Street, Walberswick, Suffolk IP18 6TZ. *T:* (01502) 723814. *Clubs:* Athenæum, Reform; Princeton (NY).

DUFFY, Most Rev. Joseph; *see* Clogher, Bishop of, (RC).

DUFFY, Joseph Michael; a Judge of the High Court, Hong Kong, 1987–96; *b* 6 Dec. 1936; *s* of John Joseph Duffy and Mary Frances Mullaney; *m* 1962, Patricia Ann Scott; one *s* two *d*. *Educ:* St Andrews Univ. (MA, LLB). Solicitor, Scotland, 1965, Hong Kong, 1976; Advocate, Scotland, 1981; QC Hong Kong, 1983. Apprentice, then Solicitor, Dundee, 1963–72; Crown Counsel and Sen. Crown Counsel, Hong Kong, 1972–76 and 1978–80 (Solicitor, Hong Kong, 1976–78); Dep. Dir and Dir of Public Prosecutions, Hong Kong, 1980–86; Solicitor-General, Hong Kong, 1986–87. *Recreations:* golf, tennis, travelling, music. *Address:* 7 Bonspiel Gardens, Broughty Ferry, Dundee DD5 2LH. *T:* (01382) 775492. *Club:* Panmure Golf.

DUFFY, Maureen Patricia, FRSL 1985; author; *b* 1933; *o c* of Grace Rose Wright. *Educ:* Trowbridge High Sch. for Girls; Sarah Bonnell High Sch. for Girls; King's College, London (BA). Chairman: Greater London Arts Literature Panel, 1979–81; Authors Lending and Copyright Soc., 1982–94; British Copyright Council, 1989–98 (Vice Chm., 1981–86; Vice-Pres., 1998–); Copyright Licensing Agency, 1996–99 (Vice-Chm., 1994–96). Pres., Writers' Guild of GB, 1985–88 (Jt Chm., 1977–78); Co-founder, Writers' Action Group, 1972–79; Vice-President: European Writers Congress, 1992–; Beauty Without Cruelty, 1975–. *Publications:* That's How It Was, 1962; The Single Eye, 1964; The Microcosm, 1966; The Paradox Players, 1967; Lyrics for the Dog Hour (poetry), 1968; Wounds, 1969; Rites (play), 1969; Love Child, 1971; The Venus Touch, 1971; The Erotic World of Faery, 1972; I want to Go to Moscow, 1973; A Nightingale in Bloomsbury Square (play), 1974; Capital, 1975; Evesong (poetry), 1975; The Passionate Shepherdess, 1977; Housespy, 1978; Memorials of the Quick and the Dead (poetry), 1979; Inherit the Earth, 1980; Gorsaga, 1981 (televised as First Born, 1988); Londoners: an elegy, 1983; Men and Beasts, 1984; Collected Poems 1949–84, 1985; Change (novel), 1987; A Thousand Capricious Chances: Methuen 1889–1989, 1989; Illuminations (novel), 1991; Occam's Razor (novel), 1993; Henry Purcell (biog.), 1994; Restitution (novel), 1998; The Making of the Myth, 2001; *visual art:* Prop art exhibn (with Brigid Brophy), 1969. *Address:* 18 Fabian Road, SW6 7TZ. *T:* (020) 7385 3598.

DUFFY, Sir Patrick; *see* Duffy, Sir A. E. P.

DUFFY, Peter Clarke, QPM 1979; Director General, Federation Against Copyright Theft, 1985–89, retired; *b* Hamilton, Scotland, 10 May 1927; *s* of Hugh Duffy and Margaret Archibald; *m* 1958, S. M. Joyce (marr. diss.); one *s* two *d*. *Educ:* Our Lady's High Sch., Motherwell. MInstAM 1983. Served Army, Western Arab Corps, Sudan Defence Force, 1945–48 (War Medal). Joined Metropolitan Police, 1949; Criminal Investigation Dept, 1954; Comdr, New Scotland Yard, 1976–83; Dir, Investigations, Fedn Against Copyright Theft, 1983–85. *Recreations:* golf, living. *Club:* Royal Automobile.

DUGDALE, family name of **Baron Crathorne**.

DUGDALE, Kathryn Edith Helen, (Lady Dugdale), DCVO 1984 (CVO 1973); JP; DL; a Lady-in-Waiting to the Queen, since 1985; *b* 4 Nov. 1923; *d* of Rt Hon. Oliver Stanley, PC, MC, MP and Lady Maureen Vane-Tempest Stewart; *m* 1956, Sir John Robert Stratford Dugdale, KCVO; two *s* two *d*. *Educ:* many and varied establishments. Served with WRNS. Temp. Woman of the Bedchamber to The Queen, 1955–60, Extra Woman of the Bedchamber 1960–72; Woman of the Bedchamber, 1972–. Pres., Shropshire Community Council. JP Salop, 1964; DL Shropshire, 1995. Employee of Greater London Fund for the Blind. *Recreations:* gardening, reading. *Address:* Tickwood Hall, Much Wenlock, Salop TF13 6NZ. *T:* (01952) 882644.

DUGDALE, Sir William (Stratford), 2nd Bt *cr* 1936; CBE 1982; MC 1943; DL; Director and Chairman, General Utilities PLC, 1988–99; *b* 29 March 1922; *er s* of Sir William Francis Stratford Dugdale, 1st Bt, and Margaret, 2nd *d* of Sir Robert Gordon Gilmour, 1st Bt, of Liberton and Craigmillar; *S* father, 1965; *m* 1st, 1952, Lady Belinda Pleydell-Bouverie (*d* 1961), 2nd *d* of 6th Earl of Radnor; one *s* three *d*; 2nd, 1967, Cecilia Mary, *e d* of Sir William Malcolm Mount, 2nd Bt; one *s* one *d*. *Educ:* Eton; Balliol Coll., Oxford. Served War of 1939–45, Grenadier Guards (Captain), Admitted as Solicitor, 1949. Director: Phoenix Assurance Co., 1968–85; Lee Valley Water Co., 1989–90; North Surrey Water Co., 1989–98; Chairman: Severn Trent Water Authority, 1974–83; National Water Council, 1982–83; Birmingham Diocesan Board of Finance, 1979–92. Steward, Jockey Club, 1985–87. Chm., Wolverhampton Racecourse PLC, 1965–91. Governor, Lady Katherine Leveson's Hosp., Temple Balsall. Mem., Warwicks CC, 1964–76; High Steward, Stratford upon Avon, 1977. JP 1951–97, DL 1955, High Sheriff 1971, Warwicks. *Publications:* contrib. DNB. *Heir:* s William Matthew Stratford Dugdale [*b* 22 Feb. 1959; *m* 1990, Paige Sullivan; two *s* two *d*]. *Address:* Blyth Hall, Coleshill, near Birmingham B46 2AD. *T:* (01675) 462203; Merevale Hall, Atherstone CV9 2HG. *T:* (01827) 713143; 24 Bryanston Mews West, W1H 7FR. *T:* (020) 7262 2510. *Clubs:* Brooks's, White's, MCC; Jockey (Newmarket).
See also Baron Hazlerigg.

DUGGAN, Patrick Gerald; actor (as **Patrick Malahide**) and writer; *b* 24 March 1945; *s* of John Cuthbert Duggan and Mary Clementine Duggan (*née* Andrews); *m* 1st, 1970, Rosemary Wright (marr. diss. 1990); one *s* one *d*; 2nd, 1993, Jo Ryan. *Educ:* Douai Sch.; Edinburgh Univ. Stage Manager, 1969, Dir of Prodns, 1970–72, Byre Th., St Andrews; joined Royal Lyceum Th., Edinburgh, as actor, 1972–76; *plays* include: The Android Circuit, Traverse and ICA, 1978; Judgement (one man show), Liverpool Playhouse, and subseq. at Edinburgh, Dublin and Amsterdam Fests, 1979; The Tempest, 1980, King Lear, 1981, Bristol Old Vic; Operation Bad Apple, Royal Court, 1982; Cock-ups, Manchester Royal Exchange, 1983; Bristol Old Vic: The Cherry Orchard, 1987; In The Ruins (one man show), transf. Royal Court, 1989–90; Clandestine Marriage, Uncle Vanya, 1990; Map of the Heart, Globe, 1991; Mutabilitie, RNT, 1998; *television* series and serials include: Minder, 1979–87; Charlie, The Pickwick Papers, 1984; The Singing Detective, 1986; The One Game, The Franchise Affair, 1988; Children of the North, 1990; The Secret Agent, 1991; The Blackheath Poisonings, 1992; The Inspector Alleyn Mysteries, 1993–94; Middlemarch, 1994; plays: Miss Julie, 1987; A Doll's House, 1991; All the King's Men, 1999; *films* include: The Killing Fields, 1984; Comfort and Joy, 1984; A Month in the Country, 1987; December Bride, 1990; A Man of No Importance, 1994; Two Deaths, 1995; Cutthroat Island, 1995; The Long Kiss Goodnight, 1996; US Marshals, 1998; The World is not Enough, 1999; Billy Elliot, 2000; Quills, 2000. Patron: Queen Margaret UC, Edinburgh, 1999–; Byre Theatre Appeal Fund, 1999–. *Publications:* screenplays as P. G. Duggan: Reasonable Force, 1988; The Writing on the Wall, 1996. *Recreations:* sailing, walking in Cornwall. *Address:* c/o ICM, Oxford House, 76 Oxford Street, W1N 0AX. *Club:* Royal Fowey Yacht.

DUGGAN, William Michael, MA; Deputy Headmaster, Taunton School, since 2001; *b* 26 Oct. 1955; *s* of Robert Michael Duggan and late Phillida Duggan (*née* Shirley); *m* 1984, Sylvia Lucy Charlotte Brown; three *d*. *Educ:* King's Sch., Canterbury; Queens' Coll., Cambridge (MA 1981). Asst Teacher, Whitgift Sch., 1978–83; Head of Classics, Manchester Grammar Sch., 1983–90; Dep. Headmaster, Warwick Sch., 1990–95; Headmaster, Batley Grammar Sch., 1995–98; Hd of Classics, St Paul's Sch., 1999–2001. *Recreation:* painting. *Address:* Taunton School, Taunton, Som TA2 6AD.

DUGGIN, Thomas Joseph; HM Diplomatic Service; Ambassador to Colombia, since 2001; *b* 15 Sept. 1947; *s* of late Joseph Duggin and of Alice Lilian (*née* Mansfield); *m* 1st, 1968 (marr. diss.); two *s*; 2nd, 1983 (marr. diss.); 3rd, 1999, Janette Mortimer (*née* David). *Educ:* Thornleigh Salesian Coll. Joined HM Diplomatic Service, 1967; Third Sec., Oslo, 1969–73; Third, later Second Sec. (Commercial), Bucharest, 1973–75; FCO, 1976–79; Second Sec., Bangkok, 1979–82; FCO, 1982–85; Head of Chancery and HM Consul, La Paz, 1985–88; Head of Chancery, Mexico City, 1989–91; High Comr, Vanuatu, 1992–95; Hd of Security Dept, then Asst Dir for Security, subseq. Hd of Security Comd, then Hd of Security Strategy Unit, FCO, 1995–2001. MSM, Order of Vanuatu, 1992. *Recreations:* tennis, golf, reading, music. *Address:* c/o Foreign and Commonwealth Office, King Charles Street, SW1A 2AH.

DUGGLEBY, (Charles) Vincent (Anstey); freelance broadcaster and financial journalist, since 1989; *b* 23 Jan. 1939; *s* of late Bernard Waldby Duggleby and Vivien Duggleby (*née* Hawkins); *m* 1964, Elizabeth Nora Frost; two *d*. *Educ:* Blundell's Sch.; Worcester Coll., Oxford (BA 1962). FRPSL 1979. Reporter, Bristol Evening Post, 1957–59; Sub-editor, Daily Express, 1960; BBC, 1963–89: sub-editor and sports presenter, 1963–67; Asst Sports Editor, 1967–70; Asst Editor, Current Affairs, 1970–80; Financial Editor, 1980–89. Mem., Royal Mint Adv. Cttee, 1987–94. Royal Philatelic Society: Mem. Council, 1979–; Hon. Treas., 1988–93; Vice-Pres., 1994–99. Numerous awards, including: Broadcasting Financial Journalist of Year, Harold Wincott Foundn, 1992; Best Personal Finance Broadcaster, ABI, 1997. *Publications:* Highlights from 21 Years of Sports Report, 1969; English Paper Money, 1975, 5th edn 1994; (with Louise Botting) Making the Most of Your Money, 1984, 2nd edn 1985. *Recreations:* philately, genealogy, classic jazz. *Address:* 41 Devonshire Place, W1N 1PE. *T:* (020) 7486 1044.

DUGUID, Andrew Alexander; Integration and Planning Executive, Global Aerospace, Lloyd's of London, since 2000; *b* 22 June 1944; *s* of Wing Comdr (retd) Alexander Gordon Duguid and Dorothy Duguid (*née* Duder); *m* 1967, Janet Hughes; two *s* one *d*. *Educ:* Whitby Dist High Sch.; Ashbury Coll., Ottawa; Sidcot Sch.; LSE (BSc Econs); Univ. of Lancaster (MA Marketing). Res. Assistant, Brunel Univ., 1967–69; Marketing Executive: Interscan Ltd, 1969–72; Ogilvy Benson and Mather, 1972–73; joined DTI as Principal, 1973; Prin. Pvte Sec. to Sec. of State for Industry, 1977–79; Asst Sec., seconded to Prime Minister's Policy Unit, 1979; returned to set up Policy Planning Unit, Dept of Industry, later DTI, 1982; Under Sec., DTI, 1985–86; Lloyd's of London: Head of Regulatory Services, 1986–88; Head of Market Services, 1988–92; Dir, Marketing Services, 1993–94; Dir, Policy and Planning, and Sec. to Council of Lloyd's, 1995–99; Dir, Devolt, 1999–2000. Non-exec. Dir, Kingsway Public Relations, 1982–85. *Publication:* (with Elliott Jaques) Case Studies in Export Organisation, 1971. *Recreations:* tennis, ski-ing, walking, canoeing. *Address:* 1 Binden Road, W12 9RJ. *T:* (020) 8743 7435. *Club:* Hartswood.

DUGUID, Prof. James Paris, CBE 1979; MD, BSc; FRCPath; Professor of Bacteriology, University of Dundee, 1967–84; Consultant, Tayside Health Board, 1963–84; *b* 10 July 1919; *s* of late Maj.-Gen. David Robertson Duguid, CB, and Mary Paris; *m* 1944, Isobel Duff; one *s* three *d*. *Educ:* Edinburgh Academy; Univ. of Edinburgh (MB ChB Hons 1942; BSc 1st Cl. Hons 1943; MD (Gold Medal) 1949); FRCPath 1966. Lectr, Sen. Lectr and Reader, Univ. of Edinburgh, 1944–62; Prof. of Bacteriology, Univ. of St Andrews, 1963–67; Director of Postgrad. Medical Educn, Univ. of Dundee, 1968–71, Dean of Faculty of Medicine, 1971–74, Mem. Univ. Court, 1977–81. Cons. Adviser in Microbiology, Scottish Home and Health Dept, 1967–85, Mem. Adv. Cttee on Medical Research, 1967–71; Member: Eastern Regional and Tayside Health Bds, 1967–77; Adv. Cttee on Laboratory Services, Scottish Health Serv. Council, 1967–74 (Chm., Epidemiology Sub-cttee, 1966–71); Scottish Health Services Planning Council, 1974–77 (Member: Adv. Cttee on New Developments in Health Care, 1976–84; Scientific Services Adv. Gp, 1975–79; Chm., Microbiology and Clin. Immunology Cttees, 1975–77); Jt Cttee on Vaccination and Immunisation, Health Services Councils, 1967–74; GMC, 1975–81; Council for Professions Supp. to Medicine, 1978–86; Independent Adv. Gp on Gruinard Island, 1986–87; Optimum Population Trust, 1993–. Hon. Mem., Pathol Soc. of GB and Ireland, 1985. Co-Editor: Jl of Pathology and Bacteriology, 1959–68; Jl of Medical Microbiology, 1968–71. *Publications:* (co-ed) Mackie and McCartney, Medical Microbiology, 11th edn 1969, 12th edn 1973, 13th edn 1978; (ed) Mackie and McCartney, Practical Medical Microbiology, 1989; scientific papers on bacterial fimbriae, adhesins, biotyping and phylogeny, airborne infection, and the action of penicillin. *Recreations:* grandchildren, gardening, atheism, population studies. *Address:* Oaklands, Merlewood Road, Inverness IV2 4NL. *T:* (01463) 220118; Hillside, Glenborrodale, Argyll PH36 4JP.

DUISENBERG, Willem Frederik, (Wim); President, European Central Bank, since 1998; *b* 9 July 1935. *Educ:* State Univ. of Groningen (PhD 1965). Scientific Asst, State Univ. of Groningen, 1961–65; IMF, 1965–69; Special Advr, 1969–70, Exec. Dir, 1981–82, Pres. and Governor, 1982–97, De Nederlandsche Bank NV; Prof. of Macro-Economics, Univ. of Amsterdam, 1970–73; Minister of Finance, Netherlands, 1973–77; MP (Socialist Party), 1977–78; Mem. and Vice-Chm. Exec. Bd, Rabobank Nederland, 1978–81; President: BIS, 1988–90, 1994–97 (also Dir); European Monetary Inst., 1997–98. Hon. Dr New Univ. of Lisbon. Commander: Order of Orange-Nassau (Netherlands); Order of Netherlands Lion; Legion of Honour (France), 1998; Grand Cross: Order of Merit (Luxembourg); Order of Merit (Senegal); Order of the Crown (Belgium); Knight Grand Cross, Royal Order of North Star (Sweden). *Publications:* Economic Consequences of Disarmament, 1965; The IMF and the International Monetary System, 1966; The British Balance of Payments, 1969; Some Remarks on Imported Inflation, 1970. *Address:* Kaiserstrasse 29, 60311 Frankfurt-am-Main, Germany. *T:* (69) 13440.

DUKAKIS, Michael Stanley; Governor, Commonwealth of Massachusetts, 1975–79, and 1983–90; *b* 3 Nov. 1933; *s* of Panos Dukakis and Euterpe Boukis-Dukakis; *m* 1963, Katharine Dickson; one *s* two *d*. *Educ:* Brookline High Sch. (Dip. 1951); Swarthmore Coll., Pa (BA 1955); Harvard Law Sch. (JD 1960). Attorney, Hill & Barlow, Boston, Mass, 1960–74; Lectr and Dir, Intergovtl Studies, John F. Kennedy Sch. of Govt, Harvard Univ., 1979–82. Moderator of public television's The Advocates, 1971–73. State Representative, Brookline, Mass, 1963–71; Democratic Candidate for the Presidency of the USA, 1988. *Publication:* (with Rosabeth Moss Kanter) Creating the Future: Massachusetts comeback and its promise for America, 1988. *Recreations:* walking, playing tennis, gardening. *Address:* 85 Perry Street, Brookline, MA 02146, USA.

DUKE, family name of **Baron Merrivale**.

DUKE, Cecil Howard Armitage; Director of Establishments and Organisation, Ministry of Agriculture, Fisheries and Food, 1965–71; *b* 5 May 1912; *s* of late John William Duke and Gertrude Beatrice (*née* Armitage); *m* 1st, 1939, Eleanor Lucy (*née* Harvie) (*d* 1992); one *s* one *d*; 2nd, 1994, Joan Gladys Haig Daly (*née* Seymour) (*d* 1997). *Educ:* Selhurst Gram. Sch.; LSE. RNVR, 1942–45 (Corvettes). Entered Civil Service, 1929; Asst Princ., 1940; Princ., 1945; Private Sec. to Lord Presidents of the Council, 1951–53; Asst Sec., Land Drainage Div. and Meat Div., 1953; Under-Sec., 1965. *Recreations:* walking, gardening, watching Sussex cricket. *Address:* 22 Fairways Road, Seaford, East Sussex BN25 4EN. *T:* (01323) 894338.

DUKE, Rt Rev. Michael Geoffrey H.; *see* Hare Duke.

DUKE, Neville Frederick, DSO 1943; OBE 1953; DFC and Two Bars, 1942, 1943, 1944; AFC 1948; MC (Czech) 1946; Managing Director, Duke Aviation; Technical Adviser and Consultant Test Pilot; *b* 11 Jan. 1922; *s* of Frederick and Jane Duke, Tonbridge, Kent; *m* 1947, Gwendoline Dorothy Fellows. *Educ:* Convent of St Mary and Judds Sch., Tonbridge, Kent. Joined Royal Air Force (cadet), 1940, training period, 1940; 92 Fighter Sqdn, Biggin Hill, 1941; Desert Air Force: 112 Fighter Sqdn, Western Desert, 1941–42, 92 Fighter Sqdn, Western Desert, 1943, Chief Flying Instructor, 73 Operational Training Unit, Egypt, 1943–44, Commanding 145 Sqdn Italy (Fighter), 1944, 28 enemy aircraft destroyed. Hawker Aircraft Ltd test flying, 1945; Empire Test Pilots Sch., 1946; RAF high speed flight, 1946 (world speed record); test flying Aeroplane and Armament Experimental Estab., Boscombe Down, 1947–48; resigned from RAF as Sqdn Leader, 1948; test flying Hawker Aircraft Ltd, 1948; Commanding 615 (County of Surrey) Sqdn, Royal Auxiliary Air Force, Biggin Hill, 1950; Chief Test Pilot, Hawker Aircraft Ltd, 1951–56 (Asst Chief, 1948–51). FRSA 1970; FRAeS 1993 (ARAeS 1948). World records: London-Rome, 1949; London-Karachi, 1949; London-Cairo, 1950. World Speed Record, Sept. 1953. Closed Circuit World Speed Record, 1953. Gold Medal Royal Danish Aero Club, 1953; Gold Medal, Royal Aero Club, 1954; two De la Vaux Medals, FAI, 1954; Segrave Trophy, 1954; Queen's Commendation, 1955. Member: RAF Escaping Soc.; United Service & Royal Aero Club (Associate). Hon. Fellow, Soc. of Experimental Test Pilots, 1991. Hon. Pres., Tangmere Mil. Aviation Mus., 1988. *Publications:* Sound Barrier, 1953; Test Pilot, 1953; Book of Flying, 1954; Book of Flight, 1958; The Crowded Sky (anthology), 1959; The War Diaries of Neville Duke, 1995. *Recreations:* sporting flying, yachting. *Clubs:* Royal Air Force; Royal Cruising, Royal Naval Sailing, Royal Lymington Yacht.

DUKE, Timothy Hugh Stewart; Chester Herald of Arms, since 1995; Registrar of the College of Arms, since 2000; *b* 12 June 1953; *s* of William Falcon Duke and Mary Cecile Duke (*née* Jackson). *Educ:* Uppingham; Fitzwilliam Coll., Cambridge (MA). Peat, Marwick, Mitchell & Co., 1974–81; Research Asst, Coll. of Arms, 1981–89; Rouge Dragon Pursuivant, 1989–95. Hon. Sec., Harleian Soc., 1994–. *Address:* College of Arms, Queen Victoria Street, EC4V 4BT. *T:* (020) 7236 7728. *Club:* Travellers.

DUKES, Alan M.; TD (FG) Kildare, since 1981; *b* 22 April 1945; *s* of James and Rita Dukes; *m* 1968, Fionnuala Corcoran; two *d*. *Educ:* Colaiste Mhuire, Dublin; University College Dublin (MA). Chief Economist, Irish Farmers' Assoc., 1967–72; Dir, Irish Farmers' Assoc., Brussels, 1973–76; Personal Advr to Comr of European Communities, 1977–80. Minister for Agriculture, 1981–82; opposition spokesman on agric., March-Dec. 1982; Minister: for Finance, 1982–86; for Justice, 1986–87; for Transport, Energy and Communications, 1996–97; opposition spokesman on envmt and local govt, 1997–. Leader, 1987–90, President, 1987–92, Fine Gael Party. Chm., Jt Oireachtas Cttee on Foreign Affairs, 1995–96. Vice-President: Internat. European Movt, 1991–96 (Pres., 1987–91, Chm., 1997–, Irish Council); European People's Party, 1987–96; Mem., Council of State, 1988–90. Adjunct Prof. of Public Admin/Management, Univ. of Limerick, 1991–. Governor: EIB, 1982–86; IMF. *Address:* (office) Dáil Eireann, Dublin 2.

DUKES, Justin Paul; Chairman, ECIC Management (formerly European Communications Industries Consortium), since 1990; *b* 19 Sept. 1941; *s* of late John Alexander Dukes and Agnes Dukes; *m* 1990, Jane Macallister; one *s* one *d*, and two *s* one *d* by a previous marriage. *Educ:* King's Coll., Univ. of Durham. Dir, Financial Times Ltd, 1975–81; Chairman: Financial Times (Europe) Ltd and Fintel Ltd, 1978–81; C. S. & P. International Inc., NY, 1980–83; Man. Dir, Channel Four TV Co., 1981–88; Chief-Exec., Galileo Co., 1988–89. Director: VTR plc, 1993–; Herald Investment Trust plc, 1994–; Aston Electronic Designs Ltd, 1997–. Pres., Inst. of Information Scientists, 1982–83; Mem. Council, Foundn for Management Educn, 1979–90. Mem., British Screen Adv. Council, 1986–88. Trustee, Internat. Inst. of Communications, 1986–91. FRTS 1986; FRSA 1986; CIMgt (CBIM 1988). Chevalier, Ordre des Arts et des Lettres (France), 1988. *Recreations:* changing institutions, walking. *Address:* Church House, Rye, E Sussex TN31 7HE.

DULBECCO, Dr Renato; Senior Clayton Foundation Investigator, since 1979, and President Emeritus, since 1993, The Salk Institute for Biological Studies (President, 1989–93); *b* Italy, 22 Feb. 1914; USA citizen; *s* of late Leonardo Dulbecco and late Maria Virdia; *m* 1963, Maureen R. Muir; one *d*; and one *d* (one *s* decd) by previous marriage. *Educ:* Univ. of Turin Medical Sch. (MD). Assistente, Univ. of Turin: Inst. Pathology, 1940–46; Anatomical Inst., 1946–47; Res. Assoc., Indiana Univ., 1947–49; Sen. Res. Fellow, 1949–52, Assoc. Prof., 1952–54, Prof. 1954–63, California Inst. Technology; Vis. Prof., Rockefeller Inst., 1962; Royal Soc. Vis. Prof. at Univ. of Glasgow, 1963–64; Salk Institute: Resident Fellow, 1963–72, Fellow, 1972–77; Distinguished Res. Prof., 1977–82; Imperial Cancer Research Fund: Asst Dir of Res., 1972–74; Dep. Dir of Res., 1974–77; Prof. of Pathology and Medicine, Univ. of Calif San Diego Med. Sch., 1977–81. MNAS; Member: Fedn of Amer. Scientists; Amer. Assoc. for Cancer Research; Cancer Center, Univ. of Calif at San Diego; Bd of Scientific Counselors, Dept of Cancer Etiology, NCI; Amer. Acad. of Arts and Scis; Internat. Physicians for Prevention of Nuclear War, Inc.; Pres., Amer.-Ital. Foundn for Cancer Res. Trustee: Amer.-Italian Foundn for Cancer Res.; La Jolla Country Day School. Foreign Member: Academia dei Lincei, 1969; Royal Society, 1974; Hon. Member: Accademia Ligure di Scienze a Lettere, 1982; Società Medico-Chirugica di Modena, 1985; Tissue Culture Assoc., 1988. Has given many lectures to learned instns. Hon. DSc Yale, 1968; Hon. LLD Glasgow, 1970; *hc* Dr Med., Vrije Universiteit Brussel, Brussels, 1978; Hon. DSc Indiana, 1984. (Jtly) Nobel Prize for Physiology or Medicine, 1975; Premio Fregene, Italy, 1988; numerous other prizes and awards. *Publications:* (jtly) Microbiology, 1967; numerous in sci. jls. *Recreation:* music. *Address:* The Salk Institute, PO Box 85800, San Diego, CA 92186-5800, USA.

DULVERTON, 3rd Baron *cr* 1929, of Batsford; **Gilbert Michael Hamilton Wills;** Bt 1897; farmer, forester and industrialist; *b* 2 May 1944; *s* of 2nd Baron and his 1st wife, Judith Betty (*d* 1983), *d* of Lt-Col Hon. Ian Leslie Melville, TD; *S* father, 1992; *m* 1st, 1980, Rosalind van der Velde-Oliver (marr. diss. 1999); one *s* one *d*; 2nd, 2000, Mrs Mary Vicary. *Educ:* Gordonstoun; RAC, Cirencester. Chm., Thwaites Ltd; Director: W Highland Woodlands Ltd; Batsford Estate Co. Trustee: Dulverton Trust; Batsford Foundn. *Heir:* *s* Hon. Robert Anthony Hamilton Wills, *b* 20 Oct. 1983.

DUMAS, Roland; Officier de la Légion d'Honneur; Croix de Guerre (1939–45); Croix du Combattant Volontaire; Minister of Foreign Affairs, France, 1988–93; *b* Limoges, Haute-Vienne, 23 Aug. 1922; *s* of Georges Dumas and Elisabeth (*née* Lecanuet); *m* 1964, Anne-Marie Lillet; two *s* one *d*. *Educ:* Lycée de Limoges; Faculté de Droit de Paris; Ecole des Sciences Politiques de Paris; Univ. of London; Ecole de langues orientales de Paris. LLL; Diplomas: in Advanced Studies in Laws; in Political Science, Paris, and London School of Economics. Counsel, Court of Appeal, Paris, 1950–; journalist; Sen. Political Dir, Journal Socialiste Limousin; Political Dir of weekly, La Corrèze Républicaine et Socialiste, 1967–; Deputy: UDSR, Haute Vienne, 1956–58; FGDS, Corrèze, 1967–68; Socialiste de la Dordogne, 1981–83, 1986–88; Minister for European Affairs, 1983–84; Govt spokesman, 1984; Minister for External Relations, 1984–86; Pres. Commn for Foreign Affairs, Nat. Assembly, 1986–87. Pres., Conseil Constitutionel, 1995–99. Grand Cross, Order of Isabel (Spain), 1982. *Publications:* J'ai vu vivre la Chine, 1960; Les Avocats, 1970; Le Droit de l'Information et de la Presse, 1981; Plaidoyer pour Roger Gilbert Lecomte, 1985; Le droit de la propriété littéraire et artistique, 1986; Le Peuple Assemblé, 1989; Le Fil et la Pelote (memoirs), 1996. *Address:* 19 quai de Bourbon, 75004 Paris, France.

DUMBELL, Dr Keith Rodney; Senior Specialist in Microbiology, Medical School, University of Cape Town, 1982–90, retired; *b* 2 Oct. 1922; *s* of late Stanley Dumbell and Dorothy Ellen (*née* Hewitt); *m* 1st, 1950, Brenda Margaret (*née* Heathcote) (*d* 1971); two *d*; 2nd, 1972, Susan (*née* Herd); two *s*. *Educ:* Wirral Gram. Sch.; University of Liverpool, MB, ChB 1944; MD (Liverpool), 1950. FRCPath 1975. Asst Lecturer, Dept of Bacteriology, University of Liverpool, 1945–47; Mem. of Scientific Staff, MRC, 1947–50; Junior Pathologist, RAF, 1950–52; Asst in Pathology and Microbiology, Rockefeller Inst. for Medical Research (Dr Peyton Rous' laboratory), 1952–53; Lecturer in Bacteriology, University of Liverpool, 1952–58; Senior Lecturer, 1958–64; Prof. of Virology, Univ. of London at St Mary's Hosp. Med. Sch., 1964–81. Vis. Prof., Univ. of Florida, 1994. Dir, WHO Collaborative Centre for Poxvirus Res., London, 1969–82; Mem., Global Commn for Certification of Smallpox Eradication, 1977–79. *Publications:* articles in various medical and scientific journals. *Address:* PO Box 1933, Somerset West, Western Cape 7129, South Africa.

DUMMETT, (Agnes Margaret) Ann, (Lady Dummett); writer; *b* 4 Sept. 1930; *d* of Arthur William Chesney and late Kitty Mary Chesney; *m* 1951, Michael Anthony Eardley Dummett (*see* Sir Michael Dummett); three *s* two *d* (and one *s* one *d* decd). *Educ:* Guildhouse Sch., Pimlico; Ware Grammar Sch. for Girls; Somerville Coll., Oxford (MA). Pres., Oxford Univ. Liberal Club, 1949. Community Relations Officer, Oxford, 1966–69; teaching in further education, 1969–71; Research Worker: Inst. of Race Relations, 1971–73; Runnymede Trust, 1975, 1977; Jt Council for the Welfare of Immigrants, 1978–84; Dir, Runnymede Trust, 1984–87. Consultant (pt-time) on Eur. policies, CRE, 1990–98. *Publications:* A Portrait of English Racism, 1973; Citizenship and Nationality, 1976; A New Immigration Policy, 1978; (with Ian Martin) British Nationality: a guide to the new law, 1982; (ed) Towards a Just Immigration Policy, 1986; chapters in: Justice First (with Michael Dummett), 1969; Colloque de la Société Française pour le Droit International, 1979; Moral Philosophy, 1979; (with Andrew Nicol) Subjects, Citizens, Aliens and Others, 1990; Free Movement, 1992; Individual Rights and the Law in Britain, 1994; (ed) Racially Motivated Crime, 1997; numerous articles and pamphlets. *Recreations:* walking about cities, theatregoing, popular music. *Address:* 54 Park Town, Oxford OX2 6SJ. *T:* (01865) 558698.

DUMMETT, Sir Michael (Anthony Eardley), Kt 1999; FBA; Wykeham Professor of Logic in the University of Oxford, 1979–92, Professor Emeritus 1992; Emeritus Fellow, All Souls College, Oxford, 1979; *b* 27 June 1925; *s* of George Herbert Dummett and Iris Dummett (*née* Eardley-Wilmot); *m* 1951, Ann Chesney (*see* A. M. A. Dummett); three *s* two *d* (one *s* one *d* decd). *Educ:* Sandroyd Sch.; Winchester Coll. (1st Schol.); Christ Church, Oxford (major hist. schol., 1942; First Class Hons, PPE 1950); DLitt Oxford, 1989. Served in Army, 1943–47: in RA and Intell. Corps (India, 1945, Malaya, 1946–47, Sgt). Asst Lectr in Philosophy, Birmingham Univ., 1950–51; Commonwealth Fund Fellow, Univ. of California, Berkeley, 1955–56; Reader in the Philosophy of Mathematics, Univ. of Oxford, 1962–74; All Souls College, Oxford: Fellow, 1950–79, Senior Research Fellow, 1974–79; Sub-Warden, 1974–76; Fellow, 1979–92, Emer. Fellow, 1992–98, Hon. Fellow, 1998, New Coll., Oxford. Vis. Lectr, Univ. of Ghana, 1958; Vis. Professor: Stanford Univ., several occasions, 1960–66; Univ. of Minnesota, 1968; Princeton Univ., 1970; Rockefeller Univ., 1973; William James Lectr in Philosophy, Harvard Univ., 1976; Alex. von Humboldt-Stiftung Vis. Res. Fellow, Münster Univ., 1981. Founder Mem., Oxford Cttee for Racial Integration, 1965 (Chm., Jan.–May 1966); Member: Exec. Cttee, Campaign Against Racial Discrimination, 1966–67; Legal and Civil Affairs Panel, Nat. Cttee for Commonwealth Immigrants, 1966–68; Chairman: Jt Council for the Welfare of Immigrants, 1970–71 (Vice-Chm., 1967–69, 1973–75); unofficial cttee of enquiry into events in Southall 23 April 1979, 1979–80; shadow board, Barclays Bank, 1981–82. FBA 1968–84, re-elected 1995. For. Hon. Mem., Amer. Acad. of Arts and Scis, 1985. Hon. PhD Nijmegen, 1983; Hon. DLitt: Caen, 1993; Aberdeen, 1993. Lakatos Award in Phil. of Sci., LSE, 1994; Rolf Schock Prize for Logic and Philosophy, Royal Swedish Acad. of Scis, 1995. *Publications:* Frege: philosophy of language, 1973, 2nd edn 1981; The Justification of Deduction, 1973; Elements of Intuitionism, 1977, rev. edn 2000; Truth and other Enigmas, 1978; Immigration: where the debate goes wrong, 1978; Catholicism and the World Order, 1979; The Game of Tarot, 1980; Twelve Tarot Games, 1980; The Interpretation of Frege's Philosophy, 1981; Voting Procedures, 1984; The Visconti-Sforza Tarot Cards, 1986; Ursprünge der analytischen Philosophie, 1988, rev. edn as Origins of Analytical Philosophy, 1993; Frege and Other Philosophers, 1991; The Logical Basis of Metaphysics, 1991; Frege: Philosophy of Mathematics, 1991; Grammar and Style for Examination Candidates and Others, 1993; The Seas of Language, 1993; Il Mondo e l'Angelo, 1993; I Tarocchi Siciliani, 1995; (jtly) A Wicked Pack of Cards, 1996; Principles of Electoral Reform, 1997; (jtly) The Tarot Mystique, 2000; contributions to: Mind and Language, 1975; Truth and Meaning, 1976; Studies on Frege, 1976; Contemporary British Philosophy, 1976; Meaning and Use, 1979; Perception and Identity, 1979; Perspectives on the Philosophy of Wittgenstein, 1981; Approaches to Language, 1983; Frege: tradition and influence, 1984; Reflections on Chomsky, 1989; Meaning and Method, 1990; contrib. entry on Frege, to Encyclopedia of Philosophy (ed P. Edwards), 1967; (with Ann Dummett) chapter on Rôle of the Government, in Justice First (ed L. Donnelly), 1969; preface to R. C. Zaehner, The City Within the Heart, 1980; articles in: Aristotelian Soc. Proceedings, Philos. Review, Bull. of London Math. Soc., Synthese, Inquiry, Econometrica, Jl of Symbolic Logic, Zeitschrift für mathematische Logik, Dublin Review, New Blackfriars, Clergy Review, Jl of Warburg and Courtauld Insts, Jl of Playing-Card Soc. *Recreations:* listening to the blues, investigating the history of card games, reading science fiction. *Address:* 54 Park Town, Oxford OX2 6SJ. *T:* (01865) 58698. *Club:* Royal Commonwealth Society.

DUMONT, Hon. Dame Ivy (Leona), DCMG 1995; DPA; Minister of Education, Bahamas, since 1995; *b* 2 Oct. 1930; *d* of Alphonso Tennyson Turnquest and Cecilia Elizabeth Turnquest; *m* 1951, Reginald Deane Dumont; one *s* one *d*. *Educ:* Univ. of Miami (BEd 1970); Nova Univ., USA (DPA 1978). Teacher, later Dep. Dir of Educn, Min. of Educn and Culture, Bahamas, 1945–75; Dep. Permanent Sec., Min. of Works and Utilities, 1975–78; Trng Officer, Personnel Manager then Gp Relations Manager, Natwest Trust Corp. (Bahamas) Ltd, then Coutts & Co., 1978–91; Minister of Health and Envmt, 1992–94. Mem. (FNM), Senate, 1992– (Govt Leader, 1992–). *Recreations:* dressmaking and design, horticulture (roses), public speaking, family. *Address:* Ministry of Education, PO Box N-3913, Nassau, Bahamas. *T:* 3228140; PO Box SS-5316, Nassau, Bahamas. *T:* 3234188.

DUMPER, Rt Rev. Anthony Charles; Hon. Assistant Bishop, diocese of Birmingham, since 1993; Hon. Tutor, Centre of Anglican Communion Studies, Selly Oak, since 1993; *b* 4 Oct. 1923; *s* of Charles Frederick and Edith Mildred Dumper; *m* 1948, Sibylle Anna Emilie Hellwig (*d* 2001); two *s* one *d*. *Educ:* Surbiton Grammar School; Christ's Coll., Cambridge (MA); Westcott House, Cambridge. Relief Worker, Germany, 1946–47; ordained, 1947; Curate, East Greenwich, 1947–49; Vicar of South Perak, Malaya, 1949–57; Archdeacon of North Malaya, 1955–64; Vicar of Penang, Malaya, 1957–64; Dean of St Andrew's Cathedral, Singapore, 1964–70; Vicar of St Peter's, Stockton on Tees, and Rural Dean of Stockton, 1970–77; Bishop Suffragan of Dudley, 1977–93. *Publication:* Vortex of the East, 1963. *Recreations:* walking, gardening. *Address:* 117 Berberry Close, Bournville, Birmingham B30 1TB.

DUMVILLE, Prof. David Norman, PhD; FRHistS; FRSAI; Professor of Palaeography and Cultural History, University of Cambridge, since 1995; Fellow, Girton College, Cambridge, since 1978; *b* 5 May 1949; *s* of late Norman Dumville and Eileen Florence Lillie Dumville (*née* Gibbs); *m* 1st, 1974, Sally Lois Hannay (*d* 1989); one *s*; 2nd, 1990, Yoko Wada. *Educ:* Emmanuel Coll., Cambridge (BA Hons, MA); Ludwig-Maximilian Universität, Munich; Univ. of Edinburgh (PhD 1976). FRHistS 1976; FRSAI 1989; FSAScot 1999. Fellow, Univ. of Wales, Swansea, 1975–77; Asst Prof. of English, Univ. of Pennsylvania, 1977–78; O'Donnell Lectr in Celtic Studies, Univ. of Oxford, 1977–78; Lectr in Anglo-Saxon, Norse and Celtic, Univ. of Cambridge, 1977–91; British Acad. Res. Reader in Humanities, 1985–87; Reader in Early Mediaeval History and Culture of British Isles, Univ. of Cambridge, 1991–95. Res. Associate, Sch. of Celtic Studies, Dublin Inst. for Advanced Studies, 1989– (Vis. Prof., 1996–97); Visiting Professor of Mediaeval Studies: UCLA, 1995; Univ. of Calif, Berkeley, 1997. Vice-Pres., Centre International de Recherche et de Documentation sur le Monachisme Celtique, 1986–. Hon. MA Pennsylvania, 1979. *Publications:* (with Kathryn Grabowski) Chronicles and Annals of Mediaeval Ireland & Wales, 1984; (with Michael Lapidge) The Annals of St Neots, 1985; The Historia Brittonum, 1985; Histories and Pseudo-Histories of the Insular Middle Ages, 1990; Wessex and England from Alfred to Edgar, 1992; Liturgy and the Ecclesiastical History of Late Anglo-Saxon England, 1992; Britons and Anglo-Saxons in the Early Middle Ages, 1993; English Caroline Script and Monastic History, 1993; Saint Patrick, 1993; The Anglo-Saxon Chronicle, 1995; The Churches of North Britain in the First Viking-Age, 1997; Three Men in a Boat (inaugural lect.), 1997; Councils and Synods of the Gaelic Early and Central Middle Ages, 1997; A Palaeographer's Review, 1999; Saint David of Wales, 2001; Pictish Matriliny Revisited, 2001. *Recreations:* travelling in North America, politics and other arguments. *Address:* Girton College, Cambridge CB3 0JG. *T:* (01223) 338999.

DUN, Peter John; HM Diplomatic Service; Head of Information Department, Foreign and Commonwealth Office, since 1996; *b* 6 July 1947; *s* of Herbert Ernest Dun and late Joyce Hannah Dun (*née* Tozer); *m* 1984, Cheng Kiak Pang; two *s*. *Educ:* Bristol Grammar Sch.; Univ. of Birmingham (BA); Univ. of Cologne; Univ. of Freiburg; Univ. of Strasbourg. British High Commn, Kuala Lumpur, 1972–76; FCO, 1976–80; UK Repn to EU, 1980–83; UK Mission to UN, 1983–87; Dep. Hd, Disarmament Dept, FCO, 1987–89; rcds, 1989; British High Commission, Islamabad, 1990–93; Foreign Policy Advr to Ext. Affairs Comr, EC, Brussels, 1993–96. *Recreations:* music, travel, maps. *Address:* c/o Foreign and Commonwealth Office, King Charles Street, SW1A 2AH. *T:* (020) 7270 3000.

DUNALLEY, 7th Baron *cr* 1800 (Ire.), of Kilboy, Tipperary; **Henry Francis Cornelius Prittie;** Probation Officer with Oxfordshire and Buckinghamshire Probation Service, since 1983; *b* 30 May 1948; *s* of 6th Baron Dunalley and of Mary Philippa, *o c* of late Hon. Philip Cary; *S* father, 1992; *m* 1978, Sally Louise, *er d* of Ronald Vere; one *s* three *d.* *Educ:* Gordonstoun Sch.; Trinity Coll., Dublin (BA); Bedford Coll., Univ. of London (CQSW). Probation Officer: Inner London Probation Service, 1977–80; Buckinghamshire Probation Service, 1980–83. *Heir: s* Hon. Joel Henry Prittie, *b* 29 April 1981. *Address:* 15 Barton Lane, Oxford OX3 9JR. *T:* (01865) 761914.

DUNANT, Sarah; novelist and broadcaster; *b* 8 Aug. 1950; *d* of David Dunant and Estelle (*née* Joseph); two *d* by Ian Willox. *Educ:* Godolphin and Latymer Girls' Sch.; Newnham Coll., Cambridge (BA Hons 1972). Actress, 1972–73; producer, Radio 4, 1974–76; freelance writer, TV and radio broadcaster and journalist, 1977–; The Late Show, BBC 2, 1989–95. *Publications:* as Peter Dunant, (with Peter Busby): Exterminating Angels, 1983; Intensive Care, 1986; as Sarah Dunant: Snow Storms in a Hot Climate, 1988; Birth Marks, 1991; Fatlands, 1993 (Silver Dagger Award); (ed) The War of the Words, 1994; Under my Skin, 1995; (ed jtly) Age of Anxiety, 1996; Transgressions, 1997; Mapping the Edge, 1999. *Recreations:* movies, travel. *Address:* c/o Clare Alexander, Gillon Aitken Associates, 29 Fernshaw Road, SW10 0TG. *T:* (020) 7351 7561.

DUNBABIN, Dr Jean Hymers; Fellow and Tutor, St Anne's College, Oxford, since 1973; Reader in Medieval History, University of Oxford, since 1997; *b* 12 May 1939; *d* of David Mackay and Peggy Mackay (*née* Stewart); *m* 1962, John Dunbabin; two *d.* *Educ:* St Leonard's Sch., St Andrews; St Hilda's Coll., Oxford (MA, DPhil 1965). Jun. Research Fellow, Somerville Coll., Oxford, 1961–63; Vice-Principal, St Anne's Coll., Oxford, 1994–97. Mem., IAS, Princeton, 1989. Ed., English Historical Rev., 2000–. *Publications:* France in the Making 843–1180, 1985, 2nd edn 2000; A Hound of God: Pierre de la Palud and the Fourteenth Century Church, 1991; Charles I of Anjou: power, kingship and state-making in thirteenth-century Europe, 1998; contributions to: The Cambridge History of Later Medieval Philosophy, 1982; The Cambridge History of Medieval Political Thought, 1988; The New Cambridge Medieval History, vol. III, 1999; contrib. various jls. *Recreations:* walking, yoga, travelling. *Address:* St Anne's College, Oxford OX2 6HS. *T:* (01865) 274872; Southernwood, Church Walk, Combe, Witney, Oxon OX29 8NQ.

DUNBAR, Alexander Arbuthnott; DL; farmer; *b* 14 March 1929; *yr s* of Sir Edward Dunbar, 9th Bt; *m* 1965, Elizabeth Susannah, *d* of Rev. Denzil Wright; one *s* one *d.* *Educ:* Wellington Coll., Berks; Pembroke Coll., Cambridge (MA); Edinburgh Sch. of Agriculture, 1980–81. Mil. Service, Lieut QO Cameron Highlanders, 1947–49. Called to the Bar, Inner Temple, 1953. Joined ICI, 1954: Asst Sec., Wilton Works, 1959–63. Joined North Eastern Assoc. for the Arts, 1963, Sec. 1964, Dir 1967; Director: Northern Arts, 1967–69; UK and British Commonwealth Branch, Calouste Gulbenkian Foundn, 1970–71; Scottish Arts Council, 1971–80. Chm., Northern Adv. Cttee, Scottish Wildlife Trust, 1986–93; Member: Arts and Disability Enquiry, Carnegie UK Trust, 1982–85; Museums and Galleries Commn Wkg Party on Museums in Scotland, 1984–86. DL Moray, 1987. *Publications:* contribs to various jls. *Recreations:* art, theatre, conservation, history, travel. *Address:* Pitgaveny, Elgin, Moray IV30 5PQ.

DUNBAR of Northfield, Sir Archibald (Ranulph), 11th Bt *cr* 1700; *b* 8 Aug. 1927; *er s* of Sir (Archibald) Edward Dunbar, 9th Bt (by some reckonings 10th Bt) and Olivia Douglas Sinclair (*d* 1964), *d* of Maj.-Gen. Sir Edward May, KCB, CMG; *S* father, 1969; *m* 1974, Amelia Millar Sommerville, *d* of Horace Davidson; one *s* two *d.* *Educ:* Wellington Coll.; Pembroke Coll., Cambridge; Imperial Coll. of Tropical Agriculture, Trinidad. Mil. Service, 2nd Lt, Cameron (att. Gordon) Highlanders, 1945–48. Entered Colonial Agricultural Service, Uganda, as Agricultural Officer, 1953; retired, 1970. Hon. Sheriff, Sheriff Court District of Moray, 1989–. Kt of Honour and Devotion, SMO Malta, 1989. *Publications:* A History of Bunyoro-Kitara, 1965; Omukama Chwa II Kabarega, 1965; The Annual Crops of Uganda, 1969; various articles in Uganda Jl. *Recreations:* swimming, military modelling, model railways, miniature ships. *Heir: s* Edward Horace Dunbar, Younger of Northfield, *b* 18 March 1977. *Address:* The Old Manse, Duffus, Elgin, Scotland IV30 5QD. *T:* (01343) 830270. *Club:* New (Edinburgh).

DUNBAR, Sir David H.; *see* Hope-Dunbar.

DUNBAR, Ian Duncan; Sheriff of Tayside Central and Fife, since 2000; *b* 31 Oct. 1948; *s* of John Duncan Dunbar and Mary Golden; *m* 1973, Sue Young. *Educ:* Lawside Acad., Dundee; Queen's Coll., Dundee (St Andrews Univ., subseq. Dundee Univ.) (LLB 1969). Apprentice Solicitor, Soutar Reid & Mill, Dundee, 1969–71; Sneddon Campbell & Munro, Perth, later Miller Sneddon, then Miller Hendry, Perth and Dundee: Asst Solicitor, 1971–72; Partner, 1972–98; Chm., 1994–98; Floating Sheriff, 1998–2000. Pres., Law Soc. of Scotland, 1993–94 (Vice Pres., 1992–93). Trustee, Perth Coll. Devlt Trust, 1995–98. *Recreations:* golf, Rugby, cooking, food, wine. *Address:* Craigrownie, Bridge of Earn, Perth PH2 9HA. *T:* (01738) 812255. *Club:* Blairgowrie Golf.

DUNBAR, Ian Malcolm, CB 1993; Director of Inmate Administration, Prison Service, Home Office, 1990–94; *b* 6 Jan. 1934; *s* of Thomas Dunbar and Rose (*née* Hook); *m* 1966, Sally Ann Hendrickson; two *s* one *d.* *Educ:* Buckhurst Hill County High Sch.; Keele Univ.; Reed Coll., Portland, USA; LSE. Joined Prison Service, 1959; Leyhill Prison, 1960; Prison Service Coll., 1965; Dep. Gov., Long Lartin, 1970; Gov., Usk Borstal and Detention Centre, 1972; Prison Dept 4 Div., Home Office, 1974; Governor: Feltham Borstal, 1978; Wakefield Prison, 1979; Wormwood Scrubs, 1983; seconded to HM Inspectorate of Prisons, 1985; Regl Dir, SW Reg., Prison Service, 1985. NI Sentence Review Comr, 1998–. *Publications:* A Sense of Direction, 1985; (with A. Langdon) Tough Justice: sentencing and penal policies in the 1990s, 1998. *Recreations:* bee-keeping, gardening, photography, walking, reading.

DUNBAR of Mochrum, Colonel Sir James Michael, 14th Bt *cr* 1694 (NS), of Mochrum, Wigtownshire; *b* 17 Jan. 1950; *s* of Sir Jean Ivor Dunbar, 13th Bt and of Rose Jeanne, *d* of Henry William Hertsch; *S* father, 1993; *m* 1st, 1978, Margaret Jacobs (marr diss. 1989; she *d* 1991); two *s* one *d*; 2nd, 1989, Margaret, *d* of Roger Gordon Talbot; one *d.* Colonel, USAF. *Heir: s* Michael Joseph Dunbar, *b* 5 July 1980. *Address:* Apt 202, 7708 Arboretum Drive, Charlotte, NC 28270, USA.

DUNBAR, John Greenwell, OBE 1999; architectural historian; Secretary, Royal Commission on the Ancient and Historical Monuments of Scotland, 1978–90; *b* 1 March 1930; *o s* of John Dunbar and Marie Alton; *m* 1974, Elizabeth Mill Blyth. *Educ:* University College Sch., London; Balliol Coll., Oxford (MA). FSA. Joined staff of Royal Commission on the Ancient and Historical Monuments of Scotland, 1953; Member: Ancient Monuments Board for Scotland, 1978–90; Regl Adv. Cttee, Forestry Commn, 1997–2000. Vice-President: Soc. for Medieval Archaeology, 1981–86; Soc. of Antiquaries of Scotland, 1983–86. Lectures: Lindsay-Fischer, Oslo, 1985; Rhind, Edinburgh, 1998. Hon. FRIAS; Hon. FSA Scot. *Publications:* The Historic Architecture of Scotland, 1966, revd edn 1978; (ed with John Imrie) Accounts of the Masters of Works 1616–1649, 1982; Sir William Burrell's Northern Tour 1758, 1997; Scottish Royal Palaces, 1999; numerous articles in archaeological jls, etc. *Address:* Patie's Mill, Carlops, By Penicuik, Midlothian EH26 9NF. *T:* (01968) 660250. *Club:* New (Edinburgh).

DUNBAR of Hempriggs, Sir Richard (Francis), 9th Bt *cr* 1706 (NS); *b* 8 Jan. 1945; *s* of Lady Dunbar of Hempriggs, Btss (8th in line) and Leonard James Blake (*d* 1989); assumed the name of Dunbar, 1965; *S* to mother's Btcy, 1997; *m* 1969, Elizabeth Margaret Jane Lister; two *d.* *Educ:* Charterhouse. Businessman. *Heir:* (to father's Btcy) *d* Emma Katherine Dunbar of Hempriggs, *b* 9 Nov. 1977. *Address:* 732 Crossway Road, Burlinghame, CA 94010, USA.

DUNBAR of Durn, Sir Robert (Drummond Cospatrick), 10th Bt *cr* 1698 (NS); Director, Merrill Lynch Investment Managers, since 1995; *b* 17 June 1958; *o s* of Sir Drummond Cospatrick Ninian Dunbar, 9th Bt, MC and of Sheila Barbara Mary, *d* of John B. de Fonblanque; *S* father, 2000; *m* 1994, Sarah Margaret, *yr d* of Robert Anthony Brooks; one *s* one *d.* *Educ:* Harrow; Christ Church, Oxford (MA). AIIMR. Allen & Overy (Private Client Dept), 1982–86; Merrill Lynch Investment Managers (formerly Mercury Warburg Investment Management), 1986–. *Heir: s* Alexander William Drummond Dunbar, Younger of Durn, *b* 1 March 1995. *Address:* 32 Westover Road, SW18 2RQ. *T:* (020) 8870 3868.

DUNBAR, Prof. Robin Ian MacDonald, PhD; FBA 1998; FRAI; Professor of Evolutionary Psychology, University of Liverpool, since 1994; *b* 28 June 1947; *s* of George MacDonald Dunbar and Betty Lilian (*née* Toon); *m* 1971, Eva Patricia Melvin; two *s* one *d.* *Educ:* Magdalen Coll., Oxford (BA 1969); Univ. of Bristol (PhD 1974). FRAI 1988. SERC Advanced Res. Fellow, King's Coll., Cambridge, 1977–80; Res. Fellow, Zool. Dept, Univ. of Cambridge, 1980–82; docent, Zool Inst., Univ. of Stockholm, 1983; Res. Fellow, Zool. Dept, Liverpool Univ., 1985–87; University College London: Lectr, Anthropol. Dept, 1987–92; Prof. of Biol Anthropol., 1992–94. Animal Procedures Cttee, Home Office, 1997–. Member: Assoc. for Study of Animal Behaviour, 1970–; British Ecol. Soc., 1979–; Galton Inst., 1988–; Assoc. for Child Psychology and Psychiatry, 1999–; Amer. Psychol Assoc., 2000–; Pres., Primate Soc., 1990–93. Co-editor, Animal Behaviour, 1994–95. *Publications:* (jtly) Social Dynamic of Galada Baboons, 1975; Reproductive Decisions, 1984; Primate Social Systems, 1988; World of Nature, 1988; The Trouble with Science, 1995; (ed) Human Reproductive Decisions, 1995; Grooming, Gossip and the Evolution of Language, 1996; (ed) The Evolution of Culture, 1999; Primate Conservation Biology, 2000; Cousins, 2000. *Recreations:* poetry, Medieval and Renaissance music, hill-walking. *Address:* School of Biological Sciences, University of Liverpool, Liverpool L69 3BX.

DUNBAR-NASMITH, Sir James (Duncan), Kt 1996; CBE 1976; RIBA; PPRIAS; FRSA, FRSE; Partner, Law & Dunbar-Nasmith, architects, Edinburgh, Forres, 1957–99; Professor Emeritus, Heriot-Watt University, since 1988; *b* 15 March 1927; *y s* of late Adm. Sir Martin Dunbar-Nasmith, VC, KCB, KCMG, DL and of late Justina Dunbar-Nasmith, CBE, DStJ. *Educ:* Lockers Park; Winchester. Trinity Coll., Cambridge (BA); Edinburgh Coll. of Art (DA). ARIBA 1954. Architekten Kammer Hessen, 1994. Lieut, Scots Guards, 1945–48. Prof. and Hd of Dept. of Architecture, Heriot-Watt Univ. and Edinburgh Coll. of Art, 1978–88. President: Royal Incorporation of Architects in Scotland, 1971–73; Edinburgh Architectural Assoc., 1967–69. Member: Council, RIBA, 1967–73 (a Vice-Pres., 1972–73; Chm., Bd of Educn, 1972–73); Council, ARCUK, 1976–84 (Vice-Chm., Bd of Educn, 1977); Royal Commn on Ancient and Historical Monuments of Scotland, 1972–96; Ancient Monuments Bd for Scotland, 1969–83 (interim Chm., 1972–73); Historic Buildings Council for Scotland, 1966–93; Council, Europa Nostra, 1986– (Vice-Pres., 1997–); Dep. Chm., Edinburgh Internat. Festival, 1981–85; Chm., Scottish Civic Trust, 1995–; Trustee, Architectural Heritage Fund, 1976–97; Theatres Trust, 1983–95. *Recreations:* music, theatre, ski-ing, sailing. *Address:* 4 Blackie House, Lady Stairs Close, Edinburgh EH1 2NY. *T:* (0131) 225 4236. *Clubs:* Royal Ocean Racing; New (Edinburgh).

DUNBOYNE, 28th Baron by Prescription, 18th Baron by Patent; **Patrick Theobald Tower Butler; His Honour The Lord Dunboyne,** VRD; a Circuit Judge, 1972–86; *b* 27 Jan. 1917; *e s* of 27th Baron Dunboyne and Dora Isolde Butler (*d* 1977), *e d* of Comdr F. F. Tower; *S* father, 1945; *m* 1950, Anne Marie, *d* of late Sir Victor Mallet, GCMG, CVO; one *s* three *d.* *Educ:* Winchester; Trinity Coll., Cambridge (MA). Pres. of Cambridge Union. Lieut Irish Guards (Suppl. Res.); served European War, 1939–44 (King's Badge) (prisoner, then repatriated); Foreign Office, 1945–46. Barrister-at-Law, Middle Temple (Harmsworth Scholar), Inner Temple, South-Eastern Circuit, King's Inns, Dublin. In practice 1949–71. Recorder of Hastings, 1961–71; Dep. Chm., Quarter Sessions: Mddx, 1963–65; Kent, 1963–71; (full-time) Inner London 1971–72. Legal Aid No 2 Area Cttee, 1954–64. Commissary Gen., Diocese of Canterbury, 1959–71. Home Sec's Ward-boundaries Comr, 1960–70. Irish Genealogical Research Society: Fellow, 1982; Pres., 1971–91; Vice-Pres., 1992–; Founder Hon. Sec., Bar Lawn Tennis Soc., 1950 (Vice-Pres. 1963–), and of Irish Peers Assoc., 1963–71 (Chm., 1987–90); Pres., Wireless Telegraphy Appeal Tribunal for Eng. and Wales, 1967–70. Mem. Council, Friends of Canterbury Cathedral, 1953–71. Lt, RNVR, 1951–58, RNR, 1958–60. *Publications:* The Trial of J. G. Haigh, 1953; (with others) Cambridge Union, 1815–1939, 1953; Butler Family History, 1966, 7th edn 1990; When the States were Young, 1997. *Recreations:* rowing, lawn tennis, chess. *Heir: s* Hon. John Fitzwalter Butler [*b* 31 July 1951; *m* 1975, Diana Caroline, *yr d* of Sir Michael Williams, KCMG; one *s* three *d*]. *Address:* 36 Ormonde Gate, SW3 4HA. *T:* (020) 7352 1837. *Clubs:* Irish; International Lawn Tennis of Great Britain (Vice-Pres., Pres. 1973–83) and (hon.) of Australia, France, Germany, Monaco, Netherlands and USA; Forty Five Lawn Tennis (Pres., 1974–91); All England Lawn Tennis (Wimbledon); Pitt, Union (Cambridge).

DUNCAN, Agnes Lawrie Addie, (Laura); Sheriff of Glasgow and Strathkelvin, since 1982; *b* 17 June 1947; *d* of late William Smith, District Clerk, and of Mary Marshall Smith McClure; *m* 1990, David Cecil Duncan, farmer, cricket coach, *y s* of late Dr and Mrs H. C. Duncan, Edinburgh; one *s.* *Educ:* Hamilton Acad.; Glasgow Univ. (LLB 1967). Admitted Solicitor, 1969; called to the Scottish Bar, 1976. Solicitor, private practice, 1969–71; Procurator Fiscal Depute, 1971–75; Standing Junior Counsel to Dept of Employment, 1982. Winner, Scottish Ladies Single handed Dinghy Championship, 1990. *Recreation:* sailing. *Address:* Glasgow Sheriff Court, 1 Carlton Place, Glasgow G5 9DA.

DUNCAN, Alan James Carter; MP (C) Rutland and Melton, since 1992; *b* 31 March 1957; 2nd *s* of late Wing Comdr J. G. Duncan, OBE and Anne Duncan (*née* Carter). *Educ:* Merchant Taylors' Sch.; St John's Coll., Oxford. Pres., Oxford Union, 1979. With Shell Internat. Petroleum, 1979–81; Kennedy Schol., Harvard Univ., 1981–82; oil trader, Marc Rich & Co., 1982–88; self-employed oil broker, 1988–. PPS to Min. of State, DoH, 1993–94, to Chm. of Cons. Party, 1995–97; a Vice Chm. of Cons. Party, 1997–98; Parly Political Sec. to Leader of the Opposition, 1997; Opposition spokesman on health,

1998–99, on trade and industry, 1999–2001, on foreign affairs, 2001–. Mem., Select Cttee on Social Security, 1993–95. Contested (C) Barnsley W and Penistone, 1987. Freeman, City of London, 1980; Liveryman, Merchant Taylors' Co., 1987. *Publications:* An End to Illusions, 1993; (with D. Hobson) Saturn's Children: how the state devours liberty, prosperity and virtue, 1995. *Address:* House of Commons, SW1A 0AA. *Club:* Beefsteak.

DUNCAN, Dr Allan George; environmental consultant, since 2000; *b* 17 Oct. 1940; *s* of Donald Allan Duncan and Annabella Duncan (*née* Thom); *m* 1972, Alison Patricia Reid; two *s* one *d*. *Educ:* Robert Gordon's Coll., Aberdeen; Aberdeen Univ. (BSc Hons 1963); New Coll., Oxford, (DPhil 1966). Research Engineer: California Univ., 1966–67; US Nat. Bureau of Standards, 1967–69; UKAEA, Harwell, 1969–79; Radiochemical Inspectorate, DoE, 1979–87 (Dep. Chief Inspector, 1984–87); HM Inspectorate of Pollution, 1987–96 (Chief Inspector, 1995–96); Hd, Radioactive Substances Regulation, EA, 1996–2000. Member: EC Network of Envmtl Regulators, 1993–; Euratom Scientific and Tech. Cttee, 1994–; Envmtl Assessment Panel, UK Accreditation Service, 1994–99. MIEMA (MIEMgt 1995). *Publications:* various contribs to scientific literature. *Recreations:* sailing, walking, North American history. *Address:* 14 Rawlings Grove, Abingdon, Oxon OX14 1SH. *T:* (01235) 529096.

DUNCAN, Prof. Archibald Alexander McBeth, FBA 1985; Professor of Scottish History and Literature, Glasgow University, 1962–93; *b* 17 Oct. 1926; *s* of Charles George Duncan and Christina Helen McBeth; *m* 1954, Ann Hayes Sawyer, *d* of W. E. H. Sawyer, Oxford; two *s* one *d*. *Educ:* George Heriot's Sch.; Edinburgh Univ.; Balliol Coll., Oxford. Lecturer in History, Queen's Univ., Belfast, 1951–53; Lecturer in History, Edinburgh Univ., 1953–61; Leverhulme Research Fellow, 1961–62. Glasgow University: Clerk of Senate, 1978–83; Dean of Faculties, 1998–2000. Mem., Royal Commn on the Ancient and Historical Monuments of Scotland, 1969–92. *Publications:* Scotland: The Making of the Kingdom, 1975; (ed and revised) W. Croft Dickinson's Scotland from the Earliest Times to 1603, 3rd edn 1977; Regesta Regum Scottorum, v, The Acts of Robert I, 1306–29, 1988; (ed, with trans. and notes), John Barbour, The Bruce, 1997. *Address:* 17 Campbell Drive, Bearsden, Glasgow G61 4NF.

DUNCAN, Rev. Canon Bruce, MBE 1993; Principal, Sarum College, since 1995; *b* 28 Jan. 1938; *s* of late Andrew Allan Duncan and of Dora Duncan (*née* Young); *m* 1966, Margaret Holmes Smith; three *d*. *Educ:* St Albans Sch.; Univ. of Leeds (BA 1960); Cuddesdon Coll., Oxford. Founder/Director: Children's Relief Internat., 1960–62; Northorpe Hall Trust, 1962–65; ordained deacon, 1967, priest, 1968; Curate, St Bartholomew, Armley, Leeds and Curate in charge, St Mary of Bethany, Leeds, 1967–69; Hon. Curate, St Mary the Less, Cambridge, 1969–70; Chaplain, Order of Holy Paraclete, Whitby, 1970–71; Chaplain to HM Ambassadors in Austria, Hungary and Czechoslovakia, based in Vienna, 1971–75; Vicar, Collegiate Church of Holy Cross and the Mother of Him Who Hung Thereon, Crediton, Devon, 1976–82; Rural Dean of Cadbury, 1976–81; Rector, Crediton and Shobrooke, 1982–86; Residentiary Canon, Manchester Cathedral and Fellow, Coll. of Christ in Manchester, 1986–95. Hon. Pres., Northorpe Hall Child and Family Trust, 1997–. FRSA 1989. *Publications:* Children at Risk (ed A. H. Denney), 1968; Sich Selbst Verstehen, 1993; Pray Your Way, Your Personality and God, 1993. *Recreations:* travel, walking. *Address:* 19A The Close, Salisbury, Wilts SP1 2EB. *T:* (01722) 324525; *e-mail:* principal@sarum.ac.uk. *Club:* Athenæum.

DUNCAN, Craig; Chief Executive (formerly Secretary), Royal College of Surgeons of England, since 1997; *b* 1 May 1951; *s* of William Sneddon Duncan and of Jessie Clark Sloan Duncan (*née* Mackie); *m* 1st, 1975, Janet Elizabeth Gillespie (marr. diss. 1988); one *s* one *d*; 2nd, 1998, Jane Alison Pavitt. *Educ:* Allan Glen's Sch., Glasgow; Univ. of Strathclyde (BA 1st Cl. Hons Geog.). Administrative Assistant: Univ. of Durham, 1973–76; Univ. of Southampton, 1976–82; Royal College of Surgeons of England, 1982–: Admin. Asst and Asst Sec., 1982–88; Asst Sec., Inst. Basic Med. Scis, 1982–86; Secretary: Hunterian Inst., 1986–88; for Ext. Affairs, 1989–97; Senate of Surgery of GB and Ireland, 1993–97. *Recreations:* music, reading, water-colour painting. *Address:* Royal College of Surgeons of England, 35–43 Lincoln's Inn Fields, WC2A 3PN. *T:* (020) 7869 6020.

DUNCAN, David Francis; HM Diplomatic Service, retired; *b* 22 Feb. 1923; *s* of late Brig. William Edmonstone Duncan, CVO, DSO, MC, and Mrs Magdalene Emily Duncan (*née* Renny-Tailyour). *Educ:* Eton; Trinity Coll., Cambridge. Served War, RA, 1941–46 (despatches). Entered Foreign (later Diplomatic) Service, 1949; Foreign Office, 1949–52; Bogotá, 1952–54; UK Delegn to ECSC, Luxembourg, 1954–55; FO, 1955–58; Baghdad, 1958; Ankara, 1958–60; FO, 1960–62; Quito, 1962–65; Phnom Penh, 1965 (as Chargé d'Affaires); FO (later Foreign and Commonwealth Office), 1965–70; Islamabad, 1970–71; Counsellor, UK Delegn to Geneva Disarm. Conf., 1971–74; Ambassador to Nicaragua, 1974–76; retired 1976. *Recreations:* walking, photography, travel. *Address:* 133 Rivermead Court, Ranelagh Gardens, SW6 3SE. *T:* (020) 7736 1576.

DUNCAN, Rev. Denis Macdonald, MA, BD; *b* 10 Jan. 1920; *s* of late Rev. Reginald Duncan, BD, BLitt and late Clarice Ethel (*née* Hodgkinson); *m* 1942, Henrietta Watson McKenzie (*née* Houston) (*d* 1993); one *s* one *d*. *Educ:* George Watson's Boys' Coll., Edinburgh; Edinburgh Univ.; New Coll., Edinburgh. Ordained, 1943; Minister of St Margaret's, Juniper Green, Edinburgh, 1943–49; Trinity Duke Street Parish Church, Glasgow, 1949–57; Founder-editor, Rally, 1956–67; Managing Editor, British Weekly, 1957–70 (Man. Dir, 1967–70); Managing Director: DPS Publicity Services Ltd, 1967–74; Arthur James Ltd (Publishers), 1983–94; broadcaster and scriptwriter, Scottish Television, 1963–68; concert promotion at Edinburgh Festival and elsewhere, 1966–; Concert series "Communication through the Arts" poetry/music anthologies (with Benita Kyle), 1970–80. Dir, Highgate Counselling Centre, 1969–86; Associate Dir and Trng Supervisor, Westminster Pastoral Foundn, 1971–79; Chm., Internat. Cttee of World Assoc. of Pastoral Care and Counselling, 1977–79; Dir, Churches' Council for Health and Healing. 1982–88; Moderator of the Presbytery of England, Church of Scotland, 1984. PhD Somerset Univ., 1989. *Publications:* (ed) Through the Year with William Barclay, 1971; (ed) Through the Year with Cardinal Heenan, 1972; (ed) Daily Celebration, vol. 1, 1972, vol. 2, 1974; Marching Orders, 1973; (ed) Every Day with William Barclay, 1973; (ed) Through the Year with J. B. Phillips, 1974; Marching On, 1974; Here is my Hand, 1977; Creative Silence, 1980; A Day at a Time, 1980; Love, the Word that Heals, 1981; The Way of Love, 1982; Victorious Living, 1982; Health and Healing: a ministry to wholeness, 1988; Be Still and Know …: 100 Daily Telegraph meditations, 1994; Solitude, stillness, serenity …: a further 75 Daily Telegraph meditations, 1997; The Road Taken: autobiographical reflections on communication, 1997; Rainbows Through the Rain: a third collection of 75 Daily Telegraph Meditations, 2000. *Recreation:* cricket. *Address:* 1 Cranbourne Road, N10 2BT. *T:* (020) 8883 1831, *Fax:* (020) 8883 8307.

DUNCAN, Geoffrey Stuart, OBE 1998; General Secretary, General Synod Board of Education and National Society for Promoting Religious Education, 1990–98; *b* 10 April 1938; *s* of Alexander Sidney Duncan and Gertude Ruth (*née* Page); *m* 1962, Shirley Bernice Matilda Vanderput; one *s* one *d*. *Educ:* Hemel Hempstead Grammar Sch.; Univ. of London (BScEcon); Univ. of Exeter (MA). Served RAEC, 1960–64. School and technical coll. teaching, 1964–72; LEA Advr and Officer, 1972–82; Schs Sec. and Dep. Sec., Gen. Synod Bd of Educn and Nat. Soc. for Promoting Religious Educn, 1982–90. Part-time WEA Tutor, 1966–70; part-time Open Univ. Counsellor, 1971–72. Dir, Urban Learning Foundn, 1990–98; Company Sec., Inst. of Consumer Scis, 2000–01. Trustee: St Gabriel's Educnl Trust, 1990–98; St Christopher's Educnl Trust, 1990–98; Winchester Shoei Coll. Foundn, 1990–. Governor, Coll. of St Mark & St John, Plymouth, 1990–. MUniv Surrey, 1998. *Publications:* contributor to: Faith for the Future, 1986; Schools for Tomorrow, 1988; various educn jls. *Recreations:* campanology, travel. *Address:* 17 Carlton Road, Seaford, East Sussex BN25 2LE. *T:* (01323) 893587.

DUNCAN, George; Chairman: Laporte plc, since 1995 (Director, since 1987); ASW Holdings PLC (formerly Allied Steel and Wire (Holdings) Ltd), since 1986; Swan Hill Group (formerly Higgs and Hill PLC), since 1993 (Director, 1992); *b* 9 Nov. 1933; *s* of William Duncan and Catherine Gray Murray; *m* 1965, Frauke Ulrike Schnuhr (separated); one *d*. *Educ:* Holloway County Grammar Sch.; London Sch. of Economics (BSc(Econ)); Wharton Sch.; Univ. of Pennsylvania (MBA). Mem., Inst. of Chartered Accountants (FCA). Chief Executive, Truman Hanbury Buxton and Co. Ltd, 1967–71; Chief Executive, Watney Mann Ltd, 1971–72; Vice-Chm., Internat. Distillers and Vintners Ltd, 1972; Chm., Lloyds Bowmaker Finance Ltd (formerly Lloyds and Scottish plc), 1976–86; Dir, Lloyds Bank Plc, 1982–87. Chairman: Humberclyde Finance Gp, 1987–89; Household Mortgage Corp., 1986–94; Rubicon Group plc, 1992–95; Alldays plc, 1999–2001; Director: BET plc, 1981–96; Haden plc, 1974–85 (Dep. Chm., 1984–85); City of London Investment Trust (formerly TR City of London Trust PLC), 1977–2000; Associated British Ports PLC, 1986– (Dep. Chm., 1998–); Newspaper Publishing plc, 1986–93; Crown House PLC, 1987; Dewe Rogerson Gp Ltd, 1987–95; Whessoe PLC, 1987–97; Calor Gp, 1990–97. Chm., CBI Companies Cttee, 1980–83; Mem., CBI President's Cttee, 1980–83. Mem., Eur. Adv. Bd, Wharton Sch., 1995–. Freeman, City of London, 1971. *Recreations:* opera, golf. *Address:* Laporte plc, Nations House, 103 Wigmore Street, W1U 1QS. *T:* (020) 7399 2400. *Club:* Brooks's.

DUNCAN, George Alexander; Fellow Emeritus of Trinity College, Dublin, since 1967; *b* 15 May 1902; *s* of Alexander Duncan and Elizabeth Linn; *m* 1932, Eileen Stone, MSc (*d* 1997), *d* of William Henry Stone and Sarah Copeland; one *d*. *Educ:* Ballymena Academy; Campbell Coll., Belfast; Trinity Coll., Dublin; University of North Carolina. BA, LLB 1923, MA 1926; Research Fellow on the Laura Spelman Rockefeller Memorial Foundation, 1924–25; Prof. of Political Economy in the University of Dublin, 1934–67; Registrar of TCD, 1951–52, and Bursar, 1952–57; Pro-Chancellor, Univ. of Dublin, 1965–72. Leverhulme Research Fellow, 1950; Visiting Fellow, Princeton Univ., 1963–64. Mem. of IFS Commissions of Inquiry into Banking, Currency and Credit, 1934–38; Agriculture, 1939; Emigration and Population, 1948. Planning Officer (temp.) in Ministry of Production, London, 1943–45; Economic Adviser to British National Cttee of Internat. Chambers of Commerce, 1941–47. Past Vice-Pres., Royal Dublin Society; Life Mem., Mont Pelerin Soc.; Founder Mem., Edmund Burke Inst., Dublin, 1993. Formerly Member: Irish National Productivity Cttee; Council Irish Management Inst.; Exec. Bd, Dublin Economic Research Inst.; Internat. Inst. of Statistics; Bd of Visitors, Nat. Mus. of Ireland. *Publications:* numerous papers in the economic periodicals. *Recreations:* travel, walking. *Address:* 7 Braemor Park, Churchtown, Dublin 14. *T:* (1) 4922442.

DUNCAN, Dr George Douglas, Regional Medical Officer, East Anglian Regional Health Authority, 1973–85; *s* of late George Forman Duncan and of Mary Duncan (*née* Davidson); *m* 1949, Isobel (*née* Reid); two *s* one *d*. *Educ:* Robert Gordon's Coll., Aberdeen; Aberdeen Univ. MB, ChB 1948; DPH 1952; FFCM 1972; BA (Hons) Open Univ., 1992. Various hosp. appts; Asst MOH Stirlingshire, Divisional MO Grangemouth, 1953–57; Asst Sen. MO, Leeds RHB, 1957–60; Dep. Sen. Admin. MO, Newcastle RHB, 1960–68; Sen. Admin. MO, East Anglian RHB, 1968–73. Member: Nat. Nursing Staff Cttee and Nat. Staff Cttee for Nurses and Midwives, 1970–74; PHLS Bd, 1973–75; Central Cttee for Community Medicine, 1974–81; Chm., English Regl MOs Gp, 1981–83; Vice-Pres., FCM RCP, 1979–83. QHP 1984–87. Hon. Mem., BPA, 1988–96; Hon. Founder Fellow, RCPCH, 1996. Hon. MA Cambridge, 1986. *Address:* 12 Storey's Way, Cambridge CB3 0DT. *T:* (01223) 363427.

DUNCAN, Very Rev. Gregor Duthie, PhD; Dean of the Diocese of Glasgow and Galloway, since 1996; Rector of St Ninian's, Pollokshields, since 1999; *b* 11 Oct. 1950; *s* of Edwin John Duncan and Janet Brown Duncan. *Educ:* Univ. of Glasgow (MA Hons 1972); Clare Coll., Cambridge (PhD 1977); Oriel Coll., Oxford (BA Hons 1983); Ripon Coll., Cuddesdon. Ordained deacon, 1983, priest, 1984; Asst Curate, Oakham with Hambleton and Egleton, and Braunston with Brooke, 1983–86; Chaplain, Edinburgh Theol Coll., 1987–89; Rector of St Columba's, Largs, 1989–99. *Recreations:* collecting gramophone records, cooking. *Address:* St Ninian's Rectory, 32 Glencairn Drive, Pollokshields, Glasgow G41 4PW. *T:* (0141) 423 1247, *Fax:* (0141) 424 3332; *e-mail:* dean@glasgow.anglican.org.

DUNCAN, Jacqueline Ann; FIDDA, FIIDA; Principal of Inchbald Schools of Design and Fine Arts, since 1960; *b* 16 Dec. 1931; *d* of Mrs Donald Whitaker; *m* 1st, 1955, Michael Inchbald, *qv* (marr. diss. 1964); one *s* one *d*; 2nd, 1974, Brig. Peter Trevenen Thwaites (*d* 1991); 3rd, 1994, Col Andrew Tobin Warwick Duncan, LVO, OBE. *Educ:* Convent of the Sacred Heart, Brighton; House of Citizenship, London. FIDDA 1991; FIIDA 1994. Founded: Inchbald Sch. of Design, 1960; Inchbald Sch. of Fine Arts, 1970; Inchbald Sch. of Garden Design, 1972. Member: Monopolies Commn, 1972–75; Whitfield Cttee on Copyright and Design, 1974–76; London Electricity Cons. Council, 1973–76; Westminster City Council (Warwick Ward), 1974–78. Mem., Vis. Cttee, RCA, 1986–90; International Society of Interior Designers: Acting Pres., London Chapter, 1987–90; Chm., 1990–92. Trustee, St Peters' Research Trust, 1987–90. JP South Westminster, 1976–2001. *Publications:* Directory of Interior Designers, 1966; Bedrooms, 1968; Design and Decoration, 1971. *Recreations:* fishing, travel. *Address:* The Manor House, Ayot St Lawrence, Herts AL6 9BP; (office) 32 Eccleston Square, SW1V 1PB.

DUNCAN, Sir James (Blair), Kt 1981; Chairman: Transport Development Group, 1975–92; Boalloy Industries Ltd, since 1992; *b* 24 Aug. 1927; *s* of late John Duncan and Emily MacFarlane Duncan; *m* 1974, Dr Betty Psaltis, San Francisco. *Educ:* Whitehill Sch., Glasgow. Qualified as Scottish Chartered Accountant. Joined Transport Development Group, 1953; Dir, 1960; Chief Exec., 1970–90; retd, 1992. Mem., LTE (part-time), 1979–82. Scottish Council: Mem. 1976–, and Chm. 1982–99, London Exec. Cttee; Vice Pres., 1983–99, Pres., 1999–. Confedn of British Industry: Mem. Council, 1980–82; Mem. 1979–90, and Chm. 1983–88, London Region Roads and Transportation Cttee; Mem., Transport Policy Cttee, 1983–92. London Chamber of Commerce: Mem. Council, 1982–; Mem., Gen. Purposes Cttee, 1983–90; Dep. Chm., 1984–86; Chm., 1986–88; Chm., Commercial Educn Trust, 1992–98. Pres., IRTE, 1984–87. FCIT (Pres., 1980–81; Spurrier Meml Lectr, 1972; Award of Merit, 1973; Herbert Crow Medal, 1978); CIMgt; FRSA 1977. Liveryman, Co. of Carmen, 1983– (Award of Merit, 1992); Freeman, Co. of Watermen & Lightermen of the River Thames, 1982. *Publications:* papers on transport matters. *Recreations:* travel, reading, walking, swimming, theatre, golf. *Address:*

17 Kingston House South, Ennismore Gardens, SW7 1NF. *T:* (020) 7589 3545. *Clubs:* Caledonian, Royal Automobile; Pacific-Union (San Francisco).

DUNCAN, Prof. James Playford, ME Adelaide, DSc Manchester; Professor of Mechanical Engineering, University of British Columbia, 1966–84, now Emeritus; Adjunct Professor, University of Victoria, 1985–87; *b* 10 Nov. 1919; *s* of late Hugh Sinclair Duncan and late Nellie Gladys Duncan; *m* 1942, Jean Marie Booth; three *s* one *d.* *Educ:* Scotch Coll., Adelaide; University of Adelaide, S Australia. Executive Engineer, Richards Industries Ltd, Keswick, S Australia, 1941–46; Senior Physics Master, Scotch Coll., Adelaide, 1946–47; Lecturer in Mechanical Engineering, University of Adelaide, 1948–49, Senior Lecturer, 1950–51 and 1953–54; Turbine Engineer, Metropolitan Vickers Electrical Co., Trafford Park, Manchester, 1952; Turner and Newall Research Fellow, University of Manchester, 1955; Lecturer in Mechanical Engineering, University of Manchester, 1956; Prof. of Mechanical Engineering, University of Sheffield, 1956–66. *Publications:* Sculptured Surfaces in Engineering and Medicine, 1983; Computer Aided Sculpture, 1989. *Recreations:* sailing, flautist. *Address:* 3568 Handley Crescent, Port Coquitlam, BC V3B 2Y5, Canada.

DUNCAN, Ven. John Finch, MBE 1991; Archdeacon of Birmingham, 1985–2001; *b* 9 Sept. 1933; *s* of John and Helen Maud Duncan; *m* 1965, Diana Margaret Dewes; one *s* two *d.* *Educ:* Queen Elizabeth Grammar School, Wakefield; University Coll., Oxford; Cuddesdon Coll. MA (Oxon). Curate, St John, South Bank, Middlesbrough, 1959–61; Novice, Society of St Francis, 1961–62; Curate, St Peter, Birmingham, 1962–65; Chaplain, Univ. of Birmingham, 1965–76; Vicar of All Saints, Kings Heath, Birmingham, 1976–85. Chairman: Copec Housing Trust, 1970–91; Focus Housing Assoc., 1991–96. *Recreations:* golf, theatre, convivial gatherings. *Address:* 66 Glebe Rise, Kings Sutton, Banbury, Oxon OX7 3PH. *Club:* Harborne Golf (Birmingham).

DUNCAN, John Spenser Ritchie, CMG 1967; MBE 1953; HM Diplomatic Service, retired; High Commissioner in the Bahamas, 1978–81; *b* 26 July 1921; *s* of late Rev. J. H. Duncan, DD and H. P. Duncan (*née* Ritchie); *m* 1950, Sheila Conacher, MB, ChB, DObstRCOG; one *d.* *Educ:* George Watson's Boys' Coll.; Glasgow Acad.; Dundee High Sch.; Edinburgh Univ. Entered Sudan Political Service, 1941. Served in HM Forces, 1941–43. Private Sec. to Governor-Gen. of the Sudan, 1954; Dep. Adviser to Governor-Gen. on Constitutional and External Affairs, 1955; appointed to Foreign (subseq. Diplomatic) Service, 1956; seconded to Joint Services Staff Coll., 1957; Political Agent, Doha, 1958; Dep. Dir-Gen., British Information Services, New York, 1959–63; Consul-Gen., Muscat, 1963–65; Head of Personnel Dept, Diplomatic Service, 1966–68; Minister, British High Commn, Canberra, 1969–71; High Comr, Zambia, 1971–74; Ambassador to Morocco, 1975–78. *Publications:* The Sudan: A Record of Achievement, 1952; The Sudan's Path to Independence, 1957. *Address:* 9 Blackford Road, Edinburgh EH9 2DT. *Club:* New (Edinburgh).

DUNCAN, Laura; *see* Duncan, A. L. A.

DUNCAN, Lindsay Vere; actress; *b* 7 Nov. 1950; *m* Hilton McRae, actor; one *s.* Central Sch. of Speech and Drama. *Television:* series: Dead Head, 1985; Traffik, 1989; GBH, 1991; A Year in Provence, 1993; Get Real, 1998; Dirty Tricks, 2000; serials: The Rector's Wife, 1994; Oliver Twist, 1999; Shooting the Past, 1999; Perfect Strangers, 2001; play, These Foolish Things, 1989; *theatre:* Les Liaisons Dangereuses, RSC, 1986 (Olivier Award); Hedda Gabler, Hampstead, 1988; Cat on a Hot Tin Roof, NT, 1988 (Evening Standard Award); A Midsummer Night's Dream, RSC; Berenice, NT, 1990; Three Hotels, Tricycle, Kilburn, 1993; The Cryptogram, Ambassadors, 1994; Ashes to Ashes, Royal Court Upstairs, 1996; The Homecoming, RNT, 1997; Celebration, and The Room, Almeida, 2000; Mouth to Mouth, Royal Court, 2001; Private Lives, Albery, 2001; *films:* Prick Up Your Ears, 1987; Manifesto, 1988; The Reflecting Skin, 1990; City Hall, 1995; A Midsummer Night's Dream, 1996; Mansfield Park, 2000; An Ideal Husband, 2000. *Address:* c/o Ken McReddie, 91 Regent Street, W1R 7TB.

DUNCAN, Peter John; MP (C) Galloway and Upper Nithsdale, since 2001; *b* 10 July 1965; *s* of late Ronald Duncan and Aureen Duncan (*née* Anderson); *m* 1994, Lorna Forbes; one *s* one *d.* *Educ:* Univ. of Birmingham (BCom Hons). Project Manager, Mackays Stores Ltd, 1985–88; Man. Dir, John Duncan & Son, 1988–2000; freelance business consultant, 1998–2000. *Recreations:* Scottish Rugby, English Test and county cricket. *Address:* 2 St Andrew Street, Castle Douglas, Kirkcudbrightshire DG7 1DE. *T:* (01556) 504265.

DUNCAN, Sean Bruce; His Honour Judge Duncan; a Circuit Judge, since 1988; *b* 21 Dec. 1942; *s* of Joseph Alexander Duncan and Patricia Pauline Duncan; *m* 1974, Dr Diana Bowyer Courtney; three *s* one *d.* *Educ:* Shrewsbury Sch.; St Edmund Hall, Oxford (MA). Called to the Bar, Inner Temple, 1966; Northern Circuit (Hon. Sec., Circuit Cttee, 1985–88); a Recorder, 1984–88. Sen. Vice Pres., Council of HM Circuit Judges, 2001 (Hon. Sec., 1996–99). Served with Cheshire Yeomanry (TA), 1963–68 (Lieut). Chairman: Old Swan Boys Club, Liverpool, 1974–79; Liverpool Youth Organisations Cttee, 1977–83; Vice-Chm., Liverpool Council of Voluntary Service, 1982–88. *Recreations:* theatre, sport, music. *Address:* c/o Queen Elizabeth II Law Courts, Derby Square, Liverpool L2 1AX. *Clubs:* Royal Liverpool Golf; Liverpool Ramblers AFC (Pres., 2000–).

DUNCAN, Stanley Frederick St Clare, CMG 1983; HM Diplomatic Service, retired; *b* 13 Nov. 1927; *yr s* of late Stanley Gilbert Scott and Louisa Elizabeth Duncan; *m* 1967, Jennifer Jane Bennett; two *d.* *Educ:* Latymer Upper Sch.; Open Univ. (Dip. European Humanities 1999). FRGS. India Office, 1946; CRO, 1947; Private Sec. to Parly Under-Sec. of State, 1954; Second Sec., Ottawa, 1954–55; Brit. Govt Information Officer, Toronto, 1955–57; Second Sec., Wellington, 1958–60; First Sec., CRO, 1960; seconded to Central African Office, 1962–64; Mem., Brit. Delegn to Victoria Falls Conf. on Dissolution of Fedn of Rhodesia and Nyasaland, 1963; First Sec., Nicosia, 1964–67; FCO, 1967–70; FCO Adviser, Brit. Gp, Inter-Parly Union, 1968–70; Head of Chancery and First Sec., Lisbon, 1970–73; Consul-General and subsequently Chargé d'Affaires in Mozambique, 1973–75; Counsellor (Political), Brasilia, 1976–77; Head of Consular Dept, FCO, 1977–80; Canadian Nat. Defence Coll., 1980–81; Ambassador to Bolivia, 1981–85; High Comr in Malta, 1985–87. Mem., UN Observer Mission to S African elections, 1994. Officer, Military Order of Christ (Portugal), 1973. *Address:* Tucksmead, Longworth, Oxon OX13 5ET.

DUNCAN-JONES, Prof. Katherine Dorothea, FRSL; Fellow, and Tutor in English Literature, Somerville College, Oxford, since 1966; Professor of English Literature, University of Oxford, since 1998; *b* 13 May 1941; *d* of late Prof. Austin Ernest Duncan-Jones and Elsie Elizabeth Duncan-Jones (*née* Phare); *m* 1971, Andrew N. Wilson, *qv* (marr. diss. 1990); two *d.* *Educ:* King Edward VI High Sch. for Girls, Birmingham; St Hilda's Coll., Oxford (BLitt, MA). Mary Ewart Res. Fellow, Somerville Coll., Oxford, 1963–65; Fellow, New Hall, Cambridge, 1965–66. Hon. Res. Fellow, UCL, 2000–. FRSL 1992; FEA 2000. Ben Jonson Discoveries Prize, 1996. *Publications:* (ed jtly) Miscellaneous Prose of Sir Philip Sidney, 1977; (ed) Sir Philip Sidney, 1989; Sir Philip Sidney: courtier poet (biog.), 1991; (ed) Shakespeare's Sonnets, 1997; Ungentle Shakespeare (biog.), 2001; contrib. numerous articles in Rev. of English Studies, TLS, and other jls. *Recreations:* swimming, theatre-going. *Address:* Somerville College, Oxford OX2 6HD. *T:* (01865) 270600.

See also R. P. Duncan-Jones, Viscount Runciman of Doxford.

DUNCAN-JONES, Richard Phare, PhD; FBA 1992; Fellow, Gonville and Caius College, Cambridge, since 1963; *b* 14 Sept. 1937; *s* of Austin Ernest Duncan-Jones and Elsie Elizabeth Duncan-Jones; *m* 1986, Julia Elizabeth Poole. *Educ:* King Edward's Sch., Birmingham; King's Coll., Cambridge (MA, PhD). Gonville and Caius College, Cambridge: W. M. Tapp Res. Fellow, 1963–67; Domestic Bursar, 1967–84; Official Fellow, 1967–; College Lectr and Dir of Studies in Classics, 1984–. Mem., Inst. for Advanced Study, Princeton, 1971–72. *Publications:* The Economy of the Roman Empire, 1974, 2nd edn 1982; Structure and Scale in the Roman Economy, 1990; Money and Government in the Roman Empire, 1994; articles in learned jls. *Recreations:* wine tasting, walking, continental cinema. *Address:* Caius College, Cambridge CB2 1TA. *T:* (01223) 332394.

See also K. D. Duncan-Jones.

DUNCAN SMITH, Rt Hon. (George) Iain; PC 2001; MP (C) Chingford and Woodford Green, since 1997 (Chingford, 1992–97); Leader of the Conservative Party, and Leader of the Opposition, since 2001; *b* 9 April 1954; *s* of late Group Captain W. G. G. Duncan Smith, DSO (Bar), DFC (2 Bars) and of Pamela Mary Duncan Smith (*née* Summers); *m* 1982, Elizabeth Wynne (*née* Fremantle); two *s* two *d.* *Educ:* HMS Conway (Cadet School); Univ. di Perugia; RMA Sandhurst; Dunchurch Coll. of Management. Scots Guards, 1975–81; ADC to Gen. Sir John Acland, 1979–81; GEC, 1981–88; Dir, Bellwinch (Property), 1988; Dir, Jane's Inf. Group, 1989–92. Vice-Chm., Fulham Cons. Assoc., 1991; contested (C) Bradford West, 1987. Opposition front bench spokesman on social security, 1997–99, on defence, 1999–2001. Member, Select Committee: on Health, 1994–95; on Nolan, 1995; on Standards and Privileges, 1996–97. Sec., Cons. Backbench Cttee on Foreign and Commonwealth Affairs, 1992–97; Vice Chm., Cons. European Affairs Cttee, 1996–97. Trustee: Lygon Alms-house, 1985–91; Whitefield Develt Trust. Freeman, City of London. *Publications:* various pamphlets on social security, European and defence issues; occasional journalism. *Recreations:* family, painting, fishing, cricket, tennis, shooting, opera, reading. *Address:* House of Commons, SW1A 0AA. *T:* (020) 7219 2664 and 3000.

DUNCANNON, Viscount; Myles Fitzhugh Longfield Ponsonby; *b* 16 Feb. 1941; *e s* and *heir* of Earl of Bessborough, *qv*; *m* 1972, Alison, *d* of William Storey, OBE; two *s* one *d.* *Heir:* *s* Hon. Frederick Arthur William Ponsonby, *b* 9 Aug. 1974. *Address:* Broadreed, Stansted Park, Rowlands Castle, Hants PO9 6DZ.

DUNCOMBE, family name of **Baron Feversham.**

DUNCOMBE, Sir Philip (Digby) Pauncefort-, 4th Bt *cr* 1859; DL; one of HM Body Guard, Honourable Corps of Gentlemen-at-Arms, since 1979 (Harbinger, 1993–97); *b* 18 May 1927; *o s* of Sir Everard Pauncefort-Duncombe, 3rd Bt, DSO, and Evelyn Elvira (*d* 1986), *d* of Frederick Anthony Denny; *S* father, 1971; *m* 1951, Rachel Moyra, *d* of Major H. G. Aylmer; one *s* two *d.* *Educ:* Stowe. 2nd Lieut, Grenadier Guards, 1946; served in Palestine, 1947–48; Malaya, 1948–49; Cyprus, 1957–59; Hon. Major, retired 1960, Regular Army Reserve. County Comdt, Buckinghamshire Army Cadet Force, 1967–70. DL Bucks 1971, High Sheriff, 1987–88. CStJ 1992. *Heir:* *s* David Philip Henry Pauncefort-Duncombe [*b* 21 May 1956; *m* 1987, Sarah, *d* of late Reginald Battrum and of Mrs Reginald Battrum; one *s* one *d*]. *Address:* Church Close, Church Lane, Great Brickhill, Bucks MK17 9AE. *T:* (01525) 261205. *Club:* Cavalry and Guards.

DUNCOMBE, Roy, VRD 1957; Chairman, Nationwide Building Society, 1989–91; *b* 7 June 1925; *s* of Joseph William Duncombe and Gladys May Duncombe (*née* Reece); *m* 1946, Joan Thornley Pickering; one *s* two *d.* *Educ:* Hinckley Grammar School. RNR, 1943–68 (Lt-Comdr (A); Pilot, Fleet Air Arm). Financial Dir, Ferry Pickering Gp, 1965–87; Chm., Anglia Building Soc., 1985–87; following merger with Nationwide Bldg Soc., Vice Chm., Nationwide Anglia Bldg Soc., 1987–89; name changed to Nationwide Bldg Soc., 1989. *Recreations:* walking, swimming, photography, ornithology. *Address:* Westways, Market Bosworth, Nuneaton, Warwickshire CV13 0LQ. *T:* (01455) 291728; 3 The Old Grammar School, Chipping Campden, Glos GL55 6HB. *T:* (01386) 841455. *Club:* Naval and Military.

DUNCUMB, Dr Peter, FRS 1977; Director, Research Centre in Super-conductivity, Cambridge University, 1988–89; *b* 26 Jan. 1931; *s* of late William Duncumb and of Hilda Grace (*née* Coleman); *m* 1955, Anne Leslie Taylor; two *s* one *d.* *Educ:* Oundle Sch.; Clare Coll., Cambridge (BA 1953, MA 1956, PhD 1957). Commnd GD Br., RAF, qualif. Pilot, 1949–50; No 22RFS Cambridge, RAFVR, 1950–54; DSIR Res. Fellow, Cambridge Univ., 1957–59; Tube Investments, subseq. TI Group, Research Laboratories: Res. Scientist and Gp Leader, 1959–67, Head, Physics Dept, 1967–72; Asst Dir, 1972–79; Dir and Gen. Manager, 1979–87. Hon. Prof., Warwick Univ., 1990–2000. Hon. Member: Microbeam Analysis Soc. of America, 1973; European Microbeam Analysis Soc., 1997. C. V. Boys Prize, Inst. of Physics, 1966; Henry Clifton Sorby Award, Internat. Metallographic Soc., 1996. *Publications:* numerous on electron microscopy and analysis in various jls. *Recreations:* photography, orienteering, family genealogy. *Address:* 5A Woollards Lane, Great Shelford, Cambridge CB2 5LZ. *T:* (01223) 843064.

DUNDAS, family name of **Viscount Melville,** and of **Marquess of Zetland.**

DUNDAS, James Frederick Trevor; Chief Executive, MEPC plc, since 1999; *b* 4 Nov. 1950; *s* of Sir Hugh Dundas, CBE, DSO, DFC, and of Hon. Lady Dundas; *m* 1979, Jennifer Daukes; one *s* two *d.* *Educ:* Eton; New Coll., Oxford (BA Hons Jurisp.). Called to the Bar, Inner Temple, 1972; Morgan Grenfell & Co. Ltd, 1972–91: Dir, 1981–91; Head, Corporate and Internat. Banking, 1987–91; Mem., Mgt Cttee, Morgan Grenfell Gp plc, 1989–91; Finance Director: Hong Kong Airport Authy, 1992–96; MEPC plc, 1997–99. Non-exec. Dir, J. Sainsbury plc, 2000–. Non-exec. Dir, Macmillan Cancer Relief, 1996– (Chm., 2001–). *Address:* c/o MEPC plc, Nations House, 103 Wigmore Street, W1H 9AB. *Club:* White's.

DUNDEE, 12th Earl of, *cr* 1660 (Scotland); **Alexander Henry Scrymgeour;** Viscount Dudhope and Lord Scrymgeour, 1641 (Scotland); Lord Inverkeithing, 1660 (Scotland); Lord Glassary (UK), 1954; Hereditary Royal Standard-Bearer for Scotland; *b* 5 June 1949; *s* of 11th Earl of Dundee, PC, and of Patricia Katherine, *d* of late Col Lord Herbert Montagu Douglas Scott; *S* father, 1983; *m* 1979, Siobhan Mary, *d* of David Llewellyn, Gt Somerford, Wilts; one *s* three *d.* *Educ:* Eton; St Andrews Univ. Contested (C) Hamilton, by-election May 1978. A Lord in Waiting (Govt Whip), 1986–89; elected Mem., H of L, 1999. *Heir:* *s* Lord Scrymgeour, *qv*. *Address:* Farm Office, Birkhill, Cupar, Fife KY15 4QP. *Clubs:* White's; New (Edinburgh).

DUNDONALD, 15th Earl of, *cr* 1669; **Iain Alexander Douglas Blair Cochrane;** Lord Cochrane of Dundonald, 1647; Lord Cochrane of Paisley and Ochiltree, 1669; Chairman, Duneth Securities and associated companies, since 1986; *b* 17 Feb. 1961; *s* of 14th Earl of Dundonald and Aphra Farquhar (*d* 1972), *d* of late Comdr George Fetherstonhaugh; *S* father, 1986; *m* 1987, Beatrice, *d* of Adolphus Russo; two *s* one *d*. *Educ:* Wellington College; RAC Cirencester. DipREM. Dir, Anglo Pacific Gp, 1995–98. Mem. Council, PITCOM, 1994–99. Hon. Consul in Scotland for Chile, 1993–. *Recreations:* shooting, fishing, skiing, sailing. *Heir: s* Lord Cochrane, *qv*. *Address:* Lochnell Castle, Ledaig, Argyll PA37 1QT.

DUNEDIN, Bishop of, since 1990; **Rt Rev. Penelope Ann Bansall Jamieson,** PhD; *b* Chalfont St Peter, Bucks, 21 June 1942; *m* 1964, Ian William Andrew Jamieson; three *d*. *Educ:* St Mary's Sch., Gerrards Cross; High Sch., High Wycombe; Edinburgh Univ. (MA 1964); Victoria Univ., Wellington (PhD 1977); Otago Univ. (BD 1983). Deacon 1982; priest 1983; Asst Curate, St James', Lower Hutt, 1982–85; Vicar, Karori West with Makara, dio. Wellington, 1985–90. *Publication:* Living at the Edge, 1997. *Address:* c/o Diocesan Office, PO Box 5445, Dunedin, New Zealand.

DUNGARVAN, Viscount; John Richard Boyle, (Jonathan); Director, E. D. & F. Man Sugar Ltd, London; *b* 3 Nov. 1945; *e s* and *heir* of Earl of Cork and Orrery, *qv*; *m* 1973, Hon. Rebecca Juliet Noble, *y d* of Baron Glenkinglas (Life Peer), PC; one *s* two *d* (of whom one *s* one *d* are twins). *Educ:* Harrow; RNC Dartmouth. Lt-Comdr RN, retd. *Recreations:* country pursuits, sailing, ski-ing, classic cars. *Address:* Lickfold House, Petworth, West Sussex GU28 9EY. *Clubs:* Boodle's; Castaways.

DUNGEY, Prof. James Wynne, PhD; Professor of Physics, Imperial College, University of London, 1965–84; *b* 30 Jan. 1923; *s* of Ernest Dungey and Alice Dungey; *m* 1950, Christine Scotland (*née* Brown); one *s* one *d*. *Educ:* Bradfield; Magdalene Coll., Cambridge (MA, PhD). Res. Fellow, Univ. of Sydney, 1950–53; Vis. Asst Prof., Penn State Coll., 1953–54; ICI Fellow, Cambridge, 1954–57; Lectr, King's Coll., Newcastle upon Tyne, 1957–59; Sen. Principal Scientific Officer, AWRE, Aldermaston, 1959–63; Res. Fellow, Imperial Coll., London, 1963–65. Fellow, Amer. Geophysical Union, 1973. Hon. Mem., European Geophysical Soc., 1994. Chapman Medal, RAS, 1982; Gold Medal for Geophysics, RAS, 1990; Fleming Medal, Amer. Geophysical Union, 1991. *Publications:* Cosmic Electrodynamics, 1958; papers on related topics. *Address:* 41 Moreton End Lane, Harpenden, Herts AL5 2HA.

DUNGLASS, Lord; Michael David Alexander Douglas-Home; *b* 30 Nov. 1987; *s* and *heir* of Earl of Home, *qv*. A Page of Honour to the Queen, 1998–2000.

DUNION, Kevin Harry, OBE 1999; Director, Friends of the Earth Scotland, since 1991; Chairman, Friends of the Earth International, 1996–99; *b* 20 Dec. 1955; *s* of Harry Dunion and Mary Leckie Bertolini; *m* 1st, 1978, Christine Elizabeth Hannam (marr. diss. 1997); two *s*; 2nd, 1997, Linda Gray. *Educ:* St Andrews High Sch., Kirkcaldy; St Andrews Univ. (MA Hons); Edinburgh Univ. (MSc Dist.). HM Inspector of Taxes, 1978–80; Administrator, Edinburgh Univ. Students' Assoc., 1980–84; Scottish Campaign Manager, OXFAM, 1984–91. Mem., Ministerial Gp for a Sustainable Scotland, Scottish Exec., 2000–; Mem. Bd, Scottish Natural Heritage, 2000–. Editor, Radical Scotland mag., 1981–85. FRSA 1997. *Publication:* Living in the Real World: the international role for Scotland's Parliament, 1995. *Recreation:* fighting lost causes. *Address:* Craignoon, 39B John Street, Cellardyke, Anstruther, Fife KY10 3BA. *T:* (01333) 312818.

DUNITZ, Prof. Jack David, FRS 1974; Professor of Chemical Crystallography at the Swiss Federal Institute of Technology (ETH), Zürich, 1957–90; *b* 29 March 1923; *s* of William Dunitz and Mildred (*née* Gossman); *m* 1953, Barbara Steuer; two *d*. *Educ:* Hillhead High Sch., Glasgow; Hutchesons' Grammar Sch., Glasgow; Glasgow Univ. (BSc, PhD). Post-doctoral Fellow, Oxford Univ., 1946–48, 1951–53; California Inst. of Technology, 1948–51, 1953–54; Vis. Scientist, US Nat. Insts of Health, 1954–55; Sen. Res. Fellow, Davy Faraday Res. Lab., Royal Instn, London, 1956–57. Overseas Fellow, Churchill Coll., Cambridge, 1968; Vis. Professor: Iowa State Univ., 1965; Tokyo Univ., 1967; Technion, Haifa, 1970; Hill Vis. Prof., Univ. of Minnesota, 1983; Fairchild Distinguished Scholar, CIT, 1985; Hooker Distinguished Vis. Prof., McMaster Univ., 1987; Alexander Todd Vis. Prof., Cambridge Univ., 1990; Oscar K. Rice Vis. Prof., Univ. of N Carolina, Chapel Hill, 1991; Robert B. Woodward Vis. Prof., Harvard Univ., 1992. Lectures: British Council, 1965; Treat B. Johnson Meml, Yale Univ., 1965; 3M Univ. of Minnesota, 1966; Reilly, Univ. Notre Dame, US, 1971; Kelly, Purdue Univ., 1971; Gerhard Schmidt Meml, Weizmann Inst. of Sci., 1973; George Fisher Baker, Cornell Univ., 1976; Centenary, Chem. Soc., 1977; Appleton, Brown Univ., 1979; H. J. Backer, Gröningen Univ., 1980; Havinga, Leiden Univ., 1980; Karl Folkers, Wisconsin Univ., 1981; A. L. Patterson Meml, Inst. for Cancer Res., Philadelphia, 1983; C. S. Marvel, Illinois Univ., 1987; Birch, Canberra, 1989; Dwyer, Sydney, 1989; Bijvoet, Utrecht Univ., 1989; Bragg, British Crystallographic Assoc., 1999. Foreign Member: Royal Netherlands Acad. of Arts and Sciences, 1979; Amer. Phil Soc., 1997; Member: Leopoldina Acad., 1979; European Acad. of Scis and Arts, 1991; Foreign Associate, US Nat. Acad. of Scis, 1988; Mem., Academia Europaea, 1989; Hon. Mem., Swiss Soc. of Crystallography, 1990; For. Hon. Mem., Amer. Acad. of Arts and Scis, 1997; Fellow AAAS, 1981. Hon. FRSC 2000. Hon. DSc: Technion, Haifa, 1990; Weizmann Inst. of Sci., 1992; Glasgow Univ., 1999. Tishler Award, Harvard Univ., 1985; Paracelsus Prize, Swiss Chem. Soc., 1986; Gregori Aminoff Prize, Swedish Royal Acad., 1990; Martin Buerger Award, Amer. Crystallographic Assoc., 1991; Arthur C. Cope Scholar Award, ACS, 1997. Jt Editor, Perspectives in Structural Chemistry, 1967–71; Mem. Editorial Bd: Helvetica Chimica Acta, 1971–85; Structure and Bonding, 1971–81. *Publications:* X-ray Analysis and the Structure of Organic Molecules, 1979; (with E. Heilbronner) Reflections on Symmetry in Chemistry . . . . and Elsewhere, 1993; papers on various aspects of crystal and molecular structure in Acta Crystallographica, Helvetica Chimica Acta, Jl Chem. Soc., Jl Amer. Chem. Soc., etc. *Recreation:* walking. *Address:* Obere Heslibachstrasse 77, 8700 Küsnacht, Switzerland. *T:* (1) 9101723; (office) Chemistry Department, ETH-Hönggerberg, 8093 Zürich, Switzerland. *T:* (1) 6322892.

DUNKEL, Arthur; Chairman, Arthur Dunkel consultancy, Geneva, since 1993; *b* 28 Aug. 1932; *s* of Walter Dunkel and Berthe Lerch; *m* 1957, Christine Müller-Cerda; one *s* one *d*. *Educ:* Univ. of Lausanne (LèsSc écon. et comm.). Federal Office for external economic affairs, 1956: successively Head of sections for OECD matters, 1960; for cooperation with developing countries, 1964; for world trade policy, 1971; Permanent Representative of Switzerland to GATT, 1973; Delegate of Federal Council for Trade Agreements, rank of Ambassador, 1976; in this capacity, head of Swiss delegations to multilateral (GATT, UNCTAD, UNIDO, etc) and bilateral negotiations in the fields of trade, development, commodities, transfer of technology, industrialisation, agriculture, etc.; Dir Gen., GATT, 1980–93. Prof. at Univs of Geneva, 1983, 1997, and Fribourg, 1987. Dr *hc* rer. pol.: Fribourg, 1980; Basle, 1992. Freedom Prize, Max Schmidheiny Foundn, 1989; Consumers Prize for World Trade, USA, 1990; Assoc. of Swiss Holding Cos Prize, 1993; Prize, Max Petitpierre Foundn, 1993. *Publications:* various articles and studies in economic, commercial, agricl and development fields. *Address:* 56 rue du Stand, 1204 Geneva, Switzerland.

DUNKELD, Bishop of, (RC), since 1981; **Rt Rev. Vincent Logan;** *b* 30 June 1941; *s* of Joseph Logan and Elizabeth Flannigan. *Educ:* Blairs College, Aberdeen; St Andrew's Coll., Drygrange, Melrose. Ordained priest, Edinburgh, 1964; Asst Priest, St Margaret's, Davidson's Mains, Edinburgh, 1964–66; Corpus Christi Coll., London, 1966–67 (DipRE); Chaplain, St Joseph's Hospital, Rosewell, Midlothian, 1967–77; Adviser in Religious Education, Archdiocese of St Andrews and Edinburgh, 1967; Parish Priest, St Mary's, Ratho, 1977–81; Episcopal Vicar for Education, Archdiocese of St Andrews and Edinburgh, 1978. *Address:* Bishop's House, 29 Roseangle, Dundee DD1 4LS. *T:* (01382) 224327.

DUNKLEY, Christopher; journalist and broadcaster; Television Critic, Financial Times, since 1973; *b* 22 Jan. 1944; 2nd *s* of late Robert Dunkley and Joyce Mary Dunkley (*née* Turner); *m* 1967, Carolyn Elizabeth, *e d* of Col A. P. C. Lyons; one *s* one *d*. *Educ:* Haberdashers' Aske's (expelled). Various jobs, incl. theatre flyman, cook, hospital porter, 1961–63; general reporter, then cinema and theatre critic, Slough Observer, 1963–65; feature writer and news editor, UK Press Gazette, 1965–68; night news reporter, then mass media correspondent and TV critic, The Times, 1968–73; Presenter, Feedback, Radio 4, 1986–98. Frequent radio broadcaster, 1963–, esp. on Kaleidoscope, Critics' Forum, Meridian, LBC. Occasional television presenter/script writer/chairman; series incl. Edition, Real Time, In Vision (all BBC2), Whistle Blowers (BBC1), This Week, Viewpoint (ITV). Critic of the Year, British Press Awards, 1976, 1986; Broadcast Journalist of the Year, 1989, Judges' Award, 1990, TV-am Awards; Best Individual Contrib. to Radio, Voice of the Listener and Viewer Awards, 1998. *Publications:* Television Today and Tomorrow: Wall to Wall Dallas?, 1985; many articles in The Listener, Television World, Stills, Electronic Media, Telegraph Magazine, etc. *Recreations:* motorcycling, extending the bookshelves in an Umbrian farmhouse, collecting almost everything, especially dictionaries, tin toys, Victorian boys' books. *Address:* 38 Leverton Street, NW5 2PG. *T:* (020) 7485 7101.

DUNLAP, Air Marshal Clarence Rupert, CBE 1944; CD; RCAF retired; *b* 1 Jan. 1908; *s* of late Frank Burns Dunlap, Truro, Nova Scotia; *m* 1935, Hester, *d* of late Dr E. A. Cleveland, Vancouver, BC; one *s*. *Educ:* Acadia Univ.; Nova Scotia Technical Coll. Joined RCAF 1928 as Pilot Officer; trained as pilot and specialised in aerial survey; later specialised in armament; Dir of Armament, RCAF HQ Ottawa on outbreak of War; commanded: RCAF Station, Mountain View, Ont., Jan.-Oct. 1942; RCAF Station, Leeming, Yorks, Dec. 1942–May 1943; 331 Wing NASAF, Tunisia, May-Nov. 1943; 139 Wing TAF, Nov. 1943–Feb. 1945; 64 Base, Middleton St George, Feb.-May 1945; Dep., AMAS, AFHQ, Ottawa, 1945–48; Air Mem. for Air Plans, AFHQ, Ottawa, 1948–49; AOC North-West Air Command, Edmonton, Alberta, 1949–51; Commandant of National Defence Coll., Kingston, Ont., 1951–54; Vice Chief of the Air Staff, AFHQ, Ottawa, 1954–58; Dep. Chief of Staff, Operations, SHAPE, Paris, 1958–62; Chief of Air Staff, AFHQ, Ottawa, 1962–64; Dep. C-in-C, N Amer. Air Def. Comd, 1964–67. Hon. DCL Acadia Univ., 1955; Hon. DEng Nova Scotia Technical Coll., 1967. *Address:* 203–1375 Newport Avenue, Victoria, BC V8S 5E8, Canada. *Clubs:* Union (Victoria); Victoria Golf.

DUNLEATH, 6th Baron *cr* 1892, of Ballywalter, co. Down; **Brian Henry Mulholland;** Bt 1945; *b* 25 Sept. 1950; *o s* of 5th Baron Dunleath and Elizabeth (*d* 1989), twin *d* of Laurence B. Hyde; *S* father, 1997; *m* 1976, Mary Joan, *y d* of Major R. J. F. Whistler; two *s* one *d*. *Educ:* Eton. Director: Dunleath Estates Ltd, 1994– (Chm., 1998–); Downpatrick Race Club Ltd, 1999–. *Recreations:* shooting, fishing, gardening. *Heir: s* Hon. Andrew Henry Mulholland, *b* 15 Dec. 1981. *Address:* (office) The Estate Office, Ballywalter Park, Newtownards, Northern Ireland BT22 2PA. *T:* (028) 4275 8264, *Fax:* (028) 4275 8818; (home) Ballywalter Park, Newtownards, Northern Ireland BT22 2PP; *e-mail:* bd@dunleath-estates.co.uk. *Clubs:* MCC; Kildare Street (Dublin).

DUNLEAVY, Prof. Patrick John, DPhil; Professor of Government, London School of Economics and Political Science, since 1989; *b* 21 June 1952; *s* of Vincent Dunleavy and Kathleen Mary Dunleavy; *m* 1974, Sheila Dorothea Squire; two *s* one *d*. *Educ:* St Mary's Grammar Sch., Sidcup; Corpus Christi Coll., Oxford (MA 1973); Nuffield Coll., Oxford (DPhil 1978). Research Fellow, Nuffield Coll., Oxford, 1976–78; Lectr in Urban Studies, Open Univ., 1978–79; London School of Economics and Political Science: Lectr in Govt, 1979–86; Reader, 1986–89. Mem. Exec., UK Political Studies Assoc., 1980–83, 1993–94 and 1999–; Academic Convenor, PSA Conf., 1994. Councillor, Bucks CC, 1981–85. Mem., Milton Keynes CHC, 1982–90. AcSS 1999. Founding Ed., Politics, 1980–82; mem. editl bd, various jls. *Publications:* Urban Political Analysis, 1980; The Politics of Mass Housing in Britain, 1981; (ed jtly) Developments in British Politics, vol. 1, 1983, vol. 2, 1986, vol. 3, 1990, vol. 4, 1993, vol. 5, 1997, vol 6, 2000; (with C. T. Husbands) British Democracy at the Crossroads, 1985; Studying for a Degree, 1987; (with B. O'Leary) Theories of the State, 1987; Democracy, Bureaucracy and Public Choice, 1991; (ed with R. A. W. Rhodes) Prime Minister, Cabinet and Core Executive, 1995; (jtly) Making Votes Count, 1997; (with M. Margetts) Government on the Web, 1999; (ed jtly) British Political Science, 2000; articles in learned jls. *Recreations:* family, gym, undermining the (old) constitution. *Address:* Department of Government, London School of Economics, Houghton Street, WC2A 2AE. *T:* (020) 7955 7178; *e-mail:* p.dunleavy@lse.ac.uk.

DUNLOP; *see* Buchanan-Dunlop.

DUNLOP, Rear-Adm. Colin Charles Harrison, CB 1972; CBE 1963; DL; *b* 4 March 1918; *s* of late Engr Rear-Adm. S. H. Dunlop, CB; *m* 1st, 1941, Moyra Patricia O'Brien Gorges (*d* 1991); two *s* (and one *s* decd); 2nd, 1995, Comdt Elizabeth Craig-McFeely, *qv*. *Educ:* Marlborough Coll. Joined RN, 1935; served War of 1939–45 at sea in HM Ships Kent, Valiant, Diadem and Orion; subseq. HMS Sheffield, 1957–59; Sec. to 1st Sea Lord, 1960–63; comd HMS Pembroke, 1964–66; Programme Evaluation Gp, MoD, 1966–68; Director, Defence Policy (A), MoD, 1968–69; Comdr, British Navy Staff, Washington, 1969–71; Chief Naval Supply and Secretariat Officer, 1970–74; Flag Officer, Medway, and Port Adm., Chatham, 1971–74, retd 1974. Director General: Cable TV Assoc., 1974–83; Nat. TV Rental Assoc., 1974–83. DL Kent 1976. *Recreations:* cricket, country pursuits. *Address:* Moonrakers, Mockbeggar Lane, Biddenden, near Ashford, Kent TN27 8ES. *T:* (01580) 291325. *Clubs:* Army and Navy; MCC, I Zingari, Free Foresters, Incogniti, RN Cricket, Band of Brothers.

DUNLOP, Elizabeth Sarah Ann, (Mrs C. C. H. Dunlop); *see* Craig-McFeely, E. S. A.

DUNLOP, Frank, CBE 1977; theatre director; Director, Edinburgh International Festival, 1983–91; *b* 15 Feb. 1927; *s* of Charles Norman Dunlop and Mary Aarons. *Educ:* Kibworth Beauchamp Grammar Sch.; University Coll., London (Fellow, 1979). BA Hons, English. Postgrad. Sch. in Shakespeare, at Shakespeare Inst., Stratford-upon-Avon; Old Vic Sch., London. Served with RAF before going to University. Director: (own young theatre co.) Piccolo Theatre, Manchester, 1954; Arts Council Midland Theatre Co., 1955; Associate

Dir, Bristol Old Vic, 1956; Dir, Théâtre de Poche, Brussels, 1959–60; Founder and Dir, Pop Theatre, 1960; Dir, Nottingham Playhouse, 1961–63; New Nottingham Playhouse, 1963–64; (dir.) The Enchanted, Bristol Old Vic Co., 1955; (wrote and dir.) Les Frères Jaques', Adelphi, 1960; Director: London Première, The Bishop's Bonfire, Mermaid, 1960; Schweyk, Mermaid, 1963; The Taming of the Shrew, Univ. Arts Centre, Oklahoma, 1965; Any Wednesday, Apollo, 1965; Too True to be Good, Edinburgh Fest., also Strand and Garrick, 1965; Saturday Night and Sunday Morning, Prince of Wales, 1966; The Winter's Tale and The Trojan Women, Edin. and Venice Festivals, also Cambridge Theatre, London, 1966; The Burglar, Vaudeville, 1967; Getting Married, Strand, 1967; A Midsummer Night's Dream and The Tricks of Scapin, Edin. Fest. and Saville Theatre, London, 1967; A Sense of Detachment, Royal Court, 1972; Sherlock Holmes, Aldwych, 1974, NY 1974; Habeas Corpus, NY 1975; The New York Idea, The Three Sisters, NY 1977; The Devil's Disciple, LA and NY, 1978; The Play's the Thing, Julius Caesar, NY, 1978; The Last of Mrs Cheyney, USA, 1978; Rookery Nook, Birmingham and Her Majesty's, 1979; Camelot, USA, 1980, London, 1996; Sherlock Holmes, Norwegian Nat. Th., Oslo, 1980; Lolita, NY, 1981; L'Elisir d'Amore, Opéra de Lyon, 1992 (filmed 1996); My Fair Lady, European tour, 1994; Carmen, Royal Albert Hall, 1997; Ecole des Femmes, Belgium, 1998; The Invisible Man, USA, 1998–99; Scapino, Tel Aviv, 1999; Napoleon at St Helena, Waterloo, 2000; Turn of the Screw, Belgium, 2001; *National Theatre:* Assoc. Dir, 1967–71 and Admin. Dir, 1968–71; productions: *Nat. Theatre:* Edward II (Brecht and Marlowe); Home and Beauty; Macrune's Guevara; The White Devil; Captain of Kopenick; *Young Vic:* Founder, 1969; Mem. Bd, 1969–; Dir, 1969–78 and 1980–83; Consultant, 1978–80; productions: (author and Dir) Scapino 1970, 1977, NY 1974, LA 1975, Australia 1975, Oslo 1975; The Taming of the Shrew, 1970, 1977; The Comedy of Errors, 1971; The Maids, Deathwatch, 1972; The Alchemist, 1972; Bible One, 1972; French Without Tears, 1973; Joseph and the Amazing Technicolor Dreamcoat (Roundhouse and Albery Theatre), 1973, NY 1976; Much Ado About Nothing, 1973; Macbeth, 1975; Antony and Cleopatra, 1976; King Lear, 1980; Childe Byron, 1981; Masquerade, 1982; *for Théâtre National de Belgique:* Pantagleise, 1970; Antony and Cleopatra, 1971; Pericles, 1972. Mem., Arts Council Young People's Panel, 1968. Governor, Central School of Arts and Crafts, 1970. Hon. Fellow of Shakespeare Inst. Hon. Dr of Theatre, Philadelphia Coll. of Performing Arts, 1978; DUniv Heriot-Watt, 1989; Dr *hc* Edinburgh, 1990. Chevalier, Order of Arts and Literature (France), 1987. *Recreations:* reading and looking. *Address:* c/o Piccolo Theatre Co., 13 Choumert Square, SE15 4RE; c/o E. Nives, Suite 1400, 157 West 57th Street, New York, NY 10019, USA. *T:* (212) 2658787.

DUNLOP, Rev. Canon Ian Geoffrey David, FSA; Canon and Chancellor of Salisbury Cathedral, 1972–92, Canon Emeritus, since 1992; *b* 19 Aug. 1925; *s* of late Walter N. U. Dunlop and Marguerite Irene (*née* Shakerley); *m* 1957, Deirdre Marcia, *d* of late Dr Marcus Jamieson; one *s* one *d*. *Educ:* Winchester Coll.; New Coll., Oxford (MA); Strasbourg Univ. (Diploma); Lincoln Theol Coll. FSA 1965. Served Irish Guards, 1944–46 (Lieut). Curate, Hatfield, 1956–60; Chaplain, Westminster Sch., 1960–62; Vicar of Bures, Suffolk, 1962–72. Member: Gen. Synod, 1975–85; Cathedrals' Adv. Commn, 1981–86. Trustee, Historic Churches Preservation Trust, 1969–. *Publications:* Versailles, 1956, 2nd edn 1970; Palaces and Progresses of Elizabeth I, 1962; Châteaux of the Loire, 1969; Companion Guide to the Ile de France, 1979, 2nd edn 1985; Cathedrals Crusade, 1981; Royal Palaces of France, 1985; Thinking It Out, 1986; (contrib.) Oxford Companion to Gardens, 1986; Burgundy, 1990; Marie-Antoinette: a portrait, 1993; Louis XIV, 1999 (Enid McLeod Prize, Franco-British Soc., 2000); weekly column in Church Times, 1970–90. *Recreations:* painting, bird watching. *Address:* Gowanbrae, The Glebe, Selkirk TD7 5AB. *T:* (01750) 20706; Hill Cottages, Marsh Lane, Felixstowe, Suffolk IP11 9RP. *T:* (01394) 286118. *Club:* Army and Navy.

DUNLOP, John Leeper, OBE 1996; racehorse trainer, since 1965; *b* 10 July 1939; *s* of Dr John Leeper Dunlop and Margaret Frances Mary Dunlop; *m* 1965, Susan Jennifer Page; two *s* (and one *s* decd). *Educ:* Marlborough Coll. Royal Ulster Rifles, 1959–61. Leading trainer, 1984; champion trainer, 1995; wins include: Shirley Heights, Derby, 1978; Circus Plume, Oaks, 1984; Salsabil, Oaks, 1990; Erhaab, Derby, 1994; One Thousand Guineas: Quick as Lightning, 1980; Salsabil, 1990; Shadayid, 1991; St Leger: Moon Madness, 1986; Silver Patriarch, 1997; Millenary, 2000. Flat Trainer of the Year, Derby Awards, 1995. *Recreations:* breeding race horses and show horses. *Address:* House on the Hill, Arundel, West Sussex BN18 9LJ. *T:* (01903) 882106. *Club:* Turf.

DUNLOP, Sir Thomas, 4th Bt *cr* 1916, of Woodbourne, co. Renfrew; *b* 22 April 1951; *o s* of Sir Thomas Dunlop, 3rd Bt and of Adda Mary Alison Dunlop (*née* Smith); *S* father, 1999; *m* 1984, Eileen, *er d* of A. H. Stevenson; one *s* one *d*. *Educ:* Rugby; Aberdeen Univ. (BSc). MICFor. *Heir: s* Thomas Dunlop, *b* 11 March 1990. *Address:* Bredon Croft, Bredons Norton, Tewkesbury, Glos GL20 7HB.

DUNLOP, William; Sheriff of North Strathclyde, since 1995; *b* 7 March 1944; *s* of William Dunlop and Catherine (*née* McKenzie); *m* 1st, 1968, Katherine Frances Howden (marr. diss. 1976); one *s* one *d*; 2nd, 1979, Janina Marthe Merecki; one *d*. *Educ:* High Sch. of Glasgow; Univ. of Glasgow (LLB 1965). Solicitor in family firm, 1968; called to the Scottish Bar, 1985; in practice at the Bar, 1985–95. Six Nations Match Comr, Scottish Rugby Union, 2000–. Governor, High Sch. of Glasgow, 1999–. *Recreations:* watching Rugby football, playing bad golf, enjoying good food and wine. *Address:* The Sheriff Court House, Paisley PA3 2HW. *T:* (0141) 887 5291. *Clubs:* Glasgow Golf; Dunaverty Golf (Kintyre).

DUNLOP, Prof. William, PhD; FRCSE, FRCOG; Professor of Obstetrics and Gynaecology, University of Newcastle upon Tyne, since 1982; President, Royal College of Obstetricians and Gynaecologists, since 2001; *b* 18 Aug. 1944; *s* of Alexander Morton Dunlop and Annie Denham Rennie (*née* Ingram); *m* 1968, Sylvia Louise Krauthamer; one *s* one *d*. *Educ:* Kilmarnock Acad.; Glasgow Univ. (MB ChB 1967); Univ. of Newcastle upon Tyne (PhD 1982). FRCSE 1971; MRCOG 1971, FRCOG 1984. Various junior posts in obstetrics and gynaecol., Glasgow Univ., 1969–74; seconded as Lectr, Univ. of Nairobi, 1972–73; on MRC scientific staff, 1974–75, Sen. Lectr, 1975–82, Univ. of Newcastle upon Tyne. Vis. Associate Prof., Medical Univ. of S Carolina, 1980. Royal College of Obstetricians and Gynaecologists: Hon. Sec., 1992–98; Chm., Exam. Cttee, 1990–92; Chm., Specialist Trng Cttee, 1999–; Hon. Treas., European Bd and Coll. of Obstetrics and Gynaecology, 1999–; Chm., Assoc. of Profs of Obstetrics and Gynaecology, 1999–. Chm., Blair-Bell Research Soc., 1989–92. Editor-in-Chief, Fetal and Maternal Medicine Rev., 1989–. *Publication:* (ed jtly) High Risk Pregnancy, 1992. *Recreations:* music, drama, literature. *Address:* Department of Obstetrics and Gynaecology, 4th Floor, Leazes Wing, Royal Victoria Infirmary, Newcastle upon Tyne NE1 4LP. *T:* (0191) 232 5131.

DUNLUCE, Viscount; Randal Alexander St John McDonnell; Fund Manager, Sarasin Investment Management Ltd, since 1998; *b* 2 July 1967; *o s* and heir of Earl of Antrim, *qv*. *Educ:* Gresham's Sch., Holt; Worcester Coll., Oxford (BA Hons). Fund Manager, NCL Investments Ltd, 1992–97. *Address:* Glenarm Castle, Glenarm, Ballymena, Co. Antrim BT44 0BD. *Clubs:* Savile, Turf, Beefsteak.

DUNMORE, 12th Earl of, *cr* 1686 (Scot.); **Malcolm Kenneth Murray;** Viscount Fincastle, Lord Murray of Blair, Moulin and Tillimet, 1686; Electrical Technical Officer, Air Services Australia, now retired; *b* 17 Sept. 1946; *er s* of 11th Earl of Dunmore and Margaret Joy (*d* 1976), *d* of P. D. Cousins; *S* father, 1995; *m* 1970, Joy Anne, *d* of A. Partridge; one *s* one *d* (both adopted). *Educ:* Launceston Technical High School (Board A Certificate and various tech. qualifs). Patron: Tasmanian Caledonian Council; Launceston Caledonian Soc.; Armorial and Heraldry Soc. of Australasia Inc.; Scottish Australian Heritage Council's annual Sydney Scottish Week; Patron and Member: St Andrew Soc., Tas; Murray Clan Soc. of Vic and Qld. Past Master, Concord Masonic Lodge, No 10 Tasmanian Constitution, 1996–97. *Recreations:* flying (Tow Master for Soaring Club of Tasmania), astronomy. *Heir: b* Hon. Geoffrey Charles Murray [*b* 31 July 1949; *m* 1974, Margaret Irene, *d* of H. Bulloch]. *Address:* PO Box 100E, East Devonport, Tas 7310, Australia. *Club:* Soaring Club of Tasmania.

DUNMORE, Helen, FRSL; poet and novelist; *b* 12 Dec. 1952; *d* of Maurice Ronald Dunmore and Betty (*née* Smith); *m* 1980, Francis Benedict David Charnley; one *s* one *d* and one step *s*. *Educ:* Univ. of York (BA Hons). FRSL 1997. Hon. DLitt Glamorgan, 1998. *Publications: poetry:* The Apple Fall, 1983; The Sea Skater, 1986 (Alice Hunt Bartlett Prize, Poetry Soc., 1987); The Raw Garden, 1988; Short Days, Long Nights: new and selected poems, 1991; Recovering a Body, 1994; Bestiary, 1997; *fiction:* Zennor in Darkness, 1993 (McKitterick Prize, Soc. of Authors, 1994); Burning Bright, 1994; A Spell of Winter, 1995 (Orange Prize for Fiction, 1996); Talking to the Dead, 1996; Love of Fat Men, 1997; Your Blue-eyed Boy, 1998; With Your Crooked Heart, 1999; Ice Cream (short stories), 2000; The Siege, 2001; *for children:* Going to Egypt, 1994; Secrets (Signal Poetry for Children Award), 1994; In the Money, 1995; Amina's Blanket, 1996; Go Fox, 1996; Fatal Error, 1996; Allie's Apples, 1997; Great-grandma's Dancing Dress, 1998; Clyde's Leopard, 1998; Brother Brother, Sister Sister, 1999; Allie's Rabbit, 1999; Zillah and Me, 2000. *Address:* c/o A. P. Watt Ltd, 20 John Street, WC1N 2DR. *T:* (020) 7405 6774.

DUNMORE, Stephen Lloyd; Chief Executive, New Opportunities Fund, since 1998; *b* 4 Dec. 1948; *s* of Leslie Alfred Dunmore and Josephine Mary Dunmore (*née* Bettles); *m* 1987, Isabel Mary Robertson; one *d*. *Educ:* Kettering Grammar Sch.; King's Coll. London (BA Hons Hist.). Urban Archaeol Officer, Ipswich BC, 1974–76; Department of the Environment: Inspector of Ancient Monuments, 1976–84; Principal, Housing, Construction Industry, Inner Cities, 1984–90; on secondment as Actg Chief Exec., Liverpool HAT, 1990–91; Principal, Citizen's Charter Unit, Cabinet Office, 1991; Regl Controller, Urban and Economic Affairs, Merseyside Task Force, 1991–94; Dir, Regeneration, Transport and Planning, Govt Office for Merseyside, 1994–98. *Recreations:* cricket, books, walking. *Address:* New Opportunities Fund, Heron House, 322 High Holborn, WC1V 7PW. *T:* (020) 7211 1760.

DUNN, Baroness *cr* 1990 (Life Peer), of Hong Kong Island in Hong Kong and of Knightsbridge in the Royal Borough of Kensington and Chelsea; **Lydia Selina Dunn,** DBE 1989 (CBE 1983; OBE 1978); Executive Director, John Swire & Sons Ltd, since 1996; Deputy Chairman, HSBC Holdings plc (formerly Hong Kong and Shanghai Banking Corporation), since 1992 (Director, since 1990); *b* 29 Feb. 1940; *d* of Yencheun Yeh Dunn and Chen Yin Chu; *m* 1988, Michael David Thomas, *qv*. *Educ:* St Paul's Convent Sch., Hong Kong; Univ. of Calif, Berkeley. MLC, Hong Kong, 1976–88 (Sen. Mem., 1985–88); MEC, 1982–95 (Sen. Mem., 1988–95). Director: John Swire & Sons (HK) Ltd, 1978–; Swire Pacific Ltd, 1981–; Hongkong and Shanghai Banking Corp., 1981–96 (Dep. Chm., 1992–96); Volvo AB, 1991–93 (Mem. Internat. Adv. Bd, 1985–91); Christie's Internat. plc, 1996–98; Christie's Fine Art Ltd, 1998–2000; Marconi (formerly GEC) plc, 1997–; Advr to Bd, Cathay Pacific Airways Ltd, 1997– (Dir, 1985–97). Chairman: Hong Kong/Japan Business Co-operation Cttee, 1988–95 (Mem., 1983–88); Hong Kong Trade Develt Council, 1983–91; Mem., Hong Kong/US Econ. Co-op. Cttee, 1984–93. Chm., Lord Wilson Heritage Trust, 1993–95. Hon. LLD: Chinese Univ. of Hong Kong, 1984; Univ. of Hong Kong, 1991; Univ. of British Columbia, 1991; Leeds Univ., 1994; Hon. DSc Univ. of Buckingham, 1995. Prime Minister of Japan's Trade Award, 1987; USA Sec. of Commerce's To Peace and Commerce Award, 1988. *Publication:* In the Kingdom of the Blind, 1983. *Recreation:* art and antiquities. *Address:* John Swire & Sons Ltd, Swire House, 59 Buckingham Gate, SW1E 6AJ.

DUNN, Anderson; Assistant Commissioner, Metropolitan Police, since 1994; *b* 6 May 1944; adopted *s* of William Rennie and Wilma Rennie (*née* Turner); *m* 1967, Margaret Docherty; one *s* one *d*. *Educ:* Queen Mary Coll., London (LLB Hons; Hon. Fellow, QMW, 1998). Joined Metropolitan Police, 1963; transf. to Thames Valley Police as Chief Supt, 1987; Asst Chief Constable, Operations, 1988–93; Dep. Chief Constable, Northants, 1993–94. *Recreations:* walking, reading, most sports. *Address:* Metropolitan Police Service, New Scotland Yard, Broadway, SW1H 0BG.

DUNN, Prof. Douglas Eaglesham, FRSL; poet and short-story writer; Professor of English, since 1991, and Director, St Andrews Scottish Studies Institute, since 1992, St Andrews University; *b* 23 Oct. 1942; *s* of William Douglas Dunn and Margaret McGowan; *m* 1st, 1964, Lesley Balfour Wallace (*d* 1981); 2nd, 1985, Lesley Jane Bathgate; one *s* one *d*. *Educ:* Univ. of Hull (BA). Became full-time writer, 1971. St Andrews University: Fellow in Creative Writing, 1989–91; Hd, Sch. of English, 1994–99. Hon. Vis. Prof., Dundee Univ., 1987–89. Mem., Scottish Arts Council, 1992–94. FRSL 1981. Hon. Fellow, Humberside Coll., 1987. Hon. LLD Dundee, 1987; Hon. DLitt Hull, 1995. Cholmondeley Award, 1989. *Publications:* Terry Street, 1969 (Somerset Maugham Award, 1972); The Happier Life, 1972; (ed) New Poems, 1972–73, 1973; Love or Nothing, 1974 (Geoffrey Faber Meml Prize, 1976); (ed) A Choice of Byron's Verse, 1974; (ed) Two Decades of Irish Writing, 1975 (criticism); (ed) The Poetry of Scotland, 1979; Barbarians, 1979; St Kilda's Parliament, 1981 (Hawthornden Prize, 1982); Europa's Lover, 1982; (ed) A Rumoured City: new poets from Hull, 1982; (ed) To Build a Bridge: celebration of Humberside in verse, 1982; Elegies, 1985 (Whitbread Poetry Prize, 1985; Whitbread Book of the Year Award, 1986); Secret Villages, 1985 (short stories); Selected Poems 1964–1983, 1986; Northlight, 1988 (poetry); New and Selected Poems 1966–1988, 1989; Andromache, 1990; (ed) The Essential Browning, 1990; (ed) Scotland: an anthology, 1991; (ed) Faber Book of 20th Century Scottish Poetry, 1992; Dante's Drum-Kit, 1993; Boyfriends and Girlfriends, 1995 (short stories); Oxford Book of Scottish Short Stories, 1995; The Donkey's Ears, 2000 (poetry); The Year's Afternoon, 2000 (poetry); contrib. to Counterblast pamphlet series, Glasgow Herald, New Yorker, TLS, etc. *Recreations:* playing the clarinet and saxophone, listening to jazz music, philately, gardening. *Address:* School of English, St Andrews University, St Andrews, Fife KY16 9AL.

DUNN, Air Marshal Sir Eric (Clive), KBE 1983; CB 1981; BEM 1951; *b* 27 Nov. 1927; *s* of late W. E. and K. M. Dunn; *m* 1951, Margaret Gray; three *d*. *Educ:* Bridlington Sch. CEng, FRAeS. RAF aircraft apprentice, 1944–47; commnd Engr Br., 1954; Staff Coll.,

1964; Jt Services Staff Coll., 1967; Sen. Engrg Officer, RAF Boulmer, 1968; MoD, 1969–70; Comd Electrical Engr, NEAF, 1971–72; Dir of Engrg Policy (RAF), 1973–75; RCDS, 1976; AO Wales, and Stn Comdr RAF St Athan, 1977; Air Officer Maintenance, RAF Support Comd, 1977–81; Air Officer Engineering, HQ Strike Comd, 1981–83; Chief Engr, RAF, 1983–86. Dir, Hellermann Deutsch, 1986–90; Engrg Consultant, Dowty Gp, 1986–90. *Recreations:* golf. *Club:* Royal Air Force.

DUNN, Hubert; *see* Dunn, W. H.

DUNN, John Churchill; broadcaster; *b* 4 March 1934; *s* of late John Barrett Jackson Dunn and of Dorothy Dunn (*née* Hiscox); *m* 1958, Margaret Jennison; two *d. Educ:* Christ Church Cathedral Choir School, Oxford; The King's School, Canterbury. Nat. Service, RAF, 1953–55. Joined BBC as studio manager, External Service, 1956; announcer/newsreader, Gen. Overseas Service, 1958, Domestic Services, 1959; worked all radio networks before joining Light Programme/Radio 2, and subseq. freelance; *radio series include:* Just For You; Housewives' Choice; Music Through Midnight; Roundabout; Jazz at Night; Saturday Sport; Sunday Sport; 4th Dimension; Breakfast Special; It Makes Me Laugh; Nat. and European Brass Band Championships; Light Music Festivals; The John Dunn Show, 1972–98; Friday Night is Music Night; numerous TV appearances. TV and Radio Industries Club Personality of the Year, 1971, 1984, 1986; Variety Club of GB Radio Personality of the Year, 1983; Daily Mail Silver Microphone, 1988; Sony Award, 1998. *Publications:* John Dunn's Curious Collection, 1982; Answers Please, 1994, rev. and expanded edn, 1995. *Recreations:* music, wine, sitting in the sun. *Address:* c/o Jo Gurnett Personal Management, 45 Queen's Gate Mews, SW7 5QN. *T:* (020) 7584 7642.

DUNN, Prof. John Montfort, FBA 1989; Professor of Political Theory, University of Cambridge, since 1987; Fellow of King's College, Cambridge, since 1966; *b* 9 Sept. 1940; *s* of Col. Henry George Montfort Dunn and Catherine Mary Dunn; *m* 1st, 1965, Susan Deborah Fyvel (marr. diss. 1971); 2nd, 1973, Judith Frances Bernal (*see* J. F. Dunn) (marr. diss. 1987); one *s* (and one *s* decd) by Dr Heather Joan Glen; 3rd, 1997, Ruth Ginette Scurr; one *d. Educ:* Winchester Coll.; King's Coll., Cambridge (BA 1962). Harkness Fellow, Graduate Sch. of Arts and Sciences, Harvard Univ., 1964–65; Official Fellow in History, Jesus Coll., Cambridge, 1965–66; Dir of Studies in History, King's Coll., Cambridge, 1966–72; Lectr in Pol Science, 1972–77, Reader in Politics, 1977–87, Cambridge Univ. Vis. Lectr, Dept of Pol Science, Univ. of Ghana, 1968–69; Visiting Professor: Dept of Civics and Politics, Univ. of Bombay, 1979–80; Faculty of Law, Tokyo Metropolitan Univ., 1983–84; Distinguished Vis. Prof., Murphy Inst. of Pol Economy, Tulane Univ., New Orleans, 1986; Benjamin Evans Lippincott Dist. Prof., Minnesota Univ., 1990; Olmsted Vis. Prof., Yale Univ., 1991. Foreign Hon. Mem., Amer. Acad. of Arts and Scis, 1991. Mem., Bd of Consultants, Kim Dae-Jung Peace Foundn for the Asia-Pacific Region, 1994–. FRSA 1993. *Publications:* The Political Thought of John Locke, 1969; Modern Revolutions, 1972; Dependence and Opportunity: political change in Ahafo, 1973; (ed) West African States: failure and promise, 1978; Western Political Theory in the Face of the Future, 1979; Political Obligation in its Historical Context, 1980; Locke, 1984; The Politics of Socialism, 1984; Rethinking Modern Political Theory, 1985; (ed) The Economic Limits to Modern Politics, 1989; (ed) Contemporary West African States, 1989; Interpreting Political Responsibility, 1990; (ed) Democracy: the unfinished journey, 1992; Contemporary Crisis of the Nation State?, 1995; The History of Political Theory, 1995; (ed with Ian Harris) Great Political Thinkers, 20 vols, 1997; The Cunning of Unreason: making sense of politics, 2000. *Address:* The Merchant's House, 31 Station Road, Swavesey, Cambridge CB4 5QJ. *T:* (01954) 231451.

DUNN, Prof. Judith Frances, PhD; FBA 1996; Research Professor, Social, Genetic and Developmental Psychiatry Research Centre, Institute of Psychiatry, University of London, since 1995; *d* of James Pace and Jean Stewart; *m* 1st, 1961, Martin Gardiner Bernal (marr. diss.); 2nd, 1973, John Montfort Dunn, *qv* (marr. diss. 1987); 3rd, 1987, Robert Plomin. *Educ:* New Hall, Cambridge (BA 1961; MA 1968); King's Coll., Cambridge (PhD 1982). MRC Develt and Integration of Behaviour Unit, and Fellow, King's Coll., Cambridge, 1978–86; Evan Pugh Professor of Human Develt, Pennsylvania State Univ., 1986–95. *Publications:* (jtly) First Year of Life: psychological and medical implications of early experience, 1979; (jtly) Siblings: love, envy and understanding, 1982; Sisters and Brothers, 1984; (ed with R. Plomin) Study of Temperament: changes, continuities and challenges, 1986; Beginnings of Social Understanding, 1988; (jtly) Separate Lives, 1990; (ed jtly) Children's Sibling Relationships, 1992; Young Children's Close Relationships, 1993; (ed jtly) Stepfamilies, 1994; (ed) Connections between Emotion and Understanding in Development, 1995. *Address:* Social, Genetic and Developmental Psychiatry Research Centre, Institute of Psychiatry, De Crespigny Park, Denmark Hill, SE5 8AF.

DUNN, Martin; Editor-in-Chief, Associated New Media, since 1996; Managing Director: DMG New Media, since 1998; DMG Front of Mind Ltd, since 2000; *b* 26 Jan. 1955. *Educ:* Dudley Grammar Sch., Worcs. Dudley Herald, 1974–77; Birmingham Evening Mail, 1977; Birmingham Post, 1978; Daily Mail, 1978–79; freelance journalist, 1979–83; New York Correspondent, The Sun, 1983–84; The Sun, London, 1984–88; Deputy Editor: News of the World, 1988–89; The Sun, 1989–91; Editor: Today, 1991–93; The Boston Herald, 1993; Editor-in-Chief, The New York Daily News, 1993–96; Editor, Channel One Television, 1996–98. *Recreations:* squash, running, golf. *Address:* DMG Front of Mind Ltd, 17–18 Margaret Street, W1N 7LE. *T:* (020) 7291 3870.

DUNN, Air Marshal Sir Patrick Hunter, KBE 1965 (CBE 1950); CB 1956; DFC 1941; FRAeS; *b* 31 Dec. 1912; *s* of late William Alexander Dunn and Jean MacFarlane Dunn (*née* Metcalfe), Ardentinny, Argyllshire; *m* 1939, Diana Ledward Smith; two *d. Educ:* Glasgow Academy; Loretto; Glasgow Univ. Commissioned, 1933, Pre-war service in flying boats; as flying instructor 500 (County of Kent) Sqdn, AAF; with the Long Range Development Unit and as instructor at the Central Flying Sch. War service included command of 80 and 274 Fighter Squadrons and 71 OTU, all in Middle East (1940–42); at Air Ministry, and in Fighter Command, Sector Commander, 1945–46. Post-war service in Air Ministry, 1947–48; Malaya, 1949–50; NATO Defence Coll., 1950–52; Fighter Command, 1953–56; ADC to the Queen, 1953–58. AOC and Commandant, RAF Flying Coll., 1956–58; Deputy Air Sec., 1959–61; AOC No. 1 Group, Bomber Command, 1961–64; AOC-in-Chief, Flying Training Command, 1964–66; retired from RAF, 1967. Director i/c Management Services, British Steel Corp., 1967–68; resigned to become Dep. Chm., British Eagle Internat. Airlines Ltd; Chm., Eagle Aircraft Services, 1969; Aviation Consultant, British Steel Corporation, 1969–76. Mem. Council, Air League, 1968–73 and 1975–79 (Dep. Chm., 1972–73; Chm., Defence Cttee, 1968–73); Member: British Atlantic Cttee, 1976–93; Atlantic Council, 1993–. Dir, Gloucester, Coventry, Cricklewood and Kingston Industrial Trading Estates, 1969–75 and 1977–81. A Trustee and Governor of Loretto, 1959–81; President: Fettesian-Lorettonian Club, 1972–75; Lorettorian Soc., 1980–81; Mem. Cttee, Assoc. of Governing Bodies of Public Schs, 1976–79. *Recreations:* tennis, sailing, shooting. *Address:* Little Hillbark, Hockett Lane, Cookham Dean, Berks SL6 9UF. *Clubs:* Royal Air Force, Hurlingham; Royal Air Force Yacht.

DUNN, Most Rev. Patrick James; *see* Auckland (NZ), Bishop of, (RC).

DUNN, Robert John; *b* 14 July 1946; *s* of late Robert and of Doris Dunn, Swinton, Lancs; *m* 1976, Janet Elizabeth Wall, BD, *d* of late Denis Wall, Dulwich; two *s. Educ:* State schs. Senior Buyer, J. Sainsbury Ltd, 1973–79. Councillor, London Borough of Southwark, 1974–78 (Opposition Minority Gp spokesman on Housing and Finance Matters). Vice-Pres., Eccles Conservative Assoc., 1974–; contested (C) Eccles, Feb. and Oct. 1974. MP (C) Dartford, 1979–97; contested (C) same seat, 1997, 2001. PPS to Parly Under-Secs of State at DES, 1981–82, to Paymaster General and Chancellor of the Duchy of Lancaster, 1982–83; Parly Under-Sec. of State, DES, 1983–88. Mem., Parly Select Cttee on the Environment, 1981–82, on Selection, 1991–97; Jt Sec., Cons backbench Educn Cttee, 1980–81; Chairman: Cons. backbench Social Security Cttee, 1988–89; Cons. backbench Transport Cttee, 1992–97; Vice-Chm., Cons. backbench Party Organization Cttee, 1989–97; Mem. Exec. Cttee, 1922 Cttee, 1988–97. President: Dartford Conservative Future (formerly Dartford Young Conservatives), 1976–; Kent Gp Young Conservatives, 1982–85; SE Area Young Conservatives, 1989–; SE Area Educn Adv. Cttee, 1982–93; Dartford branch, Kent Assoc. for the Disabled, 1983–. *Recreations:* canvassing, American politics. *Club:* Dartford Rotary (Hon. Mem.).

DUNN, Rt Hon. Sir Robin Horace Walford, Kt 1969; MC 1944; PC 1980; a Lord Justice of Appeal, 1980–84; *b* 16 Jan. 1918; *s* of late Brig. K. F. W. Dunn, CBE, and of Ava, *d* of Brig.-Gen. H. F. Kays, CB; *m* 1941, Judith (*d* 1995), *d* of late Sir Gonne Pilcher, MC; one *s* one *d* (and one *d* decd); *m* 1997, Joan, *e d* of Sir Cecil Stafford-King-Harman, 2nd Bt and *widow* of Captain George Dennehy. *Educ:* Wellington; Royal Military Academy, Woolwich (Sword of Honour). First Commissioned, RA, 1938; RHA, 1941; Staff Coll., 1946; retired (hon. Major), 1948. Served War of 1939–45; France and Belgium, 1939–40; Western Desert and Libya, 1941–42; Normandy and NW Europe, 1944–45 (wounded thrice, despatches twice, MC); Hon. Col Comdt, RA, 1980–84, Hon. Col 1984–. Called to Bar (Inner Temple), 1948; Master of the Bench, Inner Temple, 1969. Western Circuit, Junior Counsel to Registrar of Restrictive Trading Agreements, 1959–62; QC 1962; Judge of the High Court of Justice, Family Division (formerly Probate, Divorce and Admiralty Division), 1969–80; Presiding Judge, Western Circuit, 1974–78. Treas., Gen. Council of the Bar, 1967–69 (Mem., 1959–63); Chm. Betting Levy Appeal Tribunal, 1964–69; Dep. Chm., Somerset QS, 1965–71; Mem., Lord Chancellor's Cttee on Legal Educn, 1968–69. *Publication:* Sword and Wig: memoirs of a Lord Justice, 1994. *Recreation:* hunting. *Address:* Lynch Mead, Allerford, Somerset TA24 8HJ. *T:* (01643) 862509. *Club:* Cavalry and Guards.

DUNN, William Francis N.; *see* Newton Dunn.

DUNN, (William) Hubert; QC 1982; **His Honour Judge Dunn;** a Circuit Judge, since 1993, a Senior Circuit Judge, since 1998; Chief Immigration Adjudicator, 1998–2001; *b* 8 July 1933; *s* of William Patrick Millar Dunn and Isabel (*née* Thompson); *m* 1971, Maria Henriqueta Theresa d'Arouje Perestrello de Moser; one *s* one *d. Educ:* Rockport, Co. Down, N Ireland; Winchester Coll.; New Coll., Oxford (Hons degree PPE) (Half-Blue fencing 1954–55). 2nd Lieut, Life Guards, 1956–57; Household Cavalry Reserve of Officers, 1957–64. Cholmondeley Scholar, Lincoln's Inn, 1958, called to Bar, 1958; Bencher, Lincoln's Inn, 1990. A Recorder, 1980–93. Fellow, Soc. for Advanced Legal Studies, 1998. *Recreations:* travel, literature. *Address:* 19 Clarendon Street, SW1V 2EN. *Club:* Boodle's.

DUNNE, Martin; JP; Lord-Lieutenant of Warwickshire, since 1997; *b* 30 March 1938; *s* of Philip Dunne, MC and Margaret Dunne (*née* Walker); *m* 1964, Alicia Juliet Barclay; three *d. Educ:* Eton; Christ Church, Oxford. High Sheriff, 1982–83, JP 1984, DL 1993, Warwicks.

See also Sir T. R. Dunne.

DUNNE, Sir Thomas (Raymond), KCVO 1995; JP; HM Lord-Lieutenant for Herefordshire, since 1998, and for Worcestershire, 1998–2001 (HM Lord-Lieutenant, County of Hereford and Worcester, 1977–98); *b* 24 Oct. 1933; *s* of Philip Dunne, MC, and Margaret Walker; *m* 1957, Henrietta Crawley; two *s* two *d. Educ:* Eton; RMA Sandhurst. Served Army, 1951–59: Royal Horse Guards. Herefordshire CC, 1962–68. President: 3 Counties Agric. Soc., 1977; W Midlands TA Assoc., 1988–98; National Vice Pres., Royal British Legion, 1982–89. Mem., West Mercia Police Authy, 1980–99; Dir, West Regional Bd, Central TV, 1981–92. Trustee, Dyson Perrins Mus. Trust, 1980–. Colonel: 4th Worcester and Sherwood Foresters (formerly 2nd Mercian Volunteers), 1987–93; 5th Bn LI, 1993–98. High Sheriff 1970, DL 1973, Herefordshire; JP Hereford and Worcester, 1977. KStJ 1978. *Address:* c/o County Hall, Spetchley Road, Worcester WR5 2NP.

See also M. Dunne.

DUNNETT, Anthony Gordon; Chief Executive, South East England Development Agency, since 1999; *b* 17 June 1953; *s* of Peter Sydney Dunnett and Margaret Eileen (*née* Johnson); *m* 1975, Ruth Elizabeth Barker; one *s* two *d. Educ:* St Dunstan's Coll.; McGill Univ. (BComm, DipCS); Exeter Univ. (MA Econs). FCIB 1981. Nat. Westminster Bank, 1975–77; Royal Bank of Canada, Montreal, 1977–80 and 1982–86, Curaçao, 1980–82; Midland Bank: Corporate Banking Dir, 1986–88; Corporate Banking Dir, Samuel Montagu, 1988–89; Corporate Dir, 1990–91; Finance Dir, Corporate and Instnl Banking, 1991–94; Dir, Industrial Develt Unit, DTI, 1994–96; Chief Exec., English Partnerships, 1996–98. Member: Steering Bd, Insolvency Service, 1994–96; Urban Task Force, 1998–; Bd, Berks Learning and Skills Council, 2001–. Dir, Countryside Maritime, 1997–. Mem., Mgt Bd, Kingsmead Homes, 1997–99. FRSA 1997; MInstD 1999. *Recreations:* local church, gardening, theatre, opera, sports (tennis, athletics). *Address:* SEEDA Headquarters, Cross Lanes, Guildford, Surrey GU1 1YA. *T:* (01483) 484224, *Fax:* (01483) 484247.

DUNNETT, Denzil Inglis, CMG 1967; OBE 1962; HM Diplomatic Service, retired; *b* 21 Oct. 1917; *s* of late Sir James Dunnett, KCIE and late Annie (*née* Sangster); *m* 1946, Ruth Rawcliffe (*d* 1974); two *s* (one *d* decd). *Educ:* Edinburgh Acad.; Corpus Christi Coll., Oxford. Served with RA, 1939–45. Diplomatic Service: Foreign Office, 1947–48; Sofia, 1948–50; Foreign Office, 1950–53; UK Delegn to OEEC, Paris, 1953–56; Commercial Sec., Buenos Aires, 1956–60; Consul, Elisabethville, 1961–62; Commercial Counsellor, Madrid, 1962–67; seconded to BoT, 1967–70; Counsellor, Mexico City, 1970–73; Ambassador to Senegal, Mauritania, Mali and Guinea, 1973–76, and to Guinea-Bissau, 1975–76; Diplomatic Service Chm., CS Selection Bd, 1976–77. London Rep., Scottish Develt Agency, 1978–82. *Publication:* Bird Poems, 1989. *Recreations:* chess, music. *Address:* 11 Victoria Grove, W8 5RW. *T:* (020) 7584 7523. *Club:* Caledonian.

DUNNETT, Dorothy, (Lady Dunnett), OBE 1992; portrait painter, since 1950, and novelist, since 1961; *b* 25 Aug. 1923; *d* of Alexander Halliday and Dorothy Eveline Millard; *m* 1946, Sir Alastair MacTavish Dunnett (*d* 1998); two *s. Educ:* James Gillespie's High Sch., Edinburgh. British Civil Service, 1940–55. Non-exec. Dir, Scottish Television plc, 1979–92. Trustee: Scottish Nat. War Meml, 1962–96; Nat. Library of Scotland, 1986–. Bd Mem., Edinburgh Book Fest., 1988–95; Hon. Vice-Pres., Scottish PEN,

1997–. FRSA 1986. Literature Award, St Andrews Presbyterian Coll., Laurinburg, USA, 1993. *Publications: historical novels:* King Hereafter, 1982; *Lymond Chronicle:* The Game of Kings, 1961; Queens' Play, 1964; The Disorderly Knights, 1966; Pawn in Frankincense, 1969; Ringed Castle, 1971; Checkmate, 1975; *House of Niccolò:* Niccolò Rising, 1986; The Spring of the Ram, 1987; Race of Scorpions, 1989; Scales of Gold, 1991; The Unicorn Hunt, 1993; To Lie with Lions, 1995; Caprice and Rondo, 1997; Gemini, 2000; *mysteries:* Dolly and the Singing Bird, 1968; Dolly and the Cookie Bird, 1970; Dolly and the Doctor Bird, 1971; Dolly and the Starry Bird, 1973; Dolly and the Nanny Bird, 1976; Dolly and the Bird of Paradise, 1983; Moroccan Traffic, 1991; *non-fiction:* (with Alastair M. Dunnett and David Paterson) The Scottish Highlands, 1988. *Recreations:* travel, orchestral music, opera, ballet. *Address:* 87 Colinton Road, Edinburgh EH10 5DF. *Clubs:* Caledonian; New (Edinburgh).

DUNNETT, Maj. Graham Thomas, TD 1964; JP; Lord-Lieutenant of Caithness, since 1995; *b* 8 March 1929; *s* of late Daniel Dunnett and Elizabeth E. Macadie, Wick; *m* 1963, Catherine Elizabeth Sinclair, Westerdale; three *s*. *Educ:* Wick High Sch.; Archbishop Holgate's Grammar Sch., York. 1st Seaforth Highlanders, Malaya, 1948–51; 11th Seaforth Highlanders, Caithness, 1951–71; Major and Company Comdr, 1964. DL 1975, Vice Lord-Lieutenant 1986, JP 1996, Caithness. *Recreations:* gardening, walking, country dancing. *Address:* Cathel Sheiling, Loch Calder, Thurso, Caithness KW14 7YH. *T:* (01847) 871220.

DUNNETT, Jack; President, Football League, 1981–86 and 1988–89 (Member, Management Committee, 1977–89); *b* 24 June 1922; *m* 1951; two *s* three *d*. *Educ:* Whitgift Middle Sch., Croydon; Downing Coll., Cambridge (MA, LLM). Served with Cheshire Regt, 1941–46 (Capt.). Admitted Solicitor, 1949. Middlesex CC, 1958–61; Councillor, Enfield Borough Council, 1958–61; Alderman, Enfield Borough Council, 1961–63; Councillor, Greater London Council, 1964–67. MP (Lab) Central Nottingham, 1964–74, Nottingham East, 1974–83; former PPS to: Minister of State, FCO; Minister of Transport. Mem. FA Council, 1977–89, Vice-Pres., 1981–86, 1988–89; Mem., Football Trust, 1982–89; Chm., Notts County FC, 1968–87; Vice-Chm., Portsmouth FC, 1989–90. *Recreation:* watching professional football. *Address:* Whitehall Court, SW1A 2EP.

DUNNETT, Stephen Bruce, PhD; Cardiff Professorial Research Fellow, School of Biosciences, Cardiff University, since 2000; *b* 28 Jan. 1950; *s* of Peter Sidney Dunnett and Margaret Eileen Dunnett (*née* Johnson); *m* 1984, Dr Sarah-Jane Richards. *Educ:* Eltham Coll.; Churchill Coll., Cambridge (BA Hons 1972; MA 1976; PhD 1981); Poly. of N London (Dip in Social Work, CQSW 1976); Birkbeck Coll., Univ. of London (BSc Hons 1978); DSc Cantab 1999. Social worker, London Borough of Southwark, 1972–78; research student, Churchill Coll., Cambridge, 1978–81; Fellow, Clare Coll., Cambridge, 1981–99; Department of Experimental Psychology, University of Cambridge: Wellcome Trust Mental Health Res. Fellow, 1982–83; Demonstrator, 1983–86; Lectr, 1986–95; Reader in Neurobiology, 1995–99; Dir, Scientific Progs, MRC Cambridge Centre for Brain Repair, 1992–99. Vis. Scientist, Univ. of Lund, Sweden, 1981–82. Spearman Medal, BPsS, 1988; Alfred Meyer Medal, British Neuropathol Soc., 1998. *Publications:* (ed with S.-J. Richards) Neural Transplantation: from molecular basis to clinical application, 1990; (ed with A. Björklund): Neural Transplantation: a practical approach, 1992; Functional Neural Transplantation, 1994; Functional Neural Transplantation II, 2000; (with R. A. Barker) Neural Repair, Transplantation and Rehabilitation, 1999; (ed jtly) Neural Transplantation Methods, 2000; (jtly) Brain Damage, Brain Repair, 2001; over 400 research papers on topics of brain function and neural transplantation. *Recreations:* marriage, flying, the Dordogne. *Address:* School of Biosciences, Cardiff University, Box 911, Museum Avenue, Cardiff CF10 3US. *Club:* Royal Society of Medicine.

DUNNILL, Prof. Peter, OBE 1999 DSc, PhD, FREng, FRSC, FIChemE; Professor of Biochemical Engineering, University College London, since 1984; Chairman, Advanced Centre for Biochemical Engineering, since 2001 (Director, 1999–2001); *b* 20 May 1938; *s* of Eric and Marjorie Dunnill; *m* 1962, Patricia Mary Lievesley; one *s*. *Educ:* University College London (BSc; DSc 1978; Fellow, 1991). Royal Instn MRC staff, 1963–64; Lectr, 1964–79, Reader, 1979–84, UCL. Member: Internat. Cttee on Econ. and Applied Microbiol., 1974–82; Scientific and Technical Cttee, Central Lab. of Nat. Blood Transfusion Service, 1978–82; Biotechnol. Directorate Management Cttee, SERC, 1982–88, 1993–94; Biotechnol. Adv. Gp to Heads of Res. Councils, 1987–90; Biotechnol. Jt Adv. Bd, 1989–92; BBSRC, 1994–96. FREng (FEng 1985). Donald Medal, IChemE, 1995; Heatley Medal, Biochem. Soc., 1997. *Publications:* c 200 pubns in learned jls. *Recreation:* music. *Address:* Advanced Centre for Biochemical Engineering, University College London, Torrington Place, WC1E 7JE. *T:* (020) 7679 7031.

DUNNING, Graham; QC 2001; *b* 13 March 1958; *s* of Maj. James E. Dunning and Jane P. Dunning (*née* Hunt); *m* 1986, Claire Abigael Williams; three *s* one *d*. *Educ:* King Edward VI Sch., Southampton; Emmanuel Coll., Cambridge (MA); Harvard Law Sch. (LLM). Called to the Bar, Lincoln's Inn, 1982; joined Essex Court Chambers, 1983; in practice at commercial bar, 1983–. *Recreations:* travel, ski-ing, golf. *Address:* Essex Court Chambers, 24 Lincoln's Inn Fields, WC2A 3ED. *T:* (020) 7813 8000. *Club:* Woking Golf.

DUNNING, Prof. John Harry, PhD; Emeritus Professor of International Business, University of Reading, since 1992; State of New Jersey Professor of International Business, Rutgers University, US, since 1989; *b* 26 June 1927; *m* 1st, 1948, Ida Teresa Bellamy (marr. diss. 1975); one *s*; 2nd, 1975, Christine Mary Brown. *Educ:* Lower Sch. of John Lyon, Harrow; University Coll. London (BSc (Econ); PhD). Sub-Lieut, RNVR, 1945–48. Research Asst, University Coll. London, 1951–52; Lectr and Sen. Lectr, Univ. of Southampton, 1952–64; University of Reading: Prof. of Economics, 1964–74; Hd of Dept of Economics, 1964–87; Esmée Fairburn Prof. of Internat. Investment and Business Studies, 1975–87; ICI Res. Prof. of Internat. Business, 1988–92. Visiting Professor: Univ. of Western Ontario, Canada, 1968–69; Univ. of California (Berkeley), 1968, 1987; Boston Univ., USA, 1976; Stockholm Sch. of Economics, 1978; HEC, Univ. of Montreal, Canada, 1980; Walker-Ames Prof., Univ. of Washington, Seattle, 1981; Seth Boyden Distinguished Prof., Rutgers Univ., 1987; Hon. Prof., Univ. of Internat. Business and Econs, Beijing, 1995. Consultant to UN, 1974–, OECD, 1975–, and EC, 1985–. Member: SE Economic Planning Council, 1966–68; Chemicals EDC, 1968–77; UN Study Gp on Multinational Corps, 1973–74. Chm., Economists Advisory Gp Ltd. Pres., Internat. Trade Assoc., 1994. Fellow, Acad. of Internat. Business (Pres., 1987–88). Hon. PhD: Uppsala, 1975; Universidad Autónoma de Madrid, 1990; Antwerp, 1997. *Publications:* American Investment in British Manufacturing Industry, 1958, 2nd edn 1998; (with C. J. Thomas) British Industry, 1963; Economic Planning and Town Expansion, 1963; Studies in International Investment, 1970; (ed) The Multinational Enterprise, 1971; (with E. V. Morgan) An Economic Study of the City of London, 1971; (ed) International Investment, 1972; (ed) Economic Analysis and the Multinational Enterprise, 1974; US Industry in Britain, 1976; (with T. Houston) UK Industry Abroad, 1976; International Production and the Multinational Enterprise, 1981; (ed with J. Black) International Capital Movements, 1982; (with J. Stopford) Multinationals: Company Performance and Global Trends, 1983; (with R. D. Pearce) The World's Largest Industrial Companies 1962–83, 1985; (ed) Multinational Enterprises, Economic Structure and International Competitiveness, 1985; Japanese Participation in British Industry, 1986; (with J. Cantwell) World Directory of Statistics on International Direct Investment and Production, 1987; Explaining International Production, 1988; Multinationals, Technology and Competitiveness, 1988; (ed with A. Webster) Structural Change in the World Economy, 1990; Multinational Enterprises and the Global Economy, 1993; The Globalization of Business, 1993; (ed with R. Narula) Foreign Direct Investment and Governments, 1996; (ed with K. Hamdani) The New Globalism and Developing Countries, 1997; Alliance Capitalism and Global Business, 1997; (ed) Governments, Globalisation and International Business, 1997; (ed) Globalization, Trade and Foreign Direct Investment, 1998; (ed) Regions, Globalisation and the Knowledge Based Economy, 2000; Global Capitalism at Bay, 2001; Selected Essays of John H. Dunning, 2002; numerous articles in learned and professional jls. *Address:* Department of Economics, University of Reading, Whiteknights Park, Reading, Berks RG6 2AA. *T:* (0118) 987 5123. *Club:* Athenæum.

DUNNING, Joseph, CBE 1977; Chairman, Lothian Health Board, 1983–84; Principal, Napier College of Commerce and Technology, Edinburgh, 1963–81, retired; *b* 9 Oct. 1920; *s* of Joseph and Elizabeth Ellen Dunning; *m* 1st, 1948, Edith Mary Barlow (*d* 1972); one *s* one *d*; 2nd, 1992, Eileen Murdoch, OBE. *Educ:* London University (BSc Hons); Durham University (MEd); Manchester College of Technology (AMCT). Metallurgical Industry and lecturing, 1936–56; Principal, Cleveland Technical College, 1956–63. MA Open Univ.; FEIS. Hon. Fellow, Napier Polytech. of Edinburgh, 1989. Hon. DEd CNAA, 1983. *Recreations:* silversmithing, photography. *Address:* 3 Barnes Green, Great Salkeld, Penrith, Cumbria CA11 9LU. *Club:* New (Edinburgh).

DUNNING, Sir Simon (William Patrick), 3rd Bt *cr* 1930; *b* 14 Dec. 1939; *s* of Sir William Leonard Dunning, 2nd Bt, and Kathleen Lawrie (*d* 1992), *d* of J. P. Cuthbert, MC; *S* father, 1961; *m* 1975, Frances Deirdre Morton, *d* of Major Patrick Lancaster; one *d*. *Educ:* Eton. *Recreations:* shooting, racing. *Address:* Low Auchengillan, Blanefield, by Glasgow G63 9AU. *T:* (01360) 770323. *Club:* Turf.

DUNNINGTON-JEFFERSON, Sir Mervyn (Stewart), 2nd Bt *cr* 1958; Company Director, since 1968; *b* 5 Aug. 1943; *s* of Sir John Alexander Dunnington-Jefferson, 1st Bt, DSO, and of Frances Isobel, *d* of Col H. A. Cape, DSO; *S* father, 1979; *m* 1971, Caroline Anna, *o d* of J. M. Bayley; one *s* two *d*. *Educ:* Eton College. Joined Charrington & Co. Ltd (Brewers), 1961; left in 1968 to become self-employed. *Recreations:* sport—cricket, skiing, golf, etc. *Heir:* *s* John Alexander Dunnington-Jefferson, *b* 23 March 1980. *Address:* 7 Bolingbroke Grove, SW11 6ES. *T:* (020) 8675 3395. *Clubs:* MCC, Queen's.

DUNRAVEN and MOUNT-EARL, 7th Earl of, *cr* 1822; **Thady Windham Thomas Wyndham-Quin;** Baron Adare, 1800; Viscount Mountearl, 1816; Viscount Adare, 1822; Bt 1871; *b* 27 Oct. 1939; *s* of 6th Earl of Dunraven and Mount-Earl, CB, CBE, MC, and Nancy (*d* 1994), *d* of Thomas B. Yuille, Halifax County, Va; *S* father, 1965; *m* 1969, Geraldine, *d* of Air Commodore Gerard W. McAleer, CBE, MB, BCh, DTM&H, Wokingham; one *d*. *Educ:* Ludgrove; Le Rosey. *Heir:* none. *Address:* Kilgobbin House, Adare, Co; Limerick, Ireland. *Club:* Kildare Street and University (Dublin).

See also Sir F. G. W. Brooke, Bt.

DUNROSSIL, 3rd Viscount *cr* 1959; **Andrew William Reginald Morrison;** Director, Brundage Management Company, San Antonio, Texas, since 1990; *b* 15 Dec. 1953; *e s* of 2nd Viscount Dunrossil, CMG and of Mavis Dawn (*née* Spencer-Payne); *S* father, 2000; *m* 1986, Carla Marie Brundage; one *s* three *d*. *Educ:* Eton (KS); University Coll., Oxford (BA Lit Hum). FCO, 1978–79; Kleinwert Benson Ltd, 1979–89. *Recreations:* clan history, theology, poetry, sports. *Heir:* *s* Hon. Callum Alasdair Brundage Morrison, *b* 12 July 1994. *Address:* 132 Park Hill Drive, San Antonio, TX 78212, USA. *T:* (office) (210) 7359393. *Clubs:* San Antonio Country; Withington Cricket (Glos).

DUNSANY, 20th Baron of, *cr* 1439; **Edward John Carlos Plunkett;** *b* 10 Sept. 1939; *o s* of 19th Baron of Dunsany and Vera Plunkett, *d* of G. de Sà Sottomaior; *S* father, 1999; *m* 1982, Maria Alice Villela de Carvalho; two *s*. *Educ:* Eton; Slade Sch. of Fine Art; Ecole des Beaux Arts, Paris. *Heir:* *s* Hon. Randal Plunkett, *b* 9 March 1983. *Address:* Dunsany Castle, Co. Meath, Eire.

DUNSTAN, (Andrew Harold) Bernard, RA 1968 (ARA 1959); painter; *b* 19 Jan. 1920; *s* of late Dr A. E. Dunstan; *m* 1949, Diana Maxwell Armfield, *qv*; three *s*. *Educ:* St Paul's; Byam Shaw Sch.; Slade Sch. Has exhibited at RA since 1945. Many one-man exhibitions; now exhibits regularly at Agnews, Bond St. Pictures in public collections include Royal Collection, London Museum, Bristol Art Gall., Nat. Gall. of NZ, Arts Council, Nat. Portrait Gall., and many in private collections. Member: NEAC; RWA (Pres., 1980–84); Pastel Soc. Chm., Artists' General Benevolent Instn, 1987–91. Trustee, RA, 1989–95. *Publications:* Learning to Paint, 1970; Painting in Progress, 1976; Painting Methods of the Impressionists, 1976; (ed) Ruskin, Elements of Drawing, 1991; The Paintings of Bernard Dunstan, 1993. *Recreation:* music. *Address:* 10 High Park Road, Kew, Richmond, Surrey TW9 4BH. *T:* (020) 8876 6633. *Club:* Arts.

DUNSTAN, Lt-Gen. Sir Donald (Beaumont), AC 1991; KBE 1980 (CBE 1969; MBE 1954); CB 1972; Governor of South Australia, 1982–91; *b* 18 Feb. 1923; *s* of late Oscar Reginald Dunstan and Eileen Dunstan; *m* 1948, Beryl June Dunningham; two *s*. *Educ:* Prince Alfred Coll., South Australia; RMC, Duntroon. Served War of 1939–45: Regimental and Staff appts in SW Pacific Area, 1942–45. Served in Korea, 1954; Instructor: RMC Duntroon, 1955–56, 1963; Staff Coll., Queenscliff, 1958; Staff Coll., Camberley, 1959–60; Dep. Comdr 1 Task Force, Vietnam, 1968–69; Comdr, 10th Task Force, Holsworthy, NSW, 1969; idc 1970; Commander Aust. Force, Vietnam, 1971; Chief of Materiel, 1972–74; GOC Field Force Comd, 1974–77; CGS, 1977–82. KStJ 1982. *Recreations:* golf, fishing. *Address:* 52 Martin Court, West Lakes, SA 5021, Australia. *Clubs:* Australian (Sydney); Royal Sydney Golf, Royal Adelaide Golf.

DUNSTAN, Rev. Prof. Gordon Reginald, CBE 1989; F. D. Maurice Professor of Moral and Social Theology, King's College, London, 1967–82, now Emeritus; Honorary Research Fellow, University of Exeter, since 1982; Chaplain to the Queen, 1976–87; *b* 25 April 1917; *yr s* of late Frederick John Menhennet and Winifred Amy Dunstan (*née* Orchard); *m* 1949, Ruby Maud (*née* Fitzer); two *s* one *d*. *Educ:* Plymouth Corp. Gram. Sch.; University of Leeds; College of the Resurrection, Mirfield. BA, 1st cl. Hist., 1938, Rutson Post-Grad. Schol. 1938, MA w dist. 1939, Leeds Univ.; FSA 1957; FKC 1974. Deacon 1941, priest 1942; Curate, King Cross, Halifax, 1941–45; Huddersfield, 1945–46; Sub Warden, St Deiniol's Library, Hawarden, 1945–49; Vicar of Sutton Courtney with Appleford, 1949–55; Lecturer, Wm Temple Coll., 1947–49; Ripon Hall, Oxford, 1953–55; Minor Canon, St George's Chapel, Windsor Castle, 1955–59; Westminster Abbey, 1959–67; Canon Theologian, Leicester Cathedral, 1966–82, Canon Emeritus, 1982–. Sec., C of E Council for Social Work, 1955–63; Sec., Church Assembly Jt Bd of Studies, 1963–66; Editor of Crucible, 1962–66; Editor of Theology, 1965–75; Dep. Priest in Ordinary to the Queen, 1959–64, Priest in Ordinary, 1964–76; Select Preacher: University of Cambridge 1960, 1977; Leeds, 1970; Hulsean Preacher, 1977. Lectures:

Prideaux, Univ. of Exeter, 1968; Moorhouse, Melbourne, 1973; Stephenson, Sheffield, 1980. Gresham's Prof. in Divinity, City Univ., 1969–71. Consultant, Lambeth Conf., 1988. Mem. Council, Canterbury and York Soc., 1950–85 (Vice-Pres., 1985–). Mem. or Sec. cttees on social and ethical problems; Vice-Pres., 1965–66, and Chm. Brit. Cttee, of Internat. Union of Family Organizations, 1964–66; Vice-Pres., London Medical Gp and Inst. of Medical Ethics, 1985–2001; Pres., Tavistock Inst. of Med. Psychology, 1991–; Member: Adv. Gp on Transplant Policy, Dept of Health, 1969; Council of Tavistock Inst. of Human Relations (Vice-Pres., 1977–82), and Inst. of Marital Studies, 1969–88; Adv. Gp on Arms Control and Disarmament, FCO, 1970–74; Adv. Cttee on Animal Experiments, Home Office, 1975–89; Council, Advertising Standards Auth., 1981–93; MRC/RCOG Voluntary Licensing Authority, 1985–91; Cttee on Ethics of Gene Therapy, DoH, 1989–93; Nuffield Council on Bioethics, 1991–95; Unrelated Live Transplant Regulatory Authy, 1990–97. Pres., Devon and Cornwall Record Soc., 1984–87; Vice-Pres., UFAW, 1985–. Founder FMedSci 1998. Hon. FRSocMed 1985; Hon. MRCP 1987; FRCOG *ad eundem* 1991; Hon. FRCGP 1993; Hon. FRCP 1995; Hon. FRCPCH 1996. Hon. DD Exeter, 1973; Hon. LLD Leicester, 1986. *Publications:* The Family Is Not Broken, 1962; The Register of Edmund Lacy, Bishop of Exeter 1420–1455, 5 vols, 1963–72; A Digger Still, 1968; Not Yet the Epitaph, 1968; The Sacred Ministry, 1970; The Artifice of Ethics, 1974; A Moralist in the City, 1974; (ed) Duty and Discernment, 1975; (ed with M. J. Seller) Consent in Medicine, 1983; (ed with M. J. Seller) The Status of the Human Embryo: perspectives from moral tradition, 1988; (ed with D. Callahan) Biomedical Ethics: an Anglo-American dialogue, 1988; (ed with E. A. Shinebourne) Doctors' Decisions: ethical conflicts in medical practice, 1989; (ed) The Human Embryo: Aristotle and the Arabic and European Traditions, 1990; (ed with P. J. Lachmann) Euthanasia, 1996. *Recreations:* small islands, *domus* and *rus*. *Address:* 208 Kingsgate, Pennsylvania Road, Exeter EX4 6DH. *T:* (01392) 276015.

DUNSTAN, Ivan, PhD; CChem, FRSC; FIQA; Director-General International, British Standards Institution, 1991–93; *b* 27 Aug. 1930; *s* of Edward Ernest and Sarah Kathleen Dunstan; *m* 1955, Monica Jane (*née* Phillips); two *s* one *d*. *Educ:* Falmouth Grammar Sch.; Bristol Univ. (BSc). Joined Scientific Civil Service, working at Explosives Research and Development Estabt, Waltham Abbey, 1954; became Supt of Gen. Chemistry Div., 1967; Warren Spring Laboratory (DTI) as Dep. Dir (Resources), 1972–74; Dir, Materials Quality Assurance, MoD (PE), 1974–79; Dir, Bldg Res. Estabt, DoE, 1979–83; Standards Dir, 1983–86, Dir-Gen., 1986–91, BSI. Chm., UK Nat. Forum for Quality Policy and Conformity Assessment, 1993–. President: RILEM, 1988; European Standards Organ, 1990; European Orgn for Testing and Certification, 1990–92; Inst. of Quality Assurance, 1997– (Vice-Pres., 1986–97); Mem., British Bd of Agrément, 1987. CIMgt (CBIM 1986). *Recreations:* golf, badminton, gardening. *Address:* 6 High Oaks Road, Welwyn Garden City, Herts AL8 7BH. *T:* (01707) 322272.

DUNSTAN, Tessa Jane; Director, Legal Services A, Department of Trade and Industry, since 2001; *b* 18 July 1944; *d* of Alfred Thomas Fripp and Kathleen Jennie (*née* Kimpton); *m* 1973, Richard James Rowley Dunstan; two *s* two *d*. *Educ:* Convent of the Sacred Heart, Woldingham, Surrey; Lady Margaret Hall, Oxford (MA). Called to the Bar, Middle Temple, 1967; Legal Asst, Solicitor's Office, BoT, 1968; Sen. Legal Asst, Solicitor's Office, DTI, 1973–84; Legal Advr, Office of Telecommunications; 1984–87; Solicitor's Office/ Legal Department, Department of Trade and Industry, 1987–: Investigations Div., 1989–98; Grade 3, Dir Legal Services D, 1998–2001; Legal Project Dir (Co. Law Review), Legal Services, DTI, 2001. *Recreations:* opera, gardening. *Address:* Shalesbrook, Forest Row, Sussex RH18 5LS. *T:* (01342) 823079.

DUNSTER, (Herbert) John, CB 1979; consultant in radiation protection; *b* 27 July 1922; *s* of Herbert and Olive Grace Dunster; *m* 1945, Rosemary Elizabeth, *d* of P. J. Gallagher; one *s* three *d*. *Educ:* University Coll. Sch.; Imperial College of Science and Technology (ARCS, BSc). FSRP 1988. Scientist, UK Atomic Energy Authority, 1946–71; Asst Dir, Nat. Radiological Protection Bd, 1971–76; Dep. Dir Gen., HSE, 1976–82; Dir, NRPB, 1982–87. Member: Internat. Commn on Radiological Protection, 1977–97 (Emer. Mem., 1997); Sci. and Tech. Cttee, Euratom, 1982–93; Sci. Adv. Cttee, IAEA, 1982–87. *Publications:* numerous papers in technical jls. *Recreations:* music, photography. *Address:* 17 Streatley Lodge, Pegasus Grange, White House Road, Oxford OX1 4QF. *T:* (01865) 202325; *e-mail:* hjohn.dunster@virgin.net.

DUNSTONE, Charles; Founder and Managing Director, The Carphone Warehouse, since 1989; *b* 21 Nov. 1964; *s* of Denis and Anne Dunstone. *Educ:* Uppingham Sch. Sales Manager, Communications Div., NEC, 1985–89. Non-executive Director: Halifax, 2000–01; Hbos, 2001–. *Recreation:* sailing. *Address:* The Carphone Warehouse, North Acton Business Park, Wales Farm Road, W3 6RS. *Clubs:* Royal Ocean Racing, Royal Thames Yacht.

DUNT, Vice Adm. Sir John (Hugh), KCB 1998; CEng, FIEE; defence consultant; *b* 14 Aug. 1944; *s* of Harris Hugh Dunt and Margaret Rea Dunt (*née* Morgan); *m* 1972, Alynne Margaret Wood; two *d*. *Educ:* Duke of York Sch., Nairobi; RNEC Manadon (BScEng). Joined RN at BRNC Dartmouth, 1963; served in HM Ships Kent, Ajax, Dundas, Collingwood, Nubian; MoD (PE); Staff, C-in-C Fleet, 1980; Naval Operational Requirements, 1980–82; HMS Invincible, 1982–84; Staff Weapon Engr Officer to FO Sea Training, 1984; Naval Staff Duties, 1985–87; RCDS 1988; Higher Command and Staff Course, Camberley, 1989; Captain, HMS Defiance, 1989–90; Dir, Defence Systems, MoD, 1991–93; Dir, Gen. Fleet Support (Ops and Plans), 1993–95; DCDS (Systems), MoD, 1995–97; Chief of Fleet Support and Mem., Admiralty Bd, 1997–2000. Gov., Royal Sch., Haslemere, 1992–. *Publications:* articles in naval and professional jls. *Recreations:* sport (cricket, squash), gardening, travel. *Address:* Woodley House, Hill Brow, Liss, Hants GU33 7QG. *Clubs:* MCC; Royal Navy Cricket (Pres., 1995–).
See also Rear Adm. P. A. Dunt.

DUNT, Rear Adm. Peter Arthur; Senior Naval Directing Staff, Royal College of Defence Studies, and Chief Naval Supply Officer, since 2000; *b* 23 June 1947; *s* of Harris Hugh Dunt and Margaret Rae Dunt; *m* 1974, Lesley Gilchrist; two *d*. *Educ:* Duke of York Sch., Nairobi; Merchant Taylors' Sch., Liverpool; BRNC, Dartmouth. Midshipman, HMS Arethusa, 1966; Sub Lieut courses, 1967–69; Captain's Sec., HMS Charybdis, 1969–71; Flag Lieut to Flag Officer, Medway, 1971–74; Dep. Supply Officer, HMS Kent, 1974; Supply Officer, HMS Aurora, 1975–77; Officer's Trng Officer, HMS Pembroke, 1977–79; Asst Sec. to Vice Chief of Naval Staff, 1979–82; Comdr, 1982; Sec. to Flag Officer, 1st Flotilla, 1982–84 (Gp Logistics Officer, HMS Hermes, Falklands Conflict); Supply Officer, BRNC, Dartmouth, 1984–86; Sec. to Dir Gen. Naval Manpower and Trng, 1986–88; Captain, 1988; Dep. Dir Naval Staff Duties, 1988; Sec. to 2nd Sea Lord, 1989–92; Captain, HMS Raleigh, 1992–94; Dir Naval Personnel Corporate Programming, 1994–97; rcds 1997; Rear Adm., 1998; COS to Second Sea Lord and C-in-C Naval Home Command, 1998–2000. *Recreations:* cricket, golf, squash, walking, gardening, DIY. *Clubs:* I Zingari, Free Forresters, Incogniti.
See also Vice Adm. Sir J. H. Dunt.

DUNTZE, Sir Daniel Evans, 9th Bt *cr* 1774, of Tiverton, Devon; *b* 11 Aug. 1960; *o s* of Sir Daniel Evans Duntze, 8th Bt and of Marietta Duntze (*née* Welsh); *S* father, 1997. *Address:* 6811 University Drive 2E, St Louis, MO 63130, USA.

DUNWICH, Viscount; Robert Keith Rous; *b* 17 Nov. 1961; *s* and *heir* of Earl of Stradbroke, *qv*.

DUNWICH, Bishop Suffragan of, since 1999; **Rt Rev. Clive Young;** *b* 31 May 1948; *s* of William Alfred Young and late Dorothy Young; *m* 1971, Susan Elizabeth Tucker. *Educ:* King Edward VI Grammar Sch., Chelmsford; St John's Coll., Durham (BA Hons); Ridley Hall, Cambridge. Ordained: deacon, 1972; priest, 1973; Assistant Curate: Neasden cum Kingsbury St Catherine, London, 1972–75; St Paul, Hammersmith, 1975–79; Priest-in-charge, 1979–82, Vicar, 1982–92, St Paul with St Stephen, Old Ford; Area Dean, Tower Hamlets, 1988–92; Archdeacon of Hackney and Vicar of Guild Church of St Andrew, Holborn, 1992–99. *Recreations:* music, gardening. *Address:* 28 Westerfield Road, Ipswich, Suffolk IP4 2UJ. *T:* (01473) 222276.

DUNWOODY, Gwyneth (Patricia); MP (Lab) Crewe and Nantwich, since 1983 (Crewe, Feb. 1974–1983); *b* 12 Dec. 1930; *d* of late Morgan Phillips and Baroness Phillips; *m* 1954, Dr John Elliott Orr Dunwoody, *qv* (marr. diss. 1975); two *s* one *d*. MP (Lab) Exeter, 1966–70; Parly Sec. to BoT, 1967–70; Mem., European Parlt, 1975–79; Front Bench Spokesman on Foreign Affairs, 1980, on Health Service, 1980–83, on Transport, 1984–85; Parly Campaign Co-ordinator, 1983–84; Member: Labour Party NEC, 1981–88; Chairmen's Panel, 1992–. Life Pres., Labour Friends of Israel (Chm., 1988–93; Pres., 1993); Vice-Pres., Socialist Internat. Women, 1986–92. Dir, Film Production Assoc. of GB, 1970–74. *Address:* c/o House of Commons, SW1A 0AA.

DUNWOODY, Dr John (Elliott Orr), CBE 1986; general practitioner; Vice-Chairman, Merton, Sutton and Wandsworth Local Medical Committee, since 1996; *b* 3 June 1929; *s* of Dr W. O. and late Mrs F. J. Dunwoody; *m* 1st, 1954, Gwyneth Patricia (*née* Phillips), *qv* (marr. diss. 1975); two *s* one *d*; 2nd, 1979, Evelyn Louise (*née* Borner). *Educ:* St Paul's Sch.; King's Coll., London Univ.; Westminster Hosp. Med. Sch. MB, BS London; MRCS, LRCP 1954. House Surgeon, Westminster (Gordon) Hosp., 1954; House Physician, Royal Berks Hosp., 1954–55; Sen. House Physician, Newton Abbot Hosp., 1955–56; Family Doctor and Medical Officer, Totnes District Hosp, 1956–66; MO, Staff Health Service, St George's Hosp., 1976–77. MP (Lab) Falmouth and Camborne, 1966–70; Parly Under-Sec., Dept of Health and Social Security, 1969–70. Vice-Chm., 1974–77, Chm., 1977–82, Kensington, Chelsea and Westminster AHA (T); Chm., Bloomsbury DHA, 1982–90. Member: Exec. Cttee, British Council, 1967–69; Council, Westminster Med. Sch., 1974–82; (co-opted) Social Services Cttee, Westminster City Council, 1975–78; Nat. Exec. Council, FPA, 1979–87 (Dep. Chm., 1980, Chm., 1981–87). Council Mem., UCL, 1982–90. Hon. Dir, Action on Smoking and Health, 1971–73. Governor, Pimlico Sch., 1972–75. *Publication:* (jtly) A Birth Control Plan for Britain, 1972. *Recreations:* travel, cooking. *Address:* 9 Cautley Avenue, SW4 9HX. *T:* (020) 8673 7471.

DUNWOODY, (Thomas) Richard, MBE 1993; National Hunt jockey, 1982–99; company director; *b* 19 Jan. 1964; *s* of George Rutherford and Gillian Mary Dunwoody; *m* 1988, Carol Ann Abraham (marr. diss.). *Educ:* Rendcomb Coll., Glos. Wins include: Grand National, on West Tip, 1986, on Miinnehoma, 1994; Cheltenham Gold Cup, on Charter Party, 1988; King George VI Chase, on Desert Orchid, 1989 and 1990, on One Man, 1995 and 1996; Champion Hurdle, on Kribensis, 1990; Breeders' Cup Steeplechase, on Highland Bud, 1989 and 1992; Champion National Hunt Jockey, 1992–93, 1993–94 and 1994–95. Record 1699 National Hunt wins, incl. ten consecutive centuries, 1999. *Publications:* (with Marcus Armytage) Hell for Leather, 1993; (with S. Magee) Duel, 1994; (with Marcus Armytage) Hands and Heels, 1997; (with David Walsh) Obsessed: the autobiography, 2000. *Recreations:* fitness, motor-racing. *Address:* Dunwoody Sports Marketing, The Litten, Newtown Road, Newbury, Berks RG14 7BB.

DUNWORTH, John Vernon, CB 1969; CBE 1955; President, International Committee of Weights and Measures, Sèvres, France, 1975–85; *b* 24 Feb. 1917; *o c* of late John Dunworth and Susan Ida (*née* Warburton); *m* 1967, Patricia Noel Boston; one *d*. *Educ:* Manchester Grammar Sch.; Clare Coll., Cambridge; Denman Baynes Research Studentship, 1937, Robins Prize, 1937; MA, PhD; Twisden Studentship and Fellowship, Trinity Coll., 1941. War Service: Ministry of Supply on Radar Development, 1939–44; National Research Council of Canada, on Atomic Energy Development, 1944–45. Univ. Demonstrator in Physics, Cambridge, 1945. Joined Atomic Energy Research Establishment, Harwell, 1947; Dir, NPL, 1964–76. Alternate United Kingdom Member on Organising Cttee of UN Atoms for Peace Confs in Geneva, 1955 and 1958. Pres., 1975–85, Vice-Pres., 1968–75, Internat. Cttee of Weights and Measures. Fellow Amer. Nuclear Soc. 1960. Chm., British Nuclear Energy Soc., 1964–70; Vice-President, Institute of Physics: Physical Soc., 1966–70. CEng 1966. Comdr (with Star), Order of Alfonso X el Sabio, Spain, 1960. *Address:* Apartment 902, Kings Court, Ramsey, Isle of Man IM8 1LP. *T:* (01624) 813003. *Club:* Athenæum.

DU PLESSIS, Barend Jacobus; Minister of Finance, Republic of South Africa, 1984–92; MP (National Party) Florida, 1974–92; Leader of National Party of Transvaal, 1989–92; *b* 19 Jan. 1940; *s* of late Jan Hendrik Du Plessis and of Martha J. W. Du Plessis (*née* Botha); *m* 1962, Antoinette (*née* Van Den Berg); three *s* one *d*. *Educ:* Potchefstroom Univ. for Christian Higher Educn (BSc); Potchefstroom Teachers' Trng Coll. (THED). Mathematics Teacher, Hoër Seunskool Helpmekaar, Johannesburg and Johannesburg Technical Coll., 1962; Engineering Div., Data Processing and Admin. Sec., SABC, 1962–68; Systems Engineering and Marketing in Banking and Finance, IBM (SA), 1968–74. Dep. Minister of Foreign Affairs and Information, 1982; Minister of Educn and Trng, 1983.

du PLESSIS, Prof. Daniel Jacob, FRCS; Vice-Chancellor and Principal, University of the Witwatersrand, 1978–83; *b* 17 May 1918; *s* of D. J. du Plessis and L. du Plessis (*née* Carstens); *m* 1946, Louisa Susanna Wicht; two *s*. *Educ:* Univ. of Cape Town (MB ChB 1941); Hon. MD, 1986; Hon. Fellow, Smuts Hall, 1986); Univ. of the Witwatersrand (ChM 1951). Served, SA Medical Corps, 1942–46. Postgraduate study, 1947–51; Surgeon and Lectr, Univ. of Cape Town, 1952–58; Prof. of Surgery, Univ. of the Witwatersrand, 1958–77 (Hon. LLD, 1984). Trustee, S African Blood Transfusion Service, 1985–. Dir, Transvaal Bd, Provincial Bldg Soc., 1984–91. Pres., S Transvaal Br., Medical Assoc. of S Africa, 1986–87; Chairman of Council: B. G. Alexander Nursing Coll., 1985–95; Bonalesedi (formerly Natalspruit) Nursing Coll., 1985–92; Member: Council, Med. Univ. of Southern Africa, 1986–95; Adv. Council for Univs and Technikons, 1984–92; Council, Johannesburg Coll. of Educn, 1984–92; Council, Univ. of Transkei, 1989–94. Governor, Amer. Coll. of Surgeons, 1988–94. Hon. FACS 1974; Hon. Fellow: Assoc. of Surgeons of GB and Ireland, 1979; Amer. Surgical Assoc., 1981; Hon. FCSSA 1982. Hon. Life Vice-President: Assoc. of Surgeons of S Africa; Surgical Res. Soc. of Southern Africa. Paul Harris Fellowship, Rotary Club, Orange Grove, Johannesburg, 1984. Hon. Mem., Alpha Omega Alpha Honor Med. Soc. (USA), 1986. Hon. DSc Med. Univ. of Southern Africa,

1995. Order for Meritorious Service Cl. 1 (Gold), RSA, 1989. *Publications:* Principles of Surgery, 1968, 2nd edn 1976; Synopsis of Surgical Anatomy, 10th edn (with A. Lee McGregor) 1969, 11th edn 1975, 12th edn (with G. A. G. Decker) 1986; numerous articles in learned jls on surgical topics, espec. on diseases of parotid salivary gland and gastric ulcers. *Address:* 17 Chateau Road, Richmond, Johannesburg, 2092, South Africa.

DUPPLIN, Viscount; Charles William Harley Hay, MA; barrister; Director of Mergers and Acquisitions, Hiscox plc, since 2000; *b* 20 Dec. 1962; *s* and *heir* of 15th Earl of Kinnoull, *qv*. *Educ:* Summer Fields; Eton; Christ Church, Oxford (Scholar); City Univ. (Dip. in Law); Inns of Court Sch. of Law. Called to the Bar, Middle Temple, 1990. Associate, Credit Suisse First Boston Ltd, 1985–88; Underwriter, Roberts & Hiscox, then Hiscox Syndicates Ltd, 1990–95; Man. Dir (Europe), Hiscox Insce Co. Ltd, 1995–2000. Non-exec. Dir, Construction & Gen. Guarantee Insce Co., 2001–. Lieut, Atholl Highlanders, 1993–. Mem., Queen's Bodyguard for Scotland (Royal Co. of Archers), 2000–. Chm., Royal Caledonian Ball, 1996– (Trustee, 1992–). Mem., Royal Philatelic Soc. *Publication:* contrib. Jl of Chem. Soc. *Recreations:* cricket, Cresta Run, Real tennis, ski-ing, philately. *Address:* 59 Scarsdale Villas, W8 6PU. *T:* (020) 7938 4265; Pitkindie House, Abernyte, Perthshire PH14 9RE. *T:* (01828) 686342. *Clubs:* White's, Turf, MCC; Royal Perth (Perth); Jockey (Vienna).

DUPRE, Sir Tumun, Kt 1993; OBE 1988; President, South Wahgi Local Government Council, Papua New Guinea, 1967–88 and since 1990 (Councillor, 1988–90); *b* 1923; *s* of Awil Dupre and Dop Amban Ai; *m* 1st, Abamp; 2nd, Kawil; 3rd, Danamp; 4th, Muru; 5th, Wai; thirteen *s* two *d*. *Educ:* no formal schooling. Government interpreter, 1948–63; Luluai (people's representative, apptd by govt), 1956–63. Rep. of Minj Dist, and MEC, W Highlands Province; Minister for Police, Justice, Village Courts, and Peace and Good Order. PNG Independence Medal, 1975; 10th Anniversary Medal, 1985; Provincial Medal, 1988. *Recreation:* village life. *Address:* c/o South Wahgi Local Government Council, Post Office Box, Minj, Papua New Guinea. *T:* 5465553.

DUPREE, Sir Peter, 5th Bt *cr* 1921; *b* 20 Feb. 1924; *s* of Sir Victor Dupree, 4th Bt and of Margaret Cross; *S* father, 1976; *m* 1947, Joan (*d* 2000), *d* of late Captain James Desborough Hunt. *Heir: cousin* Thomas William James David Dupree, *b* 5 Feb. 1930. *Address:* 15 Hayes Close, Chelmsford, Essex CM2 0RN.

Du QUESNAY, Heather Le Mercier, CBE 1996; Director, National College for School Leadership, since 2000; *b* 10 Nov. 1947; *d* of Eric William and Agnes Elizabeth Openshaw; *m* 1969, Ian Mark Le Mercier Du Quesnay; two *d*. *Educ:* Univ. of Birmingham (BA, Cert Ed). Teacher, 1972–78, Dep. Head, 1978–83, Bartley Green Girls' Sch., Birmingham; Educn Officer, Cambs CC, 1983–89; Dep. Co. Educn Officer, Essex CC, 1989–90; Dir of Educn, Herts CC, 1991–96; Exec. Dir of Educn, 1996–2000, Interim Chief Exec., 2000, Lambeth BC. FRSA 1994. Hon. DEd de Montfort, 1997. *Publications:* essays and articles in educ. jls and newspapers. *Recreations:* walking, food, wine, family. *Address:* National College for School Leadership, Jubilee Campus, University of Nottingham, Wollaton Road, Nottingham NG8 1BB.

DURAND, Sir Edward (Alan Christopher David Percy), 5th Bt *cr* 1892, of Ruckley Grange, Salop; radio producer and writer; *b* 21 Feb. 1974; *s* of Rev. Sir (Henry Mortimer) Dickon (Marion St George) Durand, 4th Bt and of Stella Evelyn Durand (*née* L'Estrange); *S* father, 1993. *Educ:* St Columba's Coll., Dublin; Milltown Inst., Dublin (Nat. Cert. in Philosophy); Univ. of Ulster at Coleraine (BA Phil.). *Recreation:* study of the paranormal. *Heir: b* David Michael Dickon Percy Durand, *b* 6 June 1978. *Address:* 14 Lower Rathmines Road, Dublin 6, Eire. *T:* (1) 4979471; Lisnalurg House, Sligo, Eire. *T:* (71) 45819.

DURANT, Sir Anthony; *see* Durant, Sir R. A. B.

DURANT, Prof. John Robert, PhD; Chief Executive, At-Bristol, since 2000; Professor of Public Understanding of Science, Imperial College, London, since 1993; *b* 8 July 1950; *s* of Kenneth Albert James Durant and Edna Kathleen Durant (*née* Norman); *m* 1st, 1977, Nirmala Naidoo (marr. diss. 1996); two *s* one *d*; 2nd, 2000, Prof. Anne Harrington. *Educ:* Queens' College, Cambridge (MA Nat. Scis; PhD Hist. of Sci.). Staff Tutor in Biological Scis, Dept of Extramural Studies, UC Swansea, 1976–82; Staff Tutor in Biol Scis, Dept of External Studies, Univ. of Oxford, 1983–89; Hd, then Dir, Sci. Communication, Sci. Mus., 1989–2000. Vis. Prof. of History and Public Understanding of Science, Imperial College London, 1989–93. *Publications:* (ed) Darwinism and Divinity, 1985; (with P. Klopfer and S. Oyama) Aggression: conflict in animals and humans reconsidered, 1988; (ed) Museums and Public Understanding of Science, 1992; (ed) Public Participation in Science, 1995; (ed) Biotechnology in the Public Sphere: a European sourcebook, 1998; articles in professional jls. *Recreations:* family, writing, broadcasting. *Address:* At-Bristol, Harbourside, Anchor Road, Bristol BS1 5DB. *T:* (0117) 915 7156, *Fax:* (0117) 915 7256; *e-mail:* john.durant@at-bristol.org.uk. *Club:* Athenæum.

DURANT, Sir (Robert) Anthony (Bevis), Kt 1991; *b* 9 Jan. 1928; *s* of Captain Robert Michael Durant and Mrs Violet Dorothy Durant (*née* Bevis); *m* 1958, Audrey Stoddart; two *s* one *d*. *Educ:* Dane Court Prep. Sch., Pyrford, Woking; Bryanston Sch., Blandford, Dorset. Royal Navy, 1945–47. Coutts Bank, Strand, 1947–52; Cons. Party Organisation, 1952–67 (Young Cons. Organiser, Yorks; Cons. Agent, Clapham; Nat. Organiser, Young Conservatives). MP (C): Reading N, Feb. 1974–1983; Reading W, 1983–97. PPS to Sec. of State for Transport and to Sec. of State for Employment, 1983–84; Asst Govt Whip, 1984–86; a Lord Comr of HM Treasury, 1986–88; Vice-Chamberlain of HM Household, 1988–90. Member: Select Cttee Parly Comr (Ombudsman), 1973–83, 1990–93; Select Cttee on Members' Interests, 1993–95; Chm., Select Cttee on Channel Tunnel Rail Link Bill, 1995–96; Mem., Exec., 1922 Cttee, 1990–97; Chairman: All Party Gp on Widows and One Parent Families, 1977–85; All Party Gp on Inland Waterways, 1992–97; Cons. Nat. Local Govt Adv. Cttee, 1981–84; Backbench Envmt Cttee, 1991–97; All Party Gp on Film Industry, 1991–97; Vice-Chm., Parly Gp for World Govt, 1979–84. Leader, UK delegn to Council of Europe, 1996–97 (Mem., 1992–96); Chm., British Br., CPA, 1988–90; Mem., Council of Europe, 1981–83, 1990–97 (Ldr, UK Delegn, 1996–97). Dir, Southern Demolition Co. Ltd, 1998–; former Consultant: The Film Production Association of Great Britain Ltd; Delta Electrical Div. of Delta Metal Co. Ltd; Allied Industrial Designers. Dir, British Industrial Scientific Film Assoc., 1967–70; Mem. Bd of Govs, BFI, 1992–98. Chm., Sports Aid Foundn (Southern Region), 1996–. Mem., Inland Waterways Adv. Council, 1975–84; President: Kennet and Avon Canal Trust, 1996–; River Thames Soc., 1996–. Freeman: City of London, 1997; Watermen and Lightermen's Co., 1998–. *Recreations:* boating, golf. *Address:* Hill House, Surley Row, Caversham, Reading RG4 8ND.

DURANTE, Viviana Paola; Guest Artist, Royal Ballet Company; *b* Italy, 8 May 1967. *Educ:* Royal Ballet School. Came to England in 1977; joined Royal Ballet Co., 1984; soloist, 1987; Principal Dancer, 1989; Guest Artist, 1999; first major rôle, Swan Lake, Covent Garden, 1988; rôles include Manon, Ondine, La Bayadère, Giselle, Kitri (in Don Quixote), Aurora, Cinderella, Juliet. Principal Dancer, American Ballet Theater, 1999. Evening Standard Ballet Award, 1989.

DURÃO BARROSO, José Manuel, MP (PSD) Lisbon, Portugal, 1985–87 and since 1995 (Viseu, 1987–95); Professor of International Relations, Universidade Lusíada (Head of Department, 1995–99); *b* 23 March 1956; *s* of Luis Barroso and Marie Elisabete Durão; *m* 1980, Maria Margarida Pinto Ribeiro de Sousa Uva Barroso; three *s*. *Educ:* Univ. of Lisbon (LLD Hons 1978); Univ. of Geneva (Master in Pol Sci. 1981); European Univ. Inst., Univ. of Geneva (Dip.). Lecturer: Faculty of Law, Lisbon Univ., 1978–; Pol Sci. Dept, Geneva Univ., 1981–85. Vis. Scholar, 1985, Vis. Prof., 1996–98, Univ. of Georgetown, Washington. Ed., Revista de Ciência Política. Secretary of State for: Home Affairs, 1985–87; Foreign Affairs and Co-operation, 1987–92; Minister for Foreign Affairs, Portugal, 1992–95. Chm., Commn for For. Affairs, Portuguese Parlt, 1995–99. Pres., PSD, 1999– (Mem., Nat. Council, 1984–; Chm., Dept for Internat. Relns). Scholarship Fellow: Swiss Confedn; CEC; Volkswagenwerk Foundn; NATO; Swiss Nat. Fund for Scientific Res. *Publications:* (jtly) Governmental System and Party System, 1980; Le Système Politique Portugais face à l'Intégration Européenne, 1983; Política de Cooperacão, 1990; Uma Certa Ideia de Europa, 1999; Uma Ideia para Portugal, 2000; contrib. to collective works, encyclopaedias and internat. scientific jls. *Address:* c/o PSD, Rua de São Caetano 9, 1249-087 Lisbon, Portugal.

DURBIN, Prof. James, FBA 2001; Professor of Statistics, University of London (London School of Economics), 1961–88, now Emeritus; *b* 30 June 1923; *m* 1958, Anne Dearnley Outhwaite; two *s* one *d*. *Educ:* Wade Deacon GS, Widnes; St John's Coll., Cambridge. Army Operational Research Group, 1943–45. Boot and Shoe Trade Research Assoc., 1945–47; Dept of Applied Economics, Cambridge, 1948–49; Asst Lectr, then Lecturer, in Statistics, London Sch. of Economics, 1950–53; Reader in Statistics, 1953–61. Visiting Professor: Univ. of North Carolina, 1959–60; Stanford Univ., 1960; Johns Hopkins Univ., 1965–66; Univ. of Washington, 1966; ANU, 1970–71; Univ. of Calif, Berkeley, 1971; Univ. of Cape Town, 1978; UCLA, 1984; Univ. of Calif, Santa Barbara, 1989; Nat. Univ. of Singapore, 1989–90; Univ. of Trento, Italy, 1991; Ohio State Univ., 1993. Research Fellow: US Bureau of the Census, 1992; Statistics Canada, 1994; Statistics NZ, 1997. Member: ESRC, 1983–86 (Chm., Res. Resources and Methods Cttee, 1982–85); Internat. Statistical Inst., 1955 (Pres., 1983–85; Hon. Mem., 1999); Bd of Dirs, Amer. Statistical Assoc., 1980–82 (Fellow, 1960); Fellow, Inst. of Mathematical Statistics, 1958; Fellow, Econometric Soc., 1967; Royal Statistical Society: Vice Pres., 1969–70 and 1972–73; Pres. 1986–87; Guy Medal in Bronze, 1966, in Silver, 1976. Dr *hc* Tucuman, Argentina, 2001. *Publications:* Distribution Theory for Tests based on the Sample Distribution Function, 1973; (with S. J. Koopman) Time Series Analysis by State Space Methods, 2001; articles in statistical journals, incl. Biometrika, Jl of Royal Statistical Society, etc. *Recreations:* travel, opera, theatre. *Address:* 31 Southway, NW11 6RX. *T:* (020) 8458 3037.

DURBIN, Leslie, CBE 1976; MVO 1943; silversmith; *b* 21 Feb. 1913; *s* of late Harry Durbin and of Lillian A. Durbin; *m* 1940, Phyllis Ethel Durbin (*see* Phyllis E. Ginger); one *s* one *d*. *Educ:* Central Sch. of Arts and Crafts, London. Apprenticed to late Omar Ramsden, 1929–39; full-time schol., 1938–39, travelling schol., 1939–40, both awarded by Worshipful Co. of Goldsmiths. Started working on own account in workshop of Francis Adam, 1940–41. RAF, Allied Central Interpretation Unit, 1941–45. Wkg partnership with Leonard Moss, 1945–75. Commissioned by Jt Cttee of Assay Offices of GB to design Silver Jubilee Hall Mark; designed regional variants of pound coin for Royal Mint, 1983. Retrospective exhibn, Leslie Durbin, 50 years of Silversmithing, Goldsmiths' Hall, 1982. Hon. LLD Cambridge, 1963. Council of Industrial Design Awards for Silver for the 70's. MVO awarded for work on Stalingrad Sword.

DURHAM; 6th Earl of, *cr* 1833; Baron Durham, 1828; Viscount Lambton, 1833; peerages disclaimed, 1970; *see under* Lambton.

DURHAM, Baron; a subsidiary title of Earldom of Durham (disclaimed 1970), used by Hon. Edward Richard Lambton, *s* and heir of Viscount Lambton, *qv*.

DURHAM, Bishop of, since 1994; **Rt Rev. Michael Turnbull;** *b* 27 Dec. 1935; *s* of George Ernest Turnbull and Adeline Turnbull (*née* Awty); *m* 1963, Brenda Susan Merchant; one *s* two *d*. *Educ:* Ilkley Grammar Sch.; Keble Coll., Oxford (MA); St John's Coll., Durham (DipTh). Deacon, 1960; priest, 1961; Curate: Middleton, 1960–61; Luton, 1961–65; Domestic Chaplain to Archibishop of York, 1965–69; Rector of Heslington and Chaplain, York Univ., 1969–76; Chief Secretary, Church Army, 1976–84; Archdeacon of Rochester, also Canon Residentiary of Rochester Cathedral and Chm., Dio. Bd for Mission and Unity, 1984–88; Bishop of Rochester, 1988–94. Mem., General Synod, C of E, 1970–75, 1987–; Vice-Chm., Central Bd of Finance, C of E, 1990–98; Member: Bd, Church Commissioners, 1989–98; Archbishops' Council, 1998–2000 (Chm., Ministry Div., 1999–2000); Archbps' Commn on Cathedrals, 1992–93; Chm., Archbps' Commn on orgn of C of E, 1994–96. Chairman: NE Constitutional Convention, 1999–; Campaign for English Regs, 2000–. Chm., Coll. of Preachers, 1990–98. Hon. DLitt Greenwich, 1994. *Publications:* (contrib.) Unity: the next step?, 1972; God's Front Line, 1979; Parish Evangelism, 1980; Learning to Pray, 1981. *Recreations:* cricket, family life. *Address:* Auckland Castle, Bishop Auckland, Co. Durham DL14 7NR. *T:* (01388) 602576, *Fax:* (01388) 605264; *e-mail:* bishdur@btinternet.com. *Clubs:* Athenæum, MCC.

DURHAM, Dean of; *see* Arnold, Very Rev. J. R.

DURHAM, Archdeacon of; *see* Willmott, Ven. T.

DURHAM, John Clive; HM Diplomatic Service, retired; Ambassador to Mongolia, 1997–99; *b* 12 July 1939; *s* of Fred Durham and Eva Lucy (*née* Sykes); *m* 1962, Sandra Kay, (Shan), Beaumont; one *s* one *d*. *Educ:* Castleford Grammar Sch.; Leeds Coll. of Commerce. Min. of Pensions and Nat. Insce, 1955–67; joined HM Diplomatic Service, 1967: FCO, 1967–69; 3rd Sec., Wellington, NZ, 1969–72; Vice-Consul, Mogadishu, 1972–74; seconded to DTI, 1974–77; 2nd, later 1st Sec. (Commercial), Khartoum, 1977–81; Consul (Commercial), Frankfurt, 1981–86; FCO, 1986–93; Consul-Gen., Brisbane, 1993–97. *Recreations:* fell walking, travel, genealogy, steam locomotion. *Address:* 31 Crescent Wood Road, SE26 6SA. *Club:* Royal Over-Seas League.

DURHAM, Sir Kenneth, Kt 1985; Chairman: Unilever, 1982–86; Kingfisher (formerly Woolworth Holdings) plc, 1986–90 (non-executive Deputy Chairman, 1985–86); Deputy Chairman, British Aerospace, 1986–90 (Board Member, 1980–90); *b* 28 July 1924; *s* of late George Durham and Bertha (*née* Aspin); *m* 1946, Irene Markham; one *s* one *d*. *Educ:* Queen Elizabeth Grammar Sch., Blackburn; Univ. of Manchester (Hatfield Schol.; BSc Hons, Physics). Flight Lieut, RAF, 1942–46. ARE, Harwell, 1950; Unilever: joined Res. Lab., Port Sunlight, 1950, Head of Lab., 1961; Head, Res. Lab., Colworth, Bedford, 1965; assumed responsibility for animal feed interests, 1970; Chm., BOCM Silcock Ltd, 1971; Dir, Unilever Ltd, 1974, Vice-Chm., 1978; Dir, Unilever NV, 1974–86. Board Mem., Delta PLC, 1984–; Dir, Morgan Grenfell Hldgs, 1986–90. Chairman: Food, Drink and Packaging Machinery EDC, NEDO, 1981–86; Trade Policy Res. Centre, 1982–89; Industry and Commerce Liaison Cttee, Royal Jubilee Trusts, 1982–87; Economic and Financial Policy Cttee, CBI, 1983–86; Priorities Bd for Govt

Agricl Depts and AFRC, 1984–87; Member: British-N America Cttee, 1982–87; British Shippers Council, 1982–86; Bd, British Exec. Service Overseas, 1982–86; Adv. Cttee, CVCP, 1984–; Governing Body, ICC UK, 1984–88; ACARD, 1984–86; European Adv. Council, NY Stock Exchange, 1985–; Council for Industry and Higher Educn, 1985–; Adv. Panel, Science Policy Res. Unit, Sussex Univ., 1985–; Adv. Bd, Industrial Res. Labs, Durham Univ., 1985–; President: ABCC, 1986–87; BAAS, 1986–87. Attended Harvard Advanced Management Program, 1962; Member: Council, PSI, 1978–85; Council, Royal Free Hosp. Sch. of Med., 1984–. Vice-President: Liverpool Sch. of Tropical Medicine, 1982–; Opportunities for the Disabled, 1982–88; Help the Aged, 1986–; Trustee: Leverhulme Trust, 1974–98; Civic Trust, 1982–. Governor, NIESR, 1983–. CIMgt (CBIM 1978); FIGD 1983. Hon. FBA 1997. Hon. LLD Manchester, 1984; Hon. DSc: Loughborough, 1984; QUB. Comdr, Order of Orange Nassau (Netherlands), 1985. *Publications:* Surface Activity and Detergency, 1960; various scientific papers. *Recreations:* walking, golf. *Club:* Athenæum.

DURHAM, Kenneth John; Headmaster, University College School, since 1996; *b* 23 Oct. 1953; *s* of John Clifford Durham and Geraldine Mary Durham (*née* Trinder); *m* 1984, Vivienne Mary Johnson. *Educ:* St John's Sch., Leatherhead; Brasenose Coll., Oxford. St Albans Sch., 1975–87, Head of Econs, 1984–87; Head of Econs, 1987–92, Dir of Studies, 1991–96, King's Coll. Sch., Wimbledon. Chautauqua Bell Tower Scholarship to USA, ESU, 1989. *Publication:* The New City, 1992. *Recreations:* reading, theatre, music, film, walking, history of Polar exploration. *Address:* 5 Redington Road, Hampstead, NW3 7QX.

DURHAM HALL, Jonathan David; QC 1995; a Recorder, since 1995; *b* 2 June 1952; *s* of Peter David Hall and Muriel Ann Hall, Sheffield; *m* 1973, Patricia Helen Bychowski (marr. diss. 1995), *d* of Stefan Bychowski, Whitehaven; one *s* one *d*; *m* 1996, J. Hilary Hart, GRSM, LRAM, *d* of late Edgar Alfred Hart, Hants. *Educ:* King Edward VII Sch., Sheffield; Nottingham Univ. (LLB Hons). Called to the Bar, Gray's Inn, 1975; joined North Eastern Circuit, 1976: Junior, 1982; Cryer, 1990–95; Asst Recorder, 1991–95. Head of Chambers, 1993–. Mem., Bar Council, 1994–95. *Recreations:* the creation and preservation of woodland, Roman Britain, the plays of Shakespeare, ski-ing, all things Portuguese. *Address:* Old Bank House, Hartshead, Sheffield S1 2EL. *T:* (0114) 275 1223; Goldsmith Chambers, Temple, EC4Y 7BL. *T:* (020) 7353 6802.

DURIE, David Robert Campbell, CMG 1995; Governor and Commander-in-Chief, Gibraltar, since 2000; *b* 21 Aug. 1944; *s* of late Frederick Robert Edwin Durie and of Joan Elizabeth Campbell Durie (*née* Learoyd); *m* 1966, Susan Frances Weller; three *d*. *Educ:* Fettes Coll., Edinburgh; Christ Church, Oxford (MA Physics). Asst Principal, 1966, Pvte Sec. to Perm. Sec., 1970, Min. of Technology; Principal, DTI, 1971; First Sec., UK Delegn to OECD, 1974; Dept of Prices and Consumer Protection, 1977; Asst Sec., 1978; Dept of Trade, 1979; Cabinet Office, 1982; DTI, 1984; Under Sec., 1985–91; Dep. Sec., 1991; Minister and Dep. UK Perm. Rep. to EC/EU, Brussels, 1991–95; Dir Gen. (formerly Dep. Sec.), Enterprise and Regions, DTI, 1995–2000. FRSA 1996. KStJ 2000. *Recreations:* moderately strenuous outdoor exercise, theatre, admiring my grand daughter. *Address:* The Convent, Gibraltar, BFPO 52.
See also Maj.-Gen. I. G. C. Durie.

DURIE, Rev. Ian Geoffrey Campbell, CBE 1991 (OBE 1987); Curate, St Mark's, Battersea Rise, since 1998; *b* 21 Aug. 1944; *s* of late Frederick Robert Edwin Durie and of Joan Elizabeth Campbell Durie (*née* Learoyd); *m* 1968, Carolyn Jane Whitehead; one *d*. *Educ:* Fettes Coll., Edinburgh; RMA, Sandhurst; St John's Coll., Cambridge (MA Mech. Sci.); St John's Theol Coll., Nottingham. Commnd, RA; Adjt, 27 Field Regt, RA, 1973; sc 1974; Battery Comd, 29 Commando Regt, RA, 1979; SO1 Plans, Falklands Is, 1984; CO, 29 Commando Regt, RA, 1984; Instr, Staff Coll., 1987; Chief Instr, Tactics, Royal Sch. of Artillery, 1988; Commander: RA 1st Armd Div., 1989; RA 1st (UK) Armd Div. Artillery Gp, Op. Desert Sabre (Gulf War), 1991; rcds, 1992; Dir, Land Warfare, 1992; Dir, RA, 1994–96, retired in rank of Maj.-Gen. Col Comdt, RA, 1996–; Rep. Col Comdt, RA, 2001–02. Ordained deacon, 1998, priest, 1999. Hon. Exec. Chm., ACCTS Mil. Ministries Internat., 1998–; Patron, Christian Discovery Trust, Scotland, 1995–. *Recreations:* golf (of sorts), garden, fishing, family. *Address:* c/o St Mark's Church, Battersea Rise, SW11 1EJ. *Club:* Army and Navy.
See also D. R. C. Durie.

DURIE, Thomas Peter, MBE 1958; GM 1951; DL; Chairman, United Bristol Healthcare NHS Trust, 1991–94; *b* 1 Jan. 1926; *s* of Col Thomas Edwin Durie, DSO, MC, late RA and Madeleine Louise Durie; *m* 1st, 1952, Pamela Mary Bowlby (*d* 1982); one *s* one *d*; 2nd, 1983, Constance Christina Mary Linton. *Educ:* Fettes Coll.; Queen's Univ., Belfast. Commissioned RA 1945, served with RHA and Airborne Forces, India, Palestine, Cyprus, BAOR; Lt Col Directing Staff, Staff Coll., Camberley; retired 1964; Courage Ltd, 1964–86 (Main Bd Dir and Group Asst Man. Dir, 1974); Chm., Bristol & Weston DHA, 1986–90. University of Bristol: Mem. Court and Council, 1982–; Chm., Buildings Cttee, 1992–96; Pro-Chancellor, 1994–. Master, Soc. of Merchant Venturers, 1988–89. DL Avon, 1992–96, Somerset, 1996. *Recreations:* gardening, music, ski-ing, tennis. *Address:* Gatesgarth, Wrington, Somerset BS40 5QA. *Club:* Army and Navy.

DURKAN, (John) Mark; Member (SDLP) Foyle, since 1998, and Deputy First Minister, since 2001, Northern Ireland Assembly; Leader, Social Democratic and Labour Party, since 2001; *b* 26 June 1960; *s* of Brendan Durkan and Isobel Durkan (*née* Tinney); *m* 1993, Jackie Green. *Educ:* St Columb's Coll., Derry; Queen's Univ., Belfast. Asst to John Hume, 1984–98. Mem. (SDLP) Derry CC, 1993–2000. Member: Forum for Peace and Reconciliation, Dublin, 1994–96; NI Forum (Talks Negotiator), 1996–98. Minister of Finance and Personnel, NI Assembly, 1999–2001. Chairperson, SDLP, 1990–95. *Address:* (office) 7B Messines Terrace, Derry BT48 7QZ. *T:* (028) 7136 0700, *Fax:* (028) 7136 0808.

DURKIN, Air Marshal Sir Herbert, KBE 1976; CB 1973; MA; CEng, FIEE; Controller of Engineering and Supply (RAF), 1976–78; *b* 31 March 1922; *s* of Herbert and Helen Durkin, Burnley, Lancs; *m* 1951, Dorothy Hope, *d* of Walter Taylor Johnson, Burnley; one *s* two *d*. *Educ:* Burnley Grammar Sch.; Emmanuel Coll., Cambridge (MA). Commissioned into Tech. Br., RAF, Oct. 1941. Served War, with No 60 Gp, until 1945. India, 1945–47, becoming ADC to AOC-in-C India; Central Bomber Estabt, 1947–50; Sqdn Ldr, 1950; Atomic Weapons Research Estabt, 1950–52; RAF Staff Coll., 1953; Chief Signals Officer, AHQ, Iraq, 1954–56; Wing Comdr, Chief Instr of Signals Div. of RAF Tech. Coll., 1956–58; Air Ministry, 1958–60; jssc, 1961; HQ, 2 ATAF, 1961–63; Gp Capt 1962; Sen. Tech. Staff Officer, HQ Signals Command, 1964–65; Comdt, No 2 Sch. of Tech. Trg, Cosford, 1965–67; Air Cdre, 1967; Director of Eng (Policy), MoD, 1967–69; IDC, 1970; AOC No 90 Group, RAF, 1971–73; Dir-Gen. Engineering and Supply Management, 1973–76. Pres., IEE, 1980 (Dep. Pres., 1979). Pres., Assoc. of Lancastrians in London, 1988–90. Freeman, City of London, 1988. *Recreation:* golf. *Address:* Willowbank, Drakes Drive, Northwood, Middlesex HA6 2SL. *T:* (01923) 823167. *Club:* Royal Air Force.

DURLACHER, Nicholas John, CBE 1995; Chairman, Elexon Ltd, since 2000; *b* 20 March 1946; *s* of late John Sidney Durlacher, MC and of Alma Gabrielle (*née* Adams); *m* 1971, Mary Caroline Mclaren; one *s*. *Educ:* Stowe; Magdalene Coll., Cambridge (BA Econs). Mem., Stock Exchange, 1970–; Partner, Wedd Durlacher, 1972–86; Director: BZW Ltd, 1986–98; BZW Futures, 1986–96; Chairman: Ennismore Smaller Cos Fund, 1999–; EMX, 2000–; BSC Co. Ltd, 2000–; Ffastfill, 2000–. Dir, 1984–96, Chm., 1992–95, LIFFE; Dir, 1987–95, Chm., 1995–2001, SFA; Dir, Investor's Compensation Scheme, 1992–2001; Chm., Balancing and Settlement Code Panel, 2000–. Trustee, British Brain and Spine Foundn, 1994–. *Recreations:* ski-ing, golf, tennis. *Address:* 10 Rutland Street, SW7 1EH. *Clubs:* White's; Hawks.

DURMAN, David John; Editor-in-Chief, IPC Magazines, 1994–99; *b* 10 July 1948; *s* of late John Durman and of Joan Durman; *m* 1973, Hilary Pamela Aldrick. *Educ:* Leeds Univ. (BA). Editor, Woman, 1988–94; Dep. Editor, Woman's Own, 1992–94. Chm., BSME, 1996. *Recreations:* reading, theatre, life. *Address:* c/o IPC Magazines, Stamford Street, SE1 9LS. *T:* (020) 7261 6401.

DURNING, Josephine Marie; Director, Transdepartmental Group, Office of Science and Technology, Department of Trade and Industry, since 1998; *b* 27 Aug. 1952; *d* of Cecil and Isobel M. Durning; *m* 1984, Paul Stephen Capella; one *s* one *d*. *Educ:* Loreto Coll., St Albans; Univ. of Keele (BA Hons Eng. and Politics 1974). Entered CS as admin trainee, 1974; Private Sec. to Parly Under-Sec. of State, Dept of Employment, 1978–79; Sec. to HSE, 1982–85; Labour Attaché, Paris, 1985–89; Head of Sen. Mgt Support Unit, Dept of Employment, 1990–91; Head of Internat. and Gen. Policy, HSE, 1991–96; with Econ. and Domestic Secretariat, Cabinet Office, 1996–98. FRSA 2000. *Recreation:* family life. *Address:* Office of Science and Technology, Department of Trade and Industry, Albany House, 94-98 Petty France, SW1H 9ST. *T:* (020) 7271 2020.

DURR, Hon. Kent Diederich Skelton; MP (NCOP) (African Christian Democratic Party) for Western Cape Province, South Africa, since 1999; *b* 28 March 1941; *s* of Dr John Michael Durr and Diana (*née* Skelton); *m* 1966, Suzanne Wiese; one *s* two *d*. *Educ:* South African Coll. Schs; Cape Town Univ. Dir, family publishing co., 1966–68; Founder and later Man. Dir, Durr Estates, 1968–84. Elected to Provincial Council of Cape, 1974; MP for Maitland, SA, 1977–91; Dep. Minister, Trade and Industry, 1984–86, Finance, 1984–88; Minister of Budget and Public Works in Ministers' Council, 1988–89; Cabinet Minister of Trade and Industry and Tourism, 1989–91; S African Ambassador to UK, 1991–94; High Comr for S Africa in London, 1994–95. Chairman: Fuel-Tech NV, 1995–97; Clean Diesel Technologies, Inc., 1995–97; Commonwealth Investment Guarantee Agency Ltd, 1997–99. Mem., SA Nat. Foundn for Conservation of Coastal Birds, 1985 (Award of Honour, 1987). Freeman: City of London, 1995; Vintners' Co., 1995. *Publications:* numerous articles in newspapers and jls on econs, foreign affairs, constitutional affairs, urban renewal, conservation and business. *Recreations:* history, field sports, conservation. *Address:* Houses of Parliament, PO Box 15, Cape Town 800, South Africa. *Club:* Kelvin Grove (Cape Town, SA).

DURRANDS, Prof. Kenneth James, CBE 1992; DGS (Birm), MSc, CEng, FIMechE, FIEE; Vice-Chancellor and Rector, University of Huddersfield, 1992–95 (Rector, The Polytechnic, Huddersfield, 1970–92; Professor, 1985); *b* 24 June 1929; *s* of A. J. Durrands, Croxton Kerrial; *m* 1956 (marr. diss. 1971); one *s*; *m* 1983, Jennifer Jones; one *s*. *Educ:* King's Sch., Grantham; Nottingham Technical Coll.; Birmingham Univ. Min. of Supply Engrg Apprentice, ROF, Nottingham, 1947–52; Techn. Engr, UKAEA, Risley, 1954–58; Lecturer in Mechanical and Nuclear Engrg, Univ. of Birmingham, 1958–61; Head of Gen. Engrg Dept, Reactor Engrg Lab., UKAEA, Risley, 1961–67; Technical Dir, Vickers Ltd, Barrow Engrg Works, 1967–70. Vis. Lectr, Manchester Univ., 1962–68. Member: DoI Educn and Training Cttee, 1973–75 (Chm., 1975–80); DoI Garment & Allied Industries Requirements Bd, 1975–79 (Chm. Computer Cttee, 1975–79); BEC Educn Cttee, 1975–79; BEC Business Studies Bd, 1976–79; Inter-Univ. and Polytech. Council, 1978–81; Yorks Consumers' Cttee, Office of Electricity Regulation, 1990–94; British Council: Higher Educn Cttee, 1981–91; Engrg and Technology Adv. Cttee, 1981–90; Cttee, CICHE, 1985–95; Council for the Accreditation of Teacher Educn, 1991–92; Hon. Sec./Treas., Cttee of Dirs of Polytechnics, 1970–79. Educn Comr, MSC, subseq. Training Commn, 1986–89. Mem. Council, IMechE, 1963–66. Preliminary Judge, Prince of Wales Award for Industrial Innovation and Production, 1982–95. Member, Court: Leeds Univ., 1970–95; Bradford Univ., 1973–95; Mem. Council, Barnsley Coll., 1996–; Governor, King's Sch., Grantham, 1999–. *Publications:* technical and policy papers. *Recreations:* gardening, squash rackets. *Address:* Church Cottage, Croxton Kerrial, Grantham, Lincolnshire NG32 1PY. *Club:* Athenæum.

DURRANT, His Honour Anthony Harrisson; a Circuit Judge, 1991–99; *b* 3 Jan. 1931; *s* of Frank Baston Durrant and Irene Maud Durrant; *m* 1956, Jacqueline Ostroumoff; one *s* two *d*. *Educ:* Sir Joseph Williamson Mathematical Sch., Rochester. Admitted Solicitor, 1956; Partner, 1960, Sen. Partner, 1976–91, Horwood & James, Aylesbury; a Recorder, 1987–91. Dep. Chm., Agricl Land Tribunal, 1987–91. Pres., Berks, Bucks and Oxon Incorp. Law Soc., 1977–78; Chm., Berks, Bucks and Oxon Jt Consultative Cttee of Barristers and Solicitors, 1985–91. *Recreations:* reading, boating.
See also A. J. Trace.

DURRANT, Jennifer Ann, RA 1994; painter; part-time Lecturer: Royal College of Art, since 1979; Royal Academy Schools, since 1991; *b* 17 June 1942; *d* of Caleb John Durrant and Winifred May (*née* Wright); *m* 1964, William Alistair Herriot Henderson (marr. diss. 1976); *m* 2000, Richard Alban Howard Oxby. *Educ:* Varndean Grammar Sch. for Girls, Brighton; Brighton Coll. of Art; Slade Sch. of Fine Art; University Coll. London (Dip. Fine Art). FRCA 1993. Postgrad. Scholar, Slade Sch. of Fine Art, 1965–66. Artist in Residence, Somerville Coll., Oxford, 1979–80. *Solo exhibitions* include: Arnolfini Gall., Bristol, 1979; Mus. of Modern Art, Oxford, 1980; Nicola Jacobs Gall., London, 1982 and 1983; Serpentine Gall., 1987; Concourse Gall., Barbican, 1992; Salander-O'Reilly Galls, NY, 1993; *group exhibitions* include: Hayward Gall., 1976, 1979, 1980 and 1990; Mus. of Fine Art, Boston, Mass and Royal Acad., 1977; Salander-O'Reilly Galls, NY, 1981; Tate Gall. and Carnegie Inst., Pittsburgh, 1982; Serpentine Gall., 1983 and 1984; Royal Acad., 1985; Mall Galls, London, 1990–92; also in provincial galls in UK, and in Europe; has exhibited at Royal Acad. Summer Exhibn, 1986, 1987 and annually, 1989–; *works in public collections* including: Arts Council, British Council; Contemporary Art Soc.; Mus. of Fine Arts, Boston, Mass; Tate Gall.; Govt Art Collection; Neue Galerie, Aachen; *commissions:* Newham Hosp.; R. P. Scherer 50th Anniv., Swindon, 1987; Thomas Neal, Covent Gdn, 1992; Glaxo UK, Stevenage, 1994. Arts Council Award, 1976; Arts Council Major Award, 1978; Gtr London Arts Assoc. Award, 1980; Athena Art Award, 1988. *Recreations:* classical music, opera, archaeology, museums, painting and sculpture, looking at nature. *Address:* 9–10 Holly Grove, SE15 5DF. *T:* (020) 7639 6424.

DURRANT, Sir William (Alexander Estridge), 8th Bt *cr* 1784, of Scottow, Norfolk; *b* 26 Nov. 1929; *o s* of Sir William Henry Estridge Durrant, 7th Bt and Georgina Beryl Gwendoline (*d* 1968), *d* of Alexander Purse; *S* father, 1994; *m* 1953, Dorothy, *d* of Ronal

Croker, Quirindi, NSW; one *s* one *d. Heir: s* David Alexander Durrant, *b* 1 July 1960. *Address:* Red Hill, Nundle Road, Nemingha, NSW 2340, Australia.

DURWARD, (Alan) Scott; JP; Director, 1985–91, and Group Chief Executive, 1989–91, Alliance & Leicester Building Society; Chairman, Girobank Plc, 1990–91; *b* 30 Aug. 1935; *o c* of late Prof. Archibald Durward, MD and Dorothy Durward; *m* 1962, Helen Gourlay; two *s. Educ:* Stowe; St John's Coll., Cambridge (MA). Imperial Tobacco Co. Ltd, 1958–65; Rowntree & Co. Ltd, 1965–67; Cheltenham & Gloucester Bldg Soc., 1967–75; Leicester Building Society: Dep. Gen. Man., 1975–77; Gen. Man., 1977–81; Dir and Chief Gen. Man., 1981–85; merger with Alliance Bldg Soc. to form Alliance & Leicester Bldg Soc., 1985; Jt Chief Gen. Manager, 1985–86; Chief Gen. Manager, 1986–89. Chm., Midland Assoc. of Bldg Socs, 1984–85; Member: Council, Bldg Socs Assoc., 1981–85 and 1987–91; Council, Eur. Fedn of Bldg Socs, 1987–91. Director: Gourlay Properties, 1985–99; John Laing plc, 1987–89; Mem. Bd, BR (London Midland), 1990–92. Dir, Leics Ambulance and Paramedic Service NHS Trust, 1993–99. General Comr for Income Tax, 1994–. Chm., Peterborough Diocesan Bd of Finance, 1993–. Mem. Council, Loughborough Univ. of Technology, 1984–97 (Treas., 1991–97). JP Leicester, 1999. *Recreations:* tennis, fishing. *Address:* The Old House, Medbourne, Market Harborough, Leics LE16 8DX. *Club:* Oxford and Cambridge.

DUTHIE, Prof. Sir Herbert Livingston, Kt 1987; MD; FRCS, FRCSEd; Provost of the University of Wales College of Medicine (formerly the Welsh National School of Medicine, University of Wales), 1979–94; *b* 9 Oct. 1929; *s* of Herbert William Duthie and Margaret McFarlane Livingston; *m* 1959, Maureen McCann; three *s* one *d. Educ:* Whitehill Sch., Glasgow; Univ. of Glasgow (MB, ChB 1952; MD Hons 1962; ChM Hons 1959). FRCSEd 1956; FRCS 1957. Served RAMC, 1954–56. Sen. House Officer, Registrar, and Lectr in Surgery, Western Infirmary, Glasgow, 1956–59; Rockefeller Travelling Fellow, Mayo Clinic, Rochester, Minn, USA, 1959–60; Lectr in Surg., Univ. of Glasgow, 1960–61; Sen. Lectr in Surg., Univ. of Leeds, 1961–63, Reader, 1964; Prof. of Surg., Univ. of Sheffield, 1964–79 (Dean, Faculty of Medicine, 1976–78). Mem., S Glam HA, 1980–94. Chm., Med. Adv. Cttee, CVCP, 1992–93. President: Surgical Res. Soc., 1978–80; Assoc. of Surgeons of GB and Ireland, 1989–90; Member: GMC, 1976–99 (Treas., 1981–94); Welsh Med. Cttee, 1980–94. Hon. LLD: Sheffield, 1990; Wales, 1995. *Publications:* articles on gastroenterological topics. *Address:* 1 The Malverns, Malvern Place, Cheltenham GL50 2JL. *T:* (01242) 583938. *Club:* Army and Navy.

DUTHIE, Prof. Robert Buchan, CBE 1984; MA Oxon, MB, ChM; FRCSE, FRCS; Nuffield Professor of Orthopædic Surgery, Oxford University, 1966–92, now Emeritus; Professorial Fellow, Worcester College, Oxford, 1966–92, now Emeritus Fellow; Surgeon, Nuffield Orthopædic Centre, Oxford, 1966–92; Civilian Consultant Adviser in Orthopaedic Surgery to Royal Navy, since 1978; *b* 4 May 1925; 2nd *s* of late James Andrew Duthie and late Elizabeth Jean Duthie, Edinburgh; *m* 1956, Alison Ann Macpherson Kittermaster, MA; two *s* two *d. Educ:* Aberdeen Grammar Sch.; King Edward VI Gram. Sch., Chelmsford; Heriot-Watt Coll., Edinburgh; University of Edinburgh Med. Sch. Robert Jones Prize 1947, MB, ChB 1948, ChM (with dist.) (Gold Medal for Thesis) 1956, University of Edinburgh; FRCSE 1953; Hon. FACS 1987. Ho. Surg., Royal Infirmary, 1948–49; Ho. Phys., Western Gen. Hosp., Edinburgh, 1949. Active service in Malaya, RAMC, 1949–51. Registrar, Royal Infirmary, Edinburgh, 1951–53; David Wilkie Res. Schol. of University of Edinburgh, 1953; Res. Fellow of Scottish Hosps Endowment Research Trust, Edinburgh, 1953–56; Res. Fellow, Nat. Cancer Inst., Bethesda, USA, 1956–57; Extern. Mem. of MRC in Inst. of Orthopædics, London and Sen. Registrar, 1957–58; Prof. of Orthopædic Surg., University of Rochester Sch. of Medicine and Dentistry and Orthopædic Surg.-in-Chief, University of Rochester Med. Centre, 1958–66. Consultant Adviser in Orthopaedics and Accident Surgery to DHSS, 1971–80. Mem., Royal Commn on Civil Liability and Compensation for Personal Injury, 1973–78; Chairman: Adv. Cttee of Res. in Artificial Limbs and Appliances, DHSS, 1975; Working Party on Orthopaedic Services to Sec. of State for Social Services, 1980–81. Governor, Oxford Sch. for Boys, 1967–91 (Chm., 1986–91). Fellow Brit. Orthopædic Assoc. (Pres., 1983–84); Pres., Internat. Soc. of Research in Orthopaedics and Trauma, 1987–90; Member: Internat. Soc. for Orthopædic Surgery and Traumatology; Orthopædic Research Soc.; Inter-urban Orthopædic Club: Internat. Orthopædic Club. Amer. Rheumatism Assoc.; Hon. Member: Portuguese Soc. of Orthopaedic Surgery and Traumatology; Japanese Orthopaedic Assoc.; Corresponding Member: Assoc. of Orthopaedic Surgery and Traumatology, Yugoslavia; German Soc. of Orthopaedics and Traumatology; Hon. Fellow, Austrian Traumatology Assoc. Hon. DSc Rochester, NY, 1982. President's Prize, Soc. Internat. de Chirurgie, 1957. Commander, SMO, Malta. *Publications:* (co-author) Textbook of Orthopædic Surgery, 8th edn, 1983, 9th edn, 1996; contribs to med. and surg. jls relating to genetics, histochemistry, transplantation, pathology, neoplasia of musculo-skeletal tissues, and clinical subjects. *Recreations:* writing, stained glass. *Address:* Barna Brow, Harberton Mead, Headington, Oxford OX3 0DB. *T:* (01865) 762745.

DUTHIE, Sir Robert Grieve, (Sir Robin), Kt 1987; CBE 1978; CA; Vice Chairman, Advisory Board for Scotland, BP Amoco, since 1990; *b* 2 Oct. 1928; *s* of George Duthie and Mary (*née* Lyle); *m* 1955, Violetta Noel Maclean; two *s* one *d. Educ:* Greenock Academy. Apprentice Chartered Accountant with Thomson Jackson Gourlay & Taylor, CA, 1946–51 (CA 1952); joined Blacks of Greenock, 1952: Man. Dir, 1962; Chairman: Black & Edgington Ltd, 1972–83; Insight Internat. Tours Ltd, 1979–94; Bruntons (Musselburgh), 1984–86; Britoil, 1988–90; Tay Residential Investment Ltd, 1989–96; Neill Clerk Gp plc, 1994–98; Director: British Assets Trust, 1977–98; Royal Bank of Scotland, 1978–99; Investors Capital Trust, 1985–94; Carclo Engineering Gp, 1986–98; British Polythene Industries (formerly Scott & Robinson), 1989–99; Devol Engineering Ltd, 1994–. Chm., Greenock Provident Bank, 1974; Dir, Greenock Chamber of Commerce, 1967–68; Tax Liaison Officer for Scotland, CBI, 1976–79. Chm., SDA, 1979–88; Member: Scottish Telecommunications Bd, 1972–77; E Kilbride Develt Corp., 1976–78; Clyde Port Authority, 1971–83 (Chm., 1977–80); Council, Inst. of Chartered Accountants of Scotland, 1973–78; Scottish Econ. Council, 1980–95; Council, Strathclyde Business Sch., 1986–94; Governing Council, Scottish Business in the Community, 1987–95. Chm., Made Up Textiles Assoc. of GB, 1972; Pres., Inverkip Soc., 1966; Mem. of Council, Royal Caledonian Curling Club, 1985–88. Commissioner: Queen Victoria Sch., Dunblane, 1972–89; Scottish Congregational Ministers Pension Fund, 1973–; Treasurer, Nelson Street Evangelical Union Congregational Church, Greenock, 1970–. Fellow, Scottish Vocational Council, 1988. CIMgt (CBIM 1976); FRSA 1983. Hon. FRIAS, 1989. Hon. Fellow, Paisley Coll., 1990. Hon. LLD Strathclyde, 1984; Hon. DTech Napier Coll., 1989. *Recreations:* curling, golf. *Address:* Fairhaven, Finnart Street, Greenock PA16 8JA. *T:* (01475) 722642.

DUTTON, Maj.-Gen. Bryan Hawkins, CB 1997; CBE 1990 (OBE 1984; MBE 1978); Director-General, Leonard Cheshire Foundation, since 1998; *b* 1 March 1943; *s* of late Ralph Dutton and Honor Badcoe (formerly Dutton, *née* Morris); *m* 1972, Angela Margaret Wilson; one *s* one *d. Educ:* Lord Weymouth Sch.; RMA Sandhurst. Commissioned, Devonshire and Dorset Regt, 1963; served NI, British Guiana, Libya, Belize, Germany, UK; Instructor, Sch. of Infantry, 1969–71; RMCS and Staff Coll., 1974–75; C-in-C's Mission to Soviet Forces in Germany, 1976–78; Co. Comdr, 1st Devonshire and Dorset, 1978–79 (despatches 1979); Planning Staff, NI Office, 1979–81; Instructor, Staff Coll., 1981–82; MA to Adjutant-Gen., 1982–84; CO 1st Bn Devonshire and Dorset Regt, 1984–87; Ops Staff, UKLF, 1987; Comdr 39 Infantry Brigade, 1987–89; Dir, Public Relations (Army), 1990–92; Dir of Infantry, 1992–94; Comdr British Forces, Hong Kong, 1994–97. Col Comdt, POW Div., 1996–99; Col, Devonshire and Dorset Regt, 1998–. Gov., Hayes Dashwood Foundn, 1999–. *Recreations:* offshore sailing, fishing, wild-life, Rugby spectator, history, classical music. *Address:* (office) 30 Millbank, SW1P 4QD. *Club:* Army and Navy. *Club:* 1993.

DUTTON, James Macfarlane; HM Diplomatic Service, retired; *b* 3 June 1922; *s* of late H. St J. Dutton and Mrs E. B. Dutton; *m* 1958, Jean Mary McAvoy; one *s. Educ:* Winchester Coll.; Balliol Coll., Oxford. Dominions Office, 1944–46; Private Sec. to Permanent Under Sec., 1945; Dublin, 1946–48; CRO, 1948–50; Asst Private Sec. to Sec. of State, 1948; 2nd Sec., New Delhi, 1950–53; CRO, 1953–55; 1st Sec., Dacca and Karachi, 1955–58, Canberra, 1958–62; Head of Constitutional and Protocol Dept, CRO, 1963–65; Canadian Nat. Defence Coll., 1965–66; Dep. High Comr and Counsellor (Commercial), Colombo, 1966–70; Head of Rhodesia Econ. Dept, FCO, 1970–72; attached CSD, 1972–73; seconded to: British Electrical & Allied Manufacturers Assoc. (Dir, Overseas Affairs), 1973–74; Wilton Park and European Discussion Centre, 1974–75; Consul-Gen., Gothenburg, 1975–78. *Recreations:* golf, trout-fishing. *Address:* Cockerhurst, Tyrrells Wood, Leatherhead, Surrey KT22 8QH.

DUTTON, Prof. Peter Leslie, FRS 1990; Professor of Biochemistry and Biophysics, since 1981 (Chairman, Department of Biochemistry and Biophysics, since 1994), and Director, Johnson Foundation for Molecular Biophysics, since 1991, University of Pennsylvania; *b* 12 March 1941; *s* of Arthur Bramwell Dutton and Mary Dutton; *m* 1965, Dr Julia R. Dwyer; two *s* one *d. Educ:* Univ. of Wales (BSc Hons Chem.; PhD Biochem.). PD Fellow, Dept of Biochem. and Soil Science, Univ. of Wales, 1967–68; University of Pennsylvania: PD Fellow, 1968–71, Asst Prof., 1971–76, Johnson Res. Foundn; Associate Prof., Dept of Biochem. and Biophysics, 1976–81; Hon. MA 1976. *Recreations:* painting (several one-man and group shows in Wales and USA), sailing. *Address:* B501 Richards Building, 37th and Hamilton Walk, University of Pennsylvania, Philadelphia, PA 19104, USA; 654 West Rose Tree Road, Media, PA 19063, USA. *T:* (215) 8980991, *Fax:* (215) 5732235. *Clubs:* Mantoloking Yacht (NJ); Corinthian Yacht (Philadelphia).

DUTTON, Reginald David Ley; *b* 20 Aug. 1916; *m* 1951, Pamela Jean (*née* Harrison); two *s* one *d. Educ:* Magdalen Coll. Sch., Oxford. Joined OUP; subseq. joined leading British advertising agency, London Press Exchange (now Lopex plc), 1937. During War of 1939–45 served in Royal Navy. Returned to agency after his service; there, he worked on many of major accounts; Dir, 1954; Man. Dir and Chief Exec., 1964–71; Chm., 1971–76; retired 1976. Pres. Inst. Practitioners in Advertising, 1969–71; Chm., Jt Ind. Council for TV Advertising Research, 1973–75; Mem. Council, BIM, 1970–74; FIPA 1960. Councillor, Canterbury CC, 1976–77. *Recreations:* fishing, amateur radio. *Address:* Butts Fold, Stalham Road, Hoveton, Norwich NR12 8DU. *T:* (01603) 783145.

DUTTON, Roger Thomas; His Honour Judge Dutton; a Circuit Judge, since 1996; *b* 24 March 1952; *s* of Donald Roger Dutton and Doreen May Dutton (*née* Ankers); *m* 1977, Elaine Alison Dixon; one *s* two *d. Educ:* Acton Sch., Wrexham; Grove Park Grammar Sch., Wrexham; Univ. of Kent (BA Hons Law 1973). Called to the Bar, Middle Temple, 1974; in practice at the Bar, 1974–96; Mem., Wales and Chester Circuit; Asst Recorder, 1988–92; Recorder, 1992–96. Liaison Judge, N Wales Magistrates, 1998–. *Recreations:* golf, walking, travel, gardening, watching cricket, soccer, Rugby Union. *Address:* The Crown Court, The Castle, Chester CH1 2AN. *T:* (01244) 317606. *Clubs:* Lansdowne; Chester City; Wrexham Golf.

DUTTON, Timothy James; QC 1998; a Recorder, since 2000; *b* 25 Feb. 1957; *s* of J. D. Dutton, MA, JP and J. R. Dutton (*née* Parsons); *m* 1987, Sappho Raschid-Dias; one *d. Educ:* Repton Sch.; Keble Coll., Oxford (BA Jurisp. 1978). Called to the Bar, Middle Temple, 1979; an Asst Recorder, 1998–2000. Advocacy teaching, for Nat. Inst. for Trial Advocacy and the Bar, UK and USA, 1987–. Chm., Inns of Court Advocacy Trng Cttee, 2000–. Member: Admin. Law Bar Assoc.; Commercial Bar Assoc. *Publications:* contribs to Lloyds List, Financial Times, (on insce law) World Policy Review Guide. *Recreations:* music (French Horn), sailing. *Address:* Fountain Court, Temple, EC4Y 9DH. *T:* (020) 7583 3335.

DUVAL, Robin Arthur Philip; Director, British Board of Film Classification, since 1999; *b* 28 April 1941; *s* of Arthur and Jane Duval; *m* 1968, Lorna Eileen Watson; four *d* (one *s* decd). *Educ:* King Edward's Sch., Birmingham; University Coll. London (BA); Univ. of Michigan. Studio manager, BBC, 1964–65; TV producer, J. Walter Thompson, 1965–68; documentary and film producer, COI, 1968–81; Principal, Home Office, 1981–83; Hd, UK Prodn, COI, 1983–85; Chief Asst, Television, IBA, 1985–90; Dep. Dir, Programmes, ITC, 1991–99. *Recreations:* music, food, Aston Villa. *Address:* British Board of Film Classification, 3 Soho Square, W1V 6HD. *T:* (020) 7440 3280.

DUVALL, Leonard, OBE 1998; Member (Lab) Greenwich and Lewisham, London Assembly, Greater London Authority, since 2000; Vice Chairman, London Development Agency, since 2000; *b* 26 Sept. 1961; *m* (separated); two *s. Educ:* Hawthorn Sch., London. Mem., Greenwich LBC, 1990–2000 (Leader of Council, 1992–2000). Chairman: London Thames Gateway Partnership, 1997–2000; Local Govt Improvement and Develt Agency, 1998–2000; Dep. Chm., Assoc. of London Govt, 1996–2000; Vice Chm., Commonwealth Local Govt Forum, 1998–. *Address:* Greater London Authority, Romney House, 43 Marsham Street, SW1P 3PY. *T:* (020) 7983 4372.

DUXBURY, Philip Thomas; Chairman, Bradford and Bingley Building Society, 1988–91; *b* 4 Sept. 1928; *s* of Tom Duxbury and Ellen Duxbury (*née* Hargreaves); *m* 1952, Katherine Mary Hagley; three *s. Educ:* Bradford Grammar School. Magnet and Southerns plc, 1944–84 (Dir, 1963; Man. Dir, 1975); Dir, Bradford and Bingley Building Soc., 1980–91. *Recreations:* DIY, travel. *Address:* Highfield House, East Morton, Keighley BD20 5SE. *T:* (01274) 564894.

DWEK, Prof. Raymond Allen, DPhil, DSc; FRS 1998; CChem, FRSC; CBiol, FIBiol; Professor of Glycobiology, and Director of Glycobiology Institute (formerly Unit), University of Oxford, since 1988; Professorial Fellow, Exeter College, Oxford, since 1988 (Fellow, 1974–88); *b* 10 Nov. 1941; *s* of Victor Joe Dwek and Alice Liniado; *m* 1964, Sandra (*née* Livingstone); two *s* two *d. Educ:* Carmel Coll.; Manchester Univ. (BSc 1st Cl. Hons Chemistry and Mercer Scholar, 1963; MSc 1964); Lincoln Coll., Oxford (DPhil 1966); Exeter Coll., Oxford (DSc 1985). CChem, FRSC 1993; CBiol, FIBiol 1999. Oxford University: Deptl Demonstrator, 1969–74, Lectr, 1976–88, Associate Hd of Dept, 1996–, Biochem. Dept; Royal Soc. Locke Res. Fellow, 1974–76; Christ Church: Res. Lectr in Physical Chemistry, 1966–68, in Biochem., 1975–76; Lectr in Inorganic Chem., 1968–75; Lectr in Biochem., Trinity Coll., 1976–84. Vis. Royal Soc. Res. Fellow,

Weizmann Inst., Rehovot, Israel, 1969; Visiting Professor: Duke Univ., NC, seconded to Inst. of Exploratory Res., Fort Monmouth, NJ, 1968; Univ. of Trieste, Italy, 1974; Univ. of Lund, Sweden, 1977; Inst. of Enzymology, Budapest, 1980. Dir and Founding Scientist, Oxford GlycoScience (formerly Oxford GlycoSystems) Ltd, 1988–. Member: Oxford Enzyme Gp, 1971–88; MRC AIDS Antiviral Steering Cttee, 1987–89; Founder Mem., Oxford Oligosaccharide Gp, 1983. Mem., editl bds. Wellcome Trust Award, for research in biochemistry related to medicine, 1994. Hon. Dr Leuven, 1996. First Scientific Leadership Award, Hepatitis B Foundn, Philadelphia, 1997; Centennial Award, Delaware Valley Coll., Penn, 1997. *Publications:* Nuclear Magnetic Resonance (NMR) in Biochemistry, 1973; (jtly) Physical Chemistry Principles and Problems for Biochemists, 1975, 3rd edn 1983; (jtly) NMR in Biology, 1977; (jtly) Biological Spectroscopy, 1984; articles in books and jls on physical chemistry, biochemistry and medicine; various patents. *Recreations:* family, Patent Law, sport, sailing, listening to music. *Address:* Exeter College, Oxford OX1 3DP. *T:* (01865) 275344; Glycobiology Institute, Department of Biochemistry, University of Oxford, South Parks Road, Oxford OX1 3QU.

DWIGHT, Reginald Kenneth; *see* John, Sir E. H.

DWORKIN, Prof. Gerald; Herbert Smith Professor of European Law and Director, Centre of European Law, King's College, University of London, 1993–97, now Professor Emeritus; *b* 8 July 1933; *s* of Louis and Rose Dworkin; *m* 1960, Celia Sharon Levin; two *s* one *d*. *Educ:* Raines Grammar Sch., London; Univ. of Nottingham (LLB 1954). Admitted solicitor of Supreme Court, 1957; Asst Lectr, Lectr, then Reader, LSE, 1958–67; Prof. of Law, Univ. of Southampton, 1968–86; Herchel Smith Prof. of Intellectual Property Law, QMW, Univ. of London, 1986–92. Visiting Professor: Univ. of Monash, 1965–67, 1980, 1987; Univ. of NSW, 1975; Nat. Univ. of Singapore, 1985, 1991, 1997; Arizona State Univ., 1985. Mem., EC Cttee, Academic Experts on Copyright Law. Member: Council, Intellectual Property Inst. (formerly Common Law Inst. of Intellectual Property); Brit. Literary and Artistic Copyright Soc.; Law Soc. Sub-cttee on Intellectual Property. Chm., British Copyright Council. FRSA 1993. Member of Board: Mod. Law Rev.; European Intellectual Property Law Rev.; Intellectual Property Jl. *Publication:* (with R. Taylor) Guide to Copyright Law, 1989. *Address:* Rosebery, 7A Branksome Wood Road, Bournemouth, Dorset BH2 6BT. *T:* (01202) 555522.
See also P. D. Dworkin.

DWORKIN, Paul David, FSS; an Assistant Director, Central Statistical Office, 1989–91; *b* 7 April 1937; *s* of Louis and Rose Dworkin; *m* 1959, Carole Barbara Burke; two *s*. *Educ:* Hackney Downs Grammar Sch., London; LSE (BScEcon 1958). FSS 1969. E Africa High Commn, Dar es Salaam, Tanganyika, 1959; E African Common Services Org., Nairobi, Kenya, 1961; Asst Statistician, BoT, 1962, Stat. 1965; Chief Statistician: DTI, 1972; Dept of Employment, 1977; Under Secretary: Depts of Trade and Industry, 1977–81; Central Statistical Office, 1982–83; Dir of Stats, Dept of Employment, 1983–89. *Recreations:* golf, bowling.
See also G. Dworkin.

DWORKIN, Prof. Ronald Myles, FBA 1979; Quain Professor of Jurisprudence, University College London, since 1998; *b* 11 Dec. 1931; *s* of David Dworkin and Madeline Talamo; *m* 1958, Betsy Celia Ross (*d* 2000); one *s* one *d*. *Educ:* Harvard Coll.; Oxford Univ.; Harvard Law Sch. Legal Sec. to Judge Learned Hand, 1957–58; Associate, Sullivan & Cromwell, New York, 1958–62; Yale Law School: Associate Prof. of Law, 1962–65; Prof. of Law, 1965–68; Wesley N. Hohfeld Prof. of Jurisprudence, 1968–69; Prof. of Jurisprudence, Oxford Univ., 1969–98, now Emeritus; Fellow of UC, Oxford, 1969–98, now Emeritus. Vis. Prof. of Philosophy, Princeton Univ., 1974–75; Prof. of Law, 1975–, Sommer Prof. of Law and Philosophy, 1984–, NY Univ. Law Sch.; Prof.-at-Large, Cornell Univ., 1976–80; Vis. Prof. of Philosophy and Law, Harvard Univ., 1977, Vis. Prof. of Philosophy, 1979–82. Member: Council, Writers & Scholars Educnl Trust, 1982–; Programme Cttee, Ditchley Foundn, 1982–. Co-Chm., US Democratic Party Abroad, 1972–76. Fellow, Amer. Acad. of Arts and Scis, 1979. Hon. QC 1998. Hon. Bencher, Middle Temple, 1999. *Publications:* Taking Rights Seriously, 1977; (ed) The Philosophy of Law, 1977; A Matter of Principle, 1985; Law's Empire, 1986; Philosophical Issues in Senile Dementia, 1987; A Bill of Rights for Britain, 1990; Life's Dominion, 1993; Freedom's Law, 1996; Sovereign Virtue, 2000; several articles in legal and philosophical jls. *Address:* 17 Chester Row, SW1W 9JF. *Club:* Oxford American Democrats (Oxford).

DWYER, Glenn N.; *see* Neil-Dwyer.

DWYER, Sir Joseph Anthony, Kt 2001; FREng; Chairman, George Wimpey PLC, 1996–99; *b* 20 June 1939. CEng, FREng (FEng 1997); FICE, FCIOB. George Wimpey: Director: Exec. Bd, 1983; Main Bd, 1988; Gp Chief Exec., 1991–98. President: CIOB; ICE. *Address:* 99 Lonsdale Road, SW13 9DA.

DYCHE, Dame Rachael (Mary), DBE 1997 (CBE 1992); Regional Director, Midlands, Conservative Party, 1993–98; *b* 29 Nov. 1945; *d* of George Henry Dyche and late Doreen Mary Dyche (*née* Rudgard). *Educ:* Burton upon Trent Tech. High Sch. Conservative Party: Agent: Burton, 1968–72; Harwich, 1972–75; Deputy Central Office Agent: Wales, 1975–76; W Midlands, 1976–85; Wessex, 1985–88; Central Office Agent, E Midlands, 1988–93. Mem., Nat. Soc. Cons. and Unionist Agents, 1968–. *Recreations:* golf, gardening, music. *Address:* 11 Acorn Close, Lubenham, Market Harborough, Leics LE16 9SP. *T:* (01858) 432379.

DYE, Maj.-Gen. Jack Bertie, CBE 1968 (OBE 1965); MC; Vice Lord-Lieutenant of Suffolk, 1983–94; Director, Volunteers, Territorials and Cadets, 1971–74; Major-General late Royal Norfolk Regiment; *b* 1919. Served War of 1939–45 (MC). Brigadier, 1966; psc. Commanded South Arabian Army, 1966–68; GOC Eastern District, 1969–71. Col Comdt, The Queen's Division, 1970–74; Col, Royal Anglian Regt, 1976–82 (Dep. Col, 1974–76). DL Suffolk, 1979.

DYER, Alexander Patrick; Chief Executive and Deputy Chairman, BOC Group plc, 1993–96; Deputy Chairman, Bunzl plc, since 1996 (Chairman 1993–96); *b* 30 Aug. 1932; *m* 1954, Shirley Shine; one *s* (and one *s* decd). *Educ:* US Military Acad. (BSc Engrg); Harvard Business Sch. (MBA). US Army, 1954–57; Esso Corp., 1959–63; Air Products, 1963–89; Gp Vice Pres., Gases, 1978–87; Exec. Vice Pres., Gas and Equipment, 1987–88; Bd Dir, 1988–89; Man. Dir, Gases, BOC Gp, 1989–93. *Recreations:* golf, skeet. *Address:* 1803 Apple Tree Lane, Bethlehem, PA 18105, USA. *Clubs:* Saucon Valley Country; Gulf Stream Golf; Weyhill Skeet; Blooming Grove Hunting and Fishing.

DYER, Charles; playwright and novelist; actor-director (as Raymond Dyer); *b* 7 July 1928; *s* of James Sidney Dyer and Florence (*née* Stretton); *m* 1959, Fiona Thomson, actress; three *s*. *Educ:* Queen Elizabeth's Sch., Barnet. *Plays:* Clubs Are Sometimes Trumps, 1948; Who On Earth!, 1951; Turtle in the Soup, 1953; The Jovial Parasite, 1954; Single Ticket Mars, 1955; Time, Murderer, Please, and Poison In Jest, 1956; Wanted—One Body!, 1958; Prelude to Fury, 1959 (also wrote theme music); Rattle of A Simple Man, 1962 (also in Berlin, Paris, NY, Rome and London), 1981, USA, 1985, 1990, Netherlands, 1988, Germany, 1993, Scandinavia, 1993, 1995; Staircase, 1966 (for RSC; also in NY, Paris (1968, 1982, 1986, 1992), Amsterdam, Berlin, Rome, 1988, 1992, Vienna, Brazil, 1992, trans-Germany, 1992–95); Mother Adam, Paris, Berlin, 1970, London, 1971, 1973, NY, 1974; The Loving Allelujah, 1974; Circling Dancers, 1979; Lovers Dancing, 1981, 1983; Futility Rites, 1981; as R. Kraselchik: Red Cabbage and Kings, 1960 (also wrote theme music); *screenplays:* Rattle, 1964; Insurance Italian Style, 1967; Staircase, 1968; Brother Sun and Sister Moon, 1970. Also directed plays for the stage and television. *Acted in: plays:* Worm's Eye View, 1948; Room For Two, 1955; Dry Rot, 1958; *films:* Cuptie Honeymoon, 1947; Britannia Mews, 1949; Road Sense, 1950; Off The Record, 1952; Pickwick Papers, 1952; Dockland Case, 1953; Strange Case of Blondie, 1953; Naval Patrol, 1959; Loneliness of the Long Distance Runner, 1962; Mouse On The Moon, 1962; Knack, 1964; Rattle of A Simple Man, 1964; How I Won The War, 1967; Staircase, 1968; *television:* Charlie in Staircase, BBC, 1986; *television series:* Hugh and I, 1964. *Publications:* (as Charles Dyer): plays: Wanted—One Body!, 1961; Time, Murderer, Please, 1962; Rattle Of A Simple Man, (Fr.) 1963; Staircase, 1966; Mother Adam, 1970; The Loneliness Trilogy, 1972; Hot Godly Wind, 1973; novels: Rattle Of A Simple Man, 1964; Charlie Always Told Harry Almost Everything, 1969 (USA and Europe, 1970); The Rising of our Herbert, 1972. *Recreations:* amateur music and carpentry. *Address:* Old Wob, Austenwood Common, Gerrards Cross, Bucks SL9 8SF.

DYER, Prof. Christopher Charles, PhD; FBA 1995; Professor of Medieval Social History, University of Birmingham, since 1991; *b* 24 Dec. 1944; *s* of Charles James Dyer and Doris Mary Dyer; *m* 1967, Jenifer Ann Dent; one *s* one *d*. *Educ:* Univ. of Birmingham (BA, PhD). Asst Lectr in History, Univ. of Edinburgh, 1967–70; Sen. Lectr and Reader, Univ. of Birmingham, 1970–90. Ford Lectr in Medieval Hist., Oxford Univ., 2000–01. President: Soc. for Medieval Archaeology, 1998–; Bristol and Glos Archaeol Soc., 2001–02; Chm., Victoria County History Cttee, 1997–. *Publications:* Lords and Peasants in a Changing Society, 1980; Standards of Living in the later Middle Ages, 1989; Everyday Life in Medieval England, 1994. *Address:* Department of History, The University, Birmingham B15 2TT. *T:* (0121) 414 5741.

DYER, Sir Henry Peter Francis S.; *see* Swinnerton-Dyer.

DYER, Lois Edith, OBE 1984; FCSP; international physiotherapy consultant; *b* 18 March 1925; *d* of Richard Morgan Dyer and Emmeline Agnes (*née* Wells). *Educ:* Middlesex Hospital. FCSP 1986. Variety of posts as physiotherapist in Britain, Southern, Central and North Africa, 1948–71; extensive travel world wide, visiting and lecturing at national and internat. conferences. First Physiotherapist Member, NHS Health Adv. Service, 1971; first Advr in Physiotherapy, DHSS, 1976–85. Mem., Camden (formerly Hampstead) CHC, 1996–. First non-medical Chm., Chartered Society of Physiotherapy, 1972–75; Founder Mem., Soc. for Res. in Rehabilitation, 1978–; Hon. Life Vice-Pres., S African Soc. of Physiotherapy. Editor-in-Chief, Physiotherapy Practice, 1985–90. *Publications:* Care of the Orthopaedic Patient (jtly), 1977; numerous papers in professional jls. *Recreations:* music, country pursuits, bird watching, bridge, ecology, wildlife, conservation. *Address:* Garden Flat, 6 Belsize Grove, NW3 4UN. *T:* (020) 7722 1794.

DYER, Mark; His Honour Judge Dyer; a Circuit Judge, since 1977; a Senior Circuit Judge, since 1996; *b* 20 Nov. 1928; *er s* of late Maj.-Gen. G. M. Dyer, CBE, DSO, and Evelyn Mary (*née* List); *m* 1953, Diana, *d* of Sir Percy Lancelot Orde, CIE; two *d*. *Educ:* Ampleforth Coll.; Christ Church, Oxford (MA). 2nd Lieut, Royal Scots Greys, 1948–49; The Westminster Dragoons (2nd CLY) TA, 1950–58, Captain. Called to the Bar: Middle Temple, 1953; Inner Temple, 1972, Bencher, 1998; part-time Lectr in Law, Univ. of Southampton, 1957–67; Dep. Chm., Isle of Wight QS, 1971; a Recorder of the Crown Court, 1972–77; Liaison Judge for Wiltshire, 1981; Hon. Recorder: Devizes, 1988; Bristol, 1996. Mem., Parole Bd, 1992–94. Member: Gen. Council of the Bar, 1965–69; Judicial Studies Bd, 1986–91. Pres., Council of HM Circuit Judges, 1992 (Hon. Sec., 1989–91). FRSA 1994. *Recreation:* wine and kindred spirits. *Address:* The Crown Court at Bristol, The Law Courts, Small Street, Bristol BS1 1DA. *Club:* Cavalry and Guards.

DYER, Dr Richard George; Director, Babraham Institute, since 1994; *b* 18 July 1943; *s* of late Comdr Charles William Dyer, RN and Dorothy Patricia Victoria Vaughan-Hogan; *m* 1st, 1967, Shirley James Foulsham (marr. diss. 1995); two *s* one *d*; 2nd, 2000, Dr Caroline Edmonds (*née* Porter). *Educ:* Churcher's Coll., Petersfield; Univ. of London (BSc 1967); Univ. of Birmingham (MSc 1968); Univ. of Bristol (PhD 1971). Research, Dept of Anatomy, Bristol Med. Sch., 1968–74; ARC Institute of Animal Physiology, subseq. AFRC Institute of Animal Physiology and Genetics Research, now Babraham Institute: Head, Dept of Neuroendocrinology, 1985–90; Head, Cambridge Station, 1989–90; Associate Dir of Inst., 1991–93; Exec. Dir, 1993–94. Teacher of Physiol., Jesus Coll., Cambridge, 1977–90; Res. Fellowships, Germany and France; Consultant for WHO, Shanghai, 1983–86. Member: AFRC Animals Res. Bd, 1992–93; AFRC Strategy Bd, 1993; BBSRC Animal Sci. and Psych. Cttee, 1994–96; Cttee, R&D Soc., 1998–; European Science Foundation: Member: Life and Envmtl Scis Standing Cttee, 1995–2000; Eur. Medical Res. Councils, 1996–2000; Exec. Bd, 1999–. Member, Board: Babraham Bioscience Technologies Ltd, 1998– (Chm., 2000–); Univ. of Cambridge Challenge Fund, 1999–. Medal, Soc. for Endocrinology, 1986; Medal, Polish Physiol. Soc., 1987. Former Member, Editorial Board: Exptl Brain Res.; Jl of Endocrinology. *Publications:* (ed with R. J. Bicknell) Brain Opioid Systems in Reproduction, 1989; numerous papers on neuroendocrine topics in learned jls. *Recreations:* finding bargains, escaping to mountains and sea, lively dinners. *Address:* Babraham Institute, Cambridge CB2 4AT. *T:* (01223) 469212.

DYET, Fergus John C.; *see* Cochrane-Dyet.

DYKE; *see* Hart Dyke.

DYKE, Gregory; Director-General, BBC, since 2000; *b* 20 May 1947; *s* of Joseph and Denise Dyke; partner, Sue Howes; one *s* one *d*; one step *s* one step *d*. *Educ:* Hayes Grammar Sch.; York Univ. (BA Politics). Varied career, 1965–83; Editor in Chief, TV-am, 1983–84; Dir of Programmes, TVS, 1984–87; London Weekend Television: Dir of Progs, 1987–91; Dep. Man. Dir, 1989–90; Man. Dir, subseq. Gp Chief Exec., 1990–94; Chm., GMTV, 1993–94; Director: Channel Four Television, 1988–92; BSkyB, 1995; Chm. and Chief Exec., Pearson Television, 1995–99; Exec. Dir, Pearson plc, 1996–99; Chm., Channel 5 Broadcasting, 1997–99. Non-exec. Dir, ITN, 1990–92. Chm., ITV Council, 1992–94. Non-exec. Dir, Manchester United FC, 1997–99. Trustee: Science Museum, 1996–; English Nat. Stadium Trust, 1997–99. *Recreations:* football, tennis, movies, theatre. *Address:* BBC, Broadcasting House, W1A 1AA.

DYKES, David Wilmer, MA, PhD; Director, National Museum of Wales, 1986–89; *b* 18 Dec. 1933; *s* of late Captain David Dykes, OBE and Jenny Dykes; *m* 1967, Margaret Anne George; two *d*. *Educ:* Swansea Grammar Sch.; Corpus Christi Coll., Oxford (MA); PhD (Wales). FRNS 1958 (Parkes-Weber Prize, 1954); FRSAI 1963; FRHistS 1965; FSA 1973. Commnd RN and RNR, 1955–62. Civil Servant, Bd of Inland Revenue, 1958–59; administrative appts, Univ. of Bristol and Univ. Coll. of Swansea, 1959–63; Dep.

Registrar, Univ. Coll. of Swansea, 1963–69; Registrar, Univ. of Warwick, 1969–72; Sec., Nat. Museum of Wales, 1972–86, Acting Dir, 1985–86. Hon. Lectr in History, University Coll., Cardiff, later Univ. of Wales Coll. of Cardiff, 1975–95. Pres., British Numismatic Soc., 1998– (Mem. Council, 1966–70 and 1997–). FRSA 1990. Liveryman: Worshipful Co. of Tin Plate Workers, 1985; Welsh Livery Guild, 1993; Freeman, City of London, 1985. KStJ 1993 (CStJ 1991; Chancellor, Priory for Wales, 1991–98; Bailiff of St Davids, 1999–). *Publications:* Anglo-Saxon Coins in the National Museum of Wales, 1977; (ed and contrib.) Alan Sorrell: Early Wales Re-created, 1980; Wales in Vanity Fair, 1989; The University College of Swansea: an illustrated history, 1992; articles and reviews in numismatic, historical and other jls. *Recreations:* numismatics, writing, gardening. *Address:* Cherry Grove, Welsh St Donats, near Cowbridge, Vale of Glamorgan CF71 7SS. *Clubs:* Athenæum; Cardiff and County (Cardiff).

DYKES, Hugh John; Associate Member, Quilter, Hilton, Goodison, Stockbrokers, since 1978; *b* 17 May 1939; *s* of Richard Dykes and Doreen Ismay Maxwell Dykes; *m* 1965, Susan Margaret Dykes (*née* Smith); three *s*. *Educ:* Weston super Mare Grammar Sch.; Pembroke Coll. Cambridge. Partner, Simon & Coates, Stockbrokers, 1968–78. MSI, 1993. Dir, Dixons Stores Far East Ltd, 1985–. Contested (C) Tottenham, 1966. MP (C) Harrow East, 1970–97; contested (C) same seat, 1997; joined LibDem party, 1997; contested (Lib Dem) London Region, Eur. Parly elecns, 1999. PPS: to three Parly Under-Secs of State for Defence, 1970; to Parly Under-Sec. of State in Civil Service Dept attached to Cabinet Office, 1973; Mem., H of C EEC Select Cttee, 1983–97. Mem., European Parlt, Strasbourg, 1974–77; Chairman: Cons. Parly European Cttee, 1979–80 (Vice-Chm., 1974–79); Commons Euro-Gp, 1988–97; Vice-Pres., Cons. Gp for EEC, 1982–86 (Chm., 1978–81). Chm., European Movement, 1990–97 (Jt Hon. Sec., 1982–87). Research Sec., Bow Gp, 1965; Chm., Coningsby Club, 1969. Governor: Royal Nat. Orthopaedic Hosp., 1975–82; N London Collegiate Sch., 1982–. Order of Merit (Germany), 1993; Médaille pour l'Europe (Luxembourg), 1993; Chevalier, Ordre National du Mérite (France), 1994. *Publications:* (ed) Westropp's "Invest £100", 1964, and Westropp's "Start Your Own Business", 1965; many articles and pamphlets on political and financial subjects. *Recreations:* music, theatre, swimming, travel. *Address:* (office) 49 Berkeley Square, W1X 5DB. *Clubs:* National Liberal, Garrick, Beefsteak.

DYKES, Richard Thornton Booth; Group Managing Director, Royal Mail, and Executive Board Member, Consignia plc (formerly The Post Office), since 1996; *b* 7 April 1945; *s* of Alan Thornton Dykes and Myra McFie Dykes (*née* Booth); *m* 1970, Janet Rosemary Cundall (marr. diss. 1995); one *s*. *Educ:* Rossall Sch. Articled clerk, Dehn & Lauderdale, solicitors, 1965–67; EO, later HEO, Min. of Labour, 1967–73; Private Sec. to Sec. of State for Employment, 1974–76; Principal, Econ. Policy Div., Dept of Employment, 1976–77; Dir, Industrial Relns, British Shipbuilders, 1977–80; Non-exec. Dir, Austin & Pickersgill Ltd, Sunderland, 1979–80; Principal Private Sec. to Sec. of State for Employment, 1980–82; Department of Employment: Hd, Unemployment Benefit Service, 1982–85; Sec., Sen. Mgt Gp, 1985–86; Hd, Inner Cities Central Unit, 1986; Post Office Counters Ltd: Gen. Manager for Gtr London, 1986–87; Dir of Ops, 1987–92; Man. Dir, 1993–96. Non-exec. Dir, Employment Service, 1998–. Member: Forensic Sci. Service Adv. Bd, Home Office, 1991–98; EDC, BITC, 1994–; Design Council, 1994–. *Recreations:* travel, hill-walking. *Address:* Royal Mail Headquarters, 148 Old Street, EC1V 9HQ. *T:* (020) 7250 2888.

DYKSTRA, Ronald Gerrit Malcolm; Senior Partner, Addleshaw Sons & Latham, solicitors, 1987–94, retired; *b* 4 March 1934; *s* of Gerrit Abe Dykstra and Margaret Kirk Dykstra (*née* McDonald); *m* 1st, 1960, Jennifer Mary Cramer (marr diss. 1985); three *s*; 2nd, 1986, Sonia Hoole. *Educ:* Edinburgh Academy. FCIArb. Admitted Solicitor, 1957; Asst Solicitor, 1957, Partner, 1961, Addleshaw Sons & Latham, Manchester. Mem., Wilmslow Green Room Soc. *Recreations:* swimming, cycling, amateur drama, walking. *Address:* 7 Racecourse Road, Wilmslow, Cheshire SK9 5LF. *T:* (01625) 525856.

DYMOCK, Rear Adm. Anthony Knox; Deputy Commander, Striking and Support Forces Southern Region, since 2000; *b* 18 July 1949; *s* of Richard Challis Dymock and Irene Mary Dymock (*née* Knox); *m* 1977, Elizabeth Mary Frewer; one *s* one *d*. *Educ:* Brighton, Hove and Sussex Grammar Sch.; Univ. of E Anglia (BA Hons Russian and Philosophy). MNI 1992. BRNC, 1969-70; served: HMS Yarmouth, 1972-74; HMS Brighton, 1974; HMS Antrim, 1981-83 (Falklands War); i/c HMS Plymouth, 1985-88; MoD, Whitehall, 1989–91; HMS London, 1991-92 (Gulf War); i/c HMS Campbeltown, 1992-93; MoD Naval Staff, 1993–96; i/c 2nd Frigate Sqdn, HMS Cornwall, 1996-98; Dep. Comdr, UK Task Gp (HMS Invincible), Gulf and Kosovo, 1998-99. Member: RYA; RNSA; British Assoc. for Shooting and Conservation. *Publications:* contribs to Naval Rev. *Recreations:* sailing, ski-ing, shooting. *Address:* COMSTRIKFORSOUTH, HQ AF South, BFPO 8. *T:* (Italy) (081) 7212222.

DYMOKE, Lt-Col John Lindley Marmion, MBE 1960; Vice Lord-Lieutenant of Lincolnshire, since 1991; 34th Hereditary Queen's Champion, 1946; *b* 1 Sept. 1926; *s* of late Lionel Marmion Dymoke and Rachel, *d* of Hon. Lennox Lindley; *m* 1953, Susan Cicely Fane; three *s*. *Educ:* Christ's Hosp. Commnd Royal Lincs Regt, 1946; Staff Coll., 1957; Armed Forces Staff Coll., USA, 1964; Coll. Chief Instructor, RMA Sandhurst, 1961–64; Comd 3rd Bn, Royal Anglian Regt, 1966–69; military service included: India, Sumatra, Malaya, Egypt, Jordan, Aden, France, Germany, USA and UK; retired 1972. Farmer and landowner, 1972–. Mem., E Lindsey DC, 1973–99. President: Lincs Br., CLA, 1995– (Chm., 1982–85); Lincs Agricl Soc., 1995. Chm., Horncastle Grammar Sch., 1979–91. Master, Grocers' Co., 1977–78. DL 1976, High Sheriff 1979, Lincs. *Recreation:* care of Scrivelsby Estate. *Address:* Scrivelsby Court, near Horncastle, Lincolnshire LN9 6JA. *T:* (01507) 523325.

DYMOKE, Rear-Adm. Lionel Dorian, CB 1974; *b* 18 March 1921; *s* of Henry Lionel Dymoke and Dorothy (*née* Briscoe); *m* 1st, 1952, Patricia Pimlott (*d* 1968); one *s*; 2nd, 1970, Iris Hemsted (*née* Lamplough). *Educ:* Nautical Coll., Pangbourne. Entered Royal Navy, 1938; Comdr 1953; Captain 1961; Rear-Adm. 1971; retired 1976. *Address:* 3 Woodland Place, Bath BA2 6EH. *T:* (01225) 464228.

DYNEVOR, 9th Baron *cr* 1780; **Richard Charles Uryan Rhys;** *b* 19 June 1935; *s* of 8th Baron Dynevor, CBE, MC; *S* father, 1962; *m* 1959, Lucy (marr. diss. 1978), *d* of Sir John Rothenstein, CBE; one *s* three *d*. *Educ:* Eton; Magdalene Coll., Cambridge. *Heir:* *s* Hon. Hugo Griffith Uryan Rhys, *b* 19 Nov. 1966.

DYSART, Countess of (11th in line), *cr* 1643; **Rosamund Agnes Greaves;** Baroness Huntingtower, 1643; *b* 15 Feb. 1914; *d* of Major Owain Greaves (*d* 1941), RHG, and Wenefryde Agatha, Countess of Dysart (10th in line); *S* mother, 1975. *Heir:* *sister* Lady Katherine Grant of Rothiemurchus [*b* 1 June 1918; *m* 1941, Colonel John Peter Grant of Rothiemurchus, MBE (*d* 1987); one *s* one *d*]. *Address:* Bryn Garth, Grosmont, Abergavenny, Gwent NP7 8LS.

DYSON, Prof. Freeman John, FRS 1952; Professor, School of Natural Sciences, Institute for Advanced Study, Princeton, New Jersey, 1953–94, Professor Emeritus since 1994; *b* 15 Dec. 1923; *s* of late Sir George Dyson, KCVO; *m* 1st, 1950, Verena Esther (*née* Huber) (marr. diss. 1958); one *s* one *d*; 2nd, 1958, Imme (*née* Jung); four *d*. *Educ:* Winchester; Cambridge; Cornell University. Operational research for RAF Bomber Command, 1943–45. Fellow of Trinity Coll., Cambridge, 1946–50, Hon. Fellow, 1989; Commonwealth Fund Fellow at Cornell and Princeton, USA, 1947–49; Mem. of Institute for Advanced Study, Princeton, USA, 1949–50; Professor of Physics, Cornell Univ., Ithaca, NY, USA, 1951–53. Mem. of National Academy of Sciences (USA), 1964; For. Associate, Acad. des Scis, Paris, 1989. Gifford Lectr, Aberdeen, 1985; Radcliffe Lectr, Oxford, 1990. Lorentz Medal, Royal Netherlands Acad. of Sciences, 1966; Hughes Medal, Royal Soc., 1968; Max Planck Medal, German Physical Soc., 1969; Templeton Prize, 2000. *Publications:* Disturbing the Universe, 1979; Weapons and Hope, 1984; Origins of Life, 1986; Infinite in All Directions, 1988; From Eros to Gaia, 1991; Imagined Worlds, 1997; The Sun, the Genome and the Internet, 1999; contrib. to The Physical Review, Annals of Mathematics, etc. *Address:* School of Natural Sciences, Institute for Advanced Study, Einstein Drive, Princeton, NJ 08540, USA.

DYSON, James, CBE 1998; FCSD; Founder and Chairman: Dyson Ltd (formerly Prototypes Ltd, then Dyson Research), since 1979; Dyson Appliances Ltd, since 1992; *b* 2 May 1947; *s* of Alec Dyson and Mary (*née* Bolton); *m* 1967, Deirdre Hindmarsh; two *s* one *d*. *Educ:* Gresham's Sch.; Royal Coll. of Art (MDes). FCSD 1996. Dir, Rotork Marine, 1970–74 (design and manufacture of Sea Truck high speed landing craft); Man. Dir, Kirk-Dyson, 1974–79 (design and manufacture of Ballbarrow wheelbarrow); developed and designed Dyson Dual Cyclone vacuum cleaner, 1979–93, Contrarotator washing machine, 2000. Mem., Design Council, 1997–; Chm., Design Mus., 1999–. Chm., Bath Coll. of Higher Educn, 1990–92; Mem. Council, RCA, 1998– (Ext. Examr, 1993–96). Trustee, Roundhouse Th., London. Dyson vacuum cleaners on permanent display in museums: Sci. Mus., V&A and Design Mus., London; Boymans Mus., Rotterdam; Powerhouse Mus., Sydney; San Francisco Mus. of Modern Art; Mus. of Scotland; Design Mus., Zurich; Mus. für angewandte Kunst, Germany. Hon. Fellow, Liverpool John Moores, 1998. Hon. DLitt Staffordshire, 1996; Hon. DSc: Oxford Brookes, Huddersfield, 1997; Bradford, 1998; UWE, Middlesex, Brunel, 1999; Bath Spa, RCA, Bath, 2000. Awards incl.: Design and Innovation Award for Ballbarrow, Building Design, 1976; Internat. Design Fair Prize, Japan, 1991; Minerva Award, CSD, 1995; Gerald Frewer Trophy, Inst. Engrg Designers, 1996; Industrial Design Prize of America, 1996; Eversheds Grand Prix Trophy, Design Council, 1996; European Design Prize, EC, 1997; Prince Philip's Designers Prize; Design Centrum Award for Design Prestige, Czech Republic, 1997; French Oscar, Livre Mondial des Inventions, 1997; Gold Award, Industrial Design Promotion Orgn, Japan, 1999; Gal. Lafayette Prix Innovation-Design, France, 1999; Mingay Most Innovative Product Award, Australia, 2000; Daily Mail Award for Excellence, 2000. *Publications:* Doing a Dyson, 1996; Against the Odds (autobiog.), 1997. *Recreations:* running, garden design, bassoon and music, fishing, cricket, tennis. *Address:* Tetbury Hill, Malmesbury, Wilts SN16 0RP. *T:* (01666) 828282. *Club:* Chelsea Arts.

DYSON, Rt Hon. Sir John (Anthony), Kt 1993; PC 2001; **Rt Hon. Lord Justice Dyson;** a Lord Justice of Appeal, since 2001; *b* 31 July 1943; *s* of late Richard Dyson and of Gisella Dyson; *m* 1970, Jacqueline Carmel Levy; one *s* one *d*. *Educ:* Leeds Grammar Sch.; Wadham Coll., Oxford (Open Classics Scholar; MA). Harmsworth Law Scholar, 1968, called to Bar, Middle Temple, 1968, Bencher, 1990; QC 1982; a Recorder, 1986–93; a Judge of the High Court of Justice, QBD, 1993–2001; Presiding Judge, Technology and Construction Court, 1998–2001. Member: Council of Legal Educn, 1992–96; Judicial Studies Bd, 1994–98. *Recreations:* piano playing, gardening, walking. *Address:* Royal Courts of Justice, Strand, WC2A 2LL.

DYSON, John Michael; Chief Master of the Supreme Court of Judicature (Chancery Division), 1992–98 (a Master, 1973–98); a Recorder, 1994–98; *b* 9 Feb. 1929; *s* of late Eric Dyson, Gainsborough and Hope Patison (*née* Kirkland). *Educ:* Bradfield Coll.; Corpus Christi Coll., Oxford. 2nd Lieut, Royal Tank Regt, 1948. Admitted Solicitor, 1956; Partner, Field Roscoe & Co., 1957 (subseq. Field Fisher & Co. and Field Fisher & Martineau). *Address:* 20 Keats Grove, NW3 2RS. *T:* (020) 7794 3389. *Club:* Oxford and Cambridge.

DYSON, Prof. Kenneth Herbert Fewster, PhD; FRHistS; FBA 1997; AcSS; Professor of European Studies, since 1982, and Co-Director, European Briefing Unit, since 1987, University of Bradford; *b* 10 Nov. 1946; *s* of Arthur Dyson and Freda Dyson; *m* 1971, Patricia Ann Holmes; two *s*. *Educ:* Scarborough Grammar Sch.; London Sch. of Econs (BSc Econ, MSc Econ); Univ. of Liverpool (PhD 1980). FRHistS 1981. Lectr in Politics, 1969–79, Sen. Lectr, 1979–81, Univ. of Liverpool. Vis. Prof. in Politics, Univ. of Konstanz, Germany, 1981–82. Chairman: Assoc. for Study of German Politics, 1978–81; Standing Conf. of Heads of European Studies, 1990–93; HEFCE Res. Assessment Panel for European Studies, RAEs 1996 and 2001; Grants Officer, Politics Section, British Acad., 1999–. FRSA 1993; AcSS 2000. Federal Service Cross (1st Cl.) (Germany), 1990. *Publications include:* Party, State and Bureaucracy in Germany, 1978; The State Tradition in Western Europe, 1980; (with S. Wilks) Industrial Crisis, 1983; European Detente, 1986; The Politics of the Communications Revolution in Western Europe, 1986; Local Authorities and New Technologies, 1987; Broadcasting and New Media Policies in Western Europe, 1988; Combatting Long-Term Unemployment, 1989; Political Economy of Communications, 1990; Politics of German Regulation, 1992; Elusive Union, 1994; Culture First, 1996; (with K. Featherstone) The Road to Maastricht, 1999; The Politics of the Euro-Zone, 2000; European States and the Euro, 2001. *Recreations:* Renaissance Florence, classical music, charity work for the disabled, walking, swimming. *Address:* Department of European Studies, University of Bradford, Bradford BD7 1DP. *T:* (01274) 383805; West Holt, 2 Carlton Drive, Heaton, Bradford BD9 4DL. *T:* (01274) 826281.

DYSON, Prof. Roger Franklin, PhD; Honorary Professor and Director of Clinical Management Unit Centre for Health Planning and Management, University of Keele, since 1989; *b* 30 Jan. 1940; *s* of John Franklin Dyson and Edith Mary Jobson; *m* 1st, 1964 (marr. diss. 1994); one *s* one *d*; 2nd, 1995, Ann Frances Naylor, *d* of late Alfred Worsfold and Mabel (*née* Burt). *Educ:* Counthill Grammar Sch., Oldham; Keele Univ. (BA Hons 1st cl. Hist. and Econs, 1962); Leeds Univ. (PhD 1971). Asst Lectr, 1963, Lectr, 1966, Adult Educn Dept, Leeds Univ.; Dep. Dir and Sen. Lectr in Ind. Relations, Adult Educn Dept, 1974, Prof. and Dir of Adult and Continuing Educn, 1976–89, Keele Univ. Consultant Advr on Ind. Relations to Sec. of State, DHSS, 1979–81. Chm., N Staffs HA, 1982–86. Mem., RSocMed. Hon. MRCP 1997. Editor, Health Manpower Management (formerly Health Services Manpower Review), 1975–91. Gold Medal, RCAnaes, 2000. *Publications:* (ed jtly) Management for Hospital Doctors, 1994; contribs to BMJ. *Recreations:* gardening, gastronomy. *Address:* 4 Huskards, Fryerning, Ingatestone, Essex CM4 0HR. *T:* (01277) 354841. *Club:* Carlton.

DYSON, Prof. Timothy Peter Geoffrey, FBA 2001; Professor of Population Studies, London School of Economics, since 1993; *b* 1 Aug. 1949; *s* of Geoffrey Dyson and

Maureen (*née* Gardner); *m* 1979, Susan Ann Borman; two *s*. *Educ:* Queen's Univ., Kingston, Ont.; London Sch. of Econs (BSc Sociol. 1971, MSc Demography 1973). Res. Officer, Inst. of Develt Studies, Univ. of Sussex, 1973–75; Res. Fellow, Centre for Population Studies, LSHTM, 1975–80; Lectr in Population Studies, 1980–88, Reader, 1988–93, LSE. *Publications:* (ed) India's Historical Demography, 1989; (ed) Sexual Behaviour and Networking, 1992; Population and Food: global trends and future prospects, 1996. *Recreation:* gardening. *Address:* Department of Social Policy, London School of Economics, Houghton Street, WC2A 2AE. *T:* (020) 7955 7662.

DYTOR, Clive Idris, MC 1982; Head Master, Oratory School, since 2000; *b* 29 Oct. 1956; *s* of (Cecil) Frederick Dytor and Maureen (Margaret) Dytor (*née* Owen); *m* 1985, Sarah Louise Payler; one *s* one *d*. *Educ:* Trinity Coll., Cambridge (MA Hons Oriental Studies); Wycliffe Hall, Oxford (MA Hons Theology). Served Royal Marines, 1980–86: officer trng, 1980–81; Troop Officer, 45 Cdo, 1981–82; Instructor, Officers' Training Wing, 1982–83; 2nd i/c Trng Team in Persian Gulf, 1983–84; Officer Recruiting Liaison Officer, 1984–86; ordained deacon 1989, priest 1990; Curate, Rushall (dio. Lichfield), 1989–92; Chaplain, Tonbridge Boys' Sch., 1992–94; received into RC Church, 1994; Housemaster, St Edward's Sch., Oxford, 1994–2000. *Recreations:* sport, music, language. *Address:* The Oratory School, Woodcote, Reading, Berks RG8 0PJ. *T:* (01491) 680207. *Clubs:* East India; Pitt (Cambridge); Leander.

DYVIG, Peter; Comdr (1st cl.), Order of the Dannebrog, 1986; Chamberlain to Her Majesty Queen Margrethe II of Denmark, 1999; *b* 23 Feb. 1934; *m* 1959, Karen Dyvig (*née* Møller); one *s* one *d*. *Educ:* Copenhagen Univ. (grad. in Law). Entered Danish For. Service, 1959; bursary at Sch. of Advanced Internat. Studies, Washington, 1963–64; First Secretary: Danish Delegn to NATO, Paris, 1965–67; Brussels, 1967–69; Min. of For. Affairs, Copenhagen, 1969–74; Minister Counsellor, Washington, 1974–76; Ambassador, Asst Under-Sec. of State, Min. of For. Affairs, Copenhagen, 1976–79; Under-Sec. for Pol. Affairs, 1980; State Sec., 1983–86; Ambassador: to UK, 1986–89; to USA, 1989–95; to France, 1995–99. Chm. Exec. Bd, European Center for Minority Issues, Flensburg, Germany, 1999–; Chm. Exec. Bd, La Maison du Danemark, Paris, 2000–. Dir, various Danish cos. *Address:* Tryggehvile Allé 9, 2920 Charlottenlund, Denmark.

E

EABORN, Prof. Colin, PhD, DSc (Wales); FRS 1970; FRSC; Professor of Chemistry, University of Sussex, since 1962; *b* 15 March 1923; *s* of Tom Stanley and Caroline Eaborn; *m* 1949, Joyce Thomas. *Educ:* Ruabon Grammar Sch., Denbighshire; U C of N Wales, Bangor (Hon. Fellow, 2000). Asst Lecturer, 1947, Lecturer, 1950, and Reader 1954, in Chemistry, Univ. of Leicester. Research Associate, Univ. of California at Los Angeles, 1950–51; Robert A. Welch Visiting Scholar, Rice Univ., Texas, 1961–62; Erskine Fellow, Univ. of Canterbury (NZ), 1965; Pro-Vice Chancellor (Science), Univ. of Sussex, 1968–72; Dist. Prof., New Mexico State Univ., 1973; Canadian Commonwealth Fellow, Univ. of Victoria, BC, 1976; Lectures: Riccoboni, Univ. of Padua, 1977; Gilman, Iowa State Univ., 1978; R. A. Welch Vis., Texas, 1983. Hon. Sec., Chemical Society, 1964–71, Vice-Pres., Dalton Div., 1971–75: Mem. Council, Royal Soc., 1978–80, 1988–89; Chm., British Cttee on Chemical Educn, 1967–69; Mem., Italy/UK Mixed Commn, 1972–80. Mem., Editl Adv. Bd, Organometallics, 1999–. Hon. DSc Sussex, 1990. F. S. Kipping Award, Amer. Chem. Soc., 1964; Organometallic Award, Chem. Soc., 1975; Ingold Lectureship and Medal, Chem. Soc., 1976; Main Gp Award, Chem. Soc., 1989. *Publications:* Organosilicon Compounds, 1960; Organometallic Compounds of the Group IV Elements, Vol. 1, Part 1, 1968; numerous research papers, mainly in Jl of Chem. Soc., Organometallics and Jl of Organometallic Chemistry (Regional Editor, 1963–95). *Address:* School of Chemistry, Physics and Environmental Science, University of Sussex, Brighton BN1 9QJ. *T:* (01273) 678124, *Fax:* (01273) 677196; *e-mail:* c.eaborn@sussex.ac.uk.

EADES, Robert Mark; His Honour Judge Eades; a Circuit Judge, since 2001; *b* 6 May 1951; *s* of John Robert Eades and Margaret Ursula Eades; *m* 1982, Afsaneh, (Sunny) , Atri; two *d*. *Educ:* Moffats Sch., Bewdley, Worcs; Leighton Park Sch., Reading; Bristol Univ. (LLB). Called to the Bar, Middle Temple, 1974; in practice as barrister, specialising in criminal law, 1974–2001. *Recreations:* gardening, tennis, watching cricket, current affairs, English domestic architecture. *Address:* Wolverhampton Combined Court Centre, Pipers Row, Wolverhampton.

EADIE, Alexander, BEM 1960; JP; *b* 23 June 1920; *m* 1st, 1941, Jemima Ritchie (*d* 1981); one *s*; 2nd, 1983, Janice Murdoch. *Educ:* Buckhaven Senior Secondary Sch. Coal-miner from 1934. Chm., Fife County Housing Cttee, 9 yrs; Chm., Fife County Educn Cttee, 18 mths; Governor, Moray House Teachers' Training Coll., Edinburgh, 5 years; Exec. Committee: Scottish Council of Labour Party, 9 yrs; NUM Scottish Area, 2 yrs; Mem., Eastern Regional Hosp. Bd (Scotland), 14 yrs. Contested Ayr, 1959 and 1964; MP (Lab) Midlothian, 1966–92. Former PPS to Miss M. Herbison, MP, Minister of Social Security, and Mem. of Parly Select Cttee on Scottish Affairs; Opposition Front Bench Spokesman on Energy (incl. N Sea Oil), 1973–74; Parly Under-Sec. of State, Dept of Energy, 1974–79; Shadow Front Bench Spokesman on Energy, 1979–92. Chm., All Party Energy Studies Gp, 1991–92; Chm., Parly Labour Party Power and Steel Gp, 1972–74; Sec., Miners' Parly Gp, 1983–92; Vice-Chm., Parly Trade Union Group, 1972–74. JP Fife, 1951. *Recreations:* bowling, gardening. *Address:* Balkerack, The Haugh, East Wemyss, Fife KY1 4SB. *T:* (01592) 713636.

See also H. S. Eadie.

EADIE, Helen S.; Member (Lab) Dunfermline East, Scottish Parliament, since 1999; *b* 7 March 1947; *d* of James Jack Miller and Elizabeth Reid Stirling Miller; *m* 1967, Robert William Eadie, *s* of Alexander Eadie, *qv*; two *d*. *Educ:* Larbert High Sch.; Falkirk Tech. Coll.; LSE. Political researcher for Harry Ewing, MP and Alex Eadie, MP; Equal Opportunities and Political Officer, GMB. Mem. (Lab) Fife Regl Council, 1987–96. Contested (Lab) Roxburgh and Berwickshire, 1997. *Address:* Scottish Parliament, Edinburgh EH99 1SP; (office) 25 Church Street, Inverkeithing, Fife KY11 1LH. *T:* (01383) 412856, *Fax:* (01383) 412855; 3 Hopeward Mews, Dalgety Bay, Fife KY11 5TB.

EADY, family name of **Baron Swinfen**.

EADY, Hon. Sir David, Kt 1997; **Hon. Mr Justice Eady;** a Judge of the High Court of Justice, Queen's Bench Division, since 1997; *b* 24 March 1943; *s* of late Thomas William Eady and of Kate Eady; *m* 1974, Catherine, *yr d* of J. T. Wiltshire, Bath, Avon; one *s* one *d*. *Educ:* Brentwood Sch.; Trinity Coll., Cambridge (Exhibnr; Pt I Moral Science Tripos, Pt II Law Tripos; MA, LLB). Called to the Bar, Middle Temple, 1966, Bencher, 1991; QC 1983; a Recorder, 1986–97. Mem., Cttee on Privacy and Related Matters (Calcutt Cttee), 1989–90. *Publication:* The Law of Contempt (with A. J. Arlidge), 1982, 2nd edn (ed with A. T. H. Smith), 1998. *Address:* Royal Courts of Justice, Strand, WC2A 2LL.

EAGLAND, (Ralph) Martin; Managing Director, Eagland Planning Associates (formerly Director, Martin Eagland Economic Development Consultancy), since 1995; *b* 1 May 1942; *s* of Norman Albert Eagland and Jessie Eagland; *m* 1963, Patricia Anne Norton; one *s* one *d*. *Educ:* Hipperholme Grammar Sch.; Leeds Sch. of Town Planning; Univ. of Bradford (MSc); Univ. of Birmingham. FRTPI, MIHT, CIMgt. Jun. planning posts, Huddersfield, Dewsbury and Halifax, 1959–67; Principal Planning Officer, City of Gloucester, 1967–72; Asst Co. Planning Officer, Northants CC, 1972–74; Chief Planner (Envmt), W Yorks CC, 1974–79, Head of Econ. Develt Unit, 1979–84; Chief Exec., Kettering Borough Council, 1984–88; Chief Exec. and Accounting Officer, Leeds Develt Corp., 1988–95. Director: Urban Regeneration Partnership, 1996–98; BURA, 2001– (Mem. Panel, 1995–). Mem., W Yorks Cttee, CoSIRA, 1985–88; Sec., Kettering Enterprise Agency, 1986–88; Mem., Electricity Consumers' Cttee, Yorks Reg., 1997. Hon. Public Relns Officer, RTPI (Yorks Br. Exec. Cttee), 1990–92. Vice-Chm., Colne and Holme Valley Jt Cttee for the Blind, 1994–99; Mem., Rotary Club of Leeds, 1992–95. *Publications:* contribs to RTPI Jl, Instn of Highways and Transportation Jl and various property jls and publications. *Recreations:* environmental studies, music, history, gardening. *T:* (office) (01484) 686859. *Club:* Yorkshire Society (Leeds).

EAGLE, Angela; MP (Lab) Wallasey, since 1992; Parliamentary Under-Secretary of State, Home Office, since 2001; *b* 17 Feb. 1961; twin *d* of André and late Shirley Eagle. *Educ:* Formby High Sch.; St John's Coll., Oxford (BA, PPE). Economic Directorate, CBI, 1984; Confederation of Health Service Employees: Researcher, 1984; Press Officer, 1986; Parly Officer, 1987–92. Parly Under-Sec. of State, DETR, 1997–98, DSS, 1998–2001. Mem., Labour Party Nat. Women's Cttee, 1989–. Mem., BFI. *Recreations:* chess (Jun. Internat. Hons), cricket, cinema. *Address:* House of Commons, SW1A 0AA. *T:* (020) 7219 4074.

See also M. Eagle.

EAGLE, Maria; MP (Lab) Liverpool, Garston, since 1997; Parliamentary Under-Secretary of State, Department for Work and Pensions, since 2001; *b* 17 Feb. 1961; twin *d* of André Eagle and late Shirley Eagle. *Educ:* Formby High Sch.; Pembroke Coll., Oxford (BA Hons); Coll. of Law, Lancaster Gate. Articles, Brian Thompson & Partners, Liverpool, 1990–92; Goldsmith Williams, Liverpool, 1992–95; Sen. Solicitor, Steven Irving & Co., Liverpool, 1994–97. Contested (Lab) Crosby, 1992. *Address:* House of Commons, SW1A 0AA.

See also A. Eagle.

EAGLEN, Jane; international opera singer (soprano); *d* of late Ronald Arthur Eaglen and of Kathleen Eaglen. *Educ:* Royal Northern Coll. of Music (vocal studies with Joseph Ward). Principal Soprano, ENO, 1983–91; major house débuts include: Donna Anna in Don Giovanni, Vienna State Opera, 1993; Brunnhilde in Die Walküre, La Scala, Milan, 1994; Norma, Seattle Opera, 1994; Amelia in Un Ballo in Maschera, Opéra National de Paris-Bastille, 1995; Brunnhilde in Ring Cycle, Lyric Opera, Chicago, 1996, Seattle, 2000–01, Metropolitan Opera, NY; Brunnhilde in Die Walküre, San Francisco Opera, 1995; Donna Anna, Metropolitan Opera, NY, 1996; other appearances include: La Gioconda, Chicago, 1999; Isolde, in Tristan and Isolde, Seattle and Chicago, 1999, Metropolitan Opera, NY, 2000. Recordings include Tosca, Norma and three solo discs of opera arias and song cycles. *Recreations:* computing, sport spectator. *Address:* c/o AOR Management Ltd, Westwood, Lorraine Park, Harrow Weald, Middx HA3 6BX. *T:* (020) 8954 7646. *Club:* Lady Taverners.

EAGLES, Lt-Col (Charles Edward) James, LVO 1988; Member, HM Body Guard of the Honourable Corps of Gentlemen-at-Arms, 1967–88 (Harbinger, 1981–86; Standard Bearer, 1986–88); *b* 14 May 1918; *o s* of late Major C. E. C. Eagles, DSO, RMLI and Esmé Field; *m* 1941, Priscilla May Nicolette, *d* of late Brig. A. F. B. Cottrell, DSO, OBE; one *s* three *d*. *Educ:* Marlborough Coll. 2nd Lieut RM, 1936; served: HMS Sussex, Mediterranean and S Atlantic, 1938–40; Mobile Naval Base Def. Orgn, UK, ME, Ceylon and India, 1940–43; 1 HAA Regt RM, India, UK and NW Europe, 1943–45; Asst Mil. Sec., 1945; Amphibious Trng Wing, 1945–47; Staff of Maj.-Gen. RM, Portsmouth, 1947–50; HMS Devonshire, 1951–52; RN Staff Course, 1952; DS, Amphibious Warfare Sch., 1952–55; HMS Afrikander, SO (Intell.), S Atlantic, 1955–57; Dep. Dir, PRORM, 1957–59; CSO, Plymouth Gp, 1960; AAG, Staff of CGRM, 1960–62; Dir, PRORM, 1962–65; retd 1965; Civil Service, MoD, 1965–83. Pres., T. S. Churchill Sea Cadet Corps, 1988–99. *Recreation:* genealogy. *Address:* The Old Brewery, Northleach, Glos GL54 3HB. *Club:* Army and Navy.

EAGLESTONE, Diana Barbara; Her Honour Judge Eaglestone; a Circuit Judge, since 1995; *b* 24 May 1949; *d* of Frank Nelson Eaglestone and Irene Eaglestone; *m* 1991, Michael Howard Redfern, *qv*; one *d*, two *d* by previous marriage, and one step *d*. *Educ:* Manchester Univ. (LLB). Called to the Bar, Gray's Inn, 1971; a Recorder, 1989–95. *Address:* Manchester Care Centre, Prince William House, Peel Cross Road, off Eccles New Road, Salford M5 2RR.

EAGLETON, Prof. Terence Francis, PhD; Thomas Warton Professor of English Literature, and Fellow of St Catherine's College, University of Oxford, since 1992; *b* 22 Feb. 1943; *s* of Francis Paul Eagleton and Rosaleen (*née* Riley); *m* 1st, 1966, Elizabeth Rosemary Galpin (marr. diss. 1976); two *s*; 2nd, 1997, Willa Murphy; one *s*. *Educ:* Trinity Coll., Cambridge (MA, PhD). Fellow in English, Jesus Coll., Cambridge, 1964–69; Oxford University: Tutorial Fellow, Wadham Coll., 1969–89; Lectr in Critical Theory, 1989–92; Fellow, Linacre Coll., 1989–92. Hon. DLitt: Salford, 1993; NUI, 1997; Santiago di Compostela, 1999. *Publications:* Criticism and Ideology, 1976; Marxism and Literary Criticism, 1976; Literary Theory: an introduction, 1983; The Function of Criticism, 1984; The Ideology of the Aesthetic, 1990; Ideology: an introduction, 1993; Heathcliff and the Great Hunger: studies in Irish culture, 1995; Crazy John and the Bishop, and other Essays on Irish Culture, 1998; The Truth about the Irish, 1999; The Idea of Culture, 2000. *Recreation:* Irish music. *Address:* St Catherine's College, Oxford OX1 3UJ. *T:* (01865) 271700. *Clubs:* Irish; United Arts (Dublin).

EAGLING, Wayne John; dancer and choreographer; Artistic Director, Dutch National Ballet, since 1991; *s* of Eddie and Thelma Eagling. *Educ:* P. Ramsey Studio of Dance Arts; Royal Ballet Sch. Sen. Principal, Royal Ballet, 1975–91; has danced lead rôles in major classics including Sleeping Beauty, Swan Lake, Cinderella; first rôle created for him was Young Boy in Triad, 1972; subsequent created rôles include: Solo Boy in Gloria; Ariel in The Tempest; Woyzeck in Different Drummer. Choreographed: The Hunting of the Snark by Michael Batt; (for Royal Ballet) Frankenstein, The Modern Prometheus, 1985; Beauty and the Beast, 1986; The Wall, Berlin, 1990; (for Dutch Nat. Ballet) Ruins of Time, 1993, Symphony in Waves, 1994, Duet, 1995, Lost Touch, 1995, Holding a Balance (for opening of Vermeer exhibn in Mauritshuis), 1996, (with Toer van Schayk) Nutcracker and Mouseking, 1996, Magic Flute, 1999, Le sacré du printemps, 2000; (for La Scala, Milan) Alma Mahler, 1994; choreographed, produced and directed various galas. *Publication:* (with Ross MacGibbon and Robert Jude) The Company We Keep, 1981.

Recreations: golf, scuba diving, tennis, antique cars. *Address:* Dutch National Ballet, Het Muziektheater, Waterlooplein 22, 1011 PG Amsterdam, The Netherlands.

EALES, Victor Henry James, CEng, MIMechE; Director of Weapons Production and Quality (Naval), 1980–81, and Head of Naval Weapons Professional and Technical Group, 1979–81, Ministry of Defence; *b* 11 Dec. 1922; *s* of William Henry and Frances Jean Eales; *m* 1949, Elizabeth Gabrielle Irene James; two *s* one *d.* *Educ:* Wimbledon Central Sch.; Guildford Technical Coll.; Portsmouth Polytechnic. Ministry of Defence: Asst Director, Weapons Production (Naval), 1970; Dep. Director, Surface Weapons Projects (Naval), 1975; Director, Weapons Production (Naval), 1979. *Recreation:* golf. *Address:* 11 Penrhyn Avenue, East Cosham, Portsmouth, Hants PO6 2AX.

EAMES, family name of **Baron Eames** (*see under* Archbishop of Armagh and Primate of All Ireland).

EAMES, Lady; Ann Christine Eames; World-Wide President, Mothers' Union, 1995–2000; *b* 21 Jan. 1943; *d* of Captain William Adrian Reynolds Daly and Olive Margaret Daly; *m* 1966, Most Rev. Robert Henry Alexander Eames, Baron Eames (*see* Archbishop of Armagh); two *s.* *Educ:* Ashleigh House Sch., Belfast; Queen's Univ., Belfast (LLB Hons, MPhil). *Recreations:* sailing, reading. *Address:* The See House, Cathedral Close, Armagh, Co. Armagh BT61 7EE. *T:* (028) 3752 2851.

EAMES, Eric James; JP; Lord Mayor of Birmingham, 1974–75, Deputy Lord Mayor, 1975–76; *b* Highley, Shropshire, 13 April 1917; *s* of George Eames; *m* (marr. diss.); one *s.* *Educ:* Highley Sch., Highley, Shropshire. Member (Lab): Birmingham City Council, 1949–92; W Midlands CC, 1974–77. Mem., Governing Board, Internat. Center for Information Co-operation and Relationship among World's Major Cities. Dir, Assoc. for Neighbourhood Democracy (formerly Councils), 1992–. Governor, Harper Adams Agric. Coll., 1953–90. JP Birmingham, 1972. *Recreations:* gardening, do-it-yourself enthusiast. *Address:* 78 Westley Road, Acocks Green, Birmingham B27 7UH. *T:* (0121) 706 7629.

EAMES, Most Rev. Robert Henry Alexander; *see* Armagh, Archbishop of, and Primate of All Ireland.

EARDLEY-WILMOT, Sir Michael (John Assheton), 6th Bt *cr* 1821, of Berkswell Hall, Warwickshire; founder and owner, Beaufort Hotel, since 1985; *b* 13 Jan. 1941; *o s* of Sir John Eardley-Wilmot, 5th Bt, LVO, DSC and of Diana Elizabeth (*née* Moore); *S* father, 1995; *m* 1st, Wendy Wolstenholme (marr. diss. 1987); two *s* one *d*; 2nd, 1987, Diana Wallis; one *d.* *Educ:* Clifton. Director: Cavenham Ltd, 1965–81; Procea Ltd, 1968–71; Bovril Ltd, 1971–74; Man. Dir, Cavenham Confectionary Ltd, 1974–81; Founder and Man. Dir, Famous Names Ltd, 1981–85. FRSA. *Recreations:* days in Barbados, nights in New York. *Heir:* *s* Benjamin John Eardley-Wilmot, *b* 24 Jan. 1974. *Address:* Beaufort Hotel, 33 Beaufort Gardens, SW3 1PP.

EARL, Belinda Jane; Director, since 1999, and Chief Executive, since 2000, Debenhams Plc; *b* 20 Dec. 1961; *d* of late Colin Lee and of Diana Lee; *m* 1985, David Mark Earl; two *s.* *Educ:* UCW, Aberystwyth (BScEcon (Econs and Business)). Controller, Fashion Div., Harrods, 1983–85; Debenhams Retail Plc: Merchandiser (Menswear), 1985–97; Trading Dir, 1997–2000. *Address:* Debenhams Plc, Welbeck Street, W1G 0AA. *T:* (020) 7408 4444.

EARL, Christopher Joseph, MD; FRCP, FRCOphth; Hon. Consultant Physician to: Neurological Department, Middlesex Hospital, since 1988 (Physician, 1971–88); National Hospital, Queen Square, since 1988 (Physician, 1958–88); Moorfields Eye Hospital, since 1988 (Physician, 1959–88); *b* 20 Nov. 1925; *s* of Christopher and Winifred Earl, Ashbourne, Derbyshire; *m* 1951, Alma Patience Hopkins, Reading; two *s* three *d.* *Educ:* Cotton Coll.; Guy's Hosp. FRCP 1964; FRCOphth 1993. House phys. and house surg., Guy's Hosp., and MO, RAF, 1948–50. Lecturer in Chemical Pathology, Guy's Hosp., 1950–52; Research Fellow, Harvard Med. Sch., and Neurological Unit, Boston City Hosp., 1952–54; Resident MO, Nat. Hosp., Queen Square, 1954–56; Chief Asst, Neurological Dept, Guy's Hosp., 1956–58; Physician, Neurological Dept, London Hosp., 1961–71; Consultant Neurologist: King Edward VII Hosp. for Officers, 1966–95; Hosp. of St John and St Elizabeth, 1967–96. Civil Consultant in Neurol., RAF, 1976–88; Consultant Advr in Neurology to CMO, DoH, 1983–88. Director: Medical Sickness Annuity & Life Assce Soc. Ltd, 1981–95 (Chm., 1993–95); Permanent Insurance Co., 1985–95. Hon. Dir of Photography, Royal Society of Medicine, 1967–73. Hon. Sec., 1968–74, Pres., 1989–90, Assoc. British Neurologists; Mem. Council, 1967–91, Vice Chm. Bd of Management, 1993–96, Med. Defence Union; Censor, 1983–85, Chm., Cttee on Neurology, 1975–85, RCP. Corresp. Mem., Amer. Neurological Assoc., 1978. *Publications:* (ed jtly) Medical Negligence: the cranium, spine and nervous system, 1999; papers in learned jls on Biochemistry and Neurology. *Recreation:* reading history. *Address:* 23 Audley Road, Ealing, W5 3ES. *T:* (020) 8997 0380. *Club:* Garrick.

EARL, Eric Stafford; Clerk to the Worshipful Company of Fishmongers, 1974–88, retired; *b* 8 July 1928; *s* of late Alfred Henry Earl and Mary Elizabeth Earl; *m* 1951, Clara Alice Alston. *Educ:* SE Essex Technical Coll.; City of London Coll. Served with RA, 1946–48. Joined Fishmongers' Co. 1948: Accountant, 1961–68; Asst Clerk, 1969–73; Actg Clerk, 1973–74; Liveryman, 1977. Clerk to Governors of Gresham's Sch., 1974–88; formerly: Sec., City and Guilds of London Art School Ltd; Sec., Atlantic Salmon Res. Trust Ltd; Mem. Exec. and Mem. Council, Salmon and Trout Assoc.; Mem., Nat. Anglers' Council (Chm., 1983–85). Hon. Sec., Shellfish Assoc. of GB, 1974–88; Jt Hon. Sec., Central Council for Rivers Protection, 1974–88; Hon. Asst River Keeper of River Thames, 1968–88; Mem. Council, Anglers' Co-operative Assoc., 1974– (Vice Chm., 1988–). Director: Hulbert Property Co. Ltd, 1975–88; Hulbert Property Holdings Ltd, 1975–88. FZS 1988. Hon. Freeman, Watermen's Co., 1984. *Recreations:* fishing, gardening, tennis, cricket. *Address:* Dolphins, Watling Lane, Thaxted, Essex CM6 2RA. *T:* (01371) 830758. *Club:* Flyfishers'.

EARL, John, FSA; Consultant, Theatres Trust, since 1996 (Director, 1986–95); *b* 11 April 1928; *s* of Philip Haywood Earl and May Florence (*née* Walsh); *m* 1952, Valerie Atkins; one *s* (one *d* decd). *Educ:* Roan Sch.; Brixton Sch. of Building. ARICS 1952; FSA 1978. Nat. Service, RE, 1947–49. London County Council: Architect's Dept, 1954–56; Historic Bldgs Section, 1956–61; MPBW (Special Services), 1961–65; Section Leader, GLC Historic Bldgs Div., 1965–86. Private consultancy, 1986–. Lectr, various bldg conservation courses, 1970–; External Examiner for conservation courses at: Heriot-Watt Univ., 1982–84; Architectl Assoc., 1984–86; RICS Coll. of Estate Mgt, 1990–95 (Chm., Adv. Bd, 1996–2000); Tutor for SPAB William Morris Craft Fellows, 1987–90. Pres., Frank Matcham Soc., 1999–. Trustee, Talawa Theatre Co., 1996–2000. FRSA 1992; IHBC 1998. Hon. Fellow, Coll. of Estate Mgt, 2001. *Publications:* (with J. Stanton) Canterbury Hall and Theatre of Varieties, 1982; Philosophy of Building Conservation, 1996; Dr Langdon-Down and the Normansfield Theatre, 1997; (architectural ed.) Theatres Trust Guide to British Theatres, 2000; contrib. numerous books and jls on building conservation and theatre buildings. *Recreation:* avoiding organised sport.

EARL, Col Timothy James, OBE 2000; Private Secretary to HRH the Princess Royal, since 1999; *b* 2 July 1943; *s* of Rowland William Earl and Elizabeth Sylvia Earl; *m* 1968, Elizabeth Mary Ghislain de Pelet; two *s* one *d.* *Educ:* Brentwood Sch.; RMA Sandhurst. Commnd 1st Bn King's Own Royal Border Regt, 1964; served British Guyana, Gulf States, Cyprus, Gibraltar and Germany; transf. to Life Guards, 1974; served Germany, Norway, Belize; CO, 1983–85; RCDS, 1985–87; MoD, 1987–90; HQ UKLF, 1990–93; Sec., Govt Hospitality Fund, 1993–99. *Recreations:* field sports, planting trees. *Address:* Haddon, Stourton Caundle, Dorset DT10 2LB. *T:* (01963) 362241; Buckingham Palace, SW1A 1AA. *Club:* Flyfishers'.

EARLE, Arthur Frederick; management and economic consultant, since 1983; *b* Toronto, 13 Sept. 1921; *s* of Frederick C. Earle and Hilda M. Earle (*née* Brown); *m* 1946, Vera Domini Lithgow; two *s* one *d.* *Educ:* Toronto; London Sch. of Economics (BSc (Econ.), PhD; Hon. Fellow 1980). Royal Canadian Navy (Rating to Lieut Comdr), 1939–46. Canada Packers Ltd, 1946–48; Aluminium Ltd cos in British Guiana, West Indies and Canada, 1948–53; Treas., Alumina Jamaica Ltd, 1953–55; Aluminium Union, London, 1955–58; Vice-Pres., Aluminium Ltd Sales Inc., New York, 1958–61; Dir, 1961–74, Dep. Chm., 1961–65, Man. Dir, 1963–65, Hoover Ltd; Principal, London Graduate Sch. of Business Studies, 1965–72. Pres., Internat. Investment Corp. for Yugoslavia, 1972–74; Pres., Boyden Consulting Group Ltd, 1974–82; Associate, 1974–82, Vice-Pres., 1975–82, Boyden Associates, Inc.; Advisor to the Pres., Canada Develt Investment Corp., 1983–86; Director: Rio Algom Ltd, 1983–92; National Sea Products Ltd, 1984–86; Bathpaul Ltd, UK, 1984–86; Monkwells Ltd, UK, 1984. Sen. Res. Fellow, Nat. Centre for Management R & D, Univ. of Western Ontario, 1987–90. Member: Commn of Enquiry, Jamaican Match Industry, 1953; Consumer Council, 1963–68; NEDC Cttee on Management Educn, Training and Develt, 1967–69; NEDC for Electrical Engineering Industry. Chm., Canadian Assoc. of Friends of LSE, 1975–96. Dir, Nat. Ballet of Canada, 1982–85. Governor: Ashridge Management Coll., 1962–65; LSE, 1968–95; NIESR, 1968–74; Governor and Mem. Council, Ditchley Foundn, 1967. Fellow, London Business Sch., 1988. Thomas Hawksley Lecture, IMechE, 1968. *Publications:* numerous, on economics and management. *Recreations:* hill climbing, model ship building. *Address:* 901–1230 Marlborough Court, Oakville, ON L6H 3K6, Canada. *T:* (905) 3377977.

EARLE, Sir George; *see* Earle, Sir H. G. A.

EARLE, Very Rev. George Hughes, SJ; MA; Assistant Director, Jesuit Refugee Service, since 2000; *b* 20 Sept. 1925; *s* of late Lieut-Col F. W. Earle, DSO, JP, Morestead House, Winchester, and late Marie Blanche Lyne-Stivens. *Educ:* Pilgrims' Sch., Winchester; Westminster Sch.; Peter Symonds' Sch., Winchester; Balliol Coll., Oxford. Served with RAF, 1943–47. Joined Soc. of Jesus, 1950. Taught at Beaumont Coll., 1955–57, and Stonyhurst Coll., 1962–63; Headmaster, Stonyhurst Coll., 1963–72; Superior of Southwell House, 1972–75; Educnl Asst to Provincial, 1972–75; Co-editor, The Way, 1974–78; Rector of St Aloysius, Glasgow, 1978–81; Superior, English Province, SJ, 1981–87; Dean of Studies, St Joseph's Theol Inst., Cedara, Natal, 1990–92; Co-ordinator of Seminaries, S African Bishops' Conf., 1993–94; Bursar, Murray House, Johannesburg, 1998–99. *Recreations:* none; wasting time. *Address:* 112 Thornbury Road, Osterley, Middx TW7 4NN.

EARLE, Sir (Hardman) George (Algernon), 6th Bt *cr* 1869; *b* 4 Feb. 1932; *S* father, 1979; *m* 1967, Diana Gillian Bligh, *d* of Col F. F. B. St George, CVO; one *s* one *d.* *Heir:* *s* Robert George Bligh Earle, *b* 24 Jan. 1970.

EARLE, Ion, TD 1946; Assistant to the Directors, Clive Discount Co., 1973–81, retired; *b* 12 April 1916; *s* of late Stephen Earle and of E. Beatrice Earle (*née* Blair White); *m* 1946, Elizabeth Stevens, US citizen; one *s* one *d.* *Educ:* Stowe Sch.; University Coll., Oxford; Université de Grenoble. Federation of British Industries, Birmingham, 1938–51, London, 1952–60; Chief Executive, Export Council for Europe, 1960–64; Dep. Dir-Gen., BNEC, 1965–71 (Dir, 1964–65); Head of Personnel, Kleinwort Benson Ltd, 1972. Royal Artillery, TA, 1939–46 (Major). *Recreations:* golf, gardening. *Address:* Apartment 23, Strand Court, Harsfold Road, Rustington, West Sussex BN16 2NT. *T:* (01903) 773350.

EARLE, Joel Vincent, (Joe); arts management consultant, since 1990; Head of Public Services, Victoria and Albert Museum, 1987–89; *b* 1 Sept. 1952; *s* of late James Basil Foster Earle and Mary Isabel Jessie Weeks; *m* 1980, Sophia Charlotte Knox; two *s.* *Educ:* Westminster Sch.; New Coll., Oxford (BA 1st Cl. Hons Chinese). Far Eastern Department, Victoria & Albert Museum: Res. Asst, 1974–77; Asst Keeper, 1977–82; Keeper, 1982–87. Consultant, Christie's, 1998–. Exhibns Co-ordinator, Japan Fest. 1991, 1990–91; *other exhibitions include:* Japan Style, V&A, 1980; Japanese Lacquer, V&A, 1980; Great Japan Exhibition, RA, 1981; The Toshiba Gall. of Japanese Art, V&A, 1986; British Design, South Coast Plaza, 1990; Visions of Japan, V&A, 1991–92; London Transport Posters, 1994; Da un antico castello inglese, Milan, 1994; Shibata Zeshin, Nat. Mus. of Scotland, 1997; Splendors of Meiji, USA, 1999; Netsuke, Mus. of Fine Arts, Boston, 2001; Serizawa: Master of Japanese Textile Design, Nat. Mus of Scotland, 2001. Trustee, Design Mus., 1988–. *Publications:* An Introduction to Netsuke, 1980, 2nd edn 1982; An Introduction to Japanese Prints, 1980; (contrib.) Japan Style, 1980; (contrib.) The Great Japan Exhibition, 1981; (trans.) The Japanese Sword, 1983; The Toshiba Gallery: Japanese art and design, 1986; Flower Bronzes of Japan, 1995; (ed) Treasures of Imperial Japan: Lacquer, 1995; (ed) The Index of Inro Artists, 1995; Shibata Zeshin, 1996; Shadows and Reflections: Japanese lacquer art, 1996; Flowers of the Chisel, 1997; R. S. Huthart Collection of Netsuke, 1998; Splendors of Meiji, 1999; Infinite Spaces: the art and wisdom of the Japanese garden, 2000; Netsuke of Iwami Province, 2000; Japanese Lacquer: The Denys Eyre Bower Collection, 2000; Netsuke: fantasy and reality in Japanese miniature sculpture, 2001; articles in learned jls. *Address:* 123 Middleton Road, E8 4LL. *T:* (020) 7923 2662; *e-mail:* joe@bunkajin.demon.co.uk.
See also T. F. Earle.

EARLE, John Nicholas Francis, (Nick); Headmaster, Bromsgrove School, 1971–85; *b* 14 Nov. 1926; *s* of John William Arthur Earle and Vivien Constance Fenton (*née* Davies); *m* 1959, Ann Veronica Lester; one *s* two *d.* *Educ:* Winchester Coll.; Trinity Coll., Cambridge. 1st cl. Maths Tripos pt 2, 1st cl. Theol. Tripos pt 1; MA. Deacon, 1952; Priest, 1953; relinquished Holy Orders, 1994. Curate, St Matthew, Moorfields, 1952–57; PARS Fellow, Union Theol Seminary, New York, 1957–58; Lectr, St Botolph, Aldgate, 1958–61; Asst Master, Dulwich Coll., 1961–71. *Publications:* What's Wrong With the Church?, 1961; Culture and Creed, 1967; Logic, 1973; Does God Make Sense?, 1998. *Recreations:* travel, gardening. *Address:* 1 Red Post Hill, Pond Mead, SE21 7BX.

EARLE, Prof. Thomas Foster, DPhil; King John II Professor of Portuguese Studies, University of Oxford, since 1996; Fellow, St Peter's College, Oxford, since 1996; *b* 5 April 1946; *s* of late James Basil Foster Earle and Mary Earle (*née* Weeks); *m* 1970, Gisèle Hilary Wilson; one *s* one *d.* *Educ:* Westminster Sch.; Wadham Coll., Oxford (BA 1967; DPhil 1976). University of Oxford: Lectr in Portuguese Studies, 1968–96; Fellow, Linacre Coll., 1968–96; Dir, Portuguese Studies, 1976–96; Chm., Centre for Study of Portuguese

Discoveries, Linacre Coll., 1989–. Founder Mem., Associação Internacional de Lusitanistas, 1984. Grande oficial, Ordem do Infante D. Henrique (Portugal), 1995. *Publications:* Theme and Image in the Poetry of Sá de Miranda, 1980 (trans. Portuguese 1985); The Muse Reborn: the poetry of António Ferreira, 1988 (trans. Portuguese 1990); (ed) Castro de António Ferreira, 1990; (with J. Villiers) Albuquerque: Caesar of the East, 1990; (ed) Poemas Lusitanos de António Ferreira, 2000; articles in collections, learned jls, etc. *Recreations:* music, gardening, walking. *Address:* Taylor Institution, St Giles', Oxford OX1 3NA. *T:* (01865) 270474.

See also J. V. Earle.

EARLES, Prof. Stanley William Edward, PhD, DScEng; FREng, FIMechE; Professor of Mechanical Engineering, King's College, University of London, 1976–94, Emeritus since 1994; *b* 18 Jan. 1929; *s* of late William Edward Earles and Winnifred Anne Cook; *m* 1955, Margaret Isabella Brown; two *d. Educ:* King's Coll., Univ. of London (BScEng, PhD, DScEng; AKC; FKC 1993). FIMechE 1976; FREng (FEng 1992). Nuffield Apprentice, Birmingham, 1944–50; King's Coll., Univ. of London, 1950–53; Scientific Officer, Royal Naval Scientific Service, 1953–55; University of London: Queen Mary College: Lectr in Mech. Eng, 1955–69; Reader in Mech. Eng, 1969–75; Prof. of Mech. Eng, 1975–76; King's College: Head, Dept of Mech. Engrg, 1976–90, 1991–94; Dean of Engrg, 1986–90; Hd of Sch. of Phys. Scis and Engrg, 1990–91. James Clayton Fund prize, IMechE, 1967; Engineering Applied to Agriculture Award, IMechE, 1980. *Publications:* papers and articles in Proc. IMechE, Jl of Mech. Eng Science, Jl of Sound and Vibration, Wear, Proc. ASME and ASLE, and Eng. *Recreations:* Real tennis, gardening, fell walking. *Address:* Woodbury, Church Lane, Wormley, Broxbourne, Herts EN10 7QF. *T:* (01992) 464616.

EARNSHAW, (Thomas) Roy, CBE 1978 (OBE 1971); Director and General Manager of Division, TBA Industrial Products Ltd, Rochdale, 1966–76; retired; *b* 27 Feb. 1917; *s* of Godfrey Earnshaw and Edith Annie (*née* Perry); *m* 1953, Edith Rushworth; two *d. Educ:* Marlborough Coll., Liverpool. MICS. Served War, Army, 1940–46: Major Lancs Fusiliers. Shipbroking, Liverpool, 1933–39; appts with subsid. cos of Turner & Newall Ltd: Turner Brothers Asbestos Co. Ltd, Rochdale (mainly Export Sales Manager), 1939–40 and 1946–53; Dir, AM&FM Ltd, Bombay, 1954–59; Export Dir, Ferodo Ltd, Chapel-en-le-Frith, 1959–66. British Overseas Trade Board: Mem. Adv. Council, 1975–82; Export Year Advr, 1976–77; Export United Advr, 1978–83. Director: Actair Holdings Ltd, 1979–83; Actair Internat. Ltd, 1979–83; Unico Finance Ltd, 1979–81. Formerly: Pres., Rochdale Chamber of Commerce; Chm., NW Region Chambers of Commerce; UK Delegate to European Chambers of Commerce. London Economic Adviser to Merseyside CC, 1980–82. Vis. Fellow, Henley Management Coll. (formerly ASC), 1981–90. Chm., Henley Crime Prevention Panel, 1992–94; Mem., Bd of Managers, Henley YMCA, 1989–91; Sec., Henley Wildlife Gp, 1994–99. FRSA. *Publication:* Glad Hearts in Export Year, 1991. *Recreations:* gardening, oil painting, hill walking, cycling. *Club:* Leander (Henley-on-Thames).

EARWICKER, Martin John, FREng, FIOA, FRAeS, FInstP; Chief Executive, Defence Science and Technology Laboratory, Office of Science and Technology, Department of Trade and Industry, since 2001; *b* 11 May 1948; *s* of George Allen Earwicker and Joan Mary Earwicker (*née* West); *m* 1970, Pauline Ann Josey; two *s. Educ:* Farnborough Grammar Sch.; Univ. of Surrey (BSc Hons Physics 1970). FIOA 1984; FRAeS 1996; FInstP 1999; FREng 2000. Various research posts, ARE, 1970–86; Dir, Science (Sea), MoD, 1986–89; Hd, Attack Weapons Dept, 1989–90, Hd, Flight Systems Dept, 1990–92, RAE; Dir, Operational Studies, 1992–93, Dir, Air Systems Sector, 1993–96, DRA; Dep. Chief Scientist (Scrutiny and Analysis), 1996–98, Dir Gen. (Scrutiny and Analysis), 1998–99, MoD; Man. Dir, Analysis, DERA, 1998–99; Hd of Science and Engrg Base Gp, OST, DTI, 1999–2001. *Publications:* contrib. Jl of Acoustical Soc. of America, Jl of Sound and Vibration. *Recreations:* cycling, woodwork, music. *Address:* Office of Science and Technology, Department of Trade and Industry, 94–98 Petty France, SW1H 9ST.

EASEN-THOMAS, Rita Margaret; *see* Donaghy, R. M.

EASMON, Prof. Charles Syrett Farrell, CBE 2000; Md, PhD; Director of Education and Training, London (formerly North Thames) Region, NHS Executive, since 1994; *b* 20 Aug. 1946; *s* of Dr McCormack Charles Farrell Easmon and Enid Winifred Easmon; *m* 1977, Susan Lynn (*née* Peach). *Educ:* Epsom Coll.; St Mary's Hospital Med. Sch. (Open Schol.; MB BS; MD); PhD London. MRCP; FRCPath. Pathology trng, St Bartholomew's Hosp., 1970–71; St Mary's Hospital Medical School: Research Asst, 1971; Lectr, 1973; Sen. Lectr, 1976; Reader and Actg Head of Dept, 1980; Personal Chair, 1983; Fleming Prof. of Med. Microbiol., 1984–92; Dean of Postgrad. Med. for NW Thames, BPMF, Univ. of London, 1992–95. Founder FMedSci 1998. *Publications:* (ed) Medical Microbiology, vol. 1 1982, vols 2 and 3 1983, vol. 4 1984; (ed) Infections in the Immunocompromised Host, 1983; (ed) Staphylococci and Staphylococcal Infections, 1983; numerous papers in learned jls. *Recreations:* music, history, fishing. *Address:* 21 Cranes Park Avenue, Surbiton, Surrey KT5 8BS.

EASON, Anthony Gordon, CBE 1995; JP; Managing Director, Hong Kong Experts Consultancy Co. Ltd, since 2000 (Executive Director, 1997–2000); *b* 30 May 1938; *s* of Aubrey Eason and Helen Eason (*née* Hajj); *m* 1962, Teresa Wong; two *d. Educ:* Chatham House Grammar Sch., Ramsgate; RMA, Sandhurst. Served RA, 1959–62. Hong Kong Civil Service: Exec. Officer, 1962–68; Admin. Service, 1968–89; Dir, Buildings and Lands, 1989–92; Sec. for Planning, Envmt and Lands, 1992–95. Mem., Supervisory Bd, HK Housing Soc., 2000–. Hon. Exec. Dir, Centre for Asian Tall Buildings and Urban Habitat, 1995–97. JP Hong Kong, 1996. *Recreations:* reading, walking, writing. *Address:* Flat C, 5th Floor, Green Valley Mansion, 51 Wong Nai Chung Road, Happy Valley, Hong Kong.

EASON, Henry, CBE 1967; JP; a Vice-President of the Institute of Bankers, 1969–75, and Consultant with special reference to overseas relationships, 1971–74 (Secretary-General, 1959–71); *b* 12 April 1910; *s* of late H. Eason and F. J. Eason; *m* 1939 (at Hexham Abbey), Isobel (*d* 1992), *d* of late Wm and Dorothy Stevenson; one *s* two *d. Educ:* Yarm (Schol.); King's Coll., University of Durham BCom (with distinction). Barrister-at-law, Gray's Inn. Served Lloyds Bank until 1939; Asst Sec., Institute of Bankers, 1939. Served War of 1939–45 and until 1946, with Royal Air Force (Wing Commander, despatches twice). Asst Dir, Military Gov. (Banking), NW Europe, 1944–46; United Nations Adviser (Banking) to Pakistan Govt, 1952; Deputy Sec., Institute of Bankers, 1956; Governor, City of London Coll., 1958–69; Mem., British National Cttee, Internat. Chamber Commerce, 1959–74. Director: Internat. Banking Summer Sch., Christ Church, Oxford, 1961, 1964, 1970; Cambridge Banking Seminar, Christ's Coll., Cambridge, 1968 and 1969. Editor, Jl Inst. of Bankers, 1959–71. Hon. Fellow, Inst. of Bankers, 1971. JP Bromley 1967. Gen. Comr of Income Tax, Bromley, 1973–76. *Publications:* contributions to professional journals. *Recreations:* golf, walking, gardening, world travel. *Address:* 12 Redgate Drive, Hayes Common, Bromley BR2 7BT. *T:* (020) 8462 1900. *Clubs:* Gresham, Bankers'; Langley Park Golf.

EASSIE, Hon. Lord; Ronald David Mackay; a Senator of the College of Justice in Scotland, since 1997; *b* 1945; *s* of Robert Ostler Mackay and Dorothy Lilian Johnson or Mackay; *m* 1988, Annette Frenkel; one *s. Educ:* Berwickshire High Sch.; Univ. of St Andrews (MA Hons); Univ. of Edinburgh (LLB). Admitted to Faculty of Advocates, 1972; Official of Court of Justice of European Communities, Luxembourg, 1979–82; QC (Scot.) 1986; Advocate Depute, 1986–90. *Recreations:* walking, ski-ing. *Address:* Parliament House, Parliament Square, Edinburgh EH1 1RQ. *Club:* New (Edinburgh).

EAST, David Albert, QPM 1982; Secretary, Welsh Rugby Union, 1989; *b* 5 June 1936; *s* of Albert East and Florence Emily East; *m* 1957, Gloria (*née* Swinden); one *d. Educ:* King Alfred Grammar Sch., Wantage, Berks; University Coll. London (LLB Hons). Berks Constabulary, 1958–65 (constable to sergeant); First Special Course, Police Coll., Bramshill, 1962 (Johnson Prize and Cert. of Distinction); Inspector, York City Police, 1965–68; UCL, 1965–68; Metropol. Police Chief Inspector to Chief Supt, 1968–75; Eight Sen. Comd Course, Bramshill, 1971; Asst Chief Constable, Avon and Somerset Constab., 1975–78; RCDS, 1978; Dep. Chief Constable, Devon and Cornwall Constab., 1978–82, Chief Constable, 1982–83; seconded to Cyprus, 1981 and to Singapore, 1982; Chief Constable, S Wales Constab., 1983–88. Chm., British Police Athletic Assoc. OStJ 1985. Police Long Service and Good Conduct Medal, 1980. *Recreations:* Rugby, cricket.

EAST, John Anthony, CBE 1996 (OBE 1982); Chief Executive, English Tourist Board, 1985–95; Chairman: Heritage Projects Ltd, since 1997; Valuelink Ltd, since 1998; *b* 25 May 1930; *s* of John East and Jessie Mary East; *m* 1st, 1957, Barbara Collins (marr. diss. 1980); two *s* one *d*; 2nd, 1982, Susan Finch (marr. diss. 1996); two *d. Educ:* Bromley Grammar School. Reuter's, 1954–58; Notley Advertising, 1958–60; Director: French Government Tourist Office, 1960–70; English Tourist Bd, 1970–95. Chm., Watermark, 1995–97. *Publications:* History of French Architecture, 1968; Gascony and the Pyrenees, 1969; articles on France and French architecture. *Recreations:* walking, gardening, studying things French. *Address:* (office) 79 Mount Street, W1Y 5HJ.

EAST, Kenneth Arthur, CMG 1971; HM Diplomatic Service, retired; Ambassador to Iceland, 1975–81; *b* 9 May 1921; *s* of H. F. East; *m* 1946, Katherine Blackley; two *s* three *d. Educ:* Taunton's Sch; Southampton Univ. Served HM Forces, 1942–46. India Office/Commonwealth Relations Office, 1946–50; Asst Private Sec. to Sec. of State; First Secretary: Ottawa, 1950–53; Colombo, 1956–60; Head of East and General Africa Dept, CRO, 1961–63; Head of Personnel Dept, CRO, 1963–64; Counsellor, Diplomatic Service Administration, 1965; Counsellor and Head of Chancery, Oslo, 1965–70; Minister, Lagos, 1970–74. *Club:* Royal Commonwealth Society.

EAST, Rt Hon. Paul Clayton; PC 1998; QC (NZ) 1995; High Commissioner for New Zealand in the United Kingdom, 1999–2002; *b* 4 Aug. 1946; *s* of Edwin Cuthbert East and Edith Pauline Addison East; *m* 1972, Marilyn Kottman; three *d. Educ:* King's Coll., Auckland; Auckland Univ. (LLB 1970); Univ. of Virginia, USA (LLM 1972). Barrister and solicitor, Auckland, 1971; Graduate Fellow, Univ. of Va Sch. of Law, 1971–72; Partner, 1974–78, Consultant, 1978–90, East Brewster, Solicitors, Rotorua. City Councillor, and Dep. Mayor of Rotorua, 1974–79 (Chm., Finance Cttee, 1977–79). MP (N) New Zealand, 1978–99 (for Rotorua, 1978–96). Opposition Spokesman, NZ Parliament: for Commerce and Customs, 1984; on Justice, Attorney-Gen. and Constitutional Affairs, 1985–90; on Health, 1986; Attorney-Gen., 1990–97; Minister: for Crown Health Enterprises, 1991–96; of State Services, 1993–97; of Defence, and of Corrections, 1996–97. Leader of House of Representatives, 1990–93. Chm., Parly Select Cttee on Official Information, 1982; Member: Nat. Exec., NZ Nat. Party, 1985–87; NZ Delegn, Council of Europe and Eur. Parlt, 1985. Chm., Rotorua Airport Cttee, 1977–79; Mem. Exec., Airport Authorities of NZ, 1974–79. Comr, Commonwealth War Graves Commn. Trustee: Rotorua Hospice; UK Antarctic Heritage Trust. Fellow, Australia/NZ Foundn, 1983. *Publications:* numerous articles. *Recreations:* ski-ing, fishing, golf. *Address:* c/o New Zealand High Commission, New Zealand House, Haymarket, SW1Y 4TQ; PO Box 608, Rotorua, New Zealand. *Club:* Travellers.

EAST, Ronald Joseph; formerly Director: Kleinwort Charter Investment Trust PLC; Kleinwort Development Fund PLC; *b* 17 Dec. 1931; *s* of Joseph William and Marion Elizabeth Emma East; *m* 1955, Iris Joyce Beckwith; two *d. Educ:* Clare Coll., Cambridge Univ. (MA). Engineering Apprenticeship, Ford Trade Sch., Ford Motor Co. Ltd, 1945–52. Troop Comdr, RA (Lieut), 1953–55. Managerial posts in economics, product planning, finance, and engineering areas of Ford Motor Co. Ltd, 1959–65; Guest, Keen & Nettlefolds Ltd: Corporate Staff Dir of Planning, 1965–70; Planning Exec., Automotive and Allied Products Sector, 1972–73; Chairman: GKN Castings Ltd, 1974–77; GKN Kent Alloys Ltd, 1974–77; GKN Shotton Ltd, 1974–77; Dir, GKN (UK) Ltd, 1974–77; Corporate Staff Dir, Group Supplies, GKN Ltd, 1976–77. Dir, Programme Analysis and Review (PAR) and Special Advisor to Chief Sec. to the Treasury, 1971–72. Chairman: Hale Hamilton Hldgs, 1981–89; Hale Hamilton (Valves), 1981–89. *Recreations:* walking, ski-ing, ethnology, dramatic art. *Address:* 12 Rutland Gate, SW7 1BB.

EAST ANGLIA, Bishop of, (RC); *no new appointment at time of going to press.*

EAST RIDING, Archdeacon of; *see* Harrison, Ven. P. R. W.

EASTCOTT, Harry Hubert Grayson, MS; FRCS; FRCOG; Consulting Surgeon, St Mary's Hospital; Consultant in Surgery and Vascular Surgery to the Royal Navy, 1957–82, now Emeritus; *b* 17 Oct. 1917; *s* of Harry George and Gladys Eastcott; *m* 1941, Doreen Joy, *e d* of Brenchley Ernest and Muriel Mittell; four *d. Educ:* Latymer Sch.; St Mary's Hosp. Medical School and Middlesex Hospital Medical Sch., University of London; Harvard Med. Sch. War of 1939–45, Junior surgical appts and service as Surgeon Lieut, RNVR up till 1946. Surg. Lieut Comdr RNVR, London Div., until 1957. MRCS; LRCP; MB, BS (Hons), 1941; FRCS 1946; MS (London), 1951. Sen. Registrar, 1950 as Hon. Cons. to St Mary's and Asst Dir Surgical Unit; Research Fellow in Surgery, Harvard Med. Sch., and Peter Bent Brigham Hosp., Boston, Mass, 1949–50; recognised teacher, 1953, and Examr, 1959, in surgery, University of London; Cons. Surgeon, St Mary's Hosp. and Lectr in Surgery, St Mary's Hosp. Med. Sch., 1955–82; Surgeon, Royal Masonic Hosp., 1964–80; Cons. Surgeon, King Edward VII Hosp. for Officers, 1965–87; Hon. Surg., RADA, 1959–; External Examr in Surgery: Queen's Univ., Belfast, 1964–67; Cambridge Univ., 1968–84; Univ. of Lagos, Nigeria, 1970–71. Editorial Sec., British Jl of Surgery, 1972–78. Royal College of Surgeons: Hunterian Prof., 1953; Mem. Court of Examrs, 1964–70; Mem. Council, 1971–83; Bradshaw Lectr, 1980; Vice-Pres., 1981–83; Cecil Joll Prize, 1984; RCS Visitor to RCOG Council, 1972–80; Mem. Court of Patrons, 1997–. FRSocMed (Hon. Sec., Section of Surgery, 1963–65, Vice-President, 1966, Pres., 1977; Pres., United Services Section, 1981–83, Hon. Mem., 1992). Fellow Medical Soc. of London (Hon. Sec., 1962–64, Vice-Pres. 1964, Pres., 1976, Fothergill Gold Medal, 1974, Trustee 1988). Pres., Assoc. of Surgeons of GB and Ireland, 1982–83. Mem., Soc. Apothecaries, 1967 (Galen Medal, 1993). Hon. FACS, 1977; Hon. FRACS, 1978; Hon. Fellow: Amer. Surgical Assoc., 1981; Amer. Heart Assoc.; Stroke Council, 1981; Hon. Member: Purkinje Med. Soc., Czechoslovakia, 1984; Internat. Union of Angiology, 1995; Europ. Soc. for Vascular Surgery, 1995. *Publications:* Arterial Surgery, 1969, 3rd edn 1992;

A Colour Atlas of Operations on the Internal Carotid Artery, 1984; various articles on gen. and arterial surgery, Lancet, Brit. Jl of Surg., etc.; contrib. chap. of peripheral vascular disease, Med. Annual, 1961–80; various chaps in textbooks on these subjects. *Recreations:* music, travel, and a lifelong interest in aeronautics. *Address:* 47 Chiltern Court, Baker Street, NW1 5SP. *T:* (020) 7935 2020. *Club:* Garrick.

EASTERLING, Prof. Patricia Elizabeth, FBA 1998; Regius Professor of Greek, Cambridge University, 1994–2001, and Fellow of Newnham College, Cambridge, 1994–2001 (Hon. Fellow, 1987–94 and since 2001); *b* 11 March 1934; *d* of Edward Wilson Fairfax and Annie Smith; *m* 1956, Henry John Easterling; one *s*. *Educ:* Blackburn High School for Girls; Newnham College, Cambridge (BA 1955, MA 1959). Asst Lectr, Univ. of Manchester, 1957–58; University of Cambridge: Asst Lectr, 1968; Lectr, 1969–87; Newnham College, Cambridge: Asst Lectr, 1958–60; Fellow and Lectr, 1960–87; Dir of Studies in Classics, 1979–87; Vice-Principal, 1981–86; Prof. of Greek, UCL, 1987–94. Townsend Lectr, Cornell Univ., 1990. Chm., Council of Univ. Classical Depts, 1990–93. President: Classical Assoc., 1988–89; Hellenic Soc., 1996–99. Mem., Academia Europaea, 1995. Hon. Fellow, UCL, 1997. Hon. DPhil: Athens, 1996; Uppsala, 2000; Hon. DLitt Bristol, 1999; Hon. DLit London, 1999. *Publications:* (with E. J. Kenney) Ovidiana Graeca, 1965; (ed) Sophocles, Trachiniae, 1982; (with B. M. W. Knox, ed and contrib.) Cambridge History of Classical Literature, vol. I, 1985; (ed with J. V. Muir) Greek Religion and Society, 1985; (ed) Cambridge Companion to Greek Tragedy, 1997; articles and reviews in classical jls. *Recreation:* hill walking. *Address:* Newnham College, Cambridge CB3 9DF. *T:* (01223) 335700.

EASTHAM, Kenneth; *b* 11 Aug. 1927; *s* of late James Eastham; *m* 1951, Doris, *d* of Albert Howarth; one *d*. Planning engr, GEC, Trafford Park. Mem., Manchester CC, 1962–80 (Dep. Leader 1975–79; Chairman: Planning Cttee, 1971–74; Educn Cttee, 1978–79); Mem., NW Econ. Planning Council, 1975–79. MP (Lab) Manchester, Blackley, 1979–97. An Opposition Whip, 1987–92. *Address:* 12 Nan Nook Road, Manchester M23 9BZ.

EASTON, David John; HM Diplomatic Service, retired; Secretary, Royal Society for Asian Affairs, since 1997; *b* 27 March 1941; *o s* of Air Cdre Sir James Easton, KCMG, CB, CBE, and Anna, *d* of Lt-Col J. A. McKenna, Ottawa; *m* 1964, Alexandra Julie, *er d* of Kenneth W. Clark (MBE 2000), London, W8; two *s* two *d*. *Educ:* Stone House, Broadstairs; Stowe (Exhbnr); Balliol Coll., Oxford (Trevelyan Schol.; BA Hons Jurisprudence 1963, MA 1973). Apprentice, United Steel Cos, Workington, 1960. TA, 1959–65; 2nd Lieut, Oxford Univ. OTC, 1962; Lieut, Inns of Court and City Yeo., 1964. Entered Foreign Office, 1963; Third Sec., Nairobi, 1965–66; Second Sec., UK Mission to UN, Geneva, 1967–70; MECAS, Lebanon, 1970–72; First Sec., FCO, 1972–73; First Sec. (Information), Tripoli, 1973–77; Defence Dept, FCO, 1977–80; First Sec. (Chancery), later Political Counsellor, Amman, 1980–83; Counsellor, FCO, 1984–86; Counsellor (Political), New Delhi, 1986–89; FCO, 1990–94; Gen. Manager, Network Security Mgt Ltd, 1994–95; Dir (Internat. Affairs), ICAEW, 1995–97. Director, Internat. Community Sch. (Jordan) Ltd, 1980–83 (Chm. 1981–83). Pres., Delhi Diplomatic Assoc., 1988–89; Chm., Lansdowne Residents' Assoc., 1990–96. FRSA 1996; FRGS 1998. *Recreations:* swimming, travel, antiques and antiquities. *Address:* (office) 2 Belgrave Square, SW1X 8PJ. *T:* (020) 7235 5122.

EASTON, James, OBE 1986; HM Diplomatic Service, retired; Feature Writer, Accordion Times, since 1992; *b* 1 Sept. 1931; *s* of John Easton and Helen Easton (*née* Whitney); *m* 1960, Rosemary Hobbin; one *s* two *d*. *Educ:* St John Cantius Catholic Sch., Broxburn. Served 3rd Hussars, 1952–55. Admiralty, 1957–60; FO, 1960; Prague, 1960–62; Paris, 1963–65; FO, 1965–68; Vice-Consul: Belgrade, 1968–71; La Paz, 1971–74; Second Sec. (Commercial), New York, 1974–78; FCO, 1978–83; First Sec., Rome, 1983–87; Counsellor (Admin) and Consul-Gen., Brussels, 1987–89. *Recreation:* music. *Address:* 6 Cedar Gardens, Sutton, Surrey SM2 5DD. *T:* (020) 8643 2432.

EASTON, Robert Alexander, PhD; Chief Executive, Delta plc, 1989–96; *b* 24 Oct. 1948; *s* of Malcolm Edward George Easton and Violet May Liddell Easton (*née* Taylor); *m* 1983, Lynden Anne Welch; two *d*. *Educ:* St Lawrence Coll.; Univ. of Manchester (BSc Hons); Univ. of Aston (PhD). Delta plc, 1974–96: Dir of Planning, 1980–83; Man. Dir, Industrial Services Div., 1984–87; Dep. Chief Exec., 1988–89. Director: G. E. Crane (Holdings), 1986–91; Elementis (formerly Harrisons & Crosfield) plc, 1991–. *Recreations:* golf, travel, medieval art and architecture.

EASTON, Sir Robert (William Simpson), Kt 1990; CBE 1980; CEng, FIMechE, FIMarE, FRINA; Chairman: Yarrow Shipbuilders Ltd, 1979–94; GEC Scotland, 1989–99; *b* 30 Oct. 1922; *s* of James Easton and Helen Agnes (*née* Simpson); *m* 1948, Jean, *d* of H. K. Fraser and Jean (*née* Murray); one *s* one *d*. *Educ:* Royal Technical Coll., Glasgow. Fairfield Shipbuilding Co., 1939–51; Manager, Yarrow & Co. Ltd, 1951–65; Yarrow Shipbuilders Ltd: Director, 1965; Dep. Managing Director, 1970; Managing Director, 1977–91; Main Board Director, Yarrow & Co. Ltd, 1970–77. Vice Pres., Clyde Shipbuilders, 1972–79; Chm., Clyde Port Authy, 1983–93. Chm., GEC Naval Systems, 1991–94; Director: Genships (Canada), 1979–80; Supermarine Consortium Ltd, 1986–90; W of Scotland Water Authy, 1995–97; Caledonian MacBrayne Ltd, 1997–2000. Chancellor, Paisley Univ., 1993–. President: Inst. of Welding, 1991–93; Inst. of Engineers and Shipbuilders, Scotland, 1997–99; Member: Council, RINA, 1983–91 (Hon. Vice Pres., 1991–); Worshipful Company of Shipwrights, 1982–96; Merchants House of Glasgow, 1989–; Incorporation of Hammermen, 1989–. *Recreations:* walking, golf, gardening. *Address:* Springfield, Stuckenduff, Shandon, Dunbartonshire G84 8NW. *T:* (01436) 820677. *Club:* Caledonian.

EASTWOOD, Basil Stephen Talbot, CMG 1999; HM Diplomatic Service; Ambassador to Switzerland, since 2001; *b* 4 March 1944; *s* of late Christopher Gilbert Eastwood, CMG and Catherine Emma (*née* Peel); *m* 1970, Alison Faith Hutchings; three *d* (and one *d* decd). *Educ:* Eton (KS); Merton College, Oxford. Entered Diplomatic Service, 1966; Middle East Centre for Arab Studies, 1967–68; Jedda, 1968–69; Colombo, 1969–72; Cairo, 1972–76; Cabinet Office, 1976–78; FCO, 1978–80; Bonn, 1980–84; Khartoum, 1984–87; Athens, 1987–91; Dir of Res. and Analysis, FCO, 1991–96; Ambassador to Syria, 1996–2000; Project Dir, Middle East Inst., 2000–01. *Address:* c/o Foreign and Commonwealth Office, SW1A 2AH.

EASTWOOD, Prof. David Stephen, DPhil; FRHistS; Chief Executive, Arts and Humanities Research Board, since 2000; *b* 5 Jan. 1959; *s* of Colin Eastwood and Elaine Clara Eastwood; *m* 1980, Jan Page; one *s* two *d*. *Educ:* Sandbach Sch., Cheshire; St Peter's Coll., Oxford (BA 1st Cl. Hons Modern Hist.; MA 1985; DPhil 1985). FRHistS 1991. Jun. Res. Fellow, Keble Coll., Oxford, 1983–87; Fellow and Tutor in Modern Hist., 1988–95, Sen. Tutor, 1992–95, Pembroke Coll., Oxford; Dep. Chair, Bd of Faculty of Modern Hist., Univ. of Oxford, 1994–95; University of Wales, Swansea: Prof. of Social Hist., 1995–2000; Hd, Dept of Hist., 1996–2000; Actg Hd, Dept of Philosophy, 1998–99; Dean, Faculty of Arts and Social Studies, 1997–99; Pro-Vice-Chancellor, 1999–2000. British Acad. Post-Doctoral Fellow, 1986–87. Literary Dir, RHistS, 1994–2000. Chair of Examrs, A Level Hist., UODLE, O&C, OCR, 1991–2000. Co-founder and non-exec. Chair, Nat. Centre for Public Policy, 1998–2000. *Publications:* Governing Rural England: tradition and transformation in local government 1780-1840, 1994; Government and Community in the English Provinces 1700-1870, 1997; (ed with L. Brockliss) A Union of Multiple Identities: the British Isles *c* 1750-*c* 1850, 1997; (ed with N. Thompson) The Social and Political Writings of William Cobbett, 16 vols, 1998; numerous papers in scholarly jls, edited vols, etc. *Recreations:* music, collecting books and CDs, current affairs, walking, watching sport. *Address:* Arts and Humanities Research Board, Whitefriars, Lewins Mead, Bristol BS1 2AE. *T:* (0117) 987 6500, *Fax:* (0117) 987 6600; 49 Wentworth Crescent, Mayals, Swansea SA3 5HT. *T:* (01792) 403338.

EASTWOOD, John Stephen; a Recorder, 1987–92; Regional Chairman of Industrial Tribunals, Nottingham Region, 1983–92; *b* 27 April 1925; *s* of Rev. John Edgar Eastwood and Elfreda Eastwood; *m* 1949, Nancy (*née* Gretton); one *s* two *d*. *Educ:* Denstone College, Uttoxeter. Solicitor. RN (Coder), 1943–46. Articles, and Asst Sol. to Leics CC, 1946–50; Asst Sol., Salop CC, 1950–53; Sen. Asst Sol., Northants CC, 1953–58; Partner, Wilson & Wilson, Solicitors, Kettering, 1958–76; Chm., Industrial Tribunals, 1976–83; Asst Recorder, 1983–87. *Recreations:* music, painting, photography, walking, gardening, exploring British Isles, grandchildren. *Address:* 59 Beatrice Road, Kettering, Northants NN16 9QS. *T:* (01536) 514906.

EASTWOOD, Noel Anthony Michael, MA; CEng, MRAeS; Chairman, InterData Group, 1981–93; *b* 7 Dec. 1932; *s* of Edward Norman Eastwood and Irene Dawson; *m* 1965, Elizabeth Tania Gresham Boyd, *d* of Comdr Thomas Wilson Boyd, CBE, DSO, DL and Irene Barbara Gresham; three *s*. *Educ:* The Leys School, Cambridge; Christ's College, Cambridge. Lieut RA, 1951–54; Pilot Officer, RAFVR, 1954–57; de Havilland Aircraft Co., 1956–60; Rio Tinto, 1960–61; AEI Group, 1961–64; Director: Charterhouse Development, 1964–69; Charterhouse Japhet, 1969–79 (Pres., Charterhouse Japhet Texas, 1974–77); Charterhouse Middle East, 1975–79; Burnett & Rolfe Ltd, 1964–69 (Chm.); Wharton Crane & Hoist, 1967–70 (Chm.); Daniel Doncaster & Son (International Nickel), 1971–81; The Barden Corp., 1971–82; Hawk Publishing (UAE), 1981–87; Oryx Publishing (Qatar), 1981–87; Falcon Publishing (Bahrain), 1981–84; Caribbean Publishing, 1981–84; IDP InterData (Australia), 1984–92 and 1995–96; European Public Policy Advisers Gp, 1987–97; Spearhead Communications, 1988–99; Seafish Falklands Ltd (Port Stanley), 1990–95; PGI Europe Ltd, 1995–99. Sec., RAeS, 1983. Member: London Cttee, Yorkshire & Humberside Development Assoc., 1975–94; Management Cttee, Offshore Europe Conf. and Exhibn, 1990–; S Atlantic Council, 1991–. Member: Much Hadham PCC, 1989–; Much Hadham Parish Council, 1995–97; St Albans Diocesan Synod, 1997–. Hon. Treas., Herts Soc., 1992–99; Mem. Exec. Cttee, CPRE, 1995–98 (Chm., SE Reg., 1995–2000; Mem., E of England Cttee, 1999–); Chairman: Thames NE Area Envmt Gp, 1997–; E England Envmtl Forum, 1999–; Mem., Thames and Chilterns Regl Cttee, Nat. Trust, 2001–. Founder, Royal Artillery Heritage Campaign, 1991. *Recreations:* ski-ing, sailing, vintage sportscars, family picnics, desert travel. *Address:* Palace House, Much Hadham, Herts SG10 6HW. *T:* (01279) 842409. *Club:* Royal Thames Yacht.

EASTWOOD, Dr Wilfred, PhD; FREng, FICE, FIStructE, FIMechE; Senior Partner, Eastwood and Partners, Consulting Engineers, 1972–2000; *b* 15 Aug. 1923; *s* of Wilfred Andrew Eastwood and Annice Gertrude Eastwood; *m* 1947, Dorothy Jean Gover; one *s* one *d*. Road Research Laboratory, 1945–46; University of Manchester, 1946–47; University of Aberdeen, 1947–53; University of Sheffield, 1954–70: Head, Dept of Civil Engrg, 1964–70; Dean, Faculty of Engrg, 1967–70. Pres., IStructE, 1976–77; Chairman: CEI, 1983–84; Commonwealth Engrg Council, 1983–85. Hon. DEng Sheffield, 1983. *Publications:* papers in Proc. ICE and Jl IStructE, etc. *Address:* 45 Whirlow Park Road, Sheffield S11 9NN. *T:* (0114) 236 4645. *Club:* Yorkshire County Cricket (Leeds).

EASTY, Prof. David Leonello, MD; FRCS, FCOphth; Professor of Ophthalmology and Head of Department of Ophthalmology, University of Bristol, 1982–99, now Professor Emeritus; *b* 1933; *s* of Arthur Victor Easty and Florence Margaret (*née* Kennedy); *m* 1963, Božana Martinović; three *d*. *Educ:* King's Sch., Canterbury; Univ. of Manchester. MD 1963; FRCS 1969; FCOphth 1988. Capt., RAMC, 1959; Med. Officer, British Antarctic Survey, 1960. Moorfield's Eye Hospital: Resident, 1966–69; Lectr, 1969–72; Consultant, Bristol Eye Hosp., 1972–82. Dir, Corneal Transplant Service Eye Bank, 1986–99. Lectures: Lang, RSocMed, 1998; Doyne, Oxford Congress of Ophthalmol., 1999; Bowman, Univ. of Bristol, 2000. Netteship Medal for Research, 1999. Member: BMA; RSocMed (Pres., Sect. of Ophthalmol., 1998–2000); Internat. Soc. for Eye Res.; Assoc. for Res. in Vision and Ophthalmology. Member: Antarctic Club; Piscatorial Soc. *Publications:* Virus Disease of the Eye, 1985; (with G. Smolim) External Eye Disease, 1985; (ed) Current Ophthalmic Surgery, 1990; (with N. Ragge) Immediate Eye Care, 1990; Oxford Textbook of Ophthalmology, 1999. *Recreations:* fishing, squash, running, opera, tennis. *Address:* 42 Clifton Park Road, Clifton, Bristol BS8 3HN. *Clubs:* Army and Navy; Clifton (Bristol).

EATES, Edward Caston, CMG 1968; LVO 1961; QPM 1961; CPM 1956; Commissioner, The Royal Hong Kong Police, 1967–69, retired; re-employed at Foreign and Commonwealth Office, 1971–76; *b* London, 8 April 1916; *o s* of late Edward Eates and Elizabeth Lavinia Issac Eates (*née* Caston); *m* 1941, Maureen Teresa McGee (*d* 1987); no *c*. *Educ:* Highgate Sch.; King's Coll., London (LLB). Asst Examr, Estate Duty Office, 1935. Army, 1939–46 (RAC): Western Desert and NW Europe; Adjt 2nd Derby Yeo., 1943; Temp. Maj. 1944; Staff Coll. Quetta (sc), 1945. Apptd to Colonial Police Service, Nigeria, 1946; Sen. Supt, Sierra Leone, 1954; Comr, The Gambia, 1957; Asst Comr, 1963, Dep. Comr, 1966, Hong Kong. *Recreations:* cricket and association football, travel, motoring. *Address:* 2 Riverside Court, Colleton Crescent, Exeter EX2 4BZ. *T:* (01392) 436434. *Clubs:* Royal Commonwealth Society, East India; Surrey County Cricket.

EATOCK TAYLOR, Prof. (William) Rodney, FREng; Professor of Mechanical Engineering, since 1989, and Head of Department of Engineering Science, since 1999, University of Oxford; Fellow of St Hugh's College, Oxford, since 1989; *b* 10 Jan. 1944; *s* of late William Taylor, Hadley Wood, Herts and Norah O'Brien Taylor (*née* Ridgeway); *m* 1971, Jacqueline Lorraine Cannon, *d* of late Desmond Cannon Brookes; two *s*. *Educ:* Rugby Sch.; King's Coll., Cambridge (BA, MA); Stanford Univ. (MS, PhD). FRINA 1986; FIMechE 1989; FREng (FEng 1990). Engineer, Ove Arup and Partners, 1968–70; University College London: Res. Asst, 1970; Lectr, 1972; Reader, 1980; Prof. of Ocean Engineering, 1984–89; Dean, Faculty of Engineering, 1988–89. Dir, Marine Technology Directorate Ltd, 1990–95; Chm., Marine Technology Trust, 1991–. Mem., Marine Technology Foresight Panel, OST, 1995–97. Gov., Queenswood Sch., 1990–. Member, Editorial Boards: Engineering Structures, 1978–; Applied Ocean Research, 1984–; Jl of Fluids and Structures, 1990–; series: Ocean Technology, 1986–; Engineering Science, 1990–98. *Publications:* numerous contribs to learned jls of structural dynamics and marine hydrodynamics. *Recreations:* walking, music. *Address:* St Hugh's College, Oxford OX2 6LE. *T:* (01865) 274900. *Club:* Athenæum.

EATON, Rt Rev. Derek Lionel; *see* Nelson, NZ, Bishop of.

EATON, Fredrik Stefan, OC 1990; Chairman, White Raven Capital Corporation; *b* 26 June 1938; *s* of late John David Eaton and Signy Hildur Eaton (*née* Stephenson); *m* 1962, Catherine Howard (Nicky) Martin; one *s* one *d. Educ:* Univ. of New Brunswick (BA). T. Eaton Co. Ltd: joined 1962; positions in Victoria, London, England and Toronto, 1962–67; Dir, 1967–; Pres. and Dir, Eaton's of Canada, 1969; Chm., Pres. and Chief Exec. Officer, 1977; Chm., 1988–91; High Comr for Canada in the UK, 1991–94. Director: Abitibi Consolidated Inc.; Baton Broadcasting, 1994–; Hollinger, 1994–; Premdor, 1994–; Eden Roc Mineral Corp. Member: CIIA; Ontario Ex-Presidents Assoc. Chm., Toronto Hosp.; Director: Bata Shoe Museum Foundn; WWF (Canada); Member: ICBP Rare Bird Club; Polite Soc. Gov., Eaton Foundn. Patron, ESU of Canada. FRSA. Chancellor, Univ. of New Brunswick, 1993–. Internat. Retailer of the Year Award, Nat. Retail Merchants Assoc., NY, 1978; McGill Univ. Management Award, 1987. Hon. LLD: New Brunswick, 1983; QUB. *Recreations:* sailing, fishing, golf. *Address:* (office) 55 St Clair Avenue West, Suite 260, Toronto, ON M4V 2Y7, Canada.

EATON, James Thompson, CBE 1992; TD 1963; Lord-Lieutenant, County Borough of Londonderry, since 1986; *b* 11 Aug. 1927; *s* of late J. C. Eaton, DL, and Mrs E. A. F. Eaton, MBE; *m* 1954, Lucy Edith Smeeton (OBE 1986); one *s* one *d. Educ:* Campbell Coll., Belfast; Royal Technical Coll., Glasgow. Man. Dir, Eaton & Co. Ltd, 1965–80. Mem., Londonderry Develt Commn, 1969–73 (Chm., Educn Cttee, 1969–73); Chm., Londonderry Port and Harbour Comrs, 1989–95 (Mem., 1977–95; Vice Chm., 1985). Served North Irish Horse (TA), 1950–67 (Major, 1961). Hon. Col, 1st (NI) Bn, ACF, 1992–98. High Sheriff, Co. Londonderry, 1982. *Recreations:* military history, gardening. *Address:* Cherryvale Park, Limavady, Co. Londonderry, Northern Ireland BT49 9AH.

EATON, Keith John, PhD; FRMetS; CEng, FIStructE; Chief Executive and Secretary, Institution of Structural Engineers, since 1999; *b* 4 May 1945; *s* of John Ernest Eaton and Phyllis Marguerite (*née* Groom); *m* 1967, Janet Marion, *d* of Geoffrey and Winifred Allanson Walker; two *d. Educ:* Bishopshalt Grammar Sch., Hillingdon, Middx; Univ. of Birmingham (BSc Civil Engrg 1966); UCL (PhD Structural Engrg 1971). FRMetS 1971; CEng 1975; FIStructE 1986. Joined BRE, 1966; Head: Wind Loading Section, 1971–77; Overseas Develt Res. Unit, 1977–84; Structural Design Div., 1984–89; European Manager, 1989–91, Dep. Dir, 1991–99, Steel Construction Inst. Mem. Council, Hon. Sec. and Hon. Treas., IStructE, 1986–92. MASCE 1991; MIM 1994. *Publications:* Wind Loading Handbook, 1971; Wing Effects on Buildings and Structures, 1977; Buildings and Tropical Windstorms, 1981; A Comparative Environmental Life Cycle Assessment of Modern Office Buildings, 1998; technical papers on wind loading, earthquake engrg, sustainability and envmtl issues in learned jls. *Recreations:* social bridge, walking, travelling, competitive motoring, being a grandfather. *Address:* Institution of Structural Engineers, 11 Upper Belgrave Street, SW1X 8BH. *T:* (020) 7235 4535.

EATON, Adm. Sir Kenneth (John), GBE 1994; KCB 1990; FREng, FIEE; Chairman, UKAEA, since 1996; Rear Admiral of the United Kingdom, since 2001; *b* 12 Aug. 1934; *s* of John and May Eaton; *m* 1959, Sheena Buttle; two *s* one *d. Educ:* Borden Grammar Sch.; Fitzwilliam Coll., Cambridge (BA). FIEE 1989; FREng (FEng 1994). HMS Victorious, 1959–61; ASWE, 1961–65; HM Ships Eagle, Collingwood and Bristol, 1965–71; Defence Communications Network, 1971–72; ASWE, 1972–76; HMS Ark Royal, 1976–78; MoD, 1978–81; ASWE, 1981–83; Dir Torpedoes, 1983–85; Dir-Gen. Underwater Weapons (Navy), 1985–87; Flag Officer, Portsmouth, and Naval Base Comdr, Portsmouth, 1987–89; Controller of the Navy, 1989–94. Chairman: Guy's and St Thomas' NHS Trust, 1995–99; National Remote Sensing Centre Ltd Infoterra, 1995–. *Recreations:* countryside, theatre, opera, classical music. *Address:* c/o Naval Secretary, Victory Building, HM Naval Base, Portsmouth PO1 3LS.

EATON, Martin Roger, CMG 1993; HM Diplomatic Service, retired; Deputy Legal Adviser, Foreign and Commonwealth Office, 1991–2000; *b* 10 Nov. 1940; *m* 1972, Sylvia White; two *s* one *d.* Admitted Solicitor, 1968; FCO, 1970; Bonn, 1977; FCO, 1981; Legal Counsellor: FCO, 1982; UKREP Brussels, 1987; FCO, 1991. *Recreations:* choral singing, gardening. *Address:* c/o Foreign and Commonwealth Office, SW1A 2AH.

EATON, Neil Duncan, FCIPS; Chief Executive, NHS Purchasing and Supply Agency, since 2000; *b* 28 May 1946; *s* of John and Bessie Eaton; *m* 1969, Ainsley Elizabeth Isles; two *d. Educ:* King Sch., Macclesfield; Manchester Coll. of Commerce (HND Business Studies); Dip. Inst. Healthcare Mgt; Dip. Chartered Inst. Purchasing and Supply. FCIPS (FInstPS 1985); MIHM 1972. Hosp. mgt and supply mgt posts, Manchester, Swindon and Wolverhampton, 1966–74; Area Supplies Officer: Tameside AHA, 1974–78; Northants AHA, 1978–83; Dir of Ops, NW Thames RHA, 1983–90; Chief Exec., Bedfordshire HA, 1990–2000. President: Chartered Inst. Purchasing and Supply, 1992–93; Health Care Supplies Assoc., 1996–2001. *Recreations:* amateur dramatics, Rugby, football. *Address:* NHS Purchasing and Supply Agency, Premier House, 60 Caversham Road, Reading RG1 7EB. *T:* (0118) 980 8601.

EATON, Robert James; Chairman, Daimler Chrysler (formerly Chairman and Chief Executive, Chrysler Corporation), 1993–2000; *b* 13 Feb. 1940; *s* of Gene and Mildred Eaton; *m* 1964, Cornelia Cae Drake; two *s. Educ:* Univ. of Kansas (BS Mech Eng). Joined General Motors, 1963, transf. to English staff, 1971; Chevrolet Div., 1975; Oldsmobile, 1979; Vice-Pres. in charge of Tech. Staffs, 1986; Pres., General Motors Europe, 1988–92; Mem., Bd of Dirs, Lotus Group, 1986–2000; Chm., Saab Auto, 1990–2000. Member: Industrial Adv. Board, Stanford Univ.; Business Roundtable and Business Council. Mem. Bd, Dama. Chm., Nat. Acad. of Engrg; FSAE. *Address:* c/o Daimler Chrysler, 1000 Chrysler Drive, Auburn Hills, MI 48326–2766, USA.

EATWELL, family name of **Baron Eatwell**.

EATWELL, Baron *cr* 1992 (Life Peer), of Stratton St Margaret in the County of Wiltshire; **John Leonard Eatwell;** President, Queens' College, Cambridge, since 1997; Lecturer, Faculty of Economics and Politics, Cambridge University, since 1977; *b* 2 Feb. 1945; *s* of Harold Jack and Mary Eatwell; *m* 1970, Hélène Seppain; two *s* one *d. Educ:* Headlands Grammar Sch., Swindon; Queens' Coll., Cambridge (BA 1967; MA 1971); Harvard Univ. (PhD 1975). Teaching Fellow, Grad. Sch. of Arts and Scis, Harvard Univ., 1968–69; Res. Fellow, Queens' Coll., Cambridge, 1969–70; Fellow, Trinity Coll., Cambridge, 1970–96; Asst Lectr, Faculty of Econs and Politics, Cambridge Univ., 1975–77. Vis. Prof. of Economics, New Sch. for Social Res., NY, 1982–96. Econ. Advr to Rt Hon. Neil Kinnock, MP, Leader of the Labour Party, 1985–92. Opposition spokesman on Treasury affairs, and on trade and industry, HoL, 1992–93; Principal Opposition spokesman on Treasury and econ. affairs, HoL, 1993–97. Chm., British Screen Finance Ltd, 1997–2000; Dir, SFA, 1997–. Trustee, Inst. for Public Policy Res., 1988– (Sec., 1988–97; Chm., 1997–2000). Chm., Crusaid, 1993–98. Non-executive Director: Anglia Television Gp, 1994–; Cambridge Econometrics Ltd, 1996–. Chm., Commercial Radio Cos Assoc., 2000–. Chm., Extemporary Dance Theatre, 1990; Governor, Contemporary Dance Trust, 1991–95; Dir, Arts Theatre Trust, Cambridge, 1991–98; Mem. Bd, Royal Opera House, 1998–. *Publications:* (with Joan Robinson) An Introduction to Modern Economics, 1973; Whatever Happened to Britain?, 1982; (ed with Murray Milgate) Keynes's Economics and the Theory of Value and Distribution, 1983; (ed with Murray Milgate and Peter Newman): The New Palgrave: A Dictionary of Economics, 4 vols, 1987; The New Palgrave Dictionary of Money and Finance, 3 vols, 1992; Transformation and Integration: shaping the future of central and eastern Europe, 1995; (ed) Global Unemployment: loss of jobs in the '90s, 1996; Not "Just Another Accession": the political economy of EU enlargement to the East, 1997; (with L. Taylor) Global Finance at Risk: the case for international regulation, 2000; Hard Budgets, Soft States: social policy choices in central and eastern Europe, 2000; articles in sci. jls and other collected works. *Recreations:* classical and contemporary dance, Rugby Union football. *Address:* Queens' College, Cambridge CB3 9ET. *T:* (01223) 335532, *Fax:* (01223) 335555; *e-mail:* president@quns.cam.ac.uk. *Club:* Harvard (New York).

EAVES, Caroline Sarah; *see* Raphael, C. S.

EAVES, Prof. Laurence, DPhil; FRS 1997; FInstP; Lancashire-Spencer Professor of Physics, University of Nottingham, since 2000 (Professor of Physics, 1986–2000); *b* 13 May 1948; *s* of Raymond Eaves and Margaret Eaves (*née* Howells); *m* 1985, Dr Ffiona Helen Gilmore. *Educ:* Rhondda Co. Grammar Sch.; Corpus Christi Coll., Oxford (BA 1st Cl. Hons Physics 1969; MA 1973; DPhil 1973). FInstP 1996. Res. Lectr, Christ Church, Oxford and Res. Fellow, Clarendon Lab., Univ. of Oxford, 1972–74; Miller Fellow, Univ. of Calif, Berkeley, 1974–75; Lectr, 1976–84, Reader, 1984–86, Dept of Physics, Univ. of Nottingham. Vis. Prof., Inst. for Solid State Physics, Univ. of Tokyo, 1995. Royal Soc. Leverhulme Sen. Res. Fellow, 1993–94; EPSRC Sen. Res. Fellow, 1994–99. Chm., Condensed Matter Div., Inst. of Physics, 1998–99. Mott Lectr, Inst. of Physics, 1988; European Physical Soc. Lectr., 1991. Guthrie Medal and Prize, Inst. of Physics, 2001. *Publications:* (jtly) numerous res. articles in Physical Rev., Physical Rev. Letters, Applied Physics Letters, Jl Physics, etc. *Address:* School of Physics and Astronomy, University of Nottingham, Nottingham NG7 2RD. *T:* (0115) 951 5136.

EAYRS, Prof. John Thomas, PhD, DSc; Sands Cox Professor of Anatomy, University of Birmingham, 1968–77; *b* 23 Jan. 1913; *e s* of late Thomas William Eayrs, AMICE, and late Florence May (*née* Clough); *m* 1941, Frances Marjorie Sharp; one *s* two *d. Educ:* King Edward's, Birmingham; University of Birmingham. In industry until 1938. War service: Pte Royal Warwicks Regt, 1939–40; 2nd Lieut Manchester Regt, 1940; Lieut 1940; Capt. 1941; Major 1942; Worcester Regt, 1943; sc Staff Coll., Camberley, 1944. University of Birmingham: Peter Thompson Prize, 1947; John Barritt Melson Memorial Gold Medal, 1947; Lectr in Anatomy, 1948; Bertram Windle Prize, 1950; Sen. Lectr 1955; Research Fellow, Calif. Inst. of Technology, 1956–57; Reader in Comparative Neurology, Birmingham, 1958; Henry Head Research Fellow, Royal Society, London, 1957–62; Prof. of Neuroendocrinology, Birmingham, 1961; Fitzmary Prof. of Physiology, London Univ., 1963–68. Governor, King Edward's Foundn, Birmingham, 1968–77. *Publications:* Scientific Papers dealing with developmental neuroendocrinology and behaviour in Jl Endocrin., Jl Anat. (London), Anim. Behav., etc. *Recreations:* genealogy, foreign travel and languages. *Address:* 51 Old Street, Upton upon Severn, Worcester WR8 0HN.

EBAN, Abba; a Member of the Knesset, 1959–88; Minister of Foreign Affairs, Israel, 1966–74; *b* 2 Feb. 1915, Cape Town, SA; *s* of Avram and Alida Solomon; *m* 1945, Susan Ambache; one *s* one *d. Educ:* Queens' Coll., Cambridge (Triple First; BA 1937; MA 1941; Hon. Fellow, 1998). Res. Fellow and Tutor for Oriental Languages, Pembroke Coll., Cambridge, 1938. Liaison officer of Allied HQ with Jewish population in Jerusalem, 1942–44; Chief Instructor, Middle East Arab Centre, Jerusalem, 1944–46; Jewish Agency, 1946–47; Liaison Officer with UN Special Commn on Palestine, 1947; UN: Representative of provisional govt of Israel, 1948; Permanent rep., 1949–59; Vice-Pres., General Assembly, 1953; Ambassador to USA, 1950–59; Minister without Portfolio, 1959–60; Minister of Educn and Culture, 1960–63; Dep. Prime Minister, 1963–66. Pres., Weizmann Inst. of Science, 1958–66; Vice-Pres., UN Conf. on Science and Technology in Advancement of New States, 1963; Mem., UN Adv. Cttee on Science and Technology for Develt. Fellow: World Acad. of Arts and Sciences; Amer. Acad. of Arts and Sciences; Amer. Acad. of Pol Science. Hon. Doctorates include: New York; Boston; Maryland; Cincinnati; Temple; Brandeis; Yeshiva; Aberdeen. TV series: Personal Witness, 1992; Civilization and the Jews, 1994; TV prog., Brink of Peace, 1997. *Publications:* The Modern Literary Movement in Egypt, 1944; Maze of Justice, 1946; Social and Cultural Problems in the Middle East, 1947; The Toynbee Heresy, 1955; Voice of Israel, 1957; Tide of Nationalism, 1959; Chaim Weizmann: a collective biography, 1962; Reality and Vision in the Middle East (Foreign Affairs), 1965; Israel in the World, 1966; My People, 1968; My Country, 1972; An Autobiography, 1978; The New Diplomacy: international affairs in the modern age, 1983; Heritage, Civilisation and the Jews, 1985; Personal Witness: Israel through my eyes, 1993; Diplomacy for the Next Century, 1998; articles in English, French, Hebrew and Arabic. *Address:* PO Box 394, Herzliya 46747, Israel.

EBAN, Anna Maeve; *see* Guggenheim, A. M.

EBBSFLEET, Bishop Suffragan of, since 2000; **Rt Rev. Andrew Burnham;** Provincial Episcopal Visitor, Province of Canterbury, since 2000; *b* 19 March 1948; *s* of David Burnham and Eileen Burnham (*née* Franks); *m* 1984, Cathy Ross; one *s* one *d. Educ:* New Coll., Oxford (BA 1969, 1971; MA 1973); Westminster Coll., Oxford (CertEd 1972); St Stephen's House, Oxford. ARCO(CHM). Ordained deacon, 1983, priest, 1984; Hon. Curate, Clifton, Southwell Dio., 1983–85; Curate, Beeston, 1985–87; Vicar, Carrington, 1987–94; Vice-Principal, St Stephen's House, Oxford, 1995–2000. Assistant Bishop: Dio. of Bath and Wells, 2001–; Dio. of Oxford, 2001–; Dio. of Exeter, 2001–; Dio. of Lichfield, 2001–. *Publication:* A Manual of Anglo-Catholic Devotion, 2000. *Recreations:* liturgy, music. *Address:* Bishop's House, Dry Sandford, Abingdon, Oxford OX13 6JP. *T:* (01865) 390746.

EBERHART, Richard (Ghormley), Professor Emeritus of English and Poet in Residence, Dartmouth College, USA; Florida Ambassador of the Arts, since 1984; *b* Austin, Minn, 5 April 1904; *s* of late Alpha La Rue Eberhart and late Lena Eberhart (*née* Lowenstein); *m* 1941, Helen Elizabeth Butcher, Christ Church, Cambridge, Mass; one *s* one *d. Educ:* Dartmouth Coll., USA (AB); St John's Coll., Cambridge Univ., England (BA, MA; Hon. Fellow, 1986); Harvard Univ. Grad. Sch. of Arts and Sciences. Taught English, 1933–41, also tutor to son of King Prajadhipok of Siam for a year. Served War in USN Reserve finishing as Lieut-Comdr, 1946; subseq. entered Butcher Polish Co., Boston, Mass, as Asst Man., finishing as Vice-Pres. (now Hon. Vice-Pres. and Mem. Bd of Directors). Founder (and first Pres.) Poets' Theatre Inc., Cambridge, Mass, 1950. Called back to teaching, 1952, and has served as Poet in Residence, Prof., or Lecturer at University of Washington, University of Conn., Wheaton Coll., Princeton, and in 1956 was apptd Prof. of English and Poet in Residence at Dartmouth Coll. Class of 1925 Chair, 1968 (being absent as Consultant in Poetry to the Library of Congress, 1959–61). Visiting Professor: Univ. of Washington, 1967, Jan.–June 1972; Columbia Univ., 1975; Distinguished Vis. Prof., Florida Univ., 1974– (President's Medallion, 1977); Regents Prof., Univ. of California, Davis, 1975; First Wallace Stevens Fellow, Timothy Dwight Coll., Yale, 1976. Shelley Memorial Prize; Bollingen Prize, 1962; Pulitzer Prize, 1966; Fellow, Acad. of Amer. Poets, 1969 (Nat. Book Award, 1977). Advisory Cttee on the

Arts, for the National Cultural Center (later John F. Kennedy Memorial Center), Washington, 1959; Member: Amer. Acad. and Inst. of Arts and Letters, 1960; Nat. Acad. of Arts and Sciences, 1967; Amer. Acad. of Arts and Letters, 1982; Elliston Lecturer on Poetry, University of Cincinnati, 1961. Poet Laureate of New Hampshire, 1979–84. Apptd Hon. Consultant in American Letters, The Library of Congress, 1963–66, reapptd, 1966–69. Hon. Pres., Poetry Soc. of America, 1972. Participant, Poetry International, London, 1973; Exhibn, Dartmouth Coll. Library, 1984. Hon. LittD: Dartmouth Coll., 1954; Skidmore Coll., 1966; Coll. of Wooster, 1969; Colgate Univ., 1974; St Lawrence Univ., 1985; Hon. DHL, Franklin Pierce, 1978. Phi Beta Kappa poem, Harvard, 1967; Hon. Mem., Alpha Chapter, Mass, 1967; New York Qly Poetry Day Award, 1980; Sarah Josepha Hale Award, Richards Library, Newport, NH, 1982; Robert Frost Medal, Poetry Soc. of America, 1986. Diploma: World Acad. of Arts and Culture, Republic of China, 1981; Internat. Poets Acad., Madras, India, 1987. Richard Eberhart Day: 14 July 1982, RI; 14 Oct. 1982, Dartmouth; Eberhart at Eighty, celebration at Univ. of Florida, 4–6 April 1984. *Publications:* (concurrently in England and America): A Bravery of Earth, 1930; Reading the Spirit, 1936; Selected Poems, 1951; Undercliff, Poems, 1946–53, also Great Praises, 1957; Collected Poems, 1930–60, 1960; Collected Verse Plays, 1962; The Quarry, 1964; Selected Poems, 1930–65, New Directions, 1965; Thirty One Sonnets, 1967; Shifts of Being, 1968; Fields of Grace, 1972 (Nat. Book Award nominee, 1973); Poems to Poets, 1975; Collected Poems 1930–1976, 1976; Collected Poems 1930–86, 1988; To Eberhart from Ginsberg: a letter about 'Howl', 1956, 1976; Of Poetry and Poets (criticism), 1979; Ways of Light, 1980; Survivors, 1980; Four Poems, 1980; New Hampshire/Nine Poems, 1980; Chocorua, 1981; Florida Poems, 1981; The Long Reach, 1984; Maine Poems, 1989; New and Collected Poems, 1990; Recorded Readings of his Poetry, 1961, 1968; four documentary films, 1972, 1975, 1986, 1987; *Festschriften:* (in New England Review, 1980) Richard Eberhart: A Celebration; (in Negative Capability, 1986) Richard Eberhart. *Recreations:* swimming, cruising, tennis, flying 7–ft kites. *Address:* 80 Lyme Road #161, Hanover, NH 03755–1230, USA. *Clubs:* Century (New York); Buck's Harbor Yacht (S Brooksville, Maine); Signet (Harvard).

EBERLE, Adm. Sir James (Henry Fuller), GCB 1981 (KCB 1979); Vice Admiral of the United Kingdom, 1994–97; Chairman, Association of Masters of Harriers and Beagles, since 1998; writer on international affairs and security; *b* 31 May 1927; *s* of late Victor Fuller Eberle and of Joyce Mary Eberle, Bristol; *m* 1950, Ann Patricia Thompson (*d* 1988), Hong Kong; one *s* two *d*. *Educ:* Clifton Coll.; RNC Dartmouth and Greenwich. Served War of 1939–45 in MTBs, HMS Renown, HMS Belfast; subseq. in Far East; qual. Gunnery Specialist 1951; Guided Missile Develt and trials in UK and USA, 1953–57; Naval Staff, 1960–62; Exec. Officer, HMS Eagle, 1963–65; comd HMS Intrepid, 1968–70; Asst Chief of Fleet Support, MoD (RN), 1971–74; Flag Officer Sea Training, 1974–75; Flag Officer Carriers and Amphibious Ships, 1975–77; Chief of Fleet Support, 1977–79; C-in-C, Fleet, and Allied C-in-C, Channel and Eastern Atlantic, 1979–81; C-in-C, Naval Home Comd, 1981–82, retired 1983. Rear Adm. of the UK, 1990–94. UK–Japan 2000 Gp, 1983–98. Vice-Pres., RUSI, 1979; Dir, RIIA, 1984–90. Chm. Council, Clifton Coll., 1984–94; Chm., Devon Rural Skills Trust, 1992–93. Freeman: Bristol, 1946; London, 1982. Hon. LLD: Bristol, 1989; Sussex, 1992. *Publications:* Management in the Armed Forces, 1972; Jim, First of the Pack, 1982; Britain's Future in Space, 1988. *Recreations:* hunting (Master of Britannia Beagles), tennis. *Address:* Lower Abbotsleigh, Blackawton, Totnes, Devon TQ9 7AF. *Clubs:* Farmers'; Society of Merchant Venturers (Bristol); All England Lawn Tennis.

EBERS, Prof. George Cornell, MD; FRCPC; Action Professor of Clinical Neurology and Head of Department of Clinical Neurology, University of Oxford, since 1999; Fellow, St Edmund Hall, Oxford, since 1999; *b* Budapest, 24 July 1946; *s* of Cornell George Ebers and Leontine Amant Ebers; *m* 1997, Sharon Vitali; one *s* one *d*. *Educ:* De La Salle Coll.; Univ. of Toronto (MD 1970). FRCPC 1977. University of Western Ontario: Asst Prof., 1977–82; Associate Prof., 1982–87; Prof., Dept of Clinical Neurol Scis, 1987–99. Numerous vis. professorships and named lectures. Member, Editorial Board: Jl Neuroimm., 1983–; Canadian Jl Neuro. Sci., 1985–; MS Res. Reports, 1987–; Jl Tropical Geog. Neurol., 1990–94; Neuroepidemiol., 1992–; Multiple Sclerosis, 1994–. FMedSci 2001. *Publications:* The Diagnosis of MS, 1984; Multiple Sclerosis, 1998; sole or jt author numerous scientific papers and articles. *Recreations:* book collecting, ornithology. *Address:* Radcliffe Infirmary, Woodstock Road, Oxford OX2 6HE. *T:* (01865) 224492. *Club:* Osler.

EBERT, Peter; producer; *b* 6 April 1918; *s* of Carl Ebert, CBE, and Lucie Oppenheim; *m* 1st, 1944, Kathleen Havinden; two *d*; 2nd, 1951, Silvia Ashmole; five *s* three *d*. *Educ:* Salem Sch., Germany; Gordonstoun, Scotland. BBC Producer, 1948–51; 1st opera production, Mefistofele, Glasgow, 1951; Mozart and Rossini guest productions: Rome, Naples, Venice, 1951, 1952, 1954, 1955: Wexford Festival: 12 prods, 1952–65; 1st Glyndebourne Fest. prod., Ariecchino, 1954, followed by Seraglio, Don Giovanni, etc.; 1st Edinburgh Fest. prod., Forza del Destino, 1955; Chief producer: Hannover State Opera, 1954–60; Düsseldorf Opera, 1960–62; directed opera class, Hannover State Conservatory, 1954–60; Head of Opera studio, Düsseldorf, 1960–62. Guest productions in Europe, USA, Canada. TV productions of Glyndebourne operas, 1955–64; 1st TV studio prod., 1963; Opera Adviser to BBC TV, 1964–65; Dir of Productions, 1965–77, Gen. Administrator, 1977–80, Scottish Opera Co. First drama prod., The Devils, Johannesburg, 1966; first musical, Houdini, London, 1966. Dir, Opera Sch., University of Toronto, 1967–68; Intendant: Stadttheater, Augsburg, 1968–73; Stadttheater Bielefeld, 1973–75; Staatstheater Wiesbaden, 1975–77. Hon. DMus St Andrews, 1979. *Publication:* In This Theatre of Man's Life: a biography of Carl Ebert, 1999. *Recreation:* building. *Address:* Col di Mura, Lippiano, 06010 (PG), Italy.

EBERTS, John David, (Jake), OC 1992; Founder, and Chief Executive, since 1985, Allied Productions (formerly Allied Filmmakers); *b* 10 July 1941; *s* of Edmond Howard Eberts and Elizabeth Evelyn MacDougall; *m* 1968, Fiona Louise Leckie; two *s* one *d*. *Educ:* McGill Univ. (BChemEng 1962); Harvard Univ. (MBA 1966). Project Engr, l'Air Liquide, Paris, 1962–64; Marketing Manager, Cummins Engine Co., Brussels, 1966–68; Vice Pres., Laird Inc., NY, 1968–71; Man. Dir, Oppenheimer and Co. Ltd, London, 1971–76; Founder, 1976, and Chief Exec., 1976–83 and 1985–86, Goldcrest Films and Television Ltd; Pres., Embassy Communications International, 1984–85. Involved in prodn of many BAFTA and Amer. Acad. award-winning films, including: Chariots of Fire; Gandhi; The Dresser; The Killing Fields, The Name of the Rose; Hope and Glory; Driving Miss Daisy; Dances with Wolves; A River Runs Through It; James and the Giant Peach; Chicken Run; The Legend of Bagger Vance. Film Producers' Award of Merit, 1986; Evening Standard Special Award, 1987. *Publication:* (with Terry Ilott) My Indecision is Final, 1990. *Recreations:* tennis, skiing, photography. *Clubs:* Queen's; North Hatley (Quebec).

EBRAHIM, Sir (Mahomed) Currimbhoy, 4th Bt *cr* 1910; BA, LLB; Advocate, Pakistan; Member, Standing Council of the Baronetage, 1961; *b* 24 June 1935; *o s* of Sir (Huseinali) Currimbhoy Ebrahim, 3rd Bt, and Alhaja Lady Amina Khanum, *d* of Alhaj Cassumali Jairajbhoy; *S* father, 1952; *m* 1958, Dur-e-Mariam, *d* of Minuchehir Ahmud Ghulamaly Nana; three *s* one *d*. *Recreations:* tennis (Karachi University No 1, 1957, No 2, 1958), cricket, table-tennis, squash, reading (literary), art, poetry writing, debate, quotation writing. *Heir:* *s* Zulfiqar Ali Currimbhoy Ebrahim [*b* 5 Aug. 1960; *m* 1984, Adila, *d* of Akhtar Halipota; one *s*].

EBRAHIM, Prof. Shaheen Brian John, FRCP, FFPHM; Professor of Epidemiology of Ageing, University of Bristol, since 1998; *b* 19 July 1952; *s* of Dr Donald William Ebrahim and Marjorie Sybil (*née* Evans); *m* 1984, Julia Lesley Shaw. *Educ:* King Henry VIII Sch., Coventry; Nottingham Univ. Med. Sch. (BMed Sci; BM BS 1975; DM 1985). FRCP 1993; FFPHM 1993. Wellcome Trust Clinical Epidemiology Trng Fellow, Nottingham Univ. Med. Sch., 1981–83; Lectr in Geriatric Medicine, Univ. of Nottingham, 1983–85; Wellcome Trust Lectr in Epidemiology, Dept of Social Medicine and Gen. Practice, St George's Hosp. Med. Sch., London, 1985–86; Cons. Physician and Sen. Lectr, Dept of Geriatric Medicine, Royal Free Hosp. Sch. of Medicine, 1987–89; Prof. of Geriatric Medicine, London Hosp. Med. Coll. and St Bartholomew's Hosp. Med. Coll., 1989–92; Prof. of Clinical Epidemiology, Royal Free Hosp. Sch. of Med., 1992–98. Vis. Prof., Christchurch Med. Sch., NZ, 1990; Nat. Heart Foundn of NZ Vis. Prof. in Stroke, 1991; Australian Veterans Vis. Prof., 1995; Vis. Prof., McMaster Univ., Canada, 1996. *Publications:* Clinical Epidemiology of Stroke, 1990, 2nd edn 1999; (ed jtly) The Health of Older Women, 1992; (with G. Bennett) Essentials of Health Care in Old Age, 1992, 2nd edn 1995; (ed jtly) Epidemiology in Old Age, 1996; scientific papers on clinical epidemiology and geriatric medicine. *Recreations:* coarse fishing, music of Velvet Underground and Don Van Vliet. *Address:* Department of Social Medicine, University of Bristol, Canynge Hall, Bristol BS8 2PR. *Club:* Royal Society of Medicine.

EBRINGER, Prof. Alan Martin, MD; FRACP, FRCP, FRCPath; Professor of Immunology, King's College, London, since 1995; *b* 12 Feb. 1936; *s* of late Bernard Ebringer and Maria Ebringer; *m* 1960, Eva Marie Ernest; two *s* one *d*. *Educ:* Melbourne High Sch.; Univ. of Melbourne (BSc Maths 1961; MB BS 1962; MD 1971). FRACP 1967; MRCP 1970, FRCP 1987; FRCPath 1997. Prosector in Anatomy, Univ. of Melbourne, 1958–; Pathology Registrar, Geelong Hosp., 1964; Research Fellow: Walter and Eliza Hall Inst., Royal Melbourne Hosp., 1965–66; Austin Hosp., 1967–69; RACP Overseas Travelling Schol., Dept of Immunol., Middx Hosp., 1970; Berkeley Fellow, Middx Hosp. and Gonville and Caius Coll., Cambridge, 1971; King's College, London: Lectr, 1972–77; Sen. Lectr, 1977–82; Reader, 1982–95; Hon. Consultant Rheumatologist, UCL Hosps (formerly Middx Hosp.), i/c of Ankylosing Spondylitis Res. Clinic, 1980–. Appeared before Phillips Inquiry into BSE, 1998. Member: British Soc. Immunol., 1970; British Soc. Rheum., 1972; Amer. Coll. Rheumatol., 1996. Vis. Lectr, Melbourne, Edinburgh, Glasgow, Sheffield, Paris, Marseilles, Brest, Madrid, Helsinki, Turku, Bratislava, Moscow, Suzdal, Innsbruk, San Antonio. Hon. FRSH 2001. *Publications:* contrib. numerous papers dealing with autoimmune diseases produced by molecular mimicry to ext. agents, esp. ankylosing spondylitis (klebsiella), rheumatoid arthritis (proteus) and bovine spongiform encephalopathy (acinetobacter). *Recreations:* languages, Karl Popper, walking. *Address:* 76 Gordon Road, W5 2AR.

EBSWORTH, Dame Ann (Marian), DBE 1992; a Judge of the High Court of Justice, Queen's Bench Division, 1992–2001; *b* 19 May 1937; *d* of late Arthur E. Ebsworth, OBE, BEM, RM and Hilda Mary Ebsworth. *Educ:* Notre Dame Convent, Worth, Sussex; Portsmouth High Sch., GPDST; London Univ. (BA Hons (History)). Called to Bar, Gray's Inn, 1962; Bencher, 1992. A Recorder of the Crown Court, 1978–83; a Circuit Judge, 1983–92. Mental Health Review Tribunal, 1975–83, 1984–90; Parole Bd, 1989–92; Civil and Family Cttee, Judicial Studies Bd, 1991–92. *Recreations:* Italian travel, medieval history, needlework.

EBSWORTH, Prof. Evelyn Algernon Valentine, CBE 1996; PhD, ScD; FRSC, FRSE; Chairman, Council for the Registration of Forensic Practitioners, since 1998; *b* 14 Feb. 1933; *s* of Brig. Wilfred Algernon Ebsworth, CB, CBE and late Cynthia (*née* Blech); *m* 1st, 1955, Mary Salter (*d* 1987); one *s* three *d*; 2nd, 1990, Rose Zuckerman. *Educ:* King's Coll., Cambridge (BA 1st Cl., 1954; PhD 1957; MA 1958; ScD 1967). FRSE 1969. Fellow, King's Coll., Cambridge, 1957–59; Res. Associate, Princeton Univ., 1958–59; Cambridge University: Demonstrator, 1959–63; Lectr, 1963–67; Fellow, 1959–67, Tutor, 1963–67, Christ's Coll.; Crum Brown Prof. of Chemistry, Edinburgh, 1967–90; Vice-Chancellor, Durham Univ., 1990–98. Corresp. Mem., Acad. of Scis, Göttingen. FRSA. *Publications:* Volatile Silicon Compounds, 1963; (with S. Cradock and D. W. H. Rankin) Structural Methods in Inorganic Chemistry, 1988; papers in learned jls. *Recreations:* opera, gardening. *Address:* 16 Conduit Head Road, Cambridge CB3 0EY.

ECCLES, family name of **Viscount Eccles** and **Baroness Eccles of Moulton**.

ECCLES, 2nd Viscount, *cr* 1964, of Chute, co. Wilts; **John Dawson Eccles;** Baron 1962; CBE 1985; Chairman, The Bowes Museum, County Durham, since 2000; *b* 20 April 1931; *er s* of 1st Viscount Eccles, CH, KCVO, PC and Sybil (*d* 1977), *d* of 1st Viscount Dawson of Penn, GCVO, KCB, KCMG, PC; *S* father, 1999; *m* 1955, Diana Catherine Sturge (*see* Baroness Eccles of Moulton); one *s* three *d*. *Educ:* Winchester Coll.; Magdalen Coll., Oxford (BA). Director: Glynwed International plc, 1972–96; Investors in Industry plc, 1974–88; Chairman: Head Wrightson & Co. Ltd, 1976–77 (Man. Dir, 1968–77); Chamberlin & Hill plc, 1982–; Acker Deboeck, corporate psychologists, 1994–; Courtaulds Textiles plc, 1995–2000 (Dir, 1992–); Director: The Nuclear Power Gp Ltd, 1968–74; Davy Internat. Ltd, 1977–81; Govett Strategic Investment Trust plc, 1996–. Member: Monopolies and Mergers Commn, 1976–85 (Dep. Chm., 1981–85); Industrial Develt Adv. Bd, 1989–93; Gen. Manager, subseq. Chief Exec., Commonwealth Develt Corp., 1985–94 (Mem., 1982–85). Chm., Bd of Trustees, Royal Botanic Gardens, Kew, 1983–91. Hon DSc Cranfield Inst. of Technology, 1989. *Recreations:* gardening, theatre. *Heir:* *s* Hon. William David Eccles [*b* 9 June 1960; *m* 1984, Claire Margaret Alison Seddon (*d* 2001); two *s* one *d*]. *Address:* 5 St John's House, 30 Smith Square, SW1P 3HF. *T:* (020) 7222 4040; Moulton Hall, Richmond, N Yorks DL10 6QH. *T:* (01325) 377227. *Club:* Brooks's.

ECCLES OF MOULTON, Baroness *cr* 1990 (Life Peer), of Moulton in the County of North Yorkshire; **Diana Catherine Eccles, (Viscountess Eccles);** DL; Chairman, Ealing, Hammersmith and Hounslow Health Authority, 1993–2000 (Chairman, Ealing District Health Authority, 1988–93); *b* 4 Oct. 1933; *d* of late Raymond Sturge and Margaret Sturge; *m* 1955, Hon. John Dawson Eccles (*see* Viscount Eccles); one *s* three *d*. *Educ:* St James's Sch., West Malvern; Open Univ. (BA). Voluntary work, Middlesbrough Community Council, 1955–58; Partner, Gray Design Associates, 1963–77. Director: Tyne Tees Television, 1986–94; J. Sainsbury, 1986–95; Yorkshire Electricity Gp, 1990–97; National & Provincial Building Soc., 1991–96; Opera North, 1998–; Indep. Nat. Dir, Times Newspapers Holdings Ltd, 1998–. Member: North Eastern Electricity Bd, 1974–85; British Railways Eastern Bd, 1986–92; Teesside Urban Devlt Corp., 1987–98; Yorkshire Electricity Bd, 1989–90. Member: Adv. Council for Energy Conservation, 1982–84; Widdicombe Inquiry into Local Govt, 1985–86; Home Office Adv. Panel on Licences for Experimental Community Radio, 1985–86; Unrelated Live Transplant Regulatory Authority, 1990–99. Vice Chairman: Nat. Council for Voluntary

Orgns, 1981–87; Durham Univ. Council, 1985– (Lay Mem., 1981–85); Chm., Tyne Tees Television Programme Consultative Council, 1982–84. Trustee, Charities Aid Foundn, 1982–89. DL N Yorks, 1998. Hon. DCL Durham, 1995. *Address:* Moulton Hall, Richmond, N Yorks DL10 6QH. *T:* (01325) 377227; 5/30 Smith Square, SW1P 3HF. *T:* (020) 7222 4040.

ECCLES, Geoffrey, OBE 1986; CEng; Regional Chairman, British Gas plc, Eastern, 1987–90; *b* 25 Dec. 1925; *s* of George William Eccles and Elsie Eccles (*née* Hepworth); *m* 1946, Marjorie Jackson; one *s*. *Educ:* Halifax and Bradford Colls of Technol. MIGasE. West Midlands Gas Board: various technical and managerial appts, incl. Asst Regl Distribution Engr, 1964; Grid Engr, 1967; Dep. Pipelines Engr, Gas Council, 1971; Pipelines Engr, British Gas Corp., 1980; Dep. Chm., Eastern Gas, 1984. *Recreations:* hill walking, reading, music. *Address:* 3 Little Gaddesden House, Little Gaddesden, Berkhamsted, Herts HP4 1PL. *T:* (01442) 842731.

ECCLES, (Hugh William) Patrick; QC 1990; **His Honour Judge Eccles;** a Circuit Judge, since 2000; *b* 25 April 1946; *s* of Gp Captain (retd) Hugh Haslett Eccles and Mary Eccles; *m* 1972, Rhoda Ann Eccles (*née* Moroney); three *d*. *Educ:* Stonyhurst Coll.; Exeter Coll., Oxford (MA). Called to the Bar, Middle Temple, 1968, Bencher, 1998; practising barrister, head of chambers, 1985–2000; a Recorder, 1987–2000; approved to sit as Dep. High Court Judge, 1997–2000. Asst Parly Boundary Comr, 1992; Legal Mem., Mental Health Review Tribunal (Restricted Patients), 2000–. Mem., County Court Rule Cttee, 1986–91. Gov., Sch. of St Helen and St Katharine, Abingdon, 1992–. *Recreations:* playing tennis, supporting Rugby and soccer, listening to opera and rock, reading, gardening. *Address:* c/o 2 Harcourt Buildings, Temple, EC4Y 9DB. *T:* (020) 7353 6961.

ECCLES, Jack Fleming, CBE 1980; retired trade union official; *b* 9 Feb. 1922; *s* of Tom and Dora Eccles; *m* 1952, Milba Hartley Williamson; one *s* one *d*. *Educ:* Chorlton High Sch.; Univ. of Manchester. BA (Com). Gen. and Municipal Workers Union: District Organiser, 1948–60; Nat. Industrial Officer, 1960–66; Regional Sec. (Lancs), 1966–86. Trades Union Congress: Gen. Council, 1973–86; Chm., 1984–85; Pres., 1985. Non-Executive Director: Remploy Ltd, 1976–90; English Industrial Estates, 1976–92; Plastics Processing ITB, 1982–88 (Chm.); British Steel plc (formerly BSC), 1986–91. *Address:* Terange, 11 Sutton Road, Alderley Edge, Cheshire SK9 7RB. *T:* (01625) 583684.

ECCLES, Patrick; *see* Eccles, H. W. P.

ECCLES-WILLIAMS, Hilary a'Beckett, CBE 1970; Vice-President, West Midlands Conservative Council, since 1985 (Deputy Chairman, 1982–85); *b* 5 Oct. 1917; *s* of late Rev. Cyril Eccles-Williams and Hermione (*née* Terrell); *m* 1941, Jeanne, *d* of W. J. Goodwin; two *s* four *d*. *Educ:* Eton; Brasenose Coll., Oxford (MA). Served War of 1939–45, Major RA (anti-tank), Dunkirk and Normandy (wounded). Consul: for Nicaragua, 1951–59; for Cuba, 1952–60; for Costa Rica, 1964–93; for Bolivia, 1965–82. Chairman of companies; Chm., 1978–82, non-exec. Dir, 1982–87, Rabone Petersen; has travelled 900,000 miles on export business. Chairman: Brit. Export Houses Assoc., 1958–59; Guardians of Birmingham Assay Office, 1979–88 (Guardian, 1970–); President: Birmingham Chamber of Commerce, 1965–66; Assoc. of Brit. Ch. of Commerce (93 Chambers), 1970–72. Comr of Income Tax, 1966–70. Chairman: Birmingham Cons. Assoc., 1976–79 (Pres., 1979–84); W Midlands Metropolitan Co. Co-ordinating Cttee, Cons. Party, 1980–86; European Parlt constituency of Birmingham S Cons. Assoc., 1978–82 (Pres., 1982–84); Latin Amer. Gp, Cons. Foreign and Overseas Council, 1986–89; President: Eur. Parlt constituency of Birmingham E Cons. Assoc., 1984–95; Sparkbrook Constituency Cons. Assoc., 1988–92; Anglo-Asian Cons. Soc., 1984–87; Cons. Party One Nation Forum, 1990–; Mem., National Union Exec. Cttee, Cons. Party, 1975–85. Mem., Brit. Hallmarking Council, 1976–88; Pres., Birmingham Consular Assoc., 1973–74; Chairman: Asian Christian Colls Assoc., 1960–66; Brit. Heart Foundn, Midland Counties, 1973–74; Golden Jubilee Appeal Cttee, Queen Elizabeth Hosp., Birmingham, 1987–90; W Midlands Macmillan Nurse Appeal, 1991–94; Mem., Nat. Council, Cancer Relief Macmillan Fund, 1992–94. Life Governor, Birmingham Univ., 1966; Trustee, Birmingham Centre for Drama, 1994–97. Liveryman, Worshipful Co. of Glaziers, 1974; Freeman, Goldsmiths' Co., 1988. Hon. Captain, Bolivian Navy, 1969. Numerous TV appearances. *Recreations:* walking, golf. *Address:* 49 Second Avenue, Frinton-on-Sea, Essex CO13 9LY. *T:* (01225) 674850. *Clubs:* Frinton Golf; Frinton Lawn Tennis.

ECCLESHARE, Julia Jessica; journalist and broadcaster; *b* 14 Dec. 1951; *d* of late Colin Forster Eccleshare and of Elizabeth Eccleshare; *m* 1977, John Lemprière Hammond, *e s* of Prof. Nicholas Geoffrey Lemprière Hammond, CBE, DSO, FBA; three *s* one *d*. *Educ:* Camden Sch. for Girls; Girton Coll., Cambridge. Editorial assistant: TLS, 1973–78; Puffin Books, 1978–79; Fiction editor, Hamish Hamilton Children's Books, 1979–82; selector of Children's Books of Year for Book Trust, 1982–92; Children's Book corresp., Bookseller, 1993–97; Children's Books Editor, Guardian, 1997–. Chm. Judges, Smarties Award, 1994–; Mem., Adv. Body, Reading is Fundamental (UK), 1996–. Contributor to BBC Treasure Islands, Night Waves, Kaleidoscope, Woman's Hour and Open Book, 1985–. Eleanor Farjeon Award, 2000. *Publications:* The Woman's Hour Guide to Children's Books, 1987; J. K. Rowling: a critical study, 2001; ed numerous anthologies. *Address:* 21 Tanza Road, NW3 2UA. *T:* (020) 7431 1295.

ECCLESTON, Harry Norman, OBE 1979; PPRE (RE 1961; ARE 1948); RWS 1975 (ARWS 1964); RWA 1991; Artist Designer at the Bank of England Printing Works, 1958–83 (appointed first full-time bank-note designer, 1967); *b* 21 Jan. 1923; *s* of Harry Norman Eccleston and Kate Pritchard, Coseley, Staffs; *m* 1948, Betty Doreen Gripton (*d* 1995); two *d*. *Educ:* Sch. of Art, Bilston; Coll. of Art, Birmingham; Royal College of Art. ATD 1947; ARCA (1st Class) 1950. Studied painting until 1942. Served in Royal Navy, 1942–46; Temp. Commn, RNVR, 1943. Engraving Sch., Royal College of Art, 1947–51; engraving, teaching, free-lance graphic design, 1951–58. Pres., Royal Soc. of Painter-Etchers and Engravers, 1975–89. Hon. RBSA 1989; Hon. NEAC, 1995. *Recreation:* reading. *Address:* 110 Priory Road, Harold Hill, Romford, Essex RM3 9AL. *T:* (01708) 340275. *Club:* Arts.

ECCLESTONE, Bernard; Chief Executive Officer, Formula One Administration Ltd; *b* Oct. 1930; *m*; one *d*; *m* Slavica; two *d*. *Educ:* Woolwich Polytechnic (BSc). Worked for a gas company; est. car and motorbike dealership, Midweek Car Auctions; racing car driver, F3; owner Connaught racing team, 1957; Manager, Jochen Rindt; owner Brabham racing team, 1970. Vice-Pres. i/c promotional affairs, Fed. Internat. de l'Automobile. *Address:* Formula One Administration Ltd, 6 Prince's Gate, SW7 1QJ.

ECCLESTONE, Jacob Andrew; Assistant General Secretary, Writers' Guild, 1999–2001; *b* 10 April 1939; *s* of late Rev. Alan Ecclestone and Delia Reynolds Abraham; *m* 1966, Margaret Joan Bassett; two *s* one *d*. *Educ:* High Storrs Grammar Sch., Sheffield; Open Univ. (BA). Journalism: South Yorkshire Times, 1957–61; Yorkshire Evening News, 1961–62; The Times, 1962–66, 1967–81; Dep. Gen. Sec., NUJ, 1981–97 (Mem., 1977, Vice-Pres. 1978, Pres., 1979, Nat. Exec.). Member: Press Council, 1977–80; Exec., NCCL, 1982–86. *Recreations:* gardening, climbing, music. *Address:* 40 Chatsworth Way, SE27 9HN. *T:* (020) 8670 8503.

ECEVIT, Bülent; Prime Minister of Turkey, 1974, 1977, 1978–79, and since 1999; Chairman, Democratic Left Party, since 1989; *b* Istanbul, 28 May 1925; *s* of late Prof. Fahri Ecevit and Nazli Ecevit; *m* 1946, Rahşan Aral. *Educ:* Robert Coll., Istanbul (BA Lit. 1944); Univ. of Ankara; SOAS, Univ. of London; Harvard Univ. (Rockefeller Foundn Fellow, 1957–58). Press and Publicity Dept, Turkish Govt, 1944–46; Press Attaché's Office, Turkish Embassy, London, 1946–50; joined Ulus (Republican People's Party newspaper) as art critic and translator, 1950; held posts of Foreign News Ed., Man. Dir, then Pol Ed.; pol columnist, 1956–61. Served Turkish army, 1951–52 (attained rank of Lt). MP (Republican People's Party), Turkey, 1957–60, 1961–80; Mem., Constituent Assembly, 1960–61; Minister of Labour, 1961–65; Sec.-Gen., 1966–71, Chm., 1972–80, Republican People's Party; Dep. Prime Minister, 1997–98. Imprisoned by mil. regime, 1980 and 1981–82. *Publications:* Left of Centre, 1966; The System Must Change, 1968; Atatürk and Revolution, 1970; Conversations, 1974; Democratic Left, 1974; Foreign Policy, 1975; Workers and Peasants Together, 1976; Poems, 1976 (trans. German, Russian, Serbian, Danish and Romanian); translations into Turkish: Gitanjali (R. Tagore), 1941; Straybirds (R. Tagore), 1943; Cocktail Party (T. S. Eliot), 1963. *Address:* (office) Başbakanlik, Bakanliklar, Ankara, Turkey; (home) Or-an, Şehri 69/5, Ankara, Turkey.

ECHENIQUE, Prof. Marcial Hernan, DArch; Professor of Land Use and Transport Studies, University of Cambridge, since 1993; Fellow, Churchill College, Cambridge, since 1972; *b* 23 Feb. 1943; *s* of Marcial Echenique and Rosa de Echenique (*née* Talavera); *m* 1963, Maria Luisa Holzmann; two *s* one *d*. *Educ:* Catholic Univ. of Chile; Univ. of Barcelona (DArch). MA Cantab 1972. MRTPI 1990; ARIBA 1997. Asst Lectr, Univ. of Barcelona, 1964–65; University of Cambridge: Research Officer, 1967–70; Lectr, 1970–80; Reader in Architecture and Urban Studies, 1980–93. Founder and Mem., Bd of Applied Res., Cambridge, 1969–83. Chm., Marcial Echenique & Partners Ltd, England, 1978–; Pres., Marcial Echenique y Compañía SA, Spain, 1988–; Member Board: Trasporti e Territorio SRL, Italy, 1992–; Autopista Vasco-Aragonesa SA, Spain, 1994–99; Tecnologica SA, Spain, 1994–96; Ferrovial-Agroman, Construcciones, Spain, 1995–2000; Dockways Ltd, Jersey, 1996–. Bank of Bilbao-Vizcaya of Spain: Mem. Bd, 1988–94; Trustee of Foundn, 1990–94. *Publications:* (ed jtly) La Estructura del Espacio Urbano, 1975; (ed jtly) Urban Development Models, 1975; (ed) Modelos Matematicos de la Estructura Espacial Urbana: aplicaciones en America Latina, 1975; (with L. Piemontese) Un Modello per lo Sviluppo del Sistema Grecia-Italia Meridionale, 1984; (jtly) Cambridge Futures, 1999. *Recreations:* music, reading, gardening. *Address:* Department of Architecture, University of Cambridge, 1 Scroope Terrace, Cambridge CB2 1PX. *T:* (01223) 332950; Farm Hall, Godmanchester, Cambs PE29 2HQ.

ECHLIN, Sir Norman David Fenton, 10th Bt *cr* 1721; Captain 14/1st Punjab Regiment, Indian Army; *b* 1 Dec. 1925; *s* of Sir John Frederick Echlin, 9th Bt, and Ellen Patricia (*d* 1971), *d* of David Jones, JP, Dublin; *S* father, 1932; *m* 1953, Mary Christine, *d* of John Arthur, Oswestry, Salop. *Educ:* Masonic Boys' School, Dublin. *Heir:* none. *Address:* Nartopa, 36 Marina Avenue, Appley, Ryde, IoW PO33 1NJ.

ECKERBERG, (Carl) Lennart, Hon. KCMG 1983; Officer of Royal Northern Star 1970; Swedish Ambassador to the Court of St James's, 1991–94; *b* 2 July 1928; *s* of late Enar Lars Eckerberg and of Dagmar Liljedahl; *m* 1965, Willia Fales; two *s* one *d*. *Educ:* Univ. of Stockholm (law degree 1953). Swedish Foreign Service in Stockholm, London, Warsaw and Washington, 1954–71; Disarmament Ambassador, Geneva, 1971; Minister Plenipotentiary, Washington, 1975; Ambassador, Dar es Salaam, 1977; Under Sec., Political Affairs, Stockholm, 1979; Ambassador, Bonn, 1983–91. Orders from Finland, Germany, Iceland, Spain and Mexico. *Recreations:* golf, tennis, bridge. *Address:* (summer) Martornsvägen 3, 230 11 Falsterbo, Sweden; (winter) 3812 Klingle Place, NW, Washington, DC 20016–5433, USA. *T:* (202) 9660594. *Clubs:* Chevy Chase (Washington); Falsterbo (Sweden).

ECKERSLEY, Sir Donald (Payze), Kt 1981; OBE 1977; farmer, since 1946; Inaugural President, National Farmers' Federation of Australia, 1979–81; *b* 1 Nov. 1922; *s* of Walter Roland Eckersley and Ada Gladys Moss; *m* 1949, Marjorie Rae Clarke; one *s* two *d*. *Educ:* Muresk Agricl Coll. (Muresk Diploma in Agriculture). Aircrew, RAAF, 1940–45. Pres., Milk Producers' Assoc., 1947–50; Farmers' Union of WA: Executive, 1962–67; Pres., Milk Sect., 1965–70; Vice-Pres., 1969–72; Gen. Pres., 1972–75; Pres., Australian Farmers' Fedn, 1975–79; Austr. Rep., Internat. Fedn of Agric., 1979–81. Pres., Harvey Shire Council, 1970–79; Director: Chamberlain John Deere, 1980–; Br. Bd. Australian Mutual Provident Soc., 1983–. Chairman: Leschenault Inlet Management Authority, 1977–80; Artificial Breeding Bd of WA, 1981–; SW Develt Authority, 1989–96; Bd, Muresk Inst. of Agric., 1984–88; Member: WA Waterways Commn, 1977–80; Nat. Energy Adv. Cttee, 1979–; Comr, WA State Housing Commn, 1982–. Mem., Senate, Univ. of WA, 1981–86. Mem., Harvey Rotary Club. JP WA, 1982–86. Hon. DTech Curtin, 1989. WA Citizen of Year award, 1976; Man of Year, Austr. Agriculture, 1979. *Publication:* (contrib.) Farm Focus: the '80s, 1981. *Recreations:* golf, fishing. *Address:* Lot 29, Korijekop Avenue, WA 6220, Australia. *T:* (8) 97291472. *Clubs:* Weld (Perth); Harvey Golf.

ECKERSLEY-MASLIN, Rear Adm. David Michael, CB 1984; retired, RN; *b* Karachi, 27 Sept. 1929; *e s* of late Comdr C. E. Eckersley-Maslin, OBE, RN, Tasmania, and Mrs L. M. Lightfoot, Bedford; *m* 1955, Shirley Ann, *d* of late Captain H. A. Martin; one *s* one *d*. *Educ:* Britannia Royal Naval Coll. Qual. Navigation Direction Officer, 1954; rcds 1977. Navigating Officer, HMS Michael, Far East Malayan Campaign, 1950–53; Australian Navy, 1954–56; BRNC Dartmouth, 1959–61; commanded HM Ships Eastbourne, Euryalus, Fife and Blake, 1966–76; Captain RN Presentation Team, 1974; Dir, Naval Operational Requirements, 1977–80; Flag Officer Sea Training, 1980–82; ACNS (Operational Planning) (Falklands), 1982; ACDS (CIS), 1982–84; Asst Dir (CIS), IMS, NATO, Brussels, 1984–86; Dir Gen., NATO Communications and Inf. Systems Agency, 1986–91. ADC to the Queen, 1980. Vice Pres., AFCEA, 1987–90 (Gold Medal, 1991). Pres., Algerines Assoc., 1997–2000. Mem. Council, Shipwrecked Mariners Soc., 1992–97. Naval Gen. Service Decoration, Palestine, 1948, and Malaya, 1951. *Recreations:* tennis, squash, cricket. *Address:* Dunningwell, Hall Court, Shedfield, near Southampton SO32 2HL. *T:* (01329) 832350. *Club:* MCC.

EDDERY, Patrick James John; jockey; *b* 18 March 1952; *s* of Jimmy and Josephine Eddery; *m* 1978, Carolyn Jane (*née* Mercer); one *s* two *d*. Rode for Peter Walwyn, 1972–80; Champion Jockey, 1974, 1975, 1976, 1977, 1986, 1988, 1989, 1990, 1991, 1993, 1996; Champion Jockey in Ireland, 1982; won the Oaks, 1974, 1979, the Derby, on Grundy, 1975, on Golden Fleece, 1982, on Quest for Fame, 1990; Prix de l'Arc de Triomphe, 1980, 1985, 1986, 1987; St Leger on Moon Madness, 1986, on Moonax, 1994, on Silver Patriarch, 1997 (his 4,000th win in GB). *Recreations:* swimming, golf, snooker. *Address:* Musk Hill Farm, Nether Winchendon, Aylesbury, Bucks HP18 0EB. *T:* (01844) 290282.

EDDEY, Prof. Howard Hadfield, CMG 1974; FRCS, FRACS, FACS; Foundation Professor of Surgery, University of Melbourne, at Austin Hospital and Repatriation General Hospital, 1967–75, now Emeritus; also Dean of Austin Hospital and Repatriation General Hospital Clinical School, 1971–75; *b* Melbourne, 3 Sept. 1910; *s* of Charles Howard and Rachel Beatrice Eddey; *m* 1940, Alice Paul (decd); two *s* one *d*. *Educ:* Melbourne Univ.; St Bartholomew's Hosp. Med. Sch. BSc, MB BS, 1934; FRCS 1938; FRACS 1941; FACS 1964; Hallett Prize of RCS, 1938. Served War, 1941–45: AAMC, Major and Surgical Specialist; served in PoW camps: Changi (Singapore); Sandakan and Kuching (Borneo). Hon. Surgeon: Prince Henry Hosp., Melbourne, 1946–47; Alfred Hosp., Melbourne, 1947; Royal Melbourne Hosp., 1947–67; Cons. Surg., 1967, Royal Melbourne and Royal Women's Hosps; Peter MacCallum Clinic. Mem. AMA, 1935; Mem., Faculty of Med., Univ. of Melbourne, 1950–75 (Mem. Convocation, 1965–67); Indep. Lectr in Surgical Anatomy, Univ. of Melb., 1950–65; Dean, Royal Melb. Hosp. Clin. Sch., 1965–67; Colombo Plan Visitor to India, 1960–65; Cons. in Surg., Papuan Med. Coll., 1965–68; Mem. Cancer Inst. Bd, 1958–67; Mem. Med. and Sci. Cttee, Anti-Cancer Council of Vic., 1958–67; Chm., Melb. Med. Postgrad. Cttee, 1963–71; Vice-Pres., Aust. Postgrad. Fedn in Med., 1965–71 (Life Governor, 1972). Mem. Council, RACS, 1967–75 (Mem. Bd of Examrs, 1958–75, Chm. Bd, 1968–73; Hon. Librarian, 1968–75). Mem. Med. Bd of Vic., 1968–77; Mem. Austin Hosp. Bd of Management, 1971–77 (Vice-Pres., 1975–77; Life Governor, 1977). Hunterian Prof., RCS, 1960; Vis. Prof. of Surg., 1962, External Examr in Surg., 1970, Univ. of Singapore; Leverhulme Fellow, Univ. of Melb., 1974; Vis. Prof. of Surg., Univ. of Hong Kong, 1974. Howard Eddey Medal, named in 1972 by RACS and awarded to most successful cand., Part I exam (surgery) for FRACS in SE Asia, in recognition of dist. service to RACS. Hon. Surgeon to HRH Prince Charles on his visit to Victoria, 1974. Melbourne and Australian Universities Lacrosse Blue. *Publications:* many, in sci. jls, particularly in relation to diseases of salivary glands and cancer of mouth. *Recreation:* reading. *Address:* 8 Villea Avenue, Grovedale, Geelong, Vic 3216, Australia. *T:* (3) 52414577.

EDDINGTON, Dr Roderick Ian; Chief Executive Officer, British Airways PLC, since 2000; *b* 2 Jan. 1950; *s* of Gil and April Eddington; *m* 1994, Young Sook Park; one *s* one *d*. *Educ:* Univ. of WA (BEng Hons; MEng Sci.); Lincoln Coll., Oxford (DPhil 1979). Res. Lectr, Pembroke Coll., Oxford, 1978–79; John Swire & Sons, 1979–96 (on secondment to Cathay Pacific Airways as Man. Dir, 1992–96); Director: Swire Pacific, 1992–97; John Swire & Sons Pty, 1997–; Exec. Chm., Ansett Australia, 1997–2000. Non-exec. Dir, News Corp., 2000–. *Recreations:* cricket, bridge. *Address:* British Airways PLC, Waterside, PO Box 365, Harmondsworth UB7 0GB. *Clubs:* Vincent's (Oxford); Melbourne; Hong Kong, Shek O (Hong Kong).

EDDLESTON, Prof. Adrian Leonard William Francis, DM; FRCP; Professor of Liver Immunology, London University, 1982–2000, now Emeritus, and Head of Guy's, King's College and St Thomas' School of Medicine of King's College London, 1998–2000; *b* 2 Feb. 1940; *s* of late Rev. William Eddleston and Kathleen Brenda (*née* Jarman); *m* 1966, Hilary Kay Radford; three *s* one *d*. *Educ:* St Peter's Coll., Oxford (BA 1961; MB BCh, MA 1964; DM 1972); Guy's Hosp. Med. Sch., London. MRCS 1965; LRCP 1965, MRCP 1967, FRCP 1979. House Surgeon, Casualty Officer, House Physician, Sen. House Officer and Jun. Med. Registrar, Guy's Hosp., 1965–67; Med. Registrar, KCH, 1967–68; King's College School of Medicine and Dentistry: Res. Fellow and Hon. Lectr in Med., 1968–70, Hon. Sen. Lectr, 1972–78, Liver Unit; Dean, Faculty of Clinical Med., 1992–97; Dean, 1997–98; Hon. Consultant Physician, KCH, 1982–2000. Mem., London Health Commn, 2000–. MRC Vis. Res. Fellow, Clin. Immunol. Lab., Minnesota Univ., 1970–72. Non-exec. Dir, King's Healthcare NHS Trust, 1990–2000; Chm., Bromley Primary Care Trust, 2001–. Mem., King's Fund Mgt Cttee, 2000–. Trustee, St Christopher's Hospice. FKC 1996. Founder FMedSci 1998. *Publications:* Immune Reactions in Liver Disease, 1979; Interferons in the Treatment of Chronic Virus Infection of the Liver, 1990; contrib. learned publications on immunology of auto-immune and virus-induced liver diseases. *Recreations:* computing, model aircraft flying. *Address:* 14 Nelson Close, Biggin Hill, Kent TN16 3LS.

EDDY, Prof. Alfred Alan; Professor of Biochemistry, University of Manchester Institute of Science and Technology, 1959–94, Emeritus since 1994; *b* 4 Nov. 1926; Cornish parentage; *s* of late Alfred and Ellen Eddy; *m* 1954, Susan Ruth Slade-Jones; two *s*. *Educ:* Devonport High Sch.; Open scholarship Exeter Coll., Oxford, 1944; BA 1st Class Hons, 1949. ICI Research Fellow, 1950; DPhil 1951. Joined Brewing Industry Research Foundation, Nutfield, 1953. *Publications:* various scientific papers. *Recreations:* walking, talking, wining and dining. *Address:* Larchfield, Buxton Road, Disley, Cheshire SK12 2LH.

EDE, Ven. Dennis; Archdeacon of Stoke-upon-Trent, 1990–97, now Emeritus; Hon. Priest-in-charge, All Saints, Tilford, diocese of Guildford, since 1997; *b* 8 June 1931; *m* 1956, Angela Horsman; one *s* two *d*. *Educ:* Univ. of Nottingham (BA Theology 1955); Barnett House, Oxford (Cert. of Social Studies); Ripon Hall, Oxford; MSocSc Birmingham, 1972. Nat. Service, RAF, 1950–52; Pilot Officer, Admin. Branch. Asst Curate, St Giles, Shelds, dio. Birmingham, 1957–60; Asst Curate-in-charge, St Philip and St James, Hodge Hill, Birmingham, 1960–64, Priest-in-charge 1964–70, Team Rector 1970–76; Part-time Chaplain, East Birmingham Hosp., 1961–76; Vicar of All Saints Parish Church, West Bromwich, dio. Lichfield, 1976–90. Mem., Gen. Synod of C of E, 1975–76, 1980–90. Diocese of Lichfield: Chm. House of Clergy, 1985–90; Chm. of Communications, 1983–97; Prebendary of Lichfield Cathedral, 1983–90; Hon. Canon, 1990–97. Chairman: Sandwell Volunteer, 1980–86; Faith in Sandwell, 1986–90; Shallowford House, 1990–97; Diocesan Clergy Retirement Cttee, 1990–97; Widows (Diocesan) Officers Cttee, 1990–97; Surrey and Sussex Churches Broadcasting Cttee, 1997–. Co-ordinator for religious bodies in Staffs in major disasters, 1990–97. *Recreations:* walking, cycling, squash, table tennis. *Address:* All Saints Vicarage, Tilford, Farnham, Surrey GU10 2DA. *T:* and *Fax:* (01252) 792333.

EDE, Jeffery Raymond, CB 1978; Keeper of Public Records, 1970–78; *b* 10 March 1918; *e s* of late Richard Arthur Ede; *m* 1944, Mercy, *d* of Arthur Radford Sholl; one *s* one *d*. *Educ:* Plymouth Coll.; King's Coll., Cambridge (MA). Served War of 1939–45, Intell. Corps (despatches); GSO2 HQ 8 Corps District, BAOR, 1945–46. Asst Keeper, Public Record Office, 1947–59; Principal Asst Keeper, 1959–66; Dep. Keeper, 1966–69. Lectr in Archive Admin., Sch. of Librarianship and Archives, University Coll., London, 1956–61; Unesco expert in Tanzania, 1963–64. Chm., British Acad. Cttee on Oriental Documents, 1972–78; Vice Pres., Internat. Council on Archives, 1976–78. Pres., Soc. of Archivists, 1974–77. FRHistS 1969. Hon. Mem., L'Institut Grand-Ducal de Luxembourg, 1977. Freeman: Goldsmiths' Company, 1979; City of London, 1979. *Publications:* Guide to the Contents of the Public Record Office, Vol. II (major contributor), 1963; articles in archival and other professional jls. *Recreation:* countryside. *Address:* Lambourn House, Apple Court Mews, Silver Street, Ilminster, Som TA19 0DW.

EDELL, Stephen Bristow; Waterways Ombudsman, since 1997; *b* 1 Dec. 1932; *s* of late Ivan James Edell and late Hilda Pamela Edell; *m* 1958, Shirley Ross Collins; two *s* one *d*. *Educ:* St Andrew's Sch., Eastbourne; Uppingham. LLB London. Legal Mem., RTPI, 1971–92. Commnd RA, 1951. Articled to father, 1953; qual. Solicitor 1958; Partner, Knapp-Fishers (Westminster), 1959–75; Law Comr, 1975–83; Partner, Crossman Block and Keith (Solicitors), 1983–87; Building Societies Ombudsman, 1987–94; PIA Ombudsman, 1994–97. Mem. Cttee, 1973–85, Vice-Pres., 1980–82, Pres., 1982–83, City of Westminster Law Soc. Oxfam: Mem., Retailing and Property Cttee, 1984–93 (Chm., 1989–93); Mem. Council, 1985–93; Mem., Exec., 1987–93. Dir, Catholic Bldg Soc., 1998–. Chm. Council, Hurstpierpoint Coll., 1997–. Makers of Playing Cards' Company: Liveryman, 1955–; Mem., Ct of Assts, 1978–; Sen. Warden, 1980–81; Master, 1981–82. FRSA. *Publications:* Inside Information on the Family and the Law, 1969; The Family's Guide to the Law, 1974; articles in Conveyancer, Jl of Planning and Environmental Law, and newspapers. *Recreations:* family life; music, opera, theatre; early astronomical instruments; avoiding gardening; interested in problems of developing countries. *Address:* The Old Farmhouse, Twineham, Haywards Heath, Sussex RH17 5NP. *T:* (01273) 832058. *Club:* City Livery.

EDELMAN, Colin Neil; QC 1995; a Recorder, since 1996; *b* 2 March 1954; *s* of late Gerald Bertram Edelman and of Lynn Queenie Edelman (*née* Tropp); *m* 1978, Jacqueline Claire Seidel; one *s* one *d*. *Educ:* Haberdashers' Aske's Sch., Elstree; Clare Coll., Cambridge (MA). Called to the Bar, Middle Temple, 1977; Asst Recorder, 1993–96. *Publications:* articles for Internat. Insurance Law Review and British Insurance Law Assoc. Jl. *Recreations:* badminton, ski-ing, walking. *Address:* Devereux Chambers, Devereux Court, WC2R 3JJ. *T:* (020) 7353 7534, *Fax:* (020) 7353 1724.

EDELMAN, Prof. Gerald Maurice, MD, PhD; Director, Neurosciences Institute, La Jolla, since 1981; Chairman, Department of Neurobiology, Scripps Research Institute, since 1992; *b* NYC, 1 July 1929; *s* of Edward Edelman and Anna Freedman; *m* 1950, Maxine Morrison; two *s* one *d*. *Educ:* Ursinus Coll. (BS); University of Pennsylvania (MD); The Rockefeller University (PhD). Med. Hse Officer, Massachusetts Gen. Hosp., 1954–55; Asst Physician, Hosp. of The Rockefeller Univ., 1957–60; The Rockefeller University, NY: Asst Prof. and Asst Dean of Grad. Studies, 1960–63; Associate Prof. and Associate Dean of Grad. Studies, 1963–66; Prof., 1966–74; Vincent Astor Distinguished Prof. of Biochem., 1974–92. Trustee, Rockefeller Brothers Fund, 1972–82; Associate, Neurosciences Res. Program, 1965– (Scientific Chm., 1980–). Mem., Adv. Bd, Basel Inst. Immunology, 1970–77 (Chm., 1975–77); Member Emeritus, Weizmann Inst. of Science, 1987 (Mem., Bd of Governors, 1971–87); non-resident Fellow and Mem. Bd Trustees, Salk Inst. for Biol. Studies, 1973–85; Member: Biophysics and Biophys. Chem. Study Section, Nat. Insts of Health, 1964–67; Sci. Council, Center for Theoretical Studies, 1970–72; Bd of Overseers, Faculty Arts and Scis, Univ. of Pa, 1976–83; Board of Trustees, Carnegie Inst. of Washington (Mem., Adv. Cttee). Member: Nat. Acad. Scis; Amer. Acad. Arts Scis; Amer. Philosophical Soc.; Fellow: AAAS; NY Acad. Scis, NY Acad. of Medicine; Member: Amer. Soc. Biol Chemists; Amer. Assoc. Immunologists; Genetics Soc. of America; Harvey Soc. (Pres., 1975–76); Amer. Chem. Soc.; Amer. Soc. Cell Biol.; Soc. for Developmental Biol.; Sigma XI; Alpha Omega Alpha; Council of Foreign Relations. Hon. Member: Pharmaceutical Soc. of Japan; Japanese Biochem. Soc.; Foreign Mem., Academie des Sciences, Institut de France. Hon. DSc: Pennsylvania, 1973; Gustavus Adolphus Coll., Minn., 1975; Paris, Cagliari, Georgetown Univ. Sch. of Med., 1989; Univ. degli Studi di Napoli Federico II, 1990; Tulane, 1991; Adelphi, NY, 1995; Miami, 1995; Hon. ScD: Ursinus Coll., 1974; Williams Coll., 1976; Hon. MD Univ. Siena, 1974; Hon. Dr Bologna, 1998. Spencer Morris Award, Univ. of Pennsylvania, 1954; Eli Lilly Award in Biol Chem., Amer. Chem. Soc., 1965; Annual Alumni Award, Ursinus College, 1969; (jtly) Nobel Prize in Physiology or Medicine, 1972; Albert Einstein Commemorative Award, Yeshiva Univ., 1974; Buchman Meml Award, Caltech, 1975; Rabbi Shai Shacknai Meml Prize in Immunology and Cancer Res., Hebrew Univ. Hadassah Med. Sch., 1977; Regents Medal of Excellence, New York State, 1984; Hans Neurath prize, Washington Univ., 1986; Sesquicentennial Commem. Award, Nat. Liby of Medicine, 1986; Cécile and Oskar Vogt award, Dusseldorf Univ., 1988; Dist. Grad. Award, Pennsylvania Univ., 1990; Personnelité de l'année, Paris, 1990; Warren Triennial Prize, Massachusetts Gen. Hosp., Boston, 1992. *Publications:* Neural Darwinism, 1987; Topobiology, 1988; The Remembered Present, 1989; Bright Air, Brilliant Fire, 1992; (with Giulio Tononi) Consciousness: how matter becomes imagination, 2000. *Recreation:* music. *Address:* Scripps Research Institute, 10550 N Torrey Pines Road, La Jolla, CA 92037, USA.

EDELMAN, Keith Graeme; Managing Director, Arsenal Football Club, since 2000; *b* 10 July 1950; *m* 1974, Susan Brown; two *s*. *Educ:* Haberdashers' Aske's Sch.; UMIST (BSc). IBM, 1971–73; Rank Xerox, 1973–78; Bank of America, 1978–83; Grand Metropolitan, 1983–84; Corporate Planning Dir and Chm., Texas Homecare, Ladbroke Group, 1984–91; Man. Dir, Carlton Communications, 1991–93; Chief Exec., Storehouse and BHS, 1993–99. Non-executive Director: Eurotunnel plc, 1995–; Eurotunnel SA, 1995–; Channel Tunnel Gp Ltd, 1995–; France-Manche SA, 1995–. *Recreations:* tennis, ski-ing. *Address:* Laurimar, 7 Linksway, Northwood, Middx HA6 2XA. *T:* (01923) 823990.

EDELSTEIN, Victor Arnold; painter; *b* 10 July 1945; *s* of Israel and Rebecca Edelstein; *m* 1973, Anna Maria Succi. Trainee Designer, Alexon, 1962–66; Asst Designer, Biba, 1966–68; formed own small dress designing co., 1968–72; Salvador, 1972–76; Designer, Christian Dior, 1976–78; founded Victor Edelstein Ltd, 1978, closed 1993. Ballet design, Rhapsody in Blue, 1989. One-man exhibitions: Sotheby's, 1996; Hopkins Thomas, Paris, 1999; Hazlitt, Gooden & Fox Gall., 2001. *Recreations:* walking, music.

EDEN, family name of **Barons Auckland, Eden of Winton** and **Henley**.

EDEN OF WINTON, Baron *cr* 1983 (Life Peer), of Rushyford in the County of Durham; **John Benedict Eden,** Bt (E) 1672 and Bt (GB) 1776; PC 1972; Chairman, Lady Eden's Schools Ltd, since 1974 (Director, 1949–70); *b* 15 Sept. 1925; *s* of Sir Timothy Calvert Eden, 8th and 6th Bt and Patricia (*d* 1990), *d* of Arthur Prendergast; *S* father, 1963; *m* 1st, 1958, Belinda Jane (marr. diss. 1974), *o d* of late Sir John Pascoe; two *s* two *d*; 2nd, 1977, Margaret Ann, Viscountess Strathallan. Lieut Rifle Bde, seconded to 2nd KEO Goorkha Rifles and Gilgit Scouts, 1943–47. Contested (C) Paddington North, 1953; MP (C) Bournemouth West, Feb. 1954–1983. Mem. House of Commons Select Cttee on Estimates, 1962–64; Vice-Chm., Conservative Parly Defence Cttee, 1963–66 (formerly: Chm., Defence Air Sub-Cttee; Hon. Sec., Space Sub-Cttee); Vice-Chm., Aviation Cttee, 1963–64; Additional Opposition Front Bench Spokesman for Defence, 1964–66; Jt Vice-Chm., Cons. Parly Trade and Power Cttee, 1966–68; Opposition Front Bench Spokesman for Power, 1968–70; Minister of State, Min. of Technology, June-Oct. 1970; Minister for Industry, DTI, 1970–72; Minister of Posts and Telecommunications, 1972–74; Mem., Expenditure Cttee, 1974–76; Chairman: House of Commons Select Cttee on European Legislation, 1976–79; Home Affairs Cttee, 1981–83. Vice-Chm., Assoc. of Conservative Clubs Ltd, 1964–67, Vice-Pres., 1970–; President: Wessex Area Council, Nat. Union of Conservative and Unionist Assocs, 1974–77; Wessex Area Young Conservatives, 1978–80. UK Deleg. to Council of Europe and to Western European Union, 1960–62; Mem., NATO Parliamentarians' Conf., 1962–66. Chm., Royal

Armouries, 1986–94. Chairman: WonderWorld plc, 1982–98; Gamlestaden plc, 1987–92; Bricom Gp, 1990–93. Pres., Independent Schs Assoc., 1969–71; a Vice-Pres., Nat. Chamber of Trade, 1974–86; Vice-Pres., Internat. Tree Foundn (formerly The Men of the Trees), 1953–98. Hon. Vice-Pres., Nat. Assoc. of Master Bakers, Confectioners & Caterers, 1978–82. Chm., British Lebanese Assoc., 1990–98. *Heir* (to baronetcies only): *s* Hon. Robert Frederick Calvert Eden, *b* 30 April 1964. *Address:* 41 Victoria Road, W8 5RH. *Clubs:* Boodle's, Pratt's.

EDEN, Prof. Colin L., PhD; Director, University of Strathclyde Graduate School of Business, since 1999; *b* 24 Dec. 1943; *s* of John and Connie Eden; *m* 1967, Christine. *Educ:* Univ. of Leicester (BSc); Univ. of Southampton (PhD). Operational Researcher, then Operational Res. Manager, then Mgt Cons., 1967–73; Lectr, then Sen. Lectr, then Reader, Sch. of Mgt, Univ. of Bath, 1974–87; Prof., Business Sch., Univ. of Strathclyde, 1988–99. Advr, SHEFC; Mem., Mgt Bd, Scottish Exams Bd and Scottish Qualifications Authy. *Publications:* Management Decision and Decision Analysis, 1976; Thinking in Organizations, 1979; Messing About in Problems, 1983; Tackling Strategic Problems, 1990; Managerial and Organizational Cognition, 1998; Making Strategy, 1998; over 150 papers in learned jls. *Recreations:* sailing, ski-ing, walking. *Address:* 199 Cathedral Street, Glasgow G4 0QU. *Club:* Clyde Cruising.

EDEN, Prof. Osborn Bryan, (Tim), FRCPE, FRCP, FRCPath, FRCPCH; Cancer Research Campaign Professor of Paediatric Oncology, University of Manchester, since 1994; *b* 2 April 1947; *s* of Eric Victor Eden and Gwendoline Eden (*née* Hambly); *m* 1970, Randi Forsgren; one *s* one *d*. *Educ:* University Coll. London (MB BS 1970). DRCOG 1972; FRCPE 1983; FRCP 1992 (MRCP 1974); FRCPath 1995; FRCPCH 1997. House physician, UCH, 1970–71; house surgeon, Portsmouth, 1971; Sen. House Officer appts, IoW, UCH, Simpson Meml Pavilion and Royal Hosp. for Sick Children, Edinburgh, 1971–73; Registrar, Paediatrics and Haematology, Royal Hosp. for Sick Children, Edinburgh, 1974–76; Fellow, Stanford Univ., Calif., 1976–77; Leukaemia Res. Fellow, Edinburgh, 1977–78; Lectr, Edinburgh Univ., 1978–79; Consultant Clinical Haematologist, Bristol Children's Hosp., 1979–82; Consultant Paediatric Haematologist, Royal Hosp. for Sick Children, Edinburgh, 1982–91; Prof. of Paediatric Oncology, St Bartholomew's Hosp., 1991–94. Chairman: UK Childen's Cancer Study Gp, 1989–92; MRC Childhood Leukaemia Working Party, 1991–2000; Member: MRC Leukaemia Steering Cttee, 1991–; Cttee on Med. Effects of Radiation in the Envmt, 1991–; Clin. Trials Cttees, CRC, 1998–; Leukaemia Res. Fund, 2000–. Chm., Scientific Cttee, Internat. Soc. of Paediatric Oncology, 1996–99. Non-exec. Dir, Manchester Children's Hosps NHS Trust, 1996–. Trustee, Malcolm Sargent Cancer Fund, 1985–. Hon. Mem., Burma Med. Assoc., 1985. *Publications:* numerous scientific papers, editorials and chapters on paediatric haematology and oncology. *Recreations:* my family, hill-walking, photography, reading, urban wildlife, politics. *Address:* 5 South Gillsland Road, Edinburgh EH10 5DE. *T:* (0131) 447 8749.

EDEN, Prof. Richard John, OBE 1978; Professor of Energy Studies, Cavendish Laboratory, University of Cambridge, 1982–89, now Emeritus; Fellow of Clare Hall, Cambridge, 1966–89, now Emeritus (Vice-President, 1987–89; Hon. Fellow, 1993); *b* 2 July 1922; *s* of James A. Eden and Dora M. Eden; *m* 1949, Elsie Jane Greaves; one *s* one *d* and one step *d*. *Educ:* Hertford Grammar Sch.; Peterhouse, Cambridge. BA 1943, MA 1948, PhD 1951. War service, 1942–46, Captain REME, Airborne Forces. Cambridge University: Bye-Fellow, Peterhouse, 1949–50; Stokes Student, Pembroke Coll., 1950–51; Clare College: Research Fellow, 1951–55; Official Fellow, 1957–66; Dir of Studies in Maths, 1951–53, 1957–62; Royal Soc. Smithson Res. Fellow, 1952–55; Sen. Lectr in Physics, Univ. of Manchester, 1955–57; Cambridge University: Lectr in Maths, 1957–64 (Stokes Lectr, 1962); Reader in Theoretical Physics, 1964–82; Head of High Energy Theoretical Physics Gp, 1964–74, Hd of Energy Res. Gp, 1974–89, Cavendish Lab. Mem., Princeton Inst. for Advanced Study, 1954, 1959, 1973, 1989; Vis. Scientist: Indiana Univ., 1954–55; Univ. of California, Berkeley, 1960, 1967; Vis. Professor: Univ. of Maryland, 1961, 1965; Columbia Univ., 1962; Scuola Normale Superiore, Pisa, 1964; Univ. of Marseilles, 1968; Univ. of California, 1969. Member: UK Adv. Council on Energy Conservation, 1974–83; Eastern Electricity Bd, 1985–93; Energy Adviser to UK NEDO, 1974–75. Syndic, CUP, 1984–95. Chm., Cambridge Energy Res. Ltd, subseq. Caminus Energy Ltd, 1985–91. Companion, Inst. of Energy, 1985. Smiths Prize, Univ. of Cambridge, 1949; Maxwell Prize and Medal, Inst. of Physics, 1970; Open Award for Distinction in Energy Economics, BIEE, 1989. *Publications:* (jtly) The Analytic S Matrix, 1966; High Energy Collisions of Elementary Particles, 1967; Energy Conservation in the United Kingdom (NEDO report), 1975; Energy Prospects (Dept of Energy report), 1976; World Energy Demand to 2020 (World Energy Conf. report), 1977; (jtly) Energy Economics, 1981; (jtly) Electricity's Contribution to UK Energy Self Sufficiency, 1984; (jtly) UK Energy, 1984; Clare College and the Founding of Clare Hall, 1998; papers and review articles on nuclear physics and theory of elementary particles. *Recreations:* painting, reading, gardening, travel. *Address:* Clare Hall, Cambridge CB3 9AL. *T:* (01223) 337231; 6 Wootton Way, Cambridge CB3 9LX. *T:* (01223) 355591.

EDEN, Tim; *see* Eden, O. B.

EDER, (Henry) Bernard; QC 1990; a Recorder, since 2000; *b* 16 Oct. 1952; *s* of Hans and Helga Eder; *m* 1976, Diana Levin; four *s* one *d*. *Educ:* Haberdashers' Aske's School, Elstree; Downing College, Cambridge (BA 1974). Called to the Bar, Inner Temple, 1975; an Asst Recorder, 1996–2000. Vis. Prof., UCL, 1999–. *Recreations:* tennis, ski-ing. *Address:* Essex Court Chambers, 24–26 Lincoln's Inn Fields, WC2A 3ED. *T:* (020) 7813 8000; *e-mail:* hbeder@aol.com.

EDES, (John) Michael, CMG 1981; HM Diplomatic Service, retired; Ambassador and Head, UK Delegation to Conventional Arms Control Negotiations, Vienna, 1989–90; *b* 19 April 1930; *s* of late Lt-Col N. H. Edes and Mrs Louise Edes; *m* 1978, Angela Mermagen; two *s*. *Educ:* Blundell's Sch.; Clare Coll., Cambridge (Scholar; BA); Yale Univ. (MA). HM Forces, 1948–49; Mellon Fellow, Yale Univ., 1952–54; FO, 1954; MECAS, 1955; Dubai, 1956–57; FO, 1957–59 (Moscow, 1959); Rome, 1959–61; FO, 1961–62; UK Delegn to Conf. on Disarmament, Geneva, 1962–65 (UK Mission to UN, NY, 1963); FO, 1965–68; Cabinet Office, 1968–69; FCO, 1969–71; Ambassador to Yemen Arab Republic, 1971–73; Mem., UK Delegn to CSCE, Geneva, 1973–74; FCO, 1974–77; RIIA, 1977–78; Paris, 1978–79; Ambassador to Libya, 1980–83; Hd, UK Delegn to Conf. on Confidence and Security Building Measures and Disarmament in Europe, Stockholm, 1983–86; Hd, UK team at conventional arms control mandate talks, 1987–89. Vis. Fellow, IISS, 1987. *Recreations:* listening to music, gardening. *Address:* c/o Lloyds TSB, 7 Pall Mall, SW1Y 5NA. *Clubs:* Athenæum; Hawks (Cambridge).

EDEY, Prof. Harold Cecil, BCom (London), FCA; Professor of Accounting, London School of Economics, University of London, 1962–80, now Emeritus; *b* 23 Feb. 1913; *s* of Cecil Edey and Elsie (*née* Walmsley); *m* 1944, Dilys Mary Pakeman Jones (*d* 2000); one *s* one *d*. *Educ:* Croydon High Sch. for Boys; LSE (Hon. Fellow, 1986). Chartered Accountant, 1935. Commnd in RNVR, 1940–46. Lectr in Accounting and Finance, LSE, 1949–55; Reader in Accounting, Univ. of London, 1955–62; Pro-Dir, LSE, 1967–70. Mem., UK Adv. Coun. on Educn for Management, 1961–65; Mem., Academic Planning Bd for London Grad. Sch. of Business Studies, and Governor, 1965–71; Chm., Arts and Social Studies Cttee, CNAA, 1965–71, and Mem. Council, 1965–73; Chm., Bd of Studies in Econs, 1966–71, Mem. Senate, 1975–80, University of London; Mem. Council, Inst. of Chartered Accountants in England and Wales, 1969–80. Hon. Freeman, 1981, Hon. Liveryman, 1986, Co. of Chartered Accountants in England and Wales. Hon. Professor, UCW, Aberystwyth, 1980–95; Patron, Univ. of Buckingham, 1984–99. Hon. LLD CNAA, 1972. Bard of the Cornish Gorsedd, 1933. Chartered Accountants Founding Socs' Centenary Award, 1987. *Publications:* (with A. T. Peacock) National Income and Social Accounting, 1954; Business Budgets and Accounts, 1959; Introduction to Accounting, 1963; (with B. S. Yamey and H. Thomson) Accounting in England and Scotland 1543–1800, 1963; (with B. V. Carsberg) Modern Financial Management, 1969; (with B. S. Yamey) Debits, Credits, Finance and Profits, 1974; (with L. H. Leigh) The Companies Act 1981, 1981; Accounting Queries, 1982; articles in various jls. *Address:* 10 The Green, Southwick, Brighton BN42 4DA.

EDGAR, (Christopher) George; HM Diplomatic Service; Ambassador to Macedonia, since 2001; *b* 21 April 1960; *s* of Dr William Macreadie Edgar and Dr Freda Elizabeth Edgar; *m* 1994, Elena Ryurikovna Nagornichnykh; two *d*. *Educ:* Trinity Coll., Cambridge Univ. (MA Philosophy). FCO, 1981–83; Moscow, 1983–86; Lagos, 1986–88; FCO, 1988–92; resigned 1992, reinstated 1995; FCO, 1995–97; Ambassador to Cambodia, 1997–2000. *Recreation:* music. *Address:* c/o Foreign and Commonwealth Office, King Charles Street, SW1A 2AH.

EDGAR, David Burman; author and playwright; Chair, MA in Playwriting Studies, since 1989, Hon. Professor, since 1992, University of Birmingham; *b* 26 Feb. 1948; *s* of Barrie Edgar and Joan (*née* Burman); *m* 1979, Eve Brook (*d* 1998); two *s*. *Educ:* Oundle Sch.; Univ. of Manchester (BA 1969). Fellow in Creative Writing, Leeds Polytechnic, 1972–74; Resident Playwright, Birmingham Rep. Theatre, 1974–75, Board Mem., 1985–; UK/US Bicentennial Arts Fellow, USA, 1978–79; Literary Consultant, 1984–88, Hon. Associate Artist, 1989, RSC; Hon. Sen. Res. Fellow, 1988–92, Prof. of Playwriting Studies, 1995–99, Birmingham Univ. Hon. Fellow, Birmingham Polytechnic, 1991; Judith E. Wilson Fellow, Clare Hall, Cambridge, 1996. Hon. MA Bradford, 1984; DUniv Surrey, 1993. *Plays:* The National Interest, 1971; Excuses Excuses, Coventry, 1972; Death Story, Birmingham Rep., 1972; Baby Love, 1973; The Dunkirk Spirit, 1974; Dick Deterred, Bush Theatre, 1974; O Fair Jerusalem, Birmingham Rep., 1975; Saigon Rose, Edinburgh, 1976; Blood Sports, incl. Ball Boys, Bush Theatre, 1976; Destiny, Other Place, 1976, Aldwych, 1977; Wreckers, 1977; Our Own People, 1977; (adaptation) The Jail Diary of Albie Sachs, Warehouse Theatre, 1978; (adaptation) Mary Barnes, Birmingham Rep., then Royal Court, 1978–79; (with Susan Todd) Teendreams, 1979; (adaptation) Nicholas Nickleby, Aldwych, 1980, Plymouth Theatre, NY, 1981; Maydays, Barbican, 1983; Entertaining Strangers, 1985, Nat. Theatre, 1987; That Summer, Hampstead, 1987; (with Stephen Bill and Anne Devlin) Heartlanders, Birmingham Rep., 1989; The Shape of the Table, NT, 1990; (adaptation) Dr Jekyll and Mr Hyde, Barbican, 1991; Pentecost, Other Place, 1994, Young Vic, 1995; (adaptation) Albert Speer, NT, 2000; The Prisoner's Dilemma, RSC, 2001; *TV and radio:* The Eagle has Landed, 1973; Sanctuary, 1973; I know what I meant, 1974; Ecclesiastes, 1977; (with Neil Grant) Vote for Them, 1989; A Movie Starring Me, 1991; Buying a Landslide, 1992; Citizen Locke, 1994; Talking to Mars, 1996; The Secret Parts, 2000; *film:* Lady Jane, 1986. *Publications:* Destiny, 1976; Wreckers, 1977; The Jail Diary of Albie Sachs, 1978; Teendreams, 1979; Mary Barnes, 1979; Nicholas Nickleby, 1982; Maydays, 1983; Entertaining Strangers, 1985; Plays One, 1987; That Summer, 1987; The Second Time as Farce, 1988; Vote for Them, 1989; Heartlanders, 1989; Edgar Shorts, 1990; Plays Two, 1990; The Shape of the Table, 1990; Plays Three, 1991, Dr Jekyll and Mr Hyde, 1992; Pentecost, 1995; (ed) State of Play, 1999; Albert Speer, 2000. *Recreation:* correspondence. *Address:* c/o Michael Imison Playwrights Ltd, 28 Almeida Street, N1 1TD.

EDGAR, George; *see* Edgar, C. G.

EDGAR, William, FREng, FIMechE; Group Director, John Wood Group plc, since 1995; Chairman and Chief Executive, Wood Group Engineering Ltd, since 1995; Chairman, J. P. Kenny Engineering Ltd, since 1995; *b* 16 Jan. 1938; *s* of William Edgar and Alice Anderson McKerrell; *m* 1961, June Gilmour; two *s*. *Educ:* Royal Coll. of Science and Technology (Strathclyde Univ.); ARCST 1961; Birmingham Univ. (MSc 1962). CEng, FIMechE 1979. Develt Engr, BSC, Motherwell and Glasgow, 1954–62; Principal Aeromech. Engr, BAC, Warton, 1963–67; Chief Develt Engr, Gen. Manager Sales and Service, Gen. Works Manager, Weir Pumps, Glasgow, 1967–73; Chief Exec., Seaforth Engineering and Corporate Develt Dir, Seaforth Maritime, Aberdeen, 1973–86; Business Develt Dir, Vickers Marine Engineering, Edinburgh, 1986–88; Exec. Chm., Cochrane Shipbuilders, Yorks, 1988–90; Chief Exec., Nat. Engrg Lab., 1990–95. Chairman: Scottish Br., IMechE, 1996–98; Offshore Contractors Assoc., 2000–. FREng 1999. *Recreations:* golf, walking, reading, soccer. *Address:* 3 Cairnie View, Westhill, Skene, Aberdeen AB32 6NB. *T:* (01224) 741958. *Clubs:* Sloane; Westhill Golf.

EDGCUMBE, family name of **Earl of Mount Edgcumbe**.

EDGE, Geoffrey; Chairman, West Midlands Enterprise Board, since 1982; *b* 26 May 1943; single. *Educ:* London Sch. of Econs (BA); Birmingham Univ. Asst Lectr in Geography, Univ. of Leicester, 1967–70; Lectr in Geog., Open Univ., 1970–74. Member: Bletchley UDC, 1972–74 (Chm. Planning Sub-cttee 1973–74); Milton Keynes DC, 1973–76 (Vice-Chm. Planning Cttee, 1973–75); Bucks Water Bd, 1973–74; W Midlands CC, 1981–86 (Chm., Econ. Develt Cttee); Walsall MBC, 1983–90 (Leader, 1988–90). MP (Lab) Aldridge-Brownhills, Feb. 1974–1979; PPS to Minister of State for Educn, Feb.–Oct. 1974, 1976–77, to Minister of State, Privy Council Office, Oct. 1974–76. Research Fellow, Dept of Planning Landscape, Birmingham Polytechnic, 1979–80; Senior Research Fellow: Preston Polytechnic, 1980–81; NE London Polytechnic, 1982–84; Hon. Res. Fellow, Birmingham Polytechnic, 1980–81; New Initiatives Co-ordinator, COPEC Housing Trust, 1984–87; Sen. Associate, P-E Inbucon, then P-E Internat., 1987–97. Associate Dir, W. S. Atkins plc, 1997–99. *Publications:* (ed jtly) Regional Analysis and Development, 1973; Open Univ. booklets on industrial location and urban development. *Recreations:* music, reading, touring. *Address:* 5 Sedgefield Close, Dudley DY1 2UU.

EDGE, Captain Sir (Philip) Malcolm, KCVO 1995; FNI; Deputy Master and Chairman, Board of Trinity House, 1988–96; *b* 15 July 1931; *s* of Stanley Weston Edge and Edith Edge (*née* Liddell); *m* 1967, (Kathleen) Anne Greenwood (*d* 1994); one *s* one *d*. *Educ:* Rockferry High School; HMS Conway. Master Mariner. Apprenticed to Shipping subsidiary of British Petroleum, 1949, and served in all ranks; in command, world wide, 1969–78. Elder Brother and Mem. Board, Trinity House, 1978; Mem., PLA, 1980–97. Dir, Standard Steamship Owners' Protection & Indemnity Assoc. Ltd, 1988–97 (Chm., 1992–97). Mem. Council, Internat. Assoc. of Lighthouse Authies, 1988–96 (Pres., 1988–90); Mem., Cttee of Management, RNLI, 1996–. Freeman, City of London, 1980; Liveryman: Hon. Co. of Master Mariners, 1980–; Shipwrights' Co., 1990–; Master, Watermen and Lightermen's Co., 1996–97. *Recreations:* sailing, family. *Address:* c/o

Trinity House, Tower Hill, EC3N 4DH. *T:* (020) 7481 6900. *Clubs:* Royal Thames Yacht; Royal Yacht Squadron (Hon.), Royal London Yacht.

EDGE, William, (3rd Bt *cr* 1937); *S* father, 1984. *Heir: s* Edward Knowles Edge. Does not use the title and his name is not on the Official Roll of Baronets.

EDGINGTON, Prof. Dorothy Margaret Doig; Professor of Philosophy, Birkbeck College, University of London, since 2001; *b* 29 April 1941; *d* of late Edward Milne and of Rhoda Milne (*née* Blair); *m* 1965, John Edgington; one *s* (one *d* decd). *Educ:* St Leonards Sch., St Andrews; St Hilda's Coll., Oxford (BA 1964); Nuffield Coll., Oxford (BPhil 1967). Lectr in Philosophy, 1968–90, Sen. Lectr, 1990–96, Birkbeck Coll., London Univ.; Prof. of Philosophy, Oxford Univ., and Fellow of UC, Oxford, 1996–2001. British Acad. Res. Reader in the Humanities, 1992–94; visiting posts: Univ. of British Columbia, 1974–75, 1990, 1992; Univ. Nacional Autónoma de México, 1985, 1988, 1990, 1995; Princeton Univ., 1986; Univ. of Calif, Berkeley, 1993. Hon. Sec., Aristotelian Soc., 1986–92 (Ed., Proc. of Aristotelian Soc., 1986–90). *Publications:* contrib. anthologies, and learned jls incl. Analysis, British Jl for Philos. of Sci., Crítica, Mind, Proc. of Aristotelian Soc., Revista Latinoamericana de Filosofía. *Address:* Birkbeck College, Malet Street, WC1E 7HX.

EDIE, His Honour Thomas Ker; a Circuit Judge, South Eastern Circuit, 1972–84; *b* 3 Oct. 1916; *s* of H. S. Ker Edie, Kinloss, Morayshire; *m* 1945, Margaret, *d* of Rev. A. E. Shooter, TD; four *s* one *d*. *Educ:* Clifton; London Univ. Called to Bar, Gray's Inn, 1941. Metropolitan Magistrate, 1961–70; Dep. Chm. Middlesex QS, 1970–71.

EDINBURGH, Bishop of, since 2001; **Rt Rev. Brian Arthur Smith;** *b* 15 Aug. 1943; *s* of late Arthur and of Doris Marion Smith; *m* 1970, Elizabeth Berring (*née* Hutchinson); two *d*. *Educ:* George Heriot's School, Edinburgh; Edinburgh Univ. (MA Mental Philosophy 1966); Fitzwilliam Coll., Cambridge (BA Theology 1968; MA 1972); Westcott House, Cambridge; Jesus Coll., Cambridge (MLitt 1973). Curate of Cuddesdon, 1972–79; Tutor in Doctrine, Cuddesdon Coll., Oxford, 1972–75; Dir of Studies, Ripon Coll., Cuddesdon, 1975–78, Senior Tutor 1978–79; Diocese of Wakefield: Priest-in-charge of Cragg Vale, 1979–85; Dir of In-Service Training, 1979–81; Dir of Ministerial Trng, 1981–87; Warden of Readers, 1981–87; Sec. of Dio. Board of Ministry, 1979–87; Hon. Canon of Wakefield, 1981–87; Proctor in Convocation, 1985–87; Archdeacon of Craven, 1987–93; Bp Suffragan of Tonbridge, 1993–2001. Vice-Chairman, Northern Ordination Course, 1985–93. Chm., Churches Together in Kent, 1999–2001. A Director, Scottish Jl of Theology, 1977–81. *Recreations:* browsing in junk shops, walking, reading, music, short-wave radio listening. *Address:* 3 Eglinton Crescent, Edinburgh EH12 5DH; Diocesan Centre, 21A Grosvenor Crescent, Edinburgh EH12 5EL. *T:* (0131) 538 7044, *Fax:* (0131) 538 7088; *e-mail:* bishop@edinburgh.anglican.org.

EDINBURGH, Dean of; *see* Morris, Very Rev. T. D.

EDINBURGH, (St Mary's Cathedral), Provost of; *see* Forbes, Very Rev. G. J. T.

EDIS, Andrew Jeremy Coulter; QC 1997; a Recorder, since 1999; *b* 9 June 1957; *s* of late Dr Peter Edis and of Barbara Edis; *m* 1984, Sandy Wilkinson; one *s* two *d*. *Educ:* Liverpool Coll.; University Coll., Oxford (MA). Called to the Bar, Middle Temple, 1980; Junior, Northern Circuit, 1983–84; Asst Recorder, 1994–99. Hd of Chambers, 14 Castle Street. *Recreations:* cricket, history, food and wine, travel. *Address:* 14 Castle Street, Liverpool L2 0NE. *T:* (0151) 236 4421. *Club:* Oxford and Cambridge.

EDIS, Richard John Smale, CMG 1994; HM Diplomatic Service; Ambassador to Algeria, since 2001; *b* 1 Sept. 1943; *s* of late Denis Edis and of Sylvia (*née* Smale); *m* 1971, Geneviève Cérisoles; three *s*. *Educ:* King Edward's Sch., Birmingham (schol.); St Catharine's Coll., Cambridge (Exhibnr; MA). British Centre, Stockholm, 1965–66; entered HM Diplomatic Service, 1966; FO, 1966–68; Third, later Second Sec., Nairobi, 1968–70; Second, later First Sec., Lisbon, 1971–74; FCO, 1974–77; First Sec., UK Mission to UN, New York, 1977–80; Alternate UK Rep. to UN Human Rights Commn, 1978–81; Asst Head of Southern African Dept, FCO, 1981–82; Counsellor 1982; on secondment to Northern Ireland Office as Asst Sec., 1982–84; Dep. Leader, UK Disarmament Delegn, Geneva, 1984–88; Comr, British Indian Ocean Territory, and Head, E Africa Dept, FCO, 1988–91; Vis. Fellow, Centre of Internat. Studies, Univ. of Cambridge, 1991–92; Ambassador to Mozambique, 1992–95; Ambassador to Tunisia, 1995–98, and Co-ordinator, EU-Mediterranean Affairs, 1997–98; Sen. Dir (Civil), RCDS, 1999–2001. Served Metropolitan Special Constabulary, 1975–92. Special Constabulary Medal, 1991. Officer, Military Order of Christ, Portugal, 1973. *Publications:* Peak of Limuria, 1993; (with J. Baker) The Story of St Catharine's College, 1997; Byzantine Tunisia, 1998; contrib. Cambridge Review of Internat. Affairs, and other academic jls. *Recreations:* history, reading. *Address:* c/o Foreign and Commonwealth Office, SW1A 2AH. *Clubs:* Travellers; The Union (Cambridge).

EDKINS, George Joseph, (John), FCA; Chief Executive, Cystic Fibrosis Trust, 1991–96; *b* 18 June 1930; *s* of late George Henry John Edkins and Olympia Edkins (*née* Izzillo); *m* 1954, Audrey Joan Paul; one *s* (and one *s* one *d* decd). *Educ:* Mitcham GS; Oxted GS. FCA 1960. Naval Fighter Intelligence, RAF, 1948–50. Gp Finance Assistant, Shell Internat. Petroleum, 1950–55; Chartered Accountant: Frazer Whiting, 1955–60; Pike-Russell & Co., 1960–70; Sen. Partner, Russell Limebeer, 1978–88; Sen. Partner, Fraser Russell, 1988–90, retd 1990. Exec. Mem. and Treas., Internat. Cystic Fibrosis Assoc., 1991–98; Council Mem., Assoc. Med. Res. Charities, 1991–96. MIMgt (Chm., 1999–). Liveryman, Co. of Butchers, 1974–. *Recreations:* charity work, sports (Rugby and cricket). *Address:* Birchwood Cottage, Mizen Way, Cobham, Surrey KT11 2RG. *T:* (01932) 863017. *Clubs:* MCC, City of London, Royal Automobile.

EDMOND, Prof. John Marmion, PhD; FRS 1986; Professor of Marine Geochemistry, Massachusetts Institute of Technology, since 1970; *b* 27 April 1943; *s* of late Andrew John Shields Edmond and Christina Marmion Edmond; *m* 1978, Massoudeh Vafai; two *s*. *Educ:* Univ. of Glasgow (BSc 1st class Hons, Pure Chemistry, 1965); Univ. of California at San Diego, Scripps Instn of Oceanography (PhD, Marine Chemistry, 1970). Massachusetts Institute of Technology: Asst Prof., 1970; Associate Prof., 1975; Full Prof., 1981. Fellow: American Geochemical Soc., 1996; European Geochemical Soc., 1996 (Urey Medal, 1999). Mackelwane Award, Amer. Geophysical Union, 1976. *Publications:* over 150 scientific papers in professional jls. *Recreations:* reading, gardening. *Address:* E34-201, Massachusetts Institute of Technology, Cambridge, MA 02139, USA. *T:* (617) 2535739, *Fax:* (617) 2538630; *e-mail:* jedmond@mit.edu.

EDMONDS, David Albert; Director General of Telecommunications, since 1998; *b* 6 March 1944; *s* of Albert and Gladys Edmonds; *m* 1966, Ruth Beech; two *s* two *d*. *Educ:* Helsby County Grammar School; University of Keele. BA Hons Political Institutions and History. Asst Principal, Min. of Housing and Local Govt, 1966–69; Private Sec. to Parly Sec., MHLG and DoE, 1969–71; Principal, DoE, 1971–73; Observer, CSSB, 1973–74; Vis. Fellow, Centre for Metropolitan Planning and Research, Johns Hopkins Univ., 1974–75; Private Sec. to Perm. Sec., DoE, 1975–77; Asst Sec., DoE, 1977–79; Principal Private Sec. to Sec. of State, DoE, 1979–83; Under Sec., Inner Cities Directorate, DoE, 1983–84; Chief Exec., Housing Corporation, 1984–91; Gen. Manager, then Man. Dir, Central Services, NatWest Gp, 1991–97. Dir, Housing Finance Corp., 1988–91; Member: Bd, English Partnerships, 2000– (Chm., Property, Planning and Projects Cttee, 2000–); Steering Bd, Radiocommunications Agency, 1998–. Pres., Internat. New Town Assoc., 1987–91; Mem. Cttee, Notting Hill Housing Trust, 1991–94. Dep. Chm., New Statesman and Society, 1988–90 (Chm., New Society, 1986–88). Chair of Trustees, Crisis, 1996–. Mem. Council, Chm., Finance Cttee, and Univ. Treas., Keele Univ., 1997–; Mem. Ct, Univ. of Surrey, 2000–. *Recreations:* theatre, opera, walking, golf. *Address:* Office of Telecommunications, 50 Ludgate Hill, EC4M 7JJ. *T:* (020) 7634 8801. *Club:* Wimbledon Park Golf (Captain, 1997–98).

EDMONDS, John Christopher, CMG 1978; CVO 1971; HM Diplomatic Service, retired; *b* 23 June 1921; *s* of late Captain A. C. M. Edmonds, OBE, RN, and late Mrs Edmonds; *m* 1st, 1948, Elena Tornow (marr. diss., 1965); two *s*; 2nd, 1966, Armine Williams. *Educ:* Kelly College. Entered Royal Navy, 1939; psc, 1946. Staff: of NATO Defence Coll., Paris, 1953–55; of C-in-C Home Fleet, 1956–57 (Comdr, 1957); of Chief of Defence Staff, 1958–59. Entered Diplomatic Service, 1959; Foreign Office, 1959–60; 1st Secretary (Commercial), Tokyo, 1960–62; FO, 1963–67; 1st Secretary and Head of Chancery, Ankara, 1967–68; Counsellor: Ankara, 1968–71; Paris, 1972–74; Head of Arms Control and Disarmament Dept, FCO, 1974–77; Leader, UK Delegn to Comprehensive Test Ban Treaty Negotiations, Geneva, with personal rank of Ambassador, 1978–81. Chm., Jt SDP-Liberal Alliance Commn on Defence and Disarmament, 1984–86. Vis. Fellow in Internat. Relations, Reading Univ., 1981–. Chm., Sonning Parish Council, 1984–90. *Recreations:* gardening, travel. *Address:* North Lodge, Sonning, Berks RG4 6ST. *Club:* Army and Navy.

EDMONDS, John Christopher Paul, CBE 1993; Chief Executive, Railtrack, 1993–97; *b* 22 April 1936; *s* of late Frank Winston Edmonds and Phyllis Mary Edmonds; *m* 1962, Christine Elizabeth Seago; one *s* one *d*. *Educ:* Lowestoft Grammar School; Trinity College, Cambridge. Nat. Service Commission, RAF, 1955–57. Joined British Rail, 1960; Chief Freight Manager, London Midland Region, 1981; Nat. Business Manager, Coal, 1982; Dir, Provincial, 1984; Gen. Manager, Anglia Region, 1987; Bd Mem., and Man. Dir, Gp Services, 1989–93. *Recreations:* gardening, music.

EDMONDS, John Walter; General Secretary, GMB (formerly General, Municipal, Boilermakers and Allied Trades Union), since 1986; *b* 28 Jan. 1944; *s* of Walter and Rose Edmonds; *m* 1967, Linden (*née* Callaby); two *d*. *Educ:* Brunswick Park Primary; Christ's Hosp.; Oriel Coll., Oxford (BA 1965, MA 1968). General and Municipal Workers' Union: Res. Asst, 1966; Dep. Res. Officer, 1967; Reg. Officer, 1968; Nat. Industrial Officer, 1972. Mem. Council, ACAS, 1992–2000. Pres., TUC, 1997–98. Chm., TU Adv. Cttee on Sustainable Develt. Director: National Building Agency, 1978–82; Unity Trust Bank, 1986–. Mem., Royal Commn on Environmental Pollution, 1979–89; a Forestry Comr, 1995–2001. Vis. Fellow, Nuffield Coll., Oxford, 1986–94. Mem. Council, Consumers' Assoc., 1991–96. Trustee: Inst. of Public Policy Research, 1988–; NSPCC, 1995–. Gov., LSE, 1986–95. Hon. LLD Sussex, 1994. FRSA. *Recreations:* cricket, carpentry. *Address:* 50 Graham Road, Mitcham, Surrey CR4 2HA. *T:* (020) 8648 9991.

EDMONDS, Robert Humphrey Gordon, CMG 1969; MBE 1944; writer; HM Diplomatic Service, retired; *b* 5 Oct. 1920; *s* of late Air Vice-Marshal C. H. K. Edmonds, CBE, DSO; *m* 1st, 1951, Georgina Combe (marr. diss.); three *s* (and one *s* decd); 2nd, 1976, Mrs Enid Balint (*d* 1994), *widow* of Dr Michael Balint; 3rd, 1998, Mrs Gillian Pawley. *Educ:* Ampleforth; Brasenose Coll., Oxford. Pres., Oxford Union, 1940. Served Army, 1940–46; attached to Political Div., Allied Commn for Austria, 1945–46. Entered Foreign Service, Dec. 1946; served Cairo, 1947; FO, 1949; Rome, 1953; Warsaw, 1957; FO, 1959; Caracas, 1962; FO, CO and FCO, 1966–69; Minister, Moscow, 1969–71; High Comr, Nicosia, 1971–72; Asst Under Sec. of State, FCO, 1974–77, retd 1978. Vis. Fellow, Glasgow Univ., 1973–74; Fellow, Woodrow Wilson Internat. Centre for Scholars, Washington, 1977; Leverhulme Res. Fellow, 1989–91; Hon. Fellow, Glasgow Inst. of Soviet and E European Studies, 1988–91. Adviser, Kleinwort Benson, 1978–83, consultant, 1984–86. Mem. Council, RIIA, 1986–92. *Publications:* Soviet Foreign Policy: the paradox of superpower, 1975; Soviet Foreign Policy: the Brezhnev years, 1983; Setting the Mould: the United States and Britain 1945–1950, 1986; The Big Three, 1990; (contrib.) Churchill, ed Blake and Louis, 1992; Pushkin: the man and his age, 1994; articles and review articles in International Affairs, TLS and Survival. *Address:* Llogan End, Travellers Rest, Illogan Downs, Redruth, Cornwall TR15 3UY. *Club:* Turf.

EDMONDS, Sheila May, MA, PhD; Fellow, and Lecturer in Mathematics, Newnham College, Cambridge, 1945–82 (Vice-Principal, 1960–81); Fellow Emerita, Newnham College, since 1982; *b* 1 April 1916; *d* of Harold Montagu Edmonds and Florence Myra Edmonds (*née* Lilley). *Educ:* Wimbledon High Sch.; Newnham Coll., Cambridge. Research Student of Westfield Coll., 1939–40, and of Newnham Coll., 1940–41; Research Fellow of Newnham Coll., 1941–43; Asst Lecturer, Newnham Coll., 1943–45. *Publications:* papers in mathematical journals. *Recreations:* travel, photography.

EDMONDS, Winston Godward, CBE 1966; ERD 1945; Managing Director, Manchester Ship Canal Co., 1961–70; *b* 27 Nov. 1912; *s* of Wilfred Bell Edmonds and Nina (*née* Godward); *m* 1st, 1940, Sheila Mary (*née* Armitage) (*d* 1990); one *s*; 2nd, 1995, Alice Teresa (*née* Verity). *Educ:* Merchant Taylors'. Joined LNER, first as traffic apprentice and then in various positions, 1930–46; Manchester Ship Canal Co.: Commercial Manager, 1947–58; Manager, 1959–61. *Recreations:* golf, philately. *Address:* Silvermead, 17 Thatcher Avenue, Torquay, Devon TQ1 2PD. *T:* (01803) 293401.

EDMONDS-BROWN, (Cedric Wilfred) George; HM Diplomatic Service, retired; *b* 24 April 1939; *s* of late Maj. W. R. E. Edmonds-Brown and E. M. Edmonds-Brown; *m* 1st, 1964, Everild A. V. Hardman (*d* 1988); one *s* two *d*; 2nd, 1990, Teiko Watanabe; one *s* one *d*. *Educ:* Dame Allan's Boys' Sch., Newcastle; King's Coll., Durham Univ. Joined CRO, 1962; Lagos, 1963; Karachi, 1964–68; Third Sec., Buenos Aires, 1968–73; FCO, 1973–76; Second Sec., Bucharest, 1976–80; First Sec. and HM Consul, Caracas, 1980–85; ODA, 1985–88; Head of Chancery, Ottawa, 1988; Dep. High Comr, Barbados, 1989–91; First Sec., Rome, 1991–95, Geneva, 1995–97; Consul, Geneva, 1997–99. *Recreations:* writing, art, travel, cricket.

EDMONDSON, family name of **Baron Sandford.**

EDMONDSON, His Honour Anthony Arnold; a Circuit Judge (formerly County Court Judge and Commissioner, Liverpool and Manchester Crown Courts), 1971–91; *b* 6 July 1920; *s* of late Arnold Edmondson; *m* 1947, Dorothy Amelia Wilson, Gateshead-on-Tyne; three *s* one *d*. *Educ:* Liverpool Univ. (LLB Hons); Lincoln Coll., Oxford (BCL Hons). Served RA (Adjutant), 1940–44; RAF (Pilot), 1944–46; thereafter RA (TA) and TARO. Called to the Bar, Gray's Inn, 1947; William Shaw Schol. 1948; practised on Northern Circuit, 1948–71; Chairman, Liverpool Dock Labour Bd Appeal Tribunal, 1955–66; Mem. Court of Liverpool Univ., 1960–. Dep. Chm., Lancashire QS, 1970–71;

Pres., S Cumbria Magistrates' Assoc., 1977–87; JP Lancs, 1970. *Recreations:* walking, fishing. *Address:* County Sessions House, Preston, Lancs PR1 2PD.

EDMONDSON, Leonard Firby; Executive Council Member, Amalgamated Union of Engineering Workers, 1966–77; *b* 16 Dec. 1912; *s* of Arthur William Edmondson and Elizabeth Edmondson; unmarried. *Educ:* Gateshead Central Sch. Served apprenticeship as engr, Liner Concrete Machinery Co. Ltd, Newcastle upon Tyne, 1929–34; worked in a number of engrg, ship-bldg and ship-repairing firms; shop steward and convener of shop stewards in several firms. AUEW: Mem., Tyne Dist Cttee, 1943–53; Tyne Dist Sec., 1953–66. CSEU: Mem., Exec. Council, 1966–78; Pres., 1976–77. Member: Shipbldg Industry Trng Bd, 1966–79; Council, ACAS, 1976–78; Royal Commn on Legal Services, 1976–79; Council on Tribunals, 1978–84; Cttee of Inquiry into Prison Services, 1978–79; Gen. Council of TUC, 1970–78. Mem., Birtley Canine Soc. *Recreation:* exhibiting Shetland sheep dogs. *Address:* 6 Kenwood Gardens, Low Fell, Gateshead, Tyne and Wear NE9 6PN. *T:* (0191) 487 9167. *Clubs:* Northern Counties Shetland Sheep Dog; Manors Social (Newcastle-upon-Tyne).

EDMONSTONE, Sir Archibald (Bruce Charles), 7th Bt *cr* 1774; *b* 3 Aug. 1934; *o* surv. *s* of Sir Charles Edmonstone, 6th Bt, and Gwendolyn Mary (*d* 1989), *d* of late Marshall Field and Mrs Maldwin Drummond; *S* father, 1954; *m* 1st, 1957, Jane (marr. diss. 1967), *er d* of Maj.-Gen. E. C. Colville, CB, DSO; two *s* one *d*; 2nd, 1969, Juliet Elizabeth, *d* of Maj.-Gen. C. M. F. Deakin, CB, CBE; one *s* one *d*. *Educ:* St Peter's Court; Stowe Sch. *Heir:* *s* Archibald Edward Charles Edmonstone [*b* 4 Feb. 1961; *m* 1988, Ursula (marr. diss.), *e d* of late Benjamin Worthington]. *Address:* Duntreath Castle, Blanefield, Stirlingshire G63 9AJ.

See also Sir A. R. J. B. Jardine, Captain Sir C. E. McGrigor.

EDMONTON, Area Bishop of, since 1999; **Rt Rev. Peter William Wheatley;** *b* 7 Sept. 1947; *er s* of late William Nobes Wheatley and Muriel (*née* Ounsted). *Educ:* Ipswich Sch. (Queen's and Foundn Schol.); Queen's Coll., Oxford (Styring Schol., MA); Pembroke Coll., Cambridge (MA); Coll. of the Resurrection, Mirfield; Ripon Hall, Oxford. Deacon 1973, priest 1974; Asst Curate, All Saints, Fulham, 1973–78; Vicar: Holy Cross with St Jude and St Peter, St Pancras, 1978–82; St James, W Hampstead, 1982–95; Priest-in-charge: St Mary, Kilburn, 1982–90; St Mary with All Souls, Kilburn, 1990–95; Curate-in-charge, All Souls, S Hampstead, 1982–90; Archdeacon of Hampstead, 1995–99. Proctor in Convocation and Mem. Gen. Synod, C of E, 1975–95. *Recreation:* music. *Address:* 27 Thurlow Road, NW3 5PP. *T:* (020) 7435 5890.

EDMONTON (Alberta), Archbishop of, (RC), since 1999; **Most Rev. Thomas Collins,** STD; *b* 16 Jan. 1947. *Educ:* St Jerome's Coll., Waterloo, Ont. (BA 1969); St Peter's Seminary, London, Ont. (BTh 1973); Univ. of Western Ontario (MA 1973); Pontifical Biblical Inst., Rome (SSL 1978); Gregorian Univ., Rome (STD 1986). Ordained deacon, 1972, priest, 1973; Associate Pastor, Holy Rosary Parish, Burlington, and Christ the King Cath., Hamilton, and teacher and Chaplain, Cathedral Boys' High Sch., Hamilton, Ont., 1973–75; Lectr, Dept of English, King's Coll., Univ. of Western Ontario, 1978–84; St Peter's Seminary: Lectr in Scripture, 1978–84; Gp Leader and Spiritual Dir, 1981–95; Associate Prof., 1985–97; Dean of Theol. and Vice-Rector, 1992–95; Rector, 1995–97; Bishop of St Paul, Alberta, 1997–99. Pres., Alberta Conf. of Catholic Bishops, 1999–; Chm., Nat. Commn of Theol., and Mem., Permt Council, Canadian Conf. of Catholic Bishops, 1999–2001. Member, Board of Directors: Caritas Health Gp, Edmonton, 1999–; Alberta Catholic Health Corp., 1999–. Chairman, Board of Governors: Newman Theol Coll., Edmonton, 1999–; St Joseph's Coll., Edmonton, 1999–. Associate Ed., Discover the Bible, 1989–94; columnist, Bread of Life mag., 1987–89. *Publications:* contrib. to Journey, Emmanuel, and Canadian Catholic Review. *Address:* 10033–84 Avenue, Edmonton, AB T6A 0L1, Canada.

EDMONTON (Alberta), Bishop of, since 1997; **Rt Rev. Victoria Matthews;** *b* 1954; *d* of late Beverley Matthews and Pauline Ritchie Matthews. *Educ:* Trinity Coll., Univ. of Toronto (BA (Hons) 1976; ThM 1987); Yale Univ. Divinity Sch. (MDiv 1979). Ordained deacon, 1979, priest, 1980; Asst Curate, St Andrew, Scarborough, 1979–83; Incumbent: Parish of Georgina, York-Simcoe, 1983–87; All Souls, Lansing, York-Scarborough, 1987–94; Suffragan Bishop of Toronto (Bishop of the Credit Valley), 1994–97. N Amer. Theol Fellow, 1976–79. *Recreations:* reading, hiking, swimming, travel. *Address:* 10035-103 Street, Edmonton, AB T5J 0X5, Canada.

EDNAM, Viscount; William Humble David Jeremy Ward; *b* 27 March 1947; *s* and *heir* of Earl of Dudley, *qv* and of Stella Viscountess Ednam, *d* of M. A. Carcano, KCMG, KBE; *m* 1st, 1972, Sarah (marr. diss. 1976), *o d* of Sir Alastair Coats, Bt, *qv*; 2nd, 1976, Debra Louise (marr. diss. 1980), *d* of George Robert and Marjorie Elvera Pinney; one *d*. *Educ:* Eton; Christ Church, Oxford.

EDSON, Ven. Michael; Archdeacon of Leicester, since 1994; *b* 2 Sept, 1942; *s* of Joseph Pratt and Elsie (*née* Edson); name changed to Edson, 1989; *m* 1968, (Ann) Frances Tuffley; three *s* one *d*. *Educ:* Univ. of Birmingham (BSc Hons 1964); Univ. of Leeds (BA Hons 1971); College of Resurrection, Mirfield. Management Consultant, 1966–68. Ordained deacon, 1972, priest, 1973; Curate, Barnstaple, Devon, 1972–77; Team Vicar, Barnstaple, 1977–82; Chaplain, N Devon Dist Hosp., 1976–82; Vicar, Roxbourne, Harrow, 1982–89; Area Dean of Harrow, 1985–89; Warden of Lee Abbey Fellowship, Devon, 1989–94. Leicester Diocesan Evangelist, 1997–. *Publications:* The Renewal of the Mind, 1988; Loved into Life, 1993. *Recreations:* hill-walking, people, writing, spirituality, art. *Address:* 13 Stoneygate Avenue, Leicester LE2 3HE. *T:* (0116) 270 4441.

EDWARD, Judge David Alexander Ogilvy, CMG 1981; QC (Scotland) 1974; FRSE; Judge of the Court of Justice of the European Communities, since 1992 (Judge of the Court of First Instance, 1989–92); *b* 14 Nov. 1934; *s* of J. O. C. Edward, Travel Agent, Perth; *m* 1962, Elizabeth Young McSherry; two *s* two *d*. *Educ:* Sedbergh Sch.; University Coll., Oxford (Hon. Fellow, 1995); Edinburgh Univ. Sub-Lt RNVR (Nat. Service); HMS Hornet, 1956–57. Admitted Advocate, 1962; Clerk of Faculty of Advocates, 1967–70, Treasurer, 1970–77. Pres., Consultative Cttee of Bars and Law Societies, EC, 1978–80; Salvesen Prof. of European Instns, 1985–89, Hon. Prof., 1990, Univ. of Edinburgh. Trustee, Nat. Library of Scotland, 1966–95; Mem. Law Adv. Cttee, British Council, 1974–88; Specialist Advr, H of L Select Cttee on EC, 1985, 1986 and 1987. Mem., Panel of Arbitrators, Internat. Centre for Settlement of Investment Disputes, 1981–89; Chm., Scottish Council for Internat. Arbitration, 1988–89 (Hon. Pres. 1989–). Director: Continental Assets Trust plc, 1985–89 (Chm.); Adam & Co. Group plc, 1983–89; Harris Tweed Association Ltd, 1984–89. Hon. Bencher, Gray's Inn, 1992. Member: Foundation Senate, Europa Universität Viadrina, Frankfurt/Oder, 1991–93; Bd of Trustees, Acad. of European Law, Trier, 1993–. Trustee: Industry and Parlt Trust, 1995–; Carnegie Trust for Univs of Scotland, 1996–. President: Johnson Soc., Lichfield, 1995; Franco-Scottish Soc., 1996–; Edinburgh Sir Walter Scott Club, 2001–02. FRSE 1990. Hon. LLD: Edinburgh, 1993; Aberdeen, 1997; Napier, 1998; Dr (*hc*) Saarbrücken, 2001. Distinguished Cross, First Class, Order of St Raymond of Penafort, Spain, 1979. *Publications:* The Professional Secret, Confidentiality and Legal Professional Privilege in the EEC, 1976; (with R. C. Lane) European Community Law: an introduction, 1991, 2nd edn 1995; articles in legal jls, etc. *Address:* Court of Justice of the EC, L-2925 Luxembourg; 20 Rue Principale, Flaxweiler, L-6925 Luxembourg; 32 Heriot Row, Edinburgh EH3 6ES. *Clubs:* Athenæum; New (Edinburgh); Royal Scottish Automobile (Glasgow).

EDWARDES, family name of **Baron Kensington**.

EDWARDES, Sir Michael (Owen), Kt 1979; Chairman: Tryhorn Investments Ltd, since 1987; Strand Partners, since 1994; Syndicated Services Co. Inc., since 1995; *b* 11 Oct. 1930; *s* of Denys Owen Edwardes and Audrey Noel (*née* Copeland); *m* 1st, 1958, Mary Margaret (*née* Finlay) (marr. diss.; she *d* 1999); three *d*; 2nd, 1988, Sheila Ann (*née* Guy). *Educ:* St Andrew's Coll., Grahamstown, S Africa; Rhodes Univ., Grahamstown (BA; Hon. LLD). Chairman: Chloride Gp PLC, 1969–77 and 1986; BL Ltd (formerly British Leyland), 1977–82; Mercury Communications Ltd, 1982–83; ICL PLC, 1984; Dunlop Hldgs plc, 1984–85; Charter PLC, 1988–96; Porth Gp, 1991–95; ARC Internat. Ltd (BVI), 1991–98; Dep. Chm., R K Carvill (Internat. Hldgs) Ltd, 1988–; Director: Hill Samuel Gp, 1980–87; Minorco SA, 1984–93; Standard Securities PLC, 1985–87; Delta Motor Corp. (Pty) Ltd, 1986–99; Flying Pictures Ltd, 1987–; Lansing Bagnall, 1987–88; Jet Press Hldgs BV, 1990–; Federal Trust Ltd, 1996–. Dir, Internat. Management Develt Inst., Washington, 1978–94. CIMgt (Vice-Chm., BIM, 1977–80); Hon. FIMechE, 1981. President: Squash Rackets Assoc., 1991–95; Veterans Squash Club of GB, 1981–94. Trustee, Thrombosis Res. Inst., 1991–. *Publication:* Back From the Brink, 1983. *Recreations:* sailing, squash, water ski-ing, tennis. *Clubs:* Royal Automobile; Jesters; Rand and Country (Johannesburg).

EDWARDS, family name of **Baron Crickhowell**.

EDWARDS, (Alfred) Kenneth, CBE 1989 (MBE 1963); Deputy Director-General, Confederation of British Industry, 1982–88; Director: Reliance Bank Ltd, since 1992; Salvation Army Trustee Co., since 1996; *b* 24 March 1926; *s* of late Ernest Edwards and Florence Edwards (*née* Branch); *m* 1949, Jeannette Lilian, *d* of David Speeks, MBE; one *s* two *d*. *Educ:* Latymer Upper Sch.; Magdalene Coll., Cambridge; University Coll. London. Served RAF, 1944–47; RAF Coll., Cranwell, 1945, FO (Pilot). Entered HMOCS, Nigeria, 1952; Provincial Administration, Warri and Benin, 1952–54; Lagos Secretariat, 1954; Sen. Asst Sec., Nigerian Min. of Communications and Aviation, 1959; retired, 1962. Secretary, British Radio Equipment Manufrs' Assoc., 1962; Gp Marketing Manager, Thorn Elec. Industries Ltd, 1965; Internat. Dir, Brookhirst Igranic Ltd (Thorn Gp), 1967; Gp Marketing Dir, Cutler Hammer Europa, 1972; Dep. Chm., BEAMA Overseas Trade Cttee, 1973; Chief Exec., BEAMA, 1976–82. CBI: Member: Council, 1974, 1976–82; Finance and Gen. Purposes Cttee, 1977–82; Vice-Chm., Eastern Reg. Council, 1974; Chm., Working Party on Liability for Defective Products, 1978–82; Mem., President's Cttee, 1979–82. Chm., Facilities & Properties Management Plc, 1989–91; Dir, Polar Electronics PLC, 1984–96. Member: Elec. Engrg EDC, 1976; Council, Elec. Res. Assoc. Ltd, 1976–82; Exec. Cttee, ORGALIME, 1976–82; Management Bd, Eur. Cttee for Develt of Vocational Training, 1988–; BSI Bd, 1978–82, 1984–89 (Chm., British Electrotechnical Cttee and Electrotechnical Divisional Council, 1981–82; Chm., Quality Policy Cttee, 1988–); BOTB, 1982–88; BTEC, 1983–89; BBC Consultative Gp on Indust. and Business Affairs, 1983–88; Bd and Exec. Cttee, Business in the Community, 1987–88; President: CENELEC, 1977–79; Liaison Cttee for Electrical and Electronic Industries, ORGALIME, 1979–82 (Chm., 1980–82); Mem. Exec. Cttee, 1982–89, and Chm. Finance Cttee, 1983–89, UNICE. Dep. Chm., Salvation Army Adv. Bd, 1995– (Mem., 1982–). Mem. Court, Cranfield Inst. of Technol., 1970–75. *Publications:* contrib. technical jls; lectures and broadcasts on industrial subjects. *Recreations:* music, books, walking. *Address:* 53 Bedford Road, Rushden, Northants NN10 0ND. *Clubs:* Athenæum, Royal Air Force.

EDWARDS, Andrew John Cumming, CB 1994; writer and consultant, since 1995; *b* 3 Nov. 1940; *s* of John Edwards and Norah Hope Edwards (*née* Bevan); *m* 1st, 1969, Charlotte Anne Chilcot (marr. diss. 1987); one *s* two *d*; 2nd, 1994, Ursula Mary Richardson; one *s*. *Educ:* Fettes Coll., Edinburgh; St John's Coll., Oxford (MA); Harvard Univ. (AM, MPA). Asst master, Malvern Coll., 1962–63; HM Treasury: Asst Principal, 1963–67; Pvte Sec. to Jt Perm. Sec., 1966–67; Principal, 1967–75; Harkness Fellow, Harvard Univ., 1971–73; Asst Sec., 1975–83; RCDS, 1979; Asst Sec., DES, 1983–85; Under Sec., 1985–89, Dir (Dep. Sec.), 1990–95, HM Treasury. Professional advr to Greenbury Cttee, 1995; conducted reviews of BM, 1996, Financial Regulation in Crown Dependencies, 1998, Finance Ministries of Bulgaria, 1999, Slovakia, 2000, and HM Land Registry, 2000–01; Mem., Financial Issues Adv. Gp for Scottish Parliament, 1998. Gov., British Inst. of Recorded Sound, 1974–79; Sec., Bd of Dirs, Royal Opera House, 1988– (Sec., Develt Bd, 1984–87). Conductor, Acad. of St Mary's, Wimbledon, 1980–. *Publications:* Nuclear Weapons, the balance of terror, the quest for peace, 1986; reports; articles on European Community Budget, regulation of trusts and companies. *Recreations:* music, walking. *Address:* 15 Highbury Road, SW19 7PR.

EDWARDS, Arthur Frank George; Vice-Chairman, Thames Water Authority, 1973–83; *b* 27 March 1920; *o s* of Arthur Edwards and Mabel (Elsie) Edwards; *m* 1946, Joyce May Simmons; one *s* one *d*. *Educ:* West Ham Grammar Sch.; Garnett Coll., London; West Ham Coll. of Technology; City of London Polytechnic (MSc 1990); King's College London (MPhil 2000). CEng, FUChemE, MSE; Hon. FIWM. Various posts with Ever Ready (GB) Ltd, 1936–50; Prodn Man., J. Burns & Co. Ltd, 1950–53; various lectrg posts, 1954–65; Organiser for science and techn. subjects, London Boroughs of Barking and Redbridge, 1965–82. Member: West Ham Co. Borough Council, 1946–65; Newham Council, 1964–86 (Mayor, 1967–68); GLC, 1964–86 (Dep. Chm., 1970–71; Chm., Public Services Cttee, 1973–77); Chm. of Governors, NE London Polytechnic, 1972–87. Hon. Prof., Moscow Univ. of Humanities, 1996. Mem., Fabian Soc. *Recreations:* reading, Association football (watching West Ham United). *Address:* 18 Wanstead Park Avenue, E12 5EN. *T:* (020) 8530 6436. *Clubs:* West Ham Supporters'; Aldersbrook Bowls.

EDWARDS, Prof. Brian, CBE 1988; FHSM; Professor of Health Care Development, University of Sheffield, since 1996 (Foundation Dean, School of Health and Related Research, 1996–99); *b* 19 Feb. 1942; *s* of John Albert Edwards and Ethel Edwards; *m* 1964, Jean (*née* Cannon); two *s* two *d*. *Educ:* Wirral Grammar Sch. FHSM 1983. Jun. Administrator, Clatterbridge Hosp., 1958–62; Dep. Hosp. Sec., Cleaver Hosp., 1962–64; National Trainee, Nuffield Centre, Leeds, 1964–66; Administrator, Gen. Infirmary, Leeds, 1966–67; Hosp. Sec., Keighley Victoria Hosp., 1967–68; Administrator, Mansfield HMC, 1969–70; Lectr, Univ. of Leeds, 1970–72; Dep. Gp Sec., Hull A HMC, 1972–74; Nuffield Travelling Fellow, USA, 1973; Dist Administrator, Leeds AHA(T), 1974–76; Area Administrator, Cheshire AHA, 1976–81; Regional Administrator, 1981–84, Regl Gen. Man., 1984–93, Trent RHA; Chief Exec., W Midlands RHA, 1993–96; Regl Dir, NHS Exec., 1994–96. Chm., Clinical Pathology Accreditation Ltd, 1992–. Vis. Lectr, Health Care Studies, 1973–93, and Associate Fellow, Nuffield Inst., 1987–93, Univ. of Leeds; Vis. Prof., Health Care Studies, Univ. of Keele, 1989; Queen Elizabeth Nuffield Fellow, Nuffield Provincial Hosps Trust, 1991; Hon. Prof., Univ. of Keele, 1993. Adviser to WHO, 1982–; Chairman: NHS Manpower Planning Adv. Gp, 1983–86; Regional

Gen. Managers Gp, 1986–87, 1991–94; NHS Patient Empowerment Gp, 1991–94; Patient's Charter Team, 1992; Council for the Professions Supplementary to Medicine, 1997–; Notts Health NHS Trust, 2001–; Member: Steering Cttee on Future of Nursing, 1988; Standing Cttee on Medical Audit, RCP, 1989–94; Ashworth Inquiry, 1997–98; Leader: Sec. of State's Task Force on Quality in NHS, 1993; UK Delegn, Hosp. Cttee for Europe, 1994–. Director: Shirehall Gp, 1996–99; Health on the Box Ltd, 1999–. Institute of Health Service Administrators: Mem., 1964–; Pres., 1982–83; Mem. Editorial Cttee, Health Care in the UK: its organisation and management, 1982–83. Trustee, Marie Curie Trust, 1996–2000. Jt Editor, Health Services Manpower Review, 1970–91; Editor, Euro Hospital Yearbook, 1998–2001. CIMgt (CBIM 1988); Hon. FRCPath 1996. DUniv UCE, 1998. *Publications:* Si Vis Pacem—preparations for change in the NHS, 1973; Profile for Change, 1973; Bridging in Health, Planning the Child Health Services, 1975; Industrial Relations in the NHS: managers and industrial relations, 1979; Manpower Planning in the NHS, 1984; Employment Policies for Health Care, 1985; Distinction Awards for Doctors, 1987; (contrib.) Doctors' Contracts, 1992; (contrib.) Public Sector Managers' Handbook, 1992; The NHS: a manager's tale, 1993, 2nd edn 1995; (contrib.) Management for Doctors, 1994; (contrib.) Managed Healthcare, 1998; (ed) NHS 50th Anniversary Lectures, 1999; conf. papers presented in UK, Norway, Germany, USA, India, USSR, Czechoslavakia, Mexico and Guyana; contrib. prof. jls. *Recreations:* golf, stage management. *Address:* 3 Royal Croft Drive, Baslow, Derbyshire DE45 1SN. *T:* (01246) 583459, *Fax:* (01246) 582583. *Clubs:* Athenæum; Baslow Cricket (Vice-Pres.); Bakewell Golf (Captain, 1991); La Manga (Spain).

EDWARDS, (Charles) Marcus; His Honour Judge Marcus Edwards; a Circuit Judge, since 1986; *b* 10 Aug. 1937; *s* of late John Basil Edwards, CBE; *m* 1st, 1963, Anne Louise Stockdale (*d* 1970), *d* of Sir Edmund Stockdale, 1st Bt; 2nd, 1975, Sandra Wates (*née* Mouroutsos); one *d* and three step *d. Educ:* Dragon Sch., Oxford; Rugby Sch.; Brasenose Coll., Oxford (scholar; BA Jurisprudence). Trooper, RAC, 1955; 2nd Lieut, Intelligence Corps, Cyprus, 1956–57. HM Diplomatic Service, 1960–65; Third Sec., 1960, Spain, 1961, FO, 1961–62, South Africa and High Commn Territories, 1962–63, Laos, 1964; Second Sec., FO, 1965, resigned. Called to the Bar, Middle Temple, 1962; practised, London, 1966–86; Mem., Midland and Oxford Circuit; a Recorder, 1985–86. Chm., Pavilion Opera, 1987–. *Recreations:* gardening, walking, talking, food and drink. *Address:* Melbourne House, South Parade, W4 1JU. *T:* (020) 8995 9146. *Club:* Beefsteak.

EDWARDS, Sir Christopher (John Churchill), 5th Bt *cr* 1866; Executive Vice-President and General Manager, RAM Electronics Corp., Fort Collins, Colorado, since 1995; *b* 16 Aug. 1941; *s* of Sir (Henry) Charles (Serrell Priestley) Edwards, 4th Bt and of Lady (Daphne) Edwards (*née* Birt); *S* father, 1963; *m* 1972, Gladys Irene Vogelgesang; two *s. Educ:* Frensham Heights, Surrey; Loughborough, Leics. Gen. Manager, Kelsar Inc., American Home Products, San Diego, Calif, 1979–84; Vice-Pres., Valleylab Inc., Boulder, Colorado, 1981–89; Dir, Ohmeda BOC Group, Louisville, 1989–92. Pres., Intermed Consultants, Westminster, Colorado, 1992–. *Heir: s* David Charles Priestley Edwards, *b* 22 Feb. 1974. *Address:* 11637 Country Club Drive, Westminster, CO 80234, USA. *T:* (303) 4693156. *Club:* Ranch Country (Westminster, Colorado).

EDWARDS, Prof. Christopher Richard Watkin, MD; FRCP, FRCPE, FMedSci; FRSE; Vice-Chancellor, University of Newcastle upon Tyne, since 2001; *b* 12 Feb. 1942; *s* of Thomas Archibald Watkin Edwards and Beatrice Elizabeth Ruby Watkin Edwards; *m* 1968, Sally Amanda Kidd; two *s* one *d. Educ:* Marlborough Coll.; Christ's Coll., Cambridge (BA, MB, BChir, MA, MD). St Bartholomew's Hospital: Lectr in Medicine, 1969–75; Sen. Lectr in Medicine and MRC Sen. Res. Fellow, 1975–80; Hon. Consultant Physician, 1975–80; University of Edinburgh: Moncrieff Arnott Prof. of Clinical Medicine, 1980–95; Dean, Faculty of Medicine, 1991–95; Provost, Faculty Group of Medicine and Veterinary Medicine, 1992–95; Principal and Prof. of Medicine, ICSM, Univ. of London, 1995–2000. Mem., MRC, 1991–95. Gov., Wellcome Trust, 1994–. Founder FMedSci 1998. Hon. DSc Aberdeen, 2000. *Publications:* (ed) Clinical Physiology, 5th edn, 1984; (ed) Essential Hypertension as an Endocrine Disease, 1985; Endocrinology, 1986; (ed) Recent Advances in Endocrinology Metabolism, vol. 3, 1989; (ed) Davidson's Principles and Practice of Medicine, 17th edn, 1995; 421 scientific papers and communications. *Recreations:* running, reading, golf, ski-ing. *Address:* University of Newcastle upon Tyne, 6 Kensington Terrace, Newcastle upon Tyne NE1 7RU. *Club:* Athenæum.

EDWARDS, David; Director, John Laing plc, 1982–99; Chairman, Londondome Ltd, 1988–93; *b* 27 Oct. 1929; *s* of Col Cyril Edwards, DSO, MC, DL and Jessie Edwards; *m* 1966, Gay Clothier; two *s* one *d. Educ:* Felsted Sch.; Trinity Hall, Cambridge (MA, LLM). Called to the Bar, Middle Temple, 1952; Harmsworth Scholar, Middle Temple, 1955; admitted Solicitor, 1958. Partner, E. Edwards Son & Noice, 1959–75; Sec., Legal Aid, 1976–86, and Dep. Sec.-Gen., 1982–86, Law Soc. Dir, Laing Properties, 1988–90. Chm., Offshore Racing Council, 1970–78; Dep. Chm., Royal Yachting Assoc., 1976–81. *Recreation:* sailing. *Address:* Olivers, Colchester, Essex CO2 0HJ. *Clubs:* Royal Ocean Racing; Royal Yacht Squadron (Cowes).

See also J. T. Edwards.

EDWARDS, (David) Elgan (Hugh), DL; **His Honour Judge Elgan Edwards;** a Circuit Judge, since 1989; *b* 6 Dec. 1943; *s* of Howell and Dilys Edwards; *m* 1982, Carol Anne Smalls; two *s* two *d. Educ:* Rhyl Grammar Sch.; University Coll. of Wales, Aberystwyth (LLB Hons 1966; Pres., Students Union, 1967). Called to the Bar, Gray's Inn, 1967; a Recorder, Wales and Chester Circuit, 1983–89; Hon. Recorder, Chester, 1997. Contested (C): Merioneth, 1970; Stockport South, Feb. 1974. Sheriff, City of Chester, 1977–78. DL Cheshire, 2000. *Recreation:* swimming. *Address:* The Crown Court, Chester Castle, Chester CH1 2AN. *T:* (01244) 317606. *Clubs:* Lansdowne; Chester City (Chester).

EDWARDS, Very Rev. David Lawrence, OBE 1995; Provost of Southwark Cathedral, 1983–94, Emeritus since 1994; *b* 20 Jan. 1929; *s* of late Lawrence Wright and Phyllis Boardman Edwards; *m* 1st, 1960, Hilary Mary (*née* Phillips) (marr. diss. 1984); one *s* three *d*; 2nd, 1984, Sybil, *d* of Michael and Kathleen Falcon. *Educ:* King's Sch., Canterbury; Magdalen Coll., Oxford. Lothian Prize, 1951; 1st cl. hons Mod. Hist., BA 1952; MA 1956. Fellow, All Souls Coll., Oxford, 1952–59. Deacon, 1954; Priest, 1955. On HQ staff of Student Christian Movement of Gt Brit. and Ireland, 1955–66; Editor and Man. Dir, SCM Press Ltd, 1959–66; Gen. Sec. of Movt, 1965–66. Curate of: St John's, Hampstead, 1955–58; St Martin-in-the-Fields, 1958–66; Fellow and Dean of King's College, Cambridge, 1966–70; Asst Lectr in Divinity, Univ. of Cambridge, 1967–70; Rector of St Margaret's, Westminster, 1970–78; Canon of Westminster, 1970–78; Sub-Dean, 1974–78; Speaker's Chaplain, 1972–78; Dean of Norwich, 1978–82. Exam. Chaplain: to Bp of Manchester, 1965–73; to Bp of Durham, 1968–72; to Bp of Bradford, 1972–78; to Bp of London, 1974–78; to Archbishop of Canterbury, 1975–78. Hulsean Lectr, 1967; Six Preacher, Canterbury Cathedral, 1969–76. Chairman: Churches' Council on Gambling, 1970–78; Christian Aid, 1971–78. Hon. Prof., King Alfred's Coll., Winchester, 1999. Hon. Fellow, South Bank Univ. (formerly Poly.), 1990. DD Lambeth, 1990. *Publications:* A History of the King's School, Canterbury, 1957; Not Angels But Anglicans, 1958; This Church of England, 1962; God's Cross in Our World, 1963; Religion and Change, 1969; F. J. Shirley: An Extraordinary Headmaster, 1969; The Last Things Now, 1969; Leaders of the Church of England, 1971; What is Real in Christianity?, 1972; St Margaret's, Westminster, 1972; The British Churches Turn to the Future, 1973; Ian Ramsey, Bishop of Durham, 1973; Good News in Acts, 1974; What Anglicans Believe, 1974; Jesus for Modern Man, 1975; A Key to the Old Testament, 1976; Today's Story of Jesus, 1976; The State of the Nation, 1976; A Reason to Hope, 1978; Christian England: vol. 1, Its story to the Reformation, 1981; vol. 2, From the Reformation to the Eighteenth Century, 1983; vol. 3, From the Eighteenth Century to the First World War, 1984; The Futures of Christianity, 1987; Essentials: a Liberal-Evangelical dialogue with John Stott, 1988; The Cathedrals of Britain, 1989; Tradition and Truth, 1989; Christians in a New Europe, 1990; The Real Jesus, 1992; What is Catholicism?, 1994; Christianity: the first two thousand years, 1997; A Concise History of English Christianity, 1998; After Death?: past beliefs and real possibilities, 1999; John Donne: a man of flesh and spirit, 2001; The Church That Could Be, 2002; *edited:* The Honest to God Debate, 1963; Collins Children's Bible, 1978; Christianity and Conservatism, 1990; Robert Runcie: a portrait by his friends, 1990. *Address:* 19 Cripstead Lane, Winchester SO23 9SF. *T:* (01962) 862597. *Club:* Athenæum.

See also M. G. Falcon.

EDWARDS, David Michael, CMG 1990; Asia Pacific Region Counsel and Vice President, Bechtel International Inc., Singapore, since 1997; *b* 28 Feb. 1940; *s* of late Ernest William Edwards and Thelma Irene Edwards; *m* 1st, 1966, Veronica Margaret Postgate (marr. diss. 1996); one *s* one *d*; 2nd, 1996, Rain Ren; one *s* one *d. Educ:* The King's Sch., Canterbury; Univ. of Bristol. LLB Hons. Admitted to Roll of Solicitors, 1964. Solicitor of Supreme Court, 1964–67; Asst Legal Adviser, Foreign Office, 1967; Legal Adviser: British Military Govt, Berlin, 1972; British Embassy, Bonn, 1974; Legal Counsellor, 1977; Dir, Legal Div., IAEA, Vienna, 1977–79; Legal Counsellor, FCO, 1979; Agent of the UK Govt in cases before European Commn and Court of Human Rights, 1979–82; Counsellor (Legal Adviser), UK Mission to UN, New York, and HM Embassy, Washington, 1985–88; Legal Counsellor, 1988–89, Dep. Legal Advr, 1989–90, FCO; Sen. Counsel, Bechtel Ltd, 1990; Law Officer (Internat. Law), Hong Kong Govt, 1990–95; Sen. Counsel, Bechtel Ltd, London, 1995–97. *Recreations:* reading, travel, antique clocks. *Address:* c/o Bechtel International Inc., One Temasek Avenue, 23–00 Millenia Tower, Singapore 039192. *T:* (65) 3321972, *Fax:* (65) 3321979. *Club:* Royal Over-Seas League.

EDWARDS, Prof. David Olaf, DPhil; FRS 1988; University Professor of Physics, Ohio State University, 1988–95, now Distinguished Professor Emeritus; *b* 27 April 1932; *s* of Robert Edwards and Margaret Edwina (*née* Larsen); *m* 1967, Wendy Lou Townsend; one *s* one *d. Educ:* Holt High Sch., Liverpool; Brasenose Coll., Oxford (BA 1st cl. Hons, 1953; Sen. Hulme Schol., 1953–56; MA; DPhil 1957). FAPS. Pressed Steel Co. Res. Fellow, Clarendon Lab., Oxford Univ., 1957–58; Ohio State University: Vis. Asst Prof., 1958–60; Asst Prof., 1960–62; Associate Prof., 1962–65; Prof., 1965–88. Visiting Professor: Imperial Coll., London, 1964; Sussex Univ., 1964, 1968; Technion, Israel, 1971–72; Ecole Normale Supérieure, Paris, 1978, 1982, 1986; Vis. Scientist, Brookhaven Nat. Lab., 1975. Consultant: Brookhaven Nat. Lab., 1975–77; Los Alamos Scientific Lab., 1979–81. Sir Francis Simon Prize, British Inst. of Phys, 1983; Dist. Schol. Award, Ohio State Univ., 1984; Special Creativity Awards, US Nat. Sci. Foundn, 1981, 1986; Oliver E. Buckley Condensed Matter Physics Prize, APS, 1990. Mem. Editl Bd, Jl of Low Temperature Physics, 1990–. *Publications:* (ed jtly) Proceedings of the Ninth International Conference on Low Temperature Physics (LT9), 1966; numerous articles on low temp. physics in scientific jls. *Recreations:* beagling (Master, Rocky Fork Beagles, 1975–90), snorkeling (Grand Cayman), crossword puzzles, reading detective stories, watching old British TV programs. *Address:* 2345 Dorset Road, Columbus, OH 43221, USA. *T:* (614) 4864553; Department of Physics, Ohio State University, 174 W 18th Avenue, Columbus, OH 43210–1106, USA. *T:* (614) 2921771, *Fax:* (614) 2927557.

EDWARDS, Prof. Dianne, CBE 1999; ScD; FRS 1996; Distinguished Research Professor in Palaeobotany, University of Wales, Cardiff, since 1996; *b* 23 Feb. 1942; *d* of William John Edwards and Enid Edwards; *m* 1965, Thomas Geoffrey Morgan (*d* 1997); one *s. Educ:* Girton Coll., Cambridge (BA, MA; PhD 1968; ScD 1989). Res. Fellow, Girton Coll., Cambridge, 1967–70; Fellow, Univ. of Wales, 1970–72; University College, Cardiff: Lectr in Botany, 1972–82; Sen. Lectr, 1982–86; Reader in Plant Sci., 1986–92; Prof. of Palaeobotany, 1992–96. Royal Soc. Leverhulme Trust Sen. Res. Fellow, 1994–95. Mem., NERC, 1998–. Corresp. Mem., Botanical Soc. of America, 1994. Trustee: Nat. Botanical Garden of Wales, 1997–; Royal Botanic Garden, Edinburgh, 1999–. Hon. Fellow, Univ. of Wales, Swansea, 1997. Ed., Botanical Jl of Linnean Soc., 1993–. *Publications:* contrib. to jls incl. Palaeontology, Rev. of Palaeobotany and Palynology, Botanical Jl Linnean Soc., Nature. *Recreations:* gardening, Mozart. *Address:* Department of Earth Sciences, Cardiff University, PO Box 914, Cardiff CF1 3YE. *T:* (029) 2087 4264. *Club:* Soroptomist International.

EDWARDS, Douglas John; Consultant, Argyll Foods Ltd (formerly Louis C. Edwards & Sons (Manchester) Ltd), 1979–84 (Joint Chairman and Managing Director, 1966–79); Chairman and Managing Director, Imexport Meats Ltd, 1979–82; *b* 18 March 1916; *s* of Louis Edwards and Catherine Edwards; *m* 1st, 1941, Emmeline H. Haslam (*d* 1964); two *s*; 2nd, 1973, Valerie Barlow-Hitchen. *Educ:* De La Salle Coll., Salford. Served in Grenadier Guards, 1940–45. Member of Lloyd's, 1965–: Joined Manchester Conservative Party, 1947; Mem. Manchester City Council, 1951–74; Alderman, 1967–74; Lord Mayor of City of Manchester, 1971–72; Greater Manchester Metropolitan CC, 1974–78; High Sheriff, 1975–76. President: Manchester Cttee, Grenadier Guards Assoc., 1968–81 (Life Mem.); Greater Manchester Youth Assoc., 1973–80; Chairman: Manchester Br., Variety Club of GB, 1969–70; Northern Cttee, Hotel and Catering Benev. Assoc., 1976–81. Governor: De La Salle Teacher Training Coll., Greater Manchester, 1972–81; De La Salle Coll., Salford, 1972–81. DL Greater Manchester, 1979–81. Freeman and Liveryman, Makers of Playing Cards Co., 1974. Polonia Restituta, First Cl., 1972. KCHS (Papal knighthood) 1993 (KHS 1986). *Recreations:* golf, sailing, shooting. *Address:* Apt 10A, The Marbella, 250 South Ocean Boulevard, Boca Raton, FL 33432, USA. *T:* (561) 3928203. *Clubs:* Carlton; Royal Thames Yacht; Lloyd's Yacht; Lancs County Cricket (Life Mem.); Cheshire Polo; Altrincham Rifle; Antibes Yacht; St Francis Yacht (Hon. Mem.), Royal Palm Yacht and Country (Boca Raton, Florida).

EDWARDS, Elgan; *see* Edwards, D. E. H.

EDWARDS, Elizabeth Alice; *see* Wilson, E. A.

EDWARDS, Very Rev. Erwyd; *see* Edwards, Very Rev. T. E. P.

EDWARDS, Frederick Edward, LVO 1992; RD 1968 and Clasp, 1977; voluntary worker; Director of Social Work, Strathclyde Region, 1976–93; *b* 9 April 1931; *s* of Reginal Thomas Edwards and Jessie Howard Simpson; *m* 1st, 1957, Edith Jocelyn Price (marr. diss. 1990); two *s* one *d*; 2nd, 1990, Mary Olds (*née* Ellis). *Educ:* St Edward's Coll., Liverpool; Univ. of Glasgow (Dip. Applied Soc. Studies 1965). BA Open Univ., 1973. FIMgt. Merchant Navy Deck Officer, 1948–58; Perm. Commn, RNR, 1953, Lt-Comdr 1963; sailed Barque Mayflower to USA, 1957. Morgan Refractories, 1958–60; Probation Service, Liverpool, 1960–69; Dir of Social Work: Moray and Nairn, 1969–74; Grampian, 1974–76. Vis. Prof., Dept of Social Policy (formerly Social Admin.) and Social Work, Univ. of Glasgow, 1988–93. Member: Scottish Marriage Guidance Council, 1970– (Chm., 1980–83); Scottish Council on Crime, 1972–75; Adv. Council on Social Work, 1976–81; Bd, Scottish Envmt Protection Agency, 1999–. Chairman: Scottish Sen. Alliance Volunteering for the Envmt, 1989–; Carnegie Third Age Prog. Cttee, 1993–96; Capability Scotland, 1997–; President: Volunteer Develt Scotland, 1994–2000; Disability Scotland, 1995–99; Trustee, New Lanark Trust, 1993–. MUniv Open, 1988; DUniv Paisley, 1993. *Recreations:* walking, natural history, reading. *Address:* Gardenfield, Ninemileburn, Midlothian EH26 9LT.

EDWARDS, Gareth Owen; QC 1985; **His Honour Judge Gareth Edwards;** a Circuit Judge, since 1991; *b* 26 Feb. 1940; *s* of Arthur Wyn Edwards and Mair Eluned Edwards; *m* 1967, Katharine Pek Har Goh; two *s* one *d*. *Educ:* Herbert Strutt Grammar Sch., Belper; Trinity Coll., Oxford (BA,BCL). Called to the Bar, Inner Temple, 1963; Army Legal Service, 1963–65; Commonwealth Office, 1965–67. Practised, Wales and Chester Circuit, 1967–; Recorder, Crown Court, 1978–91. *Recreations:* climbing, chess. *Address:* 58 Lache Lane, Chester CH4 7LS. *T:* (01244) 677795. *Club:* Army and Navy.

EDWARDS, Gareth Owen, MBE 1975; retired 1978 as Welsh Rugby footballer; chairman of leisure company in S Wales; *b* 12 July 1947; *s* of Granville and Anne Edwards; *m* 1972, Maureen Edwards; two *s*. *Educ:* Pontardawe Tech. Sch.; Millfield Sch.; Cardiff College of Educn. Rugby Football: 1st cap for Wales, 1967 (*v* France); Captain of Wales on 13 occasions; youngest Captain of Wales (at 20 years), 1968; British Lions Tours: 1968, 1971, 1974; Barbarians, 1967–78. Member of Cardiff RFC, 1966–; a record 53 consecutive caps, to 1978. *Publications:* Gareth: an autobiography, 1978; (jtly) Rugby Skills, 1979; Rugby Skills for Forwards, 1980; Gareth Edwards on Fishing, 1984; Rugby, 1986; Gareth Edwards' 100 Great Rugby Players, 1987. *Recreations:* fishing, golf. *Address:* 211 West Road, Nottage, Porthcawl, Mid-Glamorgan CF36 3RT. *T:* (01656) 785669.

EDWARDS, Sir George (Robert), OM 1971; Kt 1957; CBE 1952 (MBE 1945); FRS 1968; FREng; DL; now retired; Chairman, British Aircraft Corporation Ltd, 1963–75; Pro-Chancellor, University of Surrey, 1964–79, now Pro-Chancellor Emeritus; *b* 9 July 1908; *m* 1935, Marjorie Annie (*née* Thurgood) (*d* 1994); one *d*. *Educ:* S West Essex Tech. Coll.; London Univ. (BScEng). Gen. engineering, 1928–35; joined Design Staff, Vickers-Aviation Ltd, Weybridge, 1935; Experimental Manager, Vickers-Armstrongs Ltd, Weybridge Works, 1940. Chief Designer, Weybridge Works, 1945; Dir, Vickers Ltd, 1955–67. Pres., Royal Aeronautical Soc., 1957–58; Vice-Pres., Royal Society of Arts, 1958–61. Mem., Royal Instn, 1971–. Pres., Surrey CCC, 1979 (Vice-Pres., 1974). DL Surrey, 1981. Hon. Fellow: RAeS 1960; IMechE; Manchester Coll. of Science and Technology; Hon. FAIAA. Hon. DSc: Southampton, 1962; Salford, 1967; Cranfield Inst. of Technology, 1970; City Univ., 1975; Stirling, 1979; Surrey, 1979; Hon. DSc(Eng) London, 1970; Hon. LLD Bristol, 1973. George Taylor Gold Medal, 1948; British Gold Medal for Aeronautics, 1952; Daniel Guggenheim Medal, 1959; Air League Founders Medal, 1969; Albert Gold Medal (RSA), 1972; Royal Medal, Royal Soc., 1974. *Publications:* various papers and lectures in Jl RAeS, Amer. Inst. of Aeronautical Sciences and Amer. Soc. of Automotive Engrs. *Recreation:* painting. *Address:* Albury Heights, White Lane, Guildford, Surrey GU4 8PR. *T:* (01483) 504488. *Club:* Athenæum.

EDWARDS, Griffith; *see* Edwards, James G.

EDWARDS, Helen, CBE 2001; Director, Active Community Unit, Home Office, since 2001; *b* 2 Aug. 1953; *d* of Charlton and Isobel Edwards; *m* 1987, David John Rounds; three *s*. *Educ:* Univ. of Sussex (BA Hons 1975); Univ. of Warwick (MA 1977; CQSW 1977). Social Worker, E Sussex CC, 1975–80; Dep. Project Dir, Save the Children Fund, 1980–83; National Association for Care and Resettlement of Offenders: Policy Develt Officer, 1983–85; Principal Officer, 1985–88; Asst Dir, 1988–93; Dir of Policy, Res. and Develt, 1993–96; Acting Chief Exec., 1996; Chief Exec., 1997–2001. Member: Morgan Cttee on Safer Communities, Home Office, 1990–91; New Deal Adv. Task Force, 1997–; Working Gp reviewing prison Bds of Visitors, 2000–; Learning and Skills Council, 2000–. Mem. Council, Inst. of Employment Studies, 1998–. Trustee, Milton S. Eisenhower Foundn, USA, 2000–. FRSA 1997. *Publications:* articles in jls on crime, social exclusion and criminal justice. *Recreation:* family and friends. *Address:* Home Office, Horseferry House, Dean Ryle Street, SW1P 2AW.

EDWARDS, Huw William Edmund; MP (Lab) Monmouth, May 1991–1992 and since 1997; *b* 12 April 1953; *s* of Rev. Dr Ifor M. Edwards and Esme Edwards. *Educ:* Eastfields High Sch., Mitcham; Manchester Polytechnic; Univ. of York (BA, MA, MPhil). Lecturer in Social Policy: Coventry (Lanchester) Poly., 1980–81; Univ. of Sheffield, 1983–84; Poly. of the South Bank, 1984–85; Manchester Poly., 1985–88. Res. Associate, Low Pay Unit, 1985–; Tutor with Open Univ., 1987–95; Sen. Lectr in Social Policy, Brighton Poly., later Univ. of Brighton, 1988–91, 1992–97. Contested (Lab) Monmouth, 1992. Member: Select Cttee on Welsh Affairs, 1991–92 and 1998–2001; Modernisation Cttee, H of C, 1997–98. Member: Parlt for Wales Campaign, 1992–; Labour campaign for Electoral Reform, 1991–; Fabian Soc., 1992–. Pres., Chepstow Mencap, 1992–; Mem. Exec., Shelter Cymru, 1988–91; Mem. Monmouth Gp, Amnesty Internat., 1969–. Patron, Gwent ME Soc., 1997–. Mem., Boro' Welsh Congregational Chapel, London. Patron, Bailey Parks Bowls Club, Abergavenny, 1997–; Vice-Pres., Monmouth Rugby Club, 1997–. *Publications:* reports on low pay in Wales and a fair electoral system for the Welsh Assembly; articles in professional jls. *Recreations:* sport, football (Member, London Welsh Veterans FC), Rugby, tennis, cricket, Welsh choral music (Member, Gwalia Male Voice Choir). *Address:* House of Commons, SW1A 0AA. *Club:* London Welsh Association.

EDWARDS, Ian Anthony; Regional Chairman of Employment (formerly Industrial) Tribunals, Southampton, since 1996; *b* 18 June 1940; *s* of Gordon Burrows Edwards and Florence Hilda Edwards; *m* 1976, Susan Joy Rooth; one *s* one *d*. *Educ:* Liverpool Inst.; Liverpool Univ. (LLB 1961); Southampton Univ. (LLM 1962). Admitted as solicitor, 1965; Partner, Paris Smith & Randall, Southampton, 1970–87; Chm., part-time, 1985–87, full-time, 1987–96, Industrial Tribunals, Southampton. *Publication:* (ed jtly) Mead's Unfair Dismissal, 5th edn, 1994. *Recreations:* leader of Crusaders, walking, music, railways. *Address:* Regional Office, Employment Tribunal, Dukes Keep, Third Floor, Marsh Lane, Southampton SO14 3EX. *T:* (023) 8071 6400.

EDWARDS, (Ifan) Prys; Director, Prys Edwards Consultancy, since 1986; *b* 11 Feb. 1942; *m* 1966, Catherine Williams; one *s* one *d*. *Educ:* Leighton Park Sch., Reading; Welsh Sch. of Architecture, Cardiff (DipArch). RIBA 1965. Principal Partner, Prys Edwards Partnership, 1966–86. Member: Wales and the Marches Postal Bd, 1974–76; Develt Bd for Rural Wales, 1976–84; BTA, 1984–92; Chairman: Wales Tourist Bd, 1984–92; Welsh Fourth Channel Authy, 1992–98. Dir, Wales Millennium Centre, 1997–. Pres., Welsh League of Youth, 1981–; Mem. Court, Nat. Eisteddfod of Wales, 1965–. *Recreations:* sailing, watching Rugby. *Address:* Bryn Aberoedd, Caemelyn, Aberystwyth SY23 2HA. *T:* (01970) 623001.

EDWARDS, Jack Trevor, CBE 1985; CEng, FICE; FCIT; Chairman, Halcrow Fox and Associates, 1986–92; Consultant, Freeman Fox & Partners, since 1986 (Senior Partner, 1979–86, retired); *b* 23 June 1920; *s* of late Col Cyril Ernest Edwards, DSO, MC, JP, and Jessie Boyd; *m* 1959, Josephine, (Sally), *d* of late S. W. Williams; one *d*. *Educ:* Felsted Sch.; City and Guilds Coll., Imperial Coll. London (BScEng, FCGI). RAF Armament and Airfield Construction Branches, Sqdn Ldr, 1941–46. Civil Engr on hydro-electric and thermal power stations, James Williamson and Partners, 1946–50; Freeman Fox & Partners: Engineer, 1951–64; Partner, 1965–79; special field: civil engrg and building works associated with thermal power stations and railways at home and overseas; major projects: Hong Kong Mass Transit Railway, opened 1980; Baghdad and Taipei Metros; Engineer to Dean and Chapter of St Paul's Cathedral, 1969–86. Mem. Council, British Consultants Bureau, 1979–85 (Chm., 1982–83). Liveryman, Worshipful Co. of Painter-Stainers, 1969–. *Publications:* Civil Engineering for Underground Rail Transport, 1990; contrib. Proc. Instn of Civil Engrs. *Recreation:* sailing. *Address:* Keepers, 77 Brentwood Road, Ingrave, Brentwood, Essex CM13 3NU. *T:* (01277) 810285. *Clubs:* Royal Cruising, Royal Burnham Yacht.

See also D. Edwards.

EDWARDS, Prof. (James) Griffith, CBE 1989; DM, DSc; FRCP, FRCPsych, FMedSci; Professor of Addiction Behaviour, Institute of Psychiatry, University of London, 1979–94, Professor Emeritus since 1994; Hon. Director, Addiction Research Unit, 1970–94 (Principal Investigator, 1967–70); Hon. Consultant, Bethlem and Maudsley Hospitals, 1967–94, Emeritus Consultant, since 1995; *b* 3 Oct. 1928; *yr s* of late Dr J. T. Edwards and late Constance Amy (*née* McFadyean); *m* 1st, 1969, Evelyn Morrison (marr. diss. 1981); one *s* one *d* (and one *d* decd); 2nd, 1981, Frances Susan Stables. *Educ:* Andover Grammar Sch.; Balliol Coll., Oxford (BA Physiology 1952; MA; Theodore Williams Schol. in Anatomy); St Bartholomew's Hosp. (Kirkes Schol. and Gold Medal); DM Oxford, 1966; DPM London, 1962; DSc London, 1990; FRCP 1976; FRCPsych 1976 (Hon. FRCPsych 1998). Served RA, 1948–49 (2nd Lieut). Jun. hosp. appts, King George, Ilford, St Bartholomew's, Hammersmith and Maudsley Hosps, 1956–62; Inst. of Psychiatry: res. worker, 1962; Lectr, 1966; Sen. Lectr, 1967; Reader, 1973. Chm., RC Psych. Special Cttee on Drug Dependence, 1983–87 (on Alcohol and Alcoholism, 1975–78); Medical Dir, Alcohol Educn Centre, 1980–83; Member: Home Office Working Party on Drunkenness Offenders, 1967–70; WHO Expert Adv. Cttee on Drug Dependence, 1969–; DoE Cttee on Drinking and Driving, 1974–75; Home Office Adv. Council on Misuse of Drugs, 1972–; DHSS Adv. Cttee on Alcoholism, 1975–78; ESRC (formerly SSRC), 1981–89; S African Adv. Cttee on Drug Abuse, 1995. Consultant Advisor: on Alcoholism, DHSS, subseq. DoH, 1986–94; Huntercombe Manor Hosp., 1995–96; ODA Consultant in Bolivia, 1987. Chm., Nat. Addiction Centre, 1991–94; Med. Advr, Phoenix House, 1990–94; Patron, Clouds House, 1996. Editor, Addiction (formerly British Jl of Addiction), 1978–96, Editor-in-Chief, 1996–; Editor-in-Chief, Internat. Research Monographs on the Addictions, 1995–. Roche Vis. Prof., Aust. and NZ, 1982; Hon. Prof., Univ. of Chile, 1992–; Vis. Prof., Amer. Coll. of Neuropsychopharmacology, 1993. Steven's Lectr and Gold Medallist, RSM, 1971; Lectures: Dent, KCL, 1980; Pollak, 1988, Okey, 1995, Inst. of Psychiatry; Maudsley, RCPsych, 2001. FMedSci 1999. Jellinek Meml Award, 1980; Evian Award, 1986; Prize, Assoc. for Med. Educn and Res. on Substance Abuse, USA, 1990; Nathan B. Eddy gold medal, Coll. on Problems of Drug Dependence, USA, 1996; Auguste Forel Prize, Internat. Order of Good Templers, 1998. *Publications:* Unreason in an Age of Reason, 1971; (jtly) Alcohol Control Policies, 1975; (ed jtly) Drugs in Socio-Cultural Perspective, 1980; (jtly) Opium and the People, 1981; Treatment of Drinking Problems, 1982 (trans. into 5 langs), 3rd edn 1997; (ed) Drug Scenes, 1987; (ed jtly) Nature of Dependence, 1990; (ed) Personal Influences and Scientific Movements, 1991; (ed) Nature of Alcohol and Drug Problems, 1992; (ed jtly) Drugs, Alcohol and Tobacco: strengthening the science and policy connections, 1993; (ed jtly) Addiction: processes of change, 1994; (ed jtly) Alcohol and Alcohol Problems, 1994; (jtly) Alcohol Policy and the Public Good, 1994; (jtly) Alcohol and Public Policy, Evidence and Issues, 1995 (trans. 8 langs); (jtly) Psychotherapy, Psychological Treatments and the Addictions, 1996; Alcohol: the ambiguous molecule, 2000; articles in jls on scientific and policy aspects of alcohol and drug dependence. *Recreations:* frequenting junk shops, putting the drink down, smoking the devils out. *Address:* 32 Crooms Hill, SE10 8ER. *T:* (020) 8858 5631; *e-mail:* (home) grifsu@crooms.freeserve.co.uk; (office) p.davis@iop.kcl.ac.uk. *Club:* Athenæum.

See also J. M. McF. Edwards.

EDWARDS, James Valentine, CVO 1978; MA; *b* 4 Feb. 1925; *s* of late Captain Alfred Harold Edwards, OBE, and Mrs Eleanor Edwards; *m* 1965, Barbara, Princess Cantacuzene, Countess Speransky, *d* of late Sir John Hanbury-Williams, CVO, and Lady Hanbury-Williams; two *d*, and one step *s* one step *d*. *Educ:* St Edmund's, Hindhead; Radley; Magdalen Coll., Oxford (MA). Served RN, 1943–47. Oxford, 1943 and 1947–49. *Address:* Almonry House, Muchelney, Langport, Somerset TA10 0DG. *T:* (01458) 252174. *Clubs:* MCC, Free Foresters; Vincent's (Oxford).

EDWARDS, Jeremy John Cary; Group Managing Director, Henderson Administration Group, 1989–95; *b* 2 Jan. 1937; *s* of late William Philip Neville Edwards, CBE, and Hon. Mrs Sheila Edwards; *m* 1st, 1963, Jenifer Graham (*née* Mould) (decd); one *s* one *d*; 2nd, 1974, April Philippa Harding (marr. diss. 1993); one *s*; 3rd, 1994, Mrs Amanda Barber. *Educ:* Ridley Coll, Ontario; Vinehall Sch., Sussex; Haileybury and Imperial Service Coll. Unilever, 1955–57; Hobson Bates & Co., 1957–59; Overseas Marketing and Advertising, 1959–61; Courtaulds, 1961–63; Vine Products, 1963–66; Loewe SA, 1966–68; Jessel Securities, 1968–70; Man. Dir, Vavasseur Unit Trust Management, 1970–74; Henderson Admin Gp, 1974–95; Jt Man. Dir, 1983–89. Non-executive Director: College Hill Associates, 1995–; Tribune Trust, 1997–; Liontrust First UK Investment Trust, 1999–. Hon. Treas., WWF (UK), 1984–; Children's Society (formerly C of E Children's Society): Mem. Council, 1987–; Vice-Chm., 1996–; Chm., E. Jewson Services to Charities Ltd, 2000–; Trustee, Haven Trust, 1998–. *Address:* 59 Dorothy Road, SW11 2JJ. *T:* (020) 7228 6055. *Clubs:* Boodle's, City of London; Brook (NY).

EDWARDS, Rev. Joel; General Director, Evangelical Alliance UK, since 1997; *b* 15 Oct. 1951; *m* 1976, Carol Munroe-Edwards; one *s* one *d*. *Educ:* London Bible Coll. (BA Theology 1975). Probation Officer, 1978–88; Gen. Sec., African and Caribbean Evangelical Alliance, 1988–92; UK Dir, Evangelical Alliance, 1992–97. Pastor, 1985–95, Associate Pastor, 1996–, Mile End New Testament Church of God. *Publications:* Lord Make Us One – But Not All the Same!, 1999; The Cradle, The Cross and The Empty Tomb, 2000. *Recreations:* swimming, sauna, reading. *Address:* Evangelical Alliance, 186 Kennington Park Road, SE11 4BT. *T:* (020) 7207 2100, *Fax:* (020) 7207 2150; *e-mail:* jedwards@eauk.org.

EDWARDS, John Charles; JP; Lord Mayor of Cardiff, 1980–81; *b* 3 April 1925; *s* of John Robert Edwards and Elsie Florence Edwards; *m* 1946, Cynthia Lorraine Bushell; one *s* two *d. Educ:* Lansdowne Road Sch., Cardiff; Ruskin Coll., Oxford. Served War of 1939–45, RM (1939–45 Star, France and Germany Star, War Medal 1939–45); TA, 1948–62, RASC (TEM). Postal Exec. Officer, GPO. Member: Cardiff CC, 1962–83 (Dep. Lord Mayor, 1978–79); S Glam CC, 1974–78; Associate Mem., Inst. of Transport Admin, 1982. Freeman of City of London, 1981. JP S Glam, 1979. Mem., St John's Council for S Glam; CStJ 1997 (OStJ 1980). *Recreations:* athletics, football. *Address:* 61 Cosmeston Street, Cathays, Cardiff CF2 4LQ. *T:* (029) 2022 1506. *Club:* Civil Service.

EDWARDS, John Coates, CMG 1989; HM Diplomatic Service, retired; Head of UK Delegation, EC Monitoring Mission in former Yugoslavia, April–Sept. 1995, April–Aug. 1996, May–Sept. 1997, April–July 1998 and March–June 1999; *b* 25 Nov. 1934; *s* of late Herbert John and Doris May Edwards; *m* 1959, Mary Harris; one *s* one *d. Educ:* Skinners' Co. Sch., Tunbridge Wells, Kent; Brasenose Coll., Oxford (MA). Military Service, 1953–55: Lieut, RA. Asst Principal: Min. of Supply, 1958; Colonial Office, 1960; Private Sec. to Parly Under Sec. of State for the Colonies, 1961; Principal: Nature Conservancy, 1962; Min. of Overseas Develt, 1965; First Sec. (Develt), and UK Perm. Rep. to ECAFE, Bangkok, Thailand, 1968; Asst Sec., Min. of Overseas Develt, 1971; Head of E Africa Develt Div., Nairobi, Kenya, 1972; Asst Sec., Min. of Overseas Develt, 1976; Head of British Develt Div. in the Caribbean, Barbados, and UK Dir, Caribbean Develt Bank, 1978; Hd, West Indian and Atlantic Dept, FCO, 1981–84; Dep. High Comr, Kenya, 1984–88; High Commissioner: Lesotho, 1988–91; Botswana, 1991–94. Chm., Kenya Soc., 1997–. JP Kent, 2000. *Address:* Fairways, Back Lane, Ightham, Sevenoaks, Kent TN15 9AU. *Clubs:* Royal Over-Seas League; Muthaiga Country (Life Mem.) (Nairobi).

EDWARDS, Prof. John Hilton, FRCP; FRS 1979; Professor of Genetics, and Fellow of Keble College, University of Oxford, 1979–95, now Emeritus; *b* 26 March 1928; *s* of late Harold Clifford Edwards, CBE, FRCS, FRCOG; *m* 1953, Felicity Clare, *d* of Dr C. H. C. Toussaint; two *s* two *d. Educ:* Univ. of Cambridge (MB, BChir). FRCP 1972. Ship's Surgeon, Falkland Islands Dependency Survey, 1952–53; Mem., MRC Unit on Population Genetics, Oxford, 1958–60; Geneticist, Children's Hosp. of Philadelphia, 1960–61; Lectr, Sen. Lectr, and Reader, Birmingham Univ., 1961–67; Hon. Consultant Paediatrician, Birmingham Regional Bd, 1967; Vis. Prof. of Pediatrics, Cornell Univ., and Sen. Investigator, New York Blood Center, 1967–68; Consultant, Human Genetics, Univ. of Iceland, 1967–; Prof. of Human Genetics, Birmingham Univ., 1969–79. *Publications:* Human Genetics, 1978; scientific papers. *Recreations:* gliding, skiing. *Address:* 78 Old Road, Headington, Oxford OX3 7LP; *e-mail:* jhe@bioch.ox.ac.uk. *Club:* Athenæum.

EDWARDS, (John) Michael, CBE 1986; QC 1981; *b* 16 Oct. 1925; *s* of Dr James Thomas Edwards and Constance Amy Edwards, *yr d* of Sir John McFadyean; *m* 1st, 1952, Morna Joyce Piper (marr. diss.); one *s* one *d*; 2nd, 1964, Rosemary Ann Moore; two *s. Educ:* Andover Grammar Sch. (schol.); University Coll., Oxford (BCL, MA). Called to the Bar, Middle Temple, 1949, Bencher, 1993; barrister-at-law, 1950–55 and 1993–2001; Asst Parly Counsel, HM Treasury, 1955–60; Dep. Legal Advr and Dir of subsid. cos trading in E Europe, Courtaulds Ltd, 1960–67; British Steel Corporation: Dir, Legal Services, 1967–71; Man. Dir, BSC (Internat.) Ltd, 1968–81; Chm. and Man. Dir, BSC (Overseas Services) Ltd, 1973–81; Provost, City of London Polytechnic, 1981–88. Dir, 1982–90, and Man. Dir, 1988–89, Bell Group Internat. Ltd; Dir, Bell Resources Ltd (Australia), 1983–88. Member: Overseas Projects Bd, 1973–81; E European Trade Council, 1973–81; Educn Assets Bd, 1988–98. Deputy Chairman: Appeal Cttee, Assoc. of Certified Accountants, 1990–95 (Chm., 1987–90); Independent Appeals Authy for Sch. Exams, 1991–99. Member: Gen. Council of Bar, 1971–79, 1980–83; Senate of Inns of Court and Bar, 1974–79, 1980–83; Gen. Cttee, Bar Assoc. for Commerce, Finance and Industry, 1967–92 (Vice-Pres., 1980–82, 1992–; Chm., 1972–74); Acad. Council, Inst. of Internat. Business Law and Practice, ICC, Paris, 1982–88. FCIArb 1984, Chartered Arbitrator, 1999 (Chm., London Br., CIArb, 2000–2001). Chairman: Eastman Dental Hosp., 1983–96 (Gov., 1981–83); Management Cttee, Eastman Dental Inst. (formerly Inst. of Dental Surgery), Univ. of London, 1984–96; Mem., Governing Body, BPMF, 1988–96. UCL Hosps Foundn Fellow, 1999. Mem., Council, Regional Opera Trust, (Kent Opera), 1981–88 (Chm., 1983–86). CIMgt (Mem. Council, BIM, 1978–81). Freeman, City of London; Mem. Court, Ironmongers' Co., 1982– (Master, 1994–95). *Recreations:* family (numerous), other people. *Address:* Verulam Chambers, Peer House, Verulam Street, Gray's Inn, WC1X 8LZ. *T:* (020) 7813 2400; *e-mail:* mestonemill@btinternet.com. *Club:* Garrick.

See also J. G. Edwards.

EDWARDS, Rear Adm. John Phillip, CB 1984; LVO 1972; CEng, FIMechE 1982; Fellow, Wadham College, Oxford, 1984–94, now Emeritus (Domestic Bursar, 1984–94; Development Director, 1994–99); *b* 13 Feb. 1927; *s* of Robert Edwards and Dilys (*née* Phillips); *m* 1951, Gwen Lloyd Bonner; three *d. Educ:* Brynhyfryd Sch., Ruthin, Clwyd; HMS Conway; Royal Naval Engrg Colls, Keyham and Manadon (King's Sword, 1947). MA 1984. Served, 1944–72: HMS King George V, Vengeance, Mauritius, Caledonia, Torquay, Lion, Diamond, Defender, HMCS Stadacona, and HMY Britannia; Mechanical Trng Estab., Portsmouth; Personnel Panel; Staff of C-in-C Fleet; SOWC; Dep. Dir, RN Staff Coll., 1972–74; Asst Dir, Dir Gen. Ships, 1974–76; RCDS, 1977; Captain of Portland Naval Base, 1978–80; Dir Gen., Fleet Support Policy and Services, 1980–83. Comdr 1964, Captain 1971, Rear Adm. 1980. Mem. (non-exec.), Welsh Office Health Policy Bd, 1985–90. President: Oxford Royal Naval Assoc., 1984–90; Oxford Royal Naval and Royal Marine Assoc., 1994–; Midland Naval Officers Assoc., 1985–95; Vice-Pres., Oxfordshire SSAFA, 1984–. Trustee, Oxford Preservation Trust, 1994–. Freeman, City of London, 1984; Liveryman, Co. of Engineers, 1984. FIMgt (FBIM 1980). Hon. FISTC 1976. *Recreation:* golf. *Address:* Wadham College, Oxford OX1 3PN. *Club:* Frilford Heath Golf.

EDWARDS, Dame Julie Andrews; *see* Andrews, Dame J.

EDWARDS, Kenneth; *see* Edwards, A. K.

EDWARDS, Dr Kenneth John Richard; Vice-Chancellor, University of Leicester, 1987–99; *b* 12 Feb. 1934; *s* of John and Elizabeth May Edwards; *m* 1958, Janet Mary Gray; two *s* one *d. Educ:* Market Drayton Grammar Sch.; Univ. of Reading (BSc 1st class 1958); University Coll. of Wales, Aberystwyth (PhD 1961; Hon. Fellow). Nat. Service, RAF, 1952–54. Fellow, Univ. of California, 1961–62; ARC Fellow, Welsh Plant Breeding Station, Aberystwyth, 1962–63, Sen. Sci. Officer, 1963–66; Cambridge University: Lectr in Genetics, 1966–84; Head of Dept of Genetics, 1981–84; Sec. Gen. of Faculties, 1984–87; St John's College: Fellow, 1971–87; Lectr, 1971–84; Tutor, 1980–84. Vis. Lectr in Genetics, Univ. of Birmingham, 1965; Vis. Prof., INTA, Buenos Aires, 1973; Leverhulme Res. Fellow, Univ. of California, 1973. Chm., CVCP, 1993–95; Member: Marshall Aid Commemoration Commn, 1991–98; Council, ACU, 1994–99; Bd, CRE, 1994–2001 (Pres., 1998–2001). Mem. Bd, USS Ltd, 1994–97. Chm. Governing Body, Inst. of Grassland and Envmtl Res., 1994–99. Hon. LLD: QUB, 1995; Leicester, 1999; Hon. DSc: Reading, 1995; Loughborough, 1995; Warwick, 2000; Hon. MA Nene Coll., 1997; Dr (*hc*) Babeş-Bolyai, Romania, 1998; Maribor, Slovenia, 2001. *Publications:* Evolution in Modern Biology, 1977; articles on genetics in sci. jls. *Recreations:* music, gardening. *Address:* 10 Sedley Taylor Road, Cambridge CB2 2PW. *T:* (01223) 245680.

EDWARDS, Linda Kay; Director, National Osteoporosis Society, since 1986; *b* 13 Feb. 1948; *d* of Richard Waldemar Sinclair Wallis (name changed by deed poll to stage name, Don Ricardo) and Evelyn Lily Wallis (*née* Ross McCandie); *m* 1972, Anthony John Edwards; one *s* one *d. Educ:* Maidenhead High Sch.; London Univ. (BA Hons English Lit. 1969). DipCAM 1972; MIPR 1972. Advertising and PR, Beechams UK Ltd, 1969–70; PR, N Thames Gas Bd, 1970–71; Regl Press and Publicity Officer, Post Office, 1971–82; PR consultant, 1982–86 (clients incl. major retailers, solicitors, architects, small businesses, charities). Trustee: Internat. Osteoporosis Foundn, 1997–; Long-Term Med. Conditions Alliance, 1999–. *Recreations:* theatre, ski-ing, chess, sheep. *Address:* National Osteoporosis Society, Manor Farm, Skinners Hill, Camerton, Bath BA2 0PJ. *T:* (01761) 471771, *Fax:* (01761) 471104; (home) Cariad, Kilmersdon, Bath BA3 5SU.

EDWARDS, Lionel Antony, (Tony), CEng, FRAeS; Head, Defence Export Services Organisation, since 1998; *b* 4 Nov. 1944; *s* of Lionel Victor and Marjorie Edwards. *Educ:* Abingdon Sch.; Univ. of Birmingham (BSc Hons 1966); Harvard Business Sch. (MBA 1972). CEng 1991; FRAeS 1991. Apprentice Engr, Rolls-Royce, Derby, 1962–68; Mfg Engr, General Electric, Lynn, Mass, 1968–71; Lectr, Harvard Univ., 1972–73; Manager/Dir, General Electric, Lynn and Cincinatti, Ohio, 1973–82; Gen. Manager, Storno A/S, Copenhagen, 1983–86; Corporate Vice-Pres., Motorola, Copenhagen, 1986–88; President: Challenger Exec. Jet Div., Montreal, 1988–89; Canadair Aerospace Gp, Montreal, 1989; Man. Dir, Lucas Aerospace Ltd, Solihull, 1989–92; Gp Man. Dir, Lucas Industries, 1992; Chief-Exec., Dowty, and Main Bd Dir, TI Gp PLC, 1992–98; Chm. and Chief Exec., Messier-Dowty, 1994–98. Chm., Defence and Aerospace Sector Panel, OST Technology Foresight Prog., 1995–97. Member: Council, SBAC, 1989–98 (Vice-Pres. 1990–91, Pres. 1991–92, Dep. Pres. 1992–93); DTI Aviation Cttee, 1992–98; Council, Air League, 1992–; Council, RAeS, 1992– (Pres., 1999–2000); NDIC, 1992–. Trustee: RAF Mus.; Swordfish Heritage Trust. *Recreations:* photography, building sports cars, preservation of historic aircraft, shooting. *Address:* Ministry of Defence, Main Building, Horseguards Avenue, SW1A 2HB.

EDWARDS, Hon. Sir Llewellyn (Roy), AC 1989; Kt 1984; FRACMA; Consultant, Jones Lang Wootton, Brisbane, since 1989; *b* 2 Aug. 1935; *s* of Roy Thomas Edwards and Agnes Dulcie Gwendoline Edwards; *m* 1st, 1958, Leone Sylvia Burley (decd); two *s* one *d*; 2nd, 1989, Jane Anne Brumfield. *Educ:* Raceview State Sch.; Silkstone State Sch.; Ipswich Grammar Sch.; Univ. of Queensland (MB, BS 1965). Qualified Electrician, 1955. RMO and Registrar in Surgery, Ipswich Hosp., 1965–68; gen. practice, Ipswich, 1968–74. MLA (L) Ipswich, Qld Parlt, 1972–83; Minister for Health, Qld, 1974–78; Dep. Premier and Treasurer, Qld, 1978–83; Dep. Med. Supt, Ipswich Hosp., 1983–85. Chairman: Ansvar Australia Insurance Ltd, 1984–94; World Expo 88 Authority 1984–89; Australian Coachline Holdings Ltd, 1992–96; Micromedical Industries, 1993–96; Multi-Function Polis Develt Corp., SA, 1995–98; Director: Westpac Banking Corp., 1984–; James Hardie Industries Pty Ltd, 1990–. Chm., Pacific Film and Television Commn, 1991–; Mem., Australia Japan Foundn Bd, 1992–. Chancellor, Univ. of Queensland, 1993– (Mem. Senate, 1984–). FRACMA 1984. Hon. FAIM 1988. Hon. LLD Queensland, 1988. *Recreations:* tennis, walking, cricket, Rugby Union. *Address:* 8 Ascot Street, Ascot, Qld 4007, Australia. *Clubs:* Brisbane (Brisbane, Qld); United Services (Qld); Ipswich (Ipswich, Qld); Brisbane Polo.

EDWARDS, Malcolm John, CBE 1985; Chairman, Coal Investments Plc, 1993–96; founded Edwards Energy Ltd, 1992; Commercial Director, British Coal (formerly National Coal Board), 1985–92; Member of the Board, British Coal, 1986–92; *b* 25 May 1934; *s* of John J. Edwards and Edith (*née* Riley); *m* 1967, Yvonne, *d* of Mr and Mrs J. A. W. Daniels, Port Lincoln, S Australia; two *s. Educ:* Alleyn's Sch., Dulwich; Jesus Coll., Cambridge (MA). Joined NCB as trainee, 1956; Industrial Sales Manager, 1962; Dir of Domestic and Industrial Sales, 1969; Dir Gen. of Marketing, 1973; responsible for coal utilisation R & D, 1984–92; Chm., British Fuels Gp, 1988–92; Dep. Chm., Inter Continental Fuels, 1989–92. Chm., Finance Cttee, Southwark Diocesan Bd of Educn, 1992–. *Publication:* (with J. J. Edwards) Medical Museum Technology, 1959. *Recreations:* book collecting, arts and crafts movement, music, gardening. *Address:* Lodge Farm, Moot Lane, Downton, Salisbury, Wilts SP5 3LN.

EDWARDS, Marcus; *see* Edwards, C. M.

EDWARDS, Michael; *see* Edwards, J. M.

EDWARDS, Dr Michael Frederick, OBE 1993; FREng, FIChemE; Principal Engineer, Unilever, since 1987; *b* 27 April 1941; *s* of H. S. Edwards and J. Edwards (*née* Wallwork); *m* 1964, Margaret Roberta Thorne; one *s* one *d. Educ:* University Coll., Swansea (BSc, PhD). FIChemE 1980; FREng (FEng 1992). Lectr in Engrg Scis, Univ. of Warwick, 1966–69; Lectr, Sen. Lectr in Chem. Engrg, 1969–81, Prof. of Chemical Engrg, 1981–87, Bradford Univ. Mem., various research council bds and cttees. *Publication:* Mixing in the Process Industries, 1985, 2nd edn 1992. *Recreations:* hill-walking, classical music. *Address:* 44 Long Meadow, Gayton, Wirral CH60 8QQ. *T:* (0151) 342 5602.

EDWARDS, Norman L.; *see* Lloyd-Edwards.

EDWARDS, Owen; Director, Sianel 4 Cymru (Welsh Fourth Channel Authority), 1981–89; *b* 26 Dec. 1933; *s* of Sir Ifan ab Owen Edwards and Eirys Mary Edwards; *m* 1st, 1958, Shân Emlyn (marr. diss. 1994); two *d*; 2nd, 1994, Rosemary Allen. *Educ:* Ysgol Gymraeg, Aberystwyth; Leighton Park, Reading; Lincoln Coll., Oxford (MA). Cataloguer, Nat. Library of Wales, 1958–60; BBC Wales: Compère, TV Programme Heddiw, 1961–66; Programme Organiser, 1967–70; Head of Programmes, 1970–74; Controller, 1974–81. Chairman: Assoc. for Film and TV in Celtic Countries, later Celtic Film and TV Assoc., 1983–85, 1989–91; Royal Nat. Eisteddfod of Wales, 1986–89 (Vice-Chm., 1985–86). Hon LLD Wales, 1989. Gold Medal, RTS, 1989; BAFTA Cymru Special Award, 1995. *Address:* 2 Riversdale, Llandaff, Cardiff CF5 2QL. *T:* (029) 2055 5392.

EDWARDS, Patricia Anne, (Mrs Roger Cox); Legal Director, Office of Fair Trading, since 1996; *b* 29 May 1944; *d* of late Maurice James Edwards and of Marion Edwards (*née* Lewis); *m* 1970, Roger Charles Cox, *qv. Educ:* Barry and Purley County Grammar Schools; King's College London (LLB). Called to the Bar, Middle Temple, 1967; Criminal Appeal Office, 1965–74; Law Officers' Dept, 1974–77; Home Office: Sen. Legal Asst, 1977–80; Asst Legal Adviser, 1980–88; Principal Asst Legal Advr, 1988–94; Dep. Parly Comr for Admin, 1994–96. *Recreations:* music, travel, reading, domestic pursuits. *Address:* Office of Fair Trading, Fleetbank House, 2–6 Salisbury Square, EC4Y 8JX.

EDWARDS, Prof. Paul Kerr, DPhil; FBA 1998; Professor of Industrial Relations, since 1992, and Director, Industrial Relations Research Unit, since 1998, Warwick University;

b 18 March 1952; *s* of Ernest Edwards and Ida Vivienne Edwards (*née* Kerr); *m* 1975, Susan Jane Martin; one *s* one *d*. *Educ:* Magdalene Coll., Cambridge (BA 1973); Nuffield Coll., Oxford (BPhil 1975; DPhil 1977). Res. posts, 1977–88, Dep. Dir, 1988–98, Indust. Relns Res. Unit, Warwick Univ. Editor, Work, Employment and Society, 1996–98. *Publications:* Strikes in the United States, 1981; (jtly) The Social Organization of Industrial Conflict, 1982; Conflict at Work, 1986; Managing the Factory, 1987; (jtly) Attending to Work, 1993; (ed) Industrial Relations, 1995; (jtly) Managers in the Making, 1997; (ed jtly) The Global Economy, National States and the Regulation of Labour, 1999. *Recreations:* tennis, sailing. *Address:* Cotswolds House, Newbold-on-Stour, Stratford-on-Avon, Warwicks CV37 8TS. *T:* (01789) 450547.

EDWARDS, Prof. Peter Philip, PhD; FRS 1996; Professor of Inorganic Chemistry, since 1991, and Professor of Chemistry and of Materials, since 1999, University of Birmingham (Head, School of Chemistry, 1996–99); *b* 30 June 1949; *s* of late Ronald Goodlass and of Ethel Mary, who later *m* Arthur Edwards; *m* 1970, Patricia Anne Clancy; two *s* one *d*. *Educ:* Univ. of Salford (BSc; PhD 1974). Fulbright Scholar and NSF Fellow, Baker Lab. of Chem., Cornell Univ., 1975–77; SERC/NATO Fellow and Ramsay Meml Fellow, Inorganic Chem. Lab., Oxford Univ., 1977–79; Cambridge University: Demonstrator in Inorganic Chem., 1979–81, Lectr, 1981–91, Univ. Chem. Labs; Dir of Studies in Chem., Jesus Coll., 1979–91; Co-Founder and Co-Dir, IRC in Superconductivity, 1988; Nuffield Sci. Res. Fellow, 1986–87; BP Venture Res. Fellow, 1988–90; Royal Soc. Leverhulme Sen. Res. Fellow, 1996–97. Vis. Prof., Cornell Univ., 1983–86. Mem., HEFCE Res. Assessment Panel, RAE for 1996 and 2001. FRSC 1988 (Vice-Pres., Dalton Div., 1995. Corday-Morgan Medal, 1985; Tilden Medal, 1992; Liversidge Medal, 1999). *Publications:* (with C. N. R. Rao): The Metallic and Non-Metallic States of Matter, 1985; Metal-Insulator Transitions Revisited, 1995. *Address:* School of Chemistry, University of Birmingham, Edgbaston, Birmingham B15 2TT. *T:* (0121) 414 4379/3530, *Fax:* (0121) 414 4442; *e-mail:* p.p.edwards@bham.ac.uk.

EDWARDS, Peter Robert; Director, Personal Investment Authority, since 1992; *b* 30 Oct. 1937; *s* of Robert and Doris Edith Edwards; *m* 1st, 1967, Jennifer Ann Boys; one *s*; 2nd, 1970, Elizabeth Janet Barrett; one *d*. *Educ:* Christ's Hospital. Chartered Accountant. Ernst & Young (and predecessor firms), 1955–90; Chief Exec., Secretan, 1990–92. Indep. Mem. Council, FIMBRA, 1990–94. Dir, Blackwall Green Ltd, 1992–96. *Recreations:* ornithology, gardening. *Address:* River House, Church Lane, Bury, Pulborough, West Sussex RH20 1PB. *T:* (01798) 831900.

EDWARDS, Prof. Philip Walter, PhD; FBA 1986; King Alfred Professor of English Literature, University of Liverpool, 1974–90, now Emeritus; *b* 7 Feb. 1923; *er s* of late R. H. Edwards, MC, and late Mrs B. Edwards; *m* 1st, 1947, Hazel Margaret (*d* 1950), *d* of late Prof. C. W. and late Mrs E. R. Valentine; 2nd, 1952, Sheila Mary, *d* of late R. S. and late Mrs A. M. Wilkes, Bloxwich, Staffs; three *s* one *d*. *Educ:* King Edward's High Sch., Birmingham; Univ. of Birmingham. MA, PhD Birmingham; MA Dublin. Royal Navy, 1942–45 (Sub-Lieut RNVR). Lectr in English, Univ. of Birmingham, 1946–60; Commonwealth Fund Fellow, Harvard Univ., 1954–55; Prof. of English Lit., TCD, 1960–66; Fellow of TCD, 1962–66; Prof. of Lit., Univ. of Essex, 1966–74; Pro-Vice-Chancellor, Liverpool Univ., 1980–83. Visiting Professor: Univ. of Michigan, 1964–65; Williams Coll., Mass, 1969; Otago Univ., NZ, 1980; Internat. Christian Univ., Tokyo, 1989; Visiting Fellow: All Souls Coll., Oxford, 1970–71; Huntington Liby, Calif., 1977, 1983. *Publications:* Sir Walter Ralegh, 1953; (ed) Kyd, The Spanish Tragedy, 1959; Shakespeare and the Confines of Art, 1968; (ed) Pericles Prince of Tyre, 1976; (ed with C. Gibson) Massinger, Plays and Poems, 1976; Threshold of a Nation, 1979; (ed jtly) Shakespeare's Styles, 1980; (ed) Hamlet Prince of Denmark, 1985; Shakespeare: a writer's progress, 1986; Last Voyages, 1988; The Story of the Voyage, 1994; Sea-Mark, 1997; numerous articles on Shakespeare and literature of his time in Shakespeare Survey, Proc. British Acad., etc. *Recreations:* walking, calligraphy. *Address:* High Gillinggrove, Gillinggate, Kendal, Cumbria LA9 4JB.

EDWARDS, Prys; *see* Edwards, I. P.

EDWARDS, His Honour Quentin Tytler; QC 1975; a Circuit Judge, 1982–97; *b* 16 Jan. 1925; *s* of Herbert Jackson Edwards and Juliet Hester Edwards; *m* 1948, Barbara Marian Guthrie; two *s* one *d*. *Educ:* Bradfield Coll.; Council of Legal Educn. Royal Navy, 1943–46. Called to Bar, Middle Temple, 1948; Bencher, 1972. A Recorder of the Crown Court, 1974–82; Chancellor: Dio. of Blackburn, 1977–90; Dio. of Chichester, 1978–99. Licensed Reader, Dio. of London, 1967; Chm., Ecclesiastical Law Soc., 1990–96; Member: Legal Adv. Commn of General Synod of Church of England, 1973–2001; Dioceses Commn, 1978–96. Pres., Highgate Literary and Scientific Instn, 1988–93. Hon. MA (Archbp of Canterbury), 1961. *Publications:* (with Peter Dow) Public Rights of Way and Access to the Countryside, 1951; (with K. Macmorran, et al) Ecclesiastical Law, 3rd edn, Halsbury's Laws of England, 1955; What is Unlawful?, 1959; (with J. N. D. Anderson, et al) Putting Asunder, 1966. *Recreations:* the open air, architecture. *Club:* Athenæum.

EDWARDS, Richard, DPhil; Member (Lab) Preseli Pembrokeshire, National Assembly for Wales, since 1999. *Educ:* Queen Elizabeth Grammar Sch., Carmarthen; Univ. of Swansea; Univ. of Birmingham. Posts in local govt and political res. Mayor of Carmarthen, 1997. Mem., ICSA. *Address:* National Assembly for Wales, Cardiff Bay, Cardiff CF99 1NA.

EDWARDS, Prof. Richard Humphrey Tudor, FRCP; Professor of Research and Development for Health and Social Care, University of Wales College of Medicine, Cardiff, and Director of Research and Development for Health and Social Care in Wales, 1996–99, now Emeritus Professor; *b* 28 Jan. 1939; *s* of Hywel Islwyn Edwards and Menna Tudor Edwards (*née* Davies); *m* 1964, Eleri Wyn Roberts; one *d* (one *s* decd). *Educ:* Llangollen Grammar Sch.; Middlesex Hosp. Med. Sch., London (BSc, PhD, MB, BS). Ho. appts, Middlesex, National Heart and Hammersmith Hosps, 1964–65; Res. Fellow, Asst Lectr, then Lectr (Wellcome Sen. Res. Fellow in Clin. Science), Hon. Cons. Physician (Respiratory Med.), Royal Postgrad. Med. Sch., Hammersmith Hosp., 1966–76; Wellcome Swedish Res. Fellow, Karolinska Inst., Stockholm, 1970; Prof. of Human Metabolism, UCH Med. Sch., 1976–84; Hd of Dept of Medicine, UCL, 1982–84; University of Liverpool: Prof. and Head of Dept of Medicine, 1984–96; Dir, Magnetic Resonance Res. Centre, 1987–96; Dir., Muscle Res. Centre, 1986–96. Hon. Consultant Physician: Royal Liverpool Univ. Hosp., 1984–96; Robert Jones and Agnes Hunt Orthopaedic Hosp., Oswestry, 1979–96. *Publications:* Clinical Exercise Testing, 1975; sci. papers on human muscle in health and disease and on various fields of medicine in Jl of Physiology, Clinical Sci., Clinical Physiol., Muscle and Nerve, etc. *Recreations:* Wales—planting trees, mountain walking, gardening, music. *Address:* Berthlwyd, Nantgwynant, Beddgelert, Gwynedd LL55 4NL. *T:* (01766) 890364.

EDWARDS, Prof. Robert Geoffrey, CBE 1988; FRS 1984; Professor of Human Reproduction, Cambridge University, 1985–89, now Emeritus; Extraordinary Fellow, Churchill College, Cambridge; *b* 27 Sept. 1925; *s* of Samuel and Margaret Edwards; *m* 1956, Ruth Eileen Fowler; five *d*. *Educ:* Manchester Central High Sch.; Univs of Wales and Edinburgh. PhD (Edin) 1955; DSc (Wales) 1962; MA (Cantab). Service in British Army, 1944–48; commnd 1946. UC North Wales, Bangor, 1948–51; Univ. of Edinburgh, 1951–57; Res. Fellow at California Inst. of Tech., 1957–58; Scientist at Nat. Inst. of Medical Research, Mill Hill, NW7, 1958–62; Glasgow Univ. 1962–63; in Dept of Physiology, Cambridge Univ., 1963–89; Ford Foundation Reader in Physiology, 1969–85. Scientific Dir, Bourn Hallam Clinics, Cambridgeshire and London, 1988–91. Founder Chm., European Soc. of Human Reproduction and Embryology, 1984–86. Visiting Scientist: in Johns Hopkins Hosp., Baltimore, 1965; Univ. of N Carolina, 1966; Visiting Professor: Free Univ., Brussels, 1984; Univ. of Hong Kong, 1998. Hon. Pres., British Fertility Soc., 1988–; Patron, UK Nat. Gamete Donation Trust, 1999. Hon. FRCOG 1985; Hon. MRCP 1986. Hon. Member: Assoc. of UK Clinical Embryologists, 1998; French Soc. for Infertility, 1983; Greek Fertility Soc., 1998; Middle East Fertility Soc., 1999. Life Fellow, Australian Fertility Soc., 1985; Hon. Fellow, Internat. Fedn of Fertility Socs, 1998. Hon. Citizen of Bordeaux, 1985. Hon. DSc: Hull, 1983; York; Dr *hc* Vrije Univ., Brussels. Spanish Fertility Soc. Gold Medal, 1985; King Faisal Award, 1989. Chief Editor, Human Reproduction, 1986–. *Publications:* A Matter of Life (with P. C. Steptoe), 1980; Conception in the Human Female, 1980; (with C. R. Austin) Mechanisms of Sex Differentiation in Animals and Man; (with J. M. Purdy) Human Conception in Vitro, 1982; (with J. M. Purdy and P. C. Steptoe) Implantation of the Human Embryo, 1985; (with M. Seppälä) In Vitro Fertilisation and Embryo Transfer, 1985; Life Before Birth, 1989; editor of several scientific textbooks on reproduction; numerous articles in scientific and medical jls, organiser of conferences, etc. *Recreations:* farming, politics, music. *Address:* Duck End Farm, Dry Drayton, Cambridge CB3 8DB. *T:* (01954) 780602.

EDWARDS, Robert John, CBE 1986; Deputy Chairman, Mirror Group Newspapers, 1985–86 (Senior Group Editor, 1984–85); *b* 26 Oct. 1925; *m* 1st, 1952, Laura Ellwood (marr. diss. 1972); two *s* two *d*; 2nd, 1977, Brigid Segrave. *Educ:* Ranelagh Sch., Bracknell. Editor, Tribune, 1951–54; feature writer, London Evening Standard, 1954–57; Dep. Editor, Sunday Express, 1957–59; Man. Editor, Daily Express, 1959–61; Editor: Daily Express, 1961, 1963–65; Evening Citizen, Glasgow, 1962–63; Sunday People, 1966–72; Sunday Mirror, 1972–84; Dir, Mirror Group Newspapers, 1976–88. Ombudsman to Today newspaper, 1990–95. Chm., Scoop of the Year Awards Panel, London Press Club, 1988–. *Publication:* Goodbye Fleet Street (autobiog.), 1988. *Address:* 14 Union Square, N1 7DH. *T:* (020) 7704 8747. *Clubs:* Garrick, Reform, Kennel, Groucho's.

EDWARDS, Robert Septimus Friar, CVO 1964; CBE 1963; *b* 21 Oct. 1910; *y s* of late Augustus C. Edwards and Amy Edwards; *m* 1946, Janet Mabel Wrigley; one *s* two *d*. *Educ:* Hereford Cathedral Sch. Chief Engineering Asst, Hereford, until 1936; Min. of Transport, Highway Engineering, 1936–43; Principal, Min. of War Transport, 1943; Mem. British Merchant Shipping Mission, Washington, DC, 1944–46. Sec. Gen. Internat. Conf. on Safety of Life at Sea, 1948; Principal Private Sec. to Minister of Transport, 1949–51; Shipping Attaché, British Embassy, Washington, DC, 1951–54; Dir of Sea Transport, 1954–57; Gen. Manager, London Airports, 1957–63; Gen. Manager, 1967–69, Dir-Gen., 1969–71, Mersey Docks and Harbour Board. Chm., Morris & David Jones Ltd, 1973–74. Called to the Bar, Middle Temple, 1941. *Address:* Dormie House, 15 Riversdale Road, West Kirby, Wirral, CH48 4EY. *T:* (0151) 625 2629.

EDWARDS, Robin Anthony, CBE 1981; Partner with Dundas & Wilson, CS (formerly Davidson & Syme, WS), 1965–96; *b* 7 April 1939; *s* of Alfred Walton Edwards and Ena Annie Ruffell; *m* 1963, Elizabeth Alexandra Mackay (marr. diss.); one *s* one *d*; *m* 1986, Janet Cant Pow. *Educ:* Daniel Stewart's Coll., Edinburgh; Edinburgh Univ. (MA, LLB (distinction), Cl. Medallist). Former Lectr in Conveyancing, Edinburgh Univ.; Admitted Member, WS Society, 1964; Mem. Council, Law Society of Scotland, 1969–84, Vice-Pres., 1978–79, Pres., 1979–80 (youngest Pres. ever, at that time). Mem., Lands Tribunal for Scotland, 1991–. *Recreations:* French travel and cuisine. *Address:* 7/6 Rocheid Park, East Fettes Avenue, Edinburgh EH4 1RP.

EDWARDS, Prof. Ronald Walter, CBE 1992; DSc; FIBiol, FIFM; Professor and Head of Department of Applied Biology, University of Wales Institute of Science and Technology, 1968–90, now Emeritus; *b* 7 June 1930; *s* of Walter and Violet Edwards. *Educ:* Solihull Sch., Warwicks; Univ. of Birmingham (BSc, DSc). FIBiol 1965; FIWEM (FIWPC 1981). Biologist, Freshwater Biol Assoc., 1953–58; Sen., Principal, and Sen. Principal Scientific Officer, Water Pollution Res. Lab., 1958–68. Chairman: Nat. Parks Rev. Panel, 1989–91; Sea Empress Envmtl Evaluation Cttee, 1996–98; Dep. Chm., Welsh Water Authority, 1983–89 (Mem., 1974–89); Member: NRA, 1988–94; NERC, 1970–73 and 1982–85; Nat. Cttee, European Year of the Environment, 1987–88; Envmt Agency, 1995–97; Council, RSPB, 1988–92; Brecon Beacons Nat. Park Cttee, 1993–95; Vice Pres., Council for Nat. Parks, 1993–; Pres., Envmtl Educn Council for Wales, 1997–; County Pres., CPRW, 1999–. Trustee, WWF-UK, 1999–. *Publications:* (co-ed) Ecology and the Industrial Society, 1968; (co-ed) Conservation and Productivity of Natural Waters, 1975; (with Dr M. Brooker) The Ecology of the River Wye, 1982; Acid Waters in Wales, 1990; (co-ed) The Sea Empress Oil Spill, 1998; about 100 papers in learned jls. *Recreations:* music, collecting Staffordshire pottery. *Address:* Talybont-on-Usk, Brecon, Powys.

EDWARDS, Prof. Sir Samuel Frederick, (Sir Sam Edwards), Kt 1975; FRS 1966; Cavendish Professor of Physics, 1984–95, Professor Emeritus since 1995 (John Humphrey Plummer Professor, 1972–84), and Pro-Vice-Chancellor, 1992–95, Cambridge University; Fellow, Gonville and Caius College, Cambridge, since 1972 (President, 1992–97); *b* 1 Feb. 1928; *s* of Richard and Mary Jane Edwards, Manselton, Swansea; *m* 1953, Merriell E. M. Bland; one *s* three *d*. *Educ:* Swansea Grammar Sch.; Gonville and Caius Coll., Cambridge (MA, PhD); Harvard University. Inst. for Advanced Study, Princeton, 1952; Univ. of Birmingham, 1953; Univ. of Manchester, 1958, Prof. of Theoretical Physics, 1963–72. Chief Scientific Adviser, Department of Energy, 1983–88. Chm., SRC, 1973–77. UK Deleg. to NATO Science Cttee, 1974–79; Mem., Planning Cttee, Max-Planck Gesellschaft, 1974–77. Vice-Pres., Institute of Physics, 1970–73 (Mem. Council, 1967–73); Mem. Council, Inst. of Mathematics and its Applications, 1976– (Vice-Pres., 1979, Pres., 1980–81). Member: Physics Cttee, SRC, 1968–73 (Chm. 1970–73); Polymer Cttee, SRC, 1968–73; Science Bd, SRC, 1970–73; Council, European Physical Soc., 1969–71 (Chm., Condensed Matter Div., 1969–71); UGC, 1971–73; Defence Scientific Adv. Council, 1973– (Chm., 1977–80); Metrology and Standards Req. Bd, Dept of Industry, 1974–77; AFRC, 1990–94; HEFCW, 1992–95. Chm., Adv. Council on R&D, Dept of Energy, 1983–88 (Mem., 1974–77); Member Council: European R&D (EEC), 1976–80; Royal Soc., 1982–83 (a Vice-Pres., 1982–83); Pres., BAAS, 1988–89 (Chm. Council, 1977–82); Foreign Mem., Académie des Sciences, France, 1989. Non-exec. Director: Lucas Industries, 1981–93; Steetley plc, 1985–93; Chm., Sen. Adv. Gp, Unilever, 1992–95; Mem., Adv. Gp, BP, 1992–98. Hon. Mem., European Physical Soc., 1996; For. Mem., Nat. Acad. of Scis, USA, 1996. FIMA; FRSC. Hon. FInstP 1996; Hon. Fellow, French Physical Soc. Hon. DTech Loughborough, 1975; Hon. DSc: Salford, Edinburgh, 1976; Bath, 1978; Birmingham, 1986; Wales, 1987; Sheffield, 1989; Dublin, 1991; Leeds, 1994; UEA, 1995; Hon. ScD Cambridge, 2001;

DUniv Strasbourg, 1986. Hon. Fellow, UC Swansea, 1994. Maxwell Medal and Prize, Inst. of Physics, 1974; High Polymer Physics Prize, Amer. Phys. Soc., 1982; Davy Medal, Royal Soc., 1984; Gold Medal, Inst. of Maths, 1986; Guthrie Medal and Prize, Inst. of Physics, 1987; Gold Medal, Rheological Soc., 1990; Louis Vaillon Moët Hennessy Prize (Science pour l'Art), 1993; Boltzmann Medal, IUPAP, 1995; Founders Polymer Prize, Inst. of Physics, 2001. *Publications:* Technological Risk, 1980; (with M. Doi) Theory of Polymer Dynamics, 1986; (with S. M. Aharoni) Networks of Liquid Crystal Polymers, 1994; contribs to learned jls. *Address:* 7 Penarth Place, Cambridge CB3 9LU. *T:* (01223) 366610. *Club:* Athenæum.

EDWARDS, Sian; freelance conductor; Music Director, English National Opera, 1993–95; *b* 27 Aug. 1959. *Educ:* Royal Northern Coll. of Music; Leningrad Conservatoire. Since 1985 has conducted many orchestras incl. LPO, RPO, Royal Scottish Orch., City of Birmingham SO, Hallé, English Chamber Orch. and Docklands Sinfonietta; conducted Orchestre de Paris and Philharmonique de Lille in France, and Pittsburgh Symphony, Philadelphia Orch., San Francisco Symphony, Los Angeles Philharmonic, Nat. Symphony, Atlanta Symphony, Minnesota Orch. in USA, and Ensemble Modern, Südwest funk Orchester, ND Radiofunkorchester in Germany; has also conducted orchestras in Canada, Belgium, Austria, Russia and Australia. Operatic début with Mahagonny (Weill), then Carmen, Scottish Opera, 1986; world première of Greek (Turnage), Munich Biennale and Edinburgh Fest., 1988; Glyndebourne: La Traviata, 1987; Katya Kabanova, 1988; New Year (Tippett), 1990; Royal Opera, Covent Garden: The Knot Garden (Tippett), 1988; Rigoletto, 1989; Il Trovatore, 1990; Madam Butterfly, 1992; English National Opera: The Gambler (Prokofiev), 1990; The Queen of Spades, 1993; La Bohème, Marriage of Figaro, Jenufa, The Mikado, Khovanshchina, 1994; Mahagonny, 1995; La Clemenza di Tito, Clara (Gefors), 1998; Eugene Onegin, 2000; The Death of Klinghoffer (John Adams), Peter Grimes, Don Giovanni, La Damnation de Faust, 2001. Recordings incl. orchestral works by Tchaikovsky, Prokofiev, Ravel, Britten and Judith Weir. *Address:* c/o Ingpen & Williams Ltd, 26 Wadham Road, SW15 2LR. *T:* (020) 8874 3222.

EDWARDS, Dr Steven, MRCVS; Chief Executive, Veterinary Laboratories Agency, Department of the Environment, Food and Rural Affairs (formerly Ministry of Agriculture, Fisheries and Food), since 2000; *b* 9 March 1948; *s* of late William Edward Edwards and of Daisy May Edwards (*née* Candelent); *m* 1976, Virginia Elizabeth Marian Lynch Evans; two *s*. *Educ:* Wolverhampton Grammar Sch.; Trinity Hall, Cambridge (MA, VetMB); Edinburgh Univ. (MSc, DVMS). MRCVS 1972. General veterinary practice, Montgomery, Powys, 1972–76; Univ. of Edinburgh, 1976–77; MAFF Veterinary Investigation Centre, Aberystwyth, 1977–78; Tech. Co-op. Officer, ODM, El Salvador, 1978–80, Bolivia, 1980; MAFF Central Veterinary Laboratory: Vet. Research Officer, 1980–92; Head of Virology Dept, 1992–98; MAFF Veterinary Laboratories Agency: Dir of Lab. Services, 1998–99, Dir of Surveillance and Lab. Services, 1999–2000. Sec. General, 1991–2000, Vice Pres., 2000–, Standards Commn, Office Internat. des Epizooties, Paris. Founder Mem., European Soc. for Vet. Virology., 1987 (Sec., 1988–94; Hon. Mem., 1997); Pres., Vet. Res. Club, London, 1995–96. *Publications:* contribs and edtl for veterinary jls, text books and conf. proceedings. *Recreations:* genealogy, railway preservation. *Address:* Veterinary Laboratories Agency, Woodham Lane, New Haw, Addlestone, Surrey KT15 3NB. *T:* (01932) 341111.

EDWARDS, Stewart Leslie, CMG 1967; Under-Secretary, Department of Trade, retired; *b* 6 Nov. 1914; *s* of late Walter James and Lilian Emma Edwards; *m* 1940, Dominica Jeanne Lavie, *d* of Joseph Lavie and Jeanne Jauréguiberry; two *s*. *Educ:* King's Sch., Canterbury; Corpus Christi Coll., Cambridge (Foundn Scholar). BA 1936; MA 1943. Appointed to War Office, 1937. Military service, 1942–44. Called to the Bar, Inner Temple, 1947. Seconded from War Office to OEEC, 1948–51; Board of Trade, 1951–65; Minister (Economic), Bonn, 1965–70; Under-Sec., DTI later Dept of Trade, 1970–74. *Recreations:* music, reading, hill-walking, wine. *Address:* B51 Résidence La Pastourelle, Bât. A, 20 Avenue Daniel-Hedde, 17200 Royan, France. *T:* 546392203.

EDWARDS, Very Rev. (Thomas) Erwyd (Pryse); Dean of Bangor, 1988–98, now Emeritus; *b* 26 Jan. 1933; *s* of Richard and Gwladys Edwards; *m* 1961, Mair (*née* Roberts); two *s*. *Educ:* St David's University College, Lampeter (BA 1956); St Michael's College, Llandaff. Curate of Caernarfon, 1958–63; Asst Chaplain, St George's Hosp., London, 1963–66; Chaplain, King's College Hosp., London, 1966–72; Vicar: Penmon, Anglesey, 1972–75; Menai Bridge, 1975–61; St David's, Bangor, 1981–85; St David's and St James's, Bangor, 1985–88; Canon of Bangor Cathedral, 1988. *Address:* 13 Carreg-y-Gad, Llanfairpwllgwyngyll, Anglesey LL61 5QF.

EDWARDS, Thomas Mowbray C.; *see* Charles-Edwards.

EDWARDS, Tony; *see* Edwards, L. A.

EDWARDS, Tracy Karen, MBE 1990; Managing Director, Tracy Edwards Associates Ltd, since 1990; *b* 5 Sept. 1962; *d* of Antony Herbert Edwards and Patricia Edwards; one *d*; *m* twice (both marrs diss.). *Educ:* Highlands Primary Sch., Berks; Arts Educnl, Tring; Gowerton Comprehensive Sch., Swansea. Assembled first all-female crew to compete in 1989 Whitbread Round the World Race (Maiden Project), 1987; set world fastest ocean record, 1997. Presenter/Commentator, TV broadcasts, incl. 1993–94 Whitbread Race. *Publications:* Maiden, 1990; Living Every Second (autobiog.), 2000. *Recreations:* riding, theatre, travel, reading, music. *Address:* c/o 14 Vernon Street, W14 0RJ. *Clubs:* Royal Ocean Racing, Mosimann's, Home House; Royal Yachting Association, Royal Southampton Yacht.

EDWARDS, William (Henry); *b* 6 Jan. 1938; *s* of Owen Henry Edwards and S. Edwards; *m* 1961, Ann Eleri Rogers; one *s* three *d*. *Educ:* Sir Thomas Jones' Comprehensive Sch.; Liverpool Univ. LLB. Solicitor. MP (Lab) Merioneth, 1966–Feb. 1974; contested (Lab) Merioneth, Oct. 1974; Prospective Parly Cand. (Lab), Anglesey, 1981–83. Mem., Historic Building Council for Wales, 1971–76. Editor, Solicitors Diary. *Recreations:* golf, Association football (from the terraces).

EDWARDS-MOSS, (Sir) David John, (5th Bt *cr* 1868); *S* father, 1988, but does not use the title.

EDWARDS-STUART, Antony James Cobham; QC 1991; a Recorder, since 1997; *b* 2 Nov. 1946; *s* of late Lt-Col Ivor Arthur James Edwards-Stuart and of Elizabeth Aileen Le Mesurier Edwards-Stuart (*née* Deck); *m* 1973, Fiona Ann, *d* of late Paul Weaver, OBE; two *s* two *d*. *Educ:* Sherborne Sch.; RMA Sandhurst; St Catharine's Coll., Cambridge. MCIArb. Called to the Bar, Gray's Inn, 1976; an Asst Recorder, 1991–97. Chm., Home Office Adv. Cttee on Service Candidates, 1995–98. Commnd 1st RTR, 1966; Adjutant: 1st RTR, 1973–75; Kent and Sharpshooters Sqn, Royal Yeomanry, 1976–77. *Recreations:* woodwork, restoring property in France, fishing, shooting. *Address:* 4 Aberdeen Park, Highbury, N5 2BN. *T:* (020) 7359 7224; Crown Office Chambers, Temple, EC4Y 7EP. *e-mail:* edwards-stuart@crownofficechambers.com.

EDWARDSON, Prof. James Alexander, PhD; Director, MRC-Newcastle University Centre Development for Clinical Brain Ageing, since 2000; Professor of Neuroendocrinology, Newcastle University, since 1982; Director, Institute for the Health of the Elderly, Newcastle University, since 1994; *b* 18 March 1942; *s* of James Thompson Hewson Edwardson and Isabel Ann Edwardson; *m* 1965, Caroline Hunter; one *s* two *d*. *Educ:* South Shields Grammar-Technical Sch. for Boys; Univ. of Nottingham (BSc Hons Zoology 1963); Inst. of Psychiatry, Univ. of London (PhD 1966). MRC Junior Res. Fellow, Inst. of Psychiatry, 1966–67; Lectr in Physiology, Aberdeen Univ., 1967–69; MRC Scientist and Lectr in Biochem., Imperial Coll., London, 1970–75; Sen. Lectr, then Reader, in Physiology, St George's Hosp. Med. Sch., 1975–79; Dir, MRC Neurochem. Pathology Unit, 1979–2000. Vice-Pres., Alzheimer's Disease Soc., 1989–. *Publications:* numerous papers on brain biochem., physiology and behaviour and on Alzheimer's Disease and related neurodegenerative disorders. *Recreations:* bird watching, religions, including the Labour Party, poetry. *Address:* 18 Leslie Crescent, Newcastle upon Tyne NE3 4AN. *T:* (0191) 285 0159, *Fax:* (0191) 284 2609.

EDZARD, Christine; film director; Managing Director, Sands Film Studios, since 1975; *b* 15 Feb. 1945; *d* of Dietz Edzard and Susanne Eisendieck, painters; *m* 1968, Richard Goodwin; one *d*, and one step *s* one step *d*. *Educ:* Ecole National de Science Politique, Paris (Econ degree). Asst designer to Lila de Nobili and Rostislav Doboujinsky, Paris; asst on Zefirelli's Romeo and Juliet, 1966; designer for Hamburg Opera, WNO and Camden Town Fest.; designer, costumes and sets and wrote (with Richard Goodwin) script of film, Tales of Beatrix Potter, 1971; directed short films, The Little Match Girl, The Kitchen and Little Ida, released as Tales from a Flying Trunk; dir, The Nightingale, 1979; wrote and directed: Biddy, 1981 (first feature film); Little Dorrit, 1987 (BAFTA Award, Best Screenplay; LA Critics Award, Best Film; Orson Welles Award, Best Director); The Fool, 1991; directed and produced, As You Like It, 1992; designed and directed, Menotti's Amahl and the Night Visitors, Spoleto Fest., 1996; wrote, designed and directed: The Nutcracker, 1997; The Children's Midsummer Night's Dream, 2000. *Address:* Sands Films, Grice's Wharf, 119 Rotherhithe Street, SE16 4NF. *T:* (020) 7231 2209, *Fax:* (020) 7231 2209; *e-mail:* CE@sandsfilms.co.uk.

EEKELAAR, John Michael, FBA 2001; Reader in Family Law, University of Oxford, since 1990; Tutorial Fellow, Pembroke College, Oxford, since 1965; *b* Johannesburg, 2 July 1942; *s* of John (Jan) Eekelaar and Delphine Eekelaar (*née* Stoughton); *m* 1978, Pia Nicole Lewis; two *d*. *Educ:* King's Coll., London (LLB); University Coll., Oxford (BCL). Rhodes Schol., 1963–65; Vinerian Schol., 1965; University of Oxford: Lectr in Law, 1966–90; Res. Fellow, Centre for Socio-Legal Studies, 1976–2000; Co-Dir, Oxford Centre for Family Law and Policy, 2000–. Pres., Internat. Soc. of Family Law, 1985–88. Gen. Ed., Oxford Jl Legal Studies, 1993–; Founding Co-ed., Internat. Jl Law Policy and the Family, 1987–. *Publications:* Family Security and Family Breakdown, 1971; Family Law and Social Policy, 1978, 2nd edn 1984 (trans German 1983); (ed jtly) Family Violence: an international and interdisciplinary study, 1978; (ed jtly) Marriage and Cohabitation in Contemporary Societies: a practical guide for social workers, health visitors and others, 1982; (jtly) The Protection of Children: state intervention and family life, 1983; (ed jtly) The Resolution of Family Conflict: comparative legal perspectives, 1984; (jtly) Maintenance after Divorce, 1986; (ed jtly) Family, State and Individual Economic Security, 1988; (ed jtly) Divorce Mediation and the Legal Process, 1988; (ed jtly) An Aging World: dilemmas and challenges for law and social policy, 1989; (jtly) The Reform of Child Care Law, 1990; Regulating Divorce, 1991; (ed jtly) Parenthood in Modern Society: social and legal issues for the Twenty-First century, 1993; (ed jtly) A Reader on Family Law, 1994; (jtly) The Parental Obligation: a study of parenthood across households, 1997; (ed jtly) The Changing Family: family law and family forms in international perspective, 1998; (jtly) Family Lawyers: the divorce work of solicitors, 2000; (ed jtly) Cross Currents: family law and policy in the US and England, 2000; contrib. articles to jls and chapters in books. *Recreation:* music. *Address:* Ridgeway Cottage, The Ridgeway, Boars Hill, Oxford OX1 5EX. *T:* (01865) 735485.

EFFINGHAM, 7th Earl of, *cr* 1837; **David Mowbray Algernon Howard;** Commander RN, retd; Baron Howard of Effingham 1554; with The Royal British Legion, since 1993; *b* 29 April 1939; *s* of Hon. John Algernon Frederick Charles Howard (*d* 1971), *yr s* of 5th Earl, and his 1st wife, Suzanne Patricia (*née* Macassey); *S* uncle, 1996; *m* 1st, 1964, Anne Mary Sayer (marr. diss. 1975); one *s*; 2nd, 1992, Mrs Elizabeth Jane Turner, *d* of late Dennis Eccleston, Eccleshall, Staffordshire and former wife of Peter Robert Easton Turner; two step *s*. *Educ:* Fettes Coll., Edinburgh; Royal Naval Coll., Dartmouth. Royal Navy, 1961–91. *Recreations:* shooting, horse racing, fishing. *Heir:* *s* Lord Howard of Effingham, *qv*. *Address:* (home) Readings Farmhouse, Blackmore End, Essex CM7 4DH. *T:* (01787) 461182; (office) Nelson House, Alington Road, St Neots, Cambs PE19 6YH. *T:* (01480) 211244, *Fax:* (01480) 211277. *Clubs:* Royal Navy, Army and Navy; Essex.
See also C. A. F. Howard.

EFFORD, Clive Stanley; MP (Lab) Eltham, since 1997; *b* 10 July 1958; *s* of Stanley Charles Efford and Mary Agnes Elizabeth Christina Caldwell; *m* 1981, Gillian Vallins; three *d*. *Educ:* Walworth Comprehensive Sch. Sen. Adventure Playground Leader; Asst to Warden, Pembroke Coll. Mission; former London taxi driver. Mem. (Lab) Greenwich LBC, 1986–98. Contested (Lab) Eltham, 1992. Prelim. FA Coach's Badge. *Recreations:* sports, reading, cinema. *Address:* (office) 132 Westmount Road, Eltham, SE9 1UT. *T:* (020) 8850 5744. *Clubs:* Burrage Road Co-op, Eltham Hill Working Man's, Woolwich Catholic.

EFSTATHIOU, Prof. George Petros, FRS 1994; Professor of Astrophysics, University of Cambridge, and Fellow of King's College, Cambridge, since 1997; *b* 2 Sept. 1955; *s* of Petros Efstathiou and Christina (*née* Parperi); *m* 1st, 1976, Helena Jane (*née* Smart) (marr. diss. 1997); one *s* one *d*; 2nd, 1998, Yvonne Nobis. *Educ:* Somerset Comprehensive Sch.; Keble Coll., Oxford (BA); Univ. of Durham (Dept of Physics) (PhD). Res. Asst, Astronomy Dept, Univ. of California, Berkeley, 1979–80; SERC Res. Asst, Inst. of Astronomy, Univ. of Cambridge, 1980–83; Jun. Res. Fellow, 1980–84, Sen. Res. Fellow, 1984–88, King's Coll., Cambridge; Institute of Astronomy, Cambridge: Sen. Asst in Res., 1984–87; Asst Dir of Res., 1987–88; Head of Astrophysics, 1988–94; Savilian Prof. of Astronomy, and Fellow, New Coll., Oxford, 1988–97; PPARC Sen. Fellow, 1994–99. Mem., PPARC, 2001–. Maxwell Medal and Prize, Inst. of Physics, 1990; Bodossaki Foundn Academic and Cultural Prize for Astrophysics, 1994; Robinson Prize in Cosmology, Univ. of Newcastle, 1997. *Publications:* articles in astronomical jls. *Recreations:* playing with his children, running. *Address:* Institute of Astronomy, Madingley Road, Cambridge CB3 0HA. *T:* (01223) 337548.

EGAN, Sir John (Leopold), Kt 1986; DL; FRAeS, FCIT, FCIPS; Chairman: Inchcape plc, since 2000; Harrison Lovegrove Ltd, since 2000; *b* 7 Nov. 1939; *m* 1963, Julia Emily Treble; two *d*. *Educ:* Bablake Sch., Coventry; Imperial Coll., London Univ., 1958–61 (BSc Hons; FIC 1985); London Business Sch., London Univ., 1966–68 (MScEcon). Petroleum Engineer, Shell International, 1962–66; General Manager, AC-Delco Replacement Parts Operation, General Motors Ltd, 1968–71; Managing Director,

Leyland Cars Parts Div., Parts and Service Director, Leyland Cars, BLMC, 1971–76; Corporate Parts Director, Massey Ferguson, 1976–80; Chm. and Chief Exec., Jaguar Cars Ltd, 1980–85, Jaguar plc, 1985–90; Chief Exec., BAA plc, 1990–99; Chm., MEPC plc, 1998–2000. Director: Foreign and Colonial Investment Trust, 1985–97; Legal & General Group, 1987–97. Chm., 1993–97, Pres., 1998–, London Tourist Bd; Dir, BTA, 1994–97. Dep. Pres., 2001–July 2002, Pres., July, 2002–, CBI. DL Warwicks, 1988. Hon. Professor: Dept of Engrg, Warwick Univ., 1990; Aston Univ., 1990. Sen. Fellow, RCA, 1987; FCIPS 1993; FRAeS 1994; FCIT 1994. Hon. FCIM 1989. Hon. Fellow: London Business Sch., 1988; Wolverhampton Poly., 1989. Dr *hc* Cranfield Inst. of Technology, 1986; Hon. DTech: Loughborough, 1987; Brunel, 1997; Hon. DBA Internat. Business Sch., 1988; Hon. LLD Bath, 1988; Hon. DSc Aston, 1992. Hon. Insignia for Technology, CGLI, 1987. Internat. Distinguished Entrepreneur Award, Univ. of Manitoba, 1989. MBA Award of the Year, 1988. *Recreations:* music, ski-ing, tennis. *Address:* Inchcape plc, 33 Cavendish Square, W1M 9HF. *Clubs:* Royal Automobile, MCC; Warwick Boat.

EGAN, Patrick Valentine Martin; Chairman, Fisons plc, 1992–94; *b* 17 July 1930; *s* of Eric and Sandy Egan; *m* 1953, Tessa Coleman; three *d. Educ:* Worth Prep. Sch., Crawley; Downside Sch., Bath. Signals Instructor, RA, 1948–50; joined Unilever, 1951; appts UK and abroad; joined main board, 1978; retired from Unilever, 1992; joined board of Fisons plc, 1985. Chairman: English Hops Ltd, 1993–; Botanix Ltd (formerly English Hop Products Ltd), 1993–; Dir, KG Fruits Ltd (formerly Kentish Garden Marketing Ltd), 1995–. Mem. Council, Lloyd's of London, 1989–92. Exec. Trustee, E Malling Trust for Horticl Res., 1996–. *Recreations:* fishing, shooting, gardening. *Address:* Whiteways, Sissinghurst, Cranbrook, Kent TN17 2JA.

EGAN, Penelope Jane; Director, Royal Society for the encouragement of Arts, Manufactures and Commerce, since 1998; *b* 18 July 1951; *d* of late Derek A. Morris and of June E. Morris; *m* 1975, David Anthony Egan; two *s. Educ:* St Paul's Girls' Sch.; Leicester Univ. (BA 1971). Mus. Asst, 1971–73, Press Officer, 1973–75, Victoria & Albert Mus.; Press Officer, Prime Minister's Office, 1975–77; Press and Publicity Officer, Crafts Council, 1977–82; Lecture Sec., 1986–95, Programme Develt Dir, 1995–97, RSA. Dir, Campaign for Learning, 1998–. Mem., Design Council, 1999–. Patron, Ben Uri Art Soc., 1998–. *Recreations:* tennis, cooking. *Address:* (office) 8 John Adam Street, WC2N 6EZ. *T:* (020) 7451 6883, *Fax:* (020) 7839 5805; *e-mail:* director@rsa-uk.demon.co.uk. *Club:* Roehampton.

EGAN, Hon. Seamus; Judge of the Supreme Court of Ireland, 1991–96; *b* 1924; *m* Ada Leahy; two *s* five *d. Educ:* Blackrock College; University College Dublin. Called to the Bar, 1945; practised on Western Circuit; Judge of the High Court, Ireland, 1984. Chm., Hepatitis C Compensation Tribunal, 1997. *Recreations:* golf, classical music, theatre; represented Connaught at tennis and table tennis. *Address:* Killowen, Shrewsbury Road, Dublin 4, Ireland.

EGAN, Rt Rev. Mgr Thomas; Vicar General, Archdiocese of Westminster, since 1993; *b* 15 Feb. 1942; *s* of Frank and Mary Egan. *Educ:* St Edmund's Coll., Ware; Inst. of Educn, London Univ. (BEd). Asst priest, Our Lady and St Joseph, Hanwell, 1967–72; Home Mission Team, 1972–73; asst priest, St Joan of Arc, Highbury, 1973–78; Parish Priest, St Pius X, St Charles Square, 1978–86; Pastoral Dir, Allen Hall Seminary, 1986–90; Parish Priest, Our Lady of Hal, Camden Town, 1990–93. *Recreations:* fishing, swimming, football. *Address:* Archbishop's House, Westminster, SW1P 1QJ. *T:* (020) 7798 9043.

EGDELL, Dr John Duncan; Consultant in Public Health Medicine (formerly Community Physician), Clwyd Health Authority, 1986–92, now Hon. Consultant, North Wales Health Authority; *b* 5 March 1938; *s* of late John William Egdell and Nellie (*née* Thompson); *m* 1963, Dr Linda Mary Flint; two *s* one *d. Educ:* Clifton Coll.; Univ. of Bristol. MB, ChB (Bristol) 1961; DipSocMed (Edin.) 1967; FFPHM 1990 (MFCM 1973; FFCM 1979). Ho. Phys. and Ho. Surg., Bristol Gen. Hosp., 1961–62; gen. practice, 1962–65; Med. Administration: with Newcastle Regional Hosp. Bd, 1966–69; with South Western Regional Hosp. Bd, 1969–74; Regional Specialist in Community Med., South Western Regional Health Authority, 1974–76; Regional Medical Postgrad. Co-ordinator, Univ. of Bristol, 1973–76; Regl MO, Mersey RHA, 1977–86; Hon. Lectr in Community Health, Univ. of Liverpool, 1980–86. *Recreations:* delving into the past, nature conservation. *Address:* Gelli Gynan Lodge, Llanarmon-yn-Ial, near Mold, Denbighshire CH7 4QX. *T:* (01824) 780345.

EGERTON, family name of **Duke of Sutherland**.

EGERTON, Maj.-Gen. David Boswell, CB 1968; OBE 1956; MC 1940; *b* 24 July 1914; *s* of Vice-Admiral W. de M. Egerton, DSO, and late Anita Adolphine (*née* David); *m* 1946, Margaret Gillian, ARCM, *d* of Canon C. C. Inge; one *s* two *d. Educ:* Stowe; RMA Woolwich. Commissioned Royal Artillery, Aug. 1934; served in India, 1935–39; ops in Waziristan, 1937; France and Belgium, 1940 (MC); Egypt 1942, Italy 1944. Technical Staff course, RMCS, 1946; BJSM, Washington, DC, 1950–52; Asst Chief Engineer in charge of ammunition development, Royal Armament R&D Estabt, 1955–58; idc 1959; Army Mem., Defence Research Policy Staff, 1959–62; Comdt, Trials Estabt Guided Weapons, RA, 1962–63; Army Mem., Air Defence Working Party, 1963–64; Dir-Gen. of Artillery, Army Dept, 1964–67; Vice-Pres., Ordnance Board, 1967–69, President, 1969–70; retired 1970. Col Comdt, RA, 1970–74. Gen. Sec., Assoc. of Recognised Eng. Lang. Schs, 1971–79. *Recreations:* gardening, travel. *Address:* Campion Cottage, Cheselbourne, Dorchester DT2 7NT. *T:* (01258) 837641. *Club:* Army and Navy.

EGERTON, Keith Robert, FRICS; Director, since 1992, and Group Chief Executive, since 1998, Taylor Woodrow plc; *b* 26 June 1942; *s* of Harold and Doris Egerton; *m* 1968, Pauline Steele; one *s* one *d.* FRICS 1988 (ARICS 1966). Development Surveyor, Laing Properties, 1970–73; Commercial Union Properties: S Area Develt Manager, 1973–75; Dir, Belgian and Dutch projects, 1975–77; Dir, 1978–82; Dir, 1977–82, Chief Exec., 1978–82, Commercial Union Property Develts Ltd; Costain plc, 1982–91: Man. Dir, 1982–85, Chief Exec., 1985–91, County & District Properties; Director: resp. for Property, 1986–90; resp. for UK, Spanish and Calif Housing Ops and Property, 1990–91; joined Taylor Woodrow plc, 1991; Man. Dir, 1991–98, and Chm., 1992–99, Taylor Woodrow Property Co. Ltd; Director: Taywood Homes, 1996–98; Monarch Develt Corp., 1998–. *Recreations:* cycling, gardening, hill walking, country pursuits, motorbikes, vintage and other interesting cars. *Address:* Venture House, 42–54 London Road, Staines, Middx TW18 4HF. *T:* (01784) 428650.

EGERTON, Sir Philip John Caledon G.; *see* Grey Egerton.

EGERTON, Sir Stephen (Loftus), KCMG 1988 (CMG 1978); Consultant, Enterprise Oil plc, since 1992; *b* 21 July 1932; *o s* of late William le Belward Egerton, ICS, and late Angela Doreen Loftus Bland; *m* 1958, Caroline, *er d* of Major and late Mrs E. T. E. Cary-Elwes, Albion House, Poringland, Norfolk; one *s* one *d. Educ:* Summer Fields; Eton; Trinity Coll., Cambridge (BA 1956, MA 1960). 2nd Lieut, 60th Rifles (KRRC), 1952–53. Entered Foreign Service, 1956; Middle East Centre for Arab Studies, Lebanon, 1956–57; Political Officer and Court Registrar, Kuwait, 1958–61; Private Sec. to Jt Parly Under-Sec. of State, FO, 1961–62; Northern Dept, FO, 1962–63; Oriental Sec. and later also Head of Chancery, Baghdad, 1963–67; First Sec., UK Mission to the UN, New York, 1967–70; Asst Head of Arabian and Near Eastern Depts, FCO, 1970–72; Counsellor and Head of Chancery, Tripoli, 1972–73; Head of Energy Dept, FCO, 1973–77; Consul-Gen., Rio de Janeiro, 1977–80; Ambassador to Iraq, 1980–82; Asst Under-Sec. of State, FCO, 1982–85; Ambassador: to Saudi Arabia, 1986–89; to Italy, 1989–92; (non-resident) to Republic of Albania, May–July 1992. Dir, 1994–99, Trustee, 1999–, St Andrew's Trust, Lambeth Palace. Pres., Soc. for Libyan Studies, 1994–98; Vice-Pres., British Sch. of Archaeology in Iraq, 1994–; Vice-Chm., Council, Keats-Shelley Meml Assoc., 1995–. Order of King Feisal bin Abdul Aziz, 1st class, 1987; Grand Cross of the Italian Republic, 1990. *Recreations:* topiary, argument. *Address:* 32 Poplar Grove, W6 7RE. *T:* (020) 7602 7876. *Clubs:* Brooks's, Greenjackets.

EGGAR, Rt Hon. Timothy (John Crommelin), (Tim); PC 1995; Vice-Chairman, ABNAMRO Corporate Finance, since 2000; Chief Executive, Monument Oil and Gas PLC, 1998–99 (Director, 1997–98); non-executive Director, GetMapping.com, since 2000; *b* 19 Dec. 1951; *s* of late John Drennan Eggar and of Pamela Rosemary Eggar; *m* 1977, Charmian Diana Minoprio; one *s* one *d. Educ:* Winchester Coll.; Magdalene Coll., Cambridge (MA). Called to the Bar, Inner Temple, 1976. European Banking Co., 1975–83; Director: Charterhouse Petroleum, 1984–85; LASMO plc, 1999–2000; Chairman: M W Kellogg, 1996–98; AGIP (UK) Ltd, 1997–98. Chm., Cambridge Univ. Cons. Assoc., 1972; Vice-Chm., Fedn of Cons. Students, 1973–74. MP (C) Enfield N, 1979–97. PPS to Minister for Overseas Develt, 1982–85; Parly Under-Sec. of State, FCO, 1985–89; Minister of State: Dept of Employment, 1989–90; DES, 1990–92; DTI (Minister for Energy, 1992–96, also for Industry, 1994–96). *Recreations:* ski-ing, simple gardening, shooting. *Address:* Nettlebed House, Nettlebed, Oxon RG9 5DD. *T:* (office) (020) 7678 1881. *Club:* Carlton.

EGGINGTON, Dr William Robert Owen; Chief Medical Adviser, Department of Health and Social Security, later Department of Social Security, 1986–92; part-time Medical Adviser, NDA, since 1999; *b* 24 Feb. 1932; *s* of Alfred Thomas Eggington and Phyllis Eggington (*née* Wynne); *m* 1961, Patricia Mary Elizabeth, *d* of Henry David and Elizabeth Grant; one *s* one *d. Educ:* Kingswood School, Bath; Guy's Hosp. MB, BS 1955, DTM&H 1960, DPH 1962, DIH 1963; MFCM 1970. House Surgeon, Guy's Hosp., 1955; House Physician, St John's Hosp., Lewisham, 1956. RAMC, 1957–73, retired as Lt-Col, Senior Specialist Army Health. DHSS, later DSS, 1973–92. Medical Adviser: War Pensions Agency, 1994–98; Benefits Agency, 1998. *Recreations:* Goss heraldic china, military history, football spectator. *Address:* 65 Frobisher Drive, Lytham St Annes, Lancs FY8 2RG.

EGGINTON, Anthony Joseph, CBE 1991; consultant; Visiting Professor, University College London, since 1991; *b* 18 July 1930; *s* of Arthur Reginald Egginton and Margaret Anne (*née* Emslie); *m* 1957, Janet Leta, *d* of late Albert and Florence Herring; two *d. Educ:* Selhurst Grammar Sch., Croydon; University Coll., London (BSc 1951; Fellow, 1992). Res. Assoc., UCL, 1951–56; AERE Harwell (Gen. Physics Div.), 1956–61; Head of Beams Physics Gp, NIRNS Rutherford High Energy Lab., 1961–65; DCSO and Head of Machine Gp, SRC Daresbury Nuclear Physics Lab., 1965–72; Head of Engrg Div., 1972–74, Under Sec. and Dir of Engineering and Nuclear Physics, 1974–78, Dir of Science and Engrg Divs, 1978–83, SRC; Science and Engineering Research Council: Dir of Engrg, 1983–88; Dir Progs, and Dep. Chm., 1988–91. Head, UK Delegn, 1978–83, Chm., 1982–83, Steering Cttee, Inst. Laue-Langevin, Grenoble. *Publications:* papers and articles in jls and conf. proceedings on particle accelerators and beams. *Recreations:* sport, cinema, music. *Address:* Carlton, 50 Burford Road, Witney, Oxon OX8 5DJ. *T:* (01993) 700697. *Club:* Lansdowne.

EGGLESTON, Anthony Francis, OBE 1968; Headmaster, Campion School, Athens, 1983–88, retired; *b* 26 Jan. 1928; *s* of late J. F. Eggleston and late Mrs J. M. Barnard, Harrow, Middx; *m* 1957, Jane Morison Buxton, JP, *d* of late W. L. Buxton, MBE and late Mrs F. M. M. Buxton, Stanmore, Middx; one *s* two *d. Educ:* Merchant Taylors' Sch., Northwood (Schol.); St John's Coll., Oxford (Sir Thomas White Schol.). BA 1949, MA 1953; 2nd cl. hons Chemistry. National Service, 1950–52; 2nd Lieut, RA, Suez Canal Zone. Asst Master, Cheltenham Coll., 1952–54; Sen. Science Master, English High Sch., Istanbul, 1954–56; Asst Master, Merchant Taylors' Sch., Northwood, 1956–62; Principal, English Sch., Nicosia, 1962–68; Headmaster, Felsted Sch., 1968–82. *Recreation:* looking at and lecturing about buildings of all periods. *Address:* Garden House, Chester Place, Norwich NR2 3DG. *T:* (01603) 616025.

EGGLESTON, Prof. James Frederick; Professor of Education, University of Nottingham, 1972–84, now Emeritus; *b* 30 July 1927; *s* of Frederick James and Anne Margaret Eggleston; *m* 1956, Margaret Snowden; three *s* two *d. Educ:* Appleby Grammar Sch.; Durham Univ. (King's Coll., Newcastle upon Tyne). BSc Hons Zoology; DipEd; FIBiol 1975. School teacher, 1953–64, Head of Biol., later Head of Sci., Hinckley Grammar Sch.; Res. Fellow, Res. Unit for Assessment and Curriculum Studies, Leicester Univ. Sch. of Educn, 1964; team leader, later consultant, Nuffield Sci. Teaching Project, 1964–68; Lectr in Educn, Leicester Univ. Sch. of Educn, 1966; apptd to Colls and Curriculum Chair of Educn, Nottingham Univ., 1973, Dean of Educn, 1975–81. *Publications:* A Critical Review of Assessment Procedures in Secondary School Science, 1965; Problems in Quantitative Biology, 1968; (with J. F. Kerr) Studies in Assessment, 1970; (jtly) A Science Teaching Observation Schedule, 1975; (jtly) Processes and Products of Science Teaching, 1976; contributions to: The Disciplines of the Curriculum, 1971; The Art of the Science Teacher, 1974; Frontiers of Classroom Research, 1975; Techniques and Problems of Assessment, 1976; (with Trevor Kerry) Topic Work in the Primary School, 1988; articles in professional jls. *Recreations:* fell walking, golf, photography. *Address:* The Old Chapel, Church Street, Fritchley, Derbys DE56 2FQ. *T:* (01773) 852870.

EGGLESTON, Prof. (Samuel) John, BScEcon, MA, DLitt; Professor, 1985–96, now Emeritus, and Chairman, 1985–91, Department of Education, University of Warwick; *b* 11 Nov. 1926; *s* of Edmund and Josephine Eggleston, Dorchester; *m* 1957, Greta Patrick; two *s* two *d. Educ:* Chippenham Grammar Sch.; LSE (BScEcon 1957); Univ. of London Inst. of Educn (MA 1965). DLitt Univ. of Keele, 1977. Teacher, Suffolk and Worcs, 1950–54; Leverhulme Scholarship, LSE, 1954–57; Teacher, Beds, and Headteacher, Oxfordshire, 1957–60; Lectr, Loughborough Coll. of Educn, 1960–63; Lectr, later Sen. Lectr, Leicester Univ., 1963–67; Keele University: Prof. and Head of Dept of Educn, 1967–84; Chm., Bd of Soc. Scis, 1976–79; Chm., Higher Degree and Res. Cttee, 1981–84. Vis. Commonwealth Fellow, Canada, 1973–74; Leverhulme Fellow, 1994–97; Vis. Res. Prof., Univ. of Central England, 1994–; Vis. Prof., Middlesex Univ., 1995–. Director: DES Res. Project, Structure and Function of Youth Service, 1968–74; Schs Council Project, Design and Craft Educn, 1968–74; DES Research Projects: Training for Multi-Racial Educn, 1978–80; Minority Gp Adolescence, 1981–84. Chairman: Council of Europe Workshop on Multi-Cultural Higher Educn, 1981–86; Education Cttee, Central Television, 1987–; Technol. Exams Cttee, RSA, 1993–; Trustees and Judges, Young Electronic Designer Awards, 1988–; Vice-Chm., Design & Technology Assoc., 1992–; Member: Council of Europe Working Party, Diversif. of Tertiary Educn, 1972–78; Cheshire Educn Cttee, 1981–83; Council, Eur. Inst. of Educn and Social Policy, 1983–93; Educnl Res. Bd, SSRC, 1973–77; Panel on Public Disorder and Sporting Events, SSRC, 1976–77; Assessment of Performance Unit, DES, Consultative Cttee, 1980–88; Res. Consultancy Cttee, DES, 1981–83; Arts Council Cttee on Trng for the Arts, 1982–87; Academic Adv. Cttee, EEC Erasmus Project, 1990–92. Hon. FEICDT 1987; Hon. FCP. Editor: Design and Technology Teaching (formerly Studies in Design Education and Craft), 1968–96; Sociological Rev., 1982–95 (Chm., Editorial Bd, 1970–82); Mentoring and Tutoring, 1993–97; Chm., Editorial Bd, European Jl of Educn (formerly Paedagogica Europaea), 1976– (Editor in Chief, 1968–76); Founding Chm., Editorial Bd, Multicultural Teaching, 1982–. Hon. FCollH 1968. DUniv Middlesex, 1994; Hon. DEd Sunderland, 1999. *Publications:* The Social Context of the School, 1967; (with G. N. Brown) Towards an Education for the 21st Century, 1969; (ed with A. R. Pemberton) International Perspectives of Design Education, 1973; (ed) Contemporary Research in the Sociology of Education, 1974; Adolescence and Community, 1976; New Developments in Design Education, 1976; The Sociology of the School Curriculum, 1977; The Ecology of the School, 1977; (ed) Experimental Education in Europe, 1978; Teacher Decision Making in the Classroom, 1979; School Based Curriculum Development, 1980; Work Experience in Secondary Schools, 1982; Education for Some, 1986; The Challenge for Teachers, 1992; Teaching Design & Technology, 1992, 3rd edn 2001; (ed) Re-education for Employment, 1992; Arts Education for a Multicultural Society, 1995; Staying on at School, 2000; (ed) Teaching Design and Technology: a guide to recent research, 2001; articles in books and jls, incl. Sociol., Brit. Jl of Sociol., New Soc., Educnl Res. *Recreations:* work in design and craft, ski-ing, travel. *Address:* Institute of Education, University of Warwick, Coventry CV4 7AL. *T:* (024) 7652 4104.

EGGLETON, Anthony, AO 1991; CVO 1970; National Director, 1995–96, Director, since 1996, CARE Australia (Secretary-General, CARE International, Brussels, 1991–95); Chief Executive Officer, Centenary of Federation Council, since 1997; *b* 30 April 1932; *s* of Tom and Winifred Eggleton; *m* 1953, Mary Walker, Melbourne; two *s* one *d*. *Educ:* King Alfred's Sch., Wantage. Journalist, Westminster Press Group, 1948–50; Editorial Staff, Bendigo Advertiser, Vic, 1950–51; Australian Broadcasting Commn, 1951–60 (Dir of ABC-TV News Coverage, 1956–60); Dir of Public Relations, Royal Australian Navy, 1960–65; Press Sec. to Prime Ministers of Australia, 1965–71 (Prime Ministers Menzies, Holt, Gorton, McMahon); Commonwealth Dir of Information, London, 1971–74; Special Advr to Leader of Opposition, and Dir of Communications, Federal Liberal Party, 1974–75; Federal Dir, Liberal Party of Australia, 1975–90; Campaign Dir, Federal Elections, 1975, 1977, 1980, 1983, 1984, 1987, 1990. Chm., Asia Pacific Democrat Union, 1998– (Exec. Sec., 1982–84, 1985–87, Dep. Chm., 1987–90, Pacific Democrat Union). Mem. Bd, Nat. Stroke Foundn, 1997–. Mem., Editl Adv. Bd, Australian Dept of Foreign Affairs, 1999–. Australian Public Relations Inst.'s 1st Award of Honour, 1968; Outstanding Service Award, Liberal Party of Australia, 1990. *Address:* 87 Buxton Street, Deakin, ACT 2600, Australia. *Clubs:* (Foundn Pres.) National Press (Canberra), Commonwealth (Canberra).

EGGLETON, Hon. Arthur C.; MP (L) York Centre, Toronto, since 1993; Minister of National Defence, Canada, since 1997; *b* 29 Sept. 1943; *m*; one *d*. Former accountant; consultant, urban mgt and policy issues; Jt Orgnr, World Urban Forum, World Bank. Toronto City Council: Mem., 1969–93; Budget Chief, 1973–80; Pres., 1975–76, 1978–80; Mayor of Toronto, 1980–91; former Member: Metropolitan Police Commn; Bd, Canadian Nat. Exhibn. Pres., Treasury Bd, and Minister responsible for Infrastructure, 1993–96; Minister for Internat. Trade, 1996–97; Vice-Chm., Cabinet Cttee on Economic Policy, 1997–. Civic Award of Merit, Toronto, 1992. *Address:* House of Commons, Ottawa, ON K1A 0A6, Canada.

EGILSSON, Ólafur; Ambassador of Iceland to China, and concurrently to Australia, Indonesia, Japan, Republic of Korea, Mongolia, New Zealand, Thailand and Vietnam, since 1998; *b* 20 Aug. 1936; *s* of Egill Kristjánsson and Anna Margrjet Thuríður Ólafsdóttir Briem; *m* 1960, Ragna Sverrisdóttir Ragnars; one *s* one *d*. *Educ:* Commercial College, Iceland (grad. 1956); Univ. of Iceland, Faculty of Law (grad. 1963). Reporter on Vísir, 1956–58, Morgunblaðið, 1959–62; publishing Exec., Almenna bókafélagið, 1963–64; Head, NATO Regional Inf. Office, Iceland, 1964–66, and Gen. Sec., Icelandic Assoc. for Western Co-operation and Atlantic Assoc. of Young Political Leaders of Iceland; Icelandic Foreign Service, 1966; Foreign Ministry, 1966–69; First Sec., later Counsellor, Icelandic Embassy, Paris, and Dep. Perm. Rep. to OECD, UNESCO, 1969–71, and Council of Europe, Strasbourg, 1969–70; Dep. Perm. Rep., N Atlantic Council and Dep. Head, Icelandic Delegn to EEC, Brussels, 1971–74; Counsellor, later Minister Counsellor, Political Div., Min. of Foreign Affairs, 1974–80; Chief of Protocol, with rank of Ambassador, 1980–83; Acting Principal Private Sec. to President of Iceland, Oct. 1981–June 1982; Dep. Perm. Under Sec. and Dir Gen. for Political Affairs, Min. of Foreign Affairs, 1983–87; Ambassador: to UK, 1986–89, and concurrently to the Netherlands, Ireland and Nigeria; to USSR, later Russia, 1990–94, and concurrently to Bulgaria, Japan, Romania and Ukraine; to Denmark, 1994–96, and also to Italy, Israel, Japan, Lithuania and Turkey; in charge of Arctic co-operation, 1996–98, also accredited to the Holy See, Turkey, Australia and NZ. Chm., Governing Bd, Icelandic Internat. Develt Agency, 1982–87; Sec., Commn revising Foreign Service Act, 1968–69. President: Nat. Youth Council of Iceland, 1963–64; Acad. Assoc. of Reykjavík, 1967–68; Executive Member: Bible Soc., 1977–87 and 1996–; History Soc., 1982–88. Commander, Icelandic Order of the Falcon, 1981; holds numerous foreign orders. *Publications:* (jtly) Iceland and Jan Mayen, 1980; (ed) Bjarni Benediktsson: Contemporaries' views, 1983; (jtly) NATO's Anxious Birth: the prophetic vision of the 1940's, 1985. *Recreations:* walking, ski-ing, music (opera), history. *Address:* Landmark Tower 1 #802, Chaoyang District, 100004 Beijing, China. *T:* 907795, *Fax:* (10) 65907801; *e-mail:* olafur.egilsson@utn.stjr.is.

EGLINGTON, Charles Richard John; Director, 1986–95, Vice-Chairman, 1990–95, S. G. Warburg Securities; *b* 12 Aug. 1938; *s* of late Richard Eglington and Treena Margaret Joyce Eglington. *Educ:* Sherborne. Dir, Akroyd & Smithers, 1978–86. Mem. Council, Stock Exchange, 1975–86, Dep. Chm., 1981–84 (Chairman: Quotations Cttee, 1978–81; Property and Finance Cttee, 1983–86); Mem., Gp of Thirty Working Cttee on Clearance and Settlement Systems, 1988–89. Governor: Sherborne Sch., 1980–; Twyford Sch., 1984–. *Recreations:* golf, cricket. *Address:* 2 Rectory Orchard, Church Road, Wimbledon, SW19 5AS. *T:* (020) 8946 3863, *Fax:* (020) 8947 3356. *Clubs:* MCC; Royal and Ancient Golf (St Andrews); Walton Heath Golf; Rye Golf.

EGLINTON and WINTON, 18th Earl of, *cr* 1507; **Archibald George Montgomerie;** Lord Montgomerie, 1448; Baron Seton and Tranent, 1859; Baron Kilwinning, 1615; Baron Ardrossan (UK), 1806; Earl of Winton (UK), 1859; Hereditary Sheriff of Renfrewshire; Chairman, Edinburgh Investment Trust plc, since 1994; *b* 27 Aug. 1939; *s* of 17th Earl of Eglinton and Winton and Ursula (*d* 1987), *er d* of Hon. Ronald Watson, Edinburgh; *S* father, 1966; *m* 1964, Marion Carolina, *o d* of John Dunn-Yarker; four *s*. *Educ:* Eton. Man. Dir, Gerrard & National Hldgs, 1972–92 (Dep. Chm., 1980–92); Chm., Gerrard Vivian Gray Ltd, 1992–94. Asst Grand Master, United Grand Lodge of England, 1989–95. *Heir: s* Lord Montgomerie, *qv*. *Address:* Balhomie, Cargill, Perth PH2 6DS.

EGLINTON, Prof. Geoffrey, PhD, DSc; FRS 1976; Professor of Organic Geochemistry, 1973–93, now Emeritus, and Senior Research Fellow, Biogeochemistry Research Centre, since 1995 (Director, 1991–96), University of Bristol; Adjunct Scientist, Woods Hole Oceanographic Institution, Massachusetts, since 1991; *b* 1 Nov. 1927; *s* of Alfred Edward Eglinton and Lilian Blackham; *m* 1955, Pamela Joan Coupland; two *s* (one *d* decd). *Educ:* Sale Grammar Sch.; Manchester Univ. (BSc, PhD, DSc). Post-Doctoral Fellow, Ohio State Univ., 1951–52; ICI Fellow, Liverpool Univ., 1952–54; Lectr, subseq. Sen. Lectr and Reader, Glasgow Univ., 1954–67; Sen. Lectr, subseq. Reader, Bristol Univ., 1967–73. Mem., NERC, 1984–90. Hon. Fellow, Plymouth Polytechnic, 1981. Gold Medal for Exceptional Scientific Achievement, NASA, 1973; Hugo Müller Silver Medal, Chemical Soc., 1974; Alfred Treibs Gold Medal, Geochem. Soc., 1981; Coke Medal, Geol Soc. of London, 1985; H. C. Urey Award, European Assoc. of Geochem., 1997; Royal Medal, Royal Soc., 1997; Martin Gold Medal, Chromatographic Soc., 1999; Goldschmidt Medal, Geochemical Soc., 2000. *Publications:* Applications of Spectroscopy to Organic Chemistry, 1965; Organic Geochemistry: methods and results, 1969; 'Chemsyn', 1972, 2nd edn 1975; contrib. Nature, Geochim. Cosmochim. Acta, Phytochem., Chem. Geol., Sci. American. *Recreations:* gardening, walking, sailing. *Address:* Oldwell, 7 Redhouse Lane, Bristol BS9 3RY. *T:* (0117) 968 3833. *Club:* Rucksack (Manchester).

EGMONT, 11th Earl of, *cr* 1733; **Frederick George Moore Perceval;** Bt 1661; Baron Perceval, 1715; Viscount Perceval, 1722; Baron Lovell and Holland (Great Britain), 1762; Baron Arden, 1770; Baron Arden (United Kingdom), 1802; *b* 14 April 1914; *o s* of 10th Earl and Cecilia (*d* 1916), *d* of James Burns Moore, Montreal; *S* father, 1932; *m* 1932, Ann Geraldine, *d* of D. G. Moodie; one *s* one *d* (and two *s* decd). *Heir: s* Viscount Perceval, *qv*. *Address:* Two-dot Ranch, Nanton, Alberta, Canada.

EGREMONT, 2nd Baron *cr* 1963, **AND LECONFIELD**, 7th Baron *cr* 1859; **John Max Henry Scawen Wyndham,** DL; *b* 21 April 1948; *s* of John Edward Reginald Wyndham, MBE, 1st Baron Egremont and 6th Baron Leconfield, and of Pamela, *d* of late Captain the Hon. Valentine Wyndham-Quin, RN; *S* father, 1972; *m* 1978, Caroline, *er d* of A. R. Nelson, Muckairn, Taynuilt, Argyll, and Hon. Lady Musker; one *s* three *d*. *Educ:* Eton; Christ Church, Oxford (MA Modern History). Mem., Royal Commn on Historical MSS, 1989–2001. Chm., Friends of the Nat. Libraries, 1985–; Trustee: Wallace Collection, 1988–2000; British Museum, 1990–2000; Nat. Manuscripts Conservation Trust, 1995– (Chm., 2000–). Pres., ACRE, 1993–99. DL W Sussex, 1988. *Publications:* (as Max Egremont) The Cousins: a biographical study of Wilfrid Scawen Blunt and George Wyndham, 1977 (Yorkshire Post First Book Award); Balfour: a life of Arthur James Balfour, 1980; Under Two Flags: the life of Major-General Sir Edward Spears, 1997; *novels:* The Ladies' Man, 1983; Dear Shadows, 1986; Painted Lives, 1989; Second Spring, 1993. *Heir: s* Hon. George Ronan Valentine Wyndham, *b* 31 July 1983. *Address:* Petworth House, Petworth, West Sussex GU28 0AE. *T:* (01798) 342447.

EHRLICH, Prof. Cyril, PhD; Professor of Economic and Social History, Queen's University, Belfast, 1974–86, now Emeritus; *b* London, 13 Sept. 1925; *s* of Henry Ehrlich and Dinah (*née* Jacobs); *m* 1954, Felicity Ruth Bell-Bonnett; two *s* one *d*. *Educ:* several grammar schools; London Sch. of Econs (BSc Econ 1950; PhD 1958). Served RAF and Army, 1943–47. Res. Asst, LSE, 1950–52; Lectr, then Sen. Lectr, Makerere Coll., Uganda, 1952–61; Queen's University, Belfast: Lectr, then Sen. Lectr and Reader, 1961–74; Dean, Econs Faculty, 1979–81. Visiting Professor in Music: Royal Holloway, London Univ., 1995–; Goldsmiths Coll., London Univ., 1998–. *Publications:* The Uganda Company, 1953; The Piano: a history, 1976, 2nd edn 1990; (contrib.) Oxford History of East Africa, Vol. II 1965, Vol. III 1976; The Music Profession in Britain since the 18th Century: a social history, 1985; Harmonious Alliance: a history of the Performing Right Society, 1989; First Philharmonic: a history of the Royal Philharmonic Society, 1995; (contrib.) The Blackwell History of Music in Britain: the Twentieth Century, 1995; (contrib.) Wigmore Hall 1901–2001: a celebration, 2001; contrib. reviews and articles in Econ. Hist. Rev., Jl African Hist., Music and Letters, Musical Times, The Times, TLS, New Grove. *Recreations:* piano, opera. *Address:* 1 St Andrew's Lane, Old Headington, Oxford OX3 9DP. *T:* (01865) 760585.

EHRMAN, John Patrick William, FBA 1970; historian; *b* 17 March 1920; *o s* of late Albert and Rina Ehrman; *m* 1948, Elizabeth Susan Anne, *d* of late Vice-Adm. Sir Geoffrey Blake, KCB, DSO; four *s*. *Educ:* Charterhouse; Trinity Coll., Cambridge (MA). Served Royal Navy, 1940–45. Fellow of Trinity Coll., Cambridge, 1947–52; Historian, Cabinet Office, 1948–56; Lees Knowles Lectr, Cambridge, 1957–58; James Ford Special Lectr, Oxford, 1976–77. Hon. Treas., Friends of the National Libraries, 1960–77; Trustee of the Nat. Portrait Gall., 1971–85; Member: Reviewing Cttee on Export of Works of Art, 1970–76; Royal Commn on Historical Manuscripts, 1973–94; Chairman: Adv. Cttee to British Library Reference Div., 1975–84; Nat. Manuscripts Conservation Trust, 1989–94; Vice-Pres., Navy Records Soc., 1968–70, 1974–76. FSA 1958; FRHistS. *Publications:* The Navy in the War of William III, 1953; Grand Strategy, 1943–5 (2 vols, UK Official Military Histories of the Second World War), 1956; Cabinet Government and War, 1890–1940, 1958; The British Government and Commercial Negotiations with Europe, 1783–1793, 1962; The Younger Pitt, vol. 1, The Years of Acclaim, 1969, vol. 2, The Reluctant Transition, 1983, vol. 3, The Consuming Struggle (Yorkshire Post Book of the Year Award), 1996. *Address:* The Mead Barns, Taynton, near Burford, Oxfordshire OX18 4UH. *Clubs:* Army and Navy, Beefsteak, Garrick.

See also W. G. Ehrman.

EHRMAN, William Geoffrey, CMG 1998; HM Diplomatic Service; Director, International Security, Foreign and Commonwealth Office, since 2000; *b* 28 Aug. 1950; *s* of J. P. W. Ehrman, *qv* and Susan (*née* Blake); *m* 1977, Penelope Anne, *d* of late Brig. H. W. Le Patourel, VC and of Babette Le Patourel; one *s* three *d*. *Educ:* Eton; Trinity Coll., Cambridge (MA). Joined Diplomatic Service, 1973; language student, Hong Kong, 1975–76; Third/Second Sec., Peking, 1976–78; First Secretary: UK Mission to UN, NY, 1979–83; Peking, 1983–84; FCO, 1985–89; Pol Advr, Hong Kong, 1989–93; Head, Near East and N Africa Dept, FCO, 1993–94; UK Mem., Bosnia Contact Gp, 1994–95; Prin. Pvte Sec. to Sec. of State for Foreign and Commonwealth Affairs, 1995–97; seconded to Unilever (China) Ltd, 1997–98; Ambassador to Luxembourg, 1998–2000. *Recreations:* sailing, walking, ski-ing. *Address:* c/o Foreign and Commonwealth Office, SW1A 2AH. *Club:* Royal Cruising.

EICHEL, Hans; Minister of Finance, Germany, since 1999; *b* Kassel, 24 Dec. 1941; *m*; two *c*. Secondary sch. teacher, Kassel, 1970–75. Mem., Kassel City Council, 1968–75; Mayor, Kassel, 1975–91; Mem. (SPD), Assembly, and Premier, Hesse Land, 1991–99. German Convention of Municipal Authorities: Mem., Presidium, 1981–91; Pres., 1985–87 and

1989–91. Joined SPD, 1964: Mem., Exec. Cttee, 1984–; Chm., Hesse, 1989–. *Address:* Ministry of Finance, Wilhelmstrasse 97, 10117 Berlin, Germany.

EICHELBAUM, Rt Hon. Sir (Johann) Thomas, GBE 1989; PC 1989; Chief Justice of New Zealand, 1989–99; Judge of Appeal, Fiji, since 1999; non-permanent Judge, Court of Final Appeal, Hong Kong, since 2000; *b* 17 May 1931; *s* of Dr Walter and Frida Eichelbaum; *m* 1956, Vida Beryl Franz; three *s*. *Educ:* Hutt Valley High School; Victoria University College (LLB). Partner, Chapman Tripp & Co., Wellington, 1958–78; QC 1978; Judge of High Court of NZ, 1982–88. Pres., NZ Law Soc., 1980–82. Chm., Royal Commn on Genetic Modification, 2000–01. *Publications:* (Editor in Chief) Mauet's Fundamentals of Trial Techniques, NZ edn, 1989; (Consulting Editor) Advocacy in New Zealand, 2000. *Recreations:* reading, music, walking. *Address:* Raumati Beach, Kapiti Coast. *Club:* Wellington (Wellington).

EIGEN, Manfred; Director at Max-Planck-Institut für biophysikalische Chemie, Göttingen, since 1964; *b* 9 May 1927; *s* of Ernst and Hedwig Eigen; *m* 1952, Elfriede Müller; one *s* one *d*. *Educ:* Göttingen Univ. Dr rer. nat. (Phys. Chem.) 1951. Research Asst, Inst. für physikal. Chemie, Göttingen Univ., 1951–53; Asst, Max-Planck-Institut für physikal. Chemie, 1953; Research Fellow, Max-Planck-Gesellschaft, 1958; Head of separate dept of biochemical kinetics, Max-Planck-Inst., 1962. Andrew D. White Prof. at Large, Cornell Univ., 1965; Hon. Prof., Technische Hochschule Braunschweig, 1965. For. Hon. Mem., Amer. Acad. of Arts and Sciences, 1964; Mem. Leopoldina, Deutsche Akad. der Naturforscher, Halle, 1964; Mem., Akad. der Wissenschaften, Göttingen, 1965; Hon. Mem., Amer. Assoc. Biol Chemists, 1966; For. Assoc., Nat. Acad. of Scis, Washington, 1966; For. Mem., Royal Soc., 1973. Dr of Science *hc*; Washington, Harvard and Chicago Univs, 1966. Has won prizes, medals and awards including Nobel Prize for Chemistry (jointly), 1967. *Publications:* numerous papers in Z. Elektrochem., Jl Phys. Chem., Trans Faraday Soc., Proc. Royal Soc., Canad. Jl Chem., ICSU Rev., and other learned jls. *Address:* Max-Planck-Institut für biophysikalische Chemie, Karl-Friedrich Bonhoeffer Institut, Postfach 2841, 37018 Göttingen-Nikolausberg, Germany.

EILLEDGE, Elwyn Owen Morris, CBE 2001; FCA; Chairman, Financial Reporting Advisory Board to HM Treasury, since 1996; Director, BG Group plc, since 1997; Senior Partner, Ernst & Young, Chartered Accountants, 1989–95; *b* 20 July 1935; *s* of Owen and Mary Elizabeth Eilledge; *m* 1962, Audrey Ann Faulkner Ellis; one *s* one *d*. *Educ:* Merton College, Oxford (BA, MA). FCA 1968. Articled with Farrow, Bersey, Gain, Vincent & Co., later Binder Hamlyn, 1959–66; Whinney Murray & Co. subseq. Ernst & Whinney, now Ernst & Young, Liberia, 1966–68; Ernst & Whinney: Audit Manager, Hamburg, 1968–71; Partner, London, 1972; Managing Partner, London office, 1983–86; Dep. Sen. Partner, 1985; Sen Partner, 1986–89; Chairman: Ernst & Whinney Internat., 1988–89; Ernst & Young Internat., 1989–95. Chm., BTR, 1996–98. *Recreations:* gardening, swimming, tennis, listening to classical music. *Address:* Whitethorn House, Long Grove, Seer Green, Beaconsfield, Bucks HP9 2QH. *Club:* Brooks's.

EILON, Prof. Samuel, FREng; Senior Research Fellow and Emeritus Professor, Imperial College of Science, Technology and Medicine, University of London, since 1989; industrial consultant on corporate performance and strategy; *b* 13 Oct. 1923; *s* of Abraham and Rachel Eilon; *m* 1946, Hannah Ruth (*née* Samuel); two *s* two *d*. *Educ:* Reali Sch., Haifa; Technion, Israel Inst. of Technology, Haifa; Imperial Coll., London. PhD London, 1955; DSc(Eng) London, 1963. FREng (Founder FEng), FIMechE, FIEE. Engr, Palestine Electric Co. Ltd, Haifa, 1946–48; Officer, Israel Defence Forces, 1948–52; CO of an Ordnance and workshop base depot (Major); Res. Asst, Imperial Coll., 1952–55; Lectr in Production Engrg, Imperial Coll., 1955–57; Associate Prof. in Industrial Engrg, Technion, Haifa, 1957–59; Imperial College: Head of Section, 1955–57; Reader, 1959–63; Head of Dept, 1959–87; Prof. of Management Sci., 1963–89. Consultant and Lectr, European Productivity Agency, Paris, 1960–62. Professorial Research Fellow, Case Western Reserve Univ., Cleveland, Ohio, 1967–68. Vis. Fellow, University Coll., Cambridge, 1970–71. Mem., Monopolies and Mergers Commn, 1990–97. Past Mem. of several cttees of IProdE and DES; Member: Council, Operational Res. Soc., 1965–67; Council, Inst. of Management Scis, 1970–72, 1980–82; Exec. Cttee, British Acad. of Management, 1985–89. Adviser, P-E Consulting Gp, 1961–71; Principal and Dir, Spencer Stuart and Associates, 1971–74; Director: Amey Roadstone Corp., subseq. ARC, 1974–88; Campari Internat., 1978–80. Chief Editor, OMEGA, Internat. Jl of Management Science, 1972–94; Deptl Editor, Management Science, 1969–77. CIMgt; Hon. FCGI 1978. Two Joseph Whitworth Prizes for papers, IMechE, 1960; Silver Medal, ORS, 1982. *Publications:* Elements of Production Planning and Control, 1962; Industrial Engineering Tables, 1962; (jtly) Exercises in Industrial Management, 1966; (jtly) Industrial Scheduling Abstracts, 1967; (jtly) Inventory Control Abstracts, 1968; (jtly) Distribution Management, 1971; Management Control, 1971, 2nd edn 1979; (jtly) Applications of Management Science in Banking and Finance, 1972; (jtly) Applied Productivity Analysis for Industry, 1976; Aspects of Management, 1977, 2nd edn 1979; The Art of Reckoning: analysis of performance criteria, 1984; Management Assertions and Aversions, 1985; (jtly) The Global Challenge of Innovation, 1991; Management Practice and Mispractice, 1992; Management Science: an anthology, 1995; Management Strategies: a critique of theories and practices, 1999; some 300 papers and articles in the field of management. *Recreations:* theatre, tennis, walking. *Address:* 1 Meadway Close, NW11 7BA. *T:* (020) 8458 6650, *Fax:* (020) 8455 0561.

EISNER, Michael D(ammann); Chairman and Chief Executive Officer, Walt Disney Co., since 1984; *b* 7 March 1942; *s* of Lester Eisner and Margaret Eisner (*née* Dammann); *m* 1967, Jane Breckenridge; three *s*. *Educ:* Lawrenceville Sch.; Denison Univ. (BA English Lit. and Theatre 1964). ABC Entertainment Corporation: Dir of Program Develt, East Coast, 1968–71; Vice President: Daytime Programming, 1971–75; Program Planning and Develt, 1975–76; Sen. Vice Pres., Prime-Time Production and Develt, 1976; Pres. and Chief Operating Officer, Paramount Pictures Corp., 1976–84. Member of Board: California Inst. of the Arts; American Film Inst. Chevalier, Légion d'Honneur (France). *Address:* Walt Disney Co., 500 South Buena Vista Street, Burbank, CA 91521, USA.

EKERT, Prof. Artur Konrad, DPhil; Professor of Physics, University of Oxford, since 1998; Fellow and Tutor, Keble College, Oxford, since 1998; *b* 19 Sept. 1961; *s* of Kazimierz and Janina Ekert; *m* 1990, Beata Wijowska. *Educ:* Jagiellonian Univ., Kraków, Poland (MSc); Wolfson Coll., Oxford (DPhil). Jun. Research Fellow, 1991–94, Res. Fellow, 1994–98, Merton Coll., Oxford. Howe Res. Fellow, Royal Soc., 1994–2000; Visiting Professor: Univ. of Innsbruck, 1994, 1998; Nat. Univ. of Singapore, 2001. Maxwell Medal and Prize, Inst. Physics, 1995. *Publications:* articles in scientific jls. *Recreations:* ski-ing, tennis. *Address:* Clarendon Laboratory, Oxford OX1 3PU; *e-mail:* artur.ekert@qubit.org.

EKINS, Prof. Roger Philip, PhD, DSc; FRS 2001; Professor of Biophysics, University of London, 1972–88, now Emeritus Professor; Head, Department of Molecular Endocrinology, University College London Medical School (formerly at Middlesex Hospital Medical School), since 1976; *b* 22 Sept. 1926; *s* of William Norman and Mathilde Therese Ekins; *m* 1st, 1947, Jane Woodger (marr. diss. 1963); two *d*; 2nd, 1990, Marisa Antonietta Sgherzi. *Educ:* Westminster City Sch.; Emmanuel Coll., Cambridge (MA); Middx Hosp. Med. Sch. (PhD 1963; DSc 1990). Middlesex Hospital Medical School: Lectr in Physics Applied to Medicine, 1949–61; Lectr, then Sen. Lectr, 1961–68, Reader and Dep. Dir, 1968–72, Inst. of Nuclear Medicine; Dir, UK Supraregl Assay Service Centre, 1972–93 (Chm., SAS Dirs' Cttee, UK Supraregl Assay Service, 1974–77). Dr *hc* Univ. Claude Bernard, Lyons, 1993. Georg von Hevesy Medal, von Hevesy Foundn, Switzerland, 1984; Dist. Clin. Chemist Award, Internat. Fedn Clin. Chem., 1993; Inaugural Edwin F. Ullman Award, Amer. Assoc. Clin. Chem., 1998. *Publications:* contrib. numerous res. papers and book chapters relating to effects of maternal hormones on fetal brain develt, and develt of microarray and other microanalytical methods for sensitive measurement of substances of biol importance (eg hormones, DNA and RNA). *Recreations:* weaving rya rugs, potting, sailing, building houses, tasting fine wines, gardening, talking to attractive women. *Address:* Department of Molecular Endocrinology, University College London Medical School, Mortimer Street, W1N 8AA. *T:* (020) 7679 9410; Pondweed Place, Friday Street, Surrey RH5 6JR.

EKSERDJIAN, David Patrick Martin, PhD; Editor, Apollo, since 1997; *b* 28 Oct. 1955; *s* of Nubar Martin Ekserdjian and Mabel Brown Ekserdjian (*née* Angus); *m* 1990, Susan Moore; one *s* one *d*. *Educ:* Westminster Sch.; Trinity Coll., Cambridge (BA Modern and Medieval Langs 1977); Courtauld Inst. of Art, Univ. of London (MA 1979; PhD 1988). Christie's Jun. Res. Fellow, Balliol Coll., Oxford, 1983–86; Lectr, Courtauld Inst. of Art, 1986–87; Slade Fellow, Corpus Christi Coll., Oxford, 1987–91; with Christie, Manson & Woods, 1991–97. Mem. Board, Courtauld Inst. of Art, 1998–. *Publications:* (introd. and notes) Vasari, Lives of the Artists, 1996; Correggio, 1997; *exhibition catalogues:* (with D. Mahon) Guercino Drawings, 1986; Old Master Paintings from the Thyssen-Bornemisza Collection, 1987; Mantegna, 1992; contrib. to Macmillan Dictionary of Art, Saurs Allgemeine Künstlerlexicon, etc. *Recreations:* wine, Real tennis, opera. *Address:* c/o Apollo, 1 Castle Lane, SW1E 6DR. *T:* (020) 7233 6640. *Clubs:* Beefsteak, Queen's.

ELAM, Caroline Mary; Editor, Burlington Magazine, since 1987; *b* 12 March 1945; *d* of John Frederick Elam and Joan Barrington Elam (*née* Lloyd). *Educ:* Colchester County High Sch.; Lady Margaret Hall, Oxford (BA); Courtauld Inst. of Art, Univ. of London. MA London and Cantab. Lectr, Fine Art Dept, Univ. of Glasgow, 1970–72; Jun. Res. Fellow, King's Coll., Cambridge, 1972–76 (Hon. Fellow, 1992); Lectr, History of Art Dept, Westfield Coll., Univ. of London, 1976–87. Fellow, Harvard Univ. Center for Renaissance Studies, Villa I Tatti, Florence, 1981–82. Member: Exec. Cttee, NACF, 1988–; Bd, Warburg Inst., 1992–97; Bd, Courtauld Inst. of Art, 1993–98. Syndic, Fitzwilliam Mus., Cambridge, 1993–. *Publications:* articles in Art History, Burlington Magazine, I Tatti Studies, Mitteilungen des Kunsthistorischen Insts in Florenz, Jl of RSA, etc. *Address:* Burlington Magazine, 14 Dukes Road, WC1H 9SZ. *T:* (020) 7388 8157.
See also J. N. Elam.

ELAM, (John) Nicholas, CMG 1994; HM Diplomatic Service, retired; *b* 2 July 1939; *s* of John Frederick Elam, OBE and Joan Barrington Elam (*née* Lloyd); *m* 1967, Florence Helen, *d* of P. Lentz; two *s* one *d*. *Educ:* Colchester Royal Grammar Sch.; New Coll., Oxford (schol.). Frank Knox Fellow, Harvard Univ., 1961–62. Entered HM Diplomatic Service, 1962; served: Pretoria and Cape Town, 1964–68; Bahrain, 1971; Brussels, 1972–76; FCO, 1976–79, Dep. Head of News Dept, 1978–79; Counsellor and Dep. British Govt Rep., Salisbury, 1979; Dep. High Comr, Salisbury (later Harare), 1980–83; Consul-General, Montreal, 1984–87; Hd of Cultural Relations Dept, FCO, 1987–94; Ambassador to Luxembourg, 1994–98. Chm., Cultural Co-operation Council, Council of Europe, 1993–94. Administrator, Caine Prize for African Writing, 1999–; Dir, Dance Umbrella, 1999–; Consultant, Serious Internat. Music Producers, 1999–; Trustee, Triangle Arts Trust, 1998–. Mem., British Council, 1994. *Recreations:* travel, the arts. *Address:* 86 Camberwell Church Street, SE5 8QZ. *Club:* Chelsea Arts.
See also C. M. Elam.

ELAND, Michael John; Commissioner and Director General, Business Services and Taxes, HM Customs and Excise, since 2000; *b* 26 Sept. 1952; *s* of George and Betty Eland; *m* 1981, Luned Rhiannon Wynn Jones; one *s* one *d*. *Educ:* Worksop Coll.; Trinity Coll., Oxford (BA Jurisp, MA). Called to the Bar, Middle Temple, 1975. Administration Trainee, HM Customs and Excise, 1975; Private Sec. to Chm., 1979–81; Cabinet Office, 1982–87; Private Sec. to Lord President of the Council (Viscount Whitelaw), 1987–88; Asst. Sec., 1988–92, Comr, 1992–97, HM Customs and Excise; Dep. Dir-Gen., Policy, Immigration and Nationality Directorate, Home Office, 1997–2000. *Recreations:* walking, theatre. *Address:* HM Customs and Excise, New King's Beam House, 22 Upper Ground, SE1 9PJ.

ElBARADEI, Dr Mohamed Mostafa; Director General, International Atomic Energy Agency, since 1997; *b* Egypt, 17 June 1942; *s* of Mostafa and Aida ElBaradei; *m* 1975, Aida ElKachef; one *s* one *d*. *Educ:* Cairo Univ. Sch. of Law (Licence en droit 1962; Dip. Advanced Studies, Admin. Law, 1964); NY Univ. Sch. of Law (LLM 1971; JSD Internat. Law 1974). Dept of Internat. Orgns, Min. of Foreign Affairs, Egypt, 1964–67; Perm. Mission of Egypt to UN, NY, 1967–71; Sen. Fellow, Center for Internat. Studies, NY Univ., 1973–74; Special Asst to Foreign Minister, Min. of Foreign Affairs, Egypt, 1974–78; Perm. Mission of Egypt to UN, Geneva, and Alternate Rep., Cttee on Disarmament, 1978–80; Sen. Fellow and Dir, Internat. Law and Orgns Prog., UN Inst. for Trng and Res., NY, 1980–84; International Atomic Energy Agency: Rep. of Dir Gen. to UN, NY, 1984–87; Dir, Legal Div. and Legal Advr, Vienna, 1987–91; Dir, Ext. Relns, Vienna, 1991–93; Asst Dir Gen. for Ext Relns, 1993–97. Adjunct Prof. of Internat. Law, NY Univ. Sch. of Law, 1981–87. Rep. of Egypt or IAEA, to UN Gen. Assembly, UN Security Council, Cttee on Disarmament, Rev. Confs of Treaty on Non-Proliferation of Nuclear Weapons, OAU, UNDP, ILO and WHO. Has lectured widely on internat. law and orgns, arms control and non-proliferation and peaceful uses of nuclear energy. *Publications:* The Right of Innocent Passage through Straits, 1974; (jtly) The International Law Commission: the need for a new direction, 1981; (jtly) Crowded Agendas, Crowded Rooms, 1981; Model Rules for Disaster Relief Operations, 1982; (jtly) The International Law of Nuclear Energy, 1993; contribs to NY Univ. Jl of Internat. Law and Politics, Leiden Jl of Internat. Law, etc. *Address:* International Atomic Energy Agency, Wagramerstrasse 5, PO Box 100, 1400 Vienna, Austria.

ELCOAT, Rev. Canon George Alastair; Vicar of Tweedmouth, Berwick-upon-Tweed, 1987–91 (Priest-in-charge, 1981–87); Chaplain to The Queen, 1982–92; Rural Dean of Norham, 1982–91; *b* 4 June 1922; *s* of George Thomas Elcoat and Hilda Gertrude Elcoat. *Educ:* Tynemouth School; Queen's College, Birmingham. Served RAF, 1941–46. Asst Master, Newcastle Cathedral Choir School, 1947–48. Deacon 1951, priest 1952; Asst Curate, Corbridge, 1951–55; Vicar: Spittal, 1955–62; Chatton with Chillingham, 1962–70; Sugley, 1970–81; RD, Newcastle West, 1977–81; Hon. Canon, Newcastle, 1979–91, Hon. Canon Emeritus, 1991–. *Recreations:* fell walking, photography, gardening, music. *Address:* 42 Windsor Crescent, Berwick-upon-Tweed, Northumberland TD15 1NT.

ELDER, Baron *cr* 1999 (Life Peer), of Kirkcaldy in Fife; **Thomas Murray Elder.** *Educ:* Kirkcaldy High Sch.; Edinburgh Univ.; Bank of England, 1972–80; Res. Asst to Shadow Trade and Industry Sec., 1980–84; Gen. Sec., Scottish Labour Party, 1988–92; Chief of Staff to Leader of Labour Party, 1992–94; Political Advr to Leader of Labour Party, 1994; Special Advr, Scottish Office, 1997–99. Contested (Lab) Ross, Cromarty & Skye, 1983. *Address:* House of Lords, SW1A 0PW.

ELDER, Dorothy-Grace; Member (SNP) Glasgow, Scottish Parliament, since 1999; *m* George Welsh; one *s* two *d.* Journalist; former columnist, Scotland on Sunday. Trustee, Yorkhill Children's Fund, Royal Hosp. for Sick Children, Glasgow. Former UK Journalist of the Year, UK Press Awards. *Address:* Scottish Parliament, Edinburgh EH99 1SP.

ELDER, Mark Philip, CBE 1989; conductor; Music Director, Hallé Orchestra, since 2000 (Music Director-Designate, 1999–2000); *b* 2 June 1947; *s* of John and late Helen Elder; *m* 1980, Amanda Jane Stein; one *d. Educ:* Bryanston Sch.; Corpus Christi Coll., Cambridge (Music Scholar, Choral Scholar; BA, MA). Music staff, Wexford Festival, 1969–70; Chorus Master and Asst Conductor, Glyndebourne, 1970–71; music staff, Covent Garden, 1970–72; Staff Conductor, Australian Opera, 1972–74; Staff Conductor, ENO, 1974, Associate Conductor, 1977, Music Dir, 1979–93; Music Dir, Rochester Philharmonic Orch., USA, 1989–94. Principal Guest Conductor: London Mozart Players, 1980–83; BBC Symphony Orchestra, 1982–85; CBSO, 1992–95. *Publication:* (with Peter Jonas and David Pountney) Power House, 1992. *Address:* c/o Ingpen and Williams Ltd, 26 Wadham Road, SW15 2LR.

ELDER, Prof. Murdoch George, MD, DSc; FRCS, FRCOG; Professor of Obstetrics and Gynaecology, University of London, at Institute of Obstetrics and Gynaecology, 1978–98, now Professor Emeritus, Imperial College School of Medicine; Chairman, Division of Paediatrics, Obstetrics and Gynaecology, Imperial College School of Medicine, 1996–98; *b* 4 Jan. 1938; *s* of late Archibald James and Lotta Annie Elder; *m* 1964, Margaret Adelaide McVicker; two *s. Educ:* Edinburgh Acad.; Edinburgh Univ. (MB ChB 1961, MD 1973). DSc London, 1994. FRCS 1968; FRCOG 1978. Junior posts, Edinburgh and Bristol, 1961–68; Lectr, Inst. of Obst. and Gyn. and Royal Univ. of Malta, 1968–71; Sen. Lectr and Reader, Charing Cross Hosp. Med. Sch., Univ. of London, 1971–78; Dean, Institute of Obstetrics and Gynaecology, RPMS, 1985–95. Green Armytage Scholarship, RCOG, 1976; WHO Travelling Scholarship, 1977; Dir, Clinical Res. Centre, WHO, 1980–94; Member: Steering Cttee on Contraception, WHO, 1980–86; WHO Scientific Ethics Res. Cttee, 1996–. Mem., Hammersmith and Queen Charlotte's Special Health Authy, 1982–90. Mem. Council, RPMS, 1979–97. Visiting Professor: UCLA, 1984 and 1997; Singapore Univ., 1987; Natal Univ., 1988. Ext Examr for DSc, PhD, Masters and MB, BS degrees of 19 univs in several countries. Silver Medal, Hellenic Obstetrical Soc., 1983; Bronze Medal, Helsinki Univ., 1996. Mem., Editl Bds, Jl of Obst. and Gyn. and Clinical Reproduction, 1985–. *Publications:* Human Fertility Control, 1979; (ed) Preterm Labour, 1980; (ed) Reproduction, Obstetrics and Gynaecology, 1988; Obstetrics and Gynaecology, 2001; Preterm Labour, 1997; chapters in books and learned articles on steroid and prostaglandin biochemistry in reproduction, clinical obstetrics, gynaecology and contraception. *Recreations:* travel, golf. *Address:* Easter Calzeat, Broughton, Biggar ML12 6HQ. *T:* (01899) 830359. *Clubs:* Roehampton; 1942.

ELDER, Air Vice-Marshal Ronald David, CBE 1991; Head of Personnel Licensing, Civil Aviation Authority, since 2000 (Head of General Aviation, 1999–2000); *b* 27 May 1946; *m* Sue; one *s* one *d. Educ:* RAF Coll., Cranwell. Commissioned RAF pilot, 1968; jun. appts and RAF Staff Coll., to 1981; Central Tactics and Trials Orgn, 1981–86; Comdr No 20 Sqdn, Laarbruch, 1986–88; Stn Comdr, Tri-National Tornado Trng Estabt, RAF Cottesmore, 1988–90; RAF Comdr, Tabuk, Saudi Arabia, 1990–91; RCDS 1991; Policy Area, Central Staff, MoD, 1991–93; Dir of Airspace Policy, CAA, 1993–98; RAF retd, 1999. FRAeS 1997. *Recreations:* Real tennis, golf, ski-ing. *Address:* Aviation House, Gatwick Airport South, West Sussex RH6 0YR. *Club:* Royal Air Force.

ELDERFIELD, Prof. Henry, PhD, ScD; FRS 2001; Professor of Ocean Geochemistry and Palaeochemistry, University of Cambridge, since 1999; Fellow, St Catharine's College, Cambridge, since 1984; *b* 25 April 1943; *s* of late Henry Elderfield and Rhoda May Elderfield (*née* Risbrough); *m* 1st, 1965, Brenda Pauline Holliday (marr. diss.); two *d*; 2nd, 1992, Marlene Wrankle. *Educ:* Sir Williams Turner's Sch., Coatham; Eston Grammar Sch.; Liverpool Univ. (BSc; PhD 1970); MA, ScD 1989, Cantab. Res. Fellow, Imperial Coll., London, 1968–69; Lectr, Univ. of Leeds, 1969–82; Asst Dir in Res., 1982–89, Reader, 1989–99, Univ. of Cambridge. Visiting Professor: Univ. of RI, 1977–78; MIT, 1988–89 (Fulbright Schol., 1988); Lady Davis Vis. Prof., Hebrew Univ., Jerusalem, 1992; Vis. Schol., Woods Hole Oceanographic Instn, 1982. Fellow: Geochem. Soc., 2000; Eur. Assoc. for Geochem., 2000; Amer. Geophysical Union, 2001; Hon. Fellow, Eur. Union of Geoscis, 2001. Prestwich Medal, Geol Soc., 1993; Plymouth Medal, 1998. *Publications:* numerous contribs to scientific jls. *Recreation:* walking. *Address:* Department of Earth Sciences, University of Cambridge, Downing Street, Cambridge CB2 3EQ. *T:* (01223) 333400; St Catharine's College, Cambridge CB2 1RL. *T:* (01223) 338300.

See also J. Elderfield.

ELDERFIELD, John, PhD; Chief Curator at Large, Museum of Modern Art, New York, since 1993; *b* 25 April 1943; *s* of late Henry Elderfield and of Rhoda May Elderfield (*née* Risbrough); *m* 1st, 1965, Joyce Davey (marr. diss.); two *s*; 2nd, 1989; Jill Elizabeth Moser (marr. diss.). *Educ:* Univ. of Manchester; Univ. of Leeds (BA 1966; MPhil 1970); Univ. of London (PhD 1975). Lectr in Hist. of Art, Winchester Sch. of Art, 1966–70; Harkness Fellow, Yale Univ., 1970–72; John Simon Guggenheim Meml Fellow, 1972–73; Lectr in Hist. of Art, Univ. of Leeds, 1973–75; Museum of Modern Art, New York: Curator of Painting and Sculpture, 1975–93; Dir, Dept of Drawings, 1980–93; Dep. Dir for Curatorial Affairs, 1996–99. Adjunct Prof. of Fine Arts, Inst. of Fine Arts, NY Univ., 1994. Editor, Studies in Modern Art, 1991–. Member, Board of Directors: Dedalus Foundn, NY, 1996–; Master Drawings Assoc., 2000–; Members Bd, Phillips Collection, Washington, 2000–. Chevalier des Arts et Lettres (France), 1989. *Publications:* Hugo Ball: the flight out of time, 1974, rev. edn 1996; The Wild Beasts: Fauvism and its affinities, 1976; European Master Paintings from Swiss Collections: Post Impressionism to World War II, 1976; The Cut-outs of Henri Matisse, 1978; Matisse in the Collection of the Museum of Modern Art, 1978; The Modern Drawing, 1983; The Drawings of Henri Matisse, 1984; Kurt Schwitters, 1985; Morris Louis, 1986; The Drawings of Richard Diebenkorn, 1988; Helen Frankenthaler, 1988; (jtly) Matisse in Morocco, 1990; Henri Matisse: a retrospective, 1992; Pleasuring Painting: Matisse's feminine representations, 1995; (jtly) Howard Hodgkin: paintings, 1995; The Language of the Body: drawings by Pierre-Paul Prud'hon, 1996; (jtly) The Art of Richard Diebenkorn, 1997; (jtly) Bonnard, 1998; (jtly) Modern Starts, 1999; (jtly) Bridget Riley: reconnaissance, 2001; (jtly) Matisse-Picasso, 2002. *Address:* Museum of Modern Art, 11 West 53 Street, New York, NY 10019–5498, USA. *T:* (212) 7089550. *Club:* Century (New York).

ELDERFIELD, Maurice; Chairman and Chief Executive, Berfield Associates Ltd, 1980–92; Chairman: Midland Industrial Leasing Ltd, 1979–90; Saga Ltd, 1979–90; Sheldon & Partners Ltd, 1981–91; *b* 10 April 1926; *s* of Henry Elderfield and Kathleen Maud Elderfield; *m* 1953, Audrey June (*née* Knight); one *s* three *d. Educ:* Southgate Grammar Sch. FCA. Fleet Air Arm, 1944–47. Thomson, Kingdom & Co., Chartered Accountants (qual. 1949), 1947–49; Personal Asst to Man. Dir, Forrestell, Land, Timber & Railway Co., 1949–57; Group Chief Accountant, Stephens Group, 1957–60; various posts, Segas, culminating in Board Mem. and Dir for Finance, 1960–73; Dir of Finance, Southern Water Authority, 1973–75; PO Board Mem. for Finance and Corporate Planning, 1975–76; Dir of Finance, Ferranti Ltd, 1977; Finance Mem., British Shipbuilders, 1977–80. Director: S. P. International Ltd, Hong Kong, 1987–90; PV Ltd, 1987–90. Chairman: Throgmorton Trust, 1972–84; Throgmorton Investment Management, 1981–84; Capital for Industry Ltd, 1980–84. *Recreations:* golf, tennis. *Address:* Hadleigh, Keeill Pharick Park, Glen Vine, Isle of Man IM4 4EW. *Club:* Gravetye Manor Country.

ELDON, 5th Earl of, *cr* 1821; **John Joseph Nicholas Scott;** Baron Eldon 1799; Viscount Encombe 1821; *b* 24 April 1937; *s* of 4th Earl of Eldon, GCVO, and Hon. Magdalen Fraser, OBE (*d* 1969), *d* of 16th Baron Lovat; *S* father, 1976; *m* 1961, Comtesse Claudine de Montjoye-Vaufrey et de la Roche, Vienna; one *s* two *d. Educ:* Ampleforth; Trinity Coll., Oxford. 2nd Lieut Scots Guards (National Service). Lieut AER. *Heir: s* Viscount Encombe, *qv.*

ELDON, David Gordon; Chairman, Hongkong and Shanghai Banking Corporation Ltd, since 1999; Director, HSBC Holdings plc, since 1999; *b* Inverness, 14 Oct. 1945; *s* of late Leslie Gordon Eldon and of Mary Forbes Eldon (*née* Smith); *m* 1975, Maria Margarita Gaus; two *s* one *d. Educ:* Duke of York's Royal Mil. Sch. Union Internat. Co., 1963–64; Commercial Banking Co. of Sydney, 1964–67; with British Bank of the Middle East, later HSBC Group, 1968–: Dist Manager, Mongkok, 1982–84; Dep. Man. Dir, Saudi British Bank, 1984–87; CEO, Malaysia, 1988–92; Exec. Dir, Internat., 1993–96; CEO, Hongkong and Shanghai Banking Corp., 1996–99. Chairman: Hang Seng Bank Ltd, 1996–; Swire Pacific Ltd, 1996; MTR Corp. Ltd, 1999–. FCIB 1986; FCIB (Hong Kong) 1995. JP 2000. *Recreations:* sports, music, reading, travel. *Address:* Hongkong and Shanghai Banking Corporation Ltd, 1 Queen's Road Central, Hong Kong. *T:* (852) 28221111. *Clubs:* Hong Kong, Hong Kong Jockey (Steward, 1996), China (Hong Kong).

ELDON, Stewart Graham, CMG 1999; OBE 1991; HM Diplomatic Service; Ambassador and Deputy Permanent Representative, UK Mission to the United Nations, New York, since 1998; *b* 18 Sept. 1953; *s* of John Hodgson Eldon and Rose Helen (*née* Stinton); *m* 1978, Christine Mary Mason; one *s* one *d. Educ:* Pocklington Sch.; Christ's Coll., Cambridge (BA Electrical Scis 1974; MSc 1976; MA 1977). AMIEE 1978. Joined HM Diplomatic Service, 1976: UK Mission to UN, NY, 1976; FCO, 1977; Third, later Second Sec., Bonn, 1978–82; First Sec., FCO, 1982; Private Sec. to Minister of State, 1983–86; First Sec., UK Mission to UN, NY, 1986–90; Asst Hd, ME Dept, FCO (also Dep. Crisis Manager, Gulf War), 1990–91; Counsellor, Eur. Secretariat, Cabinet Office, 1991–93; Fellow, Center for Internat. Affairs, Harvard Univ., 1993–94; Counsellor (Political), UK Delegn to NATO, Brussels, 1994–97; Dir (Confs), FCO, 1997–98. *Publications:* contrib. RIIA paper and to RIIA jl. *Recreations:* music, travel, science fiction, breaking computers. *Address:* c/o Foreign and Commonwealth Office, King Charles Street, SW1A 2AH. *Club:* Harvard (New York).

ELEY, Bridget Katharine C.; *see* Cracroft-Eley.

ELEY, Prof. Daniel Douglas, OBE 1961; ScD, PhD Cantab; MSc, PhD Manchester; FRS 1964; CChem, FRSC; Professor of Physical Chemistry, University of Nottingham, 1954–80, now Emeritus; Dean of Faculty of Pure Science, 1959–62; *b* 1 Oct. 1914; *s* of Daniel Eley and Fanny Allen Eley, *née* Ross; *m* 1942, Brenda May Williams, MA, MB, BChir (Cantab) (*d* 1992), 2nd *d* of Benjamin and Sarah Williams, Skewen, Glam; one *s. Educ:* Christ's Coll., Finchley; Manchester Univ.; St John's Coll., Cambridge. Manchester Univ.: Woodiwiss Schol. 1933, Mercer Schol. 1934, Darbishire Fellow 1936, DSIR Sen. Award 1937; PhD 1937; PhD 1940, ScD 1954, Cambridge. Bristol Univ.: Lectr in Colloid Chemistry, 1945; Reader in Biophysical Chemistry, 1951. Leverhulme Emeritus Fellow, 1981. Lectures: Reilly, Univ. of Notre Dame (USA), 1950; Royal Aust. Chem. Inst., 1967; Sir Jesse Boot Foundn, Nottingham Univ., 1955, 1981; Sir Eric Rideal, Soc. of Chem. Industry, 1975. Mem. Council of Faraday Soc., 1951–54, 1960–63; Vice-Pres., 1963–66. Corresp. Mem., Bavarian Acad. of Sciences, 1971. Meetings Sec., British Biophysical Soc., 1961–63, Hon. Sec., 1963–65, Hon. Mem., 1983. Scientific Assessor to Sub-Cttee on Coastal Pollutions, House of Commons Select Cttee on Science and Technology, 1967–68. Medal of Liège Univ., 1950. *Publications:* (ed) Adhesion, 1961; papers in Trans Faraday Soc., Proc. Royal Soc., Jl Chem. Soc., Biochem. Jl, etc. *Recreations:* hill walking, gardening, reading. *Address:* Brooklands, 35 Brookland Drive, Chilwell, Nottingham NG9 4BD; Chemistry Department, Nottingham University, University Park, Nottingham NG7 2RD.

ELFER, His Honour David Francis; QC 1981. a Circuit Judge, 1996–2000; *b* 15 July 1941; *s* of George and Joy Elfer; *m* 1968, Karin Ursula Strub; two *s*; *m* 1988, Alexandra Smith-Hughes; one *s. Educ:* St Bede's Coll., Manchester; Emmanuel Coll., Cambridge (MA). Called to the Bar, Inner Temple, 1964, Bencher, 1989; a Recorder, 1978–96. Bar Col rep. for W Circuit, 1987–89. *Recreation:* music. *Address:* c/o South Eastern Circuit Office, New Cavendish House, 18 Maltravers Street, WC2R 3EU.

ELGIN, 11th Earl of, *cr* 1633, **AND KINCARDINE**, 15th Earl of, *cr* 1647; **Andrew Douglas Alexander Thomas Bruce,** KT 1981; CD 1981; JP; Lord Bruce of Kinloss, 1604, Lord Bruce of Torry, 1647; Baron Elgin (UK), 1849; 37th Chief of the Name of Bruce; Lord-Lieutenant of Fife, 1987–99; late Scots Guards; Lieutenant, Royal Company of Archers, HM Body Guard for Scotland; Hon. Colonel, Elgin Regiment, Canada; *b* 17 Feb. 1924; *e s* of 10th Earl of Elgin, KT, CMG, TD and Hon. Katherine Elizabeth Cochrane (DBE 1938) (*d* 1989), *er d* of 1st Baron Cochrane of Cults; *S* father, 1968; *m* 1959, Victoria, *o d* of Dudley Usher, MBE and Mrs Usher of Larach Bhan, Kilchrennan, Argyll; three *s* two *d. Educ:* Eton; Balliol College, Oxford (BA Hons, MA Hons). Served War of 1939–45 (wounded). Dir, Royal Highland and Agricultural Soc., 1973–75; Pres., Scottish Amicable Life Assurance Soc., 1975–94. Chm., Nat. Savings Cttee for Scotland, 1972–78; Mem., Scottish Post Office Bd (formerly Scottish Postal Bd), 1980–96. Chm., Scottish Money Management Assoc., 1981–95. Lord High Comr, Gen. Assembly of Church of Scotland, 1980–81. Regent, RCSE, 1997–. County Cadet Commandant, Fife, 1952–65. Hon. Col, 153(H) Regt RCT(V), TAVR, 1976–86. JP 1951, DL 1955, Fife. Grand Master Mason of Scotland, 1961–65. Brigade Pres. of the Boys' Brigade, 1966–85; Pres., Royal Caledonian Curling Club, 1968–69. Hon. LLD: Dundee, 1977; Glasgow, 1983; Hon. DLitt St Mary's, Halifax, NS. Freeman: Bridgetown, Barbados; Regina; Port Elgin; Winnipeg; St Thomas, Ont; Moose Jaw. Order of Merit (Norway), 1994. *Heir: s* Lord Bruce, *qv. Address:* Broomhall, Dunfermline KY11 3DU. *T:* (01383) 872222, *Fax:* (01383) 872904; *e-mail:* lord.elgin@virgin.net. *Clubs:* Beefsteak, Caledonian, Pratt's; New (Edinburgh); Royal Scottish Automobile (Pres.) (Glasgow).

See also Hon. J. M. E. Bruce.

ELIAS, Gerard; QC 1984; a Recorder of the Crown Court, since 1984; *b* 19 Nov. 1944; *s* of late Leonard Elias and Patricia Elias, JP; *m* 1970, Elisabeth Kenyon; three *s*. *Educ:* Cardiff High School; Exeter University (LLB). Barrister; called to the Bar, Inner Temple, 1968, Bencher, 1993; Wales and Chester Circuit (Circuit Treasurer, 1990–92; Leader, 1993–95); Asst Comr, Boundary Commission for Wales, 1981–83, 1985–; Chancellor, dio. of Swansea and Brecon, 1999–. Mem., Bar Council, 1985–89, 1993–95; Dir, Bar Mutual Insurance Fund, 1987–97. Governor and Mem. Council, Malvern Coll., 1988–96. Mem. Governing Body, Ch in Wales, 2000–. Chairman: Disciplinary Cttee, ECB (formerly TCCB), 1996–; Glam CCC, 1998– (Mem. Exec. Cttee, 1986–93; Dep. Chm., 1993–98). *Recreations:* music, cricket. *Address:* 13 The Cathedral Green, Llandaff, Cardiff, South Glamorgan CF5 2EB. *T:* (029) 2057 8857. *Club:* Cardiff and County.
See also P. Elias.

ELIAS, Hon. Sir Patrick, Kt 1999; **Hon. Mr Justice Elias;** a Judge of the High Court, Queen's Bench Division, since 1999; *b* 28 March 1947; *s* of late Leonard and Patricia Mary Elias; *m* 1970, Wendy; three *s* one *d*. *Educ:* Cardiff High Sch.; Univ. of Exeter (LLB 1969); King's Coll., Cambridge (MA; PhD 1973). Called to the Bar, Inner Temple, 1973, Bencher, 1995; QC 1990. Fellow of Pembroke Coll., Cambridge, 1973–84; Lectr, Univ. of Cambridge, 1975–84. *Publications:* (jtly) Labour Law: cases and materials, 1979; Editor, Harvey on Industrial Relations and Employment Law, 1976; (with Keith Ewing) Trade Union Democracy, Members' Rights and the Law, 1987. *Recreations:* literature, music, sport. *Address:* Royal Courts of Justice, Strand, WC2A 2LL.
See also G. Elias.

ELIAS, Rt Hon. Dame Sian (Seerpoohi), GNZM 1999; PC 1999; Chief Justice of New Zealand, since 1999; *b* 12 March 1949; *m* 1970, Hugh Alasdair Fletcher, *qv*; two *s*. *Educ:* Diocesan High Sch. for Girls; Auckland Univ. (LLB Hons 1972); Stanford Univ., Calif (JSM 1972). Admitted to Bar of NZ, 1970; Tutor, Law Sch., Univ. of Auckland, 1970; part-time Barrister, 1975–81; in full-time practice as Barrister, 1981–95; QC 1988; Judge of the High Court of NZ, 1995–99. Mem., NZ Law Commn, 1985–89. Commemoration Medal (NZ), 1990. *Recreations:* chess, piano. *Address:* Chief Justice's Chambers, High Court, PO Box 1091, Wellington, New Zealand. *T:* (4) 9158139. *Clubs:* Northern (Auckland); Wellington (Wellington).

ELIASSEN, Kjell, Hon. GCMG 1981; Commander with Star, Royal Order of Saint Olav, 1982; Norwegian Ambassador to Germany, 1994–98; *b* 18 Aug. 1929; *s* of Carl August Eliassen and Bergljot (*née* Store); *m* 1953, Vesla Skretting; one *s* one *d*. *Educ:* Oslo Univ. (law degree). Entered Norwegian Foreign Service 1953; served Belgrade, Moscow, London; Counsellor, Min. of Foreign Affairs, 1963–67; Moscow, 1967–70; Dep. Dir-Gen., Min. of Foreign Affairs, 1970–72; Dir-Gen., 1972–77; Ambassador to Yugoslavia, 1977–80; Perm. Under-Sec., Min. of Foreign Affairs, 1980–84; Ambassador: to USA, 1984–89; to UK, 1989–94. Numerous foreign decorations. *Address:* Generallunden 21, 0382 Oslo, Norway.

ELIBANK, 14th Lord *cr* 1643 (Scotland); **Alan D'Ardis Erskine-Murray;** Bt (Nova Scotia) 1628; personnel consultant; Deminex UK Oil and Gas, 1981–86; *b* 31 Dec. 1923; *s* of Robert Alan Erskine-Murray (*d* 1939) and Eileen Mary (*d* 1970), *d* of late John Percy MacManus; *S* cousin, 1973; *m* 1962, Valerie Sylvia (*d* 1997), *d* of late Herbert William Dennis; two *s*. *Educ:* Bedford Sch.; Peterhouse, Cambridge (MA Law). Barrister-at-Law. RE, 1942–47; Cambridge Univ., 1947–49; Practising Barrister, 1949–55; Shell International Petroleum Co., 1955–80. *Recreations:* golf, tennis. *Heir: s* Master of Elibank, *qv*. *Clubs:* Carlton, MCC.

ELIBANK, Master of; Hon. Robert Francis Alan Erskine-Murray; *b* 10 Oct. 1964; *s* and *heir* of 14th Lord Elibank, *qv*; *m* 1996, Antonia, *yr d* of Roger Carrington; two *d*. *Educ:* The Grove, Harrow School; Reading Univ. (BA (Hons) History and Politics, 1987). *Recreations:* soccer, tennis and photography. *Address:* 15 Ouseley Road, SW12 8ED.

ELIOT, family name of **Earl of St Germans**.

ELIOT, Lord; Jago Nicholas Aldo Eliot; *b* 24 March 1966; *s* and *heir* of Earl of St Germans, *qv*.

ELIOT, Simon Flowerdew, MA; Headmaster, Sherborne School, since 2000; *b* 20 July 1952; *s* of late Geoffrey Philip Eliot and of Margery Hope Eliot-Sutton; *m* 1983, Olivia Margaret Cicely Roberts; one *s* one *d*. *Educ:* Radley Coll.; Queens' Coll., Cambridge (MA). Sedgwick Forbes (Marine), 1974–75; Asst Master, Radley Coll., 1975–76; Winchester College: Asst Master, 1976–2000; Housemaster, 1988–2000. *Recreations:* history, theatre, music, horse racing. *Address:* Abbey Grange, Hospital Road, Sherborne, Dorset DT9 3JF. *T:* (01935) 810410.

ELIOTT OF STOBS, Sir Charles (Joseph Alexander), 12th Bt *cr* 1666 (NS); *b* 9 Jan. 1937; *s* of Charles Rawdon Heathfield Eliott (*d* 1972) and Emma Elizabeth Harris; *S* cousin, 1989; *m* 1959, Wendy Judith, *d* of Henry John Bailey; one *s* four *d* (and one *s* decd). *Educ:* St Joseph's Christian Brothers' College, Rockhampton. *Heir: s* Rodney Gilbert Charles Eliott [*b* 15 July 1966; *m* 1988, Andrea Therese Saunders; one *s* one *d*]. *Address:* 27 Cohoe Street, Toowoomba, Queensland 4350, Australia.

ELIS-THOMAS, family name of **Baron Elis-Thomas**.

ELIS-THOMAS, Baron *cr* 1992 (Life Peer), of Nant Conwy in the County of Gwynedd; **Dafydd Elis Elis-Thomas;** Member (Plaid Cymru) Merionnydd Nant Conwy, and Presiding Officer, National Assembly for Wales, since 1999; *b* 18 Oct. 1946; name changed from Thomas to Elis-Thomas by deed poll, 1992; *m* 1st, 1970, Elen M. Williams (marr. diss.); three *s*; 2nd, 1993, Mair Parry Jones. *Educ:* Ysgol Dyffryn Conwy; UC North Wales. Research worker, Bd of Celtic Studies, 1970; Tutor in Welsh Studies, Coleg Harlech, 1971; Lectr, Dept of English, UC North Wales, 1974. MP (Plaid Cymru) Merioneth, Feb. 1974–1983, Merionnydd Nant Conwy, 1983–92. Pres., Plaid Cymru, 1984–91. Mem., Arts Council for Wales; Chairman: Welsh Lang. Bd, 1993–99; Screen Wales; a Gov., BFI, 1997–2000. Part-time freelance broadcaster, BBC Wales, HTV, 1970–73; has also broadcast on S4C and Radio Wales. *Recreations:* hill walking, camping. *Address:* National Assembly for Wales, Cardiff Bay, Cardiff CF99 1NA.

ELKAN, Prof. Walter; Professor of Economics, and Head of Economics Department, Brunel University, 1978–88, now Emeritus Professor; *b* Hamburg, 1 March 1923; *s* of Hans Septimus Elkan and Maud Emily (*née* Barden); *m* Susan Dorothea (*née* Jacobs) (marr. diss. 1982); one *s* two *d*. *Educ:* Frensham Heights; London Sch. of Economics. BSc (Econ), PhD. Army, 1942–47; Research Asst, LSE, 1950–53; Sen. Res. Fellow, E African Inst. of Social Research, 1954–58; Vis. Res. Assoc., MIT and Lectr, N Western Univ., 1958; Lectr in Econs, Makerere UC, 1958–60; Lectr in Econs, Durham Univ., 1960; Prof. of Econs, 1966–78, and rotating Head of Dept, 1968–78, Durham Univ. Vis. Res. Prof., Nairobi Univ., 1972–73. Member: Council, Overseas Develt Inst.; Econ. and Social Cttee, EEC, 1982–86; Bd of Management, Sch. of Hygiene and Trop. Med., 1982–86; Econ. and Social Cttee for Overseas Res., 1977–92; Associate, Inst. of Development Studies. Former Pres., African Studies Assoc.; former Member: Northern Economic Planning Council; REconS. Sometime consultant to Govts of Basutoland, Mauritius, Solomon Is, Fiji, Kenya and others. *Publications:* An African Labour Force, 1956; Migrants and Proletarians, 1960; Economic Development of Uganda, 1961; Introduction to Development Economics, 1973, 2nd edn 1995; articles mainly on contemp. African econ. history in econ. and other social science jls; ILO, UNESCO, IBRD and British Govt reports. *Recreation:* music. *Address:* 98 Boundary Road, NW8 0RH. *T:* (020) 7624 5102.

ELKES, Prof. Joel, MD, ChB; FACP, FAPA; psychiatrist and pharmacologist; Distinguished Service Professor Emeritus, The Johns Hopkins University, since 1975; Distinguished University Professor Emeritus, University of Louisville; Founding Fellow, 1989 and Senior Scholar-in-Residence, since 1993, Fetzer Institute, Kalamazoo; *b* 12 Nov. 1913; *s* of Dr Elchanan Elkes and Miriam (*née* Malbin); *m* 1943, Dr Charmian Bourne; one *d*; *m* 1975, Josephine Rhodes, MA. *Educ:* private schools; Lithuania and Switzerland; St Mary's Hosp., London; Univ. of Birmingham Med. Sch. (MB, ChB 1947; MD Hons 1949). MRCS, LRCP 1941. University of Birmingham: Sir Halley Stewart Research Fellow, 1942–45; Lectr, Dept of Pharmacology, 1945–48; Senior Lectr and Actg Head of Dept, 1948–50; Prof. and Chm., Dept of Experimental Psychiatry, 1951–57 (first dept of its kind in the world); Clinical Professor of Psychiatry, George Washington Univ. Med. Sch., Washington, 1957–63; Chief of Clinical Neuropharmacology Research Center, Nat. Inst of Mental Health, Washington, 1957–63; Dir, Behavioral and Clinical Studies Center St Elizabeth's Hosp., Washington, 1957–63; Henry Phipps Prof. and Dir, Dept of Psychiatry and Behavioural Scis, Johns Hopkins Univ. Sch. of Medicine, and Psychiatrist-in-Chief, Johns Hopkins Hosp., 1963–74; Samuel McLaughlin Prof.-in-residence, McMaster Univ., 1975; Professor of Psychiatry: McMaster Univ., 1976–80; Univ. of Louisville, 1980–84 (Director: Div. of Behavioral Medicine, 1982; Arts in Medicine Prog.). Dir, Foundns Fund for Research in Psychiatry, 1964–68; Consultant, WHO, 1957. Vis. Fellow, New York Univ. and New England Med. Center, Boston, 1950; Benjamin Franklin Fellow, RSA, 1974. Lectures: Harvey, 1962; Salmon, 1963; Jacob Bronowski Meml, 1978, etc. President: (first) Amer. Coll. of Neuropsychopharmacology, 1962; Amer. Psychopathological Assoc., 1968; Chairman: Bd, Israel Inst. of Psychobiol., 1961–; Foundns Fund Prize Bd for Res. in Psychiatry, 1977–81; Board Member: Inst. for Advancement of Health, 1982; Govs, Hebrew Univ. of Jerusalem; Govs, Haifa Univ. Formerly Member: Council, Internat. Collegium N Psychopharm; Central Council, Internat. Brain Research Organisation, UNESCO (Chm., Sub-Cttee on Educn); RSM. Life Fellow, Amer. Psych. Assoc.; Charter Fellow, RCPsych, GB; Fellow: Amer. Acad. of Arts and Scis; Amer. Coll. of Psychiatry; Amer. Coll. of Neuropsychopharmacol (Joel Elkes Internat. Award estab. 1986); Amer. Acad. of Behavioral Medicine Res. and Soc. of Behavioral Medicine; Fetzer Inst., 1990; Fellow and Mem. Exec. Cttee, World Acad. of Art and Sci., 1985; Former Member: Physiological Soc., GB; Pharmacological Soc., GB; Amer. Soc. for Pharmacology and Experimental Therapeutics; Sigma Xi; Scientific Assoc.; Acad. of Psychoanalysis. Hon. DPhil Hebrew Univ. of Jerusalem, 1989. Hans Selye Internat. Award, 1994; (jtly) First Internat. Pioneer Award in Psychopharmacology, Glasgow Congress, 1998; Lifetime-Achievement Award, Louisville Cathedral Heritage Foundn, 2000. Two internat. symposia in his honour, 1984, 1985; Joel Elkes Res. Labs, Dept of Psychiatry, Johns Hopkins Univ., dedicated 1989; Elkes Cottage, Fetzer Inst., dedicated 1998. *Publications:* papers to various jls and symposia. *Recreation:* painting. *Address:* Fetzer Institute, 9292 WKL Avenue, Kalamazoo, MI 49009, USA. *Club:* Cosmos (Washington).

ELKIN, Alexander, CMG 1976; international law consultant, retired; *b* St Petersburg, 2 Aug. 1909; *o c* of Boris and Anna Elkin; *m* 1937, Muriel Solomons, Dublin. *Educ:* Grunewald Gymnasium and Russian Academic Sch., Berlin; Univs of Berlin, Kiel and London. DrJur Kiel 1932, LLM London 1935. Called to the Bar, Middle Temple, 1937; practised at English Bar, 1937–39; BBC Monitoring Service, 1939–42; war-time govt service, 1942–45; Associate Chief, Legal Service, UN Interim Secretariat, London, 1945–46; Asst Dir, UN European Office, Geneva, 1946–48; Legal Adviser to UNSCOB, Salonica, 1948; Dep. Legal Adviser, later Legal Adviser, OEEC, then OECD, Paris, 1949–61; UNECA Legal Consultant, formation of African Develt Bank and Econ. Council for Africa, 1962–64; Actg Gen. Counsel of ADB, 1964–65; UNDP Legal Consultant, formation of Caribbean Develt Bank, 1967–68; Special Adviser on European Communities Law, FCO, 1970–79. Legal consultancies for: WHO, 1948; IBRD, 1966; W Afr. Regional Gp, 1968; OECD, 1975. Lectured: on Europ. payments system and OEEC/OECD activs, Univ. of the Saar, 1957–60, and Univ. Inst. of Europ. Studies, Turin, 1957–65; on drafting of treaties, UNITAR Seminars, The Hague, Geneva and NY, for legal advisers and diplomats, 1967–84; on language and law, Univ. of Bath, 1979–96; Univ. of Bradford, 1979–84. Hon. Vis. Prof., Bradford Univ., 1982–84. Mem., RIIA. Hon. LLD Bath, 1990. Ford Foundn Leadership Grant, 1960. *Publications:* contrib. European Yearbook, Jl du Droit Internat., Revue Générale de Droit Internat. Public, Survey of Internat. Affairs 1939–1946, Travaux pratiques de L'Institut de Droit Comparé de la Faculté de Droit de Paris, etc. *Recreations:* reading, visiting art collections, travel. *Address:* 70 Apsley House, Finchley Road, NW8 0NZ. *Club:* Travellers.

ELKIN, Sonia Irene Linda, OBE 1981 (MBE 1966); Director for Regions and Smaller Firms, Confederation of British Industry, 1985–92; *b* 15 May 1932; *d* of Godfrey Albert Elkin and Irene Jessamine Archibald. *Educ:* Beresford House Sch., Eastbourne. Association of British Chambers of Commerce, 1950–66; Lloyds Bank Overseas Dept, 1966–67; Confederation of British Industry, 1967–92. Commissioner, Manpower Services Commission, 1982–85. Non-executive Director: Greggs, 1992–; Kall Kwik Printing (UK), 1993–95. Mem. Review Cttee, ICAEW, 1997–. *Publications:* What about Europe?, 1967; What about Europe Now?, 1971. *Club:* Oxford and Cambridge (Lady Associate).

ELKINGTON, Prof. Andrew Robert, CBE 1996; FRCS; FRCOphth; Professor of Ophthalmology, University of Southampton, 1990–98, now Emeritus; Consultant Ophthalmic Surgeon, Southampton General Hospital, 1974–98; *b* 12 Dec. 1935; *s* of late Dr George Ernest Elkington, MC, FRCS, Newport, Salop and Kathleen Mary Elkington (*née* Budgen); *m* 1964, Patricia Kathleen Wright, *er d* of late R. M. Wright, MC and Bar and Joan Wright; four *s*. *Educ:* Repton Sch., Derbys; Clare Coll., Cambridge (MA); St Thomas' Hosp. (BChir, MB). FRCS 1969; FRCOphth 1988; DRCOG 1965; DO 1968. Moorfields Eye Hospital: Hse Surgeon and Sen. Resident Officer, 1967–70; Chief Clinical Asst, 1970–74; Sen. Registrar in Ophthalmol., Westminster Hosp., 1970–74. European Vis. Prof., RSocMed, 1992–93. Examnr, DO, 1977–83 (Chm., Examng Bd, 1981–83); Mem., Ct of Examnrs (Ophthalmol.), RCS, 1984–89 (Chm., 1988–89); Ext. Examnr, RCPSG (Ophthalmol.), 1984–89; Examnr in ophthalmol., Univs. of Glasgow, 1991, Leicester, 1992, Bristol, 1987, London, 1988, Nottingham, 1993; Examnr to Ophthalmic Nursing Bd, 1980–. Section of Ophthalmology, Royal Society of Medicine: Mem. Council, 1980–92; Hon. Sec., 1980–83; Vice Pres., 1983–86; Pres., 1990–92; Faculty of Ophthalmologists, subseq. Royal College of Ophthalmologists: Mem. Council, 1985–88; Hon. Sec., 1986–91; Vice-Pres., 1991–94; Pres., 1994–97; Ophthalmological Society of UK: Mem. Council, 1979–82; Vice Pres., 1987–88; Member: Council, RCS, 1994–96; GMC, 1994–98 (Mem., Educn Cttee, 1994–98). Chm., British Council for Prevention of Blindness, 2000–; Member: Council, Oxford Ophthalmol. Congress, 1982–98; Senate,

Royal Surgical Colls, 1994–96; Conf. and Scottish Conf. of Med. Royal Colls and their Faculties, 1994–96; Standing Med. Adv. Cttee, 1994–97. Govt of Hong Kong Commnd Trainer in ophthalmol., 1991. Mem., Bd of Govs, Moorfields Eye Hosp., 1988–94. *Publications:* (jtly) Clinical Optics, 1984, 3rd edn 1999; Ophthalmology for Nurses, 1986; ABC of Eyes, 1988, 3rd edn 1999; Aids to Ophthalmology, 1989; contribs on trauma, glaucoma and retinal detachment to ophthalmic jls. *Recreations:* wildlife, tending vegetables. *Club:* Travellers.

ELLACOMBE, Air Cdre John Lawrence Wemyss, CB 1970; DFC 1942 (Bar 1944); FBIM; *b* Livingstone, N Rhodesia, 28 Feb. 1920; *s* of Dr Gilbert H. W. Ellacombe; *m* 1951, Wing Officer Mary Hibbert, OBE, WRAF; one *s* two *d. Educ:* Diocesan Coll., Rondebosch, Cape. War of 1939–45: RAF, 1939; Fighter Comd and Two ATA Force, 1940–45 (Pilot, Battle of Britain). Aden, 1946–48; RAF Staff Coll., 1948–49; Fighter Command, 1949–57; BJSM, Washington, 1959. JSSC, 1959–60; Gp Captain, CO RAF Linton on Ouse, to Nov 1962; CFE, to Aug. 1965; Defence Operational Analysis Estabt, West Byfleet, 1965–68; Air Cdre, Commander Air Forces Gulf, 1968–70; Dir of Ops (Air Defence and Overseas), MoD (Air), 1970–73; St Thomas' Hospital: Dir, Scientific Services, 1973–80; Administrator to Special Trustees, 1980–85. *Recreations:* photography, golf, cricket. *Address:* 33 The Drive, Northwood, Middlesex HA6 1HW. *Club:* Royal Air Force.

ELLEN, Eric Frank, QPM 1980; LLB; Chairman and Director, First Approach Ltd, since 1999; Board Member, International Chamber of Commerce Commercial Crime Services, 1999 (Executive Director, 1994–99; First Director: International Maritime Bureau, 1981–99; Counterfeiting Intelligence Bureau, 1985–99; Commercial Crime Bureau, 1992–99; Regional Piracy Centre, Kuala Lumpur, 1992–99); Consultant, ICC, since 1999; *b* London, 30 Aug. 1930; *s* of late Robert Frank Ellen and of Jane Lydia Ellen; *m* 1949, Gwendoline Dorothy Perkins; one *s* one *d. Educ:* Wakefield Central Sch., East Ham; Holborn Coll. of Law, Univ. of London (LLB Hons, London Univ. Certificate in Criminology). CIMgt (FBIM 1978). Joined PLA Police, 1951; Sgt 1956; Inspector 1961; Chief Insp. 1972; Supt and Chief Supt 1973; attended 11th Sen. Comd Course, Bramshill Police Coll., 1974; Dep. Chief Constable 1975; Chief Constable, 1975–80. Adviser on security to Ports Div. of Dept of Environment; advised Barbados Govt on formation of Barbados Port Authy Police Force, 1983; reviewed port security at Jeddah and Dammam. Sec., Internat. Assoc. of Airport and Seaport Police, 1980–88 (Pres., 1977–78 and 1978–79); Founder, Chm. and Life Mem., EEC Assoc. of Airport and Seaport Police, 1975–78; Chm., Panel on Maritime Fraud, Commonwealth Secretariat, 1982–90; Consultant, Commercial Crime Unit. Member: Internat. Assoc. of Ports and Harbours Standing Cttee on Legal Protection of Port Interests, 1977–79 (Chm., Sub-Cttee on Protection of Ports against Sabotage and Terrorism, 1977–79); Cttee of Conservative Lawyers, 1985–; Shipbrokers Cttee on Maritime Fraud; British Acad. of Forensic Sciences; Hon. Soc. of Middle Temple. Police Long Service and Good Conduct Medal, 1974. Freeman of the City of London, 1978. Police Medal Republic of China, 1979. *Publications:* (co-author) International Maritime Fraud, 1981; (ed) Violence at Sea, 2nd edn, 1987; (ed) Piracy at Sea, 1989; (ed) Ports at Risk, 1993; (ed) Shipping at Risk: the rising tide of organised crime, 1998; A Guide to the Prevention of Money Laundering, 1998; professional articles on marine fraud and counterfeiting, terrorism, piracy and port policing, money laundering and fraud in commerce (has lectured on these topics at seminars in over 50 countries). *Recreations:* golf, swimming. *Address:* 38 Tyle Green, Hornchurch, Essex RM11 2TB. *Club:* Wig and Pen.

ELLEN, Patricia Mae Hayward; *see* Lavers, P. M.

ELLEN, Susan Caroline; Managing Director, United Racecourses (Holdings) Ltd, since 1996; *b* 15 Dec. 1948; *d* of late Albert John Davies and of (Winnifred) Ivy (Caroline) (*née* Emberton); *m* 1974, Simon Tudor Ellen; two *d. Educ:* Cardiff High Sch.; Malvern Girls' Coll.; Bristol Univ. (BSc Politics and Sociol.); Dip HSM. With NHS, 1970–77; joined BUPA, 1977: Dir, 1990–95; Man. Dir, BUPA Health Services, 1990–95. Non-executive Director: Asda Gp plc, 1992–98; Birmingham Midshires Building Soc., 1996–2000. Member: Financial Reporting Rev. Panel, 1992–98; Financial Reporting Council, 1995–96. *Recreations:* family, racing, the arts. *Address:* Sandown Park Racecourse, Portsmouth Road, Esher, Surrey KT10 9AJ. *T:* (01372) 463072.

ELLENBOROUGH, 8th Baron *cr* 1802; **Richard Edward Cecil Law;** Director: Towry Law & Co., 1958–96; Towry Law Group, 1958–96; *b* 14 Jan. 1926; *s* of 7th Baron and Helen Dorothy, *o d* of late H. W. Lovatt; *S* father, 1945; *m* 1st, 1953, Rachel Mary (*d* 1986), *o d* of late Major Ivor Hedley; three *s*; 2nd, 1994, Mrs Frances Kimberley. *Educ:* Eton Coll.; Magdalene Coll., Cambridge. Partner, McAnally Montgomery, stockbrokers, 1969–78. Pres., Nat. Union of Ratepayers' Associations, 1960–90. *Heir: s* Major the Hon. Rupert Edward Henry Law, Coldstream Guards, retd [*b* 28 March 1955; *m* 1981, Hon. Grania, *d* of Baron Boardman, *qv*; two *s* one *d*]. *Address:* Withypool House, Observatory Close, Church Road, Crowborough, East Sussex TN6 1BN. *T:* (01892) 663139. *Club:* Turf.

ELLERAY, Anthony John; QC 1993; a Recorder, since 1999; *b* 19 Aug. 1954; *s* of late Alexander John Elleray and of Sheila Mary Elleray (*née* Perkins); *m* 1982, Alison Elizabeth Potter; one *s* one *d. Educ:* Bishop's Stortford Coll.; Trinity Coll., Cambridge (MA). Called to the Bar, Inner Temple, 1977. *Recreations:* pictures, garden, wine. *Address:* 4 Ralli Courts, West Riverside, Manchester M3 5FT. *T:* (0161) 833 2722. *Club:* Manchester Tennis and Racquets.

ELLERTON, Sir Geoffrey (James), Kt 1992; CMG 1963; MBE 1956; Chairman, Local Government Boundary Commission for England, 1983–92; *b* 25 April 1920; *er s* of late Sir Cecil Ellerton; *m* 1946, Peggy Eleanor, *d* of late F. G. Watson; three *s. Educ:* Highgate Sch.; Hertford Coll., Oxford (MA). Military Service, 1940–45. Apptd Colonial Administrative Service as District Officer, Kenya, 1945. Acted as Minister for Internal Security and Defence, 1960 and 1962. Retired as Permanent Sec., Prime Minister's Office and Sec. to the Cabinet, at time of Kenya's Independence, Dec. 1963. Sec. to the Maud and Mallaby Cttees on Management and Staffing in Local Government, 1964. Joined Elder Dempster Lines, 1965, Chm., 1972–74; an Exec. Dir, Ocean Transport & Trading Ltd, 1972–80; Dir, Overseas Containers Ltd, 1975–80; Chm., Globe Management Ltd, 1981–83; Dir, Globe Investment Trust PLC, 1983–86. Mem. Council, Liverpool Univ., 1974–78; a Vice-Pres., Liverpool Sch. of Tropical Medicine, 1978–87. Hakluyt Society: Mem. Council, 1984–86; Hon. Treas., 1986–94; Trustee, 1994–. Chm., Central Council, Royal Over-Seas League, 1995–2000. *Recreations:* opera, books. *Address:* Briar Hill House, Broad Campden, Chipping Campden, Glos GL55 6XB. *T:* (01386) 841003. *Clubs:* Brooks's, Royal Over-Seas League, MCC.

ELLES, family name of **Baroness Elles**.

ELLES, Baroness *cr* 1972 (Life Peer), of the City of Westminster; **Diana Louie Elles;** *b* 19 July 1921; *d* of Col Stewart Francis Newcombe, DSO and Elisabeth Chaki; *m* 1945, Neil Patrick Moncrieff Elles, *qv*; one *s* one *d. Educ:* private Schs, England, France and Italy; London University (BA Hons). Served WAAF, 1941–45. Barrister-at-law. Care Cttee worker in S London, 1956–72. UK Delegn to UN Gen. Assembly, 1972; Mem., UN Sub-Commn on Prevention of Discrimination and Protection of Minorities, 1973–75; UN special rapporteur on Human Rights, 1973–75; Mem., British delegn to European Parlt, 1973–75. Mem., Cripps Cttee on legal discrimination against women; Chm., Sub-cttee of Women's Nat. Adv. Cttee (Conservative Party) on one-parent families (report publ. as Unhappy Families); Internat. Chm., European Union of Women, 1973–79; Chm., Cons. Party Internat. Office, 1973–78; Opposition front bench spokesman on foreign and Eur. affairs, H of L, 1975–79; Mem., H of L Europ. Communities Select Cttee, 1989–94 (Chm., Law and Institutions Sub-Cttee, 1992); Mem, 1996 IGC Sub-Cttee, 1995. European Parliament: MEP (C) Thames Valley, 1979–89; EDG spokesman on NI, 1980–87; Vice-Pres., 1982–87; Chm., Legal Affairs Cttee, 1987–89. Vice-Pres., UK Assoc. of European Lawyers, 1985–. Of Counsel, Van Bael and Bellis, Brussels, 1989–. Mem. Council, Caldecott Community, 1990–97; Mem. Res. Council, Europ. Univ. Inst., Florence, 1986–95; Trustee: Cumberland Lodge, 1982–96; Industry and Parlt Trust, 1985–96; Chm. Bd of Govs, British Inst., Florence, 1996 (Gov., 1986–96, Vice Chm., Bd of Govs, 1994–96, Life Gov., 1997); Gov., Reading Univ., 1986–96. Hon. Bencher, Lincoln's Inn, 1993. *Publications:* The Housewife and the Common Market (pamphlet), 1971; Human Rights of Aliens, 1980; articles, etc. *Address:* 75 Ashley Gardens, SW1P 1HG; Villa Fontana, Ponte del Giglio, Lucca, Italy.

ELLES, James Edmund Moncrieff; Member (C) South East Region, England, European Parliament, since 1999 (Oxford and Buckinghamshire, 1984–94; Buckinghamshire and Oxfordshire East, 1994–99); *b* 3 Sept. 1949; *s* of N. P. M. Elles, *qv* and Baroness Elles, *qv*; *m* 1977, Françoise Le Bail (marr. diss. 1997); one *s* one *d. Educ:* Ashdown House; Eton College; Edinburgh University. External Relations Div., EEC, 1976–80; Asst to Dep. Dir Gen. of Agriculture, EEC, 1980–84. EPP spokesman on the Budget, 1994–99; Vice-Pres., EPP-ED Gp, 1999–; Substitute Mem., Foreign Affairs Cttee and Budgetary Control Cttee, European Parlt. Founder, Transatlantic Policy Network. Co-founder, European Internet Foundn. Co-founder, EU Baroque Orch. *Address:* c/o European Parliament, Rue Wiertz, 1047 Brussels, Belgium. *T:* (2) 2845951, *Fax:* (2) 2849951; *e-mail:* jelles@europarl.eu.int. *Clubs:* Carlton; Royal and Ancient Golf (St Andrews).

ELLES, Neil Patrick Moncrieff; Chairman, Value Added Tax Appeals Tribunal, 1972–92; *b* 8 July 1919; *s* of Edmund Hardie Elles, OBE and Ina Katharine Hilda Skene; *m* 1945, Diana Louie Newcombe (*see* Baroness Elles); one *s* one *d. Educ:* Eton; Christ Church, Oxford (MA). War Service, RAF, 1939–45. Called to the Bar, Inner Temple, 1947; Sec., Inns of Court Conservative and Unionist Taxation Cttee, 1957–71; Mem., Special Study Gp, Commn on Law of Competition, Brussels, 1962–67. *Publications:* The Law of Restrictive Trade Practices and Monopolies (with Lord Wilberforce and Alan Campbell), 1966; Community Law through the Cases, 1973. *Recreations:* fishing, listening to music, the cultivation of vines. *Address:* 75 Ashley Gardens, SW1P 1HG. *T:* (020) 7828 0175; Villa Fontana, Ponte del Giglio, Lucca, Italy. *Clubs:* Flyfishers', MCC.

ELLETSON, Harold Daniel Hope; *b* 8 Dec. 1960; *m* 1987, Fiona Margaret Ferguson; one *s. Educ:* Eton Coll.; Exeter Univ.; Voronezh Univ., USSR; Poly. of Central London; Bradford Univ. Mem. (C) Lancashire CC, 1984–88; worked in journalism and public affairs, 1984–88; CBI and Illingworth Morris plc, 1988–90; consultant to cos trading in Eastern Europe, 1990–. Contested (C) Burnley, 1987. MP (C) Blackpool North, 1992–97; contested (C) Blackpool North and Fleetwood, 1997. *Publication:* The General Against the Kremlin—Alexander Lebed: power and illusion, 1998.

ELLINGTON, Prof. Charles Porter, PhD; FRS 1998; Professor of Animal Mechanics, University of Cambridge, since 1999; Fellow of Downing College, Cambridge, since 1979; *b* 31 Dec. 1952; *s* of Dr Charles Porter Ellington and Margaret Moselle Ellington; *m* 1977, Dr Stephanie Katharine Lindsay Buckley; two *s. Educ:* Duke Univ. (BA 1973); Downing Coll., Cambridge (MA 1979; PhD 1982). Cambridge University: Demonstrator and Lectr in Zoology, 1979–97; Reader in Animal Mechanics, 1997–99. Editor, Jl of Experimental Biology, 1990–94. Scientific Medal, Zoological Soc., 1990. *Publications:* (ed with T. J. Pedley) Biological Fluid Dynamics, 1995; (ed with J. D. Altringham) Designs for Life: the science of biomechanics, 1999; papers on mechanics and physiology of insect flight. *Recreations:* gardening, wood- and metal-working. *Address:* Department of Zoology, University of Cambridge, Downing Street, Cambridge CB2 3EJ. *T:* (01223) 336668, 336600.

ELLINGWORTH, Richard Henry; HM Diplomatic Service, retired; *b* 9 March 1926; *e s* of Vincent Ellingworth and Dora Ellingworth (*née* Church); *m* 1952, Joan Mary, *e d* of Sir Percival Waterfield, KBE, CB and Lady Waterfield; one *s* three *d. Educ:* Uppingham; Aberdeen Univ.; Magdalen Coll., Oxford (Demy); Exeter Univ. (certificates in French, 1989, Theology, 1991, and Russian, 1993). Served War of 1939–45: RA, and Intelligence Corps, 1944–47. Oxford, 1947–50 (first Lit. Hum.); HM Embassy, Japan, 1951–55; FO, 1955–59; HM Embassy: Belgrade, 1959–63; Japan, 1963–68 (Olympic Attaché, 1964); Head of Oil Dept., FCO, 1969–71; Research Associate, Internat. Inst. for Strategic Studies, 1971–72; Counsellor, Tehran, 1972–75; seconded to Dept of Energy, 1975–77. Course Dir (European Training), Civil Service Coll., 1978–83. Mem., Farningham Parish Council, 1979–83; pt-time Agent, Sevenoaks Liberal Assoc., 1983–84; Hon. Organiser, Farningham, Royal British Legion, 1982–87. *Publications:* (with A. N. Gilkes) An Anthology of Oratory, 1946; Japanese Economic Policy and Security, 1972. *Recreations:* gardening, music. *Address:* 29 Carlton Mews, Wells BA5 1SG. *Club:* National Liberal.

See also Sir J. C. King, Bt.

ELLIOT; *see* Elliot-Murray-Kynynmound, family name of Earl of Minto.

ELLIOT, Aydua Helen S.; *see* Scott-Elliot.

ELLIOT, Sir Gerald (Henry), Kt 1986; FRSE; Chairman, Christian Salvesen plc, 1981–88; *b* 24 Dec. 1923; *s* of late Surg. Captain J. S. Elliot, RN, and Magda Salvesen; *m* 1950, Margaret Ruth Whale (MBE 1993), *d* of Rev. J. S. Whale; two *s* one *d. Educ:* Marlborough Coll.; New Coll., Oxford (BA PPE 1948). FRSE 1978. Captain FF Rifles, Indian Army, 1942–46. Christian Salvesen Ltd, 1948–88, Dep. Chm. and Man. Dir, 1973–81. Dir, Scottish Provident Instn, 1971–89, Chm., 1983–89; Chairman: Chambers and Fargus, 1975–79; Scottish Br., RIIA, 1973–77 (Sec., 1963–73); FAO Fishery Industries Develt Gp, 1971–76; Forth Ports Authority, 1973–79; Scottish Arts Council, 1980–86. Chairman: Scottish Unit Managers Ltd, 1984–88; Martin Currie Unit Trusts, 1988–90; Biotal, 1987–90. Sec., National Whaling Bd, 1953–62; Mem., Nat. Ports Council, 1978–81. Chm., Scottish Div., Inst. of Dirs, 1989–92; Vice-Chm., Scottish Business in the Community, 1987–89. Chairman: Prince's Scottish Youth Business Trust, 1987–94; Scottish Opera, 1987–92 (Vice-Pres., 1994–99). A Vice-Pres., RSE, 1988–91. Pres., UN 50 Scotland, 1993–95. Trustee: David Hume Inst., 1985–98 (Chm., 1985–95); Nat. Museums of Scotland, 1987–91; The Prince's Trust, 1992–94; Edinburgh Fest. Th., 1995–98; Pres., Edinburgh Univ. Develt Trust, 1990–94. Member Court: Edinburgh Univ., 1984–93; Regents, RCSE, 1990–99. Dr *hc* Edinburgh, 1989; Hon. LLD Aberdeen, 1991. Consul for Finland in Edinburgh, 1957–89; Dean, Consular Corps in Edinburgh-

Leith, 1986–88. Kt 1st Cl., Order of White Rose of Finland, 1975. *Publications:* A Whaling Enterprise, 1998; papers on control of whaling and fishing, arts administration and economic management. *Address:* 39 Inverleith Place, Edinburgh EH3 5QD. *T:* (0131) 552 3005.

ELLIOT, Prof. Harry, CBE 1976; FRS 1973; Emeritus Professor of Physics, University of London; Professor of Physics at Imperial College, London, 1960–80 (Assistant Director of Physics Department, 1963–71); *b* 28 June 1920; *s* of Thomas Elliot and Hannah Elizabeth (*née* Littleton), Weary Hall, Cumberland; *m* 1943, Betty Leyman; one *s* one *d*. *Educ:* Nelson Sch., Wigton; Manchester Univ. MSc, PhD. Served War, Signals Branch, RAF, incl. liaison duties with USAAF and USN, 1941–46. Manchester University: Asst Lectr in Physics, 1948–49; Lectr in Physics, 1949–54; Imperial College, London: Lectr in Physics, 1954–56; Sen. Lectr in Physics, 1956–57; Reader in Physics, 1957–60; Sen. Res. Fellow, 1982–87. Member: Science Research Council, 1971–77 (Chm., Astronomy, Space and Radio Bd, 1974–77); Council, Royal Soc., 1978–79; Science Adv. Cttee, ESA, 1979–80 (Chm., 1980–81). Hon. Prof., Universitad Mayor de San Andres, 1957; Hon. ARCS, 1965. Fellow, World Acad. of Arts and Scis, 1978. Holweck Prize and Medal, Inst. of Physics and Société Française de Physique, 1976. *Publications:* papers on cosmic rays, solar physics and magnetospheric physics in scientific jls; contrib. scientific reviews and magazine articles. *Recreation:* painting. *Address:* Rosan, Broadwater Down, Tunbridge Wells, Kent TN2 5PE.

ELLIOT, Iain Fleming, OBE 2000; PhD; Director, East-West Insight, since 2000; *b* 24 May 1943; *s* of John Darling Elliot and Isabel Elliot (*née* MacLean); *m* 1970, Dr Elisabeth Mary Robson; one *s* one *d*. *Educ:* Univ. of Glasgow (MA); Univ. of Sussex (MA); Univ. of Bradford (PhD 1974). Res. student, Univ. of Leningrad, 1967–68; res. asst and Lectr, Univ. of Bradford, 1969–70; Sen. Lectr, Univ. of Brighton, 1971–88; leader writer and specialist on Soviet affairs, The Times, 1982–86; Associate Dir, with responsibility for Russian broadcasting, Radio Liberty; Chief Ed. and Dir, analytic research, RFE/RL Research Inst., Munich, 1987–93; Dir, Britain-Russia Centre, and British East-West Centre, 1993–2000. Ed., Soviet Analyst, 1972–88. *Publications:* The Soviet Energy Balance, 1974; (ed jtly) Demise of the USSR, 1995; contrib. books, jls and newspapers on Soviet and Russian affairs. *Address:* 42 Preston Park Avenue, Brighton, Sussex BN1 6HG. *T:* (01273) 556156. *Club:* Athenæum.

ELLIOT, (Robert) John, WS; Deputy Keeper of HM Signet, since 1999; Chairman, Lindsays WS, Edinburgh, since 1994; *b* 18 Jan. 1947; *s* of Robert Thomas Elliot and Barbara Elliot; *m* 1971, Christine Anne Glencross; one *s* one *d*. *Educ:* Craigflower Prep. Sch., Dunfermline; Loretto Sch., Musselburgh; Edinburgh Univ. (LLB). WS 1971; Admitted solicitor, 1971; with Lindsays WS, Edinburgh, 1969–: Partner, 1973–; Man. Partner, 1988–94. Pres., Law Soc. of Scotland, 1997–98 (Mem. Council, 1990–99). Chm. Scottish Cttee, Council on Tribunals, 1998–. *Recreations:* golf, politics, argument, wine, literature. *Address:* 11 Atholl Crescent, Edinburgh EH3 8HE. *T:* (0131) 477 8700.

ELLIOT, Virginia Helen Antoinette, MBE 1986; trainer of National Hunt jockeys and horses; former equestrian event rider; *b* 1 Feb. 1955; *d* of late Col Ronald Morris Holgate, RM and of Heather Holgate; *m* 1st, 1985, Hamish Julian Peter Leng (marr. diss. 1989), *s* of Gen. Sir Peter Leng, *qv*; 2nd, 1993, Michael Elliot. *Educ:* Bedgebury Park, Goudhurst, Kent. Three day event equestrian team trainer, 1996 Olympic Games. Three day event wins: Junior European Champion, 1973 (Dubonnet); Mini Olympics, 1975 (Jason); Burghley, 1983 (Priceless), 1984 (Nightcap), 1985 (Priceless), 1986 (Murphy Himself), 1989 (Master Craftsman); Badminton, 1985 (Priceless), 1989 (Master Craftsman), 1993 (Houdini); European Championship, 1985 (Priceless), 1987 (Nightcap), 1989 (Master Craftsman); World Championship, 1986 (Priceless); Team Silver Olympic Medal, 1984 and 1988; Bronze Individual Olympic Medal, 1984 (Priceless), and 1988 (Master Craftsman). *Publications:* (with Genevieve Murphy) Ginny, 1986; (with Nancy Roberts) Priceless, 1987; (with Genevieve Murphy) Ginny and Her Horses, 1987; (with Genevieve Murphy) Training the Event Horse, 1990; High Hurdle, 1997; *novels:* Winning, 1995; Race against Time, 1996. *Recreations:* ski-ing, cooking, art, theatre. *Address:* Holliers, Middle Barton, Oxon OX5 3QH.

ELLIOT-MURRAY-KYNYNMOUND, family name of **Earl of Minto**.

ELLIOTT, family name of **Baron Elliott of Morpeth**.

ELLIOTT OF MORPETH, Baron *cr* 1985 (Life Peer), of Morpeth in the County of Northumberland and of the City of Newcastle-upon-Tyne; **Robert William Elliott,** Kt 1974; DL; Vice-Chairman, Conservative Party Organisation, 1970–74; *b* 11 Dec. 1920; *s* of Richard Elliott; *m* 1956, Jane Morpeth; one *s* four *d* (of whom two are twin *d*). *Educ:* Morpeth Grammar Sch. Farmer, 1939–, at Low Heighley, Morpeth, Northumberland. MP (C) Newcastle-upon-Tyne North, March 1957–1983; Parliamentary Private Secretary: to joint Parliamentary Secs, Ministry of Transport and Civil Aviation, April 1958–Oct. 1959; to Under-Sec., Home Office, Nov. 1959–60; to Minister of State, Home Office, Nov. 1960–61; to Sec. for Technical Co-operation, 1961–63; Asst Govt Whip (unpaid), 1963–64; Opposition Whip, 1964–70; Comptroller of the Household, June-Sept. 1970. Chm., Select Cttee on Agric., Fisheries and Food, 1980–83. DL Northumberland, 1985. *Address:* Crown House, Kings Cliffe, Peterborough PE8 6XQ. *T:* (01780) 470888. *Clubs:* Carlton; Northern Counties (Newcastle upon Tyne).

ELLIOTT, Hon. Lord; Walter Archibald Elliott, MC 1943; Chairman, Scottish Land Court, 1978–92; President, Lands Tribunal for Scotland, 1971–92; *b* 6 Sept. 1922; 2nd *s* of late Prof. T. R. Elliott, CBE, DSO, FRS, Broughton Place, Broughton, Peeblesshire; *m* 1954, Susan Isobel Mackenzie Ross, Kaimend, North Berwick; two *s*. *Educ:* Eton; Trinity Coll., Cambridge; Edinburgh Univ. Active service in Italy and North West Europe with 2nd Bn Scots Guards, 1943–45 (MC); demobilised, Staff Capt., 1947. Barrister-at-law, Inner Temple, 1950; Advocate at Scottish Bar, 1950; QC (Scotland) 1963. Chm., Med. Appeal Tribunals, 1971–78. Ensign, Royal Company of Archers (Queen's Body Guard for Scotland). *Publications:* Us and Them: a study of group consciousness, 1986; Esprit de Corps, 1996. *Recreations:* gardening, travelling. *Address:* Morton House, Fairmilehead, Edinburgh EH10 7AW. *T:* (0131) 445 2548. *Clubs:* New, Arts (Edinburgh).

ELLIOTT, Anthony Michael Manton, (Tony Elliott); Founder, 1968 and Chairman, Time Out Group; *b* 7 Jan. 1947; *s* of late Katherine and Alan Elliott; *m* 1st, 1976, Janet Street-Porter, *qv* (marr. diss. 1978); 2nd, 1989, Jane L. Coke; three *s* (incl. twins). *Educ:* Stowe; Keele Univ. Time Out Group publishing activities include: Time Out London; i-D; Modern Painters; Time Out New York; Time Out Paris; timeout.com; annual guides. Time Out Trust formed 1989. Director: Roundhouse Trust, 1998–; Somerset House Trust, 1999–; Photographers' Gall., 1999–; Soho Th. Co., 2000–. Gov., BFI, 1997– (Chm., Production Bd, 1998–2000). *Recreations:* travel, watching television, cinema going, eating out with friends, reading newspapers and magazines, being with family. *Address:* Time Out Group, Universal House, 251 Tottenham Court Road, W1P 0AB. *T:* (020) 7813 3000, *Fax:* (020) 7813 6001.

ELLIOTT, Brent; *see* Elliott, W. B.

ELLIOTT, Rev. Dr Charles Middleton; Fellow, Dean and Chaplain of Trinity Hall, since 1990, Affiliated Lecturer in Theology, since 1991, in Social and Political Sciences, since 1993, University of Cambridge; *b* 9 Jan. 1939; *s* of Joseph William Elliott and Mary Evelyn Elliott; *m* 1962, Hilary Margaret Hambling; three *s* (one *d* decd). *Educ:* Repton; Lincoln and Nuffield Colls, Oxford (MA, DPhil). Deacon, 1964; priest, 1965. Lectr in Econs, Univ. of Nottingham, 1963–65; Reader in Econs, Univ. of Zambia, 1965–69; Asst Sec., Cttee on Society, Develt and Peace, Vatican and World Council of Churches, 1969–72; Sen. Lectr in Develt Econs, Univ. of E Anglia, 1972–73; Dir, Overseas Develt Gp, UEA, 1973–77; Minor Canon, Norwich Cathedral, 1974–77; Prof. of Develt Policy and Planning, and Dir, Centre of Develt Studies, Univ. of Wales, 1977–82; Director of Christian Aid, 1982–84; Asst Gen. Sec., BCC, 1982–84; Benjamin Meaker Prof., Bristol Univ., 1985–86; Sen. Consultant, ODI, 1986–87. G. E. M. Scott Fellow, Univ. of Melbourne, 1984–85; Hon. Vis. Prof. of Christian Ethics, Univ. of Edinburgh, 1985–87; Vis. Prof. in Theology, KCL, 1986–88. Chm., Indep. Gp on British Aid, 1981–89. Prebendary of Lichfield Cathedral, 1987–95. *Publications:* The Development Debate, 1972; Inflation and the Compromised Church, 1973; Patterns of Poverty in the Third World, 1975; Praying the Kingdom: an introduction to political spirituality, 1985 (Biennial Collins Prize for Religious Lit., 1985); Comfortable Compassion, 1987; Praying through Paradox, 1987; Signs of Our Times, 1988; Sword and Spirit, 1989; Memory and Salvation, 1995; Strategic Planning for Churches: an appreciative approach, 1997; Locating the Energy for Change: an introduction to appreciative inquiry, 1999; articles in Jl of Develt Studies, Econ. Hist. Rev., Theology, World Health Forum, World Develt, Lancet, BMJ and in Proc. Royal Soc. *Recreations:* sailing, fly-fishing, walking, chatting to rural craftsmen. *Address:* 11 Perowne Street, Cambridge CB1 2AY.

ELLIOTT, (Charles) Thomas, CBE 1994; PhD; FRS 1988; Tom Elliott Consultancy Ltd, since 1999; *b* 16 Jan. 1939; *s* of Charles Thomas and Mary Jane Elliott; *m* 1962, Brenda Waistell; one *s* two *d*. *Educ:* Washington Grammar Sch.; Manchester Univ. (BSc 1960; PhD 1965). Univ. of Manchester: Research student, 1960–63; Asst Lectr/Lectr, 1963–67 (research on dielectric breakdown); joined RSRE 1967, to study electrical transport in semiconductors; Vis. Scientist, MIT, Lincoln Lab., USA, 1970–71; research into infrared detectors, 1972–; DCSO, RSRE, 1986–91; CSO (Individual Merit), DRA, Electronics Sector, 1991–96; Chief Scientist, DERA, 1996–99. Part-time Prof. of Physics, Heriot-Watt Univ., 1999–. Rank Prize for optoelectronics and IEE Electronics Div. Premium Award, 1982; Churchill Medal, Soc. of Engineers, 1986; MacRobert Award for Engineering, 1991; Paterson Medal, Inst. of Physics, 1997. *Publications:* numerous papers and patents. *Recreations:* reading, golf, music. *Address:* Weardale, 8 Hall Green, Malvern, Worcs WR14 3QX. *T:* (01684) 562474.

ELLIOTT, Maj.-Gen. Christopher Haslett, CBE 1994; Defence Services Secretary, since 2001; *b* 26 May 1947; *s* of Lt-Col Blethyn Elliott and Zara Elliott; *m* 1970, Annabel Melanie Emerson; four *d*. *Educ:* Kelly Coll., Tavistock; Mons Officer Cadet Sch.; Staff Coll., Camberley (psc). Commnd into S Wales Borderers, 1966: regtl duty appts, 1966–80 (despatches, NI, 1975); Army Staff Coll., Camberley, 1980; COS, Berlin Inf. Bde, 1981–83; Mem., Directing Staff, Army Staff Coll., Camberley, 1985–87; CO, 1st Bn, Royal Regt of Wales, 1987–90; Comdr, British Forces Belize, 1990–93; Dir, Army Recruiting, MoD, 1993–94; Comdr, Brit. Mil. Adv. and Trng Team, S Africa, 1994–97; GOC UKSC (Germany), 1997–2001. Col Comdt POW Div., 1999–; Col, Royal Regt of Wales, 1999–. *Recreations:* fly-fishing, rough shooting, walking, watersports. *Club:* Army and Navy.

See also N. B. Elliott.

ELLIOTT, Maj. Gen. Christopher Leslie, CB 1999; MBE 1969; Director-General Development and Doctrine, since 2000; *b* 18 March 1947; *s* of Peter Archibald Elliott and Evelyn Sarah (*née* Wallace); *m* 1970, Margaret Bennett; two *d*. *Educ:* Pocklington Sch., York; RMA, Royal Mil. Coll. of Sci. (BSc Hons Eng); Cranfield Inst. of Technol. (MPhil). Commnd RE, 1967; OC 48 Field Sqn RE, 1980; CO, 21 Engr Regt, 1986–88; ACOS 1 (BR) Corps, 1988–90; Comdr, 6th Armd Bde, 1990–91; Dir of Studies, Staff Coll., Camberley, 1991–92; Dir, Mil. Ops, 1993–95; UK Mil. Advr to Chm., Internat. Conf. on former Yugoslavia, 1995–96; Dir Gen. Army Trng and Recruiting, and Chief Exec., Army Trng and Recruiting Agency, 1996–99; COS, HQ QMG, 1999–2000. Comr, Royal Hosp., Chelsea, 1996–. Trustee, Army Central Fund, 1998–2000. Col Comdt, RE, 2000–. Mem. Senate, Cranfield Univ., 1996–99; Mem. Adv. Council, RMCS, 2000–. Pres., Jt Services Paragliding and Hang-gliding Assoc., 1993–; Vice-Cdre, Army Sailing Assoc., 1993–94. *Publication:* (contrib.) Blast Damage to Buildings, 1995. *Recreations:* sailing, paragliding, reading. *Address:* Trenchard Lines, Upavon, Pewsey, Wilts SN9 6BE. *Clubs:* Royal Ocean Racing, Royal Cruising (Mem. Cttee, 2000–); Royal Engineer Yacht (Chatham) (Cdre, 1995–96); Royal Lymington Yacht.

ELLIOTT, Sir Clive (Christopher Hugh), 4th Bt *cr* 1917, of Limpsfield, Surrey; Senior Officer, Migratory Pests, Plant Protection Service, Food and Agriculture Organization of the UN, Rome, since 1995; *b* Moshi, Tanganyika, 12 Aug. 1945; *s* of Sir Hugh Elliott, 3rd Bt, OBE and of Elizabeth Margaret, *d* of A. G. Phillipson; *S* father, 1989; *m* 1975, Marie-Thérèse, *d* of H. Rüttimann; two *s*. *Educ:* Dragon Sch., Oxford; Bryanston Sch., Dorset; University Coll., Oxford (BA Hons Zoology); Univ. of Cape Town, S Africa (PhD Zoology 1973). University of Cape Town: Research Officer, FitzPatrick Inst. of Ornithology, 1968–71; first Officer i/c National Unit for Bird-ringing Admin, 1972–75; ornithologist/ecologist, crop protectionist/project manager, FAO: Chad, 1975–78; Tanzania, 1978–86; Kenya, 1986–89; Country Projects Officer, Eastern and Southern Africa, FAO, 1989–95. Mem., Field Staff Assoc. of FAO (Chm., 1992). *Publications:* (ed jtly with R. L. Bruggers) Quelea Quelea: Africa's Bird Pest, 1989; contrib. to books and jls on ornithology. *Recreations:* tennis, fishing, bird-watching, wildlife conservation, Africa's development. *Heir:* *s* Ivo Antony Moritz Elliott, *b* 9 May 1978. *Address:* FAO/AGPP, Via delle terme di Caracalla, Rome, Italy. *Club:* British Ornithologists' Union.

ELLIOTT, Sir David (Murray), KCMG 1995; CB 1987; Director General (Internal Market), General Secretariat of Council of European Union, 1991–95; *b* 8 Feb. 1930; *s* of late Alfred Elliott, ISM, and Mabel Kathleen Emily Elliott (*née* Murray); *m* 1956, Ruth Marjorie Ingram; one *d* (one *s* decd). *Educ:* Bishopshalt Grammar Sch.; London Sch. of Economics and Political Science (BScEcon); Kitchener Scholar. National Service, RAF, 1951–54; Gen. Post Office, 1954–57; seconded to Federal Ministry of Communications, Nigeria, 1958–62; GPO, 1962–69 (Clerk in Waiting, 1964–69); Asst Secretary: Min. of Posts and Telecommunications, 1969–74 (Dep. Leader, UK Delegn to Centenary Congress, UPU, Lausanne, 1974); Dept of Industry, 1974–75; Counsellor at UK Representation to the European Communities, Brussels, 1975–78; Under Sec., European Secretariat, Cabinet Office, 1978–82; Minister and Dep. UK Perm. Rep. to the Eur. Communities, Brussels, 1982–91. Advr on EU affairs under UK Know-How Fund and EU PHARE progs, 1995–98. Member Board: CARE UK, 1995–2001; CARE Internat., 1998–2001. *Address:* 31 Ailsa Road, St Margarets, Twickenham, Middlesex TW1 1QJ. *Club:* Travellers.

ELLIOTT, David Stewart Innes; Chief Executive, Royal Albert Hall, since 1998; *b* 6 April 1945; *s* of late John Innes Elliott, CBE and Edith Agnes Elliott; *m* 1978, Patricia Nicholson; two *s*. *Educ:* Whitgift Sch.; Oriel Coll., Oxford (MA). Commercial Evaluation Dept, 1966–68, Market and Commercial Analyst, 1969–70, Vickers Ltd; Corporate Finance Dept, Baring Brothers & Co. Ltd, 1970–80 (Asst Dir, 1978); Exec. Vice-Pres., Baring Brothers Inc., NY, 1981–84; Finance Dir, ENO, 1985–90; Dir of Finance and Admin, 1991–93, Dep. Chief Exec., 1994–97, Royal Albert Hall. Chm., Benesh Inst. of Choreology, 1997–; Mem. Exec. Cttee, Royal Acad. Dancing, 1997–. Hon. Treas., Lyric Th. Hammersmith, 1999–. *Recreations:* opera, theatre, looking at pictures, ski-ing. *Address:* c/o Royal Albert Hall, Kensington Gore, SW7 2AP.

ELLIOTT, David Stuart; Director, Mori Art Museum, Tokyo; *b* 29 April 1949; *s* of Arthur Elliott and May Elliott; *m* 1974, Julia Alison (separated); two *d*. *Educ:* Loughborough Grammar Sch.; Durham Univ. (BA Hons Mod. Hist.); Univ. of London (MA Hist. of Art, Courtauld Inst.). Asst Stage Manager, Phoenix Theatre, Leicester, 1966; Asst, City Art Gallery, Leicester, 1971; Regional Art Officer, Arts Council, 1973–76; Director: Mus. of Modern Art, Oxford, 1976–96; Moderna Museet, Stockholm, 1996–2001. Visitor, Ashmolean Mus., Oxford, 1992–2000. Pres. of Jury, La Biennale des Arts, Dakar, 2000. Contribs to radio and TV. Hon. DA Oxford Brookes, 1998. NACF Award, 1988. Orden de Mayo (Argentina), 2001. *Publications:* Alexander Rodchenko, 1979; José Clemente Orozco, 1980; New Worlds: Russian Art and Society 1900–1937, 1986; (ed jtly) Eisenstein at 90, 1988; (ed jtly) 100 Years of Russian Art 1889–1989, 1989; (ed jtly) Alexander Rodchenko: Works on Paper, 1991; (ed jtly) Engineers of the Human Soul: Soviet Socialist Realism, 1992; Photography in Russia 1840–1940, 1992; (ed) Art from Argentina 1920–1994, 1994; (ed jtly) Wounds: between democracy and redemption in contemporary art, 1998; (ed jtly) After the Wall: art and culture in post-Communist Europe, 1999; Organising Freedom: Nordic art of the '90s, 2000; contribs to arts magazines. *Recreations:* keeping fit, travelling. *Address: e-mail:* artcenter@mori.co.jp.

ELLIOTT, Frank Abercrombie, MD, FRCP; Emeritus Professor of Neurology, University of Pennsylvania, since 1979; Consultant, Elliott Neurology Centre, Pennsylvania Hospital, Philadelphia, since 1975; *b* 18 Dec. 1910; *s* of Arthur Abercrombie Elliott and Kathleen Gosselin; *m* 1st, 1940, Betty Kathleen Elkington; two *d*; 2nd, 1970, Mrs Josiah Marvel (*née* Hopkins). *Educ:* Rondebosch; Univ. of Cape Town. Univ. entrance schol., 1928; Lewis Memorial schol., 1930–34; MB, ChB Cape Town, with Hons and Gold Medal; Hiddingh Travelling Fellowship, 1936–39. House Surg. and House Phys. to professorial units, Cape Town; House Physician, British Postgrad. Sch. of Medicine and Nat. Hosp. for Nervous Diseases, London; Resident MO, Nat. Heart Hosp. RAMC, 1943–48, Lt-Col; Adviser in Neurology, India and War Office. FRCP 1948; FACP 1973. Physician to Charing Cross Hosp., 1947–58; to Moorfields Eye Hospital, 1949–58; Prof. of Neurology, Univ. of Pennsylvania, 1963–78. Lecturer and Examiner, London Univ. Member: Assoc. of British Neurologists, Assoc. of British Physicians; Internat. Soc. of Internal Medicine; Am. Acad. of Neurology; Philadelphia Neurological Soc. *Publications:* (ed) Clinical Neurology, 1952; Clinical Neurology, 1964 (2nd edn, 1971); papers on neurological subjects and the origins of aggressive behaviour. *Address:* 3339 Schoolhouse Lane, Philadelphia, PA 19144, USA. *Club:* Philadelphia.

ELLIOTT, Frank Alan, CB 1991; Permanent Secretary, Department of Health and Social Services, Northern Ireland, 1987–97; *b* 28 March 1937; *s* of Frank Elliott and Doreen Allen; *m* 1964, Olive Lucy O'Brien; one *s* two *d*. *Educ:* Royal Belfast Academical Inst.; Trinity Coll., Dublin (BA (Mod.) 1st cl.). Entered NI Civil Service, 1959; Principal, Min. of Health, 1966, Asst Sec., 1971; Sen. Asst Sec., Dept of Health and Social Services, 1975, Under Sec., 1981. Chm., Chief Execs' Forum, 1997–. DUniv Ulster, 1998. *Publication:* Curing and Caring: 50 years of health and personal social services in NI, 1998. *Recreations:* music and the arts, motoring.

ELLIOTT, George, FRICS; Senior Partner, Edmond Shipway and Partners, 1985–93; *b* 20 Aug. 1932; *s* of Harry Elliott and Nellie Elizabeth Elliott; *m* 1st, 1958, Winifred Joan (marr. diss. 1990); one *s* one *d*; 2nd, 1992, Hazel Ann Willis. *Educ:* Sir George Monoux Grammar Sch.; SW Essex Technical Coll. FRICS 1966. Founder Partner, Edmond Shipway, 1963; Chief Exec., British Urban Develt Services Unit, 1975–78. *Recreations:* travel, naval history. *Address:* 66 Bruce Street, Nedlands, WA 6009, Australia. *T:* (8) 93864581.

ELLIOTT, Hugh Percival, CMG 1959; retired, 1967; *b* 29 May 1911; *s* of late Major P. W. Elliott, IA; *m* 1951, Bridget Rosalie (*d* 1981), *d* of late Rev. A. F. Peterson. *Educ:* St Lawrence Coll., Ramsgate; Hertford Coll., Oxford. Joined Colonial Administrative Service, Nigeria, 1934; seconded Colonial Office, 1946; Supervisor, Colonial Service Courses, London, 1948–50; Senior District Officer, 1954; Permanent Sec., 1956; Adviser, Govt of Eastern Nigeria, 1962–67. Many visits to Ethiopia, Zimbabwe, Kenya, Uganda and Nigeria to support the initiatives for Moral Re-Armament by African friends, 1968–. Companion, Order of the Niger, Nigeria, 1964. *Publications:* Darkness and Dawn in Zimbabwe, 1978; Dawn in Zimbabwe, 1980. *Recreations:* the countryside, watercolour painting, Africa. *Address:* Hall Grange, Shirley Church Road, Croydon CR9 5AL.

ELLIOTT, Prof. James Philip, PhD; FRS 1980; Professor of Theoretical Physics, University of Sussex, 1969–94, now Professor Emeritus; *b* 27 July 1929; *s* of James Elliott and Dora Kate Smith; *m* 1955, Mavis Rosetta Avery; one *s* two *d*. *Educ:* University College, Southampton; London External degrees: BSc 1949, PhD 1952. Senior Scientific Officer, AERE Harwell, 1951–58; Vis. Associate Prof., Univ. of Rochester, USA, 1958–59; Lecturer in Mathematics, Univ. of Southampton, 1959–62; Reader in Theoretical Physics, Univ. of Sussex, 1962–69. Fellow of former Physical Soc. Rutherford Medal, Inst. of Physics, 1994. *Publications:* Symmetry in Physics, 1979; contribs include: The Nuclear Shell Model, Handbuch der Physik, vol 39, 1957; many papers, mostly published in Proc. Roy. Soc. and Nuclear Phys. *Recreations:* gardening, sport and music. *Address:* 36 Montacute Road, Lewes, Sussex BN7 1EP. *T:* (01273) 474783.

ELLIOTT, Prof. John; Professor of Education, University of East Anglia, since 1987; *b* 20 June 1938; *s* of Alfred George Lewis Elliott and Mary Doris Elliott (*née* Greason); *m* 1st, 1967, Jean Marion Walford (marr. diss. 1993); three *d*; 2nd, 1998, Anne Christine O'Hanlon. *Educ:* Ashford Grammar Sch.; City of Portsmouth Trng Coll.; Bishop Otter Coll., Chichester; London Univ. Inst. of Educn (Dip. Phil. Ed. 1970; MPhil 1980). Horticultural researcher, E Malling Res. Stn, 1956–59; sch. teacher, 1962–67, Educnl Researcher, Schs Council, 1967–72; Lectr in Applied Educnl Res., UEA, 1972–76; Tutor in Curriculum Studies, Cambridge Inst. of Educn, 1976–84; University of East Anglia: Reader, 1984–87; Dean, Sch. of Educn and Professional Develt, 1992–95; Dir, Centre for Applied Res. In Educn, 1996–99. Adv. Prof., Hong Kong Inst. of Educn, 2001–. Mem., Norfolk Learning and Skills Council, 2001–. FRSA 1992. *Publications:* Action Research for Educational Change, 1991; The Curriculum Experiment, 1999; (ed with H. Altrichter) Images of Educational Change, 2000; contrib. numerous papers to learned jls. *Recreations:* golf, countryside, reading, cinema and theatre. *Address:* Centre for Applied Research in Education, University of East Anglia, Norwich NR4 7TJ. *T:* (01603) 592859; 19 Catton Grove Road, Norwich NR3 3NJ.

ELLIOTT, John Dorman; Chairman, Australian Product Traders Pty Ltd, since 1992; Deputy Chairman, Foster's Brewing Group (formerly Elders IXL Ltd), 1990–92 (Chairman and Chief Executive, 1985–90); *b* 3 Oct. 1941; *s* of Frank Faithful Elliott and Anita Caroline Elliott; *m* 1st, 1965, Lorraine Clare (*née* Golder); two *s* one *d*; 2nd, 1987, Amanda Mary Drummond Moray (*née* Bayles); one *d*. *Educ:* Carey Baptist Grammar School, Melbourne; BCom (Hons) 1962, MBA Melbourne 1965. With BHP, Melbourne, 1963–65; McKinsey & Co., 1966–72; formed consortium and raised $30 million to acquire Henry Jones (IXL), and became Man. Dir, 1972; Elder Smith Goldsbrough Mort merged with Henry Jones (IXL) to form Elders IXL, 1981; Elders IXL acquired Carlton & United Breweries, 1983, largest takeover in Aust. history. Pres., Liberal Party of Australia, 1987–90. Pres., Carlton FC, 1983–. *Recreations:* football, tennis, Royal tennis. *Address:* 1 Towers Road, Toorak, Vic 3142, Australia. *T:* (3) 996211411. *Clubs:* Melbourne, Australian, Savage (Melbourne); Royal Melbourne Tennis, Royal South Yarra Tennis.

ELLIOTT, Sir John (Huxtable), Kt 1994; FBA 1972; Regius Professor of Modern History, and Fellow of Oriel College, Oxford, 1990–97 (Hon. Fellow, Oriel College, 1997); *b* 23 June 1930; *s* of late Thomas Charles Elliott and Janet Mary Payne; *m* 1958, Oonah Sophia Butler. *Educ:* Eton College; Trinity College, Cambridge (MA, PhD). Fellow of Trinity Coll., Cambridge, 1954–67, Hon. Fellow, 1991; Asst Lectr in History, Cambridge Univ., 1957–62; Lectr in History, Cambridge Univ., 1962–67; Prof. of History: KCL, 1968–73; Inst. for Advanced Study, Princeton, NJ, 1973–90. Mem., Scientific Cttee, Prado Mus., 1996–. King Juan Carlos Vis. Prof., New York Univ., 1988. Wiles Lectr, QUB, 1969; Trevelyan Lectr, Cambridge Univ., 1982–83. FKC 1998. Corresp. Fellow, Real Academia de la Historia, Madrid, 1965; Fellow, Amer. Acad. Arts and Scis, 1977. Mem., Amer. Philosophical Soc., 1982; Corresponding Member: Hispanic Soc. of America, 1975 (Hon. Fellow, 1997); Real Academia Sevillana de Buenas Letras, 1976; Royal Acad. of Letters, Barcelona, 1992; Nat. Acad. of History, Venezuela, 1992. Dr *hc* Universidad Autónoma de Madrid, 1983; Genoa, 1992; Barcelona, 1994; Valencia, 1998; Hon. DLitt: Portsmouth, 1993; Warwick, 1995; Hon. DHL: Brown, 1996; Lleida, 1999. Medal of Honour, Universidad Internacional Menéndez y Pelayo, 1987; Medalla de Oro al Mérito en las Bellas Artes, Spain, 1990; Premio Antonio de Nebrija, Univ. of Salamanca, 1993; Prince of Asturias Prize for Social Scis, 1996; Gold Medal, Spanish Inst., NY, 1997; Balzan Prize for History 1500–1800, Internat. Balzan Foundn, 1999. Visitante Ilustre de Madrid, 1983; Comdr, 1984, Grand Cross, 1988, Order of Alfonso X El Sabio; Comdr, 1987, Grand Cross, 1996, Order of Isabel la Católica; Cross of St George (Catalonia), 1999. *Publications:* The Revolt of the Catalans, 1963; Imperial Spain, 1469–1716, 1963; Europe Divided, 1559–1598, 1968; The Old World and the New, 1492–1650, 1970; (ed with H. G. Koenigsberger) The Diversity of History, 1970; (with J. F. de la Peña) Memoriales y Cartas del Conde Duque de Olivares, 2 vols, 1978–80; (with Jonathan Brown) A Palace for a King, 1980; Richelieu and Olivares, 1984 (Leo Gershoy Award, Amer. Hist. Assoc., 1985); The Count-Duke of Olivares, 1986 (Wolfson Lit. Prize for History); Spain and its World 1500–1700, 1989; (ed) The Hispanic World, 1991; (ed with Laurence Brockliss) The World of the Favourite, 1999. *Recreation:* looking at paintings. *Address:* Oriel College, Oxford OX1 4EW; 122 Church Way, Iffley, Oxford OX4 4EG. *T:* (01865) 716703.

ELLIOTT, Mark, CMG 1988; HM Diplomatic Service, retired; *b* 16 May 1939; *s* of William Rowcliffe Elliott, CB, and Karin Tess Elliott (*née* Classen); *m* 1964, Julian Richardson; two *s*. *Educ:* Eton Coll. (King's Scholar); New Coll., Oxford. HM Forces (Intell. Corps), 1957–59. FO, 1963; Tokyo, 1965; FCO, 1970; Private Sec. to Perm. Under-Sec. of State, 1973–74; First Sec. and Head of Chancery, Nicosia, 1975–77; Counsellor, 1977–81, Head of Chancery, 1978–81, Tokyo; Hd of Far Eastern Dept, FCO, 1981–85; Under-Sec. on secondment to N Ireland Office, 1985–88; Ambassador to Israel, 1988–92; Dep. Under-Sec. of State, FCO, 1992–94; Ambassador to Norway, 1994–98. Grand Cross, Order of Merit (Norway), 1994. *Recreations:* fell walking, nature, music, photography.

ELLIOTT, Dr Michael, CBE 1982; FRS 1979; Lawes Trust Senior Fellow, Rothamsted Experimental Station, since 1989; *b* 30 Sept. 1924; *s* of Thomas William Elliott and Isobel Constance (*née* Burnell); *m* 1950, Margaret Olwen James; two *d*. *Educ:* Skinners Co.'s Sch., Tunbridge Wells, Kent; The Univ., Southampton (BSc, PhD); King's Coll., Univ. of London (DSc; FKC 1984). FRSC. Postgrad. res., University Coll., Southampton, 1945–46, and King's Coll., Univ. of London, 1946–48; Rothamsted Experimental Station: Organic Chemist, Dept of Insecticides and Fungicides, 1948–85; SPSO 1971–79; DCSO 1979–83 (Hd of Dept of Insecticides and Fungicides, 1979–83, and Dep. Dir, 1980–83); Hon. Scientist and Consultant, Chemistry of Insecticides, 1983–85. Vis. Res. Scientist, Div. of Entomology, Univ. of Calif at Berkeley, 1969, 1974 and 1986–88; Vis. Prof., Imperial Coll. of Sci. and Tech., 1978–. For. Associate, US Nat. Acad. of Scis, 1996. Hon. DSc Southampton, 1985. Burdick and Jackson Internat. Award for Res. in Pesticide Chemistry, 1975; Holroyd Medal and Lectureship, Soc. of Chem. Ind., 1977; John Jeyes Medal and Lectureship, Chem. Soc., 1978; Mullard Medal, Royal Soc., 1981; Grande Médaille de la Société Française de Phytiatrie et de Phytopharmacie, 1983; Fine Chemicals and Medicinals Gp Award, RSC, 1984; British Crop Protection Council Award, 1986; Wolf Foundn Prize in Agriculture, 1989; Prix de la Fondation de la Chimie, Paris, 1989; Envmt Medal, SCI, 1993. *Publications:* Synthetic Pyrethroids, 1977; papers on chemistry of insecticides and relation of chemical structure with biological activity; chapters in books on insecticides. *Recreations:* photography, designing insecticides. *Address:* 45 Larkfield, Ewhurst, Cranleigh, Surrey GU6 7QU. *T:* (01483) 277506; *e-mail:* elliott161@aol.com.

ELLIOTT, Michael Alwyn; theatre consultant; actor, producer and director; *b* 15 July 1936; *s* of W. A. Edwards and Mrs J. B. Elliott (assumed stepfather's name); *m* Caroline Margaret McCarthy; two *s* one *d*. *Educ:* Raynes Park Grammar School. AMP INSEAD, 1976. Journalist, 1955–59; Public Relations, Avon Rubber Co. Ltd, 1959–63; Marketing, CPC International, 1963–68; Kimberly-Clark Ltd: Product Manager, 1968; Marketing Manager, 1969; Marketing and Development Manager, 1975; General Manager, 1976; Director, 1977; Gen. Administrator, Nat. Theatre, 1979–85; Dir of Admin, Denton, Hall, Solicitors, 1985–88; Head, Theatres Div., Bill Kenwright Ltd, 1992–93. Theatre Consultant: Gardner Arts Centre, 1988–99; Thorndike Th., 1992–95; Yvonne Arnaud Th., 1994–97. Mem., Executive Council, SWET, 1980–85. Stage appearances incl: Anagnos in The Miracle Worker, Comedy, then Wyndhams, 1994; Dr Grimwig in Oliver, London Palladium, 1996; Corin in As You Like It, Shakespeare's Globe, 1997; O'Hara in Maddie, Lyric, 1997; television: The Bill, 1999; The Tenth Kingdom, 2000; Dogma, 2000; Baddiel Syndrome, 2001; Tales from the Tower, 2001. *Recreations:* golf, walking, ski-ing. *Address:* The Coach House, 51A Frant Road, Tunbridge Wells, Kent TN2 5LE. *T:* and *Fax:* (01892) 530615.

ELLIOTT, Michael Norman; *b* 3 June 1932; *m* 1979, Julia Perry. *Educ:* Brunel College of Technology. Formerly res. chemist in food industry. Mem., Ealing Borough Council, 1964–86 (former Leader of Council and Chm., Educn Cttee). MEP (Lab) London W, 1984–99; contested (Lab) London Region, 1999. Formerly: Member: Civil Liberties Parly Cttee (Lab party spokesperson); Parly Cttee of Inquiry into Racism and Xenophobia; Parly

Jt Cttees with Poland and with Malta; Substitute Mem., Econ. and Monetary Cttee; Pres., Parly Intergroup for Animal Welfare and Conservation. Pres., Local Authority Aircraft Noise Council. Member: CND, 1961–; Friends of the Earth, 1985–. Hon. Fellow, Ealing Coll. of Higher Educn, 1988. *Address:* 4 Fern Dene, Ealing, W13 8AN.

ELLIOTT, Michele; Founder, and Director, Kidscape Children's Charity, since 1984; *b* 7 Jan. 1946; *d* of James Irmiter and Ivy (*née* Dashwood); *m* 1968, Edward Elliott; two *s*. *Educ:* Univ. of S Florida (MA *summa cum laude* 1967); Univ. of Florida (MA *cum laude* 1969). Educational Psychologist: Booker Washington Sch., Fla, 1969–71; Amer. Sch. in London, 1971–84. Winston Churchill Fellow, 1991. Chairman: Home Office Working Gp on prevention of sexual abuse, 1988; WHO Cttee on prevention of sexual abuse, 1989. Hon. PhD Post Univ., Conn, 1993. *Publications:* Preventing Child Sexual Assault: a practical guide to talking with children, 1985, 2nd edn 1987 (trans. Norwegian); Kidscape Primary Kit, 1986, 3rd edn 2001; Under Fives Programme, 1987, 4th edn 1999; Keeping Safe, 1988, 2nd edn 1995 (trans. German, French, Chinese, Czech, Norwegian, Polish, Slovenian, Russian); The Willow Street Kids, 1986, 2nd edn 1997; Dealing with Child Abuse, 1989; Teenscape, 1990, 2nd edn 1995; Feeling Happy Feeling Safe, 1991, 2nd edn 1999; Bullying: a practical guide to coping for schools, 1991, 2nd edn 1997; Protecting Children: a training package, 1992; Bullies Meet the Willow Street Kids, 1993, 2nd edn 1997; (ed) Female Sexual Abuse of Children: the ultimate taboo, 1993, 2nd edn 1997; (with J. Kilpatrick) How to Stop Bullying: a Kidscape training guide, 1994, 2nd edn 1997 (trans. Japanese); 501 Ways to be a Good Parent, 1996 (trans. Russian, Estonian, Chinese, Polish, German); 101 Ways to Deal with Bullying: a guide for parents, 1997 (trans. Japanese, Chinese); Bullying: wise guide, 1998; (with G. Shenton) Bully Free, 1999; 601 Ways to be a Good Parent, 1999; numerous contribs to learned jls. *Recreations:* piano, cycling, walking, dancing. *Address:* Kidscape, 2 Grosvenor Gardens, SW1W 0DH. *T:* (020) 7730 3300.

ELLIOTT, Nicholas Blethyn; QC 1995; *b* 11 Dec. 1949; *s* of Col Blethyn William Treharne Elliott, late South Wales Borderers, and Zara Elliott; *m* 1976, Penelope, (Nemmy), Margaret Longbourne Browne; two *s*. *Educ:* Kelly Coll.; Bristol Univ. (LLB Hons). Called to the Bar, Gray's Inn, 1972. Asst Boundary Comr, 2000–. *Publication:* (ed jtly) Banking Litigation, 1999. *Recreations:* tennis, cycling, swimming, bridge, rock and roll dancing. *Address:* Old Whistley Farmhouse, Potterne, Devizes, Wilts SN10 5TD.

See also Maj. Gen. C. H. Elliott.

ELLIOTT, Oliver Douglas; British Council Representative in Yugoslavia, 1979–85; *b* 13 Oct. 1925; *y s* of late Walter Elliott and Margherita Elliott, Bedford; *m* 1954, Patience Rosalie Joan Orpen; one *s*. *Educ:* Bedford Modern Sch.; Wadham Coll., Oxford (MA); Fitzwilliam House, Cambridge. Served RNVR (Sub-Lt), 1944–47. Colonial Educn Service, Cyprus, 1953–59; joined British Council, 1959; served Lebanon, 1960–63; Dep. Rep., Ghana, 1963; Dir, Commonwealth I Dept, 1966; Dir, Service Conditions Dept, 1970; Dep. Educn Advr, India, 1973; Representative in Nigeria, 1976–79. *Recreation:* golf.

ELLIOTT, Paul; Principal Finance Officer, Department for Environment, Food and Rural Affairs (formerly Ministry of Agriculture, Fisheries and Food), 1996–2001; *b* 27 Oct. 1949; *s* of John and Winifred Elliott; *m* 1995, Sharon Amanda Jordan; one *s* one *d*. *Educ:* Clare Coll., Cambridge (Hons Modern Langs). Joined MAFF, 1971; Private Secretary: to Perm. Sec., 1974–75; to Minister, 1975–76; First Sec. (Agriculture), Bonn, 1984–89; Head, Milk Div., 1989–94; Rural White Paper Team, 1994–95. *Recreations:* music, photography, cricket, computers, travel. *Address:* Department for Environment, Food and Rural Affairs, 3–8 Whitehall Place, SW1A 2HH. *T:* (020) 7270 8092.

ELLIOTT, Paul; theatrical producer; Managing Director, Paul Elliott Ltd; Joint Director, Triumph Entertainment Ltd; Managing Director, E&B Productions, 1964–2000; *b* 9 Dec. 1941; *s* of late Lewis Arthur Elliott and Sybil Elliott; *m* 1st, 1971, Jenny Logan (marr. diss. 1986); one *s*; 2nd, 1987, Linda Hayden; one *s* one *d*. *Educ:* Bournemouth Sch. Actor, 1958–63; appeared in Dixon of Dock Green, 1961–62. *London productions* include: Run for Your Wife, Criterion, Whitehall, Aldwych, 1983–92; The King and I, Adelphi, 1973; Grease, New London, 1973; The Pleasure of His Company, and I Do, I Do, Phoenix, 1974; Hedda Gabler, Aldwych, 1975; Hello Dolly, Theatre Royal, 1979; Buddy, Victoria Palace, Strand, 1989; The Pirates of Penzance, Palladium, 1990; Jolson, Victoria Palace, 1996 (Olivier Award, Best Musical, 1996); The Goodbye Girl, Albery, 1997; Kat and the Kings, Vaudeville, 1998 (Olivier Award, Best Musical, 1999); Annie, Victoria Palace, 1998; Stones in His Pockets, Duke of York's, 2000 (Olivier and Evening Standard Awards, Best Comedy); numerous pantomime prodns annually throughout UK; London *pantomimes* include: Aladdin, Shaftesbury, 1983; Snow White and the Seven Dwarfs, Strand, 1990; Jack and the Beanstalk, Piccadilly, 1991; Babes in the Wood, Sadler's Wells; *New York productions:* The Hollow Crown; Brief Lives; Run for Your Wife, 1989; Buddy, 1990; Stones in His Pockets, 2001; touring prodns in UK and overseas incl. USA, Canada, Australia, NZ, Japan, Hong Kong, Zimbabwe, India and Europe. Dir, SOLT, 1996–. Award for Contribution to Provincial Theatre, Theatre Managers Assoc., 1996. *Recreation:* watching sport! *Address:* 11 Aldwych, WC2B 4DA. *T:* (020) 7836 2795.

ELLIOTT, Ven. Peter; Archdeacon of Northumberland, since 1993; *b* 14 June 1941; *s* of James Reginald and Hilda Elliott; *m* 1967, Evelyn Embleton; one *d*. *Educ:* Queen Elizabeth Grammar Sch., Horncastle; Hertford Coll., Oxford (MA Mod. History); Lincoln Theological Coll. Assistant Curate: All Saints, Gosforth, 1965–68; St Peter, Balkwell, 1968–72; Vicar: St Philip, High Elswick, 1972–80; North Gosforth, 1980–87; Embleton with Rennington and Rock, 1987–93. RD of Alnwick, 1989–93; Hon. Canon, Newcastle Cathedral, 1990–93. Mem., English Heritage Cathedrals and Churches Adv. Cttee, 1998–. *Recreations:* water-colour painting, travel, railway timetables, food, wine, gardening. *Address:* 80 Moorside North, Fenham, Newcastle upon Tyne NE4 9DU. *T:* (0191) 273 8245, *Fax:* (0191) 226 0286.

ELLIOTT, Sir Randal (Forbes), KBE 1977 (OBE 1976); President, New Zealand Medical Association, 1976; *b* 12 Oct. 1922; *s* of Sir James Elliott and Lady (Ann) Elliott (*née* Forbes), MBE; *m* 1949, Pauline June Young; one *s* six *d*. *Educ:* Wanganui Collegiate Sch.; Otago Univ. MB, ChB (NZ), 1947; DO, 1953; FRCS, FRACS. Group Captain, RNZAF. Ophthalmic Surgeon, Wellington Hospital, 1953–. Chm. Council, NZ Med. Assoc. GCStJ 1987 (KStJ 1978). *Publications:* various papers in medical jls. *Recreations:* sailing, skiing, mountaineering. *Address:* Herbert Gardens, 186 The Terrace, Wellington 6001, New Zealand. *T:* (4) 721375. *Club:* Wellington (NZ).

ELLIOTT, Robert Anthony K.; *see* Keable-Elliott.

ELLIOTT, Sir Roger (James), Kt 1987; FRS 1976; Secretary to the Delegates and Chief Executive of Oxford University Press, 1988–93; Professor of Physics, Oxford University, 1989–96, now Emeritus; Fellow of New College, Oxford, 1974–96, now Emeritus; *b* Chesterfield, 8 Dec. 1928; *s* of James Elliott and Gladys Elliott (*née* Hill); *m* 1952, Olga Lucy Atkinson; one *s* two *d*. *Educ:* Swanwick Hall Sch., Derbyshire; New Coll., Oxford (MA, DPhil; Hon. Fellow, 1999). Research Fellow, Univ. of California, Berkeley, 1952–53; Research Fellow, UKAEA, Harwell, 1953–55; Lectr, Reading Univ., 1955–57; Fellow of St John's College, Oxford, 1957–74, Hon. Fellow, 1988; University Reader, Oxford, 1964–74; Wykeham Prof. of Physics, 1974–89; Senior Proctor, 1969; Delegate, Oxford Univ. Press, 1971–88. Chm., Computer Bd for Univs and Research Councils, 1983–87; Vice-Chm., Parly Office of Sci. and Technol., 1990–93; Member: Adv. Bd for Res. Councils, 1987–90; (part-time) UKAEA, 1988–94; British Council Bd, 1990–98. Non-exec. Dir, Blackwell Ltd, 1996– (Chm., 1999–); Chm., ICSU Press, 1997–. Chm., Disability Information Trust, 1998–. Physical Sec. and Vice-Pres., Royal Soc., 1984–88; Pres., Publishers Assoc., 1993–94 (Treas., 1990–92). Visiting Prof., Univ. of California, Berkeley, 1961; Miller Vis. Prof., Univ. of Illinois, Urbana, 1966; Vis. Dist. Prof., Florida State Univ., 1981; Vis. Dist. Prof., Michigan State Univ., 1997–2000. Hon. DSc: Paris, 1983; Bath, 1991; Essex, 1993. Maxwell Medal, 1968, Guthrie Medal, 1990, Inst. of Physics. *Publications:* Magnetic Properties of Rare Earth Metals, 1973; Solid State Physics and its Applications (with A. F. Gibson), 1973; papers in Proc. Royal Soc., Jl Phys., Phys. Rev., etc. *Address:* 11 Crick Road, Oxford OX2 6QL. *T:* (01865) 273997. *Club:* Athenæum.

ELLIOTT, Sir Ronald (Stuart), Kt 1981; Director: International Board, Security Pacific National Bank, USA, 1983–91; Security Pacific Australia Ltd, 1985–91; *b* 29 Jan. 1918; *s* of Harold J. W. Elliott and Mercedes E. Manning; *m* 1944, Isabella Mansbridge Boyd; one *s* one *d*. *Educ:* C of E Grammar Sch., Ballarat, Victoria. ABIA; FAIM. Commonwealth Banking Corporation: Sec., 1960–61; Dep. Manager for Queensland, 1961–63; Chief Manager, Foreign Div., 1963–64; Chief Manager, Queensland, 1964–65; Gen. Manager, Commonwealth Develt Bank of Australia, 1966–75; Dep. Man. Dir, 1975–76, Man. Dir, 1976–81, Commonwealth Banking Corp.; Chm., Australian European Finance Corp. Ltd, 1976–81. Director: Australian Bd, Internat. Commodities Clearing House Ltd, 1981–88; Brambles Industries, 1981–90. Mem., Sci. and Industry Forum, Australian Acad. of Sci., 1978–81. Dir., Australian Opera, 1980–87; Mem., Australian Film Develt Corp., 1970–75. *Recreations:* golf, reading, music, particularly opera. *Address:* PO Box 1401, Armidale, NSW 2350, Australia. *T:* (2) 67722387. *Clubs:* Union, Australian Golf (Sydney) (Pres., 1982–87, Capt., 1987–88); Armidale Golf.

ELLIOTT, Thomas; *see* Elliott, C. T.

ELLIOTT, Timothy Stanley; QC 1992; *b* 2 April 1950; *s* of John Edwin Elliott and Annie Elizabeth Stanley (*née* Lowe); *m* 1973, Katharine Barbara Lawrance; one *s* one *d*. *Educ:* Marlborough Coll.; Trinity Coll., Oxford (Exhibnr, MA Lit. Hum. 1973). Called to the Bar, Middle Temple, 1975. *Address:* 10 Essex Street, WC2R 3AA. *T:* (020) 7240 6981.

ELLIOTT, Walter Archibald; *see* Elliott, Hon. Lord.

ELLIOTT, (William) Brent, PhD; Librarian and Archivist, Royal Horticultural Society, since 1982; *b* 10 Jan. 1952; *s* of William Alfred and Annie Irene Elliott; *m* 1981, Dr Frances Margaret Clegg; one *s*. *Educ:* Univ. of BC (BA 1973; MA 1974); King's Coll., London (PhD 1978). Asst Librarian, RHS, 1977–82. Ed., Garden Hist. (Jl Garden Hist. Soc.), 1984–88. English Heritage: Member: Gardens Cttee, 1985–89; Historic Landscapes Panel, 1989–93; Historic Parks and Gardens Adv. Cttee, 1994–. Member: Council, Garden Hist. Soc., 1979–89; Main Cttee, Victorian Soc., 1983–93 (Chm., Cemeteries Sub-cttee, 1980–89). FLS 1995. Veitch Meml Medal, RHS, 1994. *Publications:* Victorian Gardens, 1986; (with A. Clayton-Payne) Victorian Flower Gardens, 1988; (with C. Brooks) Mortal Remains, 1989; Waddesdon Manor: the gardens, 1994; Treasures of the Royal Horticultural Society, 1994; The Country House Garden, 1995. *Recreations:* visiting parks, gardens and cemeteries, gardening, reading. *Address:* c/o Royal Horticultural Society, 80 Vincent Square, SW1P 2PE. *T:* (020) 7821 3050.

ELLIS, family name of **Baron Seaford**.

ELLIS, Dr Adrian Foss, FREng; Director of Field Operations, Health and Safety Executive, since 1996; *b* 15 Feb. 1944; *s* of Henry James Ellis and Marjorie Foss Ellis (*née* Smith); *m* 1st, 1968, Lesley Maxted Smith (*d* 1970); 2nd, 1973, Hilary Jean Miles; two *d* one *s*. *Educ:* Dean Close Sch., Cheltenham; Univ. of London (1st cl. Hons Chem. Eng.); Loughborough Univ. of Technology (PhD). FIChemE 1977; FInstE 1977; FREng (FEng 1995). Student Apprentice, Richard Thomas & Baldwins, 1962–66; British Steel Corp., 1966–71; DoE (Alkali and Clean Air), 1971–83; Health and Safety Executive: Major Hazards Assessment Unit, 1983–86; Dep. Chief Inspector (Chemicals), 1986; Regl Dir, 1990; Dir of Technology and Dir of Hazardous Installations Policy, 1990; Dir of Technology and Health Scis Div., 1991–96. ILO Consultant on major hazards control in India, Pakistan, Thailand, Indonesia. Vis. Prof., Dept of Applied Energy, Cranfield Univ. (formerly Inst. of Technology), 1992–99. Vice Pres. and Sec. Gen., Internat. Assoc. of Labour Inspection, 1999–. Mem. Council, IChemE, 1993–97. *Publications:* papers on risk assessment and major hazards control. *Recreations:* bridge, Swindon Town FC, exploring car boot sales. *Address:* Health and Safety Executive, Daniel House, Trinity Road, Bootle, Merseyside L20 7HE. *T:* (0151) 951 4702. *Club:* Athenæum.

ELLIS, Alice Thomas; *see* Haycraft, A. M.

ELLIS, Andrew Steven, OBE 1984; international consultant; technical adviser on democracy and governance issues; Associate Director, GJW-BSMG Worldwide; *b* 19 May 1952; *s* of late Peter Vernon Ellis and Kathleen Dawe; *m* 1st, 1975, Patricia Ann Stevens (marr. diss. 1987); 2nd, 1990, Helen Prudence Drummond. *Educ:* Trinity Coll., Cambridge (BA Mathematics); Univ. of Newcastle upon Tyne (MSc Statistics); Newcastle upon Tyne Polytechnic (BA Law). Proprietor, Andrew Ellis (Printing and Duplicating), Newcastle upon Tyne, 1973–81; freelance Election Agent/Organizer, 1981–84; Sec.-Gen., Liberal Party, 1985–88; Chief Exec., Social and Liberal Democrats, 1988–89; freelance political consultant, 1989–93. Consultant Nat. Agent, Welsh Liberal Party, 1984–88. Contested (L): Newcastle upon Tyne Central, Oct. 1974, Nov. 1976, 1979; Boothferry, 1983; Leader, Liberal Gp, Tyne & Wear CC, 1977–81; Vice-Chm., Liberal Party, 1980–86. Tech. Advr to Chm., Palestine Central Election Commn, 1994–96; Co-ordinator, OSCE Observation Mission for Registration of Voters, Bosnia and Hercegovina, 1997; designer of Eur. Commn electoral assistance to Cambodia, 1997–98; Sen. Advr on constitutional, electoral and decentralisation issues, Nat. Democratic Inst., Indonesia, 1998–. *Publications:* Algebraic Structure (with Terence Treeby), 1971; Let Every Englishman's Home Be His Castle, 1978. *Recreation:* travel. *Address:* (office) 110 St Martin's Lane, WC2N 4RG; 2 Chesham Street, Kemptown, Brighton BN2 1NA; Cendana 5.02, Apartemen Eksecutif Menteng Jalan Pegangsaan Barat 8, 10320 Jakarta, Indonesia. *Club:* National Liberal.

ELLIS, Arthur John, CBE 1986; Chairman, Fyffes Group Ltd, since 1984 (Chief Executive Officer, 1969–95); *b* 22 Aug. 1932; *s* of Arthur Ellis and Freda Jane Ellis; *m* 1956, Rita Patricia Blake; two *s* one *d*. *Educ:* Chingford Jun. High Sch.; South West Essex Technical Coll. FCCA; FCMA; FCIS; MBCS. Joined Fyffes Gp Ltd, Finance and Admin Dept, 1954; Chief Financial Officer, 1965; Financial Dir, 1967; Dir, Fyffes plc, 1991–. Chm., Nat. Seed Develt Organisation Ltd, 1982–87. Chm., Intervention Bd for Agricl

Produce, later Intervention Bd Exec. Agency, 1986–95. *Recreations:* golf, reading, gardening. *Clubs:* Reform, Farmers'.

ELLIS, His Honour Arthur Robert Malcolm; DL; a Circuit Judge (formerly Judge of County Courts), 1971–86; *b* 27 June 1912; *s* of David and Anne Amelia Ellis, Nottingham; *m* 1938, Brenda Sewell (*d* 1983); one *d. Educ:* Nottingham High Sch. Admitted Solicitor, 1934; called to the Bar, Inner Temple, 1953. Chm., Nottingham Council of Social Service, 1950–55; Dep. Chm., E Midland Traffic Area, 1955–71; Chm., Ministry of Pensions and National Insurance Tribunal, Sutton-in-Ashfield, Notts, 1961–64, resigned; Chm., Min. of Pensions and Nat. Insce Tribunal, Notts, 1964–71; Chm., Medical Appeals Tribunal, 1971–76. Chm., Notts QS, 1963–71 (Dep.-Chm., 1962–63); Chm., Derbyshire QS, 1966–71 (Dep.-Chm., 1965–66). DL Notts, 1973. *Recreations:* golf, bridge, reading. *Address:* Byways, 5 Manvers Grove, Radcliffe-on-Trent, Notts NG12 2FT. *Club:* United Services (Nottingham).

ELLIS, Bryan James; Under-Secretary, Department of Health and Social Security, later Department of Social Security, 1977–93; *b* 11 June 1934; *s* of late Frank and Renée Ellis; *m* 1960, Barbara Muriel Whiteley; one *s* one *d. Educ:* Merchant Taylors' Sch.; St John's Coll., Oxford (BA Lit.Hum. 1957; MA 1960); Open Univ. (BA Hist. 1998). Sec., Oxford Union Soc., 1956. Joined Min. of Pensions and National Insurance as Asst Principal, 1958; Principal, 1963; Asst Sec., DHSS, 1971; served in CSSB as Chm., 1986, and in OPCS as Dep. Dir, 1987–90. Chm., Assoc. of First Div. Civil Servants, 1983–85. Chm., Trustees of Leopardstown Park Hosp., Dublin, 1979–84. *Publication:* Pensions in Britain 1955–75, 1989. *Recreations:* walking, bridge. *Address:* 8 The Chestnuts, Walton-on-Thames KT12 1EE. *Club:* MCC.

ELLIS, Carol Jacqueline, (Mrs Ralph Gilmore), CBE 1995; QC 1980 (practises as Miss Ellis); Consultant Editor, Weekly Law Reports, since 1990; The Law Reports, since 1996; *b* 6 May 1929; *d* of Ellis W. Ellis and Flora Bernstein; *m* 1957, Ralph Gilmore (*d* 1996); two *s. Educ:* Abbey Sch., Reading; La Ramée, Lausanne; Univ. of Lausanne; University Coll. London (LLB). Called to the Bar, Gray's Inn, 1951; supernumerary law reporter for The Law Reports, The Times, and other legal jls, 1952; law reporter to The Law Reports and Weekly Law Reports, 1954; Asst Editor, Weekly Law Reports, 1969; Managing Editor, The Law Reports and Weekly Law Reports, 1970; Editor: Weekly Law Reports, 1976–90; The Law Reports, 1976–96. Mem., Inner London Probation Cttee, 1989–95. JP W Central Div. Inner London, 1972–98. *Recreations:* travel, music, theatre. *Address:* 11 Old Square, Lincoln's Inn, WC2A 3TS. *T:* (020) 7403 0341.

ELLIS, David Raymond; His Honour Judge Ellis; a Circuit Judge, since 1995; *b* 4 Sept. 1946; *s* of Raymond Ellis and Ethel Ellis (*née* Gordon); *m* 1974, Cathleen Margaret Hawe; one *s* one *d. Educ:* St Edward's Sch., Oxford; Christ Church, Oxford (MA Jurisprudence). Called to the Bar, Inner Temple, 1970; barrister, 1970–95; a Recorder, 1991–95. Chm., Lord Chancellor's SE London Adv. Cttee, 2000–. *Recreations:* travel, theatre, boating, the garden. *Address:* Croydon Combined Court Centre, The Law Courts, Altyre Road, Croydon CR9 5AB. *Club:* Leander (Henley).

ELLIS, Diana; QC 2001; a Recorder, since 1998; *d* of Evan Henry Ellis and Irene Sarah Jeanette Ellis (*née* Behrens); *m* 2001, Geoffrey Keith Watts. *Educ:* London Sch. of Econs (Dip. Social Admin); LLB Hons London. Teacher, Italia Conti Stage Sch., 1971–74, called to the Bar, Inner Temple, 1978; in practice as barrister, 1978–, specialising in criminal and internat. law. *Recreations:* reading, theatre, travel, socialising. *Address:* 3 Gray's Inn Square, Gray's Inn, WC1R 5AH. *T:* (020) 7520 5600.

ELLIS, (Dorothy) June; Headmistress, The Mount School, York, 1977–86; Clerk to Central Committee, Quaker Social Responsibility and Education, 1987–90; *b* 30 May 1926; *d* of Robert Edwin and Dora Ellis. *Educ:* La Sagesse, Newcastle upon Tyne; BSc Pure Science, Durham; DipEd Newcastle upon Tyne. Assistant Mistress: Darlington High Sch., 1947–49; Rutherford High Sch., 1949–50; La Sagesse High Sch., 1950–53; Housemistress, 1953–61, Sen. Mistress, 1961–64, St Monica's Sch.; Dep. Head, Sibford Sch., 1964–77. Clerk, 1986–90, Mem., 1990–98, Swerford Parish Council. Mem. Cttee, Bray d'Oyley Housing Assoc., 1993–96. Mem. Council, Woodbrooke Coll., 1987–93; Governor: Ellerslie Sch., Malvern, 1987–92; Friends' Sch., Saffron Walden, 1990–93. *Recreations:* walking, gardening, home-making. *Address:* Willowside, Swerford, Oxford OX7 4BQ. *T:* (01608) 737334.

ELLIS, Rear-Adm. Edward William, CB 1974; CBE 1968; *b* 6 Sept. 1918; *s* of Harry L. and Winifred Ellis; *m* 1945, Dilys (*née* Little); two *s*. Joined RN, 1940; War service afloat in HM Ships Broadwater and Eclipse, and liaison duties in USS Wichita and US Navy destroyer sqdn; psc 1952; Staff of Flag Officer Flotillas, Mediterranean, 1954–55; Sec. to 4th Sea Lord, 1956–58; Sec. to C-in-C South Atlantic and South America, 1959–60; HM Ships Bermuda and Belfast, 1960–62; Head of C-in-C Far East Secretariat, 1963–65; Sec. to C-in-C Portsmouth and Allied C-in-C Channel, 1965–66; Sec. to Chief of Naval Staff and 1st Sea Lord, 1966–68; Cdre RN Barracks Portsmouth, 1968–71; Adm. Pres., RNC Greenwich, 1972–74. Comdr 1953; Captain 1963; Rear-Adm. 1972. Private Sec. to Lord Mayor of London, 1974–82. Freeman of the City of London, 1974; Liveryman, Shipwrights' Co., 1980. OStJ 1981. Commander, Royal Order of Danebrog, 1974. *Recreations:* fishing, gardening. *Address:* South Lodge, Minstead, Lyndhurst, Hants SO43 7FR. *Club:* Army and Navy.

ELLIS, Eileen Mary, RDI 1984; freelance textile designer; *b* 1 March 1933; *m* 1954, Julian Ellis; one *s* two *d. Educ:* Leicester, Central and Royal Colleges of Art. Des RCA 1957; FCSD (FSIAD 1976). Designer of contract and decorative woven furnishing fabrics, carpets and wall coverings; designed for Ascher & Co., 1957–59; Partner, Orbit Design Group, 1960–73; formed Weaveplan as design consultancy, 1973; apptd design consultant: Tintawn Carpets, 1969; Abbotsford Fabrics, 1982; Botany Weaving Mill, Ireland, 1984; Earlys of Witney, 1994. Projects include work for British Airways, BAA. Vis Lectr, RCA, 1994. Textile Inst. Design Medal, 1985. *Recreations:* country life, reading. *Address:* Weaveplan, The Glasshouse, 11/12 Lettice Street, SW6 4EH. *T:* (020) 7736 3085.

ELLIS, Prof. George Francis Rayner, PhD; FRSSAf; Professor of Applied Mathematics, University of Cape Town, 1973–87 and since 1989; President, Royal Society of South Africa, 1992–96; *b* 11 Aug. 1939; *s* of George Rayner Ellis and Gwendoline Hilda Ellis (*née* MacRobert); *m* 1st, 1963, Jane Mary Sue Parkes; one *s* one *d*; 2nd, 1978, Mary MacDonald Wheeldon. *Educ:* Univ. of Cape Town (BSc Hons 1960; Fellow, 1982); St John's Coll., Cambridge (PhD 1964). FRSSAf 1983. Lectr, Cambridge Univ., 1968–73; Prof., Scuola Internazionale Superiore di Studi Avanzati Trieste, 1987–89. Vis. Prof., Univs of Texas, Hamburg, Chicago, Alberta, and QMC London. Pres., Internat. Soc. of General Relativity and Gravitation, 1987–91. Clerk, S Africa Yearly Meeting of Quakers, 1982–86; Chairman: Quaker Service, W Cape, 1978–86; Quaker Peace Work Cttee, W Cape, 1989–. Hon. DSc: Haverford Coll., 1995; Natal Univ., 1998. Herschel Medal, Royal Soc. of S Africa, 1978; Medal, SA Assoc. for Advancement of Science, 1993. Star of S Africa Medal, 1999. *Publications:* (with S. W. Hawking) The Large Scale Structure of Space-Time, 1973; (with D. Dewar) Low Income Housing Policy, 1979; Before the Beginning, 1993; (with N. Murphy) On the Moral Nature of the Universe, 1996. *Recreations:* mountain climbing, gliding. *Address:* Department of Applied Mathematics, University of Cape Town, Rondebosch 7700, Cape Town, South Africa; 3 Marlow Road, Kenilworth, Cape Town 7700, South Africa. *T:* 7612313. *Club:* Mountain of South Africa (Cape Town).

ELLIS, Prof. Hadyn Douglas, PhD, DSc; CPsych, FBPsS; Professor of Psychology, since 1988, and Head of Department, since 1989, and Deputy Vice-Chancellor, since 2001, Cardiff University; *b* 25 Oct. 1945; *s* of A. Douglas Ellis and Myrtle M. Ellis (*née* Oliver); *m* 1966, Diane Margaret Newton; three *s. Educ:* St Julian's High Sch., Newport, Mon; Reading Univ. (BA; PhD 1971); Aberdeen Univ. (DSc 1988). CPsych 1986; FBPsS 1986. Lectr, 1970–79, Sen. Lectr, 1979–86, Aberdeen Univ.; Prof. of Applied Psychol., UWIST, 1986–88; Cardiff University: Dean, Grad. Studies, 1995–; Pro Vice-Chancellor (Res.), 1995–99 and 2000–01. Member: Bd, QAA, 1997–2000; Council, ESRC, 2000– (Chm., Trng Bd, 2000–). *Publications:* (jtly) Perceiving and Remembering Faces, 1981; (jtly) Identification Evidence, 1982; (jtly) Aspects of Face Processing, 1986; (with A. Young) Handbook of Face Processing, 1989; (with N. Macrae) Validation in Psychology, 2001; contrib. articles to psychol., psychiatry and neurol. jls. *Recreations:* France, wine, French wine. *Address:* Llwynarthen House, Castleton, Cardiff CF3 2UN. *T:* (01633) 680213.

ELLIS, Prof. Harold, CBE 1987; MA, MCh, DM; FRCS; FRCOG; Clinical Anatomist, University of London, at Guy's campus, since 1993; *b* 13 Jan. 1926; *s* of Samuel and Ada Ellis; *m* 1958, Wendy Mae Levine; one *s* one *d. Educ:* Queen's Coll. (State Scholar and Open Scholar in Natural Sciences), Oxford; Radcliffe Infirmary, Oxford. BM, BCh, 1948; FRCS, MA, 1951; MCh 1956; DM 1962; FRCOG *ad eundem*, 1987; Hon. FACS 1989. House Surgeon, Radcliffe Infirmary, 1948–49; Hallett Prize, RCS, 1949. RAMC, 1949–51. Res. Surgical Officer, Sheffield Royal Infirm., 1952–54; Registrar, Westminster Hosp., 1955; Sen. Registrar and Surgical Tutor, Radcliffe Infirm., Oxford, 1956–60; Sen. Lectr in Surgery, 1960–62, Hon. Consultant Surgeon, 1960–89, Westminster Hosp.; Prof. of Surgery, Univ. of London, 1962–89; Clinical Anatomist, Univ. of Cambridge and Fellow, Churchill Coll., Cambridge, 1989–93. Hon. Consultant Surgeon to the Army, 1978–89. Mem. Council, RCS, 1974–86. Member: Association of Surgeons; British Soc. of Gastroenterol.; Surgical Research Soc.; Council: RSocMed; British Assoc. of Surgical Oncology; Associé étranger, L'Academie de Chirurgie, Paris, 1983. *Publications:* Clinical Anatomy, 1960; Anatomy for Anaesthetists, 1963; Lecture Notes on General Surgery, 1965; Principles of Resuscitation, 1967; History of the Bladder Stone, 1970; General Surgery for Nurses, 1976; Intestinal Obstruction, 1982; Notable Names in Medicine and Surgery, 1983; Famous Operations, 1984; Wound Healing for Surgeons, 1984; Maingot's Abdominal Operations, 1985; Research in Medicine, 1990; Cross-sectional Anatomy, 1991; Surgical Case-Histories from the Past, 1994; (ed) French's Index of Differential Diagnosis, 1996; A History of Surgery, 2000; numerous articles on surgical topics in medical journals. *Recreation:* medical history. *Address:* 16 Bancroft Avenue, N2 0AS. *T:* (020) 8348 2720.

ELLIS, Herbert; *see* Ellis, W. H. B.

ELLIS, John; Member, Local Government Planning Executive, since 2000; Steel Worker, British Steel plc, Scunthorpe, 1980–89; *b* Hexthorpe, Doncaster, 22 Oct. 1930; *s* of George and Hilda Ellis; *m* 1953, Rita Butters; two *s* two *d. Educ:* Rastrick Gram. Sch., Brighouse. Laboratory technician, Meteorological Office, 1947–63; Vice-Chm., Staff side, Air Min. Whitley Council, 1961–63; Member Relations Offr, Co-op. Retail Services, Bristol/Bath Region, 1971–74. Member: Easthampstead RDC, 1962–66; Bristol City Council, 1971–74; Humberside County Council, 1987–96; N Lincs Council, 1995– (Vice Chm., Housing Cttee, 1998–99; Chm., Planning Cttee, 1999–). Chairman: Humberside Social Service Council, 1992–94 (Vice-Chm., 1990–92); Social Services Children's Cttee, 1991–94; Member: Scunthorpe HA, 1988–91 (Chm., Jt Consultative Cttee, 1988–2000); NRA (formerly Lincs Land Drainage Cttee), 1988–96 (Member: Anglian Regl Flood Defence cttee; Lincs Flood Defence cttee). Contested (Lab) Wokingham, 1964; MP (Lab) Bristol North-West, 1966–70, Brigg and Scunthorpe, Feb. 1974–1979; PPS to Minister of State for Transport, 1968–70; an Asst Govt Whip, 1974–76. Formerly Mem., Select Cttee on Nationalised Industries. JP, North Riding Yorks, 1960–61. *Publication:* (jtly) Fabian pamphlet on MPs from Unions. *Recreations:* gardening, watching cricket. *Address:* 102 Glover Road, Scunthorpe DN17 1AS.

ELLIS, John, CB 1985; independent technical consultant; Head of Royal Armament Research and Development Establishment, Chertsey, 1984–85, retired; *b* 9 Jan. 1925; *s* of Frank William and Alice Ellis; *m* 1958, Susan Doris (*née* Puttock). *Educ:* Leeds Univ. BSc, 1st cl. hons. Mech. Eng; CEng, MIMechE. Hydro-Ballistic Research Estabt, Admty, 1945–47; David Brown & Sons Ltd, Huddersfield, 1948; RAE, Min. of Supply (Structures Dept, Armament Dept, Weapons Dept), 1948–68; MVEE (formerly FVRDE), MoD, 1968–84; Dir, MVEE, Chertsey, 1978–84, when MVEE and RARDE amalgamated. *Recreations:* motoring, golf. *Address:* Foresters, 1 Kitchers Close, Sway, Lymington, Hants SO41 6DS. *T:* (01590) 682410.

ELLIS, John Norman, OBE 1995; industrial relations consultant, with Talking People, since 1995; Secretary to Council of Civil Service Unions, 1992–95; *b* 22 Feb. 1939; *s* of Margaret and Albert Ellis; *m* 1st; one *s* one *d*; 2nd, Diane Anderson; two step *s. Educ:* Osmondthorpe; Leeds Secondary Modern; Leeds College of Commerce. Post Office Messenger and Postman, 1954–58; Clerical Officer and Executive Officer, MPBW, 1958–67; Civil and Public Services Association: Asst Sec., 1968–82; Dep. Gen. Sec., 1982–86; Gen. Sec., 1986–92. Member: Gen. Council, TUC, 1988–92 (Mem. Economic, Social Services, Industrial Welfare, Public Services and Pensions Specialists Cttees); Inst. of Employment Rights; Industrial Tribunals Panel; Exec. Cttee, Civil Service Pensioners' Alliance; Adv. Bd, Durham Univ. Business Sch. Chm., Caterham Br., Lab. Party, 1997– (Vice-Chm., 1996). Mem. Bd and Vice Chm., Tandridge Leisure Ltd. *Recreations:* reading, watching sport, gardening, listening to music, dog walking. *Address:* 26 Harestone Valley Road, Caterham, Surrey CR3 6HD.

ELLIS, Prof. John Romaine; Professor of Automobile Engineering, 1960–82 and Director, 1960–76, School of Automotive Studies, Cranfield; *b* 30 Sept. 1922; *m* 1947, Madelaine Della Blaker; one *s* one *d. Educ:* Tiffin Sch., Kingston-on-Thames. Royal Aircraft Establishment, 1944–56; Fairey Aviation Company, 1946–48; Royal Military Coll. of Science, Shrivenham, near Swindon, Wilts, 1949–60. *Recreations:* golf, music. *Address:* Upper Watkins, Lower Road, Edington, Wilts BA13 4QW.

ELLIS, John Russell; transport consultant, since 1997; *b* 21 May 1938; *s* of Percy Macdonald Ellis and Winifred Maud (*née* Bunker); *m* 1962, Jean Eileen Taylor; two *d. Educ:* Rendcomb Coll., Cirencester; Pembroke Coll., Oxford (BA Hons PPE). Joined BR as Grad. Management Trainee, 1962; various posts, 1963–80; Chief Freight Manager, 1980–83, Divl Manager, 1983–84, Asst Gen. Manager, 1984–85, Eastern Region; Dep. Gen. Manager, Southern Region, 1985–87; Gen. Manager, ScotRail, 1987–90; Gen. Manager, Southern Region, 1990–91; Dep. Man. Dir, InterCity, 1992–93; Dir,

Production, Railtrack, 1993–95; Man. Dir, ScotRail, 1995–97. *Recreations:* hockey, cricket, walking, gardening, music. *Address:* St Anne's, Chipping Campden, Glos GL55 6AL. *T:* (01386) 841253.

ELLIS, Dr Jonathan Richard, FRS 1985; Senior Staff Physicist, Theoretical Studies Division, CERN, Geneva, since 1994 (Leader, 1988–94); *b* 1 July 1946; *s* of Richard Ellis and Beryl Lilian Ellis (*née* Ranger); *m* 1985, Maria Mercedes Martinez Rengifo; one *s* one *d. Educ:* Highgate Sch.; King's Coll., Cambridge. BA; PhD. Postdoctoral research, SLAC, Stanford, 1971–72; Richard Chase Tolman Fellow, Caltech, 1972–73; Staff Mem., CERN, Geneva, 1973–. Maxwell Medal, Inst. of Physics, 1982. *Recreations:* movies, reading, travel, hiking in the mountains. *Address:* 5 Chemin du Ruisseau, Tannay, 1295 Mies, Vaud, Switzerland. *T:* (22) 7764858.

ELLIS, June; *see* Ellis, D. J.

ELLIS, Laurence Edward, MA; Rector, The Edinburgh Academy, 1977–92; *b* 21 April 1932; *s* of Dr and Mrs E. A. Ellis; *m* 1961, Elizabeth Ogilvie; two *s* one *d. Educ:* Winchester Coll.; Trinity Coll., Cambridge (MA). AFIMA. 2/Lieut Rifle Bde, 1950–52. Marlborough Coll., 1955–77 (Housemaster, 1968). FRSA. *Publications:* (part-author) texts on school maths, statistics, computing, and calculating; articles in jls. Lay Reader, Salisbury, 1961–. *Recreations:* writing, music, woodwork. *Address:* Glendene, Wick Lane, Devizes, Wilts SN10 5DW.

ELLIS, Martin Arthur; costs mediator/costs consultant; Taxing Master of the Supreme Court, 1990–2000, Costs Judge, 1999–2000; *b* 10 Jan. 1933; *s* of Walter Ellis and Phoebe Alicia Ellis; *m* 1961, Moira Herbert; two *s. Educ:* Beckenham Grammar School. Solicitor, admitted 1956; 2nd Lieut, 4th Regt, Royal Horse Artillery, 1957–58; Partner, Simmons & Simmons, 1973–90. *Recreations:* sport, golf, cricket. *Address:* Field House, North Road, Sandwich Bay, Kent CT13 9PJ. *T:* (01304) 619375. *Clubs:* MCC; Kent CC, The Addington Golf, Royal St George's Golf.

ELLIS, Mary; actress; singer; authoress; *b* New York City, 15 June 1900; *m* 1st, L. A. Bernheimer (decd); 2nd (marr. diss.); 3rd, Basil Sydney (marr. diss.); 4th, J. Muir Stewart Roberts (decd). *Educ:* New York. Studied art for three years; studied singing with Madame Ashforth. First Stage appearance, Metropolitan Opera House, New York, in Sœur Angelica, 1918; with Metropolitan Opera House, 1918–22; first appearance dramatic stage, as Nerissa in Merchant of Venice, Lyceum, New York, 1922; was the original Rose Marie (in the musical play, Rose Marie), Imperial, 1924; The Dybbuk, New York, 1925–26; Taming of the Shrew, 1927, and many New York leads followed; first appearance on London stage, as Laetitia in Knave and Quean, Ambassadors', 1930; after appearance in Strange Interlude in London, remained in London, giving up US citizenship in 1946; London: Strange Interlude, 1932; Double Harness, 1933; Music in the Air, 1934; Glamorous Night, Drury Lane, 1935; Innocent Party, St James's, 1937; Dancing Years, Drury Lane, 1939. From 1939–43: doing hospital welfare work and giving concerts for troops. Re-appeared on stage as Marie Foret in Arc de Triomphe, Phœnix, London, 1943; Old Vic (at Liverpool Playhouse), 1944 (Ella Rentheim in John Gabriel Borkman; Linda Valaine in Point Valaine; Lady Teazle in The School for Scandal); Maria Fitzherbert in The Gay Pavilion, Piccadilly, 1945; Season at Embassy: Mrs Dane's Defence, also tour and première of Ian Hay's Hattie Stowe, 1946–47; post-war successes include: Playbill, Phœnix, 1949; Man in the Raincoat, Edinburgh, 1949; If this be Error, Hammersmith, 1950. Stratford-on-Avon Season, 1952: Volumnia in Coriolanus. London: After the Ball (Oscar Wilde-Noel Coward), Globe, 1954–55; Mourning Becomes Electra, Arts, 1955–56; Dark Halo, Arts, 1959; Look Homeward Angel, Pembroke Theatre, Croydon, 1960, Phœnix, 1962; Yvonne Arnaud, Guildford: Silver Cord (revival), 1971; Mrs Warren's Profession, 1972. *Films:* Bella Donna, 1934; Hollywood, 1935–36: Paris in the Spring; The King's Horses; Fatal Lady; Glamorous Night, 1937; Gulliver's Travels, 1961. Since 1972 has devoted time to writing, radio and television; has made several major television appearances, also many radio programmes and interviews; television, 1956–: Shaw's Great Catherine, Van Druten's Distaff Side, Memoirs of Sherlock Holmes and numerous others. Theatre lectures in USA, 1977. *Publications:* Those Dancing Years (autobiog.), 1982; Moments of Truth, 1986. *Recreations:* painting, travel, writing. *Address:* c/o Chase Manhattan Bank, 125 London Wall, EC2Y 5AJ.

ELLIS, Dr Norman David; Under Secretary, British Medical Association, 1980–2000 (Senior Industrial Relations Officer, 1978–82); *b* 23 Nov. 1943; *s* of late George Edward Ellis and late Annie Elsie Scarfe; *m* 1966, Valerie Ann Fenn, PhD; one *s. Educ:* Minchenden Sch.; Univ. of Leeds (BA); MA (Oxon), PhD. Research Officer, Dept of Employment, 1969–71; Leverhulme Fellowship in Industrial Relations, Nuffield Coll., Oxford, 1971–74; Gen. Sec., Assoc. of First Division Civil Servants, 1974–78. *Publications:* (with W. E. J. McCarthy) Management by Agreement, 1973; Employing Staff, 1984; (with J. Chisholm) Making sense of the Red Book, 1993, 3rd edn 1997; (ed with T. Stanton) Making sense of Partnerships, 1994; Making sense of General Practice, 1994; (with J. Lindsay) Making sense of Pensions and Retirement, 1995; General Practitioners' Handbook, 1997; GP Employment Handbook, 1998; (with D. Grantham) Staff Pensions in General Practice, 1998; various contribs to industrial relations literature. *Recreations:* maritime history, reading, travel, swimming. *Address:* 33 Foxes Dale, SE3 9BH. *T:* (020) 8852 6244.

ELLIS, Osian Gwynn, CBE 1971; harpist; Professor of Harp, Royal Academy of Music, London, 1959–89; *b* Ffynnongroew, Flints, 8 Feb. 1928; *s* of Rev. T. G. Ellis, Methodist Minister; *m* 1951, Rene Ellis Jones, Pwllheli; two *s. Educ:* Denbigh Grammar Sch.; Royal Academy of Music. Has broadcast and televised extensively. Has given recitals/concertos all over the world; shared poetry and music recitals with Dame Peggy Ashcroft, Paul Robeson, Burton, C. Day-Lewis, etc. Mem., Melos Ensemble; solo harpist with LSO, 1961–94. Former Mem., Music and Welsh Adv. Cttees, British Council. Works written for him include Harp Concertos by Hoddinott, 1957 and by Mathias, 1970, Jersild, 1972, Robin Holloway, 1985; chamber works by Gian Carlo Menotti, 1977; William Schuman, 1978; from 1960 worked with Benjamin Britten who wrote for him Harp Suite in C (Op. 83) and (for perf. with Sir Peter Pears) Canticle V, Birthday Hansel, and folk songs; accompanied the late Sir Peter Pears on recital tours, Europe and USA, 1974–; records concertos, recitals, folk songs, etc. Film, The Harp, won a Paris award; other awards include Grand Prix du Disque and French Radio Critics' Award. FRAM 1960. Hon. DMus Wales, 1970. *Publication:* Story of the Harp in Wales, 1991. *Address:* 90 Chandos Avenue, N20 9DZ. *T:* (020) 8445 7896; Arfryn, Ala Road, Pwllheli, Gwynedd LL53 5BN. *T:* (01758) 612501.

ELLIS, Prof. Reginald John, PhD; FRS 1983; Professor of Biological Sciences, University of Warwick, 1976–96, now Emeritus; *b* 12 Feb. 1935; *s* of Francis Gilbert Ellis and Evangeline Gratton Ellis; *m* 1963, Diana Margaret Warren; one *d. Educ:* Highbury County Sch.; King's Coll., London (BSc, PhD). ARC Fellow, Univ. of Oxford, 1961–64; Lectr in Botany and Biochemistry, Univ. of Aberdeen, 1964–70; Sen. Lectr, 1970–73, Reader, 1973–76, Dept of Biol Sciences, Univ. of Warwick; SERC Senior Res. Fellow, 1983–88. Sen. Vis. Fellow, St John's Coll., Oxford, 1992–93; Vis. Prof., Oxford Centre for Molecular Scis, 1997–. Mem. EMBO, 1986. LRPS 1987. Tate & Lyle Award (for contribs to plant biochem.), 1980. *Publications:* 150 papers in biochem. jls. *Recreations:* photography, hill walking. *Address:* 44 Sunningdale Avenue, Kenilworth, Warwicks CV8 2BZ. *T:* (01926) 856382.

ELLIS, Richard Peter; Principal Assistant Treasury Solicitor, Legal Advisory Division, Ministry of Defence, 1988–91; *b* 25 Oct. 1931; *s* of late Comdr Thomas Ellis, RN and Kathleen Mary Ellis (*nee* Lewis); *m* 1963, Penelope Jane, *yr d* of late Captain J. B. Hall, RN; two *s* two *d. Educ:* Sherborne; RMA Sandhurst. Commissioned Royal Irish Fusiliers, 1952; served 1st Bn, BAOR, Berlin, Korea, Kenya; resigned commission 1957. Called to the Bar, Lincoln's Inn, 1960; Practised Common Law Bar, 1960–65, Oxford Circuit; Treasury Solicitor's Dept, 1965–91. *Recreations:* country pursuits, travel, reading. *Address:* c/o Lloyds TSB, Somerton, Somerset TA11 7NB. *Club:* Army and Navy.

ELLIS, Prof. Richard Salisbury, FRS 1995; Professor of Astronomy, California Institute of Technology, since 1999; Director, Palomar Observatory, since 2000; Professor of Observational Astrophysics, University of Cambridge, since 2000; *b* 25 May 1950; *s* of late Capt. Arthur Ellis, MBE and of Marion Ellis (*née* Davies); *m* 1972, Barbara Williams; one *s* one *d. Educ:* Abergele GS; University Coll. London (BSc Hons 1971; Fellow, 1998); Wolfson Coll., Oxford (DPhil 1974) FRAS 1974; FInstP 1998. Durham University: Sen. Demonstrator in Physics, 1974–77; Res. Asst, 1977–81; Lectr in Astronomy, 1981–83; Principal Res. Fellow, Royal Greenwich Observatory, 1983–85; Prof. of Astronomy, Durham Univ., 1985–93; SERC Sen. Res. Fellow, 1989–94; Cambridge University: Plumian Prof. of Astronomy and Exptl Philosophy, 1993–99; Dir, Inst. of Astronomy, 1994–99; Professorial Fellow, Magdalene Coll., 1994–99. Chm., SERC Large Telescope Panel, 1986–90; Mem., Anglo-Australian Telescope Bd, 1991–95. Associate, Canadian Inst. of Advanced Res., 1993–; Member: Space Telescope Science Inst. Council, 1995–; Gemini Telescopes Bd, 1996–98. Visiting Professor: Space Telescope Science Inst., 1985; Anglo-Australian Observatory, 1991; CIT, 1991, 1997; Princeton, 1992; Carnegie Observatory, 1998. Lectures: J. L. Bishop, Princeton, 1992; Halley, Oxford, 1993; Cormack, RSE, 1996; Lockyer, RAS, 1997; Sackler, Harvard, 1998; Bakerian, Royal Soc., 1998; Poynting, Birmingham, 1998; Grubb Parsons, Durham, 1999; Rosenblum, Jerusalem, 1999. *Publications:* Epoch of Galaxy Formation, 1988; Observational Tests of Cosmological Inflation, 1991; Large Scale Structure in the Universe, 1999; numerous articles in astronomical jls. *Recreations:* exploration, photography, music, ski-ing. *Address:* Astronomy Department, Mailstop 105–24, California Institute of Technology, Pasadena, LA 91125, USA. *T:* (626) 3952598; Institute of Astronomy, Madingley Road, Cambridge CB3 0HA. *T:* (01223) 337548.

ELLIS, (Robert) Thomas; *b* 15 March 1924; *s* of Robert and Edith Ann Ellis; *m* 1949, Nona Harcourt Williams; three *s* one *d. Educ:* Universities of Wales and Nottingham. Works Chemist, ICI, 1944–47; Coal Miner, 1947–55; Mining Engineer, 1955–70; Manager, Bersham Colliery, N Wales, 1957–70. MP Wrexham, 1970–83 (Lab, 1970–81; SDP, 1981–83). Contested: Clywd South West (SDP) 1983, (SDP/Alliance) 1987; Pontypridd (SLD) Feb. 1989. Mem., European Parlt, 1975–79. *Publication:* Mines and Men, 1971. *Recreations:* golf, reading, music. *Address:* 3 Old Vicarage, Ruabon, Wrexham LL14 6LG. *T:* (01978) 821128.

ELLIS, Ven. Robin Gareth; Archdeacon of Plymouth, 1982–2000; *b* 8 Dec. 1935; *s* of Walter and Morva Ellis; *m* 1964, Anne Ellis (*née* Landers); three *s. Educ:* Worksop Coll., Notts; Pembroke Coll., Oxford (BCL, MA). Curate of Swinton, 1960–63; Asst Chaplain, Worksop Coll., 1963–66; Vicar of Swaffham Prior and Reach, and Asst Director of Religious Education, Diocese of Ely, 1966–74; Vicar of St Augustine, Wisbech, 1974–82; Vicar of St Paul's, Yelverton, 1982–86. *Recreations:* cricket, theatre, prison reform. *Address:* 24 Lyndhurst Road, Exmouth, Devon EX8 3DT. *T:* (01395) 272891.

ELLIS, Roger Wykeham, CBE 1984; Director, Asquith Court Schools Ltd, since 1992; *b* 3 Oct. 1929; *s* of Cecil Ellis, solicitor, and Pamela Unwin; *m* 1964, Margaret Jean Stevenson; one *s* two *d. Educ:* St Peter's Sch., Seaford; Winchester Coll.; Trinity Coll., Oxford (Schol., MA). Royal Navy, 1947–49. Asst Master, Harrow Sch., 1952–67, and Housemaster of the Head Master's House, 1961–67; Headmaster of Rossall Sch., 1967–72; Master of Marlborough College, 1972–86. Graduate Recruitment Manager, Barclays Bank, 1986–91. Chm., HMC, 1983. Member: Harrow Borough Educn Cttee, 1956–60; Wilts County Educn Cttee, 1975–86. Governor: Campion Sch., Athens, 1981–; Cheam Sch., 1975–93 (Chm. of Govs, 1987–93); Hawtreys Sch., 1975–86; Sandroyd Sch., 1982–86; Fettes Coll., 1983–94; St Edward's Sch., Oxford, 1985– (Chm., 1992–99); Harrow Sch., 1987–97. Trustee, Hanover Foundn, 2001–. *Publication:* Who's Who in Victorian Britain, 1997. *Recreations:* golf, fishing. *Address:* 18 North Avenue, Ealing, W13 8AP. *Clubs:* East India; Denham Golf.

ELLIS, Sir Ronald, Kt 1978; BSc Tech; FREng, FIMechE; Chairman, EIDC Ltd, 1981–93; *b* 12 Aug. 1925; *s* of William Ellis and Besse Brownbill; *m* 1st, 1956, Cherry Hazel Brown (*d* 1978); one *s* one *d*; 2nd, 1979, Myra Ann Royle. *Educ:* Preston Grammar Sch.; Manchester Univ. (BScTech Hons 1949). FIMechE 1949; FCIT 1975; FREng (FEng 1981). Gen. Man., BUT Ltd, 1954; Gen. Sales and Service Man., 1962, Gen. Man., 1966, Leyland Motors Ltd; Man. Dir, British Leyland Truck and Bus, 1968; Dir, British Leyland Motor Corp. Ltd, 1970. Head of Defence Sales, MoD, 1976–81. Chm., Bus Manufacturers Hldg Co., 1972–76. Dir of corp. develt, Wilkinson Sword Gp, 1981–82; Pres. and Man. Dir, Industrial Div., 1982–85, Dir, Internat. Gp, 1981–86, Allegheny International. Director: Yarrow & Co., 1981–86; Redman Heenan Internat., 1981–86; Bull Thompson Associates, 1987–89; IDRH Ltd, 1987–89; R. L. Holdings Ltd, 1989–90. Vice-Pres., SMMT, 1972–73; Dir, ROFs, 1976–81. Mem., Engineering Council, 1988–92. Governor, UMIST, 1970–92, Vice-Pres., 1983–92, Hon. Fellow, 1981. Freeman, City of London, 1984. *Recreation:* fishing.

ELLIS, Ven. Timothy William, DPhil; Archdeacon of Stow and Lindsey, since 2001; *b* 26 Aug. 1953; *s* of Albert and Betty Ellis; *m* 1976, Susan Weston; two *s* one *d. Educ:* King's Coll., London (AKC 1975); York Univ. (DPhil 1998). Ordained deacon, 1976, priest, 1977; Asst Curate, St John, Old Trafford, 1976–80; Vicar, St Thomas, Pendleton and Chaplain to Salford Coll. of Technol., 1980–87; Vicar, St Leonard, Norwood, 1987–2001; Priest i/c, St Hilda, Shiregreen, 1994–97; RD Ecclesfield, 1994–99. Sec., 1988–94, Chm., 1999–2001, Sheffield DAC. Hon. Canon, Sheffield Cathedral, 2000–01. *Recreations:* Sheffield Wednesday FC, wine, foreign travel, golf. *Address:* The Archdeacon's House, Hackthorn, Lincoln LN2 3PF. *T:* (01673) 860382.

ELLIS, Tom; *see* Ellis, R. T.

ELLIS, Vernon James; International Chairman, Accenture (formerly Andersen Consulting), since 1999; *b* 1 July 1947; *s* of Norman and Phyllis Ellis; *m* 1972, Hazel Marilyn Lucas; one *s* one *d. Educ:* Magdalen Coll. Sch., Oxford; Magdalen Coll., Oxford (MA Hons PPE 1969). FCA 1982. Andersen Consulting: Partner, 1969; Man. Partner, UK, 1986–89; Man. Partner, Andersen Consulting Europe, ME, Africa and India, 1989–99. Member: Bd, Prince of Wales Business Leaders Forum, 1997– (Chm. Bd,

2001–); Adv. Council, European Movt, 1997–; Business Adv. Council, Britain in Europe, 1998–; Council, World Economic Forum, 1999–. Trustee, Centre for European Reform, 1998–. UK private sector delegate, G8 DOTForce, 2000–01. Member: Develt Cttee, Magdalen Coll., Oxford, 1999–; Adv. Council, Saïd Business Sch., Univ. of Oxford, 1996–; Foundn Bd, Internat. Inst. of Mgt Develt, Lausanne, 1996–; Industry and Commerce Cttee, SCF, 1996–. Mem. Bd, ENO, 2001–; Mem. Bd, 1996–, Pres., 2000–, Classical Opera Co. (Chm., 1996–2000). *Publications:* (jtly) Britain, Business and Europe, 1998; Reconnecting Europe, 1999; eEurope Takes Off, 1999. *Recreations:* music, opera, theatre, gardening, wine, cooking, photography. *Address:* Accenture, 60 Queen Victoria Street, EC4N 4TW; *e-mail:* vernon.j.ellis@accenture.com.

ELLIS, Dr (William) Herbert (Baxter), AFC 1954; Medical Adviser, Department of Health and Social Security, 1972–92; Underwriting Member of Lloyd's; *b* 2 July 1921; *er s* of William Baxter Ellis and Georgina Isabella Ellis (*née* Waller); *m* 1st, 1948, Margaret Mary Limb (marr. diss.); one *s* one *d*; 2nd, 1977, Mollie Marguerite Clarke (marr. diss.); 3rd, 1994, Jean Stanley Stawell Gross, *widow* of Ken Gross. *Educ:* Oundle Sch.; Durham Univ. (MD, BS). Royal Navy, 1945–59: Surg. Comdr, Fleet Air Arm Pilot. Motor industry, 1960–71; research into human aspects of road traffic accidents, 1960–71; Dir-Gen., Dr Barnardo's, 1971–73; dir of various companies. Industrial Medical Consultant: Wellworthy, 1979–87; Telephone Manufacturing Co., 1980–87; Plessey Co., 1981–87. Part-time Mem., Employment Medical Adv. Service, 1973–81. Freeman, City of London, 1994; Liveryman, Apothecaries' Soc., 1997. St John Ambulance: Chief Comdr, 1989–91; County Surgeon, 1979–87, Comdr, 1987–89, Glos Br.; Chm., St John Fellowship, 2001–. KStJ 1989 (CStJ 1988). Gilbert Blane Medal, RCP, 1954. *Publications:* Physiological and Psychological Aspects of Deck Landings, 1954; Hippocrates, RN—memoirs of a naval flying doctor (autobiog.), 1988; Why Not Live a Little Longer?, 1997; various on the human factor in industrial management. *Recreations:* memories of walking, observing humanity, mending fences. *Address:* Little Dalling, Rocks Lane, High Hurstwood, East Sussex TN22 4BH. *T:* (01825) 733139; 415 Dandaro Village, PO Borrowdale, Harare, Zimbabwe. *T:* 91317481. *Clubs:* Army and Navy, Naval and Military.

ELLIS-REES, Hugh Francis, CB 1986; Regional Director, West Midlands, Departments of the Environment and Transport, 1981–89; *b* 5 March 1929; *s* of late Sir Hugh Ellis-Rees, KCMG, CB and Lady (Eileen Frances Anne) Ellis-Rees; *m* 1956, Elisabeth de Mestre Gray; three *s* one *d. Educ:* Ampleforth Coll.; Balliol Coll., Oxford. Served Grenadier Guards, 1948–49. Joined War Office, 1954; DoE, 1970; Cabinet Office, 1972–74; Under Sec., DoE, 1974. Mem., Black Country Develt Corp., 1990–98.

ELLISON, Dame Jillian Paula Anne, (Dame Jill), DBE 2001; Director of Nursing, Birmingham Heartlands and Solihull NHS Trust (Teaching) (formerly East Birmingham Hospital), since 1990; *b* 31 Jan. 1955; *d* of Joseph Ellison and Mollie Yvonne Ellison (*née* North). *Educ:* St Margaret's Sch., Bushey; Birmingham Poly. (HVCert 1980); MA UCE. Trained at Mddx Hosp. Sch. of Nursing, 1973–76 (SRN); Staff Nurse: Middx Hosp., London, 1976–77; Hadassah Hosp., Israel, 1978–79; (Intensive Care) Charing Cross Hosp., 1979–80; Sandwell Health Authority: Health Visitor, 1980–85; Nurse Manager, 1985–87; Dist Sen. Nurse, 1987–90. *Recreation:* walking, cycling. *Address:* Birmingham Heartlands Hospital, Bordesley Green East, Birmingham B9 5SS. *T:* (0121) 424 1323.

ELLISON, Rt Rev. John Alexander; *see* Paraguay, Bishop of.

ELLISON, Lawrence J., (Larry); Chief Executive Officer, since 1977, and Chairman, since 1996, Oracle Corporation (President, 1977–96); *b* New York City, 1944; *s* of Florence Spellman; adopted by Louis and Lillian Ellison: *Educ:* High Sch., Chicago; Univ. of Illinois. Formerly computer programmer, Calif; posts with Amdahl Inc., 1967–71, and Ampex Corp., 1972–77; Founder (with Bob Miner), Oracle, 1977. Dir, Apple Computer Inc., 1997–. *Address:* Oracle Corporation, 500 Oracle Parkway, Redwood City, CA 94065, USA.

ELLISON, Sir Ralph Henry C.; *see* Carr-Ellison, Sir R. H.

ELLMAN, Louise Joyce; MP (Lab and Co-op) Liverpool Riverside, since 1997; *b* 14 Nov. 1945; *d* of late Harold and Annie Rosenberg; *m* 1967, Geoffrey David Ellman; one *s* one *d. Educ:* Manchester High Sch. for Girls; Hull Univ. (BA Hons); York Univ. (MPhil). Worked in further educn and on Open Univ., 1970–76. Member: Lancs CC, 1970–97 (Leader, Lab Gp, 1977–97; Leader, Council, 1981–97; Chm., 1981–85; Hon. Alderman, 1998–); W Lancs DC, 1974–87; Local Govt Adv. Cttee, Labour Party's NEC, 1977–; Regl Exec., NW Labour Party, 1985– (Chm., 1993–98). A Vice Pres., LGA, 1997–. Contested (Lab) Darwen, 1979. Mem., Select Cttee on Envmt, Transport and Regl Affairs, 1997–. Chm., PLP Regl Govt Gp, 1999–. Vice-Chm., Lancashire Enterprises, 1982–97; Founder Mem., Co-operative Enterprises NW, 1979–; Founder Chm., NW Regl Assoc., 1992–93; Mem., NW Partnership, 1993–97. Youngest mem., Lancs CC, 1970; youngest mem. and first woman to be Chm., 1981. *Recreations:* theatre, travel. *Address:* House of Commons, SW1A 0AA.

ELLORY, Prof. (John) Clive, PhD; Professor of Human Physiology, since 1996, and Head of Physiology Department, since 1994, University of Oxford; Fellow of Corpus Christi College, Oxford, since 1985; *b* 16 April 1944; *s* of Ronald and Muriel Ellory; *m* 1969, Jane Metcalfe; one *s* one *d. Educ:* Latymer Upper Sch.; Univ. of Bristol (BSc Biochemistry 1964; PhD Zoology 1967); MA 1975, ScD 1995, Cantab; MA 1985, DSc 1996, Oxon. SO, 1967–71, SSO, 1971–75, PSO, 1975, Inst. of Animal Physiology, Babraham; Lectr, Dept of Physiology, Univ. of Cambridge, 1975–84; Fellow, Queens' Coll., Cambridge, 1975–84; Reader in Human Physiology, Univ. of Oxford, 1985–96. Vis. Associate Prof., Yale, and Guest Fellow, Silliman Coll., 1971; Vis. Associate Prof., 1975, Vis. Prof., 1982, Univ. of Illinois; Investigator, US Antarctic Res. Program, McMurdo, Antarctica, 1980; Vis. Prof., Univ. of Nice, 1985, 1993; Royal Soc. Israel Res. Prof., Technion, Haifa, 1994. FMedSci 1999. *Publications:* jointly: Membrane Transport in Red Cells, 1977; Red Cell Membranes: a methodological approach, 1982; The Binding and Transport of Anions in Living Tissues, 1982; The Sodium Pump, 1985; Patronage and Plate at Corpus Christi College, Oxford, 1999. *Recreations:* food, antique silver, hill walking. *Address:* Corpus Christi College, Merton Street, Oxford OX1 4JF. *T:* (01865) 276760.

ELLSWORTH, Robert; Chairman, Hamilton Technology Ventures LP, since 2000; Deputy Secretary of Defense, USA, 1975–77; *b* 11 June 1926; *s* of Willoughby Fred Ellsworth and Lucile Rarig Ellsworth; *m* 1956, Vivian Esther Sies; one *s* one *d. Educ:* Univs of Kansas (BSME) and Michigan (JD). Active service, US Navy, 1944–46, 1950–53 (Lt-Comdr). Mem. United States Congress, 1961–67; Asst to President of US, 1969; Ambassador and Permanent Representative of US on N Atlantic Council, 1969–71; Asst Sec. of Defense (Internat. Security Affairs), 1974–75. Vice Pres., IISS, 1998– (Mem., 1973–; Chm. Council, 1990–96). Licensed Lay Reader, Episcopal Dio. of Washington. Hon. LLD: Ottawa, 1969; Boston, 1970. Knight of Honour, Johanniter Orden, Berlin, 1996. *Recreations:* single sculling, swimming, music. *Address:* Apt 708A, 3900 Cathedral Avenue NW, Washington, DC 20016–5299, USA. *Clubs:* Brook (New York); Army and Navy (Washington).

ELLWOOD, Peter Brian, CBE 2001; Chief Executive, Lloyds TSB Group plc, since 1997 (Deputy Group Chief Executive, 1995–97); *b* 15 May 1943; *s* of Isaac and Edith Ellwood; *m* 1968, Judy Ann Windsor; one *s* two *d. Educ:* King's Sch., Macclesfield. FCIB. Barclays, Bristol, 1961–89; Controller, Barclaycards Ops, 1983–85; Chief Exec., Barclaycard, 1985–89; Chief Exec., Retail Banking, TSB, 1989–92; Chief Exec., TSB Bank, 1992–95; Gp Chief Exec., TSB Gp, 1992–95; Chm., Visa International, 1994–99. Dir, Sears, 1994–97; non-exec. Dir, Royal Philharmonic Orchestra Ltd, 1996–. Trustee, Royal Theatre, Northampton, 1982–. Mem. Court, Nene Coll., Northampton, 1989–. CIMgt; FRSA. Hon. LLD Leicester, 1994; DUniv Central England, 1995. *Recreations:* theatre, music. *Address:* Lloyds TSB Group plc, 71 Lombard Street, EC3P 3BS.

ELLY, (Richard) Charles; His Honour Judge Elly; a Circuit Judge, since 1998; Partner, Reynolds, Parry-Jones & Crawford, solicitors, 1968–98; *b* 20 March 1942; *s* of Harold Elly and Dora Ellen Elly (*née* Luing); *m* 1967, Marion Rose Blackwell; one *s* one *d. Educ:* Sir William Borlase's Sch., Marlow; Hertford Coll., Oxford (MA); Coll. of Law, London. Admitted solicitor, 1966. Secretary: Southern Assoc. of Law Socs, 1975–82; Berks, Bucks and Oxon Br., Law Soc., 1975–82 (Pres., 1988–89); Law Society: Mem. Council, 1981–97; Dep. Vice-Pres., 1992–93; Vice-Pres., 1993–94; Pres., 1994–95. Mem., Lord Chancellor's Adv. Cttee on Legal Educn and Conduct, 1997–98. Mem., Berks CC, 1980–81. Chairman: Maidenhead Deanery Synod, 1972–79; High Wycombe and Dist CAB, 1983–88. President: Cookham Soc., 1987–97; Hertford Coll. Lawyers Assoc., 1995–98; Criminal Law Solicitors Assoc., 1995–98. Governor: Coll. of Law, 1984–2000; Sir William Borlase's Sch., 1995– (Chm., 1996–2001). FRSA 1995. Hon. LLD Kingston, 1994. *Recreations:* bird-watching, theatre, walking, gardening. *Address:* Reading County Court, Friar Street, Reading, Berks RG1 1HE. *Club:* Oxford and Cambridge.

ELMES, Caroline Myfanwy Tonge, CMG 2001; HM Diplomatic Service; Ambassador to Angola, since 1998; *b* 20 Sept. 1948. Second Sec., FCO, 1975; First Secretary: Czechoslovakia, 1978–81; FCO, 1981–85; (Econ.), Rome, 1985–89; Dep. High Comr and Head of Chancery, Sri Lanka, 1989–92; Dep. Head of Mission, Czechoslovakia, 1992–95; Head of S Asia Dept, FCO, 1995–98; language trng, 1998. *Address:* c/o Foreign and Commonwealth Office, King Charles Street, SW1A 2AH.

ELMES, Dr Peter Cardwell, Director, Medical Research Council Pneumoconiosis Unit, Llandough Hospital, Penarth, 1976–81, retired from MRC 1982; Consultant in Occupational Lung Diseases, since 1976; *b* 12 Oct. 1921; *s* of Florence Romaine Elmes and Lilian Bryham (*née* Cardwell); *m* 1957, Margaret Elizabeth (*née* Staley); two *s* one *d. Educ:* Rugby; Oxford Univ. (BM, BCh 1945); Western Reserve Univ., Cleveland, Ohio (MD 1943). MRCP 1951. Mil. Service, RAMC, 1946–48. Trng posts, Taunton and Oxford, 1948–50; Registrar, then Sen. Registrar in Medicine, Hammersmith Hosp., 1950–58; Dept of Therapeutics, Queen's Univ., Belfast: Sen. Lectr, 1959–63; Reader, 1963–67; Prof. of Therapeutic Sciences, 1967–71; Whitla Prof. of Therapeutics and Pharmacology, 1971–76. Member: Medicines Commn, 1976–79; Industrial Injuries Adv. Council, 1982–87; Indep. Scientific Cttee on Smoking and Health, 1982–92. Chm., Ruperra Castle Conservation Trust, 1997–; Vice Chm., Welsh Historic Gardens Trust, 1997–. *Publications:* contrib. med. jls on chronic chest disease, treatment and control of infection, occupational lung disease asbestosis, and mesothelioma. *Recreations:* working on house and garden, saving castles and historic gardens. *Address:* Dawros House, St Andrews Road, Dinas Powys, Vale of Glamorgan CF64 4HB. *T:* (029) 2051 2102, *Fax:* (029) 2051 5975.

ELMS, Marsha Marilyn; JP; MA; Headteacher, Kendrick Girls' School, since 1993; *b* 11 June 1946; *d* of James F. Carey and Carolyn M. Carey; *m* 1968, Richard A. Elms; one *s* one *d. Educ:* Tottenham County Grammar Sch.; Bedford Coll., London Univ. (BA); Brunel Univ. (PGCE 1969); Reading Univ. (MA 1988). Featherstone High School, Southall: teacher, 1969–90; Head, Liberal Studies Faculty, 1973–75; Dep. Head, 1990; Dep. Headteacher, Magna Carta Sch., Staines, 1990–93; acting Headteacher, Ashmead Sch., Reading, Summer term 1998. Mem., SHA, 1994–. JP Middx 1982. *Publications:* articles for SHA and in educnl jls. *Recreations:* family, holidays, ski-ing, Spurs supporter, food. *Address:* Roseneath, Altwood Bailey, Maidenhead, Berks SL6 4PQ. *T:* (01628) 620085.

ELMSLIE, Maj.-Gen. Alexander Frederic Joseph, CB 1959; CBE 1955; psc; CEng; FIMechE; FCIT; *b* 31 Oct. 1905; *er s* of Captain A. W. Elmslie, RAEC and Florence Edith Elmslie (*née* Kirk); *m* 1931, Winifred Allan Wright; one *d* one *s. Educ:* Farnham Grammar Sch.; RMC Sandhurst; Staff Coll., Camberley. Commissioned in Royal Army Service Corps, 29 Jan. 1925, and subsequently served in Shanghai, Ceylon, E Africa and Singapore; Lieutenant 1927; Captain 1935; served War of 1939–45 (despatches) in Madagascar, India (Combined Ops) and Europe (SHAEF); Major, 1942; Lt-Col 1948; Temp. Brig. 1943; Brig. 1953; Maj.-Gen. 1958. Dep. Dir of Supplies and Transport, War Office, 1953–55; Dir of Supplies and Transport, GHQ Far East Land Forces, 1956–57; Inspector, RASC, War Office, 1957–60, retired. Chairman Traffic Commissioners: NW Traffic Area, 1962–64; SE Traffic Area, 1965–75. Hon. Col 43 (Wessex) Inf. Div. Coln, RASC, TA, 1960–64; Col Comdt, RASC, 1964–65; Col Comdt, Royal Corps of Transport, 1965–69. Fellow, Royal Commonwealth Soc. *Address:* 9 Stanmer House, Furness Road, Eastbourne, E Sussex BN21 4EY.

ELNASHAI, Prof. Amr Salah-Eldin, PhD; FREng; FASCE, FIStructE; Professor of Earthquake Engineering, and Associate Director, Mid-America Earthquake Centre, University of Illinois at Urbana-Champaign, since 2001; *b* 8 May 1954; *s* of Salah-Eldin Hamed Elnashai and Bitedal Rizk Agiz; *m* 1st, Maha Dabbous; one *s*; 2nd, Neveen Elnashai; one *s. Educ:* Cairo Univ. (BSc); Imperial Coll., London (MSc, DIC 1980; PhD 1984). FASCE 1997; FIStructE 1997; FREng 2001. Lectr, Cairo Univ., 1977–78; Res. Asst, Imperial Coll., London, 1980–84; Sen. Engr, Wimpey Offshore, 1984–85; Imperial College, London University: Lectr, 1985–89; Reader, 1989–92; Prof. of Earthquake Engrg, 1992–2001; Principal Consultant, EQE Internat. Ltd, 1995–2001; Dir, Newmark Labs, Univ. of Ill, 2001–. *Publications:* numerous refereed jl papers and keynote papers; also contrib. tech. magazine articles, book chapters and tech. reports, incl. earthquake field mission reports, on analysis, testing and design of structures subjected to earthquake loading. *Recreations:* squash, scuba diving. *Address:* Civil and Environmental Engineering Department, University of Illinois at Urbana-Champaign, Urbana, IL 61801, USA.

ELPHICK, Michael John; actor; *b* 19 Sept. 1946; *s* of Herbert Frederick Elphick and Joan Mary (*née* Haddow); one *d. Educ:* Lancastrian Sch. for Boys, Chichester; Central Sch. of Speech and Drama. *Theatre* includes: The Changing Room, Royal Court; Hamlet, Royal Court; The Ticket of Leave Man, National; Pygmalion, Albery, 1997; *films* include: Blind Terror; Phyliss Dixie; The Knowledge; The Elephant Man; Quadrophenia; The Curse of the Pink Panther; Gorky Park, 1983; Privates on Parade, 1983; Little Dorritt, 1987; The Krays; Buddy's Song, 1992; *television* includes: The Nearly Man; Holding On; Blue

Remembered Hills; Bloomfield; Private Schultz, 1982; Smiley's People; Oxbridge Blues, 1984; David Copperfield, 1999; *series:* Pull the Other One, 1984; Three Up, Two Down, 1985–88; Boon, 1986–93; Harry, 1993–94. *Publication:* Absolute Beginner's Guide to Cookery. *Recreation:* boats. *Address:* c/o ICM, Oxford House, 76 Oxford Street, W1N 0AX. *T:* (020) 7636 6565, *Fax:* (020) 7323 0101. *Clubs:* Groucho, Gerry's.

ELPHIN, Bishop of, (RC), since 1994; **Most Rev. Christopher Jones,** DD; *b* 3 March 1936; *s* of Christopher Jones and Christina Hanley. *Educ:* Maynooth Coll. (BA Classics 1958); UC Galway, NUI (Higher DipEd 1963); UC Dublin, NUI (DipSoc 1973). Ordained priest, 1962; Teacher, St Muireadach's, Ballina, 1962–65; Teacher, 1965–71, Spiritual Dir, 1972–79, Summerhill Coll., Sligo; Archivist, Diocesan Office, 1971–72; Dir, Sligo Social Service Council, 1973–87; Curate, Rosses Point, Sligo, 1979–87; Administrator, Cathedral Parish, Sligo, 1987–94. Freeman, Sligo City, 1995. *Publication:* Child, Adolescent and Adult in Family and Community, 1976, 2nd edn 1978. *Recreations:* walking, golfing, music, reading. *Address:* St Mary's, Sligo, Ireland. *T:* (71) 62670, (71) 50106. *Clubs:* Strandhill Golf; Co. Sligo Golf.

ELPHINSTONE, family name of **Lord Elphinstone**.

ELPHINSTONE, 19th Lord *cr* 1509; **Alexander Mountstuart Elphinstone;** Baron (UK) 1885; *b* 15 April 1980; *e s* of 18th Lord Elphinstone and of Willa Mary Gabriel, 4th *d* of Major David Chetwode; *S* father, 1994. *Educ:* Belhaven Hill Sch.; Eton Coll. *Heir: b* Hon. Angus John Elphinstone, *b* 7 July 1982.

ELPHINSTONE of Glack, Sir John, 11th Bt *cr* 1701, of Logie Elphinstone and Nova Scotia; Land Agent, retired; *b* 12 Aug. 1924; *s* of Thomas George Elphinston (*d* 1967), and of Gladys Mary Elphinston, *d* of late Ernest Charles Lambert Congdon; *S* uncle, 1970; *m* 1953, Margaret Doreen, *d* of Edric Tasker; four *s*. *Educ:* Eagle House, Sandhurst, Berks; Repton; Emmanuel College, Cambridge (BA). Lieut, Royal Marines, 1942–48. Chartered Surveyor; Land Agent with ICI plc, 1956–83; Consultant, Gandy & Son, Northwich, 1983–88. Past Pres., Cheshire Agricultural Valuers' Assoc.; Past Chm., Land Agency and Agric. Div., Lancs, Cheshire and IoM Branch, RICS; Mem., Lancs River Authority, 1970–74. *Recreations:* country pursuits, cricket. *Heir: s* Alexander Elphinston [*b* 6 June 1955; *m* 1986, Ruth, *er d* of Rev. Robert Dunnett; three *s* one *d*].

ELPHINSTONE, Sir John (Howard Main), 6th Bt *cr* 1816, of Sowerby, Cumberland; *b* 25 Feb. 1949; *o s* of Sir Douglas Elphinstone, 5th Bt and of Helen Barbara Elphinstone (*née* Main); *S* father, 1995; *m* 1990, Diana Barbara Quilliam, *d* of Dr B. Q. Callow. *Educ:* Loretto Sch., Midlothian. Career in food hygiene and quality control in food and associated businesses, 1988–. *Heir: cousin* Henry Charles Elphinstone, *b* 7 July 1958. *Address:* Garden Cottage, 6 Amherst Road, Sevenoaks, Kent TN13 3LS. *T:* (01732) 459077.

ELRINGTON, Prof. Christopher Robin, FSA, FRHistS; Editor, Victoria History of the Counties of England, 1977–94; Professor of History, Institute of Historical Research, University of London, 1992–94, now Professor Emeritus; *b* 20 Jan. 1930; *s* of late Brig. Maxwell Elrington, DSO, OBE, and Beryl Joan (*née* Ommanney); *m* 1951, Jean Margaret (*née* Buchanan), RIBA; one *s* one *d*. *Educ:* Wellington Coll., Berks; University Coll., Oxford (MA); Bedford Coll., London (MA). FSA 1964; FRHistS 1969. Asst to Editor, Victoria County History, 1954; Editor for Glos, 1960; Dep. Editor, 1968. British Acad. Overseas Vis. Fellow, Folger Shakespeare Library, Washington DC, 1976. Mem., Adv. Bd for Redundant Churches, 1982–96. Pres., Bristol and Glos Archaeol Soc., 1984–85. Hon. Gen. Editor, 1962–72, Pres., 1983–, Wilts Record Soc.; Hon. Gen. Editor, Glos Record Series, 1995–. *Publications:* Divers Letters of Roger de Martival, Bishop of Salisbury, 2 vols, 1963, 1972; Wiltshire Feet of Fines, Edward III, 1974; articles in Victoria County History and in learned jls. *Address:* 34 Lloyd Baker Street, WC1X 9AB. *T:* (020) 7837 4971.

ELS, Theodore Ernest, (Ernie); South African golfer; *b* 17 Oct. 1969; *s* of Cornelius, (Nils), and Hester Els; *m* 1998, Liezl Wehmeyer; one *d*. *Educ:* Delville Sch.; Jan de Klerk Tech. Coll. Professional golfer, 1989–; winner: Jun. World Championship, USA, 1984; South African Open, 1992, 1996, 1998; US Open, 1994, 1997; World Match Play Championship, 1994, 1995, 1996; European Order of Merit, 1995; South African PGA Championship, 1995; Million Dollar Challenge, Sun City, 1999; Nedbank Golf Challenge, Sun City, 2000. *Address:* 46 Chapman Road, Klippoortjie 1401, South Africa.

ELSDEN, Sidney Reuben, BA, PhD (Cambridge); Professor of Biology, University of East Anglia, 1965–85; *b* 13 April 1915; *er s* of late Reuben Charles Elsden, Cambridge; *m* 1st, 1942, Frances Scott Wilson (*d* 1943); 2nd, 1948, Erica Barbara Scott, *er d* of late Grahame Scott Gardiner, Wisbech, Cambs; twin *s*. *Educ:* Cambridge and County High Sch. for Boys; Fitzwilliam House, Cambridge (Exhibn, Goldsmiths' Co.). Lecturer, Biochemistry, University of Edinburgh, 1937–42; Mem. Scientific Staff of ARC Unit for Animal Physiology, 1943–48; Sen. Lectr in Microbiology, 1948–59, West Riding Prof. of Microbiology, 1959–65, Sheffield Univ.; Hon. Dir, ARC Unit for Microbiology, Univ. of Sheffield, 1952–65; Dir, ARC Food Research Inst., 1965–77. Visiting Prof. of Microbiology, Univ. of Illinois, Urbana, Ill, USA, 1956. Pres., Soc. for General Microbiology, 1969–72, Hon. Mem. 1977. Hon. DSc Sheffield, 1985. *Publications:* contribs to scientific jls on metabolism of micro-organisms. *Recreations:* gardening, angling. *Address:* 26a The Street, Costessey, Norwich NR8 5DB.

ELSE, Martin Thomas; Chief Executive, Royal Free Hampstead NHS Trust, since 1994; *b* 21 May 1953; *s* of late Richard Else and of Lilian Margaret Else (*née* Stickells); *m* 1978, Jennifer Louise Bridges; one *s* one *d*. *Educ:* Farnborough Grammar Sch.; Univ. of Salford (BSc Econ); Southampton Coll. of Technol.; London Business Sch. (Sloan Fellowship with Dist.). CPFA (IPFA 1979). Finance trainee, City and Hackney HA, 1975–79; Principal Finance Planning Manager, 1979–82, Principal Asst Treas., 1982–83, NE Thames RHA; Dep. Treas., 1983–86, Dir of Finance, 1986–90, Hampstead HA; Dir of Finance and Dep. Chief Exec., Royal Free Hampstead NHS Trust, 1990–94. Royal Free Hospital: Hon. Sec., Treas., and Special Trustee, 1986–; Trustee, Appeal Trust, 1988–92; Chm., Cancerkin Mgt Cttee, 1990–94; Trustee, Hampstead Wells and Campden Trust, 1996–. *Recreations:* football, golf, horseracing. *Address:* Chief Executive's Office, Royal Free Hospital, Pond Street, Hampstead, NW3 2QG. *T:* (020) 7830 2176.

ELSMORE, Sir Lloyd, Kt 1982; OBE 1977; JP; Mayor of Manukau City, 1968–84; *b* 16 Jan. 1913; *s* of George and Minnie Elsmore; *m* 1935, Marie Kirk; two *s* two *d*. *Educ:* Greymouth High Sch. Commenced grocery business on own account, 1933; President: Grocers' Assoc., 1949, 1950, 1952, Life Member, 1954; NZ Grocers' Federation, 1955, Life Member, 1959. Mem., Auckland Harbour Bd, 1971–83. Local Body involvement, 1953–; Mayor of Ellerslie Borough Council, 1956–62. *Recreations:* boating, fishing, gardening. *Address:* 47 Park Avenue, Pakuranga Park, Pakuranga, Manukau City, New Zealand. *Club:* Rotary (Pakuranga).

ELSOM, Cecil Harry, CBE 1976; Consultant, EPR Partnership (formerly Elsom Pack & Roberts, Architects), since 1980 (Senior Partner, 1947–80); *b* 17 Jan. 1912; *s* of Julius Israelson and Leah Lazarus; name changed by deed poll to Elsom, 1930; *m* 1940, Gwyneth Mary Buxton Hopkin (*d* 1997); two *s*. *Educ:* Upton Cross Elem. Sch.; West Ham Polytechnic; Northern Polytechnic Architectural School. FRIBA. Started practice by winning competition for town hall, Welwyn Garden City, 1933; partner in Lyons Israel & Elsom, 1936; won two more competitions, Town Hall, Consett, Co. Durham and Health Clinic in Bilston, Staffs. Served with Ordnance Corps, RE, 1940–46, ending war as Captain. Began new practice, as Sen. Partner, Elsom Pack & Roberts, 1947. Works include housing, schools and old people's homes for GLC, Lambeth BC and Westminster CC; office buildings and flats for Church Commissioners, Crown Estate Commissioners, BSC, LWT (Eternit Prize for offices, Victoria St, 1977); stores in Wolverhampton, Guildford and London for Army & Navy Stores; town centres in Slough, Chesterfield, Derby and Tamworth (three Civic Trust Awards, four Commendations). Adviser to DoE on Lyceum Club, Liverpool; Assessor for Civic Trust Awards, 1980. Pres., Nightingale House Old People's Home, 1973–93. Liveryman, Clockmakers' Co., 1979. FSA 1979. *Recreation:* horology. *Address:* 14 Ferrings, College Road, Dulwich, SE21 7LU. *Club:* Arts.

ELSON, Anthony Kenneth; Chief Executive, Kirklees Metropolitan Borough Council, since 1998; *b* 15 June 1948; *s* of William and Elsie Elson; *m* 1971, Joy Waterworth. *Educ:* Birmingham Univ. (BSc 1st cl. Hons Exptl Physics 1969); Liverpool Univ. (BPhil Applied Social Studies 1972); CQSW. Social Worker, 1972–76; Principal Lectr in Social Work, Worcester Coll. of Further Educn, 1976–78; Social Services, Birmingham City Council: Team Manager, 1978–81; Area Manager, 1981–83; Asst Dir, 1983–88; Kirklees Metropolitan Borough Council: Dir of Social Services, 1988–89; Exec. Dir (Housing and Social Services), 1989–97; Exec. Dir (Social Services and Educn), 1997–98. *Address:* PO Box B24, Civic Centre, Market Street, Huddersfield HD1 1WG. *T:* (01484) 226600; *e-mail:* tony.elson@kirkleesmc.gov.uk.

ELSON, Graham Peel; Chief Executive, South West One, political and public affairs company, since 1998; *b* 21 Aug. 1949; *s* of George Ernest Elson and Rhoda (*née* Atkinson); *m* 1975, Jane Rosamunde Isaac. *Educ:* Palmers Endowed Sch. for Boys, Grays, Essex; NE London Polytechnic (BA Business Studies). Brand Manager, Rank Hovis McDougall Foods, 1972–74; Gen. Manager, Wilkinson Sword Gp, 1974–85. Councillor and Leader, Oxfordshire CC, 1985–89; Councillor, Mid Devon DC, 1999–. Gen. Sec., Liberal Democrats, 1989–97. *Recreations:* boating, gardening, supporting West Ham United FC. *Address:* 1 Penstone Barns, Hele, Exeter EX5 4QA. *Club:* National Liberal.

ELSTEIN, David Keith; Chairman: Xios Transcast Corporation, since 2001; Silicon.com, since 2001; Senior Adviser, Arthur D. Little, since 2001; *b* 14 Nov. 1944; *s* of late Albert Elstein and Millie Cohen; *m* 1978, Jenny Conway; one *s*. *Educ:* Haberdashers' Aske's; Gonville and Caius Coll., Cambridge (BA, MA). BBC: The Money Programme, Panorama, Cause for Concern, People in Conflict, 1964–68; Thames Television: This Week, The Day Before Yesterday, The World At War, 1968–72; London Weekend Television: Weekend World, 1972; Thames Television, 1972–82: This Week (ed., 1974–78); Exec. Producer, Documentaries; founded Brook Prodns, 1982: Exec. Producer, A Week in Politics, 1982–86; Exec. Producer, Concealed Enemies, 1983; Man. Dir, Primetime Television, 1983–86; Dir of Programmes, Thames Television, 1986–92; Hd of Programmes, BSkyB, 1993–96; Chief Exec., Channel 5 Broadcasting, 1996–2001. Dir, Civilian Content plc, 2001–. Chairman: Nat. Film and Television Sch., 1996–; British Screen Adv. Council, 1997–. Visiting Professor: Stirling Univ., 1995–; Broadcast Media, Oxford Univ., 1999; Westminster Univ., 2001–. *Recreations:* theatre, cinema, bridge, politics, reading.

ELSTOB, Peter (Frederick Egerton); Vice-President: International PEN, since 1981 (Secretary-General, 1974–81); English PEN, since 1978; Managing Director, Archive Press Ltd, since 1964 (co-founder 1963); writer and entrepreneur; *b* London, 22 Dec. 1915; *e s* of Frederick Charles Elstob, chartered accountant, RFC, and Lillian Page, London; *m* 1st, 1937, Medora Leigh Smith (marr. diss. 1953); three *s* one *d* (and one *d* decd); 2nd, 1953, Barbara Zacheisz (*d* 1992); one *s* one *d*. *Educ:* private schs, London, Paris, Calcutta; state schs, NY and NJ; Univ. of Michigan, 1934–35. Reporter, salesman, tourist guide, 1931–36; volunteer, Spanish Civil War, 1936 (imprisoned and expelled); RTR, 1940–46 (despatches); founded Yeast-pac Co. Ltd with A. B. Eiloart, 1938, Dir, 1938–70, Man. Dir, 1970–93; with A. B. Eiloart: bought Arts Theatre Club, London, 1941; founded Peter Arnold Studios (artists' and writers' colony, Mexico), 1951–52, and Archives Designs Ltd, 1954–62; Director: MEEC Prodns (Theatre), 1946–54; Peter Arnold Properties, 1947–61; City & Suffolk Property Ltd, 1962–70; ABC Expedns, 1957–61; Manager, Small World Trans-Atlantic Balloon Crossing, 1958–59. Chm., Dorking Divl Lab. Party, 1949–50. Mem., Burley Br., RBL, 1996–. Bulgarian Commemorative Medal, 1982; Normandy Freedom Medal, 1994. *Publications:* (autobiog.) Spanish Prisoner, 1939; (with A. B. Eiloart) The Flight of the Small World, 1959; novels: Warriors for the Working Day, 1960; The Armed Rehearsal, 1964; Scoundrel, 1986; military history: Bastogne the Road Block, 1968; The Battle of the Reichswald, 1970; Hitler's Last Offensive, 1971; Condor Legion, 1973; (ed) The Survival of Literature, 1979; (ed series) PEN International Books; PEN Broadsheet, 1977–82. *Recreations:* playing the Stock Exchange, travelling. *Address:* Ponds Cottage, Burley Lawn, Ringwood, Hants BH24 4DL. *T:* (01425) 403406. *Clubs:* Savage, Garrick, PEN, Society of Authors.

ELSTON, Christopher David; Chief Executive, London Bullion Market Association, 1995–99; *b* 1 Aug. 1938; *s* of Herbert Cecil Elston and Ada Louisa (*née* Paige); *m* 1964, Jennifer Isabel Rampling; one *s* two *d*. *Educ:* University Coll. Sch., Hampstead; King's Coll., Cambridge (BA Classics, 1960, MA 1980); Yale Univ. (MA Econs, 1967). Bank of England, 1960–95: seconded to Bank for Internat. Settlements, Basle, Switzerland, 1969–71; Private Sec. to Governor of Bank of England, 1974–76; Asst to Chief Cashier, 1976–79; seconded to HM Diplomatic Service, as Counsellor (Financial), British Embassy, Tokyo, 1979–83; Advr, later Sen. Advr (Asia and Australasia), 1983–94. Advr, KorAm Bank London Br., 1995–2000. Ordinary Mem. Council and Chm. Business Gp, Japan Soc., 1997–2000. *Recreations:* music, golf, walking, garden. *Address:* 23 Grasmere Avenue, Harpenden, Herts AL5 5PT. *T:* (01582) 760147.

ELTIS, Walter Alfred, DLitt; Emeritus Fellow of Exeter College, Oxford, since 1988; *b* 23 May 1933; *s* of Rev. Martin Eltis and Mary (*née* Schnitzer); *m* 1959, Shelagh Mary, *d* of Rev. Preb. Douglas Owen; one *s* two *d*. *Educ:* Wycliffe Coll.; Emmanuel Coll., Cambridge (BA Econs 1956); Nuffield Coll., Oxford. MA Oxon 1960; DLitt Oxon 1990. Nat. Service, Navigator, RAF, 1951–53. Res. Fellow, Exeter Coll., Oxford, 1958–60; Lectr in Econs, Exeter and Keble Colls, Oxford, 1960–63; Fellow and Tutor in Econs, Exeter Coll., Oxford, 1963–88; National Economic Development Office: Econ. Dir, 1986–88; Dir Gen., 1988–92; Chief Economic Advr to Pres., BoT, 1992–95. Vis. Reader in Econs, Univ. of WA, 1970; Visiting Professor: Univ. of Toronto, 1976–77; European Univ., Florence, 1979; Reading Univ., 1992–; Gresham Prof. of Commerce, Gresham Coll., 1993–96. Mem. Council, 1987–93, Chm., Social Scis Cttee, 1987–88, CNAA; Member Council: European Policy Forum, 1992–; Foundn for Manufacturing and Industry, 1993–96. Vice-Pres., European Soc. of Hist. of Econ. Thought, 2000–. Gov., Wycliffe Coll., 1972–88. Gen. Ed., Oxford Economic Papers, 1975–81. *Publications:* Economic Growth: analysis and policy, 1966; Growth and Distribution, 1973; (with R.

Bacon) The Age of US and UK Machinery, 1974; (with R. Bacon) Britain's Economic Problem: too few producers, 1976, 3rd edn (as Britain's Economic Problem Revisited), 1996; The Classical theory of Economic Growth, 1984, 2nd edn 2000; (with P. Sinclair) Keynes and Economic Policy, 1988; Classical Economics, Public Expenditure and Growth, 1993; (ed with S. M. Eltis) Condillac: commerce and government, 1997; Britain, Europe and EMU, 2000; contribs to econ. jls. *Recreations:* chess, music. *Address:* Danesway, Jarn Way, Boars Hill, Oxford OX1 5JF. *T:* (01865) 735440. *Clubs:* Reform (Chm., 1994–95), Royal Automobile.

ELTON, family name of **Baron Elton**.

ELTON, 2nd Baron *cr* 1934, of Headington; **Rodney Elton,** TD 1970; Deputy Chairman, Andry Montgomery Ltd, 1978–79 and since 1986; *b* 2 March 1930; *s* of 1st Baron Elton and of Dedi (*d* 1977), *d* of Gustav Hartmann, Oslo; *S* father, 1973; *m* 1958, Anne Frances (divorced, 1979), *e d* of late Brig. R. A. G. Tilney, CBE, DSO, TD; one *s* three *d*; *m* 1979, S. Richenda Gurney (CVO 1998), *y d* of late Sir Hugh Gurney, KCMG, MVO, and Lady Gurney. *Educ:* Eton; New Coll., Oxford (MA). Farming, 1954–64. Assistant Master, Loughborough Grammar Sch., 1962–67; Assistant Master, Fairham Comprehensive School for Boys, Nottingham, 1967–69; Lectr, Bishop Lonsdale College of Education, 1969–72. Contested (C) Leics, Loughborough, 1966, 1970. Cons. Whip, House of Lords, Feb. 1974–76, an Opposition spokesman, 1976–79; Parly Under Sec. of State, NI Office, 1979–81, DHSS, 1981–82, Home Office, 1982–84; Minister of State: Home Office, 1984–85; DoE, 1985–86. House of Lords: Mem., Delegated Powers Scrutiny Cttee, 1993–96; a Dep. Chm. of Cttees, 1997–; elected Mem., 1999; a Dep. Speaker, 1999–; Mem., Lord Privy Seal's Cttee on Neill Report, 2001. Chm., FIMBRA, 1987–90; Mem., Panel on Takeovers and Mergers, 1987–90. Formerly Director: Overseas Exhibition Services Ltd; Building Trades Exhibition Ltd. Mem. Exec. Cttee, Assoc. of Cons. Peers, 1986–93, 1994–97 (Dep. Chm., 1991–93). Dep. Sec., Cttee on Internat. Affairs, Synod of C of E, 1976–78. Reader, Oxford dio., C of E, 1998–. Mem. Boyd Commn to evaluate elections in Rhodesia, 1979; Chm., Cttee of Enquiry into discipline in schools, 1988. Chm., Intermediate Treatment Fund, 1990–93; Vice-Pres., Inst. of Trading Standards Administrators, 1990–; Member of Council: CGLI, 1987–91 (now Hon. Mem.; Chm., Quality and Standards Cttee, 1999–); Rainer Foundn, 1990–96; Founding Chm., DIVERT Trust, 1993–; Pres., Building Conservation Trust, 1990–95; Trustee: City Parochial Foundn, 1990–97; Trust for London, 1990–97. Late Captain, Queen's Own Warwickshire and Worcs Yeo.; late Major, Leics and Derbys (PAO) Yeo. Lord of the Manor of Adderbury, Oxon. *Heir:* *s* Hon. Edward Paget Elton, *b* 28 May 1966. *Address:* House of Lords, SW1A 0PW. *Clubs:* Pratt's, Beefsteak, Cavalry and Guards.

See also Master of Gray.

ELTON, Sir Arnold, Kt 1987; CBE 1982; MS; FRCS; Consultant Surgeon, Northwick Park Hospital and Clinical Research Centre, 1970–85; *b* 14 Feb. 1920; *s* of late Max Elton and of Ada Elton; *m* 1952, Billie Pamela Briggs; one *s*. *Educ:* University Coll. London (exhibnr; MB BS 1943); UCH Med. Sch. (MS 1951); Jun. and Sen. Gold Medal in Surgery. LRCP 1943; MRCS 1943, FRCS 1946. House Surg., House Physician and Casualty Officer, UCH, 1943–45; Sen. Surgical Registrar, Charing Cross Hosp., 1947–51 (Gosse Res. Schol.); Consultant Surgeon: Harrow Hosp., 1951–70; Mount Vernon Hosp., 1960–70; British Airways, 1981–95. First Chm., Med. Staff Cttee, Chm., Surgical Div. and Theatre Cttee, Mem., Ethical Cttee, Northwick Park Hosp. Mem., Govt Wkg Party on Breast Screening for Cancer, 1985–. Mem., Tricare Europe Preferred Provider Network, 1997–. Med. Dir, 1997–, Dep. Chm., 2000–, Medical Marketing Internat. Gp plc; Chairman and Executive Director: Healthy Living (UK) Ltd, 1997–; Healthy Living (Durham) Ltd, 1998–; Universal Lifestyle Ltd, 1999–; Health Exec., Bovis Lend Lease, 2001–. Examiner: GNC; RCS, 1971–83; Surgical Tutor, RCS, 1970–82. Pres., Cons. Med. Soc., 1992–97, now President Emeritus (Nat. Chm., 1975–92; Eur. Rep., 1994–; Chm., Eur. Gp; Ed., Eur. Bull., 1994–); Mem., Cons. Central Council and Nat. Exec. Cttee, 1976–93. Founder Officer, British Assoc. of Surgical Oncology, 1972–; Member: Europ. Soc. of Surgical Oncology, 1994–; World Fedn Surgical Oncology Socs, 1994–; Ct of Patrons, RCS, 1986–; Dir and Co-ordinator, RCS Exchange of Surgeons with China, 1994–. Mem. and UK Chm., Internat. Med. Parliamentarians Orgn, 1996–. Chm., Med. and Sci. Div., World Fellowship Duke of Edinburgh's Award, 1997–. International Advisor: World Fedn Surgical Oncology Socs, 1998–; PPP/Colombia, subseq. HCA, Gp of Hosps, 1998–; Med. Advr, Virgin Active (Healthy Living Centres), 1997–. Fellow, Assoc. of Surgeons of GB; FRSocMed; FICS. Freeman, City of London; Liveryman: Apothecaries' Soc.; Carmen's Co. Jubilee Medal, 1977. *Publications:* contribs to med. jls. *Recreations:* tennis, music, cricket. *Address:* 58 Stockleigh Hall, Prince Albert Road, NW8 7LB; The Consulting Rooms, Wellington Hospital, Wellington Place, NW8 9LE. *T:* (020) 7935 4101. *Clubs:* Carlton, Royal Automobile, MCC.

ELTON, Benjamin Charles; author and performer; *b* 3 May 1959; *s* of Prof. Lewis Richard Benjamin Elton, *qv* and Mary Elton (*née* Foster); *m* 1994, Sophie Gare; two *s* one *d* (of whom one *s* one *d* are twins). *Educ:* Godalming Grammar Sch.; S Warwicks Coll. of Further Educn; Manchester Univ. (BA Drama). First professional appearance, Comic Strip Club, 1981; writer for television: Happy Families, 1985; Filthy Rich and Catflap, 1986; jointly: The Young Ones, 1982, 1984; Blackadder II, 1987; Blackadder the Third, 1988; Blackadder goes Forth, 1989; The Thin Blue Line, 1995, 1996; writer and performer: Friday Live, 1987–88; Saturday Live, 1987; The Man from Auntie, 1990, 1994; Stark, 1993; The Ben Elton Show, 1998; writer and director: Gasping, Theatre Royal, Haymarket, 1990; Silly Cow, Theatre Royal, Haymarket, 1991; Popcorn, Apollo, 1997; Maybe Baby (film), 2000; writer, The Beautiful Game (musical), 2000; actor: Much Ado About Nothing (film), 1993; numerous tours as a stand-up comic, 1986, 1987, 1989, 1993, 1996–97. *Publications: novels:* Stark, 1989; Gridlock, 1991; This Other Eden, 1993; Popcorn, 1996; Blast from the Past, 1998; Inconceivable, 1999; Dead Famous, 2001; *plays:* Gasping, 1990; Silly Cow, 1991; Popcorn, 1996; Blast from the Past, 1998. *Recreations:* walking, reading, socialising. *Address:* c/o Phil McIntyre, 2nd Floor, 35 Soho Square, W1V 5DG. *Club:* Groucho.

ELTON, Sir Charles (Abraham Grierson), 11th Bt *cr* 1717; film and television producer; *b* 23 May 1953; *s* of Sir Arthur Hallam Rice Elton, 10th Bt, and Margaret Ann (*d* 1995), *d* of Olafur Bjornson; *S* father, 1973; *m* 1990, Lucy Lauris, *d* of late Lukas Heller; one *s* one *d*. *Educ:* Eton Coll.; Reading Univ. Publishing, 1976–79; BBC, 1979–84; Director: Curtis Brown, 1984–91; First Choice Productions, 1991–. *Heir:* *s* Abraham William Elton, *b* 27 Sept. 1995. *Address:* Clevedon Court, Somerset BS21 6QU; 24 Maida Avenue, W2 1ST. *Club:* Garrick.

ELTON, Dr George Alfred Hugh, CB 1983; consultant in biochemistry, since 1985; *b* 27 Feb. 1925; *s* of Horace and Violet Elton; *m* 1951, Theodora Rose Edith Kingham; two *d*. *Educ:* Sutton County Sch.; London Univ. (evening student). BSc 1944, PhD 1948, DSc 1956; FRSC (FRIC 1951); CChem 1974; Eur Chem 1993; FIFST 1968; FIBiol 1976; CBiol 1984. Mem. Faculty of Science, and Univ. Examnr in Chemistry, Univ. of London, 1951–58; Dir, Fog Res. Unit, Min. of Supply, 1954–58; Reader in Applied Phys. Chemistry, Battersea Polytechnic, 1956–58; Dir, British Baking Industries Res. Assoc., 1958–66; Dir, Flour Milling and Baking Res. Assoc., 1967–70; Ministry of Agriculture, Fisheries and Food: Chief Sci. Adviser (Food), 1971–85; Head of Food Science Div., 1972–73; Dep. Chief Scientist, 1972; Under-Sec. 1974; Chief Scientist (Fisheries and Food), 1981–85. Vis. Prof., Surrey Univ., 1982–97. Consultant: FAO, 1992; Internat. Life Scis Inst., USA, 1997–2001. Chairman: National Food Survey Cttee, 1978–85; Adv. Bd, Inst. of Food Res. (Bristol), 1985–88; Scientific Advr, BFMIRA, 1986–92; Scientific Governor: British Nutrition Foundn, 1971–; Internat. Life Scis Inst. (Europe), 1987–97; Vice-Chm., EEC Scientific Cttee for Food, 1987–92; Member: Cttee on Medical Aspects of Food Policy, 1971–85; UK Delegn, Tripartite Meetings on Food and Drugs, 1971–85; AFRC (formerly ARC), 1981–85; NERC, 1981–85; Fisheries Res. and Develt Bd, 1982–85; Adv. Bd for Research Councils, 1981–84; Council: Chemical Soc., 1972–75; BIBRA, 1990–2000 (Chm., 1993–95; Vice-Pres., 1996–2000). Co-inventor, Chorleywood Bread Process (Queen's Award to Industry 1966); Silver Medallist, Royal Soc. of Arts, 1969. Hon. DSc Reading, 1984; DUniv Surrey, 1991. *Publications:* research papers in jls of various learned societies. *Recreation:* golf. *Address:* Green Nook, Bridle Lane, Loudwater, Rickmansworth, Herts WD3 4JH. *Club:* MCC.

ELTON, John; *see* Elton, P. J.

ELTON, Prof. Lewis Richard Benjamin, MA, DSc; CPhys; FSRHE; Professor of Higher Education, London University at University College, since 1994, College Professor, since 1999; University Professor of Higher Education, University of Surrey, 1987–90, now Emeritus; *b* 25 March 1923; *yr s* of late Prof. Victor Leopold Ehrenberg, PhD, and Eva Dorothea (*née* Sommer); *m* 1950, Mary, *d* of late Harold William Foster and Kathleen (*née* Meakin); three *s* one *d*. *Educ:* Stepanska Gymnasium, Prague; Rydal Sch., Colwyn Bay; Christ's Coll., Cambridge (Exhibr; BA 1945, MA 1948); Univ. Correspondence Coll., Cambridge, and Regent Street Polytechnic (Certif.Ed Cantab 1945; BSc (External) 1st Cl. Hons Maths 1947); University Coll. London (Univ. Research Studentship; PhD 1950). Asst Master, St Bees Sch., 1944–46; Asst Lectr, then Lectr, King's Coll., London, 1950–57; Head of Physics Dept, Battersea Coll. of Technology, 1958–66; University of Surrey: Prof. of Physics, 1964–71; Head of Physics Dept, 1966–69; Prof. of Sci. Educn, 1971–86; Hd, Inst. of Educnl Develt (formerly Educnl Technol.), 1967–84; Associate Head, Dept of Educnl Studies, 1983–86. Sen. Fulbright Award, 1955–56; Research Associate: MIT, 1955–56; Stanford Univ., 1956; Niels Bohr Inst., Copenhagen, 1962; Visiting Professor: Univ. of Washington, Seattle, 1965; UCL, 1970–77; Univ. of Sydney, 1971; Univ. of Sao Paulo, 1975; Univ. of Science, Malaysia, 1978, 1979; Univ. of Malaya, 1982, 1983; Asian Inst. of Technology, 1985, 1986; Fundaçao Armando Alvares Penteado, São Paulo, 1985–89. Higher Educn Advr, DfEE (formerly DoE), 1989–96. Member: Governing Body, Battersea Coll. of Technology, 1962–66; Council, Univ. of Surrey, 1966–67, 1981–83; Council for Educational Technology of UK, 1975–81; Army Educn Adv. Bd, 1976–80; Convener, Standing Conf. of Physics Profs, 1971–74; Chairman: Governing Council, Soc. for Research into Higher Educn, 1976–78 (Fellow, 1987). Vice-Pres., Assoc. for Educnl and Trng Technology, 1976–95. Fellow, Amer. Physical Soc., 1978. FRSA. Hon. Life Mem., Staff and Educnl Develt Assoc., 1994. Hon. LittD Kent, 1997. Univ. of Surrey Art Gall. named Lewis Elton Gall., 1997. *Publications:* Introductory Nuclear Theory, 1959, 2nd edn 1965 (Spanish edn 1964); Nuclear Sizes, 1961 (Russian edn 1962); Concepts in Classical Mechanics, 1971; (with H. Messel) Time and Man, 1978; Teaching in Higher Education: appraisal and training, 1987 (Japanese edn 1989); contribs to sci. jls on nuclear physics, higher education, science educn, med. educn, and educnl technology. *Recreation:* words. *Address:* 3 Great Quarry, Guildford, Surrey GU1 3XN. *T:* (01483) 576548.

See also B. C. Elton.

ELTON, Michael Anthony; Director General, National Association of Pension Funds, 1987–95; *b* 20 May 1932; *s* of late Francis Herbert Norris Elton and of Margaret Helen Elton (*née* Gray); *m* 1955, Isabel Clare, *d* of late Thomas Gurney Ryott and Clare Isabel Ryott; two *s* two *d*. *Educ:* Peter Symonds Sch.; Brasenose Coll., Oxford (Class. Mods 1952, BA 1st cl. Jurisp. 1954; MA, BCL 1955). Articled to Sir Andrew Wheatley, Clerk of Hants County Council, 1954; solicitor; Cumberland CC, 1958–61; Surrey CC, 1961–65; Asst Clerk, Bucks CC, 1965–70, Dep. Clerk of the Peace, 1967–70; Chief Exec., Assoc. of British Travel Agents, 1970–86; Dir Gen., European Fedn for Retirement Provision, 1987–91. FRSA. CIMgt. *Publications:* (with Gyles Brandreth) Future Perfect: how to profit from your pension planning, 1988; Travelling to Retirement: plus ça change, plus c'est la même chose, 1989; articles in professional jls. *Recreations:* tennis, golf, music, oil painting, bridge, gardening. *Address:* 80 Old Kennels Lane, Oliver's Battery, Winchester, Hants SO22 4JT. *T:* (01962) 868470.

ELTON, (Peter) John, MC 1944; Director, British Alcan Aluminium (formerly Alcan Aluminium (UK) Ltd), 1962–99; *b* 14 March 1924; 2nd *s* of Sydney George Elton; *m* 1948, Patricia Ann Stephens; two *d*. *Educ:* Eastbourne Coll.; Clare Coll., Cambridge. Indian Army: 14th Punjab Regt, 1942–45 (twice wounded). Hons Degree, Econs and Law, Cambridge. Man. Dir, Alcan Aluminium (UK) Ltd, 1967–74, Exec. Chm. 1974–76, non-Exec. Chm., 1976–78; Chm., Alcan Booth Industries Ltd, 1968–76; Director: Alcan Aluminium Ltd, 1972–77; Hill Samuel Group, 1976–87; Consolidated Goldfields, 1977–88; Spillers, 1978–80; TVS Entertainment, 1988–90. *Recreations:* sailing, gardening. *Address:* Salternshill Farm, Buckler's Hard, Beaulieu, Hants SO42 7XE. *T:* (01590) 616206. *Clubs:* Bucks; Royal Lymington Yacht.

ELVIDGE, John William; Head, Scottish Executive Education Department, since 1999; *b* 9 Feb. 1951; *s* of Herbert William Elvidge and Irene Teresa Elvidge. *Educ:* Sir George Monoux Sch., Walthamstow; St Catherine's Coll., Oxford (BA English Lang. and Lit.). Joined Scottish Office, 1973: Principal, 1978–84; Asst Sec., 1984–88; Dir, Scottish Homes, 1988–89 (on secondment); Asst Sec., 1989–93; Under Sec., 1993–98; Dep. Hd, Econ. and Domestic Secretariat, Cabinet Office, 1998–99 (on secondment). *Recreations:* painting, film, theatre, music, modern novels, food and wine. *Address:* Scottish Executive Education Department, Victoria Quay, Edinburgh EH6 6QQ.

ELVIN, David John; QC 2000; *b* 30 April 1960; *s* of Walter and Margaret Elvin; *m* 1985, Helen Julia Shilling. *Educ:* A. J. Dawson Grammar Sch.; Hertford Coll., Oxford (BA 1st Cl. Hons Jurisprudence 1981, BCL 1982). Called to the Bar, Middle Temple, 1983. Asst Comr, Boundary Commn, 2000–. *Publications:* Unlawful Interference with Land, 1995; contrib. articles to Law Qly Rev., Judicial Rev., Jl of Planning and Envmt Law. *Recreations:* music (playing, singing, listening), opera, history. *Address:* 4 Bream's Buildings, EC4A 1AQ. *T:* (020) 7430 1221.

ELVIN, Herbert Lionel; Emeritus Professor of Education; Director of the University of London Institute of Education, 1958–73 (Professor of Education in Tropical Areas, 1956–58, Hon. Fellow, 1993); Director, Department of Education, UNESCO, Paris, 1950–56; *b* 7 Aug. 1905; *e s* of late Herbert Henry Elvin; *m* 1934, Mona Bedortha (*d* 1997), *d* of Dr C. S. S. Dutton, San Francisco; one *s*. *Educ:* elementary schs; Southend High Sch.; Trinity Hall, Cambridge (1st Class Hons, History and English; Hon. Fellow, 1980). Commonwealth Fellow, Yale Univ., USA, Fellow of Trinity Hall, Cambridge, 1930–44; Temporary Civil Servant (Air Min., 1940–42, MOI, 1943–45); Principal, Ruskin Coll.,

Oxford, 1944–50. Parliamentary candidate (Lab), Cambridge Univ., 1935; Formerly: Pres., English New Education Fellowship; Pres., Council for Education in World Citizenship; Chm., Commonwealth Educn Liaison Cttee. Member: Cttee on Higher Education; Govt of India Educn Commn; University Grants Cttee, 1946–50; Central Advisory Council for Education (England) and Secondary School Examinations Council. *Publications:* Men of America (Pelican Books), 1941; An Introduction to the Study of Literature (Poetry), 1949; Education and Contemporary Society, 1965; The Place of Commonsense in Educational Thought, 1977; (ed) The Educational Systems in the European Community, 1981; Encounters with Education, 1987. *Recreations:* formerly most games indifferently, athletics (half-mile, Cambridge *v* Oxford, 1927). *Address:* 4 Bulstrode Gardens, Cambridge CB3 0EN. *T:* (01223) 358309.

ELVIN, Violetta, (Violetta Prokhorova), (Signora Fernando Savarese); ballerina; a prima ballerina of Sadler's Wells Ballet, Royal Opera House, London (now The Royal Ballet), 1951–56; Director, Ballet Company, San Carlo Opera, Naples, 1985–87; *b* Moscow; 3 Nov. 1925; *d* of Vassilie Prokhorov, engineer, and Irena Grimouzinskaya, former actress; *m* 1st, 1944, Harold Elvin (divorced 1952), of British Embassy, Moscow; 2nd, 1953, Siegbert J. Weinberger, New York; 3rd, 1959, Fernando Savarese, lawyer; one *s*. *Educ:* Bolshoi Theatre Sch., Moscow. Trained for ballet since age of 8 by: E. P. Gerdt, A. Vaganova, M. A. Kojuchova. Grad, 1942, as soloist; made mem. Bolshoi Theatre Ballet; evacuated to Tashkent, 1943; ballerina Tashkent State Theatre; rejoined Bolshoi Theatre at Kuibishev again as soloist, 1944; left for London, 1945. Joined Sadler's Wells Ballet at Covent Garden as guest-soloist, 1946; later became regular mem. Has danced all principal rôles, notably, Le Lac des Cygnes, Sleeping Beauty, Giselle, Cinderella, Sylvia, Ballet Imperial, etc. Danced four-act Le Lac des Cygnes, first time, 1943; guest-artist Stanislavsky Theatre, Moscow, 1944, Sadler's Wells Theatre, 1947; guest-prima ballerina, La Scala, Milan, Nov. 1952–Feb. 1953 (Macbeth, La Gioconda, Swan Lake, Petrouchka); guest artist, Cannes, July 1954; Copenhagen, Dec. 1954; Teatro Municipal, Rio de Janeiro, May 1955 (Giselle, Swan Lake, Les Sylphides, Nutcracker, Don Quixote and The Dying Swan); Festival Ballet, Festival Hall, 1955; guest-prima ballerina in Giselle, Royal Opera House, Stockholm (Anna Pavlova Memorial), 1956; concluded stage career when appeared in Sleeping Beauty, Royal Opera House, Covent Garden, June 1956. *Appeared in films:* The Queen of Spades, Twice Upon a Time, Melba. Television appearances in Russia and England. Has toured with Sadler's Wells Ballet, France, Italy, Portugal, United States and Canada. *Recreations:* reading, painting, swimming. *Address:* Marina di Equa, 80066 Seiano, Bay of Naples, Italy. *T:* (81) 8798520.

ELWEN, Christopher; His Honour Judge Elwen; a Circuit Judge, since 1995; *b* 14 Sept. 1944; *s* of Kenneth Spence Elwen and Joan Marie Elwen; *m* 1967, Susan Elizabeth Allan; one *s* one *d*. *Educ:* Quarry Bank High Sch., Liverpool; Univ. of Liverpool (LLB). Called to the Bar, Gray's Inn, 1969; Wm Brandts Sons & Co. Ltd, 1970–72; Cripps Warburg Ltd, 1972–75; Holman Fenwick & Willan, 1975–89; admitted solicitor, 1976; Stephenson Harwood, 1989–95; a Recorder, 1993–95. *Recreations:* painting, golf, mediaeval history, walking. *Address:* c/o One St Paul's Churchyard, EC4M 8SH. *T:* (020) 7329 4422.

ELWES, Henry William George; JP; Lord-Lieutenant of Gloucestershire, since 1992; *b* 24 Oct. 1935; *s* of John Hargreaves Elwes, MC, Major, Scots Guards (killed in action, N Africa, 1943) and late Isabel Pamela Ivy Beckwith, *g d* of 7th Duke of Richmond and Gordon, KG, GCVO, CB; *m* 1962, Carolyn Dawn Cripps; two *s* (and one *s* decd). *Educ:* Eton; RAC, Cirencester. Served Army, Lieut, Scots Guards, 1953–56. Member: Cirencester RDC, 1959–74; Glos CC, 1970–91 (Vice-Chm., 1976–83 and 1991; Chm., 1983–85). Regl Dir, Lloyds Bank, 1985–91. Mem., Nat. Jt Council for Fire Brigades, 1979–91; Director: Colesbourne Estate Co., 1969–; Cirencester Friendly Soc. (formerly Cirencester Benefit Soc. Trustee Co.) Ltd, 1974–2000. Pres., Western Woodland Owners Ltd. Patron, Pres. and Mem. of many Glos trusts and societies. Gloucestershire: High Sheriff, 1979–80; DL 1982; JP 1992; Hon. Alderman. Hon. Lay Canon, Gloucester Cathedral, 2001–. Confrèrie des Chevaliers du Tastevin. KStJ 1992. *Address:* Colesbourne Park, near Cheltenham, Glos GL53 9NP.

ELWES, Sir Jeremy (Vernon), Kt 1994; CBE 1984; Chairman, St Helier NHS Trust, 1990–99; *b* 29 May 1937; *s* of late Eric Vincent Elwes and Dorothea Elwes, OBE (*née* Bilton); *m* 1963, Phyllis Marion Relf, 2nd *d* of George Herbert Harding Relf and late Rose Jane Relf (*née* Luery); one *s*. *Educ:* Wirral Grammar Sch.; Bromley Grammar Sch.; City of London Coll. ACIS 1963. Technical Journalist, Heywood & Co., 1958–62; Accountant and Co. Sec., Agricultural Press, 1962–70; Sec. and Dir, East Brackland Hill Farming Development Co., 1967–70; IPC Business Press: Pensions Officer, 1966–70; Divl Personnel Manager, 1970–73; Manpower Planning Manager, 1973–78; Exec. Dir (Manpower), 1978–82; Personnel Dir, Business Press Internat., then Reed Business Publishing, 1982–93; Human Resources Dir, Reed Publishing Europe, 1993–94. Director: Periodicals Trng Council, 1986–92; Sutton Enterprise Agency Ltd, 1987–94 (Chm., 1987–90). Chairman: Cons. Political Centre Nat. Adv. Cttee, 1981–84; Cons. SE Area, 1986–90; Mem., Nat. Union Exec. Cttee, 1972–94; Co-ordinator, Specialist Gps, Cons. Pty, 2000–; Hon. Sec., Cons. Med. Soc., 1996–2000. Mem. Exec. Cttee, GBGSA, 1996–99, 2000–; Dir and Trustee, Eur. Sch. of Osteopathy, 1999–. Pres., Sevenoaks Div., St John Ambulance, 2000–. Chm. of Governors, Walthamstow Hall. FRSA 1994. Liveryman, Stationers' and Newspapermakers' Co., 1991– (Master and Wardens Cttee, 1999–; Chm., Livery Cttee, 2000–). Chevalier, Ordre des Chevaliers Bretvins (Chancelier to 1992). *Recreations:* wine and food, reading, walking, golf. *Address:* Crispian Cottage, Weald Road, Sevenoaks, Kent TN13 1QQ. *T:* (01732) 454208. *Club:* Nizels Golf and Leisure (Captain, Veterans, 1998–99).

ELWOOD, Sir Brian (George Conway), Kt 1990; CBE 1985; Chief Ombudsman of New Zealand, since 1994; *b* 5 April 1933; *s* of Jack Philip Elwood and Enid Mary Elwood; *m* 1956, Dawn Barbara Elwood (*née* Ward); one *s* two *d*. *Educ:* Victoria Univ., Wellington (LLB); Trinity Coll., London (ATCL). Barrister and Solicitor, 1957. Chairman: Local Govt Commn, NZ, 1985–92; Survey Industry Review Commn, 1990–92; Comr, Wellington Area Health Bd, 1991–92. Mayor, Palmerston North City, 1971–85. Internat. Pres., Internat. Ombudsman Inst., 1999– (Regl Vice Pres., 1996–98). Hon. Mem., NZ Inst. of Surveyors. Hon. DLitt Massey, 1994. Medal for Distinguished Public Service, Lions Club Internat., 1985. *Recreations:* golf, fishing, gardening. *Address:* 38 Leeward Drive, Whitby, Wellington, New Zealand. *T:* (4) 2359255. *Club:* Wellington.

ELWORTHY, Sir Peter (Herbert), Kt 1988; farmer; *b* 3 March 1935; *s* of Harold Herbert Elworthy and June Mary Elworthy (*née* Batchelor); *m* 1960, Fiona Elizabeth McHardy; two *s* two *d*. *Educ:* Waihi Prep. Sch.; Christ's Coll.; Lincoln Agric. Coll. Nuffield Scholarship, UK, 1970; McMeekan Meml Award, 1978; Bledisloe Award, Lincoln, 1987. FNZIAS. Director: Reserve Bank of NZ, 1985–99; Landcorp, 1986–88; BP NZ Ltd, 1986–; Ascot Management Corp. (NZ) Ltd, 1991–94; Enerco NZ Ltd, 1992–95; Huttons Kiwi Ltd, 1992–96; Skellerup Gp Ltd, 1993–96; Chm., Timaru Port Co., 1988–97. Mem., NZ Adv. Cttee on Overseas Aid, 1986–89 (Chm., 1988–89). President: NZ Deer Farmers Assoc., 1974–81; Federated Farmers of NZ, 1984–87; Chairman: Ravensdown Co-op, 1977–82; NZ Farmlands Ltd, 1989–92; Electricity Distribution Reform Unit, 1990–92; The Power Co., 1990–97; Rural Electrical Reticulation Council, 1990–96; Southland Electric Power Supply, 1990–97; QEII National Trust, 1987–93; NZ Rural Property Trust, 1988–89; Opihi (SC) River Develt Co, 1992–; NZ Rural Properties Ltd, 1992–2000; Seabil (NZ) Ltd, 1994–96; Dir, Sky City Ltd, 1992–. Trustee: Lincoln Univ. Foundn, 1989–; Waitingi Foundn, 1990–; NZ Inst. Econ. Res. (Inc.), 1991–; Allan Duff Charitable Foundn, 1994–; Chm., Salvation Army Inaugural Community Support Cttee, 1994–96; Patron, Internat. Organic Agric. Conf., Lincoln, 1994–. NZ Commemoration Medal, 1990. *Recreations:* riding, fishing, flying (licensed pilot), tennis, reading. *Address:* Craigmore Farm, Maungati, 2RD, Timaru, New Zealand. *T:* (3) 6129809. *Clubs:* Farmers'; Christchurch (Canterbury, NZ); Wellington (Wellington).

ELWORTHY, Air Cdre Hon. Sir Timothy (Charles), KCVO 2001 (CVO 1995); CBE 1986; Her Majesty's Senior Air Equerry, 1995–2001; Director of Royal Travel, 1997–2001; Extra Equerry to the Queen, since 1991; *b* 27 Jan. 1938; *e s* of Marshal of the RAF Baron Elworthy, KG, GCB, CBE, DSO, LVO, DFC, AFC and late Audrey Elworthy; *m* 1st, 1961, Victoria Ann (marr. diss.), *d* of Lt Col H. C. W. Bowring; two *d*; 2nd, 1971, Anabel, *d* of late Reginald Harding, OBE; one *s*. *Educ:* Radley; RAF Coll., Cranwell. CO 29 (Fighter) Sqn, 1975 (Wing Comdr); PSO to AO Commanding-in-Chief, Strike Comd, 1979; CO RAF Stn Leuchars, 1983 (Gp Capt.); RCDS, 1986; Dir, Operational Requirements, (Air), MoD, 1987 (Air Cdre); Captain of The Queen's Flight, 1989–95. Liveryman, GAPAN, 1995. QCVSA 1968. *Recreations:* country pursuits, wine, travel. *Address:* Coates House, Swyncombe, Henley-on-Thames, Oxon RG9 6EG. *Club:* Boodle's.

ELY, 8th Marquess of, *cr* 1801; **Charles John Tottenham;** Bt 1780; Baron Loftus, 1785; Viscount Loftus, 1789; Earl of Ely, 1794; Baron Loftus (UK), 1801; Headmaster, Boulden House, Trinity College School, Port Hope, Ontario, 1941–81; *b* 30 May 1913; *s* of G. L. Tottenham, BA (Oxon), and Cécile Elizabeth, *d* of J. S. Burra, Bockhanger, Kennington, Kent; *g s* of C. R. W. Tottenham, MA (Oxon), Woodstock, Newtown Mount Kennedy, Co. Wicklow, and Plâs Berwyn, Llangollen, N Wales; *S* cousin, 1969; *m* 1st, 1938, Katherine Elizabeth (*d* 1975), *d* of Col W. H. Craig, Kingston, Ont; three *s* one *d*; 2nd, 1978, Elspeth Ann (*d* 1996), *o d* of late P. T. Hay, Highgate. *Educ:* Collège de Genève, Internat. Sch., Geneva; Queen's Univ., Kingston, Ont (BA). Career as Schoolmaster. *Recreation:* gardening. *Heir: e s* Viscount Loftus, *qv*. *Address:* Trinity College School, Port Hope, ON L1A 3W2, Canada. *T:* (905) 8855209.

ELY, Bishop of, since 2000; **Rt Rev. Anthony John Russell,** DPhil; *b* 25 Jan. 1943; *s* of Michael John William and Beryl Margaret Russell; *m* 1967, Sheila Alexandra, *d* of Alexander Scott and Elizabeth Carlisle Ronald; two *s* two *d*. *Educ:* Uppingham Sch; Univ. of Durham (BA); Trinity Coll., Oxford (DPhil); Cuddesdon Coll., Oxford. Deacon 1970, Priest 1971; Curate, Hilborough Group of Parishes, 1970–73; Rector, Preston on Stour, Atherstone on Stour and Whitchurch, 1973–88; Chaplain, Arthur Rank Centre (Nat. Agricl Centre), 1973–82, Director, 1983–88; Chaplain to the Queen, 1983–88; Area Bp of Dorchester, 1988–2000. Canon Theologian, Coventry Cathedral, 1977–88. Mem., Gen. Synod, 1980–88. Chaplain, Royal Agricl Soc., 1982–91, Vice-Pres., 1991–; Hon. Chaplain, RABI, 1983–. Comr, Rural Devlt Commn, 1991–99. Trustee, Rural Housing Trust, 1983–. *Publications:* Groups and Teams in the Countryside (ed), 1975; The Village in Myth and Reality, 1980; The Clerical Profession, 1980; The Country Parish, 1986; The Country Parson, 1993. *Address:* The Bishop's House, Ely, Cambs CB7 4DW. *T:* (01353) 662749.

ELY, Dean of; *see* Higgins, Very Rev. M. J.

ELY, Archdeacon of; *see* Watson, Ven. J. J. S.

ELY, Keith; *see* Ely, S. K.

ELY, Philip Thomas; Senior Partner, Paris Smith & Randall, Southampton, 1981–98 (Partner, 1961–98); *b* 22 March 1936; *s* of Eric Stanley Ely and Rose Josephine Ely; *m* 1966, Diana Mary (*née* Gellibrand); two *s* three *d*. *Educ:* Douai Sch.; LLB (external) London Univ. Admitted Solicitor, 1958. National Service, RN, 1958–60 (commnd, 1959). Articled Hepherd Winstanley & Pugh, Southampton, 1953–58; joined Paris Smith & Randall, Southampton, as Asst Solicitor, 1960. Law Society: Mem. Council, 1979–93; Vice-Pres., 1990–91; Pres., 1991–92; Hampshire Incorporated Law Society: Asst Hon. Sec., 1961–66; Hon. Sec., 1966–74; Hon. Treasurer, 1974–79; Pres., 1979. Appointed by HM Treasury to conduct enquiry into powers of Inland Revenue to call for papers of tax accountants, 1994. Mem., Legal Services Commn (formerly Legal Aid Bd), 1996– (Chm., Regl Legal Services Cttees, London and Reading, 1998–); Chm., Police Disciplinary Appeals Tribunal, 1996–. Hon. LLD Southampton, 1992. *Recreations:* fly-fishing, gardening, music, reading. *Address:* Orchard Cottage, Crawley, Winchester, Hants SO21 2PR. *T:* (01962) 776379.

ELY, (Sydney) Keith; Managing Director, Corporate Culture Plc, since 2000 (Director, 1988 and since 2000); *b* 17 April 1949; *s* of Charles Rodenhurst Ely and Dorothy Mary Ely (*née* Rowlands); *m* 1st, 1970, Patricia Davies (marr. diss. 1994); three *d*; 2nd, 1994, Jo Ann Beroiz. *Educ:* Maghull Grammar Sch.; Open Univ. (BA). Journalist: Liverpool Daily Post & Echo, 1968–78; Reuters, 1978–80; Daily Post, Liverpool: Business Editor, 1980–84; Acting Asst Editor, 1984; Systems Devlt, 1985–86; Features Editor, 1987; Dep. Editor, 1987; Editor, 1989–95; Man. Dir, Trinity Weekly Newspapers Ltd, 1995–96; Editor and Gen. Manager, Channel One TV, Liverpool, 1996–97; Regl Ops Dir, Liverpool Daily Post & Echo Ltd, 1998–2000 (Dir, 1989–95 and 1998–2000). *Recreations:* music, computing. *Address:* Parkside, 1A Blundell Drive, Southport, Merseyside PR8 4RG.

ELYSTAN-MORGAN, family name of Baron Elystan-Morgan.

ELYSTAN-MORGAN, Baron *cr* 1981 (Life Peer), of Aberteifi in the County of Dyfed; **Dafydd Elystan Elystan-Morgan; His Honour Judge Elystan-Morgan;** a Circuit Judge, since 1987; *b* 7 Dec. 1932; *s* of late Dewi Morgan and late Mrs Olwen Morgan; *m* 1959, Alwen, *d* of William E. Roberts; one *s* one *d*. *Educ:* Ardwyn Grammar Sch., Aberystwyth; UCW, Aberystwyth. LLB Hons Aberystwyth, 1953. Research at Aberystwyth and Solicitor's Articles, 1953–57; admitted a Solicitor, 1957; Partner in N Wales (Wrexham) Firm of Solicitors, 1958–68; Barrister-at-law, Gray's Inn, 1971; a Recorder, 1983–87. MP (Lab) Cardiganshire, 1966–Feb. 1974; Chm., Welsh Parly Party, 1967–68, 1971–74; Parly Under-Secretary of State, Home Office, 1968–70; front-bench spokesman on Home Affairs, 1970–72, on Welsh Affairs, 1972–74, on Legal and Home Affairs, House of Lords, 1981–85. Contested (Lab): Cardigan, Oct. 1974; Anglesey, 1979. Pres., Welsh Local Authorities Assoc., 1967–73. *Address:* Carreg Afon, Dolau, Bow Street, Dyfed SY24 5AE.

EMANUEL, Aaron, CMG 1957; Consultant to OECD, 1972–81; *b* 11 Feb. 1912; *s* of Jack Emanuel and Jane (*née* Schaverien); *m* 1936, Ursula Pagel; two *s* one *d*. *Educ:* Henry

Thornton Sch., Clapham; London Sch. of Economics (BSc Econ.). Economist at International Institute of Agriculture, Rome, 1935–38; Board of Trade, 1938; Ministry of Food, 1940; Colonial Office, 1943; Ministry of Health, 1961; Dept. of Economic Affairs, 1965; Under Secretary: Min. of Housing and Local Govt, 1969; Dept of the Environment, 1970–72. Chm., West Midlands Econ. Planning Bd, 1968–72; Vis. Sen. Lectr, Univ. of Aston in Birmingham, 1972–75. *Publication:* Issues of Regional Policies, 1973. *Address:* 119 Salisbury Road, Moseley, Birmingham B13 8LA. *T:* (0121) 449 5553.

EMANUEL, David, FCSD; Joint Partner/Director, Emanuel, since 1977; *b* 17 Nov. 1952; *s* of John Lawrence Morris Emanuel and late Elizabeth Emanuel; *m* 1975, Elizabeth Weiner (*see* E. Emanuel) (separated 1990); one *s* one *d. Educ:* Cardiff Coll. of Art (Diploma); Harrow Sch. of Art (Diploma); Royal College of Art (MA). Final Degree show at RCA, 1977. Emanuel (couture business) commenced in Mayfair, W1, 1977; The Emanuel Shop (retail), London, SW3, 1986–90; ready-to-wear business partnership in USA, 1988; formed David Emanuel Couture, 1990. Designed: wedding gown for the Princess of Wales, 1981; ballet productions, incl. Frankenstein, the Modern Prometheus, Royal Opera House, Covent Garden, 1985 and La Scala, Milan, 1987; uniforms for Virgin Atlantic Airways, 1990; prodns for theatre, film, TV and operatic recitals. Television presenter, fashion shows, 1994–. FCSD (FSIAD 1984). Hon. FWCMD 2000. *Publication:* (with Elizabeth Emanuel) Style for All Seasons, 1983. *Recreations:* horse-riding, jet-ski-ing, tennis, opera. *T:* (020) 7482 6486, *Fax:* (020) 7267 6627. *Clubs:* White Elephant; Royal Ascot Tennis (Berks).

EMANUEL, Elizabeth Florence, FCSD; fashion designer; *b* 5 July 1953; *d* of Samuel Charles Weiner and Brahna Betty Weiner; *m* 1975, David Leslie Emanuel, *qv* (separated 1990); one *s* one *d. Educ:* City of London Sch. for Girls; Harrow Sch. of Art (Diploma with Hons); Royal Coll. of Art (MA 1977; DesRCA 1977). FCSD 1984. Emanuel (couture) commenced in Mayfair, W1, 1977; The Emanuel Shop (retail), London, SW3, 1986–90; launched internat. fashion label, Elizabeth Emanuel, 1991; set up Elizabeth Emanuel Enterprises, 1999. Designed: wedding gown for the Princess of Wales, 1981; range of wedding dresses for Berkertex, 1995; ballet productions, incl. Frankenstein, the Modern Prometheus, Royal Opera House, Covent Garden, 1985 and La Scala, Milan, 1987; costumes for film The Changeling, 1995; uniforms for: Virgin Atlantic Airways, 1990; Britannia Airways, 1995; prodns for theatre and operatic recitals. *Publication:* (with David Emanuel) Style for All Seasons, 1983. *Recreations:* ballet, films, writing. *Address:* 49 Dorset Street, W1H 3FH.

EMANUEL, Richard Wolff, MA, DM Oxon, FRCP; Physician to Department of Cardiology, Middlesex Hospital, 1963–87; Lecturer in Cardiology, Middlesex Hospital Medical School, 1963–87; Physician to National Heart Hospital, 1963–90; Lecturer to National Heart and Lung Institute (formerly Institute of Cardiology), 1963–90; *b* 13 Jan. 1923; *s* of Prof. and Mrs J. G. Emanuel, Birmingham; *m* 1950, Lavinia Hoffmann; three *s. Educ:* Bradfield Coll.; Oriel Coll., Oxford; Middlesex Hospital. House Appts at Middx Hospital, 1948 and 1950. Captain RAMC, 1948–50; Med. Registrar, Middx Hosp., 1951–52; Sen. Med. Registrar, Middx Hosp., 1953–55; Sen. Med. Registrar, Nat. Heart Hosp., 1956–58; Fellow in Med., Vanderbilt Univ., 1956–57; Sen. Med. Registrar, Dept of Cardiology, Brompton Hosp., 1958–61; Asst Dir, Inst. of Cardiology and Hon. Asst Physician to Nat. Heart Hosp., 1961–63. Advr in Cardiovascular Disease to Sudan Govt, 1969–; Civil Consultant in Cardiology, RAF, 1979–89. Vis. Lecturer: Univ. of Med. Sciences and Chulalongkorn Univ., Thailand; Univ. of the Philippines; Univ. of Singapore; Univ. of Malaya; Khartoum Univ.; St Cyre's Lectr, London, 1968; Ricardo Molina Lectr, Philippines, 1969. Has addressed numerous Heart Socs in SE Asia. Member: British Cardiac Soc., 1955– (Asst Sec., 1966–68; Sec., 1968–70; Mem. Council, 1981–85); Council, British Heart Foundn, 1967–73, 1979–92 (Chm., Cardiac Care Cttee, 1987–92); Cardiol Cttee, RCP, 1967–85 (Sec., 1972–79; Chm., 1979–85); Brit. Acad. of Forensic Sciences (Med.); Assoc. of Physicians of GB and Ireland; Chest, Heart and Stroke Assoc., 1978–91. FACC; Hon. Fellow, Philippine Coll. of Cardiology; Hon. Mem., Heart Assoc. of Thailand. Gov., National Heart and Chest Hosps Bd, 1972–75; Mem. Trustees and Exec. Cttee, Gordon Meml Coll. Trust Fund, 1987–. Mem., Editl Cttee, British Heart Journal, 1964–72. Grand Comdr of Most Distinguished Order of Crown of Pahang, 1990. *Publications:* various articles on diseases of the heart in British and American jls. *Recreations:* XVIIIth century glass, fishing. *Address:* 47 Wimpole Street, W1M 7DG; 6 Lansdowne Walk, W11 3LN. *T:* (020) 7727 6688. *Club:* Oriental.

EMBLING, John Francis, CB 1967; Deputy Under-Secretary of State, Department of Education and Science, 1966–71; *b* 16 July 1909; *m* 1940, Margaret Gillespie Anderson; one *s. Educ:* University of Bristol. Teaching: Dean Close, 1930; Frensham Heights, 1931; Lecturer: Leipzig Univ., 1936; SW Essex Technical Coll., 1938 (Head of Dept, 1942); Administrative Asst, Essex LEA, 1944; Ministry of Education: Principal, 1946; Asst Secretary, 1949; Under-Secretary of State for Finance and Accountant-General, Dept of Education and Science, 1960–66. Research Fellow in Higher Educn, LSE, 1972–73, Univ. of Lancaster, 1974–76. Mem. Council, Klagenfurt Univ., 1972–. Grand Cross, Republic of Austria, 1976.

EMBREY, Derek Morris, OBE 1986; CEng, FIEE, FIMechE; consultant electrical engineer, since 1991; Chairman, Turnock Ltd (formerly George Turnock Ltd), since 1998; Group Technical Director, AB Electronic Products Group PLC, 1973–91; *b* 11 March 1928; *s* of Frederick and Ethel Embrey; *m* 1951, Frances Margaret Stephens (marr. diss. 1995); one *s* one *d. Educ:* Wolverhampton Polytechnic (Hon. Fellow, 1987). Chief Designer (Electronics), Electric Construction Co. Ltd, 1960–65, Asst Manager Static Plant, 1965–69; Chief Engineer, Abergas Ltd, 1969–73. Member: Engineering Council, 1982–87; Welsh Industrial Develt Adv. Bd, 1982–85; NACCB, 1985–87; Council, IERE, 1984–88 (Vice Pres., 1985–88); National Electronics Council, 1985–99; Welsh Adv. Bd, 1986–90 (Chm., 1987–90). Vis. Prof., Univ. of Technology, Loughborough, 1978–84 (External Examr, Dept of Mechanical Engrg, 1984–88); Visiting Lecturer: Loughborough Univ., 1988–97; Birmingham Univ., 1989–2000. Member: Council, UWIST, Cardiff, 1984–88; Bd, Inst. of Transducer Technol., Southampton Univ., 1986–2000; Council, IEE, 1992–95 (Chm., Management and Design Divl Bd, 1993–94); Air Cadet Council, 1988–95; Regl Civilian Chm., ATC, Wales, 1988–95; Dir and Mem. Council, BTEC, 1993–96. Freeman, City of London, 1986; Liveryman, Scientific Instrument Makers' Co., 1986–; founder Liveryman, Welsh Livery Guild, 1994. *Publications:* contribs to various jls. *Recreations:* flying and navigating powered aircraft, gliding, music, archaeology. *Address:* 21 Rockfield Glade, Penhow, Caldicot, Monmouthshire NP26 3JF. *T:* (01633) 400995; *e-mail:* dme235@aol.com. *Clubs:* Royal Air Force; Birmingham Electric.

EMBUREY, John Ernest; Director of Coaching, Middlesex County Cricket Club, since 2001; *b* 20 Aug. 1952; *s* of John Alfred Emburey and Rose Alice Emburey (*née* Roff); *m* 1980, Susan Elizabeth Anne Booth; two *d. Educ:* Peckham Manor. Professional cricketer: Middx CCC, 1971–95; England Test cricketer, 1978–95; 64 Test matches (Captain, 1988); 63 one-day internationals; Manager, England A Team tour to Pakistan, 1995; Chief Coach and Manager, Northants CCC, 1996–98; coach, England A Team tour, Zimbabwe and S Africa, 1999; player/coach, Berks CCC, 2000. *Publications:* Emburey (autobiog.), 1986; Spinning in a Fast World, 1989. *Recreations:* golf, reading. *Address:* c/o Middlesex County Cricket Club, Lord's Cricket Ground, NW8 8QZ. *Club:* Harlequins Rugby Football.

EMECHETA, Buchi; writer and lecturer, since 1972; *b* 21 July 1944; *d* of Alice and Jeremy Emecheta; *m* 1960, Sylvester Onwordi; two *s* three *d. Educ:* Methodist Girls' High Sch., Lagos, Nigeria; London Univ. (BSc Hons Sociol.). Librarian, 1960–69; Student, 1970–74; Youth Worker and Res. Student, Race, 1974–76; Community Worker, Camden, 1976–78. Visiting Prof., 11 Amer. univs, incl. Penn. State, Pittsburgh, UCLA, Illinois at Urbana-Champaign, 1979; Sen. Res. Fellow and Vis. Prof. of English, Univ. of Calabar, Nigeria, 1980–81; lectured: Yale, Spring 1982; London Univ., 1982. Proprietor, Ogwugwn Afo Publishing Co. Included in twenty 'Best of Young British', 1983. Member: Arts Council of GB, 1982–83; Home Sec's Adv. Council on Race, 1979. Hon. DLitt Fairleigh Dickensons' Univ., NJ, 1992. *Publications:* In the Ditch, 1972; Second Class Citizen, 1975; The Bride Price, 1976; The Slave Girl, 1977; The Joys of Motherhood, 1979; Destination Biafra, 1982; Naira Power, 1982; Double Yoke, 1982; The Rape of Shavi, 1983; Head Above Water (autobiog.), 1984; Gwendolen, 1989; Kehinde, 1994; *for children:* Titch the Cat, 1979; Nowhere to Play, 1980; The Moonlight Bride, 1981; The Wrestling Match, 1981; contribs to New Statesman, TLS, The Guardian, etc. *Recreations:* gardening, going to the theatre, listening to music, reading. *Club:* Africa Centre.

EMERSON, Michael Ronald, MA; FCA; Ambassador and Head of Delegation of the European Communities to the Commonwealth of Independent States, 1991–96; *b* 12 May 1940; *s* of late James Emerson and Priscilla Emerson; *m* 1966, Barbara Brierley; one *s* two *d. Educ:* Hurstpierpoint Coll.; Balliol Coll., Oxford (MA (PPE)). Price Waterhouse & Co., London, 1962–65; Organisation for Economic Cooperation and Development, Paris: several posts in Develt and Economics Depts, finally as Head of General Economics Div., 1966–73; EEC, Brussels: Head of Division for Budgetary Policy, Directorate-General II, 1973–76; Economic Adviser to President of the Commission, 1977; Dir for Nat. Economies and Economic Trends, 1978–81; Dir for Macroecon. Analyses and Policies, 1981–86; Dir, Economic Evaluation of Community Policies, Directorate-General II, 1987–90. Fellow, Centre for Internat. Affairs, Harvard Univ., 1985–86. Hon. DLitt Keele, 1993; Hon. DCL Kent, 1993. *Publications:* (ed) Europe's Stagflation, 1984; What Model for Europe, 1987; The Economics of 1992, 1988; One Market, One Money, 1991; contribs to various economic jls and edited volumes on internat. and European economics. *Address:* 128 avenue de Tervuren, 1150 Brussels, Belgium. *T:* (2) 7361283.

EMERSON, Dr Peter Albert, MD; FRCP; Hon. Consultant Physician, Chelsea and Westminster Hospital (formerly Westminster and Charing Cross Hospitals), since 1988; *b* 7 Feb. 1923; *s* of Albert Emerson and Gwendoline (*née* Davy); *m* 1947, Ceris Hood Price; one *s* one *d. Educ:* The Leys Sch., Cambridge; Clare Coll., Univ. of Cambridge (MA); St George's Hosp., Univ. of London (MB, BChir 1947; MD 1954). FRCP 1964; Hon. FACP 1975. House Physician, St George's Hosp., 1947; RAF Med. Bd, 1948–52 (Sqdn Leader); Registrar, later Sen. Registrar, St George's Hosp. and Brompton Hosp., London, 1952–57; Asst Prof. of Medicine, Coll. of Medicine, State Univ. of New York, Brooklyn, USA, 1957–58; Consultant Phys., Westminster Hosp., 1959–88; Civilian Consultant Phys. in Chest Diseases to RN, 1974–88; Dean, Westminster Medical Sch., London, 1981–84. Hon. Consultant Phys., King Edward VII Hosp., Midhurst, 1969–88. Royal Coll. of Physicians: Asst Registrar, 1965–71; Procensor and Censor, 1978–80; Vice-Pres. and Sen. Censor, 1985–86; Mitchell Lectr, 1969. *Publications:* Thoracic Medicine, 1981; articles in med. jls and chapters in books on thoracic medicine and the application of decision theory and expert systems to clinical medicine. *Recreations:* tennis, restoring old buildings. *Address:* 3 Halkin Street, SW1X 7DJ. *T:* (020) 7235 8529. *Club:* Royal Air Force.

EMERTON, Baroness *cr* 1997 (Life Peer), of Tunbridge Wells in the co. of Kent and of Clerkenwell in the London Borough of Islington; **Audrey Caroline Emerton,** DBE 1989; DL; DStJ; RGN, RM, RNT; Chief Commander, St John Ambulance, since 1998; Chairman, Brighton Health Care NHS Trust, 1994–2000 (Vice Chairman, 1993–94); *b* 10 Sept, 1935; *d* of late George Emerton and of Lily (*née* Squirrell). *Educ:* Tunbridge Wells GS; St George's Hosp.; Battersea Coll. of Technol. Sen. Tutor, Experimental 2 year and 1 year Course, St George's Hosp., SW1, 1965–68; Principal Nursing Officer, Educn, Bromley HMC, 1968–70; Chief Nursing Officer, Tunbridge Wells and Leybourne HMC, 1970–73; Regl Nursing Officer, SE Thames RHA, 1973–91. St John Ambulance, Kent: Co. Nursing Officer, 1967–85; Co. Comr, 1985–88; St John Ambulance: Chief Nursing Officer, 1988–98; Chm. of Med. Bd, 1993–96; Chief Officer, Care in the Community, 1996–97; Chief Officer, Nursing and Social Care, 1997–98. Lay Mem., GMC, 1996–. Pres., Assoc. of Nurse Administrators, 1979–82; Hon. Vice Pres., RCN, 1994–99. Chairman: English Nat. Bd for Nursing, Midwifery and Health Visiting, 1983–85; UKCC, 1985–93. Trustee, Kent Community Housing Trust, 1993–99. DL Kent, 1992. Hon. DCL Kent, 1989; Hon. DSc Brighton, 1997; DUniv Central England, 1997; Hon. DSci Kingston, 2001. *Address:* House of Lords, SW1A 0PW.

EMERTON, Rev. Prof. John Adney, FBA 1979; Regius Professor of Hebrew, Cambridge, 1968–95, Emeritus Professor since 1995; Fellow of St John's College, since 1970; Honorary Canon, St George's Cathedral, Jerusalem, since 1984; *b* 5 June 1928; *s* of Adney Spencer Emerton and Helena Mary Emerton; *m* 1954, Norma Elizabeth Bennington; one *s* two *d. Educ:* Minchenden Grammar Sch., Southgate; Corpus Christi Coll., Oxford; Wycliffe Hall, Oxford. BA (1st class hons Theology), 1950; 1st class hons Oriental Studies, 1952; MA 1954. Canon Hall Jun. Greek Testament Prize, 1950; Hall-Houghton Jun. Septuagint Prize, 1951, Senior Prize, 1954; Houghton Syriac Prize, 1953; Liddon Student, 1950; Kennicott Hebrew Fellow, 1952. Corpus Christi Coll., Cambridge, MA (by incorporation), 1955; BD 1960; DD 1973. Deacon, 1952; Priest, 1953. Curate of Birmingham Cathedral, 1952–53; Asst Lecturer in Theology, Birmingham Univ., 1952–53; Lecturer in Hebrew and Aramaic, Durham Univ., 1953–55; Lecturer in Divinity, Cambridge Univ., 1955–62; Reader in Semitic Philology and Fellow of St Peter's Coll., Oxford, 1962–68. Visiting Professor: of Old Testament and Near Eastern Studies, Trinity Coll., Toronto Univ., 1960; of Old Testament, Utd Theol Coll., Bangalore, 1986; Fellow, Inst. for Advanced Studies, Hebrew Univ. of Jerusalem, 1982–83. Select Preacher before Univ. of Cambridge, 1962, 1971, 1986. President: Internat. Orgn for the Study of the Old Testament, 1992–95 (Sec., 1971–89); SOTS, 1979. Mem. Editorial Bd, Vetus Testamentum, 1971–97. Corresp. Mem., Akademie der Wissenschaften, Göttingen, 1990. Hon. DD Edinburgh, 1977. Burkitt Medal for Biblical Studies, British Acad., 1991. *Publications:* The Peshitta of the Wisdom of Solomon, 1959; The Old Testament in Syriac: Song of Songs, 1966; (ed) Studies in the Historical Books of the Old Testament, 1979; (ed) Prophecy: essays presented to Georg Fohrer, 1980; (ed) Studies in the Pentateuch, 1990; Editor, Congress Volumes (International Organization for Study of the Old Testament): Edinburgh 1973, 1974; Göttingen 1977, 1978; Vienna 1980, 1981; Salamanca 1983, 1985; Jerusalem 1986, 1988; Leuven 1989, 1991; Paris 1992, 1995; Cambridge 1995, 1997; articles in Journal of Semitic Studies, Journal of Theological

Studies, Palestine Exploration Qly, Theology, Vetus Testamentum, Zeitschrift für die Alttestamentliche Wissenschaft. *Address:* 34 Gough Way, Cambridge CB3 9LN.

EMERY, Prof. Alan Eglin Heathcote, MD, PhD, DSc; FRSE, FRCP, FRCPE; FRSocMed; FLS; Chief Scientific Advisor, European Neuromuscular Center, Baarn, The Netherlands, since 1999 (Research Director, and Chairman, Research Committee, 1990–99); Professor of Human Genetics, University of Edinburgh and Hon. Consultant Physician, Lothian Health Board, 1968–83, now Emeritus Professor and Honorary Fellow; Hon. Visiting Fellow, Green College, Oxford, since 1986; *b* 21 Aug. 1928; *s* of Harold Heathcote Emery and Alice Eglin. *Educ:* Chester Coll.; Manchester Univ. (BSc double 1st cl. hons; John Dalton Prize); Johns Hopkins Univ., Baltimore (PhD). MD (Hons), DSc; FRIPHH 1965; FRCPE 1970; MFCM 1974; FRSE 1972; FLS 1985; FRSocMed 1992. Formerly Resident in Medicine and Surgery, Manchester Royal Infirmary; Fellow in Medicine, Johns Hopkins Hosp., Baltimore, 1961–64; Reader in Medical Genetics, Univ. of Manchester, 1964–68 and Hon. Consultant in Medical Genetics, United Manchester Hosps; Sen. Res. Fellow, Green Coll., Oxford, 1985–86. Visiting Professor: Univ. of NY, 1968; Heidelberg, 1972; Hyderabad, 1975; California (UCLA), 1980; Padua, 1984; Medical Coll., Peking, 1985; RPMS, 1986; Duke Univ. (N Carolina), 1987; Cape Town, 1988; Univ. of London (Inst. of Neurology), 1988; St George's Univ., Grenada, 1991; Polish Acad. Sci., 1995. Lectures: Harveian, 1970; Woodhull, Royal Instn, 1972; Honeyman-Gillespie, 1972; New Ireland, 1977; Telford, 1980; Lewis Hurwitz, 1982; Boerhaave, 1984; Wilfred Card, 1985; Jenner, 1997. Pres., British Clinical Genetics Soc., 1980–83; Council Mem., British Genetic Soc. (Mem. cttees on trng in genetics, 1976, 1979 and 1983 and NHS services, 1978, 1980, 1983 and 1989); Member: Sci. Cttee, Internat. Congr. Neuromusc. Dis., 1990–; Exec. Cttee, Res. Gp, World Fedn of Neurology, 1996–; Exec. Bd, World Muscle Soc., 1999–; Vice Pres., Musc. Dystrophy Campaign, GB, 1999–. Advr, Asian and Oceanian Res. Centre, Tokyo, 2000–. Member: Assoc. of Physicians, 1976; Soc. of Authors, 1989; Royal Soc. of Lit., 1993; Osler Club, 2001. Hon. Mem., Gaetano Conte Acad., Italy, 1991. Hon. Fellow: Muscular Dystrophy Assoc. of Brazil, 1982; Assoc. of British Neurologists, 1999; Netherlands Genetic Soc., 1999; Hon. FACMG 1993. For. Associate, Royal Soc. of South Africa, 1989. Hon. MD: Naples, 1993; Würzburg, 1995. Nat. Foundn (USA) Internat. Award for Research, 1980; Wilfred Card Medal, 1985; Gaetano Conte Award and Medal, Gaetano Conte Acad., 2000; Pro Finlandiae Gold Medal, Univ. of Helsinki, 2000; Elsevier Sci. Award, 2001. Exec. Editor, Procs B, RSE, 1986–90. *Publications:* Elements of Medical Genetics, 1968, 10th edn 1998; Methodology in Medical Genetics, 1976, 2nd edn 1986; Recombinant DNA—an introduction, 1984, 2nd edn (with S. Malcolm) 1995; Duchenne Muscular Dystrophy, 1987, 2nd edn 1993; Muscular Dystrophy: the facts, 1994, 2nd edn 2000; The History of a Genetic Disease, 1995; editor: Modern Trends in Human Genetics, vol. 1, 1970, vol. 2, 1975; Antenatal Diagnosis of Genetic Disease, 1973; Registers for the Detection and Prevention of Genetic Disease, 1976; Principles and Practice of Medical Genetics, 1983, 3rd edn as Emery & Rimoin's Principles and Practice of Medical Genetics, 1997; Psychological Aspects of Genetic Counselling, 1984; Diagnostic Criteria for Neuromuscular Disorders, 1994, 2nd edn 1997; Neuromuscular Disorders: clinical and molecular genetics, 1998; numerous scientific papers. *Recreations:* fly fishing, marine biology, oil painting. *Address:* (office) Lt Gen van Heutszlaan 6, 3743 JN Baarn, The Netherlands; *e-mail:* enmc@euronet.nl; Department of Neurology, Royal Devon and Exeter Hospital, Exeter EX2 5DW; (home) Ingleside Court, Upper West Terrace, Budleigh Salterton, Devon EX9 6NZ. *T:* (01395) 445847, *Fax:* (01395) 443855.

EMERY, Eleanor Jean, CMG 1975; HM Diplomatic Service, retired; *b* 23 Dec. 1918; *d* of Robert Paton Emery and Nellie Nicol (*née* Wilson). *Educ:* Western Canada High Sch., Calgary, Alberta; Glasgow Univ. MA Hons in History, 1941. Dominions Office, 1941–45; Asst Private Sec. to Sec. of State, 1942–45; British High Commn, Ottawa, 1945–48; CRO, 1948–52; Principal Private Sec. to Sec. of State, 1950–52; First Sec., British High Commn, New Delhi, 1952–55; CRO, 1955–58; First Sec., British High Commn, Pretoria/Cape Town, 1958–62; Head of South Asia Dept, CRO, 1962–64; Counsellor, British High Commn, Ottawa, 1964–68; Head of Pacific Dependent Territories Dept, FCO, 1969–73; High Comr, Botswana, 1973–77. Chm., UK Botswana Soc., 1984–88, Vice-Chm., 1981–84 and 1988–92. Governor, Commonwealth Inst., 1980–85. *Recreations:* walking, gardening. *Address:* 17 Winchmore Drive, Cambridge CB2 2LW. *Club:* Royal Commonwealth Society.
See also J. M. Zachariah.

EMERY, Fred; author and broadcaster; Presenter, Panorama, BBC TV, 1978–80 and 1982–92; *b* 19 Oct. 1933; *s* of Frederick G. L. Emery and Alice May (*née* Wright); *m* 1958, E. Marianne Nyberg; two *s*. *Educ:* Bancroft's Sch.; St John's Coll., Cantab (MA). RAF fighter pilot, 266 & 234 Squadrons, National Service, 1953. Radio Bremen, 1955–56; joined The Times, 1958, Foreign Correspondent, 1961; served in Paris, Algeria, Tokyo, Indonesia, Vietnam, Cambodia, Malaysia and Singapore until 1970; Chief Washington Corresp., 1970–77; Political Editor, 1977–81; Home Editor, 1981–82; Exec. Editor (Home and Foreign), and Actg Editor, 1982. Reporter, Watergate (TV series), 1994 (Emmy Award, 1995). *Publication:* Watergate: the corruption and fall of Richard Nixon, 1994. *Recreations:* skiing, hill walking, tennis. *Address:* 5 Woodsyre, SE26 6SS. *T:* (020) 8761 0076. *Club:* Garrick.

EMERY, George Edward, CB 1980; Director General of Defence Accounts, Ministry of Defence, 1973–80, retired; *b* 2 March 1920; *s* of late Frederick and Florence Emery; *m* 1946, Margaret (*née* Rice); two *d*. *Educ:* Bemrose Sch., Derby. Admiralty, 1938; Min. of Fuel and Power, 1946; Min. of Supply, 1951; Min. of Aviation, 1959; Min. of Technology, 1967; Principal Exec. Officer, 1967; Asst Sec., Min. of Aviation Supply, 1970; Ministry of Defence: Asst Sec., 1971; Exec. Dir, 1973; Under-Sec., 1973. *Address:* 3 The Orchard, Freshford, Bath BA2 7WX.

EMERY, Joan Dawson, (Mrs Jack Emery); *see* Bakewell, J. D.

EMERY, Joyce Margaret; *see* Zachariah, J. M.

EMERY, Lina, (Mrs Ralph Emery); *see* Lalandi-Emery, L.

EMERY, Rt Hon. Sir Peter (Frank Hannibal), Kt 1982; PC 1993; MA; FCIPS; *b* 27 Feb. 1926; *s* of late F. G. Emery, Highgate; *m* 1st, 1954 (marr. diss.); one *s* one *d*; 2nd, 1972, Elizabeth, *y d* of late G. J. R. Monnington; one *s* one *d*. *Educ:* Scotch Plains, New Jersey, USA; Oriel Coll., Oxford (MA). Joint Founder and First Secretary of the Bow Group. MP (C): Reading, 1959–66; Honiton, March 1967–1997; Devon E, 1997–2001. Parliamentary Private Secretary in Foreign Office, War Dept and Min. of Labour, 1960–64; Jt Hon. Secretary, 1922 Cttee, 1964–65; Opposition Front Bench Spokesman for Treasury, Economics and Trade, 1964–66; Parliamentary Under-Secretary of State: DTI, 1972–74. Dept of Energy, 1974. Member: Select Cttee on Industry and Trade, 1979–87; Select Cttee on Procedure, 1972–97 (Chm., 1983–97); Select Cttee on Modernisation of H of C, 1997–2001; Select Cttee on Foreign Affairs, 1997–2001. Jt Vice-Chm., Conservative Finance Cttee, 1970–72; Chairman: Cons. Housing and Construction Cttee, 1974–75. Member, Delegation to CPA Conference: Westminster, 1961; Canada, 1962; Fiji, 1981; Leader, Delegn to Kenya, 1977; Delegate: Council of Europe and WEU, 1962–64, 1970–72; North Atlantic Assembly, 1983–2001 (Chairman: Science and Technology Cttee, 1985–89; Sup. Cttee on Mil. Technol.; Rapporteur, 1989–93; Vice Chm., 1993–97); Deleg. and Treas., OSCE (formerly CSCE), 1992–2000. Chm., Winglaw Gp, 1984–2000; Director: Property Growth Insurance, 1966–72; Phillips Petroleum-UK Ltd, 1963–72; Institute of Purchasing and Supply, 1961–72; Secretary-General, European Federation of Purchasing, 1962–72; Chairman, Consultative Council of Professional Management Organisations, 1968–72. Founding Chm., Nat. Asthma Campaign, 1990–; Mem. Adv. Bd, Center for Strategic and Internat. Studies, Washington DC, 1990–. *Recreations:* sliding down mountains, tennis, cricket, golf and bridge (Capt., H of C team, 1984–). *Address:* Tytherleigh Manor, near Axminster, Devon EX13 7BD. *T:* (01460) 220309; 8 Ponsonby Terrace, SW1P 4QA. *T:* (020) 7222 6666. *Clubs:* Carlton, Portland; Leander (Henley-on-Thames).

EMERY, Richard James; Chief Executive, UKTV Ltd, since 1998; *b* 21 July 1946; *s* of Frederick Harold Emery and Hilda Emery (*née* Newson); *m* 1st, 1978, Patricia Moore (marr. diss. 1993); one *s*, and one step *s*; 2nd, 1995, Hazel Susan Challis; one step *s* two step *d*. *Educ:* Reading Blue Coat Sch. Sales Controller: Anglia Television, 1976; TVS Ltd, 1982; Sales Dir, Central Independent Television Ltd, 1984; Jt Man. Dir and Founder, TSMS Ltd, 1989; Commercial Dir, ITN Ltd, 1991; Dir, Market Strategy, ITV Network Centre, 1993; Man. Dir, BBC Worldwide TV, 1994; Chief Operating Officer, BBC Worldwide Ltd, 1997. *Recreations:* Rugby, walking, reading, boating. *Address:* UKTV Ltd, 160 Great Portland Street, W1; The Four Sycamores, Mill Road, Shiplake, Henley-on-Thames. *T:* (0118) 940 3407.

EMERY-WALLIS, Frederick Alfred John, CBE 1999; DL; FSA; Member (C), since 1973, Chairman, since 1999, Hampshire County Council; Vice-President, Southern Tourist Board, since 1988 (Chairman, 1976–88); *b* 11 May 1927; *o s* of Frederick Henry Wallis and Lillian Grace Emery Coles; *m* 1960, Solange, *o d* of William Victor Randall, London, and Albertine Beaupère, La Guerche-sur-l'Aubois; two *d*. *Educ:* Blake's Academy, Portsmouth. Royal Signals SCU4 (Middle East Radio Security), 1945–48. Portsmouth City Council, 1961–74; Lord Mayor, 1968–69; Alderman, 1969–74; Vice-Chm., 1975–76, Leader, 1976–93 and 1997–99, Hants CC. Chm., Recreation Cttee, 1982–85, Mem., Exec. and Policy Cttees, ACC, 1974–93; Mem., LGA, 1997–. Chairman: Portsmouth Develt and Estates Cttee, 1965–74; Portsmouth Papers Editorial Bd, 1966–82; S Hampshire Plan Adv. Cttee, 1969–74; Portsmouth South Cons. and Unionist Assoc., 1971–79, 1982–85; Portsmouth Record Series Adv. Panel, 1982–; Hampshire Archives Trust, 1986–; Exec. Cttee, Hampshire Sculpture Trust, 1988–; Director: Warrior Preservation Trust, 1988–91; WNO, 1990–99; Learning Through Landscapes Trust, 1991–; Member: Economic Planning Council for the South East, 1969–74; SE Regl Cultural Consortium; British Library Adv. Council, 1979–84, 1986–91; Council, British Records Assoc., 1979–; Library and Information Services Council, 1980–83; Mary Rose Develt Trust, 1980–90; Arts Council of GB Reg. Adv. Bd, 1984–88; Hampshire Gardens Trust, 1984–99; Nat. Council on Archives, 1992–94; English Heritage Archives, Libraries and Information Adv. Cttee, 1999–; Victoria County History Cttee, 1993–. President: Hampshire Field Club, 1971–74; Hatrics, the Southern Information Network, 1978–. Gov., Univ. of Portsmouth, 1991–96 (Mem., 1961–92, Vice-Chm., 1967–75, Portsmouth Polytechnic); Chm. of Govs, Portsmouth High Sch. for Girls, 1982–92. Trustee: New Theatre Royal, Portsmouth, 1982–92; Royal Naval Mus., Portsmouth, 1987–; Royal Marines Mus., Portsmouth, 1993–94. Vice-Pres., British Records Assoc., 1996–. Pres., Portsmouth YMCA, 1978–88. DL Hants 1988. Hon. Fellow, Portsmouth Polytechnic, 1972. FSA 1980. Hon. FRIBA 1985; Hon. FLA 1996. *Publications:* various publications concerning history and develt of Portsmouth and Hampshire. *Recreations:* book collecting, music. *Address:* Froddington, Craneswater Park, Portsmouth PO4 0NR. *T:* (023) 9273 1409.

EMLYN, Viscount; James Chester Campbell; *b* 7 July 1998; *s* and *heir* of Earl Cawdor, *qv*.

EMLYN JONES, John Hubert, CBE 1986 (MBE (mil.) 1941); FRICS; JP; Member of the Lands Tribunal, 1968–86; *b* 6 Aug. 1915; *s* of late Ernest Pearson Jones and Katharine Cole Jones (*née* Nicholas); *m* 1954, Louise Anne Montague, *d* of late Raymond Ralph Horwood Hazell; two *s* one *d*. *Educ:* Dulwich. FRICS 1939. Served War, RE, 1939–46: Major 1943. Partner, Rees-Reynolds and Hunt, and Alfred Savill & Sons, Chartered Surveyors, 1950–68. President: Rating Surveyors Assoc., 1965–66 (Hon. Mem. 1968); Climbers' Club, 1966–69 (Hon. Mem. 1970); Alpine Club, 1980–82. Mem. Council, RICS, 1964–69. Mem. Bureau, 1964–72, Treasurer 1967–69, Fédération Internationale des Géomètres. Mem., expedns to Himalayas: Annapurna, 1950; Ama Dablam, 1959 (Leader). High Sheriff, Bucks, 1967–68, JP 1968. *Publications:* articles and revs in mountaineering jls. *Recreations:* mountaineering, music. *Address:* Ivinghoe Manor, Leighton Buzzard, Beds LU7 9EH. *T:* (01296) 668202. *Clubs:* Garrick, Alpine.

EMMERSON, David, CBE 1989; AFC 1982; Vice Chairman, New Support Options Ltd, since 2000; *b* 6 Sept. 1939; *s* of late Alfred Robert and Sarah Helen Emmerson; *m* 1961, Martha (Marie) Katherine Stuart. *Educ:* Colchester Royal Grammar Sch. Operational and instructional flying, 1959–73; Canadian Staff Coll. and Air Staff Ottawa, 1974–76; Policy Staff, MoD, 1976–77; Air Staff, Washington, 1978–80; OC 206 Sqn, 1981–82; Gp Capt. Ops, Northwood, 1983; Stn Comdr, RAF Kinloss, 1984–85; RCDS, 1986; Principal Staff Officer to CDS, 1987–88; Chief of Staff, HQ 18 Gp, Northwood, 1989–90; retired in rank of Air Vice-Marshal. Chief Executive, Elizabeth FitzRoy Homes, 1991–2000; Chm., Assoc. for Residential Care, 1995; non-executive Director: New Dimensions Ltd, 2000–; North Hants Hosps NHS Trust, 2000–. *Recreations:* travel, world politics, all sports. *Club:* Royal Air Force.

EMMERSON, Rt Rev. Ralph; an Assistant Bishop, Diocese of Ripon, since 1986; *b* 7 June 1913; *s* of Thomas and Alys Mary Emmerson; *m* 1st, 1942, Ann Hawthorn Bygate (*d* 1982); no *c*; 2nd, 2000, Elizabeth Anne Firth. *Educ:* Leeds Grammar Sch.; King's Coll., London (BD, AKC); Westcott House, Cambridge. Leeds Educn Authority Youth Employment Dept, 1930–35; Curate, St George's, Leeds, 1938–41; Priest-in-Charge, Seacroft Estate, 1941–48; Rector of Methley and Vicar of Mickletown, 1949–56; Vicar of Headingley, 1956–66; Hon. Canon of Ripon Cath., 1964; Residentiary Canon and Canon Missioner for Dio. Ripon, 1966–72; Bishop Suffragan of Knaresborough, 1972–79; Asst Bishop, Dio. Wakefield, 1980–86. *Address:* Flat 1, 15 High Saint Agnesgate, Ripon HG4 1QR. *T:* (01765) 601626.

EMMETT, Bryan David; Chairman, EAGA Group, 1998–2000 (Director, EAGA Ltd, 1991–2000); *b* 15 Feb. 1941; *m* 1960, Moira Miller (marr. diss. 1994); one *s*. *Educ:* Tadcaster Grammar Sch. Clerical Officer, Min. of Labour, and National Service, 1958–59; Exec. Officer, War Dept, 1959–64; Asst Principal, MOP, 1965–69 (Asst Private Sec. to Ministers of Power, 1968–69); Principal, Electricity Div., DTI, 1969–74; Department of Energy: Principal, and Private Sec. to Minister of State, 1974–75; Asst Sec., and Principal Private Sec. to Sec. of State for Energy, 1975–76; Asst Sec., Petroleum Engrg Div., 1977–80; Under Sec., and Principal Estab. Officer, 1980–81; Principal Estab. and Finance

Officer, 1981–82; Chief Exec., Employment Div., MSC, 1982–85; Department of Energy: Head, Energy Policy Div., 1985–86; Head of Oil Div., 1986–87; Dir Gen., Energy Efficiency Office, 1987–88; seconded as Chief Exec., Educn Assets Bd, Leeds, 1988–90; compulsorily retired, 1991. Subpostmaster, Greenham Court PO and Store, Newbury, 1995–98. Adminr, EAGA Charitable Trust, 1993–95. Mem. (Lib Dem, 1997–2000, C, 2000), Newbury DC, later West Berks Council (Chm., Lib Dem Gp, May–Sept. 1998). *Recreations:* National Hunt racing, horseriding, golf. *Address:* Trevlyn, Limes Avenue, Burghclere, Newbury, Berks RG20 9HE.

EMMOTT, William John, (Bill); Editor, The Economist, since 1993; *b* 6 Aug. 1956; *s* of Richard Anthony Emmott and Audrey Mary Emmott; *m* 1st, 1982, Charlotte Crowther (marr. diss.); 2nd, 1992, Carol Barbara Mawer. *Educ:* Latymer Upper Sch., Hammersmith; Magdalen Coll., Oxford (BA Hons PPE); Nuffield Coll., Oxford. The Economist: Brussels corresp., 1980–82; Economics corresp., 1982–83; Tokyo corresp., 1983–86; Finance Editor, 1986–88; Business Affairs Editor, 1989–93; Editorial Dir, Economist Intelligence Unit, May–Dec. 1992. Member: European Exec. Cttee, Trilateral Commn, 1999–; BBC World Service Governors' Consultative Gp, 2000–. Hon. LLD Warwick, 1999. *Publications:* The Pocket Economist (with Rupert Pennant-Rea), 1983; The Sun Also Sets, 1989; Japan's Global Reach, 1992; Kanryo no Taizai, 1996. *Address:* The Economist Newspaper, 25 St James's Street, SW1A 1HG. *T:* (020) 7830 7000; *e-mail:* be@economist.com. *Clubs:* Reform, Lansdowne.

EMMS, David Acfield, OBE 1995; MA; Director, The London Goodenough Trust (formerly London House) for Overseas Graduates, 1987–95; *b* 16 Feb. 1925; *s* of late Archibald George Emms and Winifred Gladys (*née* Richards); *m* 1950, Pamela Baker Speed; three *s* one *d*. *Educ:* Tonbridge Sch.; Brasenose Coll., Oxford. BA Hons Mod. Langs Oxford, 1950, Diploma in Education, 1951; MA 1954. Rugby football, Oxford *v* Cambridge, 1949, 1950. Served War of 1939–45, RA, 1943–47. Undergraduate, 1947–50; Asst Master, Uppingham Sch. (Head of Mod. Languages Dept, CO, CCF Contingent), 1951–60; Headmaster of: Cranleigh School, 1960–70; Sherborne School, 1970–74; Master, Dulwich Coll., 1975–86. Chm., HMC, 1984; Pres., ISCO, 2001. Dep. Chm., E-SU, 1984–89; Chm., Jt Educnl Trust, 1987–90; Mem. Cttee, GBA, 1989–92. Vice-Chm. Council and Dep. Pro-Chancellor, City Univ., 1989–91; Governor: Bickley Park, 1978–81; Feltonfleet, 1967–86; Brambletye, 1982–88; St Felix Sch., Southwold, 1981–88; Portsmouth Grammar Sch., 1987–98; Tonbridge, 1988–2000; St. George's, Montreux, 1989–2000; St Dunstan's Coll., 1992–97. President: Alleyn Club, 1985; Brasenose Soc., 1987. Mem. Council, Fairbridge Soc., 1984–96. FRSA 1988. Freeman, City of London; Master, Skinners' Co., 1987–88. Hon. Col, 39th (City of London) Signal Regt (Special Communications) (Volunteers), 1988–91. Chm., RNLI, Chichester, 1998–. *Publication:* HMC Schools and British Industry, 1981. *Recreations:* radical gardening, travel. *Clubs:* East India, Devonshire, Sports and Public Schools; Vincent's (Oxford).

EMMS, Peter Fawcett; public administration consultant in former communist countries, since 1995; *b* 25 April 1935; *s* of late Reginald Emms and Hetty Emms; *m* 1960, Carola Wayne; three *d*. *Educ:* Derby Sch., Derby; Magdalen Coll., Oxford, 1956–59 (John Doncaster Open Schol. in Mod. Langs; MA French and German). National Service, Jt Services Russian Course, 1954–56. Assistant Master: Abingdon Sch., 1959–62; Rugby Sch., 1962–74; Vis. Master, Groton Sch., Mass, 1967–68; Hd of Mod. Langs 1969–71, Housemaster of Town House 1971–74, Rugby Sch.; joined DoE as Principal, 1974, with posts in Road Safety, Construction Industries and Housing; Asst Sec., 1979; Hd of Greater London Housing, 1979–81; seconded to DES, Further and Higher Educn Br., 1981–83; Hd of Housing Management Div., and of Estate Action Unit, 1983–87; Nuffield Leverhulme Travelling Fellowship, 1987–88; Hd, Dept of Transport Internat. Transport Div., Mem., Central Rhine Commn, 1988–89; Under Sec., 1989; Regl Dir, Eastern Reg., DoE and Dept of Transport, 1989–94; Leader, Know How Fund adv. team to Ukrainian govt, 1994–95. *Publications:* Social Housing: a European dilemma?, 1990; (contrib.) Changing Housing Finance Systems, 1991. *Recreation:* the civilizations of Europe. *Address:* 28 Sherard Court, 3 Manor Gardens, N7 6FA; 71800 Vauban, France.

EMPEY, Dr Duncan William, FRCP; Medical Director, Barts and The London (formerly Royal Hospitals) NHS Trust, since 1994; Consultant Physician, London Chest Hospital and Royal London Hospital, since 1979; *b* 9 Sept. 1946; *s* of Henry Gordon Empey and Katherine Isobel (*née* Hooper); *m* 1972, Gillian Mary Charlesworth; three *d*. *Educ:* Christ's Coll., Finchley; University Coll. London; Westminster Hosp. Med. Sch. (MB, BS). MRCS 1969; FRCP 1983 (LRCP 1969). NIH Fogarty Internat. Res. Fellow, Cardiovascular Res. Inst., San Francisco, 1974–75; Hon. Lectr, London Hosp. Med. Coll., 1975–79; Hon. Sen. Registrar, London Hosp., 1975–79; Hon. Sen. Lectr, St Bartholomew's and Royal London Sch. of Medicine and Dentistry, 1995–; Hon. Consultant Physician, King Edward VII Hosp. for Officers, 1995–. Med. Dir, NHS Executive (N Thames) Trust Unit, 1997–98. Ed., British Jl of Diseases of the Chest, 1984–88. Sec.-Gen., European Soc. for Clinical Respiratory Physiol., 1979–84. *Publications:* (jtly) Lung Function for the Clinician, 1981; papers on asthma, chronic bronchitis, pulmonary circulation, tuberculosis and cystic fibrosis. *Recreation:* equestrianism. *Address:* 18 Upper Wimpole Street, W1G 6LX. *T:* (020) 7935 2977, *Fax:* (020) 7935 2740. *Clubs:* Savage, Groucho's.

EMPEY, Sir Reginald (Norman Morgan), Kt 1999; OBE 1994; Member (UU) Belfast East, since 1998, and Minister of Enterprise, Trade and Investment, since 1999, Northern Ireland Assembly; Member, Belfast City Council, since 1985; *b* 26 Oct. 1947; *s* of Samuel Frederick Empey and Emily Winifred (*née* Morgan); *m* 1977, Stella Ethna Donnan; one *s* one *d*. *Educ:* The Royal Sch., Armagh; Queen's Univ., Belfast (BSc (Econ)). Cons. & Unionist Assoc., QUB, 1967; Publicity Officer, 1967–68, Vice-Chm., 1968–72, Ulster Young Unionist Council; Chm., Vanguard Unionist Party, 1974–75; Mem., E Belfast, NI Constitutional Convention, 1975–76. Dep. Lord Mayor, 1988–89, Lord Mayor of Belfast, 1989–90 and 1993–94. Member: Belfast Harbour Comrs, 1985–89; Eastern Health and Social Services Bd, 1985–86; Ulster Unionist Council, 1987– (Hon. Sec., 1990–96; Vice-Pres., 1996–); Bd, Laganside Corp., 1992–; Police Authy for NI, 1992–; European Cttee of the Regions for NI, Brussels, 1994–; Standing Adv. Commn on Human Rights, 1994–96. *Recreations:* walking, gardening. *Address:* Knockvale House, 205 Sandown Road, Belfast BT5 6GX. *T:* (028) 9052 1335; Parliament Buildings, Stormont, Belfast BT4 3ST.

EMPEY, Most Rev. Walton Newcombe Francis; *see* Dublin, Archbishop of, and Primate of Ireland.

EMSLIE, family name of **Baron Emslie**.

EMSLIE, Baron *cr* 1980 (Life Peer), of Potterton in the District of Gordon; **George Carlyle Emslie;** PC 1972; MBE 1946; FRSE 1987; Lord Justice-General of Scotland and Lord President of the Court of Session, 1972–89; *b* 6 Dec. 1919; *s* of late Alexander and Jessie Blair Emslie; *m* Lilias Ann Mailer Hannington (*d* 1998); three *s*. *Educ:* The High School of Glasgow; The University of Glasgow (MA, LLB). Commissioned A&SH, 1940; served War of 1939–45 (despatches): North Africa, Italy, Greece, Austria, 1942–46; psc Haifa, 1944; Brigade Major (Infantry), 1944–46. Advocate, 1948; Advocate Depute (Sheriff Courts), 1955; QC (Scotland) 1957; Sheriff of Perth and Angus, 1963–66; Dean of Faculty of Advocates, 1965–70; Senator of Coll. of Justice in Scotland and Lord of Session, 1970–72. Chm., Scottish Agricultural Wages Bd, 1969–73; Mem., Council on Tribunals (Scottish Cttee), 1962–70. Vice-Chm., Bd of Trustees, Nat. Library of Scotland, 1975–. Hon. Bencher: Inner Temple, 1974; Inn of Court of N Ireland, 1981. Hon. LLD Glasgow, 1973. *Recreation:* golf. *Address:* 47 Heriot Row, Edinburgh EH3 6EX. *T:* (0131) 225 3657. *Clubs:* New (Edinburgh); The Honourable Company of Edinburgh Golfers.
See also Hon. G. N. H. Emslie, Hon. Lord Kingarth.

EMSLIE, Hon. Derek Robert Alexander; *see* Kingarth, Hon Lord.

EMSLIE, Hon. (George) Nigel (Hannington); QC (Scot.) 1986; Dean, Faculty of Advocates, since 1997; *b* 17 April 1947; *s* of Lord Emslie, *qv*; *m* 1973, Heather Ann Davis; one *s* two *d*. *Educ:* Edinburgh Acad.; Trinity Coll., Glenalmond; Gonville and Caius Coll., Cambridge (BA); Edinburgh Univ. (LLB). Admitted to Faculty of Advocates, 1972; Standing Junior Counsel: to Forestry Commn in Scotland and to Dept of Agric. and Fisheries for Scotland, 1981–82; to Inland Revenue in Scotland, 1982–86. Part-time Chm., Med. Appeal Tribunals, 1988–97. *Address:* 20 Inverleith Place, Edinburgh EH3 5QB. *T:* (0131) 552 4091. *Clubs:* Hawks (Cambridge); New (Edinburgh).
See also Hon. Lord Kingarth.

EMSLIE, Prof. Ronald Douglas, FDSRCS; Dean of Dental Studies, Guy's Hospital Medical and Dental Schools, 1968–80, retired; Professor of Periodontology and Preventive Dentistry, University of London, 1970–80, now Emeritus; *b* 9 March 1915; *s* of late Alexander G. H. Emslie and Elizabeth Spence; *m* 1951, Dorothy, *d* of William A. Dennis, Paris, Ill, USA; four *s*. *Educ:* Felsted Sch.; Guy's Hosp. Dental Sch., London (BDS); Univ. of Illinois, Chicago (MSc). FDSRCS Eng., 1950; DRD (Edin), 1978. Served War: Surg. Lt (D) RNVR, 1943–46; Surg. Lt Comdr (D) RNVR, 1946. Half-time Asst in Dept of Preventive Dentistry, Guy's Hosp., 1946–48, also in private practice with Mr E. B. Dowsett; Research Fellow, Univ. of Illinois, Chicago, 1948–49; Head of Dept of Preventive Dentistry, Guy's Hosp., 1949–55; Reader in Preventive Dentistry, Univ. of London (Guy's Hosp. Dental Sch.), 1956–62; Prof. of Preventive Dentistry, Univ. of London (Guy's Hosp. Dental Sch.), 1963–70. Pres., Brit. Soc. of Periodontology, 1959–60; Chm., Dental Health Cttee of BDA, 1963–69; Member: Internat. Dental Fedn; Internat. Assoc. for Dental Research; Dental Educn Adv. Council (Chm., 1978–80); Bd of Faculty of Dental Surgery, RCS, 1966–81 (Vice-Dean, 1976–77); Fluoridation Soc. (Chm. 1970–80); Bd of Studies in Dentistry, Univ. of London (Chm., 1975–77). Past Pres., Odontological Section, RSM; Vis. Lectr, Univ. of Illinois, 1956; Nuffield Grant to study dental aspects of facial gangrene, in Nigeria, Sept.-Dec. 1961; Sci. Advr, Brit. Dental Jl, 1961–80 (Sci. Asst Ed., 1951–61); Consultant in Periodontology to RN, 1971–80. Fellow, BDA. Hon. Fellow, UMDS, 1995. *Publications:* various contribs to dental literature. *Recreations:* tennis, sailing, old motor cars. *Address:* Little Hale, Woodland Way, Kingswood, Surrey KT20 6NW. *T:* (01737) 832662.

ENCOMBE, Viscount; John Francis Thomas Marie Joseph Columba Fidelis Scott; *b* 9 July 1962; *s* and *heir* of 5th Earl of Eldon, *qv*; *m* 1993, Charlotte, *d* of Bob de Vlaming; one *s* one *d*.

ENDERBY, Prof. John Edwin, CBE 1997; FRS 1985; H. O. Wills Professor of Physics, University of Bristol, 1981–96, now Emeritus; *b* 16 Jan. 1931; *s* of late Thomas Edwin Enderby and Rheita Rebecca Hollinshead (*née* Stather); *m* Susan, *yr d* of late Harold Vincent Bowles, OBE and of Colleen Bessie Bowles; one *s* two *d*, and one *d* (one *s* decd) of previous marriage. *Educ:* Chester Grammar Sch.; London Univ. (BSc, PhD). Lecturer in Physics: Coll. of Technology, Huddersfield, 1957–60; Univ. of Sheffield, 1960–67; Reader in Physics, Univ. of Sheffield, 1967–69; Prof. in Physics and Head of the Dept, Univ. of Leicester, 1969–76; Prof. of Physics, Bristol Univ., 1976–81; Head of Dept of Physics, and Dir, H. H. Wills Physics Lab., Bristol Univ., 1981–94; Directeur-Adjoint, Institut Laue-Langevin, Grenoble, 1985–88. Fellow, Argonne Nat. Lab., Ill., USA, 1989–91; Visiting Fellow, Battelle Inst., 1968–69; Visiting Professor: Univ. of Guelph, Ont., 1978; Univ. of Leiden, 1989. Humphrey Davy Lectr, Royal Soc., 1997. Member: Physics Cttee, SRC, 1974–77; Neutron Beam Res. Cttee, SRC, 1974–80 and 1988–91 (Chm., 1977–80 and 1988–91); PPARC, 1994–98. Chm., Physics Panel, 2001 RAE, HEFCE, 1999–2001. Chm., Liquids Bd, Eur. Physical Soc., 1991–96. Member: Council, Institut Laue-Langevin, Grenoble, 1973–80; Council, Royal Soc., 1990–92 (Physical Sec. and Vice-Pres., 1999–). MAE 1989. FInstP 1970 (Chm., SW Br., 1979–83; Guthrie Medal, 1995). Associate Editor, Philosophical Magazine, 1975–81; Editor, Proc. Royal Soc. A, 1989–94; Editor in Chief, Jl of Physics Condensed Matter, 1997–. *Publications:* (jointly): Physics of Simple Liquids, 1968; Amorphous and Liquid Semiconductors, 1974; many publications on the structure and properties of liquids in: Phil. Mag. Adv. Phys, Jl Phys, Proc. Royal Soc., etc. *Recreations:* gardening, woodwork, watching Association football. *Address:* H. H. Wills Physics Laboratory, Tyndall Avenue, Bristol BS8 1TL. *T:* (0117) 928 8737; 7 Cotham Lawn Road, Bristol BS6 6DU. *T:* (0117) 973 3411.

ENDICOTT, Grattan, OBE 1998; Chief Executive and Secretary to the Trustees, Foundation for Sport and the Arts, since 1991; *b* 12 Jan. 1924; *s* of late Cecil George Endicott and Annette Rose Endicott; *m* 1st, 1944, Paolina Cicoria (marr. diss. 1955); two *s*; 2nd, 1961, Jean Thurgeson (marr. diss. 1981). *Educ:* Rhyl Co. Grammar Sch. Served RN, 1941–46; Principal Linguist, Navy Sub-Commn, Allied Commn, Rome, 1944–46. Personnel Asst, ICI, 1946–57; Littlewoods Pools: Asst Permutation Manager, 1957–66; Hd, Permutation Services, 1966–89. Sec., Laws Cttee, World Bridge Fedn, 1997– (Vice-Chm., 1992–96); Pres., Merseyside and Cheshire Contract Bridge Assoc. *Publication:* European Bridge League Commentary on the Laws of Duplicate Contract Bridge 1987, 1992. *Recreation:* competition (duplicate) bridge. *Address:* 14 Elmswood Court, Mossley Hill, Liverpool L18 8DJ. *T:* and *Fax:* (0151) 724 1484. *Club:* Liverpool Bridge.

ENFIELD, Viscount; William Robert Byng; computer systems developer, My Business, Newcastle, since 2000; *b* 10 May 1964; *s* and *heir* of 8th Earl of Strafford, *qv*; *m* 1994, Karen Elizabeth, *d* of S. Graham Lord, Leyland, Preston; twin *s* one *d*. *Educ:* Winchester Coll.; Durham Univ. *Heir:* *s* Hon. Samuel Peter Byng, *b* 17 July 1998. *Address:* 7 Church Street Villas, Durham DH1 3DW.

ENFIELD, Harry; comedy actor and writer; *b* 30 May 1961; *m* 1997, Lucy Lyster; two *s*. *Educ:* York Univ. (BA Hons Politics). TV programmes include: Sir Norbert Smith: a life, 1989 (Silver Rose of Montreux, Emmy Award); Smashie and Nicey: the end of an era, 1994 (Silver Rose of Montreux); Norman Ormal, 1998; Kevin's Guide to Being a Teenager, 1999; series: Harry Enfield's Television Programme, 1990, 1992; Harry Enfield's Guide to the Opera, 1993; Harry Enfield and Chums, 1994 (Writers Guild Award) and 1997 (Silver Rose of Montreux); St Albion Parish Council, 1998, 1999; Harry Enfield's Brand Spanking New Show, 2000; also appeared regularly in: Saturday Night Live, 1986; Friday Night Live, 1988; Gone to the Dogs, 1991; Men Behaving Badly, 1992; film: Kevin and Perry Go Large, 2000. Top BBC 1 Comedy Personality, British Comedy Awards, 1998. *Publication:* Harry Enfield and his Humorous Chums, 1997.

Address: c/o PBJ Management Ltd, 7 Soho Square, W1D 3DQ. *T:* (020) 7287 1112, *Fax:* (020) 7287 1191; *e-mail:* general@pbjmgt.co.uk.

ENGEL, Matthew Lewis; Chief Washington Correspondent, The Guardian, since 2001; Consultant Editor, Wisden Cricketers' Almanack, since 2001 (Editor, 1993–2000); *b* 11 June 1951; *s* of Max David and late Betty Ruth Engel; *m* 1990, Hilary Davies; one *s* one *d. Educ:* Manchester Univ. (BA Econ). Reporter, Chronicle and Echo, Northampton, 1972–75; Reuters, 1977–79; The Guardian, 1979–: cricket corresp., 1982–87; feature writer, sports columnist, occasional political and foreign corresp., 1987–2001; columnist, 1998–. Mem., Nothing Writers. Sports Writer of the Year, What the Papers Say, 1985; Sports Journalist of the Year, British Press Awards, 1991. *Publications:* Ashes '85, 1985; (ed) Guardian Book of Cricket, 1986; (ed) Sportswriter's Eye, 1989; (ed) Sportspages Almanac, 1990, 1991, 1992; (with A. Radd) History of Northamptonshire CCC, 1993; Tickle the Public, 1996. *Recreation:* whingeing. *Address:* c/o The Guardian, 1730 Rhode Island Avenue, NW, Washington, DC 20036, USA. *Clubs:* Cricket Writers'; Northamptonshire CCC (Vice-Pres.).

ENGEL, Dame Sister Pauline Frances, DBE 1995 (CBE 1986); Vicar for Education, Diocese of Auckland (RC), New Zealand, since 1994; *b* 10 Sept. 1930; *d* of John Edmond Engel and Eileen Frances Engel (*née* McDavitt). *Educ:* St Mary's Coll., Wellington; Univ. of Auckland (MA Hons). Registered Teacher. Entered Sisters of Mercy Congregation, 1960; Dep. Principal, McAuley High Sch., 1978–79; Principal, Carmel Coll., 1983–91. Gen. Exec. Sec. to Major Superiors Conference, NZ, 1992–93. Sisters of Mercy Leadership Council, 1995–2000. *Publication:* The Abolition of Capital Punishment in New Zealand 1935–61, 1976. *Recreations:* classical music, reading. *Address:* Mount Carmel Convent, Box 31142, Milford, Auckland 9, New Zealand; Pompallier Diocesan Centre, Private Bag 47–904, Ponsonby, Auckland 2, New Zealand. *T:* (9) 3784380.

ENGESET, Jetmund, FRCSE; FRCSG; Consultant Surgeon, Grampian Health Board, since 1987; Surgeon to the Queen in Scotland, since 1985; *b* 22 July 1938; *s* of Arne K. Engeset and Marta Engeset; *m* 1966, Anne Graeme (*née* Robertson); two *d. Educ:* Slemdal and Ris Skole, Oslo, Norway; Oslo University; Aberdeen University (MB ChB, ChM Hons). House Officer (Surgical and Medical), Aberdeen Royal Infirmary, 1964–65; Aberdeen University: Res. Assistant, Dept of Surgery, 1965–67; Surgical Registrar, 1967–70; Lectr in Surgery, 1970–74; Sen. Lectr in Surgery, 1974–87; Head of Dept of Surgery, 1982–85 (seconded to Salgrenska Hosp. Surgical Unit, Gothenburg, Sweden, 1972–74). *Publications:* papers on microcirculation, vascular surgery, organ preservation and tissue transplantation. *Recreations:* skiing, angling, squash, gardening. *Address:* Pine Lodge, 315 North Deeside Road, Milltimber, Aberdeen, Aberdeenshire AB13 0DL. *T:* (01224) 733753.

ENGLAND, Angela Catherine; *see* Finnerty, A. C.

ENGLAND, Prof. George Leslie, DScEng; CEng, FICE, FINucE; Professor of Mechanics and Structures, Imperial College, London, 1989–2000; *b* 9 Oct. 1935; *s* of John Edward Philip England and Rose Gladys England; *m* 1968, W. Margaret Landon. *Educ:* East Barnet Grammar Sch.; King's Coll., London (Sambrooke Schol.; BScEng 1st Cl. Hons; Jameson Prize (Eng); Eng. Soc. Centenary Prize, Tennant Medal (Geol); PhD 1961; DScEng 1974). King's College, London: Lectr, 1961; Reader in Engrg Mechanics, 1975; Dean, 1983–85; Vice-Dean, 1985–86; Prof. of Mechanics and Structures, 1986–89. Consultant to: HSE, NII, 1971; UN Develt Project, Central Soils and Materials Res. Station, India, 1992. Mem., British Orthop. Res. Soc.; MASCE. *Publications:* contribs to learned jls on time-dependent service-life performance of concrete structures and behaviour of structures at high temperatures. *Recreations:* landscape gardening, mountain walking. *Address:* Civil Engineering Department, Imperial College of Science, Technology and Medicine, SW7 2BU.

ENGLAND, Glyn, BSc(Eng); FREng, FIEE, FIMechE, CIMgt; Director, The Wind Fund plc, 1994–2000; *b* 19 April 1921; *m* 1942, Tania Reichenbach; two *d. Educ:* Penarth County Sch.; Queen Mary Coll., London Univ. (BSc (Eng)); London School of Economics. Department of Scientific and Industrial Research, 1939. War service, 1942–47. Chief Ops Engr, CEGB, 1966–71; Dir-Gen., SW Region, 1971–73; Chm., SW Electricity Bd, 1973–77; part-time Mem., 1975–77, Chm., 1977–82, CEGB. Director: F. H. Lloyd (Hldgs), 1982–87; Triplex Lloyd, 1987–90; Chm., Windcluster Ltd, 1991–96. Consultant, World Bank, 1983–89. Mem., British Nat. Cttee, World Energy Conf., 1977–82; Vice-Pres., Internat. Union of Producers and Distributors of Electrical Energy, 1981–82. Mem., Bd of Dirs, UK CEED, 1984–96. Chairman: Council for Envmtl Conservation, 1983–88; Bd of Trustees, Silvanus Trust (formerly Dartington Action Res. Trust), 1985–94; Woodlands Initiatives, later Silvanus Services Ltd, 1988–96. Pres., Mendip Soc., 1999–. Sometime Labour Mem., Herts CC; Mem. Council, Magistrates' Assoc. JP Welwyn, Herts, 1962–71. Hon. DSc Bath, 1981. *Publications:* (with Rex Savidge) Landscape in the Making; papers on: Economic Growth and the Electricity Supply Industry, Security of Electricity Supplies, Planning for Uncertainty, Railways and Power (IMechE Tritton Lecture), Efficiency Audits, Industrial Ecology. *Recreation:* actively enjoying the countryside. *Address:* Woodbridge Farm, Ubley, Bristol BS40 6PX. *T:* (01761) 462479.

ENGLAND, Prof. Philip Christopher, FRS 1999; Professor of Geology, Oxford University, since 1999; Fellow, University College, Oxford, since 2000; *b* 30 April 1951; *s* of Anthony Christopher England and Margaret Jean England; *m* 1978, Pamela Anne Shreeve; one *s* two *d. Educ:* Bristol Univ. (BSc Physics 1972); DPhil Geophysics, Oxford, 1976. NERC Research Fellow, 1977–79, IBM Res. Fellow, 1979–81, Dept Geodesy and Geophysics, Univ. of Cambridge; Asst, then Associate Prof., Harvard Univ., 1981–86; Lectr in Geophysics, Oxford Univ., 1986–99; Fellow, Exeter Coll., Oxford, 1986–2000. Fellow, Amer. Geophysical Union, 1996. *Publications:* contribs to earth science jls. *Recreations:* family, music.

ENGLAND, Rear-Adm. Timothy John, FIEE; maritime and transport consultant, since 1997; Chief Staff Officer (Support) to Commander-in-Chief Fleet, 1992–94; *b* Llandudno, 6 Feb. 1942; *s* of Wilfred James England and Kathleen Helen England (*née* Stacey); *m* 1966, Margaret Ann Cullen; one *s* one *d. Educ:* Trinity Sch. of John Whitgift, Croydon; RNEC Manadon. BScEng ext. London Univ. CEng. Joined RN at BRNC Dartmouth as Weapon Engineering specialist, 1960; served HM Ships Alert, Collingwood, London, Salisbury; Staff of DG Ships; HM Dockyard, Devonport; HMS Bristol; Staff of C-in-C Fleet; Directorate of Naval Operational Requirements, 1978–80; Weapon Engineer Officer, HMS Invincible, incl. Falklands Campaign, 1981–82; Staff Weapon Engineer Officer to FO Sea Training, 1982–84; Defence Operational Requirements, 1984–86; RCDS 1987; Fleet Weapon Engineer Officer, 1988–89; WRNS Sea Service Implementation Team Leader, 1990; Captain, RNEC, Manadon, 1990–92. Harbour Master, River Hamble, 1995–96. MInstD. *Publications:* articles in Naval and professional jls. *Recreations:* sailing/cruising, photography, information technology. *Address:* 14 East Hill Close, Fareham, Hants PO16 8SE.

ENGLE, Sir George (Lawrence Jose), KCB 1983 (CB 1976); QC 1983; First Parliamentary Counsel, 1981–86; *b* 13 Sept. 1926; *m* 1956, Irene, *d* of late Heinz Lachmann; three *d. Educ:* Charterhouse (scholar); Christ Church, Oxford (Marjoribanks and Dixon schols, MA). Served RA, 1945–48 (2nd Lt, 1947). Firsts in Mods and Greats; Cholmeley Schol., Lincoln's Inn, 1952. Called to Bar, Lincoln's Inn, 1953, Bencher, 1984. Joined Parly Counsel Office, 1957; seconded as First Parly Counsel, Fedn of Nigeria, 1965–67; Parly Counsel, 1970–80; Second Parly Counsel, 1980–81; with Law Commn, 1971–73. Pres., Commonwealth Assoc. of Legislative Counsel, 1983–86. Chm. Council, Kipling Soc., 1999–2001. *Publications:* Law for Landladies, 1955; (ed jtly) Cross on Statutory Interpretation, 2nd edn 1987, 3rd edn 1995; contributor to: Ideas, 1954; O Rare Hoffnung, 1960; The Oxford Companion to English Literature, 1985. *Recreations:* books, travel, theatre, bricolage. *Address:* 32 Wood Lane, Highgate, N6 5UB. *T:* (020) 8340 9750.

ENGLEFIELD, Dermot John Tryal; Librarian, House of Commons, 1991–93; *b* 27 Aug. 1927; *o s* of Major Henry Wotton Englefield and Blanchfield Bernardine Englefield (*née* O'Halloran); *m* 1962, Dora, *o d* of Josip and Maca Grahovac, Karlovac, Croatia; one *s* one *d. Educ:* Mount St Mary's Coll.; Trinity Coll. Dublin (MA); Sarah Purser Scholarship (Hist. of Art) 1951. ALA 1966. Served RAF, 1946–48. St Marylebone Ref. Liby, 1952–54; House of Commons Liby, 1954–93; Asst Librarian (Parly Div.), 1967; Dep. Librarian, 1976. H of C corresp. to European Centre of Parly Res. and Documentation, 1977–93; Consultant to: Council of Europe, 1970; European Parlt, 1973; proposed Scottish Assembly, 1978; NI Assembly, 1982; Hong Kong Legislative Council, 1988; Romanian Parlt, 1993; Slovakian Parlt, 1993; Eur. Parlt, 1993–94; Swaziland, 1994, 1995; Malaŵi, 1994; Kenya, 1996; Zimbabwe, 1996; Ghana, 1996; Slovakia, 1996–97; Palestine, 1997, 1998–2000; Croatia, 1998. Member: Parly Libraries Sect., IFLA (Sec., 1981–85; Chm., 1985–89); Study of Parlt Gp, 1970– (Chm., 1987–90). Dir of Studies, RIPA Internat., 1994–99. Gov., Dulwich Coll., 1985–99. Editor for Industry and Parlt Trust, 1984–. Silver Jubilee Medal, 1977. *Publications:* The Printed Records of the Parliament of Ireland 1613–1800, 1978; Parliament and Information, 1981; Whitehall and Westminster, 1985; The Study of Parliament Group, 1985; (jtly) Facts About the British Prime Ministers, 1995; *edited:* (with G. Drewry) Information Sources in Politics and Political Science, 1984; Commons Select Committees, 1984; Today's Civil Service, 1985; Legislative Libraries and Developing Countries, 1986; Local Government and Business, 1987; Parliamentary Libraries and Information Services, 1990; Workings of Westminster, 1991; Getting the Message Across: the media, business and government, 1992; Guidelines for Legislative Libraries, 1993; chapters in books and contribs to jls. *Recreations:* travel, theatre. *Address:* 19 Woodhall Drive, Dulwich SE21 7HJ. *T:* and *Fax:* (020) 8693 1471. *Clubs:* Arts, Authors'.

ENGLEHART, Robert Michael; QC 1986; a Recorder, since 1987; *b* 1 Oct. 1943; *s* of G. A. F. and K. P. Englehart; *m* 1971, Rosalind Mary Foster; one *s* two *d. Educ:* St Edward's Sch., Oxford; Trinity Coll., Oxford (MA); Harvard Law School (LLM); Bologna Centre (Dip. in Internat. Relns). Assistente, Univ. of Florence, 1968. Called to the Bar, Middle Temple, 1969 (Astbury Scholar; Bencher, 1995); practising barrister, 1969–. Chairman: London Common Law and Commercial Bar Assoc., 1990–91; Jt Regulations Cttee, Inns of Court and Bar Council, 2000–. Trustee, Free Representation Unit, 1991–. *Publication:* (contrib.) Il Controllo Giudiziario: a comparative study of civil procedure, 1968. *Recreations:* shooting, cricket, windsurfing. *Address:* Blackstone Chambers, Blackstone House, Temple, EC4Y 9BW. *T:* (020) 7583 1770. *Clubs:* Garrick, MCC.

ENGLISH, Hon. Bill; *see* English, Hon. S. W.

ENGLISH, Cyril; President, Nationwide Housing Trust, 1991–97 (Chairman, 1987–90); Director, Nationwide, then Nationwide Anglia, Building Society, 1978–90 (Deputy Chairman, 1989–90); *b* 18 Feb. 1923; *s* of Joseph and Mary Hannah English; *m* 1945, Mary Brockbank; two *d. Educ:* Ashton-under-Lyne Grammar School. ALCM; CIMgt. Joined Nationwide Building Society, 1939; Asst Secretary, 1961; Asst General Manager, 1967; General Manager, 1971; Deputy Chief General Manager, 1974; Chief Gen. Manager, 1981–85. *Recreations:* golf, music. *Address:* Ashton Grange, Cedar Drive, Pangbourne, Berks RG8 7BH. *T:* (0118) 984 3841. *Club:* Calcot Park Golf (Reading).

ENGLISH, Gerald; Australian Artists Creative Fellow, 1994–99; *b* 6 Nov. 1925; *m* 1954, Jennifer Ryan; two *s* two *d*; *m* 1974, Linda Jacoby; one *s. Educ:* King's Sch., Rochester. After War service studied at Royal College of Music and then began career as lyric tenor; subsequently travelled in USA and Europe, appeared at Sadler's Wells, Covent Garden and Glyndebourne and recorded for major gramophone companies; Professor, Royal Coll. of Music, 1960–77; Director, Opera Studio, Victorian Coll. for the Arts, Melbourne, 1977–89.

ENGLISH, Michael; Member: Lambeth Borough Council, since 1990; London Fire and Civil Defence Authority, 1992–2000; *b* 24 Dec. 1930; *s* of late William Agnew English; *m* 1976, Carol Christine Owen; one *s* one *d. Educ:* King George V Grammar Sch., Southport; Liverpool Univ. (LLB). Joined Labour Party, 1949; Rochdale County Borough Council, 1953–65 (Chairman Finance Cttee until 1964). Employed until 1964 as Asst Manager of department concerned with management services in subsidiary of large public company. Chm., Lambeth CHC, 1993–94. Pres., SE London Valuation Panel, 1996–. Contested (Lab) Shipley Div., WR Yorks, 1959; MP (Lab) Nottingham West, 1964–83. Parliamentary Private Secretary, Board of Trade, 1966–67; Chairman: Parly Affairs Gp of Parly Lab. Party, 1970–76; Gen. Sub-Cttee of House of Commons Expenditure Cttee, 1974–79; Chm., E Midlands Gp, PLP, 1976–78; formerly Mem., Chairmen's Panel, Treasury and Civil Service, Procedure (Finance) and Sound Broadcasting Cttees, House of Commons. Chm., E Midlands Regional Lab. Party, 1979–80. *Recreation:* reading history. *Address:* 12 Denny Crescent, Kennington, SE11 4UY. *T:* (020) 7735 6070.

ENGLISH, Hon. Simon William, (Bill); MP (Nat.) Clutha-Southland, New Zealand, since 1996; *b* 30 Dec. 1961; *s* of Mervyn English and Norah (*née* O'Brien); *m* 1987, Dr Mary Scanlon; five *s* one *d. Educ:* St Patrick's Coll., Silverstream; Otago Univ. (BCom); Victoria Univ. of Wellington (BA Hons English Lit.). Sheep farmer, Dipton, until 1987; Policy Analyst, NZ Treasury, 1987–89; MP (Nat.) Wallace, 1990–96; Parly Under-Sec. for Health and Crown Health Enterprises, 1993–96; Minister for Crown Health Enterprises, Associate Minister of Educn and Mem., Cabinet, Feb.–Dec. 1996; Minister of Health, 1996–99; Associate Minister of Revenue, 1997–99; Associate Treas., 1998–99; Minister of Finance and Minister of Revenue, 1999. Dep. Leader, National Party, 2001. *Recreations:* Rugby, running. *Address:* Parliament Buildings, Wellington, New Zealand. *T:* (4) 4719999.

ENGLISH, Sir Terence (Alexander Hawthorne), KBE 1991; DL; FRCS; FRCP; Master of St Catharine's College, Cambridge, 1993–2000; Consultant Cardiothoracic Surgeon, Papworth and Addenbrooke's Hospitals, Cambridge, 1973–95; *b* 3 Oct. 1932; *s* of late Arthur Alexander English and Mavis Eleanor (*née* Lund); *m* 1963, Ann Margaret, *e* *d* of late Frederick Mordaunt Dicey and Ann Gwendoline (*née* Smartt); two *s* two *d*. *Educ:* Hilton Coll., Natal; Witwatersrand Univ. (Transvaal Chamber of Mines Scholarship, 1951–54; BSc(Eng) 1954); Guy's Hosp. Med. Sch. (MB, BS 1962); MA Cantab 1977. FRCSE 1967; FRCS 1967; FRCP 1990. House appointments, Guy's Hosp., 1962–63; Demonstrator, Anatomy Dept, Guy's Hosp., 1964–65; Surgical Registrar: Bolingbroke Hosp., 1966; Brompton Hosp., 1967–68; Res. Fellow, Dept of Surgery, Univ. of Alabama, 1969; Sen. Registrar, Brompton, National Heart and London Chest Hosps, 1968–72; Dir, Papworth Heart Transplant Res. Unit, 1980–88; non-exec. Dir, Papworth Hosp. NHS Trust, 1997–2001. Chief Med. Advr, BUPA, 1991–99. Mem., Audit Commn, 1993–98. Chm., Asia Healthcare plc, 1995–98. Member: British Cardiac Soc., 1973–; British Transplantation Soc., 1980–; Soc. of Thoracic and Cardiovascular Surgeons, 1972– (Exec. Council, 1975–77); Thoracic Soc., 1971– (Exec. Council, 1978–81). Member: Council, British Heart Foundn; Specialists Adv. Cttee in Cardiothoracic Surgery, 1980–87; GMC, 1983–89; Standing Med. Adv. Cttee, 1989–92; Jt Consultants Cttee, 1989–92; Supraregional Services Adv. Gp, 1990–92; Clinical Standards Adv. Gp, 1991–94. President: Internat. Soc. of Heart Transplantation, 1984–85; Soc. of Perfusionists of GB and Ireland, 1985–86; RCS, 1989–92 (Mem. Council, 1981–93; Court of Patrons, 1994; Trustee, Hunterian Mus., 1996–); Cardiothoracic Sect., RSM, 1992–93; BMA, 1995–96. Upjohn Lectr, Royal Soc., 1988. Capt., Guy's Hosp. RFC, 1959–60. Gov., Leys Sch., Cambridge, 1993–2001. Trustee, Northwick Park Inst. for Med. Res., 1996–. Member Council: Winston Churchill Meml Trust, 1995–; Univ. of Cambridge, 1998. Hon. Freeman, Barbers' Co., 1993. DL Cambs, 1996. FACC 1986. Hon. FRCSCan 1990; Hon. FRACS 1991; Hon. FCSSA 1991; Hon. FRCS (Thailand) 1991; Hon. FCP&S (Pakistan), 1991; Hon. FRCAnaes, 1991; Hon. FDSRCS 1992; Hon. FACS 1992; Hon. FRCSI 1992; Hon. FCOphth 1993; Hon. Fellow: St Catharine's Coll., Cambridge, 1992; Hughes Hall, Cambridge, 1993; UMDS, Guy's and St Thomas' Hosps, 1993. Hon. DSc: Sussex, 1992; Hull, 1996; Hon. MD: Nantes, 1992; Mahidol, Thailand, 1993. Man of the Year, RADAR, 1980; Clement Price Thomas Award, RCS, 1986. *Publications:* (jtly) Principles of Cardiac Diagnosis and Treatment: a surgeons' guide, 1992; chapter on Surgery of the Thorax and Heart in Bailey and Love's Short Practice of Thoracic Surgery, 1980; numerous articles in medical jls on matters relating to the practice of heart transplantation and cardiothoracic surgery. *Recreations:* reading, music, walking, classic cars. *Address:* Rhea House, Church Street, Harston, Cambridge CB2 5NP. *Clubs:* Athenæum; Hawks (Cambridge) (Chm.).

ENGLISH, Terence Michael; a District Judge (Magistrates' Courts) (formerly Metropolitan Stipendiary Magistrate), since 1986; Chairman, Inner London Juvenile Court Panel, since 1989; a Recorder, 1994–97; *b* 3 Feb. 1944; *s* of John Robert English and Elsie Letitia English; *m* 1966, Ivy Joan Weatherley (*d* 1997); one *s* one *d*. *Educ:* St Ignatius' Coll., London N15; London Univ. (external LLB 1967). Admitted Solicitor of the Supreme Court, 1970. Assistant, Edmonton PSD, 1962–71; Dep. Clerk to Justices, Bullingdon, Bampton E, Henley and Watlington PSDs, 1972–76; Clerk to the Justices: Newbury and Hungerford and Lambourn PSDs, 1977–85; Slough and Windsor PSDs, 1985–86. Chm., Family Panel, 1991–92. *Recreations:* golf, philately.

ENNIS, Catherine Mary, (Mrs J. A. Higham); concert organist; Organist, St Lawrence Jewry-next-Guildhall, EC2, since 1985; *b* 20 Jan. 1955; *d* of Séamus and Margaret Ennis; *m* 1988, John Arthur Higham; two *s* one *d*, and [illegible] step *s* two step *d*. *Educ:* Christ's Hosp., Hertford; Kingsway Further Educn Coll.; St Hugh's Coll., Oxford (MA). Internat. concert organist; recitals, Europe and USA, 1977–; Dir of Music, St Marylebone Parish Church, 1978–90; Asst Organist, Christ Church Cathedral, Oxford, 1984–86; Professor: RAM, 1982–90; GSM, 1985–86. Estabd and Editor-in-Chief, London Organ Concerts Guide, 1995–. Trustee, Nicholas Danby Trust, 1999–. Presenter, recitalist, concerto soloist and conductor on radio and TV; has made several commercial recordings. Prizewinner: GSM, 1973; Manchester Internat. Organ Comp., 1981 and 1983. *Publications:* contribs to organ jls. *Recreations:* opera, cricket, cooking, children. *Address:* c/o The Vestry, St Lawrence Jewry-next-Guildhall, EC2V 5AA.

ENNIS, Jeffrey; MP (Lab) Barnsley East, since Dec. 1996; *b* 13 Nov. 1952; *s* of William Ennis and Jean Ennis; *m* 1980, Margaret Angela Knight; three *s*. *Educ:* Redland Coll.; Univ. of Bristol (BEd Hons). Teacher: Elston Hall Jun. Sch., Fordhouses, Wolverhampton, 1976–78; Burngreave Middle Sch., Sheffield, 1978–79; Hillsborough Primary Sch., Sheffield, 1979–96. Barnsley Metropolitan Borough Council: Councillor (Lab), 1980–97; Dep. Leader, 1988–95; Leader, 1995–96. PPS to Minister for Public Health, DoH, 1997–99, to Minister for Employment, 1999–2001. Mem., Educn and Skills Select Cttee, 2001–. Member: Co-op Party; TGWU; Chm., Brierley Lab. Pty Br., 1998–. *Recreations:* most sports, especially swimming, hill-walking, caravanning. *Address:* 74 Church Street, Brierley, Barnsley S72 9JG. *T:* (01226) 716178; House of Commons, SW1A 0AA.

ENNISKILLEN, 7th Earl of, *cr* 1789 (Ire.); **Andrew John Galbraith Cole;** Baron Mountflorence 1760; Viscount Enniskillen 1776; Baron Grinstead (UK) 1815; pilot and company director; Captain Irish Guards, 1965; *b* 28 April 1942; *s* of 6th Earl of Enniskillen, MBE and Sonia (*d* 1982), *d* of Major Thomas Syers, RA; *S* father, 1989; *m* 1964, Sarah, *o d* of Maj.-Gen. J. Keith-Edwards, CBE, DSO, MC, Nairobi; three *d*. *Educ:* Eton. Man. Dir, Kenya Airways, 1979–81; Exec. Vice-Chm., AAR Health Services, 1991–. *Heir: unde* Arthur Gerald Cole [*b* 15 Nov. 1920; *m* 1949, Prudence Tobina, *d* of late A. R. A. Cartright; three *s* one *d*].

ENRIGHT, Dennis Joseph, OBE 1991; CLit 1998; freelance writer; *b* 11 March 1920; *s* of late George and Grace Enright; *m* 1949, Madeleine Harders; one *d*. *Educ:* Leamington Coll.; Downing Coll., Cambridge. MA Cantab; DLitt Alexandria. Lecturer in English, University of Alexandria, 1947–50; Organising Tutor, University of Birmingham Extra-Mural Dept, 1950–53; Vis. Prof., Kōnan Univ., Japan, 1953–56; Vis. Lecturer, Free University of Berlin, 1956–57; British Council Professor, Chulalongkorn Univ., Bangkok, 1957–59; Prof. of English, Univ. of Singapore, 1960–70; Hon. Prof. of English, Univ. of Warwick, 1975–80. Dir, Chatto and Windus, 1974–82. Co-Editor, Encounter, 1970–72. FRSL 1961. Cholmondeley Poetry Award, 1974; Queen's Gold Medal for Poetry, 1981. Hon. DLitt Warwick, 1982; DUniv. Surrey, 1985. *Publications: poetry:* The Laughing Hyena, 1953; Bread Rather Than Blossoms, 1956; Some Men Are Brothers, 1960; Addictions, 1962; The Old Adam, 1965; Unlawful Assembly, 1968; Selected Poems, 1969; Daughters of Earth, 1972; The Terrible Shears, 1973; Rhyme Times Rhyme (for children), 1974; Sad Ires, 1975; Paradise Illustrated, 1978; A Faust Book, 1979; Collected Poems, 1981; Instant Chronicles, 1985; Collected Poems 1987, 1987; Selected Poems 1990, 1990; Under the Circumstances, 1991; Old Men and Comets, 1993; Collected Poems 1948–1998, 1998; *novels:* Academic Year, 1955; Heaven Knows Where, 1957; Insufficient Poppy, 1960; Figures of Speech, 1965; The Way of the Cat, 1992; *novels for children:* The Joke Shop, 1976; Wild Ghost Chase, 1978; Beyond Land's End, 1979; *non-fiction:* The Apothecary's Shop, 1957; English Critical Texts (co-editor), 1962; Conspirators and Poets, 1966; Shakespeare and the Students, 1970; Man is an Onion, 1972; (ed) A Choice of Milton's Verse, 1975; Samuel Johnson: Rasselas, 1976; (ed) The Oxford Book of Contemporary Verse 1945–1980, 1980; A Mania for Sentences, 1983; (ed) Fair of Speech: the uses of euphemism, 1985; The Alluring Problem: an essay on irony, 1986; Fields of Vision: essays on literature, language and television, 1988; Interplay: a kind of commonplace book, 1995; Play Resumed: a journal, 1999; Signs and Wonders: selected essays, 2001; *travel:* The World of Dew: Japan, 1955; Memoirs of a Mendicant Professor, 1969; *translations:* The Poetry of Living Japan (co-editor), 1957; The Sayings of Goethe, 1996; *anthologies:* (ed) The Oxford Book of Death, 1983; (ed) The Faber Book of Fevers and Frets, 1989; (ed jtly) The Oxford Book of Friendship, 1991; The Oxford Book of the Supernatural, 1994; contributor to: Scrutiny, Encounter, London Review of Books, TLS, etc. *Recreations:* reading, writing, television, listening to music. *Address:* 35A Viewfield Road, SW18 5JD.

ENSOM, Donald, FRICS, FCIArb; Chartered Surveyor; Consultant, Debenham Tewson & Chinnocks, 1986–92 (Partner, 1962–86); *b* 8 April 1926; *s* of Charles R. A. W. Ensom and Edith (*née* Young); *m* 1951, Sonia (*née* Sherrard); one *s* one *d*. *Educ:* Norbury Manor Sch., Croydon. Qualified as Chartered Surveyor, 1951; FRICS 1958; FCIArb 1970. Served RA, 1943–47. Partner, Nightingale, Page & Bennett/Debenham Tewson & Chinnocks (after merger), 1958–86. Chm., Bldg Conservation Trust, 1981–83; Royal Institution of Chartered Surveyors: Pres., Bldg Surveyors Div., 1975–76; Chm., Professional Practice Cttee, 1978–83; Hon. Sec., 1983–90; Vice-Pres., 1988–90. Pres., Land Economy Soc., Univ. of Cambridge, 1990–91. *Publications:* (jtly) Party Walls, 1993; (jtly) The Party Wall Act Explained, 1997; numerous professional papers. *Recreations:* reading, opera and music, transport history, crossword puzzles, freemasonry. *Address:* 8 The Oast House, Grange Road, Cambridge CB3 9AP. *Clubs:* East India, Royal Over-Seas League, Chartered Surveyors (1913), Pyramus and Thisbe (Chm. 1987–89).

ENSOR, David, OBE 1986; Managing Director, Croydon Advertiser Ltd, 1979–85; *b* 2 April 1924; *s* of Rev. William Walters and Constance Eva Ensor; *m* 1947, Gertrude Kathleen Brown; two *s*. *Educ:* Kingswood Sch., Bath; London Coll. of Printing. Served Royal Signals, 1942–46, Captain; ADC to GOC Bengal Dist. Managing Director: George Reveirs, 1947–59; Charles Skipper & East, 1959–69; Knapp Drewett & Sons, 1969–79; Chairman: Methodist Newspaper Co., 1975–94; Methodist Publishing House, 1981–96. A Vice-Chm., Press Council, 1987–90 (Mem., 1982–90); Mem. Council, Newspaper Soc., 1979–94. Pres., London Printing Industries Assoc., 1976. Vice-Pres., Methodist Conf., 1981. *Address:* Milborne Lodge, Dinton Road, Fovant, Salisbury, Wilts SP3 5JW. *T:* (01722) 714521.

ENSOR, George Anthony; His Honour Judge Ensor; a Circuit Judge, since 1995; *b* 4 Nov. 1936; *s* of George and Phyllis Ensor; *m* 1968, Jennifer Margaret Caile, MB, ChB; two *d*. *Educ:* Malvern College; Liverpool University (LLB). Solicitor, 1961 (Atkinson Conveyancing Medal, 1962; Rupert Bremner Medal, 1962); Partner, 1962–92, Sen. Partner, 1992–95, Rutherfords, later Weightman Rutherfords, Solicitors, Liverpool; a Recorder, 1983–95. Deputy Coroner, City of Liverpool, 1966–95; part-time Chairman, Industrial Tribunals, 1975–95; Asst Parly Boundary Comr, 1992–95. Mem., Judicial Studies Bd, 1987–89; President, Liverpool Law Society, 1982. Trustee, Empire Theatre (Merseyside) Trust, Ltd, 1986–. Dir, Liverpool FC, 1985–93. *Recreations:* golf, theatre. *Address:* c/o Courts of Justice, Crown Square, Manchester M60 9FD. *Clubs:* Artists (Liverpool); Formby Golf; Waterloo Rugby Union.

ENSOR, Michael de Normann, CMG 1980; OBE 1958; Head, East Africa Development Division, Overseas Development Administration, 1975–80; *b* 11 June 1919; *s* of Robert Weld Ensor and Dr Beatrice Ensor; *m* 1945, Mona Irene Blackburn; two *s*. *Educ:* Bryanston School; St. John's Coll., Oxford. Military service, 1940; Colonial Service, Gold Coast/Ghana Civil Service, 1940–58; Secretary, Foundation for Mutual Assistance in Africa South of the Sahara, 1958–64; Dept of Technical Cooperation/Min. of Overseas Development/Overseas Development Administration, 1964–80. Chairman: Paragon Management Co., 1983–86; Overseas Service Pensioners' Benevolent Soc., 1986–91. *Address:* Flat 1, 12 The Paragon, Blackheath, SE3 0NZ. *T:* (020) 8852 5345. *Clubs:* Travellers; Royal Blackheath Golf.

ENTWISTLE, John Nicholas McAlpine; DL; Consultant Solicitor, Davies Wallis Foyster, since 1992; President, British Chambers of Commerce, 1998–2000; *b* 16 June 1941; *s* of Sir (John Nuttall) Maxwell Entwistle and Lady (Jean Cunliffe McAlpine) Entwistle; *m* 1968, Phillida Gail Sinclair Burgess; one *s* one *d*. *Educ:* Uppingham Sch. Admitted Solicitor, 1963. Asst Attorney, Shearman & Sterling, NY, 1963–64; Partner, Maxwell Entwistle & Byrne, Solicitors, 1966–91. Regl Dir, Midshires Building Soc., 1977–87; non-exec. Dir, Rathbone Brothers plc, 1992–98. Founder Dir, Merseyside TEC, 1990–91; Dep. Dist Chm., Appeals Service, 1999– (pt-time Chm., Social Security Appeals Tribunal, 1992–99); pt-time Immigration Adjudicator, 2000–. Member: Parole Bd, 1994–2000; Criminal Injuries Compensation Appeals Panel, 2000–; Disciplinary Cttee, Mortgage Compliance Bd, 1999–; Chancellor of Exchequer's Standing Cttee on Preparation for EMU, 1998–2000. Trustee, Nat. Museums and Galls on Merseyside, 1990–97 (Chm., Develt Trust, 1991–95). Gen. Comr for Income Tax, 1978–83. Contested (C) Huyton, 1970. DL Merseyside, 1992. *Recreations:* collecting and painting pictures, gardening, fishing, shooting. *Address:* Low Crag, Crook, Cumbria LA8 8LE. *T:* (015395) 68268, *Fax:* (015395) 68769; *e-mail:* jentwistle@nascr.net.

ENTWISTLE, Prof. Kenneth Mercer; Professor of Metallurgy and Materials Science, University of Manchester Institute of Science and Technology, 1962–90, now Emeritus; *b* 3 Jan. 1925; *s* of William Charles and Maude Elizabeth Entwistle; *m* 1949, Alice Patricia Mary Johnson; two *s* two *d*. *Educ:* Urmston Grammar Sch.; Univ. of Manchester (BSc Elect. Eng. 1945, MSc 1946, PhD 1948). FIM, CEng. University of Manchester: Lectr in Metallurgy, 1948; Sen. Lectr, 1954; Reader, 1960; Dean, Faculty of Technology, 1976–77; Pro-Vice-Chancellor, 1982–85; Vice-Principal, UMIST, 1972–74. Chairman: Materials Cttee, CNAA, 1972–74; Educn Cttee, Instn of Metallurgists, 1977–79; Metallics Sub-Cttee, SRC, 1979–81; Mem., UGC, 1985–89 (Chm., Technology Sub-Cttee, 1985–89); Engrg Advr to Chief Exec. of UFC, 1989–92. Comp. UMIST, 1991. Hon. Fellow, Sheffield Polytechnic, 1971. *Publications:* numerous papers in scientific jls. *Recreations:* Scottish dancing, choral singing. *Address:* Greenacre, Bridge End Lane, Prestbury, Macclesfield, Cheshire SK10 4DJ. *T:* (01625) 829269; *e-mail:* ken.entwistle@man.ac.uk. *Club:* Athenæum.

EÖTVÖS, Peter; composer and conductor; *m* 1st, 1968, Piroska Molnar (marr. diss. 1975); one *s*; 2nd, 1976, Pi-Hsien Chen (marr. diss. 1994); one *d*; 3rd, 1995, Maria Mezei. *Educ:* Acad. of Music, Budapest; Musik Hochschule, Cologne. Composer, chamber music, electronic music, opera and orchestral music; conductor and musical director, Ensemble Intercontemporain, Paris, 1979–91; principal guest conductor, BBC Symphony Orchestra, 1985–88; first Guest Conductor, Budapest Fest. Orch., 1992–95; Chief Conductor, Radio Chamber Orch. Hilversum, 1994–. Professor: Musikhochschule Karlsruhe, 1992–98; Musikhochschule Köln, 1998–; Founder, Internat. Eötvös Inst., for young conductors and composers, 1991. *Recreations:* walking, pipe smoking, jazz. *Address:* International Eötvös Institute, Naarderweg 56, 1261 BV Blaricum, Netherlands.

EPHRAUMS, Maj.-Gen. Roderick Jarvis, CB 1977; OBE 1965; Major-General Royal Marines, Commando Forces, 1976–78, retired; *b* 12 May 1927; *s* of Hugh Cyril Ephraums and Elsie Caroline (*née* Rowden); *m* 1955, Adela Mary (*née* Forster); two *s* one *d*. *Educ:* Tonbridge. Commnd 2nd Lieut, RM, 1945; HMS Mauritius, 1946–48; 3 Commando Bde, RM, 1952–54; Staff Coll., Camberley, 1960; Bde Major, 3 Commando Bde, 1962–64; CO, 45 Commando RM, 1969–71; Royal Coll. of Defence Studies, 1972; Comdr, 3 Commando Bde, 1973–74; NATO Defense Coll., Rome, 1975. A Col Comdt, RM, 1985–, Rep. Col Comdt, 1987 and 1988. DL Angus, 1985–98. CStJ 1993. *Recreations:* painting, gardening. *Club:* Army and Navy.

EPSTEIN, Sir (Michael) Anthony, Kt 1991; CBE 1985; FRS 1979; Fellow, Wolfson College, Oxford, 1986;–2001, then Hon. Fellow; Professor of Pathology, 1968–85 (now Emeritus), and Head of Department, 1968–82, University of Bristol; Hon. Consultant Pathologist, Bristol Health District (Teaching), 1968–82; *b* 18 May 1921; *yr s* of Mortimer and Olga Epstein; *m* 1950, Lisbeth Knight (separated 1965); two *s* one *d*. *Educ:* St Paul's Sch., London; Trinity Coll., Cambridge (Perry Exhibr, 1940); Middlesex Hosp. Medical Sch. MA, MD, DSc, PhD; FRCPath. Ho. Surg., Middlesex Hosp., London, and Addenbrooke's Hosp., Cambridge, 1944; Lieut and Captain, RAMC, 1945–47; Asst Pathologist, Bland Sutton Inst., Mddx Hosp. Med. Sch., 1948–65, with leave as: Berkeley Travelling Fellow, 1952–53; French Govt Exchange Scholar at Institut Pasteur, Paris, 1952–53; Vis. Investigator, Rockefeller Inst., NY, 1956; Reader in Experimental Pathology, Mddx Hosp. Med. Sch., 1965–68; Hon. Consultant in Experimental Virology, Mddx Hosp., 1965–68. Member: Cttee, Pathological Soc. of GB and Ire., 1969–72 (Hon. Mem., 1987); Council, and Vice-Pres., Pathology Section of RSM, 1966–72 (Hon. Mem., 1988); Study Gp on Classification of Herpes Viruses, of Internat. Commn for Nomenclature of Viruses, 1971–81; Scientific Adv. Bd, Harvard Med. Sch.'s New England Regional Primate Center, 1972–96; Cancer Research Campaign MRC Jt Cttee, 1973–77, 1982–87 (Chm. 1983–87); Cttee, British Soc. for Cell Biology, 1974–77; MRC, 1982–86 (Mem. 1979–84, Chm. 1982–84, Cell Bd; Mem., 1984–85, Chm., 1985–88, Tropical Medicine Res. Bd); Council, Royal Soc., 1983–85, 1986–91 (Foreign Sec. and a Vice-Pres., 1986–91; Assessor on MRC, 1987–91); Medical and Scientific Panel, Leukaemia Research Fund, 1982–85; Scientific Adv. Cttee, Lister Inst., 1984–87; Expert Working Party on Bovine Spongiform Encephalopathy, DoH, 1988; Exec. Bd, ICSU, 1990–93 (Chm., Cttee on Sci. in Central and Eastern Europe, 1992–95); Exec. Council, ESF, 1990–93; Program Adv. Gp, World Bank China Key Studies Project, 1992–97; Special Rep. of Dir Gen. UNESCO for Sci. in Russia, 1992. Discovered in 1964 a new human herpes virus, now known as Epstein-Barr virus, which causes infectious mononucleosis and is also causally implicated in some forms of human cancer (Burkitt's lymphoma and nasopharyngeal carcinoma). Fellow, UCL, 1992. Founder FMedSci 1998. Mem., Academia Europaea, 1988. Mem. d'honneur, Belgian Soc. for Cancer Res., 1979. Hon. Professor: Sun Yat-Sen Med. Univ., Guangzhou, 1981; Chinese Acad. of Preventive Medicine, Beijing, 1988. Hon. Fellow, Queensland Inst. of Med. Research, 1983; Hon. FRCP 1986; Hon. FRSE 1991; Hon. FRCPA 1995. Hon. MD: Edinburgh, 1986; Charles Univ., Prague, 1998; Hon. DSc Birmingham, 1996. Paul Ehrlich and Ludwig Darmstaedter Prize and Medal, Paul Ehrlich Foundn, W Germany, 1973; Markham Skerrit Prize, 1977; (jtly) Bristol-Myers Award, NY, 1982; Leeuwenhoek Prize Lectr, Royal Soc., 1983; Prix Griffuel, Assoc. pour la recherche sur le cancer, Paris, 1986; Samuel Weiner Distinguished Visitor Award, Univ. of Manitoba, 1988; John H. Lattimer Award, Amer. Urol Assoc., 1988; Internat. Award, Gairdner Foundn, Toronto, 1988; Royal Medal, Royal Soc., 1992. *Publications:* over 230 scientific papers in internat. jls on tumour cell structure, viruses, tumour viruses, Burkitt's lymphoma, and the EB virus. Jt Founder Editor, The Internat. Review of Experimental Pathology (vols 1–28, 1962–86); (ed jtly) The Epstein-Barr Virus, 1979; (ed jtly) The Epstein-Barr Virus: recent advances, 1986; (ed jtly) Oncogenic γ-herpesviruses: an expanding family, 2001. *Address:* Nuffield Department of Clinical Medicine, University of Oxford, John Radcliffe Hospital, Oxford OX3 9DU. *T:* (01865) 221334, *Fax:* (01865) 222901.

ERAUT, Prof. Michael Ruarc, PhD; Professor of Education, University of Sussex, since 1986; *b* 15 Nov. 1940; *s* of Lt-Col Ruarc Bertrand Sorel Eraut and Frances Mary (*née* Hurst); *m* 1964, (Mary) Cynthia Wynne; two *s*. *Educ:* Winchester Coll. (Scholar); Trinity Hall, Cambridge (Scholar; BA Nat. Sci.; PhD Chem.). Fulbright Scholar, 1965–67; Res. Assistant, 1965–66, Vis. Asst Prof., 1966–67, Univ. of Illinois, Chicago; University of Sussex: Fellow, 1967–71; Sen. Fellow, 1971–73; Dir, Centre for Educnl Technol., 1973–76; Reader in Educn, 1976–86; Dir, Inst. of Continuing and Professional Educn, 1986–91. Chm. of Corporation, Lewes Tertiary Coll., 1992–97. *Publications:* (with N. Mackenzie and H. C. Jones) Teaching and Learning: new methods and resources in higher education, 1970, 3rd edn 1976 (trans. French, German, Spanish and Portuguese); In-Service Education for Innovation, 1972; The Analysis of Curriculum Materials, 1975 (trans. German 1976); Accountability in the Middle Years of Schooling, 1980; (with B. Connors and E. Hewton) Training in Curriculum Development and Educational Technology in Higher Education, 1980; (with T. Becher and J. Knight) Policies for Educational Accountability, 1981; Curriculum Development in Further Education, 1985; (with J. Burke) Improving the Quality of YTS, 1986; Local Evaluation of INSET, 1988; (ed) International Encyclopaedia of Educational Technology, 1989; (with G. Cole) Business Education: a handbook for schools, 1990; Education and the Information Society, 1991; (with C. Nash and M. Fielding) Flexible Learning in Schools, 1991; (with G. Cole) Assessing Competence in the Professions, 1993; Developing Professional Knowledge and Competence, 1994; Learning to Use Scientific Knowledge in Education and Practice Settings, 1995; Assessment of NVQs, 1996; Development of Knowledge and Skills in Employment, 1998; Evaluation of Vocational Training of Science Graduates in the NHS, 1998; (with B. Du Boulay) Developing the Attributes of Medical Professional Judgement and Competence, 1999; (with S. Steadman and J. James) Evaluation of Higher Level S/NVQs, 2001; chapters in books and numerous conference papers. *Recreations:* music, travel. *Address:* 49 St Anne's Crescent, Lewes, E Sussex BN7 1SD. *T:* (01273) 475955.

ERDMAN, Edward Louis, FSVA; FRSA; Founder, 1934, Chairman, 1934–74, and Senior Consultant, 1974–2000, Edward Erdman, Surveyors, later Erdman Lewis International, then Colliers Erdman Lewis; *b* 4 July 1906; *s* of David and Pauline Erdman; *m* 1949, Pamela (*née* Mason); one *s*. *Educ:* former Grocers' Co. Sch. TA KRRC, 1937; war service, N Africa and Italy, 1939–45. Re-opened practice, 1945. WPHT Housing Association (subseq. re-named Sanctuary Housing Association): Mem., Central Council, 1974; Chm., 1978–87; Pres. 1987; Mem., Property Adv. Panel to Treasury, 1975–77. FRSA 1957. *Publication:* People and Property, 1982.

EREMIN, Prof. Oleg, MD, FRCSE, FRACS, FMedSci; Special Professor in Surgery, University of Nottingham, at Queen's Medical Centre, Nottingham, since 1998; Consultant Breast Surgeon and Lead Clinician, Lincoln NHS Trust, since 1999; *b* 12 Nov. 1938; *s* of Theodor and Maria Eremin; *m* 1963, Jennifer Mary Ching; two *s* one *d*. *Educ:* Christian Brothers' Coll., St Kilda, Melbourne; Univ. of Melbourne. MB BS 1964; MD 1985. FRACS 1971; FRCSE 1983. Clinical posts: Royal Melbourne Hosp., 1965–72; Norfolk and Norwich Hosps, 1972–74; Research Asst-Associate, Dept of Pathology, Univ. of Cambridge, 1974–80; Sen. Lectr, Dept Clinical Surgery, Univ. of Edinburgh, 1981–85; Regius Prof. of Surgery, Univ. of Aberdeen, 1985–98. Hon. Professorial Fellow, Rowett Res. Inst., 1992. Founder FMedSci 1998. *Publications:* articles in surgical, oncological and immunological jls. *Recreations:* music, sport, reading. *Address:* Orchard House, 51A Washdyke Lane, Nettleham, Lincoln LN2 2PX. *T:* (01522) 750669.

ERICKSON, Prof. Charlotte Joanne; Paul Mellon Professor of American History, University of Cambridge, 1983–90, now Professor Emeritus; Fellow of Corpus Christi College, Cambridge, since 1982; *b* 22 Oct. 1923; *d* of Knut Eric Erickson and Lael A. R. Johnson; *m* 1952, G. L. Watt; two *s*. *Educ:* Augustana Coll., Rock Island, Ill (BA 1945); Cornell Univ., Ithaca, NY (MA 1947; PhD 1951). Instructor in History, Vassar Coll., Poughkeepsie, NY, 1950–52; Research Fellow, NIESR, 1952–55; Lillian Gilmore Fellow, Cornell Univ., April-Sept. 1954; Asst Lectr, 1955, Lectr, 1958, Sen. Lectr, 1966, Reader, 1975, Prof., 1979–82, in Economic History, London School of Economics. Guggenheim Fellow, Washington, DC, 1966–67; Sherman Fairchild Distinguished Scholar, Calif Inst. of Technology, 1976–77; MacArthur Fellow, John D. and Dorothy MacArthur Foundn, Chicago, 1990–95. Hon. DHumLet Augustana College, 1977. *Publications:* British Industrialists, Steel and Hosiery 1850–1950, 1958; American Industry and the European Immigrant 1860–1885, 1969; Invisible Immigrants, The Adaptation of English and Scottish Immigrants in Nineteenth Century America, 1972; Leaving England: essays on British emigration in the Ninteenth Century, 1994; articles in professional jls and collective works. *Recreations:* music, gardening. *Address:* Corpus Christi College, Cambridge CB2 1RH; 8 High Street, Chesterton, Cambridge CB4 1NG.

ERICKSON, Prof. John, FRSE 1982; FBA 1985; University Endowment Fellow, and Director, Centre for Defence Studies, University of Edinburgh, 1988–96; Hon. Fellow, Defence Studies and Professor Emeritus, since 1996; *b* 17 April 1929; *s* of Henry Erickson and Jessie (*née* Heys); *m* 1957, Ljubica (*née* Petrović); one *s* one *d*. *Educ:* South Shields High Sch.; St John's Coll., Cambridge (MA). Research Fellow, St Anthony's Coll., Oxford, 1956–58; Lectr, Dept of History, St Andrews Univ., 1958–62; Lectr, Sen. Lectr and Reader, Dept of Government, Univ. of Manchester, 1962–67; Edinburgh University: Reader, Lectr in Higher Defence Studies, 1967; Prof. of Politics (Defence Studies), 1969–88. Visiting Professor: Russian Res. Center, Univ. of Indiana, 1967; Texas A&M Univ., 1981; Dept. of History, Yale Univ., 1987. Pres., Assoc. of Civil Defence and Emergency Planning Officers, 1981–. FRSA 1991; Hon. Fellow, Aerospace Acad., Ukraine, 1995. *Publications:* The Soviet High Command 1918–1941, 1962, repr. 2001; Storia dello Stato Maggiore Sovietico, 1963; (ed) The Military-Technical Revolution, 1966; (ed) The Armed Services and Society, 1970; Soviet Military Power, 1971; The Road to Stalingrad, 1975 (reprinted, 1998); (ed) Soviet Military Power and Performance, 1979; The Road to Berlin, 1983; (ed) Barbarossa, The Axis and the Allies, 1994; (jtly) The Soviet Armed Forces 1918–1992: a research guide to Soviet sources, 1996; (jtly) The Russian Front 1941–1945, 1999; (introd) Invasion 1940, 2000; (jtly) The Eastern Front in Photographs, 1941–1945, 2001. *Recreations:* military models and music. *Address:* 13 Ravelston House Road, Edinburgh EH4 3LP. *T:* (0131) 332 1787. *Club:* Scottish Arts (Edinburgh).

ERIKSSON, Sven-Göran; Head Coach, England Football Team, since 2001; *b* Torsby, Sweden, 5 Feb. 1948. Former footballer (defender); clubs include Torsby IF, Sifhalla and KB Karlsgoba (all Sweden); managerial posts: Asst Manager, 1976, Manager, 1977–78, Degerfors, Sweden; Manager: IFK Gothenburg, Sweden, 1979–82; Benfica, Portugal, 1982–84; AS Roma, Italy, 1984–87; AC Fiorentina, Italy, 1987–89; Benfica, 1989–92; Samporia, Italy, 1992–97; SS Lazio, Italy, 1997–2000 (winners: Italian Cup, 1998; Italian Super Cup, 1998; UEFA Cup Winners Cup, 1999; UEFA Super Cup, 1999; Italian Championship, 2000). *Address:* c/o Football Association, 25 Soho Square, W1D 4FA.

ERLEIGH, Viscount; Julian Michael Rufus Isaacs; *b* 26 May 1986; *s* and *heir* of Marquess of Reading, *qv*.

ERMISCH, Prof. John Francis, FBA 1995; Professor, Institute for Social and Economic Research (formerly ESRC Research Centre on Micro-Social Change), University of Essex, since 1994; *b* 1 July 1947; *s* of Elmer and Frances Ermisch; *m* 1977, Dianne M. Monti. *Educ:* Univ. of Wisconsin (BSc); Univ. of Kansas (MA, PhD). Res. Economist, US Dept of Housing and Urban Develt, 1974–76; Res. Fellow, Centres for Environmental Studies and for the Study of Social Policy, London, 1976–78; Sen. Res. Fellow, PSI, 1978–86; Sen. Res. Officer, NIESR, 1986–91; Bonar-Macfie Prof., Univ. of Glasgow, 1991–94. *Publications:* Lone Parenthood: an economic analysis, 1991; The Political Economy of Demographic Change, 1983; contribs to economic and demographic jls. *Recreations:* films, tennis, golf. *Address:* Institute for Social and Economic Research, University of Essex, Wivenhoe Park, Colchester CO4 3SQ. *T:* (01206) 872335.

ERNE, 6th Earl of, *cr* 1789; **Henry George Victor John Crichton;** JP; Baron Erne 1768; Viscount Erne (Ireland), 1781; Baron Fermanagh (UK), 1876; Lord Lieutenant of Co. Fermanagh, Northern Ireland, since 1986; *b* 9 July 1937; *s* of 5th Earl and Lady Katharine Cynthia Mary Millicent (Davina) Lytton (who *m* 1945, Hon. C. M. Woodhouse, later 5th Baron Terrington, DSO, OBE; she *d* 1995), *yr d* of 2nd Earl of Lytton, KG, PC, GCSI, GCIE; *S* father, 1940; *m* 1958, Camilla Marguerite (marr. diss. 1980), *er d* of late Wing-Comdr Owen G. E. Roberts and Mrs Roberts; one *s* four *d*; *m* 1980, Mrs Anna Carin Hitchcock (*née* Bjork). *Educ:* Eton. Page of Honour to the Queen, 1952–54 (to King George VI, 1952). Lieut, North Irish Horse, 1959–66. Member: Royal Ulster Agricultural Society; Royal Forestry Society. JP Co. Fermanagh. *Recreations:* sailing, fishing, shooting. *Heir:* *s* Viscount Crichton, *qv*. *Address:* Crom Castle, Newtownbutler, Co. Fermanagh BT92 8AP. *T:* (01365) 738208. *Clubs:* White's; Lough Erne Yacht.

ERNST, Prof. Edzard, MD, PhD; Professor of Complementary Medicine, University of Exeter, since 1993; *b* 30 Jan. 1948; *s* of Wolfgang Ernst and Erika (*née* Tillwichs); *m* 1983, Danielle Johnson (*née* Le Mignon). *Educ:* Maximilian Ludwig Univ., Munich (MD 1978; PhD 1985). University of Munich: Sen. House Officer, 1977–79; Registrar, then Sen. Registrar, 1981–89; Res. Assistant, St George's Hosp., London, 1979–81; Prof. of Physical Medicine and Rehabilitation, Univ. of Hanover, 1989; Prof. of Physical Medicine and Rehabilitation, Univ. of Vienna, 1990–93. Vis. Prof., RCPS, Canada, 1999. Member: Medicines Commn, British Medicines Control Agency; Scientific Cttee on Herbal Medicinal Products, Irish Medicines BD. Editor-in-Chief, Focus on Alternative and Complementary Therapies. *Publications include:* Meyler's Side Effects of Drugs, 2000; (contrib.) Oxford Textbook of Medicine, 2001; Desk Top Guide to Complementary and Alternative Medicine, 2001; numerous articles in med. jls. *Recreations:* music, writing. *Address:* (office) 25 Victoria Park Road, Exeter EX2 4NT. *T:* (01392) 430802.

ERNST, Prof. Richard Robert; Professor of Physical Chemistry, Swiss Federal Institute of Technology (ETH-Z), since 1976; *b* 14 Aug. 1933; *s* of Prof. Robert Ernst, architect, and Irma Ernst (*née* Brunner); *m* 1963, Magdalena Kielholz; one *s* two *d*. *Educ:* Winterthur schools; ETH-Zentrum (DipChemEng 1956; PhD 1962). Mil. Service, 1956–57. Scientist, Instrument Div., Varian Associates, Calif., 1963–68; Swiss Federal Institute of Technology (ETH-Z): Lectr in Phys. Chem., 1968–70 (Group Leader in Magnetic

Resonance Spectroscopy); Asst Prof., 1970; Associate Prof., 1972–76; Pres., Research Council, 1990. Mem. Bd, Spectrospin AG (Vice-Pres., 1989). Fellow, Amer. Phys. Soc.; For. Mem., Royal Soc., 1993; Member: internat. scientific bodies; editl bds of learned jls. Hon. doctorates: ETH Lausanne; Technical Univ., Munich; Zürich; Antwerp; Cluj-Napoca; Montpellier. Numerous medals and prizes, Swiss and foreign; Nobel Prize in Chemistry, 1991; Wolf Prize, 1991; Louisa Gross Horwitz Prize, 1991. *Address:* Laboratorium für Physikalische Chemie, ETH-Zentrum, 8092 Zürich, Switzerland. *T:* (1) 6324368; Kurlistasse 24, 8404 Winterthur, Switzerland. *T:* (52) 2427807.

ERNSTING, Air Vice-Marshal John, CB 1992; OBE 1959; PhD; FRCP, FFOM, FRAeS; Hon. Civil Consultant in Aviation Medicine to RAF, since 1993; *b* 21 April 1928; *s* of late Reginald James Ernsting and Phyllis May Josephine Ernsting (*née* Allington); *m* 1st, 1952, Patricia Mary Woolford (decd); two *s* one *d*; 2nd, 1970, Joyce Marion Heppell. *Educ:* Chislehurst and Sidcup County Grammar Sch. for Boys; Guy's Hosp. Med. Sch. (BSc 1949; MB BS 1952; PhD 1964). MFOM 1981, FFOM 1993; MRCP 1985. Guy's Hosp., 1952–53; Guy's-Maudsley Neurosurgical Unit, 1953–54; RAF Medical Branch, 1954; Lectr in Physiology, Guy's Hosp. Med. Sch., 1961–85; RAF Consultant in Aviation Physiology, 1964; RAF Consultant Adviser in Aviation Medicine, 1971–89; Dep. Dir and Dir of Research, 1976–88, Comdt, 1988–92, RAF Inst. of Aviation Medicine; Dean of Air Force Medicine, 1990–91; Sen. Consultant (RAF) 1991–93, retd. QHS, 1989–93. Visiting Professor: Guy's Hosp. Med. Sch., 1985–90; KCL, 1987–; Imperial Coll., 1993–96; Hon. Dir of Studies MSc in Human and Applied Physiology, 1984–, and Hd, Aerospace Medicine and Physiology, 1998–, KCL. *Publications:* (ed) Aviation Medicine, 1978, 3rd edn 1999; papers and chapters in books on aviation physiology and aviation medicine. *Recreations:* music, reading, travel. *Address:* White Gables, 2A Greenways, Fleet, Hants GU52 7UG. *T:* (01252) 621788. *Club:* Royal Air Force.

ERRÁZURIZ, (Talavera) Hernán; Senior Partner, Errázuriz and Co., Attorneys at Law, since 1972; Professor of Law, University of Chile, since 1996; *b* 14 Feb. 1941; *s* of Ladislao Errázuriz Pereira and Amelia Talavera Balmaceda; *m* 1964, Carmen Cruzat Amunategui; three *s* five *d*. *Educ:* German Sch. and Military Sch. Santiago; Univ. of Chile (Law degree, 1965); New York Sch. of Law. Admitted to legal practice, 1965; Sen. Partner, Errázuriz & Co. (estab. 1905 by grandfather); Legal Advr, Chilean Copper Corp., 1962–68; University of Chile: Prof. of Economic law, 1968–93; Dir, Inst. of Internat. Studies, 1974–83; Ambassador to UK, 1993–96. Legal Advr to Confedn of Chilean Entrepeneurs, 1973–76. President: Assoc. of Chilean Industries, 1968–73; Latin American Assoc. of Industries, 1970–72; Chilean Council of Econ. Law, 1988–; Mem., Cttee of Foreign Investment of Chile, 1968–73. Mem., Internat. Gp of Lawyers, SGL, 1988–93. President: Liberal Youth Party, 1960–64; Chilean Liberal Party (PAC), 1991–93. *Publications:* Chilean Economic Law 1968–1974; The Chilean Economy in a Democratic Framework, 1984. *Recreations:* horse riding, theatre, opera. *Address:* Burgos 88, Santiago, Chile. *Clubs:* Royal Automobile; De La Union (Santiago); Los Leones Golf (Santiago).

ERRINGTON, Viscount; Alexander Rowland Harmsworth Baring; *b* 5 Jan. 1994; *s* and *heir* of Earl of Cromer, *qv*.

ERRINGTON, Col Sir Geoffrey (Frederick), 2nd Bt *cr* 1963; OBE 1998; Chairman Harefield Hospital NHS Trust, 1991–98; *b* 15 Feb. 1926; *er s* of Sir Eric Errington, 1st Bt, JP, and Marjorie (*d* 1973), *d* of A. Grant Bennett; *S* father, 1973; *m* 1955, Diana Kathleen Forbes, *o d* of late E. Barry Davenport, Edgbaston, Birmingham; three *s*. *Educ:* Rugby Sch.; New Coll., Oxford. psc 1958. GSO 3 (Int.), HQ 11 Armd Div., 1950–52; GSO 3, MI3 (b), War Office, 1955–57; Bde Major 146 Inf. Bde, 1959–61; Coy Comdr, RMA Sandhurst, 1963–65; Military Assistant to Adjutant-General, 1965–67; CO 1st Bn, The King's Regt, 1967–69; GSO 1, HQ 1st British Corps, 1969–71; Col. GS, HQ NW District, 1971–74; AAG MI (Army), MoD, 1974–75; retired 1975. Col, The King's Regt, 1975–86; Chm., The King's and Manchester Regts Assoc., 1971–86. Director: Personnel Services, British Shipbuilders, 1977–78; Executive Appointments, 1979–90 (Chm., 1982–90). Employer Bd Mem., Shipbuilding ITB, 1977–78. Chm., Assoc. for Prevention of Addiction, Community Drug and Alcohol Initiatives, 1994–98 (Vice-Chm., 1991–94); Mem. Gen. Cttee, Not Forgotten Assoc., 1991–. Hon. Dir, Britain–Australia Soc., 1998–. Chm., Woodroffe's Club, 1988–94. Freeman, City of London, 1980; Liveryman: Broderers' Co.; Coachmakers' and Coach Harness Makers' Co. FRSA 1994. *Recreations:* music, travelling, gardening. *Heir:* *s* Robin Davenport Errington [*b* 1 July 1957; *m* 2001, Margerita Dudek; one *s*]. *Address:* Stone Hill Farm, Sellindge, Ashford, Kent TN25 6AJ; 203A Gloucester Place, NW1 6BU. *Clubs:* Boodle's, Oxford and Cambridge.
See also S. G. Errington.

ERRINGTON, Sir Lancelot, KCB 1976 (CB 1962); Second Permanent Secretary, Department of Health and Social Security, 1973–76; *b* 14 Jan. 1917; *e s* of late Major L. Errington; *m* 1939, Katharine Reine, *o d* of late T. C. Macaulay; two *s* two *d*. *Educ:* Wellington Coll.; Trinity Coll., Cambridge. Entered Home Office, 1939. Served RNVR, 1939–45. Transferred to Ministry of National Insurance, 1945; Principal Private Sec. to Minister of National Insurance, 1951; Asst Sec., 1953; Under-Sec., 1957–65; Cabinet Office, 1965–68; Min. of Social Security, 1968; Asst Under-Sec. of State, DHSS, 1968–71, Dep. Under-Sec. of State, 1971–73. *Recreation:* sailing. *Address:* St Mary's, Fasnacloich, Appin, Argyll PA38 4BJ. *T:* (01631) 730331.

ERRINGTON, Stuart Grant, CBE 1994; JP; DL; Chairman, National Association of Citizens' Advice Bureaux, 1989–94; *b* 23 June 1929; *yr s* of Sir Eric Errington, 1st Bt and late Marjorie Lady Errington; *m* 1954, Anne, *d* of late Eric and Eileen Baedeker; two *s* one *d*. *Educ:* Rugby; Trinity College, Oxford (MA). National Service, 2nd Lieut Royal Artillery, 1947–49. Ellerman Lines, 1952–59; Astley Industrial Trust, 1959–70; Exec Dir, 1970, Man. Dir, 1977, Chm., 1985, Mercantile Credit Co., Chm. and Chief Exec., Mercantile Gp, 1988–89. Chairman: Equipment Leasing Assoc., 1976–78; European Fedn of Leasing Assocs, 1978–80; Finance Houses Assoc., 1982–84; Director: Barclays Merchant Bank, Barclays Bank UK, 1979–86; Kleinwort Overseas Investment Trust, 1982–98; Municipal Mutual Insurance, 1989–; Northern Electric, 1989–96; Nationwide Building Soc., 1989–97; Associated Property Owners Ltd, 1998–. Mem., 1989–, Vice-Chm., 1995–, Council, Royal Holloway (formerly RHBNC), London Univ. Chm., Sportsmatch England Award Panel, Dept of Nat. Heritage, 1992–. Chm., Berks and Oxfordshire Magistrates' Courts Cttee, 1989–. JP Windsor Forest, 1970; DL Berks, 2000. *Recreations:* fishing, golf, splitting logs. *Address:* Earleywood Lodge, Ascot SL5 9JP. *T:* (01344) 621977. *Club:* Boodle's.

ERRITT, (Michael) John (Mackey), CB 1991; Deputy Director, Central Statistical Office, 1989–91; *b* 15 Feb. 1931; *s* of late William Albert Erritt, MBE, and Anna Erritt; *m* 1957, Marian Elizabeth Hillock; two *s*. *Educ:* St Andrews Coll., Dublin; Prince of Wales Sch., Nairobi; Queen's Univ., Belfast. BSc(Econ). Research Officer, Science and Industry Cttee, 1953; Asst Statistician, Central Statistical Office, 1955; Statistician: Board of Trade, 1960; Treasury, 1964; Board of Trade, 1967; Chief Statistician: Inland Revenue, 1968; Central Statistical Office, 1973; Depts of Industry, Trade and Prices and Consumer Protection, 1975; MoD, 1979; Asst Under-Sec. of State (Statistics), MoD, 1981; Asst Dir, Central Statistical Office, 1985. *Publications:* articles in official, academic and trade jls. *Recreations:* gardening, travel, grandfathering. *Address:* Green Tiles, 14 Brook Lane, Lindfield, Sussex RH16 1SG.

ERROLL, 24th Earl of, *cr* 1452; **Merlin Sereld Victor Gilbert Hay;** Lord Hay, 1429; Baron of Slains, 1452; Bt 1685; 28th Hereditary Lord High Constable of Scotland, *cr* 1314; Celtic title, Mac Garadh Mor; 33rd Chief of the Hays (from 1171); Senior Great Officer, Royal Household in Scotland; computer consultant; *b* 20 April 1948; *er s* of 23rd Countess of Erroll and Sir Iain Moncreiffe of that Ilk, 11th Bt, CVO, QC; *S* mother, 1978 (and to baronetcy of father, 1985); *m* 1982, Isabelle Astell, *o d* of late T. S. Astell Hohler, MC; two *s* two *d*. *Educ:* Eton; Trinity College, Cambridge. Page to the Lord Lyon, 1956. Lieut, Atholl Highlanders, 1974. Chm., Cost Reduction Consultants Ltd, 1995–. Elected Mem., H of L, 1999; Member: Library and Computers Sub-Cttee, 1999–; Bd, POST, 2000–. Prime Warden, Fishmongers' Co., 2000–01. Hon. Col, RMP TA, 1992–97. OStJ 1977. Member, Queen's Body Guard for Scotland, Royal Company of Archers, 1978. Patron, Keepers of the Quaich. *Recreations:* country pursuits. *Heir:* *s* Lord Hay, *qv*. *Address:* Woodbury Hall, Sandy, Beds SG19 2HR. *T:* (01767) 650251; *e-mail:* errollm@parliament.uk. *Clubs:* White's, Pratt's; Puffin's (Edinburgh).

ERSHAD, Lt-Gen. Hussain Muhammad; Leader, Jatiya Party, Bangladesh; *b* 1 Feb. 1930; *s* of late Makbul Hussain, Advocate, and of Mojida Begum; *m* 1956, Begum Raushad Ershad; one *s* one adopted *d*. *Educ:* Carmichael Coll., Rangpur; Dhaka Univ. (BA 1st Div.). Staff Course, Defence Service Command and Staff Coll., Quetta, Pakistan, 1966; War Course, National Defence Coll., New Delhi, India, 1975. Infantry Regimental Service, 1953–58; Adjt, E Bengal Regimental Centre (Basic Inf. Trng Centre), 1960–62; E Pakistan Rifles, 1962–65; Bde Major/Dep. Asst Adjt and Quarter Master General, 1967–68; CO, Inf. Bn, 1969–71; Adjt General, Bangladesh Army, 1973–74; Dep. Chief of Army Staff, Bangladesh Army, Chm., Coordination and Control Cell for National Security, 1975–78; Chief of Army Staff, Bangladesh Army, 1978–86; C-in-C, Bangladesh Armed Forces, 1982; Chief Martial Law Administrator, Bangladesh, 1982–86; President: Council of Ministers, 1982–90; Bangladesh, 1983–90; Minister of Defence, Estabt, Health and Population Control, 1986–90. Chm., National Sports Control Bd. *Publications:* poems in Bengali contributed occasionally to literary jls. *Address:* Jatiya Dal, c/o Jatiya Sangsad, Dhaka, Bangladesh. *Club:* Kurmitola Golf (Dhaka).

ERSKINE; *see* St Clair-Erskine.

ERSKINE, family name of **Earls of Buchan** and **Mar and Kellie**.

ERSKINE, Sir David; *see* Erskine, Sir T. D.

ERSKINE, Ralph; *see* Erskine, T. R.

ERSKINE, Ralph, CBE 1978; architect; own practice (in Sweden since 1939); *b* 24 Feb. 1914; *s* of late George and Mildred Erskine; *m* 1939, Ruth Monica Francis; one *s* two *d*. *Educ:* Friends' Sch., Saffron Walden, Essex; Regent Street Polytechnic (architecture). ARIBA 1936; AMTPI 1938; SAR 1965. Won number of prizes in arch. comps in Sweden; one year's study at Academy for Fine Arts, Sweden 1945. *Work executed:* town plans, workers' houses; co-operative housing and industrial housing; flats; hostels; factories; ski-hotel; shopping centre; school; town hall; hall of residence at Clare Coll., Cambridge; churches; housing estates at Newmarket and Killingworth; clearance scheme, Byker, Newcastle upon Tyne; design of new town, Resolute Bay, Canada; University Library, Allhuset and Sports Hall, Stockholm Univ.; London Ark, Hammersmith. Lecturing: in America, Canada, Japan and many countries in Europe. Hon. Dr, Lund Univ., Sweden, 1975; Hon. DLitt, Heriot-Watt Univ., 1982. For. Mem., Royal Acad. of Arts, Sweden, 1972; Hon. Mem., Bund Deutscher Architekten, 1983. Hon Fellow of AIA, 1966; SAR's Kasper Sahlin prize for 1971 and 1981; Ytong Prize, 1974; Guld medal, Litteris et Artibus, 1980; Canadian Gold Medal, RAIC, 1983; Wolf Prize for Architecture, 1984; Royal Gold Medal, RIBA, 1987. *Publications:* for several arch. magazines, on building in northern climates, etc. *Relevant publication:* Ralph Erskine, by Mats Egelius, 1978. *Recreations:* ski-ing, skating, swimming, yachting, ice yachting. *Address:* Box 156, Gustav III's väg 4, 17802 Drottningholm, Sweden. *T:* 7590352.

ERSKINE, Sir (Thomas) David, 5th Bt *cr* 1821; JP; Vice Lord-Lieutenant, Fife Region, 1981–87; Convener, Fife County Council, 1970–73; *b* 31 July 1912; *o* surv. *s* of Sir Thomas Wilfred Hargreaves John Erskine, 4th Bt, and late Magdalen Janet, *d* of Sir Ralph Anstruther, 6th Bt of Balcaskie; *S* father, 1944; *m* 1947, Ann, *er d* of late Lt-Col Neil Fraser-Tytler, DSO, MC, and late Christian Helen Fraser-Tytler, CBE; two *s* (and one *d* decd). *Educ:* Eton; Magdalene Coll., Cambridge. Employed by Butterfield & Swire, London and China, in 1934 and served with them in China, 1935–41. Joined HM Forces in India and commissioned into Indian Corps of Engineers. Served with them in Mid-East, India and Malaya, being demobilised in 1945 with rank of Major. JP Fife, 1951; DL Fife, 1955–81. *Heir:* *s* Thomas Peter Neil Erskine [*b* 28 March 1950; *m* 1972, Catherine, *d* of Col G. H. K. Hewlett; two *s* two *d*]. *Address:* West Newhall House, Kingsbarns, Fife KY16 8QD. *T:* (01333) 450228. *Club:* New (Edinburgh).

ERSKINE, (Thomas) Ralph, CB 1986; First Legislative Counsel, Northern Ireland, 1979–93; *b* 14 Oct. 1933; *m* 1966, Patricia Joan Palmer; one *s* one *d*. *Educ:* Campbell College; Queen's University, Belfast. Called to the Bar, Gray's Inn, 1962. *Publications:* (with Arthur Bauer and Klaus Herold) Funkpeilung als allierte Waffe gegen deutsche U-Boote 1939–1945, 1997; contribs to Cryptologia, Annals of the History of Computing, legal jls, etc. *Recreations:* ski-ing, gardening, researching modern naval history. *Address:* c/o Office of the Legislative Counsel, Parliament Buildings, Belfast BT4 3SW.

ERSKINE CRUM, Douglas Vernon, CBE 1994; Chief Executive, Ascot Racecourse, since 1994; *b* 31 May 1949; *s* of Lt-Gen. Vernon Forbes Erskine Crum, CIE, MC and Rosemary Aimée Douglas Dawson; *m* 1980, Jacqueline Margaret Wilson; one *s* two *d*. *Educ:* Eton. Commissioned Scots Guards 1970; Staff Coll., Camberley, 1982; Brigade Major, Household Div., 1987–89; CO 2 SG, 1989–91; ACOS Ops, HQ N Ireland, 1991–92; Comdr 3 Inf. Brigade, 1992–94; retired 1994. *Recreations:* most sports. *Address:* Ascot Racecourse, Ascot, Berks SL5 7JN. *T:* (01344) 621093.

ERSKINE-HILL, Sir (Alexander) Roger, 3rd Bt *cr* 1945, of Quothquhan, Co. Lanark; *b* 15 Aug. 1949; *s* of Sir Robert Erskine-Hill, 2nd Bt and of Christine Alison, *o d* of late Capt. (A) Henry James Johnstone of Alva, RN; *S* father, 1989; *m* 1984, Sarah Anne Sydenham (marr. diss. 1994), *er d* of late Dr R. J. Sydenham Clarke and of Mrs Charles Clarke; one *s* one *d*; *m* 2000, Gillian Elizabeth Borlace Mitchell, *d* of David Surgey. *Educ:* Eton; Aberdeen Univ. (LLB). Director: Map Marketing Ltd, 1988–; Venture Vision Ltd, 1998–; Avian Communications Ltd, 2001–. *Heir:* *s* Robert Benjamin Erskine-Hill, *b* 6 Aug. 1986. *Address:* The Old Coach House, Woodlands Road, Blairgowrie, Perthshire PH10 6LD.

ERSKINE-HILL, Prof. (Henry) Howard, PhD, LittD; FBA 1985; Professor of Literary History, since 1994, and Fellow of Pembroke College, since 1980, Cambridge University;

b 19 June 1936; *s* of late Henry Erskine-Hill and Hannah Lilian Poppleton. *Educ:* Ashville Coll.; Nottingham Univ. (BA, PhD); MA Cantab; LittD Cantab 1988. University of Wales, Swansea: Tutor, 1960; Asst Lectr, 1961; Lectr in Eng. Lit., 1962; Sen. Fellow, 1964–65; University of Cambridge: Lectr in English, 1969–84; Reader in Literary Hist., 1984–94; Fellow, 1969–80, Tutor, 1970–76, Jesus Coll.; Tutor for Graduates, Pembroke Coll., 1983–84. Olin Fellow, Nat. Humanities Center, NC, USA, 1988–89. Taught at British Council seminars in Britain, 1962–69; invited lectr, univs of Alberta, Adelaide, Berkeley (Calif), Bristol, Davis (Calif), Essex, Flinders (S Australia), Liverpool, London, Monash, Nantes, Oxford, Saskatchewan, Stanford, Singapore, Wales (Swansea), Victoria (BC), Warwick, W Australia and York; also at David Nichol Smith Seminar, Canberra, Inter-Univ. Centre, Dubrovnik, Inst. of Hist. Res., London, and Herzog-August Library, Wolfenbüttel. *Publications:* (ed) Alexander Pope: Horatian Satires and Epistles, 1964; Pope: The Dunciad, 1972; The Social Milieu of Alexander Pope, 1975; (ed with Anne Smith) The Art of Alexander Pope, 1978; (ed with Graham Storey) Revolutionary Prose of the English Civil War, 1983; The Augustan Idea, 1983; (ed with Richard A. McCabe) Presenting Poetry, 1995; Poetry and the Realm of Politics, 1996; Poetry of Opposition and Revolution, 1996; (introd and ed) Alexander Pope: world and word, 1998; (ed) Alexander Pope, Selected Letters, 2000; contributions to: Renaissance and Modern Essays, ed G. R. Hibbard, 1966; English Drama: forms and Development, ed Marie Axton and Raymond Williams, 1977; Ideology and Conspiracy, ed Eveline Cruickshanks, 1982; jls incl. Essays in Criticism, Eighteenth-Century Studies, Jl of the Warburg and Courtauld Insts, Modern Language Review, Rev. of English Studies, Renaissance and Modern Studies. *Recreation:* fell walking. *Address:* Pembroke College, Cambridge CB2 1RF. *T:* (01223) 338100. *Club:* Oxford and Cambridge.

ERSKINE-HILL, Sir Roger; *see* Erskine-Hill, Sir A. R.

ERSKINE-MURRAY, family name of **Lord Elibank**.

ERVINE, David Walter; Member (PU) Belfast East, Northern Ireland Assembly, since 1998; *b* 21 July 1953; *s* of Walter and Elizabeth Ervine; *m* 1972, Jeanette Cunningham; two *s*. *Educ:* Orangefield Boys' Sec. Sch. Mem. (PU), Belfast CC, 1997–. Averell Harriman Peace Award, 1998; J. F. Kennedy Courage in Democracy Award, 1998. *Recreations:* restaurants, spectator sports. *Address:* Northern Ireland Assembly, Parliament Buildings, Belfast BT4 3XX. *Club:* Raven (Belfast).

ERZINÇLIOĞLU, Dr Zakaria; forensic entomologist; writer and scientific consultant, since 1995; *b* 30 Dec. 1951; *s* of Zakaria Ahmet Erzinçlioğlu and Kadria Sanna Erzinçlioğlu (*née* Shuhdi); *m* 1984, Sharon Wynne Davies; one *s* two *d*. *Educ:* Wolverhampton Poly. (BSc 1975); Univ. of Durham (PhD 1984). Zool Recorder, Zool Soc. of London, 1976–81; mature res. student and part-time demonstrator, Dept of Zool., Univ. of Durham, 1981–84; Department of Zoology, University of Cambridge: Field Studies Council Res. Associate, 1984–88; Field Studies Council Res. Officer, 1988–90; Sen. Res. Associate, 1990–92; Independent Investigator, 1992–94; Affiliated Researcher, 1995–; Dir, Forensic Sci. Res. Centre, Univ. of Durham, 1994–95. Hon. Lectr, Univ. of London, 1990–. Member, Council: Linnean Soc., 1990–93; Zool Soc., 1997–98; Sec. and Co-Founder, British Zool Soc., 1999–. Mem., NT Wicken Fen Mgt Cttee, 1991–94. Campaigner for criminal justice reform. Trustee, Bosnia-Herzegovina Heritage Rescue Foundn, 1995–96; Mem., Adv. Cttee, Centre for Albanian Studies, 1998–. John Hull Grundy Medal for Medical Entomology, RAMC, 1994. *Publications:* Blowflies, 1996; (jtly) Suspicious Death Scene Investigation, 1996; Maggots, Murder and Men, 2000; Every Contact Leaves a Trace, 2001; contrib. numerous papers to learned jls. *Recreations:* reading history and biography, visiting sites of historical interest. *Address:* 28 Harlton Road, Little Eversden, Cambridge CB3 7HB. *T:* (01223) 263897.

ESAKI, Leo; Chairman, Science and Technology Promotion Foundation of Ibaraki, Japan, since 1998; Director-General, Tsukuba International Congress Centre, since 1998; President, Shibaura Institute of Technology, since 2000; *b* 12 March 1925; *s* of Soichiro Esaki and Niyoko Ito; *m* 1986, Masako Kondo (one *s* two *d* by previous *m*). *Educ:* Univ. of Tokyo. MS 1947, PhD 1959. Sony Corp., Japan, 1956–60; IBM Research, 1960–92; IBM Fellow, 1967–92. Dir, IBM-Japan, 1976–92. Pres., Univ. of Tsukuba, Japan, 1992–98. Research in tunnelling in semiconductor junctions which led to the discovery of the Esaki tunnel diode; subsequently research on man-made semiconductor superlattice in search of predicted quantum mechanical effect. Sir John Cass sen. vis. res. fellow, London Poly, 1982. Councillor-at-Large, Amer. Phys. Soc., 1971–75; Dir, Amer. Vacuum Soc., 1972–76; Member: Japan Academy, 1975; Max-Planck-Ges., 1989; For. Associate, Nat. Acad. of Sciences, USA, 1976; For. Associate, Nat. Acad. of Engineering, USA, 1977; Corresp. Mem., Academia Nacional De Ingenieria, Mexico, 1978. Nishina Meml Award, 1959; Asahi Press Award, 1960; Toyo Rayon Foundn Award, 1961; Morris N. Liebmann Meml Prize, 1961; Stuart Ballantine Medal, Franklin Inst., 1961; Japan Academy Award, 1965; (jtly) Nobel Prize for Physics, 1973; Science Achievement Award, US-Asia Inst., 1983; Centennial Medal, IEEE, 1984; Internat. Prize for New Materials, Amer. Physical Soc., 1985; Distinguished Foreign-born Individual Award, Internat. Center, NY, 1986; IEEE Medal of Honor, 1991; Japan Prize, 1998. Order of Culture (Japan), 1974; Grand Order of Rising Sun, First Class (Japan), 1998. *Publications:* numerous papers in learned jls. *Address:* Shibaura Institute of Technology, 3-9-14 Shibaura, Minato-ku, Tokyo 108-8548, Japan.

ESCHENBACH, Christoph; pianist and conductor; Music Director: Orchestre de Paris, since 2000; Ravinia Festival, since 1994; NDR Symphony Orchestra, since 1998; *b* 20 Feb. 1940. *Educ:* Hamburg Conservatory; State Music Conservatory, Cologne. Winner: Internat. Piano Competition, Munich, 1962; Concours Clara Haskil, 1965. Canadian début, Montreal Expo, 1967; US début, Cleveland Orch., 1969; has toured Europe, N and S America, USSR, Israel, Japan; and has performed as pianist with leading orchs incl. Concertgebouw Amsterdam, Orch. de Paris, London Symphony, Berlin Philharmonic, and Cleveland Orch.; festivals incl. Salzburg, Lucerne, Bonn, and Aix-en-Provence. Chief Conductor, Tonhalle Orch., Zürich, and Artistic Dir, Tonhalle-Gesellschaft, Zürich, 1982–86; Music Dir, Houston SO, 1988–99, now Conductor Laureate; Artistic Dir, Schleswig-Holstein Music Fest., 1999–; Co-Artistic Dir, Pacific Music Fest., 1992–98; guest appearances with NY Philharmonic, Boston Symphony, Chicago Symphony, Cleveland Orch., Pittsburgh Symphony, Los Angeles Philharmonic, London Symphony, BBC Philharmonia, Berlin Philharmonic, Bavarian Radio Symphony Munich, Munich Philharmonic, Vienna Symphonic, Czech Philharmonic and New Japan Philharmonic. *Address:* c/o M. L. Falcone, 155 West 68th Street, New York, NY 10023, USA.

ESCOTT COX, Brian Robert; *see* Cox.

ESCUDIER, Prof. Marcel Paul, PhD, DSc(Eng); FREng, FIMechE; Harrison Professor of Mechnical Engineering, University of Liverpool, since 1989; *b* 17 July 1942; *s* of late Isabel Kate Escudier; *m* 1st, 1966, Sonja Kennedy Allen (marr. diss. 1973); 2nd, 1973, Agnes Margaret Simko; one *s*. *Educ:* Sir Walter St John's Grammar Sch., London; Imperial Coll., London Univ. (BScEng; DIC; PhD 1967); DSc(Eng) 1990. ACGI 1963; FIMechE 1995; FREng 2000. Res. Associate, MIT, 1967–69; Asst Prof., Univ. of Southern Calif, 1969–73; Mem., Plasmaphysics Res. Gp, 1973–74, Leader, Fluid Mechanics Res. Gp, 1974–86, Brown Boveri Res. Centre, Switzerland; Hd, Fluid Mechanics Res. Dept, Schlumberger Cambridge Res. Ltd, Cambridge, 1986–88; Hd, Dept of Mech. Engrg, Univ. of Liverpool, 1990–97. *Publications:* The Essence of Engineering Fluid Mechanics, 1998; contrib. papers on vortex flows, non-Newtonian fluid flow, etc, to scientific jls. *Recreations:* gardening, cooking, motor racing (non participatory). *Address:* Silverburn, Park Road, Willaston, Neston CH64 1TJ. *T:* (0151) 327 2949.

ESDALE, Patricia Joyce, (Mrs G. P. R. Esdale); *see* Lindop, P. J.

ESER, Prof. Dr Günter Otto; Director General, International Air Transport Association, Montreal/Geneva, 1985–92; *b* 10 Sept. 1927; *s* of Ernst Eser and Martha Siering; *m* 1976, Florida Huisman; two *s*. *Educ:* Bonn Univ.; Federal Acad. of Finance, Siegburg; Harvard (Management Programme). Auditor, Fed. German Min. of Finance, 1953–55; Lufthansa German Airlines, 1955–84: Head, Persian subsidiary, Teheran; Head, Munich Dist Office for Southern Germany; Sales Dir, Germany; Gen. Man., N and Central America; Mem., Chief Exec. Bd. Member: Adv. Bd, Europäische Reiseversicherung, 1978–; Adv. Bd, Amer. Univ., 1982–. Vis. Prof., Pace Univ., NY, 1978. Bundesverdienstkreuz 1st Class (FRG), 1985; Commendatore Officiale (Italy), 1967. *Recreations:* trekking, ocean-fishing, literature, music. *Address:* ch. de Sodome, 1271 Givrins, Vaud, Switzerland.

ESHER, 4th Viscount *cr* 1897; **Lionel Gordon Baliol Brett;** Baron 1885; CBE 1970; MA; PPRIBA; DistTP; Rector and Vice-Provost, Royal College of Art, 1971–78; *b* 18 July 1913; *o s* of 3rd Viscount Esher, GBE; *S* father, 1963; *m* 1935, Christian, *e d* of late Col Ebenezer Pike, CBE, MC; five *s* one *d*. *Educ:* Eton (Scholar); New Coll., Oxford (Scholar); BA (1st Class), 1935; Hon. Fellow, 1980; RIBA Ashpitel Prizeman, 1939. Served War in RA, 1940–45; France and Germany, 1944–45 (despatches); Major. Architect Planner, Hatfield New Town, 1949–59; major housing projects: Hatfield, Stevenage, Basildon; consultant architect: Downside Abbey; Maidenhead Town Centre; Abingdon Town Centre; Portsmouth City Centre; York City Centre; Santiago, Chile and Caracas, Venezuela (both for UNDP); principal buildings include: (with Francis Pollen): High Comr's House, Lagos; 82 and 190 Sloane St, London; Pall Mall Ct, Manchester; Downside Sch. extensions; Exeter Coll., and Oxenford Hall, Oxford; (with Teggin & Taylor) Civic Offices, Portsmouth. Lecture tours: USA 1953; India, 1954; Australia, 1959; S America, 1970. Governor, Museum of London, 1970–77; Member: Royal Fine Art Commn, 1951–69; Adv. Bd for Redundant Churches (Chm., 1977–83); Advisory Council, Victoria and Albert Museum, 1967–72; Arts Council of GB, 1972–77 (Chm., Art Panel); Environment Panel, British Rail, 1977–85; National Trust (Chm., Thames and Chilterns Reg., 1979–83); Vice-Pres., RIBA, 1962–65; Pres., 1965–67; Trustee, Soane Museum, 1976–94. Hon. DLitt Strathclyde Univ., 1967; Hon. DUniv York, 1970; Hon. DSc Edinburgh, 1981. Hon. Fellow: Amer. Inst. of Architects, 1967; Portsmouth Polytechnic, subseq. Portsmouth Univ., 1984; Chartered Inst. of Designers, 1975. *Publications:* Houses, 1947; The World of Architecture, 1963; Landscape in Distress, 1965; York: a study in conservation, 1969; Parameters and Images, 1970; (with Elisabeth Beazley) Shell Guide to North Wales, 1971; A Broken Wave, 1981; The Continuing Heritage, 1982; Our Selves Unknown (autobiog.), 1985; The Glory of the English House, 1991; Collected Poems, 2000. *Recreation:* landscapes. *Heir:* *s* Hon. Christopher Lionel Baliol Brett [*b* 23 Dec. 1936; *m* 1st, 1962, Camilla Charlotte (marr. diss. 1970), *d* of Sir (Horace) Anthony Rumbold, 10th Bt, KGMG, KCVO, CB; one *s* two *d*; 2nd, 1971, Valerie Harrington; two *s* twin *d*]. *Address:* Snowball Hill, Russell's Water, Henley on Thames RG9 6EU. *Club:* Arts.

See also Sir R. G. Beckett, Bt.

ESIRI, Prof. Margaret Miriam, DM; FRCPath; Professor of Neuropathology, Departments of Neuropathology and Neurology, Oxford University, since 1996; Professorial Fellow, St Hugh's College, Oxford, since 1988; *b* 5 Oct. 1941; *d* of William Alfred Evans and Doreen Mary (*née* Bates); *m* 1963, Frederick Obukowho Uruemuowho Esiri; two *s* one *d*. *Educ:* Croydon High Sch. (GPDST); St Hugh's Coll., Oxford (BSc, MA, DM). FRCPath 1988. University of Oxford: preregistration med. and surgical posts and scholarship for trng in research methods, 1967–69; Jun. Res. Fellow in Neuropathology, 1970–72; trng posts in Histopathology, 1973–79; MRC Sen. Clinical Fellow in Neuropathology, 1980–85; Consultant Neuropathologist, Radcliffe Infirmary, 1986–88; Clinical Reader in Neuropathology, 1988–96. *Publications:* (with J. Booss) Viral Encephalitis, 1986; (with D. R. Oppenheimer) Diagnostic Neuropathology, 1989, 2nd edn 1996; (ed with J. H. Morris) The Neuropathology of Dementia, 1997. *Recreation:* assisting in my husband's clinic in Nigeria. *Address:* Neuropathology Department, Radcliffe Infirmary, Oxford OX2 6HE. *T:* (01865) 224403; *e-mail:* margaret.esiri@dneuro.ox.ac.uk.

ESKDAILL, Lord; Walter John Francis Montagu Douglas Scott; *b* 2 Aug. 1984; *s* and *heir* of Earl of Dalkeith, *qv*. A Page of Honour to HM The Queen, 1996–99.

ESKENAZI, Giuseppe, (J. E. Eskenazi); Managing Director, Eskenazi Ltd, since 1969; *b* 8 July 1939; *s* of late Isaac Eskenazi and of Lea Eskenazi; *m* 1963, Laura (*née* Bandini); one *s* one *d*. *Educ:* King's School, Sherborne; The Polytechnic, Regent Street; University College London. Art dealer, primarily Chinese and Japanese, 1962–; Eskenazi Ltd founded by father in 1960. Member: Exec. Cttee, Asia House, 1993–; Council, Oriental Ceramic Soc., 1998–; Adv. Bd, Bard Grad. Center for Studies in the Decorative Arts, NY, 2000–. Trustee, Asia House Trust (London), 2000–. *Publications:* numerous exhibition catalogues. *Recreations:* sailing, diving, opera. *Address:* 12 Carlyle Square, Chelsea, SW3 6EX. *T:* (020) 7352 7461; Eskenazi, 10 Clifford Street, W1X 1RB. *T:* (020) 7493 5464.

ESLER, Gavin William James; presenter: BBC News 24, since 1997; BBC World, since 1998; BBC Radio Four, since 2000; *b* 27 Feb. 1953; *s* of William John Esler and Georgena Esler; *m* 1979, Patricia Margaret Warner; one *s* one *d*. *Educ:* George Heriot's Sch., Edinburgh; Kent Univ. (BA English and American Lit); Leeds Univ. (MA Anglo-Irish Lit. (Dist.)). Reporter, Belfast Telegraph, 1975–76; BBC: Reporter and Presenter, Northern Ireland, 1977–82; Reporter, Newsnight, 1982–88; Washington Corresp., 1989; Chief N America Corresp., 1989–97; presenter, Newsnight, 1997. Columnist, The Scotsman, 1998–. Hon. MA Kent, 1995. RTS Award, 1989. FRSA 2000. *Publications:* The United States of Anger: the people and the American dream, 1997; novels: Loyalties, 1990; Deep Blue, 1992; The Blood Brother, 1995. *Recreations:* hiking, ski-ing, camping, especially in the American West. *Address:* BBC News 24, BBC Television Centre, Wood Lane, Shepherds Bush, W12 7RJ.

ESMONDE, Sir Thomas (Francis Grattan), 17th Bt *cr* 1629 (Ire.), of Ballynastragh, Wexford; MD; Consultant Neurologist, Royal Victoria Hospital, Belfast, since 1996 (Senior Registrar in Neurology, 1992–96); *b* 14 Oct. 1960; *s* of Sir John Henry Grattan Esmonde, 16th Bt and of Pamela Mary, *d* of late Francis Stephen Bourke, FRCPI; *S* father, 1987; *m* 1986, Pauline Loretto Kearns; one *s* two *d*. *Educ:* Sandford Park Secondary School, Ranelagh, Dublin; Medical School, Trinity College, Dublin (MB, BCh, BAO 1984; MD 1995). MRCPI, MRCP (UK) 1987. Junior House Officer, Whiteabbey Hosp., 1984–85; SHO, Royal Victoria, Musgrave Park and Whiteabbey Hosps, 1985–87,

Altnagelvin Hosp., Londonderry, 1987–88; Med. Registrar, Royal Gwent Hosp., Newport, 1988–89; Registrar in Neurology, Univ. Hosp. of Wales, 1989–90; Clinical Res. Fellow, Dept of Neurosci., Western General Hosp., Edinburgh, 1990–92. *Recreations:* chess, fishing. *Heir: s* Sean Vincent Grattan Esmonde, *b* 8 Jan. 1989. *Address:* 6 Nutley Avenue, Donnybrook, Dublin 4, Ireland. *T:* 2693040.

ESPIE, Sir Frank (Fletcher), Kt 1979; OBE 1971; FTS, FIMM, MAIMM, MAIME; company director, retired; *b* 8 May 1917; *s* of late Frank Fancett Espie and Laura Jean Espie; *m* 1st, 1941, Madeline Elizabeth Robertson (decd); one *s* three *d*; 2nd, 1985, Jean Primrose Angove. *Educ:* St Peter's Coll., Adelaide; Univ. of Adelaide (BEng). FTS 1978; FIMM 1958. CRA Ltd: Dir, 1968; Dep. Chm., 1974–79; non-exec. Dir, 1979–85; Bougainville Copper Ltd: Gen. Man., 1965; Man. Dir, 1969; Chm., 1971–79; non-exec. Dir, 1979–85. Director: ICI Aust. Ltd, 1979–87; Tubemakers of Australia, 1980–87; Westpac Banking Corporation, 1981–90; Woodside Petroleum, 1981–89. Chairman: Nat. Petroleum Adv. Cttee, 1979–87; Australian Mineral Foundn Inc., 1988–91. Member: Exec. Cttee, Aust. Mining Industry Council, 1973–81 (Pres., 1978–80); Council: Australasian Inst. of Mining and Metallurgy, 1970–88 (Pres., 1975; Inst. Medal, 1980); Aust. Acad. of Technological Scis, 1980–90. *Recreations:* swimming, golf. *Address:* 31 Grandview Grove, Toorak Gardens, SA 5065, Australia. *Clubs:* Melbourne, Athenæum, Royal Melbourne Golf (Melbourne); Union (Sydney); Adelaide (Adelaide).

ESPLEN, (Sir) John Graham, (3rd Bt *cr* 1921, of Hardres Court, Canterbury, but does not use the title); *b* 4 Aug. 1932; *s* of Sir William Graham Esplen, 2nd Bt and of Aline Octavia, *d* of late A. Octavius Hedley; *S* father, 1989; *m*; one *s* three *d*. *Educ:* Harrow; St Catharine's Coll., Cambridge. *Heir: s* William John Harry Esplen [*b* 24 Feb. 1967; *m* 1996, Helen Chesser; one *s* one *d*].

ESPLIN, Air Vice-Marshal Ian (George), CB 1963; OBE 1946; DFC 1943; retired (voluntarily) 1965; *b* 26 Feb. 1914; *s* of late Donald Thomas Esplin and Emily Freame Esplin; *m* 1944, Patricia Kaleen Barlow; one *s* one *d*. *Educ:* Sydney Univ.; Oxford Univ. BEc 1936; MA 1939. Rowing Blue, 1934 and 1935. NSW Rhodes Schol., 1937. Entered RAF from Oxford, 1939. Served War of 1939–45, as Pilot in Night-Fighters; destroyed three enemy aircraft at night; also served at CFS and in HQ, SEAC; Air Min. (Policy), 1945; Comd RAF Desford, 1947; Dep. Senior Personnel Staff Officer, HQ Reserve Comd, 1948; Directing Staff, RAF Staff Coll., 1950–51; Comd first Jet All Weather Wing, Germany (No 148), 1952–54; Air War Coll. Course, 1954; Dep. Dir of Operational Requirements, Air Min., 1955–58; Comd RAF Wartling, 1958–60; Dir of Operational Reqts, 1960–62; Comdr, RAF Staff and Air Attaché, Washington, DC, 1963–65; Dean, Air Attaché Corps, 1964–65. *Recreations:* golf, swimming. *Address:* 141 The Villas, 15 Hale Road, Mosman, NSW 2088, Australia. *Clubs:* Vincent's (Oxford); Leander (Henley-on-Thames); Elanora Country (Sydney).

ESQUIVEL, Rt Hon. Manuel; PC 1986; Prime Minister of Belize, 1984–89 and 1993–98; Member, House of Representatives, Belize, 1984–98; Leader, United Democratic Party, 1982–98; *b* 2 May 1940; *s* of John and Laura Esquivel; *m* 1971, Kathleen Levy; one *s* two *d*. *Educ:* Loyola Univ., New Orleans (BSc Physics); Bristol Univ. (Cert Ed.). Instructor in Physics, St John's Coll., Belize City, 1967–82. Member: Belize City Council, 1974–80; Nat. Senate, 1979–84; Leader of the Opposition, Belize, 1989–93. Chm., Utd Democratic Party, 1976–82. Hon. DHL Loyola Univ., 1986. *Recreation:* electronics. *Address:* PO Box 1344, Belize City, Belize.

ESSAAFI, M'hamed; Grand Officier, Order of Tunisian Republic, 1963; Disaster Relief Co-ordinator and Under Secretary General, United Nations, 1982–92; *b* 26 May 1930; *m* 1956, Hedwige Klat; one *s* one *d*. *Educ:* Sadiki Coll., Tunis; Sorbonne, Paris. Secretariat of State for For. Affairs, 1956; 1st Sec., Tunisian Embassy, London, 1956; 1st Sec., Tunisian Embassy, Washington, 1957; Secretariat of State for For. Affairs, Tunis: Dir of Amer. Dept, 1960; America and Internat. Confs Dept, 1962; Ambassador to London, 1964–69; Ambassador to Moscow, 1970–74; Ambassador to Bonn, 1974–76; Sec.-Gen., Ministry of Foreign Affairs, Tunis, 1969–70 and 1976–78; Ambassador to Belgium and EEC, 1978–79; Permanent Rep. of Tunisia to the UN, and Special Rep. of the Sec.-Gen., 1980–81, Chef de Cabinet 1982. *Address:* rue de la Mosquée BH20, La Marsa, Tunis, Tunisia.

ESSAYAN, Michael; QC 1976; *b* 7 May 1927; *s* of late Kevork Loris Essayan and Rita Sirvarte (*née* Gulbenkian); *m* 1956, Geraldine St Lawrence Lee Guinness, *d* of K. E. L. Guinness, MBE; one *s* one *d*. *Educ:* France; Harrow; Balliol Coll., Oxford (1st Cl. Class. Hon. Mods 1949, 1st Cl. Lit. Hum. 1951, MA). Served with RA, 1945–48 (Palestine, 1947–48). Iraq Petroleum Co., London and ME, 1951–56. Called to the Bar, Middle Temple 1957 (Bencher 1983), joined Lincoln's Inn *ad eundem* 1958. Mem., Gen. Council of the Bar, 1987–88. Mem., Bd of Administration, Calouste Gulbenkian Foundn, Lisbon, 1981–, Hon. Pres., 1992–. Comdr, Order of Merit (Portugal), 1993. *Publications:* The New Supreme Court Costs (with M. J. Albery, QC), 1960; (ed with Hon. Mr Justice Walton) Adkin's Landlord and Tenant, 15th, 16th, 17th and 18th edns. *Recreations:* wine and wife. *Address:* 6 Chelsea Square, SW3 6LF. *T:* (020) 7352 6786. *Club:* Brooks's.

ESSER, Robin Charles; Executive Managing Editor, Daily Mail, since 1998; editorial and media consultant, since 1990; *b* 6 May 1935; *s* of late Charles and Winifred Eileen Esser; *m* 1959, Irene Shirley Clough (decd); two *s* two *d*; 1981, Tui (*née* France); two *s*. *Educ:* Wheelwright Grammar School, Dewsbury; Wadham College, Oxford (BA Hons, MA). Edited Oxford Univ. newspaper, Cherwell, 1954. Commissioned, King's Own Yorkshire Light Infantry, 1956. Freelance reporter, 1957–60; Daily Express: Staff Reporter, 1960; Editor, William Hickey Column, 1963; Features Editor, 1965; New York Bureau, 1969; Northern Editor, 1970; Exec. Editor, 1985; Consultant Editor, Evening News, 1977; Editor, Sunday Express, 1986–89; Gp Editl Consultant, Express Newspapers, 1989–90. *Publications:* The Hot Potato, 1969; The Paper Chase, 1971. *Recreations:* lunching, sailing, tennis, reading. *Clubs:* Garrick, Hurlingham.

ESSERY, David James, CB 1997; Under Secretary, Scottish Office Home (formerly Home and Health) Department, 1991–97; *b* 10 May 1938; *s* of Lawrence and Edna Essery; *m* 1963, Nora Sim; two *s* one *d*. *Educ:* Royal High Sch., Edinburgh. Entered Dept of Health for Scotland, 1956; Private Sec. to Minister of State, Scottish Office, 1968; Principal, Scottish Develt Dept, 1969; Assistant Secretary: Scottish Economic Planning Dept, 1976; Scottish Develt Dept, 1981–85; Under Sec., Scottish Office Agric. and Fisheries Dept, 1985–91. *Recreations:* reading, music, cricket, hill walking. *Address:* 41 Minto Street, Edinburgh EH9 2BR.

ESSEX, 10th Earl of, *cr* 1661; **Robert Edward de Vere Capell;** Baron Capell, 1641; Viscount Malden, 1661; *b* 13 Jan. 1920; *s* of Arthur Algernon de Vere Capell (*d* 1924) and Alice Mabel (*d* 1951), *d* of James Currie, Wimbledon; *S* kinsman, 1981; *m* 1942, Doris Margaret, *d* of George Frederick Tomlinson, Morecambe; one *s*. *Heir: s* Viscount Malden, *qv*.

ESSEX, David Albert, OBE 1999; singer, actor and composer; *b* 23 July 1947; *s* of Albert Cook and Doris Cook (*née* Kemp); *m* 1971, Maureen Annette Neal; one *s* one *d*. *Educ:* Shipman Secondary Sch., E London. Music industry début, 1965; acting début, touring repertory co.; Jesus, in Godspell, Wyndhams, 1972 (Most Promising Newcomer Award, Variety Club of GB); Che Guevara, in Evita, Prince Edward, 1978; Byron, in Childe Byron, Young Vic, 1981; Fletcher Christian, in Mutiny, Piccadilly, 1985 (also wrote score); She Stoops to Conquer, Queen's, 1993; annual Christmas appearances in own musical version of Robinson Crusoe. Films include: That'll Be the Day, 1973; Stardust, 1974; Silver Dream Racer (also wrote score), 1979; Shogun Mayeda, 1991. Many best-selling singles and albums; first concert tour of UK, 1974; tours, 1975–, incl. Europe, USA, Australia, and a world tour; TV and radio appearances, incl. BBC TV series, The River, 1988. Mem. Council, VSO (Ambassador, 1990–92). Patron, Gypsy Council. *Address:* c/o London Management, 2-4 Noel Street, W1V 3RB; c/o Mel Bush Organisation, 5 Stratfield Saye, 20-22 Wellington Road, Bournemouth BH8 8JN.

ESSEX, Francis; author, producer and composer; *b* 24 March 1929; *s* of Harold and Beatrice Essex-Lopresti; *m* 1956, Jeanne Shires; one *s* (and one *s* decd). *Educ:* Cotton Coll., N Staffs. Light Entertainment Producer, BBC Television, 1954–60; Sen. Prod., ATV Network Ltd, 1960–65; Controller of Progs, Scottish Television, 1965–69; ATV Network Ltd: Prodn Controller, 1969–76; Mem., Bd of Dirs, 1974; Dir of Production, 1976–81. Chm., Children's Network Cttee, ITV, 1976–81. Chm., Conservatives Abroad, Javea, 1990–92. Wrote and presented, The Bells of St Martins, St Martin's Theatre, 1953; devised and directed, Six of One, Adelphi, 1964; author, Jolson, Victoria Palace, 1995; *television film scripts include:* Shillingbury Tales; Gentle Flame, Silent Scream; Cuffy series; *scores:* Luke's Kingdom; Seas Must Live; The Lightning Tree; Maddie With Love, etc; writer of plays and songs. Fellow, Royal Television Soc., 1974. British Acad. Light Entertainment Award, 1964; Leonard Brett Award, 1964, 1981; Olivier Award for Best Musical, 1996. *Publications:* Shillingbury Tales, 1983; Skerrymor Bay, 1984. *Recreations:* tennis, gardening. *Address:* Punta Vista, Buzon No 1, Aldea de las Cuevas, 03759 Benidoleig, Prov. de Alicante, Spain.

ESSEX, Susan Linda, (Sue); Member (Lab) Cardiff North, since 1999, and Minister (formerly Secretary) for the Environment, since 2000, National Assembly for Wales; *b* 29 Aug. 1945; *m* 1967, Richard Essex; one *s* one *d*. *Educ:* Leicester Univ. (BA). MRTPI. Lectr in Planning, Univ. of Wales, Cardiff, 1992–99. Member (Lab): Cardiff City Council, 1983–96 (former Leader); Cardiff County Council, 1995–99. Mem., Countryside Council for Wales, 1994–99. *Address:* 29 Lon-y-Dail, Rhiwbina, Cardiff CF4 6DZ; National Assembly for Wales, Cardiff Bay, Cardiff CF99 1NA.

ESSEX-CATER, Dr Antony John, LRCP, MRCS; FFPHM; FRAI; Medical Officer of Health, States of Jersey, Channel Islands, 1974–88; Venereologist, General Hospital, Jersey, 1974–88; Vice President, National Association for Maternal and Child Welfare, since 1988 (Chairman, 1975–88); *b* 28 Sept. 1923; *s* of Herbert Stanley Cater and Helen Marjorie Essex; *m* 1947, Jane Mary Binning; three *s* one *d*. *Educ:* Solihull Sch.; King's Coll., Univ. of London; Charing Cross Hosp.; School of Hyg. and Trop. Med., Univ. of London. Bygott Postgrad. Schol., Univ. of London, 1952–53. DPH, DIH, DCH; FRSH; AFOM. Medical Br., RAF, 1948–50. Dep. MOH, Swansea, 1950–58, Admin. MOH, Birmingham, 1958–61; Dep. MOH, Manchester, 1961–68; County MOH, Monmouthshire, 1968–74. Part-time Lectr in Child Health, Univ. of Birmingham, 1958–61; Council of Europe Medical Fellow, 1968. Short-term Consultant, WHO, 1988–89. Mem. Exec. Cttee 1958, Vice-Chm. 1969, Nat. Assoc. for Maternal and Child Welfare; Member: Public Health Lab. Services Bd, 1969–75; Steering Cttee, Nat. Health Service Reorganization (Wales), 1971–72; Founder Fellow and Mem. First Bd, Fac. of Community Med., Royal Colls of Physicians of UK, 1972–73. Member: BMA; Med. Soc. for Study of Venereal Diseases. *Publications:* Synopsis of Public Health and Social Medicine, 1960, 2nd edn 1967; Manual of Public Health and Community Medicine, 3rd edn 1979; numerous papers on medical and allied subjects. *Recreations:* literary, music, sport. *Address:* Honfleur, La Vallette, Mont Cambrai, St Lawrence, Jersey, CI JE3 1JP. *T:* (01534) 872438. *Club:* Society of Authors.

ESSIG, Philippe Louis Charles Marie; Officier de l'Ordre National du Mérite, 1984; Commandeur de la Légion d'Honneur, 1994; international consultant, since 1991; Chairman, Board of Transmanche-Link, 1988–91; *b* 19 July 1933; *s* of Jean Essig and Germaine Olivier; *m* 1960, Isabelle Lanier; one *s* three *d*. *Educ:* Lycée Janson-de Sailly; Ecole Polytechnique; Engineer, Ponts et Chaussées. Engr, Dakar-Niger railway, 1957–59; Asst Dir, Régie du chemin de fer Abidjan-Niger, 1960–61; Dir, Régie des chemins de fer du Cameroun, 1961–66; Régie autonome des transports parisiens (RATP): Chief Engr, Research Dept, 1966–71; Chief Op. Officer, Ops Dept, 1971–73; Man. Dir, Railways, Paris, 1973–81; Gen. Man., 1982–85; Pres., SNCF, 1985–88. Sec. of State for Housing, 1988. Officier de l'Ordre de la Valeur Camerounaise, 1966. *Recreations:* walking, ski-ing, shooting. *Address:* 5 Avenue Fourcault de Pavant, 78000 Versailles, France.

ESSLIN, Martin Julius, OBE 1972; Professor of Drama, Stanford University, California (for two quarters annually), 1977–88, now Emeritus; *b* 8 June 1918; *s* of Paul Pereszlenyi and Charlotte Pereszlenyi (*née* Schiffer); *m* 1947, Renate Gerstenberg; one *d*. *Educ:* Gymnasium, Vienna; Vienna Univ.; Reinhardt Seminar of Dramatic Art, Vienna. Joined BBC, 1940; Producer and Scriptwriter, BBC European Services, 1941–55; Asst Head, BBC European Productions Dept, 1955; Asst Head, Drama (Sound), BBC, 1961; Head of Drama (Radio), BBC, 1963–77. Awarded title Professor by Pres. of Austria, 1967; Vis. Prof. of Theatre, Florida State Univ., 1969–76. Hon. DLitt Kenyon Coll., Ohio, 1978. Ehrenkreuz für Kunst und Wissenschaft, 1st cl. (Austria), 1998. *Publications:* Brecht, A Choice of Evils, 1959; The Theatre of the Absurd, 1962, 8th edn 2001; (ed) Beckett (anthology of critical essays), 1965; Harold Pinter, 1967; The Genius of the German Theatre, 1968; Reflections, Essays on Modern Theatre (NY), 1969 (UK, as Brief Chronicles, 1970); The Peopled Wound: the plays of Harold Pinter, 1970, rev. edn as Pinter: a study of his plays, 1973, 4th edn as Pinter: the Playwright, 1982, 6th edn 2000; (ed) The New Theatre of Europe, 1970; Artaud, 1976; An Anatomy of Drama, 1976; (ed) Illustrated Encyclopaedia of World Theatre, 1977; Mediations, Essays on Brecht, Beckett and the Media, 1981; The Age of Television, 1982; The Field of Drama, 1987; trans. Horváth, Judgement Day, 1986. *Recreations:* reading, book collecting. *Address:* 64 Loudoun Road, NW8 0NA. *T:* (020) 7722 4243; Ballader's Plat, Winchelsea, Sussex TN36 4EN. *T:* (01797) 226 392. *Club:* Garrick.

ESSWOOD, Paul Lawrence Vincent; singer (counter-tenor); Professor, Royal Academy of Music, since 1985; *b* West Bridgford, Nottingham, 6 June 1942; *s* of Alfred Walter Esswood and Freda Garratt; *m* 1st, 1966, Mary Lillian Cantrill, ARCM (marr. diss.); two *s*; 2nd, 1990, Aimée Désirée Blattmann; one *s* one *d*. *Educ:* West Bridgford Grammar Sch.; Royal Coll. of Music (ARCM). Lay-Vicar, Westminster Abbey, 1964–71. Prof., RCM, 1973–85; Specialist in baroque performance; first broadcast, BBC, 1965; co-founder: Pro Cantione Antiqua; A Cappella Male Voice Ensemble for Performance of Old Music, 1967; joined The Musicke Companye, 1998; operatic debut in Cavalli's L'Erismena, Univ. of California, Berkeley, 1968; debut at La Scala, Milan with Zurich

Opera in L'Incoronazione di Poppea and Il Ritorno d'Ulisse, 1978; Scottish Opera debut in Dido and Aeneas, 1978; world premieres: Penderecki's Paradise Lost, Chicago Lyric Opera, 1979; Philip Glass's Echnaton, Stüttgart Opera, 1984; Herbert Willi's Schlafes Bruder, Zurich Opera, 1996; performed in major festivals: Edinburgh, Leeds Triennial, English Bach, Vienna, Salzburg, Zurich, Hamburg, Berlin, Naples, Israel, Lucerne, Flanders, Wexford, Holland. Has made over 150 recordings for major cos, incl. solo recitals of Purcell, Schumann, English lute songs, Benjamin Britten folk songs and Canticle II (Abraham and Isaac). Debut as conductor, Chichester Fest., 2000. Hon. RAM 1990. *Recreations:* gardening (organic), apiculture. *Address:* Jasmine Cottage, 42 Ferring Lane, Ferring, West Sussex BN12 6QT. *T:* and *Fax:* (01903) 504480.

ESTEVE-COLL, Dame Elizabeth Anne Loosemore, DBE 1995; Vice-Chancellor, University of East Anglia, 1995–97; *b* 14 Oct. 1938; *o d* of P. W. and Nora Kingdon; *m* 1960, José Alexander Timothy Esteve-Coll (*d* 1980). *Educ:* Darlington Girls High Sch.; Birkbeck Coll., London Univ. (BA 1976). Head of Learning Resources, Kingston Polytechnic, 1977; University Librarian, Univ. of Surrey, 1982; Keeper, National Art Library, 1985, Dir, 1988–95, V&A Museum. *Recreations:* reading, music, foreign travel. *Address:* c/o 27 Ursula Street, SW11 3DW; c/o Le Colombier, Puylaurens, 81570 Semalens, Tarn, France.

ESTEY, Hon. Willard Zebedee, CC 1990; Counsel, McCarthy Tétrault, Toronto, since 1988; Chancellor, Wilfrid Laurier University, Waterloo, Ont, 1990–95; *b* 10 Oct. 1919; *s* of James Wilfred Estey and Muriel Baldwin Estey; *m* 1946, Marian Ruth McKinnon; three *s* one *d.* *Educ:* Univ. of Saskatchewan (BA, LLB); Harvard Law Sch. (LLM). Served Canadian Army and RCAF, 1939–45. Mem., Bar of Sask., 1942 and of Ont, 1947; QC Ont 1960. Prof., Coll. of Law, Univ. of Sask., 1946–47; Lectr, Osgoode Hall Law Sch., 1947–51. Practised law, Toronto, 1947–72. Pres., Canadian Bar Assoc., Ont, 1972. Mem. Court of Appeal, 1973, and Chief Justice of High Court, Supreme Court of Ont, 1975; Chief Justice of Ontario, 1976; Justice of Supreme Court of Canada, 1977–88. Commissioner: Steel Profits Inquiry, Royal Commn of Inquiry, 1974; Air Canada Inquiry, 1975; Inquiry into certain banking operations, 1985–86. Special Advr to Chm., Bank of Nova Scotia, 1990–94. Pres., Ballard Foundn. Formerly: Chm., Press Council of Ontario; Hockey Canada. Hon. LLD: Wilfrid Laurier Univ., Waterloo, Ont, 1977; Univ. of Toronto, 1979; Univ. of W Ont, 1980; Law Soc. of Upper Canada, 1981; Univ. of Saskatchewan, 1984; Univ. of Lethbridge, 1985. *Address:* 70 Rosehill Avenue, Toronto, ON M4T 2W7, Canada.

ESTRIN, Prof. Saul, DPhil; Professor of Economics, since 1994, Director, CIS Middle Europe Centre, since 1997, and a Deputy Dean, since 1998, London Business School; *b* 7 June 1952; *s* of Maurice Estrin and Irene Estrin (*née* Redhouse); *m* 1985, Jennifer Ann Lockwood; one *s* three *d.* *Educ:* St John's Coll., Cambridge (BA 1974; MA 1977); Univ. of Sussex (DPhil 1979). Lectr, Southampton Univ., 1977–84; Lectr, 1984–89, Sen. Lectr, 1989–90, in Econs, LSE, 1984–90; Associate Prof. of Econs, London Business Sch., 1990–94. *Publications:* Self-Management: economic theory and Yugoslav practice, 1984; (jtly) Introduction to Microeconomics, 4th edn, 1993; (ed jtly) Competition and Competition Policy, 1993; Privatisation in Central and Eastern Europe, 1994; (ed jtly) Essential Readings in Economics, 1995; Foreign Direct Investment in Central and Eastern Europe, 1997; numerous academic papers. *Recreation:* family. *Address:* London Business School, Sussex Place, NW1 4SA. *T:* (020) 7262 5050; *e-mail:* sestrin@lbs.ac.uk.

ETCHELLS, (Dorothea) Ruth, MA, BD; Principal, St John's College with Cranmer Hall, University of Durham, 1979–88 (Hon. Fellow, St John's College, Durham, 1991); *b* 17 April 1931; *d* of late Walter and Ada Etchells. *Educ:* Merchant Taylor's School for Girls, Crosby, Liverpool; Universities of Liverpool (MA) and London (BD). Head of English Dept, Aigburth Vale High Sch., Liverpool, 1959; Lectr in English, 1963, Sen. Lectr in English and Resident Tutor, 1965, Chester College of Education; Trevelyan College, Univ. of Durham: Resident Tutor and part-time Lectr in English, 1968; Vice Principal, 1972; Sen. Lectr, 1973; Mem. Council, Durham Univ., 1985–88. Examining Chaplain to Bishop of Bath and Wells, 1984–88. Member: Gen. Synod, 1985–95; Doctrine Commn, 1986–91; Crown Appointments Commn, 1987–96; Bishop's Council and Standing Cttee of Durham Diocesan Synod, 1975–97 (Chm., House of Laity, 1988–94); Hon. Vice-Pres., CMS, 1992–. Vice-Chm., Durham FHSA, 1990–96 (Chm., Med. Services Cttee, 1990–). Mem., Governing Council, Ridley Coll., Cambridge, 1988–; Mem., Governing Body, Durham High Sch., 1995–. Trustee, Anvil, 1983–92; Mem. Trustees, Hosp. of God, Greatham, 1995–99. DD Lambeth, 1992. *Publications:* Unafraid To Be, 1969; The Man with the Trumpet, 1970; A Model of Making, 1983; (ed) Poets and Prophets, 1988; Praying with the English Poets, 1990; Just as I am: personal prayers for every day, 1994; Set My People Free: a lay challenge to the Churches, 1996; A Reading of the Parables of Jesus, 1998. *Recreations:* friends, quiet, country walking, pets, painting and work in stained glass. *Address:* 12 Dunelm Court, South Street, Durham DH1 4QX. *T:* (0191) 3841497.

ETHERINGTON, David Charles Lynch; QC 1998; a Recorder, since 2000; *b* 14 March 1953; *s* of late Charles Henry Etherington and of Beryl Etherington (*née* Croft). *Educ:* Keble Coll., Oxford (BA 1976, MA 2001; Special DPSA (Distinction) 1977). Called to the Bar, Middle Temple, 1979; Asst Recorder, 1997–2000. Vice-Chm., Professional Conduct Cttee, Bar Council, 2000–. *Publication:* practical res. paper on prof. ethics. *Recreations:* reading, music, theatre. *Address:* 18 Red Lion Court, EC4A 3EB. *T:* (020) 7520 6000.

ETHERINGTON, Stuart James; Chief Executive, National Council for Voluntary Organisations, since 1994; *b* 26 Feb. 1955; *s* of Ronald Etherington and Dorothy Etherington (*née* West). *Educ:* Sondes Place Sch., Dorking; Brunel Univ. (BSc Politics 1977); Essex Univ. (MA Soc. Sci. Planning 1981); SOAS (MA Internat. Relns and Diplomacy 1992); London Business Sch. (MBA 1999). Social Worker, London Borough of Hillingdon, 1977–79; Sen. Res. Officer, Joseph Rowntree Meml Trust, Circle 33, 1980–82; Policy Advr, BASW, 1982–84; Dir, Good Practices in Mental Health, 1984–87; Dir, Public Affairs, 1987–91, Chief Exec., 1991–94, RNID. Mem. Council, ESRC, 1998–. Trustee: CAF, 1995–; BITC, 1995–. Mem., RIIA, 1997. FRSA 1995. Hon. DSocSc Brunel, 2000. *Publications:* Mental Health and Housing, 1984; Emergency Duty Teams, 1985; The Sensitive Bureaucracy, 1986; Social Work and Citizenship, 1987. *Recreations:* reading biographies, theatre, opera, watching cricket. *Address:* National Council for Voluntary Organisations, Regents Wharf, 8 All Saints Street, N1 9RL. *T:* (020) 7713 6161; 40 Walnut Tree Road, Greenwich, SE10 9EU. *T:* (020) 8305 1379. *Clubs:* National Liberal, Reform; Surrey CC.

ETHERINGTON, William; MP (Lab) Sunderland North, since 1992; *b* 17 July 1941; *m* 1963, Irene; two *d.* *Educ:* Monkwearmouth Grammar Sch.; Durham Univ. Apprentice fitter, Austin & Pickersgill shipyard, 1957–63; fitter, Dawdon Colliery, 1963–83; full-time NUM official, 1983–92. Mem., NUM, 1963– (Vice-Pres., NE Area, 1988–92). Mem., UK delegn to Council of Europe and WEU, 1997–. Secretary: Miners' Parly Gp, 1994–; All-Party Anti-Fluoridation Gp, 1998–. *Address:* House of Commons, SW1A 0AA.

ETHERINGTON-SMITH, (Raymond) Gordon (Antony), CMG 1962; HM Diplomatic Service, retired; *b* 1 Feb. 1914; *o s* of late T. B. Etherington-Smith and Henriette de Pitner; *m* 1950, Mary Elizabeth Besly (*d* 1989); one *s* three *d.* *Educ:* Downside; Magdalen Coll., Oxford; Sch. of Oriental and African Studies, London Univ. Entered FO, 1936. Served at: Berlin, 1939; Copenhagen, 1939–40; Washington, 1940–42; Chungking, 1943–45; Kashgar, 1945–46; Moscow, 1947; Foreign Office, 1947–52; Holy See, 1952–54; Counsellor, Saigon, 1954–57; The Hague, 1958–61; Office of UK Commissioner-Gen. for South-East Asia, Singapore, 1961–63; Ambassador to Vietnam, 1963–66; Minister, and Dep. Commandant, Berlin, 1966–70; Ambassador to Sudan, 1970–74. *Publication:* Maximilian's Lieutenant, 1993. *Recreations:* physical and mental exercise. *Address:* The Coach House, 25A West Street, Wilton, Salisbury, Wilts SP2 0LD. *T:* (01722) 743429. *Club:* Oriental.

ETHERTON, Hon. Sir Terence (Michael Elkan Barnet), Kt 2001; FCIArb; **Hon. Mr Justice Etherton;** a Judge of the High Court, Chancery Division, since 2001; *b* 21 June 1951; *s* of Alan Kenneth Etherton and Elaine Myrtle (*née* Maccoby). *Educ:* Holmewood House Sch., Tunbridge Wells; St Paul's Sch., London (Sen, Foundn Schol.); Corpus Christi Coll., Cambridge (Open Exhibnr; MA (History and Law); LLM). FCIArb 1993. Called to the Bar, Gray's Inn, 1974 (Uthwatt Schol., 1972; Holker Sen. Award, 1974; Arden Atkin and Mould Prize, 1975; Bencher 1998); in practice, 1975–2000; QC 1990; a Dep. High Court Judge, 2000. Mem., Bar Council, 1978–81; CKt 2001hm., Young Barristers' Cttee of Bar Council, 1980–81; Mem., Lord Rawlinson's Cttee on the Constitution of the Senate of the Inns of Court and the Bar, 1985–86; Vice Chm., Chancery Bar Assoc., 1999–2001. Mem., Mental Health Review Tribunal, 1994–99; Chairman: Broadmoor Hosp. Authy, 1999–2001; West London Mental Health NHS Trust, 2000–01; Dir (non-exec.), Riverside Mental Health NHS Trust, 1992–99 (Chm., Ethics Forum, 1994–99). Claims Adjudicator, Savings and Investment Bank (IOM) Depositors' Compensation Scheme, 1993–94. Chm., DoE/MAFF Indep. Review Panel on designation of nitrate vulnerable zones under EC Nitrate Directive, 1995 (report published, 1995). Mem. Council, RHBNC, 1992– (Chm., Academic Staff Dismissal Appeals Tribunal, 1994–). Blundell Meml Lect., 1996. FRSA 2000. Captain, Cambridge Univ. Fencing Team, 1971–72; Mem., GB Sen. Internat. Fencing Team (Sabre), 1977–80 (World Championships, 1977, 1978, 1979); England Sabre Team Gold Medal, Commonwealth Fencing Championships, 1978; selected for Moscow Olympics, GB Fencing Team, 1980. *Address:* Royal Courts of Justice, Strand, WC2A 2LL. *Club:* Hawks (Cambridge).

ETIANG, Paul Orono, BA London; Third Deputy Prime Minister, since 1996, and Minister for Disaster Preparedness and Refugees, since 1998, Uganda; *b* 15 Aug. 1938; *s* of late Kezironi Orono and Mirabu Achom Orono; *m* 1967, Zahra Ali Foum; two *s* two *d.* *Educ:* Makerere Univ. Coll. Uganda Admin. Officer, 1962–64; Asst Sec., Foreign Affairs, 1964–65; 3rd Sec., 1965–66, 2nd Sec., 1966–67, Uganda Embassy, Moscow; 1st Sec., Uganda Mission to UN, New York, 1968; Counsellor, 1968–69, High Commissioner, 1969–71, Uganda High Commission, London; Chief of Protocol and Marshal of the Diplomatic Corps, Uganda, 1971; Permanent Sec., Uganda Min. of Foreign Affairs, 1971–73; Minister of State for Foreign Affairs, 1973; Minister of State in the President's office, 1974; Minister of Transport and Communications, July 1976, of Transport, Communications and Works, Mar. 1977, of Transport and Works, 1978; an Asst. Sec.-Gen., OAU, Addis Ababa, 1978–87; Minister for Regl Co-operation, March–Dec. 1988; Minister: of Commerce, 1989–91; of Information, 1991–96; of Labour and Social Services, 1996–98. *Recreations:* chess, classical music, billiards. *Address:* Ministry for Disaster Preparedness and Refugees, PO Box 5261, Kampala, Uganda.

ETTEDGUI, Joseph; fashion designer and retailer; Joint Founder and Chairman, Joseph Ltd; *b* Casablanca; *m* Isabelle; one *d.* Came to London, 1960; with brother opened hairdressing salon and clothes shop, King's Road, Chelsea; has opened over 20 Joseph shops, incl. outlets in London, Manchester, Leeds, and in USA, France and Germany. Contemporary Collection Award, British Fashion Awards, 2000. *Address:* Joseph Ltd, 315 Brompton Road, SW3 2DY.

EUROPE, Suffragan Bishop in; *see* Gibraltar in Europe, Suffragan Bishop of.

EUSTACE, Dudley Graham, FCA; Chairman, Smith & Nephew plc, since 2000; *b* 3 July 1936; *s* of Albert and Mary Eustace; *m* 1964, Carol Diane Zakrajsek; two *d.* *Educ:* Cathedral Sch., Bristol; Univ. of Bristol (BA Econ). FCA 1972. John Barritt & Son, Hamilton, Bermuda, 1962; Internat. Resort Facilities, Ont, 1963; Aluminium Securities Ltd, Montreal, 1964–65; Aluminium Co. of Canada Ltd, Vancouver, 1966–69, Montreal, 1969–73; Alcan Aluminio America Latina, Buenos Aires, 1973–76, Rio de Janeiro, 1976–79; Empresa Nacional del Aluminio, Madrid, 1979–83; Alcan Aluminium Ltd, Montreal, 1983–84; British Alcan Aluminium PLC, Gerrards Cross, Bucks, 1984–87; BAe, 1987–92 (Finance Dir, 1988–92); Chief Financial Officer, 1992–97, Vice Pres., 1992, Exec. Vice Pres. and Dep. Chm., 1992–99, Philips Electronics NV, Eindhoven. Chm., Sendo Hldgs PLC, 2000–; Mem. Adv. Council, Bayerische Landesbank, Munich, 1995–99; Member, Supervisory Board: Aegon NV, 1997–; Hagemeyer NV, 1999–; KLM Royal Dutch Airlines, 1999–; Charterhouse Vermogensbeheer BV, 1999–; K. P. N. NV, 2000–; Mem. Bd, sonae.com SGPS, 1999. Member: Council, ECGD, 1988–92; Board, Assoc. for Monetary Union in Europe, 1992–99. Liveryman, Chartered Accountants' Co., 1991. *Recreations:* gardening, reading. *Address:* 10 Lindsay Square, SW1V 3SB.

EUSTON, Earl of; James Oliver Charles FitzRoy, MA, FCA; *b* 13 Dec. 1947; *s* and *heir* of 11th Duke of Grafton, *qv*; *m* 1972, Lady Clare Kerr, BA, *d* of Marquess of Lothian, *qv*; one *s* four *d.* *Educ:* Eton; Magdalene Coll., Cambridge (MA). Dir, Smith St Aubyn & Co. (Holdings) plc, 1980–86; Executive Director: Enskilda Securities, 1982–87; Jamestown Investments, 1987–91; Finance Director: Central Capital Hldgs, 1988–91; Capel-Cure Myers Capital Management, 1988–97. *Heir: s* Viscount Ipswich, *qv.* *Address:* 6 Vicarage Gardens, W8 4AH; The Racing Stables, Euston, Thetford, Norfolk IP24 2QT.

EVANS; *see* Parry-Evans and Parry Evans.

EVANS, family name of **Baroness Blackstone** and **Barons Evans of Parkside, Evans of Temple Guiting, Evans of Watford** and **Mountevans.**

EVANS OF PARKSIDE, Baron *cr* 1997 (Life Peer), of St Helens, in the co. of Merseyside; **John Evans;** Chairman of Labour Party, 1991–92; *b* 19 Oct. 1930; *s* of late James Evans, miner and Margaret (*née* Robson); *m* 1959, Joan Slater; two *s* one *d.* *Educ:* Jarrow Central School. Apprentice Marine Fitter, 1946–49 and 1950–52; Nat. Service, Royal Engrs, 1949–50; Engr, Merchant Navy, 1952–55; joined AUEW (later AEU), 1952; joined Labour Party, 1955; worked in various industries as fitter, ship-building and repairing, steel, engineering, 1955–65, 1968–74. Mem. Hebburn UDC, 1962, Leader 1969, Chm. 1972; Sec./Agent Jarrow CLP, 1965–68. MP (Lab) Newton, Feb. 1974–1983, St Helens, North, 1983–97. An Asst Govt Whip, 1978–79; Opposition Whip, 1979–80; PPS to Leader of Labour Party, 1980–83; opposition spokesman on employment, 1983–87. Mem., European Parlt, 1975–78; Chm., Regional Policy,

Planning and Transport Cttee, European Parlt, 1976–78. Mem., Lab Party NEC, 1982–96. *Recreations:* watching football, reading, gardening. *Address:* 6 Kirkby Road, Culcheth, Warrington, Cheshire WA3 4BS. *Clubs:* Labour (Earlestown); Daten (Culcheth).

EVANS OF TEMPLE GUITING, Baron *cr* 2000 (Life Peer), of Temple Guiting in the co. of Gloucestershire; **Matthew Evans,** CBE 1998; Chairman, Faber & Faber Ltd, since 1981 (Managing Director, 1972–93); *b* 7 Aug. 1941; *s* of late George Ewart Evans, and Florence Ellen Evans; *m* 1st, 1966, Elizabeth Amanda (*née* Mead) (marr. diss. 1991); two *s*; 2nd, 1991, Caroline (*née* Michel); two *s* one *d*. *Educ:* Friends' Sch., Saffron Walden; LSE (BScEcon). Bookselling, 1963–64; Faber & Faber, 1964–. Chairman: National Book League, 1982–84; English Stage Company, 1984–90; Library and Information Commn, 1995–99 (Chm. Working Gp on New Library: The People's Network, 1997); Re:source (Museums, Libraries and Archives Council), 2000–. Dir, Which? Ltd, 1997–. Member: Council, Publishers Assoc., 1978–84; Literary Adv. Panel, British Council, 1986–97; DCMS Adv. Panel for Public Appts, 1996–; Arts Council Nat. Lottery Adv. Panel, 1997–99; Univ. for Industry Adv. Gp, 1997; Sir Richard Eyre's Working Gp on Royal Opera House, 1997; Arts and Humanities Res. Bd, 1998–. Mem., Franco-British Soc., 1981–. Governor, BFI, 1982–97 (Vice Chm., 1996–97). FRSA 1990; Hon. FRCA 1999; Hon. FLA 1999. *Recreation:* cricket. *Address:* c/o Faber & Faber, 3 Queen Square, WC1N 3AU. *Club:* Groucho (Founder Mem., and Dir, 1982–97).

EVANS OF WATFORD, Baron *cr* 1998 (Life Peer), of Chipperfield in the co. of Hertfordshire; **David Charles Evans;** Chairman, Centurion Press Group, since 1971; *b* 30 Nov. 1942; *s* of Arthur and Phyllis Evans; *m* 1966, June Scaldwell; one *s* one *d*. *Educ:* Hampden Secondary Sch.; Watford Coll. Apprentice printer, Stone and Cox Ltd, 1957. Founded: Centurion Press Ltd, 1971; (with Susanne Lawrence) Personnel Publications Ltd, 1975; Centurion Press bv, 1975; Dir, Union Income Benefit Hldgs, 2001; Chairman: Centurion Media Gp bv, 1974; Personnel Publications Ltd, 1981; Centurion Publishing Ltd, 1995. Freeman, Marketors' Co., 1991. *Publications:* articles on marketing, print management and purchasing. *Recreations:* theatre, music, reading, travel, food, walking. *Address:* Centurion Press Group, 34/36 High Street, Rickmansworth, Herts WD3 1ER. *Club:* Morton's.

EVANS, A. Briant; Hon. Consulting Gynæcological Surgeon, Westminster Hospital and Chelsea Hospital for Women; Hon. Consulting Obstetric Surgeon, Queen Charlotte's Maternity Hospital; *b* 26 June 1909; *e s* of late Arthur Evans, OBE, MD, MS, FRCS; *m* 1939, Audrey Marie, *er d* of late Roland Eveleigh Holloway; three *s*. *Educ:* Westminster Sch.; Gonville and Caius Coll., Cambridge; Westminster Hosp. MA, MB, BCh Cantab; FRCS; FRCOG. Sometime Examiner in Obstetrics to Univs of Cambridge and London and to Royal College of Obstetricians and Gynæcologists. Temp. Lieut-Col RAMC, served in Egypt, Italy and Austria; OC No. 9 Field Surgical Unit. *Address:* Chilton House, Chilton, Aylesbury, Bucks HP18 2LR.

EVANS, Alun; *see* Evans, T. A.

EVANS, Alun S.; *see* Sylvester-Evans.

EVANS, Alun Trevor Bernard; Secretary to Inquiry into lessons to be learned from foot and mouth disease outbreak of 2001, Cabinet Office, since 2001; *b* 8 Dec. 1958; *s* of Thomas Francis Evans and late Marjorie Gladys Evans (*née* Macken); *m* 1986, Ingrid Elisabeth Dammers; two *d*. *Educ:* County Sch., Ashford, Middx; Essex Univ. (BA Hons); Birmingham Univ. (MPhil 1983). Civil Servant, Dept of Employment, subseq. DfEE, 1983–98: Private Sec. to Paymaster Gen. and Minister for Employment, 1986; Asst Regl Dir, Eastern Reg., 1992–93; Hd, Nuclear Safety Policy Div., HSE, 1993–94; Principal Private Sec. to Sec. of State for Employment, 1994–95, to Sec. of State for Educn and Employment, 1995–98; Hd, Strategic Communications Unit, Prime Minister's Office, 1998–2000; Dir of Communications, DETR, then DTLR, 2000–01. *Recreations:* political history, family, cricket, running, art, opera. *Address:* Cabinet Office, 70 Whitehall, SW1A 2AS. *Clubs:* Occasionals, Mandarins Cricket.
See also R. J. E. Evans.

EVANS, Amanda Louise Elliot, (Mrs A. S. Duncan); freelance writer, editor and editorial consultant, since 1997; *b* 19 May 1958; *d* of Brian Royston Elliot Evans and June Annabella (*née* Gilderdale); *m* 1989, Andrew Sinclair Duncan; one *s* two *d*. *Educ:* Tonbridge Girls' Grammar Sch. Editorial writer, Interiors magazine, 1981–83; Consultant Editor, Mitchell Beazley Publishers, 1983–84; freelance writer and stylist on A la carte, Tatler, Country Homes & Interiors, Sunday Times, 1984–86; Dep. Editor, April–Oct. 1986, Editor, 1986–96, Homes & Gardens. *Publications:* Homes and Gardens Bedrooms, 1997; Making the Most of Living Rooms, 1998. *Recreations:* mountain walking, opera, camping. *Address:* 98 Addison Gardens, W14 0DR. *T:* (020) 7603 1574.

EVANS, Anne Celia; *see* Segall, A. C.

EVANS, Dame Anne (Elizabeth Jane), DBE 2000; soprano; *b* 20 Aug. 1941; *d* of late David and Eleanor, (Nellie), Evans; *m* 1st, 1962, John Heulyn Jones (marr. diss. 1981); 2nd, 1981, John Philip Lucas. *Educ:* Royal Coll. of Music; Conservatoire de Genève. Début, Annina in La Traviata, Grand Théâtre, Geneva, 1967; UK début, Mimi in La Bohème, Coliseum, 1968; Principal soprano, ENO, 1968–78; subseq. major rôles at Metropolitan Opera House, NY, San Francisco Opera, Deutsche Oper, Berlin, Dresden State Opera, Vienna State Opera, Paris Opéra, Rome Opera, Théâtre de la Monnaie, Brussels, Teatro Colón, Buenos Aires, Royal Opera House, Covent Garden, WNO, Scottish Opera; rôles include: Brünnhilde in Der Ring des Nibelungen (incl. Bayreuth Fest., 1989–92), Isolde in Tristan und Isolde, Sieglinde in Die Walküre, Elsa in Lohengrin, Elisabeth in Tannhäuser, Senta in Der fliegende Holländer, Leonore in Fidelio, Cassandre in Les Troyens, Chrysothemis in Elektra, Marschallin in Der Rosenkavalier, Ariadne in Ariadne auf Naxos; recitals incl. Edinburgh Fest., Wigmore Hall; Last Night of the Proms, 1997. FWCMD 1996. *Recreations:* cooking, gardening. *Address:* c/o Ingpen & Williams Ltd, 26 Wadham Road, SW15 2LR.

EVANS, Anthony; *see* Evans, D. A.

EVANS, Sir Anthony (Adney), 2nd Bt *cr* 1920; *b* 5 Aug. 1922; *s* of Sir Walter Harry Evans, 1st Bt, and Margaret Mary, *y d* of late Thomas Adney Dickens; *S* father, 1954; married; two *s* one *d*. *Educ:* Shrewsbury; Merton Coll., Oxford.

EVANS, Anthony Clive Varteg, FIL; Head Master, King's College School, Wimbledon, since 1997; *b* 11 Oct. 1945; *s* of Edward Varteg Evans and Doris Lilian Evans; *m* 1968, Danielle Jacqueline Nicole Bégasse (*d* 1997); two *s*. *Educ:* De la Salle Grammar Sch., London; St Peter's Coll., Oxford (MA); University Coll. London (MPhil); Inst. of Educn, London Univ. (Advanced DipEd). FIL 1975. Assistant Master: Eastbourne Coll., 1967–72; Winchester Coll., 1972–77; Hd of Mod. Langs and Hd of Humanities, Dulwich Coll., 1977–83; Headmaster, Portsmouth Grammar Sch., 1983–97. Headmasters' and Headmistresses' Conference: Mem., 1985–94, Chm., 1990–94, Acad. Policy Cttee; Mem., Common Entrance Cttee, 1988–90; Mem., Cttee, 1989–97; Chm., 1996; Mem., HMC/GSA Univ. Cttee, 1993– (Co-Chm., 1993–95). Member: Admiralty Interview Bd, 1985–97; Nat. Curriculum Council, 1989–91; ISC Council, 1996–2000; Chm., ISC Adv. Council, 1997–99; Co-Chm., ISC Unity Cttee, 1997–99. Governor: Mall Sch., Twickenham, 1997–; Sevenoaks Sch., 2000–; Ecole Saint-Georges, Montreux, 2000–. Fellow, Winchester Coll., Hants, 1997. *Publication:* Souvenirs de la Grande Guerre, 1985. *Recreations:* France, theatre, Southampton FC, avoiding dinner parties. *Address:* King's College School, Wimbledon, SW19 4TT. *T:* (020) 8255 5353. *Club:* East India.

EVANS, Prof. Anthony Glyn, PhD; FRS 2001; Gordon Wu Professor of Mechnical and Aerospace Engineering, and Director, Princeton Materials Institute, Princeton University, since 1998; *b* 4 Dec. 1942; *s* of William Glyn Evans and Annie May Evans; *m* 1967, Trisha Cross; three *d*. *Educ:* Imperial Coll., London (BSc 1964; PhD 1967). Member, Technical Staff, AERE, 1967–71; Nat. Bureau of Standards, 1971–74; Gp Leader, Rockwell Internat. Sci. Center, 1974–78; Prof., Dept of Materials Sci. and Mineral Engrg, Univ. of Calif, Berkeley, 1978–85; Alcoa Prof. and Chair, Materials Dept, UCSB, 1985–94; Gordon McKay Prof. of Materials Engrg, Div. of Applied Scis, Harvard Univ., 1994–98. Member: NAE, 1995; Amer. Acad. Arts and Scis, 2000. *Publications:* Metal Foams: a design guide, 2000; contribs to numerous scientific pubns in fields of materials and mechanical engrg. *Address:* 40 Montadale Drive, Princeton, NJ 08540, USA. *T:* (609) 2584762.

EVANS, Rt Hon. Sir Anthony (Howell Meurig), Kt 1985; RD 1968; PC 1992; arbitrator; a Lord Justice of Appeal, 1992–2000; *b* 11 June 1934; *s* of late His Honour David Meurig Evans and Joy Diedericke (*née* Sander); *m* 1963, Caroline Mary Fyffe Mackie, *d* of late Edwin Gordon Mackie; one *s* two *d*. *Educ:* Bassaleg Sec. Grammar Sch., Mon; Shrewsbury Sch.; St John's Coll., Cambridge (BA 1957; LLB 1958). Nat. Service, RNVR, 1952–54 (Lt-Comdr RNR). Called to Bar, Gray's Inn, 1958 (Arden Scholar and Birkenhead Scholar; Bencher, 1979; Treas., 2000); QC 1971; a Recorder, 1972–84; a Presiding Judge, Wales and Chester Circuit, 1986–88; a Judge of the High Court of Justice, QBD, 1984–92; Judge in charge of the Commercial Court, 1991–92. Mem. Melbourne, Vic, Bar, 1975–84, Hon. Mem., 1985. Dep. Chm., Boundary Commn for Wales, 1989–92. Pres., Bar Musical Soc., 1998–. Hon. Fellow, Internat. Acad. of Trial Lawyers, 1985; FCIArb 1986 (Patron, Wales Br., 1988; Hon. Pres., 1998–2000). A Vice President: British Maritime Law Assoc., 1992–; Assoc. of Average Adjusters, 1997–. Freeman, 2000, Liveryman, 2001, Shipwrights' Co. *Publication:* (Jt Editor) The Law of the Air (Lord McNair), 1964. *Recreations:* sailing, music. *Address:* Essex Court Chambers, 24 Lincoln's Inn Fields, WC2A 3ED. *Clubs:* Royal Yacht Squadron; Royal Welsh Yacht.

EVANS, Prof. Anthony John, PhD, FLA; Professor in Department of Information and Library Studies (formerly Library and Information Studies), 1973–95, now Emeritus Professor, and Director, Alumni Office, 1992–95, Loughborough University of Technology; *b* 1 April 1930; *s* of William John and Marian Audrey (*née* Young); *m* 1954, Anne (*née* Horwell); two *d*. *Educ:* Queen Elizabeth's Hosp., Bristol (Pres., Old Boys' Soc., 1999); Sch. of Pharmacy and University College, Univ. of London. BPharm, PhD. Lectr in Pharm. Eng. Sci., Sch. of Pharmacy, Univ. of London, 1954–58; Librarian, Sch. of Pharmacy, Univ. of London, 1958–63; University Librarian, 1964–91, and Dean, Sch. of Educnl Studies, 1973–76, Loughborough Univ. of Technology. Pres., IATUL, 1970–75 (Bd Mem. and Treasurer, 1968–70; Hon. Life Mem., 1976–); Mem. Exec. Bd, IFLA, 1983–89 (Treas., 1985–89; Consultative Cttee, 1968–76; Standing Cttee on Sci. and Tech. Libraries, 1977–87; Standing Cttee on Univ. Libraries, 1989–93; Chm., Cttee on Access to Information and Freedom of Expression, 1995–97); Pres., Commonwealth Library Assoc., 1994–96; ASLIB: Vice-Pres., 1985–88; Mem. Council, 1970–80, 1985–88; Internat. Relations Cttee, 1974–85; Annual Lecture, 1985; BSI: Mem. Bd, 1984–86; Chm., Documentation Standards Cttee, 1980–86 (Mem., 1976–86); Member: Inf. Systems Council, 1980–86. Member: Adv. Cttee, Sci. Ref. Library, 1975–83; Vice-Chancellors and Principals Cttee on Libraries, 1972–77; Jt UNESCO/ICSU Cttee for establishment of UNISIST, 1968–71; Internat. Cttee, LA, 1985–96; Adv. Council to Bd of Dirs of Engineering Information Inc., USA, 1986–91; Chm., Adv. Gp on Documentation Standards, ISO, 1983–85; consultancy work for British Council, ODA, UNESCO, UNIDO, World Bank in Africa, Asia and Latin America, especially China, Kenya and Mexico. Pres., Jaguars (Notts Wheelchair Basketball Club), 1997–. Hon. FLA 1990. Medal IFLA, 1989. *Publications:* (with D. Train) Bibliography of the tabletting of medicinal substances, 1964, suppl. 1965; (with R. G. Rhodes and S. Keenan) Education and training of users of scientific and technical information, 1977; articles in librarianship and documentation. *Recreations:* genealogy, sport, canal cruising. *Address:* The Moorings, Mackleys Lane, North Muskham, Newark, Notts NG23 6EY. *T:* (01636) 700174; *e-mail:* ajevans@moorings99.freeserve.co.uk.

EVANS, Anthony Thomas; a District Judge (Magistrates' Courts) (formerly Metropolitan Stipendiary Magistrate), since 1990; *b* 29 Sept. 1943; *s* of late Emlyn Roger Evans and Dorothy Evans; *m* 1st, 1965, Gillian Celia Mather (*d* 1988); one *s*; 2nd, 1991, Margaret Elizabeth Ryles (*née* Howorth); one step *s* one step *d*. *Educ:* Bishop Gore Grammar Sch., Swansea; Univ. of Manchester (LLB 1965; LLM 1968). Asst Lectr, Univ. of Manchester, 1965–68; admitted Solicitor, 1971; Partner: Haye & Reid, 1971–85; Evans & Co., 1985–89; sole practitioner, 1989–90. Chairman: Inner London Family Courts, 1991–; Inner London Youth Courts, 1993–. Mem., British Acad. of Forensic Scis, 1994. *Recreations:* reading, music, theatre. *Address:* c/o Chief Magistrate's Office, Bow Street Magistrates' Court, WC2E 7AS.

EVANS, (Arthur) Mostyn; General Secretary, Transport and General Workers Union, 1978–85; Member, TUC General Council, 1977–85; *b* 13 July 1925; *m* 1947, Laura Bigglestone; two *s* three *d* (and one *s* decd). *Educ:* Cefn Coed Primary Sch., S Wales; Church Road Secondary Modern Sch., Birmingham. District Officer, Birmingham, Chem. and Eng. Industries, 1956; Regional Officer, Midlands, 1960; Nat. Officer, Eng., 1966; National Secretary: Chem., Rubber, and Oil Industries, 1969; Engineering Industries, 1969; (Automotive Section), TGWU, 1969–73; Nat. Organiser, TGWU, 1973–78. Part-time Mem., Nat. Bus Co., 1976–78; Member: BOTB, 1978–79; NEDC, 1978–84; Exec., ITF, 1980–; Council, ACAS, 1982–; Pres., ICEF, 1982– (Vice-Pres., 1980–82). Councillor (Lab), Borough of Kings Lynn and W Norfolk, 1991– (Mayor, 1996–97; Hon. Alderman, 2000). *Recreation:* music. *Address:* Cheney House, Cheney Hill, Heacham, King's Lynn, Norfolk PE31 7BX. *T:* (01485) 70477.

EVANS, Briant; *see* Evans, A. B.

EVANS, Christina Hambley; *see* Brown, Tina.

EVANS, Christopher; radio and television presenter; Chairman: Ginger Media Group, since 1997; Ginger Productions, since 1993; *b* 1 April 1966; *m* (marr. diss.); one *d*; *m* 2001, Billie Piper. Started broadcasting career with Piccadilly Radio, Manchester; *radio:* producer and presenter, GLR; presenter: Radio One Breakfast Show, BBC, 1995–97; Virgin Radio Breakfast Show, 1997–2001; *televison:* presenter, Power Station, BSB Channel; Channel 4: co-presenter, The Big Breakfast, 1992–93; devised, wrote and presented, Don't Forget Your Toothbrush, 1993 (BAFTA Award, 1995); TFI Friday,

1997–2000. Chm., Virgin Radio, 1997–2001. Radio Personality of the Year, TRIC, 1997. *Address:* Ginger Productions, 131–151 Great Titchfield Street, W1P 8DP. *T:* (020) 7577 7100.

EVANS, Rev. Prof. Christopher Francis, FBA 1991; MA; Professor of New Testament Studies, King's College, London, 1962–77, now Emeritus Professor, University of London; *b* 7 Nov. 1909; 2nd *s* of Frank and Beatrice Evans; *m* 1941, Elna Mary Pasco (*d* 1980), *d* of Walter and Elizabeth Burt; one *s*, and one step *d* (one step *s* decd). *Educ:* King Edward's Sch., Birmingham; Corpus Christi Coll., Cambridge. Asst Curate, St Barnabas, Southampton, 1934–38; Tutor Schol. Canc. Linc., 1938–44; Chaplain and Divinity Lecturer, Lincoln Training Coll., 1944–48; Chaplain, Fellow and Lecturer in Divinity, Corpus Christi Coll., Oxford, 1948–58, Emeritus Fellow, 1977; Lightfoot Prof. of Divinity in the University of Durham and Canon of Durham Cathedral, 1959–62; Vis. Fellow, Trevelyan Coll., Durham, 1982–83. Select Preacher, University of Oxford, 1955–57; Proctor in Convocation for University of Oxford, 1955–58; Exam. Chaplain: to Bishop of Bristol, 1948–58; to Bishop of Durham, 1958–62; to Archbishop of Canterbury, 1962–74; to Bishop of Lichfield, 1969–75. FKC, 1970. Hon. DLitt Southampton, 1977; Hon. DD Glasgow, 1987. *Publications:* Christology and Theology, 1961; The Lord's Prayer, 1963; The Beginning of the Gospel, 1968; Resurrection and the New Testament, 1970; (ed jtly) The Cambridge History of the Bible: vol. I, From the Beginnings to Jerome, 1970; Is 'Holy Scripture' Christian?, 1971; Explorations in Theology 2, 1977; The Theology of Rhetoric, 1988; Saint Luke, 1990; contribs to Journal of Theological Studies, Theology and Religious Studies, to Studies in the Gospels and to Christian Faith and Communist Faith. *Recreation:* fishing. *Address:* 4 Church Close, Cuddesdon, Oxford OX44 9HD. *T:* (01865) 874406.

EVANS, Dr (Christopher) Paul; Director, Urban Policy Unit, Department for Transport, Local Government and the Regions (formerly Department of the Environment, Transport and the Regions), since 1997; *b* 25 Dec. 1948; *s* of Colwyn and Margery Evans; *m* 1971, Margaret Beckett; two *d*. *Educ:* St Julian's High Sch., Newport; Trinity Coll., Cambridge (MA, DipArch, PhD). Department of the Environment, subseq. of the Environment, Transport and the Regions, now Department for Transport, Local Government and the Regions, 1975–: Private Sec. to Permanent Sec.,1978–80; Principal, 1980; Asst Sec., 1985; Under Sec., 1993. *Address:* Department for Transport, Local Government and the Regions, Eland House, Bressenden Place, SW1E 5DU. *T:* (020) 7944 3770; *e-mail:* paul.evans@dtlr.gsi.gov.uk.

EVANS, Sir Christopher (Thomas), Kt 2001; OBE 1995; PhD; CBiol, FIBiol; CChem, FRSC; Founder and Chairman, Merlin Ventures Ltd; *b* 29 Nov. 1957; *s* of Cyril and Jean Evans; *m* 1985, Judith Anne; two *s* two *d*. *Educ:* Imperial Coll., London (BSc 1979; ARCS 1979); Univ. of Hull (PhD). CBiol 1994, FIBiol 1994; CChem 1995; FRSC 1995. Postdoctoral Res., Univ. of Michigan, 1983; Alleix Inc., Toronto, 1984–86; Genzyme Biochemicals Ltd, Maidstone, 1986–87; Founder and Director: Enzymatix Ltd, 1987–; Chiroscience plc, 1992–; Celsis Internat. plc, 1992– (Chm., 1998–); Cerebrus Ltd, 1995–; Founder, Director and Chairman: Toad Innovations plc, 1993–; KinderTec Ltd, 1995–; Merlin Scientific Services Ltd, 1995–; Enviros Ltd, 1995–; Cyclacel Ltd, 1996–; Director: Microscience Ltd, 1997; Spacetrac Ltd, 1997. Founder: Merlin Fund, 1996; Merlin Biosciences Fund. Mem., Prime Minister's Council for Sci. and Technol. Hon. Prof., Univs of Manchester, Liverpool and Exeter, and Imperial Coll., London; Fellow, Bath Univ.; Hon. Fellow: UWCC, 1996; Univ. of Wales Swansea, 1996. Hon. DSc: Hull, 1995; Nottingham, 1995; East Anglia, 1998; Cranfield, 1998; Bath, 2000. Henderson Meml Medal, 1997; SCI Centenary Medal, 1998; RSC Interdisciplinary Medal, 1999 FRSA 1995. *Publications:* numerous scientific papers and patents. *Recreations:* wife, Rugby, gym, fly-fishing, electric guitar. *Address:* Merlin Biosciences, 12 St James's Square, SW1Y 4RB. *T:* (020) 7849 7765.

EVANS, Air Vice-Marshal Clive Ernest, CBE 1982; DL; Senior Directing Staff (Air), Royal College of Defence Studies, 1988–91, retired; *b* 21 April 1937; *s* of Leslie Roberts Evans and Mary Kathleen Butcher; *m* 1963, Therese Goodrich; one *s* one *d*. *Educ:* St Dunstan's Coll., Catford. Flying training, RAF, 1955–56; graduated as pilot, 1956, as qualified flying instr, 1960; served on Vampires, Jet Provosts, Canberras, Lightnings and F111s (exchange tour with USAF), 1960–72; RAF Staff Coll., 1972; PSO to Controller Aircraft, 1973; OC No 24 Sqn (Hercules), 1974–76; Nat. Defence Coll., 1976–77; DS RAF Staff Coll., 1977–79; Head of RAF Presentation Team, 1979–81; OC RAF Lyneham, 1981–83; RCDS, 1984; COS and Dep. Comdr, British Forces Falkland Is, 1985; Dep. Air Sec., 1985–88. Chm., MoD Retired Officer Selection Bds. Pres., Surrey Wing, ATC. DL Greater London, 1997. *Recreations:* reading, cricket, golf, gardening. *Address:* 43 Purley Bury Close, Purley, Surrey CR8 1HW. *T:* (020) 8660 8115. *Club:* Royal Air Force.

EVANS, Colin Rodney; Director, Weapon Systems Research Laboratory, Defence Science and Technology Organisation, Adelaide, 1989–91; *b* 5 June 1935; *s* of John Evans and Annie (*née* Lawes); *m* 1963, Jennifer MacIntosh; two *d*. *Educ:* Bridlington Sch.; Woolwich Polytechnic; Imperial Coll., London. BSc(Eng); HND; MIMechE. Scientific Officer, ARDE (now RARDE), 1959–60; Lectr, RNC, Greenwich, 1960–61; Scientific Officer, then Sen. Scientific Officer and PSO, ARDE, 1961–69; SO to Chief Scientist (Army), MoD, 1969–71; British Defence Staff, Washington, 1971–73; SPSO, RARDE, 1973–79; Dep. Dir, Scientific and Technical Intell., MoD, 1979–81; seconded to Sir Derek Rayner's study team on efficiency in govt, 1981; RCDS, 1982; Dep. Dir (1), RARDE, 1983–84; Asst Under Sec. of State, MoD, Dep. Dir (Vehicles) and Hd of RARDE (Chertsey), 1985–89. President: Kent Squash Rackets Assoc., 1992–; Maudslay Soc., 1993–99. *Recreations:* squash, tennis, bird watching, stamp collecting. *Address:* c/o HSBC, 105 Mount Pleasant, Tunbridge Wells TN1 1QP.

EVANS, Dr (Daniel) John (Owen); Head of Music Planning, BBC Radio 3, since 2000; *b* 17 Nov. 1953; *s* of John Leslie Evans and Avis Evans (*née* Jones). *Educ:* Gowerton Boys' Grammar Sch.; University Coll., Cardiff (BMus 1975; MA 1976; PhD 1984). ATCL 1974. First Res. Schol., Britten-Pears Liby and Archive, Aldeburgh, Suffolk, 1980–84; Music Producer, BBC Radio 3, 1985–89; Sen. Producer, BBC Singers, 1989–92; Chief Producer, Series, BBC Radio 3, 1992–93; Head of Music Dept, BBC Radio 3, 1993–97; Head of Classical Music, BBC Radio, 1997–2000. Artistic Director: Volte Face Opera, 1986–89; Covent Garden Chamber Orch., 1990–94; Mem., South Bank Music Adv. Panel, 1994–. Chm., IMZ Audio Gp, 1996–. Exec. Trustee, Peter Pears Award, 1989–92; Trustee, Masterprize composing competition, 1996–. Prix Italia Award and Charles Heidsieck Award, 1989; Royal Philharmonic Soc. Award, 1994; Sony Radio Award, 1997. *Publications:* (with D. Mitchell) Benjamin Britten: pictures from a life 1913–1976, 1978; (ed) Benjamin Britten: his life and operas, by Eric Walter White, rev. edn 1982; contributions to: A Britten Companion, 1984; A Britten Source Book, 1987; ENO, Royal Opera Hse and Cambridge Opera guides on Britten's Peter Grimes, Gloriana, The Turn of the Screw and Death in Venice. *Recreations:* theatre, musicals, cooking, entertaining, travel. *Address:* 114 Lauderdale Mansions, Lauderdale Road, Maida Vale, W9 1NF. *T:* (020) 7286 1876.

EVANS, Dr David; *see* Evans, Dr W. D.

EVANS, David, CBE 1992; Director-General, National Farmers' Union, 1985–96 (Deputy Director-General, 1984–85); Director, Federation of Agricultural Co-operatives UK, since 1995; *b* 7 Dec. 1935; *yr s* of William Price Evans and late Ella Mary Evans; *m* 1960, Susan Carter Connal, *yr d* of late Dr John Connal and Antoinette Connal; one *s* one *d*. *Educ:* Welwyn Garden City Grammar Sch.; University Coll. London (BScEcon). Joined Min. of Agriculture, Fisheries and Food, 1959; Private Sec. to Parliamentary Sec. (Lords), 1962–64; Principal, 1964; Principal Private Sec. to Ministers, 1970–71; Asst Sec., 1971; seconded to Cabinet Office, 1972–74; Under-Sec., MAFF, 1976–80; joined NFU as Chief Economic and Policy Adviser, 1981. Mem., EU Econ. and Social Cttee, 1998–. Director: ACT Ltd, 1996–; Drew Associates Ltd, 1997–. *Address:* 6 Orchard Rise, Kingston upon Thames, Surrey KT2 7EY. *T:* (020) 8942 7701.

EVANS, Rev. Canon David; Rector of Heyford with Stowe-Nine-Churches, 1989–2001, of Flore, 1996–2001, and Brockhall, 1997–2001; *b* Llanglydwen, Carmarthenshire, 15 Feb. 1937; *o s* of late Rev. W. Noel Evans, JP, and Frances M. Evans; *m* 1962, Jenifer Margaret (*née* Cross); three s. *Educ:* Sherborne; Keble Coll., Oxford (MA); Wells Theological Coll. (BD London). 2nd Lieut, Royal Signals, 1956–57. Minor Canon, Brecon Cath., and Asst Curate, Brecon St Mary with Battle, 1964–68; Bishop's Chaplain to Students, UC, Swansea, and Asst Curate, Swansea St Mary with Holy Trinity, 1968–71; Bishop of Birmingham's Chaplain for Samaritan and Social Work, 1971–75; Dir, Samaritans of Swansea, 1969–71, of Birmingham, 1971–75; Jt Gen. Sec., 1975–84, Gen. Sec., 1984–89, The Samaritans; Licensed Priest, Dio. of Oxford, 1975–89; RD of Daventry, 1995–2000. Chaplain, Northamptonshire Police, 1990–2001. Non-Residentiary Canon, Peterborough Cath., 1997–2001. Mem., Church in Wales Liturgical Commn, 1969–75. *Recreations:* music, railways, bird-watching. *Address:* Curlew River, The Strand, Starcross, Exeter EX6 8PA. *T:* (01626) 891712.

EVANS, Prof. David Alan Price, FRCP; Senior Consultant Physician (formerly Director of Medicine), Department of Medicine, Riyadh Armed Forces Hospital, Saudi Arabia, since 1983; Emeritus Professor of Medicine, Liverpool University, since 1994; *b* 6 March 1927; *s* of Owen Evans and Ellen (*née* Jones). *Educ:* Univ. of Liverpool (MD, PhD, DSc); Johns Hopkins Univ. RAMC, Jun. Med. Specialist, BMH Kure, Field Hosp. Korea, BMH Singapore and BMH Kinrara, Malaysia, 1953–55; Capt. RAMC, 1954–55. House Physician and House Surg. 1951–52, and Med. Registrar, 1956–58 and 1959–60, United Liverpool Hosps; Res. Fellow, Div. of Med. Genetics, Dept of Medicine, Johns Hopkins Hosp., 1958–59; Lectr 1960–62, Sen. Lectr 1962–68, Personal Chair, 1968–72, Dept of Medicine, Univ. of Liverpool; Prof. and Chm., Dept of Medicine and Dir, Nuffield Unit Medical Genetics, Univ. of Liverpool, 1972–83; Cons. Physician, Royal Liverpool Hosp. (formerly Royal Liverpool Infirmary) and Broadgreen Hosp., Liverpool, 1965–83. Visiting Professor: Karolinska Univ., Stockholm, 1968; Johns Hopkins Univ, 1972. Lectures: Poulson Meml, Oslo Univ., 1972; first Sir Henry Dale, and Medallist, Johns Hopkins Univ., 1972; first Walter Idris Jones, Univ. of Wales, 1974; Watson Smith, RCP, 1976. Member: BMA, 1951; Assoc. of Physicians of GB and Ireland, 1964. University of Liverpool: Roberts Prize, 1959; Samuels Prize, 1965; Thornton Prize, Eastern Psychiatric Assoc., 1964. Life Mem., Johns Hopkins Soc. of Scholars, 1972. Scientific Ed., Saudi Med. Jl, 1983–93; Mem. Edtl Bd, Internat. Jl of Clinical Pharmacology Res., 1980–. *Publications:* Genetic Factors in Drug Therapy, 1993; medical and scientific, principally concerned with genetic factors determining responses to drugs. *Address:* 28 Montclair Drive, Liverpool L18 0HA. *T:* (0151) 722 3112; C123 Riyadh Armed Forces Hospital, PO Box 7897, Riyadh 11159, Saudi Arabia. *T:* (1) 4791000, *Fax:* (1) 4784057; *e-mail:* dapevans@kfshhub.kfshrc.edu.sa.

EVANS, (David) Anthony; QC 1983; a Recorder of the Crown Court, since 1980; *b* 15 March 1939; *s* of Thomas John Evans, MD and May Evans; *m* 1974, Angela Bewley, *d* of John Clive Bewley, JP and Cynthia Bewley; two *d*. *Educ:* Clifton Coll., Bristol; Corpus Christi Coll., Cambridge (BA). Called to the Bar, Gray's Inn, 1965; in practice at the Bar, Swansea, 1965–84, London, 1984–. DTI Inspector, 1988–92. *Recreations:* sport of all kinds. *Address:* Carey Hall, Neath, W Glamorgan SA10 7AU. *T:* (01639) 643859; 8 Coleherne Mews, SW10 9EA. *T:* (020) 7370 1025. *Address:* 9–12 Bell Yard, WC2A 2JR. *T:* (020) 7400 1800. *Clubs:* Turf, MCC; Cardiff and County (Cardiff); Swansea Cricket and Football (Swansea); Downhill Only (Wengen).

EVANS, Prof. (David) Ellis, DPhil; FBA 1983; Jesus Professor of Celtic, University of Oxford, 1978–96, now Emeritus, and Fellow of Jesus College, 1978–96, now Emeritus; *b* Llanfynydd, 23 Sept. 1930; *yr s* of David Evans and Sarah Jane (*née* Lewis); *m* 1957, Sheila Mary, *er d* of David and Evelyn Jeremy; two *d*. *Educ:* Llandeilo Grammar Sch.; University Coll. of Wales, Aberystwyth (Hon. Fellow, 1992), and University Coll., Swansea (Hon. Fellow, 1985) (BA Wales, 1952; MA Wales, 1954); Jesus Coll., Oxford (Meyricke Grad. Scholar, 1952–54; DPhil 1962, MA 1978; Hon. Fellow, 1997). University College of Swansea: Asst Lectr in Welsh, 1957; Lectr, 1960; Reader, 1968; Prof. of Welsh Lang. and Lit. and Head of Dept of Welsh, 1974; Hon. Prof., 1990; Chm., Faculty of Medieval and Modern Langs, Oxford Univ., 1985–86. Lectures: Sir John Rhys Meml, British Acad., 1977; Rudolf Thurneysen Meml, Univ. of Bonn, 1979, 1994; O'Donnell, Univ. of Wales, 1980; G. J. Williams Meml, UC Cardiff, 1986; Sir Thomas Parry-Williams Meml, UCW, Aberystwyth, 1990. Pres. and Organizing Sec., Seventh Internat. Congress of Celtic Studies, Oxford, 1983; President: Cymdeithas Dafydd ap Gwilym, 1978–96; Irish Texts Soc., 1983–92 (Mem. Council, 1978–); Cambrian Archaeol Assoc., 1990–91; Vice President: N Amer. Congress of Celtic Studies, Ottawa, 1986; Nat. Liby of Wales, 1987–91 (Mem. Court and Council, 1974–91); Hon. Soc. of Cymmrodorion, 1999– (Mem. Council, 1984–98). Chairman: Welsh Dialect Studies Group, 1977–80; Council for Name Studies of GB and Ireland, 1980–84 (Mem. Council, 1962–); Member: Bd of Celtic Studies, Univ. of Wales, 1968–96; Internat. Cttee of Onomastic Sciences, 1975–; Welsh Arts Council, 1981–87; Royal Commn on Ancient and Hist. Monuments in Wales, 1984–96; Court, University of Wales, 1978–; Court, UC Swansea, 1980–; Court, Univ. of Wales Coll. of Cardiff, 1983–; UNESCO Internat. Cttee for the Study of Celtic Cultures, 1984– (Provisional Cttee, 1981–83); Celtic Commn, Austrian Acad. of Scis, 1987–98; Welsh Cttee, UFC, 1989–92. Editor, Lang. and Lit. Section, Bull. of Bd of Celtic Studies, 1972– (Editor-in-Chief, 1988–93); Editor-in-Chief, Studia Celtica, 1994–96; Mem. Editorial Bd: Geiriadur Prifysgol Cymru/A Dictionary of the Welsh Language, 1973–; Nomina, 1980–85; Welsh Acad. English-Welsh Dictionary, 1981–95. Hon. Mem., Druidic Order of Gorsedd of Bards, 1976–; Correspondant étranger, Etudes celtiques, 1982; For. Hon. Mem., Amer. Acad. of Arts and Scis, 1992; Hon. MRIA 2000 . Hon. DLitt Wales, 1993. *Publications:* Gaulish Personal Names: a study of some continental Celtic formations, 1967; Gorchest y Celtiaid yn yr Hen Fyd, 1975; (ed) Cofiant Agricola, Rheolwr Prydain, 1975; Termau Gwleidyddiaeth, 1976; (ed) Proc. 7th Internat. Congress of Celtic Studies, Oxford (1983), 1986; (ed with R. Brinley Jones) Cofio'r Dafydd, 1987; (consultant ed.) Dictionary of Celtic Mythology, ed James MacKillop, 1998; *contributed:* Swansea and its Region, ed W. G. V. Balchin, 1971; Homenaje a Antonio Tovar, 1972; (contrib.) The Anatomy of Wales, ed R. Brinley Jones, 1972; Indogermanisch und Keltisch, ed K. H. Schmidt, 1977; Aufstieg und Niedergang der römischen Welt, ed H. Temporini and W. Haase, 1983; Proc. 6th Internat. Congress of Celtic Studies, Galway (1979), 1983; Geschichte und Kultur der Kelten, ed K. H. Schmidt, 1986; Y Gwareiddiad Celtaidd, ed Geraint Bowen, 1987; Cell Gymysg o'r Genedlaethol, 1989; Britain 400–600: Language and History, 1990; Cof Cenedl, 1992; Lengua y Cultura en la Hispania Prerromana, 1993; (jtly) The Celtic Languages, ed M. J. Ball, 1993; Indogermanica et Caucasica, ed R. Bielmeier, 1994; The World of the Celts, ed M. Aldhouse Green, 1995; Die grosseren altkeltischen Sprachdenkmäler, 1996; Irish Texts Society: the first hundred years, 1998; contrib. colloquia and Festschriften; articles and revs in learned journals. *Recreations:* music, flowers. *Address:* 2 Price Close, Bicester, Oxon OX26 4JH. *T:* (01869) 246469.

EVANS, Air Chief Marshal Sir David (George), GCB 1979 (KCB 1977); CBE 1967 (OBE 1962); Bath King of Arms, 1985–99; Deputy Chairman, NAAFI, 1991–2001 (Director, 1984–2001; President of Council, 1981–83); *b* Windsor, Ont, Canada, 14 July 1924; *s* of William Stanley Evans, Clive Vale, Hastings, Sussex; *m* 1949, Denise Marson Williamson-Noble, *d* of late Gordon Till, Hampstead, London; two *d* (and two step *s*). *Educ:* Hodgson Sch., Toronto, Canada; North Toronto Collegiate. Served War, as Pilot, in Italy and NW Europe, 1944–45. Sqdn Pilot, Tactics Officer, Instructor, 1946–52; Sqdn Comdr, Central Flying Sch., 1953–55; RAF Staff Coll. course, 1955; OC No 11 (F) Sqdn, in Germany, 1956–57; Personal Staff Officer to C-in-C, 2nd Allied TAF, 1958–59; OC Flying, RAF, Coltishall, 1959–61; Coll. of Air Warfare course, 1961; Air Plans Staff Officer, Min. of Defence (Air), 1962–63; OC, RAF Station, Gutersloh, Germany, 1964–66; IDC, 1967; AOC, RAF Central Tactics and Trials Organisation, 1968–70; ACAS (Ops), 1970–73; AOC No 1 (Bomber) Group, RAF, 1973–76; Vice-Chief of Air Staff, 1976–77; C-in-C, RAF Strike Command, and UK NATO Air Forces, 1977–80; VCDS (Personnel and Logistics), 1981–83. Mil. Advr and Dir, BAe, 1983–92, and dir several BAe subsids; Chairman: BAe Canada Ltd, 1987–92; Arabian Gold, later Finngold Resources, plc, 1989–99; Dir, Intermin Resource Corp. Ltd, 1986 (Chm., 1989–93); Chairman: Officers Pensions Soc. Ltd; OPS Investment Co. Ltd; Trustees, OPS Widows' Fund; Dir, Airshow Canada. Queen's Commendation for Valuable Service in the Air (QCVSA), 1955. CIMgt (CBIM 1978; Mem. Bd of Companions, 1983–; Dep. Chm., 1989–). *Recreations:* rep. RAF at Rugby football and winter sports (President: RAF Winter Sports Assoc.; Combined Services Winter Sports Assoc.); has rep. Gt Brit. at Bobsleigh in World Championships, Commonwealth Games and, in 1964, Olympic Games. *Address:* Royal Bank of Canada Europe Ltd, 71A Queen Victoria Street, EC4V 4DE. *Club:* Royal Air Force.

EVANS, David Howard; QC 1991; a Recorder, since 1992; *b* 27 July 1944; *s* of David Hopkin Evans and Phoebe Dora Evans (*née* Reading); *m* 1973, Anne Celia Segall, *qv*; two *s*. *Educ:* London Sch. of Economics (BSc Econ 1965; MSc 1967); Wadham Coll., Oxford (BA 1970). Asst Economic Adviser, HM Treasury, 1967–68; called to the Bar, Middle Temple, 1972; Asst Recorder of the Crown Court, 1987. *Recreations:* tennis, swimming, listening to music. *Address:* Queen Elizabeth Buildings, Temple, EC4Y 9BS. *T:* (020) 7583 5766. *Clubs:* Roehampton; Riviera Golf.

EVANS, David John; Chairman, Broadreach Group (formerly Broadreach Services) Ltd, since 1990; *b* 23 April 1935; *s* of Violet Edith Evans and Arthur Thomas Evans; *m* 1956, Janice Hazel (*née* Masters); two *s* one *d*. *Educ:* Raglan Road School; Tottenham Tech. College. Professional cricketer (Glos and Warwicks) and footballer (Aston Villa); founded Exclusive Office Cleaning Ltd, 1960; Chm. and Man. Dir, Brengreen (Holdings), first co. with contract for refuse collection and street cleansing services (Southend-on-Sea Borough Council), 1960–86 (Brengreen (Holdings) acquired by BET plc, 1986). MP (C) Welwyn, Hatfield, 1987–97; contested (C) same seat, 1997. Parliamentary Private Secretary: to Minister of State for Industry, DTI, 1990–91; to Minister for Corporate Affairs, DTI, 1991–92; to Minister of State for Local Govt and Inner Cities, DoE, 1992–93; to Sec. of State for Wales, 1993. Member: Select Cttee on Deregulation, 1995–97; Exec., 1922 Cttee, 1993–97; Cons. Party Bd of Treasurers, 1996–97. Chm., Luton Town Football and Athletic Co. Ltd, 1984–89 (Dir, 1977–90); Mem. Council, Lord's Taverners, 1978–96 (Chm., 1982–84; Chm., Finance Cttee, 1992–96). *Address:* Little Radley, Mackerye End, Harpenden, Herts AL5 5DS. *T:* (01582) 460302. *Clubs:* MCC, Lord's Taverners.

EVANS, David Julian; Director, Eastern India, British Council, since 1999; *b* 12 May 1942; *s* of David Thomas Evans and Brenda Muriel Evans (*née* Bennett); *m* 1967, Lorna Madeleine Jacques; three *s*. *Educ:* Foster's Sch., Sherborne; Queen Mary Coll., London Univ. (BA Hist. 1963). Teacher, Rajasthan, VSO, 1963–64; Mgt Trainee, J. Sainsbury Ltd, 1964–65; British Council: seconded to VSO, 1965–67; Sierra Leone, 1967–70; Dep. Rep., Wales, 1970–72; educn trng course, UC, Cardiff, 1972–73; Enugu, Nigeria, 1973–76; Dir, Istanbul, 1976–80; Dir Gen's Dept, 1980–81; Dep. Dir, Germany, 1981–85; Dir, Youth Exchange Centre, 1985–88; Dir, Drama and Dance, 1988–89; Dep. Dir, Arts Div., and Head, Arts Projects, 1989–94; Dir, USA, and Cultural Counsellor, British Embassy, Washington, 1994–98; Hd of Global Advice, Facilities Gp, 1999. *Recreations:* the arts, history, travel, walking. *Address:* British Council, 5 Shakespeare Sarani, Calcutta 700071, India. *T:* (33) 2825370; *e-mail:* david.evans@in.britishcouncil.org.

EVANS, David Lloyd C.; *see* Carey Evans.

EVANS, David Marshall; QC 1981; **His Honour Judge Marshall Evans;** a Circuit Judge, since 1987; Designated Civil Judge, Liverpool Group, since 1998; *b* 21 July 1937; *s* of Robert Trevor and Bessie Estelle Evans; *m* 1961, Alice Joyce Rogers; two *s*. *Educ:* Liverpool Coll.; Trinity Hall, Cambridge (MA, LLM); Law Sch., Univ. of Chicago (JD). Called to the Bar, Gray's Inn, 1964. Teaching Fellow, Stanford University Law Sch., 1961–62; Asst Professor, Univ. of Chicago Law Sch., 1962–63; Lectr in Law, University Coll. of Wales, Aberystwyth, 1963–65; joined Northern Circuit, 1965; a Recorder, 1984–87. Mem., Vis. Cttee, Univ. of Chicago Law Sch., 1995–98. *Recreations:* walking, photography, visual arts, bird-watching, motorsport. *Address:* Queen Elizabeth II Law Courts, Derby Square, Liverpool L2 1XA. *T:* (0151) 473 7373. *Clubs:* Athenæum, Artists' (Liverpool).

EVANS, David Milne; Cabinet Office, 1977–81; *b* 8 Aug. 1917; *s* of Walter Herbert Evans, MSc and Florence Mary Evans (*née* Milne); *m* 1946, Gwynneth May (*née* Griffiths), BA. *Educ:* Charterhouse (Scholar); Gonville and Caius Coll., Cambridge (Schol.; Wrangler, Math. Tripos). Administrative Class, Home Civil Service (War Office), 1939. Served in Army (Major, RA), 1940–45. Asst Sec., 1954; Imp. Def. Coll., 1954; Asst Under-Sec. of State, MoD, 1967–77 (Under-Sec., CS Dept, 1972). Coronation Medal, 1953; Silver Jubilee Medal, 1977. *Address:* 1 Church Rise, Walston Road, Wenvoe, Cardiff, South Glamorgan CF5 6DE. *T:* (029) 2059 7129.

EVANS, David Morgan, FSA; General Secretary, Society of Antiquaries of London, since 1992; *b* 1 March 1944; *s* of David Morgan Evans and Elizabeth Margaret Evans (*née* Massey); *m* 1973, Sheena Gilfillan (*née* Milne); three *d*. *Educ:* Kings Sch., Chester; UC Cardiff (BA 1966). MIFA 1983; FSA 1987. Insp. of Ancient Monuments, Wales, 1969–77, England, 1977–92, DoE and English Heritage. *Publications:* articles on heritage and law, heritage management. *Recreations:* walking, gardening, Montgomeryshire, opera. *Address:* Society of Antiquaries of London, Burlington House, Piccadilly, W1J 0BE. *T:* (020) 7734 0193.

EVANS, Rt Rev. David Richard John; General Secretary, South American Mission Society, since 1993; an Assistant Bishop, diocese of Birmingham, since 1997; *b* 5 June 1938; *s* of William Henry Reginald Evans and Beatrix Catherine Mottram; *m* 1964, Dorothy Evelyn Parsons; one *s* two *d*. *Educ:* Caius College, Cambridge (Hons degree in Mod. Langs and Theology, 1963; MA 1966). Curate, Christ Church, Cockfosters, 1965–68; Missionary Pastor and Gen. Sec., Argentine Inter-Varsity Christian Fellowship, in Buenos Aires, Argentina, 1969–77; Chaplain, Good Shepherd Church, Lima, Peru, 1977–82; Bishop of Peru, 1978–88 (with delegated jurisdiction of Bolivia from 1980); Assistant Bishop: dio. of Bradford, 1988–93; dios of Chichester, Canterbury and Rochester, 1994–97. Internat. Co-ordinator, Evangelical Fellowship of the Anglican Communion, 1989–. *Publication:* En Diálogo con Dios, 1976. *Recreations:* golf, philately. *Address:* Allen Gardiner House, 12 Fox Hill, Birmingham B29 4AG. *T:* (0121) 472 5731; *e-mail:* gensec@samsgb.org.

EVANS, Hon. Sir (David) Roderick, Kt 2001; **Hon. Mr Justice Evans;** a Judge of the High Court, Queen's Bench Division, since 2001; *b* 22 Oct. 1946; *s* of Thomas James and Dorothy Evans; *m* 1971, Kathryn Rebecca Lewis; three *s* one *d*. *Educ:* Bishop Gore Grammar School, Swansea; University College London (LLB 1967; LLM 1968). Called to the Bar, Gray's Inn, 1970; a Recorder, 1987–92; QC 1989; Resident Judge: Merthyr Tydfil Crown Ct, 1994–98; Swansea Crown Ct, 1998–99; Cardiff Crown Court, 1999–2001; Recorder of Cardiff, 1999–2001. Mem., Criminal Cttee, Judicial Studies Bd, 1998–. *Recreations:* reading, walking. *Address:* Royal Courts of Justice, Strand, WC2A 2LL.

EVANS, Delyth; Member (Lab) Mid and West Wales, National Assembly for Wales, since May 2000; *b* 17 March 1958; *d* of David Gwynne Evans and Jean Margaret Evans; partner, Edward Richards; one *s* one *d*. *Educ:* Ysgol Gyfun Rhydfelen, Pontypridd; University Coll. of Wales, Aberystwyth (BA Hons French); Centre for Journalism Studies, Cardiff. Journalist, HTV Wales and BBC Radio 4, 1985–91; policy advr and speechwriter to John Smith, MP, Leader of Labour Party, 1992–94; Mgt Consultant, Adrian Ellis Associates, 1995–98; Special Advr to First Sec., Nat. Assembly for Wales, 1999–2000. *Recreations:* keeping fit, reading, the arts, family activities. *Address:* National Assembly for Wales, Cardiff Bay, Cardiff CF99 1NA. *T:* (029) 2089 8449.

EVANS, Derek; *see* Evans, John D.

EVANS, Eben, OBE 1976; Controller, Books Division, British Council, 1976–80; *b* 1 Nov. 1920; *s* of John Evans and Mary Evans; *m* 1946, Joan Margaret Howells; two *s* two *d*. *Educ:* Llandovery Grammar Sch.; University Coll. of Wales, Aberystwyth (BA 1948). Served War, 1941 46 (Army, Captain). Appointed to British Council, 1948; Cardiff, 1948–55; Thailand, 1955–59; Gambia, 1959–62; Ghana, 1962–64; Personnel Dept, London, 1964–68; Representative: Algeria, 1968–73; Yugoslavia, 1973–76. *Recreations:* walking, music. *Address:* Gorddinog Isaf, Llanfairfechan, Gwynedd LL33 0HS.

EVANS, Edward Stanley Price, FRTPI; City Planning Officer, Liverpool, 1974–84, retired; *b* 13 April 1925; *s* of late Bernard James Reuben Evans and of Nellie Evans; *m* 1948, Eva Magdalena Emma Fry; one *s* (and one *s* decd). *Educ:* Wolverhampton Grammar Sch.; Nottingham Coll. of Art and Crafts (DipTP). FRTPI 1966 (MTPI 1954). Chief Town Planning Officer, Norwich, 1957; City Planning Officer, Nottingham, 1966–74. Member: DoE Environmental Bd, 1977–79; DoE Panel of Local Plan Inspectors, 1985–94. *Recreations:* travel, gardening, bridge (social).

EVANS, Ven. Eifion; *see* Evans, Ven. D. E.

EVANS, Ellis; *see* Evans, D. E.

EVANS, Emrys; *see* Evans, W. E.

EVANS, Ena Winifred; Headmistress, King Edward VI High School for Girls, Birmingham, 1977–96; *b* 19 June 1938; *d* of Frank and Leonora Evans. *Educ:* The Queen's Sch., Chester; Royal Holloway Coll., Univ. of London (BSc); Hughes Hall, Cambridge (CertEd). Asst Mistress, Bolton Sch. (Girls' Div.), 1961–65; Bath High School (GPDST): Head of Mathematics Dept, 1965–72; Second Mistress, 1970–72; Dep. Head, Friends' Sch., Saffron Walden, 1972–77. Pres., GSA, 1987–88. Mem., Central Birmingham DHA, 1988–90. Mem. Council: Aston Univ., 1989–98; Queen's Coll., Birmingham, 1996–; Birmingham Univ., 2000–. FRSA 1986. Hon. DSc Aston, 1996. *Recreation:* music. *Address:* 26 Weoley Hill, Selly Oak, Birmingham B29 4AD.

EVANS, Fabyan Peter Leaf; His Honour Judge Fabyan Evans; a Circuit Judge, since 1988; *b* 10 May 1943; *s* of late Peter Fabyan Evans and Catherine Elise Evans; *m* 1967, Karen Myrtle (*née* Balfour), *g d* of 1st Earl Jellicoe; two *s* one *d*. *Educ:* Clifton College. Called to the Bar, Inner Temple, 1969. A Recorder, 1985–88. Resident Judge, Middx Guildhall Crown Court, 1995–. Chairman: Area Criminal Justice Liaison Cttee, London and Surrey, 1997–2000; London Area Criminal Justice Strategy Cttee, 2000–. *Recreations:* golf, sailing, singing. *Club:* Brooks's.

EVANS, Hon. Gareth (John), AO 2001; QC (Vic and ACT) 1983; President and Chief Executive, International Crisis Group, since 2000; *b* 5 Sept. 1944; *m* 1969, Merran Anderson; one *s* one *d*. *Educ:* Melbourne Univ. (law and arts); Oxford Univ. (PPE). Lectr in Law, 1971–74, Sen. Lectr, 1974–76, Melbourne Univ.; practising Barrister, 1977–78. Senator (Lab) for Victoria, 1978–96; Shadow Attorney-General, 1980–83; Attorney-General, 1983–84; Minister for Resources and Energy, 1984–87, for Transport and Communications, 1987–88, for Foreign Affairs, 1988–96; Dep. Leader of Govt in Senate, 1987–93, Leader, 1993–96; MP (ALP) Holt, Vic, 1996–99; Dep. Leader of Opposition and Shadow Treasurer, Australia, 1996–98. *Publications:* (ed) Labor and the Constitution, 1972; (ed) Law, Politics and the Labor Movement, 1980; (ed) Labor Essays, 1980, 1981, 1982; (jtly) Australia's Constitution, 1983; (jtly) Australia's Foreign Relations, 1991, 2nd edn 1995; Co-operating for Peace, 1993. *Recreations:* reading, writing, opera, golf, football. *Address:* 149 Avenue Louise, Level 16, Brussels 1050, Belgium.

EVANS, Gareth Robert William; QC 1994; a Recorder, since 1993; *b* 19 Jan. 1947; *s* of David M. J. Evans and Megan Evans; *m* 1971, Marion Green; one *s* one *d*. *Educ:* Caerphilly Grammar Sch.; Birmingham Poly.; LLB Hons London. Called to the Bar, Gray's Inn, 1973. *Recreations:* Rugby, reading poetry, outdoor pursuits. *Address:* 5 Fountain Court, Steelhouse Lane, Birmingham B4 6DR. *T:* (0121) 606 0500.

EVANS, George James; Sheriff of Tayside, Central and Fife at Cupar, since 1997; *b* 16 July 1944; *s* of Colin Evans and Caroline Catherine Kennedy MacPherson Harris; *m* 1973, Lesley Jean Keir Cowie; two *d*. *Educ:* Ardrossan Acad.; Glasgow Univ. (MA Hons); Edinburgh Univ. (LLB). Advocate, 1973; Standing Jun. Counsel, Dept of Energy, Scotland, 1982; Sheriff of Glasgow and Strathkelvin at Glasgow, 1983–97. *Publications:* contribs to legal periodicals. *Recreations:* art, literature, history, choral and individual singing, tennis. *Address:* Catherine Bank, Bridgend, Ceres KY15 5LS. *T:* (01334) 652121.

EVANS, Dr Gillian Rosemary, FRHistS; Lecturer in History, University of Cambridge, since 1980; *b* Birmingham, 26 Oct. 1944; *d* of late Arthur Raymond Evans and Gertrude Elizabeth (*née* Goodfellow). *Educ:* King Edward VI High Sch. for Girls, Birmingham; St Anne's Coll., Oxford (MA 1966; DipEd 1967); Grad. Centre for Medieval Studies, Univ. of Reading (PhD 1974); DLitt Oxon 1983; LittD Cantab 1983. FRHistS 1978. Asst Mistress, Queen Anne's Sch., Caversham, 1967–72; Res. Asst, Univ. of Reading, 1974–78; Lectr in Theol., Univ. of Bristol, 1978–80; British Acad. Res. Reader, 1986–88. Mem. Council, Univ. of Cambridge, 1997–. Vis. lectureships in USA and Canada and various European countries. Consulting Editor: Dictionary of Biblical Interpretation in English; Encyclopaedia of Medieval, Renaissance and Reformation Christian Thought; Jl Hist. of Biblical Interpretation; Jl of ADR, Mediation and Negotiation. Member: Faith and Order Adv. Gp, Gen. Synod of C of E, 1986–96; Archbp's Gp on Episcopate, 1987–90; English Anglican–Roman Catholic Cttee, 1997–. Officer, Council for Acad. Freedom and Acad. Standards, 1994–; Mem., Cttee for Auctores Britannici Medii Aevi, Brit. Acad., 1980–. Hon. DLitt: Nottingham Trent, 2001; Southampton Inst. of Higher Educn, 2001. FRSA 1996. *Publications* include: Anselm and Talking About God, 1978; Anselm and a New Generation, 1980; Old Arts and New Theology, 1980; The Mind of St Bernard of Clairvaux, 1983; Alan of Lille, 1983; Augustine on Evil, 1983; The Anselm Concordance, 1984; The Logic and Language of the Bible, 2 vols, 1984–85; The Thought of Gregory the Great, 1986; (ed) Christian Authority, 1988; Problems of Authority in the Reformation Debates, 1992; Philosophy and Theology in the Middle Ages, 1994; The Church and the Churches, 1994; Method in Ecumenical Theology, 1996; The Reception of the Faith, 1997; Calling Academia to Account, 1998; The Medieval Epistemology of Error, 1998; Discipline and Justice in the Church of England, 1999; Bernard of Clairvaux, 2000; (ed) Managing the Church, 2000; (ed) A History of Pastoral Care, 2000; (ed) The Medieval Theologians, 2001; (jtly) Universities and Students, 2001; contribs to jls, etc on medieval intellectual history, ecumenical theology, higher educn issues. *Recreation:* painting. *Address:* Faculty of History, University of Cambridge, West Road, Cambridge CB3 9EF. *T:* (01223) 335331. *Clubs:* Royal Commonwealth Society, Nikaean.

EVANS, Dame Glynne; *see* Evans, Dame M. G. D.

EVANS, Gwynfor; Honorary President, Plaid Cymru, since 1982 (President, 1945–81, Vice-President, 1943–45); *b* 1 Sept. 1912; *s* of Dan Evans and Catherine Mary Richard; *m* 1941, Rhiannon Prys Thomas; four *s* three *d*. *Educ:* Gladstone Road Elementary Sch.; County Sch., Barry; University of Wales, Aberystwyth (Fellow, 1994); St John's Coll., Oxford. Qual. Solicitor, 1939. Hon. Sec. Heddychwyr Cymru (Welsh Pacifist movement), 1939–45; Chm. Union of Welsh Independents, 1954. MP (Plaid Cymru) Carmarthen, July 1966–1970 and Oct. 1974–1979. Contested (Plaid Cymru) Carmarthen, 1979 and 1983. Mem., Carmarthen CC, 1949–74. Past Mem. Welsh Broadcasting Council. Hon. Fellow, Trinity Coll., Carmarthen, 1997. Hon. LLD Wales, 1973; Soc. of Cymmrodorion Medal, 1984. *Publications:* Plaid Cymru and Wales, 1950; Rhagom i Ryddid, 1964; Aros Mae, 1971; Wales can Win, 1973; Land of My Fathers, 1974; A National Future for Wales, 1975; Diwedd Prydeindod, 1981; Bywyd Cymro, 1982; Seiri Cenedl, 1986; Welsh Nation Builders, 1987; Pe Bai Cymru'n Rhydd, 1989; Fighting for Wales, 1990; Heddychiaeth Gristnogol yng Nghymru, 1991; Cymru o Hud, 1992; For the Sake of Wales, 1996; The Fight for Freedom, 2000; Gwlad yr Hud, 2000. *Address:* Talar Wen, Pencarreg, Llanybydder, Dyfed SA40 9QQ. *T:* (01570) 480907.

EVANS, Harold Matthew; author and editor; *b* 28 June 1928; *s* of late Frederick and late Mary Evans; *m* 1st, 1953, Enid (marr. diss. 1978), *d* of late John Parker and of Susan Parker; one *s* two *d*; 2nd, 1981, Christina Hambley Brown (*see* Tina Brown); one *s* one *d*. *Educ:* St Mary's Road Central Sch., Manchester; Durham Univ. BA 1952, MA Dunelm 1966. Ashton-under-Lyne, Lancs, Reporter Newspapers, 1944–46 and 1949; RAF, 1946–49; Durham Univ., 1949–52; Manchester Evening News, 1952; Commonwealth Fund Fellow in Journalism, Chicago and Stanford Univs, USA, 1956–57; Asst Ed, Manchester Evening News, 1958–61; Ed., Northern Echo, 1961–66; Editor-in-Chief, North of England Newspaper Co., 1963–66; Sunday Times: Chief Asst to Editor, 1966; Managing Editor, 1966; Editor, 1967–81; Editor, The Times, 1981–82; Editor-in-Chief, Atlantic Monthly Press, NY, 1984–86; Founding Editor, Condé-Nast Traveler Magazine, 1986–90; Editl Dir, 1984–86, Contributing Editor, 1986–, US News and World Report, Washington; Vice-Pres. and Sen. Editor, Weidenfeld & Nicolson, NY, 1986–87; Pres. and Publisher, Random House Trade Gp, 1990–97; Editl Dir and Vice-Chm., NY Daily News Inc., US News & World Report, Atlantic Monthly, and Fast Company, 1998–99. Member, Executive Board: Times Newspapers Ltd, 1968–82 (Mem. Main Bd, 1978); International Press Inst., 1974–80; Director: The Sunday Times Ltd, 1968–82; Times Newspapers Ltd, 1978–82. Writer and Presenter, Evans on Newspapers, BBC TV, 1981. Hon. Vis. Prof. of Journalism, City Univ., 1978; Vis. Prof., Inst. of Public Affairs, Duke Univ., N Carolina, 1984. Fellow, Freedom Forum. Hon. FSIAD. Internat. Editor of the Year, 1975; Gold Medal Award, Inst. of Journalists, 1979; Hood Medal, RPS, 1981; Editor of the Year, 1982; Lotos Club Medal, NY, 1993. DUniv Stirling, 1982; Hon. DCL Durham, 1998. *Publications:* The Active Newsroom, 1961; Editing and Design (five volumes): vol. 1, Newsman's English, 1972; vol. 5, Newspaper Design, 1973; vol. 2, Newspaper Text, 1974; vol. 3, Newspaper Headlines, 1974; vol. 4, Pictures on a Page, 1977; Good Times, Bad Times, 1983, 3rd edn 1994; (jointly): We Learned To Ski, 1974; The Story of Thalidomide, 1978; (ed) Eye Witness, 1981; How We Learned to Ski, 1983; Front Page History, 1984; The American Century, 1998. *Recreations:* swimming, music, chess, Sunday in the park with George and Isabel. *Address:* Suite 1143, Little, Brown & Co., 1271 Avenue of the Americas, New York, NY 10020, USA. *Clubs:* Garrick, Royal Automobile; Century, Yale (New York).

EVANS, Sir Haydn T.; *see* Tudor Evans.

EVANS, Prof. (Henry) John, CBE 1997; PhD; FRCPE, FRCSE; FIBiol; FRSE; Director, Medical Research Council Human Genetics (formerly Clinical and Population Cytogenetics) Unit, Edinburgh, 1969–94; *b* 24 Dec. 1930; *s* of David Evans and Gwladys Evans (*née* Jones); *m* 1st, 1957, Gwenda Rosalind (*née* Thomas) (*d* 1974); 2nd, 1976, Roslyn Rose (*née* Angell); four *s*. *Educ:* Llanelli Boys Grammar Sch.; UCW, Aberystwyth (BSc, PhD 1955). FRSE 1969; FIBiol 1982; FRCPE 1988; FRCSE 1992. Res. Scientist, MRC Radiobiology Unit, Harwell, 1955–65, Head of Cell Biology Section, 1962–65; Vis. Fellow, Brookhaven Nat. Laboratory, Brookhaven, NY, USA, 1960–61; Prof. of Genetics, Univ. of Aberdeen, 1965–69. Chm., Assoc. Radiation Research, 1970–72; Mem., MRC Biological Res. Bd, 1968–72; Council Mem., MRC, 1978–82. Member: Cttee on Biological Effects of Ionizing Radiation, US Nat. Acad. Sci., 1972; Genetic Manipulation Adv. Gp, 1976–80; DHSS Cttee, Mutagenicity of Foods and Chemicals, 1978–96; Nat. Radiology Protection Bd, 1982–94; Lister Scientific Adv. Council, 1982–90; Sci. Council, Internat. Agency for Research on Cancer, 1982–86 (Chm., 1985–86); Scientific Cttee, CRC, 1983–95 (Chm., 1990–95; Vice Counsellor, 1995–); Chief Scientist Cttee, SHHD, 1983–87; Council, Imperial Cancer Res. Fund, 1985–90; Cttee on Med. Aspects of Radiation in the Environment, DHSS, 1985–94; Scientific Rev. Cttee, Alberta Heritage Foundn for Med. Res., 1986–98; Internat. Commn for Protection of Envmt from Mutagens and Chemicals, 1986–91; Radiation Waste Management Adv. Cttee, DoE, 1988–92; Human Genome Orgn, 1990–95; Hong Kong Cancer Inst., 1994–. Member, Board of Governors: Beatson Inst. Cancer Res., 1985–99 (Chm., 1991–99); Lister Inst. of Preventive Medicine, 1988–; Inveresk Res. Foundn, 1988–89; Caledonian Res. Foundn, 1989– (Chm., 1999–); Inst. Cancer Res., 1990–94. Hon. Prof., Univ. of Edinburgh; Vis. Prof., Kyoto Univ., Japan, 1981; Boerhaave Prof., Univ. of Leiden, 1994–95. Hon. Fellow: UK Clinical Cytogenetics Soc., 1984; UK Environmental Mutagen Soc., 1984; Russian Med. Genetics Soc., 1992. Hon. DSc Edinburgh, 1996. Lectures include: Douglas Lea Meml, 1979; Railford Robinson, Adelaide, 1981; Honeyman-Gillespie, 1984; Woodhull, Royal Instn, 1992. Lilly Prize, 1985, Ballantyne Prize, 1990, RCPE; Frank Rose Meml Prize, CRC, 1993; Frits Sobels Award, Eur. Envmtl Mutagen Soc., 1995. *Publications:* papers on radiation cytology, mutagenesis, chromosome structure and human cytogenetics in various internat. jls; editor of various books and jls in the field of genetics and radiobiology. *Recreations:* golf, music, fishing. *Address:* 45 Lauder Road, Edinburgh EH9 1UE. *T:* (0131) 667 2437. *Club:* New (Edinburgh).

EVANS, (Henry) Nicholas; a District Judge (Magistrates' Courts) (formerly Metropolitan Stipendiary Magistrate), since 1994; *b* 7 Nov. 1945; 3rd *s* of Gilbert Arthur Evans and Muriel Elaine Evans (*née* Oxford); *m* 1980, Diana Claire Smith; one *s* one *d*. *Educ:* Highgate Sch. Called to the Bar, Middle Temple, 1971, Lincoln's Inn, *ad eundem*, 1975. *Address:* Bow Street Magistrates' Court, WC2E 7AS. *Club:* Bar Yacht.

EVANS, Prof. (Hubert) Roy, PhD; FREng; FICE, FIStructE; Vice-Chancellor, University of Wales, Bangor, since 1995; *b* 27 May 1942; *s* of David James Evans and Sarah Ann Evans; *m* 1966, Eira John; two *s* two *d*. *Educ:* Llandysul Grammar Sch.; University Coll. of Swansea (BSc, MSc; PhD 1967). Res. Fellow, University Coll. of Swansea, 1966–67; Asst Engr, Freeman Fox & Partners, 1967–69; University College, Cardiff, later University of Wales College of Cardiff: Lectr, 1969–75; Sen. Lectr, 1975–79; Reader, 1979–83; Prof. of Civil and Structural Engrg, 1983–95; Hd of Dept, 1984–95; Dean, 1987–88; Dep. Principal, 1990–93 and 1994–95. Vis. Prof., Univ. of W Virginia, 1983. FREng (FEng 1992). Hon. Fellow: UC, Swansea, 1995; Univ. of Wales, Cardiff, 1998. Telford Premium, 1976, 1979 and 1987, George Stephenson Medal, 1980, ICE; Henry Adams Bronze Medal, IStructE, 1976; Medal, Acad. of Scis, Czech Republic, 1995. *Publications:* numerous contribs in field of structural engrg and plate structures. *Recreations:* hill-walking, gardening, cricket, soccer. *Address:* 16 Victoria Terrace, Beaumaris, Isle of Anglesey LL58 8BU. *T:* (01248) 810261.

EVANS, Huw Prideaux, CB 1993; Financial Advisor, International Monetary Fund, since 2000; *b* 21 Aug. 1941; *s* of late Richard Hubert Evans and Kathleen Annie Evans; *m* 1966, Anne (*née* Bray) (marr. diss.); two *s*. *Educ:* Cardiff High Sch.; King's Coll., Cambridge (MA); London Sch. of Econs and Polit. Science (MSc). Economist: HM Treasury, 1964–72; European Commn, 1972–73; Asst Econ. Sec., Hong Kong Govt, 1973–75; Sen. Econ. Adviser, 1976–79, Under Sec., 1980–89, Dep. Sec., 1989–94, HM Treasury; UK Exec. Dir, IMF and World Bank, and Econ. Minister, Washington, 1994–97; Special Adviser: Bank of England, 1997–98; FSA, 1998–99. *Address:* International Monetary Fund, 700 19th Street NW, Washington, DC 20007, USA. *Club:* Oxford and Cambridge.

EVANS, Iain Richard, FCA; Chairman, LEK Consulting (formerly The L/E/K Partnership), since 1991; *b* 17 May 1951; *s* of late Alan Caradog Crawshay Evans and Barr Hargreave Bell (*née* Dalglish); *m* 1st, 1973, Zoe Dorothy Valentine; two *s*; 2nd, 1988, Jayne Doreen Almond; one *d*. *Educ:* John Lyon Sch.; Rotherham Sixth Form Coll.; Bristol Univ. (BSc Hons 1972); Harvard Univ. Grad. Sch. of Business Admin (MBA with High Distinction, Baker Scholar, Loeb Rhoades Fellow, 1978). ACA 1975, FCA 1977. Arthur Young McClelland Moores & Co., 1972–76; Bain & Co., 1978–83, Partner 1982; Founding Partner, L/E/K Partnership, 1983. Non-exec. Dir, Hyder (formerly Welsh Water Authy, then Welsh Water) plc, 1989–98 (Dep. Chm., 1992–93; Chm., 1993–98). *Recreations:* tennis, golf, fishing, marine paintings. *Address:* LEK Consulting, Adelphi Building, 1–11 John Adam Street, WC2N 6BW. *T:* (020) 7930 1244. *Club:* Stoke Poges Golf.

EVANS, Dr (Ian) Philip, OBE 1999; FRSC; Head Master, Bedford School, since 1990; *b* 2 May 1948; *s* of Joseph Emlyn Evans and Beryl Evans; *m* 1972, Sandra Veronica Waggett; two *s*. *Educ:* Ruabon Boys' Grammar Sch.; Churchill College, Cambridge (BA 1970; MA 1973; 1st cl. hons Nat. Scis Tripos); Imperial College of Science and Technology (PhD, DIC). CChem, FRSC 1997. Post-Doctoral Fellow, Res. Sch. of Chemistry, ANU, 1973–75; Asst Master, St Paul's Sch, 1975–90 (Head of Chemistry Dept, 1984–90). Member: Schs Exams and Assessment Council, 1991–93; SCAA, 1993–97; Qualifications and Curriculum Authority, 1997–99. Chief Examr, A-level Chem., Univ. of London Schs Exam. Bd, 1987–90. Mem. Council, Nat. Trust, 1999–2001. *Publications:* (with S. V. Evans) Anyone for Science?, 1994; contribs to books; papers in learned jls. *Recreations:* music, cricket, poetry, wine. *Address:* Bedford School, De Parys Avenue, Bedford MK40 2TU. *T:* (01234) 362200. *Club:* East India.

EVANS, James, CBE 1995; Chairman, Bristol United Press, 1997–2000; *b* 27 Nov. 1932; *s* of late Rex Powis Evans and Louise Evans; *m* 1961, Jette Holmboe; two *d*. *Educ:* Aldenham School; St Catharine's College, Cambridge (MA). Called to the Bar, Gray's Inn, 1959; admitted Solicitor, 1972; recalled to the Bar, Gray's Inn, 1991, Bencher, 1993. Commissioned 26th Field Regt RA, 1951–53. Legal Dept, Kemsley Newspapers Ltd, 1956–59; practised at Bar, 1959–65; Legal Adviser: Thomson Newspapers Ltd, 1965–73; Times Newspapers Ltd, 1967–73; Sec. and Mem. Exec. Bd, 1973–78, Dir, 1978–86, Thomson Organisation Ltd; Dir, 1977–81, Chm., 1980–81, Times Newspapers Ltd; Chm., Thomson Withy Grove Ltd, 1979–84; International Thomson Organisation plc: Dir, 1978; Jt Dep. Man. Dir, 1982–84; Man. Dir and Chief Exec., 1985–86; Chm., 1986; Chm. and Chief Exec., 1982–84, Dir, 1982–96, Thomson Regional Newspapers Ltd; Dir, Liverpool Daily Post and Echo Ltd, 1996–97. Dir, 1983–90, Chm., 1987–89, Press Assoc.; Dir, Reuters Holdings, 1984–92. Mem., Monopolies and Mergers Commn, 1989–97. Dir, Press Standards Bd of Finance, 1990–2000. Trustee, Visnews, 1985–95. Member: Council, Newspaper Soc., 1984–2001 (Vice-Pres., 1998–99; Pres., 1999–2000); Press Council, 1987–90; Council of Legal Educn, 1992–94. Mem., Home Office Deptl Cttee on Official Secrets Act (Franks Cttee), 1971. *Recreations:* various. *Address:* 6 Fishpool Street, St Albans, Herts AL3 4RT. *T:* (01727) 853064. *Club:* Garrick.

EVANS, James Humphrey R.; *see* Roose-Evans.

EVANS, Jane Elizabeth; *see* Collins, J. E.

EVANS, Jeremy David Agard; Director, Public Affairs, British Rail, 1990–97; *b* 20 June 1936; *s* of Arthur Burke Agard Evans and Dorothy (*née* Osborne); *m* 1964, Alison Mary (*née* White); one *s* two *d*. *Educ:* Whitgift Sch.; Christ's Coll., Cambridge (BA Hons). Ministry of Power: Asst Principal, 1960–64 (Private Sec. to Parly Sec., 1963–64); Principal, 1964–69; Sloan Fellow, London Business Sch., 1969–70; Principal, 1970–73, and Private Sec. to Minister for Industry, 1971–73, DTI; Asst Sec., DTI, 1973, Dept of

Energy, 1974 (Offshore Supplies Office, 1973); seconded as Sec. to BNOC on its foundn, 1976–78; a Man. Dir, 1978; Man. Dir Corporate Develt, and Sec., 1980–82, Mem. Bd 1981–82; Dir, Britoil plc, 1982–88. Mem., GDC, 1989–94. Gov., St Piers Sch., 1998–. *Recreations:* opera, ski-ing, walking, golf. *Address:* Dormans House West, Dormans Park, East Grinstead, West Sussex RH19 2LY. *T:* (01342) 870518.

EVANS, (Jeremy) Roger; Member (C) Havering and Redbridge, London Assembly, Greater London Authority, since 2000; *b* 23 June 1964; *s* of Ronald Evans and Doris Valentine Evans. *Educ:* Univ. of Sheffield (BSc Hons 1985); Westminster Univ. (CPE); Inns of Court School of Law. Various managerial rôles, Royal Mail, 1985–95; law student, 1995–98; called to Bar, Middle Temple, 1997; legal advr, Spring Gp, 1998–2000. Mem. (C) Waltham Forest LBC, 1990– (Leader, Cons. Gp, 1994–98). *Recreations:* badminton, swimming, public speaking. *Address:* Greater London Authority, Romney House, 43 Marsham Street, SW1P 3PY.

EVANS, Jillian; Member (Plaid Cymru) Wales, European Parliament, since 1999; *b* 8 May 1959; *d* of Horace Burge and Valma Burge; *m* 1992, Syd Morgan. *Educ:* UCW, Aberystwyth (BA Hons Welsh); MPhil CNAA, 1986. Res. Asst, Poly. of Wales, Treforest, 1980–85; self-employed administrator, 1986–89; Admin./Public Affairs Officer, 1989–93, Project Officer, 1994–97, NFWI Wales; Wales Regl Organiser, Child, Infertility Support Network, 1997–99. *Address:* 72 Tyntyla Road, Llwynypia, Rhondda CF40 2SR. *T:* (01443) 434232.

EVANS, John; *see* Evans, D. J. O.

EVANS, Prof. John; *see* Evans, Prof. H. J.

EVANS, Dr John; *see* Evans, Dr N. J. B.

EVANS, Prof. John, PhD; Professor of Chemistry, University of Southampton, since 1990; *b* 2 June 1949; *s* of Leslie and Eleanor Evans; *m* 1972, Hilary Jane Fulcher; two *d. Educ:* Rutherford Grammar Sch., Newcastle upon Tyne; Imperial Coll. London (BSc 1970; ARCS); Sidney Sussex Coll., Cambridge (PhD 1973). Research Fellow, Princeton Univ., 1973–74; Cambridge University: ICI Res. Fellow, 1974–75; Royal Soc. Pickering Res. Fellow, 1975–76; Southampton University: Res. Fellow, 1976–78; Lectr, 1978–84; Sen. Lectr, 1984–87; Reader, 1987–90; Dean of Science, 1997–2000. Science and Engineering Research Council: Chm., Synchrotron Radiation Cttee, 1991–94; UK Deleg. to Council of European Synchrotron Radiation Facility, 1991–94 (Mem., Scientific Adv. Cttee, 1995–98); Mem., Facilities Commn, 1993–94; Vice Chm., Diamond Scientific Adv. Cttee, 2000–. Royal Society of Chemistry: Sec. and Treas., Dalton Div., 1993–96; Council Mem., 1994–97. Tilden Lectr, RSC, 1994. Editor, Inorganic Chemistry Series, Oxford Chemistry Primers Text Book Series, 1991–2000. Meldola Medal, RSC, 1978. *Publications:* contrib. scientific jls, incl. Jl RSC. *Recreations:* cycling, watching football, travel. *Address:* Department of Chemistry, University of Southampton, Southampton SO17 1BJ. *T:* (023) 8059 3307.

EVANS, Maj.-Gen. John Alan Maurice, CB 1989; Vice-Chairman, AEI Cables, 1993–96 (Managing Director, 1992–93); *b* 13 Feb. 1936; *s* of John Arthur Mortimer Evans and Margaret (*née* Lewis); *m* 1958, Shirley Anne May; one *s* one *d. Educ:* Grammar schs in Wales and England; RMA Sandhurst; Trinity Coll., Cambridge (MA). Various Staff and RE appointments; CO, 22 Engr Regt, 1976–78; Comd, Berlin Inf. Bde, 1980–82; RCDS, 1983; Comdt, RMCS, Shrivenham, 1985–87; Sen. Army Mem., RCDS, 1988–90. Col Comdt, RE, 1991–96. With GEC Wire and Cables Gp, 1990. Pres., Inst. of Royal Engineers, 1990–93. *Recreations:* music, reluctant DIY, travel. *Address:* East Mead, Homington Road, Coombe Bissett, Salisbury SP5 4ND. *Club:* Army and Navy.

EVANS, John Alfred Eaton; Headmaster, Brentwood School, 1981–93; *b* 30 July 1933; *s* of John Eaton Evans and Millicent Jane Evans (*née* Righton); *m* 1958, Vyvyan Margaret Mainstone; two *s* one *d. Educ:* Bristol Grammar Sch.; Worcester Coll., Oxford. MA (Lit. Hum.). Nat. Service, 1952–54, commnd RAOC. Assistant Master: Blundell's Sch., 1958–63; Rugby Sch., 1963–73; Housemaster: Phillips Acad, Andover, Mass, USA, 1968–69; Rugby Sch., 1973–81. Chm., London Div., HMC, 1993. Member selection panels: CMS, 1983–91; Admiralty, 1985–96; Army Scholarship Bd, 1990–; ABM, 1992–. Chm. Trustees, Crescent Sch., Rugby, 1968–78; Governor: Colfe's Sch., 1993–; Prior Park Coll., 1998–; Mem. Adv. Bd, St Christopher's Sch., Burnham-on-Sea, 1994–97. FRSA 1983. *Publications:* various articles on community service in education. *Recreations:* cricket, Rugby fives, piano, singing, drama, walking. *Address:* Manor Farm House, Easton, near Wells, Somerset BA5 1EB. *Clubs:* East India, Devonshire, Sports and Public Schools; Vincent's (Oxford); Jesters; Cryptics Cricket.

EVANS, Prof. John Davies, OBE 1996; FBA 1973; Director, University of London Institute of Archæology, and Professor of Archæology in the University of London, 1973–89, now Professor Emeritus; *b* 22 Jan. 1925; *o s* of Harry Evans and Edith Haycocks; *m* 1957, Evelyn Sladdin. *Educ:* Liverpool Institute High Sch. (open schol. in English to Pemb. Coll.); Pembroke Coll., Cambridge. War Service, 1943–47. BA 1948, MA 1950, PhD 1956, LittD 1979; Dr *hc* Lyon 2, 1983. Fellow of British Institute of Archæology at Ankara, 1951–52; Research Fellow of Pembroke Coll., Cambridge, 1953–56; Prof. of Prehistoric Archæology, London Univ., 1956–73. President: Prehistoric Soc., 1974–78; Council for British Archæology, 1979–82; Member: Permanent Council, Internat. Union of Prehistoric and Protohistoric Scis, 1975– (Pres., 1982–86); Royal Commn on Historical Monuments (England), 1985–92; Chairman: Area Archaeol Adv. Cttee for SE England, 1975–79; Treasure Trove Reviewing Cttee, Dept of Nat. Heritage, 1988–96. FSA 1955 (Dir, 1975–80, 1983–84, Pres., 1984–87); Member: German Archaeological Inst., 1979– (Corr. Mem., 1968–79); Instituto Italiano di Preistoria e Protostoria, 1983–. *Publications:* Malta (Ancient Peoples and Places Series), 1959; (with Dr A. C. Renfrew) Excavations at Saliagos, near Antiparos, 1968; The Prehistoric Antiquities of the Maltese Islands, 1971; papers and reports in archæological journals. *Recreations:* walking, listening to music. *Address:* Melbury Cottage, 5 Love Lane, Shaftesbury, Dorset SP7 8BG.

EVANS, (John) Derek, CBE 2001; Chief Conciliator, Advisory, Conciliation and Arbitration Service, 1992–2001; *b* 11 Sept. 1942; *s* of late Leslie and Mary Evans; *m* 1964, Betty Wiseman; two *d. Educ:* Roundhay Sch., Leeds. FIPD. Dept of Employment, 1962–74; Advisory, Conciliation and Arbitration Service: Midlands, 1974–78; Head Office, 1978–82; Dir, Wales, 1982–88; Dir, Adv. Services, 1988–91; Dir, Conciliation and Arbitration, 1991–92. Industrial Fellow, Kingston Univ., 1994. *Recreations:* golf, driving, music. *Address:* 2 Tamarisk Rise, Wokingham, Berks RG40 1WG. *T:* (0118) 978 9655. *Club:* Sand Martins Golf (Berks).

EVANS, His Honour John Field; QC 1972; a Circuit Judge, 1978–93; *b* 27 Sept. 1928; 2nd *s* of late John David Evans, Llandaff, and Lucy May Evans (*née* Field). *Educ.* Cardiff High Sch.; Exeter Coll., Oxford (MA). Pilot Officer, RAF, 1948–49. Called to Bar, Inner Temple, 1953; Dep. Chm., Worcestershire QS, 1964–71; a Recorder of the Crown Court, 1972–78.

EVANS, Sir John G.; *see* Grimley Evans.

EVANS, John Kerr Q.; *see* Quarren Evans.

EVANS, John Marten Llewellyn, CBE 1956 (MBE 1945); JP; Official Solicitor to the Supreme Court of Judicature, 1950–70; *b* 9 June 1909; *s* of late Marten Llewellyn Evans, Solicitor, and Edith Helena (*née* Lile); *m* 1943, Winifred Emily, *y d* of late Austin Reed; one *s* one *d. Educ:* Rugby Sch.; Trinity Coll., Oxford. Admitted Solicitor, 1935; Legal Asst to the Official Solicitor, 1937. Served War of 1939–45, Major RA. Senior Legal Asst to the Official Solicitor, 1947; Asst Master in Lunacy, 1950. Vice-Chm., Austin Reed Group Ltd, 1969–77. Master of Worshipful Company of Cutlers, 1967–68. JP City of London, 1969. *Recreations:* the theatre, cricket, golf, tennis.

EVANS, John Robert, CC 1978; OOnt 1991; MD, DPhil, FRCP, FRCPC, FRSC; Vice Chairman, NPS-Allelix Inc., since 1999; Chairman: Torstar Corporation, since 1993; Alcan Inc., since 1995; *b* 1 Oct. 1929; *s* of William Watson Evans and Mary Thompson; *m* 1954, Gay Glassco; four *s* two *d. Educ:* Univ. of Toronto (MD); University Coll., Oxford (Rhodes Schol.; DPhil; Hon. Fellow, 1990). MACP; FRCP 1980. Jun. interne, Toronto Gen. Hosp., 1952–53; Hon. Registrar, Nat. Heart Hosp., London, 1955; Asst Res.: Sunnybrook Hosp., Toronto, 1956; Toronto Gen. Hosp., 1957; Ontario Heart Foundn Fellow, Hosp. for Sick Children, Toronto, 1958; Chief Res. Physician, Toronto Gen. Hosp., 1959; Research Fellow, Baker Clinic Research Lab., Harvard Med. Sch., 1960; Markle Schol. in Acad. Med., Univ. of Toronto, 1960–65; Associate, Dept of Med., Faculty of Med., Univ. of Toronto, 1961–65; Asst Prof., 1965–66; Dean, Faculty of Med., McMaster Univ., 1965–72, Vice-Pres., Health Sciences, 1967–72; Pres., Univ. of Toronto, 1972–78 (Pres. Emeritus, 1995); Dir, Dept of Population, Health and Nutrition, IBRD, Washington, 1979–83; CEO, Allelix Inc. (Biotechnology), 1983–89. Member: Council RCP (Can.), 1972–78; Inst. of Medicine, Nat. Acad. Sci., USA, 1972– (Mem. Council, 1976–80); Adv. Cttee Med. Res., WHO, 1976–80. Chairman: Trustees, Rockefeller Foundn, 1987–95; Canada Foundn for Innovation, 1997–; Walter & Duncan Gordon Charitable Foundn, Toronto, 1997–2000. Dir, MDS Health Gp Ltd, Toronto. Fellow, LSHTM, 1988. Hon. LLD: McGill, 1972; Dalhousie, 1972; McMaster, 1972; Queen's, 1974; Wilfred Laurier, 1975; York, 1977; Yale, 1978; Toronto, 1980; Calgary, 1996; Hon. DSc: Meml Univ. of Newfoundland, 1973; Montreal, 1977; Royal Mil Coll., Kingston, 1989; DU: Ottawa, 1978; Limbourg, 1980; Hon. DHL Johns Hopkins, 1978. *Recreations:* ski-ing, fishing, farming. *Address:* 58 Highland Avenue, Toronto, ON M4W 2A3, Canada.

EVANS, John Roger W.; *see* Warren Evans.

EVANS, Sir John (Stanley), Kt 2000; QPM 1990; DL; Chief Constable, Devon and Cornwall Constabulary, since 1989; *b* 6 Aug. 1943; *s* of late William Stanley and of Doris Evans; *m* 1965, Beryl Smith; one *s* one *d. Educ:* Wade Deacon Grammar Sch., Widnes; Liverpool Univ. (LLB Hons 1972). Liverpool City, then Merseyside Police, 1960–80; Asst Chief Constable, Greater Manchester Police, 1980–84; Dep. Chief Constable, Surrey Constabulary, 1984–88. Pres., ACPO, 1999–2000 (Mem., various cttees incl. Terrorism and Allied Matters). Chm., Police Athletic Assoc., 1996–. DL Devon, 2000. *Recreations:* most sport (ran London Marathon, 1988, 1989), service and charitable activities. *Address:* Police Headquarters, Middlemoor, Exeter, Devon EX2 7HQ. *T:* (01392) 452011.

EVANS, Very Rev. (John) Wyn, FSA, FRHistS; Dean and Precentor of St Davids Cathedral, since 1994; *b* 4 Oct. 1946; *o s* of late Ven. David Eifion Evans and Iris Elizabeth (*née* Gravelle); *m* 1997, Diane Katherine, *d* of George and Kathleen Baker. *Educ:* Ardwyn Grammar Sch., Aberystwyth; University Coll., Cardiff (BA); St Michael's Theol Coll., Llandaff (BD); Jesus Coll., Oxford. FSA 1989; FRHistS 1994. Deacon 1971, priest 1972; Curate, St Davids, 1971–72; Minor Canon, St Davids Cathedral, 1972–75; grad. student, Jesus Coll., Oxford, 1975–77, permission to officiate Oxford diocese, 1975–77; Diocesan Adviser on Archives, St Davids, 1976–82; Rector, Llanfallteg with Castell Dwyran and Clunderwen with Henllan Amgoed and Llangan, 1977–82; Exam. Chaplain to Bishop of St Davids, 1977; Diocesan Warden of Ordinands, 1978–83; Chaplain and Lectr, Trinity Coll., Carmarthen, 1982–90; Diocesan Dir of Educn, 1982–92; Hon. Canon, St Davids Cathedral, 1988–90, Canon (4th Cursal), 1990–94; Dean of Chapel, Trinity Coll., Carmarthen, 1990–94; Head, Dept of Theology and Religious Studies, 1991–94. Mem. Court, Nat. Liby of Wales, 1998–. Mem., Rep. Body, Ch in Wales, 1999–. Mem., Gorsedd of Bards (White Robe), 1997–. *Publications:* (with Roger Worsley) St Davids Cathedral 1181–1981, 1981; contribs to jls, including Jl Welsh Ecclesiastical History, Carmarthen Antiquary, Diwinyddiaeth. *Recreations:* reading, music, antiquities. *Address:* The Deanery, The Close, St Davids, Dyfed SA62 6RH. *T:* (01437) 720202. *Club:* Oxford and Cambridge.

EVANS, (John) Wynford, CBE 1995; Chairman: Bank of Wales, 1995–2001 (Director, since 1989); South Wales Electricity plc (formerly South Wales Electricity Board), 1984–95; *b* 3 Nov. 1934; *s* of late Gwilym Everton and Margaret Mary Elfreda Evans; *m* 1957, Sigrun Brethfeld; three *s. Educ:* Llanelli Grammar Sch.; St John's Coll., Cambridge (MA). FBCS. Served RAF (Flying Officer), 1955–57. IBM, 1957–58; NAAFI, W Germany, 1959–62; Kayser Bondor, 1962–63; various posts, inc. Computer and Management Services Manager, S Wales Electricity Bd, 1963–76; ASC, Henley, 1968; Dep. Chm., London Electricity Bd, 1977–84. Dir, 1992 Nat. Garden Festival Ltd, 1987–88. Member: Milton Keynes IT Adv. Panel, 1982–84; Welsh Regional Council, CBI, 1984–99 (Chm., 1991–93); Council, CBI, 1988–97. Chm., SE Wales Cttee, Industry Year 1986. Dep. Chm., Prince of Wales Cttee, 1989–96. Mem., 1985–90, Dep. Chm., 1995–2001, Nat. Trust Cttee for Wales; Member: Hon. Soc. of Cymmrodorion, 1978–; Civic Trust Bd for Wales, 1984–88; Welsh Language Bd, 1988–89; Council, Nat. Mus. and Galls of Wales, 2000–. Dir, Welsh Nat. Opera Ltd, 1988–93; Trustee and Dep. Chm., Cardiff Bay Opera House Trust, 1994–97; Trustee, Nat. Botanic Garden of Wales, 1998–2001. Mem. Council Europa Nostra, 1996– (Chm., Heritage Awards Panel, 2001–). Mem. Court, Cranfield Inst. of Technol., 1980–88; Governor, Polytechnic of Wales, 1987–88. Liveryman, Tin Plate Workers alias Wireworkers' Co.; Mem., Welsh Livery Guild. High Sheriff, S Glamorgan, 1995–96. Hon. Druid, Gorsedd of Bards of Island of Britain, 1999–. FInstD 1988; FRSA. *Recreations:* fishing, cross-country ski-ing, golf, riding. *Address:* Hafod Wen, St Fagans, Cardiff CF5 6EF. *Clubs:* Flyfishers', London Welsh; Cardiff and County, Radyr Golf (Cardiff).

EVANS, John Yorath Gwynne; Deputy Director (Air), Royal Aircraft Establishment, 1972–76, retired; medical engineering consultant, 1980–88; *b* 10 Feb. 1922; *s* of Randell and Florence Evans, Carms; *m* 1948, Paula Lewis, *d* of late Roland Ford Lewis; two *s* one *d. Educ:* UCW Aberystwyth. Royal Aircraft Estabt, 1942; attached to RAF, Germany, 1945–46; Supt Wind Tunnels, RAE Bedford, 1958; Head of Aerodynamics Dept, RAE, 1971. *Publications:* contrib. various sci. and techn. jls. *Recreations:* sailing, travel, reading. *Address:* Rushmoor Cottage, Tilford, Farnham, Surrey GU10 2EP. *T:* (01252) 792275.

EVANS, Jonathan; Company Secretary of Consignia (formerly Secretary to the Post Office), since 1999; *b* 21 April 1952; *s* of Alec H. Evans and Beryl Evans; *m* 1978, Gillian

Eileen Blundell; one *s* two *d*. *Educ:* King Edward VI Sch., Nuneaton; Durham Univ. (BSc Maths 1974). Joined Post Office, 1974; mgt trainee, 1974–76; Ops Exec., Midlands Postal Bd, 1976–82; Personal Asst to Chm., 1982–84; Asst Head Postmaster, Leicester, 1984–86; Asst Personnel Dir, PO Counters Ltd, 1986–92; Dir of Orgn, 1992–93; Gen. Manager, Midlands Region, 1993–95; Network Dir, 1995–99. *Recreations:* music, campanology, cricket. *Address:* c/o Consignia, 148 Old Street, EC1V 9HQ. *T:* (020) 7250 2298. *Club:* Warwickshire County Cricket.

EVANS, Jonathan Peter; solicitor; Member (C) Wales, European Parliament, since 1999; *b* 2 June 1950; *s* of David John Evans and late Harriet Mary Drury; *m* 1975, Margaret Thomas; one *s* two *d*. *Educ:* Lewis Sch., Pengam; Howardian High Sch., Cardiff; Coll. of Law, Guildford and London. Admitted Solicitor of Supreme Court, 1974; Leo Abse & Cohen, Cardiff: Partner, 1974–92; Man. Partner, 1987–92; Dir of Insce, Eversheds, 1997–99, consultant, 1999–; Dir, NFU Mutual Insce Gp, 2000–. Dep. Chm., Tai Cymru (Welsh Housing Corp.), 1988–92. Contested (C): Ebbw Vale, Feb. and Oct., 1974; Wolverhampton NE, 1979; Brecon and Radnor, 1987. MP (C) Brecon and Radnor, 1992–97; contested (C) Brecon and Radnorshire, 1997. PPS to Minister of State, NI Office, 1992–94; Parly Under-Sec. of State, DTI, 1994–95 (Minister for Corporate Affairs, 1994–95, for Competition and Consumer Affairs, 1995); Parly Sec., Lord Chancellor's Dept, 1995–96; Parly Under-Sec. of State, Welsh Office, 1996–97; Chief Cons. Party Spokesman for Wales, 1997–98. Sec., Cons. Parly Agric. Cttee, 1992–94; Vice-Chm., Cons. Parly Party Orgn Cttee, 1992–94; Hon. Consultant on law and policy, NSPCC, 1991–94; Dep. Chm., Welsh NSPCC Council, 1991–94; Pres., Cardiff and Dist NSPCC, 1992–94. FRSA 1995. *Recreations:* watching Rugby Union, cricket and ice-hockey; reading. *Address:* c/o European Parliament, Rue Wiertz, 1047 Brussels, Belgium. *Clubs:* Farmers; Cardiff and County (Cardiff); London Welsh RFC.

EVANS, Rt Rev. Kenneth Dawson; Assistant Bishop of Guildford, 1986–90; *b* 7 Nov. 1915; *s* of late Dr Edward Victor Evans, OBE; *m* 1939, Margaret (*d* 2001), *d* of J. J. Burton; one *s*. *Educ:* Dulwich Coll.; Clare Coll., Cambridge. Ordained, 1938; Curate of: St Mary, Northampton, 1938–41; All Saints', Northampton, 1941–45; Rector of Ockley, 1945–49; Vicar of Dorking, 1949–63; Archdeacon of Dorking and Canon Residentiary of Guildford Cathedral, 1963–68; Bishop Suffragan of Dorking, 1968–85. Hon. Canon of Guildford, 1955–63 and 1979–85. Mem., Bishop's Finance Commn, 1957. *Address:* 3 New Inn Lane, Burpham, Guildford, Surrey GU4 7HN. *T:* (01483) 567978.

EVANS, Kim; Executive Director of Arts, Arts Council of England, since 1999; *b* 3 Jan. 1951; *d* of Jon Evans and Gwendolen (*née* McLeod). *Educ:* Putney High Sch.; Our Lady of Sion Convent; Warwick Univ. (BA Hons Eng. and Amer. Lit.); Leicester Univ. (MA Hons Victorian Lit. and Society). Press Asst, Design Council, 1973–74; Asst Editor, Crafts mag., 1974–76; Chief Sub-Editor, Harpers & Queen, 1976–78; South Bank Show, LWT: researcher, 1978–82; Producer/Dir, 1982–89; BBC Television: Producer, Omnibus, 1989–92; Asst Hd, Music and Arts, 1992–93; Head of Music and Arts, subseq. of Arts, BBC TV, then of BBC Arts and Classical Music, 1993–99. Huw Wheldon Award for Best Arts Prog., BAFTA, 1993. *Recreations:* travelling, dreaming, cinema, reading. *Address:* Arts Council of England, 14 Great Peter Street, SW1P 3NQ. *T:* (020) 7333 0100, *Fax:* (020) 7973 6590.

EVANS, Lewis Jones; Chairman, Post Office Board, Wales and the Marches, 1997–2000; *b* 14 Feb. 1938; *s* of Evan Jones Evans and Jane Jones Evans (*née* Morgans); *m* 1961, Siân, *e d* of Rev. Harri Hughes, Penclawdd; two *s* one *d*. *Educ:* Tregaron County Sch.; Trinity Coll., Carmarthen (DipEd). FCIB 1986. Schoolmaster, 1960–62; Lloyds Bank plc, 1962–90: branch and head office appts incl. Manager, Llanelli Br., 1970–73; Sen. Manager, Newcastle upon Tyne, 1982–84; Regl Dir and gen. mgt, 1984–90; Dir, Lloyds Develt Capital Ltd, Alex Lawrie Factors Ltd, and Internat. Factors Ltd, 1989–90; Dep. Man. Dir, 1990–91, Man. Dir, 1991–96, Girobank; Dir, Alliance and Leicester Building Soc., 1991–96. Mem. Council, British Bankers' Assoc., 1992–96. Member: Wales Tourist Bd, 1996–; Wales Adv. Bd, BITC, 1996–2000 (Chairman: Professional Firms Gp, Cardiff, 1996–99; Community Loan Fund for Wales, 1997–2000; Mem. Council, UK Local Investment Fund, 1997–2000); Chm., Cardiff Business Link, 1998–. Member: Council, Royal Nat. Eisteddfod of Wales, 1999– (Chm., Resources and Finance Cttee, 1999–); Council, CBI for Wales, 1997–2000; Dir, Cardiff Bay Opera Trust Ltd, 1994–97. Jt Chm., Action Res. Project on the Underachievement of Boys, 1996–; Chm., NPFA Cymru, 2000–. Hon. Vice-Pres., London Welsh Trust and Assoc., 1994–2000. Hon. Treas. and Mem. Council, Univ. of Wales, Lampeter, 1993–99; University of Wales: Mem. Court, 1996–; Mem. Audit Cttee, 1997–; Gov., Univ. of Glamorgan, 1999–. CIMgt 1994; FRSA 1994. Liveryman, Welsh Livery Guild, 1994. Hon. Druid, Gorsedd of Bards, Isle of Britain, 1994. *Recreations:* family, music, sport. *T:* (01446) 773890, *Fax:* (01446) 775529. *Clubs:* Royal Automobile; Cardiff and County (Cardiff); Crawshays Rugby Football; Glamorgan CC.

EVANS, Lindsay; *see* Evans, W. L.

EVANS, Lloyd Thomas, AO 1979; DSc, DPhil; FRS 1976; FAA; Hon. Research Fellow, Commonwealth Scientific and Industrial Research Organization Division of Plant Industry, Canberra, Australia, since 1992; *b* 6 Aug. 1927; *s* of C. D. Evans and G. M. Fraser; *m* 1954, Margaret Honor Newell; two *s* one *d* (and one *d* decd). *Educ:* Wanganui Collegiate Sch., NZ; Univ. of NZ (BSc, MAgrSc, DSc); Univ. of Oxford (DPhil). FAA 1971. Rhodes Scholar, Brasenose Coll., Oxford, 1950–54; Commonwealth Fund Fellow, Calif Inst. of Technol., 1954–56; res. scientist, CSIRO Div. of Plant Industry, Canberra, 1956–92 (Chief, Div. of Plant Industry, 1971–78). National Acad. of Sciences (USA) Pioneer Fellow, 1963; Overseas Fellow, Churchill Coll., Cambridge, 1969–70; Vis. Fellow, Wolfson Coll., Cambridge, 1978. President: ANZAAS, 1976–77; Aust. Acad. of Science, 1978–82. Member, Board of Trustees: Internat. Foundn for Sci., Stockholm, 1982–87; Internat. Rice Res. Inst., Philippines, 1984–89; Internat. Center for Improvement of Wheat and Maize, 1990–95. Mem., Norwegian Acad. of Sci. and Letters, 1990. Hon. Member: Royal Soc., NZ, 1986; RASE, 1987. Hon. LLD Canterbury, 1978. *Publications:* Environmental Control of Plant Growth, 1963; The Induction of Flowering, 1969; Crop Physiology, 1975; Daylength and the Flowering of Plants, 1976; Wheat Science: today and tomorrow, 1981; Policy and Practice, 1987; Crop Evolution, Adaptation and Yield, 1993; Feeding the Ten Billion: plants and population growth, 1998; more than 200 scientific papers in jls. *Recreations:* windsurfing, chopping wood, Charles Darwin. *Address:* 3 Elliott Street, Canberra, ACT 2612, Australia. *T:* (2) 62477815.

EVANS, Hon. Dame Lois (Marie) B.; *see* Browne-Evans.

EVANS, Dame (Madelaine) Glynne (Dervel), DBE 2000; CMG 1992; DPhil; HM Diplomatic Service; Ambassador to Portugal, since 2001; *b* 23 Aug. 1944. *Educ:* Univ. of St Andrews (MA Hons 1st cl. 1966); University Coll. London (DPhil 1971). Res. Fellow, Centre for Latin American Studies, Univ. of Liverpool, 1969–70; Vis. Lectr, Coll. of William and Mary, Williamsburg, 1970–71; Second Sec., FCO, 1971; Buenos Aires, 1972; First Sec., FCO, 1975; on loan to UN Secretariat, NY, 1978; First Sec., UKMIS NY, 1979; First Sec., subseq. Counsellor, FCO, 1982; Counsellor and Dep. Hd of Mission, Brussels, 1987; Head of UN Dept, FCO, 1990–96; Res. Associate, IISS, 1996–97; Ambassador to Chile, 1997–2000; Dist. Vis. Scholar, NATO Defense Coll., Rome, 2000–01. *Publications:* The International Response to Crises in the African Great Lakes, 1997; articles on internat. peacekeeping. *Address:* c/o Foreign and Commonwealth Office, SW1A 2AH.

EVANS, Prof. Margaret, PhD; FLA; Pro Vice-Chancellor, De Montfort University, since 2000; *b* 29 April 1946; *d* of late Roderick McKay Campbell McCaskill and Gladys May McCaskill (*née* Ireland); *m* 1st, 1967, Anthony Howell (marr. diss.); two *d*; 2nd, 1978, Alan Fearn (marr. diss.); 3rd, 1985, Herbert Kinnell (marr. diss.); 4th, 1989, Gwynne Evans. *Educ:* Nottingham Poly. (BA CNAA); Leicester Poly. (MBA CNAA); Loughborough Univ. (PhD); Nottingham Univ. (PGCE). FLA 1994; FIInfSc 1995. Librarian: Nottingham City Libraries, 1964–65; Notts Co. Libraries, 1967–69; Sutton in Ashfield Libraries, 1971–73; antiquarian bookseller, 1973–75; Loughborough University: Lectr, 1979–88; Sen. Lectr, 1988–94; Prof. of Information Studies, 1994–2000; Hd of Dept of Information and Liby Studies, 1994–98; Dean, Sci. Faculty, 1998–2000. *Publications:* (ed) Planned Public Relations for Libraries, 1989; (ed) The Learning Experiences of Overseas Students, 1990; (ed) Managing Fiction in Libraries, 1991; All Change?: public library management strategies for the 1990's, 1991; (jtly) Managing Library Resources in Schools, 1994; (jtly) Continuity and Innovation in the Public Library, 1996; (jtly) Marketing in the Not-for-profit Sector, 1997; reports and articles. *Recreations:* Jamie, Lizzie, animals. *Address:* De Montfort University, The Gateway, Leicester LE1 9BH. *T:* (0116) 257 7010.

EVANS, Mark; QC 1995; a Recorder, since 1996; *b* 21 March 1946; *s* of Rev. Clifford Evans and Mary (*née* Jones); *m* 1971, Dr Barbara Skew (marr. diss. 1995); one *s* one *d*. *Educ:* Christ Coll., Brecon; King's Coll., London (LLB Hons). Called to the Bar, Gray's Inn, 1971; practice in Bristol, 1973–; founded St John's Chambers, 1978. *Recreations:* music, vintage cars. *Address:* Queen Square Chambers, 56 Queen Square, Bristol BS1 4PR. *T:* (0117) 921 1966; 24 Old Buildings, Lincoln's Inn, WC2A 3UJ. *T:* (020) 7831 8912. *Club:* Savages (Bristol).

EVANS, Mark Armstrong, CVO 1994; Director, British Council, Austria, 1996–2000; *b* 5 Aug. 1940; *s* of late Charles Tunstall Evans, CMG, Birmingham, and Kathleen Armstrong, Newcastle; *m* 1965, Katharine, *d* of Alfred Bastable, Brecon; one *s* one *d*. *Educ:* Marlborough Coll.; Clare Coll., Cambridge (BA 1962; MA 1966); Moscow State Univ.; Bristol Univ. (PGCE 1964). Head, Russian and German, Chichester High Sch. for Boys, 1964–69; apptd to British Council, 1969; Bahrain, 1969–71; Frankfurt, 1971–73; MECAS, Lebanon, 1973–74; Dir, UAE in Dubai, 1974–77; temp. posting, Kabul, 1977; Asst Dir, Educnl Contracts, 1977–79; Dep. Rep. and Cultural Attaché, France, 1979–85; Head, Office Services, 1985–88; Dir, Canada, and Cultural Counsellor, Ottawa, 1988–92; Dir, and Cultural Counsellor, Russia, 1992–96. Mem., RSAA, 1972; Adv. Bd, Österreich Institut, 1999–. Gov., RNLI, 1995. Mem., Bluebell Railway Preservation Soc., 1997–. *Recreations:* building models, gardening, household chores. *Address:* High Field, North Chailey, Sussex BN8 4JD. *Club:* Union (Cambridge).

See also D. M. A. Stokes.

EVANS, Prof. Martin John, PhD, ScD; FMedSci; FRS 1993; Director, Cardiff School of Biosciences, and Professor of Mammalian Genetics, University of Cardiff, since 1999; *b* 1 Jan. 1941; *s* of Leonard Wilfred Evans and Hilary Joyce (*née* Redman); *m* 1966, Judith Clare Williams, MBE; two *s* one *d*. *Educ:* St Dunstan's Coll., Catford; Christ's Coll., Cambridge (BA Pt II in Biochem., MA); PhD London 1969; ScD Cambridge, 1996. University College London: Res. Assistant, Dept of Anatomy and Embryology, 1963–66; Asst Lectr, 1966–69; Lectr, 1969–78; Cambridge University: Lectr, Dept of Genetics, 1978–91; Reader, 1991–94; Prof. of Mammalian Genetics, 1994–99. Discovered embryonic stem cells, 1981. Founder FMedSci 1998. *Publications:* numerous contribs to scientific works. *Recreations:* family, walking, golf, Norfolk terriers. *Address:* Cardiff School of Biosciences, Biomedical Sciences Building, Cardiff University, Museum Avenue, PO Box 911, Cardiff CF10 3US. *T:* (029) 2087 4120.

EVANS, Michael; *see* Evans, T. M.

EVANS, Michael Nordon, CMG 1964; Permanent Secretary, Ministry of Health and Housing, Kenya, 1960–64, retired; *b* 27 April 1915; *s* of late Christmas and Lilian Margaret Louise Evans, Tunbridge Wells; *m* 1st, 1939, Mary Stockwood; one *d*; 2nd, 1951, Mary Josephine Suzette van Vloten; one *d*. *Educ:* Eastbourne Coll.; Queens' Coll., Cambridge. Apptd District Officer in Colonial Administrative Service, Kenya, 1939; African Courts Officer, Kenya, 1953; Dep. Commissioner for Local Government, 1954; Permanent Sec., 1958. *Recreation:* now reading only. *Address:* Hugon Lodge, 13 Hugon Road, Claremont, Western Cape, 7700, Republic of South Africa. *Clubs:* Hawks (Cambridge); Kelvin Grove (Cape Town).

EVANS, Michael Stephen James; Defence Editor, The Times, since 1998; *b* 5 Jan. 1945; *s* of Reginald and Beatrix Evans; *m* 1971, Robyn Nicola Coles; three *s*. *Educ:* Christ's Hosp.; QMC, London Univ. (BA Hons English). Reporter, 1968–69, News Editor, Loughton office, 1969–70, Express and Independent; Daily Express: Reporter, Action Line consumer column, 1970–72; Reporter, 1972–77; Home Affairs Correspondent, 1977–82; Defence and Diplomatic Correspondent, 1982–86; The Times: Whitehall Correspondent, 1986–87; Defence Correspondent, 1987–98. *Publications: fiction:* A Crack in the Dam, 1978; False Arrest, 1979; *non-fiction:* Great Disasters, 1981; South Africa, 1987; The Gulf Crisis, 1988. *Recreations:* cricket, golf, tennis, playing piano. *Address:* The Times, 1 Pennington Street, E1 9XN. *T:* (020) 7782 5921.

EVANS, Mostyn; *see* Evans, Arthur M.

EVANS, Nicholas; *see* Evans, H. N.

EVANS, Nicholas Henry Robert; Director General, Defence Logistics (Finance and Business Planning), Ministry of Defence, since 2000; *b* 21 July 1950; *s* of Ivor Robert Evans and Esther Jane Evans; *m* Sally Vera Carter; two *s*. *Educ:* Reading Sch.; St John's Coll., Oxford (MA Hons Modern History). Joined MoD, 1971; posts in RN, Army and Air Force policy, planning and finance, incl. Private Sec. to Under-Sec. of State for the Army, 1974–75, and Civil Advr to GOC NI, 1975–77; Asst Private Sec. to Sec. of State, 1981–84; Head: Naval Manpower and Trng, 1985–87; Mgt Services Div., 1987–90; Next Steps Implementation Team, 1990–92; Resources and Progs (Air), 1992–95; Asst Under-Sec. of State (Quartermaster), 1995–99; Exec. Dir (Finance), Defence Procurement Agency, 1999–2000. *Recreations:* keeping the house up, the garden down and the children in. *Address:* Defence Logistics Organisation, Spur 6, Ensleigh, Bath BA1 5AB. *T:* (1225) 467016.

EVANS, Nigel Martin; MP (C) Ribble Valley, since 1992; *b* 10 Nov. 1957; *s* of late Albert Evans and of Betty Evans. *Educ:* Swansea Univ. (BA Hons). Retail Newsagent, family business, 1979–90. West Glamorgan County Council: Councillor (C), 1985–91; Dep. Leader, 1989. Chm., Welsh Cons. Candidates Policy Gp, 1990; Pres., Cons. NW Parly

Gp, 1991. Contested (C): Swansea West, 1987; Pontypridd, Feb. 1989; Ribble Valley, March 1991. PPS to Sec. of State for Employment, 1993–94, to Chancellor of Duchy of Lancaster, 1994–95; Opposition front bench spokesman on Welsh and constitutional affairs, 1997–2001; Shadow Welsh Sec., 2001–. Mem., Select Cttee on Transport, 1993, on Envmnt, 1996–97, on Public Service, 1996–97; Secretary: NW Gp of Cons. MPs, 1992–; Manufacturing Cttee; All-Party Tourism Cttee; Chm., All-Party Music Gp, 1996–97; Co-Chm., All-Party Drugs Gp, 1997–. Vice-Chm., Cons. Party (Wales), 1999–. Director: Made in the UK Ltd; Small Business Bureau. *Recreations:* tennis, swimming, theatre, tourism, new technology, defence, broadcasting. *Address:* Brooklyn Cottage, Main Street, Pendleton, Clitheroe, Lancs BB7 1PT. *T:* (01200) 443875. *Clubs:* Carlton, Royal Over-Seas League.

EVANS, Dr (Noel) John (Bebbington), CB 1980; Deputy Secretary, Department of Health and Social Security, 1977–84; *b* 26 Dec. 1933; *s* of William John Evans and Gladys Ellen (*née* Bebbington); *m* 1st, 1960, Elizabeth Mary Garbutt (marr. diss.); two *s* one *d*; 2nd, 1974, Eileen Jane McMullan. *Educ:* Hymers Coll., Hull; Christ's Coll., Cambridge (scholar; 1st cl., Nat. Sci. Tripos); Westminster Medical Sch., London; London Sch. of Hygiene and Tropical Med. (Newsholme prize, Chadwick Trust medal and prize). MA, MB, BChir; FRCP, DPH (Dist.), FFPHM. Called to Bar, Gray's Inn, 1965. House officer posts at: Westminster, Westminster Children's, Hammersmith, Central Middlesex and Brompton Hosps, 1958–60; Medical Registrar and Tutor, Westminster Hosp., 1960–61; Asst MoH, Warwickshire CC, 1961–65; Dept of Health and Social Security (formerly Min. of Health), 1965–84, DCMO 1977–82; Sir Wilson Jameson Travelling Fellowship, 1966. Chairman: Welsh Cttee on Drug Misuse, 1986–91; Nat. Biological Standards Bd, 1988– (Mem., 1975–); UK Transplant Support Service Authority, 1991–98; Member: Welsh Cttee, Countryside Commn, 1985–89; Welsh Health Promotion Authority, 1987–89. Conducted Review of External Advice to DoH, reported 1995. Privy Council Mem., Council of Royal Pharmaceutical Soc., 1988–. *Publications:* The Organisation and Planning of Health Services in Yugoslavia, 1967; Health and Personal Social Service Research in Wales, 1986; (with P. Benner) Isle of Man Health Services Inquiry, 1986; (with P. Cunliffe) Study of Control of Medicines, 1987; Postgraduate Medical and Dental Education in Wales, 1991; contribs to med. jls. *Recreations:* canals, photography. *Address:* Providence House, Wyre Lane, Long Marston, Stratford-upon-Avon, Warwickshire CV37 8RQ. *T:* (01789) 721509.

EVANS, Ven. Patrick Alexander Sidney; Archdeacon of Maidstone, 1989–Feb. 2002; Archdeacon of Canterbury, and a Canon Residentiary, Canterbury Cathedral, from Feb. 2002; *b* 28 Jan. 1943; *m* 1969, Jane Kemp; two *s* one *d*. *Educ:* Clifton College, Bristol; Lincoln Theological Coll. Curate: Holy Trinity, Lyonsdown, Barnet, 1973–76; Royston, 1976–78; Vicar: Gt Gaddesden, 1978–82; Tenterden, 1982–89; RD of West Charing, 1988–89; Diocesan Dir of Ordinands, Canterbury, 1989–94. Selector, ABM, 1992–95. Mem., Gen. Synod, 1996–; Chairman: Bd of Mission, 1994–95, and Pastoral Cttee, 1994–, dio. of Canterbury; Canterbury & Rochester Council for Social Responsibility, 1997–. *Address:* (until Feb. 2002) The Old Rectory, The Street, Pluckley, Kent TN27 0QT. *T:* (01233) 840291; (from Feb. 2002) 29 The Precincts, Canterbury, Kent CT1 2EP. *T:* (01227) 865238.

EVANS, Paul; *see* Evans, C. P.

EVANS, Peter, CBE 1986; National Secretary, General Workers' Trade Group, Transport & General Workers' Union, 1974–90; *b* 8 Nov. 1929; *m* 1st, 1957, Christine Pamela (marr. diss.); one *d*; 2nd, 1975, Gillian Rosemary (decd); two *s* one *d*; 3rd, 1980, Joy Elizabeth. *Educ:* Culvert Road Secondary School, Tottenham. London bus driver, 1955–62; District Officer, TGWU, 1962–66; Regional Trade Group Sec., Public Services, 1966–74. *Recreations:* talking, swimming in deep water, golf. *Address:* 54 Aldwick Felds, Aldwick, Bognor Regis, W Sussex PO21 3TT. *T:* (01243) 821304. *Clubs:* Victoria, Players' Theatre; Selsey Golf.

EVANS, Prof. Peter Angus, DMus; FRCO; Professor of Music, University of Southampton, 1961–90; *b* 7 Nov. 1929; *y s* of Rev. James Mackie Evans and Elizabeth Mary Fraser; *m* 1953, June Margaret Vickery. *Educ:* West Hartlepool Grammar Sch.; St Cuthbert's Soc., University of Durham. BA (1st cl. hons Music), 1950; BMus, MA 1953; DMus 1958; FRCO 1952. Music Master, Bishop Wordsworth's Sch., Salisbury, 1951–52; Lecturer in Music, University of Durham, 1953–61. Conductor: Palatine Opera Group, 1956–61; Southampton Philharmonic Soc., 1965–90. Hon. GSM 1998. *Publications:* Sonata for Oboe and Piano, 1953; Three Preludes for Organ, 1955; Edns of 17th Century Chamber Music, 1956–58; The Music of Benjamin Britten, 1979, 3rd edn 1996; contributor to Die Musik, in Geschichte und Gegenwart, to A Concise Encyclopædia of Music, 1958, to New Oxford History of Music, 1974, to New Grove Dictionary of Music, 1981, and to Blackwell History of Music in Britain, 1995; writer and reviewer, especially on twentieth century music. *Address:* Pye's Nest Cottage. Parkway, Ledbury, Herefordshire HR8 2JD. *T:* (01531) 633256.

EVANS, Philip; *see* Evans, I. P.

EVANS, Sir Richard (Harry), Kt 1996; CBE 1986; Chairman: BAE SYSTEMS (formerly British Aerospace plc), since 1998 (Chief Executive, 1990–98); United Utilities, since 2000; *b* 1942; *m*; three *d*. *Educ:* Royal Masonic Sch. Joined Civil Aviation section, Min. of Transport, 1960; Min. of Technology, 1961; Govt Contracts Officer, Ferranti, 1967; British Aerospace (formerly British Aircraft Corporation): Contracts Officer, 1969, Commercial Dir, 1978, Asst Man. Dir, 1981, Dep. Man. Dir, 1983, Warton Div.; Mktg Dir, 1987; Chairman: British Aerospace (Dynamics), 1988; BAe (Military Aircraft), 1988; Royal Ordnance; Dir, Panavia, 1981. *Address:* BAE SYSTEMS PLC, Stirling Square, 6 Carlton Gardens, SW1Y 5AD.

EVANS, Richard Jeremy; racing correspondent, Daily Telegraph, since 1999; *b* 28 June 1953; *s* of late George Evans and of Helen Maud Evans; *m* 1976, Alison Mary Thom. *Educ:* Ipswich Sch., Suffolk. Journalist: East Anglian Daily Times, 1974–78; Cambridge Evening News, 1978–79; with The Times, 1979–99 (Racing Correspondent, 1991–99). Racing Journalist of the Year, Horserace Writers' Assoc., 1995. *Recreations:* golf, croquet, wine. *Address:* Marymead House, Chieveley, Berks RG20 8UX. *T:* (01635) 247256; *e-mail:* richard.j.evans@btinternet.com.

EVANS, Prof. Richard John, FBA 1993; FRHistS, FRSL; Professor of Modern History, University of Cambridge, and Fellow of Gonville and Caius College, Cambridge, since 1998; *b* 29 Sept. 1947; *s* of late Ieuan Trefor Evans and of Evelyn Evans (*née* Jones); *m* 1976, Elín Hjaltadóttir (marr. diss. 1993); lives with Christine L. Corton; two *s*. *Educ:* Forest Sch., London; Jesus Coll., Oxford (Open Schol.; 1st Cl. Hons Mod. Hist. 1969; Stanhope Hist. Essay Prize 1969; Hon. Fellow, 1998); St Antony's Coll., Oxford (MA, DPhil 1973); Hamburg Univ. (Hanseatic Schol.); LittD East Anglia, 1990. Lectr in History, Univ. of Stirling, 1972–76; University of East Anglia: Lectr, 1976; Prof. of European History, 1983–89; Birkbeck College, London: Prof. of History, 1989–98; Vice-Master, 1993–97; Acting Master, 1997. Vis. Associate Prof. of European History, Columbia Univ., 1980; Vis. Fellow, Humanities Res. Centre, ANU, Canberra, 1986; Alexander von Humboldt Fellow, Free Univ. of Berlin, 1981, 1985, 1989. FRHistS 1978; FRSL 2000. Wolfson Literary Award for History, 1987; William H. Welch Medal, Amer. Assoc. for Hist. of Medicine, 1989; Medaille für Kunst und Wissenschaft der Hansestadt Hamburg, 1993; Fraenkel Prize in Contemporary History, Inst. of Contemp. Hist., 1994. *Publications:* The Feminist Movement in Germany 1894–1933, 1976; The Feminists, 1977; (ed) Society and Politics in Wilhelmine Germany, 1978; Sozialdemokratie und Frauenemanzipation im deutschen Kaiserreich, 1979; (ed jtly) The German Family, 1981; (ed) The German Working Class, 1982; (ed jtly) The German Peasantry, 1986; (ed jtly) The German Unemployed, 1987; Comrades and Sisters, 1987; Rethinking German History, 1987; Death in Hamburg, 1987; (ed) The German Underworld, 1988; (ed) Kneipengespräche im Kaiserreich, 1989; In Hitler's Shadow, 1989; Proletarians and Politics, 1990; (ed jtly) The German Bourgeoisie, 1992; Rituals of Retribution: capital punishment in Germany 1600–1987, 1996; Rereading German History, 1997; In Defence of History, 1997; Tales from the German Underworld, 1998. *Recreations:* playing the piano (Beethoven, Chopin), reading (not history books), gardening, cooking for friends. *Address:* Gonville and Caius College, Cambridge CB2 1TA.

EVANS, Richard Llewellyn; consultant for personal social services, since 1999; *b* 1 June 1949; *s* of Robert Ellis Evans and Sarah Christine (*née* Cassidy); *m*; one *s* one *d*. *Educ:* Chiswick Poly.; Dundee Univ. (Dip. Social Work; CQSW; Dip. TMHA). Aircraft engr, BAC, 1964–69; Surrey County Council: Instructor, 1969–72; Dep. Manager, 1972–73; Trng Officer, Lothian Regl Council, 1973–77; Manager, Emergency Duty Team, Wilts CC, 1977–79; Principal Officer, Lothian Regl Council, 1979–81; Develt Officer, London Boroughs' Regl Children's Planning Cttee, 1981–83; Avon County Council: Asst Dir of Social Services, 1983–90; Dir, Social Services, 1990–94; Dir of Social Services, Birmingham CC, 1994–99. Hon. Fellow, Birmingham Univ. *Recreations:* music, cinema, entertaining. *Address:* 51 Waverley Road, Bristol BS6 6ET. *T:* (0117) 923 9182, *Fax:* (0117) 923 8959.

EVANS, Sir Richard (Mark), KCMG 1984 (CMG 1978); KCVO 1986; HM Diplomatic Service, retired; Emeritus Fellow, Wolfson College, Oxford (Senior Research Fellow, 1988–95); *b* 15 April 1928; *s* of late Edward Walter Evans, CMG; *m* 1960, Margaret Elizabeth Sessinger (marr. diss. 1970); *m* 1973, Rosemary Grania Glen Birkett; two *s*. *Educ:* Dragon Sch., Oxford; Repton Sch.; Magdalen Coll., Oxford (BA 1949; MA 1992). Joined HM Foreign (now Diplomatic) Service: Third Sec., London, 1952–55; Third Sec., Peking, 1955–57; Second Sec., London, 1957–62; First Sec.: Peking, 1962–64; Berne, 1964–68; London, 1968–70; Counsellor, 1970; Head of Near Eastern Dept, FCO, 1970–72, Head of Far Eastern Dept, 1972–74; Fellow, Centre for Internat. Affairs, Harvard Univ., 1974–75; Commercial Counsellor, Stockholm, 1975–77; Minister (Economic), Paris, 1977–79; Asst Under-Sec. of State, 1979–82, Dep. Under-Sec. of State, 1982–83, FCO; Ambassador to People's Republic of China, 1984–88. Non-exec. Dir, New Asian Land Fund Ltd, 2000–. Master, Ironmongers' Co., 1999–2000. *Publication:* Deng Xiaoping and the Making of Modern China, 1993. *Recreations:* travel, reading, music. *Address:* Sevenhampton House, Sevenhampton, near Highworth, Wilts SN6 7QA. *Club:* Oxford and Cambridge.

EVANS, Sir Robert, Kt 1994; CBE 1987; FREng; FIMechE, FInstE; Chairman, British Gas plc, 1989–93 (Chief Executive, 1983–92 and Member of the Board, 1983–89); *b* 28 May 1927; *s* of Gwilym Evans and Florence May Evans; *m* 1950, Lilian May (*née* Ward); one *s* one *d*. *Educ:* Old Swan Coll., Liverpool; Blackburn Coll.; City of Liverpool Coll. (Tech.). FREng (FEng 1991). D. Napier & Son Ltd, 1943–49; North Western Gas Bd, 1950–56; Burmah Oil Co., 1956–62; Dir of Engrg, Southern Gas Bd, 1962–70; Dep. Dir (Ops), Gas Council, 1972; Dir of Operations, British Gas, 1972–75; Dep. Chm., North Thames Gas, 1975–77; Chm., E Midlands Gas Region, 1977–82; Man. Dir, Supplies, British Gas Corp., 1982–83. President: Instn of Gas Engrs, 1981–82; Inst. of Energy, 1991–92; Pipeline Industries Guild, 1990–92. Chm., Nat. Council for Hospice and Specialist Palliative Care Services. FInstE (MInstE 1988); Hon. FIGasE 1961; CIMgt (CBIM 1983); Hon. FCGI. Freeman, City of London, 1974; Mem., Engineers' Co., 1984. *Recreations:* reading, golf.

EVANS, Robert John Emlyn; Member (Lab) London Region, European Parliament, since 1999 (London North West, 1994–99); *b* 23 Oct. 1956; *s* of T. F. Evans and late Marjorie Evans. *Educ:* County Sch., Ashford, Middlesex; Shoreditch Coll. of Educn; Inst. of Educn, London Univ. (BEd 1978; MA 1993). Teacher: Thames Ditton Middle Sch., 1978–83; Woodville Middle Sch., Leatherhead, 1983–85; Dep. Headteacher, Town Farm Middle Sch., 1985–89; Headteacher, Crane Jun. Sch., Hanworth, Hounslow, 1990–94. European Parliament: Member: Youth, Culture, Educn and Media Cttee, 1994–; Rules of Procedure Cttee, 1994–99 (Vice Pres., 1997–99); Cttee on Citizens' Freedoms and Rights, Justice and Home Affairs, 1999– (Vice Pres., 1999–); Mem. Delegn for Relns with Countries of S Asia, 1994–, with Romania, 1997–. Contested (Lab): Berkshire East, 1987; Uxbridge, 1992; London South and Surrey, European Parly election, 1989. Member: NUT (Pres., Leatherhead Br., 1984–85); GMB; Nat. Exec., Socialist Educnl Assoc., 1989–98; League Against Cruel Sports, 1976– (Hon. EP Consultant, 1997–). DUniv Brunel, 1998. *Recreations:* cricket, hockey, swimming, cycling, ski-ing, cinema, psephology, mowing the lawn, theatre, travel, history of education. *Address:* European Parliament, Rue Wiertz, 1047 Brussels, Belgium; Labour European Office, 16 Charles Square, N1 6HP. *T:* (020) 7253 1782, *Fax:* (020) 7490 2143. *Clubs:* MCC; Ruskin House Labour (Croydon); Ashford Hockey, Ashford Cricket (Middlesex); Middlesex County Cricket, Incogniti Cricket.

See also A. T. B. Evans.

EVANS, Prof. Robert John Weston, PhD; FBA 1984; Fellow, Oriel College, since 1997 and Regius Professor of Modern History, since 1997, Oxford; *b* 7 Oct. 1943; *s* of Thomas Frederic and Margery Evans (*née* Weston), Cheltenham; *m* 1969, Kati Róbert; one *s* one *d*. *Educ:* Dean Close School; Jesus College, Cambridge (BA 1st Cl. with distinction 1965, PhD 1968). Oxford University: Fellow, Brasenose Coll., 1968–97; Lectr, 1969–90; Reader in Modern History of E Central Europe, 1990–92; Prof. of European History, 1992–97. Mem., Inst. for Advanced Study, Princeton, 1981–82. Fellow: Hungarian Acad. of Scis., 1995; Austrian Acad. of Scis, 1997. František Palacký Medal, Czechoslovakia, 1991. Jt Editor, English Historical Review, 1985–95. *Publications:* Rudolf II and his World, 1973; The Wechel Presses, 1975; The Making of the Habsburg Monarchy, 1979 (Wolfson Literary Award for History, 1980; Anton Gindely Preis, Austria, 1986); (ed with H. Pogge von Strandmann) The Coming of the First World War, 1988; (ed with T. V. Thomas) Crown, Church and Estates: Central European politics, 1991; (ed with H. Pogge von Strandmann) The Revolutions in Europe, 1848–9, 2000. *Recreations:* music, walking, natural (and unnatural) history. *Address:* Oriel College, Oxford OX1 4EW; Rowan Cottage, 45 Sunningwell, Abingdon, Oxon OX13 6RD.

EVANS, Maj.-Gen. Robert Noel, CB 1981; Postgraduate Dean and Commandant, Royal Army Medical College, 1979–81; *b* 22 Dec. 1922; *s* of William Evans and Norah Moynihan; *m* 1950, Mary Elizabeth O'Brien; four *s* one *d*. *Educ:* Christian Brothers Sch.,

Tralee, Co. Kerry; National University of Ireland (MB, BCh, BAO 1947). DTM&H 1961; FFARCS 1963. Commnd RAMC 1951; Consultant Anaesthetist, 1963; CO BMH Rinteln, 1969–71; ADMS 4th Div., 1971–73; DDMS HQ BAOR, 1973–75; Comdt, RAMC Trng Centre, 1975–77; DMS, HQ BAOR, 1977–79; QHP 1976–81. Col Comdt, RAMC, 1981–86. MFCM 1978. OStJ 1978. *Recreations:* gardening, walking, music. *Address:* 32 Folly Hill, Farnham, Surrey GU9 0BH. *T:* (01252) 726938.

EVANS, Hon. Sir Roderick; *see* Evans, Hon. Sir D. R.

EVANS, Roger; *see* Evans, J. R.

EVANS, Roger Kenneth; barrister; a Recorder, since 2000; *b* 18 March 1947; *s* of late G. R. Evans of Mere, Wilts and Dr A. M. Evans; *m* 1973, June Rodgers, MA, barrister; two *s*. *Educ:* The Grammar Sch., Bristol; Trinity Hall, Cambridge (MA). President: Cambridge Union, 1970; Cambridge Georgian Gp, 1969; Chm., Cambridge Univ. Conservative Assoc., 1969. Called to the Bar: Middle Temple, 1970 (Astbury Schol.); Inner Temple, *ad eundem*, 1979; in practice, 1970–94, 1997–; an Asst Recorder, 1998–2000. Contested (C): Warley West, Oct. 1974, 1979; Ynys Môn, 1987; Monmouth, May 1991. MP (C) Monmouth, 1992–97; contested (C) same seat, 1997, 2001. Parly Under-Sec. of State, DSS, 1994–97. Member: Welsh Affairs Select Cttee, 1992–94; Ecclesiastical Cttee of Parlt, 1992–97. Chairman: Friends of Friendless Churches, 1998–; Prayer Book Soc., 2001– (Vice-Pres., 1995–2001); Mem., Ecclesiastical Law Soc., 1988–. Freeman, City of London, 1976. *Recreations:* gardening, architectural history. *Address:* 2 Harcourt Buildings, Temple, EC4Y 9DB; *e-mail:* revans@harcourtchambers.law.co.uk. *Clubs:* Carlton, Coningsby (Chm., 1976–77; Treas., 1983–87); Abergavenny Constitutional, Chepstow Conservative, Monmouth Conservative, Usk Conservative.

EVANS, Roger W.; *see* Warren Evans.

EVANS, Roy; *see* Evans, H. R.

EVANS, Roy Lyon, OBE 1993; General Secretary, Iron and Steel Trades Confederation, 1985–93; *b* 13 Aug. 1931; *s* of David Evans and Sarah (*née* Lyon); *m* 1960, Brenda Jones; one *s* two *d*. *Educ:* Gowerton Grammar Sch., Swansea. Employed in Tinplate Section of Steel Industry, 1948. Iron and Steel Trades Confederation: Divl Organiser, NW Area, 1964–69; Divl Organiser, W Wales Area, 1969–73; Asst Gen. Sec., 1973–85. Mem., Gen. Council, TUC, 1985–93. Jt Sec., Jt Industrial Council for the Slag Industry, 1975–85; Mem., ECSC Consultative Cttee, 1985–93 (Pres., 1986–88); Hon. Sec., British Section, IMF, 1985–93 (Pres., Iron and Steel Dept (World), 1986). Member: Jt Accident Prevention Adv. Cttee, 1974–93 (Chm., 1983); NEC of Labour Party, 1981–84. Bd Mem., British Steel (Industry) Ltd, 1986–94. *Recreations:* reading, walking.

EVANS, Russell Wilmot, MC 1945; Chairman, Rank Organisation, 1982–83; *b* 4 Nov. 1922; *s* of William Henry Evans and Ethel Williams Wilmot; *m* 1956, Pamela Muriel Hayward (*d* 1989); two *s* one *d*. *Educ:* King Edward's Sch., Birmingham; Birmingham Univ. LLB Hons. Served HM Forces, 1942–47; commnd Durham LI, 1942, Major, 1945. Admitted Solicitor, Birmingham, 1949; Solicitor with Shakespeare & Vernon, Birmingham, 1949–50; Asst Sec., Harry Ferguson, 1951; Sec., Massey-Ferguson (Hldgs) and UK subsids, 1955–62; Dir, gp of private cos in construction industry, 1962–67; joined Rank Organisation, 1967: Dep. Sec., 1967–68; Sec., 1968–72; Dir, 1972–83; Man. Dir, 1975–82; Dep. Chm., 1981; Dir, principal subsid. and associated cos incl. Rank Xerox, 1975–83; Fuji Xerox, 1976–83; Chm., Rank City Wall, 1976–83. Director: Eagle Star Holdings, 1982–87; Oxford Economic Forecasting Ltd, 1986–96; Medical Cyclotron Ltd, 1988–. *Recreations:* tennis, golf, photography. *Address:* Walnut Tree, Roehampton Gate, SW15 5JR. *T:* (020) 8876 2433. *Clubs:* English-Speaking Union, Roehampton (Dir 1971–87, Chm., 1984–87, Pres., 1991–).

EVANS, Ruth Elizabeth; Chairman, Inquiry into Paediatric and Cardiac Services, Royal Brompton and Harefield NHS Trust, 1999–2001; *b* 12 Oct. 1957; *d* of Peter Evans and Dr Anne Evans; one *d*. *Educ:* Girton Coll., Cambridge (MA Hist.). Dir, Maternity Alliance, 1981–86; Dep. Dir, then Actg Dir, Nat. Assoc. for Mental Health (MIND), 1986–90; Gen. Sec., War On Want, 1990; Mgt Consultant, 1990–91; Dir, Nat. Consumer Council, 1992–98. Non-exec. Dir, Liverpool Victoria Gp, 1999–. Member: Central R&D Cttee, NHS, 1995–99; Chm., Standing Adv. Gp on Consumer Involvement, NHS R&D Prog., 1995–99; Member: Human Genetics Commn, 2000–; Ind. Rev. Panel for advertising of medicines for human use, 1999–; UK Round Table on Sustainable Develt, 1995–99; Expert Panel on Sustainable Develt, DETR, 1998–99; Commn on Taxation and Citizenship, Fabian Soc., 1998–2000; BBC Licence Fee Review Panel, DCMS, 1999; Bd, Financial Services Ombudsman Scheme, subseq. Financial Ombudsman Service, 1999–; Panel of Ind. Assessors, Office of Comr for Public Appts, 1999–2001. Lay Mem., GMC, 1999–. Trustee, Money Advice Trust, 1994–2000 (Chm., Adv. Gp of UK money advice agencies, 1994–2000). *Recreations:* writing, music, swimming. *Address:* 24 Falkland Road, NW5 2PX. *T:* (020) 7482 0420, *Fax:* (020) 7482 6087.

EVANS, Sally Anne; Deputy Legal Adviser, Home Office, 1995–2000; *b* 20 March 1948; *d* of Arthur Francis Gardiner Austin and late Joy Austin (*née* Ravenor); *m* 1977, Richard Maurice Evans. *Educ:* High Sch. for Girls, Darlington; Univ. of Manchester (LLB Hons 1970). Called to the Bar, Gray's Inn, 1971; Barclays Bank DCO, then Barclays Bank Internat. Ltd, 1970–72; Western American Bank Ltd, 1972–73; Legal Adviser's Br., Home Office, 1974–2000. *Recreations:* theatre, cooking, summer gardening.

EVANS, Sarah Hauldys; Headmistress, King Edward VI High School for Girls, since 1996; *b* 4 March 1953; *d* of Nancy and Wyndham Evans; *m* 1989, Andrew Romanis Fowler; one *s*. *Educ:* King James' Grammar Sch., Knaresborough; Univ. of Sussex (BA Hons English); Univ. of Leicester (MA Victorian Studies); Univ. of Leeds (PGCE). English Teacher, Leeds Girls' High Sch., 1976–84; Dep. Head, Fulneck Girls' Sch., 1984–89; Head, Friends' Sch., Saffron Walden, 1989–96. *Recreations:* the arts. *Address:* King Edward VI High School for Girls, Edgbaston Park Road, Birmingham B15 2UB.

EVANS, Stephen Nicholas, OBE 1994; HM Diplomatic Service; Counsellor and Head of South Asian Department, Foreign and Commonwealth Office, since 1998; *b* 29 June 1950; *s* of Vincent Morris Evans and late Doris Mary Evans (*née* Braham); *m* 1975, Sharon Ann Holdcroft; one *s* two *d*. *Educ:* King's Coll., Taunton; Bristol Univ. (BA). Royal Tank Regt (Lieut), 1971–74; FCO, 1974; language student (Vietnamese), SOAS, 1975; FCO, 1976; First Sec., Hanoi, 1978–80; FCO, 1980–82; language training (Thai), Bangkok, 1982–83; First Sec., Bangkok, 1983–86; FCO, 1986–90; First Sec. (Political), Ankara, 1990; Counsellor (Econ., Commercial, Aid), Islamabad, 1993–96; seconded to UN Special Mission to Afghanistan, 1996–97; Counsellor and Head of OSCE and Council of Europe Dept, FCO, 1997–98. *Recreations:* military and naval history, golf, cycling. *Address:* c/o Foreign and Commonwealth Office, SW1A 2AH. *T:* (020) 7270 3000. *Club:* Athenæum.

EVANS, (Thomas) Alun, CMG 1994; HM Diplomatic Service, retired; Overseas Political and Security Risk Adviser, British Airways, since 1995; *b* 8 June 1937; *s* of late Thomas Evans and Mabel Elizabeth (*née* Griffiths); *m* 1964, Bridget Elisabeth, *d* of Peter Lloyd, *qv* and Nora Kathleen Williams (*née* Patten); three *s*. *Educ:* Shrewsbury Sch.; University Coll., Oxford (MA). Army, 1956–58. Entered HM Foreign Service, 1961; Third Sec., Rangoon, 1962–64; Second Sec., Singapore, 1964–66; FO, 1966–70; First Sec., Geneva, 1970–74; FCO, 1974–79; Counsellor: Pretoria, 1979–82; FCO, 1983–95. *Recreations:* music, travel. *Address:* c/o British Airways, Waterside (HDB2), PO Box 365, Harmondsworth UB7 0GB. *T:* (020) 8738 6892. *Club:* Travellers.

EVANS, His Honour (Thomas) Michael; QC 1973; a Circuit Judge, 1979–98; *b* 7 Sept. 1930; *s* of late David Morgan Evans, Barrister, and of Mary Gwynydd Lloyd; *m* 1957, Margaret Valerie Booker; one *s* four *d*. *Educ:* Brightlands Prep. Sch., Newnham, Glos; Marlborough Coll., Wilts; Jesus Coll., Oxford (MA (Juris.)). Called to the Bar, Gray's Inn, 1954; Wales and Chester Circuit, 1955; a Recorder of the Crown Court, 1972–79. Legal Chm., Mental Health Review Tribunal for Wales, 1970. Chancellor, Diocese of St Davids, 1986–. Pres., Provincial Court, Church in Wales, 1997–. *Recreations:* walking, gardening, genealogy. *Address:* The Old Rectory, Reynoldston, Gower, Swansea SA3 1AD. *T:* (01792) 390129.

EVANS, Prof. Timothy William, MD, PhD; FRCP, FRCA; Professor of Intensive Care Medicine, Imperial College of Science, Technology and Medicine, University of London, since 1996; Head, Unit of Critical Care, National Heart and Lung Institute, since 1993; Consultant in Intensive Care and Thoracic Medicine, Royal Brompton Hospital, since 1987; *b* 29 May 1954; *s* of Philip Charles Evans and Mary Elizabeth Norah Evans (*née* Else); *m* 1987, Josephine Emer MacSweeney, Consultant in Neuroradiology, *d* of Prof. James MacSweeney; three *s* one *d*. *Educ:* High Storrs Grammar Sch., Sheffield; Univ. of Manchester (BSc Hons 1976; MB ChB Hons 1979; MD 1990); Univ. of Sheffield (PhD 1985; DSc 1997). MRCP 1982, FRCP 1993; FRCA 2000. House Officer, Univ. Dept of Neurosurgery, 1979–80, Renal and Gen. Medicine Dept, 1980, Manchester Royal Infirmary; Senior House Officer: Professorial Med. Unit, Royal Hallamshire Hosp., Univ. of Sheffield, 1980–81; in Gen. Medicine and Gastroenterology, Hammersmith Hosp./RPMS, 1981–82; in Thoracic Medicine, Brompton Hosp., 1982; Trent RHA Res. Fellow, and Hon. Med. Registrar, Acad. Div. of Medicine, Univ. of Sheffield, 1982–84; MRC Travelling Fellow, Cardiovascular Res. Inst., Univ. of Calif, San Francisco, 1984–85; Sen. Registrar in Thoracic and Gen. Medicine, Brompton and King's Coll. Hosps, 1985–86; Doverdale Fellow in Intensive Care and Hon. Sen. Registrar, Brompton Hosp., 1986–87; Cons. Physician, Chelsea and Westminster Hosp., 1988–. Hon. Cons. in Intensive Care Medicine, HM Forces, 1998–. Member: Adv. Gp on Intensive Care Services, Nat. Audit Commn, 1998–99; Nat. Expert Gp, Adult Critical Care Services, NHS Exec., 1999–2000. Member: BMA Grants Cttee, 1989–94; British Lung Foundn Grants Cttee, 1992–95; BHF Grants Cttee, 2002–; Council, British Thoracic Soc., 1993–96; Thoracic Medicine Cttee, 1994–, Gen. Medicine Cttee, 1996–, RCP; Council, European Intensive Care Soc., 1997–. FMedSci 1999. Member, Editorial Board: Thorax, 1991–94; Intensive Care Medicine, 1996–99; Amer. Jl of Respiratory and Critical Care Medicine, 1997–; Amer. Jl of Physiology, 2000–. *Publications:* jointly: Interpretation for MRCP, 1988; Respiratory Medicine, 1989; Slide The Drug Treatment of Respiratory Disease, 1994; Acute Respiratory Distress in Adults, 1996; Recent Advances in Critical Care 5, 1996; (ed jtly) Acute Lung Injury, 1997; more than 200 articles on scientific and clinical aspects of intensive care medicine. *Recreations:* flying, housework. *Address:* Department of Anaesthetics and Intensive Care Medicine, Royal Brompton Hospital, Sydney Street, SW3 6NP. *T:* (020) 7351 8523, *Fax:* (020) 7351 8524; *e-mail:* t.evans@rbh.nthames.nhs.uk.

EVANS, Prof. Trevor, FRS 1988; Personal Professor, University of Reading, 1968–92, Emeritus Professor, 1992; *b* 26 April 1927; *s* of late Henry and Margaret Evans; *m* Patricia Margaret Booth (*née* Johnson); two *s* and two step *s*. *Educ:* Bridgend Grammar Sch.; Univ. of Bristol (BSc, PhD, DSc). FInstP. Physicist: British Nylon Spinners, 1955–56; Tube Investments Res. Lab., 1956–58; Physics Department, University of Reading, 1958–92: Res. Physicist, 1958–61; successively, Lectr, Reader, Personal Prof., 1961–92; Hd of Dept, 1984–88; Warden of Wantage Hall, Reading Univ., 1971–84. For. Associate, RSSAf 1995. *Publications:* papers in Proc. Royal Soc. and Phil. Mag., almost entirely concerning synthetic and natural diamond. *Recreation:* pottering in the garden. *Address:* Aston, Tutts Clump, Reading, Berks RG7 6JZ. *T:* (0118) 974 4498.

EVANS, Dr Trevor John; Chief Executive and Secretary, Institution of Chemical Engineers, since 1994 (General Secretary, 1976–94); *b* 14 Feb. 1947; *o s* of late Evan Alban Evans and of Margaret Alice Evans (*née* Hilton); *m* 1973, Margaret Elizabeth (*née* Whitham); three *s* one *d*. *Educ:* King's Sch., Rochester; University Coll., London (BSc (Eng) 1968, PhD 1972; Fellow, 1997); CEng, FIChemE. Res. Officer, CSIR, Pretoria, 1968–69; Ford Motor Co., Aveley, Essex, 1972–73; Institution of Chemical Engineers: Asst Sec., Technical, 1973–75; Dep. Sec., 1975–76. Member: Bd, Council of Science and Technology Institutes, 1976–87; Exec. Cttee, Commonwealth Engineers Council, 1976–; Steering Cttee, DTI Action for Engrg Prog., 1995–96; Jt Hon. Sec., European Fedn of Chem. Engrg, 1976–. Mem. Ct, ICSTM, 1998–. FIMgt; FRSA. Kurnakov Meml Medal, USSR Acad. of Scis, 1991; Titanium Achema Plaque, 1997. *Publications:* scientific papers and general articles in Chemical Engrg Science, The Chem. Engr, etc. *Recreations:* home renovation, drama. *Address:* The Institution of Chemical Engineers, 165–189 Railway Terrace, Rugby, Warwicks CV21 3HQ. *T:* (01788) 578214.

EVANS, Very Rev. Trevor Owen; Dean of Bangor, since 1998; *b* 10 July 1937; *s* of John James Pierce Evans and Elizabeth Jane Evans; *m* 1962, Ann Christine Stephens; one *s* one *d*. *Educ:* Dolgellau Boys' Grammar Sch.; UCW, Aberystwyth (BSc); Coll. of the Resurrection, Mirfield. Ordained deacon, 1961, priest, 1962; Diocese of Bangor: Curate, Barmouth, 1961–64; Curate, 1964–70, Vicar, 1970–75, Llandudno; Vicar, Llanidloes, 1975–89; RD, Arwystli, 1976–89; Preb. and Canon of Bangor Cathedral, 1982–98; Rector of Trefdraeth, 1989–90; Dir of Ministry, 1989–98; Rector of Llanfair PG with Penmynydd, 1990–98, also with Llanddaniel-Fab and with Llanedwen, 1997–98; Surrogate, 1978–98. *Recreations:* hill-walking, wood-turning, ornithology, geology, geomorphology. *Address:* The Deanery, Cathedral Close, Bangor, Gwynedd LL57 1LH. *T:* (01248) 370693, *Fax:* (01248) 352466.

EVANS, Valerie Jean, CBE 1991; FIBiol; Soroptimist International Representative to Economic Commission of Europe region of United Nations, since 1999; human rights activist; *b* 26 July 1930; *d* of Connie and Wilfred Evans. *Educ:* Wales; Bedford Coll., London Univ. (BSc). Science teacher, 1952–67; HM Inspectorate of Schools, 1967–90: specialist in science and develt of secondary school curriculum; Divl Staff Inspector, E and W Midlands Div., Birmingham, 1977–90. Soroptimist Internat. UK rep. on Women's Nat. Commn, 1994–97; Co-Chair, 1997–98, Chair, 1998–99, Women's Nat. Commn; Chair, Gender Stats Users Gp, 2000–. Trustee or member, numerous educnl advisory bodies. *Recreations:* reading, music, china, paintings, cooking, gardens, wine. *Address:* Coombe, 84 Salisbury Road, Moseley, Birmingham B13 8JY.

EVANS, Sir Vincent; *see* Evans, Sir W. V. J.

EVANS, Maj.-Gen. William Andrew, CB 1993; DL; Secretary, Council of TAVRAs, 1993–2001; *b* 5 Aug. 1939; *s* of late Maj.-Gen. Roger Evans, CB, MC and Eileen (*née* Stanton); *m* 1964, Virginia Susan, *e d* of late William Robert Tomkinson and Helen Mary Tomkinson, MBE; two *d*. *Educ:* Sherborne; RMA Sandhurst; Christ Church, Oxford (MA). Commnd 5th Royal Inniskilling Dragoon Guards, 1959; served in BAOR, Middle East, Cyprus, Libya, N Ireland; Staff Coll., Bracknell, 1971; Army Instructor, RAF Cranwell, 1974–75; Instructor, Army Staff Coll., 1978–80; CO 5th Royal Inniskilling Dragoon Guards, 1980–82 (despatches, 1981); Col, Asst Dir (Policy), Defence Policy Staff, 1982–83; Comdr 4 Armd Bde, 1983–85; RCDS 1986; DCS, HQ BAOR, 1987–89; GOC Eastern Dist, 1989–92, retired. Pres., Essex, Army Benevolent Fund, 1997–; Vice Chm., Royal Dragoon Guards Regtl Assoc., 1992–; Member Council: ACFA, 1993–2001; Union Jack Club, 1995–. Pres., Army Cricket Assoc., 1989–91; Chm., Combined Services Cricket Assoc., 1990. Mem., Court, Essex Univ., 1994–. Liveryman, Broderers' Co., 1992–. DL Essex, 1998. *Recreations:* fishing, birdwatching. *Address:* Lyston House, Sudbury, Suffolk. *Club:* Cavalry and Guards.

EVANS, Dr (William) David; Director, Competitiveness, Department of Trade and Industry, since 1998; *b* 20 April 1949; *s* of late Harold Evans and Gladys Evans (*née* Webber); *m* 1980, Elizabeth Crowe; three *s* one *d*. *Educ:* Haberdashers' Aske's School, Elstree; St Catherine's College, Oxford (BA 1971; DPhil 1974; Senior Scholar). FRAS 1975. Dept of Energy, 1974–80; First Sec., Science and Technology, British Embassy, Bonn, 1980–83; Asst Sec., 1984–89, Chief Scientist, 1989–92, Dept of Energy; Department of Trade and Industry: Hd of Envmt Div., 1992–94; Hd of Technology and Innovation Div., 1994–96; Dir, Technol. and Standards, later Technol. and Standards Directorate, 1996–98. Member: NERC, 1989–92; EPSRC, 1994–98; PPARC, 1994–98; Assessor, SERC, ACORD, 1989–92. Senator, Engrg Council, 1996–98. *Publications:* scientific papers in professional jls. *Recreations:* music, reading, history of technology. *Address:* Department of Trade and Industry, 1 Victoria Street, SW1H 0ET.

EVANS, (William) Emrys, CBE 1981; Senior Regional Director, Wales, Midland Bank Ltd, 1976–84; *b* 4 April 1924; *s* of late Richard and Mary Elizabeth Evans; *m* 1946, Mair Thomas; one *d*. *Educ:* Llanfair Caereinion County Sch. FCIB. Served War, RN, 1942–46 (despatches 1944). Entered Midland Bank Ltd, 1941; Asst Gen. Manager (Agric.), 1967–72; Reg. Dir, S Wales, 1972–74; Reg. Dir, Wales, 1974–76. Director: Executive Secondment Ltd, 1983–90 (Vice Chm., 1983–90); Align-Rite Ltd, 1984–; Chm., Menter a Busnes, 1988–99; Chm. and Founder Trustee, Sefydliad Addysg Menter a Busnes, 1998–. Chairman: Welsh Cttee for Economic and Industrial Affairs, 1984–91; Midland Bank Adv. Council for Wales, 1984–. Director: Develt Corp. for Wales, 1973–77; Welsh Industrial Develt Adv. Bd, 1975–86; Develt Bd for Rural Wales, 1976–89; Royal Welsh Agricl Soc., 1973– (Chm., Mgt Bd, 1999–); Mem. Council, CBI, Wales, 1975–86 (Chm., 1979–81). Pres., Royal Nat. Eisteddfod of Wales, 1980–83 (Fellow, 1997). Vice President: Tenovus Cancer Res. Unit, 1980–; Kidney Res. Unit for Wales Foundn, 1980–; Barnardos, 1989– (Chm., Dr Barnardo's Centenary in Wales Appeal, 1988); Trustee: Catherine and Lady Grace James Foundn, 1973–; John and Rhys Thomas James Foundn, 1973 ; Welsh Sports Aid Trust, 1980–98 (Vice Chm., 1988–98); Llandovery Coll., 1982–93; Council for the Protection of Rural Wales, 1991–; Children's Hosp. for Wales Appeal Ltd, 1999–; Treas., Lloyd George Statue Appeal Trust, 1998–. Pres., Welsh Sports Aid Foundn, 1996– (Gov., 1980–; Chm., 1988–94); Member: Council for the Welsh Lang., 1973–78; Design Council Wales Adv. Cttee, 1981–86; Prince of Wales Cttee, 1975–87; Dairy Produce Quota Tribunal, 1984–92; NPFA, Cymru, 1998–. Vice Pres., Cardiff Business Club, 1975–; Pres., Cwlwm Busnes, 1995–. Pres., Welsh Congregational Church in Wales, 1989 (Treasurer, 1975–86); Sec., Ebenezer Welsh Cong. Ch, Cardiff, 1990–. Treasurer, Mansfield Coll., Oxford, 1977–89 (Trustee, 1989–95); Member, Court and Council: UC Swansea (now Univ. of Wales, Swansea), 1972–96 (Chm. Council, 1982–96; Fellow, 1997); UC Aberystwyth, 1979–84; Univ. of Wales, 1980– (Treas., 1998–99). Hon. LLD Wales, 1983. FRSA 1982. High Sheriff, S Glamorgan, 1985–86. *Recreations:* golf, gardening, music. *Address:* Maesglas, Pen-y-turnpike, Dinas Powis, Vale of Glamorgan CF64 4HH. *T:* (029) 2051 2985, *Fax:* (029) 2051 1091. *Club:* Cardiff and County (Cardiff).

EVANS, (William) Lindsay; DL; freelance television actor and presenter, since 1991; Trustee, National Heritage Memorial Fund, 1992–99; Chairman, Committee for Wales, Heritage Lottery Fund, 1998–99; *b* 22 March 1933; *o s* of John Evans and Nellie (*née* Davies). *Educ:* Swansea GS; Univ. of Wales (BA, MA, DipEd); Jesus Coll., Oxford (MLitt 1961). School teacher, Middlesex CC, 1958–60; freelance newsreader, BBC, 1960–61; Asst Master, Llandovery Coll., 1961–65; Lectr in Drama, Bangor Normal Coll., 1965–67; Prin. Lectr and Hd of Drama Dept, Cartrefle Coll., Wrexham, 1967–91. Lectr, summer schools, Extra-Mural Dept, UCNW, Bangor, 1967–70. Member: Exec. Cttee, N Wales Arts Assoc., 1973–76; Welsh Arts Council, 1982–88; Historic Bldgs Council for Wales, 1977–99; Welsh Cttee, NT, 1984–90. DL Clwyd, 1999. Author of numerous radio and television plays and documentaries in English and Welsh. *Publications:* Y Gelltydd (novel), 1980; The Castles of Wales, 1998; (contrib.) Everyman's Guide to England & Wales, 2000; articles on aspects of built envmt. *Recreations:* friends, music, discovering places and buildings. *Address:* 100 Erddig Road, Wrexham LL13 7DR.

EVANS, Sir (William) Vincent (John), GCMG 1976 (KCMG 1970; CMG 1959); MBE 1945; QC 1973; Barrister-at-Law; a Judge of the European Court of Human Rights, 1980–91; *b* 20 Oct. 1915; *s* of Charles Herbert Evans and Elizabeth (*née* Jenkins); *m* 1947, Joan Mary Symons; one *s* two *d*. *Educ:* Merchant Taylors' Sch., Northwood; Wadham Coll., Oxford (Hon. Fellow 1981). 1st Class Hons, Jurisprudence, 1937; BCL, 1938; MA, 1941; elected Cassel Scholar, Lincoln's Inn, 1937; called to Bar, Lincoln's Inn, 1939 (Hon. Bencher, 1983). Served in HM Forces, 1939–46. Legal Adviser (Lt-Col) to British Military Administration, Cyrenaica, 1945–46; Asst Legal Adviser, Foreign Office, 1947–54; Legal Counsellor, UK Permanent Mission to the United Nations, NY, 1954–59; Legal Counsellor, FO, 1959–60; Dep. Legal Adviser, FO, 1960–68; Legal Adviser, FCO, 1968–75, retired. Chm., Bryant Symons & Co. Ltd, 1964–85. Chm., European Cttee on Legal Cooperation, Council of Europe, 1969–71; UK Rep. Council of Europe Steering Cttee on Human Rights, 1976–80 (Chm., 1979–80); Mem., Human Rights Cttee set up under Internat. Covenant on Civil and Political Rights, 1977–84 (Vice-Chm., 1979–80); Mem., Permanent Court of Arbitration, 1987–97. Vice-Pres., British Inst. of Human Rights, 1992–; Member: Adv. Bd, Centre for Internat. Human Rights Law, Univ. of Essex, 1983–94; Council of Management, British Inst. of Internat. and Comparative Law, 1969–; Diplomatic Service Appeals Bd, 1976–86; Sch. Cttee, Merchant Taylors' Co., 1985–93. Pres., Old Merchant Taylors' Soc., 1984–85; Vice-Pres., Hon. Soc. of Cymmrodorion, 1987–. DUniv Essex, 1986. *Recreation:* gardening. *Address:* (home) 4 Bedford Road, Moor Park, Northwood, Mddx HA6 2BB. *T:* (01923) 824085. *Club:* Athenæum.

EVANS, Very Rev. Wyn; *see* Evans, Very Rev. J. W.

EVANS, Wynford; *see* Evans, J. W.

EVANS-ANFOM, Emmanuel, FRCSE 1955; Commissioner for Education and Culture, Ghana, 1978–88; Member, Council of State, 1979; Chairman, National Education Commission, since 1984; *b* 7 Oct. 1919; *m* 1952, Leonora Francetta Evans (*d* 1980); three *s* one *d*; *m* 1984, Elise Henkel. *Educ:* Achimota School; Edinburgh University (MB; ChB; DTM&H; Alumnus of the Year Award, 1996). House Surgeon, Dewsbury Infirmary, 1948–49; Medical Officer, Gold Coast Medical Service, 1950–56, Specialist Surgeon, 1956–67; Senior Lecturer, Ghana Medical School, 1966–67; Vice-Chancellor, Univ. of Science and Technology, Kumasi, 1967–74. Mem., WHO Expert Panel on Med. and Paramed. Educn, 1972–; Chairman: Nat. Council for Higher Educn, 1974–78; W African Exams Council, 1991–94; Chairman: Med. and Dental Council; Akrofi-Christaller Centre for Mission Res. and Applied Theology, 1986–; Inter-church and Ecumenical Relations Cttee, Presbyterian Church of Ghana, 1990–. Titular Mem., Internat. Assoc. Surgeons; Past President: Ghana Medical Assoc.; Assoc. of Surgeons of W Africa; FICS. Fellow: Ghana Acad. Arts and Sciences, 1971 (Pres., 1987–91); African Acad. of Scis, 1986. Chm., Ghana Hockey Assoc. Pres., Ghana Boys' Brigade Council, 1987–. Hon. DSc Salford, 1974. *Publications:* Aetiology and Management of Intestinal Perforations, Ghana Med. Jl, 1963; Traditional Medicine in Ghana: practice problems and prospects, 1986. *Recreations:* hockey, music, art. *Address:* PO Box M135, Accra, Ghana.

EVANS-BEVAN, Sir Martyn Evan, 2nd Bt *cr* 1958; *b* 1 April 1932; *s* of Sir David Martyn Evans-Bevan, 1st Bt, and of Eira Winifred, *d* of late Sidney Archibald Lloyd Glanley; *S* father, 1973; *m* 1957, Jennifer Jane Marion, *d* of Robert Hugh Stevens; four *s*. *Educ:* Uppingham. Entered family business of Evan Evans Bevan and Evans Bevan Ltd, 1953; High Sheriff of Breconshire, 1967; Liveryman, Worshipful Co. of Farmers; Freeman, City of London. *Recreations:* shooting and fishing. *Heir:* *s* David Gawain Evans-Bevan [*b* 16 Sept. 1961; *m* 1987, Philippa, *y d* of Patrick Sweeney; one *s* one *d*]. *Address:* Felinnewydd, Llandefalle, Brecon, Powys LD3 0NE. *Club:* Carlton.

EVANS-FREKE, family name of **Baron Carbery**.

EVANS-LOMBE, Hon. Sir Edward (Christopher), Kt 1993; **Hon. Mr Justice Evans-Lombe;** a Judge of the High Court of Justice, Chancery Division, since 1993; *b* 10 April 1937; *s* of Vice-Adm. Sir Edward Evans-Lombe, KCB, and Lady Evans-Lombe; *m* 1964, Frances Marilyn MacKenzie, DL; one *s* three *d*. *Educ:* Eton; Trinity Coll., Cambridge (MA). National Service, 1955–57: 2nd Lieut Royal Norfolk Regt. Called to the Bar, Inner Temple, 1963, Bencher, 1985. Standing Counsel to Dept of Trade in Bankruptcy matters, 1971; QC 1978; a Recorder, 1982–93. Chm., Agricultural Land Tribunal, S Eastern Region, 1983–93. *Recreations:* fishing, ornithology, amateur archaeology. *Address:* Royal Courts of Justice, Strand, WC2A 2LL. *Club:* Norfolk (Norwich).

EVANS O'ROURKE, Sarah Louise; Director for Resources and General Affairs, Secretariat General of European Commission, since 2000; *b* 3 Jan. 1948; *d* of John Desmond O'Rourke and Margaret Brenda (*née* Shelley, now Camou); *m* 1974, Richard Frederick Evans; one *s* one *d*. *Educ:* University Coll. London (LLB Hons 1969); Univ. of Notre Dame du Lac, USA (Cert. Amer. Law 1970). Trainee, Bank of America, London, 1971–72; Res. Asst, Brunel Univ., 1973; joined European Commn, 1974: DG XV Financial Instns and Fiscal Affairs, 1974–78; DG V Employment, Social Affairs and Educn, 1983–88; Asst to Head of Service, Task Force Human Resources, Educn, Trng and Youth, 1989–93; Head of Unit for Personnel and Admin, DG V Employment, Indust. Relns and Social Affairs, 1994–96; Dir for Rights and Obligations, DG IX Personnel and Admin, 1996–99; Principal Advr and Mem. of Cabinet of Pres., Eur. Commn, 1999–2000. *Recreations:* reading, swimming, gardening. *Address:* European Commission, Rue de la Loi 200, 1049 Brussels, Belgium.

EVANS-TIPPING, (Sir) David Gwynne, (5th Bt *cr* 1913, of Oaklands Park, Awre, Co. Gloucester); *b* 25 Nov. 1943; *e s* of Sir Francis Loring Gwynne-Evans, 4th Bt (who assumed name of Evans-Tipping, 1943–58), and of his 1st wife, Elisabeth Fforde, *d* of J. Fforde-Tipping; *S* father, 1993, but does not use the title. *Educ:* Trinity Coll., Dublin (BAgricSci). *Heir:* *b* Christopher Evan Evans-Tipping [*b* 27 Feb. 1946; *m* 1974, Fenella Catherine Morrison; one *s* one *d*].

EVATT, Hon. Elizabeth Andreas, AC 1995 (AO 1982); Member: United Nations Human Rights Committee, 1993–2000; Human Rights and Equal Opportunity Commission, Australia, 1995–98; *b* 11 Nov. 1933; *d* of Clive Raleigh Evatt, QC and Marjorie Hannah (*née* Andreas); *m* 1960, Robert J. Southan, *qv*; one *d* (one *s* decd). *Educ:* Sydney Univ. (LLB); Harvard Univ. (LLM). Called to the Bar: NSW, 1955; Inner Temple, 1958. Chief Judge, Family Court of Australia, 1976–88. Dep. Pres., Australian Conciliation and Arbitration Commn, 1973–89; Chairperson, Royal Commn on Human Relationships, 1974–77; Dep. Pres., Australian Ind. Relns Commn, 1989–94; Pres., Australian Law Reform Commission, 1988–93 (Mem., 1993–94). Member: UN Cttee on Elimination of Discrimination against Women, 1984–92 (Chairperson, 1989–91); World Bank Admin. Tribunal, 1998–. Chancellor, Univ. of Newcastle, 1988–94. Hon. LLD: Sydney, 1985; Macquarie, 1989; Queensland, 1992; Flinders, 1994; Univ. of NSW, 1996; Hon. Dr Newcastle, 1988. *Publication:* Guide to Family Law, 1986, 2nd edn 1991. *Recreation:* music. *Address:* Unit 2003, 184 Forbes Street, Darlinghurst, NSW 2010, Australia. *Club:* Royal Corinthian Yacht.

EVE, family name of **Baron Silsoe**.

EVELEIGH, Rt Hon. Sir Edward Walter; PC 1977; Kt 1968; ERD; MA; a Lord Justice of Appeal, 1977–85; *b* 8 Oct. 1917; *s* of Walter William and Daisy Emily Eveleigh; *m* 1940, Vilma Bodnar; *m* 1953, Patricia Helen Margaret Bury (decd); two *s* (and one *s* decd). *m* 1996, Nell A. Cox. *Educ:* Peter Symonds; Brasenose Coll., Oxford (Hon. Fellow 1977). Commissioned in the Royal Artillery (Supplementary Reserve), 1936; served War of 1939–45 (despatches, 1940). Called to Bar, Lincoln's Inn, 1945, Bencher 1968, Treas., 1988; QC 1961. Recorder of Burton-on-Trent, 1961–64, of Gloucester, 1964–68; Chm., QS, County of Oxford, 1968–71 (Dep. Chm., 1963–68); a Judge of the High Court of Justice, Queen's Bench Div., 1968–77; Presiding Judge, SE Circuit, 1971–76. Mem., General Council of the Bar, 1965–67. Mem., Royal Commn on Criminal Procedure, 1978–80; Chm., Statute Law Soc., 1985–89; President: British-German Jurists' Assoc., 1974–85; Bar Musical Soc., 1980–89. Hon. Citizen: Texas, 1980; Austin, 1985; Dallas, 1985. *Club:* Garrick.

EVELEIGH, Air Vice-Marshal Geoffrey Charles, CB 1964; OBE 1945; RAF retired; *b* 25 Oct. 1912; *s* of Ernest Charles Eveleigh, Henley-on-Thames; *m* 1939, Anthea Josephine (*d* 1998), *d* of F. H. Fraser, Ceylon; one *s* one *d*. *Educ:* Brighton Coll.; RAF Coll., Cranwell. Joined RAF, 1932; served War of 1939–45 in Bomber Command and No 2 Group; Dep. Chief of Air Staff, Royal New Zealand Air Force, 1955–57; Air Commodore, 1957; Dir-Gen. of Signals, Air Ministry, 1959–61; Air Vice-Marshal, 1961; Air Officer, Administration, Fighter Command, 1961–64; retd 1965. *Address:* 22 Rosehill Park, Emmer Green, Reading RG4 8XE. *Club:* Royal Air Force.

EVENNETT, David Anthony; Commercial Liaison Manager, Bexley College, since 1997; *s* of Norman Thomas Evennett and Irene Evennett; *m* 1975, Marilyn Anne Smith; two *s*. *Educ:* Buckhurst Hill County High School for Boys; London School of Economics and Political Science (BSc (Econ) Upper Second Hons, MSc (Econ)). School Master, Ilford County High School for Boys, 1972–74; Marine Insurance Broker, Lloyd's, 1974–81; Mem., Lloyd's, 1976–92; Dir, Lloyd's Underwriting Agency, 1982–91. Consultant, J & H Marsh and McLennan (UK), then Marsh (UK), Ltd, 1998–2000. Redbridge Borough Councillor, 1974–78. Contested (C) Hackney South and Shoreditch, 1979; MP (C) Erith and Crayford, 1983–97; contested (C) Bexleyheath and Crayford, 1997, 2001. PPS to Minister of State, Dept of Educn, 1992–93, to Sec. of State for Wales, 1993–95, to Sec. of State for Educn and Employment, 1996–97. Mem., Select Cttee on Educn, Science and the Arts, 1986–92. Mem., Bow Gp, 1971–; Vice-Chm., H of C Motor Club, 1992–97 (Sec., 1985–86). Vice-Pres., Hackney S and Shoreditch Cons. Assoc., 1985–97. *Recreations:* my family, reading, history, theatre and cinema. *Address:* c/o Bexleyheath and Crayford Conservative Association, 17 Church Road, Bexleyheath, Kent DA7 4DD. *Club:* Bexleyheath Conservative.

EVENS, Ven. Robert John Scott; Archdeacon of Bath, since 1996; *b* 29 May 1947; *s* of Reginald Evens and Sheila (*née* Scott); *m* 1972, Sue Hayes; one *s* one *d*. *Educ:* Maidstone Grammar Sch.; Trinity Coll., Bristol (DipTh); ACIB. Nat. Westminster Bank, 1964–74; ordained deacon, 1977, priest, 1978, Assistant Curate: St Simon's, Southsea, 1977–79; St Mary's, Portchester, 1979–83; Vicar, St John's, Locks Heath, 1983–96; RD of Fareham, 1993–96. *Recreations:* caravanning in France, gardening, walking with Sue. *Address:* 56 Grange Road, Saltford, Bristol BS31 3AG. *T:* (01225) 873609.

EVERALL, Mark Andrew; QC 1994; a Recorder, since 1996; *b* 30 June 1950; *s* of late John Everall, FRCP and of Pamela Everall; *m* 1978, Anne Perkins; two *d*. *Educ:* Ampleforth Coll., York; Lincoln Coll., Oxford (MA). Called to the Bar, Inner Temple, 1975, Bencher, 1998; Asst Recorder, 1993–96. *Publication:* (ed jtly) Rayden and Jackson on Divorce and Family Matters, 17th edn 1997. *Recreations:* walking, music, architecture. *Address:* 1 Mitre Court Buildings, Temple, EC4Y 7BS. *T:* (020) 7797 7070.

EVERARD, John Vivian; HM Diplomatic Service; Ambassador to Uruguay, since 2001; *b* 24 Nov. 1956; *s* of William Ralph Everard and Margaret Nora Jennifer Everard (*née* Massey); *m* 1990, Heather Ann Starkey. *Educ:* King's Sch., Chester; King Edward VI Sch., Lichfield; Emmanuel Coll., Cambridge (BA 1978; MA 1986); Peking Univ.; Manchester Business Sch. (MBA 1986). Joined HM Diplomatic Service, 1979: FCO, 1979–81; Third (later Second) Sec., Peking, 1981–83; Second Sec., Vienna, 1983–84; Manchester Business Sch., 1984–86; Metapraxis Ltd, 1986–87; FCO, 1987–90; First Sec., Santiago, 1990–93; Chargé d'Affaires, Minsk, 1993; Ambassador, Belarus, 1993–95; OSCE Mission to Bosnia and Hercegovina, 1995–96; Dep. Hd, Africa (Equatorial) Dept, FCO, 1996–98; Counsellor (Political, Econ. and Develt), Peking, 1998–2001. *Recreations:* reading, travel, cats, cycling. *Address:* c/o Foreign and Commonwealth Office, King Charles Street, SW1A 2AH.

EVERARD, Sir Robin (Charles), 4th Bt *cr* 1911; Management Consultant, since 1976; *b* 5 Oct. 1939; *s* of Sir Nugent Henry Everard, 3rd Bt and Frances Audrey (*d* 1975), *d* of J. C. Jesson; *S* father, 1984; *m* 1963, Ariel Ingrid, *d* of late Col Peter Cleasby-Thompson, MBE, MC; one *s* two *d*. *Educ:* Sandroyd School; Harrow; RMA Sandhurst. Short service commn, Duke of Wellington's Regt, 1958–61. Money Broker; Managing Director, P. Murray-Jones, 1962–76; Consultant, 1976–91. *Heir: s* Henry Peter Charles Everard, *b* 6 Aug. 1970. *Address:* Church Farm, Shelton, Long Stratton, Norwich NR15 2SB.

EVERARD, Simon, TD 1968; DL; Chairman, Alliance and Leicester plc (formerly Alliance and Leicester Building Society), 1994–98; *b* 30 Oct. 1928; *s* of Charles Miskin Everard and Monica Mary Everard (*née* Barford); *m* 1955, Joceline Margaret Holt (*d* 2000); three *s* one *d*. *Educ:* Uppingham Sch.; Clare Coll., Cambridge (Hons History). Served TA, Leics Yeomanry, subseq. Leics and Derbys Yeomanry. Ellis & Everard: joined 1952; Chm., 1980–90 and 1991–92; joined Leicester Temperance Building Soc., 1967; merged with Leicester Permanent Bldg Soc., 1974, with Alliance Bldg Soc., 1984; Dep. Chm., 1984–94. Non-Exec. Dir, Croda International, 1991–. DL Leics, 1984. *Recreations:* shooting, tennis, golf, bridge. *Address:* Sludge Hall, Cold Newton, Billesdon, Leics LE7 9DA. *Club:* Cavalry and Guards.

See also T. J. Everard.

EVERARD, Timothy John, CMG 1978; HM Diplomatic Service, retired; Secretary General, Order of St John, 1988–93; *b* 22 Oct. 1929; *s* of late Charles M. Everard and late Monica M. Everard (*née* Barford); *m* 1955, Josiane Romano; two *s* two *d*. *Educ:* Uppingham Sch.; Magdalen Coll., Oxford. BA (Mod. Langs). Banking: Barclays Bank DCO, 1952–62, in Egypt, Sudan, Kenya, Zaire. Entered Foreign (later Diplomatic) Service: First Sec., FO, 1962–63; First Sec., Commercial, Bangkok, 1964–66; resigned to take up directorship in Ellis & Everard Ltd, 1966–67. Rejoined Foreign and Commonwealth Office, Oct. 1967: First Sec., FO, 1967–68; Bahrain, 1969–72 (First Sec. and Head of Chancery, HM Political Residency); seconded to Northern Ireland Office, FCO, April-Aug. 1972; Consul-Gen., then Chargé d'Affaires, Hanoi, 1972–73; Economic and Commercial Counsellor, Athens, 1974–78; Commercial Counsellor, Paris, 1978–81; Minister, Lagos, 1981–84; Ambassador to GDR, 1984–88. Trustee, Dresden Trust, 1994–. Vice Pres., Eurodefense UK, 1998–. KStJ 1988. *Recreations:* golf, tennis. *Address:* Leagues, Burnt Oak, Crowborough, Sussex TN6 3SD. *Club:* Reform.

See also S. Everard.

EVERED, David Charles; Second Secretary, Medical Research Council, 1988–96; *b* 21 Jan. 1940; *s* of late Thomas Charles Evered and Enid Christian Evered; *m* 1st, 1964, Anne Elizabeth Massey Lings, (Kit) (*d* 1998), *d* of John Massey Lings, Manchester; one *s* two *d*; 2nd, 2000, Sheila May Pusinelli, *d* of Charles Cecil Lennox Pusinelli and Margaret Chalona Pusinelli, Thornton-le-Dale, Yorks. *Educ:* Cranleigh Sch., Surrey; Middlesex Hosp. Med. Sch. (BSc 1961, MB 1964, MRCP 1967, MD 1971). Junior hospital appointments, London and Leeds, 1964–70; First Asst in Medicine, Wellcome Sen. Res. Fellow and Consultant Physician, Univ. of Newcastle upon Tyne and Royal Victoria Infirmary, 1970–78; Dir, Ciba Foundn, 1978–88. Member: British Library Medical Information Review Panel, 1978–80; Council, St George's Hosp. Med. Sch. 1983–91; Cttee, Assoc. of Med. Res. Charities, 1981–84, 1987–88 (Vice-Chm., 1987–88); COPUS, Royal Soc., 1986–88; Media Resource Service Adv. Cttee, NY, 1986–; NW Thames RHA, 1988–90; Hammersmith & Queen Charlotte's SHA, 1989–94; Bd, Hammersmith Hosps NHS Trust, 1995–96; Council, Internat. Agency for Res. into Cancer (Lyon), 1988–96; Council, RPMS, 1994–96; Vice-Pres., Science Cttee, Louis Jeantet Fondation de Médecine, 1984–91; Chairman: Anglia & Oxford Res. Ethics Cttee, 1997–99; Nuffield Orthopaedic Centre NHS Trust, 1998–. FRCP 1978; FIBiol 1978; FRSocMed; Scientific Fellow, Zool Soc. of London (Mem. Council, 1985–89). Member: Soc. for Endocrinology; Eur. Thyroid Assoc. (Mem. Exec. Cttee, 1977–81, Sec.-Treas., 1983–89). *Publications:* Diseases of the Thyroid, 1976; (with R. Hall and R. Greene) Atlas of Clinical Endocrinology, 1979, 2nd edn 1990; (with M. O'Connor) Collaboration in Medical Research in Europe, 1981; numerous papers on medicine, education and science policy. *Recreations:* reading, history, tennis, Real tennis, gardening. *Address:* Whitehall Cottage, Whitehall Lane, Checkendon, S Oxfordshire RG8 0TR.

EVERETT, Bernard Jonathan, CVO 1999; HM Diplomatic Service; Consul-General, São Paulo and Director of Trade and Investment for Brazil, since 2000; *b* 17 Sept. 1943; *s* of late Arnold Edwin Everett and of Helene May Everett (*née* Heine); *m* 1970, Maria Olinda, *d* of Raul Correia de Albuquerque and Maria de Lourdes Gonçalves de Albuquerque; two *s* one *d* (and one *d* decd). *Educ:* King's Coll. Sch., Wimbledon; Lincoln Coll., Oxford (BA 1965). Researcher, Reader's Digest, 1965; entered HM Diplomatic Service, 1966; Third, later Second Sec., Lisbon, 1967; FCO, 1971; Consul, Luanda, 1975; FCO, 1976; Head of Chancery, Lusaka, 1978; Consul (Commercial), Rio de Janeiro, 1980; Asst Head, Information Dept, FCO, 1983; on secondment as Head, Sub-Saharan Africa Br., DTI, 1984; Ambassador to Guatemala, 1987–91; Consul-General, Houston, 1991–95; High Comr, Mozambique, 1996–2000. *Recreations:* sport, performing arts, horses. *Address:* c/o Foreign and Commonwealth Office, SW1A 2AH.

EVERETT, Charles William Vogt; Director, Fire and Emergency Planning, Home Office, since 1999; *b* 15 Oct. 1949; *s* of Dr Thomas Everett and Ingeborg Everett (*née* Vogt); *m* 1978, Elizabeth Vanessa Ellis; three *s*. *Educ:* Bryanston Sch.; Reading Univ. Admin. trainee, Lord Chancellor's Dept, 1971; Asst Private Sec. to Lord Chancellor, 1974–76; Dept of Transport, 1982–84; Lord Chancellor's Dept, 1984–99; Asst Sec., 1984; Under Sec., 1991; Head of Policy and Legal Services Gp, 1991–94; Dir, Finance and Admin, then Resource and Support Services, The Court Service, 1994–99. *Address:* Home Office, Horseferry House, Dean Ryle Street, SW1P 2AW.

EVERETT, Christopher Harris Doyle, CBE 1988; MA; Director General and Secretary, Daiwa Anglo-Japanese Foundation, 1990–2000; *b* 20 June 1933; *s* of late Alan Doyle Everett, MBE, MS, FRCS, and Annabel Dorothy Joan Everett (*née* Harris); *m* 1955, Hilary (Billy) Anne (*née* Robertson); two *s* two *d*. *Educ:* Winchester College; New College, Oxford. MA (Class. Mods and Lit. Hum.). Grenadier Guards, Nat. Service, 1951–53. HM Diplomatic Service, 1957–70: posts included Beirut, Washington and Foreign Office; Headmaster: Worksop Coll., 1970–75; Tonbridge Sch., 1975–89. Chm., 1986, Vice-Chm., 1987, HMC. Mem., Extended Interview Bds for Police, Fire and Prison Services. JP Tonbridge and W Malling, 1976–89. Hon. FCP 1988. *Recreations:* reading, walking, tennis. *Address:* Lavender House, 12 Madeira Park, Tunbridge Wells, Kent TN2 5SX. *T:* (01892) 525624.

EVERETT, Douglas Hugh, MBE 1946; FRS 1980; Leverhulme Professor of Physical Chemistry, University of Bristol, 1954–82, now Emeritus; Dean of Faculty of Science, 1966–68; Pro-Vice-Chancellor, 1973–76; *b* 26 Dec. 1916; *e s* of late Charles Everett and Jessie Caroline; *m* 1942, Frances Elizabeth Jessop (*d* 1999); two *d*. *Educ:* Grammar Sch., Hampton-on-Thames; University of Reading; Balliol Coll., Oxford. Wantage Scholar, Reading Univ., 1935–38; Kitchener Scholar, 1936–39; BSc, 1938; Ramsay Fellow, 1939–41; DPhil 1942. Special Scientific Duties, WO, 1942–45. ICI Fellow, Oxford Univ., 1945–47; Chemistry Lecturer, Dundee Univ. Coll., 1947; MA 1947; Fellow, Lecturer and Tutor, Exeter Coll., Oxford, 1947–48; Prof. of Chemistry, Dundee Univ. Coll., University of St Andrews, 1948–54. Chm., Internat. Union of Pure and Applied Chemistry Commn on Colloid and Surface Chemistry, 1969–73. FRSE 1950; DSc 1956. Mem., Building Research Board, DSIR, 1954–61; a Vice-Pres., Faraday Soc., 1958–61, 1963–65, 1968–70, Pres., 1976–78; Mem. Chemical Soc. Council, 1961–64, 1972–74 (Tilden Lectr, 1955; Award in Colloid and Surface Chemistry, 1971); Pres., Section B, BAAS, 1979–80; a Vice-Pres. and Gen. Sec., BAAS, 1983–88; Pres., Internat. Assoc. of Colloid and Interface Scientists, 1988–90. *Publications:* Introduction to Chemical Thermodynamics, 1959, 2nd edn, 1971; Basic Principles of Colloid Science, 1988; (with W. Rudzinski) Adsorption of Gases on Heterogeneous Surfaces, 1991; papers on Physical Chemistry in scientific jls. *Recreations:* walking, painting. *Address:* School of Chemistry, The University, Bristol BS8 1TS; 35 Downleaze, Bristol BS9 1LX.

EVERETT, Eileen, (Mrs Raymond Everett); *see* Diss, E.

EVERETT, Oliver William, CVO 1991 (LVO 1980); Librarian, Windsor Castle and Assistant Keeper of The Queen's Archives, since 1985; *b* 28 Feb. 1943; *s* of Charles Everett, DSO, MC and Judy Rothwell; *m* 1965, Theffania Vesey Stoney; two *s* two *d*. *Educ:* Felsted Sch.; Western Reserve Acad., Ohio, USA; Christ's Coll., Cambridge; Fletcher Sch. of Law and Diplomacy, Mass, USA. HM Diplomatic Service, 1967–81: First Sec., New Delhi, 1969–73; Head of Chancery, Madrid, 1980–81; Asst Private Sec. to HRH The Prince of Wales, 1978–80; Private Sec. to HRH The Princess of Wales, 1981–83, and Comptroller to TRH The Prince and Princess of Wales, 1981–83; Dep. Librarian, Windsor Castle, 1984. *Recreations:* skiing, rackets, windsurfing, baseball. *Address:* Garden House, Windsor Castle, Berks SL4 1NG. *T:* (01753) 833711. *Clubs:* Chelsea Arts, Roxburghe.

EVERETT, Rupert; actor. *Educ:* Ampleforth Coll.; Central Sch. of Speech and Drama. Trained with Glasgow Citizens' Theatre, 1979–82; *stage* includes: Glasgow Citizens' Theatre: Waste of Time; Don Juan; Heartbreak House; The Vortex, 1988, transf. Garrick, 1989; The Picture of Dorian Gray, 1993; The Milk Train Doesn't Stop Here Anymore, 1994, transf. Lyric, Hammersmith, 1997; Another Country, Greenwich, transf. Queen's, 1982; Mass Appeal, Lyric, Hammersmith; L'importance d'être Constant, Théâtre de Chaillot, Paris, 1996; Some Sunny Day, Hampstead, 1996; *films* include: A Shocking Accident, 1982; Another Country, 1984; Dance with a Stranger, 1985; Duet for One, 1986; The Comfort of Strangers, 1990; Inside Monkey Zetterland, 1992; Prêt-à-Porter, 1994; The Madness of King George, 1995; My Best Friend's Wedding, 1997; B Monkey, 1998; An Ideal Husband, 1999; Shakespeare in Love, 1999; A Midsummer Night's Dream, 1999; The Next Best Thing, 2000; *television* includes: The Far Pavilions, 1982. *Publications:* Hello Darling, Are You Working?, 1992; The Hairdressers of St Tropez, 1995. *Address:* c/o ICM, 8942 Wilshire Boulevard, Beverly Hills, CA 90211, USA.

EVERETT, Thomas Henry Kemp; Deputy Special Commissioner of Income Tax, since 2000 (Special Commissioner of Income Tax, 1983–2000); *b* 28 Jan. 1932; *s* of late Thomas Kemp Everett and Katharine Ida Everett (*née* Woodward); *m* 1954, June (*née* Partridge); three *s*. *Educ:* Queen Elizabeth Hospital, Bristol; Univ. of Bristol (LLB Hons 1957). Solicitor (Hons), admitted 1960; Partner, Meade-King & Co., 1963–83. Clerk to General Commissioners, Bedminster Div., 1965–83. Chairman: Service 9, 1972–75; Bristol Council of Voluntary Service, 1975–80; St Christopher's Young Persons' Residential Trust, 1976–83; Mem., Governing Council, St Christopher's School, Bristol, 1983–89; Gov., Queen Elizabeth Hosp., 1974–92 (Vice-Chm. Govs, 1980–91); Pres., Queen Elizabeth Hosp. Old Boys' Soc., 1990–91. *Recreations:* music, motoring, gardening. *Address:* 15–19 Bedford Avenue, WC1B 3AS. *T:* (020) 7631 4242.

EVERHART, Prof. Thomas Eugene, PhD; President, and Professor of Electrical Engineering and Applied Physics, California Institute of Technology, 1987–97, now President Emeritus and Professor Emeritus; *b* 15 Feb. 1932; *s* of William E. Everhart and Elizabeth A. Everhart (*née* West); *m* 1953, Doris A. Wentz; two *s* two *d*. *Educ:* Harvard

Coll. (AB 1953); Univ. of California (MSc 1955); Clare Coll., Cambridge (PhD 1958). Department of Electrical Engineering and Computer Science, University of California, Berkeley: Asst Prof., 1958–62; Associate Prof., 1962–67; Prof., 1967–78; Dept Chm., 1972–77; Dean, Coll. of Engrg, Cornell Univ., 1979–84; Chancellor, Univ. of Illinois, Urbana-Champaign, 1984–87; Pro-Vice-Chancellor, Cambridge Univ., 1998. Director: General Motors Corp., 1989–; Hewlett-Packard Co., 1991–99; Reveo Inc., 1994–; Saint Gobain, 1996–; Raytheon Co., 1998–; Hughes Electronics Corp., 1999–; Agilent Technologies, 1999–. Mem., NAE (USA), 1978; Foreign Mem., Royal Acad. of Engrg, 1990. Hon. LLD: Ill Wesleyan, 1990; Pepperdine, 1990; Hon. DEng Colo Sch. of Mines, 1990. Centennial Medal, IEEE, 1984; Benjamin Garver Lamme Award, 1989, Centennial Medal, 1993, ASEE; Clark Kerr Award, Univ. of Calif., Berkeley, 1992. *Publication:* Microwave Communications, 1968. *Recreations:* hiking, fishing, ski-ing. *Address:* President Emeritus, Mail Code 202–31, California Institute of Technology, Pasadena, CA 91125, USA. *T:* (818) 3953174. *Clubs:* Athenæum (CIT), California (LA).

EVERITT, Prof. Alan Milner, PhD; FRHistS; FBA 1989; Hatton Professor and Head of Department of English Local History, University of Leicester, 1968–82, now Professor Emeritus (Associate Professor, 1982–84); *b* 17 Aug. 1926; *s* of Robert Arthur Everitt and Grace Beryl Everitt (*née* Milner). *Educ:* Sevenoaks Sch.; Univ. of St Andrews (MA 1951); Inst. of Historical Res., London Univ. (Carnegie Scholar; PhD 1957). FRHistS 1969. Editorial Assistant, ACU, 1951–54; Department of English Local History, University of Leicester: Res. Assistant, 1957–59; Res. Fellow in Urban Hist., 1960–65; Lectr in Eng. Local Hist., 1965–68. Lectures: Gregynog, Univ. of Wales, 1976; Helen Sutermeister, UEA, 1982; James Ford Special, Univ. of Oxford, 1983; W. G. Hoskins, Univ. of Leicester, 1999. *Publications:* The County Committee of Kent in the Civil War, 1957; Suffolk and the Great Rebellion 1640–1660, 1960; The Community of Kent and the Great Rebellion 1640–60, 1966, 3rd edn 1986; Change in the Provinces: the seventeenth century, 1969; The Pattern of Rural Dissent: the nineteenth century, 1972; Perspectives in English Urban History, 1973; (with Margery Tranter) English Local History at Leicester 1948–1978, 1981; Landscape and Community in England, 1985; Continuity and Colonization: the evolution of Kentish settlement, 1986; (with John Chartres) Agricultural Markets and Trade 1500–1750, 1990; contribs to: The Agrarian History of England and Wales; Past and Present, Trans of RHistS, Agricl Hist. Rev., Urban History Yearbook, Jl of Histl Geog., Jl of Transport Hist., Archaeologia Cantiana, Local Historian, TLS, Nomina, and other learned publications. *Address:* Fieldedge, Poultney Lane, Kimcote, Lutterworth, Leics LE17 5RX.

EVERITT, Anthony Michael; writer; Secretary-General, Arts Council of Great Britain, 1990–94 (Deputy Secretary-General, 1985–90); *b* 31 Jan. 1940; *s* of late Michael Anthony Hamill Everitt and Simone Dolores Cathérine (*née* de Vergriette; she *m* 2nd, John Brunel Cohen). *Educ:* Cheltenham Coll.; Corpus Christi Coll., Cambridge (BA Hons English, 1962). Lectured variously at National Univ. of Iran, Teheran, SE London Coll. of Further Educn, Birmingham Coll. of Art, and Trent Polytechnic, 1963–72; The Birmingham Post: Art Critic, 1970–75; Drama Critic, 1974–79; Features Editor, 1976–79; Director: Midland Gp Arts Centre, Nottingham, 1979–80; E Midlands Arts Assoc., 1980–85. Vis. Prof., Performing and Visual Arts, Nottingham Trent Univ., 1996–. Chairman: Ikon Gall., Birmingham, 1976–79; Birmingham Arts Lab., 1977–79; Vice-Chm., Council of Regional Arts Assocs, 1981–85; Member: Drama Panel, 1974–78, and Regional Cttee, 1979–80, Arts Council of GB; Cttee for Arts and Humanities, 1986–87, Performing Arts Cttee, 1987–92, CNAA; General Adv. Council, IBA, 1987–90. Hon. Fellow, Dartington Coll. of Arts, 1995. *Publications:* Abstract Expressionism, 1974; In from the Margins, 1996; Joining In, 1997; The Governance of Culture, 1997; The Creative Imperative, 2000; Cicero: a turbulent life, 2001; contribs to The Guardian, Financial Times, Studio Internat., Country Life, etc. *Address:* Westerlies, Anchor Hill, Wivenhoe, Essex CO7 9BL.

EVERITT, Prof. Barry John, PhD; Fellow, Downing College, Cambridge, since 1976; Professor of Behavioural Neuroscience, Department of Experimental Psychology, University of Cambridge, since 1997; *b* 19 Feb. 1946; *s* of Frederick John Everitt and Winifred Everitt; *m* 1st, 1966, Valerie Sowter (marr. diss. 1978); one *s*; 2nd, 1979, Dr Jane Carolyn Sterling; one *d*. *Educ:* Univ. of Hull (BSc Zool. 1967); Univ. of Birmingham (PhD 1970); MA Cantab. MRC Res. Fellow, Univ. of Birmingham Med. Sch., 1970–73; MRC Travelling Res. Fellow, Karolinska Inst., Sweden, 1973–74; Department of Anatomy, University of Cambridge: Demonstrator, 1974–79; Lectr, 1979–91; Reader in Neurosci., 1991–97; Dir of Studies in Medicine, Downing Coll., Cambridge, 1978–98. Ciba-Geigy Sen. Res. Fellow, Karolinska Inst., 1982–83; Vis. Prof., Univ. of Calif, San Francisco, 2000; Lectures: EBBS Review, Madrid, 1993; Grass, Texas, 1997; Swammerdam, Amsterdam, 1999; Swedish Neurosci. Review, 1999; Hillarp, Miami, 1999. Editor-in-Chief: Physiol. and Behavior, 1994–99; European Jl Neurosci., 1997–. Chairman: MRC Res. Studentships and Trng Awards Panel, 1995–97; Human Sci. Frontier Prog. Fellowships Cttee, 1994–96; Scientific Adv. Bd, Astra Arcus, Sweden, 1998–. President: Brit. Assoc. Psychopharmacology, 1992–94; Eur. Brain and Behaviour Soc., 1998–2000. Foreign Corresp. Mem., Amer. Coll. of Neuropsychopharmacology, 1999. *Publications:* Essential Reproduction, 1980, 5th edn 1999; over 250 papers in scientific jls. *Recreations:* opera, wine, cricket. *Address:* Downing College, Cambridge CB2 1DQ. *T:* (01223) 333583, 334845.

EVERITT, Caroline Mary; *see* Ludlow, C. M.

EVERITT, William Howard, FREng; FIMechE, FIEE; Group Managing Director, Technology, T & N plc, 1995–96; *b* 27 Feb. 1940; *s* of H. G. H. Everitt and J. S. Everitt; *m* Antha Cecilia; two *s*. *Educ:* Leeds Univ. (BSc). Director of Operations, IBM Europe, 1974; Managing Director: Wellworthy, AE, 1975–76; Bearings, AE, 1977–79; AE plc, 1983–86 (Dir, 1978); Dir, T & N plc, 1987–96; Man. Dir, Automotive, T & N, 1990–93. Non-exec. Dir, Domino Printing Services plc, 1997–. FREng (FEng 1988). *Recreation:* golf. *Address:* Horley House, Hornton Lane, Horley, near Banbury, Oxon OX15 6BL. *T:* (01295) 730603.

EVERSON, John Andrew; education consultant; *b* 26 Oct. 1933; *s* of Harold Leslie Everson and Florence Jane Stone; *m* 1961, Gilda Ramsden; two *s*. *Educ:* Tiffin Boys' Sch., Kingston-upon-Thames; Christ's Coll., Cambridge (MA); King's Coll., London (PGCE). Teacher: Haberdashers' Aske's Sch., Elstree, 1958–65; City of London Sch., 1965–68; Schools Inspectorate, DES, later Dept for Educn, 1968–92; Chief Inspector for Secondary Educn, 1981–89; seconded to Peat Marwick McLintock, 1989; Chief Inspector for Teacher Training, 1990–92. *Publications:* (with B. P. FitzGerald) Settlement Patterns, 1968; (with B. P. FitzGerald) Inside the City, 1972. *Recreations:* opera, walking, theatre, chess. *Address:* 74 Longdown Lane North, Epsom, Surrey KT17 3JF. *T:* (01372) 721556. *Club:* Athenæum.

EVERT, Christine Marie; American tennis player, retired 1989; founder, Chris Evert Charities Inc., 1989; *b* 21 Dec. 1954; *d* of James and Colette Evert; *m* 1st, 1979, John Lloyd (marr. diss. 1987); 2nd, 1988, Andy Mill; three *s*. *Educ:* St Thomas Aquinas High Sch., Fort Lauderdale. Amateur tennis player, 1970–72, professional player, 1972–89. Semi-finalist in US Open at age of 16; won numerous titles, including: Wimbledon: 1974, 1976, 1981 (doubles, 1976); French Open: 1974–75, 1979–80, 1983, 1985–86; US Open: 1975–78, 1980, 1982; Australian Open: 1982, 1984. Represented USA in Wightman Cup, 1971–73, 1975–82, and in Federation Cup, 1977–82. Pres., Women's Tennis Assoc., 1982–91. *Address:* c/o IMG, 1360 East 9th Street, Suite 100, Cleveland, OH 44114, USA; 7200 West Camino Real, Suite 310, Boca Raton, FL 33433, USA.

EVERY, Sir Henry (John Michael), 13th Bt *cr* 1641, of Egginton, Derbyshire; Partner, Deloitte & Touche, Chartered Accountants, Birmingham; *b* 6 April 1947; *s* of Sir John Simon Every, 12th Bt and of Janet Marion, *d* of John Page; *S* father, 1988; *m* 1974, Susan Mary, *er d* of Kenneth Beaton, JP, Eastshotte, Hartford, Cambs; three *s*. *Educ:* Malvern College. FCA. Qualified as Chartered Accountant, 1970; worked in South Africa, 1970–74; Partner, Josolyne Layton-Bennett, Birmingham, 1979–81; merged with BDO Binder Hamlyn, 1982, then with Touche Ross, 1994, to form Deloitte & Touche. Pres., Birmingham and West Midlands Dist Soc. of Chartered Accountants, 1995–96 (Chm., Dist Trng Bd, 1991–93). Mem., Egginton Parish Council, 1987–. Mem. Cttee, Lunar Soc., 1993–. Trustee, Nat. Meml Arboretum, 1996–; Patron, Derby Heritage Develt Trust, 1998–. FRSA 1996. *Recreations:* tennis, National Trust, gardening; supporter of Nottingham Forest FC. *Heir:* *s* Edward James Henry Every, *b* 3 July 1975. *Address:* Cothay, Egginton, Derby DE65 6HJ.

EVES, David Charles Thomas, CB 1993; Deputy Director General and HM Chief Inspector of Factories, Health and Safety Executive; *b* 10 Jan. 1942; *s* of Harold Thomas Eves and Violet Eves (*née* Edwards); *m* 1964, Valerie Ann Carter; one *d*. *Educ:* King's Sch., Rochester; University Coll., Durham. Teacher, Kent CC, 1963–64; HM Inspector of Factories, Min. of Labour, 1964; Under Sec., 1985–89, Dep. Sec., and Dep. Dir Gen., 1989–, HSE; HM Chief Inspector of Factories, 1985–88, 1992–; Dir, Resources and Planning Div., HSE, 1988–89. International Association of Labour Inspection: Vice Pres., 1993–99; Sec. Gen., 1996–99; Technical Advr, 1999–. FIOSH (Hon. Vice Pres., 1992–). *Recreations:* sailing, fishing, music, would-be painter, wood turner. *Address:* Health and Safety Executive, Rose Court, 2 Southwark Bridge, SE1 9HS. *T:* (020) 7717 6450, *Fax:* (020) 7717 6616. *Club:* Athenæum.

EVETTS, Prof. Jan Edgar, PhD; Professor of Device Materials, University of Cambridge, since 1998; Fellow of Pembroke College, Cambridge, since 1965. *Educ:* Pembroke Coll., Cambridge (BA 1961; MA 1965; PhD 1966). Department of Materials Science and Metallurgy, University of Cambridge: formerly Lectr; Reader in Device Materials, 1993–98. Royal Soc. Armourers and Brasiers' Co. Award (jtly), 1993. *Publications:* (ed) High Temperature Superconductivity, 1991; (ed) Critical Currents: symposium proceedings, 1992; (ed) Concise Encyclopaedia of Magnetic and Superconducting Materials, 1992. *Address:* Pembroke College, Cambridge CB2 1RF.

EVISON, Dame (Helen June) Patricia, DBE 1993 (OBE 1980); freelance actress on stage, film, radio and television in New Zealand and Australia; *b* 2 June 1924; *d* of Rev. Ernest Oswald Blamires and Annie (*née* Anderson); *m* 1948, Roger Douglas Evison; two *s* one *d*. *Educ:* Solway Coll., Masterton; Victoria Univ. (BA 1943); Auckland Teachers Training Coll. (postgrad. course 1944); Auckland Univ. (DipEd 1944); LTCL (speech) 1942). Directors course, Old Vic Theatre Centre, 1947–48 (first NZ bursary); Assistant to Michel Saint-Denis, Young Vic Theatre Co., 1947–48; freelance director, Wellington, 1949–52; tutor for NZ Opera and NZ Ballet Schs, 1953–79. *Theatre includes:* Happy Days, 1964, 1974; Father's Day, 1966; The Killing of Sister George, 1968; An Evening with Katherine Mansfield (one-woman show), 1972; Awatea, 1974; Home, 1976; Juno and the Paycock, 1977; Hot Water, 1983; Last Days in Woolloomooloo, 1983; Ring Round the Moon, 1990; Steel Magnolias, 1991; Lettice and Lovage, 1993; The Cripple of Inishmaan, 1999; *films:* Tim, 1979 (Best Supporting Actress, Aust. Film Inst, 1979); The Earthling, 1981; Starstruck, 1982; Bad Blood, 1982; The Silent One, 1983; The Clinic, 1983; What the Moon Saw, 1988; Moonrise, 1992; *television:* All Earth to Love, 1963; Pukemanu, 1971 (Cummings award for Best NZ Actress, 1972); Pig in a Poke, 1974 (Logie award for best individual acting perf., 1974); They Don't Clap Losers, 1974; Close to Home (series), 1975–82; The Emigrants, 1977; A Town Like Alice, 1982; Flying Doctors (series), 1984–87. Charter Member: Wellington Zonta Club; Zonta Club for Port Nicholson. *Publication:* Happy Days in Muckle Flugga (autobiog.), 1998. *Recreations:* music, watching cricket and soccer, reading, swimming, travel. *Address:* 11 Beerehaven Road, Seatoun Heights, Wellington 6003, New Zealand. *T:* (4) 3888766.

EWANS, Sir Martin Kenneth, KCMG 1987 (CMG 1980); HM Diplomatic Service, retired; Chairman, Children's Aid Direct, since 1996; *b* 14 Nov. 1928; *s* of late John Ewans; *m* 1953, Mary Tooke; one *s* one *d*. *Educ:* St Paul's; Corpus Christi Coll., Cambridge (major scholar, MA). Royal Artillery, 1947–49, 2nd Lt. Joined Commonwealth Relations Office, 1952; Second Sec., Karachi, 1954–55; First Sec.: Ottawa, 1958–61; Lagos, 1962–64; Kabul, 1967–69. Counsellor, Dar-es-Salaam, 1969–73; Head of East African Dept, FCO, 1973–77; Minister, New Delhi, 1978–82; Sen. Civilian Instructor, RCDS, 1982–83; High Commissioner: in Harare, Zimbabwe, 1983–85; Nigeria, 1986–88. Chm., CSSB, 1989–95. Dir, Casalee SA, 1989–94. *Publications:* Bharatpur, Bird Paradise, 1989; The Battle for the Broads, 1992; Afghanistan: a new history, 2001. *Recreations:* bird watching, writing. *Address:* 26 Gladstone Street, SE1 6EY.

EWART, Sir (William) Michael, 7th Bt *cr* 1887, of Glenmachen, Co. Down and of Glenbank, Co. Antrim; *b* 10 June 1953; *o s* of Sir (William) Ivan (Cecil) Ewart, 6th Bt and Pauline Preston (*d* 1964); *S* father, 1995. *Educ:* Radley. *Recreations:* racing, ski-ing, travel. *Heir:* none. *Address:* Hill House, Hillsborough, Co; Down BT26 6AE. *Club:* Naval.

EWBANK, Sir Anthony (Bruce), Kt 1980; Judge of the High Court of Justice, Family Division, 1980–95; *b* 30 July 1925; *s* of late Rev. Harold Ewbank and Gwendolen Ewbank (*née* Bruce); *m* 1958, Moya McGinn; four *s* one *d*. *Educ:* St John's Sch., Leatherhead; Trinity Coll., Cambridge, Natural Sciences Tripos (MA). Sub Lieut RNVR, 1945–47. Maths Master, Stamford School, 1947–50; Physics Master, Epsom Coll., 1950–53. Permanent RNVR, 1951–56. Called to Bar, Gray's Inn, 1954; Bencher, 1980. Junior Counsel to Treasury in Probate matters, 1969; QC 1972; a Recorder of the Crown Court, 1975–80. Chm., Family Law Bar Assoc., 1978–80. *Address:* Beech Down, Elmhurst Road, Goring on Thames, Oxon RG8 9BN.

EWBANK, Prof. Inga-Stina; Professor of English Literature, University of Leeds, 1985–97, now Emeritus; *b* 13 June 1932; *d* of Gustav and Ingeborg Ekeblad; *m* 1959, Roger Ewbank; one *s* two *d*. *Educ:* Högre Allänna Läroverket för Flickor, Gothenburg; Univs of Carleton (BA), Gothenburg (Fil.kand.), Sheffield (MA) and Liverpool (PhD). William Noble Fellow, Univ. of Liverpool, 1955–57; Res. Fellow at Shakespeare Inst., Univ. of Birmingham, 1957–60; Univ. of Liverpool: Asst Lectr, 1960–63; Lectr, 1963–70; Sen. Lectr, 1970–72; Reader in English Literature, Bedford Coll., Univ. of London, 1972–74, Hildred Carlile Prof., 1974–84. Vis. Lectr, Univ. of Munich, 1959–60; Vis. Assoc. Prof., Northwestern Univ., 1966; Visiting Professor: Harvard Univ., 1974; Univ. of Maryland, 1981; Georgetown Univ., 1982; Columbia Univ., 1984, 1987. Mem., Univ. Grants Cttee, Hong Kong, 1982–97. Hon. DPhil Oslo, 1997; Hon. Dr jur Lingnan (Hong

Kong), 1999. Bauhinia Silver Star (Hong Kong), 1999. *Publications:* Their Proper Sphere: A Study of the Brontë Sisters as Early-Victorian Female Novelists, 1966; Shakespeare, Ibsen and the Unspeakable (Inaugural Lecture), 1975; (with Peter Hall) Ibsen's John Gabriel Borkman: An English Version, 1975; The Wild Duck, 1991; (ed jtly) Shakespeare's Styles, 1980; The Arts of Performance in Elizabethan Drama, 1991; Three Chamber Plays by August Strindberg, 1997; Anglo-Scandinavian Cross-currents, 1999; Five Ibsen Plays (trans.), 2001; chapters in: A New Companion to Shakespeare Studies, 1971; The Cambridge Companion to Shakespeare Studies, 1986; The Cambridge Companion to Ibsen Studies, 1994, and other books; contrib. Shakespeare Survey, Ibsen Yearbook, Rev. Eng. Studies, Mod. Lang. Rev., English Studies, etc. *Recreations:* same as work: reading, theatre; children. *Address:* 19 Woodfield Road, Ealing, W5 1SL. *T:* (020) 8997 2895.

EWBANK, Ven. Walter Frederick; Archdeacon Emeritus and Canon Emeritus of Carlisle Cathedral; *b* Poona, India, 29 Jan. 1918; *er s* of late Sir Robert Benson Ewbank, CSI, CIE, and Frances Helen, *d* of Rev. W. F. Simpson; *m* 1st, 1941, Ida Margaret (*d* 1976), 3rd *d* of late John Haworth Whitworth, DSO, MC, Inner Temple; three *d*; 2nd, 1976, Mrs Josephine Alice Williamson (*née* Cartwright), MD, ChB, FRCOG. *Educ:* Shrewsbury Sch.; Balliol Coll., Oxford (Classical Scholar, 1936; 1st, Classical Hon. Mods, 1938; 2nd, Hon. Sch. of Theology, 1946; BA and MA 1946); Bishops' Coll., Cheshunt, 1946; BD Oxon 1952. Friends' Ambulance Unit, 1939–42; agricl labourer, 1942–45; deacon, 1946; priest, 1947; Asst Curate, St Martin's, Windermere, 1946–49; Dio. Youth Chaplain and Vicar of Ings, 1949–52; Chap. to Casterton Sch. and Vicar of Casterton, 1952–62; Domestic Chap. to Bp of Carlisle, and Vicar of Raughtonhead, 1962–66; Vicar of St Cuthbert's, Carlisle, and Chap. to Corporation, 1966–71; Rural Dean of Carlisle, 1970–71; Archdeacon of Westmorland and Furness and Vicar of Winster, 1971–77; Archdeacon of Carlisle, 1977–84; Administrator of Church House, Carlisle and Chm., Diocesan Glebe Cttee, 1977–84; Canon Residentiary of Carlisle Cathedral, 1977–82; Hon. Canon, 1966–77 and 1982–84. Proctor in Convocation and Mem. Ch Assembly, 1957–70; Member: Canon Law Standing Commn, 1968–70; Faculty Jurisdiction Commn, 1979–83; Diocesan Director: of Ordinands, 1962–70; of Post Ordination Trng, 1962–66; Vice-Chm., Diocesan Synod, 1970–79; Chm., Diocesan Board of Finance, 1977–82. Chm., Carlisle Tithe Barn Restoration Cttee, 1968–70. Winter War Remembrance Medal (Finland), 1940. *Publications:* Salopian Diaries, 1961; Morality without Law, 1969; Charles Euston Nurse—A Memoir, 1982; Thomas Bloomer—A Memoir, 1984; Poems of Cumbria and of the Cumbrian Church, 1985; Ellen Margaret Cartwright—A Memoir, 1991; Memories of the Border Regiment in the First World War, 1991; Faith of Our Fathers, 1992; articles in Church Quarterly Review. *Recreation:* classical studies. *Address:* 7 Castle Court, Castle Street, Carlisle CA3 8TP.
See also Baron Renfrew of Kaimsthorn.

EWENS, Prof. Warren John, PhD; FRS 2000; Professor of Biology, University of Pennsylvania, since 1972; *b* 23 Jan. 1937; *s* of John and Gwendoline Ewens; *m* 1st, 1961, Helen Wiley (marr. diss.); one *s* one *d*; 2nd, 1981, Kathryn Gogolin. *Educ:* Trinity Coll., Melbourne Univ. (MA); Australian Nat. Univ. (PhD 1964). Professor, Department of Mathematics: La Trobe Univ., 1967–72; Monash Univ., 1977–96. *Publications:* Population Genetics, 1969; Mathematical Population Genetics, 1979; Probability and Statistics in Bioinformatics, 2000. *Recreations:* tennis, bridge, reading. *Address:* c/o Department of Biology, University of Pennsylvania, PA 19104-6018, USA. *T:* (215) 8987109.

EWER, Maj.-Gen. Graham Anderson, CB 1999; CBE 1991; Chief Executive, Institute of Logistics and Transport, since 1999; *b* 22 Sept. 1944; *s* of late Robert and Maud Ewer; *m* 1969, Mary Caroline Grant; two *d*. *Educ:* Truro Cathedral Sch.; RMA, Sandhurst. FILT 1999 (MILog 1994); FCIT 1999 (MCIT 1994). Commnd RCT, 1965; served Germany, UK and ME, 1966–75; Army Staff Coll., 1976; Lt Col, Directing Staff, Army Staff Coll., 1984; CO, 8 Regt RCT, Munster, 1985–87; Col, DCS, G1/4 HQ 1st Armd Div., Verden, Germany and Gulf War, 1988–91; Comdt, Army Sch. of Transportation, 1991; Col, Logistic Support Policy Secretariat, 1992; Brig. 1993; Comd, Combat Service Support Gp, Germany and Guetersloh Garrison, 1993–94; Dir, Logistic Planning (Army), 1995; ACDS (Logistics), 1996–99. FIMgt 1994. *Publications:* contrib. Blackadder's War, ed M. S. White, 1995; contrib. to various jls. *Recreations:* sailing, motor cycling, military history. *Address:* c/o HSBC, 17 Boscawen Street, Truro, Cornwall TR1 2QZ. *Club:* Army and Navy.

EWIN, Sir David Ernest Thomas F.; *see* Floyd Ewin.

EWING; *see* Orr-Ewing and Orr Ewing.

EWING, family name of **Baron Ewing of Kirkford**.

EWING OF KIRKFORD, Baron *cr* 1992 (Life Peer), of Cowdenbeath in the District of Dunfermline; **Harry Ewing;** DL; Chairman, Fife Healthcare NHS Trust, 1996–98; *b* 20 Jan. 1931; *s* of Mr and Mrs William Ewing; *m* 1954, Margaret Greenhill; one *s* one *d*. *Educ:* Foulford Primary Sch., Cowdenbeath; Beath High Sch., Cowdenbeath. Contested (Lab) East Fife, 1970; MP (Lab) Stirling and Falkirk, Sept. 1971–Feb. 1974, Stirling, Falkirk and Grangemouth, Feb. 1974–83, Falkirk East, 1983–92. Parly Under-Sec. of State, Scottish Office, with special responsibility for devolution, 1974–79. Chm., Ewing Inquiry into availability of housing for wheelchair and other disabled, 1993 (report, 1994). Jt Chm., Scottish Const. Convention, 1990–96. Mem. Educn Cttee, Church of Scotland, 1999–. Nat. Hon. Pres., Girls' Brigade, Scotland, 1993–; Nat. Hon. Mem., UCW; Hon. President: Bowhill Peoples Burns' Club, 1980–; E Fife Male Voice Choir, 1998–; Patron: Scotland Patients Assoc.; Scottish Fisheries Mus. DL Fife, 1995. DUniv Stirling, 1998. Paul Harris Fellow, Rotary Internat., 1999. *Recreation:* gardening. *Address:* Gowanbank, 45 Glenlyon Road, Leven, Fife KY8 4AA. *T:* (01333) 426123.

EWING, Annabelle Janet; solicitor; MP (SNP) Perth, since 2001; *b* 20 August 1960; *d* of Stewart Martin Ewing and Winifred Margaret Ewing, *qv*. *Educ:* Craigholme Sch., Glasgow; Univ. of Glasgow (LLB Hons); Bologna Center, Johns Hopkins Univ.; Europa Inst., Amsterdam Univ. Apprentice lawyer, Ruth Anderson and Co., 1984–86; admitted solicitor, 1986; Legal Service, EC, 1987; Associate, Lebrun de Smedt and Dassesse, Brussels, 1987–89; Associate, 1989–92, Partner, 1993–96, Akin Gump, Brussels; Special Counsel, McKenna and Cuneo, Brussels, 1996; lawyer, EC, 1997; Partner, Ewing & Co., solicitors, 1998–. *Address:* Ewing & Co., 52 Queen's Drive, Glasgow G42 8DD; c/o House of Commons, SW1A 0AA.
See also F. S. Ewing.

EWING, Fergus Stewart; Member (SNP) Inverness East, Nairn and Lochaber, Scottish Parliament, since 1999; *b* 23 Sept. 1957; *s* of Stewart Martin Ewing and Winifred Margaret Ewing, *qv*; *m* 1983, Margaret McAdam (*see* M. A. Ewing). *Educ:* Loretto Sch.; Glasgow Univ. (LLB). Solicitor, 1981; with Leslie Wolfson & Co., Solicitors, Glasgow, 1979–85; Partner, Ewing & Co., Solicitors, Glasgow, 1985–2000. Joined SNP, 1975; Mem., Nat. Exec. Contested (SNP) Inverness, Nairn and Lochaber, 1992, 1997. *Recreations:* reading, music, running. *Address:* Burns Cottage, Tulloch's Brae, Lossiemouth, Morayshire IV31 6QY.

EWING, Margaret Anne; Member (SNP) Moray, Scottish Parliament, since 1999; *b* 1 Sept. 1945; *d* of John and Peggie McAdam; *m* 1983, Fergus Stewart Ewing, *qv*. *Educ:* Univs of Glasgow and Strathclyde. MA Glasgow 1967, BA Hons Strathclyde 1973. Asst Teacher, Our Lady's High, Cumbernauld, 1968–70; St Modan's High, Stirling: Special Asst Teacher, 1970–73; Principal Teacher, Remedial Educn, 1973–74. MP (SNP): East Dunbartonshire, Oct. 1974–1979; Moray, 1987–2001. contested (SNP) Strathkelvin and Bearsden, 1983. Sen. Vice-Chm., SNP, 1984–87; Leader, SNP Parly Gp, 1987–99. *Recreations:* the arts in general, folk music in particular. *Address:* Burns Cottage, Tulloch's Brae, Lossiemouth, Morayshire IV31 6QY. *T:* (01343) 812222.

EWING, Maria Louise; soprano; *b* Detroit, 27 March 1950; *y d* of Norman Ewing and Hermina Ewing (*née* Veraar); *m* 1982, Sir Peter Hall, *qv* (marr. diss. 1990); one *d*. *Educ:* High School; Cleveland Inst. of Music. Studied with Marjorie Gordon, Eleanor Steber, Jennie Tourel, Otto Guth. First public performance, Meadowbrook, 1968 (Rigoletto); débuts Metropolitan Opera and La Scala, 1976; sings at Covent Garden, Glyndebourne, Salzburg, Paris, Metropolitan Opera, LA Opera, La Scala and other major venues; rôles include Blanche, Carmen, Cherubino, Dorabella, Lady Macbeth, Mélisande, La Périchole, Poppea, Rosina, Salomé, Susanna, Tosca, Zerlina; concerts and recitals.

EWING, Mrs Winifred Margaret; Member (SNP) Highlands and Islands, Scottish Parliament, since 1999; *b* 10 July 1929; *d* of George Woodburn and Christina Bell Anderson; *m* 1956, Stewart Martin Ewing, CA; two *s* one *d*. *Educ:* Queen's Park Sen. Sec. Sch.; University of Glasgow (MA, LLB). Qual. as Solicitor, 1952. Lectr in Law, 1954–56; Solicitor, practising on own account, 1956–. Sec., Glasgow Bar Assoc., 1961–67, Pres., 1970–71. MP (SNP): Hamilton, Nov. 1967–70; Moray and Nairn, Feb. 1974–1979; contested (SNP) Orkney and Shetland, 1983. MEP (SNP), 1975–99, elected Mem. for Highlands and Is, 1979–99; Vice-Pres., Animal Welfare Intergp, EP, 1989–99. President: Scottish National Party; European Free Alliance, 1991–; Mem., Lomé Assembly, 1981–. Pres., Glasgow Central Soroptimist Club, 1966–67. FRSA 1990. DUniv Open, 1993; Hon. LLD Glasgow, 1995. Freeman, City of Avignon; Comptroller of Scottish Privileges, Veere, Netherlands. *Address:* Goodwill, Milton Duff, Morayshire IV30 8TL. *T:* (01343) 541154, *Fax:* (01343) 540011.
See also A. J. Ewing, F. S. Ewing.

EWINGTON, John, OBE 1996; General Secretary, Guild of Church Musicians, since 1979; Consultant, Carroll & Partners Ltd, since 2001; *b* 14 May 1936; *s* of William and Beatrice Ewington; *m* 1967, Hélène Mary Leach; two *s*. *Educ:* South East Essex County Technical Sch., Dagenham. ACertCM 1968; Dip Church Music, Goldsmiths' Coll., 1988. Nat. Service, RN, 1954–56. Admin. Assistant, Inst. of London Underwriters, 1953–67; Underwriting Asst, P.C.W. Agencies, Lloyd's, 1967–86; Sen. Broker, 1986–97, Consultant, 1997–2000, HSBC Gibbs. Director of Music and Organist: Blechingley Parish Church, 1966–97; St Mary Woolnoth, 1970–93 (also Sen. Ch Warden, 1973–93); St Katharine Cree, 1998–; Dir, City Singers, 1976–. Vice Chm. of Govs, Oxted Sch., 1984–. Freeman, City of London, 1980. FGCM 1988. Hon. FCSM 1990; Hon. FFCM 1998. *Publications:* articles on church music in jls. *Recreations:* church music, cooking, eating out. *Address:* Hillbrow, Godstone Road, Blechingley, Surrey RH1 4PJ. *T:* (01883) 743168, *Fax:* (01883) 740570; *e-mail:* JohnMusicsure@aol.com. *Club:* Nikaean.

EWINS, Prof. David John, FREng; FIMechE; Professor of Vibration Engineering, since 1983, Director, Centre of Vibration Engineering, Mechanical Engineering Department, since 1990, and Pro-Rector, International Relations, since 2001, Imperial College of Science, Technology and Medicine; Temasek Professor, and Director, Centre for Mechanics of Microsystems, Nanyang Technological University, Singapore, since 1999; *b* 25 March 1942; *s* of W. J. and P. Ewins; *m* 1964, Brenda Rene (*née* Chalk) (marr. diss. 1997); three *d*. *Educ:* Kingswood Grammar Sch., Bristol; Imperial Coll., London (BScEng, ACGI, DScEng); Trinity Coll., Cambridge (PhD). MASME; FIMechE 1990; FREng (FEng 1995). Res. Asst for Rolls-Royce Ltd, Cambridge Univ., 1966–67; Lectr, then Reader, in Mech. Engrg, Imperial Coll., 1967–83; formed Modal Testing Unit at Imperial Coll., 1981; Dir, Rolls-Royce sponsored Centre of Vibration Engrg, Imperial Coll., 1990–. Sen. Lectr, Chulalongkorn Univ., Bangkok, 1968–69; Maître de Conférences, INSA, Lyon, 1974–75; Visiting Professor: Virginia Poly and State Univ., USA, 1981; ETH, Zürich, 1986; Inst. Nat. Polytechnique de Grenoble, 1990; Nanyang Technol Univ., Singapore, 1994, 1997; Hon. Professor: Nanjing Aero Inst., 1988; Shandong Polytechnic Inst., 1991. Partner, ICATS, 1989–. Consultant to: Rolls-Royce, 1969–; MoD, 1977–, and other organisations in Europe, S America and USA. Chm., then Pres., Dynamic Testing Agency, 1990–99. Governor: Cranleigh Sch., 1990–95; Parmiter's Sch., 1993–96. *Publications:* Modal Testing: theory and practice, 1984, 9th edn 1996; Modal Testing: theory, practice and application, 2000; (ed with D. J. Inman) Structural Dynamics, 2000; papers on vibration engrg in technical jls in UK, USA, France. *Recreations:* music (esp. piano duets), hill walking, travel, good food, French, bridge. *Address:* Imperial College, Exhibition Road, SW7 2BX. *T:* (020) 7594 7068.

EWINS, Peter David, CB 2001; FREng; FRAeS; Chief Executive, Meteorological Office, since 1997; *b* 20 March 1943; *s* of John Samuel Ewins and Kathleen Ewins; *m* 1968, Barbara Irene Howland; two *s* one *d*. *Educ:* Imperial College London (BSc Eng); Cranfield Inst. of Technology (MSc). FREng (FEng 1996); FRAeS 1996. Joined RAE Farnborough, 1966, research on structl applications of composite materials; section head, 1974; staff of Chief Scientist, RAF, MoD, 1978; Head of Helicopters Res. Div., RAE, 1981; seconded to Cabinet Office (Civil Service personnel policy), 1984; Dir, Nuclear Projects, MoD, 1987; Dir, ARE, MoD (PE), 1988; Man. Dir (Maritime and Electronics), 1991, Man. Dir, Command and Maritime Systems Gp, 1992, Man. Dir (Ops), 1993–94, DRA; Chief Scientist, MoD, 1994–97. Mem. Council, Royal Acad. of Engrg, 1999–. *Publications:* technical papers on structural composite materials in learned jls. *Recreations:* horticulture, bee-keeping, walking. *Address:* Meteorological Office, London Road, Bracknell, Berks RG12 2SZ.

EWUSIE, Prof. Joseph Yanney; Chief Policy Adviser and Hon. Fellow, Ghana Council for Scientific and Industrial Research, since 1994; *b* 18 April 1927; *s* of Samuel Mainsa Wilson Ewusie and Elizabeth Dickson; *m* 1st, 1959, Stella Turkson (*d* 1989); four *s*, and one adopted *d*; 2nd, 1992, Emma (*née* Ghampson) (marr. diss. 1997); 3rd, 1998, Ruth (*née* Ohene Parry). *Educ:* Winneba Anglican Sch.; Mfantsipim Sch.; University Coll. of the Gold Coast; Univ. of Cambridge. BSc (London), PhD (Cantab). Lectr in Botany, Univ. of Ghana, 1957–62; Gen. Sec. (Chief Exec.), Ghana Academy of Sciences (highest learned and res. org. in Ghana), 1963–68; University of Cape Coast: Associate Prof. of Botany, 1969–72, Prof., 1973–79; Head, Dept of Botany, 1969–73; Dean, Faculty of Science, 1971–74; Pro-Vice Chancellor, 1971–73; Vice Chancellor, 1973–78. Vis. Prof./Prof., Univs of Nairobi and Ahmadu Bello, Nigeria, 1979–80; Sec.-Gen., Pan African Inst. for Development, 1980–83; Professor of Biology: Univ. of Swaziland, 1984–90; Univ. of Bophuthatswana, 1989–92. Mem. Exec. Cttee, ICSU, 1964–67. Founder and First Pres., Bophuthatswana Assoc. for Scientific Advancement, 1990; first Pres., Ghana Inst. of

Biology, 1994 (Fellow 1995). Member: Bimillenium Foundn, Washington DC, 1984–; NY Acad. of Sciences, 1984–. FWA 1963. Co-Founder and First Editor, Swaziland Jl of Sci. and Technol. Hon. DSc Cape Coast, 1994. Medal (Govt of Hungary) for internat. understanding between Ghana and Hungary, 1964; Dipl. of Merit, Internat. Acad. of Science, Letters and Arts, Rome, 1968; Dipl. of Honour, Internat. Inst. of Community Service, 1975; Ghana Scientist of the Year, Ghana Science Assoc., 1985. *Publications:* School Certificate Biology for Tropical Schools, 1964, 4th edn 1974; Tropical Biological Drawings, 1973; Elements of Tropical Ecology, 1980; Phenology in Tropical Ecology, 1992. *Address:* PO Box LG 696, Legon-Accra, Ghana.

EXETER, 8th Marquess of, *cr* 1801; **William Michael Anthony Cecil;** Baron Burghley 1571; Earl of Exeter 1605; *b* 1 Sept. 1935; *s* of 7th Marquess of Exeter and Edith Lilian Csanady de Telegd (*d* 1954); *S* father, 1988; *m* 1st, 1967, Nancy Rose (marr. diss. 1992), *d* of Lloyd Arthur Meeker; one *s* one *d*; 2nd, 1999, Barbara Anne, *d* of Eugene Magat. *Educ:* Eton. Rancher and businessman in 100 Mile House, BC, Canada, 1954–. *Publications:* (jtly) Spirit of Sunrise, 1979; The Long View, 1985; The Rising Tide of Change, 1986; Living at the Heart of Creation, 1990. *Heir: s* Lord Burghley, *qv*. *Address:* 880 Pinecrest Terrace, Ashland, OR 97520, USA. *T:* (541) 488 3646, *Fax:* (541) 488 0003; The Courtyard, Mickleton, Glos GL55 6SF, *T:* (01386) 438525; *e-mail:* mcecil@mind.net.

EXETER, Bishop of, since 2000; **Rt Rev. Michael Laurence Langrish;** *b* 1 July 1946; *s* of Douglas Frank and Brenda Florence Langrish; *m* 1968, Esther Vivien (*née* Rudd); one *s* two *d*. *Educ:* King Edward Sch., Southampton; Birmingham Univ. (BSocSc 1967; PGCE 1968); Fitzwilliam Coll., Cambridge (BA 1973; MA 1978); Ridley Hall, Cambridge. Lectr in Educn, Mid-West State Coll. of Educn, Nigeria, 1969–71. Ordained deacon, 1973, priest, 1974; Asst Curate, Stratford-upon-Avon with Bishopston, 1973–76; Chaplain, Rugby Sch., 1976–81; Vicar, Offchurch and Diocesan Dir of Ordinands, 1981–87; Team Rector, Rugby Team Ministry, 1987–93; Bishop Suffragan of Birkenhead, 1993–2000. Examining Chaplain to the Bishop of Coventry, 1982–89; Chm., ACCM Vocations Cttee, 1984–91; Chm., House of Clergy, Coventry Diocesan Synod, 1988–93; Hon. Canon, Coventry Cathedral, 1990–93. *Recreations:* walking, gardening, local history, theatre, railways, music. *Address:* The Palace, Exeter EX1 1HY. *T:* (01392) 272362. *Clubs:* Athenæum; Royal Commonwealth Society.

EXETER, Dean of; *see* Jones, Very Rev. K. B.

EXETER, Archdeacon of; *see* Tremlett, Ven. A. F.

EXMOUTH, 10th Viscount *cr* 1816; **Paul Edward Pellew;** Bt 1796 (Pellew of Treverry); Baron 1814; Marqués de Olias (Spain *cr* 1652); *b* 8 Oct. 1940; *s* of 9th Viscount Exmouth and Maria Luisa (*d* 1994), *d* of late Luis de Urquijo, Marqués de Amurrio, Madrid; *S* father, 1970; *m* 1st, 1964 (marr. diss. 1974); one *d*; 2nd, 1975, Rosemary Countess of Burford (marr. diss. 2000); twin *s*. *Educ:* Downside. Formerly cross bencher, House of Lords. Contested (UK Ind) Teignbridge, 2001. *Heir: er twin s* Hon. Edward Francis Pellew, *b* 30 Oct. 1978. *Address:* The Coach House, Canonteign Falls, Exeter, Devon EX6 7NT; *e-mail:* PaulExmouth@cs.com.

EXNER, Most Rev. Adam; *see* Vancouver, Archbishop of.

EXTON, Clive; scriptwriter and playwright; *b* 11 April 1930; *s* of late J. E. M. Brooks and Marie Brooks (*née* Rolfe); *m* 1951, Patricia Fletcher Ferguson (marr. diss. 1957); two *d*; *m* 1957, Margaret Josephine Reid; one *s* two *d*. *Educ:* Christ's Hospital. *TV plays:* No Fixed Abode, 1959; The Silk Purse; Where I Live; Some Talk of Alexander; Hold My Hand, Soldier; I'll Have You to Remember; The Big Eat; The Trial of Doctor Fancy; Land of my Dreams; The Close Prisoner; The Bone Yard; Conceptions of Murder (series); Are You Ready for the Music?; The Rainbirds; Killers (series); Stigma; Henry Intervenes; (with Tom Stoppard) The Boundary; The Crezz (series); Dick Barton—Special Agent (series); Wolf to the Slaughter, A Guilty Thing Surprised, Shake Hands for Ever (dramatizations of novels by Ruth Rendell); Jeeves and Wooster (Writers' Guild Award, 1992); Something's Got to Give; The Long Run Home; The Man Who Could Write Miracles; many scripts and script consultant for Agatha Christie's Poirot. *Stage plays:* Have You Any Dirty Washing, Mother Dear?; Twixt; Murder is Easy; Dressing Down; The Windsor Not. *Films:* Night Must Fall; Isadora; Entertaining Mr Sloane; Ten Rillington Place; Running Scared; Doomwatch; The House in Nightmare Park; The Awakening. *Publications:* No Fixed Abode (in Six Granada Plays, anthol.), 1960; Have You Any Dirty Washing, Mother Dear? (in Plays of the Year, vol. 37), 1970. *Recreation:* panification. *Address:* c/o Rochelle Stevens & Co., 2 Terret's Place, N1 1QZ. *T:* (020) 7359 3900. *Club:* Groucho.

EYERS, Patrick Howard Caines, CMG 1985; LVO 1966; HM Diplomatic Service, retired; *b* 4 Sept. 1933; *s* of late Arthur Leopold Caines Eyers and Nora Lilian Eyers; *m* 1960, Heidi, *d* of Werner Rüsch, Dipl. Ing, and Helene (*née* Feil); two *s* one *d*. *Educ:* Clifton Coll.; Gonville and Caius Coll., Cambridge (BA Hons 1957); Institut Universitaire de Hautes Etudes Internationales, Geneva. RA, 1952–54. Asst Editor, Grolier Soc. Inc., New York, 1957; HM Foreign (now Diplomatic) Service, 1959; ME Centre for Arabic Studies, 1960; Dubai, 1961; Brussels, 1964; FO, 1966; Aden, 1969; Abidjan, 1970; British Mil. Govt, Berlin, 1971; FCO, 1974; Counsellor, Bonn, 1977; Head, Republic of Ireland Dept, FCO, 1981; RCDS, 1984; Ambassador: to Zaire, the Congo, Rwanda and Burundi, 1985–87; to Algeria, 1987–89; to GDR, 1990; to Jordan, 1991–93. Officer, Order of Leopold, Belgium, 1966. *Recreations:* music, skiing, sailing. *Address:* c/o Barclays Bank, 86 Queens Road, Bristol BS6 1RB. *Club:* Hurlingham.

EYNON, Prof. John Marles, OBE 1990; RIBA; FSA; Professor of Architecture, University of Wales, and Head, Welsh School of Architecture, 1980–87, now Professor Emeritus; *b* 3 Jan. 1923; *s* of Philip Stanley Eynon and Gwendoline Eynon (*née* Marles); *m* 1950, Yvonne Marie, *e d* of Claire Faber (*née* Vermuse) and Vivian Valdemar Faber. *Educ:* Welsh Sch. of Architecture, Univ. of Wales (MA, Dip. Arch.) ARIBA 1950, FRIBA 1963, FSA 1974. Military service: Captain RE, regtl duties, wounded, training, staff work. Chartered and Registered Architect, 1950; with Alwyn Lloyd & Gordon, later Alex Gordon & Partners, 1950–70; private practice and consultancy (historic buildings and conservation), 1970–. Lectr, Sen. Lectr, Prof. of Architecture, Welsh Sch. of Architecture, Univ. of Wales, 1956–87. Member: Historic Buildings Council for Wales, 1970–95; Welsh Arts Council, 1978–89; Craft Cttee for Wales (Chm.), Craft Council, 1970–89; Cambrian Archaeol. Assoc., 1969–; Assoc. of Artists and Designers in Wales, 1970–98; Royal Welsh Agricl Soc., 1977; Llandaff Diocesan Adv. Cttee, Church in Wales, 1988–; Cardiff Castle Management Cttee, 1990–. Prince of Wales Awards, 1976, 1977; Europa Nostra Award, 1985. *Publications:* contribs to learned jls. *Recreation:* painter (retrospective exhibition, Cardiff, 1976). *Address:* 39 Waterloo Road, Penylan, Cardiff CF3 7BJ. *T:* (029) 2048 5098.

EYRE, Brian Leonard, CBE 1993; DSc; FRS 2001; FREng; CPhys; Chairman, Council for the Central Laboratory of the Research Councils, since 2000 (Member, since 1998); *b* 29 Nov. 1933; *s* of Leonard George and Mabel Eyre; *m* 1965, Elizabeth Caroline (*née* Rackham); two *s*. *Educ:* Greenford Grammar Sch.; Univ. of Surrey (BSc, DSc). FREng (FEng 1992); FIM; FInstP. Research Officer, CEGB, 1959–62; Gp Leader, UKAEA, Harwell, 1962–79; Prof., Materials Science, Univ. of Liverpool, 1979–84; United Kingdom Atomic Energy Authority: Dir, Fuel and Engrg Technology, Risley, 1984–87; Mem. Bd, 1987–96; Dep. Chm., 1989–96; Chief Exec., 1990–94; Dep. Chm., AEA Technology plc, 1996–97. Mem., PPARC, 1996–2000. Visiting Professor: Univ. of Illinois, 1969–70; Univ. of Wisconsin, 1976; Univ. of Liverpool, 1984–; UCL, 1995–; Univ. of Oxford, 1996–; Vis. Fellow, Wolfson Coll., Oxford, 1996–. Mem. Council, Foundn of Sci. and Technology, 1994–. *Publications:* over 150 papers in Procs Royal Soc., Philosophical Magazine, Acta Metallurgica, etc. *Recreations:* sailing, walking, mountaineering. *Address:* Materials Department, University of Oxford, Parks Road, Oxford OX1 3PH. *Club:* Athenæum.

EYRE, Hon. Dean Jack; New Zealand High Commissioner to Canada, 1968–73 and 1976–80; *b* Westport, NZ, 1914; *m*; two *s* one *d*. *Educ:* Hamilton High Sch.; Auckland University Coll. Served War of 1939–45, Lieut in RNVR. Electrical importer and manufacturer. MP (Nat) North Shore, 1949–66; Minister of Customs, Industries and Commerce, 1954–57; Minister of Social Security and Tourist and Health Resorts, 1956–57; Minister of Housing, State Advances and Defence, New Zealand, 1957; Minister in Charge of Police, 1960–63; Minister of Defence, 1960–66; Minister i/c Tourism, 1961–66. *Recreations:* yachting, fishing. *Address:* 517 Wilbrod Street, Ottawa, ON K1N 5R4, Canada. *Clubs:* Royal New Zealand Yacht Squadron, Northern (Auckland); Royal Ottawa Golf.

EYRE, Maj.-Gen. Sir James (Ainsworth Campden Gabriel), KCVO 1986 (CVO 1978); CBE 1980 (OBE 1975); Director, Westminster Associates International Ltd, since 1989; *b* 2 Nov. 1930; *s* of late Edward Joseph Eyre and Hon. Dorothy Elizabeth Anne Pelline (*née* Lyon-Dalberg-Acton); *m* 1967, Monica Ruth Esther Smyth; one *s* one *d*. *Educ:* Harvard Univ. (BA, LLB). Commissioned RHG, 1955; Commanding Officer, The Blues and Royals, 1970–73; GSO 1 HQ London District, 1973–75; Officer Commanding Household Cavalry and Silver Stick, 1975–78; Col GS HQ Northern Ireland, 1978–80; Sec., Chiefs of Staff Cttee, MoD, 1980–82; Dir of Defence Programmes Staff (Concepts), MoD, 1982–83; GOC London Dist and Maj. Gen. Comdg Household Div., 1983–86. Comdr SMOM Pro Merito Militensis with Sword, 1999. *Recreations:* racing, shooting. *Address:* Somerville House, East Garston, Berks RG17 7EX. *Club:* Turf.
See also P. G. A. Eyre.

EYRE, James Henry Robert; Director, Wilkinson Eyre (formerly Chris Wilkinson) Architects Ltd, since 1989; *b* 24 Jan. 1959; *s* of late Michael Robert Giles Eyre and of Susan Bennett; *m* 1983, Karen Fiona Turner; one *s* one *d*. *Educ:* Oundle Sch.; Liverpool Univ. (BA Hons 1980). AA Dip. 1983; RIBA 1985. Architect, Michael Hopkins & Partners, 1980–85; joined Chris Wilkinson Architects, 1985, Partner, 1986–; *projects include:* Stratford Market Depot for Jubilee Line Extension, 1996; South Dock Footbridge for LDDC, 1997; Hulme Arch, Manchester, 1997; Gateshead Millennium Bridge; Stratford Station for Jubilee Line Extension; Making the Modern World gall., Science Mus. *Publications:* (contrib.) The Architecture of Bridge Design, 1997; (jtly) Bridging Art and Science, 2001; contribs World Architecture, Architects Jl. *Recreations:* travel, game fishing, sketching. *Address:* (office) Transworld House, 100 City Road, EC1Y 2BJ. *T:* (020) 7608 7900.

EYRE, Patrick Giles Andrew; Master of the Supreme Court, Queen's Bench Division, since 1992; *b* 11 March 1940; *s* of late Edward Joseph Eyre and Hon. Dorothy Elizabeth Anne Pelline Lyon-Dalberg-Acton; *m* 1977, Victoria Mary Bathurst Barthorp; one *s*, and one step *d*. *Educ:* Downside; Trinity Coll., Oxford (MA). Farmer, 1965–72. Called to the Bar, Inner Temple, 1974. *Publications:* articles on law, computers, horses and country pursuits. *Recreations:* books, horses, hunting, music. *Address:* Royal Courts of Justice, Strand, WC2A 2LL.
See also Maj.-Gen. Sir J. A. C. G. Eyre.

EYRE, Sir Reginald (Edwin), Kt 1984; President, Birmingham Heartlands Business Forum, since 2000; Consultant, Eyre & Co., solicitors, since 1992; *b* 28 May 1924; *s* of late Edwin Eyre and Mary Eyre (*née* Moseley); *m* 1978, Anne Clements; one *d*. *Educ:* King Edward's Camp Hill Sch., Birmingham; Emmanuel Coll., Cambridge (MA). RNVR, 1942–45 (Sub-Lt). Admitted a Solicitor, 1950; Senior Partner, Eyre & Co., solicitors, Birmingham, 1951–91. Chairman: Birmingham Heartlands Develt Corp. (formerly Birmingham Heartlands Ltd (East Birmingham Urban Develt Agency)), 1987–98; Birmingham Cable Corp. Ltd, 1988–99; Dep. Chm., Commn for New Towns, 1988–92. Hon. Consultant, Poor Man's Lawyer, 1948–58. Conservative Political Centre: Chm., W Midlands Area, 1960–63; Chm., National Advisory Cttee, 1964–66. Contested (C) Birmingham (Northfield) 1959; MP (C) Birmingham Hall Green, May 1965–87. Opposition Whip, 1966–70; a Lord Comr of the Treasury, June-Sept. 1970; Comptroller of HM Household, 1970–72; Parliamentary Under-Secretary of State: DoE, 1972–74; Dept of Trade, 1978–82; Dept of Transport, 1982–83. A Vice Chm., Cons. Party Organisation, 1975–79; Founder Chm., Cons. Parly Urban Affairs Cttee, 1974–79. Freeman, City of Birmingham, 1991. DUniv UCE, 1997. *Publication:* Hope for our Towns and Cities, 1977. *Address:* c/o Eyre & Co., 1041 Stratford Road, Hall Green, Birmingham B28 8AS. *Club:* Carlton.

EYRE, Richard Anthony; Chairman, RDF Media, since 2001; *b* 3 May 1954; *s* of Edgar Gabriel Eyre and Marjorie (*née* Corp); *m* 1977, Sheelagh Colquhoun; one *s* one *d*. *Educ:* King's Coll. Sch., Wimbledon; Lincoln Coll., Oxford (MA); Harvard Business Sch. (AMP). Media buyer, Benton & Bowles, 1975–79; TV airtime salesman, Scottish TV, 1979–80; media planner, Benton & Bowles, 1980–84; Media Director: Aspect, 1984–86; Bartle Bogle Hegarty, 1986–91; Chief Executive: Capital Radio plc, 1991–97; ITV, 1997–2000; Pearson Television, 2000–01; Dir, Strategy and Content, RTL Gp, 2000–01. FRSA 1997. *Recreations:* music, church, cooking. *Address:* RDF Media, 140 Kensington Church Street, W8 4BN. *Club:* Thirty.

EYRE, Sir Richard (Charles Hastings), Kt 1997; CBE 1992; theatre, film and TV director; Artistic Director, Royal National Theatre, 1988–97 (Associate Director, 1981–88); a Governor, BBC, since 1995; *b* 28 March 1943; *m* 1973, Susan Elizabeth Birtwistle, *qv*; one *d*. *Educ:* Sherborne Sch.; Peterhouse, Cambridge (BA). Asst Dir, Phoenix Theatre, Leicester, 1966; Lyceum Theatre, Edinburgh: Associate Dir, 1967–70; Dir of Productions, 1970–72; freelance director: Liverpool, 7:84 Co., West End; tours for British Council: W Africa, 1971; SE Asia, 1972; Artistic Dir, Nottingham Playhouse, 1973–78; Prod./Dir, Play for Today, BBC TV, 1978–80; Director: The Churchill Play, Nottingham, 1974; Comedians, Old Vic and Wyndhams, 1976; Touched, Nottingham, 1977; Hamlet, Royal Court, 1980; Edmond, Royal Court, 1985; Kafka's Dick, Royal Court, 1986; National Theatre: Guys and Dolls, 1982, revived 1996 (SWET Director of the Year, 1982, Standard Best Director, 1982, Critics' Circle Best Dir Award, 1997); The Beggar's Opera, and Schweyk in the Second World War, 1982; The Government Inspector, 1985; Futurists, 1986 (Best Production Award, Time Out, 1986); The

Changeling, Bartholomew Fair, 1988; Hamlet, The Voysey Inheritance, 1989; Racing Demon, Richard III, 1990; White Chameleon, Napoli Milionaria, Murmuring Judges, 1991; Night of the Iguana, 1992; Macbeth, The Absence of War, 1993; Johnny on a Spot, Sweet Bird of Youth, 1994; La Grande Magia, 1995; Skylight, 1995, transf. Wyndham's, then NY, 1996, UK tour, then Vaudeville, 1997; The Prince's Play, John Gabriel Borkman (Critics' Circle Best Dir Award, 1997), 1996; Amy's View, 1997, NY, 1999; King Lear (Olivier Award, 1998), The Invention of Love (Evening Standard Award, 1997), 1997; The Judas Kiss, Playhouse, transf. NY, 1998; (also trans.) The Novice, Almeida, 2000. *Opera:* La Traviata, Covt Gdn, 1994. *Films:* The Ploughman's Lunch (Evening Standard Award for Best Film, 1983), Loose Connections, 1983; Laughterhouse, 1984, released as Singleton's Pluck, USA, 1985 (TV Prize, Venice Film Fest.); *for television:* The Imitation Game, Pasmore, 1980; Country, 1981; The Insurance Man, 1986 (Special Prize, Tokyo TV Fest., 1986); Past Caring, 1986; Tumbledown, 1988 (BAFTA Award for best single drama, Italia RAI Prize, RTS Award, Press Guild Award, Tokyo Prize); v., 1988 (RTS Award); Suddenly Last Summer, 1992; The Absence of War, 1995; King Lear, 1998 (Peabody Award, 1999); writer and presenter, Changing Stages (series), 2000. Cameron Mackintosh Vis. Prof. of Contemporary Theatre, Oxford Univ., 1997. Hon. Fellow: Goldsmiths' Coll., 1993; KCL, 1994. Hon. DLitt: Nottingham Trent, 1992; South Bank, 1994; DUniv Surrey, 1998; Hon. DDra RSAMD, 2000. STV Awards for Best Production, 1969, 1970 and 1971; De Sica Award, Sorrento Film Fest., 1986; Laurence Olivier and South Bank Show Awards for Outstanding Achievement, 1997; Lifetime Achievement Awards, Critics' Circle, and Directors' Guild, 1997. Officier de l'ordre des Arts et des Lettres (France), 1998. *Publications:* Utopia and Other Places, 1993; The Eyre Review (report of inquiry into running of Royal Opera House), 1998; (with Nicholas Wright) Changing Stages: a view of British theatre in the twentieth century, 2000. *Address:* c/o Judy Daish Associates, 2 St Charles Place, W10 6EG. *T:* (020) 8964 8811.

EYRE, Very Rev. Richard Montague Stephens; Priest-in-Charge, St Andrew's, Pau, France, since 2001; *b* 1929; *s* of Montague Henry and Ethel Mary Eyre; *m* 1963, Anne Mary Bentley; two *d. Educ:* Charterhouse; Oriel Coll. and St Stephen's House, Oxford. MA Oxon. Deacon 1956, priest 1957; Curate, St Mark's Church, Portsea, 1956–59; Tutor and Chaplain, Chichester Theological Coll., 1959–62; Chaplain, Eastbourne Coll., 1962–65; Vicar of Arundel, 1965–73; Vicar of Good Shepherd, Brighton, 1973–75; Archdeacon of Chichester, 1975–81; Treasurer of Chichester Cathedral, 1978–81; Dean of Exeter, 1981–95. Mem., Gen. Synod of C of E, 1985–95. *Publication:* Faith in God?, 1990. *Recreations:* golf, music, travel, gardening. *Address:* Hathersage, Enmore Road, Enmore, Bridgwater, Som TA5 2DP. *Club:* Oxford and Cambridge.

EYRE, Susan Elizabeth, (Lady Eyre); *see* Birtwistle, S. E.

EYSENCK, Prof. Michael William; Professor and Head of Department of Psychology, Royal Holloway (formerly Royal Holloway and Bedford New College), University of London, since 1987; *b* 8 Feb. 1944; *s* of late Prof. Hans Jürgen Eysenck and Margaret Malcolm Eysenck (*née* Davies); *m* 1975, Mary Christine Kabyn; one *s* two *d. Educ:* Dulwich Coll.; University College London (BA Psych, 1st cl. Hons; Rosa Morrison Medal for outstanding arts graduate, 1965); Birkbeck Coll., London (PhD Psych). Asst Lectr, Lectr and Reader in Psychology, Birkbeck Coll., Univ. of London, 1965–87. Vis. Prof., Univ. of S Florida, Tampa, 1980. Chm., Cognitive Psych. Section, BPsS, 1982–87. Editor, European Jl of Cognitive Psych., 1989–91. *Publications:* Human Memory, 1977; (with H. J. Eysenck) Mindwatching, 1981; Attention and Arousal: cognition and performance, 1982; A Handbook of Cognitive Psychology, 1984; (with H J Eysenck) Personality and Individual Differences, 1985; (with J. T. Richardson and D. W. Piper) Student Learning: research in education and cognitive psychology, 1987; (with H. J. Eysenck) Mindwatching: why we behave the way we do, 1989; Happiness: facts and myths, 1990; (ed) The Blackwell Dictionary of Cognitive Psychology, 1990; International Review of Cognitive Psychology, 1990; (with M. T. Keane) Cognitive Psychology: a student's handbook, 1990; Anxiety: the cognitive perspective, 1992; (with M. Weller) The Scientific Basis of Psychiatry, 1992; (with A. Gale) Handbook of Individual Differences: biological perspectives, 1992; Principles of Cognitive Psychology, 1993; Perspectives on Psychology, 1994; Individual Differences: normal and abnormal, 1994; Simply Psychology, 1996; Anxiety and Cognition: a unified theory, 1997; Psychology: an integrated approach, 1998; Psychology: a student's handbook, 2000; numerous book chapters and contribs to Qly Jl of Exptl Psychology, Jl of Exptl Psychology, Jl of Abnormal Psychology, British Jl of Clin. Psychology, Jl of Personality and Social Psychology, Psychol Bull., and others. *Recreations:* travel, tennis, golf, walking, bridge, boules. *Address:* Department of Psychology, Royal Holloway, University of London, Egham Hill, Egham, Surrey TW20 0EX. *T:* (01784) 443530, *Fax:* (01784) 434347.

EYTON, Anthony John Plowden, RA 1986 (ARA 1976); RWS 1988 (ARWS 1985); RWA 1984; RCA 1993; NEAC 1985; *b* 17 May 1923; *s* of late Captain John Seymour Eyton, ICS, author, and Phyllis Annie Tyser; *m* 1960, Frances Mary Capell, MA (marr. diss.); three *d. Educ:* Twyford Sch.; Canford Sch.; Dept of Fine Art, Reading Univ.; Camberwell Sch. of Art (NDD). Served War, 1939–45, Cameronians (Scottish Rifles), Hampshire Regt, and Army Educn Corps. Abbey Major Scholarship in Painting, 1950–51. Elected Mem., London Gp, 1958. One Man Exhibitions: St George's Gall., 1955; Galerie de Seine, 1957; New Art Centre, 1959, 1961, 1968; New Grafton Gall., 1973; William Darby Gall., 1975; Newcastle Polytechnic Art Gall., 1978; Browse & Darby, 1978, 1981, 1985, 1987, 1990, 1993, 1996, 2000; Austin Desmond Gall., 1990; A. T. Kearney Ltd, 1997; Retrospective Exhibn, S London Art Gall., Towner Art Gall., Eastbourne, and Plymouth Art Gall., 1981; Hong Kong and the New Territories exhibn, Imperial War Museum, 1983 (subsequent to commission); work included in British Painting 1945–77, RA. Work in public collections: Tate Gall.; Arts Council; Plymouth Art Gall.; Towner Art Gall., Eastbourne; Carlisle Art Gall.; DoE; RA; Government Picture Coll.; BR; Contemp. Art Soc.; Guildhall Art Gall. Fellowship awarded by Grocers' Co. (for work and travel in Italy), 1974. Hon. Mem., Pastel Soc., 1986; Hon. ROI 1988. Prize, John Moore's Exhibn, Liverpool, 1972; First Prize, Second British Internat. Drawing Biennale, Middlesbrough, 1975; Charles Wollaston Award, RA, 1981. *Recreation:* gardening. *Address:* c/o Browse & Darby Ltd, 19 Cork Street, W1X 1HB.

EZRA, family name of **Baron Ezra**.

EZRA, Baron *cr* 1983 (Life Peer), of Horsham in the County of West Sussex; **Derek Ezra,** Kt 1974; MBE 1945; Chairman: MICROPOWER Ltd, since 2000; *b* 23 Feb. 1919; *s* of David and Lillie Ezra; *m* 1950, Julia Elizabeth Wilkins. *Educ:* Monmouth Sch.; Magdalene Coll., Cambridge (MA, Hon. Fellow, 1977). Army, 1939–47. Joined NCB, 1947; representative of NCB at Cttees of OEEC and ECE, 1948–52; Mem. of UK Delegn to High Authority of European Coal and Steel Community, 1952–56; Dep. Regional Sales Manager, NCB, 1956–58; Regional Sales Manager, 1958–60; Dir-Gen. of Marketing, NCB, 1960–65; NCB Bd Mem., 1965–67; Dep. Chm., 1967–71; Chm., 1971–82. Chairman: Associated Heat Services plc, 1966–99; J. H. Sankey & Son Ltd, 1977–82; Petrolex PLC, 1982–85; Throgmorton Trust PLC, 1984–91 Sheffield Heat and Power Ltd, 1985–2000; Associated Gas Supplies Ltd, 1987–95; Energy and Technical Services Gp plc, 1990–99; Director: British Fuel Co., 1966–82; Solvay SA, 1979–90; Redland PLC, 1982–89; Supervisory Bd, Royal Boskalis Westminster NV, 1982–85. Industrial Advr, Morgan Grenfell & Co. Ltd, 1982–88. Chm., NICG, 1972 and 1980–81; President: Nat. Materials Handling Centre, 1979; Coal Industry Soc., 1981–86 (Chm., 1961); W European Coal Producers' Assoc., 1976–79; BSI, 1983–86; Economic Res. Council, 1985–; Inst. of Trading Standards Admin, 1987–92; Vice-Pres., BIM, 1978 (Chm., 1976–78); Chm., British Iron and Steel Consumers' Council, 1983–86; Member: BOTB, 1972–82 (Chm., European Trade Cttee); Cons. Cttee, ECSC, 1973–82 (Pres., 1978 79); Adv. Council for Energy Conservation, 1974–79; Adv. Bd, Petrofina SA, 1982–90; Internat. Adv. Bd, Creditanstalt Bankverein, 1982–90; Energy Commn, 1977–79; Ct of Governors, Administrative Staff Coll., 1971–82; Internat. Adv. Bd, Banca Nazionale del Lavoro, 1984–; Governor, London Business Sch., 1973–82. Pres., Keep Britain Tidy Gp, 1985–89 (Chm., 1979–85). Hon. DSc Cranfield, 1979; Hon. LLD Leeds, 1982. Bronze Star (USA), 1945; Grand Officer, Italian Order of Merit, 1979; Comdr, Luxembourg Order of Merit, 1981; Officer of Légion d'Honneur, 1981. *Publications:* Coal and Energy, 1978; The Energy Debate, 1983. *Address:* House of Lords, Westminster, SW1A 0PW. *T:* (020) 7219 3180.

F

FABER, David James Christian; Director, Freestream Aircraft Ltd, since 1998; *b* 7 July 1961; *s* of Julian Tufnell Faber, *qv*; *m* 1st, 1988, Sally Elizabeth Gilbert (marr. diss. 1996); one *s*; 2nd, 1998, Sophie Amanda Hedley; one *d*. *Educ:* Summer Fields, Oxford; Eton Coll.; Balliol Coll., Oxford (MA Mod. Langs). Conservative Central Office, 1985–87 (Personal Asst to Dep. Chm., 1985–86); Dir, Sterling Marketing Ltd, 1987– (Chm., 1991–). Contested (C) Stockton North, 1987; MP (C) Westbury, 1992–2001. PPS to Min. of State, Foreign Office, 1994–96, to Sec. of State for Health, 1996–97; Opposition frontbench spokesman on foreign and commonwealth affairs, 1997–98. Member: Social Security Select Cttee, 1992–97; Culture, Media and Sport Select Cttee, 1998–2001; Public Accounts Cttee, 2000–01; Sec., Cons. back bench Educn Cttee, 1992–94. Trustee: Rehabilitation for Addicted Prisoners Trust; Clouds House. *Recreations:* taking my son to Stamford Bridge, cricket, golf. *Address:* 14 Headfort Place, SW1X 7DH. *Clubs:* White's, Pratt's, MCC (Mem. Cttee, 1997–2000, 2001–); Vincent's (Oxford); Royal St George's Golf, Sunningdale Golf; Trevase Golf; St Moritz Tobogganing.

FABER, Diana; Her Honour Judge Faber; a Circuit Judge, since 2000; *b* 23 Oct. 1955; *d* of T. G. Faber and Mrs D. Swan. *Educ:* Putney High Sch.; University Coll. London (LLB Hons). Called to the Bar, Gray's Inn, 1977; practised at Common Law Bar, 1977–82; admitted solicitor, 1983; joined Richards Butler, 1982, Partner, 1988–94; a Law Comr, 1994–2000; a Recorder, 1998–2000. *Publications:* (General Ed.) Multimodal Transport: avoiding legal problems, 1997; numerous articles in legal and commercial jls and newspapers. *Recreations:* theatre, reading, walking.

FABER, Julian Tufnell; Chairman: Willis Faber Ltd, 1972–77; Cornhill Insurance plc, 1986–88 (Director, 1972–88); *b* 6 April 1917; *s* of late Alfred and Edith Faber; *m* 1944, Lady (Ann) Caroline, *e d* of 1st Earl of Stockton, OM, PC, FRS, and late Lady Dorothy Macmillan; three *s* one *d* (and one *s* decd). *Educ:* Winchester; Trinity Coll., Cambridge. Joined Willis, Faber & Dumas Ltd, 1938. Served Welsh Guards (Major 2nd Bn), 1939–45. Director: Willis, Faber & Dumas Ltd, 1952; Willis, Faber & Dumas (Agencies) Ltd, 1965; Taisho Marine & Fire Insurance Co. (UK) Ltd, 1972 (Chm.); Willis Faber (Middle East) SAL, 1973; Morgan Grenfell Ltd, 1974–77; Allianz International Insurance Co., 1974. Former Mem. Bd of Governors, Summer Fields Sch., Oxford. Member: MCC Cttee, 1981–84; Kent CCC Cttee, 1977–84. *Address:* Fisher's Gate, Withyham, E Sussex TN7 4BB; Flat 4, 17 Sloane Court West, SW3 4TD. *Clubs:* White's, City of London, MCC.
See also D. J. C. Faber.

FABER, Michael Leslie Ogilvie; Professorial Fellow, Institute of Development Studies, Sussex University, since 1982 (Director, 1982–87); *b* 12 Aug. 1929; *s* of George and Kathleen Faber; *m* 1956, Diana Catriona Howard; two *s* twin *d*. *Educ:* Avon Old Farms, USA; Eton; Magdalen Coll., Oxford (MA); Univ. of Michigan. MA Cantab. Served 11th Hussars, PAO, Germany, 1948–49. Merchant Seaman, 1953–54. Claims Adjuster, Amer. Internat. Underwriters, Japan and Korea, 1954; Foreign Correspondent for Sunday Times, Observer, and Economist in FE, ME, N and Central Africa, 1954–60; Lectr in Econs, UCRN, 1958–60; community develt worker with Danilo Dolci in Sicily, 1961; Lectr in Econs, UWI, 1962–63; Sen. Economist and Under-Sec., Govt of Zambia, 1964–67; Dept of Applied Econs, Cambridge, 1968; Overseas Develt Gp, UEA, 1969–78; Dir, Tech. Assistance Gp, Commonwealth Secretariat, 1972–75 and 1978–82. Member: Council, Overseas Develt Inst., 1982–; Bd, Commonwealth Develt Corp., 1988–97. Pres., UK Chapter, Soc. for Internat. Develt, 1986–91. Leader, UNDP/IBRD Mission to PNG, 1972; specialist negotiator of debt and resource agreements. *Publications:* Economic Structuralism and its Relevance, 1965; (with J. Potter) Towards Economic Independence, 1971; (ed with Dudley Seers) The Crisis in Economic Planning, 1972; (with R. Brown) Mining Agreements: law and policy, 1977; (with R. Brown) Changing the Rules of the Game, 1980; Conciliatory Debt Reduction: why it must come and how it could come, 1988; Beware of Debtspeak, 1988. *Address:* Rodmell Hill Cottage, Mill Lane, Rodmell, E Sussex BN7 3HS. *Clubs:* Brooks's; Lewes Golf.

FABER, Sir Richard (Stanley), KCVO 1980; CMG 1977; FRSL; HM Diplomatic Service, retired; Ambassador to Algeria, 1977–81; *b* 6 Dec. 1924; *er s* of late Sir Geoffrey Faber and Enid, *d* of Sir Henry Erle Richards, KCSI, KC; unmarried. *Educ:* Westminster Sch.; Christ Church, Oxford (MA). RNVR, 1943–46. 1st cl. Lit. Hum. Oxon; Pres., Oxford Union Soc., 1949. Joined HM Foreign (subseq. Diplomatic) Service, 1950; service in FO and in Baghdad, Paris, Abidjan, Washington; Head of Rhodesia Political Dept, FCO, 1967–69; Counsellor: The Hague, 1969–73; Cairo, 1973–75; Asst Under Sec. of State, FCO, 1975–77. Hon. Treas., RSL, 1986–91. *Publications:* Beaconsfield and Bolingbroke, 1961; The Vision and the Need: Late Victorian Imperialist Aims, 1966; Proper Stations: Class in Victorian Fiction, 1971; French and English, 1975; The Brave Courtier (biog. of Sir William Temple), 1983; High Road to England, 1985; Young England, 1987; A Brother's Murder, 1992; A Chain of Cities (autobiog.), 2000. *Address:* 18 Regent Hill, Brighton BN1 3ED. *Club:* Travellers.
See also T. E. Faber.

FABER, Thomas Erle, PhD; Chairman, Geoffrey Faber Holdings Ltd (formerly Faber & Faber (Publishers) Ltd), since 1977 (Director since 1969); Fellow of Corpus Christi College, Cambridge, since 1953; *b* 25 April 1927; *s* of Sir Geoffrey Faber; *m* 1st, 1959, Penelope (*d* 1983), *d* of Clive Morton, actor; two *s* two *d*; 2nd, 1986, Dr Elisabeth van Houts; one *s* one *d*. *Educ:* Oundle Sch.; Trinity Coll., Cambridge (MA, PhD). University of Cambridge: Res. Fellow, Trinity Coll., 1950–53; Univ. Demonstr, 1953–58; Armourers' and Brasiers' Fellow, 1958–59; Lectr in Physics, 1959–93; Treasurer, Corpus Christi Coll., 1963–76. *Publications:* Introduction to the Theory of Liquid Metals, 1972; Fluid Dynamics for Physicists, 1995; papers on superconductivity, liquid metals and liquid crystals. *Recreations:* walking, local history. *Address:* The Old Vicarage, Thompson's Lane, Cambridge CB5 8AQ. *T:* (01223) 356685.
See also Sir R. S. Faber.

FABER, Trevor Martin; His Honour Judge Faber; a Circuit Judge, since 2001; *b* 9 Oct. 1946; *s* of Harry Faber and Millicent Faber (*née* Waxman); *m* 1985, Katrina Sally Clay. *Educ:* Clifton Coll.; Merton Coll., Oxford (MA). Called to the Bar, Gray's Inn, 1970; in practice, Midland and Oxford Circuit, 1970–2001; a Recorder, 1989–2001. *Recreations:* music, sport, theatre, literature, cooking. *Address:* The Crown Court, Queen Elizabeth II Law Courts, 1 Newton Street, Birmingham B4 7NA. *Club:* Vincent's (Oxford).

FABIAN, Prof. Andrew Christopher, FRS 1996; Royal Society Research Professor, Institute of Astronomy, University of Cambridge, since 1982; Fellow of Darwin College, Cambridge, since 1983 (Vice-Master, since 1997); *b* 20 Feb. 1948; *s* of John Archibald and Daphne Monica Fabian; *m* 1st, 1971 (marr. diss. 1991); one *s* one *d*; 2nd, 1991, Dr Carolin Susan Crawford; two *s*. *Educ:* Daventry Grammar Sch.; King's Coll., London (BSc Physics); University Coll. London (PhD). SRC post doctoral research asst, University Coll. London, 1972–73; Institute of Astronomy, Cambridge: SRC post doctoral Fellow, 1973–75; SRC PDRA, 1975–77; Radcliffe Fellow in Astronomy, 1977–81. *Publications:* contribs to Monthly Notices RAS, Astrophys. Jl, Nature, etc. *Address:* Institute of Astronomy, Madingley Road, Cambridge CB3 0HA.

FABIAN, (Andrew) Paul; HM Diplomatic Service, retired; Chief Secretary, Turks and Caicos Islands, 1990–91; *b* 23 May 1930; *s* of late Andrew Taggart Fabian and Edith Mary Whorwell; *m* 1st, Elisabeth Vivien Chapman; one *s* two *d*; 2nd, 1983, Eryll Francesca Dickinson. *Educ:* Mitcham County School; Reading; St Paul's; Wadham College, Oxford (scholar; MA). Singapore Engineer Regt, 1953–54; Tanganyika, 1955–64 (on secondment to Foreign Office, serving at Usumbura, 1961–64); HM Diplomatic Service, 1964; served Lusaka, Ankara, New Delhi, FCO (Hd of Guidance), Islamabad, Karachi; High Comr, Nuku'alofa, Tonga, 1987–90. Proof-reader (part-time). *Publication:* Delhi Post Bedside Book (ed), 1977. *Recreations:* chess, reading, bird-watching. *Address:* La Guionie, 24600, France. *Clubs:* Oxford and Cambridge; Tunbridge Wells Chess.

FABIANI, Linda; Member (SNP) Central Scotland, Scottish Parliament, since 1999; *b* 14 Dec. 1956; *d* of late Giovanni Aldo Fabiani and of Claire Fabiani (*née* Smith, now Nutley). *Educ:* Napier Coll., Edinburgh (SHND); Glasgow Univ. (Dip Housing 1988). MCIH 1988. Admin. Sec., Yoker Housing Assoc., Glasgow, 1982–85; Housing Officer, Clydebank Housing Assoc., 1985–88; Develt Manager, Bute Housing Assoc., Rothesay, 1988–94; Dir, E Kilbride Housing Assoc., 1994–99. Dep. shadow spokesperson on social justice, Scottish Parlt, 1999–. *Recreations:* reading, theatre, music, holidays. *Address:* Scottish Parliament, Edinburgh EH99 1SP. *T:* (0131) 348 5698.

FABIUS, Laurent; Finance Minister and Deputy Prime Minister, France, since 2000; Deputy for Seine Maritime, French National Assembly, 1978–81, re-elected 1981, 1986, 1993, 1997 (President, 1988–92, 1997–2000); *b* 20 Aug. 1946; *s* of André Fabius and Louise Fabius (*née* Mortimer); *m* 1981, Françoise Castro; two *s*. *Educ:* Lycée Janson-de-Sailly; Lycée Louis-le-Grand; Ecole Normale Supérieure, Paris; Institut d'Etudes Politiques, Paris (Agrégé des lettres); Ecole Nationale d'Administration. Conseil d'Etat, 1973–81; Nat. Sec., Parti Socialiste (responsible for the press), 1979–81; Junior Minister, Ministry of Economy and Finance (responsible for the budget), 1981–83; Minister of Industry and Research, 1983–84; Prime Minister of France, 1984–86; MEP, 1989–92; First Sec., Socialist Party, 1992–93; Pres., Socialist Gp, Nat. Assembly, 1995–97. Mem., Conseil d'Etat, 1981–93. First Dep. Mayor, 1977–95 and 2000–, Mayor, 1995–2000, Grand Quevilly. *Publications:* La France inégale, 1975; Le Coeur du Futur, 1985; C'est en allant vers la mer, 1990; Les Blessures de la Vérité, 1995. *Address:* Ministry of Finance, 139 rue de Bercy, 75012 Paris, France; 15 place du Panthéon, 75005 Paris, France.

FABRICANT, Michael Louis David; MP (C) Lichfield, since 1997 (Mid-Staffordshire, 1992–97); *b* 12 June 1950; *s* of late Isaac Nathan Fabricant and of Helena (*née* Freed). *Educ:* Loughborough Univ. (BA Law and Econs); Univ. of Sussex (MSc Systems). CEng, FIEE. FIMgt. Postgrad. doctoral res., mathematical econs, London Univ., Oxford Univ. and Univ. of S California, LA. Formerly: Broadcaster, current affairs, BBC Radio; Man. Dir, Commercial Radio Gp; Founder Dir, Internat. Broadcast Electronics and Investment Gp, 1979–91. PPS to Financial Sec., HM Treasury, 1996–97. Member, Select Committee: Nat. Heritage, 1993–96, 1997–; Culture, Media and Sport, 1997–99, 2001–; Home Affairs, 1999–2001; Information, 2001–; Mem., European Legislation Scrutiny Cttee B, 1993–97; Dep. Chm., All Party Cable and Satellite Gp, 1997–99 (Treas., 1995–97); Vice Chairman: All Party Gp on Smoking and Health, 1997–; All Party Anglo-German Gp, 1997–; All Party Gp on Film Industry, 1997–; Joint Chairman: All Party Internet Gp, 1998–; Royal Marines All Party Parly Gp, 1999–; Dep. Chm., Cons. Parly Media Cttee, 1992–96. *Publications:* various newspaper articles and pamphlets. *Recreations:* fell-walking, reading, music (Mozart to rock), ski-ing, listening to the Archers. *Address:* House of Commons, SW1A 0AA. *Club:* Rottingdean (Sussex).

FACER, Roger Lawrence Lowe, CB 1992; Deputy Under-Secretary of State, Ministry of Defence, 1988–93; *b* 28 June 1933; *s* of late John Ernest Facer and Phyllis Facer; *m* 1960, Ruth Margaret, *o d* of late Herbert Mostyn Lewis, PhD, Gresford, Clwyd; three *d*. *Educ:* Rugby; St John's Coll., Oxford (MA); Univ. of London (MA). HM Forces, 2nd Lieut, East Surrey Regt, 1951–53. War Office, 1957; Asst Private Sec. to Secretary of State, 1958; Private Sec. to Permanent Under-Sec., 1958; Principal, 1961; Cabinet Office, 1966; Ministry of Defence, 1968–93: Private Sec. to Minister of State (Equipment), 1970; Asst Sec., 1970; Internat. Inst. for Strategic Studies, 1972–73; Counsellor, UK Delegn, MBFR Vienna, 1973–75; Private Sec. to Sec. of State for Defence, 1976–79; Asst Under-Sec. of

State, 1979–81; Under Sec., Cabinet Office, 1981–83; Rand Corporation, Santa Monica, USA, 1984; Asst Under-Sec. of State, MoD, 1984–87. Dir Gen., Carroll Inst., 1993–95. *Publications:* Weapons Procurement in Europe—Capabilities and Choices, 1975; Conventional Forces and the NATO Strategy of Flexible Response, 1985; articles in Alpine Garden Soc. Bulletin. *Recreations:* Alpine gardening, hill-walking, opera. *Address:* Kennett Lodge, Hambledon, Hants PO7 4SA.

FACK, Robbert; Commander, Order of Orange-Nassau, 1979; Chevalier, Order of Netherlands Lion, 1971; Netherlands diplomat, retired; Ambassador of the Netherlands to the Court of St James's, 1976–82; also, concurrently, Ambassador to Iceland, 1976–82; *b* 1 Jan. 1917; *m* 1943, Patricia H. Hawkins; four *s*. *Educ:* Univ. of Amsterdam. Military service, 1937–45. Min. of Foreign Affairs, The Hague, 1945–46; New York (UN), 1946–48; Min. of Foreign Affairs, 1948–50; Rome, 1950–54; Canberra, 1954–58; Bonn, 1958–63; Min. of Foreign Affairs, 1963–68; Ambassador-at-large, 1968–70; Perm. Rep. to UN, New York, 1970–74. Holds various foreign decorations. *Publication:* Gedane Zaken (Finished Business), (reminiscences), 1984. *Address:* The Old Rectory, Horton, near Chipping Sodbury, S Glos BS37 6QU. *Club:* Dutch.

FAGAN, (Florence) Mary; JP; Lord-Lieutenant of Hampshire, since 1994; *b* 11 Sept. 1939; *o d* of Col George Vere-Laurie, JP, DL, Carlton Hall, Newark, Notts; *m* 1960, Capt. Christopher Fagan, Grenadier Guards; one *s* (and one *s* decd). *Educ:* St Elphin's Sch., Matlock; Southover Manor, Sussex. Dir, Andover Dist Community Health Care NHS Trust, 1993–94; Chm., Countess of Brecknock Hospice and Home Care Service Appeal, Andover, 1989–; Vice-Pres., Hospital Saving Assoc., 1990–. Former Mem., Sch. Adv. Cttee, N Hants. President: ESU, 1994–; Hants Council of Community Service, 1994–; Hants and IoW Youth Options, 1994–; Hants Br., Army Benevolent Fund, 1994–; Vice-President: Southern Regl Assoc. for the Blind, 1994–; Mary Rose Trust, 1994–; Fortune Centre of Riding Therapy, 1994–; Patron: Rowans Hospice, Portsmouth, 1994–; Hants Music Trust, 1994–; Hants Br., BRCS, 1994–; Trustee: Andover Med. Fund, 1994–; Marwell Zoo Park, 1994–; Hants Gardens Trust, 1994–. Hon. Col, ACF, 1998–; Hon. Captain, RNR, 2001–. Freeman, Saddlers' Co., 1962, Liveryman, 1996–. JP Hants, 1994. Hon. DLitt Southampton, 1997; Hon. Dr jur Portsmouth, 2000. DStJ 1994 (Pres. Council, Hants, 1994–; former County Pres., Hants). *Recreations:* country activities. *Address:* Deane Hill House, Deane, near Basingstoke, Hants RG25 3AX. *T:* (01256) 780591.

FAGAN, Maj.-Gen. Patrick Feltrim, CB 1990; MBE (mil.) 1966; FRICS 1971; FRGS 1966; *b* 8 Dec. 1935; *s* of Air Cdre Thomas Patrick Feltrim Fagan and Hon. Isabel Mairi, *yr d* of 15th Baron Arundell of Wardour; *m* 1967, Veronica Thompson (*née* Lorant), *widow* of Captain C. J. C. Thompson, RE; two *s*. *Educ:* Stonyhurst Coll.; RMA, Sandhurst; University Coll. London (MSc (Hons) 1969). FBIM 1971. Commnd RE, 1955; served in Gibraltar, Germany, Aden and Oman. Internat. Scientific Expedn to Karakoram, 1961–62; UAE-Oman Border Survey, 1964; Jt Services Expedn to S Georgia, 1964–65; Ordnance Survey, 1969–73; Geographic Advr, AFCENT, 1979–83; Chief Geographic Officer, SHAPE, 1983–85; Dir, Survey Operations and Prodn, 1985–87; Dir Gen. of Military Survey, 1987–90. Member: Council, RGS, 1987–92 and 1993–95 (Vice-Pres., 1990–92); Council, BSES, 1987–90; Cttee of Management, Mt Everest Foundn, 1989–95 (Chm., 1992–94); Nat. Cttee for Photogrammetry and Remote Sensing, 1987–91; Adv. Bd, Inst. of Engrg, Surveying and Space Geodesy, Nottingham Univ., 1987–91; Council, RICS Land Surveyors, 1988–91; RICS Pres.'s Disciplinary and Appeals Tribunal, 1989–95, Dep. Pres., Army R U, 1989–91. Col Comdt, RE, 1991–96, Rep. Col Comdt, 1992. Chm., James Caird Soc., 2000–. *Publications:* articles on surveying and mapping in Geographical Jl, Photogrammetric Record, Survey Rev., Chartered Surveyor, and on ski mountaineering in subject jls. *Recreations:* mountain sports, boats, cricket, reading, photography, music, travel. *Clubs:* Royal Over-Seas League, Alpine (Vice Pres., 1999–), Alpine Ski (Pres., 1995–98), Eagle Ski (Pres., 1988–90), MCC, Geographical.

FAGE, Prof. John Donnelly, MA, PhD; Professor of African History, 1963–84, now Emeritus, Pro-Vice-Chancellor, 1979–84, and Vice-Principal 1981–84, University of Birmingham; *b* 3 June 1921; *s* of late Arthur Fage, CBE, FRS, and Winifred Eliza Donnelly; *m* 1949, Jean, *d* of late Fred Banister, MBE; one *s* one *d*. *Educ:* Tonbridge Sch.; Magdalene Coll., Cambridge (scholar, MA, PhD). Served War, Pilot with RAFVR (Flt Lt), 1941–45. Bye-Fellow, Magdalene Coll., Cambridge, 1947–49; Lectr and Sen. Lectr, Univ. Coll. of the Gold Coast, 1949–55; Prof. of History, 1955–59, and Dep. Principal, 1957–59; Lectr in African History, SOAS, Univ. of London, 1959–63. Visiting Prof., Univ. of Wisconsin, Madison, 1957, and Smith Coll., Northampton, Mass, 1962; Dir, Centre of West African Studies, Univ. of Birmingham, 1963–82, Dep. Dean, Faculty of Arts, 1973–75, Dean, 1975–78; Founding Hon. Sec., African Studies Assoc. of the UK, 1963–66 (Vice-Pres. 1967–68, Pres. 1968–69); Council Mem., Internat. African Inst., 1965–75, and Consultative Dir, 1975–80; Member: UNESCO Scientific Cttee for Gen. History of Africa, 1971–80; Culture Adv. Cttee of UK Nat. Commn for UNESCO, 1967–85 (Chm., 1978–85); Co-ordinating Council of Area Studies Associations, 1980–86 (Vice-Chm. 1980–84, Chm., 1984–86); Chm., Birmingham Jt Cttee for Adult Educn Inf. and Advice Services, 1985–88. FRHistS. Hon. Fellow, SOAS, Univ. of London. Editor (with Roland Oliver), The Jl of African History, 1960–73; Gen. Editor (with Roland Oliver), The Cambridge History of Africa, 8 vols, 1975–86. *Publications:* An Introduction to the History of West Africa, 1955, 3rd edn 1962; An Atlas of African History, 1958, 2nd edn, 1978; Ghana, a Historical Interpretation, 1959; A Short History of Africa (with Roland Oliver), 1962, 6th edn 1988; A History of West Africa, 1969, reprinted 1993; (ed) Africa Discovers Her Past, 1970; (ed with Roland Oliver) Papers on African Prehistory, 1970; A History of Africa, 1978, 3rd edn 1995; A Guide to Sources for Western Africa, 1987, 2nd edn 1994; articles in historical and Africanist jls. *Recreations:* doing things to houses and gardens. *Address:* Hafod Awel, Pennal, Machynlleth, Powys SY20 9DP. *T:* (01654) 791207. *Club:* Athenæum.

FAGGE, Sir John William Frederick, 11th Bt *cr* 1660; *b* 28 Sept. 1910; *s* of late William Archibald Theodore Fagge (*b* of 9th Bt) and Nellie (*d* 1924), *d* of H. T. D. Wise; *S* uncle, 1940; *m* 1940, Ivy Gertrude (*d* 1992), *d* of William Edward Frier, 15 Church Lane, Newington, Kent; one *s* one *d*. *Heir: s* John Christopher Fagge [*b* 30 April 1942; *m* 1974, Evelyn Joy Golding]. *Address:* c/o 11 Forbes Road, Faversham, Kent ME13 8QF.

FAHEY, Hon. John Joseph; MP (L) Macarthur (NSW), since 1996; Minister for Finance, since 1996, and for Administration, since 1997, Australia; *b* 10 Jan. 1945; *s* of Stephen Fahey and Annie (*née* Fahey); *m* 1968, Colleen Maree McGurren; one *s* two *d*. *Educ:* St Anthony's Convent, Picton, NSW; Chevalier Coll., Bowral, NSW; Univ. of Sydney Law Extension Cttee (Dip. Law). Practised law, Camden, NSW, 1971–86. New South Wales government: MP (L): Camden, 1984–88; Southern Highlands, 1988–96; Minister for Ind. Relns and Minister assisting the Premier, 1988–90; Minister for Ind. Relns, Further Educn, Trng and Employment, 1990–92; Premier, 1992–95; Treasurer, 1992–93; Minister for Econ. Devel, 1993–95. *Recreations:* tennis, Rugby, cricket, gardening, reading. *Address:* 39 John Street, Camden, NSW 2570, Australia.

FAINT, John Anthony Leonard; Director (International), Department for International Development, since 1997; *b* 24 Nov. 1942; *s* of Thomas Leonard Faint and Josephine Rosey Faint (*née* Dunkerley); *m* 1978, Elizabeth Theresa Winter. *Educ:* Chigwell Sch.; Magdalen Coll., Oxford (BA Lit.Hum. 1965); MA Development Economics, Fletcher Sch., Mass, 1969. Ministry of Overseas Development (later Overseas Development Administration), London, 1965–71 (study leave in Cambridge, Mass, 1968–69); First Secretary (Aid), Blantyre, Malawi, 1971–73; ODM/ODA, London, 1974–80; Head of SE Asia Develt Div., Bangkok, 1980–83; Head of Finance Dept, ODA, FCO, 1983–86; Alternate Exec. Dir, World Bank, Washington, 1986–89; Head, E Asia Dept, 1989–90, Under Sec., Internat. Div., 1990–91, ODA; on secondment as UK Dir, EBRD, 1991–92; Under Sec. (Eastern Europe), ODA, 1991–93; Under Sec. (Eastern Europe and Western Hemisphere), ODA, later DFID, 1993–97. *Recreations:* music, bridge, chess, computers. *Address:* Department for International Development, 1 Palace Street, SW1E 5HE.

FAIR, Donald Robert Russell, OBE (mil.) 1945; Board Member, Central Electricity Generating Board, 1975–77; *b* 26 Dec. 1916; *s* of Robert Sidney Fair and Mary Louie Fair; *m* 1941, Patricia Laurie Rudland; one *s*. *Educ:* Roan Sch., Blackheath; King's Coll., London Univ. (BSc, AKC). CEng, FInstE; CPhys, FInstP. Served War of 1939–45, RAF (Wing Comdr; despatches 1944; USAAF Commendation 1944). Lectr, RMA Sandhurst, 1948–50; UKAEA, 1950–62; Central Electricity Generating Bd, 1962–77. *Recreations:* sailing, cricket. *Address:* 22 Carlton Leas, The Leas, Folkestone, Kent CT20 2DJ. *T:* (01303) 250573.

FAIR, (James) Stuart, CBE 1997; WS; Chairman, Dundee Incubator Ltd, since 1997; Consultant, Thorntons, WS, Dundee, 1991–97; *b* 30 Sept. 1930; *s* of James Stuart Fair and Margaret Fair (*née* McCallum); *m* 1957, Anne Lesley Cameron; two *s* one *d*. *Educ:* Perth Acad.; St Andrews Univ. (MA); Edinburgh Univ. (LLB); MSc in Criminal Justice, Napier Univ., 2000. Admitted solicitor, 1956; Sen. Partner, Thorntons, WS, 1984–91; Hon. Sheriff, Dundee, 1978–; Temp. Sheriff, 1988–98. Clerk to General Comrs of Income Tax, Dundee Div., 1975–96. Chairman: Dundee Port Authy, 1992–96; Dundee Teaching Hosps NHS Trust, 1993–96. Pres., Dundee & Tayside Chamber of Commerce and Industry, 1980–81; Dep. Chm., Tayside Cttee on Medical Research Ethics, 1990–95. Dean, Faculty of Procurators and Solicitors in Dundee, 1977–79. Chm. Court, Univ. of Dundee, 1988–93; Trustee, Sir James Caird's Travelling Scholarships Trust, 1988– (Administrator and Sec., 1993–96). Mem., Develt Adv. Bd, Nat. Museums of Scotland, 1999–. Trustee, Dundee Heritage Trust, 2000–. Hon. LLD Dundee, 1994. *Address:* Beechgrove House, 474 Perth Road, Dundee DD2 1LL. *T:* (01382) 669783. *Club:* New (Edinburgh).

FAIRBAIRN, Alasdair Chisholm; Chief Executive, Sea Fish Industry Authority, since 1997; *b* 23 Jan. 1940; *s* of late Douglas Chisholm Fairbairn, CBE and Agnes Fairbairn (*née* Arnott); *m* 1964, Charlotte Henriette Tichelman; two *s* one *d*. *Educ:* Trinity Coll., Glenalmond, Perthshire; Corpus Christi Coll., Cambridge (MA Hons). Man. Dir, Conimex BV, Netherlands, 1975–78; Reckitt & Colman plc: Chief Manager, Planning and Evaluation, 1978–80; Regl Dir, 1980–84; Dir, LR Overseas Ltd, 1984–91; Chief Exec., Potato Mktg Bd, 1991–97. MInstD (Edinburgh). *Recreations:* walking, computers, dabbling in stock market. *Address:* (office) 18 Logie Mill, Logie Green Road, Edinburgh EH7 4HG. *T:* (0131) 558 3331. *Club:* Royal Over-Seas League.

FAIRBAIRN, Sir Brooke; *see* Fairbairn, Sir J. B.

FAIRBAIRN, Carolyn Julie; Director of Strategy, BBC, since 2000; *b* 13 Dec. 1960; *d* of David Ritchie Fairbairn, *qv*; *m* 1991, Peter Harrison Chittick; one *s* two *d*. *Educ:* Wycombe High Sch. for Girls; Bryanston (Schol.); Gonville and Caius Coll., Cambridge (Hon. Sen. Scholar, BA); Univ. of Pennsylvania (Thouron Schol., MA); INSEAD, Fountainebleau (MBA). Economist, World Bank, Washington, 1984–85; financial writer, The Economist, 1985–87; Mgt Consultant, McKinsey & Co., London and Paris, 1988–94; Mem., Prime Minister's Policy Unit, 1995–97; Dir of Strategy, BBC Worldwide, 1997–99. *Recreations:* tennis, travel. *Address:* 24 St Thomas Street, Winchester, Hants SO23 9HJ. *Club:* Soho House.

FAIRBAIRN, David Ritchie, OBE 1990; Chairman, Headstrong Inc., since 2001; *b* 4 July 1934; *s* of G. F. Fairbairn; *m* 1958, Hon. Susan Hill, *d* of Baron Hill of Luton, PC; one *s* two *d*. *Educ:* Mill Hill Sch.; Gonville and Caius Coll., Cambridge (BAEcon). FBCS; FIDPM, FInstD. President, Cambridge Union Soc. Overseas Marketing Manager, Arthur Guinness Son & Co. Ltd, 1960; President, Guinness-Harp Corp., New York, 1964; Marketing Dir, Guinness Overseas Ltd, 1969; Man. Dir, Dataset Ltd (ICL), 1970; Manager, Retail and Distribution Sector, International Computers Ltd, 1975; Dir of Marketing, EMI Medical Ltd, 1976; Dir, Nat. Computing Centre, 1980–86; Man. Dir, James Martin Associates UK, 1985–89; Gp Man. Dir, James Martin Associates Ltd, 1989–92; Man. Dir, JMA Information Engineering Ltd, 1992–94; Vice-Chm., James Martin Holdings Ltd, 1994–99; Chm., James Martin Worldwide plc, 1999–2000; Vice Pres., Europe, Texas Instruments Inc., 1993–94. Pres., Inst. of Data Processing Management, 1982– (Vice-Pres., 1980–82). Vice-Chm., Parly IT Cttee, 1982. Member: Patent Office Steering Bd, 1989–2000; Telecommunications Panel, Monopoly and Mergers Commn, 1991–99. Freeman, City of London, 1990. FRSA. *Recreations:* sailing, water ski-ing, ski-ing. *Address:* 11 Oak Way, West Common, Harpenden, Herts AL5 2NT. *T:* (01582) 715820, *Fax:* (01582) 468339.

See also C. J. Fairbairn.

FAIRBAIRN, Sir (James) Brooke, 6th Bt *cr* 1869, of Ardwick; *b* 10 Dec. 1930; *s* of Sir William Albert Fairbairn, 5th Bt, and Christine Renée Cotton, *d* of late Rev. Canon Robert William Croft; *S* father, 1972; *m* 1st, 1960, Mary Russell (*d* 1992), *d* of late William Russell Scott, MB, ChB, FFARCS; two *s* one *d*; 2nd, 1997, Rosemary Anne Victoria, *d* of late Edwin Henderson, FRCSE. *Educ:* Stowe. Proprietor of J. Brooke Fairbairn & Co., textile converters and wholesalers dealing in furnishing fabrics. Upper Bailiff, Weavers' Co., 1992–93. *Heir: s* Robert William Fairbairn [*b* 10 April 1965; *m* 1990, Sarah, *e d* of Roger Griffin, BVSc, MRCVS; two *s* two *d*]. *Address:* Barkway House, Bury Road, Newmarket, Suffolk CB8 7BT. *T:* (01638) 662733; J. Brooke Fairbairn & Co., The Railway Station, Newmarket CB8 9WT. *T:* (01638) 665766.

FAIRBAIRN, John Sydney; DL; Chairman, Esmée Fairbairn Charitable Trust, since 1988; *b* 15 Jan. 1934; *s* of late Sydney George Fairbairn, MC and Angela Maude Fairbairn (*née* Fane); *m* 1968, Mrs Camilla Fry (*d* 2000), *d* of late G. N. Grinling; one *s* two *d*, and two step *s* two step *d*; *m* 2001, Felicity, Lady Milford. *Educ:* Eton; Trinity College, Cambridge (MA). FCA. National Service, 2nd Lieut 17/21 Lancers, 1952–54. Monkhouse Stoneham & Co., 1957–60; joined M & G Group, 1961: Dir, 1974–99; Dep. Chm., 1979–89; non-exec. Dir, 1989–99. Chm., Central European Growth Fund plc, 1994–. Dep. Chm., Lautro, 1986–89; Chm., Unit Trust Assoc., 1989–91. Trustee: Monteverdi Trust, 1991–96; Royal Pavilion, Art Gall. and Museums of Brighton, 1993–; Comeback, 1993–99; Dulwich Picture Gall., 1994–96; Council Mem. and Treasurer, King's College London, 1972–84 (Fellow 1978); Council Member: Univ. of Buckingham, 1986–95; Policy Studies Inst., 1991–97. DUniv Buckingham, 1992. DL

West Sussex, 1996. *Address:* Child & Co., 1 Fleet Street, EC4Y 1BD. *Clubs:* White's, Brooks's, MCC; Piltdown Golf.

FAIRCLOUGH, Anthony John, CMG 1990; Hon. Director General, European Commission (formerly Commission of the European Communities), since 1989; *b* 30 Aug. 1924; *m* 1957, Patricia Monks; two *s*. *Educ:* St Philip's Grammar Sch., Birmingham; St Catharine's Coll., Cambridge (Scholar 1944, BA Cantab 1945, MA 1950). Ministry of Aircraft Production and Ministry of Supply, 1944–48; Colonial Office, 1948–65; Secretary, Nyasaland Commn of Inquiry, 1959; Private Secretary to Minister of State for Commonwealth Relations and for the Colonies, 1963–64; Assistant Secretary, 1964; Head of Pacific and Indian Ocean Dept, Colonial Office, subseq. Commonwealth Office, 1964–68; Head of W Indian Dept, FCO, 1968–70; Head of New Towns 1 Div., DoE, 1970–72; Under-Sec., 1973; Head of Planning, Minerals and Countryside Directorate, 1973, of Planning, Sport and Countryside Directorate, 1973–74; Dir, Central Unit on Environmental Pollution, 1974–78; Dir, Internat. Transport, Dept of Transport, 1978–81; Dir for the Environment, CEC, 1981–85; Actg Dir Gen. for the Environment, Consumer Protection and Nuclear Safety, CEC, 1985–86; Dep. Dir-Gen. for Develt, CEC, 1986–89. Senior UK Commissioner at Sessions of South Pacific Commn, 1965–67; Minister's Deputy, European Conf. of Mins of Transport, 1978–81; Chm., Environment Cttee, OECD, 1976–79; British Channel Tunnel Co., 1978–81; British Co-Chm., Jt UK/USSR Cttee established under UK/USSR Agreement on cooperation in field of Environmental Protection, 1974–78; Special Advr, EC, 1989–94; Capacity 21 Advr, UNDP, 1993–; Sen. Adviser, Envmtl Resources Mgt, 1989–; Chm., Network for Envmtl Technology Transfer, asbl, Belgium, 1989–; Dir, Groundwork Foundn, 1989–95. Consultant to European Orgn for Res. and Treatment of Cancer, 1989–95. Member: Royal Soc.'s British Nat. Cttee on Problems of Environment, 1974–78; EDC for Internat. Freight Movement, 1978–80; Governing Body, Chiswick Sch., 1973–79. CompICE, 1989–93. FRSA. *Address:* 6 Cumberland Road, Kew, Richmond, Surrey TW9 3HQ; Appt 12, 32 Quai aux Briques, 1000 Brussels, Belgium.

FAIRCLOUGH, Rt Hon. Ellen Louks; PC (Can.) 1957; CC 1995 (OC 1979); FCA 1965; UE; Member of Progressive Conservative Party, Canada; *b* Hamilton, Ont, 28 Jan. 1905; *d* of Norman Ellsworth Cook and Nellie Bell Louks; *m* 1931, David Henry Gordon Fairclough; one *s*. *Educ:* Hamilton Public and Secondary Schs. Certified Public Accountant, public practice, 1935–57 (Fellow, Chartered Accountants of Ontario, 1965). Hamilton City Council, Alderman, 1946–49; Controller, 1950. Elected to House of Commons as Progressive Conservative mem. for Hamilton West, 1950; re-elected at gen. elections, 1953, 1957, 1958, 1962, defeated in 1963 election. Sec. of State for Canada, 1957–58; Minister of Citizenship and Immigration, 1958–62; Postmaster-Gen., 1962–63. Chancellor, Royal Hamilton College of Music, 1978–80. Mem. Bd, Ontario Bicentennial Commn, 1983–84; Hon. Treas. and Exec. Dir, Chedoke-McMaster Hosps Foundn, 1982–86; Patron: Huguenot Soc. of Canada, 1969–; United Empire Loyalists Assoc., Hamilton Br., 1980–. Internat. Treasurer, Zonta Internat. HQ, Chicago, 1972–76 (Hon. Life Mem.). Ontario Govt Bldg named Ellen Fairclough Bldg, 1982. LLD (*hc*) McMaster Univ., 1975. *Publication:* Saturday's Child (memoirs), 1996. *Recreations:* music, reading and photography. *Clubs:* Albany (Toronto); Hamilton, Zonta I (Hamilton); Faculty (McMaster).

FAIRCLOUGH, Sir John (Whitaker), Kt 1990; FREng, FBCS; Chief Scientific Adviser to Cabinet Office, 1986–90; *b* 23 Aug. 1930; *m* 1954, Margaret Ann (*d* 1996); two *s* one *d*. *Educ:* Manchester Univ. (BScTech). Ferranti, 1954; IBM: Poughkeepsie Lab., US, 1957; Hursley Lab., UK, 1958; Director of Development, IBM UK Ltd, 1964; Asst Gen. Manager and Dir Data Processing, IBM UK, 1968; Dir, Raleigh Development Lab., USA, 1970; System Develt Div. Vice Pres., Raleigh, USA, 1972; System Communication Div. Vice Pres. and Man. Dir, Director of Development, Hursley Lab., UK, 1974; System Product Div. Vice Pres. and Man. Dir, Hursley Lab., UK, 1982; Dir of Manufacturing & Development, IBM UK Ltd, and Chm., IBM UK Laboratories Ltd, 1983. Chairman: Systematica Ltd, 1990–92; Rothschild Ventures Ltd, 1990–98; Southampton Holdings Ltd, 1996–; Smart Chemical Co. Ltd, 1998–; Opsys plc, 1998–; non-executive Director: Oxford Instruments Gp, 1990–98; N. M. Rothschild & Sons Ltd, 1990–97; Infolink plc, 1991–93; DSC (Europe), 1992–98; DSC Communication Corp., 1992–98; Lucas Industries, 1992–96; Psion plc, 1995–2000; Southampton Innovation Ltd, 1996–; Southampton Hldgs Ltd, 1997–. Chairman: Engineering Council, 1991–96 (Mem., 1982–90); CEST, 1990–95; Prince Charles' Innovation Initiative, 1991–97. Pres., BCS, 1987; Vice Pres., UMIST, 1992–95; Dep. Chm., Council, Southampton Univ., 1996–2001. Trustee, Mental Health Foundn, 1997–98. Freeman, City of London, 1989. Fellow, Nat. Acad. of Engrg, USA, 1990. FCGI 1997. Hon. FICE 1995; Hon. FIEE 1996; Hon. FIMechE 1996. Hon. Fellow: Portsmouth Polytechnic, 1991; Manchester Metropolitan Univ., 1992. Hon. DSc: Southampton, 1983; Cranfield, 1987; Manchester, 1988; Aston, 1990; Polytechnic of Central London, 1991; City, 1992; Hon. DTech Loughborough, 1990. Mensford Gold Medal, IProdE, 1989; Gold Medal Award of Merit, Co. of Carmen, 1995; President's Award, Engrg Council, 1996. *Recreations:* gardening, carpentry. *Address:* 3 Clockhouse Close, SW19 5NT.

FAIRCLOUGH, Oliver Noel Francis; Keeper of Art, National Museums and Galleries of Wales, Cardiff, since 1998; *b* 27 March 1950; *s* of late Arthur Basil Rowland Fairclough and Jean McKenzie Fairclough (*née* Fraser); *m* 1977, Caroline Mary Latta; one *s* two *d*. *Educ:* Bryanston Sch.; Trinity Coll., Oxford (BA); Univ. of Keele (MA). AMA 1978. Asst, Liverpool Mus., 1971–74; Asst Keeper, Art, 1975–79, Dep. Keeper, Applied Art, 1979–86, Birmingham Museums and Art Gall.; Asst Keeper, Applied Art, Nat. Mus. of Wales, 1986–98. Lectr and author. Mem., various adv. bodies and learned socs. *Publications:* (with E. Leary) Textiles by William Morris, 1981; The Grand Old Mansion, 1984; (with M. Evans) Companion Guide to the National Art Gallery, 1993, 2nd edn 1997; contribs to exhibn catalogues; contrib. to Burlington Mag. and other art Jls. *Recreations:* walking, travel, architectural history, naval and military history. *Address:* 21 Clive Place, Penarth, Vale of Glamorgan CF64 1AW. *T:* (029) 2070 3789.

FAIREY, Michael Edward; Deputy Group Chief Executive, Lloyds TSB Group plc, since 1998; *b* 17 June 1948; *s* of late Douglas and Marjorie Fairey; *m* 1973, Patricia Ann Dolby; two *s*. *Educ:* King Edward VI Grammar Sch., Louth. ACIB 1974. Barclays Bank, 1967–92: Asst Dir, Watford Gp, 1986; Ops Dir, Barclaycard, 1986–88; Exec. Dir, Barclays Card Services, 1988–92; Dir, Retail Credit, and Gp Credit Dir, TSB Gp, 1992; Gp Dir, Credit and Ops, 1993–96; IT and Ops Dir, 1996–97, Gp Dir, Central Services, 1997–98, Lloyds TSB Gp. *Recreations:* tennis, opera, football. *Address:* Lloyds TSB Group plc, 71 Lombard Street, EC3P 3BS.

FAIREY, Michael John, CB 1989; Chief Executive, The Royal London Hospital and Associated Community NHS Trust, 1991–94; *b* 20 Sept. 1933; *s* of late Ernest John Saunder Fairey and Lily Emily (*née* Pateman); *m* 1st, 1958 (marr. diss. 1989); two *s* one *d*; 2nd, 1990, Victoria Frances Hardman. *Educ:* Queen Elizabeth's Sch., Barnet; Jesus Coll., Cambridge (MA). Served RA, 1952–53. Jun. Administrator, St Thomas' Hosp., 1957–60; Gp Develt Sec., Westminster Hosp., 1960–62; Deputy House Governor, The London Hosp., 1962, House Governor 1972; Regional Administrator, NE Thames RHA, 1973; Dir, Planning and Inf., NHS Management Bd, DHSS, later Dept of Health, 1984–89; Dir of Information Systems, NHS Management Exec., Dept of Health, 1989–91. Sec., London Hospital Med. Coll., 1994–96. Gov., St Catherine's Sch., Ware, 1995– (Chm., 1997–2000). *Publications:* various articles in med. and computing jls. *Recreations:* church music, history of medieval exploration, Rugby football. *Club:* Athenæum.

FAIRFAX, family name of **Lord Fairfax of Cameron**.

FAIRFAX OF CAMERON, 14th Lord *cr* 1627; **Nicholas John Albert Fairfax;** Director, Aquatask Ltd, since 1997; *b* 4 Jan. 1956; *e s* of 13th Lord and of Sonia, *yr d* of late Capt. Cecil Gunston, MC; *S* father, 1964; *m* 1982, Annabel, *er d* of late Nicholas and of Sarah Gilham Morriss; three *s*. *Educ:* Eton; Downing Coll., Cambridge (LLB in international law subjects, 1981). Called to the Bar, Gray's Inn, 1977. Director: Thomas Miller P and I, and Thomas Miller Defence, 1987–90; Sedgwick Marine & Cargo Ltd, 1995–96. *Recreations:* sailing, motorcycling. *Heir:* *s* Hon. Edward Nicholas Thomas Fairfax, *b* 20 Sept. 1984. *Address:* 10 Orlando Road, SW4 0LF. *Club:* Royal Yacht Squadron (Cowes).

FAIRFAX, James Oswald, AO 1993; Chairman, John Fairfax Ltd, Sydney, 1977–87; *b* 27 March 1933; *s* of Sir Warwick Oswald Fairfax and late Marcie Elizabeth Fairfax (*née* Wilson). *Educ:* Geelong Grammar School; Balliol College, Oxford (MA; Hon. Fellow, 1992). Director, John Fairfax, 1957–87; Chm., Amalgamated Television Services Pty Ltd, 1975–87 (Dir, 1958); Chm., David Syme & Co., 1984–87 (Dir, 1977). Member: Bd of Management, Royal Alexandra Hosp. for Children, 1967–85 (Bd, Children's Med. Res. Foundn, 1986–88); Council, International House, Sydney Univ., 1967–79; Internat. Council, Museum of Modern Art, NY, 1971–99; Council, Australian Nat. Gallery, 1976–84; Dir, Art Exhibns Australia Ltd, 1994–98. Gov., Qld Art Gall. Foundn, 1995–; Life Governor: Art Gallery of NSW, 1991; Australian Nat. Gall. Foundn, 1992. Life Member: Nat. Trust of NSW, 1957; Nat. Gall. of Vic., 1992. *Publication:* My Regards to Broadway: a memoir, 1991. *Address:* Retford Park, Old South Road, Bowral, NSW 2576, Australia; Stanbridge Mill, Gussage All Saints, near Wimborne, Dorset BH21 5EP. *Clubs:* Garrick; Union, Australian (Sydney); Melbourne (Melbourne).

FAIRFAX-LUCY, Sir Edmund (John William Hugh Cameron-Ramsay-), 6th Bt *cr* 1836; painter, chiefly of still-life and interiors; *b* 4 May 1945; *s* of Sir Brian Fulke Cameron-Ramsay-Fairfax-Lucy, 5th Bt and Hon. Alice Caroline Helen Buchan (*d* 1993), *o d* of 1st Baron Tweedsmuir, PC, GCMG, GCVO, CH; *S* father, 1974; *m* 1994, Erica, *d* of Warren Loane, Crocknaerieve, Enniskillen; two *s*. *Educ:* City and Guilds of London Art Sch.; Royal Academy Schs of Art. Regular exhibitor, RA Summer Exhibn, 1967–; one-man shows, numerous mixed exhibitions. *Heir:* *s* Patrick Samuel Thomas Fulke Fairfax-Lucy, *b* 3 April 1995. *Address:* Charlecote Park, Warwick CV35 9ER.

FAIRHALL, Hon. Sir Allen, KBE 1970; MHR (L) Paterson, NSW, 1949–69; *b* 24 Nov. 1909; *s* of Charles Edward and Maude Fairhall; *m* 1936, Monica Clelland, *d* of James and Ellen Ballantyne; one *s*. *Educ:* East Maitland Primary and High Sch.; Newcastle Tech. Inst. Founded commercial broadcasting stn 2KO, 1931; Supervising Engr, Radio and Signals Supplies Div., Min. of Munitions, 1942–45; Pres., Austr. Fedn of Commercial Broadcasting Stns, 1942–43. Mem. Australian Delegn to UN Gen. Assembly, 1954; Minister for Interior and Works, 1956–58; Minister for Supply, 1961–66; Minister for Defence, 1966–69. Mem. Newcastle CC, 1941. FRSA 1970. Hon. DSc Newcastle, NSW, 1968. *Recreations:* amateur radio, deep sea fishing. *Address:* 7 Parkway Avenue, Newcastle, NSW 2300, Australia. *T:* (2) 49292295. *Clubs:* Tattersall's, National (Sydney); Newcastle (Newcastle).

FAIRHAVEN, 3rd Baron *cr* 1929 and 1961 (new creation); **Ailwyn Henry George Broughton;** JP; Vice Lord-Lieutenant, Cambridgeshire, 1977–85; *b* 16 Nov. 1936; *s* of 2nd Baron Fairhaven and Hon. Diana Rosamond (*d* 1937), *o d* of late Captain Hon. Coulson Fellowes; *S* father, 1973; *m* 1960, Kathleen Patricia, *d* of Col James Henry Magill, OBE; three *s* two *d* (and one *s* decd). *Educ:* Eton; RMA, Sandhurst. Royal Horse Guards, 1957–71. Mem., Jockey Club, 1977– (Steward, 1981–82, Sen. Steward, 1985–89). DL Cambridgeshire and Isle of Ely, 1973; JP South Cambridgeshire, 1975. KStJ 1992. *Recreations:* gardening, cooking. *Heir:* *s* Major Hon. James Henry Ailwyn Broughton [*b* 25 May 1963; *m* 1990, Sarah Olivia, *d* of H. D. F. Creighton, *qv*; one *s* two *d*]. *Address:* Anglesey Abbey, Cambridge CB5 9EJ. *T:* (01223) 811746. *Club:* White's.

FAIRLEY, John Alexander; Chairman: Highflyer Productions, since 1996; Channel 4 Racing, since 1997; *s* of Alexander Miller Fairley and Madge Irene Fairley; *m*; three *d*. *Educ:* Merchant Taylors' Sch., Crosby; Queen's Coll., Oxford (MA). Midshipman, RNVR. Journalist: Bristol Evening Post, 1963; London Evening Standard, 1964; Producer: BBC Radio, 1965–68; Yorkshire TV, 1968–78; freelance writer and broadcaster, 1979–84; Dir of Programmes, Yorkshire TV, 1984–92; Managing Director: Yorkshire TV Programmes, 1992–93; Yorkshire TV, 1993–95; Chief Exec., UK TV, 1995–96; Chairman: ITV Broadcast Bd, 1995; K Max Radio, 1995–97. Trustee, Injured Jockeys Fund, 1999–. FRTS 1994. *Publications:* (jtly) The Monocled Mutineer, 1978; (jtly) Arthur C. Clarke's Mysterious World, 1980, and subseq. vols, 1984, 1987; Great Racehorses In Art, 1984; Racing In Art, 1990; (jtly) The Cabinet of Curiosities, 1991; The Art of the Horse, 1995. *Recreations:* writing, racing, hunting. *Address:* Trainer's House, Eddlethorpe, Malton, Yorks YO17 9QS; 539 Willoughby House, Barbican, EC2Y 8BN.

FAIRLIE-CUNINGHAME, Sir Robert (Henry), 17th Bt *cr* 1630, of Robertland, Ayrshire; *b* 19 July 1974; *o s* of Sir William Henry Fairlie-Cuninghame, 16th Bt and of Janet Menzies, *d* of R. M. Saddington; *S* father, 1999. *Heir:* *cousin* David Hastings Fairlie-Cuninghame [*b* June 1937; *m* 1963, Susan Gai White; one *s* one *d*]. *Address:* 29a Orinoco Street, Pymble, NSW 2073, Australia.

FAIRTLOUGH, Gerard Howard, CBE 1989; Director, Cantab Pharmaceuticals plc, since 1990; *b* 5 Sept. 1930; *s* of late Maj.-Gen. Eric V. H. Fairtlough, DSO, MC, and A. Zoë Fairtlough (*née* Barker); *m* 1954, Elizabeth A. Betambeau; two *s* two *d*. *Educ:* Cambridge Univ. (BA Biochemistry, Pt II). Royal/Dutch Shell Group, 1953–78; Managing Director, Shell Chemicals UK Ltd, 1973–78; Divisional Director, NEB, 1978–80; Chief Exec., Celltech Ltd, 1980–90. Chairman: Coverdale Orgn, 1974–93; Therexsys Ltd, 1992–96; Landmark Inf. Gp Ltd, 1994–97. Mem., SERC, 1989–94. Hon. DSc: City, 1987; CNAA, 1990. *Publication:* Creative Compartments, 1994. *Recreations:* walking, yoga, theatre. *Address:* Greenways, Ryall, Bridport, Dorset DT6 6EN. *T:* (01297) 489333.

FAIRWEATHER, Brig. Claude Cyril, CB 1967; CBE 1965 (OBE 1944); TD 1944; JP; Vice Lord-Lieutenant, County of Cleveland, 1977–82; Chairman, North of England TA&VRA, 1968–71; *b* 17 March 1906; *s* of Nicholas Fairweather, Middlesbrough; *m* 1930, Alice Mary, *e d* of late Sir William Crosthwaite; one *s* one *d*. *Educ:* St Peter's Sch., York. 2nd Lieut, Royal Corps of Signals, 1928; Lt-Col 1941; Col 1943; Brig. 1945. Chm., North Riding T&AFA, 1950–53 and 1962–68; Mem., TA Advisory Cttee and TA Exec.

Cttee, 1968–71. Chm., St John Council, N Yorks (Vice-Pres., N Yorks St John Amb. Bde); Hon. Col, 34 (N) Signal Regt (V), 1967–75; Chairman: N Riding Co. Cadet Cttee, 1947–52; St Luke's HMC, Middlesbrough, 1959–74; Cleveland AHA, 1973–76. Retd Company Dir. Hon. Trust Representative for Cleveland, Royal Jubilee Trusts, 1977–81. DL 1949, JP 1963, NR Yorks. KStJ 1978. *Recreations:* golf, cricket, Rugby football. *Address:* Broomcroft House, Ecceshall Road South, Sheffield S11 9PY. *T:* (0114) 235 2352, *Fax:* (0114) 235 2351. *Clubs:* Army and Navy; Cleveland (Middlesbrough); Royal and Ancient (St Andrews).

FAIRWEATHER, Clive Bruce, OBE 1990; HM Chief Inspector of Prisons for Scotland, since 1994; *b* 21 May 1944; *s* of George Fairweather and Helen Fairweather (*née* Henderson); *m* 1980, Ann Beatrice Dexter; one *s* one *d*. *Educ:* George Heriot's Sch.; RMA Sandhurst. Army Staff Coll., 1975–76; CO, Scottish Infantry Depot, 1984–87; Instr, RAF Staff Coll., 1987; CO, 1st Bn King's Own Scottish Borderers, 1987–89; Divl Col, Scottish Div., 1991–94. *Publication:* (jtly) Women Offenders: a safer way, 1998. *Recreations:* gliding, piano. *Address:* Scottish Executive, Saughton House, Broomhouse Drive, Edinburgh EH11 3XD. *T:* (0131) 244 8481. *Club:* Special Forces.

FAIRWEATHER, Prof. Denys Vivian Ivor, MD; FRCOG; Secretary-General of International Federation of Gynaecology and Obstetrics, 1985–94; Professor and Head of Department of Obstetrics and Gynaecology, 1966–90, and Vice-Provost, 1984–90, University College London; Pro-Vice-Chancellor for Medicine and Dentistry, University of London, 1989–92; *b* 25 Oct. 1927; *s* of late Albert James Ivor Fairweather and Gertrude Mary Forbes; *m* 1956, (Gwendolen) Yvonne Hubbard; one *s* two *d*. *Educ:* Forfar Acad.; Websters Seminary, Kirriemuir; St Andrews Univ. (MB, ChB 1949; MD 1966). FRCOG 1967 (MRCOG 1958). Served RAF Med. Br., 1950–55, Sqn Leader. Sen. Lectr, Univ. of Newcastle upon Tyne, 1959–66; Fulbright Scholar, Western Reserve Univ., USA, 1963–64; Dean, Faculty of Clinical Science, UCL, 1982–84; Vice Provost (Medicine) and Head, University Coll. London Sch. of Medicine, later University Coll. and Mddx Sch. of Medicine of UCL, 1984–89; Hon. Fellow, UCL, 1985. Member: GMC, 1988–92; Internat. Med. Adv. Panel, IPPF, 1988–94; Vice Pres., FPA, 1985–98 (Patron, 1998–). Hon. FAARM 1969; Hon. FACOG 1993. Freeman, City of Krakow, 1989. Dist. Service Award, FIGO, 1997. *Publications:* Amniotic Fluid Research and Clinical Applications, 1973, 2nd edn 1978; Labour Ward Manual, 1985; over 160 pubns in scientific jls, on perinatal mortality, rhesus disease, genetics, antenatal diagnosis, very low birthweight, medical education. *Recreations:* gardening, fishing, do-it-yourself. *Address:* 37 Lyndhurst Avenue, Mill Hill, NW7 2AD.

FAIRWEATHER, Eric John, FCIB; Head of Asset Finance, Co-operative Bank PLC, since 1999; *b* 9 Nov. 1942; *s* of late John Walter William Fairweather and Lilian Emma Fairweather; *m* 1st, 1966, Frances Mary Ewer (marr. diss.); two *d*; 2nd, 1991, Deborah Chubb; two *s*. *Educ:* Carlisle Grammar Sch. Entered Midland Bank at Carlisle, 1961; Manager, Corporate Finance Div., 1978–81; Sen. Asst Man., Poultry and Princes Street, 1981–84; on secondment as Dir, Industrial Develt Unit, DTI (Under Sec.), 1984–86; Manager, UK Business Sector, Midland Bank, 1986; Manager, Central Management and Planning, 1986–87; Corporate Banking Area Manager, Manchester, 1987–93; Area Manager: Manchester, 1993–94; Sheffield, 1994–95; Regl Gen. Manager, NW, Co-operative Bank, 1995–98. Director: Sheffield TEC, 1994–95; Wigan Borough Partnership, 1996–. *Recreations:* classical music, Association football (Bolton Wanderers), golf. *Address:* Co-operative Bank, PO Box 101, 1 Balloon Street, Manchester M60 4EP.

FAIRWEATHER, Dr Frank Arthur; consultant in toxicology and pathology; *b* 2 May 1928; *s* of Frank and Maud Harriet Fairweather; *m* 1953, Christine Winifred Hobbs; two *s*. *Educ:* City of Norwich Sch.; Middlesex Hospital. MB, BS 1954; MRCPath 1963, FRCPath 1975; FIBiol 1972. Clinical house appts, Ipswich Gp of Hosps, 1955–56; Pathologist, Bland Sutton Inst. of Pathology, and Courtauld Inst. of Biochem., Middlesex Hosp., Soho Hosp. for Women, 1956–60; Jt Sen. Registrar in Histopathology, Middlesex and West Middlesex Hosps, 1961–62; Chief Med. Adviser and Cons. Pathologist, Benger Labs, 1962–63; Chief Pathologist and Nuffield Scholar, British Industrial Biological Res. Assoc., Carshalton, and Hon. Sen. Lectr, RCS, 1963–65; Associate Res. Dir, Wyeth Labs, Taplow, 1965–69; Sen. Med. Officer, DHSS, and Principal Med. Officer, Cttee on Safety of Medicines, 1969–72; SPMO, DHSS, 1972–82; Head of Safety and Envmt Res. Div., Unilever, 1982–93. Mem., EEC Scientific Cttee for Food, 1976–84 (Chm., Sci. Cttee for Cosmetology); Consultant Adviser in Toxicology to DHSS, 1978–81; Dir, DHSS Toxicological Lab., St Bartholomew's Hosp., 1978–82, Hon. Dir, 1982–84; Hon. Prof. of Toxicology, Dept of Biochemistry, Univ. of Surrey, 1978–84; Hon. Prof. of Toxicology and Pathology, Sch. of Pharmacy, Univ. of London, 1982–88. Chief Examiner in Toxicology, Inst. of Biology, 1989–. Chm., BIBRA, 1987–93. Hon. FFOM 1991. QHP, 1977–80. *Publications:* various toxicological and medical papers. *Recreations:* angling, gardening, water colours. *Address:* Fairland, Wayford, Stalham, Norwich NR12 9LH. *T:* and *Fax:* (01692) 582588.

FAIRWEATHER, Sir Patrick (Stanislaus), KCMG 1992 (CMG 1986); HM Diplomatic Service, retired; Senior Adviser, Schroder Salomon Smith Barney (formerly Schroders), since 1996; Director, Butrint Foundation, since 1997; *b* 17 June 1936; *s* of John George Fairweather and Dorothy Jane (*née* Boanus); *m* 1962, Maria (*née* Merica); two *d*. *Educ:* Ottershaw Sch., Surrey; Trinity Coll., Cambridge (Hons History). National Service in Royal Marines and Parachute Regt, 1955–57. Entered FCO, 1965; 2nd Secretary, Rome, 1966–69; FCO, 1969–70; 1st Secretary (Economic), Paris, 1970–73; FCO, 1973–75; 1st Sec. and Head of Chancery, Vientiane, 1975–76; 1st Sec., UK Representation to EEC, Brussels, 1976–78; Counsellor (Economic and Commercial), Athens, 1978–83; Head of European Community Dept (Internal), FCO, 1983–85; Ambassador to Angola, 1985–87; Asst Under-Sec. of State, FCO, 1987–90; Dep. Under-Sec. of State (ME/Africa), FCO, 1990–92; Ambassador to Italy and (non-resident) to Albania, 1992–96. *Recreations:* travel, gardening, photography, sailing. *Club:* Garrick.

FAIRWOOD, Ian Stuart; a District Judge, since 1996; a Recorder, since 2001; *b* 16 May 1951; *s* of George Centenus Fairwood and Kathleen Florence Fairwood; *m* 1976, Hilary Joan Middleton; two *s*. *Educ:* Carlton Cavendish Secondary Modern; UCL (LLB). Bar Sch., 1974–75; called to the Bar, Middle Temple, 1974; Dep. Dist Judge, 1993–96; NE Circuit. *Recreations:* golf, tennis, ski-ing, gardening. *Address:* Pilmoor House, Pilmoor, York YO61 2QF. *T:* (01423) 360395. *Club:* Notts County (Nottingham).

FAITH, (Irene) Sheila; JP; dental surgeon; *b* 3 June 1928; *yr d* of late I. Book; *m* 1950, Dennis Faith. *Educ:* Central High School, Newcastle upon Tyne; Durham Univ. LDS 1950. Practised as schools dental surgeon, Northumberland. Member: Northumberland CC, 1970–74 (Mem., Health and Social Services Cttees; Rep., S Northumberland Youth Employment Bd); Newcastle City Council, 1975–77 (Mem., Educn Cttee). Vice-Chm., Jt Consultative Cttee on Educn for District of Newcastle during local govt reorganisation, 1973–74. Mem., Parole Bd, 1991–94. Contested (C) Newcastle Central, Oct. 1974; MP (C) Belper, 1979–83. Mem., Select Cttee on Health and Social Services, 1979–83; Sec., Conservative backbench Health and Social Services Cttee, 1982–83. MEP (C) Cumbria and Lancs N, 1984–89; Member: Transport Cttee, 1984–87; Cttee on Energy, Res. and Technol., 1987–89. Mem., Exec. Cttee, Cons. Medical Soc., 1981–84; Pres., Cumbria and Lancs N Cons. Euro Constituency Council, 1989–95; Dep. Chm., Hampstead and Highgate Cons. Assoc., 1991–92. Has served as Chm. or Mem. several school governing bodies and Manager of Community Homes and with CAB, Newcastle upon Tyne. JP: Northumberland County, 1972–74; Newcastle upon Tyne, 1974–78; Inner London, 1978–. *Recreations:* reading, music. *Address:* 52 Moor Court, Westfield, Gosforth, Newcastle upon Tyne NE3 4YD. *T:* (0191) 285 4438. *Club:* Royal Society of Medicine.

FAKLEY, Dennis Charles, OBE 1973; retired; *b* 20 Nov. 1924; *s* of Charles Frederick and Ethel May Fakley; *m* 1976, Louise Grace Swindell. *Educ:* Chatham House Grammar Sch., Ramsgate; Queen Mary Coll., Univ. of London (BSc Special Physics). Royal Naval Scientific Service, 1944–63; Min. of Defence, 1963–84. *Recreations:* reading, cricket. *Address:* 14 Coval Gardens, SW14 7DG. *T:* (020) 8876 6856.

FALCON, David; international public management consultant, since 1992; *b* 3 Jan. 1946; *s* of Arnold and Barbara Falcon; *m* 1st, 1967 (marr. diss. 1991); two *s*; 2nd, 1998, Simoné Mondesir. *Educ:* Helston County Grammar Sch.; University College London (BSc); Lancaster Univ. (MA); Univ. of Pennsylvania. Research Associate, Univ. of Lancaster, 1969–72; Lectr, Leeds Polytechnic, 1972–74; Sen. Lectr, Sheffield Polytechnic, 1974–76; Asst Dir, Sen. Asst Dir, Dep. Dir of Education, Humberside CC, 1976–85; Dir of Education, ILEA, 1985–88; Dir-Gen., RIPA, 1988–92. FRSA. *Publications:* articles in educn and management jls. *Recreations:* music, opera, photography, travel. *Address:* 10 Grace House, Sydenham Avenue, SE26 6UJ. *T:* (020) 8676 7837, *Fax:* (020) 8676 7838.

FALCON, Michael Gascoigne, CBE 1979; JP, DL; Chairman: Norwich Union Insurance Group, 1981–94 (Director, 1963–94; Vice Chairman, 1979–81); Norwich Winterthur Holdings Ltd, 1984–94; Norfolk and Norwich Health Care NHS Trust, 1994–97; *b* 28 Jan. 1928; *s* of late Michael Falcon and Kathleen Isabel Frances Gascoigne; *m* 1954, April Daphne Claire Lambert; two *s* one *d*. *Educ:* Stowe Sch., Bucks; Heriot-Watt Coll., Edinburgh. National Service, Grenadier Gds and Royal Norfolk Regt, 1946–48. Head Brewer and Jt Man. Dir, E. Lacon & Co. Ltd, Great Yarmouth, 1952–68; Exec. Dir, Edgar Watts, Willow Merchants, 1968–73; Chairman: National Seed Develt Orgn Ltd, 1972–82; Pauls & Whites PLC, 1976–85 (Dir, 1973–85); Eastern Counties Regional Bd, Lloyds Bank Plc, 1979–91 (Dir, 1972–91); Director: Securicor (East) Ltd, 1969–72; Lloyds Bank UK Management Ltd, 1979–85; Matthew Brown plc, 1981–87; National Bus Properties Ltd, 1983–86; Greene King & Sons PLC, 1988–96; British Railways (Anglia) Bd, 1988–92. Chm., Norwich HA, 1988–94. Trustee, E Anglian Trustee Savings Bank, 1963–75. Chm., Trustees, John Innes Foundn, 1990–98. Mem., Norwich Prison Bd of Visitors, 1969–82. JP 1967, High Sheriff 1979, DL 1981, Co. of Norfolk; High Steward, Great Yarmouth, 1984–. CStJ 1986. Hon. LLD Nottingham, 1988. *Recreation:* country pursuits. *Address:* Keswick Old Hall, Norwich, Norfolk NR4 6TZ. *T:* (01603) 454348. *Clubs:* Norfolk (Norwich); Royal Norfolk and Suffolk Yacht (Lowestoft).
See also Ven. D. L. Edwards.

FALCONER, family name of **Baron Falconer of Thoroton**.

FALCONER OF THOROTON, Baron *cr* 1997 (Life Peer), of Thoroton in the co. of Nottinghamshire; **Charles Leslie Falconer;** QC 1991; Minister of State for Housing, Planning and Regeneration, Department for Transport, Local Government and the Regions, since 2001; *b* 19 Nov. 1951; *s* of John Leslie Falconer and late Anne Mansel Falconer; *m* 1985, Marianna Catherine Thoroton Hildyard, *d* of Sir David Hildyard, KCMG, DFC; three *s* one *d*. *Educ:* Trinity Coll., Glenalmond; Queens' Coll., Cambridge. Called to the Bar, Inner Temple, 1974, Bencher, 1997. Solicitor-General, 1997–98; Minister of State, Cabinet Office, 1998–2001. *Address:* Department for Transport, Local Government and the Regions, Eland House, Bressenden Place, SW1E 5DU.

FALCONER, Alexander, (Alex); *b* Dundee, 1 April 1940; *s* of John Falconer, labourer, and Margaret McFarlane Falconer, canteen assistant; *m* Margaret Cavell Falconer, chef; one *s* one *d*. Former foundry worker; served with RN, 1959–68; insulator, Rosyth dockyard, 1969–84. Shop Steward, TGWU, 1970–84; Chm., Fife Fedn of Trades Councils. MEP (Lab) Mid Scotland and Fife, 1984–99. Mem., CND. *Address:* Forthview, 2 Greenacres, Kingseat, Fife KY12 0RW.

FALCONER, Prof. Douglas Scott, FRS 1973; FRSE 1972; *b* 10 March 1913; *s* of Gerald Scott Falconer and Lillias Harriet Gordon Douglas; *m* 1942, Margaret Duke; two *s*. *Educ:* Edinburgh Academy; Univ. of St Andrews (BSc); Univ. of Cambridge (PhD, ScD). Scientific Staff of Agricultural Research Council, 1947–68; Prof. of Genetics, Univ. of Edinburgh, and Dir, ARC Unit of Animal Genetics, 1968–80. *Publications:* Introduction to Quantitative Genetics, 1960, 4th edn 1996; papers in scientific jls.

FALCONER, Hon. Sir Douglas (William), Kt 1981; MBE 1946; a Judge of the High Court of Justice, Chancery Division, 1981–89; *b* 20 Sept. 1914; *s* of late William Falconer, S Shields; *m* 1st, 1941, Joan Beryl Argent (*d* 1989), *d* of late A. S. Bishop, Hagley, Worcs; one *s* one *d*; 2nd, 1997, Constance M. F. Drew. *Educ:* South Shields; King's Coll., Durham Univ.; BSc (Hons) Physics, 1935. Served War of 1939–45 (Hon. Major): commissioned E Yorks Regt, 1939. Called to Bar, Middle Temple, 1950, Bencher 1973; QC 1967. Apptd to exercise appellate jurisdiction of BoT, later DoT, under Trade Marks Act, 1970–81; Member: of Departmental Cttee to review British trade mark law and practice, 1972–73; Standing Adv. Cttee on Patents, 1975–79; Standing Adv. Cttee on Trade Marks, 1975–79; Senate of Four Inns of Court, 1973–74; Senate of Four Inns of Court and the Bar, 1974–77; Chm., Patent Bar Assoc., 1971–80. *Publications:* (Jt Editor) Terrell on the Law of Patents (11th and 12th edns), 1965 and 1971. *Recreations:* music, theatre. *Address:* Ridgewell House, West Street, Reigate, Surrey RH2 9BZ. *T:* (01737) 244374.

FALCONER, Peter Serrell, FRIBA, FRSA; Founder of The Falconer Partnership, Architects and Consultants, and of Handling Consultants Ltd, Stroud and Johannesburg; *b* 7 March 1916; *s* of Thomas Falconer, FRIBA, and Florence Edith Falconer; presumed heir to the Barony (1206) and Lordship (1646) of Halkerton, vacant since 1966; *m* 1941, Mary Hodson; three *s* one *d*. *Educ:* Bloxham Sch., Banbury. Commenced practice in Stroud, as partner in Ellery Anderson Roiser & Falconer, 1944; Sen. Partner of Peter Falconer and Partners, 1959–82 (with br. office in Adelaide, SA, 1970). Specialist in materials handling and industrial architecture; Mem., Materials Handling Inst. *Publications:* Building and Planning for Industrial Storage and Distribution, 1975; contributor to: Architectural Review; Architects' Jl; Material Handling magazines. *Recreations:* restoring historic buildings, garden planning, motor sport. *Address:* St Francis, Lammas Park, Minchinhampton, Stroud, Glos GL6 9HA. *T:* (01453) 882188.

FALCONER, Prof. Roger Alexander, PhD, DEng, DSc(Eng); FREng; FICE; FCIWEM; Halcrow Professor of Environmental Water Management, Cardiff School of Engineering, Cardiff University, since 1997; *b* 12 Dec. 1951; *s* of late Cyril Thomas Falconer and Winifred Mary Matilda Falconer (*née* Rudge); *m* 1977, Nicola Jane Wonson; two *s* one *d*. *Educ:* King's Coll., London (BSc(Eng)); Univ. of Washington, USA (MScEng); Imperial Coll., London (PhD 1976; DIC 1976); Univ. of Birmingham (DEng

1992); Univ. of London (DSc(Eng) 1994). CEng 1982; Eur Ing 1990; FCIWEM 1990; FICE 1992; FREng (FEng 1997). Assistance Engr, Sir M. MacDonald and Partners, Cambridge, 1976–77; Lectr in Hydraulic Engrg, Dept of Civil Engrg, Univ. of Birmingham, 1977–86; University of Bradford: Prof. of Water Engrg and Leader, Envmtl Hydraulics Res. Gp, 1987–97; Dep. Hd, 1987–94, Hd, 1994–97, Dept of Civil and Envmtl Engrg. Adv. Prof., Tongji Univ., China, 1987–; Guest Prof., Tianjin Univ., China, 1999–. Member Council: CIWEM, 1997–; Internat. Assoc. for Hydraulic Res., 1999–; ICE, 2000–. FASCE 1993; FCGI 1997. FRSA 1992. Ippen Award, Internat. Assoc. Hydraulic Res., 1991; Telford Premium, ICE, 1994; Silver Medal, Royal Acad. of Engrg, 1999. *Publications: edited:* (jtly) Hydraulic and Environmental Modelling of Coastal, Estuarine and River Waters, 1989; Water Quality Modelling, 1992; (jtly) Hydraulic and Environmental Modelling: coastal waters, 1992; (jtly) Hydraulic and Environmental Modelling: estuarine and river waters, 1992; (jtly) Wetland Management, 1994; numerous papers on envmtl water mgt in jls and internat. conf. proc. *Recreations:* music, walking, travel. *Address:* Cardiff School of Engineering, Cardiff University, PO Box 925, Newport Road, Cardiff CF24 0YB. *T:* (029) 2087 4280; Hatherton, Radyr Court Road, Llandaff, Cardiff CF5 2QF. *T:* and *Fax:* (029) 2057 6935.

FALDO, Nicholas Alexander, MBE 1988; professional golfer; President, Faldo Design; *b* 18 July 1957; *s* of George and Joyce Faldo; *m*; one *s* two *d*. *Educ:* Welwyn Garden City. Won English Amateur Golf Championship, 1975; Professional golfer, 1976; Mem., Ryder Cup team, 1977–97; many championship titles include: Open, Muirfield, 1987, 1992, St Andrews, 1990; US Masters, 1989, 1990, 1996; French Open, 1983, 1988, 1989; GA Europ. Open, 1992; World Match Play Championship, 1992; Irish Open, 1991, 1992, 1993. *Publications:* Golf: the winning formula, 1989; In Search of Perfection, 1994; A Swing for Life, 1995. *Recreations:* fly fishing, motor sports; *e-mail:* nfdo@faldodesign.com.

FALETAU, 'Inoke Fotu; *see* 'Akau'ola.

FALKENDER, Baroness *cr* 1974 (Life Peer), of West Haddon, Northants; **Marcia Matilda Falkender,** CBE 1970; Private and Political Secretary to Lord Wilson of Rievaulx, 1956–83 (at 10 Downing Street, 1964–70 and 1974–76); *b* March 1932; *d* of Harry Field. *Educ:* Northampton High School; Queen Mary Coll., Univ. of London. BA Hons Hist. Secretary to Gen. Sec., Labour Party, 1955–56. Member: Prime Minister's Film Industry Working Party, 1975–76; Interim Cttee on Film Industry, 1977–82; British Screen Adv. Council, 1985–. Chm., Canvasback Productions, 1989–91. Director: Peckham Building Soc., 1986–91; South London Investment and Mortgage Corp., 1986–91; General Mediterranean Holding Group (UK). Political columnist, Mail on Sunday, 1982–88. Trustee, Silver Trust, 1988–. Mem., External Relations Cttee, QMW (formerly QMC), London Univ., 1987–97; Governor, QMW, 1987–93. FRSA. *Publications:* Inside Number 10, 1972; Downing Street in Perspective, 1983. *Address:* House of Lords, SW1A 0PW. *Club:* Reform.

FALKINER, Sir Benjamin (Simon) Patrick, 10th Bt *cr* 1778, of Annemount, Cork; *b* 16 Jan. 1962; *s* of Sir Edmond Charles Falkiner, 9th Bt and of his 1st wife, Janet Iris, *d* of Arthur Edward Bruce Derby; *S* father, 1997; *m* 1998, Linda Louise Mason; one *s* one *d*. *Educ:* Queen Elizabeth's Grammar Sch. for Boys, Barnet. *Heir: b* Matthew Terence Falkiner, *b* 9 Jan. 1964. *Address:* 29 Glebeland, Hatfield, Herts AL10 8AA.

FALKINGHAM, Ven. John Norman; Warden, Community of the Holy Name, 1969–85; *b* 9 Feb. 1917; 2nd *s* of Alfred Richard Falkingham and Amy Grant (*née* Macallister); *m* 1947, Jean Dorothy Thoren; two *d*. *Educ:* Geelong Gram. Sch., Corio, Vic.; Trinity Coll., Univ. of Melbourne. BA (Hons) Melbourne 1940; ThL (1st Cl. Hons), ThD 1978, Australian Coll. of Theol.; prizes for Divinity and Biblical Greek. Deacon, 1941; Priest, 1942. Curate of Holy Trinity, Surrey Hills, Vic., 1941–44; Chaplain, Trinity Coll., Univ. of Melbourne, 1944–50; Incumbent, St Paul's, Caulfield, Vic., 1950–61. Exam. Chaplain to Archbishop of Melbourne, 1947–61; Lectr in Theol. Faculty, Trinity Coll., Melbourne, 1950–60; Canon of St Paul's Cath., Melbourne, 1959–61; Dean of Newcastle, NSW, 1961–75; Rector of St Paul's, Manuka, ACT, 1975–82; Canon of St Saviour's Cath., Goulburn, 1976–81; Archdeacon of Canberra, 1981–82, Archdeacon Emeritus, 1982. Sec., Liturgical Commn of Gen. Synod, 1966–78; Mem. Bd of Delegates, Aust. Coll. of Theology, 1962–88; Lecturer: Canberra Coll. of Ministry, 1975–84; St Mark's Library, Canberra, 1982–87; Chm., Bd of Dirs, Canberra C of E Girls' Grammar Sch., 1983–90. *Publications:* articles in various jls. *Recreation:* walking. *Address:* 4 Serra Place, Stirling, ACT 2611, Australia.

FALKLAND, 15th Viscount *cr* 1620 (Scot.), of Falkland, Co. Fife; **Lucius Edward William Plantagenet Cary;** Lord Cary 1620; Premier Viscount of Scotland on the Roll; *b* 8 May 1935; *s* of 14th Viscount Falkland, and Constance Mary (*d* 1995), *d* of late Captain Edward Berry; *S* father, 1984; *m* 1st, 1962, Caroline Anne (marr. diss. 1990), *o d* of late Lt-Comdr Gerald Butler, DSC, RN, and late Mrs Patrick Parish; one *s* two *d* (and one *d* decd); 2nd, 1990, Nicole, *o d* of late Milburn Mackey; one *s*. *Educ:* Wellington Coll.; Alliance Française, Paris. Late 2nd Lieut 8th Hussars. Export marketing consultant, formerly Chief Executive, C. T. Bowring Trading (Holdings) Ltd. Mem., H of L Select Cttee on Overseas Trade, 1984–85. Dep. Whip, Lib Dem, H of L, 1989–; spokesman on culture, media and sport (formerly nat. heritage), 1995–; elected Mem., H of L, 1999. *Recreations:* golf, motorcycling, cinema. *Heir: s* Master of Falkland, *qv*. *Address:* c/o House of Lords, SW1A 0PW. *Clubs:* Brooks's; Sunningdale Golf.

FALKLAND, Master of; Hon. Lucius Alexander Plantagenet Cary; late Captain, 2nd Battalion, Scots Guards; *b* 1 Feb. 1963; *s* and *heir* of 15th Viscount Falkland, *qv*; *m* 1993, Linda, *d* of Raymond Purl, Colorado City, USA; one *s*. *Educ:* Loretto School; RMA Sandhurst. *Recreations:* ski-ing, golf. *Club:* Cavalry and Guards.

FALL, Sir Brian (James Proetel), GCVO 1994; KCMG 1992 (CMG 1984); HM Diplomatic Service, retired; Principal, Lady Margaret Hall, Oxford, 1995–Sept. 2002; *b* 13 Dec. 1937; *s* of John William Fall, Hull, Yorkshire, and Edith Juliette (*née* Proetel); *m* 1962, Delmar Alexandra Roos; three *d*. *Educ:* St Paul's Sch.; Magdalen Coll., Oxford; Univ. of Michigan Law Sch. Served HM Forces, 1955–57. Joined HM Foreign (now Diplomatic) Service, 1962; served in Foreign Office UN Dept, 1963; Moscow, 1965; Geneva, 1968; Civil Service Coll., 1970; FO Eastern European and Soviet Dept and Western Organisations Dept, 1971; New York, 1975; Harvard Univ. Center for Internat. Affairs, 1976; Counsellor, Moscow, 1977–79; Head of Energy, Science and Space Dept, FCO, 1979–80; Head of Eastern European and Soviet Dept, FCO, 1980–81; Prin. Private Sec. to Sec. of State for Foreign and Commonwealth Affairs, 1981–84; Dir, Cabinet, Sec. Gen. of NATO, 1984–86; Asst Under-Sec. of State (Defence), FCO, 1986–88; Minister, Washington, 1988–89; High Comr to Canada, 1989–92; Ambassador to Russian Fedn, and to Republics of Armenia, Georgia, Moldova and Turkmenistan, 1992–95, also to Azerbaijan, Belarus, Kazakhstan, Kyrgyzstan and Uzbekistan, 1992–93. *Address:* (until Sept. 2002) Lady Margaret Hall, Oxford OX2 6QA; (from Oct. 2002) 2 St Helena Terrace, Richmond, Surrey TW9 1NR.

FALL, David William; HM Diplomatic Service; Estate Modernisation Manager (formerly Estate Sales Programme Manager), Foreign and Commonwealth Office, since 2000; *b* 10 March 1948; *s* of George William Fall and Susan Fall; *m* 1973, Margaret Gwendolyn Richards; three *s*. *Educ:* St Bartholomew's Grammar Sch., Newbury; New Coll., Oxford (MA Mod. Hist.). VSO, Papua-New Guinea, 1970–71; joined FCO, 1971; language student, later 2nd then 1st Sec., Bangkok, 1973–77; seconded to Cabinet Office, 1977–78; FCO, 1978–80; 1st Sec., Cape Town and Pretoria, 1981–85; FCO, 1985–90; Counsellor, 1989; Head of Narcotics Control and AIDS Dept, FCO, 1989–90; Dep. Hd of Mission, Bangkok, 1990–93; Dep. High Comr, Canberra, 1993–97; Ambassador to Socialist Republic of Vietnam, 1997–2000. *Recreations:* cartooning, jogging, walking, golf, reading, Monty Python. *Address:* c/o Foreign and Commonwealth Office, King Charles Street, SW1A 2AH.

FALLA, Paul Stephen; *b* 25 Oct. 1913; *s* of Norris Stephen Falla and Audrey Frances Stock, Dunedin, New Zealand; *m* 1958, Elizabeth Shearer; one *d*. *Educ:* Wellington and Christ's Colls, NZ; Balliol Coll., Oxford (Scholar). Appointed to Foreign Office, 1936; served HM Embassies, Warsaw, 1938–39, Ankara, 1939–43, Tehran, 1943; Foreign Office, 1943–46; UK Delegation to UN, New York, 1946–49; Foreign Office, 1949–67 (Dep. Dir of Research, 1958–67). Member: Exec. Cttee, Translators' Assoc., Soc. of Authors, 1971–73 and 1984–86 (Vice-Chm., 1973); Council, Inst. Linguists, 1975–81 (FIL 1984); Cttee, Translators' Guild, 1975–81. Fellow, Inst. of Translation and Interpreting, 1989. Scott Moncrieff prize, 1972 and 1981; Schlegel-Tieck Prize, 1983. *Publications:* (ed) The Oxford English-Russian Dictionary, 1984; about 50 book translations from French, German, Dutch, Russian, Polish and other languages, 1967–. *Recreation:* reading (history, philosophy, poetry, language matters). *Address:* 63 Freelands Road, Bromley, Kent BR1 3HZ. *T:* (020) 8460 4995. *Club:* Travellers.

FALLAS, Diana Elizabeth Jane; *see* Burrell, D. E. J.

FALLE, Sir Sam, KCMG 1979 (CMG 1964); KCVO 1972; DSC 1945; HM Diplomatic Service, retired; *b* 19 Feb. 1919; *s* of Theodore and Hilda Falle; *m* 1945, Merete Rosen; one *s* three *d*. *Educ:* Victoria Coll., Jersey, CI. Served Royal Navy, 1937–48; joined Foreign (subseq. Diplomatic) Service, 1948; British Consulate, Shiraz, Iran, 1949–51; British Embassy, Tehran, 1952; British Embassy, Beirut, 1952–55; FO, 1955–57; British Embassy, Baghdad, 1957–61; Consul-Gen., Gothenburg, 1961–63; Head of UN Dept, FO, 1963–67; with Lord Shackleton's mission to Aden 1967; Deputy High Comr, Kuala Lumpur, 1967–69; Ambassador to Kuwait, 1969–70; High Comr, Singapore, 1970–74; Ambassador to Sweden, 1974–77; High Comr in Nigeria, 1977–78; Delegate, Commn of the European Communities, Algiers, 1979–82; carried out evaluation of EEC aid to Zambia, 1983–84, and Swedish aid to Swaziland, 1986. Hon. Fellow, Univ. of St Andrews, 1997. Kt Grand Cross, Order of Polar Star, Sweden, 1975. *Publication:* My Lucky Life (memoirs), 1996. *Recreations:* swimming, ski-ing. *Address:* Hornsved Slättna 3, 57033 Mariannelund, Sweden. *T:* (496) 50012.

FALLICK, Prof. Anthony Edward, PhD; FRSE; Professor of Isotope Geosciences, University of Glasgow, since 1996; Director, Scottish Universities Environmental Research Centre, since 1999; *b* 21 April 1950; *s* of Edward Henry Fallick and Helen Fallick (*née* Murray); partner, Dr Charlotte Bryant; one *d*. *Educ:* Univ. of Glasgow (BSc Hons Natural Philosophy 1971; PhD Nuclear Geochem. 1975). Research Fellow, McMaster Univ., 1975–78; Vis. Schol., Cambridge Univ., 1978–80; Res. Fellow, 1980–85, Lectr, 1985–90, Reader, 1990–96, Univ. of Glasgow. FRSE 1993; FRSA 1997; FMinSoc 1998 (Schlumberger Medal, 1998). *Publications:* contrib. numerous articles and papers to peer-reviewed jls and symposia vols. *Recreations:* wine, song. *Address:* SUERC, Scottish Enterprise Technology Park, E Kilbride, Glasgow G75 0QF. *T:* (01355) 223332. *Club:* Four Forty Five (Hamilton, Ont.).

FALLON, Her Honour Hazel Rosemary; a Circuit Judge, 1978–96; *b* 7 Jan. 1931; *d* of late Arthur Henry Counsell and Elsie Winifred Counsell; *m* 1980, Peter Fallon, *qv*. *Educ:* Clifton High Sch.; Switzerland; Univ. of Bristol (LLB). Called to the Bar, Gray's Inn, 1956; Western Circuit, 1956–96; a Recorder of the Crown Court, 1976–77. Legal Dept, Min. of Labour, 1959–62. Mem. of Council, Univ. of Bristol, 1992–97. Hon. LLD UWE, 1996. *Recreations:* reading, swimming, travel, gardening. *Address:* c/o The Law Courts, Small Street, Bristol BS1 1DA.

FALLON, Ivan Gregory; Chief Executive Officer, Independent News & Media of South Africa, since 1997; Chairman, iTouch plc, since 2000; *b* 26 June 1944; *s* of Padraic and Dorothea Fallon; *m* 1st, 1967, Susan Mary Lurring (marr. diss. 1997); one *s* two *d*; 2nd, 1997, Elizabeth Rees-Jones. *Educ:* St Peter's Coll., Wexford; Trinity Coll., Dublin (BBS). Irish Times, 1964–66; Thomson Provincial Newspapers, 1966–67; Daily Mirror, 1967–68; Sunday Telegraph, 1968–70; Deputy City Editor, Sunday Express, 1970–71; Sunday Telegraph, 1971–84: City Editor, 1979–84; Dep. Editor, Sunday Times, 1984–94; Editl Dir, Argus Gp, 1994–97; Dep. Chief Exec. and Editl Dir, Independent Newspapers Holdings Ltd, 1995–97. Director: N. Brown Group plc, 1994–; Independent Newspapers plc, Ireland, 1995–. Member: Council, Univ. of Buckingham, 1982–94; Council of Governors, United Med. and Dental Schs of Guy's and St Thomas's Hosps, 1985–94; Trustee: Project Trust, 1984–94; Generation Trust, Guy's Hosp., 1985–94. FRSA 1989. *Publications:* (with James L. Srodes) DeLorean: the rise and fall of a dream-maker, 1983; (with James L. Srodes) Takeovers, 1987; The Brothers: the rise of Saatchi and Saatchi, 1988; Billionaire: the life and times of Sir James Goldsmith, 1991; Paper Chase, 1993; The Player: the life of Tony O'Reilly, 1994. *Recreations:* walking, tennis. *Address:* Prospect House, Klein Constantia Road, Constantia, Cape Town, South Africa. *T:* (21) 4884015, (11) 6332115. *Clubs:* Beefsteak, Political Economy; Rand (Johannesburg).

See also P. M. Fallon.

FALLON, Kieren; flat race jockey; *b* Crusheen, Co. Clare, 22 Feb. 1965; *s* of Frank and Maureen Fallon; *m* 1993, Julie Bowker; one *s* two *d*. Winner: Lincoln Handicap, on High Premium, 1993; 1,000 Guineas, on Sleepytime, 1997, on Wince, 1999; Oaks, on Reams of Verse, 1997, on Ramruna, 1999; Grosser Preis von Baden, Germany, on Borgia, 1997; Prix de la Forêt, France, on Tomba, 1998; Derby, on Oath, 1999; Kildangan Stud Irish Oaks, on Ramruna, 1999; Tattersalls Gold Cup, Ireland, on Shiva, 1999; 2,000 Guineas, on King's Best, 2000, on Golan, 2001. Champion Jockey, 1997, 1998, 1999. *Address:* c/o Jockey Club, 42 Portman Square, W1H 0EM.

FALLON, Martin; *see* Patterson, Harry.

FALLON, Michael; MP (C) Sevenoaks, since 1997; *b* 14 May 1952; *s* of late Martin Fallon, OBE, FRCSI and of Hazel Fallon; *m* 1986, Wendy Elisabeth, *e d* of Peter Payne, Holme-on-Spalding Moor, Yorks; two *s*. *Educ:* St Andrews Univ. (MA Hons 1974). European Educnl Res. Trust, 1974–75; Opposition Whips Office, House of Lords, 1975–77; EEC Officer, Cons. Res. Dept, 1977–79; Jt Man. Dir, European Consultants Ltd, 1979–81; Dir, Quality Care Homes plc, 1992–97; Chief Exec., Quality Care Develts Ltd, 1996–97; Director: Just Learning Ltd, 1996–; Bannatyne Fitness Ltd, 1999–2000. Sec., Lord Home's Cttee on future of House of Lords, 1977–78; Assistant to Baroness

Elles, 1979–83. MP (C) Darlington, 1983–92; contested (C) Darlington, 1992. PPS to Sec. of State for Energy, 1987–88; an Asst Govt Whip, 1988–90; a Lord Comr of HM Treasury, 1990; Parly Under-Sec. of State, DES, 1990–92; Opposition spokesman on trade and industry, 1997, on Treasury matters, 1997–98. Mem., Treasury Select Cttee, 1999–. Member: HEFCE, 1993–97; Adv. Council, Social Market Foundn, 1994–; Govt's Deregulation Task Force, 1994–97. Dir, Internat. Care and Relief, 1997–. Gov., Whitefield Schs, 1994–99. *Publications:* The Quango Explosion (jtly), 1978; Sovereign Members?, 1982; The Rise of the Euroquango, 1982; Brighter Schools, 1993; contribs to journals. *Recreation:* ski-ing. *Address:* House of Commons, SW1A 0AA. *Club:* Academy.

FALLON, Padraic Matthew; Chairman, Euromoney Institutional Investor (formerly Euromoney Publications) PLC, since 1992; *b* 21 Sept. 1946; *s* of Padraic Fallon, poet and Dorothea (Don) (*née* Maher); *m* 1972, Gillian Elizabeth Hellyer; one *s* three *d*. *Educ:* St Peter's Coll., Wexford; Blackrock Coll., Co. Dublin; Trinity Coll., Dublin (BBS, MA). Reporter: Thomson Newspapers City office, 1969–70; Daily Mirror, 1970–72; Daily Mail City pages, 1972–74; Managing Editor, Middle East Money, Beirut, 1974; Editor, Euromoney, 1974–85; Euromoney Publications, subseq. Euromoney Instit Investor, PLC: Dir, 1975–; Man. Dir, 1985–89; Chief Exec., 1989–92. Non-exec. Dir, Allied Irish Banks plc, 1988–; Dir, Daily Mail & General Trust plc, 1999–. Dir, TCD, Foundn, 2000–. FRSA. *Recreation:* country sports. *Address:* Euromoney Institutional Investor PLC, Nestor House, Playhouse Yard, EC4V 5EX. *T:* (020) 7779 8888; 20 Lower Addison Gardens, W14 8BQ. *T:* (020) 7602 1253. *Clubs:* Garrick, Flyfishers; Kildare Street and University (Overseas Member) (Dublin).

See also I. G. Fallon.

FALLON, His Honour Peter; QC 1971; a Circuit Judge, 1979–96; a Senior Circuit Judge, 1980–96; *b* 1 March 1931; *s* of Frederick and Mary Fallon; *m* 1st, 1955, Zina Mary (*née* Judd); one *s* two *d*; 2nd, 1980, Hazel Rosemary Counsell (*see* Her Honour H. R. Fallon). *Educ:* Leigh Grammar Sch.; St Joseph's Coll., Blackpool; Bristol Univ. (LLB Hons). Called to Bar, Gray's Inn, 1953. Commissioned in RAF for three years. A Recorder of the Crown Court, 1972–79; Hon. Recorder of Bristol, 1995–96. Chm., Cttee of Inquiry into the Personality Disorder Unit, Ashworth Special Hosp., 1997–99. *Publications:* Crown Court Practice: Sentencing, 1974; Crown Court Practice: Trial, 1978; contrib. Proc. RSM. *Recreations:* golf, fishing, painting. *Address:* c/o The Law Courts, Small Street, Bristol BS1 1DA.

FALLOWS, Albert Bennett, CB 1987; FRICS; Hon. FSVA; Chief Valuer, Inland Revenue Valuation Office and Commissioner of Inland Revenue, 1984–88; *b* 7 Dec. 1928; *s* of Bennett and May Fallows; *m* 1955, Maureen James; two *d*. *Educ:* Leek High School. Private practice, surveying, 1945–56; local govt service, Staffs and Hants, 1956–75; joined CS, 1975; Board of Inland Revenue: Superintending Valuer, North West, Preston, 1977–80; Asst Chief Valuer, 1980–83; Dep. Chief Valuer, 1983. Hon. FSVA 1987. *Address:* 110 Whitedown Lane, Alton, Hants GU34 1QR. *T:* (01420) 82818.

FALLOWS, Prof. David Nicholas, PhD; FBA 1997; Professor of Music, University of Manchester, since 1997; *b* 20 Dec. 1945; *yr s* of late William John Fallows and of Winifred Joan Fallows (*née* Sanderson); *m* 1976, Paulène Oliver (separated 1996); one *s* one *d*. *Educ:* Shrewsbury Sch.; Jesus Coll., Cambridge (BA 1967); King's Coll., London (MMus 1968); Univ. of Calif at Berkeley (PhD 1978). Assistant, Studio der Frühen Musik, Munich, 1968–70; Lectr, Univ. of Wisconsin-Madison, 1973–74; Lectr, 1976–82, Sen. Lectr, 1982–92, Reader in Music, 1992–97, Univ. of Manchester. Vis. Associate Prof., Univ. of N Carolina, Chapel Hill, 1982–83; Prof. invité de musicologie, Ecole Normale Supérieure, Paris, 1993. Vice-President: Internat. Musicological Soc., 1997–Aug. 2002; Royal Musical Assoc., 2000–. Corresp. Mem., Amer. Musicol Soc., 1999. Reviews Editor, Early Music, 1976–95, 1999–2000; Gen. Editor and Founder, Royal Musical Assoc. Monographs, 1982–98; Member, Editorial Board: Musica Britannica, 1985–; Jl of Royal Musical Assoc., 1986–88; Basler Jahrbuch für historische Musikpraxis, 1988–; Early Music History, 1991–; Muziek en Wetenschap, 1992–; Early English Church Music, 1994–. Chevalier, Ordre des Arts et des Lettres (France), 1994. *Publications:* Dufay, 1982, 2nd edn 1987; (jtly) Chansonnier de Jean de Montchenu, 1991; (ed jtly) Companion to Medieval and Renaissance Music, 1992, 2nd edn 1997; The Songs of Guillaume Dufay, 1995; (ed and introd) Oxford Bodleian Library MS Canon Misc. 213 (Late Medieval and Early Renaissance music in facsimile, vol. 1), 1995; Songs and Musicians in the Fifteenth Century, 1996; The Songbook of Fridolin Sicher, 1996; A Catalogue of Polyphonic Songs 1415–1480, 1999. *Address:* 10 Chatham Road, Manchester M16 0DR. *T:* (0161) 881 1188; *e-mail:* david.fallows@man.ac.uk.

FALLOWS, Geoffrey Michael; Headteacher, Camden School for Girls, 1989–2000; *b* 28 Sept. 1941; *er s* of Rt Rev. William Gordon Fallows and Edna (*née* Blakeman); *m* 1968, Carolyn (*d* 2000), *d* of Dr William Brian Littler, CB and Pearl Littler (*d* 2000); two *d*. *Educ:* Shrewsbury Sch.; Wadham Coll., Oxford (MA); London Univ. Inst. of Education (PGCE). Vis. Classics Fellow, Marlboro Coll., Vermont, 1964–65; Asst Master, Latymer Upper Sch., 1966–69; Head of Classics, Crown Woods Sch., 1969–75; Dep. Head, Camden Sch. for Girls, 1975–89. Dir, Huron Univ., USA, in London, 1998–. Exec. Sec., Jt Assoc. of Classical Teachers, 1978–81. Co-founder, Omnibus magazine, 1981. FRSA 1994. *Recreations:* theatre, gardening, Lake District. *Address:* 53 Byng Road, Barnet, Herts EN5 4NW. *T:* (020) 8449 2980, *Fax:* (020) 8440 7629; *e-mail:* geoffreyfallows@compuserve.com.

FALMOUTH, 9th Viscount, *cr* 1720; **George Hugh Boscawen;** 26th Baron Le Despencer, 1264; Baron Boscawen-Rose, 1720; Lord-Lieutenant of Cornwall, 1977–94; *b* 31 Oct. 1919; 2nd but *e* surv. *s* of 8th Viscount Falmouth; *S* father, 1962; *m* 1953, Elizabeth Price Browne, DL; four *s*. *Educ:* Eton Coll.; Trinity Coll., Cambridge. Served War, 1939–46, Italy. Capt., Coldstream Guards. DL Cornwall, 1968. *Heir:* s Hon. Evelyn Arthur Hugh Boscawen [*b* 13 May 1955; *m* 1st, 1977, Lucia Vivian-Neal (marr. diss. 1995), *e d* of R. W. Vivian-Neal; one *s* one *d*; 2nd, 1995, Katharine Maley; two *s* one *d*].

See also Rt Hon. R. T. Boscawen.

FALVEY, Dr David Alan, FGS; Executive Director, British Geological Survey, NERC, since 1998; *b* Sydney, 19 Dec. 1945; *s* of late Keith Falvey and Ella Falvey (*née* Hendley); *m* 1969, Margaret Kaye (*d* 1984); one *s* one *d*; *m* 1986, Gillian Tidey. *Educ:* Univ. of Sydney (BSc Hons 1967); Univ. of New South Wales (PhD 1972). FGS 1998. Explorationist, Shell Develt, Australia, 1972–74; Lectr, then Sen. Lectr, Univ. of Sydney, 1974–82; Chief, Marine Div., Bureau of Mineral Resources, 1982–89; Associate Dir, Petroleum and Marine Geoscis, Australian Geol Survey Orgn, 1989–94; Dir, Ocean Drilling Program, Jt Oceanographic Instns, Washington, 1994–98. *Publications:* numerous scientific contribs to learned jls. *Recreation:* golf. *Address:* British Geological Survey, Keyworth, Nottingham NG12 5GG. *T:* (0115) 936 3226. *Clubs:* Royal Canberra Golf; Cotgrave Place Golf (Notts).

FANE, family name of **Earl of Westmorland**.

FANE, Andrew William Mildmay, FCA; Deputy Chairman, Historic Buildings and Monuments Commission (English Heritage), since 2001; *b* 9 Aug. 1949; *s* of late Robert William Augustus Fane and of Elinor Valerie Fane (*née* Borthwick); *m* 1989, Clare Lucy Marx, FRCS. *Educ:* Radley Coll.; Emmanuel Coll., Cambridge (MA Law). FCA 1974. Chief Exec., Whitburgh Investments Ltd, 1982–92; Dir and Dep. Chm., Borthwicks plc, 1988–92. Non-exec. Dir, E Suffolk Local Health Services NHS Trust, 1994–99 (Vice Chm., 1997–99). Councillor, RBK&C, 1987–94 (Chm., Planning Cttee). Member: E Anglia Regl Cttee, NT, 1994–; Royal Commn on Histl Monuments of England, 1999–; English Heritage: Mem., 1995–2001; Chairman: Historic Bldgs and Areas Adv. Cttee, 1995–2001; London Adv. Cttee, 1999– (Mem., 1994–); Historic Built Envmt Adv. Cttee, 2001–. Chm., Special Trustees, Gt Ormond St Hosp., 1999– (Special Trustee, 1994–). Chm., Bd of Govs, Framlingham Coll., Suffolk, 2001– (Gov., 1995–). Mem., Develt Cttee, Emmanuel Coll., Cambridge, 1994–. *Recreation:* conservation. *Address:* Hoo House, Woodbridge, Suffolk; 64 Ladbroke Road, W11 3NR. *T:* (020) 7221 2748.

FANE TREFUSIS, family name of **Baron Clinton**.

FANNER, His Honour Peter Duncan; a Circuit Judge, 1986–95; *b* 27 May 1926; *s* of late Robert William Hodges Fanner, solicitor, and Doris Kitty Fanner; *m* 1949, Sheila Eveline England; one *s* one *d*. *Educ:* Pangbourne Coll. Admitted Solicitor of the Supreme Court, 1951 (holder Justices' Clerks' Society's prize). Served War of 1939–45, Pilot in Fleet Air Arm, Lieut (A) RNVR, 1944–47. Asst Clerk to Bromley Justices, 1947–51; Dep. Clerk to Gore Justices, 1951–56; Clerk to Bath Justices, 1956–72; Metropolitan Stipendiary Magistrate, 1972–86; a Dep. Circuit Judge, 1974–80; a Recorder, 1980–86. Mem. Council of Justices' Clerks' Society, 1966–72; Assessor Mem. of Departmental Cttee on Liquor Licensing, 1971–72. Chm., Bath Round Table, 1963–64. *Publications:* Stone's Justices' Manual; contrib. to Justice of the Peace, The Magisterial Officer, The Lawyer's Remembrancer. *Recreations:* travel, railways. *Address:* c/o The Law Courts, Small Street, Bristol BS1 1DA. *T:* (0117) 976 3030.

FANSHAWE OF RICHMOND, Baron *cr* 1983 (Life Peer), of South Cerney in the County of Gloucestershire; **Anthony Henry Fanshawe Royle,** KCMG 1974; *b* 27 March 1927; *s* of Sir Lancelot Royle, KBE; *m* 1957, Shirley Worthington; two *d*. *Educ:* Harrow; Sandhurst. Captain, The Life Guards (Germany, Egypt, Palestine and Transjordan), 1945–48; 21st SAS Regt (TA), 1948–51, M Sqn, 1950–51. Joined Sedgwick Collins, 1948; Dir, 1984–99, Chm., 1993–97, Sedgwick Gp. MP (C) Richmond, 1959–83; Parliamentary Private Secretary: to Under-Sec. of State for the Colonies, 1960; to Sec. of State for Air, 1960–62; to Minister of Aviation, 1962–64; Vice-Chm., Cons. Parly Foreign Affairs Cttee, 1965–67; Tory Whip, 1967–70; Parly Under-Sec. of State for Foreign and Commonwealth Affairs, 1970–74. Vice-Chm., Cons. Party Orgn, 1979–84 (Chm., Internat. Office, 1979–84). Mem., Assembly of Council of Europe and WEU, 1965. Chm., Wilkinson Sword Gp, 1980–83; Director: Westland Gp, 1985–94; Xerox UK (formerly Rank Xerox UK), 1988–2001; TI Group, 1990–99. Vice Pres., Franco-British Council, 1975–99. Develt Trustee, Nat. Army Mus., 1981–. Esteemed Family Order (1st cl.), Brunei, 1975. *Address:* House of Lords, SW1A 0PW. *Clubs:* Pratt's, White's, Brooks's.

See also T. L. F. Royle.

FANSHAWE, Col David, OBE 1977; Lieutenant, HM Body Guard of the Honourable Corps of Gentlemen-at-Arms, since 2000; *b* 1 Nov. 1933; *s* of late Major Richard Gennys Fanshawe and of Ruth Violet Mary, now Ruth, Baroness Dulverton, *o d* of Sir Walter Farquhar, 5th Bt; *m* 1963, Sheila McNeill; three *s*. *Educ:* Stowe; RMA Sandhurst. Commnd Grenadier Guards, 1954: served Europe, USA, Africa, Far East, and Middle East; Comdr, Guards Independent Parachute Co., 1967–70; Adjutant, RMA Sandhurst, 1970–73; CO 2nd Bn Grenadier Guards, 1974–76; Regtl Comdr, Grenadier Guards, 1978–80; Defence Attaché, Sudan and Somalia, 1981–83. Mem., HM Body Guard of Hon. Corps of Gentlemen-at-Arms, 1986– (Clerk of Cheque and Adjt, 1998–2000). Dir, Hedley Foundn, 1983–98. *Recreations:* sailing, ornithology, alpine dendrology. *Address:* Upper Mill, Sydling St Nicholas, Dorchester, Dorset DT2 9PD. *T:* (01300) 341230. *Club:* Cavalry and Guards.

FANTONI, Prof. Barry Ernest; novelist, broadcaster, cartoonist, jazz musician; Member of editorial staff of Private Eye, since 1963; Professor of Communications and Media Studies, University of Salerno, since 1997; Director, All This Time Theatre Co., since 1998; *b* 28 Feb. 1940; *s* of late Peter Nello Secondo Fantoni and of Sarah Catherine Fantoni; became Italian citizen, 1997; *m* 1972, Teresa Frances, (Tessa), Reidy. *Educ:* Archbishop Temple Sch.; Camberwell Sch. of Arts and Crafts (Wedgwood Scholar). Cartoonist of The Listener, 1968–88; contrib. art criticism to The Times, 1973–77; record reviewer, Punch, 1976–77; Diary cartoonist, The Times, 1983–90; Dir, Barry Fantoni Merchandising Co., 1985–93; designer of film and theatre posters and illustrator of book jackets; mural for Queen Elizabeth II Conf. Centre, London, 1985; film and television actor; An Evening with Barry Fantoni (one-man show for stage), 1991–; plays: Jeanne, performed Battersea Arts Centre, 1997; Modigliani, My Love, Paris, 1999; presenter and writer, Barry Fantoni's Chinese Horoscopes, BBC Radio 4 series, 1986. One-man shows: Woodstock Gall., London, 1963; Comara Gall., LA, 1964; Brunel Univ., 1974; Times cartoon exhibition, Charlotte Lampard Gall., 1990; retrospective: Cadogan Contemporary Gall., 1991; two-man shows (with Peter Fantoni): Langton Gall., London, 1977; Annexe Gall., London, 1978; Katherine House Gall., 1983; Fulford Cartoon Gall., 1983; New Grafton Gall., 1985; Green & Stone, Cirencester, 1986; work exhibited: AIA Gall., London, 1958, 1961 and 1964; D and AD Annual Exhibn, London, 1964; Royal Acad. Summer Exhibn, 1963 (as Stuart Harris, with William Rushton), 1964, 1975 and 1978 (with Richard Napper); Tate Gall., 1973; Bradford Print Biennale, 1974; National Theatre, 1977; Browse and Darby, 1977; Gillian Jason Gall., 1983; Three Decades of Art Schools, RA, 1983. Musical compositions include: popular songs (also popular songs with Marianne Faithfull and with Stanley Myers); The Cantors Crucifixion (musical improvisation for 13 instruments), 1977; (with John Wells) Lionel (musical), 1977; (with Barry Booth) We Are Your Future (official Unicef anthem), 1996; Mass of the Holy Spirit, 1999; Rooms of the House, 2001. Created Barry Fantoni's Jazz Circus, 1992 (a performance jazz trio). Male TV Personality of the Year, 1966. Editor, St Martin's Review, 1969–74; weekly columnist on Chinese Horoscopes: Today, 1986–87; Woman, 1987–88; Plus magazine, 1989; The Guardian, 1990. *Publications:* (with Richard Ingrams) Private Pop Eye, 1968; (as Old Jowett, with Richard Ingrams) The Bible for Motorists, 1970; Tomorrow's Nicodemus, 1974; (as Sylvie Krin, with Richard Ingrams) Love in the Saddle, 1974; Private Eye Cartoon Library 5, 1975; (as E. J. Thribb, with Richard Ingrams) So Farewell Then…and Other Poems, 1978; Mike Dime, 1980; (as Sylvie Krin, with Richard Ingrams) Born to be Queen, 1981; Stickman, 1982; (ed) Colemanballs, 1982; (ed) Colemanballs 2, 1984; The Times Diary Cartoons, 1984; Barry Fantoni's Chinese Horoscope, annually 1985–, retitled Barry Fantoni's Complete Chinese Horoscope, 1991; (ed) Colemanballs 3, 1986; Barry Fantoni Cartoons: a personal selection from The Times and The Listener, 1987; The Royal Family's Chinese Horoscopes, 1988; (ed) Colemanballs 4, 1988; Chinese Horoscope Guide to Love, Marriage and Friendship, 1989; (ed) Colemanballs 5, 1990; (ed) Colemanballs 6, 1992; (ed) Colemanballs 7, 1994;

(ed) A Hundred Years of Neasden Football Club, 1995; (ed) Colemanballs 8, 1996; (ed) Colemanballs 9, 1998; Colemanballs 10, 2000; *illustrations for:* How To Be a Jewish Mother, 1966; The BP Festivals and Events in Britain, 1966; (with George Melly) The Media Mob, 1980; The Best of Barry Fantoni Cartoons, 1990. *Recreations:* road running, animal welfare. *Address:* c/o The Marsh Agency, 11–12 Dover Street, W1X 3PD. *T:* (020) 7399 2800, *Fax:* (020) 7399 2801. *Club:* Chelsea Arts (Chm., 1978–80).

FARAGE, Nigel Paul; Member (UK Ind) South East Region, England, European Parliament, since 1999; *b* 3 April 1964; *s* of Guy Farage and Barbara Stevens; *m* 1st, 1988 (marr. diss. 1997); two *s*; 2nd, 1999, Kirsten Mehr; one *d*. *Educ:* Dulwich Coll. Commodity Broker: Drexel Burnham Lambert, 1982–86; Credit Lyonnais Rouse Ltd, 1986–93; Refco Overseas Ltd, 1994–. UK Independence Party: Founder Mem., 1993; Chm., 1998–2000; Spokesman, 2000–. Contested (UK Ind): Eastleigh, June 1994; Salisbury, 1997; Itchen, Test & Avon, EP elecns, 1994. *Recreations:* military history 1914–18, sea angling, proper English pubs. *Address:* 1 Darwin Villas, Single Street, Berrys Green, Westerham, Kent TN16 3AA. *T:* (home) (01959) 570034; (office) (020) 7702 4419. *Club:* East India.

FARHI, Nicole, (Lady Hare); fashion designer; Founder, 1983 and Designer, Nicole Farhi Co.; *b* 25 July 1946; *d* of Ephraim Farhi and Marcelle (*née* Babani); one *d* by Stephen Marks; *m* 1992, Sir David Hare, *qv*. *Educ:* Lycée Calmette, Nice; Cours Berçot Art Sch., Paris. First designed for Pierre d'Albi, 1968; founded French Connection with Stephen Marks, 1973; launched Nicole Farhi For Men, 1989; opened Nicole's Restaurant, 1994. Best Contemporary Designer, British Fashion Awards, 1995, 1996 and 1997. *Recreation:* sculpture. *Address:* 16 Foubert's Place, W1V 1HH. *T:* (020) 7287 8787.

FARINGDON, 3rd Baron *cr* 1916; **Charles Michael Henderson;** Bt 1902; Partner, Cazenove & Co., 1968–96; Chairman, Witan Investment Trust (formerly Witan Investment Company) plc, since 1980; a Lord in Waiting to the Queen, since 1998; *b* 3 July 1937; *s* of Hon. Michael Thomas Henderson (*d* 1953) (2nd *s* of Col Hon. Harold Greenwood Henderson, CVO, and *g s* of 1st Baron) and Oonagh Evelyn Henderson, *er d* of late Lt-Col Harold Ernest Brassey; *S* uncle, 1977; *m* 1959, Sarah Caroline, *d* of late J. M. E. Askew, CBE; three *s* one *d*. *Educ:* Eton College; Trinity College, Cambridge (BA). Treasurer, Nat. Art Collections Fund, 1984–91; Chm., RCHME, 1994–99; Comr, English Heritage, 1998–2001. Chm. Bd of Governors, Royal Marsden Hosp., 1980–85; Mem. Bd of Management, 1980–2000, Fellow, 2000, Inst. of Cancer Res. *Heir: s* Hon. James Harold Henderson [*b* 14 July 1961; *m* 1986, Lucinda, *y d* of late Desmond Hanson, Knipton, Lincs; two *s* one *d*]. *Address:* Buscot Park, Faringdon, Oxon SN7 8BU.

FARISH, Hon. William Stamps, III; Ambassador of the United States of America to the Court of St James's, since 2001; *b* Houston, Tex, 1938; *m* Sarah Sharp; one *s* three *d*. *Educ:* Univ. of Virginia. Formerly: Stockbroker, Underwood, Neuhaus & Co., Houston; Pres., Navarro Exploration Co.; Founding Director: Eurus Inc., NY; Capital Nat. Bank, Houston; Pres., W. S. Farish & Co., Houston. Owner, Lane's End Farm, Versailles, Ky, 1980–; formerly Chairman: Churchill Downs Inc., Ky; Exec. Cttee, Breeders Cup Ltd; Vice-Chm., US Jockey Club; Dir, Thoroughbred Breeders and Owners Assoc. *Address:* Embassy of the United States of America, 24 Grosvenor Square, W1A 1AE.

FARLEY, Prof. Francis James Macdonald, FRS 1972; Professor Emeritus, Royal Military College of Science (Dean, 1967–82); *b* 13 Oct. 1920; *er s* of late Brig. Edward Lionel Farley, CBE, MC; *m* 1945, Josephine Maisie Hayden; three *s* one *d*; *m* 1977, Margaret Ann Pearce. *Educ:* Clifton Coll.; Clare Coll., Cambridge. MA 1945; PhD 1950; ScD Cantab 1967; FInstP. Air Defence Research and Development Establishment, 1941–45 (first 3cm ground radar, Doppler radar); Chalk River Laboratories, 1945–46; Research Student, Cavendish Lab., Cambridge, 1946–49; Auckland Univ. Coll., NZ, 1950–57; attached AERE, 1955; CERN, Geneva, 1957–67 (muon g-2 experiment). Vis. Lectr, Univ. of Bristol, 1965–66; Vis. Scientist, CERN, 1967– (muon storage ring, tests of relativity); Vis. Sen. Res. Physicist, Yale Univ., 1984–92; Visiting Professor: Swiss Inst. of Nuclear Research, 1976–77; Reading, 1982–86; Consultant, Centre Antoine Lacassagne, Nice, 1986–92. Rep. NZ at UN Conf. on Atomic Energy for Peaceful Purposes, 1955. Governor: Clifton Coll., to 1994; Welbeck Coll., 1970–82; Member Court: Univ. of Bath, 1974–82; Cranfield Inst. of Technology, 1989–93. Hon. Mem., Instn of Royal Engineers. Hon. Fellow, TCD, 1986. Hughes Medal, Royal Soc., 1980. *Publications:* Elements of Pulse Circuits, 1955; Progress in Nuclear Techniques and Instrumentation, Vol. I, 1966, Vol. II, 1967, Vol. III, 1968; scientific papers on nuclear physics, electronics, high energy particle physics, wave energy. *Recreations:* gliding (FAI gold and diamond), ski-ing. *Address:* Le Masage, chemin de Saint Pierre, 06620 Le Bar sur Loup, France. *T:* 493424512, *Fax:* 493429407; *e-mail:* farley@bnl.gov.

FARLEY, Henry Edward, (Rob); Group Deputy Chief Executive, Royal Bank of Scotland Group, 1986–90; Director, Nationwide Building Society, 1990–97; *b* 28 Sept. 1930; *s* of late William and Frances Elizabeth Farley; *m* 1955, Audrey Joyce Shelvey; one *s* one *d*. *Educ:* Harrow County Sch. for Boys. FCIB (FIB 1966). Entered National Bank, 1947; Head of UK Banking, 1978, Dir, 1981, Williams & Glyn's Bank; Chairman: Williams & Glyn's Bank (IOM) Ltd, 1973–76; Joint Credit Card Co. Ltd, 1982–84; Royal Bank of Scotland Gp Insce, 1988–90; Mem. Bd, Mastercard International Inc., 1982–84; Director: Royal Bank of Scotland Group plc, 1985–90; Royal Bank of Scotland, 1985–90 (Man. Dir, 1985–86); Charterhouse Japhet, 1985–86; Charterhouse Development, 1985–86; Charterhouse plc, 1986–90; Chm., Royscot Finance Gp, 1987–90; Dep. Chm., Supervisory Bd of CC Bank, Germany, 1989–90. Director: EFT-POS (UK) Ltd, 1986–88; A. T. Mays Gp, 1987–90; (Alternate) Citizens Financial Gp (USA), 1989–90; John Maunders Gp, 1989–; Banque Rivaud, Paris, 1990–97; High Table Ltd, 1991–95; Davenham Gp, 1992–97. Mem. Develt Bd, Special Olympics, 1997–. Member: Council, Inst. of Bankers, 1985–90; APACS Council, 1983–90; Exec. Cttee, British Bankers Assoc., 1983–90. Gov., 1990–, and Vice-Chm. Council, 1994–2000, UMIST; Dir, UMIST Foundn, 1999–; Mem. Bd, Manchester Federal Sch. of Business and Management, 1994–99. FRSA 1995. Liveryman, Marketors' Co., 1987– (Dir, Marketors' Hall Ltd, 1992–95). *Publications:* The Clearing Banks and Housing Finance, 1983; Competition and Deregulation: branch networks, 1984; The Role of Branches in a Changing Environment, 1985; Deregulation and the Clearing Banks, 1986. *Recreations:* all forms of rough sport, travel, modern literature. *Address:* 13 Montagu Square, W1H 1RB. *Clubs:* Bankers', MCC; Racquets; Pickwick Bicycle; St James (Manchester).

FARLEY, Prof. Martyn Graham, CEng, FRAeS, FIMechE, FIEE; engineering and management consultant, 1976–95; Emeritus Professor, Royal Military College of Science, Shrivenham and Cranfield Institute of Technology, since 1986; *b* 27 Oct. 1924; *s* of Herbert Booth Farley and Hilda Gertrude (*née* Hendey); *m* 1948, Freda Laugharne; two *s* one *d*. *Educ:* Merchant Venturers Tech. Coll., Bristol; Bristol Aeroplane Co. Tech. Coll. CEng, FRAeS 1968; FIMechE 1969; FIEE (FIProdE 1975); FIIM 1988; CIMgt (CBIM 1980). Engine Div., Bristol Aeroplane Co.: Design Apprentice, 1939–45; Engine Design, 1945–46; Develt Engr, 1946–51; Bristol Aero Engines Ltd: Sen. Designer, Gas Turbine Office, 1951–55; Asst Chief Develt Engr, 1955–59; Bristol Siddeley Engines: Asst Chief Mech. Engr, 1959–62; Chief Develt Engr, Small Engines Div., 1962–65, Chief Engr, 1965–67; Small Engines Div., Rolls-Royce: Chief Engr, 1967–68; Gen. Works Manager, 1968–72; Manufg and Prodn Dir, 1972–74; HQ Exec. to Vice-Chm. of Rolls-Royce (1971) Ltd, 1974–75; Prof. and Head of Dept of Management Sciences, RMCS, 1975–84; Vice-Chm., Sch. of Management and Maths, RMCS Faculty of Cranfield Inst. of Technology, 1984–86. Dir, World Tech Ventures, 1984–86; Chairman: RECSAM Components Ltd, 1986–89; Harwell Computer Power Ltd, 1991–93. Vis. Res. Prof., Luton Univ., 1992–98. Royal Aeronautical Society: Mem. Council, 1972–92; Vice Pres., 1980–83; Pres., 1983–84; Dir, Aeronautical Trusts, 1975–88; Hon. Treasurer, 1984–88. Vice Pres., Instn of Indust. Engrs, 1981–92; Pres., IProdE, 1984–85 (Mem. Council, 1973–; Chm. Council, 1978–80; Vice-Pres., 1982–83); Chm., British Management Data Foundn Ltd, 1978–92; Founder Chm., Alliance of Manufg and Management Orgns, 1981; Member: EEF Manufg Trng Cttee, 1975–91; Guggenheim Medal Bd of Award, 1983; Adv. Council, RN Engrg Coll., Manadon, 1988–95; Court, Brunel Univ., 1977–80, Loughborough Univ., 1977–83, Cranfield Inst. of Technol., 1977–, Bath Univ., 1983–, Luton Univ., 1995–98. External Examiner: RAF Cranwell, RNEC and RMCS, 1979–; RNEC and Plymouth Univ., 1988–95. Mem., Sen. Awards Cttee, 1979–99, Fellows Cttee, 1992–, and Hon. Mem. Council, 1985–99, City and Guilds of London Inst.; Hon. CGIA 1981 (Pres., CGIA Assoc., 1984–98, Hon. Life Pres., 1998); Hon. FCGI 1990; Designer and Project Co-ordinator, EITB Manufg Fellowships, 1977–91. Hon. FIIPE 1979; Hon. Member: Amer. Inst. of Indust. Managers, 1979; Australian Inst. of Indust. Engrs, 1981; Amer. Soc. of Manufg Engrs, 1985 (elected Charter Fellow, 1986). Freeman, City of London, 1981; Mem., Co. of Coachmakers and Coach Harness Makers. Hon. DSc RNEC and Plymouth Univ., 1994. Internat. Archimedes Award, Amer. Soc. of Prof. Engrs, 1979; First Shuttle Contributions Medal, 1981; Educn Gold Medal Award, ASME, 1983; Amer. Instn Advanced Engr Medal, 1984; NASA/Rocketdyne Tech. Award, 1984; Internat. Engr of Year Award, LA Council of Engrs and Scientists, 1984; California State Engrg Commendation, 1985; NASA Contribs Award, 1985; W. B. Johnson Award, ASME, 1988. *Publications:* articles and technical pubns; procs of conferences. *Address:* Willow End, Vicarage Lane, Shrivenham, Swindon, Wilts SN6 8DT. *T:* (01793) 782319. *Clubs:* Athenæum, Advanced Class; Shrivenham (Shrivenham); Ariel Rowing (Bristol).

FARLEY, Mary-Rose Christine, (Mrs R. D. Farley); *see* Bateman, M.-R. C.

FARLEY, Rob; *see* Farley, H. E.

FARMBROUGH, Rt Rev. David John; Bishop Suffragan of Bedford, 1981–93; Hon. Assistant Bishop, diocese of St Albans, since 1994; *b* 4 May 1929; 2nd *s* of late Charles Septimus and late Ida Mabel Farmbrough; *m* 1955, Angela Priscilla Hill, DL; one *s* three *d*. *Educ:* Bedford Sch.; Lincoln Coll., Oxford (BA 1951, MA 1953); Westcott House, Cambridge, 1951–53. Deacon, 1953, priest, 1954; Curate of Bishop's Hatfield, 1953–57; Priest-in-charge, St John's, Hatfield, 1957–63; Vicar of Bishop's Stortford, 1963–74; Rural Dean of Bishop's Stortford, 1973–74; Archdeacon of St Albans, 1974–81. Mem., Gen. Synod, 1972–81; Chm., and Treas., Clergy Orphan Corp., 1995–97. Chm. Govs, St Margaret's Sch., Bushey, 1999–2001. *Publications:* In Wonder, Love and Praise, 1966; Belonging, Believing, Doing, 1971. *Recreation:* gardening. *Address:* St Michael Mead, 110 Village Road, Bromham, Beds MK43 8HU. *T:* (01234) 825042.

FARMER, Bruce; *see* Farmer, E. B.

FARMER, Dr (Edwin) Bruce, CBE 1997; FREng; FIM; Chairman: The Morgan Crucible Co. plc, since 1998; Scottish & Southern Energy plc, since 2000 (Deputy Chairman, 1999–2000); *b* 18 Sept. 1936; *s* of Edwin Bruce Farmer and Doris Farmer; *m* 1962, Beryl Ann Griffiths; one *s* one *d*. *Educ:* King Edward's, Birmingham; Univ. of Birmingham (BSc, PhD). CEng 1994; FIM 1994; FREng (FEng 1997). Dir and Gen. Manager, Brico Metals, 1967–69; Man. Dir, Brico Engineering, 1970–76; Man. Dir, Wellworthy, 1976–81; The Morgan Crucible Co.: Dir, 1981–83; Chm., Thermal Ceramics Div., 1981–83; Man. Dir and Chief Exec., 1983–97. Chairman: Allied Colloids Gp, 1996–98; Southern Electric plc, 1998; Devro plc, 1998–2001; Bodycote Internat., 1999–2002; Director: Scapa Gp plc, 1993–99; Foreign & Colonial Smaller Cos PLC, 1999–. Member: Council, CBI, 1990–; Adv. Bd, Imperial Coll. Management Sch., 1991–; Finance Cttee, ICRF, 1997–; Court, Surrey Univ., 1998–. Pres., Inst. of Materials, 1999– (Sen. Vice-Pres., 1997–99). CIMgt 1984; FRSA 1995. Freeman, City of London, 1994; Liveryman, Scientific Instrument Makers' Co., 1995–. *Recreations:* music, cricket, hill walking. *Address:* The Morgan Crucible Co., Morgan House, Windsor, Berks SL4 1EP. *T:* (01753) 837204; Weston House, Bracken Close, Wonersh, Surrey GU5 0QS. *Club:* Athenæum.

FARMER, George Wallace; President, Immigration Appeal Tribunal, 1991–97 (Vice President, 1982–91); *b* 4 June 1929; *s* of George Lawrence Farmer and Blanche Amy (*née* Niccolls); *m* 1961, Patricia Mary Joyce; three *d*. *Educ:* The Lodge, Barbados; Harrison Coll., Barbados. Called to the Bar, Middle Temple, 1950. Private practice, Barbados, 1950–52; Magistrate, Barbados, 1952–56; Resident Magistrate, Uganda, 1956–63, Sen. Resident Magistrate, 1963–64; Dir of Public Prosecutions, Uganda, 1964–65; attached to Cottle Catford & Co., Solicitors, Barbados, 1965–67; Legal Manager, Road Transport Industry Trng Bd, 1967–70; Adjudicator, Immigration Appeals, 1970–82. *Recreation:* enjoying the company of grandchildren. *Address:* 40 South Croxted Road, West Dulwich, SE21 8BD. *T:* (020) 8670 4828.

FARMER, Hugh Robert Macdonald, CB 1967; *b* 3 Dec. 1907; *s* of late Charles Edward Farmer and late Emily (*née* Randolph); *m* 1st, 1934, Penelope Frances (*d* 1963), *d* of late Capt. Evelyn Boothby, RN; one *s* three *d*; 2nd, 1966, Jean (*d* 1988), *widow* of Peter Bluett Winch. *Educ:* Cheam Sch.; Eton Coll.; New Coll., Oxford. House of Commons: Asst Clerk, 1931; Sen. Clerk, 1943; Clerk of Private Bills and Taxing Officer, and Examr of Petitions for Private Bills, 1958–60; Clerk of Cttees, 1960–65; Clerk/Administrator, 1965–72, retired 1972. *Recreation:* reading. *Address:* The Old Rectory, Iping, Midhurst, West Sussex GU29 0PF. *T:* (01730) 815923. *Club:* MCC.

FARMER, Michael; *see* Farmer, P. M.

FARMER, Paul Roy; District Judge (Magistrates' Courts) (formerly Provincial Stipendiary Magistrate), Dorset, since 1998; *b* 4 Dec. 1946; *s* of Charles Harry Farmer and Joan Farmer (*née* Mead); *m* 2nd, 1997, Christine Gillian Jago (*née* Pearce); one *d* from previous marriage. *Educ:* St Austell County Grammar Sch.; UWIST (LLB (ext.) London). Admitted Solicitor, 1971; articled Clerk, 1969–71, Asst Solicitor, 1971–74, Partner, 1974–78, Stephens and Scown, Solicitors; Dep. Justices' Clerk, 1978–86, Justices' Clerk 1986–98, PSDs (Falmouth and Kerrier, Pydar, Truro, S Powder, 1986–98, E Penwith, Isles of Scilly, Penwith, 1991–98); acting Stipendiary Magistrate for Hampshire and Devon, 1994–98. Pres., Devon and Cornwall Justices' Clerks Soc., 1993–94. Associate Editor, Magistrates' Courts Practice, 1997–. *Recreations:* golf, Rugby Union, cricket, music. *Address:* The Law Courts, Park Road, Poole, Dorset BH15 2RH. *T:* (01202) 711820. *Club:* Ferndown Golf.

FARMER, Peter John; Circuit Administrator, North-Eastern Circuit, since 1994; *b* 5 Nov. 1952; *s* of Alec and Norah Farmer; *m* 1986, Christine Ann Tetley. *Educ:* King Edward VI Sch., Southampton; Gonville and Caius College, Cambridge (Maths; MA); London Univ. (Cert. Psych.). Joined HM Customs and Excise, 1975; HM Treasury, 1979; Lord Chancellor's Dept, 1981; Circuit Principal, Leeds, 1983; Asst Sec., 1987; Asst Public Trustee, 1988; Public Trustee and Accountant Gen. of Supreme Court, 1991. FIMgt; MInstD. *Recreations:* English folk dancing, hill walking, choral music. *Address:* North-Eastern Circuit Office, West Riding House, Albion Street, Leeds LS1 5AA. *T:* (0113) 251 1200.

FARMER, (Pryce) Michael; QC 1995; **His Honour Judge Farmer**; a Circuit Judge, since 2001; *b* 20 May 1944; *er s* of Sarah Jane Farmer; *m* 1975, Olwen Mary, *d* of late Rev. Griffith John Roberts and of Margaret Morris Roberts; one *s* one *d*. *Educ:* Ysgol Dyffryn Nantlle, Penygroes; King's Coll., London (BA Hons); Inns of Court Sch. of Law. Schoolmaster, St David's Coll., Llandudno, 1968–71; called to the Bar, Gray's Inn, 1972; practice, Wales and Chester Circuit, 1973–; Junior, Wales and Chester Circuit, 1992; Asst Recorder, 1993–95; a Recorder, 1995–2001. Head of Chambers, Sedan House, Chester, 1995. Wales and Chester Circuit Regl Rep., Public Affairs Cttee, Bar Council, 1997–. Chm., Special Review Cttee, Ynys Môn CC, 1998–99. Contested (Plaid Cymru) Conwy, Feb. and Oct. 1974. *Recreations:* listening to classical music, reading, gardening, watching Rugby football. *Address:* Goldsmith Building, Temple, EC4Y 7BL. *T:* (020) 7353 7881; Sedan House, Stanley Place, Chester CH1 2LU. *T:* (01244) 348282. *Clubs:* Reform; Rygbi yr Wyddgrug (Mold).

FARMER, Robert Frederick, OBE 1985; General Secretary, Institute of Journalists, 1962–87; Member of Council, Media Society, 1982–90 (Secretary, 1973–82); *b* 19 Aug. 1922; *s* of Frederick Leonard Farmer and Gladys Farmer (*née* Winney); *m* 1958, Anne Walton. *Educ:* Saltley Grammar Sch., Birmingham. Served War of 1939–45, Royal Armoured Corps, 1941–52 (commissioned 3rd Carabiniers, despatches, Burma campaign). Secretariat: Instn of Plant Engineers, 1952–59; Instn of Civil Engineers, 1959–62. Consultative Mem., Press Council, 1962–87; Mem., Cttee on Defamation, 1971–75. *Recreation:* art history. *Address:* c/o Institute of Journalists, Suite 2, Dock Offices, Surrey Quays, Lower Road, SE16 2XL.

FARMER, Sir Thomas, Kt 1997; CBE 1990; DL; Chairman and Chief Executive, Kwik-Fit, since 1984; *b* 10 July 1940; *s* of John Farmer and Margaret (*née* Mackie); *m* 1966, Anne Drury Scott; one *s* one *d*. *Educ:* St Mary's Primary Sch., Edinburgh; Holy Cross Acad., Edinburgh. Founder, Kwik-Fit, 1971. Chairman: Scottish BITC, 1990–; Investors in People Scotland, 1991–97; Member Board: Scottish Enterprise, 1990–96; Investors in People, 1993–. DL Edinburgh, 1996. KCSG 1997. *Recreations:* tennis, swimming, ski-ing. *Address:* (office) 17 Corstorphine Road, Edinburgh EH12 6DD. *T:* (0131) 337 9200.

FARNCOMBE, Charles Frederick, CBE 1977; FRAM; Musical Director: Handel Opera Society, 1955–85; Malcolm Sargent Festival Choir, since 1985; *b* 29 July 1919; *o s* of Harold and Eleanor Farncombe, both of London; *m* 1963, Sally Mae (*née* Felps), Riverside, Calif, USA; one *d*. *Educ:* London Univ., 1936–40 (Archibald Dawnay Scholarship in Civil Engrg, 1936; BSc Hons (Eng) 1940); Royal Sch. of Church Music, 1947–48; Royal Academy of Music, 1948–51 (RAM, Mann Prize). Civil Engr to John Mowlem & Co. 1940–42. Served War, 1942–47, as Captain in REME, in 21st Army Gp. Freelance Conductor: formed Handel Opera Soc. 1955; Musical Dir, 1968–79, Chief Conductor, 1970–79, Royal Court Theatre, Drottningholm, Sweden; Chief Guest Conductor, 1979–85, Chief Conductor, annual Handel Fest., 1985–95, Badisches Staatstheater, Karlsruhe, 1979–; Guest Conductor, Komische Oper Berlin, 1994–. AMICE 1945 (resigned later); FRAM 1963 (ARAM 1962); Hon. Fellow, Royal Swedish Acad. of Music, 1972. Hon DMus: Columbus Univ., Ohio, USA, 1959; Yankton Univ., S Dakota, 1959; City Univ., 1988. Gold Medal of the Friends of Drottningholm, 1971; Gold Medal, Karlsruhe Handel Fest. Cttee, 1992. Kt Comdr, Order of North Star, Sweden, 1982. *Recreations:* cajoling singers, swimming, farm on Offa's Dyke. *Address:* 32 Trinity Court, 170A Gloucester Terrace, W2 6HS.

FARNDON, Prof. John Richard, MD; FRCS; Professor of Surgery, University of Bristol, since 1988; Hon. Consultant Surgeon, Bristol Royal Infirmary, since 1988; *b* 16 Feb. 1946; *s* of George Arthur Farndon and Margaret Cooper; *m* 1972, Christine Brenda Louet; two *s* one *d*. *Educ:* Woodhouse Grammar Sch., Sheffield; Univ. of Newcastle upon Tyne (BSc, MB BS, MD). Surgical training posts in Newcastle upon Tyne, 1971–79; Peel Travelling Fellow and Internat. Res. Fellow, Duke Univ., USA, 1979–81; Sen. Lectr in Surgery, Univ. of Newcastle upon Tyne and Consultant to Royal Infirmary, Newcastle, 1981–88. James IV Travelling Fellow, 1984; Hunterian Prof., RCS, 1985; Travelling Fellow, Australasian Coll. of Surgeons, 1985; British Council Scholar to India, 1991; Dist. Visitor, RCS of Australia, 1993; Penman Vis. Prof., Univ. of Cape Town, 1995. Ext. Examiner, Chinese Univ. of Hong Kong, 1994. Vice-Pres., Assoc. of Surgeons of GB and Ireland, April 2002–. Hon. Fellow, Assoc. of Surgeons in India, 1997; Hon. FRCSE. Consultant to World Jl of Surgery, 1991–; Editor, British Jl of Surgery, 1992– (Chm. Editl Bd, April 2002–). *Publications:* (ed with G. Keen) Operative Surgery and Management, 3rd edn 1992; (ed) Breast and Endocrine Surgery, 1997; numerous papers and chapters on surgical endocrinology and oncology. *Recreations:* gardening, Betjeman Society (founder member), classical music. *Address:* Department of Surgery, Bristol Royal Infirmary, Marlborough Street, Bristol BS2 8HW. *T:* (0117) 926 0601. *Clubs:* Royal Society of Medicine; Clifton (Bristol).

FARNELL, Graeme, FMA; Managing Director, Heritage Development Ltd, since 1996; *b* 11 July 1947; *s* of Wilson Elliot Farnell and Mary Montgomerie Wishart Farnell (*née* Crichton); *m* 1969, Jennifer Gerda (*née* Huddlestone); one *s*. *Educ:* Loughborough Grammar Sch.; Edinburgh Univ. (MA); London Film Sch. (DipFilm Studies). FMA 1989; FSAScot 1976; MBIM. Asst Keeper, Mus. of East Anglian Life, 1973–76; Curator, Inverness Mus. and Art Gall., 1976–79; Dir, Scottish Museums Council, 1979–86; Dir Gen., Museums Assoc., 1986–89; Man. Dir, The Development (formerly Museum Development) Co. Ltd, 1989–94; Publishing Ed., IMS Publications, 1994–96; Publisher: New Heritage (formerly Heritage Development) magazine, 1996–; Heritage Business (formerly Heritage Insider) newsletter, 1998–; Heritage Retail mag., 1999–. *Publications:* (ed) The American Museum Experience, 1986; The Handbook of Grants, 1990, 2nd edn, 1993; (ed) The European Heritage Directory, 1998; contribs to Museums Jl, Internat. Jl of Mus. Management and Curatorship, Museum (Unesco), Industrial Soc. *Recreations:* baroque opera, travel. *Address:* 8 Faraday Drive, Shenley Lodge, Milton Keynes, Bucks MK5 7DA. *T:* (01908) 660629.

FARNELL, John Bernard Patrick; Director, Conservation Policy, Fisheries Directorate-General, European Commission, since 2001; *b* 24 Aug. 1948; *s* of James Farnell and Laura (*née* O'Connell); *m* 1976, Susan Mary Janus; two *s*. *Educ:* Downside Sch.; Christ's Coll., Cambridge (MA Hist.); London Sch. of Econs (MSc Econ). Economist, BEA, 1970–72; CBI, 1973–74; with European Commission, 1975–: Ext. Relns, 1975–77; Fisheries, 1977–82; Industry, 1982–93 (Internat. Questions Unit, 1982–87; Head: Standardisation and Certification Unit, 1987–93; Tech. Legislation Unit, 1993); Hd, Operation of Internal Mkt and Econ. Analysis Unit, Directorate-Gen. of Internal Mkt and Financial Services, 1993–97; Dir, Horizontal Measures and Markets, Fisheries Directorate-General, 1997–2001. *Publications:* Public and Private Britain, 1975; (with James Elles) In Search of a Common Fisheries Policy, 1984. *Recreations:* opera, fly-fishing, crosswords. *Address:* 33 Rue de Châtelain, 1050 Brussels, Belgium.

FARNHAM, 13th Baron *cr* 1756; **Simon Kenlis Maxwell;** Bt (NS) 1627; *b* 12 Dec. 1933; *s* of Hon. Somerset Arthur Maxwell, MP and Angela Susan (*née* Roberts); *S* brother, 2001; *m* 1964, Karol Anne, *d* of Maj.-Gen. G. E. Prior-Palmer, CB, DSO; two *s* one *d* (of whom one *s* one *d* are twins). *Educ:* Eton. Late Lt, 10th Royal Hussars. *Heir: s* Hon. Robin Somerset Maxwell [*b* 15 Sept. 1965; *m* 1993, Tessa Shepherd; one *s* one *d*]. *Address:* The Dower House, Westcote, near Chipping Norton, Oxon OX7 6SF.

FARNINGHAM, Alexander Ian, DSC; Managing Director, Industrial Relations and Personnel, British Shipbuilders, 1977–80; *b* 3 Nov. 1923; *s* of Alexander Farningham and Janet Leask Broadley; *m* 1st, 1949, Lois Elizabeth Halse (marr. diss. 1981); one *s* two *d*; 2nd, 1981, Susan Wyllie. *Educ:* Glebelands Primary Sch., Dundee; Morgan Academy, Dundee; St Andrews Univ. (MA). Served FAA, 1941–46 (Lieut (A); DSC), RNVR. *Recreations:* walking, birdwatching, photography. *Address:* 1 John Smith Place, Kintyre Street, Tarbert, Argyll PA29 6UW. *T:* (01880) 820029.

FARNSWORTH, Ian Ross; Director: Coutts & Co., 1992–97 (Deputy Chairman and Chief Executive, 1992–95); New Sadler's Wells Ltd, since 1996; *b* 15 Feb. 1938; *s* of Frederick Sutcliffe and Winifred Ruby Bryan; *m* 1964, Rosalind Amanda Baker; one *s* one *d*. *Educ:* Nottingham High Sch. ACIB. Westminster Bank, later National Westminster Bank: joined 1954; seconded Nat. Bank of N America, 1979–80; Exec. Vice-Pres., NatWest N America, 1981–84; Asst Gen. Manager, NatWest, 1987–88; Dir, European Businesses, 1988–90; Gen. Manager, NatWest, 1990–91; Dep. Chm., Coutts & Co. AG, Zürich, 1991–94; Mem., Supervisory Bd, F. van Lanschot Bankiers, Holland, 1991–95. Chm., Willowbrite Ltd, 1997–; Dir, Megalomedia plc, 1997–. Dir, PEC Concerts Ltd, 1995–2000; Gov., Sadler's Wells Foundn, 1995–. Mem., Develt Cttee, Univ. of Herts, 1996–. Liveryman, Information Technologists' Co., 1994–. *Recreations:* music, golf. *Address:* 15 Dellcroft Way, Harpenden, Herts AL5 2NQ. *T:* (01582) 712518.

FARNWORTH, John David; His Honour Judge Farnworth; a Circuit Judge, since 1991; *b* 20 June 1935; *s* of George Arthur Farnworth and Mary Lilian Farnworth; *m* 1964, Carol Gay Mallett; one *s* two *d*. *Educ:* Bedford Sch.; St Edmund Hall, Oxford (BA). Bigelow Teaching Fellow, Univ. of Chicago Law Sch., 1958–59. Admitted Solicitor, 1962; a Recorder, 1986–91. *Recreations:* golf, cricket, snooker, art galleries. *Clubs:* MCC; Bedfordshire Golf.

FAROOKHI, Imtiaz; Chief Executive, National House-Building Council, since 1997; *b* 17 Jan. 1951; *s* of Mumtaz and Anwar Farookhi; *m* 1983, Margaret Maclean; one *s* one *d*. *Educ:* King Alfred Sch.; Acton Tech. Coll.; Univ. of Kent at Canterbury; Birkbeck Coll., London Univ. Asst Chief Exec., Hackney LBC, 1983-88; Head of Co-ordination, Wakefield MDC, 1988–89; Dir of Policy and Admin, Southwark LBC, 1988–91; Chief Exec., Leicester CC, 1991–96. Member: DEMOS Adv. Council, 1995–; QMW Public Policy Adv. Bd, 1995–; Envmt Agency, 1995–97; Bd, BURA, 1998–; British Bd of Agrément, 1999–. FRSA 1994. *Publications:* articles in jls. *Recreation:* family life. *Address:* (office) Buildmark House, Chiltern Avenue, Amersham, Bucks HP6 5AP. *T:* (01494) 434477. *Club:* QPR Supporters'.

FARQUHAR, Charles Don Petrie, OBE 1999; JP; DL; engineer; *b* 4 Aug. 1937; *s* of late William Sandeman Farquhar and Annie Preston Young Farquhar; *m*; two *d*. *Educ:* Liff Road and St Michael's Primary Schs, Dundee; Stobswell Secondary Sch., Dundee. Served with Royal Engineers (Trng NCO); subseq. supervisory staff, plant engrg, NCR Ltd, Area Manager, Community Industry, Dundee/Fife, 1972–91. City Councillor, Dundee, 1965–74 (ex-Convener, Museums, Works and Housing Cttees); Mem., Dundee DC, 1974–96 (Chm., Leisure and Recreation Cttees, 1992–96); Lord Provost and Lord Lieutenant of City of Dundee, 1975–77; Mem., Dundee City Council, 1995– (Chm., Leisure Services Cttee). Chairman: Dundee Dist Licensing Bd, Dundee Dist Licensing Cttee, 1984–93; Cttee for Employment of Disabled People (formerly Disabled Adv. Cttee), Tayside and Fife, 1979–94. JP Dundee, 1974; DL Dundee, 1977. *Recreations:* fresh-water angling, gardening, numismatics, do-it-yourself. *Address:* 2 Killin Avenue, Dundee DD3 6EB. *T:* (01382) 229369.

FARQUHAR, Prof. Graham Douglas, PhD; FRS 1995; FAA; Professor of Biology, and Leader, Environmental Biology Group, Research School of Biological Sciences, Australian National University, Canberra, since 1988; *b* 8 Dec. 1947. *Educ:* Australian Nat. Univ. (BSc 1968; PhD 1973); Queensland Univ. (BSc Hons Biophysics 1969). FAA 1988. Dept of Energy Plant Res. Lab., Michigan State Univ., 1973–76; Australian National University: Res. Fellow, 1976–80; Sen. Res. Fellow, 1980–; Fellow, 1980–83; Sen. Fellow, 1983–88. *Publications:* (ed jtly) Stomatal Function, 1987; (ed jtly) Perspectives of Plant Carbon and Water Relations for Stable Isotopes, 1993; numerous research texts. *Address:* Environmental Biology Group, Research School of Biological Sciences, Australian National University, GPO Box 475, Canberra, ACT 2601, Australia. *T:* (2) 61255052, *Fax:* (2) 61244919.

FARQUHAR, Margaret (Elizabeth), CBE 1999; JP; Lord Provost and Lord-Lieutenant of Aberdeen, 1996–99; *b* Aberdeen, 1930; *née* Burnett; *m* 1951, William Farquhar (*d* 1993); one *s* one *d*. *Educ:* Ruthrieston Secondary Sch., Aberdeen; Webster's Coll., Aberdeen. Clerical work: N of Scotland Coll. of Agric., 1947–48; Charles Michie, haulage contractor, 1948–51; Cordiners Sawmills, 1963–65; William Walker, haulage contractor, 1969–77. Member (Lab): Aberdeen DC, 1971–96 (Vice-Chm., 1994–96); Aberdeen CC, 1995–99. Mem., Planning Cttee, 1985–86, 1988–92, Aberdeen Council rep., 1992–99, COSLA. Dir, Grampian Enterprise, 1991–92. Member: Mgt Cttee, Aberdeen CAB, 1986–; Mgt Cttee, Northfield Community Centre, 1993–. Labour Party: Sec., Bridge of Don Br., 1980–81; Sec. and Chm., Cummings Pk Br., 1971–79; Chm., Aberdeen Women's Council, 1971–72. Hon. Pres., Grampian Girls' Bde, 1988–. JP Aberdeen, 1972. Hon. LLD: Aberdeen, 1996; Robert Gordon, 1998. Paul Harris Fellowship, Rotary Internat., 1998. *Recreations:* working with the elderly and the young, bowling, driving, watching television.

FARQUHAR, Sir Michael (Fitzroy Henry), 7th Bt *cr* 1796, of Cadogan House, Middlesex; farmer; *b* 29 June 1938; *s* of Sir Peter Walter Farquhar, 6th Bt, DSO, OBE, and Elizabeth Evelyn (*d* 1983), *d* of Francis Cecil Albert Hurt; *S* father, 1986; *m* 1963, Veronica Geraldine Hornidge; two *s*. *Educ:* Eton; Royal Agricultural College. *Recreations:* fishing, shooting. *Heir: s* Charles Walter Fitzroy Farquhar, *b* 21 Feb. 1964. *Address:* Manor Farm, West Kington, Chippenham, Wilts SN14 7JG. *T:* (01249) 782671. *Club:* White's.

FARQUHAR MUNRO, John; *see* Munro.

FARQUHARSON of Invercauld, Captain Alwyne Arthur Compton, MC 1944; JP; Head of Clan Farquharson; *b* 1 May 1919; *er s* of late Major Edward Robert Francis

Compton, JP, DL, Newby Hall, Ripon, and Torloisk, Isle of Mull, and Sylvia, *y d* of A. H. Farquharson; recognised by Lord Lyon King of Arms as Laird of Invercauld (16th Baron of Invercauld; *S* aunt 1941), also as Chief of name of Farquharson and Head of Clan, since 1949; assumed (surname) Compton as a third forename and assumed surname of Farquharson of Invercauld, by warrant granted in Lyon Court, Edinburgh, 1949; *m* 1st, 1949, Frances Strickland Lovell (*d* 1991), *d* of Robert Pollard Oldham, Seattle, Washington, USA; 2nd, 1993, Patricia Gabrielle Estelle Parry de Winton, *d* of Henry Norman Simms-Adams, Brancaster Hall, Norfolk. *Educ:* Eton; Magdalen Coll., Oxford. Joined Royal Scots Greys, 1940. Served War, 1940–45, Palestine, N Africa, Italy, France (wounded); Captain 1943. County Councillor, Aberdeenshire, 1949–75, JP 1951. *Address:* Invercauld, Braemar, Aberdeenshire AB35 5TS. *T:* (01339) 741213.

See also R. E. J. Compton.

FARQUHARSON, Angus Durie Miller, OBE 1995; JP; FRICS; Lord-Lieutenant of Aberdeenshire, since 1998 (Vice Lord-Lieutenant, 1987–98); *b* 27 March 1935; *s* of Dr Hugo Miller and Elsie (*née* Duthie); adopted surname of Farquharson, 1961; *m* 1961, Alison Mary Farquharson of Finzean, *o d* of W. M. Farquharson-Lang, CBE, 14th Laird of Finzean; two *s* one *d*. *Educ:* Glenalmond; Downing Coll., Cambridge (BA 1956; MA). FRICS 1985. Factor, farmer, forester, chartered surveyor. Member: Council, Scottish Landowners Fedn, 1980–88; Regl Adv. Cttee, Forestry Commn, 1980–94 (Chm., North Conservancy, 1993–94); Red Deer Commn, 1986–92; Nature Conservancy Cttee for Scotland, 1986–91; SNH NE Cttee, 1992–94. Elder, 1969–, and Gen. Trustee, 1994–, Church of Scotland. Hon. Pres., Kincardine Deeside Scouts, 1985; Dir, Lathallan Sch., 1982–98. Aberdeenshire: DL 1984; JP 1998. *Recreations:* gardening, shooting, local history, nature conservation. *Address:* Finzean House, Finzean, Banchory, Aberdeenshire AB31 6NZ. *T:* (01330) 850229. *Club:* New (Edinburgh).

FARQUHARSON of Whitehouse, Captain Colin Andrew; JP; FRICS; chartered surveyor and land agent; Lord Lieutenant of Aberdeenshire, 1987–98 (Vice Lord Lieutenant, 1983–87); JP; *b* 9 Aug. 1923; *s* of late Norman Farquharson of Whitehouse; *m* 1st, 1948, Jean Sybil Mary (*d* 1985), *d* of late Brig.-Gen. J. G. H. Hamilton, Skene, DSO, JP, DL; two *d* (and one *d* decd); 2nd, 1987, Clodagh, *widow* of Ian Houldsworth, Dallas Lodge, Moray, and *d* of Sir Kenneth Murray, Geanies, Ross-shire; three step *s* two step *d*. *Educ:* Rugby. FLAS 1956, FRICS 1970. Served Grenadier Guards, 1942–48: ADC to Field Marshal Sir Harold Alexander (later (1st) Earl Alexander of Tunis), 1945. Member, Queen's Body Guard for Scotland (Royal Company of Archers), 1964–. Chartered surveyor and land agent in private practice in Aberdeenshire, 1953–; Director, MacRobert Farms (Douneside) Ltd, 1971–87. Member, Bd of Management for Royal Cornhill Hosps, 1962–74; Chm., Gordon Local Health Council, 1975–81; Mem., Grampian Health Bd, 1981–89. DL 1966, JP 1969, Aberdeenshire. *Recreations:* shooting, fishing, farming. *Address:* Whitehouse, Alford, Aberdeenshire AB33 8DP. *Clubs:* MCC; Royal Northern and University (Aberdeen).

See also Master of Arbuthnott.

FARQUHARSON, Rt Hon. Sir Donald (Henry), Kt 1981; PC 1989; DL; a Lord Justice of Appeal, 1989–95; *b* 1928; *yr s* of Charles Anderson Farquharson, Logie Coldstone, Aberdeenshire, and Florence Ellen Fox; *m* 1960, Helen Mary, *er d* of Comdr H. M. Simpson, RN (retd), Abbots Brow, Kirkby Lonsdale, Westmorland; three *s* (one *d* decd). *Educ:* Royal Commercial Travellers Sch.; Keble Coll., Oxford (MA; Hon. Fellow, 1989). Called to Bar, Inner Temple, 1952; Bencher, 1979. Dep. Chm., Essex QS, 1970; a Recorder of the Crown Court, 1972–81; QC 1972; Judge, High Court of Justice, QBD, 1981–89; Presiding Judge, SE Circuit, 1985–88. A Legal Assessor to GMC and GDC, 1978–81; Chairman: Disciplinary Cttee of Bar, 1983–85; Judicial Studies Bd, 1992–94 (Mem., 1984–85); Criminal Justice Consultative Council, 1992–94. DL Essex, 1990. *Recreations:* opera, walking. *Address:* Bay Tree House, Bures, Suffolk CO8 5JG.

FARQUHARSON, Very Rev. Hunter Buchanan; Provost, St Ninian's Cathedral, Perth, since 1999; *b* 19 July 1958; *s* of Cameron Bruce Farquharson and Thelma Alice Buchanan Farquharson. *Educ:* Birmingham Sch. of Speech (ALAM, LLAM); Edinburgh Theol Coll. (General Ministerial Exams; Luscombe Scholar, 1989). Deacon 1988, priest 1989; Curate, West Fife Team, 1988–91; Rector, St Luke's, Glenrothes, 1991–97; Leader of Central Fife Team, 1995–97; Rector, Holy Trinity, Dunfermline and Leader of West Fife Team, 1997–99. Chm., Perth and Kinross Assoc. of Voluntary Services, 2000. *Recreations:* showing and breeding flat-coated retrievers, fishing, hill-walking. *Address:* St Ninian's House, 40 Hay Street, Perth PH1 5HS. *T:* (01738) 626874; *e-mail:* HBF1@compuserve.com. *Clubs:* Flat-coated Retriever Society; Scottish Kennel (Edinburgh).

FARQUHARSON, Sir James (Robbie), KBE 1960 (CBE 1948; OBE 1944); retired, and is now farming; *b* 1 Nov. 1903; *s* of Frank Farquharson, Cortachy, Angus, Scotland, and Agnes Jane Robbie; *m* 1933, Agnes Binny Graham (*d* 1992); two *s*. *Educ:* Royal Technical College, Glasgow; Glasgow Univ. BSc Glasgow 1923. Asst Engineer, LMS Railway, 1923–25; Asst Engineer, Kenya and Uganda Railway, 1925–33; Senior Asst Engineer, Kenya and Uganda Railway, 1933–37; Asst to Gen. Manager, Tanganyika Railways, 1937–41; Chief Engineer, Tanganyika Railways, 1941–45; General Manager, Tanganyika Railways, 1945–48; Deputy General Manager, East African Railways, 1948–52; Gen. Manager, Sudan Railways, 1952–57; Gen. Manager, East African Railways and Harbours, 1957–61; Asst Crown Agent and Engineer-in-Chief of Crown Agents for Overseas Governments and Administrations, 1961–65. Chm., Millbank Technical Services Ordnance Ltd, 1973–75. Fellow, Scottish Council for Develt and Industry, 1986–. *Publication:* Tanganyika Transport, 1944. *Recreation:* cricket. *Address:* Kinclune, by Kirriemuir, Angus DD8 5HX. *T:* (01575) 574710. *Club:* Nairobi (Kenya).

FARQUHARSON, Jonathan, CBE 1997; Charity Commissioner, 1985–96; *b* 27 Dec. 1937; *s* of Alan George Farquharson and Winifred Mary Farquharson (*née* Wilson); *m* 1963, Maureen Elsie Bright; two *d*. *Educ:* St Albans School; Manchester Univ. (LLB). Solicitor, 1962; with D. Herbert, Banbury, 1962–64; Charity Commission, 1964–96. FRSA. *Recreations:* geology, photography, reading, record collecting, gardening. *Address:* 30 Ennerdale Road, Formby, Merseyside L37 2EA. *T:* (01704) 871820.

FARQUHARSON, Robert Alexander, CMG 1975; HM Diplomatic Service, retired; *b* 26 May 1925; *s* of late Captain J. P. Farquharson, DSO, OBE, RN, and late Mrs Farquharson (*née* Prescott-Decie); *m* 1955, Joan Elizabeth, *o d* of Sir (William) Ivo Mallet, GBE, KCMG; two *s* one *d* (and one *s* decd). *Educ:* Harrow; King's Coll., Cambridge. Served with RNVR, 1943–46. Joined Foreign (now Diplomatic) Service, 1949; 3rd Sec., Moscow, 1950; FO, 1952; 2nd Sec., Bonn, 1955; 1st Sec., Panama, 1958; Paris, 1960; FO, 1964; Counsellor, Dir of British Trade Develt, S Africa, 1967; Minister, Madrid, 1971; Consul-Gen., San Francisco, 1973; Ambassador to Yugoslavia, 1977–80. Lay Canon of Salisbury Cathedral, 2000–. Lord of the Manor of Bockleton. *Address:* The Old Rectory, Tollard Royal, Wilts SP5 5PS. *Club:* Flyfishers'.

FARR, Clarissa Mary, (Mrs John Goodbody); Principal, Queenswood School, Hatfield, since 1996; *b* 30 June 1958; *d* of late Alan Farr and of Wendy Farr; *m* 1993, John Goodbody; one *s* one *d*. *Educ:* Bruton Sch. for Girls; Exeter Univ. (BA Hons Eng. Lit., MA); Bristol Univ. (PGCE). Teacher: Farnborough Sixth Form Coll., 1981–83; Filton High Sch., 1983–86; Head of Sixth Form, Shatin Coll., Hong Kong, 1986–89; Sen. Mistress, Leicester GS, 1990–92; Dep. Head, Queenswood Sch., 1992–96. *Recreations:* running, swimming, theatre, travel. *Address:* Queenswood, Brookmans Park, Hatfield, Herts AL9 6NS. *T:* (01707) 602500.

FARR, Dennis Larry Ashwell, CBE 1991; FMA; Director, Courtauld Institute Galleries, 1980–93; *b* 3 April 1929; *s* of late Arthur William Farr and Helen Eva Farr (*née* Ashwell); *m* 1959, Diana Pullein-Thompson (writer), *d* of Captain H. J. Pullein-Thompson, MC, and Joanna (*née* Cannan); one *s* one *d*. *Educ:* Luton Grammar Sch.; Courtauld Inst. of Art, London Univ. (BA, MA). Asst Witt Librarian, Courtauld Inst. of Art, 1952–54; Asst Keeper, Tate Gallery, 1954–64; Curator, Paul Mellon Collection, Washington, DC, 1965–66; Sen. Lectr in Fine Art, and Dep. Keeper, University Art Collections, Univ. of Glasgow, 1967–69; Dir, City Museums and Art Gallery, Birmingham, 1969–80. Fred Cook Meml Lecture, RSA, 1974. Hon. Art Adviser, Calouste Gulbenkian Foundation, 1969–73; Member: British Council Fine Arts Adv. Cttee, 1971–80; Wright Cttee on Provincial Museums and Galleries, 1971–73; Museums Assoc. Council, 1971–74 (Vice-Pres., 1978–79, 1980–81; Pres., 1979–80; Instnl Councillor, 1991–93); Art Panel, Arts Council, 1972–77; ICOM (UK) Exec. Bd, 1976–85; Cttee, Victorian Soc., 1980–95; Exec. Cttee, Assoc. of Art Historians, 1981–87 (Chm. of Assoc., 1983–86); History of Art and Design Bd, CNAA, 1981–87; Comité Internat. d'Histoire de l'Art, 1983–94 (Hon. Mem., 1994); Registration Cttee, Museums and Galls Commn, 1993–99. Trustee, Birmingham Mus. and Art Gall. Appeal Fund, 1980– (Chm. Trustees, 1978–80); Secretary: Home House Soc. Trustees, 1986–90; Samuel Courtauld Trust, 1990–93. Guest Curator, Francis Bacon: a retrospective, USA tour, 1999. Hon. Sec., CS Riding Club, 1958–60. FRSA 1970; FMA 1972. Hon. DLitt Birmingham, 1981. JP Birmingham, 1977–80. Gen. Editor, Clarendon Studies in the History of Art, 1985–. *Publications:* William Etty, 1958; (with M. Chamot and M. Butlin) Catalogue of the Modern British School Collection, Tate Gallery, 1964; British Sculpture since 1945, 1965; New Painting in Glasgow, 1968; Pittura Inglese 1660–1840, 1975; English Art 1870–1940, 1978, 2nd edn 1984; (contrib.) British Sculpture in the Twentieth Century, 1981; (with W. Bradford) The Courtauld Collection (catalogue for exhibns in Tokyo and Canberra), 1984; (with W. Bradford) The Northern Landscape (catalogue for exhibn in New York), 1986; (contrib.) In Honor of Paul Mellon, Collector and Benefactor, 1986; (jtly) Impressionist and Post-Impressionist Masterpieces: the Courtauld Collection, 1987; (ed and contrib.) 100 Masterpieces from the Courtauld Collections: Bernardo Daddi to Ben Nicholson, 1987; (jtly) The Oxford Dictionary of Art, 1988; (with Eva Chadwick) Lynn Chadwick: Sculptor, a complete catalogue 1947–88, 1990, 2nd edn 1998; (ed and contrib.) Thomas Gambier Parry as Artist and Collector, 1993; (ed and contrib.) Francis Bacon: a retrospective, 1999; articles in: Apollo, Burlington Magazine, TLS, etc. *Recreations:* riding, reading, music, foreign travel. *Address:* Orchard Hill, Swan Barn Road, Haslemere, Surrey GU27 2HY. *T:* (01428) 641880. *Club:* Athenæum.

See also Denis Cannan. J. M. W. Pullein-Thompson.

FARR, Jennifer Margaret; Vice Lord-Lieutenant of Nottinghamshire, since 1999; *b* 20 July 1933; *d* of late Charles Percival Holliday and Vera Margaret Emily (*née* Burchell); *m* 1956, Sydney Hordern Farr (*d* 1981); two *s* one *d*. *Educ:* Nottingham Girls' High Sch.; Middlesex Hosp.; Royal Victoria Hosp., Newcastle upon Tyne. Physiotherapist, Nottingham City Hosp., 1954–56. National Society for Prevention of Cruelty to Children: Nat. Council Mem., 1973–94; a Nat. Vice-Pres., 1994–; Chairman: Nottingham Br., 1983–98; Notts Full Stop Appeal, 1999–. Pres., League of Friends, Queen's Med. Centre, 1999–. Member: Nottingham Convent Council, 1992–98; Southwell 2000 Appeal, 1992–96. Pres., Thurgarton Cricket Club, 1981–99. JP Notts, 1979–89; DL 1993, High Sheriff 1998–99, Notts. *Recreations:* bridge, gardening, music, sports, theatre, family life. *Address:* Lanesmeet, Epperstone, Notts NG14 6AU. *T:* (0115) 966 4584. *Club:* Sloane.

FARR, Air Vice-Marshal Peter Gerald Desmond, CB 1968; OBE 1952; DFC 1942; retired; Director, Brain Research Trust, 1973–83; *b* 26 Sept. 1917; *s* of late Gerald Farr and Mrs Farr (*née* Miers); *m* 1949, Rosemarie (*d* 1983), *d* of late R. S. Haward; two *s* one *d*. *Educ:* Tonbridge Sch. Commnd in RAF, 1937; served War of 1939–45, Middle East, India and Burma; OC, No 358 Sqdn, 1944–45; OC, RAF Pegu, 1945–46; OC, 120 Sqdn, 1950–51; Dep. Dir, Jt Anti-Submarine Sch., 1952–54; OC, RAF Idris, 1954–55; Directing Staff, Jt Services Staff Coll., 1959; SASO, Malta, 1960–63; OC, RAF Kinloss, 1963–64; Air Officer Administration: RAF Germany, 1964–68; Strike Comd, 1969–72. *Recreations:* golf, music. *Address:* c/o Lloyds TSB, Great Missenden, Bucks HP16 0AT. *Club:* Royal Air Force.

FARRAN, Rt Rev. Brian George; an Assistant Bishop of Perth, Western Australia, since 1992 (Goldfields Region, 1992–98; Northern Region, since 1998); *b* 15 Dec. 1944; *s* of George Farran and Dorothy Barnes; *m* 1971, Robin Jeanne Marsden; one *s* two *d*. *Educ:* ANU (BA); St John's Theol Coll., Morpeth (ThL); Deakin Univ. (BLitt). Ordained deacon, 1967, priest, 1968; Curate: St Phillips, O'Connor, 1968; St Alban's, Griffith, 1969–71; Rector: Ch of the Epiphany, Lake Cargelligo, 1972–75; St Barnabas, N Rockhampton, 1975–79; St Saviour's, Gladstone, 1979–82; Dean of St Paul's Cathedral, Rockhampton, Queensland, 1983–89; Regl Dir, Australian Bd of Missions, Province of Victoria, 1989–92. Vice Chm., Gen. Bd of Religous Educn, Anglican Ch of Australia, 1984–. *Recreations:* gardening, music, films, reading. *Address:* (office) GPO Box 42, Joondalup, WA 6919, Australia; (home) 3 Murray Place, Duncraig, WA 6023, Australia.

FARRANCE, Roger Arthur, CBE 1988; Chief Executive, Electricity Association, 1990–93; Chairman: Electricity Association Services Ltd, 1991–93; Electricity Association Technology Ltd, 1991–93; *b* 10 Nov. 1933; *s* of Ernest Thomas Farrance and Alexandra Hilda May (*née* Finch); *m* 1956, Kathleen Sheila (*née* Owen); one *d*. *Educ:* Trinity School of John Whitgift, Croydon; London School of Economics (BScEcon). CCIPD; CompIEE. HM Inspector of Factories, Manchester, Doncaster and Walsall, 1956–64; Asst Sec., West of England Engineering Employers' Assoc., Bristol, 1964–67; Industrial Relations and Personnel Manager, Foster Wheeler John Brown Boilers Ltd, 1967–68; Dep. Director, Coventry and District Engineering Employers' Assoc., also Coventry Management Trng Centre, 1968–75; Electricity Council: Dep. Industrial Relations Adviser (Negotiating), 1975–76; Industrial Relations Adviser, 1976–79; Mem., 1979–88; Dep. Chm., 1989–90. Chm., Power Aid Logistics, 1993–94. Dir, Caswell Bay Court Mgt Co. Ltd, 2000–. Member Council: ACAS, 1983–89; CBI, 1983–93 (Chm., Health and Safety Policy Cttee, 1990–93); Mem., Directing Cttee, Union Internationale des Producteurs et Distributeurs d'Energie Electrique, 1991–94 (Chm., Human Factors Cttee, 1991–94). President: IPM, 1991–93; Electricity Supply Industry Ambulance Centre, St John's Amb. Assoc., 1979–93; St John's 210 (London Electricity) Combined Div., 1989–94. Chairman: Devonshire House Management Trustees, 1989–94; Management Bd, Electrical and Electronics Industry Benevolent Assoc., 1987–93. FRSA 1985. Councillor (C), London Borough of Merton, 1994–98. Freeman, City of London, 1985; Liveryman, Basketmakers' Co., 1986–. OStJ 1983. *Recreations:* photography, music, cycling, walking. *Address:* The Rise, Heol-y-Parc, Pentyrch, Cardiff CF15 9NB.

FARRAND, Rt Hon. Dame Brenda Marjorie; *see* Hale, Rt Hon. Dame B. M.

FARRAND, Julian Thomas, LLD; Chairman, Leasehold Valuation Tribunals and RACs for London Area, Rent Assessment Panel, since 1984; *b* 13 Aug. 1935; *s* of J. and E. A. Farrand; *m* 1st, 1957, Winifred Joan Charles (marr. diss. 1992); one *s* two *d*; 2nd, 1992, Brenda Marjorie Hoggett (*see* Rt Hon. Dame Brenda Hale). *Educ:* Haberdashers' Aske's Sch.; University Coll. London (LLB 1957, LLD 1966). Admitted Solicitor, 1960. Asst Lectr, then Lectr, KCL, 1960–63; Lectr, Sheffield Univ., 1963–65; Reader in Law, QMC, 1965–68; Prof. of Law, 1968–88, Dean of Faculty of Law, 1970–72, 1976–78, Manchester Univ. Vis. Prof., UCL, 1990–. A Law Comr, 1984–88; Insce Ombudsman, 1989–94; Pensions Ombudsman, 1994–2000. Chairman: Gtr Manchester and Lancs Area, Rent Assessment Panel, 1973–90 (Vice-Pres., 1977–84); Supplementary Benefit Appeals Tribunal, 1977–80; Nat. Insce Local Tribunal, 1980–83; Social Security Appeal Tribunal, 1983–88; Govt Conveyancing Cttee, 1984–85. Chm., Pensions Compensation Bd, 1996–2001. Non-exec. Dir, First Title plc, 1996–. Mem., ADR Chambers (UK) Ltd, 2000–. Hon. Prof. of Law, Essex Univ., 2000–. FCIArb 1994. Hon. QC 1994. Hon. LLD Sheffield, 1990. *Publications:* (ed with Dr J. Gilchrist Smith) Emmet on Title, 15th edn 1967 to 19th edn (as sole editor) 1986; Contract and Conveyance, 1963–64, 4th edn 1983; (ed) Wolstenholme and Cherry, Conveyancing Statutes, 13th edn (vols 1–6) 1972; The Rent Acts and Regulations, 1978, 2nd edn (with A. Arden) 1981; (novel) Love at all Risks, 2001. *Recreations:* chess, bridge, wine, fiction. *Address:* 87 Barnsbury Street, Islington, N1 1EJ.

FARRAR, Rex Gordon, LVO 1975; HM Diplomatic Service, retired; Regional Director (Tokyo), 1985–90, Consultant, since 1990, De La Rue Co. plc; *b* 22 Aug. 1925; *s* of late John Percival Farrar and Ethel Florence Farrar (*née* Leader); *m* 1978, Masako (*née* Ikeda); one *s* one *d*. *Educ:* Latymer's Sch., Edmonton; London Univ. (BA Hons History). Served Royal Navy, 1944–47. Joined HM Diplomatic Service, 1947; served, New Orleans, 1953–57; Jakarta, 1960–63; Caracas, 1964–68; San Salvador, 1968–71; Tokyo, 1971–75; Rangoon, 1978–80; Consul-Gen. and Dir of Trade Promotion, Osaka, Japan, 1980–85. *Recreations:* golf, tennis, studying Japanese. *Club:* Kobe (Japan).

FARRAR-HOCKLEY, Gen. Sir Anthony Heritage, GBE 1982 (MBE 1957); KCB 1977; DSO 1953 and bar 1964; MC 1944; author (military history), defence consultant and lecturer; Commander-in-Chief Allied Forces Northern Europe, 1979–82; ADC General to the Queen, 1981–83; retired 1983; *b* 8 April 1924; *s* of late Arthur Farrar-Hockley and Agnes Beatrice (*née* Griffin); *m* 1945, Margaret Bernadette Wells (*d* 1981); two *s* (and one *s* decd); *m* 1983, Linda Wood. *Educ:* Exeter Sch. War of 1939–45 (despatches, MC): enlisted under-age in ranks of The Gloucestershire Regt and served until Nov. 1942; commissioned into newly forming 1st Airborne Div., campaigning in Greece, Italy, S France, to 1945 (despatches 1943). Palestine, 1945–46; Korea, 1950–53 (despatches 1954); Cyprus and Port Said, 1956; Jordan, 1958; College Chief Instructor, RMA Sandhurst, 1959–61; commanded parachute bn in Persian Gulf and Radfan campaign, 1962–65; Col GS to Dir of Borneo Ops, 1965–66; Comdr, 16 Parachute Bde, 1966–68; Defence Fellowship, Exeter Coll., Oxford, 1968–70 (BLitt); DPR (Army), 1970; Comdr, Land Forces, N Ireland, 1970–71; GOC 4th Armoured Div., 1971–73; Dir, Combat Development (Army), 1974–77; GOC SE District, 1977–79. Colonel Commandant: Prince of Wales's Div., 1974–80; Parachute Regt, 1977–83; Col, The Gloucestershire Regt, 1978–84. Pres., UK–Korea Forum, 1991–99. FRSA 1997. *Publications:* The Edge of the Sword, 1954; (ed) The Commander, 1957; The Somme, 1964; Death of an Army, 1968; Airborne Carpet, 1969; War in the Desert, 1969; General Student, 1973; Goughie: the Life of General Sir Hubert Gough, GCB, GCMG, KCVO, 1975; Opening Rounds, 1988; The British Part in the Korean War, vol. I: A Distant Obligation, 1990, vol. II: An Honourable Discharge, 1995; Army in the Air, 1994; contributor: (and associate ed.) The D-Day Encyclopaedia, 1994; Oxford Illustrated History of the British Army, 1994; Oxford Companion to the Second World War, 1995; DNB. *Recreations:* cricket, badminton, sailing, walking. *Address:* c/o National Westminster Bank, 30 Wellington Street, Aldershot, Hants GU11 1EB. *Club:* Savage.

See also Maj.-Gen. C. D. Farrar-Hockley.

FARRAR-HOCKLEY, Maj.-Gen. Charles Dair, MC 1982; Secretary General, Chartered Institute of Arbitrators, since 1999; *b* 2 Dec. 1946; *s* of Gen. Sir Anthony Farrar-Hockley, *qv*; *m* 1969, Vicki King; two *s* one *d*. *Educ:* Exeter Sch. Commissioned Parachute Regt, 1967; Staff Coll., 1978–79; BM, Berlin, 1979–81; Co. Comdr, 2nd Para Bn, 1982, incl. Falkland Islands campaign; MA to Sec. to Chiefs of Staff Cttee, SHAPE, 1983; Directing Staff, Staff Coll., 1984; CO 3rd Para Bn, 1984–86; Special Briefer to COS, SHAPE, 1987; Higher Command and Staff Course, and Service Fellowship, KCL, 1988; Comdr 19 Inf. Bde, 1989–91; RCDS, 1992; Comdr Inf. Training, 1993–95; British Liaison Officer to Czech Chief of Defence, 1995–96; GOC 2nd Div., 1996–99. Chm. of Trustees, Airborne Forces Museum, 1993–; Trustee, Airborne Forces Security Fund, 1998–; Patron, Second World War Experience Centre, 1999–. Freeman, City of London, 1991. *Publications:* articles on causes and effects of human migration. *Recreations:* cricket, cooking, wine, photography. *Address:* c/o Personal Banking Office, National Westminster Bank, Farnborough, Hants GU14 7YU.

FARRELL, David Anthony; QC 2000; a Recorder, since 2000; *b* 27 May 1956; *s* of Joseph Anthony Farrell and Valerie Mabel Farrell; *m* 1981, Sandra Nicole Hibble; four *s* one *d*. *Educ:* Ashby-de-la-Zouch Grammar Sch.; Manchester Univ. (LLB Hons 1977). Called to the Bar, Inner Temple, 1978; Asst Recorder, 1996–2000. *Recreations:* tennis, sailing, walking, music. *Address:* 36 Bedford Row, WC1R 4JH. *T:* (020) 7421 8000.

FARRELL, James Aloysius; Sheriff of Lothian and Borders at Edinburgh, since 1986; *b* 14 May 1943; *s* of James Stoddart Farrell and Harriet Louise McDonnell; *m* 1st, 1967, Jacqueline Allen (marr. diss.); two *d*; 2nd, 1996, Patricia McLaren. *Educ:* St Aloysius College; Glasgow University (MA); Dundee University (LLB). Admitted to Faculty of Advocates, 1974; Advocate-Depute, 1979–83; Sheriff: Glasgow and Strathkelvin, 1984; S Strathclyde, Dumfries and Galloway, 1985. *Recreations:* sailing, hillwalking, cycling. *Address:* 8B Merchiston Park, Edinburgh EH10 4PN.

FARRELL, Michael Arthur; *b* 27 April 1933; *s* of Herbert and Marjorie Farrell; *m* 1st, 1957, Myra Shilton (*d* 1973); two *d*; 2nd, 1976, Beryl Browne. *Educ:* Beverley Grammar Sch., Yorks; Holly Lodge Grammar Sch., Birmingham. Design Draughtsman, 1949–51; Nat. Service, RASC, 1951–53; Planning Engineer, 1953–61; Representative, 1961–74; Sales Manager, Lillywhites Cantabrian, 1974–80; Sales Executive, En-Tout-Cas, 1980–82; Gen. Sec., AAA, subseq. British Athletic Fedn, 1982–91; Export Sales Dir, Cantabrian Athletics Ltd, 1992–93; consultant, 1994–96; restaurateur, 1996–99. *Recreations:* painting, walking, cycling.

FARRELL, Sir Terence, (Sir Terry), Kt 2001; CBE 1996 (OBE 1978); Principal, Terry Farrell & Partners, since 1980; *b* 12 May 1938; *s* of Thomas and Molly Farrell (*née* Maguire); *m* 1st, 1960, Angela Rosemarie Mallam; two *d*; 2nd, 1973, Susan Hilary Aplin; two *s* one *d*. *Educ:* St Cuthbert's Grammar Sch., Newcastle; Newcastle Univ. (BArch, 1st class hons); Univ. of Pennsylvania (MArch, MCP). ARIBA 1963; MRTPI 1970; FCSD (FSIAD 1981). Harkness Fellow, Commonwealth Fund, USA, 1962–64. Partner in Farrell Grimshaw Partnership, 1965–80. Major projects include: redevelt of Charing Cross Station; Edinburgh Internat. Conf. Centre; British Consulate-Gen., Hong Kong; Vauxhall Cross (MI6), London; Kowloon Station, Hong Kong; Internat. Centre for Life, Newcastle; Deep Aquarium, Hull. *Exhibitions:* RIBA Heinz Gall., London, 1987; RIBA, London, 1995. Comr, English Heritage, 1990–96. Vis. Prof., Univ. of Westminster, 1998–2001. Hon. FRIAS 1996; Hon. FAIA 1998. Hon. DCL Newcastle, 2000. *Publications:* Architectural Monograph, 1985; Urban Design Monograph, 1993; articles in numerous British and foreign jls; *relevant publications:* Terry Farrell: selected and current works, 1994; Ten Years: Ten Cities: the work of Terry Farrell & Partners 1991–2001. *Recreations:* walking, swimming. *Address:* (office) 7 Hatton Street, NW8 8PL.

FARRELL, Timothy Robert Warwick; Organist, Liberal Jewish Synagogue, St John's Wood, since 1975; *b* 5 Oct. 1943; *m* 1st, 1975, Penelope Walmsley-Clark (marr. diss. 1995); one *s*; 2nd, 1996, Jane Emmanuel. *Educ:* Diocesan Coll., Cape Town; Royal Coll. of Music, London; Paris, etc. FRCO, ARCM (piano and organ). Asst Organist, St Paul's, Knightsbridge, 1962–66; Asst Organist, St Paul's Cath., 1966–67; Sub-organist, Westminster Abbey, 1967–74; Organ Tutor at Addington Palace, RSCM, 1966–73; Organist, Choirmaster and Composer, HM Chapels Royal, 1974–79. Broadcaster, recordings, electronic and orchestral music, etc. *Recreations:* golf, walking, sailing, flying. *Address:* Liberal Jewish Synagogue, 28 St John's Wood Road, NW8 7HA. *T:* (020) 7286 5181.

FARRELLY, (Christopher) Paul; MP (Lab) Newcastle-under-Lyme, since 2001; *b* Newcastle-under-Lyme, 2 March 1962; *s* of late Thomas Farrelly and of Anne Farrelly (*née* King); *m* 1998, Victoria Parry; one *s*. *Educ:* St Edmund Hall, Oxford (BA Hons PPE). Manager, Corporate Finance Div., Barclays de Zoete Wedd, 1984–90; Corresp., Reuters Ltd, 1990–95; Dep. City and Business Ed., Independent on Sunday, 1995–97; City Ed., The Observer, 1997–2001. *Recreations:* Rugby, football, writing. *Address:* House of Commons, SW1A 0AA. *T:* (020) 7219 8262. *Clubs:* Trentham Rugby Union Football, Finchley Rugby Football; Holy Trinity Catholic (Newcastle-under-Lyme).

FARREN, Dr Sean; Member (SDLP) Antrim North, since 1998, and Minister of Higher and Further Education, Training and Employment, since 1999, Northern Ireland Assembly; *m* 1967, Patricia Clarke; one *s* three *d*. *Educ:* National Univ. of Ireland (BA 1960; HDE 1961); Essex Univ. (MA 1970); Univ. of Ulster (DPhil 1989). Teacher, Sierra Leone, Switzerland, Ireland, 1961–68; University Lectr in Educn, Univ. of Ulster, 1970–98. Fellow, Saltzburg Internat. Seminar, 1989. Contested (SDLP) Antrim N, 2001. *Publications:* The Politics of Irish Education 1920–1965, 1995; (with Robert Mulvihill) Paths to a Settlement in Northern Ireland, 1999; contributed to: Motivating the Majority—Modern Languages, Northern Ireland, 1991; Whose English, 1994; Irish Educational Documents, Vol. III, 1995; Language, Education and Society in a Changing World, 1996; A New History of Ireland, Vol. VII, 1998; Fiction, Multi-media and Intertextuality in Mother Tongue Education, 1998; contribs to Aspects of Educn, History of Educn, Etudes Irlandaises, Lang. Culture and Curriculum, Oxford Internat. Rev., Southeastern Pol Rev.; res. reports. *Recreations:* reading, swimming, cycling, theatre. *Address:* 30 Station Road, Portstewart, Co. Derry BT55 7DA. *T:* (028) 7083 3042.

FARRER, (Arthur) Mark; DL; Partner, Farrer & Co., 1968–99; *b* 25 March 1941; *s* of Hugh Frederick Francis Farrer and Elizabeth Mary Cross; *m* 1969, Zara Jane Thesiger; one *d*. *Educ:* Eton. Admitted solicitor, 1966. Chairman: Essex Water Co., 1992–96 (Dir, 1986–96; Dep. Chm., 1987); Suffolk Water Co., 1992–96 (Dir, 1990–96); Dir, Lyonnaise Europe, 1989–96. Mem. Council, Lloyd's, 1988–91; Chm., Assoc. of Lloyd's Members Ltd, 1991–92. DL Essex, 1996. *Publications:* articles in learned jls. *Recreations:* gardening, salmon fishing, the steam railway. *Address:* The Brick House, Finchingfield, Essex CM7 4LB. *T:* (01371) 810283; 56 Sangomore, Durness by Lairg, Sutherland IV27 4PZ. *Clubs:* Brooks's; Celer et Audax (Winchester).

FARRER, His Honour Brian Ainsworth; QC 1978; a Circuit Judge, 1985–2001; *b* 7 April 1930; *s* of A. E. V. A. Farrer and Gertrude (*née* Hall); *m* 1960, Gwendoline Valerie (*née* Waddoup), JP; two *s* one *d*. *Educ:* King's Coll., Taunton; University Coll., London (LLB). Called to the Bar, Gray's Inn, 1957. A Recorder, 1974–85. *Recreations:* golf, music, chess, bridge. *Clubs:* Aberdovey Golf; Sutton Coldfield Golf.

FARRER, Sir (Charles) Matthew, GCVO 1994 (KCVO 1983; CVO 1973); Private Solicitor to the Queen, 1965–94; Partner in Messrs Farrer & Co., Solicitors, 1959–94; *b* 3 Dec. 1929; *s* of late Sir (Walter) Leslie Farrer, KCVO, and Hon. Lady Farrer; *m* 1962, Johanna Creszentia Maria Dorothea Bennhold; one *s* one *d*. *Educ:* Bryanston Sch.; Balliol Coll., Oxford (MA). A Trustee, British Museum, 1989–99; Comr, Royal Commn on Historical Manuscripts, 1991–; Mem., British Library Bd, 1994–2000. Trustee, Lambeth Palace Library, 1991–. Pres., Selden Soc., 2001–. *Recreations:* travel, reading. *Address:* 6 Priory Avenue, Bedford Park, W4 1TX. *T:* (020) 8994 6052.

FARRER, Rt Rev. David; *see* Farrer, Rt Rev. R. D.

FARRER, David John; QC 1986; a Recorder, since 1983; *b* 15 March 1943; *s* of John Hall Farrer and Mary Farrer; *m* 1969, Hilary Jean Bryson; two *s* one *d*. *Educ:* Queen Elizabeth's Grammar Sch., Barnet; Downing Coll., Cambridge (MA, LLB). Called to the Bar, Middle Temple, 1967, Bencher, 1998; in practice, 1968–; Mem., Bar Council, 1986–; Chm., Bar Services Cttee, 1989–. Contested (L): Melton, 1979; Rutland and Melton, 1983. *Recreations:* tennis, cricket, Liberal Party politics. *Address:* 7 Bedford Row, WC1R 4BU. *T:* (020) 7242 3555; The Grange, Hoby, Melton Mowbray, Leics LE14 3DT. *T:* (01664) 434232. *Club:* National Liberal.

FARRER, Mark; *see* Farrer, A. M.

FARRER, Sir Matthew; *see* Farrer, Sir C. M.

FARRER, Rt Rev. (Ralph) David; *see* Wangaratta, Bishop of.

FARRER, William Oliver, CVO 1991; Senior Partner, Farrer & Co., Solicitors, 1976–91 (Partner, 1955–91); *b* 23 June 1926; *s* of John Oliver Farrer, MC, and Winifred Millicent Farrer; *m* 1st, 1955, Margery Hope Yates (*d* 1976); two *s* one *d*; 2nd, 1979, Hazel Mary Andrew. *Educ:* Eton Coll.; Balliol Coll., Oxford (MA). Lieut, Coldstream Guards, 1945–48. Admitted a Solicitor, 1953; Solicitor to the Duchy of Lancaster, 1984–91; Mem., Solicitors' Disciplinary Tribunal, 1986–94. Dir, Sotheby's, 1992–96. Mem. Council, Inst. of Cancer Res., 1994–2001. *Recreations:* golf, music. *Address:* Popmoor, Fernhurst, Haslemere, Surrey GU27 3LL. *T:* (01428) 642564. *Clubs:* Brooks's, MCC; Royal and Ancient (St Andrews); Honourable Company of Edinburgh Golfers.

FARRIMOND, Herbert Leonard, CBE 1977; retired; Adviser, The Associated Octel Company Ltd, 1982–88; Chairman, H. L. Farrimond & Associates Ltd, 1978–88; *b* 4 Oct. 1924; *s* of late George and Jane Farrimond, Newcastle upon Tyne; *m* 1951, Patricia Sara (*née* McGrath); one *s*. *Educ:* St Cuthbert's Grammar Sch., Newcastle upon Tyne; Durham

Univ. BA (Hons) Politics and Economics. Lieut RM, 1943–46. Australian Dept of Labour and Nat. Service, 1948–50; Imperial Chemical Industries Ltd, and Imperial Metal Industries Ltd, 1950–68; Upper Clyde Shipbuilders Ltd, 1968–69; Dir of Personnel, Dunlop Ltd, 1970–72; Mem., British Railways Bd, 1972–77. Director: British Rail Engineering Ltd; British Rail Shipping and Internat. Services Div.; Transmark Ltd (Chm.); Portsmouth and Sunderland Newspapers Ltd, 1978–80; Chm., British Transport Hotels, 1976–78. Adviser to industrial and commercial cos, 1978–88. Mem. Council, Advisory, Conciliation and Arbitration Service, 1974–78. Part-time Mem., British Waterways Bd, 1980–82. Governor, British Transport Staff Coll. Ltd, 1972–77. FCIT; FIPD. *Recreations:* golf, gardening, music. *Address:* 9 Ardgare, Shandon, Helensburgh, Argyle and Bute G84 8NW. *T:* (01436) 820803.

FARRINGTON, family name of **Baroness Farrington of Ribbleton**.

FARRINGTON OF RIBBLETON, Baroness *cr* 1994 (Life Peer), of Fulwood in the County of Lancashire; **Josephine Farrington;** a Baroness in Waiting (Government Whip), since 1997; *b* 29 June 1940; *m* 1960, Michael James Farrington; three *s.* Lancashire County Council: Mem., 1977; Chm., 1992; Chm., Educn Cttee, 1981–91. Association of County Councils: Chm., Policy Cttee, 1993–94; Leader, Labour Gp, 1987–94; Vice-Chm., 1990–94; Chm., 1994–96. Mem., Consultative Council for Local Govt Finance, 1987–. UK Rep., Cttee of the Regions, 1994– (Chm., Educn and Trng Cttee, 1994–). Pres., Council of Europe Cttee for culture, educn and the media, 1989–94. UK European Woman of the Year, 1994. *Address:* 114 Victoria Road, Fulwood, Preston, Lancs PR2 4NN. *T:* (01772) 718836.

FARRINGTON, Rev. Canon Christine Marion; Vicar of St Mark's, Cambridge, since 1996; Chaplain to the Queen, since 1998; *b* 11 June 1942; *d* of late Wilfred Bourne Farrington and of Doris Violet Farrington. *Educ:* Cheshunt Grammar Sch.; Birkbeck Coll., London (BA Hons); Univ. of Nottingham (Dip. in Applied Social Studies); Univ. of Middlesex (MA in Deviancy and Social Policy); St Albans MTS. Ordained deaconess 1982, deacon, 1987, priest, 1994. Asst librarian, 1960–62; primary school teacher, 1962–65; probation officer, Hemel Hempstead, 1967–71; social work lectr, Middlesex Poly., 1971–79; sen. probation officer, Harrow, 1979–86; asst prison chaplain, 1986–87; Asst Dir of Pastoral Studies, Lincoln Theol Coll., 1986–87; Deacon, Salisbury Cathedral, 1987–93; Dir, Sarum Christian Centre, 1987–93; Co-Diocesan Dir of Ordinands and Dir of Women's Ministry, Dio. of Ely, 1993–; Hon. Canon, Ely Cathedral, 1993–. Hon. Chaplain: Wolfson Coll., Cambridge, 1993–; St John Ambulance Bde, Cambs, 2000–. *Recreations:* gardening, walking, entertaining, reading, theatre and concerts. *Address:* St Mark's Vicarage, Barton Road, Cambridge CB3 9JZ. *T:* (01223) 363339.

FARRINGTON, Prof. David Philip, PhD; FBA 1997; Professor of Psychological Criminology, University of Cambridge, since 1992; *b* 7 March 1944; *s* of William Farrington and Gladys Holden (*née* Spurr); *m* 1966, Sally Chamberlain; three *d. Educ:* Clare Coll., Cambridge (BA, MA, PhD Psychology). On staff of Cambridge Univ. Inst. of Criminology, 1969–: Reader in Psychol Criminology, 1988–92; Fellow, Darwin Coll., Cambridge, 1980–83. Mem., Parole Bd for England and Wales, 1984–87. Chm., Div. of Criminological and Legal Psychology, British Psychological Soc., 1983–85; President: British Soc. of Criminology, 1990–93; Europ. Assoc. of Psychology and Law, 1997–99; Amer. Soc. of Criminology, 1998–99. Vice-Chm., US Nat. Acad. of Scis Panel on Violence, 1989–92; Co-Chairman: US Office of Juvenile Justice and Delinquency Prevention Study Gp on Serious and Violent Juvenile Offenders, 1995–97, on Very Young Offenders, 1998–2000; High Security Psychiatric Services Commng Bd, Network on Primary Prevention of Adult Antisocial Behaviour, DoH, 1997. Chm., UK Dept, Health Adv. Cttee, Nat. Prog. on Forensic Mental Health, 2000–. FMedSci 2000. Sellin-Glueck Award, Amer. Soc. of Criminology, 1984. *Publications:* Who Becomes Delinquent?, 1973; The Delinquent Way of Life, 1977; Behaviour Modification with Offenders, 1979; Psychology, Law and Legal Processes, 1979; Abnormal Offenders, Delinquency and the Criminal Justice System, 1982; Aggression and Dangerousness, 1985; Reactions to Crime, 1985; Prediction in Criminology, 1985; Understanding and Controlling Crime, 1986; Human Development and Criminal Behaviour, 1991; Offenders and Victims, 1992; Integrating Individual and Ecological Aspects of Crime, 1993; Psychological Explanations of Crime, 1994; Building a Safer Society, 1995; Understanding and Preventing Youth Crime, 1996; Biosocial Bases of Violence, 1997; Serious and Violent Juvenile Offenders, 1998; Antisocial Behaviour and Mental Health Problems, 1998; Evaluating Criminology and Criminal Justice, 1998; Sex and Violence, 2001; Offender Rehabilitation in Practice, 2001; Child Delinquents, 2001; Costs and Benefits of Preventing Crime, 2001. *Address:* Institute of Criminology, 7 West Road, Cambridge CB3 9DT. *T:* (01223) 335384.

FARRINGTON, Sir Henry Francis Colden, 7th Bt *cr* 1818; RA retired; *b* 25 April 1914; *s* of Sir Henry Anthony Farrington, 6th Bt, and Dorothy Maria (*d* 1969), *o d* of Frank Farrington; *S* father, 1944; *m* 1947, Anne, *e d* of late Major W. A. Gillam, DSO; one *s* one *d. Educ:* Haileybury. Retired from Army, 1960 (Major; now Hon. Col). *Heir: s* Henry William Farrington, ARICS [*b* 27 March 1951; *m* 1979, Diana Donne Broughton, *yr d* of Geoffrey Broughton, Somerset; two *s*]. *Address:* Higher Ford, Wiveliscombe, Taunton, Somerset TA4 2RL. *T:* (01984) 623219.

FARROW, Christopher John; Chairman, Aga Foodservice Group, since 2001; *b* 29 July 1937; *s* of late Thomas and Evangeline Dorothea Farrow; *m* 1961, Alison Brown; one *s* one *d. Educ:* Cranleigh Sch.; King's Coll., Cambridge (BA). Board of Trade, 1961; Harkness Fellowship and visiting scholar, Stanford Univ., USA, 1968–69; Private Sec. to Pres. of BoT and Minister for Trade, 1970–72; Dept of Trade and Industry, 1972–74; Cabinet Office, 1975–77; Dept of Industry, 1977–83; Asst Dir, Bank of England, 1983–87; Dir, Kleinwort, Benson Ltd, 1987–92; Dir-Gen., British Merchant Banking and Securities Houses, then London Investment Banking, Assoc., 1993–99. Director: London Metal Exchange Ltd, 1987–99 (Vice Chm., 1997–99); Glynwed International, 1993–2001 (Chm., 2000–01). Member: Engrg Council, 1984–86; Financial Reporting Review Panel, 1992–. *Recreation:* gardening. *Address:* 45 Alleyn Park, SE21 8AT.

FARROW, Christopher John; Managing Director, North, Welsh Development Agency, since 1998; *b* 19 Nov. 1947; *s* of Sydney A. Farrow; *m* 1980, Susan Thomas; three *d. Educ:* Claysmore Sch., Dorset; Univ. of London (BA Hons); Polytechnic of Central London (DipTP Dist.). London Borough of Newham, 1974–81; Dir, LDDC, 1981–91; Chief Exec., Merseyside Develt Corp., 1991–98. Director: Greenland Dock Develt Co., 1985–90; Mersey Partnership, 1992–98. MRTPI. FRSA 1993. *Publications:* planning papers on urban develt and economy. *Address:* Welsh Development Agency, Unit 7, St Asaph Business Park, Glascoed Road, St Asaph LL17 0LJ.

FARROW, Mia (Villiers); actress; *b* 9 Feb. 1945; *d* of late John Villiers Farrow and Maureen O'Sullivan; *m* 1970, André Previn (marr. diss. 1979), *qv*; three *s* two *d*; one *s* by Woody Allen, *qv. TV series:* Peyton Place, 1965; *films:* Secret Ceremony, 1968; Rosemary's Baby, 1969; John and Mary, 1970; The Public Eye, 1972; The Great Gatsby, 1974; Full Circle, Death on the Nile, A Wedding, 1978; Hurricane, 1980; A Midsummer Night's Sex Comedy, 1982; Zelig, 1983; Broadway Danny Rose, 1984; The Purple Rose of Cairo, 1985; Hannah and her Sisters, 1986; Radio Days, 1987; September, 1988; Another Woman, 1989; Crimes and Misdemeanours, 1990; Alice, 1990; Husbands and Wives, 1992; Shadows and Fog, 1992; Miami Rhapsody, 1995; Reckless, 1995; *stage:* The Importance of Being Earnest, NY, 1963; Mary Rose, Shaw, 1973; The Three Sisters, Greenwich, 1974; The House of Bernarda Alba, Greenwich, 1974; Peter Pan, 1975; The Marrying of Ann Leete, RSC, 1975; The Zykovs, Ivanov, RSC, 1976; A Midsummer Night's Dream, Leicester, 1976; Romantic Comedy, NY, 1979. David Donatello Award, Italy, 1969; Best Actress awards: French Academy, 1969; San Sebastian, 1969; Rio de Janeiro, 1970. *Publication:* What Falls Away (memoirs), 1997. *Address:* Bridgewater, CT, USA.

FARTHING, Bruce; *see* Farthing, R. B. C.

FARTHING, Prof. Michael John Godfrey, MD; FRCP; Professor of Medicine and Executive Dean, Faculty of Medicine, University of Glasgow, since 2000; *b* 2 March 1948; *s* of Dennis Jack Farthing and Joan Margaret Farthing (*née* Godfrey); *m* 1979, Alison Mary McLean; two *s. Educ:* Henry Thornton Sch., London; University Coll., London (BSc); UCH Med. Sch. (MB BS); MD London 1981. FRCP 1988. Res. Fellow, St Mark's Hosp., 1974; Med. Registrar, Addenbrooke's Hosp., 1975–77; Res. Fellow and Hon. Lectr, 1977–80, Wellcome Tropical Lectr, 1980–83, St Bart's Hosp.; Vis. Asst Prof., Tuft's Univ. Sch. of Medicine, 1981–83; St Bartholomew's Hospital Medical College, subseq. St Bartholomew's and Royal London Hospital School of Medicine and Dentistry, QMW: Wellcome Sen. Lectr, 1983–91; Prof. and Head of Dept of Gastroenterology, 1990–2000; Dir, Digestive Diseases Res. Centre, 1990–2000; Dean, Faculty of Clin. Medicine, 1995–97. Hon. Consultant: St Mark's Hosp., 1987–; St Luke's Hosp. for Clergy, 1990–; to the Army, 1991–. Non-exec. Dir, E London and City HA, 1998–2000. Chm., Cttee on Publication Ethics, 1997–. Hon. Sec., British Soc. of Gastroenterology, 1990–94; Pres., Eur. Assoc. of Gastroenterology and Endoscopy, 1998–. Founder FMedSci 1998. Editor, Gut, 1996–. *Publications:* Enteric Infection: mechanisms, manifestations and management, vol. 1 1989, vol. 2 1995; Clinical Challenges in Gastroenterology, 1996; many papers on intestinal disorders. *Recreations:* theatre, modern literature, jazz, running, watersports. *Address:* Faculty of Medicine, University of Glasgow, 11 Southpark Terrace, Glasgow G12 8LG.

See also S. F. G. Farthing.

FARTHING, (Richard) Bruce (Crosby); Chairman, 1999–2000, President, since 2001, Maritime London; *b* 9 Feb. 1926; *s* of late Col Herbert Hadfield Farthing and late Marjorie Cora (*née* Fisher); *m* 1st, 1959, Anne Brenda Williams (marr. diss. 1986), LLB, barrister, *d* of late Thomas Williams, solicitor; one *s* one *d*; 2nd, 1986, Moira Roupell, *o d* of late Lt-Col R. A. Curties and late Ida Curties. *Educ:* Alleyns Sch., (Dulwich and Rossall) St Catharine's Coll., Cambridge (MA). Commissioned RA and RHA, 1944–48. Called to Bar, Inner Temple, 1954; Govt Legal Service, 1954–59; joined Chamber of Shipping of the United Kingdom, 1959; Asst General Manager, 1966; Secretary, Cttee of European Shipowners and Cttee of European National Shipowners' Assocs, 1967–74; Secretary-General, Council of European and Japanese National Shipowners' Assocs (CENSA), 1974–76; Director, 1976–80, Dep. Dir-Gen., 1980–83, General Council of British Shipping. Rapporteur, Sea Transport Commn, ICC, 1976–96; Consultant Dir, Internat. Assoc. of Dry Cargo Shipowners, 1984–99. Freeman, City of London, 1979; Liveryman, Shipwrights' Co., 1982–; Mem. Court of Common Council (Aldgate Ward), 1981–. Pres., Aldgate Ward Club, 1985 (Vice-Pres., 1984). Governor: City of London Sch., 1983– (Dep. Chm., 1988–89, 1993–94, Chm., 1990–93); SOAS, 1985–2000; GSM, 2001–; Mem. Council, City Univ., 1994–98. Mem. Court, Hon. Irish Soc., 1992–94. Trustee, Nautical Museums Trust, 1983–2001. Mem., British Cttee, Registro Italiano Navale, 1997–. Chm., King of Norway Reception Cttee, 1988. FIMgt. Commander, Royal Norwegian Order of Merit, 1988. *Publications:* ed, Vol. 20, Aspinalls Maritime Law Cases, 1961; International Shipping, 1987, 3rd edn 1997. *Recreations:* sailing, music, gardening. *Address:* 44 St George's Drive, SW1V 4BT; Snaylham House, Icklesham, E Sussex TN36 4AT. *Clubs:* MCC, Royal Ocean Racing; Rye Golf.

FARTHING, Stephen Frederick Godfrey, RA 1998; Executive Director, New York Academy of Art, since 2000; *b* 16 Sept. 1950; *s* of Dennis Jack Farthing and Joan Margaret (*née* Godfrey); *m* 1975, Joni Elizabeth Jackson; one *d. Educ:* St Martin's Sch. of Art; Royal Coll. of Art; British Sch. at Rome. Lectr in Painting, Canterbury Coll. of Art, 1977–79; Tutor in Painting, RCA, 1980–85; Head of Painting, W Surrey Coll. of Art and Design, Farnham, 1985–90; Ruskin Master of Drawing, Oxford Univ., and Professorial Fellow, St Edmund Hall, Oxford, 1990–2000, now Emeritus Fellow. Artist in Residence, Hayward Gall., London, 1989. *One-man shows* include: Nat. Mus. of Modern Art, Kyoto; Museo Carrillo Gil, Mexico City; Arnolfini, Bristol; Edward Totah Gall., London. British School at Rome: Mem., Council, 1998–; Chm., Arts Faculty, 1998–. *Publication:* The Intelligent Persons Guide to Modern Art, 2000. *Recreations:* watercolours, tennis. *Address:* New York Academy of Art, 111 Franklin Street, New York, NY10013, USA. *T:* (212) 966 0300.

See also M. J. G. Farthing.

FARVIS, Prof. William Ewart John, CBE 1978 (OBE 1972); BSc, BSc(Eng), CEng, Hon. FIEE; FRSE; engineering consultant; Professor Emeritus of Electrical Engineering, University of Edinburgh (Professor, 1961–77); *b* 12 Dec. 1911; *o s* of late William Henry Farvis and Gertrude Anne Farvis; *m* 1939, Margaret May Edmonstone Martin; one *s* one *d. Educ:* Queen Elizabeth's Hosp., Bristol; Bristol and London Univs. Lectr, University Coll., Swansea, 1937–40 and 1945–48; Air Ministry, Telecommunications Res. Estab., 1940–45; Lectr/Sen. Lectr, Edinburgh Univ., 1948–61, Prof. and Head of Dept of Electrical Eng., 1961–77, Chairman, Sch. of Engineering Sci. 1972–75. Mem., British Nat. Cttee for Radio Science, 1960–66; Science Research Council: Mem., Electrical and Systems Cttee, 1968–72; Engineering Board, 1972–75 and 1976–81; Polytechnics Cttee, 1975–78; Chm., Solid-state Devices Panel, 1972–75; Electrical and Systems Cttee 1972–75; Advanced Ground Transport Panel 1975–80; Mem. Council, 1976–81. Mem. Council, IEE, 1972–75 and 1976–79; Hon. FIEE 1987. Editor, Microelectronics Journal, 1976–78. *Recreation:* music. *Address:* 14 Cluny Terrace, Edinburgh EH10 4SW. *T:* (0131) 447 4939. *Club:* Athenæum.

FASHAM, Dr Michael John Robert, FRS 2000; Senior Principal Scientific Officer, Southampton Oceanography Centre, since 1993; *b* 29 May 1942; *s* of Ronald Henry Alfred Fasham and Hazel Grace Fasham (*née* Day); *m* 1967, Jocelyn Mary Hart; one *s. Educ:* Kilburn Grammar Sch.; Birmingham Univ. (BSc; PhD 1968). Sen. Geophysicist, Wimpey Labs, 1967–68; SSO, Nat. Inst. Oceanography, 1968–73; PSO, Inst. Oceanographic Scis, 1973–93. *Publications:* (ed) Flows of Energy and Materials in Marine Ecosystems: theory and practice, 1984; (ed jtly) Towards a Model of Ocean Biogeochemical Processes, 1993; contrib. papers to oceanographic jls. *Recreations:* genealogy, British history, gardening. *Address:* White Cottage, Hill Road, Grayshott, Hindhead, Surrey GU26 6HL. *T:* (01428) 606119.

FASSETT, Kaffe; textile designer; *b* 7 Dec. 1937; *s* of William Elliot Fassett and Madeleine Fassett. Self-educated. Retrospective exhibitions: Tokyo, 1986; V&A Museum, 1989;

Copenhagen, Stockholm, Oslo, Melbourne, Toronto and Helsinki, 1990; Vancouver, Holland, 1993; Osaka, Iceland, 1996; Minneapolis, 1997. *Publications:* Glorious Knitting, 1985; Glorious Needlepoint, 1987; Kaffe Fassett at the V & A, 1988, 4th edn, as Glorious Colour, 1991; Family Album, 1989; Glorious Inspiration, 1991; Kaffe's Classics, 1994; Glorious Interiors, 1995; Patchwork, 1997; Mosaics, 1999. *Address:* c/o Random Century, 20 Vauxhall Bridge Road, SW1V 2SA.

FATAYI-WILLIAMS, Hon. Atanda, GCON 1983; CFR 1980; Chief Justice of Nigeria, 1979–83; *b* 22 Oct. 1918; *s* of Alhaji Issa Williams and Alhaja Ashakun Williams; *m* 1948, Irene Violet Lofts; three *s*. *Educ:* Methodist Boys' High Sch., Lagos, Nigeria; Trinity Hall, Cambridge (BA 1946, LLM 1947, MA 1949; Hon. Fellow 1983). Called to the Bar, Middle Temple, 1948. Private practice, Lagos, 1948–50; Crown Counsel, Lagos, 1950–55; Dep. Comr for Law Revision, Western Nigeria, 1955–58; Chief Registrar, High Court of Western Nigeria, 1958–60; High Court Judge, 1960–67; Justice of Appeal, Western State Court of Appeal, 1967–69; Justice, Supreme Court of Nigeria, 1969–79. Mem., Council of State, 1983–84, 1990–. Chairman: Ports Arbitration Bd, 1971; All Nigeria Law Reports Cttee, 1972–75; Body of Benchers, 1979–80; Legal Practitioners' Privileges Cttee, 1979–83; Federal Judicial Service Commn, 1979–83; Judiciary Consultative Cttee, 1979–83; National Archives Cttee, 1979–83; Presidential Cttee on Medical Doctors' Remuneration, 1990; Bd of Trustees, The Van Leer Nigerian Educn Trust, 1973–85; Crescent Bearers, Lagos, 1978–84; Council of Legal Educn, 1984–. Mem., Nigerian Inst. of Internat. Affairs, 1972–97. Trustee, Nigerian Youth Trust, 1979–84. Hon. Fellow, Nigerian Inst. of Advanced Legal Studies, 1983; Life FRSA 1949. Presidential Award for outstanding service to the Judiciary, Nigeria, 1992. *Publications:* (ed) Western Nigeria Law Reports, 1955–58; (with Sir John Verity) Revised Laws of the Western Region of Nigeria, 1959; Sentencing Processes, Practices and Attitudes, as seen by an Appeal Court Judge, 1970; Faces, Cases and Places (autobiog.), 1983. *Recreations:* reading, swimming, walking. *Address:* 8 Adetokunbo Ademola Street, Victoria Island, Lagos, Nigeria. *T:* (1) 611315. *Clubs:* Athenæum, Oxford and Cambridge; Metropolitan (Lagos).

FATEH, Abul Fazal Muhammad Abul; Hon. Representative of Royal Commonwealth Society in Bangladesh, 1985–94; *b* 28 Feb. 1926; *s* of Abdul Gafur and Zohra Khatun; *m* 1956, Mahfuza Banu; two *s*. *Educ:* Dhaka, Bangladesh. MA (English Lit.); special course, LSE, 1949–50. Carnegie Fellow in Internat. Peace, 1962–63. Entered Pakistan Foreign Service, 1949; 3rd Secretary: Paris, 1951–53; Calcutta, 1953–56; 2nd Sec., Washington, DC, 1956–60; Dir, Min. of Foreign Affairs, Karachi, 1961–65; 1st Sec., Prague, 1965–66; Counsellor, New Delhi, 1966–67; Dep. High Comr for Pakistan, Calcutta, 1968–70; Ambassador of Pakistan, Baghdad, 1971; Adviser to Actg President of Bangladesh, Aug. 1971; Foreign Sec., Bangladesh, Jan. 1972; Ambassador of Bangladesh to France and Spain, 1972–75; Permanent Deleg. to UNESCO, 1972–76; High Comr for Bangladesh in London, 1976–77; Ambassador, Algeria, 1977–82. Leader, Bangladesh Delegation: Commonwealth Youth Ministers' Conf., Lusaka, 1973; Meeting of UN Council on Namibia, Algiers, 1980; Ministerial Meeting of Non-aligned Countries Co-ordination Bureau on Namibia, Algiers, 1981. Chm., Commonwealth Human Ecology Council Symposium, 1977. Mem., Poetry Soc., 1994–99. *Address:* 9a Linhope Street, NW1 6ES.

FATT, Prof. Paul, FRS 1969; Emeritus Professor, University of London, since 1989. Professor of Biophysics, University College, London, 1976–89 (Reader, 1956–76); Fellow, UCL, 1973. *Publications:* papers in various scientific jls. *Address:* 25 Tanza Road, NW3 2UA. *T:* (020) 7435 9802.

FAULKNER, family name of **Baron Faulkner of Worcester**.

FAULKNER OF DOWNPATRICK, Lady; Lucy (Barbara Ethel) Faulkner, CBE 1985; *b* 1 July 1925; *d* of William John Forsythe and Jane Ethel Sewell; *m* 1951, Arthur Brian Deane Faulkner (MP (NI) 1949–73; PC 1959; *cr* Baron Faulkner of Downpatrick, 1977) (killed in a hunting accident, 1977); two *s* one *d*. *Educ:* Aubrey House; Bangor Collegiate Sch.; Trinity College Dublin. BA (Hons History). Journalist, Belfast Telegraph, 1947; Personal Secretary to Sir Basil Brooke, Prime Minister of N Ireland, 1949. Nat. Governor for NI, BBC, 1978–85; Chm., Broadcasting Council for NI, 1981–85; Researcher, 1977, Trustee 1980–, Ulster Historical Foundation; Mem., NI Tourist Bd, 1985–91. Governor, Linenhall Library, 1982–. Hon. LLD QUB, 1994. *Recreations:* hunting and dressage, genealogy, book collecting. *Address:* Toberdoney, Farranfad, Downpatrick BT30 8NH. *T:* (028) 4481 1712.

FAULKNER OF WORCESTER, Baron *cr* 1999 (Life Peer), of Wimbledon in the London Borough of Merton; **Richard Oliver Faulkner;** Director, Cardiff Millennium Stadium plc, since 1997; Strategy Adviser, Incepta Group plc, since 1999; *b* 22 March 1946; *s* of late Harold Ewart and Mabel Faulkner; *m* 1968, Susan Heyes; two *d*. *Educ:* Merchant Taylors' Sch., Northwood; Worcester Coll., Oxford (MA PPE). Research asst and journalist, Labour Party, 1967–69; PRO, Construction Ind. Trg Bd, 1969–70; Editor, Steel News, 1971; Account dir, F. J. Lyons (PR) Ltd, 1971–73; Dir, PPR International, 1973–76; communications advisor: to Leader of the Opposition and Labour Party (unpaid), gen. elections, 1987, 1992, 1997; to the Bishop at Lambeth, 1990; Govt relations adviser: rly trade unions, 1975–76; C. A. Parsons & Co., 1976–77; Pool Promoters Assoc., 1977–99; British Rlys Bd, 1977–97; Prudential Assurance Co., 1978–88; IPU, 1988–90; Southampton City Council, 1989–91; CAMRA, 1989; Barclays de Zoete Wedd, 1990–92; Standard Life Assurance, 1990–99; S Glam CC, 1991–96; Cardiff CC, 1996–99; Cardiff Bay Develt Corp., 1993–98; Littlewoods Orgn, 1994–99; FSA, 1998–99; Actg Hd of Communications, SIB, 1997; Jt Man. Dir, Westminster Communications Gp, 1989–97; Dep. Chm., Citigate, Westminster, 1997–99. Dept Liaison Peer, DETR, 2000–01, Cabinet Office, 2001–; Treas., All Party Railways Gp, 2000–; Sec., British-Norwegian Parly Gp, 2000–; Vice-Chm., British-Caribbean Parly Gp, 2000–; British-Taiwanese Parly Gp, 2001–; Jt Treas., British-Swedish Parly Gp. 2001–. Football Trust: Foundn Trustee, 1979–82; Sec., 1983–86; First Dep. Chm., 1986–98; Chm., Sports Grounds Initiative, 1995–2000; Vice Chm., Govt's Football Task Force, 1997–99; Member: Sports Council, 1986–88; Football League enquiry into membership schemes, 1984, anti-hooliganism cttee, 1987–90; Dir, Brighton and Hove Albion Football Club, 1997–; former Dir, Wimbledon and Crystal Palace Football Clubs; Chm., Women's Football Assoc., 1988–91. Vice-Chm., 1986–99, Vice-Pres., 2000–, Transport 2000 Ltd. Chm., Worcester Coll. Appeal, 1996–. Mem., Merton Borough Council, 1971–78; contested (Lab) Devizes 1970, Feb. 1974, Monmouth, Oct. 1974, Huddersfield W, 1979. Co-founder, parly jl The House mag. *Recreations:* collecting Lloyd George memorabilia, tinplate trains, watching Association Football, travelling by railway. *Address:* House of Lords, SW1A 0PW; *e-mail:* faulknerro@parliament.uk.
See also D. E. R. Faulkner.

FAULKNER, David Ewart Riley, CB 1985; Senior Research Associate, University of Oxford Centre for Criminological Research, since 1992; *b* 23 Oct. 1934; *s* of Harold Ewart and Mabel Faulkner; *m* 1961, Sheila Jean Stevenson; one *s* one *d*. *Educ:* Manchester Grammar Sch.; Merchant Taylors' Sch., Northwood; St John's Coll., Oxford (MA Lit Hum). Home Office: Asst Principal, 1959; Private Sec. to Parly Under-Sec. of State, 1961–63; Principal, 1963; Jt Sec. to Inter-Party Conf. on House of Lords Reform, 1968; Private Sec. to Home Sec., 1969–70; Asst Sec., Prison Dept, 1970, Establishment Dept, 1974, Police Dept, 1976; Asst Under-Sec. of State, 1976; Under Sec., Cabinet Office, 1978–80; Home Office; Asst Under-Sec. of State, Dir of Operational Policy, Prison Dept, 1980–82; Dep. Under-Sec. of State, 1982; Head of Criminal and Res. and Statistical Depts, 1982–90; Principal Estab. Office, 1990–92. Fellow, St John's Coll., Oxford, 1992–99. Chm., Howard League for Penal Reform, 1999–. Member: UN Cttee on Crime Prevention and Control, 1984–91; Adv. Bd, Helsinki Inst. for Crime Prevention and Control, 1988–93; Council, Magistrates' Assoc., 1992–98; Council, Justice, 1993–97; Commn on the Future of Multi-Ethnic Britain, 1998–2000. Trustee, Mental Health Foundn, 1992–96, and other charities. *Publications:* Darkness and Light, 1996; Crime, State and Citizen, 2001; contribs to jls. *Recreations:* railways, birds. *Address:* c/o Centre for Criminological Research, 12 Bevington Road, Oxford OX2 6LH.
See also Baron Faulkner of Worcester.

FAULKNER, Sir Dennis; *see* Faulkner, Sir J. D. C.

FAULKNER, Prof. Douglas, WhSch, BSc, PhD; FREng, FRINA, FIStructE, FSNAME; RCNC; consulting structural engineer and naval architect, since 1995; Head of Department of Naval Architecture and Ocean Engineering, University of Glasgow, 1973–95, now Emeritus Professor; *b* 29 Dec. 1929; *s* of Vincent and Florence Faulkner; *m* 1st, 1954, Jenifer Ann Cole-Adams (marr. diss. 1986); three *d*; *m* 2nd, 1987, Isobel Parker Campbell. *Educ:* Sutton High Sch., Plymouth; HM Dockyard Technical Coll., Devonport; RNC, Greenwich. Aircraft Carrier Design, 1955–57; Production Engrg, 1957–59; Structural Research at NCRE, Dunfermline, 1959–63; Asst Prof. of Naval Construction, RNC, Greenwich, 1963–66; Structural Adviser to Ship Dept, Bath, 1966–68; Naval Construction Officer att. to British Embassy, Washington DC, 1968–70, and Mem. Ship Research Cttee, Nat. Acad. of Scis, 1968–71; Res. Associate and Defence Fellow, MIT, 1970–71; Structural Adviser to Ship Dept, Bath, and to the Merrison Box Girder Bridge Cttee, 1971–73. UK Rep., Standing Cttee, Internat. Ship Structures Congress, 1973–85. Chm., Conoco-ABS cttee producing a design code for Tension Leg Platforms offshore, 1981–83; Dir, Veritec Ltd, 1985–88; Mem. Bd of Govs, BMT Quality Assessors Ltd, 1990–93. Technical Assessor, Lord Donaldson of Lymington's Assessment, MV Derbyshire, Dept of Transport, 1995–97; Ind. Expert Witness, re-opened formal investigation into loss of MV Derbyshire, 2000. President: Instn of Engrs and Shipbuilders in Scotland, 1995–97; Whitworth Soc., 1997–98. FREng (FEng 1981). FRSA 1983–99. Consulting Editor, Jl of Marine Structures, 1990–99 (Editor, 1987–90). Hon. DSc Technical Univ. of Gdansk, 1993. David W. Taylor Medal, SNAME, 1991; William Froude Medal, RINA, 1993; Peter the Great Medal, St Petersburg Univ. of Ocean Technology, 1993. *Publications:* (ed jtly) Integrity of Offshore Structures, 1981; Integrity of Offshore Structures—3, 1987; Integrity of Offshore Structures—4, 1990; Integrity of Offshore Structures—5, 1993; chapters in Ship Structural Design Concepts (Cornell Maritime Press), 1975; papers related to structural design of ships, in Trans RINA, Jl of Ship Res., Behaviour of Offshore Structures, etc. *Recreations:* hill walking, swimming, music, chess. *Address:* 4 Murdoch Drive, Milngavie, Glasgow G62 6QZ. *T:* (0141) 956 5071.

FAULKNER, Graham John; Chief Executive, National Society for Epilepsy, since 2000; *b* 26 Sept. 1948; *s* of William and Edna Faulkner; *m* 1st, 1975, Jennifer Barkway (marr. diss. 1998); one *s* one *d*; 2nd, 1999, Dorothy, (Dee), Napier. *Educ:* UC of Swansea (BSc Hons Psychol. 1970); Univ. of Leicester (postgrad. res.); Univ. of Birmingham (CQSW 1984; MSocSc). Local Govt O R Unit, RIPA, 1973–75; Planning Dept, 1975–77, Social Services Dept, 1977–85, Warwickshire CC; Dir, Retirement Security Ltd, 1985–92; Dir and Gen. Sec., Leonard Cheshire Foundn, 1992–98; Chief Exec., Rehab UK, 1999–2000. *Publications:* contributor to: White Media and Black Britain, 1975; Solving Local Government Problems, 1981; This Caring Business, 1988; contrib. jls and res. reports. *Recreations:* theatre, music, watching Coventry City! *Address:* 9 Parry Cottages, Chesham Lane, Chalfont St Peter, Bucks SL9 0RN. *T:* (01494) 874293.

FAULKNER, Gregory; *see* Faulkner, L. G.

FAULKNER, Sir (James) Dennis (Compton), Kt 1991; CBE 1980; VRD 1960; DL; Chairman, Marlowe Cleaners Ltd, since 1973; *b* 22 Oct. 1926; *s* of James and Nora Faulkner; *m* 1952, Janet Cunningham (*d* 1994); three *d*. *Educ:* College of St Columba, Co. Dublin. Served RNVR, 1946–71; UDR, 1971–92 (Col Comdt, 1986–92). Chairman: Belfast Collar Co. Ltd, 1957–63; Belfast Savings Bank, 1960–61; NI Develt Agency, 1978–82; Board Member: Gallaher NI, 1980–89 (Chm., 1982–89); Northern Bank Ltd, 1983–96; Chm., Ladybird (NI) Ltd, 1963–88; Dir, Giants Causeway and Bushmills Railway Co. Ltd, 1999–.Farming, 1946–. Mem., Strangford Lough Management Cttee, 1992– (Chm., 1992–97); Chm., Ulster, North Down and Ards Hosp. Trust, 1993–94. Pres., RBL NI, 1992–2000. DL County Down, 1988. *Recreations:* sailing, hunting, ocean racing. *Address:* Northern Ireland. *Clubs:* Royal Ocean Racing, Royal Cruising; Royal Yacht Squadron; Ocean Cruising; Irish Cruising; Strangford Lough Yacht; Cruising Club of America (New York).

FAULKNER, John Richard Hayward; theatre and management consultant; international impresario; *b* 29 May 1941; *s* of Richard Hayward Ollerton and Lilian Elizabeth (*née* Carrigan); *m* 1970, Janet Gill (*née* Cummings) (*d* 1994); two *d*, and two step *d*; *m* 2001, Christie Dickason; two step *s*. *Educ:* Archbishop Holgate's Sch., York; Keble Coll., Oxford (BA). Worked with a number of theatre companies, Prospect Productions, Meadow Players, Century Theatre, Sixty-Nine Theatre Co., Cambridge Theatre Co., toured extensively, UK, Europe, Indian Sub-Continent, Australia, 1960–72; Drama Director: Scottish Arts Council, 1972–77; Arts Council of GB, 1977–83; Head, Artistic Planning, Nat. Theatre, 1983–88. Mem., Assessors' Panel, Nat. Lottery Dept, Arts Council, 1996–. Director: Minotaur Films, 1988–; Visionhaven Ltd, 1991–; New Zoo Develts Ltd, 1992–. Member: Pubns & Communication Commn, Orgn Internat. des Scénographes, Techniciens et Architectes de Théâtre, 1994– (Chm., 1999–2001); Internat. Soc. for the Performing Arts, 1997–; Council, Assoc. of British Theatre Technicians, 1998–2001 (sometime Chm.); Sec., Pleasance Theatre Trust, 1997–. Trustee: The Arts Educational Schools, 1986–92; The Arts for Nature, 1990–99; Performing Arts Labs, 1991–2001; Pension Scheme for Admin. and Tech. Staff in the Arts, 1996–; Orange Tree Th. Trust, 1998– (Jt Chm., 1999–). *Recreations:* intricacies and wildernesses. *Address:* 28 Ellesmere Road, Chiswick W4 4QH. *T:* (020) 8995 3041.

FAULKNER, (Leo) Gregory; HM Diplomatic Service; Ambassador to Chile, since 2000; *b* 21 Sept. 1943; *s* of late James and of Teresa Faulkner; *m* 1970, Fiona Hardie (*née* Birkett); three *d*. *Educ:* Manchester Univ. (BA Hons Spanish). FCO, 1968–72; Lima, 1972–76; Lagos, 1976–79; EC Internal Dept, FCO, 1979–82; Head of Chancery, Madrid, 1982–84; Head, Internat. Telecoms Br., DTI, 1984–86, on secondment; Commercial Counsellor, The Hague, 1986–90; Dep. Head of Mission, Buenos Aires, 1990–93; Head, Latin America Dept, FCO, 1993–96; High Commissioner, Trinidad and Tobago, 1996–99. *Recreations:* tennis, golf, watching cricket, football and Rugby. *Address:* c/o Foreign and Commonwealth Office, SW1A 2AH. *Club:* Canning.

FAULKNER, Most Rev. Leonard Anthony; *see* Adelaide, Archbishop of, (RC).

FAULKS, Edward Peter Lawless; QC 1996; a Recorder, since 2000; *b* 19 Aug. 1950; *s* of His Honour Peter Faulks, MC; *m* 1990, Catherine Frances Turner, *d* of Lindsay Turner and Anthea Cadbury; two *s*. *Educ:* Wellington Coll.; Jesus Coll., Oxford (MA). FCIArb. Called to the Bar, Middle Temple, 1973; Literary Agent, Curtis Brown, 1980–81; Asst Recorder, 1996–2000. *Publication:* (contributing ed.) Local Authority Liabilities, 1998. *Recreation:* cricket. *Address:* 33 Ladbroke Grove, W11 3AY; 1 Serjeant's Inn, Fleet Street, EC4Y 1BQ. *T:* (020) 7415 6666. *Club:* Garrick.
See also S. C. Faulks.

FAULKS, Esmond James; His Honour Judge Faulks; a Circuit Judge, since 1993; *b* 11 June 1946; *s* of Hon. Sir Neville Faulks, MBE, TD and Bridget Marigold (*née* Bodley); *m* 1972, Pamela Margaret Ives; one *s* one *d*. *Educ:* Uppingham Sch.; Sidney Sussex Coll., Cambridge (Exhibitioner; MA). Called to the Bar, Inner Temple, 1968; a Recorder, 1987–93. *Recreations:* country pursuits. *Address:* c/o Combined Court Centre, Quayside, Newcastle upon Tyne NE1 2TH.

FAULKS, Sebastian Charles; author and journalist; *b* 20 April 1953; *s* of His Honour Peter Ronald Faulks, MC and of Pamela (*née* Lawless); *m* 1989, Veronica Youlten; two *s* one *d*. *Educ:* Wellington Coll.; Emmanuel Coll., Cambridge. Editor, New Fiction Society, 1978–81; Daily Telegraph, 1978–82; feature writer, Sunday Telegraph, 1983–86; Literary Editor, Independent, 1986–89; Dep. Editor, 1989–90, Associate Editor, 1990–91, Independent on Sunday; columnist: The Guardian, 1992–98; London Evening Standard, 1997–99; Mail on Sunday, 1999–2000. Writer and presenter, Churchill's Secret Army (television), 2000. FRSL 1995. *Publications:* A Trick of the Light, 1984; The Girl at the Lion d'Or, 1989; A Fool's Alphabet, 1992; Birdsong, 1993; The Fatal Englishman, 1996; Charlotte Gray, 1998; (ed with Jörg Hensgen) The Vintage Book of War Stories, 1999; On Green Dolphin Street, 2001; contribs to newspapers and magazines. *Address:* c/o Gillon Aitken Associates, 29 Fernshaw Road, SW10 0TG.
See also E. P. L. Faulks.

FAULL, David Wenlock, OBE 1993; Consultant, Winckworth & Pemberton, since 1990 (Senior Partner, 1985–90); *b* 25 Feb. 1929; *s* of Eldred Faull and Mary Jessie Faull (*née* Wenlock). *Educ:* Taunton School. Qualified Solicitor, 1954; joined Winckworth & Pemberton, 1978; Diocesan Registrar: St Albans, 1960–79; Chelmsford, 1960–89; Southwark, 1960–93; London, 1969–97; Dep. Registrar, Dio. of Europe, 1980; Legal Sec., Bishop of Rochester, 1960–98; Registrar, Dio. Rochester, 1997–98; Chapter Clerk and Solicitor to St Paul's Cathedral, 1981–2000. Mem., Legal Adv. Commn, C of E, 1988–94. Mem., Solicitors' Disciplinary Tribunal, 1992–2001. Chm., Ecclesiastical Law Assoc., 1988–90; Treasurer, Ecclesiastical Law Soc., 1986–95. Founder Mem., Paddington Church's Housing Assoc., 1961; Board Member: Hastoe (formerly Sutton and Hastoe) Housing Assoc., 1987–; Wyvern Housing Assoc., 2000–. Chm., Christian Children's Fund (GB), 1992–98. Mem., Co. of Parish Clerks, 1991. MA Lambeth 1997. *Recreations:* walking, theatre, Cornish history. *Address:* Lanteglos House, St Thomas Street, Wells BA5 2UZ. *T:* (01749) 675334. *Club:* Athenæum.

FAULL, Jonathan Michael Howard; Director General, Press and Communication (formerly Head of Press and Communication Service), since 1999, and Spokesman, since 2000, European Commission; *b* 20 Aug. 1954; *s* of Gerald Faull and June Faull (*née* Shepherd); *m* 1979, Sabine Garrel; two *s*. *Educ:* Univs of Sussex and Geneva (BA); Coll. of Europe, Bruges (MA). European Commission, 1978–: Administrator, then Principal Administrator, various depts, 1978–87; Asst to Dir Gen., Directorate Gen. for Competition, 1987–89; Mem., Cabinet of Sir Leon Brittan, Vice-Pres., EC, 1989–92; Directorate General for Competition: Hd, Unit IV/D/3, Transport and Tourism, 1992–93; Hd, Unit IV/E/1, Co-ordination and Gen. Policy, 1993–95; Dir, Competition Policy, Co-ordination, Internat. Affairs and Relns with other Instns, 1995–99; Dep. Dir Gen. of Competition, 1999. Prof. of Law, Free Univ. of Brussels, 1989–; Vis. Lectr, Inst. d'Etudes Politiques, Paris, 1992–95; Vis. Fellow, Centre for Eur. Legal Studies, Cambridge Univ., 1997–. Mem., editl or adv. boards of various law jls, incl. Common Market Law Reports, Eur. Business Law Rev., UK Competition Law Reports, and World Competition Review; EC corresp., Eur. Law Review, 1980–89. *Publications:* contrib. articles on various topics of EC law and policy. *Address:* Rue de la Loi, Wetstraat 200, 1049 Brussels, Belgium. *T:* (322) 2958658.

FAULL, Very Rev. Vivienne Frances; Dean of Leicester, since 2000; *b* 20 May 1955; *d* of William Baines Faull and Pamela June Faull (*née* Dell); *m* 1993, Dr Michael Duddridge. *Educ:* Queen's Sch., Chester; St Hilda's Coll., Oxford; St John's Coll., Nottingham; Open Univ. Ordained deaconess, 1982, deacon, 1987, priest, 1994. Teacher, N India, 1977–79; youth worker, Everton, 1979; Deaconess, St Matthew and St James, Mossley Hill, 1982–85; Chaplain: Clare Coll., Cambridge, 1985–90; Gloucester Cathedral, 1990–94; Canon Pastor, 1994–2000, Vice Provost, 1995–2000, Coventry Cathedral. *Address:* 21 St Martin's, Leicester LE1 5DE.

FAURE WALKER, Edward William; Vice Lord-Lieutenant, Hertfordshire, since 2001; farmer; *b* 14 Sept. 1946; *s* of Lt Col Henry W. Faure Walker and Elizabeth A. C. Faure Walker (*née* Fordham); *m* 1974, Louise Mary Robinson; two *s* one *d*. *Educ:* Eton; RMA, Sandhurst. Commnd Coldstream Guards, 1966–74 (C-in-C's Commendation for Courage and Leadership 1971). Farmer at Sandon Bury, 1974–. Chm., 1980–2000, Pres., 2000–, Herts Assoc. for Young People; Trustee, UK Youth, 1998–. Chm., Boxworth Exptl Husbandry Farm, 1988–93. DL 1985, High Sheriff 2000–01, Herts. *Recreations:* country sports, running, mountaineering, reading, travelling, being at home with family. *Address:* Sandon Bury, Sandon, Buntingford, Herts SG9 0QY. *T:* (01763) 287224. *Club:* Alpine.

FAUSET, Ian David; Executive Director, Defence Procurement Agency, Ministry of Defence, since 1999; *b* 8 Dec. 1943; *s* of late George William Fauset and Margaret Fauset (*née* Davies); *m* 1972, Susan, *d* of Donald and Gwendolen Best; two *s* one *d*. *Educ:* Chester City Grammar Sch.; King Edward VI Sch., Lichfield; University of London (BSc); UCW Aberystwyth (Dip. Statistics). CEng, FRAeS. Dept of Chief Scientist (RAF), MoD, 1968–78; Head of Air Studies, Defence Optl Analysis Orgn, Germany, 1978–82; fast jet aircraft and helicopter projects, MoD (PE), 1982–87; Civilian Management (Specialists), MoD, 1987–89; Project Dir, Tornado Aircraft, 1989, EH 101 Helicopter, 1989–91, MoD (PE); Asst Under-Sec. of State, Civilian Mgt (Personnel), MoD, 1991–96; Dir Gen. Aircraft Systems 2, MoD (PE), 1996–99. Non-exec. Dir, GEC Avery, 1991–94. *Recreations:* bridge, cricket, tennis, squash, rowing (mainly watching now). *Address:* Ministry of Defence, Abbey Wood #2, Bristol BS34 8JH. *Club:* Royal Air Force.

FAUVELLE, Major Michael Henry; barrister-at-law; *b* 12 Aug. 1920; *s* of Victor Edmond Fauvelle and Brigid Mary Fauvelle (*née* Westermann); *m* 1964, Marie-Caroline, *e d* of Count and Countess Stanislas d'Orsetti, Château de la Grènerie, Jarzé, France; one *s* one *d*. *Educ:* Stonyhurst Coll.; Royal Military Coll., Sandhurst. Commissioned, 2/Lieut The South Lancashire Regt, 1939, T/Major 1944; active service in N Africa, Italy and Palestine (wounded three times, arguably five); Staff employment as GSO 3 (Ops), Gibraltar, 1947; Staff Captain Q HQ Palestine, 1947–48; Staff Captain A HQ BMM to Greece and HQ 2 Inf. Bde, 1948–50; Adjt 1st Bn, 1951; Major 1952; retired, 1953. Called to the Bar, Lincoln's Inn, 1955; Western Circuit and Hampshire Sessions, 1955–; Dep. Recorder, Oxford, Bournemouth and Reading, 1971; a Dep. Circuit Judge, 1972–79; a Recorder, 1979–92; Hd of Chambers at 17 Carlton Crescent, Southampton, 1975–82. Pres., Pensions Appeal Tribunals for England and Wales, 1987–93 (a Chm., 1983–93; Dep. Pres., 1984–87). Lord Chancellor's Legal Visitor, 1983–90. *Recreations:* travel by sea, forestry, avoiding stress. *Address:* Tadley Cottage, Wherwell, Hampshire SP11 7JU. *T:* (01264) 860217, *Fax:* (01264) 861254. *Club:* Home Guard (Wherwell, Hants).

FAVELL, Anthony Rowland; solicitor; *b* 29 May 1939; *s* of Arnold Rowland Favell and Hildegard Favell; *m* 1966, Susan Rosemary Taylor; one *s* one *d*. *Educ:* St Bees School, Cumbria; Sheffield University (LLB). MP (C) Stockport, 1983–92; PPS to Rt Hon. John Major, MP, 1986–90. Contested (C) Stockport, 1992. Chm., Tameside and Glossop Acute Services NHS Trust, 1993–97. Part-time Chairman: Mental Health Review Tribunals, 1995–; FHSA Appeal Tribunals, 1996–; Mem., Criminal Injuries Appeal Panel, 2000–. *Recreations:* music, gardening, hill walking, dry stone walling. *Address:* Skinners Hall, Edale, Hope Valley S33 7ZE. *T:* (01433) 670281. *Club:* Lansdowne.

FAWCETT, John Harold, CMG 1986; HM Diplomatic Service, retired; *b* 4 May 1929; *yr s* of late Comdr Harold William Fawcett, OBE, RN, and of late Una Isobel Dalrymple Fawcett (*née* Gairdner); *m* 1961, Elizabeth Shaw; one *s*. *Educ:* Radley (Scholar); University Coll., Oxford (Scholar). 1st cl. Hon. Mods 1951, 2nd cl. Lit. Hum. 1953. Nat. Service, RN (Radio Electrician's Mate), 1947–49. British Oxygen Co., 1954–63 (S Africa, 1955–57). Entered Foreign Service, 1963; FO, 1963–66; 1st Sec. (Commercial), Bombay, 1966–69; 1st Sec. and Head of Chancery, Port-of-Spain, 1969–70; Asst, Caribbean Dept, FCO, 1971–72; Head of Icelandic Fisheries Unit, Western European Dept, FCO, 1973; Amb. to Democratic Republic of Vietnam, 1974; Counsellor and Head of Chancery, Warsaw, 1975–78; Dep. High Comr, Wellington, 1978–86; Counsellor (Commercial and Economic, 1978–83, Political and Economic, 1983–86), and Head of Chancery 1983–86, Wellington; Amb. to Bulgaria, 1986–89. Mem., 1998–, Chm., 2000–, Dent Parish Council. Mem., 1989–94, Lay Chm., 1994–99, Ewecross Deanery Synod, dio. of Bradford. Trustee: Bradford Dio. Church Buildings Fund, 1996–99; Sedbergh and Dist Community Trust, 1998–. Chm., Morecambe Bay Gp, CS Pensioners' Alliance, 1994–2000. Clerk, 1989–94, Chm. of Govs, 1994–2001, Dent Grammar Sch. Educnl Foundn; Governor, Dent C of E Primary Sch., 1994–99. *Recreations:* gardening, collecting books, mathematical models. *Address:* Strait End, Dent, Cumbria LA10 5QL. *Clubs:* Savile, MCC; Wellington Racing (Wellington); Royal Bombay Yacht.

FAWCETT, Kay-Tee; *see* Khaw, Kay-Tee.

FAWCUS, Maj.-Gen. Graham Ben, CB 1991; Chief of Staff and Head of UK Delegation, Live Oak, SHAPE, 1989–91, retired; *b* 17 Dec. 1937; *s* of late Col Geoffrey Arthur Ross Fawcus, RE and Helen Sybil Graham (*née* Stronach); *m* 1966, Diana Valerie, *d* of Dr P. J. Spencer-Phillips of Bildeston, Suffolk; two *s* one *d*. *Educ:* Wycliffe College; RMA Sandhurst (Sword of Honour); King's College, Cambridge (BA 1963, MA 1968). Commissioned RE, 1958; served UK, Cyprus, BAOR, MoD; OC 39 Field Squadron RE, BAOR, 1973–74; MoD, 1975–76; GSO1 (DS), Staff College, 1977–78; CO 25 Engineer Regt, BAOR, 1978–81; Cabinet Office, 1981; Comdt, RSME, 1982–83; ACOS, HQ 1 (Br) Corps, 1984–85; Chief, Jt Services Liaison Orgn, Bonn, 1986–89. Col Comdt RE, 1991–2000. Chm., RE Widows Soc., 1992–2000. Gov., Wycliffe Coll., 1995–. *Recreations:* ski-ing, tennis, Scottish country dancing, furniture restoration. *Address:* Flowton Hall, Flowton, Ipswich, Suffolk IP8 4LH.

FAWCUS, Sir (Robert) Peter, KBE 1964 (OBE 1957); CMG 1960; Overseas Civil Service, retd; *b* 30 Sept. 1915; *s* of late A. F. Fawcus, OBE; *m* 1943, Isabel Constance (*née* Ethelston) (*d* 2001); one *s* one *d*. *Educ:* Charterhouse; Clare Coll., Cambridge. Served RNVR, 1939–46 (Lt-Comdr). Joined Colonial Service (District Officer, Basutoland), 1946; Bechuanaland Protectorate: Govt Sec., 1954; Resident Commissioner, 1959; HM Commissioner, 1963–65; retd 1965. *Publication:* Botswana: the road to independence, 2000. *Address:* Dochart House, Killin, Perthshire FK21 8TN.

FAWCUS, Simon James David; His Honour Judge Fawcus; a Circuit Judge, since 1985; *b* 12 July 1938; *s* of late Ernest Augustus Fawcus and of Jill Shaw; *m* 1966, Joan Mary (*née* Oliphant); one *s* four *d*. *Educ:* Aldenham Sch.; Trinity Hall, Cambridge (MA). Called to the Bar, Gray's Inn, 1961; in practice on Northern Circuit, 1962–85; a Recorder, 1980–85. Pres., Council of Circuit Judges, 1996. *Recreations:* real tennis and other lesser sporting activities, music (listening). *Address:* Courts of Justice, Crown Square, Manchester M3 3FL. *Clubs:* MCC; Manchester Tennis and Racquet, Big Four (Manchester); Circuit Judges Golfing Soc.; Wilmslow Golf.

FAWKES, Sir Randol (Francis), Kt 1977; Attorney-at-Law, 1948–89; *b* 20 March 1924; *s* of Edward Ronald Fawkes and Mildred Fawkes (*née* McKinney); *m* 1951, Jacqueline Fawkes (*née* Bethel); three *s* one *d*. *Educ:* public schools in the Bahamas. Called to the Bar, Bahamas, 1948. A founder: Citizen Cttee, 1949; People's Penny Savings Bank, 1951. Elected Mem. (Progressive Liberal Party), House of Assembly, 1956; promoted law establishing Labour Day as Public Holiday, 1961. Founder, Pres. 1955, and now Vice Pres., Bahamas Fedn of Labour (led 19 day general strike which resulted in major labour and political reforms, 1958). Represented Labour Party at constitutional confs in London, 1963 and 1968; addressed UN Cttee of 24 on preparation of Bahamas for independence, 1966. Gen Sec., Bahamas Assoc. of former Mems of Parlt, 1990. *Publications:* You Should Know Your Government, 1949; The Bahamas Government, 1962; The New Bahamas, 1966; The Faith That Moved The Mountain: a memoir of a life and the times, 1977; Majority of One: the first 450 of the PLP–Labour Coalition, 1987. *Recreations:* swimming, music, Bible tract writing. *Address:* PO Box N-7625, John F. Kennedy Drive, Nassau, NP, Bahamas. *T:* (328) 3277.

FAWKES, Wally; cartoonist, since 1945; *b* 21 June 1924; *m* 1st, 1949, Sandra Boyce-Carmichelle; one *s* two *d*; 2nd, 1965, Susan Clifford; one *s* one *d*. *Educ:* Sidcup Central Sch.; Sidcup Sch. of Art; Camberwell Sch. of Art. Came from Vancouver, BC, to England, 1931. Joined Daily Mail, 1945; started Flook strip, 1949, transferred to The Mirror, 1984. Political cartoons for: Spectator, 1959–; Private Eye, and New Statesman, 1965–; Observer, 1965–95; Punch, 1971–92; Today, 1986–87; London Daily News, 1987; Times mag., 1995–96; Sunday Telegraph, 1996–; cartoons for Daily Express, 1994–; covers for The Week, 1997–. Co-Founder, Humphrey Lyttelton Band, 1948. Hon. DLitt Kent, 2001. *Publications:* World of Trog, 1977; Trog Shots, 1984; Trog: 40 Graphic Years, 1987; collections of Flook strips. *Recreations:* playing jazz (clarinet and soprano saxophone), cooking, cricket. *Address:* 44 Laurier Road, NW5 1SJ. *T:* (020) 7267 2979. *Clubs:* MCC, Middlesex County Cricket.

FAY, Dr Christopher Ernest, CBE 1999; FREng; Chairman: Advisory Committee on Business and the Environment, since 1999; Expro International Group plc, since 1999; *b*

4 April 1945; *s* of Harry Thomas Fay and Edith Margaret Fay (*née* Messenger); *m* 1971, Jennifer Olive Knight; one *s* two *d*. *Educ:* Leeds Univ. (BSc Civil Eng. 1967; PhD 1970). CEng 1974; FICE 1994 (MICE 1973; Hon. FICE 1998); FInstPet 1994; FREng (FEng 1996). Joined Shell Internat. Petroleum Co., 1970, as offshore design engr; Shell-BP Develt Co., Nigeria, 1971–74; Head, Engrg Planning and Design and Offshore Construction, Sarawak Shell Berhad, Malaysia, 1974–78; Develt Manager, Dansk Undergrunds Consortium, Copenhagen, on secondment from Dansk Shell, 1978–81; Technical Manager, Norske Shell Exploration and Production, Stavanger, 1981–84; Dir, Exploration and Production, Norway, 1984–86; Gen. Manager and Chief Exec., Shell Cos, Turkey, 1986–89; Man. Dir, Shell UK Exploration and Production and a Man. Dir, Shell UK, 1989–93; Chm. and Chief Exec., Shell UK, 1993–98. Non-executive Director: BAA, 1998–; Stena Internat., 1999–; Stena Drilling Ltd, 1999–; Anglo American plc, 1999–. Member: CBI President's Cttee, 1993–98; INSEAD UK Cttee, 1993–95; British Cttee, Det. Norske Veritas, 1994–95 and 1996–; Bd, Oil, Gas and Petrochemicals Supplies (formerly Oil and Gas Projects and Supplies) Office, 1994–98; Exec. Cttee, British Energy Assoc., 1994–98; Chm., Oil Industries Emergency Cttee, 1993–98. Gov., Motability, 1999– (Mem. Council, 1993–98). CIMgt 1994. FRSE 1996; FRSA 1994. *Recreations:* gardening, ski-ing, golf, tennis. *Address:* Merrifield, Links Road, Bramley, Guildford GU5 0AL. *Clubs:* Sunningdale Golf, Bramley Golf.

FAY, His Honour Edgar Stewart; QC 1956; FCIArb; a Circuit Judge (formerly an Official Referee of the Supreme Court of Judicature), 1971–80; *b* 8 Oct. 1908; *s* of late Sir Sam Fay; *m* 1st, Kathleen Margaret, *e d* of late C. H. Buell, Montreal, PQ, and Brockville, Ont; three *s*; 2nd, Jenny Julie Henriette (*d* 1990), *yr d* of late Dr Willem Roosegaarde Bisschop, Lincoln's Inn; one *s*; 3rd, Eugenia Bishop, *yr d* of late Piero Biganzoli, Milan. *Educ:* Courtenay Lodge Sch.; McGill Univ.; Pembroke Coll., Cambridge (MA). Called to Bar, Inner Temple, 1932; Master of the Bench, 1962. FCIArb 1981. Recorder: of Andover, 1954–61; of Bournemouth, 1961–64; of Plymouth, 1964–71; Dep. Chm., Hants QS, 1960–71. Member: Bar Council, 1955–59, 1966–70; Senate of Four Inns of Court, 1970–72. Chm., Inquiry into Crown Agents, 1975–77. *Publications:* Why Piccadilly?, 1935; Londoner's New York, 1936; Discoveries in the Statute Book, 1937; The Life of Mr Justice Swift, 1939; Official Referees' Business, 1983. *Address:* 95 Highgate West Hill, N6 6NR. *T:* (020) 8348 5780.

FAY, Sir (Humphrey) Michael (Gerard), Kt 1990; Principal, Fay, Richwhite & Co. Ltd, Merchant Bankers, since 1974 (Joint Chief Executive, 1990–96); *b* 10 April 1949; *s* of James and Margaret Fay; *m* 1983, Sarah Williams; one *s* two *d*. *Educ:* St Patrick's Coll., Silverstream, Wellington; Victoria Univ., Wellington (LLB 1971). Jt Chief Exec., Capital Markets, 1986–90; Dir, Bank of New Zealand, 1989–92. Chairman: Australia/NZ Bicentennial Commn, 1988; Expo 1988 Commn, 1987–88; Expo 1992 Commn, 1989–; NZ Ireland Fund, 1995–98. Hon. Consul General for Thailand, 1996–98. Chm., NZ Americas Cup Challenges, 1987, 1988, 1992. Chm., Manu Samoa Rugby Club, 1997–. *Recreations:* horse breeding and racing, fishing, swimming, running, golf. *Address:* 108 Route de Florissant, Geneva, Switzerland. *T:* (022) 839 3370. *Clubs:* Royal New Zealand Yacht Squadron, Auckland Racing, Mercury Bay Boating.

FAY, Margaret; Managing Director, Tyne Tees Television, since 1997; *b* 21 May 1949; *d* of Oswald and Joan Allen; *m* 1st, 1968, Matthew Stoker (marr. diss. 1978); one *s*; 2nd, 1982, Peter Fay (marr. diss. 1993). *Educ:* South Shields Grammar Sch. for Girls. Joined Tyne Tees TV, 1981; Dir of Ops, 1995–97. Dir, Newcastle Gateshead Initiative, 1999–; non-exec. Dir, Darlington Building Soc., 2000–. Gov., Teesside Univ., 1998–. *Recreations:* travel, theatre, wine. *Address:* Tyne Tees Television, City Road, Newcastle upon Tyne NE1 2AL. *T:* (0191) 269 3502.

FAY, Sir Michael; *see* Fay, Sir H. M. G.

FAYERS, Norman Owen; City Treasurer and Director of Financial Services, Bristol City Council, 1990–96; *b* 8 Jan. 1945; *s* of Claude Lance Fayers and Winifred Joyce (*née* Reynolds); *m* 1966, Patricia Ann Rudd; two *s*. *Educ:* Northgate Grammar Sch. for Boys, Ipswich; BA Open Univ. CPFA 1967; IRRV 1990; FMAAT 1999. Ipswich CBC, 1961–66; Eastbourne CBC, 1966–70; Group Accountant (Educn), Royal Borough of Kingston upon Thames, 1970–73; Chief Accountant, RBK & C, 1973–77; Chief Officer, Finance, London Borough of Ealing, 1977–90. Chartered Institute of Public Finance and Accountancy: Mem. Council, 1991–92; Pres., S Wales and W England Reg., 1993–95 (Vice Pres., 1991–93); Mem. Council, Assoc. of Accounting Technicians, 1992–2001. *Recreations:* golf, music, bridge. *Address:* Holly Hill, Ruffet Road, Kendleshire, Winterbourne, Bristol BS36 1AN. *T:* (01454) 250280. *Club:* Kendleshire Golf.

FAYRER, Sir John (Lang Macpherson), 4th Bt *cr* 1896; Research Officer, Moray House Institute, since 1991; *b* 18 Oct. 1944; *s* of Sir Joseph Herbert Spens Fayrer, 3rd Bt, DSC, and Helen Diana Scott (*d* 1961), *d* of late John Lang; *S* father, 1976. *Educ:* Edinburgh Academy; Scottish Hotel School, Univ. of Strathclyde. *Publication:* Child Development from Birth to Adolescence, 1992; ed reports of Scotplay confs, 1993, 1994. *Heir:* none.

FAZIO, Antonio; Governor, Bank of Italy, since 1993; *b* 11 Oct. 1936; *m* Maria Cristina Rosati; one *s* four *d*. *Educ:* Univ. of Rome (BSc *summa cum laude* Econs and Business 1960); MIT. Asst Prof. of Demography, Univ. of Rome, 1961–66; Consultant to Res. Dept, Bank of Italy, 1961–66; Bank of Italy: Dep. Head, subseq. Head, Unit of Econometric Res., 1966–72; Dep. Dir, Monetary Sector, 1972, Head, 1973–79, Res. Dept; Central Manager for Economic Res., 1980–82; Dep. Dir Gen., 1982–93. Chm., Italian Foreign Exchange Office, 1993–; Member: Bd of Dirs, BIS, 1993–; Governing Council, Eur. Central Bank (formerly Eur. Monetary Inst.), 1993–. Hon. Dr Econs and Business, Bari, 1994; Hon. DHL: Johns Hopkins, 1995; Hon. Dr Pol Sci. Macerata, 1996. Ezio Tarantelli Prize for most original theory in Economic Policy, 1995; Saint Vincent Prize for Economics, 1997. Kt Grand Cross, Order of Merit (Italy), 1993. *Publications:* scientific articles, mainly on monetary theory and monetary policy issues. *Address:* Bank of Italy, Via Nazionale 91, 00184 Rome, Italy. *T:* (6) 47921.

FEACHEM, Prof. Richard George Andrew, CBE 1995; PhD, DSc; FREng; Director, Institute for Global Health, University of California, since 1999; *b* 10 April 1947; *s* of Charles George Paulin Feachem and Margaret Flora Denise Greenhow; *m* 1st, 1970, Zuzana Sedlarova (marr. diss. 1999); one *s* one *d*; 2nd, 1999, Neelam Sekhri. *Educ:* Wellington Coll.; Univ. of Birmingham (BSc 1969); Univ. of NSW (PhD 1974); DSc (Med) London, 1991. MICE 1980; FIWEM 1987; FICE 1990; FREng (FEng 1994). Volunteer, Solomon Is, 1965–66; Research Fellow: Univ. of NSW, 1970–74; Univ. of Birmingham, 1974–76; London School of Hygiene and Tropical Medicine: Lectr and Sen. Lectr, 1976–82; Reader, 1983–87; Prof. of Tropical Envmtl Health, 1987–95; Dean, 1989–95; Sen. Advr, Human Develt, 1995–97, Dir, Health, Nutrition and Population, 1997–99, World Bank. Vis. Prof., LSHTM, 1995–; Adjunct Professor: Johns Hopkins Univ., 1996–; George Washington Univ., 1997–. Consultant, WHO, 1982–83; Principal Public Health Specialist, World Bank, 1988–89; Chairman, Advisory Committee: World Develt Report, 1992–93; TB Programme, WHO, 1992–95; Member: Adv. Cttee, Caribbean Epidemiology Centre, 1990–95; Mgt Cttee, Inst. of Child Health, 1989–91; Bd on Internat. Health, US Nat. Acad. of Scis, 1992–97; Bd, Internat. AIDS Vaccine Initiative, 1996–; Adv. Cttee, Aust. Nat. Centre for Epidemiology and Public Health, 1996–; Commn on Macroeconomics and Health, 2000–. Member Council: RSTM&H, 1978–81; VSO, 1991–; Water Aid, 1994–95; Patron, Assoc. for Promotion of Healthcare in former Soviet Union, 1992–96. Trustee Internat. Centre for Diarrhoeal Diseases Research, Bangladesh, 1985–89. Hon. FFPHM 1990. Member, Editorial Board: Transactions of the RSTM&H, 1979–88; Jl of Tropical Medicine and Hygiene, 1979–96; Current Issues in Public Health, 1993–; Health and Human Rights, 1993–; Tropical Medicine and Internat. Health, 1996–; Editor-in-Chief, WHO Bulletin, 1999–. *Publications:* Water, Wastes and Health in Hot Climates, 1977; Subsistence and Survival: rural ecology in the Pacific, 1977; Water, Health and Development, 1978; Evaluation for Village Water Supply Planning, 1980; Sanitation and Disease, 1983; Environmental Health Engineering in the Tropics, 1983; Evaluating Health Impact, 1986; Disease and Mortality in Sub-Saharan Africa, 1991; The Health of Adults in the Developing World, 1992; over 140 papers in scientific jls. *Recreations:* mountaineering, ski-ing. *Address:* 121 Creedon Circle, Alameda, CA 94502, USA. *T:* (510) 5211365. *Club:* Travellers.

FEARN, family name of **Baron Fearn.**

FEARN, Baron *cr* 2001 (Life Peer), of Southport in the County of Merseyside; **Ronald Cyril Fearn, (Ronnie),** OBE 1985; *b* 6 Feb. 1931; *s* of James Fearn and Martha Ellen Fearn; *m* 1955, Joyce Edna Dugan; one *s* one *d*. *Educ:* King George V Grammar School. FCIB. Banker with Williams Deacons Bank, later Williams & Glyn's Bank, later Royal Bank of Scotland. MP (L 1987–88, LibDem 1988–92 and 1997–2001) Southport; contested (Lib Dem) Southport, 1992. Lib Dem spokesman on health and tourism, 1988–89, on local govt, 1989–90, on transport, housing and tourism, 1990–92. Mem., Select Cttee on Culture, Media and Sport, 1997–2001. Councillor, Sefton MBC, 1974–. *Recreations:* badminton, amateur dramatics, athletics. *Address:* House of Lords, SW1A 0PW; Norcliffe, 56 Norwood Avenue, Southport, Merseyside PR9 7EQ. *T:* (01704) 228577.

FEARN, John Martin, CB 1976; Secretary, Scottish Education Department, 1973–76, retired; *b* 24 June 1916; *s* of William Laing Fearn and Margaret Kerr Fearn; *m* 1947, Isobel Mary Begbie, MA, MB, ChB; one *d*. *Educ:* High Sch. of Dundee; Univ. of St Andrews; Worcester Coll., Oxford. Indian Civil Service, Punjab, 1940–47; District Magistrate, Lahore, 1946; Scottish Home Dept, 1947; Under-Sec., 1966; Under-Sec., Scottish Educn Dept, 1968. Chairmen's Panel, CSSB, 1977–85. *Recreation:* golf. *Address:* 10/8 St Margaret's Place, Edinburgh EH9 1AY. *T:* (0131) 447 5301. *Club:* New (Edinburgh).

FEARN, Sir (Patrick) Robin, KCMG 1991 (CMG 1983); HM Diplomatic Service, retired; Associate Director, Centre for Political and Diplomatic Studies, Oxford, since 2000; *b* 5 Sept. 1934; *s* of late Albert Cyprian Fearn and Hilary (*née* Harrison); *m* 1961, Sorrel Mary Lynne Thomas; three *s* one *d*. *Educ:* Ratcliffe Coll.; University Coll., Oxford (BA Hons, Mod. Langs). Nat. Service, Intelligence Corps, 1952–54. Overseas marketing, Dunlop Rubber Co. Ltd, 1957–61; entered Foreign Service, 1961; FO, 1961–62; Third, later Second Sec., Caracas, 1962–64; Havana, 1965; First Sec., Budapest, 1966–68; FCO, 1969–72; Head of Chancery, Vientiane, 1972–75; Asst Head of Science and Technol. Dept, FCO, 1975–76; Counsellor, Head of Chancery and Consul Gen., Islamabad, 1977–79; Head of S America Dept, FCO, 1979–82; Head of Falkland Islands Dept, FCO, 1982; RCDS, 1983; Ambassador to Cuba, 1984–86; Asst Under-Sec. of State (Americas), FCO, 1986–89; Ambassador to Spain, 1989–94. Dir, Foreign Service Prog., Oxford Univ., and Vis. Fellow, UC, Oxford, 1995–99. Trustee, Imperial War Mus., 2001–. Chm., Anglo-Spanish Soc., 1999–. Mem. Council, Univ. of Bath, 2000–. *Recreations:* tennis, music, reading, family life. *Address:* c/o Barclays Bank, 9 Portman Square, W1A 3AL. *Club:* Oxford and Cambridge.

FEARNLEY, David; Vice Lord-Lieutenant, West Yorkshire, 1992–2001; *b* 20 Dec. 1924; *s* of late Wilfred Fearnley and Elizabeth (*née* Walker); *m* 1947, Patricia Bentley; one *s* one *d*. *Educ:* Pocklington Sch., York; Univs of Bradford and Leeds. Served RN, War of 1939–45. Joined family firm, Walter Walker & Sons Ltd, 1945; Dir, 1955; Man. Dir, 1960; co. purchased by Allied Textiles, 1971; Dir, Allied Textiles plc, 1971–99. Chm., Louis Latour Ltd, 1990–; Director: WW Gp Ltd, 1990–99; Sharrow Bay Hotel, 1999–. Gen. Comr of Inland Revenue, Wakefield Div., 1973–2000 (Chm., 1987–99). Mem. Bd, Wakefield Prison, 1979–94. Fellow, Woodard Corp., 1989–95. High Sheriff, W Yorks, 1982–83. *Recreations:* fell walking, wine, tennis (playing), Rugby football (watching). *Address:* The Grange, Hopton, Mirfield, W Yorks WF14 8EL. *Clubs:* Garrick; Leeds (Leeds).

FEARON, Prof. Douglas Thomas, MD; FRS 1999; FRCP; Wellcome Trust Professor of Medicine, University of Cambridge, since 1993; *b* 16 Oct. 1942; *s* of late Dr Henry Dana Fearon and of Frances Hudson (*née* Eubanks); *m* 1st, 1972, Margaret Andrews (marr. diss. 1975); 2nd, 1977, Clare MacIntyre (*née* Wheless); one *s* one *d*. *Educ:* Williams Coll. (BA 1964); Johns Hopkins Med. Sch. (MD 1968). FRCP 1994. Major, US Army Med. Corps, 1970–72 (Bronze Star and Army Commendation Medal, 1972). Med. Res., Johns Hopkins Hosp., 1968–70; Helen Hay Whitney Foundn Post-Doctoral Res. Fellow, 1974–77; Harvard Medical School: Res. Fellow in Medicine, 1972–75; Instr. in Medicine, 1975–76; Asst Prof., 1976–79, Associate Prof., 1979–84, Prof., 1984–87, of Medicine; Prof. of Medicine, and Director, Div. of Rheumatology and of Grad. Prog. in Immunology, Johns Hopkins Univ. Sch. of Medicine, 1987–93. Principal Res. Fellow, Wellcome Trust, 1993–; Hon. Consultant in Medicine, Addenbrooke's Hosp., 1993–. Member: Scientific Adv. Bd, Babraham Inst., 1998; Scientific Bd, Ludwig Inst. for Cancer Res., 1998–. Founder FMedSci 1998. Hon. MA Harvard, 1984. Merit Award, NIH, 1991. *Publications:* articles on immunology in learned jls. *Recreation:* golf. *Address:* Salix, Conduit Head Road, Cambridge CB3 0EY. *T:* (01223) 570067. *Club:* Country (Brookline, USA).

FEAST, Prof. William James, FRS 1996; Courtaulds Professor of Polymer Chemistry, Durham University, since 1989; Director, Interdisciplinary Research Centre in Polymer Science and Technology, since 1994; *b* 25 June 1938; *s* of William Edward Feast and Lucy Mary Feast (*née* Willis); *m* 1967, Jenneke Elizabeth Catherina van der Kuijl, Middleburg, Netherlands; two *d*. *Educ:* Sheffield Univ. (BSc 1960); Birmingham Univ. (PhD 1963). Lectr, 1965, Sen. Lectr, 1976, Prof., 1986, Durham University. Gillette Internation Res. Fellow, Leuven, Belgium, 1968–69; Vis. Prof., Max Planck Institut für Polymerforschungs, 1984–88. *Publications:* numerous res. papers, reviews in learned jls. *Recreations:* walking, gardening, theatre, fine arts. *Address:* Interdisciplinary Research Centre in Polymer Science and Technology, Durham University, South Road, Durham DH1 3LE. *T:* (0191) 374 3105; *e-mail:* w.j.feast@durham.ac.uk.

FEATES, Prof. Francis Stanley, CB 1991; PhD; CEng, FIChemE; FRSC; CChem; Professor of Environmental Engineering, University of Manchester Institute of Science and Technology, 1991–95; *b* 21 Feb. 1932; *s* of Stanley James Feates and Dorothy Marguerite Jenny Feates (*née* Orford); *m* 1953, Gwenda Grace Goodchild; one *s* three *d*. *Educ:* John Ruskin Sch., Croydon; Birkbeck Coll. London (BSc Special Chem.; PhD).

FRSC 1972; FIChemE 1991; CEng 1991. Wellcome Res. Foundn, 1949–52; Chester-Beatty Cancer Res. Inst., Univ. of London, 1952–54. Chemistry Lectr, Goldsmiths' Coll., London, 1954–56; AERE, Harwell, UKAEA, 1956–78; Argonne Nat. Lab., Univ. of Chicago, Illinois, 1965–67; Department of the Environment: Dir, Nuclear Waste Management, 1978–83; Chief Radiochemical Inspector, 1983–86; Chief Inspector, Radioactive Substances, HM Inspectorate of Pollution, 1986–88; Dir and Chief Inspector, HM Inspectorate of Pollution, 1989–91. Consultant to EC (formerly EEC) on nuclear matters, 1991–. Director: Sir Alexander Gibb & Partners, 1991–94; Siemens Plessey Controls Ltd, 1991–92; Grundon Waste Management, 1991–92. Expert Mem., Scientific and Technical Cttee, EEC, Brussels, 1989–92; Member: Steering Cttee, Nuclear Energy Agency, OECD, Paris, 1988–91; Steering Bd, Lab. of Govt Chemist, 1991–94; Observer Mem., NRPB, 1988–91. Founder Editor, Jl of Hazardous Materials, 1975–85. *Publications:* Hazardous Materials Spills Handbook, 1982; Integrated Pollution Management, 1995; numerous scientific papers on pollution issues, nuclear power, electrochemistry, thermodynamics, waste management, electron microscopy. *Recreations:* walking, cycling, travel. *Address:* Rylands, 18 Mill Lane, Benson, Wallingford, Oxon OX10 6SA. *T:* (01491) 201180.

FEATHER, Prof. John Pliny, FLA; Professor of Information and Library Studies, Loughborough University, since 1988; *b* 20 Dec. 1947; *m* 1971, Sarah, *d* of late Rev. A. W. Rees and Mrs S. M. Rees. *Educ:* Heath Sch., Halifax; Queen's Coll., Oxford (BLitt, MA); MA Cambridge, PhD Loughborough. FLA 1986. Asst Librarian, Bodleian Liby, Oxford, 1972–79; Munby Fellow in Bibliography, Cambridge Univ., 1977–78; Loughborough University: Lectr, then Sen. Lectr, 1979–88; Head, Dept of Inf. and Liby Studies, 1990–94; Dean of Educn and Humanities, 1994–96; Pro-Vice-Chancellor, 1996–2000. Vis. Prof., UCLA, 1982. Pres., Oxford Bibliographical Soc., 1988–92. Mem., many nat. and internat. professional cttees; consultancy and teaching in many countries and for UNESCO, EEC and British Council, 1977–. FRSA 1994. *Publications:* The Provincial Book Trade in Eighteenth-Century England, 1985; A Dictionary of Book History, 1987; A History of British Publishing, 1988; Preservation and the Management of Library Collections, 1991, 2nd edn 1996; Index to Selected Bibliographical Journals 1971–1985, 1991; Publishing, Piracy and Politics: a history of copyright in the British book trade, 1994; The Information Society, 1994, 3rd edn 2000; articles and reviews in academic and professional jls, conf. procs, etc. *Recreations:* photography, music, travel, cooking. *Address:* 36 Farnham Street, Quorn, Leicestershire LE12 8DR. *Club:* Athenæum.

FEATHERSTONE, Hugh Robert, CBE 1984 (OBE 1974); FCIS, FCIT; Director-General, Freight Transport Association, 1969–84; *b* 31 March 1926; *s* of Alexander Brown Featherstone and Doris Olive Martin; *m* 1948, Beryl Joan Sly; one *s* one *d*. *Educ:* Minchenden Sch., Southgate, London. FCIS 1956; FCIT 1970. Served War, RNVR, 1943–46 (Sub-Lt). Assistant Secretary: Nat. Assoc. of Funeral Dirs, 1946–48; Brit. Rubber Develt Bd, 1948–58; Asst Sec. 1958–60, Sec. 1960–68, Traders Road Transport Assoc. *Publications:* contrib. to jls concerned with transport and admin. *Recreations:* golf, gardening, languages, travel, bridge, cookery.

FEATHERSTONE, Lynne (Choona); Member (Lib Dem), London Assembly, Greater London Authority, since 2000; *b* 20 Dec. 1951; *d* of Joseph and Gladys Ryness; *m* 1982, Stephen Featherstone (separated 1996), two *d*. *Educ:* South Hampstead High Sch., Oxford Poly. (Dip. in Communications and Design). Various design posts, 1975–80; Man. Dir, own design co., Inhouse Outhouse Design, 1980–87; strategic design consultant, 1987–97. Dir, Ryness Electrical Supplies Ltd, 1991–. Mem. (Lib Dem), Haringey LBC, 1998– (Leader of the Opposition, 1998–). Contested (LibDem) Hornsey and Wood Green, 2001. *Publication:* (as Lynne Choona Ryness) Marketing and Communication Techniques for Architects, 1992. *Recreations:* tennis, food, architecture, writing. *Address:* 250 Muswell Hill Broadway, N10 3SH. *T:* (020) 8340 5459.

FEATHERSTONE, Simon Mark; HM Diplomatic Service; Head, European Union Department (External), Foreign and Commonwealth Office, since 1998; *b* 24 July 1958; *s* of David and Nora Featherstone; *m* 1981, Gail Teresa Salisbury; one *s* two *d*. *Educ:* Whitgift Sch., Croydon; Lincoln Coll., Oxford (BA Hons Law, MA). FCO, 1980; Chinese lang. trng, SOAS and Hong Kong, 1981–83; Second Sec., Peking, 1984; First Sec., FCO, 1987; on loan to Cabinet Office, 1988; First Sec. (Envmt), UK Perm. Rep. to EC, Brussels, 1990; Consul-Gen., Shanghai, 1994; Counsellor (Political), Peking, 1996. *Recreations:* tennis, running, computers, church activities. *Address:* c/o Foreign and Commonwealth Office, King Charles Street, SW1A 2AH.

FEAVER, William Andrew; writer and art critic; *b* 1 Dec. 1942; *s* of Rt Rev. Douglas Russell Feaver; *m* 1st, 1964, Victoria Turton (marr. diss.); one *s* three *d*; 2nd, 1985, Andrea Rose; two *d*. *Educ:* St Albans School; Nottingham High School; Keble College, Oxford. Teacher: South Stanley Boys' Modern Sch., Co. Durham, 1964–65; Newcastle Royal Grammar Sch., 1965–71; Sir James Knott Res. Fellow, Newcastle Univ., 1971–73; art critic: The Listener, 1971–75; Financial Times, 1974–75; art adviser, Sunday Times Magazine, 1974–75; art critic, The Observer, 1975–98. Critic of the Year, UK Press Awards, 1984. *Publications:* The Art of John Martin, 1975; When We Were Young, 1976; Masters of Caricature, 1981; Pitmen Painters, 1988. *Recreation:* painting. *Address:* 1 Rhodesia Road, SW9 9EJ. *T:* (020) 7737 3386.

See also W. Horbury.

FEDDEN, (Adye) Mary, (Mrs J. O. Trevelyan), OBE 1997; RA 1992; RWA; painter; *b* 14 Aug. 1915; *d* of Harry Vincent Fedden and Ida Margaret Fedden; *m* 1951, Julian Otto Trevelyan, Sen. Hon. RA (*d* 1988). *Educ:* Badminton Sch., Bristol; Slade Sch. of Art (Schol). Exhibns yearly in London and provinces, 1948–; paintings in collections of the Queen, Prince Hassan of Jordan, Tate Gall., city art galls in UK, NZ, Malta, USA, and in private collections in England and overseas. Tutor: Royal College of Art, 1956–64; Yehudi Menuhin Sch., 1964–74. Pres., Royal West of England Acad., 1984–88. Hon. DLitt Bath, 1996. *Publications:* books illustrated: The Green Man, by Jane Gardam, 1998; Birds, introd. Mel Gooding, 1999. *Relevant publication:* Mel Gooding, Mary Fedden, 1995. *Recreation:* reading. *Address:* Durham Wharf, Hammersmith Terrace, W6 9TS.

FEDIDA, Sam, OBE 1980; independent consultant, information systems, retired; inventor of Prestel, viewdata system (first public electronic information service); *b* 1918; *m* 1942, Joan Iris Druce. Served Royal Air Force, Radar Officer, 1940–46. Became Asst Dir of Research, The English Electric Company; started research for the Post Office, 1970; Prestel first in use 1979, as public service; MacRobert Award, Council of Engineering Instns, 1979; Prestel sold in Europe, USA, Far East. *Address:* Constable Cottage, 23 Brook Lane, Felixstowe, Suffolk IP11 7JP.

FEE, John Fitzgerald; Member (SDLP) Newry & Armagh, Northern Ireland Assembly, since 1998; *b* 7 Dec. 1963; *s* of Patrick and Deirdre Fee; *m* 1995, Collette Byrne. *Educ:* St Patrick's Primary Sch., Crossmaglen; St Colman's Coll., Newry; Queen's Univ., Belfast. Member: Rural Develt Council for NI, 1990–94; European Cttee of the Regions, 1998–. Mem. (SDLP) Newry and Mourne DC, 1989–. Editor, Creggan Historical Jl, 1986–87. *Recreations:* traditional Irish music, local history, golf, reading. *Address:* Aras Ceílí, Crossmaglen, Co. Armagh, N Ireland BT35 9BF. *T:* (028) 3086 8824.

FEESEY, Air Vice-Marshal John David Leonard, AFC 1977; retired, 1999; *b* 11 Oct. 1942; *s* of Leonard Ewart Feesey and Maisie Veronica Lillian Feesey; *m* 1968, Glenda Doris Barker; two *s*. *Educ:* Oldershaw Grammar Sch., Wallasey, Cheshire. RAF Officer Cadet, 1961; commnd General Duties Br., 1962; RAF pilot (Hunter, Harrier), 1962–83; OC No 1 (Fighter) Sqdn (Harrier), 1983–86; Stn Comdr, RAF Wittering, 1986–88; Comnd Exec. Officer, HQ AAFCE, 1989–91; Dir Airspace Policy, 1991–93, Dir Gen., Policy and Plans, 1993–96, HQ NATS; Dep. Comdr, Combined Air Ops Centre 4, 1996–98. Vice-Pres., CCF Assoc., 1999–. *Recreations:* hill walking, fishing, gardening. *Club:* Royal Air Force.

FEILDEN, Sir Bernard (Melchior), Kt 1985; CBE 1976 (OBE 1969); FRIBA 1968 (ARIBA 1949); Consultant, Feilden and Mawson, Chartered Architects (Partner, 1956–77); Member, Cathedrals Advisory Commission for England, since 1981; *b* 11 Sept. 1919; *s* of Robert Humphrey Feilden, MC, and Olive Feilden (*née* Binyon); *m* 1st, 1949, Ruth Mildred Bainbridge (*d* 1994); two *s* two *d*; 2nd, 1995, Christina Matilda Beatrice Murdoch. *Educ:* Bedford Sch. Exhibr, Bartlett Sch. of Architecture, 1938 (Hon. Fellow, UCL, 1985). Served War of 1939–45: Bengal Sappers and Miners. AA Diploma (Hons), 1949; Bratt Colbran Schol., 1949. Architect, Norwich Cathedral, 1963–77; Surveyor to the Fabric: York Minster, 1965–77; St Paul's Cathedral, 1969–77; Consultant Architect, UEA, 1969–77. Dir, Internat. Centre for the Preservation and Restoration of Cultural Property, Rome, 1977–81. Hoffman Wood Prof. of Architecture, Leeds Univ., 1973–74. Member: Ancient Monuments Bd (England), 1964–77; Council, RIBA, 1972–77; Cathedrals Fabric Commn, 1990–95; Cathedrals Fabric Cttees, Bury St Edmunds, Ely and Norwich, 1990–. President: Ecclesiastical Architects' and Surveyors' Assoc., 1975–77; Guild of Surveyors, 1976–77. FSA 1969; FRSA 1973; Hon. FAIA 1987. Corresp. Mem., Architectes en Chef, France. DUniv York, 1973; Hon. DLitt: Gothenburg, 1988; East Anglia, 1989. Aga Khan Award for Architecture, 1986. Order of St William of York, 1976. *Publications:* The Wonder of York Minster, 1976; Introduction to Conservation, 1979; Conservation of Historic Buildings, 1982; Between Two Earthquakes, 1987; Guidelines for Conservation (India), 1989; Guidelines for Management of World Cultural Heritage Sites, 1993; articles in Architectural Review, Chartered Surveyor, AA Quarterly. *Recreations:* painting, fishing. *Address:* The Old Barn, Hall Farm Place, Bawburgh, Norwich, NR9 3LW. *T:* (01603) 747472. *Club:* Norfolk (Norwich).

See also G. B. R. Feilden.

FEILDEN, Geoffrey Bertram Robert, CBE 1966; MA Cantab; FRS 1959; FREng, FIMechE, Hon. FIStructE; Hon. FIQA; Hon. MIED; Principal Consultant, Feilden Associates, since 1981; *b* 20 Feb. 1917; *s* of Robert Humphrey Feilden, MC, and Olive Feilden (*née* Binyon); *m* 1st, Elizabeth Ann Gorton; one *s* two *d*; 2nd, Elizabeth Diana Angier (*née* Lloyd). *Educ:* Bedford Sch.; King's Coll., Cambridge (Scholar). Lever Bros. and Unilever Ltd, 1939–40; Power Jets Ltd, 1940–46; Ruston and Hornsby Ltd, 1946–59; Chief Engineer, Turbine Dept, 1949; Engineering Dir, 1954; Man. Dir, Hawker Siddeley Brush Turbines Ltd, and Dir of Hawker Siddeley Industries Ltd, 1959–61; Gp Technical Dir, Davy-Ashmore Ltd, 1961–68; Dep. Dir Gen., British Standards Instn, 1968–70, Dir Gen. 1970–81. Director: Averys Ltd, 1974–79; Plint & Partners Ltd, 1982–2001. Member: Cttees and Sub-Cttees of Aeronautical Research Council, 1947–62; BTC Res. Adv. Council, 1956–61; Council for Sci. and Indust. Res. of DSIR, 1961–65; Design Council (formerly CoID), 1966–78 (Dep. Chm., 1977–78); Central Adv. Council for Science and Technology, 1970–71; Vis. Cttee to RCA, 1968–84 (Chm., 1977–84); Res. Develt and Engrg Cttee, Industrial Develt Bd for NI, 1983–86; Chm., UK Panel for CODATA (formerly British Nat. Cttee on Data for Sci. and Technol.), 1988–97 (UK Deleg. to CODATA, 1989–97); Pres., European Cttee for Standardisation, 1977–79. Member, Royal Society Delegation: to USSR, 1965; Latin America, 1968; People's Republic of China, 1975; Leader, BSI Delegn to People's Republic of China, 1980. Technical Adviser to Govt of India, 1968. DSIR Visitor to Prod. Engineering Res. Assoc. of Gt Brit., 1957–65, and to Machine Tool Industry Res. Assoc., 1961–65. Member Council: Royal Society (a Vice-Pres., 1967–69); IMechE, 1955–61, 1969–80; Univ. of Surrey, 1977–78. Trustee: Maurice Lubbock Meml Fund, 1973–2001; Smallpeice Trust, 1981–88. FREng (Founder FEng 1976); Senior Fellow, RCA, 1986. Hon. DTech Loughborough, 1970; Hon. DSc QUB, 1971. MacRobert Award for innovation (jt winner), 1983; Hodgson Prize, RAeS, 1994. *Publications:* Gas Turbine Principles and Practice (contributor), 1955; First Bulleid Memorial Lecture (Nottingham Univ.), 1959; Report, Engineering Design, 1963 (Chm. of Cttee); numerous papers and articles on engineering subjects. *Recreations:* sailing, ski-ing, driving kitchen and garden machines. *Address:* 1 Hambutts Mead, Painswick, Glos GL6 6RP. *T:* (01452) 812112. *Club:* Athenæum.

See also Sir B. M. Feilden.

FEILDEN, Sir Henry (Wemyss), 6th Bt *cr* 1846; *b* 1 Dec. 1916; *s* of Col Wemyss Gawne Cunningham Feilden, CMG (*d* 1943) (3rd *s* of 3rd Bt) and Winifred Mary Christian (*d* 1980), *d* of Rev. William Cosens, DD; *S* cousin, Sir William Morton Buller Feilden, 5th Bt, 1976; *m* 1943, Ethel May, 2nd *d* of John Atkinson, Annfield Plain, Co. Durham; one *s* two *d*. *Educ:* Canford Sch.; King's Coll., London. Served War, RE, 1940–46. Clerical Civil Service, 1960–79. *Recreations:* watching cricket, reading. *Heir:* *s* Henry Rudyard Feilden, BVetSc, MRCVS [*b* 26 Sept. 1951; *m* 1st, 1982, Anne Shepperd (marr. diss. 1996); one *s*; 2nd, 1998, Geraldine, *d* of Major G. R. Kendall; one *s*]. *Address:* Little Dene, Heathfield Road, Burwash, Etchingham, East Sussex TN19 7HN. *T:* (01435) 882205. *Club:* MCC.

FEILDING, family name of **Earl of Denbigh**.

FEINBERG, Peter Eric; QC 1992; a Recorder, since 1994; *b* 26 Oct. 1949; *s* of Leon and May Feinberg; *m* 1988, Tini Flannery; two *s*. *Educ:* Bradford Grammar Sch.; University College London (LLB Hons). Called to the Bar, Inner Temple, 1972; Asst Recorder, 1990. Pres., Mental Health Tribunals, 1995–. *Recreations:* opera, music, jogging, Czech Republic. *Address:* 2–4 Tudor Street, EC4Y 0AA. *T:* (020) 7797 7111. *Club:* Lambs.

FEINSTEIN, Prof. Charles Hilliard, PhD; FBA 1983; Professor of Economic History, University of Oxford, 1989–99, now Emeritus; Fellow, All Souls College, Oxford, 1989–99, now Emeritus; *b* 18 March 1932; *s* of Louis and Rose Feinstein; *m* 1st, 1958, Ruth Loshak; one *s* three *d*; 2nd, 1980, Anne Digby. *Educ:* Parktown Boys' High Sch., Johannesburg; Univ. of Witwatersrand (BCom 1950); Fitzwilliam Coll., Cambridge (PhD 1958). CA (SA) 1954. Cambridge University: Research Officer, Dept of Applied Econs, 1958–63; Univ. Lectr in Faculty of Econs, 1963–78; Clare College: Fellow, 1963–78, Hon. Fellow, 1994; Sen. Tutor, 1969–78; Prof. of Econ. and Social History, 1978–87, and Head, Dept of Econ. and Related Studies, 1981–86, Univ. of York; Reader in Recent Social and Econ. History, and Professorial Fellow, Nuffield Coll., 1987–89, Univ. of Oxford. Harvard University: Vis. Res. Fellow, Russian Res. Centre, 1967–68; Vis. Scholar, Dept of Econ., 1986–87; Vis. Lectr, Univ. of Delhi, 1972; W. D. Wilson Vis.

Fellow, Univ. of Cape Town, 1994; Visiting Professor: CIT, 1997; Univ. of Keio, 2001. Vice-Pres., British Acad., 1991–93 (Mem. Council, 1990–93); Mem. Council: Royal Economic Soc., 1980–94; Economic History Soc., 1980–99; Mem., Economic Affairs Cttee, SSRC, 1982–86 (Chm., 1985–86). Governor, NIESR, 1985–. Man. Editor, The Economic Jl, 1980–86. *Publications:* Domestic Capital Formation in the United Kingdom 1920–1938, 1965; (ed) Socialism, Capitalism and Economic Growth, Essays presented to Maurice Dobb, 1967; National Income, Expenditure and Output of the United Kingdom 1855–1965, 1972; (ed) York 1831–1981, 1981; (jtly) British Economic Growth 1856–1973, 1982; (ed) The Managed Economy: Essays in British Economic Policy and Performance since 1929, 1983; Studies in Capital Formation 1750–1920, 1988; (ed) Banking, Currency and Finance in Europe between the Wars, 1995; (jtly) The European Economy between the Wars, 1997; (ed) Chinese Technology Transfer in the 1990s, 1997; (jtly) Making History Count, 2001. *Recreations:* reading, looking for second-hand books. *Address:* Treetops, Harberton Mead, Headington, Oxford OX3 0DB.

FELDMAN, family name of **Baron Feldman.**

FELDMAN, Baron *cr* 1995 (Life Peer), of Frognal in the London Borough of Camden; **Basil Feldman,** Kt 1982; a Party Treasurer, Conservative and Unionist Party, since 1996; Chairman, Better Made in Britain Campaign, since 1983; *b* 23 Sept. 1926; *s* of late Philip and Tilly Feldman; *m* 1952, Gita Julius; two *s* one *d. Educ:* Grocers' School. National Union of Conservative and Unionist Associations: Mem., 1975–98, Chm., 1991–96, Exec. Cttee; Vice-Chm., 1982–85, Chm., 1985–86; Vice-Pres., 1986–98; Jt Nat. Chm., Cons. Party's Impact 80s Campaign, 1982–87; Chm., Team 1000, 1989–93; Member: Policy Gp for London, 1975–81, 1984–87; Nat. Campaign Cttee, 1976 and 1978; Adv. Cttee on Policy, 1981–86; Cttee for London, 1984–87; Greater London area: Dep. Chm., 1975–78; Chm., 1978–81; Pres., 1981–85; Vice Pres., 1985–; Vice-Pres., Greater London Young Conservatives, 1975–77; President: Richmond and Barnes Cons. Assoc., 1976–84; Hornsey Cons. Assoc., 1978–82; Patron, Hampstead Cons. Assoc., 1981–86. Contested GLC Elections, Richmond, 1973; Member: GLC Housing Management Cttee, 1973–77; GLC Arts Cttee, 1976–81. Mem., Free Enterprise Loan Soc., 1977–84. Chairman: Martlet Services Gp Ltd, 1973–81; Solport Ltd, 1980–85; The Quality Mark, 1987–92. Chairman: Market Opportunities Adv. Gp, DTI, 1991–93; Shopping Hours Reform Council, 1988–93 (Pres., 1993–95); Better Business Opportunities, 1990–; Watchpost Ltd, 1983–; Dir, Young Entrepreneurs Fund, 1985–95. Underwriting Mem. of Lloyd's, 1979–96. Membre Consultatif, Institut Internat. de Promotion et de Prestige, Geneva (affiliated to Unesco), 1978–. Member: Post Office Users National Council, 1978–81 (Mem., Tariffs Sub-Cttee, 1980–81); English Tourist Board, 1986–96; Chairman: Clothing EDC (NEDO), 1978–85; Maker/User Working Party (NEDO), 1988–89. Gov., Sports Aid Foundn, 1990–. Chairman: London Arts Season 1993–97; Festival of Arts and Culture, 1995; Salzburg Festival Trust, London, 2001– (Vice Chm., 1997–2001); Mem., Internat. Council, Los Angeles Philharmonic, 1995–. Freeman, City of London, 1984. FRSA 1987. *Publications:* Some Thoughts on Jobs Creation (for NEDO), 1984; Constituency Campaigning: a guide for Conservative Party workers; several other Party booklets and pamphlets. *Recreations:* golf, tennis, theatre, opera, travel. *Club:* Carlton.

FELDMAN, Prof. David John; Legal Adviser to Joint Select Committee on Human Rights, Houses of Parliament, since 2000; Professor of Law, University of Birmingham, since 2000 (on leave of absence); *b* 12 July 1953; *s* of late Alec Feldman and of Valerie Feldman (*née* Michaelson); *m* 1983, Naomi Jill Newman; one *s* one *d. Educ:* Brighton, Hove and Sussex Grammar Sch.; Exeter Coll., Oxford (BCL, MA). Lectr in Law, 1976–89, Reader, 1989–92, Bristol Univ.; Barber Prof. of Jurisprudence, Univ. of Birmingham, 1992–2000 (Dean of Law, 1997–2000). Vis. Fellow, ANU, 1989. *Publications:* Law Relating to Entry, Search and Seizure, 1986; Criminal Confiscation Orders: the new law, 1988; (ed) Criminal Investigation: reform and control, 1991; Civil Liberties and Human Rights in England and Wales, 1993, 2nd edn 2001; (ed jtly) Corporate and Commercial Law: modern developments, 1996; contrib. articles on public law, human rights and criminal procedure. *Recreations:* music, dog-walking, cooking, history, theatre. *Address:* Committee Office, House of Lords, SW1A 0PW. *T:* (020) 7219 3033. *Club:* Oxford and Cambridge.

FELDMAN, Prof. Stanley, FRCA; Professor of Anaesthetics, Charing Cross and Westminster Medical School, University of London, 1989–95; *b* 10 Aug. 1930; *s* of Israel and Lilly Feldman; *m* 1957, Carole Bowman; one *s* one *d. Educ:* London Univ. (BSc 1950); Westminster Med. Sch. (MB BS 1955). FRCA (FFARCS 1962). Fellow, Univ. of Washington, Seattle, 1957–58; Westminster Hospital: Registrar, 1958–62; Consultant Anaesthetist, 1962–89; Sen. Lectr, RPMS, 1963–66. Postgrad. Advr in Anaesthetics, RCS, 1966–72; Res. Consultant, Royal Nat. Orthopaedic Hosp. NHS Trust, 1995–98. Vis. Prof., Stanford Univ., 1967–68. Hon. Member: Australasian Soc. Anaesthetists; Spanish Portuguese Soc. Anaesth.; Belgian Soc. Anaesth.; Netherlands Soc. Anaesthetists; Israeli Soc. Anaesth. Editor, Review of Anaesthetic Pharmacology, 1992–97. *Publications:* Anatomy for Anaesthetists, 1963, 6th edn 1991; Scientific Foundations of Anaesthesia, 1971, 4th edn 1990; Muscle Relaxants, 1973, 2nd edn 1981; Drug Mechanisms in Anaesthesia, 1981, 2nd edn 1993; Neuromuscular Block, 1997. *Recreations:* sailing, travel. *Address:* 28 Moore Street, SW3 2QW. *Club:* Royal Society of Medicine.

FELDSTEIN, Prof. Martin Stuart; Professor, Harvard University, since 1969; *b* 25 Nov. 1939; *m* Kathleen Foley; two *d. Educ:* Harvard Coll. (AB *summa cum laude* 1961); Oxford Univ. (BLitt 1963, MA 1964, DPhil 1967). Nuffield College, Oxford University: Research Fellow, 1964–65; Official Fellow, 1965–67; Hon. Fellow, 1998; Lectr in Public Finance, Oxford Univ., 1965–67; Harvard University: Asst Professor, 1967–68; Associate Professor, 1968–69. President, National Bureau of Economic Research, 1977–82 and 1984–; Chm., Council of Economic Advrs, 1982–84. Director: American International Gp; J. P. Morgan; TRW; Columbia-HCA. Member: Amer. Philosophical Soc.; Amer. Acad. of Arts and Scis; Trilateral Commn; Council on Foreign Relations. Corresp. FBA, 1998. *Publications:* (ed) The American Economy in Transition, 1980; Hospital Costs and Health Insurance, 1981; Inflation, Tax Rules, and Capital Formation, 1983; Capital Taxation, 1983; Effects of Taxation on Capital Formation, 1986; United States in the World Economy, 1988; International Economic Co-operation, 1988; American Economic Policy in the 1980s, 1994; International Capital Flows, 1999. *Address:* National Bureau of Economic Research, 1050 Massachusetts Avenue, Cambridge, MA 02138, USA.

FELL, Sir David, KCB 1995 (CB 1990); Chairman, Northern Bank, since 1998; *b* 20 Jan. 1943; *s* of Ernest Fell and Jessie (*née* McCreedy); *m* 1967, Sandra Jesse (*née* Moore); one *s* one *d. Educ:* Royal Belfast Academical Instn; The Queen's University of Belfast (BSc: Pure and Applied Mathematics, also (1st Cl. Hons) Physics). Sales Manager, Rank Hovis McDougall Ltd, 1965–66; Teacher, 1966–67; Research Associate, 1967–69; Civil Servant, 1969–97: Dept of Agriculture (NI), 1969–72; Dept of Commerce (NI), 1972–82 (Under Secretary, 1981); Under Secretary, Dept of Economic Development (NI), 1982; Dep. Chief Exec., Industrial Develt Bd for NI, 1982–84; Permanent Sec., Dept of Economic Develt (NI), 1984–91; Hd of NICS, and Second Perm. Under Sec. of State, NI Office, 1991–97. Chairman: Boxmore Internat. plc, 1998–2000; Nat. Irish Bank, 1999–; Harland & Wolff Properties Ltd, 2001–; Titanic Quarter Ltd, 2001–; non-executive Director: Dunloe Ewart plc, 1998–; Nat. Australia Gp (Europe) Ltd, 1998–; Fred Olsen Energy ASA, 1999–; Chesapeake Corp. (USA), 2000–. Chairman: Opera NI, 1998–99; Prince's Trust Volunteers (NI), 1998–99; Prince's Trust (NI), 1999–; Pres., Extern Orgn, 1998–. Mem. Council, Industrial Soc., 1998–. CIMgt; FRSA; FCIB. *Recreations:* music, reading, golf, Rugby Union. *Address:* Northern Bank Ltd, Head Office, PO Box 183, Donegall Square West, Belfast BT1 6JS. *Club:* Old Instonians (Belfast).

FELL, Richard Taylor, CVO 1996; HM Diplomatic Service; High Commissioner, New Zealand, Governor (non-resident) of Pitcairn, Henderson, Ducie and Oeno Islands, and High Commissioner (non-resident), Samoa, since 2001; *b* 11 Nov. 1948; *s* of late Eric Whineray Fell and Margaret Farrer Fell (*née* Taylor); *m* 1981, Claire Gates; three *s. Educ:* Bootham Sch., York; Bristol Univ. (BSc); Univ. of London (MA). Joined HM Diplomatic Service, 1971; Ottawa, 1972–74; Saigon, 1974–75; Vientiane, 1975; First Sec. and Chargé d'Affaires *ai*, Hanoi, 1979; First Sec., UK Delegn to NATO, 1979–83; First Sec. and Head of Chancery, Kuala Lumpur, 1983–86; FCO, 1986–88; on secondment to Thorn EMI, 1988–89; Counsellor, Ottawa, 1989–93; Dep. Hd of Mission, Bangkok, 1993–96; Counsellor, FCO, 1997–2000; Acting Consul-Gen., Toronto, 2000; RCDS, 2001. *Publication:* Early Maps of South-East Asia, 1988. *Recreations:* antiques, reading, sport. *Address:* c/o Foreign and Commonwealth Office, SW1A 2AH.

FELL, Robert, CB 1972; CBE 1966; Commissioner of Banking, Hong Kong, 1984–87; *b* 6 May 1921; *s* of Robert and Mary Ann Fell, Cumberland; *m* 1946, Eileen Wicks; two *s* one *d. Educ:* Whitehaven Grammar School. War Office, 1939; military service, 1940–46 (despatches); BoT, 1947; Trade Comr, Qld, 1954–59; Asst Sec., Tariff Div., 1961; Commercial Counsellor, Delhi, 1961–66; Under-Sec. i/c export promotion, 1967–71; Sec., ECGD, 1971–74; Chief Exec., The Stock Exchange, 1975–82; Comr for Securities, Hong Kong, 1981–84. Mem., British Overseas Trade Board, 1972–75; Pres., City Branch, BIM, 1976–82. FRSA. *Recreations:* Rugby football (watching), gardening. *Address:* 60 The Drive, Craigweil, Aldwick, Bognor Regis PO21 4DT. *Club:* Travellers.

FELLGETT, Prof. Peter Berners, PhD; FRS 1986; Professor of Cybernetics, University of Reading, 1965–87, now Emeritus; *b* 11 April 1922; *s* of Frank Ernest Fellgett and Rose, (Rowena), (*née* Wagstaffe); *m* 1947, Janet Mary (*d* 1998), *o d* of late Prof. G. E. Briggs, FRS and Mrs Nora Briggs; one *s* two *d. Educ:* The Leys Sch., Cambridge; Univ. of Cambridge (BA 1943, MA 1947, PhD 1952). Isaac Newton Student, Cambridge Observatories, 1950–51; Lick Observatory, Calif, 1951–52; Cambridge Observatories, 1952–59; Royal Observatory, Edinburgh, 1959–65. *Publications:* approx. 75 pubns in learned jls and 32 gen. articles. *Recreations:* making musical instruments, high quality audio, gardening, fun-running, not being interrupted and not being hurried. *Address:* Little Brighter Farm, St Kew Highway, Bodmin, Cornwall PL30 3DU.

See also R. Fellgett.

FELLGETT, Robin, PhD; Director (formerly Deputy Director), Financial Sector, HM Treasury, since 1998; *b* 1 Oct. 1950; *s* of Peter Fellgett and late Mary Briggs; *m* 1976, Patti Douglas; one *s* one *d. Educ:* Univ. of Warwick (PhD Maths 1976); Birkbeck Coll., London Univ. (MSc Econs 1984); INSEAD (AMP 1995). BP Chemicals, 1969; Asst Prof., Univ. of Maryland, 1976–78; MSC, 1979; CSD 1979–83; joined HM Treasury, 1983: held posts in expenditure, privatisation and internat. finance. *Recreations:* music, travel, relaxation. *Address:* HM Treasury, Allington Towers, 19 Allington Street, SW1E 5EB. *Clubs:* Jazz Café, Forum.

FELLNER, Christine; Social Security and Child Support Commissioner, since 1999; *b* 1 April 1946; *d* of Gustav Michael Fellner and Gwyneth Mary Fellner (*née* Hughes). *Educ:* Chiswick Co. Grammar Sch.; St Anne's Coll., Oxford (BA Jurisp., BCL). Lectr in Law, Southampton Univ., 1969–72; solicitor, 1974–81; called to the Bar, Middle Temple, 1981; in practice as barrister, 1981–95; occasional lectr, QMW and City Univ. Business Sch., 1984–92; Chm. (part-time), Social Security, Medical and Disability Appeal Tribunals, 1986–95; Chm., Independent Tribunal Service, 1995–99. *Publications:* The Future of Legal Protection for Industrial Design, 1985; Industrial Design Law, 1995; contribs to periodicals on intellectual property. *Address:* Office of the Social Security and Child Support Commissioners, Harp House, 83 Farringdon Street, EC4A 7DH. *T:* (020) 7353 5145.

FELLNER, Eric; film producer; Co-Chairman, Working Title Films, since 1992; *b* 10 Oct. 1959; *m* (marr. diss.); three *s. Educ:* Cranleigh Sch.; Guildhall Sch. of Music and Drama. *Films include*: Sid and Nancy, 1986; Pascali's Island, 1988; The Rachel Papers, 1989; Hidden Agenda, 1990; A Kiss Before Dying, Liebestraum, 1991; Wild West, 1992; Posse, Romeo is Bleeding, 1993; Four Weddings and a Funeral, The Hudsucker Proxy, 1994; Loch Ness, French Kiss, Dead Man Walking, 1995; Fargo, 1996; Bean, The Borrowers, 1997; Elizabeth, The Big Lebowski, 1998; Notting Hill, Plunkett & Macleane, 1999; O Brother, Where Art Thou?, Billy Elliot, The Man Who Cried, 2000; Bridget Jones's Diary, Captain Corelli's Mandolin, The Man Who Wasn't There, 40 Days and 40 Nights, Long Time Dead, 2001; About A Boy, Ali G Indahouse, The Guru, My Little Eye, 2002. Four Academy Awards; thirteen BAFTA awards. *Address:* Working Title Films, Oxford House, 76 Oxford Street, WID 1BS. *T:* (020) 7307 3000; Working Title Films, 4th Floor, 9720 Wilshire Boulevard, Beverly Hills, CA 90212, USA. *T:* (310) 777 3100.

FELLNER, Dr Peter John; Chief Executive, Celltech Group (formerly Celltech Chiroscience) plc, since 1999; *b* 31 Dec. 1943; *s* of late Hans Julius Fellner and of Jessica (*née* Thompson); *m* 1st, 1969, Sandra Head (*née* Smith); one *d* and one step *s*; 2nd, 1982, Jennifer Mary Zabel (*née* Butler); two step *s. Educ:* Sheffield Univ. (BSc Biochem. 1965); Trinity Coll., Cambridge (PhD 1968). Post-doctoral Res. Fellow, 1968–70, Associate Prof., 1970–73, Strasbourg Univ.; Searle UK Research Laboratories: Sen. Res. Investigator, 1973–77; Dir of Chem., 1977–80; Dir of Res., 1980–84; Dir of Res., Roche UK Res. Centre, 1984–86; Man. Dir, Roche UK, 1986–90; Chief Exec., Celltech plc, 1990–99. Director: Colborn Dawes Ltd, 1986–90; British Biotechnol. Gp plc, 1988–90; Synaptica Ltd, 1999–. Mem., MRC. *Recreation:* country walking. *Address:* Celltech Group plc, 216 Bath Road, Slough, Berks SL1 4EN. *T:* (01753) 777101.

FELLOWES, family name of **Barons De Ramsey** and **Fellowes.**

FELLOWES, Baron *cr* 1999 (Life Peer), of Shotesham in the county of Norfolk; **Robert Fellowes,** GCB 1998 (KCB 1991; CB 1987); GCVO 1996 (KCVO 1989; LVO 1983); QSO 1999; PC 1990; Chairman, Barclays Private Banking, since 2000 (Vice-Chairman, 1999–2000); *b* 11 Dec. 1941; *s* of Sir William Fellowes, KCVO; *m* 1978, Lady Jane Spencer, *d* of 8th Earl Spencer, LVO; one *s* two *d. Educ:* Eton. Scots Guards (short service commission), 1960–63. Director, Allen Harvey & Ross Ltd, Discount Brokers and Bankers, 1968–77; Asst Private Sec. to the Queen, 1977–86, Dep. Private Sec., 1986–90; Private Sec. to the Queen and Keeper of the Queen's Archives, 1990–99. Non-exec. Dir, South African Breweries, 1999–. Vice-Chm., Commonwealth Inst., 2000–; Trustee,

Rhodes Trust, 2000–. *Recreations:* reading, watching cricket, golf, shooting. *Address:* House of Lords, SW1A 0PW. *Clubs:* White's, Pratt's, Royal Over-Seas League, MCC.

FELLOWS, Derek Edward, FIA; Executive Director, Securities and Investments Board, 1989–91; *b* 23 Oct. 1927; *s* of late Edward Frederick Fellows and of Gladys Fellows; *m* 1948, Mary Watkins; two *d. Educ:* Mercers' Sch. FIA 1956. Entered Prudential Assurance Co. Ltd, 1943; Gp Pensions Manager, 1973–81; Chief Actuary, 1981–88; Man. Dir, Gp Pension Div., 1984–88; Dir, Prudential Corp. plc, 1985–88; non-exec. Dir, Countrywide Assured (formerly Hambro Guardian Assurance, then Hambro Assured), 1992–99. Mem., Occupational Pensions Bd, 1974–78; Chm., Bd of Trustees, South Bank Centre Retirement Plan, 1993–2001; Trustee, C of E Pensions Bd, 1998–. Church Comr, 1996– (Mem., Audit Cttee, 1994–). FPMI 1976; Vice Pres., Inst. of Actuaries, 1980–83. *Publications:* contrib. Jl of Inst. of Actuaries. *Recreations:* music, theatre, gardening, bridge. *Club:* Actuaries'.

FELLOWS, Edward Frank; Editorial Consultant, Fellows Media Ltd, publishers, since 1999; *b* 25 Sept. 1930; *s* of Edward Fellows and Gladys Nora Fellows; *m* 1962, Christine Woolmore; three *s. Educ:* Ewell primary and secondary schs; Epsom Sch. of Art (schol.); Merrist Wood Agricl Inst. Nat. Service, CRMP, 1949. Joined editorial staff of Farmer and Stockbreeder, 1957; Editor, Power Farming, 1974; Dep. Editor, Farmers Weekly, 1982; Editor, Crops, 1984; Editor, Farmers Weekly, 1987–90; Editor-in-Chief, Reed Farmers Publishing Group, 1990–91; Features Editor, Shell Agriculture, 1993–94; Editor, Farming OPUS, 1995–97. Hon. Mem., Falkland Islands Assoc., 1983–. *Publication:* Tim Chooses Farming, 1962. *Recreations:* indoor rowing, Bernese mountain dogs, walking, photography, gardening, reading. *Address:* Fresh Winds, Slad, Stroud, Glos GL6 7QD. *T:* (01452) 814072, *Fax:* (01452) 812814; *e-mail:* ted@tedfellows.demon.co.uk.

FELLOWS, Jeffrey Keith; Technical Consultant, BAE Systems, since 1999; *b* 17 Sept. 1940; *s* of Albert and Hilda May Fellows; *m* 1965, Mary Ewins; one *s. Educ:* Handsworth Grammar Sch.; Birmingham Univ. (BSc (Phys) Hons 1962). Royal Aircraft Establishment: joined Weapons Dept, 1962, Sect. Leader, 1973; Div. Leader, Systems Assessment Dept, 1976; Head of: Combat Mission Systems Div., 1981; Flight Systems Dept, 1983; seconded to BNSC as Dir (Projects and Technol.), 1986; Dep. Dir (Mission Systems), RAE, Farnborough, 1988–89; Asst Under Sec. of State, MoD, 1989–95; Technical Planning Dir, BAe plc, 1995–99; retired. *Publications:* various, for AGARD, IBA, US Nat. Space Foundn, etc. *Recreations:* tennis, aeromodelling.

FELLOWS, John Walter, CEng, FICE, FIHT; independent transportation consultant, since 1996; *b* 27 July 1938; *s* of William Leslie Fellows and Lavinia Keziah (*née* Chilton); *m* 1964, Maureen Joyce Lewis; two *s. Educ:* Dudley Technical High Sch.; Wolverhampton Polytechnic; Birmingham Univ. (MSc). FICE 1990; FIHT 1989. Civil Engineer (pupil), Contractors Wilson Lovatt & Sons Ltd, 1954–59; Civil Engineer: CBs of Wolverhampton, Coventry and Dudley, 1959–69; joined Department of Transport, 1969: Asst Sec., Highway Maintenance Div., 1984–88; Dir, SE, 1988–90; Regl Dir (SE), DoE/DoT, 1990–94; Bd Dir, Highway Agency, 1994–96. *Publications:* papers to ICE and IHT. *Recreations:* boating, sailing, golf, music, theatre. *Address:* 17 Chinthurst Park, Shalford, Guildford, Surrey GU4 8JH. *T:* (01483) 565823.

FELLS, Prof. Ian, CBE 2000; FREng, FRSE; Professor of Energy Conversion, University of Newcastle upon Tyne, since 1975; *b* 5 Sept. 1932; *s* of late Dr Henry Alexander Fells, MBE and Clarice Fells, Sheffield; *m* 1957, Hazel Denton Scott; four *s. Educ:* King Edward VII School, Sheffield; Trinity College, Cambridge. MA, PhD. FInstE, FIChemE; FREng (FEng 1979); FRSE 1996. Chief Wireless Officer, British Troops in Austria, 1951–52; Lectr and Dir of Studies, Dept of Fuel Technology and Chem. Engineering, Univ. of Sheffield, 1958–62; Reader in Fuel Science, King's Coll., Univ. of Durham, 1962; Public Orator, Univ. of Newcastle upon Tyne, 1970–73. Lectures: Brough, Paisley Coll., 1977; Allerdale Wylde, Cumbria Science Socs, 1986; Fawley, Southampton Univ., 1987; Robert Spence, RSC, 1988 and 1990; Charles Parsons' Meml, Royal Soc., 1988; Clancey, City Univ., 1992; Erasmus Darwin, Lichfield Sci. and Engrg Soc., 1994; Idris Jones Meml, Cardiff, 2000. Pres., Inst. of Energy, 1978–79; Scientific Advr, World Energy Council, 1990–; Special Advisor: to H of L Select Cttee for the European Communities, 1991–92; to H of C Select Cttee on Envmt, 1993–94, and on Trade and Industry, 1995–96. Member: Electricity Supply Res. Council, 1979–90; Sci. Consultative Gp, BBC, 1976–81; Exec., David Davies Inst. of Internat. Affairs, 1975–; CNAA, 1987–93. Trustee, Internat. Centre for Life, 1995–. Hatfield Meml Prize, 1974; Beilby Meml Medal and Prize, 1976; Faraday Award and Lect., 1993, Collier Medal and Lect., 1999, Royal Soc.; Melchett Medal and Lect., Royal Instn, 1999. Participator in TV series: Young Scientist of the Year; The Great Egg Race; Men of Science; Earth Year 2050; Take Nobody's Word For It; QED; The Human Element. *Publications:* Energy for the Future, 1973, 2nd edn 1986; UK Energy Policy Post-Privatisation, 1991; Energy for the Future, 1995; World Energy 1923–98 and Beyond, 1998; contribs to professional jls. *Recreations:* sailing, cross-country ski-ing, energy conversation. *Address:* 29 Rectory Terrace, Newcastle upon Tyne NE3 1YB. *T:* (0191) 285 5343. *Club:* Naval and Military.

FELWICK, Wing Comdr David Leonard, RAF retired; Director of Trading (Food), John Lewis Partnership and Managing Director, Waitrose Ltd, since 1991; *b* 9 Nov. 1944; *s* of Leonard Felwick and Mary J. Felwick (*née* Rolling); *m* 1970, Lynne Margaret Yeardley; two *s. Educ:* Devonport High Sch., Plymouth; RAF Coll., Cranwell. Served RAF, 1962–82. Joined John Lewis Partnership, 1982; Man. Dir, John Lewis, Welwyn, 1985–87; Dir of Selling, Waitrose Ltd, 1987–91. MInstD 1985. *Recreations:* ski-ing, shooting, tennis, golf. *Address:* John Lewis Partnership, 171 Victoria Street, SW1E 5NN. *T:* (020) 7828 1000. *Club:* Royal Air Force.

FENBY, Jonathan Theodore Starmer, CBE 2000; journalist and writer; Associate Editor, Sunday Business, since 2000; *b* 11 Nov. 1942; *s* of late Charles Fenby and June (*née* Head); *m* 1967, Renée Wartski; one *s* one *d. Educ:* West House Sch., Birmingham; King Edward VI Sch., Birmingham; Westminster Sch.; New Coll., Oxford (BA). Reuters, 1963–77, Ed., Reuters World Service, 1973–77; correpondent in France and Germany, Economist, 1982–86; Asst Ed. and Home Ed., The Independent, 1986–88; Dep. Ed., The Guardian, 1988–93; Editor: The Observer, 1993–95; South China Morning Post and Sunday Morning Post, Hong Kong, 1995–99. Chevalier, Ordre Nat. du Mérite (France), 1992. *Publications:* Fall of the House of Beaverbrook, 1979; Piracy and the Public, 1983; International News Services, 1986; On the Brink: the trouble with France, 1998; Comment peut-on être français, 1999; Dealing with the Dragon: a year in the new Hong Kong, 2000. *Recreations:* walking, belote, jazz. *Address:* 101 Ridgmount Gardens, Torrington Place, WC1E 7AZ.

FENDALL, Prof. Neville Rex Edwards, MD; Professor of International Community Health, School of Tropical Medicine, University of Liverpool, 1971–81, now Emeritus Professor; Visiting Professor of Public Health, Boston University, since 1982; *b* 9 July 1917; *s* of Francis Alan Fendall and Ruby Inez Matthews; *m* 1942, Margaret Doreen (*née* Beynon). *Educ:* University College Hosp. (MD, BSc); London Sch. of Hygiene and Tropical Med. (DPH); FFPHM. Colonial Medical Service, 1944–64, Nigeria, Malaya, Singapore, Kenya; Brit. Mil. Admin, 1945–46; Dir of Med. Services, Kenya; Staff Mem., Rockefeller Foundn, 1964–66; Regional Dir, Population Council Inc., New York, 1966–71. Mem., Panel of Experts, WHO, 1957–83; Consultant: World Bank; UN Fund for Population Activities; ODM; Cento; Internat. Develt Res. Centre, Canada; APHA; USAID; Overseas govts; Vis. Consultant, Univ. of Hawaii. Adjunct Prof. of Community Health, Univ. of Calgary, 1983–88; Visiting Lecturer: Harvard, 1966–83; Inst. of Tropical Medicine, Marseilles; Univ. of Glasgow; Univ. of Bradford; Commonwealth Foundn Travelling Lectr, 1976; Dist. Fellow, Boston Univ. Center for Internat. Health, 1992. Mem., Acad. of Med., Physical and Nat. Scis, Guatemala, 1986–. Patron, Commonwealth Human Ecology Council, 1994–. Langley Meml Prize, UNCAST, 1963; Gold Medal, Mrigendra Medical Trust, Nepal, 1983; Fendall Prize, Center for Internat. Health, Boston, USA, 1996. *Publications:* Auxiliaries in Health Care, 1972 (English, French, Spanish edns); (with J. M. Paxman and F. M. Shattock) Use of Paramedicals for Primary Health Care in the Commonwealth, 1979; (with F. M. Shattock) Restraints and Constraints to Development, 1983; contribs on primary health care, epidemiology, population dynamics, in various books and jls. *Recreations:* gardening, travel. *Address:* The Coach House, Mill Street, Ludlow, Shropshire SY8 1BB. *Clubs:* Royal Commonwealth Society (Life Mem.); Athenæum (Liverpool).

FENDER, Sir Brian (Edward Frederick), Kt 1999; CMG 1985; Chief Executive, Higher Education Funding Council for England, 1995–2001; *b* 15 Sept. 1934; *s* of late George Clements and of Emily Fender; *m* 1st, 1956; one *s* three *d*; 2nd, 1986, Ann Linscott. *Educ:* Carlisle Grammar Sch.; Sale County Grammar Sch.; Imperial College London (ARCS, BSc 1956; DIC, PhD 1959; FIC 1997); MA Oxon 1963; CChem, FRSC. Research Instructor, Univ. of Washington, Seattle, 1959–61; Senior Research Fellow, Nat. Chem. Lab. (now NPL), 1961–63; University of Oxford: Dept Demonstrator in Inorganic Chemistry, 1963–65; Lectr, 1965–84; Senior Proctor, 1975–76; Mem., Hebdomadal Council, 1977–80; St Catherine's College: Fellow, 1963–84 (Hon. Fellow 1986); Sen. Tutor, 1965–69; Chm., Management Cttee, Oxford Colls Admissions Office, 1973–80; Vice-Chancellor, Univ. of Keele, 1985–95. Institut Laue-Langevin, Grenoble: Asst Dir, 1980–82; Dir, 1982–85; Mem., Steering Cttee, 1974–77; Mem., Scientific Council, 1977–80. Member: SERC, 1985–90; CERN Review Cttee, 1986–87; Chairman: Science Board, SERC, 1985–90 (Mem., 1974–77); Neutron Beam Res. Cttee, 1974–77 (Mem., 1969–71); Science Planning Group for Rutherford Lab. Neutron Scattering Source, 1977–80; Member: Defence Meteorol Bd, 1991–; BTG plc (formerly British Technol. Gp) Bd, 1992–; Adv. Cttee, Tate Gall., Liverpool, 1988–93; West Midlands Arts Bd, 1995–. Pres., NFER, 1999–. Member Council: Chem. Soc., 1973–76; CVCP, 1988–95. CIMgt (CBIM 1989). Hon. Fellow, Univ. of Wales, Cardiff, 1996. DUniv Keele, 1996. *Publications:* scientific articles on neutron scattering and solid state chemistry. *Recreation:* modern art. *Club:* Athenæum.

FENECH-ADAMI, Hon. Dr Edward, KUOM 1990; LLD; MP Malta, since 1969; Prime Minister of Malta, 1987–96, and since 1998; Leader of Nationalist Party, since 1977; *b* Birkirkara, Malta, 7 Feb. 1934; *s* of late Luigi Fenech-Adami and Josephine (*née* Pace); *m* 1965, Mary (*née* Sciberras); four *s* one *d. Educ:* St Aloysius Coll., Malta; Royal Univ. of Malta (BA 1955, LLD 1958). Entered legal practice in Malta, 1959. Mem. Nat. Exec., Nationalist Party, 1961, Asst Gen. Sec., 1962–75, Pres., Gen. and Admin. Council, 1975–77; Shadow Minister for Labour and Social Services, 1971–77; Leader of the Opposition, 1977–82, 1983–87, 1996–98; Foreign Minister, 1989–90. Vice-Pres., European Union of Christian Democrat Parties, 1979–. Editor, Il-Poplu (Party Newspaper), 1962–69. *Address:* Office of the Prime Minister, Auberge de Castille, Valletta, Malta. *T:* 242560, *Fax:* 249888; Nationalist Party, Herbert Ganado Street, Hamrun HMR 08, Malta. *T:* 243641/2/3, *Fax:* 243640.

FENHALLS, Richard Dorian; Chief Executive, Strand Partners Ltd, since 1993; *b* 14 July 1943; *s* of Roydon Myers and Maureen Rosa Fenhalls; *m* 1967, Angela Sarah Allen; one *s* one *d. Educ:* Hilton Coll., Univ. of Natal (BA); Christ's Coll., Cambridge (MA, LLM). Attorney, S Africa, 1969. Goodricke & Son, Attorney, S Africa, 1969–70; Citibank, 1970–72; Senior Vice President: Marine Midland Bank, 1972–77; American Express Bank, 1977–81; Dep. Chm. and Chief Exec., Guinness Mahon & Co. Ltd, 1981–85; Chief Exec., Henry Ansbacher Hldgs, 1985–93; Chm., Henry Ansbacher & Co. Ltd, 1985–93. *Recreations:* sailing, ski-ing, veteran cars. *Address:* The Moat House, Portsmouth Road, Fisher's Pond, near Eastleigh, Hants SO50 7HF. *Clubs:* Royal Ocean Racing, Royal Thames Yacht; Royal Southern Yacht (Hamble); Veteran Car of GB.

FENLON, Dr Iain Alexander, FSA; Fellow, King's College, Cambridge, since 1976; Reader in Historical Musicology, University of Cambridge, since 1996; *b* 26 Oct. 1949; *s* of Albert Fenlon and Joan (*née* Rainey); *m* 1993, Nicoletta Guidobaldi. *Educ:* Reading Univ. (BA); Birmingham Univ. (MA); St Catharine's Coll., Cambridge; King's Coll., Cambridge (MA; PhD 1977). FSA 1989. Hayward Research Fellow, Birmingham Univ., 1974–75; Fellow, Villa I Tatti (Harvard Univ. Center for Italian Renaissance Studies), Florence, 1975–76; King's College, Cambridge: Jun. Res. Fellow, 1976–79; Sen. Res. Fellow, 1979–83; Vice-Provost, 1986–91; University of Cambridge: Asst Lectr, 1979–84; Lectr, 1984–96. Vis. Scholar, Harvard Univ., 1984–85; Visiting Fellow: All Souls Coll., Oxford, 1991–92; New Coll., Oxford, 1992; British Acad. Res. Reader, 1996–98; Visiting Professor: Ecole Normale Supérieure, Paris, 1998–99; Univ. of Bologna, 1999–2000. Founding Ed., Early Music History, 1981–. Dent Medal, Internat. Musicological Soc./Royal Musical Assoc., 1984. *Publications:* Music and Patronage in Sixteenth-Century Mantua, 2 vols, 1980, 1982; (ed) Music in Medieval and Early Modern Europe, 1981; (with J. Haar) The Early Sixteenth-Century Italian Madrigal, 1988; (with P. Miller) The Song of the Soul: understanding Poppea, 1992; Music, Print and Culture in Early Sixteenth-Century Italy, 1995; Giaches de Wert: letters and documents, 1999; articles in various musicol jls, TLS, London Review of Books, etc. *Recreations:* travel, wine. *Address:* King's College, Cambridge CB2 1ST. *T:* (01223) 331100.

FENN, Sir Nicholas (Maxted), GCMG 1995 (KCMG 1989 CMG 1980); HM Diplomatic Service, retired; Chairman, Marie Curie Cancer Care, since 2000 (Chief Executive, 1997–2000); *b* 19 Feb. 1936; *s* of late Rev. Prof. J. Eric Fenn and of Kathleen (*née* Harrison); *m* 1959, Susan Clare (*née* Russell); two *s* one *d. Educ:* Kingswood Sch., Bath; Peterhouse, Cambridge (MA). Pilot Officer, RAF, 1954–56. Third Sec., British Embassy, Rangoon, 1959–63; Asst Private Sec. to Sec. of State for Foreign Affairs, 1963–67; First Secretary: British Interests Sect., Swiss Embassy, Algiers, 1967–69; Public Relations, UK Mission to UN, NY, 1969–72; Dep. Head, Energy Dept, FCO, 1972–75; Counsellor, Peking, 1975–77; Head of News Dept and FCO Spokesman, 1979–82; Spokesman to last Governor of Rhodesia, 1979–80; Ambassador: Rangoon, 1982–86; Dublin, 1986–91; High Comr, India, 1991–96. Jt Chm., Anglo-Irish Encounter, 1998–. Vice-Pres., Leprosy Mission, 1996–; Trustee, Sightsavers Internat., 1996–; Gov., Jawaharlal Nehru Meml Trust, 1997–. *Recreation:* sailing. *Address:* Marie Curie Cancer Care, 89 Albert Embankment, SE1 7TP. *T:* (020) 7599 7777. *Club:* Oxford and Cambridge.

FENNELL, Hon. Sir (John) Desmond (Augustine), Kt 1990; OBE 1982; a Judge of the High Court of Justice, Queen's Bench Division, 1990–92; *b* 17 Sept. 1933; *s* of late Dr A. J. Fennell, Lincoln; *m* 1966, Susan Primrose, *d* of late J. M. Trusted; one *s* two *d*. *Educ:* Ampleforth; Corpus Christi Coll., Cambridge. Served with Grenadier Guards, 1956–58. Called to the Bar, Inner Temple, 1959, Bencher, 1983; Dep. Chm., Bedfordshire QS, 1971; a Recorder of the Crown Court, 1972–89; QC 1974; Leader, Midland and Oxford Circuit, 1983–88; a Judge of the Courts of Appeal of Jersey and Guernsey, 1984–89; a Judge of the Employment Appeal Tribunal, 1991–92. Vice-Chm., 1988, Chm., 1989, Gen. Council of the Bar. Inspector, King's Cross Underground fire, 1988. Chm., Stoke Mandeville Burns and Reconstructive Surgery Res. Trust, 1994–. Chm., Buckingham Div. Cons. Assoc., 1976–79 (Pres., 1983–89). *Clubs:* Boodle's, Pilgrims.

FENNER, Prof. Frank John, AC 1989; CMG 1976; MBE 1944; FRCP 1967; FRS 1958; FAA 1954; Visiting Fellow, John Curtin School of Medical Research, Australian National University, since 1983 (University Fellow, 1980–82); *b* 21 Dec. 1914; *s* of Charles and Emma L. Fenner; *m* 1944, Ellen Margaret Bobbie Roberts (*d* 1995); one *d* (and one *d* decd). *Educ:* Thebarton Technical High Sch.; Adelaide High Sch.; Univ. of Adelaide. MB, BS (Adelaide) 1938; MD (Adelaide) 1942; DTM (Sydney) 1940. Served as Medical Officer, Hospital Pathologist, and Malariologist, AIF, 1940–46; Francis Haley Research Fellow, Walter and Eliza Hall Inst. for Medical Research, Melbourne, 1946–48; Rockefeller Foundation Travelling Fellow, 1948–49; Prof. of Microbiology, 1949–67, Dir, John Curtin Sch. of Med. Research, 1967–73, Prof. of Environmental Studies and Dir, Centre for Resource and Environmental Studies, 1973–79, ANU; Overseas Fellow, Churchill Coll., Cambridge, 1962–63. Fogarty Schol., Nat. Insts of Health, USA, 1973–74, 1982–83. Chm., Global Commn for Certification of Smallpox Eradication, WHO, 1978–80. For. Associate, Nat. Acad. of Scis, USA, 1977; David Syme Prize, Univ. of Melbourne, 1949; Harvey Lecture, Harvey Soc. of New York, 1957; Royal Society: Leeuwenhoek Lecture, 1961, Florey Lecture, 1983; Copley Medal, 1995; Australian Acad. of Science: Matthew Flinders Lecture, 1967; Burnet Lecture, 1985. Hon. MD Monash, 1966; Dr *hc* Liège, 1992; Hon. DSc: Oxford Brookes Univ., 1995; ANU, 1996. Mueller Medal, Australian and New Zealand Assoc. for the Advancement of Science, 1964; Britannica Australia Award for Medicine, 1967; ANZAC Peace Award, 1980; ANZAAS Medal, 1980; Stuart Mudd Award, Internat. Union of Microbiol Socs, 1986; Japan Prize (Preventive Medicine), Sci. & Technol. Foundn of Japan, 1988; Albert Einstein World Award for Science, 2000. *Publications:* The Production of Antibodies (with F. M. Burnet), 1949; Myxomatosis (with F. N. Ratcliffe), 1965; The Biology of Animal Viruses, 1968, 2nd edn 1974; Medical Virology (with D. O. White), 1970, 4th edn 1994; Classification and Nomenclature of Viruses, 1976; (with A. L. G. Rees) The Australian Academy of Science: the First Twenty-five Years, 1980; (jtly) Veterinary Virology, 1987, 2nd edn 1993; (jtly) Smallpox and its Eradication, 1988; (with Z. Jezek) Human Monkeypox, 1988; (with A. Gibbs) Portraits of Viruses: a history of virology, 1988; (jtly) The Orthopoxviruses, 1989; History of Microbiology in Australia, 1990; The Australian Academy of Science: the first forty years, 1995; (with B. Fantini) The Biological Control of Vertebrate Pests, 1999; (with D. R. Curtis) History of the John Curtin School of Medical Research 1948–1998, 2001; numerous scientific papers, dealing with virology, epidemiology, bacteriology, environmental problems and history of science. *Recreations:* gardening, tennis. *Address:* 8 Monaro Crescent, Red Hill, Canberra, ACT 2603, Australia. *T:* (2) 62959176; *e-mail:* fenner@jcsmr.anu.edu.au.

FENNER, Dame Peggy (Edith), DBE 1986; DL; *b* 12 Nov. 1922; *m* 1940, Bernard Fenner; one *d*. *Educ:* LCC School, Brockley; Ide Hill, Sevenoaks. Contested (C) Newcastle-under-Lyme, 1966. MP (C) Rochester and Chatham, 1970–Sept. 1974 and 1979–83, Medway, 1983–97; contested (C) Medway, 1997. Parly Sec., MAFF, 1972–74 and 1981–86. Mem., British Delegn to European Parlt, Strasbourg, 1974; UK rep. to Council of Europe and WEU, 1987–97. Member: West Kent Divisional Exec. Educn Cttee, 1963–72; Sevenoaks Urban District Council, 1957–71 (Chairman, 1962 and 1963); Exec. of Kent Borough and Urban District Councils Assoc., 1967–71; a Vice-Pres, Urban District Councils Assoc., 1971. DL Kent, 1992. *Recreations:* reading, travel, theatre, gardening.

FENNESSY, Sir Edward, Kt 1975; CBE 1957 (OBE 1944); BSc; FIEE, FRIN; *b* 17 Jan. 1912; *m* 1st, 1937, Marion Banks (*d* 1983); one *s* one *d*; 2nd, 1984, Leonora Patricia Birkett, *widow* of Trevor Birkett. *Educ:* Queen Mary Coll., London (Hon. Fellow, QMW, 1998). Telecommunications Research, Standard Telephones and Cables, 1934–38; Radar Research, Air Min. Research Station, Bawdsey Manor, 1938. War of 1939–45: commissioned RAFVR, 1940; Group Captain, 1945; staff No 60 Group, RAF, 1940–45; resp. for planning and construction radar systems for defence of UK, and Bomber Ops. Joined Bd of The Decca Navigator Co., 1946; Managing Director: Decca Radar Ltd, 1950–65; The Plessey Electronics Group, 1965–69. Chairman: British Telecommunications Research Ltd, 1966–69; Electronic Engineering Assoc., 1967–68; Man. Dir, Telecommunications, 1969–77, and Dep. Chm., 1975–77, Post Office Corp. Chairman: IMA Microwave Products Ltd, 1979–83; LKB Biochrom, 1978–87; British Medical Data Systems, 1981–91; Dep. Chm., LKB Instruments, 1978–87. Pres., Royal Institute of Navigation, 1975–78. DUniv Surrey, 1971. *Address:* Northbrook, Littleford Lane, Shamley Green, Surrey GU5 0RH. *T:* (01483) 892444. *Club:* Royal Air Force.

FENNEY, Roger Johnson, CBE 1973 (MBE (mil.) 1945); Chairman, Special Trustees, Charing Cross Hospital, 1980–88; *b* 11 Sept. 1916; *s* of James Henry Fenney and Annie Sarah Fenney; *m* 1942, Dorothy Porteus (*d* 1989); two *d*. *Educ:* Cowley Sch., St Helens; Univ. of Manchester (BA Admin 1939). Served War, 1939–46: Gunner to Major, Field Artillery; served N Africa and Italy (mentioned in despatches). Secretary, Central Midwives Board, 1947–82; Governor, Charing Cross Hosp., 1958–74 (Chm., Clinical Res. Cttee, 1970–80; Mem. Council, Med. Sch., 1970–80); Governor, Hammersmith Hosp., 1956–74; Chm., W London Hosp., 1957–68; First Nuffield Fellow for Health Affairs, USA, 1968; Dep. Chm., Kennedy Inst. of Rheumatol., 1970–77. Member: Exec., Arthritis and Rheumatism Council, 1978–98; Ealing, Hammersmith and Hounslow AHA, 1974–79; Field Dir, Jt Study Gp (FIGO/ICM), Accra, Yaounde, Nairobi, Dakar, San José and Bogotá, 1972–76. *Address:* 11 Gilray House, Gloucester Terrace, W2 3DF. *T:* (020) 7262 8313.

FENTEM, Prof. Peter Harold, FRCP; Emeritus Professor, University of Nottingham, 1997 (Stroke Association Professor of Stroke Medicine, 1992–97); Hon. Consultant, Nottingham City Hospital NHS Trust (formerly Nottingham Health Authority), 1976–97; *b* 12 Sept. 1933; *s* of Harold and Agnes Fentem; *m* 1958, Rosemary Hodson; two *s* two *d*. *Educ:* Bury Grammar Sch.; Univ. of Manchester (BSc 1st cl. hons 1955; MSc 1956; MB ChB Hons 1959). FRCP 1989. Hosp. appts, Manchester Royal Inf., 1959–60; Demonstrator in Path., Univ. of Manchester, 1960–61; Manchester and Cardiff Royal Infs, 1961–64; Lectr in Physiol., St Mary's Hosp. Med. Sch., 1964–68; University of Nottingham: Sen. Lectr in Physiol., 1968; Reader, 1975; Prof. of Physiol., 1975–92; Dean of Medicine, 1987–93. Chm., BSI Tech. Sub-Cttee on Compression Hosiery, 1978–89; Sci. Sec., Fitness and Health Adv. Gp, Sports Council, 1981; Civil Consultant to RAF, 1983–2000; Hon. Consultant to Army, 1989–97; Member: Army Personnel Res. Cttee, 1983–93 (Chm., Applied Physiol. Panel, 1986–93); GMC, 1988–93; Trent RHA, 1988–90; DoH Physical Activity Task Force, 1993–96; Nat. Alliance for Physical Activity, 1997–99; Nat. Heart Forum, 1997–. Trustee: Age Concern Essex, 1999–; Stroke Assoc., 2000–. *Publications:* (jt author): Exercise: the facts, 1981; Work Physiology, in Principles and Practice of Human Physiology, 1981; The New Case for Exercise, 1988; Benefits of Exercise: the evidence, 1990; (Adv. Editor) Physiology Integrated Clinical Science, 1983. *Recreations:* gardening, walking.

FENTON, Prof. Alexander, CBE 1986; DLitt; Professor of Scottish Ethnology and Director, School of Scottish Studies, University of Edinburgh, 1990–94, now Professor Emeritus; Director, European Ethnological Research Centre, Edinburgh, since 1989; *b* 26 June 1929; *s* of Alexander Fenton and Annie Stirling Stronach; *m* 1956, Evelyn Elizabeth Hunter; two *d*. *Educ:* Turriff Academy; Aberdeen Univ. (MA); Cambridge Univ. (BA); Edinburgh Univ. (DLitt). Senior Asst Editor, Scottish National Dictionary, 1955–59; Asst Keeper, Nat. Museum of Antiquities of Scotland, 1959–75, Dep. Keeper, 1975–78, Director, 1978–85; Res. Dir, Nat. Museums of Scotland, 1985–89. Mem., Ancient Monuments Bd for Scotland, 1979–94. Hon. Prof. of Antiquities to Royal Scottish Acad., 1996–. Member: Royal Gustav Adolf Acad., Uppsala, Sweden, 1978; Royal Danish Acad. of Scis and Letters, 1979; Soc. Royale des Lettres de Lund, Sweden, 1998; Jury, Europa Preis für Volkskunst (FVS Foundation, Hamburg) 1975–96. Hon. DLitt Aberdeen, 1989. Co-editor, Tools and Tillage (Copenhagen), 1968–; Editor: Review of Scottish Culture, 1984–; Scottish Studies, 1992–99. *Publications:* The Various Names of Shetland, 1973, 2nd edn 1977; Scottish Country Life, 1976, 3rd edn 1999; (trans.) S. Steensen Blicher, En Landsbydegns Dagbog (The Diary of a Parish Clerk, 1976); The Island Blackhouse, 1978; The Northern Isles: Orkney and Shetland, 1978, 2nd edn 1997; (with B. Walker) The Rural Architecture of Scotland, 1981; The Shape of the Past, 2 vols, 1985; (trans.) S. Weöres, Ha a Világ Rigó Lenne (If All the World were a Blackbird), 1985; Wird's an' Wark 'e Seasons Roon, 1987; Country Life in Scotland, 1987; The Turra Coo: a legal episode in the popular culture of NE Scotland, 1989; Scottish Country Life, 1989; Craiters—or Twenty Buchan Tales, 1995; numerous articles in learned jls. *Address:* 132 Blackford Avenue, Edinburgh EH9 3HH. *T:* (0131) 667 5456. *Club:* New (Edinburgh).

FENTON, Ernest John; Director General, Association of Investment Trust Companies, 1993–97; *b* 14 Oct. 1938; *s* of Forbes Duncan Campbell Fenton and Janet Burnfield Fenton (*née* Easson); *m* 1965, Ann Ishbel Ramsay; one *s* two *d*. *Educ:* Harris Acad., Scotland. CA 1961; AIIMR 1972. Partner, W. Greenwell & Co., 1968–87; Chm. and Chief Exec., Greenwell Montagu Stockbrokers, 1987–92. Non-executive Director: Fleming Income & Capital Investment Trust PLC, 1991–; Cotesworth & Co. Ltd (Lloyd's Managing Agents), 1994–; Renaissance US Growth and Income Trust PLC, 1996–. Farmer, Kent and Sussex, 1973–. Mem. Investment Cttee, CRC, 1995–98. MSI 1986; MInstD 1994. FRSA 1993. *Recreations:* shooting, curling. *Address:* Dundale Farm, Bells Yew Green, Tunbridge Wells, Kent TN3 9AQ. *Club:* City of London.

FENTON, James Martin, FRSL; writer; Professor of Poetry, University of Oxford, 1994–99; *b* 25 April 1949; *s* of Rev. Canon J. C. Fenton, *qv* and Mary Hamilton (*née* Ingoldby). *Educ:* Durham Choristers Sch.; Repton Sch.; Magdalen Coll., Oxford (MA; Hon. Fellow, 1999). FRSL 1983. Asst Literary Editor, 1971, Editorial Asst, 1972, New Statesman; freelance correspondent in Indo-China, 1973–75; Political Columnist, New Statesman, 1976–78; German Correspondent, The Guardian, 1978–79; Theatre Critic, Sunday Times, 1979–84; Chief Book Reviewer, The Times, 1984–86; Far East Corresp., 1986–88, columnist, 1993–95, The Independent. *Publications:* Our Western Furniture, 1968; Terminal Moraine, 1972; A Vacant Possession, 1978; A German Requiem, 1980; Dead Soldiers, 1981; The Memory of War, 1982; (trans.) Rigoletto, 1982; You Were Marvellous, 1983; (ed) The Original Michael Frayn, 1983; Children in Exile, 1984; Poems 1968–83, 1985; (trans.) Simon Boccanegra, 1985; The Fall of Saigon, in Granta 15, 1985; The Snap Revolution, in Granta 18, 1986; (ed) Cambodian Witness: the autobiography of Someth May, 1986; (with John Fuller) Partingtime Hall (poems), 1987; All the Wrong Places: adrift in the politics of Asia, 1988; Manila Envelope, 1989; (ed) Underground in Japan, by Rey Ventura, 1992; Out of Danger (poems), 1993; Leonardo's Nephew, 1998; The Strength of Poetry, 2001. *Address:* Peters Fraser & Dunlop, Drury House, 34–43 Russell Street, WC2B 5HA.

FENTON, Rev. Canon John Charles; Canon of Christ Church, Oxford, 1978–91, Hon. Canon, 1991–92, now Hon. Canon Emeritus and Emeritus Student; *b* 5 June 1921; *s* of Cornelius O'Connor Fenton and Agnes Claudine Fenton. *Educ:* S Edward's Sch., Oxford; Queen's Coll., Oxford (BA 1943, MA 1947, BD 1953); Lincoln Theol Coll. Deacon 1944, priest 1945. Asst Curate, All Saints, Hindley, Wigan, 1944–47; Chaplain, Lincoln Theol Coll., 1947–51, Sub-Warden, 1951–54; Vicar of Wentworth, Yorks, 1954–58; Principal: Lichfield Theol Coll., 1958–65; S Chad's Coll., Durham, 1965–78. *Publications:* Preaching the Cross, 1958; The Passion according to John, 1961; Crucified with Christ, 1961; Saint Matthew (Pelican Commentaries), 1963; Saint John (New Clarendon Bible), 1970; What was Jesus' Message?, 1971; (with M. Hare Duke) Good News, 1976; Finding the Way through John, 1988; Sunday Readings, 1991; Affirmations, 1993; Finding the Way through Mark, 1995; The Matthew Passion, 1996; Galatians, 1996, with 1 & 2 Thessalonians, 1999 (People's Bible Commentary); contrib. Theol., Jl of Theol Studies, and Church Times. *Recreations:* walking, camping, gardening. *Address:* 8 Rowland Close, Wolvercote, Oxford OX2 8PW. *T:* (01865) 554099.

FENWICK, Very Rev. Jeffery Robert; Dean of Guernsey, 1989–95; *b* 8 April 1930; *s* of Stanley Robert and Dorothy Fenwick; *m* 1955, Pamela Frances (*née* Galley); one *s* two *d*. *Educ:* Torquay and Selhurst Grammar Schools; Pembroke Coll., Cambridge (MA); Lincoln Theol Coll. Deacon 1955, priest 1956, Liverpool; Curate, St Thomas the Martyr, UpHolland, 1955; Priest-in-charge, Christ the King, Daramombe, Mashonaland, 1958; Secretary, USPG, Oxford, 1964; Rector, Gatooma 1965, Salisbury East 1967, Mashonaland; Dean, Bulawayo, Matabeleland, 1975; Canon Residentiary, Worcester Cathedral, 1978; Librarian and Treasurer, 1978–89. Examining Chaplain, Mashonaland and Matabeleland, 1966–78; Archdeacon of Charter, 1970–75, of Bulawayo 1975–78. Hon. Canon of Winchester Cathedral, 1989–95, now Emeritus. Chm., Cathedrals Finance Conf. for England, 1983–89. Chm., Britain-Zimbabwe Soc., 1996–. *Publications:* Chosen People, 1971; (contrib.) The Pattern of History, 1973. *Recreations:* painting, music, gardening, walking. *Address:* 4 Moffat Avenue, Hillside, Bulawayo, Zimbabwe. *T:* (9) 46240.

FENWICK, John James; DL; Deputy Chairman, Fenwick Ltd, 1972–79 and since 1997 (Managing Director, 1972–82; Chairman, 1979–97); Director, Northern Rock plc (formerly Northern Rock Building Society), 1984–99; *b* 9 Aug. 1932; *e s* of James Frederick Trevor Fenwick; *m* 1957, Muriel Gillian Hodnett; three *s*. *Educ:* Rugby Sch.; Pembroke Coll., Cambridge (MA). Chairman: Northumberland Assoc. of Youth Clubs, 1966–71; Retail Distributors Assoc., 1977–79; Vice Chm., National Assoc. of Citizens Advice Bureaux, 1971–79; Regional Dir, Northern Bd, Lloyds Bank, 1982–85. Member: Newcastle Diocesan Bd of Finance, 1964–69; Retail Consortium Council, 1976–79; Post

Office Users' Nat. Council, 1980–82; Civic Trust for NE, 1979–96. Governor: Royal Grammar Sch., Newcastle upon Tyne, 1975–2000 (Chm. Govs, 1987–); St Paul's Girls' Sch., 1988– (Chm. Govs, 1995–2000); Moorfields Eye Hosp., 1981–86; Royal Shakespeare Theatre, 1985–. Master, Mercers' Co., 1991–92. DL Tyne and Wear, 1986. Hon. DCL Northumbria, 1993. *Recreations:* travel, reading, walking. *Address:* 63 New Bond Street, W1A 3BS. *Clubs:* Garrick, MCC.

FENWICK, Justin Francis Quintus; QC 1993, a Recorder, since 1999; *b* 11 Sept. 1949, *s* of David and Maita Fenwick; *m* 1975, Marcia Mary Dunn; one *s* three *d. Educ:* Ampleforth Coll., York; Clare Coll., Cambridge (MA Mod. Langs and Architectural Hist.). Commnd Grenadier Guards, 1968; Adjt, 2nd Battalion, 1977–79; Temp. Equerry to HRH the Duke of Edinburgh, 1979–81. Called to the Bar, Inner Temple, 1980, Bencher, 1997. Dir, 1997–, Chm., 1999–, Bar Mutual Indemnity Fund Ltd. *Recreations:* wine, shooting, reading. *Address:* 4 New Square, Lincoln's Inn, WC2A 3RJ. *T:* (020) 7822 2000. *Clubs:* Garrick, Travellers.

FENWICK, Peter Brooke Cadogan, FRCPsych; Consultant Neuropsychiatrist: Radcliffe Infirmary, Oxford, since 1989; Maudsley Hospital, 1977–96, now Emeritus; Chairman, Scientific and Medical Network, since 1987; *b* 25 May 1935; *s* of Anthony Fenwick and Betty (*née* Darling); *m* 1963, Elizabeth Roberts; one *s* two *d. Educ:* Stowe Sch.; Trinity Coll., Cambridge (BA 1957; MB BChir 1960); DPM London 1966. FRCPsych 1986. House Officer, St Thomas' Hosp., 1960–62; SHO in Psychiatry, Middlesex Hosp., 1962–64; MRC Fellow, Nat. Hosp., 1964–66; Registrar, then Sen. Registrar, Maudsley Hosp., 1967–74; Consultant Neurophysiologist: Westminster Hosp., 1974–77; St Thomas' Hosp., 1974–96, now Hon. Consulting Neurophysiologist; Hon. Cons. Neurophysiologist, Broadmoor Special Hosp., 1972–; Hon. Sen. Lectr, Inst. of Psychiatry, London Univ., 1974–. Forensic expert on automatism and sleep disorders; has given expert neuropsychiatric evidence in many civil and criminal legal cases. Consultant, Music and the Brain documentary series, 1986. Ver Hayden de Lancey Prize, Cambridge Univ., 1987. *Publications:* with Elizabeth Fenwick: The Truth in the Light, 1995; The Hidden Door, 1997; Past Lives, 1999; over 200 contribs to learned jls. *Recreations:* flying, hill walking, wind and water turbines, the study of consciousness. *Address:* 42 Herne Hill, SE24 9QP. *T:* (020) 7274 3154.

FENWICK, Very Rev. Dr Richard David; Dean of Monmouth, since 1997; *b* 3 Dec. 1943; *s* of Ethel May and William Samuel Fenwick; *m* 1975, Dr Jane Elizabeth Hughes; one *s* one *d. Educ:* Glantâf Secondary Modern Sch.; Monkton House; Canton High Sch., Cardiff; Univ. of Wales, Lampeter (BA, MA, PhD); Trinity Coll., Dublin (MusB, MA); Fitzwilliam Coll., Cambridge; Ridley Hall, Cambridge. FLCM; FTCL. Ordained deacon, 1968, priest, 1969; Assistant Curate: Skewen, 1968–72; Penarth with Lavernock, 1972–74; Priest-Vicar, Succentor and Sacrist of Rochester Cathedral, 1974–78; Minor Canon, 1978–83, Succentor, 1979–83, Warden of the Coll. of Minor Canons, 1981–83, St Paul's Cathedral; Vicar, St Martin's, Ruislip, 1983–90; Priest-Vicar of Westminster Abbey, 1983–90; Canon Residentiary and Precentor, 1990–97, Sub-Dean, 1996–97, Guildford Cathedral. Chm., Liturgical Commn of the Church in Wales, 1998–. Warden, Guild of Church Musicians, 1998–. Liveryman, Musicians' Co.; Master's Chaplain, Co. of Gold and Silver Wyre Drawers. OStJ 2001. *Publications:* contribs to various musical and theol jls. *Recreations:* travel, reading, music. *Address:* The Deanery, Stow Hill, Newport, Monmouthshire NP20 4ED. *T:* (01633) 263338.

FERGUS, Hon. Sir Howard (Archibald), KBE 2001 (CBE 1995; OBE 1979); PhD; Deputy Governor, Montserrat, since 1976; Professor, University of West Indies, since 2001; *b* 22 July 1937; *s* of Simon and Priscilla Fergus; *m* 1970, Eudora Edgecombe; one *s* two *d. Educ:* Univ. of W Indies (BA, PhD 1984); Univ. of Bristol (CertEd); Univ. of Manchester (MEd). Primary sch. teacher, 1955–64; secondary sch. teacher, 1964–70; Chief Educn Officer, Montserrat, 1970–74; Lectr, 1974–81, Sen. Lectr, 1981–2001, Sch. of Continuing Studies, Univ. of WI. Mem. and Speaker, Legislative Council, Montserrat, 1975–2001. Supervisor of Elections, 1978–. *Publications:* Montserrat: history of a Caribbean colony, 1994; Gallery Montserrat: prominent people in our history, 1996; Montserrat Versus Volcano, 1996; Lara Rains and Colonial Rites (poetry), 1998; Volcano Song: poems of an island in agony, 2000; Montserrat in the Twentieth Century: trials and triumphs, 2001; contrib. several book chapters and articles to learned jls. *Recreations:* reading, writing, poetry. *Address:* University of West Indies, PO Box 256 Manjack, Montserrat, W Indies. *T:* 4913924; (home) Olveston, Montserrat, W Indies. *T:* 4912414, *Fax:* 4918924.

FERGUSON, Sir Alexander Chapman, Kt 1999; CBE 1995 (OBE 1984); Manager, Manchester United Football Club, 1986–May 2002; *b* 31 Dec. 1941; *s* of Alexander and Elizabeth Ferguson; *m* 1966, Catherine Holding; three *s. Educ:* Govan High Sch., Glasgow. Footballer; played for: Queen's Park, 1958–60; St Johnstone, 1960–64; Dunfermline Athletic, 1964–67; Glasgow Rangers, 1967–69; Falkirk, 1969–73; Ayr United, 1973–74; numerous championship wins as Manager of St Mirren, 1974–78, of Aberdeen, 1978–86 (League Cup, 1985); wins with Manchester United: Premier Div., 1992–93, 1993–94, 1995–96, 1996–97, 1998–99; FA Cup, 1990, 1994, 1996, 1999; European Cup Winners Cup, 1983, 1991; European Cup, 1999; Super Cup, 1983, 1991; League Cup, 1992; Charity Shield, 1990, 1993, 1994, 1996, 1997. *Publications:* A Light in the North, 1984; Six Years at United, 1992; Just Champion, 1993; A Year in the Life, 1995; (with David Meek) A Will to Win, 1997; (with Hugh McIlvanney) Managing My Life: my autobiography, 1999; The Unique Treble: achieving our goals, 2000. *Recreations:* golf, snooker. *Address:* Manchester United Football Club, Old Trafford, Manchester M16 0RA. *T:* (0161) 872 1661.

FERGUSON, Dr Archibald Thomas Graham, CPhys, FInstP; Nuclear Weapons Safety Advisor, Ministry of Defence, 1994–97; *b* 27 Dec. 1928; *s* of Francis Ferguson and Annie Orr Ferguson (*née* Graham); *m* 1956, Margaret Watson; two *d. Educ:* Irvine Royal Acad.; Glasgow Univ. (MA 1950; PhD 1954). CPhys 1974; FInstP 1974. United Kingdom Atomic Energy Authority, Harwell Laboratory, 1953–93: Nuclear Physics Div., 1953–65; Gp Leader, High Voltage Lab., 1961–81; on secondment to Neils Bohr Inst., Copenhagen, 1965–66; Head: Scientific Admin, 1982–85; Nuclear Physics Div., 1985–90; Safety, Culham and Harwell, 1990–93. *Publications:* contrib. numerous articles in learned jls; conf. proceedings. *Recreations:* sailing, gardening.

FERGUSON, Duncan George Robin, FIA; Senior Partner, B & W Deloitte, and Partner, Deloitte & Touche, since 2001; *b* 12 May 1942; *s* of Dr R. L. Ferguson and K. I. Ferguson; *m* 1966, Alison Margaret Simpson; one *s* one *d* (and one *s* decd). *Educ:* Fettes Coll., Edinburgh; Trinity Coll., Cambridge (MA Maths and Econs 1964; DipAgSci (Agricl Econs) 1965). FIA 1970. Actuarial student, Bacon & Woodrow, 1965–69; Actuary and Asst Gen. Manager, Metropolitan Life, Cape Town, 1969–72; Actuary and Dir, Nation Life, 1972–75; Dir, Internat. Div., Eagle Star, 1975–88; Partner, 1988, Sen. Partner, 1994–2000, Bacon & Woodrow. Pres., Inst. of Actuaries, 1996–98. *Publications:* Unit Linked Life Assurance in South Africa, 1972; Life Assurance Solvency and Insolvency, 1976; Business Projections: a critical appraisal, 1980; Review of Law Relating to Insolvent Life Assurance Companies and Proposals for Reform, 1984; Reasonable Expectations of Policy Holders, 1984. *Address:* B & W Deloitte, Stonecutter Court, Stonecutter Street, EC4A 4TR. *T:* (020) 7415 0300.

FERGUSON, Ernest Alexander; Under-Secretary and Accountant-General, Department of Employment, 1973–77; *b* 26 July 1917; *s* of William Henry and Lilian Ferguson; *m* 1940, Mary Josephine Wadsworth; two *s. Educ:* Priory Sch., Shrewsbury; Pembroke Coll., Cambridge (Scholar, 1935–39; MA 1944). Served War, RA (Captain), 1940–45. Entered Ministry of Labour, 1945, Principal, 1948, Asst Sec., 1962. Chm., Central Youth Employment Executive, 1967–69; Sec. to NEDC, 1971–73; Dep. Chm., Central Arbitration Cttee, 1977–87. *Recreations:* sport, hill walking, reading. *Address:* 164 Balcombe Road, Horley, Surrey RH6 9DS. *T:* (01293) 785254. *Club:* Civil Service.

FERGUSON, Air Vice-Marshal Gordon MacArthur, CB 1993; CBE 1990; Chairman, Suffolk Probation Board, since 2001; *b* 15 April 1938; *s* of James Miller Ferguson and late Elizabeth Thomson Ferguson (*née* Barron); *m* 1966, Alison Mary Saxby; one *s* one *d. Educ:* King Edward VI Sch., Southampton. Commissioned, RAF, 1960; served Mobile Air Movements, RAF Pergamos and Nicosia, HQ 38 Group, RAF Stafford and Fylingdales, MoD Supply Policy, HQ 2nd ATAF; RAF Staff Coll., 1977; OC Tac Supply Wing, 1977–79; MoD Supply Policy, 1979–81; Air Warfare Course, 1981; MoD Supply Policy, 1981–85; Dep. Dir, Supply Management, 1985–87, Dir, 1987–89; Dir, AMSO Reorgn Implementation Team, 1989–91; AOA, HQ Strike Comd, 1991–94. Trustee, Royal Patriotic Fund Corp., 1995–. *Recreations:* golf, bridge, gardening. *Address:* Lilley Cottage, Turnpike Hill, Withersfield, Suffolk CB9 7RY. *Club:* Royal Air Force.

FERGUSON, Iain William Findlay; QC (Scot.) 2000; *b* 31 July 1961; *s* of James Thomas Ferguson and Catherine Doris (*née* Findlay); *m* 1992, Valérie Laplanche; two *s. Educ:* Univ. of Dundee (LLB Hons; DipLP). Admitted Faculty of Advocates, 1987; Standing Junior Counsel: MoD (Army), 1991–98; Scottish Exec., Planning, 1998–2000. *Recreations:* cycling, Rugby, cooking. *Address:* 16 McLaren Road, Edinburgh EH9 2BN. *T:* (0131) 667 1751.

FERGUSON, Sir Ian Edward J.; *see* Johnson-Ferguson.

FERGUSON, John Alexander; HM Senior Chief Inspector of Schools in Scotland, 1981–87, retired; *b* 16 Oct. 1927; *s* of George Ferguson and Martha Crichton Dykes; *m* 1953, Jean Stewart; two *s* one *d. Educ:* Royal Coll. of Science and Technology, Univ. of Glasgow (BSc Hons, Diploma). Teacher, Airdrie Central Sch., 1950–51; Lectr, 1951–55, Head of Dept of Engrg, 1955–61, Coatbridge Technical Coll.; HM Inspector of Schs, 1961–72, Asst Sec., 1972–75, Scottish Educn Dept; HM Depute Sen. Chief Inspector of Schs, 1975–81. *Recreations:* golf, bridge. *Clubs:* Craigmillar Park Lawn Tennis, Carlton Bridge (Edinburgh); Luffness New Golf.

FERGUSON, John McIntyre, CBE 1976; FREng; FIEE, FIMechE; engineering consultant, 1973, retired 1986; *b* 16 May 1915; *s* of Frank Ferguson and Lilian (*née* Bowen); *m* 1941, Margaret Frances Tayler; three *s. Educ:* Armstrong Coll., Durham Univ. BScEng (1st Cl. Hons). English Electric Co., Stafford: Research, 1936; Chief Engr, 1953; Dir Engrg, Heavy Electric Products, 1965; Dir of Engrg, GEC Power Engrg Co., 1969. Member: Metrication Bd, 1969–76; Science Res. Council, 1972–76; UGC, 1977–82. President: IEE, 1977–78; IEETE, 1979–81. FREng (FEng 1978). Hon. FIEEIE. Hon. DSc Birmingham, 1983. *Recreations:* golf, sailing. *Address:* 11 Appledore Close, Baswich, Stafford ST17 0EW. *T:* (01785) 664700.

FERGUSON, Prof. Mark William James, CBE 1999; PhD; Professor, School of Biological Sciences, University of Manchester, since 1984; *b* 11 Oct. 1955; *s* of late James Ferguson and of Elenor Gwendoline Ferguson; *m* (marr. diss.); two *d. Educ:* Queen's Univ., Belfast (BSc 1st Cl. Hons Anatomy 1976; BDS 1st Cl. Hons Dentistry 1978; PhD Anatomy and Embryology 1982). FFDRCSI 1990; FDSRCSE 1998. Winston Churchill Travelling Fellow, 1978; Lectr in Anatomy, QUB, 1979–84; Head, Dept of Cell and Structural Biology, 1986–92, Dean, Sch. of Biol Scis, 1994–96, Univ. of Manchester. Founder and Chm. of Bd, Manchester Biotechnology Ltd, 1997–99; Founder, Pres. and CEO, Renovo Ltd, 1998–. Chm., Health and Life Scis Panel, Tech. Foresight Prog., OST, 1994–99; Member: Lord Sainsbury's Biotech. Cluster Cttee, DTI, 1999; Biol Sub Cttee, Cttee of Safety of Medicines, 1999–; Genome Valley Steering Gp, DTI, 2000–01; Preclinical Medicine, Anatomy, Physiol. and Pharmacol. Panel, RAE2001, HEFCE. Pres., Med. Scis Section, BAAAS, 1997. Gov., Res. into Ageing, 1995–. Steeger Vis. Prof. and Lectr, NY Univ. Med. Center, 1992; Teale Lecture, RCP, 1994; Broadhurst Lecture, Harvard Med. Sch., 1996; Distinguished Lectr, Amer. Soc. of Human Genetics, 1998; British Council lecture tour, India, 1999. Founder FMedSci 1998. John Tomes Prize and Medal, 1990, Charles Tomes Prize and Medal, 1998, RCS; Carter Medal, Clin. Genetics Soc., 1997; Internat. Assoc. for Dental Res. Award, 2000. *Publications:* The Structure, Development and Evolution of Reptiles, 1984; Egg Incubation: its effects on embryonic development in birds and reptiles, 1991; (ed) Gray's Anatomy, 38th edn, 1995; more than 250 scientific papers and contribs to books on wound healing, prevention of scarring, cleft palate and sex determination. *Recreations:* travel, wildlife, reading, antiques, scientific research. *Address:* School of Biological Sciences, University of Manchester, 3.239 Stopford Building, Oxford Road, Manchester M13 9PT. *T:* (0161) 275 6775.

FERGUSON, Martin John, AM 1996; MP (ALP) Batman, Australia, since 1996; *b* 12 Dec. 1953; *s* of Laurie John Ferguson and Mary Ellen Clare Ferguson (*née* Bett); *m* 1981, Patricia Jane Waller; one *s* one *d. Educ:* St Patrick's Convent, Guildford; St Patrick's Coll., Strathfield; Sydney Univ. (BEc Hons). Federated Miscellaneous Workers Union of Australia: Federal Research Officer, 1975–81; Asst Gen. Sec., 1981–84; Gen. Sec., 1984–90; Pres., ACTU, 1990–96. Opposition spokesman, Australian Parliament: on employment and trng, 1996–98; on population, 1997–99; on immigration, 1997–98; on regl develt, infrastructure, transport and regl services, 1999–; Asst to Ldr of Opposition on multicultural affairs, 1997–98. Mem., Governing Body, ILO, 1990–96. Member: Trade Develt Council, 1990–96; Econ. Planning Adv. Council, 1990–96; Australian Govt's Agric. Food Council, 1992–96; Exec. Bd, Construction Ind. Develt Agency, 1992–96. Mem. Bd, Nat. Liby of Australia, 1999–. *Address:* 48 High Street, Northcote, Vic 3070, Australia. *T:* (3) 94824644, *Fax:* (3) 94890984.

FERGUSON, Prof. Michael Anthony John, PhD; FRS 2000; FRSE; Professor of Molecular Parasitology, University of Dundee, since 1994; *b* 6 Feb. 1957; *s* of Dr Anthony John Alexander Ferguson and Pamela Mary (*née* Gray); *m* 1st, 1982, Sheila Duxbury (marr. diss. 1988); 2nd, 1992, Dr Maria Lucia Sampaio Güther; one *s. Educ:* St Peter's Sch., York; UMIST (BSc Hons Biochem. 1979); Charing Cross Hosp. Med. Sch., Univ. of London (PhD Biochem. 1982). Post-doctoral Research Fellow: Rockefeller Univ., NY, 1982–85; Oxford Univ., 1985–88; Res. Fellow, Pembroke Coll., Oxford, 1986–88; University of Dundee: Lectr, 1988–91; Reader, 1991–94. FRSE 1994. Colworth Medal, Biochemical Soc., 1991. *Recreation:* travel. *Address:* Division of Biological Chemistry and Molecular Microbiology, Wellcome Trust Biocentre, University of Dundee, Dundee DD1 5EH. *T:* (01382) 344219.

FERGUSON, Niall Campbell D.; *see* Douglas Ferguson.

FERGUSON, Patricia Josephine; Member (Lab) Glasgow Maryhill, Scottish Parliament, since 1999; *b* 24 Sept. 1958; *d* of John Ferguson and Andrewina Ferguson (*née* Power); *m* 1988, William Gerard Butler, *qv. Educ:* Garnethill Convent Secondary Sch., Glasgow; Glasgow Coll. of Technology (part-time) (SHNC Public Admin.). Greater Glasgow Health Board: Admin. Trainee, 1976–78; Administrator, 1978–83; Sec., Greater Glasgow SE Local Health Council, 1983–85; Administrator: Capital Services, Lanarkshire Health Bd, 1985–90; Scottish TUC, 1990–94; Organiser, South West of Scotland Lab. Party, 1994–96; Scottish Officer, Scottish Lab. Party, 1996–99. Dep. Presiding Officer, Scottish Parlt, 1999–. *Recreations:* reading, driving, travel. *Address:* Unit 1A, Firhill House, 55 Firhill Road, Glasgow G20 7SD. *T:* (0141) 946 1300, *Fax:* (0141) 946 1412.

FERGUSON, Ven. Paul John; Archdeacon of Cleveland, since 2001; *b* 13 July 1955; *s* of Thomas and Joyce Ferguson; *m* 1982, Penelope Hewitt-Jones; two *s* one *d. Educ:* Birkenhead Sch.; New Coll., Oxford (BA 1976, MA 1980); Westminster Coll., Oxford (PGCE); King's Coll., Cambridge (BA 1984, MA 1988); Westcott Hse, Cambridge. FRCO 1975. Ordained deacon, 1985, priest 1986; Curate, St Mary's Chester, 1985–88; Chaplain and Sacrist, 1988–92, Precentor, 1992–95, Westminster Abbey; Precentor and Residentiary Canon, York Minster, 1995–2001. *Publications:* (jtly) Sing His Glory, 1997; reviews, articles on music and liturgy. *Recreations:* cycling, swimming, flying. *Address:* 2 Langbaurgh Road, Hutton Rudby, Yarm TS15 0HL. *T:* (01642) 706095.

FERGUSON, Richard; QC 1986; QC (NI) 1973; SC (Ireland) 1983; *b* 22 Aug. 1935; *o s* of late Wesley Ferguson and Edith Ferguson (*née* Hewitt); *m* 1st, Janet Irvine Magowan (marr. diss.); three *s* one *d*; 2nd, Roma Felicity Whelan; one *s. Educ:* Rainey Sch., Magherafelt; Methodist Coll., Belfast; Trinity Coll., Dublin (BA); Queen's Univ. of Belfast (LLB). Called to NI Bar, 1956, to Bar of England and Wales, Gray's Inn, 1972 (Bencher, 1994). Chairman: NI Mental Health Review Tribunal, 1973–84; Criminal Bar Assoc. of England and Wales, 1993–95. MP (OU) S Antrim, 1969–70. FRGS 1980. *Recreations:* drinking pints of Guinness, watching the Arsenal. *Address:* 2–4 Tudor Street, EC4Y 0AA. *T:* (020) 7797 7111. *Club:* Kildare Street and University (Dublin).

FERGUSON, Susan Margaret D.; *see* Douglas Ferguson.

FERGUSON, William James, OBE 1996; FEAgS; farmer; Vice Lord-Lieutenant of Aberdeenshire, since 1998; Chairman, Aberdeen Milk Company, since 1994; *b* 3 April 1933; *s* of William Adam Ferguson and Violet (*née* Wiseman); *m* 1961, Carroll Isabella Milne; one *s* three *d. Educ:* Turriff Acad.; North of Scotland Coll. of Agriculture (Cert. of Agric.). Nat. Service, 1st Bn Gordon Highlanders, serving in Malaya, 1952–54. Chm., North of Scotland Coll. of Agric., 1986–91; Vice Chm., Scottish Agricl Colls, 1991–97. Former Chm., Grampian Farm Wildlife Adv. Gp; Member: Rowett Res. Inst., 1980–82; Technical Cttee, Crichton Royal Dairy Farm, Dumfries, 1980–83; Macaulay Inst. of Soil Res., 1983–85; Scottish Farm Bldgs Investigation Unit, 1984–86; Scottish Country Life Mus., 1986–96. FRAgS 1995. DL Aberdeenshire, 1988. *Recreations:* golf, ski-ing, field sports. *Address:* Rothiebrisbane, Fyvie, Turriff, Aberdeenshire AB53 8LE. *Club:* Farmers'.

FERGUSON DAVIE, Sir Michael, 8th Bt *cr* 1847, of Creedy, Devonshire; stockbroker; Consultant, Madoff Securities Ltd, since 1995; Partner, Footloose, since 1997; *b* 10 Jan. 1944; *er s* of Sir John Ferguson Davie, 7th Bt and (Joan) Zoë (Charlotte), *d* of Raymond Hoole, Vancouver, BC; *S* father, 2000; *m* 1st, 1968, (Margaret) Jean (marr. diss. 1992), *d* of Douglas Macbeth; one *s* decd; 2nd, 2001, Sarah, *d* of John Seyfried and Lady Cathleen Hudson (*née* Eliot), and former wife of Peter M. Smith; two step *s. Educ:* St Edward's Sch., Oxford. Grenfell & Co. (later Grenfell & Colegrave), 1961–79; Fielding Newson-Smith & Co., 1979–86; Dir, NatWest Markets, 1986–95. *Recreations:* writing, bridge, Real tennis. *Heir: b* Julian Anthony Ferguson Davie [*b* 6 July 1950; *m* 1976, Louise, *d* of John Marsden; three *s*]. *Address:* 63 Hillgate Place, SW12 9ES. *T:* (020) 8675 3593. *Clubs:* City of London, MCC.

FERGUSON FLATT, Very Rev. Roy Francis; *see* Flatt.

FERGUSON-SMITH, Prof. Malcolm Andrew, FRS 1983; FRSE 1978; Professor of Pathology and Professorial Fellow, Peterhouse, University of Cambridge, 1987–98, now Emeritus Fellow; Director, Cambridge University Centre for Medical Genetics, 1989–98; *b* 5 Sept. 1931; *s* of John Ferguson-Smith, MA, MD, FRCP and Ethel May (*née* Thorne); *m* 1960, Marie Eva Gzowska; one *s* three *d. Educ:* Stowe Sch.; Univ. of Glasgow (MB ChB 1955). MRCPath 1966, FRCPath 1978; MRCPGlas 1972, FRCPGlas 1974. Registrar in Lab. Medicine, Dept of Pathology, Western Infirmary, Glasgow, 1958–59; Fellow in Medicine and Instructor, Johns Hopkins Univ. Sch. of Medicine, 1959–61; Lectr, Sen. Lectr and Reader in Med. Genetics, Univ. of Glasgow, 1961–73, Prof. of Med. Genetics, 1973–87; Hon. Consultant: in Med. Paediatrics, Royal Hosp. for Sick Children, Glasgow, 1966–73; in Clin. Genetics, Yorkhill and Associated Hosps, 1973–87; in Med. Genetics, Addenbrooke's NHS Trust, 1987–98; Director: W of Scotland Med. Genetics Service, 1973–87; E Anglian Regl Clin. Genetics Service, 1987–95. President: Clinical Genetics Soc., 1979–81; Eur. Soc. of Human Genetics, 1997–98; Internat. Soc. for Prenatal Diagnosis, 1998–Aug. 2002. Mem., Johns Hopkins Univ. Soc. of Scholars, 1983; Foreign Mem., Polish Acad. of Scis, 1988. Founder FMedSci 1998. Hon. DSc Strathclyde, 1992. Bronze Medal, Univ. of Helsinki, 1968; Makdougall-Brisbane Prize, RSE, 1988; San Remo Internat. Prize for Genetic Res., 1990; Baschirotto Award, Eur. Soc. of Human Genetics, 1996. Editor, Prenatal Diagnosis, 1980–. *Publications:* (ed) Early Prenatal Diagnosis, 1983; (jtly) Essential Medical Genetics, 1984, 5th edn 1997; (ed) Prenatal Diagnosis and Screening, 1992; papers on cytogenetics, gene mapping, human genetics and prenatal diagnosis in med. jls. *Recreations:* swimming, sailing, fishing. *Address:* 16 Rustat Road, Cambridge CB1 3QT. *T:* (01223) 246277; Department of Clinical Veterinary Medicine, Cambridge University, Madingley Road, Cambridge CB3 0ES.

FERGUSSON, Adam (Dugdale); consultant on European affairs, since 1989; *b* 10 July 1932; *yr s* of Sir James Fergusson of Kilkerran, 8th Bt, LLD, FRSE, and Frances Dugdale; *m* 1965, Penelope, *e d* of Peter Hughes, Furneaux Pelham Hall; two *s* two *d. Educ:* Eton; Trinity Coll., Cambridge (BA History, 1955). Glasgow Herald, 1956–61: Leader-writer, 1957–58; Diplomatic Corresp., 1959–61; Statist, 1961–67: Foreign Editor, 1964–67; Feature-writer for The Times on political, economic and environmental matters, 1967–77. Special Advr on European Affairs, FCO, 1985–89. European Parliament: Member (C) West Strathclyde, 1979–84; Spokesman on Political Affairs for European Democratic Gp, 1979–82; Vice-Chm., Political Affairs Cttee, 1982–84; Mem., Jt Cttee of ACP/EEC Consultative Assembly, 1979–84; contested (C) London Central, European elecn, 1984. Vice-Pres., Pan-European Union, 1981–; Mem., Scotland Says No Referendum Campaign Cttee, 1978–79. Dir, Murray International Trust PLC, 1995–. Gov., Howick Trust, 1976–; Vice-Pres., Bath Preservation Trust, 1997–. *Publications:* Roman Go Home, 1969; The Lost Embassy, 1972; The Sack of Bath, 1973; When Money Dies, 1975; various pamphlets; articles in national and internat. jls and magazines. *Address:* 15 Warwick Gardens, W14 8PH. *T:* (020) 7603 7900.

FERGUSSON, Alexander Charles Onslow; Member (C) Scotland South, Scottish Parliament, since 1999; *b* 8 April 1949; *s* of Lt Col Rev. Simon Charles David Fergusson and Auriole Kathleen Fergusson (*née* Hughes Onslow); *m* 1974, Jane Merryn Barthold; three *s. Educ:* Eton Coll.; West of Scotland Agricl Coll. (ONDA). Farmer, 1971–99. JP S Ayrshire, 1997–99; DL Ayrshire and Arran, 1997–99. *Recreations:* curling, Rugby, folk music. *Address:* Grennan, Dalry, Kirkudbrightshire DG7 3PL.

FERGUSSON of Kilkerran, Sir Charles, 9th Bt *cr* 1703; *b* 10 May 1931; *s* of Sir James Fergusson of Kilkerran, 8th Bt, and Frances (*d* 1988), *d* of Edgar Dugdale; *S* father, 1973; *m* 1961, Hon. Amanda Mary Noel-Paton, *d* of Lord Ferrier, ED; two *s. Educ:* Eton; Edinburgh and East of Scotland Coll. of Agriculture. *Heir: s* Adam Fergusson, [*b* 29 Dec. 1962; *m* 1989, Jenifer, *yr d* of Adam Thomson; one *s* two *d*].

FERGUSSON, Sir Ewen (Alastair John), GCMG 1993 (KCMG 1987); GCVO 1992; HM Diplomatic Service, retired; King of Arms, Most Distinguished Order of St Michael and St George, since 1996; *b* 28 Oct. 1932; *er s* of late Sir Ewen MacGregor Field Fergusson; *m* 1959, Sara Carolyn, *d* of late Brig-Gen. Lord Esmé Gordon Lennox, KCVO, CMG, DSO and *widow* of Sir William Andrew Montgomery-Cuninghame, 11th Bt; one *s* two *d. Educ:* Rugby; Oriel Coll., Oxford (MA; Hon. Fellow, 1988). Played Rugby Football for Oxford Univ., 1952 and 1953, and for Scotland, 1954. 2nd Lieut, 60th Rifles (KRRC), 1954–56. Joined Foreign (later Diplomatic) Service, 1956; Asst Private Sec. to Minister of Defence, 1957–59; British Embassy, Addis Ababa, 1960; FO, 1963; British Trade Development Office, New York, 1967; Counsellor and Head of Chancery, Office of UK Permanent Rep. to European Communities, 1972–75; Private Sec. to Foreign and Commonwealth Sec., 1975–78; Asst Under Sec. of State, FCO, 1978–82; Ambassador to S Africa, 1982–84; Dep. Under-Sec. of State (Middle East and Africa), FCO, 1984–87; Ambassador to France, 1987–92. Chairman: Coutts & Co. Gp, 1993–99; Savoy Hotel, 1995–98 (Dir, 1993–98; Co-Chm., Internat. Adv. Bd, Savoy Gp, 1999–). Director: British Telecom, 1993–99; Sun Alliance Gp, 1993–95. Chm., Govt Wine Adv. Cttee, 1993–. Governor, Rugby Sch., 1985– (Chm. Govs, 1995–); Trustee: Nat. Gall., 1995–; Henry Moore Foundn, 1998– (Chm., 2001–). Hon. LLD Aberdeen, 1995. Grand Officier, Légion d'Honneur (France), 1992. *Address:* 111 Iverna Court, W8 6TX. *T:* (020) 7938 1136; Les Baumeriaux, 84340 Entrechaux, France. *T:* 490460496. *Clubs:* Royal Automobile, Beefsteak; Jockey (Paris).

FERGUSSON, George Duncan; HM Diplomatic Service; HM Consul General, Boston, since 1999; *b* 30 Sept. 1955; *s* of Baron Ballantrae, KT, GCMG, GCVO, DSO, OBE; *m* 1981, Margaret Sheila Wookey; one *s* three *d. Educ:* Ballantrae Jun. Secondary Sch.; Hereworth Sch., NZ; Eton Coll.; Magdalen Coll., Oxford. Murray and Tait, Solicitors, 1977–78; joined Northern Ireland Office, 1978; seconded to NI Dept of Commerce, 1979–80; Private Sec. to Min. of State for NI, 1982–83; First Sec., Dublin, 1988–91; joined Diplomatic Service, 1990; FCO, 1991–93; First Sec., Seoul, 1994–96; FCO, 1996–99; Head: Republic of Ireland Dept, 1997–99; Devolved Admins Dept, 1999. *Address:* c/o Foreign and Commonwealth Office, King Charles Street, SW1A 2AH.

FERGUSSON, Sir James Herbert Hamilton C.; *see* Colyer-Fergusson.

FERGUSSON, Kenneth James, CEng, FIMechE; Chief Executive, Coal Authority, 1997–2001; *b* 11 Jan. 1938; *s* of Robert Brown Millar Fergusson and Agnes Tattersall Fergusson; *m* 1961, Beryl Foster; two *s* one *d. Educ:* Robert Gordon's Coll., Aberdeen; Harrow County Grammar Sch.; Imperial Coll., London (BSc 1st cl. Hons Engrg); Harvard Business Sch. (AMP). CEng 1966; FIMechE 1976; FIMM 1999. ICI Agricl Div., 1959–68; RTZ Gp 1968–86: Geschäftsführer, Duisburger Kupferhütte, 1981–85; Man. Dir, Rio Tinto Zimbabwe, 1985–86; Project Dir, European Transonic Windtunnel, Cologne, 1986–88; Man. Dir, Docklands Light Railway, 1988–90; Chief Exec., Hub Power Co., Karachi, 1992–93; Regl Dir, BESO, 1995–97. Trustee, Industrial Trust, 1998–. FIMgt 1984; MInstD 1987; FRSA 1998. Freeman, City of London, 1990; Liveryman, Co. of Engineers, 1995. *Recreations:* advanced motoring and motorcycling, swimming, archaeology, gardening, music, current affairs, travel. *Address:* 24F Thorney Crescent, Morgans Walk, SW11 3TT. *T:* (020) 7585 1294.

FERLEGER BRADES, Susan Deborah; Director, Hayward Gallery, London, since 1996; *b* 7 July 1954; *d* of Alvin Ferleger and Beatrice Ferleger (*née* Supnick); *m* 1979, Peter Eric Brades; one *s. Educ:* Courtauld Inst. of Art (MA); Univ. of Mass, Amherst (BA 1976; magna cum laude; Phi Beta Kappa); Barnard Coll., Columbia Univ., NY. Curatorial Co-ordinator, Solomon R. Guggenheim Mus., NY, 1975–79; Nat. Endowment for Arts Fellowship, 1975–76; Researcher, British Sculpture in the Twentieth Century, Whitechapel Art Gall., London, 1979–80; Hayward Gallery: Exhibn Organiser, Arts Council of GB, S Bank Centre, 1980–88; Sen. Exhibn Organiser, Exhibns Dept, S Bank Centre, 1988–93 (Public Art Programme Co-ordinator, 1990); Dep. Dir, Hayward Gall., S Bank Centre, 1993–96. Purchaser, Arts Council Collection, 1983–. Trustee, IVAM Centre Julio Gonzalez, Valencia, 2000–; Patron, Nat. Children's Art Day, 2001. *Address:* Hayward Gallery, Belvedere Road, SE1 8XX. *T:* (020) 7921 0873, *Fax:* (020) 7401 2664; *e-mail:* sbrades@hayward.org.uk.

FERMAN, James Alan; Director (formerly Secretary), British Board of Film Classification (formerly British Board of Film Censors), 1975–99; *b* New York, 11 April 1930; *m* 1956, Monica Sophie (*née* Robinson); one *s* one *d. Educ:* Great Neck High Sch., NY; Cornell Univ. (BA Hons); King's Coll., Cambridge (MA Hons). Actor, writer and univ. lectr until 1957; author/adaptor, Zuleika (musical comedy), Saville Theatre, 1957; television director of drama and documentaries, 1957–75: trained on Armchair Theatre, then 7½ years in ITV, then freelance, chiefly at BBC, 1965–75; principal director: The Planemakers (SFTA Award, 1963); Miss Hanago; The Pistol; Kafka's America (Critics' Circle Award, 1966); Before the Party (BAFTA Award, 1970); also stage producer; wrote and dir., Drugs and Schoolchildren, documentary film series for teachers and social workers. Part-time Lectr in Community Studies, Polytechnic of Central London, 1973–76 (Dir and Chm., Community Mental Health Prog., in-service trng for social workers, health workers, teachers, etc, organised jtly with MIND); Educn Adviser, Standing Conf. on Drug Abuse; Vice-Pres., Assoc. for Prevention of Addiction. Chm. and organiser, internat. confs on standards in screen entertainment, BBFC, 1982–97. *Recreations:* theatre, music, reading, hill-walking.

FERMOR, Patrick Michael Leigh, DSO 1944; OBE (mil.) 1943; CLit 1991; author; Hon. Citizen of Herakleion, Crete, 1947, Gytheion, Laconia, 1966, and of Kardamyli, Messenia, 1967; *b* 11 Feb. 1915; *s* of late Sir Lewis Leigh Fermor, OBE, FRS, DSc, and Eileen, *d* of Charles Taaffe Ambler; *m* 1968, Hon. Joan Eyres-Monsell, *d* of 1st Viscount Monsell, PC, GBE. *Educ:* King's Sch., Canterbury. After travelling for four years in Central Europe, Balkans and Greece, enlisted in Irish Guards, 1939; "I" Corps, 1940; Lieut, British Mil. Mission, Greece, 1940; Liaison Officer, Greek GHQ, Albania; campaigns of Greece and Crete; 2 years in German occupied Crete with Resistance, commanded some minor guerilla operations; team-commander in Special Allied Airborne Reconnaissance Force, N Germany, 1945. Dep.-Dir British Institute, Athens, till middle 1946; travelled in Caribbean and Central American republics, 1947–48. Corres. Mem.,

Athens Acad., 1980. Hon. DLitt: Kent, 1991; Amer. Sch. of Greece, 1993; Warwick Univ., 1996. Municipality of Athens Gold Medal of Honour, 1988; Prix Jacques Audiberti, Ville d'Antibes, 1992. Chevalier, l'Ordre des Arts et des Lettres (France), 1995. *Publications:* The Traveller's Tree (Heinemann Foundation Prize for Literature, 1950, and Kemsley Prize, 1951); trans. Colette, Chance Acquaintances, 1952; A Time to Keep Silence, 1953; The Violins of Saint Jacques, 1953; Mani, 1958 (Duff Cooper Meml Prize; Book Society's Choice); (trans.) The Cretan Runner (George Psychoundakis), 1955; Roumeli, 1966; A Time of Gifts, 1977 (W. H. Smith & Son Literary Award, 1978); Between the Woods and the Water, 1986 (Thomas Cook Travel Book Award, 1986; Internat. PEN/Time Life Silver Pen Award, 1986); Three Letters from the Andes, 1991. *Recreation:* travel. *Address:* c/o Messrs John Murray, 50 Albemarle Street, W1X 4BD. *Clubs:* White's, Travellers, Pratt's, Beefsteak, Special Forces, Puffins.

FERMOR-HESKETH, family name of **Baron Hesketh**.

FERMOY, 6th Baron *cr* 1856; **Patrick Maurice Burke Roche;** *b* 11 Oct. 1967; *s* of 5th Baron Fermoy and of Lavinia Frances Elizabeth, *o d* of late Captain John Pitman; *S* father, 1984; *m* 1998, Tessa Fiona Ledger; two *d*. *Educ:* Eton. A Page of Honour to the Queen Mother, 1982–85. Commnd, Blues and Royals, 1987–95; Capt. With Bass Taverns, 1996–99; Dir, Arrow Pubs Ltd, 1999–. *Recreations:* horses, scuba diving. *Heir: b* Hon. (Edmund) Hugh Burke Roche, *b* 5 Feb. 1972. *Address:* Nethercote House, Nethercote, Rugby, Warwickshire CV23 8AS.

FERNANDO, Most Rev. Nicholas Marcus; *see* Colombo, Archbishop of, (RC).

FERNEYHOUGH, Prof. Brian John Peter; composer; William H. Bonsall Professor of Music, Stanford University, since 2000; *b* 16 Jan. 1943; *s* of Frederick George Ferneyhough and Emily May (*née* Hopwood); *m* 1990, Stephany Jan Hurtik. *Educ:* Birmingham Sch. of Music; RAM; Sweelinck Conservatory, Amsterdam; Musikakademie, Basle. Mendelssohn Schol., 1968; Stipend: City of Basle, 1969; Heinrich-Strobel-Stiftung des Südwestfunks, 1972; Composition teacher, Musikhochschule, Freiburg, 1973–86 (Prof., 1978–86); Principal Composition Teacher, Royal Conservatory, The Hague, 1986–87; Prof. of Music, UCSD, 1987–99. Guest Artist, Artists' Exchange Scheme, Deutsche Akad. Austauschdienst, Berlin, 1976–77; Lectr, Darmstadt Summer Sch., 1976–96 (Comp. course co-ordinator, 1984–94); Guest Prof., Royal Conservatory, Stockholm, 1981–83, 1985; Vis. Prof., Univ. of Chicago, 1986; Fellow, Birmingham Conservatoire, 1996. Master Class, Civica Scuola di Musica di Milano, 1985–87. Mem., ISCM Internat. Jury, 1977, 1988. Prizes, Gaudeamus Internat. Comp., 1968, 1969; First Prize, ISCM Internat. Comp., Rome, 1974; Koussevitsky Prize, 1978; Royal Philharmonic Soc. Award, 1996. Chevalier, l'Ordre des Arts et des Lettres, 1984. *Compositions include:* Sonatas for String Quartet, 1967; Epicycle, for 20 solo strings, 1968; Firecycle Beta, for large orch. with 5 conductors, 1971; Time and Motion Studies I–III, 1974–76; Unity Capsule, for solo flute, 1975; Funérailles, for 7 strings and harp, 1978; La Terre est un Homme, for orch., 1979; 2nd String Quartet, 1980; Lemma-Icon-Epigram, for solo piano, 1981; Carceri d'Invenzione, for various ensembles, 1981–86; 3rd String Quartet, 1987; Kurze Schatten II, for guitar, 1988; La Chute d'Icare, for clarinet ensemble, 1988; Trittico per G. S., 1989; 4th String Quartet, 1990; Bone Alphabet, for percussionist, 1991; Terrain, for violin and eight instruments, 1992; On Stellar Magnitudes, for voice and ensemble, 1994; String Trio, 1995; Incipits, for viola, percussion and small ensemble, 1996; Kranichtänze II, for piano, 1996; Maisons Noires, for ensemble, 1997; Unsichtbare Farben, for solo violin, 1999; Doctrine of Similarity, for choir and instruments, 2000; Opus Contra Naturem, for speaking pianist, 2000; Stele for Failed Time, for choir and electronics, 2001. *Publications:* Collected Writings, 1996; articles in Contrechamps, Musiktexte, and Contemp. Music Rev. *Recreations:* reading, wine, cats. *Address:* Department of Music, Braun Music Center, Stanford University, Stanford, CA 94305–3076, USA.

FERNIE, Prof. Eric Campbell, CBE 1995; FSA 1973; FRSE; Director, Courtauld Institute of Art, University of London, since 1995; *b* Edinburgh, 9 June 1939; *s* of Sydney Robert and Catherine Reid Fernie; *m* 1964, Margaret Lorraine French; one *s* two *d*. *Educ:* Univ. of the Witwatersrand (BA Hons Fine Arts); Univ. of London (Academic Diploma). FRSE 1993. Lectr, Univ. of the Witwatersrand, 1963–67; University of East Anglia: Lectr and Sen. Lectr, 1967–84; Dean, Sch. of Fine Art and Music, 1977–81; Public Orator, 1982–84; Watson Gordon Prof. of Fine Art, Univ. of Edinburgh, 1984–95 (Dean, Faculty of Arts, 1989–92). Chm., Ancient Monuments Bd for Scotland, 1989–95; Trustee: Nat. Galleries of Scotland, 1991–97; Scotland Inheritance Fund, 1992–; Samuel Courtauld Trust, 1995–; Heather Trust for the Arts, 1997–; Comr, English Heritage, 1995–; Mem., RCHM of England, 1997–99. Vice-Pres., Soc. of Antiquaries of London, 1992–95. *Publications:* An Introduction to the Communar and Pitcaner Rolls of Norwich Cathedral Priory (with A. B. Whittingham), 1973; The Architecture of the Anglo-Saxons, 1983; An Architectural History of Norwich Cathedral, 1993; Art History and its Methods, 1995; The Architecture of Norman England, 2000; contribs to British and overseas architectural jls. *Address:* Flat 10, 8 Northburgh Street, Clerkenwell, EC1V 0AY. *T:* (020) 7608 3262.

FEROZE, Sir Rustam Moolan, Kt 1983; MD; FRCS, FRCOG; retired; (first) President, European Association of Obstetrics and Gynaecology, 1985–88, now Hon. President; Consulting Obstetrician, Queen Charlotte's Maternity Hospital; Consulting Surgeon, Chelsea Hospital for Women; *b* 4 Aug. 1920; *s* of Dr J. Moolan-Feroze; *m* 1947, Margaret Dowsett; three *s* one *d*. *Educ:* Sutton Valence Sch.; King's Coll. and King's Coll. Hospital, London. MRCS, LRCP 1943; MB, BS 1946; MRCOG 1948; MD (Obst. & Dis. Wom.) London 1952; FRCS 1952; FRCOG 1962; Hon. FRCSI 1984; Hon. FRACOG 1985; Hon. FACOG 1986. Surg.-Lt, RNVR, 1943–46. King's Coll. Hosp., 1946; RMO, Samaritan Hosp. for Women, 1948; Sen. Registrar: Hosp. for Women, Soho Sq., and Middlesex Hosp., 1950–53; Chelsea Hosp. for Women, and Queen Charlotte's Maternity Hosp., 1953–54; Consultant Obstetrician and Gynaecologist, King's Coll. Hosp., 1952–85. Dean, Inst. of Obstetrics and Gynaecology, Univ. of London, 1954–67; Dir, Postgrad. Studies, RCOG, 1975–80; Pres., RCOG, 1981–84; Chm., Conf. of Royal Colls and Faculties, 1982–84. McIlrath Guest Prof., Royal Prince Alfred Hosp., Sydney, 1970. Lectures: Soc. of Obstetrics and Gynaecology of Canada, Winnipeg, 1978; Bartholomew Mosse, Dublin, 1982; Shirodkar Meml, Bombay, 1982; Charter Day, National Maternity Hosp., Dublin, 1984. Past Examiner: RCOG; Univs of London, Cambridge, Birmingham and Singapore. *Publications:* contributor: Integrated Obstetrics and Gynaecology for Postgraduates, 1981; Gynaecological Oncology, 1981, rev. edn 1992; Bonney's Gynaecological Surgery, 1986; contribs to med. jls. *Recreations:* Bonsai, music. *Address:* 9 Arbor Close, Beckenham, Kent BR3 6TW. *Club:* Royal Automobile.

FERRAN, Brian; Chief Executive, Arts Council of Northern Ireland, 1991–2000; *b* 19 Oct. 1940; *s* of late Bernard and Susan Ferran; *m* 1963, Denise Devine; one *s* one *d*. *Educ:* St Columb's Coll., Derry (ATD); Courtauld Inst., London Univ. (BA 1973); Queen's Univ., Belfast (DBA 1975). Art Teacher, Derry, 1963–66; Visual Arts Dir, Arts Council of NI, 1966–91. Commissioner: Paris Biennale, 1980; São Paolo Biennial, 1985; Orgnr, exhibn of NI artists, Houston Internat. Fest. and US tour, 1990. HRUA 1980; HRHA 1998. Leverhulme European Award, 1969; Douglas Hyde Gold Medal for historical painting, 1965, 1976; Conor Prize, Royal Ulster Acad., 1979. *Publication:* Basil Blackshaw: painter, 1995. *Recreation:* visiting museums. *Address:* 46 Myrtlefield Park, Belfast BT9 6NF. *T:* (028) 9066 3790, *Fax:* (028) 9050 7167; *e-mail:* brianferran@ntlworld.com.

FERRANTI, Sebastian Basil Joseph Ziani de; *see* de Ferranti.

FERRERO-WALDNER, Benita Maria; Federal Minister for Foreign Affairs, Austria, since 2000; *b* 5 Sept. 1948; *d* of Bruno and Emilie Waldner; *m* 1993, Prof. Francisco Ferrero Campos. *Educ:* Univ. of Salzburg (DIur). Export Dept, Paul Kiefel, Freilassing, Germany, 1971–72; Dir for Export Promotion, Gerns and Ghaler, Freilassing, 1972–78; Sales Dir for Europe, P. Kaufmann Inc., NY, 1978–81; Chief Mgt Asst, Gerns and Gahler, 1981–83; Special Consultancy, Austrian Embassy, Madrid, 1984; Federal Ministry for Foreign Affairs: Depts of Econ. Affairs, Political Affairs and Consular Affairs, 1984–86; First Sec., Dakar, 1986; Dept for Devlt Co-operation, 1986–87; Counsellor for Econ. Affairs, 1987–90, Minister-Counsellor, Dep. Chief of Mission and Chargé d'Affaires, 1990–93, Paris; Dep. Chief of Protocol, 1993; Chief of Protocol, Exec. Office of Sec. Gen., UN Secretariat, NY, 1994–95; State Sec. for Foreign Affairs, 1995–2000. Grand Decoration of Honour in Silver with Sash (Austria), 1999; holds numerous foreign decorations, including: Grand Cross: Order of Isabel la Católica (Spain), 1995; Royal Order of Merit (Norway), 1996; 2nd Cl., Order of Merit (FRG), 1997; SMO (Malta), 1999. *Publications:* Globale Ethik, 1998; Zukunft der Entwicklungszusammenarbeit, 1999. *Recreations:* reading, travelling, theatre, concerts, swimming, yoga. *Address:* Ministry of Foreign Affairs, Ballhausplatz 2, 1014 Vienna, Austria. *T:* (1) 531153350.

FERRERS, 13th Earl *cr* 1711; **Robert Washington Shirley;** Viscount Tamworth 1711; Bt 1611; PC 1982; DL; High Steward of Norwich Cathedral, since 1979; *b* 8 June 1929; *o s* of 12th Earl Ferrers and Hermione Morley (*d* 1969); *S* father, 1954; *m* 1951, Annabel Mary, *d* of late Brig. W. G. Carr, CVO, DSO; two *s* two *d* (and one *d* decd). *Educ:* Winchester Coll. (Fellow, 1988); Magdalene Coll., Cambridge. MA (Agric.). Lieut Coldstream Guards, 1949 (as National Service). A Lord-in-waiting, 1962–64, 1971–74; Parly Sec., MAFF, 1974; Jt Dep. Leader of the Opposition, House of Lords, 1976–79; Dep. Leader of House of Lords, 1979–83, 1988–97; Minister of State: MAFF, 1979–83; Home Office, 1988–94; DTI, 1994–95; DoE (Minister for the Envmt and Countryside), 1995–97; elected Mem., H of L, 1999. Mem., Armitage Cttee on political activities of civil servants, 1976. Chm., TSB of Eastern England, 1977–79; Mem., TSB Central Bd, 1977–79; Director: Central TSB, 1978–79; TSB Trustcard Ltd, 1978–79; Norwich Union Insurance Group, 1975–79 and 1983–88. Chairman: RCHM(Eng.), 1984–88; British Agricl Export Council, 1984–88; Mem. Council, Food From Britain, 1984–88; Director: Economic Forestry Gp, 1985–88; Chatham Historic Dockyard Trust, 1984–88. Mem. Council, Hurstpierpoint Coll., 1959–68. DL Norfolk, 1983. *Heir: s* Viscount Tamworth, *qv*. *Address:* Ditchingham Hall, Bungay, Suffolk NR35 2LE. *Club:* Beefsteak.

FERRIER, Prof. Robert Patton, FRSE 1977; Professor of Natural Philosophy, University of Glasgow, since 1973; *b* 4 Jan. 1934; *s* of William McFarlane Ferrier and Gwendoline Melita Edwards; *m* 1961, Valerie Jane Duncan; two *s* one *d*. *Educ:* Glebelands Sch. and Morgan Academy, Dundee; Univ. of St Andrews (BSc, PhD). MA Cantab, FInstP. Scientific Officer, AERE Harwell, 1959–61; Res. Assoc., MIT, 1961–62; Sen. Asst in Res., Cavendish Lab., Cambridge, 1962–66; Fellow of Fitzwilliam Coll., Cambridge, 1965–73; Asst Dir of Res., Cavendish Lab. 1966–71; Lectr in Physics, Univ. of Cambridge, 1971–73; Guest Scientist, IBM Res. Labs San José, Calif, 1972–73. Chm., SERC Semiconductor and Surface Physics Sub-Cttee, 1979–. *Publications:* numerous papers in Phil. Mag., Jl Appl. Physics, Jl Physics, etc. *Recreations:* do-it-yourself, tennis, gardening, reading novels. *Address:* Glencoe, 31 Thorn Road, Bearsden, Glasgow G61 4BS. *T:* (0141) 570 0769, (office) (0141) 330 5388.

FERRIS, Hon. Sir Francis (Mursell), Kt 1990; TD 1965; **Hon. Mr Justice Ferris;** Judge of the High Court of Justice, Chancery Division, since 1990; Judge of Restrictive Practices Court, since 1995; *b* 19 Aug. 1932; *s* of Francis William Ferris and Elsie Lilian May Ferris (*née* Mursell); *m* 1957, Sheila Elizabeth Hester Falloon Bedford; three *s* one *d*. *Educ:* Bryanston Sch.; Oriel Coll., Oxford (BA (Modern History) 1955, MA 1979; Hon. Fellow, 2000). Served RA, 1951–52; 299 Field Regt (RBY QOOH and Berks) RA, TA 1952–67, Major 1964. Called to the Bar, Lincoln's Inn, 1956, Bencher, 1987; practice at Chancery Bar, 1958–90; Standing Counsel to Dir Gen. of Fair Trading, 1966–80; QC 1980; a Recorder, 1989–90. Member: Bar Council, 1966–70; Senate of Inns of Court and the Bar, 1979–82. *Recreation:* gardening. *Address:* Royal Courts of Justice, Strand, WC2A 2LL. *Club:* Marlow Rowing.

FERRIS, Paul Frederick; author and journalist; *b* 15 Feb. 1929; *o c* of late Frederick Morgan Ferris and of Olga Ferris; *m* 1st, 1953, Gloria Moreton (marr. diss. 1995); one *s* one *d*; 2nd, 1996, Mary Turnbull. *Educ:* Swansea Gram. Sch. Staff of South Wales Evening Post, 1949–52; Womans Own, 1953; Observer Foreign News Service, 1953–54. *Publications: novels:* A Changed Man, 1958; Then We Fall, 1960; A Family Affair, 1963; The Destroyer, 1965; The Dam, 1967; Very Personal Problems, 1973; The Cure, 1974; The Detective, 1976; Talk to Me About England, 1979; A Distant Country, 1983; Children of Dust, 1988; The Divining Heart, 1995; Infidelity, 1999; *non-fiction:* The City, 1960; The Church of England, 1962; The Doctors, 1965; The Nameless: abortion in Britain today, 1966; Men and Money: financial Europe today, 1968; The House of Northcliffe, 1971; The New Militants, 1972; Dylan Thomas, 1977, rev. edn 1999; Richard Burton, 1981; Gentlemen of Fortune: the world's investment bankers, 1984; (ed) The Collected Letters of Dylan Thomas, 1986, rev. edn 2000; Sir Huge: the life of Huw Wheldon, 1990; Sex and the British: a 20th century history, 1993; Caitlin, 1993; Dr Freud, 1997; *television plays:* The Revivalist, 1975; Dylan, 1978; Nye, 1982; The Extremist, 1984; The Fasting Girl, 1984. *Address:* c/o Curtis Brown Ltd, Haymarket House, 28/29 Haymarket, SW1Y 4SP. *T:* (020) 7396 6600.

FERRIS, Rt Rev. Ronald Curry; *see* Algoma, Bishop of.

FERSHT, Prof. Alan Roy, MA, PhD; FRS 1983; Herchel Smith Professor of Organic Chemistry, and Fellow, Gonville and Caius College, Cambridge since 1988; Hon. Director, Cambridge Centre for Protein Engineering (formerly MRC Unit for Protein Function and Design), since 1989; *b* 21 April 1943; *s* of Philip and Betty Fersht; *m* 1966, Marilyn Persell; one *s* one *d*. *Educ:* Sir George Monoux Grammar Sch.; Gonville and Caius Coll., Cambridge (MA, PhD). Res. Fellow, Brandeis Univ., 1968; Scientific Staff, MRC Lab. of Molecular Biology, Cambridge, 1969–77; Fellow, Jesus Coll., Cambridge, 1969–72; Eleanor Roosevelt Fellow, Stanford Univ., 1978; Wolfson Res. Prof. of Royal Society, Dept of Chemistry, Imperial Coll. of Science and Technology, 1978–89; Dir, Cambridge IRC in Protein Engineering, 1989–96. Lectures: Smith Kline & French, Berkeley, 1984; Edsall, Harvard, 1984; B. R. Baker, Univ. of California at Santa Barbara, 1986; Frank Mathers, Univ. of Indiana, 1986; Cornell Biotechnol Program, 1987; Ferdinand Springer, FEBS, 1988–89; Calvin, Berkeley, 1990; Walker, Edinburgh, 1990; Max Tishler Prize, Harvard Univ., 1991–92; Jubilee, Biochemical Soc., E. Gordon Young Meml, Canada, and Brändström, Gothenberg, 1993; Sternbach, Yale, 1994; Sunner Meml, Lund, 1994; Heatley, Oxford, Chan, Berkeley, Rudin, Columbia, and Hofmann,

German Chemical Soc., 1995; Herriott, Johns Hopkins, Fritz Lipmann, German Biol Chem. Soc., and Merck-Frosst, Montreal, 1996. Mem., EMBO, 1980; MAE 1989. Hon. For. Mem., Amer. Acad. of Arts and Sci., 1988; For. Associate, Nat. Acad. of Scis, USA, 1993. Essex County Jun. Chess Champion, 1961; Pres., Cambridge Univ. Chess Club, 1964 (Half Blue, 1965). FEBS Anniversary Prize, 1980; Novo Biotechnology Prize, 1986; Charmian Medal, RSC, 1986; Gabor Medal, Royal Soc., 1991; Harden Medal, Biochemical Soc., 1993; Feldberg Foundn Prize, 1996; Distinguished Service Award, Miami, 1997. *Publications:* Enzyme Structure and Mechanism, 1977, 2nd edn 1984; papers in scientific jls. *Recreations:* chess, horology. *Address:* University Chemical Laboratory, Lensfield Road, Cambridge CB2 1EW. *T:* (01223) 336341, *Fax:* (01223) 336445; 2 Barrow Close, Cambridge CB2 1AT.

FESSEY, Mereth Cecil, CB 1977; Director, Business Statistics Office, 1969–77, retired; *b* Windsor, Berks, 19 May 1917; *s* of late Morton Fessey and Ethel Fessey (*née* Blake), Bristol; *m* 1945, Grace Lilian, *d* of late William Bray, Earlsfield, London; one *s* two *d*. *Educ:* Westminster City Sch.; LSE, Univ. of London. London Transport, 1934; Army, 1940; Min. of Transport, 1947; Board of Trade, 1948; Statistician, 1956; Chief Statistician, 1965. Statistical Adviser to Syrian and Mexican Govts, 1979; Consultant, Statistical Office, Eur. Communities, 1990–95. Chm. of Council, Inst. of Statisticians, 1970–73; Vice Pres. and Mem., Council, Royal Statistical Soc., 1974–78; Chm., Cttee of Librarians and Statisticians, LA/Royal Stat. Soc., 1978–97. Hon. FLA 1984. *Publications:* articles and papers in: Economic Trends; Statistical News; Jl of Royal Statistical Soc.; The Statistician; Annales de Sciences Economiques Appliquées, Louvain; etc. *Recreations:* chess, walking. *Address:* Undy House, Undy, Caldicot, Monmouthshire NP26 3BX. *T:* (01633) 880478.

FETHERSTON-DILKE, Capt. Charles Beaumont; RN retired; Vice Lord-Lieutenant, Warwickshire, 1990–96; *b* 4 April 1921; *s* of late Dr Beaumont Albany Fetherston-Dilke, MBE and Phoebe Stella (*née* Bedford); *m* 1943, Pauline Stanley-Williams; one *s* one *d*. *Educ:* RNC, Dartmouth. Entered RN, 1935; served throughout War of 1939–45 and Korean War, 1952–54 (underwater warfare specialist); Comdr 1955; Danish Naval Staff, 1955–58; Directing Staff, RN Tactical Sch., 1958–60; staff of C-in-C S Atlantic and S America Station, 1960–61; Captain 1961; Naval Dep. to UK Nat. Mil. Rep., SHAPE, 1962–64; comd HMS St Vincent, 1964–66; Defence Policy Staff, MOD, 1966–68; retired 1968. Warwickshire: JP 1969–91; CC, 1970–81 (Chm., 1978–80); Chm., CLA, 1984–87; High Sheriff 1974; DL 1974. SBStJ 1986 (Mem. Council, 1977–92). Seigneur de Vangalême, Jersey. *Publication:* A Short History of Maxstoke Castle, 1985. *Recreations:* country pursuits. *Address:* Keeper's Cottage, Maxstoke, Coleshill, Warwicks B46 2QA. *T:* (01675) 465100. *Club:* Army and Navy.
See also M. S. Fetherston-Dilke.

FETHERSTON-DILKE, Mary Stella, CBE 1968; RRC 1966; Organiser, Citizens' Advice Bureau, 1971–83, retired; *b* 21 Sept. 1918; *d* of late B. A. Fetherston-Dilke, MBE. *Educ:* Kingsley Sch., Leamington Spa; St George's Hospital, London (SRN). Joined QARNNS, 1942; Matron-in-Chief, QARNNS, 1966–70, retired. OStJ 1966. *Recreation:* antiques. *Address:* 12 Clareville Court, Clareville Grove, SW7 5AT.
See also C. B. Fetherston-Dilke.

FETTIPLACE, Prof. Robert, FRS 1990; Steenbock Professor of Neural and Behavioral Sciences, University of Wisconsin, since 1991; *b* 24 Feb. 1946; *s* of George Robert Fettiplace and Maisie Fettiplace (*née* Rolson); *m* 1977, Merriel Cleone Kruse. *Educ:* Nottingham High Sch.; Sidney Sussex Coll., Cambridge (BA 1968; MA 1972; PhD 1974). Research Fellow: Sidney Sussex Coll., Cambridge, 1971–74, Stanford Univ., 1974–76; Elmore Res. Fellow, Cambridge, 1976–79; Howe Sen. Res. Fellow, Royal Soc., 1979–90. *Publications:* contribs to Jl Physiology and other learned jls. *Recreations:* bird watching, listening to music. *Address:* Department of Physiology, University of Wisconsin, 273 Medical Sciences Building, 1300 University Avenue, Madison, WI 53706, USA. *T:* (608) 2629320.

FEVERSHAM, 6th Baron *cr* 1826; **Charles Antony Peter Duncombe;** free-lance journalist; *b* 3 Jan. 1945; *s* of late Col Antony John Duncombe-Anderson and G. G. V. McNalty; *S* (to barony of) kinsman, 3rd Earl of Feversham (the earldom having become extinct), 1963; *m* 1st, 1966, Shannon (*d* 1976), *d* of late Sir Thomas Foy, CSI, CIE; two *s* one *d*; 2nd, 1979, Pauline, *d* of John Aldridge, Newark, Notts; one *s*. *Educ:* Eton; Middle Temple. Chairman: Standing Conf. of Regional Arts Assocs, 1969–76; Trustees, Yorkshire Sculpture Park, 1981–; President: Yorkshire Arts Assoc., 1987–91 (Chm., 1969–80); Soc. of Yorkshiremen in London, 1974; The Arvon Foundn, 1976–86; Yorks and Cleveland Local Councils Assoc., 1977–99; Nat. Assoc. of Local Councils, 1986–99. Governor, Leeds Polytechnic, 1969–76. *Publications:* A Wolf in Tooth (novel), 1967; Great Yachts, 1970. *Heir: s* Hon. Jasper Orlando Slingsby Duncombe, *b* 14 March 1968. *Address:* Duncombe Park, Helmsley, York YO62 5EB.

FEWSON, Prof. Charles Arthur, OBE 2001; PhD; FRSE; FIBiol; Professor of Microbial Biochemistry, University of Glasgow, since 1982. (Director, Institute of Biomedical and Life Sciences, 1994–2000); *b* 8 Sept. 1937; *s* of Arthur Fewson and Brenda Margaret Fewson; *m* 1965, Margaret Christina Rose Moir; two *d*. *Educ:* Hymers Coll., Hull; Nottingham Univ. (BSc); Bristol Univ. (PhD 1961). FRSE 1979; FIBiol 1983. Res. Fellow, Cornell Univ., NY, 1961–63; Department of Biochemistry, University of Glasgow: Lectr, 1963–68; Sen. Lectr, 1968–79; Reader, 1979–82. FRSA 1995. *Publications:* numerous scientific papers and reviews on microbial and plant biochemistry. *Recreation:* hill-walking. *Address:* West Medical Building, University of Glasgow, Glasgow G12 8QQ. *T:* (0141) 330 2802.

FFOLKES, Sir Robert (Francis Alexander), 7th Bt *cr* 1774; OBE 1990; *b* 2 Dec. 1943; *o s* of Captain Sir (Edward John) Patrick (Boschetti) ffolkes, 6th Bt, and Geraldine (*d* 1978), *d* of late William Roffey, Writtle, Essex; *S* father, 1960. *Educ:* Stowe Sch.; Christ Church, Oxford. *Address:* Coast Guard House, Morston, Holt, Norfolk NR25 7BH. *Club:* Turf.

FFOWCS WILLIAMS, Prof. John Eirwyn, FREng; Rank Professor of Engineering, University of Cambridge, 1972–Sept. 2002; Master, Emmanuel College, Cambridge, 1996–Sept. 2002 (Professorial Fellow, 1972–96); *b* 25 May 1935; *m* 1959, Anne Beatrice Mason; two *s* one *d*. *Educ:* Friends Sch., Great Ayton; Derby Techn. Coll.; Univ. of Southampton. BSc; MA, ScD Cantab 1986; PhD Southampton. CEng, FREng (FEng 1988); FRAeS, FInstP, FIMA, FInstAcoust, Fellow Acoustical Soc. of America, FAIAA. Engrg Apprentice, Rolls-Royce Ltd, 1951–55; Spitfire Mitchell Meml Schol. to Southampton Univ., 1955–60 (Pres., Students' Union, 1957–58); Aerodynamics Div., NPL, 1960–62; Bolt, Beranek & Newman Inc., 1962–64; Reader in Applied Maths, Imperial Coll. of Science and Technology, 1964–69; Rolls Royce Prof. of Theoretical Acoustics, Imperial Coll., 1969–72. Chairman: Concorde Noise Panel, 1965–75; Topexpress Ltd, 1979–89; Dir, VSEL Consortium plc, 1987–95. Chm., Noise Research Cttee, ARC, 1969–76. FRSA. Honour Prof., Beijing Inst. of Aeronautics and Astronautics, 1992–. Foreign Hon. Mem., Amer. Acad. Arts and Scis, 1989; Foreign Associate, NAE, USA, 1995. Gov., Felsted Sch., 1980–94. AIAA Aero-Acoustics Medal, 1977; Rayleigh Medal, Inst. of Acoustics, 1984; Silver Medal, Société Française d'Acoustique, 1989; Gold Medal, RAeS, 1990; Per Bruel Gold Medal, ASME, 1997. *Publications:* (with A. P. Dowling) Sound and Sources of Sound, 1983; articles in Philosophical Trans Royal Soc., Jl of Fluid Mechanics, Jl IMA, Jl of Sound Vibration, Annual Reviews of Fluid Mechanics, Random Vibration, Financial Times; (jtly) film on Aerodynamic Sound. *Recreations:* friends and cigars. *Address:* Emmanuel College, Cambridge CB2 3AP. *Club:* Athenæum.

FFRENCH, family name of **Baron ffrench**.

FFRENCH, 8th Baron *cr* 1798; **Robuck John Peter Charles Mario ffrench;** Bt 1779; *b* 14 March 1956; *s* of 7th Baron ffrench and of Sonia Katherine, *d* of late Major Digby Cayley; *S* father, 1986; *m* 1987, Dörthe Marie-Louise, *d* of Captain Wilhelm Schauer; one *d*. *Educ:* Blackrock, Co. Dublin; Ampleforth College, Yorks. *Heir: uncle* John Charles Mary Joseph Francis ffrench [*b* 5 Oct. 1928; *m* 1963, Sara-Primm, *d* of James A. Turner; three *d*].

FFRENCH-CONSTANT, Prof. Charles Kenvyn, PhD; FRCP; Professor of Neurological Genetics, University of Cambridge, since 1999; Fellow of Pembroke College, Cambridge, since 1999; Hon. Consultant in Medical Genetics, since 1996; *b* 5 Nov. 1954; *m* Jennifer Wimperis, DM, FRCP, FRCPath; one *s* one *d*. *Educ:* Pembroke Coll., Cambridge (BA 1976; BChir 1979; MA 1980; MB 1980); University College London (PhD 1986). MRCP 1982, FRCP 1999. Lucille Markey Postdoctoral Fellow, MIT, 1986–88; Wellcome Trust Sen. Res. Fellow, Wellcome/CRC Inst. of Develtl Biol., Cambridge Univ., 1991–96. *Publications:* papers on develtl biol. *Recreation:* fishing. *Address:* Department of Medical Genetics, Addenbrooke's Hospital, Cambridge CB2 2QQ; 420 Unthank Road, Norwich NR4 7QH.

FFYTCHE, Timothy John, LVO 1997; FRCS; Surgeon–Oculist to the Queen, since 1999; Consultant Ophthalmologist, Moorfields Eye Hospital, since 1975; Hospital for Tropical Diseases, since 1988; Consultant Ophthalmic Surgeon to King Edward VIIth Hospital for Officers, since 1980; *b* 11 Sept. 1936; *s* of late Louis ffytche and Margaret (*née* Law); *m* 1961, Bärbl, *d* of late Günther Fischer; two *s*. *Educ:* Lancing Coll.; St George's Hosp., London. MB, BS; DO 1961; FRCS 1968. Registrar, Moorfields Eye Hosp., 1966–69; Wellcome Lectr, Hammersmith Hosp., 1969–70; Sen. Registrar, Middlesex Hosp., 1970–73; Ophthalmic Surgeon, St Thomas Hosp., 1973–99; Surgeon-Oculist to HM Household, 1980–99. Sec., OSUK, 1980–82. Mem., Medical Adv. Bd, LEPRA, 1982–; Vice-Pres., Ophthalmol Sect., RSocMed, 1985–88; UK rep. to Internat. Fedn of Ophthalmic Socs, 1985–89; Mem., Adv. Cttee to Internat. Council of Ophthalmology, 1985–. Founder, Ophthalmic Aid to Eastern Europe, 1990–; Chm., European Sect., Internat. Agency for Prevention of Blindness, 1999– (Co-Chm., 1994–99). Clayton Meml Lectr, LEPRA, 1984. Editorial Committee: Ophthalmic Literature, 1968–82; Transactions of OSUK, 1984–89, Eye, 1989–96; European Jl of Ophthalmology, 1990–. *Publications:* articles on retinal diagnosis and therapy, retinal photography and the ocular complications of leprosy, in The Lancet, British Jl of Ophthalmol., Trans OSUK, Proc. Roy. Soc. Med., Leprosy Review and other specialist jls. *Recreations:* travel, occasional fishing. *Address:* 149 Harley Street, W1N 2DE; (home) 1 Wellington Square, SW3 4NJ.

FICKLING, Benjamin William, CBE 1973; FRCS, FDS RCS; Honorary Consultant Dental Surgeon, since 1974, formerly Dental Surgeon: St George's Hospital, SW1, 1936–74; Royal Dental Hospital of London, 1935–74; Mount Vernon Centre for Plastic and Jaw Surgery (formerly Hill End), 1941–74; *b* 14 July 1909; *s* of Robert Marshall Fickling, LDS RCS, and Florence (*née* Newson); *m* 1943, Shirley Dona, *er d* of Albert Latimer Walker, FRCS; two *s* one *d*. *Educ:* Framlingham; St George's Hosp. Royal Dental Hospital. William Brown Senior Exhibition, St George's Hosp., 1929; LDS RCS, 1932; MRCS, LRCP, 1934; FRCS 1938; FDS RCS 1947; MGDSRCS 1979; Dip. in Gen. Dental Practice, RCS, 1992. Lectures: Charles Tomes, RCS, 1956; Everett Magnus, Melbourne, 1971; Webb-Johnson, RCS, 1978. Examiner (Chm.), Membership in Gen. Dental Surgery, 1979–83; formerly Examiner: in Dental Surgery, RCS; Univ. of London and Univ. of Edinburgh. Dean of Faculty of Dental Surgery, 1968–71, and Mem. Council, Royal College of Surgeons, 1968–71 (Vice-Dean, 1965; Colyer Gold Medal, 1979); Fellow Royal Society of Medicine (Pres. Odontological Section, 1964–65); Pres., British Assoc. of Oral Surgeons, 1967–68; Mem. GDC, 1971–74. Director: Med. Sickness Annuity and Life Assurance Soc. Ltd, 1967–86; Permanent Insurance Co. Ltd, 1974–86; Medical Sickness Finance Corp. Ltd, 1977–86. Civilian Dental Consultant to RN, 1954–76. *Publications:* (joint) Injuries of the Jaws and Face, 1940; (joint) Chapter on Faciomaxillary Injuries and Deformities in British Surgical Practice, 1951. *Address:* 29 Maxwell Road, Northwood, Middx HA6 2YG. *T:* (01923) 822035. *Club:* Ski Club of Great Britain.

FIDDICK, Peter Ronald; journalist and broadcaster; *b* 21 Oct. 1938; *s* of Wing-Comdr Ronald Fiddick and Phyllis (*née* Wherry); *m* 1966, Jane Mary Hodlin; one *s* one *d*. *Educ:* Reading Sch.; Magdalen Coll., Oxford (BA English Lang. and Lit.). Journalist, Liverpool Daily Post, 1962–65; Leader writer, Westminster Press, 1965–66; Asst Editor, Nova, 1968; The Guardian: reporter, 1966–67 and 1969; Asst Features Editor, 1970–75; Television Columnist, 1971–84; Media Editor, 1984–88; Editor: The Listener, 1989–91; Television (RTS), 1991–; Research (Market Res. Soc.), 1992–99; RADA, The Magazine, 1993–; Media Columnist, Adnap, 1997–. Newspaper Reviewer, BBC Breakfast News, 1989–; Media Critic, BBC Radio Arts Programme, 1990–. FRTS 1992; Associate, RADA. Wrote and presented television series: Looking at Television, 1975–76; The Television Programme, 1979–80; Soviet Television—Fact and Fiction, 1985. *Publication:* (with B. Smithies) Enoch Powell on Immigration, 1969. *Recreations:* music, food, Saturdays.

FIDLER, Prof. (John) Kelvin, PhD; CEng, FIEE; Vice-Chancellor and Chief Executive, University of Northumbria at Newcastle, since 2001; *b* 11 May 1944; *s* of Samuel Fidler and Barbara Fidler (*née* Goodall); *m* 1966, Jadwiga Sorokowska (marr. diss. 1995); one *s* one *d*. *Educ:* Harrow Co. Sch. for Boys; King's Coll., Univ. of Durham (BSc); Univ. of Newcastle upon Tyne (PhD 1968). CEng 1972; FIEE 1982. Sen. Res. Associate, Univ. of Newcastle upon Tyne, 1968–69; Lectr, 1969–74, Sen. Lectr, 1974–1980, Reader, 1980–83, Univ. of Essex; Professor of Electronics: Open Univ., 1984–88; Univ. of York, 1989–2001. *Publications:* Computer Aided Circuit Design, 1978; Introductory Circuit Theory, 1980, 2nd edn 1989; Continuous Time Active Filter Design, 1998; numerous contribs on electronics to learned jls. *Recreations:* walking, motor-biking, ham radio, cooking. *Address:* Vice-Chancellor's Office, University of Northumbria at Newcastle, Ellison Place, Newcastle upon Tyne NE1 8ST. *T:* (0191) 227 4002.

FIDLER, Prof. Peter Michael, MBE 1993; Vice-Chancellor and Chief Executive, University of Sunderland, since 1999. *Educ:* Univ. of Salford (MSc). Town planner. Formerly: Dean, Dept of Built Envmt, UWE; Dep. Vice-Chancellor (Academic Affairs), Oxford Brookes Univ. *Address:* University of Sunderland, Langham Tower, Ryhope Road, Sunderland SR2 7EE.

FIDLER-SIMPSON, John Cody; *see* Simpson.

FIELD, Brig. Anne, CB 1980; CBE 1996; Deputy Controller Commandant, Women's Royal Army Corps, 1984–92 (Director, 1977–82); Chairman of Council, 1991–97, and Life Vice President, 1999, WRAC Association (Vice President, 1984–97); *b* 4 April 1926; *d* of Captain Harold Derwent and Annie Helena Hodgson. *Educ:* Keswick Sch.; St George's, Harpenden; London Sch. of Economics. Joined ATS, 1947; commissioned: ATS, 1948; WRAC, 1949; Lt-Col, 1968; Col, 1971. Hon. ADC to the Queen, 1977–82. Dep. Col Comdt, AGC, 1992–94. Dir, London Regl Bd, Lloyds Bank, 1982–91 (Dep. Chm., 1990–91). Special Comr, Duke of York's Royal Mil. Sch., 1989–. Chm., ATS and WRAC Benevolent Fund, 1984–97. Patron, ATS Dinner Club, 1996–. Freeman, City of London, 1981; Liveryman, Spectacle Makers' Co., 1990. CIMgt (FBIM 1978). *Address:* c/o Lloyds TSB, PO Box 1190, 7 Pall Mall, SW1Y 5NA. *Club:* Army and Navy.

FIELD, Arnold, OBE 1965; aerospace consultant/technical journalist; Joint Field Commander, National Air Traffic Services, 1974–77; *b* 19 May 1917; *m* 1943, Kathleen Dulcie Bennett; one *s* one *d*. *Educ:* Sutton Coldfield Royal Sch.; Birmingham Technical Coll. RAF, 1940–46 (Sqdn Ldr). Civil Air Traffic Control Officer, 1946; Centre Supt, Scottish Air Traffic Control Centre, 1954; Centre Supt, London Air Traffic Control Centre, 1957; Divisional Air Traffic Control Officer, Southern Div., 1963; Dir, Civil Air Traffic Ops, 1969. Master, Guild of Air Traffic Control Officers, 1958; Pres., Internat. Fedn of Air Traffic Control Officers, 1970; Mem., Aviation/Space Writers' Assoc., 1986–. Gp Editor, Internat. Defence Newsletter, Law Enforcement Industry Digest, 1988–. *Publications:* The Control of Air Traffic, 1981; International Air Traffic Control, 1985; From Take-off to Touchdown—A Passenger's Guide, 1984; articles in Interavia, Times Supplement, Flight, Controller. *Recreations:* vintage cars, flying. *Address:* Footprints, Stoke Wood, Stoke Poges, Bucks. SL2 4AU. *T:* (01753) 642710. *Club:* Bentley Drivers (Long Crendon).

FIELD, Barry John Anthony, TD 1984; *b* 4 July 1946; *s* of Ernest Field and late Marguerite Eugenie Field; *m* 1969, Jaqueline Anne Miller; one *s* one *d*. *Educ:* Collingwood Boys' Sch.; Mitcham Grammar Sch.; Bembridge Sch.; Victoria Street Coll. Chm., J. D. Field & Sons Ltd, 1993–94 (Dir, 1981–94); Dir, Great Southern Cemetery & Crematorium Co. Ltd, 1969–94. Councillor, Horsham Dist. Council, 1983–86 (Vice-Chm., Housing, 1984–85, Chm., Housing, 1985–86); Mem., IoW CC, 1986–89. MP (C) Isle of Wight, 1987–97. Chm., H of C Deregulation Cttee, 1995–97. Major RCT TA; Liveryman, Turners' Co.; Mem., Watermen and Lightermen's Co. *Recreations:* sailing, theatre, ski-ing. *Address:* Medina Lodge, 25 Birmingham Road, Cowes, Isle of Wight PO31 7BH. *T:* (01983) 292871. *Club:* Island Sailing (Cowes).

FIELD, Dr Clive Douglas; Director of Scholarship and Collections, British Library, since 2001; *b* 27 June 1950; *o s* of Joseph Stanley Field and Lily Field (*née* Battams); *m* 1972, Verena Duss; one *s*. *Educ:* Dunstable Grammar Sch.; Wadham Coll., Oxford (BA Modern History 1971; MA 1975; DPhil Modern History 1975); Westminster Coll., Oxford (PGCE 1975), SSRC Post-Doctoral Fellow, Wadham Coll., Oxford, 1975–77; Asst Librarian, 1977–87, Sub-Librarian, 1987–90, John Rylands Univ. Liby of Manchester; Dep. Librarian, 1990–95, Librarian and Dir of Inf. Services, 1995–2001, Univ. of Birmingham (Associate Mem., Dept of Modern History, 1992–2001). Project Director: Ensemble: towards a distributed nat. liby resource for music, 1999–July 2002; Revelation: unlocking research resources for 19th and 20th century church history and Christian theology, 2000–July 2002. Chairman, Bd of Dirs, Consortium of Univ. Res. Libraries, 2000–01 (Mem., 1996–2001); Member: Jt Inf. Systems Cttee, Cttee on Electronic Inf., 1999–2001; Midlands Metropolitan Area Network Mgt Cttee, 1999–2001; Bd of Dirs, Birmingham Res. Park Ltd, 1999–2001. Editor, The People Called Methodists microfiche project, 1988–. *Publications:* professional papers; articles, bibliographies and reviews on the social history of religion in Great Britain since 1689, with special reference to religious statistics, religious practice, and the history of Methodism. *Recreations:* historical research and writing, visiting (incl. virtually) secondhand bookshops. *Address:* British Library, 96 Euston Road, NW1 2DB. *T:* (020) 7412 7530, *Fax:* (020) 7412 7093; *e-mail:* clive.field@bl.uk.

FIELD, (Edward) John, CMG 1991; HM Diplomatic Service, retired; High Commissioner, Sri Lanka, 1991–96; *b* 11 June 1936; *s* of late Arthur Field, OBE, MC, TD, and Dorothy Agnes Field; *m* 1960, Irene Sophie du Pont Darden; one *s* one *d*. *Educ:* Highgate Sch.; Corpus Christi Coll., Oxford; Univ. of Virginia. Courtaulds Ltd, 1960–62; FCO, 1963–: 2nd, later 1st Sec., Tokyo, 1963–68; Amer. Dept, FCO, 1968–70; Cultural Attaché, Moscow, 1970–72; 1st Sec. (Commercial), Tokyo, 1973–76; Asst Head, S Asian Dept, FCO, 1976–77; Dept of Trade, 1977–79 (Head, Exports to Japan Unit); Counsellor: (Commercial), Seoul, 1980–83; at Harvard Univ., 1983–84; UK Mission to UN, 1984–87; Minister, Tokyo, 1988–91. *Recreations:* tennis, riding, listening to music. *Address:* 21 Dawson Place, W2 4TH; Jericho Farm, 19637 Governor Darden Road, Courtland, VA 23837, USA. *Clubs:* Travellers; Tokyo (Tokyo).

FIELD, Rt Hon. Frank; PC 1997; MP (Lab) Birkenhead, since 1979; *b* 16 July 1942; *s* of late Walter and of Annie Field. *Educ:* St Clement Danes Grammar Sch.; Univ. of Hull (BSc (Econ)). Director: Child Poverty Action Gp, 1969–79; Low Pay Unit, 1974–80. Minister of State (Minister for Welfare Reform), DSS, 1997–98. Chairman: Select Cttee on Social Services, 1987–90; Select Cttee on Social Security, 1991–97. *Publications:* (ed, jtly) Twentieth Century State Education, 1971; (ed, jtly) Black Britons, 1971; (ed) Low Pay, 1973; Unequal Britain, 1974; (ed) Are Low Wages Inevitable?, 1976; (ed) Education and the Urban Crisis, 1976; (ed) The Conscript Army: a study of Britain's unemployed, 1976; (jtly) To Him Who Hath: a study of poverty and taxation, 1976; (with Ruth Lister) Wasted Labour, 1978 (Social Concern Book Award); (ed) The Wealth Report, 1979; Inequality in Britain: freedom, welfare and the state, 1981; Poverty and Politics, 1982; The Wealth Report—2, 1983; (ed) Policies against Low Pay, 1984; The Minimum Wage: its potential and dangers, 1984; Freedom and Wealth in a Socialist Future, 1987; The Politics of Paradise, 1987; Losing Out: the emergence of Britain's underclass, 1989; An Agenda for Britain, 1993; (jtly) Europe Isn't Working, 1994; (jtly) Beyond Punishment: pathways from workfare, 1994; Making Welfare Work, 1995; How to Pay for the Future: building a stakeholders welfare, 1996; Stakeholder Welfare, 1997; Reforming Welfare, 1997; Reflections on Welfare Reform, 1998; The State of Dependency: welfare under Labour, 2000; Making Welfare Work: reconstructing welfare for the millennium, 2001. *Address:* House of Commons, SW1A 0AA. *T:* (020) 7219 5193.

FIELD, Maj.-Gen. Geoffrey William, CB 1993; OBE 1983 (MBE 1976); Resident Governor and Keeper of the Jewel House, HM Tower of London, since 1994; *b* 30 Nov. 1941; *s* of William Edwin Field and Ellen Campbell Field (*née* Forsyth); *m* 1966, Janice Anne Olsen; one *s* two *d*. *Educ:* Daniel Stewart's College, Edinburgh; RMA Sandhurst; RMCS Shrivenham; Australian Staff College; RCDS. Commissioned RE 1961; OC 59 Indep. Cdo Sqn, RE, 1976–78; CO 36 Engr Regt, 1980–83 (comd RE, Falkland Islands, 1982); Asst Dir Defence Policy, MoD, 1983–85; Comd 11 Engr Gp, 1986–87; Dir Defence Programmes, MoD, 1989–90; Dir Gen., Logistic Policy (Army), 1990–93; Engr-in-Chief (Army), 1993–94. Colonel Commandant: RPC, 1991–93; RLC, 1993–96; RE, 1996–; Hon. Col, RE Vols (Specialist Units), 1992–96. Comr, Royal Hosp., Chelsea, 1990–93. Dir, Historic Royal Palaces Enterprises, 1998–. Trustee, Ulysses Trust, 1994–; Gov., St Katharine's and Shadwell Trust, 1999–. Freeman, City of London, 1995. *Recreation:* golf. *Address:* Queen's House, HM Tower of London, EC3N 4AB. *T:* (020) 7488 5630. *Club:* Rye Golf.

FIELD, Dr Ian Trevor, CBE 1994; Secretary General, World Medical Association, 1994–97; *b* 31 Oct. 1933; *s* of late Major George Edward Field, MBE, IA, and Bertha Cecilia Field; *m* 1960, Christine Mary Osman, JP; three *s*. *Educ:* Shri Shivaji School, Poona; Bournemouth School; Guy's Hosp. Med. School. MB, BS; FFPHM; FFOM. Royal Engineers, 1952–54; Med. Sch., 1954–60; house posts, 1960–62; general practice, 1962–64; Asst Sec., later Under Sec., BMA, 1964–75; SMO, 1975–78, SPMO/Under Sec., 1978–85, DHSS, (Internat. Health and Communicable Disease Control, later NHS Regional Orgn); Chief Med. and Health Services Advr, ODA, 1978–83; Dep. Sec., 1985–89, Sec., 1989–93, BMA. Member: Council, Liverpool Sch. of Trop. Med., 1979–83, 1993–96; Bd of Management, London Sch. of Hygiene and Trop. Med., 1979–83; Council, Royal Vet. Coll., 1982–88; WHO Global Adv. Cttee on Malaria Control, 1979–82 (Chm., 1981). Liveryman, Soc. of Apothecaries, 1971– (Ct of Assistants, 1986–; Master, 1998–99). *Publications:* contribs to medical jls. *Recreations:* military history, opera, watching cricket and rugby. *Address:* 10 Rockwells Gardens, SE19 1HW.

FIELD, Brig. Jill Margaret, CBE 1992; RRC 1988; Matron-in-Chief (Army) and Director of Defence Nursing Services, 1989–92; *b* 20 June 1934; *d* of late Major Charles Euston Field, Royal Signals, and Mrs Eva Gladys Field (*née* Watson). *Educ:* High School for Girls, Southend-on-Sea; St Bartholomew's Hosp., London (SRN). Joined QARANC, 1957; appointments include: service in Mil. Hosps in UK, BAOR, N Africa, Cyprus, Singapore; Instructor, QARANC Trng Centre, 1971–74; Liaison Officer QARANC, MoD, 1980–83; Matron, BMH Hannover, 1984–85; Dep. Medical (Nursing), BAOR, 1985–87; Matron, Cambridge Mil. Hosp., Aldershot and Chief Medical (Nursing) SE and SW Dist, 1987–89. QHNS 1989–92. *Recreations:* gardening, reading, music.

FIELD, John; *see* Field, E. J.

FIELD, Prof. John Edwin, OBE 1987; PhD; FRS 1994; Professor of Applied Physics, Department of Physics, University of Cambridge, since 1994; Head of Physics and Chemistry of Solids Section, Cavendish Laboratory, Cambridge, since 1987; Fellow of Magdalene College, Cambridge, since 1964; *b* 20 Sept. 1936; *s* of William Edwin Field and Madge (*née* Normansell); *m* 1963, Ineke Tjan; two *s* one *d*. *Educ:* Univ. of London (BSc); Univ. of Cambridge (PhD 1962). Graduate Tutor, Magdalene Coll., Cambridge, 1974–87; Asst Lectr, 1966–71, Lectr, 1971–90, Reader, 1990–94, Dept of Physics, Univ. of Cambridge. Hon. DSc Univ. of Luleå, Sweden, 1989. Duddell Medal, Inst. of Physics, 1990. *Publications:* (ed) The Properties of Diamond, 1979, 2nd edn 1991; (ed) The Properties of Natural and Synthetic Diamond, 1992; (ed) 3 conf. proc.; over 300 scientific papers. *Recreations:* mountain walking, running, ski-ing. *Address:* 1 Babraham Road, Cambridge CB2 2RB. *T:* (01223) 575847.

FIELD, Sir Malcolm (David), Kt 1991; Chairman, Civil Aviation Authority, since 1996; *b* 25 Aug. 1937; *s* of Stanley Herbert Raynor Field and Constance Frances (*née* Watson); *m* (marr. diss.); one *d*; *m* 2001, Anne Charlton. *Educ:* Highgate Sch.; London Business Sch. National Service, commnd Welsh Guards (2nd Lieut), 1955–57 (served in Cyprus and Germany). PA to Dir, ICI (Paints Div.), 1957; joined family wholesale newspaper distributors business, 1960 (taken over by W. H. Smith, 1963); Wholesale Dir, 1970–82, Man. Dir, Retail Gp, 1978–82, Gp Man. Dir, 1982–93, Chief Exec., 1994–96, W. H. Smith. Chairman: Bd of Management, NAAFI, 1986–93 (Mem., Bd of Management, 1973–86; Dep. Chm., 1985–86); Sofa Workshop, 1998–; Non-executive Director: MEPC, 1989–99; Scottish & Newcastle Breweries, 1993–98; Phoenix Group Ltd, 1995–97; Stationery Office, 1996–2001; Walker Greenbank, 1997–. Mem. Council, RCA, 1991–; Mem. Bd, English Nat. Ballet Sch., 1997–; Gov., Highgate Sch., 1994– (Dep. Chm., 1999–). CIMgt (CBIM 1988); CRAeS 1997; FRSA 1989. *Recreations:* watching cricket, tennis, golf, restoring an orangery and garden in Devon, reading biographies, collecting modern art. *Address:* 15 Eaton Square, SW1W 9DD. *T:* (020) 7245 0453. *Clubs:* Garrick, MCC.

FIELD, Mark Christopher; MP (C) Cities of London and Westminster, since 2001; *b* 6 Oct. 1964; *s* of late Maj. Peter Field and of Ulrike Field (*née* Peipe); *m* 1994, Michele Louise Acton. *Educ:* Reading Sch.; St Edmund Hall, Oxford (MA Hons Juris.); Coll. of Law, Chester. Trainee solicitor, Richards Butler, 1988–90; Solicitor, Freshfields, 1990–92; employment consultant, 1992–94; Man. Dir, Kellyfield Consulting (publishing/recruiting firm), 1994–. Councillor (C), RBK&C, 1994–. *Recreations:* cricket, soccer, listening to popular/rock music, ensuring that my wife is not the weakest in a foursome at bridge. *Address:* House of Commons, SW1A 0AA. *T:* (020) 7219 8160, (office) (020) 7730 8181; 67 Elizabeth Street, SW1W 9PJ.

FIELD, Marshall Hayward, CBE 1985; Consultant to Bacon & Woodrow, 1986–2000; *b* 19 April 1930; *s* of Harold Hayward Field and Hilda Maud Field; *m* 1960, Barbara Evelyn Harris (*d* 1998); two *d*. *Educ:* Dulwich College. FIA 1957. With Pearl Assce, 1948–58; Phoenix Assurance: Actuary, 1964–85; Gen. Manager, 1972–85; Dir, 1980–85. Director: TSB Trust Co. Ltd, 1985–89; TSB Gp, 1990–95; Ark Life Assurance Co., Dublin, 1991–. Institute of Actuaries: Hon. Sec., 1975–77; Vice-Pres., 1979–82; Pres., 1986–88; Vice Pres., International Actuarial Assoc., 1984–90; Chm., Life Offices' Assoc., 1983–85. Mem., Fowler Inquiry into Provision for Retirement, 1984; Consultant, Marketing of Investments Bd Organising Cttee, 1985–86. Mem., Dulwich Picture Gall. Cttee, 1985–94; Trustee, Dulwich Picture Gall., 1994–; Governor: Dulwich Coll. Estates, 1973–95 (Chm., 1988–90); Dulwich Coll., 1987–97; James Allen's Girls' School, 1981–95. Mem., Ct of Assistants, Actuaries' Co., 1989– (Master, 1996–97). *Recreations:* theatre, architecture. *Address:* 12 Gainsborough Court, College Road, SE21 7LT; Bembridge, Isle of Wight.

FIELD, Hon. Michael Walter; consultant on professional development and change management, Tasmanian Training Consortium; Chairman, Tasmanian Innovations Advisory Board, since 1999; *b* 28 May 1948; *s* of William Field and Blanche (*née* Burrows); *m* 1975, Janette Elizabeth Mary Fone; one *s* two *d*. *Educ:* Railton Primary Sch., Tasmania; Devonport High Sch., Tasmania; Univ. of Tasmania (BA Pol. Sci./History). Teacher, 1971–75; Community Develt Officer, 1975–76. Government of Tasmania: MHA (Lab) Braddon, 1976–97; Minister for Transport, Main Roads, Construction and Local Govt, 1979–82; Shadow Minister for: Transport, 1982–83; Education and Ind. Relns, 1982–86; State Development, 1992–97; Dep. Leader of Opposition and Shadow Minister for Forestry, Ind. Relns and Energy, 1986–88; Leader of the Opposition, 1988–89 and 1992–97; Premier, Treas. and Minister for State Develt and Finance, 1989–92; Shadow Minister for Educn, Trng, and Youth Affairs, 1996–97. Board Member: John Curtin House Ltd, 1997–; Leadership Adv. Gp, Ortus Star Inc., 1998–; Tasmanian Electricity Code Change Panel, 1999–. Hon. LLD Tasmania, 2000. *Recreations:* running, reading, music. *Address:* 16 Osprey Road, Eaglehawk Neck, Tas 7179, Australia. *T:* (3) 62503448; *e-mail:* field@tassie.net.au.

FIELD, Patrick John; QC 2000; a Recorder, since 2001; *b* 19 March 1959; *s* of Michael Edward and Patricia Field; *m* Helen McCubbin; one *s* two *d*. *Educ:* Wilmslow Co. Grammar Sch.; King's Coll. London (LLB Hons). Called to the Bar, Gray's Inn, 1981; Northern Circuit, 1982–. *Recreations:* fishing, shooting, travel. *Address:* Deans Court Chambers, 24 St John Street, Manchester M3 4DF. *T:* (0161) 214 6000.

FIELD, Richard Alan; QC 1987; a Deputy High Court Judge, since 1998; a Recorder, since 1999; *b* 17 April 1947; *s* of Robert Henry Field and Ivy May Field; *m* 1968, Lynne Hauskind; two *s* two *d*. *Educ:* Ottershaw Sch.; Bristol Univ. (LLB); London School of Economics (LLM with Dist.). Asst Prof., Univ. of British Columbia, 1969–71; Lectr in Law, Hong Kong Univ., 1971–73; Associate Prof., McGill Univ., Montreal, 1973–77; called to the Bar, Inner Temple, 1977, Bencher, 1998. *Publications:* articles and book reviews in UBC Law Rev., Hong Kong Law Jl, McGill Law Jl. *Recreations:* cricket, opera, theatre. *Address:* 1 Essex Court, Temple, EC4Y 9AR. *Clubs:* Garrick, Roehampton.

FIELD, Stuart, FRCR; Consultant Radiologist, Kent and Canterbury Hospital, since 1974; Director, Kent Breast Screening Programme, since 1988; *b* 22 June 1944; *s* of Walter Frederick William Field and Maisie Marlow; *m* 1968, Margaret Shirley Dawes; two *d*. *Educ:* Watford Grammar Sch. (Head Boy); Gonville and Caius Coll., Cambridge (BA 1st Cl. Hons Natural Sci. Tripos, MA, MB BChir). DMRD 1972 ; FRCR 1974. Houseman to Professorial Med. and Surgical Units, 1969–70, Registrar in Radiol., 1970–74, KCH. Royal College of Radiologists: Dean, Faculty of Clinical Radiology, 1991–93, Vice-Pres., 1993; Pres. Kent Postgrad. Med. Centre, 1994–2000; Hon. Prof., Kent Inst. of Medicine and Health Scis, Univ. of Kent at Canterbury, 1998–. Mem., DoH Adv. Cttee for Breast Cancer Screening, 1994–. Chm., Breast Gp, 1997–99. Hon. Mem., Romanian Radiol. Soc., 1993. *Publications:* numerous chapters in textbooks of radiol. on the plain abdominal radiograph in the acute abdomen; contrib. articles on breast cancer screening and other radiol topics to specialist radiol. jls. *Recreations:* gardening, walking, DIY, classical music, the family. *Address:* Department of Diagnostic Radiology, Kent and Canterbury Hospital, Ethelbert Road, Canterbury, Kent CT1 3NG. *T:* (01227) 766877.

FIELD, William James; *b* 22 May 1909; *s* of late Frederick William Field, Solicitor; unmarried. *Educ:* Richmond County Sch.; London Univ; abroad. Joined Labour Party, 1935; Parliamentary Private Sec. to Sec. of State for War, May–Oct. 1951 (to Under-Sec. for War, 1950–51); Chm. South Hammersmith Divisional Labour Party, 1945–46; contested Hampstead Div., General Election, 1945; MP (Lab) North Paddington, Nov. 1946–Oct. 1953. Mem. Hammersmith Borough Council, 1945–53, and Leader of that Council, 1946–49; a Vice-Pres. of Assoc. of Municipal Corporations, 1952–53; for several years, mem. Metropolitan Boroughs' Standing Joint Cttee and of many local govt bodies. Volunteered for Army, Sept. 1939 and served in ranks and as officer in Intelligence Corps and RASC.

FIELD-FISHER, Thomas Gilbert, TD 1950; QC 1969; a Recorder of the Crown Court, 1972–87; *b* 16 May 1915; *s* of Caryl Field-Fisher, Torquay; *m* 1945, Ebba, *d* of Max Larsen, Linwood, USA. *Educ:* King's Sch., Bruton; Peterhouse, Cambridge. BA 1937, MA 1942. Called to Bar, Middle Temple, 1942, Bencher, 1976. Served Queen Victoria's Rifles, KRRC, 1939–47; BEF 1940 (POW; despatches). Judge Advocate Gen.'s Dept, 1945–47 (i/c War Crimes Dept, CMF); joined Western Circuit, 1947. Mem., Bar Council, 1962–66; Deputy Chairman: SW Agricultural Land Tribunal, 1967–82; Cornwall QS, 1968–71; Chm., Maria Colwell Inquiry, 1973–74. Actg Deemster, IOM, 1989–90. Vice-Chm., London Council of Social Service, 1966–79; Vice-Pres., London Voluntary Service Council, 1979–. Mem., Home Secretary's Adv. Cttee on Animal Experiments, 1980–89. Vice-President: UFAW, 1989–99; Dogs' Home, Battersea, 1995– (Chm., 1982–95); Founder and Chm., Assoc. of British Dogs' Homes, 1985–. Pres., Cornwall Magistrates' Assoc., 1985–97. Autumn Reader, Middle Temple, 1991. *Publications:* Animals and the Law, 1964; Rent Regulation and Control, 1967; Dog Problem: a lawyer's view, 1989; A Dog's Life–Sam, 1997; contribs to Halsbury's Laws of England, 3rd and 4th edns, Law Jl, and other legal publications. *Recreations:* tennis, dogs, collecting watercolours, MG cars, gardening. *Address:* 38 Hurlingham Court, SW6 3UW. *T:* (020) 7736 4627; 2 King's Bench Walk, Temple, EC4Y 7DE. *T:* (020) 7353 1746. *Clubs:* Hurlingham, International Lawn Tennis of Great Britain.

FIELDEN, Frank, MA (Dunelm); Secretary, Royal Fine Art Commission, 1969–79; *b* 3 Oct. 1915; *s* of Ernest and Emma Fielden, Greenfield, Yorks; *m* 1939, Margery Keeler; two *d*. *Educ:* University of Manchester. Graduated, 1938. Served 1939–45 with Royal Engineers (Special Forces), France, N Africa, Italy, Germany. Town Planning Officer to Nigerian Government, 1945–46; Lecturer and Sen. Lectr, University of Durham, 1946–59; Prof. of Architecture, Univ. of Strathclyde, 1959–69. Mem., Royal Fine Art Commn for Scotland, 1965–69. RIBA Athens Bursar, 1950, Bronze Medallist 1960. Chairman: Soc. of Architectural Historians of Great Britain, 1965–67; Richmond Soc., 1971–74. *Publications:* articles in professional journals and national press. *Recreations:* music, gardening. *Address:* 28 Caledonian Road, Chichester, W Sussex PO19 2LQ.

FIELDER, Prof. Alistair Richard, FRCS, FRCP, FRCOphth; Kennerley Bankes Professor of Ophthalmology, Imperial College of Science, Technology and Medicine, since 1995; Hon. Consultant Ophthalmologist: St Mary's Hospital NHS Trust, since 1995; Hammersmith Hospitals NHS Trust, since 1995; Hillingdon Hospital NHS Trust, since 1996; *b* 3 Sept. 1942; *s* of late Alfred Emmanuel Hugh Fielder and of Elizabeth Rachel Fielder (*née* Hutchinson); *m* 1965, Gillian Muriel Slough; one *s* three *d*. *Educ:* St George's Hosp. Med. Sch., London Univ. (MB BS 1966). FRCS 1974; FRCOphth (FCOphth 1988); MRCP 1991, FRCP 1994; FRCPCH 1999. RSO, Moorfields Eye Hosp., 1973–76; Consultant Ophthalmologist, Derby Hosps, 1977–82; Reader in Ophthalmology, Leicester Univ., 1982–88; Prof. of Ophthalmology, Birmingham Univ., 1988–95. Vice Pres., 1995–99, Sen. Vice Pres., 1997–99, Royal Coll. of Ophthalmologists; British Rep., Societas Ophthalmogica Europæa, 1998–. Trustee: RNIB, 1990– (Mem. Exec. Cttee, 1990–); British Council for the Prevention of Blindness, 1990– (Chm., 1995–); British Retinitis Pigmentosa Soc., 1992–; Nat. Fedn of Families with Visually Impaired Children (LOOK), 2000–. *Publications:* scientific articles and contribs to books on the developing visual system and paediatric ophthalmology. *Recreation:* dreaming about canal boats. *Address:* 18 Melrose Gardens, W6 7RW. *T:* (020) 7602 4790. *Club:* Royal Society of Medicine.

FIELDHOUSE, Brian; DL; Chief Executive, West Sussex County Council, 1990–95; *b* 1 May 1933; *s* of late Harry and Florence Fieldhouse; *m* 1959, Sonia J. Browne; one *s* one *d*. *Educ:* Barnsley Holgate Grammar Sch.; Keble Coll., Oxford (MA PPE). IPFA 1960. Formerly, Treasurer's Departments: Herts CC; Hants CC; Flints CC; County Treasurer: Lincs parts of Lindsey CC, 1970–73; W Sussex CC, 1973–90. Comr, Public Works Loans Bd, 1988–92. Principal Financial Advr, ACC, 1980–85. Pres., Soc. of Co. Treasurers, 1983. Dir, Chichester Fest. Theatre, 1995–97. Sec., Rees Jeffreys Road Fund, 1995–. DL West Sussex, 1996. FRSA 1984. *Recreations:* hill farming, theatre going. *Address:* 13 The Avenue, Chichester PO19 4PX. *Club:* Farmers'.

FIELDHOUSE, Prof. David Kenneth, FBA 1996; Vere Harmsworth Professor of Imperial and Naval History, Cambridge University, 1981–92; Fellow, Jesus College, Cambridge, 1981–92, subseq. Emeritus; *b* 7 June 1925; *s* of Rev. Ernest Fieldhouse and Clara Hilda Beatrice Fieldhouse; *m* 1952, Sheila Elizabeth Lyon; one *s* two *d*. *Educ:* Dean Close Sch., Cheltenham; Queen's Coll., Oxford (MA, DLitt). War Service: RN, Sub-Lt (A), 1943–47. History master, Haileybury Coll., 1950–52; Lectr in Modern History, Univ. of Canterbury, NZ, 1953–57; Beit Lectr in Commonwealth History, Oxford Univ., 1958–81; Fellow, Nuffield Coll., Oxford, 1966–81. *Publications:* The Colonial Empires, 1966, 2nd edn, 1982; The Theory of Capitalist Imperialism, 1967, 2nd edn 1969; Economics and Empire, 1973, 2nd edn 1984; Unilever Overseas, 1978; Colonialism 1870–1945, 1981; Black Africa 1945–80, 1986; Merchant Capital and Economic Decolonization, 1994; The West and the Third World, 1999. *Recreations:* music, golf, sailing, reading fiction. *Address:* Jesus College, Cambridge CB5 8BL. *T:* (01223) 339339.

FIELDING, Sir Colin (Cunningham), Kt 1986; CB 1981; Chairman, Microturbo Ltd, since 1988; consultant in defence systems, information technology and electronics, since 1986; *b* 23 Dec. 1926; *s* of Richard Cunningham and Sadie Fielding; *m* 1953, Gillian Aerona (*née* Thomas); one *d*. *Educ:* Heaton Grammar Sch., Newcastle upon Tyne; Durham Univ. BSc Hons Physics. British Scientific Instruments Research Assoc., 1948–49; RRE Malvern, 1949–65; Asst Dir of Electronics R&D, Min. of Technology, 1965–68; Head of Electronics Dept, RRE Malvern, 1968–73; RCDS, 1973–74; Dir of Scientific and Technical Intelligence, MoD, 1975–77; Dir, Admiralty Surface Weapons Estabt, 1977–78; Dep. Controller, R&D Estabts and Res. A, and Chief Scientist (RN), MoD, 1978–80; Dep. Chief of Defence Procurement (Nuclear), and Dir, AWRE, MoD, 1980–82; Controller of R&D Estabts, Res. and Nuclear Progs, MoD, 1982–86. Dir, Cray Research (UK), 1988–. *Publications:* papers in Proc. IEE, Proc. IERE, Nature. *Recreations:* yachting, tennis, music, golf. *Address:* Cheviots, Rosemount Drive, Bickley, Kent BR1 2LQ.

FIELDING, Fenella Marion; actress; *b* London, 17 Nov. 1934. *Educ:* North London Collegiate School. Began acting career in 1954; *plays include:* Cockles and Champagne, Saville, 1954; Pay the Piper, Saville, 1954; Jubilee Girl, Victoria Palace, 1956; Valmouth, Lyric, Hammersmith, 1958, Saville, 1959, and Chichester Fest., 1982; Pieces of Eight, Apollo, 1959; Five Plus One, Edinburgh Fest., 1961; Twists, Arts, 1962 (Best Revue Performance of the Year in Variety); Doctors of Philosophy, New Arts, 1962; Luv, New Arts, 1963; So Much to Remember—The Life Story of a Great Lady, Establishment, transf. to Vaudeville, 1963; Let's Get a Divorce, Mermaid, transf. to Comedy, 1966; The Beaux Stratagem and The Italian Straw Hat, Chichester Fest., 1967; The High Bid, Mermaid, 1967; Façade, Queen Elizabeth Hall, 1970; Colette, Ellen Stewart, NY, 1970 (first appearance in NY); Fish Out of Water, Greenwich, 1971; The Old Man's Comforts, Open Space, 1972; The Provok'd Wife, Greenwich, 1973; Absurd Person Singular, Criterion, 1974, transf. to Vaudeville, 1975; Fielding Convertible, Edinburgh Fest., 1976; Jubilee Jeunesse, Royal Opera House, 1977; Look After Lulu, Chichester Fest., transf. to Haymarket, 1978; A Personal Choice, Edinburgh Fest., 1978; Fenella on Broadway, W6, Studio, Lyric, Hammersmith, 1979; Wizard of Oz, Bromley, 1983; The Jungle Book, Adelphi, 1984; The Country Wife, Mermaid, 1990; A Dangerous Woman, New End Th., 1998; Blithe Spirit, Salisbury, 1999; *films include:* Drop Dead, Darling; Lock Up Your Daughters; Carry On Screaming; Carry On Regardless; Doctor in Clover; Doctor in Distress; Doctor in Trouble; No Love for Johnnie; Robin Hood; Guest House Paradiso; *television series:* That Was The Week That Was; A Touch of Venus; Ooh La La; Stories from Saki; Dean Martin and the Gold-Diggers; Comedy Tonight; Rhyme and Reason; numerous appearances in UK and USA. *Recreations:* reading, diarising. *Address:* c/o Barry Langford, 17 Westfields Avenue, SW13 0AT.

FIELDING, Prof. Kenneth Joshua, DPhil; Saintsbury Professor of Education, 1966–84, part-time 1984–87, now Emeritus and Fellow, since 1984, University of Edinburgh; *b* 19 July 1924; *s* of Joshua Douglas Fielding and Edith Llewelyn Fielding; *m* 1956, Jean Arnold Ferguson (*d* 1994); one *d* decd. *Educ:* Gt Yarmouth Grammar Sch.; University Coll., Oxford (Open Schol.; MA 1948; DPhil 1953). Served Royal Signals, 1943–46. William Noble Fellow, Univ. of Liverpool, 1951–53; Lectr, 1954, Sen. Lectr, 1956–57, Malayan Coll. of Educn, Kirkby, Liverpool; Cheshire Coll. of Educn, Alsager; Vice Principal, City of Liverpool Coll. of Educn, 1957–66. Bobst Vis. Prof., New York Univ., 1973. Sen. Ed., Collected Letters of Thomas and Jane Welsh Carlyle, 39 vols, 1970–; Ed., The Carlyle Newsletter, 1–9, 1979–88. *Publications:* Charles Dickens: a survey, 1954; Charles Dickens: a critical introduction, 1958, enlarged 1965; (ed) The Speeches of Charles Dickens, 1960, enlarged 1985; (ed jtly) The Letters of Charles Dickens, vol. 1, 1970, vol. 5, 1981; Joint editor: Carlyle Past and Present: original essays, 1976; Carlyle's The French Revolution, 1989; Carlyle's Reminiscences, 1997; Jane Carlyle, The Simple Story of My Own First Love, 2001; contrib. to numerous books and jls, on Dickens, Carlyle and other Victorians. *Recreations:* reading, walking. *Address:* 67 Grange Loan, Edinburgh EH9 2EG. *T:* (0131) 667 5154; University of Edinburgh, 22A Buccleuch Place, Edinburgh EH8 9JX.

FIELDING, Sir Leslie, KCMG 1988; Vice-Chancellor, University of Sussex, 1987–92; *b* 29 July 1932; *o s* of late Percy Archer Fielding and of Margaret (*née* Calder Horry); *m* 1978, Dr Sally P. J. Harvey, FSA, FRHistS, sometime Fellow of St Hilda's Coll., Oxford; one *s* one *d*. *Educ:* Queen Elizabeth's Sch., Barnet; Emmanuel Coll., Cambridge (First in History; MA; Hon. Fellow 1990); School of Oriental and African Studies, London; St Antony's Coll., Oxford (MA; Vis. Fellow, 1977–78). Served with Royal Regt of Artillery, 1951–53. Entered HM Diplomatic Service, 1956; served in: Tehran, 1957–60; Foreign Office, 1960–64; Singapore, 1964; Phnom Penh (Chargé d'Affaires), 1964–66; Paris, 1967–70; Dep. Head of Planning Staff, FCO, 1970–73; seconded for service with European Commn in Brussels, 1973; Dir (External Relns Directorate Gen.), 1973–77; permanent transfer 1979; Head of Delegn of Commn in Tokyo, 1978–82; Dir-Gen. for External Relns, 1982–87. UK Mem., High Council of European Univ. Inst. in Florence, 1988–92. Chm., Nat. Curriculum Geography Wkg Gp, 1989–90. Adviser: IBM Europe, 1989–95; Panasonic Europe, 1990–96. Hon. Pres., Univ. Assoc. for Contemporary European Studies, 1990–2000; Founder Mem., Japan–EC Assoc., then Europe-Japan Business Forum, 1988–98; Mem., UK–Japan 2000 Gp, 1993–. Mem. Ct, Univ. of Sussex, 2000–. Mem., Gen. Synod, C of E, 1990–92. Admitted to office of Reader by Bishop of Exeter, 1981; served dios of Exeter, Tokyo, Gibraltar, Chichester and Hereford. FRSA 1989; FRGS 1991 (Mem. Council, 1992–95). Hon. Fellow, Sussex European Inst., 1993. Hon. LLD Sussex, 1992. Grand Officer, Order of St Agatha (San Marino), 1987; Knight Commander Order of the White Rose (Finland), 1988; Grosse Silbenes Ehrenzeichen mit dem Stern (Austria), 1989. *Publications:* Europe as a global partner: the external relations of the European Community, 1991; (contrib.) Travellers' Tales, 1999; articles on internat. relations, higher educn and ecclesiastical matters. *Recreations:* life in the country, theology. *Address:* 5 St Julian's Avenue, Ludlow, Shropshire SY8 1ET. *Clubs:* Brooks's, Travellers.

FIELDING, Richard Walter; Chairman, Richard Fielding Ltd, 1992–2000; *b* 9 July 1933; *s* of late Walter Harrison Fielding, MBE, and Marjorie Octavia Adair (*née* Roberts); *m* 1st, 1961, Felicity Ann Jones (*d* 1981); one *s* three *d*; 2nd, 1983, Jacqueline Winifred Digby (*née* Hussey). *Educ:* Clifton Coll., Bristol. National Service, Royal Engineers (Lieut), 1951–53. Broker to Dir, Bland Welch & Co. Ltd, 1954–68; Dir to Man. Dir, C. E. Heath & Co. Ltd, 1968–75; Founder and Chm., Fielding and Partners, 1975–86; Chairman: C. E. Heath PLC, 1987–92; Sharelink PLC, 1993–95. Chm., Syndicate Capital Trust, 1996–98 (Dir, 1993–96); Dir, Hambros Insurance Services, 1993–98. High Sheriff, Dorset, 1997. *Recreations:* hunting, country sports. *Address:* 48 Gloucester Street, SW1V 4EH.

FIELDS, Terence; *b* 8 March 1937; *s* of late Frank Fields; *m* 1962, Maureen Mongan; two *s* two *d*. Served RAMC, 1955–57. Fireman, Merseyside County Fire Bde, 1957–83. Former Vice-Chm., Bootle Constit. Lab. Party; former Mem., NW Regl Exec. Cttee, Lab. Party. MP Liverpool, Broad Green, 1983–92 (Lab, 1983–91, Ind, 1991–92); contested (Soc. Lab) Liverpool, Broad Green, 1992. *Address:* 20 John Hunter Way, Bootle, Merseyside L30 5RJ.

FIELDSEND, Sir John (Charles Rowell), KBE 1998; Member, Court of Appeal, Falkland Islands and British Antarctic Territory, 1985–99; President, Court of Appeal, Gibraltar, 1991–97 (Member, since 1986); Chief Justice (non-resident), British Indian Ocean Territory, 1987–99 (Principal Legal Adviser, 1984–87); *b* 13 Sept. 1921; *s* of C. E. Fieldsend, MC, and Phyllis (*née* Brucesmith); *m* 1945, Muriel Gedling; one *s* one *d*. *Educ:* Michaelhouse, Natal; Rhodes University Coll., Grahamstown, SA (BA 1942, LLB 1947). Served RA, 1943–45. Called to the Bar, S Rhodesia, 1947; advocate in private practice, 1947–63; QC S Rhodesia, 1959; Pres., Special Income Tax Court for Fedn of Rhodesia and Nyasaland, 1958–63; High Court Judge, S Rhodesia, 1963, resigned 1968; Asst Solicitor, Law Commn, 1968–78, Sec., 1978–80; Chief Justice: of Zimbabwe, 1980–83; of Turks and Caicos Islands, 1985–87. *Recreations:* home-making, travel. *Address:* Great Dewes, Ardingly, Sussex RH17 6UP.

FIENNES, family name of **Baron Saye** and **Sele**.

FIENNES, Very Rev. Hon. Oliver William Twisleton-Wykeham-; Dean of Lincoln, 1969–89, Dean Emeritus since 1989; *b* 17 May 1926; *yr s* of 20th Baron Saye and Sele, OBE, MC, and Hersey Cecilia Hester, *d* of late Captain Sir Thomas Dacres Butler, KCVO; *m* 1956, Juliet, *d* of late Dr Trevor Braby Heaton, OBE; two *s* two *d*. *Educ:* Eton; New College, Oxford; Cuddesdon College. Asst Curate, New Milton, Hants, 1954; Chaplain, Clifton College, Bristol, 1958; Rector of Lambeth, 1963. Church Comr, 1977–88. Chairman: Pilgrims Assoc., 1986–89; St Matthew Housing (formerly St Matthew Soc.), 1994–. World Fellow, Thanksgiving Square, Dallas, 1980; Pres., Lincoln Br., Inst. of Advanced Motorists, 1973–; Chm., Radio Lincolnshire Adv. Cttee, 1992–95. Governor, Marlborough Coll., 1970–89. Nat Patron, E-SU in USA, 1987. ChStJ 1971; KStJ 1996. *Recreations:* cricket, travel, country activities. *Address:* Home Farm House, Colsterworth, Grantham, Lincs NG33 5HZ. *T:* (01476) 860811.

FIENNES, Ralph Nathanial; actor; *b* 22 Dec. 1962; *s* of Mark Fiennes and late Jennifer Fiennes (*née* Lash). *Educ:* Bishop Wordsworth's Sch., Salisbury; RADA. *Theatre* includes: Open Air Theatre, Regent's Park: Twelfth Night, Ring Round the Moon, 1985; A Midsummer Night's Dream, 1985, 1986; Romeo and Juliet, 1986; Royal National Theatre: Six Characters in Search of an Author, Fathers and Sons, Ting Tang Mine, 1987; Royal Shakespeare Company: The Plantagenets, Much Ado About Nothing, 1988; Playing With Trains, 1989; Troilus and Cressida, King Lear, 1990; The Man Who Came to Dinner, 1991; Almeida Theatre: Hamlet, 1995 (also Hackney Empire and Belasco, NY); Ivanov, 1997; Richard II, Coriolanus (transf. NY), 2000; *films:* Wuthering Heights, 1992; Baby of Macon, 1993; Schindler's List, 1993; Quiz Show, 1994; Strange Days, 1995; The English Patient, 1997; Oscar and Lucinda, 1998; The Avengers, 1998; Onegin, 1999 (also exec. producer); Sunshine, 2000; The End of the Affair, 2000; *television* includes: A Dangerous Man, 1991; The Cormorant, 1992. *Recreation:* books. *Address:* c/o Larry Dalzell Associates, 91 Regent Street, W1R 7TB. *T:* (020) 7287 5131.

FIENNES, Sir Ranulph Twisleton-Wykeham-, 3rd Bt *cr* 1916; OBE 1993; *b* 7 March 1944; *s* of Lieut-Col Sir Ranulph Twisleton-Wykeham-Fiennes, DSO, 2nd Bt (died of wounds, 1943) and Audrey Joan (*d* 1995), *yr d* of Sir Percy Newson, 1st Bt; *S* father 1944; *m* 1970, Virginia Pepper (first female member of Antarctic Club, 1985; first woman to be awarded Polar Medal, 1987). *Educ:* Eton. Liveryman, Vintners' Company, 1960. French Parachutist Wings, 1965. Lieut, Royal Scots Greys, 1966, Captain 1968 (retd 1970). Attached 22 SAS Regt, 1966, Sultan of Muscat's Armed Forces, 1968 (Dhofar Campaign Medal, 1969; Sultan's Bravery Medal, 1970). T&AVR 1971, Captain RAC. Leader of British expeditions: White Nile, 1969; Jostedalsbre Glacier, 1970; Headless Valley, BC, 1971; (Towards) North Pole, 1977; Transglobe (first surface journey around the world's polar axis), 1979–82, reached South Pole, 15 Dec. 1980, reached North Pole, 11 April 1982; North Polar Unsupported Expeditions: reached 84°48´N on 16 April 1986; reached 88°58´N on 14 April 1990 (Furthest North Unsupported record); South Polar Unsupported Expedition: first crossing of Antarctic Continent and longest polar journey in history (1,345 miles), 1992–93. Hon. MRIN 1997. Hon. DSc Loughborough, 1986; DUniv Birmingham, 1995. Elected to Guinness Hall of Fame, 1987. Livingstone Gold Medal, RSGS, 1983; Explorers' Club of New York Medal (and Hon. Life Membership), 1983; Founder's Medal, RGS, 1984; Polar Medal, 1987, clasp 1995; ITN Award, for the Event of the Decade, 1990; Millennium Award for Polar Exploration, British Chapter, Explorers' Club. *Film:* (cameraman) To the Ends of the Earth, 1983. *Publications:* A Talent for Trouble, 1970; Ice Fall in Norway, 1972; The Headless Valley, 1973; Where Soldiers Fear To Tread, 1975; Hell on Ice, 1979; To the Ends of the Earth, 1983; (with Virginia Fiennes) Bothie, the Polar Dog, 1984; Living Dangerously (autobiog.), 1987, rev. and expanded 1994; The Feather Men, 1991; Atlantis of the Sands, 1992; Mind Over Matter, 1993; The Sett, 1996; Fit for Life, 1998; Beyond the Limits, 2000; The Secret Hunters, 2001. *Recreations:* langlauf, photography. *Heir:* none. *Address:* Greenlands, Exford, Som TA24 7NU. *T:* (01643) 831350.

FIENNES-CLINTON, family name of **Earl of Lincoln**.

FIFE, 3rd Duke of, *cr* 1900; **James George Alexander Bannerman Carnegie;** Lord Carnegie of Kinnaird (Scot.), 1616; Earl of Southesk and Lord Carnegie of Kinnaird and Leuchars (Scot.), 1633; Bt (NS), 1663; Baron Balinhard, 1869; Earl of Macduff, 1900; *b* 23 Sept. 1929; *o s* of 11th Earl of Southesk (*d* 1992), and Princess Maud (*d* 1945); *S* aunt, HRH Princess Arthur of Connaught (Dukedom of Fife), 1959; *m* 1956, Hon. Caroline Cicely Dewar (marr. diss. 1966; she *m* 1980, Gen. Sir Richard Worsley), *er d* of 3rd Baron Forteviot, MBE; one *s* one *d*. *Educ:* Gordonstoun. Nat. Service, Scots Guards (Malayan Campaign), 1948–50. Royal Agricultural College. Clothworkers' Company, and Freeman City of London. Pres. of ABA, 1959–73, Vice-Patron, 1973–94; Ship's Pres., HMS Fife, 1967–87; a Vice-Patron, Braemar Royal Highland Soc.; a Vice-Pres., British Olympic Assoc. *Heir: s* Earl of Southesk, *qv*. *Address:* (seat) Kinnaird Castle, Brechin, Angus DD9 6TZ; (home) Elsick House, Stonehaven, Kincardineshire AB39 3NT. *Club:* Turf.

FIFOOT, Paul Ronald Ninnes, CMG 1978; HM Diplomatic Service, retired; *b* 1 April 1928; *o s* of late Ronald Fifoot, Cardiff; *m* 1952, Erica, *er d* of late Richard Alford, DMD; no *c*. *Educ:* Monkton House Sch., Cardiff; Queens' Coll., Cambridge. BA 1948, MA 1952. Military Service, 1948–50. Called to Bar, Gray's Inn, 1953; Crown Counsel, Tanganyika, 1953; Asst to the Law Officers, 1960; Legal Draftsman (later Chief Parliamentary Draftsman), 1961; retd from Tanzania Govt Service, 1966; Asst Legal Adviser, Commonwealth Office, 1966; Legislative Counsel, Province of British Columbia, 1967; Asst Legal Adviser, Commonwealth (later Foreign and Commonwealth) Office, 1968; Legal Counsellor, 1971; Agent of the UK Govt in cases before the European Commn and Court of Human Rights, 1971–76; Counsellor (Legal Advr), UK Mission to UN, NY, 1976–79; Legal Counsellor, FCO, 1979–84; Dep. Leader, UK Delegation to 3rd UN Conference on the Law of the Sea, 1981–82; Leader, UK Delegation to Preparatory Commn for Internat. Sea Bed Authority, 1983–84; Dep. Legal Advr, FCO, 1984–88. Special Legal Advr/Consultant, FCO, 1988, 1990, and 1992–2001; consultant and constitutional advr to various overseas govts, 1988–2001; consultant, Council on Tribunals, 1988–89. *Publications:* articles and reviews in journals, etc. *Address:* Zebrato, Lynwood Avenue, Epsom, Surrey KT17 4LQ.

FIGES, Prof. Orlando Guy, PhD; Professor of History, Birkbeck College, London University, since 1999; *b* 20 Nov. 1959; *s* of John Figes and Eva Figes (*née* Unger); *m* 1990, Stephanie Palmer; two *d*. *Educ:* Gonville and Caius Coll., Cambridge (BA History 1982); Trinity Coll., Cambridge (PhD 1987). Fellow, 1984–99, Dir of Studies in History, 1988–98, Trinity Coll., Cambridge; University Lectr in History, Cambridge, 1987–99. *Publications:* Peasant Russia Civil War: the Volga countryside in revolution 1917–21, 1989, 2nd edn 1991; A People's Tragedy: the Russian Revolution 1891–1924, 1996 (Wolfson History Prize, W. H. Smith Lit. Award, NCR Book Award, Los Angeles Times Book Prize, 1997); (with B. Kolonitskii) Interpreting the Russian Revolution: the language and symbols of 1917, 1999. *Recreations:* soccer, music, gardening, wine. *Address:* Birkbeck College, Malet Street, WC1E 7HX.

FIGG, Sir Leonard (Clifford William), KCMG 1981 (CMG 1974); HM Diplomatic Service, retired; *b* 17 Aug. 1923; *s* of late Sir Clifford Figg and late Lady (Eileen) Figg (*née* Crabb); *m* 1955, Jane Brown, *d* of late Judge Harold Brown; three *s*. *Educ:* Charterhouse; Trinity Coll., Oxford. RAF, 1942–46 (Flt-Lt). HM Diplomatic Service, 1947; served in: Addis Ababa, 1949–52; FO, 1952–58; Amman, 1958–61; FO, 1961–67; Counsellor, 1965; Deputy Consul-General, Chicago, 1967–69; DTI, 1970–73; Consul General and Minister, Milan, 1973–77; Asst Under Sec. of State, FCO, 1977–80; Ambassador to Ireland, 1980–83. Mem. Council, Cooperation Ireland, 1985–95. A Vice-Chm., British Red Cross Soc., 1983–88; a Vice-Pres., Bucks Red Cross, 1988–96. President: Aylesbury Divl Conservative Assoc., 1985–95; Bucks Assoc. of Youth Clubs, 1987–; Chiltern Soc., 1990–; Bucks and Oxfordshire East Euro Constituency Cons. Assoc., 1998; Chm., Bucks Farming and Wildlife Adv. Gp, 1991–2000. *Recreations:* forestry, reading, tennis. *Address:* Court Field House, Great Missenden, Bucks HP16 9PP. *Club:* Brooks's.

FIGGIS, Sir Anthony (St John Howard), KCVO 1996; CMG 1993; HM Diplomatic Service, retired; HM Marshal of the Diplomatic Corps, since 2001; *b* 12 Oct. 1940; *s* of Roberts Richmond Figgis and Philippa Maria Young; *m* 1964, Miriam Ellen Hardt; two *s* one *d*. *Educ:* Rugby Sch.; King's Coll., Cambridge (Mod Langs). Joined HM Foreign (later Diplomatic) Service, 1962; Third Sec., Belgrade, 1963–65; Commonwealth Office, 1965–68; Second Sec., Polit. Residency, Bahrain, 1968–70; FCO, 1970–71; First Sec. (Commercial), Madrid, 1971–74; CSCE delegn, Geneva, 1974–75; FCO, 1975–79; Madrid: Head of Chancery, 1979–80; Commercial Counsellor, 1980–82; Counsellor, Belgrade, 1982–85; Head of E European Dept, FCO, 1986–88; Counsellor and Head of Chancery, Bonn, 1988–89; Dir of Res., subseq. of Res. and Analysis, FCO, 1989–91; Asst Under-Sec. of State, FCO, and HM Vice-Marshal of the Diplomatic Corps, 1991–96; Ambassador to Austria, 1996–2000. Freeman, City of London, 1996. *Recreations:* fly-fishing, tennis, music (piano). *Address:* Clock Tower House, St James's Palace, SW1A 1BN.

FIGGIS, His Honour Arthur Lenox; a Circuit Judge (formerly Judge of County Courts), 1971–92; *b* 12 Sept. 1918; *s* of late Frank Fernesley Figgis and late Frances Annie Figgis; *m* 1953, Alison, *d* of late Sidney Bocher Ganthony and late Doris Ganthony; two *s* three *d*. *Educ:* Tonbridge; Peterhouse, Cambridge (MA). Served War, 1939–46, Royal Artillery. Barrister-at-Law, Inner Temple, 1947. *Recreations:* rifle shooting half-blue, 1939, and shot for Ireland (Elcho Shield), 1935–39; walking. *Address:* The Forge, Shamley Green, Guildford, Surrey GU5 0UB. *T:* (01483) 898360.

FIGURES, Sir Colin (Frederick), KCMG 1983 (CMG 1978); OBE 1969; HM Diplomatic Service, retired; Deputy Secretary, Cabinet Office, 1985–89; *b* 1 July 1925; *s* of Frederick and Muriel Figures; *m* 1956, Pamela Ann Timmis; one *s* two *d*. *Educ:* King Edward's Sch., Birmingham; Pembroke Coll., Cambridge (MA). Served Worcestershire Regt, 1943–48. Joined Foreign Office, 1951; attached Control Commn, Germany, 1953–56; Amman, 1956–58; FCO, 1958–59; Warsaw, 1959–62; FCO, 1962–66; Vienna, 1966–69; FCO, 1969–85 (Dep. Sec.). *Recreations:* watching sport, gardening, beachcombing. *Address:* c/o HSBC, 130 New Street, Birmingham B2 4JU. *Club:* Old Edwardians (Birmingham).

FILBEY, Air Vice-Marshal Keith David, CBE 1993; Air Officer Commanding No 2 Group, since 2000; *b* 16 Dec. 1947; *s* of Sqn Ldr (rtd) Cecil Hayward Filbey and Barbara Filbey; *m* 1982, Anne Feaver; one *s* one *d*. *Educ:* Brentwood Sch.; Royal Air Force Coll., Cranwell. Royal Air Force: Pilot, 214 Sqn, 1969–76; Flt Comdr 51 Sqn, 1976–78; Personnel Officer, 1978–79; RAF Staff Coll., 1980; Staff Officer, HQ 1 Gp, 1981–83; OC, 216 Sqn, 1983–86; staff appts, MoD and HQ 1 Gp, 1986–90; OC, RAF Brize Norton, 1990–92; RCDS, 1993; Dep. Chief of Assessments Staff, Cabinet Office, 1993–96; Dir, Air Ops, 1997; Sen. DS (Air), RCDS, 1998–99; AOC No 38 Gp, 2000. Mem., Air League, 1999–. Pres., RAF Cricket Assoc., 2000. 7RAeS 2000. Upper Freeman, GAPAN, 2000–. *Recreations:* cricket, tennis, golf, choral music. *Address:* HQ No 2 Group, RAF High Wycombe, Bucks HP14 4UE. *Clubs:* Royal Air Force, Innominate; Adastrian Cricket (Pres.).

FILBY, Ven. William Charles Leonard; Archdeacon of Horsham, since 1983; *b* 21 Jan. 1933; *s* of William Richard and Dorothy Filby; *m* 1958, Marion Erica, *d* of Prof. Terence Wilmot Hutchison, *qv*; four *s* one *d*. *Educ:* Ashford County Grammar School; London Univ. (BA); Oak Hill Theological Coll. Curate, All Souls, Eastbourne, 1959–62; Curate-in-charge, Holy Trinity, Knaphill, 1962–65; Vicar, Holy Trinity, Richmond-upon-Thames, 1965–71; Vicar, Bishop Hannington Memorial Church, Hove, 1971–79; Rector of Broadwater, 1979–83; RD of Worthing, 1980–83; Hon. Canon of Chichester Cathedral, 1981–83. Proctor in Convocation, 1975–90. Chm., Redcliffe Missionary Trng Coll., Chiswick, 1970–91; Mem., Keswick Convention Council, 1973–93; Pres., Chichester Diocesan Evangelical Union, 1978–84; Chairman: Diocesan Stewardship Cttee, 1983–89; Sussex Churches Broadcasting Cttee, 1984–96; Diocesan Cttee for Mission and Renewal, 1989–93; Diocesan Industrial Mission Adv. Panel, 1989–; Diocesan Gp, Archbishops' Commn on Rural Areas, 1998–. Bishops Advr for Hosp. Chaplains,

1986–98. Governor: St Mary's Hall, Brighton, 1984–; UC, Chichester (formerly W Sussex Inst. of Higher Educn), 1985–. *Recreations:* sport, music. *Address:* The Archdeaconry, Itchingfield, Sussex RH13 7NX. *T:* (01403) 790315.

FILDES, (David) Christopher, OBE 1994; financial journalist; *b* 10 Nov. 1934; *s* of late David Garland Fildes and of Shelagh Fildes (*née* Jones), Manley, Cheshire; *m* 1st, 1969, Susan Patricia Mottram (*d* 1978); one *d* decd; 2nd, 1986, Frederica Bement Lord (*d* 1992); one step *d. Educ:* Clifton; Balliol Coll., Oxford. Financial journalist, 1963–; columnist, editor and broadcaster (The Times, Spectator, Daily Mail, Euromoney, Evening News, Investors Chronicle, Business Prog.); financial columnist: Euromoney, 1969–98; Daily Telegraph and Spectator, 1984–. Director: The Spectator (1828) Ltd, 1990–; London Mozart Players, 2000–. Member: Council, GDST, 1999–; Rly Heritage Cttee, 1999–. Hon. LittD Sheffield, 1999. Wincott Award for financial journalism, 1978 and 1986. *Recreations:* racing, railways. *Address:* 4 Scarsdale Villas, W8 6PR. *Clubs:* Garrick, City of London.

FILER, Denis Edwin, CBE 1992; TD 1965 and 1977; FREng, FIMechE, FIChemE; Chairman, Innvotec Corporate Ventures Ltd (formerly Electra Innvotec Corporate Ventures Ltd), since 2000 (Director, since 1989); *b* 19 May 1932; *s* of Francis and Sarah Filer; *m* 1957, Pamela Armitage; one *s* two *d. Educ:* Manchester Central Grammar Sch.; Manchester Univ. (Hons BSc Mech. Eng.); BA Open 1987. Commissioned REME (Nat. Service); served in Germany; REME TA, 1955–: Col, 1975–77; Hon. Col, 1978–87. ICI: Works Maintenance Engineer, 1960–67; Project Manager, Manchester, 1967–71; Project Manager, Holland (ICI Europa), 1971–73; Div. Maintenance Advisor, Organics Div., 1973; Plastics Div., Wilton Works: Works Engineer, 1973–76; Engineering Manager, 1976–78; Engineering & Production Dir, 1978–81; Dir of Engrg, 1981–88; Dir.-Gen., Engrg Council, 1988–95 (Mem., 1986–88; Chm., Continuing Educn and Trng Cttee; Mem., Standing Cttee for Industry). Chairman: Rolinx, 1978–81; Adwest Gp, then Adwest Automotive plc, 1994–97 (Dir, 1991–97); Director: Bexford, 1978–80; Engineering Services Wilton, 1978–81; Eur. Adv. Dir, Callidus Technologies Inc., 1991–99. Member: Council, IMechE, 1983–89 (Vice-Pres., 1987–89, 1996–98; Dep. Pres., 1998–2000; Pres., 2000–01; Chm., Process Industries Div. Bd, 1985–87); Board, Lloyd's Register of Quality Assurance, 1986–88, Gen. Cttee, Lloyd's Register, 1988–95. Gov., Univ. of Hertfordshire, 1996–. FREng (FEng 1985). *Recreations:* tennis, sport, reading. *Address:* Brambles, Watton Green, Watton-at-Stone, Hertford SG14 3RB. *T:* (01920) 830207. *Club:* Army and Navy.

FILER, (Douglas) Roger, FCA; Managing Director, D & S Travel Supplies Ltd, since 1997; *b* 25 Feb. 1942; *s* of Horace Filer and Raie (*née* Behrman); *m* 1979, Vivienne Sara Green; one *s* one *d. Educ:* Clifton Coll.; St John's Coll., Oxford (MA); FCA 1970. Called to the Bar, Gray's Inn, 1979. Joined Association Television Group, 1967; Chief Accountant, Ambassador Bowling, 1967–69; Financial Controller, Bentray Investments, 1969–70; Financial Dir, M. Berman then Bermans & Nathans, 1971–73; Financial Controller, Stoll Theatres Corp./Moss Empires, 1974; Dir, 1982–92, Man. Dir, 1990–92, Stoll Moss Theatres; Man. Dir, Maybox Gp, subseq. Mayfair Theatres and Cinemas Ltd, 1993–96. *Recreations:* music, history, walking. *Address:* Four Brim Hill, Hampstead Garden Suburb, N2 0HF. *T:* (020) 8455 7392.

FILKIN, family name of **Baron Filkin**.

FILKIN, Baron *cr* 1999 (Life Peer), of Pimlico in the City of Westminster; **David Geoffrey Nigel Filkin,** CBE 1997; a Lord in Waiting (Government Whip), since 2001; *b* 1 July 1944; *s* of Donald Geoffrey and Winifred Filkin; *m* 1974, Elizabeth Tompkins (*see* Elizabeth Filkin) (marr. diss. 1994); three *d. Educ:* King Edward VI Sch., Five Ways, Birmingham; Clare Coll., Cambridge (MA Hist.); Manchester Univ. (DipTP); Birmingham Univ. (postgrad. study). Formerly MRTPI. Teacher on VSO, Ghana, 1966–67; Planner, Redditch Develt Corp., 1969–72; Manager, Brent Housing Aid Centre, London Borough of Brent, 1972–75; Dep. Chief Exec., Merseyside Improved Houses, 1975–79; Borough Housing Officer, Ellesmere Port and Neston Council, 1979–82; Dir of Housing, London Borough of Greenwich, 1982–88; Chief Exec., Reading BC, 1988–91; Sec., ADC, 1991–97. Dir, New Local Govt Network, 1995–2001. Chm., All Party Parly Business Services Gp; 2000. Chm., Beacon Council Adv. Panel, 1999–2001. Adviser: on local govt, Joseph Rowntree Foundn, 1997–2001; H of C Envmt Cttee, 1998. Founder and Chm., The Parlt Choir (APPG), 2000–. *Publications:* pamphlets, papers and articles on housing and local govt policy. *Recreations:* music, walking, swimming. *Address:* c/o House of Lords, SW1A 0PW. *T:* (020) 7932 0031.

FILKIN, Elizabeth; Parliamentary Commissioner for Standards, since 1999; *b* 24 Nov. 1940; *d* of Frances Trollope and John Tompkins; *m* 1974, David Geoffrey Nigel Filkin (marr. diss. 1994); three *d*; *m* 1996, Michael John Honey, *qv. Educ:* Birmingham Univ. (BSocSci). Organiser, Sparkbrook Assoc., 1961–64; Whyndham Deedes Fellowship, Israel, 1964; Res. Asst, Res. Associate, Lectr, Birmingham Univ., 1964–68; Lectr and Community Worker, Nat. Inst. for Social Work, 1968–71; Community Work Services Officer, London Borough of Brent, 1971–75; Lectr in Social Studies, Liverpool Univ., 1975–83; Chief Exec., Nat. Assoc. of CABx, 1983–88; Dir of Community Services, 1988–90, Asst Chief Exec., 1990–92, LDDC; Revenue Adjudicator, 1993–95; The Adjudicator, Inland Revenue, Customs and Excise, and Contribs Agency, 1995–99. Non-executive Director: Britannia Bldg Soc., 1992–98; Hay Management Consultants, 1992–98; Logica, 1995–98; Weatherall, Green & Smith, 1997–99. Chm., Lord Chancellor's Adv. Cttee on Legal Aid, 1991–94. Mem., Audit Commn, 1999–. Mem. Council, Univ. of E London, 1997–. *Publications:* The New Villagers, 1968; What a Community Worker Needs to Know, 1974; Community Work and Caring for Children, 1979; Caring for Children, 1979; (ed) Women and Children First, 1984. *Recreations:* walking, swimming. *Address:* House of Commons, SW1A 0AA. *T:* (020) 7219 0320.

FILLEUL, Peter Amy, MA; Head Master, William Hulme's Grammar School, Manchester, 1974–87; *b* 7 Aug. 1929; *s* of J. C. Filleul and L. A. Mundy; *m* 1963, Elizabeth Ann Talbot; one *s* one *d. Educ:* Victoria Coll., Jersey; Bedford Sch.; (Exhibnr) Exeter Coll., Oxford (MA, DipEd). Royal Air Force, 1952–55 (Sword of Merit, RAF Spitalgate, 1952). Portsmouth GS, 1955–65; Stationers' Company's Sch., 1965–68; Cardiff High Sch. (Head Master), 1969–74. *Recreations:* rifle shooting, fishing. *Address:* Kirkliston, Midvale Close, Upper Midvale Road, St Helier, Jersey, Channel Islands JE2 3ZJ. *T:* (01534) 759941.

FILLINGHAM, David James; Director, NHS Modernisation Agency, since 2001; *b* 28 March 1960; *s* of Thomas Fillingham and Irene Fillingham (*née* Webster); *m* 1982, Janet Green; two *d. Educ:* Cowley High Sch.; Peterhouse, Cambridge (MA History 1982); Henley Coll. (MBA 1993). Personnel Officer, Pilkington plc, 1982–84; Personnel Manager, 1984–88, Product Develt Manager, 1988–89, Pilkington Glass; Regl Personnel Manager, Mersey RHA, 1989–91; Gen. Manager, Wirral FHSA, 1991–93; Chief Executive: St Helens and Knowsley HA, 1993–97; N Staffordshire Hosp. NHS Trust, 1997–2001. MIPM 1986. *Publications:* various articles in mgt jls and health service pubns. *Recreations:* going to the cinema, hill-walking, watching Rugby League. *Address:* (office) Richmond House, 79 Whitehall, SW1A 2NS; Springfield, Millbrow, St Helens, Merseyside WA10 4QQ. *T:* (01744) 29600.

FILMER-SANKEY, Dr William Patrick, FSA; Senior Engineer, Alan Baxter & Associates, since 2000; *b* 13 Oct. 1957; *s* of Patrick Hugh Filmer-Sankey and Josephine Filmer-Sankey; *m* 1981, Caroline Frances Sparrow; one *s* one *d. Educ:* Downside Sch.; New Coll., Oxford (BA Hons Mod. Hist. 1979); Inst. of Archaeology, Oxford (Dip. European Archaeol. 1981; DPhil 1989). Associate Archaeol Consultant, Oxford Archaeological Associates Ltd, 1990–93. Dir, Snape Historical Trust, 1987–95; Hon. Sec., 1994–2000, Vice Pres., 2000–, British Archaeol Assoc.; Dir, Victorian Soc. 1993–2000. FSA 1997; FRSA 1998. Editor, Anglo-Saxon Studies in Archaeology and History, 1991–94. *Publications:* From the Dust of the Earth Returning: excavations of the Anglo-Saxon cemetery at Snape, Suffolk, 1990; (contrib.) Maritime Celts, Frisians and Saxons, 1991; (contrib.) The Age of Sutton Hoo, 1992; articles and papers. *Recreations:* archaeology, ornithology, sailing, deer stalking, Germany. *Address:* 57 Lavington Road, Ealing, W13 9LS. *T:* (020) 8579 0425.

FILOCHOWSKI, Julian, OBE 1998; Director, Catholic Fund for Overseas Development, since 1982; *b* 9 Dec. 1947; *s* of Tadeusz Filochowski and Jean Filochowski (*née* Royce). *Educ:* St Michael's Coll., Leeds; Churchill Coll., Cambridge (MA Econs). Economic Planning Advr, Min. of Finance, Belize, 1969–70; Central America Regl Co-ordinator, British Volunteer Prog., 1970–73; Co-ordinator, Educn Dept, Catholic Inst. for Internat. Relations, 1973–82. *Publications:* Reflections on Puebla, 1980; Archbishop Romero, Ten Years On, 1991. *Recreations:* swimming, reading, walking. *Address:* CAFOD, 2 Romero Close, Stockwell Road, SW9 9TY. *T:* (020) 7733 7900.

FINCH, Hilary Ann; Music Critic, The Times, since 1980; *b* 2 May 1951; *d* of Francis Richard Finch and Hilda Grace (*née* Davey). *Educ:* Univ. of Exeter (MA); Hughes Hall, Cambridge (PGCE). Asst to Arts Editor, TES, 1976–80; feature writer, The Times, 1980–; freelance writer and broadcaster, 1980–. *Recreations:* travel, walking in Iceland, Nordic art and literature. *Address:* 22 Rocks Lane, Barnes, SW13 0DB. *T:* (020) 8878 5664.

FINCH, Prof. Janet Valerie, CBE 1999; DL; PhD; Vice-Chancellor, Keele University, since 1995; *b* 13 Feb. 1946; *d* of Robert Bleakley Finch and Evelyn Muriel (*née* Smith); *m* 1st, 1967, Geoffrey O. Spedding (marr. diss. 1982); 2nd, 1994, David H. J. Morgan. *Educ:* Merchant Taylors' Sch. for Girls, Crosby; Bedford Coll., London (BA Hons Sociol.); Univ. of Bradford (PhD Sociol. 1975). Lectr, Endsleigh Coll., Hull, 1974–76; Lancaster University: Lectr, then Sen. Lectr, 1976–88; Prof. of Social Relations, 1988–95; Pro-Vice-Chancellor, 1992–95. Non-exec. Dir, NW Regl HA, 1992–96; Mem. Bd, Quality Assce Agency, 1997–. Chm., Preston CRC, 1980–85. Economic and Social Research Council: Mem., 1993–97; Chm., Res. Grants Bd, 1994–97. Chm. Exec., Brit. Sociol. Assoc., 1983–84. DL Staffs, 1999. Hon. DLitt UWE, 1997. *Publications:* Married to the Job, 1983; Education as Social Policy, 1984; Research and Policy, 1986; Family Obligations and Social Change, 1989; Negotiating Family Responsibilities, 1993; Wills, Inheritance and Families, 1996; Passing On, 2000. *Recreations:* theatre-going, hill-walking in the Languedoc. *Address:* Vice-Chancellor's Office, Keele University, Staffs ST5 5BG. *Club:* University Women's.

FINCH, (John) Russell, FCIArb; Stipendiary Magistrate and Coroner, Guernsey, since 1997; Lieutenant-Bailiff (Judge) of the Royal Court of Guernsey, since 1999; *b* 15 Feb. 1950; *s* of Reginald John Peter Fergusson Finch and Winifred Joan Finch (*née* Woods); *m* 1990, Anne Elizabeth Sergeant (*née* Lowe), *widow* of Peter Sergeant; one step *s. Educ:* Southern Grammar Sch. for Boys, Portsmouth; Queen Mary Coll., London (LLB); Univ. de Caen; Open Univ. (BA Hons, DipEurHum). FCIArb 1999. Articled to Clerk to Fareham and Gosport Justices, 1972–74; admitted solicitor, 1974; Court Clerk, 1974–75; Principal Asst, Aylesbury Gp of Magistrates' Courts, 1975–79; joined Dept of DPP, 1979; served on S, Metropolitan and Police Complaints Divs, 1979–86; Asst Br. Crown Prosecutor, Inner London CPS (Sen. Principal), 1986–88; joined Chambers of HM's Procureur (Attorney-Gen.) for Guernsey, 1988; Advocate, Royal Court of Guernsey, 1993; Crown Advocate, 1994. Chm., Guernsey Inf. Exchange, 1999–. Mem., US Naval Inst., Annapolis. *Publications:* Practical Police Prosecuting, 1977; contrib. articles to various jls on magisterial law and practice. *Recreations:* chess (mainly correspondence), history, listening to opera recordings. *Address:* Magistrate's Chambers, Royal Court House, St Peter Port, Guernsey GY1 2PB. *T:* (01481) 725277; *e-mail:* russell.finch@gov.gg. *Clubs:* Royal Commonwealth Society, Royal Over-Seas League.

FINCH, Karen Solveig Sinding Møller, OBE 1976; FIIC; Founder, 1975, and Principal, 1975–86, Textile Conservation Centre, Hampton Court Palace, subseq. at Winchester College of Art, Southampton University; *b* 8 May 1921; *d* of Søren Møller and Ellen Sinding Møller, Viborg, Denmark; *m* 1946, Norman Frank Finch (*d* 1996); one *d. Educ:* Kunsthaandvarkerskolen, Copenhagen. FIIC 1962. Royal Sch. of Needlework, 1946–48; conservation work, V&A Mus., 1954–59; Independent Textile Conservation Services (based on textiles as historic documents), 1960–75; teacher, hist. of textile techniques, Courtauld Inst. of Art, 1969–86 (jtly inaugurated postgrad. course in textile conservation, 1973), Hon. Sen. Lectr, 1975–86. Dedication of Karen Finch Liby and Ref. Collection, Winchester Coll., 1993. Mem. Council, Leather Conservation Centre, UC Northampton (formerly Nene Coll.), 1978–. Emeritus Mem., Embroiderers' Guild, 1980. Hon. DLitt Southampton, 1999. Award for Lifetime Service to the Arts, NACF, 1987; Festschrift from colleagues and friends, 1999. *Publications:* Caring for Textiles, 1977; The Care and Preservation of Textiles, 1985, 2nd edn 1991; contrib. papers and articles to textile related societies and to professional jls. *Recreations:* family and friends, reading, the arts, TV. *Address:* 7 Western Gardens, Ealing, W5 3RS. *T:* (020) 8992 1979.

FINCH, Robert Gerard; Partner, Linklaters, since 1974; *b* 20 Aug. 1944; *s* of Brig. J. R. G. Finch; *m* 1971, Patricia Ann Ross; two *d. Educ:* Felsted Sch. Articled Clerk, Monro Pennefather & Co., 1963; joined Linklater & Paines, 1969; Head of Property Dept, 1996–99. A Church Comr. Alderman, 1992, Sheriff, 1999–2000, City of London; Liveryman: Solicitors' Co., 1986– (Master, 1999–2000); Innholders' Co., 1991–; Hon. Freeman, Envmtl Cleaners' Co., 1998; Hon. Liveryman, Chartered Surveyors' Co. Hon. FRICS 1999. *Recreations:* sailing, ski-ing, climbing. *Address:* (office) 1 Silk Street, EC2Y 8HQ. *Club:* Ski Club of GB, Alpine Ski, City Livery; Itchenor Sailing (W Sussex).

FINCH, Russell; *see* Finch, J. R.

FINCH, Stephen Clark, OBE 1989; independent consultant, since 1989; *b* 7 March 1929; *s* of Frank Finch and Doris Finch (*née* Lloyd), Haywards Heath; *m* 1975, Sarah Rosemary Ann, *d* of Adm. Sir Anthony T. F. G. Griffin, GCB; two *d. Educ:* Ardingly; Sch. of Signals; RMCS. FInstAM; FIMgt; FCMA. Commnd Royal Signals 1948; served Korea, UK and BAOR; retired 1968. Joined British Petroleum Co. Ltd, 1968: Gp Telecommunications Manager, 1968–81; Sen. Adviser, Regulatory Affairs, 1981–84; Asst Co-ordinator, Inf. Systems Admin, 1984–89. Member: Adv. Panel on Licensing Value Added Network

Services, 1982–87; Competition (formerly Monopolies and Mergers) Commn, 1985–2000. Member: Inst. of Administrative Management, 1968– (Mem. Council, 1981–84; Medallist, 1985); Telecommunications Managers Assoc., 1968– (Exec. Cttee, 1971–91; Chm., 1981–84; Regulatory Affairs Exec., 1984–87; Dir, External Affairs, 1988–91); Council, Internat. Telecommunications Users Gp, 1981–94 (Chm., 1987–89). Member: City of London Deanery Synod, 1981– (Lay Chm., 1994–); London Diocesan Synod, 1994– (Bishop's Council, 1994–); London DAC for Care of Churches, 1995–; Oxford Churches Trust, 1996– (Sec., 1997–). *Publications:* occasional contribs to learned jls. *Recreations:* sailing, skiing, swimming, opera. *Address:* 97 Englefield Road, Canonbury N1 3LJ. *T:* (020) 7226 2803. *Club:* National.

FINCH HATTON, family name of **Earl of Winchilsea and Nottingham**.

FINCH-KNIGHTLEY, family name of **Earl of Aylesford**.

FINCHAM, Prof. John Robert Stanley, FRS 1969; FRSE 1978; Arthur Balfour Professor of Genetics, University of Cambridge, 1984–91, now Emeritus; Professorial Fellow, Peterhouse, Cambridge, 1984–91, now Emeritus Fellow; Hon. Fellow, Division of Biology, University of Edinburgh, since 1992; *b* 11 Aug. 1926; *s* of Robert Fincham and Winifred Emily Fincham (*née* Western); *m* 1950, Ann Katherine Emerson; one *s* three *d*. *Educ:* Hertford Grammar Sch.; Peterhouse, Cambridge. BA 1946, PhD 1950, ScD 1964. Bye-Fellow of Peterhouse, 1949–50; Lectr in Botany, University Coll., Leicester, 1950–54; Reader in Genetics, Univ. of Leicester, 1954–60; Head of Dept of Genetics, John Innes Inst., 1960–66; Prof. of Genetics, Leeds Univ., 1966–76; Buchanan Prof. of Genetics, Univ. of Edinburgh, 1976–84. Vis. Associate Prof. of Genetics, Massachusetts Inst. of Technology, 1960–61. Pres., Genetical Soc., 1978–81. Editor, Heredity, 1971–78. *Publications:* Fungal Genetics (with P. R. Day), 1963, 4th edn, 1979; Microbial and Molecular Genetics, 1965; Genetic Complementation, 1966; Genetics, 1983; (jtly) Genetically Engineered Organisms, 1991; Genetic Analysis, 1995; papers in Biochemical Jl, Jl Gen. Microbiol., Jl Biol. Chem., Heredity, Jl Molecular Biol., Genet. Res. *Recreations:* listening to music, walking. *Address:* 20 Greenbank Road, Edinburgh EH10 5RY.

FINDLAY, Alastair Donald Fraser, FCIWEM; Chief Executive, North of Scotland Water Authority, 1995–2000; *b* 3 Feb. 1944; *s* of late Rev. Donald Fraser Findlay and Isobel Ellis Findlay (*née* Louden); *m* 1969, Morag Cumming Peden; one *s* three *d*. *Educ:* Pitlochry High Sch.; Kelso High Sch.; Univ. of Edinburgh (MA (Hons) Mental Philosophy). FCIWEM 1996. Asst Principal, Dept of Agriculture and Fisheries for Scotland, 1966–70; Private Sec. to Jt Parly Under Sec. of State, Scottish Office, 1970–71; Principal, Scottish Office, 1971–74; on loan to FCO as First Sec. (Agric. and Food), The Hague, 1975–78; Asst Sec., Higher Educn Div., Scottish Educn Dept, 1979–82; Fisheries Div., 1982–85, Livestock Products Div., 1985–88, Dept of Agric. and Fisheries for Scotland; Under Sec., IDS, then Scottish Office Industry Dept, 1988–93; Fisheries Sec., Scottish Office Agric. and Fisheries Dept, 1993–95. Trustee, Lloyds TSB Foundn for Scotland, 1998–. *Recreations:* golf, walking, motor cars, Rugby spectating. *Club:* Royal Commonwealth Society.

FINDLAY, Donald Russell; QC (Scot.) 1988; *b* 17 March 1951; *s* of James Findlay and Mabel Findlay (*née* Muirhead); *m* 1982, Jennifer Edith (*née* Borrowman). *Educ:* Harris Academy, Dundee; Univ. of Dundee (LLB 1st cl. Hons); Univ. of Glasgow (MPhil). Mem., Faculty of Advocates, 1975–; Lectr in Law, Heriot Watt Univ., 1976–77. Mem., Lothian Health Bd, 1987–91. Vice Chm., Glasgow Rangers FC, 1992–99 (Dir, 1991–99). Vice Chairman: N Cunninghame Cons. and Unionist Assoc., 1989–92; Leith Cons. and Unionist Assoc., 1985–88. Rector, St Andrews Univ., 1993–99. Vice Pres., Assoc. for Internat. Cancer Res., 1996–. Columnist, Scottish Daily Express, 1995–97; radio and television broadcaster. FRSA 1997. *Publications:* Three Verdicts (novel), 1998; contribs to Scots Law Times and various medico-legal publications. *Recreations:* Glasgow Rangers FC, Egyptology, malt whisky, photography, cooking, drinking claret, politics, ethics; challenging authority. *Address:* Faculty of Advocates, Parliament House, Edinburgh EH1 1RF. *T:* (0131) 226 2881. *Clubs:* Royal Scottish Automobile (Glasgow); Royal Burgess Golfing Society, Glasgow Rangers Bond.

FINDLAY, Ian Herbert Fyfe; Chairman, Lloyd's, 1978 and 1979 (Deputy Chairman, 1977); *b* 5 Feb. 1918; *s* of Prof. Alexander Findlay, CBE, Aberdeen, and Alice Mary (*née* de Rougement); *m* 1950, Alison Mary Ashby; two *s* one *d*. *Educ:* Fettes Coll., Edinburgh. Served War, Royal Artillery, 1939–46. Mem. of Lloyd's, 1946. Chm., Price Forbes (Holdings) Ltd, 1967; Dep. Chm., Sedgwick Forbes Holdings Ltd, 1972, Chm., 1974–77. Mem. Cttee, Lloyd's Insurance Brokers Assoc., 1961–65 and 1966–69; Chm., Non-Marine Cttee, 1967–68; Chm. of Assoc., 1969–70; Mem., Cttee of Lloyd's, 1971–74, 1976–79; Chm., British Insurance Brokers Assoc., 1980–82. Trustee, St George's English Sch., Rome, 1980–91; Vice-Pres., Guide Dogs for the Blind, 1987– (Chm., 1981–87); Governor, Brighton Coll., 1981–88. Pres., Senior Golfers' Soc., 1990–93. *Recreations:* golf, postal history. *Address:* West Cottage, 1 The Close, Eliot Vale, Blackheath, SE3 0UR. *T:* (020) 8318 4644. *Clubs:* City of London; Royal and Ancient Golf (St Andrews); Royal St George's (Sandwich); Addington (Surrey).

FINDLAY, Richard Martin; Entertainment Law Partner, Tods Murray, WS, since 1990; Lead Partner, T2M (Tods Total Media), since 2000; *b* 18 Dec. 1951; *s* of Ian Macdonald Semple Findlay and Kathleen Lightfoot or Findlay. *Educ:* Gordon Schs, Huntly; Univ. of Aberdeen (LLB). Trainee Solicitor, Wilsone & Duffus, Advocates, Aberdeen, 1973–75; Asst Solicitor, Maclay Murray & Spens, Glasgow, 1975–79; Partner, Ranken & Reid, SSC, Edinburgh, 1979–90. Member: Business in the Arts Placement Scheme, 1994–; Theatrical Management Assoc., 1996–. Director: Gallus Theatre Co. Ltd, 1996–98; Dance Base Ltd, 1997–98; Royal Lyceum Theatre Co. Ltd, 1999–; Audio Description Film Fund Ltd, 2000–. Dir, Lothian Gay and Lesbian Switchboard Ltd, 1998–. Member: Internat. Assoc. of Entertainment Lawyers, 1990–; Internat. Entertainment & Multimedia Law & Business Network, 1995–; Scottish Media Lawyers Soc., 1995–; IBA, 1993–; BAFTA, 1990– (Mem. Mgt Cttee, BAFTA (Scotland), 1998–); Writers' Guild, 1993–; New Producers Alliance, 1993–98; Inst. of Art and Law, 1996–98. Trustee, Peter Darrel Trust, 1996–. Part-time Lectr on Law of Film, Napier Univ., 1997–. Man. Editor, i-2-i–the business journal for the international film industry (formerly Internat. Film Business, Finance and Law Rev.), 1995–; Scotland Ed., Methuen Amateur Theatre Handbook. *Recreations:* theatre, film, music, photography, Scottish culture, kilt wearing, the Internet. *Address:* 66 Queen Street, Edinburgh EH2 4NE. *T:* (0131) 226 4771, *Fax:* (0131) 300 2202.

FINE, Anne; writer; Children's Laureate, since 2001; *b* 7 Dec. 1947; *d* of Brian Laker and Mary Baker; *m* 1968, Kit Fine (marr. diss. 1991); two *d*. *Educ:* Northampton High School for Girls; Univ. of Warwick (BA Hons History and Politics). Guardian Children's Fiction Award, 1990; Carnegie Medal, 1990, 1993; Children's Author of the Year, Publishing News, 1990, 1993. *Publications: for older children:* The Summer House Loon, 1978; The Other Darker Ned, 1978; The Stone Menagerie, 1980; Round Behind the Icehouse, 1981; The Granny Project, 1983; Madame Doubtfire, 1987; Goggle-Eyes, 1989; The Book of the Banshee, 1991; Flour Babies, 1992 (Whitbread Award, 1993); Step by Wicked Step, 1995; The Tulip Touch, 1996 (Whitbread Award, 1997); *for younger children:* Scaredy-Cat, 1985; Anneli the Art Hater, 1986; Crummy Mummy and Me, 1988; A Pack of Liars, 1988; Stranger Danger, 1989; Bill's New Frock, 1989; The Country Pancake, 1989; A Sudden Puff of Glittering Smoke, 1989; A Sudden Swirl of Icy Wind, 1990; Only a Show, 1990; Design-a-Pram, 1991; A Sudden Glow of Gold, 1991; The Worst Child I Ever Had, 1991; The Angel of Nitshill Road, 1991; Same Old Story Every Year, 1992; The Chicken Gave it to Me, 1992; The Haunting of Pip Parker, 1992; How To Write Really Badly, 1996; Press Play, 1996; Jennifer's Diary, 1997; Loudmouth Louis, 1998; Roll Over, Roly, 1999; Charm School, 1999; Bad Dreams, 2000; Very Different, 2001; *picture book:* Poor Monty, 1991; *novels:* The Killjoy, 1986; Taking the Devil's Advice, 1990; In Cold Domain, 1994; Telling Liddy, 1997; All Bones and Lies, 2001. *Recreations:* reading, walking. *Address:* c/o David Higham Associates, 5–8 Lower John Street, W1R 4HA.

FINE, Prof. Leon Gerald, FRCP, FRCPGlas, FACP, FMedSci; Professor and Head of Department of Medicine, University College London, since 1991 and Head of Department of Medicine, Royal Free and University College Medical School, since 1998; *b* 16 June 1943; *s* of Matthew Fine and Jeanette (*née* Lipshitz); *m* 1966, Brenda Sakinovsky; two *d*. *Educ:* Univ. of Cape Town, SA (MB, ChB). FACP 1978; FRCP 1986; FRCPGlas 1993. Internship and Residency in Internal Medicine, Tel Aviv Univ. Med. Sch., Israel, 1967–70; Asst Prof. of Medicine, Albert Einstein Coll. of Medicine, NY, 1975–76; University of Miami School of Medicine: Asst Prof., 1976–78; Associate Prof., 1978–82; Prof. of Medicine and Chief, Div. of Nephrology, UCLA, 1982–91; Hd of Dept of Medicine, UCL Med. Sch., 1991–98. Founder FMedSci 1998. Editor, Exptl Nephrology, 1993–. *Publications:* contribs in professional jls on pathophysiology of chronic renal disease, renal growth control, renal growth responses to acute and chronic injury, and genetic manipulation of the kidney. *Recreations:* collecting rare books on the history of medicine and fine printing, book-binding. *Address:* Department of Medicine, University College London, The Rayne Institute, 5 University Street, WC1E 6JJ. *T:* (020) 7679 6186; *e-mail:* l.fine@ucl.ac.uk. *Club:* Athenæum.

FINER, Dr Elliot Geoffrey, CChem, FRSC; Director General, Chemical Industries Association, since 1996; *b* 30 March 1944; *s* of Reuben and Pauline Finer; *m* 1970, Viviane Kibrit; two *s*. *Educ:* Royal Grammar Sch., High Wycombe; Cheadle Hulme Sch.; East Barnet Grammar Sch.; St Catharine's Coll., Cambridge (BA 1965); Univ. of East Anglia (MSc 1966; PhD 1968). CChem, FRSC 1993. Unilever Research, Welwyn, 1968–75; Dept of Energy, 1975–90; Dir for Industry and Commerce, 1983–86, Dir Gen., 1988–90, Energy Efficiency Office; Under Secretary, 1988; Head of Management Develt Gp, Cabinet Office, 1990–92; Head of Enterprise Initiative Div., 1992, Head of Chemicals and Biotechnology Div., 1992–95, DTI. Dir, Spillers Foods Ltd, 1989–92. Mem., BBSRC, 1994–95. Pres., Assembly of European Chemical Industry Fedns, 1998–2000. *Publications:* scientific papers and articles on nuclear magnetic resonance spectroscopy and its applications, esp. to phospholipid systems, in learned jls. *Recreations:* home and family, reading, DIY, music. *Address:* Chemical Industries Association, Kings Buildings, Smith Square, SW1P 3JJ.

FINESTEIN, His Honour Israel, MA; QC 1970; a Circuit Judge, 1972–87; *b* 29 April 1921; *y c* of late Jeremiah Finestein, Hull; *m* 1946, Marion Phyllis, *er d* of Simon Oster, Hendon, Mddx. *Educ:* Kingston High School, Hull; Trinity Coll., Cambridge (Major Scholar and Prizeman; MA 1946). Called to the Bar, Lincoln's Inn, 1953. Former Pres., Mental Health Review Tribunal. President: Jewish Hist. Soc. of England, 1973–75, 1994–95; Bd of Deps of British Jews, 1991–94; former Chm., London Jewish Mus. Pres., Norwood Child Care, 1983–90. Hon. LLD Hull. *Publications:* Short History of the Jews of England, 1956; Jewish Society in Victorian England, 1993; Anglo-Jewry in Changing Times 1840–1914, 1999. *Recreation:* reading history. *Address:* 18 Buttermere Court, Boundary Road, NW8 6NR.

FINESTEIN, Jonathon Eli; a District Judge (Magistrates' Courts) (formerly Stipendiary Magistrate), Lancashire, since 2000; a Recorder, since 1996 (an Assistant Recorder, 1992–96); *b* 9 April 1950; *s* of Gustav Finestein and Esther Finestein; *m* 1985, Elaine March; one *d*. *Educ:* Hull Grammar Sch.; Leeds Univ. (LLB). Called to the Bar, Gray's Inn, 1973; practice in Hull; Asst Stipendiary Magistrate, 1989–92; Stipendiary Magistrate for Lancs and Merseyside, 1992–2000. *Recreations:* watching all sports, walking. *Address:* Preston Magistrates' Court, 52 Lawson Street, Preston PR1 2RD. *T:* (01772) 208000.

FINGLAND, Sir Stanley (James Gunn), KCMG 1979 (CMG 1966); HM Diplomatic Service, retired; High Commissioner to Kenya, 1975–79; UK Permanent Representative to the UN Environment Programme 1975–79, and to UN Centre for Human Settlements, 1979; *b* 19 Dec. 1919; *s* of late Samuel Gunn Fingland and late Agnes Christina (*née* Watson); *m* 1946, Nellie (*née* Lister); one *s* one *d*. *Educ:* Royal High Sch., Edinburgh. TA 1938. War service, 1939–46 as Major, Royal Signals; served N Africa, Sicily, Italy, Egypt. Commonwealth Relations Office, 1948–; British High Commission, India, 1948–51; Australia, 1953–56; Adviser on Commonwealth and External Affairs to Governor-Gen., Nigeria, 1958–60; British High Commission, Nigeria, 1960; Adviser on Commonwealth and External Affairs to Governor-Gen., Fedn of The W Indies, 1960–61, and to the Governor of Trinidad and Tobago, 1962; British Dep. High Commissioner: Trinidad and Tobago, 1962–63; Rhodesia, 1964–66; High Comr, Sierra Leone, 1966–69; Asst Under-Sec. of State, FCO, 1969–72; Ambassador to Cuba, 1972–75. *Recreation:* fishing.

FINGLETON, David Melvin; Metropolitan Stipendiary Magistrate, 1980–95; *b* 2 Sept. 1941; *s* of Laurence Fingleton and Norma Phillips (*née* Spiro); *m* 1975, Clare, *yr d* of late Ian Colvin. *Educ:* Aldwickbury Sch., Harpenden; Stowe Sch.; University Coll., Oxford (Exhibnr; BA Hons Modern History, MA). Called to Bar, Middle Temple, 1965; South Eastern Circuit. Member: Bd, Trinity Coll. of Music, 1986–98; Trinity Coll. of Music Corp., 1986–; Trustee, Samuel Butler's Educnl Foundn, 1968–. Music Correspondent, Contemporary Review, 1969–92; Opera and Ballet Critic, Tatler and Bystander, 1970–78; Stage Design Corresp., Arts Review, 1976–95; Associate Editor, Music and Musicians, 1977–80; Music Critic: Evening News, 1979–80; Daily Express, 1982–98; Restaurant Critic, Spectator, 1996–99. *Publications:* Kiri, 1982; articles in Contemp. Rev., Tatler and Bystander, Music and Musicians, Arts Rev., Evening News, Daily Express, Spectator. *Recreations:* listening to and writing about music, village life in France, gastronomy. *Address:* c/o John Johnson Agency, Clerkenwell House, 45/47 Clerkenwell Green, EC1R 0HT. *Clubs:* Garrick, MCC.

FINGRET, Peter; His Honour Judge Fingret; a Circuit Judge, since 1992; *b* 13 Sept. 1934; *s* of late Iser and Irene Fingret; *m* 1st, 1960, June Moss (marr. diss. 1980); one *s* one *d*; 2nd, 1980, Dr Ann Lilian Mary Hollingworth (*née* Field). *Educ:* Leeds Modern Sch.; Leeds Univ. (LLB Hons); Open Univ. (BA). President, Leeds Univ. Union, 1957–58. Admitted Solicitor, 1960. Partner: Willey Hargrave & Co., Leeds, 1964–75; Fingret, Paterson & Co., Leeds, 1975–82. Stipendiary Magistrate for Co. of Humberside sitting at Kingston-upon-Hull, 1982–85; Metropolitan Stipendiary Magistrate, 1985–92; a Recorder, 1987–92; a Pres., Mental Health Rev. Tribunal, 1993–. Chm., Lord

Chancellor's Adv. Cttee on JPs for Inner London Commn Area, 1997–. Councillor, Leeds City Council, 1967–72; Member: Court, Univ. of Leeds, 1975–85; Cttee, Leeds Internat. Piano Competition, 1981–85. *Recreations:* golf, music, theatre. *Address:* Southwark Crown Court, 1 English Grounds, SE1 2HU. *Club:* Garrick.

FINK, Prof. George, FRCPE; FRSE; Vice-President of Research, Pharmos Corporation, since 1999; Director, MRC Brain Metabolism Unit, 1980–99, Hon. Professor since 1984, University of Edinburgh; *b* 13 Nov. 1936; *s* of John H. Fink and Therese (*née* Weiss); *m* 1959, Ann Elizabeth Langsam; one *s* one *d. Educ:* Melbourne High Sch.; Univ. of Melbourne (MB BS 1960; MD 1978); Hertford Coll., Univ. of Oxford (DPhil 1967). FRSE 1989; FRCPE 1998. Jun. and sen. house officer, Royal Melbourne and Alfred Hosps, Victoria, Australia, 1961–62; Demonstrator in Anatomy, Monash Univ., Victoria, 1963–64; Nuffield Dominions Demonstrator, Oxford Univ., 1965–67; Sen. Lectr in Anatomy, Monash Univ., 1968–71; Univ. Lectr 1971–80, Official Fellow in Physiology and Med., Brasenose Coll., 1974–80, Oxford Univ. Royal Soc.-Israel Acad. Exchange Fellow, Weizmann Inst., 1979; Walter Cottman Fellow and Vis. Prof., Monash Univ., 1985, 1989; Arthur Fishberg Prof., Mt Sinai Med. Sch., NY, 1988. Prosector in Anatomy, Melbourne Univ., 1956; Wolfson Lectr, Univ. of Oxford, 1982; first G. W. Harris Lectr, Physiol Soc., Cambridge, 1987. Pres., European Neuroendocrine Assoc., 1991–95; Member: Council, European Neuroscience Assoc., 1980–82, 1994–98; Mental Health Panel, Wellcome Trust, 1984–89; Steering Cttee, British Neuroendocrine Group, 1984–88 (Trustee, BNG, 1990–); Co-ordinating Cttee, ESF Network on Neuroimmunomodulation, 1990–93. Chm., 5 Year Assessment Biomed. Prog., 1991–96; Monitor, EU Biomed. 2 Prog., 1995. Trustee, Jl of Neuroendocrinology, 1990–. *Publications:* (ed with L. J. Whalley) Neuropeptides: Basic and Clinical Aspects, 1982; (ed with A. J. Harmar and K. W. McKerns) Neuroendocrine Molecular Biology, 1986; (ed with A. J. Harmar) Neuropeptides: A Methodology, 1989; (Ed. in Chief) Encyclopedia of Stress, 2000; numerous scientific publications mainly on neuroendocrinology and neuroendocrine molecular biology. *Recreations:* ski-ing, diving. *Address:* Pharmos Ltd, Kiryat Weizmann, Rehovot 76326, Israel. *T:* (8) 9409679, *Fax:* (8) 9409686; *e-mail:* gfink@pharmos.com.

FINKELSTEIN, Daniel William, OBE 1997; Director, Policy Unit, Conservative Central Office, since 1999; *b* 30 Aug. 1962; *s* of Prof. Ludwik Finkelstein, *qv*; *m* 1993, Dr Nicola Ruth, *d* of Henry and Frances Connor; one *s. Educ:* Hendon Prep. Sch.; University College Sch.; London School of Economics (BSc Econs 1984); City Univ. (MSc 1986). Journalist, Network magazine, 1987–89; Editor, Connexion, 1989–92; Dir, Social Market Foundn, 1992–95; Dir, Conservative Res. Dept, 1995–98; Associate Editor, New Moon magazine, 1990–97. Res. Asst, RCA, 1984–87; Political Advr to Dr David Owen, MP, 1986–91. Contested: (SDP) Brent E, 1987; (C) Harrow W, 2001. Mem., Nat. Cttee, SDP, 1986–90. Founder and Bd Mem., Enterprise Europe, 1990– (Chm., 1990–95). *Publications:* (with Craig Arnall) The Open Network and its Enemies, 1990; Conservatives in Opposition: Republicans in the US, 1994. *Recreations:* US political memorabilia, Chinese food. *Address:* Conservative Central Office, 32 Smith Square, SW1P 3HH. *T:* (020) 7896 4226. *Clubs:* Carlton, Reform.

FINKELSTEIN, Prof. Ludwik, OBE 1990; DSc; FREng; FIEE; CPhys, FInstP; Professor of Measurement and Instrumentation, City University, 1980–97, now Emeritus; *b* 6 Dec. 1929; *s* of Adolf and Amalia Finkelstein; *m* 1957, Mirjam Emma, *d* of Dr Alfred and Dr Margarethe Wiener; two *s* one *d. Educ:* Univ. of London (BSc, MSc). DSc City Univ., 1989; MA Leo Baeck Coll., 1996. Physicist, Technical Staff, Electronic Tubes Ltd, 1951–52; Scientist, Instrument Br., NCB Mining Res. Estabt, 1952–59; Northampton Coll., London, and City University, London: Lectr, 1959–61; Sen. Lectr, 1961–63; Principal Lectr, 1963–67; Reader, 1967–70; Prof. of Instrument and Control Engineering, 1970–80; Head of Dept of Systems Science, 1974–79; Head of Dept of Physics, 1980–88; Dean, Sch. of Electrical Engrg and Applied Physics, 1983–88; Dean, Sch. of Engrg, 1988–93; Pro-Vice-Chancellor, 1991–94. Visiting Prof., Delft Univ. of Technology, 1973–74. Pres., Inst. of Measurement and Control, 1980 (Vice-Pres., 1972–75, 1977–79; Hartley Silver Medal, 1980); Chm., Management and Design Div., IEE, 1984–85 (Management and Design Divl Premium (jtly), 1984). FREng (FEng 1986). Hon. FInstMC 1991. Hon. Dr St Petersburg Technical Univ., 1994; Hon. DCL City, 1999. *Publications:* papers in learned jls and conference proc. *Recreations:* books, conversation, Jewish studies. *Address:* City University, Northampton Square, EC1V 0HB. *T:* (020) 7477 8139; 9 Cheyne Walk, Hendon NW4 3QH. *T:* (020) 8202 6966.

See also D. W. Finkelstein.

FINLAY OF LLANDAFF, Baroness *cr* 2001 (Life Peer), of Llandaff in the County of South Glamorgan; **Ilora Gillian Finlay,** FRCP, FRCGP; Vice-Dean, School of Medicine, University of Wales College of Medicine, since 2000; first Medical Director, Holme Tower Marie Curie Centre, Cardiff, since 1987; *b* 23 Feb. 1949; *d* of Charles Beaumont Benoy Downman and Thaïs Helèna Downman (*née* Barakan); *m* 1972, Andrew Yule Finlay; one *s* one *d. Educ:* Wimbledon High Sch.; St Mary's Hosp. Med. Sch., Univ. of London (MB, BS 1972). DObstRCOG 1974; DCH 1975. MRCS; FRCGP 1992; FRCP 1999. GP, 1981-86. Consultant in Palliative Medicine, Velindre NHS Trust, Cardiff, 1994–. Course Dir, Dip. and MSc in Palliative Medicine, UWCM. Non-exec. Dir, Gwent HA, 1995–2001. Pres., Medical Women's Fedn, 2001–02. Governor, Howell's Sch., Llandaff, GDST. Ed., Palliative Care Today. *Publication:* (ed) Medical Humanities, 2001. *Address:* House of Lords, SW1A 0PW; Velindre NHS Trust, Cardiff CF14 2TP.

FINLAY, Alexander William; retired; *b* 28 Nov. 1921; *s* of late Robert Gaskin Finlay and late Alice Finlay; *m* 1949, Ona Margaret Lewis; no *c. Educ:* Tottenham County School. Flt-Lt RAF, 1941–47; various posts, BOAC and British Airways, 1947–78, Planning Dir, 1971–78, retd. Chm., Soc. for Long Range Planning, 1978–79; Mem. Council, Sussex Trust for Nature Conservation, 1982–89; Trustee, Charitable Trust, 1983–. Active interest in support for crime victims, 1989–. FCIT. *Recreations:* conservation, photography, gardening. *Club:* Royal Air Force.

FINLAY, Sir David (Ronald James Bell), 2nd Bt *cr* 1964, of Epping, Co. Essex; *b* 16 Nov. 1963; *s* of Sir Graeme Bell Finlay, 1st Bt, ERD and of June Evangeline, *y d* of Col Francis Collingwood Drake, OBE, MC, DL; *S* father, 1987; *m* 1998, Camilla, *d* of Peter Acheson; one *s. Educ:* Marlborough College; Bristol Univ. (BSc Hons Economics/ Philosophy). Peat Marwick McLintock, 1986–91; Hill Samuel Financial Services, 1992–94; Gerrard Vivian Gray, 1994–97; Greig Middleton, 1997; Cater Allen Asset Management, 1998–. Freeman, City of London, 1991. *Recreations:* ski-ing, shooting. *Heir: s* Tristan James Bell Finlay, *b* 5 April 2001.

FINLAY, Frank, CBE 1984; actor; *b* Farnworth, Lancs, 6 Aug. 1926; *s* of Josiah Finlay; *m* 1954, Doreen Shepherd; two *s* one *d. Educ:* St Gregory the Great, Farnworth; RADA (Sir James Knott Schol.). *Stage:* repertory, 1950–52 and 1954–57; Belgrade, Coventry, 1958; Epitaph for George Dillon, NY, 1958; Royal Court, 1958, 1959–62: Sugar in the Morning; Sergeant Musgrave's Dance; Chicken Soup with Barley, Roots, I'm Talking About Jerusalem; The Happy Haven; Platonov; Chips with Everything, Royal Court, transf. to Vaudeville Theatre, 1962 (Clarence Derwent Best Actor Award); Chichester Festival, 1963: St Joan; The Workhouse Donkey; with National Theatre Co. 1963–70: St Joan, 1963; Willie Mossop in Hobson's Choice, and Iago in Othello (both also Chichester Fest., 1964, Berlin and Moscow, 1965), The Dutch Courtesan (also Chichester Fest.), 1964; Giles Corey in The Crucible, Dogberry in Much Ado About Nothing, Mother Courage, 1965; Joxer Daly in Juno and the Paycock, Dikoy in The Storm, 1966; Bernard in After Haggerty, Aldwych, Criterion, Jesus Christ in Son of Man, Leicester Theatre and Round House (first actor ever to play Jesus Christ on stage in English theatre), 1970; Kings and Clowns (musical), Phoenix, 1978; Filumena, Lyric, 1978, US tour, 1979–80, and NY, 1980; The Girl in Melanie Klein, 1980; The Cherry Orchard, tour and Haymarket, 1983; Mutiny (musical), Piccadilly, 1985–86; Beyond Reasonable Doubt, Queen's, 1987, Australian tour, 1988–89, UK tour, 1989–90; Black Angel, King's Head, Islington, 1990; A Slight Hangover, 1991, The Heiress, 1992, Bromley and UK tour; The Woman in Black, UK tour, 1993–94; Peter Pan, Chichester and UK tour; Gaslight, Richmond, 1995; The Handyman, Chichester, 1996; *with National Theatre Co.:* Peppino in Saturday, Sunday, Monday, 1973; Sloman in The Party, 1973; Freddy Malone in Plunder, Ben Prosser in Watch It Come Down, Josef Frank in Weapons of Happiness, 1976; Amadeus, 1982; *films include,* 1962–: The Longest Day, Private Potter, The Informers, A Life for Ruth, Loneliness of the Long Distance Runner, Hot Enough for June, The Comedy Man, The Sandwich Man, A Study in Terror, Othello (nominated for Amer. Acad. award; best actor award, San Sebastian, 1966), The Jokers, I'll Never Forget What's 'Is Name, The Shoes of the Fisherman, Deadly Bees, Robbery, Inspector Clouseau, Twisted Nerve, Cromwell, The Molly Maguires (in Hollywood), Assault, Victory for Danny Jones, Gumshoe, Shaft in Africa, Van Der Valk and the Girl, Van Der Valk and the Rich; Van Der Valk and the Dead; The Three Musketeers; The Ring of Darkness, The Wild Geese, The Thief of Baghdad, Sherlock Holmes—Murder by Decree; Enigma; Return of the Soldier; The Ploughman's Lunch, 1982; La Chiave (The Key), Italy, 1983; Sakharov, 1983; Christmas Carol, Arch of Triumph, 1919, 1984; Lifeforce, 1985; Casanova, 1986; The Return of the Musketeers, 1988; Cthulhu Mansion, 1992; Charlemagne, 1993; The Sparrow, 1993; *TV appearances include:* Julius Caesar, Les Misérables, This Happy Breed, The Lie (SFTA Award), Casanova (series), The Death of Adolf Hitler, Don Quixote (SFTA Award), Voltaire, Merchant of Venice, Bouquet of Barbed Wire (series) (Best Actor Award), 84 Charing Cross Road, Saturday Sunday Monday, Count Dracula, The Last Campaign, Napoleon in Betzi, Dear Brutus, Tales of the Unexpected, Tales from 1001 Nights, Aspects of Love—Mona, In the Secret State, Verdict on Erebus (NZ), King of the Wind, Mountain of Diamonds (series), Stalin (US), Sherlock Holmes, How Do You Want Me (series), The Sins (series). Hon. Fellow, Bolton Inst., 1992. *Address:* c/o Ken McReddie, 91 Regent Street, W1R 7TB. *Club:* Garrick.

FINLAY, Rt Rev. Terence Edward; *see* Toronto, Bishop of.

FINLAY, Thomas Aloysius; Chief Justice of Ireland, 1985–94; *b* 17 Sept. 1922; *s* of Thomas A. Finlay and Eva Finlay; *m* 1948, Alice Blayney; two *s* three *d. Educ:* Xavier Sch., Dublin; Clongowes Wood Coll.; University Coll. Dublin. BA Legal and Political Science, NUI. Called to the Bar, King's Inns, 1944 (Bencher, 1972); Hon. Bencher: Inn of Court of NI, 1985; Middle Temple, 1986. Mem., Dáil Éireann, 1954–57; Sen. Counsel, 1961; Judge of the High Court, 1972, Pres. of the High Court, 1974. *Recreations:* fishing, shooting, conversation. *Address:* 22 Ailesbury Drive, Dublin 4. *T:* (1) 693395.

FINLAY-MAXWELL, David Campbell, MBE 1994; PhD; CEng, MIEE; FTI, FSDC; Director, D. F. Maxwell Co., since 1991; *b* 2 March 1923; *s* of Luke Greenwood Maxwell and of Lillias Maule Finlay; *m* 1954, Constance Shirley Hood; one *s* one *d. Educ:* St Paul's; Heriot-Watt Coll. (Edinburgh Univ.) (Electronic and Control Engrg). CEng 1950; MIEE 1950; FTI 1974; FSDC 1985. PhD Leeds, 1983. Major Royal Signals, 1945. Harvard Univ. Advanced Management Programme, 1968. Man. Dir, 1946–86, Chm., 1960–89, Dir, 1993–98, John Gladstone & Co.; Chm. and Man. Dir, John Gladstone & Co. (Engrg), 1948–89. Chairman: Manpower Working Party, NEDO, 1970–73; Wool Industries Res. Assoc., 1974–77; Textile Res. Council, 1977–82; Wool Textile EDC, 1977–79, UK Rep., Consultative Cttee for R&D, Brussels, 1979–84. EEC Reviewer, ESPRIT Prog., 1986–2001. Dir, Wool Foundn (Internat. Wool Secretariat), 1985–. Member: Council, Textile Inst., 1972–74; British Textile Council, 1977–85; Textile Industry and Dyeing Adv. Cttee, Leeds Univ. Council, 1974–95; Soc. of Dyers and Colourists, 1950–. Pres., Comitextil Sci. Res. Cttee, Brussels. Hon. Lectr, Leeds Univ. Hon. Organiser for UK, Technical Volunteer Helpers for Blind. *Recreations:* radio propagation, satellite tracking. *Address:* D. F. Maxwell Co., Tarrens, The Green, Pirbright, Surrey GU24 0JT. *Club:* Special Forces.

FINLAYSON, George; HM Diplomatic Service, retired; *b* 22 April 1943; *s* of late George Finlayson and Alison Boath (*née* Barclay); *m* 1966, Patricia Grace Ballantine; two *s. Educ:* Tynecastle High Sch., Edinburgh. Joined HM Diplomatic Service, 1965; Reykjavik, 1967–69; Prague, 1969–71; Lagos, 1971 75; FCO, 1975 78; 2nd Sec., New Delhi, 1978–81; 1st Sec., FCO, 1981–83; 1st Sec. and Head of Chancery, Montevideo, 1983–87; Consul (Commercial) and Dep. Dir for Trade Promotion, New York, 1987–90; Dep. High Comr, Dhaka, 1990–93; Consul-Gen., Melbourne, 1994–98; High Comr to Malaŵi, 1998–2001. *Recreations:* golf, tennis, drawing, painting.

FINLAYSON, George Ferguson, CMG 1979; CVO 1983; HM Diplomatic Service, retired; *b* 28 Nov. 1924; *s* of late G. B. Finlayson; *m* 1st, 1951, Rosslyn Evelyn (*d* 1972), *d* of late E. N. James; one *d*; 2nd, 1982, Anthea Judith, *d* of late F. D. Perry. *Educ:* North Berwick High Sch. Royal Air Force, 1943–47. Apptd HM Foreign (later Diplomatic) Service, 1949; 2nd Sec. (Inf.), HM Embassy, Rangoon, 1952–54; FO, 1955–59; First Sec., 1959; HM Consul, Algiers, 1959–61; First Sec., HM Embassy, Bamako, 1961–63; HM Consul (Commercial), New York, 1964–68; Counsellor, 1968; Counsellor (Commercial), British High Commn, Singapore, 1969–72; Head of Trade Relations and Exports Dept, FCO, 1972–73; Counsellor (Commercial) Paris, 1973–78; Consul-General: Toronto, 1978–81; Los Angeles, 1981–84. *Recreations:* travel, walking, tennis, swimming. *Address:* 141b Ashley Gardens, SW1P 1HN. *T:* (020) 7834 6227. *Club:* Oriental.

FINLEY, Gerald Hunter; baritone; *b* Montreal, 30 Jan. 1960; *s* of Eric Gault Finley and Catherine Rae Finley (*née* Hunter); *m* 1990, Louise Winter, opera singer; two *s. Educ:* Glebe Collegiate Inst., Ottawa; Univ. of Ottawa; Royal Coll. of Music (ARCM 1980); King's Coll., Cambridge (BA 1983; MA 1986); Nat. Opera Studio. St Matthew's Church Choir, Ottawa, 1970–79; Ottawa Choral Soc., 1976–79; Ontario Youth Choir, 1977–78; King's Coll. Choir, 1981–83; Glyndebourne Chorus, 1986–88; *débuts:* Figaro in Le Nozze di Figaro, Downland Opera, 1984; Antonio in Le Nozze di Figaro, Nat. Arts Centre Opera, 1987; Graf Dominik in Arabella, Glyndebourne, 1989; Graf in Capriccio, Chicago Lyric Opera, 1994; Figaro in Le Nozze di Figaro, LA Music Centre, 1994, Royal Opera House, Covent Garden, 1995; Valentin in Faust, Opéra de Paris, 1997; Papageno in Die Zauberflöte, NY Met., 1998; Mr Fox in Fantastic Mr Fox, LA Opera, 1998; Harry Heegan in The Silver Tassie, ENO, 2000; appears regularly at Glyndebourne Opera Fest. Vis. Prof., Royal Coll. of Music, 2000. Numerous opera and recital recordings. John

Christie Award, Glyndebourne, 1989; Juno Award, Canadian Acad. of Recording Arts, 1998; Singer's Award, Royal Philharmonic Soc., 2000. *Recreations:* gardening, rollerblading. *Address:* c/o IMG Artists Europe, 616 Chiswick High Road, W4 5RX. *T:* (020) 8233 5800; c/o IMG Artists, 420 West 45th Street, New York, NY 10036, USA. *T:* (212) 5415640. *Club:* Royal Commonwealth Society.

FINLEY, Michael John; Governor, International Press Foundation, 1988–97; *b* 22 Sept. 1932; *s* of late Walter Finley and of Grace Marie Butler; *m* 1955, Sheila Elizabeth Cole (*d* 1992); four *s*; *m* 2001, Maureen Elizabeth Crocker. *Educ:* King Edward VII Sch., Sheffield. Editor, 1964–69, Sheffield Morning Telegraph (formerly Sheffield Telegraph); Chief Editorial Dir, 1972–79, and Dir and Gen. Man., 1979–82, Kent Messenger Gp; Exec. Dir, Periodical Publishers Assoc., 1983–88; Dir, Internat. Fedn of Periodical Publishers, 1989–92. Hon. Mem. and Past Chm., Parly and Legal Cttee, Guild of British Newspaper Editors. Chm., Inst. of Dirs (Kent branch), 1980–83. Member: BBC Regional Adv. Council, 1967–69; BBC Gen. Adv. Council, 1971–77; Exec. Cttee, Internat. Fedn of Periodical Publishers, 1983–89; Bd, Fedn of Periodical Publishers in EEC, 1984–92; Bd, Internat. Press Centre, London, 1984–88; Gov., Cranbrook Sch., 1978–98. *Publication:* contrib. Advertising and the Community, 1968. *Recreations:* golf, Rugby (spectator), snooker, walking. *Address:* The Belvedere, Benenden, Kent TN17 4DB.

FINN, Leo Peter; Chief Executive, Northern Rock PLC, 1997–2001; *b* 13 July 1938; *s* of Thomas Leo Finn and Jenny Finn (*née* Davison); *m* 1963, Alice Patricia Harold; two *s* two *d*. *Educ:* Carlisle Grammar Sch.; Newcastle upon Tyne Polytechnic (BA Hons). FCIB. Sec., 1982–89, Exec. Dir, 1989–91, Dep. Man. Dir, 1991–97, Northern Rock Building Soc.; Dir, Bellway plc, 1995–. Trustee, Northern Rock Foundn, 1997–. *Recreations:* walking, opera, cooking. *Address:* Ratten Row Gate, Caldbeck, Cumbria CA7 8EE. *T:* (01697) 478521.

FINNEGAN, Prof. Ruth Hilary, OBE 2000; DPhil; FBA 1996; Visiting Research Professor, Open University, since 1999 (Professor in Comparative Social Institutions, 1988–99); *b* 31 Dec. 1933; *d* of Tom Finnegan and Agnes (*née* Campbell); *m* 1963, David John Murray; three *d*. *Educ:* Mount Sch., York; Somerville Coll., Oxford (BA 1956; Dip in Anthropology 1959; BLitt 1960; Hon. Fellow, 1997); Nuffield Coll., Oxford (DPhil 1963). Teacher, Malvern Girls' Coll., 1956–58; Lectr in Social Anthropol., UC of Rhodesia and Nyasaland, 1963–64; Lectr in Sociol., 1965–67, Sen. Lectr, 1967–69, Ibadan Univ.; Open University: Lectr in Sociol., 1969–72; Sen. Lectr in Comparative Social Instns, 1972–75 and 1978–82; Reader, 1982–88; Reader in Sociol. and Head of Sociol. Discipline, Univ. of S Pacific, Suva, 1975–78. Vis. Prof., Univ. of Texas at Austin, 1989. Fellow, Folklore Soc., 1995; Associate Mem., Finnish Lit. Soc., 1989; Folklore Fellow, Finnish Acad. of Sci. and Letters, 1991. *Publications:* Survey of the Limba people of northern Sierra Leone, 1965; Limba stories and story-telling, 1967; Oral literature in Africa, 1970, 1976; Oral poetry, 1977, 2nd edn 1992; Literacy and orality, 1988; The hidden musicians, 1989; Oral traditions and the verbal arts, 1992; Tales of the City, 1998; *edited:* The Penguin Book of Oral Poetry, 1978, reissued as A World treasury of oral poetry, 1982; *edited jointly:* Modes of thought, 1973; Essays on Pacific literature, 1978; Conceptions of inquiry, 1981; New approaches to economic life, 1985; Information technology: social issues, 1987; From family tree to family history, 1994; Sources and methods for family and community historians, 1994; South Pacific oral traditions, 1995; contrib. to learned jls. *Recreations:* singing in local choirs, walking. *Address:* Faculty of Social Sciences, Open University, Milton Keynes MK7 6AA. *T:* (01908) 654458.

FINNERTY, Angela Catherine, (Mrs Mark England); Her Honour Judge Finnerty; a Circuit Judge, since 2000; *b* 22 March 1954; *d* of late Michael Peter Finnerty and of Mary Elizabeth Finnerty; *m* 1978, Mark England; one *s* one *d*. *Educ:* Bury Convent Grammar Sch.; Leeds Univ. (LLB 1st Cl. Hons); Coll. of Law, London. Called to the Bar, Middle Temple, 1976; in practice as barrister, 1976–2000; Head, Family Team, and child care specialist, Park Lane Chambers, Leeds, 1977–2000. *Recreations:* family life, travel. *Address:* Bradford Combined Court Centre, Exchange Square, Bradford BD1 1JA.

FINNEY, Albert; actor, stage and film; film director; *b* 9 May 1936; *s* of Albert Finney, turf accountant, and Alice (*née* Hobson); *m* 1957, Jane Wenham, actress (marr. diss.); one *s*; *m* 1970, Anouk Aimée (marr. diss.). Associate Artistic Dir, English Stage Co., 1972–75; a Dir, United British Artists, 1983–86. *Stage:* London appearance in The Party, New, 1958; Cassio in Othello, and Lysander, Stratford-on-Avon, 1959; subsequently in: The Lily White Boys, Royal Court, 1960; Billy Liar, Cambridge Theatre, 1960; Luther, in Luther: Royal Court Theatre and Phoenix Theatre, 1961–62; New York, 1963; Armstrong in Armstrong's Last Goodnight, Miss Julie and Black Comedy, Chichester, 1965, Old Vic, 1966; A Day in the Death of Joe Egg, NY, 1968; Alpha Beta, Royal Court and Apollo, 1972; Krapp's Last Tape, Royal Court, 1973; Cromwell, Royal Court, 1973; Chez Nous, Globe, 1974; Uncle Vanya, and Present Laughter, Royal Exchange, Manchester, 1977; Orphans, Hampstead, transf. to Apollo, 1986; J. J. Farr, Phoenix, 1987; Another Time, Wyndham's, 1989, Chicago, 1991; Reflected Glory, Vaudeville, 1992; Art, Wyndham's, 1996; *National Theatre:* Love for Love, 1965; Much Ado About Nothing, 1965; A Flea in Her Ear, 1966; Hamlet, 1975; Tamburlaine, 1976; The Country Wife, 1977; The Cherry Orchard, Macbeth, Has "Washington" Legs?, 1978; *Directed for stage:* The Freedom of the City, Royal Court, 1973; Loot, Royal Court, 1975; *Directed for stage and appeared in:* The Biko Inquest, Riverside, 1984; Serjeant Musgrave's Dance, Old Vic, 1984; *Films include:* Saturday Night and Sunday Morning; Tom Jones; Night Must Fall; Two for the Road; Scrooge; Murder on the Orient Express; Wolfen; Loophole; Looker; Shoot the Moon; Annie; The Dresser; Under the Volcano; Orphans; Millers Crossing; The Playboys; Rich in Love; The Browning Version; A Man of No Importance; The Run of the Country; Washington Square; Sympatico, 1998; Delivering Milo, 1999; Erin Brockovich, 2000; Breakfast of Champions, 2000; founded Memorial Films, 1965: co-produced with Michael Medwin: Charlie Bubbles (also actor/dir); If ...; Bleak Moments; Spring and Port Wine; Gumshoe (also actor); In Loving Memory; O Lucky Man; The Day; Alpha Beta (also actor); The Engagement; Law and Disorder; Memoirs of a Survivor; *TV films:* John Paul II; The Endless Game; The Image; A Rather English Marriage; *serials:* The Green Man, 1990; Karaoke, 1996; Nostromo, 1997; My Uncle Silas, 2001. Hon. LittD: Sussex, 1965; Salford, 1979. *Address:* c/o Michael Simkins, 45/51 Whitfield Street, W1P 6AA.

FINNEY, Prof. David John, CBE 1978; MA, ScD Cantab; FRS 1955; FRSE; consultant biometrician; Professor of Statistics, University of Edinburgh, 1966–84; Director, Agricultural and Food Research Council (formerly Agricultural Research Council) Unit of Statistics, 1954–84; *b* Latchford, Warrington, 3 Jan. 1917; *e s* of late Robert G. S. Finney and late Bessie E. Whitlow; *m* 1950, Mary Elizabeth Connolly; one *s* two *d*. *Educ:* Lymm and Manchester Grammar Schools; Clare Coll., Cambridge; Galton Laboratory, Univ. of London. Asst Statistician, Rothamsted Experimental Station, 1939–45; Lecturer in the Design and Analysis of Scientific Experiment, University of Oxford, 1945–54; Reader in Statistics, University of Aberdeen, 1954–63, Professor, 1963–66. Dir, ISI Res. Centre, Netherlands, 1987–88. Vis. Prof. of Biomathematics, Harvard Univ., 1962–63; Vis. Scientist, Internat. Rice Res. Inst., 1984–85. United Nations FAO expert attached to Indian Council of Agricultural Research, 1952–53; FAO Key Consultant, Indian Agricl Stats Res. Inst., 1984–90. Scientific Consultant, Cotton Research Corporation, 1959–75. Chm., Computer Bd for Univs and Research Councils, 1970–74 (Mem., 1966–74); Member: Adverse Reactions Sub-Cttee, Cttee on Safety of Medicines, 1963–81; BBC General Adv. Council, 1969–76. Trustee, Drug Safety Res. Trust, Bursledon Hall, Southampton, 1986–97. President of Biometric Society, 1964–65 (Vice-President, 1963, 1966); Fellow: Royal Statistical Soc. (Pres., 1973–74); American Statistical Assoc.; Mem., Internat. Statistical Inst.; Hon. Fellow Eugenics Society; Hon. Mem., Société Adolphe Quetelet. Weldon Memorial Prize, 1956; Paul Martini Prize, Deutsche Ges. für Medizinische Dokumentation und Statistik, 1971. Dr *hc*, Faculté des Sciences Agronomiques de l'Etat à Gembloux, Belgium, 1967; Hon. DSc: City, 1976; Heriot-Watt, 1981; Hon. Dr Math Waterloo (Ont), 1989. *Publications:* Probit Analysis, 1947 (3rd edn 1971); Biological Standardization (with J. H. Burn, L. G. Goodwin), 1950; Statistical Method in Biological Assay, 1952 (3rd edn 1978); An Introduction to Statistical Science in Agriculture, 1953 (4th edn 1972); Experimental Design and its Statistical Basis, 1955; Tecnica y Teoria en el diseño de Experimentos, 1957; An Introduction to the Theory of Experimental Design, 1960; Statistics for Mathematicians: An Introduction, 1968; Statistics for Biologists, 1980; about 300 papers in statistical and biological journals. *Recreations:* travel (active), music (passive), and the 3 R's. *Address:* 13 Oswald Court, South Oswald Road, Edinburgh EH9 2HY. *T:* and *Fax:* (0131) 667 0135; *e-mail:* djf@freeuk.com.

FINNEY, James; Chairman, Staff Commission for Education and Library Boards, 1981–85; Permanent Secretary, Department of Manpower Services for Northern Ireland, 1976–80, retired; *b* 21 Jan. 1920; *s* of James and Ellen Finney, Co. Armagh; *m* 1956, Barbara Ann Bennett, Wargrave, Berks; one *s* three *d*. *Educ:* Royal Belfast Academical Instn; Trinity Coll., Dublin Univ. BA 1st cl. Mods 1942. Royal Engrs, 1943–46. Min. of Educn for N Ireland, 1946–76. *Recreation:* gardening. *Address:* 2A Fort Road, Dundonald, Belfast, N Ireland BT16 1XR. *T:* (028) 9048 3428.

FINNEY, Rt Rev. John Thornley; Bishop Suffragan of Pontefract, 1993–98; *b* 1 May 1932; *s* of Arthur Frederick and Elaine Mary Finney; *m* 1959, Sheila Elizabeth Russell; three *d*. *Educ:* Charterhouse; Hertford College, Oxford (BA Jurisp.; Dip. Theol.). Ordained 1958; Curate, All Saints, Headington, 1958–61; Curate in Charge, Aylesbury, 1961–65; Rector, Tollerton, Notts, 1965–71; Vicar, St Margaret's, Aspley, Nottingham, 1971–80; Adviser in Evangelism to Bishop of Southwell, 1980–89; Officer for Decade of Evangelism, 1990–93. Manager, Research Project in Evangelism, BCC, 1989–92. Chm. Council, Lee Abbey, 1999–. *Publications:* Saints Alive!, 1983; Understanding Leadership, 1989; The Well Church Book, 1991; Church on the Move, 1992; Finding Faith Today, 1992; Stories of Faith, 1995; Recovering the Past: Celtic and Roman mission, 1996; Fading Splendour?, 2000. *Recreations:* golf, growing old gracefully. *Address:* Greenacre, Crow Lane, South Muskham, Newark, Notts NG23 6DZ. *T:* and *Fax:* (01636) 679791.

FINNEY, Sir Thomas, Kt 1998; CBE 1992 (OBE 1961); *b* Preston, 5 April 1922; *s* of late Alf and Margaret Finney; *m* 1945, Elsie Noblett; one *s* one *d*. *Educ:* Deepdale County Primary Sch.; Deepdale Modern Sch. Joined plumbing firm of Pilkington's as apprentice, 1936. Professional footballer with Preston North End, 1940–42, 1946–60, for whom he played 433 league games and scored 187 goals; 76 appearances for England, 1946–58; Pres., Preston North End FC, 1975–76. Chm., Preston HA, 1985–88. Freeman, Borough of Preston, 1979. Hon. Fellow, Lancashire Poly., 1988. Hon. LLD Lancaster Univ., 1988. Footballer of the Year, Football Writers' Assoc., 1954, 1957.

FINNIE, (James) Ross, CA; Member (Lib Dem) West of Scotland, Scottish Parliament, since 1999; Minister for Environment and Rural Development (formerly for Rural Affairs), since 1999; *b* 11 Feb. 1947; *s* of late James Ross Finnie and Elizabeth Main Finnie; *m* 1971, Phyllis Sinclair; one *s* one *d*. *Educ:* Greenock Acad. Director: James Finlay Bank Ltd, 1975–86; Singer & Friedlander Ltd, 1986–91; Partner, Ross Finnie & Co., Chartered Accountants, 1991–99. Mem., Exec. Cttee, Scottish Council (Develt and Industry), 1976–87. Member (L then Lib Dem): Inverclyde DC, 1977–96; Inverclyde Council, 1995–99. Chm., Scottish Lib Party, 1982–86. Contested: (L) Renfrewshire W, 1979; (L/All) Stirling, 1983. *Address:* Scottish Parliament, Edinburgh EH99 1SP; (home) 91 Octavia Terrace, Greenock PA16 1PY. *T:* (01475) 631495, *Fax:* (01475) 636755.

FINNIS, Prof. John Mitchell, DPhil; FBA 1990; Professor of Law and Legal Philosophy, Oxford University, since 1989; Fellow and Praelector in Jurisprudence, since 1966, Stowell Civil Law Fellow, since 1973, University College, Oxford; *b* 28 July 1940; *s* of Maurice and Margaret Finnis; *m* 1964, Marie Carmel McNally; three *s* three *d* (and one *d* decd). *Educ:* St Peter's Coll., Adelaide, SA; St Mark's Coll., Univ. of Adelaide (LLB 1961); University Coll., Oxford (Rhodes Scholar for SA, 1962; DPhil 1965). Called to the Bar, Gray's Inn, 1970. Associate in Law, Univ. of Calif at Berkeley, 1965–66; Rhodes Reader in Laws of British Commonwealth and United States, Oxford Univ., 1972–89; Prof. and Head of Dept of Law, Univ. of Malaŵi, 1976–78; Biolchini Prof. of Law, Univ. of Notre Dame, USA, 1995–. Huber Distinguished Vis. Prof., Boston Coll. Law Sch., 1993–94. Special Adviser to Foreign Affairs Cttee, House of Commons, on role of UK Parlt in Canadian Constitution, 1980–82; Consultor, Pontifical Commn, Iustitia et Pax, 1977–89; Member: Pontifical Council de Iustitia et Pace, 1990–95; Catholic Bishops' Jt Cttee on Bio-Ethical Issues, 1981–88; Internat. Theol Commn, The Vatican, 1986–92. Governor, Linacre Centre, London, 1981–96, 1998– (Vice-Chm., 1987–96). *Publications:* Commonwealth and Dependencies, in Halsbury's Laws of England, 4th edn, Vol. 6, 1974, revised 1991; Natural Law and Natural Rights, 1980; Fundamentals of Ethics, 1983; (with Joseph Boyle and Germain Grisez) Nuclear Deterrence, Morality and Realism, 1987; Moral Absolutes, 1991; Aquinas: moral, political, and legal theory, 1998. *Address:* University College, Oxford OX1 4BH. *T:* (01865) 276602.

FINNISSY, Michael Peter; composer; Professor of Composition, University of Southampton, since 1999; *b* 17 March 1946; *s* of George Norman Finnissy and Rita Isolene Finnissy (*née* Parsonson). *Educ:* Hawes Down Jun. Sch.; Bromley Tech. High Sch.; Beckenham and Penge Grammar Sch.; Royal Coll. of Music. Lectr, Music Dept, London Sch. of Contemporary Dance, 1969–74; Artist-in-Residence, Victorian Coll. of the Arts, Melbourne, Australia, 1982–83; Lectr, Dartington Summer Sch., 1981, 1990, 1992–; Consultant Tutor in Composition, Winchester Coll., 1988–; Res. Fellow in Music, Univ. of Sussex, 1989–99; Mem., Composition Faculty, Royal Acad. of Music, 1990–; KBC Prof. of New Music, Katholieke Univ., Leuven, 1999–2001. Pres., ISCM, 1990–96 (Hon. Mem., 1998–). *Compositions include:* Eighteen Songs, 1963–76; World (vocal/orchestral), 1968–74; Tsuru-Kame (stage work), 1971–73; Mysteries (stage work), 1972–79; Verdi Transcriptions (piano), 1972–88; Cipriano (choral), 1974; Seven Piano Concertos, 1975–81; Pathways of Sun & Stars (orchestral), 1976; English Country-Tunes (piano), 1977; Alongside (orchestral), 1979; Sea and Sky (orchestral), 1979–80; Kelir (choral), 1981; The Undivine Comedy (stage work), 1985–88; Thérèse Raquin (stage work), 1992; Folklore (piano), 1993–94; Liturgy of S Paul (vocal), 1993–95; Shameful Vice (stage work), 1994; Speak its Name! (orchestral), 1996; The History of Photography in Sound (piano), 1993–2000. *Address:* c/o Oxford University Press, Walton Street, Oxford OX2 6DP. *T:* Oxford (01865) 556767.

FIORINA, Carleton S., (Carly); President and Chief Executive Officer, Hewlett-Packard Co., since 1999; *b* Austin, Texas, 6 Sept. 1954; *Educ:* Stanford Univ. (BA 1976); Univ. of Maryland (MBA 1980); Sloan Sch. of Mgt, MIT (MSc 1989); UCLA. Joined AT&T, 1980: posts included account exec., Sen. Vice-Pres. of Global Mktg, and Pres., Atlantic and Canadian Region; Lucent Technologies (formerly subsid. of AT&T), 1996–99: Vice-Pres. of Corp. Ops; Pres., Global Service Provider Business. Formerly Director: Kellogg Co.; Merck & Co. Inc.; non-exec. Dir, Cisco Systems Inc., 2001–. Mem., US China Bd of Trade. *Address:* Hewlett-Packard Co., 3000 Hanover Street, Palo Alto, CA 94304, USA.

FIRMSTON-WILLIAMS, Peter, CBE 1987 (OBE 1979); Chairman, Flowers and Plants Association, 1984–89; *b* 30 Aug. 1918; *s* of late Geoffrey and Muriel Firmston-Williams; *m* Margaret Beaulah; one *s* one *d*. *Educ:* Harrow. Served War, Infantry, Green Howards Regt, 1939–45 (Captain). J. Lyons & Co. Ltd, 1945–53; Marketing Director, United Canners Ltd, 1953–55; Associated British Foods Ltd, Director, Store Operations, Fine Fare, 1958–61; Fitch Lovell Ltd, Man. Dir, Key Markets Ltd, 1962–71; Associated Dairies Group Ltd, Man. Dir, ASDA Stores, and Dir, Associated Dairies, 1971–81, retired; Director: Woolworth Hdgs (formerly Paternoster Stores), 1981–85 (non-exec. Dir, 1985–86; Dep. Chm., 1982–85); Bredero Properties Ltd, 1986–; Chm., Bayfleet Hldgs Ltd, 1988–. Chairman: Covent Garden Market Authority, 1982–88; Retail Consortium, 1984–86. *Recreations:* golf, water skiing, gardening. *Address:* Oak House, 12 Pembroke Road, Moor Park, Northwood, Mddx HA6 2HR. *T:* (01923) 823052.

FIRNBERG, David; Principal, DFA Ltd, since 1989; *b* 1 May 1930; *s* of L. B. Firnberg and K. L. E. Firnberg; *m* 1957, Sylvia Elizabeth du Cros; one *s* three *d*. *Educ:* Merchant Taylors' Sch., Northwood. Went West, 1953–56; Television Audience Measurement Ltd, 1956–59; ICT/ICL, 1959–72; David Firnberg Associates Ltd, 1972–74; Dir, Nat. Computing Centre Ltd, 1974–79; Eosys Ltd: Man. Dir, 1980–88; Chm., 1989–91; Chm., The Networking Centre Ltd, 1985–91; Chief Exec., Strategic Planning Soc., 1995–97. President: UK Assoc. of Project Managers, 1978–84 (Hon. Fellow 1984); British Computer Soc., 1983–84 (Chm., IT Support for Disabled People project, 1989–91); Chairman: UK Council for Computing Develt, 1990–91; Steering Cttee, RSA Design Bursaries for Communications and Computing, 1989–94; Member: Foundn for Sci. and Technology, 1987–; Council, PITCOM, 1989–; Quality Audit Steering Council, Higher Educn Quality Council, 1992–97. Freeman, City of London, 1987. FBCS 1973; FInstD 1982; FRSA 1978. *Publications:* Computers Management and Information, 1973; Cassell's New Spelling Dictionary, 1976; Cassell's Spelling Dictionary, 1984; historical vignettes. *Address:* Mastings, Main Street, Preston Bissett, Buckingham MK18 4JR. *T:* (01280) 848772; *e-mail:* david.firnberg@btinternet.com. *Club:* Wig and Pen.

FIRTH, Andrew Trevor; Regional Chairman, Industrial Tribunals, Yorkshire/ Humberside, 1982–88 (Chairman, Industrial Tribunals, 1972–82); *b* 4 June 1922; *s* of Seth Firth and Amy Firth; *m* 1946, Nora Cornforth Armitage; one *s* two *d*. *Educ:* Prince Henry's Grammar Sch.; Leeds Univ. (LLB). Served RA, 6th Airborne Div., Normandy, 1944, Lieut; Intelligence Officer, Potsdam Conf., 1945, Captain; Rhine Army Coll., 1946, Major. Partner, later Sen. Partner, Barret Chamberlain & McDonnell, Solicitors, Harrogate, Otley, Leeds, 1948–72. Pres., Harrogate and Dist Law Soc., 1965–66; Area Chm., Law Soc. Legal Aid Cttee, Yorkshire, 1969–72. Bronze Star Medal, USA, 1945. *Recreations:* Chippendale Soc. (Chm., 1972–87; Pres., 1999–), golf, grandchildren. *Address:* Chevin Close, Birdcage Walk, Otley, West Yorkshire LS21 3HB. *Club:* Otley Golf.

FIRTH, Colin; actor; *b* 10 Sept. 1960; *s* of David and Shirley Firth; one *s* by Meg Tilly; *m* 1997, Livia Guiggioli. *Educ:* Montgomery of Alamein Sch., Winchester; London Drama Centre. *Stage* includes: Another Country, Queen's, 1983; The Lonely Road, Old Vic, 1985; The Elms, Greenwich, 1987; The Caretaker, Almeida, 1991; Chatsky, Almeida, 1993; Three Days of Rain, Donmar Warehouse, 1999; *films* include: Another Country, 1983; A Month in the Country, 1986; Valmont, 1988; Wings of Fame, 1989; The Hour of the Pig, 1992; Circle of Friends, 1995; The English Patient, 1996; Fever Pitch, 1997; Shakespeare in Love, 1999; The Secret Laughter of Women, 1999; My Life So Far, 2000; Relative Values, 2000; Bridget Jones's Diary, 2001; *television* includes: Dutch Girls, 1984; Tumbledown, 1987; Out of the Blue, 1990; The Deep Blue Sea, 1994; Pride and Prejudice, 1995; Nostromo, 1996; The Turn of the Screw, 1999; Donovan Quick, 2000. *Address:* c/o ICM Ltd, Oxford House, 76 Oxford Street, W1N 0AX. *T:* (020) 7636 6565.

FIRTH, (David) Colin; Headmaster, Cheadle Hulme School, 1977–89, retired; *b* 29 Jan. 1930; *s* of Jack and Muriel Firth; *m* 1954, Edith Scanlan; three *s* one *d*. *Educ:* Rothwell Grammar Sch.; Sheffield Univ. (BSc, DipEd). Royal Signals, 1952–54; Stand Grammar Sch., 1954–57; East Barnet Grammar Sch., 1957–61; Bristol Grammar Sch., 1961–73; The Gilberd Sch., 1973–77. Treasurer, Penrith Music Club, 1995–. *Publications:* A Practical Organic Chemistry, 1966; Elementary Thermodynamics, 1969; (jtly) Introductory Physical Science, 1971. *Recreations:* golf, fell walking, talking about gardening, singing. *Address:* Hill House, Fell Lane, Penrith, Cumbria CA11 8BJ.

FIRTH, Mrs Joan Margaret, CB 1995; PhD; Chair, Bradford Health Authority, 1998–2000 (Vice Chair, 1996–98); Deputy Director of NHS Finance, Department of Health, 1990–95; *b* 25 March 1935; *d* of Ernest Wilson and Ann (*née* Crowther); *m* 1955, Kenneth Firth. *Educ:* Lawnswood High Sch., Leeds; Univ. of Leeds (1st Cl. BSc Colour Chemistry; PhD Dyeing of Wool). Research Asst, Leeds Univ., 1958–60; Head of Science, Selby High Sch., 1960–62; Sen. Lecturer in General Science, Elizabeth Gaskell Coll., Manchester, 1962–66; Lectr in Organic Chemistry, Salford Univ., 1966–67; joined Civil Service as Direct Entry Principal, 1967; Asst Sec., 1974; Under-Sec., DHSS, 1981; Under-Sec., Social Security Div. C, DHSS, later DSS, 1987–90. Member: ESRC, 1988–92; Training Bd, 1990–92. Mem., Audit Cttee, Inst. Cancer Res., 1994–98. *Publications:* contrib. Jl Textile Inst., 1958. *Recreations:* wine, walking.

FIRTH, Paul James; a District Judge (Magistrates' Courts), Lancashire, since 2001; *b* 2 June 1951; *s* of Albert and Violet Firth; *m* 1979, Ann Barbara Whitehead; one *s*. *Educ:* Bradford Grammar Sch.; Queen's Coll., Oxford (Hastings Exhibnr; MA 1973). Admitted solicitor, 1980; Trainee Court Clerk, Keighley Magistrates' Court, 1973–74; Trainee Court Clerk, Court Clerk, then Sen. Court Clerk, Leeds Magistrates' Court, 1975–81; Dep. Clerk to Justices (Legal), Manchester City Magistrates' Court, 1981–86; Clerk to Justices, Rotherham Magistrates' Court, 1986–95; Actg Stipendiary Magistrate, 1991–95; Stipendiary Magistrate, subseq. Dist Judge (Magistrates' Cts), Merseyside, 1995–2001. *Recreations:* beginners' golf, various sports (reduced to watching, especially Bradford City), reading anything except law books. *Address:* Preston Magistrates' Courts, Lawson Street, Preston PR1 2RD. *T:* (01772) 208000. *Club:* Yorkshire CC.

FIRTH, Rt Rev. Peter James; Bishop Suffragan of Malmesbury, 1983–94; *b* 12 July 1929; *s* of Atkinson Vernon Firth and Edith Pepper; *m* 1955, Felicity Mary Wilding; two *s* two *d* (and one long-term foster *d*). *Educ:* Stockport Grammar School; Emmanuel Coll., Cambridge (Open Exhibnr, MA, DipEd); St Stephen's House Theol Coll., Oxford. Ordained, 1955; Assistant Curate, St Stephen's, Barbourne in Worcester, 1955–58; Priest-in-charge, Church of the Ascension, Parish of St Matthias, Malvern Link, Worcs, 1958–62; Rector of St George's, Abbey Hey, Gorton in Manchester, 1962–66; Religious Broadcasting Assistant, North Region, BBC, 1966–67; Religious Broadcasting Organiser and Senior Producer, Religious Programmes, BBC South and West, Bristol, 1967–83. Religious Advr to HTV West, 1983–. Pres., Religious Drama Soc. of GB, 1994–. Trustee, Bristol Cancer Health Centre, 1995–. Governor: Millfield Sch., 1994–. Clifton Coll., 1995–; Internat. Radio Festival winner, Seville, 1975. *Publications:* Lord of the Seasons, 1978; The Love that moves the Sun, 1996. *Recreations:* theatre, photography, music, travel, Manchester United. *Address:* 7 Ivywell Road, Bristol BS9 1NX. *T:* (0117) 968 5931.

FIRTH, Prof. Sir Raymond (William), Kt 1973; CNZM 2001; MA; PhD; FBA 1949; Professor of Anthropology, University of London, 1944–68, now Emeritus; *b* 25 March 1901; *s* of late Wesley Hugh Bourne Firth and Marie Elizabeth Jane Cartmill; *m* 1936, Rosemary (*d* 2001), *d* of late Sir Gilbert Upcott, KCB; one *s*. *Educ:* Auckland Grammar Sch.; Auckland University College; London School of Economics (Hon. Fellow, 1970). Anthropological research in British Solomon Islands, including one year on Tikopia, 1928–29; Lecturer in Anthropology, University of Sydney, 1930–31; Acting Professor of Anthropology, University of Sydney, 1931–32; Lecturer in Anthropology, London School of Economics, 1932–35; Reader, 1935–44; Hon. Secretary Royal Anthropological Institute, 1936–39 (President 1953–55); Research in peasant economics and anthropology in Malaya, as Leverhulme Research Fellow, 1939–40; served with Naval Intelligence Division, Admiralty, 1941–44; Secretary of Colonial Social Science Research Council, Colonial Office, 1944–45; Academic Advr, ANU, 1948–52; Fellow, Center for Advanced Study in the Behavioral Sciences, Stanford, 1958–59; Prof. of Pacific Anthropology, Univ. of Hawaii, 1968–69. Visiting Professor: British Columbia, 1969; Cornell, 1970; Chicago, 1971; Graduate Center, City Univ. of New York, 1971; Univ. of California, Davis 1974, Berkeley 1977; Auckland, 1978. Life Pres., Assoc. of Social Anthropologists, 1975. Foreign Hon. Member American Academy of Arts and Sciences, 1963; Hon. Member Royal Society, NZ, 1964; Foreign Member: American Philosophical Society, 1965; Royal Soc., NSW; Royal Danish Academy of Sciences and Letters, 1966; Internat. Union of Anthropol and Ethnol Sciences, 1983; European Assoc. of Social Anthropologists, 1990. Social research surveys: W Africa, 1945; Malaya, 1947; New Guinea, 1951; Tikopia, 1952, 1966; Malaya, 1963. Hon. degrees: DPh Oslo, 1965; LLD Michigan, 1967; LittD East Anglia, 1968; Dr Letters ANU, 1969; DHumLett Chicago, 1968; DSc British Columbia, 1970; DLitt Exeter, 1972; DLit Auckland, 1978; PhD Cracow, 1984; DSc Econ London, 1984. *Publications:* The Kauri Gum Industry, 1924; Primitive Economics of the New Zealand Maori, 1929 (new edn, 1959); Art and Life In New Guinea, 1936; We, The Tikopia: A Sociological Study of Kinship in Primitive Polynesia, 1936; Human Types, 1938 (new edn, 1975); Primitive Polynesian Economy, 1939 (new edn, 1964); The Work of the Gods in Tikopia, 1940 (new edn, 1967); Malay Fishermen: Their Peasant Economy, 1946 (enlarged edn, 1966); Elements of Social Organization, 1951 (new edn 1971); Two Studies of Kinship in London (ed), 1956; Man and Culture: An Evaluation of the Work of Malinowski (ed), 1957; Social Change in Tikopia, 1959; History and Traditions of Tikopia, 1961; Essays on Social Organization and Values, 1964; (with B. S. Yamey) Capital Saving and Credit in Peasant Societies, 1964; Tikopia Ritual and Belief, 1967; Rank and Religion in Tikopia, 1970; (with J. Hubert and A. Forge) Families and Their Relatives, 1970; Symbols Public and Private, 1973; Tikopia-English Dictionary, 1985; Tikopia Songs, 1990; Religion: a humanist interpretation, 1996. *Recreations:* Romanesque art, early music. *Address:* 33 Southwood Avenue, N6 5SA. *Club:* Athenæum.

FIRTH, Tazeena Mary; designer; *b* 1 Nov. 1935; *d* of Denis Gordon Firth and Irene (*née* Morris). *Educ:* St Mary's, Wantage; Chatelard Sch. Theatre Royal, Windsor, 1954–57; English Stage Co., Royal Court, 1957–60; partnership in stage design with Timothy O'Brien estabd 1961; output incl.: The Bartered Bride, The Girl of the Golden West, 1962; West End prodns of new plays, 1963–64; London scene of Shakespeare Exhibn, 1964; Tango, Days in the Trees, Staircase, RSC, and Trafalgar at Madame Tussaud's, 1966; All's Well that Ends Well, As You Like It, Romeo and Juliet, RSC, 1967; The Merry Wives of Windsor, Troilus and Cressida (also Nat. Theatre, 1976), The Latent Heterosexual, RSC, 1968; Pericles (also Comédie Française, 1974), Women Beware Women, Bartholomew Fair, RSC, 1969; Measure for Measure, RSC, Madame Tussaud's in Amsterdam, and The Knot Garden, Royal Opera, 1970; Enemies, Man of Mode, RSC, 1971; La Cenerentola, Oslo, Lower Depths, and The Island of the Mighty, RSC, As You Like It, OCSC, 1972; Richard II, Love's Labour's Lost, RSC, 1973; Next of Kin, NT, Summerfolk, RSC, and The Bassarids, ENO, 1974; John Gabriel Borkman, NT, Peter Grimes, Royal Opera (later in Paris), The Marrying of Ann Leete, RSC, 1975; Wozzeck, Adelaide Fest., The Zykovs, RSC, and The Force of Habit, NT, 1976; Tales from the Vienna Woods, Bedroom Farce, NT, and Falstaff, Berlin Opera, 1977; The Cunning Little Vixen, Göteborg, Evita, London (later in USA, Australia, Vienna), A Midsummer Night's Dream, Sydney Opera House, 1978; Peter Grimes, Göteborg, The Rake's Progress, Royal Opera, 1979; Turandot, Vienna State Opera, 1983. Designed independently: The Two Gentlemen of Verona, RSC, 1969; Occupations, RSC, 1971; The Rape of Lucretia, Karlstad, 1982; Katherina Ismailova, Göteborg, 1984; La Traviata, Umeå, The Trojan Woman, Göteborg, and Bluebeard's Castle, Copenhagen, 1985; Il Seraglio, Göteborg, 1986; The Magic Flute, Rigoletto, Umeå, 1987; Romeo and Juliet, Malmö, 1988; The Rake's Progress, Göteborg, and, Dido and Aeneas, Copenhagen, 1989; From the House of the Dead, Göteborg, and, Barbarians, RSC, 1990; Macbeth, Göteborg, 1990; Lady Macbeth of Mtsensk, Copenhagen, La Bohème, Malmö, and Il Seraglio, Stockholm, 1991; Don Giovanni, Prague, 1991; Rigoletto, Oslo, and Carmen, Copenhagen, 1992; Carmen, Stockholm, Drot og Mask, Copenhagen, Magic Flute, Prague and Peter Grimes, Copenhagen, 1993; Vox Humana, Göteborg, 1994; Don Giovanni, Japan, Dido and Aeneas, and Oh Come Ye Sons of Art, Dröttningholm, Bluebeard's Castle, and Jenůfa, Göteborg, 1995; Peter Grimes, Göteborg and Finnish Nat. Opera, and Jenůfa, Copenhagen, 1998. (Jtly) Gold Medal for Set Design, Prague Quadriennale, 1975. *Recreations:* sailing, walking.

FISCHEL, David Andrew; Chief Executive, Liberty International (formerly TransAtlantic Holdings) plc, since 2001; *b* 1 April 1958. ACA 1983. Touche Ross & Co., 1980–85; with TransAtlantic Holdings, later Liberty International, 1985–: Man. Dir, 1992–2001. *Address:* c/o Liberty International plc, 40 Broadway, SW1H 0BT. *T:* (020) 7960 1200.

FISCHEL, Robert Gustav; QC 1998; *b* 12 Jan. 1953; *s* of Bruno Rolf Fischel and Sophie Fischel (*née* Kruml); *m* 1st, 1989, Louise Kim Halsall (marr. diss. 1997); 2nd, 1999, Anna Louise, *d* of Patrick Landucci. *Educ:* City of London Sch.; Univ. of London (LLB). Called to the Bar, Middle Temple, 1975; in practice at the Bar, 1975–. *Recreations:* cooking, horse riding, ski-ing, travel. *Address:* 5 King's Bench Walk, Temple, EC4Y 7DN. *Clubs:* Royal Over-Seas League, Wig and Pen.

FISCHER, August Antonios; Chairman and Chief Executive Officer, Axel Springer Verlag AG, Germany, since 1998; Director, Ringier America Inc., USA, since 1995; *b* 7

Feb. 1939; *s* of August Fischer and Elisabeth Fischer (*née* Zanola); *m* 1961, Gillian Ann Streete; one *s* one *d*. *Educ:* Univ. of Zurich, Switzerland (BA Business Admin). E. I. Du Pont de Nemours & Co., 1962–78; Napp Systems (Europe) Ltd, 1978–81; Napp Systems Inc., 1981–88; News International plc, 1989–95 (Chief Exec., 1994–95); Dir, Ringier AG, Switzerland, 1995–97. *Address:* 58 Egerton Crescent, SW3 2ED.

FISCHER, Dr Edmond Henri; Professor Emeritus, University of Washington, since 1990; *b* Shanghai, China, 6 April 1920; *s* of Oscar Fischer and Renee Tapernoux; *m* 1963, Beverley Bullock; two *s*. *Educ:* Univ. of Geneva (Licencié ès Sciences 1943; Diplôme d'Ingenieur 1944; DSc 1947). Asst, Labs of Organic Chem., Univ. of Geneva, 1946–47; Fellow, Swiss Nat. Foundn, 1948–50; Res. Fellow, Rockefeller Foundn, 1950–53; Res. Associate, Div. of Biol., CIT, 1953; University of Washington: Asst Prof. of Biochem., 1953–56; Associate Prof., 1956–61; Prof., 1961–90. Associate, Neurosciences Res. Prog., Neuroscience Res. Inst., La Jolla, Calif, 1995–. Member: Biochem. Section, NIH, 1959–64; Editl Adv. Bd, Biochemistry, Jl of ACS, 1961–66 (Associate Editor, 1966–92); Adv. Bd, ACS, 1962; Sci. Adv. Bd, Friedrich Miescher Inst. CIBA-GEIGY, 1976–84 (Chm., 1981–84); Council, Amer. Soc. Biol Chemists, 1980–83; Scientific Council on Basic Sci., Amer. Heart Assoc., 1977–80; Bd of Scientific Govs, Scripps Res. Inst., 1987–; Scientific Adv. Cttee, Muscular Dystrophy Assoc., 1980–89; Scientific Adv. Bd, Basel Inst. for Immunology, 1996–; Bd Govs, Weizmann Inst. of Sci., Israel, 1997–; Chm., Task Force, Muscular Dystrophy Assoc. Res. Centres, 1985–89. Member: Amer. Soc. Biol Chemists; ACS; Amer. Acad. of Arts and Scis, 1972; AAAS 1972; NAS 1973; Amer. Assoc. of Univ. Profs. Pres., Pole Universitaire de Montpellier, 1993–96. Hon. PhD: Montpellier 1985; Basel 1988; Med. Coll. of Ohio, 1993; Indiana, 1993; Ruhr-Univ., 1994. Numerous awards, medals and prizes; Nobel Prize in Physiology or Medicine, 1992. *Publications:* numerous. *Recreations:* playing classical piano, private pilot. *Address:* Department of Biochemistry, Box 357350, University of Washington, Seattle, WA 98195–7350, USA. *T:* (206) 5431741.

FISCHER, Prof. Ernst Otto; Professor of Inorganic Chemistry, Munich Technical University; *b* Munich, 10 Nov. 1918; *s* of Prof. Karl T. Fischer and Valentine (*née* Danzer); unmarried. *Educ:* Tech. Univ., Munich. Dip. Chem., 1949; Dr rer. nat., 1952, Habilitation 1954. Associate Prof. of Inorganic Chem., Univ. of Munich, 1957, Prof. 1959, Prof. and Dir, Inorganic Chem. Inst., Tech. Univ., Munich, 1964. Member: Bavarian Acad. of Sciences; Akad. deutscher Naturforscher Leopoldina, 1969; Austrian Acad. of Scis, 1976; Accad. dei Lincei, Italy, 1976; Göttingen Akad. der Wissenschaften, 1977; Rheinisch-Westfälische Akad. der Wissenschaften, 1987; Soc. of German Chemists, etc; Centennial For. Fellow, Amer. Chem. Soc., 1976. Hon. Dr rer. nat.: Munich, 1972; Erlangen, 1977; Veszprem, 1983; Hon. DSc Strathclyde, 1975. Has received many prizes and awards including the Nobel Prize for Chemistry, 1973 (jointly with Prof. Geoffrey Wilkinson) for their pioneering work, performed independently, on the chem. of organometallic "sandwich compounds". *Publications:* (with H. Werner) Metall-pi-Komplexe mit di- und oligoolefinischen Liganden, 1963 (trans. as Metal pi-Complexes Vol. 1, Complexes with di- and oligo-olefinic Ligands, 1966–); numerous contribs to learned jls on organometallic chem., etc. *Recreations:* art, history, travel. *Address:* 16 Sohnckestrasse, 81479 München, Germany.

FISCHER, Iván; conductor; Music Director: Kent Opera, since 1984; Lyons Opera House, since 1999; *b* Budapest, 20 Jan. 1951; *s* of Sándor Fischer and Éva Boschán; two *d*. *Educ:* Béla Bartók Music Conservatory, Budapest; Wiener Hochschule für Musik; Mozarteum, Salzburg. Music Dir, Northern Sinfonia, Newcastle, 1979–82; Principal Guest Conductor, Cincinnati SO, 1989–96; Founder and Music Dir, Budapest Fest. Orch., 1983. Début in London with RPO, 1976; concert tours with LSO, to Spain, 1981, USA, 1982, world tour, 1983; concerts with orchestras, including: Berlin Philharmonic, Concertgebouw; Munich Philharmonic; Israel Philharmonic; Orch. de Paris; Orch. of Age of Enlightenment; LA and NY Philharmonics; Cleveland; Philadelphia; San Francisco Symphony; Chicago Symphony; opera prodns in London, Paris, Vienna. Has made recordings. Patron, British Kódaly Acad.; Founder, Hungarian Mahler Soc. Premio Firenze, 1974; Rupert Foundn Award, BBC, 1976; Gramophone Award for Best Orchestral Recording of Year, 1998; Crystal Award, World Econ. Forum, 1998. Golden Medal Award (Hungary), 1998. *Address:* Andrássy ut 27, 1061 Budapest, Hungary.

FISCHER, Joschka; Minister of Foreign Affairs and Deputy Chancellor, Germany, since 1998; Leader, Green Party; *b* 12 April 1948; *m*. State of Hesse: Minister for the Envmt and Energy, 1985–87; Mem., Landtag, 1987–91 (Chm., Green Party); Minister for the Envmt, Energy and Fed. Affairs, and Dep. to Minister-Pres., 1991–94; Mem., Bundestag, 1983–85, 1994–; Dep. Mem., Bundesrat, 1985–87; Parly spokesman, Alliance' 90/Green Party, Bundestag, 1994–98. *Address:* Ministry of Foreign Affairs, Werderscher Markt 1, 10117 Berlin, Germany; Bundeshaus, Platz der Republik, 11011 Berlin, Germany.

FISCHER, Hon. Timothy Andrew; MP (Nat.) Farrer, New South Wales, since 1984; Deputy Prime Minister of Australia, and Minister for Trade, 1996–99; Leader, National Party of Australia, 1990–99; *b* 3 May 1946; *s* of J. R. Fischer; *m* 1992, Judy, *d* of Harry Brewer; two *s*. *Educ:* Xavier Coll., Melbourne. Platoon Comdr and Transport Officer, RAR, 1967; Nat. Service, S Vietnam, 1968–69. Primary producer, Boree Creek, 1964–65, 1970. MLA Sturt, 1971–80, Murray, 1980–84, NSW; Nat. Party Whip, NSW, 1981–84; Shadow Minister: for Veterans' Affairs, 1985–90; for Energy and Resources, 1990–93; for Trade, 1993–96; Chm., Internat. Relns Mgt Gp, 1993–94. *Recreations:* chess, tennis, trekking, bushwalking in Bhutan. *Address:* Parliament House, Canberra, ACT 2600, Australia; PO Box 10, Boree Creek, NSW 2652, Australia.

FISCHER-DIESKAU, Dietrich; baritone; *b* Berlin, 28 May 1925; *s* of Dr Albert Fischer-Dieskau; *m* 1949, Irmgard Poppen (*d* 1963); three *s*. *Educ:* High Sch., Berlin; Music Academy, Berlin. First Baritone, Städtische Oper, Berlin, 1948–78, Hon. Mem., 1978–; Mem., Vienna State Opera, 1957–63. Extensive Concert Tours of Europe and USA; soloist in Festivals at Edinburgh, Salzburg, Bayreuth, Vienna, Berlin, Munich, Holland, Luzern, Prades, etc. Opera roles include: Wolfram, Jochanaan, Almaviva, Marquis Posa, Don Giovanni, Falstaff, Mandryka, Wozzeck, Danton, Macbeth, Hans Sachs. Many recordings. Prof., Music Acad., Berlin, 1983; Member: Acad. of Arts, Berlin; Acad. of Fine Arts, Munich; Hon. RAM, 1972; Honorary Member: Wiener Konzerthausgesellschaft, 1962; Königlich-Schwedische Akad., 1972; Acad. Santa Cecilia, Rome; Royal Philharmonic Soc., 1985. Hon. DMus Oxford, 1978; Dr *hc*: Sorbonne, 1980; Yale, 1980. Kunstpreis der Stadt Berlin, 1950; Internationaler Schallplattenpreis, since 1955 nearly every year; Orfeo d'oro, 1955 and 1966; Bayerischer Kammersänger, 1959; Edison Prize, 1961, 1964, 1966, 1970; Naras Award, USA, 1962; Mozart-Medaille, Wien, 1962; Berliner Kammersänger, 1963; Electrola Award, 1970; Léonie Sonning Music Prize, Copenhagen, 1975; Golden Gramophone Award, Germany, 1975; Ruckert-Preis, Schweinfurth, 1979; President's Prize, Charles Gros Acad., Paris, 1980; Ernst Von Siemen Prize, 1980; Artist of the Year, Phonoakademie, Germany, 1980; Gold Medal, Royal Philharmonic Soc., 1988. Bundesverdienstkreuz (1st class), 1958, Grosses Verdienstkreuz, 1974, Stern zum Grossen Bundesverdienstkreuz, 1986; Pour le mérite, Deutschland (FRG), 1984; Chevalier de la Légion d'Honneur (France), 1990. *Publications:* Texte Deutscher Lieder, 1968 (The Fischer-Dieskau Book of Lieder, 1976); Auf den Spuren der Schubert-Lieder, 1971; Wagner und Nietzsche, 1974; Robert Schumann—Wort und Musik, 1981; Töne sprechen, Worte klingen, 1985; Nachklang, 1987; Wenn Musik der Liebe Nahrung ist: Künstlerschicksale im 19 Jahrhundert, 1990; Weil nicht alle Blütenträume reifen (Reichardt), 1991; Johann Friedrich Reichardt: Kapellmeister dreier Preussenkönige, 1992; Fern die Klage des Fauns (Debussy), 1993; Carl Friedrich Zelter (biog.), 1997.

FISCHLER, Dr Franz; Member, European Commission, since 1995; *b* 23 Sept. 1946; *s* of Josef Fischler and Theodora Fischler; *m* 1973, Adelheid Hausmann; two *s* two *d*. *Educ:* Univ. for Soil Sci., Vienna (Dr in Natural Scis 1978). Univ. Asst, Dept of Regl Agricl Planning., Inst. for Farm Mgt, Vienna, 1973–79; Tyrol Chamber of Agriculture: Mem., 1979–84; Dir, 1985–89; elected Mem., Nationalrat, 1990, 1994; Fed. Minister of Agric. and Forestry, 1989–94. Grosse Goldene Ehrenzeichen am Bande (Austria), 1993. *Address:* European Commission, Rue de la Loi 200, 1049 Brussels, Belgium. *T:* (2) 2959625.

FISH, David Thomas; QC 1997; a Recorder, since 1994; *b* 23 July 1949; *s* of Tom Fish and Gladys (*née* Durkin); *m* 1989, Angelina Brunhilde Dennett; one *s* one *d*. *Educ:* Ashton-under-Lyne Grammar Sch.; London Sch. of Econs (LLB). Called to the Bar, Inner Temple, 1973. *Recreations:* horse-racing, golf. *Address:* Deans Court Chambers, 24 St John Street, Manchester M3 4DF. *T:* (0161) 214 6000.

FISH, Prof. Francis, OBE 1989; BPharm, PhD; FRPharmS; Dean, School of Pharmacy, 1978–88 (Hon. Fellow, 1992), Professor of Pharmacy, 1988, Professor Emeritus, 1989, University of London; *b* 20 April 1924; *s* of William Fish and Phyllis (*née* Griffiths); *m* 1949, Hilda Mary Brown; two *s*. *Educ:* Houghton-le-Spring Grammar Sch.; Technical Coll., Sunderland (now Univ. of Sunderland). BPharm (London) 1946; PhD (Glasgow) 1955. FPS 1946. Asst Lectr, 1946–48, Lectr, 1948–62, Royal Coll. of Science and Technology, Glasgow; University of Strathclyde: Sen. Lectr, 1962–69; Reader in Pharmacognosy and Forensic Science, 1969–76; Personal Prof., 1976–78; Dean, Sch. of Pharmaceutical Sciences, 1977–78; Supervisor, MSc course in Forensic Science, 1966–78. Mem. Editorial Bd, Jl Pharm. Pharmacol., 1964–70 and 1975–78. Member: Pharm. Soc. Cttee on Pharmacognosy, 1963–74; British Pharm. Codex Pharmacognosy Sub-Cttee A, 1968–73; Brit. Pharm. Conf. Sci. Cttee, 1973–78 (Science Chm., 1977); Brit. Pharmacopoeia Pharmacognosy Panel, 1974–77; Council, Forensic Science Soc., 1974–77 (Vice-Pres., 1981–82); Professional and Gen. Services Cttee, Scottish Council on Alcoholism, 1976–78; British Pharmacopœia Commn, 1980–91; Cttee on Safety of Medicines, 1980–83 (Mem., Herbal Sub-Cttee, 1978–80; Mem., Chemistry, Pharmacy and Standards Sub-Cttee, 1980–92); Univ. of London Senate, 1981–88; DHSS Standing Pharmaceutical Adv. Cttee, 1982–88; UGC Panel on Studies Allied to Medicine, 1982–89 (Chm., 1984–89); Nuffield Foundn Cttee of Inquiry into Pharmacy, 1983–86; Cttee on Review of Medicines, 1984–91; UGC Medical Subcttee, 1984–89. Chm., Post Qualification Bd for NHS Pharmacists in Scotland, 1989–92. Mem., Governing Body, Wye College, 1985–88. Harrison Meml Medal, 1982; Charter Gold Medal, RPSGB, 1987. *Publications:* (with J. Owen Dawson) Surgical Dressings, Ligatures and Sutures, 1967; research pubns and review articles in Pharmaceut., Phytochem. and Forensic Sci. jls. *Recreations:* gardening, golf. *Address:* Grianan, Hazel Avenue, Crieff, Perthshire PH7 3ER.

FISH, Jocelyn Barbara, DCNZM 2001; CBE 1991; voluntary community worker, since 1959; farming partner, 1959–90; *b* 29 Sept. 1930; *d* of John Arthur Green and Edna Marion Green (*née* Garton); *m* 1959, Robert John Malthus Fish; one *s* two *d*. *Educ:* Hamilton High Sch., New Zealand; Auckland Univ. (BA); Auckland Teachers' College (cert.). Secondary school teacher, NZ and UK, 1953–59. Nat. Pres., Nat. Council of Women of NZ, 1986–90; (various offices) NZ Fedn of Univ. Women, and Anglican Women; Chm. Policy Cttee, survey, NZ Women - family, employment and education, Centre for Population Studies, Univ. of Waikato, 1995–98. NZ Deleg., UN Conf. on Women, Nairobi, 1985. Member: Film Censorship Bd of Review, 1981–84; Nat. Commn for Australian Bicentenary, 1987–88; Nat. Commn for UNESCO, 1989–94; Broadcasting Standards Authority, 1989–91; Transport Accident Investigation Commn, 1990–95; Hamilton Dist Legal Services Cttee, 1992–97; NZ Dental Council Complaints Assessment Cttee, 1995–2001. Member, Board: Waikato Br., Fedn of Univ. Women, 1991–99 (Chm.); Hamilton Community Law Centre Trust, 1994–2000 (Chm.); Hamilton Combined Christian Foodbank Trust, 1997–99; Waikato Anglican Social Services Trust, 2000– (Chm.). Councillor, Piako County Council, 1980–89. JP 1984. NZ Sesquicentenary Commemoration Medal, 1990; NZ Suffrage Commemeration Medal, 1993. *Recreations:* music, literature, family, travel, watching politics. *Address:* 63 Gilbass Avenue, Hamilton, New Zealand. *T:* (7) 839 1512.

FISH, John, OBE 1996; Under-Secretary, Head of Establishment General Services Division, Department of Industry, 1974–80; *b* 16 July 1920; *m* 1948, Frances; two *s*. *Educ:* Lincoln School. BA Open Univ., 1989. Entered Customs and Excise, 1937; Exchequer and Audit Dept, 1939; War service, Pilot in RAF, 1940–46; Exchequer and Audit Dept, 1946; BoT, 1949; Principal, 1950; Min. of Materials, 1951; Volta River Preparatory Commn, Accra, 1953; BoT, 1956; Asst Sec., 1960; Min. of Health, 1962; BoT, 1965; DTI, 1970; Under-Sec., 1973; Dept of Industry, 1974. Civil Service Retirement Fellowship: Mem. Cttee of Mgt, 1985–95; Trustee, 1998–2001; formerly Sec., Vice Chm., Chm. and Pres., Warwicks Br. *Address:* The Green, Stockton, Southam, Warwicks CV47 8JF. *T:* (01926) 812833. *Club:* Civil Service.

FISH, Peter Stuart; His Honour Judge Fish; a Circuit Judge, since 1994; *b* 18 Dec. 1938; *s* of Geoffrey Chadwick Fish and Emma (*née* Wood); *m* 1963, Nola Ann Worrall; two *s* one *d* (and one *d* decd). *Educ:* Rydal Sch.; Trinity Hall, Cambridge (MA). Admitted solicitor, 1963; practised in Southport, 1964–87; Dist Registrar, subseq. Dist Judge, Manchester, 1987–94; a Recorder, 1991–94. *Recreations:* music, gardening, golf. *Address:* c/o Circuit Administrator's Office, Quay Street, Manchester M60 9FD.

FISHBURN, (John) Dudley; Chairman, HFC Bank, since 1998; company director; *b* 8 June 1946; *s* of John Eskdale Fishburn and Bunting Fishburn; *m* 1981, Victoria, *y d* of Sir Jack Boles, *qv*; two *s* two *d*. *Educ:* Eton Coll.; Harvard Univ. (BA). Exec. Editor, The Economist, 1979–88. MP (C) Kensington, July 1988–1997. Parliamentary Private Secretary: FCO, 1989–90; DTI, 1990–93. Non-executive Director: First NIS Regional Fund, 1994–; Household Internat. Inc. (USA), 1995–; Cordiant plc, 1996–; Henderson Smaller Cos Investment Trust, 1996–; Philip Morris Inc. (USA), 1999–; Advr, J. P. Morgan, 1988–96. Chm., Standing Cttee on Social Scis, 1993–96, Library Cttee, 1996–, Harvard Univ.; Mem., Bd of Overseers, Harvard Univ., 1990–96; Pres., Harvard Club of London, 1970–90. Governor, English National Ballet, 1989–95; Chm. Trustees, Open Univ., 1995–2001; Member Executive Committee: Nat. Trust, 1993– (Hon. Treas., 1996–); Prison Reform Trust, 1993–2000; Liver Res. Trust, 1995–; Dulwich Picture Gall. Council, 1997–2001; Royal Oak Foundn (USA), 1997–; Gov., Peabody Trust, 2000–. Editor, The Economist's World in 1993, and annually until 2000; Associate Editor, The Economist, 1989–. Parly Radical of the Year, 1992. *Recreations:* sailing, cooking. *Address:* 7 Gayfere Street, SW1P 3HN. *Club:* Brooks's.

FISHER, family name of **Baron Fisher** and **Baroness Fisher of Rednal**.

FISHER, 3rd Baron *cr* 1909, of Kilverstone; **John Vavasseur Fisher,** DSC 1944; JP; Director, Kilverstone Latin-American Zoo and Wild Life Park, 1973–91; *b* 24 July 1921; *s* of 2nd Baron and Jane (*d* 1955), *d* of Randal Morgan, Philadelphia, USA; *S* father, 1955; *m* 1st, 1949, Elizabeth Ann Penelope (marr. diss. 1969), *yr d* of late Herbert P. Holt, MC; two *s* two *d*; 2nd, 1970, Hon. Mrs Rosamund Anne Fairbairn, *d* of 12th Baron Clifford of Chudleigh. *Educ:* Stowe; Trinity Coll., Cambridge. Member: Eastern Gas Bd, 1962–71; East Anglia Economic Planning Council, 1971–77. DL Norfolk, 1968–82; JP Norfolk, 1970. *Heir: s* Hon. Patrick Vavasseur Fisher [*b* 14 June 1953; *m* 1977, Lady Karen Carnegie, *d* of 13th Earl of Northesk; three *s* four *d* (of whom one *s* one *d* are twins)]. *Address:* Marklye, Rushlake Green, Heathfield, Sussex TN21 9PN. *T:* (01435) 830270.
See also Baron Clifford of Chudleigh.

FISHER OF REDNAL, Baroness *cr* 1974 (Life Peer), of Rednal, Birmingham; **Doris Mary Gertrude Fisher;** JP; Member of the European Parliament, 1975–79; Member, Warrington and Runcorn (formerly Warrington) Development Corporation, 1974–89; *b* 13 Sept. 1919; *d* of late Frederick J. Satchwell, BEM; *m* 1939, Joseph Fisher (*d* 1978); two *d*. *Educ:* Tinker's Farm Girls Sch.; Fircroft Coll.; Bournville Day Continuation Coll. Member: Birmingham City Council, 1952–74; Labour Party, 1945–; UNESCO study group; Nat. Pres. Co-operative Women's Guild, 1961–62. Contested Ladywood, Birmingham, 1969 by-election; MP (Lab) Birmingham, Ladywood, 1970–Feb. 1974. Member: Gen. Medical Council, 1974–79; New Towns Staff Commn, 1976–79; Birmingham Civic Housing Assoc. Ltd, 1982–; Vice-President: Assoc. of Municipal Authorities, 1980–97; Assoc. of Dist Councils, 1982–97; Inst. of Trading Standards Admin. Pres., Birmingham Royal Inst. for the Blind, 1980–; Chm., W Midlands Macmillan Fund, 1995. Patron, St Basil's Centre for Young Homeless, Birmingham. Guardian, Birmingham Assay Office, 1979–89; Mem., Hallmarking Council, 1989–. Chm. Governors, Baskerville Special Sch., 1981–87; Governor, Hunter's Hill Special Sch., 1988–94. JP Birmingham 1961. Hon. Alderman, 1974, Birmingham District Council. DUniv UCE, 1998. *Recreations:* swimming, walking. *Address:* 60 Jacoby Place, Priory Road, Birmingham B5 7UW. *T:* (0121) 471 2003.

FISHER, Andrew Charles; Chief Executive, Coutts Group, since 2000; *b* 22 June 1961; *s* of Harold Fisher and Jessie Fisher (now Stanley); *m* 1987, Bernadette Johnson; two *s*. *Educ:* Birmingham Univ. (BSc Hons Econs). Mktg Manager, Unilever PLC, 1982–87; Principal (Partner Designate), Coopers & Lybrand Mgt Consultancy, 1987–91; Divl Sales and Mktg Dir, Standard Chartered Bank, Equitor Div., 1991–94; Man. Dir, Rangeley Co. Ltd, 1994–97; Strategic Advr, NatWest Wealth Mgt, 1997–98; Gp Commercial Dir, Coutts NatWest Gp, 1998–2000. *Recreations:* ski-ing, golf, squash, scuba diving. *Address:* Barngates House, Church Lane, Binfield, Berks RG42 5NS. *T:* (01344) 454044. *Clubs:* Mosimann's; Wentworth Golf.

FISHER, Arthur J.; *see* Jeddere-Fisher.

FISHER, Carol Ann; Chief Executive, Central Office of Information, since 1999; *b* 13 April 1954; *d* of Joseph and Gladys Fisher. *Educ:* Univ. of Birmingham (BA Hons Medieval and Modern Hist.). Brand Manager, Bisto, RHM Foods, 1979–81; Sen. Mktg Manager and various other posts, Grand Metropolitan Brewing, 1982–88; Mktg Dir, Holsten Distributors, 1989–94; Gen. Manager, Mktg and Commercial, Courage Internat., 1994–95; Man. Dir, CLT-UFA UK Radio Sales, 1996–98. Member: Women in Advertising and Communications (Pres., 2000–2001); Mktg Soc. *Recreations:* walking, long haul travel. *Address:* Central Office of Information, Hercules Road, SE1 7DU. *T:* (020) 7261 8210.

FISHER, (Christopher) Mark; Human Resources Director, Department for Work and Pensions (formerly Department of Social Security), since 2000; *b* 8 Oct. 1960; *s* of Christopher Forsyth Fisher and (Nadia) Ruth Reeve Fisher (*née* Angel); *m* 1997, Helen, *d* of Marie Fitzgibbon, Manchester. *Educ:* King Edward's Sch., Bath; Lady Margaret Hall, Oxford (BA Hons PPE). Jun. posts, DHSS, 1983–87; Principal: Social Security Policy Gp, DSS, 1988–90; Econ. Secretariat, Cabinet Office, 1990–92; speech writer for Sec. of State for Social Security, 1992; mgt posts, 1993–97, Personnel and Communications Dir, 1997–2000, Benefits Agency. *Recreations:* good company, railways, canals. *Address:* Laithe Croft, Totties Lane, Holmfirth, W Yorks HD7 1UL. *T:* (01484) 686790.

FISHER, David Paul; QC 1996; a Recorder, since 1991; *b* 30 April 1949; *s* of late Percy Laurence Fisher and Doris Mary Fisher; *m* 1st, 1971, Cary Maria Cicely Lamberton (*d* 1977); one *d*; 2nd, 1979, Diana Elizabeth Dolby. *Educ:* Felsted Sch. Called to the Bar, Gray's Inn, 1973; Asst Recorder, 1987. Member: Gen. Council of the Bar, 1997–2000; Advocacy Studies Bd, 1997–. *Recreations:* travel, sport, gardening, cinema. *Address:* 6 King's Bench Walk, Temple, EC4Y 7DR. *T:* (020) 7583 0410.

FISHER, David Richard; Strategy Director, EDS (on secondment from Ministry of Defence), since 2001; *b* 13 May 1947; *s* of William Horace and Margaret Catherine Fisher; *m* 1970, Sophia Josephine Hibbard; two *d*. *Educ:* Reading Sch.; St John's Coll., Oxford (BA 1969, 1st cl. LitHum, 1st cl. Hon. Mods). Ministry of Defence, 1970–: Private Sec. to successive RAF Ministers, 1973–74; naval programme and budget, 1976–79; Defence Budget, 1981–83; Vis. Res. Fellow, Nuffield Coll., Oxford, 1983–84; Head, Resources and Progs (Air), 1984–88; Defence Counsellor, UK Delegn to NATO, Brussels (on loan to FCO), 1988–92; Asst Under-Sec. of State (Systems), MoD, 1992–97; Dep. Hd, Defence and Overseas Secretariat, Cabinet Office, 1997–99 (on secondment); Dir, Defence Trng Review, MoD, 1999–2001. Mem., Management Cttee, Council on Christian Approaches to Defence and Disarmament. *Publications:* Morality and the Bomb, 1985; (contrib.) Ethics and European Security, 1986; (contrib.) Just Deterrence, 1990; (contrib.) Some Corner of a Foreign Field, 1998; (contrib.) The Crescent and the Cross, 1998; contribs to jls on defence and ethical issues. *Recreations:* philosophy, gardening. *Address:* EDS, Lansdowne House, Berkeley Square, W1X 5DH. *T:* (020) 7569 5870. *Clubs:* National Liberal, Royal Commonwealth Society.

FISHER, Desmond (Michael); Director, Provincial Publishers Ltd; *b* 9 Sept. 1920; *e s* of Michael Louis Fisher and Evelyn Kate Shier; *m* 1948, Margaret Elizabeth Smyth; three *s* one *d*. *Educ:* St Columb's Coll., Derry; Good Counsel Coll., New Ross, Co. Wexford; University Coll., Dublin (BA (NUI)). Asst Editor, Nationalist and Leinster Times, Carlow, 1945–48; Foreign Editor, Irish Press, Dublin, 1948–51; Economic Correspondent, Irish News Agency, Dublin, 1951–54; London Editor, Irish Press, 1954–62; Editor, Catholic Herald, 1962–66; Radio Telefis Eireann: Dep. Head of News, 1967–73; Head of Current Affairs, 1973–75; Dir of Broadcasting Devel, 1975–83; Nationalist and Leinster Times, Carlow: Ed. and Man. Dir, 1984–89; Exec. Dir, 1989–92; Chm., 1992–2001. *Publications:* The Church in Transition, 1967; Broadcasting in Ireland, 1978; The Right to Communicate: a status report, 1981; The Right to Communicate: a new human right, 1983; contributor to The Economist, The Furrow, Irish Digest and to various Irish, US and foreign magazines. *Address:* Louvain 22, Dublin 14. *T:* (1) 2884608.

FISHER, Donald, CBE 1987; County Education Officer, Hertfordshire, 1974–90; *b* 20 Jan. 1931; *s* of John Wilfred and Mabel Fisher; *m* 1953, Mavis Doreen (*née* Sutcliffe); one *s* two *d*. *Educ:* Heckmondwike Grammar Sch.; Christ Church, Oxford (MA). Teacher, Hull GS, 1954–59; Admin. Asst, Cornwall LEA, 1959–61; Asst Educn Officer, W Sussex LEA, 1961–64; Headmaster: Helston GS, 1964–67; Midhurst GS, 1967–72; Dep. Educn Officer, W Sussex LEA, 1972–74. Chm., Assoc. of Educn Officers, 1982; Pres., Soc. of Educn Officers, 1984. Gov., Univ. of Hertfordshire, 1993–. Hon. DEd Hatfield Polytechnic, 1989. *Publications:* (contrib.) Educational Administration, 1980, 3rd edn 1989; articles and book reviews in Education. *Recreations:* playing with grandchildren, reading. *Address:* 74 The Ryde, Hatfield, Herts AL9 5DL. *T:* (01707) 271428.

FISHER, Dudley Henry, CBE 1990; DL; CPFA; Chairman, Wales Region, British Gas Corporation, 1974–87, retired; *b* 22 Aug. 1922; *s* of Arthur and Mary Fisher; *m* 1st, 1946, Barbara Lilian Sexton (*d* 1984); one *s* two *d*; 2nd, 1985, Jean Mary Livingstone Miller, *d* of late Dr and Mrs Robert Brown Miller, Cowbridge, S Glam. *Educ:* City of Norwich Sch. Various accountancy positions in Local Govt and Eastern Electricity Bd, 1938–53. War service, RAF, 1942–46 (pilot; Flt Lt). Northern Gas Bd, 1953; Wales Gas Board: Asst Chief Accountant, Dep. Chief Accountant, Chief Accountant, Dir of Finance, 1956–69; Dep. Chm., 1970. Member: Adv. Cttee on Local Govt Audit, 1979–82; Audit Commn for Local Authorities in England and Wales, 1983–88; Broadcasting Council for Wales, 1986–90; Hon. Treasurer, British National Cttee, 1980–89, and Chm., Admin. Cttee, 1986–89, World Energy Conf. Chairman: Welsh Council, CBI, 1987–89; Wales Festival of Remembrance Cttee, 1996–; Dep. Chm., Inst. of Welsh Affairs, 1991–95. Mem. Council, 1983–88, Treas., 1987–88, UC Cardiff; Member of Council: Univ. of Wales Cardiff (formerly Univ. of Wales Coll. of Cardiff), 1988–2001; Univ. of Wales Coll. of Medicine, 1992–; Chm., Audit Cttee, Univ. of Wales, 1994–96. Governor, United World Coll. of the Atlantic, 1988–96. Trustee, Help the Aged, 1987–97; Vice Chm., HelpAge Internat., 1993–97. Liveryman, Welsh Livery Guild, 1996–. High Sheriff, 1988–89, DL 1991, S Glam. *Recreations:* golf, gardening, reading. *Address:* Norwood Edge, 8 Cyncoed Avenue, Cardiff CF23 6SU. *T:* (029) 2075 7958. *Clubs:* Royal Air Force; Cardiff and County (Cardiff).

FISHER, Rt Rev. Edward George K.; *see* Knapp-Fisher.

FISHER, Elisabeth Neill; Her Honour Judge Fisher; a Circuit Judge, since 1989; *b* 24 Nov. 1944; *d* of Kenneth Neill Fisher and Lorna Charlotte Honor Fisher. *Educ:* Oxford High Sch. for Girls (GPDST); Cambridge Univ. (MA). Called to the Bar, Inner Temple, 1968. A Recorder, 1982–89. Mem. Senate, Inns of Court, 1983–86. Member: Criminal Cttee, Judicial Studies Bd, 1995–98; Criminal Justice Consultative Council, 1992–99. Chm., Home Sec.'s Adv. Bd on Restricted Patients, 1998–. DUniv UCE, 1997. *Address:* Queen Elizabeth II Law Courts, Newton Street, Birmingham B4 7NA.

FISHER, Sir George Read, Kt 1967; CMG 1961; Mining Engineer; President, MIM Holdings Ltd, 1970–75; *b* 23 March 1903; *s* of George Alexander and Ellen Harriett Fisher; *m* 1st, 1927, Eileen Elaine Triggs (*d* 1966); one *s* three *d*; 2nd, 1973, Marie C. Gilbey. *Educ:* Prince Alfred Coll., Adelaide; Adelaide Univ. (BE). Formerly Gen. Manager of Operations for Zinc Corporation Ltd, Broken Hill, NSW; Chm., Mount Isa Mines Ltd, 1953–70. *Recreations:* shooting and bowling. *Address:* c/o MIM Holdings Ltd, GPO Box 1433, Brisbane, Qld 4001, Australia. *Clubs:* Queensland, Brisbane (Brisbane).

FISHER, Hon. Sir Henry (Arthur Pears), Kt 1968; President, Wolfson College, Oxford, 1975–85, Hon. Fellow, 1985; *b* 20 Jan. 1918; *e s* of late Lord Fisher of Lambeth, PC, GCVO; *m* 1948, Felicity (BA Hons, Open Univ., 1987), *d* of late Eric Sutton; one *s* three *d*. *Educ:* Marlborough; Christ Church, Oxford (Schol.); Gaisford Greek Prose Prize, 1937; 1st Cl. Hon. Mods 1938; BA 1942; MA 1943. Served Leics Regt, 1940–46; Staff Coll., Quetta, 1943; GSO2, 1943–44; GSO1 HQ 14th Army, 1945. Hon. Lieut-Col 1946 (despatches). Fellow of All Souls Coll., 1946–73, 1991–, Emeritus, 1976–91, Estates Bursar, 1961–66, Sub-Warden, 1965–67. Barrister, Inner Temple, 1947, Bencher, 1966; QC 1960; Recorder of Canterbury, 1962–68; a Judge of the High Court of Justice, Queen's Bench Div., 1968–70; Director: J. Henry Schroder Wagg & Co. Ltd, 1970–75; Schroder International Ltd, 1973–75; Thomas Tilling plc, 1970–83; Equity and Law Life Assurance Soc. plc, 1975–87; Equity and Law plc, 1987. Mem., Gen. Council of the Bar, 1959–63, 1964–68, Vice-Chm., 1965–66, Chm., 1966–68; Vice-Pres., Senate of the Four Inns of Court, 1966–68; Vice-Pres., Bar Assoc. for Commerce, Finance and Industry, 1973–. Pres., Howard League, 1983–91; Chairman: Cttee of Inquiry into Abuse of the Social Security System, 1971; City Cttee on Company Law, 1974–76; Cttee of Inquiry into self-regulation at Lloyd's, 1979–80; Appeal Cttee, Panel on Take-overs and Mergers, 1981–87; Jt Commn on the Constitution (set up by Social Democratic and Liberal Parties), 1981–83; Investment Management Regulatory Orgn, 1986–89. Conducted inquiry into Confait case, 1976–77. Member: Private Internat. Law Cttee, 1961–63; Coun. on Tribunals, 1962–65; Law Reform Cttee, 1963–66; Council, Marlborough Coll., 1967–83 (Chm., 1977–82); BBC Programmes Complaints Commn, 1972–79; Governing Body, Imperial Coll., 1973–88 (Chm., 1975–88) (FIC 1974); Trustee, Pilgrim Trust, 1965–92 (Chm., 1979–83, 1989–92). Hon. Mem., Lloyd's, 1983. Hon. Fellow, Darwin Coll., Cambridge, 1984. Hon. LLD Hull, 1979. *Recreation:* music. *Address:* Garden End, Cross Lane, Marlborough, Wilts SN8 1LA. *T:* (01672) 515420. *Club:* Travellers.

FISHER, Joan; Headteacher, King Edward VI Camp Hill School for Girls, Birmingham, since 1992; *b* 24 Sept. 1939; *d* of R. and A. R. Bowler; *m* 1969, Ronald William Fisher; four *d* (incl. triplets). *Educ:* Univ. of Leeds (BA Modern Langs); Univ. of York (Schoolteacher Fellowship); Inst. of Educn, London (MA). Teacher in comprehensive schs, Yorkshire and Surrey, 1962–89: Holme Valley GS, 1962–66; Middlesbrough Girls' High, 1966–69; Acklam High, 1970–72; Framwelgate Moor, 1972–73; Glebelands, 1974–82; Tomlinscote, 1982–89; Dep. Headteacher, Westcliff High Sch. for Girls, 1989–92. FRSA 1997. *Publications:* teaching materials for German, including: Achtung! Achtung!, 1985; Begegnungen, 1985; Lesekiste, A, 1987, B, 1988; Pack's An!, 1991. *Address:* King Edward VI Camp Hill School for Girls, Vicarage Road, Kings Heath, Birmingham B14 7QJ. *T:* (0121) 444 2150.

FISHER, Mark; MP (Lab) Stoke-on-Trent Central, since 1983; *b* 29 Oct. 1944; *s* of Sir Nigel Fisher, MC and of Lady Gloria Flower; *m* 1971, Ingrid Geach (marr. diss. 1999); two *s* two *d*. *Educ:* Eton College; Trinity College, Cambridge (MA). Documentary film producer and script writer, 1966–75; Principal, Tattenhall Centre of Education, 1975–83. Mem., Staffs CC, 1981–85 (Chm., Libraries Cttee, 1981–83). Contested (Lab) Leek, 1979. An Opposition Whip, 1985–87; Opposition spokesman on the arts, 1987–92, 1993–97, on Citizen's Charter, 1992–93; Parly Under-Sec. of State, Dept for Culture, Media and Sport, 1997–98. Mem., Treasury and CS Select Cttee, 1983–85. Dep. Pro-Chancellor, Keele Univ., 1989–97. Vis. Fellow, St Antony's Coll., Oxford, 2000–01. Member: BBC Gen. Adv. Council, 1988–95; Council, PSI, 1989–95; Museums and Galls Commn, 1999–. Trustee, Britten-Pears Foundn, 1998–. Hon. FRIBA 1992; Hon. FRCA 1993. Author of stage plays: Brave New Town, 1974; The Cutting Room, 1990. *Publications:* City Centres, City Cultures, 1988; (ed jtly) Whose Cities?, 1991; A New

London, 1992. *Address:* House of Commons, SW1A 0AA; 110 Victoria Street, Hartshill, Stoke-on-Trent ST4 6DU. *T:* (01782) 713813.

FISHER, Mark; *see* Fisher, C. M.

FISHER, Maurice, RCNC; General Manager, HM Dockyard, Rosyth, 1979–83; retired; *b* 8 Feb. 1924; *s* of William Ernest Fisher and Lily Edith (*née* Hatch); *m* 1955, Stella Leslie Sumsion; one *d. Educ:* St Luke's Sch., Portsmouth; Royal Dockyard Sch., Portsmouth; Royal Naval Coll., Greenwich. Constructor-in-Charge, HM Dockyard, Simonstown, 1956–60; Staff of Director of Naval Construction, 1960–63; Staff of C-in-C Western Fleet, 1963–65; Dep. Supt, Admiralty Experiment Works, Haslar, 1965–68; Dep. Prodn Manager, HM Dockyard, Devonport, 1968–72; Personnel Manager, HM Dockyard, Portsmouth, 1972–74; Planning Manager, 1974–77, Prodn Manager, 1977–79, HM Dockyard, Devonport. *Recreation:* game fishing. *Address:* 1 Hamble Springs, Bishops Waltham, Hants SO32 1SF.

FISHER, Rt Rev. Brother Michael, SSF, **(Reginald Lindsay Fisher)**; Assistant Bishop, Diocese of Ely, 1985–96; *b* 6 April 1918; *s* of late Reginald Watson Fisher and Martha Lindsay Fisher. *Educ:* Clapham Central School; Bolt Court; Westcott House, Cambridge. Member, Society of St Francis, 1942. Deacon 1953, priest 1954, dio. Ely; Licence to officiate: Diocese of Ely, 1954–62; Newcastle, 1962–67; Sarum, 1967–79; Bishop Suffragan of St Germans, 1979–85; Bishop to HM Prisons, 1985. Minister Provincial, 1967–79, Minister-Gen., 1985–91, SSF. MA Lambeth, 1978. *Publications:* For the Time Being (autobiog.), 1993; A Word In Time (sermons and addresses), 1997. *Recreations:* painting, music, cinema, people. *Address:* 15 Botolph Lane, Cambridge, Cambs CB2 3RD. *T:* (01223) 321576.

FISHER, Prof. Michael Ellis, FRS 1971; Distinguished University Professor and Regents' Professor, Institute for Physical Science and Technology, University of Maryland, since 1993 (Wilson H. Elkins Distinguished Professor, 1987–93); *b* 3 Sept. 1931; *s* of Harold Wolf Fisher and Jeanne Marie Fisher (*née* Halter); *m* 1954, Sorrel Castillejo; three *s* one *d. Educ:* King's Coll., London. BSc 1951, PhD 1957, FKC 1981. Flying Officer (Educn), RAF, 1951–53; London Univ. Postgraduate Studentship, 1953–56; DSIR Sen. Research Fellow, 1956–58. King's Coll., London: Lectr in Theoretical Physics, 1958–62; Reader in Physics, 1962–64; Prof. of Physics, 1965–66; Cornell University: Prof. of Chemistry and Maths, 1966–73; Horace White Prof. of Chemistry, Physics and Maths, 1973–89; Chm., Dept of Chemistry, 1975–78. Guest Investigator, Rockefeller Inst., New York, 1963–64; Vis. Prof. in Applied Physics, Stanford Univ., 1970–71; Walter Ames Prof., Univ. of Washington, 1977; Vis. Prof. of Physics, MIT, 1979; Sherman Fairchild Disting. Scholar, CIT, 1984; Vis. Prof. in Theoretical Physics, Oxford, 1985; Lorentz Prof., Leiden, 1993; Vis. Prof., Nat. Inst. of Sci. and Technol., USA, 1994; Phi Beta Kappa Vis. Scholar, 1994. Lectures: Buhl, Carnegie-Mellon, 1971; 32nd Richtmyer Meml, 1973; 17th Fritz London Meml, 1975; Morris Loeb, Harvard, 1979; H. L. Welsh, Toronto, 1979; Bakerian, Royal Soc., 1979; Welch Foundn, Texas, 1979; Alpheas Smith, Ohio State Univ., 1982; Laird Meml, Univ. of Western Ontario, 1983; Fries, Rensselaer Polytechnic Inst., NY, 1984; Amos de-Shalit Meml, Weizmann Inst., Rehovoth, 1985; Cherwell-Simon, Oxford, 1985; Marker, Penn. State Univ., 1988; Nat. Sci. Council, Taiwan, 1989; Hamilton Meml, Princeton Univ., 1990; 65th J. W. Gibbs, Amer. Math. Soc., Condon, Univ. of Colorado, and M. S. Green Meml, Temple Univ., 1992, R. and B. Sackler, Tel Aviv, 1992; Lennard-Jones, RSC, 1995; G. N. Lewis, UC Berkeley, 1995; Hirschfelder, Wisconsin Univ., 1995; Baker, in Chemistry, Cornell Univ., 1997; F. G. Brickwedde, in Physics, Johns Hopkins Univ., 1998; Michelson, Case Western Reserve Univ., 1999. Mem. Council and Vice-Pres., Royal Soc., 1993–95. Mem., Amer. Philos. Soc., 1993. John Simon Guggenheim Memorial Fellow, 1970–71, 1978–79; Fellow, Amer. Acad. of Arts and Scis, 1979; FAAAS 1986; For. Associate, National Acad. of Sciences, USA, 1983; For. Mem., Brazilian Acad. of Scis, 1996. Hon. FRSE 1986; Hon. Fellow, Indian Acad. of Scis, Bangalore, 2000. Hon. DSc Yale, 1987; Hon. DPhil Tel Aviv, 1992. Irving Langmuir Prize in Chemical Physics, Amer. Phys. Soc., 1970; Award in Phys. and Math. Scis, NY Acad. of Scis, 1978; Guthrie Medal, Inst. of Physics, 1980; Wolf Prize in Physics, State of Israel, 1980; Michelson-Morely Award, Case-Western Reserve Univ., 1982; James Murray Luck Award, National Acad. of Sciences, USA, 1983; Boltzmann Medal, Internat. Union of Pure and Applied Physics, 1983; Lars Onsager Medal, Norwegian Inst. of Technol., 1993; Onsager Meml Prize, Amer. Phys. Soc., 1995; Hildebrand Award, Amer. Chem. Soc., 1995. *Publications:* Analogue Computing at Ultra-High Speed (with D. M. MacKay), 1962; The Nature of Critical Points, (Univ. of Colorado) 1964, (Moscow) 1968; contribs to Proc. Roy. Soc., Phys. Rev., Phys. Rev. Lett., Jl Sci. Insts, Jl Math. Phys., Arch. Rational Mech. Anal., Jl Chem. Phys., Commun. Math. Phys., Rept Prog. Phys., Rev. Mod. Phys., Physica, etc. *Recreations:* Flamenco guitar, travel. *Address:* Institute for Physical Science and Technology, University of Maryland, College Park, MD 20742–2431, USA. *T:* (301) 4054820.

FISHER, Nancy Kathleen; *see* Trenaman, N. K.

FISHER, Peter Antony Goodwin, FRCP; Consultant Physician, since 1986, Director of Research, since 1996, and Clinical Director, since 1998, Royal London Homoeopathic Hospital; *b* 2 Sept. 1950; *s* of Antony Martin Fisher and Eve Fisher; *m* 1997, Nina Oxenham; two *d. Educ:* Tonbridge Sch.; Emmanuel Coll., Cambridge (BA 1972, MA 1975; MB BChir 1975); Westminster Hosp. Med. Sch. FFHom 1986 (Vice Pres., 1991); FRCP 1997. Med. Dir, Royal London Homoeopathic Hosp., 1998–99. FRSocMed 1984. Editor, British Homeopathic Jl, 1986–. *Publications:* Alternative Answers to Arthritis and Rheumatism, 1999; numerous scientific articles on homeopathy. *Recreation:* gardening. *Address:* Royal London Homoeopathic Hospital, Great Ormond Street, WC1N 3HR. *T:* (020) 7833 7223.

FISHER, Rev. Canon Peter Timothy; Principal, The Queen's Foundation for Ecumenical Theological Education (formerly The Queen's College), Birmingham, since 1994; *b* 7 July 1944; *s* of late Rev. James Atherton Fisher; *m* 1968, Elizabeth Lacey; two *s. Educ:* City of London Sch.; Durham Univ. (BA, MA); Cuddesdon Coll., Oxford. Ordained deacon, 1970, priest 1971; Curate, St Andrew's, Bedford, 1970–74; Chaplain, Surrey Univ., 1974–78; Sub-Warden, Lincoln Theol Coll., 1978–83; Rector, Houghton-le-Spring, 1983–94. Hon. Canon, Birmingham Cathedral, 2000–. *Recreations:* piano and water-colours, both strictly incognito. *Address:* The Queen's Foundation for Ecumenical Theological Education, Somerset Road, Edgbaston, Birmingham B15 2QH. *T:* (0121) 454 1527.

FISHER, Roger Anthony, FRCO(CHM); Organist and Master of Choristers, Chester Cathedral, 1967–96; *b* 18 Sept. 1936; *s* of Leslie Elgar Fisher and Vera Althea (*née* Salter); *m* 1st, 1967, Susan Mary Green (marr. diss. 1983); one *d*; 2nd, 1985, Gillian Rushforth (*née* Heywood). *Educ:* Bancroft's Sch., Woodford Green, Essex; Royal Coll. Music; Christ Church, Oxford (Organ schol.; MA). FRCO(CHM); ARCM; ATCL. Organist, St Mark's, Regent's Park, 1957–62; Asst Organist, Hereford Cathedral, 1962–67; Asst Lectr in Music, Hereford Coll. of Educn, 1963–67. Music Critic, Liverpool Echo, 1976–79; Associate Editor, Organist's Rev., 1996–. Recital tours, 1967–, incl. N America, Europe and Scandinavia. Recordings in GB and Europe; BBC broadcasts as organist and with Chester Cathedral Choir. Conductor, choral socs and orchestras; Organ Consultant to churches and cathedrals. Geoffrey Tankard Prize for Solo Organ, RCM, 1959. *Publications:* articles about the organ and related subjects in several periodicals. *Recreations:* railway interests, walking, cycling, motoring. *Address:* The Old Chapel, Trelogan, Holywell, Clwyd CH8 9BD.

FISHER, Thomas Gilbert F.; *see* Field-Fisher.

FISHLOCK, Dr David Jocelyn, OBE 1983; Editor, since 1991, and Publisher, since 1992, R&D Efficiency; *b* 9 Aug. 1932; *s* of William Charles Fishlock and Dorothy Mary Turner; *m* 1959, Mary Millicent Cosgrove; one *s. Educ:* City of Bath Boys' Sch. (now Beechen Cliff Sch.); Bristol Coll. of Technol. FIBiol 1988; Companion, Inst. of Energy, 1987. National Service, REME, 1955–58. Westinghouse Brake & Signal Co. Ltd, 1948–55; McGraw-Hill, 1959–62; New Scientist, 1962–67; Science Editor, Financial Times, 1967–91. Columnist: Nuclear Europe Worldscan, 1981–; Business in East Anglia, 1997–; Erotic Review, 1998–. Glaxo Travelling Fellow, 1978; Associate Fellow, Centre for Res. in Innovation & Competitiveness, 1998–. Member: R&D Soc., 1994–; Scientific Instrument Soc., 1994–; Foundn for Sci. and Technol., 1998–. Hon. DLitt Salford, 1982; Hon. DSc Bath, 1993. Chemical Writer of the Year Award, BASF, 1982; Worthington Pump Award, 1982; British Press Award, 1986. Silver Jubilee Medal, 1977. *Publications:* The New Materials, 1967; Man Modified, 1969; The Business of Science, 1975; The Business of Biotechnology, 1982; (with Elizabeth Antébi) Biotechnology: strategies for life, 1986. *Recreations:* writing, reading, collecting old medical/pharmaceutical equipment. *Address:* Traveller's Joy, Copse Lane, Jordans, Bucks HP9 2TA. *T:* (01494) 873242. *Club:* Athenæum.

FISHLOCK, Trevor; journalist and author; roving foreign correspondent, The Daily Telegraph, 1986–89 and 1993–96; *b* 21 Feb. 1941; *m* 1978, Penelope Symon. *Educ:* Churcher's Coll., Petersfield; Southern Grammar Sch., Portsmouth. Portsmouth Evening News, 1957–62; freelance and news agency reporter, 1962–68; The Times: Wales and W England staff correspondent, 1968–77; London and foreign staff, 1978–80; S Asia correspondent, Delhi, 1980–83; New York correspondent, 1983–86; Moscow correspondent, Daily Telegraph, 1989–91; roving foreign correspondent, The Sunday Telegraph, 1991–93. Fellow, World Press Inst., St Paul, Minnesota, 1977–78. Mem., Council for the Welsh Language, 1973–77. David Holden Award for foreign reporting (British Press Awards), 1983; Internat. Reporter of the Year (British Press Awards), 1986. *Publications:* Wales and the Welsh, 1972; Talking of Wales, 1975; Discovering Britain: Wales, 1979; Americans and Nothing Else, 1980; India File, 1983; The State of America, 1986; Indira Gandhi (for children), 1986; Out of Red Darkness: reports from the collapsing Soviet Empire, 1992; My Foreign Country: Trevor Fishlock's Britain, 1997; Cobra Road: an Indian journey, 1999. *Recreation:* sailing. *Address:* 7 Teilo Street, Cardiff CF11 9JN. *Club:* Travellers.

FISHWICK, Avril, OBE 1997; Vice Lord-Lieutenant of Greater Manchester, 1988–98; *b* 30 March 1924; *yr d* of Frank Platt and Charlotte Winifred Young; *m* 1950, Thomas William Fishwick; two *d. Educ:* Woodfield; High Sch. for Girls, Wigan; Liverpool Univ. (LLB 1946; LLM 1947). Admitted Solicitor 1949. War service, Foreign Office, Bletchley Park, 1942–45; Partner, Frank Platt & Fishwick, 1958–94. Chm., Envmtl Res. and Consultancy Unit (ERCU Ltd) Tidy Britain (formerly Tidy Britain Enterprises Ltd), 1990–2000; Dir, Northern Adv. Bd, National Westminster Bank, 1984–92. Member: Wigan and Leigh HMC, 1960–73 (Mem., Exec. Council, 1966–73); NW RHA, 1985–88; Chm., Wigan AHA, 1973–82. Local President: Civic Trust, 1976–91; RSPCA, 1974–99; Little Theatre, 1985–91; Drumcroon Arts Centre, 1995–; Hon. Mem., Soroptimists Internat., 1973–; Mem., Groundwork Trust, 1986–93. Trustee: Skelton Bounty, 1985–; Gtr Manchester Police Community Charity, 1986–98; Friends of Rosie, 1995–. Mem. Court, Manchester Univ., 1984–. DL 1982, High Sheriff 1983–84, Gtr Manchester. Hon. MA Manchester, 1993. Paul Harris Fellow, Rotary Internat., 1995; Queen Mother's Birthday Award for Envmtl Improvement, 1996. *Recreations:* family, natural history. *Address:* 6 Southfields, Richmond Road, Bowdon, Altrincham, Cheshire WA14 2TY. *T:* (0161) 941 6660.

FISK, David John, CB 1999; ScD, PhD; FREng; Under Secretary, since 1987, Chief Scientist, since 1988, and Director, Central Strategy Directorate, since 1999, Department for Transport, Local Government and the Regions (formerly Department of the Environment, then Department of the Environment, Transport and the Regions); *b* 9 Jan. 1947; *s* of late John Howard Fisk and of Rebecca Elizabeth Fisk (*née* Haynes); *m* 1972, A. Anne Thoday; one *s* one *d. Educ:* Stationers' Company's Sch., Hornsey; St John's Coll., Cambridge (BA, MA, ScD); Univ. of Manchester (PhD). FCIBSE 1983 (Hon. FCIBSE 1998); FREng (FEng 1998); FInstP 1999. Joined Building Res. Estabt (traffic noise res.), 1972; Higher Sci. Officer, 1972–73; Sen. Sci. Officer (energy conservation res.), 1973–75; PSO, 1975–78; SPSO, Hd Mechanical and Elec. Engrg Div., 1978–84; Department of the Environment: Asst Sec., Central Directorate of Environmental Protection, 1984–87; Dep. Chief Scientist, 1987–88; Director: Air, Climate and Toxic Substances Directorate, 1990–95; Envmt & Internat. Directorate, 1995–98. Vis. Prof., Univ. of Liverpool, 1988–. Dir, Watford Palace Th., 2000–. *Publications:* Thermal Control of Buildings, 1981; numerous papers on technical innovation, bldg sci., systems theory and economics. *Recreations:* modern theatre, music. *Address:* c/o Department for Transport, Local Government and the Regions, Great Minster House, 76 Marsham Street, SW1P 4DR.

FISON, Sir (Richard) Guy, 4th Bt *cr* 1905; DSC 1944; *b* 9 Jan. 1917; *er s* of Sir William Guy Fison, 3rd Bt; *S* father, 1964; *m* 1952, Elyn Hartmann (*d* 1987); one *s* one *d. Educ:* Eton; New Coll., Oxford. Served RNVR, 1939–45. Entered Wine Trade, 1948; Master of Wine, 1954; Dir, Saccone & Speed Ltd, 1952–82; Chairman: Saccone & Speed Internat., 1979–82; Percy Fox & Co. Ltd, 1982–83; Wine Devlt Bd, 1982–83; Fine Vintage Wines Plc, 1985–95; Pres., Wine and Spirit Assoc., 1977–78. Hon. Freeman, 1976, Renter Warden, 1981–82, Upper Warden, 1982–83, Master, 1983–84, Vintners' Co. *Heir: s* Charles William Fison, *b* 6 Feb. 1954. *Address:* Medwins, Odiham, Hants RG29 1NE. *T:* (01256) 704075.

FITCH, Douglas Bernard Stocker, FRICS; FAAV; MRAC; Director, Land and Water Service, Agricultural Development and Advisory Service, Ministry of Agriculture, Fisheries and Food, 1980–87, retired; *b* 16 April 1927; *s* of William Kenneth Fitch and Hilda Barrington; *m* 1952, Joyce Vera Griffiths; three *s. Educ:* St Albans Sch.; Royal Agricl Coll. (Dip. 1951). FRICS 1977. Served Army, RE, 1944–48. Joined Land Service, MAFF, 1951; Divl Surveyor, Guildford, 1971; Regional Surveyor, SE Reg., 1979. Mem., European Faculty of Land Use and Devlt, 1985– (Prof., Rural Planning and Natural Resource Mgt, 1985–97). Royal Institution of Chartered Surveyors: Mem., Agric. Divl Council, 1980–87; Mem., Gen. Council, 1980–86. Internat. Fedn. of Surveyors deleg., 1988–91, and Chm., Standing Conf. on Marine Resource Management, 1985–89. Chm. Adv. Cttee, Centre for Rural Studies, 1990–96; Mem., Bd of Governors, Royal Agricl

Coll., 1981–2001. *Recreation:* golf. *Address:* 71 Oasthouse Crescent, Hale, Farnham, Surrey GU9 0NP. *T:* (01252) 716742. *Clubs:* Farmers', Civil Service.

FITCH, Rodney Arthur, CBE 1990; PPCSD (FSIAD 1976); Founder and Chief Executive, Rodney Fitch, specialist design consultants, London, Singapore, Bangkok and Hong Kong, since 1994; *b* 19 Aug. 1938; *s* of late Arthur and Ivy Fitch; *m* 1965, Janet Elizabeth, *d* of Sir Walter Stansfield, CBE, MC, QPM; one *s* four *d*. *Educ:* Willesden Polytechnic, Sch. of Building and Architecture; Central School of Arts and Crafts (Theatre, TV Design); Hornsey School of Art (Interior and Furniture Design). Trainee designer, Hickman Ltd, 1956–58; National Service, RAPC, 1958–60; Charles Kenrick Associates, 1960–62; Conran Design Gp Ltd, 1962–69; C.D.G. (Design Consultants) Ltd, 1969–71; Founder, 1971 (resigned 1994), Fitch and Company, subseq. Fitch-RS and Fitch, a multi-discipline design practice; formerly Chm., Fitch (Design Consultants). Mem., Design Council, 1988–94. Dir Bd, City of London Fest. of Arts, 1996–. Dep. Chm., Court of Govs, London Inst., 1989–; Mem. Council, RCA, 1989–94; Trustee, V & A Museum, 1991–2001. CSD (formerly SIAD): Pres., 1988–90; Vice-Pres., 1982–86; Hon. Treas., 1984–87; Past Pres., Designers and Art Dirs Assoc., 1983. FRSA 1976. *Publications:* (with L. Knobel) Fitch on Retail Design, 1990; regular contributor to design publications. *Recreations:* cricket, tennis, opera, theatre, his family. *Address:* (office) Northumberland House, 155 Great Portland Street, W1W 6QP.

FITCHEW, Geoffrey Edward, CMG 1993; Chairman and First Commissioner, Building Societies Commission, and Chief Registrar of Friendly Societies, since 1994; *b* 22 Dec. 1939; *s* of Stanley Edward Fitchew and Elizabeth Scott; *m* 1966, Mary Theresa Spillane; two *s*. *Educ:* Uppingham School; Magdalen Coll., Oxford (MA); London Sch. of Economics (MScEcon). Asst Principal, HM Treasury, 1964; Private Sec. to Minister of State, 1968–69; Principal, 1969; Gwilym Gibbon Research Fellow, Nuffield Coll., Oxford, 1973–74; Asst Sec., Internat. Finance Div., HM Treasury, 1975–77; Counsellor (Economics and Finance), UK Perm. Rep. to EEC, 1977–80; Asst Sec., HM Treasury, 1980–83; Under Sec., HM Treasury, 1983–86; Dir-Gen. (for Banking, Financial Services and Company Law), Directorate Gen. XV, EC, Brussels, 1986–93; Dep. Sec, Cabinet Office, 1993–94. Vice-Chm., Internat. Commn on Holocaust Era Insurance Claims, 1999–. *Recreations:* tennis, golf. *Address:* Building Societies Commission, 25 North Colonnade, Canary Wharf, E14 5HS.

FITT, family name of **Baron Fitt**.

FITT, Baron *cr* 1983 (Life Peer), of Bell's Hill in the County of Down; **Gerard Fitt;** *b* 9 April 1926; *s* of George Patrick and Mary Ann Fitt; *m* 1947, Susan Gertrude Doherty (*d* 1996); five *d* (and one *d* decd). *Educ:* Christian Brothers' Sch., Belfast. Merchant Seaman, 1941–53; various positions, 1953–. Councillor, later Alderman, Belfast Corp., 1958–81; MP (Eire Lab), Parlt of N Ireland, Dock Div. of Belfast, 1962–72; Mem. (SDLP), N Belfast, NI Assembly, 1973–75, NI Constitutional Convention, 1975–76; Dep. Chief Exec., NI Exec., 1974; elected MP (Repub. Lab) Belfast West, 1966, a founder and Leader, Social Democratic and Labour Party, and MP (SDLP), 1970–79, when resigned Leadership; MP (Socialist), 1979–83. Contested (Socialist) Belfast West, 1983. *Recreation:* full-time politics. *Address:* House of Lords, SW1A 0PW.

FITTALL, Betty Daphne C.; *see* Callaway-Fittall.

FITTALL, William Robert; Associate Political Director, Northern Ireland Office, since 2000; *b* 26 July 1953; *s* of Arthur Fittall and Elsie Fittall; *m* 1978, Barbara Staples; two *s*. *Educ:* Dover Grammar Sch.; Christ Church, Oxford (MA). Entered Home Office, 1975; Private Sec. to Minister of State, 1979–80; Principal, 1980; Ecole Nationale d'Administration, Paris, 1980–81; Broadcasting Dept, 1981–85; Private Sec. to Home Sec., 1985–87; Asst Sec., 1987; Sec., Review of Parole System, 1987–88; Prison Service HQ, 1988–91; Principal Private Sec. to Sec. of State for NI, 1992–93; Police Dept, Home Office, 1993–95; Asst Under Sec. of State, 1995; Chief of Assessments Staff, Cabinet Office, 1995–97; Dir, Crime Reduction and Community Progs, Home Office, 1997–2000. Anglican Lay Reader, 1977–. *Recreations:* playing church organs, watching sport, reading. *Address:* c/o Northern Ireland Office, 11 Millbank, SW1P 4PN.

FITTER, Richard Sidney Richmond; *b* 1 March 1913; *o s* of Sidney and Dorothy Fitter; *m* 1938, Alice Mary (Maisie) Stewart (*d* 1996), *e d* of Dr R. S. Park, Huddersfield; two *s* one *d*. *Educ:* Eastbourne Coll.; LSE. BSc (Econ). Research staff: PEP, 1936–40; Mass-Observation, 1940–42; Operational Research Section, Coastal Command, 1942–45; Sec., Wild Life Cons. Special Cttee of Hobhouse Cttee on Nat. Parks, 1945–46; Asst Editor, The Countryman, 1946–59; Open Air Corresp., The Observer, 1958–66; Dir, Intelligence Unit, Council for Nature, 1959–63; Editor, Kingfisher, 1965–72. Vice-Pres., Fauna and Flora Preservation Soc., 1988– (Hon. Secretary, 1964–81; Chm., 1983–87); Member: Species Survival Commn (formerly Survival Service Commn), Internat. Union for Cons. of Nature, 1963– (Chm., Steering Cttee, 1975–88); Conservation Adv. Cttee, World Wildlife Fund Internat., 1977–79; Scientific Authority for Animals, DoE, 1965–81; Trustee, World Wildlife Fund, UK, 1977–83; Past Pres., Berks, Bucks and Oxfordshire Naturalists' Trust; Chm., Council for Nature, 1979; Vice Chm., Falkland Is Foundn, later Falklands Conservation, 1986–94 (Vice Pres., 1994–); Vice-Pres., Galapagos Conservation Trust, 1995–; President: London Natural Hist. Soc., 1998–2000; Wild Flower Soc., 2000–; Minister's Representative, Southern Council for Sport and Recreation, 1980–82; formerly Hon. Treasurer and Hon. Sec., British Trust for Ornithology; Chm., Gen. Purposes Cttee, Royal Soc. for Protection of Birds; Editor, The London Naturalist; and council or cttee mem. of numerous nat. history and conservation bodies. Scientific FZS. Christopher Cadbury Medal, RSNC, 1998; Peter Scott Medal, British Naturalists' Assoc., 1998. Officier, Order of the Golden Ark, The Netherlands, 1978; author and naturalist. *Publications:* London's Natural History, 1945; London's Birds, 1949; Pocket Guide to British Birds, 1952; Pocket Guide to Nests and Eggs, 1954; (with David McClintock) Pocket Guide to Wild Flowers, 1956; The Ark in Our Midst, 1959; Six Great Naturalists, 1959; Guide to Bird Watching, 1963; Wildlife in Britain, 1963; Britain's Wildlife: rarities and introductions, 1966; (with Maisie Fitter) Penguin Dictionary of Natural History, 1967; Vanishing Wild Animals of the World, 1968; Finding Wild Flowers, 1972; (with H. Heinzel and J. Parslow) Birds of Britain and Europe, with North Africa and the Middle East, 1972; (with A. Fitter and M. Blamey) Wild Flowers of Britain and Northern Europe, 1974; (with Sir Peter Scott) The Penitent Butchers, 1979; (with M. Blamey) Handguide to the Wild Flowers of Britain and Northern Europe, 1979; (with M. Blamey) Gem Guide to Wild Flowers, 1980; (with N. Arlott and A. Fitter) The Complete Guide to British Wildlife, 1981; (ed with Eric Robinson) John Clare's Birds, 1982; (with A. Fitter and J. Wilkinson) Collins Guide to the Countryside, 1984; (with A. Fitter and A. Farrer) Grasses, Sedges, Rushes and Ferns of Britain and Northern Europe, 1984; (ed) The Wildlife of the Thames Counties, 1985; Wildlife for Man, 1986; (with R. Manuel) Field Guide to the Freshwater Life of Britain and NW Europe, 1986; (with A. Fitter) Guide to the Countryside in Winter, 1988. *Recreations:* botanising, observing wild and human life, exploring new habitats, reading. *Address:* Danewood, 9 Coppice Avenue, Great Shelford, Cambridge CB2 5AQ. *T:* (01223) 843573. *Club:* Athenæum.

FITZALAN-HOWARD, family name of **Lady Herries of Terregles** and of **Duke of Norfolk**.

FITZALAN-HOWARD, Maj.-Gen. Lord Michael, GCVO 1981 (KCVO 1971; MVO 1952); CB 1968; CBE 1962; MC 1944; DL; Extra Equerry to the Queen, since 1999; Her Majesty's Marshal of the Diplomatic Corps, 1972–81; *b* 22 Oct. 1916; 2nd *s* of 3rd Baron Howard of Glossop, MBE, and Baroness Beaumont (11th in line), OBE. *b* of 17th Duke of Norfolk, *qv*; granted title and precedence of a Duke's son, 1975; *m* 1st, 1946, Jean (*d* 1947), *d* of Sir Hew Hamilton-Dalrymple, 9th Bt; one *d*; 2nd, 1950, Margaret (*d* 1995), *d* of Capt. W. P. Meade-Newman; four *s* one *d*; 3rd, 1997, Victoria Winifred Baring, *widow* of Sir Mark Baring, KCVO. *Educ:* Ampleforth Coll.; Trinity Coll., Cambridge. Joined Scots Guards, 1938. Served in: North West Europe, 1944–45; Palestine, 1945–46; Malaya, 1948–49; Egypt, 1952–53; Germany, 1956–57 and 1961–66; Commander Allied Command Europe Mobile Forces (Land), 1964–66; Chief of Staff, Southern Command, 1967–68; GOC London Dist, and Maj.-Gen. comdg The Household Division, 1968–71. Colonel: The Lancs Regt (Prince of Wales's Volunteers), 1966–70; The Queen's Lancashire Regiment, 1970–78; Colonel of The Life Guards, 1979–99; Gold Stick to the Queen, 1979–99; Joint Hon. Col, Cambridge Univ. OTC, 1968–71. Chm. Council, TAVR Assocs, 1973–81, Pres., 1981–84; Patron, Council, TA&VRA, 1984–; Hon. Recorder, British Commonwealth Ex-Service League, 1991–2001. DL Wilts, 1974. Freeman, City of London, 1985. *Address:* Fovant House, Fovant, Salisbury, Wilts SP3 5LA. *T:* (01722) 714617. *Clubs:* Buck's, Pratt's.

FITZGERALD, family name of **Duke of Leinster**.

FitzGERALD, Sir Adrian (James Andrew Denis), 6th Bt *cr* 1880, of Valencia, Co. Kerry; 24th Knight of Kerry; *b* 24 June 1940; *o s* of Major Sir George FitzGerald, 5th Bt, MC and of Angela Dora (*née* Mitchell); *S* father, 2001. *Educ:* Harrow. Hotelier, 1983–90. Mem. (C) Council, Royal Borough of Kensington and Chelsea, 1974– (Mayor, 1984–85; Chm., Educn and Libraries Cttee, 1995–98; Chm., Highways and Traffic Cttee, 1999–2001). Dep. Leader, London Fire and Civil Defence Authty, 1989–90. Chm., Anglo-Polish Soc., 1989–92; Vice-Chm., London Chapter, Irish Georgian Soc., 1990; Pres., Benevolent Soc. of St Patrick, 1997–. Kt of Honour and Devotion, SMO, Malta. *Publication:* (contrib.) Education, Church and State, ed M. R. O'Connell, 1992. *Heir:* *cousin* Peter Desmond FitzGerald [*b* 22 May 1910; *m* 1945, Elizabeth Norman; one *s* three *d* (and one *d* decd)]. *Clubs:* Pratt's; Kildare Street and University (Dublin).

FitzGERALD, Rev. (Sir) Daniel Patrick, SSC, (4th Bt *cr* 1903, of Geraldine Place, St Finn Barr, Co. Cork, but does not use the title); *b* 28 June 1916; *S* brother, Rev. (Sir) Edward Thomas FitzGerald (3rd Bt), 1988. Roman Catholic priest. *Heir:* *cousin* John Finnbarr FitzGerald [*b* 1918; *m* 1949, Margaret Hogg; one *s* one *d*].

FITZ-GERALD, Desmond John Villiers, (29th Knight of Glin); Irish Agent, Christie, Manson & Woods Ltd, since 1975; *b* 13 July 1937; *s* of Desmond Windham Otho Fitz-Gerald, 28th Knight of Glin (*d* 1949), and Veronica (who *m* 2nd, 1954, Ray Milner, CC (Canada), QC, Edmonton, Alta, and Qualicum Beach, Vancouver Island, BC), 2nd *d* of late Ernest Amherst Villiers, MP, and of Hon. Elaine Augusta Guest, *d* of 1st Baron Wimborne; *m* 1st, 1966, Louise Vava Lucia Henriette (marr. diss. 1970), *d* of the Marquis de la Falaise, Paris; 2nd, 1970, Olda Ann, *o d* of T. V. W. Willes, 39 Brompton Sq., SW3; three *d*. *Educ:* Stowe Sch.; University of British Columbia (BA 1959); Harvard Univ. (MA 1961). FSA 1970; MRIAI 1996. Asst Keeper, 1965–72, Dep. Keeper, 1972–75, Dept of Furniture and Woodwork, V&A. Pres., Irish Georgian Soc., 1991–; Chm., Irish Georgian Foundn, 1990– (Dir, 1974–); Vice-President: Stowe House Restoration Trust, 1999–; Bath Preservation Trust, 1999–; Director: Houses, Castles and Gardens of Ireland (formerly Historic Irish Tourist Houses Assoc., then Irish Heritage Properties), 1977–2000 (Chm., 1982–86); Castletown Foundn, 1979–; Irish Architectural Archive, 1987–; Great Gardens of Ireland Restoration Prog., 1998–2001. *Publications:* (ed) Georgian Furniture, 1969; (with Maurice Craig) Ireland Observed, a handbook to the buildings and antiquities, 1970; The Music Room from Norfolk House, 1972; (with Edward Malins) Lost Demesnes: Irish Landscape Gardening 1660–1845, 1976; (with Anne Crookshank) The Painters of Ireland, 1978; Irish Furniture, 1978; (jtly) Vanishing Country Houses of Ireland, 1988; (jtly) The Watercolours of Ireland, 1994; *catalogues*, all jointly: Irish Houses and Landscapes, 1963; Irish Architectural Drawings, 1965; Irish Portraits 1660–1860, 1969; Mildred Anne Butler, 1981; articles and reviews on architecture and the decorative arts in many Art periodicals. *Address:* Glin Castle, Glin, Co. Limerick, Ireland. *TA:* Knight Glin. *T:* (068) 34077 and 34173, *Fax:* (068) 34364; 52 Waterloo Road, Dublin 4, *T:* (1) 680765, *Fax:* (1) 680271. *Clubs:* Beefsteak, White's, Soc. of the Dilettanti; Kildare Street and University (Dublin).

FITZGERALD, Edward Hamilton; QC 1995; *b* 13 Aug. 1953; *s* of Carrol James Fitzgerald and Cornelia (*née* Claiborne); *m* 1988, Rebecca Fraser; three *d*. *Educ:* Downside; Corpus Christi Coll., Oxford (BA 1st cl. Hons Lit. Hum. 1975); MPhil Cantab 1979. Called to the Bar, Inner Temple, 1978. Times Justice Award, 1998. *Recreations:* reading history and novels, visiting the seaside, travel. *Address:* (chambers) 11 Doughty Street, WC1N 2DG. *T:* (020) 7404 1313.

FITZGERALD, Frank, CBE 1989; PhD; FREng; consultant, since 1992; Director, Sheffield Forgemasters Ltd, 1993–98; *b* 11 Nov. 1929; *s* of George Arthur Fitzgerald and Sarah Ann (*née* Brook); *m* 1956, Dorothy Eileen Unwin; two *s* one *d*. *Educ:* Barnsley Holgate Grammar Sch.; Univ. of Sheffield (BScTech; PhD). FInstE 1965, FIChemE 1984; FREng (FEng 1977); FIM 2000. Ministry of Supply, RAE, Westcott, Bucks, 1955; United Steel Cos, Swinden Laboratories, Rotherham, 1960–68; British Steel plc (formerly British Steel Corporation), 1968–92: Process Res. Manager, Special Steels Div., 1970; Head Corporate Advanced Process Laboratory, 1972; Director, R&D, 1977; Man. Dir, Technical, 1981–92; Dir, 1986–92; Chairman: British Steel Corp. (Overseas Services), subseq. British Steel Consultants, 1981–89; British Steel Stainless, 1989–91. Hon. DEng Sheffield, 1993. Hadfield Medal, Iron and Steel Inst., for work on application of combustion and heat transfer science to industrial furnaces, 1972; Melchett Medal, Inst. of Energy, 1988; Bessemer Gold Medal, Inst. of Metals, 1991; Esso Energy Award, Royal Soc., 1991. *Publications:* papers in learned jls on heat and mass transfer and metallurgical processes. *Recreation:* rock climbing and mountaineering. *Clubs:* Alpine; Climbers'.

FITZGERALD, Garret, PhD; Barrister-at-Law; Member of the Dáil (TD) (FG) for Dublin South East, 1969–92; Taoiseach (Prime Minister of Ireland), June 1981–March 1982 and 1982–87; *b* Dublin, 9 Feb. 1926; *s* of late Desmond FitzGerald (Minister for External Affairs, Irish Free State, 1922–27, and Minister for Defence, 1927–32) and Mabel FitzGerald (*née* McConnell); *m* 1947, Joan (*d* 1999), *d* of late Charles O'Farrell; two *s* one *d*. *Educ:* St Brigid's Sch., Bray; Coláiste na Rinne, Waterford; Belvedere Coll., University Coll., and King's Inns (Hon. Bencher, 1993), Dublin. Called to the Bar, 1947. Aer Lingus (Irish Air Lines), 1947–58; Rockefeller Research Asst, Trinity Coll., Dublin, 1958–59; College Lectr, Dept of Political Economy, University Coll., Dublin, 1959–87. Member: Seanad Eireann (Irish Senate), 1965–69; Dáil Cttee on Public Accounts, 1969–73; Minister for Foreign Affairs, Ireland, 1973–77; Leader and President, Fine Gael Party,

1977–87; Leader of the Opposition, 1977–June 1981, and March-Dec. 1982. President: Council of Ministers, EEC, Jan.–June 1975; European Council, July–Dec. 1984; Irish Council of Eur. Movement, 1977–81 and March–Dec. 1982; Mem., Internat. Exec. Cttee of Eur. Movement, 1972–73; Vice-Pres., Eur. People's Party, 1979–87; Member: Trilateral Commission, 1977–81, 1987–; Adv. Bd, Centre for Economic Policy Res., 1992–97; Internat. Adv. Bd, RILA Inc., 1999–. Mem., Oireachtas Library Cttee, 1965–69; Governor, Atlantic Inst. of Internat. Relations, Paris, 1972–73; Mem. Bd, Internat. Peace Acad., NY, 1990–; Chm., Council of Patrons, Saferworld, 1992–; Member: Senate of National Univ. of Ireland, 1973– (Chancellor, 1997–); Authy, Radio Telefis Eireann, 1995–2000. Formerly: Irish Correspondent of BBC, Financial Times, Economist and other overseas papers; Economic Correspondent, Irish Times; also Managing Dir, Economist Intelligence Unit of Ireland; Economic Consultant to Fedn of Irish Industries and Construction Industry Fedn, and Rep. Body for Guards. Past Member: Exec. Cttee and Council, Inst. of Public Admin; Council, Statistical and Social Inquiry, Soc. of Ireland; Senate Electoral Law Commn; Workmen's Compensation Commn; Transport Advisory Cttee for Second Programme; Cttee on Industrial Organisation; Gen. Purposes Cttee of Nat. Industrial Economic Council. Director: Trade Develt Inst., Dublin, 1987–; Point Holdings Ltd, 1996–; Election.com, 1999–. Weekly columnist, Irish Times, 1991–. Lectures: Radcliffe, Warwick Univ., 1980; Richard Dimbleby, BBC, 1982; Heinz, Pittsburgh Univ., 1980; Dunbar, Tulane Univ., 1987; Bass, Univ. of Ulster, 1988; Gaitskell, Nottingham Univ., 1988; Centenary Reckitt, London, 1988; Boston Coll., 1988, 1989; Schumann, UC, Cork, 1989; Morrell, Univ. of York, 1989; Mackintosh, Edinburgh Univ., 1990; Williamson, Univ. of Stirling, 1990; White, QUB, 1990; 2500 Anniv. of Democracy, Manchester Univ., 1993; Lloyd George, Criccieth, 1996. Hon. LLD: New York, 1974; St Louis, 1974; St Mary's, Halifax, NS, 1985; Keele, 1986; Boston Coll., 1987; Westfield Coll., Mass, 1990; Hon. DCL: Oxon, 1987; NUI, 1991; Dublin, 1998; QUB, 2000. Grand Cordon, Order of Al-Kaubar Al-Undari (Jordan), 1975; Grand Officier, Ordre de la République (Tunisia), 1976; Grand Cross (1st Cl.), Order of Merit (FRG), 1986; Order of Christ (Portugal), 1986; Grand Cordon, Order of Rising Sun (Japan), 1989; Comdr, Légion d'Honneur (France), 1995. *Publications:* State-sponsored Bodies, 1959; Planning in Ireland, 1968; Towards a New Ireland, 1972; Unequal Partners (UNCTAD), 1979; Estimates for Baronies of Minimum Level of Irish Speaking Amongst Successive Decennial Cohorts 1771–1781 to 1861–1871, 1984; All in a Life: an autobiography, 1991. *Address:* 37 Annavilla, Dublin 6, Ireland. *T:* 4962600, *Fax:* (1) 4962126; *e-mail:* garretfg@iol.ie. *Clubs:* Reform; Royal Irish Yacht (Dun Laoghaire).

FITZGERALD, Hon. Gerald Edward, AC 1991; mediator, dispute resolution consultant; Chairman, Law and Justice Foundation, since 2001; *b* Brisbane, 26 Nov. 1941; *m* 1968, Catherine Glynn-Connolly; one *s* two *d*. *Educ:* Univ. of Queensland (LLB). Admitted Queensland Bar, 1964; QC Queensland 1975 and subseq. QC NSW and Victoria; Judge of Federal Court of Australia, 1981–84; Judge of Supreme Court of ACT, 1981–84; Pres., Court of Appeal, Supreme Court of Qld, 1991–98; Judge of Ct of Appeal, Supreme Ct of NSW, 1998–2001. Presidential Mem., Administrative Appeals Tribunal, 1981–84; Mem., Australian Law Reform Commn, 1981–84; Chairman, Commission of Inquiry: into possible illegal activities and associated police misconduct, Qld, 1987–89; into the Conservation, Management and Use of Fraser Is. and the Gt Sandy Reg., Qld, 1990–91; Chm., Litigation Reform Commn, Qld, 1991–92. Chm., Australian Heritage Commn, 1990–91. Chairman: Nat. Inst. for Law, Ethics and Public Affairs, 1992–95; Key Inst. for Ethics, Law, Justice and Governance, 1999–; Vis. Scholar, New York Univ. Sch. of Law, 1997; Professorial Fellow, Univ. of Melbourne Law Sch., 1999–. Chancellor, Sunshine Coast UC, 1994–98. Dep. Chm., Gov. Bd, Mater Health Services, 1995–98. DUniv: Qld Univ. of Technol., 1995; Sunshine Coast, 1999. *Recreations:* tennis, reading, music. *Address:* Level 7, Wentworth Chambers, 180 Phillip Street, Sydney, NSW 2000, Australia. *T:* (2) 9361 5003, *Fax:* (2) 9357 1637; Level II, Inns of Court, 107 North Quay, Brisbane, Qld 4000, Australia. *T:* (7) 3371 7509, *Fax:* (7) 3870 3726; *e-mail:* tonyfitzgerald@pacific.net.au. *Club:* Brisbane (Brisbane).

FITZGERALD, Kaarene Noelle, AC 1999; Executive Director, Sudden Infant Death Research Foundation, Australia, since 1977; *b* 12 Dec.; *d* of Leslie George Stout and Muriel Joyce Stout (*née* James); *m* (marr. diss. 1992); two *s* two *d* (and one *s* decd). *Educ:* Mt Maunganui Coll., NZ; PioPio High Sch., NZ. Director: SIDSaustralia, 1986–; SIDS Internat., 1987–94 and 1998–; Chm./Founder, SIDS Global Strategy Task Force, 1992–. Trustee, Monash Inst. Reproduction and Develt, 1993–. Mem. Bd and Newsletter Ed., Order of Australia Cttee (Vic Br.), 1999–. Speaker in many countries on infant mortality, mktg and mgt. *Publications:* contrib. to jls on infant mortality, mktg and mgt. *Recreations:* Formula One motor racing, horse racing, polo. *Address:* 26 Washington Avenue, East Malvern, Vic 3145, Australia; SIDS, 1227 Malvern Road, Malvern, Vic 3144, Australia. *T:* (3) 98229611; *e-mail:* kaarene@sidsaustralia.org.au. *Clubs:* Victoria Racing, Victoria Amateur Turf, Victoria Polo (Mem. Bd, 1997–), Royal Automobile (Melbourne).

FITZGERALD, Dr Michael; Senior Fellow, Strategic Initiatives, research and consultancy group, Washington, since 1999; Chief Executive, Learning Review.com; Director, mike fitzgerald associates Ltd; *b* 4 May 1951; *s* of Richard Michael Fitzgerald and Janet Kilpatrick Costine Fitzgerald; two *s*. *Educ:* St Mary's Coll., Liverpool; Selwyn Coll., Cambridge (MA); Univ. of Leicester (PhD). Univ. of Leicester, 1973–75; taught social sciences, and criminology, Open Univ., 1975–87; Coventry Polytechnic, 1987–91; Vice-Chancellor, Thames Valley Univ., 1991–98. Vice-Chair, CVCP, 1997–98. Trustee, Paul Hamlyn Foundn, 1996–. FRSA. *Publications:* 8 books on criminology. *Recreations:* rock music, football, cricket, crime fiction, channel surfing. *T:* (020) 8994 4564; *e-mail:* mike-fitzgerald@email.msn.com. *Clubs:* Reform, Chelsea Arts.

FitzGERALD, Michael Frederick Clive; QC 1980; *b* 9 June 1936; *s* of Sir William James FitzGerald, MC, QC, and Mrs E. J. Critchley; *m* 1966, Virginia Grace Cave (marr. diss. 1992); one *s* three *d*. *Educ:* Downside; Christ's Coll., Cambridge, 1956–59 (MA). 2nd Lieut 9th Queen's Royal Lancers, 1954–56. Called to the Bar, Middle Temple, 1961, Bencher, 1987. Leader, Parly Bar, 1997–. *Recreations:* opera, field sports. *Address:* 49 Cheval Place, SW7 1EW. *Club:* Boodle's.

FitzGERALD, Niall William Arthur; Chairman, Unilever PLC, since 1996 (Vice-Chairman, 1994–96); *b* 13 Sept. 1945; *s* of William FitzGerald and Doreen Chambers; *m* 1970, Monica Cusack; two *s* one *d*. *Educ:* St Munchins Coll., Limerick; University College Dublin (MComm). FCT 1986. Unilever, 1968–: North America, 1978–80; Chief Exec. Officer, Foods, S Africa, 1981–85; Group Treasurer, 1985–86; Financial Dir, 1987–89; Exec. Dir, 1987–96; Director: Unilever Foods, 1990–91; Unilever Detergents, 1992–96; Merck Inc.; Telefonaktiebolaget LM Ericsson. Chm., CBI Europe Cttee, 1995–2001; Member: EU-China Business Council, 1997; US Business Council, 1998; Trilateral Commn, 1999; Council: Co-operation Ireland; World Econ. Forum, 1999–; Mem., President Mbeki's Internat. Adv. Council. Gov., NIESR, 1997–. Trustee, Leverhulme Trust, 1996–. FRSA. *Recreation:* observing humanity. *Address:* Unilever, Blackfriars, EC4P 4BQ. *T:* (020) 7822 5252. *Clubs:* Royal Automobile; Wisley Golf.

FITZGERALD, Prof. Patrick John; Adjunct Professor of Law, Carleton University, Ottawa, since 1996 (Professor of Law, 1971–96); *b* 30 Sept. 1928; *s* of Dr Thomas Walter and Norah Josephine Fitzgerald; *m* 1959, Brigid Aileen Judge; two *s* one *d*. *Educ:* Queen Mary's Grammar Sch., Walsall; University Coll., Oxford. Called to the Bar, Lincoln's Inn, 1951; Ontario Bar, 1984. Fellow, Trinity Coll., Oxford, 1956–60. Professor of Law: Leeds Univ., 1960–66; Univ. of Kent at Canterbury, 1966–71. Visiting Prof., University of Louisville, 1962–63. Consultant, Law Reform Commn of Canada, 1973–92. *Publications:* Criminal Law and Punishment, 1962; Salmond on Jurisprudence (12th edn), 1966; This Law of Ours, 1977; Looking at Law, 1979, 4th edn 1994; (ed) Crime, Justice and Codification, 1986. *Recreations:* music, golf, bridge. *Address:* 246–3310 Southgate Road, Ottawa, ON K1V 8X4, Canada.

FitzGERALD, Presiley Lamorna, (Mrs R. K. FitzGerald); *see* Baxendale, P. L.

FitzGERALD, Rowanne; *see* Pasco, R.

FitzGERALD, Susanna Patricia; QC 1999; *d* of Frederick Patrick FitzGerald, FRCSI, PPICS and Zina Eveline FitzGerald (*née* Moncrieff), FRCP; *m* 1983, Wendell, (Nick), Clough; two *s*. *Educ:* Benenden Sch.; Bristol Univ. (LLB Hons). Called to the Bar, Inner Temple, 1973; in practice at the Bar, 1973–; specialises in liquor, gaming, lotteries, betting and public entertainment licensing law. Dir, Business in Sport and Leisure. Trustee, Gamcare. *Publication:* (contributing ed.) Law of Betting, Gaming and Lotteries, 2nd edn; (contrib.) Gambling and Public Policy, 1991. *Recreations:* renovating old houses, ski-ing. *Address:* 1 Essex Court, Temple, EC4Y 9AR. *T:* (020) 7583 2000.

FitzGERALD, Sylvia Mary Denise, FLS; Head of Library and Archives (formerly Chief Librarian and Archivist), Royal Botanic Gardens, Kew, 1979–99; *b* 7 May 1939; *d* of Audoen Aengus FitzGerald and Doris Winifred (*née* Dickinson). *Educ:* Our Lady of Sion Sch., Worthing; Open Univ. (BA Hons 1977). ALA 1962. Assistant: Science Mus. Liby, 1956–57; Brit. Mus. (Natural Hist.) Zool. Liby, 1957–63; Assistant Librarian: Patent Office Liby, 1963–65; MAFF, 1965–67; Librarian-in-charge: MAFF Food & Nutrition Liby, 1967–72; MAFF Tolworth Liby for State Vet. Service and Vertebrate Pest Control, 1972–78. FLS 1992. *Publications:* contrib. State Librarian, Aslib Prog., Archives, etc. *Recreations:* friends, music. *Address:* 139 London Road, Ewell, Epsom, Surrey KT17 2BT.

FITZGERALD-LOMBARD, Rt Rev. Charles, OSB, **(James Michael Hubert Fitzgerald-Lombard)**; Abbot of Downside, 1990–98; *b* 29 Jan. 1941; *s* of late Col James C. R. Fitzgerald-Lombard and of Winifred (*née* Woulfe Flanagan). *Educ:* Downside; Collegio Sant Anselmo, Rome; King's Coll., London (MPhil). Monk of Downside Abbey, 1962–; ordained priest, 1968; Teacher and Tutor, Downside Sch., 1968–75; Bursar and Sec. to the Trustees, 1975–90. Dep. Chm., Union of Monastic Superiors, 1998. Titular Abbot of Glastonbury, 1999–. *Publications:* Prayers and Meditations, 1967, 3rd edn 1974; A Guide to the Church of St Gregory the Great, Downside Abbey, 1981, 3rd edn 1993; English and Welsh Priests 1801–1914, 1993. *Recreations:* electrical and telecommunications engineering, historical research, swimming. *Address:* Downside Abbey, Stratton-on-the-Fosse, Bath BA3 4RH.

FitzGIBBON, Louis Theobald Dillon; Comte Dillon in France; political writer; *b* 6 Jan. 1925; *s* of Comdr Francis Lee-Dillon FitzGibbon, RN, and Kathleen Clare (*née* Atchison), *widow* of Hon. Harry Lee-Dillon; *m* 1st, 1950, Josephine Miriam Maud (*née* Webb) (marr. diss.); 2nd, 1962, Madeleine Sally (*née* Hayward Surry) (*d* 1980); one *s* two *d*; 3rd, 1980, Joan Elizabeth Jevons (marr. diss. 1994). *Educ:* St Augustine's Abbey Sch.; Royal Naval Coll., Dartmouth. Royal Navy, 1942–54 (incl. War of 1939–45 and service in ex-German U-1171); Polish interpreter's course, 1950–52. Dir, De Leon Properties Ltd, 1954–72. Solicitor's articled clerk, 1960–63; Anglo-Polish Conf., Warsaw, 1963. Personal Asst to the then Rt Hon. Duncan Sandys, MP (later Lord Duncan-Sandys), 1967–68; Gen. Sec., British Council for Aid to Refugees, 1968–72; United Nations (UNHCR) Mission to South Sudan, 1972–73; Dir of a medical charity, 1974–76; Exec. Officer, Nat. Assoc. for Freedom, 1977–78; Gen. Sec. of a trade assoc., 1978–80; Hon. Sec., British Horn of Africa Council, 1984–92. Mem., RIIA, 1982, 1988. Won first Airey Neave Meml Scholarship (proj. on Somalia), 1981. Hon. Secretary: Jt Cttee for Preservation of Historic Portsmouth, 1956–61; Katyn Memorial Fund, 1971–77; Area Pres., St John Amb. Brigade (Hants East), 1974–76. SMHO Malta, 1985 (Kt of Honour and Devotion and Officer of Merit). Polish Gold Cross of Merit, 1969; Order of Polonia Restituta (Polish Govt in Exile) (Officer, 1971; Comdr, 1972; Kt Comdr, 1976); Officer, Order of Merit (FRG), 1990; Katyn Meml Medal Bronze, USA, 1977; Laureate van de Arbeid, Netherlands, 1982. *Publications:* Katyn—A Crime without Parallel, 1971; The Katyn Cover-up, 1972; Unpitied and Unknown, 1975; Katyn—Triumph of Evil (Ireland), 1975; The Katyn Memorial, 1976; Katyn Massacre (paper) 1977, 3rd edn 1989; Katyn (USA), 1979; Katyn (in German), 1979; The Betrayal of the Somalis, 1982 (commnd by Japan-Somalia Friendship Assoc. in Japanese, 1989); Straits and Strategic Waterways in the Red Sea, 1984; Ethiopia Hijacks the Hijack, 1985; The Evaded Duty, 1985. *Recreations:* politics, writing, reading, history, languages. *Address:* Flat 2, 8 Portland Place, Brighton BN2 1DG. *T:* (01273) 685661.

FitzHARRIS, Viscount; James Hugh Carleton Harris; *b* 29 April 1970; *s* and *heir* of Earl of Malmesbury, *qv*; *m* 1997, Jemima, *e d* of Captain M. Fulford-Dobson, RN; one *s* one *d*. *Heir: s* Hon. James Michael Oswald Harris, *b* 26 April 1999.

FITZHARRIS, Ven. Robert Aidan; Louisa Archdeacon of Doncaster, since 2001; *b* 19 Aug. 1946; *s* of John Joseph and Margaret Louis Fitzharris; *m* 1971, Lesley Margaret Mary Rhind; three *d*. *Educ:* St Anselm's Coll., Birkenhead; Sheffield Univ. (BDS 1971) Lincoln Theol Coll. (Gen. Ministerial Exam. 1989). General dental practice, 1971–87; part-time Clinical Asst to Prof. of Child Dental Health, Charles Clifford Dental Hosp., Sheffield, 1978–85. Ordained deacon, 1989, priest, 1990; Asst Curate, Dinnington, 1989–92; Vicar of Bentley, 1992–2001; Substitute Chaplain, HMP Moorland, 1992–2001; Area Dean, Adwick-le-Street, 1995–2001. Hon. Associate Chaplain, Doncaster Royal Infirmary and Mexbrough Montague Hosp. Trust, 1995–2001; Hon. Canon, Sheffield Cathedral, 1998. Chm., Sheffield Diocesan Strategy Gp, 1999–2001. *Recreations:* cooking, sharing red wine and Provençal sun with my wife. *Address:* Fairview House, 14 Armthorpe Lane, Doncaster DN2 5LZ. *T:* (01302) 325787.

FITZHERBERT, family name of **Baron Stafford**.

FitzHERBERT, Giles Eden, CMG 1985; HM Diplomatic Service, retired; *b* Dublin, 8 March 1935; *e s* of late Captain H. C. FitzHerbert, Irish Guards, and Sheelah, *d* of J. X. Murphy; *m* 1st, 1962, Margaret Waugh (*d* 1986); two *s* three *d*; 2nd, 1988, Alexandra Eyre; three *s* one *d*. *Educ:* Ampleforth Coll.; Christ Church Oxford; Harvard Business Sch. 2nd Lieut, 8th King's Royal Irish Hussars, 1957–58. Vickers da Costa & Co., 1962–66. First Secretary: Foreign Office, 1966; Rome, 1968–71; FCO, 1972–75; Counsellor: Kuwait, 1975–77; Nicosia, 1977–78; Head of Eur. Community Dept (Ext.), FCO, 1978–82; on sabbatical leave, LSE, 1982; Inspector, FCO, 1983; Minister, Rome, 1983–87; Ambassador to Venezuela and concurrently (non-resident) to the Dominican Republic, 1988–93. Contested (L) Fermanagh and South Tyrone, Gen. Elect., 1964. *Address:*

Woodbrook House, Killann, Co. Wexford, Ireland. *Clubs:* Beefsteak; Kildare Street and University (Dublin).

FitzHERBERT, Sir Richard (Ranulph), 9th Bt *cr* 1784, of Tissington, Derbyshire; *b* 2 Nov. 1963; *s* of Rev. David Henry FitzHerbert, MC (*d* 1976) and of Charmian Hyacinthe, *yr d* of late Samuel Ranulph Allsopp, CBE; *S* uncle, 1989; *m* 1993, Caroline Louise, *d* of Major and Mrs Patrick Shuter; one *s* one *d*. *Educ:* Eton College. President: Derbys Community Foundn, 1995–; Derbys Rural Community Council, 1996–; Chm., E Midlands HHA, 1999–; Mem. Exec. Cttee, Derbys Br., CLA (Chm., 1998). *Recreations:* cricket, shooting, restoring family estate. *Heir: s* Frederick David FitzHerbert, *b* 23 March 1995. *Address:* Tissington Hall, Ashbourne, Derbys DE6 1RA; *e-mail:* tisshall@dircon.co.uk. *Clubs:* White's, MCC; Stansted Hall Cricket, Parwich Royal British Legion Cricket.

FitzHUGH, Edmund Francis Lloyd, OBE 1995; JP; DL; farmer, landowner; Deputy Chairman, Local Government Boundary Commission for Wales, since 1995; Chairman, North East Wales NHS Trust, since 1999; *b* 2 Feb. 1951; *s* of late Godfrey Edmund FitzHugh and Burness Grace FitzHugh (*née* Clemson); *m* 1975, Pauline Davison; two *s*. *Educ:* Eton; Shuttleworth Agricl Coll. Chm., Bd of Mgt, Royal Welsh Agricl Soc., 1991–98. JP Wrexham 1990; DL Clwyd 1996. *Recreations:* church music, wining and dining. *Address:* Plas Power, Ruthin Road, Wrexham LL11 3BS. *T:* (01978) 263522.

FITZMAURICE; *see* Petty-Fitzmaurice, family name of Marquess of Lansdowne.

FITZPATRICK, Brian; Member (Lab) Strathkelvin and Bearsden, Scottish Parliament, since June 2001; *b* 9 June 1961; *s* of Patrick Fitzpatrick and Kathleen (*née* Strong); *m* 1986, Marie Macdonald; one *s* two *d*. *Educ:* Univ. of Glasgow (LLB Juris 1984). Called to Scottish Bar, 1993; Solicitor, Glasgow, Edinburgh and London, 1984–92; Mem., Faculty of Advocates, 1993–. Hd of Policy, First Minister's Policy Unit, Scottish Parlt, 1999–2000. *Recreations:* swimming, cinema, reading, poetry, travel, wine. *Address:* (constituency office) 110A Maxwell Avenue, Bearsden, Glasgow G61 1HU. *T:* (0141) 942 9662.

FITZPATRICK, Gen. Sir (Geoffrey Richard) Desmond, GCB 1971 (KCB 1965; CB 1961); GCVO 1997; DSO 1945; MBE 1943; MC 1939; *b* 14 Dec. 1912; *o s* of late Brig.-Gen. Sir Richard Fitzpatrick, CBE, DSO, and Lady (G. E.) Fitzpatrick; *m* 1st, 1944, Mary Sara (*d* 1996), *o d* of Sir Charles Campbell, 12th Bt; one *s* one *d*; 2nd, 1998, Lettice, *o d* of late Capt. Edward Stafford-King-Harman and *widow* of Major George Errington. *Educ:* Eton; RMC Sandhurst. Commissioned The Royal Dragoons, 1932. Served in Palestine, 1938–39 (MC); War of 1939–45 (despatches, MBE, DSO); in Middle East, Italy, NW Europe. Bt. Lieut-Col 1951; Col 1953; ADC to the Queen, 1959; Maj.-Gen. 1959; Asst Chief of Defence Staff, Ministry of Defence, 1959–61; Dir Mil. Ops, War Office, 1962–64; Chief of Staff, BAOR, 1964–65; Lt-Gen. 1965; GOC-in-C, N Ire., 1965–66; Vice-Chief of Gen. Staff, 1966–68; Gen. 1968; C-in-C, BAOR, and Commander N Army Gp 1968–70; Dep. Supreme Allied Comdr, Europe, 1970–73; ADC (General) to the Queen, 1970–73. Lieutenant-Governor and C-in-C, Jersey, 1974–79. Col, The Royal Dragoons, 1964–69; Dep. Col, 1969–74, Col, 1979–98, The Blues and Royals, and Gold Stick to the Queen, 1979–98; Col Comdt, RAC, 1971–74. *Address:* Belmont, Otley, Suffolk IP6 9PF. *Clubs:* Cavalry and Guards; Royal Yacht Squadron.

FITZPATRICK, James; MP (Lab) Poplar and Canning Town, since 1997; an Assistant Government Whip, since 2001; *b* 4 April 1952; *s* of James Fitzpatrick and Jean Fitzpatrick (*née* Stones). *Educ:* Holyrood Sch., Glasgow. Trainee, Tytrak Ltd, Glasgow, 1970–73; driver, Mintex Ltd, 1973–74; Firefighter, London Fire Brigade, 1974–97. PPS to Sec. of State for Health, 1999–2001. Mem., NEC, Fire Bdes Union, 1988–97. Non-exec. Dir, Fire Protecti. on Assoc. Mem. Exec., Gtr London Lab. Party, 1988–2000 (Chm., 1991–2000). Fire Bde Long Service and Good Conduct Medal, 1994. *Recreations:* golf, cycling, reading, football (West Ham Utd), television and films. *Address:* House of Commons, SW1A 0AA. *T:* (020) 7219 5085.

FITZPATRICK, James Bernard, CBE 1983; JP; DL; Immigration Appeal Adjudicator, 1990–April 2002; Member, Criminal Injuries Compensation Appeals Panel, since 2000; *b* 21 April 1930; *s* of late B. A. Fitzpatrick and Mrs J. E. Fitzpatrick; *m* 1965, Rosemary, *d* of late Captain E. B. Clark, RD and bar, RNR and late Mrs K. E. Clark, Claughton; one *s* one *d*. *Educ:* Bootle Grammar Sch.; London Univ. (LLB). Admitted Solicitor, 1962; FCIT 1973; CIMgt. Joined Mersey Docks and Harbour Bd, 1951: various management posts from 1965; Personnel and Industrial Relns Dir, 1971, on formation of Mersey Docks and Harbour Co.; Jt Man. Dir, 1974; Dep. Chief Exec., 1975; Man. Dir and Chief Exec., 1977; Chm., 1984–87. Director: Plan Invest Group plc, 1984–91; Teesside Hldgs, 1992–95; Mem., 1979–89, Chm., 1988–89, Merseyside Enterprise Forum. Chairman: Nat. Assoc. of Port Employers, 1979–82 (Vice-Chm., 1973–79); Employers' Assoc. of Port of Liverpool, 1974–83; Member: Liverpool Dock Labour Bd, 1974–76 (Chm., 1976); Exec. Council, British Ports Assoc., 1976–87 (Dep. Chm., 1985–87); Nat. Dock Labour Bd, 1978–84. Chairman: Liverpool HA, 1986–91; Royal Liverpool Univ. Hosp. NHS Trust, 1991–95; Royal Liverpool and Broadgreen Univ. Hosps NHS Trust, 1995–96. Chm., The Appeals Service, 1992–2000. Mem. Council, Industrial Soc., 1989–92. Liverpool University: Mem. Council, 1988–89, 1991–98; Chm., Inst. of Irish Studies, 1990–98. FRSA. JP Liverpool 1977. DL Merseyside, 1985. Hon. Fellow, Liverpool John Moores Univ. (formerly Liverpool Polytechnic), 1988. *Recreations:* fell walking, gardening, music, reading. *Address:* Waen Ffynnon, Pentre Coch, Ruthin, Denbighshire LL15 2YF. *T:* (01824) 703425. *Clubs:* Oriental, Pilgrims.

FITZPATRICK, Air Marshal Sir John (Bernard), KBE 1984; CB 1982; Royal Air Force, retired; *b* 15 Dec. 1929; *s* of Joseph Fitzpatrick and Bridget Fitzpatrick; *m* 1954, Gwendoline Mary Abbott; two *s* one *d*. *Educ:* RAF Apprentice Sch., Halton; RAF Coll. Cranwell. Officer Commanding: No 81 Sqdn, 1966–68; No 35 Sqdn, 1971–72; Gp Captain Plans to AOC No 18 Gp, 1973; OC, RAF Scampton, 1974–75; RCDS, 1976; Dir of Ops (Strike), RAF, 1977–79; SASO, HQ Strike Command, 1980–82; Dir Gen. of Organisation, RAF, 1982–83; AOC No 18 Gp, RAF, and Comdr Maritime Air Eastern Atlantic and Channel, 1983–86. Ind. Panel Inspector, Depts of the Envmt and Transport, 1986–99. *Recreations:* walking, reading, diy. *Club:* Royal Air Force.

FITZPATRICK, John Ronald; Solicitor and Parliamentary Officer, Greater London Council, 1977–85, Consultant, 1985–86; *b* 22 Sept. 1923; *s* of Henry Fitzpatrick and Mary Lister; *m* 1952, Beryl Mary Newton; two *s* one *d*. *Educ:* St Bede's Coll., Manchester; Univ. of Manchester (LLB). Admitted Solicitor, 1947; LMRTPI 1951. Asst Solicitor: Burnley, 1947; Stockport, 1948–51; Asst/Principal Asst Solicitor, Mddx CC, 1951–65; Asst Clerk/Asst Dir-Gen., GLC, 1965–69; Asst Dir, 1969–72, Dir, 1972–77, Planning and Transportation, GLC. *Recreations:* golf, bridge. *Address:* Courtlands, 2 Langley Grove, New Malden, Surrey KT3 3AL. *T:* (020) 8942 8652.

FITZPATRICK, Prof. Raymond Michael, PhD; Professor of Public Health and Primary Care, University of Oxford, since 1996; Fellow, Nuffield College, Oxford, since 1986; *b* 8 Oct. 1950; *s* of James Fitzpatrick and Maureen Fitzpatrick; *m* 1979, Mary Boulton. *Educ:* UC, Oxford (BA); Bedford Coll., London Univ. (MSc; PhD 1986). Lecturer: Bedford Coll., London Univ., 1978–86; Oxford Univ., 1986–. Mem., MRC, 1998– (Chm., Health Services and Public Health Res. Bd, 1998–). *Publications:* (jtly) The Experience of Illness, 1984; (ed with G. Albrecht) Quality of Life in Health Care, 1994; (jtly) Understanding Rheumatoid Arthritis, 1995; (ed jtly) Health Services Research Methods, 1998. *Recreations:* music, theatre. *Address:* Nuffield College, Oxford OX1 1NF. *T:* (01865) 278500.

FitzROY, family name of **Duke of Grafton** and of **Baron Southampton**.

FitzROY NEWDEGATE, family name of **Viscount Daventry**.

FITZSIMONS, Anthony; *see* Fitzsimons, P. A.

FITZSIMONS, Prof. James Thomas, FRS 1988; Professor of Medical Physiology, University of Cambridge, 1990–95, now Emeritus Professor; Fellow of Gonville and Caius College, Cambridge, since 1961 (President, since 1997); *b* 8 July 1928; *s* of Robert Allen Fitzsimons, FRCS and Dr Mary Patricia (*née* McKelvey); *m* 1961, Aude Irène Jeanne, *d* of Gén. Jean Etienne Valluy, DSO and Marie (*née* Bourdillon); two *s* one *d*. *Educ:* St Edmund's Coll., Ware; Gonville and Caius Coll., Cambridge (1st cl. Pts I and II, Nat. Sci. Tripos; BA 1949; BChir 1953; MB 1954; MA 1954; PhD 1960; MD 1967, Sir Lionel Whitby Medal; ScD 1979); Charing Cross Hosp. House appts, Leicester Gen. and Charing Cross Hosps, 1954–55; RAF, Inst. of Aviation Medicine, 1955–57 (Flight Lieut); Cambridge University: MRC Scholar, Physiol. Lab., 1957–59; Univ. Demonstrator in Physiol., 1959–64, Lectr, 1964–76, Reader, 1976–90; Gonville and Caius College: Tutor, 1964–72; Coll. Lectr in Physiol, 1964–93; Dir of Studies in Medicine, 1978–93. Visiting Professor: CNRS Lab. des Régulations Alimentaires, Coll. de France, 1967; Inst. of Neurol Scis, Univ. of Pennsylvania, 1968, 1972; CNRS Lab. de Neurobiol., Coll. de France, 1975; Lectures: Stevenson Meml, Univ. of Western Ontario, 1979; Halliburton, KCL, 1982. Royal Soc. rep., British Nat. Cttee for Physiol. Scis, 1976–82; Mem., Physiol. Soc. Cttee, 1972–76 (Chm., 1975–76); Mem., IUPS Commn on Physiol. of Food and Fluid Intake, 1973–80 (Chm., 1979–80). Member, Editorial Boards: Jl of Physiol., 1977–84; Neuroendocrinology, 1979–84; Editor, Biological Reviews, 1984–95. Hon. MD Lausanne, 1978. Dist. Career Award, Soc. for Study of Ingestive Behavior, 1998. *Publications:* The Physiology of Thirst and Sodium Appetite, 1979; scientific papers in professional jls. *Recreations:* Irish language and literature, cats, music, photography, grandchildren. *Address:* Physiological Laboratory, Downing Street, Cambridge CB2 3EG. *T:* (01223) 333836; 91 Thornton Road, Girton, Cambridge CB3 0NR. *T:* (01223) 276874.

FITZSIMONS, Lorna; MP (Lab) Rochdale, since 1997; *b* 6 Aug. 1967; *d* of late Derek Fitzsimons and of Barbara Jean Taylor; *m* 2000, Stephen Benedict Cooney; one step *s* one step *d*. *Educ:* Wardle High Sch.; Rochdale Coll. of Art and Design; Loughborough Coll. of Art and Design (BA Hons Textile Design 1988; a Vice Pres., Students' Union, 1988–89). National Union of Students: part-time Nat. Exec. Officer, 1989–90; Vice Pres., Educn, 1990–92; Pres., 1992–94; Rowland Public Affairs: Account Manager, 1994–95; Account Dir, 1995–96; Associate Dir, 1996–97. Chair, Student Forum, EU, 1990–94; Mem., Quality Cttee, FEFC, 1993–94. Member National Executive: Fabian Soc., 1996–; Lab. Co-ordinating Cttee, 1995–97, Campaign of Electoral Reform, 1997, Labour Party; Chair, Women's Cttee, PLP, 1997. Governor: Wardle High Sch., 1982–83; Loughborough Coll. of Art and Design, 1988–89; Sheffield Hallam Univ., 1995–96. *Recreations:* watching films, cooking, walking, travelling, dancing or listening to music. *Address:* c/o House of Commons, SW1A 0AA. *T:* (020) 7219 3000.

FITZSIMONS, P. Anthony; Chairman, Ruton Management Ltd, since 1994; *b* 16 March 1946; two *s*. *Educ:* LSE (BSc Econ.). Rank Xerox: Australia, 1972–75; Southern Europe, 1975–76; Australasia, Middle East, 1976–79; Regional Control Dir, London, 1979–81; Grand Metropolitan: Finance Systems and Strategy Dir, Brewing and Retail Div., 1981–83; Man. Dir, Host Group, 1983–85; Man. Dir, Personal Banking, Citibank, 1985–89; Chief Exec. and Man. Dir, Bristol & West Bldg Soc., 1989–93. Chm., Avon TEC. *Recreations:* squash, riding, music, sailing. *Address:* Hill House, Hannington, Wilts SN6 7RS.

FITZWALTER, 21st Baron *cr* 1295; **(Fitzwalter) Brook Plumptre;** JP; Hon. Captain, The Buffs; *b* 15 Jan. 1914; *s* of late George Beresford Plumptre, Goodnestone, Canterbury, Kent; *S* uncle, 1943 (FitzWalter Barony called out of abeyance in his favour, 1953); *m* 1951, Margaret Melesina, *yr d* of (Herbert) William Deedes, JP, Galt, Hythe, Kent; five *s*. *Educ:* Diocesan Coll., Rondebosch, Cape; Jesus Coll., Cambridge. Served War of 1939–45, with the Buffs (Royal East Kent Regt) in France, Belgium, UK and India; attached RIASC, as Capt. JP Kent, 1949. Landowner and farmer; succeeded to family estate, 1943. *Heir: s* Hon. Julian Brook Plumptre [*b* 18 Oct. 1952; *m* 1988, Sally, *o d* of late I. M. T. Quiney; three *s*]. *Address:* Goodnestone Park, Canterbury, Kent CT3 1PL. *T:* (01304) 840218.

FIVET, Edmond Charles Paul, FRCM; Principal, Welsh College of Music and Drama, since 1989; *b* 12 Feb. 1947; *s* of Paul Fivet and Lorna (*née* Edwards); *m* 1st, 1969, Christine Partington (marr. diss. 1976); one *s* one *d*; 2nd, 1978, Elizabeth Page. *Educ:* Royal Coll. of Music; Coll. of St Mark and St John; City Univ. (MA); Open Univ. (BA). FRCM 1988. Registrar, 1973–83, Dir, 1983–86, Jun. Dept, Royal Coll. of Music; Music Dir, Audi Jun. Musician, 1986–98. Member: Music Cttee, Welsh Arts Council, 1991–94; Steering Cttee, NYO of Wales, 1991–; Music Cttee, Cardiff Internat. Fest., 1992–95; Council, Arts Council of Wales, 2000–; Vice-Pres., Richmond upon Thames Arts Council, 1986–98. Member: Assoc. of European Conservatoires, 1989–; Fedn of British (formerly Cttee of Principals of) Conservatoires, 1990–; Heads of Higher Educn, Wales, 1996–. FRSA 1990. Gov., Dartington Coll. of Arts, 1997–. *Recreations:* golf, music, theatre, reading, current affairs. *Address:* Welsh College of Music and Drama, Castle Grounds, Cathays Park, Cardiff CF10 3ER. *T:* (029) 2039 1334. *Club:* Parc Golf (Coedkernew); Aldeburgh Golf.

FLACK, Bertram Anthony, CMG 1979; HM Diplomatic Service, retired; *b* 3 Feb. 1924; *y s* of Dr F. H. Flack and Alice Cockshut, Nelson, Lancs; *m* 1948, Jean W. Mellor; two *s* two *d*. *Educ:* Epsom Coll.; Liverpool Univ. (LLB Hons). Enlisted Gren. Gds, 1942; commissioned E Lancashire Regt, 1943; served in NW Europe (Captain). Joined Foreign Service, 1948; served Karachi, 1948–50; Alexandria, 1950–52; Stockholm, 1955–58; Accra, 1958–61; Johannesburg, 1964–67; Dep. High Comr, E Pakistan, 1967–68; Inspector, Diplomatic Service, 1968–70; Head of Communications Dept, FCO, 1971–73; Commercial Counsellor, Stockholm, 1973–75; Canadian Nat. Defence Coll., 1975–76; Dep. High Comr, Ottawa, 1976–79; High Comr, Repub. of Uganda, 1979–80. *Recreations:* cricket, golf. *Address:* Ripple Cottage, Douglas Street, Castletown, Isle of Man IM9 1AY.

FLACK, Rt Rev. John Robert; *see* Huntingdon, Bishop Suffragan of.

FLAGG, Rt Rev. John William Hawkins; an Hon. Assistant Bishop of Southwell, since 1992; *b* 16 April 1929; *s* of Wilfred John and Emily Flagg; *m* 1954, Marjorie Lund (*d* 1999); two *s* four *d*. *Educ:* All Nations Christian Coll.; Clifton Theological Coll. Agricultural missionary, Chile, 1951; Chaplain and Missionary Superintendent, St Andrew's, Asunción, Paraguay, 1959–64; Archdeacon, N Argentine, 1964–69; Diocesan Bishop of Paraguay and N Argentine, 1969–73; Asst Bishop for Chile, Peru and Bolivia, 1973–77; Bishop, Diocese of Peru, 1977; Asst Bishop, Diocese of Liverpool, 1978–86; Vicar, St Cyprian's with Christ Church, Edge Hill, 1978–85; Priest-in-Charge of Christ Church, Waterloo, 1985–86; Gen. Sec., S American Missionary Soc., 1986–93; Hon. Asst Bishop of Rochester, 1986–92. Member of Anglican Consultative Council, 1974–79; Presiding Bishop of Anglican Council of South America (CASA), 1974–77. Diocesan Advr in rural ministry, and stewardship, 1993–96, and overseas relns, 1994–96, Southwell. *Publication:* From Ploughshare to Crook, 2000. *Address:* 8 Ransome Close, Beacon Heights, Notts NG24 2LQ; *e-mail:* bishop.bill@southwell.anglican.org.

FLANAGAN, Andrew Henry; Chief Executive, SMG (formerly Scottish Media Group) plc, since 1997; *b* 15 March 1956; *s* of Francis Desmond Flanagan and Martha Donaldson Flanagan; *m* 1992, Virginia Walker; one *s* one *d*. *Educ:* Glasgow Univ. (BAcc). CA. Touche Ross, 1976–79; Price Waterhouse, 1979–81; Financial Control Manager, ITT, 1981–86; Finance Dir, PA Consulting Gp, 1986–91; Gp Finance Dir and Chief Financial Officer, BIS Ltd, 1991–94; Finance Dir, Scottish Television plc, 1994–96; Man. Dir, Scottish Television plc, 1996–97. *Recreations:* golf, ski-ing, television. *Club:* Royal Automobile.

FLANAGAN, Barry, OBE 1991; RA 1991 (ARA 1987); sculptor; *b* 11 Jan. 1941. *Educ:* Birmingham Coll. of Arts and Crafts; St Martin's Sch. of Art. Teacher, St Martin's Sch. of Art and Central Sch. of Art and Design, 1967–71. One-man exhibitions include: Rowan Gall., 1966, 1968, 1970–74; Fischbach Gall., NY, 1969; Galleria del Leone, Venice, 1971; Mus. of Modern Art, NY, Mus. of Modern Art, Oxford, 1974; Hogarth Galls, Sydney, 1975; Centro de Arte y Communicación, Buenos Aires, 1976; Van Abbemuseum, Eindhoven, Arnolfini Gall., Bristol, Serpentine Gall. (tour), 1977–79; Galerie Durand-Dessert, Paris, 1980, 1982, 1988; Waddington Galls, 1980–81, 1983, 1985, 1990–94; Inst. of Contemporary Arts (prints and drawings), 1981–82; British Pavilion, XL Venice Biennale, and tour, 1982–83; Centre Georges Pompidou, Paris, 1983; Pace Gall., NY, 1983, 1994; Fuji Television Gall., Tokyo, 1985, 1991; Tate Gall., 1986; Laing Art Gall., Newcastle upon Tyne, Mus. of Contemporary Art, Belgrade, City Gall., Zagreb, Mus. of Modern Art, Ljubljana (tour), 1987–88; Madrid and Nantes, 1993–94; Gallagher Gall., RHA, 1995. Work includes: outdoor sculpture for Sint Pietersplein, Ghent, 1980; Camdonian sculpture, Lincoln's Inn Fields, 1980; bronze sculptures, Baby Elephant and Hare on Bell, Equitable Life Tower West, NY, 1984; bronze sculpture, Nine Foot Hare, Victoria Plaza, London, 1984; bronze sculpture, The Boxing Ones, Capability Green, Luton Hoo Estate, Beds, 1986; bronze sculpture, Kouros horse, Stockley Park, Uxbridge, 1987; two bronze Leaping Hare sculptures for Kawakyo Co., Osaka, 1990. Choreographed two pieces for dance gp, Strider, 1972. Judge, Bath Sculpture Competition, 1985. *Address:* c/o Waddington Galleries, 11 Cork Street, W1X 1PD.

FLANAGAN, Michael Joseph; Director, Finance and Planning, Cheshire Constabulary, since 1995; *b* 21 Nov. 1946; *s* of Daniel and Margaret Constance Flanagan; *m* 1968, Patricia Holland; two *s* one *d*. *Educ:* St Joseph's Coll., Blackpool; Southampton Coll. of Higher Educn. IPFA 1972; DMS 1983. Trainee Accountant, Lancs CC, 1965–69; Preston County Borough, 1969–70; Southampton City Council, 1970–72; Accountant, 1972, Asst Dir of Finance, 1981–87, Telford Develt Corp.; Dir of Finance and Tech. Services, 1987–90, Chief Exec., 1990–95, Develt Bd for Rural Wales. *Recreations:* sport, esp. football, golf, tennis; family activities. *Address:* Tan-y-Fron, Pantyffridd, Berriew, Powys SY21 8BH. *Club:* Lancs CC.

FLANAGAN, Sir Ronald, Kt 1999; OBE 1996; Chief Constable, Royal Ulster Constabulary, since 1996; *b* 25 March 1949; *s* of John Patrick Flanagan and Henrietta Flanagan; *m* 1968, Lorraine Nixon; three *s*. *Educ:* Belfast High Sch.; Univ. of Ulster (BA, MA); Graduate: FBI Nat. Acad., 1987; FBI Nat. Exec. Inst., 1996. Joined Royal Ulster Constabulary, as Constable, 1970: Sergeant, Belfast, 1973; Inspector, Londonderry, 1976, Belfast, 1977–81; Detective Inspector, 1981; Detective Chief Inspector, 1983; Detective Superintendent, Armagh, 1987; Chief Superintendent, Police Staff Coll., Bramshill, 1990; Asst Chief Constable, Belfast, 1992; Actg Dep. Chief Constable, 1995, affirmed Feb. 1996. *Recreations:* walking, Rugby, reading (particularly Yeats' poetry), music (particularly Van Morrison), but very varied taste. *Address:* RUC Headquarters, Brooklyn, Knock Road, Belfast BT5 6LE. *Club:* Royal Ulster Yacht (Bangor, Co. Down).

FLANNERY, Martin Henry; *b* 2 March 1918; *m* 1949; one *s* two *d*. *Educ:* Sheffield Grammar Sch.; Sheffield Teachers' Trng College. Served with Royal Scots, 1940–46. Teacher, 1946–74 (Head Teacher, 1969–74). MP (Lab) Hillsborough, Sheffield, Feb. 1974–1992. Chairman: Tribune Group, 1980–81; PLP's NI Cttee, 1983–92; PLP Consultant MP for NUT, 1974–92. *Recreations:* music, rambling. *Address:* 530 Manchester Road, Sheffield S10 5PQ.

FLATHER, family name of **Baroness Flather**.

FLATHER, Baroness, *cr* 1990 (Life Peer), of Windsor and Maidenhead in the Royal County of Berkshire; **Shreela Flather;** JP; DL; Councillor, Royal Borough of Windsor and Maidenhead, 1976–91 (first ethnic minority woman Councillor in UK), Mayor, 1986–87 (first Asian woman to hold this office); *b* Lahore, India; *née* Shreela Rai; *m* Gary Flather, *qv*; two *s*. *Educ:* University Coll. London (LLB; Fellow 1992). Called to the Bar, Inner Temple, 1962. Infant Teacher, ILEA, 1965–67; Teacher of English as a second lang., Altwood Comp. Sch., Maidenhead, 1968–74, Broadmoor Hosp., 1974–78. Chairman: Consortium for Street Children Charities, 1992–94; Disasters Emergency Cttee, 1993–96; Vice Chm., Refugee Council, 1991–94; Member: W Metropolitan Conciliation Cttee, Race Relations Bd, 1973–78; Cttee of Inquiry (Rampton, later Swann Cttee) into Educn of Children from Ethnic Minority Gps, 1979–85; Comr, CRE, 1980–86 (Chm., Educn, Housing and Services Cttee, and Welsh Consultative Cttee, 1980–86); UK Rep., EC Commn into Racism and Xenophobia, 1994–95. Member: Police Complaints Board, 1982–85; HRH Duke of Edinburgh's Inquiry into British Housing, 1984–85; Lord Chancellor's Legal Aid Adv. Cttee, 1985–88; Social Security Adv. Cttee, 1987–90; Econ. and Social Cttee, EC, 1987–90; Carnegie Inquiry into the Third Age, 1990–93; H of L Select Cttee on Med. Ethics, 1993–94; Chm., Alcohol Educn and Res. Council, 1996–; Dir, Marie Stopes Internat., 1996–. President: Cambs, Chilterns and Thames Rent Assessment Panel, 1983–97; Community Council for Berks, 1991–98; Member: Thames and Chilterns Tourist Bd, 1987–88; Berks FPC, 1987–88; Jt Pres., FPA, 1995–98; Vice-Pres., BSA, 1988–91. Member: Cons. Women's Nat. Cttee (formerly Cons. Women's Nat. Adv. Cttee), 1978–89; Exec. Cttee, Anglo-Asian Cons. Soc., 1979–83; NEC, Cons. Party, 1989–90; Sec., Windsor and Maidenhead Cons. Gp, 1979–83. Chm., Star FM, 1992–97; Director: Daytime Television, 1978–79; Thames Valley Enterprise, 1990–93; Meridian Broadcasting, 1991–2001; Cable Corp., 1997–2000; Kiss FM, 2000–; Pres., Global Money Transfer, 1997–2001. Member: BBC S and E Regl Adv. Cttee, 1987–89; Cttee of Management, Servite Houses Ltd, 1987–94; LWT Prog. Adv. Bd, 1990–94. Member: Bd of Visitors, Holloway Prison, 1981–83; Broadmoor Hosp. Bd, 1987–88 (Chm., Ethics Cttee, 1993–97; Equal Opportunities Cttee, 1994–97; Pres., League of Friends, 1991–98); Dir, Hillingdon Hosp. Trust, 1990–98. Chm., Memorial Gates Trust, 1998–; Member Council: Winston Churchill Meml Trust, 1993–; St George's Hse, Windsor Castle, 1996–; Mem., UK Adv. Council, Asia House, 1996–; Trustee: Berks Community Trust, 1978–90; Borlase Sch., Marlow, 1991–97; Rajiv Gandhi UK Foundn, 1993–. Governor: Commonwealth Inst., 1993–98; Altwood Comp. Sch., Maidenhead, 1978–86; Slough Coll. of Higher Educn, 1984–89; Mem. Council, Atlantic Coll., 1994–98. Pres., Alumni Assoc., 1998–2000, Lay Mem., Council, 2000–, UCL. Sec./Organiser Maidenhead Ladies' Asian Club, 1968–78; Chm., New Star Boys' Club, 1969–79; Vice Chairman: Maidenhead CAB, 1982–88; Maidenhead CRC, 1969–72; formerly Vice Chairman: Maidenhead Police Consultative Cttee; Maidenhead Volunteer Centre. FRSA 1999. JP Maidenhead, 1971; DL Berks, 1994. DUniv Open, 1994. Asian of the Year, 1996. *Publication:* Stepping Stones (Adult English Training Scheme), 1973. *Recreations:* travel, cinema, swimming. *Address:* House of Lords, SW1A 0PW. *T:* (020) 7219 5353.

FLATHER, Gary Denis, OBE 1999; QC 1984; a Recorder, since 1986; a Deputy High Court Judge, since 1997; *b* 4 Oct. 1937; *s* of late Denis Flather and of Joan Flather; *m* Shreela Flather (*see* Baroness Flather); two *s*. *Educ:* Oundle Sch.; Pembroke Coll., Oxford (MA). Called to the Bar, Inner Temple, 1962, Bencher, 1995 (Mem., Scholarships Cttee). National Service, Second Lieut 1st Bn York and Lancaster Regt, 1956–58; Lieut Hallamshire Bn, TA, 1958–61. Asst Parly Boundary Comr, 1982–90; Asst Recorder, 1983–86. Mem., Panel of Chairmen: for ILEA Teachers' Disciplinary Tribunal, 1974–90 (Chm., Disciplinary ILEA Tribunal, William Tyndale Jun. Sch. teachers, 1976); for Disciplinary Tribunal for London Polytechnics, 1982–90; a Chairman: Police Disciplinary Appeals, 1987–; MoD (Police) Disciplinary Appeals, 1992–; Legal Mem., Mental Health Review Tribunal (restricted patients), 1987–; a Financial Services Act Inspector, employees of Coutts Bank, 1987–88; a legal assessor: GMC and GDC, 1987–95; RCVS, 2000–; Chairman: Statutory Cttee, RPharmS, 1990–2000 (Hon. MRPharmS); Disciplinary Cttee, Chartered Inst. of Marketing, 1993–. Bar Council: Chm., Disability Panel, 1992–; Member: Chambers Arbitration Panel, 1995; Equal Opportunities Cttee, 1998–. Dir, W. Fearnehough (Bakewell) Ltd, 1991–. Pres., Maidenhead Rotary Club, 1990–91. Vice-Pres., Community Council for Berks, 1987–; Littlewick Green Show, 1997–. Trustee: ADAPT, 1995–; Disabled Living Foundn, 1997–. Escort to the Mayor of the Royal Borough of Windsor and Maidenhead, 1986–87. *Recreations:* travel, music, golden retrievers, coping with multiple sclerosis, being with friends. *Address:* 4/5 Gray's Inn Square, Gray's Inn, WC1R 5AY. *T:* (020) 7404 5252, *Fax:* (01628) 675355; *e-mail:* garyflather@care4free.net.

FLATT, Very Rev. Roy Francis Ferguson; Dean of Argyll and the Isles, since 1999; Rector of Christ Church, Lochgilphead, with St Columba's, Poltalloch (Kilmartin), and All Saints, Inveraray, since 1983; *b* 4 Sept. 1947; *s* of Ray and Trixie Flatt; *m* 1978, Andrina Ferguson; two *s*. *Educ:* King Edward VI Grammar Sch., Bury St Edmunds; Scottish Sch. of Librarianship, Univ. of Strathclyde; Coates Hall, Edinburgh. Deacon 1980, priest 1981; Curate, St Andrews, Elie and Earlsferry and Pittenweem, dio. St Andrews, 1980–82; Diocesan Supernumerary, 1982–83. *Recreations:* reading, sketching, playing solitaire on the PC. *Address:* Bishopton House, Lochgilphead, Argyll PA31 8PY. *T:* (01546) 602315.

FLAUX, Julian Martin; QC 1994; a Recorder, since 2000; *b* 11 May 1955; *s* of Louis Michael Flaux and Maureen Elizabeth Brenda Flaux; *m* 1983, Matilda Christian (*née* Gabb); three *s*. *Educ:* King's Sch., Worcester; Worcester Coll., Oxford (BCL, MA). Called to the Bar, Inner Temple, 1978; in practice, 1979–. *Recreations:* opera, reading, walking. *Address:* 7 King's Bench Walk, Temple, EC4Y 7DS. *T:* (020) 7583 0404.

FLAVELL, Prof. Richard Anthony, PhD; FRS 1984; Chairman and Professor of Immunobiology, and Professor of Biology, Yale University School of Medicine, and Investigator of the Howard Hughes Medical Institute, since 1988; *b* 23 Aug. 1945; *s* of John T. and Iris Flavell; *m* Madlyn (*née* Nathanson); one *d*; two *s* of former *m*. *Educ:* Dept of Biochemistry, Univ. of Hull (PhD 1970); Univ. of Amsterdam (Royal Soc. Eur. Fellow); Univ of Zürich (Post-doctoral Fellow). Wetenschappelijk Medewerker, Univ. of Amsterdam, 1973–79; Head, Lab. of Gene Structure and Expression, NIMR, Mill Hill, 1979–82; Pres., Biogen Res. Corp., 1982–88; Principal Res. Officer and CSO, Biogen Gp, 1984–88. Darwin Trust Vis. Prof., 1995. Mem., EMBO, 1978–. MRI 1984–; Mem., Amer. Assoc. of Immunologists, 1990–. Anniversary Prize, FEBS, 1980; Colworth Medal, Biochem. Soc., 1980. *Publications: chapters in:* Handbook of Biochemistry and Molecular Biology ed Fasman, 3rd edn 1976; McGraw-Hill Yearbook of Science and Technology, 1980; Eukaryotic Genes: their structure, activity and regulation, ed jtly with it Maclean and Gregory, 1983; articles in numerous scientific jls, incl. Nature, Cell, Proc. Nat. Acad. Sci., EMBO Jl, Jl Exp. Med. Sci., Science, and Immunity; contrib. Proceedings of symposia. *Recreations:* music, tennis, horticulture. *Address:* Section of Immunobiology, Yale University School of Medicine, 310 Cedar Street, New Haven, CT 06520, USA; *e-mail:* richard.flavell@qm.yale.edu.

FLAVELL, Dr Richard Bailey, CBE 1999; FRS 1998; Chief Scientific Officer, Ceres Inc., since 1998; *b* 11 Oct. 1943; *s* of Sidney Flavell and Emily Gertrude Flavell (*née* Bailey); *m* 1966, Hazel New; two *d*. *Educ:* Univ. of Birmingham (BSc 1964); Univ. of East Anglia (PhD 1967). Research Associate, Univ. of Stanford, California, 1967; Plant Breeding Institute, 1969–88 (Head, Molecular Genetics Dept, 1985–88); Dir, John Innes Inst., subseq. Centre, and John Innes Prof. of Biology, UEA, 1988–98; Chm. Mgt Cttee, AFRC Inst. of Plant Sci. Res., 1990–94. Hon. Prof., King's College London, 1986–90. Fellow, EMBO, 1990; Pres., Internat. Soc. for Plant Molecular Biology, 1993–95. *Publications:* scientific papers and books. *Recreations:* music, gardening. *Address:* Ceres Inc., 3007 Malibu Canyon Road, Malibu, CA 90265, USA. *T:* (310) 3178930; *e-mail:* rflavell@ceres-inc.com.

FLAXEN, David William; statistics consultant; *b* 20 April 1941; *s* of late William Henry Flaxen and Beatrice Flaxen (*née* Laidlow); *m* 1969, Eleanor Marie Easton; two *d*. *Educ:* Manchester Grammar Sch.; Brasenose Coll., Oxford (MA Physics); University Coll. London (DipStat). Teacher, Leyton County High School for Boys, 1963; cadet statistician, 1963–64; statistical posts, Central Statistical Office and Min. of Labour, 1964–71; United Nations Adviser: Swaziland, 1971–72; Ghana, 1985–86; Statistician, Dept of Employment, 1973–75; Chief Statistician: Dept of Employment, 1975–76; Central Statistical Office, 1976–77 and 1981–83; Inland Revenue, 1977–81; Asst Dir (Under Sec.), Central Statistical Office, 1983–89; Dir of Statistics, Dept of Transport, 1989–96. *Publications:* contribs to articles in Physics Letters, Economic Trends, Dept of Employment Gazette, etc. *Recreations:* bridge, wine, cooking, music. *Address:* 65 Corringham Road, NW11 7BS. *T:* (020) 8458 5451, *Fax:* (020) 8731 6270; *e-mail:* dflaxen@easynet.co.uk.

FLECK, Prof. Norman Andrew, PhD; CEng, FIM; Professor of Mechanics of Materials, Cambridge University, since 1997; Fellow of Pembroke College, Cambridge, since 1982; *b* 11 May 1958; *s* of William and Roberta Fleck; *m* 1983, Vivien Christine Taylor; one *s* one *d.* *Educ:* Jesus Coll., Cambridge (BA 1979; MA 1981); PhD Cantab 1982. FIM 1997. Maudslay Res. Fellow, Pembroke Coll., Cambridge, 1983–84; Lindemann Fellow, Harvard Univ., 1984–85; Cambridge University: Lectr in Engineering, 1985–94; Reader in Mechanics of Materials, 1994–97; Dir, Cambridge Centre for Micromechanics, 1996–. *Publications:* (jtly) Metal Foams: a design guide, 2000; numerous papers in mechanics and materials jls. *Recreations:* running, ski-ing, wine, church. *Address:* Cambridge University Engineering Department, Trumpington Street, Cambridge CB2 1PZ. *T:* (01223) 332650.

FLECKER, James William, MA; Headmaster, Ardingly College, 1980–98; Recruitment Manager, Students Partnership Worldwide, since 1998; *b* 15 Aug. 1939; *s* of Henry Lael Oswald Flecker, CBE, and Mary Patricia Flecker; *m* 1967, Mary Rose Firth; three *d.* *Educ:* Marlborough Coll.; Brasenose Coll., Oxford (BA, now MA Lit. Hum., 1962). Asst Master: Sydney Grammar Sch., 1962–63; Latymer Upper Sch., 1964–67; (and later Housemaster), Marlborough Coll., 1967–80. *Recreations:* hockey, cricket, flute playing, children's operas. *Address:* 34 Burnaby Street, SW10 0PL. *T:* (020) 7376 3777.

FLEET, Dr Andrew James, FGS; Keeper of Mineralogy, Natural History Museum, since 1996; *b* 14 June 1950; *s* of late Rupert Stanley Fleet and of Margaret Rose Fleet (*née* Aitken); *m* 1976, Susan Mary Adamson; one *s* one *d.* *Educ:* Bryanston Sch.; Chelsea Coll., Univ. of London (BSc; PhD 1977). FGS 1976. UNESCO Fellow in Oceanography, Open Univ., 1975–79; Lectr in Geochem., Goldsmiths' Coll., Univ. of London, 1979–80; Research and Exploration, BP, 1980–95, Head, Petroleum Geochem. Res., 1987–95. Vis. Prof. in Geol., ICSTM, 1997–. Special Pubns Ed., 1993–2000, Mem. Council, 1997–2000, Geol Soc. *Publications:* edited jointly: Marine petroleum source rocks, 1987; Lacustrine petroleum source rocks, 1988; Petroleum migration, 1991; Coal and coal-bearing strata as oil-prone source rocks?, 1994; Muds and mudstones: physical and fluid flow properties, 1999; Petroleum Geology of Northwest Europe: proceedings of the 5th conference, 1999; contrib. papers in scientific jls on petroleum and sedimentary geochemistry and marine geology. *Recreations:* archaeology, family, cooking. *Address:* Department of Mineralogy, Natural History Museum, Cromwell Road, SW7 5BD. *T:* (020) 7938 9226.

FLEET, Stephen George, PhD; FInstP; Master, Downing College, Cambridge, since 2001; Deputy Vice-Chancellor, University of Cambridge, since 2001; *b* 28 Sept. 1936; *er s* of late George Fleet and Elsie Fleet, Lewes, Sussex. *Educ:* Brentwood Sch.; Lewes County Grammar Sch.; St John's Coll., Cambridge (Scholar; MA; PhD 1962). FInstP 1972. Res. Physicist, Mullard Res. Labs, Surrey, 1961–62; University of Cambridge: Demonstr in Mineralogy, 1962–67; Lectr in Mineralogy, 1967–83; Registrary, 1983–97, now Emeritus; Fellow: Fitzwilliam House, 1963–66; Fitzwilliam Coll., 1966–73 (Jun. Bursar, 1967–73; Dir of Studies in Physical Sciences, 1971–74; Hon. Fellow, 1997); Downing Coll., 1974–2000 (Bursar, 1974–83; Pres., 1983–85; Vice-Master, 1985–88, 1991–94 and 1997–2000); Mem., Council of Senate, 1975–82; Mem., Financial Bd, 1979–83; Chm., Bd of Exams, 1974–83; Chm., Bursars' Cttee, 1980–83; President: Fitzwilliam Soc., 1977, 1999; Downing Assoc., 1991. Member: Finance Cttee, Internat. Union of Crystallography, 1987–; Jt Negotiating Cttee, Universities Superannuation Scheme, 1992–. Treasurer: Cambridge Commonwealth Trust, 1983–; Cambridge Overseas Trust, 1988–; Cambridge Housing Soc., 1999–; Gates Cambridge Trust, 2000–; Chairman of Trustees: Foundn of Edward Storey, 1984–88, 1999–; Strangeways Res. Lab., 1997–; Trustee, Mineralogical Soc. of GB, 1977–87; Mem., Cttee of Management, Charities Property Unit Trust, 1983–88. FRSA 1995. *Publications:* res. pubns in scientific jls. *Recreations:* books, music, history of Sussex. *Address:* Downing College, Cambridge CB2 1DQ. *T:* (01223) 334843. *Clubs:* Athenæum, Royal Over-Seas League.

FLEGG, Dr James John Maitland, OBE 1997; FIHort; Director, External Affairs, Horticulture Research International, East Malling, 1995–97, now consultant, horticulture and environment; Chairman, Meiosis Ltd, since 2000; *b* Hong Kong, 23 April 1937; *s* of Jack Sydney Flegg and Lily Elizabeth (*née* Spooner); *m* 1976, Caroline Louise Coles; two *s.* *Educ:* Melbourne, Australia; Gillingham Grammar Sch.; Imperial Coll. of Science and Technol. (BSc, PhD). ARCS 1962; FIHort 1993. Nematologist, E Malling Res. Stn, 1956–66; MAFF, 1966–68; Dir, Brit. Trust for Ornithology, Tring, 1968–75; Hd, Zool. Dept, E Malling Res. Stn, 1976–87; Dir of Inf. Services, 1987–95, and Hd of Stn, 1990–95, Horticulture Res. Internat., East Malling. Presenter, Country Ways, Meridian TV. Sec., European Soc. of Nematologists, 1965–68; Mem. Council, RSPB, 1978–83; Pres., Kent Ornithol Soc., 1986–. MBOU 1966. Chm., Romney Marsh Res. Trust, 1990–2000. Freeman, City of London; Liveryman, Co. of Fruiterers. *Publications:* books include: In Search of Birds, 1983; Oakwatch, 1985; Birdlife, 1986; Field Guide to the Birds of Britain and Europe, 1990; Poles Apart, 1991; Deserts, 1993; Classic Birds (60 Years of Bird Photography): a biography of Eric Hosking, 1993; Photographic Field Guide to the Birds of Australia, 1996; numerous papers and articles on nematological, ornithological and envmtl topics. *Recreations:* wildlife, rural history, environmental affairs, photography, gardening, music, communication. *Address:* Horticulture Research International, E Malling, Kent ME19 6BJ. *T:* (01732) 843833; Divers Farm, E Sutton, Maidstone, Kent ME17 3DT.

FLEISCHMANN, Prof. Martin, FRS 1986; FRSC 1980; Research Professor: Department of Chemistry, University of Southampton, since 1983; University of Utah, since 1988; *b* 29 March 1927; *s* of Hans Fleischmann and Margarethe Fleischmann (*née* Srb); *m* 1950, Sheila Flinn; one *s* two *d.* *Educ:* Worthing High School; Imperial College of Science and Technology. ARCS 1947; BSc 1948; PhD 1951. ICI Fellow, King's College, Univ. of Durham, 1952–57; Lectr, then Reader, Univ. of Newcastle upon Tyne, 1957–67; Electricity Council Faraday Prof. of Electrochemistry, Univ. of Southampton, 1967–77; Senior Fellowship, SERC, 1977–82. Pres., Internat. Soc. of Electrochemistry, 1970–72; Palladium Medal, US Electrochemical Soc., 1985. *Publications:* numerous papers and chapters in books. *Recreations:* ski-ing, walking, music, cooking. *Address:* Bury Lodge, Duck Street, Tisbury, Wilts SP3 6LJ. *T:* (01747) 870384.

FLEMING, Anne Elizabeth; Head of Content, MAAS Media Online, British Universities Film and Video Council, since 2001; *b* 12 Aug. 1944; *d* of Harry Gibb Fleming and Agnes Wilkie Fleming (*née* Clark); partner, Taylor Downing. *Educ:* Univ. of Edinburgh (MA Hons English Lit. and Lang.). Films Administrator, Edinburgh Film Fest., 1966, 1967, 1968, 1969; teacher of English as a foreign lang., Acad. of Langs, Catania, Sicily, 1967–68; Imperial War Museum; Res. Asst, Dept. of Film Programming, 1970–72; Res. Asst, Dept. of Film, 1972–73; Dep. Keeper, 1973–83, Keeper, 1983–90, Dept of Film; Dep. Curator, 1990–97, Curator, 1997–2000, BFI Nat. Film and TV Archive. *Publications:* contribs to catalogues and data-bases. *Recreations:* cinema, reading, walking, cooking, growing herbs. *Address:* British Universities Film and Video Council, 77 Wells Street, W1T 3QJ. *T:* (020) 7393 1500.

FLEMING, Ven. David; Chaplain-General to HM Prisons and Archdeacon of Prisons, 1993–2001; Chaplain to the Queen, since 1995; *b* 8 June 1937; *s* of John Frederick Fleming and Emma (*née* Casey); *m* 1966, Elizabeth Anne Marguerite Hughes; three *s* one *d.* *Educ:* Hunstanton County Primary School; King Edward VII Grammar School, King's Lynn; Kelham Theological Coll. National Service with Royal Norfolk Regt, 1956–58. Deacon 1963; Asst Curate, St Margaret, Walton on the Hill, Liverpool, 1963–67; priest 1964; attached to Sandringham group of churches, 1967–68; Vicar of Great Staughton, 1968–76; Chaplain of HM Borstal, Gaynes Hall, 1968–76; RD of St Neots, 1972–76; RD of March, 1977–82; Vicar of Whittlesey, 1976–85; Priest-in-Charge of Pondersbridge, 1983–85; Archdeacon of Wisbech, 1984–93; Vicar of Wisbech St Mary, 1985–88. Hon. Canon of Ely Cathedral, 1982–. Chm. of House of Clergy, Ely Diocesan Synod, 1982–85. *Recreations:* tennis, chess, extolling Hunstanton. *Address:* Fair Haven, 123 Wisbech Road, Littleport, Ely, Cambs CB6 1JJ. *Club:* Whittlesey Rotary.

FLEMING, Prof. George, PhD; FREng, FICE; FRSE; Professor of Civil Engineering, University of Strathclyde, since 1985; Managing Director, EnviroCentre, since 1983; *b* Glasgow, 16 Aug. 1944; *s* of Felix and Catherine Fleming; *m* 1966, Irene MacDonald Cowan; two *s* one *d.* *Educ:* Univ. of Strathclyde (BSc 1st cl. Hons; PhD 1969). FICE 1982; FREng (FEng 1987); FRSE 1992; FASCE 2000. Res. Fellow, Stanford Univ., 1967; University of Strathclyde: Res. Asst, 1966–69; Lectr, 1971–76; Sen. Lectr, 1976–82; Reader, 1982–85; Dir and Vice Pres., Hydrocomp Internat., 1969–77. Consultant, Watson Hawkesley, 1980–92. Member: Overseas Projects Bd, DTI, 1991–95; Scottish Exports Forum, 1996–; Chm., Bd of Trustees, Telford Challenge, 1998–. Pres., ICE, 1999–2000; Mem., Smeatonian Soc. of Civil Engrs, 1998. Hon. Mem., British Hydrol Soc. *Publications:* Computer Simulation in Hydrology, 1971; The Sediment Problem, 1977; (ed) Recycling Derelict Land, 1991; (contrib.) Geochemical Approaches to Environmental Engineering of Metals, 1996; (contrib.) Energy and the Environment: geochemistry of fossil, nuclear and renewable resources, 1998. *Recreations:* farming, DIY, travelling. *Address:* Department of Civil Engineering, University of Strathclyde, John Anderson Building, 107 Rottenrow, Glasgow G4 0NG. *T:* (0141) 553 4169.

FLEMING, Prof. Graham Richard, PhD; FRS 1994; Professor, Department of Chemistry, University of California, Berkeley, and Director, Physical Biosciences Division, Laurence Berkeley National Laboratory, since 1997; *b* 3 Dec. 1949; *s* of Maurice Norman Henry Fleming and Lovima Ena Winter; *m* 1977, Jean McKenzie; one *s.* *Educ:* Bristol Univ. (BSc Hons); Royal Instn (PhD London). Res. Fellow, CIT, 1974–75; Univ. Res. Fellow, Univ. of Melbourne, 1975–76; Leverhulme Fellow, Royal Instn, 1977–79; University of Chicago: Asst Prof., 1979–83; Associate Prof., 1983–85; Prof., 1985–87; Arthur Holly Compton Dist. Service Prof., Dept of Chem., 1987–97. Fellow, Amer. Acad. of Arts and Scis, 1991. *Publications:* Chemical Applications of Ultrafast Spectroscopy, 1986; numerous articles in learned jls. *Recreation:* mountaineering. *Address:* Department of Chemistry, B84 Hildebrand #1460, University of California, Berkeley, CA 94720–1460, USA. *T:* (510) 6432735, *Fax:* (510) 6426340; *e-mail:* fleming@cchem.berkeley.edu.

FLEMING, Grahame Ritchie; QC (Scot.) 1990; Sheriff of Lothian and Borders, since 1993; *b* 13 Feb. 1949; *s* of Ian Erskine Fleming and Helen Ritchie Wallace or Fleming; *m* 1984, Mopsa Dorcas Robbins; one *d.* *Educ:* Forfar Acad.; Univ. of Edinburgh (MA, LLB). Admitted Faculty of Advocates, 1976. Standing Jun. Counsel to Home Office in Scotland, 1986–89. *Recreations:* food, travel, supporting the Scottish Rugby team. *Address:* Sheriff's Chambers, Sheriff Court House, Court Square, Linlithgow EH49 7EQ.

FLEMING, Prof. Ian, FRS 1993; Professor of Organic Chemistry, University of Cambridge, since 1998 (Reader in Organic Chemistry, 1986–98); Fellow of Pembroke College, Cambridge, since 1964; *b* 4 Aug. 1935; *s* of David Alexander Fleming and Olwen Lloyd Fleming (*née* Jones); *m* 1st, 1959, Joan Morrison Irving (marr. diss. 1962); 2nd, 1965, Mary Lord Bernard. *Educ:* Pembroke Coll., Cambridge (MA, PhD 1963; ScD 1982). Cambridge University: Res. Fellow, Pembroke Coll., 1962; Univ. Demonstrator, 1964–65; Asst Dir of Research, 1965–80; Univ. Lectr, 1980–86. *Publications:* (with D. H. Williams) Spectroscopic Methods in Organic Chemistry, 1966, 5th edn 1995; (with D. H. Williams) Spectroscopic Problems in Organic Chemistry, 1967; Selected Organic Syntheses, 1973; Frontier Orbitals and Organic Chemical Reactions, 1976; Pericyclic Reactions, 1998; numerous papers in chem. jls. *Recreations:* watching movies, reading, music. *Address:* Pembroke College, Cambridge CB2 1RF. *T:* (01223) 336372.

FLEMING, John Bryden; retired; *b* 23 June 1918; *s* of W. A. Fleming, advocate, and Maria MacLeod Bryden; *m* 1st, 1942, Janet Louise Guthrie (*d* 1981); one *s* three *d*; 2nd, 1998, Valerie Howard (*née* Forbes). *Educ:* Edinburgh Academy; Univs of Edinburgh and London. MA Hons Geog. Edinburgh, BScEcon London. Army, 1940–46, RASC and REME. Planning Officer, Dept of Health for Scotland, 1946; Principal, 1956; Asst Sec., Scottish Develt Dept, 1963, Under Sec., 1974–78; Sec., Scottish Special Housing Assoc., 1978–83. *Recreations:* gardening, hill walking. *Address:* The Old Parsonage, Cambridge Street, Alyth, Perthshire PH11 8AW. *T:* (01828) 632027. *Club:* Royal Commonwealth Society.

FLEMING, John Marley; Vice President, Sales and Marketing, Saab Automobile, Sweden, 1993–94; *b* 4 April 1930; *s* of David A. Fleming and Mary L. Fleming (*née* Marley); *m* 1961, Jeanne (*née* Retelle); one *s* two *d.* *Educ:* Harvard Coll., Cambridge, Mass, USA (BA); Harvard Business Sch., Boston, Mass (MBA). Lieut US Navy, 1952–55. Dist Manager, Frigidaire Sales Corp., 1957–63; Sales Promotion Manager, Ford Motor Co., 1963–68; Vice-Pres., J. Walter Thompson Co., 1969; Dir of Marketing, Oldsmobile Div., GMC, 1970–76; Dir of Sales, Adam Opel AG, West Germany, 1977–79; Dir of Commercial Vehicles, 1980–81, and Chm. and Man. Dir, 1982–85, Vauxhall Motors Ltd; Vice Pres., Sales, General Motors, Europe, 1986–87; Gen. Dir, Marketing and Product Planning, Cadillac Motor Car Div., General Motors, 1988–91. *Recreations:* ski-ing, sailing, golf. *Clubs:* Abenaqui Country (New Hampshire); Lemon Bay Golf (Florida).

FLEMING, Raylton Arthur; freelance journalist specialising in international affairs, music and Mallorca; editorial adviser, Majorca Daily Bulletin; *b* 1 Sept. 1925; *s* of Arthur and Evelyn Fleming; *m* 1967, Leila el Doweini; one *s.* *Educ:* Worksop Coll. Associate Producer, World Wide Pictures Ltd, 1952; Head of Overseas Television Production, Central Office of Information, 1957; Dep. Dir, Films/Television Div., COI, 1961; Asst Controller (Overseas) COI, 1968; Actg Controller (Overseas), 1969; Dir, Exhibns Div. COI, 1971; Controller (Home), COI, 1972–76; Controller (Overseas), COI, 1976–78; Dir of Inf., UN Univ., Japan, 1978–83; Dir, UN Univ. Liaison Office, NY, 1983–84; Liaison Officer, UN Univ., World Inst. for Develt Econs Res., Helsinki, 1984–86. *Recreations:* music, opera. *Address:* Camino del Castillo, 07340 Alaro, Mallorca, Spain.

FLEMING, Renée L.; soprano; *b* 14 Feb. 1959; *d* of Edwin Davis Fleming and Patricia (Seymour) Alexander; *m* 1989, Richard Lee Ross (marr. diss. 2000); two *d.* *Educ:* Potsdam State Univ. (BM Music Educn 1981); Eastman Sch. of Music (MM 1983). Studied at Juilliard American Opera Center, 1983–84, 1985–87; Fulbright Schol., Frankfurt, 1984–85. *Débuts* include: Spoleto Fest., Charleston and Italy, 1986; Houston Grand Opera, 1988; NYC Opera, 1989; Covent Garden, 1989; San Francisco Opera, 1991; Met. Opera, Paris Opera, Bastille, 1991; Teatro Colon, Buenos Aires, 1991; La Scala, Milan, 1993; Lyric Opera, Chicago, 1993. Winner, Met. Opera Nat. Auditions, 1988; George London Prize, 1988; Richard Tucker Award, 1990; Solti Prize, 1998; Grammy Award, 1999. *Address:* c/o M. L. Falcone, Public Relations, 155 West 68th Street, Suite 1114, New York, NY 10023–5817, USA. *T:* (212) 5804302.

FLEMING, Robert, (Robin); DL; Chairman, Robert Fleming Holdings, 1990–97; *b* 18 Sept. 1932; *s* of late Major Philip Fleming and Joan Cecil Fleming (*née* Hunloke); *m* 1962, Victoria Margaret Aykroyd; two *s* one *d*. *Educ:* Eton College; Royal Military Academy, Sandhurst. Served The Royal Scots Greys, 1952–58. Joined Robert Fleming, 1958; Director: Robert Fleming Trustee Co., 1961– (Chm., 1985–91); Robert Fleming Investment Trust, 1968–; Robert Fleming Holdings, 1974–97 (Dep. Chm., 1986–90); Glenshee Chairlift Co. Ltd, 1995–. High Sheriff, 1980, DL 1990, Oxfordshire. *Recreations:* most country pursuits, esp. stalking and fishing; most types of music, esp. Scottish traditional. *Address:* Church Farm, Steeple Barton, Bicester, Oxon OX6 3QR. *T:* (01869) 347177; Black Mount, Bridge of Orchy, Argyll PA36 4AH. *T:* (01838) 400237.

FLEMING, Roderick John; Managing Partner, Fleming Family & Partners; Chairman, Robert Fleming Holdings Ltd, 2000 (Director, since 1994; Deputy Chairman, 1999–2000); *b* 12 Nov. 1953; *s* of Richard Evelyn Fleming and Hon. Dorothy Charmian Fleming; *m* 1979, Diana Julia Wake; twin *d*. *Educ:* Eton Coll.; Magdalen Coll., Oxford (MA History). Trainee: Cazenove, 1974–75; Morgan Guaranty, NY, 1975–76; Corporate Finance Dept, Robert Fleming, 1976–80; joined Jardine Fleming, Singapore, 1980, Man. Dir, 1982–84; Dir, Jardine Fleming Internat. Ltd, with responsibility for internat. corporate finance, Jardine Fleming, Tokyo, 1984–86; International Portfolios Gp, Robert Fleming: joined, 1986; estbd Product Develt Gp, 1989; Product Develt Gp Dir, 1990–; Director: Capital Mkts, 1991–, Corporate Finance UK, 1993–, Robert Fleming; Robert Fleming Trustee Co. Ltd, 1991–2000; Dover Corp., 1995–; Ian Fleming (Glidrose) Pubns Ltd, 1996– (Chm., 2000–). *Recreation:* country pursuits. *Address:* Fleming Family & Partners, Ely House, 37 Dover Street, W1S 4NJ. *Clubs:* White's, Mark's.

FLEMING, Thomas Kelman, (Tom), CVO 1998; OBE 1980; *b* 29 June 1927; *s* of late Rev. Peter Fleming and Kate Ulla Fleming (*née* Barker). *Educ:* Daniel Stewart's Coll., Edinburgh. Actor, writer, producer and broadcaster; toured India with Edith Evans, 1945; RN, 1945–47; co-founder and Dir, Edinburgh Gateway Co., 1953–65; RSC, 1962–64, toured Europe, USA, USSR; founder and Dir, Royal Lyceum Theatre Co., 1965–66; Dir, Scottish Mil. Tattoo, Washington, 1976; Governor, Scottish Theatre Trust, 1980–82; Dir, Scottish Theatre Co., 1982–87; numerous Edinburgh Festival performances and productions. Member: Drama Adv. Panel, British Council, 1983–89; Lamp of Lothian Collegiate Trust, 1970–95; Scottish Internat. Educn Trust, 1996–. Pres., Edinburgh Sir Walter Scott Club, 2000. Hon. Mem., Royal Scottish Pipers' Soc.; Hon. Life Mem., Saltire Soc. Hon. FRSAMD 1986. DUniv Heriot-Watt, 1984; Hon. DLitt Queen Margaret UC, 1999. *Films include:* King Lear; Mary Queen of Scots; Meetings with Remarkable Men; *television:* title rôles include, 1952–: Redgauntlet; Rob Roy; Jesus of Nazareth; Henry IV; Weir of Hermiston; Reith; over 2000 broadcasts, 1944–; *television and radio:* BBC commentator, royal events, incl. Queen's Coronation, 1953, Silver Jubilee, 1977, and Queen's Birthday Parades, 1970–94; Cenotaph service, 1961, 1965–99; D Day, VE Day and VJ Day commems, 1994, 1995; also funeral services of HRH Duke of Windsor, King Frederick IX of Denmark, HRH Duke of Gloucester, Cardinal Heenan, Viscount Montgomery of Alamein, Pope John Paul I, Earl Mountbatten of Burma, President Tito, Princess Grace of Monaco, King Olav V of Norway and Diana, Princess of Wales. Proposed Immortal Memory of Robert Burns, Kremlin, 1991. Andrew Fletcher of Saltoun Award for services to Scotland, 2000. *Publications:* It's My Belief, 1953; So That Was Spring (poems), 1954; Miracle at Midnight (play), 1954; Voices out of the Air, 1981; (contrib.) BBC Book of Memories, 1991; (contrib.) A Scottish Childhood, 1998. *Recreations:* noticing, remembering and wondering. *Address:* c/o Peters, Fraser & Dunlop (Artists), Drury House, 34/43 Russell Street, WC2B 5HA. *T:* (020) 7344 1010. *Clubs:* Royal Commonwealth Society; Scottish Arts (Hon. Mem.) (Edinburgh).

FLEMMING, John Stanton, CBE 2001; FBA 1991; Warden, Wadham College, Oxford, since 1993; *b* 6 Feb. 1941; *s* of Sir Gilbert Nicolson Flemming, KCB, and late Virginia Coit; *m* 1963, Jean Elizabeth (*née* Briggs); four *c*. *Educ:* Rugby Sch.; Trinity Coll., Oxford (Hon. Fellow, 1994); Nuffield Coll., Oxford. BA Oxon 1962, MA 1966. Lecturer and Fellow, Oriel Coll., Oxford, 1963–65 (Hon. Fellow, 1993); Official Fellow in Economics, 1965–80, Emeritus Fellow, 1980, and Bursar, 1970–79, Nuffield Coll., Oxford. Bank of England: Chief Adviser, 1980–84; Economic Adviser to the Governor, 1984–88; Exec. Dir, 1988–91; Chief Economist, EBRD, 1991–93. Member: Nat. Freight Corp., 1978–80; Adv. Bd on Research Councils, 1986–91; Royal Commn on Envmtl Pollution, 1995–; Chairman: Economic Affairs Cttee, SSRC, 1981–84; Hansard Soc./Eur. Policy Forum Commn on Regulation of Privatised Utilities, 1995–96; Mgt Cttee, NIESR, 1996–. Vice-Pres., Royal Economic Soc., 1998– (Mem. Council, 1980–98; Treas., 1993–98); British Academy: Mem. Council, 1993–; Vice Pres., 1994–95; Hon. Treas., 1995–. Associate Editor: Oxford Economic Papers, 1970–73; Review of Economic Studies, 1973–76; Editor, Economic Jl, 1976–80. *Publications:* Inflation, 1976; contrib. economic jls. *Address:* Wadham College, Oxford OX1 3PN.

FLESCH, Michael Charles; QC 1983; *b* 11 March 1940; *s* of Carl and late Ruth Flesch; *m* 1972, Gail Schrire; one *s* one *d*. *Educ:* Gordonstoun Sch.; University College London (LLB 1st Cl. Hons). Called to the Bar, Gray's Inn, 1963 (Lord Justice Holker Sen. Schol.), Bencher, 1993. Bigelow Teaching Fellow, Univ. of Chicago, 1963–64; Lectr (part-time) in Revenue Law, University Coll. London, 1965–82. Practice at Revenue Bar, 1966–. Chairman: Taxation and Retirement Benefits Cttee, Bar Council, 1985–93; Revenue Bar Assoc., 1993–95. Governor of Gordonstoun Sch., 1976–96. *Publications:* various articles, notes and reviews concerning taxation, in legal periodicals. *Recreation:* all forms of sport. *Address:* (home) 38 Farm Avenue, NW2 2BH. *T:* (020) 8452 4547; (chambers) Gray's Inn Chambers, Gray's Inn, WC1R 5JA. *T:* (020) 7242 2642, *Fax:* (020) 7831 9017. *Clubs:* MCC, Arsenal FC, Brondesbury Lawn Tennis and Cricket.

FLESHER, Timothy James; a Deputy Chairman, Inland Revenue, since 1999 (a Commissioner, since 1998); *b* 25 July 1949; *s* of James Amos Flesher and Evelyn May Flesher (*née* Hale); *m* 1986, Margaret McCormack; two *d*. *Educ:* Hertford Coll., Oxford (BA). Lectr, Cambridge Coll. of Arts and Technol., 1972–74; Admin Trainee/HEO, Home Office, 1974–79; Sec. to Prisons Bd, 1979–82; Private Sec. to Prime Minister, 1982–86; Home Office: Head of: After Entry and Refugee Div., 1986–89; Personnel Div., 1989–91; Probation Service Div., 1991–92; Dir of Admin, OFSTED, 1992–94; Dep. DG (Ops), Immigration and Nationality Directorate (formerly Dept), Home Office, and Chief Inspector, Immigration Service, 1994–98. *Address:* (office) Somerset House, Strand, WC2R 1LB. *T:* (020) 7438 6543.

FLETCHER; *see* Aubrey-Fletcher.

FLETCHER, Alan Gerard, RDI 1972; designer; freelance practice, since 1993; *b* Nairobi, Kenya, 27 Sept. 1931; *s* of Bernard Fletcher and Dorothy Murphy; *m* 1956, Paola Biagi; one *d*. *Educ:* Christ's Hosp. Sch.; Central Sch. of Arts and Crafts; Royal Coll. of Art (ARCA); Sch. of Architecture and Design, Yale Univ. (Master of Fine Arts). FCSD (FSIAD 1964). Designer, Fortune Magazine, New York, 1958–59; freelance practice, London, 1959–62; Partner: Fletcher Forbes Gill, 1962–65; Crosby Fletcher Forbes, 1965–72; Founding Partner, Pentagram Design, 1972–92. Pres., Designers and Art Dirs Assoc., 1973; Internat. Pres., Alliance Graphique Internat., 1982–85. Sen. Fellow, RCA, 1989. Designers and Art Dirs Assoc. Gold Award for Design, 1974, and President's Award for Outstanding Contribn to Design, 1977; One Show Gold Award for Design, New York, 1974; Design Medal, SIAD, 1983; Prince Philip Prize for Designer of the Year, 1993; Hall of Fame, Amer. Art Directors, 1994. *Publications:* (jtly) Graphic Design: a visual comparison, 1963; (also illus.) Was Ich Sah, 1967; (jtly) A Sign Systems Manual, 1970; (jtly) Identity Kits, 1971; (jtly) Living by Design, 1978; (jtly) Ideas on Design, 1987; (jtly) Pentagram, The Compendium, 1993; Beware Wet Paint, 1995. *Address:* 12 Pembridge Mews, W11 3EQ. *T:* (020) 7229 7095, *Fax:* (020) 7229 8120.

FLETCHER, Alan Philip; QC 1984; *b* 28 June 1914; *s* of late Philip Cawthorne Fletcher, MC and Edith Maud Fletcher; *m* 1945, Annette Grace Wright; three *s* one *d*. *Educ:* Marlborough College; Trinity College, Oxford. MA; hockey blue, 1936 and 1937. War service, Army, England and India, 1939–45, ending as acting Lt-Col; called to the Bar, Inner Temple, 1940; bencher; Junior Counsel, Inland Revenue (Rating Valuation), 1969–84. Member (C): Hendon BC, 1954–65; Barnet LBC, 1964–74 (Leader, 1965–73). *Recreation:* architectural and garden history. *Address:* 26 Hollies Close, Royston, Herts SG8 7DZ. *T:* (01763) 248580.

See also Area Bishop of Dorchester, P. J. Fletcher, R. A. Fletcher.

FLETCHER, Ann Elizabeth Mary, (Mrs Michael Fletcher); *see* Leslie, A. E. M.

FLETCHER, Prof. Anthony John; Director and General Editor, Victoria County History and Professor of English Social History, University of London, since 2001; *b* 24 April 1941; *s* of John Molyneux Fletcher and Delle Clare Chenevix-Trench; *m* 1967, Tresna Dawn Russell (marr. diss. 1999); two *s*. *Educ:* Wellington Coll.; Merton Coll., Oxford (BA 1962). History Master, King's Coll. Sch., Wimbledon, 1964–67; Lect, Sen. Lectr, then Reader in History, Sheffield Univ., 1967–87; Prof. of Modern History, Durham Univ., 1987–95; Prof. of History, Essex Univ., 1995–2000. Auditor, QAA (formerly HEQC), 1994–. Pres., Ecclesiast. Hist. Soc., 1996–97; Vice-Pres., RHistS, 1997–2001 (Mem. Council, 1992–96). Convenor, History at the Univs Defence Gp, 1997–2000; Chair, QAA History Subject Benchmarking Gp, 1998–99. *Publications:* Tudor Rebellions, 1967; A County Community in Peace and War, 1975; The Outbreak of the English Civil War, 1981; (ed jtly) Order and Disorder in Early Modern England, 1985; Reform in the Provinces, 1986; (ed jtly) Religion, Culture and Society in Early Modern Britain, 1994; Gender, Sex and Subordination in England 1500–1800, 1995; (ed jtly) Childhood in Question: children, parents and the state, 1999; articles and reviews in learned jls. *Recreations:* theatre, opera, travel, walking, gardening. *Address:* Old Farm, South Newington, Banbury, Oxon OX14 5JW.

FLETCHER, Dr Archibald Peter; Medical Director, IMS International; Director, PMS International; Partner in Documenta Biomedica; *b* 24 Dec. 1930; *s* of Walter Archibald Fletcher and Dorothy Mabel Fletcher; *m* 1972, Patricia Elizabeth Samson (*née* Marr); three *s* two *d*. *Educ:* Kingswood Sch.; London Hosp. Med. Coll.; St Mary's Hosp. Med. Sch., London Univ. MB, BS; PhD (Biochemistry). Sen. Lectr in Chemical Pathology, St Mary's Hosp., London, 1961–69; Head of Biochemistry, American Nat. Red Cross, USA, 1970–73; Med. Dir, Upjohn, Scandinavia; PMO, Medicines Div., DHSS, 1977; Med. Assessor to Cttee on Safety of Medicines; Chief Sci. Officer and SPMO, DHSS, 1978–79; Res. Physician, Upjohn International Inc., Brussels, 1979. *Publications:* numerous papers in scientific and medical journals on glycoproteins, physical chemistry, metabolism of blood cells and safety evaluation of new drugs. *Recreations:* gardening, golf. *Address:* Hall Corner Cottage, Little Maplestead, Halstead, Essex CO9 2RU. *T:* (01787) 475465. *Clubs:* Wig and Pen, Royal Society of Medicine.

FLETCHER, Augustus James Voisey, OBE 1977; GM 1957; HM Diplomatic Service, retired; Foreign and Commonwealth Office, 1982–89; *b* 23 Dec. 1928; *s* of James Fletcher and Naomi Fletcher (*née* Dudden); *m* 1956, Enyd Gwynne Harries; one *s* one *d*. *Educ:* Weston-super-Mare Grammar Sch.; Oriental Language Institute, Malaya. Colonial Service, Palestine, 1946–48, Malaya, 1948–58; Min. of Defence, 1958–64; FCO, 1964–: Hong Kong (seconded HQ Land Forces), 1966–70; FCO, 1970–73; Hong Kong, 1973–76; FCO, 1976–79; Counsellor, New Delhi, 1979–82. *Recreations:* trout fishing, walking, food/wine, theatre. *Club:* Travellers.

FLETCHER, Rt Rev. Colin William; *see* Dorchester, Area Bishop of.

FLETCHER, David Edwin, MBE 1986; Executive Director, Transpennine Campaign, since 1988; environmental consultant and regional development specialist; *b* 15 July 1933; *s* of Edwin and Winifred Fletcher; marr. diss. 1990; two *d*. *Educ:* Hebden Bridge Grammar Sch.; Calder High Sch.; Sheffield Univ. (BSc Jt Hons); Leeds Univ. (PGCE); Bradford Univ. (MSc). Schoolmaster and Head of Biology, Bingley GS, 1957–60, Calder High Sch., 1960–69; Manchester Polytechnic: Sen. Lectr, 1970–74; Principal Lectr, 1974–80; Head, Envmt and Geographical Dept, 1980–88. Mem., Hebden Royd UDC, 1967–74 (Chm., Planning Cttee, 1969–74). Founder Chairman: Calder Civic Trust, 1965–75; Pennine Heritage Envmtl Trust, 1979–; Dir, Adv. Services, Civic Trust NW, 1970–76. Commissioner: Countryside Commn, 1988–96; Rural Develt Commn, 1993–2000. Chm., Action for Market Towns, 1998–; Member: NW Council for Sport and Recreation, 1972–78; Yorks and Humber Cttee, Heritage Lottery Fund, 2001–. *Publications:* ASK – Amenity, Society Knowhow, 1976; Industry Tourism, 1988; England's North West: a strategic vision for a European region, 1992; research and consultancy reports; contribs to acad. jls; environmental pamphlets. *Recreations:* walking, ski-ing, travel, meeting interesting people in interesting situations, restoring and finding new uses for wonderful old mills in the Pennines. *Address:* c/o Transpennine, Birchcliffe, Hebden Bridge, W Yorks HX7 8DG. *T:* (01422) 844450.

FLETCHER, Dr David John, CEng, FIEE; Chief Executive, British Waterways, since 1996; *b* 12 Dec. 1942; *s* of late John Fletcher and of Edna Fletcher; *m* 1967, Irene Mary Luther; one *s* one *d*. *Educ:* The Crypt Grammar Sch., Gloucester; Univ. of Leeds (BSc (Elect. Eng, High Frequency Electronics), DEng). General Electric Company, 1965–95: GEC Applied Electronics Labs, Stanmore, 1965–80; Gen. Manager, Stanmore Unit, Marconi Space and Defence Systems, 1980–84; Man. Dir, Marconi Defence Systems, 1984–87; GEC Marconi, 1987–95 (Dep. Chm., 1993–95). Chm., Assoc. of Inland Navigation Authorities, 1997–. Director Trustee, Nat. Coal Mining Mus., 1997–; Trustee, Waterways Trust, 1999–. Member: Rare Breed Survival Trust; Nat. Trust. *Recreations:* boating, classic cars. *Address:* British Waterways, Willow Grange, Church Road, Watford, Herts WD1 3QA.

FLETCHER, Geoffrey Scowcroft; artist and author; *o s* of Herbert Fletcher and Annie Talence Fletcher; *m* Mary Jean Timothy. *Educ:* University Coll., London Univ. (Dip. in Fine Art). Abbey Major Schol., British Sch. at Rome, 1948. Drawings appeared in Manchester Guardian, 1950; London drawings and articles featured in The Daily Telegraph, 1958–. Author of television features on unusual aspects of London; has been instrumental in saving a number of metropolitan buildings from demolition. Drawings and paintings in various public and private collections in England and abroad, including: exhibn of paintings and drawings in possession of Islington Council, 1972, 1978; exhibns of drawings and paintings, 1981, 1986, Lancashire industrial drawings and paintings, 1992–93, paintings, drawings and pubns, 1996, Bolton Art Gall.; *acquisitions:* drawings and sketchbooks, British Museum, 1990; oil paintings and sketchbooks, Guildhall Art Gall., 1990–97; drawings and sketchbooks, Ashmolean Mus., 1991–92; oil paintings and drawings, Bury Art Gall., 1993–94; watercolours, Whitworth Art Gall., Manchester, 1996; London and Continental oil paintings, Guildhall Art Gall., 1998; oil paintings and drawings, Blackpool Art Gall., 1999–2000. Geoffrey Fletcher Room, decorated with the artist's drawings, opened Selfridge Hotel, London, 1973. Designed enamel box for St Paul's Cathedral Appeal, 1972; *exhibitions:* drawings, Miles Gall., St James's, 1980; East End Drawings and Paintings, Limehouse, 1984; London drawings, Guildhall, City of London, 1988; Genoese drawings, for City of Genoa promotion, London, 1988; paintings, Guildhall Art Gall., 1999–2000. *Publications:* The London Nobody Knows (filmed, 1968), 1962, 3rd edn 1996; Down Among the Meths Men, 1966; Geoffrey Fletcher's London, 1968; City Sights, 1963; Pearly Kingdom, 1965; London's River, 1966; Elements of Sketching, 1966 (Amer. edn, 1968); London's Pavement Pounders, 1967; London After Dark, 1969; Changing London (Drawings from The Daily Telegraph), 1969; The London Dickens Knew, 1970; London Souvenirs, 1973; Paint It In Water Colour, 1974; Italian Impressions, 1974; Sketch It In Black and White, 1975; London: a private view, 1989; The Spitalfields Prints, 1990; Daily Telegraph Series: London Prints, 1975, London Colour Prints, 1978, London Portraits, 1978, London at My Feet, 1979; London Alleys, 1980. *Address:* c/o Cassell plc, Wellington House, 125 Strand, WC2R 0BB; c/o R. Davis-Poynter, 118 St Pancras, Chichester, W Sussex.

FLETCHER, Hugh Alasdair; Chairman: CGNU Australia Holdings Ltd (formerly CGU Insurance Australia), since 1998; New Zealand Insurance, since 1998; *b* 28 Nov. 1947; *s* of Sir James Muir Cameron Fletcher, *qv*; *m* 1970, Sian Seerpoohi Elias (*see* Rt Hon. Dame Sian Elias); two *s*. *Educ:* Auckland Univ. (MCom Hons, BSc); Stanford Univ., USA (MBA 1972). Fletcher Holdings: Asst to Ops Res., 1969–70; PA to Man. Dir, 1972–76; Dep. Man Dir, 1976–79; Chief Exec. Officer, 1979–81; Fletcher Challenge Ltd: non-exec. Dir, 1981–; Man. Dir, 1981–87; CEO, 1987–97. Non-exec. Chm., Air New Zealand Ltd, 1985–89; Director: Infrastructure Auckland, 1998–; Australasian Adv. Bd, Merrill Lynch, 1998–2000; Rubicon, 2001–. Chairman: NZ Thoroughbred Marketing, 1998–2000; Ministerial Inquiry into Telecommunications, 2000; Member: Prime Minister's Enterprise Council, 1992–97; Asia Pacific Adv. Cttee, New York Stock Exchange, 1995–; World Business Council for Sustainable Develt, Geneva, 1993–96; Adv. Cttee, UN Office for Project Services, 2000–. Mem. Council, Univ. of Auckland, 2000–. *Recreations:* horse riding, horse breeding and racing, chess, Go. *Address:* PO Box 11468, Ellerslie, New Zealand.

FLETCHER, Sir James Muir Cameron, Kt 1980; ONZ 1997; FCA; Managing Director, 1942–79, Chairman, 1972–80, Fletcher Holdings Ltd; *b* Dunedin, NZ, 25 Dec. 1914; *s* of Sir James Fletcher; *m* 1942, Margery Vaughan, *d* of H. H. Gunthorp; three *s*. *Educ:* Waitaki Boys' High School; Auckland Grammar School. South British Insurance Co., 1931–37; then Fletcher Construction Co. and Fletcher Holdings; Pres. and Dir, Fletcher Challenge Ltd, 1981–90. *Address:* Fletcher Challenge Ltd, Private Bag 92114, Auckland, New Zealand; 119 St Stephens Avenue, Parnell, Auckland, NZ.

See also H. A. Fletcher.

FLETCHER, John Edwin; His Honour Judge Fletcher; a Circuit Judge, since 1986; *b* 23 Feb. 1941; *s* of late Sydney Gerald Fletcher and Cecilia Lane Fletcher; *m* 1st, 1971, Felicity Jane Innes Dick (marr. diss.); 2nd, 1996, Mrs Susan Kennedy-Hawkes. *Educ:* St Bees Sch., Cumbria; Clare Coll., Cambridge (MA). Called to the Bar, Inner Temple, 1964; Midland and Oxford Circuit, 1965–86; a Recorder, 1983–86. Mem. Panel of Chairmen, Medical Appeal Tribunals, 1981–86. *Recreations:* walking, photography.

FLETCHER, Kim Thomas; Editorial Director, Hollinger Telegraph New Media, since 2000; *b* 17 Sept. 1956; *s* of Jack Fletcher and Agnes Fletcher (*née* Coulthwaite); *m* 1991, Sarah Sands; one *s* one *d*, and one step *s*. *Educ:* Heversham Grammar Sch., Westmorland; Hertford Coll., Oxford (BA Law); UC Cardiff (Dip. Journalism Studies). Reporter, The Star, Sheffield, 1978–81; Sunday Times, 1981–86: Home Affairs Corresp., 1984; Labour Corresp., 1985–86; Home Affairs Corresp., Daily Telegraph, 1986–87; Sunday Telegraph, 1988–98: News Editor, 1991–95; Dep. Editor, 1995–98; Editor, Independent on Sunday, 1998–99. *Recreation:* family life. *Address:* (office) Hollinger Telegraph New Media, 1 Canada Square, E14 5DT. *T:* (020) 7538 5000; (home) 37 Caithness Road, W14 0JA. *T:* (020) 7602 4217; *e-mail:* kimfletcher@dial.pipex.com. *Club:* Groucho.

FLETCHER, Sir Leslie, Kt 1983; DSC 1945; FCA; Deputy Chairman, RMC Group, 1991–96 (Director, 1983–96); *b* 14 Oct. 1922; *s* of Ernest and Lily Fletcher; *m* 1947, Audrey Faviell Jackson; one *s* one *d*. *Educ:* Nether Edge Secondary Sch., Sheffield. FCA 1952. Served War, RNVR (FAA), 1942–46 (Lieut). Helbert Wagg & Co. Ltd (subseq. J. Henry Schroder Wagg & Co. Ltd), 1955–71, Dir 1966–71; Chm., Glynwed Internat., 1971–86; Dep. Chm., Standard Chartered PLC, 1983–89 (Dir, 1972–89); Chairman: Westland Group, 1989–94; Rank Orgn, 1992–95 (Dir, 1984–95). Mem. Council, CBI, 1976–86. *Recreations:* gardening, golf, photography. *Address:* Hafod, The Green, Sherfield-on-Loddon, Hook, Hants RG27 0EN. *Clubs:* Brooks's, MCC, Royal Automobile; Royal & Ancient Golf (St Andrews).

FLETCHER, Malcolm Stanley, MBE 1982; FREng; FICE; Consultant, Sir William Halcrow & Partners Ltd, Consulting Civil Engineers, since 1996; *b* 25 Feb. 1936; *s* of Harold and Clarice Fletcher; *m* 1965, Rhona Christina Wood; one *s* two *d*. *Educ:* Manchester Grammar Sch.; Manchester Univ. (MSc); Imperial Coll., London (DIC). FGS 1968; FICE 1976; FREng (FEng 1993). Pupil, Binnie & Partners, 1957–60; Sir William Halcrow & Partners, 1968–96: Partner, 1985–96; Chm., 1990–96. Resident Engineer: Jhelum Bridge, Pakistan, 1965–67; Guiliana Bridge, Libya, 1968–74; Design Team Leader, Orwell Bridge, Ipswich, 1976–82; Dir of Design, Second Severn Crossing, 1988–96; Adviser: Dartford River Crossing, 1985–90; Lantau Fixed Crossing, Hong Kong, 1990. *Recreation:* cycling. *Address:* Burderop Park, Swindon, Wilts SN4 0QD. *T:* (01793) 812479.

FLETCHER, Comdt Marjorie Helen (Kelsey), CBE 1988; Director, Women's Royal Naval Service, 1986–88; *b* 21 Sept. 1932; *d* of late Norman Farler Fletcher and Marie Amelie Fletcher (*née* Adams). *Educ:* Avondale High Sch.; Sutton Coldfield High Sch. for Girls. Solicitor's Clerk, 1948–53; joined WRNS as Telegraphist, 1953; progressively, 3rd Officer to Chief Officer, 1956–76; Supt, 1981; served in Secretarial, Careers Advisor, Intelligence and Staff appts; ndc 1979; Directing Staff, RN Staff Coll., 1980–81; psc 1981; Internat. Mil. Staff, NATO HQ, 1981–84; Asst Dir, Dir Naval Staff Duties, 1984–85. ADC to the Queen, 1986–88. *Publication:* The WRNS, 1989. *Recreations:* reading, needlework.

FLETCHER, Michael John; Sheriff of Tayside Central and Fife, since 2000; *b* 5 Dec. 1945; *s* of Walter Fletcher and Elizabeth Fletcher (*née* Pringle); *m* 1968, Kathryn Mary Bain; two *s*. *Educ:* High Sch. of Dundee; Univ. of St Andrews (LLB). Admitted solicitor, 1968; apprenticeship, Kirk Mackie & Elliot, SSC, Edinburgh, 1966–68; Asst, then Partner, Ross Strachan & Co., Dundee, 1968–88; Partner, Hendry & Fenton, later Miller Hendry, Dundee, 1988–94; Sheriff of South Strathclyde, Dumfries and Galloway, 1994–99; Sheriff of Lothian and Borders, 1999–2000. Lectr (part-time) in Civil and Criminal Procedure, Univ. of Dundee, 1974–94. Editor, Scottish Civil Law Reports, 1999–. *Publication:* (jtly) Delictual Damages, 2000. *Recreations:* golf, badminton, gardening. *Address:* Sheriff Court House, Tay Street, Perth PH2 8NL. *T:* (01738) 620546.

FLETCHER, Neil; Head of Education, Culture and Tourism, Local Government Association, since 1998; *b* 5 May 1944; *s* of Alan and Ruth Fletcher; *m* 1967, Margaret Monaghan; two *s*. *Educ:* Wyggeston Sch., Leicester; City of Leeds Coll. of Educn (Teachers' Cert.); London Univ. (BA Hons); London Business Sch. (MBA 1994). Charter FCP 1990. Schoolteacher, 1966–68; Lectr, 1969–76; Admin. Officer, 1976–91, Educn Officer, 1991–93, NALGO; Educn Officer, UNISON, 1993–94; mgt consultant, 1995–98. Member: Camden Bor. Council, 1978–86 (Dep. Leader, 1982–84); ILEA, 1979–90 (Chair, Further and Higher Educn Sub-Cttee, 1981–87; Leader, 1987–90); Chair: Council of Local Educn Authorities, 1987–88, 1989–90; Educn Cttee, AMA, 1987–90 (Vice-Chair, 1986–87). Governor: London Inst., 1986–99; LSE, 1990–; City Literary Inst., 1996–. FRSA 1989. *Recreations:* cricket, soccer, theatre, cookery, walking. *Address:* 42 Narcissus Road, NW6 1TH. *T:* (020) 7435 5306, *Fax:* (020) 7813 9011; *e-mail:* neil.fletcher@lga.gov.uk.

FLETCHER, Philip John; Director General of Water Services, since 2000; *b* 2 May 1946; *s* of Alan Philip Fletcher, *qv* and Annette Grace Fletcher (*née* Wright); *m* 1977, Margaret Anne Boys; one *d* (and one *d* decd). *Educ:* Marlborough College; Trinity College, Oxford (MA). Asst Principal, MPBW, 1968; Department of the Environment: Private Sec. to Permanent Sec., 1978; Asst Sec., Private Sector Housebuilding, 1980, local govt expenditure, 1982–85; Under Secretary: Housing, Water and Central Finance, 1986–90; Planning and Develt Control, 1990–93; Chief Exec., PSA Services, 1993–94, and Dep. Sec., Property Holdings, 1994; Dep. Sec., Cities and Countryside Gp, 1994–95; Receiver for the Metropolitan Police District, 1996–2000. Reader, Church of England. *Recreation:* walking. *Address:* Office of Water Services, Centre City Tower, 7 Hill Street, Birmingham B5 4UA. *T:* (0121) 625 1300, *Fax:* (0121) 625 1348.

See also Area Bishop of Dorchester.

FLETCHER, Richard George Hopper, CMG 1996; HM Diplomatic Service, retired; Vice-President, Government Relations and External Affairs, Europe, Nortel Networks, since 1998; *b* 8 Nov. 1944; *s* of George Hopper Fletcher, CBE, FCA and Kathleen Mary Parsons; *m* 1967, Celia Rosemary Soord; two *d*. *Educ:* Leys Sch., Cambridge; Balliol Coll., Oxford. Joined Foreign Office, 1966–67; Athens, 1968; Nicosia, 1969–72; First Sec., Bucharest, 1973–76; FCO, 1977–83; Counsellor: Athens, 1984–88; FCO, 1989–98. *Recreations:* forestry, gardening, bridge, golf. *Clubs:* Athenæum; Wimbledon Park Golf.

FLETCHER, Robin Anthony, OBE 1984; DSC 1944; DPhil; Warden of Rhodes House, Oxford, 1980–89; Professorial Fellow, Trinity College, Oxford, 1980–89, now Emeritus; *b* 30 May 1922; *s* of Philip Cawthorne Fletcher, MC, and Edith Maud Fletcher (*née* Okell); *m* 1950, Jinny May (*née* Cornish); two *s*. *Educ:* Marlborough Coll.; Trinity Coll., Oxford (MA, DPhil). Served Royal Navy (Lieut RNVR), 1941–46. University Lecturer in Modern Greek, 1949–79; Domestic Bursar, Trinity Coll., Oxford, 1950–74; Senior Proctor, 1966–67; Member, Hebdomedal Council, 1967–74. Represented England at hockey, 1949–55 and GB, 1952 Olympic Games (Bronze Medal). *Publications:* Kostes Palamas, Athens, 1984; various articles. *Recreations:* sport, music. *Address:* Binglea, Quoyloo, Stromness, Orkney KW16 3LU. *Clubs:* Naval; Vincent's (Oxford).

See also A. P. Fletcher.

FLETCHER, Prof. Ronald Stanley, FRAeS; Professor of Thermal Power, since 1972, and Deputy Vice-Chancellor, since 1994, Cranfield University (formerly Cranfield Institute of Technology); *b* 12 Dec. 1937; *s* of Reginald and Dorothy Fletcher; *m* 1965, Pamela Alys, *d* of Gwilym and Alys Treharne; one *s* twin *d*. *Educ:* Imperial College, London Univ. (PhD, DIC); UMIST (BSc Tech). FRAeS 1994. Senior Engineer, Northern Research & Engineering Corp., Cambridge, USA, 1965–70; Consultant, Northern Research & Engineering Corp., Herts, 1970–72; Cranfield Institute of Technology: Head of Mechanical Engineering, 1977–87; Dean of Engineering, 1982–85; Pro-Vice-Chancellor, 1985–93; Head of Cranfield Campus, 1989–94; Chairman: Cranfield Mgt Develt Ltd, 1993–; Cranfield Aerospace Ltd, 1996–98. Visiting Professor: Cairo, 1975; Brazil, 1977; China (Beijing Inst. of Aero. and Astro.), 1979. Member: ARC, 1974–77; Governing Body, AFRC Inst. of Engrg Res. (formerly Nat. Inst. of Agricl Engrg), 1978–93 (Chm., Finance Cttee, 1982–86); Council, British Hydro. Res. Assoc., 1979–89; AGARD (NATO) Propulsion and Energetics Panel, 1980–99 (Chm., 1997–98); Scientific Bd, Univ. de Technologie de Compiègne, 1989–94; Conseil Scientifique, Inst. Méditerranéen de Technologie, 1989–94. Governor, Bedford Modern Sch., 1986–89. Médaille Gustave Trasenter, Liège, 1990; Prix Formation Etranger, Acad. Nat. de l'Air et de l'Espace, France, 1991. Chevalier, 1990, Officier, 1994, Ordre des Palmes Académiques (France). *Publications:* papers on combustion. *Recreations:* sailing, music. *Address:* 34 Brecon Way, Bedford MK41 8DD. *T:* (01234) 358483. *Club:* Parkstone Yacht.

FLETCHER, Stuart Barron; Chief Executive, Pembrokeshire and Derwen (formerly Pembrokeshire) NHS Trust, since 1994; *b* 28 July 1945; *s* of Arthur Barron Fletcher and Bertha Fletcher; *m* 1970, Dilys Roberts; two *s* one *d*. *Educ:* King George V Grammar Sch., Southport; Oriel Coll., Oxford (MA). MHSM, DipHSM. Entered Health Service as Nat. Trainee Administrator, 1968; NHS posts include: Hosp. Sec., Broadgreen Hosp., Liverpool, 1972–74; Area Gen. Administrator, St Helens and Knowsley HA, 1974–78; Dist Administrator, E Birmingham HA, 1978–82; Chief Exec., N Staffs HA, 1982–91; Regl Man. Dir, subseq. Chief Exec., W Midlands RHA, 1992–93. Member: NHS Trng Authy, 1985–91; NHS Trng Adv. Bd, 1991–93. Pres., IHSM, 1991–92 (Mem., Nat. Council, 1981–95). *Recreations:* Rugby, fell walking, photography, theatre. *Address:* 5 Douglas James Close, Haverfordwest, Pembrokeshire SA61 2UF. *T:* (01437) 760103.

FLETCHER-VANE, family name of **Baron Inglewood**.

FLEW, Prof. Antony Garrard Newton; Emeritus Professor, University of Reading, since 1983; *b* 11 Feb. 1923; *o s* of Rev. Dr R. N. Flew; *m* 1952, Annis Ruth Harty; two *d*. *Educ:* St Faiths Sch., Cambridge; Kingswood Sch., Bath; Sch. of Oriental and African Studies, London; St John's Coll., Oxford (John Locke Schol., MA); DLitt Keele, 1974. Lecturer: Christ Church, Oxford, 1949–50; Univ. of Aberdeen, 1950–54; Professor of Philosophy: Univ. of Keele, 1954–71; Univ. of Calgary, 1972–73; Univ. of Reading, 1973–82; (part-time) York Univ., Toronto, 1983–85; Distinguished Res. Fellow (part-time), Social Philosophy and Policy Center, Bowling Green State Univ., Ohio, 1986–91. Many temp. vis. appts. Gavin David Young Lectr, Adelaide, 1963; Gifford Lectr, St Andrews, 1986. A Vice-Pres., Rationalist Press Assoc., 1973–88; Chm., Voluntary Euthanasia Soc., 1976–79. Fellow, Acad. of Humanism, 1983–. *Publications:* A New Approach to Psychical Research, 1953; Hume's Philosophy of Belief, 1961; God and Philosophy, 1966; Evolutionary Ethics, 1967; An Introduction to Western Philosophy,

1971; Crime or Disease?, 1973; Thinking About Thinking, 1975; The Presumption of Atheism, 1976; Sociology, Equality and Education, 1976; A Rational Animal, 1978; Philosophy: an introduction, 1979; The Politics of Procrustes, 1981; Darwinian Evolution, 1984; Thinking About Social Thinking, 1985; Hume, Philosopher of Moral Science, 1986; (with G. Vesey) Agency and Necessity, 1987; The Logic of Mortality, 1987; Power to the Parents, 1987; Equality in Liberty and Justice, 1989; Atheistic Humanism, 1993; Shephard's Warning: setting schools back on course, 1994; Philosophical Essays of Antony Flew, 1998; How to Think Straight, 1998; articles in philosophical and other jls. *Recreations:* walking, climbing, house maintenance. *Address:* 26 Alexandra Road, Reading, Berks RG1 5PD. *T:* (0118) 926 1848. *Club:* Union Society (Oxford).

FLIGHT, Howard Emerson; MP (C) Arundel and South Downs, since 1997; Joint Chairman, Investec Guinness Flight Ltd, since 1998; *b* 16 June 1948; *s* of late Bernard Thomas Flight and of Doris Mildred Emerson Flight; *m* 1973, Christabel Diana Beatrice Norbury; one *s* three *d*. *Educ:* Brentwood Sch.; Magdalene Coll., Cambridge (MA Hist. Pt 1, Econs Pt 2); Univ. of Michigan (MBA 1971). Investment Adviser: N. M. Rothschild & Sons, 1970–73; Cayzer Ltd, 1973–77; Wardley Ltd (Hong Kong Bank), Hong Kong and India, 1977–79; Investment Dir, Guinness Mahon Co. Ltd, 1979–87; Jt Man. Dir, Guinness Flight Global Asset Mgt, 1987–97; Dep. Chm., Guinness Flight Hambro, 1997–98. Contested (C) Bermondsey, Feb. and Oct. 1974. Mem., Social Security Select Cttee, 1998–. Jt Chm., All Party H of C Hong Kong Cttee, 1998–. FRSA. *Publication:* All You Need to Know About Exchange Rates, 1988. *Recreations:* classical music, antiques, gardening, ski-ing. *Address:* House of Commons, SW1A 0AA. *T:* (020) 7219 6949. *Clubs:* Carlton, Winchester House.

FLINDALL, Jacqueline; JP; Regional Nursing Officer, Wessex Regional Health Authority, 1983–85; *b* 12 Oct. 1932; *d* of Henry and Lilian Flindall. *Educ:* St Davids Sch., Ashford, Mddx; University Coll. Hosp., London (DipN). SRN, SCM, UCH, 1950–54; Midwifery, St Luke's Mat. Hosp., Guildford and Watford, 1955; exchange student, Mount Sinai Hosp., NY, 1956; Ward Sister and Clinical Teacher, UCH, 1957–63; Asst Matron, Wexham Park Hosp., 1964–66; Dep. Supt of Nursing, Prince of Wales and St Anne's, 1967–69; Chief Nursing Officer: Northwick Park Hosp., 1969–73; Oxfordshire HA, 1973–83. Associate Consultant, PA Management Consultants, 1986–94. Non-exec. Dir, Royal Nat. Orth. Hosp. NHS Trust, Stanmore, 1991–95. Vice Chm., Hosp. Chaplaincies Council, 1997. Professional Organization Mem., RCN; Hon. FRCN 1983. JP Oxford, 1982, Salisbury, 1987; Mem., Wilts Magistrates' Courts Cttee, 1995–. *Recreation:* painting.

FLINT, Prof. Anthony Patrick Fielding, PhD, DSc; FIBiol; Professor of Animal Physiology, Department of Physiology and Environmental Science, University of Nottingham, since 1993; *b* 31 Aug. 1943; *s* of Maurice Fielding Flint and Patricia Joan (*née* Ince); *m* 1967, Chan Mun Kwun; two *s*. *Educ:* Hill Crest Sch., Swanage; King's Sch., Bruton; Univ. of St Andrews (Queen's Coll., Dundee) (BSc 1966); Univ. of Bristol (PhD 1969; DSc 1984). FIBiol 1982. Res. Fellow, Univ. of Western Ontario, 1969–72; Sen. Res. Biochemist in Obs and Gyn., Welsh Nat. Sch. of Medicine, Cardiff, 1972–73; Lectr, Nuffield Dept of Obs and Gyn., Oxford Univ., 1973–77; Staff Mem., AFRC Inst. of Animal Physiology and Genetics Res., Cambridge, 1977–87; Dir of Science and Dir of Inst. of Zool., Zool Soc. of London, 1987–93. Special Lectr, 1985–87, Special Prof. in Molecular Biol., 1987–93, Univ. of Nottingham Sch. of Agric.; Visiting Professor: Dept of Biology, UCL, 1989–; Biosphere Scis Div., KCL, 1989–. Member: Cttee, Soc. for Study of Fertility, 1981–89 (Sec., 1985–89); Steering Cttee, WHO Task Force on Plants for Fertility Regulation, 1982–87 (Chm., 1985). Member: Council of Management, Journals of Reproduction and Fertility Ltd, 1981–87 (Mem. Exec. Cttee, 1983–87); Bd of Scientific Editors, Jl of Endocrinology, 1983–87. Medal, Soc. for Endocrinology, 1985. *Publications:* (ed jtly) Embryonic Diapause in Mammals, 1981; Reproduction in Domestic Ruminants, 1991; papers in physiol, endocrinol and biochemical jls. *Recreations:* playing Bach on the organ or cello, coasting in small ships. *Address:* Department of Physiology and Environmental Science, University of Nottingham, Sutton Bonington, Loughborough, Leics LE12 5RD.

FLINT, Caroline Louise; MP (Lab) Don Valley, since 1997; *b* 20 Sept. 1961; *d* of Wendy Flint (*née* Beasley); *m* (marr. diss. 1990); one *s* one *d*; *m* Phil Cole; one step *s*. *Educ:* Univ. of East Anglia (BA Hons American History and Lit.). Mgt Trainee, 1983–84, Policy Officer, 1984–86, GLC; Head of Women's Unit, NUS, 1988–89; Principal Officer, Lambeth, 1989–93; Sen. Researcher and Political Officer, GMB, 1994–97. PPS to Minister of State (Minister for Europe), FCO, 2001–. *Recreations:* cinema, tennis, family and friends. *Address:* House of Commons, SW1A 0AA. *T:* (020) 7219 4407.

FLINT, Charles John Raffles; QC 1995. *Educ:* Trinity College, Cambridge (BA 1973; MA 1980). Called to the Bar, Middle Temple, 1975, Bencher, 2001; Junior Counsel to the Crown (Common Law), 1991–95. *Address:* Blackstone Chambers, Blackstone House, Temple, EC4Y 9BW.

FLINT, Prof. David, TD; MA, BL, CA; Professor of Accountancy, 1964–85, (Johnstone Smith Chair, 1964–75), and Vice-Principal, 1981–85, University of Glasgow; *b* 24 Feb. 1919; *s* of David Flint, JP, and Agnes Strang Lambie; *m* 1953, Dorothy Mary Maclachlan Jardine; two *s* one *d*. *Educ:* Glasgow High Sch.; University of Glasgow. Served with Royal Signals, 1939–46, Major (despatches). Awarded distinction final examination of Institute of Chartered Accountants of Scotland, 1948. Lecturer, University of Glasgow, 1950–60; Dean of Faculty of Law, 1971–73. Partner, Mann Judd Gordon & Co. Chartered Accountants, Glasgow, 1951–71. Hon. Prof. of Accountancy, Stirling Univ., 1988–91. Hon. Pres. Glasgow Chartered Accountants Students Soc., 1959–60; Chm., Assoc. of Univ. Teachers of Accounting (now British Accounting Assoc.), 1969. Mem. Council, Scottish Business Sch., 1971–77; Vice-Pres., Scottish Economic Soc., 1977–99; Vice-Pres., Inst. of Chartered Accountants of Scotland, 1973–75, Pres., 1975–76; Pres., European Accounting Assoc., 1983–84; Member: Management and Ind. Rel. Cttee, SSRC, 1970–72 and 1978–80; Commn for Local Authy Accounts in Scotland, 1978–80. *Publications:* A True and Fair View in Company Accounts, 1982; Philosophy and Principles of Auditing: an introduction, 1988; Professionalism and Ethics in Auditing, 1999. *Recreation:* golf. *Address:* 16 Grampian Avenue, Auchterarder, Perthshire PH3 1NY.

FLINT, Michael Frederick, FSA; consultant; *b* 7 May 1932; *s* of Frederic Nelson La Fargue Flint and Nell Dixon Smith; *m* 1st, 1954, Susan Kate Rhodes (marr. diss.) two *s* one *d*; 2nd, 1984, Phyllida Margaret Medwyn Hughes. *Educ:* St Peter's Sch., York; Kingswood Sch., Bath. Admitted Solicitor 1956; Denton Hall & Burgin, subseq. Denton Hall Burgin & Warrens, then Denton Wilde Sapte: Articled Clerk, 1951–56; Asst Solicitor, 1956–60; Partner, 1960–66 and 1972–93; Man. Partner, 1979–82; Chm., 1990–93; Consultant, 1993–2000. Paramount Pictures Corporation: Asst Vice-Pres., 1967; Vice-Pres., 1968–70; Consultant, Henry Ansbacher & Co., 1970; Chm., London Screen Enterprises, 1970–72 (Exec. Producer, feature film, Glastonbury Fayre, 1972). Director: Portman Entertainment Group Ltd, 1995–; Renaissance Films Ltd, 1999–. Consultant, London Economics Ltd, 1999–. Dir, and Chm. Council, 1995–99, Intellectual Property Inst. (formerly Council of Common Law Inst. of Intellectual Property; founder Mem.); Chm., Intellectual Property, Entertainment and Telecommunications Cttee, Internat. Bar Assoc., 1985–90. Vice-Pres., Brit. Archaeol Assoc., 1988–. Member: BAFTA, 1984–; RTS, 1990–; British Screen Adv. Council, 1991– (Dep. Chm., 1995–); Council, Aldeburgh Productions, 1998–. Chairman: Orford Mus., 1997–; Alde and Ore Assoc., 2000–. FSA 1965. *Publications:* A User's Guide to Copyright, 1979, 5th edn 2000; (jtly) Television by Satellite: Legal Aspects, 1987; (jtly) Intellectual Property: The New Law, 1989. *Recreations:* painting, golf, opera. *Address:* Green Lane House, Castle Green, Orford, Suffolk IP12 2NF. *Clubs:* Savile, Groucho; Aldeburgh Golf; Orford Sailing.

FLINT, Rachael H.; *see* Heyhoe Flint.

FLOISSAC, Rt Hon. Sir Vincent (Frederick), Kt 1992; CMG 1985; OBE 1973; PC 1992; Chief Justice and President of the Court of Appeal, Eastern Caribbean Supreme Court, 1991–96; *b* 31 July 1928; *m* 1954, Marilyn (*née* Bristol); twin *d*. *Educ:* St Mary's Coll., St Lucia; UCL (LLM 1953). Called to the Bar, Gray's Inn, 1952 (Hon. Bencher, 1992); in practice, St Lucia, 1953–91; QC (St Lucia) 1969; Mem., Seychelles Ct of Appeal, 1988–91. Nominated Mem. and Dep. Speaker, St Lucia House of Assembly, 1969–75; first Pres., Senate of St Lucia, 1979; Acting Governor Gen., St Lucia, 1987–88. Mem., Judicial Cttee, Privy Council, 1992–. Chm., St Lucia Central Water Authority, 1965–72; Dir, St Lucia Co-op Bank Ltd, 1960–91. *Recreations:* football, table tennis, tennis. *Address:* c/o Floissac Fleming & Associates, PO Box 722, Castries, St Lucia, West Indies.

FLOOD, David Andrew; Organist and Master of the Choristers, Canterbury Cathedral, since 1988; *b* 10 Nov. 1955; *s* of Frederick Flood and June Flood (*neé* Alexander); *m* 1976, Alayne Nicholas; two *s* two *d*. *Educ:* Royal Grammar School, Guildford; St John's Coll., Oxford (MA); Clare Coll., Cambridge (PGCE). FRCO(CHM). Assistant Organist, Canterbury Cathedral, 1978–86; Organist and Master of Choristers, Lincoln Cathedral, 1986–88. Mem., Royal Soc. of Musicians, 1996–; Hon. Sen. Mem., Darwin Coll., Univ. of Kent, 1989–. Hon. FGCM 2000. *Recreations:* motoring, cooking, travel. *Address:* 6 The Precincts, Canterbury, Kent CT1 2EE. *T:* (01227) 865242; *e-mail:* davidf@canterbury-cathedral.org.

FLOOD, Prof. John Edward, OBE 1986; DSc, PhD; CEng, FIEE; FInstP; Professor of Electrical Engineering, 1965–90, now Emeritus, and Head of Department of Electrical and Electronic Engineering, 1967–81 and 1983–89, University of Aston in Birmingham; *b* 2 June 1925; *s* of Sydney E. Flood and Elsie G. Flood; *m* 1949, Phyllis Mary Groocock; two *s*. *Educ:* City of London Sch.; Queen Mary Coll., Univ. of London (BSc 1945; PhD 1951; DSc 1965). CEng, FIEE 1959; FIERE 1967; FInstP 1987. Admiralty Signals Estab., 1944–46; Standard Telephone and Cables Ltd, 1946–47; PO Res. Stn, 1947–52; Siemens Brothers Ltd, 1952–57; Chief Engr, Advanced Develt Labs, AEI Telecommunications Div., 1957–65; Dean, Faculty of Engrg, 1971–74, and Sen. Pro-Vice-Chancellor, 1981–83, Univ. of Aston in Birmingham. Chairman: IEE Professional Gp on Telecommunications, 1974–77; IEE S Midland Centre, 1978–79; Univs Cttee on Integrated Sandwich Courses, 1981–82; BSI Cttee on Telecommunications, 1981–92; Member: British Electrotechnical Council, 1981–86; Monopolies and Mergers Commn, 1985–98. FCGI 1991 (CGIA 1962). Freeman, City of London, 1957. *Publications:* Telecommunication Networks, 1975, 2nd edn 1997; Transmission Systems, 1991; Telecommunications Switching, Traffic and Networks, 1995; papers in scientific and technical jls; patents. *Recreations:* swimming, wine-making. *Address:* 60 Widney Manor Road, Solihull, West Midlands B91 3JQ. *T:* (0121) 705 3604. *Club:* Royal Over-Seas League.

FLOOD, Prof. John Lewis, PhD; Deputy Director, University of London Institute of Germanic Studies, since 1979; Professor of German, University of London, since 1993; *b* 22 Sept. 1938; *s* of late William Henry Flood and Ethel Mary Flood (*née* Daffern); *m* 1973, Ann Matthews, BA, ALA, *d* of Edward Matthews; three *s*. *Educ:* Alderman Newton's Grammar Sch., Leicester; Univ. of Nottingham (BA 1961; MA 1963); Univ. of Munich; Univ. of Kiel; PhD London 1980. Lektor for English, Univ. of Erlangen–Nuremberg, 1963–64; Asst Lectr in German, Univ. of Nottingham, 1964–65; King's College London: Asst Lectr in German, 1965–67; Lectr, 1967–72; Sen. Lectr, 1972–79; Reader in German, Univ. of London, 1980–93. Chm., Panel for German, Dutch and Scandinavian Langs, RAEs 1996 and 2001, HEFCE. Hon. Sec., Conf. of Univ. Teachers of German in GB and Ireland, 1971–92. Hon. Treas., Henry Sweet Soc. for Hist. of Linguistic Ideas, 1984–; Vice-Pres., Bibliographical Soc., 1993–; Mem. Council, Philological Soc., 1998–. Fellow, Centre for the Book, British Library, 1993–94. Corresp. Mem., Historical Commn, Börsenverein des Deutschen Buchhandels, Frankfurt am Main, 1995–. Jacob und Wilhelm Grimm Prize, GDR, 1988. *Publications:* (ed) Modern Swiss Literature, 1985; (ed) Ein Moment des erfahrenen Lebens, 1987; (ed) Mit regulu bithuungan, 1989; (ed) Kurz bevor der Vorhang fiel, 1990; (ed) Common Currency?, 1991; Die Historie von Herzog Ernst, 1992; (ed) The German Book 1450–1750, 1995; Johannes Sinapius 1505–1560, 1997; (with M. Davies) Proper Words in Proper Places: studies in lexicology and lexicography, 2001; contrib. numerous essays in scholarly books and jls. *Recreation:* writing. *Address:* University of London Institute of Germanic Studies, 29 Russell Square, WC1B 5DP. *T:* (020) 7862 8969.

FLOOD, John Martin, CEng; FRAeS; non-executive Director, Hunting Engineering Ltd, 1994–99; *b* 3 Oct. 1939; *s* of late Harry Flood and Rita Flood (*née* Martin); *m* 1962, Irene Edwards; one *s*. *Educ:* Merchant Taylors' School, Crosby; Leeds Univ. (BSc Physics, 1st cl.). CEng 1991; FRAeS 1991. Graduate Apprentice, English Electric, Stevenage, 1962; joined RAE, 1963; Asst Dir, Dir Air Guided Weapons and on Army Chief Scientist staff, 1978–83; joined RAE, 1983; Head, Attack Weapons and Defensive Systems Depts, RAE, 1985–89; Dep. Dir (Mission Systems), RAE, 1989–91; Technical Dir, RAE, 1991–92; Dir, Weapon Systems Sector, 1991–93, Technical Dir, 1993–94, DRA. *Recreations:* bird watching, walking, theatre, reading (political biography). *Address:* Freshfield, Church Lane, Ewshot, Farnham, Surrey GU10 5BD.

FLOOD, Michael Donovan, (Mik); arts consultant, since 1997; President, Informal European Theatre Meeting, since 1998; Chairman, Lux Centre for Film, Video & Digital Arts, since 1998; *b* 7 May 1949; *s* of late Gp Capt. Donovan John Flood, DFC, AFC and of Vivien Ruth (*née* Alison); *m* 1975, Julie Ward (marr. diss. 1989); one *d*. *Educ:* St George's Coll., Weybridge; Llangefni County Sch., Anglesey. Founder and Artistic Dir, Chapter Arts Centre, Cardiff, 1970–81; Develt Dir, Baltimore Theater Project, USA, 1981–82; Administrator, Pip Simmons Theatre Gp, 1982–83; Arts consultancy, 1983–85; Dir, Watermans Arts Centre, Brentford, 1985–90; Dir, ICA, 1990–97. Producer of large-scale events: Woyzeck, Cardiff, 1976; Deadwood, Kew Gdns, 1986; Offshore Rig, River Thames, 1987. Member: Film Cttee, Welsh Arts Council, 1976–80; Exec. Cttee, SE Wales Arts Assoc., 1980–81; Co-Founder, Nat. Maritime Mus. Assoc. of Arts Centres, 1976. Bd Dir, Pip Simmons Theatre Gp, 1977–83. Mem., Ct of Govs, RCA, 1990–97. Silver Jubilee Medal, 1977. *Publications:* book reviews in nat. newspapers; contribs on arts and cultural politics to British and European periodicals. *Recreations:* sailing, ichthyology, travel. *Address:* 1 Marshall House, Dorncliffe Road, SW6 5LF. *T:* (020) 7736 8668, *Fax:* (020) 7384 3770; *e-mail:* mik@mikflood.com. *Club:* Groucho.

FLOOD, Philip James, AO 1992; High Commissioner for Australia in the United Kingdom, 1998–2000; *b* 2 July 1935; *s* of Thomas and Maxine Flood; *m* 1990, Carole, *d* of Cuthbert and Nicole Henderson; two *s* one *d*. *Educ:* North Sydney Boys' High Sch.; Univ. of Sydney (BEc Hons). Australian Embassy and Mission to EC, Brussels, 1959–62; Australian Embassy and Mission to OECD, Paris, 1966–69; Asst Sec., Dept of Foreign Affairs, 1971–73; High Comr, Bangladesh, 1974–76; Minister, Washington, 1976–77; Special Trade Rep., 1977–80; First Asst Sec., Dept of Trade, 1980–84; Dep. Sec., Dept of Foreign Affairs and Trade, 1985–89; Ambassador to Indonesia, 1989–93; Dir Gen., Australian Internat. Develt Assistance Bureau, 1993–95; Sec., Dept of Foreign Affairs and Trade, 1996–98. Order of Merit (Indonesia), 1993. *Recreations:* reading, music, theatre, walking, swimming. *Address:* 96 Jervois Street, Deakin, ACT 2600, Australia. *Clubs:* Commonwealth (Canberra); Royal Canberra Golf.

FLOOK, Adrian John; MP (C) Taunton, since 2001; *b* 9 July 1963; *s* of John Harold Julian Flook and late Rosemary Ann Flook (*née* Richardson). *Educ:* King Edward's Sch., Bath; Mansfield Coll., Oxford (MA Hons Mod. Hist.). Stockbroker, Warburg Securities, and others, 1985–98; Financial Dynamics (business communications consultancy), 1998–. *Address:* House of Commons, SW1A 0AA; 20A Staplegrove Road, Taunton, Som TA1 1DQ. *T:* (01823) 286106; *e-mail:* taunton@tory.org. *Club:* Wellington and District Conservative (Somerset).

FLORENCE, Prof. Alexander Taylor, CBE 1994; PhD, DSc; FRSE; FRPharmS, FRSC; Dean, School of Pharmacy, University of London, since 1989; *b* 9 Sept. 1940; *s* of late Alexander Charles Gerrard Florence and of Margaret Florence; *m* 1964, Elizabeth Catherine McRae (marr. diss. 1995); two *s* one *d*; *m* 2000, Dr Florence Madsen, *d* of Bernard Madsen, Paris. *Educ:* Royal Coll. of Science and Technology, Glasgow and Univ. of Glasgow (BSc Hons 1962; PhD 1965); DSc Strathclyde, 1984. FRSC 1977; FRPharmS 1987. University of Strathclyde: MRC Jun. Res. Fellow, 1965–66; Lectr in Pharmaceutical Chemistry, 1966–72; Sen. Lectr in Pharm. Chem., 1972–76; J. P. Todd Prof. of Pharmacy, 1976–88. Member: Cttee on Safety of Medicines, 1983–98 (Mem., Sub-cttee on Chemistry, Pharmacy and Standards of Cttee on Safety of Medicines, 1972–98); Nuffield Inquiry into Pharmacy, 1984–86. Pres., Eur. Assoc. of Faculties of Pharmacy, 1997–; Vice President: Internat. Pharmaceutical Fedn, 1998–2000 (Høst-Madsen Medal, 1996); Controlled Release Soc., 2000–. FRSE 1987; FRSA 1989. British Pharmaceutical Conf. Science Award, 1972; Harrison Meml Medal, Royal Pharmaceutical Soc., 1986; Scheele Prize, Swedish Acad. of Pharmaceutical Scis, 1993; GlaxoSmithKline Internat. Achievement Award, 2001. Co-Editor in Chief, Jl of Drug Targeting, 1993–97; Editor-in-Chief (Europe), Internat. Jl of Pharmaceutics, 1997–. *Publications:* Solubilization by Surface Active Agents, 1968; Physicochemical Principles of Pharmacy, 1981, 3rd edn 1998; Surfactant Systems, 1983; (ed) Materials Used in Pharmaceutical Formulation, 1985; (ed) Formulation Factors in Adverse Reactions, 1990; (ed jtly) Liposomes in Drug Delivery, 1992; pubns on drug delivery and targeting, surfactants and drug absorption, and polymeric systems. *Recreations:* music, writing, painting. *Address:* School of Pharmacy, University of London, 29/39 Brunswick Square, WC1N 1AX. *T:* (020) 7753 5819.

FLOREY, Prof. Charles du Vé; Professor of Public Health Medicine (formerly Community Medicine), University of Dundee, 1983–99; *b* 11 Sept. 1934; *s* of Howard Walter Florey and Mary Ethel Florey; *m* 1966, Susan Jill Hopkins; one *s* one *d*. *Educ:* Univ. of Cambridge (MD); Yale Univ. (MPH). FFCM 1977; FRCPE 1986. Instructor, 1965, Asst Prof., 1966–69, Yale Univ. School of Medicine; Mem. Scientific Staff, MRC, Jamaica, 1969–71; St Thomas's Hospital Medical School, London: Sen. Lectr, 1971–78; Reader, 1978–81; Prof., 1981–83. Pres., Internat. Epidemiol Assoc., 1999–Aug. 2002. *Publications:* (with S. R. Leeder) Methods for Cohort Studies of Chronic Airflow Limitation, 1982; (jtly) Introduction to Community Medicine, 1983; A European Concerted Action: maternal alcohol consumption and its relation to the outcome of pregnancy and child development at eighteen months, 1992; (ed) Epilex: a multilingual lexicon of epidemiological terms, 1993; (jtly) The Audit Handbook: improving health through clinical audit, 1993; (jtly) The Pocket Guide to Grant Applications, 1998. *Recreations:* photography, sailing, walking, computing. *Address:* Teesdale, Knowle Drive, Sidmouth, Devon EX10 8HW.

FLOUD, Mrs Jean Esther, CBE 1976; MA, BSc(Econ); Principal, Newnham College, Cambridge, 1972–83, Hon. Fellow, 1983; *b* 3 Nov. 1915; *d* of Annie Louisa and Ernest Walter McDonald; *m* 1938, Peter Castle Floud, CBE (*d* 1960), *s* of late Sir Francis Floud, KCB, KCSI, KCMG, and formerly Keeper of Circulation, Victoria and Albert Museum; two *d* (one *s* decd). *Educ:* public elementary and selective secondary schools; London School of Economics (BScEcon), Hon. Fellow, 1972. Asst Dir of Educn, City of Oxford, 1940–46; Teacher of Sociology in the University of London (London School of Economics and Inst. of Educn), 1947–62; Official Fellow of Nuffield College, Oxford, 1961–72, Hon. Fellow, 1983; Hon. Fellow, Darwin Coll., Cambridge, 1986. Member: Franks Commission of Inquiry into the University of Oxford, 1964–66; University Grants Cttee, 1969–74; Social Science Research Council, 1970–73; Exec. Cttee, PEP, 1975–77; Adv. Bd for the Res. Councils, 1976–81; Council, Policy Studies Inst., 1979–83. Hon. LittD Leeds, 1973; Hon. DLitt City, 1978. *Publications:* (with A. H. Halsey and F. M. Martin) Social Class and Educational Opportunity, 1956; (with Warren Young) Dangerousness and Criminal Justice, 1981; papers and reviews in sociological jls. *Recreations:* books, music. *Address:* Elderwick House, The Ridings, Shotover, Oxford OX3 8TB.

FLOUD, Prof. Roderick Castle; Provost, London Guildhall University (formerly City of London Polytechnic), since 1988; *b* 1 April 1942; *s* of late Bernard Francis Castle Floud, MP and Ailsa (*née* Craig); *m* 1964, Cynthia Anne (*née* Smith); two *d*. *Educ:* Brentwood Sch.; Wadham Coll., Oxford (Hon. Fellow, 1999); Nuffield Coll., Oxford. MA, DPhil. Asst Lectr in Economic History, UCL, 1966–69; Lectr in Economic History, Univ. of Cambridge and Fellow of Emmanuel Coll., Cambridge, 1969–75; Prof. of Modern History, Birkbeck Coll., Univ. of London, 1975–88. Vis. Prof. of European History and of Economics, Stanford Univ., Calif, 1980–81. Research Associate, Nat. Bureau of Economic Research, USA, 1978–; Research Programme Dir, Centre for Economic Policy Research, 1983–88. Member: Council: ESRC, 1993–97; UUK (formerly CVCP), 1997– (Pres., 2000–); Convenor, London Higher Educn Consortium, 1999–. Mem., Lord Chancellor's Adv. Council on Public Records, 1978–84. Mem. Bd, London Develt Partnership, 1998–. Member: Tower Hamlets Coll. Corp., 1997–; Council, Gresham Coll., 1998–. Treas., Oxford Union Soc., 1966. Freeman: City of London, 1995; Information Technologists' Co., 1996. Hon. Fellow, Birkbeck Coll., 1994. Hon. DLitt City, 1999. *Publications:* An Introduction to Quantitative Methods for Historians, 1973, 2nd edn 1980; (ed) Essays in Quantitative Economic History, 1974; The British Machine Tool Industry 1850–1914, 1976; (ed) The Economic History of Britain since 1700, 1981, 2nd edn 1994; (ed) The Power of the Past, 1984; (jtly) Height, Health and History, 1990; The People and the British Economy 1830–1914, 1997; (ed) Health and Welfare during Industrialisation, 1997; (ed) London Higher, 1998; articles in Economic History Review, Social Science History, etc. *Recreations:* family, walking, music. *Address:* London Guildhall University, 31 Jewry Street, EC3N 2EY. *T:* (020) 7320 1310; *e-mail:* floud@lgu.ac.uk; 21 Savernake Road, NW3 2JT. *T:* (020) 7267 2197. *Club:* Athenæum.

FLOWER, family name of **Viscount Ashbrook**.

FLOWER, Antony John Frank, (Tony), MA, PhD; Senior Fellow, Institute of Community Studies, since 1996 (Acting Director, 2001); Consultant, Joseph Rowntree Reform Trust Ltd, since 1993; *b* 2 Feb. 1951; *s* of late Frank Robert Edward Flower and Dorothy Elizabeth (*née* Williams). *Educ:* Chipping Sodbury Grammar Sch.; Univ. of Exeter (BA Hons Philosophy and Sociology; MA Sociology); Univ. of Leicester (PhD Mass Communications). Graphic Designer, 1973–76; Co-founder with Lord Young of Dartington, and first Gen. Sec., Tawney Soc., 1982–88; Dir, Res. Inst. for Econ. and Social Affairs, 1982–92. Co-ordinator, Argo Venture (Nat. Space Mus.), 1984–, Dir, Argo Trust, 1986–95; Director: Healthline Health Inf. Service, 1986–88; Health Information Trust, 1987–88 (Trustee, 1988–90); Environmental Concern Centre in Europe, 1990–92; Dep. Dir, Inst. of Community Studies and of Mutual Aid Centre, 1994–96. Mem. Adv. Bd, The Earth Centre, 1990–, Consultant, 1996–; Sec., Ecological Studies Inst., 1990–92. Associate: Redesign Ltd, 1989–92; Nicholas Lacey & Partners (Architects), 1989–; Consultant: CIRIA, 1992–96; Rocklabs Geochemical Analysis CC, 1993–; Cambridge Female Educn Trust, 1999–. Co-ordinator, Campaign for Educnl Choice, 1988–89. Trustee: Gaia, 1988–; Mutual Aid Centre, 1990–; Inst. of Community Studies, 1993–; Tower Hamlets Summer Univ. Trust, 1995–; Education Extra, 1995–; Patron, Nat. Space Science Centre, 1996–. Mem., Council for Social Democracy, 1982–84; Dir of Develt, Green Alliance, 1991–92. Associate: Open Coll. of the Arts, 1988–; Inst. for Public Policy Res., 1989–95; Family Covenant Assoc., 1994–. Editor, Tawney Journal, 1982–88; Co-founder and Man. Editor, Samizdat Magazine, 1988–90. FRSA 1991. *Publications:* Starting to Write: a course in creative writing, 1990; (ed jtly) The Alternative, 1990; (ed jtly) Young at Eighty: the prolific public life of Michael Young, 1995. *Recreations:* collecting junk, sailing, making and restoring musical instruments. *Address:* (office) 18 Victoria Park Square, E2 9PF. *T:* (020) 8980 6263.

FLOWER, Rear-Adm. Edward James William, CB 1980; Director, Post-Design (Ships), Ministry of Defence (Navy), 1977–80, retired; *b* 1923; *m*; three *d*. Joined RN, 1941; served in HM Ships Norfolk, Duke of York, Liverpool, Whitby, Urchin and Tenby; Canadian Nat. Defence Coll., 1966; Fleet Marine Engineering Officer, Western Fleet, 1967–69; commanded RN Nuclear Propulsion Test and Trng Estab., 1970–71; MoD (Navy), 1971–75; Flag Officer Portsmouth, and Port Admiral, Portsmouth, 1975–76; Dir of Engrg (Ships), MoD, 1976–77. *Address:* Fairmount, Hinton Charterhouse, Bath BA3 6AZ.

FLOWER, Robert Philip; JP; HM Diplomatic Service, retired; Counsellor, Foreign and Commonwealth Office, 1994–96; *b* 12 May 1939; *s* of Philip Edward Flower and Dorothy Agnes Elizabeth (*née* Beukers); *m* 1964, Anne Daveen Tweddle; two *s*. *Educ:* Christ's Hosp.; Magdalene Coll., Cambridge (BA). Called to the Bar, Middle Temple, 1964. FCO, 1967–; served in Malawi, Malaysia, UK Delegn to NATO, Bonn and London; Dep. Head of Mission, The Hague, 1990–93. JP Cumbria, 1998. *Recreations:* fell-walking, reading, music. *Address:* Lambfold, High Lorton, Cockermouth, Cumbria CA13 9UQ.

FLOWERS, family name of **Baron Flowers**.

FLOWERS, Baron *cr* 1979 (Life Peer), of Queen's Gate in the City of Westminster; **Brian Hilton Flowers,** Kt 1969; FRS 1961; Chancellor, Manchester University, 1994–2001; Chairman, Nuffield Foundation, 1987–98 (a Managing Trustee, 1982–98); *b* 13 Sept. 1924; *o s* of late Rev. Harold J. Flowers, Swansea; *m* 1951, Mary Frances, *er d* of late Sir Leonard Behrens, CBE; two step *s*. *Educ:* Bishop Gore Grammar Sch., Swansea; Gonville and Caius Coll. (Exhibitioner), Cambridge (MA); Hon. Fellow, 1974; University of Birmingham (DSc). Anglo-Canadian Atomic Energy Project, 1944–46; Research in nuclear physics and atomic energy at Atomic Energy Research Establishment, Harwell, 1946–50; Dept of Mathematical Physics, University of Birmingham, 1950–52; Head of Theoretical Physics Div., AERE, Harwell, 1952–58; Prof. of Theoretical Physics, 1958–61, Langworthy Prof. of Physics, 1961–72, Univ. of Manchester; on leave of absence as Chm., SRC, 1967–73; Rector of Imperial Coll. of Sci. and Technol., 1973–85; Vice-Chancellor, Univ. of London, 1985–90. Chairman: Royal Commn on Environmental Pollution, 1973–76; Standing Commn on Energy and the Environment, 1978–81; Univ. of London Working Party on future of med. and dent. teaching resources, 1979–80; Cttee of Vice-Chancellors and Principals, 1983–85; Select Cttee on Science and Technology, H of L, 1989–93 (Mem., 1980–93, 1994–98, 1999–). President: Inst. of Physics, 1972–74; European Science Foundn, 1974–80; Nat. Soc. for Clean Air, 1977–79; Parly and Scientific Cttee, 1993–97. Chm., Computer Bd for Univs and Research Councils, 1966–70. Member: Council, RPMS, 1990–97 (Vice Chm., 1991–97); Bd of Management, LSHTM, 1992–95 (Chm., 1994–95). Gov., Middx Univ., 1992–2001. Founding Mem. and Mem. Exec. Council, Academia Europaea, 1988. Founder Mem., SDP, 1981. FInstP 1961; Hon. FInstP 1996; Hon. FCGI, 1975; Hon. MRIA (Science Section), 1976; Hon. FIEE, 1975; Hon. FRCP 1992; Sen. Fellow, RCA, 1983; Hon. Fellow: UMIST, 1985; Royal Holloway, London Univ., 1996; Univ. of Wales, Swansea, 1996; Corresp. Mem., Swiss Acad. of Engrg Sciences, 1986. MA Oxon, 1956; Hon. DSc: Sussex, 1968; Wales, 1972; Manchester, 1973; Leicester, 1973; Liverpool, 1974; Bristol, 1982; Oxford, 1985; NUI, 1990; Reading, 1996; London, 1996; Hon. DEng Nova Scotia, 1983; Hon. ScD Dublin, 1984; Hon. LLD: Dundee, 1985; Glasgow, 1987; Manchester, 1995. Rutherford Medal and Prize, 1968, Glazebrook Medal and Prize, 1987, IPPS; Chalmers Medal, Chalmers Univ. of Technol., Sweden, 1980. Officier de la Légion d'Honneur, 1981 (Chevalier, 1975). *Publications:* (with E. Mendoza) Properties of Matter, 1970; An Introduction to Numerical Methods in C++, 1995; contribs to scientific periodicals on structure of the atomic nucleus, nuclear reactions, science policy, energy and the environment. *Recreations:* music, walking, computing, gardening. *Address:* 53 Athenaeum Road, N20 9AL. *T:* (020) 8446 5993.

FLOYD, Christopher David; QC 1992; *b* 20 Dec. 1951; a Recorder, since 2000; *s* of David and Hana Floyd; *m* 1974, Rosalind Jane Arscott; one *s* two *d*. *Educ:* Westminster Sch.; Trinity Coll., Cambridge (MA Nat. Scis and Law). Called to the Bar, Inner Temple, 1975, Bencher, 2001; called to the Bar of Republic of Ireland, 1988. An Asst Recorder, 1994–2000; a Dep. High Court Judge (Patents Court), 1998–. Dep. Chm., Copyright Tribunal, 1995–. Member: Bar Council Chm.'s Arbitration/Conciliation Panel, 1996–; Bar Council Professional Conduct and Complaints Cttee, 1998–; Chm., Intellectual Property Bar Assoc., 1999–. *Recreations:* Austin Sevens, cricket, ski-ing, walking. *Address:* 11 South Square, Gray's Inn, WC1R 5EU. *T:* (020) 7405 1222.

FLOYD, Sir Giles (Henry Charles), 7th Bt *cr* 1816; Director, Burghley Estate Farms, since 1958; *b* 27 Feb. 1932; *s* of Sir John Duckett Floyd, 6th Bt, TD, and of Jocelin Evadne (*d* 1976), *d* of late Sir Edmund Wyldbore Smith; *S* father, 1975; *m* 1st, 1954, Lady Gillian

Moyra Katherine Cecil (marr. diss. 1978), 2nd *d* of 6th Marquess of Exeter, KCMG; two *s*; 2nd, 1985, Judy Sophia Lane, *er d* of late W. L. Tregoning, CBE, and D. M. E. Tregoning. *Educ:* Eton College. High Sheriff of Rutland, 1968. *Heir: er s* David Henry Cecil Floyd [*b* 2 April 1956; *m* 1981, Caroline, *d* of John Beckly, Manor Farm, Bowerchalke, Salisbury, Wilts; two *d*]. *Address:* Tinwell Manor, Stamford, Lincs PE9 3UD. *T:* (01780) 762676. *Clubs:* Turf, Farmers'.

FLOYD, Keith; cook, broadcaster; *b* 28 Dec. 1943; *s* of late Sydney Albert Floyd and of Winnifred Margaret Floyd; *m* 1995, Theresa Mary (*née* Smith); one *s* one *d* by prev. marriages. *Educ:* Wellington Sch. Commnd, 3rd RTR 1963; journalist, 1961–; broadcaster, 1986–. *Publications:* Floyd's Food, 1981; Floyd on Fish, 1985; Floyd on Fire, 1986; Floyd on France, 1987; Floyd on Britain and Ireland, 1988; Floyd in the Soup, 1988; A Feast of Floyd, 1989; Floyd's American Pie, 1989; Floyd on Oz, 1991; Floyd on Spain, 1992; Floyd on Hangovers, 1992; Far Flung Floyd, 1993; Floyd on Italy, 1994; The Best of Floyd, 1995; Floyd on Africa, 1996; Floyd's Barbies, 1997; Floyd's Fjord Fiesta, 1998; Floyd Uncorked, 1998; Floyd Around the Med, 1999; Out of the Frying Pan (autobiog.), 2000. *Recreations:* Rugby, fishing, drinking, gardening. *Address:* c/o Stan Green Management, PO Box 4, Dartmouth, Devon TQ6 0YD. *T:* (01803) 770046, *Fax:* (01803) 770075; *e-mail:* sgm@clara.co.uk.

FLOYD EWIN, Sir David Ernest Thomas, Kt 1974; LVO 1954; OBE 1965; MA; Lay Administrator, 1939–44, Registrar and Receiver, 1944–78, Consultant to the Dean and Chapter, since 1978, St Paul's Cathedral; Notary Public; *b* 17 Feb. 1911; 7th *s* of late Frederick P. Ewin and Ellen Floyd; *m* 1948, Marion Irene, *d* of William R. Lewis; one *d*. *Educ:* Eltham. MA (Lambeth) 1962. Chairman: Tubular Exhibn, subseq. Tubular Edgington, Group, 1978–91; Stonebert Ltd and subsids, 1985–91. Freeman, City of London, 1948; Member of Court of Common Council for Ward of Castle Baynard, 1963–96 (Dep., 1972–96); Vice-Pres., Castle Baynard Ward Club, 1972–96 (Chm. 1962 and 1988); Chm., Gresham Cttee, 1975–76, Benevolent Cttee, 1991–96, Corp. of London; Member: Lord Mayor and Sheriffs Cttee, 1976, 1978, 1984 (Chm., 1987); Court of Assts, Hon. Irish Soc., 1976–79; Surrogate for Province of Canterbury; Trustee: City Parochial Foundn, 1967–90 (Chm., Pensions Cttee, 1978–90); St Paul's Cathedral Trust, 1978–; Temple Bar Trust, 1979–96; Dep. Chm., City of London's Endowment Trust for St Paul's Cathedral, 1982–. Hon. Dir, British Humane Assoc.; Governor and Member of Court: Sons of the Clergy Corp.; St Gabriel's Coll., Camberwell, 1946–72. Past Master, Scriveners' Co.; Sen. Past Master, Guild of Freemen of the City of London; Liveryman, Wax Chandlers' Co.; Gold Staff Officer at Coronation of HM Queen Elizabeth, 1953. KStJ 1970 (OStJ 1965). *Publications:* A Pictorial History of St Paul's Cathedral, 1970; The Splendour of St Paul's, 1973; numerous papers and articles. *Recreations:* tennis, gardening, fishing. *Address:* 13 Seaborne Court, Alta Vista Road, Paignton, S Devon TQ4 6DP. *T:* (01803) 523993; Chapter House, St Paul's Churchyard, EC4M 8AD. *T:* (020) 7248 2705. *Clubs:* City Livery, Guildhall.

FLUCK, Peter Nigel; freelance artist; sculptor of abstract kinetics, since 1994; founded (with Roger Law) Spitting Image, 1982; *b* 7 April 1941; *s* of Herbert William Fluck and Ada Margaret (*née* Hughes); *m* 1963, Anne-Cécile de Bruyne; one *d* one *s*. *Educ:* Cambs High Sch. for Boys; Cambridge Sch. of Art. Artist-reporter, illustrator, 1961–70; cartoonist and caricaturist, 1970–82; Luck & Flaw (with Roger Law), 1974–82; Spitting Image (18 TV series), 1982–94. Exhibn, Chaotic Constructions (with Tony Myatt) Tate Gall., St Ives and Edin. Fest., 1997, (expanded) RIBA, 1999. *Recreation:* finding time to go fishing. *Address:* White Feather, Cadgwith, Cornwall TR12 7LB. *T:* (01326) 290546.

FLUGGE, Klaus; Founder, Publisher and Managing Director, Anderson Press Ltd, since 1976; *b* 29 Nov. 1934; *s* of Werner and Emmi Flügge; *m* 1964, Joëlle; one *s*. *Educ:* German Book Trade Sch., Leipzig (Dip.). Asst to Pres., Abelard-Schuman, NY, 1959–61; Man Dir, Abelard-Schuman Ltd, 1963–76. Eleanor Farjeon Award for distinguished services to children's books, 1999. *Recreations:* book collecting, jazz, swimming. *Address:* c/o Andersen Press Ltd, 20 Vauxhall Bridge Road, SW1V 2SA. *T:* (020) 7840 8701. *Club:* Groucho.

FLYNN, Desmond James; Deputy Inspector General, Insolvency Service, Department of Trade and Industry, since 1989; *b* 21 March 1949; *s* of James Joseph Flynn and Kathleen Eithne Flynn (*née* Fagan); *m* 1975, Kumari Ramdewar; one *s* one *d*. *Educ:* Univ. of E Anglia (BA Hons 1974). Trainee examr, Official Receiver, London, 1968–71; Examr, Official Receiver, Birmingham, 1976–1980; Asst Official Receiver, Birmingham and London, 1980–86; Principal, Internat. Trade Policy Div., DTI, 1986–88; Principal Inspector of Official Receivers, 1988–9. *Publication:* (contrib.) Insolvency Law: theory and practice, ed H. Ratak, 1993. *Recreations:* reading, golf. *Address:* The Insolvency Service, 21 Bloomsbury Street, WC1B 3QW. *T:* (020) 7291 6720. *Club:* Royston Golf.

FLYNN, Douglas Ronald; Chief Executive Officer, Aegis Group plc, since 1999; *b* 8 June 1949; *s* of Ronald Norman Flynn and Rhona Ellen Flynn; *m* 1975, Lynne Cecily Harcombe; two *s*. *Educ:* Newcastle Boys' High Sch., Australia; Univ. of Newcastle, Australia (BEng Hons 1972); MBA Melbourne Univ. 1979. Australian Sales Manager, ICI Australia, Melbourne, 1975–80; Gen. Manager, ICI Explosives, Hong Kong, 1980–82; Regl Manager, Perth, 1982–85, Manager Strategic Planning, Melbourne, 1985–86, ICI Australia Ltd; Deloitte Haskins & Sells, 1986–87; Chief Exec., Hobart, Davies Bros Ltd, 1987–90; Man. Dir, News Ltd Suburban Newspapers, Sydney, 1990–94; Dep. Man. Dir, News Internat. Newspapers, London, 1994–95; Man. Dir, News Internat. plc, 1995–99. *Recreation:* sailing. *Address:* c/o Aegis Group plc, 43-45 Portman Square, W1H 6LY. *T:* (020) 7070 7700. *Clubs:* Tasmanian (Hobart); Royal Hong Kong Yacht, Royal Sydney Yacht Squadron.

FLYNN, Prof. Frederick Valentine, MD (Lond), FRCP, FRCPath; Professor of Chemical Pathology in University of London at University College School of Medicine, 1970–89, now Professor Emeritus; Civil Consultant in Chemical Pathology to Royal Navy, 1978–92; *b* 6 Oct. 1924; *e s* of Frederick Walter Flynn and Jane Laing Flynn (*née* Valentine); *m* 1955, Catherine Ann, *o d* of Dr Robert Walter Warrick and Dorothy Ann Warrick (*née* Dimock); one *s* one *d*. *Educ:* University Coll. London; University Coll. Hosp. Med. Sch. (Fellow, UCL, 1974). Obstetric Ho. Surg. and various posts, incl. Research Asst and Registrar, Dept of Clin. Pathology, UCH, 1947–60; Associate in Clin. Path., Pepper Laboratory of Clin. Medicine, Univ. of Pennsylvania, and British Postgrad. Med. Fedn Travelling Fellow, 1954–55; Consultant Chemical Pathologist, UCH, 1960–70. Chairman: Assoc. of Clin. Biochemists Sci. and Technical Cttee, 1968–70; Dept of Health's Adv. Gp on Scientific and Clinical Applications of Computers, 1971–76; Organising Cttee for 1st, 2nd and 3rd Internat. Confs on Computing in Clinical Labs, 1972–80; Research Cttee, NE Thames RHA, 1984–88; Member: Min. of Health Lab. Equipment and Methods Adv. Gp, 1966–71; Min. of Technol. Working Party on Lab. Instrumentation, 1966–67; BMA Working Party on Computers in Medicine, 1968–69; Dept of Health's Adv. Cttee on Med. Computing, 1969–76, and Laboratory Develts Adv. Gp, 1972–75; MRC Working Party on Hypogammaglobulinaemia, 1959–70; MRC Adv. Panel on Applications for Computing Facilities, 1973–77; NW Thames RHA Sci. Cttee, 1973–74; Med. Lab. Techns Bd, Council for Professions Supplementary to Medicine, 1984–88; NHS Supraregional Assay Services Bd, 1990–92; Sir Jules Thorn Charitable Trust: Mem. Med. Adv. Cttee, 1983–97; Trustee, 1988–; Section of Pathology, RSM: Mem. Council, 1968–72, 1986–93; Vice-Pres., 1971–72, 1989–91; Royal Coll. of Pathologists: Chm., Panel of Examrs in Chem. Path., 1972–82; Mem. Council, 1973–83 and 1984–87; Vice-Pres., 1975–78; Treas., 1978–83; Dir of Continuing Med. Educn, 1992–97; College Medal, 1995; Association of Clinical Pathologists: Chm., Working Party on Data Processing in Labs, 1964–67; Mem. Council, 1988–90; Pres.-elect, 1988–89; Pres., 1989–90. *Publications:* numerous contribs to med. and sci. books and jls. *Recreations:* photography, woodwork, gardening. *Address:* 20 Oakleigh Avenue, Whetstone, N20 9JH. *T:* (020) 8445 0882.

FLYNN, John Gerrard, CMG 1992; HM Diplomatic Service, retired; Ambassador to Venezuela, and concurrently (non-resident) to the Dominican Republic, 1993–97; *b* 23 April 1937; *s* of late Thomas Flynn and Mary Chisholm; *m* 1973, Drina Anne Coates; one *s* one *d*. *Educ:* Glasgow Univ. (MA). Foreign Office, 1965; Second Sec., Lusaka, 1966; First Sec., FCO, 1968; seconded to Canning House as Asst Dir-Gen., 1970; First Sec. (Commercial) and Consul, Montevideo, 1971; FCO, 1976; Chargé d'Affaires, Luanda, 1978; Counsellor and Consul-Gen., Brasilia, 1979; Counsellor, Madrid, 1982; High Comr, Swaziland, 1987; Ambassador to Angola and (non-resident) to São Tomé and Principe, 1990–93. British Special Rep. for Sierra Leone, 1998. Chairman: Anglo Latin American Foundn, 1998–; Anglo-Venezuelan Soc., 1999–; British Venezuelan Chamber of Commerce, 1999–. *Recreations:* hill-walking, golf. *Club:* Travellers.

FLYNN, Padraig; Member, European Commission (formerly Commission of the European Communities), 1993–99; *b* 9 May 1939; *m* 1963, Dorothy Tynan; one *s* three *d*. *Educ:* St Gerald's Secondary Sch., Castlebar, Co. Mayo; St Patrick's Trng Coll., Dublin (DipEd). Mayo County Council: Mem., 1967–87; Vice-Chm., 1975–77. TD (FF), 1977–93; Minister of State, Dept of Transport and Power, 1980–81; Minister for: Gaeltacht, Mar.–Oct. 1982; Trade, Commerce and Tourism, Oct.–Dec. 1982; spokesman on trade, commerce and tourism, 1982–87; Minister for: the Envmt, 1987–91; Justice, Feb.–Dec. 1992; Industry and Commerce, Nov.–Dec. 1992. Mem., Irish Nat. Teachers' Orgn, 1957–. Mem., Gaelic Athletic Assoc., 1959–. *Recreations:* golf, reading, world affairs. *Address:* Carrowbrinogue Lodge, Castlebar, Co. Mayo, Ireland.

FLYNN, Paul Phillip; MP (Lab) Newport West, since 1987; *b* 9 Feb. 1935; *s* of late James Flynn and Kathleen Williams; *m* 1st, 1962, Anne Harvey (marr. diss. 1984); one *s* (one *d* decd); 2nd, 1985, Samantha Morgan, *d* of Douglas and Elsie Cumpstone; one step *s* one step *d*. *Educ:* St Illtyd's Coll., Cardiff. Steelworker, 1955–84; Researcher, 1984–87. Mem., Gwent CC, 1974–82. Contested (Lab) Denbigh, Oct. 1974. Frontbench spokesman on Wales, 1987, on social security, 1988–90. Mem., Gorsedd of Bards, 1991. Campaign for Freedom of Information Parly Award, 1991. *Publications:* Commons Knowledge: how to be a backbencher, 1997; Baglu 'Mlaen, 1998; Dragons led by Poodles, 1999. *Address:* House of Commons, SW1A 0AA. *Club:* Ringland Labour (Newport, Gwent).

FLYNN, Most Rev. Thomas; *see* Achonry, Bishop of, (RC).

FO, Dario; Italian playwright and actor; *b* 24 March 1926; *s* of Felice Fo and Pina (*née* Rota); *m* 1954, Franca Rame; one *s*. *Educ:* Acad. of Fine Arts, Milan. Joined a small theatre gp, 1950; wrote satirical radio series, Poer nano (Poor Dwarf), 1951, and performed selections from it, Teatro Odeon, Milan; appeared in Cocorico, Teatro Odeon, Milan, 1952; jt founder and performer, Il Dito Nell'Occhio (revue co.), 1953–55 (toured nationally); screenwriter, Rome, 1955–58; performer and writer, theatre gp, Compagnia Fo-Rame, 1958–68; artistic dir, Chi l'ha visto? (TV musical revue), 1959; performer and writer, Canzonissima (TV variety show); returned to theatre work, 1963; jt founder, theatre co-operative, Nuova Scena, 1968 (toured, 1968–69); jt founder, theatre gp, la Comune, 1970; Tricks of the Trade (TV series), 1985. *Plays include:* Gli Arcangeli non Giocano a Flipper, 1959 (Archangels Don't Play Pinball); Isabella, Tre Caravelle e un Cacciabelle, 1963 (Isabella, Three Sailing Ships and a Con Man); Mistero Buffo, 1969; Morte Accidentale di un Anarchico, 1970 (Accidental Death of an Anarchist); Non Si Paga, Non Si Paga!, 1974 (Can't Pay! Won't Pay!); (with Franca Rame) Tutta Casa Letto e Chiesa, 1977 (All House, Bed and Church); Storia Della Tigre ed Altre Storie, 1979 (Tale of a Tiger and Other Stories); Clacson, Trombette e Pernacchi, 1980 (Trumpets and Raspberries); (with Franca Rame) Coppia Aperta, 1983 (Open Couple); Il Papa e La Strega, 1989 (The Pope and the Witch); (with Franca Rame) L'Eroina – Grassa e' Bello, 1991; Johan Padan a la Descoverta de le Americhe, 1991; Discorsi sul Ruzzante, 1993; Il Diavolo con le Zinne, 1997; his plays have been translated into many languages and performed in many countries. Nobel Prize for Literature, 1997. *Publications:* The Tricks of the Trade, 1991; many plays. *Address:* CTFR Srl, Corso di Porta Romana 132, 20122 Milan, Italy.

FOAKES, Prof. Reginald Anthony; Professor of English, University of California at Los Angeles, 1983–93, now Emeritus; *b* 18 Oct. 1923; 2nd *s* of William Warren Foakes and Frances (*née* Poate); *m* 1st, 1951, Barbara (*d* 1988), *d* of Harry Garratt, OBE; two *s* two *d*; 2nd, 1993, Mary (*d* 1996), *d* of Albert White. *Educ:* West Bromwich Grammar Sch.; Birmingham Univ. (MA, PhD). Fellow of the Shakespeare Inst., 1951–54; Lectr in English, Durham Univ., 1954–62; Sen. Lectr, 1963–64; University of Kent at Canterbury: Prof. of Eng. Lit., 1964–82, now Emeritus Prof. of Eng. and Amer. Lit.; Dean, Faculty of Humanities, 1974–77. Commonwealth Fund (Harkness) Fellow, Yale Univ., 1955–56; Visiting Professor: University Coll., Toronto, 1960–62; Univ. of California, Santa Barbara, 1968–69; UCLA, 1981. *Publications:* (ed) Shakespeare's King Henry VIII, 1957; The Romantic Assertion, 1958; (ed with R. T. Rickert) Henslowe's Diary, 1961; (ed) The Comedy of Errors, 1962; (ed) The Revenger's Tragedy, 1966; (ed) Macbeth and Much Ado About Nothing, 1968; Romantic Criticism, 1968; Coleridge on Shakespeare, 1971; Shakespeare, the Dark Comedies to the Last Plays, 1971; (ed) The Henslowe Papers, 2 vols, 1977; Marston and Tourneur, 1978; (ed) A Midsummer Night's Dream, 1984; Illustrations of the English Stage 1580–1642, and Visitor's Guide, 1985; (ed) S. T. Coleridge, Lectures 1808–19: On Literature, 2 vols, 1987; (ed) Troilus and Cressida, 1987; (ed) Coleridge's Criticism of Shakespeare, 1989; Hamlet versus King Lear: cultural politics and Shakespeare's art, 1993; (ed) King Lear, 1997; (with Mary Foakes) The Columbia Dictionary of Quotations from Shakespeare, 1998. *Address:* Department of English, University of California at Los Angeles, 405 Hilgard Avenue, Los Angeles, CA 90095, USA.

FOALE, Air Cdre Colin Henry; *b* 10 June 1930; *s* of late William Henry Foale and Frances M. (*née* Muse); *m* 1954, Mary Katherine Harding, Minneapolis, USA; one *s* one *d* (and one *s* decd). *Educ:* Wolverton Grammar Sch.; RAF Coll., Cranwell. 1951–74: 13 Sqdn Pilot, Egypt; 32 Sqdn Flt Comdr; Fighter Flt, RAF Flying Coll., Manby; Officer and Aircrew Selection, Hornchurch; OC 73 Sqdn, Cyprus (Sqdn Ldr); Staff Coll., Bracknell; Air Staff, HQ RAF Germany (Wing Comdr); Jt Services Staff Coll., Latimer; OC 39 Sqdn, Malta; SO Flying, MoD (PE) (Gp Captain); Stn Comdr, Luqa, Malta, 1974–76; RCDS, 1977 (Air Cdre); Dir of Public Relations (RAF), 1977–79; retired at own request, 1979. Trng Advr to Chm., Conservative Party, 1980–81; Pilot to Cttee for Aerial Photography, Univ. of Cambridge, 1981–90. FIMgt, FIWM. *Publication:* Waystation to the Stars, 1999. *Recreations:* sailing, swimming, flying, travel, music, drama, writing. *Address:* 37 Pretoria Road, Cambridge CB4 1HD; St Catharine's College, Cambridge. *Club:* Royal Air Force.

See also C. M. Foale.

FOALE, (Colin) Michael, PhD; Assistant Director (Technical), since 1998, and Chief of Expedition Corps, Astronaut Office, since 1999, Johnson Space Center, US National Aeronautics and Space Administration; *b* 6 Jan. 1957; dual UK/US nationality; *s* of Air Cdre Colin Henry Foale, *qv*; *m* 1987, Rhonda Butler; one *s* one *d*. *Educ:* King's Sch., Canterbury; Queen's Coll., Cambridge (1st Cl. Hons Nat. Sci. Tripos 1978; PhD Lab. Astrophysics 1982; Hon. Fellow, 1998). National Aeronautics and Space Administration (US): Payload Officer, 1983–87; Astronaut, 1987–; Space Shuttle Missions: Atlas 1, 1992; Atlas 2, 1993; Space Suit Test, 1995; Russian Space Station Mir, May–Oct. 1997; Hubble Telescope Repair, 1999; Comdr, Space Stn Expedn 8, 2003. Hon. FRAeS 1997. DUniv: Kent, 2000; Lincs and Humberside, 2000. Founder's Medal, Air League, 1993; Barnes Wallis Award, GAPAN, 1994. *Recreations:* flying, wind surfing, diving, ski-ing, theoretical physics, programming children's computer software. *Address:* c/o NASA JSC, Houston, TX 77058, USA; c/o 37 Pretoria Road, Cambridge CB4 1HD.

FOCKE, Paul Everard Justus; QC 1982; **His Honour Judge Focke;** a Circuit Judge, since 1997; *b* 14 May 1937; *s* of late Frederick Justus Focke and Muriel Focke; *m* 1973, Lady Tana Marie Alexander, *er d* of 6th Earl of Caledon; two *d*. *Educ:* Downside; Exeter Coll., Oxford; Trinity Coll., Dublin. National Service, 1955–57; Territorial Army, 1957–66, Cheshire Yeomanry (Captain). Called to the Bar, Gray's Inn, 1964 (Bencher, 1992), to the Bar of NSW and to the NZ Bar, 1982; QC NSW 1984; a Recorder, 1986–97. Dir, Bar Mutual Indemnity Fund, 1988–97. *Recreations:* travelling, aeroplanes. *Address:* Central Criminal Court, Old Bailey, EC4M 7EM. *T:* (020) 7248 3277. *Clubs:* Pratt's, Turf, Beefsteak, Cavalry and Guards.

FODEN, (Arthur) John; Chairman, Scottish Provident Institution, since 1998; *b* 4 Oct. 1939; *s* of Air Vice-Marshal Arthur Foden, CB, CBE and Constance Muriel Foden (*née* Corkill); *m* 1963, Virginia Caroline Field; two *d*. *Educ:* Abingdon Sch., Oxon. Joined Whitbread and Co. Ltd, 1959, Industrial Relns Manager, 1967; PA Consulting Group, 1967–95: Gp Human Resources Dir, 1975–79; Chief Executive: PA Germany, 1979–80; PA Personnel Services, 1980–85; Chief Exec., 1985–92; Chm., 1986–95. Non-executive Director: Media Audits Ltd, 1992–; Scottish Provident Instn, 1995–. *Publication:* Paid to Decide, 1991. *Recreations:* house restoration, surfing, cooking. *Address:* 7 Melville Street, Edinburgh EH3 7YZ. *T:* (0131) 527 1100.

FOËX, Prof. Pierre, DPhil; FRCA, FANZCA, FMedSci; Nuffield Professor of Anaesthetics, 1991–Sept. 2002, and Fellow of Pembroke College, since 1991, University of Oxford; *b* 4 July 1935; *s* of Georges and Berthe Foëx; *m* 1958, Anne-Lise Schürch; two *s*. *Educ:* Univ. of Geneva (DM); professional qualifying Swiss State Exam. in Medicine and Surgery, 1960; DPhil Oxon 1973. FRCA (FFARCS 1985); FANZCA 1993. University Hospital, Geneva: Asst, 1961–62 and Chef de Clinique, 1962–63, Dept of Neurology; Asst, 1963–65, Chef de Clinique-adjoint, 1966–68 and Chef de Clinique, 1969–70, Dept of Medicine; Nuffield Department of Anaesthetics, University of Oxford: Res. Fellow, 1970–71; Lectr, 1971–73; Univ. Lectr, 1973–76; Clinical Reader and Hon. Consultant (Clinical Physiology), 1976–91; Emer. Fellow, Worcester Coll., Oxford, 1993 (Fellow, 1976–91). Mem., Exec. Cttee, Anaesthetic Res. Soc., 1982–86; Senator, European Acad. of Anaesthesiology, 1988–99 (Vice-Pres., 1991–93); Mem. Council, RCAnaes, 1996–. Vis. Prof., univs in Australia, Canada, Europe, NZ, USA. Founder FMedSci 1998. *Publications:* Anaesthesia for the Compromised Heart, 1989; Principles and Practice of Critical Care, 1997; Cardiovascular Drugs in the Perioperative Period, 1999; chapters and papers on cardiac physiology, cardiovascular physiology applied to anaesthesia, myocardial ischaemia, cardiovascular pharmacology, anaesthesia and hypertension. *Recreations:* walking, foreign travel. *Address:* Nuffield Department of Anaesthetics, Radcliffe Infirmary, Woodstock Road, Oxford OX2 6HE. *T:* (01865) 224770.

FOGARTY, Christopher Winthrop, CB 1973; Deputy Secretary, Overseas Development Administration, Foreign and Commonwealth Office, (formerly Ministry of Overseas Development), 1976–81; *b* 18 Sept. 1921; *s* of late Philip Christopher Fogarty, ICS, and late Hilda Spenser Fogarty; *m* 1961, Elizabeth Margaret Ince (*d* 1972). *Educ:* Ampleforth Coll.; Christ Church, Oxford. War Service (Lieut RA), 1942–45. Asst Principal, 1946, Principal, 1949, HM Treasury; Permanent Sec., Min. of Finance of Eastern Nigeria, 1956; Asst Sec., HM Treasury, 1959, Under-Sec., 1966; Treasury Rep., S Asia and FE, 1967–72; Dep. Sec., HM Treasury, and Dir, European Investment Bank, 1972–76. *Address:* 7 Hurlingham Court, Ranelagh Gardens, SW6 3SH. *Clubs:* Royal Commonwealth Society, Travellers; Royal Selangor Golf.

FOGDEN, Michael Ernest George, CB 1994; Chairman, National Blood Authority, since 1998; Chief Executive, The Employment Service, Department of Employment, then Department for Education and Employment, 1987–96; *b* 30 May 1936; *s* of late George Charles Arthur and of Margaret May Fogden; *m* 1957, Rose Ann Diamond; three *s* one *d*. *Educ:* High Sch. for Boys, Worthing. Nat. Service, RAF, 1956–58. Ministry of Pensions and National Insurance, later Department of Health and Social Security: Clerical Officer, 1958–59; Exec. Officer, 1959–67, Private Sec. to Parly Sec., 1967–68; Asst Private Sec. to Sec. of State for Social Services, 1968–70; Principal, 1970–76; Asst Sec., 1976–83; Under Sec., 1983–84; Under Sec., Dept of Employment, then DFEE, 1984–96. Dep. Chm., Civil Service Appeal Bd, 1999–. Chm., First Div. Assoc. of Civil Servants, 1980–83. Chairman: London Council, RIPA, 1989–93; Public Management Forum (formerly London Inst. of Public Admin), 1994–98; Exec. Cttee, Public Mgt and Policy Assoc., 1998–; Investigation and Disciplinary Bd, Accountancy Foundn, 2001–. FRSA. *Recreations:* gardening, talking, music. *Address:* 59 Mayfield Avenue, Orpington, Kent BR6 0AH. *T:* (01689) 77395. *Club:* Royal Commonwealth Society.

FOGEL, Prof. Robert William; Charles R. Walgreen Distinguished Service Professor of American Institutions, University of Chicago, since 1981; *b* 1 July 1926; *s* of Harry G. Fogel and Elizabeth (*née* Mitnik); *m* Enid C. Morgan; two *s*. *Educ:* Cornell, Columbia and Johns Hopkins Univs. AB Cornell 1948; AM Columbia 1960; PhD Johns Hopkins 1963. Instructor, Johns Hopkins Univ., 1958–59; Asst Prof., Univ. of Rochester, 1960–64; Assoc. Prof., Univ. of Chicago, 1964–65; Prof., Econs and History, Univ. of Chicago, 1965–75, Univ. of Rochester, 1968–75. Taussig Research Prof., Harvard Univ., 1973–74; Pitt Prof. of Amer. History and Instns, Cambridge Univ., 1975–76; Harold Hitchings Burbank Prof. of Econs and Prof. of History, Harvard Univ., 1975–81. President: Economic History Assoc., 1977–78; Soc. Sci. Hist. Assoc., 1980–81; American Econ. Assoc.; Mem., Europ. Acad. of Sci. Fellow: Econometric Soc., 1971; Amer. Acad. of Arts and Scis, 1972; Nat. Acad. of Scis, 1973; FAAAS, 1978; FRHistS 1975; Corresponding FBA, 1991. Hon. DSc: Rochester, 1987; Palermo, 1994; Brigham Young, 1995; SUNY Binghampton, 1999. Phi Beta Kappa, 1963; Arthur H. Cole Prize, Economic History Assoc., 1968; Schumpeter Prize, Harvard Univ., 1971; Bancroft Prize, Columbia Univ., 1975; Gustavus Myers Prize, 1990; (jtly) Nobel Prize for Economics, 1993. *Publications:* The Union Pacific Railroad: a case in premature enterprise, 1960; Railroads and American Economic Growth: essays in econometric history, 1964 (Spanish edn 1972); (jtly) The Reinterpretation of American Economic History, 1971 (Italian edn 1975); (jtly) The Dimension of Quantitative Research in History, 1972; (jtly) Time on the Cross: the economics of American Negro slavery, 1974 (Japanese edn 1977, Spanish edn 1981); Ten Lectures on the New Economic History, 1977; (jtly) Which Road to the Past? Two Views of History, 1983; Without Consent or Contract: the rise and fall of American slavery, vol. 1, 1989, vols 2–4 (jtly), 1992; The Fourth Great Awakening and the Future of Egalitarianism, 2000; numerous papers in learned jls. *Address:* (office) 1101 E 58th Street, Chicago, IL 60637, USA.

FOGG, Alan, MBE 1994; Chairman, Royal Philanthropic Society, 1982–90; former Director, PA International; *b* 19 Sept. 1921; *o s* of John Fogg, Dulwich; *m* 1948, Mary Marsh; two *s* one *d*. *Educ:* Repton; Exeter Coll., Oxford (MA, BSc). Served with RN, 1944–47. *Publications:* (with Barnes, Stephens and Titman) Company Organisation: theory and practice, 1970; various papers on management subjects. *Recreations:* travel, gardening, youth charities. *Address:* Albury Edge, Merstham, Surrey RH1 3DB. *T:* (01737) 642023.

FOGG, Cyril Percival, CB 1973; Director, Admiralty Surface Weapons Establishment, Ministry of Defence (Procurement Executive), 1973–75, retired; *b* 28 Nov. 1914; *s* of Henry Fogg and Mabel Mary (*née* Orton); *m* 1st, 1939, Margaret Amie Millican (*d* 1982); two *d*; 2nd, 1983, June Adele McCoy. *Educ:* Herbert Strutt Sch., Belper; Gonville and Caius Coll., Cambridge (MA, 1st cl. Mechanical Sciences Tripos). Research Staff, General Electric Co., 1936–37; various positions in Scientific Civil Service from 1937 with Air Ministry, Ministries of Aircraft Production, Supply, Aviation and Technology. Head of Ground Radar Dept, RRE Malvern, 1956–58; Dir Electronics R&D (Ground), 1959–63; Imperial Defence Coll., 1961; Dir of Guided Weapons Research, 1963–64; Dir-Gen. of Electronics R&D, Min. of Aviation, 1964–67; Dep. Controller of Electronics, Min. of Technology, later MoD (Procurement Executive), 1967–72. *Address:* 10 Miles Cottages, Taylors Lane, Bosham, Chichester, West Sussex PO18 8QG.

FOGG, Prof. Gordon Elliott, (Tony), CBE 1983; FRS 1965; Professor and Head of the Department of Marine Biology, University College of North Wales, Bangor, 1971–85, now Professor Emeritus; *b* 26 April 1919; *s* of Rev. L. C. Fogg; *m* 1945, Elizabeth Beryl Llechid-Jones (*d* 1997); one *s* one *d*. *Educ:* Dulwich Coll.; Queen Mary Coll., London; St John's Coll., Cambridge. BSc (London), 1939; PhD (Cambridge), 1943; ScD (Cambridge), 1966. Sea-weed Survey of British Isles, 1942; Plant Physiologist, Pest Control Ltd, 1943–45; successively Asst Lectr, Lectr and Reader in Botany, University Coll., London, 1945–60; Rockefeller Fellow, 1954; Prof. of Botany, Westfield Coll., Univ. of London, 1960–71. Trustee: BM (Natural Hist.), 1976–85; Royal Botanic Gardens, Kew, 1983–89. Member: Royal Commn on Environmental Pollution, 1979–85; NERC, 1981–82. Royal Soc. Leverhulme Vis. Prof., Kerala, 1969–70; Leverhulme Emeritus Fellow, 1986. Botanical Sec., Soc. for Experimental Biology, 1957–60; President: British Phycological Soc., 1961–62; International Phycological Soc., 1964; Inst. of Biology, 1976–77; Chm. Council, Freshwater Biol Assoc., 1974–85; Joint Organizing Sec., X International Botanical Congress. Visiting research worker, British Antarctic Survey, 1966, 1974, 1979; Biological Gen. Sec., British Assoc., 1967–72, Pres., Section K, 1973. Fellow, Queen Mary and Westfield Coll., London (formerly QMC), 1976. Hon. LLD Dundee, 1974. *Publications:* The Metabolism of Algae, 1953; The Growth of Plants, 1963; Algal Cultures and Phytoplankton Ecology, 1965, 3rd edn (with B. Thake), 1987; Photosynthesis, 1968; (jointly) The Blue-green Algae, 1973; (with D. Smith) The Explorations of Antarctica, 1990; A History of Antarctic Science, 1992; The Biology of Polar Habitats, 1998; papers in learned jls. *Recreations:* water colour painting, walking. *Address:* Bodolben, Llandegfan, Menai Bridge, Isle of Anglesey LL59 5TA. *T:* (01248) 712916. *Club:* Athenæum.

FOGGON, George, CMG 1961; OBE 1949 (MBE 1945); Director, London Office, International Labour Organisation, 1976–82, retired; *b* 13 Sept. 1913; *s* of late Thomas and Margaret Foggon; *m* 1st, 1938, Agnes McIntosh (*d* 1968); one *s*; 2nd, 1969, Audrey Blanch. Joined Min. of Labour, 1930. Served War of 1939–45 (MBE), Wing-Comdr, RAFVR, 1941–46. Seconded to FO, 1946; on staff of Mil. Gov., Berlin, 1946–49; Principal, CO, 1949; Asst Sec., W African Inter-Territorial Secretariat, Gold Coast (now Ghana), 1951–53; Comr of Labour, Nigeria, 1954–58; Labour Adviser: to Sec. of State for Colonies, 1958–61; to Sec. for Techn. Co-op., 1962–64; to Min. of Overseas Development, 1965–66; Overseas Labour Advr, FO later FCO, 1966–76, retd. *Recreations:* reading, photography. *Address:* 3 Castle Hill House, Wylam, Northumberland NE41 8JG. *T:* (020) 7828 1492. *Clubs:* Athenæum, Oriental.

FOKINE, Yuri Evgenievich; Rector, Diplomatic Academy, Ministry of Foreign Affairs, Russian Federation, since 2000; *b* 2 Sept. 1936; *s* of Evgeni G. Fokine and Ekaterina I. Fokine; *m* 1958, Maya E. Klimova; one *s* (one *d* decd). *Educ:* Moscow State Inst. for Internat. Relations (grad 1960). Entered Diplomatic Service, 1960; posts in USSR Perm. Mission to UN, Dept of Internat. Orgns, USSR Foreign Min., and Secretariat, USSR Foreign Min.; Dep. Perm. Rep. to UN, 1976–79; Ministry of Foreign Affairs: Dep. Sec.-Gen., 1979–80; Sec.-Gen. and Mem. of Collegium, 1980–86; Ambassador to Cyprus, 1986–90; Dir, 2nd Eur. Dept, Min. of Foreign Affairs, 1990–95; Ambassador to Norway, 1995–97, to UK, 1997–2000. Grand Gold Cross, Order of Merit (Austria), 1995; Royal Order of Merit (Norway), 1997; also national decorations. *Publications:* articles in jls. *Recreations:* art, ballet, reading, tennis. *Address:* Diplomatic Academy, 53/2 Ostozhenka, Moscow 119021, Russia.

FOLDES, Prof. Lucien Paul; Professor of Economics, University of London, at London School of Economics and Political Science, 1979–96, then Emeritus; *b* 19 Nov. 1930; *s* of Egon and Marta Foldes. *Educ:* Bunce Court Sch.; Monkton Wyld Sch.; London School of Economics (BCom, MScEcon, DBA). National Service, 1952–54. LSE: Asst Lecturer in Economics, 1954–55; Lectr, 1955–61; Reader, 1961–79. Rockefeller Travelling Fellow, 1961–62. *Publications:* articles in Rev. of Economic Studies, Economica, Jl of Mathematical Economics, Stochastics, Mathematical Finance, and others. *Recreation:* mathematical analysis. *Address:* London School of Economics, Houghton Street, WC2A 2AE. *T:* (020) 7405 7686.

FOLEY, family name of **Baron Foley**.

FOLEY, 8th Baron *cr* 1776; **Adrian Gerald Foley;** *b* 9 Aug. 1923; *s* of 7th Baron and Minoru (*d* 1968), *d* of late H. Greenstone, South Africa; *S* father, 1927; *m* 1st, 1958, Patricia Meek (marr. diss. 1971); one *s* one *d*; 2nd, 1972, Ghislaine Lady Ashcombe (*d* 2000). *Heir:* *s* Hon. Thomas Henry Foley, *b* 1 April 1961. *Address:* c/o Marbella Club, Marbella, Malaga, Spain. *Club:* White's.

FOLEY, Hugh Smith; Principal Clerk of Session and Justiciary, Scotland, 1989–97; *b* 9 April 1939; *s* of late John Walker Foley and Mary Hogg (*née* Smith); *m* 1966, Isobel King Halliday; two *s*. *Educ:* Dalkeith High Sch. (Joint Dux). Student Actuary, Standard Life Assce Co., 1956–59; nat. service, RAF, 1959–61; entered Scottish Court Service, Court of Session Br., 1962; Asst Clerk of Session, 1962–71; Depute Clerk of Session, 1972–80;

seconded to Sheriff Court, Edinburgh, 1980–81; Prin. Sheriff Clerk Depute, Glasgow, 1981–82; Sheriff Clerk, Linlithgow, 1982; Dep. Prin. Clerk of Session, 1982–86; Sen. Dep. Principal Clerk, 1986–89. Member: Lord President's Cttee on Procedure in Personal Injuries Litigation in Court of Session, 1978–79; Lothian Valuation Appeal Cttee, 1997–. *Recreations:* walking, painting, golf. *Address:* 63 Acredales, Linlithgow EH49 6HY.

FOLEY, Johanna Mary, (Jo); journalist; *b* 8 Dec. 1945; *d* of John and Monica Foley. *Educ:* St Joseph's Convent, Kenilworth; Manchester Univ. (BA Jt Hons English and Drama, 1968). Sen. Asst Editor, Woman's Own, 1978; Woman's Editor, The Sun, 1980; Editor, Woman, 1982; Exec. Editor (Features), The Times, 1984–85; Man. Editor, The Mirror, 1985–86; Editor: Observer Magazine, 1986–87; Options, 1988–91. Editor of the Year, British Soc. of Magazine Editors, 1983. *Recreations:* eating, reading, cinema, opera.

FOLEY, John Dominic; His Honour Judge Foley; a Circuit Judge, since 1994; *b* 17 Jan. 1944; *s* of Cyril Patrick Foley and Winifred Hannah (*née* McAweeny); *m* 1978, Helena Frances McGowan (marr. diss. 1986); two *d. Educ:* St Brendan's Coll., Bristol; Exeter Univ. (LLB Hons). Called to the Bar, Inner Temple, 1968; Western Circuit, 1969–; Asst Recorder, 1986–89; Recorder, 1990–93. Vice-Pres., Immigration Appeal Tribunal, 1998–. *Recreations:* Rugby (formerly 1st XV, Exeter Univ.), cricket, travel, rock. *Clubs:* Clifton Rugby Football, Bristol Rugby Football; Somerset County Cricket.

FOLEY, Lt-Gen. Sir John (Paul), KCB 1994 (CB 1991); OBE 1979; MC 1976; Lieutenant Governor and Commander-in-Chief, Guernsey, Channel Islands, since 2000; *b* 22 April 1939; *s* of Henry Thomas Hamilton Foley, MBE and Helen Constance Margaret Foley (*née* Pearson); *m* 1972, Ann Humphries; two *d. Educ:* Bradfield College; Mons OCS; Army Staff College (psc). Lieut, Royal Green Jackets, 1959; RMCS and Army Staff Coll., 1970–71; Regimental Duty, 1972–74; Chief of Staff, 51 Inf. Bde, Hong Kong, 1974–76; Instructor, Army Staff Coll., 1976–78; CO 3rd Bn RGJ, 1978–80; Comdt Jun. Div., Staff Coll., 1981–82. Arms Dir, MoD, 1983–85; RCDS 1986; Chief, British Mission to Soviet Forces in Germany, 1987–89; ACDS, MoD, 1989–92; Comdr, British Forces Hong Kong, and Maj.-Gen. Brigade of Gurkhas, 1992–94; Chief of Defence Intelligence, MoD, 1994–97. Col Comdt, 1st Bn, Royal Green Jackets, 1991–94, The Light Div., 1994–. Chm., British Greyhound Racing Bd, 1999–2000. Mem., Royal Patriotic Fund Corp., 2000–. Liveryman, Skinners' Co., 1972– (Mem. Court, 1995–2000). KSLJ 2000. *Recreations:* tennis, walking, shooting, reading. *Address:* Office of the Lieutenant Governor, Guernsey GY1 1GH. *Club:* Boodle's.

FOLEY, Maurice (Anthony), CMG 1987; Deputy Director General, Directorate General for Development, Commission of the European Communities, 1973–86; *b* 9 Oct. 1925; *s* of Jeremiah and Agnes Foley; *m* 1952, Katherine, *d* of Patrick and Nora O'Riordan; three *s* one *d. Educ:* St Mary's Coll., Middlesbrough. Formerly: electrical fitter, youth organiser, social worker. Member: ETU, 1941–46; Transport and General Workers Union, 1948–; Royal Arsenal Co-operative Soc. MP (Lab) West Bromwich, 1963–73; Joint Parliamentary Under-Sec. of State, Dept of Economic Affairs, 1964–66; Parly Under-Secretary: Home Office, 1966–67; Royal Navy, MoD, 1967–68; FCO, 1968–70.

FOLEY, Sir Noel; *see* Foley, Sir T. J. N.

FOLEY, Rt Rev. Ronald Graham Gregory; appointed Bishop Suffragan of Reading, 1982, Area Bishop, 1985, retired 1989; Assistant Bishop, Diocese of York, since 1989; *b* 13 June 1923; *s* of Theodore Gregory Foley and Cessan Florence Page; *m* 1944, Florence Redman; two *s* two *d. Educ:* King Edward's Grammar Sch., Aston, Birmingham; Wakefield Grammar Sch.; King's Coll., London; St John's Coll., Durham BA Hons Theol., LTh. Curate, South Shore, Blackpool, 1950; Vicar, S Luke, Blackburn, 1954; Dir of Educn, Dio. of Durham, and Rector of Brancepeth, 1960; Chaplain, Aycliffe Approved Sch., 1962; Vicar of Leeds, 1971–82; Chaplain to the Queen, 1977–82. Hon. Canon: Durham Cathedral, 1965–71; Ripon Cath., 1971–82. Dir, Yorks Electricity Bd, 1976–82. Chm. of Trustees, Dorothy Kerin Trust, Burrswood, 1983–89. *Publication:* (jtly) Religion in Approved Schools, 1969. *Recreations:* journalism, reading detective stories, watching other people mow lawns. *Address:* Ramsey Cottage, 3 Poplar Avenue, Kirkbymoorside, York YO6 6ES. *T:* (01751) 432439.

FOLEY, Sir (Thomas John) Noel, Kt 1978; CBE 1967; Chairman: CSR Ltd, 1980–84; Allied Manufacturing and Trading Industries (AMATIL) Ltd, 1955–79 (retired); *b* 1914; *s* of late Benjamin Foley, Brisbane. *Educ:* Brisbane Grammar Sch., Queensland; Queensland Univ. (BA, BCom). Chairman: Bank of NSW, 1978–82; Westpac Banking Corp., 1982–87. Founding Pres., WWF, Australia, 1978–80. DUniv Sydney. *Address:* 15 Bass Place, St Ives, NSW 2075, Australia.

FOLEY, Thomas Stephen, Hon. KBE 1995; American Ambassador to Japan, 1997–2001; Partner, Akin, Gump, Strauss, Hauer & Feld, 1995–97 and since 2001; *b* 6 March 1929; *s* of Ralph E. Foley and Helen Marie (*née* Higgins); *m* 1968, Heather Strachan. *Educ:* Gonzaga High Sch.; Gonzaga Univ.; Washington Univ. (BA 1951; LLB 1957). Partner, Higgins and Foley, 1957–58; Lectr in Law, Gonzaga Univ., 1958–60; Dep. Prosecuting Attorney, Spokane County, 1958–60; Asst Attorney Gen., Washington State, 1960–61; Special Counsel, Senate Interior and Insular Affairs Cttee, 1961–64; Mem. of 89th–101st Congresses from 5th Dist Washington (Democrat), 1964–95. Chm., 1975–80, Vice-Chm., 1981–86, Agriculture Cttee. Chm., House Democratic Caucus, 1976–80; House Majority Whip, 1981–87; Majority Leader, 1987–89; Speaker, US House of Representatives, 1989–95. Mem., Bd of Advrs, Yale Univ. Council; Dir, Council on Foreign Relations. *Address:* (office) 1333 New Hampshire Avenue NW, Washington, DC 20036, USA.

FOLJAMBE, family name of **Earl of Liverpool**.

FOLKESTONE, Viscount; William Pleydell-Bouverie; *b* 5 Jan. 1955; *s* and *heir* of 8th Earl of Radnor, *qv*; *m* 1996, Melissa, *d* of James Stanford, *qv*; two *s* one *d. Educ:* Harrow; Royal Agricultural Coll., Cirencester.

FOLLETT, Barbara; *see* Follett, D. B.

FOLLETT, Sir Brian (Keith), Kt 1992; DL; FRS 1984; Chairman, Arts and Humanities Research Board, since 2001; *b* 22 Feb. 1939; *s* of Albert James Follett and Edith Annie Follett; *m* 1961, Deb (*née* Booth); one *s* one *d. Educ:* Bournemouth Sch.; Univ. of Bristol (BSc 1960, PhD 1964); Univ. of Wales (DSc 1975). Res. Fellow, Washington State Univ., 1964–65; Lectr in Zool., Univ. of Leeds, 1965–69; Lectr, subseq. Reader and Prof. of Zool., University Coll. of N Wales, Bangor, 1969–78; Bristol University: Prof. of Zool., 1978–93, AFRC Res. Prof., 1989–93; Hd of Dept of Zool., 1978–89; Chm., Sch. of Biol Scis, 1989–93; Vice-Chancellor, Warwick Univ., 1993–2001. Chairman: ESRC-British Acad. Working Party on the Future of Funding Res. in the Humanities, 1992; Adv. Bd, British Library, 2000–; Member: Biol Sci. Cttee, SERC, 1981–84; AFRC, 1984–88 (Mem., Animals Cttee, 1984–88); Biol Sci. Cttee, UGC, 1985–88; UFC, 1989–93; HEFCE, 1992–96 (Chm., Libraries Review Gp, 1992–97); Council, BBSRC, 1994–2001 (Chm., Sci. and Engrg Bd, 1994–97); Royal Commn on Envmtl Pollution, 2000–. Trustee, BM (Natural Hist.), 1989–98. Biol Sec. and Vice-Pres., Royal Soc., 1987–93; Member of Council: Soc. for Study of Fertility, 1972–87 (Prog. Sec., 1976–78; Treas., 1982–87); Soc. for Endocrinology, 1974–77; Bristol Zoo, 1978–93; Wildfowl Trust, Slimbridge, 1983–86; Zool Soc. of London, 1983–86. Pres. ASE, 1997. Lectures: Amoroso, Soc. for Study of Fertility, 1985; Annual Zool., Liverpool Univ., 1991; Barrington Meml, Nottingham Univ., 1992. Mem., Academia Europaea, 1988. DL West Midlands, 2000. Hon. FLA 1997. Hon. Fellow, UCNW, Bangor, 1990. Hon. LLD: Wales, 1992; Calgary, 2001; Hon. DSc: Univ. Teknologi, Malaysia, 1999; Leicester, 2001. Scientific Medal, 1976, Frink Medal, 1993, Zool Soc. of London; Dale Medal, Soc. of Endocrinology, 1988. Editorial Bds: Jl of Endocrinology, 1971–78; Gen. & Comparative Endocrinology, 1974–82; Jl of Biol. Rhythms, 1986–; Proc. of Royal Soc., 1987–90. *Publications:* over 260 scientific papers on biol. clocks and reproductive physiology. *Address:* Arts and Humanities Research Board, 10 Carlton House Terrace, SW1Y 5AH.

FOLLETT, (Daphne) Barbara; MP (Lab) Stevenage, since 1997; *b* 25 Dec. 1942; *d* of late William Vernon Hubbard and Charlotte Hubbard (*née* Goulding); *m* 1st, 1963, Richard Turner (marr. diss. 1971); two *d*; 2nd, 1971, Gerald Stonestreet (marr. diss. 1974); 3rd, 1974, Leslie Broer (marr. diss. 1985); one *s*; 4th, 1985, Ken Follett, *qv*; one step *s* one step *d. Educ:* London Sch. of Economics (BSc Econ); Open Univ. Teacher, Berlitz Sch. of Language, Paris, 1963–64; Jt Manager, fruit farm, Stellenbosch, S Africa, 1966–77; acting Regl Sec., S African Inst. of Race Relations, Cape Town, 1970; Regl Manager (Cape and Namibia), 1971–74, Nat. Health Educn Dir, 1975–78, Kupugani; Asst Course Orgnr and Lectr, Centre for Internat. Briefing, Farnham, 1980–84; freelance lectr and consultant, 1984–92. Vis. Fellow, Inst. of Public Policy Research, 1993. Contested (Lab): Woking, 1983; Epsom and Ewell, 1987. Founder Member: EMILY's List UK, 1992– (also Dir); Women's Movt for Peace, S Africa, 1976; Women's Network, Labour Party (Mem., Steering Cttee, 1988–); Member: Fawcett Soc., 1993; Nat. Alliance of Women's Orgns, 1993; Nat. Women's Network, 1993. *Recreations:* photography, Scrabble. *Address:* House of Commons, SW1A 0AA. *T:* (020) 7219 2649, *Fax:* (020) 7219 1158.

FOLLETT, Ken; author, since 1977; *b* 5 June 1949; *s* of Martin Dunsford Follett and late Lavinia Cynthia (Veenie) Follett (*née* Evans); *m* 1st, 1968, Mary Elson (marr. diss. 1985); one *s* one *d*; 2nd, 1985, Barbara Broer (*see* D. B. Follett). *Educ:* Harrow Weald Grammar Sch.; Poole Tech. Coll.; University Coll. London (BA; Fellow 1994). Trainee journalist, S Wales Echo, 1970–73; Reporter, London Evening News, 1973–74; Everest Books: Editl Dir, 1974–76; Dep. Man. Dir, 1976–77. Mem. Council, Nat. Literary Trust, 1996–; Chm., Nat. Year of Reading, 1998–99. Pres., Dyslexia Inst., 1998–. *Publications include:* Eye of the Needle (Edgar Award, Mystery Writers of Amer.), 1978; Triple, 1979; The Key to Rebecca, 1980; The Man from St Petersburg, 1982; On Wings of Eagles, 1983; Lie down with Lions, 1986; The Pillars of the Earth, 1989; Night over Water, 1991; Mrs Shiblak's Nightmare (pamphlet), 1992; A Dangerous Fortune, 1993; A Place Called Freedom, 1995; The Third Twin, 1997; The Hammer of Eden, 1998; Code to Zero, 2000; various articles, screenplays and short stories. *Recreations:* bass guitarist in a blues band; Labour Party supporter and campaigner. *Address:* The Old Rectory, Old Knebworth Lane, Stevenage, Herts SG3 6PT. *Club:* Groucho.

FONAGY, Prof. Peter, PhD; FBA 1997; Freud Memorial Professor of Psychoanalysis, University of London, at University College, since 1992; Director of Research: Anna Freud Centre, since 1989; Menninger Clinic, Kansas, since 1995; *b* 14 Aug. 1952; *s* of Ivan Fonagy and Judith (*née* Barath); *m* 1990, Dr Anna Higgitt; one *s* one *d. Educ:* UCL (BSc Hons 1974; PhD 1980). Dip. Clin. Psych. 1980. Lectr, 1977–88, Sen. Lectr, 1988–92, in Psychology, Univ. of London; Dir, Sub-Dept of Clin. Health Psychology, UCL, 1995–; Adjunct Prof. of Clin. Psychology, Kansas Univ., 1995–; Menninger Clinic: Co-ordinating Dir, Child and Family Center, 1995, Clin. Protocols and Outcome Center, 1996–; Vorhees Distinguished Prof., 1995. Visiting Professor: Hebrew Univ. of Jerusalem, 1993; Univ. of Haifa, 1993, 1995; Cornell Med. Coll., NY, 1994; Marie and Scott S. Smith Chair in Child Develt, Karl Menninger Sch. of Psychiatry and Mental Health Scis, Kansas, 1999–. Mem., 1988–, and Trng and Supervising Analyst, 1995–, British Psycho-Analytical Soc. *Publications:* (with A. Higgitt) Personality Theory and Clinical Practice, 1985; (with A. D. Roth) What Works for Whom?, 1996; papers, contribs books. *Recreations:* ski-ing, theatre, gardening. *Address:* Sub-Department of Clinical Health Psychology, University College London, Gower Street, WC1E 6BT. *T:* (020) 7679 1791; *e-mail:* p.fonagy@ucl.ac.uk.

FONTAINE, André Lucien Georges; Managing Editor and Publisher, le Monde, 1985–91; *b* 30 March 1921; *s* of Georges Fontaine and Blanche Rochon Duvigneaud; *m* 1943, Belita Cavaillé; two *s* one *d. Educ:* Paris Univ. (diplomes études supérieures droit public et économie politique, lic.lettres). Joined Temps Présent, 1946; le Monde, 1947: Foreign Editor, 1951; Editor, 1969. Editorialist, Radio Luxemburg, 1980–91. Chm. Adv. Gp, Internat. Strategy for the 9th Plan, 1982–84; Mem. Bd, Institut Français des Relations Internationales, 1982–92; Vice-Chm., French section, Franco-British Council, 2000–. Mem. Bd, Bank Indosuez, 1983–85. Grand Officer, Order of Dom Enrique (Portugal); Commander: German Merit; Italian Merit; Greek Phoenix; Officer, Orders of Vasa (Sweden), Leopold (Belgium) and Lion (Finland); Kt, Danebrog (Denmark) and Crown of Belgium; Order of Tudor Vladimirescu (Romania). Atlas' Internat. Editor of the Year, 1976. *Publications:* L'Alliance atlantique à l'heure du dégel, 1960; Histoire de la guerre froide, vol. 1 1965, vol. 2 1966 (English trans., History of the Cold War, 1966 and 1967); La Guerre civile froide, 1969; Le dernier quart du siècle, 1976; La France au bois dormant, 1978; Un seul lit pour deux rêves, 1981; (with Pierre Li) Sortir de l'Hexagonie, 1984; L'un sans l'autre, 1991; Après eux, le dèluge, 1995. *Address:* 25 bis rue Claude-Bernard, 75242 Paris Cedex 05, France.

FONTAINE, Nicole Claude Marie; President, European Parliament, since 1999 (Member (UDF), France, since 1984); *b* 16 Jan. 1942; *d* of Jean Garnier and Geneviève Garnier (*née* Lambert); *m* 1964, Jean-René Fontaine; one *d. Educ:* Faculté de Droit, Paris (law degree, 1962); Inst. d'Etudes Politiques, Paris (Dip. 1964); DenD 1969. Teacher, 1963–64; Catholic Education Secretariat, France: Legal Advr, 1965; Dep. Sec.-Gen., 1972–81; Chief Rep., 1981–84. Member: Nat. Educn Council, France, 1975–81; Economic and Social Council, France, 1980–84. European Parliament: Vice Pres., 1989–94; First Vice Pres., 1994–99; Member: Legal Affairs and Citizens' Rights Cttee, 1984–89; Women's Rights Cttee, 1984–89; Culture, Youth, Educn, Media and Sport Cttee, 1989–; Israel Delegn, 1989–97; Perm. Mem., Conciliation Cttee, 1994–; Chm., Delegn to COSAC. Mem., Governing Council and Exec. Cttee, Nouvelle UDF. *Publications:* Les établissements d'enseignement privé associés à l'Etat par contrat, 1980; Les députés européens: qui sont-ils? que font-ils?, 1994; L'Europe de vos initiatives, 1997; Le traité d'Amsterdam, 1998. *Address:* European Parliament, Rue Wiertz, 1047 Brussels, Belgium.

FOOKES, Baroness *cr* 1997 (Life Peer), of Plymouth in the co. of Devon; **Janet Evelyn Fookes,** DBE 1989; DL; *b* 21 Feb. 1936; *d* of late Lewis Aylmer Fookes and Evelyn Margery Fookes (*née* Holmes). *Educ:* Hastings and St Leonards Ladies' Coll.; High Sch. for

Girls, Hastings; Royal Holloway Coll., Univ. of London (BA Hons; Hon. Fellow, 1998). Teacher, 1958–70. Councillor for County Borough of Hastings, 1960–61 and 1963–70 (Chm. Educn Cttee, 1967–70). MP (C): Merton and Morden, 1970–74; Plymouth, Drake, 1974–97. Mem., Speaker's Panel of Chairmen, 1976–97; Second Dep. Chm. of Ways and Means and Dep. Speaker, H of C, 1992–97. Sec., Cons. Parly Educn Cttee, 1971–75; Chairman: Educn, Arts and Home Affairs Sub-Cttee of the Expenditure Cttee, 1975–79; Parly Gp for Animal Welfare, 1985–92 (Sec., 1974–82); Member: Unopposed Bills Cttee, 1973–75; Services Cttee, 1974–76; Select Cttee on Home Affairs, 1984–92. Chm., Cons. West Country Mems Cttee, 1976–77, Vice-Chm., 1977. Fellow, Industry and Parlt Trust, 1978. Pres., Hastings and Rye Cons. Assoc., 1998–. Member: Council, RSPCA, 1975–92 (Chm., 1979–81); Nat. Art Collections Fund; Council, SSAFA, 1980–98 (Vice-Pres., 1998–); Council, Stonham Housing Assoc., 1980–92; Commonwealth War Graves Commn, 1987–97; Council of Mgt, Coll. of St Mark and St John, 1989–. Pres., Hastings, St Leonards on Sea, Bexhill and Dist Br., NSPCC, 2000–. Patron, Plymouth Workroute Appeal, 1998–. Member: RHS; Nat. Trust. DL E Sussex, 2001. Hon. DLitt Plymouth, 1993. *Recreations:* theatre, gardening, gymnasium exercises, swimming, yoga. *Address:* House of Lords, SW1A 0PW.

FOOT, David Lovell, CB 1998; FICFor; Head of Forestry Authority, 1995–99; *b* 20 May 1939; *s* of late John Bartram Lovell Foot, MBE and of Bertha Lilian Foot; *m* 1964, Verena Janine Walton; one *s* one *d*. *Educ:* John Lyon Sch., Harrow; Edinburgh Univ. (BSc Hons 1961). FICFor 1980. Dist Officer, Forestry Commn, 1961–64; Silviculturist, Dept of Forestry and Game, Govt of Malawi, 1964–70; Forestry Commission: various appts in S Scotland, N Wales and E Scotland, 1970–86; Comr, 1986–99. Trustee, Woodland Trust, 1999–. *Recreations:* walking, fishing, photography. *Address:* 36 Coltbridge Terrace, Edinburgh EH12 6AE. *T:* (0131) 337 3874.

FOOT, Sir Geoffrey (James), Kt 1984; Chairman and Commissioner, Hydro Electric Commission of Tasmania, 1987–89 (Associate Commissioner, 1984–87); *b* 20 July 1915; *s* of James P. Foot and Susan J. Foot; *m* 1940, Mollie W. Snooks; two *s* one *d*. *Educ:* Launceston High Sch. AASA; ACIS. MLC, Tasmania, 1961–72 (Leader for Govt, 1969–72). Chairman: Tasmania Permanent Bldg Soc., 1982–85; Launceston Gas Co., 1982–84; Gas Corp. of Tasmania, 1984–87. Mem., Lilydale Commn—Local Govt, 1983–85. Mem. Council, Univ. of Tas, 1970–85. Freeman, City of Launceston, 1990. Hon. LLD Tasmania, 1988. *Recreations:* reading, music. *Address:* 85 Arthur Street, Launceston, Tas 7250, Australia. *T:* (03) 63340573.

FOOT, Rt Hon. Michael; PC 1974; *b* 23 July 1913; *s* of late Rt Hon. Isaac Foot, PC; *m* 1949, Jill Craigie (*d* 1999). *Educ:* Forres Sch., Swanage; Leighton Park Sch., Reading; Wadham Coll., Oxford (Exhibitioner). Pres. Oxford Union, 1933; contested (Lab) Mon, 1935; MP (Lab): Devonport Div. of Plymouth, 1945–55; Ebbw Vale, Nov. 1960–1983; Blaenau Gwent, 1983–92; Sec. of State for Employment, 1974–76; Lord President of the Council and Leader of the House of Commons, 1976–79; Leader of the Opposition, 1980–83. Mem., Labour Party Nat. Exec. Cttee, 1971–83; Deputy Leader of the Labour Party, 1976–80, Leader of the Labour Party 1980–83. Asst Editor, Tribune, 1937–38; Acting Editor, Evening Standard, 1942; Man. Dir, Tribune, 1945–74, Editor, 1948–52, 1955–60; political columnist on the Daily Herald, 1944–64; former Book Critic, Evening Standard. Hon. Fellow, Wadham Coll. 1969. *Publications:* Guilty Men (with Frank Owen and Peter Howard), 1940; Armistice 1918–39, 1940; Trial of Mussolini, 1943; Brendan and Beverley, 1944; Still at Large, 1950; Full Speed Ahead, 1950; Guilty Men (with Mervyn Jones), 1957; The Pen and the Sword, 1957; Parliament in Danger, 1959; Aneurin Bevan: Vol. I, 1897–1945, 1962; Vol. II, 1945–60, 1973; Debts of Honour, 1980; Another Heart and Other Pulses, 1984; Loyalists and Loners, 1986; The Politics of Paradise, 1988; H. G.: the history of Mr Wells, 1995; Dr Strangelove, I Presume, 1999. *Recreations:* Plymouth Argyle supporter, chess, reading, walking. *Address:* c/o Tribune, 9 Arkwright Road, NW3 6AN.

FOOT, Michael Colin, OBE 1984; freelance teacher and lecturer, English as a foreign language; *b* 3 Feb. 1935; *s* of William Reginald Foot and Elsie (*née* Collins); *m* 1964, Heather Pearl Foot (*née* Beaton); two *s* two *d*. *Educ:* Taunton's Sch., Southampton; University Coll., Leicester (BA London); Leicester Univ. (PGCE); Univ. of Essex (MA 1994). Lycée Champollion, Grenoble, 1959–60; Ashlyn's Sch., Berkhamsted, 1960–63. Served RAF, 1963–66. British Council: Asst Rep., Chile, 1966–71; Hd of Overseas Recruitment, Personnel Div., 1971–75; Dep. Rep., Nigeria, 1975–78; Dep. Dir, Personnel, 1978–81; Rep., Bangladesh, 1981–83; Dir, Personnel, 1984–85; Controller, Personnel, 1986–89; Dir, Australia, 1989–93; retd 1993. *Recreations:* reading, theatre, music, botany, swimming. *Address:* c/o HSBC, Bitterne, Southampton SO9 3RZ. *Club:* Royal Air Force.

FOOT, Michael David Kenneth Willoughby; Managing Director and Head of Financial Supervision, Financial Services Authority, since 1998; *b* 16 Dec. 1946; *s* of Kenneth Willoughby Foot and Ruth Joan (*née* Cornah); *m* 1972, Michele Annette Cynthia Macdonald; one *s* two *d*. *Educ:* Pembroke Coll., Cambridge (MA); Yale Univ., USA (MA). Joined Bank of England, 1969; manager, 1978; sen. man., 1985; seconded to IMF, Washington, as UK Alternate Exec. Dir, 1985–87; Head: Foreign Exchange Div., 1988–90; European Div., 1990–93; Banking Supervision Div., 1993–94; Dep. Dir, Supervision and Surveillance, 1994–96; Exec. Dir, Bank of England, 1996–98. *Publications:* contrib. essays on monetary econs to books and jls. *Recreations:* choral singing, tennis, voluntary youth work. *Address:* Financial Services Authority, 25 North Colonnade, Canary Wharf, E14 5HS.

FOOT, Michael Richard Daniell, CBE 2001; TD 1945; historian; *b* 14 Dec. 1919; *s* of late R. C. Foot and Nina (*née* Raymond); *m* twice; one *s* one *d*; 3rd, 1972, Mirjam Michaela Romme (*see* M. M. Foot). *Educ:* Winchester (scholar); New Coll., Oxford (scholar). Served in Army, 1939–45 (Major RA, parachutist, wounded). Taught at Oxford, 1947–59; research, 1959–67; Prof of Modern Hist., Manchester, 1967–73; Dir of Studies, European Discussion Centre, 1973–75. Fellow, St Deiniol's Liby, Hawarden, 2001. French Croix de Guerre, 1945; Officer, Order of Orange Nassau (Netherlands), 1989. *Publications:* Gladstone and Liberalism (with J. L. Hammond), 1952; British Foreign Policy since 1898, 1956; Men in Uniform, 1961; SOE in France, 1966; (ed) The Gladstone Diaries: vols I and II, 1825–1839, 1968; (ed) War and Society, 1973; (ed with Dr H. C. G. Matthew) The Gladstone Diaries: vols III and IV, 1840–1854, 1974; Resistance, 1976; Six Faces of Courage, 1978; (with J. M. Langley) MI9, 1979; SOE: an outline history, 1984; Art and War, 1990; (ed) Holland at war against Hitler, 1990; (ed with I. C. B. Dear) Oxford Companion to the Second World War, 1995; SOE in the Low Countries, 2001. *Recreations:* reading, talking. *Address:* Martins Cottage, Nuthampstead, Royston, Herts SG8 8ND. *Clubs:* Savile, Special Forces.

FOOT, Dr Mirjam Michaela, DLitt; FSA; Professor of Library and Archive Studies, University College London, since 2000; *b* 11 Oct. 1941; *d* of Carl Paul Maria Romme and Anthonia Maria Wiegman; *m* 1972, Michael Richard Daniell Foot *qv*. *Educ:* Amsterdam Univ. (BA, MA, DLitt 1979). FSA 1986. Asst Lectr, Bedford Coll., Univ. of London, 1965–66; British Library: Asst Keeper, Rare Book Collection, 1966–84; Curator, Preservation Service, 1984–87; Dep. Dir, Hd of W European Collections and Hd of Acquisitions, 1987–90; Dir of Collections and Preservation, 1990–99. Associate, Clare Hall, Cambridge, 1970–72. Ed., British Liby Jl, 1977–85. Bibliographical Society: Hon. Sec., 1975–94; Vice-Pres., 1990–2000; Pres., 2000–. Hon. Fellow, Designer Bookbinders, 1986. *Publications:* The Henry Davis Gift: Vol I: Studies in the History of Bookbinding, 1978; Vol II: North European Bindings, 1983; Pictorial Bookbindings, 1986; (with H. M. Nixon) The History of Decorated Bookbinding in England, 1992; Studies in the History of Bookbinding, 1993; The History of Bookbinding as a Mirror of Society, 1998; contrib. articles in Book Collector, The Liby, British Liby Jl, Revue française d'histoire du livre, Proc. and Bulletins of Assoc. Internat. de Bibliophilie, Paper Conservator. *Recreations:* music, reading, walking, gardening. *Address:* School of Library, Archive and Information Studies, University College London, Gower Street, WC1E 6BT. *T:* (020) 7679 3753; Martins Cottage, Bell Lane, Nuthampstead, Herts SG8 8ND.

FOOT, Paul Mackintosh; writer; journalist; with Private Eye, since 1993; *b* 8 Nov. 1937; *m*; three *s*; one *d*. Editor of Isis, 1961; President of the Oxford Union, 1961. TUC delegate from Nat. Union of Journalists, 1967 and 1971. Contested (Socialist Workers Party) Birmingham, Stechford, March 1977. Editor, Socialist Worker, 1974–75; with The Daily Mirror, 1979–93. What The Papers Say Awards: Journalist of the Year, 1972, 1989; Journalist of the Decade (1990s), 2000; Campaigning Journalist of the Year, British Press Awards, 1980; (with Tim Laxton) George Orwell Prize for Journalism, 1994. *Publications:* Immigration and Race in British Politics, 1965; The Politics of Harold Wilson, 1968; The Rise of Enoch Powell, 1969; Who Killed Hanratty?, 1971; Why You Should Be a Socialist, 1977; Red Shelley, 1981; The Helen Smith Story, 1983; Murder at the Farm: who killed Carl Bridgewater?, 1986; Who Framed Colin Wallace?, 1989; Words as Weapons, 1990; Articles of Resistance, 2000; contrib. Counterblasts, 1989. *Address:* c/o Private Eye, 6 Carlisle Street, W1V 5RG.

FOOT, Prof. Philippa Ruth, FBA 1976; Griffin Professor, University of California at Los Angeles, 1988–91, now Emeritus (Professor of Philosophy, 1974–91); *b* 3 Oct. 1920; *d* of William Sydney Bence Bosanquet, DSO, and Esther Cleveland Bosanquet, *d* of Grover Cleveland, Pres. of USA; *m* 1945, M. R. D. Foot (marr. diss. 1960), *qv*; no *c*. *Educ:* St George's Sch., Ascot; privately; Somerville Coll., Oxford (BA 1942, MA 1946). Somerville Coll., Oxford: Lectr in philosophy, 1947; Fellow and Tutor, 1950–69; Vice-Principal, 1967–69; Sen. Res. Fellow, 1970–88; Hon. Fellow, 1988. Formerly Vis. Prof., Cornell Univ., MIT, Univ. of California at Berkeley, Princeton Univ., City Univ. of NY; Fellow, Center for Advanced Studies in Behavioral Scis, Stanford, 1981–82. Pres., Pacific Div., Amer. Philos. Assoc., 1982–83. Fellow, Amer. Acad. of Arts and Scis, 1983. Hon. Dr Sofia, 2000. *Publications:* Theories of Ethics (ed), 1967; Virtues and Vices, 1978; articles in Mind, Aristotelian Soc. Proc., Philos. Rev., New York Rev., Philosophy and Public Affairs. *Address:* 15 Walton Street, Oxford OX1 2HG. *T:* (01865) 557130.

FOOT, Prof. Rosemary June, PhD; FBA 1996; John Swire Senior Research Fellow in International Relations, St Antony's College, Oxford, since 1990; Professor of International Relations, University of Oxford, since 1997; *b* 4 June 1948; *d* of Leslie William Foot, MBE and Margaret Lily Frances Foot; *m* 1996, Timothy C. S. Kennedy. *Educ:* Univ. of Essex (BA Hons Govt 1972); SOAS, London Univ. (MA Area Studies (Far East) 1973); LSE (PhD Internat. Relns 1977). Lectr in Internat. Relns, Univ. of Sussex, 1978–90. Fulbright Scholar and American Council of Learned Socs Fellow, E Asian Inst., Columbia Univ., NY, 1981–82. *Publications:* The Wrong War: American policy and the dimensions of the Korean conflict 1950–1953, 1985; A Substitute for Victory: the politics of peacemaking at the Korean Armistice talks, 1990; (ed jtly) Migration: the Asian experience, 1994; The Practice of Power: US relations with China since 1949, 1995; (ed jtly) Hong Kong's Transitions 1842–1997, 1997; Rights Beyond Borders: the global community and the struggle over human rights in China, 2000. *Recreations:* walking, music, sailing. *Address:* St Antony's College, Oxford OX2 6JF. *T:* (01865) 284754.

FOOTE, Prof. Peter Godfrey; Emeritus Professor of Scandinavian Studies, University of London; *b* 26 May 1924; 4th *s* of late T. Foote and Ellen Foote, Swanage, Dorset; *m* 1951, Eleanor Jessie McCaig, *d* of late J. M. McCaig and Margaret H. McCaig; one *s* two *d*. *Educ:* Grammar Sch., Swanage; University Coll., Exeter; Univ. of Oslo; University Coll., London. BA London 1948; MA London 1951; Fil. dr *hc* Uppsala, 1972; dr phil. *hc* Univ. of Iceland, 1987. Served with RNVR, 1943–46. University College London: Asst Lectr, Lectr and Reader in Old Scandinavian, 1950–63; Prof. of Scandinavian Studies, 1963–83; Fellow, 1989. Jt Sec., Viking Soc., 1956–83 (Pres., 1974–76; 1990–92; Hon. Life Mem., 1983). Member: Royal Gustav Adolfs Academy, Uppsala, 1967; Kungl. Humanistiska Vetenskapssamfundet, Uppsala, 1968; Vísindafélag Islands, 1969; Vetenskapssocieteten, Lund, 1973; Kungl. Vetenskaps-samhället, Göteborg; Det kongelige Norske Videnskabers Selskab, 1977; Societas Scientiarum Fennica, 1979; Det norske Videnskapsakademi, 1986; Hon. Member: Isl. Bókmenntafélag, 1965; Thjóðvinafélag Ísl. í Vesturheimi, 1975; Félag íslenzkra fræða, 1995; Corresp. Mem., Kungl. Vitterhets Hist. och Antikvitets Akad., Stockholm, 1971. Crabtree Orator, 1968. Commander with star, Icelandic Order of the Falcon, 1984 (Comdr, 1973); Knight, Order of Dannebrog (Denmark); Comdr, Royal Order of North Star (Sweden), 1977; Comdr, Royal Order of Merit (Norway), 1993. *Publications:* Gunnlaugs saga ormstungu, 1957; Pseudo-Turpin Chronicle in Iceland, 1959; Laing's Heimskringla, 1961; Lives of Saints: Icelandic manuscripts in fascimile IV, 1962, and XIX, 1990; (with G. Johnston) The Saga of Gisli, 1963; (with D. M. Wilson) The Viking Achievement, 1970, 2nd edn 1980; Aurvandilstá (selected papers), 1984; papers in Saga-Book, Arv, Studia Islandica, Islenzk Tunga, etc. *Recreations:* bell-ringing, walking. *Address:* 18 Talbot Road, N6 4QR. *T:* (020) 8340 1860.

FOOTMAN, John Richard Evelegh; Director of Personnel, Bank of England, since 1999; *b* 6 Sept. 1952; *s* of Jack and Joyce Footman; *m* 1983, Elaine Watkiss; two *s* three *d*. *Educ:* Clifton Coll., Bristol. Joined Bank of England, 1969; Private Sec. to Gov., 1986–89; Head of Information, 1989–94; Sec., 1994–97; Dep. Dir, 1997–99. *Address:* Bank of England, EC2R 8AH. *T:* (020) 7601 5765.

FOOTS, Sir James (William), Kt 1975; AO 1992; mining engineer; Chairman: MIM Holdings Ltd, 1970–83 (Director, 1956–87); Westpac Banking Corporation, 1987–89 (Director, 1971–89); *b* 12 July 1916; *m* 1939, Thora H.Thomas; one *s* two *d*. *Educ:* Melbourne Univ. (BME). President: Austr. Inst. Mining and Metallurgy, 1974; Austr. Mining Industry Council, 1974 and 1975; 13th Congress, Council of Mining and Metallurgical Institns, 1986. Fellow, Australian Acad. of Technol Scis. University of Queensland: Mem. Senate, 1970–92; Chancellor, 1985–92. Hon. DEng Univ. of Qld, 1982. *Address:* 79/1 Moore Street, Taringa, Qld 4068, Australia.

FOOTTIT, Rt Rev. Anthony Charles; *see* Lynn, Bishop Suffragan of.

FOPP, Dr Michael Anton; Director, Royal Air Force Museum, since 1988; *b* 28 Oct. 1947; *s* of Sqdn Ldr Desmond Fopp and Edna Meryl (*née* Dodd); *m* 1968, Rosemary Ann Hodgetts; one *s*. *Educ:* Reading Blue Coat Sch.; City Univ., London (MA 1984; PhD 1989). FIMgt; FMA; FRAeS. Dep. Keeper 1979–82, Keeper 1982–85, Battle of Britain Mus.; Co. Sec., Hendon Mus. Trading Co. Ltd, 1983–85; Dir, London Transport Mus.,

1985–88. Hon. Sec. 1976–86, Chm. 1986–88, Soc. of Friends of RAF Mus. President: London Underground Rly Soc., 1987–88; Internat. Assoc. of Transport Museums, 1992–98. Chairman: Museums' Documentation Assoc., 1995–98; London Transport Flying Club Ltd, 1986–97. Freeman: City of London, 1984; Guild of Air Pilots and Navigators, 1987. *Publications:* The Boeing Washington, 1980; The Battle of Britain Museum Guide, 1980; The Bomber Command Museum Guide, 1982; The RAF Museum Guide, 1985; (ed) A Junior Guide to the RAF Museum, 1985; (ed) Battle of Britain Project Book, 1989; Royal Air Force Museum, 1992; (ed) High Flyers, 1993; Managing Museums and Galleries, 1997; The Implications of Emerging Technologies for Museums and Galleries, 1997; various articles on aviation, museums and management, in magazines and jls. *Recreations:* flying, computers, Chinese cookery, building light aircraft. *Address:* Royal Air Force Museum, Hendon, NW9 5LL. *T:* (020) 8205 2266. *Clubs:* Royal Air Force; Air Squadron.

FORAY, Prof. Cyril Patrick; High Commissioner for Sierra Leone in the United Kingdom, 1993–95 and 1996–2000; *b* 16 March 1934; *s* of Michael Kelema Foray and Mary Bridget Foray (*née* Alie); *m* 1958, Arabella Williams; two *s* two *d*. *Educ:* St Edward's Secondary Sch., Freetown, Sierra Leone; Fourah Bay Coll., Freetown; St Cuthbert's Soc.; Durham Univ.; UCLA. Asst Master, St Edward's Secondary Sch., Freetown, 1958–60, Sen. Asst Master, 1960–62; part-time Lectr, Dept of Hist., Fourah Bay Coll., 1959–60; Lectr, Njala UC, 1964–67; Department of History, Fourah Bay College: Temp. Lectr, 1968–69 and 1972–73; Lectr, 1973–77; Actg Hd, 1975–77; Hd of Dept, 1977–85; Sen. Lectr, 1977–81; Associate Prof., 1981–85; Vice Principal, 1984–85; Prof. and Principal, 1985–93. University of Sierra Leone: Public Orator, 1976–85; Dean, Faculty of Arts, 1978–82; Pro-Vice Chancellor, 1988–90. MP Bo Town I constituency, Sierra Leone, 1969–73; Minister of: Ext. Affairs, 1969–71; Health, May–Sept. 1971. *Publications:* Historical Dictionary of Sierra Leone, Vol. 12, 1977; articles on Sierra Leone in Encyclopaedia Africana, 1979; The Road to the One Party—The Sierra Leone Experience, 1988. *Recreations:* cricket, lawn tennis. *Address:* 2 Leicester Road, Freetown, Sierra Leone.

FORBES, family name of **Lord Forbes** and of **Earl of Granard**.

FORBES, 22nd Lord *cr* 1445 or before; **Nigel Ivan Forbes,** KBE 1960; JP, DL; Premier Lord of Scotland; Representative Peer of Scotland, 1955–63; Major (retired) Grenadier Guards; Chairman, Rolawn Ltd, 1975–98; *b* 19 Feb. 1918; *o s* of 21st Lord and Lady Mabel Anson (*d* 1972), *d* of 3rd Earl of Lichfield; *S* father, 1953; *m* 1942, Hon. Rosemary Katharine Hamilton-Russell, *o d* of 9th Viscount Boyne; two *s* one *d*. *Educ:* Harrow; RMC Sandhurst. Served War of 1939–45 (wounded); Adjt, Grenadier Guards, Staff Coll. Military Asst to High Comr for Palestine, 1947–48. Minister of State, Scottish Office, 1958–59. Member: Inter-Parly Union Delegn to Denmark, 1956; Commonwealth Parly Assoc. Delegn to Canada, 1961; Parly Delegn to Pakistan, 1962; Inter-Parly Union Delegn to Hungary, 1965; Inter-Parly Union Delegn to Ethiopia, 1971. Director: Grampian Television PLC, 1960–88; Blenheim Travel Ltd, 1981–88; Dep. Chm., Tenant Caledonian Breweries Ltd, 1964–74. Mem., Aberdeen and District Milk Marketing Bd, 1962–72; Mem. Alford District Council, 1955–58; Chm., River Don District Bd, 1962–73. Pres., Royal Highland and Agricultural Society of Scotland, 1958–59; Member: Sports Council for Scotland, 1966–71; Scottish Cttee, Nature Conservancy, 1961–67; Chm., Scottish Br., Nat. Playing Fields Assoc., 1965–80; Pres., Scottish Scout Assoc., 1970–88. Pres., Books Abroad, 1982–; Chm., Alford Car Transport Service, 2000–. Patron, Friends of Insch Hosp., 1992–. JP 1955, DL 1958, Aberdeenshire. *Recreations:* wildlife, travel, photography. *Heir:* *s* Master of Forbes, *qv*. *Address:* Balforbes, Alford, Aberdeenshire AB33 8DR. *T:* (01975) 562516, *Fax:* (01975) 562898. *Club:* Army and Navy.

FORBES, Viscount; Jonathan Peter Hastings Forbes; *b* 24 Dec. 1981; *e s* and *heir* of Earl of Granard, *qv*.

FORBES, Master of; Hon. Malcolm Nigel Forbes; DL; landowner; *b* 6 May 1946; *s* and *heir* of 22nd Lord Forbes, *qv*; *m* 1st, 1969, Carole Jennifer Andrée (marr. diss. 1982), *d* of N. S. Whitehead, Aberdeen; one *s* one *d*; 2nd, 1988, Jennifer Mary Gribbon, *d* of I. P. Whittington, Tunbridge Wells. *Educ:* Eton; Aberdeen Univ. Director, Instock Disposables Ltd, 1974–; Chm., Castle Forbes Collection Ltd, 1996–. DL Aberdeenshire, 1996. *Address:* Castle Forbes, Alford, Aberdeenshire AB33 8BL. *T:* (01975) 562574; 3 Steeple Close, SW6 3LE. *T:* (020) 7736 0730.

FORBES, Anthony David Arnold William; Joint Senior Partner, Cazenove & Co., 1980–94; *b* 15 Jan. 1938; *s* of late Lt-Col D. W. A. W. Forbes, MC, and Diana Mary (*née* Henderson), later Marchioness of Exeter; *m* 1st, 1962, Virginia June Ropner; one *s* one *d*; 2nd, 1973, Belinda Mary Drury-Lowe. *Educ:* Eton. Served Coldstream Guards, 1956–59. Joined Cazenove & Co., 1960; Member of Stock Exchange, subseq. MSI, 1965–. Director: Carlton Communications Plc, 1994–; The Merchants Trust PLC, 1994–; Royal & Sun Alliance Insurance Gp (formerly Royal Insurance Hldgs plc), 1994– (Dep. Chm., 1998–); RTZ Pension Investment Ltd, 1994–2000; Watmoughs (Hldgs) PLC, 1994–98; Phoenix Group Ltd, 1995–97; Rio Tinto Pension Fund Trustees Ltd, 2000–. Chairman: Hospital and Homes of St Giles, 1975–; Wellesley House Educnl Trust, 1983–94; Hon. Trustee, Royal Botanic Gardens Kew Foundn, 1992–; Trustee, Botanic Gardens Conservation Internat., 1992–. Governor: Cobham Hall, 1975–94; Royal Choral Soc., 1979–. FRSA 1993. Hon. DBA De Montfort Univ., 1994. *Recreations:* music, shooting, gardening. *Address:* 57 Hollywood Road, SW10 9HX. *T:* (020) 7351 1565.

FORBES, Bryan; film director and author; *b* 22 July 1926; *m* 1955, Nanette Newman, *qv*; two *d*. *Educ:* West Ham Secondary Sch. Studied at RADA, 1941; entered acting profession, 1942, and (apart from war service) was on West End stage, then in films here and in Hollywood, 1948–60. Formed Beaver Films with Sir Richard Attenborough, 1959; wrote and co-produced The Angry Silence, 1960. Subseq. wrote, dir. and prod. numerous films; *films include:* The League of Gentlemen, Only Two Can Play, Whistle Down the Wind, 1961; The L-Shaped Room, 1962; Séance on a Wet Afternoon, 1963; King Rat (in Hollywood), 1964; The Wrong Box, 1965; The Whisperers, 1966; Deadfall, 1967; The Madwoman of Chaillot, 1968; The Raging Moon, 1970; The Tales of Beatrix Potter, 1971; The Stepford Wives, 1974 (USA); The Slipper and the Rose, 1975 (Royal Film Perf., 1976); International Velvet, 1978; (British segment) The Sunday Lovers, 1980; Better Late Than Never, 1981; The Naked Face, 1983; (narrator and co-dir) I am a Dancer, 1971. *Stage:* Directed: Macbeth, Old Vic, 1980; Killing Jessica, Savoy, 1986, The Living Room, Royalty, 1987; directed and acted in Star Quality, Th. Royal, Bath, 1983. *Television:* produced and directed: Edith Evans, I Caught Acting Like the Measles, Yorkshire TV, 1973; Elton John, Goodbye Norma Jean and Other Things, ATV 1973; Jessie, BBC, 1980; The Endless Game, C4, 1989; acted in: December Flower, Granada, 1984; First Among Equals, Granada, 1986. Man. Dir and Head of Production, ABPC Studios, 1969–71; Man. Dir and Chief Exec., EMI-MGM, Elstree Studios, 1970–71; Dir, Capital Radio Ltd, 1973–97. Member: BBC Gen. Adv. Council, 1966–69; BBC Schs Council, 1971–73; President: Beatrix Potter Soc., 1982–96; Nat. Youth Theatre, 1984–; Writers' Guild of GB, 1988–91. Hon. DLit London, 1992; Hon. DLitt Sussex, 1999. Won British Acad. Award, 1960; Writers' Guild Award (twice); numerous internat. awards. *Publications:* Truth Lies Sleeping, 1950; The Distant Laughter, 1972; Notes for a Life, 1974; The Slipper and the Rose, 1976; Ned's Girl: biography of Dame Edith Evans, 1977; International Velvet, 1978; Familiar Strangers, 1979; That Despicable Race, 1980; The Rewrite Man, 1983; The Endless Game, 1986; A Song at Twilight, 1989; A Divided Life, 1992; The Twisted Playground, 1993; Partly Cloudy, 1995; Quicksand, 1996; The Memory of All That, 1999; contribs to: The Spectator, New Statesman, Queen, and other periodicals. *Recreations:* running an art gallery, reading, landscape gardening, photography. *Address:* The Gallery, Station Approach, Virginia Water, Surrey GU25 4DP.

See also Sir John Leon, Bt.

FORBES, Prof. Charles Douglas, MD, DSc; Professor of Medicine, University of Dundee, since 1987; *b* 9 Oct. 1938; *s* of late John Forbes and Dr Annie Forbes (*née* Stuart); *m* 1965, Jannette MacDonald Robertson; two *s*. *Educ:* Univ. of Glasgow (MB ChB 1961; MD 1972; DSc 1986). Trng grades, Dept of Materia Medica, Univ. of Glasgow, 1961–65; Lectr in Medicine, Makerere Univ., Uganda, 1965–66; Registrar in Haemophilia, Royal Infirmary, Glasgow, 1966–68; American Heart Fellow/Fullbright Fellow, Cleveland, Ohio, 1968–70; Sen. Lectr, then Reader, Univ. of Glasgow, 1970–87. *Publications:* (with W. F. Jackson) Colour Atlas and Text of Clinical Medicine, 1993; (jtly) Haemophilia, 1997; articles and research papers on blood coagulation and thrombosis. *Recreations:* gardening, walking, DIY. *Address:* East Chattan, 108 Hepburn Gardens, St Andrews, Fife KY16 9LT. *T:* (01334) 472428.

See also J. S. Forbes.

FORBES, Colin, RDI 1974; Partner, Pentagram Design, since 1972; *b* 6 March 1928; *s* of Kathleen and John Forbes; *m* 1961, Wendy Schneider; one *s* two *d*. *Educ:* Sir Anthony Browne's, Brentwood; LCC Central Sch. of Arts and Crafts. Design Asst, Herbert Spencer, 1952; freelance practice and Lectr, LCC Central Sch. of Arts and Crafts, 1953–57; Art Dir, Stuart Advertising, London, 1957–58; Head of Graphic Design Dept, LCC Central Sch. of Arts and Crafts, 1958–61; freelance practice, London, 1961–62; Partner: Fletcher/Forbes/Gill, 1962–65; Crosby/Fletcher/Forbes, 1965–72. Mem., Alliance Graphique Internationale, 1965– (Internat. Pres. 1976–79); Pres., Amer. Inst. Graphic Arts, 1984–86. *Publications:* Graphic Design: visual comparisons, 1963; A Sign Systems Manual, 1970; Creativity and Communication, 1971; New Alphabets A to Z, 1973; Living by Design, 1978; Pentagram: the compendium, 1993. *Address:* Forbes Farm, 2879 Horseshoe Road, Westfield, NC 27053, USA. *T:* (336) 3513941.

FORBES, Donald James, MA; Headmaster, Merchiston Castle School, 1969–81; *b* 6 Feb. 1921; *s* of Andrew Forbes; *m* 1945, Patricia Muriel Yeo; two *s* one *d*. *Educ:* Oundle; Clare Coll., Cambridge (Mod. Lang. Tripos). Capt. Scots Guards, 1941–46; 1st Bn Scots Guards, 1942–46, N Africa, Italy. Asst Master, Dulwich Coll., 1946–55; Master i/c cricket, 1951–55; Headmaster, Dauntsey's Sch., 1956–69. Diploma in Spanish, Univ. of Santander, 1954; Lectr in Spanish, West Norwood Tech. Coll., 1954–55. *Recreations:* cricket, Rugby football, tennis, Rugby fives, curling, golf; history, literature; instrumental and choral music. *Address:* 33 Coates Gardens, Edinburgh EH12 5LG. *Clubs:* Hawks (Cambridge); HCEG (Muirfield).

FORBES, Very Rev. Graham John Thomson; Provost, St Mary's Cathedral, Edinburgh, since 1990; *b* 10 June 1951; *s* of J. T. and D. D. Forbes; *m* 1973, Jane T. Miller; three *s*. *Educ:* George Heriot's School, Edinburgh; Univ. of Aberdeen (MA); Univ. of Edinburgh (BD). Curate, Old St Paul's Church, Edinburgh, 1976–82; Provost, St Ninian's Cathedral, Perth, 1982–90. HM (Lay) Inspector of Constabulary, 1995–98. Member: Parole Bd for Scotland, 1990–95; Scottish Consumer Council, 1995–98; GMC, 1996–; Scottish Criminal Cases Rev. Commn, 1999–; Clinical Standards Bd for Scotland, 1999–; Historic Bldgs Council (Scotland), 2000–. *Recreations:* running, fly-fishing. *Address:* 8 Lansdowne Crescent, Edinburgh EH12 5EQ. *T:* (home) (0131) 225 2978; (office) (0131) 225 6293.

FORBES, Major Sir Hamish (Stewart), 7th Bt *cr* 1823, of Newe; MBE 1945; MC 1945; Welsh Guards, retired; *b* 15 Feb. 1916; *s* of Lt-Col James Stewart Forbes (*d* 1957) (*g s* of 3rd Bt) and Feridah Frances Forbes (*d* 1953), *d* of Hugh Lewis Taylor; *S* cousin, 1984; *m* 1st, 1945, Jacynthe Elizabeth Mary, *d* of late Eric Gordon Underwood; one *s* three *d*; 2nd, 1981, Mary Christine, MBE, *d* of late Ernest William Rigby. *Educ:* Eton College; Lawrenceville, USA; SOAS. Served Welsh Guards, France, Germany, Turkey, 1939–58. Calmic Chemicals, Gillette, and Shell-Mex BP, 1959–64. Gen. Sec., Church Lads' Bde, 1964–73; Mem., Church Lads' and Church Girls' Bde Incorporated Soc., 1978–92; Vice-Pres., Church Lads' and Church Girls' Bde Assoc., 2000– (pres., 1974–2000). Patron, Lonach Highland and Friendly Soc., 1984–. KStJ 1984 (Sec., Order of St John, 1973–83). *Recreations:* shooting, sculpture. *Heir:* *s* James Thomas Stewart Forbes [*b* 28 May 1957; *m* 1986, Kerry Lynne, *o d* of Rev. Lee Toms; two *d*]. *Address:* Newe, Strathdon, Aberdeenshire AB36 8TY. *T:* (019756) 51431. *Clubs:* Turf, Chelsea Arts, Pilgrims.

FORBES, Adm. Ian Andrew, CBE 1994; Deputy Supreme Allied Commander Atlantic, since 2002; *b* 24 Oct. 1946; *s* of James and late Winifred Forbes; *m* 1975, Sally, *d* of late Ronald Statham and of Cynthia Statham; two *d*. *Educ:* Eastbourne Coll.; BRNC. Sea-going appointments, 1969–84: HM Ships Hermes, Upton, HM Yacht Britannia, USS W. H. Stanley; RAF Staff Coll., 1982–83; HM Ships Whitby, Kingfisher (CO), Apollo, Juno, Glamorgan, Diomede (CO), 1984–86; Chatham (CO), 1989–91; MoD, 1991–94; RCDS 1994; HMS Invincible (CO), 1995–96; MA to UN Higher Rep., Sarajevo, 1996–97; Comdr, UK Task Gp and Comdr, Anti-Submarine Warfare Striking Force, 1997–2000; Flag Officer Surface Flotilla, 2000–01. QCVS 1996. *Recreations:* tennis, history, travel, gardening. *Address:* c/o Naval Secretary, Victory Building, HM Naval Base, Portsmouth PO1 3LS. *Club:* Army and Navy.

FORBES, James, FCA; Chairman, Tate & Lyle Group Pension Fund, 1978–85; Forestry Commissioner, 1982–88; *b* 2 Jan. 1923; *s* of Donald Forbes and Rona Ritchie Forbes (*née* Yeats); *m* 1948, Alison Mary Fletcher Moffat; two *s*. *Educ:* Christ's Hospital; Officers' Training School, Bangalore. Chartered Accountant. Commissioned Indian Army, 1942; released 1947, Hon. Major. Peat Marwick Mitchell Co., 1952–58; Chief Accountant, L. Rose, 1958; Group Operational Research Manager, Schweppes, 1960, Group Chief Accountant, 1963 (Dir, subsid. cos); Sec. and Financial Adviser, Cadbury Schweppes (on formation), 1969, Main Board Dir, 1971, Group Finance Dir to April 1978; Senior Exec. Dir, Tate & Lyle, 1978, Vice-Chm., 1980–84. Non-executive Director: British Transport Hotels, 1978–83; British Rail Investments, 1980–84; Steetley plc, 1984–89; Compass Hotels, 1984–99; Lautro Ltd, 1986–90. Mem. Council, Inst. of Chartered Accountants, 1971–88 (Treasurer, 1984–86). Gov., Christ's Hosp., 1983– (Chm. and Treas., Council of Almoners, 1987–96). Mem., Highland Society. FInstD. *Recreation:* golf. *Address:* Lower Ridge, Courts Mount Road, Haslemere, Surrey GU27 2PP. *Clubs:* Caledonian, Royal Commonwealth Society.

FORBES, James Alexander, CEng; Chief Executive, Scottish and Southern Energy plc, since 1998; *b* 6 Aug. 1946; *s* of James A. Forbes and Verna Kelman; *m* 1969, Jean Clark; four *s*. *Educ:* Paisley Coll. of Tech. (BSc (1st cl. hons) Elect. Engrg); Loughborough Univ.

of Tech. (MSc Electro-heat). MIEE. Scottish Power: Student Apprentice, 1964; Commercial Engr, 1973–84; Area Commercial Officer, 1984–86; Mktg Manager, 1986–89; Northern Electric: Commercial Dir, 1989–90; Distrib. Dir, 1990–91; Southern Electric: Ops Dir, 1991–94; Man. Dir, Electricity, 1994–96; Chief Operating Officer, 1996; Chief Exec., 1996–98. *Recreation:* golf. *Address:* Scottish and Southern Energy plc, 200 Dunkeld Road, Perth PH1 3AQ.

FORBES of Craigievar, Sir John (Alexander Cumnock), 12th Bt *cr* 1630 (NS), of Craigievar, Aberdeenshire; JP; equestrian photo-journalist; *b* 29 Aug. 1927; *s* of Rear-Adm. the Hon. Arthur Lionel Ochoncar Forbes-Sempill (*d* 1962), *y s* of 17th Lord Sempill, and of Mary Cutting Holland (*d* 1940), *o d* of Arthur J. Cumnock; *S* kinsman, 1991; *m* 1st, 1956, Penelope Grey-Pennington (marr. diss. 1963); 2nd, 1966, Jane Carolyn, *o d* of C. Gordon Evans. *Educ:* Cheam; Stowe; Sandhurst. Captain, Seaforth Highlanders, 1945–49. Director: Garrick Theatre, 1951–65; The Cinema, Newton Stewart, 1966–94; Auchendon Centre of Equitation Ltd, later ACE, 1972–94. Scottish showjumping correspondent, Horse and Hound, 1994–. Baillie, Newton Stewart Town Council, 1965–76. Founder Convenor, Cree Valley Community Council, 1976. Chm. PR and Promotions, Scottish Br., BSJA. JP Wigtown, 1978. *Heir: kinsman* Andrew Iain Forbes, *b* 28 Nov. 1945. *Address:* Benevean, Kendoon, St John's Town of Dalry, Castle Douglas DG7 3UB. *Club:* Naval and Military.

FORBES, Vice-Adm. Sir John Morrison, KCB 1978; *b* 16 Aug. 1925; *s* of late Lt-Col R. H. Forbes, OBE, and late Gladys M. Forbes (*née* Pollock); *m* 1950, Joyce Newenham Hadden; two *s* two *d*. *Educ:* RNC, Dartmouth. Served War: HMS Mauritius, Verulam and Nelson, 1943–46. HMS Aisne, 1946–49; Gunnery course and staff of HMS Excellent, 1950–51; served in RAN, 1952–54; Staff of HMS Excellent, 1954–56; HMS Ceylon, 1956–58; Staff of Dir of Naval Ordnance, 1958–60; Comdr (G) HMS Excellent, 1960–61; Staff of Dir of Seaman Officers' Appts, 1962–64; Exec. Officer, Britannia RN Coll., 1964–66; Operational Comdr and 2nd in Comd, Royal Malaysian Navy, 1966–68; Asst Dir, Naval Plans, 1969–70; comd HMS Triumph, 1971–72; comd Britannia RN Coll., Dartmouth, 1972–74; Naval Secretary, 1974–76; Flag Officer, Plymouth, Port Adm., Devonport, Comdr, Central Sub Area, Eastern Atlantic, and Comdr, Plymouth Sub Area, Channel, 1977–79. Naval ADC to the Queen, 1974. Kesatria Manku Negara (Malaysia), 1968. *Recreations:* country pursuits. *Address:* c/o National Westminster Bank, Waterlooville, Portsmouth, Hants. *Clubs:* Army and Navy, RN Sailing Association.

FORBES, John Stuart; Sheriff of Tayside, Central and Fife at Dunfermline, since 1980; *b* 31 Jan. 1936; *s* of late John Forbes and Dr A. R. S. Forbes; *m* 1963, Marion Alcock; one *s* two *d*. *Educ:* Glasgow High Sch.; Glasgow Univ. (MA, LLB). RA, TA, 1958–63 (Lieut). Solicitor, 1959–61; Advocate, Scottish Bar, 1962–76; Standing Counsel, Forestry Commn, 1972; Sheriff of Lothian and Borders, 1976–80. Pres., Glasgow Juridical Soc., 1963–64. Life Trustee, Carnegie, Dunfermline and Hero Fund Trusts, 1985–; Trustee, Carnegie UK Trust, 1990–. *Recreations:* tennis, golf. *Address:* Inglewood, Old Perth Road, Milnathort, Kinross KY13 9YA. *Club:* Edinburgh Sports.

See also C. D. Forbes.

FORBES, Nanette; *see* Newman, N.

FORBES, Hon. Sir Thayne (John), Kt 1993; **Hon. Mr Justice Thayne Forbes;** a Judge of the High Court of Justice, Queen's Bench Division, since 1993; Judge in charge of Technology and Construction Court, since 2001; *b* 28 June 1938; *s* of late John Thomson Forbes and Jessie Kay Robertson Stewart; *m* 1960, Celia Joan; two *s* one *d*. *Educ:* Winchester College (Quirister); Wolverton Grammar Sch.; University College London (LLB, LLM). Served Royal Navy (Instructor Lieutenant), 1963–66. Called to Bar, Inner Temple, 1966, Governing Bencher, 1991; QC 1984; a Recorder, 1986–90; a Circuit Judge (Official Referee), 1990–93; Presiding Judge, Northern Circuit, 1995–99. *Recreations:* music, reading, sailing, bird watching, astronomy, beekeeping. *Address:* Royal Courts of Justice, Strand, WC2A 2LL.

FORBES, Sir William (Daniel) Stuart-, 13th Bt *cr* 1626 (NS), of Pitsligo and of Monymusk, Aberdeenshire; *b* 21 Aug. 1935; *s* of William Kenneth Stuart-Forbes (*d* 1946), 3rd *s* of 10th Bt, and of Marjory Gilchrist; *S* uncle, 1985; *m* 1956, Jannette (*d* 1997), *d* of late Hori Toki George MacDonald; three *s* two *d*; *m* 2001, Betty Dawn Ward, *d* of William Henry Gibson and Ellen Dorothy Neilson *Heir: s* Kenneth Charles Stuart-Forbes [*b* 26 Dec. 1956; *m* 1981, Susan, *d* of Len Murray; one *s* two *d*]. *Address:* 169 Budge Street, Blenheim, New Zealand.

FORBES, Captain William Frederick Eustace; Vice Lord-Lieutenant of Stirling and Falkirk, 1984–96; Forestry Commissioner, 1982–88; *b* 6 July 1932; *er s* of late Lt-Col W. H. D. C. Forbes of Callendar, CBE and Elizabeth Forbes; *m* 1st, 1956, Pamela Susan (*d* 1993), *er d* of Lord McCorquodale of Newton, KCVO, PC; two *d*; 2nd, 1995, Venetia, Hon. Lady Troubridge, *widow* of Sir Peter Troubridge, 6th Bt. *Educ:* Eton. Regular soldier, Coldstream Guards, 1950–59; farmer and company director, 1959–. Chairman: Scottish Woodland Owners' Assoc., 1974–77; Nat. Playing Fields Assoc., Scottish Branch, 1980–90. *Recreations:* country pastimes, golf, cricket, travel. *Address:* Earlstoun Lodge, Dalry, Castle Douglas, Kirkcudbrightshire DG7 3TY. *T:* (01644) 430213. *Clubs:* MCC; New (Edinburgh); Royal and Ancient Golf.

FORBES-LEITH of Fyvie, Sir George Ian David, 4th Bt *cr* 1923, of Jessfield, co. Midlothian; *b* 26 May 1967; *e s* of Sir Andrew George Forbes-Leith, 3rd Bt and Jane Kate (*née* McCall-McCowan); *S* father, 2000; *m* 1995, Camilla Frances Ely; two *s* one *d*. *Educ:* RAC, Cirencester. *Recreations:* shooting, ski-ing, fishing. *Heir: s* Alexander Philip George Forbes-Leith, *b* 4 Feb. 1999. *Address:* The Neuk, Fyvie, Turriff AB53 8RD. *T:* (01651) 891246.

FORBES-MEYLER, John William, OBE 1990; HM Diplomatic Service, retired; Ambassador to Ecuador, 1997–2000; *b* 3 July 1942; *s* of late J. J. C. Forbes and of Moira Patricia (*née* Garvey, who later; *m* James Robert Meyler (now decd)); changed name by Deed Poll, 1963 to Forbes-Meyler; *m* 1st, 1964, Margaret Goddard (marr. diss. 1979); one *d*; 2nd, 1980, Mary Read (*née* Vlachou); one step *s*. *Educ:* grammar sch., etc. Joined HM Diplomatic Service, 1962: CRO, 1962–64; Lagos, 1964–68; Chicago, 1968–69; Boston, 1969–70; FCO, 1970–71; NY, 1971–72; FCO, 1972–75; Athens, 1975–80; FCO, 1980–83; 1st Sec. (Econ.), Bonn, 1983–86; on loan to MoD, 1986–88; Deputy Head of Mission: Bogota, 1988–92; Vienna, 1992–96. *Recreations:* walking, music, reading. *Club:* Special Forces.

FORD, Rev. Adam; Chaplain, St Paul's Girls' School, London, 1976–2001 (Head of Lower School, 1986–92); *b* 15 Sept. 1940; *s* of John Ford and Jean Beattie Ford (*née* Winstanley); *m* 1969, Veronica Rosemary Lucia Verey (marr. diss. 1993); two *s* two *d*. *Educ:* Minehead Grammar Sch.; King's Coll., Univ. of London (BD Hons, AKC 1964); Lancaster Univ. (MA Indian Religion 1972). Asst, Ecumenical Inst. of World Council of Churches, Geneva, 1964; Curate, Cirencester Parish Church, Glos, 1965–69; Vicar of Hebden Bridge, W Yorkshire, 1969–76; Priest-in-Ordinary to the Queen, 1984–90. Regular contributor to Prayer for the Day, Radio 4, 1978–; writer and narrator, Whose World?, series of TV progs on sci. and religion, 1987. Hon. FRAS 1960. *Publications:* Spaceship Earth, 1981; Weather Watch, 1982; Star Gazers Guide to the Night Sky (audio guide to astronomy), 1982; Universe: God, Man and Science, 1986; The Cuckoo Plant, 1991; Mr Hi-Tech, 1993; Faith and Science, 1999; articles in The Times and science jls on relationship between science and religion, also on dialogue between religions; regular contrib. Church Times. *Recreations:* dry stone walling, astronomy, searching for neolithic flints. *Address:* 55 Bolingbroke Road, Hammersmith, W14 0AH. *T:* (020) 7602 5902.

FORD, Sir Andrew (Russell), 3rd Bt *cr* 1929, of Westerdunes, Co. of East Lothian; Lecturer, Wiltshire College (formerly Chippenham College), since 1974; *b* 29 June 1943; *s* of Sir Henry Russell Ford, 2nd Bt, TD and Mary Elizabeth (*d* 1997), *d* of late Godfrey F. Wright; *S* father, 1989; *m* 1968, Penelope Anne, *d* of Harry Relph; two *s* one *d*. *Educ:* Winchester; New Coll., Oxford (half-blue, athletics, 1962); Loughborough Coll. (DLC); London Univ. (BA external); Birmingham Univ. (MA external). Schoolmaster: Blairmore Sch., Aberdeens, 1967–71; St Peter's Sch., Cambridge, NZ, 1971–74. *Heir: s* Toby Russell Ford, *b* 11 Jan. 1973. *Address:* 20 Coniston Road, Chippenham, Wilts SN14 0PX. *T:* (01249) 655442.

FORD, Anna; broadcaster, BBC, since 1989; *b* 2 Oct. 1943; *d* of John Ford and Jean Beattie Winstanley; *m* 1st, 1970, Dr Alan Holland Bittles (marr. diss. 1976); 2nd, 1981, Charles Mark Edward Boxer (*d* 1988); two *d*. *Educ:* Minehead Grammar Sch.; White House Grammar Sch., Brampton; Manchester Univ. (BA Hons Econ 1966; DipAdultEd 1970). Work for students' interests, Manchester Univ., 1966–69; Lectr, Rupert Stanley Coll. of Further Educn, Belfast, 1970–72; Staff Tutor, Social Sci., NI Reg., Open Univ., 1972–74; presenter and reporter, Granada TV, 1974–76; BBC Man Alive, 1976–77; BBC Tomorrow's World, 1977–78; newscaster, ITN, 1978–80; TV am, 1980–82; freelance broadcasting and writing, 1982–86; BBC news and current affairs, 1989–. Trustee, Royal Botanic Gardens, Kew, 1995–. Chancellor, Univ. of Manchester, 2001–. Hon. LLD Manchester, 1998; DUniv Open. *Publication:* Men: a documentary, 1985. *Recreations:* talking, writing, drawing. *Address:* BBC TV Centre, Wood Lane, W12 7RJ. *T:* (020) 8624 9991.

FORD, Anthony; *see* Ford, J. A.

FORD, Antony, CMG 1997; HM Diplomatic Service; Ambassador to Austria, since 2000; *b* Bexley, 1 Oct. 1944; *s* of late William Ford and Grace Ford (*née* Smith); *m* 1970, Linda Gordon Joy; one *s* one *d*. *Educ:* St Dunstan's Coll., Catford; UCW, Aberystwyth (BA). Joined HM Diplomatic Service, 1967; Third, later Second, Sec., Bonn, 1968–71; Second Sec., Kuala Lumpur, 1971–73; First Secretary: FCO, 1973–77; Washington, 1977–81; FCO, 1981–84; Counsellor: East Berlin, 1984–87; FCO, 1987–90; Consul-Gen., San Francisco, 1990–94; Chm., CSSB, on secondment to RAS Agency, 1994–96; Minister, Berlin, 1996–99; on secondment to Andersen Consulting, 1999–2000. *Recreations:* reading, golf, cricket. *Address:* c/o Foreign and Commonwealth Office, King Charles Street, SW1A 2AH.

FORD, Benjamin Thomas; DL; *b* 1 April 1925; *s* of Benjamin Charles Ford and May Ethel (*née* Moorton); *m* 1950, Vera Ada (*née* Fawcett-Fancet); two *s* one *d*. *Educ:* Rowan Road Central Sch., Surrey. Apprenticed as compositor, 1941. War Service, 1943–47, Fleet Air Arm (Petty Officer). Electronic Fitter/Wireman, 1951–64; Convener of Shop Stewards, 1955–64. Pres., Harwich Constituency Labour Party, 1955–63; Mem., Clacton UDC, 1959–62; Alderman Essex CC, 1959–65; JP Essex, 1962–67. MP (Lab) Bradford N, 1964–83; contested (Lab Ind.) Bradford N, 1983. Mem., H of C Select Cttee (Services), 1970–83 (Chm., Accom. and Admin Sub-Cttee, 1979–83); Chm., Jt Select Cttee on Sound Broadcasting, 1976–77; Chairman: British-Portuguese Parly Gp, 1965–83; British-Argentinian Parly Gp, 1974–81; British-Brazilian Parly Gp, 1974–79; British-Malaysian Parly Gp, 1975–83; British-Venezuelan Parly Gp, 1977–83; All-Party Wool Textile Parly Gp, 1974–83; Vice-Chairman: British-Latin American Parly Gp, 1974–79; PLP Defence Cttee, 1979–82; Mem. Exec. Cttee, IPU British Gp, 1971–83 (Chm., 1977–79); Sec., British-Namibian Parly Gp, 1980–83. Chm., Leeds NW Lib Dems, 1988–91; Pres., Leeds Fedn of Lib Dems, 1991–97. Bd Mem., Bradford & Northern Housing Assoc., 1975–95 (Chm., Yorks and Humberside Regl Cttee). Pres., English Shooting Council, 1996– (Chm., 1982–96); Mem. Council, Nat. Rifle Assoc., 1968–94 (Vice-Pres., 1984–); President: Yorks and Humberside Region, Mencap, 1986–91; Bradford Civic Soc., 1988–96. Freeman, City of London, 1979; Liveryman, Gunmakers' Co., 1978–99. DL W Yorks, 1982. Hon. FAIA 1983. Grand Officer, Order of the Southern Cross (Brazil), 1976. *Publication:* Piecework, 1960. *Recreations:* music, shooting, family, reading. *Address:* 9 Wynmore Crescent, Bramhope, Leeds LS16 9DH. *Club:* Idle Working Men's.

FORD, Colin John, CBE 1993; Partner, ArtConnect, since 1998; lecturer, writer and broadcaster on films, theatre and photography; exhibition organiser; *b* 13 May 1934; *s* of John William and Hélène Martha Ford; *m* 1st, 1961, Margaret Elizabeth Cordwell (marr. diss.); one *s* one *d*; 2nd, 1984, Susan Joan Frances Grayson; one *s*. *Educ:* Enfield Grammar Sch.; University Coll., Oxford (MA). Manager and Producer, Kidderminster Playhouse, 1958–60; Gen. Man., Western Theatre Ballet, 1960–62; Vis. Lectr in English and Drama, California State Univ. at Long Beach and UCLA (Univ. Extension), 1962–64; Dep. Curator, Nat. Film Archive, 1965–72. Organiser, 30th Anniv. Congress of Internat. Fedn of Film Archives, London, 1968; Dir, Cinema City Exhibn, 1970; Programme Dir, London Shakespeare Film Festival, 1972; Keeper of Film and Photography, Nat. Portrait Gall., 1972–81; founding Hd, Nat. Mus. of Photography, Film and Television, 1982–93; Dir, Nat. Mus. of Wales, then Nat. Museums & Galls of Wales, 1993–98. Hon. FRPS 1999. Hon. MA Bradford, 1989. *Film:* Masks and Faces, 1966 (BBC TV version, Omnibus, 1968). *Publications:* (with Roy Strong) An Early Victorian Album, 1974, 2nd edn 1977; The Cameron Collection, 1975; (principal contrib.) Oxford Companion to Film, 1975; (ed) Happy and Glorious: Six Reigns of Royal Photography, 1977; Rediscovering Mrs Cameron, 1979; People in Camera, 1979; (with Brian Harrison) A Hundred Years Ago (Britain in the 1880s), 1983; Portraits (Gallery of World Photography), 1983; (ed) The Story of Popular Photography, 1988; Lewis Carroll, 1998; André Kertész and the Avant Garde, 1999; (with Karl Steinorth): You Press the Button, We Do the Rest: the birth of snapshot photography, 1988; Lewis Carroll: photographs, 1991; Ferenc Berko: 60 Years of Photography, 1991; articles in many jls. *Recreations:* travel, music, small boats. *Address:* 7 Gentleman's Row, Enfield EN2 6PT.

FORD, Prof. David Frank, PhD; Regius Professor of Divinity and Fellow of Selwyn College, Cambridge University, since 1991; *b* 23 Jan. 1948; *s* of George Ford and Phyllis (*née* Woodman); *m* 1982, Deborah Perrin Hardy, *d* of Rev. Canon Prof. Daniel Wayne Hardy, *qv*; one *s* two *d* (and one *d* decd). *Educ:* Trinity Coll. Dublin (BA (Mod) 1970); St John's Coll., Cambridge (MA 1976; PhD 1977); Yale Univ. (STM 1973); Tübingen Univ. Lectr in Theology, Birmingham Univ., 1976–91. Chm., Faculty Bd of Divinity, Cambridge Univ., 1993–95. Mem., CUP Syndicate, 1993–. Pres., Soc. for Study of Theology, 1997–98. *Publications:* Barth and God's Story: biblical narrative and the theological method of Karl Barth in the Church Dogmatics, 1981; (with Daniel W.

Hardy) Jubilate: Theology in praise, 1984; (with Frances M. Young) Meaning and Truth in 2 Corinthians, 1987; (ed) The Modern Theologians, vols I and II, 1989; (ed jtly) Essentials of Christian Community, 1996; The Shape of Living, 1997; Self and Salvation: being transformed, 1999; Theology: a very short introduction, 1999. *Recreations:* gardening, poetry, drama, sports (especially ball games). *Address:* Divinity School, St John's Street, Cambridge CB2 1TW. *T:* (01223) 332592.

FORD, Sir David (Robert), KBE 1988 (OBE 1976); LVO 1975; Hong Kong Commissioner in London, 1980–81 and 1994–96; Chairman, Council for the Protection of Rural England, since 1998; *b* 22 Feb. 1935; *s* of William Ewart and Edna Ford; *m* 1st, 1958, Elspeth Anne (*née* Muckart) (marr. diss. 1987); two *s* two *d*; 2nd, 1987, Gillian Petersen (*née* Monsarrat). *Educ:* Tauntons School. National Service, 1953–55; regular commn, RA, 1955; regimental duty, Malta, 1953–58; Lieut, UK, 1958–62; Captain, Commando Regt, 1962–66; active service: Borneo, 1964; Aden, 1966; Staff Coll., Quetta, 1967; seconded to Hong Kong Govt, 1967; retired from Army (Major), 1972. Dep. Dir, Hong Kong Govt Information Service, 1972–74, Dir, 1974–76; Dep. Sec., Govt Secretariat, Hong Kong, 1976; Under Sec., NI Office, 1977–79; Sec. for Information, Hong Kong Govt, 1979–80; RCDS, 1982; Hong Kong Government: Dir of Housing, 1983–84; Sec. for Housing, 1985; Sec. for the Civil Service, 1985–86; Chief Sec., 1986–93. *Recreations:* tennis, fishing, rare breeds, cattle and sheep. *Address:* Culverwell Farm, Branscombe, Devon EX12 3DA.

FORD, Rt Rev. Douglas Albert; Bishop of Saskatoon, 1970–81; *b* 16 July 1917; *s* of Thomas George Ford and Elizabeth Eleanor (Taylor), both English; *m* 1944, Doris Ada (Elborne); two *s* one *d*. *Educ:* primary and secondary schs, Vancouver; Univ. of British Columbia (BA); Anglican Theological Coll. of BC (LTh); General Synod (BD). Deacon, 1941; Priest, 1942; Curate, St Mary's, Kerrisdale, 1941–42; St George's, Vancouver, 1942–44; Vicar of Strathmore, 1944–49; Rector of Okotoks, 1949–52; Vermilion, 1952–55; St Michael and All Angels, Calgary, 1955–62; St Augustine, Lethbridge, 1962–66; Dean and Rector, St John's Cath., Saskatoon, 1966–70; Asst Bishop of Calgary, 1981–87; Incumbent of All Saints', Cochrane, dio. Calgary, 1981–85. Hon. DD: Coll. of Emmanuel and St Chad, Saskatoon, 1970; Anglican Theological Coll. of BC, Vancouver, 1971. *Address:* 126 Hawkstone Manor NW, Calgary, AB T3G 3X2, Canada.

FORD, Sir Edward (William Spencer), GCVO 1998 (KCVO 1957; MVO 1949); KCB 1967 (CB 1952); ERD 1987; OStJ 1976; MA; FRSA; DL; Secretary and Registrar of the Order of Merit, since 1975; Secretary to the Pilgrim Trust, 1967–75; *b* 24 July 1910; 4th (twin) *s* of late Very Rev. Lionel G. B. J. Ford, Headmaster of Repton and Harrow and Dean of York, and of Mary Catherine, *d* of Rt Rev. E. S. Talbot, Bishop of Winchester and Hon. Mrs Talbot; *m* 1949, Virginia (*d* 1995), *er d* of 1st and last Baron Brand, CMG, and *widow* of John Metcalfe Polk, NY; two *s*. *Educ:* Eton (King's Schol.); New Coll., Oxford (Open Scholar; Hon. Fellow, 1982). 1st Class Hon. Mods; 2nd Class Lit. Hum. (Greats). Law Student (Harmsworth Scholar) Middle Temple, 1934–35; Tutor to King Farouk of Egypt, 1936–37; called to Bar, Middle Temple, 1937 and practised 1937–39; 2nd Lieut (Supplementary Reserve of Officers) Grenadier Guards, 1936; Lieut 1939; served in France and Belgium, 1939–40 (despatches), and in Tunisia and Italy, 1943–44 (despatches), Brigade Major 10th Infantry and 24th Guards Brigades; Instructor at Staff Coll., Haifa, 1944–45. psc†. Asst Private Secretary to King George VI, 1946–52, and to the Queen, 1952–67; Extra Equerry to the Queen, 1955. Dir, London Life Assoc., 1970–83. Mem., Central Appeals Adv. Cttee, BBC and IBA, 1969–72, 1976–78; Mem., Council, St Christopher's Hospice, Sydenham, 1980–90 (Pres., 1990–2000); Chairman: UK/USA Bicentennial Fellowships Cttee, 1975–80; St John Council for Northamptonshire, 1976–82; Grants Cttee, Historic Churches Preservation Trust, 1977–90. Trustee: York Glaziers' Trust, 1977–; Butler Trust, 1986–90; Hon. Treas., Children's Country Holidays Fund, 1958–73, Vice-Pres., 1973–; Governor, The Ditchley Foundn, 1966–89. Mem. Ct of Assts, Goldsmiths' Co., 1979–, Prime Warden, 1979. High Sheriff Northants 1970, DL 1972. *Address:* Canal House, 23 Blomfield Road, W9 1AD. *T:* (020) 7286 0028. *Clubs:* White's, Beefsteak, Pratt's, MCC.

FORD, Geoffrey; *see* Ford, M. G.

FORD, Air Marshal Sir Geoffrey (Harold), KBE 1979; CB 1974; FREng; Secretary, The Institute of Metals, 1985–88; *b* 6 Aug. 1923; *s* of late Harold Alfred Ford, Lewes, Sussex; *m* 1951, Valerie, *d* of late Douglas Hart Finn, Salisbury; two *s*. *Educ:* Lewes County Grammar Sch.; Bristol Univ. (BSc). Served War of 1939–45: commissioned, 1942; 60 Gp, 1943; Italy and Middle East, 1944–46. 90 (Signals) Gp, 1946–49; Bomber Development, 1954–57; Air Ministry, 1958–61; RAF Technical Coll., 1961–62; Min. of Aviation, 1963–64; Chief Signals Officer, RAF Germany, 1965–68; MoD, 1968–72; RCDS, 1972; AO Engineering, Strike Command, 1973–76; Dir-Gen. Engineering and Supply Management, RAF, 1976–78; Chief Engr (RAF), 1978–81. Dir, The Metals Soc., 1981–84. FIEE (Council, 1977–82); FREng (FEng 1987). *Address:* c/o Barclays Bank, Lewes, East Sussex BN7 2JP. *Club:* Royal Air Force.

FORD, George Johnson; DL; Member, Cheshire County Council, 1962–87 (Chairman, 1976–82); *b* 13 March 1916; *s* of James and Esther Ford; *m* 1941, Nora Helen Brocklehurst; three *s* one *d*. *Educ:* Chester Coll. Qualified estate agent, 1938. FAI 1938. Member, Runcorn RDC, 1953 (Chm., 1962); Mem. Bd, Warrington and Runcorn Develt Corp., 1981–87 (Runcorn Develt Corp., 1964–81). Mem., West Mercia Cttee, Nat. Trust, 1982. Pres., Frodsham Conservative Assoc., 1962–; Vice Pres., Eddisbury Parly Div., 1984. DL Cheshire, 1979. *Recreations:* horse racing, music and drama. *Address:* Windmill Bank, Manley, Warrington, Cheshire WA6 9DZ. *T:* (01928) 740447. *Club:* City (Chester).

FORD, Gerald Rudolph; President of the United States of America, Aug. 1974–Jan. 1977; lawyer; company director; *b* Omaha, Nebraska, 14 July 1913; (adopted) *s* of Gerald R. Ford and Dorothy Gardner; *m* 1948, Elizabeth (*née* Bloomer); three *s* one *d*. *Educ:* South High Sch., Grand Rapids; Univ. of Michigan (BA); Law Sch., Yale Univ. (LLB). Served War: US Navy (Carriers), 1942–46. Partner in law firm of Ford and Buchen, 1941–42; Member, law firm of Butterfield, Keeney and Amberg, 1947–49; subseq. with Amberg, Law and Buchen. Member US House of Representatives for Michigan 5th District, 1948–73; Member: Appropriations Cttee, 1951; Dept of Defense Sub-Cttee, etc; House Minority Leader, Republican Party, 1965–73; Vice President of the United States, Dec. 1973–Aug. 1974. Attended Interparly Union meetings in Europe; Mem. US-Canadian Interparly Gp. Advr to Bd, American Express Co.; Adv. Dir, Chase Bank of Texas; Hon. Mem. Bd, Citigroup Inc. Holds Amer. Pol. Sci. Assoc.'s Distinguished Congressional Service Award, 1961; several hon. degrees. Delta Kappa Epsilon, Phi Delta Phi. *Publications:* (with John R. Stiles) Portrait of an Assassin, 1965; A Time to Heal, 1979; Humor and the Presidency, 1987. *Recreations:* outdoor sports (formerly football), ski-ing, tennis, golf. *Address:* PO Box 927, Rancho Mirage, CA 92270, USA.

FORD, Dr Gillian Rachel, (Mrs N. I. MacKenzie), CB 1981; FRCP, FFPHM; Medical Director, Marie Curie Cancer Care (formerly Marie Curie Memorial Foundation), 1990–97; *b* 18 March 1934; *d* of Cecil Ford and Grace Ford; *m* 1988, Prof. Norman I. MacKenzie. *Educ:* Clarendon Sch., Abergele; St Hugh's Coll., Oxford; St Thomas' Hosp., London. MA, BM, BCh; FFCM 1976; FRCP 1985. Junior hospital posts, St Thomas', Oxford, Reading, 1959–64; Medical Officer, Min. of Health, 1965, Sen. Med. Officer, 1968; SPMO, 1974–77, Dep. Chief MO (Dep. Sec.), 1977–89, DHSS, later Dept of Health; on secondment as Dir of Studies, St Christopher's Hospice, Sydenham, 1985–88; Med. Sec., Standing Cttee on Postgrad. Med. Educn., 1989–90. Vice Pres., St Christopher's Hospice, 1999–; Vice Chm., Hospice in the Weald, 1999–. *Publications:* papers on health services research, terminal care, audit, palliative medicine and care in sundry med. publications. *Recreations:* music, ski-ing, children's literature, gardening. *Address:* 9 Ryecotes Mead, Dulwich Common, SE21 7EP. *T:* (020) 8693 6576.

FORD, Glyn; *see* Ford, J. G.

FORD, Harrison; actor; *b* Chicago, 13 July 1942; *m* 1st, Mary Ford (marr. diss. 1978); two *s*; 2nd, 1983, Melissa Mathison, screenwriter; one *s* one *d*. *Educ:* Ripon Coll., Wis. *Films* include: Dead Heat on a Merry-Go-Round, 1966; Journey to Shiloh, 1968; Getting Straight, 1970; The Conversation, 1974; American Graffiti, 1974; Star Wars, 1977; Force 10 from Navarone, 1978; Apocalypse Now, 1979; The Frisco Kid, 1979; The Empire Strikes Back, 1980; Raiders of the Lost Ark, 1981; Blade Runner, 1982; Return of the Jedi, 1983; Indiana Jones and the Temple of Doom, 1984; Witness, 1985; Mosquito Coast, 1986; Frantic, 1988; Indiana Jones and the Last Crusade, 1989; Presumed Innocent, 1990; Regarding Henry, 1991; The Fugitive, 1992; Patriot Games, 1992; Clear and Present Danger, 1994; Sabrina, 1995; Devil's Own, 1996; Air Force One, 1997; Six Days, Seven Nights, 1998; Random Hearts, 1999; What Lies Beneath, 2000; numerous TV appearances, including The Virginian, Gunsmoke, Ironside. *Address:* 10279 Century Woods Drive, Los Angeles, CA 90067, USA.

FORD, Prof. Sir Hugh, Kt 1975; FRS 1967; FREng; Professor of Mechanical Engineering, 1969–80, Professor Emeritus, since 1980, Pro-Rector, 1978–80, University of London (Imperial College of Science and Technology); Chairman, Sir Hugh Ford & Associates Ltd, since 1982; *b* 16 July 1913; *s* of Arthur and Constance Ford; *m* 1st, 1942, Wynyard (*d* 1991), *d* of Major F. B. Scholfield; two *d*; 2nd, 1993, Mrs Thelma Jensen. *Educ:* Northampton Sch.; City and Guilds Coll., Univ. of London. DSc (Eng); PhD. Practical trng at GWR Locomotive Works, 1931–36; researches into heat transfer, 1936–39; R&D Engrg, Imperial Chemical Industries, Northwich, 1939–42; Chief Engr, Technical Dept, British Iron and Steel Fedn, 1942–45, then Head of Mechanical Working Div., British Iron and Steel Research Assoc., 1945–47; Exec. Dir, Paterson Engrg Ltd, 1947–48; Reader in Applied Mechanics, Univ. of London (Imp. Coll. of Science and Technology), 1948–51, Prof., 1951–69; Head of Dept of Mech. Engineering, 1965–78. Mem. Bd of Governors, Imperial Coll., 1982–89. Technical Dir, Davy-Ashmore Group, 1968–71; Director: Ford & Dain Research Ltd, 1972–93; Alfred Herbert Ltd, 1972–79; Air Liquide UK Ltd, 1979–95; Ricardo Consulting Engrs Ltd, 1980–88; Chm., Adv. Bd, Prudential Portfolio Managers, 1985–88; Mem., Adv. Bd, Brown and Root (UK), 1983–92. John Player Lectr, 1973, Hugh Ford Management Lectr, 1988, IMechE. First Pres., Inst. of Metals, 1985–87 (merger of Inst. of Metallurgists and Metals Soc.); President: Section 6, British Assoc., 1975–76; Welding Inst., 1983–85; Founder Fellow, Fellowship (later Royal Acad.) of Engineering, 1976 (Vice-Pres., 1981–83, Mem. Council, 1986–92); Member: Council, IMechE (Vice-Pres., 1972, 1975, Sen. Vice-Pres., 1976, Pres., 1977–78); SRC, 1968–72 (Chm. Engineering Bd); Council, Royal Soc., 1973–74; ARC, 1976–81. FICE; Whitworth Schol.; FCGI; FIC 1982; Sen. Fellow, RCA, 1987. Foreign Mem., Finnish Acad. of Technology, 1979. Hon. MASME, 1980; Hon. FIMechE 1984; Hon. FIChemE 1987. Hon. DSc: Salford, 1976; QUB, 1977; Aston, 1978; Bath, 1978; Sheffield, 1984; Sussex, 1990. Thomas Hawksley Gold Medallist, IMechE, 1948, for researches into rolling of metals; Robertson Medal, Inst. of Metals, 1954; James Alfred Ewing Gold Medal, ICE, 1982; James Watt Internat. Gold Medal, 1985. *Publications:* Advanced Mechanics of Materials, 1963; papers to Royal Soc., IMechE, Iron and Steel Inst., Inst. of Metals, foreign societies, etc. *Recreations:* gardening, music, model engineering. *Address:* 18 Shrewsbury House, Cheyne Walk, SW3 5LN; Shamley Cottage, Stroud Lane, Shamley Green, Surrey GU5 0ST. *Club:* Athenæum.

FORD, James Allan, CB 1978; MC 1946; *b* 10 June 1920; 2nd *s* of Douglas Ford and Margaret Duncan (*née* Allan); *m* 1948, Isobel Dunnett; one *s* one *d*. *Educ:* Royal High School, Edinburgh; University of Edinburgh. Served 1940–46, Capt. Royal Scots. Entered Civil Service, 1938; Asst Sec., Dept of Agriculture and Fisheries for Scotland, 1958; Registrar Gen. for Scotland, 1966–69; Principal Establishment Officer, Scottish Office, 1969–79. A Trustee, Nat. Lib. of Scotland, 1981–91. *Publications:* The Brave White Flag, 1961; Season of Escape, 1963; A Statue for a Public Place, 1965; A Judge of Men, 1968; The Mouth of Truth, 1972. *Address:* 6 Hillpark Court, Edinburgh EH4 7BE. *T:* (0131) 336 5398. *Club:* Royal Scots (Edinburgh).

FORD, (James) Glyn; Member (Lab) South West Region, England, European Parliament, since 1999 (Greater Manchester East, 1984–99); *b* 28 Jan. 1950; *s* of late Ernest Benjamin Ford and Matilda Alberta Ford (*née* James); *m* 1st, 1973, Hazel Nancy Mahy (marr. diss. 1992); one *d*; 2nd, 1992, Daniela Zannelli; one *s*. *Educ:* Marling; Reading Univ. (BSc Geol. with Soil Sci.); UCL (MSc Marine Earth Sci.); Manchester Univ. Undergraduate Apprentice, BAC, 1967–68; Course Tutor in Oceanography, Open Univ., 1976–78; Teaching Asst, UMIST, 1977–78; Res. Fellow, Sussex Univ., 1978–79; Manchester University: Res. Asst, 1976–77; Res. Fellow, 1979; Lectr, 1979–80; Sen. Res. Fellow, Prog. of Policy Res. in Engrg Sci. and Technol., 1980–84; Hon. Vis. Res. Fellow, 1984–. Vis. Prof., Tokyo Univ., 1983. Tameside Borough Council: Mem., 1978–86; Chairman: Environmental Health and Control Cttee, 1979–80; Educn Services Cttee, 1980–85. Mem., Lab Party NEC, 1989–93 (Member: Sci. and Technol. Policy Sub-Cttee, 1981–83; Review Gp on Trade Union/Labour Party Links, 1992–93). European Parliament: Chm., Cttee of Inquiry into Growth of Racism and Fascism in Europe, 1984–86; Vice-Chm., Sub-Cttee on Security and Disarmament, 1987–89; first Vice-Pres., Group of Party of European Socialists, 1989–93; Vice Chm., Delgn, Japanese Diet, 1992–94, 1996–99; Leader, 1989–93, Dep. Leader, 1993–94, Eur. PLP. Mem., Consultative Cttee on Racism and Xenophobia, Council of Ministers of EU, 1994–98. Contested (Lab), Hazel Grove, 1987. *Publications:* (with C. Niblett and L. Walker) The Future for Ocean Technology, 1987; Fascist Europe, 1992; The Evolution of a European, 1994; Changing States, 1996; contribs to learned jls on sci. and technol. policy. *Recreations:* Japan, travel, writing. *Address:* (office) 1 Newfoundland Court, Newfoundland Street, Bristol BS2 9AP. *T:* (0117) 924 6399, *Fax:* (0117) 924 8599. *Clubs:* Groucho, Soho House.

FORD, John; *see* Ford, S. J.

FORD, (John) Anthony, OBE 1998; Director, Crafts Council, 1988–99 (Deputy Director, 1985–88); *b* 28 April 1938; *s* of Frank Everatt Ford and Dorothy Mary Ford; *m* 1st, 1963, Caroline Rosemary Wharrad (marr. diss.); one *d*; 2nd, 1984, Sandra Edith Williams. *Educ:* Epsom Coll.; St Edmund's Hall, Oxford (MA). Admitted Solicitor, 1963. Dir, Art Services Grants, 1974–79; Crafts Council, 1979–99. Mem., Visual Arts Adv. Cttee, British Council, 1988–99. Vice-Pres. for Europe, World Crafts Council, 1987–93

(Advr, 1993–). Mem., Fabric Adv. Cttee, Rochester Cathedral, 1990–. Member: Court, RCA, 1989–99; Court of Govs, London Inst., 1993–2000. Trustee: Craft Pottery Charitable Trust, 1991–; Idlewild Trust, 2000–. FRSA 1989. *Recreations:* theatre, cinema. *Address:* 78 Shelgate Road, SW11 1BQ. *T:* (020) 7223 5711.

FORD, Sir John (Archibald), KCMG 1977 (CMG 1967); MC 1945; HM Diplomatic Service, retired; *b* 19 Feb. 1922; *s* of Ronald Mylne Ford and Margaret Jesse Coghill, Newcastle-under-Lyme, Staffs; *m* 1956, Emaline Burnette (*d* 1989), Leesville, Virginia; two *d*. *Educ:* St Michael's Coll., Tenbury; Sedbergh Sch., Yorks; Oriel Coll., Oxford. Served in Royal Artillery, 1942–46 (temp. Major); demobilised, 1947. Joined Foreign (subseq. Diplomatic) Service, 1947. Third Sec., British Legation, Budapest, 1947–49; Third Sec. and a Resident Clerk, FO, 1949–52; Private Sec. to Permanent Under-Sec. of State, FO, 1952–54; HM Consul, San Francisco, 1954–56; seconded to HM Treasury, 1956–59; attended Course at Administrative Staff Coll., 1959; First Sec. and Head of Chancery, British Residency, Bahrain, 1959–61; Asst, FO Personnel Dept, 1961–63; Asst, FO Establishment and Organisation Dept, 1963; Head of Diplomatic Service Establishment and Organisation Dept, 1964–66; Counsellor (Commercial), Rome, 1966–70; Asst Under-Sec., FCO, 1970–71; Consul-Gen., New York, and Dir-Gen., British Trade Develt in USA, 1971–75; Ambassador to Indonesia, 1975–78; British High Comr in Canada, 1978–81. Lay Administrator, Guildford Cathedral, 1982–84. Mem., Exec. Cttee, VSO, 1982–87; Chm. of Trustees, Voluntary and Christian Service, 1985–88; Chm., AIDS Care Educn and Trng, 1989–93; Trustee: World in Need, 1987–95; Opportunity Trust, 1991–96; Opportunity Internat. (USA), 1994–95. *Publications:* Honest to Christ, 1988; The Answer is the Christ of AD 2000, 1996; Introducing the Young to the Christ of AD 2000, 1999; Searching for the Christ of AD 2000 in Saint John's Gospel, 1999; Seeking the Christ of AD 2000 through Francis of Assisi and Brother Lawrence, 1999; Praying in the Mystical Body of the Christ of AD 2000, 1999; Spiritual Exercises for AD 2000, 1999; Looking for the Christ of AD 2000 in the Recorded Sayings of Jesus, 2000. *Recreations:* walking, gardening, sailing. *Address:* Loquats, Guildown, Guildford, Surrey GU2 5EN; Admiral 633, 8750 South Ocean Drive, Jensen Beach, Florida 34957, USA. *Club:* Vanbrugh (Guildford).

FORD, (John) Peter, CBE 1969; Chairman and Managing Director, International Joint Ventures Ltd; *b* 20 Feb. 1912; *s* of Ernest and Muriel Ford; *m* 1939, Phoebe Seys, *d* of Herbert McGregor Wood, FRIBA; one *s* two *d*. *Educ:* Wrekin Coll.; Gonville and Caius Coll., Cambridge. BA (Hons Nat. Sci. Tripos) 1934; MA Cantab 1937. Cambridge Univ. Air Sqdn, 1932–35 (Pilot's A Licence, 1933–). Air Ministry (subsequently FO, RAFVR), 1939–40; Coventry Gauge and Tool Co. Ltd (Asst to Chm.), 1941–45; Gen. Man., Brit. Engineers Small Tools and Equipment Co. Ltd, and Gen. Man. Scientific Exports (Gt Brit.) Ltd, 1945–48; Man. Dir, Brush Export Ltd, Associated British Oil Engines (Export) Ltd and National Oil Engines (Export) Ltd, and Dir of other associated cos of The Brush Group, 1949–55; Dir, Associated British Engineering Ltd and subsidiaries, 1957–58; Man. Dir, Coventry Climax International Ltd, 1958–63; Director: Plessey Overseas Ltd, 1963–70; Bryant & May (Latin America) Ltd, 1970–73; Chm., Metra Martech Ltd, 1988–2000. Chm. Institute of Export, 1954–56, 1965–67; President: Soc. of Commercial Accountants, 1970–74 (Vice-Pres., 1956–70); Inst. of Company Accountants, 1974–75; Member: Council, London Chamber of Commerce, 1951–72 (Dep. Chm., 1970–72; Vice-Pres., 1972–); London Ct of Arbitration, 1970–73; FBI, Overseas Trade Policy Cttee, 1952–63; Council, British Internal Combustion Engine Manufacturers Assoc., 1953–55; BNEC Cttee for Exports to Latin America, 1964–71 (Chm. 1968–71); NEDO Cttee for Movement of Exports, 1972–75; British Overseas Trade Adv. Council, 1975–82. Chm., British Shippers' Council, 1972–75 (Dep. Chm., 1971–72). Chm., British Mexican Soc., 1973–77; Vice-Pres., Hispanic and Luso Brazilian Council, 1980–. Freeman of City of London, 1945; Mem. Ct of Assistants, Ironmongers' Co. (Master, 1981); Governor: Wrekin Coll., 1953–57; Oversea Service Coll., 1966–86. CEng, CIMechE, CIMarE, MIEE. Order of Rio Branco (Brazil), 1977. *Publications:* contributor to technical press and broadcaster on international trade subjects. *Recreations:* Athletics (Cambridge Univ. and Internat. Teams, 1932–35; held various county championships, 1932–37; Hon. Treas, 1947–58, Vice-Pres., 1990–, Achilles Club; Pres., London Athletic Club, 1964–66). *Address:* 40 Fairacres, Roehampton Lane, SW15 5LX. *T:* (020) 8876 2146. *Clubs:* Oxford and Cambridge, MCC; Hawks (Cambridge); Royal Wimbledon Golf.

FORD, Margaret Anne; Chief Executive Officer, Good Practice Ltd, since 2000; Chairman, Eglinton Management Centre, since 2000 (Managing Director, 1993–2000); *b* 16 Dec. 1957; *d* of Edward and Susan Garland; *m* 1990, David Arthur Bolger; one *s* one *d* by a previous marriage. *Educ:* Glasgow Univ. (MA Hons, MPhil). Scottish Organiser, BIFU, 1982–87; Managing Consultant, Price Waterhouse & Co., 1987–90; Dir, Scottish Homes, 1990–93; Chm., Lothian Health Bd, 1997–2000. Non-executive Director: Scottish Prison Service, 1994–98; Waverley Care Trust, 1997–99; Ofgem, 2000–. Member: Scottish Economic Council, 1997–; Exec., Scottish Council Develt and Industry, 1997. *Recreations:* family, sport, fine art, travel. *Address:* 6 Bramdean Place, Edinburgh EH10 6JS; 7 Dunan, Isle of Skye IV49 9AJ.

FORD, (Martin) Geoffrey; Librarian, since 1990, and Director of Information Services, since 1999, University of Bristol; *b* 24 Jan. 1942; *s* of George Frederick Ford and Muriel (*née* Dowding); *m* 1974, Elizabeth Jill Barker. *Educ:* Sir Joseph Williamson's Mathematical Sch., Rochester; Leicester Univ. (BSc 1963); Sheffield Univ. (DipLib 1965; MSc 1973). ALA 1967. Liby Asst, Leicester Univ., 1963–64; Durham University: Asst Librarian, 1965–67; Sen. Res. Asst, 1968–69; Res. Associate, Bristol Univ., 1969–72; Asst Dir, Liby Res. Unit, Lancaster Univ., 1972–75; Sen. Res. Officer and Dir, Centre for Res. on User Studies, Sheffield Univ., 1976–78; Southampton University: Sub-librarian, 1978–87; Dep. Librarian, 1987–89. Member: Adv. Council, British Library, 1995–2000 (Member: Res. Cttee, 1990–94; Adv. Cttee on Bibliographic Services, 1991–94); SCONUL Council, 1992–2001 (Vice Chm., 1996–98; Chm., 1998–2000); Vice-Chm., SW Regl Liby System, 1999– (Chm., 1998–99). (Jtly) Robinson Medal, LA, 1972. *Publications:* Review of Methods for Determining the Use of Library Stock, 1990; res. reports, articles and reviews in learned jls. *Recreations:* travelling on trains, gentle walking, naval and transport history. *Address:* University Library, Tyndall Avenue, Bristol BS8 1TJ. *T:* (0117) 928 8004.

FORD, Peter; *see* Ford, J. P.

FORD, His Honour Peter; a Circuit Judge, 1990–2000; *b* 30 Sept. 1930; *s* of late Rev. Cecil Henry Ford and Gwyneth Kathleen Ford (*née* Hall); *m* 1961, Jenifer Dekenah, Cape Town; one *d*. *Educ:* Ellesmere Coll.; Univ. of Manchester (LLB). Called to the Bar, Gray's Inn, 1952. In practice as barrister, Northern Circuit, 1952–55; legal advr in industry, 1956–59; in practice as barrister, Patent Bar, 1959–79; Mem., Bds of Appeal, European Patent Office, Munich, 1979–90; Chm., Legal Bd of Appeal, 1985–90; nominated Judge of Patents County Court, 1990. Reader in C of E, 1955–. MRI 1958; FRSA 1953. *Publications:* various articles in legal jls. *Recreations:* music, foreign languages, travel.

FORD, Peter George Tipping; Secretary, Medical Protection Society, 1983–90; *b* 18 Sept. 1931; *s* of late Raymond Eustace Ford, CBE; *m* 1958, Nancy Elizabeth Procter; four *d*. *Educ:* Epsom College; St Bartholomew's Hosp. Med. Coll., Univ. of London (MB, BS); MRCGP, DObst RCOG. Nat. Service, RAMC, 1957–59. Gen. practice, Hythe, 1960–68; Asst Sec., Med. Protection Soc., 1968–72, Dep. Sec., 1972–83. Sec., Jt Co-ordinating Cttee, UK Defence Organizations, 1985–89. Mem., Soc. of Apothecaries. FRSocMed. Medal of Honour, Med. Defence Soc. of Queensland, 1984. *Publications:* contribs to medico-legal periodicals. *Recreations:* baroque choral music, gardening, bridge. *Address:* Braeside Cottage, Cannongate Road, Hythe, Kent CT21 5PT. *T:* (01303) 267896.

FORD, Peter John, CBE 1998; Chairman: Reliance Integrated Services, since 2000; London Transport, 1994–98; *b* 21 Nov. 1938; *s* of John Frederick Arthur Ford and Hazel Mary Ford; *m* 1966, Olivia Mary Temple; two *s* two *d*. *Educ:* King's Sch., Canterbury; Christ Church, Oxford (MA Chem.); Harvard Business Sch. (MBA). With Shell Chemical Co., 1961–65; McKinsey & Co., NY, 1967–70; Exec. Dir, Sterling Guarantee Trust, 1970–85; Exec. Dir, P&OSNCo., 1985–93. Dir, Countrywide Assured Gp, 1994–. Pres., Sheffield Chamber of Commerce, 1985–86; Dep. Pres., London Chamber of Commerce and Industry, 1998–2000. Governor: Kingston Univ., 1993–; Collingwood Coll., 2001–. *Recreations:* walking, music. *Address:* 16 The Drive, Wimbledon, SW20 8TG. *T:* (020) 8944 7207. *Club:* Royal Automobile.

FORD, Peter William; HM Diplomatic Service; Ambassador to Bahrain, since 1999; *b* 27 June 1947; *s* of Alec and Gertrude Ford; *m* 1st, 1974, Aurora Garcia Mingo (marr. diss. 1992); 2nd, 1992, Alganesh Haile Beyene. *Educ:* Helsby Grammar Sch.; Queen's Coll., Oxford (BA Hons). FCO, 1971–72; Beirut, 1972–73; Second, then First, Sec., Cairo, 1974–78; Eur. Integration Dept, FCO, 1978–80; First Sec., Paris, 1980–85; Asst Hd, EC Dept, FCO, 1985–87; Counsellor (Commercial), Riyadh, 1987–90; Vis. Fellow, Harvard Univ., 1990–91; Dep. High Comr and Counsellor (Econ. and Commercial), Singapore, 1991–94; Hd, Near East and N Africa Dept, FCO, 1994–99. *Recreations:* sport, reading, travel. *Address:* c/o Foreign and Commonwealth Office, King Charles Street, SW1A 2AH.

FORD, Gen. Sir Robert (Cyril), GCB 1981 (KCB 1977; CB 1973); CBE 1971 (MBE 1958); Vice-Chairman, Commonwealth War Graves Commission, 1989–93 (Commissioner, 1981–93); *b* 29 Dec. 1923; *s* of late John Stranger Ford and Gladys Ford, Yealmpton, Devon; *m* 1949, Jean Claudia Pendlebury, *d* of late Gp Capt. Claude Pendlebury, MC, TD, FLAS, FRICS, and Muriel Pendlebury, Yelverton, Devon; one *s*. *Educ:* Musgrave's Coll. War of 1939–45: commissioned into 4th/7th Royal Dragoon Guards, from Sandhurst, 1943; served with Regt throughout NW European campaign, 1944–45 (despatches) and in Egypt and Palestine, 1947–48 (despatches). Instructor, Mons OCS, 1949–50; Training Officer, Scottish Horse (TA), 1952–54; Staff Coll., Camberley, 1955; GSO 2 Mil. Ops, War Office, 1956–57; Sqdn Ldr 4/7 RDG, 1958–59; Bde Major, 20th Armoured Bde, 1960–61; Brevet Lt-Col, 1962; Sqdn Ldr, 4/7 RDG, 1962–63; GSO1 to Chief of Defence Staff, 1964–65; commanded 4/7 RDG in S Arabia and N Ireland, 1966–67; Comdr, 7th Armd Bde, 1968–69; Principal Staff Officer to Chief of Defence Staff, 1970–71; Cmdr Land Forces, N Ireland, 1971–73; Comdt, RMA Sandhurst, 1973–76; Military Secretary, 1976–78; Adjutant-General, 1978–81; ADC General to the Queen, 1980–81; Governor, Royal Hosp., Chelsea, 1981–87. Colonel Commandant: RAC, 1980–82; SAS Regt, 1980–85; Col 4th/7th Royal Dragoon Gds, 1984–88. President: Services Kinema Corp., 1978–81; Army Boxing Assoc., 1978–81. Chm., 1981–87, and Pres., 1986–97, Army Benevolent Fund; Chm., Royal Cambridge Home for Soldiers' Widows, 1981–87; Nat. Pres., Forces Help Soc. and Lord Roberts Workshops, 1981–91. Governor, Corps of Commissionaires, 1981–94. Freeman, City of London, 1981. CIMgt. *Recreations:* watching cricket, tennis, war studies, theatre. *Clubs:* Cavalry and Guards, MCC.

FORD, Robert Stanley; HM Diplomatic Service, retired; *b* 30 Nov. 1929; *s* of late Robert Hempstead Ford and Janet Mabel Elliot; *m* 1957, Cynthia Valerie Arscott, *d* of late Ronald Prowse Arscott, Bexhill-on-Sea, Sussex; one *s* two *d*. *Educ:* Daniel Stewart's Coll., Edinburgh; Univ. of Edinburgh (MA). Joined HM Diplomatic Service, 1949; HM Forces, 1949; FCO, 1951; Third Sec., Moscow, 1955; Consul, Dakar, 1958; FCO, 1959; Information Officer, NY, 1963; First Sec., Managua, 1965; Consul, Naples, 1968; FCO, 1972; Consul-Gen., Madrid, 1978; FCO, 1982; Counsellor (Admin), Paris, 1984–86. *Recreations:* music, photography, gardening, travel. *Address:* 20 Heatherbank, Haywards Heath, W Sussex RH16 1HY. *T:* (01444) 455321.

FORD, Robert Webster, CBE 1982; HM Diplomatic Service, retired; *b* 27 March 1923; *s* of late Robert Ford; *m* 1956, Monica Florence Tebbett; two *s*. *Educ:* Alleyne's Sch. Served RAF, 1939–45. Served with British Mission, Lhasa, Tibet and Political Agency in Sikkim and Bhutan, 1945–47; joined Tibetan Govt Service, 1947; advised on and installed Tibet's first radio communication system and broadcasting stn; travelled extensively in Northern and Eastern Tibet, 1947–50; taken prisoner during Chinese Occupation of Tibet, 1950; imprisoned in China, 1950–55; free-lance writer and broadcaster on Chinese and Tibetan affairs, 1955; entered Foreign Service, 1956; 2nd Sec., Saigon, 1957–58; 1st Sec. (Information), Djakarta, 1959; Washington, 1960–62; FO, 1962–67; Consul-Gen., Tangier, 1967–70; Counsellor, 1970; Consul-General; Luanda, 1970–74; Bordeaux, 1974–78; Gothenburg, 1978–80; Geneva, 1980–83. *Publication:* Captured in Tibet, 1956, repr. 1990. *Recreations:* ski-ing, gardening, travelling. *Address:* Cedar Garth, Latimer Road, Monken Hadley, Barnet, Herts EN5 5NU. *Clubs:* Royal Commonwealth Society, Royal Geographical Society.

FORD, Roy Arthur, MA; Director of Visits, Canterbury Cathedral, 1986–90; *b* 10 May 1925; *s* of Arthur Ford and Minnie Elizabeth Ford; *m* 1965, Christine Margaret Moore; two *s*. *Educ:* Collyer's Sch., Horsham; Corpus Christi Coll., Cambridge (Scholar; 1st Cl. Pts I and II, History Tripos; BA 1949, MA 1971). Asst Master: Uppingham Sch., 1951–54; Tonbridge Sch., 1954–66; Uppingham Sch., (also Head of History and Sixth Form Master), 1966–71; Headmaster: Southwell Minster Grammar Sch., 1971–75; King's Sch., Rochester, 1975–86. *Recreations:* walking, travel, music. *Address:* North Street Farmhouse, Sheldwich, Kent ME13 0LN. *T:* (01795) 537614.

FORD, (Sydney) John, CBE 1999; PhD; Chairman, Ofwat CSC Wales, since 2001; Chief Executive, Driver and Vehicle Licensing Agency 1995–2000; *b* 23 Aug. 1936; *s* of Sidney James Ford and Barbara Ford (*née* Essenhigh); *m* 1st, 1960, Beryl Owen (marr. diss. 1990); two *s*; 2nd, 1990, Morag Munro. *Educ:* Bromsgrove High Sch.; Swansea Grammar Sch.; UC Swansea, Univ. of Wales (BSc Maths; PhD Maths; Hon. Fellow, 1999). British Aluminium Co. plc, 1966–82 (Dir, 1977–82; Man. Dir, 1982); Dep. Man. Dir, British Alcan Aluminium plc, 1982–85; UK Ops Dir, Williams Hldgs plc, 1985–88; Dir, European Distrib., Christian Salvesen plc, 1988–93; Chief Exec., Driving Standards Agency, 1993–94. *Recreations:* Rugby referee and coach, art, photography. *Address:* Shenval, 1 Evertons Close, Droitwich Spa WR9 8AE. *T:* (01905) 776000.

FORD, William Clay, Jr; Chairman, since 1999, and Chief Executive, since 2001, Ford Motor Company (Director, since 1988); *b* Detroit, 3 May 1957; *m. Educ:* Princeton Univ. (BA 1979); MIT (Alfred P. Sloan Fellow, 1983–84, MBA 1984). Ford Motor Company: Product Planning Analyst, Advanced Vehicle Develt, Design Center, then Manufg Engr, Automobile Assembly Div., subseq. NY Zone Manager, Ford Div., 1979–82; Mktg Strategy Analyst, N Amer. Automobile Ops, and Advertising Specialist, Ford Div., 1982–83; Internat. Finance Specialist, 1984–85; Planning Manager, Car Product Develt, 1985–86; Dir, Commercial Vehicle Mktg, Ford of Europe, 1986–87; Chm. and Man. Dir, Ford of Switzerland, 1987–89; Manager, Heavy Truck Engrg and Manufg, Ford Truck Ops, 1989–90; Dir, 1990–91, Exec. Dir, 1991–92, Business Strategy, Ford Auto Gp; Gen. Manager, Climate Control Div., 1992–94; Vice Pres., Commercial Truck Vehicle Center, Ford Automotive Ops, 1994–95; Chm., Finance Cttee, 1995–99. Vice Chm., Bd of Dirs, Greater Downtown Partnership, Detroit. Chm., Bd of Trustees, Henry Ford Mus. and Greenfield Village; Trustee: Henry Ford Health System; Detroit Renaissance; Conservation Internat.; Vice Chm., Detroit Lions (prof. football team); Member: Global Leaders for Tomorrow, World Econ. Forum; NFL Finance Cttee; NFL Properties Cttee. *Address:* Ford Motor Company, 1 American Road, Dearborn, MI 48126–2798, USA. *T:* (313) 3223000.

FORDE, Hon. Harold McDonald, CH (Barbados) 1994; MD; consultant physician; High Commissioner for Barbados in UK, 1984–86; *b* 10 Jan. 1916; *s* of Gertrude and William McDonald Forde; *m* 1949, Alice Leslie; one *s* two *d. Educ:* Harrison College, Barbados; University College London; University College Hospital (MB BS 1942; MD); DPH, DTM&H. MO, Colonial Med. Service, Belize, 1947–52; First Lectr, Dept. of Medicine, Univ. of West Indies, Jamaica, 1952–57; Consultant Physician, Barbados, 1957–78; Med. Supt, Barbados Gen. Hosp., 1961–64; Senior Lectr, Dept of Medicine, Univ. of West Indies, 1967–78 (Associate Dean, 1967–73); Mem. Senate, Univ. of W Indies, 1973–75; Chief Med. Officer, Commonwealth of Bahamas, 1978–79; Consultant Physician, Barbados, 1980–84; Chief Med. Officer, Life of Barbados, 1973–84. Mem. Privy Council, Barbados, 1980–85; Senior Fellow, Commonwealth Fund, 1976; Tech. Expert, Commonwealth Fund for Tech Co-Opn, 1978–79; Governor, Commonwealth Foundn, 1984. Hon. Vice-President: West India Cttee; Commonwealth Inst. Past Dist Gov., Lions Clubs Internat., 1973 (Life Mem., 1988; Melvin Jones Fellow, 1992). Mem., NY Acad. of Scis. Hon. FRCP 1971; Hon. FRCPE 1972; Hon. FACP 1975. Silver Jubilee Medal, 1977. *Publications:* articles in WI med. jls. *Recreations:* cricket, soccer, bridge, chess, athletics, music. *Address:* Bethesda Medical Centre, Black Rock, St Michael, Barbados, WI. *Club:* Royal Commonwealth Society.

FORDE, (Mary Marguerite) Leneen, AC 1993; Chancellor, Griffith University, Queensland, since 2000; Governor of Queensland, 1992–97; *b* 12 May 1935; *d* of John Alfred Kavanagh and Evlyn Philomena Kavanagh (*née* Bujold); *m* 1st, 1955, Francis Gerard Forde (*d* 1966), *s* of Rt Hon. Francis Michael Forde, PC; three *s* two *d*; 2nd, 1983, (Albert) Angus McDonald (*d* 1999). *Educ:* Lisgar Collegiate, Ottawa (Dip.); Univ. of Queensland (LLB). Student Med. Lab. Technician, Ottawa Gen. Hosp., 1952–53; Med. Lab. Technician, Drs Rousell and Gagne, Ottawa, 1953–54; Haematol. Dept, Royal Brisbane Hosp., 1954–56; part-time lab. work, 1956–66; articled Law Clerk, Alexander McGillivray, 1969–70; Solicitor, Cannan & Peterson, 1971–74; Partner, Sly, Weigall Cannan & Peterson, 1974–92. Chm., Royal Commn of Inquiry into Abuse of Children in Queensland Instns, 1998–99. Board Member: St Leo's Coll., 1998–2000; Brisbane Coll. of Theol., 1999–2000; Brisbane City Council Arts and Envmt Trust, 1999–2000; Qld Ballet, 2000–; Qld Govt Forde Foundn, 2000–. Founder, Qld Women Lawyers' Assoc., 1976; Member: Qld Law Soc., 1971–; Women Chiefs of Enterprises Internat., 1989–; Zonta Club of Brisbane Inc., 1971–; President: Zonta Internat., 1990–92; Scout Assoc. of Aust., 1997–. Patron, Nat. Pioneer Women's Hall of Fame, 1999–. Paul Harris Fellow, Rotary Club of Brisbane, 1990; Woman of Substance Award, Qld Girl Guides' Assoc., 1990; Queenslander of the Year, 1991. DUniv: Griffith, 1992; Qld Univ. of Technology, 1993; Australian Catholic, 2000; Southern Qld, 2000; Hon. DLitt Queensland, 1996. DStJ 1992. *Publication:* Queensland Annual Law Review, 1991, 1992. *Recreations:* theatre, art, music, ballet, surfing.

FORDER, Ven. Charles Robert; Archdeacon Emeritus, Diocese of York, since 1974; *b* 6 Jan. 1907; *s* of late Henry Forder, Worstead, Norfolk; *m* 1933, Myra, *d* of late Harry Peat, Leeds; no *c. Educ:* Paston Sch., North Walsham; Christ's Coll. and Ridley Hall, Cambridge. Exhibitioner of Christ's Coll. and Prizeman, 1926; 1st Cl. Math. Trip. Part I, 1926, BA (Sen. Opt. Part II) 1928, MA 1932; Ridley Hall, 1928. Curate: St Peter's, Hunslet Moor, 1930–33; Burley, 1933–34; Vicar: Holy Trinity, Wibsey, 1934–40; St Clement's, Bradford, 1940–47; Organising Sec., Bradford Church Forward Movement Appeal, 1945–47; Vicar of Drypool, 1947–55; Rector of Routh and Vicar of Wawne, 1955–57; Canon, and Prebendary of Fenton, York Minster, 1957–76; Rector of Sutton-on-Derwent, 1957–63; Rector of Holy Trinity, Micklegate, York, 1963–66; Archdeacon of York, 1957–72. Chaplain to HM Prison, Hull, 1950–53; Proctor in Convocation, 1954–72; Organising Sec., Diocesan Appeal, 1955–76; Church Comr, 1958–73. *Publications:* A History of the Paston Grammar School, 1934, 2nd edn 1975; The Parish Priest at Work, 1947; Synods in Action, 1970; Churchwardens in Church and Parish, 1976; contrib. to Encyclopædia Britannica. *Recreations:* reading and writing. *Address:* Dulverton Hall, St Martin's Square, Scarborough YO11 2DQ. *T:* (01723) 379534.

FORDHAM, His Honour (John) Jeremy; a Circuit Judge, 1986–99; a Deputy Circuit Judge, since 1999; *b* 18 April 1933; *s* of John Hampden Fordham, CBE and Rowena Langran; *m* 1962, Rose Anita (*née* Brandon), *d* of Philip Brandon, Wellington, New Zealand; one *s* one *d. Educ:* Gresham's Sch.; Univ. of New Zealand. LLB (NZ). Merchant Navy, 1950–55 (2nd Mate (Foreign Going) Cert.); labourer, fireman etc, 1955–60; Barrister and Solicitor, New Zealand, 1960–64; called to Bar, Inner Temple, 1965; practised 1965–71, 1976–78; Sen. Magistrate, Gilbert and Ellice Islands, 1971–75; a Metropolitan Stipendiary Magistrate, 1978–86; a Recorder, 1986. Legal Chm., Immigration Appeal Tribunal, 1999–. *Recreations:* boats, games. *Club:* Garrick.

FOREMAN, Michael, RDI 1985; AGI; writer and illustrator; *b* 21 March 1938; *s* of Walter and Gladys Mary Foreman; *m* 1st, 1959, Janet Charters (marr. diss. 1966); one *s*; 2nd, 1980, Louise Phillips; two *s. Educ:* Notley Road Secondary Modern Sch., Lowestoft; Royal College of Art, London (ARCA 1st Cl. Hons and Silver Medal). Freelance, 1963–; six animated films produced, 1967–68. Awarded Aigle d'Argent, Festival International du Livre, Nice, 1972; (jtly) Kurt Maschler Award, 1982; Graphics Prize, Bologna, 1982; Kate Greenaway Medal, Library Assoc., 1983 and 1989. *Publications:* author and illustrator: The Perfect Present, 1966; The Two Giants, 1966; The Great Sleigh Robbery, 1968; Horatio, 1969; Moose, 1971; Dinosaurs and all that Rubbish, 1972 (Francis Williams Prize, 1972); War and Peas, 1974; All The King's Horses, 1976; Panda and his Voyage of Discovery, 1977 (Francis Williams Prize, 1977); Trick a Tracker, 1980; Panda and the Odd Lion, 1981; Land of Dreams, 1982; Panda and the Bunyips, 1984; Cat and Canary, 1984; Panda and the Bushfire, 1986; Ben's Box, 1986; Ben's Baby, 1987; The Angel and the Wild Animal, 1988; War Boy (autobiog.), 1989; Oneworld, 1990; World of Fairytales, 1990; The Boy Who Sailed with Columbus, 1991; Jack's Fantastic Voyage, 1992; War Game, 1993; Grandfather's Pencil, 1993; Dad, I Can't Sleep, 1994; Surprise, Surprise, 1994; After the War Was Over, 1995; Seal Surfer, 1996; The Little Reindeer, 1996; Look! Look!, 1997; Angel and the Box of Time, 1997; Jack's Big Race, 1998; Chicken Licken, 1998; Little Red Hen, 1999; Rock-a-Doodle Do, 1999; Cat in the Manger, 2000; Saving Sinbad, 2001; illustrator of many books by other authors. *Recreations:* football, travelling. *Address:* 5 Church Gate, SW6 3LD. *Club:* Chelsea Arts.

FOREMAN, Sir Philip (Frank), Kt 1981; CBE 1972; DL; FREng, FIAE, FIMechE; Member Council, 1986–98, Chairman, 1988–91, and President, 1994–98, British Standards Institution; *b* 16 March 1923; *s* of late Frank and Mary Foreman; *m* 1971, Margaret Cooke; one *s. Educ:* Soham Grammar Sch., Cambs; Loughborough Coll., Leics. (DLC (Hons)). Royal Naval Scientific Service, 1943–58. Short Bros, 1958–88: Man. Dir, 1967–88; Chm., 1983–88. Director: Simon Engrg Ltd, 1987–94 (Dep. Chm., 1992; Chm., 1993); Progressive Bldg Soc., 1987–2000 (Chm., 1990–2000); Ricardo Group (formerly Ricardo International) plc, 1988–97 (Chm., 1992–97); Consultant, Foreman Associates, 1988–. Member: Design Council, 1986–92; NI Economic Council, 1972–88; Chm., Teaching Co. Management Cttee, 1987–90; Trustee, Scotch-Irish Trust, 1980–. Mem. Senate, QUB, 1993–. Pres., IMechE, 1985–86. FREng (FEng 1982); FIAE 1997; Fellow: Irish Management Inst., 1986; Irish Inst. of Engrs, 1987; MInstD 1987; CIMgt. FRSA 1978. A Freeman, City of London, 1980; Liveryman, Engineers' Co., 1992–. DL Belfast, 1975. Hon. FRAeS 1983. Hon. DSc QUB, 1976; Hon. DTech Loughborough, 1983; DUniv Open, 1985. *Publications:* papers to: Royal Aeronautical Soc.; Instn of Mechanical Engineers. *Recreation:* gardening. *Address:* Ashtree House, 26 Ballymenoch Road, Holywood, Co. Down BT18 0HH. *T:* (028) 9042 5673.

FORESTER; *see* Weld Forester, family name of Baron Forester.

FORESTER, 8th Baron *cr* 1821; **George Cecil Brooke Weld Forester;** DL; Director: Linley Farms, since 1974; Sipolilo Estates, since 1977; *b* 20 Feb. 1938; *s* of 7th Baron Forester and Marie Louise Priscilla (*d* 1988), *d* of Col Sir Herbert Perrott, 6th Bt, CH, CB; *S* father, 1977; *m* 1967, Hon. Elizabeth Catherine Lyttelton, 2nd *d* of 10th Viscount Cobham, KG, PC, GCMG, GCVO, TD; one *s* three *d. Educ:* Eton; Royal Agricultural College, Cirencester (MRAC). Director: Pett Hammett, 1977–99; Lady Forester Hosp. Trust, 1994–; Bridgnorth Home Care Co-op., 1994–; Callkilo, 1996–99; Telford Drive, 1996–. Member: CLA (Mem. Minerals Working Party, 1980–98; Mem. Council, 1987–96; Mem. Exec., 1990–95); W Midlands Council for Sport and Recreation, 1991–95. President: The Greenwood Trust, 1990–; Shropshire Farming and Wildlife Adv. Gp, 1991–97; Midlands Flyfishers, 1999; Shropshire Cricket League, 1999. Former Chairman: Shropshire CLA; Shropshire Tree Council; Forestry Commn Regl Adv. Cttee. DL Shropshire, 1995. *Recreations:* fishing, silviculture, fine arts, the environment. *Heir: s* Hon. Charles Richard George Weld Forester, *b* 8 July 1975. *Address:* Willey Park, Broseley, Salop TF12 5JJ. *T:* (01952) 882146.

FORESTIER-WALKER, Sir Michael (Leolin), 6th Bt *cr* 1835; Teacher, Feltonfleet School, since 1975; *b* 24 April 1949; *s* of Lt-Col Alan Ivor Forestier-Walker, MBE (*d* 1954) (*g s* of 2nd Bt), and Margaret Joan Forestier-Walker (*née* Marcoolyn) (*d* 1988); *S* cousin, 1983; *m* 1988, Elizabeth Hedley, *d* of Joseph Hedley, Bellingham, Northumberland; one *s* one *d. Educ:* Wellington College, Crowthorne; Royal Holloway College, London Univ. (BA Hons). *Recreations:* sailing, electronics. *Heir: s* Joseph Alan Forestier-Walker, *b* 2 May 1992. *Address:* Bibury, 116 Hogshill Lane, Cobham, Surrey KT11 2AW.

FORFAR, Prof. John Oldroyd, MC; Professor of Child Life and Health, University of Edinburgh, 1964–82, now Professor Emeritus; *b* 16 Nov. 1916; *s* of Rev. David Forfar, MA and Elizabeth Edith Campbell; *m* 1942, Isobel Mary Langlands Fernback, MB, ChB, DPH, AFOM; two *s* one *d. Educ:* Perth Acad.; St Andrews Univ. BSc 1938, MB, ChB 1941, St Andrews; DCH (London) 1948; FRCPE 1953 (MRCPE 1948); MD (Commendation) St Andrews, 1958; FRCP 1964 (MRCP 1947); FRSE 1975; FRCPGlas 1979 (MRCPGlas 1978). House Officer, Perth Royal Infirmary, 1941; RAMC, 1942–46: Med. Off., 47 Royal Marine Commando, 1943–45 (MC 1944; despatches, 1945); Registrar and Sen. Registrar, Dundee Royal Infirmary, 1946–48; Sen. Lectr in Child Health, St Andrews Univ., 1948–50; Sen. Paediatric Phys., Edinburgh Northern Gp of Hosps, and Sen. Lectr in Child Life and Health, Edinburgh Univ., 1950–64; Consultant Paediatrician, Royal Hosp. for Sick Children and Royal Infirm., Edinburgh, 1964–82. Chairman: Scottish Assoc. of Voluntary Child Care Organisations, 1965–69; Medical Gp, Assoc. of British Adoption Agencies, 1966–76; Jt Paediatric Cttee of Royal Colls of Physicians and British Paediatric Assoc., 1979–85; President: Scottish Paediatric Soc., 1972–74; Assoc. of Clinical Professors and Heads of Departments of Paediatrics, 1980–83; Pres., BPA, 1985–88. Vice-President: Gt Ormond St Wishing Well Appeal, 1987–89; Royal Hosp. for Sick Children Appeal, 1992–95; Trustee, Malcolm Sargent Cancer Fund for Children, 1975–84. Fellow, Amer. Coll. of Nutrition, 1977; Hon. Member: Australian Coll. of Paediatrics, 1986; Faculty of Paediatrics, RCPI, 1986. Hon. FRCPCH 1997. James Spence Medallist, BPA, 1983. *Publications:* (ed) Textbook of Paediatrics, 1973, 5th edn 1998; Child Health in a Changing Society, 1988; The British Paediatric Association 1928–1988, 1989; contribs to general medical and to paediatric jls and books. *Recreations:* walking, writing. *Address:* 9 Ravelston Heights, Edinburgh EH4 3LX. *T:* (0131) 315 2184.

FORGAN, Elizabeth Anne Lucy, OBE 1999; writer and broadcaster; Director: Most Media Ltd, since 1998; Guardian Media Group, since 1998; Webcam Media Group, Berlin, since 2000; *b* 31 Aug. 1944; *d* of Thomas Moinet Forgan and Jean Margaret Muriel. *Educ:* Benenden Sch.; St Hugh's Coll., Oxford (BA). Journalist: Teheran Journal, 1967–68; Hampstead and Highgate Express, 1969–74; Evening Standard, 1974–78; The Guardian, 1978–81; Channel Four TV: Sen. Commissioning Editor, 1981–86; Dep. Dir of Progs, 1987; Dir of Progs, 1988–93; Man. Dir, Network Radio BBC, 1993–96. Chm., Arrowhead Productions, 1997–. Member: Human Fertilisation and Embryology Authority, 1990–98; Council, RSA, 1997–98; Churches Conservation Trust, 1998–2001 (Chm., 1999–2001); Chm., Nat. Heritage Meml Fund and Heritage Lottery Fund, 2001–. Trustee: Media Trust, 1997–2001; Child Psychotherapy Trust, 1997–2001; Phoenix Trust, 1997–2001. FRTS 1988; FRSA 1989. Hon. DLitt Keele, 1994; Hon. MA Salford, 1995. Chevalier de l'ordre des arts et des lettres, 1990. *Recreations:* church music, cheap novels, Scottish islands. *Address:* Most Media Ltd, 112 Regent's Park Road, NW1 8UG. *Club:* Reform.

FORGE, Andrew Murray; artist, writer; Professor of School of Art, University of Yale, Conn, USA (Dean, 1975–83); *b* Hastingleigh, Kent, 10 Nov. 1923; *s* of Sidney Wallace Forge and late Joanna Ruth Forge (*née* Bliss); *m* 1950, Sheila Deane (marr. diss.); three *d*; *m* 1974, Ruth Miller. *Educ:* Downs Sch.; Leighton Park; Camberwell Sch. of Art (NDD). Sen. Lectr, Slade Sch., UCL, 1950–64; Head of Dept of Fine Art, Goldsmith's Coll., 1964–70. Trustee: Tate Gallery, 1964–71 and 1972–74; National Gallery, 1966–72; Member: Nat. Council for Diplomas in Art and Design, 1964–72; Jt NCDAD/NACEA Cttee, 1968–70; Calouste Gulbenkian Foundn Cttee to report on future of conservation studies in UK, 1970–72; Pres., London Group, 1964–71. Trustee, Amer. Acad. in Rome, 1983–. *Publications:* Klee, 1953; Vermeer, 1954; Soutine, 1965; Rauschenberg, 1972;

(with C. Joyes) Monet at Giverny, 1975; (ed) The Townsend Journals, 1976; (with Robert Gordon) Monet, 1983; (with Dawn Adès) Francis Bacon, 1985; (jtly) The Last Flowers of Manet, 1986; (with R. Gordon) Degas, 1988. *Recreation:* travel. *Address:* Malthouse, Elmsted, near Ashford, Kent TN25 5JZ.

FORMAN, Sir Denis, Kt 1976; OBE 1956; Chairman, Granada Television, 1974–87; Deputy Chairman, Granada Group, 1984–90 (Director, 1964–90); *b* 13 Oct. 1917; *s* of late Rev. Adam Forman, CBE, and Flora Smith; *m* 1st, 1948, Helen de Mouilpied (*d* 1987); two *s*; 2nd, 1990, Moni, *widow* of James Cameron, CBE; one step *s* one step *d*. *Educ:* at home; Loretto; Pembroke Coll., Cambridge. Served War, 1940–45: Argyll and Sutherland Highlanders; Commandant, Orkney and Shetland Defences Battle Sch., 1942 (wounded, Cassino, 1944). Chief Production Officer, Central Office of Information Films, 1947; Dir, British Film Inst., 1948–55 (Chm., Bd of Governors, 1971–73); Granada TV Ltd, 1955–87: Dir, 1959; Jt Man. Dir, 1965–81; Chm., Novello & Co., 1971–88. Dep. Chm., Royal Opera Hse, Covent Gdn, 1983–91 (Dir, 1981–91); Chm., Scottish Film Production Fund, 1990–93; Mem. Council, RNCM, 1975–84 (Hon. Mem., RNCM, 1981; Hon. FRNCM 1993). Fellow, BAFTA, 1977. DUniv: Stirling, 1982; Keele, 1990; DU Essex, 1986; Hon. LLD: Manchester, 1983; Lancaster, 1989. Ufficiale dell'ordine Al Merito della Repubblica Italiana. *Publications:* Mozart's Piano Concertos, 1971; Son of Adam (autobiog.), 1990; To Reason Why (autobiog.), 1991; (ed) The Good Opera Guide, 1994; Persona Granada: some memories of Sidney Bernstein and the early days of Independent Television (autobiog.), 1997; The Good Wagner Guide, 2000. *Recreation:* music. *Address:* Flat 2, 15 Lyndhurst Gardens, NW3 5NT. *Clubs:* Garrick, Savile, Oriental.

See also M. B. Forman.

FORMAN, (Francis) Nigel; *b* 25 March 1943; *s* of late Brig. J. F. R. Forman and Mrs P. J. M. Forman; *m*. *Educ:* Dragon Sch., Oxford; Shrewsbury Sch.; New Coll., Oxford; College of Europe, Bruges; Kennedy Sch. of Govt, Harvard; Sussex Univ. Information Officer, CBI, 1970–71; Conservative Research Dept, 1971–76. Contested (C) Coventry NE, Feb. 1974. MP (C) Carshalton, March 1976–1983, Carshalton and Wallington, 1983–97; contested (C) Carshalton and Wallington, 1997. PPS to Lord Privy Seal, 1979–81 and to Minister of State, FCO, 1979–83, to Chancellor of the Exchequer, 1987–89; Parly Under Sec. of State, Dept for Educn, 1992. Member: Select Cttee on Science and Technology, 1976–79; Select Cttee on Foreign Affairs, 1990–92; Vice-Chairman: Cons. Finance Cttee, 1983–87; All Party Social Sci. and Policy Cttee, 1984–97; Secretary: Cons. Education Cttee, 1976–79; Cons. Energy Cttee, 1977–79. Mem. Exec., 1922 Cttee, 1990–92. Mem., ESRC, 1991–92. Chm., GB–E Europe Centre; Hon. Dir, Job Ownership Ltd. *Publications:* Towards a More Conservative Energy Policy, 1977; Another Britain, 1979; Mastering British Politics, 1985, 4th edn 1999; (with John Maples) Work to be Done, 1985.

FORMAN, Air Vice-Marshal Graham Neil, CB 1989; Director of Legal Services, Royal Air Force, 1982–89; *b* 29 Nov. 1930; *s* of Stanley M. Forman and Eva Forman (*née* Barrett); *m* 1957, Valerie Fay (*née* Shaw); one *s* two *d*. *Educ:* Boston Grammar School; Nottingham Univ. Law School; Law Society's School of Law; admitted solicitor 1953. Commissioned RAF Legal Branch, 1957; served HQ Far East Air Force, Singapore, 1960–63 and 1965–68; Dep. Dir, RAF Legal Services, HQ Near East Air Force, Cyprus, 1971–72 and 1973–76; Dep. Dir, RAF Legal Services, HQ RAF Germany, 1978; Dep. Dir, Legal Services (RAF), 1978–82. *Recreations:* reading, New Orleans jazz music, watching cricket. *Address:* c/o Lloyds TSB, High Street, Bembridge, Isle of Wight PO35 5SD. *Clubs:* Royal Air Force, MCC; Middlesex CC (Life Mem.).

FORMAN, Sir John Denis; *see* Forman, Sir Denis.

FORMAN, Michael Bertram, TD 1945; Director of Personnel and Organisation, TI Group plc, 1973–84; retired; *b* 28 March 1921; *s* of late Rev. A. Forman, CBE, and Flora Smith; *m* 1947, Mary Railston-Brown, *d* of late Rev. W. R. Railston-Brown; four *d*. *Educ:* Loretto Sch., Musselburgh; Manchester Coll. of Technology. TA commn, 7th KOSB, 1939. War Service in Inf. and Airborne Forces, 1939–46: UK, Holland, Germany (POW), India. Labour Management, Courtaulds Ltd, 1946–53; Dir, Inst. of Personnel Management, 1953–56; Head of Staff Planning, NCB, 1956–59; Chief Staff Officer, SW Div., NCB, 1959–62; TI Group plc (formerly Tube Investments Ltd): Personnel Relations Adviser and Dep. Dir of Personnel, 1962–68; Personnel Dir, Steel Tube Div., 1968–73. Mem. NBPI, 1968–70; Chm., CSAB, 1984–90. CCIPD. FRSA. *Recreations:* reading, gardening, fishing, shooting. *Address:* Meikleholmside, Annan Water, Moffat, Dumfriesshire DG10 9LS. *T:* (01683) 220376. *Club:* Savile.

See also Sir D. Forman.

FORMAN, Miloš; film director; *b* Čáslav, 18 Feb. 1932; *m* Martina; four *s*. *Educ:* Acad. of Music and Dramatic Art, Prague. Director: Film Presentations, Czechoslovak Television, 1954–56; Laterna Magika, Prague, 1958–62. Co-chm. and Prof., Film Div., Columbia Univ. Sch. of Arts, 1978–. Films directed include: Talent Competition; Peter and Pavla, 1963 (Czech. Film Critics' Award; Grand Prix, Locarno, 1964; Prize, Venice Festival, 1965); A Blonde in Love (Grand Prix, French Film Acad., 1966); The Fireman's Ball, 1967; Taking Off, 1971; (co-dir) Visions of Eight, 1973; One Flew Over the Cuckoo's Nest, 1975 (Academy Award, 1976; BAFTA Award, 1977); Hair, 1979; Ragtime, 1982; Amadeus, 1985 (Oscar Award, 1985); Valmont, 1988; The People vs Larry Flynt, 1996 (Golden Globe Award, 1997); Man on the Moon, 2000. *Publication:* Turnaround: a memoir, 1993. *Address:* c/o Robert Lantz, The Lantz Office, 888 Seventh Avenue, New York, NY 10106–0084, USA.

FORMAN, Nigel; *see* Forman, F. N.

FORMAN, Roy; Managing Director and Chief Executive, Private Patients Plan Ltd, 1985–94; *b* 28 Dec. 1931; *s* of Leslie and Ena Forman; *m* 1954, Mary (*née* Nelson); three *s* one *d*. *Educ:* Nunthorpe Grammar Sch., York; Nottingham Univ. (BA Hons). RAF, 1953–56. Business economist, 1956–61; electricity supply industry, 1961–80: Chief Commercial Officer, S Wales Elec. Bd, 1972–76; Commercial Adviser, Electricity Council, 1976–80; Private Patients Plan Ltd: Gen. Manager, Marketing and Sales, 1980–81; Marketing Dir, 1981–85; Man. Dir, Age Concern Enterprises Ltd, 1995–96; Director: General Healthcare Group PLC, 1994; Reliastar Reinsurance Group (UK) Ltd, 1997. FRSA 1992. *Recreations:* music, walking, reading. *Address:* The Beacon Cottage, Cripps Corner Road, Staplecross, East Sussex TN32 5QR.

FORMARTINE, Viscount; George Ian Alastair Gordon; *b* 4 May 1983; *s* and *heir* of Earl of Haddo, *qv*.

FORRES, 4th Baron *cr* 1922; **Alastair Stephen Grant Williamson,** Bt 1909; MARAC; Chairman, Agriscot Pty Ltd; Director, Jaga Trading Pty Ltd; *b* 16 May 1946; *s* of 3rd Baron Forres and of Gillian Ann Maclean, *d* of Major John Maclean Grant, RA; *S* father, 1978; *m* 1969, Margaret, *d* of late G. J. Mallam, Mullumbimby, NSW; two *s*. *Educ:* Eton. Alderman, Orange City Council, 1987–. Pres., Big Brother Movt, 1986–. Patron, Sydney Scottish Week, 1981–. *Heir:* *s* Hon. George Archibald Mallam Williamson, *b* 16 Aug. 1972. *Clubs:* Union, Australian Jockey, Sydney Turf (Sydney).

FORREST, Prof. Sir (Andrew) Patrick (McEwen), Kt 1986; Regius Professor of Clinical Surgery, University of Edinburgh, 1970–88, now Professor Emeritus; *b* 25 March 1923; *s* of Rev. Andrew James Forrest, BD, and Isabella Pearson; *m* 1955, Margaret Beryl Hall (*d* 1961); one *s* one *d*; *m* 1964, Margaret Anne Steward; one *d*. *Educ:* Dundee High Sch.; Univ. of St Andrews. BSc 1942; MB, ChB 1945; ChM hons, University Gold Medal, 1954; MD hons, Rutherford Gold Medal, 1958; FRCSE 1950; FRCS 1952; FRCSGlas 1962; FRSE 1976; FIBiol 1986; FRCPE 1999. Surg.-Lt RNVR, 1946–48. Mayo Foundation Fellow, 1952–53; Lectr and Sen. Lectr, Univ. of Glasgow, 1955–62; Prof. of Surgery, Welsh Nat. Sch. of Medicine, 1962–70. Hon. Consultant Surgeon: Royal Inf. of Edinburgh, until 1988; Royal Prince Alfred Hosp., Sydney; Civilian Consultant to RN, 1977–88. Chief Scientist (pt-time), SHHD, 1981–87. McIlrath Vis. Prof., Royal Prince Alfred Hosp., Sydney, 1969; Nimmo Vis. Prof., Royal Adelaide Hosp., 1973; McLauchlin-Gallie Prof., RCP of Canada, 1974; numerous other visiting professorships; Vis. Scientist, Nat. Cancer Inst., 1989–90; Associate Dean, Internat. Med. Coll., Kuala Lumpur, 1993–96. Eponymous lectures include: Lister Meml, Canadian Med. Assoc., 1970; Inaugural Bruce Wellesley Hosp., Toronto, 1970; Inaugural Peter Lowe, RCP Glas., 1980. Member: Medical sub-cttee, UGC, 1967–76; MRC, 1974–79; Scientific Adv. Cttee, Cancer Res. Campaign, 1974–83; ABRC, 1982–85. Asst Editor and Editor, Scottish Med. Jl, 1957–61; Hon. Secretary: Scottish Soc. for Experimental Medicine, 1959–62; Surgical Research Soc., 1963–66, Pres., 1974–76; Chairman: British Breast Gp, 1974–77; Working Gp on Breast Cancer Screening (reported, 1986); Scottish Cancer Foundn, 1998–. Member Council: Assoc. of Surgeons of GB and Ireland, 1971–74 (Pres., 1988–89); RCSE, 1976–84, 1986–89; Member: Internat. Surgical Gp, 1963–; James IV Assoc. of Surgeons Inc., 1981–; Scottish Hosp. Endowments Res. Trust, 1990–94. Hon. Fellow, Amer. Surgical Assoc., 1981; Hon. FACS 1978; Hon. FRACS 1987; Hon. FRCR 1988; Hon. FRCSCan 1989; Hon. FFPHM 2001. Hon. DSc: Wales, 1981; Chinese Univ. of Hong Kong, 1986; Hon. LLD Dundee, 1986. Lister Medal, RCS, 1987; Gold Medal, Netherlands Surgical Assoc., 1988; Gimbernat Prize, Catalan Soc. of Surg., 1996; Breast Cancer Award, European Inst. of Oncology, 2000. *Publications:* (ed jtly) Prognostic Factors in Breast Cancer, 1968; (jtly) Principles and Practice of Surgery, 1985; Breast Cancer: the decision to screen, 1991; various papers in surgical jls, mainly on gastro-intestinal disease and breast cancer. *Address:* 19 St Thomas Road, Edinburgh EH9 2LR. *T:* (0131) 667 3203, *Fax:* (0131) 662 1193.

FORREST, John Richard, DPhil; FREng; FIEE; Director, 3i Group plc, since 1997; *b* 21 April 1943; *s* of late John Samuel Forrest, FRS and Ivy May Olding; *m* 1973, Jane Patricia Robey Leech; two *s* one *d*. *Educ:* Sidney Sussex Coll., Cambridge (MA); Keble Coll., Oxford (DPhil). Research Associate and Lectr, Stanford Univ., Calif, 1967–70; Lectr, later Prof., Electronic and Elect. Engrg Dept, University Coll. London, 1970–84; Technical Dir, Marconi Defence Systems Ltd, 1984–86; Dir of Engrg, IBA, 1986–90; Chief Exec., 1990–94, Dep. Chm., 1994–96, National Transcommunications Ltd; Chairman: Brewton Group, 1994–99; Human IT Ltd, 2000–. Director: Egan Internat., 1994–; Drake Automation, 1996–99; Loughborough Sound Images, 1996–98; Screen, 1997–2000; Tricorder Technology, 1997–; Blue Wave Systems Inc., 1998– (Chm., 2000–); Globecast (Northern Europe) Ltd, 1998–2000; Printable Field Emitters Ltd, 1999–2000; Morgan Howard Internat. Gp Ltd, 1999–2000. Chm., UK Govt Spectrum Mgt Adv. Gp, 1998–; Member: UK Adv. Bd, Stanford Res. Inst. Internat., 1996–98; EC IT Rev. Bd, 1995–99; Steering Bd, Eur. Digital Video Broadcast Initiative, 1995–97. Sen. Vice-Pres., Royal Acad. of Engrg, 1999– (FEng 1985; Hon. Sec. for Electrical Engrg, and Mem. Council, 1995–97; Vice-Pres., 1997–99); Vice-President: IEE, 1992–95; RTS, 1994–97. Mem. Council, Brunel Univ., 1996–99. FRSA 1986; FRTS 1990; FInstD 1991. Hon. Fellow, BKSTS. Hon. DSc City, 1992; Hon. DTech Brunel, 1995. Chevalier de l'ordre des arts et des lettres, 1990. *Publications:* papers and contribs to books on phased array radar, satellite communications, broadcasting and optoelectronics. *Recreations:* travel, sailing, mountain walking, literature, study of mankind. *Address:* 15 Carlyle Court, Chelsea Harbour, SW10 0UQ. *T:* (020) 7376 5731, *Fax:* (020) 7351 3620; *e-mail:* johnforrest@compuserve.com.

FORREST, Prof. Sir Patrick; *see* Forrest, Prof. Sir A. P. M.

FORREST, Peter; Deputy Chairman, Dawson International plc, since 2000 (Director, since 1994); *b* 2 May 1938; *s* of Leonard and Dora Jane Forrest; *m* 1st, 1963, Joy Thornton (marr. diss. 1992); three *s*; 2nd, 1994, Evie Tindal; two step *s*. *Educ:* Batley Grammar Sch.; Dewsbury Technical Coll. ATI. Man. Dir, Dundee Textiles Ltd, 1975–80; Director: Courtaulds Northern Weaving Div., 1975–80; Legler Industria Tessile, Bergamo, Italy, 1980–91; Dawson International plc: Premier Fibres & Yarns Div., 1991–95; Man. Dir, Todd & Duncan Ltd, 1991–95; Man. Dir, 1995–98; Chief Exec., 1998–2000. *Recreations:* sailing, reading, classical music. *Address:* Whinfield House, Kinross, Tayside KY13 8AU. *Club:* Royal Highland Yacht.

FORREST, Rev. Canon Robin Whyte; Dean of Moray, Ross and Caithness, 1992–98; Canon of St Andrew's Cathedral, Inverness, 1986–98, now Hon. Canon; Rector of Forres, 1979–98; *b* 1933. *Educ:* Edinburgh Theol Coll., 1958. Ordained deacon, 1961, priest, 1962; Asst Curate, St Mary, Glasgow, 1961–66; Rector: Renfrew, 1966–70; Motherwell, 1970–79, with Wishaw, 1975–79; Nairn, 1979–92. Synod Clerk, Moray, 1991–92. *Address:* Landeck, Cummingston, Elgin, Moray IV30 5XY. *T:* (01343) 835539.

FORREST, Rear-Adm. Sir Ronald (Stephen), KCVO 1975; JP; DL; *b* 11 Jan. 1923; *s* of Stephen Forrest, MD, and Maud M. McKinstry; *m* 1st, 1947, Patricia (*d* 1966), *e d* of Dr and Mrs E. N. Russell; two *s* one *d*; 2nd, 1967, June (*née* Weaver), *widow* of Lieut G. Perks, RN; one step *s* one step *d*. *Educ:* Belhaven Hill; RNC, Dartmouth. War Service at Sea, Lieut 1943 (despatches 1944); Comdr 1955; CO HMS Teazer, 1956; on loan to Pakistan Navy, 1958–60; Captain 1963; jssc 1963; Chief Staff Officer to Adm. Comdg Reserves, 1964; comd Dartmouth Trng Sqdn, 1966; Dir, Seaman Officers Appointments, 1968; CO, HMS London, 1970; Rear-Adm. 1972; Defence Services Secretary, 1972–75. Chm. Council, Devon Co. Agricl Assoc., 1991–98 (Pres., 1990–91). County Comr, St John Amb. Bde, Devon, 1976–81, Comdr, 1981–87. Naval Gen. Service Medal, 1949. KStJ 1987 (CStJ 1983). JP Honiton, 1978; DL Devon, 1985. Chevalier, Ordre du Mérite Agricole (France), 1990. *Recreation:* gardening. *Address:* Higher Seavington, Stockland, near Honiton, Devon EX14 9DE. *Clubs:* Naval, Army and Navy.

FORREST, Surgeon Rear-Adm. (D) William Ivon Norman, CB 1970; Director of Naval Dental Services, Ministry of Defence, 1968–71; *b* 8 June 1914; *s* of late Eng. Lt James Forrest; *m* 1942, Mary Margaret McMordie Black (*d* 1996); three *s*. *Educ:* Christ's Hospital. Guy's Hospital, 1931–36. LDS, RCS. Dental House Surgeon, Guy's Hosp., 1936–37. Royal Navy: Surg. Lieut (D), 1937; Surg. Lt-Comdr (D), 1943; Surg. Comdr (D), 1950; Surg. Capt. (D), 1960; Surg. Rear-Adm. (D), 1968. Consultant in Dental Surgery, 1963. *Recreations:* gardening, photography, bewilderment. *Address:* 32 St Peters Court, Hylton Road, Petersfield, Hants GU32 3JH. *T:* (01730) 260041.

FORRESTER, David Michael; education and training consultant; Director, Further Education and Youth Training, Department for Education and Employment, 1995–2001; *b* 22 June 1944; *s* of late Reginald Grant Forrester and Minnie Forrester (*née* Chaytow); *m* 1st, 1978, Diana Douglas (marr. diss. 1983); 2nd, 1993, Helen Mary Williams, *qv*; one *s* one *d*. *Educ:* St Paul's Sch.; King's Coll., Cambridge (BA Hons 1st Cl. 1966, MA); Kennedy Sch. of Govt, Harvard Univ. (an inaugural Kennedy Scholar, 1966–67). DES, 1967; Private Sec. to Parly Under Sec., 1971–72; Principal, DES, 1972–76; HM Treasury, 1976–78; Asst Sec., DES, 1979–85; DTI, 1985–87; Under Sec., DES, subseq. DFE, then DFEE, 1988; Hd of Further Educn Br., 1994–95. FRSA 1999. *Recreations:* cricket, squash, music, esp. opera, mountain walking. *Address:* 340 Liverpool Road, N7 8PZ. *T:* (020) 7607 1492. *Club:* Pretenders'.

FORRESTER, Rev. Prof. Duncan Baillie; Professor of Theology and Public Issues, 2000–2001, Professor of Christian Ethics and Practical Theology, 1978–2000, and Dean, Faculty of Divinity, 1996–99, University of Edinburgh (Principal, New College, 1986–96); Director, Edinburgh University Centre for Theology and Public Issues, 1984–2000; *b* 10 Nov. 1933; *s* of Rev. Prof. William Forrester and Isobel McColl or Forrester; *m* 1964, Rev. Margaret R. McDonald or Forrester (Minister of St Michael's Parish Church, Edinburgh); one *s* one *d*. *Educ:* Madras Coll., St Andrews; Univ. of St Andrews (MA Hons Mod. Hist. and Pol. Sci.); Univ. of Chicago (Grad., Dept of Politics); Univ. of Edinburgh (BD); DPhil Sussex. Part-time Asst in Politics, Univ. of Edinburgh, 1957–58; Asst Minister, Hillside Church and Leader of St James Mission, 1960–61; Church of Scotland Missionary to S India, 1962, Lectr, then Prof. of Politics, Madras Christian Coll., Tambaram, 1962–70; ordained as Presbyter of Church of S India; part-time Lectr in Politics, Univ. of Edinburgh, 1966–67; Chaplain and Lectr in Politics and Religious Studies, Sch. of African and Asian Studies, Univ. of Sussex, 1970–78. Lectures: Lee, Edinburgh, 1980; Hensley Henson, Oxford, 1988; Bernard Gilpin, Durham, 1992; F. D. Maurice, KCL, 1995; Bishop Butler, Bristol, 1996; Richard Hooker, Exeter, 1999; Von Hügel, Cambridge, 2000; Ferguson, Manchester, 2002. Chm., Edinburgh Council of Social Service, 1983–87. President: Soc. for the Study of Theol., 1991–93; Soc. for the Study of Christian Ethics, 1991–94; Church Service Soc., 1999–2001. Member: Faith and Order Commn, WCC, 1983–96; Center of Theol Inquiry, Princeton, 1992–; Nuffield Council on Bioethics, 1996–. FRSA 2000; Hon. Fellow, Harris Manchester Coll., Oxford, 2001. Hon. DTheol Univ. of Iceland, 1997; Hon. DD: Glasgow, 1999; St Andrews, 2000. Templeton UK Award, 1999. *Publications:* chapters on Luther, Calvin and Hooker, in History of Political Philosophy, ed Strauss and Cropsey, 1963, 3rd edn 1986; Caste and Christianity, 1980; (with J. I. H. McDonald and G. Tellini) Encounter with God, 1983; (ed with D. Murray) Studies in the History of Worship in Scotland, 1984; Christianity and the Future of Welfare, 1985; (ed with D. Skene and co-author) Just Sharing, 1988; Theology and Politics, 1988; Beliefs, Values and Policies: conviction politics in a secular age, 1989; (ed jtly) Worship Now, Book 2, 1989; (ed) Theology and Practice, 1990; The True Church and Morality, 1997; Christian Justice and Public Policy, 1997; Truthful Action: explorations in practical theology, 2000; On Human Worth, 2001; articles on Indian politics and religion, ethics and political theology. *Recreations:* hill-walking, ornithology. *Address:* 25 Kingsburgh Road, Edinburgh EH12 6DZ. *T:* (0131) 337 5646.

FORRESTER, Giles Charles Fielding; His Honour Judge Forrester; a Circuit Judge, since 1986; *b* 18 Dec. 1939; *s* of Basil Thomas Charles Forrester and Diana Florence Forrester (*née* Sandeman); *m* 1966, Georgina Elizabeth Garnett; one *s* one *d*. *Educ:* Rugby School; Grenoble Univ.; Trinity College, Oxford (MA Jurisp.). Account Exec., Pritchard Wood and Partners (Advertising Agents), 1962–66. Called to the Bar, Inner Temple, 1966; practised, SE Circuit, 1966–86; a Recorder of the Crown Court, 1986. Mem., HAC Infantry Bn, 1963–67, Veteran Mem., 1994–; Pres., HAC RFC, 1994–98. Mem. Council, Magistrates' Assoc., 1998–. Freeman, City of London, 1997; Freedom, Weavers' Co., 1998. *Recreations:* a wide variety, mainly sporting. *Address:* c/o The Central Criminal Court, City of London, EC4M 7EH. *T:* (020) 7248 3277. *Clubs:* Roehampton; Royal Western Yacht; St Enedoc Golf; New Zealand Golf (Weybridge).

FORRESTER, Helen Mary; *see* Williams, H. M.

FORRESTER, Ian Stewart; QC (Scot.) 1988; *b* 13 Jan. 1945; *s* of late Alexander Roxburgh Forrester and Elizabeth Richardson Forrester (*née* Stewart); *m* 1981, Sandra Anne Therese Keegan, Louisiana lawyer; two *s*. *Educ:* Kelvinside Acad., Glasgow; Univ. of Glasgow (MA 1965; LLB 1967); Tulane Univ. of Louisiana (MCL 1969). Mem., British Univs debating team, 1966; Commonwealth expedn to India, 1967. Admitted Faculty of Advocates, Scots Bar, 1972; admitted Bar of State of NY, following order of NY Court of Appeals, 1977; admitted English Bar, Middle Temple, 1996. With Maclay, Murray & Spens, 1968–69; Davis Polk & Wardwell, 1969–72; Cleary Gottlieb Steen & Hamilton, 1972–81; estab. indep. chambers, Brussels, 1981; co-founder, Forrester & Norall, 1981 (Forrester Norall & Sutton, 1989; White & Case/Forrester Norall & Sutton, 1998), practising before European Commn and Courts. Chm., British Conservative Assoc., Belgium, 1982–86. Hon. Vis. Prof., European Law, Univ. of Glasgow, 1991–. Mem., European Adv. Bd, Tulane Univ., 1992–. Elder, St Andrew's Church of Scotland, Brussels, 1992–. *Publications:* numerous articles on EEC customs, dumping and trade law, competition law, German civil and commercial codes. *Recreations:* politics, wine, cooking, restoring old houses. *Address:* White & Case, 1 Place Madou, Box 34, 1210 Brussels, Belgium; Advocates' Library, Parliament House, Edinburgh EH1 1RF; Blackstone Chambers, Blackstone House, Temple, EC4Y 9BW. *Clubs:* Athenæum; International Château Ste-Anne (Brussels); Royal Yacht Club of Belgium.

FORRESTER, John Stuart; *b* 17 June 1924; *s* of Harry and Nellie Forrester; *m* 1945, Gertrude H. Weaver. *Educ:* Eastwood Council Sch.; City Sch. of Commerce, Stoke-on-Trent; Alsager Teachers' Training Coll. Teacher, 1946–66. MP (Lab) Stoke-on-Trent, N, 1966–87. Sec., Constituency Labour Party, 1961–84. Mem., Speaker's Panel of Chairmen, 1982–87; Member: NUT, 1949–87; APEX, 1942–43, 1946–49, 1984–. Councillor, Stoke-on-Trent, 1970–2000. Freedom of Stoke-on-Trent, 1992. *Address:* 13 Cadeby Grove, Milton, Stoke-on-Trent ST2 7BY.

FORRESTER, Prof. John Vincent, MD; FRCSE, FRCOphth, FRCSGlas; Cockburn Professor of Ophthalmology, University of Aberdeen, since 1984; *b* 11 Sept. 1946; *m* Anne Gray; two *s* two *d*. *Educ:* St Aloysius Coll., Glasgow; Glasgow Univ. (MD Hons). Various hosp. appts, Glasgow, 1971–78; MRC Travelling Fellow, Columbia Univ., NY, 1976–77; Consultant Ophthalmologist, Southern Gen. Hosp., Glasgow, 1979–83. Spinoza Prof., Univ. of Amsterdam, 1997. Ed., British Jl Ophthalmol., 1992–2000. *Recreation:* family. *Address:* Department of Ophthalmology, University of Aberdeen Medical School, Foresterhill, Aberdeen AB25 2ZD. *T:* (01224) 553782.

FORRESTER, Maj.-Gen. Michael, CB 1969; CBE 1963 (OBE 1960); DSO 1943 and Bar, 1944; MC 1939 and Bar, 1941; retired 1970; *b* 31 Aug. 1917; 2nd *s* of late James Forrester, formerly of Kirklinton, Cumbria and Elsie (*née* Mathwin), Chilworth, Hants; *m* 1947, Pauline Margaret Clara (marr. diss. 1960), *d* of late James Fisher, Crossmichael; two *s*. *Educ:* Haileybury. 2nd Lieut, SRO, Queen's Royal Regt, 1936, Regular Commn, 1938; served in Palestine (Arab Rebellion), 1938–39; served War of 1939–45 in Palestine, Egypt, Greece, Crete, Western Desert, Syria, N Africa, Italy and France; Intell. Officer, GHQ Cairo, 1940; GSO3 (Ops) British Military Mission, Greece, 1940–41; GSO3 (Ops), HQ Western Desert Force and HQ 13 Corps, 1941–42; Staff Coll., Haifa, 1942; Bde Major, 132 Inf. Bde, 1942 (despatches); GSO2 (Ops), HQ 13 Corps and HQ 18 Army Gp, 1943; Comdr, 1st/6th Bn, Queen's Royal Regt, 1943–44; wounded, Normandy; GSO1 (Ops), HQ 13 Corps, 1945–46; Mil. Asst to Supreme Allied Comdr Mediterranean, 1947; Mil. Asst to Comdr Brit. Army Staff and Army Mem., Brit. Jt Services Mission, Washington, DC, 1947–50; Co. Comdr, 2nd Bn Parachute Regt, Cyprus and Canal Zone, 1951–52; Dirg Staff, Staff Coll., Camberley, 1953–55; GSO1 (Ops), GHQ East Africa, 1955–57; transf. to Parachute Regt, 1957; Comdr, 3rd Bn Parachute Regt, 1957–60 (incl. Jordan, 1958); Col, Military Operations (4), War Office, 1960–61; Comdr, 16 Parachute Bde Gp, 1961–63; Imp. Def. Coll., 1964; GOC 4th Div., BAOR, 1965–67; Dir of Infantry, MoD, 1968–70. Col Comdt, The Queen's Division, 1968–70. Lay Co-Chm., Alton Deanery Synod, 1984–88; Mem., Winchester Diocesan Synod, 1988–91. Vice-Pres., UK Crete Veterans' Assoc., 1993–. Hon. Citizen, Canea, Crete, 1966. *Address:* Hammonds, West Worldham, near Alton, Hants GU34 3BH. *T:* (01420) 84470.

FORRESTER, Prof. Peter Garnett, CBE 1981; Professor Emeritus, Cranfield Institute of Technology; *b* 7 June 1917; *s* of Arthur Forrester and Emma (*née* Garnett); *m* 1942, Marjorie Hewitt (*d* 2000), Berks; two *d*. *Educ:* Manchester Grammar Sch.; Manchester Univ. (BSc, MSc). Metallurgist, Thomas Bolton & Son Ltd, 1938–40; Research Officer, later Chief Metallurgist, Tin Research Inst., 1940–48; Chief Metallurgist and Research Man., Glacier Metal Co. Ltd, 1948–63; Dep. Principal, Glacier Inst. of Management, 1963–64; Consultant, John Tyzack & Partners, 1964–66; Prof. of Industrial Management, Coll. of Aeronautics, Cranfield, 1966; Dir, Cranfield Sch. of Management, 1967–82, Dean of Faculty, 1972; Pro-Vice-Chancellor, Cranfield Inst. of Technol., 1976–82. Chm., Conf. of Univ. Management Schs, 1976–77. Chm., Rye and Winchelsea Centre, Nat. Trust, 1991–93. Mem., Bd of Trustees, European Foundation for Management Develt, 1976–82. CIMgt. Hon. DSc Cranfield Inst. of Technol., 1983. Burnham Medal, BIM, 1979. *Publications:* The British MBA, 1986; papers and reports on management educn; numerous scientific and technological papers on metallurgy, bearing materials, tribology. *Recreations:* sailing, walking. *Address:* Strawberry Hole Cottage, Ewhurst Lane, Northiam, near Rye, Sussex TN31 6HJ. *T:* (01797) 252255.

FORRESTER-PATON, His Honour Douglas Shaw; QC 1965; a Circuit Judge (formerly a Judge of County Courts), 1970–86; *b* 1921; 3rd *s* of late Alexander Forrester-Paton, JP; *m* 1948, Agnete, *d* of Holger Tuxen; one *s* two *d*. *Educ:* Gresham's Sch., Holt; Queen's Coll., Oxford (BA). Called to Bar, Middle Temple, 1947; North East Circuit. Served RAF, 1941–45. Recorder: Middlesbrough, 1963–68; Teesside, 1968–70. *Address:* 11 The Dorkings, Great Broughton, Middlesbrough TS9 7NA. *T:* (01642) 712301; 5 King's Bench Walk, Temple, EC4Y 7DB.

FORSTER, Charles Ian Kennerley, CBE 1964; Under-Secretary, Department of Trade and Industry, 1970–72, retired; *b* 18 July 1911; *s* of Douglas Wakefield Forster; *m* 1942, Thelma Primrose Horton (marr. diss. 1974); one *s* one *d*; *m* 1975, Mrs Loraine Huxtable. *Educ:* Rossall Sch. FIA 1936. With Sun Life Assurance Soc., 1928–39, and 1946. Served RA, 1939–45. Statistics Branch, Admty, 1946–54; Ministry of Power, 1954 (Chief Statistician, 1955–65, Dir of Statistics, 1965–69); Min. of Technology, 1969. Energy consultant to NCB, 1972–81, retd. *Publications:* contribs to Jls of Inst. of Actuaries and Inst. of Actuaries Students Soc., Trans VII World Power Conf., Trans Manchester Statistical Soc., Statistical News. *Recreations:* bridge, stamps. *Address:* 140 Watchfield Court, Chiswick, W4 4NE. *T:* (020) 8994 3128.

FORSTER, David Oakley A.; *see* Arnold-Forster.

FORSTER, Donald, CBE 1988; Managing Director, 1945–81, and Chairman, 1981–86, B. Forster & Co. Ltd, Leigh (textile manufacturing company); *b* 18 Dec. 1920; *s* of Bernard and Rose Forster; *m* 1942, Muriel Steinman; one *s* two *d*. *Educ:* N Manchester Grammar School. Served War, RAF pilot (Flt Lieut), 1940–45. Mem., Skelmersdale Develt Corp., 1980–82; Chairman: Warrington/Runcorn Develt Corp., 1982–86; Merseyside Develt Corp., 1984–87. *Recreations:* golf, music, paintings. *Address:* The Dingle, South Downs Drive, Hale, Cheshire WA14 3HR. *T:* (0161) 926 9145. *Clubs:* Whitefield Golf, Dunham Forest Country, Coombe Hill Golf; The Lakes (USA).
See also L. C. Goldstone.

FORSTER, Margaret; author; *b* 25 May 1938; *d* of Arthur Gordon Forster and Lilian (*née* Hind); *m* 1960, Edward Hunter Davies, *qv*; one *s* two *d*. *Educ:* Carlisle and County High Sch. for Girls; Somerville Coll., Oxford (BA). FRSL. Teacher, Barnsbury Girls' Sch., Islington, 1961–63. Member: BBC Adv. Cttee on Social Effects of Television, 1975–77; Arts Council Literary Panel, 1978–81. Chief non-fiction reviewer, Evening Standard, 1977–80. *Publications: non-fiction:* The Rash Adventurer: the rise and fall of Charles Edward Stuart, 1973; William Makepeace Thackeray: memoirs of a Victorian gentleman, 1978; Significant Sisters: grassroots of active feminism 1839–1939, 1984; Elizabeth Barrett Browning: a biography, 1988; (ed, introd. and prefaces) Elizabeth Barrett Browning: selected poems, 1988; Daphne du Maurier, 1993; Hidden Lives (memoir), 1995; Rich Desserts and Captains Thin: a family and their times 1831–1931, 1997; Precious Lives, 1998; Good Wives? Mary, Fanny, Jennie and Me, 1845–2001, 2001; *novels:* Dame's Delight, 1964; Georgy Girl, 1965 (filmscript with Peter Nichols, 1966); The Bogeyman, 1965; The Travels of Maudie Tipstaff, 1967; The Park, 1968; Miss Owen-Owen is At Home, 1969; Fenella Phizackerley, 1970; Mr Bone's Retreat, 1971; The Seduction of Mrs Pendlebury, 1974; Mother, can you hear me?, 1979; The Bride of Lowther Fell, 1980; Marital Rites, 1981; Private Papers, 1986; Have the Men Had Enough?, 1989; Lady's Maid, 1990; The Battle for Christabel, 1991; Mothers' Boys, 1994; Shadow Baby, 1996; The Memory Box, 1999. *Recreations:* walking on Hampstead Heath, reading contemporary fiction. *Address:* 11 Boscastle Road, NW5 1EE. *T:* (020) 7485 3785; Grasmoor House, Loweswater, near Cockermouth, Cumbria CA13 0RU. *T:* (01900) 85303.

FORSTER, Neil Milward; Chairman: Air UK Ltd, 1982–90; Air UK Group Ltd, 1990–97; *b* 29 May 1927; *s* of Norman Milward Forster and Olive Christina Forster (*née* Cockrell); *m* 1954, Barbara Elizabeth Smith; one *s* two *d*. *Educ:* Hurstpierpoint College, Sussex; Pembroke College, Cambridge. BA Law and Economics; Fellow Inst. of Transport. Joined Clan Line Steamers, 1952; Chm., Calcutta Liners Conf., 1962–66; Director: Clan Line, 1967; Group and Associated cos, British & Commonwealth Shipping Co., 1974–78; British and Commonwealth Hldgs PLC, 1974–88 (Gp Man. Dir, 1982–86); S African Marine Corp., 1977–99; KLM UK, 1997–99. Chairman: Europe/SA Shipping Confs, 1977–87; UK S Africa Trade Assoc., 1985–87. Rep. England and GB at hockey, 1951–58. *Recreations:* golf, gardening. *Address:* The Orchard, Upper Slaughter, Cheltenham, Glos GL54 2JB. *T:* (01451) 822025. *Clubs:* Oriental, MCC.

FORSTER, Rt Rev. Peter Robert; *see* Chester, Bishop of.

FORSYTE, Charles; *see* Philo, G. C. G.

FORSYTH, family name of **Baron Forsyth of Drumlean.**

FORSYTH OF DRUMLEAN, Baron *cr* 1999 (Life Peer), of Drumlean in Stirling; **Michael Bruce Forsyth,** Kt 1997; PC 1995; Vice Chairman, Investment Banking Europe, JP Morgan, since 1999; *b* 16 Oct. 1954; *s* of John T. Forsyth and Mary Watson; *m* 1977, Susan Jane Clough; one *s* two *d*. *Educ:* Arbroath High School; St Andrews University (MA). Pres., St Andrews Univ. Cons. Assoc., 1972–75; Nat. Chm., Fedn of Cons. Students, 1976–77. Dir, Flemings, 1997–99. MP (C) Stirling, 1983–97; contested (C) same seat, 1997. PPS to Sec. of State for Foreign and Commonwealth Affairs, 1986–87; Parly Under-Sec. of State, 1987–90, Minister of State, 1990–92, Scottish Office; Minister of State: Dept of Employment, 1992–94; Home Office, 1994–95; Sec. of State for Scotland and Lord Keeper of the Great Seal of Scotland, 1995–97. Chm., Scottish Cons. Party, 1989–90. Mem., Westminster City Council, 1978–83. Mem. Develt Bd, Nat. Portrait Gall., 1999–. *Recreations:* photography, gardening, mountaineering, ski-ing, amateur astronomy. *Address:* House of Lords, SW1A 0PW.

FORSYTH OF THAT ILK, Alistair Charles William; JP; FSCA, FSAScot; FInstPet; Baron of Ethie; Chief of the Name and Clan of Forsyth; *b* 7 Dec. 1929; *s* of Charles Forsyth of Strathendry, FCA, and Ella Millicent Hopkins; *m* 1958, Ann, OStJ, *d* of Col P. A. Hughes, IA; four *s*. *Educ:* St Paul's Sch.; Queen Mary Coll., London. FInstPet 1973; FSCA 1976; FSAScot 1979. National Service, 2nd Lieut The Queen's Bays, 1948–50; Lieut The Parachute Regt, TA, 1950–54. Chm., Hargreaves Reiss & Quinn Ltd, 1981–99. Mem., Standing Council of Scottish Chiefs, 1978–. Freeman, City of London, 1993; Liveryman, Scriveners' Co., 1993–. CStJ 1982 (OStJ 1974). JP NSW, 1965; JP Angus, 1987. KHS 1992. *Club:* New (Edinburgh).

FORSYTH, Bill; film director and script writer; *b* Glasgow, 1947; one *s* one *d*. *Educ:* National Film School. *Films directed:* That Sinking Feeling, 1980; Gregory's Girl, 1981; Local Hero, 1983; Comfort and Joy, 1984; Housekeeping, 1988; Breaking In, 1990; Being Human, 1993; Gregory's Two Girls, 1999. TV film, Andrina, 1981. BAFTA Award: best screenplay, 1982; best dir, 1983. Hon. DLitt Glasgow, 1984; DUniv Stirling, 1989. *Address:* c/o A. D. Peters, The Chambers, Chelsea Harbour, SW10 0XF.

FORSYTH, Bruce; *see* Forsyth-Johnson, B. J.

FORSYTH, Frederick, CBE 1997; author; *b* 25 Aug. 1938; *m* 1st, 1973, Carole Cunningham; two *s*; 2nd, 1994, Sandy Molloy. *Educ:* Tonbridge Sch. RAF, 1956–58. Reporter, Eastern Daily Press, Norfolk, 1958–61; joined Reuters, 1961: Reporter, Paris, 1962–63; Chief of Bureau, E Berlin, 1963–64; joined BBC, 1965; radio and TV reporter, 1965–66; Asst Diplomatic Correspondent, BBC TV, 1967–68; freelance journalist, Nigeria and Biafra, 1968–69. *Publications: non fiction:* The Biafra Story, 1969, 2nd edn 1977; *fiction:* The Day of the Jackal, 1971 (filmed, 1973); The Odessa File, 1972 (filmed, 1975); The Dogs of War, 1974 (filmed, 1981); The Shepherd, 1975; The Devil's Alternative, 1979; No Comebacks (short stories), 1982; Emeka, 1982; The Fourth Protocol, 1984 (filmed, 1987); The Negotiator, 1988; The Deceiver, 1991; (ed) Great Flying Stories, 1991; The Fist of God, 1993; Icon, 1996; The Phantom of Manhattan, 1999; The Veteran and Other Stories, 2001. *Address:* c/o Bantam Books, 62/63 Uxbridge Road, W5 5SA.

FORSYTH, Jennifer Mary; Under-Secretary, HM Treasury and Department of Transport, 1975–83, retired; Councillor (Lab) Kensington and Chelsea, 1986–98 (Dep. Mayor, 1997–98); *b* 7 Oct. 1924; *o d* of late Matthew Forsyth, theatrical director, and late Marjorie Forsyth. *Educ:* Frensham Heights; London Sch. of Economics and Political Science (Pres. of Students' Union, 1944–45) (BScEcon). Joined Home Finance Div., HM Treasury, 1945; UN Economic Commn for Europe, 1949–51; Information Div., HM Treasury, 1951–53; Principal, Estabts, Overseas Finance and Planning Divs, 1954–62; UK Treasury Delegn, Washington, 1962–64; Assistant Secretary: DEA, 1965–69; Social Services Div., HM Treasury, 1969–75; Under Secretary: Home, Transport and Education Gp, HM Treasury, 1975–80; Dept of Transport (Roads), 1980–83. Governor: Frensham Heights, 1965–76; Thomas Jones Primary Sch., 1990–2001. *Recreations:* going to the theatre and to the Mediterranean. *Address:* Flat 4, One Ladbroke Square, W11 3LX.

FORSYTH, Prof. Murray Greensmith, FRHistS; Professor of Politics, University of Leicester, 1990–94, now Emeritus; *b* 30 Oct. 1936; *s* of Maj. Henry Russell Forsyth and Marie Elaine Forsyth; *m* 1964, Marie Denise Edelin de la Praudière; one *s* two *d*. *Educ:* Wellington Coll.; Balliol Coll., Oxford (BA Mod. Hist. 1959; MA 1964); College of Europe, Bruges. FRHistS 1991. Research Officer, Political and Econ. Planning, London, 1960–64; University of Leicester: Lectr in Politics, 1964–70; Reader in Internat. Politics, 1971–90; Dir, Centre for Federal Studies, 1988–94; Prof. of Govt and Pol Sci., Hong Kong Baptist Univ., 1995–97. British Acad. Wolfson Fellow, Paris, 1977; Bradlow Fellow, S African Inst. of Internat. Affairs, 1983; Vis. Prof., Coll. of Europe, Bruges, 1993–94; Robert Schuman Vis. Prof., Fudan Univ., Shanghai, 1998. Pres., European Consortium for Regl and Federal Studies, 1993–94. *Publications:* The Parliament of the European Communities, 1964; (jtly) Economic Planning and Policies in Britain, France and Germany, 1968; (ed jtly) The Theory of International Relations, 1970; Unions of States: the theory and practice of confederation, 1981; Reason and Revolution: the political theory of the Abbé Sieyes, 1987; (ed jtly) The Political Classics: Plato to Rousseau, 1988; (ed) Federalism and Nationalism, 1989; (trans.) The Spirit of the Revolution of 1789, 1989; (ed jtly) The Political Classics: Hamilton to Mill, 1993, Green to Dworkin, 1996. *Recreations:* collecting prints and watercolours, browsing in second-hand bookshops. *Address:* Blackmore House, Blackmore Park Road, Malvern, Worcs WR14 3LF. *T:* (01684) 560901. *Club:* Travellers.

FORSYTH-JOHNSON, Bruce Joseph, (Bruce Forsyth), OBE 1998; entertainer and comedian; *b* 22 Feb. 1928; *m* 1st, 1953, Penny Calvert; three *d*; 2nd, 1973, Anthea Redfern (marr. diss. 1982); two *d*; 3rd, 1983, Wilnelia Merced; one *s*. *Educ:* Higher Latimer Sch., Edmonton. Started stage career as Boy Bruce—The Mighty Atom, 1942; after the war, appeared in various double acts and did a 2 yr spell at Windmill Theatre; first television appearance, Music Hall, 1954; resident compère, Sunday Night at the London Palladium, 1958–60; own revue, London Palladium, 1962; leading role, Little Me, Cambridge Theatre, 1964; début at Talk of the Town (played there 7 times); compèred Royal Variety Show, 1971, and on subseq. occasions; London Palladium Show, 1973 (also Ottawa and Toronto) and 1980; commenced Generation Game, BBC TV series, 1971 (completed 7 series), and 1990–95; compèred Royal Windsor to mark BBC Jubilee Celebrations, 1977; One Man Show, Theatre Royal, Windsor, and Lakeside, 1977; Bruce Forsyth's Big Night, ITV, 1978; Play Your Cards Right, ITV, 1980–87, 1994–2000; Slinger's Day, ITV, 1986, 1987; You Bet!, 1988; Takeover Bid, BBC, 1990–91; Bruce's Guest Night, BBC, 1992–93; Bruce's Price is Right, 1996–2000. Films include: Star; Can Hieronymous Merkin Ever Forget Mercy Humppe and Find True Happiness?; Bedknobs and Broomsticks; The Magnificent 7 Deadly Sins; Pavlova. Numerous records. Show Business Personality of the Year, Variety Club of GB, 1975; TV Personality of the Year, Sun Newspaper, 1976 and 1977; Male TV Personality of the Year, TV Times, 1975, 1976, 1977 and 1978; Favourite Game Show Host, TV Times, 1984; BBC TV Personality of the Year, 1991. *Publication:* Bruce: the autobiography, 2001. *Recreation:* golf (handicap 10, Wentworth Golf Club). *Address:* Straidarran, Wentworth Drive, Virginia Water, Surrey GU25 4NY. *Clubs:* White Elephant, Crockfords, Empress, Tramp.

FORSYTHE, Air Cdre James Roy, (Paddy), CBE 1966; DFC; Director of Development, 1976–81, Joint Chief Executive, 1981–86, Look Ahead Housing Association Ltd; *b* 10 July 1920; *s* of W. R. and A. M. Forsythe; *m* 1st, 1946, Barbara Mary Churchman (*d* 1983); two *s* two *d*; 2nd, 1989, Mrs W. P. Newbery. *Educ:* Methodist Coll., Belfast; Queen's Univ., Belfast. Bomber Comd, 1944–45; OC, Aberdeen Univ. Air Sqdn, 1952–54; psa 1955; Principal Staff Officer to Dir-Gen. Orgn (RAF), 1956–58; OC, 16 Sqdn, 1958–60; Directing Staff, Coll. of Air Warfare, Manby, 1960–62; Head of RAF Aid Mission to India, 1963; Stn Comdr, RAF Acklington, 1963–65; Dep. Dir Air Staff Policy, MoD, 1965–68; Dir Public Relations, Far East, 1968–70; Dir Recruiting, RAF, 1971–73; Dir, Public Relations, RAF, 1973–75. Chm., RAF RU, 1972, 1973, 1974; Chm., Combined Services RU, 1974; Vice-Pres., 1979, Chm., 1988–90, Pres., 1990–92, London Irish RFC. Chm., League of Friends, Royal Brompton Hosp., 1992–98. MIPR. *Recreations:* Rugby, golf. *Address:* 104 Earls Court Road, W8 6EG. *T:* (020) 7937 5291. *Club:* Royal Air Force.

FORSYTHE, Dr (John) Malcolm; Chairman, South West Kent Primary Care Trust (formerly Tunbridge Wells Primary Care Group), since 1998; *b* 11 July 1936; *s* of late Dr John Walter Joseph Forsythe and Dr Charlotte Constance Forsythe (*née* Beatty); *m* 1961, Delia Kathleen Moore (marr. diss. 1984); one *s* three *d*; *m* 1985, Patricia Mary Barnes. *Educ:* Repton Sch., Derby; Guy's Hosp. Med. Sch., London Univ. BSc(Hons), MB, BS, MSc; DObstRCOG, FRCP; FFPHM. Area Medical Officer, Kent AHA, 1974–78; SE Thames Regional Health Authority: Dir of Planning, 1985–89; Regl MO, 1978–92; Regl Dir of Public Health and Service Develt, 1989–92; Professorial Fellow in Public Health, Kent Univ., 1992–2001; Sen. Lectr, King's Coll. Sch. of Medicine and Dentistry, 1992–2001. Hon. Consultant, Univ. of Kent Health Services Res. Unit, 1977–92. Vis. Prof., Univ. of N Carolina, Chapel Hill, 1973, 1976, 1993; Adjunct Prof., Univ. of St Georges, Grenada, 1995–; Jack Masur Fellow, Amer. Hosp. Assoc., 1976. Head, UK Deleg., Hospital Cttee, EEC, 1980–85, 1989–90; Consultant, Urwick Orr Ltd; Chm., GMC Wkg Pty on Performance Assessment in Public Health Medicine, 1995–97; Member: Resource Allocation Wkg Pty and Adv. Gp on Resource Allocation, 1975–78; Technical Sub Gp, Review of Resource Allocation Working Party Formula, 1986–87; DHSS Med. Manpower Planning Review, 1986–88; NHS Computer Policy Cttee, 1981–85; Standing Med. Adv. Cttee to Sec. of State, 1982–86; PHLS Bd, 1986–95; Central Council for Postgrad. Med. Educn, 1986–88; Health Services Res. Cttee, MRC, 1988–91; Bd of Governors, UMDS of Guy's and St Thomas', 1982–92; Delegacy, King's Coll. Hosp. Med. and Dental Schs, 1978–95. External Examiner to Univ. of London, 1987–89. Member: Bd of Management, Horder Centre for Arthritis, Crowborough, 1992– (Chm., 1996–2000); Tech. Bd, BUPA Ltd, 1992–. Trustee, Sick Doctors Trust, 1996–. Vice-Pres., Epidemiology Sect., RSM, 2001– (Pres., 1998–2000). Mem., Hyde Housing Assoc., 1999–. Silver Core Award, IFIP, 1977. *Publications:* (ed jtly) Information Processing of Medical Records, 1969; Proceedings of First World Conference on Medical Informatics, 1975. *Recreations:* tennis, music, ornithology. *Address:* Buckingham House, 1 royal Chase, Tunbridge Wells, Kent TN4 8AX. *T:* (01892) 522359; South West Kent Primary Care Trust, Allen Gardiner Cottage, Pembury Road, Tunbridge Wells, Kent TN2 3QQ. *T:* (01892) 616351. *Clubs:* Royal Society of Medicine; Chasers.

FORSYTHE, Air Cdre Paddy; *see* Forsythe, Air Cdre J. R.

FORSYTHE, William; choreographer; Director: Frankfurt Ballet, since 1984; Theater am Turm, since 1999 (Artistic Director, 1996–99); *b* NYC, 1949; *m*; one *s* one *d*. *Educ:* Jacksonville Univ., Florida; Joffrey Ballet Sch., NY. Joined Stuttgart Ballet as dancer, 1973, subseq. choreographer. *Works choreographed* include: Urlicht, 1976; Flore Subsimplici, 1978; Orpheus, 1979; Gänge, 1983; Artifact, 1984; Steptext, 1985; Impressing the Czar, 1988; Limb's Theorem, 1991; The Loss of Small Detail, 1991; Herman Schmerman, 1992; Firstext, 1995; Eidos: Telos, 1995; In The Middle, Somewhat Elevated, 1987; The The, 1998; Work within Work, 1998; Quartette, 1998; Woundwork, 1999; Endless House, 1999; Die Befragung des Robert Scott, 2000; Kammer Kammer, 2000; works performed by NYC Ballet, San Francisco Ballet, Nat. Ballet of Canada, Royal Ballet, Royal Swedish Ballet, etc. *Address:* Ballett Frankfurt, Untermainanlage 11, 60311 Frankfurt am Main, Germany.

FORT, Mrs Jean; Headmistress of Roedean School, Brighton, 1961–70; *b* 1915; *d* of G. B. Rae; *m* 1943, Richard Fort (*d* 1959), MP Clitheroe Division of Lancs; four *s* one *d*. *Educ:* Benenden Sch.; Lady Margaret Hall, Oxford (MA, DipEd). Asst Mistress, Dartford County Sch. for Girls, 1937–39; WVS Headquarters staff, 1939–40; Junior Civil Asst, War Office, 1940–41; Personal Asst to Sir Ernest Gowers, Sen. Regional Comr for Civil Def., London, 1941–44. *Address:* 6 King's Close, Henley-on-Thames, Oxon RG9 2DS.

FORT, Dame Maeve (Geraldine), DCMG 1998 (CMG 1990); DCVO 1999; HM Diplomatic Service, retired; High Commissioner, South Africa, 1996–2000; *b* 19 Nov. 1940; *d* of late F. L. Fort. *Educ:* Trinity College, Dublin (MA); Sorbonne, Paris. Joined Foreign Service, 1963; UKMIS, NY, 1964; CRO, 1965; seconded to SEATO, Bangkok, 1966; Bonn, 1968; Lagos, 1971; Second, later First Sec., FCO, 1973; UKMIS, NY, 1978; Counsellor, FCO, 1982; RCDS, 1983; Counsellor, Hd of Chancery and Consul-Gen., Santiago, 1984–86; Head of W African Dept, FCO, 1986–89, and Ambassador (non-resident) to Chad, 1987–89; Ambassador to: Mozambique, 1989–92; Lebanese Republic, 1992–96. *Address:* c/o Foreign and Commonwealth Office, King Charles Street, SW1A 2AH.

FORTE, family name of **Baron Forte.**

FORTE, Baron *cr* 1982 (Life Peer), of Ripley in the county of Surrey; **Charles Forte,** Kt 1970; FRSA; President, Forte (formerly Trusthouse Forte) PLC, 1992–96 (Chairman, 1982–92, Executive Chairman, 1978–81; Deputy Chairman, 1970–78, and Chief Executive, 1971–78); *b* 26 Nov. 1908; *m* 1943, Irene Mary Chierico; one *s* five *d*. *Educ:* Alloa Academy; Dumfries Coll.; Mamiani, Rome. Fellow and Mem. Exec. Cttee, Catering Inst., 1949; Member: Small Consultative Advisory Cttee to Min. of Food, 1946; London Tourist Board. Hon. Consul Gen. for Republic of San Marino. FIMgt (FBIM 1971). Grand Officier, Ordine al Merito della Repubblica Italiana; Cavaliere di Gran Croce della Repubblica Italiana; Cavaliere del Lavoro (Italy). *Publications:* Forte (autobiog.), 1986; articles for catering trade papers. *Recreations:* golf, fishing, shooting, fencing, music. *Address:* c/o House of Lords, SW1A 0PW. *Clubs:* Carlton, Caledonian.
See also Hon. Sir R. J. V. Forte, Hon. O. Polizzi.

FORTE, Hon. Sir Rocco (John Vincent), Kt 1995; FCA; Chairman, RF Hotels Ltd, since 1996; *b* 18 Jan. 1945; *s* of Lord Forte, *qv*; *m* 1986, Aliai, *d* of Prof. Giovanni Ricci, Rome; one *s* two *d*. *Educ:* Downside Coll.; Pembroke Coll., Oxford (MA). Trusthouse

Forte, subseq. Forte: Dir of Personnel, 1973–78; Dep. Chief Exec., 1978–82; Jt Chief Exec., 1982–83; Chief Exec., 1983–92; Chm., 1992–96. Pres., BHA. Dir, BTA, 1986–97. *Address:* (office) Savannah House, 11 Charles II Street, SW1Y 4QU.

See also Hon. Olga Polizzi.

FORTESCUE, family name of **Earl Fortescue**.

FORTESCUE, 8th Earl *cr* 1789; **Charles Hugh Richard Fortescue;** Baron Fortescue, 1746; Viscount Ebrington, 1789; *b* 10 May 1951; *s* of 7th Earl and his 1st wife, Penelope Jane (*d* 1959), *d* of Robert Evelyn Henderson; *S* father, 1993; *m* 1974, Julia, *er d* of Air Commodore J. A. Sowrey; three *d. Heir: uncle* Hon. Martin Denzil Fortescue [*b* 5 Jan. 1924; *m* 1954, Prudence Louisa (*d* 1992), *d* of Sir Charles Samuel Rowley, 6th Bt, TD; two *s* two *d*; *m* 1994, Mrs Caroline Loftie].

FORTESCUE, (John) Adrian, LVO 1972; Director General, Justice and Home Affairs, European Commission, since 1999; *b* 16 June 1941; *s* of T. V. N. Fortescue, *qv*; *m* 1st, 1978, Jillian Sarah Montague-Evans (marr. diss. 1987); one *s*; 2nd, 1989, Marie Wolfcarius. HM Diplomatic Service, 1964–94: MECAS, 1964; served Amman, FCO and Paris, 1966–72; on loan to EC, 1973–75; FCO, 1976–79; Washington, 1979–81; Head of Presidency Unit, ECD, FCO, 1981–82; Counsellor, Budapest, 1983–84; on loan to Commn of Eur. Communities, 1985–94 (Chef de Cabinet to Lord Cockfield, Vice-Pres., 1985–88); Dep. Dir Gen., Secretariat Gen., EC, 1994–99. *Address:* 44 Avenue Beau-Séjour, 1180 Brussels, Belgium.

FORTESCUE, Hon. Seymour Henry; Chief Executive, Banking Code Standards Board, since 1999; *b* 28 May 1942; *s* of 6th Earl Fortescue, MC, TD and late Sybil, *d* of 3rd Viscount Hardinge, CB; *m* 1st, 1966, Julia Mary Blair Pilcher (marr. diss. 1990); one *s* one *d*; 2nd, 1990, Jennifer Ann Simon; one *d. Educ:* Eton Coll.; Trinity Coll., Cambridge (MA); London Business Sch. (MSc). With Barclays Bank plc, 1964–91: Local Dir, Luton, 1972–77; Hd, Mktg, 1977–80; Chief Exec., Barclaycard, 1980–85; Dir, UK Personal Sector, 1986–91; Dir, Voluntary Income, ICRF, 1991–96; Chief Exec., HEA, 1996–99. Hon. Treas., LEPRA, 1985–96; Chm., Educnl Low-Priced Sponsored Texts, 2001–. Governor, Oundle Sch., 1999–. Mem., Court of Assistants, Grocers' Co., 1987– (Master, 1997–98). *Recreations:* gardening, travel, opera, country activities. *Address:* 22 Clarendon Street, SW1V 4RF. *T:* (020) 7834 2146; The Old School House, Denchworth, Wantage, Oxon OX12 0DX. *T:* (01235) 868592.

FORTESCUE, Trevor Victor Norman, (Tim), CBE 1984; Secretary-General, Food and Drink Industries Council, 1973–83; *b* 28 Aug. 1916; *s* of Frank Fortescue; *m* 1st, 1939, Margery Stratford (marr. diss. 1975), *d* of Dr G. H. Hunt; two *s* one *d*; 2nd, 1975, Anthea Maureen, *d* of Robert M. Higgins. *Educ:* Uppingham Sch.; King's Coll., Cambridge. BA 1938; MA 1945. Colonial Administrative Service, Hong Kong, 1939–47 and Kenya, 1949–51 (interned by Japanese, 1941–45); FAO, UN, Washington, DC, 1947–49 and Rome, 1951–54; Chief Marketing Officer, Milk Marketing Bd of England and Wales, 1954–59; Manager, Nestlé Gp of Cos, Vevey, Switz., 1959–63 and London, 1963–66. MP (C) Liverpool, Garston, 1966–Feb. 1974; an Asst Govt Whip, 1970–71; a Lord Comr of HM Treasury, 1971–73. Chairman: Conference Associates Ltd, 1978–87; Standing Cttee, Confedn of Food and Drink Industries of European Community (CIAA), 1982–84; Pres., British Food Manufg Industries Res. Assoc., 1984–92; Member: Meat Promotion Rev. Body, 1984; Council, British Industrial Biol. Res. Assoc., 1980–83. Develt Manager (with A. M. Fortescue), Winchester Cathedral, 1989–90; Dir, Winchester Cathedral Enterprises Ltd, 1990–2000. Trustee, Uppingham Sch., 1957–63; Patron and Trustee, The Quest Community, Birmingham, 1971–85. *Publications:* Lovelines, 1987; Lovelines from Winchester, 1996. *Recreation:* marriage to Anthea. *Address:* Waynflete House, 25 St Swithun Street, Winchester, Hants SO23 9JP. *T:* (01962) 854693.

See also J.A. Fortescue.

FORTEVIOT, 4th Baron *cr* 1917 of Dupplin, Perthshire; **John James Evelyn Dewar;** Bt 1907; farmer, landowner; *b* 5 April 1938; *s* of 3rd Baron Forteviot, MBE, and Cynthia Monica Starkie (*d* 1986); *S* father, 1993; *m* 1963, Lady Elisabeth Waldegrave, 3rd *d* of 12th Earl Waldegrave, KG, GCVO; one *s* three *d. Educ:* Eton. Nat. Service, Black Watch (RHR), 1956–58. John Dewar & Sons Ltd, 1959–62; ADC to Governor General of NZ, 1962–63; John Dewar & Sons, 1963–98. *Recreations:* fishing, shooting, birdwatching, travel. *Heir: s* Hon. Alexander John Edward Dewar [*b* 4 March 1971; *m* 1997, Donryn (*née* Clement); one *s*]. *Clubs:* Boodle's, Royal Perth Golfing and Country and City.

FORTEY, Dr Richard Alan, FRS 1997; Merit Researcher, Natural History Museum, since 1986; *b* 15 Feb. 1946; *s* of Frank Allen Fortey and Margaret Fortey (*née* Wilshin); *m* 1st, 1968, Bridget Elizabeth Thomas (marr. diss.); one *s*; 2nd, 1977, Jacqueline Francis; one *s* two *d. Educ:* Ealing Grammar Sch.; King's Coll., Cambridge (BA, MA; PhD 1971; ScD 1986). Res. Fellow, 1970–73, SSO, 1973–77, BM (Natural Hist.); PSO, Natural Hist. Mus., 1978–86. Howley Vis. Prof., Meml Univ. of Newfoundland, 1977–78; Vis. Prof. of Palaeobiology, Univ. of Oxford, 2000–. Member: Geol Soc. of London, 1972–; Brit. Mycological Soc., 1980–. Lyell Medal, Geol Soc., 1996; Frink Medal, Zool Soc. of London, 2001. *Publications:* Fossils: the key to the past, 1982, 2nd edn 1992; The Hidden Landscape, 1993; Life: an unauthorized biography, 1997; Trilobite!, 2000; (as Roderick Masters) The Roderick Masters Book of Money Making Schemes, 1981. *Recreations:* mushrooms and toadstools, East Anglia, cacti, conviviality. *Address:* Natural History Museum, South Kensington, Cromwell Road, SW7 5BD. *T:* (020) 7942 5493.

FORTH, Rt Hon. Eric; PC 1997; MP (C) Bromley and Chislehurst, since 1997 (Mid Worcestershire, 1983–97); *b* 9 Sept. 1944; *s* of late William and Aileen Forth; *m* 1st, 1967, Linda St Clair (marr. diss. 1994); two *d*; 2nd, 1994, Mrs Carroll Goff; one step *s. Educ:* Jordanhill Coll. Sch., Glasgow; Glasgow Univ. (MA Hons Politics and Econs). Chm., Young Conservatives', Constituency CPC, 1970–73; Member: Glasgow Univ. Cons. Club, 1962–66; Brentwood UDC, 1968–72. Contested (C) Barking, Feb. and Oct. 1974. Member (C), North Birmingham, European Parlt, 1979–84; Chm., Backbench Cttee, European Democ. Gp, European Parlt, 1979–84. PPS to Minister of State, DES, 1986–87; Parly Under Sec. of State: DTI, 1988–90; Dept of Employment, 1990–92; DFE, 1992–94; Minister of State, DFE, later DFEE, 1994–97; Shadow Leader of H of C, 2001–. Member: H of C Commn, 2000–; Select Committee: on Employment, 1986; on Standards and Privileges, 1999–2001; on Procedure, 1999–2001; Chm., Cons. Backbench European Affairs Cttee, 1987–88 (Vice-Chm., 1983–86). Chm., Cons. Way Forward, 1997–. *Publication:* Regional Policy—A Fringe Benefit?, 1983. *Recreations:* cinema, reading, biographies, travel. *Address:* House of Commons, SW1A 0AA. *Club:* Bromley Conservative.

FORTIER, Most Rev. Jean-Marie, Archbishop of Sherbrooke (RC), 1968–96, now Emeritus; *b* 1 July 1920. *Educ:* Laval University, Quebec. Bishop Auxiliary, La Pocatière, PQ, 1961–65; Bishop of Gaspé, PQ, 1965–68. Elected Pres., Canadian Catholic Conference, 1973–75. Prés. de l'Assemblée des Evêques du Québec, 1984–89. *Publication:* contrib. to Dictionnaire d'Histoire et de Géographie. *Address:* 2 rue Port-Dauphin, QC G1R 5K5, Canada. *T:* (418) 6923935.

FORTUNE, John; scriptwriter and actor; *b* 30 June 1939; *s* of Hubert William George Wood and Edna Maude Fortune; *m* 1st, 1962, Susannah Waldo (marr. diss. 1976); one *s* one *d*; 2nd, 1995, Emma Burge. *Educ:* Cathedral Sch., Bristol; King's Coll., Cambridge (MA). Has worked in theatre and television since 1961; *television* includes: writer and performer: Not So Much a Programme, More a Way of Life; BBC3; The Late Show; Rory Bremner; Rory Bremner … Who Else?; Bremner, Bird and Fortune; writer: Roger Doesn't Live Here Anymore; Round and Round. *Publications:* (with John Wells) A Melon for Ecstasy, 1971; (with Eleanor Bron) Is Your Marriage Really Necessary?, 1972; (with John Bird) The Long Johns, 1996. *Recreation:* lounging about. *Address:* c/o Richard Stone Partnership, 2 Henrietta Street, WC2E 8PS. *T:* (020) 7497 0849.

FORTY, Prof. Arthur John, CBE 1991; PhD, DSc; FRSE; FRSA; Principal and Vice-Chancellor, Stirling University, 1986–94; *b* 4 Nov. 1928; *s* of Alfred Louis Forty and Elisabeth Forty; *m* 1950, Alicia Blanche Hart Gough; one *s. Educ:* Headlands Grammar Sch.; Bristol Univ. (BSc; PhD 1953; DSc 1967). FRSE 1988, FRSA 1989. Served RAF, 1953–56. Sen. Res. Scientist, Tube Investments Ltd, 1956–58; Lectr, Univ. of Bristol, 1958–64; University of Warwick: Foundn Prof. of Physics, 1964–86; Pro-Vice-Chancellor, 1970–86. Visiting scientist: Gen. Electric Co., USA; Boeing Co.; Nat. Bureau of Standards, Washington, USA. Member: SRC Physics Cttee, 1969–73; SRC Materials Cttee, 1970–73; Computer Bd, 1982–85; University Grants Committee: Mem., 1982–86, Vice-Chm., 1985–86; Chairman: Physical Sciences Sub-cttee, 1985–86; Equipment Sub-cttee, 1985–86; Chairman: Jt ABRC, Computer Bd and UGC Working Party on Future Facilities for Advanced Res. Computing (author, Forty Report), 1985; Management Cttee for Res. Councils' Supercomputer Facility, 1986–88; UFC Cttee for Information Systems (formerly Computer Bd for Univs and Res. Councils), 1988–91; Jt Policy Cttee for Advanced Res. Computing, 1988–94; Cttee of Scottish Univ. Principals, 1990–92; Edinburgh Parallel Computing Centre, 1994–97; Adv. Cttee, Scottish Science Liby, 1995–; Member: British Library Bd, 1987–94; Bd of Trustees, Nat. Liby of Scotland, 1995–; Academic Adv. Bd, Univ. of the Highlands and Islands, 1999–. Chm., ICIAM 99 Ltd, 1995–96. Hon. Fellow, Edinburgh Univ., 1994. Hon. LLD St Andrew's, 1989; DUniv Stirling, 1995. *Publications:* papers in Proc. Royal Soc., Phil Magazine and other learned jls. *Recreations:* sailing, gardening, the ancient metallurgy of gold. *Address:* Port Mor, St Fillans, by Crieff, Perthshire. *Club:* Royal Over-Seas League.

FORWELL, Prof. George Dick, OBE 1993; PhD; FRCP; Chief Administrative Medical Officer, 1973–93, and Director of Public Health, 1989–93, Greater Glasgow Health Board; *b* 6 July 1928; *s* of Harold C. Forwell and Isabella L. Christie; *m* 1957, Catherine F. C. Cousland; two *d. Educ:* George Watson's Coll., Edinburgh; Edinburgh Univ. (MB, ChB 1950; PhD 1955). MRCPE 1957, DIH 1957, DPH 1959, FRCPE 1967, FFCM 1972, FRCPGlas 1974, FRCP 1985. House Officer and Univ. Clin. Asst, Edinburgh Royal Infirm., 1950–52; RAF Inst. of Aviation Med., 1952–54; MRC and RCPE grants, 1954–56; pneumoconiosis field res., 1956–57; Grad. Res. Fellow and Lectr, Edinburgh Univ. Dept of Public Health and Social Med., 1957–60; Asst Dean, Faculty of Med., Edinburgh Univ., 1960–63; Dep. Sen. and Sen. Admin. MO, Eastern Reg. Hosp. Bd, Dundee, 1963–67; PMO, Scottish Home and Health Dept, 1967–73. Vis. Prof., Dept of Public Health, Glasgow Univ., 1990–93; Hon. Prof., Sch. of Biol and Med. Scis, St Andrews Univ., 1993–98. QHP, 1980–83. Mem., GMC, 1984–89. *Publications:* papers on clin. res. and on health planning and services, in med. and other jls. *Recreation:* running. *Address:* 20 Irvine Crescent, St Andrews, Fife KY16 8LG. *Club:* Royal Air Force.

FORWOOD, family name of **Baroness Arlington**.

FORWOOD, Nicholas James; QC 1987; **Hon. Judge Forwood**; Judge, Court of the First Instance, European Community, since 1999; *b* 22 June 1948; *s* of Lt-Col Harry Forwood and Wendy Forwood (*née* French-Smith); *m* 1971, Sally Diane Gerrard, *e d* of His Honour Basil Harding Gerrard; one *s* three *d. Educ:* Stowe Sch.; St John's Coll., Cambridge (Open Schol., MA, Pt I Mechanical Scis Tripos (1st Cl. Hons), Pt II Law Tripos). Called to the Bar, Middle Temple, 1970, Bencher, 1998. Member: Law Adv. Cttee, British Council, 1985–91; Internat. Relations (formerly Internat. Practice) Cttee, Bar Council, 1994–99. Chm., Permanent Delegn of CCBE to European Courts, 1997–99. *Recreations:* ski-ing, golf, sailing, opera. *Address:* Court of the First Instance of the EC, rue du Fort Niedergrünewald, 2925 Luxembourg. *T:* 43031; 14 rue de Bourglinster, 6112 Junglinster, Luxembourg. *Club:* Oxford and Cambridge.

FORWOOD, Sir Peter Noel, 4th Bt *cr* 1895; *b* 15 Oct. 1925; *s* of Arthur Noel Forwood, 3rd *s* of 1st Bt, and Hyacinth Forwood (*née* Pollard); *S* cousin, 2001; *m* 1950, Roy Murphy; six *d. Educ:* Radley. Served 1939–45 War, Welsh Guards. *Heir:* none. *Address:* Newhouse Farm, Shillinglee, Chiddingfold Godalming, Surrey GU8 4SZ.

FOSKETT, David Robert; QC 1991; FCIArb; a Recorder, since 1995; *b* 19 March 1949; *s* of Robert Frederick Foskett and Ruth (*née* Waddington); *m* 1975, Angela Bridget Jacobs; two *d. Educ:* Warwick Sch.; King's Coll., London (LLB Hons; Pres., Faculty of Laws, 1969–70; Pres., Union Soc., 1970–71; Mem., Delegacy, 1970–72). FCIArb 1992. Called to the Bar, Gray's Inn, 1972, Bencher, 1999; Mem., Midland and Oxford Circuit; Asst Recorder, 1992–95; a Dep. High Ct Judge, 1998–. Mem., Civil Procedure Rule Cttee, 1997–2001. President: KCL Assoc., 1997–2000; Old Warwickian Assoc., 2000. *Publications:* The Law and Practice of Compromise, 1980, 5th edn 2001; Settlement Under the Civil Procedure Rules, 1999; various articles. *Recreations:* theatre, reading poetry and composing verse, bird watching, cricket, golf. *Address:* 1 Crown Office Row, Temple, EC4Y 7HH. *T:* (020) 7797 7500. *Clubs:* Athenæum, MCC; Woking Golf.

FOSKETT, Douglas John, OBE 1978; FLA; Director of Central Library Services and Goldsmiths' Librarian, University of London, 1978–83; *b* 27 June 1918; *s* of John Henry Foskett and Amy Florence Foskett; *m* 1948, Joy Ada (*née* McCann); one *s* two *d. Educ:* Bancroft's Sch.; Queen Mary Coll., Univ. of London (BA 1939); Birkbeck Coll., Univ. of London (MA 1954). Ilford Municipal Libraries, 1940–48; RAMC and Intell. Corps, 1940–46; Metal Box Co. Ltd, 1948–57; Librarian, Univ. of London Inst. of Educn, 1957–78. Chairman of Council, Library Assoc., 1962–63, Vice-Pres., 1966–73, Pres., 1976; Hon. Library Adviser, RNID, 1965–90; Mem., Adv. Cttee on Sci. and Techn. Information, 1969–73; Mem. and Rapporteur, Internat. Adv. Cttee on Documentation, Libraries and Archives, UNESCO, 1968–73; Cons. on Documentation to ILO and to European Packaging Fedn; Cttee Mem., UNISIST/UNESCO and EUDISED/Council of Europe Projects; Member: Army Educn Adv. Bd, 1968–73; Library Adv. Council, 1975–77. Visiting Professor: Univ. of Michigan, 1964; Univ. of Ghana, 1967; Univ. of Ibadan, 1967; Brazilian Inst. for Bibliography and Documentation, 1971; Univ. of Iceland, 1974. FLA 1949, Hon. FLA, 1975; Hon. Fellow, Polytechnic of North London, 1981. *Publications:* Assistance to Readers in Lending Libraries, 1952; (with E. A. Baker) Bibliography of Food, 1958; Information Service in Libraries, 1958, 2nd edn 1967; Classification and Indexing in the Social Sciences, 1963, 2nd edn 1974; Science, Humanism and Libraries, 1964; Reader in Comparative Librarianship, 1977; Pathways for Communication, 1984; contrib. to many professional jls. *Recreations:* books, travel, writing, cricket. *Address:* 23 St Helen's Court, St Helen's Parade, Southsea, Portsmouth PO4 0RR. *T:* (023) 9282 9808. *Clubs:* MCC; Sussex CC.

FOSS, Kathleen, (Kate); Member of Board, since 1983 and Chairman, since 1989, Direct Mail Services Standards Board; *b* 17 May 1925; *d* of George Arden and May Elizabeth Arden; *m* 1951, Robert Foss; one *s*. *Educ:* Northampton High Sch.; Whitelands Coll. (Teaching Dip.). Teacher: Northants, 1945–47; Mddx, 1947–53 (Dep. Head); Westmorland, 1953–60 (History specialist). Chairman: Consumers in European Community Gp (UK), 1979–82; Insurance Ombudsman Bureau, 1986– (Mem. Council, 1984–91); Member: Nat. Consumer Council, 1980–83; Consumers' Consultative Cttee, Brussels, 1981–86; Law Commn Standing Cttee on Conveyancing, 1985–88; Data Protection Tribunal Panel, 1986–99; Council for Licensed Conveyancers, 1986–88. Vice Pres., Keep Britain Tidy Gp, 1982–88 (Vice-Chm., 1979–82); Mem. Exec., National Fedn of Women's Insts, 1969–81 (National Treasurer, 1974–78); Chm., Bd of Dirs, WI Books Ltd, 1981–89. *Recreations:* golf, bridge. *Address:* 1 Elbow Lane, Undercliffe, Bradford BD2 4PB. *T:* (01274) 630442.

FOSTER; *see* Hylton-Foster.

FOSTER, family name of **Baron Foster of Thames Bank**.

FOSTER OF THAMES BANK, Baron *cr* 1999 (Life Peer), of Reddish in the county of Greater Manchester; **Norman Robert Foster,** OM 1997; Kt 1990; RA 1991 (ARA 1983); RWA 1994; RDI 1988; RIBA, FCSD, FAIA; architect; Chairman Partner, Foster and Partners, London, Berlin, Singapore; *b* Reddish, 1 June 1935; *s* of late Robert Foster and Lilian Smith; *m* 3rd, 1996, Dr Elena Ochoa; one *s*. *Educ:* Univ. of Manchester Sch. of Architecture (DipArch 1961, CertTP); Yale Univ. Sch. of Architecture (Henry Fellow, Jonathan Edwards Coll., March 1962). Founded: Foster Associates, 1967; Foster and Partners, 1992; in collab. with Dr Buckminster Fuller, 1968–83; Cons. Architect, UEA, 1978–87. Mem. Council: AA, 1969–70, 1970–71 (Vice Pres., 1974); RCA, 1981. Taught at: Univ. of Pennsylvania; AA, London; Bath Acad. of Arts; London Polytechnic; Visiting Professor: Bartlett Sch. of Architecture, 1998; Harvard Univ. Grad. Scho. of Design, 2000. External Examr, 1971–73 and Mem. Visiting Bd of Educn, RIBA. Major projects include: Head Office for Willis Faber & Dumas, Ipswich, 1975 (First Trustees', Medal, RIBA, 1990); Sainsbury Centre for Visual Arts, UEA, Norwich, 1977; UK headquarters for Renault, 1983; Nomos Furniture System, 1985; new HQ, Hongkong and Shanghai Banking Corp., Hong Kong, 1986; King's Cross London Master Plan, 1988; Stockley Park, Uxbridge, 1989; Millennium Tower, Tokyo, 1990; RA Sackler Galls, 1991; Terminal Zone, Stansted Airport, 1991; ITN HQ, 1991; Century Tower, Tokyo, 1991; inner harbour, Duisburg, 1991–; Barcelona Telecoms Tower, 1992; Micro-Electronics Centre, Duisburg, 1993–97; Arts Centre, Nîmes, 1993; school, Fréjus, 1993; German Parlt bldg (Reichstag), Berlin, 1993 and 1999; Bilbao Metro System, 1995; Univ. of Cambridge Faculty of Law, 1996; American Air Mus., Duxford, 1997; HQ for Commerzbank, Frankfurt, 1997; Hong Kong Internat. Airport, 1998; Congress Centre, Valencia, 1998; BM redevelt, 2000. Work exhibited: Antwerp, Barcelona, Berlin, Bordeaux, Hanover, London, Lyon, Manchester, Madrid, Milan, Munich, NY, Nîmes, Paris, Seville, Tokyo, Valencia, Zurich; permanent collections: MOMA, NY, Centre Georges Pompidou, Paris. IBM Fellow, Aspen Conference, 1980; Hon. Prof., Buenos Aires, 1997; Hon. FAIA 1980; Hon. FREng; Hon. FIStrustE; Hon. FRIAS 2000; Hon. Fellow, Inst. of Art and Design, Kent; Hon. Mem., Bund Deutscher Architekten, 1983; Member: Internat. Acad. of Architecture, Sofia; French Order of Architects; Eur. Acad. of Scis and Arts; Foreign Member: Royal Acad. of Fine Arts, Sweden; Amer. Acad. of Arts and Scis; Associate, Académie Royale de Belgique, 1990. Hon. Dr: E Anglia, Bath, Valencia, Humberside, Manchester, RCA, Eindhoven, Oxford, London, Negev, London Inst. Practice awards: over 200 for design excellence, including: R. S. Reynolds Internat. Awards, USA, 1976, 1979, 1986; 23 RIBA Awards and Commendations; 8 Financial Times Awards for outstanding Industrial Architecture; 9 Structural Steel Awards; Internat. Design Award; RSA Award, 1976; Ambrose Congreve Award, 1980; 5 Civic Trust Awards; 2 IStructE Special Awards; Premio Compasso d'Oro Award, 1987; 5 Interiors Awards (USA); 8 British Construction Industry Awards; 4 Aluminium Imagination Awards; Best Building of the Year Award, Royal Fine Art Commn/Sunday Times, 1992, 1993, Royal Fine Art Commn/BSkyB, (jtly) 1998; 3 BCO Awards; Queen's Award for Export, 1995; Regl Arch. Award, AIA, 1995. Personal awards include: RIBA Gold Medal, 1983; Kunstpreis, Berlin, 1989; Japan Design Foundn Award, 1987; Mies van der Rohe Award, Barcelona, 1991; Gold Medal, French Acad. of Arch., 1991; Brunner Meml Award, AAIL, 1992; Gold Medal, AIA, 1994; MIPIM Man of the Year, 1996; Building Award Personality of the Year, 1996; Best Internat. Promotion of Barcelona Award, 1997; Silver Medal, CSD, 1997; Berliner Zeitung Kultur-preis, 1998; special prize for positive contribution to British-German relations, German-British Forum, 1998; Pritzker Architecture Prize, 1999; special prize, 4th Internat. Biennial of Architecture, São Paulo, 1999; Visual Arts Award, South Bank Show, 2001. Officer, Order of Arts and Letters (France), 1994; Order of North Rhine Westphalia. *Relevant publications:* The Work of Foster Associates, 1979; Norman Foster, 1988; Norman Foster Foster Associates Buildings and Projects, vol 2, 1971–78, 1989, vol 3, 1978–85, 1989, vol. 1, 1964–73 (Norman Foster Team Four and Foster Associates Buildings and Projects), 1991, vol. 4, 1985–89, 1996; (by Kenneth Powell) Stansted: Norman Foster and the architecture of flight, 1992; Norman Foster Sketches, 1992; Foster Associates, 1992; Foster and Partners, 1996; Sir Norman Foster, 1997; The Master Architect Series II: Norman Foster, 1997; Norman Foster 30 Colours, 1998; The Norman Foster Studio, 2000; On Foster...Foster On, 2000. *Recreations:* running, flying, ski-ing. *Address:* (office) Riverside Three, 22 Hester Road, SW11 4AN. *T:* (020) 7738 0455, *Fax:* (020) 7738 1107; *e-mail:* enquiries@fosterandpartners.com.

FOSTER, Alicia Christian, (Jodie); American film actress and director; *b* 19 Nov. 1962; *d* of Lucius Foster and Evelyn Foster (*née* Almond); one *s*. *Educ:* Yale Univ. (BA Eng. Lit. 1985). *Films* include: Napoleon and Samantha, 1972; Kansas City Bomber, 1972; Tom Sawyer, 1973; Alice Doesn't Live Here Anymore, 1975; Taxi Driver, 1976; Bugsy Malone, 1976; The Little Girl Who Lives Down the Lane, 1977; Candleshoe, 1977; Foxes, 1980; Carny, 1980; Hotel New Hampshire, 1984; Siesta, 1987; Five Corners, 1988; The Accused, 1988 (Academy Award for Best Actress, 1989); Little Man Tate, 1991 (also dir); The Silence of the Lambs, 1991 (Academy Award for Best Actress, 1992); Shadows and Fog, 1991; Sommersby, 1993; Maverick, 1994; Nell, 1994 (also prod.); dir and prod., Home for the Holidays, 1995; Contact, 1997; Anna and the King, 1999; *television* includes: Mayberry, 1969; Bonanza; Paper Moon, 1974–75. *Address:* EGG Pictures Production Co., 5555 Melrose Avenue, Jerry Lewis Building Annex, Los Angeles, CA 90038, USA.

FOSTER, Prof. Allan (Bentham); Professor of Chemistry, University of London, 1966–86, now Emeritus; *b* 21 July 1926; *s* of late Herbert and Martha Alice Foster; *m* 1949, Monica Binns; two *s*. *Educ:* Nelson Grammar Sch., Lancs; University of Birmingham. Frankland Medal and Prize, 1947; PhD, 1950; DSc, 1957. University Res. Fellow, University of Birmingham, 1950–53; Fellow of Rockefeller Foundn, Ohio State Univ., 1953–54; University of Birmingham: ICI Res. Fellow, 1954–55; Lectr, 1955–62; Sen. Lectr, 1962–64; Reader in Organic Chemistry, 1964–66; Institute of Cancer Research: Head of Chemistry Div., Chester Beatty Res. Inst., 1966–82; Head, Drug Metabolism Team, Drug Develt Sect., 1982–86. Sec., British Technol. Gp, New Cancer Product Develt Adv. Bd, 1986–91. FChemSoc (Mem. Coun., 1962–65, 1967–70); Corresp. Mem., Argentinian Chem. Soc. Editor, Carbohydrate Research, 1965–92. *Publications:* numerous scientific papers mainly in Jl Chem. Soc., Carbohydrate Research and cancer jls. *Recreations:* golf, gardening, theatre. *Address:* 1 Pine Walk, Carshalton Beeches, Surrey SM5 4ES. *T:* (020) 8642 4102. *Club:* Banstead Downs.

FOSTER, Andrew Kevin; Director of Human Resources, Department of Health, since 2001; *b* 3 March 1955; *s* of Kevin William Foster and late Doreen Foster; *m* 1981, Sara Gillian Daniels; one *s* two *d*. *Educ:* Millfield Sch.; Keble Coll., Oxford (BA Hons PPE, MA). Mktg Manager, Rowntree Mackintosh plc, 1976–81; Dir, Worldcrest Ltd, 1981–. Chairman: W Lancs NHS Trust, 1993–96; Wigan & Leigh NHS Trust, 1996–2001; Policy Dir, NHS Confedn, 1998–2001. *Recreations:* hockey, golf. *Address:* Department of Health, Richmond House, 79 Whitehall, SW1A 2NS. *T:* (020) 7210 5834.

FOSTER, Sir Andrew (William), Kt 2001; Controller, Audit Commission, since 1992; *b* 29 Dec. 1944; *s* of George William and Gladys Maria Foster; *m* 1967, Christine Marquiss (marr. diss); one *s* one *d*. *Educ:* Abingdon School; Newcastle Polytechnic (BSc Sociol.); LSE (Postgrad. Dip. Applied Social Studies). Social Worker, London, 1966–71; Area Social Services Officer, 1971–75; Asst Dir of Social Services, Haringey, 1975–79; Dir of Social Services, Greenwich, 1979–82, N Yorks, 1982–87; Regional Gen. Manager, Yorks RHA, 1987–91; Dep. Chief Exec., NHS Management Exec., 1991–92. Hon. DCL Northumbria at Newcastle, 1996. *Recreations:* golf, walking, travel, theatre, food, wine. *Address:* Audit Commission, 1 Vincent Square, SW1P 2PN.

FOSTER, Ann; *see* Knowles, P. A.

FOSTER, Brendan, MBE 1976; television athletics commentator, since 1981; Managing Director, Nova International Ltd, since 1987; *b* 12 Jan. 1948; *s* of Francis and Margaret Foster; *m* 1972; one *s* one *d*. *Educ:* St Joseph's Grammar Sch., Hebburn, Co. Durham; Sussex Univ. (BSc); Carnegie Coll., Leeds (DipEd). School Teacher, St Joseph's Grammar Sch., Hebburn, 1970–74; Sports and Recreation Manager, Gateshead Metropolitan Bor. Council, 1974–81; UK Man. Dir, Nike Internat., 1981–87; Chm., Nike (UK), 1981–86; Man. Dir, Nike Europe, 1985–87; Vice Pres. Marketing, Nike Inc. Oregon, USA, 1986–87. Commonwealth Games: Bronze medal: 1500 metres, 1970; 5000 m, 1978; Silver medal, 5000 m, 1974; Gold medal, 10,000 m, 1978; European Games: Bronze medal, 1500 m, 1971; Gold medal, 5000 m, 1974; Olympic Games: Bronze medal, 10,000 m, 1976; World Records: 2 miles, 1973; 3000 metres, 1974. BBC Sports Personality of the Year, 1974. Hon. Fellow, Sunderland Polytechnic, 1977; Hon. MEd Newcastle, 1978; Hon. DLitt Sussex, 1982. *Publications:* Brendan Foster, 1978; Olympic Heroes 1896–1984, 1984. *Recreations:* running (now only a recreation), sport (as spectator).

FOSTER, Prof. Brian, DPhil; CPhys, FInstP; Professor of Experimental Physics, University of Bristol, since 1996; *b* 4 Jan. 1954; *s* of John and Annie Foster; *m* 1983, Sabine Margot Koch; two *s*. *Educ:* Wolsingham Secondary Sch.; Queen Elizabeth Coll., Univ. of London (BSc 1975); St John's Coll., Oxford (DPhil 1978). CPhys, FInstP 1992. Research Associate: Rutherford Appleton Lab., 1978–82; Imperial Coll. of Science and Technology, 1982–84; Bristol University: Lectr, 1984–92; SERC, subseq. PPARC, Advanced Fellow, 1991–97; Reader, 1992–96. Chm., Nuclear and Particle Physics Div., Inst. of Physics, 1989–93; Recorder, Physics Section, BAAS, 1994–97;; Mem., PPARC, 2001–(Mem., 1995, and Chm., 1996–99, Particle Physics Cttee; Jt Chm., Science Cttee, 1996–99); Member: various adv. cttees, CERN, 1993–; Extended Scientific Council, Deutsches Elektronen-Synchrotron, 1998–. Spokesman, ZEUS Collaboration, 1999–. Alexander von Humboldt-Stiftung Res. Prize Winner, 1999–2000. *Publications:* (ed) Topics in High Energy Particle Physics, 1988; (ed jtly) Forty Years of Particle Physics, 1988; (ed and contrib.) Electron-Positron Annihilation Physics, 1990; numerous papers in learned jls, articles on science in popular press, particularly the Independent. *Recreations:* squash, violin playing, history and politics, gardening. *Address:* H. H. Wills Physics Laboratory, Royal Fort, Tyndall Avenue, Bristol BS8 1TL;; Nikischstrasse 4, 22761 Hamburg, Germany. *T:* (40) 87082563.

FOSTER, Sir Christopher (David), Kt 1986; MA; Chairman, RAC Foundation, since 1999; *b* 30 Oct. 1930; *s* of George Cecil Foster and Phyllis Joan Foster (*née* Mappin); *m* 1958, Kay Sheridan Bullock; two *s* three *d*. *Educ:* Merchant Taylors' Sch.; King's Coll., Cambridge (Scholar). Economics Tripos 1954; MA 1959. Commnd into 1st Bn Seaforth Highlanders, Malaya, 1949. Hallsworth Research Fellow, Manchester Univ., 1957–59; Senior Research Fellow, 1959–64, Official Fellow and Tutor, 1964–66, Hon. Fellow, 1992, Jesus Coll., Oxford; Dir-Gen. of Economic Planning, MoT, 1966–70; Head of Unit for Res. in Urban Economics, LSE, 1970–76; Prof. of Urban Studies and Economics, LSE, 1976–78; a Dir and Head of Econ. and Public Policy Div., Coopers & Lybrand Associates, 1978–84; a Dir, Public Sector Practice Leader and Economic Advr, Coopers & Lybrand, 1984–86; Commercial Adviser to British Telecom, 1986–88; Sen. Public Sector and Econs Partner, Coopers & Lybrand Deloitte, later Coopers & Lybrand Associates, 1988–94; Advr to Chm., Coopers & Lybrand Associates, 1994–99. Governor, 1967–70, Dir, 1976–78, Centre for Environmental Studies; Visiting Professor: of Economics, MIT, 1970; LSE, 1978–86. Special Economic Adviser (part time), DoE, 1974–77; Special Advr on BR Privatisation to Sec. of State for Transport, 1992–94; Mem. Bd, Railtrack, 1994–2000. Member: (part time), PO Bd, 1975–77; Audit Commn, 1983–88; ESRC, 1985–89; Chm., NEDO Construction Industry Sector Gp, 1988–92. Chm., Cttee of Inquiry into Road Haulage Licensing, 1977–78; Mem., Cttee of Inquiry into Civil Service Pay, 1981–82; Economic Assessor, Sizewell B Inquiry, 1982–86. Member: Econ. and Financial Cttee, CBI, 1987–94; LDDC, 1988–96. Chairman: Circle 33 Housing Assoc, 1986–90; Construction Round Table, 1993–97; Vice-Chm., RAC, 1998–99 (non-exec. Dir, 1994–98). Gov., RSC, 1991–. *Publications:* The Transport Problem, 1963; Politics, Finance and the Role of Economics: an essay on the control of public enterprise, 1972; (with R. Jackman and M. Perlman) Local Government Finance, 1980; Privatisation, Public Ownership and the Regulation of Natural Monopoly, 1993; (with F. J. Plowden) The State Under Stress, 1996; papers in various economic and other journals. *Address:* 6 Holland Park Avenue, W11 3QU. *T:* (020) 7727 4757. *Clubs:* Reform, Royal Automobile.

FOSTER, Christopher Norman; Keeper of the Match Book, since 1983, and Executive Director, since 1993, The Jockey Club; *b* 30 Dec. 1946; *s* of Maj.-Gen. Norman Leslie Foster, CB, DSO; *m* 1981, Anthea Jane Sammons; two *s*. *Educ:* Westminster Sch. ACA 1969, FCA 1979. Cooper Brothers & Co., Chartered Accountants, 1965–73; Weatherbys, 1973–90; Vice Chm., Internat. Fedn of Horseracing Authorities, 2000. Governor, Westminster Sch., 1990–. *Recreations:* racing, shooting, fishing, gardening. *Address:* The Old Vicarage, Great Durnford, Salisbury, Wilts SP4 6AZ. *Club:* MCC.

FOSTER, Rt Rev. Christopher Richard James; *see* Hertford, Bishop Suffragan of.

FOSTER, Hon. Dennis (Haley), CVO 1983; CBE 1981; JP; Chief Secretary, Cayman Islands, 1976–86; *b* 26 March 1931; *s* of late Arnold and Agatha Foster; *m* 1955, Reba

Raphael Grant; one *d. Educ:* Munro Coll., Kingston, Jamaica. Joined Cayman Is Civil Service, 1950; seconded as Asst Administrator, Turks and Caicos Is, 1959; Dist Comr, Lesser Is, 1960; Asst Administrator, Cayman Is, 1968. *Recreation:* gardening. *Address:* PO Box 860, George Town, Grand Cayman, Cayman Islands, WI. *T:* (94) 92236.

FOSTER, Rt Hon. Derek; PC 1993; DL; MP (Lab) Bishop Auckland, since 1979; *b* 25 June 1937; *s* of Joseph and Ethel Maud Foster; *m* 1972, Florence Anne Bulmer; three *s* one *d. Educ:* Bede Grammar Sch., Sunderland; Oxford Univ. (BA Hons PPE). In industry and commerce, 1960–70; Youth and Community Worker, 1970–73; Further Educn Organiser, Durham, 1973–74; Asst Dir of Educn, Sunderland Borough Council, 1974–79. Councillor: Sunderland Co. Borough, 1972–74; Tyne and Wear County Council, 1973–77 (Chm. Econ. Develt Cttee, 1973–76). Chm., North of England Develt Council, 1974–76. North Regional Whip, 1981–82; opposition front bench spokesman on social security, 1982–83; PPS to Leader of Opposition, 1983–85; Opposition Chief Whip, 1985–95; opposition front bench spokesman on the Duchy of Lancaster, 1995–97. Mem., Select Cttee on Trade and Industry, 1980–82, on Employment, 1997– (Chm., 1997–2001), on Educn and Employment, 1997– (Jt Chm., 1997–2001). Member: H of C Liaison Cttee, 1997–; Parly Ecclesiastical Cttee, 1997–; Registration of Political Parties Adv. Gp, 1998–; Exec. Mem., British American Parly Gp, 1997–. Chairman: PLP Employment Cttee, 1980–81; PLP Econ. and Finance Cttee, 1981–82. Mem. (ex officio) Lab. Party NEC, 1985–95. Fellow, Industry and Parlt Trust. Chm., Bishop Auckland Develt Co., 2001–. Chairman: Manufg Industry Gp, 1998–; N Regl Electronic Economy Prog.; non-exec. Dir, Northern Informatics, 1998–. Vice Chm., Youthaid, 1979–86; Chairman: Northern Region Information Soc. Initiative, 1996; Pioneering Care Partnership, 1997–; Nat. Prayer Breakfast, 1997–99; former Vice-Pres., Christian Socialist Movt; Mem., Nat. Adv. Bd, Salvation Army. Trustee: Auckland Castle, 1996–; Nat. e^2 Learning Foundn, 2001–. Mem., Fabian Soc. DL Durham, 2001. *Recreations:* brass bands, choirs, uniformed member Salvation Army. *Address:* 3 Linburn, Rickleton, Washington, Tyne and Wear NE38 9EB. *T:* (0191) 4171580.

FOSTER, Donald Michael Ellison; MP (Lib Dem) Bath, since 1992; *b* 31 March 1947; *s* of late Rev. J. A. Foster and Iris Edith (*née* Ellison); *m* 1968, Victoria, 2nd *d* of Major Kenneth Pettegree, OBE, TD and Jean Pettegree; one *s* one *d. Educ:* Lancaster Royal Grammar Sch.; Univ. of Keele (BA Hons; Cert Ed 1969); Univ. of Bath (MEd 1982). CPhys, MInstP 1970). Science teacher, Sevenoaks Sch., Kent, 1969–75; Science Curriculum Proj. Dir, Avon LEA, 1975–81; Science Educn Lectr, Bristol Univ., 1981–89: Head, Science Educn Centre; teacher trainer; organiser of link with Univ. of Zambia; Managing Consultant, Pannell Kerr Forster, 1989–92. Mem., Avon CC, 1981–89 (Leader, Liberal Gp; Chm., Educn Cttee, 1987–89). Mem. Exec. Cttee, ACC, 1985–89. Contested (L/All) Bristol East, 1987. Lib Dem spokesman: on envmt, 1999–2001; on transport and the regions, 1999–; on local govt, 2001–. Mem., Select Cttee on Educn and Employment, 1996–99. Treas., All-Party Yugoslav Gp, 1994–97. Vice-Chm., British Assoc. for Central and Eastern Europe, 1994–97. Pres., Nat. Campaign for Nursery Educn, 1999– (Vice-Chm., 1993–99); Hon. Pres., British Youth Council, 1992–99; Trustee: Open Sch., 1992–99; Educn Extra, 1992–99. Hon. Fellow, Bath Coll. of Further Educn, 1994. *Publications:* Resource-based Learning in Science, 1979; Science with Gas, 1981; (jtly) Aspects of Science, 1984; (jtly) Reading about Science, 1984; (jtly) Nuffield Science, 1986; (ed) Teaching Science 11–13, 1987; science curriculum resources and educn papers. *Recreations:* watching all forms of sport (former rower and Rugby player), reading, films, music. *Address:* House of Commons, SW1A 0AA. *T:* (020) 7219 5001; 26 Ambra Vale, Cliftonwood, Bristol BS8 4RW. *T:* (0117) 929 1272. *Club:* National Liberal.

FOSTER, Ian Hampden; a Master of the Supreme Court, Queen's Bench Division, since 1991; a Recorder, since 1998; *b* 27 Feb. 1946; *s* of Eric Hampden Foster and Irene Foster (*née* Warman); *m* 1975, Fiona Jane, *d* of Rev. J. N. and Mrs Robertson-Glasgow; one *s* one *d. Educ:* Battersea Grammar Sch.; Univ. of Exeter (LLB Hons 1968). Called to the Bar, Inner Temple, 1969; practice at common law bar, 1969–91. Adv. Editor, Atkin's Court Forms, 1991–; Jt Editor, Supreme Court Practice, 1993–98. *Recreations:* gardening, watching cricket. *Address:* Royal Courts of Justice, Strand, WC2A 2LL. *Club:* Norfolk (Norwich).

FOSTER, Jacqueline; Member (C) North West Region, England, European Parliament, since 1999; *b* 30 Dec. 1947; *d* of late Samuel and of Isabella Renshaw; *m* 1975, Peter Laurance Foster (marr. diss. 1981). *Educ:* Prescot Girls' Grammar Sch., Lancashire. Cabin Services, BEA, then British Airways, 1969–81; Area Manager, Austria, Horizon, 1981–85; Cabin Services, British Airways, 1985–99; Founder Mem. and Exec. Officer, Cabin Crew '89 (Airline Trade Union), 1989–99. European Parliament: Chm., Cons. backbench cttee, 1999–; Mem. Industry and Transport (Aviation) Cttees, 1999–. *Recreations:* ski-ing, ice skating, travel. *Address:* European Parliament, Rue Wiertz, 1047 Brussels; NW Conservative European Office, 9 Montford Enterpise Centre, Wynford Square, Salford M5 2SN. *Club:* Carlton.

FOSTER, Joan Mary; Under Secretary, Department of Transport, Highways Planning and Management, 1978–80, retired; *b* 20 January 1923; *d* of John Whitfield Foster and Edith Foster (*née* Levett). *Educ:* Northampton School for Girls. Entered Civil Service (HM Office of Works), Oct. 1939; Ministry of Transport, 1955; Asst Secretary, 1970. *Recreations:* gardening, cooking, good wine. *Address:* 3 Hallfields, Shouldham, King's Lynn, Norfolk PE33 0DN. *T:* (01366) 347809.

FOSTER, Joanna Katharine; Chair: The BT Forum, since 1997 (Director, 1995–97); National Work-Life Forum, since 1998; *b* 5 May 1939; *d* of late Michael and of Lesley Mead; *m* 1961, Jerome Foster; one *s* one *d. Educ:* Benenden School; Univ. of Grenoble. Sec. and Editl Asst, Vogue Magazine, London and NY, 1958–59; journalist, San Francisco Chronicle, 1959; Management Adviser, Industrial Soc., 1966–72; Dir, Centre Actif Bilingue, Fontainebleau, 1972–79; Press Attachée and Editor, INSEAD, Fontainebleau, 1972–79; Educn and Trng Dir, Corporate Services, Western Psychiatric Inst. and Clinic, Univ. of Pittsburgh, 1980–82; Management Adviser, 1982–85, Head of Pepperell Unit, 1985–88, Mem. Council, 1990–, Industrial Soc.; Chair: Equal Opportunities Commn, 1988–93; UK Council, UN Internat. Year of the Family 1994, 1993–95. Pres., European Commn Adv. Cttee on Equal Opportunities, 1991–92 (Vice Pres., 1990, 1991, 1993); Member: Nat. Adv. Council for Careers and Educnl Guidance, 1993–94; Sec. of State for Employment's Women's Issues Adv. Gp, 1991–93; Target Team for Business in the Community's Opportunity 2000 Initiative, 1992–99; Govt Adv. Gp on Work-Life Balance, 2000–. Chair, Adv. Cttee, European Public Policy Inst., Warwick Univ., 1993–95. Chm., Lloyds TSB (formerly TSB) Foundn, 1997– (Dep. Chm., 1991–97). Dir, WNO, 1990–94; Mem., Central TV Adv. Bd, 1991–95; Mem., Adv. Bd, Econ. Regl Analysis, 1997–; Dir, Pennell Initiative for Women's Health, 1997–. Pres., Relate, 1993–96. Trustee, Employment Policy Inst., 1995–98. Governor: Oxford Brookes Univ., 1993– (Dep. Chm., 1998–); Birkbeck Coll., Univ. of London, 1996–98. Hon. Fellow, St Hilda's Coll., Oxford, 1988. Hon. DLitt Kingston, 1993; DU Essex, 1993; Hon. LLD: Oxford Brookes, 1993; West of England, 1993; Strathclyde, 1994; Salford, 1994; Bristol, 1996. *Recreations:* family, friends, food. *Address:* Confessor's Gate, Islip, Oxford OX5 2SN. *Clubs:* Reform, Forum UK.

FOSTER, Jodie; *see* Foster, A. C.

FOSTER, John Graham; District Judge (Magistrates' Court), South Yorkshire, since 2001; *b* 28 April 1947; *s* of James Beaumont Foster and Margaret Foster; *m* 1971, Susan Boothroyd; three *s. Educ:* Woodhouse Grove Sch.; Sheffield Univ. (LLB Hons). Admitted Solicitor, 1973; in private practice with Morrish & Co., Solicitors, Leeds, 1970–2001 (Partner 1975–2001); Dep. Dist Judge, 1997–2001. *Recreations:* after dinner speaking, theatre, films, music, sport, especially badminton and cricket. *Address:* c/o Rotherham Magistrates' Court, The Statutes, PO Box 15, Rotherham S60 1YW. *T:* (01709) 839339.

FOSTER, Sir John (Gregory), 3rd Bt *cr* 1930; Consultant Physician, George, Cape Province, until 2001; *b* 26 Feb. 1927; *s* of Sir Thomas Saxby Gregory Foster, 2nd Bt, and Beryl, *d* of late Dr Alfred Ireland; *S* father, 1957; *m* 1956, Jean Millicent Watts; one *s* three *d. Educ:* Michaelhouse Coll., Natal. South African Artillery, 1944–46; Witwatersrand Univ., 1946–51; MB, BCh 1951; Post-graduate course, MRCPE 1955; Medical Registrar, 1955–56; Medical Officer, Cape Town, 1957. DIH London, 1962; FRCPE 1981. *Recreation:* outdoor sport. *Heir:* *s* Saxby Gregory Foster [*b* 3 Sept. 1957; *m* 1989, Rowen Audrey, *d* of R. A. Ford; two *s*]. *Address:* 7 Caledon Street, PO Box 1325, George 6530, Cape Province, South Africa. *T:* (44) 8743333, *Fax:* (44) 8732507. *Club:* Johannesburg Country (S Africa).

FOSTER, (John) Peter, OBE 1990; Surveyor of the Fabric of Westminster Abbey, 1973–88, now Emeritus; *b* 2 May 1919; *s* of Francis Edward Foster and Evelyn Marjorie, *e d* of Sir Charles Stewart Forbes, 5th Bt of Newe; *m* 1944, Margaret Elizabeth Skipper; one *s* one *d. Educ:* Eton; Trinity Hall, Cambridge. BA 1940, MA 1946; ARIBA 1949. Commnd RE 1941; served Norfolk Div.; joined Guards Armd Div. 1943, served France and Germany; Captain SORE(2) 30 Corps 1945; discharged 1946. Marshall Sisson, Architect: Asst 1948, later Partner; Sole Principal 1971; Surveyor of Royal Academy of Arts, 1965–80. Partner with John Peters of Vine Press, Hemingford Grey, 1957–63. Art Workers' Guild: Mem., 1971; Master, 1980; Trustee, 1985. Pres., Surveyors Club, 1980. Member: Churches Cttee for Historic Building Council for England, 1977–84; Adv. Bd for Redundant Churches, 1979–91; Exec. Cttee, Georgian Gp, 1983–91; Fabric Cttee, Canterbury Cathedral, 1987–91 (Chm., 1990); Council, Ancient Monuments Soc., 1988–; Fabric Cttee, Ely Cathedral, 1990–. Chm., Cathedral Architects Assoc., 1987–90; Pres., Assoc. for Studies in Conservation of Historic Buildings, 2001. Governor, Suttons Hosp., Charterhouse, 1982–2000. FSA 1973; FRSA 1994. CStJ 1987. *Publication:* Holiday Painter: watercolours 1935–1998, 2000. *Recreations:* painting, books, travel. *Address:* Harcourt, Hemingford Grey, Huntingdon, Cambs PE28 9BJ. *T:* (01480) 462200. *Club:* Athenæum.

FOSTER, Jonathan Rowe; QC 1989; a Recorder, since 1988; a Deputy High Court Judge, since 1994; *b* 20 July 1947; *s* of Donald Foster and Hilda Eaton; *m* 1978, Sarah Ann Mary da Cunha; four *s. Educ:* Oundle Sch.; Keble Coll., Oxford. Called to the Bar, Gray's Inn, 1970, Bencher, 1998. Treas., Northern Circuit, 1992–97. Member: Criminal Injuries Compensation Bd, 1995–; Criminal Injuries Compensation Appeal Panel, 1996–. Gov., Ryleys' Sch., 1990–. *Recreations:* outdoor pursuits, bridge. *Address:* (chambers) 18 St John Street, Manchester M3 4EA. *T:* (0161) 278 1800. *Clubs:* St James's (Manchester); Hale Golf, Bowdon Lawn Tennis; Treaddur Bay Sailing.

FOSTER, Lawrence; conductor; Music Director, Barcelona Symphony Orchestra and National Orchestra of Catalonia, since 1996; *b* Los Angeles, 23 Oct. 1941; *s* of Thomas Foster and Martha Wurmbrandt. *Educ:* Univ. of California, LA; studied under Fritz Zweig, Bruno Walter and Karl Böhm. Asst Conductor, Los Angeles Philharmonic, 1965–68; British début, Royal Festival Hall, 1968; Covent Garden début, Troilus and Cressida, 1976; Chief Guest Conductor, Royal Philharmonic Orchestra, 1969–74; Music Dir and Chief Conductor, Houston Symphony Orchestra, 1971–78; Chief Conductor, Orchestre National (later Orchestre Philharmonique) of Monte Carlo, 1978–95; Gen. Music Dir, Duisberg concert series, 1982–86; Prin. Guest Conductor, Düsseldorf Opera, 1982–86; Music Director: Lausanne Chamber Orch., 1985–90; Aspen Fest., 1991–; Guest Conductor: Deutsche Oper Berlin; LA Music Centre Opera; LA Philharmonic Orch.; Hallé Orch.; Pittsburgh, Chicago, Montreal, and Jerusalem Symphony Orchs; Orchestre de Paris. *Recreations:* reading European history, films. *Address:* c/o Harrison/Parrott, 12 Penzance Place, W11 4PA.

FOSTER, Michael Jabez; DL; MP (Lab) Hastings and Rye, since 1997; *b* Hastings, 26 Feb. 1946; *s* of Dorothy Foster; *m* 1969, Rosemary, *d* of Eric and Hilda Kemp; two *s. Educ:* Hastings Secondary Sch.; Hastings Grammar Sch.; Leicester Univ. (LLM). Admitted Solicitor, 1980; ACIArb 1997. Partner, 1980–99, Consultant, 1999–, Fynmores, solicitors, Bexhill-on-Sea; specialist in employment law. Member: Hastings CBC, 1971–74 (Ldr, Lab. Gp, 1973); Hastings BC, 1973–79, 1983–87 (Ldr, Lab. Gp and Dep. Ldr of Council, 1973–79); E Sussex CC, 1973–77, 1981–97 (Dep Leader, Lab Gp, 1984–93); Mem., Sussex Police Authy, 1991–96; Mem., E Sussex AHA, later Hastings HA, 1974–91. Contested (Lab) Hastings, Feb. and Oct. 1974, 1979. PPS to Attorney General, 1999–. DL E Sussex, 1993. *Address:* House of Commons, SW1A 0AA.

FOSTER, Michael John; MP (Lab) Worcester, since 1997; *b* 14 March 1963; *s* of Brian and Edna Foster; *m* 1985, Shauna Ogle; one *s* two *d. Educ:* Great Wyrley High Sch., Staffs; Wolverhampton Poly. (BA Hons Econs 1984); Univ. of Wolverhampton (PGCE 1995). ACMA. Management Accountant, Jaguar Cars, 1984–91; Lectr, Worcester Coll. of Technology, 1991–97. PPS to Minister of State for Lifelong Learning and Higer Educn, Dept of Edcn and Skills, 2001–. Mem., Educn Select Cttee, 1999–2001. *Recreations:* most sports, gardening. *Address:* House of Commons, SW1A 0AA. *T:* (020) 7219 6379. *Club:* Worcestershire County Cricket.

FOSTER, Peter; *see* Foster, J. P.

FOSTER, Maj.-Gen. Peter Beaufoy, MC 1944; Major-General Royal Artillery, British Army of the Rhine, 1973–76; retired June 1976; *b* 1 Sept. 1921; *s* of F. K. Foster, OBE, JP, Allt Dinas, Cheltenham; *m* 1947, Margaret Geraldine, *d* of W. F. Henn, sometime Chief Constable of Glos; two *s* one *d* (and one *s* decd). *Educ:* Uppingham School. Commnd RA, 1941; psc 1950; jssc 1958; OC Para. Light Battery, 1958–60; DAMS MS5, WO, 1960–63; Mil. Assistant to C-in-C BAOR, 1963–64; CO 34 Light Air Defence Regt RA, 1964–66; GSO1, ASD5, MoD, 1966–68; BRA Northern Comd, 1968–71; Comdt Royal Sch. of Artillery, 1971–73. Col Comdt, RA, 1977–82; Regimental Comptroller, RA, 1985–86. Vice President: RA Assoc., 1986–; RHA Assoc., 1994–. Chapter Clerk, Salisbury Cathedral, 1978–85. *Recreations:* shooting, gardening, beagling, walking, reading. *Address:* Sherborn House, High Street, Chipping Campden, Glos GL55 6HB.

FOSTER, Peter Martin, CMG 1975; HM Diplomatic Service, retired; *b* 25 May 1924; *s* of Capt. Frederick Arthur Pearce Foster, RN and Marjorie Kathleen Sandford; *m* 1947,

Angela Hope Cross; one *s* one *d.* *Educ:* Sherborne; Corpus Christi Coll., Cambridge. Army (Horse Guards), 1943–47; joined Foreign (now Diplomatic) Service, 1948; served in Vienna, Warsaw, Pretoria/Cape Town, Bonn, Kampala, Tel Aviv; Head of Central and Southern Africa Dept, FCO, 1972–74; Ambassador and UK Rep. to Council of Europe, 1974–78; Ambassador to German Democratic Republic, 1978–81. Dir, Council for Arms Control, 1984–86; Chm., Internat. Social Service of GB, 1985–90. *Address:* Rew Cottage, Abinger Lane, Abinger Common, Surrey RH5 6HZ. *T:* (01306) 730114.

FOSTER, Richard Scot; Director, Welfare to Work, Employment Service, Department for Work and Pensions (formerly at Department for Education and Employment), since 1998; *b* 26 March 1950; *s* of Frank Walter Foster and Betty Lilian Foster; *m* 1997, Susan Warner Johnson; one *s* one *d.* *Educ:* Devonport High Sch.; Pembroke Coll., Cambridge (MA Hons Moral Scis). Joined Dept of Employment, 1973; Sec., MSC, 1975–77; Private Sec. to Minister, 1977–78; on secondment to FCO, Stockholm, 1981–84; Industrial Relations policy, 1984–86; Head of Strategy Unit, 1986–88; Director: Finance and Planning, Employment Service, 1988–90; Trng Commn (SW), 1990–92; London and SE, Employment Service, 1992–98. *Recreations:* ski-ing, climbing, opera, theatre, tennis. *Address:* Torrens, Cavendish Road, Weybridge, Surrey KT13 0JW. *T:* (01932) 855672. *Club:* Ski of GB.

FOSTER, Robert; Secretary, Competition Commission, since 2001; *b* 12 May 1943; *s* of David and Amelia Foster; *m* 1967, Judy Welsh; one *s* one *d.* *Educ:* Oundle Sch.; Corpus Christi Coll., Cambridge (BA 1964; MA 1967). CEng, FIEE 1993; FRAeS 1996. Development Engineer: Parkinson Cowan, 1964–66; Automation Ltd, 1966–71; Exec. Engineer, Post Office Telecommunications, 1971–76; DTI, 1977–92; Under Sec., OST, Cabinet Office, 1992–93, DTI, 1993–2000. *Recreations:* theatre, tennis, squash, music. *Address:* 9 Holmdene Avenue, SE24 9LB.

FOSTER, Prof. Robert Fitzroy, (Roy), PhD; FRSL; FRHistS; FBA 1989; Carroll Professor of Irish History, University of Oxford, since 1991; *b* 16 Jan. 1949; *s* of Frederick Ernest Foster and Elizabeth (*née* Fitzroy); *m* 1972, Aisling O'Conor Donelan; one *s* one *d.* *Educ:* Newtown Sch., Waterford; St Andrew's Sch., Middletown, Delaware, USA; Trinity Coll., Dublin (MA; PhD 1975). FRHistS 1979; FRSL 1992. Lectr, 1974, Reader, 1983, Professor of Modern British Hist., 1988–91, Birkbeck Coll., London Univ. Alistair Horne Fellow, St Antony's Coll., Oxford, 1979–80; British Acad. Res. Reader in the Humanities, 1987–89; Fellow, Inst. for Advanced Study, Princeton, and Vis. Fellow, Dept of English, Princeton Univ., 1988–89. Hon. DLitt: Aberdeen, 1997; QUB, 1998. Irish Post Community Award, 1982; Sunday Independent/Irish Life Arts Award, 1988. *Publications:* Charles Stewart Parnell: the man and his family, 1976, 2nd edn 1979; Lord Randolph Churchill: a political life, 1981, 3rd edn 1987; Political Novels and Nineteenth Century History, 1983; Modern Ireland 1600–1972, 1988; (ed) The Oxford Illustrated History of Ireland, 1989; (ed) The Sub-Prefect Should Have Held His Tongue and other essays, by Hubert Butler, 1990; Paddy and Mr Punch: connections in English and Irish history, 1993; The Story of Ireland, 1995; W. B. Yeats: a life, Vol. 1 The Apprentice Mage 1865–1914, 1997 (James Tait Black Prize for biog., 1998); The Irish Story: telling tales and making it up in Ireland, 2001; numerous essays and reviews. *Recreation:* recreation. *Address:* Hertford College, Oxford OX1 3BW. *Club:* Kildare Street and University (Dublin).

FOSTER, Sir Robert (Sidney), GCMG 1970 (KCMG 1964; CMG 1961); KCVO 1970; Governor-General and Commander-in-Chief of Fiji, 1970–73 (Governor and C-in-C, 1968–70); retired 1973; *b* 11 Aug. 1913; *s* of late Sidney Charles Foster and late Jessie Edith (*née* Fry); *m* 1947, Margaret (*née* Walker) (*d* 1991); no *c.* *Educ:* Eastbourne Coll.; Peterhouse, Cambridge. MA. Appointed Cadet, Administrative Service, Northern Rhodesia, 1936; District Officer, N Rhodesia, 1938. War Service, 2nd Bn Northern Rhodesia Regt, 1940–43, Major. Provincial Commissioner, N Rhodesia, 1957; Sec., Ministry of Native Affairs, N Rhodesia, 1960; Chief Sec., Nyasaland, 1961–63; Dep. Governor, Nyasaland, 1963–64; High Comr for W Pacific, 1964–68. KStJ 1968. Officer of the Legion of Honour, 1966. *Recreation:* self-help. *Address:* 18 Windmill Lane, Histon, Cambridge CB4 9JF. *Clubs:* Royal Over-Seas League; Leander (Henley); Hawks (Cambridge).

FOSTER, Roy; *see* Foster, Robert Fitzroy.

FOSTER, Samuel; Member (UU) Fermanagh and South Tyrone, since 1998, and Minister for the Environment, since 1999, Northern Ireland Assembly; *b* 7 Dec. 1931; *s* of late Samuel and Margaret Foster; *m* 1952, Dorothy Claire Brown; two *s* one *d.* *Educ:* Enniskillen Tech. Coll.; Ulster Poly., Belfast (CQSW). Compositor and proof reader, 1946–66; Sen. Educn Welfare Officer, Western Educn and Liby Bd, 1967–78; social worker: Wirral Social Services, 1979; Western Health and Social Services, 1980–96. Co. Comdr, UDR, 1970–78 (Major). Mem. (UU), Fermanagh DC, 1981–2001 (Chm., 1995–97). Mem. for Fermanagh and S Tyrone, NI Forum for Political Dialogue, 1996–98. Mem., Police Authy for NI, 1982–85. *Publication:* Recall: a little history of Orangeism and Protestantism in Fermanagh—King William Prince of Orange and all that … (booklet), 1990. *Recreations:* sport, especially soccer, table tennis, historical aspects, debate. *Address:* 35 Derrychara Road, Enniskillen, Co. Fermanagh BT74 6JF. *T:* (028) 6632 3594. *Club:* Fermanagh Unionist (Enniskillen).

FOSTER, Simon Ridgeby; farmer; *b* 1 Sept. 1939; *s* of Sir Ridgeby Foster and of Lady Nancy Foster (*née* Godden); *m* 1st, 1966, Mairi Angela Chisholm (marr. diss.); one *s* two *d*; 2nd, 1990, Philippa Back. *Educ:* Shrewsbury Sch.; Jesus Coll., Cambridge (MA Hist.); London Business Sch. (Sloane Fellow); Wye Coll., London Univ. (MSc Sustainable Agric. 1995). Pres. and Dir. Gen., Dunlop France, 1983–88; Dir, SMMT, 1988–91; Man. Dir, Toyota GB, 1991–93. Médaille d'Allier, 1987. *Publication:* Politique Industrielle, 1990. *Recreations:* farming, Dutch sailing barges.

FOSTER, Thomas Ashcroft; *b* 27 May 1934; *s* of Thomas Lawrence Foster and Ada May Foster (*née* Ashcroft); *m* 1959, Beryl Wilson; two *d.* *Educ:* Rivington and Blackrod Grammar Sch.; Univ. of Leicester (Dip. Social Studies 1957); University Coll. of South Wales and Momouthshire (Dip. Applied Social Studies 1963); Univ. of Sheffield (MA 2001). Youth Employment Asst, Derbyshire CC, 1957–59; Child Care Officer, Manchester City Council, 1959–62; Senior Mental Welfare Officer, Carlisle City Council, 1963; Student Supervisor, Children's Dept, Glamorgan CC, 1963–67; Area Children's Officer, Lancs CC, 1967–71; Divl Dir, Social Services, Cheshire CC, 1971–73; Dir, Social Services, Tameside Met. Borough Council, 1973–86; Dir of Social Services, Lancs CC, 1986–90. Mem., Cttee of Inquiry into Mental Handicap Nursing and Care, 1975–79; Social Services Adviser, AMA, 1983–86. Sen. Vice-Pres., Assoc. of Dirs of Social Servs, 1990 (Hon. Sec., Mental Health sub-cttee, 1991–95). Hon. Lectr, Univ. of Lancaster, 1990–2000. *Recreations:* theatre, archaeology, walking.

FOTHERBY, Gordon; Deputy Solicitor, HM Customs and Excise, since 1993; *b* 15 Nov. 1950; *m* 1974, Victoria Eloise. *Educ:* Hull GS; Sheffield Univ. (LLB Hons 1972). Called to the Bar, Inner Temple, 1973; Capt., Army Legal Corps, 1973–77; Solicitor's Office, HM Customs and Excise, 1977–. Asst Sec., Legal, 1986–93; on secondment to EC, 1989–91. *Address:* c/o Solicitor's Office, HM Customs and Excise, New King's Beam House, SE1 9PJ.

FOTHERGILL, Alastair David William; Series Producer, BBC Natural History Unit, since 1998; *b* 10 April 1960; *s* of David and Jaqueline Fothergill; *m* 1994, Melinda Jane Barker; two *s.* *Educ:* Harrow Sch.; St Andrews Univ.; Durham Univ. (BSc). Joined BBC Natural History Unit, 1983, Head, 1992–98. *Publications:* Life in the Freezer, 1993; The Blue Planet, 2001. *Recreations:* fly-fishing, walking, diving. *Address:* 5 Caledonia Place, Clifton, Bristol BS8 4DH. *T:* (0117) 973 1312.

FOTHERGILL, Dorothy Joan; Director, Postal Pay and Grading, 1974–83, retired; *b* 31 Dec. 1923; *d* of Samuel John Rimington Fothergill and Dorothy May Patterson. *Educ:* Haberdashers' Aske's Sch., Acton; University Coll. London. BA (Hons) History. Entered Civil Service as Asst Principal, 1948; Principal, Overseas Mails branch, GPO, 1953; UPU Congress, Ottawa, 1957; Establishments work, 1958–62; HM Treasury, 1963–65; Asst Sec., Pay and Organisation, GPO, 1965; Director: Postal Personnel, 1970; London Postal Region, 1971. *Recreations:* gardening, walking, theatre. *Address:* 38 Andrewes House, Barbican, EC2Y 8AX.

FOTHERGILL, Richard Humphrey Maclean; Director, The Ceres Trust, 1988–97; *b* 21 March 1937; *s* of late Col C. G. Fothergill, RM, and Mrs E. G. Fothergill; *m* 1962, Angela Cheshire Martin; three *d.* *Educ:* Sandle Manor, Fordingbridge; Clifton Coll., Bristol; Emmanuel Coll., Cambridge (BA Hons Nat. Sci. Tripos, 1958). Commnd RASC, National Service, 1959–61. Contemporary Films Ltd, 1961; Head of Biology, SW Ham Technical Sch., 1961–69; Res. Fellow, Nat. Council for Educnl Technol., 1970–72; Founder and Head of PETRAS (Educnl Develt Unit), Newcastle upon Tyne Polytechnic, 1972–80; Dir, Microelectronics Educn Prog., DES, 1980–86; Dir, CET, 1986–87. Co-founder, Sec. and Treasurer, Standing Conf. on Educnl Develt Services in Polytechnics, 1974–80; Member: London GCE Bd and Schools Council Science Cttee, 1968–72; Standards and Specifications Cttee, CET, 1972–80. *Publications:* A Challenge for Librarians, 1971; Resource Centres in Colleges of Education, 1973; (with B. Williams) Microforms in Education, 1977; Child Abuse: a teaching package, 1978; (with I. Butchart) Non-book Materials in Libraries: a practical guide, 1978, 3rd edn 1990; (with J. S. A. Anderson) Microelectronics Education Programme: policy and guidelines, 1983; Implications of the New Technology for the School Curriculum, 1988; The Fothergills: a first history, 1998; articles in Visual Educn, Educn Libraries Bull., Educnl Media Internat., and Educnl Broadcasting Internat. *Recreations:* reading, television, films, walking. *Address:* 17 Grenville Drive, Brunton Park, Newcastle upon Tyne NE3 5PA. *T:* (0191) 236 3380. *Club:* National Film Theatre.

FOU TS'ONG; concert pianist; *b* 10 March 1934; *m* 1st, 1960, Zamira Menuhin (marr. diss. 1970); one *s*; 2nd, 1973, Hijong Hyun (marr. diss. 1976); 3rd, 1987, Patsy Toh; one *s.* *Educ:* Shanghai and Warsaw. Debut, Shanghai, 1953. Concerts all over Eastern Europe including USSR up to 1958. Arrived in Great Britain, Dec. 1958; London debut, Feb. 1959, followed by concerts in England, Scotland and Ireland; subsequently has toured all five Continents. Hon. DLitt Hong Kong, 1983. *Recreations:* many different ones. *Address:* 62 Aberdeen Park, N5 2BL. *T:* (020) 7226 9589, *Fax:* (020) 7704 8896.

FOULDS, (Hugh) Jon; Chairman: L Huntsworth plc, since 2000; Halifax plc (formerly Halifax Building Society), 1990–99 (Director, 1986–99); Deputy Chairman, 3i Group plc (formerly Investors in Industry), 1988–92 (Director and Chief Executive, 1976–88); *b* 2 May 1932; *s* of late Dr E. J. Foulds and Helen Shirley (*née* Smith); *m* 1st, 1960, Berry Cusack-Smith (marr. diss. 1970); two *s*; 2nd, 1977, Hélène Senn, *d* of Edouard Senn, Paris. *Educ:* Bootham Sch., York. Director: Brammer plc, 1980–91 (Chm., 1988–90); London Smaller Companies (formerly London Atlantic) Investment Trust, 1983–95; Pan-Holdings SA, 1986–; Eurotunnel plc, 1988–96; Mercury Asset Management Gp plc, 1989–98. Mem. Bd of Banking Supervision, Bank of England, 1993–96. Hon. MA Salford, 1987. *Recreations:* tennis, ski-ing, shooting, pictures. *Address:* 28 Grosvenor Crescent Mews, SW1X 7EX. *Clubs:* Garrick, Hurlingham; Cercle Interallié (Paris).

FOULGER, Keith, BSc(Eng); CEng, MIMechE; FRINA, RCNC; Chief Naval Architect, Ministry of Defence, 1983–85, retired; *b* 14 May 1925; *s* of Percy and Kate Foulger; *m* 1951, Joyce Mary Hart; one *s* one *d.* *Educ:* Univ. of London (Mech. Eng.); Royal Naval Coll., Greenwich. Asst Constructor, 1950; Constructor, 1955; Constructor Commander: Dreadnought Project, 1959; C-in-C Western Fleet, 1965; Chief Constructor, 1967; Asst Director, Submarines, 1973; Deputy Director: Naval Construction, 1979; Naval Ship Production, 1979–81; Submarines, Ship Dept, 1981–83; Asst Under-Sec. of State, 1983. *Recreations:* enjoying increasing grandfatherhood, travel, gardening, photography. *Address:* Lindley, North Road, Bathwick, Bath BA2 6HW.

FOULIS, Sir Iain (Primrose Liston), 13th Bt *cr* 1634, of Colinton; Bt 1661, of Ravelston, but for the attainder; Language Tutor, Madrid, 1966–83; *b* 9 Aug. 1937; *s* of Lieut-Colonel James Alistair Liston-Foulis, Royal Artillery (killed on active service, 1942), and Mrs Kathleen de la Hogue Moran (*d* 1991), 2nd *d* of Lt-Col. John Moran, Indian Army and Countess Olga de la Hogue, *yr d* of Marquis de la Hogue, Mauritius; *S* cousin, Sir Archibald Charles Liston Foulis, 12th Bt, 1961. *Educ:* Hodder; St Mary's Hall; Stonyhurst Coll.; Cannington Farm Inst., Somerset (Dip. Agr.); Madrid (Dip. in Spanish). National Service, 1957–59; Argyll and Sutherland Highlanders, Cyprus, 1958 (Gen. Service Medal). Landowner, 1961–. Language Teacher, Estremadura and Madrid, 1959–61; Trainee, Bank of London and South America, 1962; Trainee, Bank of London and Montreal (in Nassau, 1963, Guatemala City, 1963–64; Managua, Nicaragua, 1964–65); Toronto (Sales), 1965–66. Mem., Standing Council of Baronets, 1988–. Life Mem., Nat. Trust for Scotland. Member: Spanish Soc. of the Friends of Castles; Friends of the St James Way. Cert. from Archbishop of Santiago de Compostela for pilgrimage on foot, Somport to Santiago, Jubilee Year, 1971. *Recreations:* swimming, walking, mountaineering, travelling, foreign languages and customs, reading, Spanish medieval history (especially Muslim Spain), car racing and rallies, country pursuits, hunting. *Address:* Juan Carlos I, I, Portal 5-2-C, San Agustin de Guadalix, 28750 Madrid, Spain. *T:* and *Fax:* (91) 8418978; Calle Universidad 28, Escalera 2, 5-D Jaca, Huesca, Spain.

FOULIS, Michael Bruce; Under Secretary, Enterprise and Lifelong Learning Department, Scottish Executive, since 1999; *b* 23 Aug. 1956; *s* of Kenneth Munro Foulis and Edith Lillian Sommerville (*née* Clark); *m* 1981, Gillian Margaret Tyson; one *s* one *d.* *Educ:* Kilmarnock Acad.; Edinburgh Univ. (BSc Geog.). Joined Scottish Office, 1978: Private Sec. to Parly Under Sec. of State, 1987–89; on secondment to Scottish Financial Enterprise as Asst Dir, 1989–91; Scottish Educn Dept, 1991–93; Principal Private Sec. to Sec. of State for Scotland, 1993–95; Hd of Div., Agric., Envmt and Fisheries Dept, 1995–97; on secondment to Cabinet Office as Dep. Hd, Devolution Team, Constitution Secretariat, 1997–98; Hd of Gp, Educn and Industry Dept, 1998–99. *Recreations:* playing cello, appreciating lithographs, moderate exercise. *Address:* Scottish Executive, Meridian Court, Cadogan Street, Glasgow G2 6AT.

FOULKES, Sir Arthur (Alexander), KCMG 2001; Ambassador (non-resident) of the Commonwealth of the Bahamas to the Peoples' Republic of China and to the Republic of Cuba, since 1999; *b* 11 May 1928; *s* of late Dr William Alexander Foulkes and Julie Blanche Foulkes (*née* Maisonneuve); *m* 1st, Naomi Louise Higgs; 2nd, Joan Eleanor Bullard. *Educ:* Public Sch., Inagua, Bahamas; Western Central Sch., Nassau, Bahamas; privately tutored in journalism. News Editor, The Tribune, 1950–62; Editor, Bahamian Times, 1962; Founder/Chm., Diversified Services (PR), 1967. MP Bahamas, 1967; Chm., Bahamas Telecommunications Corp., 1967; Cabinet Minister, 1968; Co-Founder, Free Nat. Movement, 1970; Mem., Senate, 1972. Delegate: Bahamas Petition to UN Cttee on Decolonization, 1965; Bahamas Constitutional Conf., London, 1972. High Comr to UK and Ambassador to France, Italy, Germany, Belgium and the EC, 1992–99. Chairman: Bahamas Broadcasting Corp., 2001–; Bahamas Parly Salaries Commn, 2001–; Bahamas Order of Merit Cttee, 2001–. *Recreations:* theatre, music, art, literature. *Address:* PO Box CB-12366, Nassau, Bahamas.

FOULKES, George; JP; MP (Lab and Co-op) Carrick, Cumnock and Doon Valley, since 1983 (South Ayrshire, 1979–83); Minister of State, Scotland Office, since 2001; *b* 21 Jan. 1942; *s* of late George and Jessie M. A. W. Foulkes; *m* 1970, Elizabeth Anna Hope; two *s* one *d*. *Educ:* Keith Grammar Sch., Keith, Banffshire; Haberdashers' Aske's Sch.; Edinburgh Univ. (BSc 1964). President: Edinburgh Univ. SRC, 1963–64; Scottish Union of Students, 1965–67; Manager, Fund for Internat. Student Cooperation, 1967–68. Scottish Organiser, European Movement, 1968–69; Director: European League for Econ. Co-operation, 1969–70; Enterprise Youth, 1970–73; Age Concern, Scotland, 1973–79. Councillor: Edinburgh Corp., 1970–75; Lothian Regional Council, 1974–79; Chairman: Lothian Region Educn Cttee, 1974–79; Educn Cttee, Convention of Scottish Local Authorities, 1975–78. Opposition spokesman on European and Community Affairs, 1984–85, on Foreign Affairs, 1985–92, on Defence, 1992–93, on Overseas Develt, 1994–97; Parly Under-Sec. of State, DFID, 1997–2001. Mem., Select Cttee on Foreign Affairs, 1981–83. Jt Chm., All Party Pensioners Cttee, 1983–97 (Sec./Treasurer 1979–83). UK Delegate to Parly Assembly of Council of Europe, 1979–81; Treas., Parliamentarians for Global Action, 1993–97 (Mem. Council, 1987–97); Member: UK Exec., CPA, 1987–97; IPU, 1989–97. Mem., Scottish Exec. Cttee, Labour Party, 1981–89. Rector's Assessor, Edinburgh Univ. Court, 1968–70, Local Authority Assessor, 1971–79. Chairman: Scottish Adult Literacy Agency, 1976–79; John Wheatley Centre, 1990–97. Mem. Exec., British/China Centre, 1987–93. Director: St Cuthbert's Co-op. Assoc., 1975–79; Co-op. Press Ltd, 1990–97. JP Edinburgh, 1975. Wilberforce Medal, City of Hull, 1998. *Publications:* Eighty Years On: history of Edinburgh University SRC, 1964; (contrib.) A Claim of Right, ed Owen Dudley Edwards, 1989. *Recreations:* boating, watching Heart of Midlothian FC. *Address:* House of Commons, SW1A 0AA.

FOULKES, Sir Nigel (Gordon), Kt 1980; Chairman: ECI International Management Ltd, 1987–91; ECI Management (Jersey) Ltd, 1986–91; Equity Capital Trustee Ltd, 1983–90; *b* 29 Aug. 1919; *s* of Louis Augustine and Winifred Foulkes; *m* 1948, Elisabeth Walker (*d* 1995), *d* of Ewart B. Walker, Toronto; one *s* one *d* of former marr. *Educ:* Gresham's Sch., Holt; Balliol Coll., Oxford (Schol., MA). RAF, 1940–45. Subsequently executive, consulting and boardroom posts with: H. P. Bulmer; P. E. Consulting Gp; Birfield; Greaves & Thomas; International Nickel; Rank Xerox (Asst Man. Dir 1964–67, Man. Dir 1967–70); Charterhouse Group Ltd (Dir, 1972–83); Dir, Charterhouse J. Rothschild plc, 1984–85; Chm., Equity Capital for Industry, 1983–86 (Vice-Chm., 1982); Dir, Bekaert Gp (Belgium), 1973–85. Chairman: British Airports Authority, 1972–77; Civil Aviation Authority, 1977–82. CIMgt; FRSA. *Club:* Royal Air Force.

FOUNTAIN, Alan; Founder, Mondial Television, 1994; Chairman, Mondialonline.com, since 1995; *b* 24 March 1946; *s* of Harold Fountain and Winifred Cecily Brown. *Educ:* Nottingham Univ. (BA Hons Philosophy). Film Officer, E Midlands Arts, 1976–79; producer, 1979–81; Channel Four TV, 1981–94 (Sen. Commissioning Editor, 1982–94); Head, Northern Media Sch., 1995–97; Programme Dir, Alfa TV, 1997–98. Professor of Cultural Industries, Middlesex Univ., 2001; Head of Studies, EAVE, 1999. *Publications:* (ed) Ruff's Guide to the Turf, 1972; contrib. film and TV pubns. *Recreations:* family, golf, watching sports. *Address:* 72 Sydney Road, N10 2RL.

FOUNTAIN, Hon. Sir Cyril (Stanley Smith), Kt 1996; Chief Justice, Supreme Court of Bahamas, 1996, retired; *b* 26 Oct. 1929; *s* of Harold Jackson Fountain and Winifred Olive Helen Fountain (*née* Smith); *m* 1954, Dorothy Alicia Hanna; two *s* one *d*. *Educ:* St Benedict's Coll., Atchison, Kansas (BA *cum laude* Econs); King's Coll. London (LLB Hons 1962). Head Teacher, Bd of Educn, Bahamas, 1955–58; articled law student to Sir Leonard J. Knowles, 1958–59; called to the Bar: Gray's Inn, 1963; Bahamas, 1963; Partner, Cash, Fountain & Co., 1963–93; Supreme Court of Bahamas: Actg Judge, April 1985 and April–Aug. 1990; Justice, 1993–94; Sen. Justice, 1994–96. MP (FNM) Long Island, Rum Cay and San Salvador, 1972–77. *Recreations:* swimming, historical reading. *Address:* PO Box N 476, Nassau, Bahamas. *T:* (home) 3936493; (office) 3222956/7.

FOURCADE, Jean-Pierre; Officier de l'ordre national du Mérite; Senator, French Republic, for Hauts-de-Seine, since 1977; *b* 18 Oct. 1929; *s* of Raymond Fourcade (Médecin) and Mme Fourcade (*née* Germaine Raynal); *m* 1958, Odile Mion; one *s* two *d*. *Educ:* Collège de Sorèze; Bordeaux Univ. Faculté de Droit, Institut des Etudes politiques (Dip.); Ecole nationale d'administration; higher studies in Law (Dip.). Inspecteur des Finances, 1954–73. Cabinet of M. Valéry Giscard d'Estaing: Chargé de Mission, 1959–61; Conseiller technique, 1962, then Dir Adjoint to chef de service, Inspection gén. des Finances, 1962; Chef de service du commerce, at Direction-Gén. du Commerce intérieur et des Prix, 1968–70; Dir-gén. adjoint du Crédit industriel et commercial, 1970; Dir-gén., 1972, and Administrateur Dir-gén., 1973; Ministre de l'Economie et des Finances, 1974–76; Ministre de l'Equipement et de l'Aménagement du Territoire, 1976–77. Mayor of Saint-Cloud, 1971–92; Conseiller général of canton of Saint-Cloud, 1973–89; Conseiller régional d'Ile de France, 1976– (Vice-Président, 1982–95); Mayor of Boulogne-Billancourt, 1995–. Président: Clubs Perspectives et Realités, 1975–82; Comité des Finances Locales, 1980; Commn des Affaires Sociales du Sénat, 1983–98; Vice-Pres., Union pour la Démocratie Française, 1978–86 (Mem. Bureau, 1986). *Publications:* Et si nous parlions de demain, 1979; La tentation social-démocrate, 1985; Remèdes pour l'Assurance-Maladie, 1989. *Address:* Palais du Luxembourg, 75291 Paris cedex 06, France; 8 Parc de Béarn, 92210 Saint-Cloud, France.

FOURNIER, Bernard; Chief Executive Officer, Xerox Ltd, 1995; *b* 2 Dec. 1938; *s* of Jean Fournier and Solange Hervieu; *m* 1st; two *s*; 2nd, 1980, Françoise Chavailler; one *s*. *Educ:* Philo Lycée (Baccalauréat); Louis Le Grand, Paris; Ecole des Hautes Etudes Commerciales, Lille. Joined: Publiart SA, 1964; Sanglier SA, 1965; Rank Xerox, 1966: Regional Manager Africa, Eastern Europe, 1980; Gen. Manager, RX France, 1981; Pres., Amer. Ops, Xerox, 1988; Man. Dir, Rank Xerox Ltd, 1989–95. *Recreations:* tennis, cooking, oenology, stamps, antiques. *Address:* c/o Xerox Ltd, Riverview, Oxford Road, Uxbridge UB8 1HS.

FOURNIER, Jean, OC 1987; CD 1972; retired diplomat; *b* Montreal, 18 July 1914; *s* of Arthur Fournier and Emilie Roy; *m* 1942, May Coote; five *s*. *Educ:* High Sch. of Québec; Laval Univ. (BA 1935, LLB 1938). Admitted to Bar of Province of Quebec, 1939. Royal Canadian Artillery (NPAM) (Lieut), 1935; Canadian Active Service Force Sept. 1939; served in Canada and overseas; discharged 1944, Actg Lt-Col. Joined Canadian Foreign Service, 1944; Third Sec., Canadian Dept of External Affairs, 1944; Second Sec., Canadian Embassy, Buenos Aires, 1945; Nat. Defence Coll., Kingston, 1948 (ndc); Seconded: to Privy Council Office, 1948–50; to Prime Minister's Office, Oct. 1950–Feb. 1951; First Sec., Canadian Embassy, Paris, 1951; Counsellor, 1953; Consul Gen., Boston, 1954; Privy Council Office (Asst Sec. to Cabinet), 1957–61; Head of European Division (Political Affairs), Dept of External Affairs, 1961–64; Chm., Quebec Civil Service Commn, 1964–71; Agent Gen. for the Province of Quebec in London, 1971–78. Mem., Canadian Metric Commn, 1981–85. Pres., Inst. of Public Administration of Canada, 1966–67; Pres., Centre Québecois de Relations Internationales; Chm. Bd, Canadian Human Rights Foundn, 1982–90; Member: Canadian Inst. of Strategic Studies; Canadian Inst. of Internat. Affairs. Freedom, City of London, 1976. Pres., Canadian Veterans Assoc. of the UK, 1976–77. *Address:* Apt 615, 4430 Ste-Catherine 0, Westmount, QC H3Z 3E4, Canada. *T:* (514) 9328633.

FOUYAS, Metropolitan Methodios, of Pisidia; former Archbishop of Thyateira and Great Britain; Greek Orthodox Archbishop of Great Britain, 1979–88; *b* 14 Sept. 1925. BD (Athens); PhD (Manchester), 1962. Vicar of Greek Church in Munich, 1951–54; Secretary-General, Greek Patriarchate of Alexandria, 1954–56; Vicar of Greek Church in Manchester, 1960–66; Secretary, Holy Synod of Church of Greece, 1966–68; Archbishop of Aksum (Ethiopia), 1968–79. Founder, Harmony of Otherness, 2000. Member, Academy of Religious Sciences, Brussels, 1974–. Dist. Lectr, Univ. of Berkeley, 1992. Estabd Foundn for Hellenism in GB, 1982; Editor, Texts and Studies: a review of the Foundn for Hellenism in GB, Vols I–X, 1982–91; Founder-Editor, Abba Salama Review of Ethio-Hellenic Studies, 10 Volumes; Editor: Ekklesiastikos Pharos (Prize of Academy of Athens), 11 Volumes; Ecclesia and Theologia, vols I-XII, 1980–93. Hon. DD: Edinburgh, 1970; Gr. Th. School of Holy Cross, Boston, 1984. Grand Cordon: Order of Phoenix (Greece); of Sellassie (Ethiopia). *Publications:* Orthodoxy, Roman Catholicism and Anglicanism, 1972, 2nd edn 1984, 3rd edn in Greek 1996; The Person of Jesus Christ in the Decisions of the Ecumenical Councils, 1976, 2nd edn in Greek 1997; History of the Church in Corinth, 1968, 2nd edn 1997; Christianity and Judaism in Ethiopia, Nubia and Meroe, 1st Vol., 1979, 2nd Vol., 1982; Theological and Historical Studies, Vols 1–13, 1979–94; Greeks and Latins, 1990, 2nd edn 1994; Hellenism, the Pedestal of Christianity, 1992; Contemporary History of the Church of Alexandria, 1993; Hellenism, the Pedestal of Islam, 1994, 2nd edn 1995; Hellenism and Judaism, 1995; The Hellenistic Jewish Tradition, 1996; Hellenic Problems, 1997; Letters of Meletius Pegas, Pope and Patriarch of Alexandria 1590–1601, 1976, 2nd edn 1998; Hellenism, the Pedestal of European Civilisation, 1999; contrib. to many other books and treatises. *Recreation:* gardening. *Address:* 9 Riga Feraiou Street, Khalandri, 15232 Athens, Greece. *T:* 6824793.

FOWDEN, Sir Leslie, Kt 1982; FRS 1964; Director of Arable Crops Research, Agricultural and Food Research Council, 1986–88; *b* Rochdale, Lancs, 13 Oct. 1925; *s* of Herbert and Amy D. Fowden; *m* 1949, Margaret Oakes; one *s* one *d*. *Educ:* University Coll., London. PhD Univ. of London, 1948. Scientific Staff of Human Nutrition Research Unit of the MRC, 1947–50; Lecturer in Plant Chemistry, University Coll. London, 1950–55, Reader, 1956–64, Prof. of Plant Chemistry, 1964–73; Dean of Faculty of Science, UCL, 1970–73; Dir, Rothamsted Exptl Station, 1973–86. Rockefeller Fellow at Cornell Univ., 1955; Visiting Prof. at Univ. of California, 1963; Royal Society Visiting Prof., Univ. of Hong Kong, 1967. Consultant Dir, Commonwealth Bureau of Soils, 1973–88. Chm., Agric. and Vet. Adv. Cttee, British Council, 1987–95; Member: Advisory Board, Tropical Product Inst., 1966–70; Council, Royal Society, 1970–72; Radioactive Waste Management Adv. Cttee, 1983–91. Royal Botanic Gardens, Kew: Mem., Scientific Adv. Panel, 1977–83; Trustee, 1983–93; Trustee, Bentham-Moxon Trust, 1994–. Foreign Member: Deutsche Akademie der Naturforscher Leopoldina, 1971; Lenin All-Union Acad. of Agricultural Sciences of USSR, 1978–92; Acad. of Agricl Scis of GDR, 1986–91; Russian Acad. of Agricl Scis, 1992–; Corresponding Mem., Amer. Soc. Plant Physiologists, 1981; Hon. Mem., Phytochemical Soc. of Europe, 1985. Hon. DSc Westminster, 1993. *Publications:* contribs to scientific journals on topics in plant biochemistry.

FOWELLS, Joseph Dunthorne Briggs, CMG 1975; DSC 1940; Deputy Director General, British Council, 1976–77, retired; *b* 17 Feb. 1916; *s* of late Joseph Fowells and Maud Dunthorne, Middlesbrough; *m* 1st, 1940, Edith Agnes McKerracher (marr. diss. 1966); two *s* one *d*; 2nd, 1969, Thelma Howes (*d* 1974). *Educ:* Sedbergh Sch.; Clare Coll., Cambridge (MA). School teaching, 1938; service with Royal Navy (Lt-Comdr), 1939–46; Blackie & Son Ltd, Educnl Publishers, 1946; British Council, 1947: Argentina, 1954; Representative Sierra Leone, 1956; Scotland, 1957; Dir Latin America and Africa (Foreign) Dept, 1958; Controller Overseas B Division (foreign countries excluding Europe), 1966; Controller Planning, 1968; Controller European Div., 1970; Asst Dir Gen. (Functional), 1972; Asst Dir Gen. (Regional), 1973–76. *Recreations:* golf, sailing. *Address:* Flat 11, Rose Tower, 62 Clarence Parade, Portsmouth PO5 2HX. *T:* (023) 9283 8220.

FOWKE, Sir David (Frederick Gustavus), 5th Bt *cr* 1814, of Lowesby, Leics; *b* 28 Aug. 1950; *s* of Lt-Col Gerrard George Fowke (*d* 1969) (2nd *s* of 3rd Bt) and of Daphne (*née* Monasteriotis); *S* uncle, 1987. *Educ:* Cranbrook School, Sydney; Univ. of Sydney (BA 1971). *Heir:* none.

FOWLER, family name of **Baron Fowler**.

FOWLER, Baron *cr* 2001 (Life Peer), of Sutton Coldfield in the County of West Midlands; **Peter Norman Fowler,** Kt 1990; PC 1979; Chairman, Aggregate Industries, since 2000; *b* 2 Feb. 1938; *s* of late N. F. Fowler and Katherine Fowler; *m* 1979, Fiona Poole, *d* of John Donald; two *d*. *Educ:* King Edward VI Sch., Chelmsford; Trinity Hall, Cambridge (MA). Nat. Service commn, Essex Regt, 1956–58; Cambridge, 1958–61; Chm., Cambridge Univ. Conservative Assoc., 1960. Joined staff of The Times, 1961; Special Corresp., 1962–66; Home Affairs Corresp., 1966–70; reported Middle East War, 1967. Mem. Council, Bow Group, 1967–69; Editorial Board, Crossbow, 1962–69; Vice-Chm., North Kensington Cons. Assoc., 1967–68; Chm., E Midlands Area, Cons. Political Centre, 1970–73. MP (C): Nottingham S, 1970–74; Sutton Coldfield, Feb. 1974–2001. Chief Opposition spokesman: Social Services, 1975–76; Transport, 1976–79; Opposition spokesman, Home Affairs, 1974–75; PPS, NI Office, 1972–74; Sec. of State for Transport, 1981 (Minister of Transport, 1979–81), for Social Services, 1981–87, for Employment, 1987–90; Opposition front bench spokesman on the envmt, transport and the regions, 1997–98, on home affairs, 1998–99. Mem., Parly Select Cttee on Race Relations and Immigration, 1970–74; Jt Sec., Cons. Parly Home Affairs Cttee, 1971–72, 1974 (Vice-Chm., 1974); Chm., Cons Parly Cttee on European Affairs, 1991–92. Special Advr to Prime Minister, 1992 Gen. Elecn; Chm., Cons. Party, 1992–94. Chairman: Midland Independent Newspapers, 1991–98; Regl Independent Media (Yorks Post gp of newspapers), 1998–; Numark Ltd, 1998–; Dir, NFC plc, 1990–97. Chm., NHBC, 1992–98. *Publications:* After the Riots: the police in Europe, 1979; political pamphlets including: The Cost of Crime, 1973; The Right Track, 1977; Ministers Decide: a memoir of the Thatcher years, 1991. *Address:* House of Lords, SW1A 0PW.

FOWLER, Prof. Alastair David Shaw, FBA 1974; Professor of English, University of Virginia, 1990–97; Regius Professor of Rhetoric and English Literature, University of Edinburgh, 1972–84, now Emeritus (University Fellow, 1985–87); *b* 17 Aug. 1930; *s* of David Fowler and Maggie Shaw; *m* 1950, Jenny Catherine Simpson; one *s* one *d. Educ:* Queen's Park Sch., Glasgow; Univ. of Glasgow; Univ. of Edinburgh; Pembroke Coll., Oxford. MA Edin. 1952 and Oxon 1955; DPhil Oxon 1957; DLitt Oxon 1972. Junior Res. Fellow, Queen's Coll., Oxford, 1955–59; Instructor, Indiana Univ., 1957–58; Lectr, UC Swansea, 1959–61; Fellow and Tutor in English Lit., Brasenose Coll., Oxford, 1962–71. Visiting Professor: Columbia Univ., 1964; Univ. of Virginia, 1969, 1979, 1985–90; Mem. Inst. for Advanced Study, Princeton, 1966, 1980; Visiting Fellow: Council of the Humanities, Princeton Univ., 1974; Humanities Research Centre, Canberra, 1980; All Souls Coll., Oxford, 1984. Lectures: Witter Bynner, Harvard, 1974; Ballard Matthews, Univ. of Wales, 1981; Coffin, UCL, 1984; Read-Tuckwell, Univ. of Bristol, 1991. Mem., Scottish Arts Council, 1976–77. Adv. Editor, New Literary History, 1972–; Gen. Editor, Longman Annotated Anthologies of English Verse, 1977–80; Mem. Editorial Board: English Literary Renaissance, 1978–; Word and Image, 1984–91, 1992–97; The Seventeenth Century, 1986–; Connotations, 1990–98; Translation and Literature, 1990–; English Review, 1990–. *Publications:* (trans. and ed) Richard Wills, De re poetica, 1958; Spenser and the Numbers of Time, 1964; (ed) C. S. Lewis, Spenser's Images of Life, 1967; (ed with John Carey) The Poems of John Milton, 1968; Triumphal Forms, 1970; (ed) Silent Poetry, 1970; (ed with Christopher Butler) Topics in Criticism, 1971; Seventeen, 1971; Conceitful Thought, 1975; Catacomb Suburb, 1976; Edmund Spenser, 1977; From the Domain of Arnheim, 1982; Kinds of Literature, 1982; A History of English Literature, 1987; The New Oxford Book of Seventeenth Century Verse, 1991; The Country House Poem, 1994; Time's Purpled Masquers, 1996; (ed) Paradise Lost, 1998; contribs to jls and books. *Address:* 11 East Claremont Street, Edinburgh EH7 4HT.

FOWLER, Beryl, (Mrs Henry Fowler); *see* Chitty, M. B.

FOWLER, Christopher B.; *see* Brocklebank-Fowler.

FOWLER, Dennis Houston, OBE 1979 (MBE 1963); HM Diplomatic Service, retired; *b* 15 March 1924; *s* of Joseph Fowler and Daisy Lilian Wraith Fowler (*née* Houston); *m* 1944, Lilias Wright Nairn Burnett; two *s* one *d. Educ:* Alleyn's Sch., Dulwich. Colonial Office, 1940; RAF, 1942–46; India Office (subseq. CRO), 1947; Colombo, 1951; Second Secretary, Karachi, 1955; CRO, 1959; First Secretary, Dar es Salaam, 1961; Diplomatic Service Administration (subseq. FCO), 1965; First Sec. and Head of Chancery, Reykjavik, 1969; FCO, 1973; First Sec., Head of Chancery and Consul, Kathmandu, 1977; Counsellor and Hd of Claims Dept, FCO, 1980–83. *Recreations:* golf, music, do-it-yourself. *Address:* 25 Dartnell Park Road, West Byfleet, Surrey KT14 6PN. *T:* (01932) 341583. *Clubs:* West Byfleet Golf; Royal Nepal Golf (Kathmandu).

FOWLER, Derek, CBE 1979; Deputy Chairman, Capita Group, 1990–2000; Chairman: Kier Group Pension Scheme, 1992–97; Railways (formerly BR) Pension Trustee Co., 1986–96; *b* 26 Feb. 1929; *s* of late George Edward Fowler and Kathleen Fowler; *m* 1st, 1953, Ruth Fox (*d* 1996); one *d*; 2nd, 1998, Nina Krzyzagorska. *Educ:* Grantham, Lincs. Financial appointments with: Grantham Borough Council, 1944–50; Spalding UDC, 1950–52; Nairobi City Council, 1952–62; Southend-on-Sea CBC, 1962–64. British Railways Board: Internal Audit Manager, 1964–67, and Management Acct, 1967–69, W Region; Sen. Finance Officer, 1969–71; Corporate Budgets Manager, 1971–73; Controller of Corporate Finance, 1973–75; Finance Mem., 1975–78; a Vice-Chm., 1981–90; Dep. Chm., 1990. Dir, Kier Gp, 1992–97. Mem., UK Accounting Standards Cttee, 1982–84. Vice-Chm., Papworth Hosp. NHS Trust, 1996–97 (Dir, 1995–97). Freeman, City of London, 1981; Liveryman, Co. of Loriners, 1981. JDipMA. *Recreation:* cartophily.

FOWLER, Sir (Edward) Michael (Coulson), Kt 1981; Mayor of Wellington, New Zealand, 1974–83; architectural consultant, since 1989; former company chairman and director; *b* 19 Dec. 1929; *s* of William Coulson Fowler and Faith Agnes Netherclift; *m* 1953, Barbara Hamilton Hall; two *s* one *d. Educ:* Christ's Coll., Christchurch, NZ; Auckland Univ. (MArch). Architect, London office, Ove Arup & Partners, 1954–56; own practice, Wellington, 1957–59; Partner, Calder Fowler Styles and Turner, 1959–89. Director: New Zealand Sugar Co., 1983–95; Cigna Insurance New Zealand Ltd, 1985–89. Chm., Queen Elizabeth II Arts Council, 1983–87. Wellington City Councillor, 1968–74. Nat. Pres., YHA of NZ, 1984–87. Medal of Honour, NZIA, 1983; Alfred O. Glasse Award, NZ Inst. of Planning, 1984. *Publications:* Wellington Sketches: Folio I, 1971, Folio II, 1974; Country Houses of New Zealand, 1972, 2nd edn 1977; The Architecture and Planning of Moscow, 1980; Eating Houses in Wellington, 1980; Wellington Wellington, 1981; Eating Houses of Canterbury, 1982; Wellington—A Celebration, 1983; The New Zealand House, 1983; Buildings of New Zealanders, 1984; Michael Fowler's University of Auckland, 1993. *Recreations:* sketching, reading, writing, history, politics. *Address:* Branches, Giffords Road, RD3 Blenheim, New Zealand. *T:* (3) 5728987; *e-mail:* michael.fowler@xtra.co.nz. *Club:* Wellington (Wellington, NZ).

FOWLER, Ian, OBE 1993; Principal Chief Clerk and Clerk to the Committee of Magistrates for the Inner London area, 1979–94; *b* 20 Sept. 1932; *s* of Major Norman William Frederick Fowler, OBE, QPM, and late Alice May (*née* Wakelin); *m* 1961, Gillian Cecily Allchin, JP; two *s* one *d. Educ:* Maidstone Grammar Sch.; Skinners Sch., Tunbridge Wells; King's Sch., Canterbury; St Edmund Hall, Oxford (MA). National Service, commnd 2nd Bn The Green Howards, 1951–53. Called to Bar, Gray's Inn, 1957; entered Inner London Magistrates Courts Service, 1959. Dep. Traffic Comr, Eastern Traffic Area, 1987–99. Councillor: Herne Bay UDC and Canterbury CC, 1961–83 (Mayor, 1976–77). Mem. Court, Univ. of Kent at Canterbury, 1976–. *Recreation:* reading. *Address:* 6 Dence Park, Herne Bay, Kent CT6 6BG.

FOWLER, John Francis, DSc, PhD; FInstP; Professor, Department of Human Oncology, University of Wisconsin, USA, 1988–94 and since 1999 (Emeritus Professor, 1994); Director of Cancer Research Campaign's Gray Laboratory, at Mount Vernon Hospital, Northwood, 1970–88; *b* 3 Feb. 1925; *er s* of Norman V. Fowler, Bridport, Dorset; *m* 1st, 1953, Kathleen Hardcastle Sutton, MB, BS (marr. diss. 1984); two *s* five *d*; 2nd, 1992, Anna Edwards, BSc, MCSP, SRP. *Educ:* Bridport Grammar Sch.; University Coll. of the South-West, Exeter. BSc 1st class Hons (London) 1944; MSc (London) 1946; PhD (London) 1955; DSc (London) 1974; FInstP 1957. Research Physicist: Newalls Insulation Co., 1944; Metropolitan Vickers Electrical Co., 1947; Newcastle upon Tyne Regional Hosp. Board (Radiotherapy service), 1950; Principal Physicist at King's Coll. Hosp., SE5, 1956; Head of Physics Section in Medical Research Council Radiotherapeutic Res. Unit, Hammersmith Hosp., 1959 (later the Cyclotron Unit); Reader in Physics, London Univ. at Med. Coll. of St Bartholomew's Hosp., 1962; Prof. of Med. Physics, Royal Postgraduate Med. Sch., London Univ., Hammersmith Hosp., 1963–70, Vice-Dean, 1967–70. Visiting Professor: in Oncology, Mddx Hosp. Med. Sch., 1977–88; Dept. of Oncol., University Hosp. of Leuven, Belgium, 1994–99; Bush Vis. Prof., Ontario Cancer Inst., Toronto, 1991. President: Hosp. Physicists Assoc., 1966–67; Europ. Soc. Radiat. Biol., 1974–76; British Inst. Radiol., 1977–78. Hon. Fellow, Amer. Coll. of Radiology, 1981; Hon. Member: Amer. Assoc. of Med. Physicists, 1983; Inst. of Physical Scis in Medicine, 1994; RCR, 1999. Hon. MD Helsinki, 1981; Hon. DSc Med. Coll. Wisconsin, 1989. Roentgen Award, BIR, 1965; Röntgen Plakette, Deutsches Röntgen Museum, 1978; Heath Meml Award, Univ. of Texas, Houston, 1981; Breur Medal, European Soc. Therapeutic Radiology and Oncology, 1983; Barclay Medal, BIR, 1985; Marie Sklodowska-Curie Medal, Polish Radiation Res. Soc., 1986; Gold Medal, Amer. Soc. Therapeutic Radiol. and Oncol., 1995. *Publications:* Nuclear Particles in Cancer Treatment, 1981; papers on radiobiology applied to radiotherapy, in Brit. Jl Radiology, Brit. Jl Cancer, Radiotherapy and Oncology, etc. *Recreations:* theatre, ballroom dancing, getting into the countryside. *Address:* K4/316, 600 Highland Avenue, Madison, WI 53792, USA.

FOWLER, Sir Michael; *see* Fowler, Sir E. M. C.

FOWLER, Neil Douglas; Editor, The Western Mail, since 1994; *b* 18 April 1956; *s* of late Arthur Vincent Fowler and Helen Pauline Fowler; *m* 1989, Carol Susan (*née* Cherry); one *d*, and one step *s. Educ:* Southend High Sch. for Boys; Univ. of Leicester (BA Social Scis). Reporter, Leicester Mercury, 1978–81; Dep. News Editor, then Asst Chief Sub-editor, Derby Evening Telegraph, 1981–84; Asst to Editor, Asst Editor, then Editor, Lincolnshire Echo, 1984–87; Editor, Derby Evening Telegraph, 1987–91; Editor, The Journal, Newcastle upon Tyne, 1991–94. Dir, Publishing NTO, 2000–. FRSA 1999. Pres., Society (formerly Guild) of Editors, 1999–2000 (Vice-Pres., 1998–99). Regional Editor of Year, Newspaper Focus magazines, 1994; BT Welsh Journalist, 1999. *Recreations:* cricket, cinema, music of Frank Zappa. *Address:* The Western Mail, Thomson House, Havelock Street, Cardiff CF10 1XR. *T:* (029) 2058 3650.

FOWLER, Peter James, CMG 1990; HM Diplomatic Service, retired; Director, Cairn Energy PLC, since 1996; *b* 26 Aug. 1936; *s* of James and Gladys Fowler; *m* 1962, Audrey June Smith; one *s* three *d. Educ:* Nunthorpe Grammar Sch., York; Trinity Coll., Oxford (BA). Army Service, 1954–56. FCO, 1962–64; Budapest, 1964–65; Lisbon, 1965–67; Calcutta, 1968–71; FCO, 1971–75; East Berlin, 1975–77; Counsellor, Cabinet Office, 1977–80; Comprehensive Test Ban Delegn, Geneva, 1980; Counsellor, Bonn, 1981–85; Head of N America Dept, FCO, 1985–88; Minister and Dep. High Comr, New Delhi, 1988–93; High Comr to Bangladesh, 1993–96. Vice-Chm., Diplomatic Service Appeal Bd, 1997–. Chm., Charles Wallace Trust (Bangladesh), 1996–; Hon. Pres., Bangladeshi-British Chamber of Commerce, 1998–; Mem. Council, RSAA, 1998–. *Recreations:* reading, South Asia, opera. *Address:* 33 Northdown Street, N1 9BL. *Clubs:* Royal Commonwealth Society, Oriental.

FOWLER, Peter Jon, PhD; Emeritus Professor, University of Newcastle upon Tyne, since 1996; *b* 14 June 1936; *s* of W. J. Fowler and P. A. Fowler; *m* 1959, Elizabeth (*née* Burley) (marr. diss. 1993); three *d. Educ:* King Edward VI Grammar Sch., Morpeth, Northumberland; Lincoln Coll., Oxford (MA 1961); Univ. of Bristol (PhD 1977). Investigator on staff of RCHM (England), Salisbury office, 1959–65; Staff Tutor in Archaeology, Dept of Extra-Mural Studies, 1965–79, and Reader in Arch., 1972–79, Univ. of Bristol; Sec., Royal Commn on Historical Monuments (England), 1979–85; Prof. of Archaeology, 1985–96, and Leverhulme Fellow, 1996–99, Univ. of Newcastle upon Tyne. Member: Historic Bldgs and Ancient Monuments Adv. Cttees, Historic Buildings and Monuments Commn, 1983–86 (Ancient Monuments Bd, 1979–83); Council, National Trust, 1983–2000; Pres., Council for British Archaeol., 1981–83 (Vice-Pres., 1979–81). Archaeological consultant, Forestry Commn, 1988–2000; Mem., Landscape Adv. Cttee, DoT, 1990–95; World Heritage consultant, ICOMOS, Paris, 2001–. Chm., Jarrow 700AD Ltd, 1991–2000. *Publications:* Regional Archaeologies: Wessex, 1967; (ed) Archaeology and the Landscape, 1972; (ed) Recent Work in Rural Archaeology, 1975; (ed with K. Branigan) The Roman West Country, 1976; Approaches to Archaeology, 1977; (ed with H. C. Bowen) Early Land Allotment in the British Isles, 1978; (with S. Piggott and M. L. Ryder) Agrarian History of England and Wales, I, pt 1, 1981; The Farming of Prehistoric Britain, 1983; Farms in England, 1983; (with P. Boniface) Northumberland and Newcastle upon Tyne, 1989; (jtly) Who Owns Stonehenge?, 1990; (with M. Sharp) Images of Prehistory, 1990; The Past in Contemporary Society: then, now, 1992; (jtly) Cadbury Congresbury 1968–73: a late/post-Roman hilltop settlement in Somerset, 1992; (with P. Boniface) Heritage and Tourism in 'the global village', 1993; (jtly) The Experimental Earthwork Project 1960–1992, 1996; (with I. Blackwell) The Land of Lettice Sweetapple, 1998; Landscape Plotted and Pieced: landscape history and local archaeology in Fyfield and Overton, Wiltshire, 2000; Farming in the First Millennium AD, 2002; contribs to learned jls. *Recreations:* writing, sport. *T:* and *Fax:* (020) 7837 5818.

FOWLER, Richard Nicholas; QC 1989; *b* 12 Oct. 1946; 2nd *s* of late Ronald Hugh Fowler and of Winifred Mary Fowler (*née* Hull). *Educ:* Bedford Sch.; Brasenose Coll., Oxford (BA). Called to the Bar, Middle Temple, 1969, Bencher, 2000. Liveryman, Goldsmiths' Co., 1989–. *Recreations:* walking, opera, dogs. *Address:* 20 Ennismore Gardens Mews, SW7 1HY. *T:* (020) 7589 7279; 4 Raymond Buildings, Gray's Inn, WC1R 5BP. *T:* (020) 7405 7211.

FOWLER, Robert Asa; Owner and Chairman, Fowler International, since 1986; Consul General for Sweden, since 1989; *b* 5 Aug. 1928; *s* of Mr and Mrs William Henry Fowler; *m* 1987, Monica Elizabeth Heden; three *s* one *d* by a previous marriage. *Educ:* Princeton Univ. (BA Econs); Harvard Business Sch. (MBA). Lieut USNR, 1950–53. Various appts with Continental Oil, 1955–75; Area Manager, Northwest Europe, Continental Oil Co., 1975–78; Chm. and Man. Dir, Conoco Ltd, 1979–81; Vice-Pres., Internat. Marketing, Conoco Inc., 1981–85. An Hon. Consul Gen. for Sweden. *Recreations:* tennis, skiing. *Address:* 49 Briar Hollow Lane 1205, Houston, TX 77027, USA. *T:* (713) 8718907. *Clubs:* Hurlingham; River, Knickerbocker (NY); Allegheny Country (Pa); Chagrin Valley Hunt (Ohio).

FOWLER, Prof. Robert Louis Herbert, DPhil; Henry Overton Wills Professor of Greek, University of Bristol, since 1996; *b* 19 May 1954; *s* of Rev. Dr Louis Heath Fowler and Helen Minto Fowler (*née* Wilson); *m* 1976, Judith Lee Evers; two *s. Educ:* Univ. of Toronto Schs; Univ. of Toronto (BA 1976, MA 1977); Wadham Coll., Oxford (DPhil 1980). Fellow, Calgary Inst. for the Humanities, 1980; Department of Classical Studies, University of Waterloo, Canada: Asst Prof., 1981–86; Associate Prof., 1986–94; Chm. of Dept, 1988–96; Prof., 1994–96. Ed., Jl Hellenic Studies, 2001–. *Publications:* The Nature of Early Greek Lyric, 1997; (ed) Early Greek Mythography, vol. I, 2000; contrib. articles to learned jls. *Recreations:* piano, golf. *Address:* Department of Classics and Ancient History, University of Bristol, 11 Woodland Road, Bristol BS8 1TB. *T:* (0117) 928 7764.

FOWLER, Prof. Robert Stewart, OBE 2001; Principal and Chief Executive, Central School of Speech and Drama, 1986–2001; *b* 1 Feb. 1932; *s* of William Fowler and Breta Bell Fowler (*née* Stewart); *m* 1965, Penelope Jessie Hobbs; two *s* one *d. Educ:* Queen's

Coll., Oxford (MA); Queen's Univ., Belfast (DipEd); Guildhall Sch. of Music and Drama (LGSM). Served RAEC, 1950–52. Asst in English, Drama and Latin, Royal Belfast Acad. Instn, 1955–58; Hd of Dept, Forest Gate Sch., 1958–60; Warden, Bretton Hall Coll., Wakefield, 1960–66; Dep. Principal and Principal Elect, Sittingbourne Coll. of Educn, 1966–76; HMI with resp. for theatre, the arts in teacher trng and staff inspector, teacher trng, 1976–86. Chief Ext. Examr (Theatre Design), Nottingham Trent Univ., 1996–98. Vis. Prof., Univ. of Central England, 1995–. Vice-Pres., European League Inst. of Arts, 1998–; Member: Bd, Univs and Colls Employers' Assoc., 1996–2000; Nat. Council for Drama Trng, 1996–2000. Panel Chm., Hong Kong Council for Academic Accreditation, 1996–2000. FRSA 1990. *Publications:* Themes in Life and Literature, 1967; (jtly) English 11/16, 5 books, 1971–73; The Hobbit Introduced for Schools, 1973; (jtly) English: a literary foundation course, 1975. *Recreations:* living, loving, life-saving, laughing, Lake District, Provence, family, friends, writing. *Address:* Lower House, Lower End, 72 Bicester Road, Long Crendon, Bucks HP18 9EF. *T:* (01844) 208224.

FOWLER, Sarah Hauldys; *see* Evans, S. H.

FOWLER HOWITT, William; *see* Howitt.

FOWLES, John; writer; *b* 31 March 1926; *s* of Robert John Fowles and Gladys May Richards; *m* 1st, 1956, Elizabeth Whitton (*d* 1990); 2nd, 1998, Sarah Smith. *Educ:* Bedford Sch.; New Coll., Oxford (Hon. Fellow, 1997). English Centre PEN Silver Pen Award, 1969; W. H. Smith Award, 1970. *Publications:* The Collector, 1963; The Aristos, 1965; The Magus, 1966, rev. edn 1977; The French Lieutenant's Woman, 1969; Poems, 1973; The Ebony Tower, 1974 (televised, 1984); Shipwreck, 1975; Daniel Martin, 1977; Islands, 1978; (with Frank Horvat) The Tree, 1979; (ed) John Aubrey's Monumenta Britannica, parts 1 and 2, 1980, part 3 and Index, 1982; The Enigma of Stonehenge, 1980; Mantissa, 1982; Thomas Hardy's England, 1984; Land, 1985; A Maggot, 1985; Wormholes: essays and occasional writings, 1998; Lyme Worthies, 2000. *Recreations:* mainly Sabine. *Address:* c/o Anthony Sheil, Gillon Aitken Associates Ltd, 29 Fernshaw Road, SW10 0TG.

FOX, Dr Alan Martin; Clerk: to Governors, Henrietta Barnett School, since 1998; to Governors, Jews Free School, since 2000; to Trustees, St Marylebone Almshouses, since 1998; *b* 5 July 1938; *s* of Sidney Nathan Fox and Clarice Solov; *m* 1965, Sheila Naomi Pollard; one *s* two *d. Educ:* Bancroft's Sch., Essex; Queen Mary Coll., London (BSc Hons II1, Physics 1959; PhD Math. Phys. 1963). ACIArb 1997, MCIArb 1999. Home Civil Service by Open Competition, 1963; Ministry of Aviation: Private Sec. to Parly Sec., 1965–67; 1st Sec. (Aviation and Defence) on loan to FCO, Paris, 1973–75; MoD, 1975–78; RCDS, 1979; MoD, 1980–98; Asst Under Sec. of State (Ordnance), 1988–92; Vis. Fellow, Center for Internat. Affairs, Harvard, 1992–93; Asst Under-Sec. of State (Quartermaster), 1994–95, (Export Policy and Finance), 1995–98. Lectr (part-time), UCL, 1998–. Member: London Rent Assessment Panel, 1999–; Compliance and Supervision Cttee, Office for the Supervision of Solicitors, 2000–; Review Cttee on Non-Competitive Contracts, 2000–. *Recreations:* playing chess, computer games, watching Rugby, cricket, TV. *Address:* 4 Woodside Avenue, N6 4SS.

FOX, Dr (Anthony) John; Director of Statistics, Department of Health, since 1999; *b* 25 April 1946; *s* of Fred Frank Fox, OBE, and Gertrude Price; *m* 1971, Annemarie Revesz; one *s* two *d. Educ:* Dauntsey's School; University College London (BSc); Imperial College London (PhD, DIC). FFPHM. Statistician: Employment Medical Adv. Service, 1970–75; OPCS, 1975–79; Prof. of Social Statistics, City Univ., 1980–88; Chief Medical Statistician, OPCS, 1988–96; Dir, Census, Population and Health Gp, ONS, 1996–99. Vis. Prof., LSHTM, 1990–. Hon. DSc City, 1997. *Publications:* Occupational Mortality 1970–72, 1978; Socio-Demographic Mortality Differentials, 1982; Health Inequalities in European Countries, 1989; (jtly) Health and Class: The early years, 1991. *Recreations:* family, tennis, bridge, theatre. *Address:* Department of Health, Skipton House, 80 London Road, SE1 6LH.

FOX, Brian Michael, CB 1998; Head of Civil Service Corporate Management (Grade 2), Cabinet Office, 1998–2000; *b* 21 Sept. 1944; *s* of Walter Frederick and Audrey May Fox; *m* 1966, Maureen Ann Shrimpton; one *d. Educ:* East Ham Grammar School for Boys. Joined CS, HM Treasury, 1963–98: Private Sec. to Financial Sec., 1967–69; secondment to 3i Gp, 1981–82; Dep. Estabt Officer, 1983–87; Head of Defence Policy and Materiel Div., 1987–89; Principal Estabt and Finance Officer, 1989–93; Dir (Grade 3), Sen. and Public Appts Gp, later Sen. CS Gp, Cabinet Office (on loan), 1994–98. *Recreations:* table tennis, badminton, soccer. *Address:* c/o Cabinet Office, Horse Guards Road, SW1P 3AL. *T:* (020) 7270 6220.

FOX, Edward; actor; *b* 13 April 1937; *s* of late Robin and Angela Muriel Darita Fox; *m* 1958, Tracy (*née* Pelissier) (marr. diss. 1961); one *d*; and one *s* one *d* by Joanna Fox. *Educ:* Ashfold Sch.; Harrow Sch. RADA training, following National Service, 1956–58; entry into provincial repertory theatre, 1958, since when, films, TV films and plays, and plays in the theatre, have made up the sum of his working life. *Theatre includes:* Knuckle, Comedy, 1973; The Family Reunion, Vaudeville, 1979; Anyone for Denis, Whitehall, 1981; Quartermaine's Terms, Queen's, 1981; Hamlet, Young Vic, 1982; Interpreters, Queen's, 1985; Let Us Go Then, You and I, Lyric, 1987; The Admirable Crichton, Haymarket, 1988; (also dir) Another Love Story, Leicester Haymarket, 1990; The Philanthropist, Wyndham's, 1991; Father, Comedy and tour, 1995; A Letter of Resignation, Comedy, 1997; The Chiltern Hundreds, Vaudeville, 1999. *Films include:* The Go-Between, 1971 (Soc. of Film and Television Arts Award for Best Supporting Actor, 1971); The Day of the Jackal, A Doll's House, 1973; Galileo, 1976; The Squeeze, A Bridge Too Far (BAFTA Award for Best Supporting Actor, 1977), The Duellists, The Cat and the Canary, 1977; Force Ten from Navarone, 1978; The Mirror Crack'd, 1980; Gandhi, 1982; Never Say Never Again, The Dresser, 1983; The Bounty, 1984; The Shooting Party, 1985; A Month by the Lake, 1996. *Television series include:* Hard Times, 1977; Edward and Mrs Simpson, 1978 (BAFTA Award for Best Actor, 1978; TV Times Top Ten Award for Best Actor, 1978–79; British Broadcasting Press Guild TV Award for Best Actor, 1978; Royal TV Soc. Performance Award, 1978–79); They Never Slept, 1991; A Dance to the Music of Time, 1997. *Recreations:* music, reading, walking. *Club:* Savile.

See also J. Fox, R. M. J. Fox, Viscount Gormanston.

FOX, Hazel Mary, (Lady Fox); Director, British Institute of International and Comparative Law, 1982–89; General Editor, International and Comparative Law Quarterly, 1987–98; *b* 22 Oct. 1928; *d* of J. M. B. Stuart, CIE; *m* 1954, Rt Hon. Sir Michael Fox, *qv*; three *s* one *d. Educ:* Roedean Sch.; Somerville Coll., Oxford (1st Cl. Jurisprudence, 1949; MA). Called to the Bar, Lincoln's Inn, 1950 (Buchanan Prize; Bencher, 1989); practised at the Bar, 1950–54 and 1994–; Fellow of Somerville Coll., Oxford, 1976–81, Hon. Fellow 1988. Vis. Lectr in Law, Oxford Univ., 1992–. Chairman: London Rent Assessment Panel, 1977–98; London Leasehold Valuation Tribunal, 1981–98; Mem., Home Office Deptl Cttee on Jury Service, 1963–65. Associate, Institut de droit international, 1997. Hon. QC 1993. JP London, 1959–77; Chm., Tower Hamlets Juvenile Court, 1968–76. *Publications:* (with J. L. Simpson) International Arbitration, 1959; (ed) International Economic Law and Developing States, Vol. I 1988, Vol. II 1992; (ed) Joint Development of Offshore Oil and Gas, vol. I 1989, vol. II 1990; (ed jtly) Armed Conflict and the New Law, vol. II: Effecting Compliance, 1993. *Address:* c/o British Institute of International and Comparative Law, 17 Russell Square, WC1B 5DR. *T:* (020) 7636 5802; *e-mail:* ICLQ@dial.pipex.com; 4/5 Grays Inn Square, WC1R 5AY. *T:* (020) 7404 5252, *Fax:* (020) 7242 7803.

FOX, James; actor; *b* 19 May 1939; *s* of late Robin and Angela Fox; changed forename from William to James, 1962; *m* 1973, Mary Elizabeth Piper; four *s* one *d. Educ:* Harrow Sch.; Central Sch. of Speech and Drama. National Service, 1959–61. Entered acting as child, 1950; left acting to pursue Christian vocation, 1970–79; returned to acting, 1980. Main films include: The Servant, 1963; King Rat, 1964; Thoroughly Modern Millie, 1965; The Chase, 1966; Isadora, 1968; Performance, 1969; A Passage to India, 1984; Runners, 1984; Farewell to the King, 1987; Finding Mawbee (video film as The Mighty Quinn), 1988; She's Been Away, 1989; The Russia House, 1990; Afraid of the Dark, 1991; The Remains of the Day, 1993; Anna Karenina, 1997; Mickey Blue Eyes, 1999; Up the Villa, 1999; Sexy Beast, 1999; The Golden Bowl, 1999; theatre includes: Uncle Vanya, NY, 1995; television includes: The Choir (serial), 1995; Gulliver's Travels, 1996. *Publication:* Comeback: an actor's direction, 1983. *Recreation:* tennis. *Address:* c/o ICM, 76 Oxford Street, W1N 0AX.

See also E. Fox, R. M. J. Fox.

FOX, John; *see* Fox, A. J.

FOX, Rt Hon. Sir (John) Marcus, Kt 1986; MBE 1963; PC 1996; *b* 11 June 1927; *s* of late Alfred Hirst Fox; *m* 1954, Ann, *d* of F. W. J. Tindall; one *s* one *d. Educ:* Wheelright Grammar Sch., Dewsbury. Mem. Dewsbury County Borough Council, 1957–65; contested (C): Dewsbury, 1959; Huddersfield West, 1966. MP (C) Shipley, 1970–97; contested (C) same seat, 1997. An Asst Govt Whip, 1972–73; a Lord Comr, HM Treasury, 1973–74; Opposition spokesman on Transport, 1975–76; Parly Under-Sec. of State, DoE, 1979–81. Mem., Parly Select Cttee on Race Relations and Immigration, 1970–72; Sec., Cons. Party's Transport Industries Cttee, 1970–72; a Vice-Chm., Cons. Party Orgn, 1976–79; Chairman: Cttee of Selection, 1984–92; 1922 Cttee, 1992–97 (a Vice-Chm., 1983–92). Chm., Nat. Assoc. of Cons. Clubs, 1988–98. *Recreations:* reading, tennis, walking. *Address:* 10 Woodvale Crescent, Oakwood Park, Bingley, West Yorks BD16 4AL.

FOX, John Rupert Anselm; a Vice President, Immigration Appeal Tribunal, since 2000; an Adjudicator, Immigration and Asylum Appeals, since 1990; *b* 10 Dec. 1935; *s* of John Arnold Fox, MBE (mil.) and Eleanor Margaret Fox (*née* Green); *m* 1965, Isabel June Mary Jermy Gwyn; three *s* one *d* (and two *s* one *d* decd). *Educ:* Stonyhurst Coll. 2nd Lieut, RASC, 1954; transf. to Cheshire Yeo., 1958; Capt. 1959; RAC Reserve of Officers, 1966. Admitted solicitor, 1960; articled to Simpson North Harley & Co., London and Liverpool, 1953, Solicitor, Liverpool, 1960–62; Partner, Whatley Weston & Fox, Worcester, Malvern and Hereford, 1963–76; Asst Dir/Legal Advr, Foreign Investment Agency of Canada, 1976–78; Partner, John Fox Solicitors, Broadway, Worcs, 1978. Under Sheriff, City of Worcester, 1965–76. Jt Sec., Liverpool River Pilots' Assoc., 1960–62. KM 1975. *Recreations:* gardening, painting. *Address:* c/o Immigration Appeal Tribunal, Field House, Breams Buildings, Chancery Lane, EC4. *T:* (020) 7862 4342. *Club:* Royal Commonwealth Society.

FOX, Kenneth Lambert, FCIPS; public sector consultant, since 1986; *b* 8 Nov. 1927; *s* of J. H. Fox, Grimsby, Lincolnshire; *m* 1959, P. E. Byrne; one *d. Educ:* City of London Coll.; Univ. of London. BSc (Hons); MIIM. Plant Man., Rowntree Gp, 1950–63; Supply Man., Ford Motor Co. (UK), 1963–67; Sen. Management Conslt, Cooper & Lybrand Ltd, 1967–70; Man. of Conslts (Europe), US Science Management Corp., 1971–72; Supply Management, British Gas Corp., 1972–75; Dir of Supplies, GLC, 1975–86. *Recreations:* tennis, painting, bird watching, DIY. *Address:* 27 Dolphin Lane, Melbourn, Royston, Herts SG8 6AE. *T:* (01763) 260573.

FOX, Dr Liam; MP (C) Woodspring, since 1992; *b* 22 Sept. 1961; *s* of William Fox and Catherine Young. *Educ:* St Bride's High Sch., E Kilbride; Univ. of Glasgow (MB ChB 1983). MRCGP 1989. General Practitioner, Beaconsfield, 1987–91; Army MO (civilian), RAEC, 1981–91; Divl Surgeon, St John's Ambulance, 1987–91. Contested (C) Roxburgh and Berwickshire, 1987. PPS to Home Sec., 1993–94; an Asst Govt Whip, 1994–95; a Lord Comr of HM Treasury (Govt Whip), 1995–96; Parly Under-Sec. of State, FCO, 1996–97; Opposition spokesman on constitutional affairs, 1997–99, on health, 1999–2001; Shadow Health Sec., 2001–. Mem., Select Cttee on Scottish Affairs, 1992; Secretary: Cons. back bench Health Cttee, 1992–93; Cons. West Country Members Group, 1992–93. *Publications:* Making Unionism Positive, 1988; (contrib.) Bearing the Standard, 1991; contrib. to House of Commons Magazine. *Recreations:* tennis, swimming, cinema, theatre. *Address:* House of Commons, SW1A 0AA. *T:* (020) 7219 4086.

FOX, Rt Hon. Sir Marcus; *see* Fox, Rt Hon. Sir J. M.

FOX, Rt Hon. Sir Michael John, Kt 1975; PC 1981; a Lord Justice of Appeal, 1981–92; *b* 8 Oct. 1921; *s* of late Michael Fox; *m* 1954, Hazel Mary Stuart (*see* Hazel Mary Fox); three *s* one *d. Educ:* Drayton Manor Sch., Hanwell; Magdalen Coll., Oxford (BCL, MA). Admiralty, 1942–45. Called to the Bar, Lincoln's Inn, 1949, Bencher, 1975; QC 1968. Judge of the High Court of Justice, Chancery Div., 1975–81.

FOX, Ven. Michael John; Archdeacon of West Ham, since 1996; *b* 28 April 1942; *s* of John and Dorothy Fox; *m* 1966, Susan Cooper; one *s* one *d. Educ:* Barking Abbey GS; Hull Univ. (BSc); Coll. of the Resurrection, Mirfield. Ordained deacon, 1966, priest, 1967; Curate: St Elizabeth, Becontree, 1966–70; Holy Trinity, S Woodford, 1970–72; Vicar: Ch. of the Ascension, Victoria Docks, and Missioner, Felsted Sch., 1972–76; All Saints, Chelmsford, 1976–88; Asst RD and RD, Chelmsford, 1982–88; Rector, St James, Colchester, 1988–93; Archdeacon of Harlow, 1993–96. Hon. Canon, Chelmsford Cathedral, 1991–. *Recreations:* walking, photography, West Ham. *Address:* 86 Aldersbrook Road, Manor Park, E12 5DH. *T:* (020) 8989 8557.

FOX, Sir Paul (Leonard), Kt 1991; CBE 1985; Chairman, Stepgrades Consultants, since 1991; *b* 27 Oct. 1925; *m* 1948, Betty Ruth (*née* Nathan); two *s. Educ:* Bournemouth Grammar Sch. Served War, Parachute Regt, 1943–46. Reporter, Kentish Times, 1946; Scriptwriter, Pathé News, 1947; joined BBC Television, 1950: Scriptwriter, Television Newsreel; Editor, Sportsview, 1953, Panorama, 1961; Head, Public Affairs, 1963, Current Affairs, 1965; Controller, BBC1, 1967–73; Dir of Progs, 1973–84, Man. Dir, 1977–88, Yorkshire Television; Man. Dir, BBC Network Television, 1988–91. Chairman: ITN, 1986–88 (Dir, 1980–86); BBC Enterprises Ltd, 1988–91; Director: Trident Television, 1973–80; Channel Four, 1985–88; World Television News, 1986–88; Thames Television, 1991–95; Barnes Television Trust, 1997–2000. Chm., Racecourse Assoc. Ltd, 1993–97; Director: British Horseracing Bd, 1993–97; Horseracing Betting Levy Bd, 1993–97. Chm., Disasters Emergency Cttee, 1996–99; Member: Royal Commn on

Criminal Procedure, 1978–80; Inquiry into Police Responsibilities and Rewards, 1992–93. Pres., RTS, 1985–92; Mem. Cttee, Nat. Mus. of Film, Photography and TV, 1985–95; Trustee, Cinema and Television Benevolent Fund, 1987–90 and 1995– (Cttee Mem., 1990–92; Pres., 1992–95). BAFTA Fellow, 1990. CIMgt (CBIM 1987). Hon. LLD Leeds, 1984; Hon. DLitt Bradford, 1991. Cyril Bennett Award, for outstanding television programming, 1984; Founders Award, Internat. Council, US Nat. Acad. of TV Arts and Scis, 1989; RTS Gold Medal, for outstanding services to television, 1992. *Recreations:* television, attending race meetings. *Address:* c/o Stepgrades Consultants, 10 Charterhouse Square, EC1M 6LQ. *Club:* Garrick.

FOX, Peter Kendrew; University Librarian, University of Cambridge, and Fellow of Selwyn College, Cambridge, since 1994; *b* 23 March 1949; *s* of Thomas Kendrew Fox and Dorothy (*née* Wildbore); *m* 1983, Isobel McConnell; two *d.* *Educ:* Baines GS, Poulton-le-Fylde; King's Coll., London (BA, AKC 1971); Sheffield Univ. (MA 1973); MA Cantab 1976; MA Dublin, 1984. ALA 1974; ALAI 1989. Cambridge University Library: grad. trainee, 1971–72; Asst Liby Officer, 1973–77; Asst Under-Librarian, 1977–78; Under-Librarian, 1978–79; Trinity College Dublin: Dep. Librarian, 1979–84; Librarian and Coll. Archivist, 1984–94. Chairman: SCONUL Adv. Cttee on Inf. Services, 1987–90; Bd of Dirs, Consortium of Univ. Res. Libraries, 1997–2000; Member: An Chomhairle Leabharlanna, Dublin, 1982–94; Cttee on Liby Co-operation in Ireland, 1983–94; Nat. Preservation Adv. Cttee, 1984–95; Mgt Cttee, Nat. Preservation Office, 1996–; Adv. Cttee for Document Supply, British Liby, 1991–95; Wellcome Trust Liby Adv. Cttee, 1996– (Chm., 2000–); Arts, Humanities and Social Scis Adv. Cttee, British Library, 2000–; Lord Chancellor's Adv. Council on Public Records, 2001–. *Publications:* Reader Instruction Methods in British Academic Libraries, 1974; Trinity College Library, Dublin, 1982; *edited:* Treasures of the Library: Trinity College Dublin, 1986; Book of Kells: commentary vol. to facsimile edn, 1990; Cambridge University Library: the great collections, 1998; Proc. Internat. Confs on Library User Education, 1980, 1982, 1984; contrib. learned jls. *Address:* University Library, West Road, Cambridge CB3 9DR. *T:* (01223) 333045.

FOX, Prof. Renée Claire, PhD; FAAAS; Annenberg Professor of the Social Sciences, University of Pennsylvania, 1969–98, now Emerita (also Professor of: Sociology in Psychiatry, 1969–98; Sociology in Medicine, 1972–98; Sociology, School of Nursing, 1978–98); Fellow, Center for Bioethics, University of Pennsylvania, since 1999; *b* 15 Feb. 1928; *d* of Paul Fred Fox and Henrietta Gold Fox. *Educ:* Smith Coll., Northampton, Mass (BA *summa cum laude* 1949); Harvard Univ. (PhD Sociol. 1954). Teaching Fellow, Harvard Univ., 1950–51; Columbia University: Res. Asst, Bureau of Applied Social Res., 1953–55; Res. Associate, 1955–58; Barnard College, New York: Lectr in Sociol., 1955–58; Asst Prof., 1958–64; Associate Prof., 1964–66; Harvard University: Lectr in Sociol., 1967–69; Res. Fellow, Center for Internat. Affairs, 1967–68; Res. Associate, Program on Technol and Soc., 1968–71; Consultant, Social Sci. Curriculum, Lincoln Center Coll., Fordham Univ., NY, 1968–70; University of Pennsylvania: Faculty Asst to Pres., 1971–72; Chm., Dept of Sociol., 1972–78. Res. Associate, Queen Elizabeth House, Internat. Develt Centre, Univ. of Oxford, 1999–. Numerous distinguished visiting appointments and lectureships; George Eastman Vis. Prof., Oxford Univ., 1996–97. Fellow, Amer. Acad. of Arts and Scis, 1971; FAAAS 1978; Mem. Inst. of Med., US NAS, 1975. Chevalier, Order of Leopold II (Belgium), 1995. *Publications:* (with W. de Craemer) The Emerging Physician: a sociological approach to the development of a Congolese medical profession, 1968; Experiment Perilous: physicians and patients facing the unknown, 1974, repr. with new epilogue, 1997; (with J. P. Swazey) The Courage to Fail: a social view of organ transplants and dialysis, 1974, rev. edn 1978; Essays in Medical Sociology: journeys into the field, 1979, 2nd edn 1988; (ed) The Social Meaning of Death, 1980; L'Incertitude Médicale, 1988; (jtly) Spare Parts: organ replacement in American society, 1992 (trans. Japanese 1999); The Sociology of Medicine: a participant observer's view, 1989 (trans. Korean 1993); In the Belgian Château: the spirit and culture of European society in the age of change, 1994 (French edn, with new epilogue, 1997); (ed jtly) Meanings and Realities of Organ Transplantation, 1996; contrib. numerous articles on medical sociology, incl. articles on organ donation and transplantation, bioethics, med. res. and educn, to scientific and learned jls worldwide. *Address:* Sociology Department, University of Pennsylvania, 3718 Locust Walk, Philadelphia, PA 19104–6299, USA. *T:* (215) 8987933; The Wellington # 1104, 135 South 19th Street, Philadelphia, PA 19103, USA. *T:* (215) 5634912.

FOX, Prof. Robert, FSA; FRHistS; Professor of the History of Science, University of Oxford, and Fellow of Linacre College, since 1988; *b* 7 Oct. 1938; *s* of Donald Fox and Audrey Hilda Fox (*née* Ramsell); *m* 1964, Catherine Mary Lilian Roper Power; three *d.* *Educ:* Doncaster Grammar Sch.; Oriel Coll., Oxford (BA 1961; MA 1965; DPhil 1967). Asst Master, Tonbridge Sch., 1961–63; Clifford Norton Junior Res. Fellow, Queen's Coll., Oxford, 1965–66; University of Lancaster: Lectr, 1966; Sen. Lectr, 1972; Reader, 1975; Prof. of History of Science, 1987. Mem., Inst. for Advanced Study, Princeton, 1974–75 and 1985; Vis. Prof. and Mem., Davis Center for Historical Studies, Princeton Univ., 1978–79; Vis. Prof., Ecole des Hautes Etudes en Scis Sociales, Paris, 1984 and 2000; Dir, Centre de Recherche en Histoire des Sciences et des Techniques, Cité des Sciences et de l'Industrie, Paris, and Dir de recherche associé, Centre Nat. de la Recherche Scientifique, 1986–88; Asst Dir, Science Museum, 1988. Pres., IUHPS, 1995–97 (Pres., Div. of History of Science, 1993–97). Chevalier de l'Ordre des Palmes Académiques (France), 1998. *Publications:* The caloric theory of gases from Lavoisier to Regnault, 1971; Sadi Carnot: Réflexions sur la puissance motrice du feu, 1978 (trans. English 1986, German 1987, Italian 1992); (ed jtly) The organization of science and technology in France 1808–1914, 1980; The culture of science in France 1700–1900, 1992; (ed jtly) Education, technology and industrial performance in Europe 1850–1939, 1993; Science, technology, and the social order in post-revolutionary France, 1995; (ed) Technological change: methods and themes in the history of technology, 1996; (ed jtly) Natural Dyestuffs and Industrial Culture in Europe 1750–1880, 1999; (jtly) Laboratories, Workshops and Sites, 1999. *Address:* Modern History Faculty, Broad Street, Oxford OX1 3BD. *T:* (01865) 277268. *Club:* Athenæum.

FOX, Dr Robert McDougall, FRCP, FRCPE; Editor, Journal of the Royal Society of Medicine, since 1996; *b* 28 Dec. 1939; *s* of Sir Theodore Fortescue Fox and Margaret Evelyn McDougall; *m* 1969, Susan Clark; two *s* one *d.* *Educ:* Univ. of Edinburgh (MB ChB). MRCP 1993, FRCP 1996; FRCPE 1990. House physician, Western Gen. Hosp., Edinburgh; house surgeon, Royal Infirmary, Edinburgh; joined staff of The Lancet, 1968: Dep. Editor, 1976–90; Editor, 1990–95. Associate Editor, Circulation, 1995–. *Recreations:* the bassoon, the hoe. *Address:* Green House, Rotherfield, Crowborough, East Sussex TN6 3QU. *T:* (01892) 853520.

FOX, Robert Michael John; theatre, film and television producer; Managing Director, Robert Fox Ltd, since 1980; *b* 25 March 1952; *s* of late Robin Fox and Angela Fox; *m* 1st, 1975, Celestia Sporborg (marr. diss. 1990); one *s* two *d*; 2nd, 1990, Natasha Richardson, *qv* (marr. diss. 1994); 3rd, 1996, Fiona Golfar; one *s* one *d.* *Educ:* Harrow. Asst Dir, Royal Court Th., 1971–73; PA, Michael White Ltd, 1973–80. *Productions* include: *theatre:* Goose Pimples, Garrick, 1981; Anyone For Denis?, Whitehall, 1981; Another Country, Queen's, 1982; The Seagull, Queen's, 1985; Chess, Prince Edward, 1986; Lettice and Lovage, Globe, 1987, NY, 1990; A Madhouse In Goa, Apollo, 1989; Burn This, Lyric, 1990; The Big Love, NY, 1991; When She Danced, Globe, 1991; The Ride Down Mount Morgan, Wyndham's, 1991; The Importance of Being Earnest, Aldwych, 1993; Vita & Virginia, Ambassadors, 1992, NY, 1994; Three Tall Women, Wyndham's, 1994; Burning Blue, Haymarket, 1995; Skylight, Wyndham's, 1995, NY, 1996, Vaudeville, 1997; Who's Afraid of Virginia Woolf?, Almeida, transf. Aldwych, 1996; Master Class, Queen's, 1997; A Delicate Balance, Haymarket, 1997; Amy's View, RNT, transf. Aldwych, 1997, NY 1999; Closer, RNT, transf. Lyric, 1998, NY 1999; The Judas Kiss (co-producer), Almeida, transf. Playhouse, NY, 1998; The Boy from Oz (co-producer), Australia, 1998; The Lady in the Van, Queen's, 1999; The Blue Room, NY, 1999; The Caretaker, Comedy, 2000; *film:* A Month by the Lake, 1996; *television:* Oscar's Orchestra, 1996. *Address:* (office) 6 Beauchamp Place, SW3 1NG. *T:* (020) 7584 6855, *Fax:* (020) 7225 1638. *Club:* Buck's.

See also E. Fox, J. Fox.

FOX, Robert Trench, (Robin), CBE 1993; Chairman, Lombard Risk Consultants, since 2000; *b* 1 Jan. 1937; *s* of Waldo Trench Fox and Janet Mary Kennedy Fox (*née* Bassett); *m* 1962, Lindsay Garrett Anderson; two *s* two *d.* *Educ:* Winchester Coll.; University Coll., Oxford (MA). FCIB. Kleinwort Benson Group, 1961–99; Vice-Chm., Kleinwort Benson Gp, 1989–97; Pres., Kleinwort Benson Asia Ltd, 1997–99. Chairman: Centro Internationale Handelsbank, 1990– (Dir, 1977–); Whiteaway Laidlaw Bank, 1997– (Dir, 1992–). Chairman: Export Guarantees Adv. Council, 1992–98; China Investment and Develt Fund; Boyer Allan Pacific Fund; Mem., Overseas Projects Bd, 1988–98. Chm. Council, City Univ. Business Sch., 1991–99. *Recreations:* sailing, shooting, theatre, reading. *Address:* Lombard Risk Consultants, 21 New Fetter Lane, EC4A 1AJ. *T:* (020) 7353 5330. *Clubs:* Brooks's; Royal Cornwall Yacht.

FOX, Robin James L.; *see* Lane Fox.

FOX, Roy, CMG 1980; OBE 1967; HM Diplomatic Service, retired; consultant with various companies; *b* 1 Sept. 1920; *s* of J. S. and A. Fox; *m* 1st, 1943, Sybil Verity; two *s* one *d*; 2nd, 1975, Susan Rogers Turner. *Educ:* Wheelwright Grammar Sch., Dewsbury; Bradford Technical Coll. Served in RNVR, 1940–46. Bd of Trade, 1947–58; British Trade Commissioner: Nairobi, 1958–60; Montreal, 1960–62; Winnipeg, 1962–64; Dep. Controller, Bd of Trade Office for Scotland, 1964–65. First Sec. Commercial, Karachi, 1965–68; Deputy High Comr, E Pakistan, 1968–70; Consul-Gen. and Comm. Counsellor, Helsinki, 1970–74; promoted to Minister, 1977; Consul-Gen., Houston, 1974–80. *Recreations:* golf, reading, tennis. *Club:* Royal Automobile.

FOX, Ruth W.; *see* Winston-Fox.

FOX, Prof. Wallace, CMG 1973; MD, FRCP, FFPHM; Professor of Community Therapeutics, Cardiothoracic Institute, Brompton Hospital, 1979–86, now Emeritus; Director, Medical Research Council Tuberculosis and Chest Diseases Unit, Brompton Hospital, 1965–86; Hon. Consultant Physician, Brompton Hospital, 1969–86; WHO Consultant, since 1961; *b* 7 Nov. 1920; *s* of Samuel and Esther Fox; *m* 1956, Gaye Judith Akker; three *s.* *Educ:* Cotham Grammar Sch., Bristol; Guy's Hosp. MB, BS (London) 1943; MRCS, LRCP, 1943; MRCP 1950; MD (Dist.) (London) 1951; FRCP 1962; FFPHM (FFCM 1976). Ho. Phys., Guy's USA Hosp., 1945–46; Resident Phys., Preston Hall Sanatorium, 1946–50; Registrar, Guy's Hosp., 1950–51; Asst Chest Physician, Hammersmith Chest Clinic, 1951–52; Mem. Scientific Staff of MRC Tuberculosis and Chest Diseases Unit, 1952–56, 1961–65; seconded to WHO, to establish and direct Tuberculosis Chemotherapy Centre, Madras, 1956–61; Dir, WHO Collaborating Centre for Tuberculosis Chemotherapy and its Application, 1976–87. Lectures: Marc Daniels, RCP, 1962; First John Barnwell Meml, US Veterans Admin, 1968; Philip Ellman, RSocMed, 1976; Martyrs Meml, Bangladesh Med. Assoc., 1977; first Quezon Meml, Philippine Coll. of Chest Physicians, 1977; Morriston Davies Meml, BTA, 1981; Mitchell, RCP, 1982; E. Merck Oration, Indian Chest Soc., 1983; A. J. S. McFadzean, Univ. of Hong Kong, 1986; Ranbaxy–Robert Koch Oration, Tuberculosis Assoc. of India, 1989. Waring Vis. Prof. in Medicine, Univ. of Colorado and Stanford Univ., 1974. Mem. Tropical Med. Research Bd, 1968–72; Mem., several MRC Cttees; Member: WHO Expert Adv. Panel on Tuberculosis, 1965–91; BCG Vaccination Sub-Cttee, Min. of Health, 1968–; Mem. Council, Chest, Heart & Stroke Assoc., 1974–90; International Union Against Tuberculosis: Mem., later Chm., Cttee of Therapy, 1964–71; Associate Mem., Scientific Cttees, 1973; Mem., Exec. Cttee, 1973–85 (Chm., 1973–77). Chm., Acid Fast Club, 1971–72. Editor, Advances in Tuberculosis Research. Life Mem., BMA, 1994; Elected Corresp. Mem., Amer. Thoracic Soc., 1962; Mem., Mexican Acad. of Medicine, 1976; Hon. Life Mem., Canadian Thoracic Soc., 1976; Corresp. Mem., Argentine Nat. Acad. of Medicine, 1977; Corresp. For. Member: Argentine Soc. of Phtisiol. and Thoracic Pathol., 1977; Coll. of Univ. Med. Phtisiologists of Argentine, 1978; Hon. Member: Argentine Med. Assoc., 1977; Singapore Thoracic Soc., 1978. Sir Robert Philip Medal, Chest and Heart Assoc., 1969; Weber Parkes Prize, RCP, 1973; Carlo Forlanini Gold Medal, Fedn Ital. contra la Tubercolosi e le Malattie Polmonari Sociali, 1976; Hon. Medal, Czech. Med. Soc., 1980; Robert Koch Centenary Medal, Internat. Union against Tuberculosis, 1982; Presidential Citation Award, Amer. Coll. of Chest Physicians, 1982; Presidential Commendation, Amer. Thoracic Soc., 1989. *Publications:* Reports on tuberculosis services in Hong Kong to Hong Kong Government: Heaf/Fox, 1962; Scadding/Fox, 1975; Fox/Kilpatrick, 1990; contribs to med. jls: on methodology of controlled clinical trials, on epidemiology and on chemotherapy, particularly in tuberculosis, and carcinoma of the bronchus. *Address:* 28 Mount Ararat Road, Richmond, Surrey TW10 6PG. *T:* (020) 8940 9662. *Club:* Athenæum.

FOX, Winifred Marjorie, (Mrs E. Gray Debros); Under-Secretary, Department of the Environment, 1970–76; *d* of Frederick Charles Fox and Charlotte Marion Ogborn; *m* 1953, Eustachy Gray Debros (*d* 1954); one *d.* *Educ:* Streatham County Sch.; St Hugh's Coll., Oxford. Unemployment Assistance Board, 1937; Cabinet Office, 1942; Ministry of Town and Country Planning, 1944; Ministry of Housing and Local Govt, 1952 (Under-Sec., 1963); Dept of the Environment, 1970; seconded to CSD as Chm., CS Selection Bd, 1971–72. *Address:* 2 The Pryors, East Heath Road, Hampstead, NW3 1BS. *T:* (020) 7435 4962.

FOX-ANDREWS, His Honour James Roland Blake; QC 1968; a Circuit Judge (Official Referee), 1985–94; *b* 24 March 1922; step *s* of late Norman Roy Fox-Andrews, QC; *m* 1950, Angela Bridget Swift (*d* 1991); two *s.* *Educ:* Stowe; Pembroke Coll., Cambridge. FCIArb. Served War, RNVR, 1940–46. Called to the Bar, Gray's Inn, 1949, Bencher, 1974. Dep. Chm., Devon QS, 1970–71; Recorder of Winchester, 1971, Hon. Recorder, 1972–2000; a Recorder of Crown Court, 1972–85. Leader, Western Circuit, 1982–84. Member: Gen. Council of the Bar, 1968–72; Senate of Inns of Court and the Bar, 1976–79. Chartered Arbitrator, 1998–. Editor, Inst. of Arbitrators Jl, 1950–54. *Publications:* (jtly) Leasehold Property (Temporary Provisions) Act, 1951; contrib. Halsbury's Laws of England, 3rd edn, building contracts, architects and engineers; (jtly)

Landlord and Tenant Act, 1954; Business Tenancies, 1970, 5th edn 1995; (jtly) Assured Tenancies, 1989. *Address:* 20 Cheyne Gardens, SW3 5QT. *T:* (020) 7352 9484; Lepe House, Exbury, Hants SO45 1AD. *T:* (023) 8089 1648. *Club:* Hurlingham.

FOX BASSETT, Nigel; Commissioner, Building Societies Commission, 1993–2001; Member Council: London First, since 1998; London Chamber of Commerce and Industry, 1993–99; *b* 1 Nov. 1929; *s* of Thomas Fox Bassett and Catherine Adriana Wiffen; *m* 1961, Patricia Anne Lambourne; one *s* one *d. Educ:* Taunton Sch.; Trinity Coll., Cambridge (MA Hons History and Law). Articled, Coward Chance, 1953; admitted Solicitor, 1956; Partner, Coward Chance, later Clifford Chance, 1960–93 (Sen. Partner, 1990–93). Dir, London First, later London First Centre, 1993–98. Member: Council, British Inst. of Internat. and Comparative Law, 1977– (Chm., Exec. Cttee, 1986–96); Council, British Gp, Internat. Assoc. for Protection of Indust. Property, 1984–89; Council, British Branch, Internat. Law Assoc., 1971–86 (Chm., Cttee on Internat. Securities Regulation, 1989–93); Business Section, Internat. Bar Assoc., 1969–93; European Gp, Law Soc., 1969–93; Cttee, Amer. Bar Assoc., 1979–93; Deleg., Banking and Finance Mission to Poland, 1989. Liveryman, City of London Solicitors' Co. Pres. Council, Taunton Sch., 1994–97 (Mem. Council, 1985–97). Mem., charitable, sports, opera concerns. *Publications:* (contrib.) Branches and Subsidiaries in the European Common Market, 1976; (contrib.) Business Law in Europe, 1982, 2nd edn 1990; articles in law professional jls. *Recreations:* shooting, beagling, cricket, art, opera. *Address:* 200 Aldersgate Street, EC1A 4JJ. *T:* (020) 7600 1000. *Clubs:* Garrick, City of London, Pilgrims, MCC; Seaview Yacht.

FOX-PITT, William; international three day event rider, since 1993; *b* 2 Jan. 1969; *s* of Oliver and Marietta Fox-Pitt; *m* 1996, Candida Channer, MRCVS. *Educ:* Eton Coll.; Goldsmiths' Coll., London Univ. (BA Hons French 1993). Three day event rider and trainer, 1993–; winner: Burghley Three Day Event, 1994; British Open Championships, 1995, 2000; team Gold Medal, 1995, team Gold and individual Bronze Medal, 1997, Open European Championships; represented GB in team at Atlanta Olympics, 1996. Board Director: Professional Event Riders' Assoc., 1998–2000; British Horse Trials Assoc., 2000–. *Recreations:* ski-ing, jogging, swimming.

FOX-STRANGWAYS, family name of **Earl of Ilchester**.

FOXALL, Colin, CBE 1995; reinsurance consultant, since 1997; *b* 6 Feb. 1947; *s* of Alfred George Foxall and Ethel Margaret Foxall; *m* 1980 (marr. diss. 2000); two *s. Educ:* Gillingham Grammar Sch., Kent. MIEx; FICM. Joined ECGD, 1966; Dept of Trade, 1974; ECGD, 1975–91: Underwriter, Eastern Bloc, 1975; Dep. Hd, For. Currency Branch, 1977; Hd, Financial Planning, 1979; Asst Sec., ME Project Gp, 1982; Under Sec., and Dir of Comprehensive Guarantee, subseq. Insce Services, Gp, 1986–91; Man. Dir and Chief Exec., NCM Credit Insurance Ltd, 1991–97; Vice-Chm., NCM (Hldg) NV, 1996–97. *Recreations:* clay target shooting, motor cycling, farming. *Address:* Brynglas Cottage, Devauden, Chepstow, Mon NP6 6NT.

FOXELL, Clive Arthur Peirson, CBE 1987; FREng; consultant; Managing Director, Engineering and Procurement, and Board Member, British Telecom, 1986–89; *b* 27 Feb. 1930; *s* of Arthur Turner Foxell and Lillian (*née* Ellerman); *m* 1956, Shirley Ann Patey Morris; one *d. Educ:* Harrow High Sch.; Univ. of London. (BSc). FREng (FEng 1985); FIEE, FInstP, FCIPS. GEC Res. Labs, 1947–68; Man., GEC Semiconductor Labs, 1968–71; Man. Dir, GEC Semiconductors Ltd, 1971–75; Dep. Dir of Research, PO, 1975–78; Dep. Dir, Procurement Exec., 1978–79; Dir of Purchasing, PO, 1980; British Telecom: Dir of Procurement, 1981–84; Senior Dir, 1984; Chief Exec., Procurement, 1984–86; Dir, British Telecommunications Systems Ltd, 1982–89. Chairman: Fulcrum Communications Ltd, 1985–86; TSCR Ltd, 1986–88; Phonepoint Ltd, 1989–93; Dir, BT&D Technologies Ltd, 1986–88. Institution of Electrical Engineers: Mem. Council, 1975–78, 1982–85, 1987–90; Vice-Pres., 1996–99; Chm., Electronics Div., 1983–84. Member: SERC (formerly SRC) Engrg Bd, 1977–80 (Chm., Silicon Working Party, 1980–81; Chm., Microelectronics, 1982–86); SERC, 1986–90; NEDC (electronics), 1987–90; ACARD Working Party on IT, 1981; Council, Foundn for Sci. and Technol., 1996–. Senator, Engrg Council, 1999–. Pres., Mobile Radio Trng Trust, 1991–95. President: IBTE, 1987–90; Inst. of Physics, 1992–94. Hon. Treas., Nat. Electronics Council, 1994–99. Bulgin Premium, IERE, 1964. Liveryman, Engineers' Co. Hon. DSc Southampton, 1994. *Publications:* Low Noise Microwave Amplifiers, 1968; Chesham Shuttle, 1996; Chesham Branch Album, 1998; The Met & GC Joint Line, 2000; articles and papers on electronics. *Recreations:* photography, steam railways. *Address:* 4 Meades Lane, Chesham, Bucks HP5 1ND. *T:* (01494) 785737.

FOXLEE, James Brazier; Under Secretary, Ministry of Agriculture, Fisheries and Food, 1971–81, retired; *b* 20 Nov. 1921; *s* of late Arthur Brazier Foxlee and late Mary Foxlee (*née* Fisher); *m* 1952, Vera June (*née* Guiver); one *s* two *d. Educ:* Brentwood Sch. Entered Min. of Agric. and Fisheries (later MAFF) as Clerical Officer, 1938. Served War, RNVR, Ordinary Seaman, 1941; commissioned, 1942; Lieut, in comd Light Coastal Forces craft and mine-sweepers. MAFF: Exec. Officer, 1946; HEO, 1948; SEO, 1950; Principal, 1955 (Welsh Dept, 1955–57; Treas., 1961–62); Asst Sec., 1965 (Regional Controller, Leeds, 1965–69). Hon. Fellow, NIAB, 1982; Hon. Mem., Arable Res. Inst. Assoc., 1990. *Recreations:* watching cricket, camping, oenology. *Address:* 14 Ware Lane, Wyton, Huntingdon, Cambs PE28 2AJ. *T:* (01480) 461854.

FOXLEY-NORRIS, Air Chief Marshal Sir Christopher (Neil), GCB 1973 (KCB 1969; CB 1966); DSO 1945; OBE 1956; Chairman: Cheshire Foundation, 1974–82, now Chairman Emeritus (Vice-Chairman, 1972–74); Battle of Britain Fighter Association, since 1978; Gardening for the Disabled, since 1980; *b* 16 March 1917; *s* of Major J. P. Foxley-Norris and Dorothy Brabant Smith; *m* 1948, Joan Lovell Hughes; no *c. Educ:* Winchester (schol.); Trinity Coll., Oxford (schol.; Hon. Fellow, 1973); Middle Temple (Harmsworth Schol.). Commissioned RAFO, 1936; France, 1940; Battle of Britain, 1940; various operational tours of duty in wartime. MA 1946. ACDS, 1963; AOC No 224 Gp, FEAF, 1964–67; Dir-Gen., RAF Organization, MoD, 1967–68; C-in-C, RAF Germany and Comdr, NATO 2nd Tactical Air Force, 1968–70; Chief of Personnel and Logistics, MoD, 1971–74; retd. Vice Pres., RUSI, 1979. Chairman: Trinity Coll. Oxford Soc., 1984–86; Ex RAF and Dependants Severely Disabled Holiday Trust, 1984. Pres., Leonard Cheshire Housing Assoc., 1978–. CIMgt. *Publications:* A Lighter Shade of Blue, 1978; various in RUSI and other service jls. *Recreations:* writing, broadcasting. *Address:* Tumble Wood, Northend Common, Henley-on-Thames RG9 6LJ. *T:* (01491) 638457. *Clubs:* Royal Air Force; Phyllis Court (Henley-on-Thames).

FOY, John Leonard; QC 1998; a Recorder, since 2000; *b* 1 June 1946; *s* of Leonard James Foy and Edith Mary Foy; *m* 1972, Colleen Patricia Austin; one *s. Educ:* Dartford GS; Birmingham Univ. (LLB Hons 1967). Called to the Bar, Gray's Inn, 1969; in practice at the Bar, 1969–. *Publications:* contribs to various legal books and jls. *Recreations:* watching West Bromwich Albion, football, Rugby, reading modern literature. *Address:* 9 Gough Square, EC4A 3DG. *T:* (020) 7353 5371.

FRACKOWIAK, Prof. Richard Stanislaus Joseph, MD, DSc; FRCP; Professor and Co-Chairman, Wellcome Department of Cognitive Neurology, and Director, Leopold Muller Functional Imaging Laboratory, Institute of Neurology, since 1994; Dean, Institute of Neurology, University College London, since 1999; *b* 26 March 1950; *s* of Joseph Frackowiak and Wanda (*née* Majewska); *m* 1972, Christine Jeanne Françoise Thepot; one *s* two *d. Educ:* Latymer Upper Sch.; Peterhouse, Cambridge (Wilhelm Brauer Open Schol.; MA); Middlesex Hosp. Med. Sch. (MB BChir; MD 1983); DSc London 1996. FRCP 1987. Sen. Lectr, 1984–90, Prof. of Neurology, 1990–94, RPMS and Hammersmith Hosp.; Consultant Neurologist: Hammersmith Hosp., 1984–95; Nat. Hosp. for Neurology and Neurosurgery, 1984–; MRC Trng Fellow, 1980–81; MRC Clinical Scientist, 1984–94; Wellcome Principal Res. Fellow, 1994–. Adjunct Prof. of Neurology, Cornell Univ. Med. Sch., NY, 1990; Visiting Professor: Wellcome Lab. of Neurobiol., UCL, 1991–95; Cath. Univ., Louvain, Belgium, 1996–97; Harvard Med. Sch., 1999. Member: Assoc. of British Neurologists, 1984; American Neurological Assoc., 1988; Soc. Française de Neurologie, 1993; Academia Europaea, 1995; L'Academie Royale de Médecine de Belgique, 1995. Founder FMedSci 1998 (Mem. Council, 2000–). Wilhelm Feldberg Foundn Prize, 1996; (jtly) Ipsen Prize for Neuronal Plasticity, Ipsen Foundn, Paris, 1997. *Publications:* (jtly) Human Brain Function, 1997; Brain Mapping: the disorders, 2000; numerous on functional anatomy and organisation of the human brain using non-invasive monitoring techniques. *Recreations:* motorcycling, reading. *Address:* Wellcome Department of Cognitive Neurology, Institute of Neurology, 12 Queen Square, WC1N 3BG. *T:* (020) 7833 7456. *Clubs:* Athenæum, Hurlingham.

FRAENKEL, Prof. Ludwig Edward, FRS 1993; Professor of Mathematics, School of Mathematical Sciences, University of Bath, since 1988; *b* 28 May 1927; *s* of Eduard David Mortier Fraenkel and Ruth (*née* von Velsen); *m* 1954, Beryl Jacqueline Margaret Currie; two *d. Educ:* Dragon Sch., Oxford; Univ. of Toronto Schs; Univ. of Toronto (BASc 1947; MASc 1948); MA Cantab 1964. SO, RAE, Farnborough, 1948–52; Res. Fellow, Univ. of Glasgow, 1952–53; Imperial College, London: Lectr, Aeronautics Dept, 1953–58, Reader 1958–61; Reader, Mathematics Dept, 1961–64; Lectr in Applied Maths, Univ. of Cambridge, 1964–75; Fellow, Queens' Coll., Cambridge, 1964–68; Prof., Maths Div., Univ. of Sussex, 1975–88. Sen. Whitehead Prize, London Math. Soc., 1989. *Publications:* An Introduction to Maximum Principles and Symmetry in Elliptic Problems, 2000; some 60 papers in jls ranging from Aeronautical Qly to Acta Mathematica. *Recreations:* ski-ing, cycling. *Address:* School of Mathematical Sciences, University of Bath, Bath BA2 7AY. *T:* (01225) 826249. *Club:* Ski of Great Britain.

FRAENKEL, Peter Maurice, FREng, FICE, FIStructE, FIHT; Founder and Senior Partner, Peter Fraenkel & Partners, since 1972; Chairman, Peter Fraenkel Maritime Ltd, since 1995; Director, Peter Fraenkel BMT Ltd, 1990–95 (Chairman, 1990–93); *b* 5 July 1915; *s* of Ernest Fraenkel and Luise (*née* Tessmann); *m* 1946, Hilda Muriel, *d* of William Norman; two *d. Educ:* Battersea Polytechnic; Imperial Coll., London. BSc(Eng). FICE 1954, FIStructE 1954, MConsE 1962; FREng (FEng 1984); FIHT 1992. Asst Engr with London firm of contractors, engaged on design and construction of marine and industrial structures, 1937–40; served in Army, 1941–42; Works Services Br., War Dept, 1942–45; Rendel, Palmer & Tritton, Cons. Engineers: Civil Engr, 1945; Sen. Engr, 1953; Partner, 1961–72. Dir, British Maritime Technology, 1990–96. Has been responsible for, or closely associated with, technical and management aspects of many feasibility and planning studies, and planning, design and supervision of construction of large civil engrg projects, incl. ports, docks, offshore terminals, inland waterways, highways, power stations and tunnels in Gt Britain, Middle East, India, Far East and Australia, including: new Oil port at Sullom Voe, Shetland; new Naval Dockyard, Bangkok; Shatin to Tai Po coastal Trunk Road, Hong Kong; comprehensive study for DoE, of maintenance and operational needs of canals controlled by Brit. Waterways Bd (Fraenkel Report), and new port at Limassol, Cyprus. James Watt Medal, 1963, Telford Gold Medal, 1971, ICE. *Publications:* (jtly) papers to Instn of Civil Engrs: Special Features of the Civil Engineering Works at Aberthaw Power Station, 1962; Planning and Design of Port Talbot Harbour, 1970. *Address:* Little Paddock, Rockfield Road, Oxted, Surrey RH8 0EL. *T:* (01883) 712927. *Club:* Athenæum.

FRAGA-IRIBARNE, Manuel; Founder-Member, People's Party (formerly People's Alliance), Spain, 1976, Leader, 1979–86; Member of the Cortes, since 1977; *b* 23 Nov. 1922; *m* 1948, María del Carmen Estévez (*d* 1996); two *s* three *d. Educ:* Insts of Coruña, Villalba and Lugo; Univs of Santiago de Compostela and Madrid. Prof. of Polit. Law, Univ. of Valencia, 1945; Prof. of Polit. Sci. and Constit. Law, Univ. of Madrid, 1953; Legal Adviser to the Cortes, 1945; entered Diplomatic Service, 1945; Sec.-Gen., Instituto de Cultura Hispánica, 1951; Sec.-Gen. in Min. of Educn, 1953; Head, Inst. of Polit. Studies, 1961; Minister of Information and Tourism, 1961–69; Ambassador to UK, 1973–75; Interior Minister, Spain, 1975–76; Leader of the Opposition, 1982–86. Pres., Galician Govt, 1989–. Holds numerous foreign orders. *Publications:* various books on law, polit. sci., history and sociology, incl. one on British Parlt. *Recreations:* shooting, fishing. *Address:* Pazo de Raxoi, Plaza del Obradoiro, Santiago de Compostela, Coruña, Spain. *T:* (81) 541215, *Fax:* (81) 541219.

FRAME, David William; Member, Baltic Exchange, since 1961 (Chairman, 1987–89); *b* 26 July 1934; *s* of William and Ursula Frame; *m* 1963, Margaret Anne Morrison; two *d. Educ:* Wellington College. Commissioned Royal Artillery, National Service. Qualified Chartered Accountant, 1960; joined Usborne & Son (London), 1961, Dir 1962; Dir, Usborne and Feedex subsid. cos and other cos. *Recreation:* golf (played for GB and Ireland in Walker Cup, 1961, for England, 1958–63). *Address:* Green Glades, Frensham Vale, Farnham, Surrey GU10 3HT. *T:* (01252) 793272. *Golf Clubs:* Royal and Ancient, Worplesdon, Trevose, Old Thorns, Plettenberg Bay.

FRAME, Frank Riddell; Adviser to the Board, HSBC Holdings plc, 1990–98; *b* 15 Feb. 1930; *s* of late William Graham Frame; *m* 1958, Maureen Willis Milligan; one *s* one *d. Educ:* Hamilton Academy; Univ. of Glasgow (MA, LLB); admitted solicitor, 1955. North of Scotland Hydro-Electric Board, 1955–60; UK Atomic Energy Authority, 1960–68; Weir Group plc, 1968–76 (Dir, 1971–76); joined Hongkong and Shanghai Banking Corp., as Gp Legal Advr, 1977, Exec. Dir, 1985, Dep. Chm., 1986–90. Chairman: South China Morning Post Ltd, 1981–87; Far Eastern Economic Review Ltd, 1981–87; Wallem Group Ltd, 1992–; Director: Marine Midland Banks Inc., 1986–90; The British Bank of the Middle East, 1986–91; Swire Pacific Ltd, 1986–90; Consolidated Press Internat. Ltd, 1988–91; Securities and Futures Commn, Hong Kong, 1989–90; Baxter Internat. Inc., 1992–2001; Edinburgh Dragon Trust plc, 1994–. DUniv Glasgow, 2001. *Publication:* (with Prof. Harry Street) The Law relating to Nuclear Energy, 1966. *Address:* 43 Shrewsbury House, Cheyne Walk, SW3 5LW. *T:* (020) 7352 3968. *Club:* Brooks's.

FRAME, Rt Rev. John Timothy, DD; Dean of Columbia and Rector of Christ Church Cathedral, Victoria, BC, 1980–95; *b* 8 Dec. 1930; *m*; three *d. Educ:* Univ. of Toronto. Burns Lake Mission, Dio. Caledonia, 1957; Hon. Canon of Caledonia, 1965; Bishop of Yukon, 1968–80. *Address:* 2173 Tull Avenue, Courtenay, BC V9N 7S1, Canada.

FRAME, Ronald William Sutherland; author; *b* 23 May 1953; *s* of Alexander D. Frame and Isobel D. Frame (*née* Sutherland). *Educ:* High Sch. of Glasgow; Univ. of Glasgow (MA Hons); Jesus Coll., Oxford (MLitt). Full-time author, 1981–; first Betty Trask Prize (jtly), 1984; Samuel Beckett Prize, 1986; Television Industries' Panel's Most Promising Writer New to TV Award, 1986. Television films: Paris, 1985; Out of Time, 1987; Ghost City, 1994; A Modern Man, 1996; M. R. James (Ghost Stories for Christmas), 2000; radio drama includes: Winter Journey, 1984; Cara, 1989; The Lantern Bearers, 1997; The Hydro (serial), 1997, 2nd series 1998, 3rd series 1999; Havisham, 1998; Maestro, 1999; Pharos, 2000; Viva Verdi!, 2001. *Publications:* Winter Journey, 1984; Watching Mrs Gordon, 1985; A Long Weekend with Marcel Proust, 1986; Sandmouth People, 1987; A Woman of Judah, 1987; Paris, 1987; Penelope's Hat, 1989; Bluette, 1990; Underwood and After, 1991; Walking My Mistress in Deauville, 1992; The Sun on the Wall, 1994; The Lantern Bearers, 1999 (Book of the Year, Saltire Soc., 2000). *Recreations:* swimming, walking. *Address:* c/o Curtis Brown Ltd, 28/29 Haymarket, SW1Y 4SP.

FRANCE, Sir Christopher (Walter), GCB 1994 (KCB 1989; CB 1984); Permanent Secretary, Ministry of Defence, 1992–95; *b* 2 April 1934; *s* of W. J. and E. M. France; *m* 1961, Valerie (*née* Larman) (*see* V. E. France); one *s* one *d*. *Educ:* East Ham Grammar Sch.; New College, Oxford (MA (PPE), DipEd). CDipAF. HM Treasury, 1959–84: Principal Private Secretary to the Chancellor of the Exchequer, 1973–76; Principal Establishment Officer, 1977–80; on secondment to Electricity Council, 1980–81; Dep. Sec., 1981; on secondment to MoD, 1981–84; Dep. Sec., 1984–86, Second Perm. Sec., 1986, Perm. Sec., 1987–92, DHSS, subseq. DoH. Staff Counsellor for Security and Intelligence Services, 1995–99. Bd Mem., Macmillan Cancer Relief, 1995–; Trustee, Nuffield (formerly Nuffield Provincial Hosps) Trust, 1998–. Chm. Council, QMW, 1995–. Founder FMedSci 1998. Freeman, Drapers' Co., 2001. Hon. Col, RMR (City of London), 1996–99. *Recreations:* supervising keeping the house up and the garden down. *Address:* c/o Barclays Premier Banking, West Kent Centre, 73–75 Calverley Road, Tunbridge Wells TN1 2UZ. *Club:* Reform.

FRANCE, Elizabeth Irene; Information Commissioner (formerly Data Protection Registrar, then Comissioner), since 1994; *b* 1 Feb. 1950; *d* of Ralph Salem and Elizabeth Joan Salem (*née* Bryan); *m* 1971, Dr Michael William France; two *s* one *d*. *Educ:* Beauchamp Sch., Leics; UCW, Aberystwyth (BScEcon Pol. Sci.). Home Office: Admin Trainee, 1971; Principal, 1977; Asst Sec., 1986; Police Dept, Criminal Justice and Constitutional Dept, IT and Pay Services, 1986–94. FRSA 1995; FICM 1999. Hon. DSc De Montfort, 1996; Hon. DLitt Loughborough, 2000. *Address:* Office of the Information Commissioner, Wycliffe House, Water Lane, Wilmslow, Cheshire SK9 5AF. *T:* (01625) 545700.

FRANCE, Prof. Peter, DPhil; FBA 1989; Professor of French, University of Edinburgh, 1980–90, now Emeritus (University Endowment Fellow, 1990–2000); *b* 19 Oct. 1935; *s* of Edgar France and Doris Woosnam Morgan; *m* 1961, Siân Reynolds; three *d*. *Educ:* Bridlington Sch.; Bradford Grammar Sch.; Magdalen Coll., Oxford (MA; DPhil). Lectr, then Reader, in French, Univ. of Sussex, 1963–80. French Editor, MLR, 1979–85. Mem., Chuvash Nat. Acad., 1991. Dr *hc* Chuvash State Univ., 1996. Officer de l'Ordre des Palmes Académiques (France), 1990. *Publications:* Racine's Rhetoric, 1965; Rhetoric and Truth in France, 1972; Poets of Modern Russia, 1982; Racine: Andromaque, 1977; Diderot, 1983; Rousseau: Confessions, 1987; trans., An Anthology of Chuvash Poetry, 1991; Politeness and its Discontents, 1992; (ed) New Oxford Companion to Literature in French, 1995; trans., Gennady Aygi, Selected Poems, 1997; (ed) Oxford Guide to Literature in English Translation, 2000. *Address:* 10 Dryden Place, Edinburgh EH9 1RP. *T:* (0131) 667 1177.

See also Rev. R. T. France.

FRANCE, Rev. Richard Thomas; Rector, Wentnor with Ratlinghope, Myndtown, Norbury, More, Lydham and Snead, diocese of Hereford, 1995–99; *b* 2 April 1938; *s* of Edgar and Doris Woosnam France; *m* 1965, Barbara Wilding; one *s* one *d*. *Educ:* Bradford Grammar School; Balliol Coll., Oxford (MA); BD London; PhD Bristol. Asst Curate, St Matthew's Church, Cambridge, 1966–69; Lectr in Biblical Studies, Univ. of Ife, Nigeria, 1969–73; Tyndale House, Cambridge: Librarian, 1973–76; Warden, 1978–81; London Bible College: Senior Lectr, 1981–88; Vice-Principal, 1983–88; Principal, Wycliffe Hall, Oxford, 1989–95. Hon. Canon Theologian, Ibadan Cathedral, 1994–. *Publications:* Jesus and the Old Testament, 1971; (ed with D. Wenham) Gospel Perspectives, vols 1–3, 1980–83; The Gospel According to Matthew: an introduction and commentary, 1985; The Evidence for Jesus, 1986; Matthew: evangelist and teacher, 1989; Divine Government, 1990; (ed with A. E. McGrath) Evangelical Anglicans, 1993; Women in the Church's Ministry, 1995; The Gospel of Mark, 2001. *Recreations:* mountains, wildlife, travel, music. *Address:* Tyn-y-Twll, Llangelynin, Llwyngwril, Gwynedd LL37 2QL. *T:* (01341) 250596.

See also P. France.

FRANCE, Valerie Edith, (Lady France), OBE 1994; MA; Headmistress, City of London School for Girls, 1986–95; *b* 29 Oct. 1935; *d* of Neville and Edith Larman; *m* 1961, Sir Christopher Walter France, *qv*; one *s* one *d*. *Educ:* St Hugh's Coll., Oxford (MA); CertEd Cantab. Deputy Headmistress, Bromley High Sch., GPDST, 1984–86; Acting Hd, Atherley Sch., Oct.–Dec. 1996. Mem., Eco-Schs Adv. Panel, 1996–2000. Member Council: Cheltenham Ladies' Coll., 1995–98; Francis Holland Schs Trust, 1997– (Chm. Council, 1999–); Mem. Court, Whitgift Foundn, 1994–97; Gov., Trinity Sch., 1997–. FRGS 1959; FRSA 1991. Freeman, City of London, 1988; Liveryman, Needlemakers' Co., 1992–. *Recreations:* family, friends, places. *Address:* c/o Barclays Premier Banking, 73–75 Calverley Road, Tunbridge Wells TN1 2UZ.

FRANCIS, Clare Mary, MBE 1978; writer; *b* 17 April 1946; *d* of Owen Francis, *qv*; *m* 1977, Jacques Robert Redon (marr. diss. 1985); one *s*. *Educ:* Royal Ballet Sch.; University Coll. London (BScEcon; Fellow, 1978). Crossed Atlantic singlehanded, Falmouth to Newport, in 37 days, 1973; Observer Transatlantic Singlehanded Race: women's record (29 days), 1976; Whitbread Round the World Race (fully-crewed), first woman skipper, 1977–78. Chm., Soc. of Authors, 1997–99. Chm., Govt Adv. Cttee on PLR, 2000–. Hon. Fellow, UMIST, 1981. *Publications: non-fiction:* Come Hell or High Water, 1977; Come Wind or Weather, 1978; The Commanding Sea, 1981; *novels:* Night Sky, 1983; Red Crystal, 1985; Wolf Winter, 1987; Requiem, 1991; Deceit, 1993 (televised, 2000); Betrayal, 1995; A Dark Devotion, 1997; Keep Me Close, 1999; A Death Divided, 2001. *Recreations:* opera, theatre, catching up. *Address:* c/o John Johnson Agency, 45–47 Clerkenwell Green, EC1R 0HT.

FRANCIS, (David) Hywel; PhD; MP (Lab) Aberavon, since 2001; *b* 6 June 1946; *s* of David Francis and Catherine Francis (*née* Powell); *m* 1968, Mair Georgina Price; one *s* one *d* (and one *s* decd). *Educ:* UC, Swansea (BA 1968; PhD 1978). Admin. Asst, TUC, 1971–72; University College, Swansea, then University of Wales Swansea: Sen. Res. Officer, 1972–74; Tutor/Lectr, Contg Educn, 1974–87; Dir, Contg Educn, 1987–99; Prof., Contg Educn, 1992–99. Chm., Wales Congress in Support of Mining Communities, 1984–86; Nat. Convenor, Yes for Wales Campaign, 1997; Special Policy Advr, Sec. of State for Wales, 1999–2000. Chm., Paul Robeson Wales Trust, 2001–; Trustee and Vice-Chm., Bevan Foundn, 2001–. Mem., Gorsedd of Bards, 1986. FRSA 1987. *Publications:* (with David Smith) The Fed: a history of the South Wales miners in the twentieth century, 1980, 2nd edn 1998; Miners against Fascism: Wales and the Spanish Civil War, 1984; contrib. hist. and educnl articles in learned jls. *Recreations:* photography, walking, reading. *Address:* House of Commons, SW1A 0AA. *T:* (020) 7219 8121. *Clubs:* Aberavon Rugby Football; Cwmavon Rugby Football.

FRANCIS, Dick, (Richard Stanley), CBE 2000 (OBE 1984); author; *b* 31 Oct. 1920; *s* of George Vincent Francis and Catherine Mary Francis; *m* 1947, Mary Margaret Brenchley (*d* 2000); two *s*. *Educ:* Maidenhead County Boys' School. Pilot, RAF, 1940–45 (Flying Officer). Amateur National Hunt jockey, 1946–48, Professional, 1948–57; Champion Jockey, season 1953–54. Racing Correspondent, Sunday Express, 1957–73. Hon. LHD Tufts, 1991. Edgar Allan Poe Grand Master Award, 1996. *Publications:* Sport of Queens (autobiog.), 1957, 3rd updated edn, 1982; Dead Cert, 1962; Nerve, 1964; For Kicks, 1965; Odds Against, 1965; Flying Finish, 1966; Blood Sport, 1967; Forfeit, 1968 (Edgar Allan Poe Award, 1970); Enquiry, 1969; Rat Race, 1970; Bonecrack, 1971; Smoke Screen, 1972; Slay-Ride, 1973; Knock Down, 1974; High Stakes, 1975; In the Frame, 1976; Risk, 1977; Trial Run, 1978; Whip Hand, 1979 (Golden Dagger Award, Crime Writers' Assoc., 1980; Edgar Allan Poe Award, 1980); Reflex, 1980; Twice Shy, 1981; Banker, 1982; The Danger, 1983; Proof, 1984; Break In, 1985; Lester, the official biography, 1986; Bolt, 1986; Hot Money, 1987; The Edge, 1988; Straight, 1989; Longshot, 1990; Comeback, 1991; (ed jtly) Great Racing Stories, 1989; Driving Force, 1992; Decider, 1993; Wild Horses, 1994; Come to Grief, 1995 (Edgar Allan Poe Award, 1996); To the Hilt, 1996; 10lb Penalty, 1997; Field of Thirteen, 1998; Second Wind, 1999; Shattered, 2000. *Recreations:* boating, travel. *Address:* c/o John Johnson Ltd, 45/47 Clerkenwell Green, EC1R 0HT.

FRANCIS, Prof. (Edward) Howel, DSc; FRSE; CGeol; FGS; Professor of Earth Sciences, University of Leeds, 1977–89; *b* 31 May 1924; *s* of Thomas Howel Francis and Gwendoline Amelia (*née* Richards); *m* 1952, Cynthia Mary (*née* Williams) (*d* 1997); one *d*. *Educ:* Port Talbot County Sch.; Univ. of Wales, Swansea (BSc, DSc; Hon. Fellow 1989). FGS 1948; FRSE 1962. Served Army, 1944–47. Geological Survey of Great Britain (now incorporated in British Geol Survey): Field Geologist, Scotland, 1949–62; Dist Geologist, NE England, 1962–67, N Wales, 1967–70; Asst Dir, Northern England and Wales, 1971–77. Geological Society of London: Murchison Fund, 1963; Mem. Council, 1972–74; Pres., 1980–82; Pres., Section C (Geol.), BAAS, 1976; Mem., Inst. of Geol., 1978. Clough Medal, Edinburgh Geol Soc., 1983; Sorby Medal, Yorks Geol Soc., 1983; Major John Sacheverell A'Deane Coke Medal, Geol Soc. of London, 1989. *Publications:* memoirs, book chapters and papers on coalfields, palaeovolcanic rocks and general stratigraphy, mainly of Britain. *Recreations:* opera, golf. *Address:* Archways, 2 Stratford Drive, Porthcawl, Bridgend, Glam CF36 3LG. *Club:* Grove Golf.

FRANCIS, Ven. Edward Reginald; Archdeacon of Bromley, 1979–94, Emeritus since 1994; *b* 31 Jan. 1929; *s* of Alfred John and Elsie Hilda Francis; *m* 1950, Joyce Noreen Atkins; three *s*. *Educ:* Maidstone and Dover Grammar Schools; Rochester Theological College. National Service, RAF, 1947–49. Insurance, including period at Chartered Insurance Inst. (ACII), 1950–59. Ordained, 1961; Chaplain, Training Ship Arethusa, and Curate of All Saints, Frindsbury, 1961–64; Vicar of St William's, Chatham, 1964–73; Vicar and Rural Dean of Rochester, 1973–78. Mem., General Synod of C of E, 1981–94. Mem., Kent Industrial Mission, 1979–89; Jt Chm., Council for Social Responsibility, Dioceses of Canterbury and Rochester, 1983–89; Dir of Continuing Ministry Educn, dio. of Rochester, 1989–94. *Recreations:* ornithology, walking, music. *Address:* 71 Ash Tree Drive, West Kingsdown, Sevenoaks, Kent TN15 6LW. *T:* (01474) 853202.

FRANCIS, Gwyn Jones, CB 1990; Director-General and Deputy Chairman, Forestry Commission, 1986–90, retired; *b* 17 Sept. 1930; *s* of Daniel Brynmor Francis and Margaret Jane Francis; *m* 1st, 1954, Margaretta Meryl Jeremy (*d* 1985); one *s* one *d* (and one *s* decd); 2nd, 1986, Audrey Gertrude (*née* Gill). *Educ:* Llanelli Grammar Sch.; University Coll. of N Wales, Bangor (BSc Hons 1952); Univ. of Toronto (MSc 1965). Served RE, 1952–54. Forestry Commission: Dist Officer, 1954; Principal, Forester Training Sch., 1962; Asst Conservator, 1969; Head, Harvesting and Marketing Div., 1976; Comr, 1983–86. Mem. Council, 1992–98, and Chm., Scottish Cttee, 1992–98, RSPB. FICFor 1982; FIWSc 1984. Hon. Fellow, Univ. of Wales, 1991. *Recreations:* bird-watching, gardening, painting. *Address:* 21 Campbell Road, Edinburgh EH12 6DT. *T:* (0131) 337 5037. *Club:* New (Edinburgh).

FRANCIS, Sir (Horace) William (Alexander), Kt 1989; CBE 1976; FREng; FICE; Director, British Railways Board, 1994–97; *b* 31 Aug. 1926; *s* of Horace Fairie Francis and Jane McMinn Murray; *m* 1949, Gwendoline Maud Dorricott; two *s* two *d*. *Educ:* Royal Technical Coll., Glasgow. Dir, Tarmac Civil Engineering Ltd, 1960; Man. Dir, Tarmac Construction Ltd, 1963; Dir, Tarmac Ltd, 1964, Vice-Chm., 1974–77; Director: Trafalgar House Ltd, 1978–85; Trafalgar House Construction Hldgs, 1979–85; Trafalgar House Oil and Gas, 1986–88; Mining (Scotland) Ltd, 1995–98; Barr Holdings Ltd, 1996–2000; Chm., Fitzpatrick Internat. Ltd, 1993–99. Member: Export Guarantees Adv. Council, 1974–80; British Overseas Trade Bd, 1977–80; Chairman: Overseas Projects Bd, 1977–80; Black Country UDC, 1987–94; Midlands Enterprise Fund, 1997–99. Mem., Engrg Council, 1995–96. Pres., ICE, 1987–88 (Vice-Pres., 1984–87). Lt-Col, Engr and Transport Staff Corps, TA, 1986. FREng (FEng 1977). FRSA 1989. Hon. LLD Strathclyde, 1988; Hon. DSc Aston, 1990. *Recreations:* golf, shooting, fishing, construction. *Address:* The Firs, Cruckton, near Shrewsbury, Shropshire SY5 8PW. *T:* (01743) 860796. *Clubs:* Army and Navy, Livery, Royal Over-Seas League.

FRANCIS, Howel; *see* Francis, E. H.

FRANCIS, Hywel; *see* Francis, D. H.

FRANCIS, Jennifer; freelance consultant in public and media affairs, since 1992; *b* 13 July 1959; *d* of Luke Faure and Clytie Jean Francis; *m* 1981; two *s*. *Educ:* St Augustine's C of E Sch., London; City Univ. DipCAM. MIPR 1989. Br. Manager, Brook Street Bureau, 1980–83; PR, Cannons Sports Club, 1983–85; freelance PR, 1985–86; Man. Dir, Networking Public Relations, then Head of African, Caribbean, Asian and Pacific Gp, Pielle Public Relations, 1986–92; PR, LAPADA, 1999. Actg Hd of Media Relations, V&A Mus., 1998; Actg Dir of Public Relations—The Show, RCA, 1999. Member: Media Adv. Gp, CRE, 1990–91; Nat. Consumer Council, 1991–94; ITC Advertising Adv. Cttee, 1992–; Prince's Youth Business Trust Ethnic Minority Adv. Gp, 1993–; Radio Authority, 1994–99; Chm., Women's Enterprise Develt Agency, 1990–93. Black Business Woman of the Year, 1989. *Publications:* contrib. to periodicals. *Recreations:* watercolours, travel, current affairs, music. *Address:* 1 Montagu Place, W1H 1RG. *T:* (020) 7935 7644.

FRANCIS, Dr John Michael, FRSE; Chairman: UK National Commission for UNESCO, since 1999; Sustainable Development, Peace and Human Rights Sector, UK

UNESCO, since 1999; *b* 1 May 1939; *s* of late William Winston Francis and of Beryl Margaret Francis (*née* Savage); *m* 1963, Eileen Sykes, Cyncoed, Cardiff; two *d. Educ:* Gowerton County Grammar Sch.; Royal Coll. of Sci., Imperial Coll. of Sci. and Tech., Univ. of London (BSc, ARCS, PhD, DIC). FRIC 1969; FRSGS 1990; FRSE 1991; FRZSScot 1992. Res. Officer, CEGB, R&D Dept, Berkeley Nuclear Labs, 1963–70; First Dir, Society, Religion and Tech. Project, Church of Scotland, 1970–74; Sen. Res. Fellow in Energy Studies, Heriot-Watt Univ., 1974–76; Scottish Office, Edinburgh, 1976–84; Dir Scotland, Nature Conservancy Council, 1984–91 (Mem., Adv. Cttee for Scotland, 1974–76); Chief Exec., NCC for Scotland, 1991–92; Asst Sec., Envmt Dept, 1992–95, Sen. Policy Advr, Home Dept, 1995–99, Scottish Office. Member: Oil Develt Council for Scotland, 1973–76; Indep. Commn on Transport, 1974; Adv. Cttee on Marine Fishfarming Crown Estate Commn, 1989–92. Chm., Francis Group (Consultants), 1992–99. Consultant on Sci., Tech. and Social Ethics, WCC, Geneva, 1971–83; Church of Scotland: Chm., Cttee on Society, Religion and Tech., 1980–94; Trustee, Society, Religion and Technol. Project Trust, 1998–; Mem., Church and Nation Cttee, 2000–. Chm., Edinburgh Forum, 1984–93. Mem. Council, Nat. Trust for Scotland, 1985–92. Mem., St Giles' Cathedral, Edinburgh. Associate, Scottish Inst. of Human Relations, 1974–94; Sen. Associate, Strathmor Gp, 1999–; Mem., Scottish Univs Policy, Res. and Advice Network, 1999–. Fellow, Inst. for Advanced Studies in the Humanities, Edinburgh Univ., 1988; Hon. Fellow, Edinburgh Univ., 2000; Vis. Fellow, Centre for Values and Social Policy, Univ. of Colorado at Boulder, 1991; UK Rep., Millennium Proj., UN Univ., 1992–. Professional Mem., World Futures Soc., Washington DC, 1991–. Mem., John Muir Trust, 1994–. *Publications:* Scotland in Turmoil, 1973; (jtly) Changing Directions, 1974; (jtly) The Future as an Academic Discipline, 1975; Facing up to Nuclear Power, 1976; (jtly) The Future of Scotland, 1977; (jtly) North Sea Oil and the Environment, 1992; (jtly) Democratic Contracts for Sustainable and Caring Societies, 2000; contribs to scientific and professional jls and periodicals, and to RSE programmes on public understanding of science. *Recreations:* writing on environmental values and the ethics of science and technology, ecumenical travels, hill walking, theatre. *Address:* 49 Gilmour Road, Newington, Edinburgh EH16 5NU. *T:* (0131) 667 3996; *e-mail:* john.m.francis@btinternet.com.

FRANCIS, Mary Elizabeth, LVO 1999; Director-General, Association of British Insurers, since 1999; *b* 24 July 1948; *d* of Frederick Henry George and Barbara Henrietta George (*née* Jeffs); *m* 1st, Dr Roger John Brown, *qv* (marr. diss.); 2nd, 1991, Prof. Peter William Francis (*d* 1999). *Educ:* James Allen's Girls' Sch., Dulwich; Newnham Coll., Cambridge (MA Hist.). Res. Asst to Prof. Max Beloff, All Souls Coll., Oxford, 1970–72; Admin. Trainee, then Principal, CS Dept and HM Treasury, 1972–82; Private Sec. to Lord Privy Seal and Minister for the Arts, 1982–84; seconded to Hill Samuel & Co. Ltd, 1984–86; Asst Sec., HM Treasury, 1986–90; Economic Counsellor, British Embassy, Washington, 1990–92; Private Sec. to Prime Minister, 1992–95; Asst Private Sec. to the Queen, 1996–99, Dep. Private Sec., Feb.–June 1999. Mem. Ct, Bank of England, 2001–. Mem. Adv. Bd, The SMART Co., 2000–; Dir, Internat. Financial Services (London), 2001–. Mem., Press Complaints Commn, 2001– (Mem., Appts Cttee, 2000–). Associate Fellow, Newnham Coll., Cambridge, 1995–98. Gov., James Allen's Girls' Sch., Dulwich, 1992–. *Recreations:* reading, swimming, looking at volcanoes. *Address:* Association of British Insurers, 51 Gresham Street, EC2V 7HQ. *T:* (020) 7600 3333.

FRANCIS, Norman; *see* Francis, W. N.

FRANCIS, Owen, CB 1960; Chairman, London Electricity Board, 1972–76; *b* 4 Oct. 1912; *yr s* of Sidney and Margaret Francis, The White House, Austwick, Yorks; *m* 1938, Joan St Leger (*née* Norman); two *d. Educ:* Giggleswick Sch., Yorks. Joined Govt Actuary's Dept, 1931. *Address:* Meadow Cottage, Stanford Dingley, Berks RG7 6LT. *T:* (0118) 974 4394. *Clubs:* Royal Yacht Squadron; Seaview Yacht; St Moritz Tobogganing.
See also C. M. Francis.

FRANCIS, Paul Richard, FRICS, FSVA; Surveyor Member, Lands Tribunal, since 1998; *b* 14 Feb. 1948; *o s* of Richard Francis and Pamela Francis (*née* Rouse); partner, Mollie Labercombe. *Educ:* King's Sch., Harrow. FSVA 1974; FRICS 2000. Midland Marts (Banbury), 1967–70; E. J. Brooks & Son, Chartered Surveyors, 1970–75; Partner, A. C. Frost & Co., 1975–86; Nat. Survey and Valuation Dir, Prudential Corp., 1986–98. Pres., ISVA, 1994–95. Chm. Adv. Bd, Cert. in Residential Estate Agency, Coll. of Estate Mgt, 1997–. *Recreations:* motor sailing, golf, shooting. *Address:* Peddars Way, Walsingham Gate, High Wycombe, Bucks HP11 1PA. *T:* (01494) 462998. *Club:* Royal Southampton Yacht.

FRANCIS, Very Rev. Peter Brereton; Warden and Chief Librarian, St Deiniol's Library, Hawarden, since 1997; *b* 18 June 1953; *s* of Richard and Pauline Francis; *m* 1st, 1976, Denise Steele (marr. diss. 1997); 2nd, Helen Grocott; one step *d. Educ:* Malvern Coll.; St Andrews Univ. (MTh 1977); Queen's Coll., Birmingham. Ordained deacon, 1978, priest, 1979; Curate, Hagley, Worcs, 1978–81; Chaplain, QMC, 1981–87; Rector, Holy Trinity, Ayr, 1987–92; Provost and Rector, St Mary's Cathedral, Glasgow, 1992–96. Dir, Gladstone Project, 1997–. *Publications:* The Grand Old Man, 2000; The Gladstone Umbrella, 2001. *Recreations:* cinema, theatre, cricket. *Address:* The Warden's Lodge, St Deiniol's Library, Hawarden, Flintshire CH5 3DF. *T:* (01244) 531659, *Fax:* (01244) 520643.

FRANCIS, Richard Mark; art historian; Senior Specialist, Twentieth Century Art, Christie's Private Sales, Christie's Inc., New York, since 1997; *b* 20 Nov. 1947; *s* of Ralph Lawrence and Eileen Francis; *m* 1976, Tamar Janine Helen Burchill; one *d. Educ:* Oakham Sch.; Cambridge Univ.; Courtauld Inst. Walker Art Gall., Liverpool, 1971–72; Arts Council of GB, 1973–80; Asst Keeper, Tate Gall., London, 1980–86; Curator, Tate Gall., Liverpool, 1986–90; Chief Curator, Mus. of Contemp. Art, Chicago, 1993–97. *Publication:* Jasper Johns, 1984. *Address:* 44 Gramercy Park North, New York, NY 10010, USA. *T:* (212) 3581744.

FRANCIS, Richard Stanley; *see* Francis, Dick.

FRANCIS, Robert Anthony; QC 1992; a Recorder, since 2000; *b* 4 April 1950; *s* of late John Grimwade Francis and of Jean Isobel Francis; *m* 1976, Catherine Georgievsky; one *s* two *d. Educ:* Uppingham Sch.; Exeter Univ. (LLB Hons). Pres., Exeter Univ. Guild of Students, 1971–72. Called to the Bar, Inner Temple, 1973. Asst Recorder, 1996–2000. Legal Assessor, Chartered Soc. of Physiotherapists, 1991. Mem. Exec. Cttee, Professional Negligence Bar Assoc., 2000–. Trustee, Peper Harow Orgn, 1992. Churchwarden, St John's Parish Church, Milford, Surrey, 1984–92. Consultant Ed., Lloyd's Law Reports: Medical, 1999–. *Recreation:* cricket. *Address:* 3 Serjeants' Inn, EC4Y 1BQ. *T:* (020) 7423 5000. *Club:* Travellers.

FRANCIS, Stewart Alexander Clement, MA; Headmaster, Colchester Royal Grammar School, 1985–2000; *b* 25 Feb. 1938; *s* of Clement Francis and Patricia Francis (*née* Stewart); *m* 1965, Valerie Stead; one *s* one *d. Educ:* St Andrew's Sch., Eastbourne; St Edward's Sch., Oxford; St John's Coll., Cambridge (MA Classics, Cert Ed). Assistant Master: Mill Hill Sch., London, 1963; Maidenhead GS, 1963–66; temp. teaching posts in S Africa and England, 1966–67; Hd, Lower Sch., Maidenhead GS, 1967–69; Hd of English and Hd of Sixth Form, William Penn Sch., Rickmansworth, 1969–74; Dep. Head, Southgate Sch., London, 1974–79; Headmaster, Chenderit Sch., Middleton Cheney, Northants, 1979–84. Mem. Court, Univ. of Essex, 1996–2000. Associate MInstD 1996; FRSA 1995. Men's squash champion, Bucks, 1970. *Recreations:* cricket and other sports, reading. *Address:* Willow Springs, 32 The Lane, West Mersea, Essex CO5 8NT. *T:* (01206) 386084. *Clubs:* MCC, Jesters Cricket.

FRANCIS, Sir William; *see* Francis, Sir H. W. A.

FRANCIS, His Honour (William) Norman; a Circuit Judge (formerly Judge of County Courts), 1969–93; *b* 19 March 1921; *s* of Llewellyn Francis; *m* 1951, Anthea Constance (*née* Kerry); one *s* one *d. Educ:* Bradfield; Lincoln Coll., Oxford (BCL, MA). Served War of 1939–45, RA. Called to Bar, Gray's Inn, 1946. Dep. Chm., Brecknock QS, 1962–71. Member: Criminal Law Revision Cttee, 1977–; Policy Adv. Cttee on Sexual Offences, 1977–85; County Court Rule Cttee, 1983–88 (Chm., 1987–88). Pres., Council of HM Circuit Judges, 1987. Chancellor, dio. of Llandaff, 1979–99. Fellow, Woodard Corp. (Western Div.), 1985–91. *Recreation:* walking. *Address:* 2 The Woodlands, Lisvane, near Cardiff CF14 0SW. *T:* (029) 2075 3070.

FRANCOIS, Mark Gino; MP (C) Rayleigh, since 2001; *b* London, 14 Aug. 1965; *m* 2000, Karen Thomas. *Educ:* Nicholas Comprehensive Sch., Basildon; Univ. of Bristol (BA 1986); King's Coll. London (MA 1987). Mgt trainee, Lloyds Bank, 1987; Consultant and Dir, Market Access Internat. Public Affairs Consultancy, 1988–95; Public Affairs Consultant, Francois Associates, 1996–2001. Mem. (C) Basildon DC, 1991–95. Mem., Envmtl Audit Cttee, H of C, 2001–. Contested (C) Brent East, 1997. Served TA, 1983–89 (Lieut). *Recreations:* reading, travel, walking, history (including military history). *Address:* (office) 25 Bellingham Lane, Rayleigh, Essex SS6 7ED; c/o House of Commons, SW1A 0AA. *T:* (020) 7219 3000. *Clubs:* Carlton; Rayleigh Conservative.

FRANÇOIS-PONCET, Jean André; Member of the French Senate (Lot-et-Garonne), since 1983 (Chairman of the Economic Committee, since 1986); *b* 8 Dec. 1928; *s* of André François-Poncet, Grand'Croix de la Légion d'Honneur, and Jacqueline (*née* Dillais); *m* 1959, Marie-Thérèse de Mitry; two *s* one *d. Educ:* Paris Law Sch.; Ecole Nationale d'Administration; Wesleyan Univ.; Fletcher Sch. of Law and Diplomacy. Joined Ministry of Foreign Affairs, 1955; Office of Sec. of State, 1956–58; Sec. Gen. of French delegn to Treaty negotiations for EEC and Euratom, 1956–58; Dep. Head, European Orgns, Ministry of Foreign Affairs, 1958–60; Head of Assistance Mission, Morocco, 1961–63; Dep. Head, African Affairs, 1963–65; Counsellor, Tehran, 1969–71. Professor, Institut d'Etudes Politiques, Paris, 1960–. Chm. 1971, Vice-Pres. 1972, Pres. and Chief Exec. 1973–75, Carnaud SA. Sec. of State for Foreign Affairs, Jan.–July 1976; Sec.-Gen. to Presidency of France, 1976–78; Minister for Foreign Affairs, 1978–81. Mem., Internat. Adv. Bd, Chase Manhattan. Pres., Comité du Bassin Adour-Garonne, 1980–. *Publication:* The Economic Policy of Western Germany, 1970. *Address:* 53 rue de Varenne, 75007 Paris, France.

FRANCOME, John, MBE 1986; writer; racing presenter, Channel 4 Television; first jockey to F. T. Winter, 1975–85; *b* 13 Dec. 1952; *s* of Norman and Lillian Francome; *m* 1976, Miriam Strigner. *Educ:* Park Senior High School, Swindon. First ride, Dec. 1970; Champion Jockey (National Hunt), 1975–76, 1978–79, 1980–81, 1981–82, 1982–83, 1983–84, 1984–85; record number of jumping winners (1,036), May 1984; retired March 1985 (1138 winners). *Publications:* Born Lucky (autobiog.), 1985; How to Make Money Betting—or at least how not to lose too much, 1986; Twice Lucky: the lighter side of steeplechasing, 1988; *novels:* Blood Stock, 1989; Stud Poker, 1990; Stone Cold, 1991; Rough Ride, 1992; Outsider, 1993; Break Neck, 1994; Dead Ringer, 1995; False Start, 1996; High Flyer, 1997; Safe Bet, 1998; Tip Off, 1999; Lifeline, 2000; Dead Weight, 2001; (with James MacGregor): Eavesdropper, 1986; Riding High, 1987; Declared Dead, 1988. *Recreations:* tennis, music. *Address:* c/o Channel 4 Television, 124 Horseferry Road, SW1P 2TX; Beechdown Farm, Sheepdrove, Lambourn, Berks RG16 7UF.

FRANK, Sir Andrew; *see* Frank, Sir R. A.

FRANK, Sir Douglas (George Horace), Kt 1976; QC 1964; Deputy Judge of the High Court, Queen's Bench Division, 1976–89; *b* 16 April 1916; *s* of late George Maurice Frank and late Agnes Winifred Frank; *m* 1979, Audrey, MA (Cantab), *yr d* of late Charles Leslie Thomas, solicitor, Neath, Glam; one *s* four *d* by former marriage. War service in Royal Artillery (TA): BEF, France, 1939–40. Called to the Bar, Gray's Inn, 1946 (Master of the Bench, 1970; Master of Moots, 1978–83; Master of Estate, 1982–84); established first Barristers' Chambers in Gray's Inn, 1966. One time Asst Commissioner, Parly Boundary Commission for England; Civil Service Comr, DoE, 1971–74; Pres., Lands Tribunal, 1974–88. Mem., Cttee Public Participation in Planning (Min. Housing and Local Govt), 1968. Conducted Brixham Marina Inquiry, 1987. Mem., Senate of Inns of Court and Bar, 1984–85. Chm., Planning and Local Govt Cttee of the Bar, 1966–73. Leader, Bar Delegn to IBA Conf., Tokyo, 1970. Hon. Pres., Anglo-American Real Property Inst., 1980–90. *Publications:* various legal. *Recreations:* theatre, music, walking. *Address:* La Mayne-Longue-Haute, Sauveterre-La-Lémance, 47500 Fumel, France. *T:* and *Fax:* 553406898; 10 South Square, Gray's Inn, WC1R 5EU. *T:* and *Fax:* (020) 7242 2937.

FRANK, Sir (Robert) Andrew, 4th Bt *cr* 1920, of Withyham, Co. Sussex; retailer; *b* 16 May 1964; *s* of Sir Robert John Frank, 3rd Bt, FRICS, and Margaret Joyce (*d* 1965), *d* of Herbert Victor Truesdale; *S* father, 1987; *m* 1990, Zoë, *er d* of S. A. Hasan. *Educ:* Ludgrove Prep. School; Eton College. *Recreations:* travel, theatre, cinema. *Heir:* none.

FRANKEL, Dr Hans Ludwig, OBE 1993; FRCP; Consultant in Spinal Injuries, since 1966 and Clinical Director, since 1993, National Spinal Injuries Centre, Stoke Mandeville Hospital; *b* 7 April 1932; *s* of late Dr Paul Frankel, CBE and Helen Frankel; *m* 1956, Mavis Anne Richardson; two *s. Educ:* Dauntsey's Sch.; University Coll. London; University Coll. Hosp. Med. Sch. (MB BS 1956). MRCS 1956; LRCP 1956, MRCP 1964, FRCP 1977. Casualty officer, Hampstead Gen. Hosp., 1957; Stoke Mandeville Hospital, 1957–: Hse Physician, 1957–58; National Spinal Injuries Centre: Registrar, 1958–62; Sen. Registrar, 1962–66; Dep. Dir, 1969–77; Mem., Exec. Bd, 1991–. Hon. Consultant, Star & Garter Home, Richmond, 1979–. Member: Editorial Board: Paraplegia; Annales de Readaptation et de Medecine Physique, Clinical Autonomic Res.; Editl Adv. Bd, Annals of Sports Medicine. Buckinghamshire Area Health Authority: Vice-Chm., 1976–77, Chm., 1978–80, Med. Adv. Cttee. International Medical Society of Paraplegia: Hon. Treas., 1966–78; Hon. Sec., 1976–87; Vice Pres., 1987–91; Chm., Scientific Cttee, 1992–. President: Brit. Cervical Spine Soc., 1990–92; Chiltern Gp, Spinal Injuries Assoc., 1989–. Mem., Exec. Cttee, Brit. Paraplegic Sports Soc., 1977–91. Chm. Trustees, Internat. Spinal Res. Trust, 1983–; Mem., Mgt Council, Brit. Neurol Res. Trust, 1989–. Numerous lectures in UK, Europe, USA and throughout the world, incl. Arnott Demonstrator, RCS 1987, Sandoz Lectr, Inst. of Neurol., London, 1988 and 1992. *Publications:* (ed) volume on Spinal Cord Injuries in Handbook of Clinical Neurology,

1992; contrib. chapters on spinal cord injuries to text books. *Recreations:* ski-ing, opera. *Address:* National Spinal Injuries Centre, Stoke Mandeville Hospital, Mandeville Road, Aylesbury, Bucks HP21 8AL. *T:* (01296) 315852.

FRANKEL, William, CBE 1970; Editor, Jewish Chronicle, 1958–77; *b* 3 Feb. 1917; *s* of Isaac and Anna Frankel, London; *m* 1st, 1939, Gertrude Freda Reed (marr. diss.); one *s* (one *d* decd); 2nd, 1973, Mrs Claire Neuman. *Educ:* elementary and secondary schs in London; London Univ. (LLB Hons). Called to Bar, Middle Temple, 1944; practised on South-Eastern circuit, 1944–55. General Manager, Jewish Chronicle, 1955–58. Special Adviser to The Times, 1977–81. Chm., Jewish Chronicle Ltd, 1991–94 (Dir, 1959–95). Pres., Mental Health Review Appeal Tribunal, 1978–89; Chm., Social Security Appeal Tribunal, 1979–89. Vis. Prof., Jewish Theological Seminary of America, 1968–69. Pres., New Israel Fund, 1997–. Vice-Pres., Inst. for Jewish Policy Res. (formerly Inst. of Jewish Affairs), 1993–; Emeritus Gov., Oxford Centre for Hebrew Studies; Mem. Bd of Govs, Cambridge Centre for Modern Hebrew Studies. Hon. Fellow, Girton Coll., Cambridge. JP Co. of London, 1963–69. *Publications:* (ed) Friday Nights, 1973; Israel Observed, 1980; (ed) Survey of Jewish Affairs (annual), 1982–92. *Address:* 30 Montagu Square, W1H 2LQ. *T:* (020) 7935 1202. *Clubs:* Savile, MCC.

FRANKL, Peter; pianist; *b* Hungary, 2 Oct 1935; *s* of Laura and Tibor Frankl; adopted British nationality, 1967; *m* 1958, Annie Feiner; one *s* one *d*. *Educ:* Liszt Ferenc Acad. of Music, Budapest. First Prize, several internat. competitions; London début, 1962; New York début, with Cleveland Orch. under George Szell, 1967; performances with Berlin Philharmonic, Amsterdam Concertgebouw, Israel Phil., Leipzig Gewandhaus, and with all London and major Amer. orchs. Vis. Prof. of Piano, Yale Univ. Sch. of Music, 1987–. Recordings include: complete works for piano by Schumann and Debussy; (with ECO) Mozart concerti; (with Tamás Vásáry) complete 4-hand works by Mozart; (with Lindsay Quartet) Brahms, Schumann, Dvorak and Martinu quintets. Officer's Cross, Order of Merit (Hungary), 1995. *Recreations:* football, opera, theatre. *Address:* 5 Gresham Gardens, NW11 8NX. *T:* (020) 8455 5228.

FRANKLAND, family name of **Baron Zouche**.

FRANKLAND, (Anthony) Noble, CB 1983; CBE 1976; DFC 1944; MA, DPhil; historian and biographer; *b* 4 July 1922; *s* of late Edward Frankland, Ravenstonedale, Westmorland; *m* 1st, 1944, Diana Madeline Fovargue (*d* 1981), *d* of late G. V. Tavernor, of Madras and Southern Mahratta Rly, India; one *s* one *d*; 2nd, 1982, Sarah Katharine, *d* of His Honour the late Sir David Davies, QC and late Lady Davies (Margaret Kennedy). *Educ:* Sedbergh; Trinity Coll., Oxford. Served Royal Air Force, 1941–45 (Bomber Command, 1943–45). Air Historical Branch Air Ministry, 1948–51; Official Military Historian, Cabinet Office, 1951–58. Rockefeller Fellow, 1953. Deputy Dir of Studies, Royal Institute of International Affairs, 1956–60; Dir, Imperial War Museum (at Southwark, 1960–82, Duxford Airfield, 1976–82, and HMS Belfast, 1978–82). Lees Knowles Lecturer, Trinity Coll., Cambridge, 1963. Historical advisor, Thames Television series, The World At War, 1971–74. Vice-Chm., British Nat. Cttee, Internat. Cttee for Study of Second World War, 1976–82. Mem., Council, Morley Coll., 1962–66; Trustee: Military Archives Centre, KCL, 1963–82; HMS Belfast Trust, 1971–78 (Vice-Chm., 1972–78); HMS Belfast Bd, 1978–82. *Publications:* Documents on International Affairs: for 1955, 1958; for 1956, 1959; for 1957, 1960; Crown of Tragedy, Nicholas II, 1960; The Strategic Air Offensive Against Germany, 1939–1945 (4 vols) jointly with Sir Charles Webster, 1961; The Bombing Offensive against Germany, Outlines and Perspectives, 1965; Bomber Offensive: the Devastation of Europe, 1970; (ed jtly) The Politics and Strategy of the Second World War (8 vols), 1974–78; (ed jtly) Decisive Battles of the Twentieth Century: Land, Sea, Air, 1976; Prince Henry, Duke of Gloucester, 1980; general editor and contributor, Encyclopaedia of 20th Century Warfare, 1989; Witness of a Century: the life and times of Prince Arthur Duke of Connaught, 1993; History at War: the campaigns of an historian, 1998; Historical Chapter in Manual of Air Force Law, 1956; contrib. to Encyclopaedia Britannica; other articles and reviews; broadcasts on radio and TV. *Address:* Thames House, Eynsham, Witney, Oxfordshire OX29 4DA. *T:* (01865) 881327. *Club:* Royal Over-Seas League.
See also M. D. P. O'Hanlon.

FRANKLIN, Albert Andrew Ernst, CVO 1965; CBE 1961 (OBE 1950); HM Diplomatic Service, retired; *b* 28 Nov. 1914; *s* of Albert John Henry Franklin; *m* 1944, Henrietta Irene Barry; two *d*. *Educ:* Merchant Taylors' Sch.; St John's Coll., Oxford. Joined HM Consular Service, 1937; served in Peking, Kunming, Chungking, Calcutta, Algiers, Marseilles, Kabul, Basle, Tientsin, Formosa, Düsseldorf and in the FO; HM Consul-General, Los Angeles, USA, 1966–74. Member of Kitchener Association. FRSA 1971. *Recreation:* chinese ceramics and paintings. *Address:* 5 Dulwich Wood Avenue, SE19 1HB. *T:* (020) 8670 2769.

FRANKLIN, George Henry, RIBA, FRTPI; Consultant, Third World planning and development; *b* 15 June 1923; *s* of late George Edward Franklin, RN, and Annie Franklin; *m* 1950, Sylvia D. Franklin (*née* Allen); three *s* one *d*. *Educ:* Hastings Grammar Sch.; Hastings Sch. of Art; Architectural Assoc. Sch. of Arch. (AADipl); Sch. of Planning and Research for Regional Develt, London (SPDip). Served War of 1939–45: Parachute Sqdn; RE, Europe; Bengal Sappers and Miners, RIE, SE Asia. Finchley Bor. Council, 1952–54; Architect, Christian Med. Coll., Ludhiana, Punjab, India, 1954–57; Physical Planning Adviser (Colombo Plan) to Republic of Indonesia, 1958–62, and Govt of Malaysia, 1963–64; Physical Planning Adviser, Min. of Overseas Develt, later Overseas Develt Admin, FCO, 1966–83 (Overseas Div., Building Research Station, 1966–73, ODM, later ODA, 1973–83). Hon. Prof., Dept of Town Planning, UWIST, 1982–88; Sen. Advr, Develt Planning Unit, UCL, 1983–. Chm., Overseas Sch., Town and Country Planning Summer Sch., 1970–75. Commonwealth Assoc. of Planners: Mem. Exec. Cttee, 1970–80; Pres., 1980–84; Hon. Sec., 1984–88; Member: Exec. Cttee, Commonwealth Human Ecology Council, 1970–90; Internat. Adv. Bd, Centre for Develt and Environmental Planning, Oxford Polytechnic, 1985–92; World Service Cttee, United Bible Socs, 1968–77. Chm., Warminster Bible Soc. Action Gp, 1991–; Vice Chm., W Wilts, Leonard Cheshire Care-at-Home (formerly Family Support) Service, 1994–96 (Chm., Warminster and Westbury Dist, 1990–94). Co-ordinator, Christian Aid, Warminster Dist, 1991–. Member Editorial Board: Third World Planning Review, 1979–91; Cities, 1983–91. FRSA; AIIA, 1955; AITP India, 1956. *Publications:* papers to internat. confs and professional jls concerning planning, building and housing in the Third World. *Recreations:* Third World, Christian, human rights and environmental issues and interests, fly-fishing. *Address:* The Manse, Sutton Veny, Warminster, Wilts BA12 7AW. *T:* (01985) 840072. *Club:* Victory Services.

FRANKLIN, Gordon Herbert, CVO 1989 (LVO 1976; MVO 1965); a Serjeant-at-Arms to HM the Queen, 1990–93; Personnel Officer, Royal Household, 1988–93, retired; *b* 1 Sept. 1933; *s* of late Herbert and Elsie Franklin; *m* 1959, Gillian Moffett; three *d*. *Educ:* Windsor County Boys' Sch. Barclays Bank, 1950. 2nd ATAF, Germany, 1952–54. Royal Household, 1956–93: Chief Clerk, Master of the Household's Dept, 1975; Chief Accountant of Privy Purse, 1982. Member: Central Finance Board and Council of Methodist Church, 1984–96; Methodist Council Exec., 1993–97. Vice-Pres., Friends of Wesley's Chapel, 1989–. Foundn Gov., Royal Sch., Great Park, Windsor, 1997–; Gov., Brigidine Sch., Windsor, 1999–. Chm., Windsor and Eton Soc., 1998–. Methodist local preacher, 1955–. Freeman, City of London, 1982; Liveryman, Painter Stainers' Co., 1983–. *Recreations:* theatre, walking, travel. *Address:* 10 Cumberland Lodge Mews, The Great Park, Windsor, Berks SL4 2JD. *Club:* Royal Over-Seas League.

FRANKLIN, John; *see* Franklin, W. J.

FRANKLIN, Sir Michael (David Milroy), KCB 1983 (CB 1979); CMG 1972; *b* 24 Aug. 1927; *o s* of late Milroy Franklin; *m* 1951, Dorothy Joan Fraser; two *s* one *d*. *Educ:* Taunton Sch.; Peterhouse, Cambridge (1st cl. hons Economics). Served with 4th RHA, BAOR. Asst Principal, Min. of Agric. and Fisheries, 1950; Economic Section, Cabinet Office (subseq. Treasury), 1952–55; Principal, Min. of Agric., Fisheries and Food, 1956; UK Delegn to OEEC (subseq. OECD), 1959–61; Private Sec. to Minister of Agric., Fisheries and Food, 1961–64; Asst Sec., Head of Sugar and Tropical Foodstuffs Div., 1965–68; Under-Sec. (EEC Gp), MAFF, 1968–73; a Dep. Dir Gen., Directorate Gen. for Agric., EC, Brussels, 1973–77; Dep. Sec., Head of the European Secretariat, Cabinet Office, 1977–81; Permanent Sec., Dept of Trade, 1982–83; Perm. Sec., MAFF, 1983–87. Director: Agricultural Mortgage Corp., 1987–93; Barclays Bank, 1988–93; Barclays PLC, 1988–93; Whessoe plc, 1988–97; Whitbread plc, 1991–98; Co-Chm., UK Adv. Bd, Rabobank, 1996–. Pres., West India Cttee, 1987–95; Chm., Europe Cttee, British Invisibles (formerly BIEC), 1993–98 (Dep. Chm., 1988–93); Member: Council, Royal Inst. for Internat. Relations, 1988–95; Internat. Policy Council on Agric., Food and Trade, 1988–98; Chm., Jt Consultative Cttee, Potato Marketing Bd, 1990–97. Governor, Henley Management Coll. (formerly Henley Administrative Staff Coll.), 1983–93; Chm., Charlemagne Inst., 1996–99; Co-Chm., Wyndham Place Charlemagne Trust, 1999–. *Publications:* Rich Man's Farming: the crisis in agriculture, 1988; Britain's Future in Europe, 1990; The EC Budget, 1992; (with Jonathan Ockenden) European Agriculture: making the CAP fit the future, 1995. *Address:* 15 Galley Lane, Barnet, Herts EN5 4AR. *Club:* Oxford and Cambridge.

FRANKLIN, Prof. Raoul Norman, CBE 1995; FREng; FInstP, FIMA; FIEE; Visiting Professor, Open University, since 1998; Vice Chancellor, 1978–98, and Professor of Plasma Physics and Technology, 1986–98, The City University, London; *b* 3 June 1935; *s* of Norman George Franklin and Thelma Brinley Franklin (*née* Davis); *m* 1961, Faith, *d* of Lt-Col H. T. C. Ivens and Eva (*née* Gray); two *s*. *Educ:* Howick District High Sch.; Auckland Grammar Sch., NZ; Univ. of Auckland (ME, DSc); Christ Church, Oxford (MA, DPhil, DSc). FInstP 1968; FIMA 1970; FIEE 1986; FREng (FEng 1990). Officer, NZ Defence Scientific Corps, 1957–75. Sen. Res. Fellow, RMCS, Shrivenham, 1961–63; University of Oxford: Tutorial Fellow, 1963–78, Dean, 1966–71, Hon. Fellow, 1980, Keble Coll.; Univ. Lectr in Engrg Science, 1966–78; Mem., Gen. Bd, 1967–74 (Vice Chm., 1971–74); Mem., Hebdomadal Council, 1971–74, 1976–78. Chairman: Associated Examining Bd, 1994–98; Assessment and Qualifications Alliance, 1998–. Consultant, UKAEA Culham, 1968–. Dep. Editor, Jl of Physics D, 1986–90. Member: UGC Equipment Sub Cttee, 1975–78; Plasma Physics Commn, IUPAP, 1971–79; Science Bd, SERC, 1982–85; Exec. Council, Business in the Community, 1982–90; Management Cttee, Spallation Neutron Source, 1983–86; Technology Educn Project, 1986–88; UK–NZ 1990 Cttee, 1988–90; Internat. Scientific Cttee, Eur. Sectional Conf. on Atomic and Molecular Processes in Ionized Gases, 1993–97. Chairman: Internat. Science Cttee, Phenomena in Ionized Gases, 1976–77; City Techology Ltd, 1978–93 (Queen's Award for Technol., 1982, 1985, for Export, 1988, 1991). Mem., London Pensions Fund Authority, 1989–95. Trustee: Ruskin School of Drawing, 1975–78; Lloyds Tercentenary Foundn, 1990–. Member Council: Gresham Coll., 1981–98; C&G, 1994–2000. Governor: Ashridge Management Coll., 1986–99; Univ. of Buckingham, 2000–. Freeman, City of London, 1981. Liveryman, Curriers' Co., 1984– (upper warden, 2001–02); Master, Guild of Preceptors, 1999–. Hon. Mem. RICS, 1992; Hon. GSMD 1993. CIMgt (CBIM 1986); FRSA. Hon. DCL City, 1999. *Publications:* Plasma Phenomena in Gas Discharges, 1976; papers on plasmas, gas discharges and granular materials. *Recreations:* tennis, walking, gardening. *Address:* 12 Moreton Road, Oxford OX2 7AX; Open University, Oxford Research Unit, Foxcombe Hall, Boars Hill, Oxford OX1 5HR. *Club:* Athenæum.

FRANKLIN, (William) John; DL; Deputy Chairman, Chartered Trust plc, 1986–97 (Director, 1982–97); Chairman: Howells Motors Ltd, 1986–89; Powell Duffryn Wagon, 1986–89; *b* 8 March 1927; *s* of late William Thomas Franklin and Edith Hannah Franklin; *m* 1951, Sally (*née* Davies); one *d*. *Educ:* Monkton House Sch., Cardiff. W. R. Gresty, Chartered Accountants, 1947–50; Peat Marwick Mitchell, Chartered Accountants, 1950–55; Powell Duffryn, 1956–86: Director, Cory Brothers, 1964; Man. Dir, Powell Duffryn Timber, 1967–70; Dir, 1970–86; Man. Dir and Chief Exec., 1976–85; Dep. Chm., Jan.–July 1986. Treas., UC of Swansea, 1989–92. DL Mid Glamorgan, 1989. *Recreation:* golf. *Address:* 80 South Road, Porthcawl, Bridgend CF36 3DA. *Club:* Royal Porthcawl Golf.

FRANKLYN, Rear-Adm. Peter Michael, CB 1999; MVO 1978; Chief Executive, Royal Hospital for Neuro-disability, since 2000; *b* 10 Sept. 1946; *s* of Roy Vernon Bolton Franklyn and Yvonne Beryl Franklyn (*née* Hooper); *m* 1977, Caroline Barbara Anne Jenks; one *s* one *d*. *Educ:* King's Coll., Taunton. Joined RN, 1963; Comdr, 1980; CO, HMS Active, 1980–82; Trng Comdr, BRNC, Dartmouth, 1982–84; SO Ops FO 3rd Flotilla, 1984–86; Captain, 1986; Naval Asst to 1st Sea Lord, 1986–88; CO, HMS Bristol, 1988–90; RCDS, 1991; Capt., Sch. of Maritime Ops, 1992–93; Dir Naval Officers' Appts (Seaman), 1993–94; Rear-Adm., 1994; Comdr, UK Task Gp, 1994–96; Flag Officer, Sea Training, 1996–97; Flag Officer, Surface Flotilla, 1997–2000. Mem., RNSA, 1993–. Younger Brother, Trinity House, 1996. *Recreations:* family, outdoor activities, antique furniture, old houses. *Address:* Royal Hospital for Neuro-disability, West Hill, Putney, SW15 3SW. *Club:* Army and Navy.

FRANKS, Sir Arthur Temple, (Sir Dick Franks), KCMG 1979 (CMG 1967); HM Diplomatic Service, retired; *b* 13 July 1920; *s* of late Arthur Franks, Hove; *m* 1945, Rachel Marianne, *d* of late Rev. A. E. S. Ward, DD; one *s* two *d*. *Educ:* Rugby; Queen's Coll., Oxford. HM Forces, 1940–46 (despatches). Entered Foreign Service, 1949; British Middle East Office, 1952; Tehran, 1953; Bonn, 1962; FCO, 1966–81. *Address:* Roefield, Alde Lane, Aldeburgh, Suffolk IP15 5DZ. *Clubs:* Travellers, Army and Navy; Aldeburgh Golf.

FRANKS, Cecil Simon; solicitor; company director; Chairman, Pryde Investments Ltd, residential property, since 1960; *b* 1 July 1935; *m* (marr. diss. 1978); one *s*. *Educ:* Manchester Grammar Sch.; Manchester Univ. (LLB). Admitted solicitor, 1958. Member: Salford City Council, 1960–74 (Leader, Cons. Gp); Manchester City Council, 1975–84 (Leader, Cons. Gp). Mem., North West RHA, 1973–75. MP (C) Barrow and Furness, 1983–92; contested (C) Barrow and Furness, 1992. Indep. Mem., Parole Bd, 1994–96. *Recreations:* ski-ing, tennis, theatre, literature. *Address:* Oak Cottage, 3 Church Brow, Bowdon, Cheshire WA14 2SF. *T:* (0161) 928 7561.

FRANKS, His Honour Desmond Gerald Fergus; a Circuit Judge, 1972–93; *b* 24 Jan. 1928; *s* of F. Franks, MC, late Lancs Fus., and E. R. Franks; *m* 1952, Margaret Leigh (*née* Daniel); one *d*. *Educ:* Cathedral Choir Sch., Canterbury; Manchester Grammar Sch.; University Coll., London (LLB). Called to Bar, Middle Temple, 1952; Northern Circuit; Asst Recorder, Salford, 1966; Deputy Recorder, Salford, 1971; a Recorder of the Crown Court, 1972. Pres., SW Pennine Br., Magistrates' Assoc., 1977–93. Chm., Selcare (Gtr Manchester) Trust, 1978–84, Vice-Pres., 1984–. *Recreations:* gardening, music, photography. *Address:* 4 Beathwaite Drive, Bramhall, Cheshire SK7 3NY.

FRANKS, Sir Dick; *see* Franks, Sir A. T.

FRANKS, Jeremy Christopher Reynell; Chief Executive and Managing Director, DAKS Simpson Group plc, since 1992; *b* 26 April 1937; *s* of late Geoffrey Charles Reynell Franks and Molly (*née* McCulluch); *m* 1959, Elizabeth Brown; one *d*. *Educ:* Lancing Coll. 2nd Lt, 1st Kings Dragoon Guards, 1956–57, Aide de Camp to British High Comr for Fedn of Malaya. Man. Dir, Simpson (Piccadilly) Ltd, 1985–86; Dir, DAKS Simpson Gp plc, 1986–87; Man. Dir, DAKS Simpson Ltd, 1987–91; Gp Man. Dir, DAKS Simpson Gp plc, 1991–92; Dir, Sankyo Seiko Co. Ltd, Japan, 1992–. Chm., British Menswear Guild, 1989–91 and 1993–95. Chm., Walpole Cttee, 1994–2000. *Recreations:* Rugby, cricket, antiques, theatre. *Address:* 30 Stanhope Terrace, W2 2UA; (office) 10 Old Bond Street, W1S 4PS. *Clubs:* Cavalry and Guards, Mark's.

FRANSMAN, Laurens François, (Laurie); QC 2000; *b* 4 July 1956; *s* of Henri Albert, (Harry), Fransman and Hannah Lena, (Helen), Fransman (*née* Bernstein); *m* 1st, 1977, Claire Frances Goodman (marr. diss. 1985); one *s*; 2nd, 1994, Helena Mary Cook; two *s*. *Educ:* King David High Sch., Johannesburg; Jerusalem Univ.; Leeds Univ. (LLB 1978). Called to the Bar, Middle Temple, 1979; in practice at the Bar, 1979–. Co-Founder, 1983 and Mem. Exec. Cttee, Immigration Law Practitioners' Assoc.; Member: Bar European Gp; Justice; Liberty. Member, Editorial Board: Immigration and Nationality Law and Practice, 1987–; Immigration and Internat. Employment Law, 1999–. *Publications:* British Nationality Law and the 1981 Act, 1982; (jtly) Tribunals Practice and Procedure, 1985; (UK contrib. Ed.) Immigration Law and Practice Reporter, 1985; (jtly) Immigration Emergency Procedures, 1986; Fransman's British Nationality Law, 1989, 2nd edn 1998; (contrib.) The Constitution of the United Kingdom, 1991; (Nationality Cons.) Halsbury's Laws of England, 4th edn, 1991; (contrib.) Strangers and Citizens, 1994; (contrib.) Citizenship and Nationality Status in the New Europe, 1998; (ed jtly and contrib.) Immigration, Nationality and Asylum under the Human Rights Act 1998, 1999; (contrib.) Immigration Law and Practice, 3rd edn 2001, 5th edn, 2001; numerous articles on law practice, procedure and policy. *Recreations:* family, guitar, ski-ing, theatre, travel. *Address:* 2 Garden Court Chambers, Middle Temple, EC4Y 9BL. *T:* (020) 7353 1633.

FRANZ, Rev. Dr Kevin Gerhard; General Secretary, Action of Churches Together in Scotland, since 1999; *b* 16 June 1953; *m* 1976, Veda Fairley; one *s* one *d*. *Educ:* Univ. of Edinburgh (MA 1974; BD 1979; PhD 1992); Edinburgh Theol Coll. Ordained deacon, 1979; priest 1980; Curate, St Martin, Edinburgh, 1979–83; Rector, St John's, Selkirk, 1983–90; Provost, St Ninian's Cathedral, Perth, 1990–99, Canon, 2000. Chm., Perth and Kinross Assoc. of Voluntary Services, 1995–. *Address:* Scottish Churches House, Dunblane FK15 0AJ.

FRASER, family name of **Barons Fraser of Carmyllie**, and **Lovat, Lady Saltoun**, and **Baron Strathalmond**.

FRASER OF CARMYLLIE, Baron *cr* 1989 (Life Peer), of Carmyllie in the District of Angus; **Peter Lovat Fraser;** PC 1989; *b* 29 May 1945; *s* of Rev. George Robson Fraser and Helen Jean Meiklejohn or Fraser; *m* 1969, Fiona Macdonald Mair; one *s* two *d*. *Educ:* St Andrews Prep. Sch., Grahamstown, S Africa; Loretto Sch., Musselburgh; Gonville and Caius Coll., Cambridge (BA Hons; LLM Hons); Edinburgh Univ. Called to Scottish Bar, 1969; QC (Scot.) 1982. Lectr in Constitutional Law, Heriot-Watt Univ., 1972–74; Standing Jun. Counsel in Scotland to FCO, 1979. Director: Total Fina Elf Exploration (UK), 1997–; Carnoustie Golf Course Hotel, 1998–; Alkane Energy, 2001–; Chm., JKX Oil and Gas plc, 1997–. Director: Internat. Petroleum Exchange, 1997– (Chm., 1999); London Metal Exchange, 1997–. Hon. Vis. Prof. of Law, Dundee Univ., 1986. Hon. Bencher, Lincoln's Inn, 1989. Chm., Scottish Conservative Lawyers Law Reform Group, 1976. Contested (C): N Aberdeen, Oct. 1974; Angus E, 1987. MP (C): S Angus, 1979–83; Angus E, 1983–87. PPS to Sec. of State for Scotland, 1981–82; Solicitor Gen. for Scotland, 1982–89; Lord Advocate, 1989–92; Minister of State: Scottish Office, 1992–95; DTI, 1995–97 (Minister for Energy, 1996–97); Dep. Leader of the Opposition, H of L, 1997–98. Patron, Queen Margaret UC, 1999–. *Recreations:* ski-ing, golf. *Address:* Slade House, Carmyllie, by Arbroath, Angus DD11 2RE. *T:* (01241) 860215. *Clubs:* Pratt's; New (Edinburgh).

FRASER, Sir Alasdair (MacLeod), Kt 2001; CB 1992; QC 1989; Director of Public Prosecutions for Northern Ireland, since 1989; *b* 29 Sept. 1946; *s* of late Rev. Dr Donald Fraser and Ellen Hart McAllister; *m* 1975, Margaret Mary Glancy; two *s* one *d*. *Educ:* Sullivan Upper School, Holywood; Trinity College Dublin (BA (Mod.); LLB); Queen's Univ., Belfast (Dip. Laws). Called to the Bar of Northern Ireland, 1970; Bencher, 1999. Director of Public Prosecutions for Northern Ireland: Court Prosecutor, 1973; Asst Dir, 1974; Senior Asst Dir, 1982; Dep. Dir, 1988. *Address:* Royal Courts of Justice, Belfast, Northern Ireland BT1 3NX. *T:* (028) 9054 6160.

FRASER, Alex; *see* Fraser, J. A.

FRASER, Andrew John, CMG 2001; Senior Adviser, Mitsubishi Corporation, since 2000; *b* 23 Oct. 1950; *s* of John and Mary Fraser; *m* 1st, 1976, Julia Savell (marr. diss. 1987); two *d*; 2nd, 1996, Jane Howard. *Educ:* Univ. of Sussex (BA); exchange schol., UCLA. Account Dir, Young and Rubicam, London, 1972–76; Man. Dir, McCann Erickson, Thailand, 1976–80; Exec. Vice Pres., Dir of Business Develt, Saatchi and Saatchi Worldwide, 1981–92; Man. Dir, cdp Europe (Dentsu Worldwide), 1992–94; Chief Exec., Invest in Britain Bureau, later INVEST.UK, 1994–2000. Dir, UK-Japan 21st Century Gp, 1998–; non-executive Director: English Partnerships, 1999–; Burson-Marsteller, 2000–. *Recreations:* sports, theatre, food and drink, conversation. *Clubs:* Royal Automobile, MCC; V&A Cricket.

FRASER, Dr Andrew Kerr, FRCPE, FFPHM; Deputy Chief Medical Officer, Scottish Executive (formerly Scottish Office), since 1997; *b* 10 Dec. 1958; *s* of Sir William (Kerr) Fraser, *qv* and of Lady Marion Fraser, *qv*; *m* 1985, Geraldine Mary Martin; three *s* one *d*. *Educ:* George Watson's Coll.; Univ. of Aberdeen (MB ChB 1981); Univ. of Glasgow (MPH 1990). FRCPE 1998; FFPHM 1999. Med. Dir, Nat. Services Div., CSA, 1993–94; Dir of Public Health, Highland Health Bd, 1994–97. *Recreations:* music, mountain walking. *Address:* Scottish Executive Health Department, St Andrew's House, Edinburgh EH1 3DG. *T:* (0131) 556 8400.

FRASER, Angus Simon James; Chairman, Benitec Ltd, since 1998; *b* 28 Feb. 1945; *s* of Baron Fraser of Kilmorack, CBE and Elizabeth Cloë Fraser (*neé* Drummond); *m* 1970, Jennifer Ann Craig; two *s* one *d*. *Educ:* Fettes Coll., Edinburgh; Selwyn Coll., Cambridge (MA); European Inst. of Business Admin (INSEAD), France (MBA); Dip. Finance Houses Assoc. Dunlop Co. Ltd, 1968–70; Mercantile Credit Co. Ltd, 1971–76; Chloride Group PLC, 1976–: Gen. Man., Malaysia, 1977–80, France, 1980–82; Man. Dir, Chloride Motive Power, 1982–83; Chm., Chloride Europe, 1983–85; Main Bd Mem., 1984; Exec. Dir, Industrial Operations, 1985–87, Corporate Operations, 1987–88; non-exec. Dir, 1988–; Man. Dir, Imperial Coll. of Sci., Technol. and Medicine, 1989–94 (Gov., 1990–94); Chief Exec., Scruttons plc, 1995–97. Non-executive Director: Kent Technology Transfer Centre, 1998–; Davies, Laing and Dick Ltd, 1998– (Chm., 2000–); Singapore Para Rubber Estates plc, 1999–. Mem. Adv. Cttee, European Business Foundn, 1991–. *Recreations:* music, opera, golf, fly-fishing, painting, gardening. *Address:* Applecote, Pilgrims Way, Boughton Aluph, Ashford, Kent TN25 4EX.

FRASER, Air Cdre Anthony Walkinshaw; consultant in public relations; *b* 15 March 1934; *s* of late Robert Walkinshaw Fraser and Evelyn Elisabeth Fraser; *m* 1st, 1955, Angela Mary Graham Shaw (marr. diss. 1990); one *s* three *d*; 2nd, 1990, Grania Ruth Eleanor Stewart-Smith. *Educ:* Stowe Sch. MIL. RAF Pilot and Flying Instructor, 1952–66; sc Camberley, 1967; MA/VCDS, MoD, 1968–70; Chief Instructor Buccaneer OCU, 1971–72; Air Warfare Course, 1973; Directing Staff, National Defence Coll., 1973; Dep. Dir, Operational Requirements, MoD, 1974–76; Comdt, Central Flying Sch., 1977–79. ADC to the Queen, 1977–79. Dir, SMMT, 1980–88. Chairman: Personal Guard, 1992–94; Chlorella Products Ltd (formerly Nature's Balance Marketing), 1994–; Dir, Nissan UK Ltd, 1989–91. President: Comité de Liaison de la Construction Automobile, 1980–83; Organisation (formerly Bureau Perm.) Internat. des Constructeurs d'Automobiles, 1983–87 (Vice-Pres., 1981–83). FRSA; FIMgt. *Recreations:* shooting, golf, fishing, languages. *Address:* 31 Grove End Road, NW8 9LY. *T:* (020) 7286 0521. *Clubs:* Boodle's, Royal Air Force, Sunningdale.

FRASER, Lady Antonia, (Lady Antonia Pinter), CBE 1999; writer; *b* 27 Aug. 1932; *d* of 7th Earl of Longford, KG, PC, and of Countess of Longford, *qv*; *m* 1st, 1956, Rt Hon. Sir Hugh Charles Patrick Joseph Fraser, MBE, MP (marr. diss. 1977, he *d* 1984); three *s* three *d*; 2nd, 1980, Harold Pinter, *qv*. *Educ:* Dragon School, Oxford; St Mary's Convent, Ascot; Lady Margaret Hall, Oxford (MA). General Editor, Kings and Queens of England series. Mem., Arts Council, 1970–72; Chairman: Soc. of Authors, 1974–75; Crimewriters' Assoc., 1985–86; Vice Pres., English PEN, 1990– (Mem. Cttee, 1979–88; Pres., 1988–89; Chm., Writers in Prison Cttee, 1985–88, 1990). Goodman Lecture, 1997. Norton Medlicott Medal, Histl Assoc., 2000. Hon. DLitt: Hull, 1986; Sussex, 1990; Nottingham, 1993; St Andrews, 1994. *Publications:* (as Antonia Pakenham): King Arthur and the Knights of the Round Table, 1954 (reissued, 1970); Robin Hood, 1955 (reissued, 1971); (as Antonia Fraser): Dolls, 1963; A History of Toys, 1966; Mary Queen of Scots (James Tait Black Memorial Prize, 1969), 1969 (reissued illus. edn, 1978); Cromwell Our Chief of Men, (in USA, Cromwell the Lord Protector), 1973; King James: VI of Scotland, I of England, 1974; (ed) Kings and Queens of England, 1975 (reissued, 1988); (ed) Scottish Love Poems, a personal anthology, 1975 (reissued, 1988); (ed) Love Letters: an anthology, 1976, rev. edn 1989; Quiet as a Nun (mystery), 1977, adapted for TV series, 1978; The Wild Island (mystery), 1978; King Charles II, (in USA, Royal Charles), 1979; (ed) Heroes and Heroines, 1980; A Splash of Red (mystery), 1981 (basis for TV series Jemima Shore Investigates, 1983); (ed) Mary Queen of Scots: poetry anthology, 1981; (ed) Oxford and Oxfordshire in Verse: anthology, 1982; Cool Repentance (mystery), 1982; The Weaker Vessel: woman's lot in seventeenth century England, 1984 (Wolfson History Award, 1984; Prix Caumont-La Force, 1985); Oxford Blood (mystery), 1985; Jemima Shore's First Case (mystery short stories), 1986; Your Royal Hostage (mystery), 1987; Boadicea's Chariot: the Warrior Queens, 1988 (paperback, The Warrior Queens, 1989, in USA The Warrior Queens, 1989); The Cavalier Case (mystery), 1990; Jemima Shore at the Sunny Grave (mystery short stories), 1991; The Six Wives of Henry VIII, 1992, reissued illus. edn, 1996 (Schloss Bauverein Preis, 1997; USA, as The Wives of Henry VIII); (ed) The Pleasure of Reading, 1992; Political Death (mystery), 1994; The Gunpowder Plot: terror and faith in 1605, 1996 (CWA Non Fiction Gold Dagger, 1996) (in USA, Treason and Faith: the story of the gunpowder plot; St Louis Literary Award, 1996); Marie Antoinette: the journey, 2001; various mystery stories in anthols, incl. Have a Nice Death, 1983 (adapted for TV, 1984); TV plays: Charades, 1977; Mister Clay, Mister Clay (Time for Murder series), 1985. *Recreations:* cats, grandchildren. *Address:* c/o Curtis Brown, Haymarket House, 28/29 Haymarket, SW1Y 4SP. *Clubs:* PEN, Biography, Vanderbilt.

FRASER, Sir Campbell; *see* Fraser, Sir J. C.

FRASER, Sir Charles (Annand), KVCO 1989 (CVO 1985; LVO 1968); DL; WS; non-executive Vice Chairman, United Biscuits (Holdings), 1986–95 (Director, 1978–95); Partner, W & J Burness, WS, Edinburgh, 1956–92; *b* 16 Oct. 1928; *o s* of late Very Rev. John Annand Fraser, MBE, TD; *m* 1957, Ann Scott-Kerr; four *s*. *Educ:* Hamilton Academy; Edinburgh Univ. (MA, LLB). Purse Bearer to Lord High Commissioner to General Assembly of Church of Scotland, 1969–88. Chairman: Morgan Grenfell (Scotland), 1985–86; Adam & Co., 1989–98; Lothian & Edinburgh Enterprise Ltd, 1991–94; NSM, 1992–94; Director: Scottish Widows' Fund, 1978–94; British Assets Trust, 1969–; Scottish Media Group plc (formerly Scottish Television Ltd), 1979–98, and other companies. Chm., Sec. of State for Scotland's Adv. Cttee on Sustainable Develt, 1995–98. Trustee, WWF (UK), 1998–2000. Mem. Council, Law Society of Scotland, 1966–72; Governor of Fettes, 1976–86; Mem. Court, Heriot-Watt Univ., 1972–78. WS 1959; DL East Lothian, 1984–. Dr *hc* Edinburgh, 1991; Hon. LLD Napier, 1992. *Recreations:* gardening, ski-ing, piping. *Address:* Shepherd House, Inveresk, Midlothian EH21 7TH. *T:* (0131) 665 2570. *Clubs:* New, Hon. Co. of Edinburgh Golfers (Edinburgh); Royal and Ancient (St Andrews).

FRASER, Christopher James; *b* 25 Oct. 1962; *s* of R. A. Fraser; *m* 1987, Lisa Margaret, *d* of B. G. Norman; one *s* one *d*. *Educ:* in Herts; Harrow Coll.; Univ. of Westminster (BA Hons). Chm., Internat. Communications Gp. Mem., Three Rivers DC, 1992–96. MP (C) Mid Dorset and N Poole, 1997–2001; contested (C) same seat, 2001. PPS to Leader of the Opposition, H of L, 1999–2001. Mem., Culture, Media and Sports Select Cttee, 1997–2001; Vice Chm., All-Party Forestry Gp, 1997–2001; Mem., Parly Info. and Technol. Cttee, 1997–2001; Sec., Culture, Media and Sport Cttee, 1997–2001; Chm., Parly Mgt Consultancy Gp, 2000–01; Vice Chm., Cons. Trade and Industry Cttee, 2000–2001. Member: IPU, 1997; CPA, 1997. Director: Small Business Bureau; Genesis Foundn. Vice Pres., Dorset Fire Safety Cttee, 1997–. Patron, Firmlink, 1995–. Appeals Chm., Pramacare, 1996–; Mem., County Cttee, Holton Lee Charity Appeal, 1997–. Mem., Soc. of Dorset Men, 1997–. Freeman, City of London, 1992. *Recreations:* breeding Kune-Kune pigs, ski-ing, sailing, golf, opera, riding, collecting 19th century watercolours and political prints, spending as much time as possible with my wife and children. *Clubs:* Athenæum, Carlton.

FRASER, Maj.-Gen. Colin Angus Ewen, CB 1971; CBE 1968; General Officer Commanding, Southern Command, Australia, 1971–74; retired March 1974; *b* Nairobi, Kenya, 25 Sept. 1918; *s* of A. E. Fraser, Rutherglen, Vic.; *m* 1942, Dorothy, *d* of A.

Champion; two *s* one *d*. *Educ:* Johannesburg; Adelaide High Sch.; RMC, Duntroon (grad. 1938); Melbourne Univ. (BA). Served War of 1939–45: UK, Middle East, Pacific. Staff Coll., Camberley, 1946; Dep. Comdr, Commonwealth Div., Korea, 1955–56; Dir, Military Trng, 1957–58; Services Attaché, Burma, 1960–62; Chief of Staff, Northern Command, Brisbane, 1964–68; Commandant, Royal Military Coll., Duntroon, 1968–69; Commander, Australian Force, Vietnam, 1970–71. *Address:* 65/1 Moore Street, Taringa, Qld 4068, Australia. *Club:* Tasmanian (Hobart).

FRASER, Gen. Sir David (William), GCB 1980 (KCB 1973); OBE 1962; retired; Vice Lord-Lieutenant of Hampshire, 1988–96; *b* 30 Dec. 1920; *s* of Brig. Hon. William Fraser, DSO, MC, *y s* of 18th Lord Saltoun and Pamela, *d* of Cyril Maude and *widow* of Major W. La T. Congreve, VC, DSO, MC; *m* 1st, 1947, Anne Balfour; one *d*; 2nd, 1957, Julia de la Hey; two *s* two *d*. *Educ:* Eton; Christ Church, Oxford. Commnd into Grenadier Guards, 1941; served NW Europe; comd 1st Bn Grenadier Guards, 1960–62; comd 19th Inf. Bde, 1963–65; Dir, Defence Policy, MoD, 1966–69; GOC 4 Div., 1969–71; Asst Chief of Defence Staff (Policy), MoD, 1971–73; Vice-Chief of the General Staff, 1973–75; UK Mil. Rep. to NATO, 1975–77; Commandant, RCDS, 1978–80; ADC General to the Queen, 1977–80. Col, The Royal Hampshire Regt, 1981–87. DL Hants, 1982. Hon. DLitt Reading, 1992. *Publications:* Alanbrooke, 1982; And We Shall Shock Them, 1983; The Christian Watt Papers, 1983; August 1988, 1983; A Kiss for the Enemy, 1985; The Killing Times, 1986; The Dragon's Teeth, 1987; The Seizure, 1988; A Candle for Judas, 1989; In Good Company, 1990; Adam Hardrow, 1990; Codename Mercury, 1991; Adam in the Breach, 1993; The Pain of Winning, 1993; Knight's Cross: a life of Field Marshal Erwin Rommel, 1993; Will: a portrait of William Douglas Home, 1995; Frederick the Great, 2000. *Recreation:* shooting. *Address:* Vallenders, Isington, Alton, Hants GU34 4PP. *T:* (01420) 23166. *Clubs:* Turf, Pratt's.

FRASER, Prof. Derek, FRHistS; Vice-Chancellor, University of Teesside, since 1992; *b* 24 July 1940; *s* of Jacob and Dorothy Fraser; *m* 1962, Ruth Spector; two *s* one *d*. *Educ:* Univ. of Leeds (BA, MA, PhD). Schoolteacher, 1962–65; Lectr, Sen. Lectr, Reader and Prof. of Modern History, Univ. of Bradford, 1965–82; Prof. of English History, UCLA, 1982–84; HMI (History and Higher Educn), 1984–88; Staff Inspector (Higher Educn), DES, 1988–90; Asst/Dep. Principal, Sheffield City Polytechnic, 1990–92. Chm., Univ. Vocational Awards Council, 1999–; Member: NACETT, 1999–2001; One NorthEast RDA, 1999–. *Publications:* The Evolution of the British Welfare State, 1973, 2nd edn 1984; Urban Politics in Victorian England, 1976; Power and Authority in the Victorian City, 1979; (ed) A History of Modern Leeds, 1980; (ed jtly) The Pursuit of Urban History, 1980; (ed) Municipal Reform and the Industrial City, 1982; (ed) Cities, Class and Communication: essays in honour of Asa Briggs, 1990; The Welfare State, 2000. *Recreations:* squash, bridge, music, spectator sports. *Address:* University of Teesside, Middlesbrough TS1 3BA. *T:* (01642) 342002.

FRASER, Donald Hamilton, RA 1985 (ARA 1975); artist; Member, Royal Fine Art Commission, 1986–99; *b* 30 July 1929; *s* of Donald Fraser and Dorothy Christiana (*née* Lang); *m* 1954, Judith Wentworth-Sheilds; one *d*. *Educ:* Maidenhead Grammar Sch.; St Martin's Sch. of Art, London; Paris (French Govt Scholarship). Tutor, Royal Coll. of Art, 1958–83, Fellow 1970, Hon. FRCA 1984. Has held 70 one-man exhibitions in Britain, Europe, N America and Japan. Work in public collections includes: Museum of Fine Arts, Boston; Albright-Knox Gall., Buffalo; Carnegie Inst., Pittsburgh; City Art Museum, St Louis; Wadsworth Athenaeum, Hartford, Conn; Hirshhorn Museum, Washington, DC; Yale Univ. Art Museum; Palm Springs Desert Museum; Nat. Gall. of Canada, Ottawa; Nat. Gall. of Vic, Melbourne; many corporate collections and British provincial galleries; Arts Council, DoE, etc. Designed Commonwealth Day issue of postage stamps, 1983. Vice-Pres. Artists Gen. Benevolent Inst., 1981– (Chm., 1981–87); Vice-Pres., Royal Over-Seas League, 1986–. Trustee: British Instn Fund, 1982–; Royal Acad., 1993–99 (Hon. Curator, 1992–99). *Publications:* Gauguin's 'Vision after the Sermon', 1969; Dancers, 1989. *Address:* Bramham Cottage, Remenham Lane, Henley-on-Thames, Oxon RG9 2LR. *T:* (01491) 574253. *Club:* Leander (Henley).

FRASER, Dame Dorothy (Rita), DBE 1987; QSO 1978; JP; Australasian Chairman, Community Systems Foundation Australasia, 1991–94 (New Zealand Director, 1975–91); *b* 3 May 1926; *d* of Ernest and Kate Tucker; *m* 1947, Hon. William Alex Fraser; one *s* one *d*. *Educ:* Gisborne High Sch. Chm., Otago Hosp. Bd, 1974–86 (Mem., 1953–56, 1962–86); Member: Nursing Council of NZ, 1981–87; Grading Review Cttee (Health Service Personnel Commn), 1984–87; Hosps Adv. Council, 1984–86; NZ Health Service Personnel Commn, 1987–88; Otago Plunket-Karitane Hosp. Bd, 1979–87; NZ Lottery Bd, 1985–90; Vice-Pres., NZ Hosp. Bds Assoc., 1981–86; Chairman: Southern Region Health Services Assoc., 1984–86; Hosp. and Specialist Services Cttee, NZ Bd of Health, 1985–88. Consultant, ADT Ltd Australasia, later Command Pacific Group, 1988–91. Chm., Otago Jt Tertiary Educn Liaison Cttee, 1988–99; Panel Chm., NZ Colls of Educn Accreditation Cttee, 1996–; Member: Council, Univ. of Otago, 1974–86; Otago High Schs Bd of Governors, 1964–85. Chm., Dunedin Airport Cttee, 1971–74; Member: Dunedin CC, 1970–74; NZ Exec. Marr. Guidance, 1969–75. Life Mem., NZ Labour Party; Gold Badge for Service to Labour Party. JP 1959. Hon. LLD Otago, 1994. Silver Jubilee Medal, 1977. *Recreations:* gardening, golf, reading. *Address:* 21 Ings Avenue, St Clair, Dunedin, New Zealand. *T:* (3) 4558663.

FRASER, Edward; *see* Fraser, J. E.

FRASER, George MacDonald, OBE 1999; author and journalist; *b* 2 April 1925; *s* of late William Fraser, MB, ChB and Anne Struth Donaldson; *m* 1949, Kathleen Margarette, *d* of late George Hetherington, Carlisle; two *s* one *d*. *Educ:* Carlisle Grammar Sch.; Glasgow Academy. Served in British Army, 1943–47: Infantryman XIVth Army, Lieut Gordon Highlanders. Newspaperman in England, Canada and Scotland from 1947; Dep. Editor, Glasgow Herald, 1964–69. FRSL 1998. *Publications:* Flashman, 1969; Royal Flash, 1970; The General Danced at Dawn, 1970; The Steel Bonnets, 1971; Flash for Freedom!, 1971; Flashman at the Charge, 1973; McAuslan in the Rough, 1974; Flashman in the Great Game, 1975; Flashman's Lady, 1977; Mr American, 1980; Flashman and the Redskins, 1982; The Pyrates, 1983; Flashman and the Dragon, 1985; The Sheikh and the Dustbin, 1988; The Hollywood History of the World, 1988; Flashman and the Mountain of Light, 1990; Quartered Safe Out Here, 1992; The Candlemass Road, 1993; Flashman and the Angel of the Lord, 1994; Black Ajax, 1997; Flashman and the Tiger, 1999; *film screenplays:* The Three Musketeers, 1974; The Four Musketeers, 1975; Royal Flash, 1975; The Prince and the Pauper, 1977; Octopussy, 1983; Red Sonja, 1985; Casanova, 1987; The Return of the Musketeers, 1989. *Recreations:* snooker, talking to wife, history, singing. *Address:* Baldrine, Isle of Man.

See also S. W. H. Fraser.

FRASER, Sir Iain (Michael Duncan), 3rd Bt *cr* 1943, of Tain, co. Ross; owner of The Elephant House chain of café/bistros, Edinburgh, since 1994; *b* 27 June 1951; *er s* of Prof. Sir James David Fraser, 2nd Bt and of Edith Maureen, *d* of Rev. John Reay, MC; *S* father, 1997; *m* 1981, Sherylle Ann Gillespie (marr. diss. 1990), Wellington, NZ; one *s* one *d*. *Educ:* Glenalmond; Edinburgh Univ. (BSc Business Studies 1974). Sales manager, Edinburgh and Hong Kong, Ben Line Containers Ltd, 1974–80; internat. traffic manager, Asia, Amerex International, 1980–84; sales/marketing management, Hong Kong, Singapore, New York and San Francisco, American President Lines, 1984–94. *Recreations:* photography, historical tourism, coffee. *Heir: s* Benjamin James Fraser, *b* 6 April 1986. *Address:* 30/7 Elbe Street, Leith, Edinburgh EH6 7HW. *T:* (0131) 555 1947.

FRASER, Lt-Comdr Ian Edward, VC 1945; DSC 1943; RD and Bar 1948; JP; Chairman, since 1947, Managing Director, 1947–65 and since 1983, Universal Divers Ltd; *b* 18 Dec. 1920; *s* of S. Fraser, Bourne End, Bucks; *m* 1943, Melba Estelle Hughes; four *s* two *d*. *Educ:* Royal Grammar Sch., High Wycombe; HMS Conway. Merchant Navy, 1937–39; Royal Navy, 1939–47; Lt-Comdr, RNR, 1951–65. Jt Man. Dir, North Sea Diving Services Ltd, 1965–76; Dir, Star Offshore Services Ltd, 1977–82. Younger Brother of Trinity House, 1980. JP Wallasey, 1957. Hon. Freeman, Metropolitan Bor. of Wirral, 1993. Officer, American Legion of Merit. *Publication:* Frogman VC, 1957. *Address:* Sigyn, 1 Lyndhurst Road, Wallasey, Merseyside CH45 6XA. *T:* (0151) 639 3355. *Clubs:* Hoylake Sailing (life mem.); New Brighton Rugby (life mem.); Leasowe Golf (life mem.; Captain, 1975).

FRASER, Sir Ian (James), Kt 1986; CBE 1972; MC 1945; Chairman, Lazard Brothers, 1980–85; Deputy Chairman: Vickers Ltd, 1980–89; TSB Group plc, 1985–91; *b* 7 Aug. 1923; 2nd *s* of late Hon. Alastair Thomas Joseph Fraser and Lady Sibyl Fraser (*née* Grimston); *m* 1st, 1958, Evelyn Elizabeth Anne Grant (*d* 1984); two *s* two *d*; 2nd, 1993, Fiona Margaret Douglas-Home. *Educ:* Ampleforth Coll.; Magdalen Coll., Oxford. Served War of 1939–45: Lieut, Scots Guards, 1942–45 (despatches, MC). Reuter Correspondent, 1946–56; S. G. Warburg & Co. Ltd, 1956–69; Dir-Gen., Panel on Take-overs and Mergers, 1969–72; Part-time Mem., CAA, 1972–74. Chairman, City Capital Markets Cttee, 1974–78; Accepting Houses Cttee, 1981–85; Member: Exec. Cttee, City Communications Centre, 1976–85; Cttee on Finance for Industry, NEDC, 1976–79; President's Cttee, CBI, 1979–81; Exec. Cttee, Jt Disciplinary Scheme of Accountancy Insts, 1979–81. Director: BOC International Ltd, 1972–85; Davy International Ltd, 1972–84; Chloride Gp Ltd, 1976–80; S. Pearson & Son Ltd, 1977–89; EMI Ltd, 1977–80; Eurafrance SA, 1979–85; Pearson-Longman Ltd, 1980–83; Chairman: Rolls-Royce Motors, 1971–80; Datastream Ltd, 1976–77. Chm., Lloyd's Syndicate 90 (1982) Names Assoc., 1990–96. Mem. Exec., Help the Hospices, 1985–90; Vice-Pres., BBA, 1981–85. Trustee, Tablet Trust, 1976–90 (Chm., Finance Cttee, 1985–90). Governor, More House Sch., 1970–75. FRSA 1970; CIMgt (FBIM 1974). Kt of Honour and Devotion, SMO of Malta, 1971. *Publication:* The High Road to England (autobiog.), 1999. *Recreations:* fishing, gardening, Scottish history. *Address:* South Haddon, Skilgate, Taunton, Somerset TA4 2DR. *T:* (01398) 331247.

FRASER, Sir (James) Campbell, Kt 1978; FRSE 1978; Chairman: Scottish Television plc, 1975–91; Director: Arlen PLC, 1991–95 (Chairman, 1993–95); Barkers Communications Scotland Ltd, 1992–95 (Chairman, 1994–95); *b* 2 May 1923; *s* of Alexander Ross Fraser and Annie McGregor Fraser; *m* 1950, Maria Harvey (*née* McLaren), JP, SRN (*d* 1995); two *d*. *Educ:* Glasgow Univ.; McMaster Univ.; Dundee Sch. of Economics. BCom. Served RAF, 1941–45. Raw Cotton Commn, Liverpool, 1950–52; Economist Intelligence Unit, 1952–57; Dunlop Rubber Co. Ltd, 1957–83: Public Relations Officer, 1958; Group Marketing Controller, 1962; Man. Dir, Dunlop New Zealand Ltd, 1967; Exec. Dir, 1969; Jt Man. Dir, 1971; Man. Dir, 1972; Chm., Dunlop Holdings, 1978–83. Director: British Petroleum, 1978–92 (Mem., Scottish Adv. Bd, 1990–97); BAT Industries, 1980–93; FFI, 1980–82; Charterhouse J. Rothschild, 1982–84; Bridgewater Paper Co., 1984–99; Alexander Proudfoot PLC, 1987–95; Tandem Inc., 1993–96; Chairman: Green Park Health Care, 1985–89; Tandem Computers Ltd, 1985–97; Internat. Adv. Bd, Wells Fargo, 1990–95; Pauline Hyde & Assocs, 1991–93; Riversoft Ltd, 1997–99. Pres., CBI, 1982–84 (Dep. Pres., 1981–82). Founder Mem., Past Chm., and Pres., 1972–84, Soc. of Business Economists; Mem. Exec. Cttee, SMMT, 1973–82. Trustee, The Economist, 1978–. Vis. Professor: Strathclyde Univ., 1980–85; Stirling Univ., 1980–88. Chm., Strathclyde Univ. Business Sch., 1976–81; Mem. Court, St Andrews Univ., 1987–90. CIMgt (CBIM 1971); FPRI 1978. Hon. LLD Strathclyde, 1979; DUniv Stirling, 1979; Hon. DCL Bishop's Univ., Canada, 1990. *Publications:* many articles and broadcasts. *Recreations:* reading, theatre, cinema, gardening, walking. *Address:* Silver Birches, 4 Silver Lane, Purley, Surrey CR8 3HG. *Club:* Caledonian.

FRASER, (James) Edward, CB 1990; Secretary of Commissions for Scotland, 1992–94; an Assistant Local Government Boundary Commissioner for Scotland, since 1997; *b* 16 Dec. 1931; *s* of late Dr James F. Fraser, TD, Aberdeen, and late Dr Kathleen Blomfield; *m* 1959, Patricia Louise Stewart; two *s*. *Educ:* Aberdeen Grammar Sch.; Univ. of Aberdeen (MA); Christ's Coll., Cambridge (BA). FSAScot. RA, 1953; Staff Captain 'Q', Tel-el-Kebir, 1954–55. Asst Principal, Scottish Home Dept, 1957–60; Private Sec. to Permanent Under Sec. of State, 1960–62, and to Parly Under-Sec. of State, 1962; Principal: SHHD, 1962–64; Cabinet Office, 1964–66; HM Treasury, 1966–68; SHHD, 1968–69; Asst Sec., SHHD, 1970–76; Asst Sec., 1976, Under Sec., 1976–81, Local Govt Finance Gp, Scottish Office; Under Sec., SHHD, 1981–91. Pres., Scottish Hellenic Soc. of Edinburgh and Eastern Scotland, 1987–93. Pres., Former Pupils' Club, Aberdeen GS, 1997–98 (Hon. Vice-Pres., 1998–). *Recreations:* reading, music, walking, Greece ancient and modern, DIY. *Address:* 59 Murrayfield Gardens, Edinburgh EH12 6DH. *T:* (0131) 337 2274. *Club:* Scottish Arts (Edinburgh).

FRASER, James Owen Arthur; a Sheriff of Grampian, Highland and Islands, since 1984; *b* 9 May 1937; *s* of James and Effie Fraser; *m* 1961, Flora Shaw MacKenzie; two *s*. *Educ:* Glasgow High Sch. (Classical Dux 1954); Glasgow Univ. (MA 1958; LlB 1961). Qualified as Solicitor, 1961; employed as solicitor, Edinburgh, 1961–65, Glasgow, 1965–66; Partner, Bird Son & Semple, later Bird Semple & Crawford Herron, Solicitors, Glasgow, 1967–84. Part-time Lectr in Evidence and Procedure, Glasgow Univ., 1976–83. Temp. Sheriff, 1983–84. *Recreation:* golf. *Address:* Sheriff Court House, Ferry Road, Dingwall IV15 9QX. *T:* (01349) 863153.

FRASER, Hon. John Allen; PC (Can.) 1979; OC 1995; OBC 1995; CD 1962; QC (Can.) 1983; Chairman, Pacific Fisheries Resource Conservation Council, Canada, since 1998; *b* Japan, 15 Dec. 1931; *m* 1960, Catherine Findlay; three *d*. *Educ:* Univ. of British Columbia (LLB 1954). Law practice, Victoria, Powell River, Vancouver, 1955–72. MP (PC) Vancouver S, 1972–94; Opposition Critic, Environment, 1972–74, Labour, 1974–79; Minister of Environment and Postmaster General, 1979–80; Opposition Critic, Environment, Fisheries, Post Office, and Solicitor-General, 1980–84; Minister of Fisheries and Oceans, 1984–85; Speaker of H of C, Canada, 1986–94; Ambassador for the Envmt, Dept of Foreign Affairs and Internat. Trade, Canada, 1994–98. Chm., Nat. Defence Minister's Monitoring Cttee on Change, 1998–. Hon. LLD: St. Lawrence Univ., 1999; Simon Fraser Univ., 1999. Hon. Lt-Col, Seaforth Highlanders of Canada, 1994–(Hon. Col). *Address:* (office) #590–800 Burrard Street, Vancouver, BC V6Z 2G7, Canada. *T:* (604) 7755621, *Fax:* (604) 7755622; *e-mail:* fraser@fish.bc.ca.

FRASER, John Denis; *b* 30 June 1934; *s* of Archibald and Frances Fraser; *m* 1960, Ann Hathaway; two *s* one *d*. *Educ:* Sloane Grammar Sch., Chelsea; Co-operative Coll.,

Loughborough; Law Soc. Sch. of Law (John Mackrell Prize). Entered Australia & New Zealand Bank Ltd, 1950; Army service, 1952–54, as Sergt, RAEC (educnl and resettlement work). Solicitor, 1960; practised with Lewis Silkin. Mem. Lambeth Borough Council, 1962–68 (Chm. Town Planning Cttee; Chm. Labour Gp). MP (Lab) Norwood, 1966–97. PPS to Rt Hon. Barbara Castle, 1968–70; Opposition front bench spokesman on Home Affairs, 1972–74; Parly Under-Sec. of State, Dept of Employment, 1974–76; Minister of State, Dept of Prices and Consumer Protection, 1976–79; opposition spokesman on trade, 1979–83, on housing and construction, 1983–87, on legal affairs, 1987–94. *Recreations:* athletics, football, music. *Address:* 12 Gough Square, EC4A 3DW.

FRASER, Rt Hon. (John) Malcolm, AC 1988; CH 1977; PC 1976; MA Oxon; Prime Minister of Australia, 1975–83; *b* 21 May 1930; *s* of late J. Neville Fraser; *m* 1956, Tamara, *d* of S. R. Beggs; two *s* two *d. Educ:* Melbourne C of E Grammar Sch.; Magdalen Coll., Oxford (MA 1952; Hon. Fellow, 1982). MHR (L) for Wannon, Vic, 1955–83; Mem. Jt Party Cttee on Foreign Affairs, 1962–66; Minister: for the Army, 1966–68; for Educn and Science, 1968–69, 1971–72; for Defence, 1969–71; Leader of Parly Liberal Party, 1975–83; Leader of the Opposition, 1975. Sen. Adjunct Fellow, Center for Strategic and Internat. Studies, Georgetown Univ., Washington, 1983–86. Chairman: UN Sec. Gen's Expert Gp on African Commodity Problems, 1989–90; CARE Australia, 1987–; Vice-Pres., CARE Internat., 1995–99 (Pres., 1990–95). Co-Chm., Commonwealth Eminent Persons Gp on S Africa, 1986. Member: InterAction Council for Former Heads of Govt (Chm., 1996–); ANZ Internat. Bd of Advice, 1987–93. Distinguished Internat. Fellow, Amer. Enterprise Inst. for Public Policy Res., 1984–86; Fellow, Center for Internat. Affairs, Harvard Univ., 1985. Mem. Council, Aust. Nat. Univ., 1964–66. Hon. Vice President: Oxford Soc., 1983; Royal Commonwealth Soc., 1983. Hon. LLD: Univ. of SC, 1981; Deakin Univ., 1989. *Recreations:* fishing, photography, vintage cars. *Address:* 44th Floor, ANZ Tower, 55 Collins Street, Melbourne, Vic 3000, Australia. *Club:* Melbourne.

FRASER, John Stewart; Chairman and Chief Executive, Ciba-Geigy plc, 1990–96; *b* 18 July 1931; *s* of Donald Stewart Fraser and Ruth (*née* Dobinson); *m* 1st, 1955, Diane Louise Witt (marr. diss. 1996); two *s* one *d*; 2nd, 1996, Lynette Ann Murray. *Educ:* Royal Melbourne Inst. of Technology. ARACI. Technical Rep., Australian Sales Manager and Australian Marketing Manager, Monsanto Australia Ltd, 1953–68; Marketing Manager, Ilford (Australia) Pty Ltd, 1968–73; Ilford Ltd, UK: Marketing Dir, 1973–78; Man. Dir and Chief Exec., 1978–84; Corporate Man. Dir, Ciba-Geigy Plastics and Additives Co., UK, 1982–84; Ciba-Geigy plc, UK: Gp Man. Dir, 1984–87; Gp Man. Dir and Chief Exec., 1987–90. Non-exec. Dir, Westminster Health Care, 1993–. Chm., Assoc. for Schools' Sci., Engrg and Technol. (formerly Standing Conf. on Schools' Sci. and Technol.), 1996–2000. Pres., Chemical Industries Assoc., 1994–95. *Recreation:* golf. *Address:* The Lodge, Forest Place, Warren Lane, Waldron, near Heathfield, East Sussex TN21 0TG.

FRASER, Julian Alexander, (Alex); Director, Logistics, HM Customs and Excise, since 2000; *b* 23 July 1959; *s* of Peter Marshall Fraser, *qv* and Ruth Fraser. *Educ:* Abingdon Sch., Oxon; Manchester Univ. (BA Hons Classics 1987). Teacher, Latin and Computer Studies, Lawrence House Sch., St Annes on Sea, Lancs, 1978–84; Database Researcher, CEDIM srl, Ancona, 1987–89; Information Consultant, Atefos SpA, Turin, 1989–90; Manager, Inf. Resource Centre, Merrill Lynch Europe Ltd, 1990–93; Asst Dir and Head of Inf. Systems, Western Merchant Bank Ltd, 1993–95; J. Henry Schroder & Co. Ltd: Manager, Inf. Centre, 1995–96; Head of Ops, European Corporate Finance Div., 1996–97; Dir and Global Head, Corporate Finance Support Services, 1997–2000. *Recreations:* equine. *Address:* HM Customs and Excise, 7th Floor East, New King's Beam House, 22 Upper Ground, SE1 9PJ. *T:* (020) 7865 5718; *e-mail:* alex.fraser@hmce.gsi.gov.uk.

FRASER, Kenneth John Alexander; international marketing consultant; *b* 22 Sept. 1929; *s* of Jack Sears Fraser and Marjorie Winifred (*née* Savery); *m* 1953, Kathleen Grace Booth; two *s* one *d. Educ:* Thames Valley Grammar Sch., Twickenham; London School of Economics (BScEcon Hons). Joined Erwin Wasey & Co. Ltd, 1953, then Lintas Ltd, 1958; Managing Director, Research Bureau Ltd, 1962; Unilever: Head of Marketing Analysis and Evaluation Group, 1965; Head of Marketing Division, 1976–79, 1981–89; Hd of Internat. Affairs, 1985–89; Hd of External Affairs, 1989–90; seconded to NEDO as Industrial Dir, 1979–81. Advr, European Assoc. of Branded Goods Manufacturers, 1991–93. Member: Consumer Protection Adv. Cttee, Dept of Prices and Consumer Protection, 1975; Management Bd, ADAS, MAFF, 1986–92; Chairman: CBI Marketing and Consumer Affairs Cttee, 1977; Internat. Chamber of Commerce Marketing Commn, 1978; Vice Chm., Advertising Assoc., 1981–90; Dir, Direct Mail Services Standards Bd, 1991–94. Mem., Advocacy Cttee, Nat. Children's Home, 1987–95. FRSA 1980. *Recreations:* walking, music, reading. *T:* (office) (020) 8949 3760.

FRASER, Rt Hon. Malcolm; *see* Fraser, Rt Hon. J. M.

FRASER, Lady Marion Anne, LT 1996; Chair of the Board, Christian Aid, 1990–97; Lord High Commissioner, then HM High Commissioner, General Assembly, Church of Scotland, 1994–95; *b* 17 Oct. 1932; *d* of Robert Forbes and Elizabeth Taylor Watt; *m* 1956, Sir William (Kerr) Fraser, *qv*; three *s* one *d. Educ:* Hutchesons' Girls' Grammar Sch.; Univ. of Glasgow (MA); Royal Scottish Academy of Music. LRAM, ARCM. Chm., Scottish Internat. Piano Comp., 1995–99. Director: Friends of Royal Scottish Academy (Founder Chm., 1986–89); Scottish Opera, 1990–94; St Mary's Music School, 1989–95. Chm., Scottish Assoc. for Mental Health, 1995–99. Pres., Scotland's Churches Scheme, 1997–. Trustee: Scottish Churches Architectural Heritage Trust, 1989–; Lamp of Lothian Collegiate Trust, 1996–; Gov., Laurel Bank Sch. for Girls, 1988–95. Hon. LLD Glasgow, 1995; DUniv Stirling, 1998. *Recreations:* family, friends, people and places. *Address:* Broadwood, Edinburgh Road, Gifford, East Lothian EH41 4JE. *Club:* New (Edinburgh).
See also A. K. Fraser.

FRASER, Murdo Mackenzie; Member (C) Scotland Mid and Fife, Scottish Parliament, since Aug. 2001; *b* 5 Sept. 1965; *s* of Sandy Fraser and Barbara MacPherson; *m* 1994, Emma Jarvis. *Educ:* Inverness Royal Acad.; Univ. of Aberdeen (LLB 1986; Dip. Legal Studies). Admitted solicitor, 1988; practised in Aberdeen and Edinburgh; Associate Partner, Ketchen and Stevens WS, Edinburgh, 1994–2001. Chairman: Scottish Young Conservatives, 1989–92; Nat. Young Conservatives, 1991–92; former Dep. Chm., Edinburgh Central Cons. Assoc. Contested (C): East Lothian, 1997; N Tayside, 2001; N Tayside, Scottish Parlt, 1999. *Recreations:* climbing, hillwalking, travel, Rangers FC. *Address:* Scottish Parliament, Edinburgh EH99 1SP. *T:* (0131) 348 5646; (office) 13 Hanover Court, North Street, Glenrothes KY7 5SB. *Club:* Perth Conservative.

FRASER, Peter Marshall, MC 1944; MA; FBA 1960; Fellow of All Souls College, Oxford, 1954–85, now Emeritus, and Acting Warden, 1985–87 (Sub-Warden, 1980–82); Lecturer in Hellenistic History, 1948–64, Reader 1964–85; *b* 6 April 1918; *y s* of late Archibald Fraser; *m* 1st, 1940, Catharine, *d* of late Prebendary Heaton-Renshaw (marr. diss.); one *s* three *d*; 2nd, 1955, Ruth Elsbeth, *d* of late F. Renfer, Bern, Switzerland; two *s*; 3rd, 1973, Barbara Ann Stewart, *d* of late L. E. C. Norbury, FRCS. *Educ:* City of London Sch.; Brasenose Coll., Oxford (Hon. Fellow 1977). Seaforth Highlanders, 1941–45; Military Mission to Greece, 1943–45. Sen. Scholar, Christ Church, Oxford, 1946–47; Junior Proctor, Oxford Univ., 1960–61; Domestic Bursar, All Souls Coll., 1962–65. Dir, British Sch. at Athens, 1968–71. Vis. Prof. of Classical Studies, Indiana Univ., 1973–74. Chm., Managing Cttee, Soc. of Afghan Studies, 1972–82; Vice Pres., Soc. for S Asian Studies, 1985–90. Ordinary Mem., German Archaeol. Soc., 1979; Corresp. Fellow, Archaeolog. Soc. of Athens, 1971 (Hon. Vice-Pres., 1999). Gen. Editor and Chm., British Acad. Cttee, Lexicon of Greek Personal Names, 1973–95. Hon. Dr. phil Trier, 1984; Hon. DLitt La Trobe, 1996. *Publications:* (with G. E. Bean) The Rhodian Peraea and Islands, 1954; (with T. Rönne) Boeotian and West Greek Tombstones, 1957; Rostovtzeff, Social and Economic History of the Roman Empire, 2nd edn, revised, 1957; Samothrace, The Inscriptions, (Vol. ii, Excavations of Samothrace), 1960; E. Löfstedt, Roman Literary Portraits, trans. from the Swedish (Romare), 1958; The Wares of Autolycus; Selected Literary Essays of Alice Meynell (ed), 1965; E. Kjellberg and G. Säflund, Greek and Roman Art, trans. from the Swedish (Grekisk och romersk konst), 1968; Ptolemaic Alexandria, 1972; Rhodian Funerary Monuments, 1977; A. J. Butler, Arab Conquest of Egypt, 2nd edn, revised, 1978; (ed with E. Matthews) A Lexicon of Greek Personal Names, vol. 1, 1987, vol. 3A, 1997, vol. 3B, 2000; (ed) Memorial Addresses of All Souls College, 1989; Cities of Alexander, 1996. *Address:* All Souls College, Oxford OX1 4AL.
See also J.A. Fraser.

FRASER, Simon James; HM Diplomatic Service; Political Counsellor, Paris, since 1999; *b* 3 June 1958; *s* of late James Stuart Fraser and of Joan Fraser; one *d. Educ:* St Paul's Sch.; Corpus Christi Coll., Cambridge (MA). Joined FCO, 1979; Second Secretary: Baghdad, 1982–84; Damascus, 1984–86; First Sec., FCO, 1986–88; Private Sec. to Minister of State, FCO, 1989–90; Policy Planning Staff, FCO, 1991–92; Asst Head, Non-Proliferation and Defence Dept, FCO, 1992–93; First Sec., Financial and Eur. Affairs, Paris, 1994–96; Dep. Chef de Cabinet of Vice-Pres. of EC, 1996–99. *Recreations:* ski-ing, football (Ipswich Town), opera, art. *Address:* c/o Foreign and Commonwealth Office, King Charles Street, SW1A 2AH; The Gatehouse, 39 rue de Faubourg St Honoré, Paris 75008, France. *Club:* Cercle de l'Union Interalliée (Paris).

FRASER, Simon William Hetherington; Sheriff of North Strathclyde at Dumbarton, since 1989; *b* 2 April 1951; *s* of George MacDonald Fraser, *qv*; *m* 1979, Sheena Janet Fraser; one *d. Educ:* Glasgow Acad.; Glasgow Univ. (LLB). Solicitor, 1973–89 (Partner, Flowers & Co., Glasgow, 1976–89). Temp. Sheriff, 1987–89. Pres., Glasgow Bar Assoc., 1981–82. *Recreations:* watching Partick Thistle, cricket. *Address:* Sheriff Court, Church Street, Dumbarton G82 1QR. *T:* (01389) 763266. *Clubs:* Avizandum (Glasgow), Glasgow Flying.

FRASER, Prof. Thomas Grant, PhD; FRHistS; Professor of History, University of Ulster, since 1991; *b* 1 July 1944; *s* of Thomas Fraser and Annie Grant Alexander; *m* 1970, Grace Frances Armstrong; one *s* one *d. Educ:* Univ. of Glasgow (MA Medieval and Modern Hist. 1966; Ewing Prize); London Sch. of Economics (PhD 1974). New University of Ulster, subseq. University of Ulster: Lectr, 1969–85; Sen. Lectr, 1985–91; Hd, Dept of Hist., 1988–94; Hd, Sch. of Hist., Philosophy and Politics, 1994–98. Fulbright Scholar-in-Residence, Indiana Univ. South Bend, 1983–84. Chm., NI Museums Council, 1998–; Nat. Trustee, Museums and Galls of NI, 1998 . FRHistS 1992; FRSA 2000. *Publications:* Partition in Ireland, India and Palestine, 1984; The USA and the Middle East since World War 2, 1989; The Arab Israeli Conflict, 1995 (Italian edn 2001); Ireland in Conflict 1922–1998, 2000. *Recreations:* travel, cooking. *Address:* 7 Circular Road, Castlerock, Co. Londonderry, Northern Ireland BT51 4XA. *T:* (028) 7084 8170.

FRASER, Veronica Mary; Diocesan Director of Education, Diocese of Worcester, 1985–93; *b* 19 April 1933; *o d* of late Archibald Fraser. *Educ:* Richmond County Sch. for Girls; St Hugh's Coll., Oxford. Head of English Department: The Alice Ottley Sch., Worcester, 1962–65; Guildford County Sch. for Girls, 1965–67 (also Librarian); Headmistress, Godolphin Sch., Salisbury, 1968–80; Adviser on Schools to Bishop of Winchester, 1981–85. Pres., Assoc. of Sen. Members, St Hugh's Coll., Oxford, 1994–98. Gov., SPCK, 1994–98.

FRASER, Prof. William Irvine, CBE 1998; MD; FRCPE, FRCPsych; Professor of Developmental Disability, University of Wales College of Medicine, since 1989; *b* 3 Feb. 1940; *s* of late Duncan Fraser and Muriel (*née* Macrae); *m* 1964, Joyce Carrol; two *s. Educ:* Greenock Acad.; Glasgow Univ. (MBChB 1963; DPM 1967; MD (with commendation) 1969). FRCPsych 1979; FRCPE 2000. Physician Superintendent, Mental Handicap Service, Fife, 1974–78; Hon. Sen. Lectr in Psychology, Univ. of St Andrews, 1973–89; pt-time Sen. Lectr, Psychiatry, Univ. of Edinburgh, 1973–89; Consultant Psychiatrist, Royal Edinburgh Hosp., 1978–89. Editor, Jl of Intellectual Disability Research, 1982–; section editor of various jls. Trustee: David Morris Fund, 1990; Bailey Thomas Charitable Fund, 1999–. Res. Medallist, Burden Inst., 1989; Fellow, Internat. Assoc. for Scientific Study of Intellectual Disability, 1997 (Dist. Achievement Award, 1996); FMedSci 2001. *Publications:* (with R. McGillivray) Care of People with Intellectual Disabilities, 1974, 9th edn, 1998; (with R. Grieve) Communicating with Normal and Retarded Children, 1981. *Recreation:* sailing. *Address:* 146 Wenallt Road, Cardiff CF14 6TQ. *T:* (029) 2052 1343. *Club:* Royal Society of Medicine.

FRASER, William James; JP; Lord Provost of Aberdeen, 1977–80; Member, City of Aberdeen District Council, 1974–96; *b* 31 Dec. 1921; *s* of late William and Jessie Fraser; *m* 1961, Mary Ann; three *s* one *d. Educ:* York Street Sch., Aberdeen; Frederick Street Sch., Aberdeen. Mem., Scottish Exec., Labour Party, 1949–74 (Chm., 1962–63). Pres., Aberdeen Trades Council, 1952. JP Aberdeen, 1950. Hon. LLD Aberdeen, 1995. *Address:* The Mill House, Brig O'Balgownie, Aberdeen AB2 8JN. *T:* (01224) 826916.

FRASER, Sir William (Kerr), GCB 1984 (KCB 1979; CB 1978); Chancellor, University of Glasgow, since 1996 (Principal and Vice-Chancellor, 1988–95); *b* 18 March 1929; *s* of A. M. Fraser and Rachel Kerr; *m* 1956, Marion Anne Forbes (*see* Lady Marion Fraser); three *s* one *d. Educ:* Eastwood Sch., Clarkston; Glasgow Univ. (MA, LLB). Joined Scottish Home Dept, 1955; Private Sec. to Parliamentary Under-Sec., 1959, and to Secretary of State for Scotland, 1966–67; Civil Service Fellow, Univ. of Glasgow, 1963–64; Asst Sec., Regional Development Div., 1967–71; Under Sec., Scottish Home and Health Dept, 1971–75; Dep. Sec., 1975–78, Permanent Under-Sec. of State, 1978–88, Scottish Office. Chm., Scottish Mutual Assce, 1999 (Dir, 1990–99). Chm., Royal Commn on the Ancient and Historical Monuments of Scotland, 1995–2000. Gov., Caledonian Res. Foundn, 1990–99. FRSE 1985. FRCPS (Hon.) 1992; FRSAMD 1995. Hon. LLD: Glasgow, 1982; Strathclyde, 1991; Aberdeen, 1993; Dr *hc* Edinburgh, 1995. *Address:* Broadwood, Edinburgh Road, Gifford, East Lothian EH41 4JE. *T:* (01620) 810319. *Club:* New (Edinburgh).
See also A. K. Fraser.

FRASER McLUSKEY, Rev. James; *see* McLuskey.

FRAWLEY, Thomas; Assembly Ombudsman for Northern Ireland and Northern Ireland Commissioner for Complaints, since 2000; *b* Limerick, 1949; *s* of Joseph and Bride Frawley; *m* 1983, Marie Mallow; two *s* one *d*. *Educ:* St Mary's Grammar Sch., Belfast; Trinity Coll., Dublin (BA). Grad. Trainee, NHS, 1971–73; Unit Administrator, Ulster Hosp., Dundonald, 1973–77; Asst Dist Administrator, Lisburn, 1977–80; Dist Administrator for Londonderry, Limavady and Strabane Dist, 1980; Chief Admin. Officer, 1980–85, Gen. Manager, 1985–2000, Western Health and Social Services Bd. Dir-Gen., Co-operation and Working Together Initiative, 1990–2000; led project to support health system in Zimbabwe, 1994. King's Fund Travel Bursary, 1983; King's Fund Internat. Fellowships, 1988 and 1992. Mem., Ministerial Adv. Bd on Health Estates, NI, 1998–2000; Chm., Rev. Gp to report on Ambulance Service, NI, 1998–2000. Trustee, NHS Confedn, 1998–2000. Mem., BITC, 1998–2000. Gov., Lumen Christi Coll., 1998–2000. *Recreations:* current affairs, sport (played Rugby and Gaelic football). *Address:* Office of the Ombudsman for Northern Ireland, 33 Wellington Place, Belfast BT1 6HN.

FRAY, Prof. Derek John, FREng; Professor of Materials Chemistry, since 1996, Head of Department of Materials Science and Metallurgy, since 2001, Cambridge University; Professorial Fellow, Fitzwilliam College, Cambridge, since 1996; *b* 26 Dec. 1939; *s* of Arthur Joseph Fray and Doris Lilian Fray; *m* 1965, Mirella Christine Kathleen Honey; one *s* one *d*. *Educ:* Emanuel Sch.; Imperial Coll., Univ. of London (BSc Eng, ARSM 1961; PhD, DIC 1965). FIMM; FREng (FEng 1989). Asst Prof. of Metallurgy, MIT, 1965–68; Gp Leader, Imperial Smelting Corp., Bristol, 1968–71; Cambridge University: Lectr, Dept of Materials Sci. and Metallurgy, 1971–91; Fitzwilliam College: Fellow, 1972–90; Tutorial and Estates Bursar, 1974–86; Bursar, 1986–88; Investment and Estates Bursar, 1988–90; Prof. of Mineral Engrg, Univ. of Leeds, 1991–96 (Head of Dept). Hon. Prof., Beijing Univ. of Sci. and Technol., 1995–; Vis. Prof., Univ. of Leeds, 1996–. Director: Cambridge Advanced Materials, 1989–; Ion Science, 1989–; Ion Science Messtechnik, 1994–; British Titanium plc, 1998–. Numerous medals and awards, UK and overseas. *Publications:* (jtly) Worked Examples in Mass Heat Transfer in Materials Technology, 1983; numerous papers and patents on extractive metallurgy and allied subjects. *Recreations:* reading, cinema, sailing. *Address:* 7 Woodlands Road, Great Shelford, Cambridge CB2 5LW. *T:* (01223) 842296.

FRAYLING, Sir Christopher (John), Kt 2001; MA, PhD; Professor of Cultural History, since 1979, Rector and Vice-Provost, since 1996, Royal College of Art, London; *b* 25 Dec. 1946; *s* of late Arthur Frederick Frayling and Barbara Kathleen (*née* Imhof); *m* 1981, Helen Snowdon. *Educ:* Repton Sch.; Churchill Coll., Cambridge (BA, MA, PhD). FCSD 1994. Churchill Research Studentship, 1968–71; Lectr in Modern History, Univ. of Exeter, 1971–72; Tutor, Dept of General Studies, Royal College of Art, 1972–73, Vis. Lectr, 1973–79; Research Asst, Dept of Information Retrieval, Imperial War Mus., 1973–74; Lectr in the History of Ideas and European Social History, Univ. of Bath, 1974–79; Royal College of Art: founder, 1979, and Head of Dept, 1979–96, Dept of Cultural History (ex General Studies); founded courses: History of Design, 1982; Conservation, 1987; Visual Arts Admin, 1991; Pro-Rector, 1993–96. Vis. Prof., Shanghai Univ. of Technol., 1991. Historian, lectr, critic; regular contributor, as writer and presenter, to radio (incl. Kaleidoscope, Stop the Week, Meridian, Critics' Forum, Third Opinion, Third Ear, Nightwaves; series: The American Cowboy; America: the movie (Silver Medal, NY Internat. Radio Fest., 1989); Britannia: the film; Print the Legend) and TV (incl. series Scene, Art of Persuasion (Gold Medal, NY Internat. Film and TV Fest., 1985), Busting the Block—or the Art of Pleasing People, Design Classics, Design Awards, Timewatch, Movie Profiles, The Face of Tutankhamun, Strange Landscape, and Nightmare: the birth of horror). Chm., Design Council, 2000–; Crafts Council: Mem., 1982–85; Mem., Educn Cttee, 1981–85; Chm., Pubns and Inf. Cttee, 1984–85. Arts Council of England (formerly of GB): Mem., 1987–2000; Mem., Art Panel, 1983–94 (Dep. Chm., 1984–87; Chm., 1987–94); Chm., Film, Video and Broadcasting Panel, 1994–97; Chm., Educn and Trng Panel, 1996–98; Mem., Photography Adv. Panel, 1983–85; Chm., Art Projects Cttee, 1986–87; Mem., Combined Arts Cttee, 1987–88; Chm., Combined Arts Cttee, 1989–95; Chm., New Collaborations Cttee, 1990–94. Mem. Adv. Bd, ICA, 1989–; Chairman: Curriculum Develt Bd, Arts Technol. Centre, 1989–94; Design Sub-Gp, Liturgical Publishing Commn, 1999–2000. Chm. of Trustees, Crafts Study Centre, Bath, 1982–; Foundn Trustee, Holbourne of Menstrie Mus., Bath, 1985–2000; Chm., Free Form Arts Trust, 1984–88; Trustee: V&A Museum, 1984– (Member: Adv. Council, 1981–83; Sen. Staff Appts Cttee, 1987–91; S Kensington Jt Planning Cttee, 1989–95; Educn and Res. Cttees, 1990–97; Chm., Bethnal Green Mus. Cttee, 1995–99; Chm., Contemporary Projects Cttee, 1999–); Koestler Trustees for Art in Prisons, 1992–99; Member: Litmus Gp for Millennium Dome, 1998–2000; Bd, Design Mus., 1999–; AHRB, 1999–. Governor, BFI, 1982–87 (Mem., 1982–86, Chm. 1984–86, Educn Cttee); Member: Art and Design Sect., Leverhulme Team on Arts in Higher Educn, 1982; Working Party on art and design advising NAB, 1985–87. Chm., Soc. of Designer-Craftsmen, 1997–. Patron: Guild of Handicraft Trust, 1989–; Parnham Trust for Makers in Wood, 1989–. FRSA 1984. Hon. DLitt NSW, 1999. Radio play, The Rime of the Bounty (Sony Radio Award, 1990). *Publications:* Napoleon Wrote Fiction, 1972; (ed) The Vampyre—Lord Ruthven to Count Dracula, 1978; Spaghetti Westerns: Cowboys and Europeans, from Karl May to Sergio Leone, 1981; The Schoolmaster and the Wheelwrights, 1983; The Royal College of Art: one hundred and fifty years of art and design, 1987; Vampyres, 1991; (ed) Beyond the Dovetail: essays on craft, skill and imagination, 1991; Clint Eastwood, 1992; The Face of Tutankhamun, 1992; (with Helen Frayling) The Art Pack, 1992; Research in Art and Design, 1994; Strange Landscape: a journey through the Middle Ages, 1995; Things to Come: a classic film, 1995; (ed jtly) Design of the Times: one hundred years of the Royal College of Art, 1996; Nightmare: the birth of horror, 1996 (Hamilton Deane Award, 1997); Tim Mara: the complete prints, 1998; Art and Design: 100 years at the Royal College of Art, 1999; Sergio Leone: something to do with death, 2000; (ed) The Hound of the Baskervilles, 2001; contribs to: Reappraisals of Rousseau—studies in honour of R. A. Leigh, 1980; Cinema, Politics and Society in America, 1981; Rousseau et Voltaire en 1978, 1981; Rousseau After Two Hundred Years: Proc. of Cambridge Bicentennial Colloquium, 1982; Eduardo Paolozzi: perspectives and themes, 1984; Eduardo Paolozzi—Lost Magic Kingdoms, 1986; Rape: an interdisciplinary study, 1987; 2D/3D—Art and Craft made and designed for the twentieth century, 1987; The Cambridge Guide to the Arts in Britain, Vol. IX (post 1945), 1988; Craft Classics since the 1940s, 1988; Eduardo Paolozzo: Noah's Ark, 1990; Ariel at Bay: reflections on broadcasting and the arts, 1990; Objects and Images: essay on design and advertising, 1992; Spellbound: art and film, 1996; Moonraker, Strangelove and Other Celluloid Dreams: the visionary art of Ken Adam, 1999; articles on film, popular culture and the visual arts/crafts in Cambridge Rev., Cinema, Film, Sight & Sound, London Magazine, New Statesman & Society, Crafts, Burlington Magazine, Art and Design, Designer, Design Week, Design, THES, TLS, Time Out, Punch, Designer, Craft History, Creative Review, Blueprint, Independent Magazine, Independent on Sunday, Culture Magazine, Listener, Times, Sunday Times, Guardian, Daily Telegraph, and various learned jls. *Recreation:* finding time. *Address:* Royal College of Art, Kensington Gore, SW7 2EU. *T:* (020) 7590 4101.

See also Rev. N. A. Frayling.

FRAYLING, Rev. Canon Nicholas Arthur; Rector of Liverpool, since 1987; Hon. Canon, Liverpool Cathedral, since 1989; *b* 29 Feb. 1944; *s* of late Arthur Frederick Frayling, OBE and Barbara Kathleen (*née* Imhof). *Educ:* Repton Sch.; Exeter Univ. (BA Theology 1969); Cuddesdon Theol Coll., Oxford. Management training, retail trade, 1962–64; Temp. Probation Officer (prison welfare), Inner London Probation and After-Care Service, 1965–66, pt-time, 1966–71. Deacon, 1971; priest, 1972; Asst Curate, St John, Peckham, 1971–74; Vicar, All Saints, Tooting Graveney, 1974–83; Canon Residentiary and Precentor, Liverpool Cathedral, 1983–87. Chaplain: St Paul's Eye Hosp., Liverpool, 1987–90; Huyton Coll., 1987–91; to High Sheriff of Merseyside, 1992–93, 1997–98 and 1999–2000. Chairman: Southwark Diocesan Adv. Cttee for Care of Churches, 1980–83; Religious Adv. Panel, BBC Radio Merseyside, 1988–; Welfare Orgns Cttee, Liverpool CVS, 1992–; Mersey Mission to Seafarers, 2000–. *Publication:* Pardon and Peace: a reflection on the making of peace in Ireland, 1996. *Recreations:* music, friends. *Address:* 25 Princes Park Mansions, Sefton Park Road, Liverpool L8 3SA. *T:* (home) (0151) 727 4692, (office) (0151) 236 5287. *Clubs:* Royal Commonwealth Society; Artists' (Hon.), Athenæum (Liverpool); Liverpool Racquet (Hon.).

See also Sir C. J. Frayling.

FRAYN, Claire, (Mrs Michael Frayn); *see* Tomalin, C.

FRAYN, Michael; writer; *b* 8 Sept. 1933; *s* of late Thomas Allen Frayn and Violet Alice Lawson; *m* 1st, 1960, Gillian Palmer (marr. diss. 1989); three *d*; 2nd, 1993, Claire Tomalin, *qv*. *Educ:* Kingston Gram. Sch.; Emmanuel Coll., Cambridge (Hon. Fellow, 1985). Reporter, Guardian, 1957–59; Columnist, Guardian, 1959–62; Columnist, Observer, 1962–68. Foreign Hon. Mem., Amer. Acad. of Arts and Scis, 2000. Hon. DLitt Cambridge, 2001. *Television:* plays: Jamie, 1968 (filmed as Remember Me?, 1997); Birthday, 1969; First and Last, 1989 (Internat. Emmy Award, 1990); A Landing on the Sun, 1994; *documentaries:* Imagine a City Called Berlin, 1975; Vienna—the Mask of Gold, 1977; Three Streets in the Country, 1979; The Long Straight, 1980; Jerusalem, 1984; Prague—the Magic Lantern, 1993; Budapest: written in water, 1996; *stage plays:* The Two of Us, 1970; The Sandboy, 1971; Alphabetical Order, 1975 (Evening Standard Drama Award for Best Comedy); Donkeys' Years, 1976 (SWET Best Comedy Award); Clouds, 1976; Liberty Hall, 1980; Make and Break, 1980 (New Standard Best Comedy Award); Noises Off, 1982 (Standard Best Comedy Award; SWET Best Comedy Award); Benefactors, 1984 (Standard Best Play Award; Laurence Olivier (formerly SWET) Award for Play of the Year; Plays and Players London Theatre Critics' Best New Play); Look Look, 1990; Here, 1993; Now You Know, 1995; Copenhagen, 1998 (Evening Standard Best Play, South Bank Show Award for Theatre, Critics' Circle Best New Play, 1998; Prix Molière, 1999; Tony Award, Best Play, 2000); Alarms and Excursions, 1998; *opera:* La Belle Vivette, 1995; *filmscripts:* Clockwise, 1986; Remember Me?, 1997. Nat. Press Award, 1970. *Publications:* collections of columns: The Day of the Dog, 1962; The Book of Fub, 1963; On the Outskirts, 1964; At Bay in Gear Street, 1967; The Original Michael Frayn, 1983; Speak After the Beep, 1995; The Additional Michael Frayn, 2000; *non-fiction:* Constructions, 1974; (with David Burke) Celia's Secret, 2000; *novels:* The Tin Men, 1965 (Somerset Maugham Award); The Russian Interpreter, 1966 (Hawthornden Prize); Towards the End of the Morning, 1967; A Very Private Life, 1968; Sweet Dreams, 1973; The Trick of It, 1989; A Landing On the Sun, 1991 (Sunday Express Book of the Year Award, 1991); Now You Know, 1992; Headlong, 1999; *translations:* Tolstoy, The Fruits of Enlightenment, 1979 (prod. 1979); Anouilh, Number One, 1984; Chekhov: The Cherry Orchard, 1978 (prod. 1978, 1989); Three Sisters, 1983 (prod. 1985); Wild Honey, 1984 (prod. 1984); The Seagull, 1986 (prod. 1986); Uncle Vanya, 1988 (prod. 1988); The Sneeze (adapted from one-act plays and short stories), 1989 (prod. 1988); Trifonov, Exchange, 1986 (prod. 1986, 1990). *Address:* c/o Greene & Heaton Ltd, 37a Goldhawk Road, W12 8QQ.

FRAYNE, Very Rev. David; Dean (formerly Provost) of Blackburn, 1992–2001, now Emeritus; *b* 19 Oct. 1934; *s* of Philip John Frayne and late Daisy Morris Frayne (*née* Eade); *m* 1961, Elizabeth Ann Frayne (*née* Grant); one *s* two *d*. *Educ:* Reigate Grammar Sch.; St Edmund Hall, Oxford (BA 1958 (2nd cl. Hons PPE); MA 1962); The Queen's Coll., Birmingham (DTh 1960). Pilot Officer, RAF, 1954–55. Ordained deacon, 1960, priest, 1961; Asst Curate, St Michael, East Wickham, 1960–63; Priest-in-charge, St Barnabas, Downham, Lewisham, 1963–67; Vicar of N Sheen, Richmond, 1967–73; Rector of Caterham, 1973–83; Vicar of St Mary Redcliffe with Temple, Bristol and St John the Baptist, Bedminster, 1983–92. Rural Dean of Caterham, 1980–83; Hon. Canon, Southwark Cathedral, 1982, Emeritus, 1983; Rural Dean of Bedminster, 1986–92; Proctor in Convocation, 1987–90; Hon. Canon of Bristol Cathedral, 1991. A Church Comr, 1994–98; Mem., Redundant Churches Cttee, 1999–. *Recreations:* walking, camping, music. *Address:* Newlands Cottage, Crown Lane, Gillingham, Dorset SP8 4HD. *T:* and *Fax:* (01747) 824065. *Club:* Oxford Society.

FRAZER, Prof. Malcolm John, CBE 1992; PhD, FRSC; education consultant; *b* 7 Feb. 1931; *m* 1st, 1957, Gwenyth Ida Biggs (marr. diss. 1990), JP, MA; three *s*; 2nd, 1991, Aleksandra Kornhauser. *Educ:* Univ. of London; BSc 1952, PhD 1955. Royal Military Coll. of Science, 1956–57; Lecturer and Head of Dept of Chemistry, Northern Polytechnic, London, 1965–72; Prof. of Chemical Educn, 1972–86, and Pro-Vice Chancellor, 1976–81, Univ. of East Anglia, Norwich; Chief Executive: CNAA, 1986–93; HEQC, 1992–93; Chm., CATE, 1993–94. Visiting Professor: Open Univ., 1993–; Univ. of Bath, 2000–. Vice-President: RSC, 1973–74; Royal Instn, 1988–91; SHRE, 1993–; Gen. Sec./Vice-Pres., Chm. Council, BAAS, 1978–91. Hon. Fellow: N London Poly., 1988; SCOTVEC, 1990; Poly. South West, 1991; Brighton Poly., 1992; Manchester Metropolitan Univ., 1993; Bolton Inst., 1994; Cardiff Inst. of Higher Educn, 1994. Hon. FCollP, 1988. Hon. Dr Leuven, 1985; Hon. DSc: Leicester, 1993; Luton, 1993; Hon. DEd: CNAA, 1992; Heriot-Watt, 1993; Hon. DLitt Glasgow Caledonian, 1993; DUniv Open, 1994. Nyholm Medal, RSC, 1982. *Publications:* textbooks on chemistry, chemical educn, and problem solving; contribs to Jl Chem. Soc., etc. *Address:* Sora, Abingdon Road, Tubney, Oxon OX13 5QQ.

FREAN, Jennifer Margaret, (Jenny), RDI 1998; Founder, and Head, First Eleven Studio, since 1986; *b* 17 April 1947; *d* of Theodore Farbridge and Isobel Farbridge (*née* Reid-Douglas); *m* 1970 (Christopher) Patrick Frean; one *d*. *Educ:* City of London Sch. for Girls; Hornsey Coll. of Art (BA Hons); Royal Coll. of Art (MA 1972). Design Consultant, Centro Design Montefibre, Milan, 1974; set up Jenny Frean Associates, textile design studio, 1975; portraitist, 1984–86; founded First Eleven Studio; working with textile manufacturers worldwide on every aspect of colour and surface decoration, 1986. *Recreations:* music (especially opera), all art forms, gardening. *Address:* 61 Camberwell Grove, SE5 8JE. *T:* (020) 7701 4245.

FREARS, Stephen Arthur; film director; *b* 20 June 1941; *s* of late Dr Russell E. Frears and Ruth M. Frears; *m* 1968, Mary K. Wilmers, *qv* (marr. diss. 1974); two *s*; lives with Anne Rothenstein; one *s* one *d*. *Educ:* Gresham's Sch., Holt; Trinity Coll., Cambridge (BA Law). Director: Gumshoe, 1971; Bloody Kids, 1980; Going Gently, 1981; Walter, 1982; Saigon, 1983; The Hit, 1984; My Beautiful Laundrette, 1985; Prick Up Your Ears,

1986; Sammy and Rosie Get Laid, 1987; Dangerous Liaisons, 1989; The Grifters, 1990; Accidental Hero, 1992; The Snapper, 1993; Mary Reilly, 1996; The Van, 1996; The Hi-Lo Country, 1999; High Fidelity, 2000; Liam, 2001; television: Fail Safe, 2000. *Recreation:* reading. *Address:* c/o Casarotto Co. Ltd, 60–66 Wardour Street, W1V 4ND. *T:* (020) 7287 4450.

FRÉCHETTE, Louise, OC 1999; Deputy Secretary General, United Nations, since 1998; *b* 16 July 1946. *Educ:* Collège Basile Moreau (BA 1966); Univ. of Montreal (LèsL Hist. 1970); Coll. of Europe, Bruges (Post-grad Dip. Econ. Studies 1978). With Dept of External Affairs, Govt of Canada, 1971–; Ambassador to Argentina and Uruguay, 1985–88; Assistant Deputy Minister: for Latin America and Caribbean, Min. of Foreign Affairs, 1988–91; for Internat. Econ. and Trade Policy, 1991–92; Ambassador to UN, 1992–94; Associate Dep. Minister, Dept of Finance, 1994–95; Dep. Minister of Defence, Canada, 1995–98. Hon. LLD St Mary's Univ., Halifax, 1993. *Recreations:* golf, reading. *Address:* Office of Deputy Secretary-General, S-3862A, United Nations, New York, NY 10017, USA. *T:* (212) 9638010.

FREDE, Prof. Michael, Dr.phil; FBA 1994; Professor of the History of Philosophy, and Fellow of Keble College, Oxford University, since 1991; *b* Berlin, 31 May 1940. *Educ:* Univ. of Göttingen (Dr.phil 1966). Philosophy Res. Assistant, Univ. of Göttingen, 1966–71; Loeb Fellow, Harvard Univ., 1971; University of California at Berkeley: Vis. Lectr, 1968–69; Asst, then Associate, Professor of Philosophy, 1971–74; Prof. of Philosophy, 1974–76; Princeton University: Prof. of Philosophy, 1976–89; Stewart Prof. of Philosophy, 1989–91. *Publication:* Essays in Ancient Philosophy, 1987. *Address:* Keble College, Oxford OX1 3PG.

FREDERICK, Sir Christopher (St John), 11th Bt *cr* 1723, of Burwood House, Surrey; *b* 28 June 1950; *s* of Sir Charles Frederick, 10th Bt and of Rosemary, *er d* of Lt-Col R. J. H. Baddeley, MC; *S* father, 2001; *m* 1990, Camilla Elizabeth, *o d* of Sir Derek Gilbey, 3rd Bt; one *s* one *d*. *Heir: s* Benjamin St John Frederick, *b* 29 Dec. 1991.

FREDERICTON, Bishop of, since 2000; **Rt Rev. William Joseph Hockin;** *b* 30 Sept. 1938; *m* 1990, Isabelle Jean Deeks. *Educ:*; Wilfred Laurier Univ., Waterloo, Ont (BA); Emmanuel Coll., Saskatoon, Sask (LTh). Ordained priest, 1963; Archdeacon of Middlesex, dio. Huron, 1984–86; Rector, St Paul's, Bloor Street, Toronto, Ont, 1986–96; Dean of Fredericton, 1996–98; Bishop Coadjutor of Fredericton, 1998–2000. *Publications:* God for Monday Morning, 1987; Twelve Stories you need to Know, 1994. *Address:* 791 Brunswick Street, Fredericton, NB E3B 1H8, Canada. *T:* (506) 4542839.

FREDMAN, Prof. Sandra Debbe; Professor of Law, University of Oxford, since 1999; Fellow and Lecturer in Law, Exeter College, Oxford, since 1988; *b* 28 July 1957; *d* of Michael Geoffrey Fredman and Naomi Pauline Fredman (*née* Greenstein); *m* 1985, Alan Leslie Stein; two *s* one *d*. *Educ:* Univ. of Witwatersrand (BA 1st Cl. Maths and Philosophy 1977); Wadham Coll., Oxford (Rhodes Schol., 1979–82; BA 1st Cl. Hons Jurisp. 1981; BCL 1st Cl. Hons 1982). Political and econs journalist, Financial Mail, S Africa, 1978–79; articled clerk, Lawford & Co., Gray's Inn, 1983–84; Lectr in Law, KCL, 1984–88. *Publications:* (with M. Nell and P. Randall) The Narrow Margin: how black and white South Africans view change in South Africa, 1983; (with B. Hepple) Labour Law and Industrial Relations in Great Britain, 1986, 2nd edn 1992; (with G. Morris) The State as Employer: labour law in the public services, 1989; Women and the Law, 1997; articles in legal jls. *Recreations:* outdoor activities, literature, theatre, travel. *Address:* Exeter College, Oxford OX1 3DP. *T:* (01865) 279600.

FREE, Prof. John Brand, CMG 1995; ScD, DSc; Hon. Professor, School of Pure and Applied Biology, University of Wales, Cardiff (formerly University College, Cardiff), 1984–98; *b* 21 Aug. 1927; *s* of Frederick Charles Free and Gladys Ellen Free; *m* 1953, Nancy Wilson Speirs; two *s* one *d*. *Educ:* Cambridge and County High Sch.; Jesus Coll., Cambridge. BA 1950, MA 1955, ScD 1982, Cantab; PhD 1954, DSc 1967, London. FIBiol 1970. Served Army, 1945–48, Suffolk Regiment: commnd RPC; seconded to High Commnd Territory Corps in ME. Rothamsted Experimental Station: ARC Scholar, 1951–54; on staff, 1954–87; SPSO 1983. NRCC Fellow, Apiculture Dept, Univ. of Guelph, Ontario, 1958–59; Nuffield/NRCC lecture tour of Canadian univs and res. centres, 1967; Leverhulme Emeritus Fellow, 1987, 1988. Visited several tropical countries for ODA and British Council to initiate and advise on bee-keeping and crop pollination projects, 1972–. Vice-Chm., Internat. Bee Res. Assoc., 1975–83 (Hon. Vice-Pres., 1993); President: Central Assoc. of Beekeepers, 1977–83; Apimondia Standing Commn on Pollination, 1985–89 (Hon. Mem. Apimondia, 1989); Chm., British Section, Internat. Union for Study of Social Insects, 1979–82 (Hon. Mem., 1988). Hon. Fellow, British Beekeepers' Assoc., 1990. *Publications:* Bumblebees (with C. G. Butler), 1959; Insect Pollination of Crops, 1970, 2nd edn 1993; The Social Organisation of Honeybees, 1977; Bees and Mankind, 1982; (ed) Honeybee Biology, 1982; Pheromones of Social Bees, 1987; (ed) Keeping Bees, 1992; *children's books:* Honeybees, 1978; Insects We Need, 1980; (with R. Dutton) Arab Village, 1980; Life Under Stones, 1981; contrib. res. papers and rev. papers to scientific jls on: social orgn of bees and their behaviour within the colony and in the field; improving honey prodn and bee pollination of agricl crops; use of pheromones (natural and synthetic) that control bee activities; insect pests of oil seed rape. *Recreations:* photography (produced many educational slide series and film-strips—mostly on insects and tropical agriculture), ancient civilisations, painting, walking. *Address:* 37 Plainwood Close, Summersdale, Chichester, West Sussex PO19 4YB. *T:* (01243) 533822.

FREEDBERG, Prof. David Adrian; Professor of Art History, Columbia University, since 1984; *b* 1 June 1948; *s* of William Freedberg and Eleonore Kupfer; one *s* one *d*. *Educ:* S African Coll. High Sch., Cape Town; Yale Univ. (BA); Balliol Coll., Oxford (DPhil). Rhodes Scholar, Oxford, 1969–72; Lectr in History of Art: Westfield Coll., Univ. of London, 1973–76; Courtauld Inst. of Art, Univ. of London, 1976–84; Slade Prof. of Fine Art, Univ. of Oxford, 1983–84. Baldwin Prof., Oberlin Coll., Ohio, 1979; Andrew W. Mellon Prof. of Fine Art, Nat. Gall. of Art, Washington, 1996–98; Vis. Mem., Inst. for Advanced Study, Princeton, NJ, 1980–81; Gerson Lectr, Univ. of Groningen, 1983; VUB-Leerstoel, Brussels Univ., 1988–89. Fellow: Amer. Acad. of Arts and Scis, 1997; Amer. Philosophical Soc., 1997. *Publications:* Dutch Landscape Prints of the Seventeenth Century, 1980; The Life of Christ after the Passion (Corpus Rubenianum Ludwig Burchard, VII), 1983; Iconoclasts and their Motives, 1985; Iconoclasm and Painting in the Revolt of the Netherlands 1566–1609, 1988; The Power of Images, 1989; (ed) The Prints of Pieter Bruegel the Elder, 1989; (ed with Jan De Vries) Art in History/History in Art: studies in seventeenth century Dutch culture, 1991; Joseph Kosuth: The Play of the Unmentionable, 1992; Peter Paul Rubens: paintings and oil sketches, 1995; The Paper Museum of Cassiano dal Pozzo: citrus fruit, 1997; articles in Burlington Magazine, Revue de l'Art, Gentse Bijdragen, Münchner Jahrbuch der Bildenden Kunst, Jl of Warburg and Courtauld Insts, Print Quarterly, Quaderni Puteani. *Address:* Department of Art History, Columbia University, Schermerhorn Hall, New York, NY 10027, USA.

FREEDMAN, Amelia, (Mrs Michael Miller), MBE 1989; FRAM 1986; Artistic Director and Founder, Nash Ensemble, since 1964; Head of Classical Music, South Bank Centre, since 1995; *b* 21 Nov. 1940; *d* of Miriam Freedman (*née* Claret) and Henry Freedman; *m* 1970, Michael Miller; two *s* one *d*. *Educ:* St George's Sch., Harpenden; Henrietta Barnet, London; RAM. LRAM (piano), ARCM (clarinet). Music teacher, 1961–72: King's Sch., Cambridge; Perse Sch. for Girls, Cambridge; Chorleywood College for the Blind; Sir Philip Magnus Sch., London. Artistic Director: Bath Internat. Fest., 1984–93; Bath Mozartfest, 1995–; Musical Adviser, Israel Fest., 1989–; Programme Adviser, Philharmonia Orch., 1992–95; chamber music consultant for various projects at South Bank Centre and Barbican, and for LSO. Hon. DMus Bath, 1993. Walter Wilson Medal, Musicians' Co., 1996; Leslie Boosey Award, PRS/Royal Philharmonic Soc., 2000. Chevalier, l'Ordre des Arts et des Lettres (France), 1984; Czech Govt Medal for services to Czech music in UK, 1986; Chevalier, l'Ordre National du Mérite (France), 1996. *Recreations:* theatre, cinema, ballet, opera; spectator sport—cricket, rugger, football; stamp-collecting, children. *Address:* 14 Cedars Close, Hendon, NW4 1TR. *T:* (020) 8203 3025, *Fax:* (020) 8203 9540.

FREEDMAN, (Benjamin) Clive; QC 1997; a Recorder, since 2000; *b* 16 Nov. 1955; *s* of Lionel and Freda Freedman; *m* 1980, Hadassa Helen Woolfson; one *s* three *d*. *Educ:* Manchester Grammar Sch.; Pembroke Coll., Cambridge (MA). Called to the Bar, Middle Temple, 1978; Mem., Northern Circuit, 1980–; an Asst Recorder, 1997–2000. *Recreations:* Manchester City FC, tennis, Test Match Special. *Address:* Littleton Chambers, 3 King's Bench Walk North, Temple, EC4Y 7HR.

FREEDMAN, Charles, CB 1983; Commissioner, Customs and Excise, 1972–84; *b* 15 Oct. 1925; *s* of late Solomon Freedman, OBE, and Lilian Freedman; *m* 1949, Sarah Sadie King; one *s* two *d*. *Educ:* Westcliff High Sch.; Cheltenham Grammar Sch.; Trinity Coll., Cambridge (Sen. Schol., BA). Entered HM Customs and Excise, 1947; Asst Sec., 1963. *Address:* 10 Cliff Avenue, Leigh-on-Sea, Essex SS9 1HF. *T:* (01702) 473148. *Club:* Civil Service.

FREEDMAN, Clive; *see* Freedman, B. C.

FREEDMAN, Dawn Angela, (Mrs N. J. Shestopal); Her Honour Judge Freedman; a Circuit Judge, since 1991; *b* 9 Dec. 1942; *d* of Julius and Celia Freedman; *m* 1970, Neil John Shestopal. *Educ:* Westcliff High Sch. for Girls; University Coll., London (LLB Hons). Called to the Bar, Gray's Inn, 1966; Metropolitan Stipendiary Magistrate, 1980–91; a Recorder, 1989–91. Mem. Parole Bd, 1992–96. Chm., Jewish Marriage Council, 1998–. Mem. Council, London Sch. of Jewish Studies, 1998–. *Recreations:* theatre, television, cooking. *Address:* Harrow Crown Court, Hailsham Drive, Harrow HA1 4TU.

FREEDMAN, Prof. Judith Anne; KPMG Professor of Tax Law, and Fellow of Worcester College, University of Oxford, since 2001; *b* 10 Aug. 1953; *d* of Harry Hill and Estella Hill; *m* 1974, Lawrence David Freedman, *qv*; one *s* one *d*. *Educ:* North London Collegiate Sch.; Lady Margaret Hall, Oxford (BA 1st Class Hons Jurisprudence, MA). Articled Clerk, Stanleys & Simpson North, 1976–78; Solicitor of Supreme Court, 1978; Solicitor, Corporate Tax Dept, Freshfields, 1978–80; Lectr in Law, Univ. of Surrey, 1980–82; London School of Economics: Lectr, Law Dept, 1982–91; Sen. Lectr, 1991–96; Reader in Law, 1996–2000; Prof. of Law, 2000–01; Sen. Res. Fellow in Company and Commercial Law, Inst. of Advanced Legal Studies, 1989–92. European Editor, Palmer's Company Law, 1991–; Jt Editor, British Tax Review, 1997– (Asst Ed., 1988–97); Mem. Editorial Cttee, Modern Law Review, 1987–. *Publications:* (jtly) Property and Marriage: an integrated approach, 1988; (ed jtly) Law and Accounting: competition and co-operation in the 1990s, 1992; Employed or Self-employed? tax classification of workers and the changing labour market, 2001. *Recreations:* family, friends, doodling. *Address:* Worcester College, Oxford OX1 2HB.

FREEDMAN, Prof. Lawrence David, CBE 1996; DPhil; FBA 1995; Professor of War Studies, King's College, London, since 1982; *b* 7 Dec. 1948; *s* of late Lt-Comdr Julius Freedman and Myra Freedman; *m* 1974, Judith Anne Hill (*see* J. A. Freedman); one *s* one *d*. *Educ:* Whitley Bay Grammar Sch. BAEcon Manchester; BPhil York; DPhil Oxford. Teaching Asst, York Univ., 1971–72; Research Fellow, Nuffield Coll., Oxford, 1974–75; Research Associate, International Inst. for Strategic Studies, 1975–76 (Mem. Council, 1984–92 and 1993–); Research Fellow, Royal Inst. of International Affairs, 1976–78; Head of Policy Studies, RIIA, 1978–82. Hon. Dir, Centre for Defence Studies, 1990–. Chm., Cttee on Internat. Peace and Security, Social Science Res. Council (US), 1993–98. FKC 1992. FRSA 1991; FRHistS 2000. *Publications:* US Intelligence and the Soviet Strategic Threat, 1977, 2nd edn 1986; Britain and Nuclear Weapons, 1980; The Evolution of Nuclear Strategy, 1981; (jtly) Nuclear War & Nuclear Peace, 1983, 2nd edn 1989; (ed) The Troubled Alliance, 1983; The Atlas of Global Strategy, 1985; The Price of Peace, 1986; Britain and the Falklands War, 1988; (jtly) Signals of War, 1990; (ed) Population Change and European Security, 1991; (ed) Britain in the World, 1991; (jtly) The Gulf Conflict 1990–1991, 1993; War: a Reader, 1994; (ed) Military Intervention in Europe, 1994; (ed) Strategic Coercion, 1998; The Politics of British Defence, 1999; Kennedy's Wars, 2000. *Recreations:* tennis, political caricature. *Address:* c/o Department of War Studies, King's College, Strand, WC2R 2LS. *T:* (020) 7873 2025.

FREEDMAN, Susan Rachel; *see* Prevezer, S. R.

FREELAND, Sir John Redvers, KCMG 1984 (CMG 1973); QC 1987; HM Diplomatic Service, retired; Judge, Arbitral Tribunal and Mixed Commission for Agreement on German External Debts, since 1988; Judge, European Court of Human Rights, 1991–98; *b* 16 July 1927; *o s* of C. Redvers Freeland and Freda Freeland (*née* Walker); *m* 1952, Sarah Mary, *er d* of late S. Pascoe Hayward, QC; one *s* one *d*. *Educ:* Stowe; Corpus Christi Coll., Cambridge. Royal Navy, 1945 and 1948–51. Called to Bar, Lincoln's Inn, 1952, Bencher, 1985; Mem. *ad eundem*; Middle Temple. Asst Legal Adviser, FO, 1954–63, and 1965–67; Legal Adviser, HM Embassy, Bonn, 1963–65; Legal Counsellor, FCO (formerly FO), 1967–70; Counsellor (Legal Advr), UK Mission to UN, NY, 1970–73; Legal Counsellor, FCO, 1973–76; Second Legal Advr, 1976–84, Legal Advr, 1984–87, FCO. Agent of UK govt, cases before European Commn of Human Rights, 1966–70. Mem., US-Chile Internat. Commn of Investigation, 1989–. Member: Exec. Cttee, David Davies Meml Inst. of Internat. Studies, 1974–; Council of Management, British Inst. of Internat. and Comparative Law, 1984–87; Cttee of Management, Inst. of Advanced Legal Studies, 1984–87; Bd of Govs, British Inst. of Human Rights, 1992–. *Club:* Travellers.

FREELAND, Mary Graham, (Mrs J. M. Freeland); *see* McGeown, M. G.

FREELING, Nicolas; writer since 1960; *b* 1927, of English parents; *m* 1954, Cornelia Termes; four *s* one *d*. *Educ:* primary and secondary schs. Hotel-restaurant cook, throughout Europe, 1945–60; novelist, 1960–. *Publications:* (numerous trans.) Love in Amsterdam, 1961; Because of the Cats, 1962; Gun before Butter, 1962; Valparaiso, 1963; Double Barrel, 1963; Criminal Conversation, 1964; King of the Rainy Country, 1965; Dresden Green, 1966; Strike Out Where Not Applicable, 1967; This is the Castle, 1968; Tsing-Boum, 1969; Kitchen Book, 1970; Over the High Side, 1971; Cook Book, 1971;

A Long Silence, 1972; Dressing of Diamond, 1974; What Are the Bugles Blowing For?, 1975; Lake Isle, 1976; Gadget, 1977; The Night Lords, 1978; The Widow, 1979; Castang's City, 1980; One Damn Thing After Another, 1981; Wolfnight, 1982; Back of the North Wind, 1983; No Part in Your Death, 1984; A City Solitary, 1985; Cold Iron, 1986; Lady Macbeth, 1987; Not as far as Velma, 1989; Sandcastles, 1989; Those in Peril, 1990; The Pretty How Town, 1992; You Who Know, 1993; Criminal Convictions, 1994; The Seacoast of Bohemia, 1994; A Dwarf Kingdom, 1996; One More River, 1997; Some Day Tomorrow, 1999; Village Book, 2001; The Janeites, 2002. *Address:* Grandfontaine, 67130 Schirmeck, France.

FREEMAN, family name of **Baron Freeman**.

FREEMAN, Baron *cr* 1997 (Life Peer); **Roger Norman Freeman;** PC 1993; MAFCA; Corporate Finance Consultant, PricewaterhouseCoopers, since 1997; Chairman: Thales plc, since 1999; British Titanium plc, since 2001; *b* 27 May 1942; *s* of Norman and Marjorie Freeman; *m* 1969, Jennifer Margaret (*née* Watson); one *s* one *d*. *Educ:* Whitgift Sch., Croydon; Balliol Coll., Oxford (MA PPE). Chartered Accountant, 1969; FCA 1979. Articled with Binder Hamlyn & Co., 1964–69 (Hons Prize, 1968); General Partner, Lehman Brothers, 1969–86. MP (C) Kettering, 1983–97; contested (C) same seat, 1997. Parliamentary Under-Secretary of State: for the Armed Forces, 1986–88; DoH, 1988–90; Minister of State: Dept of Transport, 1990–94; MoD, 1994–95; Chancellor of the Duchy of Lancaster, 1995–97. A Vice-Chm., Cons. Party, July–Dec. 1997. President: British Internat. Freight Assoc., 1999–; TAVRA Council, 1999–. *Publications:* Professional Practice, 1968; Fair Deal for Water, 1985; (ed) UK Rail Privatisation 1992–1997, 2000. *Address:* House of Lords, SW1A 0PW. *Clubs:* Carlton, Kennel.

FREEMAN, Catherine; Director, Dove Productions, since 1989; *b* 10 Aug. 1931; *d* of Harold Dove and Eileen Carroll; *m* 1st, 1958, Charles Wheeler, *qv*; 2nd, 1962, John Freeman, *qv*; two *s* one *d*. *Educ:* Convent of the Assumption; St Anne's Coll., Oxford (MA Hons). Joined BBC as trainee producer, 1954; Producer/director: Panorama, Brains Trust, Monitor, Press Conference, 1954–58; joined Thames Television as Sen. Producer in Features Dept, 1976; Editor, Daytime progs, 1976–82; originator and series producer of Citizen 2000 for Channel 4; Controller, Documentaries, Features and Religion, 1982–86; Controller, Features and Religion, 1986–89. Member: Devlin Cttee on Identification Procedures, 1974–76; Literature Panel, Arts Council, 1981–84; Broadcasting, Film and Video panel, Arts Council, 1986–88. Director: ICA, 1983–93; One World Broadcasting Trust, 1990–95. *Address:* Davis Cottage, Torriano Cottages, NW5 2TA.

FREEMAN, David Charles; Founder/Director of Opera Factory; freelance opera and theatre director; *b* 1 May 1952; *s* of Howard Wilfred Freeman and Ruth Adair Nott; *m* 1985, Marie Angel; one *s* one *d*. *Educ:* Sydney Univ., NSW (BA Hons). Opera Factory Sydney, 1973–76; Opera Factory Zürich, 1976–95: directed 20 prodns, appearing in 5, writing the text of 4; Opera Factory London, 1981–98: directed 21 prodns (8 televised by Channel Four), writing text of two; founded Opera Factory Films, 1991; Associate Artist, ENO, 1981–: prodns include world première of The Mask of Orpheus, 1986; directed: Goethe's Faust, Pts I and II, Lyric, Hammersmith, 1988; (also adapted) Malory's Morte d'Arthur, Lyric, Hammersmith, 1990; The Winter's Tale, Shakespeare's Globe (opening prodn), 1997; Madam Butterfly, 1998, Tosca, 1999, Aida, 2001, Royal Albert Hall; opera prodns in New York, Houston, Paris, Germany and St Petersburg. Chevalier de l'Ordre des Arts et des Lettres, France, 1985.

FREEMAN, David John; Founder, 1952, and Senior Partner, 1952–92, D. J. Freeman, Solicitors, subseq. Consultant; *b* 25 Feb. 1928; *s* of late Meyer Henry and Rebecca Freeman; *m* 1950, Iris Margaret Alberge (*d* 1997); two *s* one *d*. *Educ:* Christ's Coll., Finchley. Lieut, Army, 1946–48. Admitted Solicitor, 1952. Dept of Trade Inspector into the affairs of AEG Telefunken (UK) Ltd, and Credit Collections Ltd, 1977. Governor, Royal Shakespeare Theatre, 1979–96. *Recreations:* reading, theatre, gardening, golf. *Address:* 43 Fetter Lane, EC4A 1JU. *T:* (020) 7583 4055. *Clubs:* Athenæum; Huntercombe Golf.

FREEMAN, Dr Ernest Allan, CEng, FIEE; CMath, FIMA; Director, Trent Polytechnic, 1981–83; *b* 16 Jan. 1932; *s* of William Freeman and Margaret Sinclair; *m* 1954, Mary Jane Peterson; two *d*. *Educ:* Sunderland Technical Coll.; King's Coll., Univ. of Durham (Mather Scholarship, 1955–57). BSc, PhD, Durham; DSc Newcastle upon Tyne; MA (Oxon) 1972. Sunderland Forge & Engineering Co. Ltd. 1949–55; English Electric Co., 1957–58; Ferranti Ltd (Edinburgh), 1958–59; Sunderland Polytechnic: Dir of Research, 1959–65; Head of Control Engrg Dept, 1965–72; Rector, 1976–80; Tutor and Fellow in Engrg, St Edmund Hall, Oxford Univ., 1972–76. FRSA. *Publications:* contribs mainly in the fields of control engrg, systems theory and computing, to Wireless Engr, Proc. IEE (Heaviside Prize, 1974), Jl of Electronics and Control, Trans AIEE, Electronic Technol., Control, Jl of Optimisation Theory and Application, Trans Soc. of Instrument Technol., Proc. Internat. Fedn for Analogue Computation, Internat. Jl of Control. *Recreations:* swimming, browsing around antique shops, playing bridge. *Address:* 12 Rolfe Place, Headington, Oxford OX3 0DS.

FREEMAN, Prof. Ernest Michael, PhD; FREng; Professor of Applied Electromagnetics, Imperial College of Science, Technology and Medicine, London University, since 1980; *b* 10 Nov. 1937; *s* of Ernest Robert Freeman and Agnes Maud Freeman; *m* 1987, Helen Anne Rigby. *Educ:* Colfe's Grammar Sch., Lewisham; King's Coll., London (BScEng; PhD 1964). Lectr, King's Coll., London, 1960–63 and 1966–70; Engrg Designer, AEI, Rugby, 1964–65; Reader: Brighton Polytechnic, 1970–73; Imperial Coll. of Science and Technology, 1973–80. Chm., Infolytica Ltd, 1978–; Vice Pres., Infolytica Corp., 1978–. FREng (FEng 1987). FRSA 1988. *Publications:* papers in learned society jls on magnetics. *Recreations:* architecture, military history, art, aristology. *Address:* Electrical Engineering Department, Imperial College of Science, Technology and Medicine, Exhibition Road, SW7 2BT. *T:* (020) 7594 6169; *e-mail:* e.freeman@ic.ac.uk.

FREEMAN, George Vincent; Under-Secretary (Legal), Treasury Solicitor's Department, 1973–76, retired; *b* 30 April 1911; *s* of Harold Vincent Freeman and Alice Freeman; *m* 1945, Margaret Nightingale; one *d*. *Educ:* Denstone Coll., Rocester. Admitted Solicitor, 1934; in private practice Birmingham until 1940. Served RN, 1940–46, Lieut RNVR. Legal Asst, Treasury Solicitor's Dept, 1946; Sen. Legal Asst 1950; Asst Treasury Solicitor 1964. *Recreation:* gardening. *Address:* 8 Shelley Close, Ashley Heath, Ringwood, Hants BH24 2JA. *T:* (01425) 477102. *Clubs:* Civil Service; Conservative (Ringwood).

FREEMAN, Hugh Lionel, FRCPsych; FFPHM; Hon. Consultant Psychiatrist, Salford Mental Health Trust (formerly Health Authority), University of Manchester School of Medicine, since 1988 (Consultant Psychiatrist, 1961–88); *b* Salford, 4 Aug. 1929; *s* of late Bernard Freeman, FBOA and Dora Doris Freeman (*née* Kahn); *m* 1957, Sally Joan Casket (*see* S. J. Freeman); three *s* one *d*. *Educ:* Altrincham Grammar Sch.; St John's Coll., Oxford (open schol.; BM BCh 1954; MA; DM 1988); MSc Salford 1980. DPM 1958; FFPHM (FFCM 1989). Captain, RAMC, 1956–58. House Surg., Manchester Royal Inf., 1955; Registrar, Bethlem Royal and Maudsley Hosps, 1958–60; Consultant Psychiatrist, Salford Royal Hosp., 1961–70; Hon. Consultant Psychiatrist: Salford Health Dept, 1961–74; Salford Social Services Dept, 1974–88. Hon. Med. Consultant, NAMH, 1963–74. Med. Advisor, NW Fellowship for Schizophrenia, 1980–88; Professional Advr, SANE, 1998–. Chairman: Psychiatric Sub-Cttee, NW Reg. Med. Adv. Cttee, 1978–83; Area Med. Cttee and Med. Exec. Cttee, Salford AHA, 1974–78. University of Manchester: Hon. Lectr, 1973–99; Mem., Univ. Court, 1989–94; Hon. Res. Fellow, UC and Middlesex Sch. of Medicine, 1989; Centre for Psychoanalytic Studies, Kent Univ., 1993. Visiting Professor: Univ. of WI, 1970; Univ. of WA, 1990; Univ. of Bern, 1995; Hungarian Medical Schools, 1996; Rockefeller Foundn Vis. Fellow, Italy, 1980; Vis. Fellow, 1986–97, Hon. Vis. Fellow, 1997, Green Coll., Oxford. Linacre Lectr, Linacre Coll., 1996. Examiner: Univ. of Manchester, United Examg Bd, 1993; RCPsych. Med. Mem., Mental Health Rev. Tribunal, 1982–93. Member: Sex Educn Panel, Health Educn Council, 1968–72; Working Party on Behaviour Control, Council for Sci. and Society, 1973–76; Minister of State's Panel on Private Practice, DHSS, 1974–75; UK Delgn to EC Conf. on Mental Health in Cities, Milan, 1980; Mental Health Act Commn, 1983–84; Home Sec's Wking Party on Fear of Crime, 1989; Historic Building Panel, City of Manchester, 1981–89. WHO Consultant: Grenada, 1970; Chile, 1978; Philippines, 1979; Bangladesh, 1981; Greece, 1985; Rapporteur: WHO Conf. on Mental Health Services in Pilot Study Areas, Trieste, 1984; WHO Workshop on Nat. Mental Health Progs, Ruanda, 1985. Editor, British Jl of Clin. and Social Psych., 1982–84; Dep. Editor, Internat. Jl of Social Psych., 1980–83; Editor: British Jl of Psych., 1983–93 (Asst Editor, 1978–83); Current Opinion in Psychiatry, 1988–93; Continuing Professional Develt Bulletin in Psychiatry, 1998–; Co-Editor, Psychiatric Bulletin, 1983; Associate Editor, Internat. Jl of Mental Health, 1981–; Asst Editor, History of Psychiatry, 1993–. Mem. Internat. Res. Seminars, US National Inst. of Mental Health: Washington, 1966; Pisa, 1977; has lectured to and addressed univs, confs and hosps worldwide; advr on and participant in radio and TV progs. Mem. Exec. Cttees, Royal Medico-Psychol Assoc., 1965–69. Royal College of Psychiatrists: Foundn Mem., 1971; Fellow 1971, Hon. Fellow 1998; Mem. Council, 1983–93; Chm., Journal Cttee; Vice-Chm., Social and Community Gp; Maudsley Lectr, 1993. FRSH (Hon. Sec., Mental Health Gp, 1973–76); Vice-Chm., 1983–87, Mem., Council, 1987–91, MIND. Corresp. Fellow, Amer. Psychiatric Assoc., 1993; Corresp. Member: US Assoc. for Clinical Psychosociol Res.; US Assoc. for Behavioral Therapies; Hon. Member: Chilean Soc. of Psych., Neurol. and Neurosurgery; Egyptian Psychiatric Assoc.; Polish Psychiatric Assoc., 1986; Hungarian Psychiatric Soc., 1991; Bulgarian Soc. for Neuroscis, 1991; Senior Common Room, Pembroke Coll., Oxford, 1981. Vice-Chm., Manchester Heritage Trust, 1983–89; Mem., Mercian Regional Cttee, NT, 1986–92. Hon. Professorial Fellow, Salford Univ., 1986. Freeman, City of London; Liveryman, Soc. of Apothecaries, 1984 (Yeoman, 1979–84). Distinguished Service Commendation, US Nat. Council of Community Mental Health Centers, 1982; 650 Anniversary Medal of Merit, Charles Univ., Prague, 1999. *Publications:* (ed jtly) Trends in the Mental Health Services, 1963; (ed) Psychiatric Hospital Care, 1965; (ed jtly) New Aspects of the Mental Health Service, 1968; (ed) Progress in Behaviour Therapy, 1969; (ed) Progress in Mental Health, 1970; (ed) Pavlovian Approach to Psychopathology, 1971; (ed jtly) Dangerousness, 1982; Mental Health and the Environment, 1985; (jtly) Mental Health Services in Europe, 1985; (ed jtly) Mental Health Services in Britain: the way ahead, 1985; (ed jtly) Interaction between Mental and Physical Illness, 1989; (ed jtly) Community Psychiatry, 1991; (ed jtly) 150 Years of British Psychiatry, 1991; La Malattie del Potere, 1994; (ed jtly) 150 Years of British Psychiatry: the aftermath, 1996; (ed jtly) Quality of Life in Mental Disorders, 1997; (ed) A Century of Psychiatry, 1999; contribs to national press and learned jls. *Recreations:* architecture, travel, music. *Address:* 21 Montagu Square, W1H 2LF. *Club:* Oxford and Cambridge.

FREEMAN, Sir James (Robin), 3rd Bt *cr* 1945; *b* 21 July 1955; *s* of Sir (John) Keith (Noel) Freeman, 2nd Bt and Patricia Denison (*née* Thomas); *S* father, 1981. *Heir:* none.

FREEMAN, Joan; *see* Freeman, S. J.

FREEMAN, Rt Hon. John, MBE 1943; PC 1966. *Educ:* Westminster Sch.; Brasenose College, Oxford (Hon. Fellow, 1968). Active service, 1940–45. MP (Lab) Watford Div. of Herts, 1945–50; Borough of Watford, 1950–55; PPS to Sec. of State for War, 1945–46; Financial Sec., War Office, 1946; Parly Under Sec. of State for War, April 1947; Leader, UK Defence Mission to Burma, 1947; Parly Sec., Min. of Supply, 1947–51, resigned. Asst Editor, New Statesman, 1951–58; Deputy Editor, 1958–60; Editor, 1961–65. British High Commissioner in India, 1965–68; British Ambassador in Washington, 1969–71. Chairman: London Weekend Television Ltd, 1971–84; LWT (Holdings) plc, 1976–84; Page & Moy (Holdings) Ltd, 1976–84; Hutchinson Ltd, 1978–82 (Director till 1984); ITN, 1976–81. Vis. Prof. of Internat. Relns, Univ. of California, Davis, 1985–90. Governor, BFI, 1976–82. Vice-Pres., Royal Television Soc., 1975–85 (Gold Medal, 1981).

FREEMAN, John; a Vice-President, Immigration Appeal Tribunal, since 2000; *b* 13 July 1951; *s* of late E. A. Freeman, FRCS and of Joan (*née* Horrell). *Educ:* Winchester Coll.; Corpus Christi Coll., Cambridge (MA); Univ. of Warwick (LLM). Practised at Bar, Midland and Oxford Circuit, 1976–83, 1986–89; Resident Magistrate, Registrar and Commissioner of High Court and Court of Appeal, actg Dir of Public, Prosecutions, Solomon Islands, 1983–86; consultant, ODA and UNHCR, 1987–92; Immigration Appeal Adjudicator, 1992–2000. *Recreation:* trying to breed Staffordshire bull terriers. *Address:* (office) Field House, 15–25 Bream's Buildings, EC4A 1DZ. *Club:* Royal Geographical Society.

FREEMAN, John Allen, OBE 1958; PhD; FRES, CBiol, FIBiol; Director, Ministry of Agriculture, Fisheries and Food's Pest Infestation Control Laboratory, 1977–79; *b* 30 Sept. 1912; *s* of Laurence Freeman and Maggie Rentoul Freeman; *m* 1945, Hilda Mary Jackson; one *s* one *d*. *Educ:* City of London Sch. (Jun. Corp. Scholar, Travers Scholar); Imperial Coll. of Science and Technol., London Univ. (BSc Special 1st Cl. Hons 1933, PhD 1938). ARCS; FRES 1943; FIBiol 1963. Min. of Agric. Scholar in Entomology, 1934–37: Hull University Coll., 1934–35; Rothamsted Exper. Stn, 1936; Cornell Univ., USA, 1936–37; Vineland Exper. Stn, Ont, Canadian Dept of Agric., 1937. Res. Asst, Imp. Coll., London, 1938–40; Jun. Scientific Officer, Dept of Science and Indust. Res. Pest Infestation Lab., 1940; seconded Min. of Food Infest. Control, 1940–47; Chief Entomologist, 1944; Sen. Sci. Officer, 1946; transf. Min. of Agric., 1947; Principal Sci. Off., 1947; seconded OECD, 1954–55, and CENTO, 1957–58; Sen. Principal Sci. Off., 1958; Dep. Chief Sci. Off., and Dep. Dir Pest Infest. Control Lab., 1971; Chief Sci. Off., 1977. Member: British Ecol Soc.; Assoc. of Applied Biol. Treasurer, Royal Entomol Soc. of London, 1977–84; Hon. Treas., Inst. of Biol, 1965–69. Pres., Royal Coll. of Science Union and Imp. Coll. Union, 1934. Has travelled professionally in N and S America, Europe, Africa, ME and Far East. Freeman of City of London, 1947. *Publications:* scientific articles, mainly on pests of stored foods. *Recreations:* gardening, photography, travel, DIY. *Address:* 5 Woodmere Way, Park Langley, Beckenham, Kent BR3 6SJ. *T:* (020) 8658 6970.

FREEMAN, John Anthony, FCA; Managing Director, Home Service Division, Prudential Corporation plc, 1984–94; *b* 27 May 1937; *o s* of late John Eric Freeman and

Dorothy Mabel Freeman; *m* 1st, 1964, Judith Dixon (marr. diss. 1984); one *s* one *d*; 2nd, 1986, Margaret Joyce (*née* Langdon-Ellis). *Educ:* Queen Elizabeth Grammar Sch., Mansfield; Birmingham Univ. (BCom). FCA 1961; FCMA 1974. Mellors Basden & Mellors, Chartered Accountants, 1958–62; Peat Marwick Mitchell, Chartered Accountants, 1962–73; National Freight Corp., 1973–77; Prudential Corp., 1977–94. *Recreations:* golf, gardening, music.

FREEMAN, Joseph William, OBE 1968; Director of Social Service, Leeds, 1970–78; *b* 8 April 1914; *s* of Thomas and Emma Freeman; *m* 1939, Louise King (*d* 1986); one *s* one *d*. *Educ:* Toynbee Hall; Morley Coll., London; Liverpool Univ. (BSc (Soc.) 1938); BA Hons Open Univ. 1983. CQSW 1970. Qual. social worker; Probation Service, Birmingham, 1938; served War of 1939–45: Army, 1940, commnd RA, 1941; Probation Service, Liverpool, 1946; Children's Officer: Warrington, 1948; Bolton, 1951; Sheffield, 1955. Organist Emeritus, St James Parish Church, Eccleston Park, 1995. *Publications:* (contrib.) Child Care Revisited, 1998; papers in social work jls. *Recreation:* music. *Address:* 15 Fairfield Gardens, Crank Road, St Helens WA11 7SL.

FREEMAN, Prof. Kenneth Charles, PhD; FRS 1998; Duffield Professor, Research School of Astronomy and Astrophysics, Mount Stromlo Observatory, Institute of Advanced Studies, Australian National University, since 1987; *b* 27 Aug. 1940; *s* of Herbert and Herta Freeman; *m* 1963, Margaret Leigh Cook; one *s* three *d*. *Educ:* Scotch Coll.; Univ. of Western Australia (BSc Hons Mathematics 1962); Trinity Coll., Cambridge (PhD 1965). FAA 1981. Res. Fellow, Trinity Coll., Cambridge, 1965–69; McDonald Postdoctoral Fellow in Astronomy, Univ. of Texas, 1966; Mount Stromlo and Siding Spring Observatories, Australian National University: Queen Elizabeth Fellow, 1967–70; Fellow, 1970–74; Sen. Fellow, 1974–81; Professorial Fellow, 1981–87. Sen. Scientist, Kapteyn Lab., Univ. of Groningen, 1976; Vis. Mem., Inst. of Advanced Study, Princeton, 1984, 1988; Distinguished Vis. Scientist, Space Telescope Science Inst., Baltimore, 1988–; Oort Prof., Univ. of Leiden, 1994. Chm., Nat. Cttee on Astronomy, Australian Acad. of Science, 1984–86 (Pawsey Medal, 1972). Hon. DSc WA, 1999. Heineman Prize, Amer. Inst. of Physics and Amer. Astronomical Soc., 1999. *Publications:* 250 articles in learned astronomical jls. *Recreations:* bushwalking, birdwatching, classical music. *Address:* Mount Stromlo Observatory, Cotter Road, Weston Creek, ACT 2611, Australia. *T:* (2) 61250264.

FREEMAN, Dr Marie Joyce, FFCM; Health Service Management Consultant, 1988–95; *b* 14 April 1934; *d* of Wilfrid George Croxson and Ada Mildred (*née* Chiles); *m* 1958, Samuel Anthony Freeman (decd); one *s*. *Educ:* Royal Free Hospital Sch. of Medicine (MB BS, DPH). Specialist in Community Medicine, Avon AHA, 1974; District MO, Southmead HA, 1982; Actg Regl MD, SW RHA, 1986–88. *Recreations:* patchwork and quilting, making miniatures, living in Provence. *Address:* Wingfield House, Darlington Place, Bath BA2 6BY. *T:* (01225) 466670; Hameau de la Lauge, 84570 Blauvac, Vaucluse, France.

FREEMAN, Michael Alexander Reykers, MD; FRCS; Consultant Orthopaedic Surgeon, The London Hospital, 1968–96; Hon. Consultant, Royal Hospitals NHS Trust, since 1996; European Editor-in-Chief, Journal of Arthroplasty, since 1996; *b* 17 Nov. 1931; *s* of Donald George and Florence Julia Freeman; *m* 1st, 1951, Elisabeth Jean; one *s* one *d*; 2nd, 1959, Janet Edith; one *s* one *d*; 3rd, 1968, Patricia; one *d* (and one *s* decd). *Educ:* Stowe Sch.; Corpus Christi Coll., Cambridge (open scholarship and closed exhibn); London Hospital Med. Coll. BA (1st cl. hons), MB BCh, MD (Cantab). FRCS 1959. Trained in medicine and surgery, London Hosp., and in orthopaedic and traumatic surgery, London, Westminster and Middlesex Hosps; co-founder, Biomechanics Unit, Imperial Coll., London, 1964; Cons. Surg. in Orth. and Traum. Surgery, London Hosp., also Res. Fellow, Imperial Coll., 1968; resigned from Imperial Coll., to devote more time to clinical activities, 1979. Special surgical interest in field of reconstructive surgery in lower limb, concentrating on joint replacement; originator of new surgical procedures for reconstruction and replacement of arthritic hip, knee, ankle and joints of foot; has lectured and demonstrated surgery, Canada, USA, Brazil, Japan, China, Australia, S Africa, continental Europe; guest speaker at nat. and internat. profess. congresses. Robert Jones Lectr, RCS, 1989. Past Member: Scientific Co-ordinating Cttee, ARC; MRC; Clin. Res. Bd, London Hosp. Bd of Governors; Brent and Harrow AHA; DHSS working parties. President: Internat. Hip Soc., 1982–85; British Hip Soc., 1989–91; British Orthopaedic Assoc., 1992–93; Eur. Fedn of Nat. Assocs of Orthopaedics and Traumatol., 1994–95. Member: BMA; Amer. Acad. Orth. Surgs; Orth. Res. Soc.; SICOT; RSM; Health Unit, IEA; SIROT; European Orth. Res. Soc. Hon. Member: Danish Orth. Assoc.; Soc. Française de Chirurg. Orth. et Traum.; Canadian Orth. Assoc. Hon. Fellow, Soc. Belge de Chirurg. Orth. et de Traum. Bacon and Cunning Prizes and Copeman Medal, CCC; Andrew Clark and T. A. M. Ross Prize in Clin. Med., London Hosp. Med. Coll.; Robert Jones Medal, Brit. Orth. Assoc. *Publications:* editor and part-author: Adult Articular Cartilage, 1973, 2nd edn 1979; Scientific Basis of Joint Replacement, 1977; Arthritis of the Knee, 1980; chapters in: Bailey and Love's Short Practice of Surgery; Mason and Currey's Textbook of Rheumatology; papers in Proc. Royal Soc., Jl Bone and Joint Surgery, and med. jls. *Recreations:* gardening, reading, surgery. *Address:* 79 Albert Street, NW1 7LX. *T:* (020) 7387 0817.

FREEMAN, Paul, ARCS, DSc (London), FRES; Keeper of Entomology, British Museum (Natural History), 1968–81; *b* 26 May 1916; *s* of Samuel Mellor Freeman and Kate Burgis; *m* 1942, Audrey Margaret Long; two *d*. *Educ:* Brentwood Sch., Essex; Imperial Coll., London. Demonstrator in Entomology, Imperial Coll., 1938. Captain, RA and Army Operational Research Group, 1940–45. Lecturer in Entomology, Imperial Coll., 1945–47. Asst Keeper, Dept of Entomology, British Museum (Nat. Hist.), 1947–64, Dep. Keeper, 1964–68. Royal Entomological Soc. of London: Vice-Pres., 1956, 1957; Hon. Sec., 1958–62; Hon. Fellow, 1984. Sec., XIIth Internat. Congress of Entomology, London, 1964. *Publications:* Diptera of Patagonia and South Chile, Pt III-Mycetophilidae, 1951; Simuliidae of the Ethiopian Region (with Botha de Meillon), 1953; numerous papers in learned jls, on taxonomy of Hemiptera and Diptera. *Recreations:* gardening, natural history. *Address:* Briardene, 75 Towncourt Crescent, Petts Wood, Orpington, Kent BR5 1PH. *T:* (01689) 827296.

FREEMAN, Paul Illife, CB 1992; PhD; Controller and Chief Executive of HM Stationery Office, and the Queen's Printer of Acts of Parliament, 1989–95; *b* 11 July 1935; *s* of late John Percy Freeman and of Hilda Freeman; *m* 1959, Enid Ivy May Freeman; one *s* one *d*. *Educ:* Victoria University of Manchester (BSc (Hons) Chemistry, PhD). Post Doctoral Fellow, Nat. Research Council of Canada, 1959–61; Research Scientist, Dupont De Nemours Co. Ltd, Wilmington, Del, USA, 1961–64; Nat. Physical Laboratory: Sen. Scientific Officer, 1964–70; Principal Scientific Officer, 1970–74; Exec. Officer, Research Requirements Bds, DoI, 1973–77; Director: Computer Aided Design Centre, 1977–83; National Engrg Lab., 1980–83; Central Computer and Telecommunications Agency, HM Treasury, 1983–88. Member: CS Coll. Advisory Council, 1983–88; Bd, NCC, 1983–88; Bd, DVLA, 1990–92; Council, UEA, 1994–. Vis. Prof. Univ. of Strathclyde, 1981–86. CIMgt 1995. *Publications:* scientific papers. *Recreations:* fishing, reading, walking, gardening. *Address:* 12 Broadway, Wilburton, Ely, Cambridgeshire CB6 3RT. *T:* (01353) 740576.

FREEMAN, Peter David Mark, CBE 2001; Principal Finance Officer, Department for International Development, 2000–01; *b* 8 Dec. 1947; *s* of Dr Victor Freeman and Ethel (*née* Halpern); *m* 1980, Anne Tyndale; two *d*. *Educ:* Merton Coll., Oxford (BA Hons); Univ. of Toronto (MA). Asst Private Sec. to Minister for Overseas Develt, 1973–75; Office of UK Exec. Dir, World Bank, 1975–78; British High Commn, Zimbabwe, 1980–83; Asst Head, Econ. Relns Dept, FCO, 1983–84; Overseas Development Administration, then Department for International Development: Head: EC Dept, 1984–88; Central and Southern Africa Dept, 1988–90; Aid Policy Dept, 1990–91; Internat. Div., 1991–93; Personnel, Orgn and Services Div., 1993–96; Dir, Africa Div., 1996–99. Mem. Audit Cttee, Sightsavers Internat., 2001–. Governor: Stanford Jun. Sch., Brighton, 1988– (Chm., 1992–96); Dorothy Stringer High Sch., Brighton, 1996–99. *Address:* 18 Montpelier Crescent, Brighton BN1 3JF.

FREEMAN, Prof. Raymond, MA, DPhil, DSc (Oxon); FRS 1979; John Humphrey Plummer Professor of Magnetic Resonance, and Fellow of Jesus College, Cambridge University, 1987–99, now Emeritus Professor; *b* 6 Jan. 1932; *s* of late Albert and Hilda Frances Freeman; *m* 1958, Anne-Marie Périnet-Marquet; two *s* three *d*. *Educ:* Nottingham High Sch. (scholar); Lincoln Coll., Oxford (open scholar). Ingénieur, Centre d'Etudes Nucléaires de Saclay, Commissariat à l'Energie Atomique, France, 1957–59; Sen. Scientific Officer, Nat. Phys. Lab., Teddington, Mddx, 1959–63; Man., Nuclear Magnetic Resonance Research, Varian Associates, Palo Alto, Calif, 1963–73; Lectr in Physical Chemistry, 1973–87, Aldrichian Praelector in Chemistry, 1982–87, and Fellow, Magdalen Coll., 1973–87, Oxford Univ. Chem. Soc. Award in Theoretical Chem. and Spectroscopy, 1978; Leverhulme Medal, Royal Soc., 1990; Longstaff Medal, RSC, 1999. Hon. DSc Durham, 1988. *Publications:* A Handbook of Nuclear Magnetic Resonance, 1987; Spin Choreography: basic steps in high resolution NMR, 1997; articles on nuclear magnetic resonance spectroscopy in various scientific journals. *Recreations:* swimming, traditional jazz. *Address:* Department of Chemistry, University of Cambridge, Lensfield Road, Cambridge CB2 1EW; Jesus College, Cambridge CB5 8BL; 29 Bentley Road, Cambridge CB2 2AW. *T:* (01223) 323958.

FREEMAN, Dr (Sally) Joan, PhD; CPsychol, FBPsS; FCP; Visiting Professor, School of Lifelong Learning and Education, University of Middlesex, since 1992; *b* 17 June 1935; *d* of late Phillip Casket and Rebecca (*née* Goldman); *m* 1957, Hugh Lionel Freeman, *qv*; three *s* one *d*. *Educ:* Broughton High Sch.; Univ. of Manchester (BSc, PhD 1980, MEd, DipEdGuidance). FBPsS 1985; CPsychol 1988; FCP 1990. Sen. Lectr in Applied Psychol., Preston Poly., 1975–81; Hon. Tutor, Dept of Educn, Univ. of Manchester, 1975–89; Hon. Lectr, Inst. of Educn, Univ. of London, 1988–94. Private psychology practice, London, 1989–. Ed., High Ability Studies, 1995–98. Dir, Gulbenkian Res. Project on Gifted Children, 1973–88. Founder Pres., European Council for High Ability, 1987–92. Mem., various cttees and projects on the educn of children of high ability, incl. Adv. Bd on Exceptionally Able Pupils, SCAA, 1994–, and Govt Adv. Gp, Gifted and Talented Children, 1998–. Vis appts, scholarships and consultancies, Italy, Bulgaria, Canada, SA, Hong Kong and Australia. College of Preceptors, now College of Teachers: Member: Bd of Examnrs, 1987–; Council, 1995–; Exec. Cttee, 1999–; Chm., Publications Bd, 1998–; British Psychological Society: Mem., Nat. Council, 1975–86; Chm., Northern Br., 1978–86; Mem., Standing Press Cttee, 1980–85. Mem., Fawcett Soc., 1984–. *Publications:* Human Biology and Hygiene, 1968, 2nd edn 1981; In and Out of School: an introduction to applied psychology in education, 1975 (trans. Portuguese, Hebrew and Spanish); Gifted Children: their identification and development in a social context, 1979; Clever Children: a parents' guide, 1983 (trans. German, Finnish and Thai); (ed) The Psychology of Gifted Children: perspectives on development and education, 1985 (trans. Spanish); Gifted Children Growing Up, 1991; Bright as a Button: how to encourage your children's talents 0–5 years, 1991 (trans. Indonesian); Quality Basic Education: the development of competence, 1992 (trans. French); (with S. Ojanen) The Attitudes and Experiences of Headteachers, Class-teachers and Highly Able Pupils Towards the Education of the Highly Able in Finland and Britain, 1994; (ed jtly) Actualising Talent: a lifelong challenge, 1995; Highly Able Girls and Boys, 1996; How to Raise a Bright Child, 1996 (trans. Russian and Chinese); Educating the Very Able: current international research, 1998 (trans. Thai); (with Z. C. Geunther) Educando os Mais Capazes: idéias e ações comprovadas, 2000; Gifted Children Grown Up, 2001; numerous academic papers and chapters in books; contrib. numerous articles and book reviews on child develt, psychol. and educn for both professional and lay jls. *Recreations:* photography, reading, travel. *Address:* 21 Montagu Square, W1H 2LF. *T:* (020) 7486 2604; *e-mail:* j.freeman@mdx.ac.uk.

FREEMAN-GRENVILLE, family name of **Lady Kinloss**.

FREER, Maj. Gen. Ian Lennox, CB 1994; CBE 1988 (OBE 1985); Principal, Lennox Freer and Associates Pty Ltd, 1997; *b* 18 May 1941; *s* of late Lt-Col George Freer, OBE and Elizabeth (*née* Tallo), Edinburgh; *m* 1970, Karla Thwaites; one *s* two *d*. *Educ:* George Watson's Coll., Edinburgh; RMA Sandhurst. Commnd Staffordshire Regt (Prince of Wales's), 1961; served UK, Kenya, Germany, Gulf States, Belize, Gibraltar; Staff Capt. to QMG, 1972–73; MA to COS, BAOR, 1975–77; SO1, Instr Staff Coll., 1980–81; CO 1st Bn, Staffords Regt, 1982–84; Div. Col, Staff Coll., 1985; Comdr, 39 Inf. Bde (NI), 1986–87; Chief, BRIXMIS (Berlin), 1989–91; Comdr, Land Forces, NI, 1991–94; GOC Wales and Western Dist, later 5th Div., 1994–96. Col, Staffords Regt, 1990–96; Col Comdt, POW Div., 1993–96. Dir, Woodleigh Sch., Vic. Resident in Australia. *Recreations:* sailing, walking, tennis. *Address:* c/o Lloyds TSB, Worldwide Service, PO Box 349, 1 Waterloo Place, SW1Y 5NJ.

FREER, Air Chief Marshal Sir Robert (William George), GBE 1981 (CBE 1966); KCB 1977; Commandant, Royal College of Defence Studies, 1980–82, retired; Director, Pilatus Britten-Norman Ltd, 1988–96; *b* Darjeeling, 1 Sept. 1923; *s* of late William Freer, Stretton, Cirencester, Glos; *m* 1950, Margaret, 2nd *d* of late J. W. Elkington and Mrs M. Elkington, Ruskington Manor, near Sleaford, Lincs; one *s* one *d*. *Educ:* Gosport Grammar Sch. Flying Instructor, S Africa and UK, 1944–47; RAF Coll., Cranwell, 1947–50; served 54 and 614 Fighter Sqdns, 1950–52; Central Fighter Estabt, 1952–54; commanded 92 Fighter Sqdn, 1955–57 (Queen's Commendation, 1955); Directing Staff, USAF Acad., 1958–60; Staff of Chief of Defence Staff, 1961–63; Station Comdr, RAF Seletar, 1963–66; DD Defence Plans (Air), MoD, 1966–67. Air ADC to the Queen, 1969–71; Dep. Comdt, RAF Staff Coll., 1969–71; SASO, HQ Near East Air Force, 1971–72; AOC 11 Group, 1972–75; Dir-Gen., Organisation (RAF), April-Sept. 1975; AOC No 18 Group, RAF, 1975–78; Dep. C-in-C, Strike Command, 1978–79. Director: Rediffusion, 1982–88; British Manufg & Res. Co., 1984–88; Rediffusion Simulation, 1985–88. Mem. Council, RAF Benevolent Fund and Chm. Mgt Bd, Princess Marina House, Rustington, 1993–96. Pres., RAF LTA, 1975–81; Mem., Sports Council, 1980–82. CIMgt (FBIM 1977); FRSA 1988–94; FRAeS 1995. *Recreations:* golf, tennis, hill-walking. *Address:* c/o Lloyds TSB,

Farnham, Surrey. *Clubs:* Royal Air Force; All England Lawn Tennis and Croquet; Hankley Common Golf.

FREER, Yve Helen Elaine; *see* Buckland, Y. H. E.

FREESON, Rt Hon. Reginald, PC 1976; Director, Reg Freeson & Associates, urban renewal consultants, since 1987; freelance writer and speaker; *b* 24 Feb. 1926; *m* (marr. diss.); one *s* one *d*; *m*. *Educ:* Jewish Orphanage, West Norwood. Served in Army, 1944–47. Middle East magazines and newspapers, 1946–48. Joined: Labour Party on return to United Kingdom, 1948; IVS, 1956; UN Assoc. Internat. Service, 1958; Co-operative Party, 1958; Fabian Society, 1960; Poale Zion–Labour Zionists, 1964 and Labour Finance and Industry Gp, 1990–2001. Journalist, 1948–64: magazines, newspaper agencies and television; John Bull, Today, News Review, Everybody's Weekly, Tribune, News Chronicle, Daily Mirror. Asst Press Officer with Min. of Works, British Railways Board. Some short story writing, research and ghosting of books and pamphlets. Editor: Searchlight, against fascism and racialism, 1964–67; Jewish Vanguard, Labour–Zionist qly, 1987–. Radio and television: housing, urban planning, race relations and foreign affairs. Elected Willesden Borough Council, 1952; Alderman, 1955; Leader of Council, 1958–65; Chm. of new London Borough of Brent, 1964–65 (Alderman, 1964–68). MP (Lab): Willesden E, 1964–74; Brent E, Feb. 1974–1987. PPS to Minister of Transport, 1964–67; Parly Secretary: Min. of Power, 1967–69; Min. of Housing and Local Govt, 1969–70; Labour front-bench spokesman: on housing and urban affairs, 1970–74; on social security, 1979–81; Minister for Housing and Construction and Urban Affairs, DoE, 1974–79; responsible for planning, land and local govt, 1976–79; Mem., Select Cttee on the Environment, 1981–84 (Chm., 1982–83). Member: Council of Europe Parly Assembly, 1984–87; Western Eur. Assembly, 1984–87. Dir, Labour Friends of Israel, 1992–93. Dir, JBG Housing Soc., 1981–83; Mem. Exec., Housing Centre Trust, 1987–98; Exec. Mem., Nat. Housing and Planning Council, 1998–. Mem., Internat. Voluntary Service and UNA International Service. Sponsor, three Willesden housing co-operatives, 1958–60. Member: CPA; London Labour Mayors' Assoc. Founder-Chairman: Willesden (then Brent) Coun. of Social Service, 1960–62; Willesden Social Action, 1961–63; Willesden Internat. Friendship Council (then Brent Community Relns Council), 1959–63 (Vice-Pres., 1967); Chairman: Warsaw Memorial Cttee, 1964–71; Poale Zion, 1984–87; Vice-Pres., Campaign for Democracy in Ulster; Founder–Sponsor, Internat. Centre for Peace in ME; Mem., Jewish Welfare Bd, 1971–74 (Mem. Exec., 1973–74); Mem., Labour Campaign for Electoral Reform, 1983–. Mem., TCPA; Life Member: YHA, 1957; Nat. Trust, 1987. Pres., Norwood (Jewish Orphanage) Old Scholars' Assoc. Writer and speaker on urban and envmtl regeneration, housing, construction industry and planning. *Publications:* policy papers, pamphlets, reports and articles for Borrie Commn on Social Justice, Lab. Party Commn on Envmt, Labour Finance and Industry Gp, Fabian Rev., Rowntree Foundn, Housing Rev., Roof, Housing and Planning Rev., Axis, Tribune, Commonweal. *Recreations:* gardening, tree planting, music, theatre, reading, country walking, community environmental action. *Address:* 159 Chevening Road, NW6 6DZ.

FREETH, Denzil Kingson, MBE 1997; *b* 10 July 1924; *s* of late Walter Kingson and late Vera Freeth. *Educ:* Highfield Sch., Liphook, Hants; Sherborne Sch. (Scholar); Trinity Hall, Cambridge (Scholar). Served War, 1943–46: RAF (Flying Officer). Pres. Union Soc., Cambridge, 1949; Chm. Cambridge Univ. Conservative Assoc. 1949; debating tour of America, 1949, also debated in Ireland; Mem. Exec. Cttee Nat. Union, 1955. MP (C) Basingstoke Division of Hants, 1955–64. PPS to Minister of State, Bd of Trade, 1956, to Pres. of the Bd of Trade, 1957–59, to Minister of Educn, 1959–60; Parly Sec. for Science, 1961–63. Mem. Parliamentary Cttee of Trustee Savings Bank Assoc., 1956–61. Mem. Select Cttee on Procedure, 1958–59. Employed by and Partner in stockbroking firms, 1950–61 and 1964–89; Mem. of Stock Exchange, 1959–61, 1965–91. Chm. Finance Cttee, London Diocesan Fund, 1986–94. Churchwarden, All Saints' Church, Margaret St, W1, 1977–96. *Recreations:* good food, wine and conversation. *Address:* 3 Brasenose House, 35 Kensington High Street, W8 5BA. *T:* (020) 7937 8685. *Clubs:* Carlton; Pitt (Cambridge).

FREETH, Hon. Sir Gordon, KBE 1978; Chairman, Australian Consolidated Minerals, 1981–90; *b* 6 Aug. 1914; *s* of late Rt Rev. Robert Evelyn Freeth and Gladys Mary Snashall; *m* 1939, Joan Celia Carew Baker; one *s* two *d*. *Educ:* Sydney Church of England Grammar Sch.; Guildford Grammar Sch.; Univ. of Western Australia. Rowed for Australia in British Empire Games, Sydney, 1938. Admitted as Barrister and Solicitor, WA, 1938; practised Law at Katanning, WA, 1939–49. Served as Pilot, RAAF, 1942–45. Elected to House of Representatives as Member for Forrest, 1949; MP 1949–69; Minister: for Interior and Works, 1958–63; for Shipping and Transport, 1963–68; Assisting Attorney-Gen., 1962–64; for Air, and Minister Assisting the Treasurer, 1968; for External Affairs, 1969; Ambassador to Japan, 1970–73; practised law in Perth, WA, 1973–77; High Comr for Australia in UK, 1977–80. *Recreations:* gardening, golf. *Address:* Tingrith, 25 Owston Street, Mosman Park, WA 6012, Australia. *Club:* Weld (Perth).

FREETH, Peter Stewart, RA 1991 (ARA 1990); RE 1991 (ARE 1987); Tutor, Etching, Royal Academy Schools, since 1966; *b* 15 April 1938; *s* of Alfred William Freeth and Olive Walker; *m* 1967, Mariolina Meliadò; two *s*. *Educ:* King Edward's Grammar School, Aston; Slade School, London (Dip Fine Art). Rome Scholar, Engraving, British Sch., Rome, 1960–62; teacher of Printmaking, Camden Inst., 1979–. One man shows: Christopher Mendez Gall., London, 1987–89; Friends' Room, Royal Acad., 1991; S Maria a Gradillo, Ravello, Italy, 1997; represented in collections: British Museum; V&A; Fitzwilliam Mus., Cambridge; Arts Council; Metropolitan Mus., NY; Nat. Gall., Washington. Mem., Royal Soc. of Painter Printmakers. Prix de Rome, Engraving, 1960. *Recreations:* music, books, yet more work. *Address:* 83 Muswell Hill Road, N10 3HT.

FREIER, Rt Rev. Philip Leslie; *see* Northern Territory (Australia), Bishop of the.

FREMANTLE, family name of **Baron Cottesloe**.

FRÉMAUX, Louis Joseph Felix; conductor; *b* 13 Aug. 1921; *m* 1st, 1948, Nicole Petibon (*d* 1999); four *s* one *d*; 2nd, 1999, Cecily Hake. *Educ:* Conservatoire National Supérieur de Musique de Paris. Chef d'Orchestre Permanent et Directeur, l'Orchestre National de l'Opéra de Monte Carlo, 1956–66; Principal Conductor, Orchestre de Lyon, 1968–71; Musical Dir and Principal Conductor, City of Birmingham Symphony Orch., 1969–78; Music Dir and Principal Conductor, 1979–81, Principal Guest Conductor, 1982–85, Sydney Symph. Orch. First concert in England, with Bournemouth Symph. Orch., 1964. Guest appearances with all symph. orchs in GB; many recordings. Hon. RAM, 1978. Hon. DMus Birmingham, 1978. Croix de Guerre, 1945, 1947; Chevalier de la Légion d'Honneur, 1969. *Recreations:* walking, photography. *Address:* 25 Edencroft, Wheeley's Road, Birmingham, B15 2LW.

FRENCH, family name of **Baron De Freyne**.

FRENCH, Prof. Anthony Philip, PhD; Professor of Physics, Massachusetts Institute of Technology, 1964–91, now Emeritus; *b* 19 Nov. 1920; *s* of Sydney James French and Elizabeth Margaret (*née* Hart); *m* 1946, Naomi Mary Livesay; one *s* one *d*. *Educ:* Varndean Sch., Brighton; Sidney Sussex Coll., Cambridge (major schol.; BA Hons 1942, MA 1946, PhD 1948). British atomic bomb project, Tube Alloys, 1942–44; Manhattan Project, Los Alamos, USA, 1944–46; Scientific Officer, AERE, Harwell, 1946–48; Univ. Demonstrator in Physics, Cavendish Laboratory, Cambridge, 1948–51, Lectr 1951–55; Dir of Studies in Natural Sciences, Pembroke Coll., Cambridge, 1949–55, Fellow of Pembroke, 1950–55; Visiting research scholar: California Inst. of Technology, 1951; Univ. of Michigan, 1954; Prof. of Physics, Univ. of S Carolina, 1955–62 (Head of Dept, 1956–62); Guignard Lectr, 1958; Vis. Prof., MIT, 1962–64; Vis. Fellow of Pembroke Coll., Cambridge, 1975. Member, Internat. Commn on Physics Educn, 1972–84 (Chm., 1975–81); Pres., Amer. Assoc. of Physics Teachers, 1985–86. FInstP 1986; Fellow, Amer. Physical Soc., 1987. Hon. ScD Allegheny Coll., 1989. Bragg Medal, Institute of Physics, 1988; Oersted Medal, 1989, Melba Newell Phillips Award, 1993, Amer. Assoc. of Physics Teachers. *Publications:* Principles of Modern Physics, 1958; Special Relativity, 1968; Newtonian Mechanics, 1971; Vibrations and Waves, 1971; Introduction to Quantum Physics, 1978; Einstein: a centenary volume, 1979; Niels Bohr: a centenary volume, 1985; Introduction to Classical Mechanics, 1986; Physics in a Technological World, 1988; Physics History from AAPT Journals II, 1995. *Recreations:* music, squash, reading, writing. *Address:* c/o Physics Department, Room 6–101, Massachusetts Institute of Technology, Cambridge, MA 02139, USA.

FRENCH, Cecil Charles John, FREng; Group Technology Director, Ricardo International, 1990–92, retired; *b* 16 April 1926; *s* of Ernest French and Edith Hannah French (*née* Norris); *m* 1st, 1956, Olive Joyce Edwards (*d* 1969); two *d*; 2nd, 1971, Shirley Frances Outten; one *s* one *d*. *Educ:* King's Coll., Univ. of London (MScEng; DSc Eng 1987); Columbia Univ., New York. FIMechE, FIMarE; FREng (FEng 1982). Graduate apprentice, CAV Ltd, 1948–50; Marshall Aid scholar, MIT, USA (research into combustion in engines), 1950–52; Ricardo Consulting Engineers, subseq. Ricardo Internat., 1952–92, Director, 1969, Vice-Chm., 1982, Man. Dir, 1989; Man. Dir, 1979–83, Chm., 1984–87, G. Cussons Ltd. President, Instn of Mechanical Engineers, 1988–89 (Vice-Pres, 1981–86, Dep. Pres., 1986–88). *Publications:* numerous articles on diesel engines in learned soc. jls world wide. *Recreations:* folk dancing, photography. *Address:* 303 Upper Shoreham Road, Shoreham-by-Sea, Sussex BN43 5QA. *T:* (01273) 452050.

FRENCH, Sir Christopher (James Saunders), Kt 1979; Judge of the High Court of Justice, Queen's Bench Division, 1982–97 (Family Division, 1979–82); Judge of Employment Appeals Tribunal, 1985–97; *b* 14 Oct. 1925; 2nd *s* of late Rev. Reginald French, MC, MA, Hon. Chaplain to the Queen, and Gertrude Emily Mary (*née* Haworth); *m* 1957, Rosina Philippa, (Wendy) (*d* 2000), *d* of Philip Godfrey Price, Abergavenny; one *s* one *d*. *Educ:* Denstone Coll. (scholar); Brasenose Coll., Oxford (scholar). Coldstream Guards, 1943–48 (Capt.). Called to the Bar, Inner Temple, 1950; QC 1966; Master of the Bench, 1975. Dep. Chm., Bucks QS, 1966–71. Recorder of Coventry, 1971–72; a Recorder, and Hon. Recorder of Coventry, 1972–79; Presiding Judge, SE Circuit, 1982–85. Member: Gen. Council of the Bar, 1963–67; Senate of Inns of Court and Bar, 1978–79; Lord Chancellor's Adv. Cttee on Trng Magistrates, 1974–80. *Publication:* (contrib.) Agency, in Halsbury's Laws of England, 4th edn, 1973. *Recreations:* walking, music, painting, fishing. *Address:* Royal Courts of Justice, Strand, WC2A 2LL. *Clubs:* Garrick, Pilgrims.

FRENCH, David; Chief Executive (formerly Director General), Commonwealth Institute, since 1997; *b* 20 June 1947; *s* of late Captain Godfrey Alexander French, CBE, RN, and Margaret Annis French; *m* 1974, Sarah Anne, *d* of Rt Rev. H. D. Halsey, *qv*; four *s*. *Educ:* Sherborne Sch.; Durham Univ. (BA). MIPD. Nat. Council of Social Service, 1971–74; Hd of Social Services Dept, RNID, 1974–78; Dir of Services, C of E Children's Soc., 1978–87; Dir, Nat. Marriage Guidance Council, then Relate, 1987–95; consultant on family policy, 1995–97. Chairman: London Corrymeela Venture, 1973–76; St Albans Internat. Organ Fest., 1985–87; Twenty First Century Foundn, 1996–. Trustee: Charity Appts, 1984–91; British Empire and Commonwealth Mus., 1999–. Mem. Governing Council, Family Policy Studies Centre, 1989–. Mem., St Albans Cathedral Council, 1996–2000. Liveryman, Glaziers' Co., 1990–. MRSocMed 1988. FRSA 1993. *Recreations:* children, challenging projects. *Address:* 21 Prospect Road, St Albans, Herts AL1 2AT. *T:* (01727) 860520/835201.

FRENCH, Air Vice-Marshal David Rowthorne, CB 1993; MBE 1976; engineering consultant, since 1994; *b* 11 Dec. 1937; *s* of Norman Arthur French and late Edna Mary French (*née* Rowthorne); *m* 1st, 1963, Veronica Margaret Mead (marr. diss. 1982); two *s* one *d*; 2nd, 1984, Philippa Anne Pym, *d* of Sir Alexander Ross; one *s* one *d*. *Educ:* Gosport County Grammar Sch.; RAF Technical Coll., Henlow. CEng, MRAeS 1969. Commnd Engr Br., RAF, 1960; various engrg appts, 1960–69; Sen. Engrg Officer, No 14 Sqn, RAF Bruggen, 1970–71; OC Airframe Systems Sqn, CSDE, RAF Swanton Morley, 1971–72; RAF Staff Coll., Bracknell, 1973; Sen. Engrg Officer, No 54 Sqn, RAF Coltishall, 1974–76; OC Engrg Wg, RAF Lossiemouth, 1976–79; Air Warfare Coll., RAF Cranwell, 1979; SO for Offensive Support Aircraft, HQ Strike Comd, 1980; Dep. Dir of Engrg Policy, MoD, 1981–82; Comd Mech. Engr, HQ RAF Germany, 1983–86; Dir of Policy, Directorate Gen., Defence Quality Assurance, MoD (PE), 1986–87; AO Wales and Stn Comdr, RAF St Athan, 1988–90; Comd Mech. Engr, HQ Strike Comd, 1990–91; AO Maintenance and Chief Exec. Maintenance Gp Defence Support Agency, RAF Support Comd, 1991–94, retd. Chairman: RAF Germany Golf, 1983–86; RAF Support Comd Golf, 1988–90; Capt., RAF Germany Golf Club, 1985–86. *Recreations:* golf, ski-ing, gardening, wine. *Address:* Milestone Piece, Yarmouth Road, Blofield, Norwich, Norfolk NR13 4LQ. *Clubs:* Royal Air Force; Royal Norwich Golf.

FRENCH, Douglas Charles; Chairman, Westminster and City Programmes, since 1997; *b* London, 20 March 1944; *s* of Frederick Emil French and late Charlotte Vera French; *m* 1978, Sue, *y d* of late Philip Arthur Phillips; two *s* one *d*. *Educ:* Glyn Grammar Sch., Epsom; St Catharine's Coll., Cambridge (MA). Called to the Bar, Inner Temple. Exec., then Dir, P. W. Merkle Ltd, 1966–73. Asst to Rt Hon. Sir Geoffrey Howe, Shadow Chancellor, 1976–79; Special Advr to Chancellor of the Exchequer, 1981–83. Contested (C) Sheffield, Attercliffe, 1979; MP (C) Gloucester, 1987–97; contested (C) same seat, 1997. PPS to Minister of State, FCO, 1988–89, ODA, 1989–90, MAFF, 1992–93, DoE, 1993–94, to Sec. of State for the Envmt, 1994–97. Chm., All Party Cttee on Building Socs, 1996–97. Initiated Building Socs (Jt Account Holders) Act 1995, and Building Socs (Distributions) Act 1997. Chm., Bow Gp, 1978–79. *Publications:* articles and reviews. *Recreations:* gardening, renovating period houses, ski-ing, squash. *Address:* 231 Kennington Lane, SE11 5QU. *Clubs:* Royal Automobile, Coningsby.

FRENCH, Philip Neville; writer and broadcaster; Film Critic, The Observer, since 1978; *b* Liverpool, 28 Aug. 1933; *s* of late John and Bessie French; *m* 1957, Kersti Elisabet Molin; three *s*. *Educ:* Bristol Grammar Sch.; Exeter Coll., Oxford (BA Law) (editor, The Isis, 1956); Indiana Univ. Nat. Service, 2nd Lieut Parachute Regt, 1952–54. Reporter, Bristol Evening Post, 1958–59; Producer, BBC N Amer. Service, 1959–61; Talks Producer, BBC

Radio, 1961–67; New Statesman: Theatre Critic, 1967–68; Arts Columnist, 1967–72; Sen. Producer, BBC Radio, 1968–90: editor of The Arts This Week, Critics' Forum and other series, writer-presenter of arts documentaries, Radio 3. Vis. Prof., Univ. of Texas, 1972. Mem., BFI Prodn Bd, 1968–74; Jury Mem., Cannes Film Fest., 1986. *Publications:* Age of Austerity 1945–51 (ed with Michael Sissons), 1963; The Movie Moguls, 1969; Westerns: aspects of a movie genre, 1974, rev. 1977; Three Honest Men: Edmund Wilson, F. R. Leavis, Lionel Trilling, 1980; (ed) The Third Dimension: voices from Radio Three, 1983; (ed with Deac Rossell) The Press: observed and projected, 1991; (ed) Malle on Malle, 1992; (ed with Ken Wlaschin) The Faber Book of Movie Verse, 1993; (with Kersti French) Wild Strawberries, 1995; (with Karl French) Cult Movies, 1999; numerous articles and essays in magazines, newspapers and anthologies. *Recreations:* woolgathering in England, picking wild strawberries in Sweden. *Address:* 62 Dartmouth Park Road, NW5 1SN. *T:* (020) 7485 1711.

FRENCH, Roger; HM Diplomatic Service; Head of Information Management Group, Foreign and Commonwealth Office, since 2001; *b* 3 June 1947; *s* of Alfred Stephen George French and Margaret (*née* Brown); *m* 1969, Angela Cooper; one *s* one *d*. *Educ:* County Grammar Sch., Dagenham. Joined Foreign and Commonwealth Office, 1965; Havana, 1970; Madrid, 1971–73; Puerto Rico, 1973–76; FCO, 1977–80; Second, later First, Sec., (Chancery), Washington, 1980–84; First Sec. (Commercial), Muscat, 1985–88; Dep. Hd of N America Dept, FCO, 1988–92; Dep. Consul-Gen., Milan, 1992–96; Counsellor (Mgt) and Consul-Gen., Washington, 1997–2001; Dep. High Comr, Nigeria, 2001. Commnd Kentucky Col, 1998. *Recreation:* music. *Address:* c/o Foreign and Commonwealth Office, King Charles Street, SW1A 2AH.

FREND, Rev. Prof. William Hugh Clifford, TD 1959 (Clasp, 1966); DD, FRSE, FSA; FBA 1983; Hon. Assistant Priest, Fulbourn group of parishes, since 1990; Professor of Ecclesiastical History, 1969–84, now Professor Emeritus, and Dean of Divinity Faculty, 1972–75, Glasgow University; *b* 11 Jan. 1916; 2nd *s* of late Rev. E. G. C. Frend, Shottermill, Surrey and late Edith (*née* Bacon); *m* 1951, Mary Grace, *d* of late E. A. Crook, FRCS; one *s* one *d*. *Educ:* Fernden Sch.; Haileybury Coll. (Schol.); Keble Coll., Oxford (Schol.). 1st cl. hons Mod. Hist., 1937; Craven Fellow, 1937; DPhil 1940; BD Cantab 1964; DD Oxon 1966. Asst Princ., War Office, 1940; seconded Cabinet Office, 1941; FO (Pol Intell.), 1942; service in N Africa, Italy and Austria, 1943–46 (Gold Cross of Merit with Swords, Polish Forces); Ed. Bd, German Foreign Min. Documents, 1947–51; Res. Fellow, Nottingham Univ., 1951; S. A. Cook Bye-Fellow, 1952, Fellow, 1956–69, Dir Studies, Archaeology, 1961–69, Bye-Fellow, 1997, Gonville and Caius Coll.; University Asst Lectr, 1953, Lectr in Divinity, 1958–69; Birkbeck Lectr in Ecclesiastical History, 1967–68. Lay Mem., CSSB 1970–72. Chm., AUT (Scotland), 1976–78. Pres., Ecclesiastical History Soc., 1972; Vice-Pres., Assoc. internat. d'Etudes patristiques, 1983–87; Président d'Honneur, Internat. Commn for Comparative Study of Ecclesiastical History (CIHEC), 1983 (Vice-Pres. 1975–80, Pres. 1980–83). Assoc. Dir, Egypt Exploration Soc. excavations at Q'asr Ibrim, Nubia, 1963–64; Guest Scholar at Rhodes Univ., 1964 and Peter Ainslie Meml Lecturer; Guest Prof., Univ. of S Africa, 1976; Vis. Prof. of Inter-religious Studies (Walter and Mary Tuohy Chair), John Carroll Univ., Cleveland, 1981; Vis. Fellow, Harvard Univ. Center for Byzantine Studies, Dumbarton Oaks, 1984. Licensed Lay Reader, 1956, Deacon, 1982, Priest, 1983, serving in Aberfoyle parish; Priest-in-Charge, Barnwell with Thurning and Luddington, 1984–90. Mem., Peterborough Diocesan Synod, 1988–90. Editor, Modern Churchman, 1963–82. British Mem., Editl Bd, Coptic Encyclopædia, 1980–91. Commission Queen's Royal Regt (TA), 1947–67. Member: NY Acad. of Scis, 1994; AAAS, 1995. FSA 1952 (Mem. Council, 1992–94); FRHistS 1954; FRSE 1979. Hon. DD Edinburgh, 1974. *Publications:* The Donatist Church, 1952; Martyrdom and Persecution in the Early Church, 1965; The Early Church, 1965; (contrib.) Religion in the Middle East, 1968; The Rise of the Monophysite Movement, 1972; Religion Popular and Unpopular in the Early Christian Centuries, 1976; (contrib.) Cambridge History of Africa, vol. ii, 1978; Town and Country in the Early Christian Centuries, 1980; The Rise of Christianity, 1984; Saints and Sinners in the Early Church, 1985; History and Archaeology in the Study of Early Christianity, 1988; (contrib.) Agostino d'Ippona: quaestiones disputatae, 1989; The Archaeology of Early Christianity: a history, 1996; articles in Jl Theol Studies, Jl Roman Studies, Jl Eccles. History, Jahrbuch für Antike und Christentum, etc. *Recreations:* archæology, gardening, writing, collecting old coins and stamps. *Address:* Clerk's Cottage, Little Wilbraham, Cambridge CB1 5LB. *Club:* Authors' (Dist. Mem., 2000).

FRENK, Prof. Carlos Silvestre, PhD; Professor of Astrophysics, University of Durham, since 1993; *b* 27 Oct. 1951; *s* of Silvestre Frenk and Alicia Mora de Frenk; *m* 1978, Susan Frances Clarke; two *s*. *Educ:* Nat. Autonomous Univ. of Mexico (BSc Theoretical Physics 1976); King's Coll., Cambridge (Math. Tripos Part III 1977); Inst. of Astronomy, Univ. of Cambridge (PhD 1981). Postdoctoral Research Fellow: Dept of Astronomy, Univ. of Calif at Berkeley, 1981–83; Astronomy Centre, Univ. of Sussex, 1983–85; Asst Res. Physicist, Inst. for Theoretical Physics, Univ. of Calif at Santa Barbara, 1984; Lectr in Astronomy, Dept of Physics, 1985–91, Reader in Physics, 1991–93, Univ. of Durham. Occasional broadcasts, radio and television, 1988–. Member: IAU, 1985; AAS, 1993. FRAS 1981. *Publications:* (ed) The Epoch of Galaxy Formation, 1989; (ed) Observational Tests of Cosmological Inflation, 1991; more than 200 scientific papers in prof. jls, incl. Nature, Astrophys. Jl, Astronomical Jl. *Recreations:* literature, ski training. *Address:* Department of Physics, University of Durham, Rochester Building, Science Laboratories, South Road, Durham DH1 3LE. *T:* (0191) 374 2141.

FRERE, Vice-Adm. Sir Richard Tobias, (Sir Toby), KCB 1994; Chairman, Prison Service Pay Review Body, since 2001; Member, Armed Forces Pay Review Body, since 1997; *b* 4 June 1938; *s* of late Alexander Stewart Frere and Patricia Frere; *m* 1968, Jane Barraclough; two *d*. *Educ:* Eton College; Britannia Royal Naval College. Joined RNVR as National Serviceman; transf. RN 1956; commissioned 1958; submarines 1960; served Canada, 1961–62, Australia, 1966–67, 1973; commanded HM Submarines Andrew, Odin and Revenge and Frigate HMS Brazen. JSSC, Canberra, 1973; RCDS London, 1982; Dir Gen. Fleet Support, Policy and Services, 1988–91; Flag Officer Submarines, and Comdr Submarines Eastern Atlantic, 1991–93; Chief of Fleet Support, 1994–97. *Recreation:* sailing. *Address:* c/o Naval Secretary, Victory Building, HM Naval Base, Portsmouth PO1 5AB. *Clubs:* Garrick, Naval, MCC.

FRERE, Prof. Sheppard Sunderland, CBE 1976; FSA 1944; FBA 1971; Professor of the Archæology of the Roman Empire, and Fellow of All Souls College, Oxford University, 1966–83, now Professor Emeritus and Emeritus Fellow; *b* 23 Aug. 1916; *e s* of late N. G. Frere, CMG; *m* 1961, Janet Cecily Hoare; one *s* one *d*. *Educ:* Lancing Coll.; Magdalene Coll., Cambridge. BA 1938, MA 1944, LittD 1976, DLitt 1977. Master, Epsom Coll., 1938–40. National Fire Service, 1940–45. Master, Lancing Coll., 1945–54; Lecturer in Archæology, Manchester Univ., 1954–55; Reader in Archæology of the Roman Provinces, London Univ. Inst. of Archæology, 1955–62; Prof. of the Archæology of the Roman Provinces, London Univ., 1963–66. Dir, Canterbury Excavations, 1946–60; Dir, Verulamium Excavations, 1955–61. Vice-Pres., Soc. of Antiquaries, 1962–66; President: Oxford Architectural and Historical Soc., 1972–80; Royal Archæological Inst., 1978–81; Soc. for Promotion of Roman Studies, 1983–86. Hon. Corr. Mem. German Archæological Inst., 1964, Fellow, 1967; Member: Royal Commn on Hist. Monuments (England), 1966–83; Ancient Monuments Board (England), 1966–82. Hon. LittD: Leeds, 1977; Leicester, 1983; Kent, 1985. Gold Medal, Soc. of Antiquaries, 1989. Editor, Britannia, 1969–79. *Publications:* (ed) Problems of the Iron Age in Southern Britain, 1961; Britannia, a history of Roman Britain, 1967, 4th edn 1999; Verulamium Excavations, vol. I, 1972, vol. II, 1983, vol. III, 1984; Excavations on the Roman and Medieval Defences of Canterbury, 1982; Excavations at Canterbury, vol. VII, 1983; (with J. K. St Joseph) Roman Britain from the Air, 1983; (with F. A. Lepper) Trajan's Column, 1988; (with J. J. Wilkes) Strageath: excavations within the Roman fort, 1989; (ed with R. Tomlin) The Roman Inscriptions of Britain, vol. II, fasc. 1, 1990, fascs 2–3, 1991, fasc. 4, 1992, fasc. 5, 1993, fasc. 6, 1994, fascs 7–8, and Epigraphic Indexes, 1995; papers in learned jls. *Recreation:* gardening. *Address:* Netherfield House, Marcham, Abingdon, Oxon OX13 6NP.

FRERE, Vice-Adm. Sir Toby; *see* Frere, Vice-Adm. Sir R. T.

FRESHWATER, Prof. Donald Cole, FREng; Professor, Louisiana State University, 1986–96; Professor Emeritus, University of Technology, Loughborough, 1987; *b* 21 April 1924; *s* of Thomas and Ethel May Freshwater; *m* 1948, Margaret D. Worrall (marr. diss. 1977); one *s* three *d*; *m* 1980, Eleanor M. Lancashire (*née* Tether). *Educ:* Brewood Grammar Sch.; Birmingham Univ. (BSc, PhD); Sheffield Univ.; Loughborough Coll. (DLC). Fuel Engineer, Min. of Fuel and Power, 1944; Chemical Engr: APV Co. Ltd, 1948; Midland Tar Distillers Co. Ltd, 1950; Lectr, Dept of Chem. Engrg, Univ. of Birmingham, 1952–57; Loughborough College (later University) of Technology: Hd, Dept of Chem. Engrg, 1957–86; Dean of Pure and Applied Science, 1982–85; Sen. Pro Vice-Chancellor, 1972–74. Visiting Professor: Univ. of Delaware, USA, 1962; Georgia Inst. of Technology, 1980–81. Chm., Chem. Engrg Gp, Soc. of Chemical Industry, 1973–75; Mem. Council, IChemE, 1982–87 (Vice Pres., 1985–87). FREng (FEng 1986). Hon. DSc Loughborough, 1989. Dow Award for Excellence in Teaching, 1996; Council Medal, IChemE, 1998. *Publications:* Chemical Engineering Data Book, 1959; People, Pipes & Processes: a history of chemical engineering, 1997; numerous papers on mass transfer, particle technology and educn in chem. engrg jls. *Recreations:* sailing, collecting watercolours. *Address:* 131 Rothley Road, Mountsorrel, Loughborough LE12 7JT. *Clubs:* Athenæum; Mountsorrel Working Men's.

FRETWELL, Elizabeth Drina, OBE 1977; professional adjudicator and vocal coach, retired 1998; operatic and dramatic soprano; *b* Melbourne, Australia, 13 Aug. 1920; *m* 1958, Robert Simmons; one *s* one *d*. *Educ:* privately. Joined National Theatre, Melbourne, 1950; came to Britain, 1955; joined Sadler's Wells, 1956; Australia, Elizabethan Opera Co., 1963; tour of W Germany, 1963; USA, Canada and Covent Garden, 1964; tour of Europe, 1965; guest soprano with Cape Town and Durban Opera Cos, South Africa, 1970; Australian Opera, 1970–87. Rôles include Violetta in La Traviata, Leonora in Fidelio, Ariadne in Ariadne auf Naxos, Senta in The Flying Dutchman, Minnie in The Girl of the Golden West, Leonora in Il Trovatore, Aida, Ellen Orford in Peter Grimes, Leonora in Forza del Destino, Alice Ford in Falstaff, Amelia in Masked Ball, Georgetta in Il Tabarro, opening season of Sydney Opera Hse, 1973. Has sung in BBC Promenade Concerts and on TV. Mem., music bd, Opera Foundn Australia, 1982. *Recreation:* rose-growing. *Address:* 47 Kananook Avenue, Bayview, NSW 2104, Australia.

FRETWELL, Sir (Major) John (Emsley), GCMG 1987 (KCMG 1982; CMG 1975); HM Diplomatic Service, retired; Political Director and Deputy to the Permanent Under-Secretary of State, Foreign and Commonwealth Office, 1987–90; *b* 15 June 1930; *s* of late Francis Thomas and Dorothy Fretwell; *m* 1959, Mary Ellen Eugenie Dubois (OBE 2001); one *s* one *d*. *Educ:* Chesterfield Grammar Sch.; Lausanne Univ.; King's Coll., Cambridge (MA). HM Forces, 1948–50. Diplomatic Service, 1953; 3rd Sec., Hong Kong, 1954–55; 2nd Sec., Peking, 1955–57; FO, 1957–59; 1st Sec., Moscow, 1959–62; FO, 1962–67; 1st Sec. (Commercial), Washington, 1967–70; Commercial Counsellor, Warsaw, 1971–73; Head of European Integration Dept (Internal), FCO, 1973–76; Asst Under-Sec. of State, FCO, 1976–79; Minister, Washington, 1980–81; Ambassador to France, 1982–87. Specialist Advr, H of L, 1992–93; Specialist Assessor, HEFC, 1995–96. Mem., Council of Lloyd's, 1991–92. Chm., Franco-British Soc., 1995–. *Recreations:* ski-ing, walking, wine. *Club:* Brooks's.

FREUD, Sir Clement (Raphael), Kt 1987; writer, broadcaster, caterer; *b* 24 April 1924; *s* of late Ernst and Lucie Freud; *m* 1950, June Beatrice, (Jill), 2nd *d* of H. W. Flewett, MA; three *s* two *d*. Apprenticed, Dorchester Hotel, London. Served War, Royal Ulster Rifles; Liaison Officer, Nuremberg war crimes trials, 1946. Trained, Martinez Hotel, Cannes. Proprietor, Royal Court Theatre Club, 1952–62. Sports writer, Observer, 1956–64; Cookery Editor: Time and Tide, 1961–63; Observer Magazine, 1964–68; Daily Telegraph Magazine, 1968–. Sports Columnist, Sun, 1964–69; Columnist: Sunday Telegraph, 1963–65; News of the World, 1965; Financial Times, 1964–; Daily Express, 1973–75; Saga magazine, 1987–; Radio Times, 1992–; Independent, 1997–; Times Diarist, 1988–98, Columnist, 1992–96. Consultant: Intercity, 1990–; Rail Gourmet, 1998–; Compass Gp, 1999–. Contested (L) Cambridgeshire NE, 1987. MP (L): Isle of Ely, July 1973–1983; Cambridgeshire NE, 1983–87. Liberal spokesman on education, the arts and broadcasting; sponsor, Official Information Bill. Chm., Standing Cttee, Liberal Party, 1982–86. Rector, Univ. of Dundee, 1974–80. Pres., Down's Children Assoc., 1988–. £5,000 class winner, Daily Mail London-NY air race, 1969; line honours, Cape Town-Rio yacht race, 1971. Award winning petfood commercial: San Francisco, Tokyo, Berlin, 1967. BBC (sound) Just a Minute, 1968–. MUniv Open, 1989. *Publications:* Grimble, 1968; Grimble at Christmas, 1973; Freud on Food, 1978; Clicking Vicky, 1980; The Book of Hangovers, 1981; Below the Belt, 1983; No-one Else has Complained, 1988; The Gourmet's Tour of Great Britain and Ireland, 1989; contributor to, New Yorker, etc (formerly to Punch). *Recreations:* racing, backgammon, pétanque. *Address:* 14 York House, Upper Montagu Street, W1H 1FR. *T:* (020) 7724 5432; Westons, Walberswick, Suffolk IP18 6UH. *Address:* Casa de Colina, Praia da Luz, Algarve. *Clubs:* MCC, Lord's Taverners', Groucho.

See also R. W. A. Curtis, L. Freud, M. R. Freud.

FREUD, Elisabeth; *see* Murdoch, E.

FREUD, Lucian, OM 1993; CH 1983; painter; *b* 8 Dec. 1922; *s* of late Ernst and Lucie Freud; *m* 1st, 1948, Kathleen Garman (marr. diss. 1952), *d* of Jacob Epstein; two *d*; 2nd, 1953, Lady Caroline Maureen Blackwood (marr. diss. 1957; she *d* 1996), *d* of 4th Marquess of Dufferin and Ava. *Educ:* Central Sch. of Art; East Anglian Sch. of Painting and Drawing. Worked on merchant ship SS Baltrover as ordinary seaman, 1942. Teacher, Slade Sch. of Art, 1948–58; Vis. Asst, Norwich Sch. of Art, 1964–65. Painted mostly in France and Greece, 1946–48; Cyclamen bathroom, 1959, Thornhill bedroom, Chatsworth House, Derbyshire. Hon. Mem., Amer. Acad. and Inst. of Arts and Letters, 1988. *Exhibitions:* Lefevre Gall., 1944, 1946; London Gall., 1947, 1948; British Council and Galérie René Drouin, Paris, 1948; Hanover Gall., 1950, 1952; British Council and Vancouver Art Gall.,

1951; British Council, Venice Biennale, 1954; Marlborough Fine Art, 1958, 1963, 1968; Anthony d'Offay, 1972, 1978 (subseq. Davis & Long, NY), 1982; Nishimura Gall., Tokyo, 1979, 1991; Thos Agnew & Sons, 1983; Scottish Nat. Gall. of Modern Art, 1988; Berggruen Gall., Paris, 1990; Saatchi Collection, 1990; Thomas Gibson Fine Art Ltd, 1991; Palazzo Ruspoli, Rome, 1991; Castello Sforzesca, Milan, 1991; Art Gall. of NSW, 1992; Tochigi Prefectural Mus. of Fine Arts, Otani Meml Art Mus., Nishinomiya, and Setaguya Art Museum, Tokyo, Japan, 1992; Whitechapel Art Gall., 1993; Metropolitan Mus. of Art, New York, 1993; Muses Nacional Centro de Arte Reina Sofia, Madrid, 1994; Astrup Fearnley Museet for Moderne Kunst, Oslo, 1994; Dulwich Picture Gall., 1994; Fondation Maeght, St Paul de Vence, 1995; Abbot Hall Art Gall., Kendal, 1996; Acquavella Contemp. Art, NY, 1996; Tel Aviv Mus. of Art, 1996; Nat. Gall. of Scotland, 1997; Tate Gall., 1998; Yale Center for British Art, 1999; Nat. Gall., 2000; *retrospectives:* Hayward Gall., 1974 (subseq. Bristol, Birmingham and Leeds), 1988 (also Washington, Paris and Berlin, 1987–88); Works on Paper, Ashmolean Mus., Oxford, 1988 (subseq. other towns in provinces and in USA); Tate Gall., Liverpool, 1992. *Works included in public collections:* London: Tate Gall.; Nat. Portrait Gall.; V & A Museum; Arts Council of GB; British Council; British Mus.; DoE; provinces: Cecil Higgins Museum, Bedford; Fitzwilliam Mus., Cambridge; Nat. Mus. of Wales, Cardiff; Scottish Nat. Gall. of Mod. Art, Edinburgh; Hartlepool Art Gall.; Walker Art Gall., Liverpool; Liverpool Univ.; City Art Gall. and Whitworth Gall., Manchester; Ashmolean Mus. of Art, Oxford; Harris Mus. and Art Gall., Preston; Rochdale Art Gall.; Southampton Art Gall.; Australia: Queensland Art Gall., Brisbane; Art Gall. of S Australia, Adelaide; Art Gall. of WA, Perth; France: Musée National d'Art Moderne, Centre Georges Pompidou, Paris; Beaverbrook Foundn, Fredericton, New Brunswick; USA: Art Inst. of Chicago; Mus. of Mod. Art, NY; Cleveland Mus. of Art, Ohio; Mus. of Art, Carnegie Inst., Pittsburgh; Achenbach Foundn for Graphic Arts and Fine Arts Mus. of San Francisco; Art Mus., St Louis; Hirshhorn Musum and Sculpture Garden, Smithsonian Instn, Washington. Rubenspreis, City of Siegen, 1997. *Relevant publications:* Lucian Freud, by Lawrence Gowing, 1982; Lucian Freud, Paintings, by Robert Hughes, 1987; Lucian Freud, works on paper, by Nicholas Penney and Robert Flynn Johnson, 1988; The Etchings of Lucian Freud: a catalogue raisonné, by Craig Hartley, 1995; Lucian Freud, by Bruce Bernard, 1996. *Address:* c/o Diana Rawstron, Goodman Derrick, 90 Fetter Lane, EC4A 1EQ.

See also Sir C. R. Freud.

FREUD, Matthew Rupert; Chairman, Freud Communications (formerly Freud Associates), since 1985; *b* 2 Nov. 1963; *s* of Sir Clement Raphael Freud, *qv*; *m* 1991, Caroline Victoria Hutton (marr. diss. 1999); two *s*; *m* 2001, Elizabeth Murdoch, *qv*; one *d*. *Educ:* St Anthony's, Westminster. Press Officer, RCA Records, 1983–85. Dir Oxygen plc, 2000–. *Recreation:* children. *Address:* China Corner, Blenheim, Oxon OX20 1PR; (office) 19/21 Mortimer Street, W1N 8DX. *T:* (020) 7291 6400. *Club:* Groucho.

FREYBERG, family name of **Baron Freyberg**.

FREYBERG, 3rd Baron *cr* 1951, of Wellington, New Zealand and of Munstead, Co. Surrey; **Valerian Bernard Freyberg;** *b* 15 Dec. 1970; *o s* of 2nd Baron Freyberg, OBE, MC, and of Ivry Perronelle Katharine, *d* of Cyril Harrower Guild, Aspall Hall, Debenham, Suffolk; *S* father, 1993. *Educ:* Eton Coll.; Camberwell Coll. of Art. Elected Mem., H of L, 1999. Mem., Design Council, 2001–. *Address:* Munstead House, Godalming, Surrey GU8 4AR.

FRICKER, His Honour (Anthony) Nigel; QC 1977; Board Member, Children and Family Court Advisory and Support Service, since 2001; a Circuit Judge, 1984–2001; *b* 7 July 1937; *s* of late Dr William Shapland Fricker and of Margaret Fricker; *m* 1960, Marilyn Ann, *d* of late A. L. Martin, Pa, USA; one *s* two *d*. *Educ:* King's School, Chester; Liverpool Univ. (LLB 1958). President of Guild of Undergraduates, Liverpool Univ., 1958–59. Called to Bar, Gray's Inn, 1960. Conf. Leader, Ford Motor Co. of Australia, Melbourne, 1960–61. Recorder, Crown Court, 1975–84; Prosecuting Counsel to DHSS, Wales and Chester Circuit, 1975–77; an asst comr, Boundary Commn for Wales, 1981–84. Member: Bar Council, 1966–70; Senate and Bar Council, 1975–78; County Court Rule Cttee, 1988–92; Family Proceedings Rule Cttee, 1997–2001. Pres., Council of HM Circuit Judges, 1997. Fellow, Internat. Acad. of Trial Lawyers, 1979–. Mem. Court: Liverpool Univ., 1977–; York Univ., 1984–. Confrérie des Chevaliers du Tastevin. *Publications:* (jtly) Family Courts: Emergency Remedies and Procedures, 1990, 3rd edn (loose-leaf) as Emergency Remedies in the Family Courts (Gen. Ed., 1990–99, Consulting Ed., 1999–); (with David Bean) Enforcement of Injunctions and Undertakings, 1991; (consulting ed.) The Family Court Practice, (annually) 1993–; contrib. legal periodicals in UK and USA (Family and Conciliation Courts Rev.). *Address:* CAFCASS, 6th Floor, 16 Palace Street, SW1E 5LX. *T:* (020) 7210 4400, *Fax:* (020) 7210 4422; Farrar's Building, Temple, EC4Y 7BD.

FRICKER, Rt Rev. Joachim Carl; a Suffragan Bishop of Toronto (Bishop of Credit Valley), 1985–95; *b* Zweibrucken, Germany, 1 Dec. 1927; *s* of Carl and Caroline Fricker; *m* 1952, Shirley Joan (*née* Gill); three *s* two *d*. *Educ:* Niagara Falls Public Schools; Univ. of Western Ontario (BA); Huron College (LTh). Ordained deacon and priest, 1952; Rector: St Augustine's, Hamilton, 1952–59; St David's, Welland, 1959–65; St James, Dundas, 1965–73; Canon of Christ's Church Cathedral, Hamilton, 1964–73; Dean of Diocese of Niagara and Rector, Christ's Church Cathedral, 1973–85. Chm., Nat. Doctrine and Worship Cttee (Anglican Church of Canada), 1989–92. Hon. DD: Huron Coll., 1974; Trinity Coll., 1987; Hon. DSL, Wycliffe Coll., 1987. *Recreations:* theatre, gardening, reading, walking. *Address:* 233 Oak Crescent, Burlington, ON L7L 1H3, Canada.

FRIEDBERGER, Maj.-Gen. John Peter William, CB 1991; CBE 1986 (MBE 1975); Chief Executive, British Helicopter Advisory Board, since 1992; *b* 27 May 1937; *s* of late Brig. John Cameron Friedberger, DSO, DL and Phyllis Grace Friedberger, JP; *m* 1966, Joanna Mary, *d* of Andrew Thorne, ERD; one *s* two *d*. *Educ:* Red House School, York; Wellington College; RMA Sandhurst. Commissioned, 10th Royal Hussars (PWO), 1956; seconded to Northern Frontier Regt, Sultan's Armed Forces, Oman, 1961–63; Australian Army Staff Coll., 1969; CO The Royal Hussars (PWO), 1975–78; RCDS, 1978–79; Comdr, Royal Brunei Armed Forces, 1982–86; ACOS, HQ Northern Army Group, 1986–88; Administrator, Sovereign Base Areas and Commander, British Forces, Cyprus, 1988–90. Hon. Colonel: The Royal Hussars (PWO), 1991–92; The King's Royal Hussars, 1992–97. FRGS 1990; ARAeS, 1992; Dato, DPKT (Negara Brunei Darussalam) 1984. *Recreation:* travel. *Address:* c/o Home HQ, The King's Royal Hussars, Peninsula Barracks, Winchester, Hants SO23 8TS. *Club:* Cavalry and Guards.

FRIEDLANDER, Frederick Gerard, (Friedrich Gerhart), PhD; FRS 1980; Reader Emeritus, University of Cambridge, since 1982; Hon. Research Fellow, Department of Mathematics, University College London; *b* Vienna, 25 Dec. 1917. *Educ:* Univ. of Cambridge (BA, PhD). Fellow of Trinity Coll., Cambridge, 1940; Temporary Experimental Officer, Admiralty, 1943; Faculty Asst Lectr, Cambridge, 1945; Lecturer: Univ. of Manchester, 1946; Univ. of Cambridge, 1954; Fellow of St John's Coll., Cambridge, 1961; Fellow of Wolfson Coll., Cambridge, 1968; Reader in Partial Differential Equations, Univ. of Cambridge, 1979. *Publications:* Sound Pulses, 1958; The Wave Equation on a Curved Space-Time, 1975; Introduction to the Theory of Distributions, 1982, 2nd edn (with M. Joshi), 1999; papers in mathematical jls. *Address:* 28 Greenlands, Cambridge CB2 2QY.

FRIEDMAN, David Peter; QC 1990; a Recorder, since 1998; *b* 1 June 1944; *s* of Wilfred Emanuel Friedman and Rosa Lees; *m* 1972, Sara Geraldine Linton. *Educ:* Tiffin Boys' School; Lincoln College, Oxford (BCL, MA). Called to the Bar, Inner Temple, 1968, Bencher, 1999. *Recreations:* good food (cooked by others), reading. *Address:* 4 Pump Court, Temple, EC4Y 7AN. *T:* (020) 7842 5555. *Club:* Lansdowne.

FRIEDMAN, Prof. Jerome Isaac, PhD; Professor of Physics, Massachusetts Institute of Technology, since 1967; *b* 28 March 1930; *m* Tania Baranovsky Friedman; two *s* two *d*. *Educ:* Univ. of Chicago (AB 1950; MS 1953; PhD Physics 1956). Research associate; Univ. of Chicago, 1956–57; Stanford Univ., 1957–60; MIT: Asst Prof. and Associate Prof., 1960–67; Dir, Nuclear Science Lab., 1980–83; Head of Dept of Physics, 1983–88. Fellow: Amer. Phys. Soc.; Nat. Acad. of Scis; Amer. Acad. of Arts and Scis. (jtly) W. H. K. Panofsky Prize for Physics, 1989; (jtly) Nobel Prize for Physics, 1990. *Publications:* numerous papers in learned jls on particle physics, esp. the division of protons and neutrons into smaller particles, leading to different types of quarks. *Address:* Department of Physics, Massachusetts Institute of Technology, Cambridge, MA 02139, USA.

FRIEDMAN, Prof. Milton, PhD; Economist, USA; Senior Research Fellow, Hoover Institution, Stanford University, since 1976; Professor Emeritus of Economics, University of Chicago, since 1982 (Professor of Economics, 1948–82); Member of Research Staff, National Bureau of Economic Research, 1948–81; Economic Columnist, Newsweek, 1966–84; *b* Brooklyn, New York, 31 July 1912; *s* of Jeno Saul and Sarah E. Friedman; *m* 1938, Rose Director; one *s* one *d*. *Educ:* Rutgers (AB), Chicago (AM), and Columbia (PhD) Univs. Associate Economist, Natural Resources Cttee, Washington, 1935–37; Nat. Bureau of Economic Research, New York, 1937–45 (on leave 1940–45). During 1941–45: Principal Economist, Tax Research Div., US Treasury Dept, 1941–43; Associate Dir, Statistical Research Gp, Div. of War Research, Columbia Univ., 1943–45. Fulbright Lecturer, Cambridge Univ., 1953–54; Vis. Prof., Econs, Columbia Univ., 1964–65, etc. Member: President's Commn on an All-Volunteer Armed Force, 1969–70; Commn on White House Fellows, 1971–73. Mem. Bd of Editors, Econometrica, 1957–65; Pres., Amer. Economic Assoc., 1967; Pres., Mont Pelerin Soc., 1970–72. John Bates Clark Medal, Amer. Econ. Assoc., 1951; Member various societies, etc., incl. Royal Economic Soc. (GB). Fellowships and awards, in USA. Holds several Hon. doctorates. Nobel Memorial Prize for Economics, 1976; Nat. Medal of Sci., USA, 1988. Grand Cordon, Sacred Treasure (Japan), 1986; US Presidential Medal of Freedom, 1988. *Publications:* Income from Independent Professional Practice (with Simon Kuznets), 1946; Sampling Inspection (with others), 1948; Essays in Positive Economics, 1953; (ed) Studies in the Quantity Theory of Money, 1956; A Theory of the Consumption Function, 1957; A Program for Monetary Stability, 1960; Capitalism and Freedom, 1962; Price Theory: a Provisional Text, 1962; A Monetary History of the United States 1867–1960 (with Anna J. Schwartz), 1963; Inflation: Causes and Consequences, 1963; The Balance of Payments: Free versus Flexible Exchange Rates (with Robert V. Roosa), 1967; Dollars and Deficits, 1968; Optimum Quantity of Money and Other Essays, 1969; Monetary vs Fiscal Policy (with Walter W. Heller), 1969; Monetary Statistics of the United States (with Anna J. Schwartz), 1970; A Theoretical Framework for Monetary Analysis, 1971; Social Security: Universal or Selective? (with Wilbur J. Cohen), 1972; An Economist's Protest, 1972; Money and Economic Development, 1973; There's No Such Thing as a Free Lunch, 1975; Price Theory, 1976; Free to Choose (with Rose Friedman), 1980; Monetary Trends in the United States and the United Kingdom (with Anna J. Schwartz), 1982; Bright Promises, Dismal Performance, 1983; (with Rose Friedman) Tyranny of the Status Quo, 1984; Money Mischief, 1992; (with Thomas S. Szasz) Friedman and Szasz on Liberty and Drugs, 1992; (with Rose Friedman) Two Lucky People: memoirs, 1998. *Recreations:* tennis, carpentry. *Address:* Hoover Institution, Stanford, CA 94305–6010, USA. *Club:* Quadrangle (Chicago).

FRIEDMANN, Jacques-Henri; Commandeur, Légion d'Honneur, 1996; Chevalier, Ordre du Mérite, 1970; Chairman, Planning Committee, Musée du Quai Branly; *b* Paris, 15 Oct. 1932; *s* of André Friedmann and Marie-Louise Bleiweiss; *m* 1962, Cécile Fleur; two *s* one *d*. *Educ:* Inst. d'Etudes Politiques, Paris (law degree). Student, Ecole Nat. d'Admin, 1957–58; Inspector of Finance, 1959; Lectr, Inst. d'Etudes Politiques, 1964–68; Special Asst 1964, Tech. Advr 1965–66, Deptl Staff of Valéry Giscard d'Estaing, Minister of Finance; Special Asst, Gen Directorate of Domestic Trade and Pricing, 1966; Actg Dep. Sec. Gen., Interministerial Cttee on Europ. Econ. Co-op., 1966–67; Hd, Finance Dept, French Planning Org., 1967–68; Chief Executive Secretary: to Jacques Chirac, Sec. of State for Econ. Affairs and Finance, 1969–70, and Minister responsible for liaison with Parlt, 1971; Hd of Dept of Gen. Inspectorate of Finances and of Central Dept of Gen. Inspectorate for the Nat. Economy, 1971–72; Advr on Econ. and Financial Affairs to Pierre Messmer, Prime Minister, then Chief Exec. Sec., 1972–74; Special Asst to Jacques Chirac, Prime Minister, 1974; Chm., Co. Générale Maritime, 1974–82; Inspector Gen. of Finance, 1980; Chm. and Man Dir, Co. Parisienne de Chauffage Urbaine, 1983–87; Special Asst to Edouard Balladur, Minister of Econ. Affairs, Finance and Privatisation, 1986–87; Chairman: Caisse d'Epargne de Paris, 1985–95; Air France, 1987–88; SAGI, 1989–93; UAP, 1993–97; Supervisory Bd, AXA, 1997–2000. *Address:* 80 avenue de Bretenil, 75015 Paris, France. *T:* 0147340459; 7 rue Anguste Vacquerie, 75016 Paris, France. *T:* 0153574123.

FRIEDMANN, Prof. Peter Simon, MD; FRCP, FMedSci; Professor of Dermatology, University of Southampton, since 1998; *b* 18 Nov. 1943; *s* of Charles Aubrey Friedmann and Atersia Friedmann (*née* Le Roux); *m* 1967, Bridget Ann Harding; one *s* one *d*. *Educ:* Trinity Coll., Cambridge (BA 1966); University Coll. Hosp., London (MB BChir 1969; MD 1977). FRCP 1984. Wellcome Trng Fellow, RCS, 1973–77; University of Newcastle upon Tyne: Lectr in Dermatology, 1977–81; Sen. Lectr, 1981–90; University of Liverpool: Prof. of Dermatology, 1990–97; Actg Hd, Dept of Medicine, 1996–97. Hon. Res. Fellow, Tufts Univ., Boston, 1985–86. Med. Advr to All-Party Parly Gp on Skin, 1996–. Chm., Scientific Cttee, Nat. Eczema Soc., 1995–. Founder FMedSci 1998. *Publications:* contrib. book chapters; numerous scientific papers. *Recreations:* music (playing flute), bird-watching, tennis, ski-ing. *Address:* Dermatology Unit, Southampton General Hospital, Tremona Road, Southampton SO16 6YD. *T:* (023) 8079 6142.

FRIEL, Brian; writer; *b* 9 Jan. 1929; *s* of Patrick Friel and Christina Friel (*née* MacLoone); *m* 1954, Anne Morrison; one *s* four *d*. *Educ:* St Columb's Coll., Derry; St Patrick's Coll., Maynooth; St Joseph's Trng Coll., Belfast. Taught in various schools, 1950–60; writing full-time from 1960. Lived in Minnesota during first season of Tyrone Guthrie Theater, Minneapolis. Member: Irish Acad. of Letters, 1972; Aosdana, 1983–. FRSL 1998. Hon. DLitt: Chicago, 1979; NUI, 1983; NUU, 1986. *Publications: collected stories:* The Saucer of Larks, 1962; The Gold in the Sea, 1966; *plays:* Philadelphia, Here I Come!, 1965; The Loves of Cass McGuire, 1967; Lovers, 1968; The Mundy Scheme, 1969; Crystal and Fox, 1970; The Gentle Island, 1971; The Freedom of the City, 1973; Volunteers, 1975; Living

Quarters, 1976; Aristocrats, 1979; Faith Healer, 1979; Translations, 1981 (Ewart-Biggs Meml Prize, British Theatre Assoc. Award); (trans.) Three Sisters, 1981; The Communication Cord, 1983; (trans.) Fathers and Sons, 1987; Making History, 1988; London Vertigo, 1989; Dancing at Lughnasa, 1990; A Month in the Country, 1990; Wonderful Tennessee, 1993; Molly Sweeney, 1995; Give Me Your Answer, Do!, 1997. *Recreations:* reading, trout-fishing, slow tennis. *Address:* Drumaweir House, Greencastle, Co. Donegal, Ireland.

FRIEL, Michael John; District Judge (Magistrates' Courts) (formerly Stipendiary Magistrate), Derbyshire, since 1997; *b* 3 Sept. 1942; *s* of Hugh and Madeline Friel; *m* 1980, Elizabeth Mary Jenkins; two *s* one *d*. *Educ:* Leeds Univ. (LLB). Admitted solicitor, 1969; Nottingham Magistrates' Court: Court Clerk, 1965–71; Dep. Clerk to the Justices, 1972–73; Clerk to the Justices: Isle of Ely, Cambs, 1973–76; Mansfield, Notts, 1976–97; also Clerk to: Worksop and E Retford Justices, 1977–97; Newark and Southwell Justices, 1986–97; Nottingham Justices, 1996–97. *Recreations:* sports (tennis, cricket, football, squash, ski-ing). *Address:* The Court House, West Bars, Chesterfield S40 1AE. *T:* (01246) 278171.

FRIEND, Rev. Frederick James; Director, Scholarly Communication, University College London, since 1997 (Librarian, 1982–97); *b* 7 April 1941; *s* of James Frederick Friend and Emily Mary Friend (*née* Giddens); *m* 1969, Margaret Rusholme; one *s* one *d*. *Educ:* Dover Grammar Sch. for Boys; King's Coll., London (BA 1963); University Coll. London (DipLib 1965); Oak Hill Coll. Asst Librarian, Manchester Univ. Library, 1965–71; Sub-Librarian, Leeds Univ., 1971–76; Dep. Librarian, Nottingham Univ., 1976–78; Librarian, Essex Univ., 1978–82. Mem. Council, 1985–88, Chm. Scholarly Communication Cttee, 1996–, SCONUL; Treas., Consortium of Univ. Res. Libraries, 1996–98. Deacon 1982, priest 1983; NSM, Dio. Oxford, 1982–. *Publications:* various articles in learned jls. *Recreations:* walking the dogs, prayer. *Address:* The Chimes, Cryers Hill Road, High Wycombe, Bucks HP15 6JS.

FRIEND, John Richard, DM; FRCOG; Consultant Obstetrician and Gynaecologist, Plymouth General Hospital, since 1973 (Medical Director, 1999–2000); Senior Vice President, Royal College of Obstetricians and Gynaecologists, 1995–98; *b* 31 Jan. 1937; *s* of George Chamings Friend and Gwendoline Mary Lewis Friend; *m* 1971, Diana Margaret Fryer; one *s* two *d* (incl. twin *s* and *d*). *Educ:* St Edward's Sch. (schol.); St Edmund Hall, Oxford (MA; BM, BCh, DM); St Thomas' Hosp. MRCOG 1968, FRCOG 1987. Queen Charlotte's Hosp. and Chelsea Hosp., 1965–66; MRC Fellow, 1969–70; Hammersmith Hosp., 1966–67; KCH, 1967–73. Hon. Consultant Gynaecologist, RN, 1987–. *Publications:* articles in jls. *Recreations:* golf, tennis. *Address:* Holme House, Stoke Hill Lane, Crapstone, Yelverton, Devon PL20 7PP. *T:* (01822) 852527. *Club:* Royal Western Yacht.

FRIEND, Lionel; conductor; *b* 13 March 1945; *s* of Moya and Norman A. C. Friend; *m* 1969, Jane Hyland; one *s* two *d*. *Educ:* Royal Grammar School, High Wycombe; Royal College of Music; London Opera Centre. LRAM; ARCM. Glyndebourne Opera, 1969–72; Welsh National Opera, 1969–72; Kapellmeister, Staatstheater, Kassel, Germany, 1972–75; Staff Conductor, ENO, 1978–89; Musical Dir, New Sussex Opera, 1989–96. Guest Conductor: BBC orchestras; Philharmonia; Royal Ballet; Opéra National, Brussels; State Symphony, Hungary; Nash Ensemble, etc. *Recreations:* reading, theatre. *Address:* 136 Rosendale Road, SE21 8LG. *T:* (020) 8761 7845.

FRIEND, Prof. Peter John, MD; FRCS; Professor of Transplantation, University of Oxford, since 1999; Fellow, Green College, Oxford, since 1999; *b* 5 Jan. 1954; *s* of John Friend and (Dorothy) Jean Friend (*née* Brown). *Educ:* Rugby Sch.; Magdalene Coll., Cambridge (MA, MB, BChir, MD); St Thomas's Hosp. Med. Sch. FRCS 1983. St Thomas' Hosp., London, W Norwich Hosp., Bedford Gen. Hosp., Addenbrooke's Hosp., Cambridge, 1978–88; Vis. Asst Prof., Indiana Univ., USA, 1988–89; Lectr in Surgery, Univ. of Cambridge and Hon. Consultant Surgeon, Addenbrooke's Hosp., 1989–99; Fellow, Magdalene Coll., Cambridge, 1993–99. *Publications:* papers on transplantation and surgery in scientific jls. *Address:* Nuffield Department of Surgery, University of Oxford, John Radcliffe Hospital, Headington, Oxford OX3 9DU.

FRIEND, Dame Phyllis (Muriel), DBE 1980 (CBE 1972); Chief Nursing Officer, Department of Health and Social Security, 1972–82; *b* 28 Sept. 1922; *d* of late Richard Edward Friend. *Educ:* Herts and Essex High Sch., Bishop's Stortford; The London Hospital (SRN); Royal College of Nursing (RNT). Dep. Matron, St George's Hospital, 1956–59; Dep. Matron, 1959–61, Matron, 1961–68, Chief Nursing Officer 1969–72, The London Hospital. *Address:* Barnmead, Start Hill, Bishop's Stortford, Herts CM22 7TA. *T:* (01279) 654873.

FRIEND, Prof. Richard Henry, FRS 1993; Cavendish Professor of Physics, University of Cambridge, since 1995; Fellow, St John's College, Cambridge, since 1977; *b* 18 Jan. 1953; *s* of John Henry Friend and Dorothy Jean (*née* Brown); *m* 1979, Carol Anne Maxwell (*née* Beales); two *d*. *Educ:* Rugby Sch.; Trinity Coll., Cambridge (MA, PhD). Res. Fellow, St John's Coll., Cambridge, 1977–80; University of Cambridge: Demonstrator in Physics, 1980–85; Lectr, 1985–93; Reader in Experimental Physics, 1993–95. Vis. Prof., Univ. of Calif, Santa Barbara, 1986–87; Vis. Fellow, Royal Instn, 1992–99; Nuffield Science Res. Fellowship, 1992–93. R&D Dir, 1996–98, Chief Scientist, 1998–, Cambridge Display Technology. Mott Lect., Inst. of Physics, 1994. C. V. Boys Prize, Inst. of Physics, 1988; Interdisciplinary Award, RSC, 1991; Hewlett-Packard Prize, European Physical Soc., 1996; Rumford Medal and Prize, Royal Soc., 1998. *Publications:* papers on chem. physics and solid-state physics in scientific jls. *Address:* Cavendish Laboratory, Madingley Road, Cambridge CB3 0HE. *T:* (01223) 337218; *e-mail:* rhf10@cam.ac.uk.

FRIES, Richard James; Chief Charity Commissioner, 1992–99; Visiting Fellow, Centre for Civil Society, London School of Economics, since 2000; *b* 7 July 1940; *s* of late Felix Theodore Fries and Joan Mary Fries (now Mrs John Harris); *m* 1970, Carole Anne Buick; one *s* two *d*. *Educ:* King's Coll., Cambridge. Home Office, 1965–92. Chm. Bd, Internat. Centre for Not-for-Profit Law, Washington, 1999–. *Recreations:* chess, walking. *Address:* London School of Economics, Houghton Street, WC2A 2AE. *T:* (020) 7955 6036.

FRINDALL, William Howard, (Bill); freelance cricket statistician, broadcaster, writer, and editor, since 1965; *b* 3 March 1939; *s* of late Arthur Howard Frindall and Evelyn Violet Frindall (*née* McNeill); *m* 1st, 1960, Maureen Doris Wesson (marr. diss. 1970); two *s* one *d*; 2nd, 1970, Jacqueline Rose Seager (marr. diss. 1980); 3rd, 1992, Deborah Margaret Brown; one *d*. *Educ:* Reigate Grammar Sch.; Kingston upon Thames Sch. of Art. Asst Prodn Manager, Lutterworth Press, 1958; Royal Air Force, 1958–65, commnd Secretarial Br., 1964. BBC cricket statistician, 1966–; Editor, Playfair Cricket Annual, 1986–; Cricket Corresp., Mail on Sunday, 1987–89; cricket statistician, The Times, 1994–; cricket archivist to Sir Paul Getty, 1996–. President: British Blind Sport, 1984–; BBC Cricket Club, 1998–. Hon. DTech Staffordshire, 1998. Statistician of the Year, Assoc. of Cricket Statisticians and Historians, 1996. *Publications:* The Wisden Book of Test Cricket, 1979, 5th edn 2000; The Wisden Book of Cricket Records, 1981, 4th edn 1998; The Guinness Book of Cricket Fact and Feats, 1983, 4th edn 1996; England Test Cricketers, 1989; Ten Tests for England, 1989; Gooch's Golden Summer, 1991; A Tale of Two Captains, 1992; Playfair Cricket World Cup Guide, 1996; Limited-Overs International Cricket: the complete record, 1997; NatWest Playfair Cricket World Cup, 1999. *Recreations:* cricket, sketching, painting, photography, philately, elementary gardening (under supervision from my wife). *Address:* Urchfont, Wiltshire. *Clubs:* MCC, Lord's Taverners; Cricket Writers'; Forty; Master's.

FRISBY, Audrey Mary; *see* Jennings, A. M.

FRISBY, Roger Harry Kilbourne; QC 1969; a Recorder, 1972–78 and 1986–95; *b* 11 Dec. 1921; 2nd *s* of late Herbert Frisby and Hylda Mary Frisby; *m* 1961, Audrey Mary (*see* A. M. Jennings) (marr. diss. 1980); two *s* one *d* (and one *s* one *d* by previous marriage); *m* 1998, Mrs Muriel Wilkinson. *Educ:* Bablake Sch.; Christ Church, Oxford; King's Coll., Univ. of London. Called to the Bar, Lincoln's Inn, 1950. *Address:* Queen Elizabeth Building, Temple, EC4Y 9BS. *T:* (020) 7583 5766. *Club:* Hurlingham.

FRISBY, Terence; playwright, actor, producer, director, author; *b* 28 Nov. 1932; *s* of William and Kathleen Frisby; *m* 1963, Christine Vecchione (marr. diss.); one *s*. *Educ:* Dobwalls Village Sch.; Dartford Grammar Sch.; Central Sch. of Speech Training and Dramatic Art. Substantial repertory acting and directing experience, also TV, films and musicals, 1957–63; appeared in A Sense of Detachment, Royal Court, 1972–73 and X, Royal Court, 1974; Clive Popkiss, in Rookery Nook, Her Majesty's, 1979, and many since. Productions: Once a Catholic (tour), 1980–81; There's a Girl in My Soup (tour), 1982; Woza Albert!, Criterion, 1983; The Real Inspector Hound/Seaside Postcard (tour), 1983–84; Comic Cuts, 1984. Has written many TV scripts, incl. series Lucky Feller, 1976; That's Love, 1988–92 (Gold Award, Houston Film Festival); film, There's A Girl in My Soup, 1970 (Writers Guild Award, Best British Comedy Screenplay). *Publications:* Outrageous Fortune (an autobiog. story), 1998; *plays:* The Subtopians, 1964; There's a Girl in My Soup, 1966; The Bandwagon, 1970; It's All Right if I Do It, 1977; Seaside Postcard, 1978; Just Remember Two Things: it's not fair and don't be late, 1989 (radio play; Giles Cooper Award, 1988); Rough Justice, 1995; Funny About Love, 2001. *Address:* c/o The Agency, 24 Pottery Lane, Holland Park, W11 4LZ. *T:* (020) 7727 1346. *Club:* Richmond Golf.

FRISCHMANN, Wilem William, CBE 1990; PhD; FREng; FIStructE; FCGI; Chairman: Pell Frischmann Group: Pell Frischmann Consulting Engineers Ltd, since 1985; Pell Frischmann Consultants Ltd, since 1986; Pell Frischmann Milton Keynes Ltd, since 1988; Pell Frischmann Engineering, since 1988; Pell Frischmann Water Ltd, since 1990; Conseco International, since 1985; *s* of Lajos Frischmann and Nelly Frischmann; *m* 1957, Sylvia Elvey; one *s* one *d*. *Educ:* Hungary; Hammersmith College of Art and Building; Imperial Coll. of Science and Technology (DIC); City University (PhD). MASCE, MSISdeFr. FIStructE 1964; FREng (FEng 1985); FCGI 1988; FConsE 1993. Engineering training with F. J. Samuely and Partners and W. S. Atkins and Partners; joined C. J. Pell and Partners, 1958, Partner, 1961. Dep. Chm., Building & Property Management Services Ltd, 1993–. Structural Engineer for Nat. Westminster Tower (ICE Telford Premium Award), Centre Point, Drapers Gardens tower (IStructE Oscar Faber Prize) and similar high buildings, leisure buildings, hotels and hospitals; Engineer for works at Bank of England, Mansion House and Alexandra Palace; particular interest and involvement in tall economic buildings, shear walls and diaphragm floors, large bored piles in London clay, deep basements, lightweight materials for large span bridges, monitoring and quality assurance procedures for offshore structures; advisory appts include: Hong Kong and Shanghai Bank HQ, Malayan Banking Berhad, Kuala Lumpur. Hon. DSc. *Publications:* The use and behaviour of large diameter piles in London clay (IStructE paper), 1962; papers to learned socs and instns, originator of concepts: English Channel free-trade port; industrial complex based on Varne and Colbart sandbanks; two-mile high vertical city. *Recreations:* ski-ing, jogging, chess, architecture, design. *Address:* (office) 5 Manchester Square, W1A 1AU. *T:* (020) 7486 3661, *Fax:* (020) 7487 4153; Haversham Grange, Haversham Close, Twickenham, Middx TW1 2JP. *Club:* Arts.

FRISK, Monica Gunnel Constance C.; *see* Carss-Frisk.

FRITCHIE, Dame Irene Tordoff, (Dame Rennie Fritchie), DBE 1996; Commissioner for Public Appointments, since 1999; Civil Service Commissioner, since 1999; *b* 29 April 1942; *d* of Charles Fredrick Fennell and Eva (*née* Tordoff); *m* 1960, Don Jamie Fritchie; one *s* (and one *s* decd). *Educ:* Ribston Hall Grammar Sch. for Girls. Admin. Officer, Endsleigh Insce Brokers, 1970–73; Sales Trng Officer, Trident Insce Ltd, 1973–76; Head of Trng Confs and Specialist Trng Advr on Women's Develt, Food and Drink ITB, 1976–80; Consultant, Social Ecology Associates, 1980–81; Dir, Transform Ltd, 1981–85; Rennie Fritchie Consultancy, 1985–89; Man. Dir, Working Choices Ltd, 1989–91; Mainstream Develt Consultancy, 1991–; Mem. Bd, Stroud and Swindon Bldg Soc., 1995–. Chair: Gloucester HA, 1988–92; South-Western RHA, 1992–94; S and W Region, NHS Executive (formerly S and W RHA), 1994–97. Member: NHS Policy Bd, 1994–97; GMC, 1996–99; Board, British Quality Foundn, 1994–99; Selection Panel, Glos Police Authy, 1994–99. Mem., Forum UK, IHSM, 1993. Pres., Pennell Initiative for Women's Health in Later Life, 1999– (Chair, 1997–99). Patron: Headway, 1989–; Healing Arts, 1995–; SHARE young persons counselling service, 1997–; Meningitis Trust, 1998–; Westbank League of Friends, 1998–; Effective Intelligence, 2000–; SPACE, 2000–; Swindon Arts Foundn; Lord Mayor's Appeal, 2000–01; Bart's Cancer Centre, 2000–. Pres., Winston's Wish (a grief support charity for children), 1996–2000. Vis. Associate Prof., York Univ., 1996–; Pro-Chancellor, Southampton Univ., 1998– (Chm. Council, 1998–2000). CIMgt 2000. Fellow, Cheltenham & Gloucester Coll. of Higher Educn, 1996–. Hon. PhD Southampton, 1996; DUniv York, 1998. *Publications:* Working Choices, 1988; The Business of Assertiveness, 1991; Resolving Conflicts in Organisations, 1998. *Recreations:* family, reading, gardening, swimming, theatre, cooking, the 'Archers'. *Address:* 172 South Block, County Hall, 1b Belvedere Road, SE1 7GE. *T:* (020) 7207 2264.

FRITH, Anthony Ian Donald; Board Member, Bristol Water Holdings plc, 1989–99; *b* 11 March 1929; *s* of Ernest and Elizabeth Frith; *m* 1952, Joyce Marcelle Boyce; one *s* one *d*. *Educ:* various grammar schs and techn. colls. CEng. Various appts in North Thames Gas Bd and Gas Light & Coke Co., 1945–65; Sales Man. 1965–67, Dep. Commercial Man. 1967–68, North Thames Gas Bd; Marketing Man., Domestic and Commercial Gas, Gas Council, 1968–72; Sales Dir, British Gas Corp., 1972–73; Chm., SW Region, British Gas, 1973–90; Mem. Bd, Bath Dist HA, 1990–94; non-exec. Dir, Wilts and Bath Health Commn, 1992–94. *Publications:* various techn. and prof. in Gas Engineering and other jls. *Recreations:* fishing, golf. *Address:* Greenacres, Hayeswood Road, Timsbury, Bath BA2 0HH.

FRITH, Prof. Christopher Donald, PhD; FRS 2000; Professor in Neuropsychology, Institute of Neurology, University College London, since 1994; *b* 16 March 1942; *s* of Donald Alfred Frith, OBE; *m* 1966, Uta Aurnhammer (*see* U. Frith); two *s*. *Educ:* Leys Sch., Cambridge; Christ's Coll., Cambridge (MA 1963); Inst. of Psychiatry, London Univ.

(Dip. Psych. 1965; PhD 1969). Res. Asst, Inst. of Psychiatry, 1965–75; MRC Scientific Staff: Clin. Res. Centre, Div. of Psychiatry, Northwick Park Hosp., 1975–92; MRC Cyclotron Unit, Hammersmith Hosp., 1992–94; Wellcome Principal Res. Fellow, Wellcome Dept of Cognitive Neurology, Inst. of Neurology, UCL, 1994–. FRSA 1996; FMedSci 1999; FAAAS 2000. Kenneth Craik Award, St John's Coll., Cambridge, 1999. *Publications:* Cognitive Neuropsychology of Schizophrenia, 1992; papers on cognitive neuropsychology in various scientific jls. *Recreations:* music, study of consciousness. *Address:* Wellcome Department of Cognitive Neurology, Institute of Neurology, University College London, Queen Square, WC1N 3BG. *T:* (020) 7833 7457.

FRITH, David Edward John; cricket author and journalist; Founder, 1979, Editor and Editorial Director, 1979–96, Wisden Cricket Monthly; *b* 16 March 1937; *s* of Edward Frith and Patricia Lillian Ethel Frith (*née* Thomas); *m* 1957, Debbie Oriel Christina Pennell; two *s* one *d. Educ:* Canterbury High Sch., Sydney. First grade cricket, Sydney, 1960–64. Editor, The Cricketer, 1972–78. Cricket Soc. Literary Award, 1970 and 1987; Cricket Writer of the Year, Wombwell Cricket Lovers Soc., 1984; Magazine Sports Writer of the Year, Sports Council, 1988. *Publications:* Runs in the Family (with John Edrich), 1969; My Dear Victorious Stod, 1977; (ed) Cricket Gallery, 1976; (with Greg Chappell) The Ashes '77, 1977; The Golden Age of Cricket 1890–1914, 1978; The Ashes '79, 1979; Thommo, 1980; The Fast Men, 1981; The Slow Men, 1984; (with Gerry Wright) Cricket's Golden Summer, 1985; (ed) England *v* Australia Test Match Records 1877–1985, 1986; Archie Jackson, 1987; Pageant of Cricket, 1987; Guildford Jubilee 1938–1988, 1988; England *v* Australia: A Pictorial History of the Test Matches since 1877, 1990; By His Own Hand, 1991; Stoddy's Mission, 1995; (ed) Test Match Year, 1997; Caught England, Bowled Australia (autobiog.), 1997; The Trailblazers, 1999; Silence of the Heart, 2001. *Recreations:* collecting cricketana, watching documentaries, culling Queensland cane toads. *Address:* 6 Beech Lane, Guildford, Surrey GU2 4ES. *T:* (01483) 532573. *Club:* MCC.

FRITH, Air Vice-Marshal Edward Leslie, CB 1973; *b* 18 March 1919; *s* of late Charles Edward Frith, ISO. *Educ:* Haberdashers' Askes School. Gp Captain, 1961; Air Cdre, 1968; Dir of Personal Services (2) RAF, MoD, 1969–71; Air Vice-Marshal, 1971; Air Officer Administration, Maintenance Comd, later Support Comd, 1971–74. *Recreations:* lawn tennis, bridge. *Clubs:* All England Lawn Tennis and Croquet, International Lawn Tennis of GB.

FRITH, Rt Rev. Richard Michael Cokayne; *see* Hull, Bishop Suffragan of.

FRITH, Hon. Royce Herbert, CM; QC (Can.) 1974; Consultant, Borden Ladner Gervais, Barristers and Solicitors; High Commissioner for Canada in the United Kingdom, 1994–96; *b* 12 Nov. 1923; *s* of George Harry Frith and Annie Beatrice (*née* Royce); *m* 1948, Elizabeth Mary Davison (*d* 1976); one *d* (one *s* decd). *Educ:* Lachine High Sch., Quebec; Parkdale Coll. Inst., Toronto; Victoria Coll., Univ. of Toronto (BA); Osgoode Hall Law Sch. (LLB); Univ. of Ottawa (Dip. d'etudes supérieures). Practiced Law, Toronto and Perth, 1949–89. Mem. (L) Senate, Ontario, 1977–94; Dep. Govt Leader, 1980–84; Dep. Leader of Opposition in Senate, 1984–91, Leader, 1991–93. Comr, Royal Commn on Bilingualism and Biculturalism, 1963–70; Legal Advr to Comr of Official Langs, 1971–77. Pres., Ontario Liberal Assoc., 1961–62. Life Mem., Law Soc. of Upper Canada. Part-time broadcaster. *Publications:* Hoods on the Hill, 1991; The Show Must Not Go On, 1993. *Recreations:* music, theatre, golf, tennis, squash. *Address:* 510–4101 Yew Street, Vancouver, BC V6L 3B7, Canada; Borden Ladner Gervais, Barristers and Solicitors, Box 48600, Vancouver, BC V7X 1T2, Canada.

FRITH, Prof. Uta, PhD; FMedSci; FBA 2001; Professor of Cognitive Development, since 1996, and Deputy Director, Institute of Cognitive Neuroscience, since 1998, University College London; *b* 25 May 1941; *d* of Wilhelm Aurnhammer and Anne (*née* Goedel); *m* 1966, Prof. Christopher Donald Frith, *qv*; two *s. Educ:* Univ. des Saarlandes (Vordiplom. Psychol. 1964); Inst. of Psychiatry, Univ. of London (Dip. Abnormal Psychol. 1966; PhD Psychol. 1968). MRC Scientific Staff: Scientist, 1968–80; Sen. Scientist, 1980–98; Special Appt, 1998–. FMedSci 2001. Hon. Dr: Göteborg, 1998; St Andrews, 2000. *Publications:* Autism: explaining the enigma, 1989, 2nd edn 2001; Autism and Asperger's Syndrome, 1991; Autism in History, 2000. *Recreations:* collecting art and antiques, tidying and polishing, enjoying my husband's cooking. *Address:* Institute of Cognitive Neuroscience, University College London, Alexandra House, 17 Queen Square, WC1N 3AR. *T:* (020) 7679 1166.

FRITSCH, Elizabeth, CBE 1995; potter; *b* Shropshire, 1940; *d* of Welsh parents; one *s* one *d. Educ:* Royal Acad. of Music; Royal Coll. of Art (Silver Medallist, 1970). Established own workshop, E London, 1985. Mem., Crafts Council (Bursary awarded, 1980). *One-woman exhibitions* include: Crafts Council, 1974; CAA, 1976; Leeds City Art Galls, 1978, touring to Glasgow, Bristol, Bolton and Gateshead City Art Galls; V & A, 1980; RCA, 1984; Besson Gall., London, 1989; Royal Mus. of Scotland, 1990; Hetjens Mus., Dusseldorf, 1990; touring to British City Art Galls, 1992; NY Crafts Council, 1993; Crafts Council, 1994; *group exhibitions* include: Oxford Gall., 1974; ICA, 1985; Kunstler Haus, Vienna, 1986; Fischer Fine Art, London, 1987; Kyoto and Tokyo Nat. Museums of Modern Art, 1988; Crafts Council, touring to Amsterdam, 1988; Sotheby's, 1988; 35 Connaught Square, London (Lord Queensberry), 1991; Stuttgart, 1991; Oriel Gall., Cardiff, 1991; *works in public collections:* V & A; Crafts Council; Lotherton Hall, Leeds City Art Galls; Royal Mus. of Scotland; Glasgow, Bolton, Bristol and Birmingham City Art Galls. Judge, Fletcher Challenge Internat. Ceramics Competition, NZ, 1990. Major influences on work: music, fresco painting, topology. Sen. Fellow, RCA, 1995. Herbert Read Meml Prize, 1970; Winner, Royal Copenhagen Jubilee Competition, 1972; Gold Medal, Internat. Ceramics Competition, Sopot, Poland, 1976. *Recreations:* music, mountains, theatre.

FRIZZELL, Edward William, CB 2000; Under Secretary, Scottish Executive (formerly Scottish Office), since 1991; Head, Scottish Executive Enterprise and Lifelong Learning Department, since 1999; *b* 4 May 1946; *s* of late Edward Frizzell, CBE, QPM and Mary McA. Russell; *m* 1969, Moira Calderwood; two *s* one *d. Educ:* Paisley Grammar School, Glasgow Univ. (MA Hons). Scottish Milk Marketing Board, 1968–73; Scottish Council (Develt and Industry), 1973–76; Scottish Office, 1976–78; First Sec., Fisheries, FCO UK Rep. Brussels, 1978–82; Scottish Office, then Scottish Executive, 1982–: SED, 1982–86; Finance Div., 1986–89; Industry Dept/SDA (Dir, Locate in Scotland), 1989–91; Chief Exec., Scottish Prison Service, 1991–99. *Recreations:* running, mountain biking, painting. *Address:* (office) Meridian Court, 5 Cadogan Street, Glasgow G2 6AT. *Club:* Mortonhall Golf.

FRODSHAM, Anthony Freer, CBE 1978; company director and management consultant, now retired; Director-General, Engineering Employers' Federation, 1975–82; *b* Peking, China, 8 Sept. 1919; *er s* of late George William Frodsham and Constance Violet Frodsham (*née* Neild); *m* 1953, Patricia Myfanwy, *o c* of late Cmdr A. H. Wynne-Edwards, DSC, RN; two *s. Educ:* Ecole Lacordaire, Paris; Faraday House Engineering Coll., London. DFH, CEng, FIMechE, FIMC, CBIM. Served War, 1940–46: Engineer Officer, RN, Asst Fleet Engr Officer on staff of C-in-C Mediterranean, 1944–46 (despatches, 1945). P-E Consulting Group Ltd, 1947–73: Man. Dir and Gp Chief Exec., 1963–72; Group Specialist Adviser, United Dominions Trust Ltd, 1973–74. Director: TACE Ltd, 1973–76; Arthur Young Management Services, 1973–79; F. Pratt Engrg Corp. Ltd, 1982–85; Greyfriars Ltd, 1984–88 (Dep. Chm., 1986–88). Chairman: Management Consultants Assoc., 1968–70; Machine Tools EDC, 1973–79; Independent Chm., Compressed Air and Allied Machinery Cttee, 1976–96; Chairman: European Business Foundn Adv. Cttee, 1982–; Council, European Business Sch., 1986–91 (Mem., 1983–91); Vice-Chm., British Export Finance Adv. Council, 1982–87; President: Inst. of Management Consultants, 1967–68; Inst. of Linguists, 1986–89; Member: CBI Grand Council, 1975–82; CBI President's Cttee, 1979–82; Engineering Industry Training Bd, 1975–79; W European Metal Working Employers' Assoc., 1975–82; Manadon Adv. Council, RNEC, 1988–94; Enterprise Counsellor, DTI, 1988–91. A General Commissioner of Tax, 1975–94. Conducted MoD Study into Provision of Engineer Officers for Armed Services, 1983. Hon. FIL 1986. Hon. DBA RNEC, 1991. *Publications:* contrib. to technical jls; lectures and broadcasts on management subjects. *Address:* 36 Fairacres, Roehampton Lane, SW15 5LX. *T:* (020) 8878 9551. *Club:* Royal Automobile.

FROGGATT, Sir Leslie (Trevor), Kt 1981; Chairman, Ashton Mining Ltd, 1981–94; *b* 8 April 1920; *s* of Leslie and Mary Helena Froggatt (*née* Brassey); *m* 1945, Jessie Elizabeth Grant; three *s. Educ:* Birkenhead Park Sch., Cheshire. Joined Asiatic Petroleum Co. Ltd, 1937; Shell Singapore, Shell Thailand, Shell Malaya, 1947–54; Shell Egypt, 1955–56; Dir of Finance, Gen. Manager, Kalimantan, Borneo, and Dep. Chief Rep., PT Shell Indonesia, 1958–62; Shell International Petroleum Co. Ltd: Area Co-ordinator, S Asia and Australia, 1962–63; assignment in various Shell cos in Europe, 1964–66; Shell Oil Co., Atlanta, 1967–69; Chm. and Chief Exec. Officer, Shell Gp in Australia, 1969–80; non-exec. Dir, Shell Australia Ltd, 1981–87. Chairman: Pacific Dunlop, 1986–90 (Vice-Chm., 1981; Dir, 1978–90); BRL Hardy, 1992–95; Director: Australian Industry Develt Corp., 1978–90; Australian Inst. of Petroleum Ltd, 1976–80, 1982–84 (Chm., 1977–79); Moonee Valley Racing Club Nominees Pty Ltd, 1977–92; Tandem Australia, 1989–98 (Chm., 1992–98). Member: Australian Nat. Airlines Commn (Australian Airlines), 1981–87 (Vice-Chm., 1984–87); Internat. Bd of Advice, ANZ Banking Gp, 1986–91; Internat. Adv. Council, Tandem Computers Inc., USA, 1988–98; Bd, CARE Australia, 1989– (Vice Chm., 1995–). *Recreations:* reading, music, racing, golf. *Address:* 20 Albany Road, Toorak, Vic 3142, Australia. *T:* (3) 98221357. *Clubs:* Melbourne, Australian, Victoria Racing, Victoria Amateur Turf, Moonee Valley Racing, Commonwealth Golf (Melbourne).

FROGGATT, Sir Peter, Kt 1985; MD; FRCP, FRCPI; Trustee, National Museums and Galleries of Northern Ireland, since 1998; Pro-Chancellor, University of Dublin, since 1985 (Senior Pro-Chancellor, since 1999); President and Vice-Chancellor, Queen's University of Belfast, 1976–86; *b* 12 June 1928; *s* of Albert Victor and Edith (*née* Curran); *m* 1958, Norma Cochrane; four *s* (and one *s* decd). *Educ:* Royal Belfast Academical Institution; Royal Sch., Armagh (Schol.); Trinity Coll., Dublin (BA; MB; BCh; BAO 1952; MA 1956; MD 1957; Welland Prize; Cunningham Medal; Begley Schol.); Queen's Univ., Belfast (DPH 1956; PhD 1967; Carnwath Prize). MRCPI 1972; FRCPI 1973; FFPHM (FFCM 1973); MRCP 1974; FFOMI 1975; FFCMI 1976; MRIA 1978; FRCP 1980. House Surgeon and Physician, Sir Patrick Dun's Hosp., Dublin, 1952–53; Nuffield Res. Student, 1955–57; Med. Officer, Short Bros and Harland Ltd, 1957–59; Queen's University, Belfast: Lectr, 1959–65; Reader, 1965–68; Prof. of Epidemiology, 1968–76; Dean, Faculty of Medicine, 1971–76; Consultant, Eastern Health and Social Services Board, 1960–76. Hon. Prof., St Bartholomew's Hosp. Med. Sch., 1986–94. Chairman: Independent Scientific Cttee on Smoking and Health, 1980–91 (Mem., 1977–80); Tobacco Products Res. Trust, 1981–97; ASME, 1987–92; Central Ethical Compliance Gp, Unilever, 1991–97. Director: AIB Gp plc, 1984–95; TSB Bank (Northern Ireland), later First Trust Bank, 1991–98. President: Biol Scis Section, British Assoc., 1987–88; BMA, 1999–2000; Member: Bd, 1983–85, Adv. Cttee, NI, 1988–94, British Council; Gen. Adv. Cttee, BBC, 1986–88; Supervisory Bd, NHS NI, 1986–92; British Occupational Health Res. Foundn, 1991–2000. Hon. Member: Soc. for Social Medicine; Soc. of Occupational Medicine. Lectures: Robert Adams, 1977, Kirkpatrick, 1984, Abrahamson, 1986, RCSI; Apothecaries, SOM, 1978; Freyer, NUI, 1984; Bayliss, RCP, 1989; Smiley, FOMI, 1989; Bartholomew Mosse, Rotunda Hosp., 1992; John Snow, Assoc. of Anaesthetists, 2001; DARE, FPHM, 2001. Trustee, Mater Infirmorum Hosp., Belfast, 1994–; Chm., Scotch-Irish Trust of Ulster, 1990–. Freeman, City of London, 1990. FSS 1963; Hon. FRCSI 1988; Hon. Fellow, Royal Acad. of Medicine in Ireland; CIMgt (CBIM 1986). Hon. LLD: Dublin, 1981; QUB, 1991; Hon. DSc NUI, 1982. Dominic Corrigan Gold Medal, RCPI, 1981. *Publications:* (jtly) Causation of Bus-driver Accidents: Epidemiological Study, 1963; (ed jtly) Nicotine, Smoking and the Low Tar Programme, 1988; articles in jls on human genetics, occupational medicine, med. history, med. educn, epidemiology and smoking policies. *Recreations:* golf, music, travel. *Address:* Rathganley, 3 Strangford Avenue, Belfast BT9 6PG.

FRÖHLICH, Prof. Albrecht, PhD; FRS 1976; Professor of Pure Mathematics, King's College, University of London, 1962–81, now Emeritus Professor; Senior Research Fellow, Imperial College, University of London, 1982–96; Emeritus Fellow, Robinson College, Cambridge (Fellow 1982–84); *b* 22 May 1916; *s* of Julius Fröhlich and Frida Fröhlich; *m* 1950, Dr Evelyn Ruth Brooks; one *s* one *d. Educ:* Realgymnasium, Munich; Bristol Univ. (BSc 1948, PhD 1951). Asst Lectr in Maths, University Coll., Leicester, 1950–52; Lectr in Maths, University Coll. of N Staffs, 1952–55; King's College, London: Reader in Pure Maths, 1955–62; Hd, Dept of Maths, 1971–81. Vis. Royal Soc.-Israeli Acad. Research Prof., 1978; George A. Miller Prof., Univ. of Illinois, 1981–82; Gauss Prof., Göttingen Acad. of Scis, 1983; vis. prof. at other univs in USA, Canada, Germany, France, Switzerland, China and India. Corres. Mem., Heidelberg Acad. of Scis, 1982. FKC 1977. Hon. DSc: Bordeaux, 1986; Bristol, 1998. Senior Berwick Prize, 1976, de-Morgan Medal, 1992, London Math. Soc.; Res. Prize, Alexander von Humboldt Foundn, 1992. *Publications:* Formal Groups, 1968; Galois Module Structure of Algebraic Integers, 1983; Class Groups and Hermitian Modules, 1984; (with M. J. Taylor) Algebraic Number Theory, 1991; papers in math. jls. *Recreations:* cooking, eating, walking, music. *Address:* Robinson College, Cambridge CB3 9AN.

FROOD, Alan Campbell, CBE 1988; Managing Director, Crown Agents for Oversea Governments and Administrations, 1978–88; Crown Agent, 1980–88; *b* 15 May 1926; *s* of James Campbell Frood, MC and Margaret Helena Frood; *m* 1960, Patricia Ann Cotterell; two *s* two *d. Educ:* Cranleigh Sch.; Peterhouse, Cambridge. Royal Navy, 1944–47 (Sub-Lt RNVR). Bank of England, 1949; Colonial Admin. Service, 1952; Bankers Trust Co., 1962; Dir, Bankers Trust Internat. Ltd, 1967; Gen. Man., Banking Dept, Crown Agents, 1975; Dir of Financial Services, Crown Agents, 1976–78. Trustee, Queen's Nursing Inst., 1986–2000 (Hon. Treas., 1973–94). *Recreations:* sailing, gardening. *Address:* The Dairy, Bystock, Exmouth, Devon EX8 5EQ. *T:* (01395) 267744.

FROSSARD, Sir Charles (Keith), KBE 1992; Kt 1983; Bailiff of Guernsey, 1982–92; Judge of the Court of Appeal, Jersey, 1983–92; a Judge of the Courts of Appeal of Jersey and Guernsey, 1992–95; *b* 18 Feb. 1922; *s* of late Edward Louis Frossard, CBE, MA, Hon. CF, Dean of Guernsey, 1947–67, and Margery Smith Latta; *m* 1950, Elizabeth Marguerite, *d* of late J. E. L. Martel, OBE; two *d. Educ:* Elizabeth Coll., Guernsey; Univ. de Caen (Bachelier en Droit; Dhc 1990). Enlisted Gordon Highlanders, 1940; commnd 1941, 17 Dogra Regt, Indian Army; seconded to Tochi Scouts and Chitral Scouts; served India and NW Frontier, 1941–46. Called to Bar, Gray's Inn, 1949, Hon. Bencher, 2000; Advocate of Royal Court of Guernsey, 1949; People's Deputy, States of Guernsey, 1958–67; Conseiller, States of Guernsey, 1967–69; HM Solicitor General, Guernsey, 1969–73; HM Attorney General, Guernsey, 1973–76; Dep. Bailiff of Guernsey, 1977–82. Member, Church Assembly and General Synod, Church of England, 1960–82. Pres., Indian Army Assoc., 1993–; Member Council: British Assoc. of Cemetaries in SE Asia, 1998–; British Commonwealth Ex-Services League, 1999–. KStJ 1985. Médaille de Vermeil, Paris, 1984. *Recreations:* hill walking, fishing. *Address:* Les Lierres, Rohais, St Peter Port, Guernsey. *T:* (01481) 722076. *Clubs:* Army and Navy, Naval and Military; United (Guernsey).

FROST, Abraham Edward Hardy, CBE 1972; Counsellor, Foreign and Commonwealth Office, 1972–78; *b* 4 July 1918; *s* of Abraham William Frost and Margaret Anna Frost; *m* 1972, Gillian (*née* Crossley); two *d. Educ:* Royal Grammar Sch., Colchester King's Coll., Cambridge (MA); London Univ. (BScEcon). FCIS. RNVR, 1940–46 (Lieut). ILO, Geneva, 1947–48; HM Treasury, 1948–49; Manchester Guardian, City Staff, 1949–51; FO (later FCO), 1951–78. *Publication:* In Dorset Of Course (poems), 1976. *Address:* Hill View, Buckland Newton, Dorset DT2 7BS. *T:* (01300) 345415.

FROST, Alan John, FIA; Chairman, Queen Mab Consultancy Ltd, since 2001; *b* 6 Oct. 1944; *s* of Edward George Frost and Ellen Lucy Jamieson; *m* 1973, Valerie Jean Bennett; two *s. Educ:* Stratford County Grammar Sch., London; Manchester Univ. (BSc Hons). FIA 1970. Pearl Assurance Co., 1966–67; Australian Mutual Provident Soc., 1967–72; Laurie, Milbank & Co., 1972–74; London & Manchester Assurance Gp, 1974–84; Sun Life Assurance Soc., 1984–86; Man. Dir, Abbey Life Assurance Co., 1986–98; Gp Chief Exec., United Assce Gp plc, 1998–2000; Dep. Chief Exec., Royal London Gp, 2000–01. Non-executive Director: INVESCO Pensions Ltd, 2001–; Teachers' Building Soc., 2001–; Bournemouth Univ., 2001–. Liveryman, Co. of Actuaries, 1986– (Mem. Ct of Assts). FIMgt 1990; MInstD. *Publications:* (with D. P. Hager) A General Introduction to Institutional Investment, 1986; (with D. P. Hager) Debt Securities, 1990; actuarial papers. *Recreations:* opera, genealogy. *Address: e-mail:* alanjohnfrost@cs.com.

FROST, Albert Edward, CBE 1983; Director, Marks & Spencer Ltd, 1976–87; Chairman: Remploy, 1983–87; Trustees, Remploy Pension Fund, 1989–98; *b* 7 March 1914; *s* of Charles Albert Frost and Minnie Frost; *m* 1942, Eugénie Maud Barlow. *Educ:* Oulton Sch., Liverpool; London Univ. Called to the Bar, Middle Temple (1st Cl. Hons). HM Inspector of Taxes, Inland Revenue, 1937; Imperial Chemical Industries Ltd: Dep. Head, Taxation Dept, 1949; Dep. Treasurer, 1957; Treasurer, 1960; Finance Dir, 1968; retd 1976. Director: British Airways Corp., 1976–80; BL Ltd, 1977–80; S. G. Warburg & Co., 1976–83; British Steel, 1980–83 (Chm., Audit and Salaries Cttees); Guinness Peat Gp, 1983–84; Chairman: Guinness Mahon Hldgs Ltd, 1983–84; Guinness Mahon & Co., 1983–84; Billingsgate City Securities, 1989–90. Mem. Council, St Thomas's Med. Sch., London, 1974– (Chm., Finance Cttee, 1978–85); Governor, United Med. Schs of Guy's and St Thomas's Hosps, 1982–98 (Dep. Chm. of Govs, 1989–97; Chm., Finance and Investment Cttees, 1982–85; Hon. Fellow, 1994). Member: Council and Finance Cttee, Morley Coll., London, 1975–85; Exec. Cttee for Develt Appeal, Royal Opera House, Covent Garden, 1975–87; Arts Council of GB, 1982–84; Vice Pres., ABSA, 1992– (Mem. Council, 1976–93; Jt Dep. Chm., 1985–92); Chairman: Robert Mayer Trust for Youth and Music, 1981–90 (Dir, 1977–90); Jury, and of Org. Cttee, City of London Carl Flesch Internat. Violin Competition, 1984–. Trustee and Treas., Loan Fund for Mus. Instruments, 1980–; Dir, City Arts Trust, 1982–93. FRSA. *Publications:* (contrib.) Simon's Income Tax, 1952; (contrib.) Gunns Australian Income Tax Law and Practice, 1960; articles on financial matters affecting industry and on arts sponsorship. *Recreations:* violinist (chamber music); swimming (silver medallist, Royal Life Saving Assoc.); athletics (county colours, track and cross country); walking; arts generally. *Club:* Royal Automobile.

FROST, Sir David (Paradine), Kt 1993; OBE 1970; interviewer, author, producer, columnist, and television presenter; Joint Founder, London Weekend Television; Chairman and Chief Executive, David Paradine Ltd, since 1966; *b* 7 April 1939; *s* of late Rev. W. J. Paradine Frost, Tenterden, Kent; *m* 1983, Lady Carina Fitzalan-Howard, 2nd *d* of Duke of Norfolk, *qv*; three *s. Educ:* Gillingham Grammar Sch.; Wellingborough Grammar Sch.; Gonville and Caius Coll., Cambridge (MA). Sec., The Footlights; Editor, Granta. Jt Founder and Dir, TV-am, 1981–93. BBC Television series: That Was the Week That Was, 1962–63 (in USA, 1964–65); A Degree of Frost, 1963, 1973; Not So Much a Programme, More a Way of Life, 1964–65; The Frost Report, 1966–67; Frost Over England, 1967; Frost Over America, 1970; Frost's Weekly, 1973; The Frost Interview, 1974; We British, 1975–76; Forty Years of Television, 1976; The Frost Programme, 1977; The Guinness Book of Records Hall of Fame, 1986, 1987, 1988; Breakfast with Frost, 1993–; Through the Keyhole, 1997–; single programmes: Margaret Thatcher: the path to power and beyond, 1995; Nick Leeson: the man who broke the bank, 1995; Norma Major Behind Closed Doors, 1996; Prince Charles, Why it Matters to Me, 1997; Forty Years with Frost, 2000; BBC Radio: David Frost at the Phonograph, 1966, 1972; Frost on Thursday, 1974; series, Pull the Other One, 1987, 1988, 1990; ITV series and programmes: The Frost Programme, 1966–67, 1967–68, 1972, 1973, 1993–95; Frost on Friday, 1968–69, 1969–70; The Sir Harold Wilson Interviews, 1976; A Prime Minister on Prime Ministers, 1977–78; Are We Really Going to be Rich?, 1978; David Frost's Global Village, 1979, 1980, 1982; The 25th Anniversary of ITV, The Begin Interview, and Elvis—He Touched Their Lives, 1980; The BAFTA Awards, and Onward Christian Soldiers, 1981; A Night of Knights: a Royal Gala, 1982; The End of the Year Show, 1982, 1983; Frost on Sunday (TV-am), 1983–92; David Frost Presents Ultra Quiz, 1984; Twenty Years On, 1985, 1986; Through the Keyhole, 1987–96; Beyond Belief, 1995, 1996, 1997; Live for Peace, 1995; A Royal Gala, 1996; A Gala Comedy Hour, 1996; The Easter Enigma, 1996; Masters of Talk, 1996–97; The Alpha Series, 2001; Hitler and Hess, 2001. US programmes include: That Was The Week That Was, 1964–1965; David Frost's Night Out in London, 1966–67; The Next President, 1968; Robert Kennedy the Man, 1968; The David Frost Show, 1969–70, 1970–71, 1971–72; The David Frost Revue, 1971–72, 1972–73; That Was the Year That Was, 1973, 1985; David Frost Presents the Guinness Book of Records, 1973–76; Frost over Australia, 1972, 1973, 1974, 1977; Frost over New Zealand, 1973, 1974; The Unspeakable Crime, 1975; Abortion—Merciful or Murder?, 1975; The Beatles—Once Upon a Time, 1975; David Frost Presents the Best, 1975; The Nixon Interviews with David Frost, 1976–77; The Crossroads of Civilization, 1977–78; Headliners with David Frost, 1978; A Gift of Song—MUSIC FOR UNICEF Concert, The Bee Gees Special, and The Kissinger Interview, 1979; The Shah Speaks, and The American Movie Awards, 1980; Show Business, This Is Your Life 30th Anniversary Special, The Royal Wedding (CBS), 1981; David Frost Presents The Internat. Guinness Book of World Records, annually 1981–86; The American Movie Awards, Rubinstein at 95, and Pierre Elliott Trudeau, 1982; Frost over Canada, 1982, 1983; David Frost Live by Satellite from London, 1983; The Search for Josef Mengele, 1985; Spitting Image: Down and Out in the White House, 1986; The Spitting Image Movie Awards, 1987; The Spectacular World of Guinness Records, 1987–88; Entertainment Tonight, 1987, 1988; The Next President with David Frost, 1987–88; ABC Presents a Royal Gala, 1988; The President and Mrs Bush Talking with David Frost, 1989; Talking with David Frost (USA), 1991–98; Interviews I'll Never Forget, 1998; David Frost, One-on-One, 1999–. Produced films: The Rise and Rise of Michael Rimmer, 1970; Charley One-Eye, 1972; Leadbelly, 1974; The Slipper and the Rose, 1975; James A. Michener's Dynasty, 1975; The Ordeal of Patty Hearst, 1978; The Remarkable Mrs Sanger, 1979; Rogue Trader, 1999. Mem., British/USA Bicentennial Liaison Cttee, 1973–76; Pres., Lord's Taverners, 1985, 1986. Companion, TRIC, 1992. Hon. Prof., Thames Valley Univ., 1994. Golden Rose, Montreux, for Frost Over England, 1967; Royal Television Society's Silver Medal, 1967; Richard Dimbleby Award, 1967; Emmy Award (USA), 1970, 1971; Religious Heritage of America Award, 1970; Albert Einstein Award, Communication Arts, 1971; MOMI Award, NY, 1998; Mus. of TV and Radio Salute, 1999. *Stage:* An Evening with David Frost (Edinburgh Fest.), 1966. LLD Emerson Coll., USA; Hon. DLitt Sussex, 1994. *Publications:* That Was the Week That Was, 1963; How to Live under Labour, 1964; Talking with Frost, 1967; To England With Love, 1967; The Presidential Debate 1968, 1968; The Americans, 1970; Whitlam and Frost, 1974; I Gave Them a Sword, 1978; I Could Have Kicked Myself, (David Frost's Book of the World's Worst Decisions), 1982; Who Wants to be a Millionaire?, 1983; (jtly) The Mid-Atlantic Companion, 1986; (jtly) The Rich Tide, 1986; (jtly) If You'll Believe That; The World's Shortest Books, 1987; David Frost: an autobiography: part one: From Congregations to Audiences, 1993; Billy Graham: thirty years of conversations with David Frost, 1997. *Address:* David Paradine Ltd, 5 St Mary Abbots Place, W8 6LS. *Fax:* (020) 7602 0411.

FROST, Ven. George; Archdeacon of Lichfield and Canon Treasurer of Lichfield Cathedral, 1998–2000; *b* 4 April 1935; *s* of William John Emson Frost and Emily Daisy Frost; *m* 1959, Joyce Pratt; four *s. Educ:* Hatfield Coll., Durham Univ. (BA 1956, MA 1961); Lincoln Theological Coll. Schoolmaster, Westcliff High School, 1956–57; labourer, Richard Thomas and Baldwin Steelworks, Scunthorpe, 1958–59; Asst Curate, St Margaret, Barking Parish Church, 1960–64; Minister, Ecclesiastical District of St Mark, Marks Gate, 1964–70; Vicar: St Matthew, Tipton, 1970–77; St Bartholomew, Penn, Wolverhampton, 1977–87; RD of Trysull, 1984–87; Archdeacon of Salop, 1987–98; Vicar of Tong, 1987–98. Prebendary of Lichfield Cathedral, 1985–87, Hon. Canon, 1987–98. *Recreations:* walking, wild flowers, photography. *Address:* 23 Darnford Lane, Lichfield, Staffs WS14 9RW. *T:* (01543) 415109.

FROST, Gerald Philip Anthony; author and journalist; Director, Trade and Welfare Unit, Institute of Economic Affairs, since 1997; *b* 8 Nov. 1943; *s* of Sidney and Flora Frost; *m* 1970, Margaret Miriam Freedman; two *s. Educ:* Univ. of Sussex (BA Hons; mature student). Junior reporter, Ilford and East London newspapers, 1960–64; reporter: Recorder Newspapers, Ilford, 1964–65; Yorkshire Post, 1965–67; Chief reporter, Morning Telegraph, 1967–68; Sub-editor: Daily Express, Manchester, 1968–69; Press Assoc., 1969–71; research staff, Centre for Policy Studies, 1974–80 (Sec. and Mem Bd, 1977–80); Chief Leader Writer, Evening Standard, 1979–80; Director: Inst. for European Defence and Strategic Studies, 1980–92; Centre for Policy Studies, 1992–95. Consultant Dir, New Atlantic Initiative, 1996–98. *Publications:* Protest and Perish: a critique of unilateralism (with P. Towle and I. Eliott), 1983; *editor and contributor:* Europe in Turmoil, 1991; In search of Stability, 1992; Hubris: the tempting of modern conservatives, 1992; Loyalty Misplaced, 1997; Unfit to Fight: the cultural subversion of the armed forces in Britain and America, 1999; contribs to British and US newspapers and jls. *Recreations:* family pursuits, reading, wine. *Address:* 36 Victoria Avenue, Surbiton, Surrey KT6 5DW. *Club:* Reform.

FROST, Jeffrey Michael Torbet; Executive Director, London & Continental Bankers, 1983–89 (Associate Director, 1982–83); *b* 11 June 1938; *s* of late Basil Frost and Dorothy Frost. *Educ:* Diocesan Coll., Cape, South Africa; Radley Coll.; Oriel Coll., Oxford; Harvard Univ. Exec. Dir, Cttee on Invisible Exports, 1976–81. Hon. Sec., Anglo-Brazilian Soc., 1977–84. Liveryman, Worshipful Co. of Clockmakers. FRSA. *Recreations:* bridge, ballet, walking. *Address:* 34 Paradise Walk, SW3 4JL. *T:* (020) 7352 8642; The Parish Room, Kintbury, near Hungerford, Berks RG17 9UP. *Club:* White's.

FROST, Michael Edward, LVO 1983; HM Diplomatic Service, retired; Consul-General, San Francisco, 1998–2001; *b* 5 July 1941; *s* of Edward Lee Frost and Ivy Beatrice (*née* Langmead); *m* 1964, Carole Ann Beigel; three *s. Educ:* Torquay Grammar Sch. FCO, 1959–62; Algiers, 1962–67; Commercial Officer, Kuala Lumpur, 1967–71; 3rd Sec., later 2nd Sec. Commercial, Bucharest, 1972–75; FCO, 1975–78; Consul (Commercial), Seattle, 1978–83; FCO, 1983–84; on secondment to ICI, 1984–87; Dep. Head of Mission, Sofia, 1987–90; Dep. Consul Gen. and Dir (Investment), British Trade and Investment Office, NY, 1991–95; Head of Migration and Visa Dept, FCO, 1995–97. *Recreations:* watercolours, golf, travel. *Address:* 25 Waldens Park Road, Woking, Surrey GU21 4RN.

FROST, Dame Phyllis Irene, AC 1992; DBE 1974 (CBE 1963); Chairman, Victorian Relief Committee, since 1973 (Member since 1964); *b* 14 Sept. 1917; *née* Turner; *m* 1941, Glenn Neville Frost (*d* 1987), LDS, BDSc, JP; three *d. Educ:* Croydon Coll., Vic.; St Duthus Coll.; Presbyterian Ladies' Coll.; Univ. of Melbourne. Dip. of Physiotherapy, 1939; studied Criminology, 1955–56. Chairman: Victorian (formerly Fairlea) Women's Prison Council, 1953–99; Aust. Contact Emergency Service, 1984–; Vice-Chairman: Victorian Assoc. for Care and Resettlement of Offenders, 1977–; Clean World Internat., 1980–92; Mem., State Disaster Welfare Cttees, Vic, 1983–; Exec. Mem., Aust. Football League Foundn, 1997–. Hon. Life Member: Aust. Crime Prevention Council, 1972; Aust. Freedom from Hunger Campaign, 1977; Nat. Council of Women of Victoria, 1979; Keep Australia Beautiful Nat. Council (former Chm.); Trustee, patron, hon. life mem., hon. convener, and life governor of many community service, health and welfare orgns. Has attended several internat. confs as Aust. delegate or representative, including: Internat. Council of Women; FAO; FFHC (Chm., 4th Session in Rome, 1969; Chm., 3rd Regional Congress for Asia and the Far East, at Canberra, 1970, and Rome, 1971). Fellow, Melvin Jones Internat. Foundn, 1991. Chm., Bd of Dirs, Brain Behaviour Res. Inst., La Trobe Univ., 1984–91. JP, Vic, 1957–84. Freedom: City of Croydon, 1989; City of Maroondah, 1997. DSocSc *hc*, Univ. of Technol., Melb., 1993. Woman of the Year, Sun News Pictorial, 1970; Humanitarian Award, Rosicrucian Order, USA, 1971; Community Service Award, Victorian Employers' Fedn, 1978; Distinguished Service to Children Award, Aust. Parents without Partners, Vic, 1984; Community Service Award, Seventh Day Adventists, 1985; Australian Achiever, Australia Day, 1998. *Address:* Llanberis, 4 Jackson Street, Croydon, Vic 3136, Australia. *T:* (3) 97232382. *Clubs:* Royal Automobile (Vic); War Widows Guild.

FROST, Ronald Edwin; Chairman, Hays plc, 1989–2001; *b* 19 March 1936; *s* of Charles Henry Frost and Doris (*née* Foggin); *m* 1959, Beryl Ward; one *s* two *d.* Founded Farmhouse Securities, 1965, Chm., 1979–81; Farmhouse Securities purchased by Hays Gp, 1981: Chief Exec., Distribn Div., 1981–83; Chief Exec. and Man. Dir, 1983–89. MInstD 1975; CIMgt (CBIM 1989). Freeman, City of London, 1983; Liveryman, Co. of

Watermen & Lightermen, 1983–. *Recreations:* farming, game shooting, sailing. *Address:* Thorncombe Park, Thorncombe Street, Bramley, Guildford, Surrey GU5 0ND. *Clubs:* Carlton, Royal Thames Yacht.

FROST, Sir Terence Ernest Manitou, (Sir Terry), Kt 1998; RA 1992; artist; Professor of Painting, University of Reading, 1977–81 (formerly Reader in Fine Art), Professor Emeritus 1981; *b* Oct. 1915; *m* 1945; five *s* one *d*. *Educ:* Leamington Spa Central Sch. Exhibitions: Leicester Galls, 1952–58; Waddington Galls, 1958–; B. Schaeffer Gallery, New York, 1960–62; Plymouth 1976; Bristol 1976; Serpentine Gall., 1977; Paris, 1978; Norway, 1979; Austin/Desmond Fine Art, 1989; Adelson Gall., New York, 1992–94; Mayor Gall., London, 1994; McGeary Gall., Brussels, 1995; Green on Red Gall., Dublin, 1995; Belgrave Gall., London, 1997; (retrospective) RA, 2000. Oil paintings acquired by Tate Gallery, National Gallery of Canada, National Gallery of NSW; also drawing acquired by Victoria and Albert Museum. Other work in public collections; Canada, USA, Germany, Australia, and in Edinburgh, Dublin, Leeds, Hull, Manchester, Birmingham, Liverpool, Bristol, etc. First glass sculpture made in Murano, Italy, 1998. Gregory Fellow in Painting, Univ. of Leeds, 1954–56. Hon. LLD CNAA, 1978. *Publications:* (illus.) 11 Poems by Federico Garcia Lorca, 1989; (jtly) Terry Frost, 1994. *Address:* Gernick Field Studio, Tredavoe Lane, Newlyn, Penzance TR18 5DL. *T:* (01736) 365902.

FROST, Thomas Pearson, FCIB; Group Chief Executive, National Westminster Bank, 1987–92; *b* 1 July 1933; *s* of James Watterson Frost and Enid Ella Crawte (*née* Pearson); *m* 1958, Elizabeth (*née* Morton); one *s* two *d*. *Educ:* Ormskirk Grammar Sch. FCIB (FIB 1976). Joined Westminster Bank, 1950; Chief Exec. Officer and Vice Chm., NBNA (later National Westminster Bank USA), 1980; National Westminster Bank: Gen. Man., Business Develt Div., 1982; Dir, 1984–93; Dep. Gp Chief Exec., 1985–87; Dep. Chm., 1992–93; Chm., London Clearing House Ltd, 1993–96. Chm., Five Oaks Investments PLC, 1995–98 (non-exec. Dir, 1993–95); non-executive Director: Freedom Food Ltd, 1994–; Fenchurch PLC, 1993–97. Member: BOTB, 1986–93; UK Adv. Bd, British-American Chamber of Commerce, 1987–93; Business in the Cities, 1988–91; Policy Adv. Cttee, Tidy Britain Gp, 1988–92; Adv. Bd, World Economic Forum, 1990–93; Chairman: CBI Business & Urban Regeneration Task Force, 1987–88; Exec. Cttee, British Bankers' Assoc., 1991–92. Trustee, British Sports Trust, 1988–92; Gov., Royal Ballet Sch., 1988–98. Fellow, World Scout Foundn, 1984. Freeman, City of London, 1978. FCIM 1987; CompOR 1987; CIMgt 1987; Companion, BITC, 1993; FRSA 1993. OStJ 1991. *Recreations:* golf, orchids, theatre. *Clubs:* Carlton, MCC; Brocket Hall Golf.

FROW, Prof. John Anthony, PhD; Regius Professor of Rhetoric and English Literature, University of Edinburgh, since 2000; *b* 13 Nov. 1948; *s* of Anthony Gaunt Frow and Nola Marjorie Frow; *m* 1970, Mayerlene Engineer (marr. diss. 1985); one *s*; partner, 1978, Christine Alavi; one *d*. *Educ:* Australian National Univ. (BA); Cornell Univ. (MA 1974; PhD 1977). Lectr in American Lit., Universidad del Salvador, Buenos Aires, 1970–75; Lectr in English Lit., then Sen. Lectr, Murdoch Univ., WA, 1975–88; Visiting Professor: Univ. of Minnesota, 1988–89; Univ. of Qld, 1989–2000. FAHA 1998. *Publications:* Marxism and Literary History, 1986; Cultural Studies and Cultural Value, 1995; Time and Commodity Culture, 1997; (jtly) Accounting for Tastes, 1999. *Address:* Department of English Literature, University of Edinburgh, Edinburgh EH8 9JX. *T:* (0131) 650 6856.

FROY, Prof. Martin; Professor of Fine Art, University of Reading, 1972–91, now Emeritus; *b* 9 Feb. 1926; *s* of late William Alan Froy and Helen Elizabeth Spencer. *Educ:* St Paul's Sch.; Magdalene Coll., Cambridge (one year); Slade Sch. of Fine Art. Dipl. in Fine Art (London). Visiting Teacher of Engraving, Slade Sch. of Fine Art, 1952–55; taught at Bath Acad. of Art, latterly as Head of Fine Art, 1954–65; Head of Painting Sch., Chelsea Sch. of Art, 1965–72. Gregory Fellow in Painting, Univ. of Leeds, 1951–54; Leverhulme Research Award, six months study in Italy, 1963; Sabbatical Award, Arts Council, 1965. Mem., Fine Art Panel, 1962–71, Mem. Council, 1969–71, Nat. Council for Diplomas in Art and Design; Trustee: National Gall., 1972–79; Tate Gall., 1975–79. Fellow, UCL, 1978. *One-Artist Exhibitions:* Hanover Gall., London, 1952; Wakefield City Art Gall., 1953; Belgrade Theatre, Coventry, 1958; Leicester Galls, London, 1961; Royal West of England Acad., Bristol, 1964; Univ. of Sussex, 1968; Hanover Gall., London, 1969; Park Square Gall., Leeds, 1970; Arnolfini Gall., Bristol, 1970; City Art Gall., Bristol (seven paintings), 1972; Univ. of Reading, 1979; New Ashgate Gall., Surrey, 1979; Serpentine Gall., 1983. *Other Exhibitions:* Internat. Abstract Artists, Riverside Mus., NY, 1950; ICA, London, 1950; Ten English Painters, Brit. Council touring exhibn in Scandinavia, 1952; Drawings from Twelve Countries, Art Inst. of Chicago, 1952; Figures in their Setting, Contemp. Art Soc. Exhibn, Tate Gall., 1953; Beaux Arts Gall., London, 1953; British Painting and Sculpture, Whitechapel Art Gall., London, 1954; Le Congrès pour la Liberté de la Culture Exhibn, Rome, Paris, Brussels, 1955; Pittsburgh Internat., 1955; Six Young Painters, Arts Council touring Exhibn, 1956; ICA Gregory Meml Exhibn, Bradford City Art Gall., Leeds, 1958; City Art Gall., Bristol, 1960; Malerei der Gegenwart ans Sudwestengland, Kunstverein, Hanover, 1962; Corsham Painters and Sculptors, Arts Council Touring Exhibn, 1965; Three Painters, Bath Fest. Exhibn, 1970; Park Square Gall., Leeds, 1978; Ruskin Sch., Univ. of Oxford, 1978; Newcastle Connection, Newcastle, 1980; Homage to Herbert Read, Canterbury, 1984. *Commissions, etc:* Artist Consultant for Arts Council to City Architect, Coventry, 1953–58; mosaic decoration, Belgrade Th., Coventry, 1957–58; two mural panels, Concert Hall, Morley Coll., London, 1958–59. *Works in Public Collections:* Tate Gall.; Mus. of Mod. Art, NY; Chicago Art Inst.; Arts Council; Contemp. Art Soc.; Royal W of England Acad.; Leeds Univ.; City Art Galls of Bristol, Carlisle, Leeds, Southampton and Wakefield; Reading Mus. and Art Gall. *Address:* Department of Fine Art, University of Reading, Earley Gate, Reading, Berks RG6 2AT.

FRUTIGER, Adrian; typeface designer; *b* 24 May 1928; *m* 1956, Simone Bickel; one *s*. *Educ:* compositor at Schlaefli Printer's, Interlaken; School of Applied Art, Zurich (Dip. in Type Design 1951). Typeface Designer and Artistic Manager, Deberny & Peignot, Paris, 1952–60; typeface designer and Studio Manager, Arcueil, Paris, 1960–92; Lecturer in type design, hist. of type and type drawing, Ecole Estienne, Paris, 1952–60; Ecole Nat. Supérieure des Arts Décoratifs, Paris, 1954–68; has designed more than 30 alphabets, incl. Univers, Frutiger, Centennial, OCR-B, Meridien, and Indian alphabet, Devanagari. Gutenberg Preis, City of Mainz, 1986; Medal, Type Dirs Club, NY, 1987; Grand Prix Nat. des Arts Graphiques, France, 1993. Officier de l'Ordre des Arts et des Lettres (France), 1993. *Publications:* Der Mensch und seine Zeichen, 1978; Signs and Symbols, 1998; Forms and Counterforms, 1998; Life Cycle, 1999. *Recreations:* walking through forest, drawing, wood cutting. *Address:* (home) Kunoweg 15, 3047 Bremgarten, Switzerland. *T:* and *Fax:* (31) 3026875; (office) Gewerbestrasse 9, PO Box 5334, 6330 Cham, Switzerland. *T:* (41) 7431105, *Fax:* (41) 7431106; *e-mail:* syndorpress@bluewin.ch.

FRY, Christopher; dramatist; *b* 18 Dec. 1907; *s* of Charles John Harris and Emma Marguerite Hammond, *d* of Emma Louisa Fry; *m* 1936, Phyllis Marjorie Hart (*d* 1987); one *s*. *Educ:* Bedford Modern Sch. Actor at Citizen House, Bath, 1927; Schoolmaster at Hazlewood Preparatory Sch., Limpsfield, Surrey, 1928–31; Dir of Tunbridge Wells Repertory Players, 1932–35; life too complicated for tabulation, 1935–39; The Tower, a pageant-play produced at Tewkesbury Fest., 1939; Dir of Oxford Repertory Players, 1940 and 1944–46, directing at Arts Theatre, London, 1945; Staff dramatist, Arts, 1947. FRSL. Hon. Fellow, Manchester Metrop. Univ. (formerly Manchester Poly.), 1988. DLitt Lambeth, 1988; Hon. DLitt: Sussex, 1994; De Montfort, 1994. Queen's Gold Medal (for Poetry), 1962; Benson Medal, RSL, 2001. *Plays:* A Phoenix Too Frequent, Mercury, 1946, St George's Theatre, 1983; The Lady's Not for Burning, Arts, 1948, Globe, 1949, Chichester, 1972; The Firstborn, Edinburgh Festival, 1948; Thor, with Angels, Canterbury Festival, 1949; Venus Observed, St James's, 1950, Chichester, 1992; The Boy with a Cart, Lyric, Hammersmith, 1950; Ring Round the Moon (translated from French of Jean Anouilh), Globe, 1950; A Sleep of Prisoners, produced St Thomas' Church, Regent Street, W1, 1951; The Dark is Light Enough, Aldwych, 1954; The Lark (trans. from French of Jean Anouilh), Lyric, Hammersmith, 1955; Tiger at the Gates (trans. from French of Jean Giraudoux), Apollo, 1955; Duel of Angels (trans. from Pour Lucrèce, of Jean Giraudoux), Apollo, 1958; Curtmantle, Edinburgh Festival, 1962; Judith (trans. from Giraudoux), Her Majesty's, 1962; A Yard of Sun, National, 1970; Peer Gynt (trans.), Chichester, 1970; Cyrano de Bergerac (trans.), Chichester, 1975; One Thing More, or Caedmon Construed, Chelmsford Cathedral, 1986. *TV:* The Brontës of Haworth, four plays, 1973 (also performed on stage, 1985); Sister Dora, 1977; The Best of Enemies, 1977. *Film Commentary* for The Queen is Crowned (Coronation film, 1953); *Film scripts:* (participation) Ben Hur; Barabbas; The Bible; The Beggar's Opera. *Publications:* The Boy with a Cart, 1939; The Firstborn, 1946; A Phoenix Too Frequent, 1946; The Lady's Not for Burning, 1949; Thor, with Angels, 1949; Venus Observed, 1950, rev. edn 1992; (trans.) Ring Round the Moon, 1950; A Sleep of Prisoners, 1951; The Dark is Light Enough, 1954; (trans.) The Lark, 1955; (trans.) Tiger at The Gates, 1955; (trans.) Duel of Angels, 1958; Curtmantle, 1961 (Heinemann Award of RSL); (trans.) Judith, 1962; A Yard of Sun, 1970; (trans.) Peer Gynt, 1970 (this trans. included in The Oxford Ibsen, vol. III, Brand and Peer Gynt, 1972); Four television plays: The Brontës at Haworth, 1954; (trans.) Cyrano de Bergerac, 1975; Can You Find Me: a family history, 1978; (ed and introd) Charlie Hammond's Sketch Book, 1980; Selected Plays, 1985; Genius, Talent and Failure, 1986 (Adam Lecture); One Thing More, or Caedmon Construed, 1987; Looking for a Language (lecture), 1992. *Address:* The Toft, East Dean, Chichester, West Sussex PO18 0JA. *Club:* Garrick.

FRY, Graham Holbrook; HM Diplomatic Service; High Commissioner, Malaysia, since 1998; *b* 20 Dec. 1949; *s* of Wing Comdr Richard Holbrook Fry and Marjorie Fry; *m* 1st, 1977, Mayko Iida (marr. diss. 1991); two *s*; 2nd, 1994, Toyoko Ando. *Educ:* Brasenose Coll., Oxford (BA 1972). Entered HM Diplomatic Service, 1972; Third, later Second, Sec., Tokyo, 1974–78; seconded to Invest in Britain Bureau, DoI, 1979–80; FCO, 1981–83; First Sec., Paris, 1983–87; FCO, 1987–88; Political Counsellor, Tokyo, 1989–93; Head, Far Eastern Dept, later Far Eastern and Pacific Dept, FCO, 1993–95; Dir, Northern Asia and Pacific, FCO, 1995–98. *Recreation:* bird-watching. *Address:* British High Commission, 185 Jalan Ampang, 50450 Kuala Lumpur, Malaysia.

FRY, Dr Ian Kelsey, DM, FRCP, FRCR; Dean, Medical College of St Bartholomew's Hospital, 1981–89; Consultant Radiologist, St Bartholomew's Hospital, 1966–87; *b* 25 Oct. 1923; *s* of Sir William and Lady Kelsey Fry; *m* 1951, Mary Josephine Casey; three *s* (one *d* decd). *Educ:* Radley Coll.; New Coll., Oxford; Guy's Hosp. Medical Sch. BM BCh 1948, DM Oxon 1961; MRCP 1956, FRCP 1972; DMRD 1961; FFR 1963; FRCR 1975. RAF Medical Services, 1949–50 (Sqdn Ldr). Director, Dept of Radiology, BUPA Medical Centre, 1973–86; Dir of Radiology, London Independent Hosp., 1986–94; Mem. Council, Royal College of Radiologists, 1979–82; Pres. and Chm. Bd, Med. Defence Union, 1993–97 (Mem. Bd, 1991–93); President, British Institute of Radiology, 1982–83. Gov., Charterhouse Sch., 1984–94. *Publications:* chapters and articles in books and jls. *Recreations:* golf, walking, racing. *Address:* The Pines, Woodlands Road, Bickley, Bromley, Kent BR1 2AE. *T:* (020) 8467 4150.

FRY, Jonathan Michael; Chairman, Christian Salvesen plc, since 1997; *b* 9 Aug. 1937; *s* of late Stephen Fry and Gladys Yvonne (*née* Blunt); *m* 1st, 1970, Caroline Mary Dunkerly (marr. diss. 1997); four *d*; 2nd, 1999, Marilyn Diana Russell. *Educ:* Repton Sch.; Trinity Coll., Oxford (Lit. Hum., MA). Engagement Manager and Consultant, McKinsey & Co., 1966–73; Unigate Foods Division: Man. Dir, 1973–76; Chm., 1976–78; Gp Planning Dir, Burmah Oil Trading Ltd, 1978–81; Chief Executive: Burmah Speciality Chemicals Ltd, 1981–87; Castrol Internat., 1987–93; Burmah Castrol: Man. Dir, 1990–93; Chief Exec., 1993–98; Chm., 1998–2000. Non-executive Director: Northern Foods plc, 1991– (Dep. Chm., 1996–); Elementis (formerly Harrisons & Crosfield), 1997– (Chm., 1997–). Control Risks Hldgs Ltd (Chm., 2000–). Mem. Council, RIIA, 1998–. *Recreations:* cricket, ski-ing, archaeology. *Address:* Beechingstoke Manor, Pewsey, Wilts SN9 6HQ. *Clubs:* MCC; Vincent's (Oxford).

FRY, Dame Margaret (Louise), DBE 1989 (OBE 1982); Chairman, National Union of Conservative and Unionist Associations, 1990–91 (a Vice-Chairman, 1987–90); *b* 10 March 1931; *d* of Richard Reed Dawe and Ruth Dora Dawe; *m* 1955, Walter William John Fry; three *s*. *Educ:* Tavistock Grammar School. Conservative Women's Advisory Committee (Western Area): Vice-Chm., 1975–78; Chm., 1978–81; Conservative Women's National Committee: Vice-Chm., 1981–82; Chm., 1984–87; Chm., W Devon Cons. Assoc., 1982–85; Patron, Torridge and W Devon Cons. Assoc., 1999– (Pres., 1992–99; Pres., Women's Cttee, 1988–93); Pres., Western Area Cons, 1995–99. *Recreations:* farming, conservation, church, sport (former member, Devon County Hockey XI). *Address:* Thorne Farm, Launceston, Cornwall PL15 9SN. *T:* (01566) 784308.

FRY, Sir Peter (Derek), Kt 1994; *b* 26 May 1931; *s* of Harry Walter Fry and late Edith Fry; *m*; one *s* one *d*; *m* 1982, Helen Claire Mitchell. *Educ:* Royal Grammar School, High Wycombe; Worcester College, Oxford (MA). Tillotsons (Liverpool) Ltd, 1954–56; Northern Assurance Co., 1956–61; Political Education Officer, Conservative Central Office, 1961–63. Member Bucks County Council, 1961–67. Consultant to Parly Monitoring Services Ltd, 1992–. Dir, Vision FM. Contested (C) North Nottingham, 1964, East Willesden, 1966. MP (C) Wellingborough, 1969–97; contested (C) same seat, 1997. Mem., Select Cttee on Transport, 1979–92; Joint Chairman: All-Party Roads Study Gp, 1974–97; Parly Road Passenger Gp, 1992–97; All-Party Aviation Gp, 1992–97; Parly Transport Forum, 1992–97; Vice. Chm., Cons. Aviation Cttee, 1994–97; Chairman: All-Party Footwear and Leather Gp, 1979–87; Anglo-Bahamas Parly Gp, 1980–97; British Slovenia Gp, 1993–97; British Macedonia Gp, 1993–97; formerly Chm., British Yugoslav Parly Gp; Vice-Chairman: British Bosnia Gp, 1993–95; British Croatia Gp, 1993–95; All-Party CSA Monitoring Gp, 1995–97; Jt Chm., All-Party Recreation and Leisure Gp, 1994–97; Vice Pres., British Southern Slav Soc. Formerly Mem., Delegn to Council of Europe/WEU. Non-exec. Chm., Nat. Bingo Game Assoc., 1998–. Played Rugby for Bucks County, 1956–58, Hon. Secretary, 1958–61. *Recreations:* watching Rugby football, reading history and biographies. *Address:* Glebe Farm House, Church Lane, Cranford, Kettering, Northants NN14 4AE. *Club:* Royal Automobile.

FRY, Richard Henry, CBE 1965; Financial Editor of The Guardian, 1939–65; *b* 23 Sept. 1900; *m* 1929, Katherine (*née* Maritz); no *c*. *Educ:* Berlin and Heidelberg Univs. *Publications:* Zero Hour, 1936; Watch Czechoslovakia, 1938; A Banker's World: the revival of the City, 1957–70, 1970; Bankers in West Africa, 1976. *Address:* Balint House, The Bishops Avenue, N2 0BG. *T:* (020) 8458 1392. *Club:* Reform.

FRY, Maj.-Gen. Robert Alan, MBE 1981; Commandant General, Royal Marines, since 2001; *b* 6 April 1951; *s* of Raymond and Elizabeth Fry; *m* 1977, Elizabeth Woolmore; two *d*. *Educ:* Bath Univ. (BScEcon); King's Coll., London (MA). Worked in commerce, NY, 1972–73; joined Royal Marines, 1973: COS, 3 Commando Bde, 1989–91; CO 45 Commando, 1995–97; Dir Naval Staff, MoD, 1997–99; Comdr 3 Commando Bde, 1999–2001. *Publications:* contrib. to RUSI Jl, US Naval Inst. Proc., Bull. d'Etudes de la Marine. *Recreations:* Welsh Rugby, cinema, photography, history. *Address:* c/o Headquarters Royal Marines, Whale Island, Portsmouth, Hants PO2 8DX. *Club:* Special Forces.

FRY, Ronald Ernest, FSS; Director of Economics and Statistics, Departments of the Environment and Transport, 1975–80, retired; *b* 21 May 1925; *s* of Ernest Fry and Lilian (*née* Eveling); *m* 1954, Jeanne Ivy Dawson; one *s* one *d*. *Educ:* Wilson's Grammar Sch., Camberwell; Birkbeck Coll., Univ. of London (BSc (Special)). MIS. Telecommunications Technician, Royal Signals, 1944–47; Scientific Asst, CEGB (London Region), 1948–52; Statistician: Glacier Metal Co., London, 1952–54; CEGB HQ, London, 1954–64; Gen. Register Office, 1965–66; Asst Dir of Research and Intelligence, GLC, 1966–69; Chief Statistician: (Social Statistics) Cabinet Office, 1969–74; (Manpower Statistics) Dept of Employment, 1974–75. *Publications:* various technical pubns in statistical and other professional jls. *Recreations:* photography, reading, motoring. *Address:* 39 Claremont Road, Hadley Wood, Barnet, Herts EN4 0HR. *T:* (020) 8440 1393.

FRY, Stephen John; writer, actor, comedian; *b* 24 Aug. 1957; *s* of Alan John Fry and Marianne Eve (*née* Newman). *Educ:* Uppingham Sch.; Queens' Coll., Cambridge (MA). *TV series:* Blackadder, 1987–89; A Bit of Fry and Laurie, 1989–95; Jeeves in Jeeves and Wooster, 1990–92; Gormenghast, 2000; *theatre:* Forty Years On, Queen's, 1984; The Common Pursuit, Phoenix, 1988; *films:* Peter's Friends, 1992; I.Q., 1995; Wilde, 1997; Cold Comfort Farm, 1997; The Tichborne Claimant, 1998; Whatever Happened to Harold Smith?, 2000; Relative Values, 2000. Columnist: The Listener, 1988–89; Daily Telegraph, 1990–. *Publications:* Me and My Girl, 1984 (musical performed in West End and on Broadway); A Bit of Fry and Laurie: collected scripts, 1990; Moab is My Washpot (autobiog.), 1997; *novels:* The Liar, 1991; The Hippopotamus, 1994; Making History, 1996; The Stars' Tennis Balls, 2000. *Recreations:* smoking, drinking, swearing, pressing wild flowers. *Address:* c/o Hamilton, Ground Floor, 24 Hanway Street, W1P 9DD. *Clubs:* Savile, Oxford and Cambridge, Groucho, Chelsea Arts.

FRY, William Norman H.; *see* Hillier-Fry.

FRYE, Michael John Ernest, CBE 1997; Chief Executive, B. Elliott plc, since 1988 (Chairman, 1987–92); *b* 2 June 1945; *s* of late Jack Frye, CBE and Daphne Page-Croft; *m* 1st, 1970, Geraldine Elizabeth Kendall; one *s*; 2nd, 1989, Valerie Patricia Harfield-Simpson; one *d*. *Educ:* Marlborough Coll.; MIT (SB Business Management, Mech. Eng. Minor). B. Elliott and subsidiaries, 1967–; Dir, Goldfields Industrial, 1973–76; Overseas Dir, B. Elliott, 1974–76, non-exec. Dir, 1976–87; Chm. and Chief Exec., Rotaflex Gp of Cos, 1975–87; Chm., Concord Lighting, 1976–87; non-exec. Dir, Thorn Lighting Group, 1993–. Chm. and Founder, Light and Health Res. Council, 1978; Member: NEDC Sub-Cttee, exports for luminaire manufrs, 1980–81; Council, Lighting Industry Fedn, 1980–87 (Vice-Pres., 1987); Illuminating Eng. Soc. of N America, 1979–; Chairman: Cttee to establish nat. lighting award, 1984–87; Lighting Div., CIBSE, 1987–88. Chairman: West London Leadership, 1990–; Business Link London, 1995–96; Dep. Chm., Park Royal Partnership, 1993–95 (Chm., 1991–92); Director: London First, 1992– (a Dep. Chm., 1996–); London Develt Partnership, 1998– (Chm., Skills Taskforce, 1998–). Chm., CBI London Reg., 1997– (Vice-Chm., 1996–97). Chm. and Mem., numerous technical and arts organisations. Hon. Prof., Thames Valley Univ., 1995. Liveryman, Turners' Co. and Lightmongers' Co. FRAeS 1994; Fellow, RSPB, 1987; FRSA 1978 (Vice Pres., 1990–; Chm., 1991–93; Dep. Chm., 1993–94). Hon. Fellow, RCA, 1987. *Recreations:* golf, tennis, chess, bird watching, collecting old or rare bird books. *Address:* B. Elliott plc, Elliott House, Victoria Road, NW10 6NY. *T:* (020) 8961 7333. *Clubs:* Boodle's, City Livery, Royal Automobile; Royal Worlington and Newmarket Golf.

FRYER, Dr Geoffrey, FRS 1972; Deputy Chief Scientific Officer, Windermere Laboratory, Freshwater Biological Association, 1981–88; *b* 6 Aug. 1927; *s* of W. and M. Fryer; *m* 1953, Vivien Griffiths Hodgson; one *s* one *d*. *Educ:* Huddersfield College. DSc, PhD London. Royal Navy, 1946–48. Colonial Research Student, 1952–53; HM Overseas Research Service, 1953–60: Malawi, 1953–55; Zambia, 1955–57; Uganda, 1957–60; Sen., then Principal, then Sen. Principal Scientific Officer, Freshwater Biological Assoc., 1960–81. H. R. Macmillan Lectr, Univ. of British Columbia, 1963; Distinguished Vis. Schol., Univ. of Adelaide, 1985; Distinguished Lectr, Biol Scis Br., Dept. Fisheries and Oceans, Canada, 1987; Hon. Prof., Inst. of Environmental and Natural (formerly Biol) Scis, Lancaster Univ., 1988–. Mem. Council, Royal Soc., 1978–80. Mem., Adv. Cttee on Science, Nature Conservancy Council, 1986–91. Pres., Yorks Naturalists' Union, 1993. Frink Medal, Zool Soc. of London, 1983; Linnean Medal for Zoology, Linnean Soc., 1987; Elsdon-Dew Medal, Parasitological Soc. of Southern Africa, 1998. *Publications:* (with T. D. Iles) The Cichlid Fishes of the Great Lakes of Africa: their biology and evolution, 1972; A natural history of the lakes, tarns and streams of the English Lake District, 1991; The Freshwater Crustacea of Yorkshire: a faunistic and ecological survey, 1993; (ed with V. R. Alexeev) Diapause in the Crustacea, 1996; numerous articles in scientific jls. *Recreations:* natural history, walking, church architecture, photography. *Address:* Elleray Cottage, Windermere, Cumbria LA23 1AW.

FUAD, Kutlu Tekin, CBE 1993; SPMB 1999; President, Court of Appeal, Negara Brunei Darussalam, 1993–2000; a non-permanent Judge, Court of Final Appeal, Hong Kong, since 1997; *b* 23 April 1926; *s* of Mustafa Fuad Bey, CMG, and Belkis Hilmi; *m* 1952, Inci Izzet; two *s* one *d*. *Educ:* Temple Grove; Marlborough Coll.; St John's Coll., Cambridge (MA). Called to the Bar, Inner Temple, 1952, Hon. Bencher, 1993. Mil. Service, Lieut KRRC, 1944–48. Colonial Legal Service, 1953–62: Magistrate, Cyprus; Resident Magistrate, Sen. Crown Counsel, Legal Draftsman, and Dir of Public Prosecutions, Uganda; Judge of the High Court, Uganda, 1963–72 (Pres., Industrial Court; Chm., Law Reform Cttee); Dir, Legal Div., Commonwealth Secretariat, 1972–80; Judge, High Court of Hong Kong, 1980–82; Justice of Appeal, 1982–88, Vice-Pres., 1988–93, Court of Appeal, Hong Kong. Comr, Supreme Ct of Negara Brunei Darussalam, 1983–86, 1988–92. Nominated by Turkey as *ad hoc* judge for case brought to ECHR, 2000. Mem., Law Reform Commn, Hong Kong, 1983–89. Pres., Hong Kong Family Law Assoc., 1986–93. Formerly Chm., Visitation Cttee, Makerere University Coll. *Recreations:* music, Rugby football, gardening. *Address:* PO Box 415, Lefkoşa, Mersin 10, Turkey; 76 Abingdon Villas, Kensington, W8 6XB. *T:* (020) 7937 8646.

FUENTES, Prof. Carlos; Professor at Large, Brown University; *b* 11 Nov. 1928; *s* of Ambassador Rafael Fuentes and Berta Fuentes; *m* 1st, 1957, Rita Macedo; one *d*; 2nd, 1973, Sylvia Lemus; one *s* one *d*. *Educ:* Law School, Nat. Univ., Mexico; Inst. des Hautes Etudes Internat., Geneva. Sec., Mexican Deleg. to ILO, Geneva, 1950; Under Director of Culture, Nat. Univ., Mexico, 1952–54; Head, Cultural Relations Dept, Min. of Foreign Affairs, Mexico, 1955–58; Ambassador to France, 1975–77; Prof. of English and Romance Languages, Univ. of Pennsylvania, 1978–83; Prof. of Comparative Literature, Harvard, 1984–86; Simón Bolivar Prof., Cambridge, 1986–87; Robert F. Kennedy Prof. of Latin American Studies, Harvard, 1987–90. Member: El Colegio Nacional, Mexico, 1974–; Mexican Nat. Commn on Human Rights, 1989–; Fellow, Wilson Center, Washington DC, 1974; Mem., Amer. Acad. and Inst. of Arts and Letters, 1986; Trustee, NY Public Library, 1987. Hon. DLitt: Wesleyan, 1982; Warwick, 1992; Hon. LLD Harvard, 1983; Hon. LittD Cambridge, 1987; DUniv Essex, 1987; Dr *hc*: Tufts, 1993; UCLA, 1993. Nat. Prize for Literature, Mexico, 1985; Miguel de Cervantes Prize, 1987; Menéndez Pelayo Prize, Univ. of Santander, 1992. Légion d'Honneur (France), 1992. *Publications:* Where the Air is Clear, 1958; The Good Conscience, 1959; The Death of Artemio Cruz, 1962; Aura, 1962; A Change of Skin, 1967 (Biblioteca Breve Prize, Barcelona); Terra Nostra, 1975 (Rómulo Gallegos Prize); Distant Relations, 1980; Burnt Water, 1982; The Old Gringo, 1984 (filmed, 1989); Cristóbal Nonato, 1987; Myself with Others: selected essays, 1988; The Campaign, 1991; Valiente Mundo Nuevo: essays, 1991; Constancia and other stories for virgins, 1991; The Buried Mirror, 1992 (televised); El Naranjo (The Orange Tree) (novellas), 1993; Geography of the Novel: essays, 1993; A New Time for Mexico, 1997; Diana, 1997; Por un Progreso Incluyente, 1997; The Crystal Frontier: a novel in nine stories, 1997; Portraits in Time (photo essay), 1998; The Years with Laura Diaz, 1999; (ed jtly) The Picador Book of Latin American Stories, 1999. *Address:* c/o Brandt & Brandt, 1501 Broadway, New York, NY 10036, USA.

FUGARD, Athol; playwright, director, actor; *b* 11 June 1932; *s* of Harold David Fugard and Elizabeth Magdalene Potgieter; *m* 1956, Sheila Meiring; one *d*. *Educ:* Univ. of Cape Town. Directed earliest plays, Nongogo, No Good Friday, Johannesburg, 1960; acted in The Blood Knot, touring S Africa, 1961; Hello and Goodbye, 1965; directed and acted in The Blood Knot, London, 1966; Boesman and Lena, S Africa, 1969; directed Boesman and Lena, London, 1971; directed Serpent Players in various prodns, Port Elizabeth, from 1963, directed co-authors John Kani and Winston Ntshona in Sizwe Bansi is Dead, SA, 1972, The Island, 1973, and London, 1973–74; acted in film, Boesman and Lena, 1972; directed and acted in Statements after an Arrest under the Immorality Act, in SA, 1972, directed in London, 1973; wrote Dimetos for Edinburgh Fest., 1975; directed and acted in, A Lesson from Aloes, SA, 1978, London, 1980 (directed, NY 1981, winning NY Critics Circle Award for Best Play); directed: Master Harold and the Boys, NY, 1982 (Drama Desk Award), Johannesburg, 1983, Nat. Theatre, 1983 (Standard award for Best Play); The Road to Mecca, Yale Repertory Theatre, 1984; (also wrote) My Children! My Africa!, NY, 1990; (also wrote) Playland, SA, 1992, NY and London, 1993; (also wrote and acted in) Valley Song, Royal Court, 1996; (also wrote and acted in) The Captain's Tiger, NY, 1999, London, 2000. Hon. DLitt: Natal, 1981; Rhodes, 1983; Cape Town, 1984; Emory, 1992; Port Elizabeth, 1993; Hon. DFA Yale, 1983; Hon. DHL Georgetown, 1984. *Films:* Boesman and Lena, 1973; The Guest, 1977; (acted in) Meetings with Remarkable Men (dir, Peter Brook), 1979; (wrote and acted in) Marigolds in August (Silver Bear Award, Berlin), 1980; (acted in) Gandhi, 1982; (co-dir and acted in) Road to Mecca, 1991. *Publications:* The Blood Knot, 1962; People Are Living There, Hello and Goodbye, 1973; Boesman and Lena, 1973; (jtly) Three Port Elizabeth Plays: Sizwe Bansi is Dead, The Island, Statements after an Arrest under the Immorality Act, 1974; Tsotsi (novel), 1980 (also USA); A Lesson from Aloes, 1981 (also USA); Master Harold and the Boys, US 1982, UK 1983; Notebooks 1960–1977, 1983 (also USA); Road to Mecca, 1985; A Place with the Pigs, 1988; Cousins: a memoir, 1994. *Recreations:* angling, skin-diving, bird-watching. *Address:* PO Box 5090, Walmer, Port Elizabeth 6065, South Africa.

FUHR, Michael John, OBE 1999; Director, London Underground Task Group, Department for Transport, Local Government and the Regions (formerly of the Environment, Transport and the Regions), since 1999; *b* 5 June 1949; *s* of late Max Fuhr and of Betty Fuhr; *m* 1975, Susan Harrington; two *d*. *Educ:* Bradford Grammar Sch.; Univ. of Surrey (BSc Hons 1973). Admin trainee, 1974, Principal, 1978, DoE; Department of Transport, then DETR, now DTLR, 1979–; Asst Sec., 1989; Project Dir, Channel Tunnel Rail Link, 1996–99. *Recreations:* most sports, photography, technology, following the variable fortunes of Bradford City AFC. *Address:* Department for Transport, Local Government and the Regions, Great Minster House, 76 Marsham Street, SW1P 4DR. *T:* (020) 7944 6001.

FUJII, Hiroaki; President, Japan Foundation, Tokyo, since 1997; *b* 21 Aug. 1933; *m* 1963, Kiyoko Shimoda; three *d*. *Educ:* Tokyo Univ.; Amherst Coll., USA (BA 1958). Entered Min. of Foreign Affairs, Japan, 1956; Dir, Econ. Affairs Div., UN Bureau, 1971–72; Private Sec. to Minister for Foreign Affairs, 1972–74; Dir, 2nd Econ. Co-operation Div., Econ. Co-operation Bureau, 1974–75; Dir, 1st N American Div., American Affairs Bureau, 1975–76; Fellow, Center for Internat. Affairs, Harvard Univ., 1976; Counsellor, Embassy of Japan, Washington, 1977–79; Ministry of Foreign Affairs: Dir, Personnel Div., Minister's Secretariat, 1979–81; Dep. Dir Gen., Asian Affairs Bureau, 1981–83; Consul-Gen., Hong Kong, 1983–85; Ministry of Foreign Affairs: Dir Gen., N American Affairs Bureau, 1985–88; Dep. Vice-Minister, 1988–89; Ambassador to: OECD, Paris, 1989–92; Thailand, 1992–94; Court of St James's, 1994–97. Hon. DCL: Durham, 1997; UEA, 1999. Kt Grand Cross (1st Cl.), Most Exalted Order of White Elephant (Thailand), 1994. *Address:* Ark Mori Building, 21st Floor, 1-12-32 Akasaka, Minato-ku, Tokyo 107-6021, Japan. *T:* (3) 55623480, *Fax:* (3) 55623492.

FULFORD, Adrian Bruce; QC 1994; a Recorder, since 2001; *b* 8 Jan. 1953; *s* of Gerald John Fulford and Marie Bettine (*née* Stevens). *Educ:* Elizabeth Coll., Guernsey; Southampton Univ. (BA Hons). Housing Advr, Shelter's Housing Aid Centre, 1974–75; called to the Bar, Middle Temple, 1978. Ed., UK Human Rights Reports, 2000–. *Publications:* (contrib.) Atkin's Court Forms, 1987; (ed) Archbold Criminal Pleadings and Practices, 1992; (jtly) A Criminal Practitioner's Guide to Judicial Review and Case Stated, 1999. *Recreations:* riding, tennis, politics, golf. *Address:* 14 Took's Court, Cursitor Street, EC4A 1JY. *Club:* Reform.

FULFORD, Prof. Michael Gordon, PhD; FSA; FBA 1994; Professor of Archaeology, since 1993 and Pro-Vice-Chancellor, since 1998, University of Reading; *b* 20 Oct. 1948; *s* of Comdr E. G. J. D. Fulford, RN (retd) and E. Z. Fulford (*née* Simpson); *m* 1972, Charlotte Jane Hobbs; one *s* one *d*. *Educ:* St Edwards Sch., Oxford; Univ. of Southampton (BA Hons 1970; PhD 1975). DES Res. Student, 1970; Research Assistant: Univ. of Southampton, 1971–72; Univ. of Oxford, 1972–74; University of Reading: Lectr in Archaeol., 1974–85; Reader, 1985–88; Leverhulme Res. Fellow, 1987; Personal Prof., 1988–93; Dean, Faculty of Letters and Social Scis, 1994–97. Chm., Archaeol. Panel, RAE 2001, HEFCE. Dalrymple Lectr, Glasgow Univ., 1996. Editor, Britannia, 1994–99. English Heritage: Chm., Hadrian's Wall Adv. Panel, 1989–97 (Mem., 1985–97); Mem., Ancient Monuments Adv. Cttee, 1991–97; Comr, RCHM, 1993–99; Mem.,

Archaeology Adv. Cttee, Nat. Mus. of Wales, 1991–99. Mem., Humanities Res. Bd, British Acad., 1995–98; Vice-Pres., Royal Archaeol Inst., 1996–. FSA 1977. *Publications:* New Forest Roman Pottery, 1975; (with B. Cunliffe) CSIR Great Britain I: Bath and the Rest of Wessex, 1982; Silchester Defences, 1984; (with D. Peacock) Excavations at Carthage: The British Mission, The Pottery and other Ceramics, Vol 1, 1984, Vol 2, 1994; The Silchester Amphitheatre, 1989; Excavations at Sabratha 1948–1951, Vol. 2, pt i (ed with M. Hall), 1989, pt ii (ed with R. Tomber), 1994; (ed jtly) Developing Landscape of Lowland Britain: the archaeology of the British gravels, 1992; (ed jtly) England's Coastal Heritage, 1997; (with J. R. Timby) Late Iron Age and Roman Silchester: excavations on the site of the Forum-Basilica 1977 and 1980–86, 2000. *Recreations:* music, walking, sailing. *Address:* Department of Archaeology, University of Reading, PO Box 218, Reading, Berks RG6 6AA. *T:* (0118) 931 8132.

FULFORD, Robert John; Keeper, Department of Printed Books, British Library (formerly British Museum), 1967–85; *b* 16 Aug. 1923; *s* of John Fulford, Southampton; *m* 1950, Alison Margaret Rees (*d* 1996); one *s* one *d.* *Educ:* King Edward VI Sch., Southampton; King's Coll., Cambridge; Charles Univ., Prague. Asst Keeper, Dept of Printed Books, British Museum, 1945–65; Dep. Keeper, 1965–67 (Head of Slavonic Div., 1961–67); Keeper, 1967–85. *Address:* 7 Tulip Tree Close, Tonbridge, Kent TN9 2SH. *T:* (01732) 350356; Maumont, 24390 Hautefort, France. *T:* 553505007.

FULFORD-DOBSON, Captain Michael, CVO 1999; JP; RN; Lord-Lieutenant of Dorset, since 1999; *b* 6 April 1931; *e s* of late Lt-Col Cyril Fulford-Dobson, OBE and Betty Bertha Fulford-Dobson (*née* Bendelack-Hudson-Barmby); *m* 1966, Elizabeth Barbara Mary Rose Tate; three *d.* *Educ:* Pangbourne Coll.; RN Coll., Dartmouth. Royal Navy, 1949–84 (served Korean War, Suez Operation, first Cod War; 3 Sea Comds); Gentleman Usher to the Queen, 1985–99, Extra Gentleman Usher, 1999–. Chm., W Dorset Hosps NHS Trust, 1991–98. Chm., Dorset Trust, 1991–2000; Pres., Dorset Br., CPRE, 1995–; Trustee, Cancer Care Dorset, 1998–. Dir, In and Out Ltd, 1993–96. Governor, Sherborne Sch., 1999–. High Sheriff of Dorset, 1994–95; JP Dorset, 1999. KStJ 1999. *Recreations:* restoration of historic buildings, cross country ski-ing, field sports. *Address:* Cerne Abbey, Dorset DT2 7JQ. *T:* (01300) 341284, *T:* and *Fax:* (01300) 341948; *e-mail:* mfd@ukonline.co.uk. *Club:* White's.

FULHAM, Bishop Suffragan of, since 1996; **Rt Rev. John Charles Broadhurst;** *b* 20 July 1942; *s* of late Charles Harold Broadhurst and of Dorothy Sylvia (*née* Prince); *m* 1965, Judith Margaret Randall; two *s* two *d.* *Educ:* Owen's Sch., Islington; King's Coll., London (AKC 1965); St Boniface Coll., Warminster; STh Lambeth, 1982. Ordained deacon, 1966, priest, 1967; Asst Curate, St Michael-at-Bowes, 1966–70; Priest-in-charge, 1970–75, Vicar, 1975–85, St Augustine, Wembley Park; Team Rector, Wood Green, 1985–96. Area Dean: Brent, 1982–85; E Haringey, 1985–91. Member: Gen. Synod of C of E, 1972–96 (Mem., Standing Cttee, 1988–96); ACC, 1991–96. Chm., Forward in Faith, 1992–. *Publications:* (ed and contrib.) Quo Vaditis, 1996; numerous contribs to jls. *Recreations:* gardening, history, travel. *Address:* 26 Canonbury Park South, N1 2FN. *T:* (020) 7354 2334, *Fax:* (020) 7354 2335; *e-mail:* bpfulham@compuserve.com.

FULLER, Anne Rosemary, OBE 2000; JP; Chairman of Council, Magistrates' Association, 1996–99 (Deputy Chairman, 1993–96); *b* 27 Sept. 1936; *d* of Ronald Clifford Dent and Clara Vera Dent (*née* Murray); *m* 1960, John Acland Fuller; two *s* one *d.* *Educ:* St Anne's Sch., Windermere; Royal Holloway Coll., Univ. of London (BA Hons 1957); KCL and LSE (Dip. in Law 1992). Market Research Executive: McCann Erickson, then Marplan, 1958–60; Bureau of Commercial Research, 1960–65; freelance market res. consultant, 1965–. Member: Nat. Forum, SCAA, 1996–97; Home Secretary's Task Force on Youth Justice, 1997–98; Compliance and Supervision Cttee, Office for Supervision of Solicitors, 1998–; Sentencing Adv. Panel, 1999–; Tribunal Mem., Disciplinary Cttee, ICAEW, 2000–. Dir and Trustee, SOVA, 2000–. JP Kingston-upon-Thames, 1975 (Dep. Chm., 1991–95); Chm., Betting Licensing Cttee, 1986–89; Mem., Magistrates' Courts Cttee, 1987–96; Chm., Youth Panel, 1990–93; Vice Pres., Magistrates' Assoc., 1999– (Mem. Council, 1984–; Vice Chm., Sentencing Cttee, 1991–93); Mem., Magistrates' Courts Consultative Council, 1993–99 (Mem., Trial Issues Gp, 1996–99); Nat. Co-ordinator, Magistrates in Community Project, 1993–97. FRSA 1997. *Publications:* (ed jtly) International Directory of Market Research Organisations, 1974, 11th edn 1994; numerous articles on magisterial matters. *Recreations:* music, theatre, cookery. *Address:* White Ridge, Ruxley Crescent, Claygate, Surrey KT10 0TX. *T:* (01372) 462609.

FULLER, Brian Leslie, CBE 1989; QFSM 1981; Commandant Chief Executive, Fire Service College, 1990–94; Chairman, BFA Developments International; *b* 18 April 1936; *s* of Walter Leslie Victor Fuller and Eliza May Fuller; *m* 1957, Linda Peters; three *s.* *Educ:* St Albans County Grammar Sch. for Boys. FIFireE 1975. Station Officer: Herts Fire Brigade, 1960–66; Warwicks Fire Brigade, 1966–68; Asst Divl Officer, Notts Fire Brigade, 1968–69; Divl Commander, Essex Fire Brigade, 1969–72; Dep. Chief Fire Officer, Glamorgan Fire Brigade, 1972–74; Chief Fire Officer: Mid Glamorgan Fire Brigade, 1974–80; Notts Fire Brigade, 1980–81; W Midlands Fire Service, 1981–90. Gen. Manager and Principal, Fire Safety Engrg Coll., Oman, 1997–2001. Hon. DSc South Bank, 1993. *Recreations:* cricket, music, reading. *Address:* Newlands, Aqueduct Lane, Alvechurch, Birmingham B48 7BP.

FULLER, Geoffrey Herbert, CEng, FRINA, FIMarE; RCNC; defence and maritime consultant; Director, British Maritime Technology Ltd, Teddington, 1985–2000 (Deputy Chairman, 1985–95); *b* 16 Jan. 1927; *s* of late Major Herbert Thomas Fuller and Clarice Christine Fuller; *m* 1952, Pamela-Maria Quarrell; one *d.* *Educ:* Merchant Taylors', Northwood, Mddx; Royal Naval Engrg Coll., Keyham; Royal Naval Coll., Greenwich. FRINA 1965; FIMarE 1974. Constructor Commander: Staff of Flag Officer (Submarines), 1958; British Navy Staff, Washington, 1960; RCDS, 1973; Support Manager Submarines, 1976; Dep. Dir, Submarines/Polaris, Ship Dept, MoD, 1979; Dir of Naval Ship Production, 1981–82; Dir, Manpower and Productivity, HM Dockyards, 1982–83; Mem. Bd, and Man. Dir, Warship Div., British Shipbuilders, 1983–85; Exec. Chm., 1984–86, Technical Adviser, 1986–87, Vickers Shipbuilding and Engrg Ltd, Barrow. Treas., RINA, 1999– (Chm. Council, 1994–96). FRSA 1995. *Address:* Casa Feliz, Weston Park, Bath BA1 4AL. *T:* (01225) 466054.

FULLER, Sir James (Henry Fleetwood), 4th Bt *cr* 1910, of Neston Park, Corsham, Wiltshire; with Fuller Smith & Turner plc, since 1998; *b* 1 Nov. 1970; *e s* of Major Sir John William Fleetwood Fuller, 3rd Bt and of Lorna Marian (*née* Kemp-Potter); *S* father, 1998; *m* 2000, Venetia, *d* of Col Robin Mactaggart; one *s.* *Educ:* Milton Abbey Sch. Commnd The Life Guards, 1991; Belize, 1993; Bosnia, 1994; Knightsbridge, 1995–98. *Heir: s* Archie Mungo Fleetwood Fuller, *b* 7 Aug. 2001. *Address:* Neston Park, Corsham, Wiltshire SN13 9TG. *T:* (01225) 810211.

FULLER, Hon. Sir John (Bryan Munro), Kt 1974; President: Arthritis Foundation of Australia, 1980–91 (Emeritus Vice-President, since 1991); Barnardo's Australia, 1985–95 (Member, Management Committee, 1980–85); *b* 22 Sept. 1917; *s* of late Bryan Fuller, QC; *m* 1940, Eileen, *d* of O. S. Webb; one *s* one *d.* *Educ:* Knox Grammar Sch., Wahroonga. Chm., Australian Country Party (NSW), 1959–64; MLC, NSW, 1961–78; Minister for Decentralisation and Development, 1965–73; NSW Minister for Planning and Environment, 1973–76; Vice-Pres. of Exec. Council and Leader of Govt in Legis. Council,1968–76; Leader of Opposition, 1976–78; Leader, various NSW Govt trade missions to various parts of the world. Pres., Assoc. of Former Mems of NSW Parlt, 1988–92. Australian Institute of Export: Federal Pres., 1986–91; Mem., Federal Council, 1985–92; Pres., NSW, 1985; Fellow, 1969; Hon. Life Fellow, 1991. Vice-Pres., Graziers Assoc. of NSW, 1965; Member: Council, Univ. of NSW, 1967–78; Cttee, United World Colls Trust, NSW, 1978–88; Bd, Foundn for Res. and Treatment Alcohol and Drug Dependence, 1980–85; Council, Nat. Heart Foundn, NSW, 1980–. Chm., Rushcutters Bay Maritime Reserve Trust, 1993–96. Nat. Patron, Australian Monarchist League, 1997–. *Recreations:* tennis, bowls. *Address:* 54/8 Fullerton Street, Woollahra, NSW 2025, Australia. *Clubs:* Australian (Sydney); Double Bay Bowling, Royal Sydney Golf, Australian Jockey.

FULLER, John Leopold, FRSL 1980; writer; Fellow of Magdalen College, Oxford, and Tutor in English, since 1966; *b* 1 Jan. 1937; *s* of late Roy Broadbent Fuller, CBE, FRSL; *m* 1960, Cicely Prudence Martin; three *d.* *Educ:* St Paul's School; New Coll., Oxford (BLitt, MA). Vis. Lectr, State Univ. of NY at Buffalo, 1962–63; Asst Lectr, Univ. of Manchester, 1963–66. *Publications:* Fairground Music, 1961; The Tree that Walked, 1967; A Reader's Guide to W. H. Auden, 1970; The Sonnet, 1972; Cannibals and Missionaries, 1972, and Epistles to Several Persons, 1973 (Geoffrey Faber Meml Prize, 1974); Squeaking Crust, 1973; The Last Bid, 1975; The Mountain in the Sea, 1975; Lies and Secrets, 1979; The Illusionists (Southern Arts Lit. Prize), 1980; The Extraordinary Wool Mill and other stories, 1980; Waiting for the Music, 1982; Flying to Nowhere (Whitbread Prize for a First Novel), 1983; The Beautiful Inventions, 1983; (ed) The Dramatic Works of John Gay, 1983; Come Aboard and Sail Away, 1983; The Adventures of Speedfall, 1985; Selected Poems 1954–1982, 1985; (with James Fenton) Partingtime Hall, 1986; Tell It Me Again, 1988; The Grey Among the Green, 1988; The Burning Boys, 1989; (ed) The Chatto Book of Love Poetry, 1990; The Mechanical Body, 1991; Look Twice, 1991; The Worm and the Star, 1993; Stones and Fires, 1996 (Forward Prize, Forward Poetry Trust, 1997); Collected Poems, 1996; A Skin Diary, 1997; W. H. Auden: a commentary, 1998; (ed) The Oxford Book of Sonnets, 2000; The Memoirs of Laetitia Horsepole, 2001. *Recreations:* correspondence chess, music. *Address:* Magdalen College, Oxford OX1 4AU. *T:* (01865) 276070.

FULLER, Rev. Canon Dr Michael Jeremy; Principal, Theological Institute of the Scottish Episcopal Church, since 2000; *b* 7 Jan. 1963; *s* of Peter Roy Fuller and Mary Eileen Fuller; *m* 1993, Sue Rigby; two *s.* *Educ:* King Edward VI Grammar Sch., Chelmsford; Worcester Coll., Oxford (BA 1985, MA 1989; DPhil 1989); Westcott House and Queens' Coll., Cambridge (BA 1991). Ordained deacon 1992, priest 1993; Curate, All Saints', High Wycombe, 1992–95; Associate Rector, St John's, Princes Street, Edinburgh, 1995–99; Canon, St Mary's Cathedral, Edinburgh, 2000–. Hon. Vis. Fellow, New Coll., Edinburgh, 1998–. *Publications:* Atoms and Icons, 1995; articles and reviews in Theology, Modern Believing, New Blackfriars, Musical Times, etc. *Recreations:* opera, reading, writing. *Address:* Theological Institute of the Scottish Episcopal Church, Old Coates House, 32 Manor Place, Edinburgh EH3 7EB. *T:* (0131) 220 2272. *Club:* New (Edinburgh).

FULLER, Michael John; Chief Executive, since 1992, Director, since 2000, Al Ahli Commercial Bank, Bahrain; Director, Ahli United Bank, since 2000; *b* 20 July 1932; *s* of Thomas Frederick and Irene Emily Fuller; *m* 1st, 1955, Maureen Rita Slade (marr. diss. 1989); two *s* two *d*; 2nd, 1990, Elizabeth Frost. *Educ:* Wallington County Grammar Sch. FCIB 1980. National Service, commnd RAF, 1950–52. Midland Bank, 1948–90: various branch, regl and head office posts; Gp Public Affairs Advr, 1977–79; Regl Dir, Southampton, 1979–81; Gen. Manager, Midland and Wales, 1981–82; Gen. Manager, Business Develt Div., 1982–85; UK Operations Dir, 1985–87; Dep. Chief Exec., 1987–89, Chief Exec., 1989–90, UK Banking Sector; Gen. Man., Nat. Bank of Abu Dhabi, 1991–92. FRSA 1994. *Recreations:* reading, travelling, rough golf, ski-ing. *Address:* c/o Al Ahli Commercial Bank, PO Box 5941, Manama, Bahrain. *Club:* Royal Air Force.

FULLER, Simon William John, CMG 1994; HM Diplomatic Service; UK Permanent Representative to the Office of the United Nations and other international organisations, Geneva, since 2000; *b* 27 Nov. 1943; *s* of late Rowland William Bevis Fuller and Madeline Fuller (*née* Bailey); *m* 1984, Eleanor Mary Breedon; three *s.* *Educ:* Wellington College; Emmanuel College, Cambridge (BA Hist.). Served Singapore and Kinshasa, 1969–73; First Sec., Cabinet Office, 1973–75; FCO, 1975–77; UK Mission to UN, New York, 1977–80; FCO, 1980–86 (Counsellor, 1984); Dep. Hd of Mission, Tel Aviv, 1986–90; Hd of NE and N African Dept, FCO, 1990–93; Hd of UK Delegn to CSCE, then OSCE, Vienna, 1993–99. *Recreations:* cooking and cricket. *Address:* c/o Foreign and Commonwealth Office, SW1A 2AH; 27 Carlisle Mansions, Carlisle Place, SW1P 1EZ. *T:* (020) 7828 6494. *Clubs:* Brooks's, MCC.

FULLERTON, Hance, OBE 1995; Chairman: Grampian University Hospitals NHS Trust, since 1996; Angle Technology Ltd, since 1996; *b* 6 Dec. 1934; *s* of late Robert Fullerton and Jessie Fullerton (*née* Smith); *m* 1958, Jeannie Reid Cowie; three *d.* *Educ:* Anderson Educnl Inst., Lerwick; Aberdeen Univ. (BSc). Technical, producn and operational mgt in paper industry, 1958–78; Gen. Manager, Aberdeen, 1978–81, Divl Dir, 1981–86, Wiggins Teape Ltd; Gen. Manager, Grampian Health Bd, 1986–91; Chief Exec., Grampian Enterprise Ltd, 1991–96. Chairman: Aberdeen Univ. Res. and Industrial Services Ltd, 1996–2000; Cordah Ltd, 1996–99. Hon. LLD Aberdeen, 1996. *Recreations:* golf, walking, reading, theatre. *Club:* Royal Northern and University (Aberdeen).

FULLERTON, William Hugh, CMG 1989; HM Diplomatic Service, retired; Ambassador to Morocco and Mauritania, 1996–99; *b* 11 Feb. 1939; *s* of late Major Arthur Hugh Theodore Francis Fullerton, RAMC, and of Mary (*née* Parker); *m* 1968, Arlene Jacobowitz; one *d.* *Educ:* Cheltenham Coll.; Queens' Coll., Cambridge (MA Oriental Langs). Shell Internat. Petroleum Co., Uganda, 1963–65; FO, 1965; MECAS, Shemlan, Lebanon, 1965–66; Information Officer, Jedda, 1966–67; UK Mission to UN, New York, 1967; FCO, 1968–70; Head of Chancery, Kingston, Jamaica, 1970–73, and Ankara, 1973–77; FCO, 1977–80; Counsellor (Economic and Commercial), 1980–83 and Consul-Gen., 1981–83, Islamabad; Ambassador to Somalia, 1983–87; on loan to MoD, 1987–88; Gov., Falkand Is, and Comr for S Georgia and S Sandwich Is, 1988–92; High Comr, British Antarctic Territory, 1988–89; Ambassador to Kuwait, 1992–96. Dir, Arab-British Centre, London, 2000–. Mem. Cttee, British Moroccan Soc.; Hon. Mem. Cttee, Centre Koutoubia, Marrakesh. Member: Friends of Kuwait; Falkland Is Assoc. FRGS 2000. Kuwait Medallion, First Class, 1995; Comdr, Ouissam Alaouite (Morocco), 1999. *Recreations:* travelling in remote areas, sailing, reading, walking. *Club:* Travellers.

FULTON, Andrew; *see* Fulton, R. A.

FULTON, Hon. (Edmund) Davie, OC 1992; PC (Canada) 1957; QC (BC) 1957; Barrister and Solicitor; Associate Counsel, Swinton & Company, Vancouver, 1983–90, retired; *b* 10 March 1916; *s* of Frederick John Fulton, KC, and Winifred M. Davie; *m* 1946, Patricia Mary, *d* of J. M. Macrae and Christine Macrae (*née* Carmichael), Winnipeg; three *d*. *Educ:* St Michael's Sch., Victoria, BC; Kamloops High Sch.; University of British Columbia; St John's Coll., Oxford. BA (BC), BA Oxon (Rhodes Scholar, elected 1936). Admitted to Bar of British Columbia, 1940. Served in Canadian Army Overseas as Company Comdr with Seaforth Highlanders of Canada and as DAAG 1st Canadian Inf. Div., 1940–45, including both Italian and Northwest Europe campaigns (despatches); transferred to R of O with rank of Major, 1945. Practised law with Fulton, Verchere & Rogers, Kamloops, BC, 1945–68, and with Fulton, Cumming, Richards & Co., Vancouver, 1968–73; Judge, Supreme Court of British Columbia, 1973–81. A Comr, 1986–92, Chm., 1990–92, Canadian Sect., Internat. Jt Commn, Ottawa. Elected to House of Commons of Canada, 1945; re-elected in 1949, 1953, 1957, 1958, 1962, 1965. Mem. Senate, University of British Columbia, 1948–57, 1969–75. Acting Minister of Citizenship and Immigration, June 1957–May 1958; Minister of Justice and Attorney Gen., Canada, June 1957–Aug. 1962; Minister of Public Works, Aug. 1962–April, 1963. Mem., Vancouver Adv. Cttee, Guaranty Trust Co. of Canada, 1983–86. Member: Law Soc. of BC, 1940–; Law Soc. of Upper Canada, 1957–; Canadian Bar Assoc., 1940–. Dir, Western Recovery Foundn, Vancouver, 1985–; Hon. Dir, Physical Medicine Res. Foundn, 1993– (Dir, 1987–93). Hon. Colonel: Rocky Mountain Rangers, 1959; 419 Sqdn, RCAF, 1993–96. Hon. LLD: Ottawa, 1960; Queen's, 1963. Human Relns Award, Canadian Council of Christians and Jews, 1985; Citation for meritorious service to country and profession, Trial Lawyers Assoc. of BC, 1986. *Address:* 4716 Paton Street, Vancouver, BC V6L 2J1, Canada. *Clubs:* Vancouver, Shaughnessy Golf and Country (Vancouver).

FULTON, Prof. John Francis; Secretary, Northern Ireland Fund for Reconciliation, since 1999; *b* 21 Sept. 1933; *s* of Robert Patrick Fulton and Anne Fulton (*née* McCambridge); *m* 1958, Elizabeth Mary Brennan; one *s* one *d*. *Educ:* St Malachy's College, Belfast; QUB (BA 1954, DipEd 1958, MA 1964); Univ. of Keele (PhD 1975). Lectr and Principal Lectr, St Joseph's Coll. of Educn, Belfast, 1961–73; Queen's University of Belfast: Lectr, Inst. of Educn, 1973–76; Prof. and Head of Dept of Educnl Studies, 1977–85; Dir, Sch. of Educn, 1985–93; Pro-Vice-Chancellor, 1987–92; Provost, Legal, Social and Educnl Scis, 1993–97; Dir of Develt, 1997–98; Prof. Emeritus, 1997. Mem., IBA, subseq. ITC, 1987–94. Member: Trng and Employment Agency, 1993–; Central Services Agency, Dept of Health and Social Services NI, 1999–; Chm., Strategy Gp for Health Services R&D, 1999–. FRSA. *Publications:* contribs to: Education in Great Britain and Ireland, 1973; Educational Research and Development in Great Britain, 1982; Willingly to School, 1987; articles in learned jls. *Recreations:* golf, music. *Address:* Northern Ireland Fund for Reconciliation, c/o Queen's University of Belfast, BT7 1NN. *T:* (028) 9027 3773.

FULTON, (Paul) Robert (Anthony); Director, Strategy and Performance, Home Office, since 2000; *b* 20 March 1951; *s* of George Alan Fulton and Margaret Fulton (*née* Foxton); *m* 1981, Lee Hong Tay. *Educ:* Nunthorpe Grammar Sch., York; Churchill Coll., Cambridge (BA Hons French and Russian). Joined Home Office, 1973; Private Sec. to Perm. Sec., 1977–78; Radio Regulatory Dept, 1978–83; Police Dept, 1984–88; Prison and Criminal Policy Depts, 1988–91; Dir of Prison Service Industries and Farms, 1991–96; Principal Finance Officer, 1996–2000. *Recreations:* music, walking, cycling, travel, languages, food and wine, photography. *Address:* Home Office, 50 Queen Anne's Gate, SW1H 9AT. *T:* (020) 7273 3902.

FULTON, (Robert) Andrew; HM Diplomatic Service, retired; Chairman, Scottish North American Business Council, since 2000; *b* 6 Feb. 1944; *s* of late Rev. Robert M. Fulton and of Janet W. Fulton (*née* Mackenzie); *m* 1970, Patricia Mary Crowley; two *s* one *d*. *Educ:* Rothesay Academy; Glasgow University (MA, LLB). Foreign and Commonwealth Office, 1968; Third later Second Secretary, Saigon, 1969; FCO, 1972; First Sec., Rome, 1973; FCO, 1977; First Sec., E Berlin, 1978; FCO, 1981; Counsellor, Oslo, 1984; FCO, 1987; UK Mission to UN, NY, 1989; FCO, 1992; Counsellor: Washington, 1995–99; FCO, 1999. Vis. Prof., Univ. of Glasgow Sch. of Law, 1999–. *Recreations:* golf, racing, reading, cinema. *Address:* 7 Crown Road South, Glasgow G12 9DJ.

FULTON, Maj. Gen. Robert Henry Gervase; Capability Manager (Information Superiority), Ministry of Defence, since 2001; *b* 21 Dec. 1948; *s* of late James Fulton and Cynthia Fulton (*née* Shaw); *m* 1975, Midge Free; two *s*. *Educ:* Eton Coll.; Univ. of East Anglia (BA Hons). Entered RM, 1972: 42 Commando, 1973–75; 40 Commando, 1976–78; Instructor, Sch. of Signals, Blandford, 1978–80; student, Army Staff Coll., Camberley, 1980–81; Instructor, Jun. Div. Staff Coll., 1981–83; 42 Commando, 1983–85; SO2 Ops, HQ Training, Reserve and Special Forces, 1985–87; SO2 Commitments, Dept of Comdt Gen., 1987–90; SO1 DS, Army Staff Coll., Camberley, 1990–92; CO, 42 Commando, 1992–94; Asst Dir, CIS Operational Requirements, MoD, 1994–95; RCDS, 1996; Comdr, 3 Commando Bde, 1997–98, Comdt Gen., 1998–2001, RM. *Recreations:* playing and watching sport, military history. *Address:* Ministry of Defence, Main Building, Whitehall, SW1A 2HB. *Clubs:* Army and Navy, MCC.

FUNG, Hon. Sir Kenneth Ping-Fan, Kt 1971; CBE 1965 (OBE 1958); JP; Chairman, KPFF Holding Ltd; Director, The Bank of East Asia Ltd, Hong Kong, 1947–97 (Chief Manager, 1963–69); Senior Consultant for External Economy, Chongqing, Sichuan Province, China, since 1985; *b* 28 May 1911; *yr s* of late Fung Ping Shan, JP; *m* 1933, Ivy (*née* Kan) Shiu-Han, OBE, JP (*d* 2001), *d* of late Kan Tong-Po, JP; four *s* one *d*. *Educ:* Government Vernacular Sch.; Sch. of Chinese Studies, Univ. of Hong Kong. Unofficial Mem., Urban Council, 1951–60; Unofficial MLC, 1959–65, MEC, 1962–72. Hon. Chairman: Sui Fung Consultants Ltd; Dransfield Hldgs Ltd (Chm., 1993–2000); Hon. Dir, Beijing Municipal Develt Centre of Sci. and Technol. of Agric., Forestry and Animal Husbandry. Pres., Chm., Mem. etc of numerous social organisations, both present and past, including: Pres., WWF, Hong Kong; Chm., Hong Kong Nat. Cttee, United World Colleges; Member: HK Br., CPA; Bd of Trustees, Duke of Edinburgh Award; Rotary Internat. (Paul Harris Fellow; 50-Year Membership Award, 1985); Internat. Council, Asia Soc., NY; Overseer Emer., Univ. of Calif. Hosp. Med. Sch., San Francisco. Comr St John Ambulance Bde (first Chinese to serve), 1953–58; first Chinese Hon. ADC to 4 successive Governors and Officers Admin. Govt (rep. StJAB). Life Mem. Court, Univ. of Hong Kong; formerly Mem. Council, Chinese Univ. of Hong Kong. JP Hong Kong, 1952. Founder Mem., Royal Asiatic Soc.; Mem. other Socs and Assocs; FRGS, Hong Kong. Hon. degrees: LLD, Chinese Univ. of Hong Kong, 1968; DSocSc, Univ. of Hong Kong, 1969. Silver Acorn, Commonwealth Scout Council (UK), 1976; Gold Dragon, Scout Assoc. of Hong Kong, 1985. KStJ 1958. Order of the Sacred Treasure, II Class (Japan), 1985; Knight Grand Officer, 1984 (Knight Commander, 1979), Internat. Order of St Hubert (Austria). *Recreations:* racing, golf, swimming. *Address:* (home) Apt 24B, 101 Repulse Bay Road, Repulse Bay, Hong Kong; (office) KPFF Holding Ltd, 620 Prince's Building, 10 Chater Road, Hong Kong. *T:* 25220311. *Clubs:* Oriental; Hong Kong, Hong Kong Jockey (Hon. Steward), Hong Kong Golf, Hongkong Country, Hongkong Squash (Life Mem.), Chinese Recreation (Hon. Pres.), American, Rotary (Hong Kong); Knickerbocker, Sky, Explorers' (New York); Bohemian (San Francisco); Tokyo, Hodogaya Country (Japan).

FUNNELL, Christina Mary; Director, Funnell Associates Consultancy, since 1997; *b* 24 Aug. 1947; *d* of Joanna Christina Beaumont (*née* Lenes) and Norman Beaumont; *m* 1970 (marr. diss. 1994); one *s* one *d*. *Educ:* Hull Univ. (BA Spec. Hons Soc. Admin. 1968). W Riding CC Social Services, 1964; Methodist Assoc. of Youth Clubs, 1965–68; London Council of Social Service, 1971; Herts CC Youth Service, 1973; Nat. Eczema Soc., 1982–96 (Dir, 1987–96; Chief Exec., Skin Care Campaign, 1995–96). Mem., Standing Adv. Gp on consumer involvement in NHS R&D prog., 1996–; Chm., Consumer Health Inf. Centre, 1997–; Organising Sec., Health Coalition Initiative, 1997–; Co-ordinator, Patient Information Forum, 2001–. Lay Member: Nat. Clin. Assessment Authy, 2001–; Shadow Nursing and Midwifery Council, 2001–. Feasibility Consultant to North Bank Estate, Muswell Hill, London, 1998–99. Member: Wesley's Chapel, 1996–; Exec., Christian Socialist Movt, 1998–; Associate Mem., Iona Community, 1997–. Trustee, Convoy of Hope. *Publications:* (contrib.) Clinical and Experimental Dermatology, 1993; (contrib.) Developing New Clinical Roles: a guide for health professionals, 2000. *Address:* 28 Queensbury Street, N1 3AD. *T:* (020) 7688 9208, *Fax:* (020) 7359 4583; *e-mail:* tinafunnell@cs.com. *Club:* New Cavendish.

FURBER, (Frank) Robert; retired solicitor; *b* 28 March 1921; *s* of late Percy John Furber and Edith Furber; *m* 1948, Anne Wilson McArthur; three *s* one *d*. *Educ:* Willaston Sch.; Berkhamsted Sch.; University College London. LLB. Articled with Slaughter and May; solicitor 1945; Partner, Clifford-Turner, 1952–86. Mem., Planning Law Cttee, Law Society, 1964–69. Chairman: Blackheath Soc., 1968–89; Blackheath Preservation Trust, 1972–2000; Film Industry Defence Organization, 1968–89; Governor: Yehudi Menuhin Sch., 1964–91; Live Music Now!, 1977–87; Berkhamsted Sch., and Berkhamsted Sch. for Girls, 1976–91 (Chm., 1986–91); Board Member: Trinity Coll. of Music, 1974–91; Nat. Jazz Centre, 1982–87; Common Law Inst. of Intellectual Property, 1982–87; Chm., Rules of Golf Cttee, Royal and Ancient Golf Club, 1976–80; Trustee, Robert T. Jones Meml Trust, 1982–86; Mem. and Hon. Sec., R & A Golf Amateurism Commn of Inquiry, 1984–85; Mem., CCPR Cttee of Enquiry into Amateurism in Sport, 1986–88. Hon. Fellow, Trinity College, London. *Publication:* A Course for Heroes, 1996. *Recreations:* golf, music, books. *Address:* 8 Pond Road, Blackheath, SE3 9JL. *T:* (020) 8852 8065. *Clubs:* Buck's; Royal Blackheath Golf, Royal St George's Golf, Royal and Ancient, Honourable Company of Edinburgh Golfers; Pine Valley (USA).

See also S. A. Coakley, R. J. Furber.

FURBER, (Robert) John; QC 1995; *b* 13 Oct. 1949; *s* of Frank Robert Furber, *qv*, and Anne Wilson Furber (*née* McArthur); *m* 1977, Amanda Cherry Burgoyne Varney; one *s* two *d*. *Educ:* Westminster Sch.; Gonville and Caius Coll., Cambridge (MA). Called to the Bar, Inner Temple, 1973. *Publications:* (ed jtly) Halsbury's Laws of England: Landlord and Tenant, 4th edn 1981, Compulsory Acquisition of Land, 4th edn reissue 1996; (ed jtly) Hill and Redman's Landlord and Tenant, 17th edn 1982, 18th edn (looseleaf) 1988–. *Address:* Wilberforce Chambers, 8 New Square, Lincoln's Inn, WC2A 3QP. *T:* (020) 7306 0102; 52 Southbrook Road, Lee, SE12 8LL. *T:* (020) 8852 5770. *Clubs:* Buck's, Beefsteak.

FURCHGOTT, Prof. Robert Francis, PhD; Emeritus Professor of Pharmacology, State University of New York Health Science Center, Brooklyn, since 1990; *b* Charleston, SC, 4 June 1916; *m* 1941; three *d*. *Educ:* Univ. of N Carolina (BS 1937); Northwestern Univ. (PhD Biochem. 1940). Medical College, Cornell University: Res. Fellow in Medicine, 1940–43; Res. Associate, 1943–47; Instructor in Physiol., 1943–48; Asst Prof. of Med. Biochem., 1947–49; Asst Prof., then Associate Prof. of Pharmacol., Med. Sch., Washington Univ., 1949–56; SUNY Health Science Center, Brooklyn: Chm., Dept of Pharmacol., 1956–83; Prof., 1956–88; Univ. Dist. Prof., 1988–. Visiting Professor: Univ. of Geneva, 1962–63; Univ. of Calif., San Diego, 1971–72; Med. Univ., SC, 1980; UCLA, 1980; Adjunct Prof. of Pharmacol., Sch. Medicine, Univ. of Miami, 1989–. Member: ACS, 1937; AAAS, 1940; Amer. Soc. Biochem., 1948; Amer. Soc. Pharmacol. and Exptl Therapeutics, 1952 (Pres., 1971–72; Goodman and Gilman Award, 1984); NAS, 1991; Harvey Soc. Hon. degrees from Univs of Lund, N Carolina, Ghent, Ohio State, Autonomous Univ. of Madrid, Mt Sinai Med. Sch., Med. Univ. of S Carolina, Med. Coll. of Ohio, Northwestern Univ. and UCL. Awards include: Res. Achievement Award, Amer. Heart Assoc., 1990; Bristol-Myers Squibb Award for Achievement in Cardiovascular Res., 1991; Medal, NY Acad. Medicine, 1992; Wellcome Gold Medal, Brit. Pharmacol. Soc., 1995; Gregory Pincus Award for Res., 1996; Lasker Award for Med. Res., 1996; Nobel Prize for Physiology or Medicine, 1998. *Address:* State University of New York Health Science Center, Department of Pharmacology, 450 Clarkson Avenue # 29, Brooklyn, NY 11203–2056, USA. *T:* (718) 2701355; 170 Westview Lane, Hewlett, NY 11557–1718, USA.

FURLONG, Mrs Monica; writer; *b* 17 Jan. 1930; *d* of Alfred Gordon Furlong and Freda Simpson; *m* 1953, William John Knights (marr. diss. 1977); one *s* one *d*. *Educ:* Harrow County Girls' Sch.; University College London. Truth, Spectator, Guardian, 1956–61; Daily Mail, 1961–68; Producer, BBC, 1974–78. Moderator, Movement for the Ordination of Women, 1982–85. Hon. DD Gen. Theol Seminary, NY, 1986; Hon. DLitt Bristol, 1995. *Publications:* Travelling In, 1971; Contemplating Now, 1971; God's A Good Man (poems), 1974; Puritan's Progress, 1975; Christian Uncertainties, 1975; The Cat's Eye (novel), 1976; Merton (biography), 1980; Cousins (novel), 1983; (ed) Feminine in the Church, 1984; Genuine Fake: a biography of Alan Watts, 1986; Thérèse of Lisieux (biog.), 1987; Wise Child (novel), 1987; (ed) Mirror to the Church, 1988; A Year and a Day (novel), 1990; A Dangerous Delight, 1991; Bird of Paradise (memoir), 1995; Flight of the Kingfisher: a journey among the Kukatja Aborigines, 1996; Visions & Longings: medieval women mystics, 1996; C of E, The State It's In, 2000; (ed jtly) Reflections on Forgiveness and Spiritual Growth, 2001. *Address:* c/o Sinclair-Stevenson, 3 South Terrace, SW7 2TB. *T:* (020) 7581 2550.

FURLONG, Ronald (John), FRCS; Hon. Consulting Orthopædic Surgeon: St Thomas' Hospital; King Edward VII Hospital for Officers; Queen Victoria Hospital, East Grinstead; and lately to the Army; *s* of Frank Owen Furlong and Elsie Muriel Taffs, Woolwich; *m* 1970, Eileen Mary Watford. *Educ:* Eltham Coll.; St Thomas's Hosp. MB, BS London 1931; MRCS, LRCP, 1931; FRCS 1934. Served with Royal Army Medical Corps, 1941–46. Home Commands, North Africa and Italy; Brigadier, Consulting Orthopædic Surgeon to the Army, 1946, Hon. Consulting Orthopædic Surgeon 1951; Orthopædic Surgeon, St Thomas' Hosp., 1946. Introd. Muller Total Hip Replacement to England, 1969; established: surgical co., Jt Replacement Instrumentation Ltd, 1970; JRI (Manufacturing) Ltd, 1974; designed and implanted first in the world Hydroxy-apatite ceramic coated total hip replacement, Queen's Award for Technol Achievement, 1993; inaug. Furlong Research Foundn, 1988. *Publications:* Injuries of the Hand, 1957; (trans.) Pauwel's Atlas of the Biomechanics of the Normal and Diseased Hip, 1978; (trans.) Pauwel's Biomechanics of the Locomotor Apparatus, 1980; (trans.) W. Braun, O. Fischer, On the Centre of Gravity of the Human Body, 1986; contrib. Jl of Bone and Joint

Surgery. *Recreations:* reading, history, archæology. *Address:* Lister House, 11–12 Wimpole Street, W1N 7AB. *T:* (020) 7637 1844. *Club:* Athenæum.

FURLONGER, Robert William, CB 1981; retired public servant, Australia; *b* 29 April 1921; *s* of George William Furlonger and Germaine Rose Furlonger; *m* 1944, Verna Hope Lewis; three *s* one *d.* *Educ:* Sydney High Sch.; Sydney Univ. (BA). Served War, AMF, 1941–45. Australian Dept of External (later Foreign) Affairs, 1945–69 and 1972–77 (IDC, 1960; Dir, Jt Intell. Org., Dept of Def., 1969–72); appointments included: High Comr, Nigeria, 1961; Aust. Perm. Rep. to the European Office of the UN, 1961–64; Minister, Aust. Embassy, Washington, 1965–69; Ambassador to Indonesia, 1972–74, and to Austria, Hungary and Czechoslovakia, 1975–77; Dir-Gen., Office of National Assessments, Canberra, 1977–81. *Address:* PO Box 548, Belconnen, ACT 2616, Australia. *T:* (2) 62531384. *Clubs:* Canberra; Royal Canberra Golf.

FURMSTON, Bentley Edwin, FRICS; Director of Overseas Surveys, Ordnance Survey, 1984–89; *b* 7 Oct. 1931; *s* of Rev. Edward Bentley Furmston and Mary Furmston (*née* Bennett); *m* 1957, Margaret (*née* Jackson); two *s* one *d.* *Educ:* The Nelson Sch., Wigton, Cumbria; Victoria Univ., Manchester (BSc Mathematics). Entered Civil Service as Surveyor, Directorate of Overseas Surveys, 1953, with service in Gambia, Swaziland, Basutoland, N Rhodesia; Sen. Surveyor, N Rhodesia, 1960; Sen. Computer, DOS, 1963; seconded to Govt of Malawi as Dep. Commissioner of Surveys, 1965; Principal Survey Officer, DOS, 1968: Overseas Supervisor, Sch. of Military Survey; Regional Survey Officer, W Africa; Asst Director (Survey), 1971; Asst Dir (Cartography), Ordnance Survey, 1973; Dep. Dir, Field Survey, Ordnance Survey, 1974; Dep. Dir (Survey), DOS, 1977; Dir, Overseas Surveys and Survey Advr, Min. of Overseas Develt, 1980. *Publications:* contribs to technical jls. *Recreations:* reading, gardening, hill walking, climbing. *Address:* The Orchards, Carter's Clay Road, Newtown, Romsey, Hants SO51 0GL.

FURMSTON, Prof. Michael Philip, TD 1966; Professor of Law, University of Bristol, 1978–98, now Emeritus; *b* 1 May 1933; *s* of Joseph Philip Furmston and Phyllis (*née* Clowes); *m* 1964, Ashley Sandra Maria Cope; three *s* seven *d.* *Educ:* Wellington Sch., Somerset; Exeter Coll., Oxford (BA 1st Cl. Hons Jurisprudence, 1956; BCL 1st Cl. Hons 1957; MA 1960). LLM Birmingham, 1962. Called to the Bar, Gray's Inn, 1960 (1st Cl. Hons), Bencher, 1989. National Service, RA, 1951–53 (2nd Lieut); Major, TA, 1966–78, TAVR. Lecturer: Univ. of Birmingham, 1957–62; QUB, 1962–63; Fellow, Lincoln Coll., Oxford, 1964–78 (Sen. Dean, 1967–68; Sen. Tutor and Tutor for Admissions, 1969–74); Univ. Lectr in Law, 1964–78, Curator, University Chest, 1976–78, Oxford; Lectr in Common Law, Council of Legal Educn, 1965–78; Dean, Faculty of Law, 1980–84 and 1995–98, Pro-Vice-Chancellor, 1986–89, Univ. of Bristol. Chm., COMEC, 1996–2000. Visiting Professor: City Univ., 1978–82; Katholieke Universiteit, Leuven, 1980, 1986, 1992 and 1999; Nat. Univ. of Singapore, 1987, 1999. Liveryman, Arbitrators' Co. Jt Editor, 1985–97, Editor, 1997–, Construction Law Reports. *Publications:* (ed) Cheshire, Fifoot and Furmston's Law of Contract, 8th edn 1972, to 13th edn 1996; Contractors Guide to ICE Conditions of Contract, 1980; Misrepresentation and Fraud, in Halsbury's Law of England, 1980, 1998; Croner's Buying and Selling Law, 1982; (ed jtly) The Effect on English Domestic Law of Membership of the European Communities and Ratification of the European Convention on Human Rights, 1983; (jtly) A Building Contract Casebook, 1984, 3rd edn 1999; (jtly) Cases and Materials on Contract, 1985, 3rd edn 1995; (ed) The Law of Tort: policies and trends in liability for damage to property, 1986; (ed) You and the Law, 1987; Croner's Model Business Contracts, 1988; (jtly) 'A' Level Law, 1988, 3rd edn 1996; Sale of Goods, 1990; Sale and Supply of Goods, 1994, 3rd edn 2000; (jtly) Commercial Law, 1995; Contract Formation and Letters of Intent, 1998; (ed) The Law of Contract, 1999. *Recreations:* chess (Member, English team, Postal Olympiads), watching cricket, collecting Austin A35s, dogs. *Address:* The Old Post Office, Shipham, Winscombe, Somerset BS25 1TQ. *T:* (01934) 842253; Faculty of Law, University of Bristol, Wills Memorial Building, Queen's Road, Bristol BS8 1RJ. *T:* (0117) 928 9000, 928 7441. *Clubs:* Reform, Naval and Military.

FURNELL, Very Rev. Raymond; Dean of York, since 1994; *b* 18 May 1935; *s* of Albert George Edward and Hetty Violet Jane Furnell; *m* 1967, Sherril Witcomb; one *s* three *d.* *Educ:* Hinchley Wood School, Surrey; Brasted Place Theological Coll.; Lincoln Theol Coll. Thomas Meadows & Co. Ltd, 1951; RAF, 1953; Lummus Co. Ltd, 1955; Geo. Wimpey & Co. Ltd, 1960; Brasted Place, 1961; Lincoln Theol Coll., 1963; Curate, St Luke's, Cannock, 1965; Vicar, St James the Great, Clayton, 1969; Rector, Hanley Team Ministry and RD, Stoke North, 1975–81; Provost, St Edmundsbury, 1981–94. Mem., Gen. Synod of C of E, 1988–; Chairman: Assoc. of English Cathedrals, 1994–; Council for the Care of Churches, 1999–. Chm. Bd, Theatre Royal, York, 1996–. Mem. Council, Liberal Club, 1999–. DUniv. *Recreations:* music, drama. *Address:* The Deanery, York YO1 2JD. *T:* (01904) 623608; *e-mail:* R.Furnell@btinternet.com. *Club:* Athenæum.

FURNER, Air Vice-Marshal Derek Jack, CBE 1973 (OBE 1963); DFC 1943; AFC 1954; *b* 14 Nov. 1921; *s* of Vivian J. Furner; *m* 1948, Patricia Donnelly; three *s.* *Educ:* Westcliff High Sch., Essex. Joined RAF, 1941; commnd as navigator, 1942; Bomber Comd (2 tours), 1942–44; Transport Comd, Far East, 1945–47; Navigation Instructor, 1948–50; trials flying, Boscombe Down, 1951–53 and Wright-Patterson, Ohio, 1953–56; Air Min., 1957; OC Ops Wing, RAF Waddington, 1958–60; Planning Staff, HQ Bomber Comd, 1961–63 and SHAPE, Paris, 1964–65; Dep. Dir Manning, MoD (Air), 1966–67; OC RAF Scampton, 1968; AOC Central Reconnaissance Estab., 1969–70; Sec., Internat. Mil. Staff, NATO, Brussels, 1970–73; Asst Air Secretary, 1973–75. Gen. Manager, 1976–81, Dir, 1977–81, Harlequin Wallcoverings. FCIPD (FIPM 1975); FIMgt (FBIM 1975). Mem., Mensa, 1989. *Recreations:* mathematical problems, music, computing. *Address:* 6 Sutherland Court Gardens, Overstrand Road, Cromer, Norfolk NR27 0DA. *T:* and *Fax:* (01263) 510255. *Club:* Royal Air Force.

FURNESS, Alan Edwin, CMG 1991; HM Diplomatic Service, retired; Ambassador to Senegal and, concurrently, to Cape Verde, Guinea, Guinea Bissau and Mali, 1993–97; *b* 6 June 1937; *s* of late Edwin Furness and Marion Furness (*née* Senton); *m* 1971, Aline Elizabeth Janine Barrett; two *s.* *Educ:* Eltham Coll.; Jesus Coll., Cambridge (BA, MA). Commonwealth Relations Office, 1961; Private Sec. to Parliamentary Under-Secretary of State, 1961–62; Third, later Second Secretary, British High Commn, New Delhi, 1962–66; First Secretary, DSAO (later FCO), 1966–69; First Sec., UK Delegn to European Communities, Brussels, 1969–72; First Sec. and Head of Chancery, Dakar, 1972–75; First Sec., FCO, 1975–78; Counsellor and Head of Chancery, Jakarta, 1978–81; Counsellor and Head of Chancery, Warsaw, 1982–85; Head of S Pacific Dept., FCO, 1985–88; Dep. High Comr, Bombay, 1989–93. Ambassador of Order of Malta to Senegal, 2000–. Knight of Magistral Grace, Order of Malta, 1999. *Recreations:* music, literature, gardening. *Address:* 40 Brunswick Court, 89 Regency Street, SW1P 4AE; BP 8766, Dakar-Yoff, Senegal. *Club:* Oxford and Cambridge.

FURNESS, Mark Richard; His Honour Judge Furness; a Circuit Judge, since 1998; *b* 28 Nov. 1948; *m* 1974, Margaretta Trevor Evans; one *s* one *d.* *Educ:* Hereford Cathedral Sch.; St John's Coll., Cambridge (BA 1970; MA 1972). Called to the Bar, Lincoln's Inn, 1970; an Asst Recorder, 1992–96; a Recorder, 1996–98. Chairman: Social Security Appeal Tribunal, 1987–94; Disability Appeal Tribunal, 1991–98. *Recreations:* gardening, motoring, literature, music, DIY, travel. *Address:* Swansea County Court, Caravella House, Quay West, Quay Parade, Swansea SA1 1SP. *Clubs:* Cardiff and County (Cardiff); Radyr Golf.

FURNESS, Michael James; QC 2000; *b* 2 Sept. 1958; *s* of late Harry Furness and of Rosemary Nancy Furness. *Educ:* Emmanuel Coll., Cambridge (MA); St Edmund Hall, Oxford (BCL). Called to the Bar, Lincoln's Inn, 1982; First Standing Jun. Counsel to Inland Revenue, 1998–2000. *Recreations:* acting (Hon. Sec., Bar Theatrical Soc.), walking. *Address:* Wilberforce Chambers, 8 New Square, Lincoln's Inn, WC2A 3QP. *T:* (020) 7306 0102.

FURNESS, Robin; *see* Furness, Sir S. R.

FURNESS, Col Simon John; Vice Lord-Lieutenant of Berwickshire, since 1990; *b* 18 Aug. 1936; 2nd *s* of Sir Christopher Furness, 2nd Bt and Violet Flower Chipchase Furness, OBE (*d* 1988), *d* of Lieut-Col G. C. Roberts, Hollingside, Durham. *Educ:* Charterhouse; RMA Sandhurst; Royal Naval Staff College. Commissioned 2nd Lieut Durham Light Infantry, 1956; served Far East, UK, Germany; active service, Borneo and NI; Comd 5th Bn LI, 1976–78, retired 1978. Dep. Col (Durham), LI, 1989–93. DL Berwickshire, 1984. *Recreations:* gardening, country sports, fine arts. *Address:* The Garden House, Netherbyres, Eyemouth, Berwickshire TD14 5SE. *T:* (018907) 50337. *Clubs:* Army and Navy; Durham County.

FURNESS, Sir Stephen (Roberts), 3rd Bt *cr* 1913, of Tunstall Grange, West Hartlepool; farmer and sporting/landscape artist (as Robin Furness); *b* 10 Oct. 1933; *e s* of Sir Christopher Furness, 2nd Bt, and Flower, Lady Furness, OBE (*d* 1988), *d* of late Col G. C. Roberts; *S* father, 1974; *m* 1961, Mary, *e d* of J. F. Cann, Cullompton, Devon; one *s* one *d.* *Educ:* Charterhouse. Entered RN, 1952; Observer, Fleet Air Arm, 1957; retired list, 1962. NCA, Newton Rigg Farm Inst., 1964. Member: Armed Forces Art Soc.; Darlington Art Soc. *Recreations:* looking at paintings, foxhunting, racing. *Heir:* *s* Michael Fitzroy Roberts Furness [*b* 12 Oct. 1962; *m* 1998, Katrine Oxtoby]. *Address:* Stanhow Farm, Great Langton, Northallerton, Yorks DL7 0TJ. *T:* (01609) 748614.

See also S. J. Furness.

FURNHAM, Prof. Adrian Frank, DSc, DPhil, DLitt; Professor of Psychology, University College London, since 1992; *b* 3 Feb. 1953; *s* of late Leslie Frank Furnham and of Lorna Audrey (*née* Cartwright); *m* 1990, Dr Alison Clare Green; one *s.* *Educ:* Natal Univ. (BA Hons, MA; DLitt 1997); LSE (MSc Econ, DSc 1991); Wolfson Coll. and Pembroke Coll., Oxford (DPhil 1982). Oxford University: Res. Officer, Dept Exptl Psychol., 1979–81; Lectr in Psychol., Pembroke Coll., 1980–82; University College London: Lectr, 1981–87; Reader, 1988–92. Visiting Lecturer: Univ. of NSW, 1984; Univ. of WI, 1986; Univ. of Hong Kong, 1994–96; Vis. Prof., Henley Mgt Coll., 1999–2001. Founder Dir, ABRA, business consultancy, 1986–. Ext. Examr at various univs. Mem., Internat. Adv. Council, Social Affairs Unit, 1995–. Dir, Internat. Soc. for Study of Individual Differences, 1996–2001. Mem., editl bd of 8 internat. scientific jls. *Publications:* books include: Culture Shock, 1986; Lay Theories, 1988; The Protestant Work Ethic, 1990; Personality at Work, 1992; Corporate Assessment, 1994; All in the Mind, 1996, 2nd edn 2001; The Myths of Management, 1996; The Psychology of Behaviour at Work, 1997; Complementary Medicine, 1997; The Psychology of Money, 1998; The Psychology of Managerial Incompetence, 1998; Children as Consumers, 1998; Personality and Social Behaviour, 1999; Body Language at Work, 1999; The Hopeless, Hapless and Helpless Manager, 2000; Designing and Analysing Questionnaires and Surveys, 2000; Children and Advertising, 2000; The Psychology of Culture Shock, 2001; Assessing Potential, 2001; 400 scientific papers; contrib. articles and columns to newspapers, incl. FT. *Recreations:* travel, theatre, arguing at dinner parties, sought after by tennis, bridge and squash players who like to win. *Address:* 45 Thornhill Square, Islington, N1 1BE. *T:* (020) 7679 6265; *e-mail:* ucjtsaf@ucl.ac.uk.

FURNISS, Air Vice-Marshal Peter, DFC 1944; TD 1964; Director of Legal Services, RAF, 1978–82; *b* 16 July 1919; *s* of John and Mary Furniss; *m* 1954, Denise Cotet; one *s* two *d.* *Educ:* Sedbergh School. Commissioned 1st Bn The Liverpool Scottish TA, Queen's Own Cameron Highlanders, 1939; seconded to RAF, 1942; Comd No 73 Fighter Sqdn, 1945–46; demobilised 1946; admitted as Solicitor, 1948; commissioned in Legal Branch, RAF, 1950; Director of Legal Services: HQ Air Forces Middle East, Aden, 1961–63; HQ Far East Air Force, Singapore, 1969–71; HQ RAF Germany, 1973–74; Dep. Dir of Legal Services (RAF), 1975–78. *Recreations:* shooting, gardening, fishing. *Address:* 18 Sevington Park, Loose, Maidstone, Kent ME15 9SB. *T:* (01622) 744620. *Club:* Royal Air Force.

FURNIVALL, Barony *cr* 1295; in abeyance. *Co-heiresses:* Hon. Rosamond Mary Dent (Sister Ancilla, OSB); *b* 3 June 1933; Hon. Patricia Mary Dent [*b* 4 April 1935; *m* 1st, 1956, Captain Thomas Hornsby (marr. diss., 1963; he *d* 1967); one *s* one *d*; 2nd, 1970, Roger Thomas John Bence; one *s* one *d*].

FURSDON, Maj.-Gen. Francis William Edward, CB 1980; MBE 1958; defence consultant and correspondent; Correspondent, Salut (South Africa), since 1995; *b* 10 May 1925; *s* of late G. E. S. Fursdon and Mrs Fursdon; *m* 1950, Joan Rosemary (*née* Worssam); one *s* one *d.* *Educ:* Westminster Sch. MLitt (Aberdeen) 1978; DLitt (Leiden) 1979. Passed AMIMechE; FIMgt. Enlisted RE, 1942; RE Course, Birmingham Univ., 1943; in ranks until commnd, 1945; 1945–67: Royal W Afr. Frontier Force, India, Burma and Gold Coast; Student RMCS; staff and regtl duty, UK, Singapore, Canal Zone and Cyprus; Staff Coll.; DAA&QMG 19 Inf. Bde, UK and Port Said; GSO2 RE Sch. of Inf.; JSSC; OC 34 Indep. Fd Sqdn, E Africa and Kuwait; Instr, Staff Coll., Camberley; Borneo; 2 i/c 38 Engr Regt; Admin. Staff Coll., Henley; CO 25 Engr Regt, BAOR, 1967–69; AA&QMG HQ Land Forces, Gulf, 1970–71; Dep. Comd and COS Land Forces, Gulf, 1971; Col Q (Qtg) HQ BAOR, 1972–73; Service Fellow, Aberdeen Univ., 1974; Dir of Def. Policy (Europe and NATO), MoD, 1974–77; Dir, Military Assistance Office, MoD, 1977–80; Mil. Adv. to Governor of Rhodesia, and later Senior British Officer, Zimbabwe, 1980, retired 1980. Dir of Ceremonies, Order of St John, 1980–94. Defence and Military Correspondent, The Daily Telegraph, 1980–86; Correspondent, Army Qly & Defence Jl, 1985–2000; Naval Correspondent, Navy Internat., 1991–94; Contributing Editor Europe, Asia-Pacific Defence Reporter, 1989–94. Freeman, City of London, 1987. KStJ 1980. *Publications:* Grains of Sand, 1971; There are no Frontiers, 1973; The European Defence Community: a History, 1980; Falklands Aftermath: picking up the pieces, 1988. *Recreations:* photography (IAC Internat. Award, 1967), gardening, travel.

FURSE, Clara Hedwig Frances; Chief Executive, London Stock Exchange plc, since 2001; *b* 16 Sept. 1957; 2nd *d* of Hermann Werner Siemens and Cornelie Siemens; *m* 1981, Richard Furse; two *s* one *d.* *Educ:* St James's Sch., W Malvern; London Sch. of Econs (BScEcon). Man. Dir, UBS, 1983–98; Gp Chief Exec., Credit Lyonnais Rouse, 1998–2000. Dep. Chm., LIFFE, 1997–99. *Address:* London Stock Exchange, Old Broad Street, EC2N 1HP.

FURST, Stephen Andrew; QC 1991; a Recorder, since 1999; *b* 8 Feb. 1951; *s* of Herbert and Viviane Furst; *m* 1979, Bridget Collins; one *s* one *d*. *Educ:* Edinburgh Academy; St Edmund Hall, Oxford (BA Hons); Leeds Univ. (LLB Hons). Called to the Bar, Middle Temple, 1975, Bencher, 2000. An Asst Recorder, 1993–99. Joint Editor, Construction Law Yearbook, 1994–. *Publication:* (ed jtly) Keating on Building Contracts, 7th edn 2000. *Recreations:* bee-keeping, watercolour painting. *Address:* Keating Chambers, 10 Essex Street, WC2A 3AA. *T:* (020) 7544 2600.

FURTADO, Peter Randall; Editor, History Today, since 1997; *b* 20 May 1952; *s* of Robert Audley Furtado and Marcelle Elizabeth Furtado (*née* Whitteridge); *m* 1st, 1977, Roberta Jane Day (marr. diss.); 2nd, 1983, (Margaret Elizabeth) Ann Swoffer; three *d*. *Educ:* Whitgift Sch., Croydon; Oriel Coll., Oxford (BA 1st Cl. Hons 1973; Dip. Hist. Art 1974). Sen. ed., Hamlyn Books, 1977–83; freelance ed., 1983–87; sen. ed., Equinox Books, 1987–91; Exec. Ed., Andromeda Books, 1991–97. Managing Editor: The Ordnance Survey Atlas of Great Britain, 1981; The Illustrated History of the 20th Century, 10 vols, 1989–92; The Cassell Atlas of World History, 1996. Chm., Bd of Dirs, Shintaido Foundn, 1994–97. *Recreations:* bricolage, family, Japanese corporal arts. *Address:* 13 Jack Straws Lane, Oxford OX3 0DL. *T:* (01865) 456068.

FYFE, family name of **Baron Fyfe of Fairfield**.

FYFE OF FAIRFIELD, Baron *cr* 2000 (Life Peer), of Sauchie in Clackmannanshire; **George Lennox Fyfe;** Chairman, Unity Trust Bank, since 2000; Chief Executive, Midlands Co-operative Society, 1995–2000 (Leicestershire Co-operative Society, 1975–95); *b* 10 April 1941; *s* of George L. and Elizabeth S. Fyfe; *m* 1965, Ann Clark Asquith (*d* 1999); one *d* (one *s* decd). *Educ:* Alloa Acad.; Co-operative Coll., Loughborough. Gen. Manager, Kirriemuir Co-operative Soc., 1966–68; Regl Manager, Scottish Co-operative Soc., 1968–72; Gp Gen. Manager, CWS, 1972–75. Director: Shoefayre Ltd, 1981(Chm., 1984–2000); CWS, 1981–2000 (Vice-Chm., 1986–89; Chm., 1989–2000); Co-operative Insce Soc. Ltd, 1982–2000; Central TV-East, 1983–92; Co-operative Bank plc, 1986–2000 (Dep. Chm., 1996–2000). Mem., E Midlands Econ. Planning Council, 1976–79. Mem. Select Cttee, EU Sub-Cttee D, H of L. JP Perthshire, 1972–75. *Recreations:* history, reading, music, classic cars. *Address:* House of Lords, SW1A 0PW.

FYFE, Maria; *b* 25 Nov. 1938; *d* of James O'Neill and Margaret Lacey; *m* 1964, James Joseph Fyfe (decd); two *s*. *Educ:* Strathclyde Univ. (BA Hons. Economic History 1975). Senior Lecturer, Central College of Commerce, Glasgow Trade Union Studies Unit, 1978–87. Mem., Labour Party, 1960–, Scottish Exec., 1981–88; Mem., Glasgow District Council, 1980–87 (Vice-Convener, Finance Cttee, 1980–84; Convener, Personnel Cttee, 1984–87). MP (Lab) Glasgow, Maryhill, 1987–2001. Dep. Shadow Minister for Women, 1988–91; Convener, Scottish Gp of Labour MPs, 1991–92; Scottish front bench spokesperson, 1992–95. Chair: Labour Deptl Cttee on Internat. Devel, 1997–2001; Labour Gp, UK Delegn to Council of Europe, 1997–2001. *Address:* 10 Ascot Avenue, Glasgow G12 0AX. *T:* (0141) 334 6737.

FYFE, Prof. William Sefton, CC (Canada) 1989; FRS 1969; Professor of Geology, University of Western Ontario, since 1972 (Dean of Science, 1986–90); *b* 4 June 1927; *s* of Colin and Isabella Fyfe; *m* 1968; two *s* one *d*. *Educ:* Otago Univ., New Zealand. BSc 1948, MSc 1949, PhD 1952; FRSC 1980. Univ. of California, Berkeley: Lecturer in Chemistry, 1952, Reader, 1958; Prof. of Geology, 1959; Royal Soc. Res. Prof. (Geochemistry), Univ. of Manchester, 1967–72. Guggenheim Fellow, 1983. Pres., IUGS, 1992–. Hon. Fellow, Geological Soc. Amer.; Corresponding Member: Brazilian Acad. of Science; Russian Acad. of Scis; Indian Acad. of Scis. Hon. DSc: Meml Univ. of Newfoundland, 1989; Lisbon, 1990; Lakehead, 1990; Guelph, 1991; Otago, 1995; Western Ontario, 1996. Mineralogical Soc. of Amer. Award, 1964; Logan Medal, Geolog. Assoc. of Canada, 1982; Willet G. Miller Medal, Royal Soc. of Canada, 1985; Arthur Holmes Medal, European Union of Geoscientists, 1989; Day Medal, Geol Soc. of America, 1990; Canada Gold Medal for Science and Engineering, 1992; Roebling Medal, Mineralogical Soc. of America. Commemoration Medal, New Zealand, 1990, Canada, 1992; Ordem Nacional do Merito Cientifico (Brazil), 1996; Wollaston Medal, Geol Soc., London, 2000. *Publications:* Metamorphic Reactions and Metamorphic Facies, 1958; The Geochemistry of Solids, 1964; Fluids in the Earth's Crust, 1978; also numerous scientific papers. *Address:* Department of Earth Sciences, University of Western Ontario, London, ON N6A 5B7, Canada.

FYFE, William Stevenson, CBE 1992 (OBE 1987); FIIM; Chairman, Greater Glasgow Health Board, 1993; *b* Glasgow, 10 June 1935; *s* of Dr Andrew Fyfe and Janet Isabella Fyfe (*née* Soutar), New Cumnock; *m* 1986, Margaret H. H. Auld; one *s* one *d*. *Educ:* Dollar Acad.; Scottish Coll. of Commerce. FIIM 1985. Town Councillor (C), Prestwick, 1967–73; Co. Councillor (C), Ayrshire, 1970–73; Ayrshire and Arran Health Board: Financial Convener, 1973–81; Chm., 1981–93. Chm., Scottish Health Services Adv. Council, 1989–93; Mem., General Whitley Council, 1989–93. *Recreation:* golf. *Address:* Cassillis View, Alloway Road, Maybole, Ayrshire KA19 8DG.

FYFIELD, Frances; novelist; solicitor; *b* 8 Nov. 1948; *d* of Dr Andrew George Hegarty and Winifred Doris Hegarty (*née* Fyfield). *Educ:* convent and grammar schools, Newcastle upon Tyne; Newcastle upon Tyne Univ. (BA English Lit. 1970); Coll. of Law. Admitted solicitor, 1973; a solicitor: for Metropolitan Police, 1973–80; for DPP, 1980–86; CPS, 1986–87; pt-time lawyer, and novelist, 1987–2000. Mem. Cttee, Royal Literary Fund. *Publications:* A Question of Guilt, 1988 (televised 1994); Shadows on the Mirror, 1989; Trial by Fire, 1990 (televised 1999); Deep Sleep (Silver Dagger Award, CWA), 1990; Shadow Play, 1991; Perfectly Pure and Good, 1992; A Clear Conscience, 1994 (Grand Prix de Literature Policière, 1998); Without Consent, 1996; Blind Date, 1998 (televised 2000); Staring at the Light, 1999; Undercurrents, 2000; *as Frances Hegarty:* The Playroom, 1990; Half Light, 1992; Let's Dance, 1995. *Recreations:* tobacco and fine wine, paintings, company, watching the sea. *Address:* c/o Rogers Coleridge White, 20 Powis Mews, W11 1JN.

FYJIS-WALKER, Richard Alwyne, CMG 1980; CVO 1976; HM Diplomatic Service, retired; Chairman, Commonwealth Institute, 1988–93; *b* 19 June 1927; *s* of Harold and Marion Fyjis-Walker; *m* 1st, 1951, Barbara Graham-Watson (marr. diss.); one *s*; 2nd, 1972, Gabrielle Josefi; one *s*. *Educ:* Bradfield Coll.; Magdalene Coll., Cambridge (MA). Army (KRRC), 1945–48. Joined Foreign (subseq. Diplomatic) Service, 1955; served: Amman, 1956; FO, 1957–61; Paris, 1961–63; Cairo, 1963–65; FCO, 1966–71; Counsellor, 1970; Ankara, 1971–74; Counsellor (Information), Washington, 1974–78; Counsellor, UK Mission to UN, NY, 1978–79; Ambassador to the Sudan, 1979–84; Ambassador to Pakistan, 1984–87. *Address:* 17 Stonefield Street, N1 0HW.

FYSH, (Robert) Michael; QC 1989; QC (NI) 1990; **His Honour Judge Fysh;** a Circuit Judge, since 2001; *b* 2 Aug. 1940; *s* of Dr Leslie Fysh and Margaret Fysh, Ashford, Kent; *m* 1971, Mary Bevan; three *s*. *Educ:* Downside Sch.; Exeter Coll., Oxford (MA). Called to the Bar, Inner Temple, 1965, Bencher, 1999; NI, 1974; NSW, 1975; Ireland, 1975; India, 1982; Pakistan, 1987; SC Trinidad and Tobago Bar, 1990; SC Dublin, 1994. A Dep. High Court Judge, Chancery Div., 1997–. *Publications:* Russell-Clarke on Registered Designs, 4th edn 1974; The Industrial Property Citator, 1982, 2nd edn 1996; (ed) The Spycatcher Cases, 1989. *Recreations:* swimming, travel. *Address:* Central London County Court, 26 Park Crescent, W1N 4HT. *Clubs:* Royal Over-Seas League; Kildare Street and University (Dublin).

FYSON, Anne Elizabeth; *see* Howells, A. E.

G

GABATHULER, Prof. Erwin, OBE 2001; FRS 1990; FInstP; Sir James Chadwick Professor of Physics, Liverpool University, 1991–2001, now Emeritus Professor (Professor of Experimental Physics, 1983–91); *b* 16 Nov. 1933; *s* of Hans and Lena Gabathuler; *m* 1962, Susan Dorothy Jones, USA; two *s* one *d. Educ:* Queen's University Belfast (BSc 1956; MSc 1957); Univ. of Glasgow (PhD 1961). Research Fellow, Cornell Univ., 1961–64; Group Leader, Research, SERC, Daresbury Lab., 1964–73; European Organisation for Nuclear Research: Vis. Scientist, EMC Experiment, 1974–77; Leader, Exp. Physics Div., 1978–80; Dir of Research, 1981–83; Hd of Physics Dept, Liverpool Univ., 1986–91 and 1996–99. Chm., Particle Physics Cttee, SERC, 1985–88; Member: Nuclear Physics Bd, 1985–88; NATO Collaborative Research Grants Panels, 1990–93; Educn and Trng Cttee, PPARC, 1994–96. Dr *hc* Univ. of Uppsala, 1982; Hon. DSc QUB, 1997. Rutherford Medal, Inst. of Physics, 1992. *Publications:* articles in research jls. *Recreations:* music, walking. *Address:* 3 Danebank Road, Lymm, Cheshire WA13 9DQ. *T:* (01925) 752753.

GABITASS, Jonathan Roger, MA; Head Master, Merchant Taylors' School, since 1991; *b* 25 July 1944; *s* of William Gabitass and Nell Gabitass (*née* Chaffe); *m* 1967, Fiona Patricia Hoy; two *d. Educ:* Plymouth Coll.; St John's Coll., Oxford (MA English Lang. and Lit., PGCE). Asst English teacher, Clifton Coll., Bristol, 1967–73; Head of English, 1973–78, Second Master, 1978–91, Abingdon Sch., Oxon. *Recreations:* Rugby football, Cornish coastal path walking, 18th and 19th Century caricature, art galleries and theatre. *Address:* Head Master's House, Merchant Taylors' School, Sandy Lodge, Northwood, Middx HA6 2HT. *Clubs:* East India; Vincent's (Oxford).

GABRIEL, Peter; singer, musician and songwriter; *b* 13 Feb. 1950; *m* 1971, Jill Moore (marr. diss.); two *d. Educ:* Charterhouse. Mem., Genesis, 1966–75; solo artist, 1975–. Founder: World of Music, Arts and Dance (annual festivals), 1982; Real World Gp, 1985; Real World Studios, 1986; Real World Records, 1989; Real World Multimedia, 1994; Jt Founder, Witness (human rights programme), 1992. *Albums* include: *with Genesis:* From Genesis to Revelation, 1969; Nursery Crime, 1971; Foxtrot, 1972; Selling England by the Pound, 1973; The Lamb Lies Down on Broadway, 1974; *solo:* Peter Gabriel I, 1977, II, 1978, III, 1980, IV, 1982; So, 1986; Us, 1992; Ovo, 2000; *film soundtracks:* Birdy, 1984; Last Temptation of Christ, 1988. *Address:* Real World, Box Mill, Box, Wilts SN13 8PL.

GADD, (John) Staffan; Chairman, Saga Securities Ltd, 1985–98; Hon. Vice President, Swedish Chamber of Commerce for UK, since 1996 (Chairman, 1993–96); *b* 30 Sept. 1934; *s* of John Gadd and Ulla Olivecrona; *m* 1st, 1958, Margaretha Löfborg (marr. diss.); one *s* one *d*; 2nd, 1990, Kay McGreeghan. *Educ:* Stockholm Sch. of Econs. MBA. Sec., Confedn of Swedish Industries, 1958–61; Skandinaviska Banken, Stockholm, 1961–69 (London Rep., 1964–67); Dep. Man. Dir, Scandinavian Bank Ltd, London, 1969–71, Chief Exec. and Man. Dir, 1971–80; Chief Exec., 1980–84, Chm., 1982–84, Samuel Montagu & Co. Ltd; Chm., Montagu and Co. AB, Sweden, 1982–86; Dir, Guyerzeller Zurmont Bank AG, Switzerland, 1983–84; Chm., J. S. Gadd Cie SA, Geneva, 1989–98; Mem. Bd, Carta Corporate Advisors AB, 1990–98. *Recreations:* shooting, ski-ing, the arts, walking, travel. *Address:* Locks Manor, Hurstpierpoint, West Sussex BN6 9JZ.

GADD, Ruth Maria; *see* Kelly, R. M.

GADDES, (John) Gordon; President, European Organisation for Conformity Assessment (formerly for Testing and Certification), since 2001 (UK Delegate, 1997; Secretary General, 1998–2001); *b* 22 May 1936; *s* of late James Graham Moscrop Gaddes and of Irene Gaddes (*née* Murray; who married E. O. Kine); *m* 1958, Pamela Jean (*née* Marchbank); one *s* one *d. Educ:* Carres Grammar Sch., Sleaford; Selwyn Coll., Cambridge (MA Hons Geography); London Univ. (BScEcon Hons). Joint Services Sch. of Languages, Russian Translator in RAF, 1955–57. Asst Lectr in Business Studies, Peterborough Technical Coll., 1960–64; Lectr in Business Studies, later Head of Business Studies, then Vice-Principal, Dacorum Coll. of Further Educn, Hemel Hempstead, 1964–69; Head of Export Services: British Standards Instn, 1969–72; Quality Assurance Dept, 1972–73; Dir, BSI Hemel Hempstead Centre, 1973–77; Commercial Dir, BSI, 1977–81; Dir, Information, Marketing and Resources, BSI, 1981–82; Dir Gen., BEAMA, 1982–97. Secretary, BSI Quality Assurance Council, 1976–80; Member: Council, 1982–97, President's Cttee, 1984–86, Production Cttee, 1984–88, CBI; NACCB, 1984–90 (Chm., Assessment Panel, 1985–90); Project Leader for ISO/UNESCO inf. network study, 1974–75; variously, consultant to UNIDO and EC; UK Rep., ORGALIME, 1982–97 (Chairman: Electrical and Electronic Inds Liaison Cttee, 1982–86; Finance and Admin Cttee, 1986–88; Exec. Cttee, 1988–90); Pres., CENELEC, 1989–91 (Dep. Pres., 1987–89, 1994–95); Chairman: Eur. Electrotechnical Sectoral Cttee for Testing and Certification, 1992–95; ASTA Certification Services, 1994–98; UK Ex Forum, 1995–97; Kennedy Mgt Develt, 1998–99. Freeman, City of London, 1991; Liveryman, Glaziers' Co., 1993. *Recreations:* swimming, golf. *Clubs:* Athenæum; Whipsnade Park Golf.

GADSBY, (Gordon) Neville, CB 1972; *b* 29 Jan. 1914; *s* of William George and Margaret Sarah Gadsby; *m* 1938, Jeanne (*née* Harris); two *s* one *d. Educ:* King Edward VI Sch., Stratford-upon-Avon; University of Birmingham. BSc 1935, DipEd 1937, Cadbury Prizeman 1937, Birmingham; FRSC, CChem. Princ. Lectr, RMCS, 1946–51; Supt, Army Operational Research Gp, 1951–55; Dep. Sci. Adviser to Army Coun., 1955–59; idc 1960; Dir of Army Operational Science and Research, 1961; Dir, Army Operational Res. Estab., 1961–64; Dir of Biol. and Chem. Defence, MoD, 1965–67; Dep. Chief Scientist (Army), MoD, 1967–68; Dir, Chemical Defence Estabt, Porton, Wilts, 1968–72; Minister, Defence R&D, British Embassy, Washington, 1972–75, retired. *Publications:* Lubrication, 1949; An Introduction to Plastics, 1950. *Recreations:* oil painting, photography. *Address:* Ruan House, Cliff Road, Sidmouth, Devon EX10 8JN. *T:* (01395) 577842.

GADSDEN, Sir Peter (Drury Haggerston), GBE 1979; Hon. AC 1988; MA; FREng; Lord Mayor of London for 1979–80; Chairman, PPP Healthcare Foundation, since 1996; *b* Canada, 28 June 1929; *er s* of late Basil Claude Gadsden, ACT, ThL, and late Mabel Florence Gadsden (*née* Drury); *m* 1955, Belinda Ann, *e d* of late Captain Sir (Hugh) Carnaby de Marie Haggerston, 11th Bt; four *d. Educ:* Rockport, Northern Ireland; The Elms, Colwall; Wrekin Coll., Wellington; Jesus Coll., Cambridge (MA; Hon. Fellow, 1988). 2nd Lieut King's Shropshire LI, attached Oxf. and Bucks LI and Durham LI, Germany, 1948–49. Man. Dir, London subsid. of Australian Mineral Sands Producer, 1964–70; Marketing Economist (Mineral Sands) to UN Industrial Development Organisation, 1969; pt-time Mem., Crown Agents for Oversea Govts and Admins, 1981–87. Director: City of London (Arizona) Corp., 1970–88 (Chm., 1985–88); Wm Jacks plc, 1984–; W. Canning plc, 1989–99 (Dep. Chm., 1990–99); PPP Healthcare Gp (formerly Private Patients Plan Ltd), 1981–96 (Chm., 1984–96; Pres., 1996–98); Chm., PPP Healthcare Medical Trust, 1996–99. Chm. City of London Br., Inst. of Dirs, 1995–99. Dir, Clothworkers' Foundn, 1978–; Hon. Mem. London Metal Exchange. President: Nat. Assoc. of Charcoal Manufacturers, 1970–86; City of London Rifle & Pistol Club (formerly Embankment Rifle Club), 1975–87; Leukaemia Res. Fund, City of London Br., 1975–86; Metropolitan Soc. for the Blind, 1979– (Council, 1972–82); Publicity Club of London, 1983–2001; Council, London World Trade Centre Assoc., 1980–92; St John Ambulance (Eastern Area), 1981–86 (Mem. Council, Shropshire Br.); British-Australasian Heritage Soc., 1986–; Australian-NZ Chamber of Commerce, 1997–2001. Sheriff, City of London, 1970–71; Common Councilman (Cripplegate Within and Without), 1969–71; Alderman, City of London (Ward of Farringdon Without), 1971–99, Sen. Alderman, 1996–99; HM Lieutenant, City of London, 1979–99; Founder Master, Engineers' Co., 1983–85; Liveryman, Clothworkers' Co. (Master 1989–90); Hon. Liveryman: Plaisterers' Co., 1975–; Marketors Co., 1978–; Fruiterers' Co., 1999–; Freeman, Shrewsbury Drapers' Co., 1998– (Patron, Shrewsbury Drapers Hall Preservation Trust, 1998–); Hon. Freeman, Actuaries' Co., 1981–; Master, Cripplegate Ward Club, 1982–83; Member: Guild of Freemen, 1963– (Master 1984–85; Hon. Asst, 1995); Company of World Traders (formerly Guild of World Traders in London), 1985– (Master, 1987–88); Royal Soc. of St George (City of London Br.), 1970–; Council, City Univ., 1985–86 (Chancellor, 1979–80); Council, Britain Australia Soc., 1978–92 (Chm., 1989–92; Vice Pres., 1992–); Bermuda Soc., 1987– (Founder Chm., 1987–89). Chairman: Britain Australia Bicentennial Cttee, 1984–88; UK Europe, Order of Australia Assoc., 1991–93; Cook Soc., 1999. Hon. Freeman, Borough of Islwyn, S Wales, 1983. Vice-President: Sir Robert Menzies Meml Trust; League of Friends, Robert Jones and Agnes Hunt, Orthopaedic Hosp., 1980–; Nuffield Nursing Homes Trust, 1984–; Commonwealth Trust, 1984–95; Shropshire Soc. in London, 1986–89; Blackwood Little Theatre, 1986–. Fellowship of Engrg Distinction Lectr, 1980; Wm Menelaus Meml Lectr, SW Inst. of Engrs, 1983; paper to MANTECH Symposium, 1983; Royal Instn Lectr, 1991. Trustee: St Bartholomew's and St Mark's Hosps, 1981–88; Britain–Australia Bicentennial Trust, 1986–; Britain-Australia Bicentennial Schooner Trust, 1986–92; Britain-Australia Soc. Educnl Trust, 1990–; Edward King Hse, Lincoln, 1988–2000; Battle of Britain Meml Trust, 1990–93; Nat. History Mus. Develt Trust, 1992–98; Shropshire Regt Museum, 2000– (Chm., Appeal, 1991–99); Ludlow Mus. Develt Trust, 2000–; Chm., London Bridge Mus. Trust, 2000–; President: Ironbridge Gorge Museum Develt Trust, 1981–; Upper Severn Navigation Trust Ltd, 1992–; Shropshire Horticultural Soc., 1992–93; Patron, Telford and Wrekin Community Trust, 1998– (Chm., Community Chest 2000, 1999–); Gov., Hereford Cathedral Perpetual Trust, 2001–; Shropshire and Mid Wales Hospice, 1998– (Vice Pres., 1989–98). Life Pres., Freemen of City of London in Islwyn, 1995. Member: Management Council, Shakespeare Theatre Trust, 1979–86; Royal Commn for the 1851 Exhibn, 1986–99; Chm. and Mem. Council, 1984–88, Vice-Pres., 1988–89, Royal Commonwealth Soc.; Patron: Museum of Empire and Commonwealth Trust, 1986–; Guild of Rahere, 1986–; Royal Soc. Project Science, 1996–. Vice-Pres., Royal Nat. Coll. for the Blind, 2001–. Governor: Hon. Irish Soc., 1984–87; The Elms, Colwall, 1993–; Wrekin Coll., 1997–99. JP, City of London, 1971 (Inner London Area of Greater London, 1969–71). Hon. FCIM; FIMM 1979; CEng 1979, FREng (FEng 1980); Hon. Mem., Instn of Royal Engrs, 1986; Hon. FRSH 1992; Hon. FRCA 1994. Hon. DSc 1979. Hon. Mem. Court, HAC, 1971–99; Hon. Col 5th (Shropshire and Hereford) Bn LI (Vol.), 1988–93 (Hon. Mem. of Mess). KStJ 1980 (OStJ 1977). Christ Church-Midnite Award, Perth, WA, 1997. Officier de l'Etoile Equatoriale de la République Gabonaise, 1970. *Publications:* articles in: InstMM Transactions, 1971; RSM Jl, 1979; Textile Institute and Industry, 1980; articles on titanium, zirconium, and hafnium in Mining Jl Annual Reviews, 1969–86. *Recreations:* walking, photography, fishing. *Address:* Cheriton, Middleton Scriven, Bridgnorth, Shropshire WV16 6AG. *T:* (01746) 789650. *Clubs:* Boodle's, City Livery (Mem. Council), United Wards, Farringdon Ward (Patron, 1971–99), City of London (Hon.), City of London Pickwick (Pres., 1999–), Light Infantry (Hon.); Bligny (Shrewsbury); Royal London Yacht (Hon.).

GAFFNEY, James Anthony, CBE 1984; FREng; FICE; *b* Bargoed, Glam, 9 Aug. 1928; *s* of James Francis and Violet Mary Gaffney; *m* 1953, Margaret Mary, 2nd *d* of E. and G. J. Evans, Pontypridd; one *s* two *d. Educ:* De La Salle Coll.; St Illtyd's Coll., Cardiff; UWIST; UC, Cardiff (Fellow, 1984). BSc (Eng) London. FREng (FEng 1979); FICE 1968; FInstHE 1970. Highway Engr, Glam CC, 1948–60; Asst County Surveyor, Somerset CC, 1960–64; Deputy County Surveyor, Notts CC, 1964–69; County Engr and Surveyor, WR Yorks, 1969–74; Dir Engrg Services, W Yorks MCC, 1974–86. President: County Surveyors' Soc., 1977–78; Instn of Highway Engrs, 1978–79; ICE, 1983–84; Vice-Pres., Fellowship of Engrg, 1989–92. Hon. DSc: Wales, 1982; Bradford, 1984. *Recreations:* golf, travel, supporting Rugby. *Address:* Drovers Cottage, 3 Boston Road, Wetherby, W Yorks LS22 5HA. *Club:* Alwoodley Golf (Leeds).

GAFFNEY, John Campion B.; *see* Burke-Gaffney.

GAGE, family name of **Viscount Gage.**

GAGE, 8th Viscount *cr* 1720 (Ire.); **Henry Nicholas Gage;** DL; Bt 1622; Baron Gage (Ire.) 1720; Baron Gage (GB) 1790; *b* 9 April 1934; *yr s* of 6th Viscount Gage, KCVO and his 1st wife, Hon. Alexandra Imogen Clare Grenfell (*d* 1969), *yr d* of 1st Baron Desborough, KG, GCVO; *S* brother, 1993; *m* 1974, Lady Diana Adrienne Beatty; two *s*. *Educ:* Eton; Christ Church, Oxford. 2nd Lt Coldstream Guards, 1953. DL East Sussex, 1998. *Recreations:* country and other pursuits. *Heir: s* Hon. Henry William Gage, *b* 25 June 1975. *Address:* Firle Place, Lewes, East Sussex BN8 6LP. *T:* (01273) 858535, *Fax:* (01273) 858188.

GAGE, Hon. Sir William (Marcus), Kt 1993; **Hon. Mr Justice Gage;** a Judge of the High Court of Justice, Queen's Bench Division, since 1993; Presiding Judge, South Eastern Circuit, 1997–2000; *b* 22 April 1938; *s* of late His Honour Conolly Gage; *m* 1962, Penelope Mary Groves; three *s*. *Educ:* Repton; Sidney Sussex Coll., Cambridge. MA. National Service, Irish Guards, 1956–58. Called to the Bar, Inner Temple, 1963, Bencher, 1991; QC 1982; a Recorder, 1985–93. Chancellor, diocese of Coventry, 1980–, of Ely, 1989–. Mem., Criminal Injuries Compensation Bd, 1987–93. *Recreations:* shooting, fishing, travel. *Address:* Royal Courts of Justice, Strand, WC2A 2LL.

GAGEBY DENHAM, Susan; *see* Denham.

GAGGERO, Joseph James, CBE 1989; Chairman, Bland Group of Shipping, Aviation and Travel Companies; *b* 20 Nov. 1927; *s* of Sir George Gaggero, OBE, JP and Mabel Andrews-Speed; *m* 1st, 1958, Marilys Healing (marr. diss. 1987); one *s* one *d*; 2nd, 1994, Christina Russo. *Educ:* Downside Sch. Dir, Gibraltar Chamber of Commerce, 1951–56; Head, Gibraltar Govt Tourist Dept, 1955–59; served on or led other Gibraltar Govt Cttees and Gibraltar Trading Assocs, 1948–. Hon. Consul Gen. for Sweden in Gibraltar, 1971–95. Director: Credit Suisse (Gibraltar) Ltd; Hovertravel; Chairman: GB Airways; Gibraltar Airways; Pres., Rock Hotel. Freeman, City of London, 1997; Liveryman, GAPAN, 1997–. KHS. Order of the North Star (Sweden). *Recreations:* travel, painting. *Address:* Cloister Building, Gibraltar. *T:* 78456. *Clubs:* Travellers; Valderrama Golf.

GAHAGAN, Michael Barclay, CB 2000; Director, Housing (formerly Housing, Private Policy and Analysis) Directorate, Department for Transport, Local Government and the Regions (formerly Department of the Environment, Transport and the Regions), since 1997; *b* 24 March 1943; *s* of Geoffrey and Doris Gahagan; *m* 1967, Anne Brown; two *s*. *Educ:* St Mary's Coll., Southampton; Univ. of Manchester (MA Econ, BA). ARICS. W. H. Robinson & Co., Chartered Surveyors, Manchester, 1964–66; DEA (NW), 1966–69; Min. of Housing and Local Govt (NW), 1969–71; DoE, Central Res. and Inner Cities Directorates, NW, SE and London Regl Offices, 1971–88; seconded to DTI Inner Cities Unit, 1988–91; Dir, Inner Cities, subseq. Cities and Countryside Policy, then Regeneration, Directorate, DoE, 1991–96. Pres., Internat. Urban Develt Assoc, 1995–99. *Recreations:* soccer, bridge, squash. *Address:* Department for Transport, Local Government and the Regions, Eland House, SW1E 5DU. *T:* (020) 7944 3260.

GAINFORD, 3rd Baron *cr* 1917; **Joseph Edward Pease;** *b* 25 Dec. 1921; *s* of 2nd Baron Gainford, TD, and Veronica Margaret (*d* 1995), *d* of Sir George Noble, 2nd Bt; *S* father, 1971; *m* 1953, Margaret Theophila Radcliffe, *d* of late Henry Edmund Guise Tyndale; two *d*. *Educ:* Eton; Gordonstoun; Open Univ. (Dip. in Eur. Humanities, 1995, BA Hons, 1997). FRGS; TechRICS. RAFVR, 1941–46. Hunting Aerosurveys Ltd, 1947–49; Directorate of Colonial Surveys, 1951–53; Soil Mechanics Ltd, 1953–58; London County Council, 1958–65; Greater London Council, 1965–78. UK Delegate to UN, 1973. Mem., Coll. of Guardians, Nat. Shrine of Our Lady of Walsingham, 1979–. Mem., Plaisterers' Co., 1976. *Recreations:* golf, music, veteran and vintage aviation. *Heir: b* Hon. George Pease [*b* 20 April 1926; *m* 1958, Flora Daphne, *d* of late Dr N. A. Dyce Sharp; two *s* two *d*]. *Address:* 1 Dedmere Court, Marlow, Bucks SL7 1PL. *T:* (01628) 484679. *Clubs:* MCC, Pathfinder.

GAINS, John Christopher, CEng, FICE; Chief Executive, John Mowlem & Co. PLC, since 1995 (Director, since 1992); *b* 22 April 1945; *s* of Albert Edward Gains and Grace (*née* Breckenridge); *m* 1969, Ann Murray (*d* 1999); one *s* one *d*. *Educ:* King Henry VIII Sch., Coventry; Loughborough Univ. (BSc). CEng 1970; FICE 1992. Joined John Mowlem & Co. PLC, 1966; Dir, Mowlem Civil Engineering, 1983–95. Non-exec. Dir, SGB plc, 1997–. *Recreations:* golf, sailing, walking. *Address:* Longridge, Farm Lane, East Markham, Newark, Notts NG22 0QH. *T:* (01777) 870616. *Clubs:* Reform; Lincoln Golf.

GAINSBOROUGH, 5th Earl of, (2nd) *cr* 1841; **Anthony Gerard Edward Noel;** Bt 1781; Baron Barham, 1805; Viscount Campden, Baron Noel, 1841; JP; *b* 24 Oct. 1923; *s* of 4th Earl and Alice Mary (*d* 1970), *e d* of Edward Eyre, Gloucester House, Park Lane, W1; *S* father, 1927; *m* 1947, Mary, *er d* of late Hon. J. J. Stourton, TD and Mrs Kathleen Stourton; four *s* three *d*. *Educ:* Georgetown, Garrett Park, Maryland, USA. Chairman: Oakham RDC, 1952–67; Executive Council RDC's Association of England and Wales, 1963 (Vice-Chairman 1962, Pres., 1965); Pres., Assoc. of District Councils, 1974–80; Vice-Chm. Rutland CC, 1958–70, Chm., 1970–73; Chm., Rutland Dist Council, 1973–76. Chm., Bd of Management, Hosp. of St John and St Elizabeth, NW8, 1970–80 (Pres., 1995–). Chm., Hosp. Mgt Trust, 1985–. Mem. Court of Assistants, Worshipful Co. of Gardeners of London, 1960 (Upper Warden, 1966; Master, 1967). Hon. FICE (Hon. FIMunE 1969). JP Rutland, 1957, Leics 1974. Knight of Malta, 1948; Bailiff Grand Cross Order of Malta, 1958; Pres. Br. Assoc., SMO, Malta, 1968–74. KStJ 1970. *Recreations:* shooting, sailing. *Heir: s* Viscount Campden, *qv*. *Address:* Horn House, Exton Park, Oakham, Rutland LE15 7QU. *T:* (office) (01780) 460772. *Clubs:* Brooks's, Pratt's; Royal Yacht Squadron (Cowes), Bembridge Sailing.

See also Earl of Liverpool, Hon. G. E. W. Noel.

GAINSBOROUGH, George Fotheringham, CBE 1973; PhD, FIEE; Barrister-at-law; Secretary, Institution of Electrical Engineers, 1962–80; *b* 28 May 1915; *o s* of late Rev. William Anthony Gainsborough and of Alice Edith (*née* Fennell); *m* 1937, Gwendoline (*d* 1976), *e d* of John and Anne Berry; two *s*. *Educ:* Christ's Hospital; King's Coll., London; Gray's Inn. Scientific Staff, Nat. Physical Laboratory, 1938–46; Radio Physicist, British Commonwealth Scientific Office, Washington, DC, USA, 1944–45; Administrative Civil Service (Ministries of Supply and Aviation), 1946–62. Imperial Defence College, 1960. Secretary, Commonwealth Engineering Conf., 1962–69; Sec.-General, World Fedn of Engineering Organizations, 1968–76. *Publications:* papers in Proc. Instn of Electrical Engineers. *Address:* Moncorbon, 41360 Savigny-sur-Braye, France. *T:* 254239925. *Club:* Athenæum.

See also Michael Gainsborough.

GAINSBOROUGH, Michael; Assistant Secretary, Royal Hospital, Chelsea, 1994–2001 (Commissioner, since 2001); *b* 13 March 1938; *s* of George Fotheringham Gainsborough, *qv*; *m* 1962, Sally (*née* Hunter); one *s* two *d*. *Educ:* St Paul's Sch.; Trinity Coll., Oxford. Air Ministry, 1959–64; Ministry of Defence, 1964–78; Defence Counsellor, UK Delegn to NATO, Brussels, FCO, 1978–81; Dir, Resources and Programmes (Strategic Systems), MoD, 1981–83; Asst Under-Sec. of State (Naval Staff), 1984, (Programmes), 1985–86, MoD; Center for Internat. Affairs, Harvard Univ., 1986–87; Asst Under-Sec. of State (Adjutant Gen.), 1987–91, (Service Personnel), 1992, MoD. Mem., Royal Patriotic Fund Corp., 1987–2000. *Recreations:* listening to music, gardening, walking. *Address:* 3 Methley Street, SE11 4AL.

GAINSFORD, Sir Ian (Derek), Kt 1995; FDSRCS, FDSRCSE; Dean of King's College School of Medicine and Dentistry, King's College London, 1988–97; Vice-Principal, King's College London, 1994–97; *b* 24 June 1930; *s* of late Rabbi Morris Ginsberg, MA, PhD, AKC, and Anne Freda; *m* 1957, Carmel Liebster; one *s* two *d*. *Educ:* Thames Valley Grammar Sch., Twickenham; King's Coll. and King's College Hosp. Med. Sch., London (BDS; FKC 1984); Toronto Univ., Canada (DDS Hons). FDSRCS 1967; FDSRCSE 1998. Junior Staff, King's College Hosp., 1955–57; Member staff, Dept of Conservative Dentistry, London Hosp. Med. Sch., 1957–70; Sen. Lectr/Consultant, Dept of Conservative Dentistry, King's College Hosp., 1970–; Dep. Dean of Dental Studies, 1973–77; Dir of Clinical Dental Services, KCH, 1977–87 (Dean of Dental Studies, KCHMS, 1977–83); Dean, Faculty of Clinical Dentistry, KCL, 1983–87. President, British Soc. for Restorative Dentistry, 1973–74; Member: BDA, 1956– (Pres., Metropolitan Br., 1981–82); Internat. Dental Fedn, 1966–; American Dental Soc. of London, 1960– (Pres., 1982); Amer. Dental Soc. of Europe, 1965– (Hon. Treas. 1971–77; Pres., 1982); GDC, 1986–94 (Chm., Educn Cttee, 1990–94; Chm., Specialist Trng Adv. Cttee, 1996–2000). Examiner for Membership in General Dental Surgery, RCS, 1979–84 (Chm., 1982–84); External Examiner: Leeds Univ. Dental Sch., 1985–87; Hong Kong Dental Sch., 1988–90; Fellow, and Mem., 1967–, Hon. Mem., 1996, Pres., 1993–94, Odontological Sect., RSM. Non-exec. Dir, SE Thames RHA, 1988–93. President: Western Marble Arch Synagogue, 1998–2000; The Maccabaeans, 2000–. Hon. Pres., British Friends of Magen David Adom, 1995–. Hon. Mem., Amer. Dental Assoc., 1983. Hon. Scientific Advr, British Dental Jl, 1982. FICD 1975; MGDS RCS 1979; FACD 1988. *Publication:* Silver Amalgam in Clinical Practice, 1965, 3rd edn 1992. *Recreations:* theatre, canal cruising. *Address:* 31 York Terrace East, NW1 4PT. *T:* (020) 7935 8659. *Clubs:* Athenæum, Royal Society of Medicine.

GAIR, Hon. George Frederick, CMG 1994; QSO 1988; Chairman, New Zealand Ambulance Board, since 1995; *b* 13 Oct. 1926; *s* of Frederick James Gair and Roemer Elizabeth Elphege (*née* Boecking); *m* 1951, Esther Mary Fay Levy; one *s* two *d*. *Educ:* Wellington Coll.; Wairarapa Coll.; Victoria and Auckland Univ. Colls (BA 1949). Journalist: NZ Herald, 1945–47; BCON, Japan, 1947–48; Sun News Pictorial, 1949–50; Auckland Star, 1950–52; Auckland PRO, 1952–57; Staff Leader of Opposition, NZ, 1958; Press Officer and Personal Asst to Chief Exec., TEAL (later Air NZ), 1960–66. MP (Nat.) North Shore, 1966–90; Parly Under-Sec. to Minister of Educn, 1969–71; Minister of: Customs, and Associate Minister of Finance, 1972; Housing, and Dep. Minister of Finance, 1975–77; Energy, 1977–78; Health, and of Social Welfare, 1978–81; Transport, Railways, and Civil Aviation, 1981–84; Dep. Leader of Opposition, 1986–87; retd 1990. High Comr for NZ in UK, 1991–94, concurrently High Comr in Nigeria and Ambassador to Republic of Ireland. Mayor, North Shore City, NZ, 1995–98. Pres., Alumni Assoc., Univ. of Auckland, 1994–97. *Recreation:* walking. *Address:* 41 Hauraki Road, Takapuna, Auckland 9, New Zealand.

GAISFORD, Rt Rev. John Scott; Bishop Suffragan of Beverley, 1994–2000; Episcopal Visitor for the Province of York, 1994–2000; Hon. Assistant Bishop of Ripon, 1996–2000; *b* 7 Oct. 1934; *s* of Joseph and Margaret Thompson Gaisford; *m* 1962, Gillian Maclean; one *s* one *d*. *Educ:* Univ. of Durham (Exhibnr, St Chad's Coll., Durham; BA Hons Theol. 1959, DipTh with Distinction 1960, MA 1976). Deacon 1960, priest 1961, Manchester; Assistant Curate: S Hilda, Audenshaw, 1960–62; S Michael, Bramhall, 1962–65; Vicar, S Andrew, Crewe, 1965–86; RD of Nantwich, 1974–85; Hon. Canon of Chester Cathedral, 1980–86; Archdeacon of Macclesfield, 1986–94. Proctor in Convocation, Mem. Gen. Synod, 1975–95; Church Commissioner, 1986–94; Member: Church of England Pensions Bd, 1982–97; Churches Conservation Trust (formerly Redundant Churches Fund), 1989–98. *Recreation:* fell walking. *Address:* 5 Trevone Close, Knutsford, Cheshire WA16 9EJ. *T:* (01565) 633531; *e-mail:* john.gaisford@cwcom.net. *Club:* Athenæum.

GAISMAN, Jonathan Nicholas Crispin; QC 1995; a Recorder, since 2000; *b* 10 Aug. 1956; *o s* of Peter and Bea Gaisman; *m* 1982, Tessa Jardine Paterson (MBE 1990); one *s* two *d*. *Educ:* Summer Fields; Eton College (King's Scholar); Worcester Coll., Oxford (BCL; MA 1st cl Hons Jurisp.). Called to the Bar, Inner Temple, 1979; Asst Recorder, 1998–2000. Director: English Chamber Orchestra and Music Soc. Ltd, 1992–96; Internat. Musicians' Seminar, Prussia Cove, 1994–. FRSA 1997. *Recreations:* the arts, travel, country pursuits. *Address:* 7 King's Bench Walk, Temple, EC4Y 7DS. *T:* (020) 7583 0404. *Clubs:* Brooks's; I Zingari.

GAITSKELL, Robert; QC 1994; PhD; CEng, FIEE, FIMechE; FCIArb; a Recorder, since 2000; Vice President, Institution of Electrical Engineers, 1998–Oct. 2001; *b* 19 April 1948; *s* of late Stanley Gaitskell and late Thelma Phyllis Gaitskell (*née* Holmes); *m* 1974, Dr Deborah Lyndall Bates; one *d*. *Educ:* Hamilton High Sch., Bulawayo, Zimbabwe; Univ. of Cape Town (BSc Eng); KCL (PhD 1998; AKC 1998). CEng 1993; FIEE 1993; FCIArb 1995; FIMechE 1998. CEDR Accredited Mediator, 1999. Grad. trainee, Reyrolle Parsons, 1971–73; Engr, Electricity Dept, Bulawayo CC, Zimbabwe, 1973–75; Electrical Engr, GEC (South Africa), 1975–76; called to the Bar, Gray's Inn, 1978; in practice at Bar in construction cases; arbitrator; Asst Recorder, 1997–2000. Lectr, Centre of Construction Law and Mgt, KCL, 1993–, and other professional bodies. Institution of Electrical Engineers: Mem. Council, 1994–; Chairman: Bd of Mgt and Design Div., 1995; Professional Gp on Engrg and the Law, 1994; Internat. Bd, 1998–99; Public Affairs Bd, 1999–2000; Professional Bd, 2000. Mem., Heilbron Cttee on Civil Procedure, 1993; Chm., IEE/IMechE Jt Cttee on Model Forms, 2001–. Senator, Engrg Council, 1998– (Chairman: Election Cttee, 1999–; Code of Conduct Cttee, 1999–). Member Committee: London Common Law and Commercial Bar Assoc., 1987–2000; Official Referees Bar Assoc., 1987–93. Legal columnist, Engrg Mgt Jl, 1994–; Mem. Editl Bd, Construction and Engrg Law Jl, 1998–. Methodist local preacher. Liveryman: Engineers' Co., 1997–; Arbitrators' Co., 2001–. *Publications:* papers and articles on law and engrg. *Recreations:* walking, theatre, travel. *Address:* Keating Chambers, 10 Essex Street, WC2R 3AA.

GAIUS, Rev. Sir Saimon, KBE 1988 (OBE 1975); *b* 6 Aug. 1920; *s* of Peni Tovarur and Miriam Ia Pea; *m* 1941, Margaret Ia Kubak; five *s* one *d* (and one *s* one *d* decd). *Educ:* Mission Sch., East New Britain; theological training, PNG and Sydney, Aust. Ordained 1960; worked as United Church Minister; Principal, Pastors' Training Coll., 1967–68; Bishop of New Guinea Island Region, 1968–77; retired as Minister of Religion, 1983. SBStJ 1976. *Recreation:* reading. *Address:* United Church, PO Box 90, Rabaul, East New Britain, Papua New Guinea.

GAJDUSEK, Daniel Carleton, MD; Director of Program for Study of Child Growth and Development and Disease Patterns in Primitive Cultures, and Laboratory of Slow Latent and Temperate Virus Infections, National Institute of Neurological Disorders (formerly of

Neurological and Communicative Disorders and Stroke), National Institutes of Health, Bethesda, Md, 1958–97; Chief, Central Nervous System Studies Laboratory, NINDS, 1970–97; *b* Yonkers, NY, 9 Sept. 1923; *s* of Karol Gajdusek and Ottilia Dobroczki; sixty adopted *s* and *d* (all from New Guinea and Micronesia). *Educ:* Marine Biological Lab., Woods Hole, Mass; Univ. of Rochester (BS *summa cum laude*); Harvard Medical Sch. (MD); California Inst. of Technology (Post-Doctoral Fellow). Residencies: Babies Hosp., NY, 1946–47; Children's Hosp., Cincinatti, Ohio, 1947–48; Children's Hosp., Boston, Mass, 1949–51; Sen. Fellow, Nat. Research Council, Calif Inst. of Tech., 1948–49; Children's Hosp., Boston, Mass, 1949–51; Research Fellow, Harvard Univ. and Sen. Fellow, Nat. Foundn for Infantile Paralysis, 1949–52; Walter Reed Army Medical Center, 1952–53; Institut Pasteur, Tehran, Iran and Univ. of Maryland, 1954–55; Vis. Investigator, Nat. Foundn for Infantile Paralysis and Walter and Eliza Hall Inst., Australia, 1955–57. Adjunct Prof., Inst. of Human Virology, Baltimore, 1996–; Guest Scientist, CNRS, Institut Alfred Fessard, Gif-sur-Yvette, France, 1998–; Visiting Professor: Human Retrovirus Lab., Univ. of Amsterdam, 1998–; Univ. of Tromsø, 1998–. Member: Nat. Acad. of Sciences, 1974; Amer. Philos. Soc., 1978; Amer. Acad. of Arts and Scis, 1978; Amer. Acad. of Neurol.; Infectious Dis. Soc. of America; Amer. Pediatric Soc.; Amer. Epidemiological Soc.; Amer. Soc. for Virology; Deutsche Akademie der Naturforscher Leopoldina, 1982; Czechoslovak, Portuguese, Australian, Russian and Sakha Acads of Science; Mexican Nat. Acad. of Medicine; Nat. Acad. of Medicine, Colombia; Royal Acad. of Medicine of Belgium. Mem., Scientific Council, Fondn pour l'Etude du Système Nerveux, Geneva, 1983–96. Discovered slow virus infections of man; studied child growth and develt and disease patterns in primitive and isolated populations, virus encephalitides, hemorrhagic fevers, hantavirus and human retrovirus infections, chronic degenerative brain diseases, cerebral amyloidoses, and aging, spontaneous generation of infectious agents by nucleating induction of infectious conformation of host precursor proteins, molecular casting. E. Meade Johnson Award, Amer. Acad. Pediatrics, 1963; DHEW Superior Service Award, 1970; DHEW Distinguished Service Award, 1975; Lucien Dautrebande Prize, Belgium, 1976; shared with Dr Baruch Blumberg Nobel Prize in Physiology or Medicine, for discoveries concerning new mechanisms for the origin and dissemination of infectious diseases, 1976; George Cotzias Meml Prize, Amer. Acad. of Neurol., 1978; Huxley Medal, RAI, 1988; Gold Medal, Slovak Acad. of Scis, 1996; Premio Gargano, Inst. di Cultura, Manfredouia, 2000; Shandong Friendship Prize, 2000. Hon. Curator, Melanesian Ethnography, Peabody Mus., Salem, Mass; Hon. Pres., World Hantavirus Soc., 1994–; Hon. Advr, Shandong Acad. Scis, 2000–. Hon. DSc: Univ. of Rochester, 1977; Med. Coll. of Ohio, 1977; Washington and Jefferson Coll., 1980; Harvard Med. Sch. (Bicentennial), 1982; Hahnemann Univ., 1983; Univ. of Medicine and Dentistry of NJ, 1987; Hon. LHD: Hamilton Coll., 1977; Univ. of Hawaii, 1986; Comenius Univ., Bratislava, 1996; Docteur *hc*: Univ. of Marseille, 1977; Univ. of Lisbon, 1991; Univ. of Las Palmas, 1996; Hon. LLD Aberdeen, 1980; Laurea *hc* Univ. of Milan, 1992. *Publications:* Acute Infectious Hemorrhagic Fevers and Mycotoxicoses in the USSR, 1953; (ed with C. J. Gibbs, Jr and M. P. Alpers) Slow, Latent and Temperate Virus Infections, 1965; Journals 1937–2000, 60 vols, 1958–2001; Smadel-Gajdusek Correspondence 1955–1958; (ed with J. Farquhar) Kuru, 1981; Viliuisk Encephalitis, 1996; over 1000 papers in major jls of medicine, microbiology, immunology, pediatrics, developmental biology, psychosexual development, neurobiology, genetics, evolution, anthropology and linguistics.

GALASKO, Prof. Charles Samuel Bernard; Professor of Orthopaedic Surgery, University of Manchester, since 1976; Consultant Orthopaedic Surgeon: Hope Hospital, since 1976 (Medical Director, 1993–96); Royal Manchester Children's Hospital, since 1976 (Manchester Children's Hospital NHS Trust); *b* 29 June 1939; *s* of David Isaac Galasko and Rose Galasko; *m* 1967, Carol Freyda Lapinsky; one *s* one *d*. *Educ:* King Edward VII Sch., Johannesburg; Univ. of Witwatersrand (MB BCh 1st Cl. Hons 1962; ChM 1969). FRCS 1966; FRCSEd 1966. Med., surg. and orth. trng, Johannesburg Gen. Hosp. and Univ. of Witwatersrand, 1963–66; House Surgeon and Surg. Registrar, Hammersmith Hosp. and RPMS, 1966–69; Lord Nuffield Schol. in Orthopaedic Surgery, Univ. of Oxford, 1969; Orth. and Trauma Registrar and Sen. Registrar, Radcliffe Infirmary and Nuffield Orth. Centre, Oxford, 1970–73; Cons. Orth. Surgeon, Dir of Orth. Surgery, and Asst Dir, Div. of Surgery, RPMS and Hammersmith Hosp., 1973–76. Member, Management Board: Royal Manchester Children's Hosp., 1989–92; Salford Royal Hosps NHS Trust, 1989–96. Hunterian Prof., RCS, 1971; Sir Arthur Sims Commonwealth Prof., 1998. Chm., Jt Cttee on Higher Surgical Trng, UK and Ire., 1997–2000. Member: Med. Sub-Cttee, British Olympic Assoc., 1988–; Internat. Cttee, 1990–93, Internat. Adv. Bd, 1994–96, SICOT (A. O. Internat. Award, 1981); President: SIROT, 1990–93; British Orthopaedic Assoc., 2000–Sept. 2001 (Vice Pres., 1999–2000; Mem. Council, 1988–91, 1998–); Vice Pres., RCS, 1999– (Mem. Council, 1991–; Chm., Trng Bd, 1995–99). Vice Pres., British Amateur Wrestling Assoc., 1996– (Chm., 1992–96; Med. Advr, 1987–); Vice-Chm., English Olympic Wrestling Assoc., 1998– (Med. Advr, 1987–). *Publications:* (ed jtly) Radionuclide Scintigraphy Orthopaedics, 1984; (ed) Principles of Fracture Management, 1984; Skeletal Metastases, 1986; (ed) Neuromuscular Problems in Orthopaedics, 1987; (ed jtly) Recent Developments in Orthopaedic Surgery, 1987 (ed jtly) Current Trends in Orthopaedic Surgery, 1988; (ed jtly) Imaging Techniques in Orthopaedics, 1989; (jtly) Competing for the Disabled, 1989; articles and contribs to books on aspects of orthopaedics and trauma. *Recreations:* sport, opera, music. *Address:* Department of Orthopaedic Surgery, Clinical Sciences Building, Hope Hospital, Eccles Old Road, Salford M6 8HD. *T:* (0161) 787 4291.

GALBRAITH, family name of **Baron Strathclyde**.

GALBRAITH, James Hunter, CB 1985; Under Secretary, Department of Employment Industrial Relations Division, 1975–85; *b* 16 July 1925; *o s* of late Prof. V. H. Galbraith, FBA, and Dr G. R. Galbraith; *m* 1954, Isobel Gibson Graham; two *s*. *Educ:* Dragon Sch.; Edinburgh Academy; Balliol Coll., Oxford. 1st Cl. Litt Hum. Fleet Air Arm (pilot), 1944–46. Entered Ministry of Labour, 1950; Private Sec. to Permanent Sec., 1953–55; Jun. Civilian Instructor, IDC, 1958–61; Private Sec. to Minister of Labour, 1962–64; Chm. Central Youth Employment Exec., 1964–67; Sen. Simon Research Fellow, Manchester Univ., 1967–68; Asst Under-Sec. of State, Dept of Employment and Productivity (Research and Planning Div.), 1968–71; Dir, Office of Manpower Economics, 1971–73; Under-Sec., Manpower Gen. Div., Dept of Employment, 1973–74; Sec., Manpower Services Commn, 1974–75. Mem., Employment Appeal Tribunal, 1986–96. Chm., Bd of Govs. Volunteer Centre UK, 1989–93. *Recreations:* rugby (Oxford Blue), golf, fishing. *Address:* The Orangery, Alde House, Aldeburgh, Suffolk IP15 5EE. *T:* (01728) 452594.

See also G. M. Moore.

GALBRAITH, Prof. John Kenneth; Paul M. Warburg Professor of Economics, Harvard University, 1949–75, now Emeritus Professor; *b* Ontario, Canada, 15 Oct. 1908; *s* of William Archibald and Catherine Galbraith; *m* 1937, Catherine M. Atwater; three *s*. *Educ:* Univ. of Guelph; California Univ. BS, MS, PhD. Tutor, Harvard Univ., 1934–39; Social Science Research Fellow, Cambridge Univ., 1937; Asst Prof. of Economics, Princeton Univ., 1939; Asst Administrator, Office of Price Administration, 1941; Deputy Administrator, 1942–43; Dir, State Dept Office of Economic Security Policy, 1945; Mem. Bd of Editors, Fortune Magazine, 1943–48. United States Ambassador to India, 1961–63 (on leave from Professorship). Reith Lecturer, 1966; Vis. Fellow, Trinity Coll., Cambridge, 1970–71 (Hon. Fellow, 1987). TV series, The Age of Uncertainty, 1977. Chm., Americans for Democratic Action, 1967–69; President: Amer. Econ. Assoc., 1972; Amer. Acad. of Arts and Letters, 1984 (Mem., 1982–). LLD Bard, 1958; Miami Univ., 1959; University of Toronto, 1961; Brandeis Univ., 1963; University of Mass, 1963; University of Saskatchewan, 1965; Rhode Island Coll., 1966; Boston Coll., 1967; Hobart and William Smith Colls, 1967; Univ. of Paris, 1975; and others. President's Certificate of Merit; Medal of Freedom. *Publications:* American Capitalism, the Concept of Countervailing Power, 1952; The Great Crash, 1929, 1955, new edn 1979; The Affluent Society, 1958, 4th edn, 1985; Journey to Poland and Yugoslavia, 1958; The Liberal Hour, 1960; Made to Last, 1964; The New Industrial State, 1967, rev. edn, 1978; Indian Painting, 1968; Ambassador's Journal, 1969; Economics, Peace and Laughter, 1971; A China Passage, 1973; Economics and the Public Purpose, 1974; Money: whence it came, where it went, 1975; The Age of Uncertainty, 1977; Almost Everyone's Guide to Economics, 1978; Annals of an Abiding Liberal, 1979; The Nature of Mass Poverty, 1979; A Life in Our Times, 1981; The Anatomy of Power, 1983; China Passage, 1983; A View from the Stands, 1987; A History of Economics, 1987; (with S. Menshikov) Capitalism, Communism and Coexistence, 1989; A Tenured Professor (novel), 1990; A Short History of Financial Euphoria, 1990; The Culture of Contentment, 1992; A Journey through Economic Time, 1994; The Good Society: the humane agenda, 1996; Letters to Kennedy, ed James Goodman, 1998; Name-Dropping: from FDR on, 1999; contribs to learned jls. *Address:* 206 Littauer Center, Harvard University, Cambridge, MA 02138, USA; 30 Francis Avenue, Cambridge, MA 02138, USA. *Clubs:* Century (NY); Federal City (Washington).

GALBRAITH, Neil, CBE 1975; QPM 1959; DL; HM Inspector of Constabulary, 1964–76, retired; *b* 25 May 1911; *s* of late Peter and Isabella Galbraith; *m* 1942, Catherine Margaret Thornton; one *s* one *d*. *Educ:* Kilmarnock Academy. Constable to Inspector, Lancs Constabulary, 1931–46. Chief Supt, Herts Constabulary, 1946–51; Asst Chief Constable, Monmouthshire Constabulary, 1951–55; Chief Constable, Leicester City Police, 1956; Chief Constable, Monmouthshire Constabulary, 1957–64. DL Gwent (formerly Monmouth), 1973. *Recreation:* living. *Address:* 7 Caringal Place, St Ives, Sydney, NSW 2075, Australia. *T:* (2) 94494404.

GALBRAITH, Samuel Laird; *b* 18 Oct. 1945. *Educ:* Glasgow Univ. (BSc Hons 1968; MB ChB Hons 1971; MD 1977); FRCSGlas 1975. Consultant in Neurosurgery, Gtr Glasgow Health Bd, 1978–87. MP (Lab) Strathkelvin and Bearsden, 1987–2001. Opposition spokesman on Scottish affairs and health, 1988–92, on employment, 1992–93; Parly Under-Sec. of State, Scottish Office, 1997–99. Scottish Parliament: Mem. (Lab) Strathkelvin and Bearsden, 1999–2001; Minister: for Children and Educn, Culture and the Arts and Sport, 1999–2000; for the Envmt, 2000–01. *Publication:* An Introduction to Neurosurgery, 1983.

GALBRAITH, William Campbell; QC 1977; *b* 25 Feb. 1935; *s* of William Campbell Galbraith and Margaret Watson or Galbraith; *m* 1959, Mary Janet Waller; three *s* (and one *s* decd). *Educ:* Merchiston Castle Sch.; Pembroke Coll., Cambridge (BA); Edinburgh Univ. (LLB). Teacher, Turkey, 1959–61; Lectr, Meshed Univ., Iran, 1961–62; admitted to Faculty of Advocates, 1962; in practice at Scottish Bar, 1962–67; Sen. State Counsel, Malaŵi, 1967–70; Parly Draftsman, London, 1970–74; Parly Counsel, Canberra, 1974; returned to practice, 1975; Parly Counsel, Scottish Law Commn, 1975–95. Chm., Nat. Health Tribunal (Scotland), 1987–95. *Recreations:* fishing, music, travel.

GALE, Baroness *cr* 1999 (Life Peer), of Blaenrhondda in the county of Mid Glamorgan; **Anita Gale;** General Secretary, Wales Labour Party, 1984–99; *b* 28 Nov. 1940; *d* of late Arthur and Lilian Gale; *m* 1959 (marr. diss. 1983); two *d*. *Educ:* Pontypridd Tech. Coll.; University Coll., Cardiff (BSc Econ). Clothing factory machinist and shop asst, 1955–69; returned to full-time educn, 1969–76; Women's Officer and Asst Organiser, Wales Labour Party, 1976–84. Member, All Party Groups on university, BBC, pro choice, maternity care, osteoporosis; Vice-Chairman: Associate Parly Gp on animal welfare; Labour Animal Welfare Soc. Pres., Treherbert and Dist. Br., RBL. *Address:* House of Lords, SW1A 0PW. *Recreations:* walking, swimming, gardening.

GALE, Audrey Olga Helen; *see* Sander, A. O. H.

GALE, Prof. Edwin Albert Merwood, FRCP; Professor of Diabetic Medicine, Bristol University, since 1997; *b* 21 March 1945; *s* of George Edwin Gale and Carole Fisher Gale; *m* 1982, Lone Brogaard; one *s* two *d*. *Educ:* Sevenoaks Sch.; Sidney Sussex Coll., Cambridge (MA, MB BChir). Sen. Lectr, 1984–92, Prof. of Diabetes, 1992–97, St Bartholomew's Hosp. *Publications:* (with R. B. Tattersall) Diabetes: clinical management, 1990; papers on causes, prediction and possible prevention of type 1 diabetes. *Recreations:* ancient coins, fossils. *Address:* 9 Carnarvon Road, Bristol BS6 7DR. *T:* (0117) 924 3123.

GALE, Prof. Ernest Frederick, FRS 1953; BSc London; BA, PhD, ScD Cantab; Professor of Chemical Microbiology, University of Cambridge, 1960–81, now Emeritus; Fellow of St John's College, Cambridge, 1949–88; *b* 15 July 1914; *s* of Nellie Annie and Ernest Francis Edward Gale; *m* 1937, Eiry Mair Jones; one *s*. *Educ:* St John's Coll. Cambridge (Scholar). Research in biochemistry, Cambridge, 1936–83; Senior Student, Royal Commn for Exhibition of 1851, 1939; Beit Memorial Fellow, 1941; Scientific Staff of Med. Research Council, 1943; Reader in Chemical Microbiology, University of Cambridge, 1948–60; Dir, Medical Research Council Unit for Chemical Microbiology, 1948–62. Herter Lecturer, Johns Hopkins Hosp., Baltimore, USA, 1948; Commonwealth Travelling Fellow, Hanna Lecturer, Western Reserve Univ., 1951; Harvey Lectr, New York, 1955; Leeuwenhoek Lectr, Royal Society, London, 1956; Malcolm Lectr, Syracuse Univ., 1967; M. Stephenson Meml Lectr, 1971; Linacre Lectr, St John's Coll., Cambridge, 1973; Squibb Lectr, Nottingham Univ., 1986. Visiting Fellow, ANU, 1964–65. Hon. Mem., Society for General Microbiology, 1978 (Meetings Sec., 1954–58; International Representative, 1963–67; Pres., 1967–69); Mem. Food Investigation Board, 1954–58; Mem. International Union of Biochemistry Commission on Enzymes, 1957–61. *Publications:* Chemical Activities of Bacteria, 1947; The Molecular Basis of Antibiotic Action, 1972, 2nd edn 1981; scientific papers in Biochem. Journal, Journal of General Microbiology, Biochimica et Biophysica Acta, etc. *Recreations:* photography, wood carving. *Address:* 59 Blake Court, Winchmore Hill, N21 1SQ. *T:* (020) 7263 0228.

GALE, (Gwendoline) Fay, AO 1989; PhD; FASSA; President: Association of Asian Social Science Research Councils, since 2001; Academy of the Social Sciences in Australia, 1998–2000; *b* 13 June 1932; *d* of Rev. George Jasper Gilding and Kathleen Gertrude Gilding; one *s* one *d*. *Educ:* Adelaide Univ. (BA 1952, Hons I 1954; PhD 1962). University of Adelaide: Lectr, 1966–71; Sen. Lectr, 1972–74; Reader, 1975–77; Prof., 1978–89; Pro-Vice-Chancellor, 1988–89; Vice-Chancellor, Univ. of WA, 1990–97. Pres., Australian Vice-Chancellors' Cttee, 1996–97. Comr, Australian Heritage Commn, 1989–95. Elin Wagner Fellow, 1971; Catherine Helen Spence Fellow, 1972. FASSA 1978. Hon. Life

Fellow, Inst. of Australian Geographers, 1994. DUniv Adelaide, 1994; Hon. DLitt WA, 1998. British Council Award, 1972; John Lewis Gold Medal, 2000; Griffith Taylor Medal, 2001. *Publications:* Race Relations in Australia: the Aboriginal situation, 1975; Urban Aborigines, 1972; Poverty among Aboriginal families in Adelaide, 1975; Adelaide Aborigines, a case study of urban life 1966–81, 1982; We are bosses ourselves: the status and role of Aboriginal women today, 1983; Tourists and the National Estate: procedures to protect Australia's heritage, 1987; Aboriginal youth and the criminal justice system: the injustice of justice, 1990; Changing Australia, 1991; Inventing Places: studies in cultural geography, 1992; Juvenile Justice: debating the issues, 1993; Tourism and the Protection of Aboriginal Cultural Sites, 1994; Cultural Geographics, 1999. *Recreations:* bush walking, music, theatre. *Address:* c/o Vice Chancellory, University of Adelaide, North Terrace, Adelaide, SA 5005, Australia.

GALE, John, OBE 1987; Director: Lisden Productions Ltd, since 1975; John Gale Productions Ltd, since 1960; Gale Enterprises Ltd, since 1960; West End Managers Ltd, since 1972; *b* 2 Aug. 1929; *s* of Frank Haith Gale and Martha Edith Gale (*née* Evans); *m* 1950, Liselotte Ann (*née* Wratten); two *s*. *Educ:* Christ's Hospital; Webber Douglas Academy of Dramatic Art. Formerly an actor; presented his first production, Inherit the Wind, London, 1960; has since produced or co-produced, in London, British provinces, USA, Australia, New Zealand and S Africa, over 80 plays, including: Candida, 1960; On the Brighter Side, 1961; Boeing-Boeing, 1962; Devil May Care, 1963; Windfall, 1963; Where Angels Fear to Tread, 1963; The Wings of the Dove, 1963; Amber for Anna, 1964; Present Laughter, 1964, 1981; Maigret and the Lady, 1965; The Platinum Cat, 1965; The Sacred Flame, 1966; An Evening with G. B. S., 1966; A Woman of No Importance, 1967; The Secretary Bird, 1968; Dear Charles, 1968; Highly Confidential, 1969; The Young Churchill, 1969; The Lionel Touch, 1969; Abelard and Héloïse, 1970; No Sex, Please—We're British, 1971; Lloyd George Knew My Father, 1972; The Mating Game, 1972; Parents' Day, 1972; At the End of the Day, 1973; Birds of Paradise, 1974; A Touch of Spring, 1975; Separate Tables, 1977; The Kingfisher, 1977; Sextet, 1977; Cause Célèbre, 1977; Shut Your Eyes and Think of England, 1977; Can You Hear Me at the Back?, 1979; Middle Age Spread, 1979; Private Lives, 1980; A Personal Affair, 1982. The Secretary Bird and No Sex, Please—We're British set records for the longest run at the Savoy and Strand Theatres respectively; No Sex, Please—We're British is the longest running comedy in the history of World Theatre and passed 6,000 performances at the Garrick Theatre in Nov. 1985. Chichester Festival Theatre: Exec. Producer, 1983–84; Director, 1984–89. President, Soc. of West End Theatre Managers, 1972–75; Chm.. Theatres National Cttee, 1979–85. Governor, 1976–, and Almoner, 1978–95, Christ's Hospital; Chm. of Govs, Guildford Sch. of Acting, 1989–2000. Member, Amicable Soc. of Blues, 1981–. Liveryman, Gold and Silver Wyredrawers Company, 1974. FRSA 1990. *Recreations:* travel, Rugby. *Address:* East Dean Cottage, East Dean, near Chichester, W Sussex PO18 0JA. *T:* (01243) 811407. *Clubs:* Garrick; London Welsh Rugby Football (Richmond) (Chairman, 1979–81).

GALE, Michael; QC 1979; a Recorder of the Crown Court, 1977–97; *b* 12 Aug. 1932; *s* of Joseph Gale and Blossom Gale; *m* 1963, Joanna Stephanie Bloom; one *s* two *d*. *Educ:* Cheltenham Grammar Sch.; Grocers' Sch.; King's Coll., Cambridge (Exhibnr; BA History and Law, 1954, MA 1958). National Service, Royal Fusiliers and Jt Services Sch. for Linguists, 1956–58. Called to the Bar, Middle Temple, 1957, Bencher, 1988; Harmsworth Law Scholar, 1958. Mem., Gen. Council of the Bar, 1987–94; Legal Assessor: GMC, 1995–; GDC, 1995–; Chm., Review and Complaints Cttee, Nat. Heritage Meml Fund and Heritage Lottery Fund, 1996–. *Recreations:* the arts and country pursuits. *Address:* 1 King's Bench Walk, Temple, EC4Y 7DB. *T:* (020) 7936 1500. *Clubs:* Oxford and Cambridge, MCC.

GALE, Michael Denis, PhD; FRS 1996; Associate Research Director, John Innes Centre, Norwich, since 1994; *b* 25 Aug. 1943; *s* of Sydney Ralph Gale and Helen Mary (*née* Johnson); *m* 1979, Susan Heathcote Rosbotham; two *d*. *Educ:* W Buckland Sch., Barnstaple; Birmingham Univ. (BSc Hons); UCW, Aberystwyth (PhD). Plant Breeding Institute, subseq. AFRC Institute of Plant Science Research, Cambridge: Researcher, 1968–86; Head, Cereals Res. Dept, and Individual Merit SPSO, Cambridge Lab., 1986–92; Head of Cambridge Lab., Norwich, 1992–94; Dir, John Innes Centre, Norwich, 1999; John Innes Prof., UEA, 2000–. Farrer Meml Bicentennial Fellow, NSW Dept of Agric., 1989; Hon. Res. Prof., Inst. of Crop Germplasm Resources, Acad. Sinica, 1992. Advr, Inst. of Genetics, Beijing, 1992. Foreign Fellow, Chinese Acad. of Engrg, 1999. Res. Medal, RASE, 1994; Rank Prize for Nutrition, 1997; Darwin Medal, Royal Soc., 1998. *Publications:* 200 scientific papers and articles on plant genetics and cytogenetics, esp. dwarfism, quality and genome res. in wheat. *Recreations:* golf, tennis. *Address:* John Innes Centre, Norwich Research Park, Colney, Norwich NR4 7UH. *T:* (01603) 450000. *Club:* Royal Norwich Golf.

GALE, Michael Sadler, MC 1945; Assistant Under-Secretary of State, Prison Department, Home Office, 1972–79; *b* 5 Feb. 1919; *s* of Rev. John Sadler and Ethel Gale; *m* 1950, Philippa, *d* of Terence and Betty Ennion; two *s* one *d* (and one *s* decd). *Educ:* Tonbridge Sch.; Oriel Coll., Oxford (Scholar, MA). Served War of 1939–45: enlisted 1939, Royal Fusiliers; commnd 1940, Queen's Own Royal W Kent Regt, Major 1944; served N Africa and NW Europe. Housemaster, HM Borstal, Rochester, 1946–48; Dep. Governor, HM Prison, Durham, 1948–49; Staff Course Tutor, Imperial Trng Sch., Wakefield, 1949–50; Principal, 1950–52; Governor, HM Prison: The Verne, 1952–57; Camp Hill, 1957–62; Wandsworth, 1962–66; Asst Dir, Prison Dept, Home Office, 1966–69; Controller, Planning and Develt, 1969–75; Controller, Operational Administration, 1975–79; Mem. Prisons Board, 1969–79. *Recreations:* walking, reading, gardening. *Address:* 5A Christchurch Road, Winchester, Hants SO23 9SR. *T:* (01962) 853836.

GALE, Roger James; MP (C) North Thanet, since 1983; *b* Poole, Dorset, 20 Aug. 1943; *s* of Richard Byrne Gale and Phyllis Mary (*née* Rowell); *m* 1st, 1964, Wendy Dawn Bowman (marr. diss. 1967); 2nd, 1971, Susan Sampson (marr. diss.); one *d*; 3rd, 1980, Susan Gabrielle Marks; two *s*. *Educ:* Southbourne Prep. Sch.; Hardye's Sch., Dorchester; Guildhall Sch. of Music and Drama (LGSM). Freelance broadcaster, 1963–72; freelance reporter, BBC Radio, London, 1972–73; Producer, Current Affairs Gp, BBC Radio (progs included Newsbeat and Today), 1973–76; Producer/Dir, BBC Children's Television, 1976–79; Producer/Dir, Thames TV, and Editor, teenage unit, 1979–83. Joined Conservative Party, 1964; Mem., Cttee, Greater London Young Conservatives, 1964–65. PPS to Minister of State for Armed Forces, 1992–94. Member: Select Cttee on Televising of Proceedings of the House, 1988–91; Home Affairs Select Cttee, 1990–92; Broadcasting Select Cttee, 1997–; All Party Parly Gp, Fund for Replacement of Animals in Med. Experiments, 1983–86; Chm., All Party Animal Welfare Gp, 1992–98; Vice Chm., Nat. Heritage backbench cttee, 1997–; Mem., Chairman's Panel, 1997–. Founding Mem., Police and Parlt Scheme, 1996. Delegate, Council of Europe, 1987–89. Contested Birmingham, Northfield, Oct. 1982 (Lab. majority, 289). Mem., Gen. Council, BBC, 1992–94. Founder, East Kent Development Assoc., 1984–86. Fellow: Industry and Parlt Trust, 1985; Parlt and Armed Forces Fellowship, 1992. *Recreations:* swimming, sailing. *Address:* House of Commons, Westminster, SW1A 0AA; *e-mail:* roger@rogergale.co.uk. *Clubs:* Farmers', Radio Academy; Kent County Cricket.

GALE, William Stuart; QC (Scot) 1993; *b* 10 June 1955; *s* of William Grimshaw Gale and Patricia Sheila (*née* Nicol); *m* 1981, Michele Marie Keklak. *Educ:* Univ. of Dundee (LLB Hons 1977); Tulane Univ., New Orleans (LLM 1978). Advocate of Scottish Bar, 1980–93; Standing Jun. Counsel to FCO in Scotland, 1987–93. *Recreation:* modern jazz.

GALES, Kathleen Emily, (Mrs Heinz Spitz); Senior Lecturer in Statistics, London School of Economics, 1966–90, retired; *b* 1927; *d* of Albert Henry and Sarah Thomson Gales; *m* 1970, Heinz Spitz. *Educ:* Gateshead Grammar Sch.; Newnham Coll., Cambridge (Exhibr); Ohio Univ. (Schol.). BA Cantab 1950, MA Ohio, 1951. Asst Statistician, Foster Wheeler Ltd, 1951–53; Statistician, Municipal Statistical Office, Birmingham, 1953–55; Res. Asst and part-time Lectr, LSE, 1955–58; Asst Lectr in Statistics, LSE, 1958–60, Lectr, 1960–66. Vis. Assoc. Prof. in Statistics, Univ. of California, 1964–65. Statistical Consultant: Royal Commn on Doctors' and Dentists' Remuneration, 1959; WHO, 1960; Turkish Min. of Health, 1963. Mem. Performing Rights Tribunal, 1974–80. *Publications:* (with C. A. Moser and P. Morpurgo) Dental Health and the Dental Services, 1962; (with B. Abel-Smith) British Doctors at Home and Abroad, 1964; (with T. Blackstone et al.) Students in Conflict: LSE in 1967, 1970; articles in Jl RSS. *Recreations:* bridge, golf, travel.

GALL, Anthony Robert S.; *see* Scott-Gall.

GALL, Henderson Alexander, (Sandy), CBE 1988; freelance writer and broadcaster; Foreign Correspondent, Independent Television News, 1963–92 (Newscaster, 1968–90); *b* 1 Oct. 1927; *s* of Henderson Gall and Jean Begg; *m* 1958, Eleanor Mary Patricia Ann Smyth; one *s* three *d*. *Educ:* Glenalmond; Aberdeen Univ. (MA). Foreign Correspondent, Reuters, 1953–63, Germany, E Africa, Hungary, S Africa, Congo; joined ITN, 1963, working in Middle East, Africa, Vietnam, Far East, China, Afghanistan; Newscaster on News at Ten, 1970–90; Producer/Presenter/Writer, documentaries on: King Hussein, 1972; Afghanistan, 1982, 1984, 1986; Cresta Run, 1984; George Adamson: lord of the lions, 1989; Richard Leakey, the man who saved the animals, 1995; Empty Quarter, 1996; Veil of Fear (Taliban rule in Afghanistan), 1996; Imran's Final Test, 1997. Chm., Sandy Gall's Afghanistan Appeal. Rector, Aberdeen Univ., 1978–81 (Hon. LLD, 1981). Sitara-i-Pakistan, 1986; Lawrence of Arabia Medal, RSAA, 1987. *Publications:* Gold Scoop, 1977; Chasing the Dragon, 1981; Don't Worry About the Money Now, 1983; Behind Russian Lines, 1983; Afghanistan: Agony of a Nation, 1988; Salang, 1989; Lord of the Lions, 1991; News from the Front, 1994; The Bushmen of Southern Africa: slaughter of the innocent, 2001. *Recreations:* golf, gardening, swimming. *Address:* Doubleton Oast House, Penshurst, Tonbridge, Kent TN11 8JA. *Clubs:* Turf, Special Forces; St Moritz Tobogganing.

GALL, Sandy; *see* Gall, H. A.

GALL, Thomas Mitchell; Hon. Mr Justice Gall; Judge of the Court of the First Instance of the High Court (formerly Judge of the High Court), Hong Kong, since 1991; *b* 20 Nov. 1942; *s* of John Berry Gall and Helen Lucy (*née* Mitchell); *m* 1966, Barbara Smart; one *s* one *d*. *Educ:* Univ. of Adelaide (LLB). Admitted barrister and solicitor, 1966; Colin D. Rowe & Co., Barristers and Solicitors, 1966–73; Hong Kong: Crown Counsel, 1973–76; Sen. Crown Counsel, 1976–78; Asst Principal Crown Counsel, 1978–81; Dist Judge, 1981–91. Hon. Sec., Council Early Childhood Educn; Chm., Childsafe Action Gp, 1992–. Vice-Chm., Criminol Soc., Hong Kong, 1992–. Gov., Winchester Internat. Sch., Hong Kong, 1989–. *Address:* High Court Building, 38 Queensway, Hong Kong.

GALLACHER, family name of **Baron Gallacher**.

GALLACHER, Baron *cr* 1982 (Life Peer), of Enfield in Greater London; **John Gallacher;** retired; *b* 7 May 1920; *s* of William Gallacher and Janet Stewart; *m* 1947, Freda Vivian Chittenden; one *s*. *Educ:* St Patrick's High School, Dumbarton; Co-operative College, Loughborough. Chartered Secretary. President: Enfield Highway Co-operative Soc., 1954–68; Inst. of Meat, 1983–86; Secretary, International Co-operative Alliance, 1963–67; Parliamentary Sec., Co-operative Union, 1974–83; Mem., Select Cttee on the European Communities, 1983–89. Chief opposition spokesman on agriculture and food, 1989–92. *Publication:* Service on the Board (a handbook for directors of retail co-operatives), 1974, 2nd edn 1976. *Recreation:* gardening. *Address:* House of Lords, SW1A 0PW. *T:* (020) 7219 3000.

GALLACHER, Bernard, OBE 1996; golf professional, Wentworth Golf Club, since 1975; *b* 9 Feb. 1949; *s* of Bernard and Matilda Gallacher; *m* 1974, Lesley Elizabeth Wearmouth; one *s* two *d*. *Educ:* St Mary's Academy, Bathgate. Golf tournaments won: Scottish Open Amateur Championship, 1967; PGA Schweppes, W. D. & H. O. Wills Open, 1969; Martini Internat., 1971, 1982; Carrolls Internat., 1974; Dunlop Masters, 1974, 1975; Spanish Open, 1977; French Open, 1979; Tournament Players Championship, 1980; Gtr Manchester Open, 1981; Jersey Open, 1982, 1984. Harry Vardon Trophy, 1969. Scottish Professional Champion , 1971, 1973, 1974, 1977, 1984. Ryder Cup Team, 1969, 1971, 1973, 1975, 1977, 1979, 1981, 1983, European Captain, 1991, 1993, 1995. Pres., Golf Foundn, 1996–2001. *Publications:* (with Mark Wilson) Teach Yourself Golf, 1988; (with Renton Laidlaw) Captain at Kiawah, 1991. *Recreations:* walking dogs, reading. *Address:* Wentworth Club, Virginia Water, Surrey GU25 4LS. *T:* (019904) 3353.

GALLACHER, John; HM Diplomatic Service, retired; *b* 16 July 1931; *s* of John Gallacher and Catherine Gallacher (*née* Crilly); *m* 1956, Eileen Agnes (*née* McGuire); one *s*. *Educ:* Our Lady's High School, Motherwell. Nat. Service, RAF, 1950–52. Kenya Police, 1953–65 (retired as Supt of Police, 1965); Libyan Govt (attached to Min. of Interior), 1965–67; FCO, 1967–70; Lagos, 1970–73; FCO, 1973–74; Kuwait, 1974–77; FCO 1977; Counsellor, FCO, 1983–84. Gp Security Advr, Gallaher Ltd, 1985–91; Rep. (Scotland), Control Risks Gp, 1992–98. *Recreations:* reading, golf, travel, gardening. *Address:* 160 Lochend Road, Gartcosh, Glasgow G69 8BB. *Club:* Royal Over-Seas League.

GALLAGHER, Edward Patrick, CBE 2001; FREng, FIEE, FCIWEM; Member Board, English Nature, since 2001; a Civil Service Commissioner, since 2001; *b* 4 Aug. 1944; *m* 1969, Helen Wilkinson; two *s*. *Educ:* Univ. of Sheffield (BEng Hons; Diploma in Business Studies; Mappin Medal, 1966; John Brown Award, 1966). MRI 1992. Systems Analyst, Vauxhall Motors, 1963–68; Corporate Planning Manager, Sandoz Products, 1968–70; Computer Services Manager, Robinson Willey, 1970–71; with Black and Decker, 1971–86: Director: Marketing Services, 1978–79; Service and Distribn, 1979–81; Business Analysis, 1981–83; Market and Product Develt, 1983–86; Amersham International: Dir of Corporate Develt, 1986–88; Divl Chief Exec., 1988–90; Mfg Dir, 1990–92; Chief Executive and Board Member: NRA, 1992–95; EA, 1995–2001. Vice-Pres., Council for Envmtl Educn, 1997–. Middlesex University: Vis. Prof., Business Sch. and Faculty of Technol., 1994–97, Sch. of Health, Biol and Envmtl Sci., 1997–; Mem., Faculty of Technol. Adv. Gp, 1994–97; Gov., 1994– (Dep. Chm., Bd of Govs, 2001–); Chairman: Audit Cttee, 1995–2001; Planning and Resources Cttee, 2001–; Governance Cttee, 2000–; Bristol University: Mem. Council, 1994–98; Mem. Finance Adv. Gp, 1994–2001;

Mem. Adv. Bd, Centre for Social and Econ. Res. on Global Envmt, UEA, 2001–. Mem. Council, 1998–, Mem., Envmt and Energy Policy Cttee, IEE, 1999–; Mem., Sustainable Develt Educn Panel, Royal Acad. of Engrg, 1999–; Chm., Health, Safety and Envmt Cttee, EEF, 2001–. Patron, Envmtl Industries Commn, 2001. Trustee, Living Again Trust, Royal Hosp. for Neurodisability (formerly Royal Hosp. and Home, Putney), 1993–. FRSA 1995; CIMgt 1996. Freeman, City of London; Liveryman, and Mem., Ct of Assts, Co. of Water Conservators. Hon. DEng Sheffield, 1996; Hon. DSc: Tomsk, 1998; Plymouth, 1998; Brunel, 1999. *Recreations:* golf, tennis, theatre, walking, guitar. *Address:* English Nature, Northminster House, Peterborough PE1 1UA.

GALLAGHER, Eileen Rose; Co-owner, co-founder, and Managing Director, Shed Productions, since 1998; *b* 26 Nov. 1959; *d* of Mathew Gallagher and Christine McAvoy. *Educ:* Glasgow Univ. (MA Hons Politics); UC Cardiff (Dip. Journalism). Freelance journalist, 1980–84; Scottish Television: Press Officer, 1984–87; Head of Programme Planning, 1987–91; Head of Broadcasting Div., 1991–92; Dir of Broadcasting, 1992–94; Man. Dir, Granada/LWT Broadcasting, then Man. Dir, LWT and Dep. Man. Dir, Granada UK Broadcasting, 1994–98; Man. Dir, Ginger TV, 1999. Director: Granada, 1995–98; LWT, 1995–. *Address:* Shed Productions, Acre House, 11–15 William Road, NW1 3ER.

GALLAGHER, (Francis George) Kenna, CMG 1963; HM Diplomatic Service, retired; *b* 25 May 1917; *er s* of late George and Johanna Gallagher. *Educ:* St Joseph's Coll.; King's Coll., University of London (LLB (Hons)). Clerical officer, Min. of Agric., 1935–38; Asst Examr, Estate Duty Office, 1938–44; served in HM Forces, 1941–45; Examr, Estate Duty Office, 1944–45; apptd a Mem., HM Foreign (subseq. Diplomatic) Service, 1945; Vice-Consul Marseilles, 1946–48; Acting Consul-Gen., there, in 1947; HM Embassy, Paris, 1948–50; FO, 1950–53; First Sec., HM Embassy, Damascus, 1953–55; acted as Chargé d'Affaires, 1953, 1954 and 1955; FO, 1955; appointed Counsellor and Head of European Economic Organisations Dept, 1960; Counsellor (Commercial), HM Embassy, Berne, 1963–65; acted as Chargé d'Affaires (Berne) in 1963 and 1964; Head of Western Economic Dept, CO, 1965–67, of Common Market Dept, 1967–68; Asst Under-Sec. of State, FCO, 1968–71; Ambassador and Head of UK Delegn to OECD, 1971–77. Consultant on Internat. Trade Policy, CBI, 1978–80. *Recreations:* music, chess. *Address:* 37 Howard Terrace, Morpeth, Northumberland NE61 1HT. *T:* (01670) 504384.

GALLAGHER, Francis Xavier, OBE 1986; HM Diplomatic Service; Head of Panel 2000 Unit, Foreign and Commonwealth Office, since 1998; *b* 28 March 1946; *s* of F. P. H. Gallagher and Carmen Gallagher (*née* Wilson); *m* 1981, Marie-France Martine Guiller; one *d*. *Educ:* Oxford Univ. (Chancellor's Essay and Matthew Arnold Meml Prizes; BA, BPhil). Tutor, Villiers Park Educnl Trust, Oxon, 1970; joined FCO, 1971: MECAS, Lebanon, 1972–74; served FCO, Beirut, Khartoum, Kuwait, NY, 1974–95; Dep. Hd of Mission, Copenhagen, 1995–98. Officier, Ordre National du Lion (Senegal), 1988. *Recreations:* music, walking. *Address:* c/o Foreign and Commonwealth Office, King Charles Street, SW1A 2AH.

GALLAGHER, James Daniel; Head of Scottish Executive Justice Department, since 2000; *s* of William Gallagher and Bridget Gallagher (*née* Hart); *m* 1978, Una Mary Green; one *s* two *d*. *Educ:* Glasgow Univ. (BSc Hons Chemistry and Nat. Phil. 1976); Edinburgh Univ. (MSc Public Policy 1986). Joined Scottish Office, 1976: Private Sec. to Minister for Home Affairs, 1979; Head of Criminal Policy and Procedure Brs, 1981–85; Sec., Mgt Gp, 1985–88; Head of Urban Policy Div., 1988–89; Private Sec. to successive Secs of State for Scotland, 1989–91; Dir (Human Resources), Scottish Prison Service, 1991–96; Hd, Local Govt Finance Gp, later Local Govt and Europe Gp, Scottish Office, 1996–99; Dep. Head of Economic and Domestic Secretariat, Cabinet Office, 1999; Policy Advr, Prime Minister's Policy Unit, 1999–2000. Director: Scottish Mutual Assurance, 1999–; Abbey National Life, 1999–. *Address:* Scottish Executive Justice Department, Saughton House, Broomhouse Drive, Edinburgh EH11 3XD.

GALLAGHER, Kenna; *see* Gallagher, F. G. K.

GALLAGHER, Sister Maire Teresa, CBE 1992 (OBE 1987); SND; Sister Superior, Convent of Notre Dame, Dumbarton, 1987–94, retired; *b* 27 May 1933; *d* of Owen Gallagher and Annie McVeigh. *Educ:* Notre Dame High Sch., Glasgow; Glasgow Univ. (MA Hons 1965); Notre Dame Coll. of Educn (Dip. 1953). Principal Teacher of History, Notre Dame High Sch., Glasgow, 1965–72; Lectr in Secondary Educn, Notre Dame Coll., 1972–74; Head Teacher, Notre Dame High Sch., Dumbarton, 1974–87. Chair, Scottish Consultative Council (formerly Scottish Consultative Cttee) on the Curriculum, 1987–91 (Mem., 1976–91; Chair: Secondary Cttee, 1983–87; Main Cttee, 1987–90); Mem., Sec. of State's Cttee of Enquiry into Teachers' Pay and Conditions of Service, 1986; Pres., Scottish Br., Secondary Heads Assoc., 1980–82. Member: Central Council, Action of Churches Together in Scotland, 1990– (Convener, 1999–Sept. 2002); Assembly, CCBI, 1990–. Fellow: SCOTVEC, 1989; Scottish Qualifications Authority, 1997. Hon. MEd CNAA, 1992. *Publications:* papers and articles in jls on teaching and management of schools. *Recreations:* homemaking skills, reading. *Address:* Sisters of Notre Dame, 67 Moorpark Avenue, Penilee, Glasgow G52 4ET. *T:* (0141) 810 4214.

GALLAGHER, Michael; *b* 1 July 1934; *s* of Michael and Annie Gallagher; *m* 1959, Kathleen Mary Gallagher; two *s* three *d*. *Educ:* Univ. of Nottingham; Univ. of Wales. Dip. General Studies. Branch Official, NUM, 1967–70; day release, Univ. of Nottingham, 1967–69; TUC scholarship, Univ. of Wales, 1970–72; Univ. of Nottingham, 1972–74. Councillor: Mansfield Borough Council, 1970–74; Nottinghamshire CC, 1973–81. Contested (Lab) Rushcliffe, general election, Feb. 1974; Member (Lab) Nottingham, European Parlt, 1979–83, (SDP) 1983–84; contested (SDP) Lancs Central, European elecn, 1984. *Recreations:* leisure, sports.

GALLAGHER, Dame Monica (Josephine), DBE 1976; *m* 1946, Dr John Paul Gallagher, KCSG, KM; two *s* two *d*. Mem. Cttee, Friends of St Mary's Cathedral, Sydney, 1994– (Chm., 1984–87 and 1998–2001; Dep. Chm., 1988–93); Pres., Flower Festival Cttee, 1987–95, Dir, Flower Fest., 1996–97, St Mary's Cathedral; Mem. Cttee, Order of British Empire Assoc., NSW, 1995– (Vice-Pres., 1985–89; Pres., 1989–92); Vice-Pres., SCF, NSW, 1992–94; Member: Dr Horace Nowland Travelling Scholarship; Australian Church Women, NSW Div.; Adv. Bd, Fest. of Light; former Mem., Nursing Adv. Cttee, Australian Catholic Univ. (formerly Catholic Coll. of Educn), Sydney. Tour Guide, St Mary's Cathedral. State Pres., NSW, and Gen. Pres., Sydney Archdiocese, Catholic Women's League, Aust., 1972–80 (Nat. Pres., 1972–74); Past President: Catholic Central Cttee for Care of Aged; Catholic Women's Club, Sydney; Associated Catholic Cttee; Austcare; Catholic Inst. of Nursing Studies. Former Member: NSW Div., UNA; UN Status of Women Cttee; Exec. Bd, Mater Misericordiae Hosp., N Sydney; Bd, Gertrude Abbott Nursing Home; Selection Cttee, Queen Elizabeth II Silver Jubilee Trust; former Chm., YWCA Appeal Cttee, Sydney. Good Citizen Award, Festival of Light, 1979; Papal Honour, Augustae Crucis Insigne pro Ecclesia et Pontifice, 1981; DCSG 2001. *Address:* Unit 92/2 Artarmon Road, Willoughby, NSW 2068, Australia.

GALLAGHER, Paul, CBE 1996; General Secretary, Amalgamated Engineering and Electrical Union, 1995–96; *b* 16 Oct. 1944; *s* of Joe and Annie Gallagher; *m* 1974, Madeleine. *Educ:* St Anne's, Droylesden, Manchester. Electrical, Electronic, Telecommunication and Plumbing Union: full-time officer, 1966–78; Exec. Councillor for Manchester and N Wales, 1978–91; Pres., 1986–91; Gen. Sec., 1992–95. Mem., HSC, 1990–96. *Recreations:* gardening, music, reading.

GALLAGHER, Thomas Joseph; Member (SDLP) Fermanagh and South Tyrone, Northern Ireland Assembly, since 1998; *b* 17 Aug. 1942; *s* of Thomas and Nellie Gallagher; *m* 1968, Eileen Carty; two *s* one *d*. *Educ:* St Joseph's Coll.; Queen's Univ., Belfast. Mem., NI Forum, 1996. Mem. (SDLP), Fermanagh DC, 1989–. Contested (SDLP) Fermanagh and S Tyrone, 2001. Mem., Western Educn and Library Bd, 1989–. *Recreations:* Gaelic games, horse racing. *Address:* Keenaghan, Belleek, Co. Fermanagh BT93 3ES. *T:* (028) 6865 8355. *Club:* Erne Gaels Gaelic Football.

GALLEN, Hon. Sir Rodney (Gerald), KNZM 2000; QC 1976; High Court Judge, New Zealand, 1983–99; *b* 12 Aug. 1933; *s* of Gerald Collins Gallen and Eva Susan Ann Gallen. *Educ:* Victoria UC, Wellington (LLB). *Recreations:* gardening, music, reading. *Address:* Birchwood RD2, Hastings, New Zealand. *T:* (6) 8778499. *Clubs:* Wellington, Hawkes Bay.

GALLEY, Robert Albert Ernest, PhD; FRSC; Director, Shell Research Ltd, Woodstock Agricultural Research Centre, Sittingbourne, Kent, 1960–69; *b* 23 Oct. 1909; *s* of John and Jane A. Galley; *m* 1st 1933, Elsie Marjorie Walton (*d* 1985); one *s* two *d*; 2nd 1988, Ann Louise Grundy (*née* Dale). *Educ:* Colfe's Gram. Sch.; Imperial Coll., London. BSc 1930, PhD 1932, FRIC 1944. Research Chemist, Wool Industries Research Assoc., 1932–34; Chemist, Dept of War Department Chemist, 1934–37; Lectr, Sir John Cass Coll., 1937–39; Prin. Exper. Officer, Min. of Supply, Chemical Inspectorate, 1939–45, Flax Establishment, 1945–46; Sen. Prin. Scientific Officer, Agric. Research Council (Sec. Interdepartmental Insecticides Cttees), 1946–50; seconded to Scientific Secretariat, Office of Lord Pres. of Council, 1950–52; Dir, Tropical Products Institute, Dept of Scientific and Industrial Research (formerly Colonial Products Laboratory), 1953–60. *Publications:* papers in Journal of Chem. Soc., Chemistry and Industry, World Crops, etc. *Recreations:* tennis, gardening, sailing. *Address:* Riversdale, 26 River Reach, Teddington, Middx TW11 9QL.

GALLEY, Roy; Director, Planning, Post Office Property Holdings, since 1998; *b* 8 Dec. 1947; *s* of Kenneth Haslam Galley and late Letitia Mary Chapman; *m* 1976, Helen Margaret Butcher; one *s* one *d*. *Educ:* King Edward VII Grammar Sch., Sheffield; Worcester Coll., Oxford (MA). North-East Postal Bd, 1969–83: started as management trainee; Asst Controller, Projects (regional manager), 1980–83; Head of Project Control, London Building and Estates Centre, Royal Mail Letters, 1987–91; Royal Mail, London: Dir, Facilities, 1992–95; Dir, Restructuring, 1995–96; Dir, Operations, 1996–98. Councillor, Calderdale Metropolitan Bor. Council, 1980–83. Chm., Kingston and Richmond (formerly Kingston and Esher) DHA, 1989–98. Chm., Yorks Young Conservatives, 1974–76; contested (C): Dewsbury, 1979; Halifax, 1987. MP (C) Halifax, 1983–87. Sec., Cons. Backbench Health Cttee, 1983–87; Mem., Social Services Select Cttee, 1984–87. Chm., Kingston and St George's Coll. of Nursing, 1993–. Fellow, British Inst. of Facilities Mgt, 1997. *Recreations:* history, European literature, theatre, music, gardening, riding. *Address:* Fairplace Farm, Nutley, Uckfield, East Sussex TN22 3HE.

GALLI, Paolo; Italian Ambassador to the Court of St James's, 1995–99; *b* 10 Aug. 1934; *s* of Carlo Galli and Bianca Metral-Lambert; *m* 1959, Maria Giuliana Calioni; two *d*. *Educ:* Univ. of Padua (law degree). Entered Italian Diplomatic Service, 1958; Minister of State's Private Office, 1958–61; Vice Consul, Cardiff, 1961–63; Second Sec., Washington, 1963–65; First Sec., Co-ordination Dept, Sec.-Gen's Office, Min. for Foreign Affairs, 1965–68; First Sec., later Counsellor and First Counsellor, London, 1968–72; First Counsellor, Warsaw, 1972–75; Min. for Foreign Affairs, Econ. Affairs Dept, 1975–79; Foreign Minister's Private Office, 1979–80; Minister-Counsellor, Dep. Perm. Rep. to EEC, Brussels, 1980–85; promoted to rank of Minister, 1985; Ambassador to Warsaw, 1986–88; Dir-Gen., Aid and Co-operation Dept, Min. for Foreign Affairs, 1988–91; promoted to rank of Ambassador, 1989; Ambassador to Tokyo, 1992–95. Cavaliere di Gran Croce, Ordine al Merito della Repubblica Italiana, 1997. *Recreations:* classical music, the arts, fencing. *Address:* c/o Italian Embassy, 14 Three Kings Yard, W1Y 2EH. *T:* (020) 7312 2200.

GALLIANO, John Charles, CBE 2001; Company Director and Couturier for Maison John Galliano, since 1984; Designer of Haute Couture and Prêt-à-Porter for Dior, since 1996; *b* 28 Nov. 1960. *Educ:* Wilson's Grammar Sch. for Boys; St Martin's Sch. of Art and Design (BA; Hon. Fellow, London Inst., 1997). Regular seasonal collections, 1985–. Designer of Haute Couture and Prêt-à-Porter for Givenchy, 1995–96. British Designer of the Year, British Fashion Council, 1987, 1994, 1995, 1997 (jtly); Telva Award for Best Internat. Designer, Mejor Creador International, 1995; VH1 Best Women's Wear Designer Award, 1998; Internat. Designer Award, Council of Fashion Designers of America, 1998. *Address:* 60 rue d'Avron, 75020 Paris, France. *T:* (1) 55251111, *Fax:* (1) 55251112.

GALLIE, Prof. Duncan Ian Dunbar, DPhil; FBA 1995; Professor of Sociology, University of Oxford, since 1996; Official Fellow, Nuffield College, Oxford, since 1985; *b* 16 Feb. 1946; *s* of Ian Gallie and Elsie (*née* Peers); *m* 1971, Martine Josephine Jurdant. *Educ:* St Paul's Sch., London (Scholar); Magdalen Coll., Oxford (Demyship; BA 1st Cl. Hons History); LSE (MSc); St Antony's Coll., Oxford (DPhil). Research Fellow, Nuffield Coll., Oxford, 1971–73; Lectr in Sociology, Univ. of Essex, 1973–79; Reader in Sociology, Univ. of Warwick, 1979–85; Dir, ESRC Social Change and Economic Life Initiative, 1985–90. Advr, Comité Nat. d'Evaluation de la Recherche, 1991; Member, Scientific Committee: IRESCO, 1989–93; IFRESI, 1993–98. Dist. Contrib. to Scholarship Award, Amer. Sociol. Assoc., 1985. *Publications:* In Search of the New Working Class, 1978; Social Inequality and Class Radicalism in France and Britain, 1983; (ed jtly) New Approaches to Economic Life, 1985; (ed) Employment in Britain, 1988; (ed jtly) Social Change and the Experience of Unemployment, 1994; (ed jtly) Trade Unionism in Recession, 1996; (jtly) Restructuring the Employment Relationship, 1998; (ed jtly) Welfare Regimes and the Experience of Unemployment in Europe, 2000; articles in learned jls. *Recreations:* travelling, music, museum gazing. *Address:* Nuffield College, Oxford OX1 1NF. *T:* (01865) 278586; 149 Leam Terrace, Leamington Spa, Warwickshire CV31 1DF. *T:* (01926) 314941.

GALLIE, Philip Roy; Member (C) Scotland South, Scottish Parliament, since 1999; Managing Consultant, PG Business Advice, since 1998; *b* 3 June 1939; *s* of George Albert Gallie and Ivy Edith Gallie (*née* Williams); *m* 1964, Marion Wands Whyte; one *s* one *d*. *Educ:* Dunfermline High Sch.; Kirkcaldy Tech. Coll. MIPlantE; TE. Apprentice elect. fitter, HM Dockyard, Rosyth, 1955–60; Elect. Engineer, Ben Line Steamers, 1960–64; Electricity Supply Industry; Kincardine, Ironbridge and Inverkip Power Stations; SSEB Central Maint. Orgn; Galloway and Lanark Hydros and Inverkip Power Station (Manager, 1989–92). Dist Councillor, Cunninghame, 1980–84. Contested (C): Cunninghame

South, 1983; Dunfermline West, 1987. MP (C) Ayr, 1992–97; contested (C) same seat, 1997, 2001. Vice-Chm., Scottish Cons. and Unionist Party, 1995–97; party spokesman on Industry and Economy, 1999–. Mem., RAFA. *Recreations:* politics, sports. *Address:* Scottish Parliament, Edinburgh EH99 1SP; 1 Wellington Square, Ayr KA7 1EN. *Club:* Ayr Rugby Football.

GALLIFORD, Rt Rev. David George; Assistant Bishop, Diocese of York, since 1991; *b* 20 June 1925; *s* of Alfred Edward Bruce and Amy Doris Galliford; *m* 1st, 1954, Enid May Drax (*d* 1983); one *d*; 2nd, 1987, Claire Margaret Phoenix. *Educ:* Bede Coll., Sunderland; Clare Coll., Cambridge (Organ Scholar, 1942, BA 1949, MA 1951); Westcott House, Cambridge. Served 5th Royal Inniskilling Dragoon Guards, 1943–47. Curate of St John Newland, Hull, 1951–54; Minor Canon of Windsor, 1954–56; Vicar of St Oswald, Middlesborough, 1956–61; Rector of Bolton Percy and Diocesan Training Officer, 1961–70; Canon of York Minster, 1969; Canon Residentiary and Treasurer of York Minster, 1970–75; Bishop Suffragan of Hulme, 1975–84; Bishop Suffragan of Bolton, 1984–91. SBStJ 1992. *Publications:* God and Christian Caring, 1973; Pastor's Post, 1975; (ed) Diocese in Mission, 1968. *Recreations:* gardening, music, composition. *Address:* Bishopsgarth, Maltongate, Thornton-le-Dale, N Yorks YO18 7SA. *T:* (01751) 474605.

GALLIGAN, Prof. Denis James, DCL; Professor of Socio-Legal Studies, and Director, Centre for Socio-Legal Studies, University of Oxford, since 1993; Fellow, Wolfson College, Oxford, since 1993; *b* 4 June 1947; *s* of John Felix Galligan and Muriel Maud Galligan; *m* 1972, Martha Louise Martinuzzi; one *s* one *d*. *Educ:* Univ. of Queensland (LLB 1970); Univ. of Oxford (BCL 1974; MA 1976; DCL 2000). Barrister, Supreme Court of Qld, 1970; called to the Bar, Gray's Inn, 1996. Rhodes Scholar, Magdalen Coll., Oxford, 1971–74; Lectr, Faculty of Law, UCL, 1974–76; Fellow, Jesus Coll., and CUF Lectr, Oxford Univ., 1976–81; Sen. Lectr, Univ. of Melbourne, 1982–84; Prof. of Law, Univ. of Southampton, 1985–92 (Dean, Law Faculty, 1987–90); Prof. of Law, Univ. of Sydney, 1990–92. Vis. Prof., Central European Univ., 1993–. Founding Academician, Acad. of Social Scis, 2000. *Publications:* Essays in Legal Theory, 1984; Law, Rights and the Welfare State, 1986; Discretionary Powers, 1986; Australian Administrative Law, 1993; Socio-Legal Readings in Administrative Law, 1995; Socio-Legal Studies in Context, 1995; Due Process and Fair Procedures, 1996; Administrative Justice in the New Democracies, 1998. *Recreations:* reading, gardening. *Address:* Wolfson College, Linton Road, Oxford OX2 6UD; The Rosery, Beckley, Oxford OX3 9UU. *T:* (01865) 284220 and 351281.

GALLINER, Peter; Director Emeritus, International Press Institute; Chairman: Peter Galliner Associates, since 1970; International Encounters, since 1995; *b* 19 Sept. 1920; *s* of Dr Moritz and Hedwig Galliner; *m* 1st, 1948, Edith Marguerite Goldschmidt; one *d*; 2nd, 1990, Helga Stenschke. *Educ:* Berlin and London. Reuters, 1942–47; Foreign Manager, Financial Times, 1947–60; Chm. and Man. Dir, Ullstein Publishing Co., Berlin, 1960–64; Vice-Chm. and Man. Dir, British Printing Corporation Publishing Gp, 1965–70; international publishing consultant, 1965–67 and 1970–75; Dir, Internat. Press Inst., Zürich/London, 1975–93. Press Freedom Award, Turkey, 1995; Europäischer Media and Communications Award, Germany, 1998. Order of Merit, 1st cl., 1961, and Comdr's Cross, 1990 (GFR); Ecomienda, Orden de Isabel la Católica (Spain), 1982. *Recreations:* reading, music. *Address:* Bregenzer Strasse 3, 10707 Berlin, Germany. *T:* (30) 8871166; 8001 Zürich, Untere Zäune 9, Switzerland. *T:* (1) 2518664. *Club:* Reform.

GALLOWAY, 13th Earl of, *cr* 1623; **Randolph Keith Reginald Stewart;** Lord Garlies, 1607; Bt 1627, 1687; Baron Stewart of Garlies (GB), 1796; *b* 14 Oct. 1928; *s* of 12th Earl of Galloway, and Philippa Fendall (*d* 1974), *d* of late Jacob Wendell, New York; *S* father, 1978; *m* 1975, Mrs Lily May Budge, DLJ (*d* 1999), *y d* of late Andrew Miller, Duns, Berwickshire. *Educ:* Harrow. KLJ. *Heir: cousin* Andrew Clyde Stewart [*b* 13 March 1949; *m* 1977, Sara, *o d* of Brig. Patrick Pollock; one *s* two *d*]. *Address:* Senwick House, Brighouse Bay, Borgue, Kirkcudbrightshire DG6 4TP.

GALLOWAY, Bishop of, (RC), since 1981; **Rt Rev. Maurice Taylor,** DD; *b* 5 May 1926; *s* of Maurice Taylor and Lucy Taylor (*née* McLaughlin). *Educ:* St Aloysius Coll., Glasgow; Our Lady's High School, Motherwell; Pontifical Gregorian Univ., Rome (DD). Served RAMC in UK, India, Egypt, 1944–47. Ordained to priesthood, Rome, 1950; lectured in Philosophy, 1955–60, in Theology 1960–65, St Peter's Coll., Cardross; Rector, Royal Scots Coll., Valladolid, Spain, 1965–74; Parish Priest, Our Lady of Lourdes, East Kilbride, 1974–81. Vice-Pres., Catholic Inst. for Internat. Relations, 1985–; Chm., Internat. Commn on English in the Liturgy, 1997–. *Publications:* The Scots College in Spain, 1971; Guatemala: a bishop's journey, 1991; El Salvador: portrait of a parish, 1992; (with Ellen Hawkes) Opening Our Lives to the Saviour, 1995; (with Ellen Hawkes) Listening at the Foot of the Cross, 1996. *Address:* Candida Casa, 8 Corsehill Road, Ayr KA7 2ST. *T:* (01292) 266750.

GALLOWAY, Alexander Kippen; Clerk of the Privy Council, since 1998; *b* 29 April 1952; *s* of late Alexander Kippen Galloway and Vera Eleanor Galloway; *m* 1973, Elaine Margaret Watkinson; three *s*. *Educ:* Birkenhead Sch.; Jesus Coll., Oxford (MA Lit.Hum.). Department of the Environment: Exec. Officer, 1974; Principal, 1982; Private Sec. to Chancellor of Duchy of Lancaster, 1982–84, to Paymaster Gen., 1982–83 and 1984–85; Secretariat, Cabinet Office, 1992–93; Asst Sec., DoE, 1994–98. *Recreations:* playing the cello, scuba diving. *Address:* Privy Council Office, 2 Carlton Gardens, SW1Y 5AA. *T:* (020) 7210 1040.

GALLOWAY, Rev. Prof. Allan Douglas; Professor of Divinity, University of Glasgow, 1968–82, now Emeritus Professor; Principal of Trinity College, Glasgow, 1972–82; *b* 30 July 1920; *s* of late William Galloway and Mary Wallace Galloway (*née* Junor); *m* 1948, Sara Louise Phillipp; two *s*. *Educ:* Stirling High Sch.; Univ. of Glasgow; Christ's Coll., Cambridge; Union Theol Seminary, New York. MA, BD, STM, PhD. Ordained, Asst Minister, Clune Park Parish, Port Glasgow, 1948–50; Minister of Auchterhouse, 1950–54; Prof. of Religious Studies, Univ. of Ibadan, Nigeria, 1954–60; Sen. Lectr, Univ. of Glasgow, 1960–66, Reader in Divinity, 1966–68. Hensley Henson Lectr in Theology, Oxford Univ., 1978; Cunningham Lectr, Edinburgh, 1979; Gifford Lectr, Glasgow, 1984. FRSE 1985. *Publications:* The Cosmic Christ, 1951; Basic Readings in Theology, 1964; Faith in a Changing Culture, 1966; Wolfhart Pannenberg, 1973; History of Christian Theology, Vol. 1, Pt III, 1986. *Recreation:* sailing. *Address:* 5 Straid Bheag, Clynder, Helensburgh, Dunbartonshire G84 0QX.

GALLOWAY, Prof. David Malcolm, PhD; FBPsS; Professor of Primary Education, University of Durham, 1992–2001 (Head of School of Education, 1993–2000); *b* 5 July 1942; *s* of Malcolm Ashby Galloway and Joan Dorah Frances Galloway (*née* Slater); *m* 1971, Christina Mary King; two *s* one *d*. *Educ:* St Edmund Hall, Oxford (BA Psychol., Phil. and Physiol. 1970; MA 1974); UCL (MSc Educnl Psychol. 1972); Sheffield City Poly (PhD 1980). FBPsS 1983. Educnl Psychologist and Sen. Educnl Psychologist, Sheffield LEA, 1972–79; Sen. Lectr, Victoria Univ. of Wellington, NZ, 1980–83; Lectr, UC Cardiff, 1983–87; Lectr and Reader in Educnl Res., Lancaster Univ., 1987–91. Chm., Assoc. for Child Psychology and Psychiatry, 1999–2001. *Publications:* books include: Schools and Persistent Absentees, 1985; (with C. Goodwin) The Education of Disturbing Children: pupils with learning and adjustment difficulties, 1987; (with A. Edwards) Primary School Teaching and Educational Psychology, 1991; (jtly) The Assessment of Special Educational Needs: whose problem?, 1994; (jtly) Motivating the Difficult to Teach, 1998; numerous articles in acad. and professional jls. *Recreations:* bee-keeping, fell search and mountain rescue. *Address:* Leases, Smardale, Kirkby Stephen, Cumbria CA17 4HQ.

GALLOWAY, George; MP (Lab) Glasgow Kelvin, since 1997 (Glasgow, Hillhead, 1987–97); *b* 16 Aug. 1954; *s* of George and Sheila Galloway; *m* 1979, Elaine Fyffe (marr. diss. 1999); one *d*; *m* Dr Amineh Abu-Zayyad. *Educ:* Charleston Primary Sch.; Harris Acad., Dundee. Engrg worker, 1973; organiser, Labour Party, 1977; Gen. Sec., War on Want, 1983–87. HQA (Pakistan), 1990; HPK (Pakistan), 1995. *Publication:* (jtly) Downfall: the Ceausescus and the Romanian revolution, 1991. *Recreations:* boxing, football, films, music. *Address:* House of Commons, SW1A 0AA. *T:* (020) 7219 4084.

GALLOWAY, Maj.-Gen. Kenneth Gardiner, CB 1978; OBE 1960; Director Army Dental Service, 1974–March 1978; *b* 3 Nov. 1917; *s* of David and Helen Galloway, Dundee and Oban; *m* 1949, Sheila Frances (*née* Dunsmor); two *d* (one *s* decd). *Educ:* Oban High Sch.; St Andrews Univ. LDS 1939, BDS 1940. Lieut Army Dental Corps, 1940; Captain 1941; Major 1948; Lt-Col 1955; Col 1963; Brig. 1972; Maj.-Gen. 1974. Served in Egypt, Palestine, Syria and Iraq, 1942–46; Chief Instructor and 2nd in comd, Depot and Training Establishment, RADC, 1956–60; Malta and BAOR, 1960–67; Asst Dir Dental Service, MoD, 1967–71; Dep. Dir Dental Service: Southern Comd, 1971–72; BAOR, 1972–74. QHDS 1971–78. Col Comdt, RADC, 1980–83. OStJ 1960. *Recreations:* tennis, golf, gardening. *Address:* Berwyn Court, Avenue Road, Farnborough, Hants GU14 7BH. *T:* (01252) 544948.

GALLOWAY, Rev. Dr Peter John, OBE 1996; JP; Vicar, Emmanuel Church, West Hampstead, since 1995 (Priest-in-Charge, 1990–95); *b* 19 July 1954; *s* of late Henry John Galloway and of Mary Selina (*née* Beshaw). *Educ:* Westminster City Sch.; Goldsmiths' Coll., Univ. of London (BA); King's Coll., London (PhD); St Stephen's House, Oxford. Ordained deacon, 1983; priest, 1984; Curate: St John's Wood, 1983–86; St Giles-in-the-Fields, 1986–90; Warden of Readers, London Episcopal Area, 1987–92. Mem., London Dio. Synod, 1997–2000. St John Ambulance: Asst Dir-Gen., 1985–91; Dep. Dir-Gen., 1991–99; Sub Dean, Priory of England, 1999–; Chm., Nat. Publications Cttee, 1988–95. Mem., Lord Chancellor's Adv. Cttee, 1994–2000. Mem. Council, 1999–, Vice Chm. Convocation, 1999–, London Univ.; Mem. Council, Goldsmiths' Coll., London Univ., 1993–99 (Hon. Fellow, 1999). Chm., Goldsmiths' Soc., 1997– (Vice-Chm., 1991–97). Gov., Soho Parish Sch., 1989–91; Chm. of Governors, Emmanuel Sch., W Hampstead, 1990–; Patron, English Schs Orch., 1998–. Freeman, City of London, 1995; Liveryman, Glaziers' Co., 1998– (Freeman, 1997). JP City of London, 1989 (Chm. Bench, 2001–). FSA 2000. KStJ 1997 (ChStJ 1992; Mem., Chapter Gen., 1996–99; Mem., Priory of England Chapter, 1999–). *Publications:* The Order of St Patrick 1783–1983, 1983; Henry Falconar Barclay Mackay, 1983; (with Christopher Rawll) Good and Faithful Servants, 1988; The Cathedrals of Ireland, 1992; The Order of the British Empire, 1996; (jtly) Royal Service, 1996; The Most Illustrious Order, 1999; A Passionate Humility: Frederick Oakeley and the Oxford movement, 1999; The Cathedrals of Scotland, 2000; The Order of St Michael and St George, 2000. *Recreations:* reading, writing, book collecting, solitude. *Address:* The Vicarage, Lyncroft Gardens, NW6 1JU. *T:* (020) 7435 1911. *Club:* Athenæum.

GALLWEY, Sir Philip Frankland P.; *see* Payne-Gallwey.

GALPIN, His Honour Brian John Francis; a Circuit Judge, 1978–93; an Official Referee, Western Circuit, 1986–93; *b* 21 March 1921; *s* of late Christopher John Galpin, DSO and late Gladys Elizabeth Galpin (*née* Souhami); *m* 1st, 1947, Ailsa McConnel (*d* 1959); one *d* decd; 2nd, 1961, Nancy Cecilia Nichols; two adopted *s*. *Educ:* Merchant Taylors' Sch.; Hertford Coll., Oxford. MA 1947. FCIArb. RAF Officer, 1941–45. Editor, Isis, 1946. Called to Bar, 1948; a Recorder of the Crown Court, 1972–78. Councillor, Metropolitan Borough of Fulham, 1950–59; Chm., Galpin Soc. for Study of Musical Instruments, 1954–72, Vice-Pres., 1974–; Pres., Madrigal Soc., 1989–91; Mem. Bach Choir, 1947–93 (Mem. Cttee, 1954–61). Pres., Old Merchant Taylors' Soc., 1988 and 1991. Trustee, Horniman Mus., 1990– (Vice-Chm., 1990–96). *Publications:* A Manual of International Law, 1950; Maxwell's Interpretation of Statutes, 10th edn 1953 and 11th edn 1962; Every Man's Own Lawyer, 69th edn 1962, 70th edn 1971, 71st edn 1981; contrib. Halsbury's Laws of England, 3rd and 4th edns, Encycl. of Forms and Precedents, Galpin Soc. Jl. *Recreations:* cricket (retired), music, chess. *Address:* St Bruno House, Charters Road, Sunningdale, Berks SL5 9QB. *Clubs:* Travellers, Pratt's.

GALPIN, Rodney Desmond; Chairman, Alpha Airports Group PLC, since 1994; *b* 5 Feb. 1932; *s* of Sir Albert James Galpin, KCVO, CBE; *m* 1956, Sylvia Craven; one *s* one *d*. *Educ:* Haileybury and Imperial Service Coll. Joined Bank of England, 1952; Sec. to Governor (Lord Cromer), 1962–66; Dep. Principal, Discount Office, 1970–74; Dep. Chief Cashier, Banking and Money Markets Supervision, 1974–78; Chief of Establishments, 1978–80; Chief of Corporate Services, 1980–82; Associate Dir, 1982–84; Exec. Dir, Bank of England, 1984–88; Chairman and Group Chief Executive: Standard Chartered plc, 1988–93; Standard Chartered Bank, 1988–93. Director: Cater Allen Holdings PLC, 1993–97; Capital Shopping Centres PLC, 1994–2000; Ascot (formerly Ascot Holdings) PLC, 1995–; P&O, 1996–. Chm., Independent Review Body (formerly Code of Banking Practice Review Cttee), 1994–99. Mem. Council, Foundn for Management Educn, 1984–86. Chm., Look Ahead Housing Assoc. Ltd, 1994–. Life Governor and Council Mem., Haileybury, 1973–; Mem. Council, Scout Assoc., 1972–. CIMgt (FBIM 1979); FCIB 1988. Freeman, City of London, 1981. OStJ. *Recreations:* tennis, gardening, music. *Address:* Alderman's Cottage, Lutmans Haven, Knowl Hill, Reading, Berks RG10 9YN. *Club:* Bankers' (Pres., 1992–93).

GALSWORTHY, Sir Anthony (Charles), KCMG 1999 (CMG 1985); HM Diplomatic Service; Ambassador to People's Republic of China, 1997–Feb. 2002; *b* 20 Dec. 1944; *s* of Sir Arthur Norman Galsworthy, KCMG, and Margaret Agnes Galsworthy (*née* Hiscocks); *m* 1970, Jan Dawson-Grove; one *s* one *d*. *Educ:* St Paul's Sch.; Corpus Christi Coll., Cambridge (MA). FCO, 1966–67; Hong Kong (language training), 1967–69; Peking, 1970–72; FCO, 1972–77; Rome, 1977–81; Counsellor, Peking, 1981–84; Head of Hong Kong Dept, FCO, 1984–86; Principal Private Sec. to Sec. of State for Foreign and Commonwealth Affairs, 1986–88; seconded to RIIA, 1988–89; Sen. British Rep., Sino-British Jt Liaison Gp, Hong Kong, 1989–93; Chief of Assessments Staff, Cabinet Office, 1993–95. Dep. Under Sec. of State, FCO, 1995–97. Scientific Associate, Natural Hist. Mus., 2001–. *Recreations:* bird-watching, wildlife. *Address:* c/o Foreign and Commonwealth Office, King Charles Street, SW1A 2AH. *Club:* Oxford and Cambridge.

GALSWORTHY, (Arthur) Michael (Johnstone), CBE 1999; DL; Chairman, Trewithen Estates Management Co. Ltd, since 1979; *b* 10 April 1944; *s* of Sir John Galsworthy, KCVO, CMG and late Jennifer Ruth Johnstone; *m* 1st, 1972, Charlotte Helena Prudence Roberts (*d* 1989); one *s* two *d*; 2nd, 1991, Sarah Christian Durnford;

one *s* one *d*. *Educ:* Radley; St Andrews Univ. (MA Hons). International Harvester Corp., 1967–69; English China Clays PLC, 1970–82; Man. Dir, Hawkins Wright Associates, 1982–86. Local Adv. Dir, Barclays Bank, 1987–98. Mem., Prince of Wales Council, 1985–; Dir, CoSIRA, 1985–88; a Develt Comr, 1987–92; Trustee, Rural Housing Trust, 1986–92; Chairman: Cornwall Rural Housing Assoc., 1985–95; Royal Cornwall Hosps NHS Trust, 1991–93; Dir, Westcountry Develt Corp., 1993–96; Chm., In Pursuit of Excellence Partnership for Cornwall, 1994–. Dir, Woodard Corp. (W Region), 1983–87. Mem., Court of Assts, Goldsmiths' Co., 1998–. Chm. Council, Order of St John for Cornwall, 1995–. FRSA 1997. DL Cornwall, 1993; High Sheriff, Cornwall, 1994. *Publications:* In Pursuit of Excellence: testimonial of business in Cornwall, 1994; The IPE Business Journal, 1996; The IPE Green Book Testimonial, 1997; A Wealth of Talent: the best of crafts in Cornwall, 1998. *Recreations:* gardening, fishing, shooting, walking. *Address:* Trewithen, Grampound Road, near Truro, Cornwall TR2 4DD. *T:* (01726) 882418; Flat 11, 6/8 Clanricarde Gardens, W2 4NA. *Clubs:* Brooks's, Farmers'.

GALTON, Raymond Percy, OBE 2000; author and scriptwriter, since 1951; *b* 17 July 1930; *s* of Herbert and Christina Galton; *m* 1956, Tonia Phillips (*d* 1995); one *s* two *d*. *Educ:* Garth Sch., Morden. *Television:* with Alan Simpson: Hancock's Half Hour, 1954–61 (adaptation and translation, Fleksnes, Scandinavian TV, film and stage); Comedy Playhouse, 1962–63; Steptoe and Son, 1962–74 (adaptations and translations: Sanford and Son, US TV; Stiefbeen and Zoon, Dutch TV; Albert och Herbert, Scandinavian TV, film and stage); Galton-Simpson Comedy, 1969; Clochemerle, 1971; Casanova '74, 1974; Dawson's Weekly, 1975; The Galton and Simpson Playhouse, 1976–77; Paul Merton in Galton and Simpson's …, 1997; with Johnny Speight: Tea Ladies, 1979; Spooner's Patch, 1979–80; with John Antrobus: Room at the Bottom, 1986–87 (Banff TV Fest. Award for Best Comedy, 1987); Get Well Soon, 1997; *films* with Alan Simpson: The Rebel, 1960; The Bargee, 1963; The Spy with a Cold Nose, 1966; Loot, 1969; Steptoe and Son, 1971; Steptoe and Son Ride Again, 1973; Den Siste Fleksnes (Scandinavia), 1974; Die Skraphandlerne (Scandinavia), 1975; with Alan Simpson and John Antrobus: The Wrong Arm of the Law, 1963; with Andrew Galton: Camping (Denmark), 1990; *theatre:* with Alan Simpson: Way Out in Piccadilly, 1966; The Wind in the Sassafras Trees, 1968; Albert och Herbert (Sweden), 1981; Fleksnes (Norway), 1983; Mordet pa Skolgatan 15 (Sweden), 1984; with John Antrobus: When Did You Last See Your Trousers?, 1986, UK tour, 1994. Awards, with Alan Simpson: Scriptwriters of the Year, 1959 (Guild of TV Producers and Directors); Best TV Comedy Series, Steptoe and Son, 1962/3/4/5 (Screenwriters Guild); John Logie Baird Award (for outstanding contribution to Television), 1964; Best Comedy Series (Steptoe and Son, Dutch TV), 1966; Best comedy screenplay, Steptoe and Son, 1972 (Screenwriters Guild); Lifetime Achievement Award, Writer's Guild of GB, 1997. *Publications:* (with Alan Simpson): Hancock, 1961; Steptoe and Son, 1963; The Reunion and Other Plays, 1966; Hancock Scripts, 1974; The Best of Hancock, 1986; The Best of Steptoe and Son, 1988. *Recreations:* reading, worrying. *Address:* The Ivy House, Hampton Court, Middx KT8 9DD. *T:* (020) 8977 1236; Tessa Le Bars Management, 54 Birchwood Road, Petts Wood, Kent BR5 1NZ. *T:* (01689) 837084.

GALVIN, Bernard Vincent Joseph, CB 1991; Secretary to the Treasury, New Zealand, 1980–86; *b* 15 March 1933; *s* of Eustace Bartholemew Galvin and Margaret Jean (*née* Lenihan); *m* 1st, 1960, Beverly Ann Snook (marr. diss. 1977); three *s* one *d*; 2nd, 1980, Margaret Clark. *Educ:* Univ. of NZ (BSc 1954); Victoria Univ. of Wellington (BA Hons 1959); Harvard Univ. (MPA 1961). Joined Treasury, NZ, 1955; Harkness Fellow, USA, 1960–61; Econ. Counsellor, NZ High Commn, London, 1965–68; Treasury Dir, 1969; Asst Sec., 1972; Dep. Sec., 1974; Perm. Head of PM's Dept, 1975–80. Chm., Econ. Develt Commn, 1986–89. Alternate Gov., World Bank, 1976–86. Chm., Ministerial Wkg Pty on Disability and Accident Compensation, 1991. Vis. Fellow, Inst. of Policy Studies, 1989–98. Mem. Council, Victoria Univ. of Wellington, 1989–98 (Treas., 1990–96). *Publications:* Policy Co-ordination, Public Sector and Government, 1991; chapters in books on NZ government; articles in public admin jls. *Recreations:* beach house, gardening, reading, walking. *Address:* 10 Jellicoe Towers, 189 The Terrace, Wellington, New Zealand. *T:* (weekdays) (4) 4728143; (weekends) (6) 3643374. *Club:* Wellington (Wellington, NZ).

GALVIN, John Rogers; General, United States Army, retired; Supreme Allied Commander, Europe, and Commander-in-Chief, US European Command, Stuttgart, 1987–92; Dean, Fletcher School of Law and Diplomacy, Tufts University, 1995–2000, now Emeritus; *b* 13 May 1929; *s* of John J. Galvin and Mary Josephine Logan; *m* 1961, Virginia Lee Brennan; four *d*. *Educ:* US Mil. Acad. (BS); Columbia Univ. (MA); US Army Command and General Staff Coll.; Univ. of Pennsylvania; US Army War Coll.; Fletcher Sch. of Law and Diplomacy (US Army War Coll. Fellowship). Platoon Leader, I Co., 65 Inf. Regt, Puerto Rico, 1955–56; Instructor, Ranger Sch., Colombia, 1956–58; Co. Comdr, 501 Airborne Battle Group, 101 Airborne Div., 1958–60; Instructor, US Mil. Acad., 1962–65; DACOS, Plans, 1st Cavalry Div., Vietnam, 1966–67; MA and Aide to Sec. of US Army, 1967–69; Comdr, 1st Bn, 8th Cavalry, 1st Cavalry Div., Vietnam, 1969–70; Dep. Sec., Jt Staff, US European Comd, Stuttgart, 1973–74; MA to SACEUR, 1974–75; Comdr, Div. Support Comd, 1975–77; COS, 3rd Inf. Div. (Mechanized), Würzburg, 1977–78; Asst Div. Comdr, 8th Inf. Div. (Mechanized), Mainz, 1978–80; Asst DCOS for Training, US Army Training and Doctrine Comd, 1980–81; Comdg Gen., 24 Inf. Div. (Mechanized), and Fort Stewart, 1981–83; Comdg Gen., VII Corps, Stuttgart, 1983–85; C-in-C, US Southern Comd, Panama, 1985–87. Olin Dist. Prof. of Nat. Security, W Point, 1992–94; Dist. Policy Analyst, Mershon Center, Ohio State Univ., 1994–95. Defense DSM, Army DSM, Navy DSM, Air Force DSM, Silver Star, Legion of Merit (with 2 Oak Leaf Clusters), DFC, Soldier's Medal, Bronze Star (with 2 Oak Leaf Clusters), Combat Infantryman Badge, Ranger Tab, foreign decorations. *Publications:* The Minute Men, 1967; Air Assault: the development of airmobility, 1969; Three Men of Boston, 1975. *Recreations:* walking, jogging. *Address:* 2714 Lake Jodeco Circle, Jonesboro, GA 30236, USA.

GALWAY, 12th Viscount *cr* 1727; **George Rupert Monckton-Arundell;** Baron Killard, 1727; Lieut Comdr RCN, retired; *b* 13 Oct. 1922; *s* of Philip Marmaduke Monckton (*d* 1965) (*g g s* of 5th Viscount) and of Lavender, *d* of W. J. O'Hara; *S* cousin, 1980; *m* 1944, Fiona Margaret, *d* of late Captain P. W. de P. Taylor; one *s* three *d*. *Heir:* *s* Hon. John Philip Monckton [*b* 8 April 1952; *m* 1980, Deborah Holmes (marr. diss.)]. *Address:* 787 Berkshire Drive, London, ON N6J 3S5, Canada.

GALWAY AND KILMACDUAGH, Bishop of, (RC), since 1993; **Most Rev. James McLoughlin;** *b* 9 April 1929; *s* of Patrick McLoughlin and Winifred (*née* McDermott). *Educ:* St Patrick's Coll., Maynooth (BA, HDipEd). Ordained priest, 1954; Professor, St Mary's Coll., Galway, 1954–65; Diocesan Secretary, 1965–83; Parish Priest, Galway Cathedral, 1983–93. *Address:* Diocesan Office, The Cathedral, Galway, Ireland. *T:* (91) 563566.

GALWAY, Sir James, Kt 2001; OBE 1977; FRCM 1983; fluteplayer; *b* 8 Dec. 1939; *s* of James Galway and Ethel Stewart Clarke; *m* 1st, 1965; one *s*; 2nd, 1972; one *s* twin *d*; 3rd, 1984, Jeanne Cinnante. *Educ:* St Paul's Sch., and Mountcollyer Secondary Modern Sch., Belfast; RCM, and Guildhall Sch. of Music, London; Conservatoire National Supérieur de Musique, Paris. First post in wind band of Royal Shakespeare Theatre, Stratford-upon-Avon; later worked with Sadler's Wells Orch., Royal Opera House Orch. and BBC Symphony Orch.; Principal Flute, London Symphony Orch., 1966, Royal Philharmonic Orch., 1967–69; Principal Solo Flute, Berlin Philharmonic Orch., 1969–75; international soloist, 1975–. Principal Guest Conductor, London Mozart Players, 1999–. Recordings of works by C. P. E. Bach, J. S. Bach, Beethoven, Corigliano, Debussy, Franck, Handel, Khachaturian, Mancini, Mozart, Nielsen, Prokoviev, Reicha, Reincke, Rodrigo, Schubert, Stamitz, Telemann and Vivaldi; also albums of flute showpieces, Australian, Irish and Japanese collections. Grand Prix du Disque, 1976, 1989. Hon. MA Open, 1979; Hon. DMus: QUB, 1979; New England Conservatory of Music, 1980. Officier des Arts et des Lettres, France, 1987. *Publications:* James Galway: an autobiography, 1978; Flute (Menuhin Music Guide), 1982; James Galway's Music in Time, 1983 (TV series, 1983); Masterclass: performance editions of great flute literature, 1987. *Recreations:* music, walking, swimming, films, theatre, TV, chess, backgammon, computing, talking to people. *Address:* c/o Kathryn Enticott, IMG Artists, 1st Floor, Lovell House, 616 Chiswick High Road, W4 5RX. *T:* (020) 8233 5800.

GAM, Rt Rev. Sir Getake, KBE 1995; Head Bishop, Evangelical Lutheran Church of Papua New Guinea, since 1982; *b* 12 August 1943; *s* of Getanuka Gam and Maluave Gam; *m* 1975, Anna Goba; two *s* three *d* and one adopted *s*. *Educ:* Martin Luther Seminary, Lae, PNG (BTh). Pastoral Ministry, Finschhafen and Panguna, Bougainville, 1971–75; teacher, Martin Luther Seminary, 1976–78; Dir, Evangelism Dept, Evangelical Lutheran Ch of PNG, 1978–81. Sec. and Treas., Lae Soccer Referees Assoc. Independence Medal (PNG), 1975. *Recreation:* football (formerly played soccer and Australian rules football). *Address:* Evangelical Lutheran Church of Papua New Guinea, Box 80, Lae, Papua New Guinea. *T:* 4723711, *Fax:* 4721056.

GAMBETTA, Dr Diego, FBA 2000; Reader in Sociology, University of Oxford and Fellow, All Souls College, Oxford, since 1995; *b* 30 Jan. 1952; *s* of Carlo Gambetta and Giovanna (*née* Giavelli); *m* 1992, Dr Valeria Pizzini; one *s* one *d*. *Educ:* Chieri, Turin; Univ. of Turin (BA Philosophy); King's Coll., Cambridge (PhD 1983). Civil servant, Regl Admin, Piedmont, Italy, 1978–84; Jun. Res. Fellow, 1984–88, Sen. Res. Fellow, 1988–91, King's Coll., Cambridge; Fellow, St Anne's Coll., Lectr in Sociology, Univ. of Oxford, 1991–95 (*ad hominem* Reader, 1993). Vis. Prof. in Social Orgn, Grad. Sch. of Business and Dept of Sociol., Univ. of Chicago, 1994. Inaugural Fellow, Italian Acad. for Advanced Studies, Columbia Univ., 1996–97. *Publications:* Were they pushed or did they jump?: individual decision mechanisms in education, 1987 (trans. Italian 1990), 2nd edn 1996; (ed) Trust: making and breaking co-operative relations, 1988 (trans. Italian 1989); The Sicilian mafia: the business of private protection (Premio Iglesias), 1993 (trans. Italian and German 1994), 2nd edn 1996; (with S. Warner) La retorica della riforma: fine del sistema proporzionale in Italia, 1994; contribs to anthologies and social scientific jls. *Recreations:* mountaineering, ski-ing, yoga, cinema. *Address:* All Souls College, Oxford OX1 4AL. *T:* (01865) 279387.

GAMBLE, Prof. Andrew Michael, PhD; FBA 2000; Professor of Politics, since 1986, and Director, Political Economy Research Centre, since 1999, University of Sheffield; *b* 15 Aug. 1947; *s* of Marcus Elkington Gamble and Joan (*née* Westall); *m* 1974, Christine Jennifer Rodway; one *s* two *d*. *Educ:* Brighton Coll.; Queens' Coll., Cambridge (BA Econs 1968); Univ. of Durham (MA Pol Theory 1969); Gonville and Caius Coll., Cambridge (PhD Social and Pol Scis 1975). University of Sheffield: Lectr in Politics, 1973–82; Reader, 1982–86; Pro-Vice-Chancellor, 1994–98. Visiting Professor: Univ. of Kobe, 1990; Univ. of Hitotsubashi, 1992; Univ. of Chuo, 1994. Mem. Exec., 1988–91, Vice-Chair, 1989–91, Political Studies Assoc. FRSA 1999. Joint Editor: New Political Economy, 1996–; Political Qly, 1997–. Mitchell Prize, 1977. *Publications:* (jtly) From Alienation to Surplus Value (Isaac Deutscher Meml Prize), 1972; The Conservative Nation, 1974; (jtly) Capitalism in Crisis, 1976; Britain in Decline, 1981, 4th edn 1994; An Introduction to Modern Social and Political Thought, 1981; (ed jtly) Developments in British Politics, vol. 1, 1983, vol. 2, 1986, vol. 3, 1990, vol. 4, 1993, vol. 5, 1997, vol. 6, 2000; (jtly) The British Party System and Economic Policy, 1984; (ed jtly) The Social Economy and the Democratic State, 1987; The Free Economy and the Strong State, 1988, 2nd edn 1994; (ed jtly) Thatcher's Law, 1989; Hayek: the iron cage of liberty, 1996; (ed jtly) Regionalism and World Order, 1996; (ed jtly) Stakeholder Capitalism, 1997; (ed jtly) Fundamentals in British Politics, 1999; (ed jtly) Marxism and Social Science, 1999; (ed jtly) The New Social Democracy, 1999; Politics and Fate, 2000; (ed jtly) The Political Economy of the Company, 2000; After Empire, 2001; articles in learned jls. *Recreations:* music, growing tomatoes. *Address:* Department of Politics, University of Sheffield, Sheffield S10 2TU. *T:* (0114) 222 1651; *e-mail:* a.m.gamble@shef.ac.uk.

See also C. S. Gamble.

GAMBLE, Dr Christine Elizabeth; Director, Royal Institute of International Affairs, 1998–2001; *b* 1950; *d* of late Albert Edward Gamble and of Kathleen Laura (*née* Wallis); *m* 1989, Edward Barry Antony Craxton. *Educ:* Royal Holloway Coll., London Univ. (BA 1st Cl. Hons; PhD 1977). English–French Cultural Orgn, 1974–75; served British Embassy, Moscow, 1975–76; with British Council, 1977–98: New Delhi, 1977–79; Stratford-on-Avon, 1979–80; Harare, 1980–82; Regl Officer for Soviet Union in London, 1982–85; Dep. Dir, Athens, 1985–87; Dir General's Dept (Corporate Planning), 1988–90; Head, Project Pursuit Dept and Dir, Chancellor's Financial Sector Scheme for Former Soviet Union, 1991–92; Dir, Visitors' Dept, 1992–93; Gen. Manager, Country Services Gp, 1993–95 and Hd, European Series, 1994–96; Cultural Counsellor, Paris and Dir, France, 1996–98. Dir, Japan 21st Century Gp, 1999–; Mem., Franco-British Council, 2000–. *Recreations:* collecting books, reading, music, theatre, gardening. *Address:* Syke Fold, Dent LA10 5RE.

GAMBLE, Prof. Clive Stephen; PhD; FBA 2000; FSA; Professor of Archaeology, since 1995, and Director, Centre for the Archaeology of Human Origins, since 1999, University of Southampton; *b* 10 March 1951; *s* of Marcus Elkington Gamble and Joan Gamble (*née* Westall); *m* 1981, Dr Elaine Lisk Morris. *Educ:* Brighton Coll.; Jesus Coll., Cambridge (BA 1972, MA 1975; PhD 1978). FSA 1981; MIFA 1987. Department of Archaeology, University of Southampton: exptl officer, 1975; Lectr, 1976–86; Sen. Lectr, 1986–90; Reader, 1990–95; British Acad. Res. Reader, 2000–02. *Publications:* The Palaeolithic Settlement of Europe, 1986; Timewalkers: the prehistory of global colonisation, 1993; (with C. Stringer) In Search of the Neanderthals, 1993; The Palaeolithic Societies of Europe, 1999; Archaeology: the basics, 2001. *Recreations:* cats, cricket, gardening. *Address:* Department of Archaeology, University of Southampton, Southampton SO17 1BJ. *T:* (023) 8059 2297.

See also A. M. Gamble.

GAMBLE, Sir David (Hugh Norman), 6th Bt *cr* 1897, of Windlehurst, St Helens, Co. Palatine of Lancashire; *b* 1 July 1966; *s* of Sir David Gamble, 5th Bt and of Dawn Adrienne, *d* of late David Hugh Gittins; *S* father, 1984. *Educ:* Shiplake College, Henley-on-Thames.

Heir: cousin Hugh Robert George Gamble [*b* 3 March 1946; *m* 1989, Rebecca Jane, *d* of Lt Comdr David Odell, RN; one *s* one *d*]. *Address:* Keinton House, Keinton Mandeville, Somerton, Somerset TA11 4DX. *T:* (01458) 223964.

GAMBLE, Richard Arthur; Non-executive Chairman, Denne Group Ltd, since 2001 (Adviser, 1999–2001); *b* 19 Sept. 1939; *s* of late Arthur Gamble and of Grace Emily Gamble (*née* Little); *m* 1966, Elizabeth Ann, *d* of Edward Godwin-Atkyns; two *s*. *Educ:* Raynes Park Co. Grammar Sch. FCA 1962. Articled clerk, W. J. Gilbert & Co., London, 1957–62; Asst Manager, Turquand Youngs & Co., 1962–66; Dir and Co. Sec., Lee Davy Gp Ltd, 1966–68; Dir and Sec., Hamilton Smith, Lloyd's Brokers, 1968–70; Finance Dir, Lowndes Lambert Internat., Lloyd's Brokers, 1970–76; European Finance Dir, Data100/Northern Telecom Systems, 1976–80; Finance Dir, McDonnell Douglas Inf. Systems and Dir, McDonnell Douglas UK, 1980–84; Dep. Chief Financial Officer, British Airways, 1984–89; Royal Insurance Holdings PLC: Gp Finance Dir, 1989–91; Gp Chief Operating Officer, 1991; Gp Chief Exec., 1992–96; Gp Chief Exec., Royal & Sun Alliance Insurance Gp plc, 1996–97. Mem. Bd, ABI, 1994–96; Chm., Policy Holders Protection Bd, 1994–98. Mem., Adv. Cttee on Business in the Envmt and Chm., Financial Services Working Gp, 1993–96. Mem., Educnl Nat. Leadership Team, BITC, 1995–. Trustee, Crimestoppers, 1995–; Pres., GB Wheelchair Basketball Assoc., 1997–; Gov., RSC, 1997–. CIMgt 1992. *Recreations:* all sport, particularly golf, walking with dogs, theatre, family. *Address:* Chart Hall Farm, Green Lane, Chart Sutton, Kent ME17 3ES. *T:* (01622) 842526.

GAMBLING, Prof. William Alexander, PhD, DSc; FRS 1983; FREng, Hon. FIEE; Royal Society Kan Tong Po Professor and Director, Optoelectronics Research Centre, City University, Hong Kong, since 1996; industrial consultant; *b* 11 Oct. 1926; *s* of George Alexander Gambling and Muriel Clara Gambling; *m* 1st, 1952, Margaret Pooley (marr. diss. 1994); one *s* two *d*; 2nd, 1994, Barbara Colleen O'Neil. *Educ:* Univ. of Bristol (BSc, DSc); Univ. of Liverpool (PhD). FIERE 1964; CEng, FIEE 1967; FREng (FEng 1979); FHKAES 2000. Lectr in Electric Power Engrg, Univ. of Liverpool, 1950–55; National Res. Council Fellow, Univ. of BC, 1955–57; Univ. of Southampton: Lectr, Sen. Lectr, and Reader, 1957–64; Dean of Engrg and Applied Science, 1972–75; Prof. of Electronics, 1964–80, Hd of Dept, 1974–79; BT Prof. of Optical Communication, 1980–95; Dir, Optoelectronics Res. Centre, 1989–95. Dir, York Ltd, 1980–97. Vis. Professor: Univ. of Colo, USA, 1966–67; Bhabha Atomic Res. Centre, India, 1970; Osaka Univ., Japan, 1977; City Univ. of Hong Kong, 1995; Hon. Professor: Huazhung Univ. of Sci. and Technol., Wuhan, China, 1986–; Beijing Univ. of Posts and Telecommunications, 1987–; Shanghai Univ., 1991–; Shandong Univ., 1999–; Hon. Dir, Beijing Optical Fibre Inst., 1987–. Pres., IERE, 1977–78 (Hon. Fellow 1983). Member: Electronics Res. Council, 1977–80 (Mem., Optics and Infra-Red Cttee, 1965–69 and 1974–80); Board, Council of Engrg Instns, 1974–79; National Electronics Council, 1977–78, 1984–95; Technol. Sub-Cttee of UGC, 1973–83; British Nat. Cttee for Radio Science, 1978–87; Nat. Adv. Bd for Local Authority Higher Educn, Engrg Working Gp, 1982–84; Engineering Council, 1983–88; British Nat. Cttee for Internat. Engineering Affairs, 1984–88; Council, Royal Acad. of Engrg, 1989–92; Chairman: Commn D, Internat. Union of Radio Science, 1984–87 (Vice-Chm., 1981–84); Nat. DTI/SERC Optoelectronics Cttee, 1988–91. Selby Fellow, Australian Acad. of Science, 1982; For. Mem., Polish Acad. of Scis, 1985. Freeman, City of London, 1988; Liveryman, Worshipful Co. of Engrs, 1988. Dr *hc* Univ. Politèchnica de Madrid, 1994; Hon. DSc Aston, 1995; Hon. DEng Bristol, 1999. Bulgin Premium, IERE, 1961, Rutherford Premium, IERE, 1964, Electronics Div. Premium, IEE, 1976 and 1978, Oliver Lodge Premium, IEE, 1981, Heinrich Hertz Premium, IERE, 1981, for research papers; J. J. Thomson Medal, IEE, 1982, Faraday Medal, IEE, 1983, Churchill Medal, Soc. of Engineers, 1984 and Simms Medal, Soc. of Engineers, 1989, for research innovation and leadership; Academic Enterprise Award, 1982; Micro-optics Award, Japan, 1989; Dennis Gabor Award, Internat. Soc. for Optical Engrg, USA, 1990; Rank Prize for Optoelectronics, 1991; Medal and Prize, Foundn for Computer and Communications Promotion, Japan, 1993; Mountbatten Medal, Nat. Electronics Council, 1993. *Publications:* papers on electronics and optical fibre communications. *Recreations:* music, reading, walking. *Address:* Optoelectronics Research Centre, City University of Hong Kong, 83 Tat Chee Avenue, Kowloon, Hong Kong. *T:* 27887828.

GAMBON, Sir Michael (John), Kt 1998; CBE 1990; actor; *b* 19 Oct. 1940; *s* of Edward and Mary Gambon; *m* 1962, Anne Miller; one *s*. *Educ:* St Aloysius School for Boys, Somers Town, London. Served 7 year apprenticeship in engineering; first appeared on stage with Edwards/MácLiammoir Co., Dublin, 1962; Nat. Theatre, Old Vic, 1963–67; Birmingham Rep. and other provincial theatres, 1967–69 (title rôles incl. Othello, Macbeth, Coriolanus); RSC Aldwych, 1970–71; Norman Conquests, Globe, 1974; Otherwise Engaged, Queen's, 1976; Just Between Ourselves, Queen's 1977; Alice's Boys, Savoy, 1978; King Lear and Antony and Cleopatra (title rôles), RSC Stratford and Barbican, 1982–83; Old Times, Haymarket, 1985; Uncle Vanya, Vaudeville, 1988; Veterans Day, Haymarket, 1989; Man of the Moment, Globe, 1990; Othello and Taking Steps, Scarborough, 1990; Tom and Clem, Aldwych, 1997; The Unexpected Man, Barbican Pit, transf. Duchess, 1998; Juno and the Paycock, Gaiety, Dublin, 1999; Cressida, Albery, 2000; The Caretaker, Comedy (Variety Club Best Actor, Critics' Circle Best Actor), 2000; National Theatre: Galileo, 1980 (London Theatre Critics' Award, Best Actor); Betrayal, 1980; Tales From Hollywood, 1980; Chorus of Disapproval, 1985 (Olivier Award, Best Comedy Performance); Tons of Money, 1986; A View from the Bridge, 1987, transf. Aldwych (Best Actor, Evening Standard Awards, Olivier Awards, and Plays and Players London Theatre Critics Awards; Best Stage Actor, Variety Club Awards); A Small Family Business, 1987; Mountain Language, 1988; Skylight, transf. Wyndhams, then NY, and Volpone (Best Actor, Evening Standard Awards), 1995. *Television* includes: The Singing Detective, 1986 (BAFTA Award, Best Actor, 1987); Maigret, 1992, 1993; Faith, 1994; Wives and Daughters, 1999 (BAFTA Award, Best Actor, 2000); Longitude, 2000 (BAFTA Award, Best Actor, 2001); Perfect Strangers, 2001. *Films* include: The Cook, The Thief, His Wife and Her Lover, 1989; The Heat of the Day, 1989; Paris by Night, 1989; A Dry White Season, 1990; Mobsters, 1992; Toys, 1992; The Browning Version, 1993; A Man of No Importance, 1994; Midnight in Moscow, 1994; The Innocent Sleep, 1995; All Our Fault, 1995; Mary Reilly, 1996; Two Deaths, 1996; Nothing Personal, 1996; The Gambler, 1996; The Wings of the Dove, 1997; Dancing at Lughnasa, 1997; Plunkett and Macleane, 1999; The Last September, 2000; Sleepy Hollow, 2000; The Insider, 2000; End Game, 2001; High Heels and Low Lifes, 2001. Trustee, Royal Armouries, 1995–. Liveryman, Gunmakers' Co. *Recreations:* flying, gun collecting, clock making. *Address:* ICM, Oxford House, Oxford Street, W1N 0AX. *Club:* Garrick.

GAMMELL, John Frederick, MC 1943; MA; *b* 31 Dec. 1921; 2nd *s* of Lieut-Gen. Sir James A. H. Gammell, KCB, DSO, MC; *m* 1947, Margaret Anne, *d* of Ralph Juckes, Fiddington Manor, Tewkesbury; two *s* one *d*. *Educ:* Winchester Coll.; Trinity Coll., Cambridge. MA 1953. Asst Master, Horris Hill, Newbury, 1940–41. War Service with KRRC, 1941–44; wounded, 1943; invalided out, 1944. Trinity Coll., Cambridge, 1946–47 (BA); Asst Master, Winchester Coll., 1944–45 and 1947–68; Exchange with Sen. Classics Master, Geelong Grammar Sch., Australia, 1949–50; Housemaster of Turner's, Winchester Coll., 1958–68; Headmaster, Repton Sch., 1968–78; Asst Sec., Cambridge Univ. Careers Service, 1978–83. *Recreation:* friends. *Address:* The Old School House, Seaton, Oakham LE15 9HR. *T:* (01572) 747835.

GAMON, Hugh Wynell, CBE 1979; MC 1944; formerly Partner, Winckworth & Pemberton (incorporating Sherwood & Co., 1991); HM Government Agent, 1970–89; *b* 31 March 1921; *s* of Judge Hugh R. P. Gamon and E. Margaret Gamon; *m* 1949, June Elizabeth, *d* of William and Florence Temple; one *s* three *d*. *Educ:* St Edward's Sch., Oxford; Exeter Coll., Oxford, 1946–48. MA 1st Cl. Hons Jurisprudence; Law Society Hons; Edmund Thomas Childe Prize. Served War, 1940–46: Royal Corps of Signals, N Africa, Italy and Palestine, with 1st Division. Articled to Clerk of Cumberland CC, 1949–51; joined Sherwood & Co., 1951; Parly Agent, 1954; Sen. Partner, Sherwood & Co., 1972; retd from Winckworth & Pemberton, 1995. *Recreation:* gardening. *Address:* Black Charles, Underriver, Sevenoaks, Kent TN15 0RY. *T:* (01732) 833036.

GANDHI, Manmohan Purushottam, MA, FREconS, FSS; Editor, Major Industries of India Annual, since 1951 (vol. 34, 1988); Director: Indian Link Chain Manufacturers Ltd; Zenith Ltd; Orient General Industries Ltd; *b* 5 Nov. 1901; *s* of late Purushottam Kahanji Gandhi, of Limbdi (Kathiawad); *m* 1926, Rambhaben, BA (Indian Women's Univ.), *d* of Sukhlal Chhaganlal Shah of Wadhwan. *Educ:* Bahauddin Coll., Junagad; Gujerat Coll., Ahmedabad; Hindu Univ., Benares. BA (History and Econs), Bombay Univ., 1923; MA (Political Econ. and Political Philosophy), Benares Hindu Univ., 1925; Ashburner Prize of Bombay Univ., 1925. Statistical Asst, Govt of Bombay, Labour Office, 1926; Asst Sec., Indian Currency League, Bombay, 1926; Sec., Indian Chamber of Commerce, Calcutta, 1926–36; Sec., Indian Sugar Mills Assoc., 1932–36; Officer-in-Charge, Credit Dept, National City Bank of New York, Calcutta, 1936–37; Chief Commercial Manager, Rohtas Industries Ltd; Dalmia Cement Ltd, 1937–39; Dir, Indian Sugar Syndicate Ltd, 1937–39; Controller of Supplies, Bengal and Bombay, 1941–43; Sec., Indian Nat. Cttee, Internat. Chamber of Commerce, Calcutta, 1929–31; Sec., Fedn of Indian Chambers of Commerce and Industry, 1928–29. Member: East Indian Railway Adv. Cttee, 1939–40; Bihar Labour Enquiry Cttee, 1937–39; UP and Bihar Power Alcohol Cttee, 1938; UP and Bihar Sugar Control Board, 1938; Western Railway Adv. Cttee, Bombay, 1950–52; Small Scale Industries Export Prom. Adv. Cttee; Technical Adviser, Indian Tariff Board, 1947. Hon. Prof., Sydenham Coll. of Commerce, 1943–50. Member: All India Council of Tech. Educn, 1948–73; All India Bd of Studies in Commerce, 1948–70; All India Bd of Management Studies, 1978–84; Indian Merchants Chamber Cttee, 1945–83; Indian Council of Agriculture Res., 1959–66; Senate and Syndicate, Bombay Univ., 1957–69; Dean, Commerce Faculty, Bombay Univ., 1966–67. Director: E India Cotton Assoc., 1953–73 and 1983–84; Bombay Oils & Oilseeds Exchange, 1972–74; Bombay Yarn Exchange, 1972–75. Member: All-India Handloom Bd, 1952–58; Central Silk Bd, 1954–60; Handloom Export Adv. Council, 1965–68; Small-Scale Industries Bd, 1965–69. National FAO Liaison Cttee, 1974–76. Hon. Metropolitan Magistrate, Bombay, 1947–84; JP 1951–68. Swadeshi Prachar Sanuti, 1930–36. *Publications:* How to Compete with Foreign Cloth (with a foreword by Mahatma Gandhi), 1931; The Indian Sugar Industry: Its Past, Present and Future, 1934; The Indian Cotton Textile Industry-Its Past, Present and Future, 1937; The Indian Sugar Industry (annually, 1935–64); The Indian Cotton Textile Industry, (annually, 1936–60); Centenary Volume of the Indian Cotton Textile Industry, 1851–1950; Problems of Sugar Industry in India, 1946; Monograph on Handloom Weaving in Indi, 1953; Some Impressions of Japan, 1955; What I learnt from the Mahatma including the Twelve Letters of Mahatma Gandhi to M. P. Gandhi, 1930–32, with reminiscences, 1998. *Recreations:* tennis (name recorded for first time in Limca Book of Records, as oldest tennis player, playing tennis at 91, 1992), badminton, billiards, bridge, cricket. *Clubs:* Radio, National Sports, Rotary, Fifty-Five Tennis, Garden (Bombay).

GANDHI, Sonia; President, Congress Party, India, since 1998; *b* Italy, 9 Dec. 1947; adopted Indian nationality, 1983; *d* of Stefano and Paola Maino; *m* 1968, Rajiv Gandhi (*d* 1991); one *s* one *d*. *Educ:* language sch., Cambridge; Art restoration course, Nat. Gall. of Modern Art, New Delhi. Pres., Rajiv Gandhi Foundn. Mem., Congress Party, 1997–. *Publications:* (ed) Freedom's Daughter, 1989; (ed) Two Alone, Two Together, 1992; Rajiv, 1992; Rajiv's World, 1994. *Address:* All India Congress Committee, 24 Akbar Road, New Delhi 110011, India.

GANDY, Christopher Thomas; HM Diplomatic Service, retired; *b* 21 April 1917; *s* of late Dr Thomas H. Gandy and late Mrs Ida Gandy (authoress of A Wiltshire Childhood, Around the Little Steeple, etc); unmarried. *Educ:* Marlborough; King's Coll., Cambridge. On active service with Army and RAF, 1939–45. Entered Foreign Office, Nov. 1945; Tehran, 1948–51; Cairo, 1951–52; FO, 1952–54; Lisbon, 1954–56; Libya, 1956–59; FO, 1960–62; apptd HM Minister to The Yemen, 1962, subsequently Counsellor, Kuwait; Minister (Commercial) Rio de Janeiro, 1966–68. Sen. Common Room Mem., St Antony's Coll., Oxford, 1973–. *Publications:* articles in Asian Affairs, Middle East International, The New Middle East, The Annual Register of World Events, Art International, Arts of Asia, Jl of Royal Asiatic Soc., British Jl of Middle Eastern Studies, and Financial Times. *Recreations:* music, gardening. *Address:* 60 Ambleside Drive, Headington, Oxford OX3 0AH. *Club:* Travellers.

GANDY, David Stewart, CB 1989; OBE 1981; Consultant, Pannone and Partners, solicitors, since 1993; Deputy Director of Public Prosecutions and Chief Executive, Crown Prosecution Service, 1987–93; *b* 19 Sept. 1932; *s* of Percy Gandy and Elizabeth Mary (*née* Fox); *m* 1956, Mabel Sheldon; one *s* one *d*. *Educ:* Manchester Grammar Sch.; Manchester Univ. Nat. Service, Intell. Corps (Germany and Austria), 1954–56. Admitted Solicitor, 1954; Asst Solicitor, Town Clerk, Manchester, 1956–59; Chief Prosecuting Solicitor: Manchester, 1959–68; Manchester and Salford, 1968–74; Gtr Manchester, 1974–85; Head of Field Management, Crown Prosecution Service, 1985–87; Acting DPP, Oct. 1991–May 1992. Mem., Home Office Assessment Consultancy Unit, 1993–. Mem. Council, Criminal Law Solicitors Assoc., 1992–2001. Lect. tour on English Criminal Justice System, for Amer. Bar Assoc., USA and Canada, 1976; Lecturer: UN Asia and FE Inst. for Prevention of Crime and Treatment of Offenders, Tokyo, 1990, 1995; Internat. Congress of Criminal Lawyers on Penal Reform, La Plata, 1995. Law Society: Mem., Criminal Law Standing Cttee, 1969–97 (Vice Chm., 1995–96); Mem., Council, 1984–96; Prosecuting Solicitors' Society of England and Wales: Mem., Exec. Council, 1966–85; Pres., 1976–78; Chm., Heads of Office, 1982–83; President: Manchester Law Soc., 1980–81; Manchester and Dist Medico-Legal Soc., 1982–84; Manchester Trainee Lawyers Gp, 1982–84. Non-exec. Dir, Mancunian Community Health NHS Trust, 1993–98. Mem. Council, Order of St John, 1978–85. *Recreations:* cricket, theatre, bridge, walking. *Address:* The Ridgeway, Broad Lane, Hale, Altrincham, Cheshire WA15 0DD. *Club:* St James's (Manchester).

GANDY, Ronald Herbert; Treasurer to the Greater London Council, 1972–77, retired; *b* 22 Nov. 1917; *s* of Frederick C. H. Gandy and Olive (*née* Wilson); *m* 1942, Patricia M. Turney; two *s* one *d*. *Educ:* Banister Court Sch. and Taunton's Sch. (now Taunton's

Coll.), Southampton. Town Clerk's Dept, Civic Centre, Southampton County Borough Council, 1936; LCC: Admin. Officer, Comptroller's (i.e. Treasurer's) Dept, 1937; Asst Comptroller, 1957; Dep. Comptroller, 1964; Dep. Treasurer, GLC, 1965; Dep. Chief Financial Officer, Inner London Educn Authority, 1967. Mem. CIPFA. *Address:* 15 Lynbury Court, Watford, Herts WD18 7HL. *T:* (01923) 224215.

GANE, Barrie Charles, CMG 1988; OBE 1978; HM Diplomatic Service, retired; Director Group Research, Group 4 Securitas, 1993–2000; *b* 19 Sept. 1935; *s* of Charles Ernest Gane and Margaret Gane; *m* 1974, Jennifer Anne Pitt; two *d* of former marriage. *Educ:* King Edward's School, Birmingham; Corpus Christi College, Cambridge. MA. Foreign Office, 1960; served Vientiane, Sarawak, Kuching and Warsaw; First Sec., Kampala, 1967; FCO, 1970; First Sec., later Counsellor, seconded to HQ British Forces, Hong Kong, 1977; Counsellor, FCO, 1982–92. *Recreations:* walking, reading. *Club:* Brooks's.

GANE, Michael, DPhil, MA; economic and environmental consultant; *b* 29 July 1927; *s* of late Rudolf E. Gane and Helen Gane; *m* 1954, Madge Stewart Taylor; one *d. Educ:* Colyton Grammar Sch., Devon; Edinburgh Univ. (BSc Forestry 1948); London Univ. (BSc Econ 1963); Oxford Univ. (DPhil, MA 1967). Asst Conservator of Forests, Tanganyika, 1948–62; Sen. Research Officer, Commonwealth Forestry Inst., Oxford, 1963–69; Dir, Project Planning Centre for Developing Countries, Bradford Univ., 1969–74; Dir, England, Nature Conservancy Council, 1974–81. *Publications:* various contribs to scientific and technical jls. *Recreations:* natural history, gardening. *Address:* Flat 6, Wentworth, 2 Crichel Mount Road, Lilliput, Poole, Dorset BH14 8LT.

GANELLIN, Charon Robin, PhD, DSc; FRS 1986; CChem, FRSC; Smith Kline and French Professor of Medicinal Chemistry, University College London, since 1986; *b* 25 Jan. 1934; *s* of Leon Ganellin and Beila Cluer; *m* 1956, Tamara Greene; one *s* one *d. Educ:* Harrow County Grammar School for Boys; Queen Mary Coll., London Univ. (BSc, PhD, DSc; Fellow, QMW, 1992). Res. Associate, MIT, 1960; Res. Chemist, then Dept Hd in Medicinal Chem., Smith Kline & French Labs Ltd, 1958–59, 1961–75; Smith Kline & French Research Ltd: Dir, Histamine Res., 1975–80; Vice-President: Research, 1980–84; Chem. Res., 1984–86. Hon. Lectr, Dept of Pharmacol., UCL, 1975–; Hon. Prof. of Medicinal Chem., Univ. of Kent at Canterbury, 1979–. Tilden Lectr and Medal, 1982, Adrien Albert Lectr and Medal, 1999, RSC. Chm., Soc. for Drug Res., 1985–87; Hon. Mem., Soc. Española de Quimica Terapeutica, 1982. Hon. DSc Aston, 1995. Medicinal Chem. Award, RSC, 1977; Prix Charles Mentzer, Soc. de Chimie Therap., 1978; Div. of Medicinal Chem. Award, ACS, 1980; Messel Medal, SCI, 1988; Award for Drug Discovery, Soc. for Drug Res., 1989; USA Nat. Inventors' Hall of Fame. 1990. *Publications:* Pharmacology of Histamine Receptors, 1982; Frontiers in Histamine Research, 1985; Dictionary of Drugs, 1990; (jtly) Medicinal Chemistry, 1993; Dictionary of Pharmacological Agents, 1997; res. papers and reviews in various jls, incl. Jl Med. Chem., Jl Chem. Soc., Brit. Jl Pharmacol. *Recreations:* music, sailing, walking. *Address:* Department of Chemistry, University College London, 20 Gordon Street, WC1H 0AJ.

GANI, Prof. David, DPhil; CChem, FRSC; FRSE; Professor of Chemistry, Birmingham University, since 1998; *b* 29 Sept. 1957; *m* Julie Margaret; four *d. Educ:* Sussex Univ. (BSc, DPhil). Southampton University: Royal Soc. Fellow, 1983–88; Lectr, then Sen. Lectr in Chemistry, 1988–90; Res. Co-ordinator, Inst. of Biomolecular Scis, 1987–90; Prof. of Chemistry, St Andrews Univ., 1990–98. Mem., Strategy Bd, BBSRC, 1997–. *Publications:* (jtly) Enzymic Catalysis, 1991; contrib. to learned jls. *Address:* School of Chemistry, Birmingham University, Edgbaston, Birmingham B15 2TT. *T:* (0121) 414 4361.

GANT, John; Director of Finance, Inland Revenue, since 2000; *b* 25 Feb. 1944; *s* of William and Barbara Gant; *m* 1967, Annette Sonia Cobb; two *s. Educ:* Univ. of Newcastle upon Tyne (BA Hons French and German). Inland Revenue: Inspector of Taxes, 1966; Dist Inspector, 1972–74; Head Office Adviser, 1974–77; Dist Inspector, 1977–81; Group Controller, 1981–83; Asst Dir, Ops, 1983–88; Regl Controller, 1988–90; Dep. Dir, Ops, 1990–92; Dir of Human Resources, 1992–2000. *Recreations:* music, theatre, travel, horse racing. *Address:* Inland Revenue, Somerset House, Strand, WC2R 1LB.

GANZ, Prof. Peter Felix; Professor of German, University of Oxford, 1972–85, now Emeritus; *b* 3 Nov. 1920; *s* of Dr Hermann and Dr Charlotte Ganz; *m* 1st, 1949, Rosemary (*née* Allen) (*d* 1986); two *s* two *d*; 2nd, 1987, Prof. Nicolette Mout, Univ. of Leiden. *Educ:* Realgymnasium, Mainz; King's Coll., London. MA 1950; PhD 1954; MA Oxon 1960. Army service, 1940–45. Asst Lectr, Royal Holloway Coll., London Univ., 1948–49; Lectr, Westfield Coll., London Univ., 1949–60; Reader in German, 1960–72; Fellow of Hertford Coll., Oxford Univ., 1963–72 (Hon. Fellow, 1977); Fellow of St Edmund Hall, 1972–85, now Emeritus Fellow; Resident Fellow, Herzog August Bibliothek, Wolfenbüttel, W Germany, 1985–88. Vis. Professor: Erlangen-Nürnberg Univ., 1964–65 and 1971 (Hon. Dr 1993); Munich Univ., 1970 and 1974. Comdr, Order of Merit, Germany, 1973. Jt Editor: Beiträge zur Geschichte der deutschen Sprache und Literatur, 1976–90; Oxford German Studies, 1978–90. *Publications:* Der Einfluss des Englischen auf den deutschen Wortschatz 1740–1815, 1957; Geistliche Dichtung des 12. Jahrhunderts, 1960; Graf Rudolf, 1964; (with F. Norman and W. Schwarz) Dukus Horant, 1964; (with W. Schröder) Probleme mittelalterlicher Überlieferung und Textkritik, 1967; Jacob Grimm's Conception of German Studies, 1973; Gottfried von Strassburgs 'Tristan', 1978; Jacob Burckhardt, Über das Studium der Geschichte, 1981; articles on German medieval literature and language in jls. *Recreations:* music, walking, travel. *Address:* Flat 2, 21 Bardwell Road, Oxford OX2 6SU; Oranje Nassaulaan 27, 2361 LB Warmond, Netherlands.

GANZONI, family name of **Baron Belstead**.

GAPES, Michael John; MP (Lab and Co-op) Ilford South, since 1992; *b* 4 Sept. 1952; *s* of Frank William Gapes and Emily Florence Gapes (*née* Jackson); *m* 1992, Frances Alison Smith. *Educ:* Staples Road Infants' Sch., Loughton; Manford County Primary Sch., Chigwell; Buckhurst Hill County High Sch., Essex; Fitzwilliam Coll., Cambridge (MA Hons Econs 1975); Middlesex Polytechnic (Dip. Indust. Relations and Trade Union Studies 1976). VSO teacher, Swaziland, 1971–72; Sec., Cambridge Students' Union, 1973–74; Chm., Nat. Orgn of Labour Students, 1976–77. Admin. Officer, Middlesex Hosp., 1977; Nat. Student Organiser, Lab. Party, 1977–80; Res. Officer, Internat. Dept, Lab. Party, 1980–88; Sen. Internat. Officer, Lab. Party, 1988–92. Contested (Lab) Ilford North, 1983. PPS to Minister of State: NI Office, 1997–99; Home Office, 2001–. Member: Foreign Affairs Select Cttee, 1992–97; Defence Select Cttee, 1999–; Chairman: PLP Children and Families' Cttee, 1994–95; UN All Party Parly Gp, 1997–; Vice Chairman: All Party Parly Gp against Anti-Semitism, 1992–; PLP Defence Cttee, 1992–95 and 1996–97. Dep. Chm., Labour Friends of Israel, 1997–. Member, Council: RIIA, 1996–99; VSO, 1997–. Vice Pres., Valentines Park Conservationists, 1998–. *Publications:* co-author of books on defence policy; Labour Party and Fabian Society pamphlets. *Recreations:* blues and jazz music, supporting West Ham United FC. *Address:* House of Commons, SW1A 0AA.

GARBUTT, Graham Bernard; Regional Director, Government Office for West Midlands, since 2001; *b* 16 June 1947; *s* of late Alfred Garbutt and of Rhoda Garbutt (*née* Jones); *m* 1986, Lyda Patricia Jadresic, MD; one *s* two *d. Educ:* Grove Sch., Market Drayton; Univ. of Bath (BSc 1970; BArch 1972); Univ. of Sheffield (MA Town and Regl Planning 1974). Urban Renewal Co-ordinator, Haringey BC, 1974–80; Policy and Prog. Planning Officer, Hackney BC, 1980–87; Dir, S Canning Town and Custom House Project, Newham BC, 1987–90; Chief Exec., Gloucester CC, 1990–2001. Occasional Consultant in town planning and housing policy, Nigeria, 1976 and 1977. Vis. Lectr, AA Grad. Sch., London, 1976–82. *Recreations:* family, visual arts, architecture, cycling, lawnmower maintenance. *Address:* Government Office for West Midlands, 77 Paradise Circus, Queensway, Birmingham B1 2DT. *T:* (0121) 212 5000; *e-mail:* rd@go-wm.gov.uk.

GARCIA, Arthur, CBE 1989; JP; Judge of the High Court, Hong Kong, 1979–89; Commissioner for Administrative Complaints, Hong Kong, 1989–94, retired; *b* 3 July 1924; *s* of late F. M. Garcia and of Maria Fung; *m* 1948, Hilda May; two *s. Educ:* La Salle Coll., Hong Kong; Inns of Court Sch. of Law. Called to the Bar, Middle Temple, 1957. Jun. Clerk, Hong Kong Govt, 1939–41; Staff Mem., British Consulate, Macao, 1942–45; Clerk to Attorney Gen., Hong Kong, 1946–47; Asst Registrar, 1951–54; Colonial Develt and Welfare Scholarship, Inns of Court Sch. of Law, 1954–57; Legal Asst, Hong Kong, 1957–59; Magistrate, 1959; Sen. Magistrate, 1968; Principal Magistrate, 1968; Dist Judge, 1971. Member: Preliminary Working Cttee, HKSAR, 1994–95; Preparatory Cttee, HKSAR, 1996–97. JP Hong Kong, 1991. *Recreations:* photography, swimming. *Address:* 15 Briar Avenue, Hong Kong. *Club:* Hong Kong Jockey (Hong Kong).

GARCÍA, Arturo; Peruvian Ambassador to the Court of St James's, 1992–95; *b* 3 May 1914; *s* of Arturo and Carmen García; *m* 1989, Rosa (*née* Peña). *Educ:* Universidad Mayor de San Marcos, Lima, Peru; Universidad Católica, Lima. Joined Foreign Service, 1939; served at Peruvian Representation to: French Cttee of Nat. Liberation, Algeria, 1944; France, 1944–48; USA, 1948–51; Cuba, 1949; Switzerland, 1951–54; Portugal, 1955–57; GB, 1957–61; France, 1961; USA, 1962–63; Ambassador: Ecuador, 1964–66; Canada, 1967–68; Chile, 1968–74; Italy and concurrently Greece, 1974–77; Ecuador, 1977–79; Minister of Foreign Affairs, Peru, 1979–80; Mem., Consultative Commn, Min. of Foreign Affairs, 1981–92. Pres., Peruvian Soc. of Internat. Law, 1986–88. Decorations from Peru, Chile, Ecuador, Spain, Italy, France and Venezuela. *Recreation:* golf. *Address:* c/o Embassy of Peru, 52 Sloane Street, SW1X 9SP. *T:* (020) 7235 4451. *Clubs:* Nacional, Lima Golf, Regatas, Ecuestre Huachipa (Peru).

GARCÍA MÁRQUEZ, Gabriel; *see* Márquez.

GARCÍA-PARRA, Jaime; Gran Cruz, Orden de San Carlos, Colombia, 1977; Gran Cruz de Boyacá, Colombia, 1981; President, J. García P. y Cía, Consultants, since 1993; *b* 19 Dec. 1931; *s* of Alfredo García-Cadena and Elvira Parra; *m* 1955, Lillian Duperly; three *s. Educ:* Gimnasio Moderno, Bogotá, Colombia; Univ. Javeriana, Bogotá; Univ. la Gran Colombia, Bogotá; Syracuse Univ., USA (MA); LSE, London (MSc). Lawyer. Minister (Colombian Delegn) to Internat. Coffee Org., 1963–66; Finance Vice-Pres., Colombian Nat. Airlines AVIANCA, 1966–69; Consultant in private practice, 1969–74; Actg Labour and Social Security Minister and Minister of Communications, 1974–75; Minister of Mines and Energy, 1975–77; Ambassador of Colombia to UK, 1977–78; Minister of Finance, Colombia, 1978–81; Exec. Dir, World Bank, 1981–82; Senator, Colombia, 1982; Pres. and Chief Exec. Officer, Acerías Paz del Río, steel and cement, 1982–90; Ambassador to USA, 1990–93. Mem., several delegns to UNCTAD and FAO Confs at Geneva, 1964, New Delhi, 1968, Rome, 1970, 1971. Hon. Fellow, LSE, 1980. Gran Cruz, Orden del Baron de Rio Branco, Brasil, 1977. *Publications: essays:* La Inflación y el Desarrollo de América Latina (Inflation and Development in Latin America), 1968; La Estrategia del Desarrollo Colombiano (The Strategy of Colombian Development), 1971; El Problema Inflacionario Colombiano (Colombia's Inflationary Problem), 1972; Petróleo un Problema y una Política (Oil—a Problem and a Policy), 1975; El Sector Eléctrico en la Encrucijada (The Electrical Sector at the Cross-Roads), 1975; Una Política para el Carbón (A Policy for Coal), 1976; La Cuestión Cafetera (The Coffee Dilemma), 1977; Política Agraria (Agrarian Policy), 1977. *Recreations:* walking, reading, poetry, tennis, cooking. *Address:* Apartado Aéreo 12025, Bogotá, Colombia. *Clubs:* Jockey, Country (Bogotá).

GARDAM, David Hill; QC 1968; *b* 14 Aug. 1922; *s* of late Harry H. Gardam, Hove, Sussex; *m* 1954, Jane Mary Gardam, *qv*; two *s* one *d. Educ:* Oundle Sch.; Christ Church, Oxford. MA 1948. War Service, RNVR, 1941–46 (Temp. Lieut). Called to the Bar, Inner Temple, 1949; Bencher 1977. *Recreations:* painting, etching, printing. *Address:* 1 Atkin Building, Gray's Inn, WC1R 5BQ. *T:* (020) 7404 0102; Haven House, Sandwich, Kent CT13 9ES. *Club:* Arts.

See also T. D. Gardam.

GARDAM, Jane Mary; novelist; *d* of William Pearson, Coatham Sch., Redcar and Kathleen Mary Pearson (*née* Helm); *m* 1954, David Hill Gardam, *qv*; two *s* one *d. Educ:* Saltburn High Sch. for Girls; Bedford Coll., London Univ. Red Cross Travelling Librarian, Hospital Libraries, 1951; Sub-Editor, Weldon's Ladies Jl, 1952; Asst Literary Editor, Time and Tide, 1952–54. FRSL 1976. *Publications:* A Long Way From Verona, 1971; The Summer After The Funeral, 1973; Bilgewater, 1977; God on the Rocks, 1978 (Prix Baudelaire, 1989; televised, 1992); The Hollow Land (Whitbread Literary Award), 1981; Bridget and William, 1981; Horse, 1982; Kit, 1983; Crusoe's Daughter, 1985; Kit in Boots, 1986; Swan, 1987; Through the Doll's House Door, 1987; The Queen of the Tambourine (Whitbread Novel Award), 1991; Faith Fox, 1996; Tufty Bear, 1996; The Green Man, 1998; The Flight of the Maidens, 2000; *non-fiction:* The Iron Coast, 1994; *short stories:* A Few Fair Days, 1971; Black Faces, White Faces (David Highams Award, Winifred Holtby Award), 1975; The Sidmouth Letters, 1980; The Pangs of Love, 1983 (Katherine Mansfield Award, 1984); Showing the Flag, 1989; Going into a Dark House, 1994; Missing the Midnight, 1997. *Recreation:* Swaledale. *Address:* Haven House, Sandwich, Kent CT13 9ES. *Clubs:* PEN, University Women's.

See also T. D. Gardam.

GARDAM, Timothy David; Director of Programmes, Channel Four, since 1998; *b* 14 Jan. 1956; *s* of David Hill Gardam, *qv* and Jane Mary Gardam, *qv*; *m* 1982, Kim Scott Walwyn; one *d. Educ:* Westminster Sch.; Gonville and Caius Coll., Cambridge (BA). Joined BBC as trainee researcher, 1977; Asst Producer, Nationwide, 1977–79; Producer, Newsnight, 1979–82; Executive Producer: Timewatch, 1982–85; Bookmark, 1984–85; Dep. Editor, Election Programmes, 1985–87; Editor: Panorama, 1987–90; Newsnight, 1990–93; Hd, Weekly Programmes, BBC News and Current Affairs, 1993–96; Controller, News, Current Affairs and Documentaries, Channel Five, 1996–98. *Recreations:* history, gardens. *Address:* Channel 4 Television, 124 Horseferry Road, SW1P 2TX.

GARDEN, Ian Harrison; barrister; Member, Crown Appointments Commission, since 1997; *b* 18 June 1961; *s* of late Norman Harrison Garden and of Jean Elizabeth Garden; *m*

1986, Alexandra Helen Grounds; two *s*. *Educ:* Sedbergh Sch.; UC Wales, Aberystwyth (LLB Hons 1982). Barrister in private practice, 1989–. Mem., Gen. Synod, C of E, 1995– (Member: Legislative Cttee, 1996–2000; Legal Adv. Commn, 2001–); Member: Bishop's Council and Standing Cttee, Dio. of Blackburn, 1996–; Archbishops' Council, 2000–; C of E Appts Cttee, 2001–. Dep. Chancellor, Dio. of Sheffield, 1999–. Member, Appeals Tribunal Panels, 1996–2001: Pastoral Measure (1983); Incumbents (Vacation of Benefices) Measure (1977); Ordination of Women (Financial Provisions) Measure (1993). Guardian, Shrine of Our Lady of Walsingham, 1996–. Gov., Quainton Hall Sch., Harrow, 1999–2001. *Recreations:* orchestral and choral conducting, organ playing, driving classic cars on the continent. *Address:* Old Church Cottage, 29 Church Road, Rufford, near Ormskirk, Lancs L40 1TA. *T:* (office) (0151) 709 4222; (home) (01704) 821303. *Clubs:* East India; Athenæum (Liverpool).

GARDEN, Prof. (Olivier) James, MD; FRCSE, FRCSGlas; Regius Professor of Clinical Surgery, University of Edinburgh, since 2000; *b* 13 Nov. 1953; *s* of James Garden and Marguerite Marie Jeanne Garden (*née* Vourch); *m* 1977, Amanda Gillian Merrills; one *s* one *d*. *Educ:* Lanark Grammar Sch.; Univ. of Edinburgh (BSc 1974; MB ChB 1977; MD 1988). FRCSGlas 1981; FRCSE 1994. Lectr in Surgery, Univ. of Glasgow, 1985; Chef de Clinique, Univ. de Paris-Sud, 1986–88; University of Edinburgh: Sen. Lectr in Surgery, 1988–98; Prof. of Hepatobiliary Surgery, 1998–2000; Head, Dept of Clin. and Surgical Scis, 1999–. Hon. Consultant Surgeon: Royal Infirmary of Edinburgh, 1988–; and Head, Scottish Liver Transplant Unit, 1992–. Ext. Examr, univs incl. Glasgow and Newcastle. Member: James IV Assoc. of Surgeons, 1996– (Hon. Sec., 1999–); Assoc. Upper Gastrointestinal Surgeons, 1996–; Internat. Hepato Pancreato Biliary Assoc., 1998–. *Publications:* Principles and Practice of Surgical Laparoscopy, 1994; Intraoperative and Laparoscopic Ultrasonography, 1995; Color Atlas of Surgical Diagnosis, 1995; A Companion to Specialist Surgical Practice (7 vols), 1997, 2nd edn 2000; Liver Metastasis: biology, diagnosis and treatment, 1998; Principles and Practice of Surgery, 2000; numerous contribs to surgical and gastroenterological jls. *Recreations:* ski-ing, golf. *Address:* 22 Moston Terrace, Edinburgh EH9 2DE. *T:* (0131) 667 3715.

GARDEN, Sir Timothy, KCB 1994 (CB 1992); Joint Editor in Chief, The Source, since 2000 (Defence Editor, 1998–99); *b* 23 April 1944; *s* of Joseph Garden and Winifred M. Garden (*née* Mayes); *m* 1965, Susan Elizabeth, *d* of Henry George Button, *qv*; two *d*. *Educ:* King's Sch., Worcester; St Catherine's Coll., Oxford (MA 1967; Hon. Fellow, 1994); Magdalene Coll., Cambridge (MPhil 1982). FRAeS 1994. Joined RAF 1963; Pilot, 3 Sqn, 1967–71; Flying Instructor, 1972–75; Army Staff Coll., 1976; PSO to Air Mem. for Personnel, 1977–79; OC 50 Sqn, 1979–81; Dir Defence Studies RAF, 1982–85; Station Comdr RAF Odiham, 1985–87; Asst Dir, Defence Programmes, 1987–88; Dir Air Force Staff Duties, 1988–90; ACAS, 1991–92; ACDS (Programmes), 1992–94; Air Marshal; Comdt, RCDS, 1994–95; retired 1996. Dir, RIIA, 1997–98. Vis. Prof., Centre for Defence Studies, KCL, 2000–. Dist. Citizen Fellow, Indiana Univ., 2001. Member of Advisory Board: NATO Defense Coll., Rome, 1996–, Internat. Studies Centre, Cambridge Univ., 1996–; Centre for Strategic Studies, Univ. of Hull, 1996–; Academic Study Gp on Israel and ME, 1996–; Königswinter Conf., 1997–; Lancaster and York Univ. Defence Research Inst., 1999–; Oxford Res. Gp, 2001–; Mem., DERA Analysis Bd, 1997–2000; Mem. Develt Council, St Catherine's Coll., Oxford, 1992–; Gov., King's Sch., Worcester, 1986–94. Dir, Asia Pacific Technol. Network, 1997–2000. Trustee, World Humanity Action Trust, 1996–2000. Member: RUSI, 1981– (Mem. Council, 1984–87; FRUSI 1996); IISS, 1982–; RIIA, 1994– (Associate Fellow, 2000–); Air League, 1997–; Council, RAeS, 1999–; Pugwash Conf., 1999–. Fellow, World Economic Forum, 1997–. Pres., CCF, 2000–. Hon. Vice Pres., RAF Rowing Assoc., 1996 (Pres., 1992–95); Hon. Pres., London and SE Reg. ATC, 1997–; Chm., RAF Oxford and Cambridge Soc., 1998–; Rippon Gp, 2000. Pres., Adastral Burns Club, 1999–. Liveryman, GAPAN, 1997 (Asst to Court), 1999–. *Publications:* Can Deterrence Last?, 1984; The Technology Trap: science and the military, 1989; contribs to books and jls on internat. relations. *Recreations:* writing, bridge, photography, computing. *Address:* Centre for Defence Studies, King's College London, Strand, WC2R 2LS. *T:* (020) 7848 2338, *Fax:* (020) 7209 0859; *e-mail:* tgarden@mac.com. *Clubs:* Beefsteak, National Liberal.

GARDINER, Barry Strachan; MP (Lab) Brent North, since 1997; *b* 10 March 1957; *s* of late John Flannegan Gardiner and Sylvia Jean Strachan; *m* 1979, Caroline Anne Smith; three *s* one *d*. *Educ:* Haileybury; St Andrews Univ. (MA Hons). Corpus Christi Coll., Cambridge. ACII. Scottish Sec., SCM, 1979–81. John F. Kennedy Schol., Harvard Univ., 1983; General Average Adjuster, 1987–97. *Publications:* articles in Philosophical Qly, Lloyd's List, Insurance Internat. *Recreations:* music, bird watching, hill walking. *Address:* 1 Chalfont Lane, Chorleywood, Rickmansworth, Herts WD3 5PR. *Club:* Royal Over-Seas League.

GARDINER, Duncan; *see* Gardiner, J. D. B.

GARDINER, Sir George (Arthur), Kt 1990; *b* 3 March 1935; *s* of Stanley and Emma Gardiner; *m* 1st, 1961, Juliet Wells (marr. diss. 1980); two *s* one *d*; 2nd, 1980, Helen Hackett. *Educ:* Harvey Grammar Sch., Folkestone; Balliol Coll., Oxford. 1st cl. hons PPE. Sec., Oxford Univ. Conservative Assoc., 1957. Chief Political Corresp., Thomson Regional Newspapers, 1964–74. Contested (C) Coventry South, 1970. MP (C) Reigate, Feb. 1974–1997; contested (Referendum) same seat, 1997. Member: Select Cttee on Home Affairs and its Sub-Cttee on Race Relations and Immigration, 1979–82; Exec., 1922 Cttee, 1987–93; Sec., Cons. European Affairs Cttee, 1976–79, Vice-Chm., 1979–80, Chm., 1980–87; Chm., 92 Gp, 1984–96; Vice-Chm., Cons. For. and Commonwealth Affairs Cttee, 1988–97. Mem. Council, Cons. Way Forward, 1991–97 (Editor, FORWARD, 1991–97). *Publications:* The Changing Life of London, 1973; Margaret Thatcher: from childhood to leadership, 1975; A Bastard's Tale, 1999. *Address:* 16 Acris Street, SW18 2QP.

GARDINER, Dame Helen (Louisa), DBE 1961 (CBE 1952); MVO 1937; *b* 24 April 1901; *y d* of late Henry Gardiner, Bristol. *Educ:* Clifton High School. Formerly in Private Secretary's Office, Buckingham Palace; Chief Clerk, 1946–61. *Recreations:* reading, gardening.

GARDINER, (John) Duncan (Broderick); author and broadcaster; Editor, Western Mail, 1974–81; *b* 12 Jan. 1937; *s* of late Frederick Keith Gardiner and Ruth Dixon; *m* 1965, Geraldine Mallen; one *s* one *d*. *Educ:* St Edward's School, Oxford. Various editorial positions in Sheffield, Newcastle, Sunday Times, London (1963–64, 1966–73) and Cardiff. *Recreations:* travel, all sport, wine and food, crosswords.

GARDINER, Sir John Eliot, Kt 1998; CBE 1990; conductor; Founder and Artistic Director, English Baroque Soloists, Monteverdi Choir, Monteverdi Orchestra, and Orchestre Révolutionnaire et Romantique; Chef fondateur, Opéra de Lyon Orchestra, since 1988 (Musical Director, 1983–88); residency at the Châtelet, Paris, since 1999; *b* 20 April 1943; *s* of Rolf Gardiner and late Marabel Gardiner (*née* Hodgkin); *m* 1981, Elizabeth Suzanne Wilcock (marr. diss. 1997); three *d*. *Educ:* Bryanston Sch.; King's Coll., Cambridge (MA History); King's Coll., London (Certif. of Advanced Studies in Music, 1966; Hon. FKC 1992). French Govt Scholarship to study in Paris and Fontainebleau with Nadia Boulanger, 1966–68. Founded: Monteverdi Choir, following performance of Monteverdi's Vespers of 1610, King's Coll. Chapel, Cambridge, 1964; Monteverdi Orchestra, 1968; English Baroque Soloists (period instruments), 1978; Orchestre Révolutionnaire et Romantique, 1990. Début: (concert), Wigmore Hall, 1966; (operatic), Sadler's Wells Opera, London Coliseum, 1969; Royal Opera House, Covent Garden, 1973; Royal Festival Hall, 1972; Glyndebourne, 1997; Guest engagements conducting major European orchestras in Paris, Brussels, Geneva, Frankfurt, Dresden, Leipzig, London and Vienna; US débuts: Dallas Symphony, 1981; San Francisco Symphony, 1982; Carnegie Hall, NY, 1988; Boston Symphony, 1991; Cleveland Orchestra 1992; European Music Festivals: Aix-en-Provence, Aldeburgh, Bath, Berlin, Edinburgh, Flanders, Holland, Salzburg, City of London, etc; concert revivals in London of major dramatic works of Purcell, Handel and Rameau; world première: (staged) of Rameau's opera Les Boréades, Aix-en-Provence, 1982; Berlioz, Messe Solenelle, Westminster Cath., 1993; Bach Cantata Pilgrimage, 1999–2001. Principal Conductor: CBC Vancouver Orchestra, 1980–83; NDR Symphony Orch., Hamburg, 1991–94. Artistic Director: Göttingen Handel Fest., 1981–90; Veneto Music Fest., 1986. Has made over 200 records ranging from Monteverdi and Mozart to Massenet, Rodrigo and Central American Percussion Music. Hon. FRAM 1992. DUniv Univ. Lumière Lyon, 1987. Grand Prix du Disque, 1978, 1979, 1980, 1992; Gramophone Awards for early music and choral music records, 1978, 1980, 1986, 1988, 1989, 1990, 1991 (Record of the Year), 1994 (Artist of the Year); Prix Caecilia, 1982, 1983, 1985; Edison Award, 1982, 1986, 1987, 1988, 1989, 1996, 1997; Internat. Record Critics Award, 1982, 1983; Deutscher Schallplattenpreis, 1986, 1994, 1997; Arturo Toscanini Music Critics Award, 1985, 1986; IRCA Prize, Helsinki, 1987; Best Choir of the Year for Monteverdi Choir, Internat. Classical Music Awards, 1992. Commandeur, Ordre des Arts et des Lettres (France), 1997 (Officier, 1988). *Publications:* (ed) Claude le Jeune Hélas! Mon Dieu, 1971; contrib. to opera handbook on Gluck's Orfeo, 1980. *Recreations:* forestry, organic farming. *Address:* c/o IMG Artists Europe, Media House, 3 Burlington Lane, W4 2TH. *T:* (020) 8233 5800, *Fax:* (020) 8233 5801.

GARDINER, Prof. John Graham, PhD; FIEE; FREng; Professor of Electronic Engineering, since 1986, and Dean of Engineering and Physical Sciences, since 1996, University of Bradford; *b* 24 May 1939; *s* of William Clement Gardiner and Ellen (*née* Adey); *m* 1962, Sheila Joyce Andrews; one *s* two *d*. *Educ:* Univ. of Birmingham (BSc 1st Cl. Hons; PhD 1964). FIEE 1988; FREng (FEng 1994). Software designer, Racal Res. Ltd, 1966–68; University of Bradford: Lectr, 1968–72; Sen Lectr, 1972–78; Reader, 1978–86; Hd, Dept of Electronic and Electrical Engrg, 1994–96. SMIEE 1995; FRSA 1997. *Publications:* (with J. D. Parsons) Mobile Communication Systems, 1989; (with B. West) Personal Communication Systems and Technologies, 1995. *Recreation:* music. *Address:* 1 Queen's Drive Lane, Ilkley, W Yorks LS29 9QS. *T:* (01943) 609581.

GARDINER, John Ralph; QC 1982; *b* 28 Feb. 1946; *s* of late Cyril Ralph Gardiner and of Mary Gardiner; *m* 1976, Pascal Mary Issard-Davies; one *d*. *Educ:* Bancroft's Sch., Woodford; Fitzwilliam Coll., Cambridge (BA (Law Tripos), MA, LLM). Called to the Bar, Middle Temple, 1968 (Harmsworth Entrance Scholar and Harmsworth Law Scholar; Bencher, 1992); practice at the Bar, 1970–; Mem., Senate of Inns of Court and Bar, 1982–86 (Treasurer, 1985–86); Chm., Taxation and Retirement Benefits Cttee, Bar Council, 1982–85. *Publications:* contributor to Pinson on Revenue Law, 6th to 15th (1982) edns. *Recreations:* tennis, cricket, squash. *Address:* 11 New Square, Lincoln's Inn, WC2A 3QB. *T:* (020) 7242 3981; Admiral's House, Admiral's Walk, Hampstead, NW3 6RS. *T:* (020) 7435 0597. *Club:* Cumberland Lawn Tennis.

GARDINER, Air Vice-Marshal Martyn John, OBE 1987; FRAeS; Military Advisor to High Representative for Bosnia and Herzegovina, since 2001; *b* 13 June 1946; *s* of late John Glen Gardiner and Edith Eleanor Gardiner (*née* Howley); *m* 1971, Anne Dunlop Thom; two *s* one *d*. *Educ:* Frimley and Camberley Grammar Sch.; Southampton Univ. (BScEng Aeronautics and Astronautics 1967). FRAeS 2000. Flying and staff appointments include: Coll. of Air Warfare, 1969–71; No 99 Sqdn, Brize Norton, 1971–75; Dept of Air Warfare, Gen. Duties Aero-Systems Course, 1976; No 72 Sqdn, Odiham, 1977–80; HQ 2 Armd Div., Germany, 1980–82; RAF Staff Coll., Bracknell, 1983; OC 32 Sqdn, RAF Northolt, 1984–87; HQ STC, 1987–88; Defence Policy and Commitments Staffs, MoD, 1988–91; OC RAF Northolt, 1991–93; SASO, HQ 38 Gp, 1994–96; COS Reaction Force Air Staff Kalkar, 1996–98; Dep. Comdr, Combined Air Ops Centre 4, Messstetten, 1998–2001. GAPAN 1994. *Recreations:* golf, ski-ing, walking, Rugby-watching. *Address:* 2 Yew Tree Road, Uxbridge, Middx UB10 0RN. *T:* (01895) 237183. *Club:* Royal Air Force.

GARDINER, Peter Dod Robin; First Deputy Head, Stanborough School, Hertfordshire, 1979–92, retired; *b* 23 Dec. 1927; *s* of late Brig. R. Gardiner, CB, CBE; *m* 1959, Juliet Wright; one *s* one *d*. *Educ:* Radley College; Trinity Coll., Cambridge. Asst Master, Charterhouse, 1952–67, and Housemaster, Charterhouse, 1965–67; Headmaster, St Peter's School, York, 1967–79. *Publications:* (ed) Twentieth-Century Travel, 1963; (with B. W. M. Young) Intelligent Reading, 1964; (with W. A. Gibson) The Design of Prose, 1971. *Recreations:* reading, music, walking, acting. *Address:* Willows, Stream Road, Upton, Didcot, Oxfordshire OX11 9JG.

GARDINER, Victor Alec, OBE 1977; consultant, film and television programme production, facilities and distribution; Director and General Manager, London Weekend Television, 1971–87; *b* 9 Aug. 1929; *m*; one *s* two *d*. *Educ:* Whitgift Middle Sch., Croydon; City and Guilds (radio and telecommunications). Techn. Asst, GPO Engrg, 1947–49; RAF Nat. Service, 1949–51; BBC Sound Radio Engr, 1951–53; BBC TV Cameraman, 1953–55; Rediffusion TV Sen. Cameraman, 1955–61; Malta TV Trng Man., 1961–62; Head of Studio Prodn, Rediffusion TV, 1962–67; Man. Dir, GPA Productions, 1967–69; Production Controller, London Weekend Television, 1969–71; Director: LWT (Hldgs) Ltd, 1976–87; London Weekend Services Ltd, 1976–87; Richard Price Television Associates, 1981–87; Chairman: Dynamic Technology Ltd, 1972–87; Standard Music Ltd, 1972–87; LWT Internat., 1981–87. Mem., Royal Television Soc., 1970– (Vice-Chm. Council, 1974–75; Chm. Papers Cttee, 1975; Chm. Council, 1976–77; Fellow, 1977). *Recreations:* music, building, gardening.

GARDNER, family name of **Baroness Gardner of Parkes**.

GARDNER OF PARKES, Baroness *cr* 1981 (Life Peer), of Southgate, Greater London, and of Parkes, NSW; **(Rachel) Trixie (Anne) Gardner;** JP; dental surgeon; Chairman, Plan International (UK) Ltd, since 1990; *b* Parkes, NSW, 17 July 1927; eighth *c* of late Hon. J. J. Gregory McGirr and late Rachel McGirr, OBE, LC; *m* 1956, Kevin Anthony Gardner, *o s* of late George and Rita Gardner, Sydney, Australia; three *d*. *Educ:* Monte Sant Angelo Coll., N Sydney; East Sydney Technical Coll.; Univ. of Sydney (BDS 1954). Cordon Bleu de Paris, Diplôme 1956. Came to UK, 1955. Member: Westminster City Council, 1968–78 (Lady Mayoress, 1987–88); GLC, for Havering, 1970–73, for Enfield-Southgate, 1977–86. Contested (C) Blackburn, 1970; N Cornwall, Feb. 1974. House of Lords: a Dep. Speaker, 1999–; Dep. Chm. of Cttees, 1999–. Chm., Royal Free Hampstead

NHS Trust, 1994–97; Vice-Chm., NE Thames RHA, 1990–94; Member: Inner London Exec. Council, NHS, 1966–71; Standing Dental Adv. Cttee for England and Wales, 1968–76; Westminster, Kensington and Chelsea Area Health Authority, 1974–82; Industrial Tribunal Panel for London, 1974–97; N Thames Gas Consumer Council, 1980–82; Dept of Employment's Adv. Cttee on Women's Employment, 1980–88; Britain–Australia Bicentennial Cttee, 1984–88; London Electricity Bd, 1984–90. British Chm., European Union of Women, 1978–82; UK Rep., UN Status of Women Commn, 1982–88. Director: Gateway Building Soc., 1987–88; Woolwich Building Soc., 1988–93. Chm., Suzy Lamplugh Trust, 1993–97. Governor: Eastman Dental Hosp., 1971–80; Nat. Heart Hosp., 1974–90. Hon. Pres., War Widows Assoc. of GB, 1984–87. JP North Westminster, 1971. DUniv Middlesex, 1997. *Recreations:* gardening, reading, travel, needlework. *Address:* House of Lords, SW1A 0PW.

GARDNER, Antony John; Registrar, Central Council for Education and Training in Social Work, 1988–92 (Principal Registration Officer, 1970–88), retired; *b* 27 Dec. 1927; *s* of David Gardner, head gardener, and Lillian Gardner; *m* 1956, Eveline A. Burden. *Educ:* Elem. school; Co-operative Coll.; Southampton Univ. Pres. Union, Southampton, 1958–59; BSc (Econ) 1959. Apprentice toolmaker, 1941–45; National Service, RASC, 1946–48; building trade, 1948–53. Tutor Organiser, Co-operative Union, 1959–60; Member and Education Officer, Co-operative Union, 1961–66. Contested (Lab): SW Wolverhampton, 1964; Beeston, Feb. and Oct. 1974; MP (Lab) Rushcliffe, 1966–70. Contested (Lab) Dorset and E Devon, Eur. Parly elecns, 1994. *Recreations:* angling, gardening and the countryside generally. *Address:* 118 Ringwood Road, Parkstone, Poole, Dorset BH14 0RW. *T:* (01202) 676683. *Club:* Parkstone Trades and Labour (Poole).

GARDNER, Brigid Catherine Brennan; Principal, St George's British International (formerly English) School, Rome, since 1994; *b* 5 May 1941; *d* of John Henthorn Cantrell Brennan and Rosamond Harriet Brennan (*née* Gardner); *m* 1963, Michael Henry Davies (marr. diss. 1980); three *d. Educ:* The Alice Ottley Sch., Worcester; Girton Coll., Cambridge (MA). English and History teacher, Harrogate High Sch., 1963–66; English teacher, Hong Kong, 1967–69; James Allen's Girls' School: Head of History, 1976–83; Dep. Head, 1981–83; Headmistress, 1984–94. Governor: Oundle Sch., 1992–94; Whitgift Foundn, 1992–94. *Recreations:* gardening, travelling, walking, reading, sailing. *Address:* St George's British International School, Via Cassia, La Storta, 00123 Roma, Italy.

GARDNER, Christopher James Ellis; QC 1994; a Recorder, since 1993; *b* 6 April 1945; *s* of James Charles Gardner and Phillis May Gardner (*née* Wilkinson); *m* 1972, Arlene Sellers; one *s* one *d. Educ:* Rossall Sch., Lancs; Fitzwilliam Coll., Cambridge (MA). Called to the Bar, Gray's Inn, 1968. FCIArb 1999; Accredited Mediator, 2000. Legal Assessor, GMC and GDC, 1992–. International Bar Association: Vice Chm., Negligence and Damages Cttee, 1999–; Sec., Barristers and Advocates Forum, 1998–. Fellow, Soc. for Advanced Legal Studies, 1999; FRSocMed 2000. *Recreations:* theatre, ballet, bell ringing, golf, cooking curries. *Address:* Lamb Chambers, Lamb Building, Temple, EC4Y 7AS. *T:* (020) 7797 8300. *Club:* Dartmouth Yacht.

GARDNER, Prof. David Pierpont, PhD; President, The William and Flora Hewlett Foundation, 1993–99; President, University of California, 1983–92; Professor of Education, University of California at Berkeley, 1983–92; *b* 24 March 1933; *s* of Reed S. Gardner and Margaret (*née* Pierpont); *m* 1958, Elizabeth Fuhriman (*d* 1991); four *d. Educ:* Brigham Young Univ. (BS 1955); Univ. of Calif, Berkeley (MA 1959, PhD 1966). Dir, Calif Alumni Foundn and Calif Alumni Assoc., Univ. of Calif, Berkeley, 1962–64. University of California, Santa Barbara: Asst Prof. of Higher Educn, 1964–69; Associate Prof. of Higher Educn, 1969–70; Prof. of Higher Educn (on leave), 1971–73; Asst to the Chancellor, 1964–67; Asst Chancellor, 1967–69; Vice Chancellor and Exec. Asst, 1969–70; Vice Pres., Univ. of Calif, 1971–73; Pres., and Prof. of Higher Educn, Univ. of Utah, 1973–83, Pres. Emeritus, 1985. Vis. Fellow, Clare Hall, Univ. of Cambridge, 1979 (Life Mem. 1979). Member: Nat. Acad. of Public Administration; Council, Amer. Philosophical Soc.; Nat. Acad. of Educn. Board of Directors: First Security Corp.; Fluor Corp.; Chm., J. Paul Getty Trust. Trustee, Tanner Lectures on Human Values. Fulbright 40th Anniversary Distinguished Fellow, Japan, 1986; Fellow, Amer. Acad. of Arts and Scis, 1986. Hon. LLD: Univ. of The Pacific, 1983; Nevada, Las Vegas, 1984; Westminster Coll., 1987; Brown, 1989; Notre Dame, 1989; Hon. DH Brigham Young, 1981; Hon. DLitt Utah, 1983; Hon. HHD Utah State, 1987; Hon. Dr Bordeaux II, 1988; Hon. DHL Internat. Christian Univ. Benjamin P. Cheney Medal, Eastern Washington Univ., 1984; James Bryant Conant Award, Educn Commn of the States, 1985; Hall of Fame Award, Calif. Sch. Bd Res Foundn, 1988. Chevalier, Légion d'Honneur (France), 1985; Knight Commander, Order of Merit (Germany), 1992. *Publications:* The California Oath Controversy, 1967; contrib. articles to professional jls. *Address:* (office) Center for Studies in Higher Education, South Hall Annex, University of California, Berkeley, CA 94720, USA.

GARDNER, Douglas Frank; Chairman, Nuffield Hospitals, since 2001; *b* 20 Dec. 1943; *s* of late Ernest Frank Gardner and Mary Gardner; *m* 1978, Adèle (*née* Alexander); one *s* two *d. Educ:* Woolverstone Hall; College of Estate Management, London Univ. (BSc). FRICS. Chief Exec., Properties Div., Tarmac plc, 1976–83; Man. Dir, 1983–93, Chm., 1993–2000, Brixton Estate plc. Gov., Nuffield Nursing Homes Trust, 1996–. *Recreations:* tennis, theatre. *Address:* 20 Cottesmore Gardens, Kensington, W8 5PR. *T:* (020) 7937 7127.

GARDNER, Rear-Adm. Herbert, CB 1976; Chartered Engineer; *b* 23 Oct. 1921; *s* of Herbert and Constance Gladys Gardner; *m* 1946, Catherine Mary Roe, Perth, WA. *Educ:* Taunton Sch.; Weymouth Coll. War of 1939–45; joined Dartmouth, 1940; RN Engineering Coll., Keyham, 1940; HMS Nigeria, Cumberland, Adamant, and 4th Submarine Sqdn, 1944; HM S/M Totem, 1945. Dept of Engr-in-Chief, 1947; HM S/M Telemachus, 1949; Admty Develt Establishment, Barrow-in-Furness, 1952; HMS Eagle, 1954; Comdr, 1956; HMS Caledonia, 1956; HMS Blackpool, 1958; Asst to Manager Engrg Dept, Rosyth Dockyard, 1960; HMS Maidstone, 1963; Capt., 1963; Dep. Manager, Engrg Dept, Devonport Dockyard, 1964; Chief Engr and Production Manager, Singapore Dockyard, 1967; Chief Staff Officer (Technical) to Comdr Far East Fleet, 1968; course at Imperial Defence Coll., 1970; Chief of Staff to C-in-C Naval Home Comd, 1971–73; Vice Pres., Ordnance Bd, 1974–76, Pres., 1976–77. *Recreations:* sailing, golf. *Address:* 41 Mayfair Street, Mount Claremont, Perth, WA 6010, Australia. *Club:* Royal Freshwater Bay Yacht (Perth).

GARDNER, James Jesse, CVO 1995; CBE 1986; DL; consultant, since 1986; Chairman, OFWAT National Consumer Council, 1993–98; *b* 7 April 1932; *s* of James and Elizabeth Rubina Gardner; *m* 1955, Diana Sotheran; three *s* one *d. Educ:* Kirkham Grammar Sch.; Victoria Univ., Manchester (LLB). Nat. Service, 1955–57. Articled to Town Clerk, Preston, 1952–55; Legal Asst, Preston Co. Borough Council, 1955; Crosby Borough Council: Asst Solicitor, 1957–59; Chief Asst Solicitor, 1959–61; Chief Asst Solicitor, Warrington Co. Borough Council, 1961–65; Stockton-on-Tees Borough Council: Dep. Town Clerk, 1966; Town Clerk, 1966–68; Asst Town Clerk, Teesside Co. Borough Council, 1968; Associate Town Clerk and Solicitor, London Borough of Greenwich, 1968–69; Town Clerk and Chief Exec. Officer, Co. Borough of Sunderland, 1970–73; Chief Exec., Tyne and Wear CC, 1973–86; Chm., Tyne and Wear PTE, 1983–86. Chief Exec., Northern Develt Co. Ltd, 1986–87; Chairman: Sunderland DHA, 1988–90; Northumbrian Water Customer Services Cttee, 1990–2001; North East Television, 1991–92; Dir, Birtley Enterprise Action Management (BEAM) Ltd, 1989–93; Sec., Northern Region Councils Assoc., 1986. Clerk to Lieutenancy, Tyne and Wear, 1974–91. Dir, Garrod Pitkin (1986) Ltd, 1991–93. Chairman: Prince's Trust Trustees, 1986–94; Prince's Trust and Royal Jubilee Trust Management Bd, 1989–93 (former Chm., Northumbria Cttee, Royal Jubilee and Prince's Trusts); Prince's Trust Events Ltd, 1987–94; Director: Threshold (formerly Prince's Trust Training & Employment Ltd), 1991–95 (Chm., 1992); NE Civic Trust, 1986–92. Chairman: Century Radio, 1993–2000; St Benedict's Hospice, Sunderland, 1993–; Trustee: Tyne Tees Telethon Trust, 1988–91; Great North Air Ambulance Service Appeal, 1991–95. DL Tyne and Wear, 1976. FRSA 1976; CIMgt 1987. Hon. Fellow, Sunderland Polytechnic, 1986. *Recreations:* golf, music, theatre, food and drink. *Address:* Wayside, 121 Queen Alexandra Road, Sunderland, Tyne and Wear SR2 9HR.

GARDNER, (James) Piers; barrister; *b* 26 March 1954; *s* of Michael Clement Gardner and Brigitte Elsa Gardner (*née* Ekrut); *m* 1978, Penelope Helen Chloros; three *s* one *d. Educ:* Bryanston Sch.; Brasenose Coll., Oxford (MA Jurisp. 1st Class). Solicitor of the Supreme Court, 1979–2000; called to the Bar, 2000. Articled and in private practice as solicitor, with Stephenson Harwood, London, 1977–80; Secretariat, European Commn of Human Rights, Council of Europe, Strasbourg, 1980–87; Exec. Dir, 1987–89, Dir, 1989–2000, British Inst. of Internat. and Comparative Law. *Recreations:* foreign property, arguing. *Address:* Monckton Chambers, Gray's Inn, WC1R 5BP. *T:* (020) 7405 7211. *Club:* Athenæum.

GARDNER, Prof. John; DPhil; Professor of Jurisprudence, University of Oxford, since 2000; Fellow, University College, Oxford, since 2000; *b* 23 March 1965; partner, Margaret Bolton. *Educ:* New Coll., Oxford (BA 1986; Vinerian Schol.; BCL 1987); Inns of Court Sch. of Law; All Souls Coll., Oxford (DPhil 1993). Called to the Bar, Inner Temple, 1988; Fellow, All Souls Coll., Oxford, 1986–91; Fellow and Tutor, Brasenose Coll., Oxford, 1991–96; Reader in Legal Philosophy, KCL, 1996–2000; Fellow, All Souls Coll., Oxford, 1998–2000. Vis. Prof., Columbia Univ. Sch. of Law, NY, 2000. *Publications:* Action and Value in Criminal Law, 1993; contrib. jls incl. Oxford Jl Legal Studies, Cambridge Law Jl, Univ. of Toronto Law Jl. *Recreation:* cooking. *Address:* University College, Oxford OX1 4BH. *T:* (01865) 276638.

GARDNER, John Linton, CBE 1976; composer; *b* 2 March 1917; *s* of late Dr Alfred Gardner, Ilfracombe, and Muriel (*née* Pullein-Thompson); *m* 1955, Jane (*d* 1998), *d* of late N. J. Abercrombie; one *s* two *d. Educ:* Eagle House, Sandhurst; Wellington Coll.; Exeter Coll., Oxford (BMus). Served War of 1939–45: RAF, 1940–46. Chief Music Master, Repton Sch., 1939–40. Staff, Covent Garden Opera, 1946–52; Tutor: Morley Coll., 1952–76 (Dir of Music, 1965–69); Bagot Stack Coll., 1955–62; London Univ. (extra-mural) 1959–60; Dir of Music, St Paul's Girls' Sch., 1962–75; Prof. of Harmony and Composition, Royal Acad. of Music, 1956–86. Conductor: Haslemere Musical Soc., 1953–62; Dorian Singers, 1961–62; European Summer Sch. for Young Musicians, 1966–75; Bromley YSO, 1970–76. Brit. Council Lecturer: Levant, 1954; Belgium, 1960; Iberia, 1963; Yugoslavia, 1967. Adjudicator, Canadian Festivals, 1974, 1980. Chm., Composer's Guild, 1963; Member: Arts Council Music Panel, 1958–62; Cttee of Management, Royal Philharmonic Soc., 1965–72; Brit. Council Music Cttee, 1968. Dir, Performing Right Soc., 1965–92 (Dep. Chm., 1983–88). Worshipful Co. of Musicians: Collard Fellow, 1962–64; elected to Freedom and Livery, 1965. Hon. RAM 1959; Hon. Mem., Royal Philharmonic Soc., 1998. Bax Society's Prize, 1958. *Works include: orchestral:* Symphony no 1, 1947; Variations on a Waltz of Carl Nielsen, 1952; Piano Concerto no 1, 1957; Sinfonia Piccola (strings), 1960; Occasional Suite, Aldeburgh Festival, 1968; An English Ballad, 1969; Three Ridings, 1970; Sonatina for Strings, 1974; Divertimento, 1977; Symphony no 2, 1984; Symphony no 3, 1989; Concerto for Oboe and Strings, 1990; Concerto for Flute and Strings, 1995; Irish Suite, 1996; *chamber:* Concerto da Camera (4 insts), 1968; Partita (solo 'cello), 1968; Chamber Concerto (organ and 11 insts), 1969; English Suite (harpsichord), 1971; Sonata Secolare for organ and brass, 1973; Sonata da Chiesa for two trumpets and organ, 1976; String Quartet no 2, 1979; Hebdomade, 1980; Sonatina Lirica for brass, 1983; Triad, 1984; Quartet for Saxes, 1985; Oboe Sonata no 2, French Suite for Sax. 4tet, 1986; String Quartet no 3, 1987; Octad, 1987; Piano Sonata no 3, 1988; Larkin Songs, 1990; Organ Sonata, 1992; Sextet for piano and wind, 1995; Easter Fantasy for organ and brass, 1997; *ballet:* Reflection, 1952; *opera:* A Nativity Opera, 1950; The Moon and Sixpence, 1957; The Visitors, 1972; Bel and the Dragon, 1973; The Entertainment of the Senses, 1974; Tobermory, 1976; *musical:* Vile Bodies, 1961; *choral:* Cantiones Sacrae 1973; (sop., chor. and orch.), 1952; Jubilate Deo (unacc. chor.), 1957; The Ballad of the White Horse (bar., chor. and orch.), 1959; Herrick Cantata (ten. solo, chor. and orch.), 1961; A Latter-Day Athenian Speaks, 1962; The Noble Heart (sop., bass, chor, and orch.), Shakespeare Quatercentenary Festival, 1964; Cantor popularis vocis, 18th Schütz Festival Berlin, 1964; Mass in C (unacc. chor.), 1965; Cantata for Christmas (chor. and chamb. orch.), 1966; Proverbs of Hell (unacc. chor.), 1967; Cantata for Easter (soli, chor., organ and percussion), 1970; Open Air (chor. and brass band), 1976; Te Deum for Pigotts, 1981; Mass in D, 1983; Cantata for St Cecilia, 1991; Stabat Mater (sop., chor., organ and timpani), A Burns Sequence (chor. and orch.), 1993; Seven Last Words, 1996; many smaller pieces and music for films, Old Vic and Royal Shakespeare Theatres, BBC. *Publications:* Robert Schumann, the man and his music, 1972; The Musical Companion, 1978; contributor to: Dublin Review, Musical Times, Tempo, Composer, Listener, Music in Education, DNB. *Recreations:* jazz, bore-watching. *Address:* 20 Firswood Avenue, Epsom, Surrey KT19 0PR. *T:* (020) 8393 7181.

GARDNER, Prof. John William; Consulting Professor, School of Education, Stanford University, since 1996; *b* 8 Oct. 1912; *s* of William Frederick and Marie (Flora) Gardner; *m* 1934, Aida Marroquin; two *d. Educ:* Stanford Univ. (AB 1935, AM 1936); Univ. of Calif. (PhD 1938). 1st Lt-Captain, US Marine Corps, 1943–46. Teaching Asst in Psychology, Univ. of Calif., 1936–38; Instructor in Psychology, Connecticut Coll., 1938–40; Asst Prof. in Psychology, Mt Holyoke Coll., 1940–42; Head of Latin Amer. Section, Federal Communications Commn, 1942–43. Carnegie Corporation of New York: Staff Mem., 1946–47; Exec. Associate, 1947–49; Vice-Pres., 1949–55; Pres., 1955–67; Pres., Carnegie Foundn for Advancement of Teaching, 1955–67; Sec. of Health, Education and Welfare, 1965–68; Chairman: Urban Coalition, 1968–70; Common Cause, 1970–77; Independent Sector, 1980–83; US Adv. Commn on Internat. Educational and Cultural Affairs, 1962–64; Pres. Johnson's Task Force on Educn, 1964; White House Conf. on Educn, 1965; President's Commn on White House Fellowships, 1977–81. Senior Fellow, Aspen Inst., 1981–; Miriam and Peter Haas Prof. in Public Service, Stanford Univ., 1989–96. Dir, Amer. Assoc. for Advancement of Science, 1963–65. Director: New York Telephone Co., 1962–65; Shell Oil Co., 1962–65; Time Inc., 1968–71; American Airlines, 1968–71; Rockefeller Brothers Fund, 1968–77; New York Foundn, 1970–76. Trustee: Metropolitan Museum of Art, 1957–65; Stanford Univ., 1968–82; Chm., Nat. Civic League, 1994–96. Benjamin Franklin Fellow, RSA, 1964.

Holds hon. degrees from various colleges and univs. USAF Exceptional Service Award, 1956; Presidential Medal of Freedom, 1964; Public Welfare Medal, Nat. Acad. of Science, 1967. *Publications:* Excellence, 1961, rev. edn 1984; (ed) Pres. John F. Kennedy's book, To Turn the Tide, 1961; Self-Renewal, 1964, rev. edn 1980; No Easy Victories, 1968; The Recovery of Confidence, 1970; In Common Cause, 1972; Know or Listen to Those who Know, 1975; Morale, 1978; Quotations of Wit and Wisdom, 1980; On Leadership, 1990. *Address:* 836 Lathrop Drive, Stanford, CA 94305, USA.

GARDNER, Norman Keith Ayliffe; *b* 2 July 1925; *s* of late Charles Ayliffe Gardner and Winifred Gardner; *m* 1951, Margaret Patricia Vinson; one *s* one *d*. *Educ:* Cardiff High Sch.; University Coll., Cardiff (BScEng); College of Aeronautics, Cranfield; Univ. of London Commerce Degree Bureau (BScEcon Hons). CEng. Flight Test Observer, RAE, 1944; Test Engr, Westland Aircraft Ltd, 1946; Development Engr, Handley Page Ltd, 1950; Engr, Min. of Aviation, 1964; Economic Adviser, Min. of Technology, 1970; Asst Dir (Engrg), DTI, 1973; Sen. Economic Adviser, 1974, Under Secretary: DoI, 1977; Dept of Employment, 1979; DTI, 1984–85. *Publications:* Decade of Discontent: the changing British economy, 1987; A Guide to United Kingdom and European Community Competition Policy, 1990, 2nd edn as A Guide to United Kingdom and European Union Competition Policy, 1996, 3rd edn 2000; The Economics of Launching Aid, in The Economics of Industrial Subsidies (HMSO), 1976; papers in Jl Instn Prodn Engrs and other engrg jls. *Recreation:* music. *Address:* 15 Chanctonbury Way, N12 7JB. *T:* (020) 8922 0847.

GARDNER, Philip John, VC 1941; MC 1941; Chairman, J. Gardner Holdings Ltd, 1955–99; *b* 25 Dec. 1914; *s* of Stanley John Gardner and Mable (*née* Puttick); *m* 1939, Renee Sherburn; one *s*. *Educ:* Dulwich Coll. Westminster Dragoons, TA, 1938–39; served 4th RTR, N Africa, 1939–42, when captured at Tobruk. Dir, J. Gardner Hldgs Ltd, 1946.

GARDNER, Piers; *see* Gardner, J. P.

GARDNER, Prof. Richard Lavenham, PhD; FRS 1979; Royal Society Henry Dale Research Professor, since 1978; Student of Christ Church, Oxford, since 1974; *b* 10 June 1943; *s* of late Allan Constant and Eileen May Gardner; *m* 1968, Wendy Joy Cresswell; one *s*. *Educ:* St John's Sch., Leatherhead; North East Surrey Coll. of Technology; St Catharine's Coll., Cambridge (BA 1st Cl. Hons Physiol., 1966; MA; PhD 1971). Res. Asst, Physiological Lab., Cambridge, 1970–73; Lectr in Developmental and Reproductive Biology, Dept of Zoology, Oxford Univ., 1973–77; Res. Student, Christ Church, Oxford, 1974–77; Hon. Dir, ICRF Develtl Biol. Unit, 1986–96. Indep. Mem., ABRC, 1990–93. Scientific Medal, Zoological Soc. of London, 1977; March of Dimes Prize in Develtl Biology, 1999. *Publications:* contribs to Jl of Embryology and Experimental Morphology, Nature, Jl of Cell Science, and various other jls and symposia. *Recreations:* ornithology, music, sailing, painting, gardening. *Address:* Christ Church, Oxford OX1 1DP.

GARDNER, Dr Rita Ann Moden; Director and Secretary, Royal Geographical Society (with the Institute of British Geographers), since 1996; *b* 10 Nov. 1955; *d* of John William Gardner and Evelyn Gardner (*née* Moden); partner, 1982, Dr Martin Eugene Frost. *Educ:* Huntingdon Grammar Sch.; Hinchingbrooke Sch.; University Coll. London (BSc 1st cl. Hons Geog.); Wolfson Coll., Oxford (DPhil 1981). Lectr in Physical Geog., St Catherine's Coll., Oxford, 1978–79; Lectr in Geog., KCL, 1979–94; Dir, Envmtl Sci. Unit and Reader in Envmtl Sci., QMW, 1994–96. Ed., Geographical Jl, 1989–93. Hon. Sec., RGS, 1991–96. Busk Medal, RGS, 1995. *Publications:* Landscape in England and Wales, 1981, 2nd edn 1994; Mega-geomorphology, 1981; Land Shapes, 1986; numerous academic papers in learned jls specialising in geomorphology, physical geog., sedimentology and Quaternary envmtl change. *Recreations:* restoration of historic vernacular buildings, contemporary architecture and furniture, gardening, horse riding, good food and wine. *Address:* Royal Geographical Society (with IBG), 1 Kensington Gore, SW7 2AR. *T:* (020) 7591 3010; *e-mail:* R.Gardner@rgs.org.

GARDNER, Sir Robert Henry B.; *see* Bruce-Gardner.

GARDNER, Roy Alan, FCCA; FRAeS; Chief Executive, Centrica plc, since 1997; *b* 20 Aug. 1945; *s* of Roy Thomas Gardner and Iris Joan Gardner; *m* 1969, Carol Ann Barker; one *s* two *d*. *Educ:* Strode's Sch., Egham. FCCA 1980; FRAeS 1992. Works Acct, later Concorde Project Acct, BAC Ltd, 1963–75; Chief Acct, Asst Finance Dir, then Finance Dir, Marconi Space & Defence Systems, 1975–84; Finance Dir, Marconi Co. Ltd, 1984–85; STC plc: Finance Dir, 1986–89; Dir, 1986–91; Man. Dir, STC Communications Ltd, 1989–91; Chief Operating Officer, Northern Telecom Europe Ltd, 1991–92; Man. Dir, GEC-Marconi Ltd, 1992–94; Dir, GEC plc, 1994; Exec. Dir, British Gas plc, 1994–97. Non-exec. Dir, 1999–, Chm., March 2002–, Manchester United plc; non-exec. Dir, Laporte plc, 1997–2001. Chm., Employers' Forum on Disability, 2000–. Mem., Council for Ind. and Higher Educn, 1996–99. Mem. Council, RUSI, 1992–96. Pres., Carers Nat. Assoc., 1998–. CIMgt. FRSA 1995. *Recreations:* golf, running. *Address:* c/o Centrica plc, Charter Court, 50 Windsor Road, Slough, Berks SL1 2HA. *Clubs:* Brooks's, Annabel's, Mark's.

GARDOM, Hon. Garde Basil; QC (Canada) 1975; Lieutenant-Governor of British Columbia, since 1995; *b* 17 July 1924; *s* of Basil Gardom and Gabrielle Gwladys (*née* Bell); *m* 1956, Theresa Helen Eileen Mackenzie; one *s* four *d*. *Educ:* Univ. of British Columbia (BA, LLB). Called to Bar of British Columbia, 1949; elected to BC Legislature as Mem. for Vancouver-Point Grey, 1966; re-elected, 1969, 1972, 1975, 1979, 1983; Govt House Leader, 1977–86; Attorney Gen. of BC, 1975–79; Minister of Intergovtl Relns, 1979–86; Chairman: Constitution Cttee, 1975–86; Legislation Cttee, 1975–86; Mem., Treasury Bd and Planning and Priorities Cttee, 1983–86; Minister responsible, Official Visits to Expo '86; Policy Cons., Office of the Premier, 1986–87; Agent General for BC in the UK and Europe, 1987–92; Dir, Crown Life Insurance Co., 1993–95. Member: Canadian Bar Assoc., 1949–; Vancouver Bar Assoc., 1949–; British Columbia Sports Hall of Fame; Phi Delta Theta Fraternity, 1943. Hon. Col, BC Regt (Duke of Connaught's Own). KStJ. *Recreation:* fishing. *Address:* 2122 SW Marine Drive, Vancouver, BC V6P 6B5, Canada. *Clubs:* Royal Over-Seas League; Union Club of BC, Vancouver Lawn Tennis and Badminton (British Columbia).

GAREL-JONES, family name of **Baron Garel-Jones**.

GAREL-JONES, Baron *cr* 1997 (Life Peer), of Watford in the co. of Hertfordshire; **William Armand Thomas Tristan Garel-Jones;** PC 1992; Managing Director, UBS Warburg (formerly Warburg Dillon Read), since 1999; *b* 28 Feb. 1941; *s* of Bernard Garel-Jones and Meriel Garel-Jones (*née* Williams); *m* 1966, Catalina (*née* Garrigues); four *s* one *d*. *Educ:* The King's Sch., Canterbury. Principal, Language Sch., Madrid, Spain, 1960–70; Merchant Banker, 1970–74; worked for Cons. Party, 1974–79 (Personal Asst to Party Chm., 1978–79). Contested (C): Caernarvon, Feb. 1974; Watford, Oct. 1974. MP (C) Watford, 1979–97. PPS to Minister of State, CSD, 1981; Asst Govt Whip, 1982–83; a Lord Comr of HM Treasury, 1983–86; Vice-Chamberlain of HM Household, 1986–88; Comptroller of HM Household, 1988–89; Treasurer of HM Household and Dep. Chief Whip, 1989–90; Minister of State, FCO, 1990–93. *Recreation:* collecting books. *Address:* House of Lords, SW1A 0PW. *Club:* Beefsteak.

GARFITT, His Honour Alan; a Circuit Judge, 1977–92, and Judge, Cambridge County Court and Wisbech County Court, 1978–92; *b* 20 Dec. 1920; *s* of Rush and Florence Garfitt; *m* 1st, 1941, Muriel Ada Jaggers; one *s* one *d*; 2nd, 1973, Ivie Maud Hudson; 3rd, 1978, Rosemary Lazell; one *s* one *d*. *Educ:* King Edward VII Grammar Sch., King's Lynn; Metropolitan Coll. and Inns of Court Sch. of Law. Served War of 1939–45, RAF, 1941–46. LLB London 1947; called to the Bar, Lincoln's Inn, 1948. Hon. Fellow, Faculty of Law, Cambridge, 1978. *Publications:* Law of Contracts in a Nutshell, 4 edns 1949–56; The Book for Police, 5 vols, 1958; jt ed, Roscoe's Criminal Evidence, Practice and Procedure, 16th edn, 1952; contribs to Jl of Planning Law, Solicitors' Jl and other legal pubns. *Recreations:* farming, gardening, DIY activities, horse riding and, as a member since 1961 and President 1978–93 of the Association of British Riding Schools (Fellow, 1989), the provision of good teaching and riding facilities for non-horse owners, dinghy sailing, boat building. *Address:* Leap House, Barcham Road, Soham, Ely, Cambs CB7 5TU.

GARING, Air Commodore William Henry, CBE 1943; DFC 1940; *b* Corryong, Victoria, 26 July 1910; *s* of late George Garing, retired grazier, and late Amy Evelyn Garing; *m* 1st, 1940 (marr. diss); one *s* one *d*; 2nd, 1954, Marjorie Irene Smith, Preston, England; two *d*. *Educ:* Corryong Higher Elementary School; Royal Melbourne Inst. of Technol.; Royal Military Coll., Duntroon, ACT. Began career as Electrical and Mechanical Engineer, 1928; entered RMC, Duntroon, 1929, as specially selected RAAF Cadet; Flying Training: Point Cook, Australia, 1931; Sch. of Air Pilotage and Specialist Navigation Sch., UK 1934–35; Seaplane Flying Instructor and Chief Navigation Instructor, Point Cook, Victoria, 1936; commanded Seaplane Squadron, Point Cook; conducted first Specialist Air Navigation Course in Australia, 1938; posted to United Kingdom in 1939; served with No 10 Aust. Sunderland Squadron, RAAF, as Flt Commander in Coastal Command, RAF, 1939; operations in N Atlantic, France and Mediterranean (DFC); flew Lord Lloyd to France for discussions with Pétain Government prior to collapse of France, 1940, and subsequently was pilot to the late Duke of Kent and to Mr Eden (later Earl of Avon), and others (Atlantic Star; despatches); arrived Australia, 1941; Senior Air Staff Officer, HQ Northern Area (extended from Neth. Indies through New Guinea, British Solomons to New Caledonia), 1941; commanded No 9 (Operational) Group RAAF, New Guinea, 1942; Milne Bay Campaign, 1942; Buna Campaign, 1942–43 (American DSC, awarded by Gen. MacArthur); 1943 (CBE, awarded for air operations SW Pacific); commanded No 1 Operational Training Unit, E Sale, Victoria, 1943–44; Director Operational Requirements, 1944; SASO to RAAF Rep., Washington, 1945–46, subseq. RAAF Rep. (1939–45 star); OC Western Area, 1947; JSSC, 1948; ADC to the King, 1951; Commandant School Land/Air Warfare, NSW, 1950; AOC Amberley, Qld, 1951; Imperial Defence Coll., London, 1952; AOC Overseas HQ, and RAAF Rep., London, 1953; AOC RAAF, Richmond, NSW, 1953–55; AOC RAAF and Commandant RAAF Staff Coll., Point Cook, Victoria, 1955–60; Air Officer, South Australia, and OC, RAAF, Edinburgh Field, Salisbury, SA, 1960–64, retired. Exec. Dir, Rothmans Nat. Sport Foundn, Sydney, Australia, 1964; Commercial Relations Manager, Alfred Dunhill Ltd, 1971–75. Holds No 1 1st cl. Air Navigators' Certificate (Australia); Air Master Navigator (RAF). Bd, Royal Freemasons Benevolent Inst.; Co-ordinator, Masonic Internat. Fest., 1977–79. FAIM 1964. *Recreations:* Alpine ski-ing, water ski-ing, yachting, shooting, flying, carpentry, landscape painting, gardening. *Clubs:* Imperial Service, Royal Automobile, New South Wales Leagues, Tattersall's (Sydney).

GARLAND, Basil; Registrar, Family Division of High Court of Justice (formerly Probate, Divorce and Admiralty Division), 1969–85; *b* 30 May 1920; *o c* of late Herbert George Garland and Grace Alice Mary Martha Garland; *m* 1942, Dora Mary Sudell Hope; one *s*. *Educ:* Dulwich Coll.; Pembroke Coll., Oxford (MA). Served in Royal Artillery, 1940–46: commnd 1941; Staff Officer, HQ RA, Gibraltar, 1943–45; Hon. Major 1946. Called to Bar, Middle Temple, 1948; Treasury Junior Counsel (Probate), 1965; Registrar, Principal Probate Registry, 1969. *Publications:* articles in Law Jl. *Recreations:* sailing, drama, painting. *Address:* Christmas Cottage, Blyth's Lane, Wivenhoe, Colchester, Essex CO7 9BG. *T:* (01206) 827566. *Club:* Bar Yacht.

GARLAND, Nicholas Withycombe, OBE 1998; Political Cartoonist, The Daily Telegraph, 1966–86 and since 1991; *b* 1 Sept. 1935; *s* of Tom and late Peggy Garland; *m*; three *s* one *d*. *Educ:* Slade School of Fine Art. Worked in theatre as stage man. and dir, 1958–64; Political Cartoonist: New Statesman, 1971–78; The Independent, 1986–91; has drawn regularly for The Spectator, 1979–; with Barry Humphries created and drew comic strip, Barry McKenzie, in Private Eye. *Publications:* (illustrated) Horatius, by T. B. Macaulay, 1977; An Indian Journal, 1983; Twenty Years of Cartoons by Garland, 1984; Travels with my Sketchbook, 1987; Not Many Dead, 1990.

GARLAND, Patrick Ewart; director and producer of plays, films, television; writer; Artistic Director, Chichester Festival Theatre, 1980–84 and 1991–94; *b* 10 April 1935; *s* of late Ewart Garland and Rosalind, *d* of Herbert Granville Fell, editor of The Connoisseur; *m* 1980, Alexandra Bastedo. *Educ:* St Mary's Coll., Southampton; St Edmund Hall, Oxford (MA; Hon. Fellow, 1997). Actor, Bristol Old Vic, 1959; Age of Kings, BBC TV, 1961; lived in Montparnasse, 1961–62; writing—two plays for ITV, 1962; Research Asst, Monitor, BBC, 1963; Television interviews with: Stevie Smith, Philip Larkin, Sir Noel Coward, Sir John Gielgud, Sir Ralph Richardson, Dame Ninette de Valois, Claire Bloom, Tito Gobbi, Marcel Marceau, 1964–78. Director and Producer, BBC Arts Dept, 1962–74; Stage Director: West End: 40 Years On, 1968, 1984; Brief Lives, 1968; Getting On, 1970; Cyrano, 1971; The Doll's House (New York and London), 1975; Billy, the Musical, 1976; Under the Greenwood Tree, 1978; Look After Lulu, 1978; Beecham, 1980; Hair (Israel), 1972; York Mystery Plays, 1980; My Fair Lady (US), 1980; Kipling (Mermaid and New York), 1984; Canaries Sometimes Sing, Albery, 1987; The Secret of Sherlock Holmes, Wyndham's, 1988; Victory (adapted from The Dynasts by Thomas Hardy), Chichester, 1989; A Room of One's Own, Hampstead, 1989, New York, 1991; Song in the Night, Lyric, Hammersmith, 1989; The Dressmaker, Windsor and tour, 1990; Tovarich, Piccadilly, 1991; Vita and Virginia, Ambassadors, 1993; The Tempest, Regent's Park Open Air, 1996; The Importance of Being Oscar, Savoy, 1997; The Mystery of Charles Dickens, Comedy, 2000; The Woman in Black, San Diego, 2001; television: Director: Talking Heads, 1998; Telling Tales, 2000; co-author, Underneath the Arches, Chichester, and Prince of Wales, 1982–83; Director, Chichester Festival Theatre: The Cherry Orchard, 1981; The Mitford Girls, 1981 (also London, 1981); On the Rocks, 1982; Cavell, 1982; Goodbye, Mr Chips, 1982; As You Like It, 1983; Forty Years On, Merchant of Venice, 1984; Tovarich, 1991; Pickwick, 1993; Pygmalion, 1994; Beatrix, 1996; Chimes at Midnight, 1998; produced: Fanfare for Elizabeth, the Queen's 60th birthday gala, Covent Garden, 1986; Celebration of a Broadcaster, for Richard Dimbleby Cancer Fund at Westminster Abbey, 1986; Thanksgiving service for Lord Olivier, 1989; Christmas Glory, ITV, annually 1997–. *Films:* The Snow Goose, 1974; The Doll's House, 1976. Creative Writing Fellowship, Bishop Otter Coll., Chichester, 1984–85. Hon. DLitt Southampton, 1994. *Publications:*

Brief Lives, 1967; The Wings of the Morning (novel), 1989; Oswald the Owl (for children), 1990; Angels in the Sussex Air: an anthology of Sussex poems, 1995; The Incomparable Rex: a memoir of Rex Harrison in the 1980s, 1998; poetry in: London Magazine, 1954; New Poems, 1956; Sussex Seams, 1996; Poetry West; Encounter; short stories in: Transatlantic Review, 1976; England Erzählt, Gemini, Light Blue Dark Blue. *Recreations:* reading Victorian novels, walking in Corsica. *Club:* Garrick.

GARLAND, Hon. Sir Patrick Neville, Kt 1985; **Hon. Mr Justice Garland;** a Judge of the High Court, Queen's Bench Division, since 1985; Senior Trial Judge, England and Wales, since 2000; *b* 22 July 1929; *s* of Frank Neville Garland and Marjorie Garland; *m* 1955, Jane Elizabeth Bird; two *s* one *d. Educ:* Uppingham Sch. (Scholar); Sidney Sussex Coll., Cambridge (Exhibnr and Prizeman; MA, LLM; Hon. Fellow, 1991). Called to Bar, Middle Temple, 1953, Bencher, 1979. Asst Recorder, Norwich, 1971; a Recorder, 1972–85; QC 1972; Dep. High Court Judge, 1981–85; a Judge of the Employment Appeal Tribunal, 1986–95; Presiding Judge, SE Circuit, 1989–93. Mem., Judges' Council, 1993–94. President: Central Probation Council (formerly Central Council of Probation Cttees), 1986–2001; Technol. and Construction Bar Assoc.; Mem., Parole Bd, 1988– (Vice-Chm., 1989–91). *Publications:* articles in legal and technical jls. *Recreations:* shooting, gardening, industrial archaeology. *Address:* c/o Royal Courts of Justice, Strand, WC2A 2LL. *Clubs:* Norfolk (Norwich); Cumberland Lawn Tennis.

GARLAND, Peter; *see* Garland, F. P. C.

GARLAND, Prof. Peter Bryan, CBE 1999; PhD; FRSE; Professor of Biochemistry, Institute of Cancer Research, University of London, 1992–99, now Emeritus Professor and Visiting Fellow (Chief Executive, 1989–99); *b* 31 Jan. 1934; *s* of Frederick George Garland and Molly Kate Jones; *m* 1959, Ann Bathurst; one *s* two *d. Educ:* Hardye's Sch., Dorchester; Downing Coll., Cambridge (BA 1st Class Hons in Physical Anthropol., 1955; BChir 1958, MB 1959; PhD 1964); King's Coll. Hosp. Med. Sch. (Burney Yeo Schol.). MRC Res. Schol., Chem. Pathol. Dept, KCH Med. Sch., and Biochem. Dept, UCL, 1959–61; British Insulin Manufacturers' Fellow, Biochem. Dept, Cambridge Univ., 1961–64; Lectr, 1964–68, Reader, 1969–70 in Biochem., Bristol Univ.; Prof. of Biochem., Dundee Univ., 1970–84; Principal Scientist and Hd, Biosciences Div., Unilever Research, 1984–87; Dir of Research, Amersham Internat., 1987–89. Vis. Prof., Johnson Res. Foundn, Philadelphia, 1967–69; Vis. Fellow, ANU, 1983. Member: MRC, 1980–84 (Chm., Cell Biol.–Disorders Bd, 1980–82); EMBO, 1981; CRC Scientific Policy Cttee, 1985–92. Director: CRC Technology Ltd, 1988–96 (Chm., 1988–91); CAT Ltd, 1990– (Chm., 1995–). FRSE 1977; Fellow, UCL, 1999. Hon. LLD Dundee, 1990. Colworth Medal, Biochem. Soc., 1970. *Publications:* numerous articles in biochemistry and biophysics. *Recreations:* sport (athletics blue, Cambridge, 1954–55), ski-ing, sailing, windsurfing, reading. *Address:* Haddow Laboratories, Institute of Cancer Research, 15 Cotswold Road, Sutton, Surrey SM2 5NG. *Clubs:* Athenæum; Bosham Sailing.

GARLAND, Peter Leslie; Regional Director, Northern and Yorkshire Region, NHS Executive, Department of Health, since 1999; *b* 21 Sept. 1946; *s* of Leslie and Stella Garland; *m* 1979, Janet Rosemary Prescott; three *d. Educ:* Bristol Cathedral Sch.; Manchester Univ. Joined DHSS, 1974; Asst Sec. 1989; Under Sec. and Dep. Dir of Finance, NHS Exec., DoH, 1993–99. *Recreations:* family, gardening. *Address:* National Health Service Executive, Northern and Yorkshire Region, Department of Health, John Snow House, Durham University Science Park, Durham DH1 3YG.

GARLAND, Hon. Sir (Ransley) Victor, KBE 1982; Chairman: Henderson Far East Income Trust PLC, since 1990 (Director, since 1984); Govett High Income Trust plc, since 1993; Director: Throgmorton Trust PLC, since 1985; Fidelity Asian Values PLC, since 1996; Chairman, South Bank Board, since 2000 (Vice Chm., 1985–2000); Director, South Bank Foundn, since 1996; *b* Perth, 5 May 1934; *m* 1960, Lynette Jamieson, BMus (Melb.); two *s* one *d. Educ:* Univ. of Western Australia. BA(Econ); FCA. Practised as Chartered Accountant, 1958–70. Chm., Glenchewton PLC, 1993–2001; Director: Prudential Corp., 1984–93; Govett Funds Inc., 1991–2000 (Pres., 1997–2000). MP for Curtin, Australian Federal Parliament, 1969–81; Minister for Supply, 1971–72; Executive Councillor, 1971–; Minister Asstg Treasurer, 1972; Chief Opposition Whip, 1974–75; Minister for Special Trade Representations, also Minister Asstg Minister for Trade and Resources, 1977–79; Minister for Business and Consumer Affairs, 1979–80; High Comr for Australia in UK, 1981–83. Govt Representative Minister: at Commonwealth Ministerial Meeting for Common Fund, London, 1978; at Ministerial Meetings of ESCAP, New Delhi, 1978; Minister representing Treas., at Ministerial Meeting of OECD, Paris, 1978; Leader, Aust. Delegn to UNCTAD V and Chm. Commonwealth Delegns to UNCTAD V, Manila, 1979; attended, with Premier, Commonwealth Heads of Govt meeting, Lusaka, 1979. Parly Adviser, Aust. Mission to UN Gen. Assembly, New York, 1973; Chairman: House of Reps Expenditure Cttee, 1976–77; Govt Members' Treasury Cttee, 1977. Councillor, Royal Commonwealth Society for the Blind, 1988–93. Freeman, City of London, 1982. *Recreations:* music (chorister, St George's Cathedral, 1942–46), reading, shooting, ski-ing. *Address:* Wilton Place, Knightsbridge, SW1X 8RL. *T:* (020) 7235 2729. *Clubs:* White's; Weld (Perth).

GARLICK, Sir John, KCB 1976 (CB 1973); Permanent Secretary, Department of the Environment, 1978–81; *b* 17 May 1921; *m* 1945, Frances Esther Munday (*d* 1992); three *d. Educ:* Westcliff High Sch., Essex; University of London. Entered Post Office Engineering Dept, 1937; Ministry of Transport, 1948; Private Secretary to Rt Hon. Ernest Marples, 1959–60; Assistant Secretary, 1960; National Economic Development Office, 1962–64; Under-Sec., Min. of Transport, 1966, later DoE; Dep. Sec., DoE, 1972–73; Dir-Gen., Highways, DoE, 1973–74; Second Permanent Sec., Cabinet Office, 1974–77. Mem., London Docklands Develt Corp., 1981–92. Dir, Abbey National plc (formerly Abbey National Building Soc.), 1981–92. Chm., Alcohol Concern, 1985–96. *Address:* 16 Astons Road, Moor Park, Northwood, Middx HA6 2LD. *T:* (01923) 824628.

GARLICK, Kenneth John; Keeper of Western Art, Ashmolean Museum, Oxford, 1968–84; Professorial Fellow of Balliol College, Oxford, 1968–84, now Emeritus; *b* 1 Oct. 1916; *s* of late D. E. Garlick and Annie Hallifax. *Educ:* Elmhurst Sch., Street; Balliol Coll., Oxford; Courtauld Inst. of Art, London. MA Oxon, PhD Birmingham; FSA, FMA. RAF Signals, 1939–46. Lectr, Bath Academy of Art, 1946–48; Asst Keeper, Dept of Art, City of Birmingham Museum and Art Gallery, 1948–50; Lectr (Sen. Lectr 1960), Barber Inst. of Fine Arts, Univ. of Birmingham, 1951–68. Governor, Royal Shakespeare Theatre, 1978–95. Hon. DLitt Birmingham, 1996. *Publications:* Sir Thomas Lawrence, 1954; Walpole Society Vol. XXXIX (Lawrence Catalogue Raisonné), 1964; Walpole Society Vol. XLV (Catalogue of Pictures at Althorp), 1976; (ed with Angus Macintyre) The Diary of Joseph Farington, Vols I-II, 1978, III-VI, 1979; Sir Thomas Lawrence, 1989; numerous articles and reviews. *Recreations:* travel, music. *Address:* 40 Ritchie Court, 380 Banbury Road, Oxford OX2 7PW. *Club:* Reform.

GARLICK, Paul Richard; QC 1996; a Recorder, since 1997; *b* 14 Aug. 1952; *s* of late Arthur Garlick and of Dorothy Garlick (*née* Allan). *Educ:* Liverpool Univ. (LLB 1973). Called to the Bar, Middle Temple, 1974; Standing Counsel to HM Customs and Excise, 1990–96; Asst Recorder, 1993–97. *Recreations:* music, cooking, ski-ing, walking, athletics. *Address:* 35 Essex Street, WC2R 3AR. *T:* (020) 7353 6381, *Fax:* (020) 7583 1786.

GARLING, David John Haldane, ScD; Reader in Mathematical Analysis, Cambridge University, 1978–99; Fellow of St John's College, Cambridge, since 1963; *b* 26 July 1937; *s* of Leslie Ernest Garling and Frances Margaret Garling; *m* 1963, Anthea Mary Eileen Dixon; two *s* one *d. Educ:* Highgate Sch.; St John's Coll., Cambridge (BA, MA, PhD; ScD 1978). Cambridge University: Asst Lectr, 1963–64; Lectr, 1964–78; Head of Dept of Pure Maths and Math. Stats, 1984–91; Pro-Proctor, 1995–96, Sen. Proctor, 1996–97, Dep. Proctor, 1997–98; Tutor, 1971–78, Pres., 1987–91, St John's Coll. Mem., SERC Mathematics Cttee, 1983–86. Exec. Sec., London Mathematical Soc., 1998– (Mem. Council, 1986–88 and 1995–98); Meetings and Membership Sec., 1995–98). *Publications:* A course in Galois Theory, 1987; papers in sci. jls. *Address:* St John's College, Cambridge CB2 1TP. *T:* (01223) 338600.

GARMOYLE, Viscount; Hugh Sebastian Frederick Cairns; with Cazenove, stockbrokers, since 1994; *b* 26 March 1965; *s* and *heir* of Earl Cairns, *qv*; *m* 1991, Juliet, *d* of Andrew Eustace Palmer, *qv*; one *s* two *d. Educ:* Eton; Edinburgh Univ. (MA Hons); London Coll. of Law. With Freshfields, solicitors, 1990–94. *Heir: s* Hon. Oliver David Andrew Cairns, *b* 7 March 1993. *Address:* 11 Lonsdale Road, W11 2BY.

GARNER, Alan, OBE 2001; author; *b* 17 Oct. 1934; *s* of Colin and Marjorie Garner; *m* 1st, 1956, Ann Cook; one *s* two *d*; 2nd, 1972, Griselda Greaves; one *s* one *d. Educ:* Alderley Edge Council Sch.; Manchester Grammar Sch.; Magdalen Coll., Oxford. Writer and presenter, documentary films: Places and Things, 1978; Images, 1981 (First Prize, Chicago Internat. Film Fest.). Mem. Internat. Editl Bd, Detskaya Literatura Publishers, Moscow, 1991–. *Publications:* The Weirdstone of Brisingamen, 1960 (Lewis Carroll Shelf Award, USA, 1970); The Moon of Gomrath, 1963; Elidor, 1965; Holly from the Bongs, 1966; The Old Man of Mow, 1967; The Owl Service, 1967 (Library Assoc. Carnegie Medal 1967, Guardian Award 1968); The Hamish Hamilton Book of Goblins, 1969; Red Shift, 1973 (with John Mackenzie, filmed 1978); (with Albin Trowski) The Breadhorse, 1975; The Guizer, 1975; The Stone Book, 1976 (Phoenix Award, Children's Lit. Assoc. of Amer., 1996); Tom Fobble's Day, 1977; Granny Reardun, 1977; The Aimer Gate, 1978; Fairy Tales of Gold, 1979; The Lad of the Gad, 1980; Alan Garner's Book of British Fairy Tales, 1984; A Bag of Moonshine, 1986; Jack and the Beanstalk, 1992; Once Upon a Time, 1993; Strandloper, 1996; The Voice That Thunders, 1997; The Little Red Hen, 1997; The Well of the Wind, 1998; Grey Wolf, Prince Jack and the Firebird, 1998; *plays:* Lamaload, 1978; Lurga Lom, 1980; To Kill a King, 1980; Sally Water, 1982; The Keeper, 1983; *dance drama:* The Green Mist, 1970; *libretti:* The Bellybag, 1971 (music by Richard Morris); Potter Thompson, 1972 (music by Gordon Crosse); Lord Flame, 1995; *screenplay:* Strandloper, 1992. *Recreation:* work. *Address:* Blackden, Cheshire CW4 8BY. *Club:* Portico Library (Manchester).

GARNER, Sir Anthony (Stuart), Kt 1984; parliamentary and public affairs consultant, since 1988; Director of Organisation, Conservative Central Office, 1976–88; *b* 28 Jan. 1927; *s* of Edward Henry Garner, MC, FIAS, and Dorothy May Garner; *m* 1967, Shirley Taylor; two *s. Educ:* Liverpool Coll. Grenadier Guards, 1945–48. Young Conservative Organiser, Yorks Area, 1948–51; Conservative Agent, Halifax, 1951–56; Nat. Organising Sec., Young Conservative Org., 1956–61; Conservative Central Office Agent for: London Area, 1961–64; Western Area, 1964–66; North West Area, 1966–76. Chm., Conservative Agents' Examination Bd, 1976–88. Pres., Conservative Agents' Benevolent Assoc., 1976–88. Director: Carroll Anglo-American Corp., 1989–94; Clifton Court Residents, 1990– (Chm., 1996–); Farnborough Aerospace Develt Corp., 1994–95; Carroll Aircraft Corp., 1994–95; British–Iranian Chamber of Commerce, 1996–2000 (Vice Chm., 1996–2000). Life Governor, Liverpool Coll., 1980. Pres., Old Lerpoolian Soc., 1995–97. *Recreations:* travelling, theatre. *Address:* The Beeches, Bottom Lane, Seer Green, Beaconsfield, Bucks HP9 2UH. *Clubs:* Carlton, St Stephen's Constitutional.

GARNER, Prof. Christopher David, PhD; FRS 1997; CChem, FRSC; Professor of Biological Inorganic Chemistry, University of Nottingham, since 1999; *b* 9 Nov. 1941; *s* of Richard Norman Garner and Chrystabel (*née* Potts); *m* 1968, Pamela Eva Kershaw; one *s* one *d. Educ:* Cheadle Hulme Warehousemen & Clerk's Orphans' Sch.; Nottingham Univ. (BSc 1st Cl. Hons Chem. 1963; PhD 1966). CChem 1982; FRSC 1982. Post-doctoral Res. Fellow, CIT, 1966–67; ICI Res. Fellow, Univ. of Nottingham, 1967–68; University of Manchester: Lectr in Chemistry, 1968–78; Sen. Lectr, 1978–84; Prof. of Inorganic Chemistry, 1984–99; Hd of Chemistry, 1988–96; Mem. Court, 1995–99; Mem. Council, 1996–99. Vis. Prof., Univ. of Lausanne, 1977; Frontiers in Chem. Res. Vis. Prof., Texas A&M Univ., 1987; Visiting Professor: Strasbourg Univ., 1990–92; Univ. of Florence, 1995; Univ. of Arizona, 1998; Sydney Univ., 2000; Wilsmore Fellow, Univ. of Melbourne, 1994; Bye Fellow and Fellow, Robinson Coll., Cambridge, 1997. Chatt Lectr, RSC, 1999. Chm., Metbio Prog., ESF, 1994–98. Founding Pres., Soc. Biol Inorganic Chem., 1996–98. Elder, URC, Bramhall, and Chm., Develt Gp, 1990–98. Tilden Medal, RSC, 1985. *Publications:* original res. papers and reviews, primarily concerned with roles of transition metals in biological systems and develt of chemical analogues for centres which occur in nature. *Recreations:* listening to classical music, theatre, dining out and in, watching sport. *Address:* School of Chemistry, Nottingham University, Nottingham NG7 2RD. *T:* (0115) 951 4188.

GARNER, Frederick Leonard; Chairman, Pearl Assurance Company Ltd, 1977–83, President, and President, Pearl Group, 1983–88, retired; *b* 7 April 1920; *s* of Leonard Frank Garner and Florence Emily Garner; *m* 1953, Giovanna Maria Anzani, Italy. *Educ:* Sutton County Sch., Surrey. Served War, RA, 1940–46. Joined Pearl Assurance Co., 1936; rejoined, 1946; sole employment, 1946–83. Director: Schroder Global Trust, 1971–89; Kleinwort Development Fund, 1981–. *Address:* 98 Tudor Avenue, Worcester Park, Surrey KT4 8TU. *T:* (020) 8337 3313. *Club:* Royal Automobile.

GARNER, John Donald, CMG 1988; CVO 1991 (LVO 1979); HM Diplomatic Service, retired; *b* 15 April 1931; *s* of late Ronald Garner and of Doris Ethel Garner (*née* Norton); *m* Karen Maria Conway; two *d. Educ:* Trinity Grammar Sch., N22. Royal Navy, National Service, 1949–51. Foreign Office, 1952–55; Third Secretary: Seoul, 1955; Bangkok, 1957; Foreign Office, 1959–63; Second Secretary: Benghazi and Tripoli, 1963–67; Sydney, 1967–69; First Sec., Tel Aviv, 1969–73; FCO, 1973–76; NDC 1976; Dep. High Commissioner, Lilongwe, 1977–80; Chargé d'affaires, Kabul, 1981–84; High Comr, The Gambia, 1984–87; Consul-Gen., Houston, 1988–91. Rep. of Sec. of State for Foreign and Commonwealth Affairs, 1996–. *Recreation:* golf. *Address:* 30 The Green, N14 6EN. *T:* (020) 8882 6808. *Club:* South Herts Golf.

GARNER, Maurice Richard; formerly specialist in the structure and governmental control of public enterprises; *b* 31 May 1915; *o s* of Jesse H. Garner; *m* 1943, Joyce W. Chapman; one *s* one *d. Educ:* Glendale County Sch.; London Sch. of Economics and Political Science. Royal Armoured Corps, 1942–45 (despatches). Inland Revenue (Tax Inspectorate), 1938–46; BoT, Asst Principal and Principal, 1947; Commercial Sec. and

UK Trade Comr in Ottawa, 1948–55; transf. to Min. of Power, 1957; Asst Sec. 1960; Under-Sec., Electricity Div., Min. of Technology, 1969, later DTI, retired 1973. Vis. Prof., Dept of Govt, LSE, 1981–85. *Recreations:* reading, oenology. *Address:* New Albany, 33 Sand Hill Lane, Leeds LS17 6AJ. *T:* (0113) 268 5115.

GARNER, Michael Scott; His Honour Judge Garner; a Circuit Judge, since 1988; *b* 10 April 1939; *s* of William Garner and Doris Mary (*née* Scott); *m* 1st, 1964, Sheila Margaret (*d* 1981) (*née* Garland); one *s* one *d*; 2nd, 1982, Margaret Anne (*née* Senior). *Educ:* Huddersfield Coll.; Manchester Univ. (LLB). Admitted Solicitor, 1965. Asst Recorder, 1978–85; a Recorder, 1985–88. *Recreations:* motoring, walking, cooking with wok in Lakeland hideaway. *Address:* Leeds Combined Court Centre, Oxford Row, Leeds LS1 3BE.

GARNETT, Ven. David Christopher; Archdeacon of Chesterfield, since 1996; *b* 26 Sept. 1945; *s* of Douglas and Audrey Garnett; *m* 1974, Susanne Crawford; two *s*. *Educ:* Giggleswick Sch.; Nottingham Univ. (BA Hons); Fitzwilliam Coll., Cambridge (BA Hons); Westcott House, Cambridge; MA Cantab. Curate of Cottingham, E Yorks, 1969–72; Chaplain, Fellow, Tutor, Selwyn Coll. and Pastoral Advr, Newnham Coll., Cambridge, 1972–77; Rector of Patterdale and Diocesan Dir of Ordinands, Carlisle, 1977–80; Vicar of Heald Green, Dio. Chester and Chaplain, St Ann's Hospice, 1980–87; Rector of Christleton and Chm., Bishop's Theol Adv. Gp, 1987–92; Team Rector, Ellesmere Port, 1992–96; Canon of Derby Cathedral, 1996–. Mem. Gen. Synod, 1990–96, 2000–. *Recreations:* poultry breeding, genetics. *Address:* The Vicarage, Baslow, Bakewell, Derbys DE45 1RY. *Club:* Poultry of Great Britain.

GARNETT, Adm. Sir Ian (David Graham), KCB 1998; Chief of Staff Supreme Headquarters Allied Powers Europe, since 2001; *b* 27 Sept. 1944; *s* of late Capt. Ian Graham Hartt Garnett, DSC, RN and Barbara Anne Langrishe (*née* Hackett); *m* 1973, Charlotte Mary Anderson; one *s* two *d*. *Educ:* Canford Sch.; BRNC, Dartmouth. Entered RN, 1962; Lt 1967; flying trng, 1968–69; HMS Hermes, 814 Sqdn, 1969–70; Loan Service, RAN, 1971–72; HMS Tiger, 826 Sqdn, 1973–74; Warfare Officer, 1974–76; Sen. Pilot, 820 Sqdn, 1977–78; Dep. Dir, JMOTS, 1978–80; in comd, HMS Amazon, 1981–82; RN staff course, 1983; Asst Dir, Operational Requirements, 1983–86; Captain Fourth Frigate Sqnd (HMS Active), 1986–88; RN Presentation Team, 1988–89; Dir Operational Requirements, 1989–92; FO Naval Aviation, 1993–95; Dep. SACLANT, 1995–98; Chief of Jt Ops, MoD, 1999–2001. Mem., Fleet Air Arm Officers Assoc., 1992–. *Recreations:* gardening, restoring furniture, walking. *Address:* Supreme Headquarters Allied Powers Europe, Belgium BFPO 26. *Club:* Royal Navy of 1765 and 1785.

GARNETT, Julia Charity, (Mrs John Garnett); *see* Cleverdon, J. C.

GARNETT, Kevin Mitchell; QC 1991; a Recorder, since 2000; a Deputy High Court Judge, since 2000; *b* 22 June 1950; *s* of Frank Raymond Garnett and Cynthia Ruby Eberstein; *m* 1980, Susan Jane Louise (*née* Diboll); one *s*. *Educ:* Bradfield Coll., Berks; University Coll., Oxford (MA). Called to the Bar, Middle Temple, 1975; Bencher, Lincoln's Inn, 2000. Asst Recorder, 1996–2000. Vice-Chm., Cartoon Art Trust, 1994–. *Publications:* (ed jtly) Williams, Mortimer and Sunnucks on Executors, Administrators and Probate, 16th edn 1982, 17th edn 1993; (ed jtly) Copinger and Skone James on Copyright, 13th edn 1991, 14th edn 1999. *Recreations:* tennis, golf, mountain walking. *Address:* 5 New Square, Lincoln's Inn, WC2A 3RJ. *T:* (020) 7404 0404. *Clubs:* National Liberal; Woking Golf.

GARNETT, Thomas Ronald, OAM 1996; MA; Head Master of Geelong Grammar School, Australia, 1961–73; *b* 1 Jan. 1915; *s* of E. N. Garnett; *m* 1946, Penelope, *d* of Philip Frere; three *s* two *d*. *Educ:* Charterhouse (Scholar); Magdalene Coll., Cambridge (Scholar; BA 1936, MA 1946). Assistant Master: Westminster School, 1936–38; Charterhouse, 1938–52; Master of Marlborough College, 1952–61. Served War of 1939–45, RAF, India and Burma, 1941–46, Squadron Leader (despatches). Cricket for Somerset, 1939. *Publications:* Stumbling on Melons, 1984; (ed) A Gardener's Potpourri, 1986; Man of Roses: Alister Clark of Glenara, 1990; The Evolution of a Gardener, 1993; A Gardener's Guide to the Climatic Zones of Australia, 1997. *Recreations:* gardening, ornithology. *Address:* 7 McGrath Street, Castlemaine, Vic 3450, Australia.

GARNHAM, Diana Anjoli; Chief Executive (formerly General Secretary), Association of Medical Research Charities, since 1991; *b* 17 Nov. 1954; *d* of George Leslie John Garnham and Monisha Vida (*née* Mander). *Educ:* Christ's Hosp., Hertford; Lady Margaret Sch., London; Univ. of Leicester (BSocSc (Politics)); King's Coll. London (MA War Studies); University Coll. of Wales, Aberystwyth. Admin. Sec., Council on Christian Approaches to Defence and Disarmament, 1983–87; Association of Medical Research Charities: Exec. Officer, 1987–89; Asst Sec.-Gen., 1989–91. Member: BBC Appeals Cttee, 1992–98; Bd, Groundwork Southwark, 1995–; NHS Standing Cttee (formerly Adv. Gp) on Consumer Involvement in NHS R&D, 1997–; COPUS, Royal Soc., 2001–. Trustee, Cae Dai Trust, 1994–; also involved in other charity sector gps. *Recreations:* music, needlework, food and drink, travel. *Address:* Association of Medical Research Charities, 61 Gray's Inn Road, WC1X 8TL. *T:* (020) 7269 8820; *e-mail:* d.garnham@amrc.org.uk.

GARNHAM, Neil Stephen; QC 2001; a Recorder, since 2001; *b* 11 Feb. 1959; *s* of Geoffrey Arthur Garnham and Cynthia Avril Rose Garnham; *m* 1991, Gillian Mary Shaw; two *s*. *Educ:* Ipswich Sch.; Peterhouse, Cambridge (MA). Called to the Bar, Middle Temple, 1982; a Jun. Counsel to the Crown, 1995–2001. *Address:* 1 Crown Office Row, Temple, EC4Y 7HH. *T:* (020) 7797 7500. *Club:* Travellers.

GARNIER, Edward Henry; QC 1995; MP (C) Harborough, since 1992; barrister; a Recorder, since 2000; *b* 26 Oct. 1952; *s* of late Col William d'Arcy Garnier and of Hon. Lavender Hyacinth (*née* de Grey); *m* 1982, Anna Caroline Mellows; two *s* one *d*. *Educ:* Wellington Coll.; Jesus Coll., Oxford (BA, MA). Called to the Bar, Middle Temple, 1976; Bencher, 2001. Vice-Pres., Hemsworth Assoc., 1987–. Contested: Wandsworth BC by-election, 1984; Tooting ILEA election, 1986; (C) Hemsworth, Gen. Election, 1987. PPS to Ministers of State, FCO, 1994–95; PPS to Attorney General and to Solicitor General, 1995–97, and to Chancellor of the Duchy of Lancaster, 1996–97; Opposition spokesman, Lord Chancellor's Dept, 1997–99; Shadow Attorney-Gen., 1999–. Mem., Home Affairs Select Cttee, 1992–95; Sec., Cons. Foreign Affairs Cttee, 1992–94. UK Election Observer: Kenya, 1992; Bosnia, 1996. Vis. Parly Fellow, St Antony's Coll., Oxford, 1996–97. Mem., Leics and Rutland Cttee, 1992–, Legal and Parly Cttee, 1994–, CLA. *Publications:* (contrib.) Halsbury's Laws of England, 4th edn, 1985; (contrib.) Bearing the Standard, 1991; (contrib.) Facing the Future, 1993. *Recreations:* cricket, shooting, opera. *Address:* House of Commons, SW1A 0AA. *T:* (020) 7219 3000. *Club:* Pratt's.

GARNIER, Rear-Adm. Sir John, KCVO 1990 (LVO 1965); CBE 1982; Extra Equerry to the Queen, since 1988; *b* 10 March 1934; *s* of Rev. Thomas Vernon Garnier and Helen Stenhouse; *m* 1966, Joanna Jane Cadbury; two *s* one *d*. *Educ:* Berkhamsted School; Britannia Royal Naval College. Joined RN 1950; served HM Yacht Britannia, 1956–57; HMS Tyne (Suez Operation) 1956; qualified navigation specialist, 1959; Naval Equerry to HM Queen, 1962–65; Comd HMS Dundas, 1968–69; Directorate of Naval Ops and Trade, 1969–71; Comd HMS Minerva, 1972–73; Defence Policy Staff, 1973–75; HMS Intrepid, 1976; Asst Dir, Naval Manpower Planning, 1976–78; RCDS 1979; Comd HMS London, 1980–81; Dir, Naval Ops and Trade, 1982–84; Commodore Amphibious Warfare, 1985; Flag Officer Royal Yachts, 1985–90. Private Sec. and Comptroller to HRH Princess Alexandra, 1991–95. Younger Brother of Trinity House, 1974. Mem., Council, Shipwrecked Fishermen and Mariners' Royal Benevolent Soc., 1996–. Gov., Sherborne Sch. for Girls, 1985–. Freeman of City of London, 1982. *Recreations:* sailing, golf, gardening, opera. *Address:* Bembury Farm, Thornford, Sherborne, Dorset DT9 6QF.

GARNOCK, Viscount; William James Lindesay-Bethune; *b* 30 Dec. 1990; *s* and *heir* of Earl of Lindsay, *qv*.

GARNON, Tudor Mansel; Chairman of Employment Tribunals, London North West, since 2001; *b* 19 Oct. 1953; *s* of David Carey Garnon and Marian Garnon; *m* 1976, Jean Davina Hewet; one *d*. *Educ:* Trinity Hall, Cambridge (MA). Admitted as solicitor, 1978; Partner, Richard Reed and Co., Solicitors, 1980–92; sole practitioner, Garnon and Co., 1993–99; Partner, McArdles, Solicitors, 2000–01. *Recreations:* various sports. *Address:* Laburnum House, 83 Tudhoe Village, Spennymoor, Co. Durham DL16 6LG. *T:* (01388) 819132.

GARNSEY, Prof. Peter David Arthur, FBA 1993; Professor of the History of Classical Antiquity, University of Cambridge, since 1997; Fellow of Jesus College, Cambridge, since 1974; *b* 22 Oct. 1938; *m* 1967, Elizabeth Franklin; one *s* two *d*. *Educ:* Sydney Univ. (BA); Rhodes Scholar, 1961; MA 1967, DPhil 1967, Oxon; PhD Cantab 1974. Jun. Fellow, University Coll., Oxford, 1964–67; Asst, then Associate, Prof., Univ. of Calif, Berkeley, 1967–73; Lectr, 1974–90, Reader in Ancient History, 1990–97, Univ. of Cambridge. *Publications:* Social Status and Legal Privilege in the Roman Empire, 1970; (ed jtly) Imperialism in the Ancient World, 1979; (ed jtly) Trade and Famine in Classical Antiquity, 1980; (ed) Nonslave Labour in the Graeco-Roman World, 1980; (jtly) Early Principate: Augustus to Trajan, 1982; (ed jtly) Trade in the Ancient Economy, 1983; (jtly) Roman Empire: economy, society and culture, 1987; Famine and Food Supply in the Graeco-Roman World, 1988; (ed) Food, Health and Culture in Classical Antiquity, 1989; Ideas of Slavery from Aristotle to Augustine, 1996; (ed jtly) Hellenistic Constructs: essays in culture, history and historiography, 1997; (ed jtly) Cambridge Ancient History XIII: the Late Empire AD325–425, 1998; Cities, Peasants and Food in Classical Antiquity, 1998; Food and Society in Classical Antiquity, 1999. *Address:* Jesus College, Cambridge CB5 8BL.

GARRARD, Rt Rev. Richard; Director of the Anglican Centre in Rome, and Archbishop of Canterbury's Representative to the Holy See, since 2001; *b* 24 May 1937; *s* of Charles John Garrard and Marjorie Louise (*née* Pow); *m* 1961, Elizabeth Ann Sewell; one *s* one *d*. *Educ:* Northampton Grammar Sch.; King's Coll., Univ. of London (BD, AKC). MIMgt. Ordained deacon, 1961, priest, 1962; Assistant Curate: St Mary's, Woolwich, 1961–66; Great St Mary's, Cambridge, 1966–68; Chaplain/Lectr, Keswick Hall Coll. of Educn, Norwich, 1968–74; Principal, Church Army Training Coll., 1974–79; Canon Chancellor, Southwark Cathedral and Dir of Training, dio. of Southwark, 1979–87; Canon Residentiary, St James's Cathedral, Bury St Edmunds and Advr for Clergy Training, dio. of St Edmundsbury and Ipswich, 1987–91; Archdeacon of Sudbury, 1991–94; Suffragan Bp of Penrith, 1994–2001. *Publications:* Lent with St Mark, 1992; A Time to Pray, 1993; Love on the Cross, 1995. *Recreations:* cats, crosswords, Italy, the fells. *Address:* The Anglican Centre in Rome, Palazzo Doria Pamphilj, Piazza del Collegio Romano 2, Int. 7, 00186 Rome, Italy.

GARRELS, John Carlyle; retired; Chairman: Monsanto Chemicals Ltd, 1965–71; Monsanto Textiles Ltd, 1970–71; formerly Director: Forth Chemicals Ltd; Monsanto Australia Ltd; Monsanto Oil Co. of UK, Inc.; British Saccharin Sales Ltd; *b* 5 March 1914; *s* of John C. and Margaret Ann Garrels; *m* 1st, 1938, Valerie Smith; one *s* two *d*; 2nd, 1980, Isabelle Rogers Kehoe. *Educ:* Univ. of Michigan (BS (Chem. Eng.)); Harvard (Advanced Management Programme). Pennsylvania Salt Mfg Co., Production Supervisor, 1936–42; Monsanto Co.: various appts, 1942–54; Asst Gen. Manager, 1955; Monsanto Chemicals Ltd: Dep. Man. Dir, 1960; Man. Dir, 1961; Chm. and Man. Dir, 1965. Pres., British Plastics Fedn, 1970, 1971. Member: National Economic Development Cttee for Chemical Industry, 1971; Council, Chemical Industries Assoc. *Recreations:* golf, shooting, fishing. *Address:* 59 Commercial Wharf, Apt 7, Boston, MA 02110–3807, USA. *Clubs:* American; Sunningdale Golf; Yacht and Country (Stuart, Fla); Fishing of America (New York).

GARRETT, Anthony David, CBE 1993; Deputy Master and Comptroller, Royal Mint, 1988–92; *b* 26 Aug. 1928; *s* of Sir William Garrett, MBE and Lady Garrett; *m* 1952, Monica Blanche Harris; three *s* one *d*. *Educ:* Ellesmere College; Clare College, Cambridge. MA. National Service, Subaltern IVth QO Hussars, 1946–48; Procter & Gamble Co., 1953–82, Vice-Pres., 1975–82; Bd Mem., 1983–87, and Man. Dir of Parcels, 1986–87, Post Office. Dir, Nat. Provident Instn, 1988–94. FRSA 1991. *Recreations:* golf, bridge, chess, walking. *Address:* 2 Harlequin Place, Harlequin Lane, Crowborough, East Sussex TN6 1HZ. *T:* (01892) 663648.

GARRETT, Sir Anthony (Peter), Kt 1997; CBE 1992; General Secretary, Association of British Dispensing Opticians, since 1999; *b* Jersey, 28 Nov. 1952; *m* 1st, 1974 (marr. diss. 1985); twin *d*; 2nd, 1989, Jane Wight Scott; two *d*. *Educ:* Canterbury Tech. High Sch. for Boys. Conservative Party Organisation, 1971–98: Constituency Agent, Rochester and Chatham, 1973–79; Cons. Central Office, 1979–98: SE Area Office, 1979–86; Asst Dir, Campaigning, 1986–92; Dir of Campaigning, 1992–98; Mem., Cons. Bd of Mgt, 1993–98. Pres., Cons. Agents' Benevolent Fund, 1992–98; Trustee, Cons. Agents' Superannuation Fund, 1992–98. *Recreations:* cricket, travel. *Address:* c/o Association of British Dispensing Opticians, 199 Gloucester Terrace, W2 6HX. *Clubs:* Carlton; Kent County Cricket (Life Mem.).

GARRETT, Godfrey John, OBE 1982; HM Diplomatic Service, retired; consultant on Central and Eastern Europe, since 1996; *b* 24 July 1937; *s* of Thomas and May Garrett; *m* 1963, Elisabeth Margaret Hall; four *s* one *d*. *Educ:* Dulwich Coll.; Cambridge Univ. (MA). Joined FO, 1961; Third Sec., Leopoldville (later Kinshasa), 1963; Second Sec. (Commercial), Prague, 1965; FCO, 1968; First Sec., Buenos Aires, 1971; FCO, 1973; First Sec., later Counsellor, Stockholm, 1981; Counsellor: Bonn, 1983; FCO, 1988; E Berlin, 1990; Prague, 1990–92; FCO, 1992–93; Head of UK Delegn to EC Monitoring Mission, Zagreb, 1993–94; Hd, OSCE Mission to Ukraine, 1995. Consultant, Control Risks Group Ltd, 1996–98. Order of the Northern Star, Sweden, 1983. *Recreations:* all outdoor activities, especially ski-ing; travel, gardening, languages. *Address:* White Cottage, Henley, Haslemere, Surrey GU27 3HQ. *T:* (01428) 652172; Mains of Glenlochy, Bridge of Brown, Tomintoul, Ballindalloch, Banff AB37 9HR. *T:* (01807) 580257.

GARRETT, Maj.-Gen. Henry Edmund Melvill Lennox, CBE 1975; *b* 31 Jan. 1924; *s* of John Edmund Garrett and Mary Garrett; *m* 1973, Rachel Ann Beadon; one step *s* one step *d*. *Educ:* Wellington Coll.; Clare Coll., Cambridge (MA). Commnd 1944; psc 1956; DAAG, HQ BAOR, 1957–60; US Armed Forces Staff Coll., 1960; OC 7 Field Sqdn RE, 1961–63; GSO2 WO, 1963–65; CO 35 Engr Regt, 1965–68; Col GS MoD, 1968–69; Comdr 12 Engr Bde, 1969–71; RCDS, 1972; Chief of Staff HQ N Ireland, 1972–75; Maj.-Gen. i/c Administration, HQ UKLF, 1975–76; Vice Adjutant General, MoD, 1976–78; Dir of Security (Army), MoD, 1978–89. Chm., Forces Help Soc. and Lord Roberts Workshops, 1991–96; Vice-President: SSAFA, 1991–96; SSAFA/Forces Help, 1997–. Col Comdt RE, 1982–90. Chm., RE Assoc., 1989–93. Chm. Governors, Royal Soldiers' Daughters Sch., 1983–86. *Recreations:* reading, walking. *Address:* c/o National Westminster Bank, 7 Hustlegate, Bradford, W Yorkshire BD1 1PP. *Club:* Army and Navy.

GARRETT, John Laurence; *b* 8 Sept. 1931; *s* of Laurence and Rosina Garrett; *m* 1959, Wendy Ady; two *d*. *Educ:* Selwyn Avenue Primary Sch., London; Sir George Monoux Sch., London; University Coll., Oxford (MA, BLitt); Grad. Business Sch. of Univ. of California at Los Angeles (King George VI Fellow). Labour Officer, chemical industry, 1958–59; Head of Market Research, motor industry, 1959–63; Management Consultant, Dir of Public Services, 1963–74, and Associate Dir, 1983–87, Inbucon Ltd. Consultant to Fulton Cttee on CS, 1966–68. Hon. Lectr in Govt, UEA, 1998–. Mem. (Lab), Norfolk CC, 1997– (spokesman on planning and transportation, 1997–98). MP (Lab) Norwich South, Feb. 1974–1983, and 1987–97; contested (Lab) same seat, 1983. PPS to Minister for Civil Service, 1974, to Minister for Social Security, 1977–79; Opposition Treasury spokesman, 1979–80; spokesman: on industry, 1980–83; on energy, 1987–88; on industry, 1988–89; on civil service, 1993–94; Campaigns Co-ordinator, Southern and Eastern England, 1989–92. *Publications:* Visual Economics, 1966; (with S. D. Walker) Management by Objectives in the Civil Service, 1969; The Management of Government, 1972; Administrative Reform, 1973; Policies Towards People, 1973 (Sir Frederic Hooper Award); Managing the Civil Service, 1980; Westminster, 1992; articles and papers on industry, management and govt. *Recreations:* theatre, dabbling, arguing. *Address:* 217 College Road, Norwich NR2 3JD.

GARRETT, Lesley, FRAM; Principal Soprano, English National Opera, since 1984; *b* 10 April 1955; *d* of Derek Arthur Garrett and Margaret Garrett (*née* Wall); *m* 1991; one *s* one *d*. *Educ:* Thorne Grammar Sch.; Royal Acad. of Music (FRAM 1995); Nat. Opera Studio (Post-grad.) Winner, Kathleen Ferrier Meml Competition, 1979. Performed with WNO, Opera North and at Wexford and Buxton Fests and Glyndebourne; joined ENO, 1984; début with Royal Opera, 1997; has appeared in opera houses in Geneva, São Paulo, Boboli Gdns, Florence, Bolshoi Theatre, Moscow and Kirov Theatre, St Petersburg; major roles include: Susanna in Marriage of Figaro; Despina in Così Fan Tutte; Musetta in La Bohème; Jenny in The Rise and Fall of The City of Mahaggony; Atalanta in Xerxes; Zerlinda in Don Giovanni; Yum-Yum in The Mikado; Adèle in Die Fledermaus; Oscar in A Masked Ball; Dalinda in Ariodante; Rose in Street Scene; Bella in A Midsummer Marriage; Eurydice in Orpheus and Eurydice; Rosina in The Barber of Seville; title rôles in The Cunning Little Vixen, and La Belle Vivette; concert hall appearances in UK and abroad include: Royal Variety Performance, 1993, Last Night of the Proms, Royal Albert Hall, Royal Fest. Hall, Centre Pompidou, Paris; numerous recordings and TV and radio appearances. Hon. DArts Plymouth, 1995. Best selling classical artist, Gramophone award, 1996. *Recreation:* watching cricket. *Address:* The Music Partnership Ltd, 41 Aldebert Terrace, SW8 1BH. *T:* (020) 7787 0361, *Fax:* (020) 7787 0364.

GARRETT, Richard Anthony, CBE 1987; company director; Chairman, National Association of Boys' Clubs, 1980–87, retired; *b* 4 July 1918; 3rd *s* of Charles Victor Garrett and Blanche Michell; *m* 1946, Marie Louise Dalglish (*d* 1999); one *s* two *d* (and one *d* decd); *m* 2000, Nancy Rae Wise. *Educ:* King's Sch., Worcester. MInstD; CIMgt (CBIM 1979). Served War, 1939–45 (despatches, 1945). Joined W.D. & H.O. Wills, 1936; Chm., ITL, retd 1979; Chm. and Man. Dir, John Player & Sons, 1968–71; Chm., Dataday Ltd, 1978–83; Director: HTV Gp plc, 1976–89 (Vice-Chm., 1978–83); Standard Commercial (formerly Standard Commercial Tobacco) Corp., 1980–95. Vice Pres., (Founder), Arts & Business (formerly Assoc. of Business Sponsorship of the Arts). Chm., Bath Festival, 1986–87; Trustee, Glyndebourne Arts Trust, 1976–88. Liveryman, Worshipful Co. of Tobacco Pipe Makers and Tobacco Blenders. *Recreations:* golf, gardening, music, opera, reading. *Address:* Marlwood Grange, Thornbury, Bristol BS35 3JD. *T:* (01454) 412630. *Clubs:* Naval and Military, MCC, XL; Bristol and Clifton Golf.

GARRETT, Terence, CMG 1990; CBE 1967; Assistant Secretary (International Affairs), Royal Society, 1991–94; *b* 27 Sept. 1929; *e s* of late Percy Herbert Garrett and Gladys Annie Garrett (*née* Budd); *m* 1960, Grace Elizabeth Bridgman Braund, *yr d* of Rev. Basil Kelly Braund; two *s* three *d*. *Educ:* Alleyn's Sch.; Gonville and Caius Coll., Cambridge (Scholar; 1st Cl. Hons, Mathematics). DipMathStat. Instructor Lieut RN, 1952–55. Lecturer, Ewell County Technical Coll., 1955–56; Sen. Lectr, RMCS, Shrivenham, 1957–62; Counsellor (Sci. and Technol.), Moscow, 1962–66 and 1970–74; Programmes Analysis Unit, Min. of Technology, 1967–70; Internat. Technological Collaboration Unit, Dept of Trade, 1974–76; Sec. to Bd of Governors and to Gen. Conf. of Internat. Atomic Energy Agency, Vienna, 1976–78; Counsellor (Science and Technology), Bonn, 1978–82; DCSO, Research and Technology Policy Div., DTI, 1982–87; Counsellor (Sci. and Technol.), Moscow, 1987–91. *Recreation:* travel. *Address:* Lime Tree Farmhouse, Chilton, Didcot, Oxon OX11 0SW. *Club:* Hawks (Cambridge).

GARRETT, Thomas John; Principal, Royal Belfast Academical Institution, 1978–90; *b* 13 Sept. 1927; *s* of late Mr and Mrs T. J. Garrett; *m* 1958, Sheenah Agnew (*d* 1991), *o d* of late Mr and Mrs G. Marshall, Drymen, Stirlingshire; one *d*. *Educ:* Royal Belfast Acad. Instn; QUB (BA); Heidelberg Univ. Asst Master: Royal Belfast Acad. Instn, 1951–54; Nottingham High Sch. for Boys, 1954–56; Sen. German Master, Campbell Coll., Belfast, 1956–73, Housemaster, 1968–73; Headmaster, Portora Royal Sch., Enniskillen, 1973–78. Member: Broadcasting Council for N Ireland, 1982–84; Northern Ireland Partnership, 1987–; Ind. Commn for Police Complaints (NI), 1990–97. Mem., Mus. and Arts Cttee, Down DC, 1996–. Mem., Bd of Govs, Bloomfield Collegiate Sch., 1992–. Pres., Old Instonians Assoc., 1996–97. *Publications:* Modern German Humour, 1969; Two Hundred Years at the Top—a dramatised history of Portora Royal School, 1977. *Recreations:* writing, hill-walking, ornithology. *Address:* Carnbeg, 44 Dunmore Road, Spa, Ballynahinch, Co. Down BT24 8PR. *T:* (028) 9756 2399. *Club:* East India.

GARRICK, Sir Ronald, Kt 1994; CBE 1986; DL; FREng; FRSE; Chairman, Weir Group, since 1999; *b* 21 Aug. 1940; *s* of Thomas Garrick and Anne (*née* McKay); *m* 1965, Janet Elizabeth Taylor Lind; two *s* one *d*. *Educ:* Royal College of Science and Technology, Glasgow; Glasgow University (BSc MechEng, 1st cl. hons). FIMechE; FREng (FEng 1984); FRSE 1992. Joined G. & J. Weir Ltd, 1962; Weir Pumps: Dir, Industrial Div., 1973; Dir Production Div., 1976; Managing Dir, 1981; Dir, 1981, Man. Dir and Chief Exec., 1982–99, Weir Group. Vis. Prof., Dept of Mech. Engrg, Univ. of Strathclyde, 1991–96. Member: Scottish Council, CBI, 1982–90; Gen. Convocation, 1985–96, Court, 1990–96, Univ. of Strathclyde; Restrictive Practices Court, 1986–96; Offshore Industry Adv. Bd, 1989–97; Scottish Economic Council, 1989–98; Scottish Business Forum, 1998–99; Dep. Chm., Scottish Enterprise Bd, 1991–96; Dearing Cttee of Inquiry into Higher Educn, 1996–97 (Chm., Scottish Cttee). Non-executive Director: Supervisory Bd, NEL, 1989–92; Strathclyde Graduate Business Sch., 1990–96; Scottish Power PLC, 1992–99; Shell UK Ltd, 1993–98; Bank of Scotland, 2000–01; Hbos, 2001–. DL Renfrewshire, 1996. DUniv: Paisley, 1993; Strathclyde, 1994; Hon. DEng Glasgow, 1998. *Recreations:* golf, reading. *Address:* c/o Weir Group, Cathcart, Glasgow G44 4EX. *T:* (0141) 637 7111.

GARRIOCH, Sir (William) Henry, Kt 1978; Chief Justice, Mauritius, 1977–78, retired; *b* 4 May 1916; *s* of Alfred Garrioch and Jeanne Marie Madeleine Colin; *m* 1964, Jeanne Louise Marie-Thérèse Desvaux de Marigny. *Educ:* Royal Coll., Mauritius. Called to the Bar, Gray's Inn, 1952. Civil Service (clerical), Mauritius, 1936–48; law student, London, 1949–52; Dist Magistrate, Mauritius, 1955; Crown Counsel, 1958; Sen. Crown Counsel, 1960; Solicitor-Gen., 1964; Dir of Public Prosecutions, 1966; Puisne Judge, 1967; Sen. Puisne Judge, 1970; Actg Governor-Gen., 1977–78. KCSG 1996. *Recreations:* reading, chess. *Address:* Lees Street, Curepipe, Mauritius. *T:* 6752708.

GARROD, Lt-Gen. Sir (John) Martin (Carruthers), KCB 1988; CMG 1999; OBE 1980; DL; UN Regional Administrator of Mitrovica, Kosovo, 1999; *b* 29 May 1935; *s* of Rev. William Francis Garrod and Isobel Agnes (*née* Carruthers); *m* 1963, Gillian Mary, *d* of late Lt-Col R. G. Parks-Smith, RM; two *d*. *Educ:* Sherborne School. Joined Royal Marines, 1953; served Malta, Cyprus, DS Officers' Training Wing, RM School of Music, Malaya, Borneo, 1955–66; Staff Coll., Camberley, 1967; HQ 17 Div., Malaya, 1968–69; HQ Farelf, Singapore, 1970–71; 40 Commando RM (Co. Comdr, Plymouth and N Ireland), 1972–73 (despatches); GSO2 Plans, Dept of CGRM, 1973–76; GSO1, HQ Commando Forces RM, 1976–78; CO 40 Commando RM, 1978–79 (OBE operational, NI); Col Ops/Plans, Dept of CGRM, 1980–82; Comdr 3 Commando Bde RM, 1983–84; ADC to the Queen, 1983–84; COS to Comdt Gen. RM, 1984–87; Comdt Gen., RM, 1987–90. Mem., EC Monitor Mission in Bosnia, 1993–94; COS to EU Adminr, Mostar, 1994–96; EU Special Envoy, Mostar, 1996; Head, 1997–98, a Dep. High Rep., 1998, Regl Office of High Representative resp. for Southern Bosnia and Hercegovina. Dep. Dir, Maastricht Referendum Campaign, 1993. Freeman, City of London, 1990; Liveryman, Plaisterers' Co., 1990. DL Kent, 1992. *Recreation:* portrait photography. *Address:* c/o Lloyds TSB, 2 High Street, Deal, Kent CT14 7AD. *Club:* East India.

GARSIDE, Charles Alexander; Proprietor, Miller Howe Hotel and Restaurant, Windermere, since 1998; Managing Director, 649 Service Ltd, since 1997; *b* 9 April 1951; *s* of John Robert Garside and Florence Garside (*née* Wilson); *m* 1st, 1972, Shirley May Reynolds (marr. diss.); 2nd, 1984, Carole Anne Short (marr. diss.); one *s* one *d*. *Educ:* Queen Elizabeth's Grammar Sch., Blackburn; Harris Coll., Preston. News Editor, London Evening News, 1979–80; News Editor, 1981–85, Asst Editor, 1986, Evening Standard; Dep. News Editor, The Times, 1987; Dep. Editor, Sunday Express, 1988–89; Asst Editor, The Times, 1989–90; Dep. Editor, 1991–92, Editor and Gen. Manager, 1992–94, Editor in Chief, 1994–97, The European. *Recreations:* fly fishing, theatres, classic cars. *Address:* Miller Howe, Rayrigg Road, Windermere, Cumbria LA23 1EY. *T:* (01539) 442536. *Club:* Travellers.

GARSIDE, Charles Roger; QC 1993; a Recorder, since 1994; *b* 13 Aug. 1948; *s* of Richard Murray Garside and Jane Garside (*née* Boby); *m* 1973, Sophie Shem-Tov; two *s* one *d*. *Educ:* Tonbridge Sch. Called to the Bar, Gray's Inn, 1971. Mem., Manchester Pedestrian Club, 1993–. *Recreations:* gardening, cricket, Rugby. *Address:* 9 St John Street, Manchester M3 4DN. *T:* (0161) 955 9000. *Clubs:* Lancashire County Cricket; Manchester Pedestrian.

GARSIDE, Prof. John, PhD, DSc(Eng); FREng, FIChemE; Professor of Chemical Engineering, since 1982 and Principal and Vice-Chancellor, since 2000, University of Manchester Institute of Science and Technology; *b* 9 Oct. 1941; *s* of Eric and Ada Garside; *m* 1965, Patricia Louise Holtom; one *s* one *d*. *Educ:* Christ's Coll., Finchley; University Coll. London (BSc(Eng), PhD, DSc(Eng); Fellow, 1994). FIChemE 1986; FREng (FEng 1988). ICI Agricl Div., 1966–69; Lectr, later Reader, UCL, 1969–81; Vice-Principal, UMIST, 1985–87. Vis. Prof., Iowa State Univ., 1976–77. Mem., various cttees and Engrg Bd, SERC, 1989–93. Institution of Chemical Engineers: Mem. Council, 1992–; Pres., 1994–95. *Publications:* (ed) Advances in Industrial Crystallization, 1991; Precipitation: basic principles and industrial application, 1992; From Molecules to Crystallizers, 2000; papers in Chem. Engrg Sci., Trans IChemE, Amer. Instn Chem. Engrs, Jl Crystal Growth, etc. *Recreations:* music, sailing, gardening. *Address:* University of Manchester Institute of Science and Technology, PO Box 88, Manchester M60 1QD. *T:* (0161) 200 4360.

GARSIDE, (Pamela) Jane, CBE 1995; JP; Chief Commissioner, The Guide (formerly Girl Guides) Association of the United Kingdom and the Commonwealth, 1990–95; *b* 20 Aug. 1936; *d* of Ronald and Nellie Whitwam; *m* 1958, Adrian Fielding Garside; two *s* (two *d* decd). *Educ:* Royds Hall Grammar Sch., Huddersfield; Yorkshire Trng Coll. of Housecraft, Leeds Inst. of Educn (Teaching Dip. 1957). Teacher, Deighton Secondary Sch., 1957–58; Co. Sec. 1959–, Dir 1964–, Highfield Funeral Service Ltd. Girl Guides: Dist Comr, Huddersfield N, 1973–77; County Comr, W Yorks S, 1977–83 (County Pres., 1996–); Chief Comr, NE England, 1984–89 (Vice-Pres., 1990–). *Recreations:* reading, gardening, music. *Address:* Lower Hall, Lascelles Hall Road, Huddersfield HD5 0BQ.

GARSIDE, Roger Ramsay; Executive Chairman, GMA Capital Markets Ltd (formerly Garside, Miller Associates), advisers to emerging financial markets, since 1990; *b* 29 March 1938; *s* of late Captain F. R. Garside and Mrs Peggie Garside; *m* 1969, Evelyne Madeleine Pierrette Guérin; three *d*. *Educ:* Eton; Clare Coll., Cambridge (BA EngLit, MA); Sloan Fellow in Management, Massachusetts Inst. of Technology. 2nd Lieut, 1/6 QEO Gurkha Rifles, 1958–59; entered HM Foreign Service, 1962; served, Rangoon, 1964–65; Mandarin Chinese Lang. Student, Hong Kong, 1965–67; Second Secretary, Peking, 1968–70; FCO, 1970–71, resigned 1971; World Bank, 1972–74; rejoined Foreign Service, 1975; served FCO, 1975; First Sec., Peking, 1976–79; on leave of absence, as Vis. Professor of East Asian Studies, US Naval Postgrad. Sch., Monterey, Calif, 1979–80; Dep. Head, Planning Staff, FCO, 1980–81; seconded, HM Treasury, 1981–82; Financial and Commercial Counsellor, Paris, 1982–87, resigned 1987; Dir, Public Affairs, Internat. Stock Exchange of UK and Rep. of Ireland (now London Stock Exchange), 1987–90. *Publication:* Coming Alive: China after Mao, 1981. *Recreations:* writing, tennis, travel. *Address:* 36 Groveway, SW9 0AR. *T:* (020) 7582 1577. *Club:* Reform.

GARSON, Cdre Robin William, CBE 1975; RN retd; Director of Leisure Services, London Borough of Hillingdon, 1975–86; *b* 13 Nov. 1921; *s* of late Peter Garson and Ada Frances (*née* Newton); *m* 1946, Joy Ligertwood Taylor (*née* Hickman); one *s* one *d*. *Educ:* School of Oriental and African Studies. Japanese Interpreter. Entered Royal Navy, 1937; served War of 1939–45, HM Ships: Resolution, Nigeria, Cyclops, and HM Submarines: Seawolf, H.33, Spark; subsequent principal appointments: In Command HM Submarines: Universal, Uther, Seraph, Saga, Sanguine, Springer, Thule, Astute, 1945–54; Chief Staff

Officer Intelligence, Far East, 1966–68; Sen. Polaris UK Rep., Washington, 1969–71; Captain 1st Submarine Sqdn, 1971–73; Commodore, HMS Drake, 1973–75; ADC to the Queen, 1974. Adviser to AMA on Arts and Recreation, 1976–86; Adviser to Sports Council, 1985–86; Mem., Library Adv. Council (England), 1977–83. Patron, RN Submarine Mus., 1990–. *Recreations:* golf, ski-ing, tennis. *Address:* Gateways, Hamilton Road West, Old Hunstanton, Norfolk PE36 6JB. *Clubs:* Army and Navy, Royal Navy of 1765 and 1785; Moor Park (Rickmansworth); Hunstanton Golf.

GARTHWAITE, Sir Mark; *see* Garthwaite, Sir W. M. C.

GARTHWAITE, Sir (William) Mark (Charles), 3rd Bt *cr* 1919, of Durham; Director, Willis Ltd (formerly Willis Faber), Lloyds Brokers, since 1997; *b* 4 Nov. 1946; *s* of Sir William Francis Cuthbert Garthwaite, 2nd Bt, DSC and of his 2nd wife, Patricia Beatrice Eden (*née* Neate); *S* father, 1993; *m* 1979, Victoria Lisette Hohler, *e d* of Gen. Sir Harry Tuzo, GCB, OBE, MC; one *s* two *d*. *Educ:* Dragon Sch.; Gordonstoun; Univ. of Pennsylvania (Wharton Sch.; BSc Econ.). Seascope Insurance Services, Lloyds Brokers, 1970–87 (Man. Dir, 1980–87); Brandram and Garthwaite Ltd, 1987–88; Director: Regis Low Ltd, Lloyds Brokers, 1988–92; Steel Burrill Jones Ltd, Lloyds Brokers, 1992–97. Chm., Lloyd's Insurance Brokers Cttee (Marine), 2000–. *Recreations:* sailing, ski-ing, trekking. *Heir: s* William Tuzo Garthwaite, *b* 14 May 1982. *Address:* 3 Hazlewell Road, SW15 6LU. *Clubs:* Turf; Royal Southampton Yacht (Southampton).

GARTON, George Alan, PhD, DSc; FRSE 1966; FRS 1978; Hon. Professorial Fellow, Rowett Research Institute, Bucksburn, Aberdeen, since 1992; Hon. Research Fellow, University of Aberdeen, since 1987; *b* 4 June 1922; *o s* of late William Edgar Garton, DCM, and late Frances Mary Elizabeth Garton (*née* Atkinson), Scarborough, N Yorks; *m* 1951, Gladys Frances Davison, BSc; two *d*. *Educ:* Scarborough High Sch.; Univ. of Liverpool (BSc: (War Service) 1944, (Hons Biochem.) 1946; PhD 1949, DSc 1959). Experimental Asst, Chemical Inspection Dept, Min. of Supply, 1942–45; Johnston Research and Teaching Fellow, Dept of Biochem., Univ. of Liverpool, 1949–50; Rowett Research Inst., Bucksburn, Aberdeen: Biochemist, 1950; Dep. Dir, 1968–83; Head of Lipid Biochem. Dept, 1963–83; Hon. Res. Associate, 1983–92; Hon. Res. Associate, Univ. of Aberdeen, 1966–86. Sen. Foreign Fellow of Nat. Science Foundn (USA), and Vis. Prof. of Biochem., Univ. of N Carolina, 1967. Chm., British Nat. Cttee for Nutritional and Food Sciences, 1982–87; Pres., Internat. Confs on Biochem. Lipids, 1982–89. Scientific Gov., British Nutrition Foundn, 1982–; a Dir, The Mother and Child Foundn, 1995–2000. SBStJ 1985. *Publications:* papers, mostly on aspects of lipid biochemistry, in scientific jls. *Recreations:* gardening, golf, foreign travel. *Address:* 2 St Devenick's Mews, Cults, Aberdeen AB15 9LX. *T:* (01224) 867012. *Clubs:* Farmers; Deeside Golf (Aberdeen).

GARTON, Rt Rev. John Henry; *see* Plymouth, Bishop Suffragan of.

GARTON, John Leslie, CBE 1974 (MBE (mil.) 1946); President, Henley Royal Regatta, since 1978; *b* 1 April 1916; *er s* of late C. Leslie Garton and Madeline Laurence; *m* 1939, Elizabeth Frances, *d* of late Sir Walter Erskine Crum, OBE; one *s* (and two *s* decd). *Educ:* Eton; Magdalen Coll., Oxford (MA). Commissioned TA, Royal Berkshire Regt, 1938. Served War, in France, 1940; psc 1943; Gen. Staff Ops Br., First Canadian Army HQ, in Europe, 1944–46; transf. to RARO, Scots Guards, 1951. Chm., Coca-Cola Bottling Co. (Oxford) Ltd, 1951–65, Coca-Cola Western Bottlers Ltd, 1966–71. Henley Royal Regatta: Steward, 1960; Mem. Cttee of Management, 1961–77; Chm., 1966–77. Amateur Rowing Association: Exec. Cttee and Council, 1948–77; Pres., 1969–77; Hon. Life Vice-Pres., 1978. Hon. Sec. and Treas., OUBC Trust Fund, 1959–69; Mem., Finance and Gen. Purposes Cttee, British Olympic Assoc., 1969–77; Thames Conservator, 1970–74; Chm., World Rowing Championships, 1975; Pres., Leander Club, 1980–83; Trustee, Leander Trust, 1982– (Chm., 1982–96). Liveryman, Grocers' Company, 1947–. High Sheriff, Bucks, 1977. *Recreations:* supporting the sport of rowing (rowed in Eton VIII, 1934, 1935, Captain of the Boats, 1935; rowed in the Boat Race for Oxford, 1938, 1939, Pres. OUBC, 1939), shooting (particularly deer-stalking), fishing. *Address:* Mill Green House, Church Street, Wargrave, Berkshire RG10 8EP. *T:* (0118) 940 2944. *Club:* Leander (elected 1936, Life Mem., 1953, Cttee, 1956, Chm. Executive, 1958–59).

GARTON, Prof. William Reginald Stephen, FRS 1969; Professor of Spectroscopy, University of London, Imperial College, 1964–79, now Professor Emeritus; Associate Head, 1970–79, and Senior Research Fellow, since 1979, Department of Physics, Imperial College; *b* Chelsea, SW3, 7 March 1912; *s* of William and Gertrude Emma Caroline Garton; *m* 1st, 1940, Margarita Fraser Callingham (marr. diss. 1976); four *d*; 2nd, 1976, Barbara Lloyd (*née* Jones) (*d* 2000). *Educ:* Sloane Sch., SW10; Chelsea Polytechnic, SW3; Imperial Coll., (Hon. Fellow 1983). BSc, ARCS 1936; DSc 1958. Demonstrator in Physics, Imperial Coll., 1936–39. Served in RAF, 1939–45. Imperial Coll.: Lectr in Physics, 1946–54; Sen. Lectr, 1954–57; Reader, 1957–64. External Examiner: Univ. of Singapore, 1972–75; Univ. of Malaya, 1986–89. Associate, Harvard Coll. Observatory, 1963–; Nuffield Fellow, Univ. of Western Ontario, 1964; Hertz Fellow, Univ. of Bonn, 1984; Leverhulme Trust Emeritus Fellow, 1987–89. W. F. Meggers Award, 1976, Fellow, 1979, Optical Soc. of America. Hon. DSc York Univ., Toronto, 1972. *Publications:* contrib. on Spectroscopy in Advances in Atomic and Molecular Physics (ed D. R. Bates), 1966 (New York); numerous papers on Spectroscopy and Atomic Physics. *Recreations:* gardening, Oriental history. *Address:* Blackett Laboratory, Imperial College, SW7 2AZ. *T:* (020) 7589 5111; Chart House, Great Chart, Ashford, Kent TN23 3AP. *T:* (01233) 621657.

GARTON ASH, Timothy John, CMG 2000; writer; Fellow of St Antony's College, Oxford, since 1990; *b* 12 July 1955; *s* of John Garton Ash and Lorna (*née* Freke); *m* 1982, Danuta Maria Brudnik; two *s*. *Educ:* Sherborne; Exeter Coll., Oxford (BA 1st Cl. Hons Mod. Hist., MA); St Antony's Coll., Oxford; Free Univ., W Berlin; Humboldt Univ., E Berlin. Foreign Editor, Spectator, 1984–90; editl writer on Central Europe, The Times, 1984–86; Fellow, Woodrow Wilson Center, Washington, 1986–87; columnist, Independent, 1988–90; Sen. Fellow, Hoover Instn, Stanford Univ. Fellow: Berlin-Brandenburg Acad. of Scis, European Acad. of Scis; Institut für die Wissenschaften vom Menschen, Vienna. Commentator of Year, What the Papers Say awards, 1989; David Watt Meml Prize, RTZ, 1990; Premio Napoli, 1995; OSCE Prize for Journalism and Democracy, 1998. Order of Merit (Poland), 1992; Bundesverdienstkreuz (FRG), 1995. *Publications:* 'Und willst Du nicht mein Bruder sein …' Die DDR heute, 1981; The Polish Revolution: Solidarity, 1983, 3rd edn 1999 (Somerset Maugham Award, 1984); The Uses of Adversity, 1989, 2nd edn 1991 (Prix Européen de l'Essai, 1989); We the People, 1990, 2nd edn 1999; In Europe's Name: Germany and the divided continent, 1993; The File: a personal history, 1997; History of the Present: essays, sketches and despatches from Europe in the 1990s, 1999, 2nd edn 2000. *Address:* St Antony's College, Oxford OX2 6JF. *T:* (01865) 274474, *Fax:* (01865) 556762.

GARVAGH, 5th Baron *cr* 1818; **Alexander Leopold Ivor George Canning;** Accredited Representative, Trade and Industry, The Cayman Islands, 1981; *b* 6 Oct. 1920; *s* of 4th Baron and Gladys Dora May (*d* 1982), *d* of William Bayley Parker; *S* father, 1956; *m* 1st, 1947, Christine Edith (marr. diss. 1974), *d* of Jack Cooper; one *s* two *d*; 2nd, 1974, Cynthia Valerie Mary, *d* of Eric E. F. Pretty, CMG, Kingswood, Surrey. *Educ:* Eton; Christ Church, Oxford. Commissioned Corps of Guides Cavalry, Indian Army, 1940; served Burma (despatches). Founder Dir, Internat. Business Services Ltd, 1947; Director: Stonehaven Tankers Ltd; Campden Research & Sales Ltd; Independent Chartering Ltd; AODC (UK) Ltd; Camco Machinery Ltd; Telomex (New York) Inc. Founder Mem., Instituto de Proprietarios Extranjeros (Spain), 1985. Mem., Baltic Exchange, 1978. Mem., British Inst. of Exports, 1957; MIMgt (MBIM 1962); FInstD 1964. Past Mem. Court, Painter Stainers Co. Consultant and contributor, Spanish Property Gazette, 1987–88. *Publications:* contrib. to The Manufacturing Optician, 1949. *Recreations:* travel, motoring, and motor sport; writing articles, short stories, etc. *Heir: s* Hon. Spencer George Stratford de Redcliffe Canning [*b* 12 Feb. 1953; *m* 1979, Julia Margery Morison Bye, *er d* of Col F. C. E. Bye, Twickenham; one *s* two *d*]. *Address:* Half Moon House, Cumberland Street, Woodbridge, Suffolk IP12 4AQ.

GARVEY, Arnold James; Editor, Horse and Hound, since 1995; *b* 7 Aug. 1946; *s* of late James Adamson Garvey and Esme Muriel (*née* Noble); *m* 1st, 1969, Kathleen Gordon (marr. diss. 1996); two *d*; 2nd, 1997, Marta-Lisà Conversi; one *s* one *d*. *Educ:* Bramston, Witham, Essex; Braintree Coll., Essex. Joined Horse and Hound, as sub-editor, 1971: Dep. Ed., 1987–94; Actg Ed., 1994–95. *Recreations:* horse riding, theatre, walking. *Address:* Horse and Hound, Room 2018, King's Reach Tower, Stamford Street, SE1 9LS. *T:* (020) 7261 6453. *Club:* Farmers'.

GARVEY, Thomas, (Tom); Deputy Director General (Environment, Nuclear Safety and Civil Protection), European Commission, 1992–98; *b* 27 May 1936; *s* of Thomas and Brigid Garvey; *m* 1961, Ellen Devine; two *s* two *d*. *Educ:* University Coll., Dublin (MA Econ). Fellow, Management Inst. Ireland. Various marketing and internal trade appts, 1958–69; Chief Exec., Irish Export Bd, 1969–76; EEC Delegate, Nigeria, 1977–80; Chief Exec., An Post (Irish Postal Service), 1980–84; Dir, Internal Market and Ind. Affairs, EEC, 1984–89; Dir, DG1 (External Relns), EC, 1990–92. Mem. Bd, Regl Envmt Centre, Budapest, 1996–; Chm., Regl Envmt Centre, Moldova, 1999–. Vis. Lectr, Grad. Sch. of Internat. and Public Affairs, Univ. of Pittsburgh, 1998–. FRSA 1990. *Publications:* various, in industrial, trade and academic jls. *Recreations:* golf, music. *Clubs:* Hibernian, United Services (Dublin).

GARVIN, Clifton Canter, Jr; Chairman of the Board and Chief Executive Officer, Exxon Corporation, 1975–86, retired; *b* 22 Dec. 1921; *s* of Clifton C. Garvin, Sr, and Esther Ames; *m* 1943, Thelma Volland; one *s* three *d*. *Educ:* Virginia Polytechnic Inst. and State Univ. MS (ChemEng) 1947. Exxon: Process Engr, subseq. Refining Operating Supt, Baton Rouge, Louisiana Refinery, 1947–59; Asst Gen. Manager, Supply Dept, Exxon Corp., 1959–60; Gen. Manager, Supply Dept, 1960–61; Manager, Production, Supply & Distribution Dept, Exxon Co., USA, 1961–62, subseq. Vice-Pres., Central Region, 1963–64; Exec. Asst to Pres. and Chm., Exxon Corp., NY, 1964–65; Pres., Exxon Chemical (US), subseq. Pres. Exxon Chemical (Internat.), 1965–68; Dir, subseq. Exec. Vice-Pres., subseq. Pres., Exxon Corp., 1968–75. Dir, Saudi Arabian Oil Co.; former Director: Citicorp and Citibank; Hosp. Corp. of America; PepsiCo, Inc.; Johnson & Johnson; J. C. Penney Co., Inc.; TRW Inc.; Americas Soc.; Member: Amer. Inst. of Chem. Engrs; Business Roundtable; Council on Foreign Relns; Business Council; Nat. Associate, White Burkett Miller Center of Public Affairs, Univ. of Virginia. Virginia Polytechnic Institute and State University: Mem. Cttee of 100—Coll. of Engrg Corporate Devélt; Bd of Visitors. *Recreations:* golf, bird watching.

GARY, Lesley; *see* Blanch, L.

GASCH, Pauline Diana, (Mrs F. O. Gasch); *see* Baynes, P. D.

GASCOIGNE, Bamber; author and broadcaster; *b* 24 Jan. 1935; *s* of late Derick Gascoigne and Midi (*née* O'Neill); *m* 1965, Christina Ditchburn. *Educ:* Eton; Magdalene Coll., Cambridge (Hon. Fellow, 1996). Commonwealth Fund Fellow, Yale, 1958–59. Theatre Critic, Spectator, 1961–63, and Observer, 1963–64; Co-editor, Theatre Notebook, 1968–74. Founded Saint Helena Press, 1977; Chm., Ackermann Publishing, 1981–85; Co-founder and Chm., HistoryWorld, 2000. Trustee: Nat. Gall., 1988–95; Tate Gall., 1993–95; Chm., Friends of Covent Garden, 1991–95; Member: Bd of Dirs, Royal Opera House, Covent Garden, 1988–95; Council, Nat. Trust, 1989–94. Sandars Lectr in Bibliography, Cambridge, 1993–94. FRSL 1976. *Theatre:* Share My Lettuce, London, 1957–58; Leda Had a Little Swan, New York, 1968; The Feydeau Farce Festival of Nineteen Nine, Greenwich, 1972; Big in Brazil, Old Vic, 1984. *Television:* presenter of: University Challenge, (weekly) 1962–87; Cinema, 1964; (also author) The Christians, 1977; Victorian Values, 1987; Man and Music, 1987–89; The Great Moghuls, 1990; Brother Felix and the Virgin Saint, 1992; deviser and presenter of Connoisseur, 1988–89; author of: The Four Freedoms, 1962; Dig This Rhubarb, 1963; The Auction Game, 1968. *Publications:* (many with photographs or watercolour illustrations by Christina Gascoigne): Twentieth Century Drama, 1962; World Theatre, 1968; The Great Moghuls, 1971; Murgatreud's Empire, 1972; The Heyday, 1973; The Treasures and Dynasties of China, 1973; Ticker Khan, 1974; The Christians, 1977; Images of Richmond, 1978; Images of Twickenham, 1981; Why the Rope went Tight, 1981; Fearless Freddy's Magic Wish, 1982; Fearless Freddy's Sunken Treasure, 1982; Quest for the Golden Hare, 1983; Cod Streuth, 1986; How to Identify Prints, 1986; Amazing Facts, 1988; Encyclopedia of Britain, 1993; Milestones in Colour Printing, 1997; World History: a narrative encyclopedia, 2000. *Address:* Saint Helena Terrace, Richmond, Surrey TW9 1NR.

GASCOIGNE, Stanley, CMG 1976; OBE 1972; Secretary to the Cabinet, Bermuda, 1972–76; Member, Senate, 1976–85, Vice-President, 1980–85; *b* 11 Dec. 1914; *s* of George William Gascoigne and Hilda Elizabeth Gascoigne; *m* 1st, 1941, Sybil Wellspring Outerbridge (*d* 1980); 2nd, 1980, Sandra Alison Lee; two *s*. *Educ:* Mt Allison Univ., Canada (BA 1937): London Univ., England (DipEd 1938): Boston Univ., USA (MEd 1951). Teacher, 1939–51; Inspector of Schools, 1951–59; Director, Marine and Ports Authority, 1959–69; Permanent Sec., Education, 1969–72. Exec. Dir, Inst. of Chartered Accountants of Bermuda, 1976–89. *Recreation:* ornithology. *Address:* #17 Panorama, South Road, Paget, DV 04, Bermuda. *T:* 2367053; *e-mail:* gascoigne@northrock.bm. *Club:* Royal Hamilton Amateur Dinghy (Bermuda).

GASCOYNE-CECIL, family name of **Marquess of Salisbury**.

GASH, Haydon Boyd W.; *see* Warren-Gash.

GASH, Prof. Norman, CBE 1989; FBA 1963; FRSL 1973; FRSE 1977; FRHistS; Professor of History, St Salvator's College, University of St Andrews, 1955–80, now Emeritus; *b* 16 Jan. 1912; *s* of Frederick and Kate Gash; *m* 1st, 1935, Ivy Dorothy Whitehorn (*d* 1995); two *d*; 2nd, 1997, Mrs Ruth Frances Jackson. *Educ:* Reading Sch.; St John's Coll., Oxford (Hon. Fellow 1987). Scholar, St John's Coll.; 1st cl. Hons Mod. Hist., 1933; BLitt, 1934; MA 1938. FRHistS 1953. Temp. Lectr in Modern European

History, Edinburgh, 1935–36; Asst Lectr in Modern History, University Coll., London, 1936–40. Served War, 1940–46: Intelligence Corps; Capt. 1942; Major (Gen. Staff), 1945. Lectr in Modern British and American History, St Salvator's Coll., University of St Andrews, 1946–53; Prof. of Modern History, University of Leeds, 1953–55; Vice-Principal, 1967–71, Dean of Faculty of Arts, 1978–80, St Andrews Univ. Hinkley Prof. of English History, Johns Hopkins Univ., 1962; Ford's Lectr in English History, Oxford Univ., 1963–64; Sir John Neale Lectr in English Hist., UCL, 1981; Wellington Lectr, Southampton Univ., 1992. Vice-Pres., Hist. Assoc. of Scotland, 1963–64. Hon. DLitt: Strathclyde, 1984; St Andrews, 1985; Southampton, 1988. *Publications:* Politics in the Age of Peel, 1953; Mr Secretary Peel, 1961; The Age of Peel, 1968; Reaction and Reconstruction in English Politics, 1832–1852, 1966; Sir Robert Peel, 1972; Peel, 1976; (jtly) The Conservatives: a history from their origins to 1965, 1978; Aristocracy and People: England 1815–1865, 1979; Lord Liverpool, 1984; Pillars of Government, 1986; (ed) Wellington: studies in the military and political career of the first Duke of Wellington, 1990; Robert Surtees and Early Victorian Society, 1993; articles and reviews in Eng. Hist. Review, Trans. Royal Historical Society, and other learned jls. *Recreations:* gardening, swimming. *Address:* Old Gatehouse, Portway, Langport, Som TA10 0NQ. *T:* (01458) 250334.

GASK, Daphne Irvine Prideaux, (Mrs John Gask), OBE 1976; JP; Member, Inner London Commission of the Peace, 1982–88; *b* 25 July 1920; *d* of Roger Prideaux Selby and Elizabeth May (*née* Stirling); *m* 1945, John Gask, MA, BM, BCh; one *s* one *d*. *Educ:* St Trinnean's, Edinburgh; Tolmers Park, Herts; Collège Brillantmont, Lausanne, Switzerland. BA Open Univ., 1979. CAB worker, 1985–. Member: Shropshire Probation and After-Care Cttee, 1960–80 (Chm., 1978–80); Exec. Cttee, Central Council of Probation and After-Care Cttees, 1964–80 (Vice-Chm., 1977–80); Royal Commn on Criminal Procedure, 1978–80; Council, Magistrates Assoc., 1968–80 (Mem. Exec. Cttee, 1976–80); Sports Council Adv. Gp, 1978–80; NACRO, 1982–; Asst Sec., L'Association Internationale des Magistrats de la Jeunesse et de la Famille, 1979–86 (Hon. Mem., 1986–; Mem. Gen. Purposes Cttee, 1986–). Served on Salop CC, 1965–77; Chm., Leisure Activities Cttee, 1974–77. Mem., W Midland Reg. Sports Council (Vice-Chm., 1970–77). Member: Council of Management, Stonham Housing Assoc., 1994–99; Family Courts' Consortium, 1996–. JP Salop, 1952. Mello Matlos medal, Brazil, 1986. *Publication:* Juvenile Delinquents and Young People in Danger in an Open Environment (research project), 1996. *Recreations:* travel, gardening, photography. *Address:* 5 The Old School House, Garrett Street, Cawsand, near Torpoint, Cornwall PL10 1PD. *T:* (01752) 822136.

GASKELL, Dr Colin Simister, CBE 1988; FREng; Chairman: Infra Red Integrated Systems Ltd, since 1997; Telemetrix plc, since 1997 (Director, since 1994); Ferranti Technologies Ltd, since 2000; *b* 19 May 1937; *s* of James and Carrie Gaskell; *m* 1961, Jill (*née* Haward); one *s* one *d*. *Educ:* Manchester Grammar Sch.; Manchester Univ. (BSc); St Edmund Hall, Oxford (DPhil). CEng, FREng (FEng 1989); FIEE (Hon. Treas., 1996–99). Research Fellow, Oxford Univ., 1960–61; Central Electricity Res. Labs, 1961–62; Microwave Associates, 1962–67; Chief Engineer, Microwave Div., Marconi Instruments, 1967–71; Technical Dir, Herbert Controls, 1971–74; Marconi Instruments: Technical Management, 1974–77; Technical Dir, 1977–79; Man. Dir, 1979–90; Gp Man. Dir, 1990–96, Chief Exec., 1996–97, 600 Group plc. CIMgt; FRSA. *Recreations:* reading, walking, theatre, family pursuits. *Address:* Infra Red Integrated Systems Ltd, Towcester Mill, Towcester, Northants NN12 6AD.

GASKELL, Joseph William; His Honour Judge Gaskell; a Circuit Judge, since 1996; *b* 5 June 1947; *s* of Joseph Gerald Gaskell and Maureen Elizabeth Jane Gaskell (*née* Thomas); *m* 1970, Rowena Gillian Case; one *s* one *d*. *Educ:* Harrow Sch.; Clare Coll., Cambridge. Called to the Bar, Inner Temple, 1970; Asst Recorder, 1990; Recorder, 1993–96; Asst Parly Boundary Comr, 1994. *Recreations:* the arts, sailing, dog walking. *Address:* The Crown Court, Cathays Park, Cardiff CF1 3PG. *Clubs:* Cardiff and County; Penarth Yacht.

GASKELL, Sir Richard (Kennedy Harvey), Kt 1989; Consultant, Lawrence Tucketts, solicitors, since 1997 (Partner, 1963–89; Senior Partner, 1989–97); President of the Law Society, 1988–89; *b* 17 Sept. 1936; *o s* of late Dr Kenneth Harvey Gaskell, MRCS, LRCP, DMRD and Jean Winsome Gaskell; *m* 1965, Judith Poland; one *s* one *d*. *Educ:* Marlborough Coll. Admitted solicitor, 1960. Chm., Nat. Cttee, Young Solicitors' Gp, 1964–65; Law Society: Mem. Council, 1969–92; Dep. Vice-Pres., 1986–87; Vice Pres., 1987–88; President: Bristol Law Soc., 1978–79; Assoc. of South Western Law Socs, 1980–81. Member: Crown Court Rules Cttee, 1977–83; Security Service Tribunal, 1989–; Intelligence Services Tribunal, 1994–; Criminal Justice Consultative Council, 1991–94; Criminal Injuries Compensation Bd, 1992–2000; Criminal Injuries Compensation Appeals Panel, 1997–; Investigatory Powers Tribunal, 2000–; Professional Conduct Cttee, GMC, 2001–. Director: Law Society Trustees Ltd, 1974–92; Bristol Waterworks Co., 1989–91; Bristol Water Hldgs plc, 1991– (Dep. Chm., 1998–). Dir, Wildfowl Trust (Hldgs) Ltd, 1980–; Mem. Council, Wildfowl and Wetlands (formerly Wildfowl) Trust, 1980–92 (Chm., 1983–87; Vice-Pres., 1992–); Chm., SS Great Britain Project Ltd, 1992–2000 (Chm. Exec. Cttee and Council, SS Great Britain). Trustee: Frenchay and Southmead Med. Trust, 1968–99; Laura Ashley Foundn, 1990–97; CLIC (UK), 1991–95. Mem. Council, 1995–, and Kt Principal, 2000–, Imperial Soc. of Kts Bachelor (Chm., 1999–2000). Mem. Court, Bristol Univ., 1973–2000. Hon. LLD Bristol, 1989; Hon. LLM Bristol Polytechnic, 1989. *Address:* Grove Farm, Yatton Keynell, Chippenham, Wilts SN14 7BS. *T:* (01249) 782289, *Fax:* (01249) 783267. *Club:* Farmers'.

GASKILL, William; freelance stage director; *b* 24 June 1930; *s* of Joseph Linnaeus Gaskill and Maggie Simpson. *Educ:* Salt High Sch., Shipley; Hertford Coll., Oxford. Asst Artistic Dir, English Stage Co., 1957–59; freelance Dir with Royal Shakespeare Co., 1961–62; Assoc. Dir, National Theatre, 1963–65, and 1979; Artistic Director, English Stage Company, 1965–72, Mem. Council, 1978–87; Dir, Joint Stock Theatre Gp, 1973–83. *Publication:* A Sense of Direction: life at the Royal Court (autobiog.), 1988. *Address:* 124A Leighton Road, NW5 2RG.

GASKIN, Catherine; author; *b* Co. Louth, Eire, 2 April 1929; *m* 1955, Sol Cornberg (*d* 1999). *Educ:* Holy Cross Coll., Sydney, Australia; Conservatorium of Music, Sydney. Brought up in Australia; lived in London, 1948–55, New York, 1955–65, Virgin Islands, 1965–67, Ireland, 1967–81. *Publications:* This Other Eden, 1946; With Every Year, 1947; Dust In Sunlight, 1950; All Else Is Folly, 1951; Daughter of the House, 1952; Sara Dane, 1955; Blake's Reach, 1958; Corporation Wife, 1960; I Know My Love, 1962; The Tilsit Inheritance, 1963; The File on Devlin, 1965; Edge of Glass, 1967; Fiona, 1970; A Falcon for a Queen, 1972; The Property of a Gentleman, 1974; The Lynmara Legacy, 1975; The Summer of the Spanish Woman, 1977; Family Affairs, 1980; Promises, 1982; The Ambassador's Women, 1985; The Charmed Circle, 1988. *Recreations:* music, reading. *Address:* Villa 139, The Manors, 15 Hale Road, Mosman, NSW 2088, Australia.

GASKIN, Prof. Maxwell, DFC 1944 (and Bar 1945); Jaffrey Professor of Political Economy, Aberdeen University, 1965–85, now Professor Emeritus; *b* 18 Nov. 1921; *s* of late Albert and Beatrice Gaskin; *m* 1952, Brenda Patricia, *yr d* of late Rev. William D. Stewart; one *s* three *d*. *Educ:* Quarry Bank Sch., Liverpool; Liverpool Univ. (MA). Lever Bros Ltd, 1939–41. Served War, RAF Bomber Comd, 1941–46. Economist, Raw Cotton Commn, 1949–50; Asst Lectr, Liverpool Univ., 1950–51; Lectr and Sen. Lectr, Glasgow Univ., 1951–65; Visiting Sen. Lectr, Nairobi Univ., 1964–65. Consultant to Sec. of State for Scotland, 1965–87. Member, Committee of Inquiry: into Bank Interest Rates (N Ire.), 1965–66; into Trawler Safety, 1967–68; Member and Chairman: Wages Councils, 1967–93; Bd of Management for Foresterhill and Associated Hosps, 1971–74; Independent Member: Scottish Agricl Wages Bd, 1972–90; EDC for Civil Engineering, 1978–84; Chm., Industry Strategy Cttee for Scotland (Building and Civil Engrg EDCs), 1974–76. Director: Offshore Med. Support Ltd, 1978–85; Aberdeen Univ. Research & Industrial Services, 1981–85. President: Section F, British Assoc., 1978–79; Scottish Economic Soc., 1981–84. *Publications:* The Scottish Banks, 1965; (co-author and ed) North East Scotland: a survey of its development potential, 1969; (jtly) The Economic Impact of North Sea oil on Scotland, 1978; (ed) The Political Economy of Tolerable Survival, 1981; articles in economic and banking jls; reports on the international coal trade. *Recreations:* music and country life. *Address:* Westfield, Ancrum, Roxburghshire TD8 6XA. *T:* (01835) 830237.

GASS, Elizabeth Periam Acland Hood, (Lady Gass); JP; Lord-Lieutenant of Somerset, since 1998 (Vice Lord-Lieutenant, 1996–98); *b* 2 March 1940; *d* of late Hon. John Acland-Hood, barrister, *yr s* of 1st Baron St Audries, PC and of Dr Phyllis Acland-Hood (*née* Hallett); *m* 1975, Sir Michael Gass, KCMG (*d* 1983). *Educ:* Cheltenham Ladies' Coll.; Girton Coll., Cambridge (MA). Somerset County Council: Member, 1985–97; Chm., Exmoor Nat. Park Cttee, 1989–93; Vice-Chm., Social Services Cttee, 1989–93. Dir, Avalon NHS Trust, 1993–96. Comr, English Heritage, 1995–2001. Member: Rail Users' Consultative Cttee for Western England, 1992–99; Nat. Trust Wessex Cttee, 1994–. Member, Council: Cheltenham Ladies' Coll., 1992–2001; Bath Univ., 1999–. Trustee, West of England Sch. for Children with Little or no Sight, 1996–. High Sheriff 1994, DL 1995, JP 1996, Somerset. *Recreations:* gardening, music. *Address:* Fairfield, Stogursey, Bridgwater, Somerset TA5 1PU. *T:* (01278) 732251, *Fax:* (01278) 732277.

GASS, James Ronald, CMG 1989; Consultant, European Economic Commission, since 1989; *b* 25 March 1924; *s* of Harold Amos Gass and Cherry (*née* Taylor); *m* 1950, Colette Alice Jeanne Lejeune; two *s* one *d*. *Educ:* Birkenhead Park High Sch.; Liverpool Univ. (BA Hons); Nuffield and Balliol Colls, Oxford. Flight Lieut Pilot, RAF, service in US, India and Burma, 1942–46. PSO, DSIR Intelligence Div., 1951–57; Special Asst to Chm., Task Force on Western Scientific Co-operation, NATO, Paris, 1957; OEEC, subsequently OECD, Paris: Head of Div., Scientific and Tech. Personnel, 1958–61; Dep. Dir for Scientific Affairs, 1961–68; Director: Centre for Educnl Res. and Innovation, 1968–89; Social Affairs, Manpower and Educn, 1974–89; retired 1989. *Recreations:* restoration of antiques, gymnastics, philosophy. *Address:* 2 avenue du Vert Bois, Ville d'Avray, 92410 Paris, France. *T:* 47095481.

GASS, Simon Lawrance, CMG 1998; CVO 1999; HM Diplomatic Service; *b* 2 Nov. 1956; *s* of late Geoffrey Gass and of Brenda Gass (*née* Lawrance); *m* 1980, Marianne Enid Stott; two *s* one *d*. *Educ:* Eltham Coll.; Reading Univ. (LLB 1977). Joined FCO, 1977; Lagos, 1979–83; Athens, 1984–87; FCO, 1987–90; Asst Private Sec. to Foreign Sec., 1990–92; Rome, 1992–95; Counsellor, FCO, 1995–98; Dep. High Comr, S Africa, 1998–2001. *Address:* c/o Foreign and Commonwealth Office, King Charles Street, SW1A 2AH.

GASSON, (Gordon) Barry, OBE 1985; ARSA; Principal, Barry Gasson, Architects; *b* 27 Aug. 1935; *s* of late Gladys Godfrey (previously Gasson) and Stanley Gasson; *m* Rosemary Mulligan; one *s* two *d*. *Educ:* Solihull Sch.; Birmingham Sch. of Architecture (Dip. Arch. 1958); RIBA (Owen Jones Student); Columbia Univ., NY (MS 1961); Q. W. Boese English Speaking Fellowship; MA Cantab 1963. ARIAS, RIBA. Lectr, Univ. of Cambridge, 1963–73; visiting critic: University Coll., Dublin, 1969–72; California State Poly., 1969; Mackintosh Sch. of Arch., 1978–85; Edinburgh Coll. of Art, 1986–92; Vis. Prof., Univ. of Manchester, 1987–95. Former Mem., Royal Fine Art Commn for Scotland. Assessor, Civic Trust Awards, RIBA student medals, nat. competitions; Chm., RIBA regional awards. Farmer (biodynamic). Designed galleries for Burrell Collection, Glasgow (won in open comp., 1972); awards: Stone Fedn, 1983; Arch. Design; RA Premier Arch., 1984; Museum of the Year; British Tourist Trophy; Sotheby Fine Art; Services in Building; Civic Trust; Eternit Internat., 1985; RIBA 1986; RSA Gold Medal, 1983; World Biennale of Arch. Gold Medal, 1987. *Publication:* contrib. to The Burrell Collection, 1983.

GASSON, John Gustav Haycraft, CB 1990; Head of Policy and Legal Services Group, Lord Chancellor's Department, 1987–91; *b* 2 Aug. 1931; *s* of late Dr and Mrs S. G. H. Gasson; *m* 1964, Lesley, *d* of L. L. Thomas, Nyamandhlovu, Zimbabwe; two *s* one *d*. *Educ:* Diocesan Coll., Rondebosch, Cape Town; Cape Town Univ. (BA); Pembroke Coll., Oxford (Rhodes Schol. Rhodesia 1953; MA, BCL). Called to the Bar, Gray's Inn, 1957; Advocate of High Court of S Rhodesia, 1959; Lord Chancellor's Dept, 1964; Sec., Law Commn, 1982–87. *Recreations:* cycling, gardening. *Address:* The White House, Candys Lane, Blandford Road, Shillingstone, Dorset DT11 0SF. *Club:* Bulawayo (Zimbabwe).

GASTON, Prof. John Stanley Hill, PhD; FRCP; Professor of Rheumatology, University of Cambridge, since 1995; *b* 24 June 1952; *s* of John Gaston, CBE and Elizabeth Gaston (*née* Gordon); *m* 1975, Christine Mary Arthur; one *s* one *d*. *Educ:* Royal Belfast Academical Instn; Lincoln Coll., Oxford (MA); Oxford Univ. Med. Sch. (BM BCh); Univ. of Bristol (PhD 1983). FRCP 1995. SHO, then Registrar posts at Hammersmith Hosp., Bristol Hosps and Torbay, 1977–80; Sir Michael Sobell Cancer Res. Fellow, Univ. of Bristol, 1980–83; MRC Travelling Fellowship, Stanford Univ. Med. Centre, 1983–85; University of Birmingham: MRC Res. Trng Fellow, 1985–87; Wellcome Sen. Res. Fellow in Clinical Sci., 1987–92; Sen. Lectr, then Reader in Rheumatology, 1992–95. Hon. Consultant in Rheumatology, S Birmingham HA, 1987–95. *Publications:* papers on immunology and immunological aspects of rheumatic diseases. *Recreations:* music, reading biographies. *Address:* University of Cambridge School of Clinical Medicine, Box 157, Level 5, Addenbrooke's Hospital, Hills Road, Cambridge CB2 2QQ. *T:* (01223) 330161; *e-mail:* jshg2@medschl.cam.ac.uk; 6 Parsonage Court, Whittlesford, Cambs CB2 4PH.

GATEHOUSE, Graham Gould; Director, Orchard Lane Initiatives Ltd, since 1995; *b* 17 July 1935; *s* of G. and G. M. Gatehouse; *m* 1960, Gillian M. Newell; two *s* one *d*; one *d* by Wanda Kwilecka. *Educ:* Crewkerne Sch., Somerset; Exeter Univ., Devon (DSA); London School of Economics (Dip. Mental Health). Served Royal Artillery, 1954–56. Somerset County Council, 1957–67; Worcestershire CC, 1967–70; Norfolk CC, 1970–73; West Sussex CC, 1973–81; Dir of Social Services, Surrey CC, 1981–95. FRSA 1987. *Recreations:* Rugby football, cricket, theatre. *Address:* Fir Tree Farm, Doncaster Road, Darfield, Barnsley, S Yorks S73 9JB.

GATEHOUSE, Sir Robert Alexander, Kt 1985; a Judge of the High Court, Queen's Bench Division, 1985–96; *b* 30 Jan. 1924; *s* of late Major-Gen. A. H. Gatehouse, DSO,

MC; *m* 1st, 1951, Henrietta Swann; 2nd, 1966, Pamela Fawcett. *Educ:* Wellington Coll.; Trinity Hall, Cambridge. Served War of 1939–45: commissioned into Royal Dragoons; NW Europe. Called to the Bar, Lincoln's Inn, 1950; Bencher, 1977; QC 1969. Governor, Wellington Coll., 1970–94. *Recreations:* music, wood sculpture. *Address:* Cross Farm, Frimley Green, Surrey GU16 6LS; Flat 9, Elm Quay Court, SW8 5DE.

GATENBY, Michael Richard Brock, FCA; Vice Chairman, Charterhouse Bank Ltd, 1989–95; *b* 5 Oct. 1944; *s* of Arthur Duncan Gatenby and Dora Ethel (*née* Brock); *m* 1990, Lesley Ann Harding; two step *s. Educ:* Haileybury; Trinity Hall, Cambridge (BA 1966). ACA 1970. With Peat Marwick Mitchell, 1966–71; Hill Samuel & Co. Ltd, 1971–85 (Dir, 1975–85); Charterhouse Bank Ltd, 1985–95: Man. Dir, 1986–89; Director: Staveley Industries plc, 1980–96; Bridport plc, 1980–99; Scholl plc, 1996–98; Philip Harris plc, 1996–97; SGB Gp plc, 1997–; Protherics (formerly Proteus International) plc, 1997–; Powell Duffryn plc, 1997–; Tarmac plc, 1999–2000. *Recreations:* golf, ski-ing. *Address:* 11 Norland Square, W11 4PX. *T:* (020) 7221 9420.

GATES, Robert M.; Director of Central Intelligence, USA, 1991–93; *b* Kansas, 25 Sept. 1943; *m* Becky; two *c. Educ:* Coll. of William and Mary (BA 1965); Indiana Univ. (MA History, 1966); Georgetown Univ. (PhD Russian and Soviet History, 1974). Joined CIA, 1966; intelligence analyst; Asst. Nat. Intell. Officer for Strategic Programs; staff, Nat. Security Council, 1974–79; rejoined CIA, 1979: admin. posts; Nat. Intell. Officer for Soviet Union; Dep. Dir for Intell., 1982–86; Chm., Nat. Intell. Council, 1983–86; Dep. Dir of Central Intell., 1986–89 (Actg Dir, 1986–87); Asst to the President, and Dep. for Nat. Security Affairs, Nat. Security Council, 1986–91. Presidential Citizens Medal; Nat. Intell. Distinguished Service Medal; Distinguished Intell. Medal, CIA; Intell. Medal of Merit; Arthur S. Flemming Award. *Publication:* From the Shadows, 1996.

GATES, Emeritus Prof. Ronald Cecil, AO 1978; FASSA; Vice-Chancellor, University of New England, 1977–85; *b* 8 Jan. 1923; *s* of Earle Nelson Gates and Elsie Edith (*née* Tucker); *m* 1953, Barbara Mann; one *s* two *d* (and one *s* decd). *Educ:* East Launceston State Sch., Tas; Launceston C of E Grammar Sch., Tas; Univ. of Tas (BCom Econs and Commercial Law); Oxford Univ. (MA PPE). FASSA 1968. Served War, 1942–45: Private, AIF. Clerk, Aust. Taxation Office, Hobart, 1941–42; Rhodes Scholar (Tas), Oxford, 1946–48; Historian, Aust. Taxation Office, Canberra, 1949–52; Univ. of Sydney: Sen. Lectr in Econs, 1952–64; Associate Prof., 1964–65; Rockefeller Fellow in Social Sciences, 1955; Carnegie Travel Grant, 1960; Prof. of Econs, Univ. of Qld, 1966–77 (Pres., Professorial Bd, 1975–77). Pres., Econ. Soc. of Australia and NZ, 1969–72. Chairman: statutory Consumer Affairs Council of Qld, 1971–73; Aust. Inst. of Urban Studies, 1975–77. Comr, Commonwealth Commn of Inquiry into Poverty, 1973–77. Chairman: Aust. Nat. Commn for Unesco, 1981–83 (Vice-Chm., 1979); Adv. Council for Inter-govt Relations, 1979–85; Internat. Relations Cttee, Cttee of Australian Vice-Chancellors, 1981–84; Local Govt Trng Council (formerly Nat. Local Govt Industry Trng Cttee), 1983–92; Armidale-Dumaresq Jt Planning Cttee, 1992–97. Pres., Australian Esperanto Assoc., 1998–2001 (Vice-Pres., 1995–98). Hon. FRAPI 1976; Hon. Fellow, Aust. Inst. of Urban Studies, 1979. Hon. DEcon Qld, 1978; Hon. DLitt New England, 1987. *Publications:* (with H. R. Edwards and N. T. Drane) Survey of Consumer Finances, Sydney 1963–65: Vol. 2, 1965; Vols 1, 3 and 4, 1966; Vols 5, 6 and 7, 1967; (jtly) The Price of Land, 1971; (jtly) New Cities for Australia, 1972; (jtly) Land for the Cities, 1973; (with P. A. Cassidy) Simulation, Uncertainty and Public Investment Analysis, 1977; *in Esperanto:* detective novels: La Septaga Murdenigmo, 1991; Kolera Afero, 1993; Morto de Sciencisto, 1994; La Vidvino kaj la Profesoro (romantic novel), 1997; short stories: Sep Krimnoveloj, 1993; Refoje Krimnoveloj Sep, 1994; Tria Kolekto da Krimnoveloj, 1996; chapters in books and articles in learned jls. *Recreations:* music, beef cattle, Esperanto, bridge. *Address:* Wangarang, Kelly's Plains Road, Armidale, NSW 2350, Australia.

GATES, William Henry, III; Chairman, since 1976, and Chief Software Architect, since 2000, Microsoft Corp.; *b* 28 Oct. 1955; *s* of William Henry and Mary Maxwell Gates; *m* 1994, Melinda French; one *s* one *d. Educ:* Lakeside High Sch., Seattle; Harvard Univ. Co-founder, Micro Soft, later Microsoft Corp., 1975. *Publications:* The Road Ahead, 1995; (with C. Hemingway) Business @ the Speed of Thought: using a digital nervous system, 1999. *Address:* Microsoft Corp., 1 Microsoft Way, Redmond, WA 98052-8300, USA.

GATFORD, Ven. Ian; Archdeacon of Derby, since 1993; *b* 15 June 1940; *s* of Frederick Ernest and Chrissie Lilian Gatford; *m* 1965, Anne Maire (*née* Whitehead); one *s* three *d. Educ:* King's Coll. London (AKC 1965); St Boniface Coll., Warminster. Management Trainee, Taylor Woodrow Gp, 1959–62; Accounts and Admin, Farr's (Construction) Ltd, 1965–66; theolog. trng, 1966–67; ordained deacon 1967, priest 1968; Curate, St Mary, Clifton, Nottingham, 1967–71; Team Vicar, Holy Trinity, Clifton, 1971–75; Vicar, St Martin, Sherwood, 1975–84; Canon Residentiary, Derby Cathedral, 1984–2000; Sub-Provost, Derby Cathedral, 1990–93. Presenter of weekly help-line programmes, BBC Radio Nottingham, 1972–84; presenter of religious affairs programmes, BBC Radio Derby, 1984–93; Chm., BBC Local Adv. Council, 1998–2001. *Recreations:* playing the piano, walking, cycling, jazz, classical music. *Address:* Derby Church House, Full Street, Derby DE1 3DR. *T:* (01332) 382233.

GATHERCOLE, Ven. John Robert; Archdeacon of Dudley, 1987–2001; *b* 23 April 1937; *s* of Robert Gathercole and Winifred Mary Gathercole (*née* Price); *m* 1963, Claire (*née* London); one *s* one *d. Educ:* Judd School, Tonbridge; Fitzwilliam Coll., Cambridge (BA 1959, MA 1963); Ridley Hall, Cambridge. Deacon 1962, priest 1963; Curate: St Nicholas, Durham, 1962–66; St Bartholomew, Croxdale, 1966–70; Social and Industrial Adviser to Bishop of Durham, 1967–70; Industrial Chaplain, Redditch, dio. Worcester, 1970–87; RD of Bromsgrove, 1978–85; Team Leader, and Sen. Chaplain, Worcs Industrial Mission, 1985–91. Member: General Synod of C of E, 1995–2001; Council for the Care of Churches, 1998–2001. *Recreations:* vintage sports cars, music. *Address:* Wisteria Cottage, Kidderminster Road, Ombersley, Worcs WR9 0EL. *T:* (01905) 620263.

GATHORNE-HARDY, family name of **Earl of Cranbrook**.

GATT, Colin, CMG 1993; Director, Managed Projects, Commonwealth Development Corporation, 1990–94; *b* 16 Aug. 1934; *s* of late William John Sim Gatt and Margaret Whyte-Hepburn; *m* 1st, 1957, Sheena Carstairs (*d* 1996); two *s* one *d*; 2nd, 1998, Susan Tessa Jennifer (*née* Lewis-Antill). *Educ:* state schs in Scotland. Engineer, 1955–71: manager, gen. manager and consultant, agricl businesses in Africa and Asia; Commonwealth Development Corporation, 1971–94: managed businesses in third world countries in Asia, Africa and Pacific regions, 1971–88; Dir, Technical Services, London, 1989–90. Independence Medal (Solomon Is), 1978. *Recreations:* reading, golf, wine, basic survival cookery. *Address:* Tudor Cottage, 29 High Street, Long Crendon, Bucks HP18 9AL. *Clubs:* Royal Over-Seas League; Oxfordshire Golf (Thame); Goring & Streatley Golf (Streatley on Thames).

GATTI, Daniele; conductor; Music Director: Royal Philharmonic Orchestra, since 1996; Teatro Communale, Bologna, since 1997; *b* Milan, 6 Nov. 1961; *m* 1990, Silvia Chiesa. *Educ:* Milan Conservatory. Founder and Music Dir, Stradivari Chamber Orch., 1986–92; débuts: La Scala, Milan, 1987–88; in USA with American Symphony Orch., Carnegie Hall, NY, 1990; Covent Gdn, 1992; Metropolitan Opera, NY, 1994–95; with RPO, 1994; with NY Philharmonic, 1995; Music Dir, Accad. di Santa Cecilia, Rome, 1992–97; Principal Guest Conductor, Covent Gdn, 1994–96; has worked with leading opera cos incl. Lyric Opera, Chicago, Staatsoper, Berlin; has conducted leading internat. orchestras incl. Toronto Symphony and LA Philharmonic, 1991; Orchestre Symphonique de Montreal, LSO, Philadelphia Orch., 1993; Cincinnati Symphony, Chicago Symphony, LPO, 1994; Berlin Philharmonic, 1997. Has toured extensively and made numerous recordings. *Recreations:* reading, walking, football, chess. *Address:* c/o Royal Philharmonic Orchestra, 16 Clerkenwell Green, EC1R 0DP.

GATTING, Michael William, OBE 1987; cricketer; Director, Ashwell Leisure Group; Consultant, Titan Travel Group; *b* 6 June 1957; *s* of William Alfred Gatting and Vera Mavis Gatting; *m* 1980, Elaine Mabbott; two *s. Educ:* John Kelly Boys' High Sch. Middlesex County Cricket team, 1975–98: début, 1975; county cap, 1977; Captain, 1988–97; retired from 1st XI, 1998; scored 77 hundreds, 8 double hundreds, 1000 runs in a season 17 times; highest score 258, 1984; also took 129 wickets and 393 catches. Test début, 1977; England Captain, 1986–88; overseas tours with England: NZ and Pakistan, 1977–78, 1983–84; W Indies, 1980–81, 1985–86; India and Sri Lanka, 1981–82, 1992–93; India, 1984–85; Australia, 1986–87; Australia and NZ, 1987–88; Australia, 1994–95; also, World Cup, 1987–88, *v* India, Pakistan, Australia and NZ; scored ten Test centuries; highest score 207, 1984–85. England A team coach, Australia tour, 1996–97, Kenya and Sri Lanka tour, 1997–98; Dir of Coaching, Middx CCC, 1998–2000; Manager: England Under 19 team, NZ tour, 1999; England A team, NZ tour, 1999. Mem., Selection Panel, ECB, 1997–99. *Publications:* Limited Overs, 1986; Triumph in Australia, 1987; Leading from the Front, 1988. *Recreations:* golf, swimming, reading, music. *Address:* c/o Middlesex County Cricket Club, Lord's Cricket Ground, St John's Wood Road, NW8 8QN. *Club:* Wig and Pen.

GATTY, Trevor Thomas, OBE 1974; HM Diplomatic Service, retired; international business consultant, arbitrator and mediator; President, TGC Group (formerly MGT International), since 1989; *b* 8 June 1930; *s* of Thomas Alfred Gatty and Lillian Gatty (*née* Wood); *m* 1st, 1956, Jemima Bowman (marr. diss. 1983); two *s* one *d*; 2nd, 1989, Myrna Saturn; one step *s* one step *d. Educ:* King Edward's Sch., Birmingham. Served Army, 1948–50, 2/Lieut Royal Warwickshire Regt, later Lieut Royal Fusiliers (TA), 1950–53. Foreign Office, 1950; Vice-Consul, Leopoldville, 1954; FO, 1958–61; Second (later First) Sec., Bangkok, 1961–64; Consul, San Francisco, 1965–66; Commercial Consul, San Francisco, 1967–68; FCO, 1968–73; Commercial Consul, Zürich, 1973–75; FCO, 1975–76; Counsellor (Diplomatic Service Inspector), 1977–80; Head, Migration and Visa Dept, FCO, 1980–81; Consul-General, Atlanta, 1981–85. Protocol Advr, Atlanta Organising Cttee for Olympic Games, 1996. Hon. British Consul for N Carolina, 1994–. *Recreations:* reading, English Springer spaniels. *Address:* 229 North Poplar Street (#15), Charlotte, NC 28202, USA. *T:* (704) 3381372; *e-mail:* tgcg@mail.org.

GATWARD, (Anthony) James; Deputy Chairman, Premium TV Ltd, since 2000; *b* 4 March 1938; *s* of George James Gatward and Lillian Georgina (*née* Strutton); *m* 1969, Isobel Anne Stuart Black, actress; three *d. Educ:* George Gascoigne Sch., Walthamstow; South West Essex Technical Coll. and Sch. of Art (drama course). Entered TV industry, 1957; freelance drama producer/director: Canada and USA, 1959–65; BBC and most ITV cos, 1966–70; partner in prodn co., acting as Exec. Prod. and often Dir of many internat. co-prodns in UK, Ceylon, Australia and Germany, 1970–78; instigated and led preparation of application for S and SE England television franchise, 1979–80 (awarded Dec. 1980); Man. Dir, 1979–84, Chief Exec., 1984–91, Television South, subseq. TVS Entertainment PLC; Dep. Chm. and Chief Exec., 1984–90, Chm., 1990–91, TVS Television; Chief Exec., 1993–96, Chm., 1996–2000, Complete Media Mgt Ltd; Chm., Digital Television Network Ltd, 1996–99. Director: Southstar, Scottish and Global TV, 1971–78; Indep. TV Publications Ltd, 1982–88; Oracle Teletext Ltd, 1982–88; Solent Cablevision Ltd, 1983–89; Channel 4 TV Co., 1984–89; Indep. TV News Ltd, 1986–91; Super Channel Ltd, 1986–88; ITV Super Channel Ltd, 1986–89; Chm., TVS Production, 1984–89; Chm. and Chief Exec., TVS N American Hldgs, 1988–91; Pres., Telso Communications Inc., 1987–90; Chairman: Telso Communications Ltd, 1987–91; Telso Overseas Ltd, 1987–91; Midem Orgn SA, 1987–89; MTM Entertainment Inc., 1988–91 (Chief Exec. Officer, 1989–91); Redgrave Theatre, 1995–98. Member: Council, Operation Raleigh; Court of the Mary Rose. Pres., SE Agricl Soc., 1992; Governor, S of England Agricl Soc. *Recreations:* sailing, music. *Address:* (office) 22 Suffolk Street, SW1Y 4HS. *Clubs:* Royal Thames Yacht; Porquerolles Yacht (Hyères).

GAU, John Glen Mackay, CBE 1989; independent producer; Chief Executive, John Gau Productions, since 1991 (Managing Director, 1981–88); *b* 25 March 1940; *s* of late Cullis William Gau and Nan Munro; *m* 1966, Susan Tebbs; two *s. Educ:* Haileybury and ISC; Trinity Hall, Cambridge; Univ. of Wisconsin. BBC TV: Assistant Film Editor, 1963; Current Affairs Producer, 1965–74; Editor, Nationwide, 1975; Head of Current Affairs Programmes, 1978–81; Dep. Chief Exec. and Dir of Programmes, British Satellite Broadcasting, 1988–90. Dir, Channel 4, 1984–88. Chm., Indep. Programme Producers' Assoc., 1983–86. Chm. Council, RTS, 1986–88 (Hon. Sec., 1993–). FRTS 1986. *Publications:* (jtly) Soldiers, 1985; Lights, Camera, Action!, 1995. *Address:* 15 St Albans Mansion, Kensington Court Place, W8 5QH. *T:* (020) 7937 4033.

GAUDRY, Roger, CC (Canada) 1968; DSc; FRSC; President, Jules & Paul-Emile Léger Foundation, 1983–95; *b* 15 Dec. 1913; *m* 1941, Madeleine Vallée; two *s* three *d. Educ:* Laval Univ. (BA 1933; BSc 1937; DSc 1940); Rhodes Scholar, Oxford Univ., 1937–39. Organic Chemistry, Laval Univ.: Lectr, 1940; Prof., 1945; Full Prof., 1950. Ayerst Laboratories: Asst Dir of Research, 1954; Dir of Research, 1957; Vice-Pres. and Dir of Research, 1963–65; Rector, Univ. of Montreal, 1965–75; Dir, 1975–88, Chm., 1984–88, Bio-Research Labs. Chm., Nordic Labs, 1975–91. Director: Corby Distilleries, 1975–89; Bank of Montreal, 1975–84; Alcan Aluminium, 1976–86; Hoechst Canada, 1977–87; SKW Canada, 1978–88; St Lawrence Starch, 1983–89. Chm., Science Council of Canada, 1972–75; President: Internat. Assoc. of Univs, 1975–80; Sci., Technology and Industry Centre of Montreal, 1988–90. Chm. Bd, UN Univ., 1974–76; Dir, Inst. de recherches cliniques, Montreal, 1975–96; Chm., Network for Neural Regeneration and Functional Recovery, 1990–94. Hon. FRCP&S (Canada), 1971. Hon. doctorates: (Laws) Univ. of Toronto, 1966; (Science) RMC of Kingston, 1966; (Science) Univ. of BC, 1967; (Laws) McGill Univ., 1967; Univ. of Clermont-Ferrand, France, 1967; (Laws) St Thomas Univ., 1968; (Laws) Brock Univ., 1969; (Civil Laws) Bishop's Univ., 1969; (Science) Univ. of Saskatchewan, 1970; (Science) Univ. of Western Ontario, 1976; (Laws) Concordia Univ., 1980; Parizeau Medal from Assoc. Canadienne Française pour l'Avancement des Sciences, 1958. KM 1976; Silver Jubilee Medal, 1977; Compagnon de Lavoisier, 1985; Grand Officier de l'Ordre du Québec, 1992; Medal of 125th Anniversary of Confederation, 1992; World Award of Educn, World Cultural Council, Mexico, 1996. *Publications:* author and co-author of numerous scientific papers in organic and biological chemistry. *Address:* 6100 chemin Deacon, apt 03-L, Montréal, QC H3S 2V6, Canada.

GAULD, William Wallace; Under-Secretary, Department of Agriculture and Fisheries for Scotland, 1972–79; *b* 12 Oct. 1919; *e s* of late Rev. W. W. Gauld, DD, of Aberdeen, and Charlotte Jane Gauld (*née* Reid); *m* 1943, Jean Inglis Gray (*d* 1999); three *d*. *Educ:* Fettes; Aberdeen Univ. MA (1st Cl. Hons Classics). Served Pioneer Corps, 1940–46 (Major 1945). Entered Dept of Agriculture for Scotland, 1947; Private Sec. to Secretary of State for Scotland, 1955–57; Asst Sec., 1958; Scottish Development Dept, 1968–72; Mem. Agricultural Research Council, 1972–79. Pres., Botanical Soc., Edinburgh, 1978–80. *Recreation:* natural history. *Address:* 1 Banks Crescent, Crieff, Perthshire PH7 3SR.

GAULIN, Jean; Vice-Chairman, President and Chief Operating Officer, Ultramar Diamond Shamrock, since 1997; *b* 9 July 1942; *m* 1981, Andrée LeBoeuf; two *s* one *d*. *Educ:* Univ. of Montreal (degrees in appl. scis and chem. eng.). Vice-Pres., Ultramar Canada, 1977–79; President: Nouveler Inc., 1980–82; Gaz Metropolitan Inc., 1982–85 (and Chief Exec.); Ultramar Canada, 1985–89; CEO, Ultramar plc, 1989–92; Chm. and CEO, Ultramar Corp., 1992–96. *Address:* Ultramar Diamond Shamrock Inc., PO Box 696000, San Antonio, TX 78269, USA.

GAULT, David Hamilton; Executive Chairman, Gallic Management Co. Ltd, 1974–93; *b* 9 April 1928; *s* of Leslie Hamilton Gault and Iris Hilda Gordon Young; *m* 1950, Felicity Jane Gribble; three *s* two *d*. *Educ:* Fettes Coll., Edinburgh. Nat. Service, commnd in RA, 1946–48; Clerk, C. H. Rugg & Co. Ltd, Shipbrokers, 1948–52; H. Clarkson & Co. Ltd, Shipbrokers: Man. 1952–56; Dir 1956–62; Jt Man. Dir 1962–72; Gp Man. Dir, Shipping Industrial Holdings Ltd, 1972–74; Chm., Jebsen (UK) Ltd, 1962–81; Chm., Seabridge Shipping Ltd, 1965–73. *Recreations:* gardening, walking. *Address:* Kent House, East Harting, near Petersfield, Hants GU31 5LS. *T:* (01730) 825206. *Clubs:* Boodle's, City.

GAULT, David Thomas, FRCS; Consultant Plastic Surgeon: Mount Vernon Hospital, since 1991; Great Ormond Street Hospital for Sick Children, since 2000; *b* 21 March 1954; *s* of William and Irene Mabel Bebe Gault; *m* 1989, Debra Hastings-Nield; two *s* two *d*. *Educ:* Edinburgh Univ. (MB ChB 1977). FRCS 1982. MRC French Exchange Fellow, 1987; Craniofacial Fellow, Hôpital des Enfants Malades, Paris, 1987; Sen. Registrar, Plastic Surgery, St Thomas' Hosp., Gt Ormond St Hosp. for Sick Children and Royal Marsden Hosp., 1988–91. Consultant: Bishops Wood Hosp., 1991–; Wellington Hosp., 1992–. Hon. Sen. Lectr, UCL, 1999–. Ethicon Foundn Travelling Schol., 1987; Wellington Foundn Schol., 1989; BAPS Travelling Bursary, 1990. *Publications:* contribs to books and articles on laser and plastic surgery, particularly on ear reconstruction and depilation laser treatment. *Recreations:* rowing, painting, sculpting, planting. *Address:* 10 Harley Street, W1N 1AA. *T:* (020) 7935 7665. *Club:* Cliveden (Taplow).

GAULT, Rt Hon. Thomas Munro, DCNZM 2001; PC 1992; **Rt Hon. Justice Gault;** Judge of Court of Appeal, New Zealand, since 1991; *b* 31 Oct. 1938; *s* of Thomas Gordon Gault and Evelyn Jane Gault (*née* Paulmeir); *m* 1963, Barbara Pauline Stewart; one *s*. *Educ:* Wellington Coll.; Victoria University Coll. (LLB); Victoria Univ. of Wellington (LLM). Solicitor of Supreme Court of NZ, 1961; A. J. Park & Son, 1961–81; practised at NZ Bar, 1981–87; QC 1984; Judge of High Court of NZ, 1987–91. Mem. of Honour, Internat. Assoc. for Protection of Industrial Property, 1990. *Recreation:* golf. *Address:* PO Box 1606, Wellington, New Zealand; 25A Benbow Street, Auckland, New Zealand. *T:* (4) 9143549. *Club:* Wellington (New Zealand).

GAULTER, Derek Vivian, CBE 1978; Chairman, Construction Industry Training Board, 1985–90; *b* 10 Dec. 1924; *s* of late Jack Rudolf Gaulter, MC and Muriel Gaulter (*née* Westworth); *m* 1st, 1949, Edith Irene Shackleton (*d* 1996); one *s* three *d*; 2nd, 2000, Marion Bowker. *Educ:* Denstone College; Peterhouse, Cambridge (MA). RNVR, Sub Lieut MTBs/Minesweepers, 1943–46. Lord Justice Holker Sen. Scholarship, Gray's Inn; called to the Bar, Gray's Inn, 1949; Common Law Bar, Manchester, 1950–55. Federation of Civil Engineering Contractors: Legal Sec., General Sec., Dep. Dir Gen., 1955–67; Dir Gen., 1967–86. Trustee, Woodland Trust, 1995–. *Recreations:* gardening, travel, photography. *Address:* Brampton House, 11 Shilton Road, Burford, Oxon OX18 4PA.

GAULTIER, Jean-Paul; fashion designer; *b* 24 April 1952; *s* of Paul Gaultier and Solange Gaultier (*née* Garrabe). *Educ:* Lycée, Arcueil, Paris. Assistant: to Pierre Cardin, 1970; to Jacques Esterel, 1971–73; designer of US collections for Pierre Cardin, 1974–75; ind. designer, 1976–82; founder, Jean-Paul Gaultier SA, 1978. Début collection, 1976; first collection for men, 1984, for children, 1988; also perfumes, 1993 and 1995. Designed costumes: for ballet, Le Défilé de Régine Chopinot, 1985; for films: The Cook, the Thief, His Wife and her Lover, 1989; Kika, 1994; La Cité des Enfants Perdus, 1995; The Fifth Element, 1996; for Madonna's Blond Ambition tour, 1990. Chevalier des Arts et des Lettres (France). *Address:* Jean-Paul Gaultier SA, 30 rue du Faubourg-Saint-Antoine, 75012 Paris, France.

GAUMOND, Most Rev. Mgr André; *see* Sherbrooke, Archbishop of (RC).

GAUNT, Jonathan Robert; QC 1991; *b* 3 Nov. 1947; *s* of late Dr Brian Gaunt and Dr Mary Gaunt (*née* Hudson); *m* 1975, Lynn Dennis; one *d*. *Educ:* St Peter's Coll.; Radley; University Coll., Oxford (BA). Called to the Bar, Lincoln's Inn, 1972, Bencher, 1998. Jt Head, Falcon Chambers, 1993–. *Publications:* (ed) Halsbury's Laws of England, Vol. 27, 4th edn 1981, rev. 1994; (ed) Gale on Easements, 16th edn 1996. *Recreations:* golf, sailing. *Address:* Falcon Chambers, Falcon Court, EC4Y 1AA. *T:* (020) 7353 2484. *Club:* North Middlesex Golf.

GAUTIER-SMITH, Peter Claudius, FRCP; Physician, National Hospitals for Nervous Diseases, Queen Square and Maida Vale, 1962–89; *b* 1 March 1929; *s* of late Claudius Gautier-Smith and Madeleine (*née* Ferguson); *m* 1960, Nesta Mary Wroth; two *d*. *Educ:* Cheltenham Coll. (Exhibnr); King's Coll., Cambridge; St Thomas's Hosp. Med. Sch. MA, MD. Casualty Officer, House Physician, St Thomas' Hosp., 1955–56; Medical Registrar, University Coll. Hosp., 1958; Registrar, National Hosp., Queen Square, 1960–62; Consultant Neurologist, St George's Hosp., 1962–75; Dean, Inst. of Neurology, 1975–82. Mem., Bd of Governors, Nat. Hosps for Nervous Diseases, 1975–89. Hon. Neurologist, Dispensaire Français, London, 1983–89. *Publications:* Parasagittal and Falx Meningiomas, 1970; papers in learned jls on neurology. *Recreations:* literary (twenty-three novels published under a pseudonym); French language; squash (played for Cambridge v Oxford, 1951; Captain, London Univ., 1954); tennis. *Clubs:* MCC; Hawks (Cambridge); Jesters.

GAUTREY, Peter, CMG 1972; CVO 1961; DK (Brunei) 1972; HM Diplomatic Service, retired; High Commissioner in Guyana, 1975–78, concurrently Ambassador (non-resident) to Surinam, 1976–78; *b* 17 Sept. 1918; *s* of late Robert Harry Gautrey, Hindhead, Surrey, and Hilda Morris; *m* 1947, Marguerite Etta Uncles; one *s* one *d*. *Educ:* Abbotsholme Sch., Derbys. Joined Home Office, 1936. Served in Royal Artillery, (Capt.), Sept. 1939–March 1946. Re-joined Home Office; Commonwealth Relations Office, 1948; served in British Embassy, Dublin, 1950–53; UK High Commission, New Delhi, 1955–57 and 1960–63; British Deputy High Commissioner, Bombay, 1963–65; Corps of Diplomatic Service Inspectors, 1965–68; High Commissioner: Swaziland, 1968–71; Brunei, 1972–75. FRSA 1972. *Recreations:* walking, music, art. *Address:* 24 Fort Road, Guildford, Surrey GU1 3TE.

GAVASKAR, Sunil Manohar; Padma Bhushan; cricketer; business executive; Chairman, Cricket Committee, International Cricket Council, since 2000; *b* 10 July 1949; *s* of Manohar Keshav Gavaskar and Meenal Manohar Gavaskar; *m* 1974, Marshniel Mehrotra; one *s*. *Educ:* St Xavier's High Sch.; St Xavier's Coll.; Bombay Univ. (BA). Represented India in cricket, 1971–88; Captain, Indian Team, 1978, 1979–80, 1980–82 and 1984–85; passed previous world records: no of runs in Test Matches, 1983; no of Test centuries, 1984; first batsman to score over 10,000 Test runs, 1987. Sheriff of Mumbai, 1994–95. *Publications:* Sunny Days, 1976; Idols, 1983; Runs 'n Ruins, 1984; One-day Wonders, 1985. *Clubs:* Cricket Club of India, Bombay Gymkhana.

GAVIN, (Alexander) Rupert; Chief Executive, BBC Worldwide, since 1998; *b* 1 Oct. 1954; *s* of late David Maitland Gavin and of Helen Gavin (who *m* 1991, Sir Hugh Hambling, Bt, *qv*); *m* 1991, Ellen Janet Miller; two *d*. *Educ:* Magdalene Coll., Cambridge (BA Hons 1975; MA). Dir and Partner, Sharps Advertising, 1981–85; Dir, Saatchi & Saatchi Gp, 1985–87; Dep. Man. Dir, Dixons Stores Gp, 1987–94; Man. Dir, Consumer Div., British Telecom, 1994–98. Dir, Ambassador Theatre Gp, 1999–. Vice-Pres., RTS, 1997–. Gov., Nat. Film and TV Sch., 1995–. Liveryman, Grocers' Co., 1986–. *Recreations:* commercial theatre, visual arts (contemporary). *Club:* Pratt's.

GAVIN, Rupert; *see* Gavin, A. R.

GAVRON, family name of **Baron Gavron**.

GAVRON, Baron *cr* 1999 (Life Peer), of Highgate in the London Borough of Camden; **Robert Gavron,** CBE 1990; Chairman, Folio Society Ltd, since 1982; Director, St Ives plc, 1964–98 (Chairman, 1964–93); Proprietor, Carcanet Press Ltd, since 1983; *b* 13 Sept. 1930; *s* of Nathaniel and Leah Gavron; *m* 1955, Hannah Fyvel (*d* 1965); two *s*; *m* 1967, Felicia Nicolette Coates (*see* F. N. Gavron) (marr. diss. 1987); two *d*; *m* 1989, Katharine Gardiner (*née* Macnair) (*see* K. S. Gavron). *Educ:* Leighton Park Sch.; St Peter's Coll., Oxford (MA; Hon. Fellow, 1992). Called to the Bar, Middle Temple, 1955. Entered printing industry, 1955; founded St Ives Gp, 1964 (public co., 1985). Director: Octopus Publishing plc, 1975–87; Electra Management Plc, 1981–91; Chm., Guardian Media Group plc, 1997–2000; Dir, National Gallery Company (formerly National Gallery Publications) Ltd, 1998– (Chm., 1996–98). Chm., Open Coll. of the Arts, 1991–96 (Trustee, 1987–96); Dir, Royal Opera House, 1992–98. Trustee: Nat. Gall., 1994–; Scott Trust, 1997–2000; IPPR, 1991– (Treas., 1994–2000). Gov., LSE, 1997–. Hon. Fellow: RCA, 1990; RSL 1996. *Publication:* (jtly) The Entrepreneurial Society, 1998. *Address:* 44 Eagle Street, WC1R 4FS. *T:* (020) 7400 4300. *Clubs:* Groucho, MCC.

GAVRON, Lady; Katharine Susan Gavron, (Kate); PhD; Chair, Carcanet Press Ltd, since 1989; *b* 19 Jan. 1955; *d* of His Honour (Maurice John) Peter Macnair, *qv* and Vickie Macnair; *m* 1st, 1975, Gerrard Gardiner (marr. diss. 1982); 2nd, 1989, Robert Gavron (*see* Baron Gavron). *Educ:* Francis Holland Sch.; London Sch. of Econs (BSc; PhD 1997). William Heinemann Ltd, 1974–88 (Dir, 1984–88); Director: Secker & Warburg Ltd, 1984–88; Virago Press Ltd, 1994–96. Trustee and Res. Fellow, Inst. Community Studies, 1992–. Dir, Mutual Aid Centre, 1996–. Trustee, Runnymede Trust, 1997–. *Address:* c/o Institute of Community Studies, 18 Victoria Park Square, E2 9PF. *Club:* Groucho.

GAVRON, Felicia Nicolette, (Nicky); Member (Lab) Enfield and Haringey, London Assembly, Greater London Authority, since 2000; Deputy Mayor of London, since 2000; *d* of Clayton English Coates and Elisabet Charlotta Horstmeyer; *m* 1967, Robert Gavron (*see* Baron Gavron) (marr. diss. 1987); two *d*. *Educ:* Worcester Girls' Grammar Sch.; Courtauld Inst. Lectr, Camberwell Sch. of Art and St Martin's Sch. of Art. Mem. (Lab) Haringey BC, 1986–. Chair: Nat. Planning Forum, 2000–; London Planning Adv. Cttee, 1994–96 and 1998–2000 (Labour Leader, 1990); Planning Cttee, LGA, 1997–99; Member: Metropolitan Police Authy, 2000–; Commn for Integrated Transport, 1999–; Advr, Urban Task Force. *Address:* Greater London Authority, Romney House, 43 Marsham Street, SW1P 3PY.

GAY, Geoffrey Charles Lytton; Consultant, Knight, Frank & Rutley, 1975–85 (Senior Partner, 1969–75); World President, International Real Estate Federation (FIABCI), 1973–75; a General Commissioner for Inland Revenue, 1953–89; *b* 14 March 1914; *s* of late Charles Gay and Ida, *d* of Sir Henry A. Lytton (famous Savoyard); *m* 1947, Dorothy Ann, *d* of Major Eric Rickman; one *s* two *d*. *Educ:* St Paul's School. FRICS. Joined Knight, Frank & Rutley, 1929. Served War of 1939–45: Durham LI, BEF, 1940; psc; Lt-Col; Chief of Staff, Sind District, India, 1943. Mem. Westminster City Council, 1962–71. Governor: Benenden Sch., 1971–86; Clayesmore Sch. Council; Mem. Council of St John, London, 1971–84; Liveryman, Broderers' Co. Licentiate, RPS, 1983; FRSA 1983. Chevalier de l'Ordre de l'Economie Nationale, 1960. OStJ 1961; KStJ 1979. *Recreations:* photography, fishing, music, theatre. *Address:* Castle View, 122 Newland, Sherborne, Dorset DT9 3DT. *T:* (01935) 816676; *e-mail:* poohbah@dial.pipex.com. *Clubs:* Carlton, MCC, Flyfishers'.

GAY, Rear-Adm. George Wilsmore, CB 1969; MBE 1946; DSC 1943; JP; Director-General of Naval Training, 1967–69; retired; *b* 1913; *s* of late Engr Comdr G. M. Gay and late Mrs O. T. Gay (*née* Allen); *m* 1941, Nancy Agnes Clark; two *s* one *d*. *Educ:* Eastman's Sch., Southsea; Nautical Coll., Pangbourne. Entered RN, 1930; Cadet Trng, 1930–32; RNEC, Keyham, 1932–35; HMS Glorious, 1935–37; Engr. Off., HMS Porpoise, 1939–41, HMS Clyde, 1941–43; HMS Dolphin, 1938 and 1943–46; HM Dockyard, Portsmouth, 1946–47; HMS Euryalus, 1947–49; Sqdn Engr Off., 1st Submarine Sqdn, HMS Forth, 1949–50; Trng Comdr, HMS Raleigh, 1951–53; Admiralty Engr Overseer, Vickers Armstrong Ltd, 1953–55; HMS Dolphin, 1956–58; Senior Officer, War Course, Royal Naval Coll., Greenwich, 1958; HM Dockyard, Malta, 1959–60; CO, HMS Sultan, Gosport, 1960–63; Chief Staff Off. Material to Flag Off. Submarines, 1963–66; Admty Interview Bd, 1966. Comdr 1947; Capt. 1958; Rear-Adm. 1967. FIMechE (MIMechE 1958). JP Plymouth 1970. *Recreations:* fishing, sailing, gardening.

GAYDON, Prof. Alfred Gordon, FRS 1953; Warren Research Fellow of Royal Society, 1945–74; Professor of Molecular Spectroscopy, 1961–73, now Emeritus, and Fellow, since 1980, Imperial College of Science and Technology, London; *b* 26 Sept. 1911; *s* of Alfred Bert Gaydon and Rosetta Juliet Gordon; *m* 1940, Phyllis Maude Gaze (*d* 1981); one *s* one *d*. *Educ:* Kingston Grammar Sch., Kingston-on-Thames; Imperial Coll., London. BSc (Physics) Imperial Coll., 1932; worked on molecular spectra, and on measurement of high temperatures, on spectra and structure of flames, and shock waves; DSc (London) 1942; Hon. Dr (University of Dijon), 1957. Rumford Medal, Royal Society, 1960; Bernard Lewis Gold Medal, Combustion Inst., 1960. *Publications:* Identification of Molecular Spectra (with Dr R. W. B. Pearse), 1941, 1950, 1963, 1965, 1976; Spectroscopy and Combustion Theory, 1942, 1948; Dissociation Energies and Spectra of Diatomic Molecules, 1947, 1953, 1968; Flames, their Structure, Radiation and Temperature (with Dr H. G. Wolfhard), 1953, 1960, 1970, 1979; The Spectroscopy of

Flames, 1957, 1974; The Shock Tube in High-temperature Chemical Physics (with Dr I. Hurle), 1963. *Recreations:* wild-life photography; formerly rowing. *Address:* Dale Cottage, Shellbridge Road, Slindon Common, Sussex BN18 0LT. *T:* (01243) 814277.

GAYOOM, Maumoon Abdul, Hon. GCMG 1997; President and Commander-in-Chief of the Armed Forces, Republic of Maldives, since 1978; *b* 29 Dec. 1937; *s* of late Abdul Gayoom Ibrahim and Khadeeja Moosa; *m* 1969, Nasreena Ibrahim; two *s* twin *d. Educ:* Al-Azhar Univ., Cairo. Res. Asst, Amer. Univ. of Cairo, 1967–69; Lectr in Islamic Studies and Philosophy, Abdullahi Bayero Coll., Ahmadu Bello Univ., 1969–71; teacher, Aminiya Sch., 1971–72; Manager, Govt Shipping Dept, 1972–73; writer and translator, Pres. Office, 1972–74; Under-Sec., Telecommunications Dept, 1974; Special Under-Sec., Office of the Prime Minister, 1974–75; Dep. Ambassador to Sri Lanka, 1975–76; Under-Sec., Dept of External Affairs, 1976; Dep. Minister of Transport, 1976; Perm. Rep. to UN, 1976–77; Minister of Transport, 1977–78; Governor, Maldives Monetary Authy, 1981–; Minister: of Defence and Nat. Security, 1982–; of Finance, 1989–93; of Finance and Treasury, 1993–. Numerous hon. degrees. *Publication:* The Maldives: a nation in peril, 1998. *Recreations:* astronomy, calligraphy, photography, badminton, cricket. *Address:* Ma. Ki'nbigasdhoshuge, Malé 20–02, Republic of Maldives; Presidential Palace, Orchid Magu, Malé 20–02, Republic of Maldives. *T:* 322100, 322200; The President's Office, Boduthakurufaanu Magu, Malé 20–05, Republic of Maldives.

GAZDAR, Prof. Gerald James Michael, FBA 1988; Professor of Computational Linguistics, University of Sussex, since 1985; *b* 24 Feb. 1950; *s* of John and Kathleen Gazdar. *Educ:* Heath Mount; Bradfield Coll.; Univ. of East Anglia (BA Phil with Econ); Reading Univ. (MA Linguistics, PhD). Sussex University: Lectr 1975–80; Reader 1980–85; Dean, Sch. of Cognitive and Computing Scis, 1988–93. Fellow, Center for Advanced Study in the Behavioral Sciences, Stanford Univ., California, 1984–85. *Publications:* (with Klein, Pullum) A Bibliography of Contemporary Linguistic Research, 1978; Pragmatics, 1979; (with Klein, Pullum) Order, Concord, and Constituency, 1983; (with Klein, Pullum, Sag) Generalized Phrase Structure Grammar, 1985; (with Coates, Deuchar, Lyons) New Horizons in Linguistics II, 1987; (with Franz, Osborne, Evans) Natural Language Processing in the 1980s, 1987; (with Mellish): Natural Language Processing in Prolog, An Introduction to Computational Linguistics, 1989; Natural Language Processing in LISP, An Introduction to Computational Linguistics, 1989; Natural Language Processing in POP-11, An Introduction to Computational Linguistics, 1989. *Address:* School of Cognitive and Computing Sciences, University of Sussex, Brighton BN1 9QH. *T:* (01273) 678029.

GAZE, Dr Raymond Michael, FRS 1972; FRSE 1964; Head, Medical Research Council Neural Development and Regeneration Group, Edinburgh University, 1984–92, Hon. Professor, since 1986; *b* 22 June 1927; *s* of late William Mercer Gaze and Kathleen Grace Gaze (*née* Bowhill); *m* 1957, Robinetta Mary Armfelt; one *s* two *d. Educ:* at home; Sch. of Medicine, Royal Colleges, Edinburgh; Oxford Univ. (MA, DPhil). LRCPE, LRCSE, LRFPSG. House Physician, Chelmsford and Essex Hosp., 1949; National Service, RAMC, 1953–55; Lectr, later Reader, Dept of Physiology, Edinburgh Univ., 1955–70; Alan Johnston, Lawrence and Moseley Research Fellow, Royal Soc., 1962–66; Head, Div. of Developmental Biol., 1970–83, Dep. Dir 1977–83, Nat. Inst. for Med. Research. Visiting Professor: of Theoretical Biology, Univ. of Chicago, 1972; of Biology, Middlesex Hosp. Med. Sch., 1972–74. *Publications:* The Formation of Nerve Connections, 1970; Editor, 1975–88, and contrib., Development (formerly Jl Embryology and Exper. Morphology); various papers on neurobiology in Jl Physiology, Qly Jl Exper. Physiology, Proc. Royal Soc., etc. *Recreations:* drawing, hill-walking, music. *Address:* 37 Sciennes Road, Edinburgh EH9 1NS. *T:* (0131) 667 6915.

GAZZARD, Prof. Brian George, FRCP; Clinical Research Director, HIV Unit, Chelsea and Westminster Hospital, since 1978; Professor of HIV Medicine, Imperial College, University of London, since 1998; *b* 4 April 1946; *s* of Edward George Gazzard and Elizabeth (*née* Hill); *m* 1970, Joanna Koeller; three *s. Educ:* Queens' Coll., Cambridge (MA); King's Coll. Hosp., London (MD 1976). FRCP 1983. Senior Registrar: Liver Unit, KCH, 1974–76; Gastroenterology Unit, St Bartholomew's Hosp., 1976–78; Consultant Physician, Westminster and St Stephen's Hosps, 1978–. Prin. UK Investigator, various collaborative AIDS studies incl. MRC Delta Trial, 1978–. *Publications:* Treatment of Peptic Ulcer, 1989; Common Symptoms in Gastroenterology, 1990; Gastroenterological Manifestations in AIDS Patients, 1992. *Recreation:* gardening. *Address:* Old Blew House, Dulwich Common, SE21 7EW. *T:* (020) 8746 8239.

GAZZARD, Roy James Albert (Hon. Major), FRIBA; FRTPI; Pro-Director, 1982–84, Director, 1984–86, Hon. Fellow, 1987, Centre for Middle Eastern and Islamic Studies, Durham University; *b* 19 July 1923; *s* of James Henry Gazzard, MBE, and Ada Gwendoline Gazzard (*née* Willis); *m* 1947, Muriel Joy Morgan; one *s* two *d* (and one *s* decd). *Educ:* Stationers' Company's Sch.; Architectural Assoc. Sch. of Architecture (Dip.); School of Planning and Research for Reg. Develt (Dip.). Commissioned, Mddx Regt, 1943; service Palestine and ME. Acting Govt Town Planner, Uganda, 1950; Staff Architect, Barclays Bank Ltd, 1954; Chief Architect, Peterlee Develt Corp., 1960; Dir of Develt, Northumberland CC, 1962; Chief Professional Adviser to Sec. of State's Environmental Bd, 1976; Under Sec., DoE, 1976–79. Prepared: Jinja (Uganda) Outline Scheme, 1954; Municipality of Sur (Oman) Develt Plan, 1975. Renter Warden, Worshipful Co. of Stationers and Newspaper Makers, 1985–86. Govt medals for Good Design in Housing; Civic Trust awards for Townscape and Conservation. *Publications:* Durham: portrait of a cathedral city, 1983; contribs to HMSO pubns on built environment. *Recreations:* Islamic art and architecture, fortifications, dry-stone walling. *Address:* 13 Dunelm Court, South Street, Durham DH1 4QX. *T:* (0191) 386 4067. *Club:* City Livery.

GEACH, Prof. Peter Thomas, FBA 1965; Professor of Logic, University of Leeds, 1966–81; *b* 29 March 1916; *o s* of Prof. George Hender Geach, IES, and Eleonora Frederyka Adolfina Sgonina; *m* 1941, Gertrude Elizabeth Margaret Anscombe, FBA (*d* 2001); three *s* four *d. Educ:* Balliol Coll., Oxford (Domus Schol.; Hon. Fellow, 1979). 2nd cl. Class. Hon. Mods, 1936; 1st cl. Lit. Hum., 1938. Gladstone Research Student, St Deiniol's Library, Hawarden, 1938–39; philosophical research, Cambridge, 1945–51; University of Birmingham: Asst Lectr in Philosophy, 1951; Lectr, 1952; Sen. Lectr, 1959; Reader in Logic, 1961. Vis. Prof., Univ. of Warsaw, 1985. Lectures: Stanton, in the Philosophy of Religion, Cambridge, 1971–74; Hägerström, Univ. of Uppsala, 1975; O'Hara, Univ. of Notre Dame, 1978. Forschungspreis, A. Von Humboldt Stiftung, 1983; Aquinas Medal, 2000. Papal medal, Pro Ecclesia et Pontifice, 1999. *Publications:* Mental Acts, 1957; Reference and Generality, 1962, 3rd rev. edn 1980; (with G. E. M. Anscombe) Three Philosophers, 1961; God and the Soul, 1969; Logic Matters, 1972; Reason and Argument, 1976; Providence and Evil, 1977; The Virtues, 1977; Truth, Love, and Immortality: an introduction to McTaggart's philosophy, 1979; Truth and Hope, 2001; articles in Mind, Philosophical Review, Analysis, Ratio, etc. *Recreations:* reading stories of detection, mystery and horror; collecting and annotating old bad logic texts. *Address:* 3 Richmond Road, Cambridge CB4 3PP. *T:* (01223) 353950. *Club:* Union Society (Oxford).

GEAKE, Jonathan Richard Barr; His Honour Judge Geake; a Circuit Judge, Northern Circuit, since 1994; *b* 27 May 1946; *s* of Michael and Margaret Geake; *m* 1978, Sally Louise Dines; three *s. Educ:* Sherborne Sch.; Fitzwilliam Coll., Cambridge (BA). Called to the Bar, Inner Temple, 1969; practised on Northern Circuit; a Recorder, 1989; Standing Counsel for Customs & Excise, 1989. *Recreations:* golf and various other sporting activities, gardening. *Address:* Crown Court, Manchester M3 3FL. *Clubs:* Knutsford Golf, St Enodoc Golf; Alderley Edge Cricket.

GEAR, Rt Rev. Michael Frederick; Bishop Suffragan of Doncaster, 1993–99; Hon. Assistant Bishop: Diocese of Rochester, since 1999; Diocese of Canterbury, since 2000; *b* 27 Nov. 1934; *s* of Frederick Augustus and Lillian Hannah Gear; *m* 1961, Daphne, *d* of Norman and Millicent Earl; two *d. Educ:* St John's College and Cranmer Hall, Durham. BA Social Studies, 1st cl., 1959; DipTh 1961. Assistant Curate: Christ Church, Bexleyheath, 1961–64; St Aldate, Oxford, 1964–67; Vicar of St Andrew, Clubmoor, Liverpool, 1967–71; Rector, Avondale, Salisbury, Rhodesia, 1971–76; Tutor, Wycliffe Hall, Oxford, 1976–80; Team Rector, Macclesfield, 1980–88; Archdeacon of Chester, 1988–93. Hon. Chaplain, Mothers' Union, 1996–99. Chairman: Cranmer Hall Cttee, St John's Coll., Durham, 1994–98; Northern Ordination Course, 1995–99; Member: Scargill Council, 1993–99; Bd, Church Army, 1993–99. *Recreations:* photography, golf, history and contemporary politics of Southern Africa. *Address:* 10 Acott Fields, Yalding, Maidstone ME18 6DQ.

GEDDES, family name of **Baron Geddes**.

GEDDES, 3rd Baron *cr* 1942; **Euan Michael Ross Geddes;** Company Director since 1964; *b* 3 Sept. 1937; *s* of 2nd Baron Geddes, KBE, and Enid Mary, Lady Geddes (*d* 1999), *d* of late Clarance H. Butler; *S* father, 1975; *m* 1st, 1966, Gillian (*d* 1995), *d* of late William Arthur Butler; one *s* one *d*; 2nd, 1996, Susan Margaret Hunter, *d* of late George Harold Carter. *Educ:* Rugby; Gonville and Caius Coll., Cambridge (MA 1964); Harvard Business School. Elected Mem., H of L, 1999. *Recreations:* golf, bridge, music, gardening, shooting. *Heir: s* Hon. James George Neil Geddes, *b* 10 Sept. 1969. *Address:* House of Lords, SW1A 0PW. *T:* (01379) 388001. *Clubs:* Brooks's; Hong Kong (Hong Kong); Noblemen and Gentlemen's Catch; Aldeburgh Golf, Hong Kong Golf.

GEDDES, Prof. Alexander MacIntosh, (Alasdair), CBE 1996; FRCP, FRCPE, FRCPath, FFPHM, FMedSci; Professor of Infection, 1991–99, and Deputy Dean, Faculty of Medicine and Dentistry, 1994–99, University of Birmingham (Professor of Infectious Diseases, 1982–91; Associate Dean, since 1999); *b* 14 May 1934; *s* of Angus and Isabella Geddes; *m* 1984, Angela Lewis; two *s. Educ:* Fortrose Acad.; Univ. of Edinburgh (MB ChB). FRCPE 1971; FRCP 1981; FRCPath 1995; FFPHM 1998. Served RAMC, Captain, 1958–60. Med. Registrar, Aberdeen Hosps, 1961–63; Sen. Registrar, City Hosp. and Royal Infirmary, Edinburgh, 1963–67; Cons. Phys., E Birmingham Hosp., 1967–91; Hon. Cons. Phys., S Birmingham Health Dist, 1991–. Examiner: MRCP (UK), 1972–; Final MB, Univs of Birmingham, Glasgow, London, Sheffield, 1975–. Forbes Vis. Fellow, Fairfield Hosp., Melbourne, Aust., 1988; Sir Edward Finch Vis. Prof., Univ. of Sheffield, 1989. Chairman: Sub-Cttee on Communicable and Trop. Diseases, Jt Cttee on Higher Med. Trng, 1984–94; Isolation Beds Working Party, DoH, 1989–95; Member: Birmingham AHA, 1977–81; Health Educn Authority, 1987–98; Sub-Cttee on Efficacy and Adverse Reactions, Cttee on Safety of Medicines, 1978–85; DHSS Expert Adv. Gp on AIDS, 1985–92; DoH (formerly DHSS) Jt Cttee on Vaccination and Immunization, 1986–95; Trop. Med. Res. Bd, MRC, 1984–88; Ministerial Inquiry into the Public Health Function, 1985–87; DoH Cttee on Safety of Medicines, 1993–96; Consultant Advr in Infectious Diseases, DoH, 1990–94; Civilian Consultant, Infectious Diseases and Tropical Medicine, RN, 1991–. Chm., Brit. Soc. for Antimicrobial Therapy, 1982–85; Chm., Communicable and Tropical Diseases Cttee, 1983–93, Censor, 1987–89, RCP; Mem., Assoc. of Physicians of GB and Ire., 1976–; President: Internat. Soc. for Infectious Diseases, 1994–96; 21st Internat. Chemotherapy Congress, 1999. Lectures: Honeyman-Gillespie, Univ. of Edinburgh, 1975; Public, Univ. of Warwick, 1980; Davidson, RCPE, 1981; Watson-Smith, 1988; Lister, RCPE, 1990. FMedSci 2000. Chm., Editorial Bd, Jl of Antimicrobial Therapy, 1975–85. *Publications:* (ed) Control of Hospital Infection, 1975, 5th edn 2000; (ed) Recent Advances in Infection, 1975, 3rd edn 1988; (contrib.) Davidson, Principles and Practice of Medicine, 16th edn 1991, 17th edn 1995; papers on infectious diseases, immunology, antibiotic therapy and epidemiology in learned jls. *Recreations:* gardening, reading. *Address:* 34 The Crescent, Solihull, West Midlands B91 1JR. *T:* (0121) 705 8844, *Fax:* (0121) 705 2314. *Club:* Athenæum.

GEDDES, Andrew Campbell; His Honour Judge Geddes; a Circuit Judge, since 1994; Designated Civil Judge, Coventry Group of Courts, since 1998; *b* 10 June 1943; *s* of Hon. Alexander Campbell Geddes, OBE, MC, TD and Hon. Margaret Kathleen Geddes (*née* Addis); *m* 1st, 1974, Jacqueline Tan Bunzl; two *s*; 2nd, 1985, Bridget Bowring; one *s* one *d. Educ:* Stowe; Christ Church, Oxford (MA). Founder, Building Products Index, 1965. Called to the Bar, Inner Temple, 1972; a Recorder, 1990; authorised to sit as High Court Judge, 1995. *Publications:* Product and Service Liability in the EEC, 1992; Public Procurement, 1993; Protection of Individual Rights under EC Law, 1995; Public and Utility Procurement, 1996; contribs to learned jls. *Recreations:* music, walking, reading, writing, gardening. *Address:* 4 Essex Court, Temple, EC4Y 9AJ. *T:* (020) 7797 7970.

GEDDES, Prof. Duncan Mackay, MD, FRCP; Professor of Respiratory Medicine, Imperial College School of Medicine, since 1996; Consultant Physician, Royal Brompton Hospital, since 1978; *b* 6 Jan. 1942; *s* of Sir Reay Geddes, KBE and Lady Geddes, (Imogen, *d* of late Captain Hay Matthey); *m* 1968, Donatella Flaccomio Nardi Dei; two *s* one *d. Educ:* Eton Coll.; Magdalene Coll., Cambridge (MA); Westminster Hosp. Med. Sch. (MB, BS 1971; MD 1978). FRCP 1982. Hon. Consultant: Royal London Hosp., 1982–; Royal Marsden Hosp., 1990–; Civilian Consultant in chest disease to the Army and Navy, 1986–. Director: Finsbury Worldwide Pharmaceutical Trust, 1995–; S R Pharma. Vice-Chm. and Chm. Council, Nat. Asthma Campaign, 1996–. Mem., Med. Adv. Bd, Transgene, France, 1997–. Pres., British Thoracic Soc., 2000–01 (Vice-Pres., 1999–2000). *Publications:* Practical Medicine, 1976; Airways Obstruction, 1981; Respiratory Medicine, 1990; Cystic Fibrosis, 1995; numerous papers in med. and scientific jls. *Recreations:* tennis, painting. *Address:* 57 Addison Avenue, W11 4QU. *Clubs:* Boodle's, Queen's.

GEDDES, Ford Irvine, MBE 1943; *b* 17 Jan. 1913; *e s* of Irvine Campbell Geddes and Dorothy Jefford Geddes (*née* Fowler); *m* 1945, Barbara Gertrude Vere Parry-Okeden; one *s* four *d. Educ:* Loretto Sch.; Gonville and Caius Coll., Cambridge (BA). Joined Anderson Green & Co. Ltd, London, 1934. Served War RE, 1939–45 (Major). Director: Bank of NSW (London Adv. Bd), 1950–81; Equitable Life Assce Soc., 1955–76 (Pres. 1963–71); British United Turkeys Ltd, 1962–69, 1976–78 (Chm., 1976–78); Chairman: P&O Steam Navigation Co., 1971–72 (a Dep. Chm., 1968–71; Dir, 1960–72); British Shipping Federation, 1965–68; Pres., Internat. Shipping Fedn, 1967–69. *Address:* 8 Kensington

Court Gardens, Kensington Court Place, W8 5QE. *Clubs:* City of London; Union (Sydney).

See also Sir N. L. J. Montagu.

GEDDES, Keith Taylor, CBE 1998; Policy Director, P. S. Communication Consultants Ltd, since 1999; *b* 8 Aug. 1952. *Educ:* Galashiels Acad.; Edinburgh Univ. (BEd 1975); Moray House Coll. of Educn (Cert. in Youth and Community work 1977); Heriot-Watt Univ. (Dip. in Housing 1986). Worker, Shelter Housing Aid (Scotland), 1977–84. Lothian Regional Council: Mem. (Lab), 1982–95; Chair, Educn Cttee, 1987–90; Leader, Labour Gp, 1990–96; Leader, City of Edinburgh Council, 1995–99. Convention of Scottish Local Authorities: Vice Chair, Educn Cttee, 1987–90; Sen. Vice Pres., 1994–96; Pres., 1996–99. Contested (Lab) Tweeddale, Ettrick and Lauderdale, 2001. Mem. Bd, Scottish Natural Heritage. Chm., Young People Speak Out. *Recreations:* hill walking, golf, watching Gala Rugby team. *Address:* 7 Howard Street, Edinburgh EH3 5JP. *T:* (0131) 624 2365.

GEDDES, Michael Dawson; Executive Director, Milton Keynes Economic Partnership, since 1995; *b* 9 March 1944; *s* of David Geddes and late Audrey Geddes; *m* 1966, Leslie Rose Webb; two *s*. *Educ:* Sherborne Sch., Dorset; Univ. of BC (Goldsmith's Exhibitioner) (BA). Cranfield Institute of Technology: Admin. Asst, 1968–71; Planning Officer, 1971–77; Develt and Estates Officer, 1977–83; Financial Controller, RMCS, 1983–84; Sec., Ashridge (Bonar Law Meml) Trust; Dir, Admin, Ashridge Management Coll. and Dir, Ashridge subsids, 1984–90; Chief Exec., Recruitment and Assessment Services Agency, 1990–95; Civil Service Comr, 1990–97. *Publications:* (with W. Briner and C. Hastings) Project Leadership, 1990; papers on resource allocation in univs and on project management. *Recreations:* golf, bridge. *Address:* 11 Main Street, Mursley, Bucks MK17 0RT. *T:* (01296) 720601.

GEDLING, Raymond, CB 1969; Deputy Secretary, Department of Health and Social Security, 1971–77; *b* 3 Sept. 1917; *s* of late John and late Mary Gedling; *m* 1956, Joan Evelyn Chapple (*d* 2000); one *s*. *Educ:* Grangefield Grammar Sch., Stockton-on-Tees. Entered Civil Service as Executive Officer, Min. of Health, 1936; Asst Principal, 1942, Principal, 1947. Cabinet Office, 1951–52; Principal Private Sec. to Minister of Health, 1952–55; Asst Sec., 1955; Under-Sec., 1961; Asst Under-Sec. of State, Dept of Educn and Science, 1966–68; Dep. Sec., Treasury, 1968–71. *Recreations:* walking, chess. *Address:* 27 Wallace Fields, Epsom, Surrey KT17 3AX. *T:* (020) 8393 9060.

GEE, Anthony Hall; QC 1990; a Recorder of the Crown Court, since 1989; *b* 4 Nov. 1948; *s* of late Harold Stephenson Gee and Marjorie Gee (*née* Hall); *m* 1975, Gillian Pauline Glover, St Annes-on-Sea; one *s* two *d*. *Educ:* Cambs High School for Boys; Chester City Grammar Sch.; Inns of Court School of Law. Called to the Bar, Gray's Inn, 1972; Mem., Northern Circuit, 1972–. Member: Medico-Legal Soc., 1996–; Criminal Bar Assoc., 1997– (N Circuit Rep.). *Recreations:* golf, ski-ing, cricket, fly-fishing. *Address:* (chambers) 28 St John Street, Manchester M3 4DJ. *T:* (0161) 834 8418. *Clubs:* Lancashire CC; Bramhall Golf; Northern Lawn Tennis (Didsbury).

GEE, David Charles Laycock; Projects Manager, Information Needs Analysis/Emerging Issues, European Environment Agency, Copenhagen, since 1995; consultant, environmental and occupational risk, since 1992; Partner, WBMG Environmental Communications, since 1992; *b* 18 April 1947; *s* of Charles Laycock Gee and Theresa Gee (*née* Garrick); *m* 1974, Vivienne Taylor Gee; four *d*. *Educ:* Thomas Linacre and Wigan Grammar Schs; York Univ. (BA Politics). MIOSH 1985. Res. Dept, AUEW, 1970–73; Educn Service, TUC, 1973–78; Nat. Health/Safety Officer, GMB, 1978–88; Occupational/Environmental Cons., 1988–89; Campaign Co-ordinator, 1989–90, Dir, 1990–91, Friends of the Earth. Fellow, Collegium Ramazzini, Italy, 1984; FRSA 1990. *Publications:* (with John Cox and Dave Leon) Cancer and Work, 1982; (with Lesley Doyal et al) Cancer in Britain, 1983; Eco-nomic Tax Reform: a primer, 1994; *contributions to:* Radiation and Health—Biological Effects of Low Level Exposure to Ionising Radiation, 1987; Transport and Health, ed Fletcher and McMichael, 1995; Ecotaxation, ed O'Riordan, 1997; The Market and the Environment, ed Sterner, 1999; The Daily Globe: environmental change, the public and the media, ed Smith, 2000; pubns for EEA and MSF. *Recreations:* family, swimming, tennis, running, entertaining, theatre, music. *Address:* Kastelsvej 15 5TV, 2100 Copenhagen, Denmark. *T:* 35262716.

GEE, David Stephenson; His Honour Judge David S. Gee; a Circuit Judge, since 1992; *b* 16 Dec. 1944; *s* of William and Marianne Gee; *m* 1972, Susan Margaret Hiley; two *s* two *d*. *Educ:* William Hulme's Grammar Sch., Manchester; Leeds Univ. (LLB Hons). Admitted Solicitor, 1970; Registrar, Manchester County Court and Dist Registry, 1982–90; Dist Judge, 1991–92; a Recorder of the Crown Court, 1991. Chairman: Selcare (Greater Manchester) Trust, 1989–95; Rhodes Foundn Scholarship Trust, 1989–. Adv. Editor, Atkins' Court Forms, 1989–; Editor, Butterworth's Family Law Service, 1990–98. *Recreations:* music, walking, reading. *Address:* c/o Circuit Administrator, 15 Quay Street, Manchester M60 9FD. *Club:* Royal Commonwealth Society.

GEE, James; Director, Counter Fraud Services, Department of Health and National Health Service, since 1998; *b* 1 Oct. 1957; *m* 1992, Lesley Ann White. *Educ:* London Sch. of Econs (BSc Econs 1978); CPE Law 1995. Civil servant, 1978–90; Counter Fraud Manager, London Boroughs of: Islington, 1990–94; Haringey, 1994–96; Lambeth, 1996–98. Advr to Social Security Select Cttee, H of C, 1995–97; Counter Fraud Advr to Minister of State for Welfare Reform, 1997–98. *Recreations:* military history, gardening. *Address:* c/o Department of Health, Hannibal House, Elephant and Castle, SE1 6TE. *T:* (020) 7972 2505. *Club:* Manchester United Football.

GEE, Mark Norman K.; *see* Kemp-Gee.

GEE, Richard; a Circuit Judge, 1991–1999; *b* 25 July 1942; *s* of John and Marie Gee; *m* 1st, 1965; three *s*; 2nd, 1995, Mrs Marilyn Gross. *Educ:* Kilburn Grammar School; University College London (LLB Hons). Admitted Solicitor, 1966; Assistant Recorder, 1983; Recorder, 1988. Mem., Main Board, Judicial Studies Board, 1988–93 (Mem., Ethnic Minorities Adv. Cttee, 1991–93). *Recreations:* golf, the arts.

GEE, Steven Mark; QC 1993; a Recorder, since 2000; *b* 24 Aug. 1953; *yr s* of Dr Sidney Gee and Dr Hilda Elman; *m* 1999, Meryll Emilie Bacri; two *s*. *Educ:* Tonbridge Sch.; Brasenose Coll., Oxford (Open Scholar; MA 1st Cl. Hons Jurisprudence; Gibbs Prize for Law). Called to the Bar, Middle Temple, 1975 (Inns of Court Prize, Harmsworth Scholar); admitted NY Bar, 1999. Standing Jun. Counsel, ECGD, DTI, 1986–93. *Publication:* Mareva Injunctions and Anton Piller Relief, 1995, 4th edn 1998. *Recreations:* marathon running, bridge. *Address:* 4 Field Court, Gray's Inn, WC1R 5EA. *T:* (020) 7440 6900. *Club:* MCC.

GEELONG, Bishop in; *see* St John, Rt Rev. A. R.

GEERING, Ian Walter; QC 1991; *b* 19 July 1947; *s* of late Wilfrid Robert Geering and of Barbara Pearce (*née* James); *m* 1975, (Alison) Diana Burne; two *s* two *d*. *Educ:* Bedford Sch.; Univ. of Edinburgh (BVMS). Called to the Bar, Inner Temple, 1974. *Recreations:* walking, reading, sailing, photography. *Address:* 3 Verulam Buildings, Gray's Inn, WC1R 5NT.

GEERING, Rev. Prof. Lloyd George, PCNZM 2001; CBE 1989; Foundation Professor of Religious Studies, Victoria University of Wellington, 1971–84, now Professor Emeritus; *b* 26 Feb. 1918; *s* of George Frederick Thomas Geering and Alice Geering; *m* 1st, 1943, Nancy McKenzie (*d* 1949); one *s* one *d*; 2nd, 1951, Elaine Parker; one *d*. *Educ:* Univ. of Otago (MA 1st Cl. Hons Maths; BD Hons OT); Melbourne Coll. of Divinity. Presbyterian Parish Minister, 1943–55; Professor of Old Testament: Emmanuel Coll., Brisbane, 1956–59; Theol Hall, Knox Coll., Dunedin, 1960–71 (Principal, 1963–71). Hon. DD Otago, 1976. *Publications:* God in the New World, 1968; Resurrection: a symbol of hope, 1971; In the World Today, 1976; Faith's New Age, 1981; Tomorrow's God, 1994; The World to Come, 1999. *Address:* 5B Herbert Gardens, 186 The Terrace, Wellington, New Zealand. *T:* (4) 4730188.

GEFFEN, Dr Terence John; Medical Adviser, Capsticks Solicitors, 1990–99; *b* 17 Sept. 1921; *s* of late Maximilian W. Geffen and Maia Geffen (later Reid); *m* 1965, Judith Anne Steward; two *s*. *Educ:* St Paul's Sch.; University Coll., London; UCH. MD, FRCP. House Phys., UCH, 1943; RAMC, 1944–47; hosp. posts, Edgware Gen. Hosp., Hampstead Gen. Hosp., UCH, 1947–55; Min. of Health (later DHSS), 1956–82, SPMO, 1972–82; Consultant in Public Health Medicine, NW Thames RHA, 1982–90. FRSocMed 1991. *Publications:* various in BMJ, Lancet, Clinical Science, etc. *Recreations:* music, reading, bridge. *Address:* 2 Stonehill Close, SW14 8RP. *T:* (020) 8878 0516.

GEHRELS, Jürgen Carlos, Hon. KBE 1997; non-executive Chairman, Siemens Holdings plc, since 1998 (Chief Executive, 1986–98); *b* 24 July 1935; *s* of Hans Gehrels and Ursula (*née* da Rocha); *m* 1963, Sigrid Kausch; one *s* one *d*. *Educ:* Technical Univs, Berlin and Munich (Dipl. Ing.). Siemens AG, Germany, 1965–79; Pres., General Numeric Corp., Chicago, USA, 1979–82; Dir, Factory Automation, Siemens AG, Germany, 1982–86. Chairman: Siemens Communication Systems Ltd, 1986–92; Siemens Financial Services Ltd, 1988–92; Siemens Controls Ltd, 1990–98; Siemens–Nixdorf Inf. Systems Ltd, 1990–98; Director: Siemens Domestic Appliances Ltd, 1987–98; Comparex Ltd, 1988–92; Alfred Engelmann Ltd, 1989–98; Plessey UK, 1989–98; Plessey Overseas, 1989–98; Siemens Holdings plc, 1990–98; Siemens Business Communication Systems Ltd, 1996–98; non-executive Director: Nammo AS, Norway, 1989–; Management Engineers, Germany, 1997–. Pres., German–British Chamber of Industry and Commerce in UK, 1997– (Chm., 1992–97). FIEE 1991. FRSA 1993. *Recreations:* golf, gardening, architecture. *Address:* Siemens plc, Siemens House, Oldbury, Bracknell, Berks RG12 8FZ. *Clubs:* Reform; Burhill Golf (Surrey).

GEHRY, Frank Owen; architect; Principal, Frank O. Gehry & Associates, since 1962; *b* Toronto, 28 Feb. 1929; *s* of late Irving and Thelma Gehry; *m* 1975, Berta Aguilera; two *s*, and two *d* by a previous marriage. *Educ:* Univ. of Southern Calif (BArch 1954); Grad. Sch. of Design, Harvard Univ. Designer, 1953–54, Planning, Design and Project Dir, 1958–61, Victor Gruen Associates, LA; Project Designer and Planner, Pereira & Luckman, LA, 1957–58. Projects include: Loyola Law Sch., 1981–84; Calif Aerospace Mus., 1984; Inf. and Computer Sci./Engrg Res. Lab., Univ. of Calif, Irvine, 1986–88; Centre for Visual Arts, Univ. of Toledo, 1992; Frederick R. Weisman Art Mus., Minneapolis, 1993; American Centre, Paris, 1994; Vitra Internat. HQ, Basel, 1994; EMR Communication and Tech. Centre, Bad Oeynhausen, Germany, 1995; Nationale Nederlanden bldg, Prague, 1996; Guggenheim Mus., Bilbao, 1997; Experience Music Project, Seattle, 2000; Weatherhead Sch. of Mgt, Case Western Reserve Univ., 2001. Charlotte Davenport Prof. of Architecture, Yale Univ., 1982, 1985, 1987–89; Eliot Noyes Prof. of Design, Harvard Univ., 1984. FAIA 1974. Prizes include: Arnold W. Brunner Meml Prize in Architecture, 1983; Gold Medal, RIBA, 2000. *Publications:* (with Thomas Hines) Franklin D. Israel: buildings and projects, 1992; (with L. William Zahner) Architectural Metals: a guide to selection, specification and performance, 1995; Individual Imagination and Cultural Conservatism, 1995. *Address:* Frank O. Gehry & Associates, 1520-B Cloverfield Boulevard, Santa Monica, CA 90404-3502, USA.

GELDER, Prof. Michael Graham; W. A. Handley Professor of Psychiatry, University of Oxford, 1969–96, now Emeritus Professor; Fellow of Merton College, Oxford, 1969–96, now Emeritus Fellow (Subwarden, 1992–94); *b* 2 July 1929; *s* of Philip Graham Gelder and Margaret Gelder (*née* Graham); *m* 1954, Margaret (*née* Anderson); one *s* two *d*. *Educ:* Bradford Grammar Sch.; Queen's Coll., Oxford. Scholar, Theodore Williams Prize 1949 and first class Hons, Physiology finals, 1950; MA, DM Oxon, FRCP, FRCPsych; DPM London (with distinction) 1961. Goldsmit Schol., UCH London, 1951. House Physician, Sen. House Physician, UCH, 1955–57; Registrar, Maudsley Hosp., 1958–61; MRC Fellow in Clinical Research, 1962–63; Sen. Lectr, Inst. of Psychiatry, 1965–67 (Vice-Dean, 1967–68); Physician, Bethlem Royal and Maudsley Hosps, 1967–68. Hon. Consultant Psychiatrist, Oxford RHA, later DHA, 1969–96; Mem., Oxford DHA, 1985–92; Dir, Oxford Mental Health Care NHS Trust, 1993–97. Dir, WHO Collaborating Centre, 1994–96. Mem., MRC, 1978–79 (Chm., 1978–79, Mem., 1975–78 and 1987–90, Neurosciences Bd). Chm., Wellcome Trust Neuroscience Panel, 1990–95 (Mem., 1984–88). Chairman: Assoc. of Univ. Teachers of Psychiatry, 1979–82; Jt Cttee on Higher Psychiatric Trng, 1981–85. Europ. Vice-Pres., Soc. for Psychotherapy Research, 1977–82. Advisor, WHO, 1992–. Mem., Assoc. of Physicians, 1983–. Mem. Council, RCPsych, 1981–90 (Vice Pres. 1982–83; Sen. Vice-Pres., 1983–84; Chm. Res. Cttee, 1986–91). Founder FMedSci 1998. Mayne Guest Prof., Univ. of Queensland, 1990. Lectures: Malcolm Millar, Univ. of Aberdeen, 1984; Yap Meml, Hong Kong, 1987; Guze, Univ. of Washington, 1993; Curran, St George's Hosp. Med. Sch., 1996; Sargant, RCPsych, 1996. Gold Medal, Royal Medico-Psychol Assoc., 1962. *Publications:* (jtly) Agoraphobia: nature and treatment, 1981; (jtly) The Oxford Textbook of Psychiatry, 1983, 3rd edn 1996; (jtly) Concise Oxford Textbook of Psychiatry, 1994; Psychiatry: an Oxford core text, 1999; (ed jtly) New Oxford Textbook of Psychiatry, 2 vols, 2000; (jtly) Shorter Oxford Textbook of Psychiatry, 2001; chapters in books and articles in medical jls. *Recreations:* photography, gardening, travel. *Address:* St Mary's, Jack Straw's Lane, Oxford OX3 0DN.

GELDOF, Bob, Hon. KBE 1986; singer; songwriter; initiator and organiser, Band Aid, Live Aid and Sport Aid fund-raising events; *b* Dublin, 5 Oct. 1954; *m* 1986, Paula Yates (marr. diss. 1996; she *d* 2000); three *d*. *Educ:* Black Rock Coll. Sometime journalist: Georgia Straight, Vancouver; New Musical Express; Melody Maker. Jt Founder, Boomtown Rats, rock band, 1975. Acted in films: Pink Floyd—The Wall, 1982; Number One, 1985. Organised Band Aid, 1984, to record Do They Know It's Christmas, sales from which raised £8 million for famine relief in Ethiopia; organised simultaneous Live Aid concerts in London and Philadelphia to raise £50 million, 1985; organised Sport Aid to raise further £50 million, 1986. Chm., Band Aid Trust, 1985–; Founder, Live Aid Foundn, USA, 1985–. Freeman: Borough of Swale, 1985; Newcastle. Hon. MA Kent, 1985; Hon. DSc(Econ) London, 1987; Hon. DPh Ghent. TV film: The Price of Progress, 1987. Awards include: UN World Hunger Award, FAO Medal; EEC Gold Medal; Irish

Peace Prize; music awards include: Ivor Novello (four times); several gold and platinum discs. Order of Two Niles (Sudan); Cavalier, Order of Leopold II (Belgium). *Publication:* Is That It? (autobiog.), 1986.

GELL-MANN, Murray; Professor and Distinguished Fellow, Santa Fe Institute, since 1993; Robert Andrews Millikan Professor of Theoretical Physics at the California Institute of Technology, 1967–93, now Emeritus; *b* 15 Sept. 1929; *s* of Arthur and Pauline Gell-Mann; *m* 1st, 1955, J. Margaret Dow (*d* 1981); one *s* one *d*; 2nd, 1992, Marcia Southwick; one step *s*. *Educ:* Yale Univ.; Massachusetts Inst. of Technology. Mem., Inst. for Advanced Study, Princeton, 1951; Instructor, Asst Prof., and Assoc. Prof., Univ. of Chicago, 1952–55; Assoc. Prof. 1955–56, Prof. 1956–66, California Inst. of Technology. Vis. Prof., Collège de France and Univ. of Paris, 1959–60. Overseas Fellow, Churchill Coll., Cambridge, 1966. Member: President's Science Adv. Cttee, 1969–72; President's Council of Advrs on Sci. and Technol., 1994–. Regent, Smithsonian Instn, 1974–88; Chm. of Bd, Aspen Center for Physics, 1973–79; Dir, J. D. and C. T. MacArthur Foundn, 1979–; Vice-Pres. and Chm. of Western Center, Amer. Acad. of Arts and Sciences, 1970–76; Member: Nat. Acad. of Sciences, 1960–; Sci. and Grants Cttee, Leakey Foundn, 1977–90; Sci. Adv. Cttee, Conservation Internat., 1993–. Santa Fe Institute: Founding Trustee, 1982–; Chm., Bd of Trustees, 1982–85; Co-Chm., Sci. Bd, 1985–2000. Member Board: California Nature Conservancy, 1984–93; Wildlife Conservation Soc., 1993–. Foreign Mem., Royal Society, 1978. Hon. ScD: Yale, 1959; Chicago, 1967; Illinois, 1968; Wesleyan, 1968; Utah, 1970; Columbia, 1977; Southern Illinois, 1993; (Nat. Resources), Florida, 1994; Southern Methodist, 1999; Hon. DSc: Cantab, 1980; Oxon, 1992; Hon. Dr,Turin, 1969. Listed on UN Envmtl Program Roll of Honor for Envmtl Achievement (Global 500), 1988. Dannie Heineman Prize (Amer. Phys. Soc.), 1959; Ernest O. Lawrence Award, 1966; Franklin Medal (Franklin Inst., Philadelphia), 1967; John J. Carty Medal (Nat. Acad. Scis), 1968; Research Corp. Award, 1969; Nobel Prize in Physics, 1969; Erice Science for Peace Prize, 1990. *Publications:* (with Yuval Ne'eman) The Eightfold Way, 1964; The Quark and the Jaguar, 1994; various articles in learned jls on topics referring to classification and description of elementary particles of physics and their interactions. *Recreations:* walking in wild country, study of natural history, languages. *Address:* Santa Fe Institute, 1399 Hyde Park Road, Santa Fe, NM 87501, USA. *T:* (505) 9848800; *e-mail:* mgm@santafe.edu. *Clubs:* Cosmos (Washington) Explorers', Century (New York); Athenæum (Pasadena).

GELLHORN, Peter, FGSM; Professor, Guildhall School of Music and Drama, 1981–92; *b* 24 Oct. 1912; *s* of late Dr Alfred Gellhorn, and late Mrs Else Gellhorn; *m* 1943, Olive Shirley (*née* Layton), 3rd *d* of 1st Baron Layton, CH, CBE; two *s* two *d*. *Educ:* Schiller Realgymnasium, Charlottenburg; University of Berlin; Berlin Music Acad. FGSM 1989. After passing final exams (with dist.) as pianist and conductor, left Germany 1935. Musical Dir, Toynbee Hall, London, E1, 1935–39; Asst Conductor, Sadler's Wells Opera, 1941–43. On industrial war service, 1943–45. Conductor, Royal Carl Rosa Opera (115 perfs), 1945–46; Conductor and Head of Music Staff, Royal Opera House, Covent Garden (over 260 perfs), 1946–53; Conductor and Chorus Master, Glyndebourne Festival Opera, 1954–61, rejoined Glyndebourne Music Staff, 1974 and 1975; Dir, BBC Chorus, 1961–72; Conductor, Elizabethan Singers, 1976–80. Has also worked at National Sch. of Opera, annually at Summer Sch. of Music at Dartington Hall; composes; wrote and arranged music for silhouette and puppet films of Lotte Reiniger (at intervals, 1933–57). Mem., Music Staff, London Opera Centre, 1973–78; Conductor, Morley Coll. Opera Gp, 1974–79; Barnes Choir, 1982–2000; Music Dir, Opera Players Ltd, 1950–2000; Mem. Staff, Opera Sch., RCM, 1980–88, conducting its opera perfs, 1981. Lectures on courses arranged by various County Councils and adult colleges; frequently adjudicates at music fests in UK and overseas. Musical Dir, Opera Barga, Italy, from foundn, 1967–69. *Recreations:* reading, walking and going to plays. *Address:* 33 Leinster Avenue, East Sheen, SW14 7JW. *T:* (020) 8876 3949. *Club:* BBC.

GELLING, Margaret Joy, OBE 1995; PhD; FBA 1998; FSA; President, English Place-Name Society, 1986–98; *b* 29 Nov. 1924; *d* of Lucy and William Albert Midgley; *m* 1952, Peter Stanley Gelling (*d* 1983). *Educ:* Chislehurst Grammar Sch.; St Hilda's Coll., Oxford (BA 1945; MA 1951; Hon. Fellow, 1993); University Coll. London (PhD 1957). FSA 1986. Temp. Civil Servant, 1945–46; Res. Asst, English Place-Name Soc., 1946–53. Hon. Reader, Univ. of Birmingham, 1981–. Vice-Pres., Internat. Council for Onomastic Scis, 1993–99. *Publications:* English Place-Name Society volumes: Oxfordshire, part 1, 1953, part 2, 1954; Berkshire, part 1, 1973, part 2, 1974, part 3, 1976; Shropshire, part 1, 1990, part 2, 1995, part 3, 2001; (jtly) The Names of Towns and Cities in Britain, 1970; Signposts to the Past, 1978, 3rd edn 1997; The Early Charters of the Thames Valley, 1979; Place-Names in the Landscape, 1984; The West Midlands in the Early Middle Ages, 1992; (jtly) The Landscape of Place-Names, 2000; papers in Medieval Archaeology, Anglo-Saxon England, etc. *Recreation:* gardening. *Address:* 31 Pereira Road, Harborne, Birmingham B17 9JG. *T:* (0121) 427 6469.

GEM, Dr Richard David Harvey, FSA; Secretary, Cathedrals Fabric Commission for England, since 1991; *b* 10 Jan. 1945. *Educ:* Eastbourne Coll.; Peterhouse, Cambridge (MA, PhD). Inspector of Ancient Monuments, DoE, 1970–80; Res. Officer, Council for Care of Churches, 1981–88; Dep. Sec., then Sec., Cathedrals Adv. Commn for England, 1988–91. Mem., RCHM, 1987–99. Pres., British Archaeol Assoc., 1983–89. MIFA. *Publications:* numerous papers on early medieval architecture in British and foreign learned jls. *Recreations:* gardening, theatre, music, foreign travel, philosphy and theology. *Address:* Church House, Great Smith Street, SW1P 3NZ. *T:* (020) 7898 1887; The Bothy, Mentmore, near Leighton Buzzard, Beds LU7 0QG.

GEMMELL, Gavin John Norman, CBE 1998; CA; Joint Senior Partner, Baillie Gifford & Co., 1989–2001; *b* 7 Sept. 1941; *s* of late Gilbert A. S. Gemmell and of Dorothy M. Gemmell (*née* Mackay); *m* 1967, Kathleen Fiona Drysdale; one *s* two *d*. *Educ:* George Watson's Coll., Edinburgh. CA 1964. Baillie Gifford & Co., 1964–2001: investment trainee, 1964–67; Partner, 1967; Partner, Pension Funds, 1973–89. Non-executive Director: Scottish Widows, 1984– (Dep. Chm., 1995–); Scottish Enterprise Edinburgh and Lothian, 1995–; Scottish Financial Enterprise, 1998–. Trustee, Nat. Galls of Scotland, 1999–. Chm., Standing Cttee, Scottish Episcopal Ch, 1997–. *Recreations:* golf, foreign travel. *Address:* 14 Midmar Gardens, Edinburgh EH10 6DZ. *T:* (0131) 447 8135; *e-mail:* gavingemmell@blueyonder.co.uk. *Clubs:* Hon. Co. of Edinburgh Golfers (Muirfield); Gullane Golf.

GEMS, Iris Pamela, (Pam); playwright; *b* 1 Aug. 1925; *d* of late James Price and Elsie Mabel Price; *m* 1949, Keith Leopold Gems; two *s* two *d*. *Educ:* Brockenhurst Grammar Sch.; Manchester Univ. *Plays* include: Dusa, Fish, Stas and Vi, 1976; Queen Christina, 1977; Piaf, 1978; Franz into April, 1978; The Treat, 1979; Pasionaria, 1981; Aunt Mary, 1982; Camille, 1985; The Danton Affair, 1986; The Blue Angel, 1991; Deborah's Daughter, 1994; I Wish You Love, 1995; Stanley, 1995 (Evening Standard Award, Best Play; Olivier award for best play, 1997); Marlene, 1997; The Snow Palace, 1998; Natalya Ivanovna, 1998; plays performed RSC, RNT, Hampstead, West End and Broadway. *Publications:* (novels) Mrs Frampton, 1986; Bon Voyage, Mrs Frampton, 1988. *Recreation:* working. *Address:* c/o Tom Erhardt, Casarotto Co. Ltd, 60–66 Wardour Street, W1V 4ND.

GENDERS, Rt Rev. Roger Alban Marson, (Father Anselm), CR; *b* 15 Aug. 1919; *yr s* of John Boulton Genders and Florence Alice (*née* Thomas). *Educ:* King Edward VI School, Birmingham; Brasenose College, Oxford (Sen. Scholar 1938, BA Lit. Hum. 1946, MA 1946). Served War, Lieut RNVR, 1940–46. Joined Community of the Resurrection, Mirfield, 1948; professed, 1952; ordained, 1952; Tutor, College of the Resurrection, 1952–55; Vice-Principal 1955, and Principal 1957–65, Codrington Coll., Barbados; Exam. Chaplain to Bishop of Barbados, 1957–65; Treasurer of St Augustine's Mission, Rhodesia, 1966–75; Archdeacon of Manicaland, 1970–75; Asst Bursar, Community of the Resurrection, Mirfield, 1975–77; Bishop of Bermuda, 1977–82; Assistant Bishop of Wakefield, 1983–89. *Publications:* contribs to Theology. *Address:* Community of the Resurrection, House of the Resurrection, Mirfield, W Yorks WF14 0BN.

GENGE, Rt Rev. Kenneth Lyle; Bishop of Edmonton (Alberta), 1988–96; Chaplain, St George's College, Jerusalem, 1996; *b* 25 Oct. 1933; *s* of Nelson Simms Genge and Grace Winifred Genge; *m* 1959, Ruth Louise Bate; two *s* one *d*. *Educ:* Univ of Saskatchewan (BA 1958); Emmanuel Coll., Saskatoon (LTh 1957; BD 1959). Parish priest, 1959–85; Conference Retreat Centre Director, 1985–88. Hon. DD Emmanuel Coll. and St Chad, 1989. *Recreations:* sports, physical fitness, music.

GENGE, Rt Rev. Mark; Bishop of Central Newfoundland, 1976–90; Pastoral Associate, St John's, Yorkmills, Ontario, 1990–92; *b* 18 March 1927; *s* of Lambert and Lily Genge; *m* 1959, Maxine Clara (*née* Major); five *d*. *Educ:* Queen's Coll. and Memorial Univ., Newfoundland; Univ. of Durham (MA); BD Gen. Synod of Canada. Deacon, Corner Brook, Newfoundland, 1951; priest, Stephenville, 1952; Durham, 1953–55; Vice-Principal, Queen's Coll., St John's, Newfoundland, 1955–57; Curate, St Mary's Church, St John's, 1957–59; Rector: Foxtrap, 1959–64; Mary's Harbour, 1964–65; Burgeo, 1965–69; Curate, Marbleton, PQ, 1969–71; Rector, South River, Port-de-Grave, 1971–73; District Sec., Canadian Bible Soc., 1973–76. Chaplain, Queen's Coll., Newfoundland, 1993–98. *Recreations:* badminton, swimming, rollerblading. *Address:* 6 Maypark Place, St John's, Newfoundland A1B 2E3, Canada.

GENN, Prof. Hazel Gillian, CBE 2000; LLD; FBA 2000; Professor of Socio-Legal Studies, University College London, since 1994; *b* 17 March 1949; *d* of Lionel Isaac Genn and Dorothy Rebecca Genn; *m* 1973, Daniel David Appleby; one *s* one *d*. *Educ:* Univ. of Hull (BA Hons 1971); CNAA (LLB 1985); Univ. of London (LLD 1992). Res. Asst, Cambridge Inst. of Criminology, 1972–74; Sen. Res. Officer, Oxford Univ. Centre for Socio-Legal Studies, 1974–85; Lectr, 1985–88, Reader, 1988–91, Prof. and Head of Law Dept, 1991–94, Queen Mary and Westfield Coll., London Univ. *Publications:* Surveying Victims, 1978; Hard Bargaining, 1987; Personal Injury Compensation: how much is enough?, 1994; Mediation in Action, 1999; Paths to Justice, 1999. *Recreations:* music, walking, spending time with my family. *Address:* Faculty of Laws, University College London, Bentham House, Endsleigh Gardens, WC1H 0EG. *T:* (020) 7679 1436.

GENSCHER, Hans-Dietrich; Member of Bundestag, 1965–98; Federal Minister for Foreign Affairs and Deputy Chancellor, Federal Republic of Germany, 1974–92 (in government of Helmut Schmidt, to Oct. 1982, then in government of Helmut Kohl); Chairman of the Free Democratic Party, 1974–85; *b* Reideburg/Saalkreis, 21 March 1927; *m* Barbara; one *d*. *Educ:* Higher Sch. Certif. (Abitur); studied law and economics in Halle/Saale and Leipzig Univs, 1946–49. Served War, 1943–45. Mem., state-level org. of LDP, 1946. Re-settled in W Germany, 1952: practical legal training in Bremen and Mem. Free Democratic Party (FDP); FDP Asst in Parly Group, 1956; Gen. Sec.: FDP Parly Group, 1959–65; FDP at nat. level, 1962–64. A Parly Sec., FDP Parly Group, 1965–69; Dep. Chm., FDP, 1969–74; Federal Minister of the Interior, Oct. 1969 (Brandt-Scheel Cabinet); re-apptd Federal Minister of the Interior, Dec. 1972. He was instrumental in maintaining pure air and water; gave a modern structure to the Federal Police Authority; Federal Border Guard Act passed; revised weapons laws, etc.; in promoting relations between West and East, prominent role in CSCE, Helsinki, 1975, Madrid, 1980–83, Stockholm, 1984–86 and in setting up conferences on Conventional Armed Forces, Confidence and Security Building Measures, Vienna, 1989; an initiator of reform process that led to the inclusion of the Single European Act 1986. Co-initiator: 'Eureka' initiative; independence process in Namibia. Promotes co-operation between EC and other regional gps, ASEAN, Central Amer. States, (San José Conferences), Golf Co-operation Council. Chm., Bd of Trustees, Franckesche Stiftungen, Halle, 1992–94. Chm., Assoc. of Friends and Patrons, State Opera, Berlin. Hon. Prof., Free Univ., Berlin, 1994. Hon. Dr: Madras, 1977, Salamanca, 1987, Athens, 1988, Seoul, 1988, Budapest, 1988; Georgetown, Washington, 1990; Kattowitz, 1992; Essex, 1993; Moscow, 1993; Warsaw, 1993; Hon. Master, German Handicrafts 1975; Hon. citizen Costa Rica, 1987; Grand Fed. Cross of Merit 1973, 1975 with star and sash; Wolfgang-Döring Medal 1976; numerous foreign decorations. *Publications:* Umweltschutz: Das Umweltschutzprogramm der Bundesregierung, 1972; Bundestagsreden, 1972; Aussenpolitik im Dienste von Sicherheit und Freiheit, 1975; Deutsche Aussenpolitik, 1977, 3rd edn 1985; Bundestagsreden und Zeitdokumente, 1979; Zukunftsverantwortung, 1990; Erinnerungen, 1995. *Recreations:* reading, walking, swimming. *Address:* PO Box 200655, 53136 Bonn, Germany.

GENT, Sir Christopher (Charles), Kt 2001; Chief Executive, Vodafone Group, since 1997; *b* 10 May 1948; *m* 1st, 1973, Lynda Marion Tobin (marr. diss. 1999); two *d*; 2nd, 1999, Kate Elizabeth Mary Lock; one *s*. *Educ:* Archbishop Tennison Grammar Sch. With Nat West Bank, 1969–71; Schroder Computer Services, 1971–79; Divl Dir, ICL and Man. Dir, Baric, 1979–84; Man. Dir, Racal Vodac and Vodata, 1985–86; Man. Dir, Vodafone Ltd, 1985–97. *Recreations:* family, politics, cricket, horseracing, golf. *Address:* The Courtyard, 2–4 London Road, Newbury, Berks RG14 1JX. *Clubs:* Carlton; Goodwood (Sussex); Royal Ascot Racing; Hampshire CC; Lord's Taverners; West Berkshire Golf.

GENT, (John) David (Wright), FIMI; Director, DC Cook Holdings plc, 1995–2001; *b* 25 April 1935; *s* of late Reginald Philip Gent and Stella Eva Parker; *m* 1970, Anne Elaine Hanson. *Educ:* Lancing Coll. Admitted a Solicitor, 1959. Joined Soc. of Motor Manufacturers as Legal Advr, 1961; Asst Sec., 1964; Sec. 1965; Dep. Dir, 1971–80; joined Lucas Industries as Gen. Man., Lucas Service UK, 1981; Gp PR Man., 1982–83; Dir, British Road Fedn, 1983–84; Dir Gen., Retail Motor Industry Fedn, 1985–95. Member: Road Transport ITB, 1985–91; Vehicle Security Installation Bd, 1994–95. FRSA 1995. Freeman, City of London, 1985; Liveryman, Coach Makers and Coach Harness Makers' Co., 1985. *Recreations:* golf, gardening. *Address:* 44 Ursula Street, SW11 3DW. *T:* (020) 7228 8126.

GENTLEMAN, David (William), RDI 1970; artist and designer; *b* 11 March 1930; *s* of late Tom and Winifred Gentleman; *m* 1st, 1953, Rosalind Dease (marr. diss. 1966; she *d* 1997); one *d*; 2nd, 1968, Susan, *d* of late George Ewart Evans; two *d* one *s*. *Educ:* Hertford Grammar Sch.; St Albans Sch. of Art; Royal College of Art. Work includes: painting in watercolour, illustration, graphic design, lithography and wood engraving; commissions include Eleanor Cross mural designs for Charing Cross underground station, 1979; historical panels for East Cloister, Westminster Abbey, 1986; illustrations and designs for many publishers; postage stamps for the Royal Mail, including, 1962–: Shakespeare, Churchill, Darwin, Ely Cathedral, Abbotsbury Swans, Millennium, etc; posters for London Transport and the National Trust; symbols for British Steel, Bodleian Library, etc. Solo exhibitions at Mercury Gallery: watercolours of: India, 1970; Carolina, 1973; Africa, 1976; Pacific, 1981; Britain, 1982; London, 1985; British coastline, 1988; Paris, 1991; India, 1994; Italy, 1997; City of London, 2000. Editions of lithographs of architecture and landscape, 1967–2000. Work in public collections incl. Tate Gall., V&A, BM and Nat. Maritime Mus. and also in private collections. Member: Nat. Trust Properties Cttee; Alliance Graphique Internat.; Council, Artists' Gen. Benevolent Instn. Master of Faculty, RDI, 1989–91. Hon. Fellow, RCA, 1981; Hon. FRIBA 1996. Hon. DDes Kingston, 1994. *Publications:* author and illustrator: Design in Miniature, 1972; David Gentleman's Britain, 1982; David Gentleman's London, 1985; A Special Relationship, 1987; David Gentleman's Coastline, 1988; David Gentleman's Paris, 1991; David Gentleman's India, 1994; David Gentleman's Italy, 1997; The Wood Engravings of David Gentleman, 2000; *for children:* Fenella in Greece, 1967; Fenella in Spain, 1967; Fenella in Ireland, 1967; Fenella in the South of France, 1967; *illustrator:* Plats du Jour, 1957; Bridges on the Backs, 1961; Swiss Family Robinson, 1963 (USA); The Shepherd's Calendar, 1964; Poems of John Keats, 1966 (USA); The Pattern Under the Plough, 1966; covers for New Penguin Shakespeare, 1968–78; The Jungle Book, 1968 (USA); Robin Hood, 1977 (USA); The Dancing Tigers, 1979; Westminster Abbey, 1987; The Illustrated Poems of John Betjeman, 1995; Inwards where all the battle is, 1997; The Key Keeper, 2001; *illustrator and editor:* The Crooked Scythe, 1993. *Address:* 25 Gloucester Crescent, NW1 7DL. *T:* (020) 7485 8824, *Fax:* (020) 7267 4541; *e-mail:* d@gentleman.demon.co.uk.

GEORGALA, Prof. Douglas Lindley, CBE 1986; PhD; FIFST; Director of Food Research, Agricultural and Food Research Council, 1988–94; External Professor, University of Leeds, since 1993; independent scientific consultant, since 1994; *b* 2 Feb. 1934; *s* of late John Michael Georgala and of Izetta Iris Georgala; *m* 1959, Eulalia Catherina Lochner; one *s* one *d*. *Educ:* South African College Sch., Cape Town; Univ. of Stellenbosch (BScAgric); Univ. of Aberdeen (PhD). FIFST 1987. Research Officer, Fishing Research Inst., Univ. of Cape Town, 1957–60; Research Microbiologist, 1960–69, Division Manager, 1969–72, Head of Laboratory, 1977–86, Unilever Colworth Laboratory; Technical Member, Unilever Meat Products Co-ordination, 1973–77; Mem., Unilever Res. Div., 1987–88; Indust. Consultant, Biotechnology Unit, DTI, 1987–88. Chairman: Fisheries Res. Bd, 1980–84; Adv. Cttee of Food Science Dept, Leeds Univ., 1984–88; Scientific and Technical Cttee, Food and Drink Fedn, 1986–88; Adv. Cttee on Microbiological Safety of Food, 1996– (Mem., 1991–; Acting Chm., 1994–95); Member: ACARD, 1980–83; Food Cttee, 1984–88, Strategy Bd, 1991–93, AFRC; Co-ordinating Cttee for Marine Science and Technol., 1988–89; Food Adv. Cttee, 1989–94; Council, Inst. of Food Science and Technology, 1992–94; Ownership Bd, Centre for Envmt, Fisheries and Agric. Sc., 1997–. Vis. Prof., UEA, Leeds and Reading Univs, 1988–94. Scientific Governor, British Nutrition Foundn, 1992–. Trustee, World Humanity Action Trust, 1999–2000. FRSA 1984. *Publications:* papers in jls of general microbiology, applied bacteriology, hygiene, etc. *Recreations:* gardening, cycling, recorded music.

GEORGE; *see* Lloyd George and Lloyd-George.

GEORGE, Andrew Henry; MP (Lib Dem) St Ives, since 1997; *b* Mullion, Cornwall, 2 Dec. 1958; *s* of Reginald Hugh George and Diana May (*née* Petherick); *m* 1987, Jill Elizabeth, *d* of Bill and Margery Marshall; one *s* one *d*. *Educ:* Helston Grammar (subseq. Comprehensive) Sch.; Sussex Univ. (BA); University Coll., Oxford (MSc). Rural Officer, Notts Rural Community Council, 1981–85; Dep. Dir, Cornwall Rural Community Council, 1985–97. Contested (Lib Dem) St Ives, 1992. *Publications:* The Natives are Revolting Down in the Cornwall Theme Park, 1986; (jtly) Cornwall at the Crossroads, 1989; A Vision of Cornwall (Cornwall Blind Assoc.), 1995; housing and planning pubns and res. reports. *Recreations:* football, Rugby, cricket, tennis, swimming, cycling, walking, singing, poetry, theatre. *Address:* House of Commons, SW1A 0AA. *T:* (020) 7219 4588; Knights' Yard, Belgravia Street, Penzance, Cornwall TR18 2EL. *T:* (01736) 360020. *Clubs:* Commons Football, Commons and Lords Rugby; Leedstown Cricket, Hayle Tennis (Cornwall).

GEORGE, Andrew Neil; HM Diplomatic Service; Counsellor (Commercial Development) Jakarta, since 2002; *b* 9 Oct. 1952; *s* of Walter George and late Madeleine George (*née* Lacey); *m* 1977, Watanalak Chaovieng; one *s* one *d*. *Educ:* Royal High Sch., Edinburgh; Univ. of Edinburgh (MA Politics and Modern History 1974). Entered HM Diplomatic Service, 1974; W Africa Dept, FCO, and Third Sec., Chad, 1974–75; SOAS, London Univ., 1975–76; Third, subseq. Second, Sec., Bangkok, 1976–80; S America Dept, 1980–81, W Africa Dept, 1981–82, Perm. Under-Sec.'s Dept, 1982–84, FCO; First Sec., Canberra, 1984–88; First Sec. and Head of Chancery, Bangkok, 1988–92; Republic of Ireland Dept, 1993–94, Eastern Dept, 1994–95, Non-Proliferation Dept, 1995–98, FCO; Ambassador to Paraguay, 1998–2001. *Recreations:* reading, golf, watching football. *Address:* c/o Foreign and Commonwealth Office, King Charles Street, SW1A 2AH.

GEORGE, Rear Adm. Anthony Sanderson, CB 1983; CEng, FIIM; Port Manager, Portsmouth, since 1987; *b* 8 Nov. 1928; *s* of Sandys Parker George and Winifred Marie George; *m* 1953, Mary Veronica Frances Bell; two *d*. *Educ:* Royal Naval Coll., Dartmouth; Royal Naval Engrg Coll., Manadon. MIMechE 1957; FBIM 1977; FIIM 1979. Sea-going appts, 1950–62; warship design, Ship Dept of MoD, 1962–64; RN Staff Coll., 1965; British High Commn, Canberra, 1966–67; MEO, HMS Hampshire, 1968–69; Staff of Flag Officer Sea Trng, 1970–71; Dep. Prodn Manager, HM Dockyard, Portsmouth, 1972–75; RCDS, 1976; CSO (Trng) to C-in-C Naval Home Comd, 1977–78; Prodn Manager, HM Dockyard, Portsmouth, 1979–81; Dir, Dockyard Prodn and Support, 1981–82; Chief Exec., Royal Dockyards, 1983–86. Chief Exec., World Energy Business, 1986. Comdr 1965, Captain 1972, Rear Adm. 1981. FIMgt. *Recreations:* sailing, swimming, walking, painting. *Address:* c/o National Westminster Bank, 5 East Street, Chichester, West Sussex PO19 1HH.

GEORGE, Sir Arthur (Thomas), AO 1987; Kt 1972; solicitor and company director; *b* 17 Jan. 1915; *s* of late Thomas George; *m* 1939, Renee (AM 1998), *d* of Anthony Freeleagus; one *d*. *Educ:* Sydney High Sch., NSW. Chm. and Man. Dir, George Investment Pty Ltd Group, 1943; Chm., Australia Solenoid Holdings Ltd, 1967. Chm., Assoc. for Classical Archæology, of Sydney Univ., 1966–. Chm., Australian Soccer Fedn., 1969–88; Comr, Australian Sports Commn, 1986–89; Member: Exec., FIFA, 1981–94; Organising Cttee, 1983 World Youth Championship. Founder, The Arthur T. George Foundation Ltd, 1972. Fellow, Confedn of Australian Sport, 1985; Hon. Fellow, Senate of Univ. of Sydney, 1985. Gold Order of Merit, FIFA, 1994. Coronation Medal; Silver Jubilee Medal, 1977. Grand Commander (Keeper of the Laws), Cross of St Marks, and Gold Cross of Mount Athos, Greek Orthodox Church; Order of Phoenix (Greece). *Recreations:* interested in sport, especially Association football, etc. *Address:* 15 Hopetoun Avenue, Vaucluse, NSW 2030, Australia.

GEORGE, Rt Hon. Bruce Thomas; PC 2001; MP (Lab) Walsall South since Feb. 1974; *b* 1 June 1942; *m* 1992, Lisa Toelle. *Educ:* Mountain Ash Grammar Sch.; UCW Swansea; Univ. of Warwick. BA Politics Wales 1964, MA Warwick 1968. Asst Lectr in Social Studies, Glamorgan Polytechnic, 1964–66; Lectr in Politics, Manchester Polytechnic, 1968–70; Senior Lectr, Birmingham Polytechnic, 1970–74. Vis. Lectr, Univ. of Essex, 1985–86. Member: Select Cttee on Violence in the Family; Select Cttee on Defence, 1979– (Chm., 1997–); Chm., All Party Parly Maritime Gp. Mem., North Atlantic Assembly, 1981– (Chm., Mediterranean Special Gp). OSCE Parliamentary Assembly: Mem., 1992–; Gen. Rapporteur, 1992–95; Chm., 1996–99; Vice Pres., 1999–. Member: RIIA; IISS; RUSI (Mem. Council). Hon. Advr, Royal British Legion. Co-founder, Sec., House of Commons FC. Fellow, Parliament and Industry Trust, 1977–78. Ed., Jane's NATO Handbook, 1988–91. *Publications:* numerous books and articles on defence and foreign affairs. *Recreations:* Association football, snooker, student of American Indians, eating Indian food. *Address:* 42 Wood End Road, Walsall, West Midlands WS5 3BG. *T:* (01922) 627898; House of Commons, SW1A 0AA.

GEORGE, Sir Charles (Frederick), Kt 1998; MD; FRCP, FFPM; Medical Director, British Heart Foundation, since 1999; Emeritus Professor of Clinical Pharmacology, University of Southampton, since 1999; *b* 3 April 1941; *s* of William and Evelyn George; *m* 1969, Rosemary Moore (marr. diss. 1973). *Educ:* Univ. of Birmingham Med. Sch. (BSc 1962; MB ChB 1965; MD 1974). MRCP 1968; FRCP 1978; FFPM 1989. Med. Registrar, United Birmingham Hosps, 1967–69; Hammersmith Hospital, London: Med. Registrar, 1969–71; Sen. Registrar, 1971–73; University of Southampton: Sen. Lectr, 1973–75; Prof. of Pharmacology, 1975–99; Dean, Faculty of Medicine, Health and Biol Scis, 1993–98. Founder FMedSci 1998.FRSA 1993. *Publications:* Topics in Clinical Pharmacology, 1980; (ed) Presystemic Drug Metabolism, 1982; (ed) Clinical Pharmacology and Therapeutics, vol. 1, 1982; (ed) Drug Therapy in the Elderly, 1998. *Recreations:* music, jogging, wind surfing. *Address:* 15 Westgate Street, Southampton SO14 2AY.

GEORGE, Charles Richard; QC 1992; a Recorder, since 1997; *b* 8 June 1945; *s* of Hugh Shaw George, CIE and Joan George (*née* Stokes); *m* 1976, Joyce Tehmina Barnard; two *d*. *Educ:* Bradfield Coll.; Magdalen Coll., Oxford (MA 1st Cl. Hons Modern History); Corpus Christi Coll., Cambridge. Asst Master, Eton Coll., 1967–72; called to the Bar, Inner Temple, 1974; called to Irish Bar, King's Inns, Dublin, 1995; speciality, Parly, Envmtl and Admin. Law; an Asst Recorder, 1994–97; Chancellor, dio. of Southwark, 1996–. Mem., Council, St Stephen's House, Oxford, 1999–. *Publication:* The Stuarts: an age of experiment, 1973. *Recreations:* tennis, architecture, travel. *Address:* Ashgrove Farm, Ashgrove Road, Sevenoaks, Kent TN13 1SU. *T:* (01732) 451875; 2 Harcourt Buildings, Temple EC4Y 9DB. *T:* (020) 7353 8415. *Club:* Athenæum.

GEORGE, Prof. Donald William, AO 1979; Vice-Chancellor and Principal, University of Newcastle, New South Wales, 1975–86; *b* 22 Nov. 1926; *s* of late H. W. George, Sydney; *m* 1950, Lorna M. Davey, Parkes, NSW; one *s* one *d*. *Educ:* Univ. of Sydney. BSc, BE, PhD, FTS, FIEE, FIMechE, FIEAust, FAIP. Lectr, Elec. Engrg, NSW Univ. of Technology, 1949–53; Exper. Officer, UKAEA, Harwell, 1954–55; Res. Officer, Sen. Res. Officer, AAEC, Harwell and Lucas Heights, 1956–59; Sen. Lectr, Elec. Engrg, Univ. of Sydney, 1960–66; Associate Prof., Elec. Engrg, Univ. of Sydney, 1967–68; P. N. Russell Prof. of Mech. Engrg, Univ. of Sydney, 1969–74. Chairman: Australian-American Educational Foundn, 1977–84; Australian Atomic Energy Commn, 1976–83. Hon. Life Trustee, Asian Inst. of Technology, 1998 (Trustee, 1978–98). Hon. DEng Newcastle, NSW, 1986; Hon. DTech Asian Inst. of Technol., Bangkok, 1999. *Publications:* numerous sci. papers and techn. reports. *Address:* Shamley Green, 170 Glenning Road, Glenning Valley, NSW 2261, Australia. *T:* (2) 43883056.

GEORGE, Rt Hon. Sir Edward (Alan John), GBE 2000; PC 1999; Governor, Bank of England, since 1993; *b* 11 Sept. 1938; *s* of Alan George and Olive Elizabeth George; *m* 1962, Clarice Vanessa Williams; one *s* two *d*. *Educ:* Dulwich Coll.; Emmanuel Coll., Cambridge (BAEcon 2nd Cl. (i); MA). Joined Bank of England, 1962; worked initially on East European affairs; seconded to Bank for International Settlements, 1966–69, and to International Monetary Fund as Asst to Chairman of Deputies of Committee of Twenty on Internat. Monetary Reform, 1972–74; Adviser on internat. monetary questions, 1974–77; Dep. Chief Cashier, 1977–80; Asst Dir (Gilt Edged Div.), 1980–82; Exec. Dir, 1982–90; Dep. Gov., 1990–93. Hon. DSc (Econ) Hull, 1993; City, 1995; Cranfield, 1997; UMIST, 1998; Buckingham, 2000; Hon. DLitt: Loughborough, 1994; Sheffield, 1999; Hon. DPhil London Guildhall, 1996; Hon. LLD: Exeter, 1997; Bristol, 1999; Herts, 1999; Cantab, 2000. *Recreations:* family, sailing, bridge. *Address:* Bank of England, Threadneedle Street, EC2R 8AH. *T:* (020) 7601 4444.

GEORGE, Henry Ridyard, CBE 1979; FInstPet; Director of Petroleum Engineering, Department of Energy, 1973–81; retired; *b* 14 May 1921; *s* of Charles Herbert George and Mary Ridyard; *m* 1st, 1948, Irene May Myers (*d* 1981); one *s*; 2nd, 1985, Gwen (*née* Gooderham), *widow* of Prof. E. O'Farrell Walsh. *Educ:* George Dixon's Secondary Sch., Birmingham; Univ. of Birmingham (1st Cl. Hons degree, Oil Engrg and Refining and Petroleum Technol., 1941). Served War, REME/IEME, 1941–46 (2nd Lieut, later Captain). Pet. Engr with Royal Dutch/Shell Gp, 1947–68: service in USA, Holland, Brunei, Nigeria and Venezuela in a variety of positions, incl. Chief Pet. Engr in last 3 countries; Dept of Energy, 1968–81. *Recreations:* gardening, golf. *Address:* Heron Bank, Aldeburgh Road, Aldringham, Leiston, Suffolk IP16 4QL. *T:* (01728) 454620.

GEORGE, Hywel, CMG 1968; OBE 1963; Fellow, Churchill College, Cambridge, since 1971 (Bursar, 1972–90); *b* 10 May 1924; *s* of Rev. W. M. George and Catherine M. George; *m* 1955, Edith Pirchl; three *d*. *Educ:* Llanelli Gram. Sch.; UCW Aberystwyth; Pembroke Coll., Cambridge; SOAS, London. RAF, 1943–46. Cadet, Colonial Admin. Service, N Borneo, 1949–52; District Officer, 1952–58; Secretariat, 1959–62; Resident, Sabah, Malaysia, 1963–66; Administrator, 1967–69, Governor, 1969–70, St Vincent; Administrator, British Virgin Is, 1971. Mem. Court and Council, Univ. of Wales, Bangor, 1999–. Panglima Darjah Kinabalu (with title of Datuk), Sabah, 1964; JMN, Malaysia, 1966. CStJ 1969. *Recreation:* walking. *Address:* 46 St Margaret's Road, Girton, Cambridge CB3 0LT. *T:* (01223) 563766; Tu Hwnt ir Afon, The Close, Llanfairfechan LL33 0AG. *T:* (01248) 681509.

GEORGE, Most Rev. Ian Gordon Combe; *see* Adelaide, Archbishop of.

GEORGE, Prof. Kenneth Desmond; Professor of Economics, 1988–98, now Emeritus, and Pro Vice-Chancellor (formerly Vice-Principal), 1993–98, University of Wales Swansea (formerly University College of Swansea); *b* 11 Jan. 1937; *s* of Horace Avory George and Dorothy Margaret (*née* Hughes); *m* 1959, Elizabeth Vida (*née* Harries); two *s* one *d*. *Educ:* Ystalyfera Grammar Sch.; University Coll. of Wales, Aberstwyth (MA). Res. Asst, then Lectr in Econs, Univ. of Western Australia, 1959–63; Lectr in Econs, University Coll. of N Wales, Bangor, 1963–64; Univ. Asst Lectr, Univ. of Cambridge, 1964–66, Univ. Lectr, 1966–73; Fellow and Dir of Studies in Econs, Sidney Sussex Coll., Cambridge, 1965–73; Prof. and Head of Dept of Econs, 1973–88, and Dep. Principal,

1980–83, UC, Cardiff; Head of Dept of Economics, 1988–95 and Dean, Faculty of Econ. and Soc. Studies, 1992–93, UC Swansea. Vis. Prof., McMaster Univ., 1970–71. Part-time Mem., Monopolies and Mergers Commn, 1978–86; Member: Ind. panel on public appointments, Welsh Office, 1996–; Parly Boundary Commn for Wales, 1998–. Editor, Jl of Industrial Economics, 1970–83; Mem. Adv. Bd, Antitrust Law and Econs Rev., 1988–92. *Publications:* Productivity in Distribution, 1966; Productivity and Capital Expenditure in Retailing, 1968; Industrial Organisation, 1971, 4th edn (with C. Joll and E. Lynk), 1992; (with T. S. Ward) The Structure of Industry in the EEC, 1975; (ed with C. Joll) Competition Policy in the UK and EEC, 1975; (with J. Shorey) The Allocation of Resources, 1978; (ed with L. Mainwaring) The Welsh Economy, 1988; articles in Econ. Jl, Oxford Econ. Papers, Aust. Econ. Papers, Jl Indust. Econs, Rev. of Econs and Stats, Oxford Bull., Scottish Jl Polit. Econ., and British Jl Indust. Relations. *Recreations:* walking, music, cricket. *Address:* Ein-Tŷ-Ni, 39 St Fagans Drive, St Fagans, Cardiff CF5 6EF. *T:* (029) 2056 2801.

GEORGE, Llewellyn Norman Havard; a Recorder of the Crown Court, 1980–91; Consultant, V. J. G. Johns & Son, Solicitors, since 1991 (Partner, 1950–91, Senior Partner, 1972–91); *b* 13 Nov. 1925; *s* of Benjamin William George, DSO, RNR, and Annie Jane George; *m* 1950, Mary Patricia Morgan (*née* Davies); one *d*. *Educ:* Cardiff High Sch.; Fishguard Grammar Sch. HM Coroner, 1965–80; Recorder, Wales and Chester Circuit, 1980–. President: West Wales Law Society, 1973–74; Pembrokeshire Law Society, 1981–83; Chairman: (No 5) South Wales Law Society Legal Aid Cttee, 1979; Agricl Land Tribunal (Wales), 1985–90 (Dep. Chm., 1983–85). Mem., Farrand Cttee, 1984–85. *Recreations:* golf, reading, chess. *Address:* Pwllderi, 3 Pantycelyn, Penyraber, Fishguard, Pembs SA65 9EH. *T:* (01348) 872040. *Clubs:* Pembrokeshire County; Newport (Pembs) Golf.

GEORGE, Patrick Herbert; artist; Emeritus Professor of Fine Art, University of London, since 1988; *b* 28 July 1923; *s* of A. H. George and N. George (*née* Richards); *m* 1st, 1953, June Griffith (marr. diss. 1980); four *d*; 2nd, 1981, Susan Ward. *Educ:* Downs Sch.; Bryanston Sch.; Edinburgh Coll. of Art; Camberwell Sch. of Art (NDD). Served War, RNVR, 1942–46. Asst, Slade Sch. of Fine Art, London, 1949–. Head, Dept of Fine Art, Nigerian Coll. of Art, Zaria, 1958–59; Slade School of Fine Art: Lectr, 1962; Reader in Fine Art, 1976; Prof. of Fine Art, Univ. of London, 1983; Slade Prof. of Fine Art, 1985–88. Works in public collections in GB and USA; one-man exhibn, Gainsborough's House, Sudbury, 1975; retrospective exhibn, Serpentine Gall., London, 1980; exhibn, Browse & Darby, 1984, 1989, 1994 and 1998; dealer, Browse & Darby. *Recreation:* make do and mend. *Address:* 33 Moreton Terrace, SW1 2NS. *T:* (020) 7828 3302; Grandfathers, Great Saxham, Bury St Edmunds, Suffolk IP29 5JW. *T:* (01284) 810997.

GEORGE, Peter John, OBE 1974; HM Diplomatic Service, retired; Counsellor and Consul General, British Embassy, Manila, 1976–79; Chargé d'Affaires *ai*, 1978; *b* 12 Dec. 1919; *s* of late Cecil John George and Mabel George; *m* 1946, Andrée Louise Perrion; one *d*. *Educ:* Sutton Grammar Sch., Plymouth. Served War, 1939–46: Captain. Home Civil Service, 1936; HM Diplomatic Service, 1966; First Secretary, Commercial: Colombo, 1967–70; Seoul, 1971–73 (Chargé d'Affaires *ai*, 1971 and 1972); Prague, 1973–76. *Recreations:* reading, golf, swimming. *Address:* St Just, Walton Park, Walton-on-Thames, Surrey KT12 3EU.

GEORGE, Sir Richard (William), Kt 1995; CVO 1998; Director, since 1972, Chairman and Managing Director, since 1982, Weetabix Ltd; *b* 24 April 1944; *m* 1984, Patricia Jane Ogden; two *s* one *d*. *Educ:* Repton Sch.; Kansas State Univ. (BSc). Joined Weetabix Ltd, 1968: Dep. Man. Dir, 1976–82; Chm., Whitworths Holdings Ltd, 1987–97. Dep. Chm., Envmt Agency, 1995–98. Member: Exec. Cttee, Assoc. of Cereal Food Mfrs, 1977– (Chm., 1983–85); Council, Food and Drink Fedn (formerly Food Mfrs Fedn), 1982– (Mem., Exec. Cttee, 1984–; Dep. Pres., 1990–92; Pres., 1993–95); Exec. Cttee, Ceereal (European Breakfast Cereal Assoc.), 1992–96 (Pres., 1994–March 1996). Chm., Governing Body, Inst. of Food Res. (formerly Adv. Bd, Inst. of Food Res.), 1993–98; Mem., Food from Britain Council, 1993–98. Mem., Council, Royal Warrant Holders' Assoc., 1983– (Pres., 1993; Hon. Treas., 1998–). Prince's Trust: Mem., Mgt Bd, 1993–99 (Vice Chm., 1996–99); Mem., Northants Cttee, 1985–94 (Chm., 1985–88, 1991–94); Pres., Northants Prince's Youth Business Trust, 1998– (Vice-Chm., 1986–98). Chm., RAF Benevolent Fund, 2001–. Hon. Air Cdre, 504 (Co. of Nottingham) Sqn (formerly Offensive Support Role Support Sqn), RAF Cottesmore, 1998–. FIGD 1983; CIMgt (CBIM 1985); FInstD 1981; FRSA 1991. Freeman, City of London, 2001; Liveryman, GAPAN, 2001– (Freeman, 1982). Hon. LLD Leicester, 1997. *Recreations:* family, golf. *Address:* Weetabix Ltd, Burton Latimer, Kettering, Northants NN15 5JR. *T:* (01536) 722181. *Clubs:* Saints and Sinners; Royal and Ancient (St Andrews).

GEORGE, Prof. Stephen Alan; Professor, Department of Politics, University of Sheffield, since 1994; *b* 14 Oct. 1949; *s* of Arthur George and Florence Lilian George (*née* Jefferson); *m* 1970, Linda Margaret Booth; one *s* one *d*. *Educ:* Univ. of Leicester (BA 1st cl. Hons Social Scis 1971; MPhil 1974). Res. Asst in European Affairs, Huddersfield Poly., 1971–72; Lectr, 1973–90, Sen. Lectr, 1991–92, Reader, 1992–94, in Politics, Univ. of Sheffield. Chair, Univ. Assoc. for Contemporary European Studies, 1996–2000. *Publications:* Politics and Policy in the European Community, 1985, 3rd edn, as Politics and Policy in the European Union, 1996; An Awkward Partner: Britain in the European Community, 1990, 3rd edn 1998; (jtly) Politics in the European Union, 2001. *Recreations:* walking, reading history, poetry and novels. *Address:* Department of Politics, University of Sheffield, Elmfield, Northumberland Road, Sheffield S10 2TU. *T:* (0114) 222 1652.

GEORGE, Timothy John Burr, CMG 1991; HM Diplomatic Service, retired; *b* 14 July 1937; *s* of late Brig. J. B. George, late RAMC and M. Brenda George (*née* Harrison); *m* 1962, Richenda Mary, *d* of late Alan Reed, FRIBA and of Ann Reed (*née* Rowntree); one *s* two *d*. *Educ:* Aldenham Sch.; Christ's Coll., Cambridge (BA). National Service, 2nd Lieut RA, 1956–58; Cambridge Univ., 1958. FCO, 1961; 3rd Secretary: Hong Kong, 1962; Peking, 1963; 2nd, later 1st Sec., FCO, 1966; 1st Sec. (Economic), New Delhi, 1969; Asst Political Adviser, Hong Kong, 1972; Asst European Integration Dept (Internal), FCO, 1974; Counsellor and Head of Chancery, Peking, 1978–80; Res. Associate, IISS, 1980–81; Counsellor and Hd of Chancery, UK Perm. Delegn to OECD, 1982–86; Hd, Republic of Ireland Dept, FCO, 1986–90; Ambassador to Nepal, 1990–95; FCO, 1996–99. Mem. Bd, CARE Internat. UK, 1998–. *Publication:* (jtly) Security in Southern Asia, 1984. *Address:* Martlets, Ogbourne St George, Marlborough, Wilts SN8 1SL. *T:* (01672) 841278.

GEORGE, William; His Honour Judge George; a Circuit Judge, since 1995; *b* 28 Sept. 1944; *s* of William Henry George and Elizabeth George; *m* 1973, Susan Isabel Pennington; two *d*. *Educ:* Herbert Strutt Grammar Sch.; Victoria Univ. of Manchester (LLB, LLM). Called to the Bar, Lincoln's Inn (Mansfield Scholar), 1968; Chancery Bar, Liverpool, 1968–95; Head, Chancery Chambers, Liverpool, 1985–95; Asst Recorder, 1990–93; Recorder, 1993–95. Chm., Northern Chancery Bar Assoc., 1992–94. *Recreations:* history (military history and the American Civil War), contemporary British art, gardening. *Address:* Queen Elizabeth II Law Courts, Derby Square, Liverpool L2 1XA. *Club:* Athenæum (Liverpool).

GEORGE, Prof. William David, FRCS; Regius Professor of Surgery, University of Glasgow, since 1999 (Professor of Surgery, 1981–99); *b* 22 March 1943; *s* of William Abel George and Peggy Eileen George; *m* 1st, 1967, Helen Marie (*née* Moran) (*d* 1986); one *s* three *d*; 2nd, 1990, Pauline (*née* Mooney). *Educ:* Reading Bluecoat Sch.; Henley Grammar Sch.; Univ. of London (MB, BS 1966; MS 1977). FRCS 1970. Jun. surgical jobs, 1966–71; Registrar in Surgery, Royal Postgrad. Med. Sch., 1971–73; Lectr in Surg., Univ. of Manchester, 1973–77; Sen. Lectr in Surg., Univ. of Liverpool, 1977–81. *Publications:* articles in BMJ, Lancet, British Jl of Surg. *Recreations:* veteran rowing, fishing, squash. *Address:* 21 Kingsborough Gardens, Glasgow G12 9NH. *T:* (0141) 339 9546. *Club:* Clyde Amateur Rowing (Glasgow).

GEORGES, Rt Hon. (Philip) Telford; PC 1986; Judge of the Court of Appeal, Grand Cayman, 1985–2000; *b* Dominica, 5 Jan. 1923; *s* of John Georges and Milutine Cox; *m* 1954, Grace Glasgow (marr. diss.); *m* 1981, Joyce Cole. *Educ:* Dominica Grammar Sch.; Toronto Univ. (BA). Called to the Bar, 1949; in private practice, Trinidad and Tobago, 1949–62; Judge of the High Court, Trinidad and Tobago, 1962–74; on secondment as Chief Justice of Tanzania, 1965–71; acting Justice of Appeal, Trinidad and Tobago, 1972; Judge of the Courts of Appeal of Bahamas, 1975–81, of Bermuda, 1975–81 and 1990–94, of Belize, 1975–81 and 1993–97; Judge of the Supreme Court, 1981–83, Chief Justice, 1983, Zimbabwe; Chief Justice of the Bahamas, 1984–89. Law Reform Comr, Bahamas, 1989–95. Prof. of Law, 1974–81, and Dean of the Faculty of Law, 1977–79, Univ. of WI at Cave Hill. Vice-Chm., Trinidad and Tobago Constitutional Reform Commn, 1971–74; Chm., Crime Commn, Bermuda, 1977–78; Mem., Admin. Tribunal, Inter-American Develt Bank, 1993–98. Mem., Judicial Cttee, OAS, 1992–95. Hon. LLD: Toronto; Dar-es-Salaam; West Indies, 1985; Dalhousie, 1995. Order of Caribbean Community, 1994; Award of Dominica, 1996. *Recreation:* walking. *Address:* Newcastle, St John, Barbados.

GERAINT, Baron *cr* 1992 (Life Peer), of Ponterwyd in the County of Dyfed; **Geraint Wyn Howells;** farmer; an Extra Lord-in-Waiting to the Queen, since 1998; *b* 15 April 1925; *s* of David John Howells and Mary Blodwen Howells; *m* 1957, Mary Olwen Hughes Griffiths; two *d*. *Educ:* Ponterwyd Primary Sch.; Ardwyn Grammar School. MP Cardigan, Feb. 1974–1983, Ceredigion and Pembroke North, 1983–92 (L 1983–88, Lib Dem 1988–92). Leader, Welsh Lib Dems, 1979–85. Dep. Speaker, H of L, 1994–99. Former Mem., British Wool Marketing Bd (Vice-Chm., 1971–83); Chm., Wool Producers of Wales Ltd, 1977–87. Pres., Royal Welsh Agricl Show Soc., 1983. FRAgS 1980. Sec., Ponterwyd Eisteddfod, 1944–2001; Mem., Gorsedd, 1976. *Recreations:* walking, sport. *Address:* Glennydd, Ponterwyd, Cardiganshire SY23 3LB. *T:* (01970) 890258.

GERARD, family name of **Baron Gerard**.

GERARD, 5th Baron *cr* 1876; **Anthony Robert Hugo Gerard;** Bt 1611; *b* 3 Dec. 1949; *er s* of Maj. Rupert Charles Frederick Gerard, MBE (*g g s* of 1st Baron), and of Huguette Reiss-Brian; *S* cousin, 1992; *m* 1976, Kathleen (marr. diss. 1997), *e d* of Dr Bernard Ryan, New York; two *s*. *Educ:* Harvard. *Heir:* *s* Hon. Rupert Bernard Charles Gerard, *b* 17 Dec. 1981. *Address:* PO Box 2308, East Hampton, NY 11937, USA.

GERARD, Ronald, OBE 1987; *b* 30 Oct. 1925; *s* of Samuel and Caroline Gerard; *m* 1952, Patricia Krieger; one *s* one *d*. *Educ:* Regent Street Polytechnic; College of Estate Management. FRICS 2000 (FSVA 1968). Royal Engineers, 1943–47, Italy and Egypt; articled to a City Chartered Surveyor, 1947–50; Principal, R. P. Gerard & Co., Surveyors and Valuers, 1952–59; Jt Man. Dir, 1959–87, Chm., 1982–87, London & Provincial Shop Centres Plc (created regional HQ buildings for many well-known public cos incl. Data General, Midland Bank, National Westminster Bank, Thomas Tilling, EMI, Rank Hovis, Honeywell, Calor Gas, Black & Decker, Chubb, Yellow Pages, Fluor plc etc.). Chm., Ronald Gerard Charitable Trust, 1983–95; has also funded many charitable enterprises, several of them eponymous, incl. medical research, facilities for the handicapped and the general public, restoration of works of art, youth cricket. President: London Community Cricket Assoc., 1992–94; London Cricket Coll., 1992–94; Middlesex Cricket Union, 1992–95; Middlesex Colts Assoc., 1995–97; Middlesex CCC, 1999–2001 (Life Vice-Pres., 1992); London Community Trust, 1992–94; Vice-President: English Schools Cricket Assoc., 1981–; Seaxe Club, 2001; Patron, Wilf Slack Young Cricketers Develt Trust, 1999; Mem. Council, Lord's Taverners, 1984–90; Trustee, Centenary Youth Trust, 1984–94. Patron, Brooklands Club, 1991. Life Vice-Pres., Enfield & Southgate Conservative Assoc., 1993. Liveryman, Glass Sellers' Co., 1990; Freeman, City of London, 1990. KStJ 1992. FRSA. Granted Arms, 1989. *Clubs:* Arts, Carlton, Buck's, MCC (Life Mem.).

GERARD-PEARSE, Rear-Adm. John Roger Southey, CB 1979; Group Personnel Manager, Jardine Matheson Co. Ltd, Hong Kong, 1980–84; *b* 10 May 1924; *s* of Dr Gerard-Pearse; *m* 1955, Barbara Jean Mercer; two *s* two *d*. *Educ:* Clifton College. Joined RN, 1943; comd HM Ships Tumult, Grafton, Defender, Fearless and Ark Royal; Flag Officer, Sea Training, 1975–76; Asst Chief, Naval Staff (Ops), 1977–79. *Recreations:* sailing, carpentry. *Address:* Enbrook, 170 Offham Road, West Malling, Kent ME19 6RF. *T:* (01732) 842375.

GERE, Richard; actor; *b* 31 Aug. 1949; *m* 1991, Cindy Crawford (marr. diss.). *Educ:* Univ. of Massachusetts. Played trumpet, piano, guitar and bass and composed music with various gps; stage performances: with Provincetown Playhouse, Seattle Rep. Theatre; Richard Farina, Long Time Coming and Long Time Gone, Back Bog Beat Bait, off-Broadway; Soon, Habeus Corpus and Grease on Broadway; A Midsummer Night's Dream, Lincoln Center; Taming of the Shrew, Young Vic, London; Bent, on Broadway (Theatre World Award); *films* include: Report to the Commissioner, 1975; Baby Blue Marine, 1976; Looking for Mr Goodbar, 1977; Days of Heaven, Blood Brothers, 1978; Yanks, American Gigolo, 1979; An Officer and a Gentleman, 1982; Breathless, Beyond the Limit, 1983; The Cotton Club, 1984; King David, 1985; Power, No Mercy, 1986; Miles From Home, 1989; Pretty Woman, Internal Affairs, 1990; Rhapsody in August, 1991; Final Analysis, 1992; Mr Jones, Sommersby, 1993; And the Band Played On, Intersection, 1994; First Knight, 1995; Primal Fear, 1996; The Jackal, Red Corner, 1998; The Runaway Bride, 1999; Autumn in New York, Dr T and the Women, 2000. Founding Chm. and Pres., Tibet House, NY. *Publication:* Pilgrim, 1997. *Address:* c/o ICM, 40 West 57th Street, New York, NY 10019, USA.

GERGIEV, Valery Abesalovich; Principal Conductor: Kirov Opera, since 1988; Rotterdam Philharmonic Orchestra, since 1995; Director, Mariinsky Theatre, St Petersburg, since 1996; *b* Moscow, 1953. *Educ:* studied conducting under Ilya Musin, Leningrad Conservatory. Kirov Opera: début, War and Peace, 1978; Asst Conductor; Artistic Director, 1988; former Chief Conductor, Armenian State Orch.; has appeared with numerous major internat. orchs, incl. Bayerische Rundfunk, Berlin Philharmonic, Boston SO, LPO, LSO, Philharmonia, NY Philharmonic, Vienna Philharmonic; tours with Kirov Opera. Principal Guest Conductor, Metropolitan Opera, NY, 1998–; Artistic Director: Stars of the White Nights Fest.; Rotterdam Philharmonic/Gergiev/Philips Fest.; Director and Founder: Mikkeli Internat. Fest., Finland; Peace to the Caucasus Fest.; Red Sea Internat. Music Fest., Eilat, Israel. Has made numerous recordings. Winner, Herbert von Karajan Conductors Competition, Berlin; Dmitri Shostakovich Award; Golden Mask Award; People's Artist of Russia. *Address:* c/o Columbia Artists Management Inc., 165 West 57th Street, New York, NY 10019, USA.

GERHARD, Dr Derek James, (Jeremy), CB 1986; Partner, The Dowding Partnership (Planning and Problem Solving for Business), since 1993; Deputy Master and Comptroller, Royal Mint, 1977–88, retired; *b* 16 Dec. 1927; *s* of late F. J. Gerhard, Banstead; *m* 1952, Dr Sheila Cooper, *d* of late Dr G. K. Cooper; three *s* two *d. Educ:* Highgate Sch.; Fitzwilliam Coll., Cambridge (MA; Hon. Fellow 1986); Reading Univ. (PhD). Commnd 3rd Carabiniers (Prince of Wales DG), 1945–48. Dept of Scientific Adviser, Air Ministry, 1952–57; transf. to DSIR, 1957; Sec., British Commonwealth Scientific Cttee, 1959–60; Asst Sci. Attaché, British Embassy, Washington, 1961–64; transf. to Admin. CS, 1964; Board of Trade, latterly leader UK Delgn to Internat. Consultative Shipping Gp, 1964–69; Head of Management Services, BoT, 1969–71; loaned to CSD (Personnel Management), 1971–73; Dept of Industry, leader UK Delgn to Internat. Tin Council, 1973–75; Air Div., DoI, 1975–77. Pres., Mint Dir's Conf., 1982–84. Mem., Welsh Council, CBI, 1984–87. Hon. Treas., CTBI (formerly CCBI), 1992–2000. *Publications:* various scientific papers. *Recreations:* gardening, woodwork. *Address:* Little Dowding, Dorking Road, Walton Heath, Surrey KT20 7TJ. *T:* (01737) 813045.

GERKEN, Ian, LVO 1992; HM Diplomatic Service; Ambassador to Ecuador, since 2000; *b* 1 Dec. 1943; *s* of late Alfred Gerken and Esther Mary (*née* Chesworth); *m* 1976, Susana Drucker; two *s*, and one step *d. Educ:* Liverpool Collegiate. Entered Foreign Office, 1962: served in Budapest, 1965; Buenos Aires, 1966–68; FCO, 1968–71; Caracas, 1971–75; FCO, 1975–79; Lima, 1979–84; UN Gen. Assembly, 1984; FCO, 1985–88; Dep. High Comr, Valletta, 1988–92; Counsellor and Dep. Head, Perm. Under Sec's Dept, FCO, 1992–95; Ambassador to El Salvador, 1995–99. *Address:* c/o Foreign and Commonwealth Office, King Charles Street, SW1A 2AH.

GERKEN, Vice-Adm. Sir Robert William Frank, KCB 1986; CBE 1975; DL; Royal Navy, retired 1987; Chairman, Corps of Commissionaires, since 1994 (Director, since 1988); *b* 11 June 1932; *s* of Francis Sydney and Gladys Gerken; *m* 1st, 1966, Christine Stephenson (*d* 1981); two *d*; 2nd, 1983, Mrs Ann Fermor. *Educ:* Chigwell Sch.; Royal Naval Coll., Dartmouth. Sea service as Lieut and Lt-Comdr, 1953–66; RN Staff Course, 1967; in command HMS Yarmouth, 1968–69; Commander Sea Training, 1970–71; Naval Staff, 1972–73; in command: Sixth Frigate Sqdn, 1974–75; HMS Raleigh, 1976–77; Captain of the Fleet, 1978–81; Flag Officer Second Flotilla, 1981–83; Dir Gen., Naval Manpower and Trng, 1983–85; Flag Officer Plymouth, Port Admiral Devonport, Comdr Central Sub Area Eastern Atlantic, Comdr Plymouth Sub Area Channel, 1985–87. Chm., Plymouth Develt Corp., 1993–96. Chairman: China Fleet Club (UK) Charitable Trust, 1987–; Mount Batten Centre Trust, 2000–. President: British Korean Veterans' Assoc. (Plymouth Br.); Plymouth Lifeboat, RNLI, 1988–; SSAFA Forces Help Plymouth, 1998–. Governor, Chigwell Sch., 1987–2000. DL Devon, 1995. Hon. DSc Plymouth, 1993. *Recreations:* hearth and boat maintenance. *Address:* 22 Custom House Lane, Mill Bay, Plymouth, Devon PL1 3TG. *T:* (01752) 665104. *Clubs:* Naval; Royal Western Yacht (Cdre, 1993–97).

GERMAN, Lt-Col David John Keeling, TD 1972; JP; Vice Lord-Lieutenant of Staffordshire, since 1995; *b* 25 May 1932; *s* of Col Guy German, DSO and Rosemary German (*née* Keeling), MBE; *m* 1961, Anita Blanche Jupp; one *s* one *d. Educ:* Winchester; RMA, Sandhurst. Served Grenadier Guards, 1952–59; Keeling & Walker Ltd, Stoke on Trent, Chem. Mfrs, 1959–90, Man. Dir, 1974–90. Served Staffs Yeomanry, 1960–70, commanded QO Mercian Yeomanry, 1972–75. Freeman, City of London. JP 1972, DL 1979, High Sheriff 1982–83, Staffs. *Recreations:* yachting, field sports, France. *Address:* The Laundry House, 49 Pool Lane, Brocton, Stafford ST17 0TY. *Clubs:* Army and Navy; Royal Yacht Squadron, Household Division Yacht.

GERMAN, Michael James, OBE 1996; Member (Lib Dem) South Wales East, and Leader of Liberal Democrats, National Assembly for Wales, since 1999; Deputy First Minister for Wales and Minister (formerly Secretary) for Economic Development, since 2000; *b* 8 May 1945; *s* of Arthur Ronald German and Molly German; *m* 1970 (marr. diss. 1996); two *d. Educ:* St Mary's Coll., London (CertEd 1966); BA Open Univ. 1972; Bristol Poly. (Postgrad. Dip. in Educn Mgt 1973). Primary sch. teacher, 1966–67; Secondary sch. teacher, Mostyn High Sch., 1967–70; Head of Music: Lady Mary High Sch., Cardiff, 1970–86; Corpus Christi High Sch., Cardiff, 1986–91; Dir, European Div., Welsh Jt Educn Cttee, 1991–99. Mem., Cardiff CC, 1983–96 (Jt Leader, 1987–91; Leader, Liberal Democrats, 1983–96). Chm., Legislation Cttee, Nat. Assembly for Wales, 1999. *Publications:* articles in political and educnl jls. *Recreations:* music, travel. *Address:* 70 Princes Street, Roath, Cardiff CF2 3SL. *T:* (029) 2049 8783.

GERMOND, Rt Rev. Brian Charles; *see* Johannesburg, Bishop of.

GEROSA, Peter Norman; Secretary, Tree Council, 1983–91; *b* 1 Nov. 1928; *s* of late Enrico Cecil and Olive Doris Gerosa; *m* 1955, Dorothy Eleanor Griffin; two *d. Educ:* Whitgift Sch.; London Univ. (Birkbeck). BA (Hons) 1st Cl., Classics. Civil Service, 1945–82; Foreign Office, 1945; Home Office, 1949; HM Customs and Excise, 1953; Min. of Transport, 1966; DoE, 1970; Under Secretary: DoE, 1972; Dept of Transport, 1977; Dir of Rural Affairs, DoE, 1981–82. *Recreations:* singing, gardening, walking. *Address:* Sunnyside, Chart Lane, Reigate, Surrey RH2 7BW. *T:* (01737) 243771.

GEROSKI, Prof. Paul Andrew; Deputy Chairman, Competition Commission, since 2001; Professor of Economics, London Business School, since 1987; *b* 18 Oct. 1952. *Educ:* Bard Coll., USA (BA); Univ. of Warwick (MA, PhD). Council Mem., REcon.S Fellow, Centre for Econ. Policy Res. Mem. editorial bds of several jls. *Publications:* Market Dynamics and Entry, 1991; (jtly) Entry and Market Contestability: an international comparison, 1991; (with K. Knight) Targeting Competitive Industries, 1991; Market Structure, Corporate Performance and Innovative Activity, 1995; (with P. Gregg) Coping with Recession, 1997; numerous papers in learned jls. *Address:* Competition Commission, New Court, 48 Carey Street, WC2A 2JT.

GERRARD, Ven. David Keith Robin; Archdeacon of Wandsworth, since 1989; *b* 15 June 1939; *s* of Eric Henry and Doris Jane Gerrard; *m* 1963, Jennifer Mary Hartley; two *s* two *d. Educ:* Royal Grammar School, Guildford; St Edmund Hall, Oxford (BA); Lincoln Theol Coll. Curate: St Olave, Woodberry Down, N16, 1963–66; St Mary, Primrose Hill, NW3, 1966–69; Vicar: St Paul, Lorrimore Square, SE17, 1969–79; St Andrew and St Mark, Surbiton, Surrey, 1979–89; RD of Kingston upon Thames, 1983–88. *Publication:* (co-author) Urban Ghetto, 1976. *Recreations:* embroidery, Proust, Yorkshire, statistics. *Address:* 68 North Side, Wandsworth Common, SW18 2QX. *T:* (020) 8874 5766.

GERRARD, John Henry, CBE 1981 (OBE 1972); MC 1944; QPM 1975; Assistant Commissioner, Metropolitan Police, 1978–81; *b* 25 Nov. 1920; *s* of Archie Reginald and Evelyn Gerrard; *m* 1943, Gladys Hefford; two *s. Educ:* Cordwainers Technical Coll. Served War, Army, 1939–46: Iceland, 1940–42; commissioned 1st Mddx Regt, 1943; NW Europe, 1944–46 (Captain). Constable to Commander, 1946–65; Comdr, West End Central, 1965–68; Comdr 'A' Dept (Public Order/Operations), 1968–70; Deputy Assistant Commissioner: 'A' (Operations), 1970–74; No 1 Area, 1974–78. Chm., Met. Police Museums Adv. Bd, 1975–81. Freeman, City of London, 1978. KStJ 1986; Comr, London Dist, SJAB, 1983–88. *Recreations:* philately, history.

GERRARD, Neil Francis; MP (Lab) Walthamstow, since 1992; *b* 3 July 1942; *m* 1968, Marian Fitzgerald (marr. diss. 1983); two *s. Educ:* Manchester Grammar Sch.; Wadham Coll., Oxford (BA Hons); Chelsea Coll., London (MEd). Teacher, Queen Elizabeth's Sch., Barnet, 1965–68; Lectr in Computing, Hackney Coll., 1968–92. Mem. (Lab) Waltham Forest BC, 1973–90 (Leader of Council, 1986–90). Contested (Lab) Chingford, 1979. Mem. Bd, Pioneer Theatres. *Address:* House of Commons, SW1A 0AA.

GERRARD, Peter Noël, CBE 1991; General Counsel, London Stock Exchange, 1991–94; *b* 19 May 1930; *oc* of Sir Denis Gerrard and of Hilda Goodwin (*née* Jones, who *m* 2nd, Sir Joseph Cantley, OBE); *m* 1957, Prudence Lipson-Ward; one *s* two *d. Educ:* Rugby; Christ Church, Oxford (MA). 2nd Lieut, XII Royal Lancers, Malaya, 1953–54. Solicitor, 1959; Partner, Lovell, White & King, 1960, Sen. Partner, 1980–88; Sen. Partner, Lovell White Durrant, 1988–91. Member: Bd of Banking Supervision, 1990–2001; City Capital Markets Cttee, 1974–91. Member: Council, Law Society, 1972–82; Bd, Inst. of Advanced Legal Studies, 1985–96; Council, St George's Hosp. Med. Sch., 1982–94. *Recreations:* music, walking. *Address:* Pightle Cottage, Ashdon, Saffron Walden, Essex CB10 2HG. *T:* (01799) 584374; Le Petit Martinaud, Gageac-Rouillac 24240, France. *T:* (5) 53234695.

GERRARD, Ronald Tilbrook, FREng, FICE, FCIWEM; Senior Partner, Binnie & Partners, Consulting Engineers, 1974–83, retired; *b* 23 April 1918; *s* of Henry Thomas Gerrard and Edith Elizabeth Tilbrook; *m* 1950, Cecilia Margaret Bremner; three *s* one *d. Educ:* Imperial Coll. of Science and Technology, Univ. of London. BSc(Eng). FCGI; FICE 1957; FIWE 1965; FREng (FEng 1979); MEIC. Served War, RE, 1939–45. Resident Engr, sea defence and hydro-electric works, 1947–50; Asst Engr, design of hydro-power schemes in Scotland and Canada, 1951–54; Binnie & Partners: Sen. Engr, 1954; Partner, 1959; resp. for hydro-power, water supply, river engrg, coast protection and indust. works in UK and overseas. Chm., Assoc. of Cons. Engrs, 1969–70; Mem. Council, ICE, 1974–77. Telford Silver Medal, ICE, 1968. *Publications:* (jtly) 4 papers to ICE. *Address:* 6 Ashdown Road, Epsom, Surrey KT17 3PL. *T:* (01372) 724834. *Club:* Athenæum.

GERRARD-WRIGHT, Maj.-Gen. Richard Eustace John, CB 1985; CBE 1977 (OBE 1971; MBE 1963); DL; Director, Territorial Army and Cadets, 1982–85, retired; *b* 9 May 1930; *s* of Rev. R. L. Gerrard-Wright; *m* 1960, Susan Kathleen Young; two *s* one *d* (and one *d* decd). *Educ:* Christ's Hospital; RMA, Sandhurst. Commnd Royal Lincolnshire Regt, 1949; served Egypt, Germany and UK, 1950–55; Malaya, 1955–58 (despatches, 1958); Instructor, RMA, Sandhurst, 1958–62 (2nd E Anglian Regt, 1960); Staff Coll., India, 1962–63; served Kenya, Aden, Malta, Malaya, 1963–70 (Royal Anglian Regt, 1964); Bn Comdr, UK, Germany, NI, 1970–73 (despatches 1973); Comdr, 39 Inf. Bde, Belfast, 1975–77; Nat. Defence Coll., Canada, 1977–78; Chief of Staff, 1 (Br) Corps, 1978–79; GOC Eastern District, 1980–82. Dep. Col, Royal Anglian Regt, 1975–80; Col Comdt, Queen's Div., 1981–84. Chief Exec. and Sec., Hurlingham Club, 1985–87. DL Cambs, 1993–97; DL Lincs 1997. *Address:* 21 Market Place, Folkingham, Sleaford, Lincs NG34 0SE. *Clubs:* Army and Navy, MCC; Free Foresters.

GERSHON, Peter Oliver, CBE 2000; FREng; Chief Executive, Office of Government Commerce, since 2000; *b* 10 Jan. 1947; *s* of late Alfred Joseph Gershon and Gerta Gershon; *m* 1971, Eileen Elizabeth Walker; one *s* two *d. Educ:* Reigate Grammar Sch.; Churchill Coll., Cambridge (MA). FIEE 1998; FRAeS 2000; FCIPS 2000; FREng 2001. Joined ICL, 1969; Mem. Mgt Bd, and Dir of Network Systems, 1985; Managing Director: STC Telecommunications Ltd, 1987–90; GPT Ltd, 1990–94; Marconi Electronic Systems Ltd, 1994–99; Chief Operating Officer, BAE Systems, 1999–2000. CIMgt 1997; MBCS 1985. *Recreations:* swimming, reading, theatre, ski-ing. *Address:* Office of Government Commerce, Fleetbank House, 2–6 Salisbury Square, EC4Y 8AE. *T:* (020) 7211 1351. *Club:* Oxford and Cambridge.

GERSHUNY, Prof. Jonathan Israel, DPhil; Professor of Economic Sociology and Director, Institute for Social and Economic Research (formerly ESRC Research Centre on Micro-social Change), University of Essex, since 1993; *b* 16 Sept. 1949; *s* of Charles and Cynthia Gershuny; *m* 1974, Esther Gershuny; one *s* one *d. Educ:* Loughborough Univ. (BSc Econs and Politics 1971); Strathclyde Univ. (MSc 1972); Sussex Univ. (DPhil 1977). Res. Officer, Dept of Transport Technology, Loughborough Univ., 1973–74; Science Policy Research Unit, Sussex University: Fellow, 1974–81; Sen. Fellow, 1981–84; Vis. Professorial Fellow, 1986–91; on secondment as pt-time Res. Fellow, Res. Unit on Ethnic Relations, Univ. of Bristol, 1978–79; University of Bath: Prof. of Sociology, 1984–89; Head: Sociology and Social Policy Gp, 1984–88; Sch. of Social Scis, 1988–89; Univ. Lectr, Dept of Social and Admin. Studies, and Fellow of Nuffield Coll., Univ. of Oxford, 1990–93. Silver Medal, Market Res. Soc., 1986. *Publications:* After Industrial Society?, 1978 (trans. German, 1981, Italian, 1985); Social Innovation and the Division of Labour, 1983 (trans. Swedish, 1986); (with I. D. Miles) The New Service Economy, 1983 (trans. Japanese, 1983, Spanish, 1988); (ed jtly) Time Use Studies World Wide, 1991; L'innovazione Sociale: tempo, produzione e consumi, 1993; (jtly) Changing Households, 1994; (ed jtly) The Social and Political Economy of the Household, 1994; Changing Times: the social and political economy of post industrial society, 2000; (ed jtly) Seven Years in the Lives of British Households, 2000. *Recreations:* coarse gardening, opera. *Address:* Institute for Social and Economic Research, Rab Butler Building, University of Essex, Wivenhoe Park, Colchester, Essex CO4 3SQ. *T:* (01206) 872734.

GERSON, John Henry Cary, CMG 1999; Vice-President, Government and Public Affairs, BP Amoco plc, since 2000; *b* 25 April 1945; *s* of late Henry and of Benedicta Joan Gerson; *m* 1968, Mary Alison, *d* of late George Ewart Evans; one *s* one *d. Educ:* Bradfield; King's Coll., Cambridge (MA). HM Diplomatic Service, 1968–99: Third Sec., FCO, 1968; language student, Hong Kong, 1969–71; Second Secretary: Singapore, 1971–73; FCO, 1973–74; First Sec. and HM Consul, Peking, 1974–77; First Sec., FCO, 1978; on loan to Home CS, 1978–79; First Sec., later Counsellor, FCO, 1979–87; Counsellor, Hong Kong, 1987–92; Vis. Fellow, Princeton Univ., 1992; Counsellor, FCO, 1992–99. *Recreations:* ornithology, sinology, literature. *Address:* BP Amoco plc, Britannic House, 1 Finsbury Circus, EC2M 7BA. *Club:* Athenæum.

GERSTENBERG, Frank Eric, MA; Principal, George Watson's College, Edinburgh, 1985–2001; *b* 23 Feb. 1941; *s* of late Eric Gustav Gerstenberg and Janie Willis Gerstenberg; *m* 1966, Valerie Myra (*née* MacLellan); one *s* twin *d. Educ:* Trinity College, Glenalmond;

Clare College, Cambridge (MA); Inst. of Education, Univ. of London (PGCE). Asst History Teacher, Kelly Coll., Tavistock, 1963–67; Housemaster and Head of History, Millfield School, 1967–74; Headmaster, Oswestry School, 1974–85. Gov., Glenalmond Coll. *Recreations:* ski-ing, golf. *Address:* Sylvan House, Goose Green, Gullane, East Lothian EH31 2AT. *Clubs:* Public Schools; New (Edinburgh).

GERSTENBERG, Richard Charles; *b* Little Falls, NY, 24 Nov. 1909; *s* of Richard Paul Gerstenberg and Mary Julia Booth; *m* 1934, Evelyn Josephine Hitchingham; one *s* one *d*. *Educ:* Univ. of Michigan (AB). General Motors Corporation: Asst Comptroller, 1949–55; Treasurer, 1956–60; Vice-Pres., in charge of financial staff, 1960–67; Exec. Vice-Pres. in charge of Finance, 1967–70; Vice-Chm. Bd and Chm. Finance Cttee, 1970–72; Chm., 1972–74; a Director, 1967–79. *Clubs:* Bloomfield Hills Country; Paradise Valley Country (Scottsdale, Arizona); Mohawk (NY) Fish and Game.

GERSTNER, Louis Vincent, Jr; Chairman and Chief Executive Officer, IBM, since 1993; *b* NY, 1 March 1942. *Educ:* Dartmouth Coll. (BA Engrg 1963); Harvard Business Sch. (MBA 1965). Dir, McKinsey & Co, Inc., 1965–78; Pres., American Express Co., 1978–89; Chm. and Chief Exec. Officer, RJR Nabisco Inc., 1989–93. Director: NY Times Co.; Bristol-Myers Squibb Co. Dir, New American Schs Develt Corp. Dir, Japan Soc., 1992–. Mem. Bd, Lincoln Center for Performing Arts. *Address:* c/o IBM, Old Orchard Road, Armonk, NY 10504–1709, USA.

GERTYCH, Prof. Zbigniew; Professor, Botanical Garden, Polish Academy of Sciences, Warsaw, since 1990; *b* 26 Oct. 1922; *s* of Tadeusz Gertych and Maria Gertych (*née* Marecka); *m* 1st, 1945, Roza (*née* Skrochowska) (decd); one *s* two *d*; 2nd, 1970, Zofia (*née* Dobrzanska). *Educ:* Uniw. Jagiellonski, Krakow. MA eng 1946, DAgric 1950. Joined Army as volunteer and participated in September campaign, 1939; during Nazi occupation took part in clandestine activities, was detained in camps and Gestapo prisons; after escape served Home Army (AK) to 1945 (wounded in partisan combat). Polish Academy of Sciences (PAN), 1946–83: Head of Pomology Dept, Dendrology Research Centre, Kórnik, 1947–53; Dir Exp. Fruit Growing Research Centre, Brzeźna, 1953–64; Dir, Research Centre, Agric. and Forestry Econ. Science, 1964–78; Vice-Dir and Dir, Vegetable Growing Inst., Skierniewice, 1964–82; Vice-Sec. and Sec., Agric. and Forestry Scis Dept, 1964–87; First Dep. Gen. Sec., 1981–83; Mem., PAN, 1976; Mem., Presidium of PAN, 1978–86; Asst Prof., 1963, Associate Prof., 1969, Prof., 1979, Jagiellonian Univ., Cracow and Polish Acad. of Scis. MP, Nowy Sacz, 1957–89; Dep. Speaker, Sejm, 1982–85 (Chm., Budget Commn, Social and Economic Council and Main Cttee, Nat. Action for School Assistance); Dep. Chm., Council of Ministers, 1985–87; Ambassador of Poland to the Court of St James's and to Republic of Ireland, 1987–90. Pres., Homo et Planta Foundn, 1991–; Mem., Supreme Council and Exec. Cttee, Internat. Soc. of Hort. Scis. Hon. Dr, Acad. of Agric. Scis, Berlin, 1974; DAgr *hc* Szczecin Univ., 1989. Cross of Valour, 1944; Comdr's Cross, Order of Polonia Restituta, 1984; other Polish decorations; numerous foreign honours and awards. *Publications:* contribs to sci. jls. *Recreations:* music, art, travels. *Address:* Botanical Garden, Polish Academy of Sciences, vl. Prawdziwka 2, POB 84, 02–973 Warsaw 34, Poland. *Club:* Rotary.

GERVAIS, Most Rev. Marcel; *see* Ottawa, Archbishop of, (RC).

GERVIS MEYRICK; *see* Meyrick.

GERY, Sir Robert Lucian W.; *see* Wade-Gery.

GESTETNER, David; President, Gestetner Holdings PLC, 1987–95; *b* 1 June 1937; *s* of Sigmund and Henny Gestetner; *m* 1961, Alice Floretta Sebag-Montefiore (*d* 2000); one *s* three *d*. *Educ:* Midhurst Grammar Sch.; Bryanston Sch.; University Coll., Oxford (MA). Gestetner Holdings: Jt Chm., 1972–86; Man. Dir, 1982–86; Jt Pres., 1986–87. Dir, Alphameric PLC, 1994–2000. *Recreation:* sailing. *Clubs:* Reform, MCC.
See also J. Gestetner.

GESTETNER, Jonathan; Chairman, Marlborough Rare Books Ltd, since 1990; *b* 11 March 1940; *s* of Sigmund and Henny Gestetner; *m* 1965, Jacqueline Margaret Strasmore; two *s* one *d*. *Educ:* Bryanston Sch.; Massachusetts Institute of Technology (BScMechEngrg). Joined Gestetner Ltd, 1962; Jt Chm., 1972–87, and Jt Pres., 1987–88, Gestetner Hldgs PLC; Director: DRS, USA, 1987–89; Klein Associates, USA, 1987–90. Member: Executive Council, Engineering Employers' London Assoc., 1972–77 (Vice-Pres., 1975–77); Maplin Development Authority, 1973–74; SSRC, 1979–82; Dir, Centre for Policy Studies, 1982–96. Mem., Educnl Council, MIT, 1973–. *Recreation:* the visual arts. *Address:* 7 Oakhill Avenue, NW3 7RD. *T:* (020) 7435 0905. *Clubs:* Brooks's, MCC.
See also David Gestetner.

GETHIN, Sir Richard (Joseph St Lawrence), 10th Bt *cr* 1665, of Gethinsgrott, Cork; engineer; public relations, Channel Tunnel Rail Link; *b* 29 Sept. 1949; *s* of Sir Richard Patrick St Lawrence Gethin, 9th Bt and of Fara, *y d* of late J. H. Bartlett; *S* father, 1988; *m* 1974, Jacqueline Torfrida, *d* of Comdr David Cox; three *d*. *Educ:* The Oratory School; RMA Sandhurst; RMCS Shrivenham; Cranfield Inst. of Technology (BSc(Eng), MSc). Joined first unit, 1971; served in Germany and UK; retd in rank of Major, 1990. MIL 1988. *Recreations:* gardening, woodwork. *Heir: cousin* Antony Michael Gethin [*b* 10 Jan. 1939; *m* 1965, Vanse, *d* of late Col C. D. Barlow, OBE, KSLI; two *s* one *d*]. *T:* (01474) 814231.

GETHING, Air Commodore Richard Templeton, CB 1960; OBE 1945; AFC 1939; *b* 11 Aug. 1911; *s* of George A. Gething, Wilmslow, Cheshire; *m* 1940, Margaret Helen, *d* of late Sir Herbert Gepp, Melbourne, Australia; one *s* one *d*. *Educ:* Malvern; Sydney Sussex Coll., Cambridge. Joined RAF, 1933; navigator and co-pilot of Vickers Wellesley aircraft which set world record for distance in straight line (flying Ismailia, Egypt to Darwin, Australia non-stop), 1938. Served War of 1939–45: Canada; UK; India; Burma. Actg Group Capt., 1943; Group Capt., 1950; Actg Air Commodore, 1956; Dir Operations, Maritime Navigation and Air Traffic, Air Ministry, 1956–60, retired. FRIN (FIN 1956). *Recreation:* gliding. *Address:* Garden Hill, Kangaroo Ground, Victoria 3097, Australia. *Club:* Royal Air Force.

GETTY, Hon. Donald Ross; PC (Can.) 1985; OC 1998; President and Chief Executive Officer, Sunnybank Investments Ltd, since 1993; Premier of Alberta, 1985–93; MLA Edmonton Whitemud, 1967–79, 1985–93; *b* 30 Aug. 1933; *s* of Charles Ross Getty and Beatrice Lillian Getty; *m* 1955, Margaret Inez Mitchell; four *s*. *Educ:* Univ. of Western Ontario (BBA 1955). MLA Alberta 1967; Minister of Federal and Intergovernmental Affairs, 1971; Minister of Energy and Natural Resources, 1975; resigned 1979; re-elected MLA, 1985. Joined Imperial Oil, 1955; Midwestern Industrial Gas, 1961; formed Baldonnel Oil & Gas, 1964 (Pres. and Man. Dir); Partner, Doherty Roadhouse & McCuaig, 1967; Pres., D. Getty Investments, 1979; Chm., Ipsco, 1981–85; former Chm. and Chief Exec., Nortek Energy Corp.; director of other cos. Played quarterback for Edmonton Eskimos Canadian Football team for 10 years. *Recreations:* horse racing, golf, hunting. *Address:* 1273 Potter Greens Drive NW, Edmonton, AB T5T 5Y8, Canada.

GETTY, Sir (John) Paul, KBE 1986; *b* 7 Sept. 1932; adopted British nationality, 1998; *s* of J. Paul Getty and Ann (*née* Rork); *m* 1st, 1956, Gail (marr. diss. 1966), *d* of Judge Harris; two *s* two *d*; 2nd, 1966, Talitha (*d* 1971), *d* of William Pol; one *s*; 3rd, 1994, Victoria, *d* of late Comdr Gerald Holdsworth. Worked in Getty Oil, Italia, 1959–70. *Recreations:* watching cricket and old movies, bibliophily. *Address:* PO Box 8799, SW1A 1ZD. *Clubs:* Garrick, Pratt's, MCC; Royal Yacht Squadron.
See also M. H. Getty.

GETTY, Mark Harris; Executive Chairman, Getty Images Inc., since 1995; *b* 9 July 1960; *s* of Sir Paul Getty, *qv* and of Gail Harris Getty; *m* 1982, Domitilla Lante Harding; three *s*. *Educ:* Taunton Sch.; St Catherine's Coll., Oxford (BA). Kidder, Peabody, Inc., 1984–88; Hambros Bank, 1990–93; Getty Images Inc., 1994–. *Address:* Getty Images, 101 Bayham Street, NW1 0AG.

GHALI, Boutros B.; *see* Boutros-Ghali.

GHEORGHIU, Angela; soprano; *b* 1965; *m* 1st, 1988, Andrei Gheorghiu (marr. diss.); 2nd, 1996, Roberto Alagna, *qv*; one step *d*. *Educ:* Bucharest Acad. Débuts: Nat. Opera, Cluj, 1990; Royal Opera, Covent Garden, 1992; Vienna State Opera, 1992; Metropolitan Opera, NY, 1993. Rôles include: Mimi in La Bohème; Violetta in La Traviata; Micaela in Carmen; title rôle in Turandot; Adina in L'elisir d'amore; Juliette in Roméo et Juliette. Numerous recordings. *Address:* c/o Royal Opera House, Covent Garden, WC2E 9DD; c/o M Levon Sayan, 76–78 avenue des Champs Elysées, 75008 Paris, France.

GHERAIEB, Abdelkrim; Ambassador of Algeria to Mali, 1996; *b* 30 July 1935; *m* Fizia Gheraieb; one *s* three *d*. *Educ:* Univ. of Algiers (LèsL); Inst. of Pol Scis, Univ. of Algiers (Diploma). Hd of Legal Services, First Nat. Assembly, 1962–65; Chm., Assoc. of Algerians in Europe, 1965–79; Ambassador to: Teheran, 1979–82; Peking, 1982–84; Beirut, 1984–86; Saudi Arabia, 1986–89; UK, 1989–91; Ambassador Councillor, Min. of For. Affairs, Algeria, 1992–93; Mediator, Touareg dispute, North Mali, 1993. Member: Assemblée Nationale Populaire, 1977; (nominated) Central Cttee, FLN Party, 1979. Médaille de la Résistance, Algerian war of liberation, 1982. Kt, Order of Cedar (Lebanon), 1986; Order of HM King Abdul Aziz (Saudi Arabia), 1989. *Address:* c/o Ministry of Foreign Affairs, 6 rue 16n-Batran, el-Mouradia, Algiers, Algeria.

GHIZ, Hon. Joseph Atallah; Justice of the Supreme Court, Prince Edward Island, since 1995; *b* 27 Jan. 1945; *s* of Atallah J. and Marguerite Farah (McKarris); *m* 1972, Rose Ellen, *d* of Douglas and Elizabeth McGowan; one *s* one *d*. *Educ:* Prince of Wales College; Dalhousie Univ. (BCom 1966, LLB 1969). LLM Harvard, 1981. Senior Partner, Scales, Ghiz, Jenkins & McQuaid, 1970–81; Crown Prosecutor, Queen's Co., 1970–72; Federal Narcotics Drug Prosecutor, 1970–79; Counsel to Commn of Inquiry into Charlottetown Police Force, 1977; private practice, 1981–86; QC (Can.) 1984. MLA (L) 6th Queens, 1982–93; Pres., Liberal Party of PEI, 1977–78, Leader, 1981–93; Premier, PEI, 1986–93. Dean, Faculty of Law, Dalhousie Univ., 1993–95. Chm., Bd of Advrs, Andersen Consulting, Canada, 1993–95; Dir, Guardian Insce Co. of Canada, 1994–95. Lectr, Univ. of Prince Edward Island, 1970–73. Mem., Canadian Council of Multiculturalism, 1972–75 (Past Regional Chm.); Dir, Canadian Civil Liberties Assoc., 1994–95. Member: Bd of Dirs, Canada's Nat. Hist. Soc., 1994–; Bd of Dirs, Canadian Liver Foundn, 1994–95. Trustee, McGill Inst. for Study of Canada, 1993–. Hon. LLD Univ. of Prince Edward Island, 1987. *Publications:* Towards a New Canada (jtly), 1978; Constitutional Impasse Over Oil and Gas, 1981. *Address:* Sir Louis Henry Davies Law Courts, 42 Water Street, PO Box 2000, Charlottetown, PE C1A 7N8, Canada. *T:* (902) 3686596, *Fax:* (902) 3686123. *Club:* The Charlottetown.

GHODSE, Prof. (Abdol) Hamid, Hon. CBE 1999; MD, PhD; FRCP, FRCPsych; Professor of Psychiatry and Addictive Behaviour, since 1987, Director, Centre for Addiction Studies, since 1992, University of London at St George's Hospital Medical School; Hon. Consultant Psychiatrist: St George's Hospital, since 1978; Springfield University Hospital, since 1978; *b* 30 April 1938; *s* of Abdol Rahim Ghods and Batool Daneshmand; *m* 1973, Barbara Bailin; two *s* one *d*. *Educ:* Esfehan, Tabriz and Tehran; American Univ., Beirut (Schol. 1958); MD Iran 1965; PhD London 1976; DPM 1974. FRCPsych 1985; FRCP 1992; MFPHM 1996, FFPHM 1997; FRCPE 1997. Lieut, Iranian Health Corps, 1965–67. Postgrad. trng, Morgannwg Hosp., Wales, and St Bartholomew's and Maudsley Hosps, London, 1968–74; res. psychiatrist, Inst. of Psychiatry, Univ. of London, 1974–78; Consultant Psychiatrist, St Thomas' Hosp., 1978–88. Mem. Council, St George's Hosp. Med. Sch., 1993–96. Co-ordinator, Higher Degrees in Psychiatry, Univ. of London, 1993–. Director: Regl Drug and Alcohol Team, SW Thames RHA, 1991–97; Medical Council on Alcoholism, 1996–; Addiction Resource Agency for Comrs, 1997–. Member: WHO Adv. Panel, 1979–; WHO Prog. Planning Wkg Gp, 1986–89; Convenor, Mem., Rapporteur and Chm. of various WHO Expert Cttees and Wkg Gps on Drug Dependence, 1980–. Advr, BNF, 1984–. Editor: Internat. Jl Social Psychiatry, 1982–2000; Substance Misuse Section, Current Opinion in Psychiatry, 1994 (Vice Pres., 2000–). Royal College of Psychiatrists: Mem., Exec. Cttee, Substance Misuse Faculty, 1981–; Chm., Substance Misuse Sect., 1990–94; Mem. Council, 1990–94; Mem., Court of Electors, 1993–99; President: Assoc. for Prevention of Addiction, 1984–90; Internat. Narcotics Control Bd, 1993–95, 1997–99 and 2000– (Mem., 1992–); European Collaborating Centres for Addiction Studies, 1995–. Hon. Sec., Assoc. of Profs of Psychiatry, 1990–; Convenor, Assoc. of European Profs of Psychiatry, 1996–; Mem., Fedn of Assocs of Clinical Profs. McLeod Prof., SA, 1990; Hon. Prof., Beijing Med. Univ., 1997; Peking Univ., 2000. *Publications:* (ed jtly) Doctors and their Health; (jtly) Misuse of Drugs, 1986, 3rd edn 1996; (jtly) Psychoactive Drugs: improving prescribing practices, 1988 (trans. 8 langs); Drugs and Addictive Behaviour: a guide to treatment, 1989, 2nd edn 1995; (ed jtly) Substance Abuse and Dependence, 1990; (ed jtly) Drug Misuse and Dependence, 1990; numerous articles on self-poisoning, substance misuse and med. educn. *Recreations:* reading, cycling. *Address:* St George's Hospital Medical School, Cranmer Terrace, SW17 0RE. *T:* (020) 7672 9944. *Club:* Athenæum.

GHOSH, Shaks; Chief Executive, Crisis, since 1997; *b* 17 Jan. 1957; *d* of Samir Ghosh and Maria Rheinhold. *Educ:* Frank Anthony Public Sch.; Calcutta Univ. (BA 1st cl. Hons Geog. 1978); Salford Univ. (MSc Urban Studies 1980). Urban Renewal Officer, Leicester CC, 1980–84; Improvement Officer, Islington LBC, 1984–86; Supported Housing Officer, Community Housing Assoc., Camden and Westminster, 1986–89; Asst Dir, Centrepoint, 1989–92; Supported Housing Manager, NFHA, 1992–94; Head of London Region/Public Affairs Manager, Nat. Housing Fedn, 1994–97. *Recreations:* gardening, travel, current affairs. *Address:* (office) 1st Floor, Challenger House, 42 Adler Street, E1 1EE. *T:* (020) 7655 8300.

GHURBURRUN, Sir Rabindrah, Kt 1981; Vice-President, Republic of Mauritius, 1992–97; *b* 27 Sept. 1929; *s* of Mrs Sookmeen Ghurburrun; *m* 1959; one *s* one *d*. *Educ:* Keble Coll., Oxford. Called to the Bar, Middle Temple; QC Mauritius, 1991; practised as Lawyer, 1959–68; High Comr for Mauritius in India, 1968–76; MLA 1976; Minister of Justice, 1976; Minister of Economic Planning and Development, 1977–82. Member: Central Board; Bar Council (Chm., 1991–92). Former President: Mauritius Arya Sabha;

Mauritius Sugar Cane Planters' Assoc.; Hindu Educn Authority; Nat. Congress of Young Socialists. Patron, Commonwealth ESU in Mauritius. Grand Order of the Star and Key, Mauritius, 1993. *Address:* 18 Dr Lesur Street, Cascadelle, Beau Bassin, Mauritius. *T:* 4546421.

GIACHARDI, Dr David John, FRSC; Secretary General and Chief Executive, Royal Society of Chemistry, since 2000; *b* 17 May 1948; *o s* of Thomas and Kathleen Giachardi; *m* 1971, Helen Margaret Fraser; one *d. Educ:* Watford Boys' Grammar Sch.; Merton Coll., Oxford (BA Chem. 1971); St John's Coll., Oxford (MA, DPhil 1974). FRSC 1990. Boston Consulting Group, 1975–79; Courtaulds, 1979–98: Dir of Research, 1982–94; Exec. Dir, 1987–98; Human Resources Dir, 1994–98; Dir of Policy and Assoc. Affairs, EEF, 1998–2000. Member: Nat. Commn on Educn, 1991–93; European Science and Technology Assembly, 1994–97; EPSRC, 1994–99; Quality Assurance Cttee, HEFCE, 1999–; Vice-Chm., Industrial R&D Adv. Cttee to Commn for EC, 1991–94. Chm. Adv. Council, ASE, 1996– (Pres., 1994); Mem. Council, Royal Instn of GB, 1995–98 (Chm., 1997–98). *Recreations:* science, golf. *Address:* Royal Society of Chemistry, Burlington House, Piccadilly, W1J 0BA. *T:* (020) 7437 8656. *Clubs:* Athenæum, Oxford and Cambridge; Brocket Hall Golf.

GIAEVER, Prof. Ivar; Institute Professor, Physics Department, Rensselaer Polytechnic Institute, Troy, New York, since 1988; Professor-at-large, University of Oslo, Norway, since 1988; *b* 5 April 1929; *s* of John A. Giaever and Gudrun (*née* Skaarud); *m* 1952, Inger Skramstad; one *s* three *d. Educ:* Norwegian Inst. of Tech.; Rensselear Polytechnical Inst. ME 1952; PhD 1964. Norwegian Army, 1952–53; Norwegian Patent Office, 1953–54; Canadian General Electric, 1954–56; General Electric, 1956–58; Staff Mem., Gen. Electric R&D Center, 1958–88. Fellow, Amer. Phys. Soc.; Member: Nat. Acad. of Sciences; Nat. Acad. of Engineering; Amer. Acad. of Arts and Scis; Norwegian Acad. of Scis; Norwegian Acad. of Technology; Norwegian Profl Engrs; Swedish Acad. of Engrg. Hon. DSc: RPI, 1974; Union Coll., 1974; Clarkson, Potsdam, NY, 1983; Trondheim, Norway; Hon. DEng, Michigan Tech. Univ., 1976; Hon. DPhys: Oslo, 1976; State Univ. of NY, 1984. Oliver E. Buckley Prize, 1964; Nobel Prize for Physics, 1973; Zworykin Award, 1974. *Publications:* contrib. Physical Review, Jl Immunology. *Recreations:* ski-ing, tennis, camping, hiking. *Address:* Physics Department, Rensselaer Polytechnic Institute, Troy, NY 12180-3590, USA. *T:* (518) 2766429, *Fax:* (518) 2762825; *e-mail:* giaevi@rpi.edu.

GIBB, Andrew Thomas Fotheringham; Partner, since 1975, Chairman, since 1996, Balfour and Manson, Solicitors, Edinburgh; President, Law Society of Scotland, 1990–91; *b* 17 Aug. 1947; *s* of Thomas Fotheringham Gibb and Isabel Gow McKenzie or Gibb; *m* 1971, Mrs Patricia Anne Eggo or Gibb; two *s. Educ:* Perth Acad.; Edinburgh Univ. (LLB Hons). Temporary Sheriff, 1989–99. Member: Lothian and Borders Legal Aid Cttee, 1977–84; Legal Aid Central Cttee, 1984–86; Council, Law Soc. of Scotland, 1981–94. Chm. Management Cttee, Lothian Allellon Soc., 1984–97 (Mem., Bd of Govs, 1984–). Session Clerk, St Ninian's Church, Corstorphine, Edinburgh. *Recreations:* music, church organist, golf. *Address:* 58 Frederick Street, Edinburgh EH2 1LS. *Club:* New (Edinburgh).

GIBB, Frances Rebecca; Legal Editor, The Times, since 1999; *b* 24 Feb. 1951; *d* of Matthew Gibb and Bettina Mary Gibb (*née* Dawson); *m* 1978, Joseph Cahill; three *s. Educ:* St Margaret's Sch., Bushey; Univ. of E Anglia (BA 1st Cl. Hons English). News researcher, Visnews, 1973; reporter, THES, 1974–78; Art Sales corresp., Daily Telegraph, 1978–80; The Times: reporter, 1980–82; Legal Corresp., 1982–99. MUniv Open, 2000. *Recreations:* my family, gardening, theatre. *Address:* The Times, 1 Pennington Street, E98 1XY. *Club:* Reform.

GIBB, Sir Francis Ross, (Sir Frank Gibb), Kt 1987; CBE 1982; BSc; FREng; FICE; Chairman and Chief Executive, Taylor Woodrow Group, 1985–89 (Joint Managing Director, 1979–85, and a Joint Deputy Chairman, 1983–85); President, Taylor Woodrow Construction, since 1985 (Chairman, 1978–85); *b* 29 June 1927; *s* of Robert Gibb and Violet Mary Gibb; *m* 1st, 1950, Wendy Marjorie Fowler (*d* 1997); one *s* two *d*; 2nd, 2000, Kirsten Harwood. *Educ:* Loughborough Coll. BSc(Eng); CEng. Dir, 1963–70, Man. Dir, then Jt Man. Dir, 1970–84; Taylor Woodrow Construction; Director: Taylor Woodrow Internat., 1969–85; Taylor Woodrow plc, 1972–89; Chm., Taywood Santa Fe, 1975–85. Jt Dep. Chm., Seaforth Maritime Ltd, 1986–89; Director: Seaforth Maritime Hldgs, 1978–89; (indep.) Energy Saving Trust Ltd, 1992–99 (Chm., 1995–98); non-executive: Eurotunnel plc, 1986–87; Babcock Internat. Group, 1989–97; Steetley plc, 1990–92; Nuclear Electric plc, 1990–94; H. R. Wallingford, 1995–; AMCO Corporation plc, 1995–99. Member: Construction Industry Adv. Cttee, HSE, 1978–81; Gp of Eight, 1979–81; Board, British Nuclear Associates, 1980–88 (Chm., Agrément Bd, 1980–82); Chm., Nat. Nuclear Corp., 1981–88. Mem. Council, CBI, 1979–80, 1985–90. Dir, Holiday Pay Scheme, 1980–84 and Trustee, Benefits Scheme, 1980–84, Building and Civil Engrg Trustees. Federation of Civil Engineering Contractors: Vice-Chm., 1978–79; Chm., 1979–80; Vice Pres., 1980–84; Pres., 1984–87; Vice-Pres., ICE, 1988–90. Freeman, City of London, 1978. Hon. FINucE 1984; Hon. FCGI 1990. Hon. DTech Loughborough, 1989. *Recreations:* ornithology, gardening, walking, music. *Address:* Ross Gibb Consultants, 11 Latchmoor Avenue, Gerrards Cross, Bucks SL9 8LJ. *Club:* Arts.

GIBB, Ian Pashley; Director of Public Services, Planning and Administration, British Library (Humanities and Social Sciences), 1985–87; *b* 17 April 1926; *s* of late John Pashley Gibb and Mary (*née* Owen); *m* 1953, Patricia Mary Butler (*d* 1993); two *s. Educ:* Latymer Upper Sch.; UCL (BA). ALA. Sen. Library Asst, Univ. of London, 1951–52; Asst Librarian, UCL, 1952–58; Dep. Librarian, National Central Library, 1958–73; British Library: Dep. Dir, Science Reference Library, 1973–75; Head of Divl Office, Reference Div., 1975–77; Dir and Keeper, Reference Div., 1977–85. Part-time Lectr, UCL, 1967–77, Hon. Research Fellow, 1977–85, Examiner, 1985–87. Hon. Treasurer, Bibliographical Soc., 1961–67; Member Council: Library Assoc., 1980–82; Friends of British Library, 1989– (Dep. Chm., 1989–93). Chm., Dacorum NT Assoc., 1993–97. *Publications:* (ed) Newspaper Preservation and Access, 2 vols, 1988; various articles. *Recreations:* music, watching cricket, walking, wine-tasting, travel especially to Austria and Greece. *Address:* The Old Cottage, 16 Tile Kiln Lane, Leverstock Green, Hemel Hempstead, Herts HP3 8ND. *T:* (01442) 256352.

GIBB, Nicolas John; MP (C) Bognor Regis and Littlehampton, since 1997; *b* 3 Sept. 1960; *s* of late John McLean Gibb and Eileen Mavern Gibb. *Educ:* Maidstone Grammar Sch.; Roundhay Sch., Leeds; Thornes House Sch., Wakefield; Univ. of Durham (BA Hons). ACA 1987. Chartered Accountant, KPMG, 1984–97. Opposition spokesman on HM Treasury, 1998–99, on trade and industry, 1999–2001. Mem., Social Security Select Cttee, 1997–98. Contested (C): Stoke-on-Trent Central, 1992; Rotherham, May 1994. *Address:* House of Commons, SW1A 0AA.

GIBB, Walter Frame, DSO 1945; DFC 1943; Chairman, 1980–84, and Managing Director, 1978–84, British Aerospace, Australia, Ltd; retired; *b* 26 March 1919; British; *m* 1944, Pauline Sylvia Reed; three *d. Educ:* Clifton Coll. Apprentice, Bristol Aero Engines, 1937. RAF, 1940–46. Test Pilot, Bristol Aircraft Ltd, 1946; Asst Chief Test Pilot, 1953; Chief Test Pilot, Bristol Aeroplane Co. Ltd, 1956–60; Product Support Manager, BAC Filton, 1960–78. World Altitude Height Record 63,668 feet in Olympus-Canberra, 1953, and second record 65,890 ft in same machine, 1955. MRAeS. JP Bristol, 1974. *Recreation:* sailing. *Address:* Merlin Haven Lodge, Wotton-Under-Edge, Glos GL12 7BA. *Clubs:* Royal Air Force; Royal Sydney Yacht Squadron.

GIBBENS, Barnaby John, OBE 1989; Chairman, Mercator Systems Ltd, since 2000; *b* 17 April 1935; *s* of late Dr Gerald Gibbens and Deirdre Gibbens; *m* 1st, 1960, Sally Mary Stephenson (marr. diss. 1990); one *s* two *d*; 2nd, 1990, Kristina de Zabala. *Educ:* Winchester College. FCA 1972. Founder, 1962, Dep. Chm., 1962–81, Chm., 1981–90, Computer Analysts & Programmers (later CAP Group, then SEMA Group); Chairman: Enterprise Systems Group Ltd, 1989–96; The Royal Tennis Court, Hampton Court Palace, 1995–2001. Chairman: Computing Services Industry Trng Council, 1984–93; IT Industry Lead Body, 1987–93; IT Trng Accreditation Council, 1991–94; IT Industry Trng Orgn, 1992–95; a Director: National Computing Centre, 1987–90; UK Skills, 1990–2001; Member: Nat. Ctte on Computer Networks, 1978; NCVQ, 1989–92; NCET, 1991–94. Pres., Computing Services Assoc., 1975. Chairman: Skin Treatment and Res. Trust, 1991–; Young IT Technician of the Year, 1993–. Founding Master, Co. of Information Technologists, 1987. Hon. Mem., C & G, 1993. FRSA 1993. *Recreations:* golf, real tennis, music, gardening. *Address:* 12 Kings Road, Wimbledon, SW19 8QN. *T:* (020) 8542 3878. *Clubs:* Savile; Wisley Golf.

GIBBERD, Dr Frederick Brian, MD; FRCP, FRCPE; Consultant Neurologist, Chelsea and Westminster Hospital, since 1965, Honorary, since 1996; Neurologist, The Lister Hospital, since 1996; *b* 7 July 1931; *s* of late George Frederick Gibberd, CBE and Margaret Erica (*née* Taffs); *m* 1960, Margaret Clare Sidey; four *d. Educ:* Aldenham Sch. (Schol.); Gonville and Caius Coll., Cambridge (Schol.; BA 1954; MA, MB BChir 1957; MD 1974); Westminster Med. Sch. (Schol.). FRCP 1972; FRCPE 1993. Nat. Service, commnd RA, 1949–51. Jun. doctor posts at Westminster, Addenbrookes, Brompton, Nat. Queen Square and Royal London Hosps, 1957–65; Consultant Neurologist, Queen Mary's Hosp., Roehampton, 1965–96. Mem., GMC, 1992–96. Chm., Westminster Hosp. Med. Cttee, 1983–86; Mem., Riverside Dist HA, 1987–90. Royal College of Physicians: Censor, 1991–92; Council Mem., 1970–72 and 1990–96; Royal Society of Medicine: Pres., Clinical Section, 1972–74; Hon. Librarian, 1975–79. Pres., Harveian Soc., 1995. Society of Apothecaries: Liveryman, 1968; Master, 1996–97. Hon. FFOM 1995. *Publications:* (contrib.) Medical Negligence, 1994; MRCP (UK) Examination Book, 1995; articles and papers on epilepsy, Parkinson's Disease, Refsum's Disease, and neurological diseases. *Recreations:* gardening, travelling, history. *Address:* Chelsea and Westminster Hospital, 369 Fulham Road, SW10 9NH. *T:* (020) 8746 8134; The Lister Hospital, Chelsea Bridge Road, SW1W 8RH. *T:* (020) 7730 8298; 2 Ferrings, Dulwich, SE21 7LU. *T:* (020) 8693 8106.

GIBBINGS, Sir Peter (Walter), Kt 1989; Chairman, Radio Authority, 1995–99; *b* 25 March 1929; *s* of late Walter White Gibbings and Margaret Russell Gibbings (*née* Torrance); *m* 1st, Elspeth Felicia Macintosh; two *d*; 2nd, Hon. Louise Barbara, *d* of 2nd Viscount Lambert, TD; one *s. Educ:* Rugby; Wadham Coll., Oxford. Called to the Bar, Middle Temple, 1953. Served in 9th Queen's Royal Lancers, 1951–52. The Observer, 1960–67 (Deputy Manager and Dir, 1965–67); Man. Dir, Guardian Newspapers Ltd, 1967–73; Dir, Manchester Guardian and Evening News Ltd, 1967–73; Chm., Guardian and Manchester Evening News plc, 1973–88; Anglia Television Gp: Dir, 1981–94; Dep. Chm., 1986–88; Chm., 1988–94. Director: Press Assoc. Ltd, 1982–88 (Chm., 1986–87); Reuters Holdings PLC, 1984–88; The Economist, 1987–99; Rothschild Trust Corp. Ltd, 1989–96; Council, UEA, 1989–96. Mem., Press Council, 1970–74; Pres., CPU, 1989–91. *Recreations:* fishing, music. *Address:* 10 The Vale, SW3 6AH.

GIBBINS, Rev. Dr Ronald Charles; Methodist Minister; Superintendent Minister, Wesley's Chapel, London, 1978–88; *s* of Charles and Anne Gibbins; *m* 1949, Olive Ruth (*née* Patchett); one *s* two *d. Educ:* London Univ. (BScSociol); Wesley Theological Coll., Bristol; Eden Theological Seminary, US (DMin). Methodist Minister: Bradford, 1948–49; Spennymoor, 1949–50; Middlesbrough, 1950–57; Basildon, 1957–64; East End Mission, London, 1964–78. *Publications:* Mission for the Secular City, 1976; The Lumpen Proletariat, 1979; The Stations of the Resurrection, 1987. *Recreations:* travel, journalism. *Address:* 27 Riverside Close, Kingston upon Thames, Surrey KT1 2JG.

GIBBON, His Honour Michael; QC 1974; a Senior Circuit Judge, 1993–99 (a Circuit Judge, 1979–99); *b* 15 Sept. 1930; 2nd *s* of late Frank and Jenny Gibbon; *m* 1956, Malveen Elliot Seager; two *s* one *d. Educ:* Brightlands; Charterhouse; Pembroke Coll., Oxford (MA). Commnd in Royal Artillery, 1949. Called to Bar, Lincoln's Inn, 1954. A Recorder of the Crown Court, 1972–79; Hon. Recorder, City of Cardiff, 1986–99; Resident Judge, Cardiff Crown Court, 1993–99. Chairman: Electoral Adv. Cttee to Home Sec., 1972; Local Govt Boundary Commn for Wales, 1978–79 (Dep. Chm., 1974–78); Lord Chancellor's Adv. Cttee for S Glam, 1990–2000; Criminal Justice Area Liaison Cttee for S and SW Wales, 1992–99; Mem., Parole Bd, 1986–88. A Chm., Bar Disciplinary Tribunal, 1988. *Recreations:* music, golf. *Clubs:* Cardiff and County (Cardiff); Royal Porthcawl Golf, Cardiff Golf.

GIBBONS, Brian Joseph, FRCGP; Member (Lab) Aberavon, National Assembly for Wales, since 1999; *b* 25 Aug. 1950. *Educ:* National Univ. of Ireland (MB BCh, BAO 1974). DRCOG 1979; Cert. FPA 1979; MRCGP 1980, FRCGP 1995. Jun. hosp. doctor, Galway, Roscommon and Sheffield, 1974–76; Calderdale GP Vocation Trng Scheme, 1977–80; GP, Blaengwynfi, 1980–99. Sec., W Glamorgan/Morgannwg LMC, 1994–99. *Address:* National Assembly for Wales, Crickhowell House, Cardiff Bay, Cardiff CF99 1WA. *T:* (029) 2089 8382. *Club:* Gwynfi Social and Athletic.

GIBBONS, Hon. Sir David; *see* Gibbons, Hon. Sir J. D.

GIBBONS, Prof. Gary William, PhD; FRS 1999; Professor of Theoretical Physics, University of Cambridge, since 1997; *b* 7 July 1946; *s* of Archibald Gibbons and Bertha Gibbons (*née* Bunn); *m* 1972, Christine Howden; two *s. Educ:* Purley County Grammar Sch.; St Catharine's Coll., Cambridge (BA 1968; MA 1972); Clare Coll., Cambridge (PhD 1973). University of Cambridge: Lectr in Maths, 1980–90; Reader in Theoretical Physics, 1990–97. *Publication:* (with S. W. Hawking) Euclidean Quantum Gravity, 1993. *Recreations:* listening to music, looking at paintings. *Address:* 52 Hurst Park Avenue, Cambridge CB4 2AE. *T:* (01223) 363036.

GIBBONS, Prof. Ian Read, FRS 1983; Research Cell Biologist, University of California, Berkeley, since 1997; *b* 30 Oct. 1931; *s* of Arthur Alwyn Gibbons and Hilda Read Cake; *m* 1961, Barbara Ruth Hollingworth; one *s* one *d. Educ:* Faversham Grammar School; Cambridge Univ. (BA, PhD). Research Fellow, 1958–63, Asst Prof., 1963–67, Harvard Univ.; Associate Prof., 1967–69, Prof. of Biophysics, 1969–97, Univ. of Hawaii. *Publications:* contribs to learned jls. *Recreations:* gardening, computer programming, music. *Address:* Department of Molecular and Cell Biology, University of California, Berkeley, 335 LSA–3200, Berkeley, CA 94720–3200, USA. *T:* (510) 6422439.

GIBBONS, Jeremy Stewart; QC 1995; a Recorder, since 1993; *b* 15 July 1949; *s* of Geoffrey Gibbons and Rosemary Gibbons (*née* Stewart); *m* 1974, Mary Mercia Bradley; two *s* one *d* (and one *d* decd); *m* 1998, Sarah Valerie Jenkins. *Educ:* Oakmount Sch., Southampton; St Edward's Sch., Oxford. Called to the Bar, Gray's Inn, 1973; Asst Recorder, 1989–93. *Recreations:* cooking, gardening, ski-ing, carpentry. *Address:* 17 Carlton Crescent, Southampton SO15 2XR. *T:* (023) 8032 0320; Au Grand Chêne, Chez Perroteau, Champagnolles 17240, Charente Maritime, France.

GIBBONS, Hon. Sir (John) David, KBE 1985; JP; Chairman: Colonial Insurance Co. Ltd, Bermuda, since 1986; Global Asset Management Ltd, since 1986; *b* 15 June 1927; *s* of late Edmund G. Gibbons, CBE, and Winifred G. Gibbons, MBE; *m* 1958, Lully Lorentzen; three *s* (and one *d* by former *m*). *Educ:* Saltus Grammar Sch., Bermuda; Hotchkiss Sch., Lakeville, Conn; Harvard Univ., Cambridge, Mass (BA). CIMgt. Mem. Govt Boards: Social Welfare Bd, 1949–58; Bd of Civil Aviation, 1958–60; Bd of Educn, 1956–59 (Chm., 1973–74); Trade Develt Bd, 1960–74. MP Bermuda, 1972–84; Minister of Health and Welfare, 1974–75, of Finance, 1975–84; Premier of Bermuda, 1977–82. Chm., Bank of N. T. Butterfield & Son Ltd, Bermuda, 1986–97. Chairman: Bermuda Monetary Authy, 1984–86; Economic Council, Bermuda, 1984–86. Mem., Law Reform Cttee, 1969–72. Mem. Governing Body, subseq. Chm., Bermuda Technical Inst., 1956–70. Trustee, Massachusetts Financial Services, 1988–. JP Bermuda, 1974. *Recreations:* tennis, golf, ski-ing, swimming. *Address:* Leeward, 5 Leeside Drive, Pembroke HM 05, Bermuda. *T:* (441) 2952396. *Clubs:* Phoenix (Cambridge, Mass); Harvard (New York); Royal Bermuda Yacht, Royal Hamilton Amateur Dinghy, Mid-Ocean, Riddells Bay Golf, Spanish Point Boat (Bermuda); Lyford Cay (Bahamas).

GIBBONS, Dr John Ernest, CBE 2000; Chief Architect, Scottish Executive, since 1999 (Director of Building and Chief Architect, Scottish Office, 1984–99); *b* Halesowen, Worcs, 20 April 1940; *s* of late John Howard Gibbons and Lilian Alice Gibbons (*née* Shale); *m* 1963, Patricia Mitchell; one *s* two *d*. *Educ:* Oldbury Grammar Sch.; Birmingham Sch. of Architecture; Edinburgh Univ. PhD; DipArch; DipTP; ARIBA; ARIAS; FSA(Scot). In private practice, 1962–65; Lectr, Birmingham Sch. of Architecture and Univ. of Aston, 1964–66; Res. Fellow, 1967–69, Lectr, 1969–72, Edinburgh Univ.; Scottish Development Department: Prin. Architect, 1972–78; Asst Dir, Building Directorate, 1978–82; Dep. Dir and Dep. Chief Architect, 1982–84. Vis. Res. Scientist, CSIRO, Melbourne, 1974–75. Member, Council: EAA and RIAS, 1977–80; ARCUK, 1984. *Publications:* contribs on architectural and planning matters to professional and technical jls. *Recreations:* reading, photography, music, travel. *Address:* Crichton House, Pathhead, Midlothian EH37 5UX. *T:* (01875) 320085. *Club:* New (Edinburgh).

GIBBONS, Ven. Kenneth Harry; Archdeacon of Lancaster, 1981–97, now Emeritus; Priest-in-charge: St Magnus the Martyr, Lower Thames Street with St Margaret, Fish Street, and St Michael, Crooked Lane, since 1997; St Clement, Eastcheap, City of London, since 1999; *b* 24 Dec. 1931; *s* of Harry and Phyllis Gibbons; *m* 1962, Margaret Ann Tomlinson; two *s*. *Educ:* Blackpool and Chesterfield Grammar Schools; Manchester Univ. (BSc); Cuddesdon Coll., Oxford. RAF, 1952–54. Ordained, 1956; Assistant Curate of Fleetwood, 1956–60; Secretary for Student Christian Movement in Schools, 1960–62; Senior Curate, St Martin-in-the-Fields, Westminster, 1962–65; Vicar of St Edward, New Addington, 1965–70; Vicar of Portsea, 1970–81; RD of Portsmouth, 1973–79; Priest-in-charge of Weeton, 1981–85; Vicar, St Michael's-on-Wyre, 1985–97; Diocesan Dir of Ordinands, Blackburn, 1982–90. Acting Chaplain to HM Forces, 1981–85. *Recreations:* gardening, cinema. *Address:* 112 Valley Road, Kenley, Surrey CR8 5BU. *T:* (020) 8660 7502. *Club:* Reform.

GIBBONS, Michael Gordon, PhD; Secretary General, Association of Commonwealth Universities, since 1996; *b* 15 April 1939; *m* 1968, Gillian Monks; one *s* one *d*. *Educ:* Concordia Univ., Montreal (BSc Maths and Physics); McGill Univ., Montreal (BEng); Queen's Univ., Ont (MSc Radio Astronomy); Manchester Univ. (PhD 1967). Department of Science and Technology Policy, University of Manchester: Lectr, 1967–72; Sen. Lectr, 1972–75; Prof., 1975–92; Hd of Dept, 1975–92; Dir, Univ./UMIST Pollution Res. Unit, 1979–86; Chm. and Founding Dir, Policy Res. in Engrg, Sci. and Technol., 1979–92; Dir, Res., Exploitation and Develt, Vice-Chancellor's Office, 1984–92; University of Sussex: Dean, Grad. Sch. and Dir, Science Policy Res. Unit, 1992–96; Mem., Senate and Mgt Cttee, 1992–96; Mem., Court and Council, 1994–96; Hon. Prof., 1994. Visiting Professor: Univ. of Montreal, 1976 and 1977–81; Univ. of Calif, Berkeley, 1992. Chm., Marinetech NW, 1981–91. Special Advr, H of C Sci. and Technol. Cttee, 1993–. Mem. Council, ESRC, 1997– (Mem., 1994–, Chm., 1997–2001, Res. Priorities Bd). Consultant, Cttee of Sci. and Technol. Policy, OECD, Paris, 1979–. Fellow, Royal Swedish Acad. of Engrg Scis, 2000. Member, Editorial Board: Technovation, 1984–; Prometheus, 1992–. Hon. LLD Ghana, 1999. *Publications:* (jtly) Wealth from Knowledge, 1972; (jtly) Future of University Research, 1981; (ed jtly) Science Studies Today, 1983; (jtly) New Forms of Communication and Collaboration between Universities and Industry, 1985; (jtly) Post-Innovation Performance: technological development and competition, 1986; (with L. Georghiou) The Evaluation of Research: a synthesis of current practice, 1987; (jtly) The New Production of Knowledge: the dynamics of science and research in contemporary societies, 1994; (jtly) Re-Thinking Science: knowledge and the public in an age of uncertainty, 2001; contrib. numerous papers and articles on science policy. *Address:* 22 Kensington Court Gardens, Kensington Court Place, W8 5QF.

GIBBONS, Sir William Edward Doran, 9th Bt *cr* 1752; JP; Director, Passenger Shipping Association, since 1994; *b* 13 Jan. 1948; *s* of Sir John Edward Gibbons, 8th Bt, and of Mersa Wentworth, *y d* of late Major Edward Baynton Grove Foster; *S* father, 1982; *m* 1972, Patricia Geraldine Archer, *d* of Roland Archer Howse; one *s* one *d*. *Educ:* Pangbourne; RNC Dartmouth; Bristol Univ. (BSc); Southampton Univ. Management Sch. (MBA 1996). MCIT. Asst Shipping and Port Manager, Sealink UK, Parkeston Quay, 1979–82; Service Manager (Anglo-Dutch), Sealink UK Ltd, 1982–85; Ferry Line Manager (Harwich–Hook), 1985–87, Gen. Manager, IoW Services, 1987–90, Sealink British Ferries. Transport and management consultant, 1990–94. Chm., Council of Travel and Tourism, 1996–2001 (Vice Chm., 1995–96); Mem. Bd, Duty Free Confedn, 1996–2000. Non-Exec. Mem., IoW DHA, 1990–94. Mem., Manningtree Parish Council, 1981–87 (Chm., 1985–87). JP: Portsmouth, 1990–94; S Westminster Div., Inner London, 1994– (Probation Liaison Justice, 1998–). *Heir: s* Charles William Edwin Gibbons, *b* 28 Jan. 1983. *Address:* 5 Yarborough Road, Southsea, Hants PO5 3DZ.

GIBBS, family name of **Barons Aldenham** and **Wraxall**.

GIBBS, Barbara Lynn; Head Teacher, British School in The Netherlands, since 2001; *b* 8 Nov. 1945; *d* of William Newill and Mabel Till; *m* 1967, John Colin Gibbs; two *d*. *Educ:* Bromley Grammar Sch. for Girls; Univ. of Hull (BSc Hons Chem.); Univ. of E Anglia (MA; PGCE). Teaching and lecturing, mainly on chem. and maths, in various educnl estabts in Yorks, Notts, Norfolk and Barnet, 1967–86; Sen. Teacher, Henrietta Barnett Sch., 1986–90; Vice Principal, Havering Sixth Form Coll., 1990–94; Head Teacher, Newstead Wood Sch. for Girls, 1994–2001. OFSTED Inspector, 1998–; Strategic Dir, Prospects Educn Services, 1999–2001; performance management consultant, 2000–. FRSA 1994; MInstD 1999. *Recreations:* music, literature, travel, swimming, Rugby Union. *Address:* British School in The Netherlands, Jan van Hooflaan 3, 2252 BG, Voorschoten, The Netherlands. *T:* (31) 71560 2222.

GIBBS, Air Vice-Marshal Charles Melvin, CB 1976; CBE 1966; DFC 1943; RAF retd; Recruiting Consultant with Selleck Associates, Colchester, 1977–86; *b* 11 June 1921; American father, New Zealand mother; *m* 1947, Emma Pamela Pollard (*d* 1991); one *d*; *m* 1999, Adrienne Ryan. *Educ:* Taumarunui, New Zealand. MECI 1980. Joined RNZAF, 1941; service in Western Desert and Mediterranean, 1942–44; Coastal Comd, 1945; India, 1946–47; commanded Tropical Experimental Unit, 1950–52; RAF Staff Coll., 1953; commanded No 118 Squadron, 1954–55; Directing Staff, RAF Staff Coll., 1956–58; Pakistan, 1958–61; Chief Instructor, RAF Chivenor, 1961–63; CO, Wattisham, 1963–66; idc 1967; Defence Policy Staff, 1968–69; Dir of Quartering, 1970–72; AOA, Germany, 1972–74; Dir-Gen. Personal Services, RAF, 1974–76. *Recreations:* fishing, golf. *Address:* 5 Kew Place, Taupo, New Zealand. *T:* (7) 3771957.

GIBBS, Rt Hon. Sir Harry (Talbot), AC 1987; GCMG 1981; KBE 1970; PC 1972; Chief Justice of Australia, 1981–87; *b* 7 Feb. 1917; *s* of late H. V. Gibbs, formerly of Ipswich, Qld; *m* 1944, Muriel Ruth (*née* Dunn); one *s* three *d*. *Educ:* Ipswich Grammar Sch., Qld; Univ. of Queensland (BA, LLM). Served War, Australia and New Guinea, 1939–45, Major (despatches). Admitted as Barrister, Qld, 1939; QC 1957; Judge of Supreme Court of Qld, 1961; Judge of Federal Court of Bankruptcy and of Supreme Court of Australian Capital Territory, 1967; Justice of High Court of Australia, 1970. Hon. Bencher, Lincoln's Inn, 1981. Hon. LLD Queensland, 1980; DUniv Griffith Univ., 1987. *Address:* 30 Lodge Road, Cremorne, NSW 2090, Australia. *T:* (2) 99091844. *Clubs:* Australian (Sydney); Queensland (Brisbane).

GIBBS, Rt Rev. John; Bishop of Coventry, 1976–85; *b* 15 March 1917; *s* of late A. E. Gibbs, Bournemouth; *m* 1943, G. Marion, *d* of late W. J. Bishop, Poole, Dorset; one *s* one *d*. *Educ:* Univ. of Bristol; Western Coll., Bristol; Lincoln Theological Coll. BA (Bristol); BD (London). In the ministry of the Congregational Church, 1943–49. Student Christian Movement: Inter-Collegiate Sec., 1949–51; Study Sec. and Editor of Student Movement, 1951–55. Curate of St Luke's, Brislington, Bristol, 1955–57; Chaplain and Head of Divinity Dept, Coll. of St Matthias, Bristol, 1957–64, Vice-Principal, 1962–64; Principal, Keswick Hall Coll. of Education, Norwich, 1964–73; Examining Chaplain to Bishop of Norwich, Hon. Canon of Norwich Cathedral, 1968–73; Bishop Suffragan of Bradwell, Dio. Chelmsford, 1973–76. Hon. Asst to Bps of Gloucester and Bristol, 1985–. Member, Durham Commn on Religious Education, 1967–70; Chairman: C of E Children's Council, 1968–71; C of E Bd of Educn Publications Cttee, 1971–79, Education and Community Cttee, 1974–76; Assoc. of Voluntary Colls, 1985–87; Further and Higher Educn Cttee, General Synod Bd of Educn, 1986–91; BCC Wkg Parties: Chm., The Child in the Church, 1973–76, Chm., Understanding Christian Nurture, 1979–81; Anglican Chm., Anglican–Lutheran European Reg. Commn, 1980–82. Chm., Cotswold Care Hospice, 1986–96. Introduced into H of L, 1982. *Recreations:* music, bird watching. *Address:* Farthingloe, Southfield, Minchinhampton, Stroud, Glos GL6 9DY.

GIBBS, Marion Olive; Headmistress, James Allen's Girls' School, Dulwich, since 1994; *b* 16 Sept. 1951; *d* of Harry Norman Smith and Olive Mabel (*née* Lewis); *m* 1st, 1976, Robert Baldock (marr. diss. 1983); 2nd, 1992, Peter Gibbs. *Educ:* Pate's Grammar Sch. for Girls, Cheltenham; Bristol Univ. (BA 1st cl. Hons Classics 1973; PGCE 1974; MLitt 1981). Assistant Mistress: City of Worcester Girls' Grammar Sch., 1974–76; Chailey Comprehensive Sch., 1977; Hd of Sixth Form, Dir of Studies and Hd of Classics, Burgess Hill Sch. for Girls, 1977–89; Hd of Sixth Form and Classics, Haberdashers' Aske's Girls' Sch., Elstree, 1989–91; HMI of Schools, 1992–94. Tutor, Open Univ., 1979–91. Member Council: Classical Assoc., 1984–87, 1995–98 (Hon. Jt Sec., 1989–92); Hellenic Soc., 1997–2000; Chm. Council, JACT, 2001–. FRSA 1997. *Publication:* Greek Tragedy: an introduction, 1989. *Recreations:* music, gardening, drama, keeping informed about the developing world. *Address:* James Allen's Girls' School, East Dulwich Grove, SE22 8TE. *T:* (020) 8693 1181.

GIBBS, Dr Richard John; Chief Executive, Kingston and Richmond (formerly Kingston and Esher) Health Authority, since 1990; *b* 15 May 1943; *s* of Leslie and Mary Gibbs; *m* 1968, Laura Wanda Olasmi; one *d*. *Educ:* Merchant Taylors' Sch., Northwood; Pembroke Coll., Cambridge (BA 1965); Warwick Univ. (PhD 1974). Teacher, City of London Sch. for Boys, 1965; Scientific Officer, Home Office, 1968; Sen. Scientific Officer, 1970, PSO, 1972, DHSS; Res. Schol., Internat. Inst. for Applied Systems Analysis, Austria, 1977; SPSO, DHSS, 1978; Central Policy Review Staff, 1980; Dir of Operational Res. (DCSO), 1982, CSO, 1985, DHSS; Under Sec. and Dir of Stats and Management, DHSS, then DoH, 1986–90. Vis. Prof., UCL, 1985. *Publications:* contribs to Jl of ORS. *Recreations:* windsurfing, cooking. *Address:* Kingston and Richmond Health Authority, 22 Hollyfield Road, Surbiton, Surrey KT5 9AL.

GIBBS, Hon. Sir Richard (John Hedley), Kt 2000; **Hon. Mr Justice Gibbs;** a Judge of the High Court of Justice, Queen's Bench Division, since 2000; *b* 2 Sept. 1941; *s* of Brian Conaway Gibbs and Mabel Joan Gibbs; *m* 1965, Janet (*née* Whittall); one *s* two *d* (and one *d* decd). *Educ:* Oundle Sch.; Trinity Hall, Cambridge (MA). Called to the Bar, Inner Temple, 1965, Bencher, 2000; a Recorder, 1981–90; QC 1984; a Circuit Judge, 1990–2000. *Address:* Royal Courts of Justice, Strand, WC2A 2LL.

GIBBS, Sir Roger (Geoffrey), Kt 1994; Chairman: The Wellcome Trust, 1989–99 (Governor, 1983–99); Fleming Family & Partners, since 2000; Director, Gerrard & National Holdings PLC (formerly Gerrard & National Discount Co. Ltd), 1971–94 (Chairman, 1975–89); *b* 13 Oct. 1934; 4th *s* of Hon. Sir Geoffrey Gibbs, KCMG, and Hon. Lady Gibbs, CBE. *Educ:* Eton; Millfield. Jessel Toynbee & Co. Ltd, 1954–64, Dir 1960; de Zoete & Gorton, later de Zoete & Bevan, Stockbrokers, 1964–71, Partner 1966. Chm., London Discount Market Assoc., 1984–86. Director: Arsenal FC, 1980–; Colville Estate Ltd, 1989–; Howard de Walden Estates Ltd, 1989–2001 (Chm., 1993–98). Member: Council, Royal Nat. Pension Fund for Nurses, 1975–; Finance Cttee, 1985–, Council, 1989–92, ICRF. Chm., St Paul's Cathedral Foundn, 2000–; Trustee, Winston Churchill Meml Trust, 2001–. Governor, London Clinic, 1983–93; Special Trustee, Guy's Hosp., 1983–92. Freeman, City of London; Liveryman, Merchant Taylors' Co. Trustee, Arundel Castle Cricket Foundn, 1987– (Chm., 1987–95). *Publication:* The Cresta Run 1885–1985, 1984. *Recreations:* travel, sport. *Clubs:* Boodle's, Pratt's; Queen's, MCC; Swinley Forest Golf (Chm., 1993–97); Vanderbilt.

GIBBS, Field Marshal Sir Roland (Christopher), GCB 1976 (KCB 1972); CBE 1968; DSO 1945; MC 1943; Lord-Lieutenant for Wiltshire, 1989–96; Chief of the General Staff, 1976–79; ADC General to the Queen, 1976–79; *b* 22 June 1921; *yr s* of late Maj. G. M. Gibbs, Parkleaze, Ewen, Cirencester; *m* 1955, Davina Jean Merry; two *s* one *d*. *Educ:* Eton Coll.; RMC Sandhurst. Commnd into 60th Rifles, 1940; served War of 1939–45 in N Africa, Italy and NW Europe. Comd 3rd Bn Parachute Regt, 1960–62; GSO1, Brit. Army Staff, Washington, 1962–63; Comdr 16 Para. Bde, 1963–66; Chief of Staff, HQ Middle

East, 1966–67; IDC 1968; Commander, British Forces, Gulf, 1969–71; GOC 1 (British) Corps, 1972–74; C-in-C, UKLF, 1974–76. Colonel Commandant: 2nd Bn The Royal Green Jackets, 1971–78; Parachute Regt, 1972–77. Constable, HM Tower of London, 1985–90. Salisbury Regional Dir, Lloyds Bank, 1979–91. Chm., Nat. Rifle Assoc., 1984–90. DL, 1980, Vice Lord-Lieutenant, 1982–89, Wilts. KStJ 1990. *Recreation:* out-of-door sports. *Address:* Patney Rectory, Devizes, Wilts SN10 3QZ. *Clubs:* Turf, Cavalry and Guards.

GIBBS, Stephen, CBE 1981; Chairman: Turner & Newall Ltd, 1979–82; Gibbs Associates Ltd (formerly Gibbs Littlewood Associates), 1984–91; *b* 12 Feb. 1920; *s* of Arthur Edwin Gibbs and Anne Gibbs; *m* 1941, Louie Pattison; one *s* one *d. Educ:* Oldbury Grammar Sch.; Birmingham Univ. (part-time). FIM. British Industrial Plastics Ltd, Oldbury, Warley, W Midlands, 1936–39. Served RASC, 1939–46. British Industrial Plastics Ltd: Technical Dept, 1946–52; General Sales Manager, 1952–56; Director, and Chm. of subsidiary cos, 1956–68; Turner & Newall Ltd, Manchester: Director, 1968–72; Man. Dir, 1972–76; Dep. Chm., 1976–79; Chm., Gascoigne Moody Associates, 1984–87. Dir, Whitford Hall & Dodderhill (formerly Whitford Hall Ltd), 1990–95. Chm., Energy Policy Cttee, CBI, 1981–83. *Address:* Corner House, 11 Dodderhill Road, Droitwich Spa, Worcs WR9 8QN.

GIBRALTAR, Dean of; *see* Robinson, Very Rev. J. K.

GIBRALTAR IN EUROPE, Bishop of, since 2001; **Rt Rev. Dr (Douglas) Geoffrey Rowell;** *b* 13 Feb. 1943; *s* of late Cecil Victor Rowell and Kate (*née* Hunter). *Educ:* Eggar's Grammar Sch., Alton, Hants; Winchester Coll.; Corpus Christi Coll., Cambridge (MA, PhD); MA, DPhil, DD Oxon; Cuddesdon Theol Coll. Ordained deacon, 1968, priest 1969; Hastings Rashdall Student and Asst Chaplain, New Coll., Oxford, 1968–72; Hon. Asst Curate, St Andrew's, Headington, 1968–71; University of Oxford: Fellow, Chaplain and Tutor in Theology, Keble Coll., 1972–94 (Emeritus Fellow, 1994–); Lectr in Theology, 1977–94; Leader, expedn to Ethiopia, 1974; Pro-Proctor, 1980–81; Suffragan Bishop of Basingstoke, 1994–2001. Canon, Chichester Cathedral, 1981–; Vis. Canon-Theologian, St James' Episcopal Cathedral, Chicago, 1988. Member: C of E Liturgical Commn, 1981–91; C of E Doctrine Commn, 1991–96, 1998– (Consultant, 1996–98); Inter-Anglican Standing Commn on Ecumenical Relations, 2000–; Anglican Co-Chm., Anglican-Oriental Orthodox Internat. Forum, 1996– (Mem., 1985, 1989, 1993); Chm., Churches Gp on Funeral Services in Cemeteries and Crematoria, 1997–. Examining Chaplain to: Bp of Leicester, 1979–90; Bp of Winchester, 1991–93. Hon. Dir, Archbp's Exam. in Theol., 1985–2001; Conservator, Mirfield Cert. in Pastoral Theol., 1987–94; Mem., Theol Colls Assessment Gp, 1993. Gov., SPCK, 1984–94, 1997– (Vice-Pres., 1994–). Member: Council of Almoners, Christ's Hosp., 1979–89; Council of Mgt, St Stephen's Hse, Oxford, 1986–; Governor: Pusey Hse, Oxford, 1979– (Pres., Govs, 1996–); Eggar's Sch., Alton, 1994–98; Chm. Council, Hse of St Gregory and St Macrina, Oxford, 1987–94. Vis. Prof., UC, Chichester (formerly Chichester Inst. of Higher Educn), 1996–. Trustee, Scott Holland Lectureship, 1979– (Chm., 1992–); Louise Ward Haskin Lectr, St Paul's, Washington, 1995. Hon. Consultant, Nat. Funerals Coll., 1995–. Mem., Internat. Editl Bd, Mortality, 1995–. FRSA 1989. Hon. DD Nashotah House, Wisconsin, 1996. *Publications:* Hell and the Victorians: a study of the 19th century theological controversies concerning eternal punishment and the future life, 1974; (ed with B. E. Juel Jensen) Rock-Hewn Churches of Eastern Tigray, 1976; The Liturgy of Christian Burial: an historical introduction, 1977; The Vision Glorious: themes and personalities of the Catholic Revival in Anglicanism, 1983; (ed) Tradition Renewed: the Oxford Movement Conference Papers, 1986; (ed and contrib.) To the Church of England, by G. Bennett, 1988; (ed with M. Dudley) Confession and Absolution, 1990; (ed) The English Religious Tradition and the Genius of Anglicanism, 1992; (ed with M. Dudley) The Oil of Gladness: anointing in the Church, 1993; The Club of Nobody's Friends 1800–2000, 2000; (contrib.) History of the University of Oxford: Nineteenth Century Oxford, pt 2, 2000; (with J. Chilcott-Monk) Flesh, Bone, Wood: entering into the mysteries of the cross, 2001; (ed jtly) Love's Redeeming Work: the Anglican quest for holiness, 2001; contributor to various books on theol subjects, to New DNB, and Oxford Dict. of the Christian Church (3rd edn); articles in Jl Theol Studies, English Hist. Rev., Jl Ecclesiastical Hist., Church Hist., Anglican and Episcopal Hist., Internationale Cardinal-Newman Studien, Studia Urbania, etc. *Recreations:* travel in remote places, reading, music. *Address:* Bishop's Lodge, Church Road, Worth, Crawley, W Sussex PO10 7RT. *T:* (01293) 883051, *Fax:* (01293) 884479; *e-mail:* bishop@eurobish.clara.co.uk.

GIBRALTAR IN EUROPE, Suffragan Bishop of, since 1995; **Rt Rev. Henry William Scriven;** *b* 30 Aug. 1951; *s* of William Hamilton Scriven and Jeanne Mary Edwards; *m* 1975, Catherine Rose Ware; one *s* one *d. Educ:* Repton Sch.; Sheffield Univ. (BA Hons); St John's Theol Coll., Nottingham. Ordained deacon, 1975, priest, 1976; Asst Curate, Holy Trinity, Wealdstone, Harrow, 1975–79; Missionary with S American Missionary Soc., N Argentina, 1979–82; Educn Associate Rector, Christ Church, Little Rock, Arkansas, 1982–83; Missionary, S American Missionary Soc., Spain, 1984–90; Chaplain, British Embassy Church of St George, Madrid, 1990–95. *Recreations:* reading, walking, tennis, music. *Address:* Diocese in Europe, 14 Tufton Street, SW1P 3QZ. *T:* (020) 7898 1160; *e-mail:* henry.scriven@europe.c-of-e.org.uk.

GIBSON, family name of **Barons Ashbourne** and **Gibson**.

GIBSON, Baron *cr* 1975 (Life Peer), of Penn's Rocks; **Richard Patrick Tallentyre Gibson;** Chairman, National Trust, 1977–86; *b* 5 Feb. 1916; *s* of Thornely Carbutt Gibson and Elizabeth Anne Augusta Gibson; *m* 1945, Elisabeth Dione Pearson; four *s. Educ:* Eton Coll.; Magdalen Coll., Oxford (Hon. Fellow, 1977). London Stock Exchange, 1937. Served with Mddx Yeo, 1939–46; N Africa, 1940–41; POW, 1941–43; Special Ops Exec., 1943–45; Political Intell. Dept, FO, 1945–46. Westminster Press Ltd, 1947–78 (Dir, 1948); Director: Whitehall Securities Corp. Ltd, 1948–60, 1973–83; Financial Times Ltd, 1957–78 (Chm., 1975–77); Economist Newspaper Ltd, 1957–78; Pearson PLC (formerly S. Pearson & Son Ltd), 1960–88 (Dep. Chm., 1969; Exec. Dep. Chm., 1975; Chm., 1978–83); Royal Exchange Assce, 1961–69; Chm., Pearson Longman Ltd, 1967–79. Hon. Treas. Commonwealth Press Union, 1957–67. Chm., Arts Council, 1972–77. Vice-Pres., RSA, 1986–90; Chm., RSA Environment Cttee, 1986–90. Trustee, Historic Churches Preservation Trust, 1958; Member: Exec. Cttee, National Trust, 1963–72; Council, Nat. Trust, 1966–86; Adv. Council, V&A Museum, 1968–75 (Chm., 1970); UK Arts Adv. Commn, Calouste Gulbenkian Foundn, 1969–72; Redundant Churches Fund, 1970–71; Exec. Cttee, Nat. Art Collections Fund, 1970–91; Bd, Royal Opera House, 1977–87; Treasurer, Sussex Univ., 1983–87; Trustee, Glyndebourne Fest. Opera, 1965–72 and 1977–86. Hon. DLitt: Reading, 1980; Keele, 1992; DUniv Sussex, 1989. *Recreations:* music, gardening, architecture. *Address:* Penn's Rocks, Groombridge, Tunbridge Wells TN3 9PA. *T:* (01892) 864244. *Clubs:* Garrick, Brooks's.

GIBSON OF MARKET RASEN, Baroness *cr* 2000 (Life Peer), of Market Rasen in the Co. of Lincolnshire; **Anne Bartell,** OBE 1998; National Secretary, (Union for) Manufacturing, Science, Finance, 1987–2000; *b* 10 Dec. 1940; *d* of Harry Tasker and Jessie Tasker (*née* Roberts); *m* 1st, 1962, John Donald Gibson (marr. diss. 1985); one *d*; 2nd, 1988, John Bartell; one step *d. Educ:* Market Rasen C of E Sch.; Caistor Grammar Sch., Lincs; Chelmsford Coll. of Further Educn, 1970–71; Univ. of Essex, 1972–76 (BA Hons II1, Govt). Sec., Penney and Porter Engrg Co., Lincoln, 1956; Cashier, Midland Bank, Market Rasen, 1959–62. Organiser, Saffron Walden Labour Party, 1966–70; Asst Sec., Organisation and Industrial Relns Dept, TUC, 1977–87. Member: TUC Gen. Council, 1989–2000; EOC, 1991–98; Dept of Employment Adv. Gp on Older Workers, 1993–96; HSC, 1996–2000. Mem., Lab. Party Nat. Constitutional Cttee, 1997–2000. EC Mem., RoSPA, 2000–. *Recreations:* Francophile, embroidery, reading, politics. *Address:* House of Lords, SW1A 0PW.

GIBSON, Charles Andrew Hamilton; His Honour Judge Gibson; a Circuit Judge, since 1996; *b* 9 July 1941; *s* of late Rev. Preb. Leslie Andrew Gibson and Kathleen Anne Frances Gibson; *m* 1969, Susan Judith Rowntree; two *d. Educ:* Sherborne Prep. Sch.; Sherborne Sch.; Hertford Coll., Oxford (MA). Called to the Bar, Lincoln's Inn, 1966; practised at the Bar, 1966–96; Asst Recorder, 1987–91; a Recorder, 1991–96. Chm., Southwark Diocesan Pastoral Cttee, 1993–. *Publication:* (with Prof. M. R. A. Hollis) Surveying Buildings, 1983, 4th edn 2000. *Recreations:* music, theatre, wine. *Address:* c/o Woolwich County Court, 165–167 Powis Street, SE18 6JW. *T:* (020) 8854 2127. *Club:* Oxford and Cambridge.

GIBSON, Charles Anthony Warneford, QC 2001; a Recorder, since 2001; *b* 25 Sept. 1960; *s* of Philip Gaythorne Gibson and Margaret Elizabeth (*née* Mellette, now Sim); *m* 1989, Mary Ann Frances Morgan; three *s* one *d. Educ:* Wellington Coll.; Durham Univ. (BA Hons); Dip. Law Poly. Central London. Called to the Bar, Inner Temple, 1984. *Recreations:* family, sport, ballet, theatre, food, comedy. *Address:* 2 Harcourt Buildings, Temple, EC4Y 9DB. *T:* (020) 7583 9020.

GIBSON, Christopher Allen Wood; QC 1995; *b* 5 July 1953; *s* of Rt Hon. Sir Ralph Brian Gibson, *qv*; *m* 1984, Alarys Mary Calvert Eaton; two *d. Educ:* St Paul's Sch.; Brasenose Coll., Oxford. FCIArb 1992. Called to the Bar, Middle Temple, 1976. *Recreations:* sailing, motorcycles, family. *Address:* 4 New Square, Lincoln's Inn, WC2A 3RJ. *T:* (020) 7242 8800. *Clubs:* Vincent's (Oxford); Emsworth Sailing; Whitstable Yacht.

GIBSON, Rev. Sir Christopher (Herbert), 4th Bt *cr* 1931, of Linconia, Argentina, and of Faccombe, Southampton; CP; *b* 17 July 1948; *o s* of Sir Christopher Herbert Gibson, 3rd Bt and of Lilian Lake Young, *d* of Dr George Byron Young; *S* father, 1994. Ordained priest, 1975. *Heir: cousin* Robert Herbert Gibson [*b* 21 Dec. 1966; *m* 1992, Catherine Grace, *d* of E. W. Pugh; one *s* one *d*]. *Address:* Passionist Community, 5700 North Harlem Avenue, Chicago, IL 60631, USA.

GIBSON, David, CB 1997; Deputy Chairman, Northern Ireland Science Park Foundation, since 1999; *b* 8 Sept. 1939; *s* of Frank Edward Gibson and Nora Jessie Gibson (*née* Gurnhill); *m* 1963, Roberta Alexandra (*née* McMaster); one *s* two *d. Educ:* King Edward VI Grammar Sch., Retford. FCCA. GPO, 1958–63; MAFF, 1963–68; Belfast City Council, 1968–72; Dept of Commerce, NI, 1972–82; Dir of Accountancy Services, 1982–85, Asst Sec., 1985–87, Under Sec., then Dep. Sec., 1987–99, Dept of Economic Develt, NI. Pres., Irish Region, Chartered Assoc. of Certified Accountants, 1982–83. Trustee, The Bytes Project, 2000–. *Recreations:* reading, music, walking. *Address:* 14 Bramble Grange, Newtownabbey, Co. Antrim BT37 0XH. *T:* (028) 9086 2237.

GIBSON, Prof. Frank William Ernest, FRS 1976; FAA; Emeritus Professor of Biochemistry, and Visiting Fellow, Australian National University, since 1989; *b* 22 July 1923; *s* of John William and Alice Ruby Gibson; *m* 1st, 1949, Margaret Isabel Nancy (marr. diss. 1979); two *d*; 2nd, 1980, Robin Margaret; one *s. Educ:* Queensland, Melbourne, and Oxford Univs. BSc, DSc (Melb.), DPhil (Oxon). Research Asst, Melbourne and Queensland Univs, 1938–47; Sen. Demonstrator, Melbourne Univ., 1948–49; ANU Scholar, Oxford, 1950–52. Melbourne University: Sen. Lectr, 1953–58; Reader in Chem. Microbiology, 1959–65; Prof. of Chem. Microbiology, 1965–66; Australian National University: Prof. of Biochem., 1967–88; Hd. of Biochem. Dept, 1967–76, Chm., Div. of Biochemical Scis, 1988, John Curtin Sch. of Medical Res.; Howard Florey Prof. of Medical Res., and Dir, John Curtin Sch. of Med. Res., 1977–79. Newton-Abraham Vis. Prof. and Fellow of Lincoln Coll., Oxford Univ., 1982–83. David Syme Research Prize, Univ. of Melb., 1963. FAA 1971. *Publications:* scientific papers on the biochemistry of bacteria, particularly the biosynthesis of aromatic compounds, energy metabolism. *Recreations:* tennis, skiing. *Address:* John Curtin School of Medical Research, Australian National University, Canberra, ACT 0200, Australia.

GIBSON, Ven. (George) Granville; Archdeacon of Auckland, Diocese of Durham, 1993–2001; *b* 28 May 1936; *s* of late George Henry Gibson and of Jessie Gibson (*née* Farrand); *m* 1958, Edna (*née* Jackson); two *s* one *d* (and one *s* decd). *Educ:* Queen Elizabeth Grammar Sch., Wakefield; Barnsley Coll. of Technology; Cuddesdon Coll., Oxford. Mining Surveyor, NCB, 1952–62; Field Officer, The Boys' Brigade, 1962–69. Ordained deacon, 1971, priest, 1972; Curate, St Paul, Cullercoats, 1971–73; Team Vicar, Cramlington, 1973–77; Vicar, St Clare, Newton Aycliffe, 1977–85; Rector of Bishopwearmouth and RD of Wearmouth, 1985–93; Hon. Canon of Durham, 1988–. Proctor in Convocation, 1980–2000; Church Comr, 1991–98 (Mem., Bd of Govs., 1993–98). Trustee, Church Urban Fund, 1991–. *Recreations:* gardening, cactus plants, grandchildren. *Address:* 12 West Crescent, Darlington DL3 7PR; *e-mail:* vengg@gibven.demon.co.uk.

GIBSON, Ian, PhD; MP (Lab) Norwich North, since 1997; *b* 26 Sept. 1938; *s* of late William and Winifred Gibson; *m* 1974, Elizabeth Frances (*née* Lubbock); two *d. Educ:* Dumfries Acad.; Edinburgh Univ. (BSc, PhD). Indiana Univ., 1963–64; Univ. of Washington, 1964–65. Lectr, 1968–71, Sen. Lectr, 1971–97 and Dean of Sch. of Biol Scis, 1991–97, UEA. Contested (Lab) Norwich N, 1992. Chairman: Parly OST, 1998–; Parly Sci. and Technol. Cttee, 1998–; All Party Parly Gp on Cancer, 1998–. Jt Manager, Parly football squad, 1999–. Governor: Hellesdon High Sch., 1992–97; Sprowston High Sch., 1995–97 (Chm.). *Publication:* Anti-sense Technology, 1997. *Recreations:* football coaching, watching, listening and questioning. *Address:* House of Commons, SW1A 0AA. *T:* (020) 7219 4419.

GIBSON, Sir Ian, Kt 1999; CBE 1990; FInstP; Senior Vice President, Nissan Motor Co. Ltd and Supervisory Board Member, Nissan Europe NV, since 2000; *b* 1 Feb. 1947; *s* of Charley Gibson and Kate Gibson (*née* Hare); *m* 1st, 1969, Joy Musker (marr. diss.); two *d*; 2nd, 1988, Susan Wilson; one *s. Educ:* UMIST (BSc Physics 1969). FInstP 1999. Ford Motor Co. and Ford Werke AG: various posts in industrial relns and gen. mgt, 1969–79; General Manager: Halewood Ops, 1979–82; Saarlouis, 1982–83; Nissan Motor Manufacturing: Dir, 1984–2000; Dep. Man. Dir, 1987–89; Man. Dir, 1989–98; Chm., UK, 1999–2000; Vice-Pres., 1994–98, Pres., 1999–2000, Nissan Europe. Dep. Chm., ASDA plc, 1994–99. Mem. Court, Bank of England, 1999–. Mem., GBN, 1998–; Advr, ANA, 2001–. CIMgt (CBIM 1990). Hon. DBA Sunderland Poly., 1990. Mensforth Gold Medal, IEE, 1998. *Recreations:* sailing and working on my boat, ski-ing, reading. *Address:*

c/o Nissan Motor Co., Washington Road, Sunderland SR5 3NS. *T:* (0191) 415 2301. *Club:* Royal Automobile.

GIBSON, John Peter; Chief Executive, Seaforth Maritime, 1986–88 (Deputy Chairman, 1978–83; Chairman, 1983–86); *b* 21 Aug. 1929; *s* of John Leighton Gibson and Norah Gibson; *m* 1954, Patricia Anne Thomas; two *s* three *d. Educ:* Caterham Sch.; Imperial Coll., London (BSc (Hons Mech. Engrg), ACGI). Post-grad. apprenticeship Rolls Royce Derby, 1953–55; ICI (Billingham and Petrochemicals Div.), 1955–69; Man. Dir, Lummus Co., 1969–73; Dir Gen. Offshore Supplies Office, Dept of Energy, 1973–76. Dir, Taylor Woodrow Construction Ltd, 1989–90. *Recreations:* gardening, handyman. *Address:* Little Stapleton, Haytor, Ilsington, Newton Abbot, Devon TQ13 9RR.

GIBSON, John Sibbald; historian; Under Secretary, Scottish Office, 1973–83, retired; *b* 1 May 1923; *s* of John McDonald Frame Gibson and Marion Watson Sibbald; *m* 1948, Moira Helen Gillespie; one *s* one *d. Educ:* Paisley Grammar Sch.; Glasgow Univ. Army, 1942–46, Lieut in No 1 Commando from 1943; Far East. Joined Admin. Grade Home Civil Service, 1947; Asst Principal, Scottish Home Dept, 1947–50; Private Sec. to Parly Under-Sec., 1950–51; Private Sec. to Perm. Under-Sec. of State, Scottish Office, 1952; Principal, Scottish Home Dept, 1953; Asst Sec., Dept of Agriculture and Fisheries for Scotland, 1962; Under Secretary: Scottish Office, 1973; Dept of Agriculture and Fisheries for Scotland, 1979. Mem., Agricl Res. Council, 1979–83. Organiser, Scottish Office Centenary Exhibn, 1985. *Publications:* Ships of the '45: the rescue of the Young Pretender, 1967; Deacon Brodie: Father to Jekyll and Hyde, 1977; The Thistle and the Crown, 1985; Playing the Scottish Card: the Franco-Jacobite invasion of 1708, 1988; (contrib.) The '45: to keep an image whole, 1988; (jtly) The Jacobite Threat: a source book, 1990; (jtly) Summer Hunting a Prince, 1992; Lochiel of the '45, 1994; Edinburgh in the '45, 1995; The Gentle Lochiel, 1998. *Recreation:* historical research. *Address:* 28 Cramond Gardens, Edinburgh EH4 6PU. *T:* (0131) 336 2931.

GIBSON, John Walter; Chief of Operational Research, SHAPE Technical Centre, 1977–84; *b* 15 Jan. 1922; *s* of late Thomas John Gibson and Catherine Gibson (*née* Gregory), Bamburgh, Northumberland; *m* 1951, Julia (*d* 2000), *d* of George Leslie Butler, Buxton, Derbyshire; two *s* one *d. Educ:* A. J. Dawson Sch., Durham; Sheffield Univ.; University Coll., London. RNVR, 1942–46. Sheffield Univ., 1940–42, 1946–47 (BSc); University Coll., London, 1947–48; Safety-in-Mines Research Estabt, 1948–53; BJSM, Washington, DC, 1953–56; Royal Armament Research and Develt Estabt, 1957–60; Head of Statistics Div., Ordnance Bd, 1961–64; Supt, Assessment Br., Royal Armament Research and Develt Estabt, 1964–66, Prin. Supt, Systems Div., 1966–69; Asst Chief Scientific Adviser (Studies), MoD, 1969–74; Under-Secretary: Cabinet Office, 1974–76; MoD, 1976–77. FSS 1953. *Address:* 7 Islestone Court, Bamburgh, Northumberland NE69 7BQ. *T:* (01668) 214501.

GIBSON, Joseph, CBE 1980; PhD; CChem, FRSC; FREng, FInstF; Coal Science Adviser, National Coal Board, 1981–83 (Member for Science, 1977–81); *b* 10 May 1916; *m* 1944, Lily McFarlane Brown; one *s* one *d. Educ:* King's Coll. (now Univ. of Newcastle upon Tyne; MSc, PhD). Res., Northern Coke Res. Lab. 1938; Head of Chemistry Dept, Sunderland Technical Coll., and Lectr, Durham Univ., 1948; Chief Scientist, Northern Div., 1958, and Yorks Div., 1964, NCB; Director: Coal Res. Estab., 1968; Coal Utilisation Res., 1975. President: Inst. of Fuel, 1975–76; BCURA, 1977–81 and 1992– (Chm. 1972–77). Lectures: Cadman Meml, 1980, 1983; Prof. Moore Meml, 1981; Brian H. Morgans Meml, 1983. Coal Science Lecture Medal, 1977; Carbonisation Sci. Medal, 1979. Hon. FIChemE. Hon. DCL Newcastle, 1981. *Publications:* jointly: Carbonisation of Coal, 1971; Coal and Modern Coal Processing, 1979; Coal Utilisation: technology, economics and policy, 1981; papers on coal conversion and utilisation. *Recreations:* bridge, gardening. *Address:* 31 Charlton Close, Charlton Kings, Cheltenham, Glos GL53 8DH. *T:* (01242) 517832.

GIBSON, Kenneth James; Member (SNP) Glasgow, Scottish Parliament, since 1999; *b* Paisley, 8 Sept. 1961; *s* of Kenneth George Gibson and Iris Gibson; *m* 1989, Lynda Dorothy Payne; two *s* one *d. Educ:* Bellahouston Acad., Glasgow; Univ. of Stirling (BA Econs). Member (SNP): Glasgow DC, 1992–96; Glasgow CC, 1995–99 (Leader of Opposition, 1998–99). Shadow Minister for Local Govt, Scottish Parlt, 1999–. Mem., SNP Nat. Exec. Cttee, 1997–; Vice-Convener for Local Govt, SNP, 1997–. *Recreations:* cinema, theatre, swimming, classical history. *Address:* Scottish Parliament, Edinburgh EH99 1SP. *T:* (0131) 348 5924.

GIBSON, Madeline; Regional Nursing Officer, Oxford Regional Health Authority, 1973–83; retired; *b* 12 March 1925; *d* of late James William Henry Davis, JP, and Mrs Edith Maude Davis; *m* 1977, Comdr William Milburn Gibson, RN (*d* 1991). *Educ:* Haberdashers' Aske's Hatcham Girls' Sch.; Guy's Hosp. (SRN); British Hosp. for Mothers and Babies, Woolwich; Bristol Maternity Hosp. (SCM). Ward Sister, then Dep. Night Supt, Guy's Hosp., 1949–53; Asst Matron, Guy's Hosp., 1953–57; Admin. Sister then Dep. Matron, St Charles' Hosp., London, 1957–61; Asst Nursing Officer, 1962–68, Chief Regional Nursing Officer, 1968–73, Oxford Regional Hosp. Bd. Formerly Mem., Central Midwives Board. *Recreations:* village community work, theatre, golf. *Clubs:* New Cavendish; North Oxford Golf.

GIBSON, Mark; Director General, Enterprise and Innovation, Department of Trade and Industry, since 2000; *b* 2 Jan. 1953; *m* 1981, Jane Norma Lindley. *Educ:* University Coll., Oxford (BA 1974); London Business Sch. (MSc). Entered Department of Trade and Industry, 1974: Dep. Project Manager, Next Steps team, Cabinet Office, 1990–92; Asst Sec. Competitiveness Unit, 1992–94; Principal Private Sec. to Pres., BoT, and Dep. Prime Minister, 1994–97; Dir, British Trade Internat., 1997–2000. *Address:* Enterprise and Innovation Directorate, Department of Trade and Industry, 1 Victoria Street, SW1H 0ET. *T:* (020) 7215 5371.

GIBSON, Air Vice-Marshal Michael John, CB 1994; OBE 1979; FRAeS; Head of Aviation Regulation Enforcement, Civil Aviation Authority, 1996–99; *b* 2 Jan. 1939; *m* 1961, Dorothy Russell; one *s* one *d. Educ:* Imperial Coll., London (BSc); Selwyn Coll., Cambridge; National Defense Univ., Washington, DC. ACGI; FRAeS. Commnd RAFVR, 1959; commnd RAF, 1961; various appointments as fighter pilot and instructor; Personal Air Sec. to Air Force Minister, 1972–73; Officer Commanding: 45 Sqdn (Hunter), 1974–76; 20 Sqdn (Jaguar), 1976–79; RAF Brawdy, 1982–84; RAF Stanley, 1984–85; Air Officer Plans, HQ Strike Comd, 1987–88; Dir, Airspace Policy, 1988–91, Dir Gen. of Policy and Plans, 1991–94, Head of Mgt Support Unit, 1994–96, NATS. *Recreation:* music (singing and church organ playing). *Address:* 12 Watling Street, Radlett, Herts WD7 7NH. *Club:* Royal Air Force.

GIBSON, Paul Alexander; Founder, 1973, and Partner, since 1973, Sidell Gibson Partnership, Architects; *b* 11 Oct. 1941; *s* of Wing-Comdr Leslie Gibson and Betty Gibson (later Betty Stephens); *m* 1969, Julia Atkinson. *Educ:* Kingswood Sch., Bath; King's Coll., London; Canterbury Sch. of Architecture; Regent Street Polytechnic Sch. of Architecture (DipArch 1968). Worked for Farrell Grimshaw Partnership, 1968–69; Lectr, North Dakota State Univ., 1969; worked for Foster Associates, 1970–73. 3 RIBA awards, Good Housing, 1986; won open competition for redevelt of Grand Buildings, Trafalgar Square, 1986; won competition for redevelt of Winchester Barracks, 1988; expansion of Jewel House, HM Tower of London, 1992–94. *Recreations:* struggling pianist, keen gardener. *Address:* Fitzroy Yard, Fitzroy Road, NW1 8TP. *T:* (020) 7722 5009.

GIBSON, Rear-Adm. Peter Cecil, CB 1968; *b* 31 May 1913; 2nd *s* of Alexander Horace Cecil Gibson and Phyllis Zeline Cecil Gibson (*née* Baume); *m* 1938, Phyllis Anna Mary Hume, *d* of late Major N. H. Hume, IMS, Brecon; two *s* one *d. Educ:* Ealing Priory; RN Engrg Coll., Keyham. RN, 1931; HMS Norfolk, EI, 1936–38; maintenance test pilot, RN Aircraft Yard, Donibristle, 1940–41; Air Engr Officer, RNAS, St Merryn, 1941–42; Staff of RANAS, Indian Ocean, E Africa, 1942–43, Ceylon, 1943–44; Staff Air Engr. Off., British Pacific Fleet, 1945–46; Aircraft Maintenance and Repair Dept, 1946–49; loan service RAN, 1950–52; Trng Off., RNAS, Arbroath, 1952–54; Engr Off., HMS Gambia, 1954–56 and as Fleet Engr. Off., E Indies, 1955–56; Staff Engr. Off., Flag Off. Flying Trng, 1957–60; Dep. Dir Service Conditions, 1960–61; Dir Engr Officers' Appts, 1961–63; Supt RN Aircraft Yard, Fleetlands, 1963–65; Dep. Controller Aircraft (RN), Min. of Aviation, 1966–67, Min. of Technology, 1967–69, retired, 1969. ADC, 1965–66. Comdr 1946; Capt. 1957; Rear-Adm. 1966. Chm. United Services Catholic Assoc., 1966–69. *Recreation:* bridge. *Address:* Pangmere, Hampstead Norreys, Thatcham, Berks RG18 0TE. *Club:* Army and Navy.

GIBSON, Rt Hon. Sir Peter (Leslie), Kt 1981; PC 1993; **Rt Hon. Lord Justice Peter Gibson;** a Lord Justice of Appeal, since 1993; *b* 10 June 1934; *s* of late Harold Leslie Gibson and Martha Lucy Gibson (*née* Diercking); *m* 1968, Katharine Mary Beatrice Hadow, PhD; two *s* one *d. Educ:* Malvern Coll.; Worcester Coll., Oxford (Scholar; Hon. Fellow, 1993). 2nd Lieut RA, 1953–55 (National Service). Called to the Bar, Inner Temple, 1960; Bencher, Lincoln's Inn, 1975; Treas., Lincoln's Inn, 1996. 2nd Jun. Counsel to Inland Revenue (Chancery), 1970–72; Jun. Counsel to the Treasury (Chancery), 1972–81; a Judge of the High Court of Justice, Chancery Div., 1981–93. A Judge of the Employment Appeal Tribunal, 1984–86. Chm., Law Commn, 1990–92. *Address:* Royal Courts of Justice, Strand, WC2A 2LL.

GIBSON, Prof. Quentin Howieson, FRS 1969; Professor of Biochemistry and Molecular Biology, Cornell University, Ithaca, NY, 1966–90, now Emeritus; *b* 9 Dec. 1918; *s* of William Howieson Gibson, OBE, DSc; *m* 1951, Audrey Jane, *yr d* of G. H. S. Pinsent, CB, CMG, and Katharine Kentisbeare, *d* of Sir George Radford, MP; one *s* three *d. Educ:* Repton. MB, ChB, BAO, Belfast, 1941, MD 1944, PhD 1946, DSc 1951. Demonstrator in Physiology, Belfast, 1941–44; Lecturer in Physiology: Belfast, 1944–46; Sheffield Univ., 1946–55; Professor of Biochem., Sheffield Univ., 1955–63; Prof. of Biophys. Chem., Johnson Research Foundn, University of Pennsylvania, 1963–66. Dist. Faculty Fellow, Rice Univ., Houston, 1996–. Fellow, Amer. Acad. of Arts and Sciences, 1971; MNAS 1982. *Recreation:* sailing. *Address:* 3 Woods End Road, Etna, NH 03750, USA.

GIBSON, Rt Hon. Sir Ralph (Brian); PC 1985; Kt 1977; a Lord Justice of Appeal, 1985–94; *b* 17 Oct. 1922; 2nd *s* of Roy and Emily Gibson; *m* 1949, Ann Chapman Ruether, Chicago; one *s* two *d. Educ:* Charterhouse; Brasenose Coll., Oxford (Hon. Fellow 1986). MA Oxon 1948. Army Service, 1941–45: Lieut, 1st KDG; Captain, TJFF. Called to Bar, Middle Temple, 1948, Bencher 1974; QC 1968. A Recorder of the Crown Court, 1972–77; Judge of the High Court of Justice, Queen's Bench Div., 1977–85. Chm., Law Commn, 1981–85. Bigelow Teaching Fellow, University of Chicago, 1948–49. Member: Council of Legal Educn, 1971–86; Parole Bd, 1979–81; Court of Ecclesiastical Causes Reserved, 1986–96; Chm., Fees Adv. Commn, C of E, 1986–97. Pres., Central Council of Probation Cttees, 1982–86. Hon. LLD Dalhousie, 1983. *Address:* 8 Ashley Gardens, SW1P 1QD. *T:* (020) 7828 9670. *Club:* Emsworth Sailing.

See also C. D. O. Barrie, C. A. W. Gibson.

GIBSON, Prof. Robert Dennis, PhD, DSc; FTS, FAIM; first Vice-Chancellor, Queensland University of Technology, since 1989; *b* 13 April 1942; *m*; one *s* two *d*; *m* 1994, Catherin Bull. *Educ:* Hull Univ. (BSc Hons); Newcastle upon Tyne Univ. (MSc, PhD); DSc CNAA 1987. FAIM 1982; FTS 1993. Asst Lectr, Maths Dept, Univ. of Newcastle upon Tyne, 1966–67; Scientific Officer, Culham Plasma Lab., UKAEA, 1967–68; Lectr in Maths, Univ. of Newcastle upon Tyne, 1968–69; Sen. Lectr, Maths and Statistics, Teesside Polytechnic, 1969–77; Head, Dept of Maths, Stats and Computing (later Sch. of Maths, Stats and Computing), Newcastle upon Tyne Polytechnic, 1977–82; Queensland Institute of Technology: Dep. Dir then Actg Dir, 1982–83; Dir, 1983–88. Mem., 1988–92, Dep. Chm., 1991–92, Aust. Res. Council; Chm., Grad. Careers Council of Aust., 2000–. DUniv USC, 1999. *Publications:* numerous research papers on various aspects of mathematical modelling. *Recreations:* jogging, cricket. *Address:* Queensland University of Technology, GPO Box 2434, Brisbane, Qld 4001, Australia. *Club:* Brisbane.

GIBSON, Prof. Robert Donald Davidson, PhD; Professor of French, University of Kent at Canterbury, 1965–94, now Emeritus (Master of Rutherford College, 1985–90); *b* Hackney, London, 21 Aug. 1927; *o s* of Nicol and Ann Gibson, Leyton, London; *m* 1953, Sheila Elaine, *o d* of Bertie and Ada Goldsworthy, Exeter, Devon; three *s. Educ:* Leyton County High Sch. for Boys; King's Coll., London; Magdalene Coll., Cambridge; Ecole Normale Supérieure, Paris. BA (First Class Hons. French) London, 1948; PhD Cantab. 1953. Asst Lecturer, St Salvator's Coll., University of St Andrews, 1954–55; Lecturer, Queen's Coll., Dundee, 1955–58; Lecturer, Aberdeen Univ., 1958–61; Prof., Queen's Univ. of Belfast, 1961–65. *Publications:* The Quest of Alain-Fournier, 1953; Modern French Poets on Poetry, 1961; (ed) Le Bestiaire Inattendu, 1961; Roger Martin du Gard, 1961; La Mésentente Cordiale, 1963; (ed) Brouart et le Désordre, 1964; (ed) Provinciales, 1965; (ed) Le Grand Meaulnes, 1968; The Land Without a Name, 1975; Alain-Fournier and Le Grand Meaulnes, 1986; (ed) Studies in French Fiction, 1988; Annals of Ashdon, 1988; The Best of Enemies, 1995; reviews and articles in: French Studies, Modern Language Review, The London Magazine, Times Literary Supplement, Encyclopædia Britannica, Collier's Encyclopædia. *Recreations:* reading, writing, talking. *Address:* Thalassa!, Cliff Road, Sidmouth, Devon EX10 8JN.

GIBSON, Robin Warwick, OBE 2001; Chief Curator, National Portrait Gallery, 1994–2001; *b* 3 May 1944; *s* of Walter Edward Gibson and Freda Mary Yates (*née* Partridge). *Educ:* Royal Masonic Sch., Bushey; Magdalene Coll., Cambridge (BA 1966). Asst Keeper, City Art Gall., Manchester, 1967–68; National Portrait Gallery: Asst Keeper, 1968–83; Curator, Twentieth Century Collection, 1983–94. Mem. Cttee, NT Foundn for Art, 1991–. *Publications:* The McDonald Collection, 1970; (jtly) British Portrait Painters, 1971; Flower Painting, 1976; The Clarendon Collection, 1977; 20th Century Portraits, 1978; Glyn Philpot, 1984; John Bellany: new portraits, 1986; (jtly) Madame Yevonde, 1990; John Bratby Portraits, 1991; The Portrait Now, 1993; (jtly) The Sitwells, 1994; (jtly) Glenys Barton, 1997; The Face in the Corner, 1998; (jtly) Painting the Century, 2000; contrib. to new DNB; various catalogue essays; articles and reviews for Burlington Mag., Museums Jl, The Independent, Folio, Modern Painters. *Recreations:* 20th century music, village organist, plants, my dog, paintings other than portraiture. *Address:*

Brookside, Hempstead, near Saffron Walden, Essex CB10 2PE; *e-mail:* robline@btinternet.com.

GIBSON, Roy; aerospace consultant, since 1980; Director General, British National Space Centre, 1985–87; *b* 4 July 1924; *s* of Fred and Jessie Gibson; *m* 1st, 1946, Jean Fallowes (marr. diss. 1971); one *s* one *d*; 2nd, 1971, Inga Elgerus. *Educ:* Chorlton Grammar Sch.; Wadham College, Oxford; SOAS. Malayan Civil Service, 1948–58; Health and Safety Br., UKAEA, 1958–66; European Space Research Orgn, 1967–75 (Dir of Admin, 1970–75); Dir Gen., European Space Agency, 1975–80. DSC (Kedah, Malaysia), 1953; Das Grosse Silberne Ehrenzeichen mit Stern (Austria), 1977. *Publications:* Space, 1992; numerous articles in aerospace technical jls. *Recreations:* music, chess, walking. *Address:* Résidence les Hespérides, 51 Allée J. de Beins, Montpellier 34000, France. *T:* 467648181. *Club:* Naval and Military.

GIBSON, Ven. Terence Allen; Archdeacon of Ipswich, since 1987; *b* 23 Oct. 1937; *s* of Fred William Allen and Joan Hazel Gibson. *Educ:* Jesus Coll., Cambridge (MA); Cuddesdon Coll., Oxford. Curate of St Chad, Kirkby, 1963–66; Warden of Centre 63, Kirkby C of E Youth Centre, 1966–75; Rector of Kirkby, Liverpool, 1975–84; RD of Walton, Liverpool, 1979–84; Archdeacon of Suffolk, 1984–87. *Address:* 99 Valley Road, Ipswich, Suffolk IP1 4NF. *T:* (01473) 250333.

GIBSON-BARBOZA, Mario, Hon. GCMG 1968; Brazilian Ambassador to the Court of St James's, 1982–86; *b* Olinda, Pernambuco, 13 March 1918; *s* of Oscar Bartholomeu Alves Barboza and Evangelina Gibson Barboza; *m* 1975, Julia Blacker Baldassarri Gibson-Barboza. *Educ:* Law School of Recife, Pernambuco (graduated in Law, 1937); Superior War College, 1951. Entered Brazilian Foreign Service, 1940; served: Houston, Washington and Brussels, 1943–54; Minister-Counsellor: Buenos Aires, 1956–59; Brazilian Mission to United Nations, New York, 1959–60; Ambassador: to Vienna, 1962–66; to Asunción, 1967–68; Secretary General for Foreign Affairs, 1968–69; Ambassador to Washington, 1969; Minister of State for External Relations, 1969–74; Ambassador: to Athens, 1974–77; to Rome, 1977–82. Several Grand Crosses of Orders of Brazil and other countries. *Recreations:* riding, reading, theatre. *Address:* c/o Ministry of Foreign Affairs, Palácio do Hamaraty, Esplanada dos Ministérios, 70.170 Brasília, DF, Brazil. *Clubs:* Athenæum, Travellers, White's; Jockey Clube Brasileiro (Rio de Janeiro).

GIBSON-CRAIG-CARMICHAEL, Sir David Peter William, 15th Bt *cr* 1702 (Gibson Carmichael) and 8th Bt *cr* 1831; *b* 21 July 1946; *s* of Sir Archibald Henry William Gibson-Craig-Carmichael, 14th Bt and Rosemary Anita (*d* 1979), *d* of George Duncan Crew, Santiago, Chile; *S* father, 1969; *m* 1973, Patricia, *d* of Marcos Skarnic, Santiago, Chile; one *s* one *d*. *Educ:* Queen's Univ., Canada (BSc, Hons Geology, 1971). *Heir: s* Peter William Gibson-Craig-Carmichael, *b* 29 Dec. 1975.

GIBSON-WATT, Baron *cr* 1979 (Life Peer), of the Wye in the District of Radnor; **James David Gibson-Watt,** MC 1943 and 2 Bars; PC 1974; DL; a Forestry Commissioner, 1976–86; Chairman, Timber Growers United Kingdom, 1987–90 (Hon. President, 1993–98); *b* 11 Sept. 1918; *er s* of late Major James Miller Gibson-Watt, DL, JP; *m* 1942, Diana (*d* 2000), 2nd *d* of Sir Charles Hambro; two *s* two *d* (and one *s* decd). *Educ:* Eton; Trinity Coll (BA). Welsh Guards, 1939–46; N African and Italian campaigns. Contested (C) Brecon and Radnor constituency, 1950 and 1951; MP (C) Hereford, Feb. 1956–Sept. 1974; a Lord Commissioner of the Treasury, 1959–61; Minister of State, Welsh Office, 1970–74. FRAgS; Pres., Royal Welsh Agric. Soc., 1976 (Chm. Council, 1976–94). Chm., Council on Tribunals, 1980–86. Mem., Historic Buildings Council, Wales, 1975–79. DL Powys, 1968; JP Rhayader, retd 1989. *Address:* Doldowlod, Llandrindod Wells, Powys. *T:* (01597) 860208. *Club:* Boodle's.

GICK, Rear-Adm. Philip David, CB 1963; OBE 1946; DSC and Bar, 1942; Chairman, Emsworth Shipyard Group, 1965–90; *b* 22 Feb. 1913; *s* of late Sir William John Gick, CB, CBE; *m* 1938, Aylmer Rowntree (*d* 1993); one *s* three *d*. *Educ:* St Lawrence Coll., Ramsgate. Joined RN, 1931; qualified as Pilot, 1936. Capt. 1952; Comd HMS Daring, RNAS, Lossiemouth, HMS Bulwark, 1952–58; Rear-Adm. 1961; Flag Officer, Naval Flying Training, 1961–64, retd. *Recreation:* sailing. *Address:* Furzefield, Bosham Hoe, West Sussex PO18 8ET. *T:* (01243) 572219.

GIDDENS, Prof. Anthony, PhD; Director, London School of Economics, since 1997; *b* 18 Jan. 1938; *s* of T. G. Giddens; *m* 1963, Jane M. Ellwood. *Educ:* Hull Univ. (BA); LSE (MA); MA 1970, PhD 1974, Cantab. Cambridge University: Lectr in Sociology, subseq. Reader, 1969–85; Prof. of Sociology, Faculty of Econs and Politics, 1985–96; Fellow, King's Coll., 1969–96. Reith Lectr, BBC, 1999. *Publications:* Capitalism and Modern Social Theory, 1971; (ed) Sociology of Suicide, 1972; Politics and Sociology in the Thought of Max Weber, 1972; (ed and trans) Emile Durkheim: Selected Writings, 1972; (ed) Positivism and Sociology, 1974; New Rules of Sociological Method, 1976; Studies in Social and Political Theory, 1976; Central Problems in Social Theory, 1979; Class Structure of the Advanced Societies, 2nd edn 1981; Contemporary Critique of Historical Materialism: vol. 1, Power, Property and State, 1981, vol. 2, Nation, State and Violence, 1985; (jtly) Classes, Power and Conflict, 1982; Profiles and Critiques in Social Theory, 1983; (ed jtly) Social Class and the Division of Labour, 1983; Constitution of Society, 1984; Durkheim, 1985; Sociology: a brief but critical introduction, 1986; Social Theory and Modern Sociology, 1987; (ed jtly) Social Theory Today, 1987; Sociology, 1989; The Consequences of Modernity, 1990; Modernity and Self-Identity, 1991; The Transformation of Intimacy, 1992; Beyond Left and Right, 1994; In Defence of Sociology, 1996; Third Way, 1998; Runaway World (Reith Lectures), 1999; (with Will Hutton) On the Edge: living with global capitalism, 2000; The Third Way and its Critics, 2000. *Recreations:* theatre, cinema, playing tennis, supporting Tottenham Hotspur. *Address:* London School of Economics, Houghton Street, WC2A 2AE.

GIDDINGS, Air Marshal Sir (Kenneth Charles) Michael, KCB 1975; OBE 1953; DFC 1945; AFC 1950 and Bar 1955; *b* 27 Aug. 1920; *s* of Charles Giddings and Grace Giddings (*née* Gregory); *m* 1946, Elizabeth McConnell; two *s* two *d*. *Educ:* Ealing Grammar Sch. Conscripted, RAF, 1940; Comd, 129 Sqdn, 1944; Empire Test Pilots Sch., 1946; Test pilot, RAE, 1947–50; HQ Fighter Command, 1950–52; RAF Staff Coll., 1953; OC, Flying Wing, Waterbeach, 1954–56; CFE, 1956–58; OC, 57 Sqdn, 1958–60; Group Captain Ops, Bomber Command, 1960–62; Supt of Flying, A&AEE, 1962–64; Dir Aircraft Projects, MoD, 1964–66; AOC, Central Reconnaissance Estabt, 1967–68; ACAS (Operational Requirements), 1968–71; Chief of Staff No 18 (M) Group, Strike Command, RAF, 1971–73; Dep. Chief of Defence Staff, Op. Requirements, 1973–76. Dir, Nat. Counties Building Soc., 1982–85. Indep. Panel Inspector, DoE, 1979–91. *Recreations:* golf, gardening, music. *Address:* 159 Long Lane, Tilehurst, Reading, Berks RG31 6YW. *T:* (0118) 942 3012.

GIDDINGS, Dr Philip James; Senior Lecturer in Politics, University of Reading, since 1998; *b* 5 April 1946; *s* of Albert Edward Robert Giddings and Irene Trustrail Giddings (*née* Dunstan); *m* 1st, 1970, Margaret Anne Mulrenan (*d* 1978); one *d*; 2nd, 1979, Myfanwy Hughes; one *s*. *Educ:* Sir Thomas Rich's Sch., Gloucester; Worcester Coll., Oxford (BA Hons PPE); Nuffield Coll., Oxford (DPhil 1970). Lectr in Public Admin, Univ. of Exeter, 1970–72; Lectr in Politics, Reading Univ., 1972–98. Member: Crown Appointments Commn, 1992–97; Archbishops' Council, 1999– (Chm., Church and World Div., 1999–). Mem., Gen. Synod of C of E, 1985– (Vice-Chm., House of Laity, 1995–2000); Lay Vice-Pres., Oxford Diocesan Synod, 1988–2000. *Publications:* Marketing Boards and Ministers, 1974; Parliamentary Accountability, 1995; (with G. Drewry) Westminster and Europe, 1996; (with R. Gregory) Righting Wrongs: the ombudsman in six continents, 2000. *Recreations:* light gardening, short walks. *Address:* 5 Clifton Park Road, Caversham, Reading, Berks RG4 7PD. *T:* (0118) 954 3892.

GIDLEY, Sandra Julia; MP (Lib Dem) Romsey, since May 2000; *b* 26 March 1957; *d* of Frank Henry and Maud Ellen Rawson; *m* 1979, William Arthur Gidley; one *s* one *d*. *Educ:* Eggars Grammar Sch., Alton; AFCENT Internat., Brunssum, Netherlands; Windsor Girls' Sch., Hamm, Germany; Bath Univ. (BPharm). MRPharmS 1979. Pharmacist, Cheltenham, 1979–80; Pharmacy Manager, Gloucester, then Cheltenham, 1980–82; locum pharmacist, 1982–92; Pharmacy Manager: Safeway, 1992–99; Tesco, 1999–2000. Mem. (Lib Dem) Test Valley BC, 1995–; Mayor of Romsey, 1997–98. *Recreations:* food, photography, badminton. *Address:* House of Commons, SW1A 0AA; 15 Sycamore Close, Romsey, Hants SO51 5SB. *T:* (01794) 517652.

GIDOOMAL, Balram, (Ram), CBE 1998; Chairman, Winning Communications Partnership Ltd, since 1992; *b* 23 Dec. 1950; *s* of late Gagandas Gidoomal and of Vasanti Gidoomal; *m* 1976, Sunita Shivdasani; two *s* one *d*. *Educ:* Aga Khan Sch., Mombasa; Christopher Wren Sch., London; Imperial Coll., London (BSc Hons Physics). ARCS 1972. Inlaks Group: Dep. Gp Chief Exec., Head Office, France, then Geneva, 1978–85; UK Gp Chief Exec. and Vice Chm., 1985–92. Board Member: Covent Gdn Mkt Authy, 1998–; English Partnerships, 2000–; London First Centre, 2001–; Dir, Far Pavilions Ltd, 1998–. Mem., Better Regulation Task Force, Cabinet Office, 1997–. Mem., Nat. Leadership Team and Chm., London Exec., Race for Opportunity, 1993–99; Founder Chm., Business Links London South, 1995–98; Director: Business Links-Nat. Accreditation Adv. Bd, 1995–2000; Business Links London, 1995–98 (Chm., CEO's Gp, 1996–98). Patron, Small Business Bureau, 1998–. Mem. Council, Britain in Europe, 1999–. Chm., S Asian Develt Partnership, 1991–. Vis. Prof., Middx Univ., 2001–. Member: Council, RSA, 1993– (Trustee, 1999–); Council, Inst. of Employment Studies, 2001–. Chm., Christmas Cracker Trust, 1989–2000. Leader, Christian Peoples Alliance, 2001–; Vice Pres., Leprosy Mission, 1999–. Gov., PPP Medical Healthcare Trust, 2000–. Trustee: Inst. of Citizenship, 2000–; Timebank, 2001–. Freeman, City of London, 1997; Mem., Co. of Inf. Technologists, 1998–. FRSA 1993. Hon. Mem., Faculty of Divinity, Cambridge Univ., 1998–. *Publications:* Sari 'n' Chips, 1993; Karma 'n' Chips, 1994; Chapatis for Tea, 1994; Lions, Princesses and Gurus, 1996; The UK Maharajahs, 1997; Hinduism: a way of life, 1997; Building on Success: the South Asian contribution to UK competitiveness, 1997; (jtly) How Would Jesus Vote?, 2001; The British and How to Deal With Them: doing business with Britain's ethnic minorities, 2001; various reports. *Recreations:* music, current affairs, swimming. *Address:* 14 The Causeway, Sutton, Surrey SM2 5RS.

GIELGUD, Maina; free-lance ballerina; ballet producer; Guest Repetiteur: English National Ballet; Tokyo Ballet; Béjant Ballet, Lausanne; Ballet du Rhin; *b* 14 Jan. 1945; *d* of Lewis Gielgud and Elisabeth Grussner. *Educ:* BEPC (French). Ballet du Marquis de Cuevas, 1962–63; Ballet Classique de France, 1965–67; Ballet du XXème Siècle, Maurice Béjart, 1967–72; London Festival Ballet, 1972–77; Royal Ballet, 1977–78; free-lance, 1978–; rehearsal director, London City Ballet, 1981–82; Artistic Dir, Australian Ballet, 1983–96; Dir, Royal Danish Ballet, Copenhagen, 1997–99. Hon. AO 1991. *Address:* 1/9 Stirling Court, 3 Marshall Street, W1V 1LQ. *T:* (020) 7734 6612.

GIESKE, Dr Friedhelm; Member, Supervisory Board, RWE AG, since 1995 (Chairman, Managing Board, 1989–95); *b* Schwege/Bohmte, near Osnabrück, 12 Jan. 1928. *Educ:* Göttingen (Dr jur 1954). Joined RWE (Rheinisch-Westfählisches Elektrizitätswerk), 1953; Dep. Mem., 1968, Mem. (Finance), 1972, Bd of Management; Bd spokesman, 1988; Chairman, Supervisory Board: Karstadt Quelle AG, Essen; MAN AG, München; National-Bank AG, Essen. *Address:* c/o RWE AG, Opernplatz 1, 45128 Essen, Germany.

GIEVE, (Edward) John (Watson), CB 1999; Permanent Under-Secretary of State, Home Office, since 2001; *b* 20 Feb. 1950; *s* of late David Watson Gieve, OBE and of Susan Gieve; *m* 1972, Katherine Vereker; two *s*. *Educ:* Charterhouse; New Coll., Oxford (BA PPE, BPhil). Dept of Employment, 1974–78; HM Treasury: Principal, Industrial Policy Div., 1979–81; Energy Div., 1981–82; Private Sec., 1982–84; Investment Controller, Investors in Industry, 1984–86 (on secondment); Public Expenditure Survey Div., 1986–88; Press Sec., 1988–89; Principal Private Sec. to Chancellor of the Exchequer, 1989–91; Under Sec., Banking Gp, 1991–94; Dep. Dir, then Dir, Budget and Public Finances, 1994–98; Dir, then Man. Dir, Public Services, 1998–2001; Man. Dir, Finance, Regulation and Industry, 2001. *Recreations:* golf (playing), football (mainly watching). *Address:* Home Office, 50 Queen Anne's Gate, SW1H 9AT.

GIFFARD, family name of **Earl of Halsbury**.

GIFFARD, Adam Edward; *b* 3 June 1934; *o s* of 3rd Earl of Halsbury, FRS; *S* father as 4th Earl, 2000, but does not use the title; *m* 1976, Joanna Elizabeth, *d* of late Frederick Harry Cole; two *d*. *Educ:* Jesus Coll., Cambridge (MA 1961); BSc Open Univ. 1995.

GIFFARD, Sir (Charles) Sydney (Rycroft), KCMG 1984 (CMG 1976); HM Diplomatic Service, retired; *b* 30 Oct. 1926; *s* of Walter Giffard and Minna Giffard (*née* Cotton); *m* 1st, 1951, Wendy Vidal (marr. diss. 1976); one *s* one *d*; 2nd, 1976, Hazel Roberts, OBE. *Educ:* Repton Sch.; Wadham Coll., Oxford (Hon. Fellow, 1991). Served in Japan, 1952; Foreign Office, 1957; Berne, 1961; Tokyo, 1964; Counsellor, FCO, 1968; Royal Coll. of Defence Studies, 1971; Counsellor, Tel Aviv, 1972; Minister in Tokyo, 1975–80; Ambassador to Switzerland, 1980–82; Dep. Under-Sec. of State, FCO, 1982–84; Ambassador to Japan, 1984–86. *Publication:* Japan Among the Powers 1890–1990, 1994. *Address:* Winkelbury House, Berwick St John, Wilts, near Shaftesbury, Dorset SP7 0EY. *Club:* Lansdowne.

See also Dr B. J. Greenhill.

GIFFARD, John William, QPM 1997; DL; Chief Constable, Staffordshire Police, since 1996; *b* 25 March 1952; *s* of late Peter Richard de Longueville Giffard and of (Mary) Roana (Borwick) Giffard; *m* 1978, Crescent Vail; two *s*. *Educ:* Eton; Univ. of Southampton (BA Hons 1973). With Staffordshire Police, 1973–91: Grad. Entrant 1973; Chief Supt, 1991; Asst Chief Constable, N Yorks Police, 1991–96. DL Staffs, 1999. *Recreations:* cricket, shooting, bridge. *Address:* Chief Constable's Office, Cannock Road, Stafford ST17 0QG. *T:* (01785) 232217. *Clubs:* MCC, I Zingari; Staffs Gents Cricket, Yorks Gents Cricket.

GIFFORD, family name of **Baron Gifford**.

GIFFORD, 6th Baron *cr* 1824; **Anthony Maurice Gifford;** QC 1982; Barrister at Law, practising since 1966; Attorney-at-Law, Jamaica, since 1990; *b* 1 May 1940; *s* of 5th Baron Gifford and Lady Gifford (*née* Margaret Allen) (*d* 1990), Sydney, NSW; *S* father, 1961; *m* 1st, 1965, Katherine Ann (marr. diss. 1988), *o d* of Dr Mundy; one *s* one *d*; 2nd, 1988, Elean Roslyn (marr. diss. 1998), *d* of Bishop David Thomas, Kingston, Jamaica; one *d*; 3rd, 1998, Tina Natalia Goulbourne, Kingston, Jamaica. *Educ:* Winchester Coll. (scholar); King's Coll., Cambridge (scholar; BA 1961). Student at Middle Temple, 1959–62, called to the Bar, 1962. Chairman: Cttee for Freedom in Mozambique, Angola and Guiné, 1968–75; Mozambique Angola Cttee, 1982–90. Chairman: N Kensington Neighbourhood Law Centre, 1974–77 (Hon. Sec., 1970–74); Legal Action Gp, 1978–83; Vice-Chm., Defence and Aid Fund (UK), 1983–. Pres., Cttee for Human Rights, Grenada, 1987–; Vice-Pres., Haldane Soc. of Socialist Lawyers, 1986–. Chairman: Broadwater Farm Inquiry, 1986; Liverpool 8 Inquiry, 1988–89. *Publication:* Where's the Justice?, 1986. *Heir: s* Hon. Thomas Adam Gifford, *b* 1 Dec. 1967. *Address:* 122–126 Tower Street, Kingston, Jamaica. *T:* 922 6056, *Fax:* 967 0225; 8 King's Bench Walk, Temple, EC4Y 7DU. *T:* (020) 7797 8888, *Fax:* (020) 7797 8880.

GIFFORD, Prof. (Charles) Henry, FBA 1983; Winterstoke Professor of English, University of Bristol, 1967–75, Professor of English and Comparative Literature, Jan.–July 1976, retired; *b* 17 June 1913; *s* of Walter Stanley Gifford and Constance Lena Gifford (*née* Henry); *m* 1938, Mary Rosamond van Ingen; one *s* one *d. Educ:* Harrow Sch.; Christ Church, Oxford. BA 1936, MA 1946. War Service, 1940–46, Royal Armoured Corps; Univ. of Bristol: Asst Lectr, 1946; Sen. Lectr, 1955; Prof. of Modern English Literature, 1963. Clark Lectr, Trinity Coll., Cambridge, 1985. Gen. Editor, Cambridge Studies in Russian Literature, 1980–84. *Publications:* The Hero of his Time, 1950; (with Charles Tomlinson) Castilian Ilexes: versions from Antonio Machado, 1963; The Novel in Russia, 1964; Comparative Literature, 1969; Tolstoy: a critical anthology, 1971; Pasternak: a critical study, 1977; Tolstoy, 1982; Poetry in a Divided World (1985 Clark Lectures), 1986; articles and reviews on English and comparative literature. *Address:* 10 Hyland Grove, Bristol BS9 3NR. *T:* (0117) 950 2504.

GIFFORD, Joshua Thomas, (Josh), MBE 1989; racehorse trainer, since 1970; *b* 3 Aug. 1941; *s* of late Thomas Gifford and Dinah Florence Gifford (*née* Newman); *m* 1969, Althea Meryl Roger-Smith; one *s* one *d*. Flat racing jockey, 1951–58; National Hunt jockey, 1958–70; rode 700 winners; champion jockey, 1962, 1963, 1967, 1968; National Hunt trainer, 1970–; winners include: Aldaniti, Grand National, 1981. *Recreation:* cricket. *Address:* The Downs, Findon, Worthing, Sussex BN14 0RR. *T:* (01903) 872226.

GIFFORD, Michael Brian; Chairman, Danka Business Systems, since 2001 (Director, since 1999); *b* 9 Jan. 1936; *s* of Kenneth Gifford and Maude Gifford (*née* Palmer); *m* Nancy Baytos-Fenton; two *s* two *d* by previous marrs. *Educ:* LSE (BSc Econ). Joined Leo Computers (later part of ICL), 1960; Man. Dir, ICL (Pacific), 1973–75; Chief Exec., Cadbury Schweppes Australia, 1975–78; Finance Dir, Cadbury Schweppes plc, 1978–83; Man. Dir and CE, Rank Orgn, 1983–96; Director: Fuji Xerox Ltd, 1984–96; English China Clays PLC, 1992–99; Gillette Co., 1993–. *Address:* Suite 354, 568 Ninth Street South, Naples, Florida 34102–6620, USA.

GIL-ROBLES GIL-DELGADO, José María; Member, European Parliament, since 1989 (President, 1997–99); *b* 17 June 1935; *m* 1963, Magdalena Casanueva (*d* 1999). *Educ:* Univ. of Deusto; Univ. of Salamanca. Legal Advr, Spanish Parlt, 1958; barrister, Madrid, Barcelona, Bilbao and Salamanca, 1959; Lectr in Law, Univ. of Complutense, 1959; Comité Director, Fedn of Christian Democrats, Spain, 1972. European Parliament: Pres., Institutional Affairs Cttee, 1991; Vice-Pres., 1994. Pres., European Movt Internat., 1999–. Freeman, City of Salamanca, 1998. Hon. Fellow, Catholic Univ. of Chile, 1998. Dr *hc* State Inst. for Internat. Relations, Moscow, 1998. Robert Schuman Medal; Gold Medal, City of Athens; Order of Francisco Morazán (Central American Parlt), 1997; Silver Medal of Galicia, 2000. Medalla del Mérito Agrícola (Spain); Grand Cross, Order of Isabel la Católica (Spain), 2000; Medal of the Republic (Uruguay), 1998; Grand Cross: Order of Merit (Chile), 1998; Order of Liberator San Martin (Argentina), 1998; Order Antonio José de Irizarri (Guatemala), 1999; Officer, Legion of Honour (France), 2000. *Publications:* Derecho de huelga, 1961; Commentarios a la ley de arrendamientos rústicos, 1981; Legislación agraria básica, 1986; Control y autonomías, 1986; Los derechos del europeo, 1993; Los Parlamentos de Europa y el Parlamento Europeo, 1997. *Recreations:* reading, golf. *Address:* European Parliament, Rue Wiertz, 1047 Brussels, Belgium. *T:* (2) 2845757.

GILBART, Andrew James; QC 1991; a Recorder, since 1996 (an Assistant Recorder, 1992–96); *b* 13 Feb. 1950; *s* of Albert Thomas Gilbart and Carol Christie Gilbart, Vinehall Sch., Robertsbridge, Sussex; *m* 1979, Morag Williamson (marr. diss. 2000); one *s* one *d. Educ:* Westminster Sch. (Queen's Scholar); Trinity Hall, Cambridge (MA). Called to the Bar, Middle Temple, 1972; Bencher, 2000; elected to Northern Circuit, 1973. Member: Planning and Envmt Bar Assoc. (formerly Local Govt, Planning and Envmtl Bar Assoc.), 1986– (Mem. Cttee, 1988–92); UK Envmtl Law Assoc., 1996–; Admin Law Bar Assoc., 1999–; Internat. Associate Mem., Amer. Bar Assoc., 1994–. *Publications:* articles in Jl of Planning and Environment Law and Local Govt Chronicle. *Recreations:* history, walking, theatre, computers. *Address:* 40 King Street, Manchester M2 6BA. *T:* (0161) 832 9082; 4 Breams Buildings, EC4A 1AQ. *T:* (020) 7353 5835.

GILBART-DENHAM, Lt-Col Seymour Vivian, CVO 1994; Crown Equerry, since 1987; *b* 10 Oct. 1939; *s* of Major Vivian Vandeleur Gilbart-Denham (killed in action, Narvik, 1940), Irish Guards and Diana Mary Beaumont; *m* 1976, Patricia Caroline Brooking; two *d*. Commissioned, Life Guards, 1960; served UK, Germany, Cyprus and Far East; Adjutant, Life Guards, 1965–67; commanded Household Cavalry Regt, 1986–87. Vice-President: Royal Windsor Horse Show, 1988–; Royal Parks Equitation Trust, 1992–; Gtr London Region, Riding for the Disabled, 1994–; Pres., Coaching Club, 2001. *Recreations:* carriage driving, shooting, ski-ing. *Address:* The Royal Mews, Buckingham Palace, SW1W 0QH. *T:* (020) 7930 4832. *Clubs:* White's, Royal Automobile.

GILBERD, Rt Rev. Bruce Carlyle; Bishop of Auckland, 1985–94; Chaplain, King's School, Remuera, 1997–2000; retired; *b* 22 April 1938; *s* of Carlyle Bond Gilberd and Dorothy Annie Gilberd; *m* 1963, Patricia Molly Tanton; two *s* one *d. Educ:* King's College, Auckland; Auckland Univ. (BSc); St John's Coll., Auckland (LTh Hons, STh). Deacon 1962, priest 1963, Auckland; Assistant Curate: Devonport, 1962–64; Ponsonby and Grey Lynn, 1965; Panmure, 1965–68; Vicar of Avondale, 1968–71; trainee Industrial Chaplain, Tees-side Industrial Mission, and Asst Curate of Egglescliffe, 1971–73; visited industrial missions in UK and Europe; Director, Interchurch Trade and Industrial Mission, Wellington, 1973–79; founding Mem., Wellington Industrial Relations Soc.; Hon. Asst Curate, Lower Hutt 1973–77, Waiwhetu 1977–79; Lectr, St John's Coll., Auckland, 1980–85; Priest-in-charge, Albany Greenhithe Mission Dist, 1995, St Thomas, Tamaki, 1996, dio. of Auckland. Pres., Christian Res. Assoc., Aotearoa, NZ, 1996–2000. Mem. Gen. Synod, NZ. Has travelled widely in UK, Europe, China, USA and S Africa. NZ Commemorative Medal, 1990. *Publication:* (ed) Christian Ministry: a definition, 1984. *Recreations:* fishing, surfing, sailing. *Address:* 81 Manaia Road, Tairua, 2853, New Zealand.

GILBERT, family name of **Baron Gilbert**.

GILBERT, Baron *cr* 1997 (Life Peer), of Dudley, in the co. of West Midlands; **John William Gilbert;** PC 1978; PhD; *b* April 1927; *m* 1963, Jean Olive Ross Skinner; two *d* of previous marriage. *Educ:* Merchant Taylors' Sch.; St John's Coll., Oxford; New York Univ. (PhD in Internat. Economics, Graduate Sch. of Business Administration). Chartered Accountant, Canada. Contested (Lab): Ludlow, 1966; Dudley, March 1968; MP (Lab) Dudley, 1970–74; Dudley E, Feb. 1974–1997. Opposition front-bench spokesman on Treasury affairs, 1972–74; Financial Secretary to the Treasury, 1974–75; Minister for Transport, DoE, 1975–76; Minister of State, MoD, 1976–79 and 1997–99. Member: Select Cttee on Expenditure, 1970–74; Select Cttee on Corporation Tax, 1973; Select Cttee on Defence, 1979–87; Select Cttee on Trade and Industry, 1987–92; Cttee on Intelligence and Security, 1994–97; Chm., PLP Defence Gp, 1981–83; Vice-Chm., Lab. Finance and Industry Group, 1983–92. Member: Fabian Soc.; RUSI; RIIA; IISS; GMB; WWF. FRGS. Hon. LLD Wake Forest, S Carolina, 1983. *Address:* House of Lords, SW1A 0PW. *Club:* Reform.

See also N. Rogerson.

GILBERT, Prof. Alan David, DPhil; Vice-Chancellor, University of Melbourne, since 1996; *b* 11 Sept. 1944; *s* of Garnet E. Gilbert and Violet Gilbert (*née* Elsey); *m* 1967, Ingrid Sara Griffiths; two *d. Educ:* ANU (BA Hons 1965; MA 1967); Oxford Univ. (DPhil History 1973). Lectr, Univ. of Papua New Guinea, 1967–69; University of New South Wales: Lectr, 1973–77; Sen. Lectr, 1977–79; Associate Prof., 1979–81; Prof. of History, 1981–88; Pro-Vice-Chancellor, 1988–91; Vice-Chancellor, Univ. of Tasmania, 1991–95. Mem., Australian Higher Educn Council, 1991–95. FASSA 1990. Hon. DLitt Tasmania, 1995. *Publications:* Religion and Society in Industrial England, 1976; The Making of Post-Christian Britain, 1980; (with R. Currie and L. Horsley) Churches and Churchgoers, 1977; (Gen. Editor) Australians: a historical library, 11 Vols, 1987. *Recreation:* golf. *Address:* Vice-Chancellor's Office, University of Melbourne, Parkville, Vic 3052, Australia. *Club:* Melbourne (Vic).

GILBERT, Francis Humphrey Shubrick; QC 1992; **His Honour Judge Gilbert;** a Circuit Judge, since 2001; *b* 25 Jan. 1946; *s* of late Comdr Walter Raleigh Gilbert, RN, DL, Compton Castle, Devon and Joan Mary Boileau Gilbert; *m* 1975, Sarah Marian Kaye, *d* of late Col Douglas Kaye, DSO, DL, Brinkley Hall, Newmarket; one *s* two *d. Educ:* Stowe; Trinity Coll., Dublin (MA). Called to the Bar, Lincoln's Inn, 1970, Bencher, 2000. A Recorder, 1994–2001. Devon County Councillor, 1977–85. Pres., Pegasus Club, 2001. *Recreations:* sailing, shooting. *Address:* The Law Courts, Small Street, Bristol BS1 1DA. *Club:* Royal Yacht Squadron.

GILBERT, Prof. Geoffrey Alan, FRS 1973; Professor of Biochemistry, University of Birmingham, 1969–85, now Emeritus; *b* 3 Dec. 1917; *s* of A. C. Gilbert and M. M. Gilbert (*née* Cull); *m* 1948, Lilo M. Gilbert (*née* Czigler de Egerszalok); two *s. Educ:* Kingsbury County Sch., Mddx; Emmanuel Coll., Cambridge; Dept of Colloid Science, Cambridge. MA, PhD, ScD (Cantab). Lectr, Chemistry Dept, Univ. of Birmingham, 1943–46. Research Fellow, Medical Sch., Harvard Univ., 1946–47. Univ. of Birmingham: Sen. Lectr, Chemistry Dept, 1947–61, Reader, 1961–69. Chm., British Biophysical Soc., 1974. Mem., Editorial Bd, Jl of Molecular Biol., 1972–87. *Publications:* articles and papers in scientific jls. *Recreations:* photography, gardening, fox-watching. *Address:* 194 Selly Park Road, Birmingham B29 7HY. *T:* (0121) 472 0755.

GILBERT, Maj.-Gen. Glyn Charles Anglim, CB 1974; MC 1944; *b* 15 Aug. 1920; *s* of late C. G. G. Gilbert, OBE, MC, and H. M. Gilbert, MBE; *m* 1943, Heather Mary Jackson (*d* 2000); three *s* one *d. Educ:* Eastbourne Coll.; RMC Sandhurst. Commnd 1939; served with 2nd Lincolns, 1940–47, NW Europe and Palestine; Instructor, Sch. of Infantry, 1948–50; 3rd Bn Para. Regt, 1951; Staff Coll., 1952; staff and regimental appts in MoD, Airborne Forces, Royal Lincolns and Para. Regt, 1952–66, Cyprus, Egypt and Malaya; idc 1966; comd Sch. of Infantry, 1967–70; GOC 3rd Div., 1970–72; Comdt, Joint Warfare Estab., 1972–74, retired. Dir, Fitness for Industry Ltd, 1980–96. *Recreation:* following the sun. *Club:* Army and Navy.

GILBERT, Ian Grant; Under Secretary, International Relations Division, Department of Health and Social Security, 1979–85; retired; *b* Kikuyu, Kenya, 18 June 1925; *s* of Captain Alexander Grant Gilbert, DCM, indust. missionary, Lossiemouth and Kenya, and Marion Patrick Cruickshank; *m* 1960, Heather Margaret Donald, PhD (*d* 1999) (biographer of Lord Mount Stephen), *y d* of Rev. Francis Cantlie and Mary Donald, Lumphanan, Aberdeenshire. *Educ:* Fordyce Acad., Banffshire; Royal High Sch. of Edinburgh; Univ. of Edinburgh (MA 1950). Served HM Forces (Captain Indian Artillery), 1943–47. Entered Home Civil Service as Asst Principal and joined Min. of National Insurance, 1950; Private Sec. to Perm. Sec., 1953, and to Parly Sec., 1955; Principal, Min. of Pensions and Nat. Ins., 1956; seconded to HM Treasury, 1962–66; Asst Sec., Min. of Social Security (later DHSS), 1967; Head of War and Civilian Disabled Branches, DHSS, 1974–79. UK Member: Social Security, Health and Social Affairs Cttees, Council of Europe, Strasbourg, 1979–85; EEC Adv. Cttee on Social Security for Migrant Workers, Brussels, 1979–85; UK Delegate, Governing Body, Internat. Soc. Security Assoc., Geneva, 1979–85; Mem., UK Delegn to World Health Assembly, Geneva, 1979–84; Clerk/Advr to Select Cttee on European Legislation, House of Commons, 1987–90. Hon. Treasurer, Presbytery of England (Church of Scotland), 1965–77; Session Clerk, Crown Court Ch. of Scotland, Covent Garden, 1975–80. A Ch. of Scotland Mem., The Churches Main Cttee, 1986–. Chm., Caledonian Christian Club, 1984–86. Clerk to Govs, St Gregory's Sch., Marnhull, 1991–. *Recreations:* keeping half-an-acre in good heart, local and natural history, choral singing, France. *Address:* Wellpark, Moorside, Sturminster Newton, Dorset DT10 1HJ. *T:* (01258) 820306. *Club:* Royal Commonwealth Society.

See also C. R. C. Donald.

GILBERT, Air Chief Marshal Sir Joseph (Alfred), KCB 1985 (CB 1983); CBE 1974; Deputy Commander-in-Chief, Allied Forces Central Europe, 1986–89; retired; *b* 15 June 1931; *s* of late Ernest and Mildred Gilbert; *m* 1955, Betty, *yr d* of late William and Eva Lishman; two *d. Educ:* William Hulme's Sch., Manchester; Univ. of Leeds (BA Hons, Econ. and Pol Science; Hon. LLD 1989). Commnd into RAF, 1952; Fighter Sqdns, 1953–61; Air Secretary's Dept, 1961–63; RAF Staff Coll., 1964; CO 92 (Lightning) Sqdn, 1965–67; jssc 1968; Sec., Defence Policy Staff, and Asst Dir of Defence Policy, 1968–71; CO, RAF Coltishall, 1971–73; RCDS, 1974; Dir of Forward Policy (RAF), 1975; ACAS (Policy), MoD, 1975–77; AOC 38 Group, 1977–80; ACDS (Policy), 1980–82; Asst Chief of Staff (Policy), SHAPE, 1983–84; Dep. C-in-C, RAF Strike Command, 1984–86. Vice Chm., Commonwealth War Graves Commn, 1993–98 (Comr, 1991–98); Trustee, Imperial War Mus., 1997–. Life Vice-Pres., RAFA, 1995. *Publications:* articles in defence jls. *Recreations:* grandchildren, Rugby, strategic affairs. *Address:* Brook House, Salisbury Road, Shrewton, Salisbury, Wiltshire SP3 4EQ. *T:* (01980) 620627. *Club:* Royal Air Force.

GILBERT, Sir Martin (John), Kt 1995; CBE 1990; DLitt; FRSL; historian; Hon. Fellow of Merton College, Oxford, since 1994 (Fellow, 1962–94); Official Biographer of Sir

Winston Churchill since 1968; *b* 25 Oct. 1936; *s* of late Peter and Miriam Gilbert; *m* 1st, 1963, Helen Constance, *yr d* of late Joseph Robinson, CBE; one *d*; 2nd, Susan, *d* of late Michael Sacher; two *s*. *Educ:* Highgate Sch.; Magdalen Coll., Oxford (MA); DLitt Oxon 1999. Nat. Service (Army), 1955–57; Sen. Research Scholar, St Antony's Coll., Oxford, 1960–62; Vis. Lectr, Budapest Univ., 1961; Res. Asst (sometime Sen. Res. Asst) to Hon. Randolph S. Churchill, 1962–67; Vis. Prof., Univ. of S Carolina, 1965; Recent Hist. Correspt for Sunday Times, 1967; Res. Asst (Brit. Empire) for BBC, 1968; Historical Adviser (Palestine) for Thames Television, 1977–78. Visiting Professor: Tel-Aviv Univ., 1979; Hebrew Univ. of Jerusalem, 1980– (Vis. Lectr 1975); UCL, 1995–96; Visiting Lecturer: Univ. of Cape Town (Caplan Centre), 1984; MoD and Acad. of Sciences, Moscow, 1985. Non-Govtl Rep., UN Commn on Human Rights (43rd Session), Geneva, 1987, (44th Session), Geneva, 1988. Mem., Prime Minister's delegn to Israel and Jordan, and to Washington, 1995. Script designer and co-author, Genocide (Acad. Award winner, best doc. feature film), 1981; Historical Consultant to Southern Pictures TV series, Winston Churchill: The Wilderness Years, 1980–81; Historical Adviser, BBC TV, for Auschwitz and the Allies, 1981–82; historical consultant, Yalta 1945, for BBC TV, 1982–83; writer and narrator, Churchill, BBC TV, 1989–91. Governor, Hebrew Univ. of Jerusalem, 1978–. Hon. Fellow, Univ. of Wales Lampeter, 1997. Hon. DLitt: Westminster Coll., Fulton, 1981; Buckingham, 1992; Gratz Coll., Penn, 2000; George Washington Univ., Washington, 2000. *Publications:* The Appeasers, 1963 (with Richard Gott), 3rd edn 2001 (trans. German, Polish, Rumanian); Britain and Germany Between the Wars, 1964; The European Powers, 1900–1945, 1965 (trans. Italian, Spanish); Plough My Own Furrow: The Life of Lord Allen of Hurtwood, 1965; Servant of India: A Study of Imperial Rule 1905–1910, 1966; The Roots of Appeasement, 1966; Recent History Atlas 1860–1960, 1966; Winston Churchill (Clarendon Biogs for young people), 1966; British History Atlas, 1968, 2nd edn 1993; American History Atlas, 1968, 3rd edn 1993; Jewish History Atlas, 1969, 5th edn 1993 (trans. Spanish, Dutch, Hebrew, Russian, Hungarian, Italian, Chinese); First World War Atlas, 1970, 2nd edn 1994; Winston S. Churchill, vol. iii, 1914–1916, 1971, companion volume (in two parts) 1973; Russian History Atlas, 1972, 2nd edn 1993; Sir Horace Rumbold: portrait of a diplomat, 1973; Churchill: a photographic portrait, 1974, 3rd edn 2000; The Arab-Israeli Conflict: its history in maps, 1974, 7th edn 2001 (trans. Spanish, Hebrew); Churchill and Zionism (pamphlet), 1974; Winston S. Churchill, vol. iv, 1917–1922, 1975, companion volume (in three parts), 1977; The Jews in Arab Lands: their history in maps, 1975, illustr. edn, 1976 (trans. Hebrew, Arabic, French, German); Winston S. Churchill, vol. v, 1922–1939, 1976, companion volume, part one, The Exchequer Years 1922–1929, 1980, part two, The Wilderness Years 1929–1935, 1981, part three, The Coming of War 1936–1939, 1982; The Jews of Russia: Illustrated History Atlas, 1976 (trans. Spanish); Jerusalem Illustrated History Atlas, 1977, 2nd edn 1994 (trans. Hebrew, Spanish); Exile and Return: The Emergence of Jewish Statehood, 1978; Children's Illustrated Bible Atlas, 1979; Final Journey, the Fate of the Jews of Nazi Europe, 1979 (trans. Dutch, Hebrew); Auschwitz and the Allies, 1981, 3rd edn 2001 (trans. German, Hebrew); Churchill's Political Philosophy, 1981; The Origin of the 'Iron Curtain' speech, 1981 (pamphlet); Atlas of the Holocaust, 1982, 3rd edn 2001 (trans. German, Hebrew, French, Japanese); Winston S. Churchill, vol. vi, Finest Hour, 1939–41, 1983 (Wolfson Award, 1983); The Jews of Hope: the plight of Soviet Jewry today, 1984 (trans. Hebrew, Japanese); Jerusalem: rebirth of a city, 1985; The Holocaust: the Jewish tragedy, 1986; Winston S. Churchill, vol vii, Road to Victory, 1986; Shcharansky: hero of our time, 1986 (trans. Dutch, Hebrew); Winston S. Churchill, vol viii, 'Never Despair', 1945–65, 1988; Second World War, 1989, 3rd edn 2000 (trans. German, Italian, Portuguese, Japanese, Polish); Churchill, A Life, 1991 (trans. Italian, Polish, Spanish); Atlas of British Charities, 1993; The Churchill War Papers, vol. 1, At the Admiralty September 1939–May 1940, 1993, vol. 2, Never Surrender, May–December 1940, 1995, vol. 3, The Ever-Widening War, 1941, 2000; In Search of Churchill, 1994; First World War, a History, 1994 (trans. Polish); The Day the War Ended: VE-Day 1945, 1995 (trans. Czech); Jerusalem in the Twentieth Century, 1996; The Boys: triumph over adversity, 1996; A History of the Twentieth Century, vol. 1, 1900–1933, 1997, vol. 2, 1933–1951, 1998, vol. 3, 1952–1999, 1999 (trans. German, Danish, Polish, Czech); Holocaust Journey, Travelling in Search of the Past, 1997 (trans. Croatian); Israel: a history, 1998 (trans. Hungarian); Never Again: an illustrated history of the Holocaust, 2000 (trans. Italian, French, German, Polish, Dutch, Lithuanian); The Jews in the Twentieth Century: an illustrated history, 2001 (trans, Danish, French, German, Czech); Five Thousand Years of Jewish History: letters to my Indian aunt, 2001; Editor: A Century of Conflict: Essays Presented to A. J. P. Taylor, 1966; Churchill, 1967, and Lloyd George, 1968 (Spectrum Books); compiled Jackdaws: Winston Churchill, 1970; The Coming of War in 1939, 1973; contribs historical articles and reviews to jls (incl. Purnell's History of the Twentieth Century, Reader's Digest). *Recreation:* drawing maps. *Address:* Merton College, Oxford OX1 4JD. *Club:* Athenæum.

GILBERT, Michael Francis, CBE 1980; TD 1950; crime writer; *b* 17 July 1912; *s* of Bernard Samuel Gilbert and Berwyn Minna Cuthbert; *m* 1947, Roberta Mary, *d* of Col R. M. W. Marsden; two *s* five *d*. *Educ:* Blundell's Sch.; London University. LLB 1937. Served War of 1939–45, Hon. Artillery Co., 12th Regt RHA, N Africa and Italy (despatches 1943). Joined Trower Still & Keeling, 1947 (Partner, 1952–83). Legal Adviser to Govt of Bahrain, 1960. Member: Arts Council Cttee on Public Lending Right, 1968; Royal Literary Fund, 1969; Council of Soc. of Authors, 1975; (Founder) Crime Writers' Assoc. (Diamond Dagger, 1994); Mystery Writers of America, Grand Master, 1987. FRSL 1999. *Publications: novels:* Close Quarters, 1947; They Never Looked Inside, 1948; The Doors Open, 1949; Smallbone Deceased, 1950; Death has Deep Roots, 1951; Death in Captivity, 1952; Fear to Tread, 1953; Sky High, 1955; Be Shot for Sixpence, 1956; The Tichborne Claimant, 1957; Blood and Judgement, 1958; After the Fine Weather, 1963; The Crack in the Tea Cup, 1965; The Dust and the Heat, 1967; The Etruscan Net, 1969; The Body of a Girl, 1972; The Ninety Second Tiger, 1973; Flash Point, 1974; The Night of the Twelfth, 1976; The Empty House, 1978; Death of a Favourite Girl, 1980; The Final Throw, 1983; The Black Seraphim, 1983; The Long Journey Home, 1985; Trouble, 1987; Paint Gold and Blood, 1989; The Queen against Karl Mullen, 1991; Roller Coaster, 1993; Ring of Terror, 1995; Into Battle, 1997; Over and Out, 1998; *short stories:* Game Without Rules, 1967; Stay of Execution, 1971; Petrella at Q, 1977; Mr Calder and Mr Behrens, 1982; Young Petrella, 1988; Anything for a Quiet Life, 1990; *plays:* A Clean Kill; The Bargain; Windfall; The Shot in Question; *edited:* Crime in Good Company, 1959; The Oxford Book of Legal Anecdotes, 1986; The Fraudsters, 1988; Prep School, 1991; has also written radio and TV scripts. *Recreations:* walking, contract bridge. *Address:* The Old Rectory, Luddesdown, Gravesend, Kent DA13 0XE. *T:* (01474) 814272. *Club:* Garrick.

See also P. W. Clarke.

GILBERT, Patrick Nigel Geoffrey; General Secretary of the Society for Promoting Christian Knowledge, 1971–92; *b* 12 May 1934; adopted *s* of late Geoffrey Gilbert and Evelyn (*née* Miller), Devon. *Educ:* Cranleigh Sch.; Merton Coll., Oxford. Lectr, S Berks Coll. of Further Educn, 1959–62; PA to Sir Edward Hulton, 1962–64; OUP, 1964–69; Linguaphone Group (Westinghouse), 1969–71 (Man. Dir in Group, 1970). World Assoc. for Christian Communication: Trustee, 1975–87; European Vice-Chm., 1975–82; representative to EEC, 1975–82, to Conf. of Eur. Churches, 1976–82, to Council of Europe, 1976–82, and to Central Cttee, 1979–84. Member: Bd for Mission and Unity of Gen. Synod, 1971–78 (Mem. Exec., 1971–76); Archbishops' Cttee on RC Relations, 1971–81; Church Inf. Cttee, 1978–81; Church Publishing Cttee, 1980–84; Council, Conf. of British Missionary Socs, 1971–78; Council, Christians Abroad, 1974–79; Exec., Anglican Centre, Rome, 1981–91 (Vice Chm. of Friends, 1984–91); British National Cttee, UNESCO World Book Congress, 1982. Greater London Arts Association: Mem. Exec., 1968–78; Hon. Life Mem., 1978; Chm., 1980–84 (Dep. Chm., 1979–80); Initiator, 1972 Festivals of London. Art Workers' Guild: Hon. Brother, 1971; Chm. Trustees and Hon. Treas., 1976–86 (Trustee, 1975). Chairman: Gp Eight Opera, 1962–72; Standing Conf. of London Arts Councils, 1975–78; Embroiderers' Guild, 1977–78 (Hon. Treas., 1974–77); Concord Multicultural Arts Trust, 1980–89; Harold Buxton Trust, 1983–92; Nikaean Club, 1984–92; Vice-President: Camden Arts Council, 1974–89 (Chm., 1970–74); Nat. Assoc. of Local Arts Councils, 1980–89 (Founder Chm., 1976–80); Mem., Arts Adv. Cttee, CRE, 1979; Steward, Artists' Gen. Benevolent Instn, 1971–93. Rep. of Archbishop of Canterbury to Inter-Church Travel, 1987–92; Consultant, Saga Travel, 1994–98. Trustee: Overseas Bishoprics Fund, 1971–92; All Saints Trust, 1978–92 (Chairman: F and GP and Investment Cttees); Schulze Trust, 1980–83 (Chm.); Dancers' Resettlement Fund, 1982–90 (Chm., Finance Cttee); Richards Trust, 1971–92; ACC Res. Fund, 1982–84; Vis. Trustee, Seabury Press, NY, 1978–80; Chm., Dancers' Resettlement Trust, 1987–90. Member, Executive: GBGSA, 1981–84, 1988–89; Assoc. of Vol. Colls, 1979–87; Member, Governing Body: SPCK India, 1971–92; SPCK Australia, 1977–92; SPCK (USA), 1984–92; SPCK NZ, 1989–92; Partners for World Mission, 1979–92; Governor: Contemp. Dance Trust, 1981–90; All Saints Coll., Tottenham, 1971–78; St Martin's Sch. for Girls, 1971–92 (Vice Chm., 1978–91; Rep. to Tertiary Educn Council, 1983–89); Ellesmere Coll., 1977–87 (Mem. ISCO Exec., 1984–86); St Michael's Sch., Petworth, 1978–88 (rep. to GBGSA); Roehampton Inst., 1978–92 (rep. to Assoc. of Vol. Colls, 1978–88; Chm., Audit Cttee, 1989–92); Pusey House, 1985–92; Patron, Pusey House Appeal, 1984–88; Fellow, Corp. of SS Mary and Nicholas (Woodard Schs), 1972–92 (Mem. Exec., 1981–92; Chm., S Div. Res. Cttee, 1972–84; Trustee, Endowment Fund; Dir, Corp. Trustee Co.). Member Development Cttee: SPAB, 1985–87; London Symphony Chorus, 1985–87; Bd Mem., Nat. Youth Dance Co., 1988–92; Mem. Council, Publishers Assoc., 1990–92. Cttee, London Europe Soc., 1985–93; Mem. Court, City Univ., 1987–93. Dir, Surrey Building Soc., 1988–93. Dep. Chm. and Chm., Exec. Cttee, Athenæum Club, 1985–89. Hon. Member: Assoc. for Develt in the Arts; Georgia Salzburger Soc., USA, 1986. JP Inner London, 1971–75. Freeman, City of London, 1966; Liveryman, Worshipful Co. of Woolmen (Master, 1985–86; Rep. to City and Guilds); Parish Clerk, All Hallows, Bread Street, 1981–93; Mem., Guild of Freemen (Court, 1991–93); Lord of the Manor of Cantley Netherhall, Norfolk. Hon. Citizen, Savannah, Georgia, 1986. FRSA 1978; FIMgt (FBIM 1982); FInstD 1982. Hon. DLitt Columbia Pacific, 1982. Order of St Vladimir, 1977. *Publications:* articles in various jls. *Recreations:* mountain walking, reading, travel, enjoying the Arts, golf. *Address:* 3 The Mount Square, NW3 6SU. *T:* (020) 7794 8893; PO Box 118, Udon Thani 41000, Thailand. *T:* (42) 347338.

GILBERT, Rev. Canon Roger Geoffrey; Rector of Falmouth, since 1986; Chaplain to the Queen, since 1995; *b* 18 June 1937; *s* of Geoffrey and Ruth Gilbert; *m* 1965, Marie-Pascale (*née* Berthelot); three *d*. *Educ:* Truro Secondary Modern Sch. for Boys; St Peter's Coll., Birmingham; King's Coll. London (BD; AKC); St Augustine's Coll., Canterbury. RAF, 1957–59. Asst Master, Hinchley Wood Sch., 1963–67; ordained deacon, 1970, priest, 1971; Asst Curate, Walton-on-Thames, 1970–74; Rector, St Mabyn with Helland, 1974–81; Priest-in-charge, Madron with Morvah, 1981–86. Hon. Canon of Truro Cathedral, 1994–; Rural Dean of Carnmarth South, 1994–2000. Fellow, Woodard Corp., 1988. *Recreations:* travel, Cornish-Breton history and culture, post-Impressionist painters, antiques, books. *Address:* The Rectory, Albany Road, Falmouth, Cornwall TR11 3RP. *T:* (01326) 314176.

GILBERT, Ronald Stuart J.; *see* Johnson-Gilbert.

GILBERT, Stuart William, CB 1983; Chairman, Upkeep (Trust for training and education in building maintenance), 1993–96 (Trustee, since 1988); *b* 2 Aug. 1926; *s* of Rodney Stuart Gilbert and Ella Edith (*née* Esgate); *m* 1955, Marjorie Laws Vallance; one *s* one *d*. *Educ:* Maidstone Grammar Sch.; Emmanuel Coll., Cambridge (Open Exhibnr and State Scholar; MA). Served RAF, 1944–47. Asst Principal, Min. of Health, 1949; Asst Private Sec.: to Minister of Housing and Local Govt, 1952; to Parly Sec., 1954; Principal, 1955; Sec., Parker Morris Cttee on Housing Standards, 1958–61, Rapporteur to ECE Housing Cttee, 1959–61; Reporter to ILO Conf. on Workers' Housing, 1960; Asst Sec., Local Govt Finance Div., 1964; Under-Sec., DoE, 1970–80 (for New Towns, 1970, Business Rents, 1973, Construction Industries, 1974, Housing, 1974, Planning Land Use, 1977); Dep. Dir, 1980–81, Dir (Dep. Sec.), 1981–86, Dept for Nat. Savings. *Recreations:* computing, music, woodwork. *Address:* 3 Westmoat Close, Beckenham, Kent BR3 5BX. *T:* (020) 8650 7213.

GILBERT, Prof. Walter; Carl M. Loeb University Professor, Department of Molecular and Cellular Biology (formerly of Cellular and Developmental Biology), Harvard University, since 1985; Joint Founder, 1978, and Director, Biogen NV (Chairman and Principal Executive Officer, 1981–84); Vice Chairman, Myriad Genetics Inc., since 1992; *b* Boston, 21 March 1932; *s* of Richard V. Gilbert and Emma (*née* Cohen); *m* 1953, Celia Stone; one *s* one *d*. *Educ:* Harvard Coll. (AB *summa cum laude* Chem. and Phys., 1953); Harvard Univ. (AM Phys., 1954); Cambridge Univ. (PhD Maths, 1957). National Science Foundn pre-doctoral Fellow, Harvard Univ. and Cambridge Univ., 1953–57, post-doctoral Fellow in Phys., Harvard, 1957–58; Harvard University: Asst Prof. in Phys., 1959–64; Associate Prof. of Biophys., 1964–68; Prof. of Biochem., 1968–72; Amer. Cancer Soc. Prof. of Molecular Biology, 1972–81; H. H. Timken Prof. of Science, 1986–87. Guggenheim Fellow, Paris, 1968–69. Member: Amer. Acad. of Arts and Sciences, 1968; National Acad. of Sciences, 1976; Amer. Phys. Soc.; Amer. Soc. of Biol Chemists; Foreign Mem., Royal Soc., 1987–. Hon. DSc: Chicago, 1978; Columbia, 1978; Rochester, 1979; Yeshiva, 1981. Many prizes and awards, incl. (jtly) Nobel Prize for Chemistry, 1980. *Publications:* chapters, articles and papers on theoretical physics and molecular biology. *Address:* Biological Laboratories, 16 Divinity Avenue, Cambridge, MA 02138, USA. *T:* (617) 495–0760; 15 Gray Gardens West, Cambridge, MA 02138. *T:* (617) 8648778.

GILBERTSON, Prof. David Dennis, FGS; Head, School of Conservation Sciences, Bournemouth University, since 2000; Emeritus Professor, University of Wales, since 1998; *b* Stratford, London, 1 Sept. 1945; *s* of late Thomas Gilbertson and of Ivy Florence Joyce Gilbertson; *m* 1970, Barbara Mary Mitchell; one *s* two *d*. *Educ:* SW Ham Tech. Sch.; Univ. of Lancaster (BA Hons 1968); Univ. of Exeter (PGCE 1969); Univ. of Bristol (PhD 1974; DSc 1991). FGS 1983. Teacher, Pretoria Sch., London, 1964–65; Res. Asst in Geology, Univ. of Bristol, 1969–71; Lectr in Geography, Plymouth Poly., 1971–74, Univ. of Adelaide, 1974–77; Sheffield University: Lectr, 1977–85; Sen. Lectr, 1985–88; Reader, 1988–92; Prof., and Hd of Res. Sch. of Archaeology and Archaeol Studies,

1992–94; Prof. of Physical Geography, Inst. of Geography and Earth Scis, and Dir, Inst. of Earth Studies, 1994–97, Univ. of Wales, Aberystwyth, 1994–98; Prof. of Envmtl Science, Nene Centre for Res., UC Northampton, 1998–2000. Vis. Prof. and Fulbright Schol., Univ. of Arizona, 1981–82; Munro Lectr, Edinburgh Univ., 1999; Vis. Schol., Adelaide Univ., 1999. Co-Dir, UNESCO Libyan Valleys Archaeol Survey, 1988–96; Chm., Univ. of Wales Subject Panel for Envmtl Studies, 1996–98. Jt Founder and Associate Ed., Applied Geography, 1981–88; Sen. UK Ed., Jl of Archaeol Sci., 1992–98. J. P. Wiseman Prize, Archaeol Inst. of Amer., 2001. *Publications:* (jtly) The Pleistocene Succession at Kenn, Somerset, 1978; (jtly) In the Shadow of Extinction, 1984; Late Quaternary Environments and Man in Holderness, 1984; (jtly) Practical Ecology, 1985; (jtly) The Chronology and Environment of Early Man: a new framework, 1985; (jtly) Farming the Desert: the UNESCO Libyan Valley survey, 1996; (jtly) The Outer Hebrides: the last 14000 years, 1996; (ed jtly) The Archaeology of Drylands: living on the margins, 2000; contribs to books, and papers in learned jls. *Recreations:* walking, railways—large and small, West Ham United, the Teign Estuary. *Address:* School of Conservation Sciences, Bournemouth University, Fern Down, Poole, Dorset BH12 5BB. *T:* (01202) 595178, *Fax:* (01202) 595255; *e-mail:* dgilbertson@bournemouth.ac.uk.

GILBEY, family name of **Baron Vaux of Harrowden.**

GILBEY, Sir Gavin; *see* Gilbey, Sir W. G.

GILBEY, Sir (Walter) Gavin, 4th Bt *cr* 1893, of Elsenham Hall, Essex; *b* 14 April 1949; *s* of Sir (Walter) Derek Gilbey, 3rd Bt and of Elizabeth Mary, *d* of Col K. G. Campbell; *S* father, 1991; *m* 1st, 1980, Mary (marr. diss. 1984), *d* of late William E. E. Pacetti; 2nd, 1984, Anna (marr. diss. 1995), *d* of Edmund Prosser. *Educ:* Eton.

GILCHRIST, Andrew Charles; General Secretary, Fire Brigade Union, since 2000; *b* 5 Dec. 1960; *s* of Edward and Shirley Gilchrist; *m* 1985, Loretta Borman; one *s* one *d*. *Educ:* Bedford Modern Sch. Bedfordshire Fire Service, 1979–96; Mem., Exec. Council, 1993–2000, Nat. Officer, 1996–2000, Fire Bde Union. *Recreations:* cycling, walking, reading. *Address:* Fire Brigade Union, Bradley House, 68 Coombe Road, Kingston-upon-Thames, Surrey KT2 7AE. *T:* (020) 8541 1765.

GILCHRIST, Archibald, OBE 1996; Managing Director, 1971–79, and Chairman, 1978–79, Govan Shipbuilders; *b* 17 Dec. 1929; *m* 1958, Elizabeth Jean Greenlees; two *s* one *d*. *Educ:* Loretto; Pembroke Coll., Cambridge (MA). Barclay Curle & Co. Ltd, Glasgow, 1954–64, various managerial posts; ultimately Dir, Swan Hunter Group; Brown Bros & Co. Ltd, Edinburgh, 1964–72: Dep. Man. Dir, 1964; Man. Dir, 1969; Man. Dir, Vosper Private, Singapore, 1980–86; Dir, Management Search Internat. Ltd, 1986–89; Pt-time Bd Mem., Scottish Legal Aid Bd, 1986–96; non-executive Director: F. J. C. Lilley plc, 1987–93; RMJM Ltd, 1988–98; Scottish Friendly Assurance Soc. Ltd (formerly Glasgow Friendly Soc.), 1988–2000; Caledonian MacBrayne Ltd, 1990–97. Vice Chm., Royal Scottish National (formerly Royal Scottish) Orchestra, 1989–94 (Dir, 1987–94). Chm. Council, St Leonard's Sch., 1989–95; Gov., Glasgow Polytechnic, 1987–93. *Recreations:* golf, shooting, fishing, music. *Address:* Inchmaholm, 35 Barnton Avenue, Edinburgh EH4 6JJ. *Clubs:* New (Edinburgh); Hon. Company of Edinburgh Golfers.

GILCHRIST, Maj. Gen. Peter; Executive Director, Defence Procurement Agency, and Master-General of the Ordnance, since 2000; *b* 28 Feb. 1952; *s* of Col David A. Gilchrist and Rosemary Gilchrist (*née* Drewe); *m* 1981, Sarah-Jane Poyntz; one *s* one *d*. *Educ:* Marlborough Coll.; Sandhurst. Commnd Royal Tank Regiment, 1972; Troop Leader, 3RTR, Germany and NI, 1972–76; aic 1977; Schools Gunnery Instructor, Lulworth, 1978–80; Ops Officer and Adjutant, 3RTR, 1980–82; Div. II, Army Staff Course (psc†), 1983–84; COS, 20th Armd Bde, 1985–87; Comdr, Indep. Recce Sqdn, Cyprus, 1986; Sqdn Comdr (Challenger), 3RTR, 1988; Mil. Sec.'s Staff, 1989; Directing Staff, RMCS, 1990–93; CO, 1st RTR, 1993–95; HCSC, 1996; Dep. DOR (Armour and Combat Support Vehicles), 1996–98; Prog. Dir, Armd Systems, MoD PE, 1998–2000. Col Comdt, RAC, 2000–; Dep. Col Comdt, RTR, 2000–. Non-exec. Dir, DERA Facilities Bd, 2000–. *Recreations:* sailing, ski-ing, field sports, gardening, DIY. *Address:* Defence Procurement Agency, Maple 2c # 1, MoD Abbey Wood, Bristol BS34 8JH. *Club:* Army and Navy.

GILDER, Robert Charles, FIA; Directing Actuary, Government Actuary's Department, 1979–83; *b* 22 April 1923; *s* of Charles Henry Gilder and Elsie May (*née* Sayer); *m* 1954, Norah Mary Hallas; two *s*. *Educ:* Brentwood School. Liverpool Victoria Friendly Soc., 1940–41 and 1946–48. Served War, RAF, 1941–46. Government Actuary's Dept, 1948–83; Actuary, 1959; Principal Actuary, 1973. FIA 1951. *Recreations:* cricket, golf, music.

GILDERNEW, Michelle; MP (SF) Fermanagh and South Tyrone, since 2001; Member (SF) Fermanagh and South Tyrone, Northern Ireland Assembly, since 1998. *Educ:* Univ. of Ulster. Press Officer, Sinn Féin, 1997. Dep. Chm., Social Develt Cttee, 1999–, Mem., Centre Cttee, 2000–, NI Assembly. *Address:* c/o House of Commons, SW1A 0AA; c/o Northern Ireland Assembly, Stormont Castle, Belfast BT4 3ST.

GILES, Ann, (Mrs Keith Giles); *see* Howard, A.

GILES, Bill; *see* Giles, W. G.

GILES, Frank Thomas Robertson; Editor, The Sunday Times, 1981–83 (Deputy Editor, 1967–81); *b* 31 July 1919; *s* of late Col F. L. N. Giles, DSO, OBE, and Mrs Giles; *m* 1946, Lady Katharine Pamela Sackville, *o d* of 9th Earl De La Warr and Countess De La Warr; one *s* two *d*. *Educ:* Wellington Coll.; Brasenose Coll., Oxford (Open Scholarship in History; MA 1946). ADC to Governor of Bermuda, 1939–42; Directorate of Mil. Ops, WO, 1942–45; temp. mem. of HM Foreign Service, 1945–46 (Private Sec. to Ernest Bevin; Mem. of Sir Archibald Clark Kerr's mission to Java); joined editorial staff of The Times, 1946; Asst Correspondent, Paris, 1947; Chief Corresp., Rome, 1950–53, Paris, 1953–60; Foreign Editor, Sunday Times, 1961–77; Dir, Times Newspapers Ltd, 1981–85. Lectures: tours, USA, 1975, FRG, 1984; Gritti, Venice, 1985. Chm., Library Cttee, Britain-Russia Centre, 1993–99. Chm., Painshill Park Trust, 1985–96; Mem., Governing Body, British Inst. of Florence, 1986–; Governor: Wellington Coll., 1965–89; Sevenoaks Sch., 1967–92. *Publications:* A Prince of Journalists: the life and times of de Blowitz, 1962; Sundry Times (autobiog.), 1986; The Locust Years: the story of the Fourth French Republic 1946–1958, 1991 (Franco-British Soc. award); (ed) Corfu, the Garden Isle, 1994; Napoleon Bonaparte, England's Prisoner, 2001. *Recreations:* going to the opera; collecting, talking about, consuming the vintage wines of Bordeaux and Burgundy. *Address:* 42 Blomfield Road, W9 2PF; Bunns Cottage, Lye Green, Crowborough, East Sussex TN6 1UY. *Clubs:* Brooks's, Beefsteak.

GILES, Rear-Adm. Sir Morgan Charles M.; *see* Morgan-Giles.

GILES, Air Comdt Dame Pauline; *see* Parsons, Air Comdt Dame P.

GILES, Robert Frederick; Senior Clerk, House of Commons, 1979–83; *b* 27 Dec. 1918; *s* of Robert and Edith Giles; *m* 1948, Mabel Florence Gentry; two *d*. *Educ:* Drayton Manor Sch., Hanwell. Min. of Agriculture, 1936–39. Royal Navy, 1939–45: CO, HMS Tango, 1942–44. Various assignments, MAF, from 1945; Regional Controller, Northern Region MAFF, 1963–68; Head, Food Standards/Food Science Div., 1968–74; Under Sec., MAFF, 1975–78; Food Standards and Food Subsidies Gp, 1975; Food Feedingstuffs and Fertilizer Standards Gp, 1977. *Recreations:* walking, theatre. *Address:* 8 The Ridings, Copthill Lane, Kingswood, Surrey KT20 6HJ. *Club:* Civil Service.

GILES, Roy Curtis, MA; Administrative Consultant, Busoga Trust, since 1991; Head Master, Highgate School, 1974–89; *b* 6 Dec. 1932; *s* of Herbert Henry Giles and Dorothy Alexandra Potter; *m* 1963, Christine von Alten; two *s* one *d*. *Educ:* Queen Elizabeth's Sch., Barnet; Jesus Coll., Cambridge (Open Scholar). Asst Master, Dean Close Sch., 1956–60; Lektor, Hamburg Univ., 1960–63; Asst Master, Eton Coll., 1963–74, Head of Modern Languages, 1970–74. Educnl Selector, ABM (formerly ACCM), 1979–92; Mem., House of Bishops' Panel on Marriage Educn, 1983–89. Mem., Council of Management, Vernon Educnl Trust (formerly Davies's Educn Services), 1975–; Governor: The Hall, Hampstead, 1976–89; Channing Sch., 1977–89. *Recreations:* music, theatre, Central Europe. *Address:* Chattan Court, Woodbury Lane, Axminster, Devon EX13 5TL. *T:* (01297) 33720.

GILES, William George, (Bill Giles), OBE 1995; Consultant Broadcast Meteorologist, BBC Weather Centre, since 2000; *b* 18 Nov. 1939; *s* of Albert William George Giles and Florence Ellen Christina Giles; *m* 1st, 1961, Eileen Myrtle Lake (marr. diss. 1991); one *s* one *d*; 2nd, 1993, Patricia Maureen Stafford. *Educ:* Queen Elizabeth's Sch., Crediton; Bristol Coll. of Sci. and Tech.; Meteorological Office Coll. Meteorological Office, 1959; radio broadcaster, 1972; television broadcaster, 1975; Head, BBC Weather Centre, 1983–2000. Prix des Scientifiques, Fest. Internat. de Meteo, Paris, 1994. *Publications:* Weather Observations, 1978; The Story of Weather, 1990. *Recreations:* gardening, golf, One Man Weather Show. *Address:* 73 Lower Icknield Way, Chinnor, Oxon OX9 4EA.

GILHOOLY, John Francis; Chief Executive, Office of the Parliamentary Counsel, since 2000; *b* 26 April 1945; *s* of Francis Gilhooly and Sarah Gilhooly (*née* Gavigan); *m* 1971, Gillian Marie (*née* Cunningham); two *s* two *d*. *Educ:* Clapham Coll. Grammar Sch. (RC); King's Coll., Cambridge (BA Econ 1970). Clerical Officer, then Exec. Officer, ODM, 1965–70; Econ. Asst, then Sen. Econ. Asst, ODA, 1970–74; Econ. Adviser, Royal Commn on the Distribution of Income and Wealth, 1974–78; HM Treasury: Econ. Adviser, then Principal, 1978–84; Asst Sec. Pay Policy, Tax Policy, Gen. Expenditure Policy, Training Review, 1984–92; Asst Dir (on loan), Capital Allowances Policy, Tax Law Rewrite, Inland Revenue, 1992–96; Mgt Advr, Office of Parly Counsel, 1996–99. *Recreations:* reading, walking, family, friends. *Address:* Office of the Parliamentary Counsel, 36 Whitehall, SW1A 2AY. *T:* (020) 7210 6605. *Clubs:* Civil Service; St Andrews' Ramblers.

GILL, Hon. Lord; Brian Gill; a Senator of the College of Justice in Scotland, since 1994; Chairman, Scottish Law Commission, since 1996; *b* 25 Feb. 1942; *s* of Thomas and Mary Gill, Glasgow; *m* 1969, Catherine Fox; five *s* one *d*. *Educ:* St Aloysius' Coll., Glasgow; Glasgow Univ. (MA 1962, LLB 1964); Edinburgh Univ. (PhD 1975). Asst Lectr, 1964–65, Lectr, 1965–69 and 1972–77, Faculty of Law, Edinburgh Univ.; Advocate, 1967; Advocate Depute, 1977–79; Standing Junior Counsel: Foreign and Commonwealth Office (Scotland), 1974–77; Home Office (Scotland), 1979–81; Scottish Education Dept, 1979–81; QC (Scot.) 1981; Chm., Industrial Tribunals, 1981–88. Called to the Bar, Lincoln's Inn, 1991. Keeper of the Advocates' Library, 1987–94; Trustee, Nat. Liby of Scotland, 1987–94. Chm., Cttee of Investigation for Scotland (Agricl Marketing), 1985–94 (Mem., Cttees for GB and for England and Wales); Dep. Chm., Copyright Tribunal, 1989–94; Member: Scottish Legal Aid Bd, 1987–90; Scottish Valuation Adv. Council, 1989–94. Chm, RSAMD, 1999–. Hon. LLD Glasgow, 1998. *Publications:* The Law of Agricultural Holdings in Scotland, 1982, 3rd edn 1997; (ed) Scottish Planning Encyclopedia, 1996; articles in legal jls. *Recreation:* church music. *Address:* 13 Lauder Road, Edinburgh EH9 2EN. *T:* (0131) 667 1888. *Clubs:* Reform, MCC.

GILL, Adrian Anthony; journalist, Restaurant Critic, Television Critic and features writer, Sunday Times; *b* 28 June 1954; *s* of George Michael Gill and Yvonne Gilan Gill; *m* 1st, 1983, Cressida Connoly; 2nd, 1991, Amber Rudd; one *s* one *d*. *Educ:* St Christopher Sch., Letchworth; St Martin's Sch. of Art; Slade Sch. of Fine Art. Sometime illustrator, muralist, graphic designer, portrait painter, artist material salesman, warehouseman, gents' outfitter, pizza chef, waiter, painter and decorator, gardener, pornography salesman, maitre d', film lectr, moonshine runner, nanny, sugar cane cutter, theatrical scene shifter, drawing master, plongeur, barman, male model, cookery teacher, writer and journalist. *Publications:* Sap Rising, 1996; The Ivy: the restaurant and its recipes, 1997; Starcrossed (fiction), 1999. *Recreation:* journalism. *Address:* c/o Sunday Times, 1 Pennington Street, E1 9XN. *Clubs:* Chelsea Arts, Gerry's.

GILL, Sir Anthony (Keith), Kt 1991; FREng; Chairman, Docklands Light Railway, 1994–99; *b* 1 April 1930; *s* of Frederick William and Ellen Gill; *m* 1953, Phyllis Cook; one *s* two *d*. *Educ:* High Sch., Colchester; Imperial Coll., London (BScEng Hons). National Service officer, REME, 1954–56. Joined Bryce Berger Ltd, 1956, subseq. Director and Gen. Manager until 1972; Lucas CAV Ltd, 1972, subseq. Director and Gen. Manager until 1978; Divisional Managing Director, Joseph Lucas Ltd, 1978; Lucas Industries: Jt Gp Man. Dir, 1980–83; Gp Man. Dir, 1984–87 and Dep. Chm., 1986–87; Chm. and Chief Exec., 1987–94. Non-executive Director: Post Office Bd, 1989–91; National Power, 1990–98; Tarmac, 1992–2000. Chm., Teaching Co. Scheme Bd, 1991–96; Member: Adv. Council on Science and Technology (formerly Adv. Council for Applied R&D), 1985–91; DTI Technology Requirements Bd, 1986–88; Engineering Council, 1988–96 (Dep. Chm., 1994–95); Nat. Trng Task Force, 1991–93. Pres., IProdE, 1986–87; Mem., Council, IMechE, 1986–92; Vice-Pres., Inst. of Management, 1993 (Chm. Council, 1996–99; Pres., 1998–99). Member Court: Univ. of Warwick, 1986–94; Cranfield Univ. (formerly Inst of Technology), 1991– (Pro-Chancellor, 1991–2001). FREng (FEng 1983); FCGI 1979; Fellow, City of Birmingham Polytechnic, 1989. Hon. FIEE. Hon. DEng Birmingham, 1990; Hon. DSc: Cranfield, 1991; Southampton, 1992; Warwick, 1992; Hon. DTech Coventry, 1992; DUniv Sheffield Hallam, 1993. *Recreations:* boating, music. *Address:* The Point House, Astra Court, Hythe Marina Village, Hythe, Southampton SO45 6DZ. *T:* (023) 8084 0165, *Fax:* (023) 8084 0175. *Clubs:* Royal Thames Yacht; Royal Southampton Yacht.

GILL, Arthur Benjamin Norman, (Ben), CBE 1996; President: National Farmers' Union, since 1998 (Deputy President, 1992–98); Confederation of European Agriculture, since 2000; *b* 1 Jan. 1950; *o s* of William Norman Gill and Annie (Nancy) Gill (*née* Almack); *m* 1973, Carolyn Davis; four *s*. *Educ:* Easingwold Primary Sch.; Barnard Castle Sch.; St John's Coll., Cambridge (MA Agric. 1971). Various posts at Namasagali Coll., Jinja, Uganda, 1972–75; i/c pig unit, Holderness, Humberside, 1975–77; running family farm, Vale of York, 1978–. National Farmers' Union: Mem. Council, 1985–; Vice-Chm., 1986–87, Chm., 1987–91, Livestock and Wool Cttee; Vice-Pres., 1991–92. Member:

AFRC, 1991–94; BBSRC, 1994–97 (Chm., Agricl Systems Directorate, 1994–97); Mem. Panel, Agric., Natural Resources and Envmt, 1994–95, Agric., Horticulture and Forestry, 1995–99, Technology Foresight, OST. Chm., Alternative Crops Technology Interactive Network, 1995–. Dir, FARM Africa, 1991–98. Mem. Council, Food from Britain, 1999–; Vice-Pres., COPA, 1999–. Vis. Prof., Leeds Univ., 1996–. Patron, Rural Stress Inf. Network, 2000. Hon. DSc: Leeds, 1997; Cranfield, 2000. *Recreation:* rowing (Founder Mem., Guy Fawkes Boat Club, York). *Address:* Agriculture House, 164 Shaftesbury Avenue, WC2H 8HL. *T:* (020) 7331 7204, *Fax:* (020) 7331 7348; Home Farm, Hawkhills, Easingwold, York YO61 3EG. *Clubs:* Farmers'; Yorkshire Agricultural Adventurers (York).

GILL, Brian; *see* Gill, Hon. Lord.

GILL, Christopher John Fred, RD 1971; butcher and farmer; Chairman, Freedom Association Ltd, since 2001; *b* 28 Oct. 1936; *m* 1960, Patricia M. (*née* Greenway); one *s* two *d*. *Educ:* Shrewsbury School. Chm., F. A. Gill Ltd, 1968–. Councillor, Wolverhampton BC, 1965–72. MP (C) Ludlow, 1987–2001. Member: Agriculture Select Cttee, 1989–95; Welsh Affairs Select Cttee, 1996–97. Vice Chairman: Cons. European Affairs Cttee, 1989–91 (Sec., 1988–89); Cons. Agric. Cttee, 1991–94 (Sec., 1990–91); Pres., Midlands W European Cons. Council, 1984–85. Member: Exec., 1922 Cttee, 1997–99; Council of Europe, 1997–99. *Address:* Billingsley Hall Farm, Bridgnorth, Shropshire WV16 6PJ.

GILL, (George) Malcolm, FCIB; Head, Banking Department, Bank for International Settlements, 1995–99 (Deputy Head, 1991–95); *b* 23 May 1934; *s* of late Thomas Woodman Gill and Alice Muriel Gill (*née* Le Grice); *m* 1966, Monica Kennedy Brooks; one *s* one *d*. *Educ:* Cambridgeshire High Sch.; Sidney Sussex Coll., Cambridge (MA). Entered Bank of England, 1957: seconded to UK Treasury Delegation, Washington DC, 1966–68; Private Sec. to Governor, 1970–72; Asst Chief Cashier, 1975; seconded to HM Treasury, 1977–80; Chief Manager, Banking and Credit Markets, 1980–82; Head of Foreign Exchange Div., 1982–88; Asst Dir, 1987–88; Chief of the Banking Dept and Chief Cashier, 1988–91. *Recreations:* reading, travel, music. *Address:* 3 Scotscraig, Radlett, Herts WD7 8LH.

GILL, Air Vice-Marshal Harry, CB 1979; OBE 1968; Director-General of Supply, Royal Air Force, 1976–79; *b* 30 Oct. 1922; *s* of John William Gill and Lucy Gill, Newark, Notts; *m* 1951, Diana Patricia, *d* of Colin Wood, Glossop; one *d*. *Educ:* Barnby Road Sch.; Newark Technical Coll. Entered RAF, 1941; pilot trng, 1942; commnd 1943; flying duties, 1943–49; transf. to Equipment Br., 1949; Officer Commanding: Supply Sqdns, RAF Spitalgate and RAF North Coates, 1949–52; HQ Staff No 93 Maintenance Unit Explosives and Fuels Supply Ops, 1952–55; Explosives and Fuels Sch., 1955–58; Staff Officer Logistics Div., HQ Allied Forces Northern Europe, 1958–61; Head of Provision Br., Air Min., 1961–64; Chief Equipment Officer, No 25 Maintenance Unit, RAF Hartlebury, 1964–66; Equipment Staff Officer, HQ Air Forces Middle East, 1966–67; Dep. Dir Supply Systems, MoD Air, 1968–70; RCDS, 1971; Comdt, RAF Supply Control Centre, 1972–73; Dir, Supply Management, MoD Air, 1973–76. Internat. rifle and pistol shot; Silver Medallist, King's Prize, Bisley, 1951. *Recreations:* shooting, fishing, tennis, cricket, gardening. *Address:* c/o Lloyds TSB, 37 Castlegate, Newark, Notts NG24 1BD. *Club:* Royal Air Force.

GILL, Maj.-Gen. Ian Gordon, CB 1972; OBE 1959 (MBE 1949); MC 1940, Bar 1945; idc, psc; Colonel, 4/7 Royal Dragoon Guards, 1973–78; *b* Rochester, 9 Nov. 1919; *s* of late Brig. Gordon Harry Gill, CMG, DSO and Mrs Doris Gill, Rochester, Kent; *m* 1963, Elizabeth Vivian Rohr, MD, MRCP (*d* 1990), *o d* of late A. F. Rohr; no *c*. *Educ:* Edinburgh House, Hants; Repton School. Commnd from SRO into 4th/7th Roy. Dragoon Guards, 1938; served with Regt in: BEF, France, 1939–40; BLA, NW Europe, 1944–45 (despatches, 1945); Palestine, 1946–48; Tripolitania, 1951–52; Instructor, Armoured Sch., 1948–50; Staff Coll., Camberley, 1952; Bde Maj., HQ Inf. Bde, 1953–55; comdg 4th/7th RDG, 1957–59; Asst Mil. Sec., HQ, BAOR, 1959–61; Coll. Comdt RMA Sandhurst, 1961–62; Imp. Def. Coll., 1963; Comdr, 7th Armoured Bde, 1964–66; Dep. Mil. Sec. 1, MoD (Army), 1966–68; Head, British Defence Liaison Staff, Dept of Defence, Canberra, 1968–70; Asst Chief of Gen. Staff (Op. Requirements), 1970–72, retired. Hon. Liveryman, Coachmakers' Co., 1974. *Recreations:* equitation, ski-ing, cricket, squash rackets. *Address:* Cheriton House, Thorney, Peterborough PE6 0QD. *Clubs:* Cavalry and Guards, MCC.

GILL, Jack, CB 1984; Chief Executive (formerly Secretary), Export Credits Guarantee Department, 1983–87; Executive Director(part-time), Government Relations, BICC plc, 1987–91; *b* 20 Feb. 1930; *s* of Jack and Elizabeth Gill; *m* 1954, Alma Dorothy; three *d*. *Educ:* Bolton Sch. Export Credits Guarantee Department: Clerical Officer, 1946; Principal, 1962; Asst Sec., 1970; Asst Sec., DTI, 1972–75; Export Credits Guarantee Department: Under Sec., 1975–79; Principal Finance Officer, 1978–79; Sec., Monopolies and Mergers Commn, 1979–81; Dep. Sec., and Dir of Industrial Develt Unit, DoI, 1981–83. Mem., BOTB, 1981–87. Consultant: NEI Power Projects Ltd, 1987–90; British Aerospace plc, 1987–89; CBI Council, 1988–91 (Chm., Public Procurement Contact Gp, 1990–91; Mem., Overseas Cttee, 1990–91). National Service, REME, 1948–50. *Recreations:* music (Bass, St Paul's Cath. Sunday Evening and Special Service Choirs, 1951–60), chess; occasional crossword setter for The Listener. *Address:* 9 Ridley Road, Warlingham, Surrey CR6 9LR. *T:* (01883) 622688.

GILL, (James) Kenneth; President, Saatchi and Saatchi Company PLC, 1985–94; *b* 27 Sept. 1920; *s* of late Alfred Charles and Isabel Gill; *m* 1948, Anne Bridgewater; one *s*. *Educ:* Highgate Sch. Served RAC, 24th Lancers and Intelligence Corps, GSO II, 1939–45. Copywriter, S. T. Garland Advertising Service, 1938–39; Chm., Garland-Compton Ltd, 1970–76; Saatchi and Saatchi Company: Chm., 1976–85; Pres. and Dir, 1985–89. FIPA. *Recreations:* the theatre, the cinema, cricket. *Address:* Davenport House, Duntisbourne Abbots, Cirencester, Glos GL7 7JN. *T:* (01285) 821468.

GILL, Kenneth; General Secretary, Manufacturing, Science, Finance, 1989–92 (Joint General Secretary, 1988–89); Chairman, Morning Star, 1984–95; *b* 30 Aug. 1927; *s* of Ernest Frank Gill and Mary Ethel Gill; *m* 1st, 1953, Jacqueline Manley; 2nd 1967, S. A. Paterson (marr. diss. 1990); two *s* one *d*; 3rd, 1997, Norma Bramley. *Educ:* Chippenham Secondary School. Engrg apprentice, 1943–48; Draughtsman Designer, Project Engr, Sales Engr in various cos, 1948–62; District Organiser, Liverpool and Ireland TASS, 1962–68; Editor, TASS Union Jl, 1968–72; Dep. Gen. Sec., 1972–74; Gen. Sec. AUEW (TASS), 1974–86, TASS—the Manufacturing Union, 1986–88. Pres., CSEU, 1988–89. Mem., Gen. Council, TUC, 1974–92 (Chm., 1985–86); Pres. of TUC, 1985–86. Mem., Commn for Racial Equality, 1981–87. Chm., Cuba Solidarity Campaign, 1992–. *Recreations:* sketching, political caricaturing. *Address:* 164 Ramsden Road, Balham, SW12 8RE. *T:* (020) 8265 3022.

GILL, Rt Rev. Kenneth Edward; Assistant Bishop of Newcastle (full time), 1980–98; *b* 22 May 1932; *s* of Fred and Elsie Gill; *m* 1957, Edna Hammond; one *s* two *d*. *Educ:* Harrogate Grammar School; Hartley Victoria Coll., Manchester. Presbyter in Church of South India, Mysore Diocese, 1958–72; Bishop of Karnataka Central Diocese, Church of South India, 1972–80. *Publications:* Meditations on the Holy Spirit, 1979; Count us Equal, 1990. *Recreation:* gardening. *Address:* 54 Merley Gate, Morpeth, Northumberland NE61 2EP. *T:* (01670) 510194, *Fax:* (01670) 518357.

GILL, Air Vice-Marshal Leonard William George, DSO 1945; Consultant in personnel planning, since 1973; Director, Merton Associates since 1979 (Chairman, 1984–94); Consultant, Randle Cooke & Associates, since 1994; Senior Consultant, MSL (formerly Austin Knight Ltd), since 1997; Managing Director, Windsor Personnel Consultants, since 1999; *b* 31 March 1918; *s* of L. W. Gill, Hornchurch, Essex, and Marguerite Gill; *m* 1st, 1943, Joan Favill Appleyard (marr. diss.); two *s* two *d*; 2nd, Mrs Constance Mary Cull. *Educ:* University Coll. Sch., London. Joined RAF, 1937; served in Far East until 1942; then UK as night fighter pilot; comd No 68 Sqdn for last 6 months of war; subseq. served in various appts incl. comd of Nos 85 and 87 night fighter Sqdns and tour on directing staff at RAF Staff Coll.; Stn Comdr No 1 Flying Trng Sch., Linton-on-Ouse, 1957–60; Dir of Overseas Ops, 1960–62; Nat. Def. Coll. of Canada, 1962–63; Dir of Organisation (Estabs), 1963–66; SASO, RAF Germany, 1966–68; Dir-Gen., Manning (RAF), MoD, 1968–73, retired. Manpower and Planning Advr, P&O Steam Navigation Co., 1973–79. Vice-Pres., RAF Assoc., 1973– (Pres. E Area, 1974–81; Vice-Chm., Central Council, 1984–88). Chm., River Thames Soc., 1994–. FIPD; FIMgt. Order of King George of Bohemia (Czech and Slovak Republic), 1991. *Recreations:* shooting, cricket, boats, amateur woodwork. *Address:* Flat 15, 35 Cranley Gardens, Kensington, SW7 3BD. *T:* (020) 7370 2716. *Clubs:* Royal Air Force; Phyllis Court (Henley).

GILL, Malcolm; *see* Gill, G. M.

GILL, Neena; Member (Lab), West Midlands Region, England, European Parliament, since July 1999; *b* 24 Dec. 1956; *d* of late Jasmer S. Gill and of Birjinder K. Gill; *m* 1992, Dr John Towner; one *s*. *Educ:* Watford High Sch.; Liverpool Poly. (Dep. Pres., Students' Union, 1979–80); London Business Sch. (BA Hons). Admin. Officer, Ealing LBC, 1981–83; Principal Housing Officer, UK Housing Trust, 1983–86; Chief Executive: ASRA Greater London Housing Assoc., 1986–90; New London Housing Gp, 1990–99. Former Director: Dalston City Partnership; Hackney Housing Partnership; former Mem., Macintyre Housing Assoc. Member: MSF; AEEU. FRSA; CIOH. *Recreations:* hill walking, football, antiques, minor bird watching, cinema, opera. *Address:* (office) 67 Birmingham Road, West Bromwich B70 6PY. *T:* (0121) 553 6642, *Fax:* (0121) 553 6603.

GILL, Peter, OBE 1980; FWCMD; dramatic author; Associate Director, Royal National Theatre, 1989–97; *b* Cardiff, 7 Sept. 1939; *s* of George John Gill and Margaret Mary Browne. *Educ:* St Illtyd's Coll., Cardiff. FWCMD 1992. Associate Dir, Royal Court Theatre, 1970–72; Dir, 1976–80, Associate Dir, 1980, Riverside Studios, Hammersmith; Dir, Royal Nat. Theatre Studio, 1984–90. Productions include: Royal Court: A Collier's Friday Night, 1965; The Local Stigmatic, A Provincial Life, 1966; A Soldier's Fortune, The Daughter-in-law, Crimes of Passion, 1967; The Widowing of Mrs Holroyd, 1968; Life Price, Over Gardens Out, The Sleepers' Den, 1969; The Duchess of Malfi, 1971; Crete & Sergeant Pepper, 1972; The Merry-go-round, 1973; Small Change, The Fool, 1976; Riverside Studios: As You Like It, 1976; Small Change, 1977; The Cherry Orchard (own version), The Changeling, 1978; Measure for Measure, 1979; Julius Caesar, 1980; Scrape off the Black, 1980; Royal National Theatre: A Month in the Country, Don Juan, Scrape off the Black, Much Ado about Nothing, 1981; Danton's Death, Major Barbara, 1982; Kick for Touch, Tales from Hollywood, Antigone (co-dir), 1983; Venice Preserv'd, Fool for Love (transf. Lyric), 1984; The Murderers, As I Lay Dying (also adapted), A Twist of Lemon, In the Blue, Bouncing, Up for None, The Garden of England (co-dir), 1985; Mean Tears, 1987; Mrs Klein, 1988 (transf. Apollo, 1989); Juno and the Paycock, 1989; Cardiff East (also wrote), 1997; Friendly Fire, 1999; Luther, 2001; other London theatres: O'Flaherty VC, Mermaid, 1966; The Way of the World, Lyric, Hammersmith, 1992; New England, Barbican Pit, 1994; Uncle Vanya, Tricycle, 1995; A Patriot for Me, Barbican, 1995; Tongue of a Bird, Almeida, 1997; Certain Young Men, Almeida, 1999; Speed the Plow, New Ambassadors, 2000; has also produced plays by Shakespeare and modern writers at Stratford-upon-Avon, Nottingham, Edinburgh and in Canada, Germany, Switzerland and USA; Music Theatre and Opera includes: Down By the Green Wood Side (co-dir), Bow Down (co-dir), Queen Elizabeth Hall, 1987; Marriage of Figaro, Opera North, 1987; Television productions include: Grace, 1972; Girl, 1973; A Matter of Taste, Fugitive, 1974; Hitting Town, 1976. *Publications:* plays: The Sleepers' Den, 1965; Over Gardens Out, 1969; Small Change, 1976; Small Change, Kick for Touch, 1985; In the Blue, Mean Tears, 1987; Cherry Orchard, 1996; The Look Across the Eyes, 1997; Cardiff East, 1997; Certain Young Men, 1999; The Seagull, 2000. *Address:* c/o Casarotto Co. Ltd, 60–66 Wardour Street, W1V 3HP.

GILL, Robin Denys, CVO 1993; Founder Trustee, and Chairman of Executive, Royal Anniversary Trust, since 1990; Chairman of Executive, The Queen's Anniversary Awards for Higher and Further Education, since 1993; *b* 7 Oct. 1927; *s* of Thomas Henry Gill and Marjorie Mary (*née* Butler); *m* 1st, 1951, Mary Hope Alexander (*d* 1986); three *s*; 2nd, 1991, Denise Spencer Waterhouse. *Educ:* Dulwich Coll.; Brasenose Coll., Oxford (MA). Unilever plc, 1949–54; British Internat. Paper Ltd, 1954–59; Founder and Man. Dir, Border TV Ltd, 1960–64; Man. Dir, ATV Corp. Ltd, 1964–69; Chairman: ITN, 1968–69; 1970 Trust Ltd, 1970–93; Ansvar Insce Co. Ltd, 1975–; Standard Ind. Trust Ltd, 1970–81; Baring Communications Equity Ltd, 1993–; various internat. venture capital funds; Director: Reed Paper Gp Ltd, 1970–75; Hewlett Packard Ltd, 1975–92; Yarrow Plc, 1979–88; Baring Hambrecht Alpine Ltd, 1986–98; SD-Scicon plc, 1988–90. Member: Nat. Adv. Bd for Higher Educn; Oxford Univ. Appts Cttee; Vis. Cttee, RCA; Cttee, Royal Family Film, 1968–70. Pres., Brasenose Soc., 1995–96. *Recreations:* golf, sport, travel, art collecting, new projects. *Address:* PO Box 1, East Horsley, Surrey KT24 6RE. *T:* (01483) 285290. *Clubs:* Vincent's (Oxford); St George's Hill Golf; Free Foresters Cricket.

GILL, Rev. Prof. Robin Morton, PhD; Michael Ramsey Professor of Modern Theology, University of Kent at Canterbury, since 1992; *b* 18 July 1944; *s* of Alan Morton Gill and Mary Grace (*née* Hammond); *m* 1967, Jennifer Margaret Sheppard; one *s* one *d*. *Educ:* Westminster Sch.; King's Coll., London (BD 1966; PhD 1969); Birmingham Univ. (MSocSc 1972). Deacon, 1968; priest, 1969; Curate, Rugby St Andrews, 1968–71; Lectr, Newton Theol Coll., PNG, 1971–72; Edinburgh University: Lectr in Christian Ethics, 1972–86; Associate Dean, Faculty of Theol., 1985–88; Sen. Lectr, 1986–88; William Leech Res. Prof. in Applied Theol., Newcastle Univ., 1988–92. Priest-in-charge: St Philip, Edinburgh, 1972–75; Ford with Etal, Northumberland, 1975–87; St Mary, Coldstream, 1987–92; Hon. Canon, Canterbury Cathedral, 1992–. *Publications:* The Social Context of Theology, 1975; Theology and Social Structure, 1977; Faith in Christ, 1978; Prophecy and Praxis, 1981; The Cross Against the Bomb, 1984; A Textbook of Christian Ethics, 1985, 2nd edn 1995; Theology and Sociology, 1987, 2nd edn 1995; Beyond Decline, 1988; Competing Convictions, 1989; Christian Ethics in Secular Worlds, 1991; Gifts of Love, 1991; Moral Communities, 1992; The Myth of the Empty

Church, 1993; A Vision for Growth, 1994; Readings in Modern Theology, 1995; (with Lorna Kendall) Michael Ramsey as Theologian, 1995; (with Derek Burke) Strategic Church Leadership, 1996; Moral Leadership in a Postmodern Age, 1997; Euthanasia and the Churches, 1998; Churchgoing and Christian Ethics, 1999; The Cambridge Companion to Christian Ethics, 2000. *Recreations:* running churches, playing the trumpet. *Address:* Cornwallis Buildings, The University, Canterbury, Kent CT2 7NF. *T:* (01227) 764000.

GILL, His Honour Stanley Sanderson; a Circuit Judge, 1972–87; *b* Wakefield, 3 Dec. 1923; *s* of Sanderson Henry Briggs Gill, OBE and Dorothy Margaret Gill (*née* Bennett); *m* 1954, Margaret Mary Patricia Grady; one *s* two *d. Educ:* Queen Elizabeth Grammar Sch., Wakefield; Magdalene Coll., Cambridge (MA). Served in RAF, 1942–46: 514 and 7 (Pathfinder) Sqdns, Flt Lt 1945. Called to the Bar, Middle Temple, 1950; Asst Recorder of Bradford, 1966; Dep. Chm., WR Yorks QS, 1968; County Court Judge, 1971. Mem., County Court Rule Cttee, 1980–84. Chm., Rent Assessment Cttee, 1966–71. *Recreations:* walking, reading, painting. *Address:* c/o Newcastle Crown Court, Newcastle upon Tyne NE1 3LA.

GILLAM, Sir Patrick (John), Kt 1998; Chairman, Standard Chartered PLC, since 1993 (Director, since 1988); *b* 15 April 1933; *s* of late Cyril B. Gillam and Mary J. Gillam; *m* 1963, Diana Echlin; one *s* one *d. Educ:* London School of Economics (BA Hons History; Hon. Fellow, 1999). Foreign Office, 1956–57; British Petroleum Co. Ltd, 1957–91; Vice-Pres., BP North America Inc., 1971–74; General Manager, Supply Dept, 1974–78; Dir, BP International Ltd (formerly BP Trading Ltd), 1978–82; Man. Dir, BP, 1981–91; Chairman: BP Shipping Ltd, 1987–88; BP Minerals Internat. Ltd/Selection Trust Ltd, 1982–89; BP Coal Ltd, 1986–88; BP Coal Inc., 1988–90; BP America Inc., 1989–91; BP Nutrition, 1989–91; BP Oil International, 1990–91; Dep. Chm., Standard Chartered PLC, 1991–93. Chairman: Booker Tate Ltd, 1991–93; Asda Gp, 1991–96; Royal & Sun Alliance Insurance Gp, 1997–. Chm., ICC UK, 1989–98; Mem. Exec. Bd, ICC Worldwide, 1991–98; Dir, Commercial Union, 1991–96. Mem., Court of Governors, LSE, 1989–; Trustee, Queen Elizabeth's Foundn for Disabled Develt Trust, 1984–. *Recreation:* gardening. *Address:* Standard Chartered PLC, 1 Aldermanbury Square, EC2V 7SB. *T:* (020) 7280 7500.

GILLAM, Stanley George, MA, MLitt; Librarian, The London Library, 1956–80; *b* 11 Aug. 1915; *s* of Harry Cosier Gillam, Oxford; *m* 1950, Pauline, *d* of Henry G. Bennett, Oxford; one *s. Educ:* Southfield Sch.; Saint Catherine's Coll., Oxford. Bodleian Library, Oxford, 1931–40 and 1946–54. Oxfordshire and Bucks Light Infantry (1st Bucks Bn), 1940–46. Asst Sec. and Sub-Librarian, The London Library, 1954–56. *Publications:* The Building Accounts of the Radcliffe Camera, 1958; The Divinity School and Duke Humfrey's Library at Oxford, 1988; The Radcliffe Camera, 1992; articles in The Bodleian Library Record and other periodicals. *Address:* Flat 5, Randolph House, 1 Hernes Road, Oxford OX2 7PT. *T:* (01865) 557827.

GILLAN, Cheryl Elise Kendall, (Mrs J. C. Leeming); MP (C) Chesham and Amersham, since 1992; *b* 21 April 1952; *d* of Major Adam Mitchell Gillan and Mona Elsie Gillan (*née* Freeman); *m* 1985, John Coates Leeming, *qv. Educ:* Cheltenham Ladies' Coll.; Coll. of Law. FCIM DipM. International Management Group, 1976–84; British Film Year, 1984–86; Ernst & Young, 1986–91; Dir, Kidsons Impey, 1991–93. PPS to Lord Privy Seal, 1994–95; Party Under-Sec. of State, DFEE, 1995–97; Opposition frontbench spokesman: on trade and industry, 1997–98; on foreign and commonwealth affairs and overseas develt, 1998–2001. Chm., Bow Group, 1987. Freeman, City of London, 1991; Liveryman, Marketors' Co., 1991. *Recreations:* golf, music, gardening, animals. *Address:* House of Commons, SW1A 0AA. *T:* (020) 7219 3000. *Club:* Royal Automobile.

GILLANDERS, Prof. Lewis Alexander; Clinical Professor in Radiology, University of Aberdeen, and Consultant in Charge, Radiology Services (Grampian Health Board), 1964–88, now Professor Emeritus in Radiology; *b* 7 Feb. 1925; *s* of Kenneth John Alexander Gillanders and Nellie May Sherris; *m* 1960, Nora Ellen Wild, MB, ChB; one *s* one *d. Educ:* Dingwall Academy; Univ. of Glasgow (graduated in medicine, 1947). Commissioned, RAMC, 1948–50; general medical practice, Scottish Highlands, 1950–52; trained in Diagnostic Radiology, Glasgow Royal Infirmary and United Birmingham Hosps, 1953–58; Consultant Radiologist, Aberdeen Teaching Hosps, 1958. Examiner in Radiology for: RCR, 1969–79, and DMRD, Univ. of Aberdeen, 1969–89; Faculty of Radiologists, RCSI, 1975–77; Univ. of Nairobi, 1978–80; Univ. of Wales, 1981–83. Member, GMC, 1979–84; Vice-Pres., RCR, 1981–83. *Publications:* chapter in Pye's Surgical Handicraft (1st edn 1884), 19th edn 1969, 20th edn 1977; papers in general medical and radiological literature, students' magazines, etc. *Recreations:* derivations and meanings; golf, do-it-yourself. *Address:* 17 Denhead, Kirk Brae, Cults, Aberdeen AB15 9QT.

GILLEN, Hon. Sir John, Kt 1999; **Hon. Mr Justice Gillen;** a Judge of the High Court of Justice, Northern Ireland, since 1999; *b* 18 Nov. 1947; *s* of John Gillen and Susan Letitia Gillen; *m* 1976, Claire; two *d. Educ:* Methodist Coll., Belfast; Queen's Coll., Oxford (BA 1969; BL). Called to the Bar, Gray's Inn, 1970; Barrister, 1970–83; QC (NI), 1983–99. *Recreations:* reading, music, sports. *Address:* Royal Courts of Justice, Chichester Street, Belfast BT1 3JF. *T:* (028) 9023 5111.

GILLES, Prof. Dennis Cyril; Professor of Computing Science, University of Glasgow, 1966–90; *b* 7 April 1925; *s* of George Cyril Gilles and Gladys Alice Gilles (*née* Batchelor); *m* 1955, Valerie Mary Gardiner; two *s* two *d. Educ:* Sidcup Gram. Sch.; Imperial Coll., University of London. Demonstrator, Asst Lectr, Imperial Coll., 1945–47; Asst Lectr, University of Liverpool, 1947–49; Mathematician, Scientific Computing Service, 1949–55; Research Asst, University of Manchester, 1955–57; Dir of Computing Lab., University of Glasgow, 1957–66. *Publications:* contribs to Proc. Royal Society and other scientific jls. *Address:* Ardbeg House, Kilmun, Dunoon, Argyll PA23 8SE. *T:* (01369) 840342.

GILLES, Prof. Chevalier Herbert Michael Joseph, MD; FRCP, FFPHM; Alfred Jones and Warrington Yorke Professor of Tropical Medicine, University of Liverpool, 1972–86, now Emeritus; *b* 10 Sept. 1921; *s* of Joseph and Clementine Gilles; *m* 1955, Wilhelmina Caruana (*d* 1972); three *s* one *d*; *m* 1979, Dr Mejra Kačić-Dimitri. *Educ:* St Edward's Coll., Malta; Royal Univ. of Malta (MD). Rhodes Schol. 1942. MSc Oxon; FMCPH (Nig.), DTM&H. Served War of 1939 45 (1939–45 Star, Africa Star, VM). Mem., Scientific Staff, MRC Lab., Gambia, 1954–58; University of Ibadan: Lectr, Tropical Med., 1958–63; Prof. of Preventive and Social Med., 1963–65; Liverpool University: Sen. Lectr, Tropical Med., 1965–70; Prof. of Tropical Med. (Personal Chair), 1970; Dean, Liverpool Sch. of Tropical Medicine, 1978–83. Vis. Prof., Tropical Medicine, Univ. of Lagos, 1965–68; Royal Society Overseas Vis. Prof., Univ. of Khartoum, Sudan, 1979–80; Hon. Prof. of Tropical Medicine, Sun-Yat-Sen Med. Coll., Guangzhou, People's Republic of China, 1984; Visiting Professor: Public Health, Univ. of Malta, 1989–; Internat. Health, Royal Colls of Surgeons, Ireland, 1994–; Tropical Medicine, Mahidol Univ., Bangkok, 1994–. Consultant Physician in Tropical Medicine, Liverpool AHA(T) and Mersey RHA, 1965–86; Consultant in Malariology to the Army, 1974–86; Consultant in Tropical Medicine to the RAF, 1978–86, to the DHSS, 1980–86. Pres., RSTM&H, 1985–87; Vice President: Internat. Fedn of Tropical Medicine, 1988–92; Liverpool Sch. of Tropical Medicine, 1991–. KStJ 1972. Title of Chevalier awarded for medical work in the tropics. Hon. MD Karolinska Inst., 1979; Hon. DSc Malta, 1984. Darling Foundn Medal and Prize, WHO, 1990; Mary Kingsley Medal, Liverpool Sch. of Tropical Medicine, 1994. *Publications:* Tropical Medicine for Nurses, 1955, 4th edn 1975; Pathology in the Tropics, 1969, 2nd edn 1976; Management and Treatment of Tropical Diseases, 1971; A Short Textbook of Preventive Medicine for the Tropics, 1973, 4th edn 2002; Atlas of Tropical Medicine and Parasitology, 1976, 4th edn 1995 (BMA Book Prize, 1996); Recent Advances in Tropical Medicine, 1984; Human Antiparasitic Drugs, Pharmacology and Usage, 1985; The Epidemiology and Control of Tropical Diseases, 1987; Management of Severe and Complicated Malaria, 1991; Hookworm Infections, 1991; *edited:* Bruce-Chwatt's Essential Malariology, 3rd edn, 1993, 4th edn 2001; Protozoal Diseases, 1999. *Recreations:* swimming, music. *Address:* 3 Conyers Avenue, Birkdale, Southport PR8 4SZ. *T:* (01704) 566664.

GILLESPIE, Dr Alan Raymond; Chief Executive, CDC Group plc, since 1999; Chairman, Ulster Bank Group, since 2001; *b* 31 July 1950; *s* of Charles Gillespie and Doreen Gillespie (*née* Murtagh); *m* 1973, (Georgina) Ruth Milne; one *s* one *d. Educ:* Grosvenor High Sch., Belfast; Clare Coll., Cambridge (BA 1972; MA 1973; PhD 1977). Citicorp International Bank Ltd, London and Geneva, 1976–86; Goldman Sachs & Co., NY, 1986–87; Goldman Sachs International, London, 1987–99 (Partner and Man. Dir, 1990–99). Non-exec. Dir, Elan Corp. plc, 1996–. Chm., NI IDB, 1998–2001; Member: NI Econ. Strategy Steering Gp, 1998–99; NI Econ. Council, 1999–. Pres., European Develt Finance Institns, 2001–. Member: Adv. Bd, Judge Inst. of Mgt Studies, Univ. of Cambridge, 1996–; Adv. Council, Prince's Trust, 1999–. Chm., Univ. Challenge Fund, NI, 1999–. DUniv Ulster, 2001. *Recreations:* golf, tennis, ski-ing. *Address:* CDC Group plc, One Bessborough Gardens SW1V 2JQ. *Clubs:* Wisley Golf, St George's Hill Lawn Tennis, Kiawah Island.

GILLESPIE, Prof. Iain Erskine, MD, MSc, FRCS; Professor of Surgery, University of Manchester, 1970–92 (Dean of Medical School, 1983–86); *b* 4 Sept. 1931; *s* of John Gillespie and Flora McQuarie; *m* 1957, Mary Muriel McIntyre; one *s* one *d. Educ:* Hillhead High Sch., Glasgow; Univ. of Glasgow. MB, ChB, 1953; MD (Hons) 1963; MSc Manchester 1974; FRCSE 1959; FRCS 1963; FRCSGlas 1970. Series of progressive surgical appts in Univs of Glasgow, Sheffield, Glasgow (again), 1953–70. Nat. service, RAMC, 1954–56; MRC grantee, 1956–58; US Postdoctoral Research Fellow, Los Angeles, 1961–62; Titular Prof. of Surgery, Univ. of Glasgow, 1969. Vis. Prof. in USA, Canada, S America, Kenya, S Africa, Australia and New Zealand. Member: Cttee of Surgical Res. Soc. of GB and Ireland, 1975–; Medical Sub-Cttee, UGC, 1975–86; Univs and Polytechnics Grants Cttee, Hong Kong, 1984–89. Non-exec. Mem., Central Manchester HA, 1991–94. President: Manchester Med. Soc., 1994–95; Manchester Lit. and Phil Soc., 1999–2001 (Mem. Council, 1995–98). *Publications:* jt editor and contributor to several surgical and gastroenterological books; numerous articles in various med. jls of GB, USA, Europe. *Recreations:* none. *Address:* 27 Athol Road, Bramhall, Cheshire SK7 1BR. *T:* (0161) 439 2811.

GILLESPIE, Ian; District Judge (Magistrates' Courts) (formerly Stipendiary Magistrate), West Midlands Area, since 1991; *b* 8 Oct. 1945; *s* of James Alexander and Margaret Cicely Gillespie; *m* 1974, Diana Mary Stevens. *Educ:* King Henry VIII Sch., Coventry. Admitted Solicitor of Supreme Court, 1973; Partner, Brindley Twist Tafft & James, Solicitors, Coventry, 1974–91; Actg Stipendiary Magistrate, Wolverhampton, 1989–91. *Recreations:* ski-ing, sailing, riding, attending concerts and ballet. *Address:* The Law Courts, North Street, Wolverhampton WV1 1RA. *T:* (01902) 773151.

GILLESPIE, Prof. John Spence; Head of Department of Pharmacology, Glasgow University, 1968–92; *b* 5 Sept. 1926; *s* of Matthew Forsyth Gillespie and Myrtle Murie Spence; *m* 1956, Jemima Simpson Ross; four *s* one *d. Educ:* Dumbarton Academy; Glasgow Univ. MB ChB (Commendation), PhD. FRCP; FRSE. Hosp. Residency (Surgery), 1949–50; Nat. Service as RMO, 1950–52; hosp. appts, 1952–53; McCunn Res. Schol. in Physiology, Glasgow Univ., 1953–55; Faulds Fellow then Sharpey Schol. in Physiology Dept, University Coll. London, 1955–57; Glasgow University: Lectr in Physiol., 1957–59; Sophie Fricke Res. Fellow, Royal Soc., in Rockefeller Inst., 1959–60; Sen. Lectr in Physiol., 1961–63; Henry Head Res. Fellow, Royal Soc., 1963–68; Vice-Principal, 1983–87, 1988–91. *Publications:* articles in Jls of Physiol. and Pharmacol. *Recreations:* gardening, painting. *Address:* 5 Boclair Road, Bearsden, Glasgow G61 2AE. *T:* (0141) 942 0318.

GILLESPIE, Prof. Ronald James, PhD, DSc; FRS 1977; FRSC; FRSC (UK); FCIC; Professor of Chemistry, McMaster University, Hamilton, Ont, 1960–88, now Emeritus; *b* London, England, 21 Aug. 1924; Canadian citizen; *s* of James A. Gillespie and Miriam G. (*née* Kirk); *m* 1950, Madge Ena Garner; two *d. Educ:* London Univ. (BSc 1945, PhD 1949, DSc 1957). FRSC 1965; FCIC 1960; FRIC; Mem., Amer. Chem. Soc. Asst Lectr, Dept of Chemistry, 1948–50, Lectr, 1950–58, UCL; Commonwealth Fund Fellow, Brown Univ., RI, USA, 1953–54; McMaster University: Associate Prof., Dept of Chem., 1958–60; Prof., 1960–62; Chm., Dept of Chem., 1962–65. Professeur Associé, l'Univ. des Sciences et Techniques de Languedoc, Montpellier, 1972–73; Visiting Professor: Univ. of Geneva, 1976; Univ. of Göttingen, 1978. Nyholm Lectr, RSC, 1979. Faraday Soc. Hon. LLD: Dalhousie Univ., 1988; Concordia Univ., 1988; Dr *hc* Montpellier, 1991; Hon. DSc McMaster, 1993. Medals: Ramsay, UCL, 1949; Harrison Meml, Chem. Soc., 1954; Canadian Centennial, 1967; Chem. Inst. of Canada, 1977; Silver Jubilee, 1978; Henry Marshall Tory, Royal Soc. of Canada, 1983. Awards: Noranda, Chem. Inst. of Canada, 1966 (for inorganic chem.); Amer. Chem. Soc. N-Eastern Reg., 1971 (in phys. chem.); Manufg Chemists Assoc. Coll. Chem. Teacher, 1972; Amer. Chem. Soc., 1973 (for distinguished service in advancement of inorganic chem.), 1980 (for creative work in fluorine chem.); Chem. Inst. of Canada/Union Carbide, 1976 (for chemical educn); Izaak Walton Killam Meml, Canada Council (for outstanding contrib. to advancement of res. in chemistry), 1987. *Publications:* Molecular Geometry, 1972 (London; German and Russian trans, 1975); (jtly) Chemistry, 1986, 2nd edn, 1989; The VSEPR Model of Molecular Geometry, 1990 (trans. Russian, 1992; Italian, 1994); (jtly) Atoms, Molecules and Reactions: an introduction to chemistry, 1994; (jtly) The Chemical Bond and Molecular Geometry: from Lewis to electron densities, 2001; papers in Jl Amer. Chem. Soc., Canadian Jl of Chem., and Inorganic Chem. *Recreations:* skiing, sailing. *Address:* Department of Chemistry, McMaster University, Hamilton, ON L8S 4M1, Canada. *T:* (905) 5259140, ext. 23307, *Fax:* (905) 5222509; *e-mail:* gillespi@mcmail.cis.mcmaster.ca.

GILLETT, Rt Rev. David Keith; *see* Bolton, Bishop Suffragan of.

GILLETT, Sir Robin (Danvers Penrose), 2nd Bt *cr* 1959; GBE 1976; RD 1965; Underwriting Member of Lloyd's; Lord Mayor of London for 1976–77; *b* 9 Nov. 1925; *o s* of Sir (Sydney) Harold Gillett, 1st Bt, MC, and Audrey Isabel Penrose Wardlaw (*d* 1962); *S* father, 1976; *m* 1950, Elizabeth Marion Grace (*d* 1997), *e d* of late John Findlay, JP,

Busby, Lanarks; two *s*; *m* 2000, Alwyne Winifred Cox, JP, *widow* of His Honour Albert Edward Cox. *Educ:* Nautical Coll., Pangbourne. Served Canadian Pacific Steamships, 1943–60; Master Mariner 1951; Staff Comdr 1957; Hon. Comdr RNR 1971. Elder Brother of Trinity House; Fellow and Founder Mem., Nautical Inst. City of London (Ward of Bassishaw): Common Councilman 1965–69; Alderman 1969–96; Sheriff 1973; one of HM Lieuts for City of London, 1975; Chm. Civil Defence Cttee, 1967–68; Pres., City of London Civil Defence Instructors Assoc., 1967–78; Vice-Pres., City of London Centre, St John Ambulance Assoc.; Pres., Nat. Waterways Transport Assoc., 1979–83; Dep. Commonwealth Pres., Royal Life Saving Soc., 1981–96; Chm. Council, Maritime Volunteer Service, 1998–2000, Gov., 2000–. Vice-Chm., PLA, 1979–84. Master, Hon. Co. of Master Mariners, 1979–80. Trustee, Nat. Maritime Mus., 1982–92. Chm. of Governors, Pangbourne Coll., 1978–92. Chancellor, City Univ., 1976–77. FIAM (Pres., 1980–84; Gold Medal, 1982); FRCM 1991. Hon. DSc City, 1976. Gentleman Usher of the Purple Rod, Order of the British Empire, 1985–2000. KStJ 1977 (OStJ 1974). Gold Medal, Administrative Management Soc., USA, 1983. Officer, Order of Leopard, Zaire, 1973; Comdr, Order of Dannebrog, 1974; Order of Johan Sedia Mahkota (Malaysia), 1974; Grand Cross of Municipal Merit (Lima), 1977. *Publication:* A Fish out of Water. *Recreation:* sailing. *Heir:* *s* Nicholas Danvers Penrose Gillett, BSc, ARCS [*b* 24 Sept. 1955; *m* 1987, Haylie (marr. diss. 1998), *er d* of Dennis Brooks]. *Address:* 4 Fairholt Street, Knightsbridge, SW7 1EQ. *T:* (020) 7589 9860. *Clubs:* City Livery, City Livery Yacht (Admiral), Guildhall, Royal Yacht Squadron, Royal London Yacht (Cdre, 1984–85), St Katharine's Yacht (Admiral).

GILLETT, Sarah, MVO, 1986; HM Diplomatic Service; Consul-General, Montreal, from Feb. 2002; *b* 21 July 1956; *d* of Sir Michael Cavenagh Gillett, KBE, CMG and late Margaret Gillett. *Educ:* St Anthony's Leweston, Sherborne; Aberdeen Univ. (MA Hons). Joined HM Diplomatic Service, 1976: Third Sec., Washington, 1984–87; Third, later Second, Sec., Paris, 1987–90; on secondment to ODA, 1990–91; Central Eur. Dept, FCO, 1991–92; Vice-Consul (Inward Investment), Los Angeles, 1992–94; SE Asia Dept, FCO, 1994–97; First Sec., Brasilia, 1997–99; Counsellor and Dep. Head of Mission, Brasilia, 1999–2001. *Recreation:* outdoor exercise. *Address:* c/o Foreign and Commonwealth Office, King Charles Street, SW1A 2AH.

GILLFORD, Lord; Patrick James Meade; Chairman, The Policy Partnership, since 1996; *b* 28 Dec. 1960; *s* and *heir* of Earl of Clanwilliam, *qv*; *m* 1st, 1989, Serena Emily (marr. diss. 1994), *d* of late Lt-Col B. J. Lockhart; one *d*; 2nd, 1995, Cara de la Peña; one *s* one *d*. *Educ:* Eton College. 1 Bn, Coldstream Guards, 1979–83. Exec., Hanson plc, 1983–90, attached Home Office as special advr to Home Sec., 1986–88; with Ian Greer & Associates, 1990–93; Man. Dir, Westminster Policy Partnership Ltd, 1993–95. Councillor (C) Royal Bor. of Kensington and Chelsea, 1990– (Chm., Traffic and Highways Cttee). Mem. Bd of Trustees, British Sch. of Osteopathy, 1997–. *Recreations:* prison reform and prison sentencing policy, free fall parachuting, sub-aqua diving, Palladian architecture, golf, fishing, motorbiking. *Heir:* *s* Hon. John Maximillian Meade, *b* 28 Jan. 1998. *Address:* 51 Causton Street, SW1P 4AT. *T:* (020) 7976 5555; *e-mail:* pgillford@policypartnership.co.uk. *Clubs:* Turf, Chatham Dining; Mill Reef (Antigua, WI); New Zealand (Weybridge).

GILLHAM, Geoffrey Charles; HM Diplomatic Service; Head, Southern European Department, Foreign and Commonwealth Office, since 2001; *b* 1 June 1954; *s* of Peter George Gee Gillham and Alison Mary (*née* Jackman); *m* 1991, Nicola Mary Brewer; one *s* one *d*. *Educ:* UWIST (BScEcon). Joined FCO, 1981: Second Sec., Caracas, 1983–85; on loan to Cabinet Office, 1986–88; FCO, 1988–89; First Secretary: Madrid, 1989–91; UK Delegn, OECD, Paris, 1991–95; later Counsellor, FCO, 1995–98; Counsellor, New Delhi, 1998–2001. *Recreations:* music, travel, sailing. *Address:* c/o Foreign and Commonwealth Office, King Charles Street, SW1A 2AH.

GILLIAM, Terry; animator, actor, writer; film director, since 1973; *b* Minneapolis, USA, 22 Nov. 1940; *s* of James H. and Beatrice Gilliam; *m* 1973, Maggie Weston; one *s* two *d*. *Educ:* Occidental Coll., LA, Calif. *Television:* resident cartoonist, We Have Ways of Making You Laugh, 1968; animator: Do Not Adjust Your Set, 1968–69; (also actor and co-writer), Monty Python's Flying Circus, 1969–74 and 1979; The Marty Feldman Comedy Machine, 1971–72; The Do-It-Yourself Film Animation, 1974; presenter, The Last Machine, 1995; *films:* co-writer, actor and animator: And Now For Something Completely Different, 1971; (also co-director) Monty Python and the Holy Grail, 1974; Monty Python's Life of Brian, 1979; Monty Python Live at the Hollywood Bowl, 1982; Monty Python's The Meaning of Life, 1983; (animator, writer) The Miracle of Flight, 1974; (writer, director) Jabberwocky, 1977; (co-writer, producer, director) Time Bandits, 1981; (co-writer, director) Brazil, 1985; (co-writer, director) The Adventures of Baron Münchhausen, 1989; (dir) The Fisher King, 1991; (dir) Twelve Monkeys, 1996; (co-writer, dir) Fear and Loathing in Las Vegas, 1998. Hon. DFA Occidental Coll., 1987; Hon. Dr RCA, 1989. *Publications:* Animations of Mortality, 1978; Time Bandits, 1981; (jtly) The Adventures of Baron Münchhausen, 1989; Fear and Loathing in Las Vegas: not the screenplay, 1998; Gilliam on Gilliam, 1999; Dark Nights and Holly Fools, 1999; *contributed to:* Monty Python's Big Red Book, 1971; The Brand New Monty Python Book, 1973, Monty Python and the Holy Grail, 1977; Monty Python's Life of Brian, 1979; Monty Python's The Meaning of Life, 1983. *Recreations:* too busy. *Address:* c/o The Casarotto Co., National House, 60–66 Wardour Street, W1V 3HP.

GILLIBRAND, Philip Martin Mangnall; District Judge (Magistrates' Courts), Inner London, since 2001; *b* 28 June 1951; *s* of late Frank Ivor Croft Gillibrand and of Marjorie Joyce Gillibrand (*née* Golding); *m* 1979, Felicity Alexandra Augusta Priefert; one *s* one *d*. *Educ:* Reading Blue Coat Sch. (Aldsworth's Hosp); Poly. of Central London (LLB Hons 1974). Called to the Bar, Gray's Inn, 1975; in practice at the Bar, London and on Western Circuit, 1975–2000: Bristol, 1982–93; Winchester, 1993–2000. *Recreations:* classic and historic motoring (Mem., Brooklands Soc.), motor racing (Mem., Mini Seven Racing Club), reading, music (Mem., Elgar Soc.), the countryside, family life. *Address:* c/o Horseferry Road Magistrates' Court, 70 Horseferry Road, SW1P 2AX.

GILLIBRAND, Sydney, CBE 1991; FREng, FRAeS; Chairman, AMEC plc, since 1997 (Director, since 1995); *b* 2 June 1934; *s* of Sydney and Maud Gillibrand; *m* 1960, Angela Ellen Williams; three *s* (and one *s* decd). *Educ:* Preston Grammar Sch.; Harris Coll., Preston; College of Aeronautics, Cranfield (MSc). FRAeS 1975 (Hon. FRAeS 1994); FREng (FEng 1987). English Electric: apprentice, Preston, 1950; Chief Stress Engr, 1966; Works Man., Preston, 1974; Special Dir, BAC (Preston) Ltd, 1974; Dir of Manufacturing, Mil. Aircraft Div., 1977; British Aerospace Aircraft Group: Div. Prodn Dir, Warton, 1978; Dep. Man. Dir, Warton Div., and Bd Mem., Aircraft Gp, 1981; Div. Man. Dir, Kingston/Brough Div., 1983, Weybridge Div., 1984; British Aerospace PLC: Man. Dir, Civil Aircraft Div., 1986; Dir, 1987–95; Vice-Chm., 1991–95; Sen. Corporate Advr, 1995–99; Chairman: British Aerospace (Commercial Aircraft) Ltd, 1988–89; Aerospace Companies, 1989–92. Director: ICL plc, 1996–; Messier-Dowty Internat. Ltd, 1998–; Powergen, 1999–; Chm., TAG Aviation (UK) Ltd, 1998–. Pres., SBAC, 1990–91. CIMgt. Silver Medal, RAeS, 1981; James Watt Gold Medal, IMechE, 1997. *Recreation:* golf. *Address:* AMEC plc, 1 Golden Lane, EC1Y 0RR. *T:* (020) 7574 3999.

GILLICK, Rev. John, SJ; MA Oxon; Spiritual Director, St Peter's National Seminary, Hammanskraal, S Africa, 1986–90, retired; *b* Wallasey, 27 March 1916; 2nd *s* of Laurence Gillick and Catherine Devine. *Educ:* St Francis Xavier's Coll., Liverpool; Heythrop and Campion Hall, Oxford (1st Cl. Hons Mod. History). Asst Master at Mount St Mary's and Beaumont. Two years writing and photography in Italy and Africa. Headmaster, Beaumont Coll., 1964–67; studied psychology at Loyola Univ., Chicago, 1967–68 (MA); Dir, Laboratories for the Training of Religious Superiors in S Africa, 1969; Dir, Fons Vitae (Pastoral Institute for Religious), 1970–84. *Publications:* Teaching the Mass, 1961; Baptism, 1962; followed by Teaching the Mass: African, 1963; Teaching the Sacraments: African, 1964; Teaching Confirmation, 1964, etc; *illustrations for:* The Breaking of Bread, 1950; The Pilgrim Years, 1956; Our Faith, 1956; The Holy Mass, 1958; Christ Our Life, 1960; Catholic Encyclopedia, 1965. *Address:* 8 The Elms, York Road, Rosebank, 7700, South Africa; c/o 114 Mount Street, W1Y 6AH.

GILLILAND, David; *see* Gilliland, J. A. D.

GILLILAND, David Jervois Thetford; practising solicitor and farmer; *b* 14 July 1932; *s* of late Major W. H. Gilliland and of Mrs N. H. Gilliland; *m* 1st, 1958, Patricia, *o d* of late J. S. Wilson and late Mrs Wilson (marr. diss. 1976); two *s* three *d*; 2nd, 1976, Jennifer Johnston, *qv*. *Educ:* Rockport Prep. Sch.; Wrekin Coll.; Trinity Coll., Dublin. BA 1954, LLB 1955. Qualified as solicitor, 1957, own practice. Mem. ITA, 1965–70; Chm., N Ireland Adv. Cttee of ITA, 1965–70. Chm., NI Heritage Gardens Cttee, 1991–; Mem. Council, Internat. Dendrology Soc., 1966–75; etc. *Recreations:* gardening, sailing, photography. *Address:* Brook Hall, 65 Culmore Road, Londonderry, Northern Ireland BT48 8JE. *T:* (028) 7135 1297.

GILLILAND, (James Andrew) David; QC 1984; **His Honour Judge Gilliland;** a Circuit Judge (Technology and Construction Court), since 1992; *b* 29 Dec. 1937; *s* of James Albin Gilliland and Mary Gilliland (*née* Gray); *m* 1961, Elsie McCully; two *s*. *Educ:* Campbell College; Queen's University Belfast. LLB (1st Class Hons) 1960. Called to the Bar, Gray's Inn, 1964 (Holt Scholar, Atkin Scholar, Macaskie Scholar); Lectr in Law, Manchester University, 1960–72; a Recorder, 1989–92. *Recreations:* music, opera, stamp collecting, wind surfing, ski-ing. *Address:* Salford County Court, Prince William House, Peel Cross Road, off Eccles New Road, Salford M5 2RR. *T:* (0161) 745 7511. *Club:* Athenæum (Liverpool).

GILLILAND, Jennifer, (Mrs David Gilliland); *see* Johnston, J.

GILLING, Lancelot Cyril Gilbert, OBE 1985; CBiol, FIBiol; FRAgS; Member, Royal Commission on Environmental Pollution, 1984–89; *b* 7 March 1920; *s* of Gilbert Joseph Gilling and Esther Marianne Gilling (*née* Clapp); *m* 1951, Brenda Copp; two *d*. *Educ:* Shebbear Coll., N Devon; Reading Univ. (BSc Agr). Pres. Union, Reading Univ., 1948–49. Lectr, Dorset Coll. of Agric., 1949–51; Head of Agric. Dept, Writtle Coll. of Agric., Essex, 1951–57; Principal, Askham Bryan Coll. of Agric. & Hortic., 1957–84. Member: Technical Develt Cttee and Educn and Gen. Purposes Cttee, Royal Agricl Soc., 1970–85; Northern Regional Panel, MAFF, 1982–88; Adv. Cttee on Agric. and Vet. Sci., British Council, 1972–86; Chm., York Agricl Soc., 1983–92 (Pres., 1981–82; Chm. Finance Cttee, 1995–2000). Vice-Chm., Sub-Cttee, Yorkshire Museum, 1985–90; Chm. and Life Vice-Pres., Yorks Philosophical Soc., 1982–88. Chairman: Yorks Wildlife Trust, 1992–94 (Mem. Council and Chm., F and GP Cttee, 1985–92); York Centre, Nat. Trust, 1988–90. Gov., Univ. Coll. of Ripon and York St John, 1976–99. Hon. Mem., CGLI. *Publications:* contribs to Agricultural Progress, Jl of Agricl Educn Assoc. and Jl of Royal Agricl Soc. *Recreations:* ornithology, travel, choral music. *Address:* The Spinney, Brandsby, York YO61 4RQ.

GILLINGHAM, (Francis) John, CBE 1982 (MBE mil. 1944); FRSE 1970; Professor of Neurological Surgery, University of Edinburgh, 1963–80, now Emeritus; at Royal Infirmary of Edinburgh and Western General Hospital, Edinburgh, 1963–80; Consultant Neuro-Surgeon to the Army in Scotland, 1966–80; *b* 15 March 1916; *s* of John H. Gillingham, Upwey, Dorset; *m* 1945, Irene Judy Jude; four *s*. *Educ:* Hardye's Sch., Dorset; St Bartholomew's Hosp. Medical Coll., London. Matthews Duncan Gold Medal, 1939, MRCS, LRCP Oct. 1939; MB, BS (London) Nov. 1939; FRCS 1947; FRCSE 1955; FRCPE 1967. Prof. of Surgical Neurol., King Saud Univ., Saudi Arabia, 1983–85, now Emeritus. Advr in Neuro-Surgery, MoD, Kingdom of Saudi Arabia, 1980–83. Hon. Consultant in Neurosurgery, St Bartholomew's Hosp., London, 1981–. Hunterian Prof., RCS, 1957; Morison Lectr, RCP of Edinburgh, 1960; Colles Lectr, College of Surgeons of Ireland, 1962; Elsberg Lectr, College of Physicians and Surgeons, NY, 1967; Penfield Lectr, Middle East Med. Assembly, 1970; Syme Derby Lectr, Univ. of Hong Kong, 1982; Adlington Syme Oration, RACS, 1983. Hon. Mem., Soc. de Neurochirurgie de Langue Française, 1964; Hon. Mem., Soc. of Neurol. Surgeons (USA), 1965; Hon. Mem., Royal Academy of Medicine of Valencia, 1967; Hon. and Corresp. Mem. of a number of foreign neuro-surgical societies; Hon. Pres., World Fedn of Neurosurgical Socs. President: Medico-Chirurgical Soc. of Edinburgh, 1965–67; European Soc. of Stereostatic and Functional Neurosurgery, 1972–76; RCSE, 1979–82 (Vice-Pres., 1974–77; Mem., Court of Regents, 1990–). FRSA 1991. Hon. FRACS 1980; Hon. FCS Sri Lanka 1980; Hon. FRCSI 1981; Hon. FRCSGlas 1982. Hon. MD Thessaloniki, 1973. Jim Clark Foundn Award, 1979; Medal of City of Gdansk, Poland, 1980. *Publications:* Clinical Surgery: Neurological Surgery, 1969; papers on surgical management of cerebral vascular disease, head and spinal injuries, Parkinsonism and the dyskinesias, epilepsy and other neurosurgical subjects. *Recreations:* sailing, travel, gardening (cactus). *Address:* Easter Park House, Easter Park Drive, Edinburgh EH4 6SN. *T:* (0131) 336 3528. *Clubs:* Bruntsfield Links Golfing Society; Nautico (Javea, Alicante).

GILLINGS, Ven. Richard John; Archdeacon of Macclesfield, since 1994; Vicar of Bramhall, since 1993; *b* 17 Sept. 1945; *s* of John Albert Gillings and Constance Ford Gillings; *m* 1972, Kathryn Mary Hill; two *s* one *d*. *Educ:* Sale GS; St Chad's Coll., Durham (BA, Dip Biblical Studies); Lincoln Theol Coll. Ordained deacon, 1970, priest, 1971; Curate, St George's, Altrincham, 1970–75; Priest i/c, then Rector, St Thomas', Stockport, 1975–83, and Priest i/c, St Peter's, Stockport, 1978–83; Rector, Birkenhead Priory, 1983–93; RD, Birkenhead, 1985–93; Hon. Canon, Chester Cathedral, 1992–94. Mem., Gen. Synod, 1980–. *Recreations:* music, cinema, theatre, railways, Rotary. *Address:* The Vicarage, Robins Lane, Bramhall, Stockport, Cheshire SK7 2PE. *T:* (0161) 439 2254.

GILLMAN, Bernard Arthur, (Gerry Gillman); General Secretary, Society of Civil and Public Servants, 1973–85; *b* 14 April 1927; *s* of Elias Gillman and Gladys Gillman; *m* 1951, Catherine Mary Antonia Harvey. *Educ:* Archbishop Tenison's Grammar Sch. Civil Service, 1946–53; Society of Civil Servants, 1953–85. Mem., Police Complaints Authy, 1986–91. *Address:* 2 Burnham Street, Kingston-upon-Thames, Surrey KT2 6QR. *T:* (020) 8546 6905. *Clubs:* Royal Over-Seas League, MCC.

GILLMAN, Derek Anthony; President, Chief Executive Officer, and the Edna S. Tuttleman Director , Pennsylvania Academy of the Fine Arts, since 2001 (Executive Director and Provost, 1999); *b* 7 Dec. 1952; *s* of Abraham Gillman and Esther Gillman; *m* 1987, Yael Joanna Hirsch; one *s* two *d*. *Educ:* Clifton Coll., Bristol; Magdalen Coll., Oxford (MA); Beijing Langs Inst.; Univ. of E Anglia (LLM). Chinese specialist, Christie's Auctioneers, London, 1977–81; Curator, Dept of Oriental Antiquities, BM, 1981–85; Keeper, Sainsbury Centre for Visual Arts, UEA, 1985–95; Dep. Dir, Internat. Art and Collection Mgt, 1995–96, Curatorial and Educn Services, 1996–99, Nat. Gall. of Victoria. Sen. Fellow, Melbourne Inst. of Asian Langs and Socs, 1998–. *Publications:* contrib. to exhibn catalogues; articles and reviews for Art, Antiquity and Law, SOAS Bull., Buddhist Forum, Apollo, Orientations, Trans Oriental Ceramic Soc. *Recreations:* reading, painting. *Address:* (office) 1301 Cherry Street, Philadelphia, PA 19107, USA.

GILLON, Karen Macdonald; Member (Lab) Clydesdale, Scottish Parliament, since 1999; *b* 18 Aug. 1967; *d* of Edith Turnbull (*née* Macdonald); *m* 1999, James Gillon; one *s*. *Educ:* Jedburgh Grammar Sch.; Birmingham Univ. (Cert. Youth and Community Work 1991). Project Worker, Terminal One youth project, Blantyre, 1991–94; Community Educn Worker, N Lanarkshire Council, 1994–97; PA to Rt Hon. Helen Liddell, MP, 1997–99. *Recreations:* sport, cooking, flower arranging, music. *Address:* Constituency Office, 11 Wellgate, Lanark ML11 9DS. *T:* (01555) 660526.

GILLON, Prof. Raanan Evelyn Zvi, FRCP; Professor of Medical Ethics, School of Medicine, Imperial College, London, 1995–99, now Emeritus (Visiting Professor, 1989–94); part-time general practitioner; NHS Senior Partner, Imperial College Medical Partnership, since 1991; *b* Jerusalem, 15 April 1941; *s* of Diana Gillon and late Meir Gillon; *m* 1966, Angela Spear; one *d*. *Educ:* Christ's Hospital; University College London (MB BS 1964); Christ Church, Oxford; Birbeck College London (BA Phil 1st cl. Hons 1979). MRCP 1974, FRCP 1988. Medical journalism, 1964–71 (Ed., Medical Tribune); part-time GP, part-time philosophy student then teacher, 1974–; Dir, Imperial Coll. Health Service, 1982–95; Dir of Teaching in Medical Ethics (for MA course), KCL, 1986–89. Vis. Prof. in Med. Ethics, KCL, 1988–91. Chm., Imperial Coll. Ethics Cttee, 1984–93. Member: BMA, 1964 (Mem. Ethics Cttee, 1998–); Archbp of Canterbury's Adv. Gp on Med. Ethics, 1999–. Mem. Governing Body, 1989–, Chm., 2000–, Inst of Medical Ethics. Ed., Jl of Med. Ethics, 1980–2001. FRSocMed 1966. Hon RCM 1986. Henry Beecher Award, Hastings Center, USA, 1999. *Publications:* Philosophical Medical Ethics, 1986; (Sen. Ed. and contrib.) Principles of Health Care Ethics, 1994; numerous papers on medical ethics. *Recreations:* enjoying the company of wife and daughter and sometimes the cats; reading moral philosophy and, intermittently, thrillers; playing (own) trumpet, or rather, Uncle Peter's trumpet, kindly lent in 1954; ski-ing, swimming, cooking, winetasting, arguing and good company. *Address:* 42 Brynmaer Road, SW11 4EW. *T:* (020) 7622 1450; (office) Imperial College Health Centre, SW7 1LU. *T:* (020) 7584 6301.

GILMORE, Brian Terence, CB 1992; *b* 25 May 1937; *s* of late John Henry Gilmore and of Edith Alice Gilmore; *m* 1962, Rosalind Edith Jean Fraser (*see* R. E. J. Gilmore). *Educ:* Wolverhampton Grammar Sch.; Christ Church, Oxford (Passmore-Edwards Prize, 1956; BA Lit. Hum.; MA 1961). CRO and Diplomatic Service Admin Office, 1958–65: Private Sec. to Perm. Sec., 1960–61, to Parly Under Sec., 1961–62; Asst Private Sec. to Sec. of State, 1962–64; British Embassy, Washington, 1965–68; Min. of Technology and DTI, 1968–72: Private Sec. to Minister of State, Industry, 1969–70, and to Lord Privy Seal and Leader of the House of Lords, 1971–72; CSD, 1972–81; Under Sec., 1979; Principal, CS Coll., 1979–81; HM Treasury, 1981–88; Principal Estabt Officer and Principal Finance Officer, 1982–84; Dep. Sec., Office of Minister for CS, Cabinet Office, 1988–92; Dep. Sec., DSS, 1992–94. Chairman: PYBT (E London), 1996–2000; Bart's and the London NHS Trust, 1999–2000. Trustee, Soc. for Promotion of Hellenic Studies, 1997–. *Recreations:* reading, music, walking, Greece. *Address:* 3 Clarendon Mews, W2 2NR. *Club:* Athenæum (Chm., 2000–).

GILMORE, Carol Jacqueline; *see* Ellis, C. J.

GILMORE, Rosalind Edith Jean, (Mrs B. T. Gilmore), CB 1995; Director, Zurich Financial Services AG, since 1998; *b* 23 March 1937; *o c* of Sir Robert Brown Fraser, OBE, and Betty Fraser; *m* 1962, Brian Terence Gilmore, *qv*. *Educ:* King Alfred Sch.; University Coll. London (BA; Fellow, 1989); Newnham Coll., Cambridge (BA, MA; Associate Fellow, 1986–95, Hon. Fellow, 1995). Asst Principal, HM Treasury, 1960–65; IBRD, 1966–67; Principal, HM Treasury, 1968–73; Prin. Pvte Sec. to Chancellor of Duchy of Lancaster, Cabinet Office, 1974; HM Treasury: Asst Sec., 1975–80; Press Sec. and Hd of Inf., 1980–82; Gen. Man., Corporate Planning, Dunlop Ltd, 1982–83; Dir of Marketing, Nat. Girobank, 1983–86; Directing Fellow, St George's House, Windsor Castle, 1986–89; re-instated, HM Treasury, and seconded to Bldg Socs Commn, 1989; Dep. Chm., 1989–91, Chm. (First Comr), 1991–94, Bldg Socs Commn; Chief Registrar of Friendly Socs, 1991–94; Industrial Assurance Comr, 1991–94; Dir of Regulation, Lloyd's of London, 1995. Chairman: Arrow Broadcasting, 1994–97; Homeowners Friendly Soc., 1996–98; Director: Mercantile Gp plc, 1986–89; London and Manchester Gp plc, 1988–89; BAT Industries, 1996–98; TU Fund Managers, 2000–; Cons. Man., FI Gp plc, 1987–89. Mem., SIB, 1993–96; Comr, Nat. Lottery Commn, 2000–. Vice Pres., Internat. Women's Forum, 1997–; Dir, Leadership Foundn, Washington, 1997–. Member: Board: Opera North, 1993–97; Moorfields Eye Hosp. NHS Trust, 1994–; Council, RCM, 1997–; Court, Cranfield Univ., 1992–. FRSA 1985; CIMgt 1992. *Publication:* Mutuality for the Twenty-first Century, 1998. *Recreations:* swimming (Half Blue, Cambridge Univ.), music, house in Greece. *Address:* 3 Clarendon Mews, W2 2NR.

GILMOUR, family name of **Baron Gilmour of Craigmillar**.

GILMOUR OF CRAIGMILLAR, Baron *cr* 1992 (Life Peer), of Craigmillar in the District of the City of Edinburgh; **Ian Hedworth John Little Gilmour;** Bt 1926; PC 1973; *b* 8 July 1926; *er s* of Lt-Col Sir John Little Gilmour, 2nd Bt, and Hon. Victoria Laura, OBE, TD (*d* 1991), *d* of late Viscount Chelsea (*e s* of 5th Earl Cadogan); *S* father, 1977; *m* 1951, Lady Caroline Margaret Montagu-Douglas-Scott, *yr d* of 8th Duke of Buccleuch and Queensberry, KT, GCVO, PC; four *s* one *d*. *Educ:* Eton; Balliol Coll., Oxford (Hon. Fellow, 1999). Served with Grenadier Guards, 1944–47; 2nd Lieut 1945. Called to the Bar, Inner Temple, 1952. Editor, The Spectator, 1954–59. MP (C) Norfolk Central, Nov. 1962–1974, Chesham and Amersham, 1974–92. Parly Under Sec. of State, MoD, 1970–71; Minister of State: for Defence Procurement, MoD, 1971–72; for Defence, 1972–74; Sec. of State for Defence, 1974; Lord Privy Seal, 1979–81. Chm., Cons. Res. Dept, 1974–75. Pres., Med. Aid for Palestinians, 1993–96. *Publications:* The Body Politic, 1969; Inside Right: a study of Conservatism, 1977; Britain Can Work, 1983; Riot, Risings and Revolution: governance and violence in 18th Century England, 1992; Dancing with Dogma: Britain under Thatcherism, 1992; (jtly) Whatever Happened to the Tories: a history of the Conservative Party since 1945, 1997. *Heir* (to baronetcy): *s* Hon. David Robert Gilmour [*b* 14 Nov. 1952; *m* 1975, Sarah Anne, *d* of M. H. G. Bradstock; one *s* three *d*]. *Address:* The Ferry House, Old Isleworth, Middx TW7 6BD. *T:* (020) 8560 6769. *Clubs:* Pratt's, White's.
See also A. C. Gilmour.

GILMOUR, Alexander Clement, CVO 1990; Director, Thames Community Foundation (formerly South West London Community Foundation), since 1995; *b* 23 Aug. 1931; *s* of Sir John Little Gilmour, 2nd Bt, and of Lady Mary Gilmour; *m* 1954, Barbara M. L. Constance Berry; two *s* one *d*; *m* 1983, Susan Lady Chetwode. *Educ:* Eton. National Service, commn in Black Watch, 1950–52. With Joseph Sebag & Co. (subseq. Carr, Sebag), 1954–82; Director: Safeguard Industrial Investments, 1974–84; Tide (UK) Ltd, 1986–87; Exec. Dir, Equity Finance Trust Ltd, 1984–86. Consultant, Grieveson Grant, 1982. Chm., Nat. Playing Fields Assoc., 1976–88 (Past-Chm. Appeals Cttee, 10 yrs). Dir, Tate Gallery Foundn, 1986–88. Governor, LSE, 1969–. *Recreations:* tennis, fishing, gardening. *Address:* c/o Drummonds Branch, Royal Bank of Scotland, 49 Charing Cross, SW1A 2DX. *Clubs:* White's; Hon. Company of Edinburgh Golfers.
See also Baron Gilmour of Craigmillar.

GILMOUR, Colonel Sir Allan (Macdonald), KCVO 1990; OBE 1961; MC 1942, and Bar 1943; Lord-Lieutenant of Sutherland, 1972–91; Chairman, Highland River Purification Board, 1994–96 (Vice-Chairman, 1986–94); *b* 23 Nov. 1916; *o s* of late Captain Allan Gilmour, of Rosehall, Sutherland, and late Mary H. M. Macdonald, of Viewfield, Portree, Skye; *m* 1941, Jean Wood; three *s* one *d*. *Educ:* Winchester Coll. Gazetted, The Seaforth Highlanders, Jan. 1939. Served War, in Middle East, France and Germany (despatches, 1945); DSC (USA) 1945. Staff Coll., 1946; Regimental and Staff Service in: Germany, Middle East, UK, Pakistan and Africa, 1946–67, incl. Instructor, Staff Coll., Quetta, on loan to Pakistan Army, 1952–54. Chief of Gen. Staff, Ghana Armed Forces, 1959–62; service in Congo, 1961–62; retired from Army, 1967. Vice-Pres., Highland TA&VRA, 1972–89, Pres., 1989–91. Chm., East Sutherland Council of Social Service, 1973–77; Mem., Highland Health Bd, 1974–81 (Chm., 1981–83); Pres., Voluntary Gps Sutherland, 1993–96. Mem., Highlands and Is Develt Consultative Council, 1975–87. Member: Highland Regl Council, 1977–96; Sutherland District Council, 1978–86 (Chm., 1974–78); Sutherland CC, 1970–74. DL Sutherland, 1971. *Recreations:* fishing, local government. *Address:* Invernauld, Rosehall, Lairg, Sutherland IV27 4EU. *T:* (01549) 441204.

GILMOUR, Col Sir John (Edward), 3rd Bt *cr* 1897; DSO 1945; TD; JP; Lord-Lieutenant of Fife, 1980–87 (Vice Lord-Lieutenant, 1979–80); Lord High Commissioner, General Assembly of the Church of Scotland, 1982 and 1983; *b* 24 Oct. 1912; *o s* of Col Rt Hon. Sir John Gilmour, 2nd Bt, GCVO, DSO, MP, and Mary Louise (*d* 1919), *e d* of late E. T. Lambert, Telham Court, Battle, Sussex; *S* father, 1940; *m* 1941, Ursula Mabyn, *yr d* of late F. O. Wills; two *s*. *Educ:* Eton; Trinity Hall, Cambridge. Served War of 1939–45 (DSO). Bt Col 1950; Captain, Royal Company of Archers (Queen's Body Guard for Scotland); Hon. Col, The Highland Yeomanry, RAC, T&AVR, 1971–75. MP (C) East Fife, 1961–79. Chm., Cons. and Unionist Party in Scotland, 1965–67. DL Fife, 1953. *Heir:* *s* John Gilmour [*b* 15 July 1944; *m* 1967, Valerie, *yr d* of late G. W. Russell, and of Mrs William Wilson; two *s* two *d*]. *Address:* Montrave, Leven, Fife KY8 5NZ. *TA:* Leven. *T:* (01333) 426159. *Club:* Royal & Ancient Golf (St Andrews).
See also Dame Anne Bryans.

GILMOUR, Nigel Benjamin Douglas; QC 1990; **His Honour Judge Gilmour;** a Circuit Judge, since 2000; *b* 21 Nov. 1947; *s* of late Benjamin Waterfall Gilmour and Barbara Mary Gilmour (subseq. Mrs E. Harborow); *m* 1972, Isobel Anne, *d* of E. Harborow; two *d*. *Educ:* Tettenhall Coll., Staffordshire; Liverpool Univ. (LLB Hons). Called to the Bar, Inner Temple, 1970; an Asst Recorder, 1984–90; a Recorder, 1990–2000. *Recreations:* wine, food. *Address:* Queen Elizabeth II Law Courts, Derby Square, Liverpool L2 1XA. *T:* (0151) 473 7373.

GILMOUR, Dr Roger Hugh, FIFST; Chief Executive, Microbiological Research Authority and Centre for Applied Microbiology and Research, Porton Down, since 1996; *b* 24 March 1942; *s* of William and Elizabeth Gilmour; *m* 1968, Margaret Jean Chisholm; one *s* one *d*. *Educ:* Ross High Sch.; Edinburgh Univ. (BSc); Heriot-Watt Univ. (PhD 1969). FIFST 1989. Griffith Laboratories: Canada, 1969; UK/Internat., 1970–79; Pres., USA, 1979–83; CEO Agricl Genetics Co. Ltd, 1983–93; Business Develt Dir, Centre for Applied Microbiol. and Res., 1994–96. Dir, MRC Collaborative Centre, 1992–99. Chm., NMT Gp plc, 1998–. *Recreations:* walking, ski-ing, gardening, cycling. *Address:* Centre for Applied Microbiology and Research, Porton Down, Salisbury, Wilts SP4 0JG. *Club:* Farmers'.

GILPIN, Ven. Richard Thomas; Archdeacon of Totnes, since 1996; *b* 25 July 1939; *s* of Thomas and Winifred Gilpin; *m* 1966, Marian Moeller; one *s* one *d*. *Educ:* Ashburton Coll.; Lichfield Theol Coll. Ordained deacon, 1963, priest, 1964; Assistant Curate: Whipton, 1963–66; Tavistock and Gulworthy, 1966–69; Vicar, Swimbridge, 1969–73; Priest-in-charge, W Buckland, 1970–73; Vicar, Tavistock and Gulworthy, 1973–91; Diocesan Dir of Ordinands, 1990–96, and Advr for Vocations, 1991–96, Exeter; Sub-Dean, Exeter Cathedral, 1992–96. Rural Dean, Tavistock, 1987–90. Prebendary, Exeter Cathedral, 1982–; Proctor in Convocation, 1995–2000. *Recreations:* family, music, art, theatre, walking. *Address:* Blue Hills, Bradley Road, Bovey Tracey, Newton Abbot, Devon TQ13 9EU. *T:* (01626) 832064, *Fax:* (01626) 834947.

GILROY, Linda; MP (Lab and Co-op), Plymouth Sutton, since 1997; *b* 19 July 1949; *d* of William Jarvie and Gwendoline Jarvie (*née* Grey); *m* 1987, Bernard Gilroy. *Educ:* Edinburgh Univ. (MA Hons History 1971); Strathclyde Univ. (Postgrad. Secl Dip. 1972), MITSA (Dip. in Consumer Affairs 1990). Dep. Dir, Age Concern Scotland, 1972–79; Regl Sec., subseq. Regl Manager, SW Office, Gas Consumers' Council, 1979–97. PPS to Minister of State for Local Govt, Dept of Transport, Local Govt and the Regions, 2000–. *Recreations:* swimming, walking, keep fit. *Address:* House of Commons, SW1A 0AA. *T:* (020) 7219 3000.

GILSENAN, Prof. Michael Dermot Cole; David B. Kriser Professor of Middle Eastern Studies and Anthropology, New York University, since 1995; *b* 6 Feb. 1940; *s* of Michael Eugene Cole Gilsenan and Joyce Russell Horn. *Educ:* Eastbourne Grammar Sch.; Oxford Univ. BA (Oriental Studies), Dip. Anth., MA, DPhil (Soc. Anthropology). Research Fellow, Amer. Univ. in Cairo, 1964–66; Research studentship, St Antony's Coll., Oxford, 1966–67; Research Fellow, Harvard Middle East Center, 1967–68; Asst Prof., Dept of Anthropology, UCLA, 1968–70; Research Lectr, Univ. of Manchester, 1970–73; Associate Fellow, St Antony's Coll., Oxford, 1970–73; Lectr, 1973–78, Reader, 1978–83, Dept of Anthropology, University College London; Mem., Sch. of Social Sci., Inst. for Advanced Study, Princeton, 1979–80; Khalid bin Abdullah al Saud Prof. for study of contemp. Arab world, and Fellow of Magdalen Coll., Oxford Univ., 1984–95, Emeritus Fellow, 1995. Anthrop. field work, Egypt, 1964–66, Lebanon, 1971–72, Japan and Singapore, 1999–2000. Mem. Editl Bds, Past and Present, History and Anthropology, and formerly of Man, and Internat. Jl of Middle Eastern Studies; Series Editor, Society and Culture in the Modern Middle East, 1987–. *Publications:* Saint and Sufi in Modern Egypt, 1973; Recognizing Islam, 1982; Lords of the Lebanese Marches, 1996. *Recreations:* music, theatre, being elsewhere. *Address:* Department of Middle Eastern Languages and Literature, 50 Washington Square South, New York, NY 10012-1073, USA.

GILSON, Rev. Nigel Langley, DFC 1944; Methodist minister, retired; President of the Methodist Conference, 1986–87; *b* 11 April 1922; *s* of Clifford Edric and Cassandra Jeanette Gilson; *m* 1951, Mary Doreen (*née* Brown); four *d.* *Educ:* Holcombe Methodist Elementary; Midsomer Norton Co. Secondary; St Catherine's Soc., Oxford Univ. (MA Hons); Wesley House and Fitzwilliam House, Cambridge Univ. (BA Hons). Served RAF, 1941–45 (Navigator (Wireless) 107 Sqdn, 1944–45), Flying Officer. Methodist Minister: Tintagel, Cornwall, 1950–52; Newark-upon-Trent, 1952–58; Rhodesia Dist, 1958–67; Chaplain, Hunmanby Hall Sch., Filey, Yorks, 1967–71; Supt Minister of Oxford Methodist Circuit, 1971–75 and 1988–89; Chm., Wolverhampton and Shrewsbury Dist, 1975–88. *Recreations:* gardening, theatre, family, community and multi-cultural activities. *Address:* 30 Spencer Avenue, Yarnton, Kidlington, Oxon OX5 1NG. *T:* (01865) 378058.

GIMBLETT, (Catherine) Margaret (Alexandra Forbes); Sheriff of North Strathclyde at Dunoon, since 1999; *b* 24 Sept. 1939; *d* of Alexander Forbes Hendry and Margaret Hendry (*née* Whitehead); *m* 1965, Iain McNicol Gimblett; one *s* one *d.* *Educ:* St Leonard's Sch., St Andrews; Edinburgh Univ. (MA); Glasgow Univ. Sec. and PA, Humphreys & Glasgow Ltd, London, 1960–63; Staff Manager, John Lewis Partnership, London, 1963–67; Partner, Alexander Hendry & Son, subseq. Russel & Aitken, Denny, Solicitors, 1972–95; Temp. Sheriff, 1992–95; Sheriff, Glasgow and Strathkelvin, 1995–99. Churchill Fellowship, 1986. *Recreations:* gardening, walking, people, taking up a challenge. *Address:* Glecknabae, Rothesay, Isle of Bute PA20 0QX.

GIMINGHAM, Prof. Charles Henry, OBE 1990; FRSE 1961; Regius Professor of Botany, University of Aberdeen, 1981–88 (Professor of Botany, since 1969); *b* 28 April 1923; *s* of late Conrad Theodore Gimingham and Muriel Elizabeth (*née* Blake), Harpenden; *m* 1948, Elizabeth Caroline, *o d* of late Rev. J. Wilson Baird, DD, Minister of St Machar's Cathedral, Aberdeen; three *d.* *Educ:* Gresham's Sch., Holt, Norfolk; Emmanuel Coll., Cambridge (Open scholarship; BA 1944; ScD 1977); PhD Aberdeen 1948. FIBiol 1967. Research Asst, Imperial Coll., Univ. of London, 1944–45; University of Aberdeen: Asst, 1946–48, Lectr, 1948–61, Sen. Lectr, 1961–64, Reader, 1964–69, Dept of Botany. Pres., British Ecological Soc., 1986–87. Vice Chm., NE Regl Bd, NCC for Scot., 1991–92; Member: Countryside Commn for Scotland, 1980–92; Sci Adv. Cttee, Scottish Natural Heritage, 1996–99 (Mem., NE Regl Bd, 1992–96); Bd of Management, Hill Farming Res. Organisation, 1981–87; Council of Management, Macaulay Inst. for Soil Research, 1983–87; Governing Body, Macaulay Land Use Res. Inst., 1987–90. Mem. Governing Body, Aberdeen Coll. of Educn, 1979–87. Founding Fellow, Inst. of Contemporary Scotland, 2000. Patron, Inst. of Ecology and Envmtl Mgt, 2000. *Publications:* Ecology of Heathlands, 1972; An Introduction to Heathland Ecology, 1975; The Lowland Heathland Management Handbook, 1992; papers, mainly in botanical and ecological jls. *Recreations:* hill walking, photography, foreign travel, history and culture of Japan. *Address:* 4 Gowanbrae Road, Bieldside, Aberdeen AB1 9AQ.

GIMSON, George Stanley; QC (Scotland) 1961; Sheriff Principal of Grampian, Highland and Islands, 1975–82; *b* 1915. *Educ:* High School of Glasgow; Glasgow Univ. TA, 1938–46; commnd, RA, 1941; attached Indian Artillery, 1941–46; POW, Singapore, River Kwai. Advocate, 1949; Standing Junior Counsel, Department of Agriculture for Scotland and Forestry Commission, 1956–61; Sheriff Principal of Aberdeen, Kincardine and Banff, 1972–74. Chairman: Pensions Appeals Tribunals, Scotland, 1971–95 (Pres., 1971–75); Medical Appeal Tribunals, 1985–91. Member, Board of Management: Edinburgh Central Hosps, 1960–70 (Chm., 1964–70); Edinburgh Royal Victoria Hosps, 1970–74 (Vice-Chm.); Dir, Scottish Nat. Orchestra Soc. Ltd, 1962–80; Trustee, Nat. Library of Scotland, 1963–76; Chm., RSSPCC, Edinburgh, 1972–76. Hon. Advr, RBL, Scotland, on captivity in FE during War of 1939–45; Chm., Scottish FE POW Assoc., 1996–. Hon. LLD Aberdeen, 1981. *Address:* 16 Royal Circus, Edinburgh EH3 6SS. *T:* (0131) 225 8055. *Club:* Royal Northern and University (Aberdeen).

GINGELL, Air Chief Marshal Sir John, GBE 1984 (CBE 1973; MBE 1962); KCB 1978; KCVO 1992; RAF, retired; Gentleman Usher of the Black Rod, Serjeant-at-Arms, House of Lords, and Secretary to the Lord Great Chamberlain, 1985–92; *b* 3 Feb. 1925; *e s* of late E. J. Gingell; *m* 1949, Prudence, *d* of late Brig. R. F. Johnson; two *s* one *d.* *Educ:* St Boniface Coll., Plymouth. Entered RAF, 1943; Fleet Air Arm, 1945–46 as Sub-Lt (A) RNVR; returned to RAF, 1951; served with Nos 58 and 542 Sqdns; CFS 1954; psc 1959; jssc 1965; comd No 27 Sqdn, 1963–65; Staff of Chief of Defence Staff, 1966; Dep. Dir Defence Ops Staff (Central Staff), 1966–67; Mil. Asst to Chm. NATO Mil. Cttee, Brussels, 1968–70; AOA, RAF Germany, 1971–72; AOC 23 Group, RAF Trng Comd, 1973–75; Asst Chief of Defence Staff (Policy), 1975–78; Air Member for Personnel, 1978–80; AOC-in-C, RAF Support Comd, 1980–81; Dep. C-in-C, Allied Forces Central Europe, 1981–84. Mem., Commonwealth War Graves Commn, 1986–91. Hon. Bencher, Inner Temple, 1990. *Recreations:* gardening, walking, music. *Club:* Royal Air Force.

GINGELL, Maj.-Gen. Laurie William Albert, CB 1980; OBE 1966 (MBE 1959); General Secretary, Officers' Pensions Society, 1979–90; *b* 29 Oct. 1925; *s* of late Major William George Gingell, MBE, MM, and of Elsie Grace Gingell; *m* 1949, Nancy Margaret Wadsworth; one *s* one *d.* *Educ:* Farnborough Grammar Sch.; Oriel Coll., Oxford. Commissioned into Royal Gloucestershire Hussars, 1945; transf. Royal Tank Regt, 1947; psc 1956; jssc 1961; Commanded: 1st Royal Tank Regt, 1966–67; 7th Armoured Bde, 1970–71; DQMG, HQ BAOR, 1973–76; Maj.-Gen. Admin, HQ UKLF, 1976–79. ADC to the Queen, 1974–76. Vice-Pres., Victory Services Club, 1997– (Chm., 1989–97). FIMgt (FBIM 1979). *Recreations:* swimming, reading. *Address:* 54 Station Road, Thames Ditton, Surrey KT7 0NS. *T:* (020) 8224 7023.

GINGER, Phyllis Ethel, (Mrs Leslie Durbin), RWS 1958 (ARWS 1952); freelance artist since 1940; *b* 19 Oct. 1907; *m* 1940, Leslie Durbin, *qv*; one *s* one *d.* *Educ:* Tiffin's Girls' Sch., Kingston on Thames. LCC three years' scholarship at Central School of Arts and Crafts, 1937–39. Water colours for Pilgrim Trust Recording Britain Scheme, 1941–42; Royal Academy Exhibitor; Drawings and Lithographs purchased by: Washington State Library, 1941; Victoria and Albert Museum, 1952; London Museum, 1954; South London Art Gallery, 1960. *Publications:* Alexander the Circus Pony, 1941; book jacket designs; book illustrations include: London by Mrs Robert Henrey, 1948; The Virgin of Aldemanbury, by Mrs Robert Henrey, 1960. *Address:* 298 Kew Road, Kew, Richmond, Surrey TW9 3DU. *T:* (020) 8940 2221.

GINGRICH, Newton Leroy, (Newt); Chief Executive Officer, Gingrich Group, since 1999; *b* 17 June 1943; *s* of late Robert Bruce Gingrich and of Kathleen (*née* Daugherty); *m* 1st, 1962, Jacqueline Battley (marr. diss. 1981); two *d*; 2nd, 1981, Marianne Ginther (marr. diss. 2000); 3rd, 2000, Callista Bisek. *Educ:* Emory Univ. (BA); Tulane Univ. (MA; PhD 1971). Taught history, W Georgia Coll., Carrollton, 1970–78; Mem. from 6th Dist of Georgia, US Congress, 1979–99 (Republican Whip, 1989–94); Speaker, US House of Representatives, 1995–99. *Publications:* (jtly) Window of Opportunity: a blueprint for the future, 1984; (jtly) 1945, 1995; To Renew America, 1995; Lessons Learned the Hard Way, 1998. *Address:* The Gingrich Group, 1301 K Street NW, Suite 800 West, Washington, DC 20005, USA.

GINNEVER, John Anthony; Director of Education, Leisure and Libraries, East Riding of Yorkshire, since 1995; *b* 24 June 1948; *s* of George Edward Ginnever and Olive Ginnever; *m* 1971, Wendy Marian Brown; one *s* one *d.* *Educ:* Hatfield Coll., Durham Univ. (BSc Hons 1970; PGCE 1971); Newcastle Univ. (MEd 1977). Teacher, 1971–77; Education Officer: Leeds MBC, 1978–82; Bucks CC, 1982–87; N Yorks CC, 1987–89; Dep. Dir of Educn, Newcastle MBC, 1989–95. Chm., UK/US Teacher Exchange Cttee, British Council, 1995–. Chm., NE Regl Adv. Cttee, Duke of Edinburgh's Award, 1998–. *Recreations:* birdwatching, hill walking, golf. *Address:* Old Minster School, Minster Moorgate, Beverley, E Riding HU17 8HP; (office) County Hall, Beverley, E Riding HU17 9BA. *T:* (01482) 392000.

GINSBURG, Ruth Bader; Associate Justice of the Supreme Court of the United States, since 1993; *b* 15 March 1933; *d* of Nathan Bader and Celia Amster Bader; *m* 1954, Martin D. Ginsburg; one *s* one *d.* *Educ:* James Madison High Sch., Brooklyn; Cornell Univ. (BA Hons 1954); Harvard Law Sch.; Columbia Law Sch. (Kent Scholar; LLB, JD 1959). Clerk, Southern Dist, NY, 1959–61; Columbia Law Sch. Project on Internat. Procedure, 1961–63; Professor: Rutgers Univ. Sch. of Law, 1963–72; Columbia Law Sch., 1972–80; Circuit Judge, Court of Appeals for Dist of Columbia, 1980–93. American Civil Liberties Union: Gen. Counsel, 1973–80; Nat. Board, 1974–80; Counsel to Women's Rights Project, 1972–80. Fellow: Amer. Bar Foundn, 1978– (Exec. Cttee and Sec., 1979–89); Amer. Acad. of Arts and Scis, 1982– (Mem. Council, Foreign Relations, 1975–). *Publications:* (with A. Bruzelius) Civil Procedure in Sweden, 1965; (with A. Bruzelius) Swedish Code of Judicial Procedure, 1968; (jtly) Text, Cases and Materials on Sex-Based Discrimination, 1974, Supp. 1978; numerous contribs to learned jls. *Address:* Supreme Court, 1 First Street NE, Washington, DC 20543, USA.

GIOLITTI, Dr Antonio; Member, Commission of the European Communities, 1977–85; Senator, Italian Parliament, 1987–92; *b* 12 Feb. 1915; *s* of Giuseppe and Maria Giolitti; *m* 1939, Elena d'Amico; one *s* two *d.* *Educ:* Rome Univ. (Dr Law); Oxford; München. Dep., Italian Parlt, 1946–76; Minister of Budget and Economic Planning, 1964, 1970–72, 1973–74. Member: Italian Communist Party, 1943–57; Italian Socialist Party, 1958–83; Exec., Italian Socialist Party, 1958–83; Sinistra Indipendente, 1987–92. *Publications:* Riforme e rivoluzione, 1957; Il comunismo in Europa, 1960; Un socialismo possibile, 1967; Lettere a Marta, 1992. *Recreations:* music, walking. *Address:* Piazza Cairoli 6, 00186 Rome, Italy.

GIORDANO, Richard Vincent, Hon. KBE 1989; Chairman, BG Group plc, since 2000 (Chairman, BG (formerly British Gas) plc, 1994–2000); *b* March 1934; *s* of late Vincent Giordano and of Cynthia Giordano (*née* Cardetta); *m* 1st, 1956, Barbara Claire Beckett; one *s* two *d*; 2nd, 2000, Susan Mary Ware. *Educ:* Harvard Coll., Cambridge, Mass, USA (BA); Columbia Univ. Law Sch. (LLB). Shearman & Sterling, 1959; Airco, Inc., 1963–78: Gp Vice Pres., 1967; Gp Pres., Chief Operating Officer and Mem. Bd, 1971; Chief Exec. Officer, Airco, Inc., 1978; BOC Group: Chief Exec. Officer, 1979–91; Gp Man. Dir, 1979–85; Chm., 1985–92; non-exec. Chm., 1994–96; Grand Metropolitan plc: Bd Mem., 1985–97; Dep. Chm., 1991–97. Mem., CEGB, 1982–92; part-time Board Member: Rio Tinto plc (formerly RTZ Corp.), 1992– (Dep. Chm., 2000–); Georgia Pacific Corp., Atlanta, Ga, 1984–; Dir, Lucas Industries, 1993–94. Hon. Dr of Commercial Science, St John's Univ., 1975. *Recreations:* ocean sailing, tennis. *Address:* c/o BG Group plc, Eagle House, 108–110 Jermyn Street, SW1Y 6RP. *Clubs:* The Links, New York Yacht (New York).

GIPPS, Dr Jonathan Henry William, OBE 2000; Director, Bristol Zoo, and Bristol, Clifton and West of England Zoological Society, since 2001; *b* 7 July 1947; *s* of late Capt. Louis H. F. P. Gipps, RN and Molly Joyce Gipps; *m* 1970, Prof. Caroline Victoria Davis; two *s.* *Educ:* Imperial Coll., Univ. of London (BSc Zool. 1973); Royal Holloway Coll., Univ. of London (PhD 1977). RN, 1966–70. Post-doctoral Research Fellow, Univ. of British Columbia, 1977–79; Lectr in Biology, Univ. of Bath, 1980–81; Res. Fellow, RHBNC, 1981–84; Educn Officer, Computer Centre, Kingston Poly., 1984–87; London Zoo: Curator of Mammals, 1987–91; General Curator, 1991–93; Dir, 1993–2001. Hon. DSc Kingston, 1993. *Publications:* (ed jtly) The Ecology of Woodland Rodents, 1981; (ed) Beyond Captive Breeding: re-introducing endangered mammals to the wild, 1989. *Recreations:* fishing, making jewellery, ski-ing, cooking, travelling. *Address:* Bristol Zoo Gardens, Guthrie Road, Bristol BS8 3HA.

GIPPSLAND, Bishop of, since 1994; **Rt Rev. Arthur Lucas Vivian Jones,** PhD; *b* 11 Dec. 1934; *s* of Arthur Edmond Jones and Mona Emily Jones; *m* 1979, Valerie Joan Maxwell; one *s* three *d.* *Educ:* St John's Coll., Morpeth, NSW (ThL); ACT (ThSchol); London Univ. (BD ext); Deakin Univ. (BA); Newcastle Univ., NSW (MA Classics); Adelaide Coll. of Adv. Educn (Grad.Dip.RE); Geneva Theol Coll. (ThD); Lambeth Diploma; LaTrobe Univ. (PhD 1998). Deacon 1966, priest 1967; Curate, Holy Trinity, Orange, NSW, 1966–69; Missionary, Panama, 1970–73 and 1977–80; Rector, St Barnabas, Orange, NSW, 1973–77; Vicar, Corangamite, Vic, 1980–82; Lectr in NT, St John's Coll., Morpeth, 1982–85; Rector, Woy Woy, NSW, 1985–89; Dean, St Paul's Cathedral, Sale, 1989–94; Diocesan Theologian, Gippsland, 1989–94. *Recreations:* golf, writing. *Address:* Bishopscourt, 4 Cranswick Crescent, Sale, Vic 3850, Australia. *T:* (3) 51442046; PO Box 28, Sale, Vic 3850, Australia.

GIRDWOOD, Prof. Ronald Haxton, CBE 1984; MD, PhD, FRCP, FRCPE, FRCPI, FRCPath; FRSE 1978; Professor of Therapeutics and Clinical Pharmacology, University of Edinburgh, 1962–82, Emeritus, since 1982; President, Royal College of Physicians of Edinburgh, 1982–85; *b* 19 March 1917; *s* of late Thomas Girdwood and Elizabeth Stewart Girdwood (*née* Haxton); *m* 1945, Mary Elizabeth, *d* of late Reginald Williams, Calstock, Cornwall; one *s* one *d.* *Educ:* Daniel Stewart's Coll., Edinburgh; University of Edinburgh; University of Michigan. MB, ChB (Hons) Edinburgh 1939; Ettles Schol., Leslie Gold Medallist, Royal Victoria Hosp.; Tuberculosis Trust Gold Medallist, Wightman, Beaney and Keith Memorial Prize Winner, 1939; MD (Gold Medal for thesis), 1954. Pres. Edinburgh Univ. Church of Scotland Soc., 1938–39. Served RAMC, 1942–46 (mentioned in Orders); Nutrition Research Officer and Officer i/c Med. Div. in India and Burma. Lectr in Medicine, University of Edinburgh, 1946; Rockefeller Research Fellow, University of Michigan, 1948–49; Cons. Phys., Chalmers Hosp., Edinburgh, 1950–51; Sen. Lectr in Med., 1951–58; Vis. Lectr, Dept of Pharmacology, Yale Univ., 1956; Reader in Med., 1958, Dean of Faculty of Medicine, 1975–79, Edinburgh Univ.; Consultant Physician, Royal Infirmary of Edinburgh, 1951–82. Sometime External Examiner for Universities of London, Sheffield, St Andrews, Dundee, Dublin, Glasgow and Hong Kong, and for Med. Colls in Singapore, Dhaka and Karachi. Chm., SE Scotland Blood Transfusion Assoc., 1970–95; Mem. Council, RCPE, 1966–70, 1978–80, Vice-Pres., 1981–82, Pres. 1982–85; Member: South-Eastern Reg. Hosp. Board (Scotland), 1965–69; Board of Management, Royal Infirmary, Edinburgh, 1958–64; Cttee on Safety of Medicines, 1972–83; Exec., Medico-Pharmaceutical Forum, 1972–74 (Vice-Chm.,

1983–85; Chm., 1985–87); Chairman: Scottish Group of Hæmophilia Soc., 1954–60; Non-Professorial Medical Teachers and Research Workers Gp Cttee (Scot.) of BMA, 1956–62; Scottish Gp of Nutrition Soc., 1961–62; Consultative Council, Edinburgh Medical Gp, 1977–82; Scottish Nat. Blood Transfusion Assoc., 1980–95; Pres. Brit. Soc. for Hæmatology, 1963–64; Member: Coun. Brit. Soc. of Gastroenterology, 1964–68; Council of Nutrition Soc., 1957–60 and 1961–64; Pres., Univ. of Edinburgh Graduates' Assoc., 1991–93 (Vice-Pres., 1989–91). British Council visitor to W African Hosps, 1963, to Middle East, 1977, to India, 1980; Visiting Prof. and WHO Consultant, India, 1965, Pakistan, 1985. Gov., St Columba's Hospice, 1985–97. Former Chm., Bd of Management, Scottish Med. Jl and Mem., Editl Bds, Blood, and British Jl of Haematology; Mem. Editl Bd, Brit. Jl of Nutrition, 1960–65. Office Bearer, Kirk of the Greyfriars, Edinburgh, 1970–. Awarded Freedom of the township of Sirajgunj, Bangladesh, 1984. Hon. FACP 1983; Hon. FRACP 1985. Cullen Prize, 1970, Lilly Lectr, 1979, RCPE; Suniti Panja gold medal, Calcutta Sch. Trop. Med., 1980; Oliver Meml Award (for services to blood transfusion), 1991. *Publications:* about 350, particularly in relation to nutrition, hæmatology, gastroenterology and medical history; (contrib.) Davidson's Principles and Practice of Medicine, all edns 1952–81; (ed with A. N. Smith) Malabsorption, 1969; (ed with S. Alstead) Textbook of Medical Treatment, 12th edn 1971 to 14th edn 1978, (ed with J. Petrie) 15th edn, 1987 (trans. Spanish, 1992); (ed) Blood Disorders due to Drugs and Other Agents, 1973; (ed) Clinical Pharmacology, 23rd edn 1976 to 25th edn 1984; Travels with a Stethoscope, 1991. *Recreations:* photography, writing. *Address:* 2 Hermitage Drive, Edinburgh EH10 6DD. *T:* (home) (0131) 447 5137. *Club:* East India, Devonshire, Sports and Public Schools.

See also J. O. Drife.

GIRET, (Josephine) Jane; QC 2001; *b* 6 June 1944; *d* of late Bernard Leslie Barker and of Josephine Mamie Barker; *m* 1985, Joseph John Bela Leslie Giret. *Educ:* Queen Anne's Sch., Caversham, Berks. Called to the Bar, Inner Temple, 1981. *Recreations:* following the English Cricket Team, Barbados, yoga. *Address:* 11 Stone Buildings, Lincoln's Inn, WC2A 3TG; 74 Alder Lodge, River Gardens, Stevenage Road, SW6 6NR. *T:* (020) 7831 6381.

GIRLING, (John) Anthony; Consultant, Girlings, Solicitors, since 2000; President of the Law Society, 1996–97; *b* 21 Aug. 1943; *s* of James William Girling, OBE and Annie Doris (*née* Reeves); *m* 1965, Lynne Margaret Davis; one *s* one *d*. *Educ:* Tonbridge Sch.; Guildford Coll. of Law. Admitted Solicitor, 1966; Girlings, Solicitors: Partner, 1968; Man. Partner, 1982–96; Chm., 1997–2000. Hon. Sec., 1974–80, Pres., 1980–81, Kent Law Soc.; Mem. for Kent, Council of Law Soc., 1980–99. Hon. Sen. Mem., Darwin Coll., Univ. of Kent, 1984. Fellow, Inst. of Advanced Legal Studies, Univ. of London, 1997–. Hon. LLD Kent, 1998. *Publications:* contrib. to Law Soc. Gazette and other legal jls. *Recreations:* golf, ski-ing, the countryside. *Address:* Girlings, Solicitors, 3 Dane John, Canterbury, Kent CT1 2UG. *T:* (01227) 768374; Maypole House, Hoath, Canterbury, Kent CT3 4LN. *Clubs:* Ski of Great Britain; Canterbury Golf.

GIROLAMI, Sir Paul, Kt 1988; FCA; Chairman, Glaxo Holdings, 1985–94; *b* 25 Jan. 1926; *m* 1952, Christabel Mary Gwynne Lewis; two *s* one *d*. *Educ:* London School of Economics (Hon. Fellow, 1989); FREconS; FIMC 1990. Chantrey & Button, Chartered Accountants, 1950–54; Coopers & Lybrand, Chartered Accountants, 1954–65; Glaxo Holdings: Financial Controller, 1965; Finance Director, 1968; Chief Exec., 1980–86. Director: Inner London Board of National Westminster Bank, 1974–89; Credito Italiano Internat. UK, 1990–93; Forte plc, 1992–96; UIS France, 1994–. Member: Bd of Dirs, Amer. Chamber of Commerce (UK), 1983–; CBI Council, 1986–93; Appeal Cttee, ICA, 1987–; Stock Exchange Listed Cos Adv. Cttee, 1987–92. Chm., Senate for Chartered Accountants in Business, 1990–. Chm. Council, Goldsmiths' Coll., Univ. of London, 1994–; Mem. Open Univ. Vis. Cttee, 1987–89. Gov., NIESR, 1992. Freeman, City of London; Liveryman, Goldsmiths' Co., 1980– (Mem., Ct of Assistants, 1986–; Prime Warden, 1995–96); Mem., Soc. of Apothecaries, 1993–. Hon. FCGI 1994; FIMgt (FBIM 1986); FRSA 1986. Hon. DSc: Aston, 1990; Trieste, 1991; Sunderland, 1991; Bradford, 1993; Hon. LLD: Singapore, 1993; Warwick, 1996; Hon. DBA Strathclyde, 1993. Centenary Medal, UK SCI, 1992; Centenary Award, UK Founding Socs, 1992. Grand Cross, Order of the Holy Sepulchre, 1994. Grande Ufficiale, Ordine al Merito della Repubblica Italiana, 1987; Cavaliere al Merito del Lavoro, Italy, 1991; Insignia of the Order of the Rising Sun, Japan, 1991; Public Service Star, Singapore, 2000. *Recreations:* reading, music.

GIROUARD, Mark, PhD; writer and architectural historian; Slade Professor of Fine Art, University of Oxford, 1975–76; *b* 7 Oct. 1931; *s* of late Richard D. Girouard and Lady Blanche Girouard; *m* 1970, Dorothy N. Dorf; one *d*. *Educ:* Ampleforth; Christ Church, Oxford (MA); Courtauld Inst. of Art (PhD); Bartlett Sch., UCL (BSc, Dip. Arc). Staff of Country Life, 1958–66; studied architecture, Bartlett Sch., UCL, 1966–71; staff of Architectural Review, 1971–75. George Lurcy Vis. Prof., Columbia Univ., NY, 1987. Member: Council, Victorian Soc., 1979– (Founder Mem. 1958; Mem. Cttee, 1958–66); Royal Fine Art Commn, 1972–96; Royal Commn on Historical Monuments (England), 1976–81; Historic Buildings Council (England), 1978–84; Commn for Historic Buildings and Monuments, 1984–90 (Mem., Buildings Adv. Cttee, 1984–86; Mem., Historic Areas Adv. Cttee, 1985–89; Mem., Historic Bldgs Cttee, 1988–90); Council, Spitalfields Historic Buildings Trust, 1983– (Chm., 1977–83); Trustee, Architecture Foundn, 1992–99. Mem., Adv. Council, Paul Mellon Centre for Studies in British Art, 1990–96. FSA 1986; Hon. FRIBA, 1980. Hon. DLitt: Leicester, 1982; Buckingham, 1991. *Publications:* Robert Smythson and the Architecture of the Elizabethan Era, 1966, 2nd edn, Robert Smythson and the Elizabethan Country House, 1983; The Victorian Country House, 1971, 2nd edn 1979; Victorian Pubs, 1975, 2nd edn 1984; (jtly) Spirit of the Age, 1975 (based on BBC TV series); Sweetness and Light: the 'Queen Anne' movement 1860–1900, 1977; Life in the English Country House, 1978 (Duff Cooper Meml Prize; W. H. Smith Award, 1979); Historic Houses of Britain, 1979; Alfred Waterhouse and the Natural History Museum, 1981; The Return to Camelot: chivalry and the English gentleman, 1981; Cities and People, 1985; A Country House Companion, 1987; The English Town, 1990; Town and Country, 1992; Windsor: the most romantic castle, 1993; Big Jim: the life and work of James Stirling, 1998; Life in the French Country House, 2000; articles in Country Life, Architect. Rev., Listener. *Address:* 35 Colville Road, W11 2BT. *Club:* Beefsteak.

GIRVAN, Hon. Sir (Frederick) Paul, Kt 1995; **Hon. Mr Justice Girvan;** a Justice of the High Court of Northern Ireland, since 1995; *b* 20 Oct. 1948; *s* of Robert Frederick Girvan and Martha Elizabeth (*née* Barron); *m* 1974, Karen Elizabeth Joyce; two *s* one *d*. *Educ:* Belfast Royal Acad.; Clare Coll., Cambridge (BA); Queen's Univ., Belfast; Gray's Inn. Called to the Bar: NI, 1971; Inner Bar (NI), 1982; Jun. Crown Counsel, NI, 1979–82. Chancellor, Archdio. of Armagh, 1999–. Chairman: Council of Law Reporting for NI, 1994–; Law Reform Adv. Cttee for NI, 1997– (Mem., 1994–). Hon. Bencher, Gray's Inn, 1999. *Recreations:* badminton, walking, swimming, reading, modern languages, gardening, cooking, golf, painting. *Address:* Royal Courts of Justice, Chichester Street, Belfast, Northern Ireland BT1 3JF. *T:* (028) 9023 5111.

GISBOROUGH, 3rd Baron *cr* 1917; **Thomas Richard John Long Chaloner;** Lieutenant of North Yorkshire, since 1996 (Lord-Lieutenant of Cleveland, 1981–96); *b* 1 July 1927; *s* of 2nd Baron and Esther Isabella Madeleine (*d* 1970), *yr d* of late Charles O. Hall, Eddlethorpe; *S* father, 1951; *m* 1960, Shane, *e d* of late Sidney Newton, London, and *g d* of Sir Louis Newton, 1st Bt; two *s*. *Educ:* Eton; Royal Agricultural Coll. 16th/5th Lancers, 1948–52; Captain Northumberland Hussars, 1955–61; Lt-Col Green Howards (Territorials), 1967–69. Mem., Rural Develt Commn, 1985–89. CC NR Yorks, 1964–74, Cleveland, 1974–77. Hon. Col, Cleveland County Army Cadet Force, 1981–92. President: British Ski Fedn, 1985–90; Assoc. of Professional Foresters, 1998–. DL N Riding of Yorks and Cleveland, 1973; JP Langbaurgh East, 1981–94. KStJ 1981. *Recreations:* field sports, ski-ing, tennis, bridge, piano. *Heir:* *s* Hon. Thomas Peregrine Long Chaloner [*b* 17 Jan. 1961; *m* 1992, Karen, *o d* of Alan Thomas]. *Address:* Gisborough House, Guisborough, Cleveland TS14 6PT. *T:* (01287) 632002. *Club:* White's.

GISCARD d'ESTAING, Valéry; Grand Croix de la Légion d'Honneur; Croix de Guerre (1939–45); President of the French Republic, 1974–81; Deputy for Puy-de-Dôme, since 1993; President: Conseil Régional d'Auvergne, since 1986; Council of European Municipalities and Regions, since 1997; *b* Coblence, 2 Feb. 1926; *s* of late Edmond Giscard d'Estaing and May Bardoux; *m* 1952, Anne-Aymone de Brantes; two *s* two *d*. *Educ:* Lycée Janson-de-Sailly, Paris; Ecole Polytechnique; Ecole Nationale d'Administration. Inspection of Finances: Deputy, 1952; Inspector, 1954; Dep. Dir, Cabinet of Président du Conseil, June-Dec. 1954. Elected Deputy for Puy-de-Dôme, 1956; re-elected for Clermont N and SW, Nov. 1958, Nov.–Dec. 1962, March 1967, June 1968, March 1973, 1984, 1986 and 1988–89; Sec. of State for Finance, 1959; Minister of Finance, Jan.-April 1962; Minister of Finance and Economic Affairs, April-Nov. 1962 and Dec. 1962–Jan. 1966; Minister of Economy and Finance, 1969–74. Pres., Nat. Fedn of Indep. Republicans, 1966–73 (also a Founder); Pres., comm. des finances de l'économie générale et du plan de l'Assemblée nationale, 1967–68; Chm., Commn of Foreign Affairs, Nat. Assembly, 1987–89, 1993–97. Mem., Eur. Parlt, 1989–93. Pres., Eur. Movt Internat., 1989–97. Mayor of Chamalières, 1967–74. Deleg. to Assembly of UN, 1956, 1957, 1958. Mem., Real Acad. de Ciencias Economicas y Financieras, Spain, 1995–. Nansen Medal, 1979. *Publications:* Démocratie Française, 1976 (Towards a New Democracy, 1977); 2 Français sur 3, 1984; Le Pouvoir et la Vie (memoirs), 1988; L'Affrontement, 1991; Le Passage (novel), 1994; Dans 5 ans l'an 2000, 1995. *Address:* 11 rue Bénouville, 75116 Paris, France; (office) 199 Boulevard Saint-Germain, 75007 Paris, France. *Clubs:* Polo (Paris); Union Interalliée.

GITTINGS, Harold John; Director, Meltemi Entertainment Ltd, 1996–2000; *b* 3 Sept. 1947; *s* of Harold William Gittings and Doris Marjorie Gittings (*née* Whiting); *m* 1988, Andrea (*née* Fisher) (*d* 1995); two step *c*. *Educ:* Duke of York's Royal Military School, Dover. ACIS. Beecham Group, 1971–73; Peat Marwick Mitchell, Hong Kong, 1973–74; N. M. Rothschild & Sons, 1974–81; Continental Bank, 1981–82; Target Group, 1982–85; Man. Dir, Touche Remnant & Co. 1986–90; Chm., Greenfield Marketing, subseq. Greenfield Gp, 1992–96. *Recreations:* travel, collecting, film. *Address:* Southcot, Clayhill, Beckley, Rye, E Sussex TN31 6SG.

GITTUS, John Henry, DSc, DTech; FREng; Senior Technical Consultant: Cox Power Holdings, since 1997; ESKOM, since 1998; Working Member, Lloyds' Nuclear Syndicate, since 1996; Senior Partner: SPA Consultants, since 1993; NUSYS Consultants, Paris, since 1994; AEA Technology, since 1996; Nycomed-Amersham, since 1999; Sumitomo Corporation, since 1999; *b* 25 July 1930; *s* of Henry Gittus and Amy Gittus; *m* 1953, Rosemary Ann Geeves; one *s* two *d*. *Educ:* BSc (1st Cl. Hons, Maths) London 1952; DSc Phys London 1976; DTech Metall Stockholm 1975. CEng, FREng (FEng 1989); FIMechE, FIS, FIM. British Cast Iron Res. Assoc., 1947–55; Mond Nickel Co., R&D Labs, Birmingham, 1955–60 (develt Nimonic series high temp. super alloys for aircraft gas turbine engines); United Kingdom Atomic Energy Authority, 1960–89: Research Manager, Springfields; Head, Water Reactor fuel develt; Head, Atomic Energy Tech. Br., Harwell; Director: Water Reactor Safety Research; Safety and Reliability Directorate, Culcheth; Communication and Information; Dir Gen., British Nuclear Forum, 1990–93. Consultant: Argonne Nat. Lab., USA, 1968; Oak Ridge Nat. Lab., 1969. Visiting Professor: Ecole Polytechnique Fédérale, Lausanne, 1976; Univ. de Nancy, 1984; Regents' Prof., UCLA, 1990–91; Prof. of Risk Mgt, Plymouth Univ., 1997–. Editor-in-Chief, Res Mechanica, 1980–91. *Publications:* Uranium, 1962; Creep, Viscoelasticity and Creep-fracture in Solids, 1979; Irradiation Effects in Crystalline Solids, 1979; (with W. Crosbie) Medical Response to Effects of Ionizing Radiation, 1989; numerous articles in learned jls. *Recreations:* old houses, old motor cars, old friends. *Address:* (office) 34 Leadenhall Street, EC3A 1AX. *T:* (020) 7265 6866; (home) The Rectory, 19 Butter Street, Alcester, Stratford-upon-Avon B49 5AL. *Club:* Royal Society of Medicine.

GIUDICE, Geoffrey Michael; Hon. Justice Giudice; Judge of the Federal Court, Australia, since 1997; President, Australian Industrial Relations Commission, since 1997; *b* 16 Dec. 1947; *s* of Rupert Emanuel Giudice and Emily Muriel Giudice; *m* 1970, Beth Hayden; three *s* one *d*. *Educ:* Xavier Coll., Melbourne; Univ. of Melbourne (BA 1970; LLB). Res. Officer, Hosp. Employees Union, 1971; IR Manager, Myer Emporium Ltd, 1972–78; Partner, Moule Hamilton and Derham, solicitors, 1979–84; Barrister, Victoria Bar, 1984–97. *Recreations:* tennis, bridge. *Address:* Australian Industrial Relations Commission, Level 42, 80 Collins Street, Melbourne, Vic 3000, Australia. *T:* (3) 96538272. *Clubs:* Athenæum (Melbourne); Melbourne Cricket, Victoria Racing.

GIULIANI, Rudolph William, Hon. KBE 2001; Mayor, City of New York, 1994–2001; *b* 28 May 1944; *m* 1984; one *s* one *d*. *Educ:* Manhattan Coll. (AB); New York Univ. (JD). Legal Clerk to US Dist Court Judge, NYC, 1968–70; Asst Attorney, S Dist, NY, 1970–73; Exec. Asst Attorney, Dept of Justice, 1973–75; Associate Dep. Attorney Gen., 1975–77; with Patterson, Belknap, Webb and Tyler, 1977–81; Associate Attorney Gen., 1981–83; US Attorney, US Dist Court, S Dist, NY, 1983–89; with White & Case, 1989–90; with Anderson Kill Olick & Oshinsky PC, 1990–93. Republican Candidate for Mayor, NY, 1989. *Address:* c/o Office of the Mayor, City Hall, New York, NY 10007, USA.

GIULINI, Carlo Maria; conductor; Music Director, Los Angeles Philharmonic Orchestra, 1978–84; *b* 9 May 1914; *m*; three *s*. *Educ:* Accademia Santa Cecilia, Rome. Début as conductor, Rome, 1944; formed Orchestra of Milan Radio, 1950; Principal Conductor, La Scala, Milan, 1953–55; début in Great Britain, conducting Verdi's Falstaff, Edinburgh Festival, 1955; closely associated with Philharmonia Orchestra, 1955–; début at Royal Opera House, Covent Garden, Don Carlos, 1958; Principal Guest Conductor, Chicago Symphony Orch., 1969–78; Music Dir, Vienna Symphony Orch., 1973–76; Music Dir, Los Angeles Philharmonic Orch., 1978–84; conducted new prodn of Falstaff in Los Angeles, at Covent Garden, and at Teatro Comunale, Florence, 1982, after 14 year absence from opera. Laureate Conductor, Swedish Radio Orch. Hon. Mem., Ges. der Musikfreunde, Vienna, 1978; Hon. DHL DePaul Univ., Chicago, 1979. Gold Medal: Bruckner Soc., 1978; International Mahler Society; Una Vita Nella Musica. *Recreation:* sailing. *Address:* c/o Signor Francesco Giulini, Via Bonnet 7, 20121 Milan, Italy.

GIVEN, Edward Ferguson, CMG 1968; CVO 1979; HM Diplomatic Service, retired; *b* 13 April 1919; *s* of James K. Given, West Kilbride, Ayrshire; *m* 1st, 1946, Philida Naomi Bullwinkle; one *s*; 2nd, 1954, Kathleen Margaret Helena Kelly. *Educ:* Sutton County Sch.; University Coll., London. Served RA, 1939–46. Entered HM Foreign Service, 1946; served at Paris, Rangoon, Bahrain, Bordeaux, Office of Political Adviser to C-in-C Far East, Singapore, Moscow, Beirut; Ambassador: United Republic of Cameroon and Republic of Equatorial Guinea, 1972–75; Bahrain, 1975–79, retired, 1979. Dir-Gen., Middle East Assoc., 1979–83. *Address:* 10 Clarendon Park, Lymington, Hants SO41 8AX. *Club:* Army and Navy.

GLADSTONE, David Arthur Steuart, CMG 1988; HM Diplomatic Service, retired; *b* 1 April 1935; *s* of late Thomas Steuart Gladstone and Muriel Irene Heron Gladstone; *m* 1961, April (*née* Brunner); one *s* one *d*. *Educ:* Eton; Christ Church, Oxford (MA History). National Service, 1954–56; Oxford Univ., 1956–59. Annan, Dexter & Co. (Chartered Accountants), 1959–60; FO, 1960; MECAS, Lebanon, 1960–62; Bahrain, 1962–63; FO, 1963–65; Bonn, 1965–69; FCO, 1969–72; Cairo, 1972–75; British Mil. Govt, Berlin, 1976–79; Head of Western European Dept, FCO, 1979–82; Consul-Gen., Marseilles, 1983–87; High Comr, Colombo, 1987–91; Chargé d'Affaires *ai*, Kiev, 1992. *Recreations:* music, theatre, cinema, dreaming, landscape gardening. *Address:* 1 Mountfort Terrace, N1 1JJ.

GLADSTONE, Sir (Erskine) William, 7th Bt *cr* 1846; KG 1999; JP; Lord-Lieutenant of Clwyd, 1985–2000; *b* 29 Oct. 1925; *s* of Charles Andrew Gladstone, (6th Bt), and Isla Margaret (*d* 1987), *d* of late Sir Walter Erskine Crum; *S* father, 1968; *m* 1962, Rosamund Anne, *yr d* of late Major A. Hambro; two *s* one *d*. *Educ:* Eton; Christ Church, Oxford. Served RNVR, 1943–46. Asst Master at Shrewsbury, 1949–50, and at Eton, 1951–61; Head Master of Lancing Coll., 1961–69. Chief Scout of UK and Overseas Branches, 1972–82; Mem., World Scout Cttee, 1977–83 (Chm., 1979–81). DL Flintshire, 1969, Clwyd, 1974, Vice Lord-Lieut, 1984; Alderman, Flintshire CC, 1970–74. Chm., Rep. Body of Church in Wales 1977–92; Chairman: Council of Glenalmond Coll. (formerly Trinity Coll., Glenalmond), 1982–86; Govs, Ruthin Sch., 1987–92 (Patron, 1998–). JP Clwyd 1982. Hon. LLD Liverpool, 1998. *Publications:* various school textbooks. *Recreations:* reading history, watercolours, shooting, gardening. *Heir: s* Charles Angus Gladstone [*b* 11 April 1964; *m* 1988, Caroline, *o d* of Sir Derek Thomas, *qv*; two *s* four *d*]. *Address:* Hawarden Castle, Flintshire CH5 3PB. *T:* (01244) 520210.

GLADWIN, family name of **Baron Gladwin of Clee**.

GLADWIN OF CLEE, Baron *cr* 1994 (Life Peer), of Great Grimsby in the County of Humberside; **Derek Oliver Gladwin,** CBE 1979 (OBE 1977); JP; Regional Secretary (Southern Region), General and Municipal Workers' Union, 1970–90; Member, Post Office Board (formerly Post Office Corporation), 1972–94; *b* 6 June 1930; *s* of Albert Victor Gladwin and Ethel Gladwin (*née* Oliver); *m* 1956, Ruth Ann Pinion; one *s*. *Educ:* Carr Lane Junior Sch., Grimsby; Wintringham Grammar Sch.; Ruskin Coll., Oxford; London Sch. of Economics. British Railways, Grimsby, 1946–52; fishing industry, Grimsby, 1952–56; Regional Officer 1956–63, Nat. Industrial Officer 1963–70, Gen. and Municipal Workers' Union. Bd Mem., BAe, 1977–91. Chm., Labour Party's Conf. Arrangements Cttee, 1974–90. Mem., Employment Appeal Tribunal, 1992–2001. Member: Council, Industrial Soc., 1968 (Mem. Exec. Cttee, 1968–91); Bd of Trustees, Diabetes UK (formerly British Diabetic Assoc.), 1995–2001; Armed Forces Pay Review Body, 1998–. Pres., Holiday Care Service, 1998–. Chm., Governing Council, Ruskin Coll., Oxford, 1979–99. Vis. Fellow, Nuffield Coll., Oxford, 1978–86. JP Surrey, 1969. *Address:* 2 Friars Rise, Woking, Surrey GU22 7JL. *T:* (01483) 714591; House of Lords, SW1A 0PW.

GLADWIN, Rt Rev. John Warren; *see* Guildford, Bishop of.

GLADWYN, 2nd Baron *cr* 1960, of Bramfield, co. Suffolk; **Miles Alvery Gladwyn Jebb;** *b* 3 March 1930; *s* of 1st Baron Gladwyn, GCMG, GCVO, CB and Cynthia (*d* 1990), *d* of Sir Saxton Noble, 3rd Bt; *S* father, 1996. *Educ:* Eton; Magdalen Coll., Oxford (MA). Served as 2nd Lieut, Welsh Guards and Pilot Officer, RAFVR. Sen. management, BOAC, later British Airways, 1961–83. *Publications:* The Thames Valley Heritage Walk, 1980; A Guide to the South Downs Way, 1984; Walkers, 1986; A Guide to the Thames Path, 1988; East Anglia, 1990; The Colleges of Oxford, 1992; Suffolk, 1995; (ed) The Diaries of Cynthia Gladwyn, 1995. *Recreation:* long-distance walking. *Heir:* none. *Address:* E1 Albany, Piccadilly, W1V 9RH. *Clubs:* Brooks's, Beefsteak.

GLAIEL, Dr Sami; Ambassador of Syria to the Court of St James's, since 2000; *b* 2 Feb. 1941; *s* of George and Milia Glaiel; *m* 1975, Ghada Khoury; one *s* one *d*. *Educ:* Damascus Univ. (BA French Lit. 1965); Warsaw Univ. (Dip. Jlism 1969; PhD Political Scis 1973). Joined Min. of Foreign Affairs, Syria, 1974: First Sec., Perm. Mission to UN, NY, 1975–81; Dep. Dir, Dept of Internat. Orgns, then Dir, Dept of America, Min. of Foreign Affairs, 1981–84; Minister Counsellor, Perm. Mission to UN, 1984–87; Ambassador and Perm. Rep. to UN, Geneva and Vienna, 1987–90; Ambassador to Venezuela and Caribbean Is, 1990–94; Dir, Africa Dept, then Econ. Dept, Min. of Foreign Affairs, 1994–99. *Address:* Embassy of Syria, 8 Belgrave Square, SW1X 8PH.

GLAISYER, Ven. Hugh; Archdeacon of Lewes and Hastings, 1991–97; *b* 20 Jan. 1930; *s* of Rev. Canon Hugh Glaisyer and Edith Glaisyer; *m* 1962, Alison Marion Heap; one *s* two *d*. *Educ:* Tonbridge Sch.; Oriel Coll., Oxford (MA 2nd cl. Hon. Mods, 2nd Cl. Theol.); St Stephen's House, Oxford. FO, RAF, 1954. Ordained, Manchester, 1956; Curate: St Augustine's, Tonge Moor, Bolton, 1956–62; Sidcup, 1962–64; Vicar, Christ Church, Milton-next-Gravesend, 1964–81; RD, Gravesend, 1974–81; Vicar, Hove, 1981–91; RD, Hove, 1982–91; Canon of Chichester Cathedral, 1982–91. *Recreations:* British shorthair cats, gardening. *Address:* Florence Villa, Hangleton Lane, Ferring, W Sussex BN12 6PP. *T:* (01903) 244688.

GLAMANN, Prof. Kristof, OBE 1985; Hon. FBA 1985; author; President, Carlsberg Foundation, 1976–93 (Director, since 1969); Chairman, Carlsberg Ltd, 1977–93 (Director, since 1969); *b* 26 Aug. 1923; *s* of Kai Kristof Glamann, bank manager, and Ebba Henriette Louise (*née* Madsen); *m* 1954, Kirsten Lise (*née* Jantzen), MA, lecturer; two *s*. *Educ:* Odense Katedral-skole; Univ. of Copenhagen (MA Hist. 1948, PhD Econ. Hist., 1958). Univ. of Copenhagen: Research Fellow, 1948–56; Associated Prof., 1956–60; Prof. of History, 1960–80. Visiting Professor: Pennsylvania, 1960; Wisconsin, 1961; LSE 1964; Vis. Overseas Fellow, Churchill Coll., Cambridge, 1971–72, 1993; Toho Gakkai, Japan, 1977; Master, 4th May and Hassager Coll., Copenhagen, 1961–81. Chm., Scand. Inst. of Asian Studies, 1967–71; Hon. Pres., Internat. Econ. Hist. Assoc., 1974 (Pres., 1970–74; Vice-Pres., 1968–70). Director: Carlsberg Brewery Ltd, UK, 1977–93; Fredericia Brewery Ltd, 1975–93; Royal Copenhagen (Holmegaard) Ltd, 1975–93; Politiken Foundn, 1990. Chm., Danish State Research Council of Humanities, 1968–70; Mem. Bd, HM Queen Ingrid's Roman Foundn, 1980; Vice-Pres., Scandinavia-Japan Sasakawa Foundn, 1985–; Member: Royal Danish Acad. of Science and Letters, 1969; Royal Danish Hist. Soc., 1961; Swedish Acad., Lund, 1963; Hist. Soc. of Calcutta, 1962; Corresp. FRHistS 1972; Founding Mem., Acad. Europaea, 1988 (Erasmus Lectr, 2000); Fellow, Royal Belgian Acad., 1989. Editor, Scand. Econ. History Review, 1961–70. Hon. LittD Gothenburg, 1974. Comdr (I), Order of the Dannebrog, 1990 (Kt 1984); Comdr, Northern Star of Sweden, 1984; Order of Orange-Nassau, Netherlands, 1984; Comdr, Falcon of Iceland, 1987; Das Grosse Verdienstkreuz, FRG, 1989; Order of Gorkha Dakshina Bahu, 3rd Cl., Nepal, 1989; Grand Comdr, Ordem do Mérito Agricola e Industrial, Portugal, 1992. *Publications:* History of Tobacco Industry in Denmark 1875–1950, 1950; Dutch-Asiatic Trade 1620–1740, 1958, 2nd edn 1981; (with Astrid Friis) A History of Prices and Wages in Denmark 1660–1800, vol. I, 1958; A History of Brewing in Denmark, 1962; Studies in Mercantilism, 1966, 2nd edn 1984; European Trade 1500–1750, 1971; The Carlsberg Foundation, 1976; Cambridge Econ. Hist. of Europe, vol. V, 1977; J. C. Jacobsen of Carlsberg, Brewer and Philanthropist, 1991; The Carlsberg Foundation since 1970, 1993; Carl Jacobsen of New Carlsberg, 1995; The Carlsberg Group since 1970, 1997; Time Out: an essay, 1998. *Recreations:* painting, walking. *Address:* Høeghsmindeparken 10, 2900 Hellerup, Denmark. *T:* 39403977, *Fax:* 39403976.

GLAMIS, Lord; Simon Patrick Bowes Lyon; *b* 18 June 1986; *s* and *heir* of Earl of Strathmore and Kinghorne, *qv*.

GLAMORGAN, Earl of; Robert Somerset; *b* 20 Jan. 1989; *s* and *heir* of Marquess of Worcester, *qv*.

GLANCY, Robert Peter; QC 1997; a Recorder, since 1999; a President, Mental Health Review Tribunal, since 1999; *b* 25 March 1950; *s* of Dr Cecil Jacob Glancy, JP and Anita Glancy; *m* 1976, Linda Simons; one *s* two *d*. *Educ:* Manchester Grammar Sch.; St John's Coll., Cambridge (MA). Called to the Bar, Middle Temple, 1972; in practice at the Bar, 1973–; Asst Recorder, 1993–99. *Publication:* (jtly) The Personal Injury Handbook. *Recreations:* theatre, cinema, reading, watching Manchester United. *Address:* 26 Litchfield Way, Hampstead Garden Suburb, NW11 6NJ. *T:* (020) 8933 1938.

GLANUSK, 5th Baron *cr* 1899; **Christopher Russell Bailey;** Bt 1852; TD 1979; consultant; *b* 18 March 1942; *o s* of 4th Baron Glanusk and Lorna Dorothy (*d* 1997), *o d* of Capt. E. C. H. N. Andrews, MBE, RA; *S* father, 1997; *m* 1974, Frances Elizabeth, *o d* of Air Chief Marshal Sir Douglas Lowe, *qv*; one *s* one *d*. *Educ:* Summerfields, Oxford; Eton Coll.; Clare Coll., Cambridge (BA 1964). Design Engr, English Electric Leo Ltd, 1964–66; Product Mkting Manager, Ferranti Ltd, 1966–78; Internat. Product Manager, Bestobell Mobrey Ltd, 1978–83; Sales Engr, STC Telecommunication Ltd, 1984–86; General Manager: Autocar Equipment Ltd, 1986–97; Woolfram Research Europe Ltd, 1997–98. Territorial Army: Captain, Berks Yeo. Signal Sqdn, 1967–76, Cheshire Yeo. Signal Sqdn, 1976–79; Maj., HQ2 Signal Bde, 1979–83. *Heir: s* Hon. Charles Henry Bailey, *b* 12 Aug. 1976. *Address:* 51 Chertsey Road, Chobham, Surrey GU24 8PD.

GLANVILLE, Alec William; Assistant Under-Secretary of State, Home Office, 1975–81, retired; *b* 20 Jan. 1921; *y s* of Frank Foster and Alice Glanville; *m* 1941, Lilian Kathleen Hetherton; one *s* one *d*. *Educ:* Portsmouth Northern Secondary Sch.; Portsmouth Municipal Coll. War service, RAMC, 1939–46. Exchequer and Audit Dept, 1939–47; General, Criminal, Police and Probation and After-care Depts, Home Office, 1947–81 (seconded to Cabinet Office, 1956–58); Private Sec. to Permanent Under Sec. of State, 1949–50; Principal Private Sec. to Sec. of State, 1960–63; Sec., Interdepartmental Cttee on Mentally Abnormal Offenders, 1972–75.

GLANVILLE, Brian Lester; author and journalist since 1949; *b* 24 Sept. 1931; *s* of James Arthur Glanville and Florence Glanville (*née* Manches); *m* 1959, Elizabeth Pamela de Boer (*née* Manasse), *d* of Fritz Manasse and Grace Manasse (*née* Howden); two *s* two *d*. *Educ:* Newlands Sch.; Charterhouse. Literary Advr, Bodley Head, 1958–62; Sunday Times (football correspondent), 1958–92; The People (sports columnist), 1992–96; The Times (football writer), 1996–98; Sunday Times, 1998–. *Publications:* The Reluctant Dictator, 1952; Henry Sows the Wind, 1954; Along the Arno, 1956; The Bankrupts, 1958; After Rome, Africa, 1959; A Bad Streak, 1961; Diamond, 1962; The Director's Wife, 1963; The King of Hackney Marshes, 1965; A Second Home, 1965; A Roman Marriage, 1966; The Artist Type, 1967; The Olympian, 1969; A Cry of Crickets, 1970; The Financiers, 1972; The History of the World Cup, 1973; The Thing He Loves, 1973; The Comic, 1974; The Dying of the Light, 1976; Never Look Back, 1980; (jtly) Underneath The Arches (musical), 1981; A Visit to the Villa (play), 1981; Kissing America, 1985; Love is Not Love, 1985; (ed) The Joy of Football, 1986; The Catacomb, 1988; Champions of Europe, 1991; Story of the World Cup, 1993; Football Memories, 1999; Dictators, 2001; *juvenile:* Goalkeepers are Different (novel), 1971; Target Man (novel), 1978; The Puffin Book of Football, 1978; The Puffin Book of Tennis, 1981. *Recreation:* playing football. *Address:* 160 Holland Park Avenue, W11 4UH. *T:* (020) 7603 6908. *Club:* Chelsea Casuals.

GLANVILLE, Philippa Jane, FSA; Academic Director, Waddesdon Manor, Buckinghamshire, since 1999; *b* 16 Aug. 1943; *d* of late Wilfred Henry Fox-Robinson and of Jane Mary (*née* Home); *m* 1968, Dr Gordon Harris Glanville; two *s*. *Educ:* Talbot Heath, Bournemouth; Girton Coll., Cambridge (MA Hist.); University Coll. London (Archives Admin). FSA 1968. Tudor and Stuart Curator, London Mus., 1966–72; Hd, Tudor and Stuart Dept, Mus. of London, 1972–80; Victoria and Albert Museum: Asst Keeper, Metalwork Dept, 1980–89; Curator, 1989–96, Chief Curator, 1996–99, Metalwork, Silver and Jewellery Dept. Consultant Curator, Gilbert Collection. Member: Council for Care of Churches, 1997–2001; Westminster Abbey Fabric Commn, 1998–. Mem. Cttee, Court Dining Res. Gp, 1989–; contributor, Henry VIII inventory project, 1992–. Liveryman, Co. of Goldsmiths, 1991–. *Publications:* London in Maps, 1972; Silver in England, 1987; Silver in Tudor and Early Stuart England, 1990; (with J. Goldsborough) Women Silversmiths 1685–1845, 1991; (ed and contrib.) Silver, 1996 2nd edn 1999; (ed with Hilary Young and contrib.) Elegant Eating, 2001; contrib. Articles in Antiquaries Jl, Burlington Mag., Silver Society Jl, etc, and in exhibn catalogues. *Address:* 144 Kew Road, Richmond TW9 2AU.

GLANVILLE-JONES, Thomas; *see* Jones.

GLASBY, (Alfred) Ian; HM Diplomatic Service, retired; Director: Trust Co. of Australia (UK) Ltd, since 1990; Truco (Australia) Europe Ltd, since 1990; *b* 18 Sept. 1931; *s* of Frederick William Glasby and Harriet Maria Glasby; *m* 1970, Herma Fletcher; one *d*. *Educ:* Doncaster Grammar Sch.; London School of Economics and Political Science (BSc). Served HM Forces, 1950–52. Home Office, 1952–68; Second Sec., CO, later FCO, 1968–71; Second, later First Sec. (Commercial and Energy), Washington, 1971–76; Dep. High Comr, Hd of Chancery and Consul, Kampala, 1976; Hd, British Interests Sect., French Embassy, Kampala, 1976–77; First Sec., Hd of Chancery and Consul, Yaoundé, 1977–81, concurrently non-resident Chargé d'Affaires, Central Afr. Empire, Gabon, and Equatorial Guinea; Asst Hd, Consular Dept, FCO, 1981–84; Dep. Consul Gen., Sydney, 1984–88; Ambassador to People's Republic of the Congo, 1988–90. Hon. Chevalier, Ordre de Mérite (Republique Populaire du Congo). *Recreations:* Rugby, cricket, international affairs, reading, gardening. *Address:* Longridge, 3 Love Lane, Shaftesbury, Dorset SP7 8BG. *T:* (01747) 850389; 5 rue du Collet, Spéracèdes, near Grasse 06530, France. *T:* 493605311. *Clubs:* Royal Commonwealth Society, Lansdowne; Australasian Pioneers, NSW Rugby (Sydney).

GLASBY, John Hamilton; Treasurer, Devon and Cornwall Police Authority, since 1993; *b* 29 March 1950; *s* of James Ronald Glasby and Lucie Lillian Glasby (*née* Baxter); *m* 1971 (marr. diss. 1989); two *s* one *d*; partner, Vivienne Amanda Lloyd. *Educ:* Univ. of Sheffield (BA); Univ. of Birmingham (MSocSc); Liverpool Poly. Mem., CIPFA, 1982. Lectr in Econs, Univ. of E Anglia, 1972–73; Economist: Central Lancs New Town, 1973–76; Shropshire CC, 1976–82; Asst Dir of Finance, Dudley Metropolitan Borough, 1982–84; Devon County Council: Dep. Co. Treas., 1984–93; Co. Treas., 1993–96; Dir of Resources, 1996–2000. Treasurer: Dartmoor Nat. Park Authy, 1997–2000; Devon Fire Authy, 1998–2000. *Recreation:* amateur author, academic and fiction. *Address:* Devon and Cornwall Police Authority, Rockeagle House, Pynes Hill Business Park, Exeter, Devon EX2 5AZ.

GLASER, Prof. Donald Arthur; Professor of Physics and of Neurobiology (formerly of Molecular and Cell Biology), University of California, since 1960; *b* 21 Sept. 1926; *s* of William Joseph and Lena Glaser. *Educ:* Case Institute of Technology (BS 1946); California Inst. of Technology (PhD 1950). University of Michigan: Instr. of Physics, 1949–53; Asst Prof., 1953–55; Associate Prof., 1955–57; Prof. of Physics, 1957–59; University of California, Berkeley: Vis. Prof., 1959–60; Prof. of Physics, 1960–; Miller Res. Biophysicist, 1962–64; Prof. of Molecular Biol., 1964–89; Prof. of Molecular and Cell Bio., 1989–. National Science Foundation Fellow, 1961; Guggenheim Fellow, 1961–62. Member: National Academy of Sciences (USA), 1962; NY Acad. of Science; Fellow Amer. Physical Soc.; FAAAS. Henry Russel Award, 1955; Charles Vernon Boys Prize, 1958; Amer. Phys. Soc. Prize, 1959; Nobel Prize for Physics, 1960. Hon. ScD Case Inst., 1959. *Publications:* chapters in: Topics in the Biology of Aging, 1965; Biology and the Exploration of Mars, 1966; Frontiers of Pattern Recognition, 1972; New Approaches to the Identification of Microorganisms, 1975; articles in Physical Review, Handbuch der Physik, Jl Molecular Biol., Pattern Recognition and Image Processing, Somatic Cell Genetics, Cell Tissue Kinetics, Computers and Biomed. Res., Proc. Nat. Acad. of Scis (USA), Suppl. to Investigative Ophthalmol & Visual Sci., Jl Opt. Soc. of Amer. A, Vision Res., Visual Neurosci., Cell Biophys, Perception, Computational Neuroscience, etc. *Address:* 229 Stanley Hall, Department of Molecular and Cell Biology, University of California, Berkeley, CA 94720, USA; 41 Hill Road, Berkeley, CA 94708, USA.

GLASER, Milton; graphic designer; *b* 26 June 1929; *s* of Eugene and Eleanor Glaser; *m* 1957, Shirley Girton. *Educ:* High Sch. of Music and Art, NY; Cooper Union Art Sch., NY; Acad. of Fine Arts, Bologna (Fulbright Schol.). Joint Founder: Pushpin Studios, 1954; New York mag., 1968 (Pres. and Design Dir, 1968–77); WBMG, pubn design co., 1983; Milton Glaser Inc., 1974; *projects* include: 600 foot mural, New Federal Office Building, Indianapolis, 1974; Observation Deck and Perm. Exhibn, Twin Towers, World Trade Center, NY, 1975; Sesame Place, Pennsylvania, 1981–83; Grand Union Co. architecture, interiors and packaging; Internat. AIDS symbol and poster, WHO, 1987; Trattoria dell'Arte, NY, 1988; New York Unearthed mus., 1990; *solo exhibitions* include: MOMA, NY, 1975; Centre Georges Pompidou, Paris, 1977; Lincoln Center Gall., NY, 1981; Posters, Vicenza Mus., 1989; Art Inst. of Boston, 1995; *work in public collections*, including: MOMA, NY; Israel Mus., Jerusalem; Nat. Archive, Smithsonian Instn, Washington; Cooper Hewitt Nat. Design Mus., NY. Member: Bd, Sch. of Visual Arts, NY, 1961–; Bd of Dirs, Cooper Union, NY; Amer. Inst. of Graphic Arts. Gold Medal, Soc. of Illustrators; St Gauden's Medal, Cooper Union; Prix Savignac, Urban Art Internat. and UNESCO, 1996; Honors Award, AIA, 1992. *Address:* Milton Glaser Inc., 207 East 32nd Street, New York, NY 10016, USA. *T:* (212) 8893161, *Fax:* (212) 2134072; *e-mail:* miltonglaser@mindspring.com.

GLASGOW, 10th Earl of, *cr* 1703; **Patrick Robin Archibald Boyle;** Lord Boyle, 1699; Viscount of Kelburn, 1703; Baron Fairlie (UK), 1897; DL; television director/producer; *b* 30 July 1939; *s* of 9th Earl of Glasgow, CB, DSC, and of Dorothea, *o d* of Sir Archibald Lyle, 2nd Bt; *S* father, 1984; *m* 1975, Isabel Mary James; one *s* one *d*. *Educ:* Eton; Paris Univ. National Service in Navy; Sub-Lt, RNR, 1959–60. Worked in Associated Rediffusion Television, 1961; worked at various times for Woodfall Film Productions; Asst on Film Productions, 1962–64; Asst Dir in film industry, 1962–67; producer/director of documentary films, Yorkshire TV, 1968–70; freelance film producer, 1971–, making network television documentaries for BBC Yorkshire Television, ATV and Scottish Television. Formed Kelburn Country Centre, May 1977, opening Kelburn estate and gardens in Ayrshire to the public. DL Ayrshire and Arran, 1995. *Recreations:* ski-ing, theatre. *Heir: s* David Michael Douglas Boyle, *b* 15 Oct. 1978. *Address:* Kelburn, Fairlie, Ayrshire KA29 0BE. *T:* (01475) 568204; (office) South Offices, Kelburn Estate, Fairlie, Ayrshire KA29 0BE. *T:* (01475) 568685.

GLASGOW, Archbishop of, (RC); *no new appointment at time of going to press.*

GLASGOW, (St Mary's Cathedral), Provost of; *see* Dines, Very Rev. P. J.

GLASGOW, Edwin John, CBE 1998; QC 1987; *b* 3 Aug. 1945; *s* of Richard Edwin, (Dick), Glasgow and Diana Geraldine Mary Glasgow (*née* Markby); *m* 1967, Janet Coleman; one *s* one *d*. *Educ:* St Joseph's Coll., Ipswich; University Coll. London (LLB). Called to the Bar, Gray's Inn, 1969, Bencher, 1994. Chm., Financial Reporting Review Panel, 1992–97. Trustee: London Opera Players, 1985–; Mary Glasgow Language Trust, 1984– (Chm.); Public Concern at Work, 1994–. Chm. Trustees, Harlequin FC. *Recreations:* family, friends, France, music. *Address:* 39 Essex Street, WC2R 3AT. *T:* (020) 7583 1111; Copper Hall, Watts Road, Thames Ditton, Surrey KT7 0BX; Entrechaux, Vaucluse, France. *Club:* Royal Automobile (Steward, 1992–).

GLASGOW AND GALLOWAY, Bishop of, since 1998; **Rt Rev. Dr Idris Jones;** *b* 2 April 1943; *s* of Edward Eric Jones and Alice Gertrude (*née* Burgess); *m* 1973, Alison Margaret Williams; two *s*. *Educ:* St David's Coll., Lampeter, Univ. of Wales (BA); Univ. of Edinburgh (LTh); NY Theol Seminary (DMin 1987); Dip. Person Centred Therapy 1994. Curate, St Mary, Stafford, 1967–70; Precentor, Dundee Cathedral, 1970–73; Team Vicar, St Hugh, Gosforth, 1973–80; Chaplain, St Nicholas Hosp. (Teaching), 1975–80; Rector, Montrose with Inverbervie, 1980–89; Canon, St Paul's Cathedral, Dundee, 1984–92; Anglican Chaplain, Dundee Univ. and Priest-in-Charge, Invergowrie, 1989–92; Team Rector, Ayr, Girvan, Maybole, 1992–98; Dir, Pastoral Studies, Theol Inst., Edinburgh, 1995–98. Lay Psychotherapist: Dundee, 1990–92; Ayr, 1995–98. *Recreations:* walking, golf, music. *Address:* Bishop's Office, Diocesan Centre, 5 St Vincent Place, Glasgow G1 2DH.

GLASGOW AND GALLOWAY, Dean of; *see* Duncan, Very Rev. G. D.

GLASHOW, Prof. Sheldon Lee, PhD; Higgins Professor of Physics, Harvard University, since 1979 (Professor of Physics, since 1966); *b* 5 Dec. 1932; *s* of Lewis and Bella Glashow; *m* 1972, Joan (*née* Alexander); three *s* one *d*. *Educ:* Cornell Univ. (AB); Harvard Univ. (AM, PhD). National Science Foundn Fellow, Copenhagen and Geneva, 1958–60; Res. Fellow, Calif Inst. of Technol., 1960–61; Asst Prof., Stanford Univ., 1961–62; Associate Prof., Univ. of Calif at Berkeley, 1962–66. Vis. Professor: CERN, 1968; Marseille, 1971; MIT, 1974 and 1980; Boston Univ., 1983; Univ. Schol., Texas A&M Univ., 1983–. Consultant, Brookhaven Nat. Lab., 1966–; Affiliated Senior Scientist, Univ. of Houston, 1983–. Pres., Sakharov Internat. Cttee, Washington, 1980–. Hon. DSc: Yeshiva, 1978; Aix-Marseille, 1982. Nobel Prize for Physics (jtly), 1979. *Publications:* articles in learned jls. *Recreations:* scuba diving, tennis. *Address:* 30 Prescott Street, Brookline, MA 02146, USA. *T:* (617) 2775446.

GLASS, Anthony Trevor; QC 1986; a Recorder of the Crown Court, since 1985; *b* 6 June 1940. *Educ:* Royal Masonic School; Lincoln College, Oxford (MA). Called to the Bar, Inner Temple, 1965, Bencher, 1995. *Address:* Queen Elizabeth Building, Temple, EC4Y 9BS. *T:* (020) 7583 5766. *Club:* Garrick.

GLASS, John Basil Caldwell; Master, Supreme Court of Judicature of Northern Ireland, 1987–98; *b* 21 May 1926; *s* of John Glass and Muriel Florence Glass (*née* Caldwell); *m* 1st, 1952, Elizabeth Charlotte Caldwell (marr. diss. 1980); four *s*; 2nd, 1980, Mary Burnell Clark (*née* Chubb). *Educ:* Methodist Coll., Belfast; Queen's Univ., Belfast (Rowing Blue, 1947) (LLB 1947). Articled to J. B. McCutcheon, Solicitor, Belfast, 1947; admitted as solicitor, 1950; in private practice as solicitor, Belfast, 1950–87. Observer of legal, political, economic and social conditions in Haiti under rule of Pres. Duvalier, 1962. Founder Mem., Alliance Party of NI, 1970 (Chm., 1970–72; Pres., 1972–74; Dep. Leader, 1976–80). Mem. (Alliance) for S Belfast, NI Assembly, 1973–74; Mem., NI Constnl Convention, 1975; Belfast City Council: Mem. for S Belfast, 1977–81; Chm., Community Services Cttee, 1977–79. Member: Belfast Educn and Library Bd, 1977–81; NI Consumer Council, 1977–85 (Chm., Legal Affairs Cttee, 1982–85); Council Mem., NI Chamber of Commerce and Industry, 1986–87. Rep. of Methodist Ch in Ireland on Exec. Cttee, World Methodist Council, visiting Jamaica, Norway, W Germany and Sweden, 1961–65. Pres., QUB Assoc., 1996–98. Founder Mem., Corrymeela Community, Ballycastle, 1965. *Publication:* contrib. A Handbook of Consumer Law, 1982. *Recreations:* reading, music, theatre, sailing, hill-walking, cycling, gardening. *Address:* The Old Curatage, 6 The Square, Hillsborough, Co. Down BT26 6AG. *T:* (028) 9268 2726.

GLASS, Norman Jeffrey, CB 2000; Director, National Centre for Social Research, since 2002 (Director Designate, 2001–March 2002); *b* 31 May 1946; *s* of Philip Harris Glass and Anne (*née* Stein); *m* 1974, Marie-Anne Verger; one *s* one *d*. *Educ:* Trinity Coll., Dublin (BA); Univ. of Amsterdam (Post Grad. Dip.). Shell Mex and BP, 1969–70; Economic Models Ltd, 1970–72; Lectr, Univ. of Newcastle upon Tyne, 1972–74; Res. Scholar, Internat. Inst. for Applied Systems Analysis, Vienna, 1974–75; Economic Adviser: DHSS, 1975–77; HM Treasury, 1977–79; Exchequer and Audit Dept, 1979–81; Sen. Econ. Advr, DHSS, 1981–86; Asst Sec., DoH, 1986–89; Dir, Analytical Services, DSS, 1989–92; Chief Economist, DoE, 1992–95; Dep. Dir (Micro-econs), HM Treasury, 1995–2001. Chm., Economic Policy Cttee, EU, 1999–2001 (Vice-Chm., 1997–99). Member: ESRC, 1992–96; Council, Royal Economic Soc., 1997–. *Publications:* articles on health econs. *Recreations:* music, languages, gardening. *Address:* National Centre for Social Research, 35 Northampton Square, EC1V 0AX.

GLASS, Philip; American composer and performer; *b* 31 Jan. 1937; *s* of Benjamin Glass and Ida Glass (*née* Gouline); *m* 1st, JoAnne Akalaitis; one *s* one *d*; 2nd, Luba Burtyk; 3rd, Candy Jernigan; 4th, Holly Critchlow. *Educ:* Peabody Conservatory; Univ. of Chicago; Juilliard Sch. of Music. Has worked as a taxi-driver, plumber and furniture mover. Composer-in-Residence, Pittsburgh Public Schs, 1962–64; studied with Nadia Boulanger, Paris, 1964–66; Musical Dir, Mabou Mines Co., 1965–74; Founder: Philip Glass Ensemble, 1968; record companies: Chatham Square Productions, 1972; Point Music, 1991; music publishers: Dunvagen, Inc., 1982. *Compositions include: operas:* Einstein on the Beach, 1976; Satyagraha, 1980; The Photographer, 1982; The Civil Wars, 1984; Akhnaten, 1984; The Juniper Tree, 1986; The Making of the Representative for Planet 8, 1986; The Fall of the House of Usher, 1988; 1000 Airplanes on the Roof, 1988; The Hydrogen Jukebox, 1990; White Raven, 1991; The Voyage, 1992; Orphée, 1993; La Belle et la Bête, 1994; Les Enfants Terribles, 1996; Monsters of Grace, 1998; *film scores:* Koyaanisqatsi, 1982; Mishima (Cannes Special Jury Prize), 1985; Powaqqatsi, 1987; The Thin Blue Line, 1989; Hamburger Hill, 1989; Mindwalk, 1990; A Brief History of Time, 1991; Anima Mundi, 1991; Candyman, 1992; Compassion in Exile, 1992; Candyman II, 1995; Jenipapo, 1995; Secret Agent, 1995; Bent, 1998; Kundun, 1998; The Truman Show (Golden Globe award for best score), 1998; Dracula, 1998; Maqoyqatsi, 2001; *theatre music:* Endgame, 1984; Cymbelline, 1989; (with Foday Musa Suso) The Screens, 1990; Henry IV, 1992; Woyzeck (Drama Desk Award), 1992; The Mysteries & What's So Funny?, 1992; In the Penal Colony, 2000; *dance music:* In the Upper Room, 1986; Witches of Venice, 1995; *instrumental works:* String Quartet no 1, 1966; Piece in the Shape of a Square, 1967; Strung Out, 1969; Music in Similar Motion, 1969; Music in Fifths, 1969; Music with Changing Parts, 1970; Music in Twelve Parts, 1974; Another Look at Harmony, 1974; North Star, 1977; Modern Love Waltz, 1979; Dance nos 1–5, 1979; Company, 1983; String Quartet no 2, 1983; String Quartet no 3, 1985; Songs from Liquid Days, 1986; Violin Concerto, 1987; The Light, 1987; Itaipu, 1988; Canyon, 1988; String Quartet no 4, 1989; Solo Piano, 1989; (with Ravi Shankar) Passages, 1990; String Quartet no 5, 1991; Low Symphony, 1992; Mattogrosso, 1992; Symphony no 2, 1994, no 3, 1995; Heroes Symphony, 1996; Symphony no 5, 1999; Concerto Fantasy, 2000; Concerto for Cello and Orchestra, 2001. Numerous awards and prizes, including: Benjamin Award, 1961; Fulbright Award, 1966–67. Officer, Order of Arts and Letters (France), 1995. *Publication:* Music by Philip Glass, ed R. T. Jones, 1987. *Address:* c/o Dunvagen Music Publishers, 632 Broadway, 9th Floor, New York, NY 10012, USA.

GLASSCOCK, John Lewis, FCIS; Director, British Aerospace PLC, 1982–87; *b* 12 July 1928; *s* of Edgar Henry and Maude Allison Glasscock; *m* 1959, Anne Doreen Baker; two *s*. *Educ:* Tiffin Sch.; University Coll. London (BA Hons). Served Royal Air Force, 1950–53. Joined Hawker Aircraft Ltd, 1953, Asst Sec., 1956, Commercial Man., 1961; Hawker Siddeley Aviation Ltd: Divl Commercial Man., 1964; Dir and Gen. Man. (Kingston), 1965–77; British Aerospace Aircraft Group: Admin. Dir, 1978; Commercial Dir, 1979; Man. Dir (Military), 1981; BAe PLC: Dep. Chief Exec., Aircraft Gp, and Man. Dir, Civil Aircraft Div., 1982–85; Commercial Dir, 1986–87. Mem. Supervisory Bd, Airbus Industrie, 1983–85. Mem. Council, SBAC, 1979–87. *Recreation:* golf. *Address:* West Meadow, The Wedges, Itchingfield, near Horsham, W Sussex RH13 7TA. *Clubs:* MCC, Royal Air Force, Royal Automobile.

GLASSER, Cyril, CMG 1999; Consultant, Sheridans, Solicitors, since 2001; *b* 31 Jan. 1942; *s* of late Phillip and Eva Glasser. *Educ:* Raine's Foundn Grammar Sch., London; London Sch. of Econs (LLB 1963; LLM 1966). Admitted solicitor, 1967; Sheridans, Solicitors: Partner, 1977–2001; Hd, Litigation Dept, 1977–99; Managing Partner, 1989–2001; Sen. Partner, 2001. Consultant on solicitors' costs to NBPI, 1967; Co-founder and Dir, Legal Action Gp, 1972–74; Legal Advr to ANC during Commn on

Rhodesian Opinion, 1972; attached to Lord Chancellor's Dept as Special Consultant, Legal Aid Adv. Cttee, 1974–77. Vis. Prof. of Law, UCL, 1987–. Mem., Wkg Party to Review Legal Aid Legislation, 1974–77; Chm., Legal Aid Provisions Wkg Party, 1975–77; Mem., Social Scis and the Law Cttee, SSRC, 1979–83. Mem. Council, Law Soc., 1997–2001; Dir, Law Soc. Trustees Ltd, 1999–. Mem., Jt Tribunal on Barristers' Fees, 1998–2001. Advr, Experts' Cttee on Efficiency of Justice, Council of Europe, 1998–2000. Trustee, Legal Assistance Trust, 1985–. FRSA 1995; Fellow, Soc. Advanced Legal Studies, 1998. Vice-Chm., Legal Practice Course Bd, 1999–2001; Member: Mgt Cttee, Inst. Judicial Admin, Birmingham Univ., 1984–; Adv. Bd, Centre of Advanced Litigation, Nottingham Trent Univ., 1991–; Gov., 1996–, Mem. Council, 1999–, LSE. Member, Editorial Board: Modern Law Rev., 1992–; Internat. Jl Evidence and Proof, 1996–; Mem., Editl Adv. Bd, Litigator, 1994–98. *Publications:* contribs to legal jls, books, etc. *Address:* Sheridans, 14 Red Lion Square, WC1R 4QL. *T:* (020) 7404 0444.

GLASSER, Prof. Stanley; Head of Music, 1969-91, (first) Professor of Music, 1990-91, Goldsmiths' College, University of London, now Emeritus Professor; composer, ethnomusicologist and music consultant; *b* 28 Feb. 1926; *s* of Joe Glasser and Assia (*née* Kagan); *m* 1st 1951, Mona Vida Schwartz (marr. diss. 1965); one *s* one *d*; 2nd, 1971, Elizabeth Marianne Aylwin; two *s*. *Educ:* King Edward VII High Sch., Johannesburg; Univ. of the Witwatersrand (BComm (Econ) 1949); studied composition with Benjamin Frankel, 1950-52, Matyas Seiber, 1952-55; ethnomusicology res. under Dr Hugh Tracey, Internat. Liby of African Music, 1954-55; King's Coll., Cambridge (Music Tripos 1958; MA 1960). Dir, King Kong (African musical), 1958-60; Lectr and Asst Dir, Music Dept, Univ. of Cape Town, 1959-63; Music Critic, Cape Times, 1959-62; Goldsmiths' College, University of London: Music Tutor, Dept of Adult Studies, 1963-65; Lectr, 1966-69; established 1st UK electronic music teaching studio, 1971; Chm., Bd of Studies in Music, Univ. of London, 1981-83. Composer-in-residence, Standard Bank Nat. Arts Fest., 2001. Internat. Cttee, ISCM, 1951-55; Chm., Composers' Guild of GB, 1975; Founder and Trustee, Rand Educn Fund, 1964-98; Trustee, Classic FM Charitable Trust, 1994-; Academic Governor, Richmond, American Internat. Univ. in London, 1980-; Music Consultant to Nat. Council for Culture, Arts & Letters, Kuwait, 1994-. Hon. Fellow, Goldsmiths Coll., 2001. Hon. DMus Richmond, American Internat. Univ., 1997. Royal Philharmonic Soc. Prizeman, 1952; George Richards Prize, 1958; Kathleen Gurner Award, Goldsmiths' Coll., 1998. *Compositions:* The Square (full-length ballet), 1961; Mr. Paljas (musical comedy, lyrics by Beryl Bloom), 1962; The Chameleon and The Lizard (choral, Zulu text by Lewis Nkosi), 1973; The Gift (one-act comic chamber opera), 1976; Lalela Zulu (a cappella male sextet, Zulu poems by Lewis Nkosi), 1977; The Ward (song cycle, poems by Ronald Duncan), 1983; Zonkizizwe (large choir, wind band and percussion), 1991; Magnificat & Nunc Dimittis (chapel double choir a cappella), 1995; Ezra (sacred drama, text by Elisabeth Ingles), 1996; Noon (tone poem for orch.), 1997; A Greenwich Symphony (choir and orch., text by Elisabeth Ingles), 1999; Concerto for flugelhorn and chamber orch., 2001. *Publications:* (with Adolf Wood) 100 Songs of Southern Africa, 1968; (contrib.) The New Grove Dictionary of Music and Musicians, 7th edn 1980; The A-Z of Classical Music, 1994; various articles and reviews on music. *Recreations:* dining with family and friends, Walt Kelly's Pogo Possum books, cowboy films. *Address:* c/o Woza Music, 46 Weigall Road, SE12 8HE. *T:* (020) 8852 1997. *Club:* Oxford and Cambridge.

GLAUERT, Audrey Marion, ScD; Fellow of Clare Hall, University of Cambridge, since 1966; Head of Electron Microscopy Department, Strangeways Research Laboratory, Cambridge, 1956–89 (Associate Director, 1979–85); *b* 21 Dec. 1925; *d* of late Hermann Glauert, FRS and Muriel Glauert (*née* Barker); *m* 1959, David Franks (marr. diss. 1979). *Educ:* Perse Sch. for Girls, Cambridge; Bedford Coll., Univ. of London. BSc 1946, MSc 1947, London; MA Cantab 1967, ScD Cantab 1970. Asst Lectr in Physics, Royal Holloway Coll., Univ. of London, 1947–50; Mem. Scientific Staff, Strangeways Res. Lab., Cambridge, Sir Halley Stewart Research Fellow, 1950–89. Chairman: British Joint Cttee for Electron Microscopy, 1968–72; Fifth European Congress on Electron Microscopy, 1972; Pres., Royal Microscopical Soc., 1970–72, Hon. Fellow, 1973. Hon. Member: French Soc. for Electron Microscopy, 1967; Microscopy (formerly Electron Microscopy) Soc. of America, 1990 (Dist. Scientist Award for Biol. Scis, 1990). JP Cambridge, 1975–88. Editor: Practical Methods in Electron Microscopy, 1972–; Jl of Microscopy, Royal Microscopical Soc., 1986–88. *Publications:* Fixation Dehydration and Embedding of Biological Specimens, 1974; (ed) The Control of Tissue Damage, 1988; Biological Specimen Preparation for Transmission Electron Microscopy, 1998; papers on cell and molecular biology in scientific jls. *Recreations:* sailing, gardening, working for prison reform. *Address:* 29 Cow Lane, Fulbourn, Cambridge CB1 5HB. *T:* (01223) 880463; Clare Hall, Herschel Road, Cambridge CB3 9AL; *e-mail:* amg44@cam.ac.uk.

GLAVES-SMITH, Frank William, CB 1975; Deputy Director-General of Fair Trading, 1973–79, retired; *b* 27 Sept. 1919; *m* 1st, 1941, Audrey Glaves (*d* 1989); one *s* one *d*; 2nd, 1990, Ursula Mary Murray. *Educ:* Malet Lambert High Sch., Hull. War Service, 1940–46 (Captain, Royal Signals). Called to Bar, Middle Temple, 1947. Board of Trade, 1947; Princ. Private Sec. to Pres. of Bd of Trade, 1952–57; Asst Secretary: HM Treasury, 1957–60; Cabinet Office, 1960–62; Bd of Trade, 1962–65; Under-Sec., BoT, 1965–69, Dept of Employment and Productivity, 1969–70, DTI, 1970–73; Dep. Sec., 1975. Mem., Export Guarantees Adv. Council, 1971–73. *Recreations:* rock-climbing, fell-walking. *Address:* 8 Grange Park, Keswick, Cumbria CA12 4AY.

GLAVIN, William Francis; President, Babson College, Wellesley, Mass, 1989–96; *b* 29 March 1932; *m* 1955, Cecily McClatchy; three *s* four *d*. *Educ:* College of the Holy Cross, Worcester, Mass (BS); Wharton Graduate Sch. (MBA). Vice-Pres., Operations, Service Bureau Corp. (subsid. of IBM), 1968–70; Exec. Vice-Pres., Xerox Data Services, 1970; Pres., Xerox Data Systems, 1970–72; Gp Vice-Pres., Xerox Corp., and Pres., Business Development Gp, 1972–74; Rank Xerox Ltd: Man. Dir, 1974–80; Chief Operating Officer, 1974–77; Chief Exec. Officer, 1977–80; Xerox Corp.: Exec. Vice-Pres. Chief Staff Officer, 1980–82; President: Reprographics and Ops, 1982–83; Business Equipment Gps, 1983–89 (Vice Chm., 1985–89). *Recreations:* golf, music, boating, tennis. *Address:* c/o Babson College, Babson Park, Wellesley, MA 02157, USA.

GLAZE, Michael John Carlisle, (James), CMG 1988; HM Diplomatic Service, retired; Deputy Secretary-General, Order of St John of Jerusalem, 1994–2001; *b* 15 Jan. 1935; *s* of late Derek Glaze and Shirley Gardner (formerly Glaze, *née* Ramsay); *m* 1965, Rosemary Duff; two step-*d*. *Educ:* Repton; St Catharine's Coll., Cambridge (open Exhibitioner, BA 1958); Worcester Coll., Oxford. Colonial Service, Basutoland, 1959–65; HMOCS, Dep. Permanent Sec., Finance, Lesotho, 1966–70; Dept of Trade (ECGD), 1971–73; FCO, 1973–75; Abu Dhabi, 1975–78; Rabat, 1978–80; Consul-Gen., Bordeaux, 1980–84; Ambassador: Republic of Cameroon, 1984–87; Angola, 1987–90; Ethiopia, 1990–94. OStJ 2000. *Recreations:* golf, grand opera, the garden. *Address:* 2 Fairhall, Colley Lane, Reigate, Surrey RH2 9JA. *Club:* Athenæum.

GLAZEBROOK, (Reginald) Mark; writer, painter and lecturer on art; *b* 25 June 1936; *s* of late Reginald Field Glazebrook; *m* 1st, 1965, Elizabeth Lea Claridge (marr. diss. 1969); one *d*; 2nd, 1974, Wanda Barbara O'Neill (*née* Osińska) (marr. diss. 2000); one *d*. *Educ:* Eton; Pembroke Coll., Cambridge (MA); Slade School of Fine Art. Worked at Arts Council, 1961–64; Lectr at Maidstone Coll. of Art, 1965–67; Art Critic, London Magazine, 1967–68; Dir, Whitechapel Art Gall., 1969–71; Head of Modern English Paintings and Drawings, P. and D. Colnaghi & Co. Ltd, 1973–75; Gallery Director and Art History Lectr, San José State Univ., 1977–79; Dir, Albemarle Gall. Ltd, London, 1986–93. One-man exhibn, Mayor Gall., London, 2000. FRSA 1971. *Publications:* (comp.) Artists and Architecture of Bedford Park 1875–1900 (catalogue), 1967; (comp.) David Hockney: paintings, prints and drawings 1960–1970 (catalogue), 1970; Edward Wadsworth 1889–1949: paintings, prints and drawings (catalogue), 1974; (introduction) John Armstrong 1893–1973 (catalogue), 1975; (introduction) John Tunnard (catalogue), 1976; Sean Scully (catalogue), 1997; articles in: London Magazine, Modern Painters, Royal Acad. Magazine, Spectator. *Recreations:* cooking, cinema, swimming. *Clubs:* Beefsteak, Chelsea Arts, Lansdowne.

GLEDHILL, Anthony John, GC 1967; Divisional Auditor, NWS plc, 1993–97; *b* 10 March 1938; *s* of Harold Victor and Marjorie Edith Gledhill; *m* 1958, Marie Lilian Hughes; one *s* one *d*. *Educ:* Doncaster Technical High Sch., Yorks. Accounts Clerk, Officers' Mess, RAF Bruggen, Germany, 1953–56. Metropolitan Police: Cadet, 1956–57; Police Constable, 1957–75; Detective Sergeant, 1976–87; Investigator, PO Investigation Dept, 1987–88. *Recreations:* football, golf, bowls, DIY, philately.

GLEDHILL, Rt Rev. Jonathan Michael; *see* Southampton, Suffragan Bishop of.

GLEDHILL, Michael Geoffrey James, QC 2001; a Recorder, since 1998; *b* 28 Dec. 1954; *s* of Geoffrey Gledhill and L. Barbara Gledhill (*née* Haigh); *m* 1988, Elizabeth Ann Miller Gordon. *Educ:* Christ Church, Oxford (MA Juris.). Called to the Bar, Middle Temple, 1976; Asst Recorder, 1995-98. *Address:* 2 Dyers Buildings, Holborn, EC1N 2JT. *T:* (020) 7404 1881.

GLEDHILL, Ruth, (Mrs Andrew Daniels); Religion Correspondent, The Times, since 1990; *b* 15 Dec. 1959; *d* of Rev. Peter Gledhill and Bridget Mary Gledhill (*née* Rathbone), Anglesey, N Wales; *m* 1996, Andrew Daniels. *Educ:* Thomas Alleyne's GS, Uttoxeter; London Coll. of Printing (HND); Birkbeck Coll., London (Cert. Religious Studies). With Uttoxeter Advertiser news service, 1980–81; Australasian Printer, Sydney, 1981–82; indentured, Birmingham Post & Mail, 1982–84; Industrial corresp., Birmingham Post, 1984; gen. news reporter and feature writer, Daily Mail, 1984–87; The Times: Home News Reporter, 1987–90; columnist, At Your Service (Times Weekend), 1993–; also writer on dance sport for sports pages, 1997–; occasional corresp. on religion and new technology for Interface, 1998–. Guest presenter: Good Worship Guide, Yorks TV, 1996; ITV Sunday Worship, 1999. Member: IJA Commn on Rise of Neo-Fascism, 1993; BBC Governors' Independent Advice Panel: Religious Programmes, 1998. Mem., London Rotary, 1997–. *Publications:* (jtly) Birmingham is Not a Boring City, 1984; (ed and introd) The Times Book of Best Sermons, annually 1995–; At A Service Near You, 1996; (ed) The Times Book of Prayers, 1997. *Recreation:* dance sport (Sussex Open Amateur Champs, 1996; Embassy Sen. Mod. Champs, America, 1997; Hants Open Amateur Champs, 1998; S of England Sen. Mod. title, 1999). *Address:* The Times, 1 Pennington Street, E1 9XN. *T:* (020) 7782 5001; (home) (01372) 745092; *e-mail:* ruth.gledhill@the-times.co.uk. *Club:* Reform.

GLEESON, Hon. Anthony Murray, AC 1992 (AO 1986); **Hon. Chief Justice Gleeson;** Chief Justice of Australia, since 1998; *b* 30 Aug. 1938; *s* of Leo John Gleeson and Rachel Alice Gleeson; *m* 1965, Robyn Paterson; one *s* three *d*. *Educ:* St Joseph's Coll., Hunters Hill; Univ. of Sydney (BA, LLB). Called to the NSW Bar, 1963; QC 1974. Tutor in Law, St Paul's Coll., Sydney Univ., 1963–65; Part-time Lectr in Company Law, Sydney Univ., 1965–74. Chief Justice of NSW, 1988–98; Lt-Gov., NSW, 1989–98. Pres., Judicial Commn, NSW, 1988–98. Mem. Council, NSW Bar Assoc., 1979–85 (Pres., 1984 and 1985). Hon. Bencher, Middle Temple, 1989. Hon. LLD Sydney, 1999; DUniv Griffith, 2001. *Recreations:* tennis, ski-ing. *Address:* High Court of Australia, Parkes Place, Parkes, ACT 2600, Australia. *Club:* Australian (Sydney).

GLEESON, Dermot James; Executive Chairman, M. J. Gleeson Group plc, since 1998; a Governor of the BBC, since 2000; *b* 5 Sept. 1949; *s* of Patrick Joseph Gleeson and Margaret Mary Gleeson (*née* Higgins); *m* 1980, Rosalind Mary Catherine Moorhead; one *s* one *d*. *Educ:* Downside; Fitzwilliam Coll., Cambridge (MA). Conservative Res. Dept, 1974–77; Mem., Cabinet of C. Tugendhat, EC, 1977–79; EEC Rep., Brussels, Midland Bank, 1979–81; Dep. Man. Dir, 1982–88, Chief Exec., 1988–98, M. J. Gleeson Gp plc. Mem. Bd, Housing Corp., 1986–92; Dir, CITB, 1996–. *Recreation:* family life, especially in the Outer Hebrides. *Address:* Hook Farm, White Hart Lane, Wood Street Village, Guildford, Surrey GU3 3EA. *Clubs:* Beefsteak, Royal Automobile.

GLEESON, Most Rev. James William, AO 1979; CMG 1958; DD 1957; FACE 1967; Archbishop Emeritus of Adelaide, (RC), since 1985; *b* 24 Dec. 1920; *s* of John Joseph and Margaret Mary Gleeson. *Educ:* St Joseph's Sch., Balaklava, SA; Sacred Heart Coll., Glenelg, SA. Priest, 1945; Inspector of Catholic Schs, 1947–52; Dir of Catholic Education for South Australia, 1952–58; Auxiliary Bishop to the Archbishop of Adelaide and Titular Bishop of Sesta, 1957–64; Coadjutor Archbishop of Adelaide and Titular Archbishop of Aurusuliana, 1964–71; Archbishop of Adelaide, 1971–85. Episcopal Chm., Young Catholic Students Movement of Australia, 1958–65. *Address:* Ennis, 28 Robe Terrace, Medindie, SA 5081, Australia. *T:* (8) 83443641.

GLEGG, Maj.-Gen. John B.; *see* Baskervyle-Glegg.

GLEN, Sir Alexander (Richard), KBE 1967 (CBE 1964); DSC 1942 (and Bar, 1945); Vice President, British Air Line Pilots' Association, since 1994 (President, 1982–94); *b* 18 April 1912; *s* of late R. Bartlett Glen, Glasgow; *m* 1st, 1936, Nina Nixon (marr. diss. 1945); one *s* decd; 2nd, 1947, Baroness Zora de Collaert. *Educ:* Fettes Coll.; Balliol Coll., Oxford. BA, Hons Geography. Travelled on Arctic Expeditions, 1932–36; Leader, Oxford Univ. Arctic Expedition, 1935–36; Banking, New York and London, 1936–39. RNVR, 1939–59, Capt. 1955. Export Council for Europe: Dep. Chm., 1960–64; Chm., 1964–66; Chairman: H. Clarkson & Co., 1965–73; Anglo World Travel, 1978–81; Dep. Chm., British Transport Hotels, 1978–83; Director: BICC, 1964–70; Gleneagles Hotels, 1980–83. Chm., BTA, 1969–77; Member: BNEC, 1966–72; Board of BEA, 1964–70; Nat. Ports Council, 1966–70; Horserace Totalisator Bd, 1976–84. Chm., Adv. Council, V&A Museum, 1978–84; Mem., Historic Buildings Council, 1976–80. Awarded Cuthbert Peek Grant by RGS, 1933; Bruce Medal by RSE, 1938; Andrée Plaque by Royal Swedish Soc. for Anthropology and Geography, 1939; Patron's Gold Medal by RGS, 1940. Polar Medal (clasp Arctic 1935–36), 1942; Norwegian War Cross, 1943; Chevalier (1st Class), Order of St Olav, 1944; Czechoslovak War Cross, 1946. *Publications:* Young Men in the Arctic, 1935; Under the Pole Star, 1937; Footholds Against a Whirlwind (autobiog.), 1975. *Recreations:* friends old and new, the arts, the world today. *Address:* The Dower House, Stanton, Broadway, Worcs WR12 7NE. *Clubs:* City of London; Explorers (NY).

GLEN, Ian Douglas; QC 1996; a Recorder, since 2000; *b* 2 April 1951; *s* of Douglas and Patricia Glen; *m* 1978, Helen O'Dowd; two *s*. *Educ:* Hutton Grammar Sch.; Wyggeston Grammar Sch.; King's Coll., London (LLB Hons). Called to the Bar, Gray's Inn, 1973. Hon. Res. Fellow, Bristol Univ., 1999. *Recreations:* seaside fairways, tranquil waters, American Pie. *Address:* Guildhall Chambers, 23 Broad Street, Bristol BS1 2HG. *T:* (0117) 927 3366. *Clubs:* India House (New York); Long Ashton Golf.

GLEN HAIG, Dame Mary (Alison), DBE 1993 (CBE 1977; MBE 1971); *b* 12 July 1918; *e d* of late Captain William James and Mary (*née* Bannochie); *m* 1943, Andrew Glen Haig (decd). *Educ:* Dame Alice Owen's Girls' School. Mem., Sports Council, 1966–82; Vice Pres., CCPR, 1982– (Chm., 1974–80); Mem., Internat. Olympic Cttee, 1982–93 (Hon. Mem., 1993–). Vice Pres., Sports Aid Foundn, 1987–; Life Pres., Disability Sport England (formerly British Sports Assoc. for the Disabled), 1991 (Pres., 1981–90); Hon. Pres., British Fencing Assoc. (formerly Amateur Fencing Assoc.), 1986– (Pres., 1974–86); Patron, Women's Sports Foundn, 1998–. British Ladies' Foil Champion, 1948–50; Olympic Games, 1948, 1952, 1956, 1960; Commonwealth Games Gold Medal, 1950, 1954, Bronze Medal, 1958; Captain, Ladies' Foil Team, 1950–57. Asst Dist Administrator, S Hammersmith Health District, 1975–82. Member: Adv. Council Women's Transport Service (FANY), 1980; Exec. Cttee, Arthritis and Rheumatism Council, 1992–. Chm. of Trustees, HRH The Princess Christian Hosp., Windsor, 1981–94; Trustee: Wishbone Trust, 1991–; Kennedy Inst., 1998–. *Recreations:* fencing, gardening. *Address:* 66 North End House, Fitzjames Avenue, W14 0RX. *T:* (020) 7602 2504; 2 Old Cottages, Holyport Street, Holyport, near Maidenhead, Berks SL6 2JR. *T:* (01628) 633421. *Club:* Lansdowne.

GLENAMARA, Baron *cr* 1977 (Life Peer), of Glenridding, Cumbria; **Edward Watson Short;** PC 1964; CH 1976; Chairman, Cable and Wireless Ltd, 1976–80; *b* 17 Dec. 1912; *s* of Charles and Mary Short, Warcop, Westmorland; *m* 1941, Jennie, *d* of Thomas Sewell, Newcastle upon Tyne; one *s* one *d*. *Educ:* Bede College, Durham; LLB London. Served War of 1939–45 and became Capt. in DLI. Headmaster of Princess Louise County Secondary School, Blyth, Northumberland, 1947; Leader of Labour Group on Newcastle City Council, 1950; MP (Lab) Newcastle upon Tyne Central, 1951–76; Opposition Whip (Northern Area), 1955–62; Dep. Chief Opposition Whip, 1962–64; Parly Sec. to the Treasury and Govt Chief Whip, 1964–66; Postmaster General, 1966–68; Sec. of State for Educn and Science, 1968–70; Lord Pres. of the Council and Leader, House of Commons, 1974–76. Dep. Leader, Labour Party, 1972–76. Mem. Council, WWF, 1983–92. President: Finchale Abbey Training Coll. for the Disabled (Durham), 1985–; North East People to People, 1989–. Chancellor, Polytechnic of Newcastle upon Tyne, 1984–92, Univ. of Northumbria at Newcastle, 1992–. Freeman, City of Newcastle upon Tyne, 2001. Hon. FCP, 1965. Hon. DCL: Dunelm, 1989; Newcastle, 1998; DUniv Open, 1989; Hon. DLitt CNAA, 1990. *Publications:* The Story of The Durham Light Infantry, 1944; The Infantry Instructor, 1946; Education in a Changing World, 1971; Birth to Five, 1974; I Knew My Place, 1983; Whip to Wilson, 1989. *Recreation:* painting. *Address:* 21 Priory Gardens, Corbridge, Northumberland NE45 5HZ. *T:* (01434) 632880.

GLENAPP, Viscount; Fergus James Kenneth Mackay; *b* 9 July 1979; *s* and *heir* of 4th Earl of Inchcape, *qv*. *Educ:* Radley Coll.; Edinburgh Univ. *Address:* c/o Manor Farm, Clyffe Pypard, Swindon, Wilts SN4 7PY.

GLENARTHUR, 4th Baron *cr* 1918; **Simon Mark Arthur;** Bt 1903; DL; Director, Millennium Chemicals Inc., since 1996; *b* 7 Oct. 1944; *s* of 3rd Baron Glenarthur, OBE, and Margaret (*d* 1993), *d* of late Captain H. J. J. Howie; *S* father, 1976; *m* 1969, Susan, *yr d* of Comdr Hubert Wyndham Barry, RN; one *s* one *d*. *Educ:* Eton. Commissioned 10th Royal Hussars (PWO), 1963; ADC to High Comr, Aden, 1964–65; Captain 1970; Major 1973; retired 1975; Royal Hussars (PWO), TA, 1976–80. British Airways Helicopters Captain, 1976–82. A Lord in Waiting (Govt Whip), 1982–83; Parly Under Sec. of State, DHSS, 1983–85, Home Office, 1985–86; Minister of State: Scottish Office, 1986–87; FCO, 1987–89; elected Mem., H of L, 1999. Sen. Exec., 1989–96, Consultant, 1996–99, Hanson PLC; Dep. Chm., 1994–97, Consultant, 1997–99, Hanson Pacific Ltd; Director: Aberdeen and Texas Corporate Finance Ltd, 1977–82; The Lewis Gp, 1993–95; Whirlybird Services Ltd, 1995–; Consultant: BAe PLC, 1989–99; Chevron UK Ltd, 1994–97; Imperial Tobacco Gp, 1996–98; Intertele Testing Services Ltd, 2001–. Chairman: St Mary's Hosp., Paddington, NHS Trust, 1991–98 (Special Trustee, St Mary's Hosp., 1991–2000); British Helicopter Adv. Bd, 1992–; Europ. Helicopter Assoc., 1996–; Dep. Chm., Internat. Fedn of Helicopter Assocs, 1996–97 and 2000– (Chm., 1997–2000). Pres., Nat. Council for Civil Protection, 1991–; Mem. Council, Air League, 1994–. Scottish Patron, Butler Trust, 1994–; Gov., Nuffield Nursing Homes Trust, 2000–; Comr, Royal Hosp., Chelsea, 2001–. Brig., Queen's Body Guard for Scotland (Royal Co. of Archers). FCIT 1999 (MCIT 1979); FRAeS 1992. Liveryman, GAPAN, 1996. DL Aberdeenshire, 1988. *Recreations:* field sports, flying, gardening, choral singing, photography, barometers. *Heir: s* Hon. Edward Alexander Arthur, *b* 9 April 1973. *Address:* PO Box 11012, Banchory AB31 6ZJ. *Clubs:* Cavalry and Guards, Pratt's.

GLENCONNER, 3rd Baron *cr* 1911; **Colin Christopher Paget Tennant;** Bt 1885; Governing Director, Tennants Estate Ltd, 1967–91; Chairman, Mustique Co. Ltd, 1969–87; *b* 1 Dec. 1926; *s* of 2nd Baron Glenconner, and Pamela Winefred (*d* 1989), 2nd *d* of Sir Richard Paget, 2nd Bt; *S* father, 1983; *m* 1956, Lady Anne Coke, VO, *e d* of 5th Earl of Leicester, MVO; one *s* twin *d* (and two *s* decd). *Educ:* Eton; New College, Oxford. Director, C. Tennant Sons & Co. Ltd, 1953; Deputy Chairman, 1960–67, resigned 1967. *Heir: g s* Cody Tennant, *b* 2 Feb. 1994. *Address:* Beau Estate, PO Box 250, Soufrière, St Lucia, West Indies. *T:* and *Fax:* 4597864.

See also Lady Emma Tennant.

GLENCROSS, David, CBE 1994; Chairman, Disasters Emergency Committee, since 1999; *b* 3 March 1936; *s* of John William and Elsie May Glencross; *m* 1965, Elizabeth Louise, *d* of John and Edith Richardson; one *d*. *Educ:* Salford Grammar School; Trinity College, Cambridge. BBC: general trainee, 1958; talks producer, Midlands, 1959; TV Midlands at Six, 1962; Staff Training section, 1964; Senior Producer, External Services, 1966; Asst Head of Programmes, N Region, 1968; Senior Programme Officer, ITA, 1970; Head of Programme Services, IBA, 1976; Dep. Dir, 1977, Dir, 1983–90, Television, IBA; Chief Exec., ITC, 1991–96; Chm., British Screen Adv. Council, 1996–97. Mem., Disasters Emergency Cttee, 1997–; Trustee: Sandford St Martin Trust, 1998–; One World Broadcasting Trust, 2000–. FRTS 1981. Hon. MA Salford, 1993. *Publications:* (contrib.) Yearbook of Media and Entertainment Law, 1996; articles on broadcasting in newspapers and jls. *Recreations:* music, reading, listening to radio, walking. *Address:* Disasters Emergency Committee, 52 Great Portland Street, W1N 5AH. *T:* (020) 7580 6550.

GLENDEVON, 2nd Baron *cr* 1964, of Midhope, Co. Linlithgow; **Julian John Somerset Hope;** opera producer; *b* 6 March 1950; *er s* of 1st Baron Glendevon and Elizabeth Mary (*d* 1998), *d* of (William) Somerset Maugham, CH; *S* father, 1996. *Educ:* Eton; Christ Church, Oxford. Resident Prod., WNO, 1973–75; Assoc. Prod., Glyndebourne Festival, 1974–81; other prodns for San Francisco Opera, Wexford and Edinburgh Festivals. *Heir: b* Hon. Jonathan Charles Hope, *b* 23 April 1952. *Address:* 17 Wetherby Gardens, SW5 0JP.

GLENDINING, Rev. Canon Alan, LVO 1979; Chaplain to the Queen, 1979–94; Hon. Canon of Norwich Cathedral, since 1977; *b* 17 March 1924; *s* of late Vincent Glendining, MS, FRCS and Freda Alice; *m* 1948, Margaret Locke, *d* of Lt-Col C. M. Hawes, DSO and Frances Cooper Richmond; one *s* one *d* (and one *d* decd). *Educ:* Radley; Westcott House, Cambridge. Newspaper publishing, 1945–58. Deacon, 1960; Priest, 1961. Asst Curate, South Ormsby Group of Parishes, 1960–63; Rector of Raveningham Group of Parishes, 1963–70; Rector, Sandringham Group of Parishes, and Domestic Chaplain to the Queen, 1970–79; Rural Dean of Heacham and Rising, 1972–76; Rector of St Margaret's, Lowestoft, and Team Leader of Lowestoft Group, 1979–85; Vicar of Ranworth with Panxworth with Woodbastwick, Bishop's Chaplain for the Broads and Senior Chaplain for Holidaymakers, 1985–89; RD of Blofield, 1987–89. *Recreation:* writing. *Address:* 7 Bellfosters, Kings Staithe Lane, Kings Lynn, Norfolk PE30 1LZ.

GLENDINNING, Hon. Victoria, (Hon. Mrs O'Sullivan), CBE 1998; FRSL; author and journalist, since 1969; *b* 23 April 1937; *d* of Baron Seebohm, TD and Evangeline, *d* of Sir Gerald Hurst, QC; *m* 1st, 1958, Prof. (Oliver) Nigel (Valentine) Glendinning (marr. diss. 1981); four *s*; 2nd, 1982, Terence de Vere White (*d* 1994); 3rd, 1996, Kevin (Patrick) O'Sullivan. *Educ:* St Mary's Sch., Wantage; Millfield Sch.; Somerville Coll., Oxford (MA Mod. Langs); Southampton Univ. (Dip. in Social Admin). Part-time teaching, 1960–69; part-time psychiatric social work, 1970–73; Editorial Asst, TLS, 1974–78. FRSL 1982 (Vice-Pres., RSL, 2000–); Pres., English Centre, PEN, 2001–. Hon. DLitt: Southampton, 1994; Ulster, 1995; Dublin, 1995; York, 2000. *Publications:* A Suppressed Cry, 1969; Elizabeth Bowen: portrait of a writer, 1977; Edith Sitwell: a unicorn among lions, 1981; Vita: a biography of V. Sackville-West, 1983; Rebecca West: a life, 1987; The Grown-Ups (novel), 1989; Hertfordshire, 1989; Trollope, 1992; Electricity (novel), 1995; (ed with M. Glendinning) Sons and Mothers, 1996; Jonathan Swift, 1998; reviews and articles in newspapers and magazines in Britain, Ireland and USA. *Address:* c/o David Higham Associates, 5–8 Lower John Street, Golden Square, W1F 9HA.

GLENDYNE, 3rd Baron *cr* 1922; **Robert Nivison;** Bt 1914; Chairman, Glenfriars Holdings Ltd, 1977–93, retired; *b* 27 Oct. 1926; *o s* of 2nd Baron and late Ivy May Rose; *S* father, 1967; *m* 1953, Elizabeth, *y d* of late Sir Cecil Armitage, CBE; one *s* two *d*. *Educ:* Harrow. Grenadier Guards, 1944–47. *Heir: s* Hon. John Nivison, *b* 18 Aug. 1960. *Address:* Craigeassie, by Forfar, Angus DD8 3SE.

See also Maj.-Gen. P. R. Leuchars, Maj.-Gen. D. J. St M. Tabor.

GLENN, Sir Archibald; *see* Glenn, Sir J. R. A.

GLENN, John H(erschel), Jr; US Senator from Ohio (Democrat), 1975–98; *b* Cambridge, Ohio, 18 July 1921; *s* of John H. and Clara Glenn; *m* 1943, Anna Castor; one *s* one *d*. *Educ:* Muskingum Coll., New Concord, Ohio. Joined US Marine Corps, 1943; Served War (2 DFC's, 10 Air Medals); Pacific Theater, 1944; home-based, Capt., 1945–46; Far East, 1947–49; Major, 1952; served Korea (5 DFC's, Air Medal with 18 clusters), 1953. First non-stop supersonic flight, Los Angeles-New York (DFC), 1957; Lieut-Col, 1959. In Jan. 1964, declared candidacy for US Senate from Ohio, but withdrew owing to an injury; recovered and promoted Col USMC, Oct. 1964; retired from USMC, Dec. 1964. Became one of 7 volunteer Astronauts, man-in-space program, 1959; made 3–orbit flight in Mercury capsule, Friendship 7, 20 Feb. 1962 (boosted by rocket; time 4 hrs 56 mins; distance 81,000 miles; altitude 160 miles; recovered by destroyer off Puerto Rico in Atlantic). Vice-Pres. (corporate develt), Royal Crown Cola Co., 1966–68, Pres., Royal Crown Internat., 1967–69. Holds hon. doctorates, US and foreign. Awarded DSM (Nat. Aeronautics and Space Admin.), Astronaut Wings (Navy), Astronaut Medal (Marine Corps), etc, 1962; Galabert Internat. Astronautical Prize (jointly with Lieut-Col Yuri Gagarin), 1963; also many other awards and citations from various countries and organizations.

GLENN, Sir (Joseph Robert) Archibald, Kt 1966; OBE 1965; BCE; FIChemE, FIE (Aust.); Managing Director, 1953–73, Chairman, 1963–73, ICI Australia; *b* 24 May 1911; *s* of late J. R. Glenn, Sale, Vic., Aust.; *m* 1st, 1939, Elizabeth M. M. (*d* 1988), *d* of late J. S. Balderstone; one *s* three *d*; 2nd, 1992, Mrs Sue Debenham (*née* Hennesey). *Educ:* Scotch Coll. (Melbourne); University of Melbourne; Harvard (USA). Joined ICI Australia Ltd, 1935; Design and Construction Engr, 1935–44; Explosives Dept, ICI (UK), 1945–46; Chief Engineer, ICI Australia Ltd, 1947–48; Controller, Nobel Group, 1948–50; General Manager, 1950–52, ICI Australia Ltd; Director: Westpac Banking Corp. (formerly Bank of NSW), 1967–84; ICI, London, 1970–75; Hill Samuel Australia Ltd, 1973–83; Westralian Sands Ltd, 1977–85; Alcoa of Australia Ltd, 1973–86; Tioxide Australia Ltd, 1973–86; Newmont Pty Ltd, 1977–88; Chairman: Fibremakers Ltd, 1963–73; Rocky Dam Pty Ltd, 1968–; IMI Australia Ltd, 1970–78; Collins Wales Pty Ltd, 1973–84; I. C. Insurance Australia Ltd, 1973–85. Chancellor, La Trobe Univ., 1967–72 (Hon. DUniv 1981); Chairman: Council of Scotch Coll., 1960–81. Ormond Coll. Council, 1976–81; Member: Manufacturing Industry Advisory Council, 1960–77; Industrial Design Council, 1958–70; Australia/Japan Business Co-operation Cttee, 1965–75; Royal Melbourne Hospital Bd of Management, 1960–70; Melbourne Univ. Appointments Bd; Bd of Management, Melbourne Univ. Engrg Sch. Foundn, 1982–88; Council, Inst. of Pacific Affairs, 1976–; Governor, Atlantic Inst. of Internat. Affairs, 1970–88. Mem., Nat. Finance Cttee, Aust. Red Cross, 1982–98. J. N. Kirby Medal, 1970. *Recreations:* golf, tennis, collecting rare books. *Address:* 8 Freemans Road, Mount Eliza, Vic 3930, Australia. *T:* (3) 97875850. *Clubs:* Australian, Melbourne, Frankston Golf, Melbourne Univ. Boat (all in Melbourne); Australian (Sydney).

GLENNIE, Angus James Scott; QC 1991; QC (Scot.) 1998; barrister and advocate, farmer; *b* 3 Dec. 1950; *yr s* of Robert Nigel Forbes Glennie and Barbara Scott (*née* Nicoll); *m* 1981, Patricia Jean Phelan, *er d* of His Honour Judge Phelan, *qv*; three *s* one *d*. *Educ:* Sherborne Sch.; Trinity Hall, Cambridge (MA Hons). Called to the Bar, Lincoln's Inn, 1974; admitted to Faculty of Advocates, 1992. *Recreations:* sailing, real tennis. *Address:* Threeburnford, Oxton, Lauder, Berwicks TD2 6PU. *T:* (01578) 750615.

GLENNIE, Evelyn Elizabeth Ann, OBE 1993; FRAM, FRCM; percussionist; *b* 19 July 1965; *d* of Isobel and Arthur Glennie; *m* 1993, Greg Malcangi. *Educ:* Ellon Acad., Aberdeen; Royal Academy of Music (GRSM Hons, LRAM, ARAM; FRAM 1992; Queen's Commendation Prize); FRCM 1991. Shell Gold Medal, 1984; studied in Japan; Leonardo da Vinci Prize, 1987; début, Wigmore Hall, 1986; soloist in Zürich, Paris, Schwetzingen, Holland, Dublin, Norway, Australia; festivals of Aldeburgh, Bath, Edinburgh, Chichester, Salisbury; percussion and timpani concertos specially written; TV and radio presenting; numerous recordings and awards. Hon. DMus: Aberdeen, 1991; Bristol, 1995; Portsmouth, 1995; Leicester, Surrey, 1997; Belfast, Essex, Durham, 1998; Hon. DLitt: Warwick, 1993; Loughborough, 1995. Grammy Award, 1988. *Publication:* Good Vibrations (autobiog.), 1990. *Recreations:* reading, walking, cycling, art. *Address:* PO Box 6, Sawtry, Huntingdon, Cambs PE17 5NE. *T:* (01480) 891772.

GLENNIE, Robert McDougall; Senior Partner, McGrigor Donald, Solicitors, since 2000; *b* 4 April 1951. *Educ:* Jordanhill Coll. Sch., Glasgow; Univ. of Strathclyde (LLB). FCIS 2000 (MCIS). Admitted Solicitor, 1978. Joined McGrigor Donald, 1976; Partner,

1980–; Managing Partner of London Office, 1989. Mem., Law Soc. of Scotland, 1977–. *Recreations:* hillwalking, cinema, tropical fruit farming. *Address:* McGrigor Donald, 63 Queen Victoria Street, EC4N 4ST. *T:* (020) 7329 3299.

GLENNY, Misha; freelance journalist, writer and broadcaster, since 1993; *b* 25 April 1958; *s* of late Michael V. G. Glenny and of Juliet Sydenham (*née* Crum); *m* 1987, Snezana Curcic (marr. diss. 2001); one *s* one *d*; one *s* with Kirsty Lang. *Educ:* Bristol Univ. (BA Drama); Charles Univ., Prague. Rights editor, Verso publishing house, London, 1983–86; Central Europe Correspondent (based in Vienna): The Guardian, 1986–89; BBC World Service, 1989–93. Sony Special Award for Broadcasting, 1993; American Overseas Pressclub Award for Best Book on Foreign Affairs, 1993. *Publications:* The Rebirth of History: Eastern Europe in the age of democracy, 1990, 2nd edn 1993; The Fall of Yugoslavia, 1992, 2nd edn 1993; The Balkans 1804–1999: nationalism, war and the great powers, 1999. *Address:* 20 Wellingtonia Court, Laine Close, Brighton, E Sussex BN1 6TD.

GLENNY, Dr Robert Joseph Ervine, CEng, FIM; Consultant to UK Government, industry, and European Economic Community, since 1983; *b* 14 May 1923; *s* of late Robert and Elizabeth Rachel Glenny; *m* 1947, Joan Phillips Reid; one *s* one *d*. *Educ:* Methodist Coll., Belfast; QUB (BSc Chemistry); London Univ. (BSc Metallurgy, PhD). CEng, 1979; FIM 1958. Res. Metallurgist, English Electric Co. Ltd, Stafford, 1943–47; National Gas Turbine Establishment, 1947–70; Materials Dept, 1947–66; Head of Materials Dept, 1966–70; Supt, Div. of Materials Applications, National Physical Lab., 1970–73; Head of Materials Dept, RAE, 1973–79; Group Head of Aerodynamics, Structures and Materials Depts, RAE, 1979–83. *Publications:* research and review papers on materials science and technology, mainly related to gas turbines, in ARC (R&M series) and in Internat. Metallurgical Rev. *Recreations:* reading, gardening, walking. *Address:* 77 Gally Hill Road, Fleet, Hants GU52 6RU. *T:* (01252) 615877.

GLENTON, Anthony Arthur Edward, CBE 2000 (MBE mil. 1982); TD 1972 (bars 1980, 1986, 1992); DL; FCA; Director, since 1988, Chairman, since 1994, Port of Tyne Authority; Senior Partner, Ryecroft Glenton, Chartered Accountants, Newcastle, since 1967; *b* 21 March 1943; *s* of late Lt-Col Eric Cecil Glenton, Gosforth, Newcastle, and of Joan Lydia Glenton (*née* Taylor); *m* 1972, Caroline Ann, *d* of Maurice George Meade-King; one *s* one *d*. *Educ:* Merchiston Castle Sch., Edinburgh. FCA 1965. Chm., Charles W. Taylor & Son Ltd, Iron Founders, S Shields, 1995-; Dir, Newcastle Bldg Soc., 1987- (Chm., 1992-97). Joined Royal Artillery, Territorial Army, 1961: Lieut Col 1984; CO 101 (Northumbrian) Field Regt RA (V), 1984-86; Col 1986; Dep. Comdr, 15 Inf. Bde, 1986-89; ADC to the Queen, 1987-89; TA Advr to GOC Eastern Dist, 1989-94; Chm., N of England RFCA, 1999- (Vice Chm., 1995-99). Chm., Northumberland Br., SSAFA Forces Help, 1989-. Freeman, City of London, 1981; Liveryman, Co. of Chartered Accountants of England and Wales, 1981. DL Northumberland, 1993. *Recreations:* shooting, sailing, contemporary art. *Address:* Whinbank, Rothbury, Northumberland NE65 7YJ. *T:* (01669) 620361; Palace Hill Cottage, St Cuthbert's Square, Holy Island of Lindisfarne, Northumberland TD15 2SP. *T:* (01289) 389312; (office) 27 Portland Terrace, Newcastle upon Tyne NE2 1QP. *T:* (0191) 281 1292. *Club:* Army and Navy.

GLENTORAN, 3rd Baron *cr* 1939, of Ballyalolly, Co. Down; **Thomas Robin Valerian Dixon,** CBE 1992 (MBE 1969); Bt 1903; *b* 21 April 1935; *er s* of 2nd Baron Glentoran, KBE, PC; *S* father, 1995; *m* 1959, Rona, *d* of Captain G. C. Colville; three *s*; *m* 1990, Margaret Rainey. *Educ:* Eton. Man. Dir, Redland (NI) Ltd, 1971–92. Mem., Millenium Fund Commn, 1994–. Elected Mem., H of L, 1999. *Recreations:* sailing, golf. *Heir: s* Hon. Daniel George Dixon [*b* 26 July 1959; *m* 1983, Leslie Hope Brooke; two *s*]. *Address:* Drumadarragh House, Ballyclare, Co. Antrim BT39 0TA; 17 Redcliffe Street, SW10 9DR. *Clubs:* Carlton; Royal Yacht Squadron, Royal Cruising.

GLENTWORTH, Viscount; Edmund Christopher Pery; Director, Deutsche Bank AG London, since 1996; *b* 10 Feb. 1963; *s* and *heir* of 6th Earl of Limerick, *qv*; *m* 1990, Emily Kate (marr. diss. 2000), *o d* of Michael Thomas; two *s*. *Educ:* Eton; New Coll., Oxford (MA); Pushkin Inst., Moscow; City Univ. (Dip. Law). Called to the Bar, Middle Temple, 1987. HM Diplomatic Service, 1987–92: FCO, 1987–88; Ecole Nationale d'Administration, Paris, 1988–89; attachment to Ministère des Affaires Etrangères, Paris, 1990; Second Sec., Senegal, 1990–91, Amman, 1991–92; lawyer: with Clifford Chance, 1992–93; with Freshfields, 1993–94; solicitor with Milbank Tweed, 1994–96; Chief Rep., Morgan Grenfell (Deutsche Bank), Moscow, 1996–98. *Recreations:* ski-ing, windsurfing. *Heir: s* Hon. Felix Edmund Pery, *b* 16 Nov. 1991. *Address:* 30 Victoria Road, W8 5RG. *T:* (020) 7937 1954; *e-mail:* edmund.glentworth@db.com.

GLESTER, John William; Chairman and Managing Director, John Glester Consultancy Services; *b* 8 Sept. 1946; *o s* of George Ernest Glester and late Maude Emily Glester; *m* 1970, Ann Gleave Taylor (*d* 1998); two *s*. *Educ:* Plaistow Grammar Sch.; Reading Univ. (BA Hons). Joined Civil Service 1968; served DEA, DoE and Merseyside Task Force; Regl Controller, NW, DoE, 1985–88; Chief Exec., Central Manchester Develt Corp., 1988–96; Trust Fund Adminr, Lord Mayor of Manchester's Emergency Appeal Fund, 1996–98; Dir (Regl Strategy), NW Regl Develt Agency, 1999–2000. Chairman: Castlefield Management Co., 1992–2001; Castlefield Heritage Trust, 1996–; Hallogen Ltd (Bridgewater Hall), 1998– (Dir, 1995–98); Dir, Langtree Gp plc, 1999–; Consultant: Lloyds Metal Group plc, 1997–98; Dunlop Heywood, 1998–99; Valley and Vale Properties, 1998–2000. Chm., Network Space Consultative Cttee, 1999–. Director: Salford Phoenix, 1987–95; Manchester Arts Fest., 1989–93; Manchester Olympic Bid Cttee, 1990–93; Manchester 2000, 1992–94; Manchester City of Drama, 1992–94; Manchester Concert Hall Ltd, 1994–; Patterson Inst. for Cancer Res., 2001–. Consultant: UMIST, 1998–; Commonwealth Games 2002, 2000–. Trustee, Amcoats Bldgs Preservation Trust, 2001–. *Recreations:* cricket, football (West Ham United in particular), music, theatre, cooking. *Address:* Bridgewater Hall, Manchester M2 3WS. *Club:* St James's (Manchester).

GLICK, Ian Bernard; QC 1987; a Recorder, since 2000; *b* 18 July 1948; *s* of late Dr Louis Glick and of Phyllis Esty Glick; *m* 1986, Roxane Eban; three *s*. *Educ:* Bradford Grammar School; Balliol College, Oxford (MA, BCL). President, Oxford Union Society, 1968. Called to the Bar, Inner Temple, 1970, Bencher, 1997. Junior Counsel to the Crown, Common Law, 1985–87; Standing Junior Counsel to DTI in Export Credit Cases, 1985–87. Chm., Commercial Bar Assoc., 1997–99. *Address:* 1 Essex Court, Temple, EC4Y 9AR.

GLICKSMAN, Brian Leslie; Treasury Officer of Accounts, HM Treasury, since 2000; *b* 14 Dec. 1945; *s* of Henry and Kitty Glicksman; *m* 1971, Jackie Strachan; two *d*. *Educ:* Ealing Grammar Sch.; New Coll., Oxford (BA Maths); Warwick Univ. (MSc Mgt Sci. and OR). OR Scientist, CSD, 1969; Principal, DoE, 1976; Asst Dir, PSA, 1984; Sec. Royal Commn on Envmtl Pollution, 1987; Divl Manager, DoE, 1992. *Address:* HM Treasury, Allington Towers, 19 Allington Street, SW1E 5EB.

GLIDEWELL, Rt Hon. Sir Iain (Derek Laing), Kt 1980; PC 1985; a Lord Justice of Appeal, 1985–95; a Judge of the Court of Appeal, Gibraltar, since 1998; *b* 8 June 1924; *s* of late Charles Norman and Nora Glidewell; *m* 1950, Hilary, *d* of late Clinton D. Winant; one *s* two *d*. *Educ:* Bromsgrove Sch.; Worcester Coll., Oxford (Hon. Fellow 1986). Served RAFVR (pilot), 1942–46. Called to the Bar, Gray's Inn, 1949 (Bencher 1977, Treas. 1995). QC 1969; a Recorder of the Crown Court, 1976–80; Judge of Appeal, Isle of Man, 1979–80; a Judge of the High Court of Justice, Queen's Bench Division, 1980–85; Presiding Judge, NE Circuit, 1982–85. Chm., Judicial Studies Bd, 1989–92; Member: Senate of Inns of Court and the Bar, 1976–79; Supreme Court Rule Cttee, 1980–84. Chm., Panels for Examination of Structure Plans: Worcestershire, 1974; W Midlands, 1975; conducted: Heathrow Fourth Terminal Inquiry, 1978; Review of CPS, 1997–98. Hon. RICS, 1982. *Recreations:* vigorous gardening, walking, theatre. *Address:* Rough Heys Farm, Henbury, Macclesfield, Cheshire SK11 9PF. *Club:* Garrick.

GLIN, Knight of; *see* Fitz-Gerald, D. J. V.

GLOAG, Ann Heron; Director, Stagecoach Holdings plc, since 1986 (Managing Director, 1986–94; Executive Director, 1986–2000); *b* 10 Dec. 1942; *d* of Iain and Catherine Souter; *m* 1st, 1965, Robin N. Gloag; one *d* (one *s* decd); 2nd, 1990, David McCleary. *Educ:* Caledonian Road Primary School; Perth High School. Trainee Nurse, Bridge of Earn Hosp., Perth, 1960–65; Ward Sister, Devonshire Royal Hosp., Buxton, 1965–69; Theatre Sister, Bridge of Earn Hosp., 1969–80; Founding Partner, Gloagtrotter, re-named Stagecoach Express Services, 1980–83; Co-Director, Stagecoach Ltd, 1983–86 (acquired parts of National Bus Co., 1987 and 1989 and Scottish Bus Group, 1991). Scottish Marketing Woman of the Year, Scottish Univs, 1989; UK Businesswoman of the Year, Veuve Cliquot and Inst of Dirs, 1989–90. *Recreations:* family, travel, charity support. *Address:* Stagecoach Group, 10 Dunkeld Road, Perth PH1 5TW.

See also B. Souter.

GLOAK, Graeme Frank, CB 1980; Solicitor for the Customs and Excise, 1978–82; *b* 9 Nov. 1921; *s* of late Frank and Lilian Gloak; *m* 1944, Mary, *d* of Stanley and Jane Thorne; one *s* one *d* (and one *s* decd). *Educ:* Brentwood School. Royal Navy, 1941–46; Solicitor, 1947; Customs and Excise: Legal Asst, 1947; Sen. Legal Asst, 1953; Asst Solicitor, 1967; Principal Asst Solicitor, 1971. Sec., Civil Service Legal Soc., 1954–62. Member: Dairy Produce Quota Tribunal, 1984–85; Agricl Wages Cttee for Essex and Herts, 1984–90 (Vice-Chm., 1987–90); Chm., Agricl Dwelling House Adv. Cttee, Essex and Herts, 1984–93. Member: Barking and Havering FPC, 1986–90; Barking and Havering FHSA, 1990–96; Barking and Havering HA, 1996–97. *Publication:* (with G. Krikorian and R. K. F. Hutchings) Customs and Excise, in Halsbury's Laws of England, 4th edn, 1973. *Recreations:* badminton, walking, watching cricket. *Address:* 31 Burses Way, Hutton, Brentwood, Essex CM13 2PL. *T:* (01277) 212748. *Clubs:* MCC; Essex County Cricket (Chelmsford).

GLOBE, Henry Brian; QC 1994; a Recorder, since 1991; *b* 18 June 1949; *o s* of Theodore Montague Globe and Irene Rita Globe; *m* 1972, Estelle Levin; two *d*. *Educ:* Liverpool Coll.; Birmingham Univ. (LLB Hons). Called to the Bar, Middle Temple, 1972; in practice on Northern Circuit, 1972– (Treas., 2001–); Standing Counsel to: DSS, 1985–94; HM Customs and Excise, 1992–94; Asst Recorder, 1987–90. Member: Bar Council, 2001–; Criminal Cttee, Judicial Studies Bd, 2001–. Chm. of Govs, King David High Sch., Liverpool, 1990–2000. *Recreations:* tennis, bridge. *Address:* Exchange Chambers, Pearl Assurance House, Derby Square, Liverpool L2 9XX. *T:* (0151) 236 7747, *Fax:* (0151) 737 2560; *e-mail:* henryglobe@btinternet.com.

GLOCER, Thomas Henry; Chief Executive Officer, Reuters Group plc, since 2001; *b* NYC, 8 Oct. 1959; *s* of Walter Glocer and Ursula Glocer (*née* Goodman); *m* 1988, Maarit Leso; one *s* one *d*. *Educ:* Columbia Coll. (BA *summa cum laude* 1981); Yale Law Sch. (JD 1984). Mergers and acquisitions lawyer, Davis Polk and Wardwell, NY, Paris and Tokyo, 1985–93; joined Reuters, 1993: mem., Legal Dept, Gen. Counsel, Reuters America Inc., NYC, 1993–96; Exec. Vice-Pres., Reuters America Inc. and CEO, Reuters Latin America, 1996–98; Chief Executive Officer: Reuters business in the Americas, 1998–2001; Reuters Inf., 2000–01. Director: NYC Investment Fund, 1999– (Mem., Exec. Cttee); Instinet Corp., 2000–. Mem., Adv. Bd, Singapore Monetary Authy, 2001–. Mem., Corporate Council, Whitney Mus. of American Art, 2000–. Author of computer software, incl. (jtly) Coney Island: a game of discovery, 1983. NY Hall of Sci. Award, 2000; John Jay Alumni Award, 2001. *Recreations:* tennis, windsurfing, ski-ing. *Address:* Reuters Group plc, 85 Fleet Street, EC4P 4AJ.

GLOSSOP, Peter; Principal Baritone, Royal Opera House, Covent Garden, until 1967, now Guest Artist; *b* 6 July 1928; *s* of Cyril and Violet Elizabeth Glossop; *m* 1st, 1955, Joyce Elizabeth Blackham (marr. diss. 1977); no *c*; 2nd, 1977, Michèle Yvonne Amos; two *d*. *Educ:* High Storrs Grammar Sch., Sheffield. Began singing professionally in chorus of Sadler's Wells Opera, 1952, previously a bank clerk; promoted to principal after one season; Covent Garden Opera, 1962–67. Début in Italy, 1964; La Scala, Milan, début, Rigoletto, 1965. Sang Otello and Rigoletto with Metropolitan Opera Company at Newport USA Festival, Aug. 1967; Rigoletto and Nabucco with Mexican National Opera Company, Sept. 1967. Guest Artist (Falstaff, Rigoletto, Tosca) with American National Opera Company, Oct. 1967. Has sung in opera houses of Bologna, Parma Catania, Vienna, 1967–68, and Berlin and Buenos Aires. Is a recording artist. Hon. DMus, Sheffield, 1970. Winner of 1st Prize and Gold Medal in First International Competition for Young Opera Singers, Sofia, Bulgaria, 1961; Gold Medal for finest performance (in Macbeth) of 1968–69 season, Barcelona; Amici di Verdi Gold Medal, 1995. *Films:* Pagliacci, Otello. *Recreations:* New Orleans jazz music, golf. *Address:* End Cottage, Hawkchurch, Axminster, Devon EX13 5TY.

GLOSTER, Elizabeth, (Mrs S. E. Brodie); QC 1989; a Judge of the Courts of Appeal of Jersey and Guernsey, since 1993; a Recorder, since 1995; *b* 5 June 1949; *d* of Peter Gloster and Betty Gloster (*née* Read); *m* 1973, Stanley Eric Brodie, *qv*; one *s* one *d*. *Educ:* Roedean Sch., Brighton; Girton Coll., Cambridge (BA Hons). Called to the Bar, Inner Temple, 1971, Bencher 1992. Mem., panel of Counsel who appear for DTI in company matters, 1982–89. Mem. Bd (non-exec.), CAA, 1992–93. *Address:* 1 Essex Court, Temple, EC4Y 9AR. *T:* (020) 7583 2000, *Fax:* (020) 7583 0118.

GLOSTER, Prof. John, MD; Hon. Consulting Ophthalmologist, Moorfields Eye Hospital; Emeritus Professor of Experimental Opthalmology, University of London; *b* 23 March 1922; *m* 1947, Margery (*née* Williams); two *s*. *Educ:* Jesus Coll., Cambridge; St Bartholomew's Hosp. MB, BChir 1946; MRCS, LRCP 1946; DOMS 1950; MD Cantab 1953; PhD London 1959. Registrar, Research Dept, Birmingham and Midland Eye Hosp., 1950–54; Mem. Staff, Ophth. Research Unit, MRC, 1954–63; Prof. of Experimental Ophthalmology, Inst. of Ophth., Univ. of London, 1975–82; Dean of the Inst. of Ophthalmology, 1975–80. Mem. Ophth. Soc. UK; Hon. Mem., Assoc. for Eye Res. *Publications:* Tonometry and Tonography, 1966; (jtly) Physiology of the Eye, System of Ophthalmology IV, ed Duke-Elder, 1968; contribs to jls. *Address:* 14 Church Place, Ickenham, Middlesex UB10 8XB.

GLOUCESTER, Bishop of, since 1993; **Rt Rev. David Edward Bentley;** *b* 7 Aug. 1935; *s* of William Bentley and Florence (*née* Dalgleish); *m* 1962, Clarice Lahmers; two *s* two *d*. *Educ:* Gt Yarmouth Grammar School; Univ. of Leeds (BA English); Westcott House, Cambridge. Deacon 1960, priest 1961; Curate: St Ambrose, Bristol, 1960–62; Holy Trinity with St Mary, Guildford, 1962–66; Rector: Headley, Bordon, 1966–73; Esher, 1973–86; Suffragan Bishop of Lynn, 1986–93. Hon. Canon of Guildford Cathedral, 1980; RD of Emly, 1977–82. Warden, Community of All Hallows, Ditchingham, 1989–93. Chairman: Guildford dio. House of Clergy, 1977–86; Guildford dio. Council of Social Responsibility, 1980–86; ACCM Candidates Cttee, 1987–91; ABM Recruitment and Selection Cttee, 1991–93; ABM Ministry Develt and Deployment Cttee, 1995–98; Deployment, Remuneration and Conditions of Service Cttee, Ministry Div., Archbishops' Council, 1999–. *Recreations:* music; sport, especially cricket; theatre, travel. *Address:* Bishopscourt, Pitt Street, Gloucester GL1 2BQ. *T:* (01452) 524598, *Fax:* (01452) 310025; *e-mail:* bshpglos@star.co.uk. *Club:* MCC.

GLOUCESTER, Dean of; *see* Bury, Very Rev. N. A. S.

GLOUCESTER, Archdeacon of; *see* Sidaway, Ven. G. H.

GLOVER, Anthony Richard Haysom; Chief Executive Officer, City Council of Norwich, 1980–88; *b* 29 May 1934; 2nd *s* of late Arthur Herbert Glover and late Marjorie Florence Glover; *m* 1960, Ann Penelope Scupham, *d* of late John Scupham, OBE; two *s* one *d*. *Educ:* Culford Sch., Bury St Edmunds; Emmanuel Coll., Cambridge (BA). HM Customs and Excise: Asst Principal, 1957; Principal, 1961; on secondment to HM Treasury, 1965–68; Asst Sec., 1969; Asst Sec., HM Treasury, 1972–76; Dep. Controller, HM Stationery Office, 1976–80. Sec., Norfolk Historic Bldgs Trust, 1991–95. University of East Anglia: Mem. Council, 1984–88; part-time Tutor, Dept. of Extra-Mural Studies, 1991–. *Recreations:* music, reading, writing, alpine gardening. *Address:* 7 Hillside Road, Thorpe St Andrew, Norwich NR7 0QG. *T:* (01603) 433508.

GLOVER, Audrey Frances, (Mrs E. C. Glover), CMG 1997; barrister; Leader, UK Delegation to UN Human Rights Commission, since 1998; *d* of Robert John Victor Lush and Frances Lucy de la Roche; *m* 1971, Edward Charles Glover, *qv*; two *s* two *d* (and one *s* decd). *Educ:* St Anne's Coll., Sanderstead, Surrey; King's Coll. London (LLB Hons). Called to the Bar, Gray's Inn, 1961; LCD, 1965–67; HM Diplomatic Service, 1967–97: joined Foreign Office, as Asst Legal Advr, 1967; Asst (Temp.), Attorney Gen's Dept, Australia, 1972–73; Advr on British Law, Liby of Congress, Washington, 1974–77; Legal Advr (Asst), FCO, 1978–85; Legal Advr, British Mil. Govt, Berlin, 1985–89; Legal Counsellor, FCO, and UK Agent to EC and Ct of Human Rights, 1990–94; Dir (with rank of Ambassador), OSCE Office of Democratic Instns and Human Rights, Warsaw, 1994–97. EU Rep., Council of Europe Cttee of Wise Persons, 1998. *Recreations:* collecting paintings, sailing, travelling, theatre. *Address:* c/o Foreign and Commonwealth Office (Georgetown, Guyana), SW1A 2AH; Oak House, Thornham, Norfolk PE36 6LY. *Club:* Brancaster Staithe Sailing (Norfolk).

GLOVER, Prof. David Moore, PhD; FRSE; Arthur Balfour Professor of Genetics, and Head, Department of Genetics, University of Cambridge, since 1999; Director, Cancer Research Campaign Cell Cycle Genetics Group, since 1989; *b* 28 March 1948; *s* of Charles David Glover and Olivia Glover; *m* 2000, Magdalena Zernicka. *Educ:* Broadway Tech. Grammar Sch., Barnsley; Fitzwilliam Coll., Cambridge (BA 2nd Cl. Biochem.); ICRF and UCL (PhD 1972). FRSE 1992. Post-doctoral Res. Fellow, Stanford Univ., Calif, 1972–75; Imperial College, London: Lectr in Biochem., 1975–81; Sen. Lectr in Biochem., 1981–83; Reader in Molecular Genetics, 1983–86; Prof. of Molecular Genetics, 1986–89; Hd, Dept of Biochem., 1988–89; Prof. of Molecular Genetics, Dept of Biochem., 1989–92, Dept of Anatomy and Physiol., 1992–99, Univ. of Dundee. Jt Dir, 1979–86, Dir, 1986–89, CRC Eukaryotic Molecular Genetics Gp. Mem., EMBO, 1978. *Publications:* Genetic Engineering: cloning DNA, 1980; Gene Cloning: the mechanics of DNA manipulation, 1984; DNA Cloning: a practical approach (3 vols), 1985, 2nd edn (jtly with B. D. Hames) 1995; (with C. J. Hutchison) The Cell Cycle, 1995; (with S. Endow) Dynamics of Cell Division, 1998; contrib. numerous scientific papers. *Recreations:* music, reading, walking. *Address:* University of Cambridge, Department of Genetics, Downing Street, Cambridge CB2 3EH. *T:* (01223) 333999.

GLOVER, Edward Charles, MVO 1976; HM Diplomatic Service; High Commissioner to Guyana and Ambassador to Suriname, since 1998; *b* 4 March 1943; *s* of Edward and Mary Glover; *m* 1971, Audrey Frances Lush (*see* A. F. Glover); two *s* two *d* (and one *s* decd). *Educ:* Goudhurst Sch. for Boys; Birkbeck Coll., London (BA Hons Hist., MPhil Hist.). Joined FO from BoT, 1967: Private Sec. to High Comr, Australia, 1971–73; Washington, 1973–77; Sec. to UK Delegn to UN Law of Sea Conf., 1978–80; on secondment to Guinness Peat Gp, 1981–83; Sect. Hd, Arms Control and Disarmament Dept, FCO, 1983–85; Senate Liaison Officer, BMG, Berlin, 1985–89; Dep. Hd, Near East and N Africa Dept, FCO, 1989–91; Hd, Mgt Rev. Staff, FCO, 1991–94; Dep. Hd of Mission and Consul-Gen., Brussels, 1994–98. Mem., RIIA, 1969–. Mem., King's Lynn Preservation Trust, 1977–. *Recreations:* tennis, reading, water-colour painting. *Address:* c/o Foreign and Commonwealth Office, King Charles Street, SW1A 2AH; Oak House, Thornham, Norfolk PE36 6LY. *Club:* Brooks's.

GLOVER, Eric; Secretary-General, Chartered Institute of Bankers (formerly Institute of Bankers), 1982–94; *b* 28 June 1935; *s* of William and Margaret Glover; *m* 1960, Adele Diane Hilliard; three *s*. *Educ:* Liverpool Institute High Sch.; Oriel Coll., Oxford (MA). Shell International Petroleum (Borneo and Uganda), 1957–63; Institute of Bankers, later Chartered Institute of Bankers, 1963–; Asst Sec., 1964–69; Dir of Studies, 1969–82. Chm., Open and Distance Learning Quality Council (formerly Council for Accreditation of Correspondence Colls), 1993–98 (Mem., 1983–); Treas., British Accreditation Council for Indep. Further and Higher Educn, 1987– (Mem., 1985–); Pres., Teachers & Trainers of Financial Services, 1998–. Chm., Intrabank Expert Witness, 1998–. Hon. Fellow, Sheffield Hallam Univ., 1992. Hon. FCIB 1994. Hon. MBA City of London Polytechnic, 1991. *Publications:* articles on banking education. *Recreations:* golf, swimming. *Address:* 12 Manor Park, Tunbridge Wells, Kent TN4 8XP. *T:* (01892) 531221.

GLOVER, Jane Alison, DPhil; FRCM; conductor; *b* 13 May 1949; *d* of late Robert Finlay Glover, TD and of Jean Glover (*née* Muir). *Educ:* Monmouth School for Girls; St Hugh's Coll., Oxford (BA, MA, DPhil; Hon. Fellow, 1991). FRCM 1993. Oxford University: Junior Research Fellow, 1973–75, Sen. Res. Fellow, 1982–91, St Hugh's Coll.; Lecturer in Music: St Hugh's Coll., 1976–84; St Anne's Coll., 1976–80; Pembroke Coll., 1979–84; elected to OU Faculty of Music, 1979. Professional conducting début at Wexford Festival, 1975; thereafter, operas and concerts for: BBC; Glyndebourne (Musical Dir, Touring Opera, 1982–85); Royal Op. House, Covent Garden (début, 1988); ENO (début, 1989); Teatro la Fenice, Venice; Royal Danish Opera; Glimmerglass Opera, NY; Australian Opera; London Symphony Orch.; London Philharmonic Orch.; Philharmonia Orch.; Royal Philharmonic Orch.; English Chamber Orch.; BBC Symphony Orch.; BBC Welsh Symphony Orch.; Scottish Nat. Orch.; Bournemouth Symphony Orch.; Bournemouth Sinfonietta; and many others in Italy, Holland, Denmark, Canada, China, Hong Kong, Austria, Yugoslavia, Germany, France, Belgium, Australia, NZ, etc; Artistic Dir, London Mozart Players, 1984–91; Principal Conductor: London Choral Soc., 1983–; Huddersfield Choral Soc., 1989–96. A Gov., BBC, 1990–95. Member: BBC Central Music Adv. Cttee, 1981–85; Music Adv. Panel, Arts Council, 1986–87. Radio and television documentaries and series, and presentation for BBC and LWT, esp. Orchestra, 1983, Mozart, 1985, Opera House, 1995, Musical Dynasties, 2000. Governor, RAM, 1985–90. Hon. DMus: Exeter, 1986; London, 1992; City, 1994; Glasgow, 1997; Hon. DLitt: Loughborough, 1988; Bradford, 1992; Brunel, 1996; DUniv Open, 1988; Hon. DMus CNAA, 1991. ABSA/Daily Telegraph Arts Award, 1990. *Publications:* Cavalli, 1978; contribs to: The New Monteverdi Companion, 1986; Monteverdi 'Orfeo' handbook, 1986; articles in Music and Letters, Proc. of Royal Musical Assoc., Musical Times, The Listener, TLS, Early Music, Opera, and others; many recordings. *Recreations:* The Times crossword puzzle, theatre, ski-ing, walking. *Address:* c/o Askonas Holt Ltd, Lonsdale Chambers, 27 Chancery Lane, WC2A 1PF. *T:* (020) 7400 1700.

GLOVER, Prof. Keith, FRS 1993; FREng, FIEEE, FInstMC; Professor of Engineering, since 1989, and Fellow of Sidney Sussex College, since 1976, University of Cambridge; *b* 23 April 1946; *s* of William Frank Glover and Helen Ruby Glover (*née* Higgs); *m* 1970, Jean Elizabeth Priestley; one *s* one *d*. *Educ:* Dartford Grammar Sch., Kent; Imperial College London (BScEng); MIT (PhD). FIEEE 1993. Development engineer, Marconi Co., 1967–69; Kennedy Meml Fellow, MIT, 1969–71; Asst Prof. of Electrical Engineering, Univ. of S California, 1973–76; Department of Engineering, University of Cambridge: Lectr, 1976–87; Reader in Control Engineering, 1987–89; Head of Inf. Engrg Div., 1993–. FREng 2000. *Publications:* (with D. C. McFarlane) Robust Controller Design using Normalized Coprime Factor Plant Descriptions, 1989; (with D. Mustafa) Minimum Entropy H-infinity Control, 1990; (jtly) Robust and Optimal Control, 1996; contribs to control and systems jls. *Address:* Faculty of Engineering, Trumpington Street, Cambridge CB2 1PZ.

GLOVER, Kenneth Frank; Assistant Under-Secretary of State (Statistics), Ministry of Defence, 1974–81, retired; *b* 16 Dec. 1920; *s* of Frank Glover and Mabel Glover; *m* 1951, Iris Clare Holmes. *Educ:* Bideford Grammar Sch.; UC of South West, Exeter; LSE (MScEcon). Joined Statistics Div., MoT, 1946; Statistician, 1950; Statistical adviser to Cttee of Inquiry on Major Ports (Rochdale Cttee), 1961–62; Dir of Econs and Statistics at Nat. Ports Council, 1964–68; Chief Statistician, MoT and DoE, 1968–74. *Publications:* various papers; articles in JRSS, Dock and Harbour Authority. *Recreations:* boating, idleness. *Address:* Little Hamlets, 26 Platway Lane, Shaldon, Teignmouth, South Devon TQ14 0AR. *T:* (01626) 872700.

GLOVER, Myles Howard; Clerk, Worshipful Company of Skinners, 1959–90; *b* 18 Dec. 1928; *yr s* of Cedric Howard Glover and Winifred Mary (*née* Crewdson); *m* 1969, Wendy Gillian, *er d* of C. M. Coleman; one *s* two *d*. *Educ:* Rugby; Balliol Coll., Oxford (MA). Called to the Bar, Lincoln's Inn, 1954. Sec., CIFE, 1991–98. Chm., Cttee of Clerks to Twelve Chief Livery Cos of City of London, 1975–81. Hon. Sec., GBA, 1967–91. Member: City & Guilds Art Sch. Cttee, 1960–71; Adv. Cttee, Gresham Coll., 1985–86; Governing Council: St Paul's Cathedral Choir Sch., 1986–90; Cambridge Tutors' Coll., 1993–94, 2000–; Governing Body, St Leonards-Mayfield Sch., 1988–93; Hon. Addtl Mem., GBA Cttee, 1991. Hon. Member: Old Tonbridgian Soc., 1986; Old Skinners' Soc., 1990 (Leopard of the Year Trophy, 1990); CIFE, 1999. Liveryman, Musicians' Co., 1954; Hon. Freeman: Fellmongers' Co., Richmond, N Yorks, 1991; Skinners' Co., 1993. *Recreation:* music. *Address:* Wisteria Cottage, 31 The Green, Woodchurch, Ashford, Kent TN26 3PF. *T:* (01233) 860288. *Club:* Savile.

GLOVER, Rt Rev. Patrick; *see* Bloemfontein, Bishop of.

GLOVER, Maj.-Gen. Peter James, CB 1966; OBE 1948; *b* 16 Jan. 1913; *s* of late G. H. Glover, CBE, Sheephatch House, Tilford, Surrey, and late Mrs G. H. Glover; *m* 1946, Wendy Archer; one *s* two *d*. *Educ:* Uppingham; Cambridge (MA). 2nd Lieut RA, 1934; served War of 1939–45, BEF France and Far East; Lieut-Col 1956; Brig. 1961; Comdt, Sch. of Artillery, Larkhill, 1960–62; Maj.-Gen. 1962; GOC 49 Infantry Division TA and North Midland District, 1962–63; Head of British Defence Supplies Liaison Staff, Delhi, 1963–66; Director, Royal Artillery, 1966–69, retd. Col Comdt, RA, 1970–78. *Address:* Garden Cottage, Wallop House, Nether Wallop, Stockbridge, Hants SO20 8HE.

GLOVER, Stephen Charles Morton; journalist; *b* 13 Jan. 1952; *s* of Rev. Prebendary John Morton Glover and Helen Ruth Glover (*née* Jones); *m* 1982, Celia Elizabeth (*née* Montague); two *s*. *Educ:* Shrewsbury Sch.; Mansfield Coll., Oxford (MA). Daily Telegraph, 1978–85: leader writer and feature writer, 1978–85; parly sketch writer, 1979–81; Independent: Foreign Editor, 1986–89; Editor, The Independent on Sunday, 1990–91; Associate Editor, Evening Standard, 1992–95; Columnist: Daily Telegraph, 1996–98; Spectator, 1996–; Daily Mail, 1998–. Dir, Newspaper Publishing, 1986–92. Vis. Prof. of Journalism, St Andrews Univ., 1992. *Publications:* Paper Dreams, 1993; (ed) Secrets of the Press, 1999. *Address:* c/o The Spectator, 56 Doughty Street, WC1N 2LL. *Club:* Beefsteak.

GLOVER, Trevor David; consultant, book and music publishing consultancy; *b* 19 April 1940; *s* of Frederick Percy and Eileen Frances Glover; *m* 1967, Carol Mary Roberts; one *s* one *d*. *Educ:* Tiffin Sch., Kingston-upon-Thames; Univ. of Hull (BA Hons English Lang. and Lit.). Newspaper reporter, BC, Canada, 1963; began publishing career as college rep. with McGraw-Hill, Sydney, 1964; Coll. Sales Manager, 1966, later Gen. Manager, Professional and Reference Book Div., McGraw-Hill, UK; joined Penguin UK, 1970; UK Sales Manager, later UK Sales and Marketing Dir; Viking Penguin, NY, 1975–76; Man. Dir, 1976–87, Chm., 1987–95, Penguin Australia; UK Man. Dir, Penguin Gp, 1987–95; Man. Dir, Boosey & Hawkes Music Publishers Ltd, 1996–2001. Pres., Australian Book Publishers Assoc., 1983–85 and 1986–87; Pres., Publishers Assoc., 1997–98. *Recreation:* choral singing. *Club:* Groucho.

GLOVER, Hon. Sir Victor (Joseph Patrick), Kt 1989; GOSK 1992; legal consultant; Chief Justice, Mauritius, 1988–94; *b* 5 Nov. 1932; *s* of Joseph George Harold Glover and Mary Catherine (*née* Reddy); *m* 1960, Marie Cecile Ginette Gauthier; two *s*. *Educ:* Collège du St Esprit; Royal Coll., Mauritius; Jesus Coll., Oxford (BA (Hons) Jurisprudence). Called to the Bar, Middle Temple, 1957. District Magistrate, 1962; Crown Counsel, 1964; Sen. Crown Counsel, 1966; Prin. Crown Counsel, 1970; Parly Counsel, 1972; Puisne Judge, 1976; Sen. Puisne Judge, 1982. Actg Governor General, July 1988, May 1989, June 1990 and Feb. 1991; Actg Pres. of the Republic, 1992. Chm., Tertiary Educn Commn, 1988–97; Pres., ESU, 1993–. Hon. Prof. of Civil Law, Univ. of Mauritius, 1986. Hon. Bencher, Middle Temple, 1991. *Publications:* Abstract of Decisions of Supreme Court of Mauritius 1966–1981, 1982, Supplement 1982–1986, 1987; The Law of Seychelles through the Cases, 1999; The New Mauritius Digest, 2000. *Recreations:* reading, swimming, bridge. *Address:* 309 Chancery House, Port Louis, Mauritius. *Clubs:* Oxford Union Society; Oxford University Boat.

GLOVER, William James; QC 1969; a Recorder of the Crown Court, 1975–91; *b* 8 May 1924; *s* of late H. P. Glover, KC and Martha Glover; *m* 1956, Rosemary D. Long; two *s*. *Educ:* Harrow; Pembroke Coll., Cambridge. Served with Royal West African Frontier Force in West Africa and Burma, 1944–47. Called to Bar, Inner Temple, 1950, Bencher, 1977. Second Junior Counsel to Inland Revenue (Rating Valuation), 1963–69. *Recreations:* photography, golf. *Address:* Arrajadere, 32170 Mont de Marrast, Le Gers, France.

GLUBE, Hon. Constance Rachelle; Chief Justice, Court of Appeal, Nova Scotia, since 1998; *b* 23 Nov. 1931; *d* of Samuel Lepofsky, QC and Pearl Lepofsky (*née* Slonemsky); *m* 1952, Richard Glube (*d* 1997); three *s* one *d*. *Educ:* McGill Univ. (BA 1952); Dalhousie Univ. (LLB 1955). Called to the Canadian Bar, 1956. Barrister and Solicitor: Kitz Matheson, 1960–64; Fitzgerald & Glube, 1964–68; City of Halifax: Sen. Solicitor, 1969–74; City Manager, 1974–77; QC (Can.) 1974; Puisne Judge, 1977–82, Chief Justice, 1982–98, Supreme Court of NS. Hon. LLD: Dalhousie Law Sch., 1983; St Mary's, 2000; Hon. LHD Mt St Vincent Univ., 1998. Award of Merit, City of Halifax, 1977; Frances Fish Award (Women Lawyers), 1997. *Recreation:* gardening. *Address:* 5920 Inglewood Drive, Halifax, NS B3H 1B1, Canada. *T:* (902) 4246932.

GLUCKMAN, Prof. Peter David, CNZM 1997; DSc; FRACP; FRS 2001; FRSNZ; Director, Liggins Institute, University of Auckland, since 2001; *b* 8 Feb. 1949; *s* of Laurie Kalman Gluckman and Ann Jocelyn Gluckman (*née* Klippel); *m* 1970, Judith Lucy Nathan; one *s* one *d*. *Educ:* Univ. of Otago (MB ChB); Univ. of Auckland (MMedSci); Univ. of Calif, San Francisco (DSc). FRCPCH; FRSNZ 1988. Res. Fellow, Univ. of Auckland, 1973-76; Res. Fellow, 1976-78, Asst Prof., 1978-80, Dept of Paediatrics, Univ. of Calif, San Francisco; University of Auckland: Sen. Res. Fellow, 1980-88, Prof. and Chair, 1988-92, Dept of Paediatrics; Dean, Faculty of Med. and Health Scis, 1992-2001. *Publications:* contrib. numerous papers to scientific jls relating to fetal physiology, neurosci. and the endocrinology of growth. *Recreation:* travel. *Address:* Liggins Institute, University of Auckland, Private Bag 92019, Auckland, New Zealand. *T:* (9) 3737599. *Club:* Northern (Auckland).

GLUCKSMANN, Dame Margaret Myfanwy Wood; *see* Booth, Dame Margaret.

GLUE, George Thomas; Director-General of Supplies and Transport (Naval), Ministry of Defence, 1973–77; *b* 3 May 1917; *s* of Percy Albert Glue and Alice Harriet Glue (*née* Stoner); *m* 1947, Eileen Marion Hitchcock; one *d*. *Educ:* Portsmouth Southern Secondary School. Admiralty: Asst Naval Store Officer, 1937; Dep. Naval Store Officer, Mediterranean, 1940; Naval Store Officer, Mediterranean, 1943; Asst Dir of Stores, 1955; Suptg Naval Store Officer, Devonport, 1960; Dep. Dir of Stores, 1963; Dir of Stores, 1970; Dir, Supplies and Transport (Naval), 1971. *Recreation:* reading. *Address:* 18 Late Broads, Winsley, near Bradford-on-Avon, Wilts BA15 2NW. *T:* (01225) 722717.

GLYN, family name of **Baron Wolverton**.

GLYN, Sir Richard (Lindsay), 10th Bt *cr* 1759, and 6th Bt *cr* 1800; *b* 3 Aug. 1943; *s* of Sir Richard Hamilton Glyn, 9th and 5th Bt, OBE, TD, and Lyndsay Mary (*d* 1971), *d* of T. H. Baker; *S* father, 1980; *m* 1970, Carolyn Ann Williams (marr. diss. 1979); one *s* one *d*. *Educ:* Eton. Co-Founder, High Lea Sch., 1982; Founder: Gaunts House Centre, 1989; Richard Glyn Foundn, 1995. *Recreation:* tennis. *Heir: s* Richard Rufus Francis Glyn, *b* 8 Jan. 1971. *Address:* Ashton Farmhouse, Wimborne, Dorset BH21 4JD. *T:* (01258) 840585.

GLYNN, Prof. Alan Anthony, MD; FRCP, FRCPath; Director, Central Public Health Laboratory, Colindale, London, 1980–88, retired; Visiting Professor of Bacteriology, London School of Hygiene and Tropical Medicine, 1983–88; *b* 29 May 1923; *s* of late Hyman and Charlotte Glynn; *m* 1962, Nicole Benhamou; two *d*. *Educ:* City of London Sch.; University Coll. London (Fellow, 1982) and UCH Med. Sch., London (MB, BS 1946, MD 1959). MRCP 1954, FRCP 1974; MRCPath 1963, FRCPath 1973. House Physician, UCH, 1946; Asst Lectr in Physiol., Sheffield Univ., 1947–49; National Service, RAMC, 1950–51; Registrar, Canadian Red Cross Meml Hosp., Taplow, 1955–57; St Mary's Hospital Medical School: Lectr in Bacteriology, 1958–61; Sen. Lectr, 1961–67; Reader, 1967–71; Prof., 1971–80; Hon. Consultant Bacteriologist, 1961–83; Visiting Prof. of Bacteriology, St. Mary's Hosp., 1980–83. Examr in Pathol., Univs of Edinburgh, 1974–76, 1983–85, Glasgow, 1975–78, and London, 1979–80. Member: DHSS Jt Cttee on Vaccination and Immunization, 1979–85; Adv. Gp, ARC Inst. for Res. in Animal Diseases. Almroth Wright Lectr, Wright-Fleming Inst., 1972; Erasmus Wilson Demonstrator, RCS, 1973. Mem. Editorial Board: Immunology, 1969–79; Parasite Immunity, 1979–87. *Publications:* papers on bacterial infection and immunity and hospital acquired infections. *Recreations:* theatre, walking. *Club:* Athenæum.
See also Prof. I. M. Glynn.

GLYNN, Prof. Ian Michael, MD, PhD, FRS 1970; FRCP; Professor of Physiology, University of Cambridge, 1986–95, now Emeritus; Fellow, Trinity College, since 1955 (Vice-Master, 1980–86); *b* 3 June 1928; 2nd *s* of late Hyman and Charlotte Glynn; *m* 1958, Jenifer Muriel, 2nd *d* of Ellis and Muriel Franklin; one *s* two *d*. *Educ:* City of London Sch.; Trinity Coll., Cambridge; University Coll. Hosp. 1st cl. in Pts I and II of Nat. Sci. Tripos; BA (Cantab) 1949; MB, BChir, 1952; MD 1970; FRCP 1987. House Phys., Central Mddx Hosp., 1952–53; MRC Scholar at Physiol. Lab., Cambridge; PhD 1956. Nat. Service in RAF Med. Br., 1956–57. Cambridge University: Res. Fellow, 1955–59, Staff Fellow and Dir of Med. Studies, 1961–73, Trinity Coll.; Univ. Demonstrator in Physiology, 1958–63; Lecturer, 1963–70; Reader, 1970–75; Prof. Membrane Physiology, 1975–86. Vis. Prof., Yale Univ., 1969. Member: MRC, 1976–80 (Chm., Physiological Systems and Disorders Bd, 1976–78); Council, Royal Soc., 1979–81; 1991–92; AFRC (formerly ARC), 1981–86. Hon. Foreign Mem., Amer. Acad. of Arts and Scis, 1984. Hon. MD Aarhus, 1988. Chm., Editorial Bd, Jl of Physiology, 1968–70. *Publications:* (with J. C. Ellory) The Sodium Pump, 1985; An Anatomy of Thought: the origin and machinery of the mind, 1999; scientific papers dealing with transport of ions across living membranes, mostly in Jl of Physiology. *Address:* Trinity College, Cambridge CB2 1TQ. *T:* (01223) 338415; Daylesford, Conduit Head Road, Cambridge CB3 0EY. *T:* (01223) 353079.
See also Prof. A. A. Glynn.

GOAD, Sarah Jane Frances; JP; Lord-Lieutenant of Surrey, since 1997; *b* 23 Aug. 1940; *er d* of Uvedale Lambert and late Diana (*née* Grey) and step *d* of Melanie Grant Lambert, Denver, Colo; *m* 1961, Timothy Francis Goad, DL; two *s* one *d*. *Educ:* St Mary's, Wantage. Worked for Faber & Faber, 1959–70; Dir, Tilburstow Farms Co. Ltd, 1963–70; Partner, Lambert Farmers, 1970–94. JP Surrey, 1974; Dep. Chm., Family Panel, 1992–97; Mem., Surrey Magistrates' Soc., 1987–93. Trustee: St Mark's Foundn, 1971–; Love Walk (home for disabled), 1984–98 (Chm. Trustees, 1989–93); Surrey Care Trust, 1987–97 (Chm. Trustees, 1995–97); Chevening Estate, 2001. Chm., Southwark Cathedral Council, 2000–. Governor: local C of E sch., 1970–90; Hazelwood Sch., 1979–84. DStJ 1997. *Recreations:* books, buildings, arts. *Address:* South Park, Blechingley, Surrey RH1 4NE.

GOAVA, Sir Sinaka (Vakai), KBE 1998 (CBE 1984; MBE 1975); Government service, Papua New Guinea and Australia, 1946–84; a part-time consultant to the Motu-Koitabu on Land Group Incorporations, since 1997; *b* 5 July 1927; *s* of James Goava Oa and Mea Tapo Dai; *m* 1949, (Hekure) Naomi Vaieke; two *s* five *d* (and twin *s* decd). *Educ:* LMS Primary Sch., Hanuabada; Administrative Coll., Port Moresby (matric. 1967). Trainee clerk and broadcaster, 1946–48; radio announcer and translator, Depts of Educn, of Dist Services and Native Affairs, and of the Administrator, PNG, 1948–63; Sen. Interpreter, House of Assembly, 1964–65; Sen. Magistrate, Local, Dist and Children's Courts, 1967–75; Sec., Land Courts Secretariat, Dept of Justice, 1976–81; Chairman: Commn of Inquiry into Land Matters, PNG, 1973–74; Commn of Inquiry into suitable form of govt for NCD, 1981; NCD Interim Commn, 1982–83 (Mem., 1982–85); 10th Independence Anniv. Cttee, PNG, 1985. Consultant, Hanuabada Village project, NCD Interim Commn and Motu-Koitabu Interim Assembly, 1986. Mem., Hanuabada Local Govt Council, 1952–54; Vice Pres., Fairfax Local Govt Council, 1954–57. Mem. Bd of Trustees, Peace Foundn Melanesia (formerly Foundn for Law, Order and Justice), 1991–. Life Mem., Public Employees Assoc. (Hon. Chm., Life Mems Gp). Public Service and Community Service Medal, PNG, 1975; Long Service and Good Conduct Medal, PNG, 1983; PNG Independence Medal, 1975, PNG 10th Independence Anniv. Medal, 1985; Silver Jubilee Medal, 1977. *Publications:* A Cross Road to Justice, 2000; judicial and govt reports; contribs to PNG press. *Recreations:* cricket, fishing, singing, dancing, reading, writing, stamp collecting. *Address:* Peace Foundation Melanesia, PO Box 4205, Boroko, National Capital District, Papua New Guinea. *T:* 3253910; (home) PO Box 689, Port Moresby, NCD, Papua New Guinea.

GOBBO, Hon. Sir James (Augustine), AC 1993; Kt 1982; CVO 2000; Chairman, National Library of Australia, since 2001; Commissioner for Italy, Victoria, since 2001; *b* 22 March 1931; *s* of Antonio Gobbo and Regina Gobbo (*née* Tosetto); *m* 1957, Shirley Lewis; two *s* three *d*. *Educ:* Xavier Coll., Kew, Victoria; Melbourne Univ. (BA Hons); Magdalen Coll., Oxford Univ. (MA; Pres., OUBC, 1955; Mem., Boat Race Crew, 1954, 1955). Called to Bar, Gray's Inn, London, 1956; Barrister and Solicitor, Victoria, Aust., 1956; signed Roll of Counsel, Victorian Bar, 1957; QC 1971; Supreme Court Judge, Victoria, 1978–94; Lt Gov., 1995–97, Governor, 1997–2000, of Victoria. Indep. Lectr in Evidence, Univ. of Melbourne, 1963–68. Comr, Victorian Law Reform Commn, 1985–88. Chairman: Aust. Refugee Council, 1977; Aust. Multicultural Affairs Council, 1987–91; Aust. Bicentennial Multicultural Foundn, 1988–97, 2001–; Palladio Foundn, 1989–97; Aust. Banking Industry Ombudsman Council, 1994–97; Electricity Industry Ombudsman Council, 1995–97; Mercy Private Hosp., Melbourne, 1977–87 (Mem. Bd, Mercy Maternity Hosp., 1972–91); Caritas Christi Hospice, 1986–97; Order of Malta Hospice Home Care, 1986–97; Italian Historical Soc. of Vic, 1980–97; Member: Council, Order of Australia, 1982–92; Nat. Population Council, 1983–87; Victorian Health Promotion Foundn, 1989–97; Victorian Community Foundn, 1992–97; Newman Coll. Council, 1970–85; Pres., CO-AS-IT, 1979–84, 1986–94. Trustee: Victorian Opera Foundn, 1983–97; WWF, Australia, 1991–97. Vice-Pres., Aust. Assoc. of SMO Malta, 1984–87, Pres., 1987–97; Pres., Scout Assoc. of Victoria, 1987–97. Hon. LLD Monash, 1995; Hon. Dr Aust. Catholic Univ., 1996; Hon. Dr Jurisprudence Bologna, 1998. Commendatore, 1973, Grand Cross, 1998, Order of Merit, Republic of Italy; Kt Grand Cross SMO Malta, 1982. *Publications:* (ed) Cross on Evidence (Australian edn), 1970–1978; various papers. *Address:* 8/25 Douglas Street, Toorak, Vic 3142, Australia. *T:* (3) 98266115.

GOBBY, Clive John; Director, South Africa and Regional Director, Southern Africa, British Council, since 2000; *b* 2 June 1947; *m* 1978, Margaret Ann Edwards. *Educ:* Bective Secondary Mod. Sch., Northampton; Northampton GS; Leicester Univ. (BA 1968). Joined British Council, 1982; Dep. Manager, Enterprises, 1992–96; Network Manager, Grant in Aid Services, 1996; Dir, Turkey, 1997–2000. *Recreations:* walking, net surfing, dog training. *Address:* British Council, PO Box 30637, Braamfontein, Johannesburg 2017, South Africa. *T:* (11) 4033316, *Fax:* (11) 3397806.

GOBLE, John Frederick; retired solicitor; *b* 1 April 1925; *o s* of John and Evileen Goble; *m* 1953, Moira Murphy O'Connor; one *s* three *d*. *Educ:* Finchley Catholic GS; Highgate Sch.; Brasenose Coll., Oxford (MA). Sub-Lieut, RNVR, 1944–46. Admitted solicitor, 1951; Herbert Smith: Partner, 1953–88; Hong Kong office, 1982–83; Sen. Partner, 1983–88. Crown Agents, 1974–82 (Dep. Chm., 1975–82); Director: British Telecommunications, 1983–91; Wren Underwriting Agencies, 1988–91. A Dep. Chm., City Panel on Takeovers and Mergers, 1989–97. Chm., St Barnabas Soc., 1992–95. Governor, Highgate Sch., 1976–96. Chm., The Friends of Highgate Sch. Soc., 1978–87; Pres., Old Cholmeleian Soc., 1983–84. KCSG 1994. *Recreations:* music, golf, wine. *Address:* 52 Chelsea Park Gardens, SW3 6AD; 3 Warren Court, Warren Road, Thurlestone, Kingsbridge, Devon TQ7 3NT. *Clubs:* Garrick, MCC, Hurlingham; New Zealand Golf (West Byfleet); Thurlestone Golf; Royal Mid-Surrey Golf; Honourable Company of Edinburgh Golfers.

GODARD, Jean-Luc; French film director; *b* 3 Dec. 1930; *s* of Paul Godard and Odile Godard (*née* Monad); *m* 1st, 1961, Anna Karina (marr. diss.); 2nd, 1967, Anne Wiazemsky. *Educ:* Collège de Nyon; Lycée Buffon; Faculté de Lettres, Paris. Former journalist and film critic: La Gazette du cinéma; Les Cahiers du cinéma. Mem., Conseil supérieur de la langue française, 1989. *Films include:* A bout de souffle, 1959 (prix Jean Vigo, 1960; Best Dir Award, Berlin Fest., 1960); Le Petit Soldat, 1960; Une femme est une femme, 1961 (Special Prize, Berlin Fest.); Les sept péchés capitaux, 1961; Vivre sa vie, 1962 (Special Prize, Venice Fest.); Les Carabiniers, 1963; Les plus belles escroqueries du Monde, 1963; Le Mépris, 1963; Paris vu par …, 1964; Une femme mariée, 1964; Alphaville, 1965; Pierrot le fou, 1965; Masculin-Féminin, 1966; Made in USA, 1966; Deux ou trois choses que je sais d'elle, 1966; La Chinoise, 1967 (Special Prize, Venice Fest.); Week-end, 1967; Loin du Vietnam, 1967; La Contestation, 1970; Ici et ailleurs, 1976; (jtly) Tout va bien, 1972; Moi je, 1974; Comment ça va?, 1975; Sauve qui peut, 1980; Passion, 1982; Prénom Carmen, 1983 (Golden Lion, Venice Fest.); Je vous salue Marie, 1985; Détective, 1985; Soigne ta droite, 1987; Le Roi Lear, 1987; Nouvelle vague, 1990; Hélas pour moi, 1993; JLG/JLG, 1995; For Ever Mozart, 1996; Eloge de l'amour, 2001. Chevalier de l'ordre national du Mérite. *Publication:* Introduction à une véritable histoire du cinéma. *Address:* (office) 26 avenue Pierre 1er de Serbie, 75116 Paris, France; 15 rue du Nord, 1180 Rouille, Switzerland.

GODBER, Sir George (Edward), GCB 1971 (KCB 1962; CB 1958); Chief Medical Officer, Department of Health and Social Security, Department of Education and Science, and Home Office, 1960–73; *b* 4 Aug. 1908; *s* of late I. Godber, Willington Manor, Bedford; *m* 1935, Norma Hathorne Rainey (*d* 1999); two *s* one *d* (and two *s* two *d* decd). *Educ:* Bedford Sch.; New Coll., Oxford (Hon. Fellow, 1973); London Hospital; London Sch. of Hygiene. BA 1930, BM 1933, DM 1939, Oxon; MRCP 1935, FRCP 1947; DPH London 1936. Medical Officer, Min. of Health, 1939; Dep. Chief Medical Officer, Min. of Health, 1950–60. Chm., Health Educn Council, 1977–78 (Mem., 1976–78). QHP, 1953–56. Scholar in Residence, NIH Bethesda, 1975. Vice-Pres., RCN, 1973. Fellow: American Hospital Assoc., and American Public Health Assoc., 1961; British Orthopaedic

Assoc.; Mem. Dietetic Assoc., 1961; Hon. Member: Faculty of Radiologists, 1958; British Pædiatric Assoc.; Royal Pharmaceut. Soc., 1973. FRCOG *ad eundem*, 1966; FRCPsych 1973; FFCM 1974; Hon. FRCS, 1973; Hon. FRCGP, 1973; Hon. FRSocMed, 1973. Hon. LLD: Manchester, 1964; Hull, 1970; Nottingham, 1973; Hon. DCL: Newcastle 1972; Oxford 1973; Hon. DSc Bath, 1979. Hon. Fellow, London Sch. of Hygiene and Tropical Medicine, 1976. Bisset Hawkins Medal, RCP, 1965; 150th Anniversary Medal, Swedish Med. Soc., 1966; Leon Bernard Foundn Medal, 1972; Ciba Foundn Gold Medal, 1970; Therapeutics Gold Medal, Soc. of Apothecaries, 1973. Lectures: Thomas and Edith Dixon Belfast, 1962; Bartholomew, Rotunda, Dublin, 1963; Woolmer, Bio-Engineering Soc., 1964; Monkton Copeman, Soc. of Apothecaries, 1968; Michael M. Davis, Chicago, 1969; Harold Diehl, Amer. Public Health Assoc., 1969; Rhys Williams, 1969; W. M. Fletcher Shaw, RCOG, 1970; Henry Floyd, Inst. of Orthopaedics, 1970; First Elizabeth Casson Meml, Assoc. of Occ. Therapists, 1973; Cavendish, W London Med.-Chir. Soc., 1973; Heath Clark, London Univ., 1973; Rock Carling, Nuffield Provincial Hosps Trust, 1975; Thom Bequest, RCSE, 1975; Maurice Bloch, Glasgow, 1975; Ira Hiscock, Yale, 1975; John Sullivan, St Louis, 1975; Fordham, Sheffield, 1976; Lloyd Hughes, Liverpool, 1977; Gale Meml, SW England Faculty RCGP, 1978; Gordon, Birmingham, 1979; Samson Gamgee, Birm. Med. Inst., 1979; W. H. Duncan, Liverpool, 1984; W. Pickles, RCGP, 1985; Green Coll., Oxford, 1988. *Publications:* (with Sir L. Parsons and Clayton Fryers) Survey of Hospitals in the Sheffield Region, 1944; The Health Service: past, present and future (Heath Clark Lectures), 1974; Change in Medicine (Rock Carling monograph), 1975; British National Health Service: Conversations, 1977; papers in Lancet, BMJ, Public Health. *Recreation:* gardening. *Address:* 21 Almoners' Avenue, Cambridge CB1 8NZ. *T:* (01223) 247491.

GODBER, John Harry; playwright, since 1981; *b* 18 May 1956; *s* of Harry Godber and Dorothy (*née* Deakin); *m* 1993, Jane Thornton; two *d.* *Educ:* Leeds Univ. (CertEd, BEd Hons, MA, MPhil). Sch. teacher, 1979–83; writing for TV, 1981–; Artistic Dir, Hull Truck Theatre Co., 1984–. *Plays include:* Up 'N' Under, 1984 (filmed, 1997); Bouncers, 1986; Teechers, 1987; On the Piste, 1993; April in Paris, 1994; Passion Killers, 1994; Shakers: the musical, 1994; Lucky Sods, 1995; Weekend Breaks, 1997; Perfect Pitch, 1998; Unleashed, 1998; Thick as a Brick, 1999; On a Night Like This, 2001. Sunday Times Play-writing Award, 1981; Olivier Award for Comedy of Year, 1984. Hon. DLitt: Hull, 1988; Humberside, 1997. *Publications:* Up 'N' Under, 1985; Bouncers, 1986; John Godber: 5 plays, 1989; On the Piste, 1991; April in Paris, 1992; Blood Sweat and Tears, 1995; Lucky Sods, 1995; Passion Killers, 1995; Gym and Tonic, 1996. *Recreations:* keep fit, reading, theatre, cinema, opera. *Address:* 64 Riverview Avenue, North Ferriby HU14 3DT.

GODDARD, Ann Felicity; QC 1982; **Her Honour Judge Goddard;** a Circuit Judge, since 1993; *b* 22 Jan. 1936; *o c* of late Graham Elliott Goddard and Margaret Louise Hambrook Goddard (*née* Clark). *Educ:* Grey Coat Hosp., Westminster; Birmingham Univ. (LLB); Newnham Coll., Cambridge (LLM and Dip. in Comparative Legal Studies). Called to the Bar, Gray's Inn, 1960; Bencher, 1990; a Recorder, 1979–93. Member: Gen. Council of the Bar, 1988–93; Criminal Justice Consultative Council, 1992–93. Pres., British Acad. of Forensic Scis, 1995–96. Freeman, 1994, Liveryman, 1996–, Clockmakers' Co. *Recreation:* travel. *Address:* Central Criminal Court, EC4M 7EH. *T:* (020) 7248 3277.

GODDARD, David Rodney, MBE 1985; Director, International Sailing Craft Association, 1966–96; *b* 16 March 1927; *s* of Air Marshal Sir Victor Goddard, KCB, CBE, and Mildred Catherine Jane, *d* of Alfred Markham Inglis; *m* 1952, Susan Ashton; three *s* one *d.* *Educ:* Bryanston School; Wanganui Collegiate Sch., New Zealand; Peterhouse, Cambridge. MA Hons Geography. Joined Royal Marines, 1944, hostilities only commn, 1946, demob. 1948. Whaling, United Whalers, 1949; Schoolmaster, 1950–52. Joined Somerset Light Infantry, 1952; active service, Malaya (mentioned in despatches, 1954); served: Germany, Kenya (King's African Rifles), Bahrein, N Ireland; retired at own request, as Major, 1968, to found and direct Internat. Sailing Craft Assoc. and Exeter Maritime Museum; Dir, Exeter Maritime Mus., 1968–88, 1991–96. *Recreations:* shooting, fishing, sailing, bird watching, photography. *Address:* The Mill, Lympstone, Exmouth, Devon EX8 5HH. *T:* (01395) 265575.

GODDARD, Harold Keith; QC 1979; barrister-at-law; a Recorder of the Crown Court, since 1978; a Deputy High Court Judge, since 1993; *b* 9 July 1936; *s* of late Harold Goddard and Edith Goddard, Stockport, Cheshire; *m* 1st, 1963, Susan Elizabeth (marr. diss.), *yr d* of late Ronald Stansfield and of Evelyn Stansfield, Wilmslow, Cheshire; two *s*; 2nd, 1983, Alicja Maria, *d* of late Czeslaw Lazuchiewicz and of Eleonora Lazuchiewicz, Lodz, Poland. *Educ:* Manchester Grammar Sch.; Corpus Christi Coll., Cambridge (Scholar; 1st Cl. Law Tripos 1957; MA, LLM). Bacon Scholar, Gray's Inn; called to the Bar, Gray's Inn, 1959. Practised on Northern Circuit, 1959–; Head of Chambers, 1983–. Mem., CICB, 1993–. Chm., Disciplinary Appeals Cttee, 1974–80, Mem. Council, 1980–, Mem. Ct of Governors, 1981, UMIST. *Recreation:* golf. *Address:* Deans Court Chambers, 24 St John Street, Manchester M3 4DF. *T:* (0161) 214 6000. *Club:* Wilmslow Golf.

GODDARD, Prof. John Burgess, OBE 1986; Henry Daysh Professor of Regional Development Studies, University of Newcastle upon Tyne, since 1975; *b* 5 Aug. 1943; *s* of Burgess Goddard and Molly Goddard (*née* Bridge); *m* 1966, Janet Patricia (*née* Peddle); one *s* two *d.* *Educ:* Latymer Upper Sch.; University Coll. London (BA); LSE (PhD). Lectr, LSE, 1968–75; Leverhulme Fellow, Univ. of Lund, 1974; University of Newcastle: Hon. Dir, Centre for Urban and Regional Develt Studies, 1978–; Dean, Faculty of Law, Envmt and Social Scis, 1994–98; Pro Vice-Chancellor, 1998–. Dir, ESRC Prog. on Inf. and Communications Technol., 1992–93. Advr, Trade and Industry Select Cttee, H of C, 1994–95. Chairman: Assoc. of Dirs of Res. Centres in Social Sciences, 1991–98; Assoc. of Res. Centres in the Social Scis, 1998–99. Member: Northern Economic Planning Council, 1976–79; Human Geography Cttee, SSRC, 1976–80; Bd, Port of Tyne Authority, 1990–93. Governor, University of Northumbria at Newcastle (formerly Newcastle upon Tyne Poly.), 1989–98. Editor, Regional Studies, 1980–85. FRSA 1992. Victoria Medal, RGS, 1992. *Publications:* Office Linkages and Location, 1973; Office Location in Urban and Regional Development, 1975; The Urban and Regional Transformation of Britain, 1983; Technological Change, Industrial Restructuring and Regional Development, 1986; Urban Regeneration in a Changing Economy, 1992; articles in professional jls.

GODDARD, Rt Rev. John William; *see* Burnley, Bishop Suffragan of.

GODDARD, Prof. Peter, ScD; FRS 1989; Professor of Theoretical Physics, University of Cambridge, since 1992; Master, St John's College, Cambridge, since 1994; *b* 3 Sept. 1945; *s* of Herbert Charles Goddard and Rosina Sarah Goddard (*née* Waite); *m* 1968, Helen Barbara Ross; one *s* one *d.* *Educ:* Emanuel Sch., London; Trinity Coll., Cambridge (BA 1966; MA, PhD 1971); ScD Cantab 1996. Res. Fellow, Trinity Coll., Cambridge, 1969–73; Vis. Scientist, CERN, Geneva, 1970–72, 1978; Lectr in Applied Maths, Univ. of Durham, 1972–74; Mem., Inst. for Advanced Study, Princeton, NJ, 1974, 1988; Cambridge University: Asst Lectr 1975–76; Lectr 1976–89; Reader in Mathematical Physics, 1989–92; Dep. Dir, Isaac Newton Inst. for Mathematical Scis, 1991–94 (Sen. Fellow, 1994–); Mem., Univ. Council, 2000–; St John's College: Fellow, 1975–94; Lectr in Maths 1975–91; Tutor 1980–87; Sen. Tutor 1983–87. Vis. Prof. of Maths and Physics, Univ. of Virginia, 1983; SERC Vis. Fellow, Imperial Coll., 1987. Mem., Inst. for Theoretical Physics, Univ. of California, Santa Barbara, 1986, 1990. Chm., Univ. of Cambridge Local Exams Syndicate, 1998–. Governor: Berkhamsted Schs, 1985–96; Emanuel Sch., 1992–; Shrewsbury Sch., 1994–; Hills Road Sixth Form Coll., Cambridge, 1999– (Chm., 2001–). Hon. Fellow, TCD, 1995. Dirac Medal and Prize, Internat. Centre for Theoretical Physics, Trieste, 1997. *Publications:* articles on elementary particle physics and mathematical physics in sci. jls. *Address:* The Master's Lodge, St John's College, Cambridge CB2 1TP. *T:* (01223) 338635.

GODDARD, Air Vice-Marshal Peter John, CB 1998; AFC 1981; FRAeS; Senior Directing Staff (Air), Royal College of Defence Studies, 1996–98; *b* 17 Oct. 1943; *s* of John Bernard Goddard and Lily Goddard; *m* 1966, Valerie White; two *s.* *Educ:* Nottingham High Sch. qwi, ndc, aws, rcds. FRAeS 1997. Joined RAF 1963; served 54 and 4 Hunter Sqns, 233 Harrier and 226 Jaguar OCUs; OC, 54 Jaguar Sqn, 1978–80; MoD, 1981–83; OC, Tri-nat. Tornado Trng Estabt, RAF Cottesmore, 1984–86; RCDS 1988; Dir, Air Armament, 1989–93; Dep. Comdr, Interim Combined Air Ops Centre 4, 1993–96. Chm., Seckford Foundn, 2000–. *Recreations:* golf, gardening, walking. *Clubs:* Royal Air Force; Felixstowe Ferry Golf.

GODDARD, Roy; independent business consultant, since 1988; Member, Independent Television Commission, 1991–97; *b* 21 Feb. 1939; *s* of Roy Benjamin Goddard and Emma Annie Coronation (*née* Beckett); *m* 1961, Sally Anne Pain; one *s* one *d.* *Educ:* Henry Thornton Grammar Sch.; Regent Street Polytechnic. Cummins Engine Co., 1964–68; Partner, Alexander Hughes & Associates, executive search consultants, 1968–70; Founder, Goddard Kay Rogers & Associates, 1970–88. Chm., Network Gp of Cos, 1992–98; Mem. Adv. Bd, Private Equity Div., Mercury Asset Mgt, 1997–2000; Dir, Mercury Private Equity, 2001–. Member: IBA, 1990–91; GMC, 1994–99. Home Office selection panel appointee, Sussex Police Authy, 1994–2000; Ind. Assessor, Legal Aid Bd, 1996–98. Hon. Vice Pres., Dyslexia Inst., 1997– (Chm., 1990–96). Freeman, City of London, 1981; Liveryman, Co. of Glaziers and Painters of Glass, 1981–. *Recreations:* squash, water gardening, reading, eating, cinema, theatre. *Address:* Newells, Brighton Road, Lower Beeding, West Sussex RH13 6NQ. *T:* (01403) 891110. *Club:* Royal Automobile.

GODDEN, Charles Henry, CBE 1982; HM Diplomatic Service, retired; Governor (formerly HM Commissioner), Anguilla, 1978–83; *b* 19 Nov. 1922; *s* of late Charles Edward Godden and Catherine Alice Godden (*née* Roe); *m* 1943, Florence Louise Williams; two *d.* *Educ:* Tweeddale Sch., Carshalton; Morley Coll., Westminster. Served Army, 1941–46. Colonial Office, 1950–66 (seconded British Honduras, 1961–64: Perm. Sec., External Affairs; Dep. Chief Sec.; Clerk of Executive Council); FCO, 1966–: First Sec., 1968; Asst Private Sec. to Sec. of State for Colonies; Private Secretary: to Minister of State, FCO, 1967–70; to Parly Under Sec. of State, 1970; First Sec. (Commercial), Helsinki, 1971–75; First Sec., Belize, 1975–76; Dep. High Comr and Head of Chancery, Kingston, 1976–78. *Recreations:* cricket, walking, reading. *Address:* Stoneleigh, Blackboys, Sussex TN22 5JL. *T:* (01825) 890410. *Clubs:* MCC, Royal Commonwealth Society.

GODDEN, Prof. Malcolm Reginald, PhD; Rawlinson and Bosworth Professor of Anglo-Saxon, and Fellow of Pembroke College, Oxford, since 1991; *b* 9 Oct. 1945. *Educ:* Devizes Grammar Sch.; Barton Peveril Sch., Eastleigh; Pembroke Coll., Cambridge (BA 1966; MA, PhD 1970). Res. Fellow, Pembroke Coll., Cambridge, 1969–72; Asst Prof., Cornell Univ., 1970–71; Lectr in English, Liverpool Univ., 1972–75; Univ. Lectr in English, and Fellow, Exeter Coll., Oxford, 1976–91. Editor, Anglo-Saxon England, 1989–. *Publications:* (ed) Ælfric's Catholic Homilies, second series, 1979; The Making of Piers Plowman, 1990; (ed jtly) The Cambridge Companion to Old English Literature, 1991; (ed jtly) Anglo-Saxon England, 2000; contribs to Anglia, English Studies, Anglo-Saxon England, Rev. of English Studies. *Address:* Pembroke College, Oxford OX1 1DW. *T:* (01865) 276444.

GODDEN, Tony Richard Hillier, CB 1975; Secretary, Scottish Development Department, 1980–87, retired; *b* 13 Nov. 1927; *o s* of late Richard Godden and Gladys Eleanor Godden; *m* 1953, Marjorie Florence Snell; one *s* two *d.* *Educ:* Barnstaple Grammar Sch.; London Sch. of Economics (BSc (Econ.) 1st cl.). Commissioned, RAF Education Branch, 1950. Entered Colonial Office as Asst Principal, 1951; Private Sec. to Parly Under-Sec. of State, 1954–55; Principal, 1956; Cabinet Office, 1957–59; transferred to Scottish Home Dept, 1961; Asst Sec., Scottish Development Dept, 1964; Under-Sec., 1969; Sec., Scottish Economic Planning Dept, 1973–80. Member: Council on Tribunals, 1988–94; Ancient Monuments Board for Scotland, 1990–95. Sec., Friends of Royal Scottish Acad., 1987–2000. *Address:* 9 Ross Road, Edinburgh EH16 5QN. *T:* (0131) 667 6556. *Club:* New (Edinburgh).

GODFRAY, Prof. (Hugh) Charles (Jonathan), PhD; FRS 2001; Professor of Evolutionary Biology, since 1995, Director, NERC Centre for Population Biology, since 1999, Imperial College, London University; *b* 27 Oct. 1958; *s* of Hugh and Annette Godfray; *m* 1992, Caroline Essil Margaret Elmslie. *Educ:* Millfield Sch., Som; St Peter's Coll., Oxford (MA; Hon. Fellow, 2001); Imperial Coll., London (PhD 1983). NERC Postdoctoral Fellow, Dept of Biol., Imperial Coll., London Univ., 1982–85; Demonstrator in Ecol., Dept of Zool., Univ. of Oxford, 1985–87; Lectr, 1987–92, Reader, 1992–95, Dept of Biol Scis, Imperial Coll., London Univ., Scientific Medal, Zool. Soc., 1994. *Publications:* Parasitoids, 1994; scientific papers in ecology and evolution. *Recreations:* natural history, gardening, opera, walking. *Address:* NERC Centre for Population Biology, Imperial College at Silwood Park, Ascot, Berks SL5 7PY. *T:* (020) 7594 2354.

GODFREY, Daniel Charles; Director General, Association of Investment Trust Companies, since 1998; Chairman, Personal Finance Education Group, since 2000; *b* 30 June 1961; *s* of Gerald Michael Godfrey, *qv*; *m* 1994, Frederiki Androulla Perewiznyk; three *s* one *d.* *Educ:* Victoria Univ. of Manchester (BA Hons Econs). Life Inspr, UK Provident, 1982–85; Mktg Manager, Schroders, 1985–88; Project Manager, Mercury Asset Mgt, 1988–90; Mktg Manager, Laurentian Life, 1990–91; Proprietor, The Sharper Image, 1991–94; Mktg Dir, Flemings, 1994–98. Mem., ICA, 1987–. *Recreations:* football (watching), children (raising). *Address:* Durrant House, 8–13 Chiswell Street, EC1Y 4YY. *T:* (020) 7282 5555.

GODFREY, Gerald Michael, CBE 2001; a Justice of Appeal, 1993–2000, and Vice-President, 2000, Court of Appeal of the High Court (formerly Supreme Court) of Hong Kong; *b* 30 July 1933; *s* of late Sidney Godfrey and late Esther (*née* Lewin); *m* 1960, Anne Sheila, *er d* of late David Goldstein; three *s* two *d.* *Educ:* Lower Sch. of John Lyon, Harrow; King's Coll., London Univ. LLB 1952, LLM 1954. FCIArb 1990. Called to the Bar: Lincoln's Inn, 1954 (Bencher 1978); Bahamas, 1972; Hong Kong, 1974; Kenya, 1978; Singapore, 1978; Malaysia, 1979; Brunei, 1979; National Service as 2nd Lt, RASC, 1955; Temp. Captain, 1956. In practice at the Chancery Bar, 1957–86; QC 1971; a Judge of the High Court, Hong Kong, 1986–93. Chm., Justice Cttee on Parental Rights and Duties and Custody Suits (Report, 1975); DoT Inspector into Affairs of Saint Piran Ltd (Report,

1981). Member: Senate of Inns of Court and the Bar, 1974–77, 1981–84 (Chm., Law Reform Cttee, 1981–83); Council of Justice, 1976–81. *Publication:* Editor, Business Law Review, 1958. *Recreations:* walking, travel. *Address:* The Garden Flat, 76 Hamilton Terrace, NW8 9UL.

See also D. C. Godfrey.

GODFREY, Rt Rev. (Harold) William; *see* Peru, Bishop of.

GODFREY, Howard Anthony; QC 1991; a Recorder, since 1992; *b* 17 Aug. 1946; *s* of late Emanuel and of Amy Godfrey; *m* 1972, Barbara Ellinger; two *s*. *Educ:* William Ellis Sch.; LSE (LLB). Asst Lectr in Law, Univ. of Canterbury, NZ, 1969. Called to the Bar, Middle Temple, 1970, *ad eundem* Inner Temple, 1984; part-time Tutor, Law Dept, LSE, 1970–72; practising on SE Circuit, 1972–; called to the Bar, Turks and Caicos Is, 1996. Fellow, Soc. for Advanced Legal Studies, 1998. *Recreations:* wine and food, travel, humour. *Address:* 2 Bedford Row, WC1R 4BU. *T:* (020) 7440 8888, *Fax:* (020) 7242 1738.

GODFREY, Louise Sarah, (Mrs Stanley Bland); QC 1991; a Recorder of the Crown Court, since 1989; *b* 17 April 1950; *d* of Philip Godfrey and Pearl (*née* Goodman); *m* 1977, Stanley Leslie Bland; two *d*. *Educ:* Tadcaster Grammar Sch.; St Hugh's Coll., Oxford (MA Jurisprudence). Called to the Bar, Middle Temple, 1972, Bencher 1998. Part-time Chm., Police Disciplinary Tribunal, 1997–; Member: Mental Health Review Tribunal, 2000–; Criminal Injuries Compensation Appeals Panel, 2000–. *Recreations:* cooking, walking. *Address:* Park Court Chambers, 16 Park Place, Leeds LS1 2SJ. *T:* (0113) 243 3277.

GODFREY, Dr Malcolm Paul Weston, CBE 1986; Chairman, Public Health Laboratory Service Board, 1989–96; *b* 11 Aug. 1926; *s* of late Harry Godfrey and Rose Godfrey; *m* 1955, Barbara Goldstein; one *s* one *d* (and one *d* decd). *Educ:* Hertford Grammar Sch.; King's Coll., London Univ. (FKC 2000); KCH Med. Sch. (MB, BS (Hons and Univ. Medal) 1950); MRCP 1955, FRCP 1972. Hosp. posts at KCH, Nat. Heart and Brompton Hosps; RAF Med. Br., 1952–54; Fellow in Med. and Asst Physician, Johns Hopkins Hosp., USA, 1957–58; MRC Headquarters Staff, 1960–74: MO, 1960; Sen. MO, 1964; Principal MO, 1970; Sen. Principal MO, 1974; Dean, Royal Postgrad. Med. Sch., 1974–83 (Mem. Council, 1974–83, 1988–96; Chm., Audit Cttee, 1995–96; Hon. Fellow, 1985); Second Sec., MRC, 1983–88. University of London: Member: Senate, 1980–83; Court, 1981–83; Chm., Jt Med. Adv. Cttee, 1979–82. Mem., Faculty Bd of Clinical Medicine, Univ. of Cambridge, 1988–89. Chm., Brit. Council Med. Adv. Cttee, 1985–90; Member: Sci. Adv. Panel CIBA Foundn, 1974–91; Ealing, Hammersmith and Hounslow AHA(T), 1975–80; NW Thames RHA, 1980–83, 1985–88; Hammersmith SHA, 1982–83; Sec. of State's Adv. Gp on London Health Services, 1980–81; GMC, 1979–81. Lay Mem., Professional Standards Dept, Gen. Council of the Bar, 1990–95. Consultant Advr, WHO Human Reproduction Programme, 1979–90; Scientific Advr, Foulkes Foundn, 1983–89. Member, Council: Charing Cross Hosp. Med. Sch., 1975–80; St Mary's Hosp. Med. Sch., 1983–88; Royal Free Hosp. Sch. of Medicine, 1991–96; KCL, 1997–; Mem., Governing Body, BPMF, 1974–89; Chm., Council of Governors, UMDS of Guy's and St Thomas' Hosps, 1996–98 (Mem., 1990–96; Trustee, UMDS, 1998–); Mem., Special Trustees, Hammersmith Hosp., 1975–83. Vice-Pres., KCL Assoc., 2000–. Trustee, Florence Nightingale Fund, 1996–. Mem., Soc. of Scholars, Johns Hopkins Univ., USA, 2000. Gov., Quintin Kynaston Sch., 2000–. Liveryman, Goldsmiths' Co., 1984– (Mem., Charity Cttee, 1998–); Mem. Court of Assts, Soc. of Apothecaries, 1979–94 (Master, 1989–90; Assistant Emeritus, 1995–). JP Wimbledon, 1972–92 (Chm. of the Bench and of Merton Magistrates' Courts Cttee, 1988–90 (Dep. Chm., 1987); Chm., Juvenile Panel, 1983–87). QHP, 1987–90. FRSA, 1989–92. Hon. Fellow, ICSM, 1999. *Publications:* contrib. med. jls on cardiac and respiratory disorders. *Recreations:* theatre, planning holidays (sometimes taking them), walking. *Address:* 17 Clifton Hill, St John's Wood, NW8 0QE. *T:* (020) 7624 6335.

GODFREY, Norman Eric; *b* 16 Aug. 1927; *s* of Cecil and Beatrice Godfrey. *Educ:* Northampton Grammar Sch.; London Sch. of Econs (BScEcon). Career mainly in HM Customs but also served in Min. of Transport/DoE, 1968–71, and Price Commn, 1976–79; Comr, HM Customs and Excise, 1979–86. *Recreations:* music, especially opera, composing, theatre, travel, walking. *Address:* 2 Belsize Avenue, NW3 4AU. *T:* (020) 7435 6085; *e-mail:* normanegodfrey@hotmail.com.

GODFREY, Peter, FCA; Senior Partner, Ernst & Whinney, Chartered Accountants, 1980–86, retired; Chairman, Accounting Standards Committee, 1984–Sept. 1986 (Member, 1983–86); *b* 23 March 1924; *m* 1951, Heather Taplin; two *s* one *d*. *Educ:* West Kensington Central Sch. Served Army, 1942, until released, rank Captain, 1947. Qual. as an Incorporated Accountant, 1949; joined Whinney Smith & Whinney, 1949; admitted to partnership, 1959; Chm., Ernst & Whinney Internat., 1981–83, 1985–86. Appointed: BoT Inspector into Affairs of Pinnock Finance Co. (GB) Ltd, Aug. 1967; DTI Inspector into Affairs of Rolls-Royce Ltd, April 1971; Mem., ODM Cttee of Inquiry on Crown Agents, April 1975. Institute of Chartered Accountants: Mem., Inflation Accounting Sub-Cttee, 1982–84; Mem., Council, 1984–86. *Recreation:* family. *Address:* 2N Maple Lodge, Lythe Hill Park, Haslemere, Surrey GU27 3TE. *T:* (01428) 656729.

GODFREY, Sarah; *see* Radclyffe, S.

GODFREY, Rt Rev. William; *see* Godfrey, Rt Rev. H. W.

GODLEY, family name of **Baron Kilbracken**.

GODLEY, Prof. Hon. Wynne Alexander Hugh; Professor of Applied Economics, University of Cambridge, 1980–93 (Director, 1970–85, Acting Director, 1985–87, Department of Applied Economics); Fellow of King's College, Cambridge, 1970–98; *b* 2 Sept. 1926; *yr s* of Hugh John, 2nd Baron Kilbracken, CB, KC and Elizabeth Helen Monteith, *d* of Vereker Monteith Hamilton; *m* 1955, Kathleen Eleonora, *d* of Sir Jacob Epstein, KBE; one *d*. *Educ:* Rugby; New Coll., Oxford; Conservatoire de Musique, Paris. Professional oboist, 1950. Joined Economic Section, HM Treasury, 1956; Dep. Dir, Economic Sect., HM Treasury, 1967–70. Dir, Investing in Success Equities Ltd, 1970–85. Official Advr, Select Cttee on Public Expenditure, 1971–73; an Economic Consultant, HM Treasury, 1975; Mem., Panel of Indep. Forecasters, 1992–95. Visiting Professor: Aalborg Univ., 1987–88; Roskilde Univ., 1995; Distinguished Scholar, Jerome Levy Econs Inst., Annandale-on-Hudson, NY, 1991–92, 1993–95, 1996–. Director: Royal Opera House, Covent Garden, 1976–87; Kent Opera, 1993–. *Publications:* (with T. F. Cripps) Local Government Finance and its Reform, 1976; The Planning of Telecommunications in the United Kingdom, 1978; (with K. J. Coutts and W. D. Nordhaus) Pricing in the Trade Cycle, 1978; (with T. F. Cripps) Macroeconomics, 1983; articles, in National Institute Review, Economic Jl, London and Cambridge Economic Bulletin, Cambridge Economic Policy Review, Economica, Jl of Policy Modelling, Manchester School, Nationalokonomisk Tidsskrift, Political Qly, New Statesman and Society, Observer, Guardian, London Review of Books, Financial Times, Challenge, Cambridge Jl of Econs, Jl of Post Keynesian Econs. *Address:* Jasmine House, The Green, Cavendish, Suffolk CO10 8BB. *T:* (01787) 281166.

GODMAN, Norman Anthony, PhD; *b* 19 April 1938; *m* 1981, Patricia (*née* Leonard) (*see* Patricia Godman). *Educ:* Westbourne Street Boys' Sch., Hessle Road, Hull; Hull Univ. (BA); Heriot-Watt Univ. (PhD 1982). Nat. Service, Royal Mil. Police, 1958–60. Shipwright to trade teacher in Scottish further and higher educn; Contested (Lab) Aberdeen South, 1979. MP (Lab) Greenock and Port Glasgow, 1983–97, Greenock and Inverclyde, 1997–2001.

GODMAN, Patricia, (Trish); Member (Lab) West Renfrewshire, Scottish Parliament, since 1999; *d* of Martin Leonard and Cathie Craig; *m* 1981, Norman Anthony Godman, *qv*; three *s* from previous marriage. *Educ:* St Gerard's Secondary Sch.; Jordanhill Coll. (CQSW 1976). Social worker, Strathclyde Reg. Member (Lab): Strathclyde Regl Council, 1994–96; Glasgow City Council, 1996–99. *Recreations:* gardening, theatre, music, cinema, reading. *Address:* Scottish Parliament, The Mound, Edinburgh EH99 1SP. *T:* (0131) 348 5837.

GODSELL, Stanley Harry; Regional Director (South West), Departments of Environment and Transport, 1978–80; retired; *b* 19 March 1920; *s* of Thomas Harry Godsell and Gladys Godsell; *m* 1946, Rosemary Blackburn (*d* 1990); one *s* (and one *s* decd). *Educ:* Alsop High Sch., Liverpool. Civil Service: PO, 1937–48; Min. of Town and Country Planning, 1948; Asst Sec., Min. of Housing and Local Govt, 1965. *Recreations:* bridge, swimming, croquet, photography. *Address:* 6 Pitch and Pay Park, Sneyd Park, Bristol BS9 1NJ. *T:* (0117) 968 3791.

GODSIFF, Roger Duncan; MP (Lab) Birmingham Sparkbrook and Small Heath, since 1997 (Birmingham, Small Heath, 1992–97); *b* 28 June 1946; *s* of late George and of Gladys Godsiff; *m* 1977, Julia Brenda Morris; one *s* one *d*. *Educ:* Catford Comprehensive Sch. Bank clerk, 1965–70; political officer, APEX, 1970–90; senior research officer, GMB, 1990–92. Mem. (Lab) Lewisham BC, 1971–90 (Mayor, 1977). Contested (Lab) Birmingham, Yardley, 1983. *Recreations:* sport – particularly football and cricket, listening to music, spending time with family. *Address:* House of Commons, SW1A 0AA. *Clubs:* Rowley Regis Labour; Charlton Athletic Supporters.

GODSMARK, Nigel Graham; QC 2001; a Recorder, since 2000; *b* 8 Dec. 1954; *s* of Derek and Betty Godsmark; *m* 1982, Priscilla Howitt; one *s* two *d*. *Educ:* Queen Mary's Grammar Sch., Basingstoke; Univ. of Nottingham (LLB 1978). Called to the Bar, Gray's Inn, 1979; Asst Recorder, 1998–2000. *Recreations:* sport (Rugby, cricket), wine, family. *Address:* 7 Bedford Row, WC1R 4BU. *T:* (020) 7242 3555.

GODWIN, Fay S.; photographer; *b* 17 Feb. 1931; *d* of Sidney Simmonds and Stella MacLean; *m* 1961, Anthony Godwin; two *s*. Writer, lecturer, and tutor of photographic workshops. *Solo exhibitions* include: Land, Serpentine Gall., and UK tour, 1985–87, Yale Center for British Art, USA, and Stanford Mus. of Art, USA; British Council internat. tour, 1984–94; Photographers' Gall., London, 1985; Nat. Mus. of Photography, Bradford, 1986, 1988; Royal Photographic Soc., Bath, 1990; Glassworks & Secret Lives, Mead Gall., Warwick Arts Centre and tour, 1995–97; A Perfect Republic of Shepherds, Wordsworth Trust, 1997; retrospective, Barbican, 2001; *work in public and private collections* including: Nat. Mus. of Photography, Bradford; British Council; Nat. Portrait Gall.; British Library; Nat. Portrait Gall., Scotland; V&A Mus.; Stanford Mus. of Art, USA. Joined: Photographers' Gall. (Print Room), 1976; Zelda Cheatle Gall., 1989; Network Photographers, 1991; Collections, 1994; Focus Gall., 2001. Pres., Ramblers' Assoc., 1987–90 (Life Vice Pres., 1990). Fellow, Nat. Mus. of Film, Photography and TV, Bradford, 1986–87. Hon. FRPS 1990. Hon. FRIAS 1992. Arts Council of GB Award, 1978; Award, Erna & Victor Hasselbad Foundn, 1995. *Publications:* (jtly) The Oldest Road, 1975; (jtly) The Oil Rush, 1976; (jtly) The Drovers' Roads of Wales, 1977; (jtly) Islands, 1978; (jtly) Remains of Elmet, 1979; (jtly) Romney Marsh and the Royal Military Canal, 1980; (jtly) Tess: the story of a guide dog, 1981; (jtly) The Whisky Roads of Scotland, 1982; Bison at Chalk Farm, 1982; (jtly) The Saxon Shore Way from Gravesend to Rye, 1983; (jtly) National Trust Book of Wessex, 1985; Land, 1985; The Secret Forest of Dean, 1986; Our forbidden land (Green Book of the Year), 1990; Elmet, 1994; The Edge of the Land, 1995; Glassworks & Secret Lives, 1999; Landmarks, 2001. *Recreations:* walking, reading, painting, looking at art and modern architecture. *Address:* c/o Photographers' Gallery, 5/8 Great Newport Street, WC2H 7HY.

GODWIN, William Henry; *b* 29 Nov. 1923; *s* of George Godwin and Dorothy (*née* Purdon); *m* Lela Milosevic; one *s* one *d*. *Educ:* Colet Court; Lycée Français de Londres; St John's Coll., Cambridge. Called to the Bar, Middle Temple, 1948. Treasury Solicitor's Office, 1948–90; Under Sec., 1977; UK Agent before Europ. Ct of Justice, 1973–85; Legal Advr to Cabinet Office, European Secretariat, 1982–85. Consultant, 1990–98.

GODWIN-AUSTEN, Dr Richard Bertram; FRCP; Consultant Neurologist, Nottingham, Derby and South Lincolnshire Hospitals, 1970-97, Consultant Emeritus, since 1997; Secretary Treasurer-General, World Federation of Neurology, since 1999; *b* 4 Oct. 1935; *s* of late Annesley Godwin-Austen, CBE and Beryl Godwin-Austen; *m* 1st, 1961, Jennifer Jane (*d* 1996), *d* of Louis Himely; one *s*; 2nd, 1997, Deidre, (Sally), *d* of FO Gerald Stark Toller. *Educ:* Charterhouse; St Thomas' Hosp., London (MB BS; MD 1968). FRCP 1976. Nat. Hosp. for Neurol., Queen Sq., 1964-70; clinical teacher in neurol., Faculty of Medicine, Univ. of Nottingham, 1970-97; Clinical Dir for Neuroservices, University Hosp., Nottingham, 1990-93. Chm., Sheffield Regl Adv. Cttee on Neurol. and Neurosurgery, 1990-93. Mem., Med. Adv. Panel, Parkinson's Disease Soc., 1970-97. Pres., Assoc. of British Neurologists, 1997-99; Vice-Pres., Eur. Fedn of Neurol Socs, 1996-2001; Mem., Eur. Bd of Neurol., 1996-2001. High Sheriff, Notts, 1994-95. *Publications:* The Neurology of the Elderly, 1990; The Parkinson's Disease Handbook, 1987, 2nd edn 1997; numerous contribs to peer-reviewed med. jls. *Recreations:* water-colour painting, sweet wines, Mexico. *Address:* Papplewick Hall, Papplewick, Nottingham NG15 8FE. *T:* (0115) 963 3491. *Clubs:* Garrick, Royal Society of Medicine.

GOEDERT, Michel, MD, PhD; FRS 2000; Member of Scientific Staff, Medical Research Council Laboratory of Molecular Biology, Cambridge, since 1984; *b* 22 May 1954; *s* of Pierre Goedert and Dr Marie-Antoinette Goedert (*née* Bové); one *s* with Dr Maria Grazia Spillantini. *Educ:* Athénée, Luxembourg; Univ. of Basel (MD 1980); Trinity Coll., Cambridge (PhD 1984). Mem., EMBO, 1997. 1st Prize, Eur. Contest for Young Scientists and Inventors, 1973; Metropolitan Life Foundn Award for Med. Res., 1996; Potamkin Prize, Amer. Acad. Neurol., 1998. *Publications:* contrib. res. papers and reviews to scientific jls. *Recreations:* reading, classical music. *Address:* MRC Laboratory of Molecular Biology, Hills Road, Cambridge CB2 2QH. *T:* (01223) 402036.

GOEHR, Prof. Alexander; composer; Professor of Music, and Fellow of Trinity Hall, University of Cambridge, 1976–99, now Emeritus Professor and Fellow; *b* 10 Aug. 1932; *s* of Walter and Laelia Goehr. *Educ:* Berkhamsted; Royal Manchester Coll. of Music; Paris Conservatoire. Lectr, Morley Coll., 1955–57; Music Asst, BBC, 1960–67; Winston Churchill Trust Fellowship, 1968; Composer-in-residence, New England Conservatory, Boston, Mass, 1968–69; Associate Professor of Music, Yale University, 1969–70; West Riding Prof. of Music, Leeds Univ., 1971–76. Artistic Dir, Leeds Festival, 1975; Vis. Prof.,

Peking Conservatoire of Music, 1980; Hon. Prof., Beijing Central Conservatsory. Reith Lectr, BBC, 1987. Mem., Bd of Dirs, Royal Opera House, 1982–84. Hon. Vice-Pres., SPNM, 1983–. Hon. Mem., Amer. Acad. and Inst. of Arts and Letters. Hon. FRMCM; Hon. FRAM 1975; Hon. FRNCM 1980; Hon. FRCM 1981. Hon. DMus: Southampton, 1973; Manchester, 1990; Nottingham, 1994; Siena, 1998; Cambridge, 2000. *Compositions include:* Songs of Babel, 1951; Fantasia Op. 4, 1954; String Quartet No. 1, 1957; La Belle Dame Sans Merci (ballet), 1958; Suite Op. 11, 1961; Hecuba's Lament, 1961; A Little Cantata of Proverbs, 1962; Concerto Op. 13, 1962; Little Symphony, 1963; Pastorals, 1965; Piano Trio, 1966; String Quartet No. 2, 1967; Romanza, 1968; Paraphrase, 1969; Symphony in One Movement, 1970; Concerto for Eleven, 1970; Concerto Op. 33, 1972; Chaconne for Wind, 1974; Lyric Pieces, 1974; Metamorphosis/Dance, 1974; String Quartet No. 3, 1976; Fugue on the notes of the Fourth Psalm, 1976; Romanza on the notes of the Fourth Psalm, 1977; Chaconne for Organ, 1979; Sinfonia, 1979; Kafka Fragments, 1979; Deux Etudes, 1981; Sonata, 1984; … a musical offering (JSB 1985), 1985; Symphony with Chaconne, 1986; …in real time, 1989; Still Lands, 1990; Bach Variations, 1990; …second musical offering (GFH 2001), 2001; *vocal:* The Deluge, 1958; Sutter's Gold, 1960; Virtutes, 1963; Arden Must Die (opera), 1966; Triptych (Naboth's Vineyard, 1968; Shadowplay, 1970; Sonata about Jerusalem, 1970); Psalm IV, 1976; Babylon the Great is Fallen, 1979; The Law of the Quadrille, 1979; Behold the Sun, 1981; Behold the Sun (opera), 1984; Eve Dreams in Paradise, 1988; Sing Ariel, 1990; The Death of Moses, 1992; Colossos or Panic, 1993; Arianna (opera), 1995; Schlussgesang, 1997; Kantan and Damask Drum (opera), 1999; Piano Quintet, 2000. *Address:* Trinity Hall, Cambridge CB2 1TJ; c/o Schott & Co. Ltd, 48 Great Marlborough Street, W1V 2BN.

GOERNE, Matthias; baritone; *b* Weimar, Germany. *Educ:* Studied under Prof. Beyer at Leipzig, Elizabeth Schwarzkopf and Dietrich Fischer-Dieskau. Début with Leipzig Radio SO; performances with Berlin Phil. Orch., Concentus Musicus, Concertgebouw; recitals in London, Amsterdam, Paris, Leipzig, Cologne and New York. Opera appearances include: Dresden Opera, and Komische Oper, Berlin, 1993; débuts, as Papageno, Salzburg Fest., 1997, Metropolitan Opera, NY, 1998; title rôle in Wozzek, Zürich, 1999. Numerous recordings. Gramophone Award; Diapason d'Or; Echo Prize, Germany; Cecilia Award, Belgium. *Address:* c/o Manfred Wichmann PRManagement, Eschenweg 8A, 22926 Ahrensburg, Germany; c/o Lothar Schacke, Künstler Sekretariat am Gasteig, Rosenheimer Strasse 52, 81669 München, Germany.

GOFF, family name of **Baron Goff of Chieveley**.

GOFF OF CHIEVELEY, Baron *cr* 1986 (Life Peer), of Chieveley in the Royal County of Berkshire; **Robert Lionel Archibald Goff,** Kt 1975; PC 1982; DCL; FBA 1987; a Lord of Appeal in Ordinary, 1986–98; Senior Law Lord, 1996–98; *b* 12 Nov. 1926; *s* of Lt-Col L. T. Goff and Mrs Goff (*née* Denroche-Smith); *m* 1953, Sarah, *er d* of Capt. G. R. Cousins, DSC, RN; one *s* two *d* (and one *s* decd). *Educ:* Eton Coll.; New Coll., Oxford (MA 1953, DCL 1972; Hon. Fellow, 1986). Served in Scots Guards, 1945–48 (commnd 1945). 1st cl hons Jurisprudence, Oxon, 1950. Called to the Bar, Inner Temple, 1951; Bencher, 1975; QC 1967. Fellow and Tutor, Lincoln Coll., Oxford, 1951–55; in practice at the Bar, 1956–75; a Recorder, 1974–75; Judge of the High Ct, QBD, 1975–82; Judge i/c Commercial List, and Chm. Commercial Court Cttee, 1979–81; a Lord Justice of Appeal, 1982–86. Chm., Sub-Cttee E (Law and Instns), H of L Select Cttee on EC, 1986–88. Chairman: Council of Legal Educn, 1976–82 (Vice-Chm., 1972–76; Chm., Bd of Studies, 1970–76); Common Professional Examination Bd, 1976–78; Court, London Univ., 1986–91; Pegasus Scholarship Trust, 1987–. High Steward, Oxford Univ., 1991–. Hon. Prof. of Legal Ethics, Univ. of Birmingham, 1980–81; Lectures: Maccabean, British Acad., 1983; Lionel Cohen Meml, Hebrew Univ. of Jerusalem, 1987; Cassel, Stockholm Univ., 1993. Member: Gen. Council of the Bar, 1971–74; Senate of Inns of Court and Bar, 1974–82 (Chm., Law Reform and Procedure Cttee, 1974–76). Chm., British Inst. of Internat. and Comparative Law, 1986–. President: CIArb, 1986–91; Bentham Club, 1986; Holdsworth Club, 1986–87. Hon. Fellow: Lincoln Coll., Oxford, 1985; Amer. Coll. of Trial Lawyers, 1997. Hon. DLitt: City, 1977; Reading, 1990; Hon. LLD: Buckingham, 1990; London, 1990; Bristol, 1996. Grand Cross (First Class), Order of Merit (Germany), 1999. *Publication:* (with Prof. Gareth Jones) The Law of Restitution, 1966. *Address:* House of Lords, Westminster, SW1A 0PW.

GOFF, Martyn, OBE 1977; Vice President, Book Trust, since 2000 (Chairman, 1992–96; Deputy Chairman, 1991–92, 1996–97); Director and Executive Chairman, Sotherans, since 1988; *b* 7 June 1923; *s* of Jacob and Janey Goff. *Educ:* Clifton College. Served in Royal Air Force, 1941–46. Film business, 1946–48; bookseller, 1948–70; Dir, NBL, later Chief Exec., Book Trust, 1970–88; Administrator, Booker Prize, 1970–. Has lectured on: music; English fiction; teenager morality; the book trade, 1946–70; fiction reviewer, 1975–88, non-fiction, 1988–, Daily Telegraph. Founder and Chm., Bedford Square Bookbang, 1971. Member: Arts Council Literature Panel, 1970–78; Arts Council Trng Cttee, 1973–78; Greater London Arts Assoc. Literature Panel, 1973–81; British Nat. Bibliography Res. Fund, 1976–88; British Library Adv. Council, 1977–82; PEN Exec. Cttee, 1978–; Exec. Cttee, Gtr London Arts Council, 1982–88; Library and Information Services Council, 1984–86; Bd, British Theatre Assoc., 1983–85; Chairman: Paternosters '73 Library Adv. Council, 1972–74; New Fiction Soc., 1975–88; School Bookshop Assoc., 1977–; Soc. of Bookmen, 1982–84 (Pres., 1997–); 1890s Soc., 1990–99; Nat. Life Story Collections, 1996–; Poetry Book Soc., 1996–99 (Mem. Bd, 1992–99); Wingate Scholarships, H. H. Wingate Foundn, 1998–; Vice-Pres., Royal Over-Seas League, 1996–; Dir, Battersea Arts Centre, 1992–97 (Trustee, 1981–85); Trustee: Cadmean Trust, 1981–99; Nat. Literacy Trust, 1993–. Judge, Glenfiddich Awards, 1993. FIAL 1958, FRSA 1979. *Publications: fiction:* The Plaster Fabric, 1957; A Season with Mammon, 1958; A Sort of Peace, 1960; The Youngest Director, 1961, new edn 1985; Red on the Door, 1962; The Flint Inheritance, 1965; Indecent Assault, 1967; The Liberation of Rupert Bannister, 1978; Tar and Cement, 1988; *non-fiction:* A Short Guide to Long Play, 1957; A Further Guide to Long Play, 1958; LP Collecting, 1960; Why Conform?, 1968; Victorian and Edwardian Surrey, 1972; Record Choice, 1974; Royal Pavilion, 1976; Organising Book Exhibitions, 1982; Publishing, 1988; Prize Writing, 1989. *Recreations:* travel, collecting paintings and sculptures, music. *Address:* 95 Sisters Avenue, SW11 5SW. *Clubs:* Athenæum, Savile, Groucho.

GOFF, Hon. Philip Bruce; MP; Minister of Foreign Affairs and Trade, and Minister of Justice, New Zealand, since 1999; *b* 2 June 1953; *s* of Bruce Charles Goff and Elaine Loyola Goff; *m* 1979, Mary Ellen Moriarty; two *s* one *d*. *Educ:* Univ. of Auckland (MA 1st Cl. Hons); Nuffield Coll., Oxford. MP (Lab): Roskill, 1981-90 and 1993-96; New Lynn, 1996-99; Mt Roskill, 1999-. Cabinet Minister, 1984-90: for Housing, Employment and Envmt, 1984-87; for Employment, Tourism, Youth Affairs and Associate Educn, 1987-89; for Educn, 1989-90. *Recreations:* squash, travel, gardening. *Address:* Parliament Buildings, Wellington, New Zealand. *T:* (4) 4719370.

GOFF, Sir Robert (William Davis-), 4th Bt *cr* 1905; Director, O'Connor & Co., Art Dealers and Property Investment Co.; *b* 12 Sept. 1955; *s* of Sir Ernest William Davis-Goff, 3rd Bt, and of Alice Cynthia Davis-Goff (*née* Woodhouse); *S* father, 1980; *m* 1978, Nathalie Sheelagh, *d* of Terence Chadwick; three *s* one *d*. *Educ:* Cheltenham College, Glos. *Recreation:* shooting. *Heir:* *s* William Nathaniel Davis-Goff, *b* 20 April 1980. *Address:* Eairy Moar Farm, Glen Helen, Isle of Man.

GOFFE, Judith Ann, FCA; independent business consultant, since 1991; Member, Independent Television Commission, since 1994; *b* 6 March 1953; *d* of Albert Edward Goffe and Jennie Lucia Goffe (*née* Da Costa); *m* 1992, Peter Alexander Rose; one *s*. *Educ:* Immaculate Conception High Sch., Kingston, Jamaica; Reading Univ. (BSc 1976). Chartered Accountant, 1981; FCA 1991. Articled clerk, Deloitte Haskins & Sells, 1977–82; Sen. Audit Manager, Blick Rothenberg & Noble, 1982–83; Investment Dir, 3i Group plc, 1984–91. Dir, Moorfields Eye Hosp. Trust, 1994–. FRSA 1994. *Recreations:* collecting contemporary ceramics and jewellery, design, travel, family, food.

GOGGINS, Paul Gerard; MP (Lab) Wythenshawe and Sale East, since 1997; *b* 16 June 1953; *s* of John Goggins and late Rita Goggins; *m* 1977, Wyn, *d* of Tom and Mary Bartley; two *s* one *d*. *Educ:* St Bede's Sch., Manchester; Birmingham Poly.; Manchester Poly. Child care worker, Liverpool Catholic Social Services, 1974–75; Officer-in-Charge, local authy children's home, Wigan, 1976–84; Project Dir, NCH Action for Children, Salford, 1984–89; Nat. Dir, Church Action on Poverty, 1989–97. Mem. (Lab) Salford MBC, 1990–98. PPS to Minister of State for Health, 1998–2000, to Sec. of State for Educn and Employment, 2000–01, to Home Sec., 2001–. *Address:* House of Commons, SW1A 0AA. *T:* (constituency) (0161) 499 7900.

GOGUEN, Prof. Joseph Amadee, PhD; Professor of Computer Science and Director, Meaning and Computation Laboratory (formerly Program in Advanced Manufacturing), University of California at San Diego, since 1996; *b* 28 June 1941; *s* of Joseph Amadee Goguen and Helen Stratton; *m* 1st, 1961, Nancy Hammer; one *s* one *d*; 2nd, 1981, Kathleen Morrow; one *d*. *Educ:* Harvard Univ. (BA); Univ. of California at Berkeley (MA, PhD). Asst Prof., Cttee on Inf. Sciences, Univ. of Chicago, 1968–73; Academic Staff, Naropa Inst., Boulder Colo, 1974–78; Prof., Computer Sci. Dept, UCLA, 1973–79; Man. Dir, Structural Semantics, Palo Alto, 1978–88; Sen. Staff Scientist, SRI Internat., Menlo Park, Calif, 1979–88; Sen. Mem., Center for Study of Language and Inf., Stanford Univ., 1984–88; Prof. of Computing Sci., Oxford Univ., 1988–96. IBM Postdoctoral Fellowship, T. J. Watson Res. Center, 1971; Sen. Vis. Fellow, Univ. of Edinburgh, 1976, 1977, 1983. Fellow, Japan Soc. for Promotion of Sci., 1999. Exceptional Achievement Award, SRI Internat., 1984. *Publications:* (ed) Theory and Practice of Software Technology, 1983; (ed jtly) Requirements Engineering: social and technical issues, 1994; (jtly) Algebraic Semantics of Imperative Programs, 1996; over 200 articles in professional jls. *Address:* Department of Computer Science and Engineering, University of California at San Diego, 9500 Gilman Drive, La Jolla, CA 92093–0114, USA.

GOH CHOK TONG; Prime Minister of Singapore, since 1990; *b* 20 May 1941; *m* Tan Choo Leng; one *s* one *d* (twins). *Educ:* Raffles Instn; Univ. of Singapore (1st cl. Hons Econs); Williams Coll., USA. Joined Admin. Service, Singapore Govt, 1964, Econ. Planning Unit, Min. of Finance; Planning and Projects Manager, Neptune Orient Lines, 1969–73, Man. Dir, 1973–77. MP for Marine Parade, 1976–; Sen. Minister of State for Finance, 1977–79; Minister: for Trade and Industry, 1979–81; for Health, 1981–85; for Defence, 1981–91; First Dep. Prime Minister, 1985–90. People's Action Party: Mem., Central Exec. Cttee, 1979–; First Organising Sec., 1979; Second Asst Sec. Gen., 1979–84; Asst Sec. Gen., 1984–89; First Asst Sec. Gen., 1989–92; Sec. Gen., 1992–. Formerly Chairman: Singapore Labour Foundn; NTUC Income, NTUC Fairprice. Medal of Honour, NTUC, 1987. *Recreations:* golf, tennis. *Address:* Prime Minister's Office, Istana Annexe, Istana, Singapore 238823.

GOHEEN, Robert Francis; educator; President Emeritus, and Senior Fellow, Public and International Affairs, since 1981, Princeton University; *b* Vengurla, India, 15 Aug. 1919; *s* of Dr Robert H. H. Goheen and Anne Ewing; *m* 1941, Margaret M. Skelly; two *s* four *d*. *Educ:* Princeton Univ. AB 1940; PhD 1948. Princeton University: Instructor, Dept of Classics, 1948–50; Asst Prof., 1950–57; Prof., 1957–72; President, 1957–72. Chm., Council on Foundns, 1972–77; US Ambassador to India, 1977–80; Dir, Mellon Fellowships in Humanities, 1982–92. Sen. Fellow in Classics, Amer. Academy in Rome, 1952–53; Dir Nat. Woodrow Wilson Fellowship Program, 1953–56. Member: Adv. Commn on Oceans and Internat. Scientific and Environmental Affairs, US State Dept; Adv. Bd, Nat. Foreign Language Center; Adv. Council, S Asia Inst., Columbia Univ.; Adv. Council, Centre for Advanced Study of India, Univ. of Pennsylvania; American Philosophical Soc.; American Academy of Arts and Sciences; Phi Beta Kappa; Trustee: Nat. Humanities Center; Bharatiya Vidya Bhavan (USA). Former Mem. Internat Adv. Bd, Chemical Bank; former Member of Board: Amer. Univ. in Beirut; Carnegie Foundn for Advancement of Teaching; Carnegie Endowment for Internat. Peace; United Bd of Christian Higher Educn in Asia; Rockefeller Foundn; Asia Soc.; Amer. Acad. in Rome; Inst. of Internat. Educn; Equitable Life; Thomson Newspapers Inc.; Dreyfus Third Century Fund; Midlantic Nat. Bank; Reza Shah Kabir Univ., Iran; Univ. Service Cttee, Hong Kong. Hon. degrees: Harvard, Rutgers, Yale, Temple, Brown, Columbia, New York, Madras, Pennsylvania, Hamilton, Middlebury, Saint Mary's (Calif), State of New York, Denver, Notre Dame, N Carolina, Hofstra, Nebraska, Dropsie, Princeton; Tusculum Coll.; Trinity Coll., USA; Coll. of Wooster; Jewish Theological Seminary of America; Ripon Coll.; Rider Coll. *Publications:* The Imagery of Sophocles' Antigone, 1951; The Human Nature of a University, 1969; articles. *Recreations:* books, golf. *Address:* 1 Orchard Circle, Princeton, NJ 08540, USA. *T:* (609) 9242751. *Clubs:* Princeton, Century Association (New York); Cosmos (Washington); Nassau, Pretty Brook (Princeton); Gymkhana, Delhi Golf (Delhi).

GOLD, Sir Arthur (Abraham), Kt 1984; CBE 1974; Chairman, Commonwealth Games Council for England, 1979–90; Honorary Secretary, British Amateur Athletic Board, 1965–77 (Life Vice President, 1977); Vice President, British Olympic Association, since 1992 (Chairman, 1988–92); *b* 10 Jan. 1917; *s* of late Mark and Leah Gold; *m* 1942, Marion Godfrey, *d* of late N. Godfrey; one *s*. *Educ:* Grocers' Company's Sch. Inst. of Motor Industry Wakefield Gold Medallist, 1945. Internat. high jumper, 1937; Athletics Team Leader Olympic Games: Mexico, 1968; Munich, 1972; Montreal, 1976; Commandant, English Commonwealth Games Team: Brisbane, 1982; Edinburgh, 1986; Auckland, 1990; Comdr, British Olympic Team, Albertville and Barcelona, 1992. Chm., Drug Abuse Adv. Cttee, Eur. Sports Conf., 1985–91; Vice-Chm., Cttee on Doping in Sport, Council of Europe, 1983–90; Member: Sports Council, 1980–88 (Chm., Drug Abuse Adv. Gp, 1981–92); Exec. Cttee, CCPR, 1982–90. President: Eur. Athletic Assoc., 1976–87 (Hon. Life Pres., 1988; Mem. Council, 1966–76); Counties Athletic Union, 1978–; UAU, 1984–; AAA, 1995–; Past President: London Athletic Club; Middlesex Co. Amateur Athletic Assoc. Hon. FCP 1987. Hon. DTech Loughborough, 1989; Hon. LLD Sheffield, 1991. Olympic Order (Silver), 1991. *Publications:* Ballet Training Exercises for Athletes, 1960; various contribs to technical books on athletics. *Recreations:* walking, talking, reading, weeding. *Address:* 49 Friern Mount Drive, Whetstone, N20 9DJ. *T:* (020) 8445 2848. *Clubs:* City Livery, MCC; London Athletic.

GOLD, Jack; film director; *b* 28 June 1930; British; *m* 1957, Denyse (*née* Macpherson); two *s* one *d*. *Educ:* London Univ. (BSc (Econs), LLB). Asst Studio Manager, BBC radio, 1954–55; Editor, Film Dept, BBC, 1955–60; Dir, TV and film documentaries and fiction, 1960–. Desmond Davies Award for services to television, BAFTA, 1976. *TV films:* Tonight; Death in the Morning (BAFTA Award, 1964); Modern Millionairess; Famine; Dispute; 90 Days; Dowager in Hot Pants; World of Coppard (BAFTA Award, 1968); Mad Jack (Grand Prix, Monte Carlo, 1971); Stocker's Copper (BAFTA Award, 1972); Arturo Ui; The Lump; Catholics (Peabody Award, 1974); The Naked Civil Servant (Italia Prize, 1976, Internat. Emmy, and Critics Award, 1976); Thank You Comrades; Marya; Charlie Muffin; A Walk in the Forest; Merchant of Venice; Bavarian Night; A Lot of Happiness (Kenneth Macmillan), 1981 (Internat. Emmy Award); Praying Mantis, Macbeth, L'Elegance, 1982; The Red Monarch, 1983; Good and Bad at Games, 1983; Sakharov, 1984 (Assoc. Cable Enterprises Award); Murrow, 1986 (Assoc. Cable Enterprises Award); Me and the Girls, 1985; Escape from Sobibor, 1987 (Golden Globe Award); Stones for Ibarra, 1988; The Tenth Man, 1989; Masterclass, 1989; Ball-trap on the Côte Sauvage, 1989; The Rose and the Jackal, 1990; She Stood Alone, 1991 (Christopher Award); The Last Romantics, 1992; Heavy Weather, 1995; Mute of Malice, 1997; Blood Money, 1997; Into the Blue, 1997; Kavanagh QC, 1998; Goodnight Mr Tom, 1998 (Silver Hugo Award, Chicago, 1998, BAFTA Award, 1999); The Remorseful Day, 2000; End of Law, 2001; *cinema:* The Bofors Gun, 1968; The Reckoning, 1969; The National Health, 1973 (Evening News Best Comedy Award); Who?, 1974; Man Friday, 1974; Aces High, 1976 (Evening News Best Film Award); The Medusa Touch, 1977; The Sailor's Return, 1978 (jt winner, Martin Luther King Meml Prize, 1980; Monte Carlo Catholic Award, 1981; Monte Carlo Critics Award, 1981); Little Lord Fauntleroy, 1981 (Christopher Award); The Chain, 1985; The Lucona Affair, 1993; Return of the Native, 1994; Spring Awakening, 1994; *theatre:* The Devil's Disciple, Aldwych, 1976; This Story of Yours, Hampstead, 1987; Danger! Memory, Hampstead, 1988; Three Hotels, Tricycle Th., 1993. *Recreations:* music, reading, tennis. *Address:* 24 Wood Vale, N10 3DP.

GOLD, John (Joseph Manson); Public Relations Consultant, 1979–90, retired; Manager of Public Relations, Hong Kong Mass Transit Railway, 1975–79; *b* 2 Aug. 1925; *m* 1953, Berta Cordeiro; one *d*. *Educ:* Clayesmore Sch., Dorset. Yorkshire Evening News, 1944–47; London Evening News, 1947–52; Australian Associated Press (New York), 1952–55; New York Corresp., London Evening News, 1955–66; Editor, London Evening News, 1967–72; Dir, Harmsworth Publications Ltd, 1967–73. Free-lance writer and lectr, Far East, 1973–75.

GOLD, Stephen Charles, MA, MD, FRCP; Consulting Physician to: the Skin Department, St George's Hospital; St John's Hospital for Diseases of the Skin; King Edward VII Hospital for Officers; Former Hon. Consultant in Dermatology: to the Army; to Royal Hospital, Chelsea; *b* Bishops Stortford, Herts, 10 Aug. 1915; *yr s* of late Philip Gold, Stansted, Essex, and late Amy Frances, *er d* of James and Mary Perry; *m* 1941, Betty Margaret, *o d* of late Dr T. P. Sheedy, OBE; three *s* one *d*. *Educ:* Radley Coll.; Gonville and Caius Coll., Cambridge; St George's Hosp. (Entrance Exhibnr); Zürich and Philadelphia. BA 1937; MRCS, LRCP 1940; MA, MB, BChir 1941; MRCP 1947; MD 1952; FRCP 1958. Served RAMC, 1941–46. Late Med. First Asst to Out-Patients, St George's Hosp., Senior Registrar, Skin Dept, St George's Hosp., Sen. Registrar, St John's Hosp. for Diseases of the Skin; Lectr in Dermatology, Royal Postgraduate Med. Sch., 1949–69. Sec., Brit. Assoc. of Dermatology, 1965–70 (Pres., 1979). FRSocMed (late Sec. Dermatological Section, Pres., 1972–73); Fellow St John's Hosp. Dermatological Soc. (Pres., 1965–66). *Publications:* St George's and Dermatology: evolution and progress, 1993; A Biographical History of British Dermatology, 1996.

GOLD, Prof. Thomas, FRS 1964; John L. Wetherill Professor of Astronomy, Cornell University, 1971–86, Professor Emeritus of Astronomy, 1987; *b* 22 May 1920; *s* of Max and Josefine Gold; *m* 1st, 1947, Merle E. Gold (*née* Tuberg); three *d*; 2nd, 1972, Carvel B. Gold (*née* Beyer); one *d*. *Educ:* Zuoz Coll., Switzerland; Trinity Coll., Cambridge (Hon. Fellow, 1986). BA Mechanical Sciences (Cambridge), 1942; MA Mechanical Sciences, Cambridge, 1946; ScD, Cambridge, 1969. Fellow Trinity Coll., Cambridge, 1947–51. British Admiralty, 1942–46; Cavendish Laboratory, Cambridge, 1946–47 and 1949–52; Med. Research Council, Zoological Lab., Cambridge, 1947–49; Sen. Principal Scientific Officer (Chief Asst), Royal Greenwich Observatory, 1952–56; Prof. of Astronomy, 1957–58, Robert Wheeler Willson Prof. of Applied Astronomy, 1958–59, Harvard Univ. Dir, Center for Radio-Physics and Space Research, Cornell Univ., 1959–81. Hon. MA (Harvard), 1957. Member: Amer. Philosophical Soc.; Nat. Acad. of Sciences; Fellow, Amer. Acad. of Arts and Sciences. Gold Medal, RAS, 1985. *Publications:* Power from the Earth, 1987; The Deep Hot Biosphere, 1999; contribs to learned journals on astronomy, physics, biophysics, geophysics. *Recreations:* ski-ing, travelling. *Address:* 7 Pleasant Grove Lane, Ithaca, NY 14850, USA.

GOLDBERG, Prof. Sir Abraham, Kt 1983; Regius Professor of the Practice of Medicine, University of Glasgow, 1978–89, now Emeritus (Regius Professor of Materia Medica, 1970–78); Consultant Physician, Western Infirmary, Glasgow, since 1959; Hon. Professorial Research Fellow in Modern History, University of Glasgow, since 1996; *b* 7 Dec. 1923; *s* of late Julius Goldberg and Rachel Goldberg (*née* Varinofsky); *m* 1957, Clarice Cussin; two *s* one *d*. *Educ:* George Heriot's Sch., Edinburgh; Edinburgh University. MB, ChB 1946, MD (Gold Medal for thesis) 1956, Edinburgh; DSc Glasgow 1966; FRCP, FRCPE, FRCPGlas, FFPM; FRSE. Nat. Service, RAMC, 1947–49. Nuffield Research Fellow, UCH Med. Sch., London, 1952–54; Eli Lilly Trav. Fellow in Medicine (MRC) in Dept of Medicine, Univ. of Utah; Lectr in Medicine 1956, Titular Prof. 1967, Univ. of Glasgow. Mem., Grants Cttee, Clinical Res. Bd, MRC, 1971–77, Chm., Grants Cttee I, Clinical Res. Bd, MRC, 1973–77. Mem., Chief Scientist Cttee, SHHD, 1977–83; Chm., Biomed. Res. Cttee, SHHD Chief Scientist Orgn, 1977–83; Chm., Cttee on Safety of Medicines, 1980–86. Mem., Editorial Bd, Jt Formulary Cttee, British Nat. Formulary, 1972–78. Foundn Pres., Faculty of Pharmaceutical Medicine, RCP, 1989–91. Editor, Scottish Medical Jl, 1962–63. Lectures: Sydney Watson Smith, RCPE, 1964; Henry Cohen, Hebrew Univ., Jerusalem, 1973; Fitzpatrick, RCP, 1988; Archibald Goodall Meml, RCPSG, 1989. Watson Prize, RCPGlas, 1959; Alexander Fleck Award, Univ. of Glasgow, 1967. Lord Provost's Award for Public Service, City of Glasgow, 1988. *Publications:* (jtly) Diseases of Porphyrin Metabolism, 1962; (ed jtly) Recent Advances in Haematology, 1971; (jtly) Disorders of Porphyrin Metabolism, 1987; (ed jtly) Pharmaceutical Medicine and the Law, 1991; papers on clinical and investigative medicine. *Recreations:* walking, swimming, writing. *Address:* 16 Birnam Crescent, Bearsden, Glasgow G61 2AU.

GOLDBERG, David Gerard; QC 1987; *b* 12 Aug. 1947; *s* of late Arthur Goldberg and of Sylvia Goldberg; *m* 1981, Alison Ninette Lunzer; one *s* one *d*. *Educ:* Plymouth Coll.; London School of Economics (LLB, LLM). Called to the Bar, Lincoln's Inn, 1971, Bencher, 1997; practice at Revenue Bar, 1972–. Chm. Trustees, Surgical Workshop for Anatomical Prosection, 1994–. *Publications:* (jtly) Introduction to Company Law, 1971, 4th edn 1987; (jtly) The Law of Partnership Taxation, 1976, 2nd edn 1979; various articles and notes in legal periodicals mainly concerning taxation and company law. *Recreations:* reading, writing letters, thinking. *Address:* Gray's Inn Chambers, Gray's Inn, WC1R 5JA. *T:* (020) 7242 2642.

GOLDBERG, Sir David (Paul Brandes), Kt 1996; DM; FRCP, FRCPsych; Professor of Psychiatry, Institute of Psychiatry, London, since 1992; Director of Research and Development, Bethlem Maudsley Trust, since 1992; *b* 28 Jan. 1934; *s* of Paul Goldberg and Ruby Dora Goldberg; *m* 1966, Ilfra Joy Pink; one *s* three *d*. *Educ:* William Ellis Sch., London; Hertford Coll., Oxford (MA 1956; DM 1970); St Thomas' Hosp.; Manchester Univ. (MSc 1974). FRCPsych 1974; FRCP 1976. Trained at Maudsley Hosp., 1962–69; Sen. Lectr, 1969–72, Prof., 1972–92, Univ. of Manchester. Visiting Professor: Medical Univ. of S Carolina, 1978–79; Univ. of WA, 1986. Founder FMedSci 1998. FKC. *Publications:* Mental Illness in the Community: the pathway to psychiatric care, 1981; Commom Mental Disorders: a biosocial model, 1991; Psychiatric Illness in Medical Practice, 1992. *Recreations:* walking, talking, travelling. *Address:* Institute of Psychiatry, de Crespigny Park, SE1 8AF.

GOLDBERG, Jonathan Jacob; QC 1989; a Recorder, since 1993; *b* 13 Nov. 1947; *s* of late Rabbi Dr and Mrs P. Selvin Goldberg; *m* 1980, Alexis Jane (marr. diss. 1991), *e d* of Sir George Martin, *qv*; one *s* one *d*. *Educ:* Manchester Grammar Sch.; Trinity Hall, Cambridge (MA, LLB). Called to the Bar, Middle Temple, 1971; Member, NY State Bar, 1985. Mem. Presidency, Internat. Assoc. of Jewish Lawyers and Jurists, 1999–. *Recreations:* music, cinema, wine, travel. *Address:* 3 Temple Gardens, Temple, EC4Y 9AU. *T:* (020) 7583 1155, *Fax:* (020) 7353 5446.

GOLDBERGER, Prof. Marvin Leonard, PhD; Professor of Physics, since 1993, and Dean of Natural Sciences, since 1994, University of California, San Diego; *b* 22 Oct. 1922; *s* of Joseph Goldberger and Mildred (*née* Sedwitz); *m* 1945, Mildred Ginsburg; two *s*. *Educ:* Carnegie Inst. of Technology (BS); Univ. of Chicago (PhD). Asst to Associate Prof., Univ. of Chicago, 1950–55; Prof., Univ. of Chicago, 1955–57; Princeton University: Higgins Prof. of Mathematical Physics, 1957–77; Chm., Dept of Physics, 1970–76; Joseph Henry Prof. of Physics, 1977–78; Pres., California Inst. of Technology, 1978–87; Dir, Inst. for Advanced Study, Princeton, NJ, 1987–91; Prof. of Physics, UCLA, 1991–93. Hon. ScD: Carnegie-Mellon, 1979; Notre Dame, Indiana, 1979; Brandeis, 1991; Hon. DHL: Hebrew Union Coll., 1980; Univ. of Judaism, 1982; Hon. LLD Occidental Coll., 1980. *Publications:* (jtly) Collision Theory, 1964; professional papers in Physical Rev. *Recreations:* jogging, cooking. *Address:* Urey Hall Annex, University of California, San Diego, 9500 Gilman Drive, La Jolla, CA 92093-0319, USA.

GOLDBLATT, Simon; QC 1972. Called to the Bar, Gray's Inn, 1953 (Bencher, 1982). *Address:* 39 Essex Street, WC2R 3AT.

GOLDEN, Surgeon Rear-Adm. Francis St Clair, OBE 1981; Consultant in Applied Physiology, and Hon. Lecturer, Portsmouth University, since 1998; *b* 5 June 1936; *s* of Harry Golden and Nora Golden (*née* Murphy); *m* 1964, Jennifer (*née* Beard); two *s* one *d*. *Educ:* Presentation Coll., Cork; University Coll., Cork (MB BCh, BAO); London Univ. (Diploma in Aviation Medicine); Leeds Univ. (PhD Physiol). GP, Kingston on Thames, 1961–63; HMS Jaguar, 1963–64; RNAS Culdrose, 1964–67; RN Air Med. Sch., 1967–73; Inst. of Naval Medicine, 1973–85; MoD, 1985–86; Fleet MO, 1986–88; MO i/c Haslar, 1988–90; Surg. Rear-Adm., Support Med. Services, 1990–93, retd. Consultant in Applied Physiol., Robens Inst., Surrey Univ., 1994–98. QHP 1990–93. Chm., Med. and Survival Cttee, RNLI, 1994–. Hon. FNI 1982. OStJ. *Publications:* papers in sci. jls and chapters in medical textbooks on immersion, drowning, hypothermia. *Recreations:* born again golfer, armchair Rugby. *Address:* 15 Beech Grove, Gosport, Hants PO12 2JE. *Clubs:* Royal Society of Medicine; Lee-on-the-Solent Golf (Capt., 1998–99).

GOLDHILL, Flora Taylor; Director of Personnel, Department of Health, since 1999; *b* 13 Feb. 1953; *d* of Thomas Kissock and Flora (*née* McKenzie); *m* 1978, Jonathan Paul Goldhill. *Educ:* Morgan Academy, Dundee; Edinburgh Univ. (MA Hons). Civil Servant, DHSS and DoH, 1976–90; Chief Exec., HFEA, 1991–96; Head, Policy Mgt Unit, DoH, 1996–98. Gov., Canonbury Primary Sch., 1994– (Vice-Chm., 1996–). *Recreations:* family, friends, walking. *Address:* Department of Health, Skipton House, 80 London Road, SE1 6LH. *T:* (020) 7972 5657.

GOLDIE, Annabel MacNicoll; DL; Member (C) Scotland West, Scottish Parliament, since 1999; Partner, Donaldson, Alexander, Russell & Haddow (formerly Dickson, Haddow & Co.), since 1978; Deputy Leader, Scottish Conservative and Unionist Party, since 1998; *b* 27 Feb. 1950; *d* of Alexander MacIntosh Goldie and Margaret MacNicoll Goldie. *Educ:* Greenock Acad.; Strathclyde Univ. (LLB). Admitted Solicitor, 1974; Notary Public, 1978. Apprentice Solicitor, McClure Naismith Brodie & Co., Glasgow, 1971–73; Asst Solicitor, Haddow & McLay, Glasgow, subseq. Dickson, Haddow & Co., 1973–77. Dep. Convener, Enterprise and Lifelong Learning Cttee, Scottish Parlt, 1999–. Mem., Royal Faculty of Procurators in Glasgow, 1982–. Dir, Prince's Scottish Youth Business Trust, 1995–. Vice-Chm., 1992–95, Dep. Chm., 1995–97 and 1997–98, Chm., March–July 1997, Scottish Cons. and Unionist Party. Vice-Chm., Adv. Bd, W Scotland Salvation Army. Mem., Charing Cross Rotary Club, Glasgow. DL Renfrew, 1993. *Recreations:* gardening badly, walking happily, watching birds usually uncomprehendingly, listening to classical music enthusiastically, if not knowledgeably. *Address:* Parliament Headquarters, George IV Bridge, Edinburgh EH99 1SP. *Club:* Royal Scottish Automobile (Glasgow).

GOLDIE, Ven. David; Archdeacon of Buckingham, since 1998; *b* 20 Dec. 1946; *s* of Frederick and Margaret Goldie; *m* 1969, (Emily) Rosemary Robson; three *d*. *Educ:* Glasgow Acad.; Glasgow Univ. (MA); Fitzwilliam Coll., Cambridge (MA); Westcott House, Cambridge. Curate: Christ Church, Swindon, 1970–73; Troon, 1973–75; Mission Priest, Irvine and Rector, Ardrossan, 1975–82; Milton Keynes: Priest Missioner, 1982–86; Vicar, Christ the Cornerstone, 1986–98; RD, 1986–90; Borough Dean, and Canon of Christ Church, Oxford, 1990–98. Mem., Gen. Synod, C of E, 1990–. *Recreations:* dog-walking, organ playing, exploring France. *Address:* 60 Wendover Road, Aylesbury, Bucks HP21 9LW. *T:* (01296) 423269.

GOLDIE, Dr Peter Lawrence; Lecturer in Philosophy, King's College, London, since 1998; *b* 5 Nov. 1946; *s* of Kenneth and Norah Goldie; *m* 1990, Sophie Hamilton; two *s* by previous marriage. *Educ:* Felsted Sch., Essex; UCL (BA 1993); Balliol Coll., Oxford (BPhil 1995; DPhil 1997). Chief Executive: Abaco Investments PLC, 1983–86; British & Commonwealth Hldgs, 1987–89; Dir, Guinness Mahon, 1973–83. Lectr in Philosophy, Magdalen Coll., Oxford, 1996–98. *Publications:* The Emotions, 2000; articles in philosophical jls. *Recreation:* physical and mental exercise.

GOLDING, Baroness *cr* 2001 (Life Peer), of Newcastle-under-Lyme in the County of Staffordshire; **Llinos Golding;** *b* 21 March 1933; *d* of Rt Hon. Ness Edwards, MP and Elina Victoria Edwards; *m* 1st, 1957, Dr John Roland Lewis; one *s* two *d*; 2nd, 1980, John Golding (*d* 1999). *Educ:* Caerphilly Girls' Grammar Sch.; Cardiff Royal Infirmary Sch. of Radiography. Mem., Soc. of Radiographers. Worked as a radiographer at various times;

Assistant to John Golding, MP, 1972–86. MP (Lab) Newcastle-under-Lyme, July 1986–2001. An Opposition Whip, 1987–92; opposition spokesman: on social security, 1992–95; on children and the family, 1993–95; on agric., fisheries and food, 1995–97. Mem., Select Cttee on Culture, Media and Sport, 1997–2001. Former Chm., All Party Parly Gp on Children; Joint Chairman: All Party Parly Gp on Homeless, 1989–99; All Party Parly Gp on Drugs Misuse, until 1998; former Treas., All Party Parly Gp on Racing and Bloodstock. Member: BBC Gen. Adv. Council, 1988–91; Commonwealth War Graves Commn, 1992–. Former Mem., Dist Manpower Services Cttee; Mem., N Staffs DHA, 1983–87. Sec., Newcastle (Dist) Trades Council, 1976–87. *Address:* House of Lords, SW1A 0PW. *Club:* Halmerend Working Men's (Audley).

GOLDING, Francis Nelson; architecture, planning and conservation consultant, since 2000; *b* 28 Jan. 1944; *s* of late Frank Edwards Golding and Ella Golding (*née* Morris). *Educ:* King's Sch., Macclesfield; Clare Coll., Cambridge (Exhibnr; BA 1966; MA 2000). Min. of Public Building and Works, 1967; DoE, 1972; Royal Commn on the Press, 1975–77; Asst Sec., DoE, 1978; English Heritage: Head of Secretariat, 1984; Head of Properties, 1986–90; Sec., ICOMOS, 1992–94; Sec., Royal Fine Art Commn, 1995–99; Chief Exec., Commn for Architecture and the Built Envmt, 1999. Hon. FRIBA 2000. *Recreations:* Chinese pots and jade, going to India. *Address:* 36–37 Featherstone Street, EC1Y 8QX. *T:* (020) 7251 5194.

GOLDING, (Harold) John, CBE 1992; PhD; FBA 1994; painter; Senior Tutor in the School of Painting, Royal College of Art, 1981–86 (Tutor, 1973); *b* 10 Sept. 1929; *s* of Harold S. Golding and Dorothy Hamer. *Educ:* Ridley Coll. (St Catherine's, Ontario); Univ. of Toronto; Univ. of London. BA; MA; PhD. Lectr, 1962–77, and Reader in History of Art, 1977–81, Courtauld Inst., Univ. of London; Slade Prof. of Fine Art, Cambridge Univ., 1976–77; Andrew W. Mellon Lectr in the Fine Arts, Nat. Gall. of Art, Washington, 1997. Trustee, Tate Gallery, 1984–91. Hon. Fellow, RCA, 1987. *Publications:* Cubism 1907–14, 1959, 3rd edn 1988; (with Christopher Green) Leger & Purist Paris, 1970; Duchamp: The Bride Stripped Bare by her Bachelors, Even, 1972; (ed with Roland Penrose) Picasso, 1881–1973, 1973; Visions of the Modern, 1994; (with Elizabeth Cowling) Picasso: sculptor/painter, 1994; Paths to the Absolute, 2000. *Address:* 24 Ashchurch Park Villas, W12 9SP. *T:* (020) 8749 5221.

GOLDING, John Anthony, CVO 1966; Queen's Messenger, 1967–80; *b* 25 July 1920; *s* of George Golding, Plaxtol, Kent; *m* 1950, Patricia May, *d* of Thomas Archibald Bickel; two *s*. *Educ:* Bedford Sch.; King's Coll., Auckland. Served with King's African Rifles and Military Administration, Somalia, 1939–46 (Captain). Entered Colonial Service, 1946; Dep. Provincial Comr, Tanganyika, 1961; Administrator, Turks and Caicos Is, 1965–67. *Publication:* Colonialism: the golden years, 1987. *Recreations:* gardening, fishing. *Address:* c/o Barclays Bank, 11 High Street, Hythe, Kent CT21 5AE.

GOLDING, Prof. Raymund Marshall, AO 1994; FNZIC; FRACI; FInstP; FTSE; Vice-Chancellor, James Cook University of North Queensland, 1986–96; *b* 17 June 1935; *s* of Austin E. Golding and Marion H. R. Golding; *m* 1962, Ingeborg Carl; two *d*. *Educ:* Auckland Univ., NZ (BSc 1957, MSc 1958); Cambridge Univ. (PhD 1963). Res. and Sen. Res. Scientist, DSIR, NZ, 1957–68; Prof. of Theoretical and Physical Chemistry, 1968–86, Mem., Bd of Sen. Sch. Studies, 1975–86, Pro-Vice-Chancellor, 1978–86, Univ. of NSW. Dir, St George Hosp., 1982–86. Chm., Aust. Marine Sci. Consortium, 1984–; Dep. Chm., Consultative Gp on Marine Industries Sci. and Technol., 1990–94. Hon. Chm., Australian Chapter, Pacific Congress on Marine Sci. and Technol., Internat., 1990–; Chm., Nat. Unit for Multidisciplinary Studies of Spinal Pain, Townsville Gen. Hosp., 1997–; Member: Educn Cttee, NSW Chiropractic Registration Bd, 1983–; Chiropractors and Osteopaths Bd of Qld, 1991–. Mem. Council, PNG Univ. of Technol., 1987–93. Chm., Aust. Fest. of Chamber Music Pty, 1990–96; Director: Tropic Line Res. Theatre Ltd, 1992–94; Townsville Enterprise Ltd, 1990–96; Aust. Tourism Res. Inst., 1990–97. Mem., Crown-of-Thorns Res. Cttee, 1986–96. Trustee, WWF (Australia), 1988–94. Hon. DSc Univ. of NSW, 1986. *Publications:* Applied Wave Mechanics, 1969; The Goldings of Oakington, 1992; contribs to books on chem. subjects; numerous research papers and articles. *Recreations:* music, photography, astronomy. *Address:* 5 Tolson Road, Mooloolah, Qld 4553, Australia. *T:* and *Fax:* (7) 54947689. *Club:* Australasian Pioneers' (Sydney).

GOLDING, Ven. Simon Jefferies, QHC 1997; Archdeacon for the Royal Navy and Principal Anglican Chaplain (Naval), since 1998; Director General, Naval Chaplaincy Service and Chaplain of the Fleet, since 2000; *b* 30 March 1946; *s* of late George William Golding and of Gladys Joyce Golding (*née* Henstridge); *m* 1968, Anne Reynolds; one *s* one *d*. *Educ:* HMS Conway Merchant Navy Cadet Sch.; Brasted Place Coll.; Lincoln Theol Coll. Navigating Officer, MN, and Lieut (X) RNR, 1963–69; ordained deacon, 1974, priest, 1975; Curate, St Cuthbert, Wilton, 1974–77; Chaplain, Royal Navy, 1977–; Chaplain of the Fleet, 1997–98. Hon. Canon, Gibraltar Cathedral, 1998. *Address:* c/o Ministry of Defence, Victory Building, HM Naval Base, Portsmouth PO1 3LS. *T:* (023) 9272 7904.

GOLDING, Terence Edward, OBE 1992; FCA; Chairman, Expocentric plc, since 2000; *b* 7 April 1932; *s* of Sydney Richard Golding and Elsie Golding; *m* 1955, Sheila Jean (*née* Francis); one *s* one *d*. *Educ:* Harrow County Grammar Sch. FCA 1967. Earls Court Ltd (Exhibition Hall Proprietors): Chief Accountant, 1960; Co. Sec., 1965; Financial Dir, 1972; Financial Dir, Olympia Ltd, and Earls Court & Olympia Ltd, 1973; Commercial Dir, Earls Court & Olympia Group of Cos, 1975; Chief Executive: Nat. Exhibn Centre, Birmingham, 1978–95; Internat. Convention Centre, Birmingham, 1990–95; Dep. Chm., Earls Court & Olympia Ltd, 1995–99. Member: Exhibition Liaison Cttee, 1979–97; Nat. Assoc. of Exhibn Hallowners, 1988–97. Director: British Exhibitions Promotion Council, 1981–83; Birmingham Convention and Visitor Bureau, 1981–93; Heart of England Tourist Bd, 1984–91; Central England, TEC, 1990–92; Birmingham Marketing Partnership, 1993–95; Chm., Exhibn Industry Fedn, 1995–97; Exhibition Venues Assoc., 1997–99. Hon. Mem. Council, Birmingham Chamber of Industry and Commerce, 1990–95. Midlander of the Year, 1990. *Recreation:* following sport. *Address:* Pinn Cottage, Pinner Hill, Pinner, Mddx HA5 3XX. *T:* (020) 8866 2610.

GOLDINGAY, Rev. Prof. John Edgar, PhD; David Allan Hubbard Professor of Old Testament Studies, Fuller Theological Seminary, Pasadena, since 1997; *b* 20 June 1942; *s* of Edgar Charles and Ada Irene Goldingay; *m* 1967, Ann Elizabeth Wilson; two *s*. *Educ:* King Edward's School, Birmingham; Keble Coll., Oxford (BA); Nottingham University (PhD). Ordained deacon 1966, priest 1967; Asst Curate, Christ Church, Finchley, 1966–69; St John's College, Nottingham: Lectr, 1970–75; Dir of Acad. Studies, 1976–79; Registrar, 1979–85; Vice-Principal, 1985–88; Principal, 1988–97. DD Lambeth, 1997. *Publications:* Songs from a Strange Land, 1978; Approaches to Old Testament Interpretation, 1981; Theological Diversity and the Authority of the Old Testament, 1987; Daniel, 1989; (ed) Signs, Wonders and Healing, 1989; Models for Scripture, 1994; Models for the Interpretation of Scripture, 1995; (ed) Atonement Today, 1995; After Eating the Apricot, 1996; To The Usual Suspects, 1998; Men Behaving Badly, 2000; Isaiah, 2001. *Recreations:* family, Old Testament, rock music. *Address:* 111 South Orange Grove, Apartment 108, Pasadena, CA 91105, USA. *T:* (626) 4050626, *Fax:* (626) 5845251; *e-mail:* JohnGold@fuller.edu.

GOLDMAN, Antony John, CB 1995; Director General, Civil Aviation, Department of the Environment, Transport and the Regions, 1996–99; *b* 28 Feb. 1940; *s* of Sir Samuel Goldman, *qv*; *m* 1964, Anne Rosemary Lane; three *s*. *Educ:* Marlborough College; Peterhouse, Cambridge (BA). International Computers Ltd, 1961–73; entered Civil Service, DoE, 1973; Private Sec. to Sec. of State for Transport, 1976–78; Asst Sec., 1977; seconded to HM Treasury, 1981–83; Under Sec., 1984. Non-exec. Dir, Hugh Baird & Sons, 1985–86. Chm., Eur. Air Traffic Control Harmonisation and Integration Prog., 1994–99; Vice-Pres., Eur. Civil Aviation Conf., 1997–99; Pres., Eurocontrol Council, 1998–99. Special Advr to H of L Select Cttee on Europe, 2001. Hon. CRAeS 1997. Eur. Regl Airlines Award, 1993. *Recreations:* music, sailing, writing doggerel.

GOLDMAN, Prof. John Michael, DM; FRCP, FRCPath, FMedSci; Professor of Leukaemia Biology and Therapy, Imperial College School of Medicine, since 1987; Chairman, Department of Haematology, Imperial College School of Medicine/Hammersmith Hospital, since 1994; Director, Leukaemia Research Fund Centre for Adult Leukaemia, since 1992; *b* 30 Nov. 1938; *s* of Carl Heinz Goldman and Berthe Goldman (*née* Brandt); *m* 1st, 1967, Jeannine Fuller (marr. diss.); one *d*; 2nd, 1972, Constance Wilson; one *s* one *d*. *Educ:* Westminster Sch. (Schol.); Magdalen Coll., Oxford (Ann Shaw Schol.; BM BCh 1963; DM 1981); St Bartholomew's Hosp., London. FRCP 1979; FRCPath 1986. Fellow in Hematology, Univ. of Miami, 1967–68; Fellow in Oncology, Massachusetts Gen. Hosp./Harvard Univ., 1968–70; mem. staff, MRC Leukaemia Unit, 1970–92, Cons. Haematologist, 1976–, Hammersmith Hosp. Ham-Wasserman Lectr, Amer. Soc. Hematology, 1997; McCredie Lectr, Leukemia Soc. Amer., 2000. Ed., Bone Marrow Transplantation, 1985–. Med. Dir, Anthony Nolan Bone Marrow Trust, 1987–; Scientific Advr, Kay Kendall Leukaemia Fund, 1991–; Chm. Adv. Cttee, Internat. Bone Marrow Transplant Registry, 1998–2001. President: Internat. Soc. For Exptl Hematology, 1984–85; Eur. Gp for Blood and Marrow Transplantation, 1990–94; Eur. Hematology Assoc., 1996–98. FMedSci 1999. Hon. MD: Louvain, 1993; Poitiers, 1995. *Publications:* contrib. scientific papers on haematology, leukaemia, lymphoma, stem cell transplantation and molecular biol. *Recreations:* reading, ski-ing, riding. *Address:* Department of Haematology, ICSM/Hammersmith Hospital, Du Cane Road, W12 0NN. *T:* (020) 8383 3238; 33 Northumberland Place, W2 5AS. *T:* (020) 7727 6092.

GOLDMAN, Sir Samuel, KCB 1969 (CB 1964); *b* 10 March 1912; *y s* of late Philip and late Sarah Goldman; *m* 1st, 1933, Pearl Marre (*d* 1941); one *s*; 2nd, 1943, Patricia Rosemary Hodges (*d* 1990). *Educ:* Davenant Foundation Sch.; Raine's Sch.; London Sch. of Economics, London Univ. Inter-Collegiate Scholar. BSc (Econ.), First Class Hons in Economics and Gladstone Memorial Prize, 1931; MSc (Econ.), 1933. Hutchinson Silver Medallist. Moody's Economist Services, 1934–38; Joseph Sebag & Co., 1938–39; Bank of England, 1940–47. Entered Civil Service, 1947, as Statistician in Central Statistical Office; transferred to Treasury, Sept. 1947; Chief Statistician, 1948; Asst Sec., 1952; Under-Sec., 1960–62; Third Sec., 1962–68; Second Perm. Sec., 1968–72. UK Alternate Executive Dir, International Bank, 1961–62. Exec. Dir, 1972–74, Man. Dir, 1974–76, Orion Bank Ltd. Chm., Henry Ansbacher Holdings Ltd and Henry Ansbacher Ltd, 1976–82. Chm., Covent Garden Market Authority, 1976–81. Hon. Fellow LSE. *Publication:* Public Expenditure Management and Control, 1973. *Recreations:* music, gardening. *Address:* 3 Little Tangley, Wonersh, Guildford, Surrey GU5 0PW. *T:* (01483) 568913.

See also A. J. Goldman.

GOLDMARK, Peter Carl, Jr; Chairman and Chief Executive Officer, International Herald Tribune, since 1998; *b* 2 Dec. 1940; *m* 1964, Aliette Misson. *Educ:* Harvard Univ. (BA Govt *magna cum laude* with Highest Hons 1962; Phi Beta Kappa). History teacher, Putney Sch., Vermont, 1962–64; US Office of Econ. Opportunity, Washington, 1965–66; City of New York: Exec. Asst to Dir of Budget, 1966–68; Asst Budget Dir for Prog. Planning and Analysis, 1968–70; Exec. Asst to Mayor, 1970–71; Sec. of Human Services, Commonwealth of Massachusetts, 1971–74; Dir of Budget, State of NY, 1975–77; Exec. Dir, Port Authy of NY and NJ, 1977–85; Sen. Vice Pres., Times Mirror Co., 1985–88; Pres., Rockefeller Foundn, 1988–97. *Address:* International Herald Tribune, 6 bis rue des Graviers, 92521 Neuilly, Cedex, France.

GOLDREIN, Iain Saville; QC 1997; a Recorder, since 1999; *b* 10 Aug. 1952; *s* of Neville Clive Goldrein, *qv*; *m* 1980, Margaret de Haas, *qv*; one *s* one *d*. *Educ:* Merchant Taylors' Sch., Crosby; Hebrew Univ., Jerusalem; Pembroke Coll., Cambridge (exhibnr, Ziegler Prize for Law; Cambridge Squire Schol. for Law). Called to the Bar, Inner Temple, 1975; Jt Head, No 7 Harrington Street (formerly Corn Exchange) Chambers, Liverpool, 1989–; Asst Recorder, 1995–99. Mem., Mental Health Review Tribunal, 1999–. Vis. Prof., Nottingham Law Sch., 1991. Mediator, Acad. of Experts, 1992 (Companion, 1992). Fellow, Soc. of Advanced Legal Studies, 1998. Jt Ed.-in-Chief, Genetics Law Monitor, 2000–. *Publications:* Personal Injury Litigation: practice and precedents, 1985; Ship Sale and Purchase, Law and Technique, 1985, 3rd edn (Editor in Chief, with C. Chance) 1998; (with K. H. P. Wilkinson) Commercial Litigation: pre-emptive remedies, 1987, 3rd edn (with K. H. P. Wilkinson and P. M. Kershaw) 1996; with Sir J. Jacob: Bullen and Leake and Jacob's Precedents of Pleadings, 13th edn 1990; Pleadings, Principles and Practice, 1990; with M. d Haas: Property Distribution on Divorce, 1983, 2nd edn 1985; Butterworths Personal Injury Litigation Service, 1988–; Structured Settlements, 1993, 2nd edn 1997; Medical Negligence: cost effective case management, 1997; (ed jtly) Insurance Disputes (loose-leaf), 1999–; (ed jtly) Civil Court Practice, 2 vols, 2000; (also ed jtly) Personal Injury Major Claims Handling: cost effective case management, 2000. *Recreations:* Classical Hebrew, history, new ideas, anything aeronautical. *Address:* 7 Harrington Street, Liverpool L2 9QA. *T:* (0151) 227 1081; 12 King's Bench Walk, Temple, EC4Y 7EL. *T:* (020) 7583 0811. *Clubs:* Athenæum, Racquets (Liverpool).

GOLDREIN, Margaret Ruth; *see* de Haas, M. R.

GOLDREIN, Neville Clive, CBE 1991; Consultant, Deacon Goldrein Green, Solicitors, 1985–92; Senior Partner, Goldrein & Co., 1953–85; *b* 28 Aug.; *s* of Saville and Nina Goldrein; *m* 1949, Dr Sonia Sumner, MB, BS Dunelm; one *s* one *d*. *Educ:* Hymers Coll., Hull; Pembroke Coll., Cambridge (MA). Served Army: commnd E Yorks Regt; served East Africa Comd (Captain). Admitted Solicitor of the Supreme Court, 1949; former Dep. Circuit Judge. Mem., Crosby Bor. Council, 1957–71; Mayor of Crosby, 1966–67, Dep. Mayor, 1967–68; Mem., Lancs CC, 1965–74; Merseyside County Council: Mem., 1973–86; Dep. Leader, Cons. Gp, 1974–77; Vice-Chm. of Council, 1977–80; Leader, 1980–81; Leader, Cons. Gp, 1981–86. Chm., Crosby Constituency Cons. Assoc., 1986–89. Area Vice-Pres., Sefton, St John Ambulance, 1980–87 (Chm., S Sefton Div., 1975–87); Member: NW Econ. Planning Council, 1966–72; Bd of Deputies of British Jews, 1966–85, 1992–; Council, Liverpool Univ., 1977–81; Council, Merseyside Chamber of Commerce, 1987– (Chairman: Envmt and Energy Cttee; Rivers Cttee, 1990–93; Police Liaison Cttee, 1994–); Regl Affairs Cttee, British Assoc. of Chambers of Commerce, 1993–97. Director: Merseyside Economic Develt Co. Ltd, 1981–87; Merseyside Waste Derived Fuels Ltd, 1983–86. Vice-Pres., Crosby Mencap, 1967–;

Chm., Crosby Hall Residential Trust Appeal, 1989–91. Chm., Liverpool Royal Court Theatre Foundn, 1994–. Governor, Merchant Taylors' Sch., Crosby, 1965–74. *Recreations:* videography, photography, music, grandchildren, freelance journalism. *Address:* Torreno, St Andrew's Road, Blundellsands, Merseyside L23 7UR. *T:* and *Fax:* (0151) 924 2065; *e-mail:* goldrein@aol.com. *Club:* Athenæum (Liverpool).

See also I. S. Goldrein.

GOLDRING, Hon. Sir John (Bernard), Kt 1999; **Hon. Mr Justice Goldring;** a Judge of the High Court, Queen's Bench Division, since 1999; *b* 9 Nov. 1944; *s* of Joseph and Marianne Goldring; *m* 1970, Wendy Margaret Lancaster Bennett; two *s. Educ:* Wyggeston Grammar Sch.; Exeter Univ. (LLB). Called to the Bar, Lincoln's Inn, 1969, Bencher, 1996. Standing Prosecuting Counsel to Inland Revenue, Midland and Oxford Circuit, 1985–87; QC 1987; a Recorder, 1987–99; a Dep. Sen. Judge, Sovereign Base Areas, Cyprus, 1991–99; a Dep. High Court Judge, 1996–99; a Judge of the Courts of Appeal of Jersey and Guernsey, 1998–99. *Recreation:* gardening. *Address:* Royal Courts of Justice, Strand, WC2A 2LL.

GOLDRING, Mark Ian; Chief Executive, Voluntary Service Overseas, since 1999; *b* 8 March 1957; *s* of Stephen and Pamela Goldring; *m* 1989, Rachel Carnegie; one *s* one *d. Educ:* Keble Coll., Oxford (BA Law 1979); LSE (MSc Social Policy and Planning in Developing Countries 1989). VSO Volunteer Teacher, Sarawak, 1979–81; Legal Researcher, Linklaters & Paines, 1982; Field Officer, Caribbean, 1983–85, Field Dir, Bhutan, 1985–88, VSO; UNDP Asst Rep., 1990–91, Oxfam Country Rep., 1991–94, Bangladesh; DFID Social Develt Advr, Pacific, 1994–95; VSO Overseas Dir, 1995–99. *Recreations:* cycling, squash, Rugby. *Address:* Voluntary Service Overseas, 317 Putney Bridge Road, SW15 2PN. *T:* (020) 8780 7235.

GOLDRING, Mary Sheila, OBE 1987; economist; presenter, Goldring Audit, Channel 4, 1992, 1993, 1994, 1995. *Educ:* Our Lady's Priory, Sussex; Lady Margaret Hall, Oxford (PPE). Air and Science correspondent, 1949–74, Business editor, 1966–74, Economist Newspaper; economist and broadcaster, 1974–; *television:* presenter: Analysis, BBC, 1977–87; Answering Back, Channel 4 interviews, 1989–91. Mem. Selection Cttee, Harkness Fellowships, 1980–86. Trustee, Science Museum, 1987–97. Fawley Foundn Lect., 1992. CRAeS 1995. Hon. DLitt UWE, 1994. Blue Circle Award for industrial journalism, 1979; Sony Radio Award for best current affairs programme (Analysis: Post-Recession Britain), 1985; Industrial Journalist Award, Industrial Soc., 1985; Outstanding Personal Contribution to Radio, Broadcasting Press Guild, 1986; Harold Wincott Award for Broadcasting, 1991; Industrial Journalist of the Year, Industrial Soc. and BP, 1991, 1995. *Publication:* Economics of Atomic Energy, 1957. *Recreation:* small-scale landscaping. *Address:* 37 Sloane Avenue, SW3 3JB.

GOLDS, Anthony Arthur, CMG 1971; LVO 1961; HM Diplomatic Service, retired; Director, British National Committee, International Chamber of Commerce, 1977–83; *b* 31 Oct. 1919; *s* of late Arthur Oswald Golds and Florence Golds (*née* Massey); *m* 1944, Suzanne Macdonald Young; one *s* one *d. Educ:* King's Sch., Macclesfield; New Coll., Oxford (Scholar). HM Forces (Royal Armoured Corps), 1939–46; CRO, 1948; 1st Sec., Calcutta and Delhi, 1951–53; Commonwealth Office, 1953–56; Head of Chancery, British Embassy, Ankara, 1957–59; Karachi, 1959–61; Counsellor in Commonwealth Office and Foreign Office, 1962–65; Head of Joint Malaysia/Indonesia Dept, 1964–65; Counsellor, HM Embassy, Rome, 1965–70; Ambassador to the Republic of Cameroon, the Republic of Gabon and the Republic of Equatorial Guinea, 1970–72; High Comr to Bangladesh, 1972–74; Senior Civilian Instructor, RCDS, 1975–76. *Recreations:* music, cricket, golf, literature. *Address:* 4 Oakfield Gardens, SE19 1HF. *T:* (020) 8670 7621. *Club:* Dulwich & Sydenham Hill Golf.

GOLDSACK, Alan Raymond; QC 1990; **His Honour Judge Goldsack;** a Circuit Judge, since 1994; *b* 13 June 1947; *s* of Raymond Frederick Goldsack, MBE and Mildred Agnes Goldsack (*née* Jones); *m* 1971, Christine Marion Clarke; three *s* one *d. Educ:* Hastings Grammar School; Leicester Univ. (LLB). Called to the Bar, Gray's Inn, 1970; a Recorder, 1988–94. *Recreations:* gardening, walking. *Address:* Sheffield Crown Court, 50 West Bar, Sheffield S3 8PH.

GOLDSACK, John Redman, MBE 1971; consultant in tropical agriculture and development, since 1993; *b* 15 Aug. 1932; 2nd *s* of late Bernard Frank and Dorothy Goldsack; *m* 1962, Madeleine Amelia Rowena, *d* of late Stanley and Grace Kibbler; two *s* one *d. Educ:* Sutton Grammar Sch., Surrey; Wye Coll., London Univ. (BScAgric); Queens' Coll., Cambridge (DipAgric); Imperial Coll. of Tropical Agric., Trinidad (DTA). Agricl Officer, HMOCS, Kenya, 1956; Hd of Soil Conservation and Planning Officer, Min. of Lands and Settlement, Kenya, 1963–67; Hd of Land Develt Div., Min. of Agriculture, Kenya, 1967–70; Asst Agric. Advr, ODM, 1970–74; Agriculture Adviser: S African Develt Div., 1974–78; ME Develt Div., 1979–81; E. African Develt Div., 1981–83; Sen. Agric. Advr, Asia Div., ODA, 1983–86; Dep. Chief Natural Resources Advr and Prin. Agriculture Advr, ODA, 1986–88; Minister and UK Perm. Rep. to UNFAO, Rome, 1988–93. Chm., Prog. Adv. Cttee, Natural Resources Systems Progs, ODA, 1995–99. *Recreations:* cricket, golf, natural history. *Address:* Bradford Peverell Farmhouse, Bradford Peverell, Dorchester, Dorset DT2 9SF. *T:* and *Fax:* (01305) 266543. *Clubs:* Farmers', MCC.

GOLDSCHMIED, Marco Lorenzo Sinnott, RIBA; President, Royal Institute of British Architects, 1999–2001; Founder Partner and Managing Director, Richard Rogers Partnership, since 1977; *b* 28 March 1944; *s* of Guido Rodolfo Goldschmied and Elinor Violet (*née* Sinnott); *m* 1969, Andrea Halvorsen; four *s* one *d. Educ:* Architectural Assoc. (AA Dip. 1969); Reading Univ. (MSc 1986). RIBA 1971. Associate Partner, Piano & Rogers, 1971–77; Vice-Pres., Richard Rogers Japan KK, 1988–; Chm., Thames Wharf Studios Ltd, 1984–. Teacher: AA, 1971; Glasgow Sch. of Art, 1999; Lectr, RIBA, 1981–99. Mem., Architects Registration Bd, 1997– (Mem., European Adv. Gp, 1998–); Trustee, Architectural Assoc., 1991–93; Chm., European Awards, 1996–99, Educn Review, 1998–99, C4 Stirling Prize, 2001, RIBA. *Projects* include: Lloyd's HQ, City of London, 1978 (Civic Trust Award, 1987; RIBA Award, 1988); Fleetguard Manufg and Distribn Centre, Quimper, France, 1979–81; Inmos Microprocessor Factory, Newport, 1982 (British Steel Design Award, 1982; RIBA Award, 1983); PA Technology Res. Centre, Princeton, 1983; Linn-Sondek HQ, Glasgow, 1985 (RIBA Award); Billingsgate Mkt Restoration and Conversion, 1988 (Civic Trust Award, 1989); Reuters Computer Centre, London, 1988 (RIBA Award, 1990); Pumping Station, Victoria Docks, 1989; Channel 4 HQ, 1994 (RIBA Award, and RFAC Award, 1995); European Court of Human Rights, Strasbourg, 1995; Learning Resource Centre, Thames Valley Univ., 1996 (RIBA Award, 1998); Europier Passenger Terminal, Heathrow, 1996 (RIBA Award, and British Steel Award, 1997); Terminal 5, Heathrow, 1990–; Bordeaux Law Courts, 1998; Lloyd's Register of Shipping HQ, 1999; Daiwa Europe Office, 1999; Millennium Dome, Greenwich, 1999; Offices and Laboratories, Gifu, Japan, 1999; Lloyd's Register of Shipping HQ, 1999. Chm., Appeal for Care of Victims of Torture, Med. Foundn, 1999–. TV and radio interviews. Hon. Mem., AIA. Hon. FRSA. *Publications:* (jtly) Architecture 98, 1998; articles in jls. *Recreations:* twentieth century history, Europe etymology, architecture, ski-ing, meditation, cooking, The Simpsons. *Address:* (office) Thames Wharf, Rainville Road, W6 9HA. *T:* (020) 7385 1235. *Club:* Reform.

GOLDSMITH, family name of **Baron Goldsmith**.

GOLDSMITH, Baron *cr* 1999 (Life Peer), of Allerton in the county of Merseyside; **Peter Henry Goldsmith;** PC 2001; QC 1987; Attorney General, since 2001; *b* 5 Jan. 1950; *s* of late Sydney Elland Goldsmith, solicitor, and of Myra Nurick; *m* 1974, Joy; three *s* one *d. Educ:* Quarry Bank High Sch., Liverpool; Gonville and Caius Coll., Cambridge (Sen. Schol., Tapp Postgrad. Schol., Schuldham Plate, 1968–71; MA); UCL (LLM 1972). Called to the Bar, Gray's Inn (Birkenhead Schol.), 1972, Bencher, 1994; Avocat, Barreau de Paris, 1997; a Jun. Counsel to the Crown, Common Law, 1985–87; a Recorder, 1991–2001. Chairman: Bar Council, 1995 (Chairman: Legal Services Cttee, 1992–94; Internat. Relations Cttee, 1996); Bar Pro Bono Unit, 1996–2001 (Pres., 2001); Financial Reporting Review Panel, 1997–99 (Mem., 1995–97); Mem. Council, 1996–2001, Co-Chm., Human Rights Inst., 1998–2001, Internat. Bar Assoc. Personal Rep. of Prime Minister to Convention to draft EU Charter of Fundamental Rights, 1999–2000. Mem., Jt Human Rights Select Cttee, 2001. Member: Council, Public Concern at Work, 1995–2001; Exec. Cttee, GB–China Centre, 1997–2001; Adv. Bd, Cambridge Centre for Commercial and Corporate Law, 1998–. Fellow, American Law Inst., 1997. *Publications:* (contrib.) Common Land, Common Bond; articles in nat., internat. and legal press. *Address:* House of Lords, SW1A 0PW.

GOLDSMITH, Alexander Benedict Hayum; Director: Cavamont Investment Advisors Ltd, since 1998; Book Runner Ltd, since 1999; *b* 10 Dec. 1960; *s* of Edward René David Goldsmith, *qv* and Gillian Marion (*née* Pretty); *m* 1990, Louisa Kate Slack; one *s. Educ:* Westminster Sch.; Jesus Coll., Cambridge (MA Social Anthropol. 1986). Researcher and fundraiser for Survival Internat., 1986; Publisher and Editor, Envmt Digest, 1987–90; Editor: Geographical Magazine, 1991–94; People and Places in Peril series, 1995; Green Futures mag., 1996–98. Trustee, Cancer Prevention Soc., 2000–. *Recreation:* walking. *Clubs:* Groucho; Travellers (Paris).

GOLDSMITH, Alexander Kinglake, (Alick); Director, Export Group for the Constructional Industries, since 1991; *b* 16 Jan. 1938; *s* of Maj.-Gen. Robert Frederick Kinglake Goldsmith, CB, CBE and Brenda (*née* Bartlett); *m* 1971, Deirdre Stafford; one *s* one *d. Educ:* Sherborne; Trinity Coll., Oxford (MA Modern History). National Service, 1956–58 (DCLI and Queen's Own Nigeria Regt). Asst Principal, CRO, 1961; Hindi student, SOAS, 1962; Third Sec., New Delhi, 1963; FCO, 1967; First Sec. (Inf.), Wellington, NZ, 1971; FCO, 1975; Head of Chancery, E Berlin, 1978; FCO, 1980; Hd of Commonwealth Co-ordination Dept, FCO, 1982; seconded to Hong Kong Govt, 1984; Consul-Gen., Hamburg, 1986–90. *Recreations:* walking, swimming. *Address:* c/o Lloyds TSB, Butler Place, SW1H 0PR. *Club:* Royal Automobile.

GOLDSMITH, Edward René David; author; Publisher, The Ecologist, since 1970 (Editor, 1970–89, and since 1997); *b* 8 Nov. 1928; *s* of late Frank B. H. Goldsmith, OBE, TD, MP (C) for Stowmarket, Suffolk, 1910–18, and Marcelle (*née* Mouiller); *m* 1st, 1953, Gillian Marion Pretty; one *s* two *d*; 2nd, 1981, Katherine Victoria James; two *s. Educ:* Magdalen Coll., Oxford (MA Hons). Adjunct Associate Prof., Univ. of Michigan, 1975; Vis. Prof., Sangamon State Univ., 1984. Contested (Ecology Party): Eye, Feb. 1974; Cornwall and Plymouth, European parly election, 1979. Hon. Right Livelihood Award, 1991. Chevalier, Légion d'Honneur, 1991. *Publications:* (ed) Can Britain Survive?, 1971; (with R. Prescott-Allen) A Blueprint for Survival, 1972; The Stable Society, 1977; (ed with J. M. Brunetti) La Médecine à la Question, 1981; (with N. Hildyard) The Social and Environmental Effects of Large Dams, vol. I, 1984, (ed) vol. II, 1986, (ed) vol. III, 1992; (ed with N. Hildyard) Green Britain or Industrial Wasteland?, 1986; (ed with N. Hildyard) The Earth Report, 1988; The Great U-Turn, 1988; (with N. Hildyard and others) 5,000 Days to Save the Planet, 1990; The Way: an ecological world view, 1992; (ed with J. Mander) The Case against the Global Economy and for a Turn Towards the Local, 1996. *Address:* 9 Montague Road, Richmond, Surrey TW10 6QW. *Clubs:* Brooks's; Travellers (Paris).

See also A. B. H. Goldsmith.

GOLDSMITH, Harvey Anthony, CBE 1996; Chief Executive, Artiste Management Productions Ltd; Managing Director, TBA Entertainment Corporation (Europe) Ltd, since 2000; *b* 4 March 1946; *s* of Sydney and Minnie Goldsmith; *m* 1971, Diana Gorman; one *s. Educ:* Christ's Coll.; Brighton Coll. of Tech. Partner, Big O Posters, 1966–67; organised first free open-air concert in Parliament Hill Fields, 1968; (with Michael Alfandary) opened Round House, Camden Town, 1968; Crystal Palace Gdn Party series of concerts, 1969–72; merged with John Smith Entertainments, 1970; formed Harvey Goldsmith Entertainments (rock tours promotions co.), 1976; acquired Allied Entertainments Gp (rock concert promotions co.), 1984; (with Mark McCormack) formed Classical Productions (to produce operas), 1986. Promoter and producer of pop, rock and classical musical events, including: *concerts:* Bruce Springsteen; The Rolling Stones; Elton John; The Who; Pink Floyd; *opera:* Aida, 1988 and 1998, Carmen, 1989, Tosca, 1991, Earls Court; Pavarotti at Wembley, 1986; Pavarotti in the Park, 1991; The Three Tenors, 1996. Dir, British Red Cross Events Ltd, 2000–; Member: London Tourist Bd, 1994– (Dir); Prague Heritage Fund, 1994–. Chairman: Concert Promoters' Assoc., 1986–; Nat. Music Fest., 1991; Co-Chm., President's Club, 1994–2000; Vice-Chm., Action Mgt Bd, Prince's Trust, 1993–; Trustee: Band Aid, 1985–; Live Aid, 1985–; Royal Opera House, 1995–; Vice-President: REACT, 1989–; Music Users' Council, 1994–; Mem., Communications Panel, BRCS, 1992–. *Recreation:* golf. *Address:* Artiste Management Productions Ltd, 2nd Floor, 32–38 Osnaburgh Street, NW1 3ND. *T:* (020) 7224 1992, *Fax:* (020) 7224 0111. *Clubs:* Royal Automobile; Hartsbourne Golf; Vale de Lobo Golf.

GOLDSMITH, John Stuart, CB 1984; Director General Defence Accounts, Ministry of Defence, 1980–84; *b* 2 Nov. 1924; *o s* of R. W. and S. E. Goldsmith; *m* 1948, Brenda; two *s* one *d. Educ:* Whitgift Middle Sch.; St Catharine's Coll., Cambridge. Royal Signals, 1943–47 (Captain). War Office, 1948; Principal, 1952; Treasury, 1961–64; Asst Sec., MoD, 1964; RCDS 1971; Asst Under-Sec. of State, MoD, 1973; Chm. Civil Service Selection Bd, 1973. *Recreations:* gardening, jazz, travel. *Address:* Cobthorne House, Church Lane, Rode, Frome BA11 6PN. *T:* (01373) 830681.

GOLDSMITH, Philip; Director (observation of the Earth and its environment), European Space Agency, Paris, 1985–93; *b* 16 April 1930; *s* of late Stanley Thomas Goldsmith and Ida Goldsmith (*née* Rawlinson); *m* 1st, 1952, Daphne (*d* 1983), *d* of William Webb; two *s* two *d*; 2nd, 1990, Gail Lorraine. *Educ:* Almondbury Grammar Sch.; Pembroke Coll., Oxford (MA). Meteorologist with the Meteorological Office, 1947–54, incl. National Service, RAF, 1948–50; Research Scientist, AERE Harwell, 1957–67; Meteorological Office: Asst Director (Cloud Physics Research), 1967–76; Dep. Director (Physical Research), 1976–82; Dir (Res.), 1982–85. President: Royal Meteorological Society, 1980–82; Internat. Commn on Atmospheric Chem. and Global Pollution, 1979–83. *Publications:* articles in scientific jls mainly on atmospheric physics and chemistry and space research related to associated environmental concerns. *Recreations:* golf, gardening, antiques, old cars. *Address:* Hill House, Broad Lane, Bracknell, Berks RG12 9BY. *Clubs:* East Berks Golf, Woodsome Hall Golf.

GOLDSMITH, Walter Kenneth, FCA; CIMgt; Chairman, PremiSys Technologies plc (formerly WML, then PremiSys, Group plc), since 1998; *b* 19 Jan. 1938; *s* of late Lionel and of Phoebe Goldsmith; *m* 1961, Rosemary Adele, *d* of Joseph and Hannah Salter; two *s* two *d. Educ:* Merchant Taylors' School. Admitted Inst. of Chartered Accountants, 1960; Manager, Mann Judd & Co., 1964; joined Black & Decker Ltd, 1966: Dir of Investment, Finance and Administration, Europe, 1967; Gen. Man., 1970; Man. Dir, 1974; Chief Executive and European Dir, 1975; Black & Decker USA, 1976–79: Corporate Vice-Pres. and Pres. Pacific Internat. Operations; Dir Gen., Inst. of Dirs, 1979–84; Chm., Korn/Ferry International Ltd, 1984–86; Gp Planning and Marketing Dir, Trusthouse Forte plc, 1985–87; Chm., Food from Britain, 1987–90; Dep. Chm., British Food & Farming Ltd, 1990–. Chairman: Ansoll Estates Ltd, 1989–98; Trident, later Flying Flowers, Ltd, 1990–99; Ewart Parsons, 1992–97; Jumbo Internat. plc (formerly Self Sealing Systems Internat.), 1995–; Royal Stafford Tableware Ltd, 1997–; ASAP Internat. Gp plc, 2000–01; Dep. Chm., MICE Gp, 1994–95; Director: Bank Leumi (UK) plc, 1984– (Member: Audit-Remuneration Cttee, 1988–; Credit Cttee, 1986–); Trusthouse Forte Inc., 1985–87; The Winning Streak Ltd, 1985–2000; Isys plc (Dep. Chm.), 1987–99; CLS Group, 1992–2000; Chambers & Newman, 1994–2000; Betterware, 1995–97 (Chm., 1990–97); Fitness First plc, 1997–; Beagle Hldgs, 1997–; Lifestyle Products Ltd, 1997–2000; Guiton Gp plc, 1998–; SCS Upholstery plc, 1998–; Mem. Adv. Bd, Kalchas, 1990–97; Advr to Rotch Property Gp, 1996–. Member: English Tourist Board, 1982–84; BTA, 1984–86; Vice-Pres., British Overseas Trade Gp for Israel, 1992–2000 (Chm., 1987–91); Chm., Governing Bd, Marketing Quality Assurance, 1990–. Treas., Leo Baeck Coll., 1987–89. Council Member: Co-operation Ireland, 1985–90; RASE, 1988–95. Trustee, Israel Diaspora Trust, 1982–92; Chm., Grange Hospice Project, 1994–99. FRSA. Liveryman, Worshipful Co. of Chartered Accountants in England and Wales, 1985. Free Enterprise Award, Aims for Industry, 1984. *Publications:* (with D. Clutterbuck): The Winning Streak, 1984; The Winning Streak Workout Book, 1985; The Winning Streak: Mark 2, 1997; (with Berry Ritchie) The New Elite, 1987. *Recreations:* boating, music. *Address:* c/o Glenmore Investments Ltd, 52 Queen Anne Street, W1M 9LA.

GOLDSTAUB, Anthony James; QC 1992; barrister; a Recorder of the Crown Court, since 1999; *b* 26 May 1949; *er s* of late Henry Goldstaub, engineer, and of Hilda (*née* Bendix); *m* 1st, 1982 (marr. diss. 1989); two *s*; 2nd, 1993, Moira Pooley; one *d. Educ:* Highgate Sch.; Nottingham Univ. (LLB 1971). Called to the Bar, Middle Temple, 1972. Common Law litigation, 1972–. *Address:* 24 The Ropewalk, Nottingham NG1 5EF. *T:* (0115) 947 2581.

GOLDSTAUB, Jane Hilary, (Mrs T. C. Goldstaub); *see* Procter, J. H.

GOLDSTEIN, Alfred, CBE 1977; FREng; consulting engineer, 1951–93; Senior Partner, Travers Morgan & Partners, 1972–85; Chairman, Travers Morgan Group, 1985–87; *b* 9 Oct. 1926; *s* of late Sigmund and Regina Goldstein; *m* 1959, Anne Milford, *d* of late Col R. A. M. Tweedy and of Maureen Evans, and step *d* of Hubert Evans; two *s. Educ:* Rotherham Grammar Sch.; Imperial Coll., Univ. of London. BSc (Eng); ACGI 1946; DIC. FICE 1959; FIStructE 1959; FIHT (FIHE 1959); MConsE 1959; FREng (FEng 1979); FCIT; FCGI 1984. Partner, R. Travers Morgan & Partners, 1951; responsible for planning, design and supervision of construction of major road and bridge projects and for planning and transport studies, incl. M23, Belfast Transportation Plan, Clifton Bridge, Nottingham, Elizabeth Bridge, Cambridge, Itchen Bridge, Southampton. Transport Consultant to Govt SE Jt Planning Team for SE Regional Plan; in charge London Docklands Redevelopment Study; Cost Benefit Study for 2nd Sydney Airport for Govt of Australia; Mem. Cttee on Review of Railway Finances, 1982; UK full mem., EC Article 83 Cttee (Transport), 1982–85; TRRL Visitor on Transport Res. and Safety, 1983–87. Member: Building Research Bd, subseq. Adv. Cttee on Building Research, 1963–66; Civil Engrg EDC on Contracting in Civil Engrg since Banwell, 1965–67; Baroness Sharp's Adv. Cttee on Urban Transport Manpower Study, 1967–69; Commn of Inquiry on Third London Airport, 1968–70; Urban Motorways Cttee, 1969–72; Genesys Bd, 1969–74; Chairman: DoE and Dept of Transport Planning and Tnspt Res. Adv. Council, 1973–79; DoE Environmental Bd, 1975–78; Mem., TRRL Adv. Cttee on Transport, 1974–80; Mem. Bd, Coll. of Estate Management, Reading Univ., 1979–92. *Publications:* papers and lectures (inc. Criteria for the Siting of Major Airports, 4th World Airports Conf., 1973; Highways and Community Response, 9th Rees Jeffreys Triennial Lecture, RTPI, 1975; Environment and the Economic Use of Energy, (Plenary Paper, Hong Kong Transport Conf., 1982); Decision-taking under Uncertainty in the Roads Sector, PIARC Sydney, 1983; Investment in Transport (Keynote address, CIT Conf., 1983); Buses: social enterprise and business (main paper, 9th annual conf., Bus and Coach Council, 1983); Public Road Transport: a time for change (Keynote address, 6th Aust. passenger trans. conf., 1985); Private Enterprise and Highways (Nat. Res. Council conf., Baltimore, 1986); The Expert and the Public: local values and national choice (Florida Univ.), 1987; Travel in London: is chaos inevitable? (LRT), 1989). *Recreations:* carpentry, music, bridge. *Address:* Kent Edge, Crockham Hill, Edenbridge, Kent TN8 6TA. *T:* (01732) 866227. *Club:* Athenæum.

GOLDSTEIN, Prof. Harvey, FBA 1996; Professor of Statistical Methods, Institute of Education, University of London, since 1977; *b* 30 Oct. 1939; *s* of Jack and Millicent Goldstein; *m* 1970, Barbara Collinge; one *s. Educ:* Oakthorpe Primary Sch., London; Hendon Grammar Sch.; Manchester Univ. (BSc Hons); University College London (Dip. Stats). Lectr in Statistics, Inst. of Child Health, 1964–71; Head of Statistics Section, Nat. Children's Bureau, 1971–76. *Publications:* (jtly) From Birth to Seven, 1972; (jtly) Assessment of Skeletal Maturity and Prediction of Adult Height, 1976; The Design and Analysis of Longitudinal Studies, 1979; (with C. Gipps) Monitoring Children, 1983; Multilevel Statistical Models, 1995; (with T. Lewis) Assessment, 1996; (with A. Leyland) Multilevel Modelling of Health Statistics, 2001. *Recreations:* playing the flute, walking, cycling, squash, tennis. *Address:* Institute of Education, 20 Bedford Way, WC1H 0AL. *T:* (020) 7612 6652.

GOLDSTEIN, Joan Delano, (Mrs Julius Goldstein); *see* Aiken, J. D.

GOLDSTEIN, Prof. Joseph Leonard; physician, genetics educator; Paul J. Thomas Professor of Medicine, and Chairman, Department of Molecular Genetics, since 1977, Regental Professor, since 1985, University of Texas Southwestern Medical (formerly Health Science) Center at Dallas (Member of Faculty, since 1972); *b* 18 April 1940; *s* of Isadore E. and Fannie A. Goldstein. *Educ:* Washington and Lee University (BS); Univ. of Texas Health Science Center at Dallas (MD). Intern, then Resident in Medicine, Mass Gen. Hosp., Boston, 1966–68; clinical associate, NIH, 1968–70; Postdoctoral Fellow, Univ. of Washington, Seattle, 1970–72. Harvey Soc. Lecture, Rockefeller Univ., 1977. Member: Sci. Rev. Bd, Howard Hughes Med. Inst., 1978–84, Med. Adv. Bd, 1985–90 (Chm., 1995–); Bd of Dirs, Passano Foundn, 1985–; Sci. Adv. Bd, Welch Foundn, 1986–; Bd of Consultants, Meml Sloan-Kettering Cancer Center, 1992–; Bd of Trustees, Rockefeller Univ., 1994–; Bd of Govs, Scripps Res. Inst., 1996–. Fellow, Salk Inst., 1983–94. Member, editorial board: Jl Clin. Investigation, 1977–82; Annual Review of Genetics, 1980–85; Arteriosclerosis, 1981–87; Jl Biol Chemistry, 1981–85; Cell, 1983–; Science, 1985–98; Genomics, 1988–; Mol. Biol. of the Cell, 1992–97; Proc. Nat. Acad. Scis, 1992–. Member: Nat. Acad. of Scis (Lounsbery Award, 1979); Amer. Acad. of Arts and Scis, and other bodies; Foreign Mem., Royal Soc., 1991. Hon. DSc: Chicago, 1982; Rensselaer Polytechnic Inst., 1982; Washington and Lee, 1986; Paris-Sud, 1988; Buenos Aires, 1990; Southern Methodist, 1993; Miami, 1996. Numerous awards from scientific instns, incl. Pfizer Award in Enzyme Chemistry, Amer. Chem. Soc., 1976; award in biol and med. scis, NY Acad. Scis, 1981; Albert Lasker Award in Basic Science (with Michael Brown), 1985; Nobel Prize (with Michael Brown) for Physiology or Medicine, 1985; Amer. Coll. of Physicians Award, 1986; US Nat. Medal of Science, 1988; Distinguished Alumni Award, NIH, 1991. *Publications:* (jtly) The Metabolic Basis of Inherited Diseases, 5th edn 1983; papers on genetics educn and science subjects. *Address:* Department of Molecular Genetics, University of Texas Southwestern Medical Center at Dallas, 5323 Harry Hines Boulevard, Dallas, TX 75390, USA; 3831 Turtle Creek Boulevard, Apt 22-B, TX 75219, USA.

GOLDSTEIN, Dr Michael, CBE 1997; FRSC; Vice-Chancellor, Coventry University, since 1992 (Director, Coventry Polytechnic, 1987–92); *b* 1 May 1939; *s* of Sarah and Jacob Goldstein; *m* 1962, Janet Sandra Skevington; one *s. Educ:* Hackney Downs Grammar School; Northern Polytechnic, London. BSc, PhD, DSc; CChem. Lectr, sen. lectr, principal lectr, Polytechnic of N London, 1963–73; Head of Dept of Chemistry, 1974–83 and Dean of Faculty of Science, 1979–83, Sheffield City Polytechnic; Dep. Dir, Coventry Lanchester Polytechnic, 1983–87. Mem., cttees and bds, CNAA, 1975–93, incl. Chm., CNAA Chem. Bd, 1978–84; Dep. Chm., Polys and Colls Admissions System, 1989–94; Member: UCAS, 1993–2001 (Dep. Chm., 1995–97; Chm., 1997–2001); Univs and Colls Employers Assoc., 1994–. Director: Coventry and Warwicks TEC, 1992–97; Coventry and Warwicks Partnerships Ltd, 1995–; City Centre Co. (Coventry) Ltd, 1997– (Vice-Chm., 1999–); Coventry and Warwicks Chamber of Commerce, Trng and Enterprise, 1997–2001; Coventry and Warwicks Learning and Skills Council, 2001–. Member: Adv. Cttee, Coventry Common Purpose, 1989–; Coventry is making it, 1992–95. Member: RSC Council, 1983–86, 1993–99; other RSC cttees, 1975–99 (Pres., Educn Div., 1993–95; Chm., Educn and Quals Bd, 1995–99). Hon. FCGI 1994. *Publications:* contribs to sci. jls, chapters in review books. *Recreations:* Coventry City FC, exercise. *Address:* 33 Frythe Close, Kenilworth CV8 2SY. *T:* (01926) 854939.

GOLDSTEIN, Simon Alfred; His Honour Judge Goldstein; a Circuit Judge, since 1987; *b* 6 June 1935; *s* of Harry and Constance Goldstein; *m* 1973, Zoë Philippa, *yr d* of late Basil Gerrard Smith, TD. *Educ:* East Ham Grammar Sch.; Fitzwilliam Coll., Cambridge (BA 1956). Educn Officer, RAF, 1957–60. Called to the Bar, Middle Temple, 1961; Dep. Circuit Judge, 1975; a Recorder, 1980–87. *Recreation:* bridge. *Address:* The Garden Flat, 15 Montagu Place, W1H 1RT. *Club:* London Duplicate Bridge.

GOLDSTEIN-JACKSON, Kevin Grierson; JP; writer; company director; *b* 2 Nov. 1946; *s* of H. G. and W. M. E. Jackson; *m* 1975, Jenny Mei Leng, *e d* of Ufong Ng, Malaysia; two *d. Educ:* Reading Univ. (BA Phil. and Sociol.); Southampton Univ. (MPhil Law). Staff Relations Dept, London Transport (Railways), 1966; Scottish Widows Pension & Life Assurance Soc., 1967; Prog. Organizer, Southern TV, 1970–73; Asst Prod., HK-TVB, Hong Kong, 1973; freelance writer/TV prod., 1973–75; Head of Film, Dhofar Region TV Service, Sultanate of Oman, 1975–76; Founder and Dir, Thames Valley Radio, 1974–77; Asst to Head of Drama, Anglia TV, 1977–81; Founder, TSW-Television South West: Programme Controller and Dir of Progs, 1981–85; Jt Man. Dir, 1981–82; Chief Exec., 1982–85. Writer of TV scripts. Dir of private cos. Gov., Lilliput First Sch., Poole, 1988–93. FRSA 1978; FIMgt (FBIM 1982); FInstD 1982; FFA 1988; FRGS 1989. Freeman, City of London, 1996. JP Poole, 1990. *Publications:* 17 books, including: The Right Joke for the Right Occasion, 1973; Experiments with Everyday Objects, 1976; Things to make with Everyday Objects, 1978; Magic with Everyday Objects, 1979; Dictionary of Essential Quotations, 1983; Jokes for Telling, 1986; Share Millions, 1989; The Public Speaker's Joke Book, 1991; The Astute Private Investor, 1994; contrib. financial and gen. pubns. *Recreations:* writing, TV, films, theatre, travel, music, walking, philosophical and sociological investigation. *Address:* c/o Alcazar, 18 Martello Road, Branksome Park, Poole, Dorset BH13 7DH.

GOLDSTONE, Prof. Anthony Howard, FRCP, FRCPE; FRCPath; Professor, University College London, since 1999; Director, North London Cancer Network, since 2000; *b* 13 Sept. 1944; *s* of Norman Goldstone and Edith Goldstone; *m* 1970, Jennifer Anne Krantz; one *s* one *d. Educ:* Bolton Sch.; St John's Coll., Oxford (BM BCh 1968; MA); University Coll. Hosp. Med. Sch. (Fellow, UCL, 1993). FRCPE 1979; FRCP 1983; FRCPath 1987. Sen. House Officer, Gastrointestinal Unit, Western General Infirmary, Edinburgh, 1969–70; Sen. Registrar in Haematology, Addenbrooke's Hosp., Cambridge, 1973–76; University College Hospital, London: Consultant Haematologist, 1976–; Dir, Bone Marrow Transplantation, 1979–; Postgrad. Dean, UCH Med. Sch., 1984–87; Chm., UCH Med. Cttee, 1986–88; Med. Dir, UCL Hosps NHS Trust, 1992–2000. Chm., NE Thames Regl Haematologists, 1988–90. Mem. Bd, European Gp for Bone Marrow Transplantation, 1990–98; Nat. Co-ordinator, UK Adult Leukaemia Trials, 1987–. President: British Soc. for Blood and Bone Marrow Transplantation, 1999–2000; British Soc. for Haematology, 2000–2001. *Publications:* (jtly) Leukaemias, Lymphomas and Allied Disorders, 1976; Examination Haematology, 1977; (jtly) Synopsis of Haematology, 1983; numerous papers on treatment of leukaemia, and bone marrow transplantation. *Recreations:* shouting at the dogs, driving fast cars, hoping Manchester City won't be relegated. *Address:* Department of Haematology, University College London Hospitals, WC1E 6AU; 67 Loom Lane, Radlett, Herts WD7 8NX. *Club:* Athenæum.

GOLDSTONE, David Joseph; Chairman since 1990, and Chief Executive since 1970, Regalian Properties Plc; *b* 21 Feb. 1929; *s* of Solomon Goldstone and Rebecca Goldstone (*née* Degotts); *m* 1957, Cynthia (*née* Easton); one *s* two *d. Educ:* Dynevor Secondary Sch., Swansea; London School of Economics and Political Science (LLB Hons; Hon. Fellow, 1995). Admitted Solicitor (Hons), 1955. Legal practice, 1955–66. Director: Swansea Sound Commercial Radio Ltd, 1974–96; Wales Millennium Centre Ltd, 1998–. Mem., London First (formerly London Forum), 1993–97; Vice Pres., London Welsh Trust Ltd, 1990–. Member Council: WNO, 1984–89; Royal Albert Hall, 1999–. Dep. Chm., London Welsh RFC, 1997– Member: Court of Govs, 1985–, Council, 1998–, LSE; Council, London Univ., 1994–. Dep. Chm., Estates (formerly Statute 32) Cttee, London Univ., 1998–. Mem. Court, 1999–, Chm. Fund Raising Cttee, 1999–, Coram Family. *Recreations:* family, reading, sport. *Address:* 18 Grosvenor Hill Court, 15 Bourdon Street, W1K 3PX. *T:* (020) 7493 9613. *Clubs:* Lansdowne, Savile, Bath & Racquets, Vanderbilt Racquet.

GOLDSTONE, Prof. Jeffrey, PhD; FRS 1977; Cecil and Ida Green Professor in Physics, Massachusetts Institute of Technology, since 1983 (Director, Center for Theoretical Physics, 1983–89); *b* 3 Sept. 1933; *s* of Hyman Goldstone and Sophia Goldstone; *m* 1980,

Roberta Gordon; one *s*. *Educ:* Manchester Grammar Sch.; Trinity Coll., Cambridge (MA 1956, PhD 1958). Trinity Coll., Cambridge: Entrance Scholar, 1951; Res. Fellow, 1956; Staff Fellow, 1962; Hon. Fellow, 2000; Cambridge University: Lectr, 1961; Reader in Math. Physics, 1976; Prof. of Physics, MIT, 1977. Vis. appointments: Institut for Teoretisk Fysik, Copenhagen; CERN, Geneva; Harvard Univ.; MIT; Inst. for Theoretical Physics, Santa Barbara; Stanford Linear Accelerator Center; Lab. de Physique Théorique, L'Ecole Normale Supérieure, Paris; Università di Roma I. Smith's Prize, Cambridge Univ., 1955; Dannie Heineman Prize, Amer. Phys. Soc., 1981; Guthrie Medal, Inst. of Physics, 1983; Dirac Medal, Internat. Centre for Theoretical Physics, 1991. *Publications:* articles in learned jls. *Address:* Department of Physics, (6–313) Massachusetts Institute of Technology, Cambridge, MA 02139, USA. *T:* (office) (617) 2536263; *e-mail:* goldston@mit.edu.

GOLDSTONE, Leonard Clement; QC 1993; a Recorder, since 1992; *b* 20 April 1949; *s* of Maurice and Maree Goldstone; *m* 1972, Vanessa, *yr d* of Donald Forster, *qv*; three *s*. *Educ:* Manchester Grammar Sch.; Churchill Coll., Cambridge (BA). Called to the Bar, Middle Temple, 1971. Treas., Northern Circuit, 1998–2001. *Recreations:* golf, bridge, music, theatre. *Address:* 28 St John Street, Manchester M3 4DJ. *T:* (0161) 834 8418; 2–4 Tudor Street, EC4Y 0AA. *T:* (020) 7797 7111. *Club:* Dunham Forest Golf and Country (Altrincham).

GOLDSTONE, His Honour Peter Walter; a Circuit Judge, 1978–97; *b* 1 Nov. 1926; *y s* of late Adolph Lionel Goldstone and Ivy Gwendoline Goldstone; *m* 1955, Patricia (*née* Alexander), JP; one *s* two *d*. *Educ:* Manchester Grammar Sch.; Manchester Univ. Solicitor, 1951. Fleet Air Arm, 1944–47. Partner in private practice with brother Julian S. Goldstone, 1951–71. Manchester City Councillor (L), 1962–65; Chm., Manchester Rent Assessment Panel, 1967–71; Reserve Chm., Manchester Rent Tribunal, 1969–71; Dep. Chm., Inner London QS, Nov. 1971; a Metropolitan Stipendiary Magistrate, 1971–78; a Recorder of the Crown Court, 1972–78. Designated Care Judge, Watford Care Centre, 1994–97. *Recreations:* walking, gardening, reading. *Address:* c/o Watford County Court, Cassiobury House, 11/19 Station Road, Watford WD1 1EZ. *T:* (01923) 249666. *Club:* MCC.

GOLDSWORTHY, Andrew Charles, (Andy), OBE 2000; artist and sculptor; *b* 25 July 1956; *s* of Frederick Goldsworthy and Muriel Goldsworthy (*née* Stangar); *m* 1982, Judith Gregson; two *s* two *d*. *Educ:* Harrogate Secondary Mod. Sch.; Harrogate High Sch.; Bradford Coll. of Art; Lancashire Poly. Has worked in Yorkshire, Cumbria and Dumfriesshire, 1978–. Hon. Fellow, Central Lancashire Univ., 1995. Hon. MA Bradford, 1993. *Publications:* Touching North, 1989; Leaves, 1989; Hand to Earth, 1990; Andy Goldsworthy, 1990; Snow and Ice Drawings, 1992; Two Autumns, 1993; Stone, 1994; Black Stones–Red Pools, 1995; Wood, 1996. *Address:* c/o Michael Hue-Williams, Fine Art Ltd, 21 Cork Street, W1X 1HB.

GOLDSWORTHY, Rt Rev. (Arthur) Stanley; permission to officiate, diocese of The Murray, SA, since 1992; *b* 18 Feb. 1926; *s* of Arthur and Doris Irene Goldsworthy; *m* 1952, Gwen Elizabeth Reeves; one *s* one *d*. *Educ:* Dandenong High School, Vic; St Columb's Theological Coll., Wangaratta. Deacon 1951, priest 1952; Curate of Wodonga, in charge of Bethanga, 1951–52; Priest of Chiltern, 1952; Kensington, Melbourne, 1955; Yarrawonga, Wangaratta, 1959; Shepparton (and Archdeacon), 1972; Parish Priest of Wodonga, and Archdeacon of Diocese of Wangaratta, 1977; Bishop of Bunbury, 1977–83; an Assisting Bishop to Primate of Australia, 1983–84; Parish Priest: St John, Hendra, Brisbane, 1983–84; Gilgandra, Bathurst, 1986–89; Tailem Bend, Meningie, SA, 1989–92, retired. Chaplain, 1956–77, Visitor, 1977–84, Community of the Sisters of the Church. *Recreations:* music, gardening. *Address:* The Theotokos Shrine, PO Box 244, Temora, NSW 2666, Australia. *T:* (2) 69774857.

GOLDSWORTHY, Rt Rev. Stanley; *see* Goldsworthy, Rt Rev. A. S.

GOLDTHORPE, John Harry, FBA 1984; Official Fellow, Nuffield College, Oxford, since 1969; *b* 27 May 1935; *s* of Harry Goldthorpe and Lilian Eliza Goldthorpe; *m* 1963, Rhiannon Esyllt (*née* Harry); one *s* one *d*. *Educ:* Wath-upon-Dearne Grammar School; University College London (BA Hons 1st Class Mod. Hist.); LSE. MA Cantab; MA Oxon. Asst Lectr, Dept of Sociology, Univ. of Leicester , 1957–60; Fellow of King's College, Cambridge, 1960–69; Asst Lectr and Lectr, Faculty of Economics and Politics, Cambridge, 1962–69. Lectures: Fuller, Univ. of Essex, 1979; Marshall, Univ. of Southampton, 1989; Aubert, Oslo Univ., 1993; Geary, Econ. and Social Res. Inst., Dublin, 1998; Cummings, McGill Univ., Montreal, 2001. MAE 1988. For. Mem., Royal Swedish Acad. of Scis, 2001. Hon. FilDr Stockholm Univ., 1990. *Publications:* (with David Lockwood and others): The Affluent Worker: industrial attitudes and behaviour, 1968; The Affluent Worker: political attitudes and behaviour, 1968; The Affluent Worker in the Class Structure, 1969; (with Keith Hope) The Social Grading of Occupations, 1974; (with Fred Hirsch) The Political Economy of Inflation, 1978; Social Mobility and Class Structure in Modern Britain, 1980, 2nd edn 1987; Order and Conflict in Contemporary Capitalism, 1984; (with Hermann Strasser) Die Analyse Sozialer Ungleichheit, 1985; (contrib.) John H. Goldthorpe: consensus and controversy (ed Clark, Modgil and Modgil), 1990; (with Robert Erikson) The Constant Flux: a study of class mobility in industrial societies, 1992; (with Christopher Whelan) The Development of Industrial Society in Ireland, 1992; Causation, Statistics and Sociology, 1999; On Sociology: numbers, narratives and the integration of research and theory, 2000; papers in Acta Sociologica, American Jl of Sociology, British Jl of Sociology, Comparative Soc. Res., Sociological Review, Sociology, European Jl of Sociology, European Sociological Rev., Rationality and Society, Sociological Methods and Res., Sociologie du Travail, Rev. Française de Sociologie. *Recreations:* lawn tennis, bird watching, computer chess. *Address:* 32 Leckford Road, Oxford OX2 6HX. *T:* (01865) 556602.

GOLLANCZ, Livia Ruth; Chairman, Victor Gollancz Ltd, 1983–89 (Governing Director, Joint Managing Director, 1965–85, Consultant, 1990–92); *b* 25 May 1920; *d* of Victor Gollancz and Ruth Lowy. *Educ:* St Paul's Girls' Sch.; Royal Coll. of Music (ARCM, solo horn). Horn player: LSO, 1940–43; Hallé Orch., 1943–45; Scottish Orch., 1945–46; BBC Scottish Orch., 1946–47; Covent Garden, 1947; Sadler's Wells, 1950–53. Joined Victor Gollancz Ltd as editorial asst and typographer, 1953; Dir, 1954. *Publication:* (ed and introd) Victor Gollancz, Reminiscences of Affection, 1968 (posthumous). *Recreations:* making music, hill walking, gardening. *Address:* 26 Cholmeley Crescent, N6 5HA. *Club:* Alpine.

GOLLIN, Prof. Alfred M., DLitt; FRSL; Professor of History, University of California, Santa Barbara, 1967–94, now Professor Emeritus (Chairman, Department of History, 1976–77); *b* 6 Feb. 1926; 2nd *s* of Max and Sue Gollin; *m* 1st, 1951, Gurli Sørensen (marr. diss.); two *d*; 2nd, 1975, Valerie Watkins (*née* Kilner). *Educ:* New York City Public Schs; City College of New York; Harvard Univ.; New Coll., Oxford (BA); St Antony's Coll., Oxford (MA); DPhil Oxon 1957; DLitt Oxon 1968. Served US Army, 1943–46; taught history at New Coll., Oxford, 1951–54; official historian for The Observer, 1952–59; Lectr, City Coll. of New York, 1959; Univ. of California, Los Angeles: Acting Asst Prof., 1959–60; Research Associate, 1960–61; Associate Prof., Univ. of California, Santa Barbara, 1966–67. Dir, Study Center of Univ. of California, UK and Ire., 1971–73; Mem., US-UK Educnl Commn, 1971–72. Fellow: J. S. Guggenheim Foundn, 1962, 1964, 1971; Amer. Council of Learned Socs, 1963, 1975; Nat. Endowment for Humanities, 1989; FRHistS 1976; FRSL 1986. *Publications:* The Observer and J. L. Garvin, 1960; Proconsul in Politics: a study of Lord Milner, 1964; From Omdurman to V. E. Day: the Life Span of Sir Winston Churchill, 1964; Balfour's Burden, 1965; Asquith, a New View, in A Century of Conflict, Essays for A. J. P. Taylor, 1966; Balfour, in The Conservative Leadership (ed D. Southgate), 1974; No Longer an Island, 1984; The Impact of Air Power on the British People and their Government 1909–14, 1989; articles and reviews in various jls. *Recreation:* swimming. *Address:* Department of History, University of California, Santa Barbara, CA 93106, USA.

GOLOMBOK, Prof. Susan Esther, PhD; Professor of Psychology, since 1992, and Director, Family and Child Psychology Research Centre, since 1989, City University; *b* 11 Aug. 1954; *d* of Bennie and Kitty Golombok; *m* 1979, Dr John Rust; one *s*. *Educ:* Hutchesons' Girls' Sch.; Univ. of Glasgow (BSc Hons 1976); Inst. of Educn, Univ. of London (MSc Child Devel 1977; PhD 1982). London University Institute of Psychiatry: Res. Psychologist, 1977–83; Lectr in Psychology, 1983–86; City University: Lectr, 1987–89; Sen. Lectr, 1989–90; Reader, 1990–92. Trustee, Laura Ashley Foundn, 1998–. Freeman, City of London, 1986. *Publications:* (with Valerie Curran) Bottling It Up, 1985; (with John Rust) Modern Psychometrics, 1989, 2nd edn 1999; (with Robyn Fivush) Gender Development, 1994; (with Fiona Tasker) Growing Up in a Lesbian Family, 1997; Parenting: what really counts?, 2000; contribs to sci. jls. *Recreations:* reading, cinema, cooking, moving house. *Address:* 133 Lauderdale Tower, Barbican, EC2Y 8BY. *T:* (020) 7588 7741.

GOMBRICH, Sir Ernst (Hans Josef), OM 1988; Kt 1972; CBE 1966; FBA 1960; FSA 1961; PhD (Vienna); MA Oxon and Cantab; Director of the Warburg Institute and Professor of the History of the Classical Tradition in the University of London, 1959–76, now Emeritus Professor; *b* Vienna, 30 March 1909; *s* of Dr Karl B. Gombrich, Vice-Pres. of Disciplinary Council of Lawyers' Chamber, Vienna, and Prof. Leonie Gombrich (*née* Hock), pianist; *m* 1936, Ilse Heller; one *s*. *Educ:* Theresianum, Vienna; Vienna Univ. Research Asst, Warburg Inst., 1936–39. Served War of 1939–45 with BBC Monitoring Service. Senior Research Fellow, 1946–48, Lectr, 1948–54, Reader, 1954–56, Special Lectr, 1956–59, Warburg Inst., Univ. of London; Durning-Lawrence Prof. of the History of Art, London Univ., at University Coll., 1956–59; Slade Prof. of Fine Art in the University of Oxford, 1950–53; Visiting Prof. of Fine Art, Harvard Univ., 1959; Slade Prof. of Fine Art, Cambridge Univ., 1961–63; Lethaby Prof., RCA, 1967–68; Andrew D. White Prof.-at-Large, Cornell, 1970–77. A Trustee of the British Museum, 1974–79; Mem., Museums and Galleries Commn (formerly Standing Commn on Museums and Galleries), 1976–82. Hon. Fellow: Jesus Coll., Cambridge, 1963; UCL, 1992. FRSL 1975; Foreign Hon. Mem., American Academy of Arts and Sciences, 1964; For. Mem., Amer. Philosophical Soc., 1968; Hon. Member: American Acad. and Inst. of Arts and Letters, 1985; Akad. der Wissenschaften zu Göttingen, 1986; Modern Lang. Assoc. of America, 1988; Deutsche Akademie für Sprache und Dichtung, 1988; Austrian Acad. of Scis, 1991; Corresponding Member: Accademia delle Scienze di Torino, 1962; Royal Acad. of Arts and Sciences, Uppsala, 1970; Koninklijke Nederlandse Akademie van Wetenschapen, 1973; Bayerische Akad. der Wissenschaften, 1979; Royal Swedish Acad. of Sciences, 1981; European Acad. of Arts, Scis and Humanities, 1980; Accademia Nazionale dei Lincei, 1983; Royal Belgian Acad. of Science, Letters and Fine Arts, 1989. Hon. FRIBA, 1971; Hon. Fellow: Royal Acad. of Arts, 1982; Bezalel Acad. of Arts and Design, 1983; Akademie der bildenden Künste, Vienna, 1999. Hon. DLit: Belfast, 1963; London, 1976; Richmond Coll., London, 1993; Hon. LLD St Andrews, 1965; Hon. LittD: Leeds, 1965; Cambridge, 1970; Manchester, 1974; Hon. DLitt: Oxford, 1969; Harvard, 1976; New York, 1986; Urbino, 1992; Hon. Dr Lit. Hum.: Chicago, 1975; Pennsylvania, 1977; DU Essex, 1977; Hon. DHL: Brandeis, 1981; Emory, 1991; Hon. DPhil Vienna, 1999; Hon. Dr RCA, 1984; Hon. Dr in Geography and History, Universidad Complutense de Madrid, 1992. W. H. Smith Literary Award, 1964; Medal of New York Univ. for Distinguished Visitors, 1970; Erasmus Prize, 1975; Ehrenkreuz für Wissenschaft und Kunst, 1st cl., Austria, 1975; Hegel Prize, 1976; Medal of Collège de France, 1977; Orden Pour le Mérite für Wissenschaften und Künste, 1977; Ehrenzeichen für Wissenschaft und Kunst, Austria 1984; Premio Rosina Viva of Anacapri, 1985; Internat. Balzan Prize, 1985; Kulturpreis der Stadt Wien, 1986; Ludwig Wittgenstein-Preis der Österreichischen Forschungsgemeinschaft, 1988; Britannica Award, Encyclopedia Britannica, 1989; Goethe Medaille, 1989; Austrian Auslands Kulturpreis, 1993; Goethe Prize, Frankfurt, 1994; Golden Medal, Vienna, 1994; Agnes and Elizabeth Mongan Prize, Villa I Tatti, 1996. Hon. Citizen, City of Mantova, 1998. *Publications:* Weltgeschichte für Kinder, 1936, rev. and enl. edn 1985; (with E. Kris) Caricature, 1940; The Story of Art, 1950, 16th edn 1995; Art and Illusion (The A. W. Mellon Lectures in the Fine Arts, 1956), 1960; Meditations on a Hobby Horse, 1963; Norm and Form, 1966; Aby Warburg, an intellectual biography, 1970; Symbolic Images, 1972; In Search of Cultural History, 1972; (jtly) Art, Perception and Reality, 1973; (ed jtly) Illusion in Nature and Art, 1973; Art History and the Social Sciences (Romanes Lect.), 1975; The Heritage of Apelles, 1976; Means and Ends (W. Neurath Lect.), 1976; The Sense of Order (Wrightsman Lect.), 1979; Ideals and Idols, 1979; The Image and the Eye, 1982; Tributes, 1984; New Light on Old Masters, 1986; Oskar Kokoschka in his Time, 1986; Reflections on the History of Art (ed R. Woodfield), 1987; Topics of Our Time, 1991; Styles of Art and Styles of Life (Reynolds Lect.), 1991; (with D. Eribon) Ce que l'image nous dit: entretiens sur l'art et la science, 1991; Gastspiele: zur Deutschen Sprache und Germanistik, 1992; On Pride and Prejudice in the Arts, 1992; Künstler, Kenner, Kunden (Wiener Vorlesungen im Rathaus), 1993; Das forschende Auge, 1994; Anthony Gormley, 1995; The Essential Gombrich (ed R. Woodfield), 1996; Shadows, 1996; Speis der Malerknaben (Wiener Vorlesungen 2), 1997; The Uses of Images, 1999; contributions to learned journals; *relevant publication:* E. H. Gombrich: a bibliography, ed J. B. Trapp, 2000. *Address:* 19 Briardale Gardens, NW3 7PN. *T:* (020) 7435 6639.

See also R. F. Gombrich.

GOMBRICH, Prof. Richard Francis, DPhil; Boden Professor of Sanskrit, Oxford University, since 1976; Fellow of Balliol College, Oxford, since 1976; Emeritus Fellow of Wolfson, 1977; *b* 17 July 1937; *s* of Sir Ernst Gombrich, *qv*; *m* 1st, 1964, Dorothea Amanda Friedrich (marr. diss. 1984); one *s* one *d*; 2nd, 1985, Sanjukta Gupta. *Educ:* Magdalen Coll., Oxford (MA, DPhil); Harvard Univ. (AM). Univ. Lectr in Sanskrit and Pali, Oxford Univ., 1965–76; Fellow of Wolfson Coll., 1966–76. Stewart Fellow, Princeton Univ., 1986–87. Pres., Pali Text Soc., 1994– (Hon. Sec., 1982–94). Hon. DLitt Kalyani Univ., West Bengal, 1991; Hon. DEd De Montfort, 1996. Sri Lanka Ranjana (Sri Lanka), 1994; Vacaspati, Tirupati (India), 1997. *Publications:* Precept and Practice: traditional Buddhism in the rural highlands of Ceylon, 1971, 2nd edn, as Buddhist Precept and Practice, 1991; (with Margaret Cone) The Perfect Generosity of Prince Vessantara, 1977; On being Sanskritic, 1978; (ed with Heinz Bechert) The World of Buddhism, 1984; Theravada Buddhism: a social history from ancient Benares to modern Colombo, 1988; (with G. Obeyesekere) Buddhism Transformed, 1988; How Buddhism Began, 1996;

contribs to oriental and anthropological journals. *Recreations:* singing, walking, photography. *Address:* Balliol College, Oxford OX1 3BJ.

GOMERSALL, Sir Stephen (John), KCMG 2000 (CMG 1997); HM Diplomatic Service; Ambassador to Japan, since 1999; *b* 17 Jan. 1948; *s* of Harry Raymond Gomersall and Helen Gomersall; *m* 1975, Lydia Veronica (*née* Parry); two *s* one *d*. *Educ:* Forest Sch., Snaresbrook; Queens' Coll., Cambridge (Mod. Langs, MA); Stanford Univ., Calif (MA 1970). Entered HM Diplomatic Service, 1970; Tokyo, 1972–77; Rhodesia Dept, FCO, 1977–79; Private Sec. to Lord Privy Seal, 1979–82; Washington, 1982–85; Econ. Counsellor, Tokyo, 1986–90; Head of Security Policy Dept, FCO, 1990–94; Dep. Perm. Rep., UK Mission to UN, 1994–98; Dir, Internat. Security, FCO, 1998–99. *Recreations:* music, composing silly songs. *Address:* c/o Foreign and Commonwealth Office, King Charles Street, SW1A 2AH.

GOMEZ, Rt Rev. Drexel Wellington; *see* West Indies, Archbishop of.

GOMEZ, Jill; singer; *b* Guyana, of Spanish and English parents. *Educ:* Royal Academy of Music (FRAM 1986); Guildhall School of Music, London. Operatic début as Adina in L'Elisir d'Amore with Glyndebourne Touring Opera, 1968 (after winning John Christie Award), then Glyndebourne Fest. Opera, 1969, and has subseq. sung leading roles, incl. Mélisande, Calisto, Anne Truelove in The Rake's Progress, Helena in A Midsummer Night's Dream; has appeared with The Royal Opera, English Opera Gp, ENO, WNO and Scottish Opera in roles including Pamina, Ilia, Fiordiligi, The Countess in Figaro, Elizabeth in Elegy for Young Lovers, Tytania, Lauretta in Gianni Schicchi, the Governess in The Turn of the Screw, Jenifer in The Midsummer Marriage, Leila in Les Pêcheurs de Perles; with Kent Opera: Tatiana in Eugene Onegin, 1977; Violetta in La Traviata, 1979; Amyntas in Il Re Pastore, 1987; Donna Anna in Don Giovanni, 1988; created the role of Flora in Tippett's The Knot Garden, 1970, at Covent Garden, and of the Countess in Thea Musgrave's Voice of Ariadne, Aldeburgh, 1974; created title role in William Alwyn's Miss Julie for radio, 1977; title rôle BBC world première, Prokoviev's Maddalena, 1979; Duchess, world première, Adès' Powder Her Face, 1995; other rôles include Donna Elvira, Cinna in Mozart's Lucio Silla, Cleopatra in Giulio Cesare, Teresa in Benvenuto Cellini, title rôle in Massenet's Thaïs, Desdemona in Otello, at Edinburgh, Wexford, and in Austria, France, Germany and Switzerland; première of Eighth Book of Madrigals, Monteverdi Fest., Zürich, 1979. Also recitalist, progs incl. A Spanish Songbook, Night and Day, and Fortunes of Love and War, perf. world-wide; concert repertoire includes Rameau, Bach, Handel (Messiah and cantatas), Haydn's Creation and Seasons, Mozart's Requiem and concert arias, Beethoven's Ninth, Berlioz's Nuits d'Eté, Brahms's Requiem, Fauré's Requiem, Ravel's Shéhérazade, Mahler's Second, Fourth and Eighth Symphonies, Strauss's Four Last Songs, Britten's Les Illuminations, Spring Symphony and War Requiem, Tippett's A Child of Our Time, Messiaen's Poèmes pour Mi, Webern op. 13 and 14 songs, and Schubert songs orch. Webern. Commissioned Cantiga—the song of Iñes de Castro (dramatic scena for soprano and orch.) from David Matthews (world première, BBC Prom., 1988). Regular engagements in France, Belgium, Holland, Germany, Scandinavia, Switzerland, Italy, Spain, Israel, America; masterclasses; festival appearances include Aix-en-Provence, Spoleto, Bergen, Versailles, Flanders, Holland, Prague, Edinburgh, Aldeburgh, Dartington, and BBC Prom. concerts. Recordings include three solo recitals (French, Spanish, and songs by Mozart), Ravel's Poèmes de Mallarmé, Handel's Admeto, Acis and Galatea, Elvira in Don Giovanni, Fauré's Pelléas et Mélisande, Handel's Ode on St Cecilia's Day, Rameau's La Danse, Britten's Les Illuminations, Canteloube's Songs of the Auvergne, Villa Lobos' Bachianas Brasilieras no 5, Samuel Barber's Knoxville—Summer of 1915, Cabaret Classics (with John Constable), Britten's Blues, Cole Porter Songs, South of the Border, A Spanish Songbook (with John Constable); première recordings: David Matthew's Cantiga, Mahler's Seven Early Songs, Britten's Quatre Chansons Françaises, Tippett's The Knot Garden, Adès' Powder her Face. *Address:* 16 Milton Park, N6 5QA.

GOMM, Richard Culling C.; *see* Carr-Gomm.

GOMME, Robert Anthony, CB 1990; Under Secretary, Department of the Environment, 1981–90, retired; *b* 19 Nov. 1930; *s* of Harold Kenelm Gomme and Alice Grace (*née* Jacques); *m* 1960, Helen Perris (*née* Moore); one *s* one *d*. *Educ:* Colfe's Grammar Sch., Lewisham; London School of Economics, Univ. of London (BScEcon 1955). National Service, Korean War, Corporal with Royal Norfolk Regt, 1951–52; Pirelli Ltd, 1955–66; NEDO, 1966–68; direct entrant Principal, Min. of Public Building and Works, 1968; Asst Sec., DoE, 1972–74, 1979–81; RCDS 1975; Cabinet Office, 1976–79; Department of the Environment: Dir of Defence Services, PSA, 1981–86; Prin. Finance Officer, 1987–90; Chief Exec., Crown Suppliers, 1990. Member: Exec. Cttee, Friends of the National Libraries, 1991–97, 1999–; Cttee, London Library, 1992–95, 1996–2000. Hon. Treas., Friends of Greenwich Park, 1992–95. *Publications:* contrib. to learned jls. *Recreations:* historical research, music, theatre, travel. *Address:* 14 Vanbrugh Fields, Blackheath, SE3 7TZ. *T:* (020) 8858 5148.

GOMMIE, Marie-Claire Geneviève; *see* Alain, M.-C. G.

GOMPERTZ, (Arthur John) Jeremy; QC 1988; a Recorder, since 1987; *b* 16 Oct. 1937; *s* of late Col Arthur William Bean Gompertz and Muriel Annie Gompertz (*née* Smith). *Educ:* Beaumont Coll.; Trinity Coll., Cambridge (MA). Called to the Bar, Gray's Inn, 1962, Bencher, 1997; in practice, South East Circuit. Chm., Mental Health Review Tribunal, 1993. Mem., Jockey Club Appeal Bd, 2001. *Recreations:* racing and breeding, travel, ski-ing. *Address:* 5 Essex Court, Temple, EC4Y 9AH. *T:* (020) 7410 2000.

GÖNCZ, Árpád, Hon. GCB 1999; Hon. KCMG 1991; President, Republic of Hungary, 1990–2000; *b* 10 Feb. 1922; *s* of Lajos Göncz and Ilona Heimann; *m* 1947, Mária Zsuzsanna Göntér; two *s* two *d*. *Educ:* Pázmány Péter Univ. (DJ 1944); Univ. of Agric. Scis. Nat. Land Bank, 1942–45; Independent Smallholders' Party: Sec. to Gen. Sec.; Leader, Independent Youth; Editor in Chief, Generation (weekly), 1947–48; jobless from 1948, worked as welder and metalsmith; sentenced to life imprisonment for political activity, 1957; released under general amnesty, 1963; freelance writer and literary translator, esp. of English works, 1963–; Pres., Hungarian Writers' Union, 1989–90; founding mem., Free Initiatives Network, Free Democratic Fedn, Historic Justice Cttee; MP, regional list, 1990; Speaker of Parliament and President *ai*, Republic of Hungary, May–Aug. 1990. József Áttila Literary Prize, 1983; Wheatland Prize, 1989; Premio Mediterraneo, 1991. *Publications:* Men of God (novel), 1974; Hungarian Medea (play), Iron Bars (play), 1979; Encounters (short stories), 1980; Balance (6 plays, incl. A Pessimistic Comedy, and Persephone), 1990; Homecoming (short stories), 1991; Shavings (essays), 1991. *Recreations:* reading, walking. *Address:* c/o Parliament, Kossuth tér 1–3, 1357 Budapest, Hungary. *T:* 269–0367.

GONZÁLEZ MÁRQUEZ, Felipe; Member for Madrid, Congress of Deputies, since 1977; Prime Minister of Spain and President, Council of Ministers, 1982–96; *b* 5 March 1942; *s* of Felipe González and Juana Márquez; *m* 1969, Carmen Romero Lopez; two *s* one *d*. *Educ:* Univ. of Seville (Law degree); Univ. of Louvaine. Opened first labour law office, Seville, 1966; Spanish Socialist Party (PSOE), 1964–: Mem., Seville Provincial Cttee, 1965–69; Mem., Nat. Cttee, 1969–70; Mem., Exec. Bd, 1970; First Sec., 1974–79, resigned; re-elected, 1979; Sec.-Gen., 1974–97. Chm., Socialist Parly Group. Chm., Global Progress Foundn (formerly Fundación Socialismo XXI), 1997–. Grand Cross: Order of Military Merit (Spain), 1984; Order of Isabel the Catholic (Spain), 1996. *Publications:* What is Socialism?, 1976; PSOE, 1977. *Address:* Gobelas 31, 28023 Madrid, Spain.

GOOBEY, Alastair R.; *see* Ross Goobey.

GOOCH, Anthony John; HM Diplomatic Service; Deputy High Commissioner and Economic and Commercial Counsellor, Singapore, since 1997; *b* 28 Nov. 1941; *s* of John Edgar Gooch and Mary Elizabeth (*née* Bricknell); *m* 1966, Jennifer Jane Harrison (*d* 1984); one *d*; *m* 1988, Cynthia Lee Barlow. *Educ:* Latymer Upper Sch.; St Catharine's Coll., Cambridge (BA Hist.). Pubns Editor, Europa Pubns, 1964–70; joined FCO, 1970: attachment to SEATO, Bangkok, 1972–74; Second, later First, Sec., FCO, 1974–80; First Secretary: (Economic), Stockholm, 1980–83; (Labour), Pretoria, 1984–88; FCO, 1988–92; (Commercial), Warsaw, 1992–96; Dir, Trade Promotion, and Consul-Gen., Warsaw, 1996–97. *Recreations:* tennis, gardening, history, film, contemporary literature. *Address:* c/o Foreign and Commonwealth Office, King Charles Street, SW1A 2AH; British High Commission, Tanglin Road, Singapore. *T:* 4740461. *Clubs:* Royal Over-Seas League; Tanglin (Singapore).

GOOCH, Graham Alan, OBE 1991; cricketer; Chief Coach, Essex County Cricket Club, since 2001; *b* 23 July 1953; *s* of late Alfred and of Rose Gooch; *m* 1976, Brenda Daniels; three *d* (incl. twins). *Educ:* Leytonstone. Batsman and bowler; first played for Essex CCC, 1973, Captain, 1986–94, retired, 1997; Member, England Test team, 1975–82 and 1986–Jan. 1995 (retired); played in S Africa, 1982; Captain of England, July 1988 and Sept. 1989–1993; 333 against India, highest score by a Test captain, 1990; 20 Test centuries; record no of runs (8900) in English Test cricket, 1995. England A team manager, Kenya and Sri Lanka tour, 1997–98; Manager, England Test tour, Australia, 1998–99. Mem., Selection Panel, ECB, 1997–99. *Publications:* Batting, 1980; (with Alan Lee) My Cricket Diary 1981, 1982; (with Alan Lee) Out of the Wilderness, 1985; Testing Times (autobiog.), 1991; (with Frank Keating) Gooch: My Autobiography, 1995. *Address:* c/o Essex County Cricket Club, County Ground, New Writtle Street, Chelmsford, Essex CM2 0PG. *T:* (01245) 252420.

GOOCH, Prof. John, PhD; FRHistS; Professor of International History, Leeds University, since 1992; *b* 25 Aug. 1945; *s* of George Gooch and Doris Evelyn (*née* Mottram); *m* 1967, Catherine Ann Staley; one *s* one *d*. *Educ:* Brockenhurst County High Sch.; King's Coll., Univ. of London (BA Hons History, class 1, 1966; PhD War Studies 1969). FRHistS 1975. Asst Lectr in History, 1966–67, Asst Lectr in War Studies, 1969, KCL; University of Lancaster: Lectr in History, 1969–81; Sen. Lectr, 1981–84; Reader in History, 1984–88; Prof. of History, 1988–92. Sec. of the Navy Sen. Res. Fellow, US Naval War Coll., 1985–86; Vis. Prof. of Military and Naval History, Yale Univ., 1988; Associate Fellow, Davenport Coll., Yale, 1988. Chm. of Council, Army Records Soc., 1983–; Vice-Pres., RHistS, 1990–94. Editor, Jl of Strategic Studies, 1978–; Gen. Editor, Internat. Relations of the Great Powers; Member of Editorial Board: European History Qly; Diplomacy and Statecraft; Terrorism and Small Wars; Security Studies; War in History. Premio Internazionale di Cultura, Città di Anghiari, 1983. Kt, Order of Vila Viçosa (Portugal), 1991. *Publications:* The Plans of War: the general staff and British military strategy *c.* 1900–1916, 1974; Armies in Europe, 1980; The Prospect of War: studies in British defence policy 1847–1942, 1981; Politicians and Defence: studies in the formulation of British defence policy 1847–1970, 1981; Strategy and the Social Sciences, 1981; Military Deception and Strategic Surprise, 1982; Soldati e Borghesi nell' Europa Moderna, 1982; Army, State and Society in Italy 1870–1915, 1989 (trans. Italian); Decisive Campaigns of the Second World War, 1989; (with Eliot A. Cohen) Military Misfortunes: the anatomy of failure in war, 1990; Airpower: theory and practice, 1995. *Recreations:* Italian food and wine. *Address:* Coverhill House, Coverhill Road, Oldham OL4 5RE. *T:* (0161) 678 8573. *Club:* Savile.

GOOCH, Sir Peter; *see* Gooch, Sir T. S.

GOOCH, Major Sir Timothy (Robert Sherlock), 13th Bt *cr* 1746, of Benacre Hall, Suffolk; MBE 1970; DL; company director; landowner; *b* 7 Dec. 1934; *y s* of Col Sir Robert Gooch, 11th Bt, KCVO, DSO and Katharine Clerveaux, *d* of Maj. Gen. Sir Edward Chaytor, KCMG, KCVO, CB; *S* brother, 1999; *m* 1963, Susan Barbara Christie, *o d* of Maj. Gen. K. C. Cooper, CB, DSO, OBE; two *d*. *Educ:* Eton; RMA Sandhurst. Commissioned, The Life Guards, 1955; served in Egypt, Aden, Oman, Germany, Malaya, Hong Kong and Northern Ireland; retd 1972. Mem., HM Body Guard, Hon. Corps of Gentlemen-at-Arms, 1986–, Standard Bearer, 2000–. DL Suffolk, 1999. *Recreations:* shooting, reading, walking. *Heir: cousin* Arthur Brian Sherlock Gooch [*b* 1 June 1937; *m* 1963, Sarah Diana Rowena Perceval Scott; two *d*]. *Address:* The Cedars, Covehithe, Wrentham, Beccles, Suffolk NR34 7JW. *T:* (01502) 675266. *Clubs:* White's, Cavalry and Guards.

GOOCH, Sir Trevor Sherlock, 5th Bt *cr* 1866, of Clewer Park, Berkshire; *b* 15 June 1915; *s* of Charles Trevor Gooch (*d* 1963; *g s* of Sir Daniel Gooch, 1st Bt), and Hester Stratford (*d* 1957), *d* of late Lt-Col Wright Sherlock; *S* kinsman, 1989; *m* 1st, 1956, Denys Anne (*d* 1976), *o d* of late Harold Victor Venables; one *s* four *d*; 2nd, 1978, Jean, *d* of late Joseph Wright. *Educ:* Charterhouse. Flt Lt, RAFVR, 1939–46. *Heir: s* Miles Peter Gooch [*b* 3 Feb. 1963; *m* 2000, Louise; one *d*]. *Address:* Jardin de la Rocque, Mont de la Rocque, St Aubin, Jersey, CI. *T:* (01534) 42980. *Club:* Royal Channel Islands Yacht (Jersey).

GOOD, Anthony Bruton Meyrick, FIPR; Founder Chairman: Good Relations Group plc, 1961–88; Good Consultancy Ltd, since 1988; Chairman, Cox & Kings Ltd, since 1975 (Director, since 1971); *b* 18 April 1933; *s* of Meyrick George Bruton Good and Amy Millicent Trussell; *m* (marr. diss.); two *d*. *Educ:* Felsted Sch. Mgt Trainee, Distillers Gp, 1950–52; Editorial Asst, Temple Press Ltd, 1952–55; PRO, Silver City Airways, 1955–60. Chairman: Flagship Gp Ltd, 1999–; Cox & Kings (India) Ltd, 1988– (Dir, 1980–); Good Relations (India) Ltd, 1988–; Legend Consultancy Ltd, 1999–; Director: IM Gp Ltd, 1977–; WinWin Business Solutions Ltd, 1999–; Miller Insurance Gp Ltd, 2000–. FIPR 1975; FInstD 1994. *Recreations:* travel, reading, theatre. *Address:* Clench House, Wootton Rivers, Marlborough, Wilts SN8 4NT. *T:* (01672) 810126, *Fax:* (01672) 810869. *Club:* Royal Automobile.

GOOD, Sir John K.; *see* Kennedy-Good.

GOOD, Ven. Kenneth Roy; Archdeacon of Richmond, since 1993; *b* 28 Sept. 1941; *s* of Isaac Edward Good and Florence Helen Good (*née* White); *m* 1970, Joan Thérèse Bennett; one *s* one *d*. *Educ:* Stamford Sch.; King's Coll., London (BD 1966; AKC). Ordained deacon 1967, priest 1968; Asst Curate, St Peter, Stockton on Tees, 1967–70; Missions to Seamen: Port Chaplain, Antwerp, 1970–74, Kobe, 1974–79; Asst Gen. Sec.,

1979–85; Vicar of Nunthorpe, 1985–93; RD of Stokesley, 1989–93. Hon. Canon, Kobe, 1985. *Recreations:* gardening, caravanning. *Address:* Hoppus House, Smith Lane, Hutton Conyers, Ripon, Yorks HG4 5DX. *T:* (01765) 604342.

GOODACRE, Kenneth, TD 1952; DL; Deputy Clerk to GLC, 1964–68; Clerk and Solicitor of Middlesex CC, 1955–65; Clerk of the Peace for Middlesex, 1959–65; *b* 29 Oct. 1910; *s* of Clifford and Florence Goodacre; *m* 1936, Dorothy (*d* 1992), *d* of Harold Kendall, Solicitor, Leeds; one *s*. *Educ:* Doncaster Grammar Sch. Admitted Solicitor, 1934; Asst Solicitor: Doncaster Corp., 1934–35; Barrow-in-Furness Corp., 1935–36; Sen. Solicitor, Blackburn Corp., 1936–39; served War of 1939–45, TA with E Lancs Regt and Staff 53 Div. (Major), and 2nd Army (Lieut-Col); released from Army Service, 1945, and granted hon. rank of Major; Dep. Town Clerk: Blackburn, 1945–49, Leicester, 1949–52; Town Clerk, Leicester, 1952–55. Partner, Gillhams, Solicitors, 1968–71; practised under name of K. Goodacre & Co., Solicitors, 1971–89. DL, Greater London (DL Middlesex, 1960–65), 1965. *Address:* 4 Chartfield Avenue, Putney, SW15 6HD. *T:* (020) 8789 0794. *Club:* Hurlingham.

GOODACRE, Peter Eliot, RD 1979, with clasp 1991; Principal, College of Estate Management, Reading, since 1992; *b* 4 Nov. 1945; *s* of Edward Leslie Goodacre and Cicely May (*née* Elliott); *m* 1971, Brita Christina Forsling; two *d*. *Educ:* Kingston Grammar Sch.; Coll. of Estate Management; Loughborough Univ. of Technology (MSc). FRICS 1980. Commnd RNR, 1965; Lt Comdr, 1979. In private practice, 1966–69; Lecturer: Coll. of Estate Mgt, 1970–73; Univ. of Reading, 1973–78, Sen. Lectr 1978–83; Vice-Principal, Coll. of Estate Mgt, 1984–92. Mem., Gen. Council, RICS, 1986– (Vice-Chm., 1997–98, Pres., 1998–July 1999, Quantity Surveyors' Divl Council). Mem., Gtr London TA&VRA (Chm., Works and Bldgs Sub-Cttee, 1997–). Freeman, City of London, 1994; Liveryman, Chartered Surveyors' Co., 1995–. FCIOB 1999. *Publications:* Formula Method of Price Adjustment for Building Contracts, 1978, 2nd edn 1987; Cost Factors of Dimensional Co-ordination, 1981; Worked Examples in Quantity Surveying Measurement, 1982. *Recreations:* home and garden. *Address:* College of Estate Management, Whiteknights, Reading, Berks RG6 6AW. *T:* (0118) 986 1101, *Fax:* (0118) 986 9878. *Clubs:* Athenæum, MCC; Phyllis Court (Henley).

GOODALL, Sir (Arthur) David (Saunders), GCMG 1991 (KCMG 1987; CMG 1979); HM Diplomatic Service, retired; Chairman, Leonard Cheshire (the Leonard Cheshire Foundation), 1995–2000 (Chairman, International Committee, 1992–95); *b* 9 Oct. 1931; *o c* of late Arthur William and Maisie Josephine Goodall; *m* 1962, Morwenna, *y d* of late Percival George Beck Peecock; two *s* one *d*. *Educ:* Ampleforth; Trinity Coll., Oxford (1st Cl. Hons Lit. Hum., 1954; MA; Hon. Fellow, 1992). Served 1st Bn KOYLI (2nd Lieut), 1955–56. Entered HM Foreign (subseq. Diplomatic) Service, 1956; served at: Nicosia, 1956; FO, 1957–58; Djakarta, 1958–60; Bonn, 1961–63; FO, 1963–68; Nairobi, 1968–70; FCO, 1970–73; UK Delegn, MBFR, Vienna, 1973–75; Head of Western European Dept, FCO, 1975–79; Minister, Bonn, 1979–82; Dep. Sec., Cabinet Office, 1982–84; Dep. Under-Sec. of State, FCO, 1984–87; High Comr to India, 1987–91. Co-Chm., Anglo-Irish Encounter, 1992–97; Chm., British–Irish Assoc., 1997–. Vis. Prof., Inst. of Irish Studies, Univ. of Liverpool, 1996–. Vice-Chm., Council, Durham Univ., 1997–2000; Chm. Governing Body, Heythrop Coll., Univ. of London, 2000–; Gov., Westminster Cathedral Choir Sch., 1994–. Pres., Irish Genealogical Res. Soc., 1992– (Fellow, 1978). Hon. LLD Hull, 1994. *Publications:* Remembering India, 1997; Ryedale Pilgrimage, 2000; contribs to: Ampleforth Jl; Tablet; Irish Genealogist; The Past. *Recreation:* painting in watercolours. *Address:* Greystones, Ampleforth, North Yorks YO62 4DU. *Clubs:* Garrick, Oxford and Cambridge.

GOODALL, David William, PhD (London); DSc (Melbourne); ARCS, DIC, FLS; FIBiol; Hon. Research Associate, Centre for Ecosystem Management, Edith Cowan University, since 1998; *b* 4 April 1914; *s* of Henry William Goodall; *m* 1st, 1940, Audrey Veronica Kirwin (marr. diss. 1949); one *s*; 2nd, 1949, Muriel Grace King (marr. diss. 1974); two *s* one *d*; 3rd, 1976, Ivy Nelms (*née* Palmer). *Educ:* St Paul's Sch.; Imperial Coll. of Science and Technology (BSc). Research under Research Inst. of Plant Physiology, on secondment to Cheshunt and East Malling Research Stns, 1935–46; Plant Physiologist, W African Cacao Research Inst., 1946–48; Sen. Lectr in Botany, University of Melbourne, 1948–52; Reader in Botany, University Coll. of the Gold Coast, 1952–54; Prof. of Agricultural Botany, University of Reading, 1954–56; Dir, CSIRO Tobacco Research Institute, Mareeba, Qld, 1956–61; Senior Principal Research Officer, CSIRO Div. of Mathematical Statistics, Perth, Australia, 1961–67; Hon. Reader in Botany, Univ. of Western Australia, 1965–67; Prof. of Biological Science, Univ. of California Irvine, 1966–68; Dir, US/IBP Desert Biome, 1968–73; Prof. of Systems Ecology, Utah State Univ., 1969–74; Sen. Prin. Res. Scientist, 1974–79, Sen. Res. Fellow, 1979–83, Land Resources Management Div., CSIRO; Hon. Fellow, CSIRO Div. of Wildlife and Ecology, 1983–98. Hon. Dr in Natural Scis, Trieste Univ., 1990. *Publications:* Chemical Composition of Plants as an Index of their Nutritional Status (with F. G. Gregory), 1947; ed, Evolution of Desert Biota, 1976; editor-in-chief, Ecosystems of the World (series), 1977–; co-editor: Productivity of World Ecosystems, 1975; Simulation Modelling of Environmental Problems, 1977; Arid-land Ecosystems: Structure, Functioning and Management, vol. 1 1979, vol. 2 1981; Mediterranean-type Shrublands, 1981; Hot Deserts, 1985; numerous papers in scientific jls and symposium vols. *Recreations:* acting, reading, walking. *Address:* Centre for Ecosystem Management, Edith Cowan University, Joondalup Drive, Joondalup, WA 6027, Australia.

GOODALL, Howard Lindsay; composer and broadcaster; President, London College of Music and Media, Thames Valley University, since 1995; *b* 26 May 1958; *s* of Geoffrey and Marion Goodall. *Educ:* New College Sch.; Stowe Sch.; Lord Williams' Sch., Thame; Christ Church, Oxford (MA 1979). ARCO 1975. Freelance composer, 1976–; Hon. Prof., Thames Valley Univ., 1994–. *TV and film themes/scores* include: Blackadder; The Red Dwarf; The Vicar of Dibley; The Thin Blue Line; 2.4 Children; Mr Bean; Rowan Atkinson in Revue; *compositions* include: The Hired Man, 1984 (Ivor Novello Award for best musical, 1985); Girlfriends, 1987; Days of Hope, 1990; Silas Marner, 1993; Missa Aedis Christi, 1993; Marlborough Canticles, 1995; In Memoriam Anne Frank, 1995; The Kissing-Dance, 1998; We are the Burning Fire, 1998. Presenter: BBC: Choir of the Year, 1990–; Channel Four: Howard Goodall's Organ Works (RTS Award for best original title music), 1997; Four Goes to Glyndebourne, 1997–98; Howard Goodall's Choir Works, 1998; Howard Goodall's Big Bangs, 2000. *Recreation:* Newcastle United Football Club. *Address:* c/o Caroline Chignell, 7 Soho Street, W1D 3DQ. *T:* (020) 7287 1112, *Fax:* (020) 7287 1191; *e-mail:* general@pbjmgt.co.uk.

GOODALL, Jane; *see* Goodall, V. J.

GOODALL, Rt Rev. Lindsay; *see* Horsham, Area Bishop of.

GOODALL, Rt Rev. Maurice John, MBE 1974; Bishop of Christchurch, 1984–90; *b* 31 March 1928; *s* of John and Alice Maud Goodall; *m* 1st, 1953, Nathalie Ruth Cummack; two *s* four *d*; 2nd, 1981, Beverley Doreen Moore. *Educ:* Christchurch Technical Coll.; College House, Univ. of NZ (BA 1950); Univ. of Canterbury (LTh 1964); Dip. Social Work (Distinction) 1977; CQSW 1982. Asst Curate, St Albans, Dio. of Christchurch, 1951–54; Vicar of: Waikari, 1954–59; Shirley, 1959–67; Hon. Asst, Christchurch, St John's 1967–69; Chaplain, Kingslea Girls' Training Centre, 1967–69; City Missioner (dio. Christchurch), 1969–76; Nuffield Bursary, 1973; Dir, Community Mental Health Team, 1976–82; Dean of Christchurch Cathedral, 1982–84. *Publications:* (with Colin Clark) Worship for Today, 1967; (contrib.) Christian Responsibility in Society (ed Yule), 1977; contribs to journals. *Recreations:* walking, reading, NZ history. *Address:* Flat 1, 50 Crofton Road, Christchurch 5, New Zealand.

GOODALL, Ralph William; Chairman, Volex Group, since 1992 (Director, since 1988); Vice Lord-Lieutenant of Lancashire, since 1999; *b* 15 Oct. 1931; *s* of James Goodall and Evelyn (*née* Hamer); *m* 1959, Marjory Audrey Ellen Flint; three *s* one *d*. *Educ:* Haileybury Coll.; Leeds Univ. (BSc Textile Inds); Pembroke Coll., Cambridge (MA Econs). CText 1967; ATI 1967; CompTI 1983. Flying Officer/Engr, RAF, 1954–56. Joined Scapa Dryers Ltd as Mgt Trainee, 1956; Scapa Group plc: Asst Gp Man. Dir, 1969–76; Gp Man. Dir and Chief Exec., 1976–86; Chm., 1986–93; Dir and Chm., Carbo (formerly Hopkinsons Gp) plc, 1992–; Dir, Manweb plc, 1993–95 (Chm., 1994–95); Chm., Inveresk PLC, 1994–2001. Pres., Textile Inst., 1985–87. Fishing trawler owner, 1968–96. Gov., Queen Elizabeth's Grammar Sch., Blackburn, 1979– (Chm., 1993–98); Council Mem., UMIST, 1992– (Dep. Chm., 1997–99); Dep. Pro Chancellor, Lancaster Univ., 1997–. Pres., Royal Lancs Agricl Soc., 1997–98. Freeman, City of London, 1986; Liveryman, Feltmakers' Co., 1986–. DL 1988, High Sheriff, 1995–96, Lancs. Hon. DEng Leeds Univ., 1990. *Recreations:* shooting, golf, walking, music. *Address:* The Old Vicarage, Hoghton, near Preston, Lancs PR5 0SJ. *Clubs:* Farmers', Oxford and Cambridge; District & Union, Pleasington Golf (Blackburn).

GOODALL, Air Marshal Sir Roderick Harvey, KBE 2001 (CBE 1990); CB 1999; AFC 1981, Bar 1987; FRAeS; Chief of Staff, Component Command Air North, NATO, since 1999; *b* 19 Jan. 1947; *s* of Leonard George Harvey Goodall and Muriel Goodall (*née* Cooper); *m* 1973, Elizabeth Susan Haines; two *d*. *Educ:* Elizabeth Coll., Guernsey; RAF Coll., Cranwell. FRAeS 1997. Commissioned 1968; served Bahrain, UK and Germany, to 1981; RAF Staff Coll., 1981; PMC Barnwood, 1982; OC 16 Sqn, Laarbruch, 1983–85; MoD, 1986–87; Station Comdr, RAF Bruggen, 1987–89; RCDS 1990; Station Comdr, RAF Detachment, Bahrain, 1990; Dir, Air Offensive and Air Force Ops, MoD, 1991–93; AOC No 2 Gp, 1994–96; COS Perm. Jt HQ, 1996–98; Leader, RAF Officers Branch Structure Review Team, 1998–99. Pres., RAF Golf Assoc., 1995–. *Recreations:* golf, photography, family. *Address:* c/o Lloyds TSB, 2 North Gate, Sleaford, Lincs NG34 7BL. *Club:* Royal Air Force.

GOODALL, (Valerie) Jane, CBE 1995; PhD; Scientific Director, Gombe Wildlife Research Institute, Tanzania, since 1967; *b* 3 April 1934; *er d* of Mortimer Herbert Morris-Goodall and Vanne Morris-Goodall (*née* Joseph); *m* 1st, 1964, Baron Hugo van Lawick (marr. diss. 1974); one *s*; 2nd, 1975, Hon. Derek Bryceson, Tanzanian MP (*d* 1980). *Educ:* Uplands Sch., Bournemouth; Cambridge Univ. (PhD 1965). Sec., Oxford Univ., 1952; worked as asst to Louis and Mary Leakey, Olduvai Gorge, 1957; engaged in res. into behaviour of chimpanzees, Gombe Stream Game Reserve, now Gombe Nat. Park, 1960–; res. in social behaviour of Spotted Hyena, Ngorongoro, 1968–69; dir. res. on behaviour of Olive Baboon, Gombe, 1972–82. Vis. Prof., Dept of Psychiatry and Program of Human Biology, Stanford Univ., 1971–75; Hon. Vis. Prof. in Zoology, Dar es Salaam Univ., 1973–; A. D. White Prof.-at-Large, Cornell Univ., 1996–. Vice-Pres., Animal Welfare Inst., BVA, 1987–; Mem. Adv. Bd, Albert Schweitzer Inst. for the Humanities, 1991–; Trustee, Jane Goodall Insts in UK, USA and Canada, and member of many other conservation and wildlife socs and foundns. Documentary films for television on research with chimpanzees incl. Fifi's Boys, BBC, 1995. Hon. FRAI 1991. Many hon. degrees. Numerous awards and prizes including: Franklin Burr Award for contrib. to Science, 1963, 1964, Centennial Award, 1988, Hubbard Medal, 1995, Nat. Geographic Soc.; Conservation Award, NY Zool Soc., 1974; Gold Medal, Soc. of Women Geographers, 1990; Kyoto Prize, 1990; Edinburgh Medal, 1991; Silver Medal, Zool Soc. of London, 1996. *Publications:* My Friends the Wild Chimpanzees, 1967; (with H. van Lawick) Innocent Killers, 1970; In the Shadow of Man, 1971; The Chimpanzees of Gombe: patterns of behaviour, 1986; Through A Window: 30 years observing the Gombe chimpanzees, 1990; (with Dale Peterson) Visions of Caliban, 1993; Jane Goodall: with love, 1994; Reason for Hope (autobiog.), 1999; contribs to learned jls; *for children:* (with H. van Lawick) Grub: the bush baby, 1972; My Life with the Chimpanzees, 1988; The Chimpanzee Family Book, 1989; Jane Goodall's Animal World: chimps, 1989; Animal Family Series, 1991. *Address:* Jane Goodall Institute (UK), 15 Clarendon Park, Lymington, Hants SO41 8AX. *Club:* Explorers' (New York).

GOODBODY, Clarissa Mary; *see* Farr, C. M.

GOODBOURN, Dr David Robin; General Secretary, Churches Together in Britain and Ireland, since 1999; *b* 1 Aug. 1948; *s* of Albert Lewis Goodbourn and Olive Mary Goodbourn (*née* Pring); *m* 1972, Evlynn Ann Cassie; one *s* one *d*. *Educ:* Sir Roger Manwood's Sch., Sandwich; Univ. of Durham (BA 1969); Univ. of Manchester (MEd 1980; PhD 1989). Sec. for Student Work, Baptist Union of GB, 1969–71; Dir, Baptist World Poverty Educn Prog., 1971–73; Tutor, Northern Baptist Coll., and Lectr, Northern Coll. (URC and Congregational), 1973–85; Adult Educn Advr, Church of Scotland, 1985–94; Asst Dir, 1994–98, then Depute Dir, 1998–99, Ch of Scotland Bd of Parish Educn, and Dean, Scottish Churches Open Coll., 1996–99. Mem., Bd and Exec., Christian Aid, 1999–. Patron, Friends of the Church in China, 1999–. *Recreations:* the usual boring walking and reading, plus a moderately educated taste for malt whisky. *Address:* Inter-Church House, 35–41 Lower Marsh, SE1 7SA. *T:* (020) 7523 2121; 145 Westcombe Hill, Blackheath, SE3 7DP.

GOODCHILD, David Hicks, CMG 1992; CBE 1973; Partner of Clifford Chance (formerly Clifford-Turner), Solicitors, 1962–91 (resident in Paris), retired; *b* 3 Sept. 1926; *s* of Harold Hicks Goodchild and Agnes Joyce Wharton Goodchild (*née* Mowbray); *m* 1954, Nicole Marie Jeanne (*née* Delamotte); one *s* one *d*. *Educ:* Felsted School. Lieut, Royal Artillery, 1944–48; articled clerk, Longmores, Hertford; qual. Solicitor, 1952; Mem., Paris Bar, 1992. HAC, 1952–56. Chairman: Hertford British Hosp. Corp., 1976–2001; Victoria Home, 1982–. Hon. Pres., Franco-British Chamber of Commerce and Industry (formerly British Chamber of Commerce in France), 1982– (Pres., British Chamber of Commerce in France, 1970–72). *Recreations:* golf, cricket. *Address:* 53 Avenue Montaigne, 75008 Paris, France. *T:* 42254927. *Clubs:* MCC, HAC; Polo (Paris); Golf de Chantilly.

GOODCHILD, David Lionel Napier, CMG 1986; a Director, Directorate-General of External Relations, Commission of the European Communities, 1985–86; *b* 20 July 1935; *s* of Hugh N. Goodchild and Beryl C. M. Goodchild. *Educ:* Eton College; King's College, Cambridge (MA). Joined Foreign Office, 1958; served Tehran, NATO (Paris), and FO, 1959–70; Dep. Political Adviser, British Mil. Govt, Berlin, 1970–72; transferred to EEC, Brussels, 1973; Head of Division, 1973, Principal Counsellor then Director, 1979–86.

Address: Orchard House, Thorpe Morieux, Bury St Edmunds, Suffolk IP30 0NW. *T:* (01284) 828181.

GOODCHILD, Marianne, (Mrs Trevor Goodchild); *see* Rigge, M.

GOODCHILD, Peter Robert Edward; Director, Green Umbrella Films, since 1998; *b* 18 Aug. 1939; *s* of Douglas Richard Geoffrey Goodchild and Lottie May Goodchild; *m* 1968, Penelope Jane Pointon-Dick; two *d.* *Educ:* Aldenham Sch., Elstree; St John 's College, Oxford (MA). CChem, FRSC 1979. General trainee, BBC, 1963; BBC TV: Director/Producer, Horizon, 1965–69, Editor, 1969–76; Editor, Special Features, 1977–80; Head, Science Features Dept, 1980–84; Head, Plays Dept, 1984–89; Exec. Producer, BBC Films, 1989–92. Director: Screen Partners, 1992–94; Stone City Films, 1995–98. Pres., Dunchideock Treacle Mines, 2000–. SFTA Mullard Award, for Horizon, 1967, 1968, 1969; BAFTA Awards: best factual series, for Horizon, 1972, 1974; best drama series, Marie Curie, 1977, Oppenheimer, 1980; Gold Award, Chicago Film Fest., for Black Easter, 1996. *Publications:* J. Robert Oppenheimer: shatterer of worlds, 1980; Edward Teller, 2002; *plays:* Chicago Conspiracy Trial, 1993 (Gold Award, NY Radio Fest., 1995); Nuremberg, 1995; In the Name of Security, 1998; Lockerbie on Trial, 2001. *Recreations:* tennis, music, painting, rowing, environmental action. *Address:* Dunchideock House, Dunchideock, Exeter, Devon EX2 9TS. *Club:* Groucho.

GOODDEN, Robert Yorke, CBE 1956; RDI 1947; Architect and Designer; Professor, School of Silversmithing and Jewellery, 1948–74, and Pro-Rector, 1967–74, Royal College of Art; *b* 7 May 1909; 2nd *s* of late Lieut-Col R. B. Goodden, OBE and Gwendolen Goodden; *m* 1st, 1936, Kathleen Teresa Burrow; 2nd, 1946, Lesley Macbeth Mitchell; two *s* two *d.* *Educ:* Harrow Sch. Trained AA Sch. of Architecture, 1926–31; AA Diploma 1932; ARIBA 1933; private practice as architect and designer, 1932–39; served RAFVR, 1940–41; RNVR, 1941–45; resumed private practice, 1946. Joint architect and designer: Lion and Unicorn Pavilion, South Bank Exhibition, 1951; Western Sculpture Rooms, Print Room Gall. and Gall. of Oriental Art, British Museum, 1969–71; designer of: domestic pressed glassware for Chance Brothers, 1934–48; Asterisk Wallpapers, 1934; sports section, Britain Can Make It Exhbn, 1946; Coronation hangings for Westminster Abbey, 1953; gold and silver plate in collections: Victoria and Albert Museum, Worshipful Co. of Goldsmiths, Royal Society of Arts, Downing Coll. and Sidney Sussex Coll., Cambridge, Royal Coll. of Art; glass for King's Coll., Cambridge, Grosvenor House, Min. of Works, and others; metal foil mural decorations in SS Canberra, 1961. Consulting Architect to Board of Trade for BIF, Olympia, 1947, Earls Ct, 1949, Olympia, 1950 and 1951. Member: Council of Industrial Design, 1955; National Council for Diplomas in Art and Design, 1961; Adv. Council, V&A Museum, 1977; Chm., Crafts Council, 1977–82. Mem. Council, Essex Univ., 1973. FSIA, 1947; Hon. Fellow, Sheffield Polytechnic, 1971. Hon. DesRCA, 1952; Hon. Dr RCA, 1974; Sen. Fellow, RCA, 1981. SIAD Design Medal, 1972. Master of Faculty, RDI, 1959–61. Liveryman, Worshipful Co. of Goldsmiths, Prime Warden 1976. *Publication:* (with P. Popham) Silversmithing, 1972. *Recreation:* daydreaming. *Address:* 16 Hatfield Buildings, Widcombe Hill, Bath, Somerset BA2 6AF.

GOODE, Charles Barrington, AC 2001; Director, since 1991, Chairman, since 1995, Australia and New Zealand Banking Group Ltd; *b* 26 Aug. 1938; *s* of Charles Thomas Goode and Jean Florence (*née* Robertson); *m* 1987, Cornelia Masters (*née* Ladd; former wife of Baron Baillieu, *qv*); one step *s.* *Educ:* Univ. of Melbourne (BCom Hons); Columbia Univ., NY (MBA). Joined Potter Partners, 1961: Partner, 1969; Sen. Partner, 1980–86; Chm., Potter Partners Gp Ltd, 1987–89; Chm., Ian Potter Foundn Ltd, 1994–. Chairman: Australian United Investment Co. Ltd, 1990–; Diversified United Investment Ltd, 1991–; Woodside Petroleum Ltd, 1999– (Dir, 1988–); Pacific Dunlop Ltd, 1987–99; Qld Investment Corp. Ltd, 1991–99; CSR Ltd, 1993–2000; Singapore Airlines Ltd, 1999–; Air New Zealand Ltd, 1999–. Member: Melbourne Cttee, Ludwig Inst. for Cancer Res., 1981–92; Exec. Cttee, Anti-Cancer Council of Victoria, 1981–84; Cttee of Mgt, Royal Victorian Eye and Ear Hosp., 1982–86; Chm., Howard Florey Inst. Exptl Physiol. and Medicine, 1997–. Pres., Inst. Public Affairs, 1984–93. Member of Council: Monash Univ., 1980–85 (Trustee, Monash Univ. Foundn, 1983–85); Australian Ballet Sch., 1980–86. Hon. LLD Melbourne. *Recreations:* tennis, golf, reading. *Address:* 294 Walsh Street, South Yarra, Vic 3141, Australia. *T:* (3) 98675792, *Fax:* (3) 98677494; Level 31, 100 Queen Street, Melbourne, Vic 3000, Australia. *T:* (3) 92734736, *Fax:* (3) 92736478. *Clubs:* Melbourne, Australian, Royal Melbourne Golf (Melbourne).

GOODE, Dr David Anthony, FLS; Head of Environment, Greater London Authority, since 2000; *b* 16 Jan. 1941; *s* of Rev. William Aubrey Goode and Vera Goode (*née* Parkinson); *m* 1966, Diana Lamble; one *s* one *d.* *Educ:* Queen's Sch., Mönchen Gladbach, Germany; Malet Lambert High Sch., Hull; Univ. of Hull (BSc Sp. Hons Geol. 1963; PhD Botany 1970); University Coll. London (Postgrad. Dip. Conservation). MIEEM 1991 (Pres., 1994–97). Peatland Officer, 1967–69, Hd, Peatland Ecology, 1969–73, Nature Conservancy; PSO, 1973–76, Asst Chief Scientist, 1976–82, NCC; Sen. Ecologist, GLC, 1982–86; Dir, London Ecology Unit, 1986–2000. Vis. Prof., UCL, 1994–; Hon. Prof., E China Normal Univ., Shanghai, 1996–2000. Member: Envmt Panel, C of E Bd for Social Responsibility, 1983–92; Terrestrial Life Scis Grants Panel, 1984–87, Expert Rev. Gp on Urban Envmtl Sci., 1993–94, NERC; Adv. Cttee, Envmtl Law Foundn, 1993–; RHS Sci. and Horticulture Cttee, 1994–; UK Biodiversity Action Plan Steering Gp, 1994–95 (Chm., Public Awareness Gp, 1994–95); UK Agenda 21 Steering Gp, 1995–2000; UK Biodiversity Gp, 1996– (Chm., Local Issues Gp, 1996–98); New Renaissance Gp, 1996–; Adv. Cttee, Darwin Initiative for Survival of the Species, 2000–; UK Local Sustainability Gp, 2001–; Council for Conservation and Envmt, RHS, 2001–. Member Board: Field Studies Council Exec., 1979–85; London Ecology Centre Trust, 1985–91; Think Green Campaign, 1985–91; Dir, Nat. Forest Co., 1998–; Chairman: Trust for Urban Ecology, 1987–91 (Pres., 1991–94); Tree Council, 1992–94 (Vice-Chm., 1991–92); London Biodiversity Partnership, 1997–. Vice-Pres., British Assoc. Nature Conservationists, 1981–85; President: Reigate Soc., 1995–2000; Ecology and Conservation Studies Soc., 1999–2001; Biol Scis Section, BAAS, 2000. Mem., British Ecol Soc., 1964– (Mem. Council, 1977–80 and 1988–92). FLS 1981 (Mem. Council, 1983–86); FRSA 1999. Heidelberg Award for Envmtl Excellence, 1999. *Publications:* Wild in London, 1986; (ed jtly) Ecology and Design in Landscape, 1986; contrib. numerous scientific papers and articles on envmtl topics. *Recreations:* photography, music, theatre, walking, ornithology, exploring the natural world. *Address:* Greater London Authority, Romney House, 43 Marsham Street, SW1P 3PY. *T:* (020) 7983 4300; *e-mail:* david.goode@london.gov.uk; 25 Vandon Court, Petty France, SW1H 9HE. *Club:* Athenæum.

GOODE, (Penelope) Cary (Anne); freelance garden designer, since 1992; *b* 5 Dec. 1947; *d* of Ernest Edgar Spink and Rachel Atcherly Spink; *m* 1987, Richard Nicholas Goode. *Educ:* Westwing Sch. Royal Ascot Enclosure Office, 1971; MoD, 1973; Manager, retail business, 1978; Domestic and Social Sec., RCOG, 1980; Educn Administrator, British Heart Foundn, 1982; Dir, Asthma Res. Council, later Nat. Asthma Campaign, 1988–92. *Recreations:* gardening, vintage cars, dogs. *Address:* Nieuport House, Almely, Hereford HR3 6LL. *T:* (01544) 322200.

GOODE, Sir Royston Miles, (Sir Roy), Kt 2000; CBE 1994 (OBE 1972); QC 1990; FBA 1988; barrister; Norton Rose Professor of English Law, Oxford University, 1990–98, now Emeritus Professor; Fellow, St John's College, Oxford, 1990–98, now Emeritus Fellow; *b* 6 April 1933; *s* of Samuel and Bloom Goode; *m* 1964, Catherine Anne Rueff; one *d.* *Educ:* Highgate School. LLB London, 1954; LLD London, 1976. Admitted Solicitor, 1955. Partner, Victor Mishcon & Co., solicitors, 1966–71, Consultant 1971–88. Called to the Bar, Inner Temple, 1988; Hon. Bencher, 1992. Queen Mary College, University of London: Prof. of Law, 1971–73; Head of Dept and Dean of Faculty of Laws, 1976–80; Crowther Prof. of Credit and Commercial Law, 1973–89; Dir and Founder, Centre for Commercial Law Studies, 1980–89. Vis. Prof., Melbourne, 1975; Aust. Commonwealth Vis. Fellow, 1975. Chairman: Advertising Adv. Cttee, IBA, 1976–80; Pension Law Rev. Cttee, 1992–93; Member: Cttee on Consumer Credit, 1968–71; Monopolies and Mergers Commn, 1981–86; Departmental Cttee on Arbitration Law, DTI, 1986–; Council of the Banking Ombudsman, 1989–92. Justice: Mem. Council, 1975; Chm. Exec. Cttee, 1994–96 (Vice-Chm., 1988–94); Mem., Council of Management, British Inst. of Internat. and Comparative Law, 1982. Hon. President: Centre for Commercial Law Studies, 1990–; Oxford Inst. of Legal Practice, 1994–. Hon. Fellow, QMW (Fellow, 1991). FRSA 1990. Hon. DSc (Econ) London, 1996. *Publications:* Hire-Purchase Law and Practice, 1962, 2nd edn 1970, with Supplement 1975; The Hire-Purchase Act 1964, 1964; (with J. S. Ziegel) Hire-Purchase and Conditional Sale: a Comparative Survey of Commonwealth and American Law, 1965; Introduction to the Consumer Credit Act, 1974; (ed) Consumer Credit Legislation, 1977; Consumer Credit, 1978; Commercial Law, 1982, 2nd edn 1995; Legal Problems of Credit and Security, 1982, 2nd edn 1988; Payment Obligations in Commercial and Financial Transactions, 1983; Proprietary Rights and Insolvency in Sales Transactions, 1985, 2nd edn 1989; Principles of Corporate Insolvency Law, 1990, 2nd edn 1997. *Recreations:* chess, reading, walking, browsing in bookshops. *Address:* c/o St John's College, Oxford OX1 3JP; 42 St John Street, Oxford OX1 2LH. *Club:* Reform.

GOODENOUGH, Sir Anthony (Michael), KCMG 1997 (CMG 1990); HM Diplomatic Service, retired; Secretary-General, Order of St John, since 2000; *b* 5 July 1941; *s* of Rear-Adm. Michael Grant Goodenough, CBE, DSO, and Nancy Waterfield (*née* Slater); *m* 1967, Veronica Mary, *d* of Col Peter Pender-Cudlip, LVO; two *s* one *d.* *Educ:* Wellington Coll.; New Coll., Oxford. *Recreation:* MA 1980. Voluntary Service Overseas, Sarawak, 1963–64; Foreign Office, 1964; Athens, 1967; Private Secretary to Parliamentary Under Secretary, 1971, and Minister of State, FCO, 1972; Paris, 1974; First Sec., FCO, 1977; Counsellor on secondment to Cabinet Office, 1980; Hd of Chancery, Islamabad, 1982; Counsellor, FCO, 1986–89; High Comr, Ghana and Ambassador (non-resident), Togo, 1989–92; Asst Under-Sec. of State (Africa and Commonwealth), FCO, 1992–95; High Comr to Canada, 1996–2000. Gov., London Goodenough Trust for Overseas Graduates, 2000–. *Recreations:* reading, walking, gardening. *Address:* 9 Thornton Hill, SW19 4HU. *Club:* Royal Over-Seas League.

GOODENOUGH, Frederick Roger; DL; FCIB; Director: Barclays PLC, 1985–89; *b* 21 Dec. 1927; *s* of Sir William Macnamara Goodenough, 1st Bt, and late Lady (Dorothea Louisa) Goodenough; *m* 1954, Marguerite June Mackintosh; one *s* two *d.* *Educ:* Eton; Magdalene Coll., Cambridge (MA). MA Oxon; FCIB (FIB 1968). Joined Barclays Bank Ltd, 1950; Local Director: Birmingham, 1958; Reading, 1960; Oxford, 1969–87; Director: Barclays Bank UK Ltd, 1971–87; Barclays Internat. Ltd, 1977–87; Barclays Bank PLC, 1979–89; Adv. Dir, Barclays Bank Thames Valley Region, 1988–89; Mem., London Cttee, Barclays Bank DCO, 1966–71, Barclays Bank Internat. Ltd, 1971–80. Supernumerary Fellow, Wolfson Coll., Oxford, 1989–95 (Hon. Fellow, 1995). Sen. Partner, Broadwell Manor Farm, 1968–; Curator, Oxford Univ. Chest, 1974–93; Trustee: Nuffield Med. Benefaction, 1968– (Chm., 1987–); Nuffield Dominions Trust, 1968– (Chm., 1987–); Nuffield Orthopaedic Trust, 1978– (Chm., 1981–); Oxford and Dist Hosps Improvement and Develt Fund, 1968– (Chm., 1982–88); Radcliffe Med. Foundn, 1987–98; Oxford Preservation Trust, 1980–89; Pres., Oxfordshire Rural Community Council, 1993–98. Governor: Shiplake Coll., 1963–74 (Chm., 1966–70); Wellington Coll., 1968–74; London Hse for Overseas Graduates, 1985–. Patron, Anglo-Ghanian Soc. (UK), 1991–. FLS (Mem. Council, 1968–75; Treasurer, 1970–75); FRSA. High Sheriff, 1987–88, DL 1989, Oxfordshire. *Recreations:* shooting, fishing, photography, ornithology. *Address:* Broadwell Manor, Lechlade, Glos GL7 3QS. *T:* (01367) 860326. *Club:* Brooks's.

GOODENOUGH, Prof. John Bannister; Virginia H. Cockrell Centennial Professor of Engineering, University of Texas at Austin, since 1986; *b* 25 July 1922; *s* of Erwin Ramsdell Goodenough and Helen Lewis Goodenough; *m* 1951, Irene Johnston Wiseman. *Educ:* Yale Univ. (AB, Maths); Univ. of Chicago (MS, PhD, Physics). Meteorologist, US Army Air Force, 1942–48; Research Engr, Westinghouse Corp., 1951–52; Research Physicist (Leader, Electronic Materials Gp), Lincoln Laboratory, MIT, 1952–76; Prof. and Hd of Dept of Inorganic Chemistry, Oxford Univ., 1976–86. Raman Prof., Indian Acad. of Science, 1982–83 (Hon. Mem., 1980–). Member: Nat. Acad., of Engrg, 1976–; Presidential Commn on Superconductivity, 1989–90. Foreign Associate, Acad. of Scis, Institut de France, 1992. Dr *hc*, Bordeaux, 1967. Von Hippel Award, Materials Res. Soc., 1989; Sen. Res. Award, Amer. Soc. of Engrg Educn, 1990; Univ. of Pennsylvania Medal for Dist. Achievement, 1996; John Bardeen Award, Minerals, Metals & Materials Soc., 1997; Olim Palladium Award, Electrochem. Soc., 1999–; Japan Prize, 2001. Associate Editor: Materials Research Bulletin, 1966–; Jl Solid State Chemistry, 1969–; Structure and Bonding, 1978–; Solid State Ionics, 1980–94; Superconductor Science and Technology, 1987–; Jl of Materials Chem., 1990–95; Chem. of Materials, 1990–; Co-editor, International Series of Monographs on Chemistry, 1979–86; Member Executive, Editorial Board: Jl of Applied Electrochem., 1983–88; European Jl of Solid State and Inorganic Chem., 1992–. *Publications:* Magnetism and the Chemical Bond, 1963; Les oxydes des métaux de transition, 1973; numerous research papers in learned jls. *Recreations:* walking, travel. *Address:* Texas Materials Institute, University of Texas at Austin, ETC 9.102, Austin, TX 78712, USA. *T:* (512) 4711646.

GOODENOUGH, Sir William (McLernon), 3rd Bt *cr* 1943, of Broadwell and Filkins, co. Oxford; Founder and Deputy Chairman, Design Bridge Ltd, since 1986; *b* 5 Aug. 1954; *o s* of Sir Richard Edmund Goodenough, 2nd Bt and Jane Isobel Goodenough (*d* 1998); *S* father, 1996; *m* 1982, Louise Elizabeth Ortmans (marr. diss. 1998); one *s* two *d.* *Educ:* Stanbridge Earls Sch.; Southampton Univ. Designer, Allied International Designers, 1980–83; Man. Dir, Allied International Designers (Singapore), 1983–86. *Recreations:* stalking, fishing, shooting, painting. *Heir: s* Samuel William Hector Goodenough, *b* 11 June 1993. *Address:* 7 Cape Yard, Kennet Street, E1W 2JU. *Club:* Boodle's.

GOODFELLOW, Prof. Julia Mary, CBE 2001; PhD; FMedSci; FIBiol; Vice-Master, since 1998, Professor of Biomolecular Sciences, since 1995, and Chairman, Department of Crystallography, since 1996, Birkbeck College, University of London; *b* 1 July 1951; *d* of Gerald Lansdall and late Brenda Lansdall; *m* 1972, Peter Neville Goodfellow, *qv*; one *s* one *d.* *Educ:* Woking Co. Sch. for Girls; Reigate Co. Sch. for Girls; Univ. of Bristol (BSc Physics); Open Univ. (PhD Biophysics 1975). NATO Res. Fellow, Stanford Univ., 1976–78; Birkbeck College, University of London: Res. Fellow, 1979–83; Lectr, then

Sen. Lectr and Reader, 1983–95. Wellcome Trust Res. Leave Fellow, 1990–93. Chm., Wellcome Trust Molecular and Cell Panel, 1995–98. Member, BBSRC, 1997–; CCLRC, 2000–. FRSA; FMedSci 2001. *Publications:* (ed) Molecular Dynamics: applications in molecular biology, 1990; (ed) Computer Modelling in Molecular Biology, 1992; (ed) Computer Simulation in Molecular Biology, 1995; numerous contribs to learned jls. *Recreations:* reading, family. *Address:* Department of Crystallography, Birkbeck College, Malet Street, WC1E 7HX. *T:* (020) 7631 6833; *e-mail:* j.goodfellow@mail.cryst.bbk.ac.uk.

GOODFELLOW, Michael Robert, PhD; Divisional Managing Director and Board Member, Defence Evaluation and Research Agency, Ministry of Defence, since 1998; *b* 7 Aug. 1948; *s* of Henry Goodfellow, MBE and Eileen Goodfellow (*née* Muff); *m* 1972, Karon Elizabeth Taylor; one *s* one *d. Educ:* St Bartholomew's Grammar Sch., Newbury; Imperial Coll., London (BSc 1st Cl. Hons Theoretical Physics 1970; ARCS 1970; DIC 1974; PhD 1974). CEng, FIEE 1988; FInstP 1999. Student Asst, Rutherford High Energy Lab., 1967; Res. Student, UKAEA, 1970–73; Sen. Analyst, Scicon Ltd, BP Gp, 1973–76; PSO, Systems Analysis Res. Unit, Depts of the Envmt and Transport, 1976–79; project manager, then staff manager, subseq. business gp manager, Sema Gp plc, 1979–95 (on secondment as Commercial Dir, DRA, 1992); Commercial Dir, DRA, MoD, 1995–98. Director, 1987–91: Yard Ltd; Sema Scientific Ltd; Dowty-Sema Ltd; Stephen Howe Ltd; VSEL-CAP Ltd; CAP-DBE Ltd; non-executive Director: Army Base Repair Orgn, MoD, 1998; Defence Aviation Repair Agency, MoD, 2000. Chm., Mgt Cttee, Surrey and NE Hants Industrial Mission, 1998–. Gov., Holy Trinity Sch., Guildford, 1989–97 (Chm., Finance Cttee). Mem., IAM. FIMgt 1998. *Recreations:* sailing, walking, gardening. *Address:* Defence Evaluation and Research Agency, Cody Building, Ively Road, Farnborough GU14 0LX. *T:* (01252) 394588, *Fax:* (01252) 394659; *e-mail:* mgoodfellow@dera.gov.uk; mike.goodfellow@btinternet.com.

GOODFELLOW, Prof. Peter Neville, DPhil; FRS 1992; Senior Vice President, Discovery Research, GlaxoSmithKline, since 2001; *b* 4 Aug. 1951; *s* of Bernard Clifford Roy Goodfellow and Doreen Olga (*née* Berry); *m* 1972, Julia Mary Lansdall (*see* J. M. Goodfellow); one *s* one *d. Educ:* Bristol Univ. (BSc 1st Cl. Hons 1972); Oxford Univ. (DPhil 1975). MRC Postdoctoral Fellow, Oxford Univ., 1975–76; Stanford University: Jane Coffin Childs Postdoctoral Fellow, 1976–78; Amer. Cancer Soc. Sen. Fellow, 1978–79; Imperial Cancer Research Fund: Staff Scientist, 1979–83; Sen. Scientist, 1983–86; Principal Scientist, 1986–92; Arthur Balfour Prof. of Genetics, Cambridge Univ., 1992–96; Sen. Vice Pres., Biopharmaceuticals and Neuroscis, then Discovery, SmithKline Beecham Pharmaceuticals, 1996–2001. Founder FMedSci 1998. *Publications:* (ed) Genetic analysis of the cell surface in Receptors and Recognition, Vol. 16, 1984; (ed jtly) The Mammalian Y Chromosome: molecular search for the sex determining gene, 1987; (ed) Cystic Fibrosis, 1989; (ed jtly) Molecular genetics of muscle disease, 1989; (ed jtly) Sex determination and the Y chromosome, 1991; (ed jtly) Mammalian Genetics, 1992; numerous reviews and contribs to learned jls. *Recreations:* soccer, science, sex. *Address:* GlaxoSmithKline, Gunnels Wood Road, Stevenage, Herts SG1 2NY.

GOODFELLOW, Mrs Rosalind Erica; JP; Moderator of the General Assembly of the United Reformed Church, 1982–83; *b* 3 April 1927; *d* of late Rev. William Griffith-Jones and Kathleen (*née* Speakman); *m* 1949, Keith Frank Goodfellow, QC (*d* 1977); two *s* one *d. Educ:* Milton Mount Coll. (now Wentworth Coll.); Royal Holloway Coll., London Univ. (BA Hons). Member: BCC Div. of Community Affairs Bd, 1980–83; Churches' Council for Covenanting, 1981–82; Chm., World Church and Mission Dept, URC, 1983; Moderator, Churches Council for Inter-faith Relations, CCBI, 1994–99. Chairman: Surrey and W Sussex CAB, 1985; Age Concern Surrey, 1990–93. Mem. Council, Brunel Univ., 1995–2000. JP Surrey (Esher and Walton PSD), 1960. *Recreation:* attending committee meetings. *Address:* 2 Judge Walk, Claygate, Surrey KT10 0RP. *T:* (01372) 467656.

GOODHART, family name of **Baron Goodhart.**

GOODHART, Baron *cr* 1997 (Life Peer), of Youlbury in the co. of Oxfordshire; **William Howard Goodhart,** Kt 1989; QC 1979; *b* 18 Jan. 1933; *s* of late Prof. A. L. Goodhart, Hon. KBE, QC, FBA and Cecily (*née* Carter); *m* 1966, Hon. Celia McClare Herbert (*see* Lady Goodhart); one *s* two *d. Educ:* Eton; Trinity Coll., Cambridge (Scholar, MA); Harvard Law Sch. (Commonwealth Fund Fellow, LLM). Nat. Service, 1951–53 (2nd Lt, Oxford and Bucks Light Infantry). Called to the Bar, Lincoln's Inn, 1957, Bencher, 1986. Dir, Bar Mutual Indemnity Fund Ltd, 1988–97. Member: Council of Legal Educn, 1986–92; Conveyancing Standing Cttee, Law Commn, 1987–89; Tax Law Review Cttee, 1994–; Cttee on Standards in Public Life, 1997–; Select Cttee on EU, H of L, 1998–; Select Cttee on Delegated Powers and Deregulation, H of L, 1998–. Chm., Cambridge Univ. Court of Discipline, 1993–2000. Member: Internat. Commn of Jurists, 1993– (Exec. Cttee, 1995–); Council, Justice, 1972– (Vice Chm., 1978–88, Chm., 1988–94, Exec. Cttee); Council, RIIA, 1999–; Vice Chm., Liaison Cttee, Human Rights Inst., 1996–; leader of Human Rights Missions: to Hong Kong, 1991; Kashmir, 1993; to Israel, and The West Bank, 1994; Kenya, 1996; Sri Lanka, 1997. Contested: Kensington: (SDP) 1983; (SDP/Alliance) 1987; (Lib Dem) July 1988; (Lib Dem) Oxford West and Abingdon, 1992. Chairman: SDP Council Arrangements Cttee, 1982–88; Lib Dem Conf. Cttee, 1988–91; Lib Dem Lawyers Assoc., 1988–91; Mem., Lib Dem Policy Cttee, 1988–97 (Vice-Chm., 1995–97). Mem. Adv. Council, Centre for Socio-Legal Studies, Oxford, 1994–. Trustee: Campden Charities, 1975–90; Airey Neave Trust, 1999–. *Publications:* (with Prof. Gareth Jones) Specific Performance, 1986, 2nd edn 1996; reports of Human Rights Missions; contribs to Halsbury's Laws of England; articles in legal periodicals. *Recreations:* walking, ski-ing. *Address:* House of Lords, SW1A 0PW. *Clubs:* Brooks's; Century Association (New York).
See also C. A. E. Goodhart, Sir P. C. Goodhart.

GOODHART, Lady; Celia McClare Goodhart; Chairman: Family Planning Association, since 1999; Executive Committee, Oxford University Society (formerly Oxford Society), since 1996; Principal, Queen's College, Harley Street, London, 1991–99; *b* 25 July 1939; *er d* of 2nd Baron Hemingford and Elizabeth (*née* Clark) (*d* 1979); *m* 1966, William Howard Goodhart (*see* Baron Goodhart); one *s* two *d. Educ:* St Michael's, Limpsfield; St Hilda's Coll., Oxford (MA; Hon. Fellow 1989). HM Civil Service, MAFF, seconded to Treasury, 1960–66; Hist. Tutor, Queen's Coll., London and Westminster Tutors, 1966–81. Contested: (SDP) Kettering, 1983; (SDP Liberal Alliance) Kettering, 1987; (SDP) Northants (for European Parlt), 1984. Chairman: SDP Envmt Policy Gp, 1985–87; Women for Social Democracy, 1986–88; Member: SDP Nat. and Policy Cttees, 1984–88; Liberal Democrats Fed. Exec. Cttee, 1988–90; Pres., E Midlands Liberal Democrats, 1988–91. Member: Elizabeth Nuffield Educnl Fund, 1972–82; St Bartholomew's Hosp. Ethical Cttee, 1974–86; Lindop Cttee on Data Protection, 1976–78; Nat. Gas Consumer Councils, 1979–82 (also Chm., N Thames Gas Consumer Council); Women's Nat. Commn, 1986–89; Code Monitoring Cttee for Mkting of Infant Formulae in UK, 1986–90; Med. Audit Cttee, RCP, 1989–92; Internat. Women's Forum and Forum UK, 1990–; Council, GSA, 1997–99 (Sec., 1994–96, Chm., 1996–99, London Reg.); Ethics Cttee, RCOG, 1999–. President: Schoolmistresses and Governesses Benevolent Instn, 1991–; London Marriage Guidance Council, 1990–95; Chm., Youth Clubs, UK, 1988–91 (Vice-Pres., 1991–); Mem., Forum UK (Chm., 2001–). Trustee: CPRE, 1987–91; Oxford Univ. Nuffield Medical Benefaction, 1988–96; Childline, 1999–. Governor: Godolphin and Latymer, 1976–86; St Michael's, Limpsfield, 1975–83; Isaac Newton Comprehensive, 1977–81; Sch. of St Helen and St Katharine, Abingdon, Northwood Coll., 1999–. FRSA 1989. *Recreation:* sociability. *Address:* 11 Clarence Terrace, NW1 4RD. *T:* (020) 7262 1319; Youlbury House, Boars Hill, Oxford OX1 5HH. *T:* (01865) 735477. *Clubs:* Reform; Cosmopolitan (New York).
See also H. T. Moggridge.

GOODHART, Prof. Charles Albert Eric, CBE 1997; PhD; FBA 1990; Norman Sosnow Professor of Banking and Finance, London School of Economics and Political Science, since 1985; *b* 23 Oct. 1936; *s* of late Prof. Arthur Goodhart, Hon. KBE, QC, FBA, and Cecily (*née* Carter); *m* 1960, Margaret, (Miffy), Ann Smith; one *s* three *d. Educ:* Eton; Trinity Coll., Cambridge (scholar; 1st Cl. Hons Econs Tripos); Harvard Grad. Sch. of Arts and Sciences (PhD 1963). National Service, 1955–57 (2nd Lieut KRRC). Prize Fellowship in Econs, Trinity Coll., Cambridge, 1963; Asst Lectr in Econs, Cambridge Univ., 1963–64; Econ. Adviser, DEA, 1965–67; Lectr in Monetary Econs, LSE, 1967–69; Bank of England: Adviser with particular reference to monetary policy, 1969–80; a Chief Adviser, 1980–85; External Mem., Monetary Policy Cttee, 1997–2000. Mem., Adv. Cttee, Hong Kong Exchange Fund, 1990–97. *Publications:* The New York Money Market and the Finance of Trade, 1900–13, 1968; The Business of Banking, 1891–1914, 1972; Money, Information and Uncertainty, 1975, 2nd edn 1989; Monetary Theory and Practice: the UK experience, 1984; The Evolution of Central Banks, 1985, rev. edn 1988; (ed jtly) The Operation and Regulation of Financial Markets, 1987; (ed) EMU and ESCB after Maastricht, 1992; (jtly) The Future of Central Banking, 1994; The Central Bank and the Financial System, 1995; (ed) The Emerging Framework of Financial Regulation, 1998; (jtly) Financial Regulation: why, how and where now?, 1998; (ed) Which Lender of Last Resort for Europe, 2000; (jtly) The Foreign Exchange Market, 2000; articles in econ. jls and papers contrib. to econ. books. *Recreation:* keeping sheep. *Address:* London School of Economics and Political Science, Houghton Street, WC2A 2AE. *T:* (020) 7955 7555.
See also Baron Goodhart, Sir P. C. Goodhart.

GOODHART, Rear-Adm. (Hilary Charles) Nicholas, CB 1972; FRAeS; *b* 28 Sept. 1919; *s* of G. C. Goodhart; *m* 1975, Molly Copsey. *Educ:* RNC Dartmouth; RNEC Keyham. Joined RN, 1933; served in Mediterranean in HM Ships Formidable and Dido, 1941–43; trained as pilot, 1944; served as fighter pilot in Burma Campaign, 1945; trained as test pilot, 1946; served on British Naval Staff, Washington, 1953–55; idc 1965; Rear-Adm. 1970; Mil. Dep. to Head of Defence Sales, MoD, 1970–73, retired. World Gliding Champion, 2-seaters, 1956; British Gliding Champion, 1962, 1967 and 1971. Freedom of London, 1945; Mem. Ct of Grocers' Co., 1975, Master, 1981. US Legion of Merit, 1958. *Recreation:* computer programming. *Address:* Cable House, Lindridge Park, Teignmouth, Devon TQ14 9TF. *T:* (01626) 779790.

GOODHART, Sir Philip (Carter), Kt 1981; *b* 3 Nov. 1925; *s* of late Prof. Arthur Goodhart, Hon. KBE, QC, FBA, and Cecily (*née* Carter); *m* 1950, Valerie Winant; three *s* four *d. Educ:* Hotchkiss Sch., USA; Trinity Coll., Cambridge. Served KRRC and Parachute Regt, 1943–47. Editorial staff, Daily Telegraph, 1950–54; Editorial staff, Sunday Times, 1955–57. Mem., LCC Educn Cttee, 1956–57. Contested (C) Consett, Co. Durham, Gen. Election, 1950; MP (C) Beckenham, March 1957–1992. Parly Under-Sec. of State, Northern Ireland Office, and Minister responsible for Dept of the Environment (NI), 1979–81; Parly Under Sec. of State, MoD, 1981. Joint Hon. Sec., 1922 Cttee, 1960–79; Mem., Cons. Adv. Cttee on Policy, 1973–79; Chairman: Cons. Parly Defence Cttee, 1972–74 (Vice-Chm., 1974–79); Cons. Parly NI Cttee, 1976–79; Parly Select Cttee on Sound Broadcasting, 1983–87; Anglo-Taiwan Parly Gp, 1987–92. Member: British Delegation to Council of Europe and WEU, 1961–63; British Delegation to UN Gen. Assembly, 1963; North Atlantic Assembly, 1964–79 and 1983–92; Leader, CPA Delegns to Australia, 1984, Sri Lanka, 1989. Member: Council, Consumers' Assoc., 1959–68, 1970–79 (Vice-Pres., 1983–); Adv. Council on Public Records, 1970–79; Exec. Cttee, British Council, 1974–79; Council, RUSI, 1973–76. Chairman: Bd of Sulgrave Manor, 1982–; Warship Preservation Trust, 1987–; Warrior Preservation Trust, 1993–97; Dir, Flagship Portsmouth, 1993–97. Order of the Brilliant Star (China), 1992. *Publications:* The Hunt for Kimathi (with Ian Henderson, GM), 1958; In the Shadow of the Sword, 1964; Fifty Ships that Saved the World, 1965; (with Christopher Chataway) War without Weapons, 1968; Referendum, 1970; The 1922: the history of the 1922 Committee, 1973; Full-Hearted Consent, 1975; various pamphlets incl.: Stand on Your Own Four Feet: a study of work sharing and job splitting, 1982; Jobs Ahead, 1984; Skip Ahead, 1985; Colonel George Washington: soldier of the King, 1993. *Recreation:* ski-ing (Chm. and Capt., Lords and Commons Ski Club, 1971–73). *Address:* 25 Abbotsbury Road, W14 8EJ. *T:* (020) 7602 8237. *Clubs:* Beefsteak, Carlton, Garrick.
See also Baron Goodhart, C. A. E. Goodhart.

GOODHART, Sir Robert (Anthony Gordon), 4th Bt *cr* 1911; Medical Practitioner, Beaminster, Dorset; *b* 15 Dec. 1948; *s* of Sir John Gordon Goodhart, 3rd Bt, FRCGP, and of Margaret Mary Eileen, *d* of late Morgan Morgan; *S* father, 1979; *m* 1972, Kathleen Ellen, *d* of late Rev. A. D. MacRae; two *s* two *d. Educ:* Rugby; Guy's Hospital Medical School, London Univ. MB BS (Lond.), MRCS, LRCP, MRCGP, DObstRCOG. Qualification, 1972. *Recreation:* Real tennis. *Heir: s* Martin Andrew Goodhart, *b* 9 Sept. 1974.

GOODHEW, Duncan Alexander, MBE 1983; Director, LEA Events & Marketing Group, since 1997; Partner, Honours Mill Restaurant, Edenbridge, Kent, since 1986; *b* 27 May 1957; *s* of late Donald Frederick Goodhew and of Dolores Perle Goodhew (*née* Venn); *m* 1984, Anne Patterson; one *s* one *d. Educ:* Millfield Sch.; North Carolina State Univ. (BA Business Mgt 1979). International swimmer, 1976–80; Captain, England and GB squads, 1978–80; competitions: Montreal Olympic Games, 1976; Commonwealth Games, 1978 (Silver Medal: 100m breast stroke; 200m breast stroke; 4×100 medley); World Championships, 1978 (Bronze Medal, 4×100 medley relay); Moscow Olympic Games, 1980 (Gold Medal, 100m breast stroke; Bronze Medal, 4×100 medley relay); Mem., 2-man and 4-man Bobsleigh teams, European Championships, 1981. Dir, Sports Aid Foundation (London) Ltd, 1981–; Trustee: Sports Aid Trust, 1984–; Teenage Cancer Trust, 1995–; City of London Sinfonia. Pres., BT Swimathon, 1987–; Vice President: Dyslexia Inst., 1994–; Youth Sport Trust, 1995–. Patron: Disability Sport, England; The Aurora Charity; Hairline International; Sparks; Cranial Facial Support Unit; James Powell Trust. Hon. Citizen, N Carolina. *Publication:* Sink or Swim (with Victoria Hislop), 2001. *Recreations:* sport (including squash, aerobics, cycling), photography, cooking. *Address:* LEA Events and Marketing Group, 59–60 Russell Square, WC1B 4HJ. *T:* (020) 7759 8500.

GOODHEW, Most Rev. Richard Henry, (Harry), AO 2001; Archbishop of Sydney and Metropolitan of New South Wales, 1993–2001; *b* 19 March 1931; *s* of Baden Powell

Richard Goodhew and Christina Delgarno Goodhew (*née* Fraser); *m* 1958, Pamela (*née* Coughlan); two *s* two *d*. *Educ:* Univ. of Wollongong (MA Hons; DLitt *hc*, 1993); Moore Theol Coll. (ThL 2nd cl. Hons, Diploma 2nd cl. Hons). Ordained 1958; Curate, St Matthew's, Bondi, NSW, 1958; Curate-in-charge, St Bede's, Beverly Hills, NSW, 1959–63; with Bush Church Aid, Ceduna, SA, 1963–66; Rector: St Paul's, Carlingford, NSW, 1966–71; St Stephen's, Coorparoo, Qld, 1971–76; Rector and Senior Canon, St Michael's Cathedral, Wollongong, 1976–79; Archdeacon of Wollongong and Camden, 1979–82; Bishop of Wollongong, Asst Bishop in dio. of Sydney, 1982–93. *Recreations:* jogging, reading, tennis, swimming. *Address:* 134A O'Briens Road, Figtree, NSW 2525, Australia. *T:* (2) 42253332.

GOODHEW, Sir Victor (Henry), Kt 1982; *b* 30 Nov. 1919; *s* of late Rudolph Goodhew, Mannings Heath, Sussex; *m* 1st, 1940, Sylvia Johnson (marr. diss.); one *s* one *d*; 2nd, 1951, Suzanne Gordon-Burge (marr. diss. 1972); 3rd, 1972, Eva Rittinghausen (marr. diss. 1981). *Educ:* King's Coll. Sch. Served War of 1939–45: RAF, 1939–46; comd Airborne Radar Unit, attached 6th Airborne Div.; Sqdn Ldr 1945. Member: Westminster City Council, 1953–59; LCC, 1958–61. Contested (C) Paddington North, 1955; MP (C) St Albans Div., Herts, Oct. 1959–83. PPS to Mr C. I. Orr-Ewing, OBE, MP (when Civil Lord of the Admiralty), May 1962–63; PPS to Hon. Thomas Galbraith, MP (Jt Parly Sec., Min. of Transport), 1963–64; Asst Govt Whip, June-Oct. 1970; a Lord Comr, HM Treasury, 1970–73. Member: Speaker's Panel of Chairmen, 1975–83; Select Cttee, House of Commons Services, 1978–83; House of Commons Commn, 1979–83; Jt Sec. 1922 Cttee, 1979–83; Vice-Chm., Cons. Defence Cttee, 1974–83. Chm., Bd of Management, Inst. of Sports Medicine, 1982– (Mem., 1967–70, 1973–82). *Recreations:* swimming, reading. *Address:* The Coach House, St Leonard's Dale, Winkfield Road, Windsor, Berks SL4 4AQ. *T:* (01753) 859073. *Clubs:* United and Cecil, 1900; Constitutional (Windsor).

GOODING, Anthony James Joseph S.; *see* Simonds-Gooding.

GOODING, Valerie Frances; Chief Executive, British United Provident Association, since 1998; *b* 14 May 1950; *d* of Frank and Gladys Gooding; *m* 1986, Crawford Macdonald; two *s*. *Educ:* Leiston GS, Suffolk; Univ. of Warwick (BA Hons 1971); Kingston Univ. (Dip. Mgt Studies 1981). British Airways: Reservations Agent, 1973–76; Mgt Trainer, 1977–80; Personnel Manager, 1980–83; Reservations Manager, 1983–86; Head of Cabin Services, 1987–92; Head of Mktg, 1992–93; Dir of Business Units, 1993–96; Dir, Asia Pacific, 1996; Man. Dir, UK, BUPA, 1996–98. Director: BAA plc, 1998–; Compass plc, 2000–. Hon. DBA Bournemouth, 1999. *Recreations:* tennis, theatre, travel, keeping fit, family life. *Address:* BUPA House, 15–19 Bloomsbury Way, WC1A 2BA.

GOODISON, Sir Alan (Clowes), KCMG 1985 (CMG 1975); CVO 1980; HM Diplomatic Service, retired; *b* 20 Nov. 1926; *o s* of late Harold and Winifred Goodison (*née* Ludlam); *m* 1956, Anne Rosemary Fitton (*d* 1994); one *s* two *d*. *Educ:* Colfe's Grammar Sch.; Trinity Coll., Cambridge (Scholar, Mod. and Medieval Langs Tripos, first cl.; MA 1951); DipTh London 1995; MA (Theol) London 1997. Army, Lieut, 1947–49. Foreign Office, Third Sec., 1949; Middle East Centre for Arab Studies, 1950; served in Cairo, Tripoli, Khartoum, Lisbon, Amman, and Bonn, with spells in Foreign Office, 1950–68; Counsellor, Kuwait, 1969–71; Head of Trg Dept and Dir, Diplomatic Service Lang. Centre, FCO, 1971–72; Head of S European Dept, FCO, 1973–76; Minister, Rome, 1976–80; Asst Under-Sec. of State, FCO, 1980–83; Ambassador, Dublin, 1983–86. Dir, Wates Foundn, 1988–92. Chm., Charities Evaluation Services, 1993–97; Trustee, Hampstead Wells and Campden Trust, 1993–. Pres., Beckenham Chorale, 1972–73. Licensed Reader of Anglican Church, 1959–62, 1966–82, 1988–; a Bishops' Selector for ABM (formerly ACCM), 1989–96; Moderator of Reader Training, Edmonton Episcopal Area, 1990–92. Mem. Council: Jerusalem and the East Mission, 1964–65; Anglican Centre, Rome, 1977–80. Grande Ufficiale dell'Ordine al Merito della Repubblica Italiana (Hon.), 1980. *Publications:* articles on devotional subjects and trans. for Encyclopaedia of Islam. *Recreations:* theology, music, theatre, reading. *Address:* 12 Gardnor Mansions, Church Row, NW3 6UR.

GOODISON, Sir Nicholas (Proctor), Kt 1982; Chairman, National Art Collections Fund, since 1986; Deputy Chairman, Lloyds TSB Group plc, 1995–2000 (Chairman, TSB Group, 1989–95); Chairman, TSB Bank plc, 1989–2000; Deputy Chairman, Corus Group plc (formerly British Steel), 1993–99 (Director, since 1989); *b* 16 May 1934; *s* of Edmund Harold Goodison and Eileen Mary Carrington (*née* Proctor); *m* 1960, Judith Abel Smith; one *s* two *d*. *Educ:* Marlborough Coll.; King's Coll., Cambridge (Scholar; BA Classics 1958, MA; PhD Architecture and History of Art, 1981). H. E. Goodison & Co., later Quilter Goodison, 1958–88: Partner, 1962; Chm., 1975–88. Director: Ottoman Bank, 1986–92; Banque Paribas (Luxembourg) SA, 1986–88; Banque Paribas Capital Markets Ltd, 1986–88; Gen. Accident, 1987–95. Mem. Council, Stock Exchange, 1968–88; Chm., Stock Exchange, 1976–88; President: Internat. Fedn of Stock Exchanges, 1985–86; British Bankers' Assoc., 1991–96; Vice Pres., Chartered Inst. of Bankers, 1989– (FCIB 1989); Member: Panel on Takeovers and Mergers, 1976–88; Council of Securities Industry, 1978–85; Securities Assoc., 1986–88. Mem. Council, Industrial Soc., 1976–2000; Chairman: Courtauld Inst. of Art, 1982–; Crafts Council, 1997–; Director: ENO, 1977–98 (Vice-Chm., 1980–98); Burlington Magazine Ltd, 1975–; Trustee, Nat. Heritage Meml Fund, 1988–97. Mem., Royal Commn on the Long Term Care of the Elderly, 1997–99. Hon. Keeper of Furniture, Fitzwilliam Museum, Cambridge; President: Furniture History Soc., 1990– (Hon. Treas., 1970–90); Antiquarian Horological Soc., 1986–93. Chm., Review Steering Gp, Nat. Record of Achievement, 1996–97; Pres., Heads, Teachers and Industry, 1999–; Member: Adv. Bd, Judge Inst. of Mgt Studies, 1999–; FEFCE, 2000–01. Governor, Marlborough Coll., 1981–97. CIMgt; FSA, FRSA, Sen. FRCA; Hon. Fellow RA, 1987; Hon. FRIBA 1992. Hon. DLitt City, 1985; Hon. LLD Exeter, 1989; Hon. DSc Aston, 1994; Hon. DArt De Montfort, 1998; Hon. DCL Northumbria, 1999. Chevalier, Légion d'Honneur, 1990. *Publications:* English Barometers 1680–1860, 1968, 2nd edn 1977; Ormolu: The Work of Matthew Boulton, 1974; many papers and articles on history of furniture, clocks and barometers. *Recreations:* history of furniture and decorative arts, opera, walking. *Address:* PO Box 2512, W1A 5ZP. *Clubs:* Athenæum, Beefsteak, Arts.

GOODLAD, Rt Hon. Sir Alastair (Robertson), KCMG 1997; PC 1992; High Commissioner to Australia, since 2000; *b* 4 July 1943; *y s* of late Dr John Goodlad and Isabel (*née* Sinclair); *m* 1968, Cecilia Barbara, 2nd *d* of late Col Richard Hurst and Lady Barbara Hurst; two *s*. *Educ:* Marlborough Coll.; King's Coll., Cambridge (MA, LLB). Contested (C) Crewe Div., 1970; MP (C) Northwich, Feb. 1974–1983, Eddisbury, 1983–99. An Asst Govt Whip, 1981–82; a Lord Commissioner of HM Treasury, 1982–84; Parly Under-Sec. of State, Dept of Energy, 1984–87; Comptroller of HM Household, 1989–90; Dep. Govt Chief Whip and Treasurer, HM Household, 1990–92; Minister of State, FCO, 1992–95; Parly Sec. to HM Treasury and Govt Chief Whip, 1995–97; Opposition frontbench spokesman on internat. devel, 1997–98. Member: Select Cttee on Agric., 1979–81; Select Cttee on Televising of Proceedings of the House, 1987–89; Jt Hon. Secretary: Cons. Party Trade Cttee, 1978–81 (Jt Vice-Chm., 1979–81); Cons. NI Cttee, 1979–81; Hon. Sec., All Party Heritage Gp, 1979–81; Chm., All Party Parly Cttee for Refugees, 1987–89. Chm., NW Area Cons. Members, 1987–89. *Address:* c/o Foreign and Commonwealth Office, SW1A 2AH. *Clubs:* Brooks's, Beefsteak, Pratt's.

GOODLAND, Judith Mary; Head Mistress, Wycombe Abbey School, 1989–98; *b* 26 May 1938; *d* of Rolf Thornton Ferro and Joan (*née* O'Hanlon); *m* 1961, A. T. Goodland (marr. diss.); one *s* two *d*. *Educ:* Howell's Sch., Denbigh; Bristol Univ. (BA Hons); Charlotte Mason Coll., Ambleside (Cert Ed). Head, Modern Languages Dept, Cartmel Priory C of E Comprehensive Sch., 1968–72; Casterton Sch., Kirkby Lonsdale, 1980–83; Headmistress, St George's Sch., Ascot, 1983–88. FRSA 1994. *Recreations:* fell walking, bridge. *Address:* 12 Starnthwaite Ghyll, Crosthwaite, Kendal, Cumbria LA8 8JN. *Club:* Lansdowne.

GOODMAN, Dame Barbara; *see* Goodman, Dame P. B.

GOODMAN, Elinor Mary; Political Editor, Channel Four News, since 1988; *b* 11 Oct. 1946; *d* of Edward Weston Goodman and Pamela Longbottom; *m* 1985, Derek John Scott, *qv*. *Educ:* private schools, secretarial college. Financial Times: Consumer Affairs Corresp., 1971–78; Political Corresp., 1978–82; Political Corresp., Channel Four News, 1982–88. *Recreations:* riding, walking.

GOODMAN, Geoffrey George, CBE 1998; Editor, British Journalism Review, since 1989; broadcaster and commentator, BBC and commercial television and radio, since 1986; *b* 2 July 1921; *s* of Michael Goodman and Edythe (*née* Bowman); *m* 1947, Margit (*née* Freudenbergova); one *s* one *d*. *Educ:* elementary schs, Stockport and Manchester; grammar schs, London; LSE (BScEcon). RAF, 1940–46. Manchester Guardian, 1946–47; Daily Mirror, 1947–48; News Chronicle, 1949–59; Daily Herald, 1959–64; The Sun (IPC), 1964–69; Daily Mirror, 1969–86 (Industrial Editor, 1969–86; Asst Editor, 1976–86). Fellow, Nuffield Coll., Oxford, 1974–76. Broadcaster, BBC Current Affairs, and LBC/IRN, later London News Radio, 1986–. Head of Govt's Counter-inflation Publicity Unit, 1975–76; Member: Labour Party Cttee on Industrial Democracy, 1966–67; Royal Commn on the Press, 1974–77; TGWU; NUJ. Hon. MA Oxon. Descriptive Writer of the Year, Nat. Press Awards, 1971; Gerald Barry Award for Journalism, Granada TV Press Awards, 1984. *Publications:* General Strike of 1926, 1951; Brother Frank, 1969; The Awkward Warrior, 1979; The Miners' Strike, 1985; The State of the Nation, 1997; contrib. London Inst. of World Affairs, 1948. *Recreations:* pottering, poetry, supporting Tottenham Hotspur FC, and climbing—but not social. *Address:* 64 Flower Lane, Mill Hill, NW7 2JL. *Club:* Savile.

GOODMAN, Prof. John Francis Bradshaw, CBE 1995; PhD; CCIPD; Frank Thomas Professor of Industrial Relations, University of Manchester Institute of Science and Technology, since 1975 (Vice-Principal, 1979–81); *b* 2 Aug. 1940; *s* of Edwin and Amy Goodman; *m* 1967, Elizabeth Mary Towns; one *s* one *d*. *Educ:* Chesterfield Grammar Sch.; London Sch. of Economics (BSc Econ; PhD); MSc Manchester. Personnel Officer, Ford Motor Co. Ltd, 1962–64; Lectr in Industrial Econs, Univ. of Nottingham, 1964–69; Industrial Relations Adviser, NBPI, 1969–70; Sen. Lectr in Industrial Relations, Univ. of Manchester, 1970–74; Chm., Manchester Sch. of Management, UMIST, 1977–79, 1987–94. Vis. Professor: Univ. of WA, 1981, 1984; McMaster Univ., 1985; Univ. of Auckland, 1996. Pres., British Univs Industrial Relations Assoc., 1983–86. Member: Council, ACAS, 1987–98; Training Bd, 1991–97, Council, 1993–97, ESRC. Dep. Chm., Central Arbitration Cttee, 1998–; Chm., Professional Football Negotiating and Consultative Cttee, 2000–. *Publications:* Shop Stewards in British Industry, 1969; Shop Stewards, 1973; Rulemaking and Industrial Peace, 1977; Ideology and Shop-floor Industrial Relations, 1981; Employment Relations in Industrial Society, 1984; Unfair Dismissal Law and Employment Practice, 1985; New Developments in Employee Involvement, 1992; Industrial Tribunals and Workplace Disciplinary Procedures, 1998; contribs to British Jl of Industrial Relations, ILR, Industrial Relations Jl, Jl of Management Studies, Personnel Management, etc. *Recreations:* hill walking (compleat Munroist, 1997), ornithology, golf, football. *Address:* Lundy Rise, Brookledge Lane, Adlington, Macclesfield, Cheshire SK10 4JX. *T:* (01625) 572480.

GOODMAN, Prof. Martin David, DPhil; FBA 1996; Professor of Jewish Studies, Oxford University, since 1996, and Fellow of Wolfson College, Oxford, since 1991; Fellow, Oxford Centre for Hebrew and Jewish Studies, since 1986; *b* 1 Aug. 1953; *s* of Cyril Joshua Goodman and Ruth (*née* Sabel); *m* 1976, Sarah Jane Lock; two *s* two *d*. *Educ:* Rugby; Trinity Coll., Oxford (MA; DPhil 1980). Kaye Jun. Res. Fellow, Oxford Centre for Postgrad. Hebrew Studies, 1976–77; Lectr in Ancient Hist., Birmingham Univ., 1977–86; Oxford University: Sen. Res. Fellow, St Cross Coll., 1986–91; Lectr in Roman Hist., Christ Church, Oxford, 1988–; Reader in Jewish Studies, 1991–96. Fellow, Inst. for Advanced Studies, Hebrew Univ. of Jerusalem, 1993. Pres., British Assoc. for Jewish Studies, 1995. Jt Ed., Jl of Jewish Studies, 1995–99; Ed., Jl of Roman Studies, 2000–. *Publications:* State and Society in Roman Galilee, 1983, 2nd edn 2000; (trans. with Sarah Goodman) Johann Reuchlin, On the Art of the Kabbalah, 1983; (ed jtly) E. Schürer, The History of the Jewish People in the Age of Jesus Christ, vol. 3, pt 1 1986, pt 2 1987; The Ruling Class of Judaea, 1987; (with G. Vermes) The Essenes according to the Classical Sources, 1989; Mission and Conversion, 1994; The Roman World 44BC–AD180, 1997; (ed) Jews in a Graeco-Roman World, 1998; (ed jtly) Apologetics in the Roman Empire, 1999. *Address:* Oriental Institute, Pusey Lane, Oxford OX1 2LE; 11 Carpenter Road, Edgbaston, Birmingham B15 2JW. *T:* (0121) 454 8609.

GOODMAN, His Honour Michael Bradley; a Circuit Judge, 1983–99; *b* 3 May 1930; *s* of Marcus Gordon Goodman and Eunice Irene May Goodman (*née* Bradley); *m* 1967, Patricia Mary Gorringe; two *d* (one *s* decd). *Educ:* Aldenham; Sidney Sussex Coll., Cambridge (MA). Called to the Bar, Middle Temple, 1953; Western Circuit; a Recorder of the Crown Court, 1972–83. Prosecuting Counsel to DHSS, 1975–83; Pres., Wireless Telegraphy Appeals Tribunal, 1977–88. Chancellor: Dio. Guildford, 1968–; Dio. Lincoln, 1970–98; Dio. Rochester, 1971–; Vicar-Gen., Province of Canterbury, 1977–83. Member: Commn on Deployment and Payment of the Clergy, 1965–67; C of E Legal Adv. Commn, 1973– (Chm., 1986–96); Faculty Jurisdiction Commn, 1980–83; General Synod, Church of England, 1977–83; Lay Chm., Dulwich Deanery Synod, 1970–73. Chairman: William Temple Assoc., 1963–66; Ecclesiastical Judges Assoc., 1987–97. President: SE London Magistrates' Assoc., 1989–96; SE London Mediation Bureau, 1999–. Governor: Liddon Trust, London, 1964–; Pusey Hse, Oxford, 1965–88. *Address:* c/o Lloyds TSB, 9 Brompton Road, SW3 1DB.

GOODMAN, Michael Jack, MA, PhD; Social Security Commissioner (formerly National Insurance Commissioner), 1979–98, and Child Support Commissioner, 1993–98, now a Deputy Commissioner; *b* 3 Oct. 1931; *s* of Vivian Roy Goodman and Muriel Olive Goodman; *m* 1958, Susan Kerkham Wherry; two *s* one *d*. *Educ:* Sudbury Grammar Sch., Suffolk; Corpus Christi Coll., Oxford (MA). PhD Manchester. Solicitor. Lectr, Gibson & Weldon, 1957; solicitor, Lincoln, 1958–60; Lectr, Law Society's Sch., 1961–63; Lectr, then Sen. Lectr in Law, Manchester Univ., 1964–70; Prof. of Law, Durham Univ., 1971–76; Perm. Chm. of Indust. Tribunals, Newcastle upon Tyne,

1976–79. Gen. Editor, Encyclopedia of Health and Safety at Work, 1974–. *Publications:* Industrial Tribunals' Procedure, 1976, 4th edn 1987; Health and Safety at Work: law and practice, 1988; contrib. Mod. Law Rev., and Conveyancer. *Recreations:* amateur radio (licence holder), The Times crossword. *Address:* Office of the Social Security Commissioners, Harp House, 83 Farringdon Street, EC4A 4DH. *T:* (020) 7353 5145.

GOODMAN, Sir Patrick (Ledger), Kt 1995; CBE 1990; Special Trade Ambassador of New Zealand, 1990; company director; President Emeritus, Goodman Fielder Ltd; *b* 6 April 1929; *s* of Athol Ledger Goodman and Delia Marion Goodman; *m* 1960, Hilary Gay Duncan; three *s*. *Educ:* St Patrick's Coll., Silverstream, NZ; Victoria University Coll., Wellington. Chairman: Heinz-Wattie, 1992–98; Quality Bakers of NZ, 1967–76; Goodman Group and subsidiaries, 1979–92; former Chm., Tourism Nelson. Founder Chm., NZ Business and Parlt Trust, 1991–92; Trustee: Founders of Nelson; Massey Univ. Agric. Foundn; Bishop Suter Art Gall. Foundn Mem., NZ Rugby Foundn. Hon. DSc Massey. *Recreations:* golf, cricket, Rugby, boating, fishing. *Address:* 52 Tudor Street, Motueka, Nelson, New Zealand. *T:* (3) 5288314.

GOODMAN, Paul Alexander Cyril; MP (C) Wycombe, since 2001; *b* 17 Nov. 1959; *s* of Abel Goodman and Irene Goodman (*née* Rubens); *m* 1999, Fiona Gill. *Educ:* Cranleigh Sch., Surrey; York Univ. (BA Hons Eng. Lit). Exec., Extel Consultancy, 1985-86; Res. Asst to Rt Hon. Tom King, MP, 1985-87; Mem., Policy Unit, Westminster CC, 1987-88; Novice, Quarr Abbey, 1988-90; Home Affairs Ed., Catholic Herald, 1991-92; Leader Writer, Daily Telegraph, 1992; reporter, Sunday Telegraph, 1992-95; Comment Ed., Daily Telegraph, 1995-2001. *Address:* House of Commons, SW1A 0AA.

GOODMAN, Dame (Pearl) Barbara, DBE 1989; QSO 1981; JP; *b* 5 Oct. 1932; *d* of late Horace Robinson and Lillie Robinson (*née* Shieff); *m* 1954, Harold Goodman (decd); two *s* one *d*. *Educ:* Parnell Sch.; St Cuthbert's Coll. Mayoress, City of Auckland, 1968–80; founding Trustee, HELP Foundn, 1980–85; Chm., Auckland Spastic Soc., 1980–84; Chm., Odyssey House Trust, 1981–92; former Mem. Exec. Cttee, NZ Fedn of Voluntary Welfare Organisations. Mem., Auckland City Council, 1989–. Mem., NZ Internat. Trade Fair Cttee, 1985–89; Chm., Auckland 1990 Trust Board, 1989–91. Guardian, NZ Women's Refuge Foundn; Patron and Mem., Aotearoa NZ Peace Foundn. Member: Cttee, Shalom Court; Women's Internat. Zionist Orgn. Vice Patron, Auckland Cricket Assoc. *Publication:* For Flying Kiwis, 1990. *Recreations:* meeting people, travel, reading, cooking, embroidery. *Address:* 22a Tohunga Crescent, Parnell, Auckland 1001, New Zealand. *T:* (9) 3790650, *Fax:* (9) 3779112. *Clubs:* Athene, Zonta (Auckland).

GOODMAN, Perry; Director (Industry and Regions), The Engineering Council, 1990–92; *b* 26 Nov. 1932; *s* of Cyril Goodman and Anne (*née* Rosen); *m* 1958, Marcia Ann (*née* Morris); one *s* one *d*. *Educ:* Haberdashers' Aske's Hampstead Sch.; University Coll., London (BSc). MIM. 2nd Lieut, Royal Corps of Signals, 1955–57; Jt Head, Chemistry Res. Lab., then Project Leader, Morgan Crucible Co. Ltd, 1957–64; Sen. Scientific Officer, DSIR, 1964–65; Principal Scientific Officer, Process Plant Br., Min. of Technology, 1965–67; 1st Sec. (Scientific), 1968–70, Counsellor (Scientific), 1970–74, British Embassy, Paris; Research Gp, DoI, 1974–79; Hd, Policy and Perspectives Unit, DoI, 1980–81; Department of Trade and Industry: Hd, Design Policy/Technical Adv. Services for Industry, 1981–86; Hd, Electrical Engrg Br., 1986–90. Mem. Bd, Northern Engrg Centre, 1990–92. FRSA 1986. *Recreations:* travel, walking, conversation. *Address:* 118 Westbourne Terrace Mews, W2 6QG. *T:* (020) 7262 0925.

GOODPASTER, Gen. Andrew Jackson; United States Army, retired; US Medal of Freedom, 1984; DSC (US); DSM (Def.) (Oak Leaf Cluster); DSM (Army) (3 Oak Leaf Clusters); DSM (Navy); DSM (Air Force); Silver Star; Legion of Merit (Oak Leaf Cluster); Purple Heart (Oak Leaf Cluster); Superintendent, United States Military Academy, West Point, New York (in grade of Lt-Gen.), 1977–81; *b* 12 Feb. 1915; *s* of Andrew Jackson Goodpaster and Teresa Mary Goodpaster (*née* Mrovka); *m* 1939, Dorothy Anderson Goodpaster (*née* Anderson); two *d*. *Educ:* McKendree Coll., Lebanon, Ill; US Mil. Academy, 1935–39 (BS); Princeton Univ., 1947–50 (MSE, MA, PhD). 11th Eng. Panama, 1939–42; Ex O, 390th Eng. Gen. Svc Regt, Camp Claiborne, La, 1942–43; Comd and Gen. Staff Sch., Ft Leavenworth, Kansas, Feb.-April 1943; CO, 48th Eng. Combat Bn, II Corps, Fifth Army, 1943–44; Ops Div., Gen. Staff, War Dept (incl. Jt War Plans Cttee, JCS, 1945–46), 1944–47; Student, Civil Eng. Course and Polit. Sc. Grad. Sch., Princeton Univ., 1947–50; Army Mem., Jt Advanced Study Cttee, JCS, 1950–51; Special Asst to Chief of Staff, SHAPE, 1951–54; Dist Eng., San Francisco Dist, Calif, July-Oct. 1954; Def. Liaison Officer and Staff Sec. to President of US, 1954–61; Asst Div. Comdr, 3rd Inf. Div., April-Oct. 1961, and CG, 8th Inf. Div., Oct. 1961–Oct. 1962, USAREUR; Sp. Asst (Policy) to Chm., JCS, Washington, DC, Nov. 1962–Jan. 1964; Asst to Chm., JCS, Washington, DC, Jan. 1964–July 1966; Dir Joint Staff, JCS, Washington, DC, Aug. 1966–Mar. 1967; Dir of Sp. Studies, Office Chief of Staff, USA, Washington, DC, April 1967–July 1967; Senior US Army Mem., Mil. Staff UN, May 1967–July 1968; Comdt, Nat. War Coll., Washington, DC, Aug. 1967–July 1968; Mem. US Delegn for Negotiations with N Vietnam, Paris (addl duty), April 1968–July 1968; Dep. Comdr, US Mil. Assistance Comd, Vietnam, July 1968–April 1969; Supreme Allied Commander Europe, 1969–74; C-in-C, US European Command, 1969–74. Sen. Fellow, Woodrow Wilson Internat. Center for Scholars, Washington DC, 1975–76; Prof. of Govt and Internat. Studies, The Citadel, Charleston, SC, 1976–77; Sen. Fellow, Eisenhower World Affairs Inst., 1998–. Pres., Inst. for Defence Analyses, Alexandria, Va, 1983–85; Chairman: American Battle Monuments Commn, 1985–90; Atlantic Council of the US, 1985–97; George C. Marshall Foundn, 1993–2000. *Publication:* For the Common Defense, 1977. *Recreations:* golf, fishing, music. *Address:* Apt 345, 6200 Oregon Avenue NW, Washington, DC 20015, USA.

GOODRICH, David, CEng, RCNC; FRINA; Chief Executive, since 1986, and Chairman, since 1997, British Maritime Technology Ltd (Deputy Chairman, 1995–97); Chairman, BMT Group Ltd, since 1995; *b* 15 April 1941; *s* of William B. Goodrich and Florence B. Goodrich; *m* 1965, Margaret R. Riley; one *s* three *d*. MBA. Shipbuilding management apprentice, 1958–63; shipbuilding designer/estimator, 1963–65; Constructor, RCNC, 1965–77; Manager, Shipbuilding Technology, 1977–79, Man. Dir, 1979–85, BSRA. FRINA (Pres., 1999–July 2002). *Publication:* paper to Royal Soc. *Recreations:* squash, walking, family. *Address:* British Maritime Technology Ltd, Orlando House, 1 Waldegrave Road, Teddington, Middx TW11 8LZ.

GOODRIDGE, Rt Rev. Sehon Sylvester; *see* Windward Islands, Bishop of.

GOODSMAN, James Melville, CBE 1993; Chairman, Michael Fraser Associates Ltd, since 1997 (Managing Director, 1995–97); Director, Michael Fraser & Co. Ltd, since 1997; *b* 6 Feb. 1947; *s* of late James K. Goodsman and Euphemia Goodsman, Elgin, Moray; *m* 1990, Victoria, *y d* of late Col Philip Smitherman and Rosemary Smitherman, CBE. *Educ:* Elgin Academy. Joined Cons. Party organisation, 1966; Agent: to Rt Hon. Betty Harvie Anderson, 1970–74; to Rt Hon. Maurice Macmillan, 1974–80; Conservative Central Office: Dep. Agent, NW Area, 1980–84; Asst Dir (Community Affairs), 1984–90; Head, Community and Legal Affairs, May-Sept. 1990; Dir, Cons. Party in Scotland, 1990–93. Director: ICP Ltd, 1997–; Capitalize Ltd, 2001–. Hon. Sec., One Nation Forum, 1986–90. Mem., Edinburgh Morayshire Club (Chm., 1996). *Publications:* contribs to Cons. party and community relations papers. *Recreation:* church music. *Address:* The Old Schoolhouse, Collessie, Fife KY15 7UU.

GOODSON, Rear-Adm. Frederick Brian, CB 1996; OBE 1982; Chairman: South Gloucestershire Primary Care Trust, since 2001; Trading Force Group, since 1999; *b* 21 May 1938; *m* 1965, Susan, (Sue), Mary Firmin; two *s* two *d*. *Educ:* Campbell Coll. Coastal Forces, 1958–60; HMS Gambia and HMS Lion, 1960–64; Aden, 1964–65; Supply Officer, HMS Diana, 1966–69; Staff, BRNC, Dartmouth, 1970–72; Exchange Service, USN, 1972–74; Comdr 1974; Exchange Service, Royal Naval Supply and Transport Service, 1975–78; Naval Sec's Dept, 1978–79; Supply Officer, HMS Invincible, 1980–81; Fleet Supply Officer, C-in-C Fleet, 1981–82; Capt. 1982; Sec., C-in-C Naval Home Comd, 1983–85; Dir, Naval Logistic Planning, 1985–87; Cdre comdg HMS Centurion, 1988–91; rcds 1992; Rear-Adm. 1993; ACDS (Logistics), 1993–96. Chm., Bath and West Community NHS Trust, 1997–2001. MInstD 1996. OStJ 1997; Chm., Wilts, St John Ambulance, 1997. *Recreations:* offshore sailing, squash, country pursuits. *Address:* North Wraxall, Wilts. *Clubs:* Bowood Golf and Country; Royal Naval Sailing Association.

GOODSON, Prof. Ivor Frederick, DPhil; Professor of Education, School of Education and Professional Development, University of East Anglia, since 1996; Susan B. Anthony Scholar in Residence and Professor, Margaret Warner Graduate School of Education and Human Development, University of Rochester, New York, since 1996; *b* 30 Sept. 1943; *s* of Frederick G. J. Goodson and Lily W. Goodson; *m* 1975, Mary L. Nuttall; one *s*. *Educ:* Forest Grammar Sch.; University Coll. London (BSc Econ); Inst. of Educn, Univ. of London; London Sch of Econs; DPhil Sussex 1979. University of Sussex: Res. Fellow, 1975–78; Dir, Eur. Schools Unit, 1978–85; University of Western Ontario: Prof., Faculty of Educn, Faculty of Grad. Studies and Centre for Theory and Criticism, 1986–96; Dir, Educnl Res. Unit, 1989–96; Hon. Prof. of Sociol., 1993–98. Founding Ed. and Man. Ed., Jl Educn Policy, 1986–. Frederica Warner Schol., Margaret Warner Grad. Sch. of Educn and Professional Develt, Univ. of Rochester, NY, 1991–96; Vis. Internat. Guest Scientist, Max Planck Inst. of Human Develt and Educn, Berlin, 1994; J. Woodrow Wilson Vis. Prof., Oppenheimer Foundn, Univ. of Witwatersrand, SA, 1996. Dist. Vis. Professorial Award, Japanese Soc. for Promotion of Sci., Univ. of Tokyo, 1993. *Publications:* School Subjects and Curriculum Change, 1983, 3rd edn 1993; The Making of Curriculum: collected essays, 1988, 2nd edn 1995; Biography, Identity and Schooling, 1991; Through the Schoolhouse Door, 1993; Studying Curriculum: cases and methods, 1994; Curriculo: teoria e historia (Brazil), 1995, 3rd edn 1999; Historia del Coriculum (Spain), 1995; Att Starka Lararnas Roster: sex essaer om lararforskning och lararforskarsamarbete (Sweden), 1996; The Changing Curriculum: studies in social construction, 1997; Studying School Subjects, 1997; Subject Knowledge: readings for the study of school subjects, 1998; Das Schulfach als Handlungsrahmen: vergleichende untersuchung zur geschichte und funktion der schulfächer (Germany), 1999; La Crisis del Cambio Curricular (Spain), 2000. *Recreations:* tennis, walking and birdwatching, jazz and rhythm and blues, Norwich City FC supporter. *Address:* Woodlands, 4a Newmarket Road, Cringleford, Norwich, Norfolk NR4 6UE. *T:* (01603) 458259; School of Education and Professional Development, University of East Anglia, Norwich, Norfolk NR4 7TJ. *T:* (01603) 592617.

GOODSON, Sir Mark (Weston Lassam), 3rd Bt *cr* 1922, of Waddeton Court, Co. Devon; *b* 12 Dec. 1925; *s* of Major Alan Richard Lassam Goodson (*d* 1941) (2nd *s* of 1st Bt) and Clarisse Muriel Weston (*d* 1982), *d* of John Weston Adamson; *S* uncle, 1986; *m* 1949, Barbara Mary Constantine, *d* of Surg.-Capt. Reginald Joseph McAuliffe Andrews, RN; one *s* three *d*. *Educ:* Radley; Jesus College, Cambridge. *Heir: s* Alan Reginald Goodson, *b* 15 May 1960. *Address:* Kilham, Mindrum, Northumberland TD12 4QS. *T:* (01890) 850217.

GOODSON, Michael John; Assistant Auditor General, National Audit Office, 1984–93; *b* 4 Aug. 1937; *s* of late Herbert Edward William Goodson and Doris Maud Goodson; *m* 1958, Susan Elizabeth (*née* Higley); one *s* one *d*. *Educ:* King Henry VIII Sch., Coventry. Joined Exchequer and Audit Dept, 1955; Asst Auditor, 1955; Auditor, 1965; Private Sec. to Comptroller and Auditor Gen., 1967–70; Sen. Auditor, 1970; Health Service Ombudsman (on secondment), 1973–76; Chief Auditor, Exchequer and Audit Dept, 1976; Dep. Dir of Audit, 1978; Dir of Audit, 1981. *Recreations:* ornithology, model engineering, caravanning. *Address:* 2 Bayley Mead, St John's Road, Boxmoor, Herts HP1 1US. *T:* (01442) 242611.

GOODSON-WICKES, Dr Charles; DL; consulting physician, company director, business consultant; Chief Executive, London Playing Fields Society, since 1998 (Chairman, 1997–98); *b* 7 Nov. 1945; *s* of late Ian Goodson Wickes, FRCP, Consultant Paediatrician and farmer, of Stock Harvard, Essex and of Monica Goodson-Wickes; *m* 1974, Judith Amanda Hopkinson, *d* of late Comdr John Hopkinson, RN, of Sutton Grange, near Stamford, Lincs; two *s*. *Educ:* Charterhouse; St Bartholomew's Hosp. (MB BS 1970). Called to the Bar, Inner Temple, 1972. Ho. Physician, Addenbrooke's Hosp., Cambridge, 1972; Surgeon-Capt., The Life Guards, 1973–77 (served BAOR, N Ireland, Cyprus); Silver Stick MO, Hsehold Cavalry, 1977; RARO, 1977–2000; re-enlisted as Lt-Col, 1991, for Gulf Campaign (served S Arabia, Iraq, Kuwait, with HQ 7 Armoured Bde). Clin. Asst, St Bart's Hosp., 1977–80; Consulting Phys., BUPA, 1977–86; Occupational Phys., 1980–94; formerly Med. advr to Barclays Bank, RTZ, McKinsey, Christie's, British Alcan, Collins, Meat & Livestock Commn etc; UK Advr, Norwegian Directorate of Health, 1983–94; Chm., Appeals Bd, Asbestos Licensing Regulations, 1982–87; Member: Med. Adv. Cttee, Industrial Soc., 1981–87; Fitness Adv. Panel, Inst. of Dirs, 1982–84. Director: Medarc Ltd, 1981–; Thomas Greg and Sons Ltd, 1992–; Nestor Healthcare Gp (formerly Nestor-BNA) plc, 1993–99; Gyrus Gp plc, 1997–; and other internat. cos. Contested (C) Islington Central, 1979. MP (C) Wimbledon, 1987–97; contested (C) same seat, 1997. Vice-Pres., Islington South and Finsbury Cons. Assoc., 1982–97. PPS to Minister of State for Housing and Planning, DoE, 1992–94, to Financial Sec. to HM Treasury, 1994–95, to Sec. of State for Transport, 1995–96. Mem., Select Cttee on Members' Interests, 1992–94; Vice-Chm., Constitutional Affairs Cttee, 1990–91; Sec., Arts and Heritage Cttee, 1990–92; Vice Chm., Defence Cttee, 1991–92; Mem., Jt Cttee, Consolidation of Bills, 1987–92; Founder Chm., All Party, British-Colombian Gp, 1995–97; Vice Chm., All Party British-Russian Gp, 1993–97; Treas., All Party British Chinese Gp, 1992–97. Fellow, Industry and Parlt Trust, 1991. Vice Chm., Cons. Foreign and Commonwealth Council, 1997–. Treas., Dr Ian Goodson Wickes Fund for Handicapped Children, 1979–88; Vice-Pres., Ex-Services Mental Welfare Soc., 1990–; Founder Chm., Countryside Alliance, 1997–99 (Chm., 1994–98, Mem., Public Affairs Cttee, 1980–87, British Field Sports Soc.); Chm., Rural Trust, 1999–. Governor, Highbury Grove Sch., 1977–85. Pte, The Parachute Regt (TA), 1963–65. Founder Chm., Essex Kit Cat Club, 1965. DL Gtr London, 1999. *Publications:* The New Corruption, 1984; (contrib.) Another Country, 1999. *Recreations:* hunting, shooting, Real tennis, gardening, travel, history. *Address:* Watergate House, Bulford, Wilts SP4 9DY. *T:* (01980) 632344; 37 St James's Place, SW1A 1NS. *T:* (020) 7629 0981; (office) Fraser House, 29

Albemarle Street, W1S 4JB. *T:* (020) 7409 1447, *Fax:* (020) 7409 1449; *e-mail:* cgwmcEdarc@aol.com. *Clubs:* Boodle's, Pratt's, MCC.

GOODWAY, Russell; Lord Mayor of Cardiff, since 1999; Member, and first Leader of the Council, since 1995, Chairman, Council's Cabinet, since 1999, County Council of the City and County of Cardiff; *b* 23 Dec. 1955; *s* of Russell Donald Goodway and Barbara Mary Goodway (*née* Vizard); *m* 1979, Susan Yvonne Witchard; one *s*. *Educ:* Barry Boys' Comprehensive Sch.; University Coll., Swansea (BA Econs and Politics 1977). Partner, Keane Goodway & Co., Accountants, 1988–2000. Dep. Chm., Millennium Stadium plc, 1996–; Bd Mem., Cardiff Bay Develt Corp., 1993–2000; Member: Porthkerry Community Council, 1977–82 (Chm., 1980–81); Rhoose Community Council, 1982–87 (Chm., 1985–86); S Glamorgan County Council: Mem., 1985–96; Chm., Property Services Cttee, 1988–89; Chm., Finance Cttee, 1989–92; Leader, and Chm. Policy Cttee, 1992–96; Dep. Chm., 1992–93; Chm., Policy Cttee, Co. Council of City and Co. of Cardiff, 1995–99. Dep. Chm., Assembly of Welsh Counties, 1994–96. *Recreations:* sport, especially Rugby and tennis, reading political biographies, music. *Address:* County Hall, Atlantic Wharf, Cardiff CF1 5UW. *T:* (029) 2087 2500.

GOODWILL, Robert; Member (C) Yorkshire and the Humber Region, European Parliament, since 1999; *b* 31 Dec. 1956; *s* of late Robert W. Goodwill and Joan Goodwill; *m* 1987, Maureen (*née* Short); two *s* one *d*. *Educ:* Bootham Sch., York; Univ. of Newcastle upon Tyne (BSc Hons Agriculture). Farmer, 1979–. Contested (C): Redcar, 1992; NW Leics, 1997; Cleveland and Richmond, 1994, Yorks S, May 1998, EP elecns. *Recreation:* steam ploughing. *Address:* Southwood Farm, Terrington, York YO60 6QB. *T:* (01653) 648459.

GOODWIN, Christine, (Mrs Richard Goodwin); *see* Edzard, C.

GOODWIN, Dr Eric Thomson, CBE 1975; retired; *b* 30 July 1913; *s* of John Edward Goodwin and Florence Goodwin; *m* 1st, 1940, Isobel Philip (*d* 1976); two *s*; 2nd, 1977, Avis Mary (*née* Thomson). *Educ:* King Edward VI Sch., Stafford; Harrow County Sch.; Peterhouse, Cambridge. BA 1934, Rayleigh Prize 1936, MA 1937, PhD 1938. Asst Lectr, Sheffield Univ., 1937–39; war service: Mathematical Lab., Cambridge, 1939–43; Admty Signal Estabt, Witley, 1943–44; Admty Computing Service, Bath, 1945; Maths Div., Nat. Physical Lab., 1945–71 (Supt 1951–71); Dep. Dir, Nat. Phys. Lab., 1971–74, retd. *Publications:* papers in learned jls on theoretical physics and numerical analysis. *Recreations:* music, reading, the countryside, philately. *Address:* 3 Arundell Place, West Street, Farnham, Surrey GU9 7HQ. *T:* (01252) 716059.

GOODWIN, Frederick Anderson; Chief Executive, Royal Bank of Scotland Group plc, since 2000 (Deputy Group Chief Executive, 1998–2000); *b* 17 Aug. 1958; *s* of Frederick Anderson Goodwin and Marylyn Marshall Goodwin (*née* Mackintosh). *Educ:* Paisley GS; Univ. of Glasgow (LLB). CA 1983, FCIBS 1996. Joined Touche Ross & Co., 1979, Partner, 1988–95; Dep. Chief Exec., 1995, Chief Exec., 1996–98, Clydesdale Bank PLC; Chief Exec., Yorkshire Bank, 1997–98. Dir, Scottish Financial Enterprise. Chm., Prince's Trust, Scotland, 1999–; Trustee, Prince's Trust. *Recreations:* restoring cars, golf. *Address:* Royal Bank of Scotland Group plc, 42 St Andrew Square, Edinburgh EH2 2YE.

GOODWIN, Prof. Guy Manning, DPhil; FRCPsych; W. A. Handley Professor of Psychiatry, and Fellow of Merton College, University of Oxford, since 1996; *b* 8 Nov. 1947; *s* of Kenneth M. Goodwin and Constance (*née* Hudson); *m* 1971, Philippa Catherine Georgeson; two *d*. *Educ:* Manchester GS; Exeter Coll., Oxford (open schol.; MA); Wolfson Coll., Oxford (Grad. Schol.; DPhil 1972); Magdalen Coll., Oxford (MB BCh 1978). FRCPE 1995–2000; FRCPsych 1995. Scholar, MRC, 1968–71; Fellow, Magdalen Coll., Oxford, 1971–76; House Physician, Nuffield Dept of Clin. Medicine, Oxford and House Surgeon, Horton Gen. Hosp., Banbury, 1978–79; Sen. House Officer, Nat. Hosp., Queen Sq., and Professorial Unit, Brompton Hosp., 1979–80; Registrar, Rotational Trng Scheme in Psychiatry, Oxford, 1980–83; MRC Clin. Trng Fellow, and Lectr, MRC Clin. Pharmacol. Unit, Oxford, 1983–86; MRC Clin. Scientist, Hon. Consultant Psychiatrist and Hon. Sen. Lectr, Edinburgh Univ., 1986–95; Prof. of Psychiatry, Edinburgh Univ., 1995–96. Res. Associate, Univ. of Washington, Seattle, 1972–74; Hobson Meml Schol., Oxford, 1975. Mem., Neuroscis and Mental Health Grants and Fellowships Cttee, Wellcome Trust, 1992–97. Pres., British Assoc. for Psychopharmacol., July 2002– (Mem. Council, 1993–97). *Publications:* contrib. learned jls on neurophysiol., psychopharmacol. and psychiatry. *Recreations:* football and opera passively, hillwalking actively. *Address:* Department of Psychiatry, Warneford Hospital, Oxford OX3 7JX.

GOODWIN, Leonard George, CMG 1977; FRCP; FRS 1976; Director, Nuffield Laboratories of Comparative Medicine, Institute of Zoology, The Zoological Society of London, 1964–80; Director of Science, Zoological Society of London, 1966–80; Consultant, Wellcome Trust, since 1984; *b* 11 July 1915; *s* of Harry George and Lois Goodwin; *m* 1940, Marie Evelyn Coates; no *c*. *Educ:* William Ellis Sch., London; University Coll. London (Fellow, 1981); School of Pharmacy, London; University Coll. Hospital. BPharm 1935, BSc 1937, MB, BS 1950, (London). MRCP 1966, FRCP 1972. Demonstrator, Sch. of Pharmacy, London, 1935–39; Head of Wellcome Labs of Tropical Medicine, 1958–63 (Protozoologist, 1939–63). Jt Hon. Sec., Royal Soc. of Tropical Medicine and Hygiene, 1968–74, Pres., 1979–81. Chairman: Trypanosomiasis Panel, ODM, 1974–77; Filariasis Steering Cttee, WHO Special Programme, 1978–82. Hon. Dir, Wellcome Museum for Med. Sci., 1984–85. Hon. FRPharmS (Hon. FPS 1977). Hon. DSc Brunel, 1986. Soc. of Apothecaries Gold Medal, 1975; Harrison Meml Medal, 1978; Schofield Medal, Guelph Univ., 1979; Silver Medal, Zoological Soc., 1980; Manson Medal, RSTM&H, 1992. Chm. Editorial Bd, Parasitology, 1980–. *Publications:* (pt author) Biological Standardization, 1950; (contrib.) Biochemistry and Physiology of Protozoa, 1955; (jointly) A New Tropical Hygiene, 1960, 2nd edn 1972; (contrib.) Recent Advances in Pharmacology, 1962; many contribs to scientific jls, mainly on pharmacology and chemotherapy of tropical diseases, especially malaria, trypanosomiasis and helminth infections. *Recreations:* Dabbling in arts and crafts especially pottery (slipware), gardening and passive participation in music and opera. *Address:* Shepperlands Farm, Park Lane, Finchampstead, Berks RG40 4QF. *T:* (0118) 973 2153.

GOODWIN, Sir Matthew (Dean), Kt 1989; CBE 1981; CA; Chairman: CrestaCare plc, since 1995 (Director, since 1994), Murray Enterprise plc, since 1988; *b* 12 June 1929; *s* of Matthew Dean Goodwin and Mary Gertrude Barrie; *m* Margaret Eileen Colvil; two *d*. *Educ:* Hamilton Acad.; Glasgow Acad. FO, RAF, 1952–54. Raeburn & Verel, Shipowners, 1954–56; Partner, Davidson Downe McGowan, CA, 1956–68; Exec. Dir, 1960–79, Chm., 1979–95, Hewden Stuart. Director: Irvine Develt Corp., 1980–90; F/S Assurance, 1980–89; Murray Ventures PLC, 1981–; Easpark Children's Home, 1989–; Chm., Scotcare Ltd, 1988–. Mem., Scottish Econ. Council, 1991–97. Jt Dep. Chm., Scottish Conservative Party, 1991– (Hon. Treas., 1982–90). *Recreations:* bridge, fishing, shooting, farming. *Address:* 87 Kelvin Court, Anniesland, Glasgow G12 0AH. *T:* (0141) 221 7331. *Club:* Western (Glasgow).

GOODWIN, Dr Neil, FHSM; Chief Executive, Manchester Health Authority, since 1994; *b* 1 March 1951; *s* of James and Dorothy Goodwin; *m* 1st, 1980, Sian Elizabeth Mary Holliday (marr. diss. 1992); two *s*; 2nd, 1998, Helen Peller, bassoonist and interior designer (marr. diss. 2001). *Educ:* North Salford County Secondary Sch.; London Business Sch. (MBA); Manchester Business Sch. (PhD 2001). FHSM 1990. NHS mgt posts, London, Manchester, Liverpool, Southport, Bromsgrove, Hertfordshire, 1969–85; General Manager, Central Middlesex Hosp., 1985–88; Chief Exec., St Mary's Hosp., subseq. St Mary's Hosp. NHS Trust, 1988–94. Founder and Hd, Public Leadership Centre, Univ. of Manchester, 2000–. Non-exec. Dir, UK Transplant Authy, 2000–. Member: Orgnl Audit Council and Accreditation Cttee, King's Fund Coll., 1993–2000; Manchester TEC Investors in People accreditation panel, 1995–99; Cabinet Office review of public sector leadership, 2000; Scientific Cttee, Eur. Health Mgt Assoc., 2000–. Hon. Vis. Res. Fellow, UMIST, 2000–. Editorial Adviser: British Jl of Health Care Mgt, 1998–; Jl of Mgt in Medicine, 1999–. Hon. Fellow, Health Services Management Unit, Univ. of Manchester, 1994–. MIMgt (MBIM 1982); FRSA. *Publications:* articles on public sector leadership, customer care in hosps, leadership develt needs of chief execs and internat. healthcare. *Recreations:* music, Coronation Street. *Address:* Gateway House, Piccadilly South, Manchester M60 7LP. *T:* (0161) 237 2011, *Fax:* (0161) 237 2264.

GOODWIN, Noël; *see* Goodwin, T. N.

GOODWIN, Peter Austin, CBE 1986; Secretary, Public Works Loan Commission, 1979–87; Comptroller General, National Debt Office, 1980–87; Director, National Investment and Loans Office, 1980–87; *b* 12 Feb. 1929; *s* of late Stanley Goodwin and Louise Goodwin; *m* 1950, Audrey Vera Webb; one *d*. *Educ:* Harrow County School. Served Royal Air Force, 1947–49. Executive Officer, Public Works Loan Commn, 1950; Principal, Civil Aviation Authority, 1973–76; Asst Secretary and Establishment Officer, Public Works Loan Commn, 1976–79. UK Mem., Gp of Experts advising on management of Pension Reserve Fund, Europ. Patent Office, 1986–87. *Recreations:* theatre, opera, ballet, country dancing, model railways. *Address:* 87 Woodmansterne Road, Carshalton Beeches, Surrey SM5 4JW. *T:* (020) 8643 3530.

GOODWIN, Prof. Phillip Bramley, PhD; Professor of Transport Policy and Director of ESRC Transport Studies Unit, University College London, since 1996; *b* 6 March 1944; *s* of Dennis and Joan Goodwin; *m* 1966, Margaret Livesey (separated); one *d*. *Educ:* Henry Thornton Grammar Sch.; UCL (BSc Econs 1965; PhD Civil Engrg 1973); MA Oxon. FCIT, FIHT. Res. Asst, LRD Ltd, 1965–66; Res., UCL, 1966–74; Transport Planner, GLC, 1974–79; Dep. Dir, 1979–81, Dir, and Reader, 1981–95, Transport Studies Unit, Univ. of Oxford. Member: Standing Adv. Cttee on Trunk Road Assessment, 1979–; Internat. Scientific Adv. Bd, Swedish Min. of Transport, 1994–. Chm., Indep. Adv. Panel for Transport White Paper, 1997–98. Non-exec. Dir, Dover Harbour Bd, 1989–. Distinguished Contrib. Award, Instn of Highways and Transportation, 1998. *Publications:* Subsidised Public Transport and the Demand for Travel, 1983; Long Distance Transportation, 1983; (jtly) Transport and the Environment, 1991; (jtly) Trunk Roads and the Generation of Traffic, 1994; Car Dependence, 1995; (jtly) Transport and the Economy, 1999; approx. 200 articles in learned jls, conf. papers, and contribs to books on transport policy and travel behaviour. *Recreation:* Isla de el Hierro. *Address:* ESRC Transport Studies Unit, University College London, Gower Street, WC1E 6BT. *T:* (020) 7679 1580.

GOODWIN, (Trevor) Noël; freelance critic, writer and broadcaster, specialising in music and dance; *b* 25 Dec. 1927; *s* of Arthur Daniel Goodwin and Blanche Goodwin (*née* Stephens); *m* 1st, 1954, Gladys Marshall Clapham (marr. diss. 1960); 2nd, Anne Myers (*née* Mason); one step *s*. *Educ:* mainly in France. BA (London). Assistant Music Critic: News Chronicle, 1952–54; Manchester Guardian, 1954–55; Music and Dance Critic, Daily Express, 1956–78; Exec. Editor, Music and Musicians, 1963–71; regular reviewer for: The Times, 1978–98; Internat. Herald Tribune, 1978–84; Opera News, 1975–90; Ballet News, 1979–86; Dance and Dancers, 1957– (Associate Editor, 1972–); Opera, 1984– (Overseas News Editor, 1985–91; Mem. Editl Bd, 1991–99). Member: Arts Council of GB, 1979–81 (Mem., 1973–81, Chm., 1979–81, Dance Adv. Panel; Mem., 1974–81, Dep. Chm., 1979–81, Music Adv. Panel; Council's rep. on Visiting Arts Unit of GB, 1979–81); Dance Adv. Panel, UK Branch, Calouste Gulbenkian Foundn, 1972–76; Nat. Enquiry into Dance Educn and Trng in Britain, 1975–80; Drama and Dance Adv. Cttee, British Council, 1973–88; HRH The Duke of Kent's UK Cttee for European Music Year 1985, 1982–84 (Chm., sub-cttee for Writers and Critics); Trustee-dir, Internat. Course for Professional Choreographers and Composers, 1975–. Pres., The Critics' Circle, 1977 (Jt Trustee, 1984–). Planned and presented numerous radio programmes of music and records for BBC Home and World Services, and contributed frequently to music and arts programmes on Radios 3 and 4. *Publications:* London Symphony: portrait of an orchestra, 1954; A Ballet for Scotland, 1979; (with Sir Geraint Evans) A Knight at the Opera, 1984; editor, Royal Opera and Royal Ballet Yearbooks, 1978, 1979, 1980; area editor and writer, New Grove Dictionary of Music and Musicians, 1981; (ed) A Portrait of the Royal Ballet, 1988; contribs to: Encyclopaedia Britannica, 15th edn, 1974; Encyclopaedia of Opera, 1976; Britannica Books of the Year, annually 1980–93; Cambridge Encyclopaedia of Russia and the Soviet Union, 1982, 2nd edn 1994; New Oxford Companion to Music, 1983; Pipers Enzyklopädie des Musiktheaters, 1986; New Grove Dictionary of Opera, 1992; Viking Opera Guide, 1993; International Dictionary of Ballet, 1993; Metropolitan Opera Guide to Recorded Opera, 1993; Penguin Opera Guide, 1995; International Encyclopedia of Dance, 1998; Larousse Dictionnaire de la danse, 2000; New DNB. *Recreation:* philately. *Address:* 76 Skeena Hill, SW18 5PN. *T:* (020) 8788 8794.

GOODWIN, Prof. Trevor Walworth, CBE 1975; FRS 1968; Johnston Professor of Biochemistry, University of Liverpool, 1966–83; *b* 22 June 1916; British; *m* 1944, Kathleen Sarah Hill; three *d*. *Educ:* Birkenhead Inst.; Univ. of Liverpool. Lectr 1944, Sen. Lectr 1949, in Biochemistry, University of Liverpool; Prof. of Biochemistry and Agricultural Biochemistry, UCW, Aberystwyth, 1959. NSF Sen. Foreign Scientist, Univ. of Calif at Davis, 1964. Chairman: British Photobiol. Gp, 1964–66; Phytochemical Soc., 1968–70; MRC Biol Grants Cttee B, 1969–73; Cttee, Biochem. Soc., 1971–74 (Mem., 1953–57, 1962–64); Brit. Nat. Cttee for Biochem., 1976–82; Royal Soc. Internat. Exchange Cttee (Panel A), 1986–89, 1994–; Member: Council, Royal Society, 1972, 1974, 1985; UGC, 1974–81; SRC Science Bd, 1975–78; ARC Grants Bd, 1975–82; Wirral Educn Cttee, 1974–84; Lawes Agricl Trust Cttee, 1977–91; Exec. Cttee, FEBS, 1975–83 (Chm., Publication Cttee, 1975–83); Vice-Pres., Comité Internat. de Photobiologie, 1967–69. Mem. Court, UCW, Aberystwyth, 1965–; Rep. of Lord Pres. of Council on Court, Univ. of N Wales, Bangor, 1983–; Royal Soc. Rep., Court, Univ. of Liverpool, 1985–92. Gov., Birkenhead Inst., 1976–79; Gov., Wirral County Grammar Sch. for Girls, 1980–94 (Chm., 1990–94). Morton Lectr, Biochem. Soc., 1983. Corresp. Mem., Amer. Soc. Plant Physiologists, 1982; Hon. Member: Phytochemical Soc. of Europe, 1983; Biochem. Soc., 1985. Diplôme d'honneur, FEBS, 1984. Ciba Medallist, Biochemical Soc., 1970; Prix Roussel, Societé Roussel Uclaf, 1982. Editor, Protoplasma, 1968–80; Mem., Editl Bd, Phytochemistry, 1966–96. *Publications:* Comparative Biochemistry of Carotenoids, 1952 (trans. Russian, 1956), 2nd edn, vol. 1 1980, vol. 2

1983; Recent Advances in Biochemistry, 1960; Biosynthesis of Vitamins, 1964 (trans. Japanese, 1966); (ed) Chemistry and Biochemistry of Plant Pigments, 1965, 3rd edn 1988; (with E. I. Mercer) Introduction to Plant Biochemistry, 1972, 2nd edn 1982 (trans. Russian, 1986); History of the Biochemical Society, 1987; (Subject Editor) Oxford Dictionary of Biochemistry and Molecular Biology, 1997; numerous articles in Biochem. Jl, Phytochemistry, etc. *Recreation:* gardening. *Address:* Monzar, 9 Woodlands Close, Parkgate, Neston CH64 6RU. *T:* (0151) 336 4494; *e-mail:* goodwinbiochemistry@bushinternet.com.

GOODWYN, Charles Wyndham, FRICS; FRPSL; Keeper, Royal Philatelic Collection, since 1995; *b* 11 March 1934; *s* of Charles Colin Goodwyn and Phylis Goodwyn; *m* 1962, Judith Elisabeth Ann Riley; two *s* two *d. Educ:* Wellington Coll.; London Univ. (LLB Hons). FRICS 1964; FCIArb 1976. Joined Wilks Head & Eve, Chartered Surveyors, 1956, Sen. Partner, 1990–95. Royal Philatelic Society: Mem., 1965–; Fellow, 1975, Hon. Fellow, 2000; Hon. Treas., 1981–82; Hon. Sec., 1982–90; Vice Pres., 1990–92; Pres., 1992–94. Medal, Royal Philatelic Soc., 1994; Signatory, Roll of Distinguished Philatelists, 1995. *Publications:* The Crown Colony of Wei Hai Wei, 1985; Royal Reform, 1999; contrib. articles to London Philatelist, etc. *Recreations:* tennis, golf, cricket. *Address:* Hinton House, 132 High Street, Amersham, Bucks HP7 0EE. *T:* (01494) 726291; *e-mail:* goodwinbiochemistry@bushinternet.com. *Clubs:* Army and Navy, MCC.

GOODY, Prof. John Rankine, FBA 1976; William Wyse Professor of Social Anthropology, University of Cambridge, 1973–84; Fellow, St John's College, Cambridge, since 1960; *b* 27 July 1919; *m*; one *s* four *d. Educ:* St Albans Sch.; St John's Coll., Cambridge; Balliol Coll., Oxford. BA 1946, Dip. Anthrop. 1947, PhD 1954, ScD 1969, Cantab; BLitt Oxon 1952. HM Forces, 1939–46. Educnl admin, 1947–49; Cambridge Univ.: Asst Lectr, 1954–59; Lectr, 1959–71; Dir, African Studies Centre, 1966–73; Smuts Reader in Commonwealth Studies, 1972. Mem., Academia Europaea, 1991; Foreign Hon. Mem., Amer. Acad. of Arts and Scis, 1980. International Prize, Fondation Fyssen, 1991. Mem., Ordre des Palmes Académiques, 1993; Officier dans l'Ordre des Arts et des Lettres (France), 2001 (Chevalier, 1996). *Publications:* The Social Organisation of the LoWiili, 1956; (ed) The Developmental Cycle in Domestic Groups, 1958; Death, Property and the Ancestors, 1962; (ed) Succession to High Office, 1966; (with J. A. Braimah) Salaga: the struggle for power, 1967; (ed) Literacy in Traditional Societies, 1968; Comparative Studies in Kinship, 1969; Technology, Tradition and the State in Africa, 1971; The Myth of the Bagre, 1972; (with S. J. Tambiah) Bridewealth and Dowry, 1973; (ed) The Character of Kinship, 1973; (ed) Changing Social Structure in Ghana, 1975; Production and Reproduction, 1977; The Domestication of the Savage Mind, 1977; (with S. W. D. K. Gandah) Une Recitation du Bagré, 1981; Cooking, Cuisine and Class, 1982; The Development of the Family and Marriage in Europe, 1983; The Logic of Writing and the Organization of Society, 1986; The Interface between the Oral and the Written, 1987; The Oriental, the Ancient and the Primitive, 1990; The Culture of Flowers, 1993; The Expansive Moment, 1995; The East in the West, 1996; Jack Goody: l'homme, l'écriture et la mort, 1996; Representations and Contradictions, 1997; Oltre i Muri: la mia prigionia in Italia, 1997; Food and Love: a cultural history of East and West, 1999; The European Family, 2000; The Power of the Written Tradition, 2000; contrib. learned jls. *Address:* St John's College, Cambridge CB2 1TP. *T:* (01223) 338638.

GOODYER, Prof. Ian Michael, MD; FRCPsych, FMedSci; Foundation Professor of Child and Adolescent Psychiatry, Cambridge University, since 1992; Fellow of Wolfson College, Cambridge, since 1993; *b* 2 Nov. 1949; *s* of Mark and Belle Goodyer; *m* 1979, Jane Elizabeth Akister; one *s* one *d. Educ:* University College London; St George's Hosp.; Oxford Univ.; Newcastle Univ.; Brown Univ. MB BS, MD London; MRCPsych 1976, FRCPsych 1990; DCH 1978. Sen. Lectr, Child/Adolescent Psych. and Consultant, Univ. of Manchester and Salford HA, 1983–87; Cambridge University: Foundn Lectr in Child Psych., 1987–92; Head, Developmental Psych. Section, 1992–. FMedSci 1999. *Publications:* Life Experiences, Development and Child Psychopathology, 1991; The Depressed Child and Adolescent: developmental and clinical perspectives, 1995, 2nd edn 2000; contribs to learned jls. *Recreations:* keeping fit, guitar. *Address:* Developmental Psychiatry Section, Douglas House, 18 Trumpington Road, Cambridge CB2 2AH. *T:* (01223) 336098.

GOOLD, Sir George William, 8th Bt *cr* 1801, of Old Court, Cork; *b* 25 March 1950; *o s* of Sir George Leonard Goold, 7th Bt and of Joy Cecelia Goold (now Joy, Lady Goold); *S* father, 1997; *m* 1973, Julie Ann Crack; two *s. Heir: s* George Leonard Powell Goold, *b* 1 Dec. 1975. *Address:* 180 Hargrave Street, Paddington, NSW 2021, Australia. *T:* (2) 93621155.

GOOLEY, Michael David William, FRGS; Founder and Chairman, Trailfinders Ltd, since 1970; *b* 13 Oct. 1936; *s* of late Denis David Gooley and Lennie Frances May Gooley (*née* Woodward); *m* 1st, 1961, Veronica Georgina Broad (marr. diss. 1970); two *d*; 2nd, 1971, Hilary Eila (marr. diss. 1981; she *d* 1993), *d* of Sir Paul Mallinson, 3rd Bt; one *s* one *d*; 3rd, 1983, Bernadette Mary Woodward (marr. diss. 1997); 4th 2000, Fiona Kathleen Leslie. *Educ:* St John's Beaumont Prep. Sch.; St George's, Weybridge; RMA, Sandhurst. Enlisted Regular Army, 1955: commnd 2nd Lieut, S Staffs Regt, 1956; joined 22 SAS, 1958; served Malaya and Arabian Peninsula; Adjt, 21 SAS, 1961–63; 1st Bn Staffords, 1963; served Kenya; 2nd tour, 22 SAS, 1964; served Malay Peninsula, Borneo and S Arabia; retd 1965. Mil. Advr to Royalist Yemini Army, 1965–69. Leader, expedition Trans Africa, 1971. Founder Trustee, Mike Gooley Trailfinders Charity, 1995. FInstD 1978; FRGS 1996. Patron, Prostate Cancer Charity, 1998–. Trustee, Special Forces Club, 1996–. *Publication:* Trans Africa Route Report, 1972. *Recreations:* travel, aviation, pragmatic entrepreneuralism, wining and dining, sport. *Address:* (office) 9 Abingdon Road, W8 6AH. *T:* (020) 7937 7909. *Club:* Wisley Golf.

GOONERATNE, Tilak Eranga; Ambassador of Sri Lanka to the Commission of the European Communities, and concurrently to Belgium, 1975–78; *b* 27 March 1919; *m* 1st, 1948, Pamela J. Rodrigo (*d* 1978); two *d*; 2nd, 1986, Ina Heyn. *Educ:* BA (London Univ.); Ceylon Law Coll. Advocate, Supreme Ct of Ceylon. Joined Ceylon Civil Service, 1943; Asst Sec., Min. of External Affairs, 1947–51; Govt Agent: Trincomalee, 1951–54; Matara, 1954–56; Registrar Gen., Marriages, Births and Deaths, 1956–58; Dir-Gen. of Broadcasting and Dir of Information, Ceylon, 1958–60; Comr Co-operative Devel, 1960–63; Dir of Economic Affairs, 1963; Dep. Sec. to Treasury, 1963–65; Pres., Colombo Plan Council for Technical Co-operation in S and SE Asia, 1964–65; Ceylon deleg. to UN Gen. Assembly, 1964–65; Dep. Sec.-Gen., Commonwealth Secretariat, London, 1965–70; High Comr in UK, 1970–75. Commonwealth Fund for Technical Co-operation: Chm., Bd of Representatives, 1975–76; Chm., Review Gp of Experts. *Publications:* An Historical Outline of the Development of the Marriage and Divorce Laws of Ceylon; An Historical Outline of the Development of the Marriage and Divorce Laws Applicable to Muslims in Ceylon; Fifty Years of Co-operative Development in Ceylon; Mrs Sirima R. D. Bandaranaike, first woman Prime Minister in the world: as I knew her. *Address:* 51 Lapworth Court, Blomfield Villas, W2 6NN. *T:* (020) 7286 4675.

GOOSE, Margaret Elizabeth; Chief Executive, Stroke Association, since 1997; *b* 10 Oct. 1945; *d* of late Leonard Charles Goose and of Gladys Muriel Goose (*née* Smith). *Educ:* Blyth Sch., Norwich; Newnham Coll., Cambridge (BA 1967; MA 1971). FHSM 1991. Gen. mgt in hosps and health authorities, 1967–82; Chief Exec., N Beds HA, 1982–92; Hd of Health and Mgt Develt Div., Nuffield Inst. for Health, Univ. of Leeds, 1993–97. Pres., IHSM, 1989–90. Hon. MFPHM 1998. *Recreations:* walking, travel, theatre, music, friends. *Address:* Stroke House, Whitecross Street, EC1Y 8JJ. *T:* (020) 7566 0300.

GOPAL, Dr Sarvepalli; Professor of Contemporary History, Jawaharlal Nehru University, New Delhi, 1972–83, now Emeritus; Fellow of St Antony's College, Oxford, 1966–96, Hon. Fellow, 1996; *b* 23 April 1923; *y c* and *o s* of Sir Sarvepalli Radhakrishnan, Hon. OM, Hon. FBA. *Educ:* Mill Hill School; Madras Univ.; Oxford Univ. MA (Madras and Oxon), BL (Madras), DPhil (Oxon), DLitt (Oxon). Lecturer and Reader in History, Andhra Univ., Waltair, 1948–52; Asst Dir, Nat. Archives of India, 1952–54; Dir, Historical Div., Min. of Extl Affairs, New Delhi, 1954–66; Commonwealth Fellow, Trin. Coll., Cambridge, 1963–64; Reader in S Asian History, Oxford Univ., 1966–71. Guest Scholar, Woodrow Wilson Center, Washington, 1992; Vis. Fellow, All Souls Coll., Oxford, 1992. Chairman: Nat. Book Trust, India, 1973–76; Indian Inst. of Advanced Study, 1992–; Madras Inst. of Develt Studies, 1995–97; Indian Inst. of Social Studies, 1995–98; Member: Indian UGC, 1973–79; UNESCO Exec. Bd, 1976–80; Vis. Prof., Leeds, 1977. Pres., Indian History Congress, 1978. Corresp. FRHistS. Hon. Professor: Tirupati, 1971; Hyderabad, 1990. Hon. DLitt: Andhra, 1975; Tirupati, 1979; Banaras, 1984; Hyderabad, 1993. Sahitya Akademi award, 1976. *Publications:* The Permanent Settlement in Bengal, 1949; The Viceroyalty of Lord Ripon, 1953; The Viceroyalty of Lord Irwin, 1957; British Policy in India, 1965; Modern India, 1967; Jawaharlal Nehru, vol. 1, 1975, vol. 2, 1979, vol. 3, 1984; Radhakrishnan, 1989; general editor, Selected Works of Jawaharlal Nehru; contribs articles to historical jls. *Recreations:* good food and travel. *Address:* 97 Radhakrishna Salai, Mylapore, Madras 4, India. *Club:* Oxford and Cambridge.

GOPALAN, Coluthur, MD, DSc; FRCP, FRCPE; FRS 1987; President, Nutrition Foundation of India, New Delhi, since 1979; *b* 29 Nov. 1918; *s* of C. Doraiswami Iyengar and Mrs Pattammal; *m* 1940, Seetha Gopalan; one *s* one *d* (and one *s* decd). *Educ:* Univ. of Madras (MD); Univ. of London (PhD, DSc). Fellow, Acad. of Med. Scis, India, 1961; FIASc 1964; FNA 1966. Dir, Nat. Inst. of Nutrition, Hyderabad, 1960–74; Dir-Gen., Indian Council of Med. Res., New Delhi, 1975–79. Hon. DSc. Banares Hindu, 1982. *Publications:* Nutritive Value of Indian Foods, 1966; Nutrition and Health Care, 1984; Use of Growth Charts for Promoting Child Nutrition: a review of global experience, 1985; Combating Undernutrition: basic issues and practical approaches, 1987; Nutrition Problems and Programmes in South East Asia, 1987; Nutrition in Developmental Transition in South East Asia, 1992; Recent Trends in Nutrition, 1993; Towards Better Nutrition: problems and policies, 1993; Nutrition Research in South East Asia: the emerging agenda for the future, 1994; over 200 contribs to sci. jls; chapters on specific topics to several books on nutrition in internat. pubns on nutrition. *Recreation:* music. *Address:* Nutrition Foundation of India, C-13, Qutab Institutional Area, New Delhi 110016, India. *T:* (11) 6857814, 6965410. *Club:* India International Centre (New Delhi).

GORAI, Rt Rev. Dinesh Chandra; Bishop of Calcutta, 1982–1999; *b* 15 Jan. 1934; *m* Binapani; two *c. Educ:* Calcutta Univ. (BA 1956). Serampore Theological Coll. (BD 1959). Ordained, 1962; Methodist Minister in Calcutta/Barrackpore, 1968–70; first Bishop, Church of N India Diocese of Barrackpore, 1970–82; Dep. Moderator, 1980, Moderator, 1983–86, Church of N India. Hon. DD: Bethel Coll., 1985; Serampore Coll., 1991. *Publications:* Society at the Cross Road, 1968; (ed) Transfer of Vision: a leadership development programme for the Church of North India 1983–1986, 1984; New Horizons in Christian Ministry, 1993. *Address:* Binapani Villa, 28 Mahatma Ghandi Road, Keorapukur M., Calcutta 700 082, India.

GORARD, Anthony John; *b* 15 July 1927; *s* of William James and Rose Mary Gorard; *m* 1954, Barbara Kathleen Hampton; one *s* three *d. Educ:* Ealing Grammar School. Chartered Accountant, 1951; Manufacturing Industry, 1952–58; Anglia Television Ltd, 1959–67, Executive Director and Member of Management Cttee; Managing Director, HTV Ltd, 1967–78; Chief Exec., HTV Gp Ltd, 1976–78; Director: Independent Television Publications Ltd, 1967–78; Independent Television News Ltd, 1973–78; Chief Exec., Cardiff Broadcasting Co. Ltd, 1979–81; Consultant, Mitchell Beazley Television, 1982–83; hotel proprietor, 1983–87; restaurant owner, 1987–94. Chm., British Regional Television Association, 1970–71. *Recreations:* tennis, rambling. *Address:* Threbs House, Bull Lane, Maiden Newton, Dorchester, Dorset DT2 0BQ. *T:* (01300) 321141.

GORBACHEV, Mikhail Sergeyevich; President: International Foundation for Socio-Economic and Political Studies (Gorbachev Foundation), since 1992; Green Cross International, since 1993; Executive President of the Soviet Union, 1990–91; *b* 2 March 1931; *m* 1953, Raisa Gorbacheva (*d* 1999); one *d. Educ:* Moscow State Univ. (law graduate); Stavropol Agric. Inst. Machine operator, 1946; joined CPSU 1952; First Sec., Stavropol Komsomol City Cttee, 1956–58, later Dep. Head of Propaganda; 2nd, later 1st Sec., Komsomol Territorial Cttee, 1958–62; Party Organizer, Stavropol Territorial Production Bd of Collective and State Farms, 1962; Head, Dept of party bodies, CPSU Territorial Cttee, 1963–66; 1st Sec., Stavropol City Party Cttee, 1966–68; 2nd Sec., 1968–70, 1st Sec., 1970–78, Stavropol Territorial CPSU Cttee; Central Committee, Communist Party of Soviet Union: Mem., 1971–91; Sec., with responsibility for agric., 1978–85; Alternate Mem., 1979–80, then Mem., Political Bureau; Gen. Sec., 1985–91. Deputy, Supreme Soviet: USSR, 1970–89 (Chm., Foreign Affairs Commn of the Soviet of the Union, 1984–85; Mem., 1985–88, Chm., 1988–89, Presidium); RSFSR, 1980–90; Deputy, Congress of Peoples' Deps, USSR, 1989; Chm., Supreme Soviet, USSR, 1989–90. Freeman of Aberdeen, 1993. Hon. Citizen of Berlin, 1992. Nobel Peace Prize, 1990; Ronald Reagan Freedom Award, 1992. Orders of Lenin, of Red Banner of Labour, Badge of Honour. *Publications:* A Time for Peace, 1985; The Coming Century of Peace, 1986; Speeches and Writings (7 vols), 1986–90; Peace has no Alternative, 1986; Moratorium, 1986; Perestroika: new thinking for our country and the world, 1987; The August Coup, 1991; December, 1991; My Stand, 1992; The Years of Hard Decisions, 1993; Life and Reforms, 1995 (UK edn, Memoirs, 1996); Reflections on the Past and Future, 1998. *Address:* (office) Leningradsky Prospekt 49, Moscow 125468, Russia. *T:* (095) 9439990, *Fax:* (095) 9439594.

GORDIMER, Nadine; author; *b* 20 Nov. 1923; *d* of Isidore Gordimer; *m* Reinhold Cassirer; one *s* one *d. Educ:* Convent Sch.; Witwatersrand Univ. Neil Gunn Fellowship, Scottish Arts Council, 1981. Hon. Member: Amer. Acad. of Art and Literature, 1979; Amer. Acad. of Arts and Sciences, 1980. DLit *hc* Leuven, Belgium, 1980; DLitt *hc:* City Coll. of NY, 1985; Smith Coll., 1985; Harvard, 1986; Yale, 1986; Columbia, 1987; New Sch. for Social Res., 1987; York, 1987; Oxford, 1994. MLA Award, USA, 1981; Malaparte Prize, Italy, 1985; Nelly Sachs Prize, W Germany, 1985; Bennett Award, USA, 1986; Nobel Prize for Literature, 1991. *Publications: novels:* The Lying Days, 1953; A World of Strangers, 1958; Occasion for Loving, 1963; The Late Bourgeois World, 1966;

A Guest of Honour, 1971 (James Tait Black Meml Prize, 1971); The Conservationist, 1974 (jtly, Booker Prize 1974; Grand Aigle d'Or, France, 1975); Burger's Daughter, 1979; July's People, 1981; A Sport of Nature, 1987; My Son's Story, 1990; None to Accompany Me, 1994; The House Gun, 1997; The Pickup, 2001; *stories:* The Soft Voice of the Serpent, 1953; Six Feet of the Country, 1956; Friday's Footprint, 1960 (W. H. Smith Lit. Award, 1961); Not for Publication, 1965; Livingstone's Companions, 1972; Selected Stories, 1975; Some Monday for Sure, 1976; A Soldier's Embrace, 1980; Something Out There, 1984; Jump, 1991; *non-fiction:* South African Writing Today (jt editor), 1967; The Essential Gesture: writing, politics and places, 1988; Writing and Being (Charles Eliot Norton Lectures), 1995; Living in Hope and History: notes from our century (essays), 1999. *Address:* c/o A. P. Watt, 20 John Street, WC1N 2DR.

GORDON, family name of **Marquess of Aberdeen and Temair, Marquess of Huntly** and of **Baron Gordon of Strathblane**.

GORDON OF STRATHBLANE, Baron *cr* 1997 (Life Peer), of Deil's Craig in Stirling; **James Stuart Gordon,** CBE 1984; Chairman, Scottish Radio Holdings, since 1996; *b* 17 May 1936; *s* of James Gordon and Elsie (*née* Riach); *m* 1971, Margaret Anne Stevenson; two *s* one *d*. *Educ:* St Aloysius' Coll., Glasgow; Glasgow Univ. (MA Hons). Political Editor, STV, 1965–73; Man. Dir, Radio Clyde, 1973–96; Chief Exec., Radio Clyde Hldgs, subseq. Scottish Radio Hldgs, 1991–96. Chairman: Scottish Exhibn Centre, 1983–89; Scottish Tourist Bd, 1998–2001 (Mem., 1997); Vice-Chm., Melody Radio, 1991–97; Member: Scottish Develt Agency, 1981–90; Scottish Adv. Bd, BP, 1990–; Director: Clydeport Hldgs, 1992–98; Johnston Press plc, 1996–. Chm., Adv. Gp on Listed Sporting Events, 1997–98; Member: Cttee of Inquiry into Teachers' Pay and Conditions, 1986; Cttee to Review Funding of BBC, 1999. Trustee, Nat. Galls of Scotland, 1998–. Chm., Glasgow Common Purpose, 1995–97. Mem. Court, Univ. of Glasgow, 1984–97. Hon. DLitt Glasgow Caledonian, 1994; DUniv Glasgow, 1998. *Recreations:* ski-ing, walking, genealogy, golf. *Address:* Deil's Craig, Strathblane, Glasgow G63 9ET. *T:* (01360) 770604. *Clubs:* New (Edinburgh); Glasgow Art (Glasgow); Buchanan Castle Golf, Prestwick Golf.

GORDON, Sir Andrew Cosmo Lewis D.; *see* Duff Gordon.

GORDON, Rt Rev. (Archibald) Ronald (McDonald); Canon and Sub-Dean of Christ Church, Oxford, 1991–96; an Assistant Bishop, diocese of Oxford, since 1991; *b* 19 March 1927; *s* of late Sir Archibald Gordon, CMG, and late Dorothy Katharine Gordon, Bridge House, Gerrards Cross, Bucks. *Educ:* Rugby Sch.; Balliol Coll., Oxford (Organ Schol., MA 1950); Cuddesdon Theol. Coll. Deacon 1952; Priest 1953; Curate of Stepney, 1952–55; Chaplain, Cuddesdon Coll., 1955–59; Vicar of St Peter, Birmingham, 1959–67; Res. Canon, Birmingham Cathedral, 1967–71; Vicar of University Church of St Mary the Virgin with St Cross and St Peter in the East, Oxford, 1971–75; Bishop of Portsmouth, 1975–84; Bishop at Lambeth (Hd of Archbp's Staff), 1984–91; an Asst Bishop, Dio. of Southwark, 1984–91; Bishop to the Forces, 1985–90. Mem., H of L, 1981–84. Fellow of St Cross Coll., Oxford, 1975; Select Preacher, Univ. of Oxford, 1985, 1993, 1997. Mem., Church Assembly and General Synod and Proctor in Convocation, 1965–71; Chm., ACCM, 1976–83. Member: Court of Ecclesiastical Causes Reserved, 1991–; Archbishops' Commn on Cathedrals, 1992–94; Adv. Bd for Redundant Churches, 1992–98. Chm., Malaŵi Church Trust, 1993–95; Pres., Oxford Mission, 1992–2001. *Recreations:* piano playing, refraining from giving advice. *Address:* 16 East St Helen Street, Abingdon, Oxon OX14 5EA. *T:* (01235) 526956.

GORDON, Boyd; fisheries consultant; Fisheries Secretary, Department of Agriculture and Fisheries for Scotland, 1982–86; *b* 18 Sept. 1926; *er s* of David Gordon and Isabella (*née* Leishman); *m* 1951, Elizabeth Mabel (*née* Smith); two *d*. *Educ:* Musselburgh Grammar School. Following military service with the Royal Scots, joined the Civil Service, initially with Min. of Labour, then Inland Revenue; Department of Agriculture and Fisheries for Scotland: joined, 1953; Principal, Salmon and Freshwater Fisheries Administration and Fisheries R&D, 1962–73; Asst Secretary, Agriculture Economic Policy, EEC Co-ordination and Agriculture Marketing, 1973–82. *Recreations:* family and church affairs, gardening, sport of all kinds, though only golf as participant now, reading, playing and writing Scottish fiddle music. *Address:* 87 Duddingston Road, Edinburgh EH15 1SP. *Club:* Civil Service.

GORDON, Brian William, OBE 1974; HM Diplomatic Service, 1949–81, retired; Commercial Counsellor, Caracas, 1980–81; *b* 24 Oct. 1926; *s* of William and Doris Margaret Gordon; *m* 1951, Sheila Graham Young; two *s* one *d*. *Educ:* Tynemouth Grammar School. HM Forces (Lieut in IA), 1944–47; joined HM Foreign Service (now Diplomatic Service), 1949; served in: Saigon; Libya; Second Sec. in Ethiopia, 1954–58 and in Peru, 1959–61; HM Consul: Leopoldville, Congo, 1962–64; New York, 1965–67; Puerto Rico, 1967–69; Consul-General, Bilbao, 1969–73; Asst Head, Trade Relations and Export Dept, FCO, 1974–77; Dep. Consul-Gen., Los Angeles, 1977–80. *Recreations:* golf, walking. *Address:* 4 Cragside, Corbridge, Northumberland NE45 5EU.

See also I. W. Gordon.

GORDON, Sir Charles (Addison Somerville Snowden), KCB 1981 (CB 1970); Clerk of the House of Commons, 1979–83; *b* 25 July 1918; *s* of late C. G. S. Gordon, TD, Liverpool, and Mrs E. A. Gordon, Emberton and Wimbledon; *m* 1943, Janet Margaret, (Jane), Beattie (*d* 1995); one *s* (one *d* decd). *Educ:* Winchester; Balliol Coll., Oxford. Served in Fleet Air Arm throughout War of 1939–45. Apptd Asst Clerk in House of Commons, 1946; Senior Clerk, 1947; Fourth Clerk at the Table, 1962; Principal Clerk of the Table Office, 1967; Second Clerk Assistant, 1974; Clerk Asst, 1976. Sec., Soc. of Clerks-at-the-Table in Commonwealth Parliaments, and co-Editor of its journal, The Table, 1952–62. *Publications:* Parliament as an Export (jointly), 1966; Editor, Erskine May's Parliamentary Practice, 20th edn, 1983 (Asst Editor, 19th edn); contribs to: The Table; The Parliamentarian. *Recreation:* dolce far niente. *Address:* 279 Lonsdale Road, Barnes, SW13 9QB. *T:* (020) 8748 6735.

GORDON, (Cosmo) Gerald (Maitland); His Honour Judge Gordon; a Circuit Judge, since 1990; *b* 26 March 1945; *s* of John Kenneth Maitland Gordon and Erica Martia Clayton-East; *m* 1973, Vanessa Maria Juliet Maxine Reilly-Morrison, LLB, AKC, barrister; two *s*. *Educ:* Eton. Called to the Bar, Middle Temple, 1966. Asst Recorder, 1982–86; Recorder, 1986–90. Royal Borough of Kensington and Chelsea: Mem. Council, 1971–90; Chm., Works Cttee, 1978–80; Chm., Town Planning Cttee, 1988; Dep. Leader, 1982–88; Mayor, 1989–90. Chairman: Edwardes Square Scarsdale and Abingdon Assoc., 1990–; N Kensington Amenity Trust, 1992–; Nicholas Freeman Meml Trust, 1996–. Liveryman, Merchant Taylors' Co. *Recreations:* planning conservation, cooking, food and wine. *Address:* c/o 36 Essex Street, WC2 3AS. *T:* (020) 7413 0353.

GORDON, Prof. David, FRCP; Professor of Medicine, and Dean, Faculty of Medicine, Dentistry, Nursing and Pharmacy (formerly Medicine, Dentistry and Nursing), University of Manchester, since 1999; Hon. Consultant Physician, Manchester Royal Infirmary, Salford Royal Hospitals and South Manchester University Hospitals, since 1999; *b* 23 Feb. 1947; *s* of late Lawrence Gordon and of Pattie Gordon (*née* Wood); *m* Dr C. Louise Jones; three *s* one *d*. *Educ:* Whitgift Sch.; Magdalene Coll., Cambridge (BA 1967, MA 1971; MB BChir 1970); Westminster Med. Sch. MRCP 1972, FRCP 1989. Clin. appts, Leicester and Cambridge, 1970–72; St Mary's Hospital Medical School: Res. Fellow, 1972–74; Lectr in Medicine, 1974–80; Sen. Lectr in Medicine, 1980–83; Hon. Sen. Lectr in Medicine, 1983–94; Hon. Cons. Physician, St Mary's Hosp., London, 1980–94; Wellcome Trust: Asst Dir, 1983–89; Prog. Dir, 1989–98; Dir of Special Initiatives, 1998–99. Member: Res. Sub-Gp, Task Force on Support of R&D in NHS, 1994; Academic Wkg Gp, HEFCE-CVCP-SCOP Cttee on Post Grad. Educn, 1995; Indep. Task Force on Clin. Academic Careers, CVCP, 1996–97; Res. Cttee, HEFCE, 1998–99; Chief Scientist Cttee, Scottish Office DoH, 1997–99. FMedSci 1999. *Publications:* papers, reviews, etc on biomed. res., sci. policy and other subjects in learned jls. *Recreations:* music (cello), books, food, finding out what is going on. *Address:* Faculty of Medicine, Dentistry, Nursing and Pharmacy, Stopford Building, University of Manchester, Oxford Road, Manchester M13 9PT. *T:* (0161) 275 5027, *Fax:* (0161) 275 5784; *e-mail:* dean.mdn.gordon@man.ac.uk.

GORDON, David Sorrell; Secretary, Royal Academy of Arts, since 1996; *b* 11 Sept. 1941; *s* of late Sholom and Tania Gordon; *m* 1st, 1963, Enid Albagli (marr. diss. 1969); 2nd, 1974, Maggi McCormick; two *s*. *Educ:* Clifton College; Balliol College, Oxford (PPE, BA 1963); LSE; Advanced Management Program, Harvard Business Sch. FCA. Articles with Thomson McLintock, 1965–68; The Economist: editorial staff, 1968–78; Production and Develt Dir, 1978–81; Gp Chief Exec., Economist Newspaper Ltd, 1981–93; Chief Exec., ITN, 1993–95. Director: Financial Times, 1983–93; eFinancial News, 1999–; Profile Books, 1996–. Dir, South Bank Bd, 1986–96; a Governor, BFI, 1983–91. Chm., Contemporary Art Soc., 1991–98; Trustee: Tate Gall., 1993–98; Architecture Foundn, 1993–; Architecture Assoc. Foundn, 1995–98. Gov., LSE, 1990–2000. *Publication:* (with Fred Hirsch) Newspaper Money, 1975. *Recreation:* collecting stereoscopic photographs. *Address:* Greenwood, 56 Duke's Avenue, Chiswick, W4 2AF. *T:* (020) 8994 3126. *Clubs:* Garrick, Arts.

GORDON, Donald; Chairman: Liberty International PLC (formerly TransAtlantic Holdings), since 1981; Capital & Counties (UK), since 1982; Capital Shopping Centres (UK), since 1994; *b* 24 June 1930; *s* of Nathan and Sheila Gordon; *m* 1958, Peggy Cowan; two *s* one *d*. *Educ:* King Edward VII Sch., Johannesburg; Univ. of Witwatersrand. Chairmanships include: Liberty Life Assoc. of Africa, SA, 1957-99; Liberty Hldgs, SA, 1968-99; Liberty Investors, SA 1971-99; Guardian Nat. Insce Co., SA, 1980-99; Directorships include: Guardbank Mgt Corp., SA, 1969-99; Standard Bank Investment Corp. SA, 1979-99 (Dep. Chm.); S African Breweries, SA, 1982-99 (Dep. Chm.); Guardian Royal Exchange (UK), 1984-94; Beverage & Consumer Ind. Hldgs, SA, 1989-99; Sun Life Corp., UK, 1992-95. Hon. DEconSc Witwatersrand, 1991. Business Man of Year Award, Financial Mail (SA), 1965; Financial Mail Achiever of the Century in SA Financial Services, 1999. *Recreations:* tennis, opera, ballet. *Address:* Liberty International PLC, 40 Broadway, SW1H 0BT. *T:* (020) 7960 1200, *Fax:* (020) 7960 1333. *Clubs:* Rand, Johannesburg Country, Plettenburg Bay Country, Houghton Golf, (SA).

GORDON, Douglas; *see* Gordon, R. D.

GORDON, Douglas Lamont; artist; *b* 20 Sept. 1966; *s* of James Gordon and Mary Clements Gordon (*née* MacDougall). *Educ:* Glasgow Sch. of Art (BA Hons 1st cl.); Slade Sch. of Art (Postgrad. Res. Dip.). *Exhibitions* include: Lisson Gall., 1993, 1995 (solo), 1998, 2000; Hayward Gall., 1996, 1997; MOMA, Oxford, 1996; 10th Sydney Biennale, 1996; Venice Biennale (Premio 2000), 1997; Tate Liverpool, 2000. Turner Prize, 1996. *Recreations:* eating, drinking, sleeping. *Address:* c/o Lisson Gallery, 67 Lisson Street, NW1 5DA.

GORDON, Eileen; *b* 22 Oct. 1946; *d* of late Charles Leatt and Margaret Rose Leatt; *m* Tony Gordon; one *s* one *d*. *Educ:* Harold Hill Grammar Sch.; Shoreditch Comp. Sch.; Westminster Coll., Oxford (CertEd). Teacher; Asst to Tony Banks, MP, 1990–97. MP (Lab) Romford, 1997–2001. Contested (Lab) Romford, 1992 and 2001. Member: Broadcasting Select Cttee, 1998–2001; Health Select Cttee, 1999–2001.

GORDON, François; *see* Gordon, J. F.

GORDON, Gerald; *see* Gordon, C. G. M.

GORDON, Sir Gerald (Henry), Kt 2000; CBE 1995; QC (Scot.) 1972; LLD; Sheriff of Glasgow and Strathkelvin, 1978–99; Temporary Judge of Court of Session and High Court of Justiciary, since 1992; Member, Scottish Criminal Cases Review Commission, since 1999; *b* 17 June 1929; *er s* of Simon Gordon and Rebecca Gordon (*née* Bulbin), Glasgow; *m* 1957, Marjorie Joseph (*d* 1996), *yr d* of Isaac and Aimée Joseph (*née* Strump), Glasgow; one *s* two *d*. *Educ:* Queen's Park Senior Secondary Sch., Glasgow; Univ. of Glasgow (MA (1st cl. Hons Philosophy with English Literature) 1950; LLB (Distinction) 1953; PhD 1960); LLD Edinburgh 1968. National Service, RASC, 1953–55 (Staff-Sgt, Army Legal Aid, BAOR, 1955). Admitted Scottish Bar 1953; practice at Scottish Bar, 1953, 1956–59; Faulds Fellow, Univ. of Glasgow, 1956–59. Procurator Fiscal Depute, Edinburgh, 1960–65. University of Edinburgh: Sen. Lectr, 1965; Personal Prof. of Criminal Law, 1969–72; Head of Dept of Criminal Law and Criminology, 1965–72; Prof. of Scots Law, 1972–76; Dean of Faculty of Law, 1970–73; Vis. Prof., 2000–. Sheriff of S Strathclyde, Dumfries and Galloway at Hamilton, 1976–77. Commonwealth Vis. Fellow and Vis. Res. Fellow, Centre of Criminology, Univ. of Toronto, 1974–75. Temporary Sheriff, 1973–76. Member: Interdepartmental Cttee on Scottish Criminal Procedure, 1970–77; Cttee on Appeals Criteria and Alleged Miscarriages of Justice Procedures, 1995–96. Hon. LLD Glasgow, 1993. *Publications:* The Criminal Law of Scotland, 1967, 2nd edn 1978; (ed) Renton and Brown's Criminal Procedure, 4th edn 1972, to 6th edn 1996; (ed) Scottish Criminal Case Reports, 1981–; various articles. *Recreations:* Jewish studies, coffee conversation, crosswords.

GORDON, Giles Alexander Esmé; Literary Agent and Director, Curtis Brown, since 1995; *b* 23 May 1940; *s* of late Alexander Esmé Gordon, RSA, FRIBA, FRIAS and Betsy Gordon (*née* McCurry); *m* 1st, 1964, Margaret Anna Eastoe (*d* 1989); one *s* one *d* (and one *s* decd); 2nd, 1990, Margaret Anne McKernan; one *s* two *d*. *Educ:* Edinburgh Academy; (briefly) Edinburgh College of Art. FRSL 1990. Trainee publisher, Oliver & Boyd, Edinburgh, 1959–63; advertising manager, Secker & Warburg, 1963–64; editor, Hutchinson, 1964–66; plays editor, Penguin Books, 1966–67; edtl dir, Victor Gollancz, 1967–73; Literary Agent, Anthony Sheil Associates, later Sheil Land Associates, 1973–95. C. Day Lewis Fellow in Writing, KCL, 1974–75. Sec. and Chm., Soc. of Young Publishers; Member: Literature Panel, Arts Council, 1968–72; Cttee of Management, Soc. of Authors; Cttee, Assoc. of Authors' Agents; Council, RSL, 1992–94; Cttee, Authors' Club, 1992–; Cttee, Soc. of Authors in Scotland, 1996–99. Lectr, Tufts Univ. in London, 1970–74; Lectr, Hollins Coll. in London, 1983–86. Theatre critic: Spectator; London Daily News; Drama; books columnist, The Times, 1993–95; columnist, Edinburgh Evening News, 1999–; restaurant critic, Caledonia, 1999–; Editor, Drama, 1984–86.

Series Editor: Bloomsbury Classics short stories, 1995–99; Clarion Tales, 1996–99. *Publications:* Pictures from an Exhibition, 1970; The Umbrella Man, 1971; About a Marriage, 1972; Girl with Red Hair, 1974; (ed with A. Hamilton) Factions, 1974; (with Margaret Gordon) Walter and the Balloon (for children), 1974; (ed) Beyond the Words, 1975; Farewell, Fond Dreams, 1975; (ed) Prevailing Spirits, 1976; 100 Scenes from Married Life, 1976; (ed with Dulan Barber) Members of the Jury, 1976; (ed jtly) You Always Remember the First Time, 1976; (ed) A Book of Contemporary Nightmares, 1977; Enemies, 1977; The Illusionist, 1978; (ed with Fred Urquhart) Modern Scottish Short Stories, 1978; Ambrose's Vision, 1980; (ed) Shakespeare Stories, 1982; (ed) English Short Stories 1940–1980, 1982; (ed with David Hughes) Best Short Stories (annually), 1986–95; (ed) English Short Stories: 1900 to the present, 1988; (ed) The Twentieth Century Short Story in English: a bibliography, 1989; Aren't We Due a Royalty Statement?, 1993; (ed with David Hughes) The Best of Best Short Stories, 1986–1995, 1995; Scotland from the Air, 1996. *Recreations:* theatre, opera, walking, travelling, eating, drinking, book collecting. *Address:* Curtis Brown, 37 Queensferry Street, Edinburgh EH2 4QS. *Clubs:* Garrick, PEN, Useless Information Society.

GORDON, Hannah Cambell Grant; actress; *b* 9 April 1941; *d* of William Munro Gordon and Hannah Grant Gordon; *m* 1970, Norman Warwick; one *s*. *Educ:* St Denis School for Girls, Edinburgh; Glasgow Univ. (Cert. Dramatic Studies); College of Dramatic Art, Glasgow (Dip. in speech and drama). FRSAMD 1980. Hon. DLitt Glasgow, 1993. Winner, James Bridie Gold Medal, Royal Coll. of Music and Dramatic Art, Glasgow, 1962. *Stage:* Dundee Rep., Glasgow Citizens Theatre, Belgrade Theatre, Coventry, Ipswich, Windsor; Can You Hear me at the Back, Piccadilly, 1979; The Killing Game, Apollo, 1980; The Jeweller's Shop, Westminster, 1982; The Country Girl, Apollo, 1983; Light Up the Sky, Old Vic, 1985; Mary Stuart, Edinburgh Fest., 1987; Shirley Valentine, Duke of York's, 1989; Hidden Laughter, Vaudeville, 1991; An Ideal Husband, Globe, 1992; The Aspern Papers, Wyndham's, 1996; *television:* 1st TV appearance, Johnson Over Jordan, 1965; series: Great Expectations, 1969; Middlemarch, 1969; My Wife Next Door, 1972; Upstairs, Downstairs, 1976; Telford's Change, 1979; Goodbye Mr Kent, 1983; Gardener's Calendar, 1986; My Family and Other Animals, 1987; Joint Account, 1989; Midsomer Murders, 1999; One Foot in the Grave (final episode), 2000; presenter, Watercolour Challenge, 1998, 1999, 2000; *films:* Spring and Port Wine, 1970; The Elephant Man, 1979; numerous radio plays. *Recreations:* tennis, gardening, cooking, walking, sailing. *Address:* c/o Conway Van Gelder Ltd, 18–21 Jermyn Street, SW1Y 6HP.

GORDON, Prof. Ian Alistair, CBE 1971; MA, PhD; Professor of English Language and Literature, University of Wellington, NZ, 1936–74, now Emeritus; *b* Edinburgh, 30 July 1908; *e s* of Alexander and Ann Gordon; *m* 1936, Mary Ann McLean Fullarton, Ayr; one *s* three *d*. *Educ:* Royal High Sch., Edinburgh; University of Edinburgh. Bruce of Grangehill Bursar, Sloan Prizeman, Gray Prizeman, Scott Travelling Scholar (Italy), Dickson Travelling Scholar (Germany), Elliot Prizeman in English Literature, Pitt Scholar in Classical and English Literature; MA (Hons Classics) 1930, (Hons English) 1932; PhD 1936. Asst Lecturer in English language and lit., University of Edinburgh, 1932; Sub-Ed., Scot. Nat. Dictionary, 1930–36; Dean: Faculty of Arts, Victoria Univ. Coll., Wellington, 1944–47, 1952, 1957–61; Faculty of Languages, 1965–68; Vice-Chancellor Univ. of New Zealand, 1947–52; Chm., Academic Bd, 1954–61. Visiting Professor: KCL 1954; Univ. of Edinburgh, 1962; Univ. of South Pacific, Fiji, 1972; France and Belgium, 1976; Univ. of Waikato, 1980; Research Associate, UCL, 1969; Res. Fellow, Auckland Univ., 1993; Vis. Fellow, Edinburgh Univ., 1974–75; Vis. Fellow in Commonwealth Literature, Univ. of Leeds, 1975. Columnist, NZ Listener, 1977–88. Member: Copyright Cttee and Tribunal, 1958; UGC, 1960–70; Chairman: English Language Institute, 1961–72; NZ Literary Fund, 1951–73; Exec. Council, Assoc. of Univs of Br. Commonwealth, 1949–50. NZ representative at internat. confs: Utrecht, 1948; Bangkok, 1960; Kampala, 1961; Karachi, 1961. Army Educ. Service, 2 NZEF, Hon. Major. Hon. LLD Bristol, 1948; Hon. DLitt NZ, 1961; DUniv Stirling, 1975. Massey Univ. Medal, 1995. *Publications:* John Skelton, Poet Laureate, 1943; New Zealand New Writing, 1943–45; The Teaching of English, a study in secondary education, 1947; English Prose Technique, 1948; Shenstone's Miscellany, 1759–1763, 1952; Katherine Mansfield, 1954; The Movement of English Prose, 1966; John Galt (biog.), 1972; Word (festschrift), 1974; Undiscovered Country, 1974; Katherine Mansfield's Urewera Notebook, 1979; Word Finder, 1979; A Word in Your Ear, 1980; (ed) Collins Concise English Dictionary, NZ edn, 1982; (ed) Collins Compact New Zealand Dictionary, 1985; Take My Word For It, 1997; Victorian Voyage, 2000; edited the following works of John Galt: The Entail, 1970; The Provost, 1973; The Member, 1975; The Last of the Lairds, 1976; Short Stories, 1978; part-author: Edinburgh Essays in Scottish Literature, 1933; Essays in Literature, 1934; The University and the Community, 1946; John Galt (bicent. vol.), 1980; Lexicographical and Linguistic Studies, 1988; The Fine Instrument, 1989; articles in research journals and other periodicals. *Address:* 58 Ardmore Road, Herne Bay, Auckland, New Zealand. *Club:* Aorangi Ski, New Zealand (former Pres.).

GORDON, Ian William; Head, Scotland Office, since 1999; *b* 27 Dec. 1952; *s* of Brian William Gordon, *qv*; *m* 1979, Alison Margaret Bunting; two *s*. *Educ:* Strathallan Sch., Perth; Downing Coll., Cambridge (BA). Joined Civil Service, 1975: Dept of Energy, 1975–81; Scottish Office, 1981–99; Industry, 1981–85; Finance, 1985–86; Educn, 1986–90; Agriculture, 1990–93; Fisheries, 1993–99 (Fisheries Sec., 1995–99). *Address:* Scotland Office, Dover House, Whitehall, SW1A 2AU.

GORDON, Isabel; *see* Allende, I.

GORDON, Maj.-Gen. James Charles Mellish, CBE 1992; General Secretary, Forces Pension Society (formerly Officers' Pensions Society), since 2000; Director, FPS Investment Co. Ltd, since 2000; Managing Trustee, FPS Widows' Fund, since 2000; *b* 3 Aug. 1941; *s* of Brig. Leonard Henry Gordon and Joyce Evelyn Mary Gordon (*née* Gurdon); *m* 1964, Rosemary Stella Kincaid; two *s* one *d*. *Educ:* Tonbridge Sch.; RMA Sandhurst. Commissioned RA 1961; served in UK, Germany, Singapore; RMCS, Shrivenham, 1972; Staff Coll., Camberley, 1973; MoD, 1974–75; Comdr, D Batt., RHA, UK and BAOR, 1976–78; MA to MGO, MoD, 1978–80; CO 45 Field Regt RA, BAOR, 1980–83; Col, ASD1, MoD, 1983–86; CRA 4th Armoured Div., BAOR, 1986–89; Dir, Mil. Ops, MoD, 1989–91; COS, HQ UKLF, 1991–94. Dir Gen., Assoc. of Train Operating Cos, 1994–99 (Director: Rail Settlement Plan Ltd; Rail Staff Travel Ltd; Nat. Rail Enquiry Service). Corporate Fellow, Industry and Parlt Trust, 1998. Mem. Council Officers' Assoc., 2000–. Mem., RYA. FCIT 1996, FILT 1999. *Recreations:* sailing, tennis, music, theatre, travel.

GORDON, (Jean) François, CMG 1999; HM Diplomatic Service; Ambassador to the Côte d'Ivoire, since 2001; *b* 16 April 1953; *s* of Michael Colin Gordon and Jeanine Marie Gordon (*née* Parizet); *m* 1977, Elaine Daniel; two *d*. *Educ:* Queen's Coll., Oxford (BA Hons Jurisprudence 1974); Université d'Aix et Marseille (Diplôme d'Etudes Supérieures 1975). Articled clerk, Ingledew Brown, 1975–78; admitted solicitor, 1979; joined HM Diplomatic Service, 1979: EU Dept, FCO, 1979–81; Second, later First Sec., Luanda, 1981–83; First Secretary: UK Delegn to UN Conf. on Disarmament, Geneva, 1983–88; UN Dept, FCO, 1988–90; (Political), Nairobi, 1990–92; Africa Dept (Southern), FCO, 1992–95; Dep. Hd, Drugs, Internat. Crime and Terrorism Dept, FCO, 1995–96; Hd, Drugs and Internat. Crime Dept, FCO, 1996; Ambassador to Algeria, 1996–99; RCDS, 2000. *Recreations:* gardening, watching African wildlife, collecting children's books, shooting small-bore rifle. *Address:* c/o Foreign and Commonwealth Office, King Charles Street, SW1A 2AH. *Club:* Muthaiga Country (Nairobi).

GORDON, John Alexander, CB 1995; CEng; FRAeS; Compliance Officer for merger undertakings, BAE SYSTEMS, since 2000; Director, Gordon Consulting; General Manager, NATO Eurofighter and Tornado Management Agency, 1996–99; *b* 7 Nov. 1940; *s* of John and Eleanor Gordon; *m* 1962, Dyanne Calder; two *d*. *Educ:* RAF Colls, Henlow and Cranwell. CEng, MIMechE; FRAeS 1990. Royal Air Force: training and education, 1958–61; Engr Br., 1961–70; Ministry of Defence, Procurement Executive, 1970–95: mil. aircraft procurement in collaboration with US and European Govts; projects incl. Harrier, Jaguar, Tornado and New European Fighter Aircraft. RAeS British Gold Medal, 1997. *Recreations:* dinghy sailing, mountain walking, equestrian activities. *Club:* Royal Air Force.

GORDON, John Keith; international environmentalist; *b* 6 July 1940; *s* of late Prof. James Edward Gordon and of Theodora (*née* Sinker); *m* 1965, Elizabeth Shanks; two *s*. *Educ:* Marlborough Coll.; Cambridge Univ. (1st Cl. Hons History). Henry Fellow, Yale Univ., 1962–63; research in Russian history, LSE, 1963–66; entered FCO, 1966; Budapest, 1968–70; seconded to Civil Service Coll., 1970–72; FCO, 1972–73; UK Mission, Geneva, 1973–74; Head of Chancery and Consul, Yaoundé, 1975–77 (concurrently Chargé d'Affaires, Gabon and Central African Republic); FCO, 1977–80; Cultural Attaché, Moscow, 1980–81; Office of UK Rep. to European Community, Brussels, 1982–83; UK Perm. Deleg. to UNESCO, Paris, 1983–85; Head of Nuclear Energy Dept, FCO, 1986–88; Imperial College, London: Academic Visitor, Centre for Envmtl Technol., 1988–90; Dep. and Policy Dir, Global Envmt Res. Centre, 1990–94. Mem., UK Nat. Commn for UNESCO; Special Advr, and UK 2002 Co-ordinator, UK-UN Envmt and Develt Forum. Contested (Lib Dem) Daventry, 1997. *Publications:* (with Caroline Fraser) Institutions and Sustainable Development, 1991; (with Tom Bigg) 2020 Vision, 1994; Canadian Round Tables, 1994; reports and articles on internat. envmtl issues. *Recreations:* jogging, sailing, reading. *Address:* 68 Hornsey Lane, N6 5LU.

GORDON, Kate; *see* Timms, V. K.

GORDON, Sir Keith (Lyndell), Kt 1979; CMG 1971; Chairman, Public Service Board of Appeal, St Lucia, 1978–88, retired; Justice of Appeal, West Indies Associated States Supreme Court, 1967–72, retired; *b* 8 April 1906; 3rd *s* of late George S. E. Gordon, Journalist, and Nancy Gordon; *m* 1947, Ethel King; one *d*. *Educ:* St Mary's Coll., St Lucia, WI; Middle Temple, London. Magistrate, Grenada, 1938; Crown Attorney, Dominica, 1942; Trinidad and Tobago: Magistrate, 1943–46 and 1949–53; Exec. Off., Black Market Board, 1946–48; Puisne Judge, Windward Islands and Leeward Islands, 1954–59; Puisne Judge, British Guiana, 1959–62; Chief Justice, West Cameroon, 1963–67. *Recreation:* gardening. *Address:* PO Box 505, Vigie, Castries, St Lucia.

GORDON, Sir Lionel Eldred Peter S.; *see* Smith-Gordon.

GORDON, Prof. Michael John Caldwell, PhD; FRS 1994; Professor of Computer Assisted Reasoning, Computer Laboratory, University of Cambridge, since 1996; *b* 28 Feb. 1948; *m* 1979, Avra Jean Cohn; two *s*. *Educ:* Bedales Sch.; Gonville and Caius Coll., Cambridge (BA Maths); King's Coll., Cambridge (Dip. Linguistics); Edinburgh Univ. (PhD). Research Associate, Stanford Univ., 1974–75; University of Edinburgh: Res. Fellow, 1975–78; SRC Advanced Res. Fellow, 1978–81; University of Cambridge: Lectr, 1981–88; Reader in Formal Methods, 1988–96; Royal Soc./SERC Industrial Fellow, SRI International, 1987–89. *Publications:* The Denotational Description of Programming Languages, 1979; Programming Language Theory and its Implementation, 1988. *Recreation:* mushroom hunting. *Address:* Computer Laboratory, University of Cambridge, William Gates Building, J J Thompson Avenue, Cambridge CB3 0FD.

GORDON, Mildred; *b* 24 Aug. 1923; *d* of Dora and Judah Fellerman; *m* 1st, 1948, Sam Gordon (*d* 1982); one *s*; 2nd, 1985, Nils Kaare Dahl. *Educ:* Raines Foundation School; Forest Teacher Training College. Teacher, 1945–85. Mem. Exec., London Labour Party, 1983–86; Jt Chm., Greater London Labour Policy Cttee, 1985–86. MP (Lab) Bow and Poplar, 1987–97. Mem., Select Cttee on Educn, Science and Arts, 1991–97; Chm., All-Party Parly Child Support Act Monitoring Group, 1995–97; Vice Chm., PLP Educn Cttee and Social Services Cttee, 1990–92, 1997. Formerly, Advr, GLC Women's Cttee. Chm., Barnet Co-op. Party, 1998–2000. Member: Bd, Tower Hamlets Business and Educn Partnership; Exec. Cttee, Gtr London Forum for the Elderly, 1999–; Nat. Council, and Exec. Cttee, London and SE Reg., National Pensioner Convention. Patron: Gtr London Pensioners' Assoc.; Dockland Singers; Danesford Trust. Founder, Schs' Public Speaking Competition, Tower Hamlets. School Governor, 1999–. Freeman, London Bor. of Tower Hamlets. *Publications:* essays and articles on education. *Recreations:* pottery, designing and making costume jewellery, painting, writing poetry. *Address:* 28 Cumbrian Gardens, NW2 1EF.

GORDON, Nadia, (Mrs Charles Gordon); *see* Nerina, N.

GORDON, Pamela Joan; Chief Executive, City of Sheffield Metropolitan District, 1989–97; *b* 13 Feb. 1936; *d* of Frederick Edward Bantick and Violet Elizabeth Bantick; *m* 1st, 1959, Wallace Henry Gordon (*d* 1980); two *s*; 2nd, 1997, Peter Charles Hoad. *Educ:* Richmond (Surrey) Grammar School for Girls; St Hilda's Coll., Oxford (MA). Variety of posts with ILEA, GLC and LCC, 1957–81; Greater London Council: Asst Dir Gen., 1981–83; Dep. Dir of Industry and Employment, 1983–85; Chief Exec., London Bor. of Hackney, 1985–89. Member: Adv. Cttee, Constitution Unit, 1995–97; Local Govt Commn for England, 1998–; Indep. Panel of Assessors for Public Appts made by DETR, 1999–; Electoral Commn, 2001–. Pres., SOLACE, 1996–97. Gov., Sheffield Hallam Univ., 1995–. Hon. Fellow, Inst. of Local Govt Studies, Birmingham Univ., 1990. Columnist, Local Government Chronicle. *Publications:* articles on management, etc, in local govt jls. *Recreations:* opera, theatre, foreign travel. *Address:* 9 Scarlett Oak Meadow, Sheffield S6 6FE. *T:* (0114) 232 3005.

GORDON, Patrick W.; *see* Wolrige-Gordon.

GORDON, Richard, (Dr Gordon Ostlere), MB BChir (Cantab); FRCA; *b* 15 Sept. 1921; *m*; two *s* two *d*. Formerly: anaesthetist at St Bartholomew's Hospital, and Oxford University; assistant editor, British Medical Jl; ship's surgeon. Mem., Punch Table. Author of: Anaesthetics for Medical Students; Doctor in the House, and 16 sequels; 32 other novels and non-fiction (adapted for 8 films and 4 plays, radio and TV, and translated into 21 langs); (ed) The Literary Companion to Medicine; TV screenplay, The Good Dr Bodkin Adams; TV series, A Gentlemen's Club; contribs to Punch.

GORDON, Richard John Francis; QC 1994; a Recorder, since 2000; *b* 26 Nov. 1948; *s* of John Bernard Basil Gordon and Winifred Josephine (*née* Keenan); *m* 1975, Jane Belinda Lucey; two *s*. *Educ:* St Benedict's Sch., Ealing; Christ Church, Oxford (Open Schol.; MA); University Coll. London (LLM). Called to the Bar, Middle Temple, 1972. Sen. Lectr in Admin. Law, KCL, 1991–93. Vis. Prof. of Law, UCL, 1994–. Editor-in-Chief, Administrative Court (formerly Crown Office) Digest, 1989–. Mem., Exec. Cttee, Admin. Law Bar Assoc., 1991–. *Publications:* The Law Relating to Mobile Homes and Caravans, 1978, 2nd edn 1985; Judicial Review: law and procedure, 1985, 2nd edn 1995; Crown Office Proceedings, 1990; Community Care Assessments, 1993, 2nd edn 1996; Human Rights in the United Kingdom, 1996; Judicial Review and Crown Office Practice, 2000; Judicial Review and the Human Rights Act, 2000; The Strasbourg Cases: leading cases from the European Human Rights Reports, 2001; contrib. to numerous legal jls on admin. law. *Recreations:* reading, writing. *Address:* Brick Court Chambers, 7–8 Essex Street, WC2R 3LD. *T:* (020) 7379 3550. *Club:* MCC.

GORDON, Robert Anthony Eagleson, CMG 1999; OBE 1983; HM Diplomatic Service; Head, South East Asia Department, Foreign and Commonwealth Office, since 1999; *b* 9 Feb. 1952; *s* of Major Cyril Vivian Eagleson, MC, RE and Clara Renata Romana Gordon (*née* Duse); *m* 1978, Pamela Jane Taylor; two *s* two *d*. *Educ:* King's Sch., Canterbury; Magdalen Coll., Oxford (MA Modern Langs). FCO 1973; Second Sec., Warsaw, 1975–77; First Sec., Santiago, 1978–83; FCO, 1983–87; First Sec., UK Deleg. to OECD, Paris, 1987–92; Counsellor and Dep. Head of Mission, Warsaw, 1992–95; Ambassador to Burma (Union of Myanmar), 1995–99. *Address:* c/o Foreign and Commonwealth Office, SW1A 2AH.

GORDON, (Robert) Douglas; HM Diplomatic Service, retired; Diplomatic Consultant, Royal Garden Hotel, since 1996; *b* 31 July 1936; *s* of Robert Gordon and Helen (*née* MacTaggart); *m* 1st, 1960, Margaret Bruckshaw (marr. diss. 1990); one *s*; 2nd, 1990, Valerie Janet Brownlee, MVO (5th class). *Educ:* Greenock Acad.; Cardiff High Sch. for Boys. FO, 1954. National Service with RM, 1955–57; commnd 2 Lieut Wilts Regt, 1957. FO, 1958; Amman, 1958; MECAS, 1959; Abu Dhabi, 1961; Vienna, 1963; Second Sec. (Commercial), Kuwait, 1966; FCO, 1969; Second, later First Sec., Hd of Chancery and Consul, Doha, 1973; Asst to Dep. Gov., Gibraltar, 1976; FCO, 1979; HM Asst Marshal of the Diplomatic Corps, 1982; First Sec. (Commercial), Washington, 1984; Consul (Commercial), Cleveland, 1986; Ambassador, 1989–90, Consul-General, 1990, Aden; High Comr, Guyana, 1990–93, and Ambassador, Republic of Suriname, 1990–93; Ambassador, Republic of Yemen, 1993–95. Chm., British-Yemeni Soc., 1999–. Freeman, City of London, 1984. Order of: Gorkha Dakshina Bahu, 5th Cl. (Nepal), 1980; King Abdul Aziz ibn Saud, 4th Cl. (Saudi Arabia), 1982; Officier, l'Ordre Nat. du Mérite (France), 1984. *Recreations:* golf, photography, walking. *Address:* Melbrook, 73 North Road, Tollesbury, Essex CM9 8RQ. *Clubs:* Royal Over-Seas League; Five Lakes Golf and Country (Tolleshunt Knights).

GORDON, Maj. Gen. Robert Duncan Seaton, CBE 1994; General Officer Commanding 2nd Division in Edinburgh, and Governor of Edinburgh Castle, since 2000; *b* 23 Nov. 1950; *s* of Col Jack Gordon and Joan Gordon (*née* Seaton); *m* 1979, Virginia Brown, Toronto; two *s*. *Educ:* Wellington Coll.; St Catharine's Coll., Cambridge (MA Modern Hist.). Commnd 17th/21st Lancers, 1970; Staff Coll., 1982; CO 17th/21st Lancers, 1990–92; Sec. to Chiefs of Staff Cttee, MoD, 1992–94 (Col); Brig. 1993; HCSC 1994; Comdr, 19th Mechanized Bde, 1994–96; rcds 1996; DPR (Army), 1997–99; Maj.-Gen. 1999; GOC 2nd Div. in York, 1999–2000. Col Comdt, RAVC, 2001–. *Recreations:* reading, moving, offshore sailing, golf. *Address:* HQ 2nd Division, Craigiehall, S Queensferry, W Lothian EH30 9TN. *Club:* Cavalry and Guards.

GORDON, Robert Ian Neilson; Director, Society of Genealogists, since 1998; *b* 29 March 1952; *s* of late Louis George Gordon and Patricia Dunella Mackay Gordon (*née* Neilson); *m* 1984, Susan Elizabeth Leigh; three *d*. *Educ:* Watford Grammar Sch.; Univ. of Sussex; Coll. of Law, Guildford and Lancaster Gate. Joined Maffey & Brentnall, solicitors, Watford, 1974, as Articled Clerk; admitted Solicitor, 1978; Partner, Brentnall & Cox, subseq. Bryan & Gordon, then Bryan, Furby & Gordon, 1978–92, Consultant, 1992–93. Mem. Exec. Cttee, Fedn of Family Hist. Socs, 1998–; Sec., Soc. of Genealogists Enterprises Ltd, 1999–; non-exec. Dir, W Herts Community Health NHS Trust, 1998–2001. Member (C): Watford BC, 1982–90 (Leader of Opposition, 1984–86, 1988–90); Herts CC, 1989–97, 2001– (Dep. Leader, 1991–93; Leader of Opposition, 1993–96; Chairman: Herts LEA, 1992–93; Herts Police Authy, 1995–97, 2001–; Exec. Mem. for Children, Schs and Families, 2001–); Mem. Exec. Council, ACC, 1991–93. Contested (C): Torfaen, 1987; Watford, 1997; Eastern Reg., England, EP, 1999. Chairman: Watford Cons. Assoc., 1990–92, 1995–96; Herts County Cons. Fedn, 1997–; Mem., Cons. Nat. Local Govt Adv. Cttee, 1991–97. Chm. Govs, Watford GS for Girls, 1998–2001. *Recreations:* choral music, walking, photography. *Address:* 22 Park Road, Watford, Herts WD17 4QN. *T:* (01923) 248826. *Club:* New Cavendish.

GORDON, Sir Robert James, 10th Bt *cr* 1706, of Afton and Earlston, Kirkcudbrightshire; farmer since 1958; *b* 17 Aug. 1932; *s* of Sir John Charles Gordon, 9th Bt and of Marion, *d* of late James B. Wright; *S* father, 1982; *m* 1976, Helen Julia Weston Perry. *Educ:* Barker College, Sydney; North Sydney Boys' High School; Wagga Agricultural Coll., Wagga Wagga, NSW (Wagga Dip. of Agric., Hons I and Dux). *Recreations:* tennis, ski-ing, swimming. *Heir:* none. *Address:* Earlstoun, Guyra, NSW 2365, Australia. *T:* (2) 67791343.

GORDON, Prof. Robert Patterson, PhD; Regius Professor of Hebrew, Cambridge University, since 1995; Fellow, St Catharine's College, Cambridge, since 1995; *b* 9 Nov. 1945; *s* of Robert Gordon and Eveline (*née* Shilliday); *m* 1970, Helen Ruth Lyttle; two *s* one *d*. *Educ:* Methodist Coll., Belfast; St Catharine's Coll., Cambridge (BA 1st Cl. Hons Oriental Studies 1968; MA 1972; PhD 1973; Tyrwhitt Scholarship and Mason Hebrew Prize, 1969). Asst Lectr in Hebrew and Semitic Langs, 1969–70, Lectr, 1970–79, Glasgow Univ.; Cambridge University: Lectr in Divinity, 1979–95; Fellow, St Edmund's Coll., 1985–89 (Tutor, 1986–89); Univ. Preacher, 1999. Macbride Sermon, Oxford Univ., 2000; Didsbury Lectures, 2001. Review Ed., Vetus Testamentum, 1998–; Ed., Hebrew Bible and its Versions, monograph series, 2001–. *Publications:* 1 and 2 Samuel, 1984; 1 and 2 Samuel: a commentary, 1986; (ed jtly) The Targum of the Minor Prophets, 1989; Studies in the Targum to the Twelve Prophets, 1994; (ed jtly) Wisdom in Ancient Israel, 1995; (ed) The Place is too Small for Us: the Israelite prophets in recent scholarship, 1995; (Consulting Ed.) New International Dictionary of Old Testament Theology and Exegesis, 1997; (ed) The Old Testament in Syriac: Chronicles, 1998; Hebrews: a new biblical commentary, 2000; contrib. to learned jls incl. Jl Jewish Studies, Jewish Qly Rev., Jl Semitic Studies, Jl for Study of OT, Jl Theol Studies, Revue de Qumran, Vetus Testamentum, and to various composite vols. *Recreations:* jogging, local history (N Ireland). *Address:* 85 Barrons Way, Comberton, Cambridge CB3 7DR. *T:* (01223) 263153; Faculty of Oriental Studies, Sidgwick Avenue, Cambridge CB3 9DA.

GORDON, Robert Smith Benzie, CB 2000; Head of Executive Secretariat, Scottish Executive (formerly Scottish Office), since 1998; *b* 7 Nov. 1950; *s* of William Gladstone Gordon and Helen Watt Gordon (*née* Benzie); *m* 1976, Joyce Ruth Cordiner; two *s* two *d*. *Educ:* Univ. of Aberdeen (MA Hons Italian Studies). Admin. trainee, Scottish Office, 1973–78; Principal, Scottish Develt Dept, 1979–85; Asst Sec., 1984; Principal Private Sec. to Sec. of State for Scotland, 1985–87; Dept of Agriculture and Fisheries for Scotland, 1987–90; Scottish Office: Mgt Orgn and Industrial Relns, 1990–91; Dir of Admin. Services, 1991–97; Under Sec., 1993; Head of Constitution Gp, 1997–98; Dep. Sec., 1998. *Address:* Scottish Executive, St Andrews House, Regent Road, Edinburgh EH1 3DG.

GORDON, Rt Rev. Ronald; *see* Gordon, Rt Rev. A. R. McD.

GORDON, Ronald Dingwall; Chairman, John Gordon & Son Ltd, since 2000; Vice Lord-Lieutenant of Nairnshire, since 1999; *b* 13 Nov. 1936; *s* of Ronald James Robertson Gordon and Mary Isabella Cardno Gordon; *m* 1961, Elizabeth Ancell Gordon; two *s* one *d*. *Educ:* Nairn Acad. Nat. Service, RAF, 1955–57. Joined John Gordon & Son, 1957; jt partner with father, 1961; sole trader, 1965–85; Man. Dir, 1985–2000. DL Nairnshire, 1991. *Recreations:* golf, fishing, gardening. *Address:* Achareidh House, Nairn IV12 4UD. *T:* (01667) 452130. *Clubs:* Royal and Ancient Golf, Royal Aberdeen Golf, Royal Dornoch Golf, Nairn Golf (Capt. 1980–82).

GORDON, Prof. Siamon, PhD; Glaxo-Wellcome Professor of Cellular Pathology, Oxford University, since 1991 (Professor of Cellular Pathology, 1989–91); Fellow, Exeter College, Oxford, since 1976; *b* 29 April 1938; *s* of Jonah and Liebe Gordon; *m* 1963, Lyndall Getz; two *d*. *Educ:* South African Coll. Sch., Cape Town; Univ. of Cape Town (MB ChB 1961); Rockefeller Univ. (PhD 1971). Res. Asst, Wright-Fleming Inst., St Mary's, London, 1964–65; Rockefeller University, NY: Res. Associate, 1965–71; Asst Prof. of Cellular Immunology, 1971–76; Adjunct Associate Prof., 1976–; Reader in Exptl Pathology, Sir Wm Dunn Sch. of Pathology, Univ. of Oxford, 1976–89, Actg Hd of Dept, 1989–90, 2000–01. University of Oxford: Chairman: Physiol Scis Bd, 1984–86; Search Cttee, E. P. Abrahams Bldg, 1999–; Member: General Bd, 1989–92; Med. Scis Div., 2000–. Mem., Lister Scientific Adv. Cttee, 1987–92. Special Fellow and Scholar, Leukaemia Soc. of America, 1971–76; Vis. Scientist, Genetics, Oxford Univ., 1974–75. *Publications:* contribs to jls of exptl medicine, immunology, cell biology, neuroscience. *Recreations:* reading biography, medical history. *Address:* Sir William Dunn School of Pathology, South Parks Road, Oxford OX1 3RE. *T:* (01865) 275534, *Fax:* (01865) 275515.

GORDON, Sir Sidney, Kt 1972; CBE 1968 (OBE 1965); GBM 1999; CA; JP; Director, Sir Elly Kadoorie & Sons, Ltd; *b* 20 Aug. 1917; *s* of late P. S. Gordon and late Angusina Gordon; *m* 1950, Olive W. F. Eldon (*d* 1992), *d* of late T. A. Eldon and late Hannah Eldon; two *d*. *Educ:* Hyndland Sch., Glasgow; Glasgow Univ. Sen. Partner, Lowe Bingham & Matthews, Chartered Accountants, Hong Kong, 1956–70. MLC, 1962–66, MEC, Hong Kong, 1965–80. Chairman: Univ. and Polytechnic Grants Cttee, 1974–76; Standing Commn on Civil Service Salaries and Conditions of Service, 1988–2000. JP Hong Kong, 1961. Hon. LLD The Chinese University of Hong Kong, 1970. *Recreation:* racing. *Address:* 7 Headland Road, Hong Kong. *T:* 28122577. *Clubs:* Oriental; Hong Kong, Hong Kong Jockey (Hon. Steward), Hong Kong Golf (Hon. Life Mem.; formerly, Pres. and Captain), Hong Kong Country, Hong Kong Cricket, Shek O Country, etc.

GORDON, Vera Kate, (Mrs E. W. Gordon); *see* Timms, V. K.

GORDON, William John, FCIB; Chief Executive (formerly Managing Director), UK Banking Services, Barclays Bank plc, 1992–98; *b* 24 April 1939; *s* of Sidney Frank Gordon and Grace Louie Gordon; *m* 1963, Patricia Rollason; two *s*. *Educ:* King Edward VI Sch., Fiveways, Birmingham. FCIB 1979. Joined Barclays Bank, 1955: branch and regl appts, 1955–80; Asst Gen. Manager, Barclaycard, 1980–83; Regl Gen. Manager, Central UK, 1983–87; Dir, UK Corporate Services, 1987–90; Gp Personnel Dir, 1990–92; Dir, 1995–98. Chm., Barclays Pension Fund Trustees Ltd, 1996–; Ind. Dir, Britannia Bldg Soc., 1999–. Mem., Herts Bridge Assoc. *Recreations:* bridge, golf, chess, music. *Address:* 9 High Elms, Harpenden AL5 2JU. *Club:* Mid Herts Golf (Wheathampstead).

GORDON-BANKS, Matthew Richard William; Director, LBJ Ltd, management consultancy, since 1989; *b* 21 June 1961; *s* of Harry and Audrey Banks; *m* 1992, Jane, *d* of Michael Miller; one *s* one *d*. *Educ:* Sheffield City Polytechnic (BA Hons History and Econs); RMA Sandhurst. 1st Bn, 51st Highland Vols, 1979–81; Commnd, The Gordon Highlanders, 1981–83; War Disablement Pension, 1983. Barclays Bank, 1984–88; Private Sec. to Cecil Franks, MP, 1988–89. Mem., Wirral BC, 1984–90 (Chairman: Schs Cttee, 1985–86; Works Cttee, 1986–87). Contested (C) Manchester Central, 1987; MP (C) Southport, 1992–97; contested (C) same seat, 1997. PPS, DoE, 1996–97. Mem., Select Cttee on Transport, 1992–97; Vice-Chm., Cons. Back bench Transport Cttee, 1993–97; Chm., Anglo-Venezuela Parly Gp, 1993–97; Sec., Anglo-UAE Parly Gp, 1993–97. FRGS 1983. *Recreations:* golf, walking, travel, reading, flying, fishing. *Address:* Gordon Castle, Fochabers, Morayshire IV32 7PQ. *Clubs:* Carlton, Caledonian, Montes.

GORDON-BROWN, Alexander Douglas, CB 1984; Receiver for the Metropolitan Police District, 1980–87; *b* 5 Dec. 1927; *s* of late Captain and Mrs D. S. Gordon-Brown; *m* 1959, Mary Hilton; three *s*. *Educ:* Bryanston Sch.; New Coll., Oxford. MA; 1st cl. hons PPE. Entered Home Office, 1951; Sec., Franks Cttee on section 2 of Official Secrets Act 1911, 1971; Asst Under-Sec. of State, Home Office, 1972–75, 1978–80; Under Sec., Cabinet Office, 1975–78. Chm., Home Office Wkg Gp on Costs of Crime, 1988. Mem., Nat. Council, 1991–97, Trustee, 1998–2000, Victim Support. *Recreations:* music, gardening, golf.

GORDON-CUMMING, Alexander Roualeyn, CMG 1978; CVO 1969; Director, Invest in Britain Bureau, Department of Industry, 1979–84; *b* 10 Sept. 1924; *s* of late Lt-Comdr R. G. Gordon-Cumming and Mrs M. V. K. Wilkinson; *m* 1st, 1965, Beryl Joyce Macnaughton Dunn (*d* 1973); one *d*; 2nd, 1974, Elizabeth Patricia Blackley (*d* 1983); one *d*; 3rd, 1999, Rosalind Diana Lynch Jones. *Educ:* Eton Coll. RAF, 1943; retd with rank of Gp Captain, 1969. Board of Trade, 1969; Dept of Trade and Industry, 1973; seconded HM Diplomatic Service, 1974–78. *Recreations:* gardening, skiing, fell walking, ballet. *Address:* Woodstock, West Way, West Broyle, Chichester, Sussex PO19 3PW. *T:* (01243) 776413. *Club:* Royal Air Force.

GORDON CUMMING, Sir William Gordon, 6th Bt *cr* 1804; Royal Scots Greys; *b* 19 June 1928; *s* of Major Sir Alexander Penrose Gordon Cumming, 5th Bt, MC, and of Elizabeth Topham, *d* of J. Topham Richardson, Harps Oak, Merstham; *S* father, 1939; *m* 1953, Elisabeth (marr. diss. 1972), *d* of Maj.-Gen. Sir Robert Hinde, KBE, CB, DSO; one *s* three *d*; *m* 1989, Sheila Bates. *Educ:* Eton; RMC, Sandhurst. Late Royal Scots Greys; retired 1952. *Heir:* *s* Alexander Penrose Gordon Cumming [*b* 15 April 1954; *m* 1991, Louisa, *e d* of E. G. Clifton-Brown]. *Address:* Altyre, Forres, Morayshire.

GORDON DAVIES, Rev. John; *see* Davies.

GORDON JONES, Air Marshal Sir Edward, KCB 1967 (CB 1960); CBE 1956 (OBE 1945); DSO 1941; DFC 1941; idc; jssc; qs; Air Officer Commanding-in-Chief, Near East Air Force, and Administrator, Sovereign Base Areas, 1966–69; Commander, British Forces Near East, 1967–69; retired 1969; *b* 31 Aug. 1914; *s* of late Lt-Col Dr A. Jones, DSO, MC, MD, DPH; *m* 1938, Margery Thurston Hatfield, BSc; two *s*. Served War of 1939–45 (despatches, DFC, DSO, OBE, Greek DFC). ACOS (Intelligence), Allied Air Forces Central Europe, 1960–61; Air Officer Commanding RAF Germany, 1961–63; Senior RAF Directing Staff, Imperial Defence Coll., 1963–65; AOC, RAF, Malta, and Dep. C-in-C (Air), Allied Forces, Mediterranean, 1965–66. Comdr Order of Orange Nassau. *Recreations:* sport (Rugby for Lancashire and RAF), music. *Address:* 20 Marlborough Court, Grange Road, Cambridge CB3 9BQ. *T:* (01223) 363029. *Club:* Royal Air Force.

GORDON-LENNOX, family name of **Duke of Richmond**.

GORDON LENNOX, Maj.-Gen. Bernard Charles, CB 1986; MBE 1968; Regimental Lieutenant-Colonel, Grenadier Guards, 1989–95; *b* 19 Sept. 1932; *s* of Lt-Gen. Sir George Gordon Lennox and Nancy Brenda Darell; *m* 1958, Sally-Rose Warner; three *s*. *Educ:* Eton; Sandhurst. 2nd Lt, Grenadier Guards, 1953; Hong Kong, 1965; HQ Household Div., 1971; Commanding 1st Bn Grenadier Guards, 1974; Army Directing Staff, RAF Staff College, 1976–77; Command, Task Force H, 1978–79; RCDS, 1980; Dep. Commander and Chief of Staff, SE District, 1981–82; GOC Berlin (British Sector), 1983–85; Sen. Army Mem., RCDS, 1986–88, retd. Dir of Regions, Motor Agents Assoc., 1988–89. *Recreations:* field sports, cricket, squash, music. *Address:* c/o The Estate Office, Gordon Castle, Fochabers, Morayshire IV32 7PQ. *Clubs:* Army and Navy, Guards' Polo (Chm., 1992–99), MCC.

GORDON LENNOX, Lord Nicholas Charles, KCMG 1986 (CMG 1978); KCVO 1989 (LVO 1957); HM Diplomatic Service, retired; a Governor, BBC, 1990–98; director of companies, since 1990; *b* 31 Jan. 1931; *yr s* of 9th Duke of Richmond and Gordon and of Elizabeth Grace, *y d* of late Rev. T. W. Hudson; *m* 1958, Mary (LVO 2001), *d* of late Brig. H. N. H. Williamson, DSO, MC; one *s* three *d*. *Educ:* Eton; Worcester Coll., Oxford (Scholar). 2nd Lieut KRRC, 1950–51. Entered HM Foreign Service, 1954; FO, 1954–57; Private Sec. to HM Ambassador to USA, 1957–61; 2nd, later 1st Sec., HM Embassy, Santiago, 1961–63; Private Sec. to Perm. Under-Sec., FO, 1963–66; 1st Sec. and Head of Chancery, HM Embassy, Madrid, 1966–71; seconded to Cabinet Office, 1971–73; Head of News Dept, FCO, 1973–74, Head of N America Dept, 1974–75; Counsellor and Head of Chancery, Paris, 1975–79; Asst Under-Sec. of State, FCO, 1979–84; Ambassador to Spain, 1984–89. Director: Foreign and Colonial Investment Trust; Sothebys; Plus Ultra Seguros (Spain); MGM Assurance. Vice-Chm., Canada Blanch Foundn, 1996–; Chm., Exec. Cttee, Historic Churches Preservation Trust, 1997–; Trustee, Pallant House Gallery, 1994–. Hon. Col, 4th Bn Royal Green Jackets, TA, 1990–95. Medal of Honour, Univ. of Madrid, 1988. Grand Cross, Order of Isabel la Católica (Spain), 1986. *Clubs:* Boodle's, Beefsteak.

GORDON-SMITH, David Gerard, CMG 1971; Director-General in Legal Service, Council of Ministers, European Communities, 1976–87; *b* 6 Oct. 1925; *s* of late Frederic Gordon-Smith, QC, and Elsie Gordon-Smith (*née* Foster); *m* 1952, Angela Kirkpatrick Pile; one *d* (and one *s* decd). *Educ:* Rugby Sch.; Trinity Coll., Oxford. Served in RNVR, 1944–46. BA (Oxford) 1948; called to Bar, Inner Temple, 1949; Legal Asst, Colonial Office, 1950; Sen. Legal Asst, 1954; CRO, 1963–65; Asst Legal Adviser, CO, 1965–66; Legal Counsellor, CO, later FCO, 1966–72; Dep. Legal Advr, FCO, 1973–76. *Address:* Kingscote, Westcott, Surrey RH4 3NX.

GORDON-SMITH, Prof. Edward Colin, FRCP, FRCPE, FRCPath, FMedSci; Professor of Haematology, St George's Hospital Medical School, London, since 1987; *b* 26 June 1938; *s* of late Gordon John Gordon-Smith and Valentine (*née* Waddington); *m* 1968, Moira Phelan; two *s*. *Educ:* Oakham Sch.; Epsom Coll.; Exeter Coll., Oxford (MA, BSc, BM BCh); Westminster Med. Sch., London (MSc). FRCP 1978; FRCPath 1987; FRCPE 1999. House Officer, Westminster Hosp., 1964; Sen. House Officer, Nuffield Dept of Medicine, Radcliffe Infirmary, Oxford, 1966; Lectr in Neurology, Churchill Hosp., Oxford, 1966–67; Registrar in Haematology, Hammersmith Hosp., 1968–69; MRC Clinical Trng Fellow, RPMS Metabolic Unit, Oxford, 1970–71; Sen. Lectr 1972–83, Reader 1983–86, RPMS. Editor, Brit. Jl of Haematology, 1983–86. President: European Bone Marrow Transplant Gp, 1980; Internat. Soc. Explt Haematology, 1990–92; British Soc. for Haematology, 1995; Vice-Pres., RCPath, 1996–99. Founder FMedSci 1998. Order of Prasidda Prabala Gorkha-Dakshin Bahu (2nd class), Nepal, 1984. *Publications:* papers on aplastic anaemia, bone marrow transplantation, inherited bone marrow disorders, culture of human bone marrow and drug induced blood disorders. *Recreations:* golf, music, gardening, arguing with the wireless. *Address:* Department of Haematology, St George's Hospital Medical School, Cranmer Terrace, Tooting, SW17 0RE. *T:* (020) 8725 5448, *Fax:* (020) 8725 0245. *Club:* Royal Society of Medicine.

GORE, family name of **Earl of Arran**.

GORE; *see* Ormsby Gore.

GORE, Albert, Jr; Vice-President of the United States of America, 1993–2001; *b* 31 March 1948; *s* of late Albert and of Pauline Gore; *m* 1970, Mary Elizabeth Aitcheson; one *s* three *d*. *Educ:* Harvard and Vanderbilt Univs. Served US Army in Vietnam, 1969–71. Reporter and editorial writer, The Tennessean, 1971–76; livestock and tobacco farmer, 1971–. Mem., US House of Representatives, 1977–85; Mem. for Tennessee, US Senate, 1985–92. Chm., US Senate Delegn to Earth Summit, Rio de Janeiro, 1992. Democrat; Presidential cand., US elections, 2000. *Publication:* Earth in the Balance: ecology and the human spirit, 1992.

GORE, (Francis) St John (Corbet), CBE 1986; FSA; *b* 8 April 1921; *s* of late Francis Gore and Kirsteen Corbet-Singleton; *m* 1st, 1951, Priscilla (marr. diss. 1975), *d* of Cecil Harmsworth King; one *s* one *d*; 2nd, 1981, Lady Mary Strachey (*d* 2000), *d* of 3rd Earl of Selborne, PC, CH. *Educ:* Wellington; Courtauld Inst. of Art. Served War, 1940–45, Captain, Royal Northumberland Fusiliers. Employed Sotheby's, 1950–55; National Trust: Adviser on pictures, 1956–86, Hon. Advr, 1986–; Historic Buildings Sec., 1973–81. Mem., Exec. Cttee, Nat. Art Collections Fund, 1964–97; Trustee: Wallace Collection, 1975–89; National Gall., 1986–94. *Publications:* Catalogue, Worcester Art Museum, Mass (British Pictures), 1974; various exhibn catalogues, incl. RA; contribs to Apollo, Country Life, etc. *Recreation:* sight-seeing. *Address:* Flat 5, 42 Sutherland Street, SW1V 4JZ. *Clubs:* Brooks's, Beefsteak.

See also Baron O'Hagan.

GORE, Frederick John Pym, CBE 1987; RA 1972 (ARA 1964); Painter; Head of Painting Department, St Martin's School of Art, WC2, 1951–79, and Vice-Principal, 1961–79; *b* 8 Nov. 1913; *s* of Spencer Frederick Gore and Mary Johanna Kerr. *Educ:* Lancing Coll.; Trinity Coll., Oxford; studied art at Ruskin, Westminster and Slade Schs. Taught at: Westminster Sch. of Art, 1937; Chelsea and Epsom, 1947; St Martin's, 1946–79. Chm., RA exhibitions cttee, 1976–87. Trustee, Imperial War Mus., 1967–84 (Chm., Artistic Records Cttee, 1972–1986). *One-man exhibitions:* Gall. Borghèse, Paris, 1938; Redfern Gall., 1937, 1949, 1950, 1953, 1956, 1962; Mayor Gall., 1958, 1960; Juster Gall., NY, 1963; RA (retrospective), 1989. *Paintings in public collections include:* Contemporary Art Soc., Leicester County Council, GLC, Southampton, Plymouth, Rutherston Collection and New Brunswick. Served War of 1939–45: Mx Regt and RA (SO Camouflage). *Publications:* Abstract Art, 1956; Painting, Some Principles, 1965; Piero della Francesca's 'The Baptism', 1969. *Recreation:* Russian folk dancing. *Address:* Flat 3, 35 Elm Park Gardens, SW10 9QF. *T:* (020) 7352 4940.

GORE, Michael Edward John, CVO 1994; CBE 1991; HM Diplomatic Service, retired; Governor, Cayman Islands, 1992–95; *b* 20 Sept. 1935; *s* of late John Gore and Elsa Gore (*née* Dillon); *m* 1957, Monica Shellish; three *d*. *Educ:* Xaverian College, Brighton. Reporter, Portsmouth Evening News, 1952–55; Captain, Army Gen. List, 1955–59; Air Ministry, Dep. Comd. Inf. Officer, Cyprus and Aden, 1959–63; CRO, later FCO, 1963; served Jesselton, 1963–66, FCO, 1966–67, Seoul, 1967–71, Montevideo, 1971–74; First Sec., Banjul, 1974–78; FCO, 1978–81; Nairobi, 1981–84; Dep. High Comr, Lilongwe, 1984–87; Ambassador to Liberia, 1988–90; High Comr to the Bahamas, 1991–92. Mem., UK Dependent, then UK Overseas, Territories Conservation Forum, 1996–; Chm., Wider Caribbean Working Gp, 1997–. Trustee, Trust for Oriental Ornithology, 1992–. Mem., Zool Photographic Club; Nature Photographers Portfolio. MBOU; FRPS. *Publications:* The Birds of Korea (with Pyong-Oh Won), 1971; Las Aves del Uruguay (with A. R. M. Gepp), 1978; Birds of the Gambia, 1981, 2nd edn 1991; On Safari in Kenya: a pictorial guide to the national parks and reserves, 1984; papers on birds and conservation; wild-life photographs in books and magazines. *Recreations:* ornithology, wildlife photography, fishing. *Address:* 5 St Mary's Close, Fetcham, Surrey KT22 9HE.

GORE, Sir Nigel (Hugh St George), 14th Bt *cr* 1621 (Ire.), of Magherabegg, Co. Donegal; grazier and farmer, since 1945; *b* 23 Dec. 1922; *yr s* of St George Richard Gore (*d* 1952, *great nephew* of Sir St George Ralph Gore, 9th Bt), and Loo Loo Ruth (*d* 1961), *d* of E. P. Amesbury; *S* nephew, 1993; *m* 1952, Beth Allison (*d* 1976), *d* of R. W. Hooper; one *d*. *Educ:* Church of England Grammar Sch., Brisbane; Gatton Agricl Coll. Served Army, 1940–45. *Heir:* *cousin* Dundas Corbet Gore [*b* 20 April 1921; *m*]. *Clubs:* Toowoomba Range Probus, Returned Soldiers League (Toowoomba).

GORE, Paul Annesley, CMG 1964; CVO 1961; *b* 28 Feb. 1921; *o s* of late Charles Henry Gore, OBE and late Hon. Violet Kathleen (*née* Annesley); *m* 1946, Gillian Mary, *d* of T. E. Allen-Stevens; two *s* (and one *s* decd). *Educ:* Winchester Coll.; Christ Church, Oxford. Military Service, 1941–46: 16/5 Lancers. Colonial Service, 1948–65; Dep. Governor, The Gambia, 1962–65. *Address:* 1 Burkitt Road, Woodbridge, Suffolk IP12 4JJ.

GORE, St John; *see* Gore, F. St J. C.

GORE-BOOTH, Hon. Sir David (Alwyn), KCMG 1997 (CMG 1990); KCVO 1997; Special Adviser to Chairman of HSBC Holdings plc, since 1999; *b* 15 May 1943; twin *s* of late Baron Gore-Booth, GCMG, KCVO; *heir-presumptive* to Sir Josslyn Gore-Booth, Bt, *qv*; *m* 1st, 1964, Jillian Sarah (*née* Valpy) (marr. diss. 1970); one *s*; 2nd, 1977, Mary Elisabeth Janet, *d* of Sir David Muirhead, KCMG, CVO; one step *s*. *Educ:* Eton Coll.; Christ Church, Oxford (MA Hons). HM Diplomatic Service, 1964–98; entered Foreign Office, 1964; Middle East Centre for Arab Studies, 1964; Third Secretary, Baghdad, 1966; Third, later Second Sec., Lusaka, 1967; FCO, 1969; Second Sec., Tripoli, 1969; FCO, 1971; First Sec., UK Permanent Representation to European Communities, Brussels, 1974; Asst Head of Financial Relations Dept, FCO, 1978; Counsellor, Jedda, 1980; Counsellor and Hd of Chancery, UK Mission to UN, NY, 1983; Hd of Policy Planning Staff, FCO, 1987; Asst Under Sec. of State (ME), FCO, 1989; Ambassador, Saudi Arabia, 1993; High Comr, New Delhi, 1996–98. Chm., ORBCOMM (ME and Central Asia), 1999–; Director: HSBC Bank Middle East, 1999–; British Arab Commercial Bank, 1999–; Egyptian-British Bank, 1999–; Middle East Internat., 1999–; Saudi-British Bank, 2000–; Group 4 Falck, 2000. Trustee, Next Century Foundn, 1997–. Mem. Adv. Bd, Centre for Internat. Studies and Diplomacy, Birmingham Univ., 1999–. *Recreations:* tennis, current affairs, the island of Hydra (Greece). *Address:* 27 Wetherby Mansions, Earl's Court Square, SW5 9BH. *T:* (020) 7373 1767, *Fax:* (020) 7373 5313. *Clubs:* Garrick, MCC, Hurlingham, Travellers; Bill's Bar (Hydra).

GORE-BOOTH, Sir Josslyn (Henry Robert), 9th Bt *cr* 1760 (Ire.), of Artarman, Sligo; landowner; *b* 5 Oct. 1950; *o s* of Sir Angus Gore-Booth, 8th Bt and Hon. Rosemary Myra Vane, *o d* of 10th Baron Barnard, CMG, OBE, MC, TD; *S* father, 1996; *m* 1980, Jane Mary, *o d* of Rt Hon. Sir Roualeyn Hovell-Thurlow-Cumming-Bruce; two *d*. *Educ:* Eton Coll.; Balliol Coll., Oxford (BA); Insead (MBA). Dir, Kiln Cotesworth Corporate Capital Fund plc, 1993–97. Patron, living of Sacred Trinity, Salford. *Recreations:* cooking, fishing, shooting. *Heir:* *cousin* Hon. Sir David Alwyn Gore-Booth, *qv*. *Address:* Selaby Hall, Gainford, Darlington, Co. Durham DL2 3HF. *T:* (01325) 730206, *Fax:* (01325) 730993; Lissadell, Sligo, Ireland. *Club:* Brooks's.

GORE-LANGTON; *see* Temple-Gore-Langton, family name of Earl Temple of Stowe.

GORE-RANDALL, Philip Allan, FCA; Managing Partner, Global Operations, Andersen (formerly Arthur Andersen), since 2001; *b* 16 Dec. 1952; *s* of late Alec Albert Gore-Randall and of Joyce Margaret Gore-Randall; *m* 1984, Prof. Alison Elizabeth While; two *s*. *Educ:* Merchant Taylors' Sch., Northwood; University Coll., Oxford (MA 1975). FCA 1978. Arthur Andersen, subseq. Andersen, 1975–: Partner, 1986–; UK Man. Partner, Assurance and Business Advisory, 1995–97, Man. Partner, Assurance and Business Advisory, Europe, Africa, Middle East and India, 1996–97; UK Managing Partner, 1997–2001. *Recreations:* classical music/opera, good food, travel. *Address:* (office) 1 Surrey Street, WC2R 2PS. *Club:* Vincent's (Oxford).

See also A. J. Randall.

GORELL, 4th Baron *cr* 1909; **Timothy John Radcliffe Barnes;** *b* 2 Aug. 1927; *e s* of 3rd Baron Gorell and Elizabeth Gorell, *d* of Alexander Nelson Radcliffe; *S* father, 1963; *m* 1954, Joan Marion, *y d* of late John Edmund Collins, MC, Sway, Hants; two adopted *d*. *Educ:* Eton Coll.; New Coll., Oxford. Lieut, Rifle Brigade, 1946–48. Barrister, Inner Temple, 1951. Sen. Executive, Royal Dutch/Shell Group, 1959–84. *Heir:* *b* Hon. Ronald Alexander Henry Barnes [*b* 28 June 1931; *m* 1957, Gillian Picton Hughes-Jones; one *s* one *d*]. *Address:* 4 Roehampton Gate, SW15 5JS. *T:* (020) 8876 5522. *Club:* Roehampton.

GORHAM, Martin Edwin; Chief Executive, National Blood Authority, since 1998; *b* 18 June 1947; *s* of Clifford Edwin Gorham and Florence Ada Gorham; *m* 1st, 1968, Jean McNaughton Kerr (marr. diss. 1998); 2nd, 1998, Sally Ann Stevens (*née* Fletcher); one step *d*. *Educ:* Buckhurst Hill County High Sch.; Queen Mary Coll., Univ. of London (BA Hons History 1968). MHSM, DipHSM 1973. NHS Mgt Trainee, 1968; Deputy Hospital Secretary: Scarborough Gen. Hosp., 1970–72; Doncaster Royal Infirmary, 1972–75; Hosp. Manager, Northern Gen. Hosp., Sheffield, 1975–83; Dep. Dist Gen. Manager, Newcastle HA, 1983–86; Gen. Manager, Norfolk and Norwich Hosp., 1986–90; Dep.

Regl Gen. Manager, SW Thames RHA, 1990–92; Chief Exec., London Ambulance Service, 1992–96; Dir of Projects, S Thames Regl Office, NHS Exec., DoH, 1996–98. *Recreations:* travel, music, books, art, ski-ing, food and wine, gardening. *Address:* National Blood Authority, Oak House, Reeds Crescent, Watford, Herts WD1 1QH. *T:* (01923) 486804; 20 Grange Road, Bishop's Stortford, Herts CM23 5NQ. *T:* (01279) 501876. *Club:* Commonwealth Trust.

GORHAM, Col Sir Richard (Masters), Kt 1995; CBE 1978; DFC 1945; JP; Chairman: The Supermart Ltd, since 1954; Gorham's Ltd, 1964–98, now Chairman Emeritus; *b* 3 Oct. 1917; *s* of late Arthur John Gorham and Muriel Irene Gorham; *m* 1948, Barbara McIntire; three *s* two *d. Educ:* Saltus Grammar Sch., Bermuda; Ridley Coll., St Catherines, Canada; Shaw Business Sch., Toronto. Served in Bermuda Volunteer Engineers, 1938, Bermuda Militia Artillery, 1942; RA, 1942; Pilot, Army Air Comd, Artillery Spotter, Captain RA, in UK, N Africa, Italy (DFC), Austria, Yugoslavia. Mem., Pembroke Vestry, 1958–64; Chm., Pembroke W Constituency, 1964; Mem., Central Cttee, United Bermuda Party, 1964; Chm., Finance Cttee, UBP, 1965–75; MLC, 1968–76; First Parly Sec. and First Parly Sec. for Finance, Bermuda, 1968–77. Dir, Bank of Bermuda, 1966–90. Financial Advisor: New Testament Church of God, 1974–; Girl Guide Assoc. of Bermuda and UK, 1989–; business consultant to service orgns, Salvation Army and numerous other charitable bodies; Founder and Chairman: Summerhave Home for Physically Handicapped, 1974–; Volunteer Independent Pension and Community Services Fund, 1976–; funded eponymous Room, Mus. of Army Flying, Middle Wallop, Hants, 1986. Mem., HAC, 1992–; Hon. Col RA, 1996–. Coronation Medal. *Recreations:* military history; formerly ocean racing, Rugby, table tennis. *Address:* Westmorland, 9 Fairylands Road, Pembroke West HM 06, Bermuda. *T:* (441) 2955321. *Clubs:* Royal Bermuda Yacht, Coral Beach, Mid-Ocean (Bermuda); Metropolitan (NYC); Fishers Island, Hay Harbor (NY).

GORHAM, Robin Stuart; HM Diplomatic Service, retired; Lecturer, Diplomatic Academy of London, Westminster University; Consultant, Commonwealth Secretariat; *b* 15 Feb. 1939; *s* of Stuart Gorham and Dorothy Gorham (*née* Stevens); *m* 1st, 1966, Barbara Fechner (marr. diss. 1991); three *d*; 2nd, 1992, Joanna Bradbury. *Educ:* Sutton Manor High Sch.; Oriel Coll., Oxford (MA). CRO, 1961–62; Ottawa, 1962–64; Centre for Econ. Studies, 1964–65; Bonn, 1965–66; Central European Dept, FCO, 1967–69; First Secretary: (External Affairs and Defence) and Dep. Hd of Chancery, Tokyo, 1970–74; (Commercial and Develt), Accra, 1974–77; ME Dept, FCO, 1977–79; Hd of Chancery, Helsinki, 1980–83; Counsellor and Dep. High Comr, Lusaka, 1983–86; rcds, 1987; Hd, W Indian and Atlantic Dept, FCO, 1988–91; Dep. Hd of Mission, Lagos, 1991–94; Head of Protocol Dept and Asst Marshal of Diplomatic Corps, FCO, 1994–98. *Recreations:* riding, swimming, music, theatre. *Address:* 28 Alma Square, St John's Wood, NW8 9PY. *T:* (020) 7286 1357; 17 Church Walk, Long Melford, Suffolk CO10 9DL. *T:* (01787) 881553.

GORING, Sir William (Burton Nigel), 13th Bt *cr* 1627; Member of London Stock Exchange since 1963; *b* 21 June 1933; *s* of Major Frederick Yelverton Goring (*d* 1938) (6th *s* of 11th Bt) and Freda Margaret (*d* 1993), *o d* of N. V. Ainsworth; S uncle, Sir Forster Gurney Goring, 12th Bt, 1956; *m* 1st, 1960, Hon. Caroline Thellusson (marr. diss. 1993), *d* of 8th Baron Rendlesham and of Mrs Patrick Barthropp; 2nd, 1993, Mrs Judith Rachel Walton Morison (*d* 1995), *d* of Rev. R. J. W. Morris, OBE; 3rd, 1998, Mrs Stephanie Bullock, *d* of George Carter. *Educ:* Wellington; RMA Sandhurst, Lieut, The Royal Sussex Regt. Master, Co. of Woolmen, 2000–01. *Recreation:* bridge. *Heir: kinsman* Richard Harry Goring [*b* 10 Sept. 1949; *m* 1972, Penelope Ann, *d* of J. K. Broadbent; three *s* three *d*]. *Address:* c/o Quilter & Co. Ltd, St Helen's, 1 Undershaft, EC3A 8BB. *Club:* Hurlingham.

GORMALLY, Michael Anthony Peter Thomas; Headmaster, Cardinal Vaughan Memorial School, Kensington, since 1997; *b* 30 Jan. 1956; *s* of Charles Gormally and Frances Edna Gormally. *Educ:* Inst. of Education, Univ. of London (BA Hons French). ACP 1986. Cardinal Vaughan Memorial School, 1981–: Asst Master, 1981–84; Hd, Modern Langs, 1984–90; Sen. Master, 1990–95; Dep. Headmaster, 1995–97. FRSA 1998. *Recreations:* reading, playing the piano, cooking. *Address:* Cardinal Vaughan Memorial School, 89 Addison Road, W14 8BZ. *T:* (020) 7603 8478.

GORMAN, Christopher Nicoll; Partner, Linklaters & Paines, Solicitors, 1972–97 (Managing Partner, 1991–95); *b* 29 Aug. 1939; *s* of late James Gorman and Louise Barbara (*née* Rackham); *m* 1967, Anne Beech (*d* 1996); one *s* one *d. Educ:* Royal Liberty Sch., Romford; St Catharine's Coll., Cambridge (MA, LLM). Admitted Solicitor, 1965. *Publications:* (ed) Nelson's Tables of Company Procedure, 6th edn 1975 to 8th edn 1983; (ed) Westby Nunn's Company Secretarial Handbook, 7th edn 1977 to 11th edn 1992. *Recreations:* books and bookshops, outdoor activity, unfinished business. *Address:* 4 Windhill, Bishop's Stortford, Herts CM23 2NG. *T:* (01279) 656028. *Clubs:* Athenæum, Royal Automobile.

GORMAN, Sir John Reginald, Kt 1998; CVO 1961; CBE 1974 (MBE 1959); MC 1944; DL; Member (UU) Down North, since 1998, and Deputy Speaker, Northern Ireland Assembly; *b* 1 Feb. 1923; *s* of Major J. K. Gorman, MC; *m* 1948, Heather, *d* of George Caruth, solicitor, Ballymena; two *s* two *d. Educ:* Rockport, Haileybury and ISC; Portora; Glasgow Univ.; Harvard Business Sch. FCIT, FIPM; MIH. Irish Guards, 1941–46, Normandy, France, Belgium, Holland, Germany (Captain, 1944–46). Royal Ulster Constabulary, 1946–60; Chief of Security, BOAC, 1960–63 (incl. Royal Tour of India, 1961); Personnel Dir and Mem. Bd of Management, BOAC, 1964–69; British Airways: Regional Man., Canada, 1969–75; Regional Man., India, Bangladesh, Sri Lanka, 1975–79; Vice-Chm. and Chief Exec., NI Housing Exec., 1979–85; Dir, Inst. of Dirs, NI, 1986–95. Dir, NI Airports Bd, 1985–92. Pres., British Canadian Trade Assoc., 1972–74; Vice-Chm., Federated Appeal of Montreal, 1973–74. Chm., Bd of Airline Representatives, India, 1977–79; Chm., Inst. of Housing (NI), 1984. Chm., NI Forum for Political Dialogue, 1996–98. DL, 1982, High Sheriff, 1987–88, Co. Down. Kt Hospitaller, SMO of St John of Malta, NI, 1997. *Recreations:* gardening, bee keeping, country pursuits. *Address:* The Forge, Jericho Road, Killyleagh, Co. Down BT30 9TE. *T:* (028) 4482 8400. *Clubs:* Cavalry and Guards; Ulster Reform (Belfast).

GORMAN, Teresa Ellen; *b* Sept. 1931; *m. Educ:* Fulham Co. Sch.; London Univ. (BSc 1st cl. Hons). Founder and manager of own company. Mem., Westminster City Council, 1982–86. MP (C) Billericay, 1987–2001. Contested (Ind.) Streatham, Oct. 1974. Founder and Chairman: Alliance of Small Firms & Self Employed People Ltd, 1974; Amarant Trust, 1986. Mem., Cons. Women's Nat. Cttee, 1983–. *Publications:* The Bastards: dirty tricks and the challenge to Europe, 1993; The Amarant Book of HRT, 1989; No, Prime Minister!, 2001; research papers for IEA, Adam Smith Inst., CPS.

GORMAN, William Moore, FBA 1978; Emeritus Fellow, Nuffield College, Oxford, since 1990 (Fellow, 1962–67 and 1979–90); *b* 17 June 1923; *s* of late Richard Gorman, Lusaka, Northern Rhodesia, and Sarah Crawford Moore, Kesh, Northern Ireland; *m* 1950, Dorinda Scott. *Educ:* Foyle Coll., Derry; Trinity Coll., Dublin (Hon. Fellow 1990). Asst Lectr, 1949, Lectr, 1951, and Sen. Lectr, 1957, in Econometrics and Social Statistics, University of Birmingham; Prof. of Economics, University of Oxford, 1962–67; Prof. of Economics, London Univ., at LSE, 1967–79. Fellow, 1961, European Chm., 1971–73, Pres. 1972, Econometric Soc. Mem., Academia Europaea, 1990; Hon. Foreign Member: Amer. Acad. of Arts and Scis, 1986; Amer. Economic Assoc., 1987. Hon. DSocSc Birmingham, 1973; Hon. DSc(SocSc) Southampton, 1974; Hon. DEconSc NUI, 1986; Hon. DSc (Econ) London, 1998. *Publications:* articles in various economic journals. *Address:* Nuffield College, Oxford OX1 1NF. *T:* (01865) 278605; Moorfield, Fountainstown, Myrtleville, Co. Cork, Ireland. *T:* Cork (21) 831174.

GORMANSTON, 17th Viscount *cr* 1478; **Jenico Nicholas Dudley Preston;** Baron Gormanston (Ire.), 1365; Baron Gormanston (UK), 1868; Premier Viscount of Ireland; *b* 19 Nov. 1939; *s* of 16th Viscount and Pamela (who *m* 2nd, 1943, M. B. O'Connor, Irish Guards; he *d* 1961, she *d* 1975), *o d* of late Capt. Dudley Hanly, and Lady Marjorie Heath (by her 1st marriage); S father, who was officially presumed killed in action, France, 9 June 1940; *m* 1st, 1974, Eva Antoine Landzianowska (*d* 1984); two *s*; 2nd, 1997, Lucy Arabella, former wife of David Grenfell and *d* of Edward Fox, *qv* and of Tracy Reed. *Educ:* Downside. *Heir: s* Hon. Jenico Francis Tara Preston, *b* 30 April 1974. *Address:* 8 Dalmeny House, 9 Thurloe Place, SW7 2RY.

GORMLEY, Antony Mark David, OBE 1998; sculptor; *b* London, 30 Aug. 1950; *s* of Arthur John Constantine Gormley and Elspeth Gormley (*née* Brauninger); *m* 1980, Vicken Parsons; two *s* one *d. Educ:* Trinity Coll., Cambridge (BA Hist. of Art); Central Sch. of Art, London; Goldsmiths' Sch. of Art, London (BA Fine Art; Hon. Fellow, Goldsmiths Coll., 1998); Slade Sch. of Fine Art (Boise travelling scholar, 1979). Mem., Arts Council of England, 1998–. Numerous *solo exhibitions* in Europe, America, Japan and Australia, 1980–, including: Whitechapel Art Gall., 1981; Louisiana Mus. of Modern Art, Denmark, 1989; American Field, US touring exhibn, 1991; Recent Iron Works, LA, 1992; Tate Gall., Liverpool, 1993; European Field, touring exhibn, 1993–95; Irish Mus. of Modern Art, Dublin, 1994; Lost Subject, White Cube, London, 1994; Escultura, Portugal, 1994; Field for the British Isles, GB tour, 1994–95 and Hayward Gall., 1996; Kohji Ogura Gall., Tokyo, 1995; Drawings, San Antonio, USA, 1995; Critical Mass, Vienna, 1995, RA, 1998; New Work, Sarajevo, 1996; Inside the Inside, Brussels, 1996; Arts 04, St Remy de Provence, France, 1996; Still Moving, retrospective tour, Japan, 1996–97; Drawings 1990–94, Ind. Art Space, London, 1996; Cuxhaven, and Total Strangers, Cologne, 1997; Neue Skulpturen, Cologne, 1998; Critical Mass, RA, 1998; Insiders, Brussels, 1999; Intimate Relations, Ontario and Cologne, 1999; European Field, Malmö, 1999; Quantum Clouds, Paris, 2000; *group exhibitions* include: British Sculpture in the 20th Century, Whitechapel Art Gall., 1981; Biennale de Venezia, Venice, 1982 and 1986; An Internat. Survey of Recent Painting and Sculpture, Mus. of Modern Art, NY, 1984; Documenta 8, Kassel, 1987; Avant-garde in the Eighties, LA Co. Mus. of Art, 1987; Starlit Waters, Tate Gall., Liverpool, 1988; GB–USSR, Kiev, Moscow, 1990; British Art Now, touring Japan, 1990; Arte Amazonas, Rio de Janeiro, 1992, Berlin, 1993, Dresden, 1993, Aachen, 1993; From Beyond the Pale, Irish Mus. of Modern Art, Dublin, 1994; Un Siècle de Sculpture anglaise, Jeu de Paume, Paris, 1996; Presence, Liverpool, 1999; Trialogo, Rome, 2000; also exhibns in Malmö, Sweden, 1996, Sydney, Lisbon and Knislinge, Sweden, 1998; work in private and public collections worldwide, including: Tate Gall., London; Scottish Gall. of Modern Art, Edinburgh; Jesus Coll., Cambridge; Art Gall. of NSW, Sydney; Louisiana Mus., Denmark; Israel Mus., Jerusalem; Sapporo Sculpture Park, Hokkaido, Japan; Mus. of Contemporary Art, LA; sculpture in public places: Out of the Dark, Kassel, Germany, 1987; Open Space, Rennes, France, 1993, Iron Man, Birmingham, 1994; Havmann, Mo I Rana, Norway, 1995; Angel of the North, Gateshead, 1998; Quantum Cloud, Greenwich, 2000. Turner Prize, 1994; South Bank Award, 1999. *Address:* 153A Bellenden Road, SE15 4DH. *T:* (020) 7639 1303, *Fax:* (020) 7639 2674; 13 South Villas, NW1 9BS. *T:* (020) 7482 7383, *Fax:* (020) 7267 8336.

GORMLY, Allan Graham, CBE 1991; Chairman, BPB Industries, since 1997 (Deputy Chairman, 1996–97; Director, since 1995); *b* 18 Dec. 1937; *s* of William Gormly and Christina Swinton Flockhart Arnot; *m* 1962, Vera Margaret Grant; one *s* one *d. Educ:* Paisley Grammar School. CA. Peat Marwick Mitchell & Co., 1955–61; Rootes Group, 1961–65; John Brown PLC, 1965–68; Brownlee & Co. Ltd, 1968–70; John Brown PLC, 1970: Finance Director, John Brown Engineering Ltd, 1970–77; Director, Planning and Control, John Brown PLC, 1977–80; Dep. Chairman, John Brown Engineers and Constructors Ltd, 1980–83; Gp Man. Dir, John Brown PLC, 1983–92; Chief Exec., Trafalgar House, 1992–94 (Dir, 1986–95); Dir, 1990–96, Dep. Chm., 1992–94, Chm., 1994–96, Royal Insce Hldgs; Dir and Dep. Chm., Royal & Sun Alliance, 1996–98. Chm., Q-One Biotech Ltd, 1999–; Director: Brixton Estates, 1994– (Chm., 2000–); European Capital Co., 1996–2000; Bank of Scotland, 1997–2001. Chm., Overseas Projects Bd, 1988–91; Dep. Chm., Export Guarantees Adv. Council, 1990–92; Member: BOTB, 1988–92; Review Body on Top Salaries, 1990–92; FCO Bd of Mgt, 2000–. *Recreations:* golf, music. *Address:* 56 North Park, Gerrards Cross, Bucks SL9 8JR.

GORRIE, Donald Cameron Easterbrook, OBE 1984; Member (Lib Dem) Central Scotland, Scottish Parliament, since 1999; *b* 2 April 1933; *s* of Robert Maclagan Gorrie and Sydney Grace Gorrie (*née* Easterbrook); *m* 1957, Astrid Margaret Salvesen; two *s. Educ:* Hurst Grange Sch., Stirling; Oundle Sch.; Corpus Christi Coll., Oxford (MA Classical Mods and Modern History). Schoolmaster, Gordonstoun Sch., 1957–60; School Master and Dir of Phys. Educn, Marlborough Coll., 1960–66; Researcher and Adult Educn Lectr in Scottish History, 1966–68; Dir of Res., 1968–71, Dir of Admin, 1971–75, Scottish Liberal Party; Founder, Edinburgh Translations Ltd, 1976 (Dir, 1976–); Jt Founder, Scoted Ltd, 1978 (Dir, 1978–84). Member (L, subseq. Lib Dem): Edinburgh Town Council, 1971–75; also Group Leader: Lothian Regl Council, 1974–96; City of Edinburgh DC, 1980–96, City of Edinburgh Council, 1995–97. MP (Lib Dem) Edinburgh West, 1997–2001. Scottish Parliament: Member: Finance Cttee; Procedures Cttee, 1999–. Member of Board/Committee: Edinburgh Fest., 1975–80, 1988–97; Royal Lyceum Theatre, 1975–97; Scottish Chamber Orch., 1988–96; Lothian Assoc. of Youth Clubs, 1975–97; Castle Rock Housing Assoc., 1973–97; Queen's Hall, Edinburgh, 1980–, and other local orgns; Convener: Diverse Attractions, 1984–99; Edinburgh City Youth Café, 1990–97. DL City of Edinburgh, 1996–99. *Recreations:* former Scottish native record holder for 880 yards, reading, music, opera, drama, visiting ruins. *Address:* 9 Garscube Terrace, Edinburgh EH12 6BW.

GORRINGE, Christopher John, CBE 1999; Chief Executive, All England Lawn Tennis and Croquet Club, Wimbledon, since 1983; *b* 13 Dec. 1945; *s* of Maurice Sydney William Gorringe and Hilda Joyce Gorringe; *m* 1976, Jennifer Mary Chamberlain; two *d. Educ:* Bradfield Coll., Berks; Royal Agricl Coll., Cirencester. ARICS. Asst Land Agent, Iveagh Trustees Ltd (Guinness family), 1968–73; Asst Sec., 1973–79, Sec., 1979–83, All England Lawn Tennis and Croquet Club. *Recreations:* lawn tennis, squash, soccer. *Address:* All England Lawn Tennis Club, Church Road, Wimbledon, SW19 5AE. *T:* (020) 8944 1066. *Clubs:* East India, Devonshire, Sports and Public Schools; All England Lawn Tennis and Croquet, International Lawn Tennis of GB, Queen's, St George's Hill Lawn Tennis, Jesters.

GORROD, Prof. John William, FRCPath; CChem, FRSC; FIBiol; Professor of Biopharmacy, King's College London, 1984–97, now Emeritus; Research Professor, Chelsea Department of Pharmacy, 1990–97; Visiting Professor of Toxicology, University of Essex, since 1997; *b* 11 Oct. 1931; *s* of Ernest Lionel and Carrie Rebecca Gorrod; *m* 1954, Doreen Mary Collins; two *s* one *d*. *Educ:* Brunel Coll. of Advanced Technology; Chelsea Coll. (DCC, PhD, DSc). FRSC 1980; FRCPath 1984; FIBiol 1998. Biochem. Asst, Inst. of Cancer Res., 1954–64; Res. Fellow, Univ. of Bari, Italy, 1964; Sen. Student, Royal Commn for Exhibn of 1851, 1965–68; University of London: Lectr 1968–80, then Reader 1980–84, in Biopharmacy, Chelsea Coll.; Hd, Chelsea Dept of Pharmacy, King's Coll., 1984–90; Chm., Univ. Bd of Studies in Pharmacy, 1986–88; Hd of Div. of Health Scis, KCL, 1988–89; FKC 1996. Dir, Drug Control and Teaching Centre, Sports Council, 1985–91. Member: Council, Internat. Soc. for Study of Xenobiotics (Pres., 2000–01); Educn Cttee, Pharmaceutical Soc. of GB, 1986–91; Assoc. for Res. in Indoor Air, 1989–95; Council, Indoor Air Internat., 1990–97; Associates for Res. in Substances of Enjoyment, 1990–92; Air Transport Users Cttee, CAA, 1990–93; Scientific Bd, Inst. of Drug and Pharmacokinetics Res., Develt and Applications, Ege Univ., Turkey, 1994–. Vis. Prof., Univs of Bologna, Bari, and Kebangsan, Malaysia; Canadian MRC Vis. Prof., Univs of Manitoba and Saskatchewan, 1988; Vis. Prof., Chinese Acad. of Preventive Medicine, 1991. Mem., Polstead Parish Council, 1999–. Hon. MPS, 1982; Corresp. Mem., German Pharm. Soc., 1985. Hon. Fellow: Greek Pharmaceutical Soc., 1987; Turkish Assoc. of Pharmacists, 1988. Gold Medal, Comenius Univ., Bratislava, 1991. Editorial Board: Xenobiotica; Europ. Jl of Metabolism and Pharmacokinetics; Toxicology Letters; Anti-Cancer Res. *Publications:* Drug Metabolism in Man (ed jtly), 1978; Biological Oxidation of Nitrogen, 1978; Drug Toxicity, 1979; Testing for Toxicity, 1981; (ed jtly) Biological Oxidation of Nitrogen in Organic Molecules, 1985; (ed jtly) Development of Drugs and Modern Medicines, 1986; (ed jtly) Metabolism of Xenobiotics, 1987; (ed jtly) Molecular Aspects of Human Disease, 1989; (ed jtly) Molecular Basis of Neurological Disorders and their Treatment, 1991; (ed jtly) Nicotine and Related Alkaloids, 1993; Analytical Determination of Nicotine and Related Compounds and their Metabolites, 1999; contribs to Xenobiotica, Europ. Jl Drug Metabolism, Jl Pharm. Pharmacol, Mutation Res., Anti-Cancer Res., Jl Nat. Cancer Inst., Drug Metabolism Revs, Med. Sci. Res., Drug Metabolism & Drug Interact., Jl of Chromatography. *Recreations:* trying to understand government policies on tertiary education, travel, books, running (slowly!), badminton. *Address:* Toxicology Unit, John Tabor Laboratories, Essex University, Wivenhoe Park, Colchester CO4 3SQ. *T:* (01206) 873331, *Fax:* (01206) 872096; *e-mail:* jgorr@essex.ac.uk; (home) The Rest Orchard, Polstead Heath, Suffolk CO6 5BG. *Clubs:* Athenæum; Hillingdon Athletic (Mddx).

GORST, Sir John (Michael), Kt 1994; Chairman, Chadwick Associates Ltd, since 1997; *b* 28 June 1928; *s* of late Derek Charles Gorst and Tatiana (*née* Kolotinsky); *m* 1954, Noël Harington Walker; five *s*. *Educ:* Ardingly Coll.; Corpus Christi Coll., Cambridge (MA). Advertising and Public Relations Manager, Pye Ltd, 1953–63; Trade Union and Public Affairs Consultant, John Gorst & Associates, 1964–95. Public relations adviser to: British Lion Films, 1964–65; Fedn of British Film Makers, 1964–67; Film Production Assoc. of GB, 1967–68; BALPA, 1967–69; Guy's Hosp., 1968–74. Founder: Telephone Users' Assoc., 1964–80 (Sec. 1964–70); Local Radio Assoc. 1964 (Sec., 1964–71). Contested (C) Chester-le-Street, 1964; Bodmin, 1966; MP (C) Hendon North, 1970–97; contested (C) Hendon, 1997. Sec., Cons. Consumer Protection Cttee, 1973–74; Member: Employment Select Cttee, 1979–87; Nat. Heritage Select Cttee, 1992–97; Vice-Chm., All Party War Crimes Cttee, 1987–97; Chairman: Cons. Media Cttee, 1987–90; British Mexican Gp, 1992–97. *Recreations:* gardening, woodwork, chess. *Club:* Garrick.

GORT, 9th Viscount *cr* 1816 (Ire.); **Foley Robert Standish Prendergast Vereker;** Baron Kiltart 1810; photographer; *b* 24 Oct. 1951; *er s* of 8th Viscount Gort and of Bettine Mary Mackenzie, *d* of Godfrey Greene; *S* father, 1995; *m* 1st, 1979, Julie Denise Jones (marr. diss. 1984); 2nd, 1991, Sharon Quayle; one *s* one *d*. *Educ:* Harrow. *Recreation:* golf. *Heir:* *s* Robert Foley Prendergast Vereker, *b* 5 April 1993. *Address:* The Coach House, Arbory Street, Castletown, Isle of Man IM9 1LJ. *T:* (01624) 822295.

GORTON, Rt Hon. Sir John (Grey); PC 1968; GCMG 1977; AC 1988; CH 1971; MA; retired; *b* 9 Sept. 1911; *m* 1st, 1935, Bettina (decd), *d* of G. Brown, Bangor, Me, USA; two *s* one *d*; 2nd, 1993, Nancy, *widow* of John Home; five step *s* one step *d*. *Educ:* Geelong Gram. Sch.; Brasenose Coll., Oxford (MA, Hon. Fellow, 1968). Orchardist. Enlisted RAAF, Nov. 1940; served in UK, Singapore, Darwin, Milne Bay; severely wounded in air ops; discharged with rank of Flt-Lt, Dec. 1944. Councillor, Kerang Shire, 1947–52 (Pres. of Shire); Mem., Lodden Valley Regional Cttee. Senator for State of Victoria, Parlt of Commonwealth of Australia, 1949–68 (Govt Leader in Senate, 1967–68); Minister for Navy, 1958–63; Minister Assisting the Minister for External Affairs, 1960–63 (Actg Minister during periods of absence overseas of Minister); Minister in Charge of CSIRO, 1962–68; Minister for Works and, under Prime Minister, Minister in Charge of Commonwealth Activities in Educn and Research, 1963–66; Minister for Interior, 1963–64; Minister for Works, 1966–67; Minister for Educn and Science, 1966–68; MHR (L) for Higgins, Vic, 1968–75; Prime Minister of Australia, 1968–71; Minister for Defence, and Dep. Leader of Liberal Party, March-Aug. 1971; Mem. Parly Liberal Party Exec., and Liberal Party Spokesman on Environment and Conservation and Urban and Regional Develt, 1973–75; Dep. Chm., Jt Parly Cttee on Prices, 1973–75. Contested Senate election (Ind.), ACT, Dec. 1975. *Address:* 32 Parsley Road, Vaucluse, NSW 2030, Australia.

See also Sir W. D. Home, Bt.

GORTVAI, Dame Rosalinde; *see* Hurley, Dame R.

GOSCHEN, family name of **Viscount Goschen**.

GOSCHEN, 4th Viscount *cr* 1900; **Giles John Harry Goschen;** a Director, Barchester Advisory, since 2000; *b* 16 Nov. 1965; *s* of 3rd Viscount Goschen, KBE, and of Alvin Moyana Lesley, *yr d* of late Harry England, Durban, Natal; *S* father, 1977; *m* 1991, Sarah Penelope, *d* of late Alan Horsnail; one *s* one *d*. *Educ:* Eton. A Lord in Waiting (Govt Whip), 1992–94; Parly Under-Sec. of State, Dept of Transport, 1994–97; elected Mem., H of L, 1999. With Deutsche Bank, 1997–2000. *Heir:* *s* Hon. Alexander John Edward Goschen, *b* 5 Oct. 2001.

GOSCHEN, Sir (Edward) Alexander, 4th Bt *cr* 1916 of Beacon Lodge, Highcliffe, co. Southampton; *b* 13 March 1949; *s* of Sir Edward Goschen, 3rd Bt, DSO and of Cynthia, *d* of Rt Hon. Sir Alexander Cadogan, OM, GCMG, KCB, PC; *S* father, 2001; *m* 1976, Louise Annette, *d* of Lt-Col R.F.L. Chance, MC and Lady Ava Chance; one *d*. *Educ:* Eton. *Heir:* *cousin* Sebastian Bernard Goschen, *b* 1 Jan. 1959.

GOSDEN, Prof. Christine Margaret, PhD; FRCPath; Professor of Medical Genetics, University of Liverpool, since 1993; Hon. Consultant, Liverpool Women's Hospital, since 1993; Member, Human Fertilisation and Embryology Authority, since 1996; *b* 25 April 1945; *d* of George G. H. Ford and Helena P. S. Ford; *m* 1971, Dr John Gosden. *Educ:* Univ. of Edinburgh (BSc Hons; PhD 1971). MRCPath, FRCPath. Res. Fellow, Univ. of Edinburgh, 1971–73; Mem., MRC Sen. Scientific Staff, MRC Human Genetics Unit, Western Gen. Hosp., Edinburgh, 1973–93; Vis. Prof. in Human Genetics, Harris Birthright Centre for Fetal Medicine, and Dept of Obstetrics and Gynaecology, King's Coll. Hosp. Sch. of Medicine and Dentistry, 1987–93. Researcher, scriptwriter, co-presenter, etc of films (incl. contrib. to TV series Dispatches (Saddam's Secret Time Bomb) and 60 Minutes, 1998) and author of articles on med. effects of chemical and biological weapons use. *Publications:* (jtly) Is My Baby All Right?, 1994; numerous scientific papers, articles and contribs to books on human genetics, fetal medicine, mental illness, childhood and adult cancers and med. effects of chemical and biological weapons. *Recreations:* campaigner for human rights, whalewatching, alpine gardening, organ and harpsichord music, modern poetry. *Address:* University Department, Liverpool Women's Hospital, Crown Street, Liverpool L8 7SS.

GOSDEN, John Harry Martin; racehorse trainer; *b* 30 March 1951; *s* of late John Montague Gosden and Peggie Gosden; *m* 1982, Rachel Dene Serena Hood; two *s* two *d*. *Educ:* Eastbourne Coll.; Emmanuel Coll., Cambridge (MA; athletics blue, 1970–73). Sussex Martletts schoolboy cricketer, 1967–68; Mem., Blackheath Rugby Club, 1969–70; Mem., British Under-23 Rowing Squad, 1973. Assistant trainer to: Noel Murless, 1974–76; Vincent O'Brien, 1976–77; trainer, USA, 1979–88: trained 8 State champions, Calif, 3 Eclipse Award winners; England, 1989–: by 2000, over 1000 UK winners; over 100 Group Stakes winners, incl. Derby, St Leger, English and French 1000 Guineas. *Recreations:* opera, ski-ing, environmental issues. *Address:* Manton House Estate, Manton, Marlborough, Wilts SN8 1PN.

GOSDEN, Prof. Roger Gordon; Research Director, Department of Obstetrics and Gynecology, McGill University, since 1999; *b* 23 Sept. 1948; *s* of Gordon Conrad Jason Gosden and Peggy (*née* Butcher); *m* 1971, Carole Ann Walsh; two *s*. *Educ:* Bristol Univ. (BSc); Darwin Coll., Cambridge (PhD 1974); Edinburgh Univ. (DSc 1989). CBiol, FIBiol 1987. MRC Fellow, Physiological Lab., Cambridge, 1973–74, 1975–76; Population Council Fellow, Duke Univ., N Carolina, 1974–75; Lectr and Sen. Lectr and Dep. Head, Dept of Physiol., Edinburgh Univ. Med. Sch., 1976–94; Prof. of Reproductive Biol., Leeds Univ., 1994–99; Hon. Consultant, Leeds Gen. Infirmary and St James's Univ. Hosp., Leeds, 1994–99. Guest Scientist: Univ. of Southern California, 1979, 1980, 1981, 1987; Univ. of Naples, 1989; Visiting Professor: Univ. of Washington, Seattle, 1999; Univ. of Leeds, 1999–. Scientific conf. organiser. Mem., Bd of Prison Visitors, Wetherby, 1996–99. Elder, Church of Scotland, 1982–. FRSA 1996. Occasional broadcasts. *Publications:* Biology of Menopause, 1985; Cheating Time, 1996; Transplantation of Ovarian and Testicular Tissues, 1996; Designer Babies, 1999; technical articles and contribs to popular press. *Recreations:* natural history, writing. *Address:* Department of Obstetrics and Gynecology, McGill University, Women's Pavilion, Royal Victoria Hospital, 687 Pine Avenue West, Montreal, QC H3A 1A1, Canada.

GOSFORD, 7th Earl of, *cr* 1806; **Charles David Nicholas Alexander John Sparrow Acheson;** Bt (NS) 1628; Baron Gosford 1776; Viscount Gosford 1785; Baron Worlingham (UK) 1835; Baron Acheson (UK) 1847; *b* 13 July 1942; *o s* of 6th Earl of Gosford, OBE, and Francesca Augusta, *er d* of Francesco Cagiati, New York; *S* father, 1966; *m* 1983, Lynnette Redmond. *Educ:* Harrow; Byam Shaw Sch. of drawing and painting; Royal Academy Schs. Chm., Artists Union, 1976–80; Mem. Visual Arts Panel, Greater London Arts Assoc., 1976–77; Council Member, British Copyright Council, 1977–80. Represented by: Barry Stern Gall., Sydney; Phillip Bacon Galls, Brisbane; Solander Gall., Canberra; Von Bertouch Gall., Newcastle, NSW. *Heir:* *u* Hon. Patrick Bernard Victor Montagu Acheson [*b* 4 Feb. 1915; *m* 1946, Judith, *d* of Mrs F. B. Bate, Virginia, USA; three *s* two *d*].

GOSKIRK, (William) Ian (Macdonald), CBE 1986; Partner, Coopers & Lybrand Deloitte, 1990–92; *b* 2 March 1932; *s* of William Goskirk and Flora Macdonald; *m* 1969, Hope Ann Knaizuk; one *d*. *Educ:* Carlisle Grammar Sch.; Queen's Coll., Oxford (MA). Served REME, 1950–52. Shell Internat. Petroleum, 1956–74; Anschutz Corp., 1974–76; BNOC, 1976–85; Man. Dir, BNOC Trading, 1980–82; Chief Exec., BNOC, 1982–85; Dir, Coopers & Lybrand Associates, 1986–90. *Recreation:* gardening.

GOSLING, Allan Gladstone; Sales Director, PSA Projects, Property Services Agency, Department of the Environment, 1991–92, retired (Operational Director, 1990–91); Consultant to TBV Consult, 1992–95; *b* 4 July 1933; *s* of late Gladstone Gosling and of Elizabeth Gosling (*née* Ward); *m* 1961, Janet Pamela (*née* Gosling); one *s* one *d*. *Educ:* Kirkham Grammar Sch.; Birmingham Sch. of Architecture. DipArch; RIBA 1961; FRIAS 1988 (RIAS 1984); FFB 1991. Asst Architect, Lancs County Council, 1950–54; Birmingham Sch. of Architecture, 1954–57; Surman Kelly Surman, Architects, 1957–59; Royal Artillery, 1959–61; Army Works Organisation, 1961–63; Min. of Housing R&D Group, 1963–68; Suptg Architect, Birmingham Regional Office, Min. of Housing, 1968–72; Regional Works Officer, NW Region, PSA, 1972–76; Midland Regional Dir, PSA, 1976–83; Dir, Scottish Services, PSA, 1983–90. *Recreations:* walking, gardening, watercolour painting, DIY. *Address:* 11 The Moorlands, Four Oaks Park, Sutton Coldfield, West Midlands B74 2RF.

GOSLING, Sir Donald, Kt 1976; Joint Chairman, National Car Parks Ltd, 1950–98; Chairman, Palmer & Harvey Ltd, since 1967; *b* 2 March 1929; *m* 1959, Elizabeth Shauna (marr. diss. 1988), *d* of Dr Peter Ingram and Lecky Ingram; three *s*. Joined RN, 1944; served Mediterranean, HMS Leander. Mem., Council of Management, White Ensign Assoc. Ltd, 1970– (Chm., 1978–83; Vice Pres., 1983–93; Pres., 1993–); Mem., Exec. Cttee, Imperial Soc. of Kts Bachelor, 1977–. Chm., Berkeley Square Ball Trust, 1982–; Trustee: Fleet Air Arm Museum, Yeovilton, 1974–2000 (Chm., Mountbatten Meml Hall Appeals Cttee, 1980); RYA Seamanship Foundn, 1981–; Vice Pres., King George's Fund for Sailors, 1993–; Patron: Submarine Meml Appeal, 1978–; HMS Ark Royal Welfare Trust, 1986–. Hon. Capt., RNR, 1993–. Younger Brother, Trinity House, 1998. Mem., Grand Order of Water Rats, 1999. *Recreations:* swimming, sailing, shooting. *Address:* (office) 21 Bryanston Street, Marble Arch, W1H 7PR. *T:* (020) 7499 7050. *Clubs:* Royal Thames Yacht, Royal London Yacht, Royal Naval Sailing Association, Thames Sailing, Royal Yacht Squadron; Saints and Sinners.

GOSLING, Justin Cyril Bertrand; Principal, St Edmund Hall, Oxford, 1982–96; *b* 26 April 1930; *s* of Vincent and Dorothy Gosling; *m* 1958, Margaret Clayton; two *s* two *d*. *Educ:* Ampleforth Coll.; Wadham Coll., Oxford (BPhil, MA). Univ. of Oxford: Fereday Fellow, St John's Coll., 1955–58; Lectr in Philosophy, Pembroke Coll. and Wadham Coll., 1958–60; Fellow in Philosophy, St Edmund Hall, 1960–82; Sen. Proctor, 1977–78. Barclay Acheson Prof., Macalester Coll., Minnesota, 1964; Vis. Res. Fellow, ANU, Canberra, 1970 (Pro-Vice-Chancellor, 1989–95). *Publications:* Pleasure and Desire, 1969; Plato, 1973; (ed) Plato, Philebus, 1975; (with C. C. W. Taylor) The Greeks on Pleasure, 1982; Weakness of the Will, 1990; articles in Mind, Phil Rev. and Proc. Aristotelian Soc. *Recreations:* gardening, intaglio printing, recorder music. *Address:* Joymount, Northcourt Lane, Abingdon, Oxon OX14 1QA.

GOSLING, Prof. Leonard Morris, PhD; CBiol, FIBiol; Professor of Animal Behaviour, University of Newcastle, since 1999; *b* 22 Jan. 1943; *s* of William Richard Gosling and Marian (*née* Morris); *m* 1977, Dr Marion Petrie; two *d*. *Educ:* Wymondham Coll., Norfolk; Queen Mary Coll., London (BSc Zool. 1965); University Coll., Nairobi (PhD 1975). CBiol, FIBiol 1989. Ministry of Agriculture, Fisheries and Food: SSO, Coypu Res. Lab., 1970–73; PSO, Mammal Ecology Gp, 1974–85; SPSO, Central Science Lab., 1986–93; Dir of Sci., Zool Soc. of London and Dir, Inst. of Zool., 1993–99. Hon. Lectr, UEA, 1978–81; Vis. Prof., UCL, 1994–. Member, Council: Mammal Soc., 1982–85; Assoc. for Study of Animal Behaviour, 1988–90 (Sec., Ethical Cttee, 1991–94); Royal Vet. Coll., 1994–99; Mem., Mgt Cttee, UCL Centre for Ecology and Evolution, 1995–99. *Publications:* (ed with M. Dawkins) Ethics in Research on Animal Behaviour, 1992; (ed with W. J. Sutherland) Behaviour and Conservation, 2000; numerous articles in learned jls and books on population biol. and behavioural ecology. *Recreations:* drawing, ditching, formerly Rugby. *Address:* Department of Psychology, University of Newcastle, Newcastle upon Tyne NE1 7RU. *T:* (0191) 222 7525; *e-mail:* l.m.gosling@ncl.ac.uk.

GOSLING, Col Richard Bennett, OBE 1957; TD 1947; DL; *b* 4 Oct. 1914; 2nd *s* of late T. S. Gosling, Dynes Hall, Halstead; *m* 1st, 1950, Marie Terese Ronayne (*d* 1976), Castle Redmond, Co. Cork; one adopted *s* one adopted *d* (one *s* decd); 2nd, 1978, Sybilla Burgers van Oyen, *widow* of Bernard Burgers, 't Kasteel, Nijmegen. *Educ:* Eton; Magdalene Coll., Cambridge (MA). CEng. Served with Essex Yeomanry, RHA, 1939–45; CO, 1953–56; Dep. CRA, East Anglian Div., 1956–58. Dir-Gen., British Agricl Export Council, 1971–73. Chairman: Constructors, 1965–68; Hearne & Co., 1971–82. Director: P-E International, 1956–76; Doulton & Co., 1962–72; Revertex Chemicals, 1974–81; Press Mouldings, 1977–92. DL 1954, High Sheriff 1982, Essex. DU Essex, 1993. French Croix de Guerre, 1944. *Recreation:* country pursuits. *Address:* Canterburys Lodge, Margaretting, Essex CM4 0EE. *T:* (01277) 353073. *Clubs:* Naval and Military, MCC; Beefsteak (Chelmsford).

GOSS, James Richard William; QC 1997; *b* 12 May 1953; *s* of His Honour Judge William Alan Belcher Goss and of Yvonne Goss (*née* Samuelson); *m* 1982, Dawna Elizabeth Davies; two *s* three *d*. *Educ:* Charterhouse; University Coll., Durham (BA). Called to the Bar, Inner Temple, 1975. *Address:* 6 Park Square East, Leeds LS1 2LW. *T:* (0113) 2459763. *Club:* Colonsay Golf.

GOSS, Prof. Richard Oliver, PhD; Professor Emeritus, Cardiff University; *b* 4 Oct. 1929; *s* of late Leonard Arthur Goss and Hilda Nellie Goss (*née* Casson); *m* 1st, Lesley Elizabeth Thurbon (marr. diss. 1983); two *s* one *d*; 2nd, 1994, Gillian Mary (*née* Page). *Educ:* Christ's Coll., Finchley; HMS Worcester; King's Coll., Cambridge. Master Mariner 1956; BA 1958; MA 1961; PhD 1979. FCIT 1970; MNI (Founder) 1972; FNI 1977; FRSA 1993. Merchant Navy (apprentice and executive officer), 1947–55; NZ Shipping Co. Ltd, 1958–63; Economic Consultant (Shipping, Shipbuilding and Ports), MoT, 1963–64; Econ. Adviser, BoT (Shipping), 1964–67; Sen. Econ. Adviser (Shipping, Civil Aviation, etc), 1967–74; Econ. Adviser to Cttee of Inquiry into Shipping (Rochdale Cttee), 1967–70; Under-Sec., Depts of Industry and Trade, 1974–80; Prof., Dept of Maritime Studies, 1980–95, Dist. Res. Prof., 1995–96, UWIST, subseq. Univ. of Wales Coll. of Cardiff, Prof. Emeritus, Univ. of Wales, Cardiff, 1996. Nuffield/Leverhulme Travelling Fellow, 1977–78. Governor, Plymouth Polytechnic, 1973–84; Mem. Council: RINA, 1969–; Nautical Inst. (from foundn until 1976); Member: CNAA Nautical Studies Bd, 1971–81; CNAA Transport Bd, 1976–78. Pres. (first), Internat. Assoc. of Maritime Economists, 1992–94. Editor and Editor-in-Chief, Maritime Policy and Management, 1985–93. Hon. PhD Piraeus, 1999. Premio Internazionale delle Comunicazioni Cristoforo Colombo, Genoa, 1991. *Publications:* Studies in Maritime Economics, 1968; (with C. D. Jones) The Economies of Size in Dry Bulk Carriers, 1971; (with M. C. Mann, et al) The Cost of Ships' Time, 1974; Advances in Maritime Economics, 1977; A Comparative Study of Seaport Management and Administration, 1979; Policies for Canadian Seaports, 1984; Port Authorities in Australia, 1987; Collected Papers, 1990; numerous papers in various jls, transactions and to conferences. *Recreations:* lock maintenance, local history, travel. *Address:* 1 Weir Gardens, Pershore, Worcs WR10 1DX. *T:* (01386) 561140.

GOSS, Hon. Wayne Keith; consultant; Managing Partner, Deloitte Touche Tohmatsu, Queensland, since 1999; *b* 26 Feb. 1951; *s* of Allan James Goss and Norma Josephine Goss; *m* 1981, Roisin Anne Hirschfeld; one *s* one *d*. *Educ:* Univ. of Queensland (LLB; MBA 1997). Admitted solicitor, 1973; Partner, Goss and Downey, 1977–83. MLA (ALP) Salisbury, 1983–86 and Logan, Queensland, 1986–98; Opposition Minister for Lands, Forestry and Police, 1983–86, for Justice, 1986–88; Leader of Opposition, 1988–89; Premier of Queensland, 1989–96; Minister for the Arts, 1989–92, for Economic and Trade Devt, 1989–96. Chairman: Qld Art Gall.; Goodwill Games Brisbane Ltd, 1998–. *Address:* 315 Indooroopilly Road, Indooroopilly, Qld 4068, Australia.

GOSSCHALK, Joseph Bernard; His Honour Judge Gosschalk; a Circuit Judge, since 1991; *b* 27 Aug. 1936; *s* of late Lionel Samuel Gosschalk and of Johanna (*née* Lion); *m* 1973, Ruth Sandra Jarvis; two *d*. *Educ:* East Ham Grammar Sch.; Magdalen Coll., Oxford (MA Jurisprudence). Called to the Bar, Gray's Inn, 1961; Asst Recorder, 1983–87; Head of Chambers, Francis Taylor Bldg, Temple, EC4, 1983–91; a Recorder, SE Circuit, 1987–91. *Recreations:* theatre, tennis, foreign travel. *Address:* The Crown Court, Bricket Road, St Albans, Herts AL1 3LB. *T:* (01727) 753220.

GOSTIN, Larry, DJur; Professor of Law, Georgetown University Law Center, since 1994; Professor of Health Policy, Johns Hopkins School of Hygiene and Public Health, since 1994; Associate Director, Harvard University/World Health Organization Collaborating Center on Health Legislation, since 1988; *b* 19 Oct. 1949; *s* of Joseph and Sylvia Gostin; *m* 1977, Jean Catherine Allison; two *s*. *Educ:* State Univ. of New York, Brockport (BA Psychology); Duke Univ. (DJur 1974). Dir of Forensics and Debate, Duke Univ., 1973–74; Fulbright Fellow, Social Res. Unit, Univ. of London, 1974–75; Legal Dir, MIND (Nat. Assoc. for Mental Health), 1975–83; Gen. Sec., NCCL, 1983–85; Harvard University: Sen. Fellow of Health Law, 1985–86; Lectr, 1986–87; Adjunct Prof. in Health Law, Sch. of Public Health, 1988–94; Exec. Dir, Amer. Soc. of Law and Medicine, 1986–94. Legal Counsel in series of cases before Eur. Commn and Eur. Court of Human Rights, 1974–. Vis. Prof., Sch. of Social Policy, McMaster Univ., 1978–79; Vis. Fellow in Law and Psychiatry, Centre for Criminological Res., Oxford Univ., 1982–83. Chm., Advocacy Alliance, 1981–83; Member: National Cttee, UN Internat. Year for Disabled People, 1981; Legal Affairs Cttee, Internat. League of Socs for Mentally Handicapped People, 1980–; Cttee of Experts, Internat. Commn of Jurists to draft UN Human Rights Declarations, 1982–; Adv. Council, Interights, 1984–; AE Trust, 1984–85; WHO Expert Cttee on Guidelines on the Treatment of Drug and Alcohol Dependent Persons, 1985; WHO Steering Cttee, Internat. Ethical Guidelines for Human Population Res., 1990–; Nat. Bd of Dirs, Amer. Civil Liberties Union, 1986– (Mem. Exec. Cttee, 1988–). Western European and UK Editor, Internat. Jl of Law and Psychiatry, 1978–81; Exec. Ed., Amer. Jl of Law and Medicine, 1986–; Ed.-in-chief, Jl of Law, Medicine and Health Care, 1986–. Hon. LLD SUNY, 1994. Rosemary Delbridge Meml Award for most outstanding contribution to social policy, 1983. *Publications:* A Human Condition: vol. 1, 1975; vol. 2, 1977; A Practical Guide to Mental Health Law, 1983; The Court of Protection, 1983; (ed) Secure Provision: a review of special services for mentally ill and handicapped people in England and Wales, 1985; Mental Health Services: law and practice, 1986; Human Rights in Mental Health: an international report for the World Federation for Mental Health, 1988; Civil Liberties in Conflict, 1988; Surrogate Motherhood: politics and privacy, 1990; AIDS and the Health Care System, 1990; Implementing the Americans with Disabilities Act: rights and responsibilities of all Americans, 1993; Rights of Persons who are HIV Positive, 1996; Human Rights and Public Health in the AIDS Pandemic, 1997; Public Health Law: power, duty, restraint, 2000; articles in learned jls. *Recreations:* family outings, walking on the mountains and fells of the Lake District. *Address:* Georgetown University Law Center, 600 New Jersey Avenue NW, Washington, DC 20001–2022, USA. *T:* (202) 6629373.

GOSWELL, Sir Brian (Lawrence), Kt 1991; FRICS; Consultant, Healey & Baker, Surveyors, since 2000; *b* 26 Nov. 1935; *s* of late Albert George Goswell and Florence Emily (*née* Barnett); *m* 1961, Deirdre Gillian Stones; two *s*. ACIArb 1980; FRICS 2000 (FSVA 1968). Mil. service, Oxford and Bucks Light Infantry, 1954–57. Joined Healey & Baker, Surveyors, 1957; Partner, 1969; Managing Partner, 1977; Dep. Sen. Partner, 1988–97; Dep. Chm., 1997. Chairman: Roux Restaurants Ltd, 1988–96; Avon City Ltd, 1989–98; Sunley Secure II PLC, 1993–99; Brent Walker Gp PLC, 1993–97; William Hill Gp Ltd, 1994–97; Pubmaster Ltd, 1994–96; Internat. Security Management Gp Ltd, 1998–. Pres., 1993–94, and Mem. Bd of Mgt, British Council for Offices; Pres., Amer. Chamber of Commerce (UK), 1994–98; Member: Adv. Bd, Fulbright Commn, 1997–; Duke of Edinburgh's Award Internat. Fellowship, 1997–. FInstD 1972; FRSA 1993. *Recreations:* cricket, horse-racing, shooting. *Address:* Pipers, Camley Park Drive, Pinkneys Green, Maidenhead, Berks SL6 6QF. *T:* (01628) 630768. *Clubs:* Carlton (Vice-Pres., Political Cttee, 1998–), United & Cecil, Cavalry and Guards, City Livery, Royal Green Jackets, MCC; Leander (Henley-on-Thames); Temple Golf.

GOTO, Mi Dori, (Midori); violinist; *b* Osaka, Japan, 25 Oct. 1971; *d* of Setsu Goto. *Educ:* Professional Children's Sch., New York; Juilliard Sch. of Music, New York; New York Univ. (BA). Début with New York Philharmonic Orch., 1982; concert and recital appearances worldwide. Founder and Pres., Midori Foundn, 1992. Numerous recordings. *Address:* c/o ICM, 40 West 57th Street, New York, NY 10019, USA.

GOTT, Haydn; a District Judge (Magistrates' Courts) (formerly Metropolitan Stipendiary Magistrate), since 1992; *b* 29 April 1946; *s* of Alan Gott and Delia Mary Gott (*née* Pugh); *m* 1975, Brigid Mary Kane; one *s* one *d*. *Educ:* Manchester Grammar Sch.; Oxford Univ. (MA). Admitted solicitor, 1972; Partner, Alexander & Partners, solicitors, 1975–92. Legal Mem., Mental Health Review Tribunal, 1986–. *Recreations:* sport, music. *Address:* Camberwell Magistrates' Court, SE5 7UP. *T:* (020) 7703 0909. *Club:* Ronnie Scott's.

GOTT, Richard Willoughby; journalist; Literary Editor, The Guardian, 1992–94; *b* 28 Oct. 1938; *s* of Arthur Gott and Mary Moon; *m* 1st, 1966, Ann Zammit (marr. diss. 1981); one adopted *s* one adopted *d*; 2nd, 1985, Vivien Ashley. *Educ:* Winchester Coll.; Corpus Christi Coll., Oxford (MA). Res. Asst, RIIA, 1962–65; Leader Writer, Guardian, 1964–66; Res. Fellow, Inst. de Estudios Internacionales, Univ. of Chile, 1966–69; Foreign Editor, Tanzanian Standard, Dar es Salaam, 1970–71; Third World corresp., New Statesman, 1971–72; The Guardian: Latin American corresp., 1972–76; Foreign News Editor, 1977–78, Features Editor, 1978–89; Asst Editor, 1988–94. Editor, Pelican Latin American Library, 1969–78; Dir, Latin American Newsletters, 1973–79. Contested (Ind.) North Hull, byelection 1966. *Publications:* The Appeasers (with Martin Gilbert), 1963; Guerrilla Movements in Latin America, 1970; Land Without Evil: Utopian journeys across the South American watershed, 1993; In the Shadow of the Liberator: Hugo Chavez and the transformation of Venezuela, 2000. *Recreation:* travelling. *Address:* 88 Ledbury Road, W11 2AH. *T:* (020) 7229 5467.

GOTTLIEB, Bernard, CB 1970; retired; *b* 1913; *s* of late James Gottlieb and Pauline (*née* Littaur); *m* 1955, Sybil N. Epstein; one *s* one *d*. *Educ:* Haberdashers' Hampstead Sch.; Queen Mary Coll., London Univ. BSc First Class Maths, 1932. Entered Civil Service as an Executive Officer in Customs and Excise, 1932. Air Ministry, 1938; Asst Private Sec., 1941, and Private Sec., 1944, to Permanent Under-Sec. of State (late Sir Arthur Street), Control Office for Germany and Austria, 1945; Asst Sec., 1946. Seconded to National Coal Board, 1946; Min. of Power, 1950; Under-Sec., 1961, Dir of Establishments, 1965–69; Under-Sec., Min. of Posts and Telecommunications, 1969–73; Secretariat, Pay Board, 1973–74, Royal Commn for Distribution of Income and Wealth, 1974–78; research with Incomes Data Services, 1978–90. Gwilym Gibbon Research Fellow, Nuffield Coll., Oxford, 1952–53. *Address:* 65 Hillfield Court, NW3 4BG. *T:* (020) 7794 3607. *Club:* Reform.

GOTTLIEB, Robert Adams; dance and book critic; Editor-in-Chief, The New Yorker, 1987–92; *b* 29 April 1931; *s* of Charles and Martha Gottlieb; *m* 1st, 1952, Muriel Higgins (marr. diss. 1965); one *s*; 2nd, 1969, Maria Tucci; one *s* one *d*. *Educ:* Columbia Coll., NY; Cambridge Univ. Simon & Schuster, publishers, 1955–68 (final positions, Editor-in-Chief and Vice-Pres.); Pres. and Editor-in-Chief, Alfred A. Knopf, publishers, 1968–87. Pres., Louis B. Mayes Foundn. *Recreations:* ballet, classic film, shopping.

GOUDIE, family name of **Baroness Goudie**.

GOUDIE, Baroness *cr* 1998 (Life Peer), of Roundwood in the London Borough of Brent; **Mary Teresa Goudie;** public affairs consultant, since 1995; *b* 2 Sept. 1946; *d* of Martin Brick and Hannah Brick (*née* Foley); *m* 1969, Thomas James Cooper Goudie, *qv*; two *s*. *Educ:* Our Lady of the Visitation; Our Lady of St Anselm. Asst Dir, Brent Peoples' Housing Assoc., 1977–80; Sec. and Organiser, Labour Solidarity Campaign, 1980–84; Director: The Hansard Soc., 1985–89; The House Magazine, 1989–90; Public Affairs Dir, WWF, 1990–95. *Publications:* various articles. *Recreations:* the Labour Party, family, gardening, travelling, art, food and wine, reading. *Address:* 53 Lancaster Grove, NW3 4HB. *T:* (020) 7435 6914. *Club:* Reform.

GOUDIE, Prof. Andrew Shaw; Professor of Geography, University of Oxford, since 1984; Fellow of Hertford College, Oxford, since 1976; *b* 21 Aug. 1945; *s* of late William and Mary Goudie; *m* 1987, Heather (*née* Viles); two *d*. *Educ:* Dean Close Sch., Cheltenham; Trinity Hall, Cambridge. BA, PhD Cantab; MA Oxon. Oxford University: Departmental Demonstrator, 1970–76; Univ. Lectr, 1976–84; Head, Dept of Geography, 1984–94; Pro-Vice-Chancellor, 1995–97; Head of Devolt Prog., 1995–97. Hon. Secretary: British Geomorphological Res. Gp. 1977–80 (Chm., 1988–89); RGS, 1981–88; Member: Council, Inst. of British Geographers, 1980–83; British Nat. Cttee for Geography, 1982–87. Dep. Leader: Internat. Karakoram Project, 1980; Kora Project, 1983. President: Geographical Assoc., 1993–94; Section E, BAAS, 1995–96. Cuthbert Peek award, RGS, 1975; Geographic Soc. of Chicago Publication award, 1982; Founder's Medal, RGS, 1991; Mungo Park Medal, RSGS, 1991. *Publications:* Duricrusts of Tropical and Sub-tropical Landscapes, 1973; Environmental Change, 1976, 3rd edn 1992; The

Warm Desert Environment, 1977; The Prehistory and Palaeogeography of the Great Indian Desert, 1978; Desert Geomorphology, 1980; The Human Impact, 1981, 5th edn 1999; Geomorphological Techniques, 1981, 3rd edn 1990; The Atlas of Swaziland, 1983; Chemical Sediments and Geomorphology, 1983; The Nature of the Environment, 1984, 4th edn 2001; (jtly) Discovering Landscape in England and Wales, 1985; The Encyclopædic Dictionary of Physical Geography, 1985, 3rd edn 2000; (jtly) Landshapes, 1989; The Geomorphology of England and Wales, 1990; Techniques for Desert Reclamation, 1990; Climate, 1997; contribs to learned jls. *Recreations:* bush life, old records, old books. *Address:* Hertford College, Oxford OX1 3BW. *T:* (01865) 271921. *Clubs:* Geographical; Gilbert (Oxford).
See also T. J. C. Goudie.

GOUDIE, Andrew William, PhD; Chief Economic Adviser, Scottish Executive (formerly Scottish Office), since 1999; *b* 3 March 1955; *s* of Britton Goudie and Joan Goudie; *m* 1978, Christine Lynne Hurley; two *s* two *d*. *Educ:* Queens' Coll., Cambridge (Wrenbury Schol.; BA Econs, MA; PhD 1992); Open Univ. (BA Maths and Stats). University of Cambridge: Research Officer, Dept of Applied Econs, 1978–85; Res. Fellow, Queens' Coll., 1981–83; Fellow and Dir of Studies, Robinson Coll., 1983–85; Sen. Economist, World Bank, Washington, 1985–90; Sen. Economic Advr, Scottish Office, 1990–95; Principal Economist, OECD Develt Centre, Paris, 1995–96; Chief Economist, DFID (formerly ODA), 1996–99. *Publications:* articles in learned jls, incl. Econ. Jl, Jl Royal Statistical Soc., Economica, Scottish Jl Political Economy. *Address:* Scottish Executive, St Andrew's House, Edinburgh EH1 3DG. *T:* (0131) 244 3430.

GOUDIE, James; *see* Goudie, T. J. C.

GOUDIE, Rev. John Carrick, CBE 1972; Assistant Minister at St John's United Reformed Church, Northwood, 1985–88, retired; *b* 25 Dec. 1919; *s* of late Rev. John Goudie, MA and late Mrs Janet Goudie, step *s* of late Mrs Evelyn Goudie; unmarried. *Educ:* Glasgow Academy; Glasgow Univ. (MA); Trinity Coll., Glasgow. Served in RN: Hostilities Only Ordinary Seaman and later Lieut RNVR, 1941–45; returned to Trinity Coll., Glasgow to complete studies for the Ministry, 1945; Asst Minister at Crown Court Church of Scotland, London and ordained, 1947–50; Minister, The Union Church, Greenock, 1950–53; entered RN as Chaplain, 1953; Principal Chaplain, Church of Scotland and Free Churches (Naval), 1970–73; on staff of St Columba's Church of Scotland, Pont Street, 1973–77; Minister of Christ Church URC, Wallington, 1977–80; on staff of Royal Scottish Corp., London, 1980–84. QHC 1970–73. *Recreations:* tennis, the theatre. *Address:* 309 Howard House, Dolphin Square, SW1V 3PF. *T:* (020) 7798 8537. *Club:* Army and Navy.

GOUDIE, (Thomas) James (Cooper); QC 1984; a Recorder, since 1986; a Deputy High Court Judge (Queen's Bench Division), since 1995; *b* 2 June 1942; *s* of late William Cooper Goudie and Mary Isobel Goudie; *m* 1969, Mary Teresa Brick (*see* Baroness Goudie); two *s*. *Educ:* Dean Close Sch.; London School of Economics (LLB Hons). FCIArb 1991. Solicitor, 1966–70; called to the Bar, Inner Temple, 1970 (Bencher, 1991). A Dep. Chm., Data Protection Tribunal (for nat. security appeals), 2000–. Chairman: Law Reform Cttee, Gen. Council of the Bar, 1995–96; Administrative Law Bar Assoc., 1994–96; Soc. of Labour Lawyers, 1994–99. Contested (Lab) Brent North, Feb. and Oct. 1974; Leader of Brent Council, 1977–78. *Publications:* (ed with M. Supperstone, and contrib.) Judicial Review, 1992, 2nd edn 1997; (ed with P. Elias, and contrib.) Butterworths Local Government Law, 1998; (ed jtly and contrib.) Local Authorities and the Human Rights Act 1998, 1999. *Address:* 11 King's Bench Walk, Temple, EC4Y 7EQ. *T:* (020) 7583 0610.
See also A. S. Goudie.

GOUGH, family name of **Viscount Gough.**

GOUGH, 5th Viscount *cr* 1849, of Goojerat, of the Punjaub, and Limerick; **Shane Hugh Maryon Gough;** Irish Guards, 1961–67; *b* 26 Aug. 1941; *o s* of 4th Viscount Gough and Margaretta Elizabeth (*d* 1977), *o d* of Sir Spencer Maryon-Wilson, 11th Bt; *S* father, 1951. *Educ:* Abberley Hall, Worcs; Winchester Coll. Mem. Queen's Bodyguard for Scotland, Royal Company of Archers. Member: Exec. Council, RNIB; Scottish Lifeboat Council, RNLI. FRGS. *Heir:* none. *Address:* Keppoch Estate Office, Strathpeffer, Ross-shire IV14 9AD. *T:* (01997) 421224; 17 Stanhope Gardens, SW7 5RQ. *Clubs:* Pratt's, White's, MCC.

GOUGH, Rear-Adm. Andrew Bankes, CB 2000; Deputy Chief Executive, Forces Group Ltd, since 2001; *b* 22 June 1947; *s* of late Gilbert Bankes Gough and of Pauline Gough; *m* 1971, Susanne Jensen, Copenhagen; two *s*. *Educ:* Bridgnorth Grammar Sch.; Britannia Royal Naval Coll. Joined RN, 1965; flying tours, 1970–76; i/c, HMS Bronington, 1976–78; 824 Naval Air Sqdn, 1978–80; i/c, 737 Naval Air Sqdn, 1980–81; SS Uganda, Falklands Task Force, 1982; HMS Glamorgan, 1982–84; JSDC, 1985; MoD, 1985–87; in command HM Ships: Broadsword, 1987–88; Beaver, 1988; Brave, 1988–89; RCDS, 1990; MoD, 1991–93; Dep. UK Mil. Rep. to NATO, 1993–96; Comdr, Standing Naval Force, Atlantic, 1996–97; ACOS (Policy/Requirements), Supreme HQ Allied Powers in Europe, 1997–2000. MNI, FIMgt. *Recreations:* military history, house restoration, Bordeaux wine. *Club:* Army and Navy.

GOUGH, (Charles) Brandon, FCA; Chairman, De La Rue plc, since 1997 (Director, since 1994); *b* 8 Oct. 1937; *s* of late Charles Richard Gough and Mary Evaline (*née* Goff); *m* 1961, Sarah Smith; one *s* two *d*. *Educ:* Douai Sch.; Jesus Coll., Cambridge (MA). FCA 1974. Joined Cooper Brothers & Co. subseq. Coopers & Lybrand, 1964, Partner 1968; Chm., 1983–94; Mem., Exec. Cttee, Coopers & Lybrand (Internat.), 1982–94 (Chm., 1985 and 1991–92); Chm., Coopers & Lybrand Europe, 1989, and 1992–94. Chm., Yorkshire Water, then Kelda Gp, 1996–2000; Govt Dir, BAe plc, 1987–88; Director: British Invisibles, 1990–94; S. G. Warburg Gp, 1994–95 (Dep. Chm., 1995); National Power, 1995–2000; George Wimpey, 1995–99; Montanaro UK Smaller Cos Investment Trust plc, 1998– (Chm., 1999–); Singer & Friedlander Gp, 1999–; Innogy Hldgs, 2000–; Partnership Council, Freshfields, 1996–2000. Mem. Council, Inst. of Chartered Accountants in England and Wales, 1981–84; Chm., CCAB Auditing Practices Cttee, 1981–84 (Mem., 1976–84); Member: Accounting Standards Review (Dearing) Cttee, 1987–88; Financial Reporting Council, 1990–96. City University Business School: Chm., City Adv. Panel, 1986–91 (Mem., 1980–91); Mem. Council, 1986–93 (Chm., 1992–93); Chm., Finance Cttee, 1988–91; Member: Council of Lloyd's, 1983–86; Cambridge Univ. Careers Service Syndicate, 1983–86; Governing Council, 1984–88, Council, 1988–94, President's Cttee, 1992–94, Business in the Community; Council for Industry and Higher Educn, 1985–93; Management Council, GB-Sasakawa Foundn, 1985–96; UK Nat. Cttee, Japan-European Community Assoc., 1989–94; CBI Task Force, Vocational Educn and Trng, 1989; CBI Educn & Trng Affairs Cttee, 1990–94; Council, Foundn for Educn Business Partnerships, 1990–91; Council, City Univ., 1991–93; Council, Prince of Wales Business Leaders Forum of Internat. Business in the Community, 1992–94. Chairman: Common Purpose Trust, 1991–97 (Trustee, 1989–97); Nat. Trng Task Force working gp on role of TECs in local econ. develt, 1991–92; Doctors' and Dentists' Pay Review Body, 1993–2001; HEFCE, 1993–97. Mem., Council of Management, Royal Shakespeare Theatre Trust, 1991–97; Trustee, GSMD Foundn, 1989–95. FRSA 1988. Hon. DSc City, 1994. Lloyd's Silver Medal, 1986. *Recreations:* music, gardening. *Address:* De La Rue plc, Jays Close, Basingstoke RG22 4BS.

GOUGH, Prof. Douglas Owen, PhD; FRS 1997; Professor of Theoretical Astrophysics, since 1993, and Director, Institute of Astronomy, since 1999, University of Cambridge; Fellow, Churchill College, Cambridge, since 1972; *b* 8 Feb. 1941; *s* of Owen Albert John Gough and Doris May Gough (*née* Camera); *m* 1965, Rosanne Penelope Shaw; two *s* two *d*. *Educ:* Hackney Downs Sch.; St John's Coll., Cambridge (BA 1962; MA 1966; PhD 1966). Res. Associate, Jt Inst. for Lab. Astrophysics, Univ. of Colo, 1966–67; Nat. Acad. of Scis Sen. Postdoctoral Resident Res. Associate, Inst. for Space Studies, NY, 1967–69; University of Cambridge: Mem., Grad. Staff, Inst. of Theoretical Astronomy, 1969–73; Lectr in Astronomy and Applied Maths, 1973–85; Reader in Astrophysics, 1985–93; Dep. Dir, Inst. of Astronomy, 1993–99. Astronome Titulaire Associé des Observatoires de France, 1977; SRC Sen. Fellow, 1978–83; Prof. Associé, Univ. of Toulouse, 1984–85; Hon. Prof. of Astronomy, QMW, Univ. of London, 1986–; Fellow Adjoint, Jt Inst. for Lab. Astrophysics, Boulder, Colo, 1986–; Scientific Co-ordinator, Inst. for Theoretical Physics, Univ. of Calif, Santa Barbara, 1990; Vis. Prof., Stanford Univ., 1996–. Lectures: James Arthur, Harvard, 1982; Sir Joseph Larmor, Cambridge Philosophical Soc., 1988; Wernher von Braun, Marshall Space Flight Center, 1991; Morris Loeb, Harvard, 1993; Halley, Oxford Univ., 1996; Bishop, Columbia Univ., 1996. FInstP 1997. For. Mem., Royal Danish Acad. of Scis and Letters, 1998. William Hopkins Prize, Cambridge Philosophical Soc., 1984; George Ellery Hale Prize, Amer. Astronomical Soc., 1994. *Publications:* mainly res. papers and reviews in scientific jls. *Recreations:* cooking, listening to music. *Address:* Institute of Astronomy, Madingley Road, Cambridge CB3 0HA. *T:* (01223) 337548.

GOUGH, Janet, MA; High Mistress, St Paul's Girls' School, 1993–98; *b* 1 Aug. 1940; *d* of Clifford Gough and Sarah (*née* Allen). *Educ:* Ludlow High Sch.; Newnham Coll., Cambridge (BA Hons, MA). St Paul's Girls' Sch., 1964–71; Manchester Grammar Sch., 1972; Worcester High Sch. for Girls, 1973; St Paul's Girls' Sch., 1973–98. Trustee, Multi A, 2000–. Governor: Dulwich Coll., 1999–; Ludlow Coll., 2001–. *Recreations:* book collecting, architecture, music. *Address:* 58 Corve Street, Ludlow, Shropshire SY8 1DU.

GOUGH, Piers William, CBE 1998; RIBA; architect; Partner, CZWG Architects, since 1975; *b* 24 April 1946; *s* of Peter Gough and Daphne Mary Unwin Banks; *m* 1991, Rosemary Elaine Fosbrooke Bates. *Educ:* Uppingham Sch., Rutland; Architectural Assoc. Sch. of Architecture. Principal works: Phillips West 2, Bayswater, 1976; Lutyens Exhibn, Hayward Gall., 1982; Cochrane Sq., Glasgow, 1987–; China Wharf, 1988, The Circle, 1990, Bermondsey; Craft, Design and Technol. Bldg, 1988, two boarding houses, 1994, Bryanston Sch.; Street-Porter House, 1988, 1–10 Summers St, 1994, Clerkenwell; Crown St Regeneration Proj., Gorbals, 1991–; Westbourne Grove Public Lavatories, 1993; Brindleyplace Café, Birmingham, 1994–97; Bankside Lofts, Southwark, 1994–99; 19th and 20th century galls, Nat. Portrait Gall., 1995–96; Soho Lofts, Wardour Street, 1995; Leonardo Centre, Uppingham Sch., 1995; The Glass Building, Camden, 1996–99; Suffolk Wharf, Camden Lock, 1996–; Green Bridge, Mile End Park, 1997–2000; Westferry Studios, Isle of Dogs, 1999–2000. Comr, English Heritage, 2000– (Mem., London Adv. Cttee, 1995–; Mem., Urban Panel, 1999–). Pres., AA, 1995–97 (Mem. Council, 1970–72, 1991–99; Trustee, 1999–). Mem., Cultural Strategy Gp, GLA, 2000–. Trustee: Chisenhale Gall., 1993–; Artangel, 1994–. Television: The Shock of the Old (series), Channel 4, 2000. FRSA 1992. DUniv Middlesex, 1999. *Publication:* English Extremists, 1988. *Recreation:* throwing parties. *Address:* CZWG Architects, 17 Bowling Green Lane, EC1R 0QB. *T:* (020) 7253 2523, *Fax:* (020) 7250 0594; *e-mail:* mail@czwgarchitects.co.uk. *Club:* Groucho.

GOULD, family name of **Baroness Gould of Potternewton.**

GOULD OF POTTERNEWTON, Baroness *cr* 1993 (Life Peer), of Leeds in the Metropolitan County of West Yorkshire; **Joyce Brenda Gould;** a Baroness in Waiting (Government Whip), 1997–98 and since 2001; *b* 29 Oct. 1932; *d* of Sydney and Fanny Manson; *m* 1952, Kevin Gould (separated); one *d*. *Educ:* Cowper Street Primary Sch.; Roundhay High Sch. for Girls; Bradford Technical Coll. Dispenser, 1952–65; Labour Party: Mem., 1951–; Asst Regional Organiser, 1969–75; Asst Nat. Agent and Chief Women's Officer, 1975–85; Dir of Organisation, 1985–93. Opposition spokesperson on women's affairs, 1995–97. Member: Council of Europe, 1993–96 (Ldr, Delegn to UN Conf. on Women, Beijing, 1995); WEU, 1993–96; CPA, 1998–; IPU, 1998–; Fellow, Parlt and Industry Trust. Mem., Ind. Commn on Voting Systems, 1998–. Sec., Nat. Jt Cttee of Working Women's Orgns, 1975–85; Vice-Pres., Socialist Internat. Women, 1978–86. President: BEA, 1998–; FPA, 1999–. *Publications:* (ed) Women and Health, 1979; pamphlets on feminism, socialism and sexism, women's right to work, and on violence in society; articles and reports on women's rights and welfare. *Recreations:* relaxing, sport as a spectator, theatre, cinema, reading. *Address:* 6 St John's Mews, Bristol Road, Brighton BN2 1BD; House of Lords, SW1A 0PW.

GOULD, Bryan Charles; Vice-Chancellor, Waikato University, New Zealand, since 1994; *b* 11 Feb. 1939; *s* of Charles Terence Gould and Elsie May Driller; *m* 1967, Gillian Anne Harrigan; one *s* one *d*. *Educ:* Auckland Univ. (BA, LLM); Balliol Coll., Oxford (MA, BCL). HM Diplomatic Service: FO, 1964–66; HM Embassy, Brussels, 1966–68; Fellow and Tutor in Law, Worcester Coll., Oxford, 1968–74. MP (Lab): Southampton Test, Oct. 1974–1979; Dagenham, 1983–94; an opposition spokesman on trade, 1983–86, on economy and party campaigns, 1986–87, on Trade and Industry, 1987–89, on the environment, 1989–92, on national heritage, 1992 (Mem. of Shadow Cabinet, 1986–92). Presenter/Reporter, TV Eye, Thames Television, 1979–83. *Publications:* Monetarism or Prosperity?, 1981; Socialism and Freedom, 1985; A Future for Socialism, 1989; Goodbye to All That (memoirs), 1995. *Recreations:* gardening, food, wine. *Address:* University of Waikato, Private Bag 3105, Hamilton, New Zealand.

GOULD, David John; Deputy Chief Executive, Defence Procurement Agency, since 2000; *b* 9 April 1949; *s* of James McIntosh Gould and Joan Vivienne Gould; *m* 1st, 1973; two *s* one *d*; 2nd, Christine Lake. *Educ:* West Buckland Sch., Barnstaple; Univ. of Sussex (Hons, French and European Studies). Joined MoD Naval Weapons Dept, 1973; Materiel Finance (Air), 1978; NATO Defence College, 1980; MoD (Air), 1981; UK Delegn to NATO, 1983; Asst Sec., Materiel Finance (Air), 1987; Head of Resources and Programmes (Air), 1990; Assistant Under-Secretary of State: (Supply and Orgn) (Air), 1992; Policy, 1993; seconded to Cabinet Office, 1993–95; Asst Under-Sec. of State, Fleet Support, 1995–99; Dir Gen., Finance and Business Plans, Defence Logistics Orgn, MoD, 1999–2000. Silver Jubilee Medal, 1977. *Recreations:* fitness, Rugby union, fly fishing, music, especially opera and lieder. *Address:* Defence Procurement Agency, MoD Abbey Wood, Bristol BS34 8JH. *T:* (0117) 913 0009; *e-mail:* dce@dpa.mod.uk.

GOULD, Donald (William), BSc (Physiol.), MRCS, DTM&H; writer and broadcaster on medical and scientific affairs; *b* 26 Jan. 1919; *s* of late Rev. Frank J. Gould; *m* 1st, 1940,

Edna Forsyth; three *s* four *d*; 2nd, 1969, Jennifer Goodfellow; one *s* one *d*. *Educ:* Mill Hill Sch.; St Thomas's Hosp. Med. Sch., London. Orthopædic House Surg., Botley's Park Hosp., 1942; Surg. Lieut, RNVR, 1942–46; Med. Off., Hong Kong Govt Med. Dept, 1946–48; Lectr in Physiol., University of Hong Kong, 1948–51, Sen. Lectr, 1951–57; King Edward VII Prof. of Physiol., University of Malaya (Singapore), 1957–60; Lectr in Physiol., St Bartholomew's Hosp. Med. Coll., London, 1960–61, Sen. Lectr, 1961–63; External Examr in Physiol., University of Durham (Newcastle), 1961–63; Dep. Ed., Medical News, 1963–65; Editor: World Medicine, 1965–66; New Scientist, 1966–69; Med. Correspondent, New Statesman, 1966–78. Chm., Med. Journalists' Assoc., 1967–71; Vice-Chm., Assoc. of British Science Writers, 1970–71. *Publications:* The Black & White Medicine Show, 1985; The Medical Mafia, 1987; Nurses, 1988; Examining Doctors, 1991; contributions to: Experimentation with Human Subjects, 1972; Ecology, the Shaping Enquiry, 1972; Better Social Services, 1973; scientific papers in physiological jls; numerous articles on medical politics, ethics and science in lay and professional press. *Recreations:* writing poems nobody will publish, listening, talking, and walking. *Address:* Taunton Cottage, Wroslyn Road, Freeland, Witney OX29 8AQ. *T:* (01993) 880280; *e-mail:* gouldilocks@amserve.net.

GOULD, Edward John Humphrey, MA; FRGS; Master, Marlborough College, since 1993; *b* Lewes, Sussex, 31 Oct. 1943; *s* of Roland and Ruth Gould; *m* 1970, Jennifer Jane, *d* of I. H. Lamb; two *d*. *Educ:* St Edward's Sch., Oxford; St Edmund Hall, Oxford (BA 1966, MA 1970, DipEd 1967). FRGS 1974. Harrow School, 1967–83: Asst Master, 1967–83; Head, Geography Dept, 1974–79; Housemaster, 1979–83; Headmaster, Felsted Sch., 1983–93. Mem., Indep. Schs Curriculum Cttee, 1985–92 (Chm., 1990–92); Chm., ISIS East, 1989–93; Mem. Council, and Policy Cttee (Chm., 2000), ISC, 2000–; Chm., HMC, 2002. FRSA 1993. JP Essex, 1989–93. *Recreations:* Rugby (Oxford Blue, 1963–66), swimming (Half Blue, 1965), rowing (rep. GB, 1967), music. *Address:* The Master's Lodge, Marlborough College, Wilts SN8 1PA. *Clubs:* East India, Devonshire, Sports and Public Schools; Vincent's (Oxford).

GOULD, Prof. Frank William; Vice-Chancellor, University of East London, 1992–2001 (Pro-Rector, North East London Polytechnic, 1988–92); *b* 12 Aug. 1937; *s* of Frank Gould and Bridget (*née* Tyler); *m* 1963, Lesley Hall; one *s* two *d*. *Educ:* University Coll. London (BA Hons); Univ. of NSW (MA). Tutor in Econs, Univ. of NSW, 1964–66; Econs Journalist, Beaverbrook Newspapers, 1966–67; Lectr in Econs, Kingston Poly., 1967–73; Principal Lectr in Econs and Dean of Faculty, Poly. of Central London, 1973–85; Asst Dir, Leeds Poly., 1985–88. Vice-Chm., Bd of Dirs, Open Learning Foundn, 1994–96; Chairman: Open Learning Foundn Enterprises, 1989–95; UEL Business Services (formerly E London Trng and Consultancy Co.), 1994–2001; Member: Bd, London East TEC, 1993–96; Bd, E London Partnership, 1997–; Adv. Council, Economic and Regl Analysis, 1997–. Dir, London Docklands Business Sch., 1994–2001. FRGS 1996. *Publications:* contribs to books and scientific jls in econs, pol sci. and social policy on govt and the economy and devolt of public expenditure. *Recreations:* horse-riding, mountain-walking, ski-ing. *Club:* Reform.

GOULD, Gail Ruth, (Mrs Philip Gould); *see* Rebuck, G. R.

GOULD, Patricia, CBE 1978; RRC 1972; Matron-in-Chief, Queen Alexandra's Royal Naval Nursing Service, 1976–80; *b* 27 May 1924; *d* of Arthur Wellesley Gould. *Educ:* Marist Convent, Paignton. Lewisham Gen. Hosp., SRN, 1945; Hackney Hosp., CMB Pt I, 1946; entered QARNNS, as Nursing Sister, 1948; accepted for permanent service, 1954; Matron, 1966; Principal Matron, 1970; Principal Matron Naval Hosps, 1975. QHNS 1976–80. OStJ (Comdr Sister), 1977. *Recreations:* gardening, photography.

GOULD, Peter John Walter; Chief Executive, Northamptonshire County Council, since 2000; Clerk to Lord-Lieutenant of Northamptonshire, since 2000; *b* 10 Feb. 1953; *s* of Morris Edwin Gould and Hilda Annette Gould; *m* 1977, June Lesley Sutton; one *s*. *Educ:* Yeovil Sch., Som; NE London Poly. (BScSoc, London Univ.). Res. Fellow, Sch. for Independent Study, NE London Poly., 1976; London Borough of Lambeth, 1977-98: Hd of Strategy, 1995; Dir of Personnel, 1996-98; Corporate Dir, Middlesborough Unitary Council, 1998-2000. *Recreations:* music, opera, flute, cooking, literature, social history. *Address:* Northamptonshire County Council, PO Box 93, County Hall, Northampton NN1 1AN. *T:* (01604) 236050.

GOULD, Philip; Founder, Philip Gould Associates, 1985; Partner, Gould Greenberg Carville Ltd, political strategy and polling, since 1997; *b* 30 March 1950; *s* of Wilfred Caleb Gould and Fennigien Anna Gould (*née* de-Jager); *m* 1985, Gail Ruth Rebuck, *qv*; two *d*. *Educ:* Knaphill Secondary Modern Sch., Woking; E London Coll.; Univ. of Sussex (BA Politics); LSE (MA with Dist. Hist. of Political Thought); London Business Sch. (Sloan Fellow (Dist.)). Account Dir, Wasey, Campbell-Ewald, 1975–79; Dir, Tinker and Partners, 1979–81; Founder, Brignull LeBas Gould, 1981–83; Mgt Dir, Doyle Dane Bernbach, 1984–85. *Publication:* The Unfinished Revolution, 1998. *Recreations:* friends, family, QPR, tennis, reading, travel. *Address:* Philip Gould Associates, Ludgate House, 245 Blackfriars Road, SE1 9UL. *T:* (020) 7890 9003.

GOULD, Robert; JP; DL; Member, Glasgow City Council, since 1995 (Leader, since 1995); *b* 8 Feb. 1935; *s* of James and Elizabeth Gould; *m* 1953, Helen Wire; two *s* two *d*. *Educ:* Albert Secondary Sch. Formerly with BR. Entered local government, 1970: Glasgow Corp., 1970–74; Mem., Strathclyde Regl Council, 1974–96 (Leader, 1992–96). JP Glasgow; DL Glasgow, 1997. *Recreations:* all sports (spectator), hill-walking. *Address:* Flat 6D, 15 Eccles Street, Springburn, Glasgow G22 6BJ. *T:* (0141) 558 9586.

GOULD, Prof. Stephen Jay, PhD; Professor of Geology, and Curator of Invertebrate Palaeontology, Museum of Comparative Geology, since 1973, and Alexander Agassiz Professor of Zoology, since 1982, Harvard University; *b* NYC, 10 Sept. 1941. *Educ:* Antioch Coll. (AB 1963); Columbia Univ. (PhD 1967). Instr in Geology, Antioch Coll., 1966; Harvard University: Asst Prof., 1967–71, Associate Prof., 1971–73, of Geology; Asst Curator, 1967–71, Associate Curator, 1971–73, of Invertebrate Palaeontology, Mus. of Comparative Zoology; Mem., Cttee of Profs, Dept of Biology, 1973–; Adjunct Mem., Dept of History of Sci., 1973–. Vincent Astor Vis. Res. Prof. of Biology, NY Univ., 1996–. Tanner Lectures, Cambridge Univ., 1984, Stanford Univ., 1989; Terry Lectures, Yale Univ., 1986; Lilly Lectr, RCP, 1993. Member: Space Exploration Council, NASA, 1989–91; Bd, British Mus. (Natural History) Internat. Foundn, 1992–; Commn on the Future, Smithsonian Instn, 1992–94; Bd of Trustees, Rockefeller Foundn, 1994–. President: Palaeontological Soc., 1985–86 (Golden Trilobite Award for excellence in palaeontological writing, 1992); Soc. for the Study of Evolution, 1990–91 (Vice Pres., 1975–76). Member: Nat. Acad. of Scis, 1989; Associé, Mus. Nat. d'Histoire Naturelle, Paris, 1989; FAAAS 1975 (Mem. Council, 1974–76); Fellow, Amer. Acad. of Arts and Scis, 1983; FRSE 1990. Mem., Bd of Editors, Science, 1986–91. Numerous hon. doctorates. Medal of Excellence, Columbia Univ., 1982; Silver Medal, Zoological Soc. of London, 1984; Distinguished Service Award, Amer. Geological Inst., 1986; Gold Medal for Service to Zoology, Linnean Soc. of London, 1992; UCLA Medal, 1992. *Publications* include: Ontogeny and Phylogeny, 1977; Ever since Darwin, 1977; The Panda's Thumb, 1980; The Mismeasure of Man, 1981 (Nat. Book Critics Circle Award, 1982); A View of Life, 1981; Hen's Teeth and Horse's Toes, 1983; The Flamingo's Smile, 1985; Illuminations: a bestiary, 1986; Time's Arrow, Time's Cycle, 1987; An Urchin in the Storm, 1987; Wonderful Life, 1989 (Rhône-Poulenc Prize, 1991); Bully for Brontosaurus, 1991; Eight Little Piggies, 1993; Dinosaur in a Haystack, 1995; Full House, 1995; Questioning the Millennium, 1997; Rocks of Ages, 1999; The Lying Stones of Marrakech, 2000. *Address:* Harvard University Museum of Comparative Zoology, Cambridge, MA 02138, USA.

GOULD, Thomas William, VC 1942; Lieutenant RNR retired; *b* 28 Dec. 1914; *s* of late Mrs C. E. Cheeseman and late Reuben Gould (killed in action, 1916); *m* 1941, Phyllis Eileen Eldridge (*d* 1985); one *s*. *Educ:* St James, Dover, Kent. Royal Navy, 1933–37; Submarines, 1937–45 (despatches); invalided Oct. 1945. Business Consultant, 1965–; company director. Pres., Internat. Submarine Assoc. of GB. *Address:* 6 Howland, Orton Goldhay, Peterborough, Cambs PE2 5QY. *T:* and *Fax:* (01733) 238918.

GOULD, Prof. Warwick Leslie; Professor of English Literature, University of London, since 1995; Director, Institute of English Studies, School of Advanced Study, University of London, since 1999; (Deputy Dean, School of Advanced Study, since 2000); *b* 7 April 1947; *s* of Leslie William Gould and Fedora Gould (*née* Green). *Educ:* Brisbane Grammar Sch.; Univ. of Queensland (BA 1st Cl. Hons English Language and Lit. 1969). Royal Holloway College, then Royal Holloway and Bedford New College, University of London: Lectr in English Language and Lit., 1973–86; Sen. Lectr, 1986–91; Reader in English Lit., 1991–95; British Acad. Res. Reader, 1992–94; Prof., 1995; Dep. Prog. Dir, 1994–97, Prog. Dir, 1997–99, Centre for English Studies, Sch. of Advanced Study, Univ. of London. University of London: Member: Senate, 1990–94; Academic Council, 1990–94; Academic Cttee, 1994–2000; Council, 1995–2000. FRSL 1997; FRSA 1998; FEA 1999. Cecil Oldman Meml Medal for Bibliography and Textual Criticism, Leeds Univ., 1993. Editor, Yeats Annual, 1983–. *Publications:* (jtly) Joachim of Fiore and the Myth of the Eternal Evangel, 1987; (ed jtly) The Secret Rose: stories by W. B. Yeats, 1981, 2nd edn 1992; (ed jtly) The Collected Letters of W. B. Yeats, Vol. II 1896–1990, 1997; (jtly) Gioacchino da Fiore e il mito dell'Evangelo eterno nella cultura europea, 2000. *Recreation:* book collecting. *Address:* Institute of English Studies, Room 308, Senate House, Malet Street, WC1E 7HU. *T:* (020) 7862 8673, *Fax:* (020) 7862 8672; *e-mail:* wgould@sas.ac.uk.

GOULDEN, Sir (Peter) John, GCMG 2001 (KCMG 1996; CMG 1989); HM Diplomatic Service, retired; Ambassador and UK Permanent Representative to North Atlantic Council and to Permanent Council of Western European Union, 1995–2001; *b* 21 Feb. 1941; *s* of George Herbert Goulden and Doris Goulden; *m* 1962, Diana Margaret Elizabeth Waite; one *s* one *d*. *Educ:* King Edward VII Sch., Sheffield; Queen's Coll., Oxford (BA 1st Cl. Hons History, 1962). FCO, 1962–2001: Ankara, 1963–67; Manila, 1969–70; Dublin, 1976–79; Head of Personnel Services Dept, 1980–82; Head of News Dept, FCO, 1982–84; Counsellor and Hd of Chancery, Office of the UK Permt Rep. to EEC, Brussels, 1984–87; Asst Under-Sec. of State, FCO, 1988–92; Ambassador to Turkey, 1992–95. *Recreations:* early music, bookbinding, opera, ski-ing.

GOULDER, Catharine Anne O.; *see* Otton-Goulder.

GOULDING, Jeremy Wynne Ruthven, MA; Headmaster, Shrewsbury School, since 2001; *b* 29 Aug. 1950; *s* of Denis Arthur and Doreen Daphne Goulding; *m* 1974, Isobel Mary Fisher; two *s* two *d*. *Educ:* Becket Sch., Nottingham; Magdalen Coll., Oxford (MA, PGCE). Asst Master and Head of Divinity, Abingdon Sch., 1974–78; Head of Divinity, 1978–83, and Housemaster, Oldham's Hall, 1983–89, Shrewsbury Sch.; Headmaster: Prior Park Coll., 1989–96; Haberdashers' Aske's Sch., 1996–2001. *Recreations:* music-making, hill-walking. *Address:* Headmaster's House, Shrewsbury School, Shropshire SY3 7BA. *T:* (01743) 280525.

GOULDING, Sir Lingard; *see* Goulding, Sir W. L. W.

GOULDING, Sir Marrack (Irvine), KCMG 1997 (CMG 1983); Warden of St Antony's College, Oxford, since 1997; *b* 2 Sept. 1936; *s* of Sir Irvine Goulding; *m* 1st, 1961, Susan Rhoda D'Albiac (marr. diss. 1996), *d* of Air Marshal Sir John D'Albiac, KCVO, KBE, CB, DSO, and of Lady D'Albiac; two *s* one *d*; 2nd, 1996, Catherine Pawlow, *d* of Alexandre Pawlow and Alla Sobkevitch de Vicens. *Educ:* St Paul's Sch.; Magdalen Coll., Oxford (1st cl. hons. Lit. Hum. 1959). Joined HM Foreign (later Diplomatic) Service, 1959; MECAS, 1959–61; Kuwait, 1961–64; Foreign Office, 1964–68; Tripoli (Libya), 1968–70; Cairo, 1970–72; Private Sec., Minister of State for Foreign and Commonwealth Affairs, 1972–75; seconded to Cabinet Office (CPRS), 1975–77; Counsellor, Lisbon, 1977–79; Counsellor and Head of Chancery, UK Mission to UN, NY, 1979–83; Ambassador to Angola, and concurrently to São Tomé e Principe, 1983–85; United Nations, New York: Under Sec.-Gen., Special Political Affairs, later Peace-Keeping Ops, 1986–93; Under Sec.-Gen., Political Affairs, 1993–97. *Recreations:* travel, birdwatching. *Address:* St Antony's College, Oxford OX2 6JF. *Club:* Royal Over-Seas League.

GOULDING, Paul Anthony; QC 2000; *b* 24 May 1960; second *s* of Byron and Audrey Goulding; *m* 1984, Rev. Canon June Osborne; one *s* one *d*. *Educ:* Latymer Sch.; St Edmund Hall, Oxford (BA 1st Cl. Jurisprudence 1981; BCL 1982; MA). Tutor in Law, St Edmund Hall, Oxford, 1982–84; called to the Bar, Middle Temple, 1984; practising barrister, 1985–. Chm., 1998–2000, Vice-Pres., 2000–, Employment Lawyers Assoc.; Mem., Mgt Cttee, Bar Pro Bono Unit, 2000–. *Publication:* European Employment Law and the UK, 2001. *Recreations:* football, Rugby, opera, ballet. *Address:* Blackstone Chambers, Blackstone House, Temple, EC4Y 9BW. *T:* (020) 7583 1770. *Clubs:* Reform; Tottenham Hotspur Members'.

GOULDING, Sir (William) Lingard (Walter), 4th Bt *cr* 1904; Headmaster of Headfort School, since 1977; *b* 11 July 1940; *s* of Sir (William) Basil Goulding, 3rd Bt, and of Valerie Hamilton (Senator, Seanad Éireann), *o d* of 1st Viscount Monckton of Brenchley, PC, GCVO, KCMG, MC, QC; *S* father, 1982. *Educ:* Ludgrove; Winchester College; Trinity College, Dublin (BA, HDipEd). Computer studies for Zinc Corporation and Sulphide Corporation, Conzinc Rio Tinto of Australia, 1963–66; Systems Analyst, Goulding Fertilisers Ltd, 1966–67; Manager and European Sales Officer for Rionore, modern Irish jewellery company, 1968–69; Racing Driver, formulae 5000, 3 and 2, 1967–71; Assistant Master: Brook House School, 1970–74; Headfort School (IAPS prep. school), 1974–76. *Recreations:* squash, cricket, running, bicycling, tennis, music, reading, computers. *Heir:* *b* Timothy Adam Goulding [*b* 15 May 1945; *m* 1971, Patricia Mohan]. *Address:* Headfort School, Kells, Co. Meath. *T:* Navan (46) 40065; Dargle Cottage, Enniskerry, Co. Wicklow. *T:* Dublin 862315.

GOULDSBROUGH, Catherine Mary; *see* Newman, C. M.

GOULSTONE, Very Rev. (Thomas Richard) Kerry; Dean of St Asaph Cathedral, 1993–2001; *b* 5 June 1936; *s* of Thomas Louis and Elizabeth Goulstone; *m* 1963, Lyneth Ann Harris; one *s* one *d*. *Educ:* Llanelli Boys' Grammar Sch.; St David's University Coll.,

Lampeter (BA); St Michael's Theol Coll., Llandaff. Deacon 1959, priest 1960, St David's; Curate: Llanbadarn Fawr, 1959–61; St Peter's, Carmarthen, 1961–64; Vicar: Whitchurch with Solva, 1964–67; Gorslas, 1967–76; Burry Port with Pwll, 1976–84; St Peter's, Carmarthen, 1984–93; Canon, St David's Cathedral, 1986–91; RD of Carmarthen, 1988–91; Archdeacon of Carmarthen, 1991–93. Chaplain, West Wales Hosp., 1984–93. *Recreations:* music, sport, collecting porcelain. *Address:* 80 Sandpiper Road, Sandy Water Park, Llanelli SA15 4SH. *T:* (01745) 583597.

GOULTY, Alan Fletcher, CMG 1998; HM Diplomatic Service; Director, Middle East and North Africa, Foreign and Commonwealth Office, since 2000; *b* 2 July 1947; *s* of Anthony Edmund Rivers Goulty and Maisie Oliphant Goulty (*née* Stein); *m* 1983, Lillian Craig Harris; one *s* by former marr. *Educ:* Bootham School, York; Corpus Christi College, Oxford (MA 1972). FCO 1968; MECAS, 1969–71; Beirut, 1971–72; Khartoum, 1972–75; FCO, 1975–77; Cabinet Office, 1977–80; Washington, 1981–85; FCO, 1985–90; Counsellor, 1987; Head of Near East and N Africa Dept, 1987–90; Dep. Head of Mission, Cairo, 1990–95; Ambassador to Sudan, 1995–99; Fellow, Weatherhead Center for Internat. Affairs, Harvard Univ., 1999–2000. Grand Cordon du Wissam Alaouite (Morocco), 1987. *Recreations:* real tennis, lawn tennis, chess, bird-watching. *Address:* Foreign and Commonwealth Office, SW1A 2AH. *Clubs:* Royal Over-Seas League, Pilgrims, MCC.

GOUNARIS, Elias; Ambassador; Permanent Representative of Greece to the United Nations, New York, since 1999; *b* 7 Sept. 1941; *s* of Panayotis and Christine Gounaris; *m* 1970, Irene Hadjilias. *Educ:* Univ. of Athens (LLM). Military Service, 1964–66; Attaché, Min. of Foreign Affairs, Athens, 1966–67; 3rd Sec., 1967; Consul, New York, 1969–73; Head, Section for Cyprus Affairs, Min. of Foreign Affairs, 1973–75; Sec., Perm. Mission of Greece to Internat. Orgns, Geneva, 1975–79; Counsellor, 1976; Dep. Chief of Mission, Belgrade, 1979–83; Head, American Desk, Min. of Foreign Affairs, 1983–87; Minister Counsellor, then Minister, Bonn, 1987–89; Minister Plenipotentiary, 1988; Ambassador to Moscow with parallel accreditation to Mongolia, 1989–93; Ambassador to UK, 1993–96; Dir Gen. for Pol Affairs, Min. of For. Affairs, Greece, 1996–99. Grand Cross: Order of the Phoenix (Greece); Order of the Lion (Finland), 1996; of Civil Merit (Spain); Commander: Order of Merit (Germany); Order of Merit (Italy), 1997; Grand Silver Badge of Honour with star (Austria). *Recreations:* jogging, classical music, reading, antique hunting. *Address:* 866 2nd Avenue, New York, NY 10017-2905, USA. *Clubs:* Brooks's; Athenean (Athens).

GOURLAY, Gen. Sir (Basil) Ian (Spencer), KCB 1973; CVO 1990; OBE 1956 (MBE 1948); MC 1944; Vice President, United World Colleges, since 1990 (Director General, 1975–90); *b* 13 Nov. 1920; *er s* of late Brig. K. I. Gourlay, DSO, OBE, MC; *m* 1948, Natasha Zinovieff; one *s* one *d*. *Educ:* Eastbourne Coll. Commissioned, RM, 1940; HMS Formidable, 1941–44; 43 Commando, 1944–45; 45 Commando, 1946–48; Instructor, RNC Greenwich, 1948–50; Adjt RMFVR, City of London, 1950–52; Instructor, RM Officers' Sch., 1952–54; psc 1954; Bde Major, 3rd Commando Bde, 1955–57 (despatches); OC RM Officers' Trng Wing, Infantry Training Centre RM, 1957–59; 2nd in Comd, 42 Commando, 1959–61; GSO1, HQ Plymouth Gp, 1961–63; CO 42 Commando, 1963–65; Col GS, Dept of CGRM, Min. of Defence, 1965–66; Col 1965; Comdr, 3rd Commando Bde, 1966–68; Maj.-Gen. Royal Marines, Portsmouth, 1968–71; Commandant-General, Royal Marines, 1971–75; Lt-Gen., 1971; Gen., 1973. Admiral, Texas Navy. Vice Patron, RM Museum. *Clubs:* Army and Navy, MCC; Royal Navy Cricket (Vice-Pres.).

GOURLAY, Gen. Sir Ian; *see* Gourlay, Gen. Sir B. I. S.

GOURLAY, Dame Janet; *see* Vaughan, Dame J.

GOURLAY, Robert Martin, (Robin); Chairman, Anglian Water plc, since 1994; *b* 21 April 1939; *s* of late Cleland Gourlay and Janice (*née* Martin); *m* 1971, Rosemary Puckle Cooper; one *s* two *d*. *Educ:* Sedbergh Sch.; St Andrews Univ. (MSc). Joined BP, 1958: Gen. Manager, BP of Greece, 1970–74; European Finance and Planning Co-ordinator, 1975–77; Asst Gen. Manager, Corporate Planning, 1978–79; Gen. Manager, Public Affairs, 1979–83; BP Australia: Dir, Refining and Marketing, 1983–86; Chief Exec., 1986–90; Chm., BP PNG, 1986–90; Dir, BP NZ, 1988–90; Chief Exec., BP Nutrition, 1990–94. Chm., Rugby Gp plc, 1994–2000 (non-exec. Dir, 1994–96); Director: Beazer Gp (formerly Beazer Homes) plc, 1995–2001; Astec (BSR) plc, 1996–99. Bd Mem., Australia Staff Coll., Mt Eliza, 1986–90; Chm., BITC, Victoria, 1988–90. Mem. Council, WaterAid, 1995–. *Recreations:* music, gardening, tennis. *Address:* c/o Anglian Water plc, Ambury Road, Huntingdon, Cambs PE29 3NZ. *T:* (01480) 323000, *Fax:* (01480) 323115.

GOURLAY, Sir Simon (Alexander), Kt 1989; President, National Farmers' Union, 1986–91; *b* 15 July 1934; *s* of David and Helga Gourlay; *m* 1st, 1956, Sally Garman; one *s*; 2nd, 1967, Caroline Mary Clegg; three *s*. *Educ:* Winchester; Royal Agricultural College. National Service, Commission 16th/5th Lancers, 1954–55. Farm manager, Cheshire, 1956–58; started farming on own account at Knighton, 1958; Man. Dir, Maryvale Farm Construction Ltd, 1977–85; Dir, Agricl Mortgage Corp., 1991–; Vice Chm., Hereford HA, 1996–2000. Chm., BFREM Ltd, 2000–; Dir, Britannica Fare Ltd, 2000–. Chm., Guild of Conservation Grade Producers, 1992–. Gov., Harper Adams Agricl Coll., 1992–99. *Recreations:* gardening, music, hill walking. *Address:* Hill House Farm, Knighton, Powys LD7 1NA. *T:* (01547) 528542.

GOVAN, Sir Lawrence (Herbert), Kt 1984; President, Lichfield (NZ) Ltd, since 1991 (Director, 1949–79; Deputy Chairman, 1979–91); *b* 13 Oct. 1919; *s* of Herbert Cyril Charles Govan and Janet Armour Govan (*née* Edmiston); *m* 1946, Clara Hiscock; one *s* three *d*. *Educ:* Christchurch Boys' High School. Started in garment industry with Lichfield (NZ) Ltd, 1935, Managing Director, 1950. Pres., NZ Textile and Garment Fedn, 1961–63, Life Mem., 1979. Pres., Canterbury Med. Res. Foundn, 1987–. *Recreations:* golf, swimming, horticulture. *Address:* 11 Hamilton Avenue, Fendalton, Christchurch 4, New Zealand. *T:* (3) 3519557. *Club:* Rotary (Christchurch) (Pres. 1963–64).

GOVENDIR, Ian John; marketing and fundraising consultant, Ian Govendir Marketing, since 1997; Marketing Manager, Jewish Care, since 2000; *b* 5 April 1960; *s* of Philip Govendir and Eve Karis Govendir (*née* Cohen). *Educ:* City of London Poly. (HND (Dist.) Business and Finance); Univ. of Lancaster (MA Mktg). Asst Product Manager, then Showroom Manager, Sony UK Ltd, 1979–83; Direct Marketing Manager, Bull Computers, 1988–92; Head of Direct Marketing/Fundraising, BRCS, 1992–94; Chief Exec., British Lung Foundn, 1994–96. Part-time Lectr in Marketing, London Guildhall Univ., 1992–. Sec., UK Coalition Trust, 1996–; Trustee, Jewish AIDS Trust, 1998–. FRSA 1996. MCIM 1990. *Recreations:* swimming, travel, cooking, gardening, preservation of national heritage, such as National Trust, architecture old and new, effect of religions on society, Middle Eastern politics. *Address:* Jewish Care, Stuart Young House, 221 Golders Green Road, NW11 9DG. *T:* (020) 8922 2762; *e-mail:* igovendirjcare@org.

GOVETT, William John Romaine; *b* 11 Aug. 1937; *s* of John Romaine Govett and Angela Mostyn (*née* Pritchard); *m* 1st, Mary Hays; two *s* one *d*; 2nd, Penelope Irwin; one *d*; 3rd, 1994, Jacqueline de Brabant. *Educ:* Sandroyd; Gordonstoun. National Service, commnd Royal Scots Greys, 1956–58. Joined John Govett & Co. Ltd, 1961; Chm., 1974–86; Dep. Chm., 1986–90. Director: Legal & General Gp, 1972–96; Govett Oriental Investment Trust, 1972–98; Govett Strategic Investment Trust, 1975–98; Scottish Eastern Investment Trust, 1977–98; Govett Amer. Smaller Cos Trust (formerly Govett Atlantic Investment Trust), 1979–98; Union Jack Oil Co., 1981–94; 3i (formerly Investors in Industry), 1984–98; Coal Investment Nominees NCB Pension Fund, 1985–96; Ranger Oil (UK), 1988–95; Govett High Income Investment Trust, 1993–; Ranger Oil (N Sea), 1995–97; Halifax Financial Services (Hldgs), 1998–; Halifax Life, 1998–; Halifax Unit Trust Mgt, 1998–; Halifax Fund Mgt, 1998–; Govett European Enhanced Investment Trust, 1999–. Chairman: Hungarian Investment Co., 1990–98; 3i Smaller Quoted Cos Trust, 1996–; Govett Mexican Horizons Investment Co. Ltd, 1991–96. Advr, Mineworkers' Pension Scheme, 1996–. Trustee: NACF, 1985–; Tate Gall., 1988–93. *Recreations:* modern art, fishing. *Address:* 33 Cork Street, W1S 3NQ.

GOW, Gen. Sir (James) Michael, GCB 1983 (KCB 1979); DL; Commandant, Royal College of Defence Studies, 1984–86; *b* 3 June 1924; *s* of late J. C. Gow and Mrs Alastair Sanderson; *m* 1946, Jane Emily Scott, *e d* of late Capt. and Hon. Mrs Mason Scott; one *s* four *d*. *Educ:* Winchester College. Enlisted Scots Guards, 1942; commnd 1943; served NW Europe, 1944–45; Mil. Div., Quadripartite Control Commn, Berlin, 1945–46; Malayan Emergency, 1949; Equerry to HRH the Duke of Gloucester, 1952–53; psc 1954; Bde Major 1955–57; Regimental Adjt Scots Guards, 1957–60; Instructor Army Staff Coll., 1962–64; comd 2nd Bn Scots Guards, Kenya and England, 1964–66; GSO1, HQ London District, 1966–67; comd 4th Guards Bde, 1968–69; idc 1970; BGS (Int) HQ BAOR and ACOS G2 HQ Northag, 1971–73; GOC 4th Div. BAOR, 1973–75; Dir of Army Training, 1975–78; GOC Scotland and Governor of Edinburgh Castle, 1979–80; C-in-C BAOR and Comdr, Northern Army Gp, 1980–83 (awarded die Plakette des deutschen Heeres); ADC Gen. to the Queen, 1981–84. Colonel Commandant: Intelligence Corps, 1973–86; Scottish Division, 1979–80. Mem., Queen's Body Guard for Scotland, Royal Company of Archers, 1964– (Ensign, 1986). UK Mem., Eurogroup US Tour, 1983. UK Kermit Roosevelt Lectr, USA, 1984. President: Royal British Legion, Scotland, 1986–96; Earl Haig Fund Scotland, 1986–96 (Vice Pres., 1996–); Nat. Assoc. of Supported Employment, 1993–; Officers' Assoc. Scotland, 1995–96 (Vice Pres., 1996–); Chairman: Scottish Ex-Services' Charitable Orgn, 1989–96; Scots at War Trust, 1992–; Patron, Disablement Income Group Scotland, 1993–. Vice-President: Royal Patriotic Fund Corp., 1983–88; Scottish Nat. Instn for War Blinded, 1995–. Chm., Queen Victoria Sch., Dunblane, 1979–80; Vice-President: Royal Caledonian Schs, Bushey, 1980–96; Royal Caledonian Schs Educnl Trust, 1996–2000. Chm., London Baroque, 1999–. County Comr, British Scouts W Europe, 1980–83 (Silver Acorn). Freeman: City of London, 1980; State of Kansas, USA, 1984; Freeman and Liveryman, Painters' and Stainers' Co., 1980. Elder of Church of Scotland, Canongate Kirk, 1988–. FSAScot 1991. DL Edinburgh, 1994. *Publications:* Trooping the Colour: a history of the Sovereign's Birthday Parade by the Household troops, 1989; Jottings in a General's Notebook, 1989; General Reflections: a military man at large, 1991; articles in mil. and hist. jls. *Recreations:* sailing, music, travel, reading. *Address:* 18 Ann Street, Edinburgh EH4 1PJ. *T:* (0131) 332 4752. *Clubs:* Pratt's, Highland Society of London; New (Edinburgh).

See also Lt-Col Sir W. H. M. Ross.

GOW, Dame Jane; *see* Whiteley, Dame J. E.

GOW, John Stobie, PhD; CChem, FRSC; FRSE 1978; Secretary-General, Royal Society of Chemistry, 1986–93; *b* 12 April 1933; *s* of David Gow and Anne Scott; *m* 1955, Elizabeth Henderson; three *s*. *Educ:* Alloa Acad.; Univ. of St Andrews (BSc, PhD). Res. Chemist, ICI, Billingham, 1958; Prodn Man., Chem. Co. of Malaysia, 1966–68; ICI: Res. Man., Agric. Div., 1968–72; Gen. Man. (Catalysts), Agric. Div., 1972–74; Res. Dir, Organics, 1974–79; Dep. Chm., Organics, 1979–84; Man. Dir, Speciality Chemicals, 1984–86. Assessor, SERC, 1988–94; Sec., CSTI, 1995–. FRSA 1980. *Publications:* papers and patents in Fertilizer Technology and Biotechnology. *Recreations:* choral music, Rugby. *Address:* 19 Longcroft Avenue, Harpenden, Herts AL5 2RD. *T:* (01582) 764889.

GOW, Gen. Sir Michael; *see* Gow, Gen. Sir J. M.

GOW, Neil; QC (Scot.) 1970; Sheriff of South Strathclyde, at Ayr, since 1976; *b* 24 April 1932; *s* of Donald Gow, oil merchant, Glasgow; *m* 1959, Joanna, *d* of Comdr S. D. Sutherland, Edinburgh; one *s*. *Educ:* Merchiston Castle Sch., Edinburgh; Glasgow and Edinburgh Univs. MA, LLB. Formerly Captain, Intelligence Corps (BAOR). Carnegie Scholar in History of Scots Law, 1956. Advocate, 1957–76. Standing Counsel to Min. of Social Security (Scot.), 1964–70. Contested (C): Kirkcaldy Burghs, Gen. Elections of 1964 and 1966; Edinburgh East, 1970; Mem. Regional Council, Scottish Conservative Assoc. An Hon. Sheriff of Lanarkshire, 1971. Pres., Auchinleck Boswell Soc. FSA (Scot.). *Publications:* A History of Scottish Statutes, 1959; Jt Editor, An Outline of Estate Duty in Scotland, 1970; A History of Belmont House School, 1979; numerous articles and broadcasts on legal topics and Scottish affairs. *Recreations:* golf, books, antiquities. *Address:* Old Auchenfail Hall, by Mauchline, Ayrshire KA5 5TA. *T:* (01290) 550822. *Clubs:* Western (Glasgow); Prestwick Golf.

GOW, Dame Wendy; *see* Hiller, Dame Wendy.

GOWAN, David John; HM Diplomatic Service; Minister, Moscow, since 2000; *b* 11 Feb. 1949; *s* of Prof. Ivor Lyn Gowan and Gwendoline Alice Gowan (*née* Pearce); *m* 1975, Marna Irene Williams; two *s*. *Educ:* Nottingham High Sch.; Ardwyn Grammar Sch., Aberystwyth; Balliol Coll., Oxford (MA Eng. Lang. and Lit.). Asst Principal, MoD, 1970–73; Home CS, 1973–75; joined HM Diplomatic Service, 1975: Second Sec., FCO, 1975–76; Russian lang. trng, 1976–77; Second, then First Sec., Moscow, 1977–80; First Sec., FCO, 1981–85; Hd of Chancery and Consul, Brasilia, 1985–88; on secondment to Cabinet Office, 1988–89; Asst Hd, Soviet Dept, FCO, 1989–90; on secondment, as Counsellor, Cabinet Office, 1990–91; Counsellor (Commercial and Know How Fund), Moscow, 1992–95; Counsellor and Dep. Hd of Mission, Helsinki, 1995–99; Counsellor, FCO, 1999; Sen. Associate Mem., St Antony's College, Oxford, 1999–2000. *Recreations:* reading, walking, travel, music, theatre. *Address:* c/o Foreign and Commonwealth Office, King Charles Street, SW1A 2AH.

GOWANS, Sir James (Learmonth), Kt 1982; CBE 1971; FRCP 1975; FRS 1963; Secretary General, Human Frontier Science Programme, Strasbourg, 1989–93; Secretary, Medical Research Council, 1977–87; *b* 7 May 1924; *s* of John Gowans and Selma Josefina Ljung; *m* 1956, Moyra Leatham; one *s* two *d*. *Educ:* Trinity Sch., Croydon; King's Coll. Hosp. Med. Sch. (MB BS (Hons) 1947; Fellow, 1979); Lincoln Coll., Oxford (BA (1st cl. Hons Physiology) 1948; MA; DPhil 1953; Hon. Fellow, 1984). MRC Exchange Scholar, Pasteur Institute, Paris, 1952–53; Research Fellow, Exeter Coll., Oxford, 1955–60 (Hon. Fellow, 1983–); Fellow, St Catherine's Coll., Oxford, 1961–87 (Hon. Fellow, 1987); Henry Dale Res. Prof. of Royal Society, 1962–77; Hon. Dir, MRC Cellular Immunology

Unit, 1963–77; Dir, 1980–86, Sen. Sci. Advr, 1988–90, Celltech Ltd. Consultant, WHO Global Prog. on AIDS, 1987–88. Member: MRC, 1965–69; Adv. Bd for Res. Councils, 1977–87; Director: Charing Cross Sunley Res. Centre, 1989–91; European Initiative for Communicators of Science, Munich, 1995–99. Royal Society: Mem. Council and a Vice-Pres., 1973–75; Assessor to MRC, 1973–75. Member: Council, St Christopher's Hospice, 1987–98; Res. Progs Adv. Cttee, Nat. MS Soc., NY, 1988–90; Awards Assembly, Gen. Motors Cancer Res. Foundn, NY, 1988–90; Chm., Scientific Adv. Cttee, Lister Inst. of Preventive Medicine, 1994–97. Non-exec. Dir, Tavistock and Portman NHS Trust, 1994–97. Delegate, OUP, 1971–77. FRSA 1994. Founder FMedSci 1998. Vis. Prof., NY Univ. Sch. of Med., 1967; Lectures: Harvey, NY, 1968; Dunham, Harvard, 1971; Bayne-Jones, Johns Hopkins, 1973; Harveian Orator, RCP, 1987. Foreign Associate, Nat. Acad. of Scis, USA, 1985. Mem., Academia Europaea, 1991. Hon. Member: Amer. Assoc. of Immunologists; Amer. Soc. of Anatomists. Hon. ScD Yale, 1966; Hon. DSc: Chicago, 1971; Birmingham, 1978; Rochester, 1987; Hon. MD: Edinburgh, 1979; Sheffield, 2000; Hon. DM Southampton, 1987; Hon. LLD Glasgow, 1988. Gairdner Foundn Award, Toronto, 1968; Paul Ehrlich Ludwig-Darmstaedter Prize, Frankfurt, 1974; Royal Medal, Royal Society, 1976; Feldberg Foundn Award, 1979; Wolf Prize in Medicine, Wolf Foundn, Israel, 1980; Medawar Prize, 1990; Galen Medal, Soc. of Apothecaries, 1991. *Publications:* articles in scientific journals. *Address:* 75 Cumnor Hill, Oxford OX2 9HX. *T:* (01865) 862304. *Club:* Garrick.

GOWANS, James Palmer; JP; DL; Lord Provost of Dundee and Lord-Lieutenant of the City of Dundee, 1980–84; *b* 15 Sept. 1930; *s* of Charles Gowans and Sarah Gowans (*née* Palmer); *m* 1950, Davina Barnett (*d* 2000); one *s* three *d* (and one *s* one *d* decd). *Educ:* Rockwell Secondary School, Dundee. With National Cash Register Co., Dundee, 1956–94. Elected to Dundee DC, May 1974; Mem., Dundee City Council, 1975–92. JP 1977; DL Dundee 1984. *Recreations:* golf, motoring. *Address:* 41 Dalmahoy Drive, Dundee DD2 3UT. *T:* (01382) 84918.

GOWANS, Gen. John; General of The Salvation Army, 1999–Nov. 2002; *b* 13 Nov. 1934; *s* of John and Elizabeth Gowans; *m* 1957, Gisèle Marie Bonhotal; two *s*. *Educ:* Halesowen Grammar Sch.; William Booth Coll. Served with Salvation Army, 1955–; commnd officer, in Liverpool, N Wales, London, Manchester, Yorkshire, Nottingham, 1955–77; Chief Sec., Paris, 1977–81; Leader for Southern California, LA, 1981–86; Territorial Commander in: France, 1986–93; Australia E and PNG, 1993–97; UK and Republic of Ireland, 1997–99. Freeman, City of London, 2000. *Publications:* O Lord!, 1977, 3rd edn 1996; libretto for ten Salvation Army musicals. *Recreations:* reading, gardening, English literature, drama. *Address:* The Salvation Army, 101 Queen Victoria Street, EC4P 4EP. *T:* (020) 7332 0101.

GOWAR, Prof. Norman William; Principal, Royal Holloway (Royal Holloway and Bedford New College), University of London, 1990–2000; *b* 7 Dec. 1940; *s* of Harold James and Constance Dawson-Gowar; *m* 1st, 1963, Diane May Parker (marr. diss.); one *s* one *d*; 2nd, 1981, Prof. Judith Margaret Greene, *d* of Lord Gordon-Walker, PC, CH. *Educ:* Sir George Monoux Grammar Sch.; City Univ. (BSc, MPhil). FIMA. English Electric Co., 1963; Lectr in Maths, City Univ., 1963; Open University: Lectr and Sen. Lectr, 1969; Prof. of Mathematics, 1983; Dir, Centre for Maths Educn, 1983; Pro-Vice Chancellor, 1977–81; Dep. Vice-Chancellor, 1985–90; Dir, Open Coll., 1986. Vis. Fellow, Keble Coll., Oxford, 1972. Member, Council: CNAA, 1979–83; NCET, 1986–91 (Chm., Trng Cttee); CVCP, 1998–2000; Mem., Fulbright Commn, 2001–. Chm. and Dir, Open Univ. Educational Enterprises Ltd, 1988–90. Dir, Surrey TEC, 1991–93. Mem., London Math. Soc. Governor: South Bank Univ. (formerly Polytechnic), 1992–95; UCS, 1993–2000; Rugby Sch., 1994–; Middlesex Univ., 2001–. Mem. Council, IMA, 1993–96. FRSA. Hon. DSc City, 1994; DUniv Open, 2001. *Publications:* Mathematics for Technology: a new approach, 1968; Basic Mathematical Structures, vol. 1, 1973, vol. 2, 1974; Fourier Series, 1974; Invitation to Mathematics, 1980; articles and TV series. *Address:* 3 Canonbury Lane, N1 2AS.

GOWDY, David Clive, CB 2001; Permanent Secretary, Department of Health, Social Services and Public Safety, Northern Ireland, since 1997; *b* 27 Nov. 1946; *s* of Samuel David Gowdy and Eileen Gowdy (*née* Porter); *m* 1973, Linda Doreen Traub; two *d*. *Educ:* Royal Belfast Academical Instn; Queen's Univ. Belfast (BA, MSc). Min. of Finance, NI, 1970; N Ireland Office, 1976; Exec. Dir, Industrial Develt Bd for NI 1985; Under Sec., Dept of Econ. Develt, NI, 1987; Under Sec, Dept of Health and Social Services, NI, 1990; Dir of Personnel, NICS, 1994. *Recreations:* music, reading, theatre, tennis. *Address:* Department of Health, Social Services and Public Safety, Castle Buildings, Stormont, Belfast BT4 3PP.

GOWENLOCK, Prof. Brian Glover, CBE 1986; PhD, DSc; FRSE; FRSC; Hon. Research Fellow, University of Exeter, since 1992; Professor of Chemistry, 1966–90, Leverhulme Emeritus Fellow, 1990–92, Heriot-Watt University; *b* 9 Feb. 1926; *s* of Harry Hadfield Gowenlock and Hilda (*née* Glover); *m* 1953, Margaret L. Davies; one *s* two *d*. *Educ:* Hulme Grammar Sch., Oldham; Univ. of Manchester (BSc, MSc, PhD). DSc Birmingham. FRIC 1966; FRSE 1969. Asst Lectr in Chemistry 1948, Lectr 1951, University Coll. of Swansea; Lectr 1955, Sen. Lectr 1964, Univ. of Birmingham; Dean, Faculty of Science, Heriot-Watt Univ., 1969–72, 1987–90. Vis. Scientist, National Res. Council, Ottawa, 1963; Erskine Vis. Fellow, Univ. of Canterbury, NZ, 1976. Mem., UGC, 1976–85, Vice-Chm., 1983–85. *Publications:* (with Sir Harry Melville) Experimental Methods in Gas Reactions, 1964; (with James C. Blackie) First Year at the University, 1964; (with Alex Anderson) Chemistry in Heriot-Watt 1821–1991, 1998; contribs to scientific jls. *Recreations:* genealogy, foreign travel. *Address:* Riccarton, 5 Roselands, Sidmouth, Devon EX10 8PB. *T:* (01395) 516864.

GOWER; *see* Leveson Gower.

GOWER, David Ivon, OBE 1992; broadcaster and journalist; *b* 1 April 1957; *s* of Richard Hallam Gower and Sylvia Mary Gower (*née* Ford); *m* 1992, Thorunn Ruth Nash; two *d*. *Educ:* King's Sch., Canterbury; UCL. Professional cricketer, 1975–93; Leicestershire, 1975–89; Hampshire, 1990–93; 117 Test matches for England, 1978–92; 8,231 Test runs (2nd highest for England), incl. 18 centuries; captained England 32 times, 1984–86, 1989; retired from 1st class cricket, Nov. 1993. PR consultant (cricket sponsorship), Nat. Westminster Bank, 1993–2000. BBC Cricket Commentator, 1994–99; Presenter: Gower's Cricket Monthly, BBC TV, 1995–98; David Gower's Cricket Weekly, BBC Radio 5, 1995–98; Internat. Cricket, Sky Sports, 1999–; panel mem., They Think It's All Over, BBC TV, 1996–. Hon. MA: Southampton Inst. (Nottingham Trent Univ.), 1993; Loughborough, 1994. *Publications:* With Time to Spare, 1979; Heroes and Contemporaries, 1983; A Right Ambition, 1986; On the Rack, 1990; Gower, The Autobiography, 1992. *Recreations:* ski-ing, safari, Cresta Run, tennis. *Address:* c/o SFX, 35/36 Grosvenor Street, W1K 4QX. *Clubs:* East India, MCC (Mem. Cttee 2000–); St Moritz Tobogganing.

GOWER, His Honour John Hugh; QC 1967; a Circuit Judge, 1972–96; a Deputy Circuit Judge, 1996–99; *b* 6 Nov. 1925; *s* of Henry John Gower, JP and Edith (*née* Brooks); *m* 1960, Shirley Mameena Darbourne; one *s* one *d*. *Educ:* Skinners' Sch., Tunbridge Wells. RASC, 1945–48 (Staff Sgt). Called to the Bar, Inner Temple, 1948, Bencher, 1995; Dep. Chm., Kent QS, 1968–71; Resident and Liaison Judge of Crown Courts in E Sussex, 1986–96. Mem., Lord Chancellor's Adv. Cttee on Legal Educn and Conduct, 1991–96 (Vice-Chm., 1994–96). Chm., Kent and Sussex Area Criminal Justice Liaison Cttee, 1992–96; Pres., E Sussex Magistrates' Assoc., 1997–99 (Vice-Pres., 1986–97). Indep. Assessor, UK Govt Review of NI Criminal Justice System, 1998–2000. Pres., Tunbridge Wells Council of Voluntary Service, 1974–88. Hon. Vice-Pres., Kent Council of Voluntary Service, 1971–86. Chm., Southdown and Eridge Hunt, 1985–91. Freeman, City of London (by purchase), 1960. *Recreations:* fishing, riding, gardening, tapestry. *Address:* The Coppice, Lye Green, Crowborough, E Sussex TN6 1UY.

GOWER ISAAC, Anthony John; *see* Isaac.

GOWERS, Andrew; Editor, Financial Times, since 2001; *b* 19 Oct. 1957; *s* of Michael and Anne Gowers; *m* 1982, Finola Clarke; one *s* one *d*. *Educ:* Trinity Sch., Croydon; Gonville and Caius Coll., Cambridge (MA 1980). Reuters, London, Brussels and Zurich, 1980–83; Financial Times, 1983–: on foreign staff, 1983–84; Agric. Corresp., 1984–85; Commodities Ed., 1985–87; ME Ed., 1987–90; Features Ed., 1990–92; Foreign Ed., 1992–94; Dep. Ed., 1994–97; Actg Ed., 1997–98; Ed.-in-Chief, FT Deutschland, 1998–2001. *Publication:* Arafat: the biography, 1990. *Recreations:* food, wine, tennis, film, music. *Address:* Financial Times, 1 Southwark Bridge, SE1 9HL. *T:* (020) 7873 3000.

GOWERS, Prof. (William) Timothy, PhD; FRS 1999; Rouse Ball Professor of Mathematics, University of Cambridge, since 1998; Fellow of Trinity College, Cambridge, since 1995; *b* 20 Nov. 1963; *s* of William Patrick Gowers and Caroline Molesworth Gowers; *m* 1988, Emily Joanna, *d* of Sir Keith (Vivian) Thomas, *qv*; two *s* one *d*. *Educ:* Eton Coll.; Trinity Coll., Cambridge (BA; PhD 1990). Res. Fellow, Trinity Coll., Cambridge, 1989–93; Lectr, 1991–94, Reader, 1994–95, UCL; Lectr, Univ. of Cambridge, 1995–98. Hon. Fellow, UCL, 1999. European Mathematical Soc. Prize, 1996; Fields Medal, 1998. *Publications:* contrib. papers in mathematical jls. *Recreation:* jazz piano. *Address:* Department of Pure Mathematics and Mathematical Statistics, Centre for Mathematical Sciences, Wilberforce Road, Cambridge CB3 0WB. *T:* (01223) 337999.

GOWING, Nicholas Keith, (Nik); Presenter: BBC World TV, BBC News, since 1996; BBC News 24, since 1997; *b* 13 Jan. 1951; *s* of Donald James Graham Gowing and Margaret Mary Gowing (*née* Elliott); *m* 1982, Judith Wastall Venables; one *s* one *d*. *Educ:* Latymer Upper Sch.; Simon Langton Grammar Sch., Canterbury; Bristol Univ. Reporter, Evening Chronicle, Newcastle upon Tyne, 1973–74; Presenter and Reporter, Granada TV, 1974–78; joined ITN, 1978; Rome Corresp., 1979; Eastern Europe Corresp., Warsaw, 1980–83; Foreign Affairs Corresp., 1983–87, Diplomatic Corresp., 1987–89, Diplomatic Editor, 1989–96, Channel 4 News. Fellow, Shorenstein Center, J. F. Kennedy Sch., Harvard Univ., 1994; Vis. Fellow, Keele Univ., 1998–. Consultant: Carnegie Commn on Preventing Deadly Conflict, 1996–97; on Wars and Information Mgt, EC Humanitarian Office, 1997–98. Vice Chair and Gov., Westminster Foundn for Democracy, 1996–; Governor: British Assoc. for Central and Eastern Europe, 1996–; Ditchley Foundn, 2000–; Member: IISS 1990; Council, 1998–, Exec. Council, 2000–, RIIA; Academic Council, Wilton Park, 1998–; Adv. Bd, Birmingham Univ. Centre for Studies in Security and Diplomacy, 1999–; Cttee, Project on Justice in Times of Transition, 1999–; Cttee, Rory Peck Trust, 1996–. *Publications:* The Wire, 1988; The Loop, 1993. *Recreations:* cycling, ski-ing, authorship, lecturing, chairing conferences. *Address:* BBC TV Centre, W12 7RJ. *T:* (020) 8225 8137; *e-mail:* nik.gowing@bbc.co.uk.

GOWING, Prof. Noel Frank Collett; Emeritus Professor of Pathology, University of London; Consultant Pathologist and Director of the Department of Histopathology, The Royal Marsden Hospital, SW3, 1957–82; Professor of Tumour Pathology (formerly Senior Lecturer), Institute of Cancer Research: The Royal Cancer Hospital, 1971–82; *b* 3 Jan. 1917; *s* of Edward Charles Gowing and Annie Elizabeth Gowing; *m* 1942, Rela Griffel; one *d*. *Educ:* Ardingly Coll., Sussex; London Univ. MRCS, LRCP 1941; MB, BS, London, 1947; MD London, 1948. Served RAMC (Capt.), 1942–46, 52nd (Lowland) Div. Lectr in Pathology, St George's Hosp. Med. Sch., 1947–52; Sen. Lectr in Pathology and Hon. Cons. Pathologist, St George's Hosp., 1952–57. Vis. Pathologist, St Vincent's Hosp., Worcester, Mass and Vis. Prof. of Pathology, Univ. of Mass, 1979. Sometime Examiner in Pathology to: Univ. of London; RCPath; Univ. of Newcastle-upon-Tyne; Univ. of Malta; Nat. Univ. of Malaysia. Lectures: Kettle Meml, RCPath, 1968; Whittick Meml, Saskatchewan Cancer Soc., 1974; Symeonidis Meml, Thessaloniki Cancer Inst., Greece, 1977. Pres., Assoc. of Clinical Pathologists, 1982–83. FRCPath (Founder Fellow, Coll. of Pathologists, 1964). *Publications:* A Colour Atlas of Tumour Histopathology, 1980; articles on pathology in medical journals. *Recreations:* gardening, astronomy.

GOWON, Gen. Dr Yakubu, PhD; jssc, psc; Chairman: National Oil and Chemical Marketing Co., Lagos, since 1996; Base Development (Nigeria) Ltd (formerly Kanawa Industries (Nigeria) Ltd), Kano, since 1987; *b* Garam, Pankshin Div., Plateau State, Nigeria, 19 Oct. 1934; *s* of Yohanna Gowon (an Angas, a Christian evangelist of CMS) and Saraya Gowon; *m* 1969, Victoria Hansatu Zakari; one *s* two *d*. *Educ:* St Bartholomew's Schs (CMS), Wusasa, and Govt Coll., Zaria, Nigeria; Warwick Univ. (BA Hons 1978; PhD). Regular Officer's Special Trng Sch., Teshie, Ghana; Eaton Hall Officer Cadet Sch., Chester, RMA, Sandhurst, Staff Coll., Camberley and Joint Services Staff Coll., Latimer (all in England). Enlisted, 1954; commissioned, 1956; served in Cameroon, 1960; Adjt, 4th Bn Nigerian Army, 1960 (Independence Oct. 1960); UN Peace-Keeping Forces, Congo, Nov. 1960–June 1961 and Jan.-June 1963 (Bde Major). Lt-Col and Adjt-Gen., Nigerian Army, 1963; Comd, 2nd Bn, Nigerian Army, Ikeja, 1966; Chief of Staff, 1966; Head of Fed. Mil. Govt, and C-in-C, Armed Forces of Fed. Republic of Nigeria, July 1966–1975; Maj.-Gen. 1967; maintained territorial integrity of his country by fighting, 1967–70, to preserve unity of Nigeria (after failure of peaceful measures) following on Ojukwu rebellion, and declared secession of the Eastern region of Nigeria, July 1967; created 12 equal and autonomous states in Nigeria, 1967; Biafran surrender, 1970; promoted Gen., 1971. Chm. Trustees, Commonwealth Human Ecology Foundn, 1986–. Is a Christian; works for internat. peace and security within the framework of OAU and UNO; Chm., Nigeria Prays. Vis. Prof., Jos Univ., 1987–. Hon. LLD Cambridge, 1975; also hon. doctorates from Univs of Ibadan, Lagos, ABU-Zaria, Nigeria at Nsukka, Benin, Ife, and Shaw Univ., USA, 1973. Holds Grand Cross, etc, of several foreign orders. *Publication:* Faith in Unity, 1970. *Recreations:* squash, lawn tennis, pen-drawing, photography, cinephotography. *Address:* National Oil and Chemical Marketing Co., 38–39 Marina, PMB 2052, Lagos, Nigeria. *Clubs:* Army and Navy, Les Ambassadeurs.

GOWRIE, 2nd Earl of, *cr* 1945; **Alexander Patrick Greysteil Hore-Ruthven;** PC 1984; Baron Ruthven of Gowrie, 1919; Baron Gowrie, 1935; Viscount Ruthven of Canberra, 1945; Director, Sotheby's Holdings Inc., 1985–98 (Chairman, Sotheby's Europe, 1987–94; Chairman, Sotheby's International, 1985–86); *b* 26 Nov. 1939; *er s* of late Capt. Hon. Alexander Hardinge Patrick Hore-Ruthven, Rifle Bde, and Pamela Margaret (as Viscountess Ruthven of Canberra, she *m* 1952, Major Derek Cooper, MC, The Life Guards), 2nd *d* of late Rev. A. H. Fletcher; *S* grandfather, 1955; *m* 1st, 1962,

Xandra (marr. diss. 1973), *yr d* of Col R. A. G. Bingley, CVO, DSO, OBE; one *s*; 2nd, 1974, Adelheid Gräfin von der Schulenburg, *y d* of late Fritz-Dietlof, Graf von der Schulenburg. *Educ:* Eton; Balliol Coll., Oxford. Visiting Lectr, State Univ. of New York at Buffalo, 1963–64; Tutor, Harvard Univ., 1965–68; Lectr in English and American Literature, UCL, 1969–72. Fine Art consultant, 1974–79. Provost, RCA, 1986–95. Chm., Arts Council of England, 1994–98. Chairman: The Really Useful Gp, 1985–90; Development Securities, 1995–99. A Conservative Whip, 1971–72; Parly Rep. to UN, 1971; a Lord in Waiting (Govt Whip), 1972–74; Opposition Spokesman on Economic Affairs, 1974–79; Minister of State: Dept of Employment, 1979–81; NI Office, 1981–83 (Dep. to Sec. of State); Privy Council Office (Management and Personnel), 1983–84; Minister for the Arts, 1983–85; Chancellor, Duchy of Lancaster, 1984–85. Freeman, City of London, 1976. *Publications:* A Postcard from Don Giovanni, 1972; (jt) The Genius of British Painting, 1975; (jt) The Conservative Opportunity, 1976; Derek Hill: an appreciation, 1987. *Recreation:* book reviewing. *Heir: s* Viscount Ruthven of Canberra, *qv*. *Address:* Development Securities, Portland House, Stag Place, SW1E 5DS. *T:* (020) 7828 4777.

GOY, David John Lister; QC 1991; *b* 11 May 1949; *s* of Rev. Leslie Goy and Joan Goy; *m* 1970; Jennifer Anne Symington; three *s*. *Educ:* Haberdashers' Aske's School, Elstree; King's College London. Called to the Bar, Middle Temple, 1973. *Publication:* VAT on Property, 1989, 2nd edn 1993. *Recreations:* running and other sports. *Address:* Gray's Inn Chambers, Gray's Inn, WC1R 5JA. *T:* (020) 7242 2642.

GOYDER, Daniel George, CBE 1996; solicitor; Consultant: Birketts, Ipswich, since 1983 (Partner, 1968–83); Linklaters & Alliance (formerly Linklaters & Paines), since 1997; *b* 26 Aug. 1938; *s* of George Armin Goyder, CBE; *m* 1962, Jean Mary Dohoo; two *s* two *d*. *Educ:* Rugby Sch.; Trinity Coll., Cambridge (MA, LLB); Harvard Law Sch. (Harkness Commonwealth Fund Fellow, LLM). Admitted Solicitor, 1962; Asst Solicitor, Messrs Allen & Overy, 1964–67. Pt-time Lectr in Law, 1981–91, Vis. Prof., 1991–97, Univ. of Essex; Vis. Prof., KCL, 1991–. Chm., St Edmundsbury and Ipswich Diocesan Bd of Finance, 1977–85; Hon. Lay Canon, St Edmundsbury Cathedral, 1987–93. Dep. Chm., Monopolies and Mergers Commn, 1991–97 (Mem., 1980–91). Leverhulme Trust Res. Grant, for research into EEC competition law, 1986. Trustee, British Liver Trust, 1996–. FRSA 1991. *Publications:* The Antitrust Laws of the USA (with Sir Alan Neale), 3rd edn 1981; EEC Competition Law, 1988, 3rd edn 1998. *Recreations:* choral singing, tennis, sport. *Address:* Manor House, Old London Road, Capel St Mary, Ipswich, Suffolk IP9 2JU. *T:* (01473) 310583. *Clubs:* Law Society; Ipswich and Suffolk (Ipswich).

GOYMER, Andrew Alfred; His Honour Judge Goymer; a Circuit Judge, since 1999; *b* 28 July 1947; *s* of late Richard Kirby Goymer and of Betty Eileen Goymer (*née* Thompson); *m* 1972, Diana Mary, *d* of late Robert Harry Shipway, MBE and of Sheila Mary Shipway; one *s* one *d*. *Educ:* Dulwich Coll.; Pembroke Coll., Oxford (Hull Schol.; MA). Called to the Bar, Gray's Inn, 1970 (Gerald Moody Entrance Schol., Holker Sen. Exhibnr, Arden Atkin and Mould Prizeman); practised, S Eastern Circuit, 1972–99; admitted to NSW Bar, 1988; Asst Recorder, 1987–91; Recorder, 1991–99. *Address:* Southwark Crown Court, 1 English Grounds, SE1 2HU. *T:* (020) 7522 7200.

GOZNEY, Richard Hugh Turton, CMG 1993; HM Diplomatic Service; Ambassador to Indonesia, since 2000; *b* 21 July 1951; *s* of Thomas Leonard Gozney and Elizabeth Margaret Lilian Gozney (*née* Gardiner); *m* 1982, Diana Edwina Baird; two *s*. *Educ:* Magdalen Coll. Sch., Oxford; St Edmund Hall, Oxford (BA Hons Geol. 1973). Teacher, Tom Mboya Rusinga Secondary Sch., Kenya, 1970; joined FO, 1973; Jakarta, 1974–78; Buenos Aires, 1978–81; FCO, 1981–84; Hd of Chancery, Madrid, 1984–88; Asst Private Sec., later Private Sec., to Foreign Sec., FCO, 1989–93; High Comr, Swaziland, 1993–96; Head of Security Policy Dept, FCO, 1996–97; Chief of Assessments Staff, Jt Intelligence Orgn, Cabinet Office, 1998–2000. *Publication:* Gibraltar and the EC, 1993. *Recreations:* bird-watching, walking, wind surfing, still learning to fish. *Address:* c/o Foreign and Commonwealth Office, King Charles Street, SW1A 2AH.

GRAAFF, Sir David (de Villiers), 3rd Bt *cr* 1911, of Cape Town; farmer, since 1964; *b* 3 May 1940; *er s* of Sir de Villiers Graaff, 2nd Bt and of Helena Le Roux Graaff (*née* Voigt); *S* father, 1999; *m* 1969, Sally Williams; three *s* one *d*. *Educ:* Diocesan Coll.; Stellenbosch Univ. (BSc Agric.); Grenoble Univ. (Premier Degré); Magdalen Coll., Oxford (BA Hons; MA). MP (Nat. Party), Wynberg, 1987–98; Dep. Minister, Trade and Industry, 1991–94. Mem., Audit Commn, 1992–94. Dir, Deciduous Fruit Bd, 1983–87. Director: Graaff's Trust, 1969–; Milnerton Estates, 1969–. Hon. Col, Cape Garrison Artillery, 2000–. *Recreation:* golf. *Heir: s* de Villiers Graaff [*b* 16 July 1970; *m* 2000, Gaedry Kriel]. *Address:* De Grendel, PO Box 15192, Panorama 7506, Cape Town, South Africa. *T:* (21) 5587030. *Clubs:* Cape Town, Royal Cape Golf.

GRABHAM, Sir Anthony (Herbert), Kt 1988; FRCS; Chairman, BMA Services, since 1982; Vice Chairman, PPP Healthcare Group plc, since 1996 (Director, PPP, 1984–96); *b* 19 July 1930; *s* of John and Lily Grabham; *m* 1960, Eileen Pamela Rudd; two *s* two *d*. *Educ:* St Cuthbert's Grammar School, Newcastle upon Tyne. MB, BS Durham. RSO, Royal Victoria Infirmary, Newcastle upon Tyne; Consultant Surgeon, Kettering and District Gen. Hosp., 1965–95. Chairman: Jt Consultants Cttee, 1984–90; Central Cttee for Hosp. Med. Services, BMA, 1975–79; Council, BMA, 1979–84; Cttee, BMJ, 1993–; Member: GMC, 1979–99; Council, World Med. Assoc., 1979–84; Hon. Sec. and Treasurer, Commonwealth Med. Assoc., 1982–86 (Vice-Pres., 1980–84). Governor, PPP Healthcare Med. Trust, 1998–. *Recreation:* survival planning. *Address:* Rothesay House, 56 Headlands, Kettering, Northants NN15 6DG. *T:* (01536) 513299. *Club:* Army and Navy.

GRABINER, family name of **Baron Grabiner**.

GRABINER, Baron *cr* 1999 (Life Peer), of Aldwych in the City of Westminster; **Anthony Stephen Grabiner;** QC 1981; a Recorder, 1990–99; a Deputy High Court Judge, since 1994; *b* 21 March 1945; *e s* of late Ralph Grabiner and Freda Grabiner (*née* Cohen); *m* 1983, Jane, *er d* of Dr Benjamin Portnoy, TD, JP, MD, PhD, FRCP, Hale, Cheshire; three *s* one *d*. *Educ:* Central Foundn Boys' Grammar Sch., London, EC2; LSE, Univ. of London (LLB 1st Cl. Hons 1966, LLM with Distinction 1967). Lincoln's Inn: Hardwicke Scholar, 1966; called to the Bar, 1968; Droop Scholar, 1968; Bencher, 1989. Standing Jun. Counsel to Dept of Trade, Export Credits Guarantee Dept, 1976–81; Jun. Counsel to the Crown, 1978–81. Chm., Ct of Govs, LSE, 1998– (Mem., 1991–; Vice-Chm., 1993–98). *Publications:* (ed jtly) Sutton and Shannon on Contracts, 7th edn 1970; contrib. Banking Documents, to Encyclopedia of Forms and Precedents, 5th edn, 1986. *Recreations:* theatre, golf. *Address:* 1 Essex Court, Temple, EC4Y 9AR. *T:* (020) 7583 2000. *Clubs:* Garrick, Royal Automobile, MCC; Hendon Golf.

GRABINER, Michael; Chief Executive, Energis plc, 1997–2001; *b* 21 Aug. 1950; *s* of Henry Grabiner and Renée (*née* Geller); *m* 1976, Jane Olivia Harris; three *s* one *d*. *Educ:* St Alban's Sch.; King's Coll., Cambridge (MA Econ; Pres., Students' Union, 1972–73). Joined Post Office, 1973: Personal Asst to Man. Dir, Telecommunications, 1976–78; London Business Sch. (Sloan Prog.), 1980; British Telecommunications: Controller, Commercial Finance Divl HQ, 1982–84; Dep. Dir, Mktg, 1984–85; General Manager: Northern London Dist, 1985–88; City of London Dist, 1988–90; Director: Quality and Orgn, 1990–92; Global Customer Service, Business Communications Div., 1992–94; BT Europe, 1994. Director: BT Telecommunications SA Spain, 1994–95; VIAG InterKom Germany, 1994–95; Telenordia Sweden, 1994–95; Albacom Italy, 1994–95; Chm., Planet Online, 1998–; non-executive Director: Metro Hldgs Ltd, 1998–; Littlewoods plc, 1998–. Mem. (Lab) Brent BC, 1978–82 (Chm., Develt Cttee, 1980–82). Dir, E London Partnership, 1994–95. Freeman, City of London, 1995; Mem., Co. of Inf. Technologists, 1995. ACMA 1979. *Address:* 35 Uphill Road, NW7 4RA. *T:* (020) 8906 2930, *Fax:* (020) 8959 5020.

See also S. Grabiner.

GRABINER, Stephen; Director, Apax Partners & Co., since 1999; *b* 30 Sept. 1958; *s* of Henry and Renée Grabiner (*née* Geller); *m* 1984, Miriam Lœbl; two *s* one *d*. *Educ:* Univ. of Sheffield (BA 1981); Manchester Business Sch. (MBA 1983). Mgt Consultant, Coopers and Lybrand, 1983–86; Telegraph plc: Mktg Dir, 1986–93; Dep. Man. Dir, 1993–94; Man. Dir, 1994–96; Exec. Dir, UK Consumer Publishing, United News and Media plc, 1996–98; Chief Exec., ONdigital, 1998–99. *Recreations:* family, tennis. *Address:* (office) 15 Portland Place, W1N 3AA. *T:* (020) 7872 6353, *Fax:* (020) 7636 7183.

See also M. Grabiner.

GRACE, John Oliver Bowman; QC 1994; *b* 13 June 1948; *s* of late Oliver Grace, MBE, TD and of Marjorie (*née* Bowman); *m* 1973, Carol S. Roundhill; two *s* one *d*. *Educ:* Marlborough; Southampton Univ. (LLB Hons). Called to the Bar, Middle Temple, 1973. *Recreations:* gardening, modern art, reading, music, cricket, church, brick-laying. *Address:* 3 Serjeants' Inn, EC4Y 1BQ. *T:* (020) 7353 5537. *Club:* 4W's (Wandsworth).

GRACEY, Howard, OBE 1998; FIA, FIAA, FPMI; consulting actuary; Senior Partner, R. Watson and Sons, 1993–95 (Partner, 1970–95); *b* 21 Feb. 1935; *s* of late Charles Douglas Gracey and Margaret Gertrude (*née* Heggie); *m* 1960, Pamela Jean Bradshaw; one *s* two *d*. *Educ:* Birkenhead Sch. FIA 1959; FIAA 1982; FPMI 1977; ASA 1978. National Service, 1960–61 (2nd Lieut). Royal Insurance Co., 1953–69. Church Comr, 1978–95; Member: Gen. Synod of C of E, 1970–97; C of E Pensions Bd, 1970–97 (Chm., 1980–97); Archbishops' Commn on orgn of C of E; Treasurer, S Amer. Missionary Soc., 1975–93 (Chm., 1994–); Pres., Pensions Management Inst., 1983–85; Chm., Assoc. of Consulting Actuaries, 1991–93. Mem. Council, St John's Coll., Nottingham, 1998–. *Recreations:* fell-walking, photography. *Address:* Holmhurst Cottage, Back Lane, East Clandon, Guildford, Surrey GU4 7SD.

GRACEY, John Halliday, CB 1984; Director General (Deputy Secretary), Board of Inland Revenue, 1981–85; Commissioner of Inland Revenue, 1973–85; *b* 20 May 1925; *s* of Halliday Gracey and Florence Jane (*née* Cudlipp); *m* 1950, Margaret Procter; three *s*. *Educ:* City of London Sch.; Brasenose Coll., Oxford (MA). Army, 1943–47. Entered Inland Revenue, 1950; HM Treasury, 1970–73. Hon. Treas., NACRO, 1987–98. *Recreations:* walking, bee-keeping. *Address:* 3 Woodberry Down, Epping, Essex CM16 6RJ. *T:* (01992) 572167. *Club:* Reform.

GRADE, Michael Ian, CBE 1998; Chairman: Pinewood-Shepperton (formerly Pinewood Studios) Ltd, since 2000; Octopus Publishing Gp, since 2000; Hemscott.NET, since 2000; Camelot Group plc, since 2002; *b* 8 March 1943; *s* of Leslie Grade and *g s* of Olga Winogradski; *m* 1st, 1967, Penelope Jane (*née* Levinson) (marr. diss. 1981); one *s* one *d*; 2nd, 1982, Hon. Sarah Lawson (marr. diss. 1991), *y d* of 5th Baron Burnham; 3rd, 1998, Francesca Mary (*née* Leahy); one *s*. *Educ:* St Dunstan's Coll., London. Daily Mirror: Trainee Journalist, 1960; Sports Columnist, 1964–66; Theatrical Agent, Grade Organisation, 1966; joined London Management and Representation, 1969, Jt Man. Dir until 1973; London Weekend Television: Dep. Controller of Programmes (Entertainment), 1973; Dir of Programmes and Mem. Bd, 1977–81; Pres., Embassy Television, 1981–84; Controller, BBC1, 1984–86; Dir of Programmes, BBC TV, 1986–87; Chief Exec., Channel Four, 1988–97; First Leisure Corporation: Dir, 1991–2000; non-exec. Chm., 1995–97; Chm., 1997–98; Chief Exec., 1997–2000. Chm., VCI plc, 1995–98; Director: ITN, 1989–93; Delfont Macintosh Theatres Ltd, 1994–99; Charlton Athletic FC, 1997–; New Millennium Experience Co., 1997–; Camelot Gp, 2000–; Digital Broadcasting Corp., 2001–. Chm. Develt Council, RNT, 1997–; Member: Council, LAMDA, 1981–93; Council, RADA, 1996–; Council, BAFTA, 1981–82, 1986–88; 300 Group; Milton Cttee; British Screen Adv. Council, 1986–97; Council, Cinema and Television Benevolent Fund, 1993–; Council, Royal Albert Hall, 1997–. Chm., Wkg Gp, Fear of Crime, 1989; Mem., Nat. Commn of Inquiry into Prevention of Child Abuse, 1994–96; Chm., Index on Censorship, 2000–. President: TV and Radio Industries Club, 1987–88; Newspaper Press Fund, 1988–89; Entertainment Charities Fund, 1994–; Vice-Pres., Children's Film Unit, 1993–; Director: Open Coll., 1989–97; Cities in Schools, 1991–96; Gate Theatre, Dublin, 1990–; Internat. Council, Nat. Acad. of Television Arts and Scis, 1991–97; Jewish Film Foundn, 1997–99. Trustee: Band Aid; Nat. Film and Television Sch., Virgin Healthcare Foundn; WWF; Dep. Chm., Soc. of Stars, 1995–; Hon. Treas., Stars Organisation for Spastics, 1986–92. FRTS 1991 (Pres., 1995–97); Fellow, BAFTA, 1994. Hon. Prof., Thames Valley Univ., 1994. Hon. LLD Nottingham, 1997. *Publication:* It Seemed Like a Good Idea at the Time (autobiog.), 1999. *Recreation:* entertainment. *Address:* (office) 29 Wardour Street, W1V 3HB. *T:* (020) 7734 4898. *Clubs:* Royal Automobile, Royal Thames Yacht.

GRADIN, Anita Ingegerd; Member, Commission of the European Communities, 1995–99; *b* 12 Aug. 1933; *d* of Ossian Gradin and Alfhild Gradin; *m* Bertil Kersfelt; one *d*. *Educ:* Grad. Fr. Sch. of Social Work and Public Admin, Stockholm. Journalist in various newspapers, 1950–63; Mem., Social Welfare Planning Cttee, Stockholm, 1963–67; MP, 1968–92; posts include: Chairperson: Council, Cttee on Educn and Financial Affairs; Cttee on Migration, Refugees and Democracy, Council of Europe; Cabinet Minister for Migration and Equality between Women and Men, 1982–86; Minister for Foreign Trade and Eur. Affairs, 1986–91; Ambassador to Austria, Slovenia and UN, 1992–95. Vice-Chairperson, Nat. Fedn of Social Democratic Women, 1975–92; Vice-Pres., Socialist Internat., 1983–92; Pres., Socialist Internat. Women, 1986–92. Pro Merito Medal, Council of Europe, 1982; Wizo Woman of the Year Award, 1986; Marisa Bellizario European Prize, Italy, 1998; King's Medal, Royal Order of Seraphim, Sweden, 1998. Pro Merito Medal, Council of Europe, 1992. Cavalieri di Gran Croce (Italy), 1991; Order of Merit (Austria) 1995. *Recreations:* swimming, walking in the woods, stamps, fishing. *Address:* Svartviksslingan 27, 16738 Bromma, Sweden; *e-mail:* gradin.kersfelt@lelia.com.

GRADY, Terence, MBE 1967; HM Diplomatic Service, retired; Ambassador at Libreville, 1980–82; *b* 23 March 1924; *s* of Patrick Grady and Catherine (*née* Fowles); *m* 1960, Jean Fischer; one *s* four *d*. *Educ:* St Michael's Coll., Leeds. HM Forces, 1942–47; Foreign Office, 1949; HM Embassy: Baghdad, 1950; Paris, 1951; Asst Private Secretary to Secretary of State for Foreign Affairs, 1952–55; HM Legation, Budapest, 1955–58; HM Embassy, Kabul, 1958–60; FO, 1960–63; Vice Consul, Elisabethville, 1963; Consul, Philadelphia, 1964–69; UK High Commission, Sydney, 1969–72; FCO, 1972–75; Head of Chancery, Dakar, 1975–77; Consul, Istanbul, 1977–80. *Recreations:* tennis, walking. *Address:* 58 The Close, Norwich NR1 4EH. *Club:* Norfolk (Norwich).

GRAEF, Roger Arthur; writer, director and producer of films; *b* NYC, 18 April 1936; UK citizen, 1995; *m* 1st, 1971, Karen Bergemann (marr. diss. 1983); one *s* one *d*; 2nd, 1986, Susan Mary Richards. *Educ:* Horace Mann Sch., NYC; Putney Sch., Vermont; Harvard Univ. (BA Hons). Directed, USA, 26 plays and operas; also directed CBS drama; Observer/Dir, Actors Studio, NYC, 1958–62; resident in England, 1962–; Director, London: Period of Adjustment (Royal Court, Wyndham's); Afternoon Men (Arts); has written, produced and directed more than 80 films; *films for television include:* The Life and Times of John Huston, Esq., 1965; (Exec. Producer) 13-part Who Is series, 1966–67 (wrote/dir. films on Pierre Boulez, Jacques Lipchitz, Walter Gropius, Maurice Béjart); Günter Grass' Berlin, 1965; Why Save Florence?, 1968; In the Name of Allah, 1970; The Space between Words, 1971–72; A Law in the Making, 1973; Inside the Brussels HQ, 1975; Is This the Way to Save our Cities?, 1975; Decision series: British Steel, etc, 1976–77, British Communism, 1978 (Royal Television Soc. Award); Pleasure at Her Majesty's, The Secret Policeman's Ball, 1977–78; Inside Europe, 1977–78; Police series, 1980–82 (BAFTA Award); Police: Operation Carter, 1981–82; Nagging Doubt, 1984; The Fifty-Minute Hour, 1984; Maybe Baby, 1985; Comic Relief, 1986; Closing Ranks, 1987; The Secret Life of the Soviet Union, 1990; Turning the Screws, 1993; Look at the State We're In, 1995; In Search of Law and Order (UK), 1995; Breaking the Cycle, 1996; In Search of Law and Order (USA), 1998; Keeping it in the Family, 1998; The Siege of Scotland Yard, 1999; Race Against Crime, 1999; Masters of the Universe, 1999; Looks That Kill, 2000; executive producer: Who's Your Father, 2000; Not Black and White, 2001; Thames Valley Revisited, 2001; Series Editor: Inside Europe, 1977–78; Signals, 1988–89; *radio:* The Illusion of Information, 2000. Mem., Develt Control Review (Dobry Cttee), Chm., Study Gp on Public Participation in Planning, and Mem., Cttee on Control of Demolition, DoE, 1974–76; Member: Commn on Child and Adolescent Mental Health, 1997–98; Prince's Trust Wkg Party on surviving damage in childhood, 1997–98; Fulbright Commn, 2000–; Advr, Oxford Probation Studies Unit, 1997–; Social Affairs Advr, Paul Hamlyn Foundn, 1999–. Chm., AIP, 1988–89; Member: Council, ICA, 1970–82; Council, BAFTA, 1976–77; Bd, Channel Four, 1980–85; Governor, BFI, 1974–78. Adviser on broadcasting to Brandt Commn, 1979–80; Media Consultant: Collins Publishing, 1983–88; London Transport (Mem. Bd, LTE, 1976–79; co-designer, new London Bus Map). Pres., Signals Internat. Trust, 1990–; Trustee: Koestler Trust for Prisoners' Art, 1995–; Butler Trust, 1997–; Divert Trust, 1999–2000; Family Policy Studies Centre, 1999. Chm., Police Scholarships Cttee. Chairman: Book Aid, 1991; Théâtre de Complicité, 1991–. Member: Collège Analytique de Securité Urbaine, 1993–98; British Soc. of Criminology; Vis. Fellow, Mannheim Centre for the Study of Criminology and Criminal Justice, LSE, 1993–. Visiting Professor: Broadcast Media, Oxford Univ., 1999–2000; Univ. of London, 2001–02. FRTS 1996. *Publications:* Daily Mail, Talking Blues, 1989; Living Dangerously, 1992; Why Restorative Justice?, 2000; contrib. Daily Telegraph, The Times (media columnist, 1992–94), Sunday Telegraph, Observer, Independent on Sunday, Mail on Sunday, Evening Standard, Police Review, The Independent, Guardian, Sunday Times, Independent on Sunday. *Recreations:* tennis, chamber music, photography, Dorset. *Address:* 72 Westbourne Park Villas, W2 5EB. *T:* (020) 7727 7868. *Clubs:* Beefsteak, Groucho, Pilgrims.

GRAF, (Charles) Philip; Chief Executive, Trinity Mirror plc, since 1999; *b* 18 Oct. 1946; *s* of Charles Henry Graf and Florence (*née* Mulholland); *m* 1970, Freda Mary Bain; three *d*. *Educ:* Methodist Coll., Belfast; Carlmont High Sch., Calif; Clare Coll., Cambridge (MA). Circulation Mktg Controller, Thomson Regl Newspapers, 1978–83; Asst Man. Dir, Liverpool Daily Post and Echo, 1983–85; Chief Exec., Trinity Paper and Packaging, 1986–90; Corporate Develt Dir, 1990–93, Chief Exec., 1993–99, Trinity plc. *Recreations:* reading, opera, watching Rugby, soccer and cricket, theatre.

GRAF, Stefanie; German tennis player, 1982–99; Founder, and Chairman, Children for Tomorrow, since 1998; *b* 14 June 1969; *d* of Peter and Heidi Graf. Has won 107 singles titles, including 22 Grand Slam titles: French Open, 1987–88, 1993, 1995–96, 1999; Australian Open, 1988–90, 1994; Wimbledon, 1988–89, 1991–93, 1995–96; US Open, 1988–89, 1993, 1995–96. Olympic Gold Medal, Seoul, 1988; Olympic Silver Medal, Barcelona, 1992; Olympic Order, 1999. *Publication:* (jtly) Wege zum Erfolg, 1999. *Address:* Steffi Graf Marketing GmbH & Co. KG, Mallaustrasse 75, 68219 Mannheim, Germany.

GRAFTON, 11th Duke of, *cr* 1675; **Hugh Denis Charles FitzRoy;** KG 1976; DL; Earl of Euston, Viscount Ipswich; Captain Grenadier Guards; *b* 3 April 1919; *e s* of 10th Duke of Grafton, and Lady Doreen Maria Josepha Sydney Buxton (*d* 1923), *d* of 1st Earl Buxton; *S* father, 1970; *m* 1946, Fortune (*see* Duchess of Grafton); two *s* three *d*. *Educ:* Eton; Magdalene Coll., Cambridge. ADC to the Viceroy of India, 1943–46. Vice-Chm. of Trustees, Nat. Portrait Gall., 1967–92; Mem., Royal Fine Art Commn, 1971–94. Chairman: Architectural Heritage Fund, 1976–94; Cathedrals Adv. Commn, 1981–91; Member: Hist. Bldgs Council for England, 1953–84; Hist. Bldgs Adv. Cttee, 1984–2001, Cathedrals and Churches Adv. Cttee, 1984–2001, English Heritage; Properties Cttee, Nat. Trust, 1981–94; President: Suffolk Preservation Soc., 1957–; SPAB, 1989–; Trustee: Sir John Soane's Mus. (Chm., 1975–97); Hist. Churches Preservation Trust (Chm., 1980–97); Tradescant Trust, 1976–99; Buildings at Risk Trust, 1986–2000; Patron, Historic Houses Assoc. President: Internat. Students House, 1972–; East Anglia Tourist Bd, 1973–93; British Soc. of Master Glass Painters. Patron, Hereford Herd Book Soc. DL Suffolk, 1973. Hon. DCL East Anglia, 1990. *Heir: s* Earl of Euston, *qv*. *Address:* Euston Hall, Thetford, Norfolk IP24 2QW. *T:* (01842) 753282. *Club:* Boodle's.

GRAFTON, Duchess of; (Ann) Fortune FitzRoy, GCVO 1980 (DCVO 1970; CVO 1965); Mistress of The Robes to The Queen since 1967; *o d* of Captain Eric Smith, MC, LLD, Lower Ashfold, Slaugham; *m* 1946, Duke of Grafton, *qv*; two *s* three *d*. Lady of the Bedchamber to the Queen, 1953–66. SRCN Great Ormond Street, 1945; Mem. Bd of Governors, The Hospital for Sick Children, Great Ormond Street, 1952–66; Patron, Nurses' League. President: W Suffolk Mission to the Deaf; W Suffolk Decorative and Fine Arts Soc.; Bury St Edmunds Br., BHF; Vice-President: Suffolk Br., Royal British Legion Women's Section; Trinity Hospice, Clapham Common, 1951–. Governor: Felixstowe Coll.; Riddlesworth Hall. Patron: Relate, W Suffolk; Guildhall String Ensemble; Clarence River Historical Soc., Grafton, NSW. JP County of London, 1949, W Suffolk, 1972–90. *Address:* Euston Hall, Thetford, Norfolk IP24 2QW. *T:* (01842) 753282.

See also Jeremy F. E. Smith, Sir John L. E. Smith.

GRAFTON, NSW, Bishop of, since 1998; **Rt Rev. Philip James Huggins;** *b* 16 Oct. 1948; *s* of Alf Huggins and Mary Nutt; *m* 1976, Elizabeth Cuming; three *s*. *Educ:* Monash Univ. (BEcon, Grad. Dip. Welfare Admin., MA). Teaching Fellow, Univ. of New England, 1971–74; ordained priest, 1977; worked in parishes, Dio. of Bendigo, 1977–80; Industrial Chaplain, dio. Melbourne, 1980–83; Univ. Chaplain, Monash Univ., 1983–89; Exec. Officer, Archbishop of Melbourne's Internat. Develt Fund, 1990–91; Rector of Williamstown, 1991–95; Archdeacon of Essendon, 1994–95; Regl Bishop, Dio. of Perth, 1995–98. ChLJ 1997. *Recreations:* varied sports, poetry, the arts. *Address:* PO Box 4, Grafton, NSW 2460, Australia. *T:* (2) 66424122.

GRAFTON, Peter Witheridge, CBE 1972; Senior Partner, G. D. Walford & Partners, Chartered Quantity Surveyors, 1978–82 (Partner 1949–78), retired; *b* 19 May 1916; *s* of James Hawkins Grafton and Ethel Marion (*née* Brannan); *m* 1st, 1939, Joan Bleackley (*d* 1969); two *d* (and one *s* one *d* decd); 2nd, 1971, Margaret Ruth Ward; two *s*. *Educ:* Westminster City Sch.; Sutton Valence Sch.; Coll. of Estate Management. FRICS. Served War of 1939–45, Queen's Westminster Rifles, Dorsetshire Regt and RE, UK and Far East (Captain). Pres., RICS, 1978–79 (Vice-Pres., 1974–78); Mem. and Past Chm., Quantity Surveyors Council; Mem. Council, Construction Industries Research and Information Assoc., 1963–69; Member: Research Adv. Council to Minister of Housing and Construction, 1967–71; Nat. Cons. Council for Building and Civil Engrg Industries, 1968–76; British Bd of Agrément, 1973–88; Chm., Nat. Jt Consultative Cttee for Building Industry, 1974–75 (Mem., 1970–77). Master, Worshipful Co. of Chartered Surveyors, 1983–84. Trustee, United Westminster Schs; Governor, Sutton Valence Sch., 1971–96 (Chm., 1976–91); Pres. and Past Chm., Old Suttonians Assoc. Contested (L) Bromley, 1950. *Publications:* numerous articles on techn. and other professional subjects. *Recreations:* golf (founder, Chm., 1962–94, Pres., 1994–, Public Schs Old Boys Golf Assoc., Co-donor Grafton Morrish Trophy; past Captain and past Pres. of Chartered Surveyors Golfing Soc.); writing. *Address:* 57 Padbrook, Limpsfield, Oxted, Surrey RH8 0DZ. *T:* (01883) 716685. *Clubs:* Reform; Tandridge Golf.

GRAFTON-GREEN, Patrick; Senior Partner, Theodore Goddard, solicitors, since 1997; *b* 30 March 1943; *s* of George Grafton-Green and Brigid Anna Grafton-Green (*née* Maxwell); *m* 1982, Deborah Susan Goodchild; two *s* two *d*. *Educ:* Ampleforth Coll., York; Wadham Coll., Oxford (MA). Joined Theodore Goddard, solicitors, 1966; qualif. as solicitor, 1969; Partner, 1973–; Indep. Mem., Mgt Cttee, 1990–92; Head, Media and Communications Dept, 1993–. *Recreations:* cricket, music, theatre. *Address:* Theodore Goddard, 150 Aldersgate Street, EC1A 4EJ. *T:* (020) 7606 8855. *Club:* MCC.

GRAHAM, family name of **Duke of Montrose** and **Baron Graham of Edmonton**.

GRAHAM, Marquis of; James Alexander Norman Graham; *b* 16 Aug. 1973; *s* and *heir* of Duke of Montrose, *qv*. *Educ:* Eton; Univ. of Edinburgh (BSc); Univ. of Cape Town (MSc). *Address:* Auchmar, Drymen, Glasgow G63 0AG.

GRAHAM OF EDMONTON, Baron *cr* 1983 (Life Peer), of Edmonton in Greater London; **Thomas Edward Graham;** PC 1998; *b* 26 March 1925; *m* 1950, Margaret, *d* of Frederick Golding; two *s*. *Educ:* elementary sch.; WEA Co-operative College. BA Open Univ., 1976. FIMgt. Newcastle-on-Tyne Co-operative Soc., 1939–52; Organiser, British Fedn of Young Co-operators, 1952–53; Educn Sec., Enfield Highway Co-operative Soc., 1953–62; Sec., Co-operative Union Southern Section, 1962–67; Nat. Sec., Co-operative Party, 1967–74. MP (Lab and Co-op) Enfield, Edmonton, Feb. 1974–1983; contested (Lab) Edmonton, 1983. PPS to Minister of State, Dept of Prices and Consumer Protection, 1974–76; a Lord Comr of HM Treasury, 1976–79; Opposition spokesman on the environment, 1980–83; Opposition Chief Whip, H of L, 1990–97. Chm., Labour Peers' Gp, 1997–. Mem. and Leader, Enfield Council, 1961–68. Chm., UK Co-operative Council, 1997–. *Address:* 2 Clerks Piece, Loughton, Essex IG10 1NR.

GRAHAM, Alastair Carew, FRSA; Head Master, Mill Hill School, 1979–92; *b* 23 July 1932; *s* of Col J. A. Graham and Mrs Graham (*née* Carew-Hunt); *m* 1969, Penelope Rachel Beaumont; two *d*. *Educ:* Winchester Coll.; Gonville and Caius Coll., Cambridge (1st Cl. Mod. and Med. Langs). Served 1st Bn Argyll and Sutherland Highlanders, 1951–53. Foy, Morgan & Co. (City), 1956–58; Asst Master, Eton, 1958; House Master, 1970–79. *Recreations:* Winchester Cathedral, walking, theatre and opera, music listening, gardening, educn for the disabled. *Address:* Longbourn, Chawton, Alton, Hants GU34 1SA.

See also Maj.-Gen. J. D. C. Graham.

GRAHAM, Sir Alexander (Michael), GBE 1990; JP; Chairman, Employment Conditions Abroad Ltd, since 1993 (Director, since 1992); Lord Mayor of London, 1990–91; *b* 27 Sept. 1938; *s* of Dr Walter Graham and Suzanne Graham (*née* Simon); *m* 1964, Carolyn, *d* of Lt-Col Alan Wolryche Stansfeld, MBE; three *d*. *Educ:* Fyvie Village Sch.; Hall Sch., Hampstead; St Paul's Sch. National Service, 1957–59; commnd Gordon Highlanders; TA 1959–67; Chm., Nat. Employers Liaison Cttee for TA and Reserve Forces, 1992–97. Joined Norman Frizzell & Partners Ltd, 1957: Dir, 1967–93; Man. Dir, 1973–90; Dep. Chm., 1990–93; Underwriting Member of Lloyd's, 1978–2000; Dir, Folgate Insce Co. Ltd, 1975– (Chm., 1995–); Chm., FirstCity Insce Brokers, 1993–98. Mercers' Co.: Liveryman, 1971–; Mem., Ct of Assistants, 1980; Master, 1983–84; Mem., Ct of Common Council, City of London, 1978–79; Alderman for Ward of Queenhithe, 1979–; Pres., Queenhithe Ward Club, 1979–. Sheriff, City of London, 1986–87; HM Lieut, City of London, 1989–. Hon. Liveryman, Co. of Chartered Secretaries and Administrators, 1992; Hon. Freeman: Insurers' Co., 1992; Merchant Adventurers of York, 1983. President: CS Motoring Assoc., 1993–; British Insurance Law Assoc., 1994–96; Vice-Pres., Insurance Inst. of London, 1978–. Governor: Hall Sch., Hampstead, 1975–93; Christ's Hosp. Sch., 1979–; King Edward's Sch., Whitley, 1979–; St Paul's Sch., 1980–93 (Vice Pres., 1988–2000, Dep. Pres., 2000–01, Pres., 2001–, Old Pauline Club; Chm., Gen. Charitable Trust, 1997–); St Paul's Girls' Sch., 1980–93; City of London Boys' Sch., 1983–85; City of London Girls' Sch., 1992–95; Mem. Council, Gresham Coll., 1983–93; Trustee, Morden College, 1988– (Chm., 1995–); Chancellor, City Univ., 1990–91. Trustee: United Response, 1988– (Chm., 1993–); Lord Mayor's 800th Anniversary Trust, 1989–2000; Temple Bar Trust, 1992–; Vice Pres., 1992–, and Hon. Life Mem., 1993, Macmillan Cancer Relief (formerly Cancer Relief Macmillan Fund); Vice Pres., Garden House Hospice, 1992–; Hon. Mem., Ct, HAC, 1979–; Mem., Exec. Cttee, Army Benevolent Fund, 1991–98; Chm. Council, Order of St John, Herts, 1993–2001; Mem., Royal Soc. of St George, 1981–; Vice Pres., Royal Soc. of St George, Herts Br., 1999–. Vice Pres., Herts Agricl Show, 1996–. Gentlemen Usher of the Purple Rod, Order of the British Empire, 2000–. FCII 1964; FBIIBA 1967; FCIS 1990; FInstD 1975; CIMgt (CBIM 1991); FRSA 1980. JP City of London, 1979. Commandeur de l'Ordre du Tastevin, 1985; Vigneron d'Honneur et Bourgeois de St Emilion, 1999. Hon. DCL City, 1990. KStJ 1990. Silver Medal, City of Helsinki, 1990; Medal, City of Santiago, 1991. Order of Wissam Alouite (Morocco), 1987; Grand Cross Order of Merit (Chile), 1991. *Recreations:* wine, calligraphy, genealogy, music, reading, silver, bridge, golf, swimming, tennis, shooting, ski-ing, avoiding gardening. *Address:* Walden Abbotts, Whitwell, Hitchin, Herts SG4 8AJ. *T:* and *Fax:* (01438) 871223. *Clubs:* Garrick, City Livery; Highland Brigade; Royal Worlington and Newmarket Golf, South Bedfordshire Golf, Lloyd's Golf (Capt. 1994, Pres., 1996).

See also Lt-Gen. Sir P. W. Graham.

GRAHAM, Sir Alistair; *see* Graham, Sir J. A.

GRAHAM, Rt Rev. Andrew Alexander Kenny; Hon. Assistant Bishop, diocese of Carlisle, since 1997; *b* 7 Aug. 1929; *o s* of late Andrew Harrison and Magdalene Graham; unmarried. *Educ:* Tonbridge Sch.; St John's Coll., Oxford (Hon. Fellow, 1986); Ely Theological College. Curate of Hove Parish Church, 1955–58; Chaplain and Lectr in Theology, Worcester Coll., Oxford, 1958–70; Fellow and Tutor, 1960–70, Hon. Fellow, 1981; Warden of Lincoln Theological Coll., 1970–77; Canon and Prebendary of Lincoln Cathedral, 1970–77; Bishop Suffragan of Bedford, 1977–81; Bishop of Newcastle, 1981–97. Chairman: ACCM, 1984–87; Doctrine Commn, 1987–95. DD Lambeth, 1995; Hon. DCL Northumbria, 1997. *Recreation:* hill walking. *Address:* Fell End, Butterwick, Penrith, Cumbria CA10 2QQ. *T:* (01931) 713147. *Clubs:* Oxford and Cambridge; Northern Counties (Newcastle).

GRAHAM, Andrew Winston Mawdsley; Master, Balliol College, Oxford, since 2001; *b* 20 June 1942; *s* of Winston Mawdsley Graham, *qv*; *m* 1970, Peggotty Fawssett. *Educ:* Charterhouse; St Edmund Hall, Oxford. MA (PPE). Economic Assistant: NEDO, 1964; Dept of Economic Affairs, 1964–66; Asst to Economic Adviser to the Cabinet, 1966–68; Economic Adviser to Prime Minister, 1968–69; Balliol College, Oxford: Fellow, 1969–2001; Tutor in Econs, 1969; Estates Bursar, 1978; Investment Bursar, 1979–83; Vice Master, 1988 and 1992–94; Acting Master, 1997–2001; Policy Adviser to Prime Minister (on leave of absence from Balliol), 1974–75; Economic Advr to Shadow Chancellor of Exchequer, 1988–92, to Leader of the Opposition, 1992–94. Tutor, Oxford Univ. Business Summer Sch., 1971, 1972, 1973 and 1976. Vis. Researcher, SE Asian Central Banks Res. and Trng Centre, Malaysia, 1984; Vis. Fellow, Griffith Univ., Brisbane, 1984; Vis. Scholar, MIT, and Vis. Fellow, Center for Eur. Studies, Harvard, 1994. Member: Wilson Cttee to Review the Functioning of Financial Institutions, 1977–80; Economics Cttee, SSRC, 1978–80; British Transport Docks Bd, 1979–82; Chm., St James Gp (Economic Forecasting), 1982–84, 1985–92. Mem., ILO/Jobs and Skills Prog. for Africa (JASPA) Mission to Ethiopia, 1982; Hd, Queen Elizabeth House/Food Studies Gp team assisting Govt of Republic of Zambia, 1984; Consultant, BBC, 1989–92; Mem. Bd, Channel Four Television Ltd, 1998–. Mem., Media Adv. Cttee, IPPR, 1994–97; Trustee, Foundn for Information Policy Res., 1998–. Sen. Fellow, Gorbachev Foundn of N America, 1999–. Mem., Council of Management, Templeton Coll., Oxford, 1990–95. Founder Mem. Editorial Bd, Library of Political Economy, 1982–. *Publications:* (ed) Government and Economies in the Postwar Period, 1990; (jtly) Broadcasting, Society and Policy in the Multimedia Age, 1997. *Recreation:* windsurfing on every possible occasion. *Address:* Balliol College, Oxford OX1 3BJ. *T:* (01865) 277710.

GRAHAM, Anne Silvia, (Lady Graham); Chairman, South Cumbria Health Authority, 1988–94; *b* 1 Aug. 1934; *o d* of late Benjamin Arthur Garcia and Constance Rosa (*née* Journeaux). *Educ:* Francis Holland Sch., SW1; LSE (LLB). Called to the Bar, Inner Temple, 1958; Yarborough-Anderson Scholar, 1959. Joined Min. of Housing and Local Govt, 1960; Dep. Legal Advr, DoE, 1978–86. Mem. Court, Lancaster Univ. *Recreations:* gardening, arts, music.

GRAHAM, Antony Richard Malise; management consultant, retired; Director, Clive & Stokes International, 1985–95; *b* 15 Oct. 1928; *s* of late Col Patrick Ludovic Graham, MC, and late Barbara Mary Graham (*née* Jury); *m* 1958, Gillian Margaret (marr. diss. 1996), *d* of late L. Bradford Cook and of Mrs W. V. Wrigley; two *s* one *d*. *Educ:* Abberley Hall; Nautical Coll., Pangbourne. Merchant Navy, 1945–55 (Master Mariner). Stewarts and Lloyds Ltd, 1955–60; PE Consulting Group Ltd, management consultants, 1960–72 (Regional Dir, 1970–72); Regional Industrial Dir (Under-Sec.), DTI, 1972–76; Dir, Barrow Hepburn Group Ltd, and Maroquinerie Le Tanneur et Tanneries du Bugey SA, 1976–81; Chm., Paton & Sons (Tillicoultry) Ltd, 1981–82; Dir, DTI, 1983–85. Contested (C) Leeds East, 1966. *Recreations:* sailing, oil painting. *Address:* Old Bank House, Haddington, E Lothian EH41 3JS.

GRAHAM, (Arthur) William; JP; Member (C) South Wales East, National Assembly for Wales, since 1999; *b* 18 Nov. 1949; *s* of late William Douglas Graham and of Eleanor Mary Scott (*née* Searle); *m* 1981, Elizabeth Hannah, *d* of late Joshua Griffiths; one *s* two *d*. *Educ:* Blackfriars; Coll. of Estate Mgt, London. FRICS 1974. Principal, Graham & Co., Chartered Surveyors, 1970–. Newport Harbour Comr, 1990– (Vice Chm., 1999–). Member: Gwent CC, 1985–89; Newport County BC, 1988– (Leader, Conservative Gp, 1992–). Chm., Educn Cttee, Nat. Assembly for Wales, 1999–. Trustee, United Reformed Church, 1981–. Gov., Rougemont Sch. Trust, 1991–. MInstD 1980. JP Newport, 1979. *Recreations:* breeder of pedigree Suffolk sheep, foreign travel. *Address:* The Volland, Lower Machen, Newport NP10 8GY. *T:* (01633) 440419.

GRAHAM, Billy; *see* Graham, William F.

GRAHAM, Dr Christopher Forbes, FRS 1981; Professor of Animal Development, and Professorial Fellow, St Catherine's College, University of Oxford, since 1985; *b* 23 Sept. 1940. *Educ:* Oxford Univ. (BA 1963, DPhil 1966). Formerly Junior Beit Memorial Fellow in Med. Research, Sir William Dunn Sch. of Pathology. Lectr, Zoology Dept, Oxford Univ., 1970–85. Member: Brit. Soc. Cell Biology; Brit. Soc. for Developmental Biology; Soc. for Experimental Biology; Genetical Soc. *Publication:* The Developmental Biology of Plants and Animals, 1976, new edn as Developmental Control in Plants and Animals, 1984. *Address:* Department of Zoology, University of Oxford, South Parks Road, Oxford OX1 3PS.

GRAHAM, Christopher Sidney Matthew; Director General, Advertising Standards Authority, since 2000; *b* 21 Sept. 1950; *s* of late David Maurice Graham and Rosemary West Graham (*née* Harris); *m* 1985, Christine Harland (*née* McLean). *Educ:* Canterbury Cathedral Choir Sch.; St Edward's Sch., Oxford; Univ. of Liverpool (Pres., Guild of Undergrads, 1971–72; BA Hons Hist. 1973). BBC News Trainee, 1973–75; Producer: General Talks, Radio, BBC Manchester, 1976–78; Television Current Affairs, BBC, Lime Grove, 1979–87; A Week in Politics, Channel 4, 1987–88; Dep. Editor, The Money Prog., BBC, 1988–89; Asst Editor, 1989–90, Man. Editor, 1990–93, BBC Television News; Man. Editor, BBC News Progs, 1994–95; Sec., BBC, 1996–99. Mem. (L), Liverpool City Council, 1971–74. Contested (L) Wilts N, 1983, 1987. *Recreations:* media, music, history. *Address:* Advertising Standards Authority, 2 Torrington Place, WC1E 7HW. *T:* (020) 7580 5555.

GRAHAM, Colin; stage director, designer, lighting designer, and author; Artistic Director, Opera Theatre of St Louis, since 1984 (Associate Artistic Director, 1979–84); *b* 22 Sept. 1931; *s* of Frederick Eaton Graham-Bonnalie and Alexandra Diana Vivian Findlay. *Educ:* Northaw Prep. Sch.; Stowe Sch.; RADA (Dip.). Dir of Productions, English Opera Gp, 1963–74; Associate Dir of Prodns, Sadler's Wells Opera/ENO, 1967–75; Dir of Prodns, 1977–84, then Associate Artist, ENO; Artistic Director: Aldeburgh Fest., 1969–89; English Music Theatre, 1975–79. Principal productions for: English Music Theatre; Royal Opera, Covent Garden; Scottish Opera; New Opera Co.; Glyndebourne Opera; BBC TV; Brussels National Opera; St Louis Opera Theatre; Santa Fe Opera; Metropolitan Opera, New York; NYC Opera; San Fransciso Opera; Chicago Lyric Opera; Washington Opera, etc; dir. world premières: of all Benjamin Britten's operas since 1954; of other contemp. composers. Theatre productions for: Old Vic Co.; Bristol Old Vic; Royal Shakespeare Co. Ordained minister, New Covenant Church, St Louis, Mo, 1987. Hon. DA: Webster Univ., 1985; Univ. of Missouri, 1992. Arts and Education Council Award, 1993. Orpheus award (Germany) for best opera production, 1973 (War and Peace, ENO); Opera America award for production, 1988 (Albert Herring, Banff Fest. Opera). *Publications:* A Penny for a Song (libretto for Richard Rodney Bennett), 1969; The Golden Vanity (libretto for opera by Britten), 1970; King Arthur (libretto for new version of Purcell opera), 1971; The Postman Always Rings Twice (libretto for opera by Stephen Paulus), 1981; Jōruri (libretto for opera by Minoru Miki), 1985; The Woodlanders (libretto for opera by Stephen Paulus), 1984; production scores for Britten's: Curlew River, 1969; The Burning Fiery Furnace, 1971; The Prodigal Son, 1973; contrib. Opera. *Recreations:* The Bible, motor cycles, movies, weight training. *Address:* PO Box 191910, Saint Louis, MO 63119, USA.

GRAHAM, David; *see* Graham, S. D.

GRAHAM, Douglas; *see* Graham, M. G. D.

GRAHAM, Rt Hon. Sir Douglas (Arthur Montrose), KNZM 1999; PC 1998; Minister of Justice, 1990–99, Minister in charge of Treaty of Waitangi Negotiations, 1991–99, and Attorney General, 1997–99, New Zealand; *b* 12 Jan. 1942; *s* of late Robert James Alister Graham and Patricia Kennedy Graham; *m* 1966, Beverley Virginia Cordell; two *s* one *d*. *Educ:* Southwell Preparatory Sch.; Auckland GS; Auckland Univ. (BL 1965). Barrister and solicitor, 1968–84; Sen. Partner, Graham & Co., Solicitors, 1972–84. MP (N) New Zealand, 1984–99, for Remuera, 1984–96; Minister of Cultural Affairs, and of Disarmament and Arms Control, 1990–96. *Publication:* Trick or Treaty?, 1997. *Recreations:* music, gardening. *Address:* Elderslie, Manuwai Lane, RD2 Drury, South Auckland, New Zealand. *T:* (9) 2948608; *e-mail:* douglas.graham@xtra.co.nz.

GRAHAM, Duncan Gilmour, CBE 1987; Senior Partner, Duncan Graham Consultants, since 1991; *b* 20 Aug. 1936; *s* of Robert Gilmour Graham and Lilias Turnbull Graham (*née* Watson); *m* 1st, 1962, Margaret Gray Graham (*née* Cairns) (marr. diss. 1991); two *s* one *d*; 2nd, 1991, Wendy Margaret Wallace. *Educ:* Hutcheson's, Glasgow; Univ. of Glasgow (MA (Hons) History); Jordanhill Coll. of Education (Teachers' Secondary Cert.). Teacher of History: Whitehill Sec. Sch., Glasgow, 1959–62; Hutcheson's, Glasgow, 1962–65; Lectr in Social Studies, Craigie Coll. of Educn, Ayr, 1965–68; Asst Dir of Educn, Renfrewshire, 1968–70; Sen. Depute Dir of Educn, Renfrewshire, 1970–74, Strathclyde Regl Council, 1974–79; Advr to COSLA and Scottish Teachers' Salaries Cttee, 1974–79; County Educn Officer, Suffolk, 1979–87; Chief Exec., Humberside CC, 1987–88; Chm. and Chief Exec., Nat. Curriculum Council, 1988–91. Advr to ACC, 1982–88; Mem., Burnham Cttee, 1983–87 and of ACAS Indep. Panel, 1986. Sec., Co. Educn Officers Soc., 1985–87; Chm., Assoc. of Educn Officers, 1985; Project Dir, DES Teacher Appraisal Study, 1985–86; Chm., Nat. Steering Gp on Teacher Appraisal, 1987–90. Member: BBC North Adv. Council, 1988–91; Lincs and Humberside Arts Council, 1988–91; Yorks and Humberside Arts, 1991–94; Council of Nat. Foundn for Educnl Res., 1984, and 1989–90; Exec. Council, Industrial Soc., 1988–90; Chm., Nat. Mathematics Wkg Gp, 1988. Mem. Exec., Caravan Club, 1997–2000. Chm., Eden Rivers Trust, 2000–. FRSA 1981. *Publications:* Those Having Torches, 1985; In the Light of Torches, 1986; Sense, Nonsense and the National Curriculum, 1992; A Lesson For Us All, 1992; Sunset on the Clyde, 1993; The Education Racket, 1996; Visiting Distilleries, 2001; many articles in nat. press and educn and local govt jls. *Recreations:* motor cycling, fly-fishing. *Address:* Parkburn, Colby, Appleby, Cumbria CA16 6BD. *T:* (01768) 352920.

GRAHAM, Elizabeth; Director of Education, London Borough of Enfield, since 1994; *b* 25 Jan. 1951. *Educ:* Knightswood Secondary Sch., Glasgow; Edinburgh Univ. (MA History); Moray House Coll. of Educn, Edinburgh (PGCE). Teacher, Stirlingshire CC, 1971–73; Head of Dept, Waltham Forest LBC, 1973–81; Professional Asst, Haringey LBC, 1982–84; Asst Educn Officer, Enfield LBC, 1984–89; Asst Dir of Educn, Redbridge LBC, 1989–94. *Recreations:* cats, the crusades. *Address:* London Borough of Enfield, PO Box 56, Civic Centre, Silver Street, Enfield EN1 3XQ. *T:* (020) 8379 3201.

GRAHAM, Euan Douglas, CB 1985; Principal Clerk of Private Bills, House of Lords, 1961–84; *b* 29 July 1924; *yr s* of Brig. Lord (Douglas) Malise Graham, CB, DSO, MC, RA; *m* 1st, Pauline Pitt-Rivers (*née* Tennant) (marr. diss. 1972); one adopted *s*; 2nd, Caroline, *d* of late K. W. B. Middleton and of Ruth, Lady Kinross; two *d*. *Educ:* Eton; Christ Church, Oxford (MA). Served RAF, 1943–47. Joined Parliament Office, House of Lords, 1950; Clerk, Judicial Office, 1950–60; Principal Clerk of Private Bills, Examiner of Petitions for Private Bills, Taxing Officer, 1960–85. *Recreations:* deer stalking, mountain bicycling. *Address:* Hill Farm, Heddington, near Calne, Wilts SN11 0PW. *Club:* Beefsteak.

GRAHAM, George; Manager, Tottenham Hotspur Football Club, 1998–2001; *b* Scotland, 30 Nov. 1944; *m* 1998, Sue Schmidt. Professional football player, 1962–77: Aston Villa, 1962–64; Chelsea, 1964–66 (League Cup, 1965); Arsenal, 1966–72 (League and FA Cups, 1971); Manchester United, 1972–74; Portsmouth, 1974–76; Crystal Palace, 1976–77; twelve Scotland caps; coach: Queen's Park Rangers, 1977; Crystal Palace, 1977–82; Manager: Millwall, 1982–86; Arsenal, 1986–95 (League Cup, 1987, 1993; League Champions, 1989, 1991; FA Cup, 1993; European Cup Winners' Cup, 1994); Leeds, 1996–98; Tottenham Hotspur, 1998–2001 (League Cup, 1999).

GRAHAM, (George) Ronald (Gibson), CBE 1986; Partner, 1968–2000, Senior Partner, Maclay, Murray & Spens, Solicitors, Glasgow, Edinburgh and London; *b* 15 Oct. 1939; *o s* of James Gibson Graham, MD, and Elizabeth Waddell; *m* 1965, Mirren Elizabeth Carnegie; three *s*. *Educ:* Glasgow Academy; Loretto Sch., Musselburgh; Oriel Coll., Oxford (MA); Glasgow Univ. (LLB). Director: Scottish Widows' Fund and Life Assce Soc., 1984–2000; Scottish Widows Bank PLC, 1995–2002. Co-ordinator of Diploma in Legal Practice, 1979–83; Clerk to Gen. Council, Glasgow Univ., 1990–96, Mem. Ct, 1996–. Mem. Council, 1977–89, Pres., 1984–85, Law Soc. of Scotland. Gov., Jordanhill Coll. of Educn, Glasgow, 1991–93. *Recreations:* fishing, golf, swimming, walking. *Address:* Carse of South Coldoch, Gargunnock, by Stirling FK8 3DF. *T:* (01786) 860397. *Clubs:* The Western, Western Baths (Glasgow).

GRAHAM, Gordon; *see* Graham, L. G.

GRAHAM, Gordon; *see* Graham, W. G.

GRAHAM, Ian James Alastair, OBE 1999; FSA; Director, Maya Corpus Progam, Peabody Museum of Archaeology, Harvard University, since 1993; *b* 12 Nov. 1923; *s* of Captain Lord Alastair Graham, RN, *y s* of 5th Duke of Montrose, and Lady Meriel Olivia Bathurst (*d* 1936), *d* of 7th Earl Bathurst; unmarried. *Educ:* Winchester Coll.; Trinity Coll., Dublin. RNVR (A), 1942–47; TCD 1947–51; Nuffield Foundn Research Scholar at The National Gallery, 1951–54; independent archaeological explorer in Central America, 1959–68; Res. Fellow, 1968–75, Asst Curator, 1975–93, Peabody Mus. of Archaeol., Harvard Univ. Occasional photographer of architecture. Hon. LHD Tulane, 1998; Hon. DLitt Dublin, 2000. MacArthur Foundn Prize Fellowship, 1981. *Publications:* Splendours of the East, 1965; Great Houses of the Western World, 1968; Archaeological Explorations in El Peten, Guatemala, 1967; Corpus of Maya Hieroglyphic Inscriptions, 18 parts, 1975–. *Address:* Chantry Farm, Campsey Ash, Suffolk IP13 0PZ; c/o Peabody Museum, Harvard University, Cambridge, MA, USA.

GRAHAM, Sir James Bellingham, 11th Bt *cr* 1662; researcher in history and art history; *b* 8 Oct. 1940; *e s* of Sir Richard Bellingham Graham, 10th Bt, OBE, and Beatrice, OBE (*d* 1992), *d* of late Michael Hamilton-Spencer-Smith, DSO, MC; *S* father, 1982; *m* 1986, Halina, *d* of Major Wiktor and Eleonora Grubert. *Educ:* Eton College; Christ Church, Oxford (MA). *Publications:* Guide to Norton Conyers, 1976, rewritten 1994; (with Halina Graham) A Guide to the Cecil Higgins Art Gallery, 1987. *Recreations:* travel, visiting historic houses and museums, early science fiction. *Heir: b* Jeremy Richard Graham [*b* 23 Jan. 1949; *m* 1976, Judith, *d* of Gerard McCann; two *s* one *d*]. *Address:* Norton Conyers, Ripon, N Yorks HG4 5EQ. *T:* (01765) 640333.

GRAHAM, Sir James (Fergus Surtees), 7th Bt *cr* 1783, of Netherby, Cumberland; farmer; *b* 29 July 1946; *s* of Sir Charles Graham, 6th Bt and of Isabel Susan Anne, *d* of Major R. L. Surtees, OBE; *S* father, 1997; *m* 1975, Serena Jane, *yr d* of Ronald Frank Kershaw; one *s* two *d. Educ:* Milton Abbey; Royal Agricl Coll., Cirencester. Lloyd's Reinsurance Broker, 1969–90. *Heir: s* Robert Charles Thomas Graham, *b* 19 July 1985.

GRAHAM, James Lowery, OBE 1991; DL; non-executive Chairman, Border Television, Carlisle, since 1999 (Managing Director, 1982–96; Deputy Chairman, 1990–96; Chief Executive Officer and Chairman, 1996–98); *b* 29 Oct. 1932; *s* of William and Elizabeth Graham; *m* 1984, Ann Routledge; two *d* by previous marr. *Educ:* Whitehaven Grammar School. Journalist, North West Evening Mail, Barrow, 1955–62; News Editor, Border Television, 1962–67; Producer, BBC, Leeds, 1967–70; BBC: Regional News Editor, North, 1970–75; Regional Television Manager, North East, 1975–80; Head of Secretariat, Broadcasting House, 1980–82; Sec., Central Music Adv. Council, 1981–82. Jt Sec., Broadcasters' Audience Res. Bd, 1980–82. Dir, Indep. Television Publications, 1982–89. Chm., Independent Television Facilities Centre Ltd, 1987–; Director: Oracle Teletext, 1988–93; Radio Borders, 1989–; Radio SW Scotland, 1989–93 (Chm., 1990–93); Bay Radio Ltd, 1992–94; Central Scotland Radio, 1993–95; Century (formerly North East) Radio, 1993–; Border Radio Holdings, 1997–; Century Radio 105, 1998–; Sunderland City Radio, 1998–; Reliance Security Gp, 1999–. Pres., Prix Italia, 1998– (ITVA rep., 1987–). Dir, Educnl Broadcasting Services Trust, 1992–. Member: BAFTA; Internat. Council, Nat. Acad. of Television Arts and Scis, NY, 1999–; European Movement; Co-operative Internationale de Recherche et d'Action en Matière de Communication (European Producers). Governor: Newcastle Polytechnic, 1975–80; Cumbria Coll. of Art and Design, 1995–. DL Cumbria 2000. FRSA 1987. MInstD; FRTS 1994. Hon. Fellow, Central Lancashire, 2001. Hon. DCL Northumbria, 1999. News Film Award, RTS, 1975; Beffroi d'Or, Lille (European regional broadcasting award), 1983; RTS Regl Broadcasting Award, 1989. *Recreations:* hill walking, ski ing, cycling. *Address:* Oak House, Great Corby, Carlisle, Cumbria CA4 8NE. *Clubs:* Reform, Groucho.

GRAHAM, Sir James (Thompson), Kt 1990; CMG 1986; farmer, since 1946; Director, 1979–89, Chairman, 1982–89, New Zealand Dairy Board, retired; *b* 6 May 1929; *s* of Harold Graham and Florence Cecily Graham; *m* 1955, Ina Isabelle Low; one *s* two *d. Educ:* New Plymouth Boys' High Sch. Dir, NZ Co-op Dairy Co., 1974–89 (Chm., 1979–82). *Recreations:* golf, tennis, bowls. *Address:* 131c Oceanbeach Road, Mount Maunganui, New Zealand. *T:* (75) 754043.

GRAHAM, John, CB 1976; Fisheries Secretary, Ministry of Agriculture, Fisheries and Food, 1967–76; *b* 17 March 1918; *s* of late John Graham; *m* 1940, Betty Ramage Jarvie; two *s* three *d. Educ:* Fettes Coll., Edinburgh; Trinity Coll., Cambridge (Schol.). Classical Tripos, MA Cantab. Entered Post Office as Asst Principal, 1939; Min. of Food, 1940.

GRAHAM, Sir John (Alexander Noble), 4th Bt *cr* 1906, of Larbert; GCMG 1986 (KCMG 1979 CMG 1972); HM Diplomatic Service, retired; Registrar, Order of Saint Michael and Saint George, 1987–2001; Director, Ditchley Foundation, 1987–92; *b* 15 July 1926; *s* of Sir John Reginald Noble Graham, 3rd Bt, VC, OBE and Rachel Septima (*d* 1984), *d* of Col Sir Alexander Sprot, 1st and last Bt; *S* father, 1980; *m* 1st, 1956, Marygold Ellinor Gabrielle Austin (*d* 1991); two *s* one *d*; 2nd, 1992, Jane, *widow* of Christopher Howells. *Educ:* Eton Coll.; Trinity Coll., Cambridge. Army, 1944–47; Cambridge, 1948–50; HM Foreign Service, 1950; Middle East Centre for Arab Studies, 1951; Third Secretary, Bahrain 1951, Kuwait 1952, Amman 1953; Asst Private Sec. to Sec. of State for Foreign Affairs, 1954–57; First Sec., Belgrade, 1957–60, Benghazi, 1960–61; FO 1961–66; Counsellor and Head of Chancery, Kuwait, 1966–69; Principal Private Sec. to Foreign and Commonwealth Sec., 1969–72; Cllr (later Minister) and Head of Chancery, Washington, 1972–74; Ambassador to Iraq, 1974–77; Dep. Under-Sec. of State, FCO, 1977–79; Ambassador to Iran, 1979–80; Deputy Under-Sec. of State, FCO, 1980–82; Ambassador and UK Permanent Representative to NATO, Brussels, 1982–86. *Heir: s* Andrew John Noble Graham, MBE, Brig. late Argyll and Sutherland Highlanders [*b* 21 Oct. 1956; *m* 1984, Susie M. B. O'Riordan, *er d* of Rear-Adm. J. P. B. O'Riordan, *qv*; one *s* three *d*]. *Address:* Salisbury Place, Church Street, Shipton under Wychwood, Oxon OX7 6BP. *Club:* Army and Navy.

GRAHAM, Sir (John) Alistair, Kt 2000; Chairman, Police Complaints Authority, since 2000; *b* 6 Aug. 1942; *s* of late Robert Graham and Dorothy Graham; *m* 1967, Dorothy Jean Wallace; one *s* one *d. Educ:* Royal Grammar Sch., Newcastle upon Tyne. FIPD (FITD 1989; FIPM 1989). Clerical Asst, St George's Hosp., Morpeth, 1961; Admin Trainee, Northern Regional Hosp. Bd, 1963; Higher Clerical Officer, Royal Sussex County Hosp., Brighton, 1964; Legal Dept, TGWU, 1965; The Civil and Public Services Association: Asst Sec., 1966; Asst Gen. Sec., 1975; Dep. Gen. Sec., 1976; Gen. Sec., 1982–86; Dir, Industrial Soc., 1986–91; Chief Executive: Calderdale & Kirklees TEC, 1991–96; Leeds TEC, 1996–2000. Chm., Shareholders' Trust FI Group, 1991–97. Vis. Fellow, Nuffield Coll., Oxford, 1984–92; Vis. Prof., Management Sch., Imperial Coll., London Univ., 1989–91. External assessor, teacher trng courses, Univ. of Huddersfield, 1993–96. Chairman: BBC S and E Regl Adv. Council, 1987–90; Training and Develt Lead Body, 1989–94; Member: Personnel Lead Body, 1991–94; BBC Educn Broadcasting Council, 1991–97; Restrictive Practices Court, 1993–99; Bd, Univ. of Huddersfield Trng and Quality Services Certification Div., 1993–96; Overview Gp on producing standards for Teachers, Teacher Trng Agency, 1996–97. Mem., TUC Gen. Council, 1982–84, 1985–86. Mem., 1988–97, Chm., Staff Cttee, 1991–97, OU Council. Trustee, Duke of Edinburgh Study Conf., 1989–92. Mem., Work, Income and Social Policy Cttee, Joseph Rowntree Foundn, 1997–2000. Bd Mem., 1989–, Chm. Finance Cttee, 1996–97, Opera North; Mem. Management Cttee, Huddersfield Contemporary Music Fest., 1992–97; Chm., Yorks Youth and Music, 1995–97. Assessor, Guildford and Woolwich Inquiry, 1990–94; Chm., Parades Commn for NI, 1997–2000. Contested (Lab) Brighton Pavilion, 1966. FRSA 1989. DUniv Open, 1999. *Recreations:* music, theatre. *Address:* (office) 10 Great George Street, SW1P 3AE.

GRAHAM, Maj.-Gen. John David Carew, CB 1978; CBE 1973 (OBE 1966); Secretary to the Administrative Trustees of the Chevening Estate, 1978–86; *b* 18 Jan. 1923; *s* of late Col J. A. Graham, late RE, and Constance Mary Graham (*née* Carew-Hunt); *m* 1956, Rosemary Elaine Adamson; one *s* one *d. Educ:* Cheltenham Coll. psc 1955; jssc 1962. Commissioned into Argyll and Sutherland Highlanders, 1942 (despatches, 1945); served with 5th (Scottish) Bn, The Parachute Regt, 1946–49; British Embassy, Prague, 1949–50; HQ Scottish Comd, 1956–58; Mil. Asst to CINCENT, Fontainebleau, 1960–62; comd 1st Bn, The Parachute Regt, 1964–66; Instr at Staff Coll., Camberley, 1967; Regtl Col, The Parachute Regt, 1968–69; Comdr, Sultan's Armed Forces, Oman, 1970–72; Indian Nat. Defence Coll., New Delhi, 1973; Asst Chief of Staff, HQ AFCENT, 1974–76; GOC Wales, 1976–78. Hon. Col, Kent ACF, 1981–88 (Chm. Kent ACF Cttee, 1979–86); Hon. Col, 203 (Welsh) Gen. Hosp., RAMC, TA, 1983–88. Freeman, City of London, 1992. OStJ 1978, and Chm., St John Council for Kent, 1978–86; CStJ 1983. Order of Oman, 1972. *Address:* Montrose, 58 Rendez-Vous Ridge East, Christ Church, Barbados, WI.

See also A. C. Graham.

GRAHAM, Sir John (Moodie), 2nd Bt *cr* 1964; Director, Kinnegar Inns Ltd, since 1981; Chairman, John Graham (Dromore) Ltd, 1966–83; *b* 3 April 1938; *s* of Sir Clarence Graham, 1st Bt, MICE, and Margaret Christina Moodie (*d* 1954); *S* father, 1966; *m* 1970, Valerie Rosemary (marr. diss. 1983), *d* of late Frank Gill, Belfast; three *d*; partner since 1980, David Galway. *Educ:* Trinity Coll., Glenalmond; Queen's Univ., Belfast. BSc, Civil Engineering, 1961. Joined family firm of John Graham (Dromore) Ltd, Building and Civil Engineering Contractors, on graduating from University. Director: Electrical Supplies Ltd, 1967–83; Concrete (NI) Ltd, 1967–83; Ulster Quarries Ltd; Graham (Contracts) Ltd, 1971–83; Fieldhouse Plant (NI) Ltd, 1976–83. Chm., Concrete Soc., NI, 1972–74; Senior Vice-Pres., Concrete Soc., 1980; Pres., Northern Ireland Leukaemia Research Fund, 1967. Mem., Lloyd's, 1977–. *Recreations:* sailing, ski-ing, photography. *Address:* Les Bordes d'Arinsal, Andorra. *T:* 837863; 2615 NE 26th Street, Fort Lauderdale, FL 33305–1608, USA. *T:* (954) 5654137; *e-mail:* sirjg@gte.net.

GRAHAM, John Strathie; Secretary and Head of Scottish Executive Rural Affairs Department (formerly Scottish Office Agriculture, Environment and Fisheries Department), since 1998; *b* 27 May 1950; *s* of Sir Norman Graham, *qv*; *m* 1979, Anne Janet Stenhouse; two *s* one *d. Educ:* Edinburgh Academy; Corpus Christi College, Oxford (BA Lit Hum). Joined Scottish Office, 1972; Private Sec. to Minister of State, 1975–76; Industrial Develt and Electricity Divs, 1976–82; Private Sec. to Sec. of State, 1983–85; Asst Sec., Planning and Finance Divs, 1985–91; Under Sec. (Local Govt), Envmt Dept, 1991–96; Prin. Finance Officer, 1996–98. *Recreations:* music, hillwalking. *Address:* Scottish Executive, Pentland House, 47 Robb's Loan, Edinburgh EH14 1TY. *T:* (0131) 244 6021.

GRAHAM, Kenneth, CBE 1987 (OBE 1971); Deputy General Secretary, Trades Union Congress, 1985–87 (Assistant General Secretary, 1977–85); Member, Council, Institute for Employment Studies (formerly of Manpower Studies), 1975–97; *b* 18 July 1922; *er s* of late Ernest Graham and Ivy (*née* Hutchinson), Cleator, Cumbria; *m* 1945, Ann Winifred Muriel Taylor. *Educ:* Workington Techn. Sch.; Leyton Techn. Coll.; Univ. of London (external). Engrg apprentice, 1938–42; Wartime Radar Research Unit, 1942–45; Air Trng Sch., qual. licensed engr, Air Registration Bd, 1947; employed in private industry, Mins of Aircraft Prodn and Supply, BOAC, and RN Scientific Service. Joined AEU, 1938: Mem. Final Appeal Court, Nat. Cttee, Divisional Chm., District Pres., etc, 1947–61; Tutor (part-time) in Trade Union Studies, Univ. of Southampton and WEA, 1958–61; joined TUC Organisation Dept, 1961, Head of TUC Organisation and Industrial Relations Dept, 1966–77. Comr, MSC, 1974–87; Member: Bd, European Foundn for Improvement of Living and Working Conditions, 1976–87; Adv. Cttee, European Social Fund, 1976–87; Council, Templeton Coll. (Oxford Centre for Management Studies), 1984–95; NCVQ, 1986–92; Board, Open Coll., 1987–97; Interim Adv. Cttee to Sec. of State for Educn and Sci., on Teachers' Pay and Conditions, 1987–89; Employment Appeal Tribunal, 1989–93; Management Bd, Univs' Staff Develt and Trng Unit, subseq. Univs' Staff Develt Unit, 1989–93; Professional Conduct Cttee, Gen. Council of the Bar, 1990–95. Mem. Bd, Remploy Ltd, 1987–92. A Vice-Pres., Airborne Forces Charities Appeal, 1990–; Hon. Friend, Airborne Forces Charitable Trust, 1996–. FRSA, 1987. Hon. LLD CNAA, 1986. Special Award of Merit, AEU, 1981; TUC Trades Councils Silver Badge for Merit, 1987; TUC Congress Gold Badge, 1987. *Publication:* contrib. Job Satisfaction: Challenge and Response in Modern Britain, 1976. *Recreations:* music, military history. *Address:* 90 Springfield Drive, Ilford, Essex IG2 6QS. *T:* (020) 8554 0839.

GRAHAM, Prof. (Lawrence) Gordon, PhD; FRSE; Regius Professor of Moral Philosophy, University of Aberdeen, since 1996; *b* 15 July 1949; *s* of William Moore Graham and Hyacinth Elizabeth (*née* Donald); *m* 1971; one *s* one *d. Educ:* Univ. of St Andrews (MA); Univ. of Durham (MA; PhD 1975). FRSE 1999. University of St Andrews: Lectr in Moral Philosophy, 1975–88; Reader, 1988–95; Dir of Music, 1991–95. Sec., Scots Philosophical Club, 1987–2001. *Publications:* Historical Explanation Reconsidered, 1983; Politics in its Place, 1986; Contemporary Social Philosophy, 1988, 4th edn 1995; The Idea of Christian Charity, 1990; Living the Good Life, 1990, 2nd edn 1994; The Shape of the Past, 1997; Ethics and International Relations, 1997; Philosophy of the Arts, 1997, 2nd edn 2000; The Internet: a philosophical inquiry, 1999; Evil and Christian Ethics, 2000. *Recreations:* music, walking, poetry. *Address:* Department of Philosophy, University of Aberdeen, Old Aberdeen AB24 3UB. *T:* (01224) 272372.

GRAHAM, (Malcolm Gray) Douglas; DL; Chairman: The Midland News Association Ltd, since 1984 (Deputy Chairman, 1978–84); Claverley Co., since 1993; Stars News Shops Ltd, since 1994; *b* 18 Feb. 1930; *s* of late Malcolm Graham and Annie Jeanette Robinson; *m* 1980, Sara Anne Elwell (*née* Anderson). *Educ:* Shrewsbury Sch. National Service, RM, 1948–50. Newspaper trng, UK and Australia, 1950–53; Dir, Express & Star (Wolverhampton) Ltd, 1957. President: Young Newspapermen's Assoc., 1969; W Midlands Newspaper Soc., 1973–74; Chm., Evening Newspaper Advertising Bureau, 1978–79. DL Shropshire, 1997. *Recreation:* shooting. *Address:* Roughton Manor, Bridgnorth, Shropshire WV15 5HE. *T:* (01746) 716209.

GRAHAM, His Honour Martin; QC 1976; a Circuit Judge, 1986–2000; *b* 10 Feb. 1929; *m* 1962, Jane Filby; one *d. Educ:* Emanuel School; Trinity College, Oxford (Scholar; MA, PPE). Called to the Bar, Middle Temple, 1952; a Recorder, 1986. Nat. Service, Officer BAOR, 1953–55. *Recreations:* swimming, tennis. *Address:* 7 Oakeshott Avenue, Highgate, N6 6NT. *Clubs:* Reform, Royal Automobile, Hurlingham.

GRAHAM, Sir Norman (William), Kt 1971; CB 1961; FRSE; Secretary, Scottish Education Department, 1964–73, retired; *b* 11 Oct. 1913; *s* of William and Margaret Graham; *m* 1949, Catherine Mary Strathie; two *s* one *d. Educ:* High Sch. of Glasgow; Glasgow Univ. Dept of Health for Scotland, 1936; Private Sec. to Permanent Under-Sec. of State, 1939–40; Ministry of Aircraft Production, 1940; Principal Private Sec. to Minister, 1944–45; Asst Sec., Dept of Health for Scotland, 1945; Under-Sec., Scottish Home and Health Dept, 1956–63. Hon. DLitt Heriot-Watt, 1971; DUniv Stirling, 1974. *Recreations:* golf, gardening. *Address:* 6 The Steading, Chesterhall, Longniddry, East

Lothian EH32 0PQ. *T:* (01875) 852130. *Club:* New (Edinburgh).
See also J. S. Graham.

GRAHAM, Sir Peter, KCB 1993 (CB 1982); QC 1990; First Parliamentary Counsel, 1991–94; *b* 7 Jan. 1934; *o s* of late Alderman Douglas Graham, CBE, Huddersfield, and Ena May (*née* Jackson); *m* 1st, Judith Mary Dunbar; two *s*; 2nd, Anne Silvia Garcia (*see* A. S. Graham); 3rd, Janet, *o d* of late William Eric Walker, Mayfield, Sussex. *Educ:* St Bees Sch., Cumberland (scholar); St John's Coll., Cambridge (scholar, 1st cl. Law Tripos, MA, LLM, McMahon Law Studentship). Served as pilot in Fleet Air Arm, 1952–55, Lieut, RNR. Called to Bar, Gray's Inn, 1958 (Holker Exhbn; H. C. Richards Prize, Ecclesiastical Law; Bencher, 1992), Lincoln's Inn, 1982; joined Parliamentary Counsel Office, 1959; Parly Counsel, 1972–86; with Law Commn, 1979–81; Second Parly Counsel, 1987–91. External Examr (Legislation), Univ. of Edinburgh, 1977–81; Consultant: in Legislative Drafting, Office of Attorney-Gen., Dublin, 1994–96; to Hassans' Gibraltar, 1997–. Mem., Tax Law Review Cttee, Inst. of Fiscal Studies, 1994–. Hon. Legal Adviser, Historic Vehicle Clubs Cttee, 1967–86. *Recreations:* vintage and classic car motoring, la bonne cuisine. *Address:* Le Petit Château, La Vallette, 87190 Magnac Laval, France. *Club:* Sette of Odd Volumes.

GRAHAM, Sir Peter (Alfred), Kt 1987; OBE 1969; FCIB, CIMgt; Chairman, Crown Agents for Oversea Governments and Administrations, 1983–90; *b* 25 May 1922; *s* of Alfred Graham and Margaret (*née* Winder); *m* 1953, Luned Mary (*née* Kenealy-Jones); two *s* two *d*. *Educ:* St Joseph's Coll., Beulah Hill. FCIB (FIB 1975); CIMgt (CBIM 1981). Served War, RNVR: Pilot, FAA. Joined The Chartered Bank of India, Australia and China, 1947; 24 yrs overseas banking career, incl. appts in Japan, India and Hong Kong; i/c The Chartered Bank, Hong Kong, 1962–70; Chm. (1st), Hong Kong Export Credit Insurance Corp., 1965–70; General Manager 1970, Dep. Man. Dir 1975, Gp Man. Dir, 1977–83, Sen. Dep. Chm., 1983–87, Chm., 1987–88, Standard Chartered Bank, London. Director: Standard Chartered Finance Ltd, Sydney (formerly Mutual Acceptance Corp.), 1974–87; First Bank Nigeria, Lagos, 1976–87; Union Bank Inc., Los Angeles, 1979–88; Singapore Land Ltd, 1988–89; Employment Conditions Abroad Ltd, 1988–94; Dolphin Hldgs Ltd, Bermuda, 1995–99; Chairman: Standard Chartered Merchant Bank Ltd, 1977–83; Mocatta Commercial Ltd, 1983–87; Mocatta & Goldsmid Ltd, 1983–87; Equatorial Bank, 1989–93; Deputy Chairman: Chartered Trust plc, 1983–85; Governing Body, ICC UK, 1985–92; Mem., Bd of Banking Supervision, 1986–87; Pres., Inst. of Bankers, 1981–83. City University: Chm., Adv. Cttee, 1981–86, Council, 1986–92, Business Sch.; Chm., Council, 1986–92; Mem., Court, 1997–2000. Formerly Chm., Exchange Banks' Assoc., Hong Kong; Mem., Govt cttees connected with trade and industry, Hong Kong. FRSA 1983. Freeman, City of London, 1982. Hon. DSc City Univ., 1985. *Recreations:* golf, tennis. *Clubs:* Naval, Royal Automobile; Hong Kong (Hong Kong); Rye Golf.

GRAHAM, Peter Donald, CMG 1997; Senior Partner, Graham, Thompson & Co., since 1950; *b* 11 Oct. 1928; *m* 1951, Jolanta Maria Poplawska (*d* 1995); one *s* one *d*. *Educ:* Queen's Coll., Nassau, Bahamas; Bishop's Coll. Sch., Lennoxville, Canada; Univ. of London (LLB). Called to the Bar, Lincoln's Inn, 1949. Mem., Bahamas House of Assembly, 1956–72; Minister of Labour and Minister of Housing, 1964–67; Dir, Central Bank of the Bahamas, 1992–. Mem., Bahamas Bar Assoc. *Recreations:* golf, tennis. *Address:* PO Box N272, Nassau, Bahamas. *Clubs:* Lyford Cay (Nassau); Nassau Lawn Tennis.

GRAHAM, Dr Peter John; Director of Strategy and Analytical Support, Health and Safety Executive, since 1999; *b* 16 Sept. 1943; *s* of John Graham and late Judy Graham; *m* 1968, Janice Head; three *s*. *Educ:* St Joseph's Coll., Stoke-on-Trent; Liverpool Univ. (BSc; PhD Maths 1968). DTI, 1969–79; 1st Sec., UK Perm. Repn, Brussels, 1979–82; DTI, 1982–84; Dept of Employment, 1984–88; Health and Safety Executive: Hazardous Substances Div., 1988–91; General Policy Br., 1991–93; Offshore Safety Div., 1993–94; Dir, Health, 1994–99. *Address:* c/o Health and Safety Executive, Rose Court, Southwark Bridge, SE1 9HS. *T:* (020) 7717 6000.

GRAHAM, Lt.-Gen. Sir Peter (Walter), KCB 1991; CBE 1981 (OBE 1978; MBE 1972); GOC Scotland and Governor of Edinburgh Castle, 1991–93, retired; *b* 14 March 1937; *s* of Dr Walter Graham and Suzanne Graham (*née* Simon); *m* 1963, Alison Mary, MB ChB, MRCGP, *d* of D. B. Morren, TD; three *s*. *Educ:* Fyvie Village School, Aberdeenshire; Hall Sch., Hampstead; St Paul's Sch.; RMA Sandhurst; psc (Aust), ocds (Can). Commissioned, The Gordon Highlanders, 1956; regtl appts, Dover, BAOR, Scotland, Kenya, 1957–62; HQ Highland Bde, 1962–63; Adjt, 1 Gordons, Kenya, Scotland, Borneo (despatches), 1963–66; Staff Capt., HQ (1 Br) Corps, 1966–67; Aust. Staff Coll., 1968; Co. Comdr, 1 Gordons, BAOR, 1969–70; Bde Maj., 39 Inf. Bde, Ulster, 1970–72; 2nd i/c 1 Gordons, Scotland, Ulster, Singapore, 1972–74; MA to Adjt-Gen., MoD, 1974–75; CO, 1 Gordons, Scotland, Ulster, 1976–78; COS, HQ 3rd Armd Div., BAOR, 1978–82; Comdr UDR, 1982–84 (despatches); Nat. Defence Coll., Canada, 1984–85; Dep. Mil. Sec., MoD, 1985–87; GOC Eastern Dist, 1987–89; Comdt, RMA, Sandhurst, 1989–91. Col, The Gordon Highlanders, 1986–94; Col Comdt, The Scottish Div., 1991–93. Mem., Royal Company of Archers, Queen's Body Guard for Scotland, 1986–. Chairman: Gordon Highlanders Regtl Trust Fund, 1986–; Mgt Cttee, The Gordon Highlanders Mus., 1994–. Burgess of Guild, City of Aberdeen, 1994. Hon. DLitt Robert Gordon Univ., Aberdeen, 1996. *Publications:* (with Pipe Major B. MacRae) The Gordon Highlanders Pipe Music Collection, Vol. 1, 1983, 3rd edn 1986, Vol. 2, 1985; (contrib.) John Baynes, Soldiers of Scotland, 1988; contrib. to Jl of RUSI. *Recreations:* stalking, hill walking, shooting, reading, pipe music, gardening under wife's directions. *Address:* c/o Army HQ Scotland, Craigiehall, W Lothian EH30 9TN.
See also Sir A. M. Graham.

GRAHAM, Prof. Philip Jeremy; Chairman, Association of Child Psychology and Psychiatry, since 2001; *b* 3 Sept. 1932; *s* of Jacob Rackham Graham and Pauline Graham; *m* 1960, Nori (*née* Burawoy); two *s* one *d*. *Educ:* Perse Sch., Cambridge; Cambridge Univ. (MA); University Coll. Hosp., London. FRCP 1973; FRCPsych 1972. Consultant Psychiatrist: Maudsley Hosp., London, 1966–68; Hosp. for Sick Children, Great Ormond Street, London, 1968–74; Prof. of Child Psychiatry, 1975–94 and Dean, 1985–90, Inst. of Child Health, London Univ.; Prof. of Child Psychiatry, Univ. of Oslo, 1994–2000; Lectr, Dept of Develtl Psychiatry, Univ. of Cambridge, 1994–2000. Chm., Nat. Children's Bureau, 1994–2000 (Chm., Child Policy Rev. Gp, 1987–89). President: European Soc. for Child and Adolescent Psychiatry, 1987–91; Psychiatry Section, RSM, 1994–95; Vice-Pres., RCPsych, 1996–98. Sen. Mem., Wolfson Coll., Cambridge, 1994–. *Publications:* A Neuropsychiatric Study in Childhood (jtly), 1970; (ed) Epidemiological Approaches to Child Psychiatry, 1977; (jtly) Child Psychiatry: a developmental approach, 1986, 3rd edn 1999; (ed) Cognitive Behaviour Therapy for Children and Families, 1998; various publications on child and adolescent psychiatry. *Recreations:* reading, play-going, tennis. *Address:* 27 St Alban's Road, NW5 1RG.

GRAHAM, Sir Ralph Stuart, 14th Bt *cr* 1629 (NS), of Esk, Cumberland; *b* 5 Nov. 1950; *s* of Sir Ralph Wolfe Graham, 13th Bt and of Geraldine, *d* of Austin Velour; *S* father, 1988; *m* 1st, 1972, Roxanne (*d* 1978), *d* of Mrs Lovette Gurzan; 2nd, 1979, Deena Vandergrift; one adopted *s*. *Heir:* *b* Robert Bruce Graham [*b* 14 Nov. 1953; *m* 1974, Denise, *d* of T. Juranich; two *s*].

GRAHAM, Robert Martin; Chief Executive, British United Provident Association, 1984–91; *b* 20 Sept. 1930; *s* of Francis P. Graham and Margaret M. Graham (*née* Broderick); *m* 1959, Eileen (*née* Hoey); two *s* two *d*. *Educ:* Dublin; ACII. Hibernian Fire and General Insurance Co. Ltd, 1948–57; Voluntary Health Insurance Board, 1957–82 (to Chief Exec.); Dep. Chief Exec., BUPA 1982. Chm., Board of Management, Meath Hosp., 1972–82; Pres., Internat. Fedn of Voluntary Health Service Funds, 1988–90 (Dep. Pres., 1986–88); Vice-Pres., Assoc. Internationale de la Mutualité, 1990– (Mem. Bd of Govs, 1978–91); Mem., Central Council, Federated Voluntary Hosps, Ireland, 1978–82. *Address:* 39 Garratts Lane, Banstead, Surrey SM7 2ED. *T:* (01737) 360771. *Clubs:* Royal Automobile, Rotary Club of London.

GRAHAM, Ronald; *see* Graham, G. R. G.

GRAHAM, Dr Ronald Cairns, CBE 1992; General Manager, Tayside Health Board, 1985–93 (Chief Administrative Medical Officer, 1973–85); *b* 8 Oct. 1931; *s* of Thomas Graham and Helen Cairns; *m* 1959, Christine Fraser Osborne; two *s* one *d*. *Educ:* Airdrie Acad.; Glasgow Univ. MB, ChB Glasgow 1956; DipSocMed Edin. 1968; FFCM 1973; FRCPE 1983. West of Scotland; house jobs, gen. practice and geriatric med., 1956–62; Dep. Med. Supt, Edin. Royal Infirmary, 1962–65; Asst Sen. Admin. MO, SE Regional Hosp. Bd, 1965–69; Dep. and then Sen. Admin. MO, Eastern Regional Hosp. Bd, 1969–73. Mem. Court, Univ. of Dundee, 1994–. *Recreations:* fishing, bowling. *Address:* 34 Dalgleish Road, Dundee DD4 7JT. *T:* (01382) 455426.

GRAHAM, Sir Samuel Horatio, Kt 1988; CMG 1965; OBE 1962; Chief Justice of Grenada, 1987–90; *b* Trinidad, 3 May 1912; *o s* of late Rev. Benjamin Graham and Mrs Graham, Trinidad; *m* 1943, Oris Gloria (*née* Teka); two *s* four *d*. *Educ:* Barbados; External Student, London Univ. BA (London) 1945; LLB (London) 1949. Teacher and journalist until called to Bar, Gray's Inn, 1949. Private practice as Barrister in Grenada, 1949–53; Magistrate, St Lucia, 1953–57; Crown Attorney, St Kitts, 1957–59; Attorney-General, St Kitts, 1960–62; Administrator of St Vincent, 1962–66; Puisne Judge, British Honduras, 1966–69; Pres., Industrial Court of Antigua, 1969–70, Associate Pres., 1981–84; Puisne Judge, Supreme Court of the Commonwealth of the Bahamas, 1973–78. Acted Chief Justice: British Honduras, Feb.–May 1968; Bahamas, Oct. 1977; Temp. Judge, Belize Court of Appeal, 1980. Judicial Mem., Bermuda Constituencies Boundaries Commn, 1979. Chairman: Grenada Develt Bank, 1985–87; Grenada Industrial Develt Corp., 1985–87. Mem., Council of Legal Educn, WI, 1971–. Chairman Inquiries into: Income Tax Reliefs; Coconut Industry, St Lucia, 1955; Legislators' Salaries, St Kitts, 1962. Acted Administrator of St Lucia, St Kitts and Dominica on various occasions. CStJ 1964. *Recreations:* bridge, swimming. *Address:* PO Box 615, St George's, Grenada, West Indies.

GRAHAM, (Stewart) David; QC 1977; Partner, Cork Gully, 1985–92; *b* 27 Feb. 1934; *s* of late Lewis Graham and of Gertrude Graham; *m* 1959, Corinne Carmona; two *d*. *Educ:* Leeds Grammar Sch.; St Edmund Hall, Oxford (MA, BCL). Called to the Bar, Middle Temple, 1957; Harmsworth Law Scholar, 1958. Mem. Council, Justice, 1976–96 (Chm., Cttee on Protection of Small Investor, 1989–92; Chm., Cttee on Insolvency, 1993–94); Mem., Insolvency Rules Adv. Cttee, 1984–86; Chm., Law, Parly and Gen. Purposes Cttee, Bd of Deputies of British Jews, 1983–88. Indep. Mem. Council, The Insurance Ombudsman Bureau, 1993–; Associate Mem., British and Irish (formerly UK) Ombudsman Assoc., 1994–2001. Vis. Fellow, Centre for Commercial Law, QMW, London, 1992–. Chm. Editorial Bd, Insolvency Intelligence, 1988–94. FRSA 1995. *Publications:* (ed jtly) Williams and Muir Hunter on Bankruptcy, 18th edn 1968, 19th edn 1979; (contrib.) Longman's Insolvency, 1986; (ed) legal textbooks. *Recreations:* biography, music, drama, travel, history of insolvency. *Address:* 6 Grosvenor Lodge, Dennis Lane, Stanmore, Mddx HA7 4JE. *T:* (020) 8954 3783.

GRAHAM, Stuart Twentyman, CBE 1981; DFC 1943; FCIS, FCIB; Chairman, Aitken Hume Bank (formerly Aitken Hume) Ltd, 1985–93; *b* 26 Aug. 1921; *s* of late Twentyman Graham; *m* 1948, Betty June Cox (*d* 1999); one *s*. *Educ:* Kilburn Grammar Sch. Served War, 1940–46: commissioned, RAF, 1942. Entered Midland Bank, 1938; Jt Gen. Manager, 1966–70; Asst Chief Gen. Manager, 1970–74; Chief Gen. Manager, 1974–81; Gp Chief Exec., 1981–82; Dir, 1974–85. Chairman: Northern Bank Ltd, 1982–85; International Commodities Clearing House Ltd, 1982–86; Director: Allied Lyons plc, 1981–92; Sheffield Forgemasters Holdings, 1983–85; Aitken Hume International, 1985–93; Scotia (formerly Efamol) Hldgs, 1985–95. *Recreations:* music, reading. *Club:* Royal Air Force.

GRAHAM, Susan Alesta; mezzo soprano; *b* 23 July 1960; *d* of Floyd Ben Graham and Betty Fort. *Educ:* Midland Lee High Sch.; Texas Technical Univ.; Manhattan Sch. of Music. Opera début in Vanessa, St Louis, 1988. Regular performances with Metropolitan Opera, 1991–, and at Salzburg Fest.; other appearances include: Royal Opera, 1994–; WNO, 1994–; Glyndebourne; Vienna State Opera; La Scala; Paris Opéra, etc. Rôles include: title rôle, Chérubin; Octavian in Der Rosenkavalier; Dorabella in Così fan tutte; Cherubino in Le Nozze di Figaro; title rôle, Arianna; title rôle, Iphigénie en Tauride; Charlotte in Werther; title rôle, Béatrice et Bénédict; Marguerite in La damnation de Faust; title rôle in world première of Monteverdi's Arianna. Numerous recitals and recordings. Metropolitan Opera Nat. Council Award, 1988. *Address:* c/o Matthew Epstein, CAMI, 165 West 57th Street, New York, NY 10019, USA.

GRAHAM, Thomas; *b* 5 Dec. 1943; *m* Joan Bagley; two *s*. Engineer with Rolls-Royce, 1965–78; Office Manager, Robertson and Ross, solicitors, 1982–87. Mem., Strathclyde Reg. Council, 1978–87. MP Renfrew and Inverclyde, 1987–97, Renfrewshire, 1997–2001 (Lab 1987–98, Ind. 1998–2001). *Address:* 265 Gilmartin Road, Linwood, Paisley PA3 3SU.

GRAHAM, Rear-Adm. Wilfred Jackson, CB 1979; *b* 17 June 1925; *s* of late William Bryce Graham and Jean Hill Graham (*née* Jackson); *m* 1951, Gillian Mary Finlayson; three *s* one *d*. *Educ:* Rossall Sch., Fleetwood, Lancs. Served War of 1939–45, Royal Navy: Cadet, 1943; specialised in gunnery, 1951; Comdr 1960; Captain 1967; IDC, 1970; Captain, HMS Ark Royal, 1975–76; Flag Officer, Portsmouth, 1976–79, retired. Dir and Sec., RNLI, 1979–87. Mem. Council, Rossall Sch., 1988–95. Gov., E. Hayes Dashwood Foundn, 1994–. FNI 1987. *Recreations:* sailing, walking. *Address:* Yarnfield Cottage, Maiden Bradley, Warminster, Wilts BA12 7HY. *Clubs:* Royal Naval Sailing Association, Royal Yacht Squadron.

GRAHAM, William; *see* Graham, A. W.

GRAHAM, William Franklin, (Billy Graham); Evangelist; *b* Charlotte, NC, 7 Nov. 1918; *s* of late William Franklin Graham and Morrow (*née* Coffey); *m* 1943, Ruth McCue Bell; two *s* three *d*. *Educ:* Florida Bible Institute, Tampa (ThB); Wheaton Coll., Ill (AB). Ordained to Baptist ministry, 1939; first Vice-Pres., Youth for Christ Internat., 1945–50; Pres., Northwestern Coll., Minneapolis, 1947–52; Evangelistic campaigns, 1946–; worldwide weekly broadcast, 1950–; many evangelistic tours of Great Britain, Europe, the Far East, South America, Australia and Russia. Chairman, Board of World Wide Pictures Inc. Holds numerous honorary degrees in Divinity, Laws, Literature and the Humanities, from American universities and colleges; also varied awards from organisations, 1954–, inc. Templeton Foundn Prize, 1982; President's Medal of Freedom Award, 1983; Congressional Gold Medal, 1996. *Publications include:* Peace with God, 1953; World Aflame, 1965; Jesus Generation, 1971; Angels—God's Secret Agents, 1975; How to be Born Again, 1977; The Holy Spirit, 1978; Till Armageddon, 1981; Approaching Hoofbeats: the four horsemen of the Apocalypse, 1983; A Biblical Standard for Evangelists, 1984; Unto the Hills, 1986; Facing Death and the Life After, 1987; Answers to Life's Problems, 1988; Hope for the Troubled Heart, 1991; Storm Warning, 1992; Just As I Am, 1997. *Recreations:* swimming, walking. *Address:* (office) 1300 Harmon Place, Minneapolis, MN 55403, USA. *T:* (612) 3380500.

GRAHAM, (William) Gordon, MC 1944 (Bar 1945); Editor, LOGOS, since 1990; Group Chairman, Butterworth Publishers, 1975–90 (Chief Executive, 1974–87); *b* 17 July 1920; *s* of Thomas Graham and Marion Hutcheson; US citizen, 1963; *m* 1st, 1943, Margaret Milne, Bombay (*d* 1946); one *d*; 2nd, 1948, Friedel Gramm (*d* 1992), Zürich; one *d*; 3rd, 1994, Betty Cottrell, USA. *Educ:* Hutchesons' Grammar Sch.; Glasgow Univ. (MA 1940). Commissioned, Queen's Own Cameron Highlanders, 1941; served in India and Burma, 1942–46: Captain 1944, Major 1945; GSO II India Office, 1946. Newspaper correspondent and publishers' representative in India, 1946–55; Internat. Sales Manager, 1956–63, Vice-Pres., 1961–63, McGraw-Hill Book Co., New York; Man. Dir, McGraw-Hill Publishing Co., UK, 1963–74; Director: W & R Chambers, Edinburgh, 1974–83; International Publishing Corp., 1975–82; Reed Publishing Gp, 1982–90; Chairman: Internat. Electronic Publishing Res. Centre Ltd, 1981–84; Publishers Database Ltd, 1982–84; Bd, R. R. Bowker Co., 1986–90; Mem. Bd, Polish Scientific Publishers, 1994–99. Chm., Soc. of Bookmen, 1972–75; Publishers Association: Mem. Council, 1972–87; Chm., Electronic Publishing Panel, 1980–83; Vice Pres., 1984–85, 1987–88; Pres., 1985–87. Member Board: British Liby, 1980–86; Eur. Foundn for Liby Co-operation, 1991–95. Trustee, Kraszna-Krausz Foundn, 1987–97 (Chm. Trustees, 1990–95). Correspondent, Christian Science Monitor, 1946–56. FRSA 1978. DUniv Stirling, 1993. *Publications:* As I Was Saying: essays on the international book business, 1994; Butterworths History of a Publishing House, 1997; articles in US and British trade press. *Recreations:* ski-ing, writing, fostering transatlantic understanding, landscape gardening, singing sentimental songs. *Address:* White Lodge, Beechwood Drive, Marlow, Bucks SL7 2DH. *T:* (01628) 483371; Juniper Acres, East Hill, Keene, NY 12942, USA.

GRAHAM, Winston Mawdsley, OBE 1983; FRSL; *b* Victoria Park, Manchester; *m* 1939, Jean Mary Williamson (*d* 1992); one *s* one *d*. Chm., Soc. of Authors, 1967–69. Books trans. into 17 languages. *Publications:* some early novels (designedly) out of print, and: Night Journey, 1941 (rev. edn 1966); The Merciless Ladies, 1944 (rev. edn 1979); The Forgotten Story, 1945 (ITV prodn, 1983); Ross Poldark, 1945; Demelza, 1946; Take My Life, 1947 (filmed 1947); Cordelia, 1949; Night Without Stars, 1950 (filmed 1950); Jeremy Poldark, 1950; Fortune is a Woman, 1953 (filmed 1956); Warleggan, 1953; The Little Walls, 1955; The Sleeping Partner, 1956 (filmed 1958; ITV prodn, 1967); Greek Fire, 1957; The Tumbled House, 1959; Marnie, 1961 (filmed 1963); The Grove of Eagles, 1963 (Book Society Choice); After the Act, 1965; The Walking Stick, 1967 (filmed 1970); Angell, Pearl and Little God, 1970; The Japanese Girl (short stories), 1971; The Spanish Armadas, 1972; The Black Moon, 1973; Woman in the Mirror, 1975; The Four Swans, 1976; The Angry Tide, 1977; The Stranger from the Sea, 1981; The Miller's Dance, 1982; Poldark's Cornwall, 1983; The Loving Cup, 1984; The Green Flash, 1986; Cameo, 1988; The Twisted Sword, 1990; Stephanie, 1992; Tremor, 1995; The Ugly Sister, 1998. BBC TV Series Poldark (the first four Poldark novels), 1975–76, second series (the next three Poldark novels), 1977; Circumstantial Evidence (play), 1979. *Recreation:* gardening. *Address:* Abbotswood House, Buxted, East Sussex TN22 4PB. *Clubs:* Savile, Beefsteak, Pratt's.

See also A. W. M. Graham.

GRAHAM, Yvonne Georgette; Headmistress, Clifton High School, Bristol, 1996–97; *b* 31 Aug. 1943; *d* of J. van Gorkom and M. E. van Gorkom-Pas; *m* 1967, Lt-Col I. G. Graham, RE (retd); two *s*. *Educ:* Alexander Hegius-Gymnasium-Deventer; Amsterdam Univ. (MA); London Univ. Various teaching posts in England, Germany and Holland, 1965–90; Headmistress, Lavant House Sch., Chichester, 1990–95. *Recreations:* reading, travel, theatre, music. *Address:* 20 Stanton Drive, Chichester, West Sussex PO19 4QN. *T:* (01243) 528111.

GRAHAM-BRYCE, Ian James, CBE 2001; DPhil; Principal and Vice-Chancellor, University of Dundee, 1994–2000, now Principal Emeritus; *b* 20 March 1937; *s* of late Alexander Graham-Bryce, FRCS, and Dame Isabel Graham-Bryce, DBE; *m* 1959, Anne Elisabeth Metcalf; one *s* three *d*. *Educ:* William Hulme's Grammar Sch., Manchester; University Coll., Oxford (Exhibnr). BA, MA, BSc, DPhil (Oxon); FRSC, CChem 1981; FRSE 1996. Research Asst, Univ. of Oxford, 1958–61; Lectr, Dept of Biochemistry and Soil Sci., UCNW, Bangor, 1961–64; Sen. Scientific Officer, Rothamsted Exper. Station, 1964–70; Sen. Res. Officer, ICI Plant Protection Div., Jealott's Hill Res. Station, Bracknell, Berks, 1970–72; Special Lectr in Pesticide Chemistry, Dept of Zoology and Applied Entomology, Imperial Coll. of Science and Technology, 1970–72 (Vis. Prof., 1976–79); Rothamsted Experimental Station: Head, Dept of Insecticides and Fungicides, 1972–79; Dep. Director, 1975–79; Dir, East Malling Res. Stn, Maidstone, Kent, 1979–86 (Trustee, Develt and Endowment Fund, 1986–); Cons. Dir, Commonwealth Bureau of Horticulture and Plantation Crops, 1979–86; Hon. Lectr, Dept of Biology, Univ. of Strathclyde, 1977–80; Hd of Envmtl Affairs Div., Shell Internat. Petroleum Maatschappij BV, 1986–94. Society of Chemical Industry, London: Pres., 1982–84; Mem. Council, 1969–72 and 1974–89; Hon. Sec., Home Affairs, 1977–80; Chm., Pesticides Gp, 1978–80; Sec., Physico-Chemical and Biophysical Panel, 1968–70, Chm., 1973–75; Mem., British Nat. Cttee for Chemistry, 1982–84. President: Assoc. of Applied Biologists, 1988 (Vice-Pres., 1985–87); Scottish Assoc. of Marine Sci., 2000–. Chm., Agrochemical Planning Gp, IOCD, 1985–88; Mem., Scientific Cttee, Eur. Chemical Industry Ecol. and Toxicol. Centre, 1988–94; Vice-Chm., Environmental Res. Wkg Gp, Industrial R&D Adv. Cttee to EC, 1988–91; Member: NERC, 1989–96 (Chm., Polar Sci. and Technol. Bd, 1995–96); Royal Commn on Envmtl Pollution, 2000–. Hon. Vice-Pres., British Crop Protection Council, (Pres., 1996–2000). Member, Board of Directors: British Council Educnl Counselling Service, 1996–98; Quality Assurance Agency for Higher Educn, 1997–98; Rothamsted Experimental Station, 2000–; Convener, Cttee of Scottish Higher Educn Principals, 1998–2000; Vice Pres., CVCP, 1999–2000. Governor: Long Ashton Res. Stn, 1979–85; Wye Coll., 1979–86, Imperial Coll., 1985–, Univ. of London; Hon. Advr, Zhejiang Wanli Univ., China, 1999–. Member, Editorial Board: Chemico-Biological Interactions, 1973–77; Pesticide Science, 1978–80; Agriculture, Ecosystems and Environment, 1978–87. FRSA 1996. Hon. LLD Dundee, 2001. British Crop Protection Council Medal, 2000. *Publications:* Physical Principles of Pesticide Behaviour, 1980; papers on soil science, plant nutrition, crop protection, and envmtl matters in sci. jls. *Recreations:* music (espec. opera), ski-ing, windsurfing. *Clubs:* Athenæum, Caledonian.

GRAHAM-CAMPBELL, Prof. James Alastair, FBA 2001; FSA, FSAScot; FRHistS; Professor of Medieval Archaeology, University of London, at University College, since 1991; *b* 7 Feb. 1947; *s* of David John Graham-Campbell and Joan Sybil Graham-Campbell (*née* Maclean). *Educ:* Eton Coll.; Trinity Coll., Cambridge (MA, PhD); Bergen Univ.; Oslo Univ.; UCL. FSA 1977. Asst Lectr in Archaeology, UC Dublin, 1971–73; Lectr, 1973–82, Reader, 1982–91, in Medieval Archaeology, UCL. Vis. Prof., Univ. of Minnesota, 1981; British Acad. Res. Reader, 1988–90; O'Donnell Lectr, Univ. of Wales, 1989; Crabtree Orator, UCL, 1990; Rhind Lectr, Soc. of Antiquaries of Scotland, 1996. Mem., Ancient Monuments Adv. Cttee, English Heritage, 1992–97. Sec., Soc. for Medieval Archaeology, 1976–82. MIFA. *Publications:* Viking Artefacts, 1980; The Viking World, 1980, 3rd edn 2001; (jtly) The Vikings, 1980; (ed) Cultural Atlas of the Viking World, 1994; The Viking-Age Gold and Silver of Scotland, 1995;(jtly) Vikings in Scotland: an archaeological survey, 1998; numerous articles in learned jls. *Recreations:* cooking, gardening, music. *Address:* Institute of Archaeology (UCL), 31–34 Gordon Square, WC1H 0PY. *T:* (020) 7679 7510. *Club:* Athenæum.

GRAHAM-DIXON, Andrew Michael; writer and presenter, Music and Arts Department, BBC Television, since 1992; Chief Arts Feature Writer, Sunday Telegraph Magazine, since 1999; *b* 26 Dec. 1960; *s* of Anthony Philip Graham-Dixon, *qv*, and Suzanne Graham-Dixon (*née* Villar); *m* 1985, Sabine Marie-Pascale Tilly; one *s* two *d*. *Educ:* Westminster Sch.; Christ Church, Oxford (MA 1st Cl. English); Courtauld Inst. Chief Art Critic, 1986–97, Chief Arts Feature Writer, 1997–99, The Independent. BP Arts Journalist of Year, 1988, 1989, 1990; Hawthornden Prize for Art Criticism, 1991; 1st Prize, Reportage Section, Montreal Internat. Fest. of Films, 1994. *Publications:* Howard Hodgkin: paintings, 1994; A History of British Art, 1996; Paper Museum: writings about paintings, mostly, 1996; Renaissance, 1999. *Recreations:* snooker, horse-racing. *Address:* Sunday Telegraph Magazine, 1 Canada Square, Canary Wharf, E14 5DT. *Club:* Camden Snooker Centre.

GRAHAM-DIXON, Anthony Philip; QC 1973; *b* 5 Nov. 1929; *s* of late Leslie Charles Graham-Dixon, QC; *m* 1956, Margaret Suzanne Villar; one *s* one *d*. *Educ:* Westminster School; Christ Church, Oxford. MA (1st Cl. Hon. Mods, 1st Cl. Lit. Hum.). RNVR, 1953–55, Lieut (SP). Called to the Bar, Inner Temple, 1956, Bencher 1982; Member of Gray's Inn, 1965–. Mem. Council, Charing Cross Hosp. Medical School, 1976–83. Chm., London Concertino Ltd, 1982–. Dep. Chm., PHLS, 1988–96 (Bd Mem., 1987–96). Gov., Bedales Sch., 1988–96. Trustee, SPNM, 1988–97 (Chm. Trustees, 1994–97). Chm., London Jupiter Orch. Trust Ltd, 2001. *Publication:* (mem. adv. bd) Competition Law in Western Europe and the USA, 1976. *Recreations:* music (especially opera), gardening. *Address:* 46A Courtfield Gardens, SW5 0NA. *T:* (020) 7373 1461; Masketts Manor, Nutley, Uckfield, East Sussex TN22 3HD. *T:* (01825) 712010.

See also A. M. Graham-Dixon.

GRAHAM HALL, Jean; *see* Hall, J. G.

GRAHAM-HARRISON, Francis Laurence Theodore, CB 1962; Deputy Under-Secretary of State, Home Office, 1963–74; *b* 30 Oct. 1914; *s* of late Sir William Montagu Graham-Harrison, KCB, KC, and Lady Graham-Harrison, *d* of Sir Cyril Graham, 5th and last Bt, CMG; *m* 1941, Carol Mary St John, 3rd *d* of late Sir Francis Stewart, CIE; one *s* three *d*. *Educ:* Eton; Magdalen Coll., Oxford. Entered Home Office, 1938. Private Secretary to Parliamentary Under-Secretary of State, 1941–43; Asst Private Secretary to Prime Minister, 1946–49; Secretary, Royal Commission on Capital Punishment, 1949–53; Asst Secretary, Home Office, 1953–57; Asst Under-Secretary of State, Home Office, 1957–63. Chm., Nat. Sound Archive Adv. Cttee, British Library, 1984–88; Trustee: Tate Gallery, 1975–82; Nat. Gallery, 1981–82. Gov., Thomas Coram Foundn, 1975–95. Chm., Exec. Finance Cttee, Dr Barnardo's, 1978–81. *Address:* 32 Parliament Hill, NW3 2TN. *T:* (020) 7435 6316.

See also R. M. Graham-Harrison.

GRAHAM-HARRISON, Robert Montagu; Director, British Development Co-operation Office, New Delhi, since 1997; *b* 16 Feb. 1943; *s* of Francis Laurence Theodore Graham-Harrison, *qv*; *m* 1977, Kathleen Patricia, *d* of John and Mary Gladys Maher; two *d*. *Educ:* Eton Coll.; Magdalen Coll., Oxford. VSO India, 1965; GLC, 1966; Min. of Overseas Development, later Overseas Development Administration, then Dept for Internat. Develt, 1967–; World Bank, Washington, 1971–73; Private Sec. to Minister for Overseas Development, 1978; Asst Sec., ODA, 1979; Hd, British Develt Div. in E Africa, Nairobi, 1982–86; Hd, E Asia Dept, ODA, 1986–89; Alternate Exec. Dir, World Bank, Washington, 1989–92; UK Exec. Dir, EBRD, 1992–97. *Address:* c/o Foreign and Commonwealth Office, King Charles Street, SW1A 2AH.

GRAHAM-MOON, Sir Peter Wilfred Giles; *see* Moon.

GRAHAM-SMITH, Sir Francis; *see* Smith.

GRAHAM-TOLER, family name of **Earl of Norbury**.

GRAHAME, Christine; Member (SNP) South Scotland, Scottish Parliament, since 1999; *b* 9 Sept. 1944; *d* of Christie and Margaret Grahame; *m* (marr. diss.); two *s*. *Educ:* Edinburgh Univ. (MA 1966; DipEd 1967; LLB 1984; DipLP 1985). Schoolteacher, secondary schs, 1967–80; solicitor, 1986–99. Convenor: Cross Party Gp, Borders Rail; Justice Cttee I, 2001–. *Recreations:* cats, trad jazz, gardening and drinking malt at the same time. *Address:* 6 Baronscourt Road, Edinburgh EH8 7ET. *T:* (0131) 652 2622.

GRAHAME-SMITH, Prof. David Grahame, CBE 1993; Rhodes Professor of Clinical Pharmacology, University of Oxford, 1972–2000; Hon. Director, Smith Kline Beecham Centre of Applied Neuropsychobiology, Oxford University, 1990–99; Fellow of Corpus Christi College, Oxford, 1972–2000, now Emeritus (Vice-President, 1998–99); *b* 10 May 1933; *s* of George E. and C. A. Smith; *m* 1957, Kathryn Frances, *d* of Dr F. R. Beetham; two *s*. *Educ:* Wyggeston Grammar Sch., Leicester; St Mary's Hosp. Medical Sch., Univ. of London. MB, BS (London) 1956; MRCS, LRCP 1956; MRCP 1958; PhD (London) 1966; FRCP 1972. House Phys., Paddington Gen. Hosp., London, 1956; House Surg., Battle Hosp., Reading, 1956–57. Captain, RAMC, 1957–60. Registrar and Sen. Registrar in Medicine, St Mary's Hosp., Paddington, 1960–61; H. A. M. Thompson Research Scholar, RCP, 1961–62; Saltwell Research Scholar, RCP, 1962–65; Wellcome Trust Research Fellow, 1965–66; Hon. Med. Registrar to Med. Unit, St Mary's Hosp., 1961–66; MRC Travelling Fellow, Dept of Endocrinology, Vanderbilt Univ., Nashville, Tennessee, USA, 1966–67; Sen. Lectr in Clinical Pharmacology and Therapeutics, St Mary's Hosp. Med. Sch., Univ. of London, 1967–71; Hon. Cons. Physician, St Mary's Hosp., Paddington, 1967–71; Hon. Dir, MRC Unit of Clin. Pharm., Radcliffe Infirmary, Oxford, 1972–93. Vis. Prof., Peking Union Medical Coll., Beijing, China, 1985–. Non-exec. Mem., Oxfordshire HA, 1992–98. Member: Cttee on Safety of Medicines, 1975–86; Jt Cttee on Vaccination and Immunisation, 1987–89; Chairman: Adv. Gp on Hepatitis, 1987–89; Adv. Council on Misuse of Drugs, 1988–98. Lilly Prize, Clinical Sect., British Pharmacol Soc., 1995. *Publications:* (with J. K. Aronson) Oxford Textbook of Clinical Pharmacology and Drug Therapy, 1984, 2nd edn 1992; papers on biochemical, therapeutic and med. matters in scientific jls. *Recreations:* horse riding, jazz. *Address:* Romney, Lincombe Lane, Boars Hill, Oxford OX1 5DY.

GRAHAMSTOWN, Bishop of, since 1987; **Rt Rev. David Hamilton Russell;** *b* 6 Nov. 1938; *s* of James Hamilton Russell and Kathleen Mary Russell; *m* 1980, Dorothea Madden; two *s.* *Educ:* Diocesan College, Rondebosch; Univ. of Cape Town (BA, PhD); Univ. of Oxford (MA). Assistant Priest, 1965–75; Chaplain to migrant workers, 1975–86; banned and house arrested by SA Government, 1977–82; Suffragan Bishop, Diocese of St John's, 1986. *Address:* 17 Durban Street, Grahamstown, South Africa; PO Box 162, Grahamstown, Eastern Cape, 6140, South Africa. *T:* (home) (46) 6222500, (office) (46) 6361996.

GRAINGER, Ian Richard Peregrine L.; *see* Liddell-Grainger.

GRAINGER, Leslie, CBE 1976; BSc; FREng; MInstF; Chairman, Mountain Petroleum PLC, 1984–88; *b* 8 Aug. 1917. Mem. for Science, NCB, 1966–77; Chairman: NCB (Coal Products) Ltd, 1975–78; NCB (IEA Services) Ltd, 1975–79; Man. Dir, Branon PLC, 1981–83; Dir, Cavendish Petroleum Plc, 1982–85 (Chm., 1982–84). *Publication:* Coal Utilisation: Technology, Economics and Policy (with J. G. Gibson), 1981. *Address:* 16 Blackamoor Lane, Maidenhead, Berks SL6 8RD. *T:* (01628) 623923.

GRAMMENOS, Prof. Constantinos Theophilos, Hon. OBE 1994; DSc; Pro Vice-Chancellor, City University, London, since 1998; Founder and Head of Department of Shipping, Trade and Finance, since 1984, Professor of Shipping, since 1986, City University Business School; *b* 23 Feb. 1944; *s* of late Commander Theophilos C. Grammenos and Argyro (*née* Spanakos); *m* 1972, Anna C. Papadimitriou; one *s.* *Educ:* Third State Sch. of Athens; Pantion Univ. (BA); Univ. of Wales (MSc); City University (DSc). National Service, Greek Navy, 1968-70. Nat. Bank of Greece, 1962-74 (shipping finance expert, head office, 1972-74); Vis. Prof., 1982-86; Actg Dean, 2000, City Univ. Business Sch. Vis. Prof., World Maritime Univ., Malmö, 1990-95. Founder and Chm., first City of London Biennial Meeting, 1999; Pres., Internat. Assoc. of Maritime Economists, 1998-; Member: Bd of Dirs, Alexander S. Onassis Public Benefit Foundn, 1995-; American Bureau of Shipping, 1966-; Baltic Exchange, 1997-. Member: Bd of Govs (Educn); Baltic Internat. Maritime Council, 1995; Bd of Trustees, Inst. of Marine Engineers Meml Trust, 2000-. Archon of Ecumenical Patriarchate of Constantinople, 1994. FRSA 1996. Seatrade Orgn Personality of the Year 1998. *Publications:* Bank Finance for Ship Purchase, 1979; various papers and studies in shipping finance. *Recreations:* music, theatre, walking. *Address:* City University Business School, Frobisher Crescent, Barbican Centre, EC2Y 8HB. *T:* (020) 7040 8670. *Club:* Travellers.

GRANADO, Donald Casimir, TC 1970; *b* 4 March 1915; *m* 1959, Anne-Marie Faustin Lombard; one *s* two *d.* *Educ:* Trinidad. Gen. Sec., Union of Commercial and Industrial Workers, 1951–53; Sec./Treas., Fedn of Trade Unions, 1952–53; Elected MP for Laventille, Trinidad, 1956 and 1961; Minister of: Labour and Social Services, 1956–61; Health and Housing, and Dep. Leader House of Representatives, 1961–63. Ambassador to Venezuela, 1963–64; High Comr to Canada, 1964–69; Ambassador to Argentina and to Brazil, 1965–69; High Comr to London, 1969–71, and Ambassador to France, Germany, Belgium, Switzerland, Italy, Holland, Luxembourg and European Common Market, 1969–71. Led Trinidad and Tobago delegations to: India, Ceylon, Pakistan, 1958; CPA in Nigeria, Israel, Uganda, 1962; UN, 1965; St Lucia, 1966; attended Heads of Commonwealth Govts Conf., Singapore, 1971; rep. Trinidad and Tobago at missions to Grenada, Jamaica, France, and inaugurations of heads of govt of Chile and Brazil. First Gen. Sec., People's National Movement. Formerly: Vice-Chm., West India Cttee, London; Governor, Commonwealth Inst; Vice-Pres., Trinidad & Tobago Contract Bridge League. President: Fidelis Youth Club; National Golf Club; Vice-Pres., Trinidad & Tobago Golf Assoc.; Pres., Potentials Sports Club (also Manager, soccer team). National Father of the Year 1981. Speaks, reads and writes French and Spanish. *Recreations:* cricket, soccer, bridge and golf; music (tape-recording), writing.

GRANARD, 10th Earl of, *cr* 1684 (Ire.); **Peter Arthur Edward Hastings Forbes;** Bt (NS) 1628; Viscount Granard, Baron Clanehugh (Ire.), 1675; Baron Granard (UK), 1806; *b* 15 March 1957; *s* of Hon. John Forbes (*d* 1982), *yr s* of 8th Earl, and of Joan, *d* of A. Edward Smith; *S* uncle, 1992; *m* 1980, Noreen Mitchell; three *s* one *d.* *Heir: s* Viscount Forbes, *qv.* *Address:* Strathallan Cliff House, Strathallan Road, Onchan, Isle of Man.

GRANATT, Michael Stephen Dreese, CB 2001; Head, Government Information and Communication Service, Cabinet Office, since 1998; *b* 27 April 1950; *s* of Arthur Maurice Granatt and Denise Sylvia Granatt (*née* Dreese); *m* 1974, Jane Veronica Bray; one *s* three *d.* *Educ:* Westminster City Sch.; Queen Mary Coll., London. Sub-ed., subseq. Dep. Chief Sub-ed., Kent & Sussex Courier, 1973–77; Prodn Ed., Industrial Relns Services, 1977–79; Asst Ed., Dept of Employment, 1979–81; Press Officer, Home Office, 1981–83; Sen. Press Officer, 1983–85, Chief Press Officer, 1985–86, Hd of Inf., 1986–89, Dept of Energy; Dir, Public Affairs and Internal Communication, Metropolitan Police Service, 1989–92; Director of Communication: DoE, 1992–94; Home Office, 1995–98; also Hd, Govt Inf. Service, 1997–98. Chm., London Emergency Press Officers' Gp, 1989–92. FRSA 1993; FIPR 2000. *Publication:* (contrib.) Disasters and the Media, 1999. *Recreations:* photography, reading science fiction, gadgets, joining-up government. *Address:* Cabinet Office, 70 Whitehall, SW1A 2AS. *T:* (020) 7270 6631. *Club:* Savage.

GRANBY, Marquis of; Charles John Montague Manners; *b* 3 July 1999; *s* and *heir* of Duke of Rutland, *qv.*

GRANDY, Marshal of the Royal Air Force Sir John, GCB 1967 (KCB 1964; CB 1956); GCVO 1988; KBE 1961; DSO 1945; RAF; Constable and Governor of Windsor Castle, 1978–88; *b* Northwood, Middlesex, 8 Feb. 1913; *s* of late Francis Grandy and Nell Grandy (*née* Lines); *m* 1937, Cecile Elizabeth Florence Rankin, CStJ (*d* 1993), *yr d* of Sir Robert Rankin, 1st and last Bt; two *s.* *Educ:* University College Sch., London. Short service commn, RAF, 1931 (perm. commn, 1936); No 54 (Fighter) Sqdn, 1932–35; Asst Adjt and Flying Instr, 604 (Middx) Sqdn., RAuxAF, 1935–36; Adjt and Flying Instr, London Univ. Air Sqdn, 1937–39; Comd No 249 (Fighter) Sqdn during Battle of Britain; Staff Duties, HQ Fighter Comd, and Wing Comdr Flying RAF Coltishall, 1941; commanded: RAF Duxford, 1942 (First Typhoon Wing); HQ No 210 Group, No 73 Op Training Unit, and Fighter Conversion Unit at Abu Sueir, 1943–44; No 341 Wing (Dakotas), SE Asia Comd, 1944–45; DSO 1945, despatches 1943 and 1945. SASO No 232 Gp, 1945; *psc* 1946; Dep. Dir Operational Training, Air Min., 1946; Air Attaché, Brussels, 1949; Comd Northern Sector, Fighter Comd, 1950; Air Staff HQ Fighter Comd, 1952–54; Comdt, Central Fighter Estab., 1954–57; *idc* 1957; Comdr, Task Force Grapple (British Nuclear Weapon Test Force), Christmas Is., 1957–58; Assistant CAS (Ops), 1958–61; Commander-in-Chief, RAF, Germany and Comdr, Second Allied TAF, 1961–63; AOC-in-C, Bomber Command, 1963–65; C-in-C, British Forces, Far East, and UK Mil. Adviser to SEATO, 1965–67; Chief of the Air Staff, 1967–71; Governor and C-in-C, Gibraltar, 1973–78. Dir, Brixton Estate Ltd, 1971–73, 1978–83; Trustee, Imperial War Museum, 1971–78 (Chm., 1978–89); Dep. Chm. Council, RAF Benevolent Fund, 1980–96; Trustee: Burma Star Assoc., 1979–96 (Vice-Pres.); Shuttleworth Remembrance Trust, 1978–88 (Chm., Aerodrome Cttee, 1980–88); RAF Church, St Clement Danes, 1971–97; Prince Philip Trust Fund, Windsor and Maidenhead, 1982–92; Past President: Officers' Assoc.; Air League; Vice-President: Officers' Pension Soc., 1971–; Nat. Assoc. of Boys' Clubs, 1971–; Life Vice-Pres., RNLI, 1988– (Vice-Pres., 1986–88, Mem. Management Cttee, 1971–); Friends of Gibraltar Heritage Soc., 1986–; Mem. Cttee, Royal Humane Soc., 1978–95; Patron, Polish Air Force Assoc. in GB, 1979–2000. PMN 1967. Hon. Liveryman, Haberdashers' Co., 1968. Freeman, City of London, 1968. KStJ 1974. *Clubs:* White's, Pratt's, Royal Air Force; Royal Yacht Squadron (Cowes); Swinley Forest Golf.

GRANGE, Kenneth Henry, CBE 1984; RDI, FCSD; industrial designer; in private practice since 1958; Founder Partner, Pentagram Design, since 1972; *b* 17 July 1929; *s* of Harry Alfred Grange and Hilda Gladys (*née* Long). *Educ:* London. Technical Illustrator, RE, 1948–50; Design Asst, Arcon Chartered Architects, 1948; Bronek Katz & Vaughn, 1950–51; Gordon Bowyer & Partners, 1951–54; Jack Howe & Partners, 1954–58. Pres., CSD, 1987–88; Master of Faculty, RDI, 1985–87. RDI 1969; FCSD (FSIAD 1959). Hon. Prof., Heriot-Watt, 1987. Hon. Dr RCA, 1985; DUniv: Heriot-Watt, 1986; De Montfort, 1998; Staffs, 1998. 10 Design Council Awards; Duke of Edinburgh Award for Elegant Design, 1963. *Recreations:* tennis, ski-ing. *Address:* 53 Christchurch Hill, NW3 1LG.

GRANT; *see* Lyall Grant.

GRANT, family name of **Baron Strathspey**.

GRANT, Alexander (Marshall), CBE 1965; Artistic Director, National Ballet of Canada, 1976–83; *b* Wellington, New Zealand, 22 Feb. 1925; *s* of Alexander and Eleather Grant. *Educ:* Wellington Coll., NZ. Arrived in London, Feb. 1946, to study with Sadler's Wells School on Scholarship given in New Zealand by Royal Academy of Dancing, London; Sadler's Wells Ballet (later Royal Ballet Company), Aug. 1946–76. Dir, Ballet for All (touring ballet company), 1971–76 (Co-director, 1970–71). Senior Principal, London Fest. Ballet, later English National Ballet, 1985–91; Guest Artist: Royal Ballet, 1985–89; Joffrey Ballet, USA, 1987–89. Frequent judge at internat. ballet competitions, notably Varna (Bulgaria), Paris, Budapest, Jackson, Mississippi and Moscow. Danced leading rôles in following: Mam'zelle Angot, Clock Symphony, Boutique Fantasque, Donald of the Burthens, Rake's Progress, Job, Three Cornered Hat, Ballabile, Cinderella, Sylvia, Madame Chrysanthème, Façade, Daphnis and Chloé, Coppélia, Petrushka, Ondine, La Fille Mal Gardée, Jabez and the Devil, Perséphone, The Dream, Jazz Calendar, Enigma Variations, Sleeping Beauty (Carabosse), A Month in the Country, La Sylphide, The Nutcracker, Napoli, Schéhérazade, Variations on a Theme of Purcell, Don Quixote; *films:* Tales of Beatrix Potter (Peter Rabbit and Pigling Bland); Steps of the Ballet. *Recreations:* gardening, cinema going, cuisine.

GRANT, Andrew Young; Chief Operating Officer (formerly Principal), Grant Leisure Group, since 1982; Chairman, Real Live Leisure Co. Ltd, since 1999; *b* 8 April 1946; *s* of Marshall Grant and Marilyn Greene (*née* Phillips); *m* 1st, 1969, Dietra (marr. diss.); one *d;* 2nd, 1973, Lindy Lange; one *d.* *Educ:* Univ. of Oregon (BSc). Personnel Manager, Universal Studios Tour, Universal City, Calif., 1967–69; Dir of Personnel, Busch Gardens, LA, 1969–71, Ops Dir, 1971–73; Gen. Manager, Squaw Valley Ski Resort, 1973–74; Gen. Manager, Busch Gardens, 1974–76; Dir, Economic Research Associates, LA, 1976–79; Dep. Dir, Zoological Soc., San Diego, 1979–83; Dir, Leeds Castle Enterprises, 1983–88; Director: Granada Studios Tour, 1987–90; Grant Leisure Developments, 1987–; Man. Dir, Zoo Operations Ltd, Zoological Soc., 1988–91; Principal, Internat. Spirit Develt Corp. Ltd (formerly Internat. Spirit Management Co.), 1995–. Member: Internat. Assoc. of Amusement Parks and Attractions, 1975–; Tourism Soc., 1988–; Tourism and Leisure Industries Sector Gp, NEDC, 1990–; Urban Land Inst., 1998–. *Recreations:* running, fishing, golf, tennis. *Address:* Grant Leisure Group, Russell Square House, 10–12 Russell Square, WC1B 5EH. *T:* (020) 7309 6200.

GRANT, Ann; HM Diplomatic Service; High Commissioner, South Africa, since 2000; *b* 13 Aug. 1948. Joined FCO, 1971; Calcutta, 1973–75; Dept of Energy, 1976–79 (on loan); Head of Chancery and Consul, Maputo, 1981–84; First Sec. (Energy), Office of UK Perm. Rep. to EU, Brussels, 1987–89, resigned; Communications Dir, Oxfam, 1989–91; rejoined FCO, 1991; Counsellor (Econ. and Social Affairs), UK Mission to UN, NY, 1992–96; Counsellor, FCO, 1996–98; Dir, African Dept, FCO, 1998–2000. *Address:* c/o Foreign and Commonwealth Office, SW1A 2AH.

GRANT, Sir Anthony, Kt 1983; solicitor and company director; *b* May 1925; *m* Sonia Isobel; one *s* one *d.* *Educ:* St Paul's Sch.; Brasenose Coll., Oxford. Army 1943–48, Third Dragoon Guards (Capt.). Admitted a solicitor, 1952. MP (C): Harrow Central, 1964–83; Cambs SW, 1983–97. Opposition Whip, 1966–70; Parly Sec., Board of Trade, June-Oct. 1970; Parliamentary Under-Secretary of State: Trade, DTI, 1970–72; Industrial Develt, DTI, 1972–74. Chm., Cons. back bench Trade Cttee, 1979–83; Mem., Foreign Affairs Select Cttee, 1980–83. A Vice-Chm., Conservative Party Organisation, 1974–76; Mem. Exec., 1922 Cttee, 1978–97. Formerly Member: Council of Europe (Chm., Econ. Cttee, 1980–87); WEU. Pres., Guild of Experienced Motorists. Trustee, Howard Foundn, 2000–. Freeman, City of London; Master, Guild of Freemen, 1979–80, 1997–98; Liveryman, Co. of Solicitors. *Recreations:* watching Rugby and cricket, playing golf; Napoleonic history. *Address:* Whiteacre, The Chase, Oxshott, Surrey KT22 0HR; 32 Beaufort Place, Cambridge CB5 8AG. *Clubs:* Carlton; Walton Heath Golf, Meridien Golf.

GRANT of Monymusk, Sir Archibald, 13th Bt *cr* 1705; *b* 2 Sept. 1954; *e s* of Captain Sir Francis Cullen Grant, 12th Bt, and of Lady Grant (Jean Margherita, *d* of Captain Humphrey Douglas Tollemache, RN), who *m* 2nd, Baron Tweedsmuir, *qv;* *S* father, 1966; *m* 1982, Barbara Elizabeth, *e d* of A. G. D. Forbes, Drumminnor Castle, Rhynie, Aberdeenshire; two *d.* *Heir: b* Francis Tollemache Grant [*b* 18 Dec. 1955; *m* 1993, Virginia, *d* of R. Scott Russell; one *s* one *d*]. *Address:* House of Monymusk, Aberdeenshire AB51 7HL. *T:* (01467) 651220.

GRANT, His Honour Brian; *see* Grant, His Honour H. B.

GRANT, Sir Clifford (Harry), Kt 1977; Chief Stipendiary Magistrate, Western Australia, 1982–90; *b* England, 12 April 1929; *m* 1962, Karen Ann Ferguson. *Educ:* Montclair, NJ, USA; Harrison Coll., Barbados; Liverpool Coll.; Liverpool Univ. (LLB (Hons) 1949). Solicitor, Supreme Court of Judicature, 1951; Comr for Oaths, 1958; in private practice, London; apptd to HM Overseas Judiciary, 1958; Magistrate, Kenya, 1958, Sen. Magistrate, 1962; transf. to Hong Kong, Crown Solicitor, 1963, Principal Magistrate, 1965; transf. to Fiji, Sen. Magistrate, 1967; admitted Barrister and Solicitor, Supreme Court of Fiji, 1969; Chief Magistrate, 1971; Judge of Supreme Court, 1972; Chief Justice of Fiji, 1974–80. Pres., Fiji Court of Appeal, and Chm., Judicial and Legal Services Commn, 1974–80; sole

Comr, Royal Commn on Crime, 1975 (report published 1976). Sometime Actg Governor-General, 1973–79. Fellow, Flinders Univ. Foundn, 1992. Fiji Independence Medal, 1970. *Publications:* articles for legal jls. *Recreations:* sociobiology, photography, literature, music. *Address:* c/o 121 Hamilton Street, Stirling, WA 6021, Australia.

GRANT, Dr David, CBE 1997; FREng, FIEE; Vice-Chancellor, Cardiff University, since 2001; *b* 12 Sept. 1947; *s* of Edmund Grant and Isobel Scorer Grant (*née* Rutherford); *m* 1974, Helen Joyce Rutter; one *s* one *d. Educ:* Univ. of Durham (PhD 1974). FIEE 1984; FREng (FEng 1997). Reyrolle Parsons Gp, 1966–77; United Technologies Corp., 1977–84; Gp Technical Dir, Dowty Gp, 1984–91; Technical Dir, GEC, then Marconi plc, 1991–2001. Mem., EPSRC, 2001–. Mensforth Internat. Gold Medal, IEE, 1996. *Recreation:* classic cars. *Address:* Cardiff University, Main Building, Park Place, Cardiff CF10 3AT.

GRANT, David James, CBE 1980; Lord-Lieutenant and Custos Rotulorum of County Durham, 1988–97; *b* 18 Jan. 1922; *s* of late Frederick Grant, MC, QC and Grace Winifred Grant (*née* McLaren); *m* 1949, Jean Margaret, *d* of Gp Capt. T. E. H. Birley, OBE; two *s* one *d. Educ:* Fettes Coll., Edinburgh; Oriel Coll., Oxford (Open Schol.; MA). Served RAFVR, Bomber Command and overseas 1940–45 (Flight Lieut). Chm., Darchem Ltd, 1963–92 (Chief Exec., 1959–88); Dep. Chm., William Baird plc, 1981–92. Chairman: Teesside Productivity Assoc., 1965–68; Northern Regl Council, CBI, 1973–75; Northern Regl Council, BIM, 1982–87; Member: Northern Econ. Planning Council, 1968–79; NE Industrial Develt Bd, 1975–84. President: N of England TA&VRA, 1990–93; N of England Anglo-Japanese Soc., 1990–97; Co. Durham, RBL, 1997–. Chm., Council, Univ. of Durham, 1985–92 (Hon. DCL, 1988); Visitor, Teeside Univ., 1995–2000. Hon. DCL Newcastle upon Tyne, 1989. Co. Durham: DL 1982; High Sheriff, 1985–86; Vice Lord-Lieut, 1987–88. KStJ 1988. CIMgt. *Recreations:* gardening, golf. *Address:* Aden Cottage, Durham DH1 4HJ. *T:* (0191) 386 7161. *Club:* Durham County.

GRANT, Donald Blane, CBE 1989; TD 1964; Partner, KMG Thomson McLintock, CA (formerly Moody Stuart & Robertson, then Thomson McLintock & Co.), 1950–86; *b* 8 Oct. 1921; *s* of Quintin Blane Grant and Euphemia Phyllis Grant; *m* 1944, Lavinia Margaret Ruth Ritchie; three *d. Educ:* High Sch. of Dundee. CA 1948. Served War, RA, 1939–46: TA Officer, retd as Major. Director: Dundee & London Investment Trust PLC, 1969–93; HAT Group PLC, 1969–86; Don Brothers Buist PLC, 1984–87. Inst. of Chartered Accountants of Scotland: Mem. Council, 1971–76; Vice Pres., 1977–79, Pres., 1979–80. Chairman: Tayside Health Bd, 1984–91; Scottish Legal Aid Bd, 1986–91. Hon. LLD Dundee, 1989. *Recreations:* shooting, fishing, golf, bridge, gardening. *Address:* Summerfield, 24 Albany Road, West Ferry, Dundee DD5 1NT. *T:* (01382) 737804. *Clubs:* Institute of Directors; New (Edinburgh); Royal and Ancient Golf (St Andrews); Panmure Golf (Carnoustie); Blairgowrie Golf (Rosemount).

GRANT, Donald David, CB 1985; Director General, Central Office of Information, 1982–85; *b* 1 Aug. 1924; *s* of Donald Herbert Grant and Florence Emily Grant, *m* 1954, Beatrice Mary Varney; two *d. Educ:* Wandsworth Sch. Served War, RNVR, Sub-Lt (A), 1942–46. Journalist, Evening Standard, Reuters, 1946–51; Dir, Sidney Barton Ltd, PR Consultants, 1951–61; Chief Information Officer, Min. of Aviation and Technology, 1961–67; Dir, Public Relations, STC Ltd, 1967–70; Director of Information: GLC, 1971–72; DTI, 1972–74; Home Office, 1974–82. Vis. Prof., Graduate Centre for Journalism, City Univ., 1986–90. *Recreation:* sailing. *Address:* Ferry View, Castle House, Southtown, Dartmouth, Devon TQ6 9BU. *T:* (01803) 833095. *Club:* Dartmouth Yacht.

GRANT, His Honour (Hubert) Brian; a Circuit Judge of Sussex and Kent (formerly Judge of County Courts), 1965–82; *b* Berlin, 5 Aug. 1917; *m* 1946, Jeanette Mary Carroll; one *s* three *d. Educ:* Trinity Coll., Cambridge (Sen. Schol.). 1st cl. hons, Law Tripos, 1939; MA. War service, 1940–44: Commandos, 1942–44. Called to Bar, Gray's Inn, 1945 (Lord Justice Holker Senior Scholar). Mem., Law Reform Cttee, 1970–73. Vice-Chm., Nat. Marriage Guidance Council, 1970–72; Founder Pres., Parenthood, 1979. FRSA 1991. *Publications:* Marriage, Separation and Divorce, 1946; Family Law, 1970; Conciliation and Divorce, 1981; The Quiet Ear, 1987; The Deaf Advance, 1990; Not Guilty, 1994. *Address:* 33 Arthur Street, Penrith CA11 7TX. *Club:* Penrith Golf.

GRANT, Ian David, CBE 1988; Crown Estate Commissioner for Scotland, since 1996; *b* Dundee, 28 July 1943; *s* of late Alan H. B. Grant and of Florence O. Grant; *m* 1968, Eileen May Louisa Yule; three *d. Educ:* Strathallan Sch.; East of Scotland College of Agriculture (Dip.). Vice Pres. 1981–84, Pres. 1984–90, National Farmers' Union of Scotland; Mem., Scottish Council, CBI, 1984–96. Bd Mem., 1988–90, Chm., 1990–98, Scottish Tourist Bd; Bd Mem., BTA, 1990–98. Director: East of Scotland Farmers Ltd, 1978–; Clydesdale Bank PLC, 1989–97; NFU Mutual Insce Soc. Ltd, 1990–; Scottish and Southern Energy plc (formerly Scottish Hydro Electric PLC), 1992– (Dep. Chm., 2000–); Scottish Exhibition Centre Ltd, 1998– (Dep. Chm., 2001–); Chm., Cairngorms Partnership, 1998–. Vice Pres., Royal Smithfield Club, 1996. FRAgS 1987. *Recreations:* travel, swimming, shooting, reading, music. *Address:* Leal House, Alyth PH11 8JQ.

GRANT, (Ian) Nicholas; Managing Director, Mediatrack plc, since 1992; *b* 24 March 1948; *s* of late Hugo and of Cara Grant; *m* 1977, Rosalind Louise Pipe; one *s* one *d. Educ:* Univ. of London (LLB); Univ. of Warwick (MA, Industrial Relns). Confederation of Health Service Employees: Research Officer, 1972–74; Head of Research and Public Relations, 1974–82; Dir of Information, Labour Party, 1982–85; Public Affairs Advr, Mirror Group Newspapers and Maxwell Communication Corp., 1985–89. Dep. Chm., Assoc. of Media Evaluation Cos, 1997–. Member: Council London Borough of Lambeth, 1978–84; Lambeth, Southwark and Lewisham AHA, 1978–82; W Lambeth DHA, 1982–83. Contested (Lab) Reigate, 1979. *Publications:* contrib. to: Economics of Prosperity, ed D. Blake and P. Ormerod, 1980; Political Communications: the general election campaign of 1983, ed I. Crewe and M. Harrop, 1985. *Recreations:* walking, reading, photography. *Address:* Mediatrack plc, 9 Lincoln's Inn Fields, WC2A 3BP. *T:* (020) 7430 0699. *Club:* Reform.

GRANT, Prof. Ian Philip, DPhil; FRS 1992; CMath; Professor of Mathematical Physics, University of Oxford, 1992–98, now Emeritus Professor; Tutorial Fellow in Mathematics, Pembroke College, Oxford, 1969–98, now Emeritus Fellow; *b* 15 Dec. 1930; *er s* of Harold Hyman Grant and Isabella Henrietta Ornstien; *m* 1958, Beryl Cohen; two *s. Educ:* St Albans Sch., Herts; Wadham Coll., Oxford (Open Scholar; MA; DPhil 1954). CMath 1992. SSO, 1957–61, PSO, 1961–64, UKAEA, Aldermaston; Res. Fellow, Atlas Computer Lab., SRC, 1964–69; Lectr in Maths, 1969–90, Reader in Mathematical Physics, 1990–92, Oxford Univ.; Res. Fellow in Maths, 1964–69, Actg Master, 1984–85, Pembroke Coll., Oxford. Visiting Professor: McGill Univ., 1976; Abo Akademi, Finland, 1977; Inst. de Fisica, Univ. Nacional Autónoma de México, 1981. Governor: Royal Grammar Sch., High Wycombe, 1981–99; St Paul's Schs, 1993–. *Publications:* papers in learned jls on relativistic quantum theory in atomic and molecular physics, and on radiative transfer theory in astrophysics and atmospheric science. *Recreations:* walking, music, theatre-going, gardening, travel. *Address:* Mathematical Institute, 24–29 St Giles', Oxford OX1 3LB. *T:* (01865) 273525; 6 Woodlands Close, Headington, Oxford OX3 7RY. *T:* (01865) 762156.

GRANT, Rt Rev. James Alexander, AM 1994; Assistant Bishop, Diocese of Melbourne, 1985–99; Dean of St Paul's Cathedral, Melbourne, 1985–99; *b* 30 Aug. 1931; *s* of late V. G. Grant, Geelong; *m* 1983, Rowena Margaret Armstrong. *Educ:* Trinity College, Univ. of Melbourne (BA Hons); Melbourne College of Divinity (BD). Deacon 1959 (Curate, St Peter's, Murrumbeena), Priest 1960; Curate, West Heidelberg 1960, Broadmeadows 1961; Leader Diocesan Task Force, Broadmeadows, 1962; Domestic and Examining Chaplain to Archbishop of Melbourne, 1966–70; Chaplain, Trinity Coll., Univ. of Melbourne, 1970–75, Fellow, 1975; Bishop Coadjutor, dio. of Melbourne, 1970–85; Chairman, Brotherhood of St Laurence, 1971–87 (Director, 1969); Pres., Diocesan Mission to Streets and Lanes, 1987–97. *Publications:* (with Geoffrey Serle) The Melbourne Scene, 1957; Perspective of a Century-Trinity College, 1872–1972, 1972. *Recreation:* historical research. *Address:* 151 Park Drive, Parkville, Vic 3052, Australia. *Club:* Melbourne (Melbourne).

GRANT, Janet; *see* Thompson, J.

GRANT, Sir (John) Anthony; *see* Grant, Sir A.

GRANT, John Donald; Consultant, Grant & Fairgrieve, since 1988; *b* 31 Oct. 1926; *s* of Ian and Eleanor Grant; *m* 1951, Helen Bain Fairgrieve Wilson, *d* of late James Wilson and of Clara Wilson; two *s. Educ:* various schs; King's Coll., Cambridge (Exhibnr; MA Nat. Sciences). National Service, REME, 1947–49; TA, London Rifle Bde, 1949–56. N Thames Gas Bd, 1949–60; Imperial Chemical Industries: Plastics Div., 1960–71; Head Office, 1971–82; Chief Exec., FIMBRA (formerly NASDIM), 1983–88. Dir, Cadogan Management Ltd, 1991–95. Chairman: Strategic Planning Soc., 1989–91; Fedn of Software Systems, 1989–91. Mem., Money Management Council, 1989–. Chm., Henley Alumni Assoc., 1996–98; Mem. Ct of Govs, Henley Mgt Coll., 1996–99. *Recreations:* opera, music, travel (particularly to islands). *Address:* 6 Bailey Mews, Auckland Road, Cambridge CB5 8DR; also in Westmorland. *Club:* Oxford and Cambridge.

GRANT, John Douglas Kelso, CMG 1999; HM Diplomatic Service; Ambassador to Sweden, since 1999; *b* 17 Oct. 1954; *s* of Douglas Marr Kelso Grant and Audrey Stevenson Grant (*née* Law); *m* 1983, Anna Maria Lindvall; one *s* two *d. Educ:* Edinburgh Acad.; St Catharine's Coll., Cambridge (BA 1976). HM Diplomatic Service: W African Dept, FCO, 1976; Stockholm, 1977–80; Russian lang. trng, 1980–81; Moscow, 1982–84; Morgan Grenfell and Co. Ltd, 1985–86; News Dept, FCO, 1986–89; UK Perm Repn to EU, 1989–93 and 1994–97; Principal Private Sec. to Sec. of State for Foreign and Commonwealth Affairs, 1997–99. *Recreations:* cross-country ski-ing, walking. *Address:* c/o Foreign and Commonwealth Office, King Charles Street, SW1A 2AH.

GRANT, John James, CBE 1960; Director, University of Durham Institute of Education, 1963–77; *b* 19 Oct. 1914; *s* of John and Mary Grant; *m* 1945, Jean Graham Stewart; two *s. Educ:* Shawlands Academy, Glasgow; Univ. of Glasgow (MA, EdB). Supply teaching, Glasgow, 1939–40. Served War: UK, India, Burma, 1940–46. Mod. Lang. Master, High Sch. of Glasgow, 1946–48; Lectr in Educn, Univ. of Durham, 1948–52; Vice-Principal, Fourah Bay Coll., Sierra Leone, 1953–55, Principal, 1955–60; Principal, St Cuthbert's Soc., Univ. of Durham, 1960–63. Hon. DCL Durham, 1960. *Recreations:* theatre, gardening. *Address:* Stokeleigh Residential Home, 19 Stoke Hill, Stoke Bishop, Bristol BS9 1JN.

GRANT, Keith Wallace; Dean, Faculty of Design, Kingston University (formerly Polytechnic), 1988–99; *b* 30 June 1934; *s* of Randolph and Sylvia Grant; *m* 1968, Deanne (*née* Bergsma); one *s* one *d. Educ:* Trinity Coll., Glenalmond; Clare Coll., Cambridge (MA). Account Exec., W. S. Crawford Ltd, 1958–62; General Manager: Covent Garden Opera Co., later Royal Opera, 1962–73; English Opera Group, 1962–73; Sec., Royal Soc. of Arts, 1973–77; Dir, Design Council, 1977–88. Member: Adv. Council, V&A Mus., 1977–83; PO Stamp Adv. Cttee, 1978–89; Exec. Bd, Internat. Council of Socs of Industrial Design, 1983–87; Chm., Nat. Lead Body for Design, 1995–98. Chm., English Music Theatre Co., 1979–92; Mem., Management Cttee, Park Lane Gp, 1988–95; Sec., Peter Pears Award for Singers, 1988–95. Governor: Central Sch. of Art and Design, 1974–77; Birmingham Polytechnic, 1981–86; Edinburgh Coll. of Art, 1982–86; Mem., Ct, Brunel Univ., 1985–89. Hon. Prof., Heriot-Watt Univ., 1987. Hon. Fellow, Univ. of Central England (formerly Birmingham Poly.), 1988. Hon. FCSD (Hon. FSIAD, 1983). *Address:* 43 St Dunstan's Road, W6 8RE. *Club:* Garrick.

GRANT, Kenneth Isaac; a District Judge (Magistrates' Courts) (formerly Metropolitan Stipendiary Magistrate), since 1999; *b* 14 Nov. 1951; *s* of late Samuel Grant and of Mercia Grant; *m* 1979, Irene Whilton; one *s* one *d. Educ:* Haberdashers' Aske's Sch., Elstree; Univ. of Sussex (BA); Coll. of Law. Admitted Solicitor, 1977; Solicitor, Darlington & Parkinson, 1977–99, Sen. Partner, 1990–99. Chm., Area Cttee, Legal Aid Bd, 1994–99 (Chm., Area 14 Regional Cttee, 1997–99). *Recreations:* theatre, opera. *Address:* Camberwell Green Magistrates' Court, 15 D'Eynsford Road, Camberwell Green, SE5 7UP. *T:* (020) 7805 6897. *Club:* Hurlingham.

GRANT, Very Rev. Malcolm Etheridge; Provost and Rector of St Andrew's Cathedral, Inverness, since 1991; *b* 6 Aug. 1944; *s* of Donald Etheridge Grant and Nellie Florence May Grant (*née* Tuffey); *m* 1984, Katrina Russell Nuttall (*née* Dunnett); one *s* one *d. Educ:* Dunfermline High School; Univ. of Edinburgh (Bruce of Grangehill Bursar, 1962; BSc (Hons Chemistry); BD (Hons New Testament); Divinity Fellowship, 1969); Edinburgh Theological College. Deacon 1969, priest 1970; Assistant Curate: St Mary's Cathedral, Glasgow, 1969; St Wulfram's, Grantham (in charge of Church of the Epiphany, Earlesfield), 1972; Team Vicar of Earlesfield, Grantham, 1972; Priest-in-charge, St Ninian's, Invergordon, 1978; Examining Chaplain to Bishop of Moray, Ross and Caithness, 1979; Provost and Rector, St Mary's Cathedral, Glasgow, 1981; Rector, St Paul's, Strathnairn, and Priest i/c, St Mary's-in-the-Fields, Culloden, 1991–97. Member, Highland Regional Council Education Cttee, 1979–81. *Address:* 15 Ardross Street, Inverness IV3 5NS. *T:* (01463) 233535.

GRANT, Prof. Malcolm John, LLD; Professor of Land Economy, University of Cambridge, since 1991; Fellow of Clare College, Cambridge, since 1991; *b* 29 Nov. 1947; *s* of Francis William Grant and Vera Jessica Grant; *m* 1974, Christine (*née* Endersbee); two *s* one *d. Educ:* Waitaki Boys' High Sch., NZ; Univ. of Otago (LLB 1970; LLM 1973; LLD 1986). Called to the Bar, Middle Temple, 1999. Lectr, subseq. Sen. Lectr in Law, Southampton Univ., 1972–86; University College London: Sen. Lectr in Law, 1986–88; Prof. of Law, and Vice-Dean, Faculty of Laws, 1988–91. Chairman: Local Govt Commn for England, 1996– (Mem., 1992–; Dep. Chm., 1995–96); Agric. and Envmt Biotechnol. Commn, 2000–. Hon. MRTPI 1993; Hon. ARICS 1995. Gen. Editor, Encyclopedia of Planning Law and Practice, 1981–; Co-Editor, Encyclopedia of Environmental Law, 1993–. *Publications:* Planning Law Handbook, 1981; Urban Planning Law, 1982, 2nd Suppl. 1990; Rate Capping and the Law, 1985, 2nd edn 1986; Permitted Development,

1989, 2nd edn 1996; (ed jtly) Concise Lexicon of Environmental Terms, 1995; Singapore Planning Law, 1999. Environmental Court Report, 2000. *Recreations:* reading, travel, music. *Address:* Clare College, Cambridge CB2 1TL; Department of Land Economy, 19 Silver Street, Cambridge CB3 9EP. *T:* (01223) 337134; 4/5 Gray's Inn Square, WC1R 5AY.

GRANT, Martin James; Chief Executive, Inn Partnerships, since 1999; *b* 29 June 1949; *s* of James and Barbara Grant; *m* 1979, Helena Kay; two *s*. *Educ:* King Henry VIII, Coventry; Nottingham Univ. (BSc). Marks and Spencer, 1971–74; Grand Metropolitan, 1974–79; Holt Lloyd, 1979–82; Imperial Foods, 1982–83; Whitbread & Co. plc, 1983–90; Allied Lyons, subseq. Allied Domecq, 1990–98: Managing Director: Ansells Ltd, 1990–95; Allied Domecq Leisure, 1995–98; Chief Exec., Vaux Gp, 1998–99. Fellow, Mktg Soc., 1995; FBII 1996. *Recreations:* military music, military history. *Address:* Oak House, Waverley Edge, Bubbenhall, Coventry CV8 3BP.

GRANT, Dame Mavis, DBE 1999; Headteacher, Canning Street Primary School, Newcastle upon Tyne, since 1999; *b* 1 Feb. 1948; *d* of Joseph S. Edgar and Edna M. Edgar (*née* Hewson); *m* 1970, Roger M. Grant. *Educ:* Northumberland Coll. of Educn (CertEd and Cert. Advanced Educn Studies). Teaching in primary schools, Herts, Northumberland and Newcastle upon Tyne, 1969–: Dep. Headteacher, Cowgate Primary Sch., Newcastle upon Tyne, 1978–84; Headteacher, Mary Trevelyan Primary Sch., Newcastle upon Tyne, 1984–99. *Recreations:* reading, theatre, travel, dining out, watching Newcastle United Football Club.

GRANT, Michael, CBE 1958 (OBE 1946); MA, LittD (Cambridge); *b* 21 Nov. 1914; *s* of late Col Maurice Harold Grant and Muriel, *d* of C. Jörgensen; *m* 1944, Anne Sophie Beskow, Norrköping, Sweden; two *s*. *Educ:* Harrow Sch.; Trinity Coll., Cambridge. Porson Prizeman, First Chancellor's Classical Medallist, Craven Student; Fellow Trinity Coll., Cambridge, 1938–49. Served War of 1939–45, Army, War Office, 1939–40, Actg Capt.; first British Council Rep. in Turkey, 1940–45; Prof. of Humanity at Edinburgh Univ., 1948–59; first Vice-Chancellor, Univ. of Khartoum, 1956–58; Pres. and Vice-Chancellor of the Queen's Univ. of Belfast, 1959–66; Pres., 1953–56, Medallist, 1962, and Hon. Fellow, 1984, Royal Numismatic Soc.; Huntington Medalist, American Numismatic Soc., 1965. J. H. Gray Lectr, Cambridge, 1955; FSA. Chairman, National Council for the Supply of Teachers Overseas, 1963–66. President: Virgil Soc., 1963–66; Classical Assoc., 1977–78. Chm., Commonwealth Conf. on Teaching of English as 2nd Language at Makerere, Uganda, 1961. Hon. LittD Dublin, 1961; Hon. LLD QUB, 1967. Gold Medal for Educn, Sudan, 1977; Premio Internazionale Le Muse, Florence, 1989. *Publications:* From Imperium to Auctoritas, 1946; Aspects of the Principate of Tiberius, 1950; Roman Anniversary Issues, 1950; Ancient History, 1952; The Six Main Aes Coinages of Augustus, 1953; Roman Imperial Money, 1954; Roman Literature, 1954; translations of Tacitus and Cicero; Roman History from Coins, 1958; The World of Rome, 1960; Myths of the Greeks and Romans, 1962; (ed) Birth of Western Civilization, 1964 (new edn as Greece and Rome, 1986); The Civilizations of Europe, 1965; The Gladiators, 1967; The Climax of Rome, 1968; The Ancient Mediterranean, 1969 (Premio del Mediterraneo, Mazara del Vallo, 1983, for Italian edn); Julius Caesar, 1969; The Ancient Historians, 1970; The Roman Forum, 1970; Nero, 1970; Cities of Vesuvius, 1971; Herod the Great, 1971; Roman Myths, 1971; Cleopatra, 1972; The Jews in the Roman World, 1973; (with J. Hazel) Who's Who in Classical Mythology, 1973 (Premio Latina for Italian edition, 1986); The Army of the Caesars, 1974; The Twelve Caesars, 1975; (ed) Greek Literature, 1976; The Fall of the Roman Empire, 1976; Saint Paul, 1976; Jesus, 1977; History of Rome, 1978; (ed) Latin Literature, 1978; The Etruscans, 1980; Greek and Latin Authors 800 BC-AD 1000, 1980; The Dawn of the Middle Ages, 1981; From Alexander to Cleopatra, 1982; History of Ancient Israel, 1984; The Roman Emperors, 1985; A Guide to the Ancient World, 1986; The Rise of the Greeks, 1987; (ed with R. Kitzinger) Civilization of the Ancient Mediterranean, 1988; The Classical Greeks, 1989; The Visible Past, 1990; Short History of Classical Civilization, 1991 (US edn, The Founders of the Western World); Greeks and Romans: a social history, 1992; Readings in the Classical Historians, 1992; The Emperor Constantine, 1993; Sayings of the Bible, 1994; Saint Peter, 1994; My First Eighty Years, 1994; The Antonines, 1994; Art in the Roman Empire, 1995; The Severans, 1996; From Rome to Byzantium: the Fifth Century, 1998; The Collapse and Recovery of the Roman Empire, 1998; Sick Caesar, 2000. *Address:* Le Pitturacce, 351 Via della Chiesa, Gattaiola, Lucca 55050, Italy. *Club:* Athenæum.

GRANT, Michael John, CEng, FICE, FCT; Chief Executive, Strategic Rail Authority, since 2001; *b* 3 Aug. 1953; *s* of Michael George Grant and Zena Grant (*née* Vernem); *m* 1979, Maureen Hampson; one *s* two *d*. *Educ:* North East London Poly. (BSc Hons Civil Engrg); City Univ. Business Sch., London (MBA Finance); Harvard Business Sch. (AMP). Trainee engr, Sir Alexander Gibb & Partners Consulting Engrs, 1971-72; Civil Engineer: DoE, 1972-78; BRB, 1978-84; Financial Analyst, Laing & Cruikshank (Stock Brokers), 1985-86; Dir of Corporate Finance and Gp Treas., Eurotunnel plc, 1987-98; Property Dir, Railtrack, 1998-99; Franchising Dir, OPRAF, 1999-2001. Former Director: Eurotunnel Finance; Eurotunnel Services; Broadgate Plaza; Railtrack Develts; Non-exec. Dir, Liverpool Vision, 1999-. *Recreations:* travel, live music, sport. *Address:* Strategic Rail Authority, 55 Victoria Street, SW1H 0EU. *T:* (020) 7654 6313.

GRANT, Nicholas; *see* Grant, I. N.

GRANT of Dalvey, Sir Patrick Alexander Benedict, 14th Bt *cr* 1688 (NS); Chieftain of Clan Donnachy; (Donnachaidh); Managing Director, Grant's of Dalvey Ltd, since 1988; *b* 5 Feb. 1953; *e s* of Sir Duncan Alexander Grant, 13th Bt, and Joan Penelope (*d* 1991), *o d* of Captain Sir Denzil Cope, 14th Bt; *S* father, 1961; *m* 1981, Dr Carolyn Elizabeth Highet, MB, ChB, DRCOG, MRCGP, *d* of Dr John Highet, Glasgow; two *s*. *Educ:* St Conleth's Coll., Dublin; The Abbey Sch., Fort Augustus; Univ of Glasgow (LLB 1981). FSAScot. Former deer-stalker, inshore fisherman. *Recreations:* professional competing piper, deerstalking, shooting. *Heir:* *s* Duncan Archibald Ludovic Grant, *b* 19 April 1982. *Address:* Tomintoul House, Flichity, Inverness-shire IV1 2XD. *Club:* New (Edinburgh).

GRANT, Peter James, CBE 1997; Chairman, Highlands and Islands Airports, 1993–2001; *b* 5 Dec. 1929; 2nd *s* of late Lt-Col P. C. H. Grant, Scots Guards, and Mrs Grant (*née* Gooch); *m* 1st, Ann, *d* of late Christopher Pleydell-Bouverie; one *s* one *d*; 2nd, Paula, *d* of late E. J. P. Eugster; one *s* two *d*. *Educ:* Winchester; Magdalen Coll., Oxford. Lieut, Queen's Own Cameron Highlanders. Edward de Stein & Co., 1952, merged with Lazard Brothers & Co. Ltd, 1960; Vice-Chm., 1983–85, Dep. Chm., 1985–88, Lazard Bros & Co.; Dir, 1973–95, Vice-Chm., 1976, Chm., 1983–95, Sun Life Assurance Soc. Chairman: Egypt Investment Co., 1996–; CDP-Concord Egyptian Direct Investment Fund Ltd, 2000–; Director: Walter Runciman plc, 1973–90; Standard Industrial Gp, 1966–72; Charrington, Gardner, Lockett & Co. Ltd, 1970–74; London Merchant Securities, 1985– (Dep. Chm., 1994–); Scottish Hydro, 1990–94; Union des Assurances de Paris International, 1989–91 (Internat. Adv. Bd, 1991–95); BNP (UK) plc, 1991–; Transatlantic Hldgs, 1992–95. Member: Industrial Develt Adv. Bd, 1985–92; CAA, 1993–95; Cromarty Firth Port Authority, 1994– (Chm., 2000). Mem. Council and Chm., Finance Cttee, British Red Cross Soc., 1972–85; Mem., Council, Inst. of Dirs, 1989–99. *Recreations:* shooting, golf, gardening. *Address:* Mountgerald, near Dingwall, Ross-shire IV15 9TT. *T:* (01349) 62244; 33 Robert Adam Street, W1M 5AH. *T:* (020) 7935 3555. *Clubs:* Boodle's, Caledonian.

GRANT, Prof. Peter Raymond, FRS 1987; Class of 1877 Professor of Zoology, Princeton University, since 1989; *b* 26 Oct. 1936; *s* of Frederick Thomas Charles and Mavis Irene Grant (now Reading); *m* 1962, Barbara Rosemary Matchett; two *d*. *Educ:* Whitgift Sch.; Cambridge Univ. (BA Hons); Univ. of British Columbia (PhD). Seessel-Anonymous Postdoctoral Fellow in Biology Dept of Yale Univ., 1964–65; Asst Prof. 1965–68, Associate Prof. 1968–73, Prof. 1973–78, McGill Univ.; Prof., Univ. of Michigan, 1977–85; Prof. of Biology, Princeton Univ., 1985–89. FLS 1986. Hon. PhD Uppsala, 1986; Hon. DSc McGill, 2000. *Publications:* Ecology and Evolution of Darwin's Finches, 1986; (with B. R. Grant) Evolutionary Dynamics of a Natural Population, 1989 (Wildlife Soc. Publication Award, 1991); contribs to Science, Nature, Proc. Royal Society, Proc. Nat. Acad. of Scis (USA), etc. *Recreations:* walking, tennis, music. *Address:* Department of Ecology and Evolutionary Biology, Princeton University, Princeton, NJ 08544-1003, USA. *T:* (609) 2585156.

GRANT, Rhoda; Member (Lab) Highlands and Islands, Scottish Parliament, since 1999; *b* 26 June 1963; *d* of Donald and Morag MacCuish; *m* 1989, (Christopher) Mark Grant. *Educ:* Open Univ. (BSc Hons Social Sci.). Administrator: Highland Regl Council, 1987–93; UNISON, 1993–99. *Address:* Scottish Parliament, Edinburgh EH99 1SP.

GRANT, Richard E.; actor and writer; *b* 5 May 1957; *m* 1986, Joan Washington; one *d*. *Educ:* Waterford-Kamhlaba, Swaziland; Univ. of Cape Town (BA English). *Films:* Withnail and I, 1986; How to Get Ahead in Advertising, 1988; Warlock, 1989; Killing Dad, 1989; Henry and June, 1989; LA Story, 1990; The Player, 1990; Hudson Hawk, 1990; Dracula, 1991; The Age of Innocence, 1991; Jack and Sarah, 1993; Prêt-à-Porter, 1994; Twelfth Night, 1995; Portrait of a Lady, 1995; Serpent's Kiss, 1996; Keep the Aspidistra Flying, 1997; Cold Light of Day, 1998; All for Love, 1998; The Match, 1998; Little Vampire, 1999; *television:* Trial and Retribution, 1999; Scarlet Pimpernel, 1999. *Publications:* With-Nails: film diaries, 1996; By Design: Hollwood novel, 1998. *Recreation:* scuba diving. *Address:* c/o ICM, Oxford House, 76 Oxford Street, W1N 0AX. *T:* (020) 7636 6565.

GRANT, Dr Richard Sturge; Ambassador for New Zealand in France, since 1999; *b* 3 Nov. 1945; *s* of Sydney Wallace Grant and Eva Grant; *m* 1973, Cherrilyn Gaye Turnbull; two *d*. *Educ:* Victoria Univ. of Wellington (MA Hons); Univ. de Clermont-Ferrand (Dr d'Univ.). Department of External Affairs, Wellington, 1968; French Govt Scholar, 1968–70; NZ Embassy, Paris, 1971–75; Min. of Foreign Affairs, 1976–78; Counsellor and Dep. Head of Mission, Vienna, 1978–81; Consul-Gen., Noumea, 1982–85; Head, European Div., Min. of Foreign Affairs, 1985–86; Consul-Gen., Sydney, 1987–90; Ambassador, Bonn, 1990–94; Dir, Australia Div., Min. of Foreign Affairs, 1994–97; High Comr for NZ in the UK, 1997–99. Vis. Scholar, John F. Kennedy Sch. of Govt, Harvard Univ., 1999. *Recreations:* tennis, cricket, reading. *Address:* New Zealand Embassy, 7ter rue Léonard de Vinci, 75116 Paris, France. *Clubs:* Royal Automobile; Wellington Golf (NZ).

GRANT, Rodney Arandall; His Honour Judge Grant; a Circuit Judge, since 1995; *b* 8 May 1944; *s* of Thomas and Olive Grant; *m* 1988, Elaine Illingworth. *Educ:* Leeds Grammar Sch.; Trinity Coll., Oxford (Minor Scholar; MA Mod. Langs). Called to the Bar, Inner Temple, 1970; NE Circuit, 1970–95; Head of Chambers, 1992–95; a Recorder, 1993–95. *Recreations:* fell walking, golf, carpentry, gardening, reading, music. *Address:* c/o Circuit Administrator, 17th Floor, West Riding House, Albion Street, Leeds LS1 5AA. *Club:* Bradford Golf.

GRANT, Lt-Gen. Sir Scott (Carnegie), KCB 1999 (CB 1995); Chief Royal Engineer, since 1999; *b* 28 Sept. 1944; *s* of Maurice and Margaret Wotherspoon Gibb Grant; *m* 1973, Catharine Susan Pawsey; one *s* one *d*. *Educ:* King's Sch., Pontefract; RMA Sandhurst; Clare Coll., Cambridge (MA). Commissioned Royal Engineers, 1965; Regtl duty Aden, Sharjah, BAOR and UK, 1965–73; Instructor, RMA, 1973–74; student, Staff Coll., 1975–76; MoD, 1977–78; Sqn Comdr, BAOR, 1979–80; Instructor, Staff Coll., 1981–82; CO 26 Engineer Regt, 1982–84; MoD, 1985; SHAPE, 1986–87; Comdr, 33 Armoured Brigade, 1988–89; RCDS 1990; Army Member, Prospect Team, 1991; Dir Gen. of Army Trng, 1991–93; Team Leader, Army Command Structure Review, 1993; GOC, UK Support Comd (Germany), 1994–95; Comdt, RCDS, 1996–98; QMG, 1998–2000. Col, The Queen's Lancashire Regt, 1993–99; Colonel Commandant: King's Div., 1997–2001; RE, 1997–. *Recreations:* 20th Century art and literature. *Clubs:* Army and Navy; Hawks (Cambridge).

GRANT PETERKIN, Maj. Gen. (Anthony) Peter, OBE 1990; Military Secretary, since 2000; *b* 6 July 1947; *s* of late Brig. James Grant Peterkin, DSO and of Dorothea Grant Peterkin; *m* 1974, Joanna, *d* of Sir Brian Young, *qv*; one *s* one *d*. *Educ:* Ampleforth; RMA Sandhurst; Durham Univ. (BA 1971; MSc 1980). Commnd Queen's Own Highlanders; ADC to CGS, 1973–74; Indian Staff Coll., 1980; Australian JSSC, 1986; CO, 1st Bn, 1987–89; MA to Mil. Sec., 1989–91; MA, UN Observer Mission, Iraq and Kuwait, 1991; Comdr, 24 Airmobile Bde, 1993–94; rcds, 1995; Dep. Mil. Sec., 1996–98; Sen. Directing Staff, RCDS, 1999; Man. Dir, OSCE Mission, Kosovo, April–Sept. 1999; GOC 5th Div., 2000. Chm., Army Rifle Assoc., 1993–. *Recreations:* travelling in Indochina, football, cleaning ditches. *Address:* Grange Hall, Forres, Moray IV36 2TR. *Club:* Army and Navy.

GRANT-SUTTIE, Sir James (Edward); *see* Suttie.

GRANTCHESTER, 3rd Baron *cr* 1953; **Christopher John Suenson-Taylor;** *b* 8 April 1951; *e s* (twin) of 2nd Baron Grantchester, CBE, QC and of Betty, *er d* of Sir John Moores, CBE; *S* father, 1995; *m* 1973, Jacqueline, *d* of Dr Leo Jaffé; two *s* two *d*. *Educ:* Winchester; LSE (BSc Econ). *Heir:* *s* Hon. Jesse David Suenson-Taylor, *b* 6 June 1977. *Address:* Lower House Farm, Back Coole Lane, Audlem, Crewe, Cheshire CW3 0ER.

GRANTHAM, Bishop Suffragan of, since 1997; **Rt Rev. Alastair Llewellyn John Redfern;** *b* 1 Sept. 1948; *s* of Victor Redfern and Audrey Joan Redfern; *m* 1974, Jane Valerie Straw; two *d*. *Educ:* Christ Church, Oxford (MA Modern Hist.); Trinity Coll., Cambridge (MA Theol.); Westcott House, Cambridge. Curate, Wolverhampton, 1976–79; Lectr in Church History, 1979–87, Vice Principal, 1985–87, Ripon Coll., Cuddesdon; Dir, Oxford Inst. for Church and Society, 1979–83; Curate, All Saints, Cuddesdon, 1983–87; Canon Theologian, Bristol Cathedral, 1987–97; Dean of Stamford, 1997–; Canon and Preb., Lincoln Cathedral, 2000–. *Publications:* Ministry and Priesthood, 1999; Being Anglican, 2000. *Recreations:* reading, walking. *Address:* Fairacre, 243 Barrowby Road, Grantham, Lincs NG31 8NP. *T:* (01476) 564722.

GRANTHAM, Roy Aubrey, CBE 1990; National Secretary, APEX Partnership (white collar section of GMB), 1989–91; *b* 12 Dec. 1926; *m* 1964 (marr. diss. 1988); two *d*. *Educ:* King Edward Grammar Sch., Aston, Birmingham. Association of Professional, Executive,

Clerical & Computer Staff: Midland area Organiser, 1949; Midland area Sec., 1959; Asst Sec., 1963; Gen. Sec., 1970–89, when APEX merged with GMB. Mem., TUC Gen. Council, 1983–92. Exec. Mem., Labour Cttee for Europe. Member: Royal Commn on Environmental Pollution, 1976–79; CNAA, 1976–79; IBA, 1984–90; former Mem., MSC, subseq. Training Commn. Director: Chrysler UK Ltd, 1977–79, Talbot UK Ltd, 1979–81; Ansvar Insce Co. Ltd, 1990–97. Governor, Henley Management Coll., 1979–91; Mem., Ditchley Foundn, 1982–97. Chm., UK Temperance Alliance, 1989–. Councillor (Lab), London Bor. of Croydon, 1994–. *Publication:* Guide to Grading of Clerical and Administrative Work, 1968. *Recreations:* walking, reading, chess. *Address:* 16 Owendale, 359 Grange Road, SE19 3BN.

GRANTLEY, 8th Baron *cr* 1782; **Richard William Brinsley Norton;** Baron of Markenfield 1782; a Director, Project and Export Finance, HSBC Investment Bank, since 1997; *b* 30 Jan. 1956; *er s* of 7th Baron Grantley, MC and of Lady Deirdre Freda Mary Hare, *e d* of Earl of Listowel, GCMG, PC; *S* father, 1995. *Educ:* Ampleforth Coll.; New Coll., Oxford (Open Schol. in Maths; BA (Law), MA). Pres., Oxford Union Soc., 1976. Cons. Res. Dept, 1977–81; Morgan Grenfell & Co. Ltd, 1981–97; Dir, Morgan Grenfell Internat., 1994–97. Contested (C) Wentworth, 1983. Councillor, RBK&C, 1982–86. Leader, UK Indep. Party, H of L, 1997. Kt SMO Malta, 1981. *Recreation:* bridge. *Heir: b* Hon. Francis John Hilary Norton, *b* 30 Sept. 1960. *Address:* 8 Halsey Street, SW3 2QH. *T:* (home) (020) 7589 7531; (office) (020) 7336 4645. *Clubs:* White's, Pratt's.

GRANVILLE, 6th Earl *cr* 1833; **Granville George Fergus Leveson Gower;** Viscount Granville 1815; Baron Leveson 1833; *b* 10 Sept. 1959; *s* of 5th Earl Granville, MC and of Doon Aileen (*née* Plunket); *S* father, 1996; *m* 1997, Anne, *o d* of Bernard Topping; one *s* one *d*. *Heir: s* Lord Leveson, *qv*. *Address:* Callernish, Lochmaddy, Isle of N Uist, Western Isles HS6 5BZ.

GRANVILLE-CHAPMAN, Lt-Gen. Sir Timothy (John), KCB 2001; CBE 1991; Adjutant General, since 2000; *b* 5 Jan. 1947; *s* of Guy Granville-Chapman and Elsa Granville-Chapman (*née* Campbell); *m* 1971, Elizabeth Stevens; one *s* one *d*. *Educ:* Charterhouse; Christ's Coll., Cambridge (BA Law 1968; MA 1972). Commissioned RA, 1968; regtl duties, 1968–77; Staff Coll., 1978–79; MA to Comdr, 1st BR Corps, 1980–82; CO 1st Regt RHA, 1985–88; Higher Command and Staff Course, 1988; Mil. Doctrine Author, 1988; Policy Staff, MoD, 1989–90; Comdr 12th Armd Bde, 1990–93; Dir, Army Staff Duties, MoD, 1994; ACGS, MoD, 1994–96; Comdt, Jt Services Comd and Staff Coll., 1997–99. Col, Dorset Yeomanry, 1997–. Gov., Harrow Sch., 1997–. *Recreations:* sailing, some country pursuits, architecture, clocks. *Address:* c/o Cox's & King's, 7 Pall Mall, SW1Y 5NA.

GRANVILLE SLACK, George; *see* Slack.

GRANZIOL, Dr Markus Johannes; Chairman and Chief Executive Officer, UBS Warburg, since 2000; Member, Group Executive Board, UBS AG, since 1998; *b* 21 Jan. 1952; *m*, Manuela Fornera; one *s* one *d*. *Educ:* Univ. of Zurich (MA Econs; PhD Econs 1980). University of Zurich: res. analyst, Inst. for Empirical Res. in Econs, 1976-85; Lectr in Macroecons and Financial Theory, Dept of Juris. and Pol Sci., 1978-90; COS, Dept III, Swiss Nat. Bank, Zurich, 1985-87; Swiss Bank Corporation, 1987-98: Man. Dir and Hd, Securities Dept, 1987-94; Man. Dir, Hong Kong and Global Hd, Equities Business, 1994-95; Jt Global Hd, Equities Business, SBC Warburg, 1995-96 (also Mem. Exec. Bd and Investment Banking Bd); Gen. Manager and Mem., Gp Exec. Bd, 1996-98; Global Hd, Equities and Fixed Income, 1998-99, CEO, Investment Banking Div., 1999-2000, Warburg Dillon Read. Vis. Schol., Grad. Sch. of Business Admin, Univ. of Chicago, 1981-82. *Publications:* contribs to scientific jls. *Recreations:* sports, piano. *Address:* UBS Warburg, 1 Finsbury Avenue, EC2M 2PP.

GRASS, Günter Wilhelm; German writer and artist; *b* Danzig, 16 Oct. 1927; *m* 1st, 1954, Anna Schwarz; three *s* (inc. twin *s*) one *d*; 2nd, 1979, Ute Grunert. *Educ:* Volksschule and Gymnasium, Danzig; Düsseldorf Kunstakademie; Hochschule für Bildende Künste, Berlin. Lecture Tour of US, 1964, and many other foreign tours. Member: Deutscher PEN, Zentrum der Bundesrepublik; Verband Deutscher Schriftsteller; Amer. Academy of Arts and Sciences. Prizes: Lyric, Süddeutscher Rundfunk, 1955; Gruppe 47, 1958; Bremen Literary, 1959 (prize money withheld); Literary, Assoc. of German Critics, 1960; Meilleur livre étranger, 1962; Georg-Büchner, 1965; Fontane, Berlin, 1968; Theodor-Heuss, 1969; Internat., Mondello, 1978; Antonio-Feltrinelli, 1982; Grinzane Cavour, 1992; Chodowiecki, 1992; Hidalgo, 1993; Bayerischen Akad. der Schönen Künste, 1994; (with Philip Roth) Karel Capek, 1994; Hans Fallada, 1995; Sonning, 1995; Thomas Mann, 1996; Asturias, 1999; Nobel Prize for Literature, 1999; medals: Ossietzky, 1968; Hermann Kesten, 1995. *Publications: novels:* Die Blechtrommel, 1959 (The Tin Drum, 1962; filmed 1979); Katz und Maus, 1961 (Cat and Mouse, 1963); Hundejahre, 1963 (Dog Years, 1965); Örtlich betäubt, 1969 (Local Anaesthetic, 1970); Aus dem Tagebuch einer Schnecke, 1972 (From the Diary of a Snail, 1974); Der Butt, 1977 (The Flounder, 1978); Das Treffen in Telgte, 1979 (The Meeting at Telgte, 1981); Kopfgeburten, 1980 (Headbirths, 1982); Die Rättin, 1986 (The Rat, 1987); Unkenrufe (The Call of the Toad), 1992; Ein weites Feld (A Wide Field), 1995; *poetry:* (also drawings) Die Vorzüge der Windhühner, 1956; (also drawings) Gleisdreieck, 1960; Ausgefragt, 1967; Ach Butt, dein Märchen geht böse aus, 1983; Novemberland, 1994; (also paintings) Fundsachen für Nichtleser, 1997; *poetry in translation:* Selected Poems, 1966; Poems of Günter Grass, 1969; In the Egg and other poems, 1978; Novemberland: selected poems 1956–1993, 1996; *drama:* Hochwasser, 1957 (Flood, 1968); Noch zehn Minuten bis Buffalo, 1958 (Only Ten Minutes to Buffalo, 1968); Onkel, Onkel, 1958 (Onkel, Onkel, 1968); Die bösen Köche, 1961 (The Wicked Cooks, 1968); Die Plebejer proben den Aufstand, 1966 (The Plebeians rehearse the Uprising, 1967); Davor, 1969; *prose:* Über das Selbstverständlische, 1968 (Speak Out!, 1969); Dokumente zur politischen Wirkung, 1971; Der Bürger und seine Stimme, 1974; Denkzettel, 1978; Aufsätze zur Literatur, 1980; Zeichnen und Schreiben, Band I, 1982, Band II, 1984; Widerstand lernen, 1984; On Writing and Politics 1967–83, 1985; Zunge Zeigen, 1988 (Show Your Tongue, 1989); Two States – One Nation?, 1990; Schreiben nach Auschwitz, 1990; Deutscher Lastenausgleich, 1990; Ein Schnäppchen namens DDR, 1990; Deutschland, einig Vaterland, 1990; Alptraum und Hoffnung, 1990; Gegen die verstreichende Zeit, 1991; Rede vom Verlust, 1992; Angestiftet, Partei zu ergreifen, 1994; Die Deutschen und ihre Dichter, 1995; Gestern, vor 50 Jahren (correspondence with Kenzaburo Öe), 1995; *graphic work:* Mit Sophie in die Pilze gegangen, 1987; Totes Holz, 1990; Brief aus Altdöbern, 1991; Vier Jahrzehnte, 1991; In Kupfer, auf Stein, 1994. *Address:* Glockengiesserstrasse 21, 23552 Lübeck, Germany.

GRATTAN, Donald Henry, CBE 1989; Chairman: Adult Continuing Education Development Unit, 1984–91; National Council for Educational Technology (formerly Council for Educational Technology), 1985–91 (Member, 1973–84); *b* St Osyth, Essex, 7 Aug. 1926; *s* of Arthur Henry Grattan and Edith Caroline Saltmarsh; *m* 1950, Valmai Dorothy Morgan; one *s* one *d*. *Educ:* Harrow Boys Grammar Sch.; King's Coll., Univ. of London. BSc 1st Cl. Hons, Mathematics Dip. in Radio-Physics. Jun. Scientific Officer, TRE, Gt Malvern, 1945–46; Mathematics Teacher, Chiswick Grammar Sch., 1946–50; Sen. Master, Downer Grammar Sch., Mddx, 1950–56. BBC: Sch. Television Producer, 1956–60; Asst Head, Sch. Television, 1960–64; Head of Further Educn, Television, 1964–70; Asst Controller, Educnl Broadcasting, 1970–72, Controller, 1972–84. Member: Open Univ. Council, 1972–84 and Univ. Delegacy for Continuing Educn, 1978–84; Vis. Cttee, Open Univ., 1987–92; Adv. Council for Adult and Continuing Educn, 1978–83; European Broadcasting Union Working Party on Educn, 1972–84; Venables' Cttee on Continuing Educn, 1976–78. Chm., Adult Literacy Support Services Fund, 1975–80. Mem., Royal TV Soc., 1982–. Chm., Marlow Soc., 1993–96. FRSA 1988. DUniv Open, 1985. Burnham Medal of BIM for services to Management Educn, 1969. *Publications:* Science and the Builder, 1963; Mathematics Miscellany (jt, BBC), 1966; numerous articles. *Recreations:* education (formal and informal), planning and organizing, people. *Address:* Delabole, Gossmore Close, Marlow, Bucks SL7 1QG. *T:* (01628) 473571.

GRATTAN-BELLEW, Sir Henry Charles, 5th Bt *cr* 1838; *b* 12 May 1933; *s* of Lt-Col Sir Charles Christopher Grattan-Bellew, 4th Bt, MC, KRRC and Maureen Peyton, *niece* and adopted *d* of late Sir Thomas Segrave, Shenfield, Essex; *S* father, 1948; *m* 1st, 1956, Naomi Ellis (marr. diss. 1966); 2nd, 1967, Gillian Hulley (marr. diss. 1973); one *s* one *d*; 3rd, 1978, Elzabé Amy (*née* Body), *widow* of John Westerveld, Pretoria, Tvl, SA. *Educ:* St Gerard's, Bray, Co. Wicklow; Ampleforth Coll., York. Publisher: Horse and Hound, SA, and Sustagen Supersport, 1977. Sports administrator, leading radio and TV commentator, hotelier, thoroughbred breeder and owner. *Heir: s* Patrick Charles Grattan-Bellew, *b* 7 Dec. 1971.

GRATWICK, Stephen; QC 1968; *b* 19 Aug. 1924; *s* of late Percival John Gratwick, Fawkham, Kent; *m* 1954, Jocelyn Chaplin, Horton Kirby, Kent; four *d*. *Educ:* Charterhouse; Balliol Coll., Oxford. Oxford 1942–44; Signals Research and Develt Estabt., 1944–47. BA (Physics) 1946; MA 1950. Called to the Bar, Lincoln's Inn, 1949, Bencher, 1976. *Recreations:* swimming, making and mending things. *Address:* Greenmantle, Parkfield, Sevenoaks TN15 0HX.

GRAVENEY, David Anthony; Chief Executive (formerly General Secretary), Professional Cricketers' Association, since 1994; *b* 2 Jan. 1953; *s* of Ken Graveney and late Jeanne Graveney; *m* 1978, Julie Anne Smith-Marriott; one *s* one *d*. *Educ:* Millfield Sch., Somerset. Gloucestershire CCC, 1972–90, Captain 1981–88; Somerset CCC, 1991; Durham CCC, 1992–94, Captain 1992–93. Treasurer, Professional Cricketers' Assoc., 1979–94. Manager: England cricket team, South Africa tour, 1990; England A team, Australia tour, 1996; England cricket team, One-Day series, Australia, 1998–99, and World Cup, 1999; Selector, England cricket team, 1995–96, Chm. of Selectors, 1997–. *Recreations:* golf, watching Rugby. *Address:* (office) 1 St Paul's Road, Clifton, Bristol BS8 1LZ.

GRAVES, family name of **Baron Graves**.

GRAVES, 9th Baron *cr* 1794 (Ire.); **Evelyn Paget Graves;** farmer, retired; *b* 17 May 1926; *s* of Alweyn Montague Graves (*d* 1956), and Kathleen Eleanor Cowle Priest (*d* 1974), and *g g s* of 2nd Baron Graves; *S* kinsman, 1994; *m* 1957, Marjorie Ann (OAM 1992), *d* of late Dr Sidney Ernest Holder; one *s* two *d* (and one *s* decd). *Heir: s* Hon. Timothy Evelyn Graves, *b* 27 March 1960. *Address:* Woodlands, 405 Mole Creek Road, Deloraine, Tas 7304, Australia. *T:* (3) 63622009. *Club:* Launceston (Tasmania).

GRAVES, Christopher James Mitchell; Director, Tudor Trust, since 1986 (Project Officer, 1985–86); *b* 6 April 1956; *s* of Desmond James Turner Graves and Mary Kathleen Graves (*née* Mitchell); *m* 1986, Amanda Patricia Mayhew; one *s* two *d*. *Educ:* Westminster Sch.; Queens' Coll., Cambridge (BA 1978, MA 1981, DipArch 1981). RIBA 1983. Architect, Trehearne, Norman, Preston & Partners, 1981–85. *Recreations:* watercolours, opera, singing, watching a failing football team. *Address:* Tudor Trust, 7 Ladbroke Grove, W11 3BD. *T:* (020) 7727 8522.

GRAVES, Rev. Dr Peter Charles; Minister, Cambridge Wesley Methodist Church, and Methodist Chaplain to the Universities in Cambridge, since 2000; *b* 23 March 1943; *s* of Walter and Eileen Graves; *m* 1976, Patricia Mary Campbell; two *s* one *d*. *Educ:* Handsworth Theol Coll., Birmingham; Union Theol Seminary, Virginia (ThM, DMin); London Univ. (Cert Ed). Minister: Enfield Circuit (St John's, Goff Oak), 1968–69; Highgate Circuit (Holly Park), 1969–72; Chaplain and Associate Lectr, Enfield Coll. of Technol., 1969–72; Chaplain and Sen. Lectr, 1972–77, Sen. Chaplain and Hd of Student Welfare, 1977–79, Middlesex Poly.; Minister: Epsom, 1979–89; Cullercoats, 1989–95; Superintendent Minister, Methodist Central Hall, Westminster, 1995–2000. Methodist Tutor, North East Ordination Course, 1990–95; Tutor, Wesley Study Centre, Cranmer Hall, Durham, 1992–95; Chaplain to Methodist MPs and Leader, Methodist Parly Fellowship, 1995–2000. Finch Lectr, High Point Univ., NC, USA, 1997. Vice Pres., Bible Soc., 1998–. Chm. Judges, Times Preacher of the Year Award, 1998–2000. Broadcaster, Premier Radio, London, 1997–. *Publications:* contrib. New Daylight. *Recreations:* travel, theatre, family life. *Address:* Wesley Methodist Church, Christ's Pieces, Cambridge CB1 1LG. *T:* (01223) 352115.

GRAVES, Rupert; actor; *b* Weston-super-Mare, 30 June 1963. *Educ:* Wyvern Comp. Sch. Early career in a circus and as a mime artist; London theatrical début, King's Head, Islington; film actor, 1986–. *Theatre includes:* Torch Song Trilogy, Albery, 1985; The Importance of Being Earnest; Candida, 1988; 'Tis Pity She's a Whore, NT, 1988; A Madhouse in Goa, Lyric, Hammersmith, 1989; Les Enfants du Paradis, Barbican, 1996; Hurlyburly, Old Vic, transf. Queen's, 1997; The Iceman Cometh, Almeida, 1998; The Caretaker, Comedy, 2000. *Films include:* A Room with a View, 1986; Maurice, 1987; A Handful of Dust,1988; The Children, The Plot to Kill Hitler, 1990; Where Angels Fear to Tread, 1991; Damage, 1992; Royal Celebration, 1993; The Madness of King George, Sheltering Desert, 1994; The Innocent Sleep, Different for Girls, 1996; Intimate Relations, Bent, Mrs Dalloway, 1997; The Revengers' Comedies, 1998; Dreaming of Joseph Lees, All My Loved Ones, 1999; Room to Rent, 2001. *Television includes:* Fortunes of War, 1987; Open Fire, Doomsday Gun, 1994; The Tenant of Wildfell Hall, 1996; Blonde Bombshell, Cleopatra, 1999. *Address:* c/o PFD, Drury House, 34–43 Russell Street, WC2B 5HA.

GRAY, family name of **Baron Gray of Contin**.

GRAY, 22nd Lord *cr* 1445; **Angus Diarmid Ian Campbell-Gray;** *b* 3 July 1931; *s* of Major Hon. Lindsay Stuart Campbell-Gray, Master of Gray, MC (*d* 1945), and Doreen (*d* 1948), *d* of late Cyril Tubbs, Thedden Grange, Alton, Hants; *S* grandmother, 1946; *m* 1959, Patricia Margaret (*d* 1987), *o d* of late Capt. Philip Alexander, Kilmorna, Lismore, Co. Waterford; one *s* three *d*; *m* 1994, Mrs Paul Williams (*née* Cecilia Wilfrida Dimsdale). *Heir: s* Master of Gray, *qv*. *Address:* Airds Bay, Taynuilt, Argyll PA35 1JR. *Clubs:* Carlton, MCC.

GRAY, Master of; Hon. Andrew Godfrey Diarmid Stuart Campbell-Gray; *b* 3 Sept. 1964; *s* and *heir* of 22nd Lord Gray, *qv*; *m* 1993, Hon. Lucy, *y d* of 2nd Baron Elton, *qv*; one *s* one *d*.

GRAY OF CONTIN, Baron *cr* 1983 (Life Peer), of Contin in the District of Ross and Cromarty; **James, (Hamish), Hector Northey Gray;** PC 1982; Lord-Lieutenant, Inverness, since 1996; parliamentary and business consultant, since 1986; non-executive Director, Allied Deals Capital Ltd, since 1998; *b* 28 June 1927; *s* of late J. Northey Gray, Inverness, and Mrs E. M. Gray; *m* 1953, Judith Waite Brydon, BSc, Helenburgh; two *s* one *d*. *Educ:* Inverness Royal Academy. Served in Queen's Own Cameron Hldrs, 1945–48. A director of private and family companies, 1950–70. MP (C) Ross and Cromarty, 1970–83; an Asst Govt Whip, 1971–73; a Lord Comr, HM Treasury, 1973–74; an Opposition Whip, 1974–Feb. 1975; Opposition spokesman on Energy, 1975–79; Minister of State: Dept of Energy, 1979–83; Scottish Office, 1983–86; Govt spokesman on Energy, H of L, 1983–86. Contested (C) Ross, Cromarty and Skye, 1983. Member, Inverness Town Council, 1965–70. DL, 1989–94, Vice Lord-Lieut, 1994–96, Lochaber, Inverness, Badenoch and Strathspey. *Recreations:* golf, cricket, walking, family life. *Address:* Achneim House, Flichity, Inverness-shire IV2 6XE.

GRAY, Alasdair James; self-employed verbal and pictorial artist; *b* 28 Dec. 1934; *s* of Alexander Gray and Amy (*née* Fleming); *m* 1st, 1961, Inge Sørensen (marr. diss.); one *s*; 2nd, 1991, Morag McAlpine. *Educ:* Glasgow Sch. of Art (Scottish Educn Dept Dip. in mural painting and design); Jordanhill Teachers' Trng Coll. (CertEd). Part-time teacher and painter, 1958–62; theatrical scene painter, 1962–63; social security scrounger, 1963–64; painter and playwright, 1965–76 (8 one-man exhibns, one retrospective; 17 TV and radio plays broadcast; 4 plays staged); Glasgow's official artist-recorder for People's Palace local history mus., 1977; Writer-in-Residence, Glasgow Univ., 1977–79. Collections of paintings owned by Collins Gall., Strathclyde Univ. and People's Palace local history mus., Glasgow Green. *Publications: novels:* Lanark, 1981; 1982 Janine, 1984; The Fall of Kelvin Walker, 1985; Something Leather, 1990; McGrotty and Ludmilla, 1990; Poor Things, 1992; A History Maker, 1994; *short story collections:* Unlikely Stories Mostly, 1983; (with J. Kelman and A. Owens) Lean Tales, 1985; Ten Tales Tall and True, 1993; Mavis Belfrage, 1996; *play:* Working Legs (a play for people without them), 1997; *polemics:* Why Scots Should Rule Scotland, 1992; Why Scots Should Rule Scotland 1997, 1997; Old Negatives (poetry), 1989; Saltire Self-Portrait no 4 (autobiog.), 1989; (ed) The Book of Prefaces, 2000; Sixteen Occasional Poems, 2000; A Short Survey of Classic Scots Writing, 2001. *Address:* c/o McAlpine, 2 Marchmont Terrace, Glasgow G12 9LT. *T:* (0141) 339 0093.

GRAY, Anthony James; *b* 12 Feb. 1936; *o s* of Prof. Sir James Gray, CBE, MC, FRS; *m* 1963, Lady Lana Mary Gabrielle Baring (*d* 1974), *d* of 3rd Earl of Cromer, KG, GCMG, MBE, PC; one *s* one *d*; *m* 1980, Mrs Maxine Redmayne, *er d* of Captain and Mrs George Brodrick. *Educ:* Marlborough Coll.; New Coll., Oxford (MA). C. T. Bowring & Co. (Insurance) Ltd, 1960–64; Sen. Investment Analyst, de Zoete & Gorton, 1965–67; Head of Investment Research and Partner, James Capel & Co., 1967–73. Member, London Stock Exchange, 1971–73. Dep. Dir, Industrial Development Unit, Dept of Trade and Industry, 1973–75; Special Industrial Advr, Dept of Industry, 1975–76; Assoc., PA Management Consultants Ltd, 1977–81; Chief Exec., Cogent Gp (technol. transfer collaboration with Assoc. of Indep. Contract Res. Orgns), 1982–88. Chm., various advanced technol. cos. Member: Foundries EDC (NEDO), 1977–79; Hammersmith and Fulham DHA, 1982–85; Research and Manufacturing Cttee, CBI, 1988–90; Science and Industry Cttee, BAAS, 1989–91. Member Council: Charing Cross Hosp. Med. Sch., 1982–84; ERA Technology Ltd (formerly Electrical Res. Assoc.), 1986–89. Gov., British American Drama Acad., 1996–99. Director: Apollo Soc., 1966–73; Nat. Trust Concert Soc., 1966–73. FInstD; FRSA. *Recreations:* fishing, music. *Address:* The Old Coach House, Reepham, Norfolk. *Clubs:* Beefsteak, Garrick.

GRAY, Cecil; *see* Gray, T. C.

GRAY, Hon. Sir Charles (Antony St John), Kt 1998; **Hon. Mr Justice Gray;** a Judge of the High Court, Queen's Bench Division, since 1998; *b* 6 July 1942; *s* of late Charles Herbert Gray and Catherine Margaret Gray; *m* 1st, 1968, Rosalind Macleod Whinney (marr. diss. 1990); one *s* one *d*; 2nd, 1995, Susan (*née* Eveleigh) (*d* 1997), former wife of Hon. Sir John Astor, MBE, ERD; 3rd, 2001, Cynthia Elizabeth Selby. *Educ:* Winchester; Trinity College, Oxford (scholar). Called to Bar, Lincoln's Inn, 1966, Bencher, 1991; QC 1984; a Recorder, 1990–98. *Recreations:* ski-ing, travel, music. *Address:* Royal Courts of Justice, Strand, WC2A 2LL. *Club:* Brooks's.

GRAY, Charles Ireland, CBE 1994; JP; Member, North Lanarkshire Council, since 1995 (Chairman, Education Committee, since 1995); *b* 25 Jan. 1929; *s* of Timothy Gray and Janet (*née* Brown); *m* 1952, Catherine Creighton Gray; three *s* two *d*. *Educ:* Coatbridge. Dept of Public Affairs, Scotrail, 1946; Mem. (later Chm.), Lanark DC, 1958–64; Mem., Lanark CC, 1964–75; founder Mem., 1975–96, first Vice-Convener, and Leader 1986–92, Strathclyde Regl Council. Leader, UK delegn to Euro Cttee of the Regions, 1994–98. Pres., Convention of Scottish Local Authorities, 1992–94. Member: Scottish Exhibn and Conf. Centre, 1986–91; Scottish Enterprise Bd, 1990–93. FRSA 1991. JP Strathclyde, 1970. *Recreations:* music, reading, politics. *Address:* 9 Moray Place, Chryston G69 9LZ. *T:* (0141) 779 2962, *Fax:* (0141) 779 3142.

GRAY, Dr Denis Everett, CBE 1983 (MBE 1972); JP; Resident Staff Tutor since 1957, and Senior Lecturer, 1967–84, Department of Extramural Studies, University of Birmingham; *b* 25 June 1926; *s* of Charles Norman Gray and Kathleen Alexandra (*née* Roberts); *m* 1949, Barbara Joyce, *d* of Edgar Kesterton. *Educ:* Bablake Sch., Coventry; Univ. of Birmingham (BA); Univ. of London; Univ. of Manchester (PhD). Tutor-organiser, WEA, S Staffs, 1953–57. Chairman: Jt Negotiating Cttees for Justices' Clerks and Justices' Clerks' Assts, 1978–86; Central Council of Magistrates' Courts Cttees, 1980–86 (Dep. Chm., 1978–80); Member: Magistrates' Courts Rule Cttee, 1982–86; Lord Chancellor's Adv. Cttee on Trng of Magistrates, 1974–84. JP Solihull, 1962; Dep. Chm., 1968–71 and 1978–82, Chm., 1971–75, Solihull Magistrates; Chm., Licensing Cttee, 1972–76. *Publication:* Spencer Perceval: the evangelical Prime Minister, 1963. *Recreations:* travel, church architecture, reading. *Address:* 11 Brueton Avenue, Solihull, West Midlands B91 3EN. *T:* (0121) 705 2935.

GRAY, Prof. Sir Denis (John Pereira), Kt 1999; OBE 1981; FRCGP; General Medical Practitioner, 1962–2000; Professor of General Practice, University of Exeter, since 1986, (Director of Postgraduate Medical School, 1987–97); President, Royal College of General Practitioners, 1997–2000; *b* 2 Oct. 1935; *s* of late Dr Sydney Joseph Pereira Gray and Alice Evelyn Gray; *m* 1962, Jill Margaret Hoyte; one *s* three *d*. *Educ:* Exeter Sch.; St John's Coll., Cambridge (MA); St Bartholomew's Hosp. Med. Sch. MB BChir. Sen. Lectr in Charge, Univ. of Exeter, 1973–86. Regional Adviser in Gen. Practice, 1975–2000; Consultant Adviser in Gen. Practice to Chief MO, DHSS, 1984–87. Mem., GMC, 1994–; Chm., Jt Cttee on Postgrad. Trng for Gen. Practice, 1994–97. Trustee, The Nuffield Trust (formerly Nuffield Provincial Hosps Trust), 1994–. Chm. Council, RCGP, 1987–90 (Hon. Editor, Journal, 1972–80, Publications, 1976–2000); Vice-Chm., 1998–2000, Chm., 2000–, Acad. of Medical Royal Colls. Editor, Medical Annual, 1983–87. Founder FMed Sci 1998. Lectures: James Mackenzie, RCGP, 1977; Pfizer, N England Faculty, RCGP, Gale Meml, SW England Faculty, RCGP, 1979; Eli Lilly, Haliburton Hume Meml, Newcastle upon Tyne and Northern Counties Med. Soc., Northcott Meml, Barnstaple, Harvard Davis, Denbigh, McConaghey Meml, Lifton, 1988; Murray Scott Meml, Aberdeen, 1990; Harben Meml, London, 1994; Sally Irvine, Ashridge Mgt Coll., 1995; Albert Wander, RSocMed, 1998; Andrew Smith, Durham, 1998; David Bruce, 1999. Gold Medal, Hunterian Soc., 1966, 1969; Sir Charles Hastings Prize, BMA, 1967, 1970; George Abercrombie Award, RCGP, 1978; Foundn Council Award, RCGP, 1980; Sir Harry Platt Prize, Modern Medicine Jl, 1981; Silver Medal, SIMG, 1989; Gold Medal, RIPH&H, 1999. *Publications:* Running a Practice (jtly), 1978, 3rd edn 1981; Training for General Practice, 1981; Forty Years On: the story of the first forty years of the RCGP, 1992; articles in Lancet, BMJ, Jl RCGP. *Recreation:* reading. *Address:* Alford House, 9 Marlborough Road, Exeter EX2 4TJ. *T:* (01392) 218080.

GRAY, Rev. Canon Dr Donald Clifford, CBE 1998; TD 1970; Canon of Westminster and Rector of St Margaret's, Westminster Abbey, 1987–98, Canon Emeritus, since 1998; Chaplain to HM The Queen, 1982–2000; Chaplain to the Speaker, House of Commons, 1987–98; *b* 21 July 1930; *s* of Henry Hackett Gray and Constance Muriel Gray; *m* 1955, Joyce (*née* Jackson); one *s* two *d*. *Educ:* Newton Heath Technical High Sch.; King's Coll., London and Warminster (AKC); Univ. of Liverpool (MPhil); Univ. of Manchester (PhD) FRHistS. Curate, Leigh Parish Church, 1956–60; Vicar: St Peter's, Westleigh, 1960–67; All Saints', Elton Bury, 1967–74; Rector of Liverpool, 1974–87; RD of Liverpool, 1975–81; Canon Diocesan of Liverpool, 1982–87. Proctor-in-Convocation for Manchester, 1964–74; Mem., Gen. Synod, 1980–87. President: Soc. for Liturgical Study, 1998– (Chm., 1978–84); Societas Liturgica, 1987–89 (Treas. 1981–87); Mem., Liturgical Commn, 1968–86; Chm., Jt Liturgical Gp, 1989–94 (Mem., 1969–96; Sec., 1980–89); Mem., Cathedrals Fabric Commn, 1991–96. Chm., Alcuin Club, 1987–. CF (TA), 1958–67; CF (T&AVR), 1967–77; QHC, 1974–77; Chaplain, Order of St John of Jerusalem, 1990 (Sub Chaplain, 1982). *Publications:* (contrib.) Worship and the Child, 1975; (contrib.) Getting the Liturgy Right, 1982; (contrib.) Liturgy Reshaped, 1982; (ed) Holy Week Services, 1983; Earth and Altar, 1986; (ed) The Word in Season, 1988; (contrib.) Towards Liturgy 2000, 1989; (contrib.) Liturgy for a New Century, 1990; Chaplain to Mr Speaker, 1991; Ronald Jasper: his life, his work and the ASB, 1997; (contrib.) They Shaped Our Worship, 1998; All Majesty and Power: royal prayers, 2000; Percy Dearmer, 2000; Memorial Services, 2001. *Recreations:* watching cricket, reading modern poetry. *Address:* 3 Barn Hill Mews, Stamford, Lincs PE9 2GN. *T:* (01780) 765024, *Fax:* (01780) 756183. *Clubs:* Army and Navy; Artists' (Liverpool).

GRAY, Prof. Douglas, FBA 1989; J. R. R. Tolkien Professor of English Literature and Language, University of Oxford, 1980–97, now Emeritus; Professorial Fellow of Lady Margaret Hall, Oxford, 1980–97, now Hon. Fellow; *b* 17 Feb. 1930; *s* of Emmerson and Daisy Gray; *m* 1959, Judith Claire Campbell; one *s*. *Educ:* Wellington College, NZ; Victoria Univ. of Wellington (MA 1952); Merton Coll., Oxford (BA 1954, MA 1960). Asst Lecturer, Victoria Univ. of Wellington, 1952–54; Oxford University: Lectr, Pembroke and Lincoln Colls, 1956–61; Fellow, Pembroke Coll., 1961–80, now Emeritus; University Lectr in English Language, 1976–80. Mem. Council, EETS, 1981–; Pres., Soc. for Study of Mediæval Langs and Lit., 1982–86. De Carle Lectr, Univ. of Otago, 1989; M. M. Bhattacharya Lectr, Calcutta Univ., 1991. Hon. LitD Victoria Univ. of Wellington, 1995. *Publications:* (ed) Spenser, The Faerie Queene, Book 1, 1969; Themes and Images in the Medieval English Religious Lyric, 1972; (ed) A Selection of Religious Lyrics, 1975; (part of) A Chaucer Glossary, 1979; Robert Henryson, 1979; (ed with E. G. Stanley): Middle English Studies presented to Norman Davis, 1983; Five Hundred Years of Words and Sounds for E. J. Dobson, 1983; (ed) The Oxford Book of Late Medieval Verse and Prose, 1985; (ed) J. A. W. Bennett, Middle English Literature, 1986; (ed jtly) From Anglo-Saxon to Early Middle English: studies presented to E. G. Stanley, 1994; Selected Poems of Robert Henryson and William Dunbar, 1998; articles on medieval literature. *Address:* Lady Margaret Hall, Oxford OX2 6QA; 31 Nethercote Road, Tackley, Oxon OX5 3AW.

GRAY, Dulcie; *see* Denison, D. W. C.

GRAY, Dr George Gowans, CBE 2000; FIMechE; Chairman, National Physical Laboratory, since 1995; *b* 21 Jan. 1938; *s* of Alexander Newlands Gray and Elizabeth Hunter Gray (*née* Gowans); *m* 1959, Grace Alicia Edmondson; one *s* two *d* (and one *s* decd). *Educ:* Linlithgow Acad.; Edinburgh Univ. (BSc Hons 1958); Corpus Christi Coll., Cambridge (PhD 1972). MIMechE 1972, FIMechE 1990. Engineer: Pratt & Whitney (Canada), 1960–63; RCA Ltd (Canada), 1963–69; Researcher, Univ. of Cambridge, 1969–71; Manager, 1972–74, Dir, 1974–87, RCA Ltd (UK); Chm., Serco Gp plc, 1987–99; Director: Misys plc, 1996–; Regus Business Centres plc, 1999– (Chm., 2000–). *Publications:* papers in engrg jls. *Recreations:* walking, reading, golf, theatre. *Address:* National Physical Laboratory, Queens Road, Teddington, Middx TW11 0LW. *Clubs:* Oxford and Cambridge; Wentworth Golf.

GRAY, George Thomas Alexander; First Legislative Counsel for Northern Ireland, since 1996; *b* 20 Jan. 1949; *s* of George Gray and Eveline Gray; *m* 1985, Mary Louise Gray; two *s*. *Educ:* Annadale Grammar Sch., Belfast; The Queen's University of Belfast (LLB 1st Cl. Hons). Called to the Bar of N Ireland; Draftsman, 1971–88, Second Legislative Counsel, 1988–96, Office of the Legislative Counsel for NI. *Recreation:* cricket. *Address:* Office of the Legislative Counsel, Parliament Buildings, Stormont, Belfast BT4 3SW. *T:* (028) 9052 1304.

GRAY, Prof. George William, CBE 1991; PhD; FRS 1983; FRSE; CChem, FRSC; Research Consultant; Visiting Professor, Southampton, since 1990; *b* 4 Sept. 1926; *s* of John William Gray and Jessie Colville (*née* Hunter); *m* 1953, Marjorie Mary (*née* Canavan); three *d*. *Educ:* Univ. of Glasgow (BSc); Univ. of London (PhD). CChem, FRSC 1972; FRSE 1989. Staff of Chem. Dept, Univ. of Hull, 1946–: Sen. Lectr, 1960; Reader, 1964; Prof. of Organic Chem., 1978; G. F. Grant Prof. of Chem., 1984–90; Emeritus Prof., 1992. Res. Co-ordinator, Merck Ltd (formerly BDH Ltd), 1990–93. Vis. Sen. Fellow, DERA, 1999. For. Associate, Engrg Acad. of Japan, 1995; Hon. Mem., Internat. Liquid Crystal Soc., 1998. Hon. DSc: Hull, 1991; Nottingham Trent, 1994; Southampton, 1996; East Anglia, 1997; Aberdeen, 2001. Clifford Paterson Prize Lectr, Royal Soc., 1985. Queen's Award for Technol Achievement, 1979; Rank Prize for Optoelectronics, 1980; Leverhulme Medal, Royal Soc., 1987; SCI Medallist, 1993; Kyoto Laureate, Inamori Foundn, 1995; Karl Ferdinand Braun Medal, Soc. for Inf. Display, 1996; Fréedericksz Medal, Russian Liquid Crystal Soc., 1997. Editor, Liquid Crystals, 1992–. *Publications:* Molecular Structure and the Properties of Liquid Crystals, 1962; (ed and jtly with P. A. Winsor) Liquid Crystals and Plastic Crystals, 1974; (ed jtly with G. R. Luckhurst) The Molecular Physics of Liquid Crystals, 1979; (with J. W. Goodby) Smectic Liquid Crystals – textures and structures, 1984; (ed) Thermotropic Liquid Crystals, 1987; (ed jtly) Handbook of Liquid Crystals, Vols 1–3, 1998; 360 pubns on liquid crystals in Jl Chem. Soc., Trans Faraday Soc., Phys. Rev., Molecular Cryst. and Liquid Cryst., Jl Chem. Phys., and Proc. IEEE. *Recreations:* gardening, philately. *Address:* Juniper House, Furzehill, Wimborne, Dorset BH21 4HD. *T:* (01202) 880164, *Fax:* (01202) 840702; *e-mail:* ggray83828@cs.com.

GRAY, Gilbert; QC 1971; a Recorder of the Crown Court, 1972–98; *b* 25 April 1928; *s* of late Robert Gray, JP, Scarborough, and of Mrs Elizabeth Gray; *m* 1954, Olga Dilys Gray (*née* Thomas), BA, JP; two *s* two *d. Educ:* Scarborough Boys' High Sch.; Leeds Univ. (LLB). Pres., Leeds Univ. Union. Called to the Bar, Gray's Inn, 1953; Bencher, 1979. Leader of NE Circuit, 1984–87. *Recreation:* sailing. *Address:* 3 Raymond Buildings, Gray's Inn, WC1R 5BH; Park Court Chambers, 16 Park Place, Leeds LS1 1SJ; Treasurer's House, York.

GRAY, (Hamish) Martin (Vincent); Chairman: Hanover Executive, since 1999; Flying Scotsman Railways, since 2000; *b* 8 June 1946; *s* of Kenneth Dunwell Gray and Helen McGeorge Gray; *m*; two *s*; *m* 2nd, 1992, Alison Margaret Wells. *Educ:* Cockburn High Sch., Leeds. FCIB. Appts with National Westminster Bank, 1963–99; Head of Group Planning, Business Develt Div., 1986–88; Asst Gen. Manager, Group Develt, 1988–89; Gen. Manager, UK Branch Business, 1990–92; Chief Exec., UK Br. Business, later NatWest UK, 1992–98; Exec. Dir, Retail and Commercial Businesses and Main Bd Dir, 1993–99. *Recreations:* fell-walking, fishing. *Address:* (office) 8 Hanover Street, W1R 9HF.

GRAY, Prof. Hanna Holborn, PhD; Harry Pratt Judson Distinguished Service Professor of History, University of Chicago, since 1993 (President, 1978–93, now President Emeritus); *b* 25 Oct. 1930; *d* of Hajo and Annemarie Holborn; *m* 1954, Charles Montgomery Gray. *Educ:* Bryn Mawr Coll., Pa (BA); Univ. of Oxford (Fulbright Schol.); Univ. of Harvard (PhD). Instructor, Bryn Mawr Coll., 1953–54; Harvard University: Teaching Fellow, 1955–57, Instr, 1957–59, Asst Prof., 1959–60, Vis. Lectr, 1963–64; Asst Prof., Univ. of Chicago, 1961–64, Associate Prof., 1964–72; Dean and Prof., Northwestern, Evanston, Ill, 1972–74; Provost, and Prof. of History, Yale Univ., 1974–78, Acting Pres., 1977–78. Hon. degrees include: LHD: Duke, 1982; Brandeis, 1983; Amer. Coll. of Greece, 1986; Univ. of Chicago, 1996; LLD: Dartmouth Coll., Yale, 1978; Brown, 1979; Rochester, Notre Dame, 1980; Michigan, 1981; Princeton, 1982; Georgetown, 1983; Columbia, 1987; Toronto, 1991; Harvard, 1995; DLitt: Oxford, 1979; Washington, 1985. *Publications:* ed (with Charles M. Gray) Jl Modern History, 1965–70; articles in professional jls. *Address:* (office) 1126 E 59th Street, Chicago, IL 60637, USA. *T:* (773) 7027799. *Clubs:* Quadrangle (Chicago); Cosmopolitan (New York City).

GRAY, Hon. Herb(ert Eser); PC 1969; MP (L) Windsor West, since 1962; Deputy Prime Minister of Canada, since 1997, and Minister responsible for Millennium Bureau of Canada, since 1998; *b* 25 May 1931; *s* of Harry and Fannie Gray; *m* 1967, Sharon Sholzberg; one *s* one *d. Educ:* McGill Univ.; Osgoode Hall Law Sch., Toronto. Mem., Ontario Bar. Government of Canada: Minister: without Portfolio (Finance), 1969–70; of Nat. Revenue, 1970–72; of Consumer and Corporate Affairs, 1972–74; of Industry, Trade and Commerce, 1980–82; of Regl Econ. Expansion, 1982; Pres., Treasury Bd, 1982–84; Opposition House Leader, 1984–90; Dep. Leader of the Opposition, 1989–90, Leader, 1990–91; Finance Critic for Official Opposition, 1991–93; Solicitor Gen. and Leader of the Govt in H of C, 1993–97. *Address:* (office) Room 209-S, Centre Block, House of Commons, Ottawa, ON K1A 0A6, Canada.

GRAY, Hugh, BSc(Soc), PhD; former International Secretary, Theosophical Society; *b* 19 April 1916; *s* of William Marshall Kemp Gray; *m* 1954, Edith Esther (*née* Rudinger) (*d* 1998); no *c. Educ:* Battersea Grammar Sch.; London Sch. of Economics. Army Service, Intelligence Corps. UNRRA and Internat. Refugee Organisation, 1945–52; Social Worker; Lectr at SOAS, University of London, 1962–66 and 1970–81; Chm., Centre for S Asian Studies, 1980–81; Gen. Sec., Theosophical Soc. in England, 1983–89. MP (Lab) Yarmouth, 1966–70. *Publications:* various articles on Indian politics and philosophy.

GRAY, Iain; Member (Lab) Edinburgh Pentlands, Scottish Parliament, since 1999; *b* Edinburgh, 7 June 1957; *s* of Robert and Catherina Gray; *m* 1997, Gillianne (*née* McCormack); one *d* and two step *d. Educ:* Inverness Royal Acad.; Edinburgh Univ. (BSc Hons). Physics teacher: Gracemount High Sch., Edin., 1978–82; Scola Agricole, Shokwe, Mozambique, 1982–83; Inveralmond High Sch., Livingston, 1983–86; Campaigns Manager, OXFAM, Scotland, 1986–99. Dep. Minister for Community Care, 1999–2000, for Justice, 2000–, Scottish Exec. *Recreations:* football (season ticket, Hibernian FC), reading, hill-walking. *Address:* Scottish Parliament, George IV Bridge, Edinburgh EH99 1SP; (constituency office) 78 Colinton Mains Drive, Edinburgh EH13 9BJ. *T:* (0131) 348 5754.

GRAY, James Whiteside; MP (C) Wiltshire North, since 1997; *b* 7 Nov. 1954; *s* of Very Rev. John R. Gray, VRD, sometime Moderator, Gen. Assembly of Church of Scotland, and of Dr Sheila Gray; *m* 1980, Sarah Ann Beale; two *s* one *d. Educ:* Hillhead Primary Sch., Glasgow; Glasgow High Sch.; Glasgow Univ. (MA Hons); Christ Church, Oxford. Grad. mgt trainee, P&O, 1977–78; Shipbroker, Anderson Hughes & Co., 1978–84; Mem., Baltic Exchange, 1978–91, 1997–; Dir, Baltic Futures Exchange, 1989–91; Man. Dir, GNI Freight Futures, 1985–92; Special Advr to Sec. of State, DoE, 1992–95; Dir, Westminster Strategy Ltd, 1995–97. Dep. Chm., Wandsworth Tooting Cons. Assoc., 1994–96. Contested (C) Ross, Cromarty and Skye, 1992. An Opposition Whip, 2000–01; Opposition front bench spokesman on defence, 2001–. Mem., Select Cttee on Envmtl Affairs, 1997–2000; Jt Chm., All-Party Minerals Gp, 1998–; Sec., Cons. Agricl Cttee, 1997–99; Vice Chm., Cons. Back bench Cttee, 1999–2000; Mem. Cttee, Parly Maritime Gp., 1997–. Vice Pres., Conservatives Against a Federal Europe, 1997–; Chm., Horse and Pony Taxation Cttee, 1999–. Graduate, Armed Forces Parly Scheme, 1997–98, Post-grad. Scheme, 2001; Fellow, Industry and Parlt Trust. Served HAC (TA), 1977–84; Vice-Pres., HAC Saddle Club; Mem., RA Foxhounds. Freeman, City of London, 1982. *Publications:* Financial Risk Management in the Shipping Industry, 1985; Futures and Options for Shipping, 1987 (Lloyds of London Book Prize); Shipping Futures, 1990. *Recreations:* countryside, riding horses. *Address:* House of Commons, SW1A 0AA. *T:* (020) 7219 6237.

GRAY, Prof. Jeffrey Alan, PhD; Professor of Psychology, Institute of Psychiatry, University of London, 1983–99, now Emeritus Professor; *b* 26 May 1934; *s* of Maurice and Dora Gray; *m* 1961; two *s* two *d. Educ:* Magdalen Coll., Oxford (BA Hons Mod. Langs 1957; BA Hons Psychology 1959); Univ. of London (DipPsych 1960; PhD 1964). FBPsS 1993. Research Worker, Inst. of Psychiatry, 1960–64; Lectr in Psychol., Dept of Exp. Psych., Oxford, 1964–83; Fellow, University Coll., Oxford, 1965–83; Travelling Fellow, MRC, and Guest Investigator, Rockefeller Univ., NY, 1968–69; Soc. Sci. Res. Fellow, Nuffield Foundn, 1975–76; Associate Prof., Univ. of Paris VI, 1979–80; Vis. Prof., Collège de France, Paris, 1998. Director: Psychology at Work Ltd, 1989–; ReNeuron Ltd, 1997–2000. Pres., Exptml Psychol. Soc., 1996–98. Presidents' Award, BPsS, 1983; Kenneth Craik Award, St John's Coll., Cambridge, 1995. *Publications:* Pavlov's Typology, 1964; The Psychology of Fear and Stress, 1971, 2nd edn 1987; The Biological Bases of Individual Behaviour, 1972; Elements of a Two-Process Theory of Learning, 1975; Pavlov, 1979; The Neuropsychology of Anxiety, 1982, and other works. *Recreation:* ski-ing. *Address:* Department of Psychology, Institute of Psychiatry, De Crespigny Park, Denmark Hill, SE5 8AF. *T:* (020) 7919 3245.

GRAY, Sir John (Archibald Browne), Kt 1973; MA, MB, ScD; FRS 1972; Member, External Scientific Staff, MRC, 1977–83: working at Marine Biological Association Laboratory, Plymouth, 1977–93; *b* 30 March 1918; *s* of late Sir Archibald Gray, KCVO, CBE; *m* 1946, Vera Kathleen Mares; one *s* one *d. Educ:* Cheltenham Coll.; Clare Coll., Cambridge (Hon. Fellow, 1976); University Coll. Hospital. BA 1939; MA 1942; MB, BChir 1942; ScD 1962. Service Research for MRC, 1943–45; Surg. Lieut, RNVR, 1945–46; Scientific Staff of MRC at Nat. Inst. for Med. Research, 1946–52; Reader in Physiology, University Coll., London, 1952–58; Prof. of Physiology, University Coll., London, 1959–66; Medical Research Council: Second Sec., 1966–68; Sec., 1968–77; Dep. Chm., 1975–77. Chm., EC Cttee for Medical Res., 1972–76; Member of Council: Marine Biol Assoc., 1969–88 (Vice-Pres., 1988–); Freshwater Biol Assoc., 1981–88 (Pres., 1983–88; Chm. of Council, 1985–88; Vice-Pres., 1988–). QHP 1968–71. FIBiol; FRCP 1974. Hon. DSc Exeter, 1985. *Publications:* papers, mostly on sensory receptors and sensory nervous system, in Jl of Physiology, Procs of Royal Soc. series B, Jl of Marine Biol Assoc., etc. *Recreations:* painting, sailing. *Address:* Seaways, Kingsway, Kingsand, near Plymouth PL10 1NG. *T:* (01752) 822745.

GRAY, (John Armstrong) Muir, CBE 1998; MD; FRCP, FRCPSGlas; FFPHM; Director, Institute of Health Sciences, University of Oxford, 1999–April 2002; *b* 21 June 1944; *yr s* of late John Gray and Nancie Gray (*née* Armstrong); *m* 1974, Jacqueline Elizabeth Rosenthal; two *d. Educ:* Jordanhill Coll. Sch.; Univ. of Glasgow (MB, ChB 1969; MD 1981); Univ. of Bristol (DPH 1973). FFPHM 1984; MRCGP 1985; FRCPSGlas 1989; FRCP 1993. House surgeon, Western Infirmary, Glasgow, 1966–70; Sen. House Officer, Aberdeen, 1970–71; SMO, City of Oxford, 1972–74; Public Health Specialist, Oxfordshire HA, 1974–91; Dir, Health Policy and Public Health, Oxford RHA, 1991–94; Dir of R&D, Anglia and Oxford RHA, then Anglia and Oxford Regl Office, NHS Exec., DoH, 1994–98. Fellow, Green Coll., Oxford, 1984–94, Fellow Emeritus, 1994. Co-ordinator: Nat. Breast Cancer Screening Prog., 1988–91; Nat. Cervical Screening Prog., 1988–94; Dir, Nat. Screening Cttee, DoH, 1999–. Dir, Nat. Electronic Library for Health Project, 1999. Advr, WHO, 1984–91. Hon. DSc UEA 1998. *Publications:* Man Against Disease, 1979; Take Care of Your Elderly Relative, 1980; Football Injuries, 1981; Prevention of Diseases in the Elderly, 1985; Evidence Based Healthcare, 1996; articles in med., epidemiology and public health jls. *Recreations:* reading, ornithology, linguistics, combating the effects of biological ageing. *Address:* (until April 2002) Institute of Health Sciences, Old Road, Oxford OX3 7LF. *T:* (01865) 226833; 59 Lakeside, Oxford OX2 8JQ. *T:* (01865) 554066.

GRAY, Prof. John Clinton, PhD; Professor of Plant Molecular Biology, University of Cambridge, since 1996; Fellow, Robinson College, Cambridge, since 1977; *b* 9 April 1946; *s* of William John Gray and Edith Grace Gray (*née* Tooke); *m* 1971, Julia Hodgetts; one *s* one *d. Educ:* Sir Joseph Williamson's Mathematical Sch., Rochester; Simon Langton Grammar Sch., Canterbury; Univ. of Birmingham (BSc 1967; PhD 1970); MA Cantab 1977. Res. Fellow, Univ. of Birmingham, 1970–73; Res. Biochemist, UCLA, 1973–75; University of Cambridge: SRC Res. Fellow, 1975–76; Demonstrator, 1976–80; Lectr, 1980–90; Reader in Plant Molecular Biol., 1990–96. Nuffield Foundn Sci. Res. Fellow, 1983–84; Royal Soc. Leverhulme Trust Res. Fellow, 1991–92. Non-exec. Dir, Horticulture Res. Internat., 1997–. Member: SERC Biol Scis Cttee, 1990–93; EMBO, 1994. Plant Sci. Advr, Gatsby Charitable Foundn, 1996–. Trustee, Sci. and Plants for Schs, 1991–. Mem., Midlands Assoc. of Mountaineers, 1967–. *Publications:* (ed with R. J. Ellis) Ribulose Bisphosphate Carboxylase-Oxygenase, 1986; papers in scientific jls. *Recreations:* growing plants, mountains. *Address:* Robinson College, Grange Road, Cambridge CB3 9AN; Department of Plant Sciences, University of Cambridge, Downing Street, Cambridge CB2 3EA. *T:* (01223) 333925; 47 Barrons Way, Comberton, Cambridge CB3 7EQ. *T:* (01223) 263325.

GRAY, John Malcolm, CBE 1996; Deputy Chairman, Harvey Nichols Group, since 1996; *b* 28 July 1934; *s* of Samuel Gray and Christina (*née* Mackay-Sim); *m* 1984, Ursula Siong Koon; three *d. Educ:* Strathallan Sch., Scotland. With Hongkong and Shanghai Banking Corp. Ltd, 1952–96, Chm., 1993–96. Dir, World Maritime Ltd, Bermuda, 1984–. Chm., Hong Kong Port Develt Bd, 1990–96. MEC, Hong Kong, 1993–95; Mem., Governor's Business Council, Hong Kong, 1993–96. *Recreations:* reading, golf. *Clubs:* Hong Kong (Hong Kong); Penang (Malaysia).

GRAY, Prof. John Michael, DPhil; FBA 2000; Director of Research, Homerton College, Cambridge, since 1994; *b* 25 March 1948; *s* of Ronald Gray and Patricia Gray (*née* Martin); *m* 1977, Susan Lendrum (marr. diss. 1985); one *d*; partner, 1985, Prof. Jean Rudduck. *Educ:* Exeter Coll., Oxford (BA); Harvard Univ. (EdM); Sussex Univ. (PGCE, DPhil 1976). Asst to Dir, Shelter, 1966–67; Res. Asst, Harvard Univ., 1970–72; teacher, ILEA, 1974–75; Res. Fellow, Edinburgh Univ., 1975–79; Sheffield University: Lectr, 1979–84; Reader, 1984–86; Prof., 1987–93; Jt Dir, Qualitative and Quantitive Studies, Educn Res. Gp, 1988–93; Res. Co-ordinator Social Scis, 1989–93. Vis. Prof., Inst. of Educn, Univ. of London, 1996–2000. Mem. Cttees, 1985–96, Chm., Wkg Party on Future of Educnl Res., 1992, ESRC. Mem. Bd and Chm., Res. Cttee, TTA, 1997–2000; Chm., Standards Cttee, Oxford, Cambridge and RSA Exams Bd, 2001–. *Publications:* jointly: Reconstructions of Secondary Education, 1983; Elton Enquiry into School Discipline, 1989; National Youth Cohort Study of England and Wales (1988–94), Good School, Bad School, 1995; Merging Traditions, 1996; Inspecting Schools, 1996; Gender and Educational Performance, 1998; Improving Schools, 1999. *Address:* Homerton College, Cambridge CB2 2PH. *T:* (01223) 507111.

GRAY, Prof. John Richard; Professor of African History, University of London, 1972–89, now Emeritus; *b* 7 July 1929; *s* of Captain Alfred William Gray, RN and of Christobel Margaret Gray (*née* Raikes); *m* 1957, Gabriella, *d* of Dr Camillo Cattaneo; one *s* one *d. Educ:* Charterhouse; Downing Coll., Cambridge (Richmond Scholar). BA Cantab 1951; PhD London 1957. Lectr, Univ. of Khartoum, 1959–61; Res. Fellow, Sch. of Oriental and African Studies, London, 1961–63, Reader, 1963–72. Vis. Prof., UCLA, 1967. Editor, Jl African History, 1968–71; Chairman: Africa Centre, Covent Garden, 1967–72; Britain-Zimbabwe Soc., 1981–84. Mem., Pontifical Cttee of Historical Sciences, 1982–. Order of St Silvester, 1966. *Publications:* The Two Nations: aspects of the development of race relations in the Rhodesias and Nyasaland, 1960; A History of the Southern Sudan, 1839–1889, 1961; (with D. Chambers) Materials for West African History in Italian Archives, 1965; (ed, with D. Birmingham) Pre-Colonial African Trade, 1970; (ed) The Cambridge History of Africa, vol. 4, 1975; (ed, with E. Fasholé-Luke and others) Christianity in Independent Africa, 1978; Black Christians and White Missionaries, 1990. *Recreation:* things Italian. *Address:* 39 Rotherwick Road, NW11 7DD. *T:* (020) 8458 3676; Picco Alto, Palazzago 24030, Bergamo, Italy. *T:* 03555 1222.

GRAY, Sir John (Walton David), KBE 1995; CMG 1986; HM Diplomatic Service, retired; Chairman: Consultancy Board, Spadel UK, since 1997; Deffrainc Ltd, since 1998; Vandemoortele UK Ltd, since 2000; *b* Burry Port, Carmarthenshire, 1 Oct. 1936; *s* of Myrddin Gray and Elsie Irene (*née* Jones), Llanelli, Carms; *m* 1957, Anthoula, *e d* of Nicolas Yerasimou, Nicosia, Cyprus; one *s* two *d. Educ:* Blundell's Sch.; Christ's Coll.,

Cambridge (MA; Scholar and Tancred Student); ME Centre, Oxford; Amer. Univ., Cairo. National Service, 1954–56. Joined Foreign Service, 1962; served: Mecas, 1962; Bahrain Agency, 1964; FO, 1967; Geneva, 1970; Sofia, 1974; Counsellor (Commercial), 1978, Counsellor and Hd of Chancery, 1980, Jedda; Hd of Maritime, Aviation and Environment Dept, FCO, 1982–85; Ambassador to Lebanon, 1985–88; Ambassador and UK Perm. Rep. to OECD, Paris, 1988–92; Ambassador to Belgium, 1992–96. Chm., OECD Information Policy Wkg Gp, 1980–82; Rapporteur, Study Team on Performance of OECD's Centre for Co-operation with Eur. Econs in Transition, 1994. Adviser: Hyder plc, 1996–99; Fortis Bank, 1998–; Burwood Corp., 1998–; MEM Group, 1999–2000. Mem., Cardiff Bay Develt Corp., 1998–2000. Mem., Commonwealth War Graves Commn, 1997–; Trustee, Nat. Botanic Gdn of Wales, 1998–; Chm., Co-ordinating Cttee, Welsh Internat. Trust, 1997–. President: Wales Council Eur. Movt, 1997–; Inst. of Dirs, Wales, 2000–; Hon. Pres., Paris Chapter, Inst. of Welsh Affairs, 1992; Member: Cttee, Anglo-Belgian Soc., 1996–; Council, Belgium–Luxemburg Chamber of Commerce, 1997–; Cttee, ME Assoc., 1998–; Cttee, British–Lebanese Assoc., 1999–; RIIA. Hon. Consul of Belgium, Cardiff, 2000–. Vice-President: Crawshays Welsh Rugby Club, 1996–; Cardiff Business Club, 1995; WEA, Llanelli, 1997–. Mem. Council, Cheltenham Coll., 1994–97; Gov., Univ. of Glamorgan, 2000–. Hon. Fellow: Cardiff Univ., 1998; UWIC, 2000. Freeman, City of London, 1997; Hon. Freeman, Gardeners' Co., 1996. *Publications:* (jtly) Wales in Europe, 1997; (contrib.) Agenda for the Assembly, 1998. *Recreations:* most spectator sports, light history, things Welsh, public speaking (Internat. Toastmasters' After Dinner Speaker of the Year, 1993). *Address:* 10 Marine Parade, Penarth, Vale of Glamorgan CF64 3BG. *Clubs:* Royal Commonwealth Society, Royal Anglo-Belgian (Chm., 1998–); Cardiff and County (Cardiff); Llanelli Rugby Football.

GRAY, Kenneth Walter, CBE 1992; PhD; FREng; FInstP, FIEE; Chairman and Chief Executive, Scipher plc, since 1996; *b* 20 March 1939; *s* of late Robert W. Gray and Ruby M. Gray; *m* 1962, Jill Henderson; two *s* one *d*. *Educ:* Blue Coat Sch.; Univ. of Wales (BSc, PhD). FInstP 1991; FIEE 1992; FREng (FEng 1996). Research on magnetic resonance, as Nat. Res. Council of Canada post-doctoral Fellow, Univ. of British Columbia, Vancouver, 1963–65; research on semiconductor devices and on radiometry, N American Rockwell Science Center, Thousand Oaks, Calif, 1965–70; research on devices and systems at Royal Signals and Radar Estabt, 1971; Supt Solid State Physics and Devices Div., 1976; Head of Physics Group, 1979; RCDS 1981; Royal Signals and Radar Establishment: CSO, MoD, Dep. Dir (Applied Physics), 1982–84; Under Sec., Dep. Dir (Information Systems), 1984; Dir of Res., 1984–86, Technical Dir, 1986–96, THORN EMI plc; Technical Dir, EMI Group plc, Aug.–Dec. 1996; Exec. Chm., Thorn Software, 1987–89; Technical Dir, Thorn Security and Electronics, 1991–93; Man. Dir, Thorn Transaction, 1993–96. Non-exec. Dir, British Steel, 1995–99. Visiting Research Fellow: Univ. of Newcastle, 1972–74; Univ. of Leeds, 1976–; Vis. Prof., Univ. of Nottingham, 1986–. Member: DTI Innovation Adv. Bd, 1988–93; SERC, 1991–94; Technology Foresight Steering Cttee, OST, 1993–97; HEFCW, 1996–. Hon. DSc Nottingham Trent, 1998. *Publications:* over 30 scientific and technical papers in various learned jls. *Recreations:* tennis, bridge. *Address:* 1a King Street, SW17 6QG.

GRAY, Kevin Adrian; a District Judge (Magistrates' Courts) (formerly Stipendiary Magistrate), Essex, since 1995; *b* 12 Oct. 1947; *s* of Kenneth Thomas Gray and Gladys Gray; *m* 1971 (separated); one *s* one *d*. *Educ:* Portsmouth Southern Grammar Sch.; Kingston Poly. (LLB Hons). Police Officer, Portsmouth City Police, later Hampshire Constabulary, 1964–71; admitted Solicitor, 1976; Sen. Partner, Gray Purdue & Co., 1977–90; sole practitioner, 1990–92; Partner, Gregsons, 1993–94; Acting Metropolitan Stipendiary Magistrate, 1993–95. *Recreations:* clay shooting, walking, cookery, fishing. *Address:* c/o Southend Magistrates' Court, 80 Victoria Avenue, Southend-on-Sea, Essex SS2 6EU. *T:* (01702) 283800.

GRAY, Prof. Kevin John, PhD, LLD, DCL; FBA 1999; Professor of Law, University of Cambridge, since 1993; Fellow, Trinity College, Cambridge, 1981–90 and since 1993; *b* 23 July 1951; *s* of Bryce Holmes Gray, Belfast, and Priscilla Margaret Gray (*née* McCullough), Lisburn; *m* 1996, Susan, *d* of late Arthur Walter David Francis and Helen Francis (*née* Waggott); two *s* by previous marriages. *Educ:* Trinity Hall, Cambridge (BA 1972 (1st Cl. Law Tripos Parts I and II); MA, PhD 1976; Yorke Prize, 1977; LLD 1991); DCL Oxford, 1994). Called to the Bar, Middle Temple, 1993. University of Cambridge: Fellow, Queens' Coll., 1975–81; Asst Lectr and Lectr in Law, 1978–90; Univ. Advocate, 1986–88; Res. Fellow, ANU, 1990; Drapers' Prof. of Law, QMW, Univ. of London, 1991–93. Vis. Fellow, ANU, 1979, 1989, 1998; Sen. Vis. Res. Fellow, St John's Coll., Oxford, 1993–94; Visiting Professor: Grad. Sch. of Law, Univ. of Osaka, 2001; Univ. of NSW, 2002. Associate Mem., Acad. Internat. de Droit Comparé, 1995. Jun. and sen. internat. athlete, 1968–69. *Publications:* Reallocation of Property on Divorce, 1977; Elements of Land Law, 1987, 3rd edn (with S. F. Gray) 2001; (with S. F. Gray) Land Law, 1999, 2nd edn 2001; other books and articles on law, legal theory, human rights, and the envmt. *Recreations:* mountaineering, rock climbing. *Address:* Trinity College, Cambridge CB2 1TQ. *T:* (01223) 314520.

GRAY, Linda Esther, (Mrs Peter McCrorie); retired as opera singer, now teaching; *b* 29 May 1948; *d* of James and Esther Gray; *m* 1971, Peter McCrorie; one *d*. *Educ:* Greenock Academy; Royal Scottish Academy of Music and Drama. Cinzano Scholarship, 1969; Goldsmith Schol., 1970; James Caird Schol., 1971; Kathleen Ferrier Award, 1972; Christie Award, 1972. London Opera Centre, 1969–71; Glyndebourne Festival Opera, 1972–75; Scottish Opera, 1974–79; Welsh Opera, 1980; English National Opera, 1979; American début, 1981; Royal Opera House: Sieglinde, 1982; Fidelio, 1983. Records: Tristan und Isolde, 1981; Wagner's Die Feen, 1983. Principal rôles: Isolde, Sieglinde, Kundry (Wagner); Tosca (Puccini); Fidelio (Beethoven). *Recreations:* cooking, swimming. *Address:* 35 Green Lane, New Malden, Surrey KT3 5BX.

GRAY, Margaret Caroline, MA Cantab; Headmistress, Godolphin and Latymer School, 1963–73; *b* 25 June 1913; *d* of Rev. A. Herbert Gray, DD, and Mrs Gray (Mary C. Dods, *d* of Principal Marcus Dods of New Coll., Edinburgh). *Educ:* St Mary's Hall, Brighton; Newnham Coll., Cambridge. Post graduate fellowship to Smith Coll., Mass, USA, 1935–36. Asst History mistress, Westcliff High Sch. for Girls, 1937–38; Head of History Dept, Mary Datchelor Girls' Sch., Camberwell, 1939–52; Headmistress, Skinners' Company's Sch., Stamford Hill, 1952–63. Chm., Nat. Advisory Centre on Careers for Women, 1970–91. Governor: Francis Holland Schs, 1974–99; Hampton Sch., 1976–88; West Heath Sch., Sevenoaks, 1974–89; Unicorn Sch., Kew, 1974–89; Chm. of Trustees, Godolphin and Latymer Bursary Fund, 1976–. Hon. Sec., RUKBA, Kingston-upon-Thames, 1973–. Elder, St John's Wood URC, 1960–. *Recreations:* gardening, motoring, walking. *Address:* 15 Fitzwilliam Avenue, Kew, Richmond, Surrey TW9 2DQ. *T:* (020) 8940 4439.

GRAY, Martin; *see* Gray, H. M. V.

GRAY, Ven. Martin Clifford; Archdeacon of Lynn, since 1999; *b* 19 Jan. 1944; *s* of John Oscar Gray and Lilian Annie Bertha Gray; *m* 1966, Pauline Jean Loader; three *s*. *Educ:* West Ham Coll. of Technology (DipChemEng; AWHCT 1967); Westcott House, Cambridge. Process Engineer, May & Baker, Norwich, 1968–70; Process Engr, Plant Supt, Project Manager, 1970–78, Dow Chemical, Kings Lynn, Norfolk and Bilbao, Spain. Deacon 1980, priest 1981; Asst Curate, St Faith's, Gaywood, Kings Lynn, 1980–84; Vicar, St Peter's, Sheringham, 1984–94; Rector, Lowestoft St Margaret Team Ministry, Suffolk, 1994–99. *Recreations:* golf, hill-walking. *Address:* Hollytree House, Whitwell Road, Sparham, Norfolk NR9 5PN.

GRAY, Lt-Gen. Sir Michael Stuart, KCB 1986; OBE 1970; DL; Lieutenant of the Tower of London, 1995–98; Defence Industries Adviser, Airborne Systems Division, Troyess Ltd (formerly Wardle Storeys plc), since 1989; Chairman of Board of Directors, Thelma Turner Homes Ltd, for people with special needs, since 1996; *b* Beverley, E Yorkshire, 3 May 1932; *e s* of late Lieut Frank Gray, RNVR, and Joan Gray (*née* Gibson); *m* 1958, Juliette Antonia Noon, Northampton; two *s* one *d*. *Educ:* Beverley Grammar Sch.; Christ's Hosp., Horsham; RMA, Sandhurst. FIMgt; FInstD; FICFM. Enlisted RA, 1950; commissioned E Yorkshire Regt, 1952; served Malaya; transf. to Parachute Regt, 1955; served Cyprus, Suez, Jordan, Greece, Bahrein, Aden, N Ireland; sc Camberley, 1963; commanded 1st Bn Parachute Regt, 1969–71; DS Staff Coll., Camberley, 1971–73; Col GS 1 Div. BAOR, 1973–75; RCDS 1976; last Comdr 16 Para Bde, 1977; Comdr 6 Field Force and COMUKMF, 1977–79; Comdr British Army Staff and Mil. Attaché, Washington, 1979–81, and Head of British Def. Staff and Def. Attaché, Washington, 1981; GOC SW District, and Maj.-Gen., UKMF(L), 1981–83; COS, HQ BAOR, 1984–85; GOC SE Dist and Comdr Jt Force HQ, 1985–88, retd. Dep. Col Comdt, Parachute Regt, 1986–90, Col Comdt, 1990–93. Hon. Colonel: 10 Para (V), 1984–88; 250 (Hull) Field Amb. RAMC (V), 1991–99. Consultant, Brittany Ferries (wrote Battlefield Tours audio tapes of Pegasus Trail, 1989 and British D-Day Trail, 1994), 1988–. Chm., Airborne Assault Normandy Trust (AAN), to preserve the history of 6 AB Division in Normandy, 1978–; Trustee: AB Forces Security Fund, 1986–; AB Forces Charities (formerly AB Forces Charities Develt Trust) (Chm., 1990–94); Pres., York Br., 1991–, Vice Pres., NI Br. and Tyneside Br., 2000–, Parachute Regt Assoc.; Vice Pres., Army Parachute Assoc. (Free Fall), 1987– (Pres., 1981–87); Normandy Veterans Association: Vice-Pres., Goole Br., 1988–; Pres., Leeds Br., 1991–; Pres., Grimsby Br., 1995–; Pres., E Yorks Cttee, King George's Fund for Sailors, 2000– (Chm., 1988–2000); Mem., Amicable Soc. of Blues, 1989–; Patron: Combined Ex-Service Assoc., Bridlington, 1988–; Yorks Air Mus., Elvington, 1999–; Friends of Airborne Forces, 2000–. Chm., Thelma Turner Charitable Trust, 1998–. Hon. Brother, Trinity House, Hull, 2000–. Freeman, City of London, 1983. DL ER of Yorks, 1997. Officier, Légion d'Honneur (France), 1994. *Recreations:* military history, travelling, DIY, photography, painting. *Address:* c/o GQ Parachutes Ltd, PO Box 77, Bridgend CF35 6XX.

GRAY, Monique Sylvaine, (Mrs P. F. Gray); *see* Viner, M. S.

GRAY, Muir; *see* Gray, J. A. M.

GRAY, Paul Edward, ScD; Hon. Chairman of the Corporation, and President Emeritus, Massachusetts Institute of Technology, since 1997; *b* 7 Feb. 1932; *s* of Kenneth Frank Gray and Florence (*née* Gilleo); *m* 1955, Priscilla Wilson King; one *s* three *d*. *Educ:* Massachusetts Inst. of Technol. (SB 1954, SM 1955, ScD 1960). Served Army, 1955–57 (1st Lieut). Massachusetts Institute of Technology: Mem., Faculty of Engrg, 1960–71, 1990–; Class of 1922 Prof. of Electrical Engrg, 1968–71; Dean, Sch. of Engrg, 1970–71; Chancellor, 1971–80; Pres., 1980–90; Mem., 1971–, Chm., 1990–97, of Corp. Director: A. D. Little Inc., Cambridge; NVEST, LP, Boston; Boeing Co., Seattle; Eastman Kodak, Rochester. Emeritus Trustee: Museum of Science, Boston; Wheaton Coll., Mass. Fellow, Amer. Acad. of Arts and Sciences; Member: National Acad. of Engrg (Treas., 1994–); Mexican National Acad. of Engrg; Life Fellow, IEEE. *Address:* Massachusetts Institute of Technology, 77 Massachusetts Avenue, Cambridge, MA 02139, USA; 100 Memorial Drive, Apt 11–4A, Cambridge, MA 02142.

GRAY, Paul Lucas, DPhil; Director of Education, Surrey County Council, since 1996; *b* 20 Jan. 1957; *s* of Alfred N. Gray and Doris J. Gray (*née* Hutchens); *m* 1982, Patricia Ann Wright. *Educ:* Univ. of Durham (BA Hons); Univ. of Birmingham (DPhil). Lectr, 1980–84, Sen. Lectr and Asst Principal, 1984–86, Merseyside; Sen. Educn Officer, Cambs CC, 1986–90; Dep. Chief Educn Officer, Devon CC, 1990–96. Chm., QCA Curriculum and Assessment Cttee, 1999–. Mem. Bd, Nat. Youth Agency, 1999–. FRSA 1997. *Recreations:* sport, music, literature, sailing. *Address:* 22 Falconhurst, The Crescent, Surbiton, Surrey KT6 4BP. *T:* (020) 8390 3839.

GRAY, Paul Richard Charles, CB 2000; Group Director, Children, Pensioners and Disabled, Department for Work and Pensions (formerly Department of Social Security), since 1999; *b* 2 Aug. 1948; *s* of Rev. Sidney Gray and Ina (*née* Maxey); *m* 1972, Lynda Elsie Braby; two *s*. *Educ:* Wyggeston Boys' Sch., Leicester; LSE (BSc Econ 1969). Dept of Econ. Affairs, 1969; HM Treasury, 1969–77; with Booker McConnell Ltd, 1977–79; HM Treasury: Principal, 1979–83; Asst Sec., 1984–87; Econ. Affairs Private Sec. to Prime Minister, 1988–90; Under Sec., Monetary Gp, 1990–93; Dir, Personnel and Support Services, 1994–95; Dir, Budget and Public Finances, 1995–98; Hd of Policy Gp, DSS, 1998–99. Dir (non-exec.), Laing Management Ltd, 1993–95. *Recreations:* family, walking, Wensleydale sheep. *Address:* Department for Work and Pensions, The Adelphi, 1–11 John Adam Street, WC2N 6HT. *T:* (020) 7962 8000.

GRAY, Paul Shapter, FRSC; Director, Environment and Climate and Marine Science and Technology Programme, European Commission, 1992–97; *b* 18 Sept. 1932; *s* of Frederick Archibald and Vera Emma Gray; *m* 1958, Diane Lillian Platt; one *s* one *d* (and one *s* decd). *Educ:* St Chad's Coll., Wolverhampton; Birmingham Univ. (BSc Hons; MSc). FRSC (FRIC 1967). Chief Chemist, Midland Tar Distillers, 1954–57; Sen. Research Fellow, Ministry of Power, 1957–59; Head of Div., Reactor Chemistry, UKAEA, Winfrith, 1959–63; Ops Controller, OECD DRAGON (high temp. gas cooled reactor expt), 1963–73; European Commission, 1973–: Dep. Head of Div., Elimination of Technical Barriers to Trade, 1977–81; Head of Service, Wood, Paper and Construction Industries, 1981–83; Head of Div., Food Law and Food Trade, 1983–91; Advr for industrial aspects of biotechnology, 1991–92. Sci. Advr, European Assoc. for Global Ocean Observing System, 1996–; Member Sci. Cttee, Royal Inst. for sustainable mgt of natural resources and promotion of clean technols, Belgium, 1997–; Mem. Mgt Bd, Belgian Nat. Orch., 1998–. Hon. DSc Birmingham, 1999. *Publications:* jointly: Radionuclides in the Food Chain, 1988; Chernobyl, 1991; EU Committees as Influential Policymakers, 1998; Food Safety Regulation, 1999; numerous pubns in scientific and economic jls. *Recreations:* music, singing, sailing, playwriting, gardening. *Address:* 67 Avenue des Chênes, 1180 Brussels, Belgium. *T:* (2) 3751432; *e-mail:* paul.gray@4thwave.be.

GRAY, Prof. Peter, MA, PhD, ScD (Cantab); FRS 1977; CChem, FRSC; Master, 1988–96, Fellow, since 1988, Gonville and Caius College, Cambridge; *b* Newport, 25 Aug. 1926; *er s* of late Ivor Hicks Gray and Rose Ethel Gray; *m* 1st, 1952, Barbara Joan Hume, PhD (*d* 1992), 2nd *d* of J. B. Hume, London; two *s* two *d*; 2nd, 1996, Rachel

Katharine, *d* of late P. A. Buxton and *widow* of C. Herzig, CBE. *Educ:* Newport, High Sch.; Gonville and Caius Coll., Cambridge (Major Schol., 1943; Prizeman, 1944, 1945 and 1946; BA 1st cl. hons Nat. Sci. Tripos, 1946; Dunlop Res. Student, 1946; PhD 1949; ScD 1963). Ramsay Meml Fellow, 1949–51; Fellow, Gonville and Caius Coll., 1949–53; ICI Fellow, 1951; University Demonstrator in Chem. Engrg, University of Cambridge, 1951–55; Physical Chemistry Dept, University of Leeds: Lectr, 1955; Reader, 1959; Prof., 1962; Head of Dept, 1965–88; Chm., Bd of Combined Faculties of Science and Applied Science, 1972–74; Hon. Vis. Prof., 1988–; University of Cambridge: Chm., Faculty of Engrg, 1989–94; Mem., Council of Senate, 1990–96; Mem., Financial Bd, 1991–94. Visiting Professor: Univ. of BC, 1958–59; Univ. of W Ont., 1969; Univ. of Göttingen, 1979, 1986; Macquarie Univ., 1980; Beijing Univ. of Technol., 1984; Univ. of Paris, 1986; Calabria Univ., 1988; H. C. Hottel Lectr, Orléans, 1990; Pierre Bruylants Lectr, Louvain, 1994; Larmor Lectr, Cambridge, 1995; Visitor, Fire Res. Orgn, 1984–90 (G. R. Nice Lectr, 1989). Mem. Council: Faraday Soc., 1965 (Vice-Pres., 1970; Treasurer, 1973; Pres., 1983–85); Chemical Soc., 1969. Pres., Cambridge Phil Soc., 1992–93. Chairman: Schiff Foundn, 1989–95; Oppenheimer Fund, 1988–95; Trustee, Edward Boyle Meml Trust, 1989–98. Hon. DSc Leeds, 1997. Meldola Medal, Royal Inst. Chem., 1956; Marlow Medal, Faraday Soc., 1959; Gold Medal, Combustion Inst., 1978; Award for Combustion, Royal Soc. of Chemistry, 1986; Italgas Prize for Chemistry, 1988. Associate Editor, Royal Society, 1983–97; Member, Editorial Board: Combustion and Flame, 1976–82; Dynamics and Stability of Systems, 1986–; Jl of Non equilibrium Thermodynamics, 1990–95; Discrete Dynamics in Nature & Soc., 1995–. *Publications:* (with S. K. Scott) Chemical Oscillations and Instabilities, 1990; numerous papers on phys. chem. subjects in scientific jls. *Recreation:* hill walking. *Address:* Gonville and Caius College, Cambridge CB2 1TA. *T:* (01223) 332400, *Fax:* (01223) 332456; 2 Fendon Close, Cambridge CB1 7RU. *T:* (01223) 212660.

GRAY, Peter Francis; Chairman, Gray & Co., since 1987; *b* 7 Jan. 1937; *s* of Revd George Francis Selby Gray; *m* 1978, Fiona Bristol; two *s*. *Educ:* Marlborough; Trinity College, Cambridge. MA; FCA. Served Royal Fusiliers, attached 4th Kings African Rifles, Uganda, 1956–58. HM Foreign Service, 1963–64; SG Warburg & Co., 1964–66; Cooper Brothers & Co., 1966–69; Samuel Montagu & Co., 1970–77; Head of Investment Div., Crown Agents for Oversea Govts & Admins, 1977–83; Man. Dir, Touche Remnant & Co., 1983–87; Chairman: Nomina, 1997–; Supervisory Bd, Postbank and Savings Bank Corp. (Hungary), 1998; Finngold Resources, 1998–; Enhanced Zero Trust, 1999–; Close Finsbury EuroTech Trust, 2000–; Director: NZ Investment Trust, 1988–; Gartmore Monthly Income Trust (formerly Gartmore Shared Equity Trust), 1993–; Foreign & Colonial Private Equity Trust, 1994–; Liberty (formerly Liberty Newport) World Portfolio SICAV, 1995–; Folio Corporate Finance Ltd, 1997–. Dep. Chm., Assoc. of Investment Trust Cos, 1985–87. *Recreations:* literature, music. *Address:* 1 Bradbourne Street, SW6 3TF. *Club:* Brooks's.

GRAY, Richard Dennis; Director, Compton Verney, since 1999; *b* 19 Sept. 1951; *s* of John Dennis and Betty Gray; *m* 1976, Cherry Elizabeth Allen; two *s*. *Educ:* Carre's Grammar Sch.; Bristol Univ. (BA History and History of Art); Manchester Univ. AMA. Asst Keeper and Keeper, Manchester City Art Galls, 1974–89; Dir, Manchester City Art Galls, 1989–98. Member: English Ceramic Circle, 1976–; Glass Circle, 1981–; Cttee, Glass Assoc., 1983–87; Cttee, Northern Ceramic Soc., 1986–89; NW Museums Service Adv. Panel, 1988–98; Bd of Management, 1994–98; Indep. Assessor, Reviewing Cttee on Export of Works of Art; Ext. Examnr, Manchester Polytechnic, 1989–92. Trustee: Spode Mus., 1989–; Rekonstruktsiya Trust, 1991–93. *Publications:* The History of Porcelain, Chapter 1, 1982; catalogues and inventories, Manchester City Art Galleries; articles and book reviews for arts jls. *Recreations:* music, fishing, walking. *Address:* Compton Verney, Warwick CV36 9HZ.

GRAY, Prof. Richard John, PhD; FBA 1993; Professor of Literature, University of Essex, since 1990; *b* 5 Jan. 1944; *s* of George Ernest Gray and Helen Gray; *m* 1st, 1965, Joyce Mary Gray (marr. diss. 1991); one *s* one *d*; 2nd, 1991, Sheona Catherine Binnie; one *s* one *d*. *Educ:* St Catharine's Coll., Cambridge (BA, MA, PhD). Sen. Res. Schol., St Catharine's Coll., Cambridge, 1966–67; Harkness Fellow, for res. in US Univs, 1967–69; Lectr, Sen. Lectr and Reader in Literature, Univ. of Essex, 1969–90. Robert E. McNair Vis. Prof. in Southern Studies, Univ. of South Carolina, 1993. Editor, Jl of Amer. Studies, 1997–. Research awards of: Amer. Philos. Soc., 1979; Internat. Communications Agency, 1981; Humanities Res. Bd, 1995, 1998. *Publications:* American Verse of the Nineteenth Century, 1973; American Poetry of the Twentieth Century, 1976; The Literature of Memory: modern writers of the American South, 1977; Robert Penn Warren: essays, 1980; American Fiction: new readings, 1983; Writing the South: ideas of an American region (C. Hugh Holman Award, Soc. for Study of Southern Lit.), 1986, 2nd edn 1997; American Poetry of the Twentieth Century, 1990; (ed) The Complete Poems of Edgar Allan Poe, 1993; The Life of William Faulkner: a critical biography, 1994; (ed) Selected Poems of Edgar Allan Poe, 1996; Southern Aberrations: writers of the American South and the problems of regionalism, 2000. *Recreations:* running, tennis, wine tasting, cycling, cinema. *Address:* Department of Literature, University of Essex, Wivenhoe Park, Colchester, Essex CO4 3SQ. *T:* (01206) 872590.

GRAY, Richard Paul; QC 1993; *b* 1 Nov. 1945; *s* of John Montgomery Gray and Margaret Elizabeth Gray (*née* Welsh); *m* 1977, Emma Serena Halpin; one *s*. *Educ:* Tonbridge Sch.; St Andrew's Univ. (LLB). Called to the Bar, Inner Temple, 1970. *Recreations:* family, gardens, games.

GRAY, Robert, CBE 1988; JP; building consultant and clerk of works; Vice Lord-Lieutenant, City of Glasgow, 1992–96; *b* 3 March 1928; *s* of John Gray and Mary (*née* McManus); *m* 1955, Mary (*née* McCartney); one *d*. *Educ:* St Mungo's Acad., Glasgow. LIOB 1970. Lecturer: Glasgow Coll. of Building, 1964–65; Anniesland Coll., 1965–70; Sen. Lectr, Cardonald Coll., 1970–84. Mem. (Lab) City of Glasgow (formerly Glasgow Dist, then Glasgow City) Council, 1974–; Lord Provost and Lord-Lieutenant of Glasgow, 1984–88. Deacon, Incorporation of Wrights of Glasgow, 1996. DL City of Glasgow, 1988. OStJ. Fellow, Glasgow Coll. of Technol., 1987. Hon. LLD Strathclyde, 1987. *Recreations:* walking, reading, music. *Address:* 106 Churchill Drive, Glasgow G11 7EZ. *T:* (0141) 357 3328. *Clubs:* Royal Scottish Automobile, Art (Glasgow).

GRAY, Hon. Sir Robert McDowall, (Sir Robin), Kt 1994; *b* 2 July 1931; *s* of Adam Gray and Elsie McDowall; *m* 1957, Mary Thomson (*d* 1981); one *s* two *d*. *Educ:* George Watson's Boys' Coll., Edinburgh. Served 4th/7th Royal Dragoon Guards, 1949–51; immigrated to NZ, as farm labourer, 1952; purchased farm, 1956; entered politics, 1978; MP (Nat.) Clutha, 1978–96; Whip, 1985, Sen. Whip, 1987; Speaker, NZ House of Reps, 1990–93; Minister of State, Associate Minister of For. Affairs and Trade, 1993–96. Chm., Parly Service Commn, 1990–93. *Address:* 3 Inglis Street, Mosgiel, Otago, New Zealand.

GRAY, Robert Walker; *see* Gray, Robin.

GRAY, Robin; Member: Local Government Commission for England, since 1996; Parliamentary Boundary Commission for England, since 1999; *b* 16 April 1944; *s* of Robert George and Jeannie Gray; *m* 1971, Kathleen Rosemary Kuhn; two *d*. *Educ:* Woking County Grammar Sch. for Boys; Birkbeck Coll., London Univ. (BA Hons). UKAEA, 1962–64; HM Treasury, 1964–70; Asst Sec. to Crowther Cttee on Consumer Credit, 1968–70; Min. of Housing and Local Govt, subseq. DoE, 1970–93; seconded to Water Resources Bd, 1973–75, to W Sussex CC, 1982–83; Sec., London and Metropolitan Govt Staff Commn, 1984–86; PSA, 1986–92; Under Sec., 1988–92; Dir of Civil Projects, 1988–89; Dir, Marketing and Planning, 1990–92; Internat. Dir, 1991–92; Business Develt Dir, PSA Projects Ltd, 1992–93. Management consultant, 1993–. *Recreations:* cricket, walking and other outdoor activities, talking. *Address:* c/o Boundary Commission for England, Room B1/04, 1 Drummond Gate, SW1V 2QQ.

GRAY, Robin, (Robert Walker Gray), CB 1977; Deputy Secretary, Department of Trade, 1975–84; retired; *b* 29 July 1924; *s* of Robert Walker Gray and Dorothy (*née* Lane); *m* 1955, Shirley Matilda (*née* Taylor); two *s* one *d*. *Educ:* John Lyon Sch., Harrow; London Sch. of Economics. BScEcons 1946; Farr Medal in Statistics. Air Warfare Analysis Section of Air Min., 1940–45; BoT, 1947; UK Delegn to OEEC, 1950–51; BoT, 1952–66; Commercial Counsellor, British High Commn, Ottawa, 1966–70; Under-Secretary: DTI, 1971–74; Dept of Prices and Consumer Protection, 1974–75; Dep. Sec., DoI, 1975. *Address:* Tansy, Brook Road, Wormley, Godalming, Surrey GU8 5UA. *T:* (01428) 682486.

GRAY, Hon. Robin (Trevor), BAgrSc; Chairman, Botanical Resources Australia Pty Ltd, since 1996; Partner, Evers Gray Consultants, since 1996; *b* 1 March 1940; *s* of late Rev. W. J. Gray; *m* 1965, Judith, *d* of late A. G. Boyd; two *s* one *d*. *Educ:* Box Hill High Sch.; Dookie Agricl Coll., Melbourne Univ. Teacher, 1961–65 (in UK, 1964); agricl consultant, Colac, Vic, 1965, Launceston, Tas, 1965–76; pt-time Lectr in Agricl Econs, Univ. of Tasmania, 1970–76. MHA (L) for Wilmot, Tas, 1976–85, for Lyons, 1985–95; Dep. Leader of the Opposition, Tasmania, 1979–81; Leader of the Opposition, 1981–82 and 1989–91; Premier of Tasmania and Treasurer, 1982–89; Minister: for Racing and Gaming, 1982–84; for Energy, 1982–88; for Forests, 1984–86; for State Develt, 1984–89; for Small Business, 1986–89; for Status of Women, 1989; for Antarctic Affairs, 1989; for Science and Technology, 1989; for Primary Industry, Fisheries and Energy, 1992–95; for the TT-Line, 1993–95. Director: Gunns Ltd, 1996–; Fujii Tasmania Pty Ltd, 1996–; AMC Search Ltd, 1996–; Tasmanian Global Investments Pty, 1997–. Trustee, Tasmanian Wool Museum, 1996–. *Recreations:* gardening, golf. *Address:* 11 Beech Road, Launceston, Tas 7250, Australia.

GRAY, Simon James Holliday; writer; *b* 21 Oct. 1936; *s* of Dr James Davidson Gray and Barbara Cecelia Mary Holliday; *m* 1965, Beryl Mary Kevern; one *s* one *d*. *Educ:* Westminster; Dalhousie Univ.; Trinity Coll., Cambridge (MA). Trinity Coll., Cambridge: Sen. Schol., Research Student and Harper-Wood Trav. Student, 1960; Supervisor in English, 1960–63; Sen. Instructor in English, Univ. of British Columbia, 1963–64; Lectr in English, QMC, London Univ., 1965–85 (Hon. Fellow, 1985). Co-dir, The Common Pursuit, Promenade Theatre, NY, 1986, and dir, Phoenix Theatre, 1988. Screenplay: A Month in the Country, 1987. *Publications: novels:* Colmain, 1963; Simple People, 1965; Little Portia, 1967, repr. 1986; (as Hamish Reade) A Comeback for Stark, 1968; Breaking Hearts, 1997; *plays:* Wise Child, 1968; Sleeping Dog, 1968; Dutch Uncle, 1969; The Idiot, 1971; Spoiled, 1971; Butley, 1971; Otherwise Engaged, 1975 (voted Best Play, 1976–77, by NY Drama Critics Circle); Plaintiffs and Defendants, 1975; Two Sundays, 1975; Dog Days, 1976; Molly, 1977; The Rear Column, 1978; Close of Play, 1979; Stage Struck, 1979; Quartermaine's Terms, 1981 (televised 1987); adap. Tartuffe (for Washington, DC; unpublished), 1982; The Common Pursuit, 1984 (televised 1992); Plays One, 1986; Melon, 1987; The Holy Terror and Tartuffe, 1990; Hidden Laughter, 1990; Cell Mates, 1995; Simply Disconnected, 1996; Life Support, 1997; Just the Three of Us, 1997; The Late Middle Classes, 1999; Japes, 2001; *television plays:* After Pilkington, 1987; Old Flames, 1990; They Never Slept, 1991; Running Late, 1992; Unnatural Pursuits, 1993; Femme Fatale, 1993; *radio plays:* The Rector's Daughter, 1992; Suffer the Little Children, 1993; With a Nod and a Bow, 1993; *non-fiction:* An Unnatural Pursuit and Other Pieces, 1985; How's That for Telling 'Em, Fat Lady?, 1988; Fat Chance, 1995; Enter a Fox: further adventures of a paranoid, 2001. *Recreations:* watching cricket and soccer, tennis, swimming. *Address:* c/o Judy Daish Associates, 2 St Charles Place, W10 6EG.

GRAY, Prof. (Thomas) Cecil, CBE 1976; KCSG 1982; MD; FRCP, FRCS, FRCA; FFARCS; FANZCA (Hon.); FFARCSI (Hon.); Professor of Anæsthesia, The University of Liverpool, 1959–76, now Emeritus; Dean of Postgraduate Medical Studies, 1966–70, of Faculty of Medicine, 1970–76; *b* 11 March 1913; *s* of Thomas and Ethel Gray; *m* 1st, 1937, Marjorie Kathleen (*née* Hely) (*d* 1978); one *s* one *d*; 2nd, 1979, Pamela Mary (*née* Corning); one *s*. *Educ:* Ampleforth Coll.; University of Liverpool (MB ChB 1937; MD 1947). General Practice, 1937–41; Anaesthetist to various hospitals, 1941–47. Active Service, Royal Army Medical Corps, 1942–44 (Captain; invalided out). Demonstrator in Anæsthesia, University of Liverpool, 1942, 1944–46; Reader in Anæsthesia, University of Liverpool, 1947–59; Hon. Cons Anæsthetist: United Liverpool Hosps, Royal Infirmary Branch; Liverpool Thoracic Surgical Centre, Broadgreen Hosp. Mem. Bd, Faculty of Anæsthetists, RCS, 1948–69 (Vice-Dean, 1952–54; Dean, 1964–67); Member Council: RCS, 1964–67; Assoc. of Anæsthetists of GB and Ire., 1948–76 (Hon. Treas. 1950–55; Pres. 1956–59; Hon. Mem., 1977–); ASME, 1972–76; FRSocMed (Mem. Council, 1958–61; Pres. Anæsthetic Section, 1955–56; Mem. Council, Sect. of Med. Educn, 1969–72; Hon. Fellow, 1979); Chm. BMA Anæsthetic Group, 1957–62; Mem., Liverpool Regional Hosp. Board, 1968–74 (Chm., Anæsthetic Adv. Cttee, 1948–70; Chm., Med. Adv. Council, 1970–74); Mem., Merseyside RHA, 1974–77; Mem., Bd of Governors, United Liverpool Hosp., 1969–74; Pres., Liverpool Medical Inst., 1974; Mem. Clinical Res. Bd, Med. Res. Council, 1965–69; Hon. Civilian Consultant in Anæsthetics to the Army at Home, 1960–78 (Guthrie Medal 1977), Emeritus Consultant to the Army, 1979–. Mem., delegn of anæsthetists to USSR, 1964. Hon. Consultant to St John's Ambulance; Member Council, Order of St John for Merseyside; Asst Dir-Gen., St John Ambulance, 1977–82; Vice-Pres., Med. Defence Union, 1956–77 (Treasurer, 1977–82); Chm., Bd of Governors, Linacre Centre for Study of Ethics of Health Care, 1973–83. Examiner in FFARCS, 1953–70; FFARCSI 1967–70: Dip. Vet. Anæsth., RCVS, 1968–76. Hon. Member: Sheffield and East Midlands Soc. of Anæsthetists; Yorks Soc. of Anæsthetists; SW Regl Soc. of Anæsthetists; Austrian Soc. of Anæsthetists; Soc. Belge d'Anesthesie et de Reanimation; Argentinian and Brazilian Socs of Anesthesiologists; Australian and Malaysian Socs of Anæsthetists; Assoc. of Veterinary Anæsthetists; W African Assoc. of Surgeons. Hon. Corresp. Mem., Sociedade das Ciencias Medical di Lisboa. Clover Lectr and Medallist, RCS, 1954; Lectures: Med. Soc. of London, 1946; Simpson-Smith Meml, W London Sch. of Med., 1956; Jenny Hartmann Meml, Univ. of Basle, 1958; Eastman, Univ. of Rochester, NY, 1958; Sir James Young Simpson Meml, RCSE, 1967; Torsten Gordh, Swedish Soc. of Anaesthetists, 1978; Kirkpatrick, Faculty of Anaesthetists, RCSI, 1981; John Gillies, Scottish Soc. of Anaesthetists, 1982; Mitchiner Meml, RAMC, 1983; Florence Elliott, Royal Victoria Hosp., Belfast, 1984. Sims Commonwealth Travelling Prof., 1961. JP City of Liverpool, 1966 (retd list). Freeman, City of London, 1984; Liveryman, Soc. of Apothecaries, 1956. OStJ 1979. Medallist,

Univ. of Liège, 1947; Henry Hill Hickman Medal, RSocMed, 1972; Hon. Gold Medal, RCS, 1978; Ralph M. Waters medal and award, Illinois Soc. of Anesthesiologists, 1978; John Snow Silver Medal, Assoc. of Anaesthetists of GB & Ire, 1982. Ed., British Jl of Anæsthesia, 1948–64. *Publications:* Modern Trends in Anæsthesia (ed jtly), 1958, 3rd edn 1967; (ed jtly) General Anæsthesia, 1959, 4th edn 1980; (ed with G. J. Rees) Paediatric Anæsthesia, 1981; many contribs to gen. med. press and specialist jls. *Recreations:* music, reading, writing. *Address:* 6 Raven Meols Lane, Formby, Liverpool L37 4DF.

GRAY, Sir William (Hume), 3rd Bt *cr* 1917; Director: Eggleston Hall Ltd; William Gray Associates; *b* 26 July 1955; *s* of William Talbot Gray (*d* 1971) (*er s* of 2nd Bt), and of Rosemarie Hume Gray, *d* of Air Cdre Charles Hume Elliott-Smith; *S* grandfather, 1978; *m* 1984, Catherine Victoria Willoughby (marr. diss. 1998), *y d* of late John Naylor and of Mrs Jerram, Wadebridge, Cornwall; one *s* two *d*; *m* 2001, Juliet Rachel, *d* of D. J. Jackson, Headlam, Co. Durham. *Educ:* Aysgarth School, Bedale, Yorks; Eton College; Polytechnic of Central London BA (Hons) Architecture; DipArch; RIBA. High Sheriff, Durham, 1998–99. *Recreation:* sport. *Heir: s* William John Cresswell Gray, *b* 24 Aug. 1986. *Address:* Eggleston Hall, Barnard Castle, Co. Durham DL12 0AG. *T:* (01833) 650553.

GRAY DEBROS, Winifred Marjorie, (Mrs E. Gray Debros); *see* Fox, W. M.

GRAYDON, Air Chief Marshal Sir Michael (James), GCB 1993 (KCB 1989); CBE 1984; FRAeS; non-executive Director, Thales plc, since 1999; Military Adviser, Airtanker; *b* 24 Oct. 1938; *s* of James Julian Graydon and Rita Mary Alkan; *m* 1963, Margaret Elizabeth Clark. *Educ:* Wycliffe Coll.; RAF Coll., Cranwell. Qualified Flying Instructor No 1 FTS, Linton-on-Ouse, 1960–62; No 56 Sqn, 1962–64; No 226 OCU, 1965–67 (Queen's Commendation); Flight Comd, No 56 Sqn, 1967–69; RAF Staff Coll., Bracknell, 1970; PSO to Dep. C-in-C Allied Forces Central Region, Brunssum, 1971–73; Operations, Joint Warfare, MoD, 1973–75; NDC, Latimer, 1976; OC No 11 Sqn, Binbrook, 1977–79; MA to CDS, MoD, 1979–81; OC RAF Leuchars, 1981–83; OC RAF Stanley, Falkland Is, 1983; RCDS, 1984; SASO 11 Gp, Bentley Priory, 1985–86; ACOS Policy, SHAPE, 1986–89; AOC-in-C, RAF Support Comd, 1989–91; AOC-in-C, RAF Strike Comd, and C-in-C, UK Air Forces, 1991–92; CAS, and Air ADC to the Queen, 1992–97. Chm., Sherwood Coalfield Regeneration Trust, 1997–. Mem., Cttee of Mgt, RNLI, 1998–; Vice-Patron, Air Cadet Council, 1999–; President: Battle of Britain Meml Trust, 1999–; The Officers' Assoc., 2000. Mem. Council, Church Schs Co., 1997– (Vice-Chm., 2000); Governor: Wycliffe Coll., 1986– (Vice-Chm., 1992–); Sutton's Hosp. in Charterhouse, 1998–. FRAeS 1993. Freeman, City of London, 1995; Liveryman, GAPAN, 1996–. *Publications:* contrib. to professional jls. *Recreations:* golf, birdwatching, reading. *Address:* c/o Lloyds TSB, Cox and King's Branch, PO Box 1190, 7 Pall Mall, SW1Y 5NA. *Clubs:* Royal Air Force; Royal & Ancient Golf (St Andrews).

GRAYLING, Christopher Stephen; MP (C) Epsom and Ewell, since 2001; *b* 1 April 1962; *s* of John Terence Grayling and Elizabeth Grayling; *m* 1987, Susan Dillistone; one *s* one *d*. *Educ:* Royal Grammar Sch., High Wycombe; Sidney Sussex Coll., Cambridge (MA Hist.). BBC News producer, 1985–88; producer and editor, Business Daily, Channel 4, 1988–91; Commissioning Editor, BBC Select, Business Develt, BBC Enterprises, 1991–93; Dir, Charterhouse Prodns, 1993; Div Dir, Workhouse Ltd, 1993–95; Dir, SSVC Gp, 1995–97; Change Consultant and Eur. Mktg Dir, Burson-Marsteller, 1997–2001. *Publications:* The Bridgewater Heritage, 1984; A Land Fit for Heroes, 1985; (jtly) Just Another Star, 1988; The Story of Joseph Holt, 1985, 2nd edn 1999. *Recreations:* golf, cricket, antiques. *Address:* House of Commons, SW1A 0AA. *T:* (020) 7219 8226.

GRAYSON, David Roger, CBE 1999 (OBE 1994); a Director, Business in the Community, since 1995; *b* 26 May 1955; *s* of Henry Eric Fitton Grayson and Patricia Grayson (*née* Clayton). *Educ:* Mount St Mary's Coll.; Downing Coll., Cambridge (MA Law); Free Univ. of Brussels (Wiener Anspach Schol.; MA 1978); Newcastle Univ. (MBA 1985). Brand Mgt, Procter and Gamble, 1978–80; Co-Founder and Dir, Project NE, 1980–86; Jt Man. Dir, Prince's Youth Business Trust, 1986–87; Business in the Community, 1987–: Jt Man. Dir, resp. for ops and staff, 1989–92; Man. Dir, Business Strategy Gp., 1992–95. Vis. Fellow, Sch. of Mgt, Imperial Coll., 1998–; Vis. Prof., London Guildhall Univ., 2000–. Chairman: Business Link Nat. Assessment Panel, DTI, 1993–97; Business Link Nat. Accreditation Bd, 1996–2000; Nat. Disability Council, 1996–2000; Mem. Bd, Strategic Rail Authority, (formerly BRB), 2000–. Internat. lectures on MBA and exec. mgt progs. Ambassador, Nat. AIDS Trust, 2000–; Trustee: AbilityNet, 2000–; Prince of Wales Innovation Trust, 2000–. Gov., Lilian Baylis Sch., Lambeth, 2000–. *Publications:* (contrib.) Mastering Enterprise, 1996; (contrib.) What If..., 2000; (jtly) Everybody's Business, 2001. *Recreations:* scuba diving, travel; happiest in, on or underwater, preferably in warm climates. *Address:* Business in the Community, 137 Shepherdess Walk, N1 7RQ. *Club:* Royal Automobile.

GRAYSON, Sir Jeremy (Brian Vincent), 5th Bt *cr* 1922, of Ravenspoint, Co. Angelsey; photographer; *b* 30 Jan. 1933; *s* of Brian Harrington Grayson (*d* 1989), 3rd *s* of 1st Bt and of Sofia Maria (*née* Buchanan); *S* uncle, 1991; *m* 1958, Sara Mary, *d* of C. F. Upton; three *s* three *d* (and one *d* decd). *Educ:* Downside. *Heir: s* Simon Jeremy Grayson, *b* 12 July 1959. *Address:* 4 Manor Farm Barns, East Stoke, Wareham, Dorset BH20 6AW. *T:* (01929) 463207.

GRAYSTON, Rev. Prof. Kenneth, MA, DLitt; Professor of Theology, Bristol University, 1965–79, now Emeritus Professor; Pro-Vice-Chancellor, Bristol University, 1976–79; *b* Sheffield, 8 July 1914; *s* of Ernest Edward and Jessie Grayston; *m* 1942, Elizabeth Alison (*d* 1995), *d* of Rev. Walter Mayo and Beatrice Aste, Elsfield, Oxon.; no *c*. *Educ:* Colfe's Grammar Sch., Lewisham; Universities of Oxford and Cambridge; DLitt Bristol 1991. Ordained Methodist Minister, 1942; Ordnance Factory Chaplain, 1942–44; Asst Head of Religious Broadcasting, BBC, 1944–49; Tutor in New Testament Language and Literature, Didsbury Coll., 1949–64; Bristol University: Special Lecturer in Hellenistic Greek, 1950–64; Dean, Faculty of Arts, 1972–74; Hon. Fellow, 1992. Select Preacher to Univ. of Cambridge, 1952, 1962, to Univ. of Oxford, 1971; Sec. Studiorum Novi Testamenti Societas, 1955–65; Chairman: Theolog. Adv. Gp, British Council of Churches, 1969–72; Christian Aid Scholarships Cttee, 1973–78. *Publications:* The Epistles to the Galatians and to the Philippians, 1957; The Letters of Paul to the Philippians and the Thessalonians, 1967; The Johannine Epistles, 1984; Dying, We Live, 1990; The Gospel of John, 1990; The Epistle to the Romans, 1997; The New Testament: which way in?, 2000; contributions to: A Theological Word Book of the Bible, 1950; The Teacher's Commentary, 1955; The Interpreter's Dictionary of the Bible, 1962; A New Dictionary of Christian Theology, 1983, etc; contrib. to Expository Times, New Testament Studies, Theology, Scottish Jl Theology, Epworth Review, etc. *Recreation:* music. *Address:* 11 Rockleaze Avenue, Bristol BS9 1NG. *T:* (0117) 968 3872.

GREATHEAD, Dr David John; Director, International Institute of Biological Control, 1985–91; Hon. Senior Research Fellow, Centre for Population Biology, Imperial College of Science, Technology and Medicine at Silwood Park; *b* 12 Dec. 1931; *s* of Harold Merriman Greathead and Kathleen May (*née* Collett); *m* 1958, Annette Helen Blankley; one *s* two *d*. *Educ:* Merchant Taylors' Sch., Middx; Imperial Coll., London Univ. (BSc, PhD, DSc). ARCS; CBiol; FIBiol. Anti-Locust Res. Centre, 1953–59; research on desert locust in Ethiopia, Somalia, Kenya, Aden Protectorates, Desert Locust Survey, 1959–61; Commonwealth (later Internat.) Institute of Biological Control: set up and managed East African Station in Uganda, res. on crop pests and weeds, 1962–73; based in UK, 1973–91; Asst Dir, 1976–85. *Publications:* A Review of Biological Control in the Ethiopian Region, 1971; A Review of Biological Control in Western and Southern Europe, 1976; (with J. K. Waage) Insect Parasitoids, 1986; (with N. L. Evenhuis) World Catalog of Bee Flies, 1999; numerous publications in learned jls. *Recreations:* natural history, walking, travelling. *Address:* Centre for Population Biology, Imperial College at Silwood Park, Ascot, Berks SL5 7PY. *T:* (01344) 872999; 6 The Walled Garden, Wargrave, Reading, Berks RG10 8LL.

GREATREX, Neil; National President and General Secretary, Union of Democratic Mineworkers, since 1993; *b* 1 April 1951; *s* of John Edward and Joyce Irene Greatrex; *m* 1972, Sheila Waterhouse; two *d*. *Educ:* Greenwood Drive Jun. Sch.; Mowlands Intermediate Sch.; Ashfield Comprehensive Sch. Bentinck Colliery, 1965–85. National Union of Mineworkers: Cttee Mem., 1970–74; Branch Treas., 1974–80; Branch Pres., 1980–85; full-time Area Official, 1985–86; Union of Democratic Mineworkers: Area Pres., 1986–88; Nat. Vice-Pres., 1988–93. *Recreations:* Do It Yourself, shooting. *Address:* Miners' Offices, Berry Hill Lane, Mansfield, Notts NG18 4JU. *T:* (01623) 626094; 2 Chestnut Avenue, Kirkby in Ashfield, Notts NG17 8BB. *T:* (01623) 758346.

GREAVES, family name of **Baron Greaves**.

GREAVES, Baron *cr* 2000 (Life Peer), of Pendle in the county of Lancashire; **Anthony Robert Greaves;** *b* 27 July 1942; *s* of Geoffrey Greaves and Moyra Greaves (*née* Brookes); *m* 1968, Heather Ann (*née* Baxter); two *d*. *Educ:* Queen Elizabeth GS, Wakefield; Hertford Coll., Oxford (BA Hons Geog.). Teacher/Lectr, 1968–74; Organising Sec., Assoc. of Liberal Councillors, 1977–85; Man. Dir, Hebden Royd Publications Ltd, (Lib Dem publications), 1985–90; second-hand book dealer, Liber Books, 1992–. Member: (L) Colne BC, 1971–74; (L then Lib Dem): Pendle BC, 1973–92 and 1994–98; Lancs CC, 1973–97. *Publication:* (with Rachael Pitchford) Merger: the inside story, 1988. *Recreations:* climbing, mountain/hill walking, wild flowers, cycling, politics. *Address:* 3 Hartington Street, Winewall, Colne, Lancashire BB8 8DB. *T:* (01282) 864346, (office) (020) 72198620.

GREAVES, Graham Charles; independent aviation consultant, since 2000; *b* 5 July 1945; *s* of Joseph Clarence Greaves and Jane Isabella Greaves; *m* 1975, Pamela Ann Ellson; two *d*. *Educ:* Loughborough Univ. (BSc Hons Transport Mgt and Planning). FCIT 1995; FILT 2000. Civil Engr, City of Birmingham, 1964–71; Professional and Technol. Officer, Civil Engr, W Midlands Regl Office, Depts of Transport and the Envmt, 1971–79; various mgt posts, HQ London, Heathrow and Gatwick, BAA, 1979–85; Ops Manager, Manchester Airport, 1985–87; Ops Dir/Man. Dir, Cardiff Airport, 1987–95; Mgt Cons., BAe and independent, 1995–98; Dir Gen. and Chief Exec., CIT, 1998–99. Vis. Lectr in civil aviation, Loughborough Univ., 1995–. MIMgt 1984. *Publication:* ACI Marketing Handbook, 1995. *Recreations:* British history, military and civil aviation, photography, cricket. *Address:* Kinfauns, St Nicholas, Vale of Glamorgan CF5 6SH. *T:* (01446) 761050.

GREAVES, James Peter, (Jimmy); TV broadcaster, since 1983; football correspondent, The Sun; *b* 20 Feb. 1940; *s* of James and Mary Greaves; *m* Irene Barden; two *s* two *d* (and one *s* decd). *Educ:* Kingswood Sch., Hainault. Professional footballer (inside forward), 1957; played for: Chelsea, 1957–61; AC Milan, 1961; Tottenham Hotspur, 1961–70 (FA Cup wins, 1962, 1967); West Ham, 1970–71; scored record 357 goals in First Division, 55 goals in FA Cup ties; played 57 times for England (scored 44 goals). *Publications* include: (with N. Giller): This one's on me, 1981; It's a funny old life, 1990. *Address:* c/o Sports Department, The Sun, 1 Virginia Street, E1 9XN.

GREAVES, Jeffrey; HM Diplomatic Service, retired; Consul General, Alexandria, 1978–81; *b* 10 Dec. 1926; *s* of Willie and Emily Greaves; *m* 1949, Joyce Mary Farrer; one *s* one *d*. *Educ:* Pudsey Grammar Sch. Served RN, 1945–48. Joined HM Foreign Service, 1948; FO, 1948; Benghazi, 1951; Vice Consul, Tehran, 1953; ME Centre for Arab Studies, 1955; Second Sec. and Vice Consul, Paris, 1960; Vice Consul, Muscat, 1962; Second Sec. and Consul, Athens, 1965; Second Sec. (Commercial), Cairo, 1968; First Sec. and Consul, Muscat, 1970; First Sec. (Com.), Bangkok, 1972; FCO, 1976. *Address:* 7 Pitchstone Court, Leeds LS12 5SZ. *T:* (0113) 257 7238.

GREAVES, John Western, CMG 1998; Business Director, Zeneca Agrochemicals, since 1997; *b* 6 Sept. 1939; *s* of Sir Western Greaves, KBE and Marjorie Nahir (*née* Wright); *m* 1965, Margaret Anne Berg; one *s* three *d*. *Educ:* Uppingham Sch.; Leeds Univ. (BSc Hons Chem. Engrg). Business Manager: ICI Argentina, Buenos Aires, 1965–73; ICI Europa, Brussels, 1973–79; ICI Plastics, 1979–81; Corporate Planning, ICI, 1981–85; Regl Exec., Latin America, Zeneca, 1992–97. Chairman: Latin American Crop Protection Assoc., 1993–96; Latin American Trade Adv. Gp, 1995–98. Dir, Bd, Inst. of Latin American Studies, London Univ., 1996–; Dep. Chm., Canning House, 1999–. *Recreations:* family, home, riding, yachting. *Address:* Bramshott Thatch, Rectory Lane, Liphook, Hants GU30 7QZ. *T:* (01428) 722243; Las Terrazas, Portals, Mallorca. *Club:* Tortugas Country (Buenos Aires).

GREAVES, Prof. Malcolm Watson, MD, PhD; FRCP; Professor of Dermatology, National University of Malaysia, Selangor, since 2001; *b* 11 Nov. 1933; *s* of Donald Watson Greaves and Kathleen Evelyn Greaves; *m* 1964, Evelyn Yeo; one *s* one *d*. *Educ:* Epsom College; Charing Cross Med. Sch. MD, PhD London. MRC Clinical Res. Fellow, UCL, 1963–66; Reader in Dermatology, Univ. of Newcastle upon Tyne, 1966–75; Prof. of Dermatology, Univ. of London, 1975–99, now Emeritus; Dean, St John's Inst. of Dermatology, UMDS of Guy's and St Thomas' Hosps, 1989–95. Vis Prof., Wake Forest Univ., NC, 1996. Visiting Consultant: Maadi Armed Forces Hosp., Cairo, 1984–98; Hamed Med. Corp., State of Qatar, 1995. Chm., Scientific Cttee and Trustee, Skin Disease Res. Fund, 1980–96; Member: Pharmacopoeia Commn, 1982–; Cttee on Safety of Medicines, DHSS, 1982–89; British Nat. Formulary expert adv. cttee, 1990–. President: European Soc. for Dermatological Research, 1984; Sect. of Dermatol., RSM, 1996; Vice-Pres., Psoriasis Assoc. of GB, 1991–; Chm., Therapy and Audit Cttee, British Assoc. of Dermatologists, 1994–96. Internat. Hon. Mem., Amer. Dermatol. Assoc., 1987; Hon. Member: Amer. Soc. for Investigative Dermatol., 1989; Malaysian Dermatol Assoc., 1995; British Assoc. of Dermatologists, 2000; Austrian Dermatological Soc., 2000; Eur. Soc. for Dermatol Res., 2000; Lithuanian Dermatol Assoc., 2000. Mem. Management Bd Exec., UMDS, 1990–95; Mem. Governing Body, Sch. of Pharmacy, Univ. of London, 1990–95. Alvin J. Cox Award for dist. research in psoriasis, 1984; Egyptian Armed Forces Award for Distinguished Med. Services, 1990; Sir Archibald Gray Gold Medal, British Assoc. of Dermatologists, 1998; Leo Von Zumbusch Gold Medal, Munich Univ., 1998. *Publications:* Pharmacology of the Skin, Vol. I, Pharmacology of Skin Systems and Autocoids in Normal and Inflamed Skin, 1989; Vol. II, Methods, Absorption, Metabolism, Toxicity, Drugs and Diseases, 1989. *Recreation:* equestrian activities. *Address:*

56 Jalan Jelujong, Damansara Heights, 50490 Kuala Lumpur, Malaysia. *Clubs:* Athenæum; Royal Selangor.

GREAVES, Prof. Melvyn Francis; Director, Leukaemia Research Fund Centre, Institute of Cancer Research, London, since 1984; *b* 12 Sept. 1941; *s* of Edward and Violet Greaves; *m* 1966, Josephine Pank; one *s* one *d*. *Educ:* City of Norwich Grammar Sch.; University Coll. London; Middlesex Hosp. Med. Sch. BSc, PhD London. FRCPath 1997. Vis Scientist, Karolinska Inst., Stockholm, 1968–69; Res. Fellow, Nat. Inst. for Med. Res., London, 1969–72; Res. Scientist, Dept of Zoology, UCL, 1972–76; Hd, Membrane Immunology Dept, Imperial Cancer Res. Fund, 1976–84. Hon. MRCP 1987. FMedSci 1999. Paul Martini Prize (Germany), 1977; Peter Debye Prize (Holland), 1981; King Faisal Internat. Prize for Medicine, 1988. *Publications:* T and B Lymphocytes, 1973; Cellular Recognition, 1975; Atlas of Blood Cells, 1981, 2nd edn 1988; Monoclonal Antibodies to Receptors, 1984; Cancer: the evolutionary legacy, 2000. contribs to bio-med. jls. *Recreations:* music, cooking, photography, natural history. *Address:* Institute of Cancer Research, Fulham Road, SW3 6JB.

GREBENIK, Eugene, CB 1976; MSc (Economics); Consultant, Office of Population Censuses and Surveys, 1977–84; *b* 20 July 1919; *s* of S. Grebenik and E. Lopatitskaya; *m* 1946, Virginia, *d* of James D. Barker; two *s* one *d*. *Educ:* abroad; London Sch. of Economics. Statistician, Dept of Economics, Univ. of Bristol, 1939–40; London Sch. of Economics: Asst. 1940–44 and Lecturer, 1944–49, in Statistics (on leave, 1944–46; served in RN, 1944; Temp. Statistical Officer, Admiralty, 1944–45; Secretariat, Royal Commn on Population, 1945–46); Reader in Demography, Univ. of London, 1949–54; Research Sec., Population Investigation Cttee, 1947–54; Prof. of Social Studies, Univ. of Leeds, 1954–69. Principal, Civil Service Coll., 1970–76 and Dep. Sec., Civil Service Dept, 1972–76. Mem., Impact of Rates Cttee, Ministry of Housing, 1963–64. Social Science Research Council: Statistics Cttee, 1966–69; Cttee on Social Science and Government, 1968–72; Population Panel, 1971–73; Member: Cttee on Governance of London Univ., 1970–72; Council, RHBNC (formerly RHC), Univ. of London, 1971–90. Pres., British Soc. for Population Studies, 1979–81. Sec.-Treasurer, Internat. Union for Scientific Study of Population, 1963–73. Hon. Fellow, LSE, 1969; Vis. Fellow, ANU, 1982–83; Hon. Vis. Prof., City Univ., 1986–89. Managing Ed., Population Studies, 1978–96 (Jt Ed., 1954–78). Olivia Schieffelin Nordberg Award, Population Council, 1997. *Publications:* (with H. A. Shannon) The Population of Bristol, 1943; (with D. V. Glass) The Trend and Pattern of Fertility in Great Britain; A Report on the Family Census of 1946, 1954; various articles in statistical and economic journals. *Address:* 16 Spindlers, Kidlington, Oxon OX5 2YP. *T:* (01865) 842697.

GREEN, Albert A.; *see* Aynsley-Green.

GREEN, Sir Allan (David), KCB 1991; QC 1987; *b* 1 March 1935; *s* of late Lionel and Irene Green; *m* 1967, Eva (*d* 1993), *yr d* of Prof. Artur Attman and Elsa Attman, Gothenburg, Sweden; one *s* one *d*. *Educ:* Charterhouse; St Catharine's Coll., Cambridge (Open Exhibnr, MA). Served RN, 1953–55. Called to the Bar, Inner Temple, 1959, Bencher, 1985; Jun. Prosecuting Counsel to the Crown, Central Criminal Court, 1977, Sen. Prosecuting Counsel, 1979, First Senior Prosecuting Counsel, 1985; a Recorder, 1979–87; DPP and Hd of Crown Prosecution Service, 1987–91. Mem., Gen. Council of the Bar, 1992. *Recreation:* music. *Address:* 2 Hare Court, Temple, EC4Y 7BH. *Club:* Athenæum.

GREEN, Andrew Curtis; farmer and horticulturist, since 1960; *b* 28 March 1936; *s* of Christopher Green and Marjorie (*née* Bennett); *m* 1966, Julia Margaret (*née* Davidson); two *s*. *Educ:* Charterhouse; Magdalene Coll., Cambridge. MA (Nat. Scis), Dip. of Agriculture. Commnd RNVR, 1954–56. Farm management, 1960–67; founded Greens of Soham farming and horticultural business, 1967; Dir, Elsoms Spalding Seed Co., 1982–; Chm., Hassy Ltd, 1983–89. Mem., AFRC, 1984–88. FLS 1978; Hon. FIHort 1986 (Industrial Mem. Council, 1988–94); FRAgS 1995. Extra Mem., Court of Skinners' Co., 1994–96. *Recreations:* sailing, fishing, shooting, ski-ing. *Address:* Kingfishers Bridge, Wicken, Ely, Cambs CB7 5XL. *Clubs:* Army and Navy, Farmers'; Hawks (Cambridge); Royal Thames Yacht.

GREEN, Sir Andrew (Fleming), KCMG 1998 (CMG 1991); HM Diplomatic Service, retired; Ambassador to Saudi Arabia, 1996–2000; *b* 6 Aug. 1941; *s* of late Gp Captain J. H. Green, RAF, and Beatrice Mary (*née* Bowditch); *m* 1968, C. Jane Churchill; one *s* one *d*. *Educ:* Haileybury and ISC; Magdalene Coll., Cambridge (MA). Served RGJ, 1962–65; joined HM Diplomatic Service, 1965; Middle East Centre for Arab Studies, 1966–68; Aden, 1968–69; Asst Political Agent, Abu Dhabi, 1970–71; First Secretary, FCO, 1972–74; Private Sec. to Minister of State, FCO, 1975, and to Parliamentary Under Sec. of State, 1976; First Secretary, UK Delegn to OECD, Paris, 1977–79; First Sec., FCO, 1980–81; Counsellor, Washington, 1982–85; Counsellor, Hd of Chancery and Consul Gen., Riyadh, 1985–88; Counsellor, FCO, 1988–90; Ambassador to Syria, 1991–94; Asst Under-Sec. of State (Middle East), FCO, 1994–96. *Recreations:* tennis, sailing, bridge, desert travel. *Address;* 89 St George's Square, SW1V 3QW.

GREEN, Andrew Michael Walter; Librarian, National Library of Wales, since 1998; *b* 30 Sept. 1952; *s* of Harry Green and Ellen Martha Kennedy Green (*née* Allan); *m* 1980, Carys Evans; two *d*. *Educ:* Hoylandswaine Primary Sch.; Queen Elizabeth Grammar Sch., Wakefield; Gonville and Caius Coll., Cambridge (BA 1973; MA 1975; Wace Medal for Classical Archaeology 1973); Coll. of Librarianship, Wales (Dip. Librarianship 1975). ALA 1977. Asst Librarian, UC, Cardiff, 1975–88; Arts and Social Studies Librarian, UWCC, 1988–89; Sub-Librarian (Services and Collection Develt), Univ. of Sheffield, 1989–92; Librarian, 1992–95, Dir of Library and Information Services, 1996–98, UC, Swansea. Vice-Chm., SCONUL, 2000–April 2002. Hon. Fellow, Univ. of Wales, Swansea, 2001. *Publications:* numerous articles on library and information studies. *Recreations:* running, cycling, walking, music, looking out of windows. *Address:* 30 Caswell Drive, Caswell, Swansea SA3 4RJ. *T:* (01792) 361260.

GREEN, Anthony Eric Sandall, RA 1977 (ARA 1971); Member, London Group, 1964; Artist (Painter); *b* 30 Sept. 1939; *s* of late Frederick Sandall Green and Marie Madeleine (*née* Dupont); *m* 1961, Mary Louise Cozens-Walker; two *d*. *Educ:* Highgate Sch., London; Slade Sch. of Fine Art, University Coll. London (Fellow, UCL, 1991). Henry Tonks Prize for drawing, Slade Sch., 1960; French Govt Schol., Paris, 1960; Gulbenkian Purchase Award, 1963; Harkness Fellowship, in USA, 1967–69. Trustee, RA, 2000. Has exhibited in: London, New York, Haarlem, Rotterdam, Stuttgart, Hanover, Helsingborg, Malmö, Tokyo, Brussels, W Berlin, Chicago and Sydney. Paintings in various public collections, including: Tate Gallery; Metropolitan Mus. of Art, N York; Olinda Museum, Brazil; Baltimore Mus. of Art, USA; Nat. Mus. of Wales; Gulbenkian Foundn; Arts Council of Gt Brit.; British Council; Victoria and Albert Mus.; Contemporary Art Soc.; Frans Hals Mus., Holland; Boymans-van Bevningen Mus., Holland; Ulster Mus., Belfast; Ikeda and Niigata Mus., Setagaya Art Mus., Metropolitan, Tokyo; Hiroshima; Fukuoka. Exhibit of the Year award, RA, 1977. *Publication:* A Green Part of the World, 1984. *Recreations:* travelling, family life. *Address:* Mole End, 40 High Street, Little Eversden, Cambridge CB3 7HE. *T:* (01223) 262292.

GREEN, Prof. Anthony Richard, PhD; FRCP, FRCPath; Professor of Haemato-Oncology, University of Cambridge and Addenbrooke's Hospital, since 1999; *b* 13 Oct. 1955; *s* of John Richard Green and Jeanne Dorothy Green; *m* 1984, Sarah Frances Rann; one *s* two *d*. *Educ:* Highgate Sch.; Queens' Coll., Cambridge; University Coll. Hosp., London (PhD 1987). FRCP 1995; FRCPath 1997. Jun. hosp. posts, London, 1980–84; Clinical Res. Fellow, ICRF, 1984–87; Lectr in Haematology, Univ. Hosp. of Wales, Cardiff, 1987–89; CRC Hamilton Fairley Travelling Fellow, Walter & Eliza Hall Inst., Melbourne, 1989–91; Wellcome Trust Sen. Clinical Fellow, Dept of Haematology, Cambridge Univ., 1991–99. *Recreations:* family, friends, hill walking, scuba diving, bird watching, reading. *Address:* Department of Haematology, Cambridge Institute for Medical Research, Hills Road, Cambridge CB2 2XY.

GREEN, Arthur; Senior Partner, Grant Thornton, 1986–88, retired; President, Institute of Chartered Accountants in England and Wales, 1987–88; *b* 15 June 1928; *s* of Arthur Henry and Elizabeth Burns Green; *m* 1952, Sylvia Myatt; one *s* one *d*. *Educ:* Liverpool Collegiate. FCA. Qualified Chartered Accountant, 1950; Partner, Bryce Hanmer & Co., Liverpool, 1954 (merged Thornton Baker; later Grant Thornton); Nat. Managing Partner, Thornton Baker, 1975–84; Chm. and Man. Dir, Grant Thornton International, 1984–85. Vice-Pres., 1985–86, Dep. Pres., 1986–87, ICA. *Recreations:* golf, tennis, theatre. *Address:* Up Yonder, Herbert Road, Salcombe, Devon TQ8 8HP. *T:* (01548) 842075.

GREEN, Arthur Edward Chase, MBE (mil.) 1955; TD (and Bar) 1950; DL; FRICS; Chartered Surveyor; Chief Estates Surveyor, Legal and General Assurance Society, 1946–71 (Surveyor, 1934–46); *b* 5 Nov. 1911; *s* of Harry Catling and Sarah Jane Green, Winchmore Hill, London; *m* 1941, Margaret Grace (*d* 1991), *yr d* of John Lancelot and Winifred Churchill, Wallington, Surrey; one *s* one *d* (and one *d* decd). *Educ:* Merchant Taylors' Sch.; Coll. of Estate Management. HAC, 1932–: King's Prize, 1938; commnd, 1939; Adjt 11 (HAC) Regt RHA, 1941–42; Western Desert, ME; PoW 1942; on release, Germany, 1945, commanded unit collecting evidence of atrocities against POWs, Brunswick area; despatches, Germany, 1945; attended Brunswick/Hanover War Crimes Trials, 1946; Territorial Efficiency Medal and bar; Court of Assistants, HAC, 1946–76, Treasurer, 1966–69, Vice-Pres., 1970–72; Metropolitan Special Constabulary, HAC Div., 1937–39 and 1946–74 (Long Service Medal and bar; Champion Shot, Met. Special Constab., 1958); Hon. Mem., Transvaal Horse Artillery. Property Advr, J. H. Schroder Wagg & Co., 1972–82; Advr, Schroder Property Fund for Pension Funds and Charities, 1972–82; Dir, Schroder Properties Ltd, 1974–82; Member: Cttee of Management, Pension Fund Property Unit Trust, 1972–82; Transcontinental Property Unit Trust, 1974–82; Advr on Policy, Post Office Staff Superannuation Fund, 1973–77, Dir, Mereacre Ltd, and Mereacre Farms Ltd (PO Staff Superann. Fund), 1977–83; Director: Franey & Co. Ltd, and subsids, 1965–76; Percy Bilton (Industrial Development) Ltd, 1972–76. Member: Chancellor of the Exchequer's Property Adv. Panel, 1975–80; Govt Cttee of Inquiry into Agriculture in GB, 1977–79 (Northfield Cttee). Chm., Elecrent Properties Ltd (Electronic Rentals Gp), 1974–83; Director: Lock Estate Ltd, 1974–82; Marlborough Property Hldgs plc, 1978–86; Studley Farms Ltd, 1980–82. Mem., TA&VR Assocs for City of London, 1970–77, and for Greater London, 1970–81. Pres., Camden and Islington Corps, 1974–75, City of London Bde (formerly City of London and Hackney Corps), 1975–, St John Ambulance. Governor: Bridewell Royal Hosp. (King Edward's Sch., Witley), 1962–88; City of London Sch., 1976–81; Queenswood Sch., 1966–78; Corp. of Sons of the Clergy, 1986 (Mem. Court of Assistants, 1966–86); Vice-Pres., Brunswick Boys' Club Trust, 1978– (Founder-Trustee, 1945–78, elected while POW, Oflag 79, Germany). City of London Court of Common Council (Bread Street Ward), 1971–81. Freedom of the City of London, 1939; Liveryman: Merchant Taylors' Co., 1946; Gunmakers' Co., 1954. DL Greater London, 1967 (Representative DL for London Borough of Islington, 1967–81). CStJ 1988. *Recreations:* various. *Address:* The Coach House, High Street, Cranleigh, Surrey GU6 8AS. *T:* (01483) 267372. *Clubs:* HAC, Guildhall, Bread Street Ward, Cordwainer Ward.

GREEN, Arthur Jackson; Under Secretary, Department of Education for Northern Ireland, 1983–87, retired; *b* 12 Nov. 1928; *s* of F. Harvey Green and Sylvia Green (*née* Marsh), MB; *m* 1957, Rosemary Bradley, MA; two *s*. *Educ:* Friends Sch., Lisburn, Co. Antrim; Leighton Park Sch., Reading; Lincoln Coll., Oxford (BA Mod. Hist.); Haverford Coll., Philadelphia (MA Philosophy). Asst Principal, NICS, 1952; Secretary: Cameron Commn, 1969; Scarman Tribunal, 1969–72; Asst Sec., NI Dept of Finance, 1972–78; Under Sec., NI Office, 1978–79; Dir, NI Court Service (Lord Chancellor's Dept), 1979–82; Fellow, Center for Internat. Affairs, Harvard Univ., 1982–83. English teacher, Poland, 1993–2000. Mem. Bd, British Council, 1992–97. *Publications:* articles on Anglo-Irish topics. *Address:* 36 St Patrick's Road, Saul, Downpatrick, N Ireland BT30 7JQ. *T:* (028) 4461 4360. *Club:* Reform.

GREEN, Barry Spencer; QC 1981; **His Honour Judge Green;** a Circuit Judge, since 1993; *b* 16 March 1932; *s* of Lionel Maurice Green, FRCS and Juliette Green; *m* 1st, 1960, Marilyn Braverman (marr. diss. 1987); two *s*; 2nd, 1988, Muriel Coplan. *Educ:* Westminster Sch.; Christ Church, Oxford (MA, BCL). Called to the Bar, Inner Temple, 1954, Bencher, 1987; a Recorder, 1979–93. Legal Mem., Mental Health Review Tribunal, 1983–93; Mem., Criminal Injuries Compensation Bd, 1988–93. Gov., City Literary Inst., 1996–. *Recreation:* tennis. *Clubs:* Garrick, Roehampton.

GREEN, Father Benedict; *see* Green, Rev. H. C.

GREEN, Rev. Bernard; General Secretary, Baptist Union of Great Britain, 1982–91; Moderator of the Free Church Federal Council, 1988–89; *b* 11 Nov. 1925; *s* of George Samuel Green and Laura Annie Agnes (*née* Holliday); *m* 1952, Joan Viccars; two *s* one *d*. *Educ:* Wellingborough Sch.; Bristol Baptist Coll.; Bristol Univ. (BA); Regent's Park Coll., Oxford, and St Catherine's Coll., Oxford (MA); London Univ. BD taken externally. Served War as coal-miner, 1944–47. Ordained as Baptist Minister, 1952; pastorates at: Yardley, Birmingham, 1952–61; Mansfield Road, Nottingham, 1961–76; Horfield, Bristol, 1976–82. Dir, Baptist Insce Co., 1982–93. Vice Pres., Churches' Council for Health and Healing, 1988–99. Regular broadcaster on BBC Radio Nottingham until 1976 and on BBC Radio Bristol until 1982. *Publications:* (jtly) Patterns and Prayers for Christian Worship, 1991; (ed jtly) Baptist Praise and Worship, 1991; Tomorrow's Man: a biography of James Henry Rushbrooke, 1997; Crossing the Boundaries: a history of the European Baptist Federation 1949–1999, 1999. *Recreations:* reading, music (listening), gardening. *Address:* 34 Mill Road, Abingdon, Oxon OX14 5NS. *T:* (01235) 521092.

GREEN, Brian Russell; QC 1997; *b* 25 July 1956; *s* of late Bertram Green and Dora Green (*née* Rinsler); *m* 1994, Yvonne Mammon; one *s* one *d*, and two step *d*. *Educ:* Ilford County High Sch. for Boys; St Edmund Hall, Oxford (BA, BCL). Called to the Bar, Middle Temple, 1980; Mem., Lincoln's Inn, 1991. Mem., Revenue Law Cttee, Law Soc., 1994–. *Recreations:* travel, hill-walking, opera, the arts. *Address:* Wilberforce Chambers, 8 New Square, Lincoln's Inn, WC2A 3QP. *T:* (020) 7306 0102.

GREEN, Prof. Brynmor Hugh, OBE 1995; Sir Cyril Kleinwort Professor of Countryside Management, University of London, Wye College, 1987–96, now Professor Emeritus; *b* 14 Jan. 1941; *s* of Albert Walter Green and Margaret Afona Green (*née* Griffiths); *m* 1965, Jean Armstrong; two *s*. *Educ:* Dartford Grammar Sch.; Univ. of Nottingham (BSc 1st Cl. Hons Botany, PhD Plant Ecol.). Lectr in Plant Ecology, Dept of Botany, Univ. of Manchester, 1965–68; Dep. Regl Officer (SE) 1968–69, Regl Officer (SE) 1969–75, Nature Conservancy Council; Lectr and Sen. Lectr, Wye Coll., 1975–87. A Countryside Comr, 1984–93. *Publications:* Countryside Conservation: landscape ecology, planning and management, 1981, 3rd edn 1996; (jtly) The Diversion of Land: conservation in a period of farming contraction, 1990; (jtly) The Changing Role of the Common Agricultural Policy: the future of farming in Europe, 1991; (jtly) Threatened Landscapes: conserving cultural environments, 2001; numerous chapters in books, conf. reports, sci. jls. *Recreations:* golf, watercolour sketching, bird-watching. *Address:* 16 The Granville, Hotel Road, St Margaret's Bay, Dover, Kent CT15 6DX. *T:* (01304) 851752.

GREEN, Candida L.; *see* Lycett Green.

GREEN, Catherine; *see* Matheson, C.

GREEN, Charles Frederick; Director, 1982–89, and Deputy Group Chief Executive, 1986–89, National Westminster Bank; *b* 20 Oct. 1930; *m* 1956, Rev. Pauline (*née* Jackson); two *s* one *d*. *Educ:* Harrow County School. FCIB (FIB 1971); FIMgt (FBIM 1982). Nat. Service, RAF, 1949–51 (Flying Officer). Joined National Provincial Bank, 1946, Secretary, 1967–70; Head of Planning, National Westminster Bank, 1970; Manager, Lombard Street, 1972; Managing Dir, Centre-file, 1974; General Manager: Business Develt Div., 1977; Financial Control Div., 1982. Chairman: CBI/ICC Multinational Affairs Panel, 1982–87; Overseas Cttee, CBI, 1987–89; Dir, Business in the Community, 1981–91 (Vice-Chm., 1985–89); Mem. Council, PSI, 1984–98 (Treas., 1984–93). Mem., General Synod, 1980–90; Vice-Chm., C of E Bd for Social Responsibility, 1983–91; Chm., Industrial and Econ. Affairs Cttee, 1986–93; Mem., Central Stewardship Cttee, Central Bd of Finance, 1991–99 (Chm., 1993–99); Trustee, Church Urban Fund, 1987–89. Chm., Co. of Glos Community Foundn, 1991–2000 (Trustee, 1990–); Vice-Chm., Dio. of Gloucester Bd of Finance, 1991–2000; Mem., Council for Charitable Support, 1989–93; Chm., Glenfall House Trust, 1996–; Trustee: Small Business Res. Trust, 1986–96; Monteverdi Choir, 1986–; Charities Aid Foundn, 1989–98; Church Housing Trust, 1992–. Governor: Westonbirt Sch., 1990–; Monkton Combe Sch., 1990–96; Mem. Council, Cheltenham & Gloucester Coll. of Higher Educn, 1993– (Vice-Chm. Council, 1994–; Fellow, 1990). FRSA 1994. Hon. FLCM 1988. Freeman, City of London, 1990. *Recreations:* opera, concert music, drama. *Address:* The Old House, Parks Farm, Old Sodbury, Bristol BS37 6PX. *Clubs:* Athenæum, National, Langbourn Ward.

GREEN, Christopher Edward Wastie, MA; FCIT; Chief Executive, Virgin Trains, since 1999; Director, Virgin Rail Group Ltd, since 1999; *b* 7 Sept. 1943; *s* of James Wastie Green and Margarita Mensing; *m* 1966, Mitzie Petzold; one *s* one *d*. *Educ:* St Paul's School, London; Oriel College, Oxford. MA Mod. Hist. British Rail: Management Trainee, 1965–67; served Birmingham, Nottingham, Hull, Wimbledon; Passenger Operating Manager, HQ, 1979–80; Chief Operating Manager, Scotland, 1980–83; Dep. Gen. Manager, Scotland, 1983–84; Gen. Manager, Scottish Region, 1984–86; Dir, Network SouthEast, 1986–91; Managing Director: InterCity, 1992–94; ScotRail, 1994–95; Chief Exec. and Comr, English Heritage, 1995–96; Director: Gibb Rail Ltd, 1996–99; Gibb Ltd, 1996–99. Director: Eurotunnel, 1995–; Connex Rail, 1998–99. Mem., Regl Council, CBI, 1986. Pres., Railway Study Assoc., 1989–90, 1997–98; Vice Pres., CIT, 1988. Mem. Adv. Bd, Cranfield Univ. Logistics and Transportation Centre, 1996–. *Recreations:* music, reading, walking, canals, architecture. *Address:* West Wing Offices, Euston Station, NW1 2HS. *T:* (020) 7904 3204, *Fax:* (020) 7320 0506.

GREEN, Prof. Christopher Kenneth, PhD; FBA 1999; Professor of History of Art, Courtauld Institute of Art; *b* 1943; *m* Charlotte Sebag-Montefiore; one *s* one *d*. *Educ:* Christ's Coll., Cambridge (BA 1966); London Univ. (MA); PhD. Courtauld Institute of Art: successively Asst Lectr, Lectr, and Reader in History of Art; Curator, Roger Fry exhibn, 1999. Leverhulme Res. Fellow, 1997-98. *Publications:* Cubism and its Enemies, 1987; (jtly) Juan Gris, 1992; European Avant-Gardes, 1995; One Man Show (novel), 1995; (ed) Art Made Modern: Roger Fry's vision of art, 1999; Art in France 1900–1940, 2000; exhibn catalogues. *Recreation:* finding calm. *Address:* Courtauld Institute of Art, Somerset House, Strand, WC2R 0RN.

GREEN, Colin Raymond; Secretary, since 1994 and Group Commercial Director, since 1999, British Telecommunications; *b* 16 April 1949; *s* of Gerald and Maisie Green; *m* 1975, Hazel Ruth Lateman; one *s* one *d*. *Educ:* Hampton Grammar Sch.; LSE (LLB Hons); Coll. of Law; WUJS Post-grad. Inst., Israel. Solicitor, 1973; Paisner & Co., 1971–74; Partner, Clintons, 1975–77; Solicitor's Office, Post Office, 1977; BT Solicitor's Office, 1981: Head, Privatisation Div., 1982–84; Head, M&A Div., 1984–85; Dir, Commercial Dept, 1985–89; Solicitor and Chief Legal Advr, 1989–94, Secretary and Chief Legal Adviser, 1989–99, BT; Mem. Exec. Cttee, 1996–. Trustee, BT Pension Scheme. Director: Vio (Worldwide) Ltd, 1998–2001; Airtel SA, 1999–2001; BT Telecomunicaciones SA, 2001–. Dir, Centre for Dispute Resolution, 1995–2000. Chm., Kingston Jt Israel Appeal Cttee, 1986–96. FRSA 1997. *Recreations:* music (playing and composing), walking, reading, theatre, football. *Address:* BT Centre, 81 Newgate Street, EC1A 7AJ. *T:* (020) 7356 5237.

GREEN, Damian Howard; MP (C) Ashford, since 1997; *b* 17 Jan. 1956; *s* of Howard and late Audrey Green; *m* 1988, Alicia Collinson; two *d*. *Educ:* Reading Sch.; Balliol Coll., Oxford (MA 1st cl. Hons. PPE). Producer, BBC Financial Unit, 1980–82; Business Producer, Channel 4 News, 1982–84; Business News Ed., The Times, 1984–85; Business Ed., Channel 4 News, 1985–87; Presenter and City Editor, Business Daily prog., Channel 4, 1987–92; Prime Minister's Policy Unit, 1992–94; Public Affairs Advr, 1994–97. Opposition spokesman: on employment and higher educn; 1998–99; on the envmt, 1999–2001; Shadow Educn Sec., 2001–. Contested (C) Brent E, 1992. Trustee, Communities Develt Foundn, 1997–. *Publications:* ITN Budget Factbook, annually 1984–86; A Better BBC, 1990; Communities in the Countryside, 1995; The Four Failures of the New Deal, 1998. *Recreations:* cricket, football, opera, cinema. *Address:* House of Commons, SW1A 0AA. *T:* (020) 7219 3000.

GREEN, David; *see* Green, G. D.

GREEN, David Charles, CBE 2001; FCIT; Executive Vice-President, Freight Transport Association, since 2001; *b* 3 June 1943; *s* of Phillip and Eileen Green; *m* 1969, Anne Patricia Ward; one *s* one *d*. *Educ:* Latymer Upper Sch. FCIT 1992; FILT (FILog 1993). Exec. Officer, Traders Road Transport Assoc., 1966–71; Freight Transport Association: Regl Controller, 1971–87; Exec. Dir, 1987–93; Dir-Gen., 1993–2000. Pres., Internat. Road Transport Union, 1995–. *Publications:* numerous articles and reports on freight transport and logistics. *Recreations:* golf, cricket, modern political history. *Address:* (office) Hermes House, St John's Road, Tunbridge Wells, Kent TN4 9UZ. *T:* (01892) 526171. *Club:* Royal Automobile.

GREEN, David George, PhD; Director, Civitas: Institute for the Study of Civil Society, since 2000; *b* 24 Jan. 1951; *s* of George Green and Kathleen Mary (*née* Ellis); *m* 1980, Catherine Walker; one *s* one *d*. *Educ:* Newcastle upon Tyne Univ. (BA Hons 1973; PhD 1980). Pt-time Lectr, Newcastle upon Tyne Poly., 1974–81; Res. Fellow, ANU, 1981–83; Res. Fellow, 1984–86, Dir, Health and Welfare Unit, 1986–2000, Inst. of Economic Affairs. Mem. (Lab), Newcastle upon Tyne CC, 1975–81. *Publications:* Power and Party in an English City, 1981; Mutual Aid or Welfare State, 1984; Working Class Patients and the Medical Establishment, 1985; Challenge to the NHS, 1986; The New Right, 1987; Everyone a Private Patient, 1988; Reinventing Civil Society, 1993; Community without Politics, 1996; From Welfare State to Civil Society, 1996; Benefit Dependency, 1998; An End to Welfare Rights, 1999; Delay, Denial and Dilution, 2000; Stakeholder Health Insurance, 2000. *Recreation:* walking.

GREEN, Prof. David Headley, FRS 1991; FAA; Director, Research School of Earth Sciences, Australian National University, since 1994 (Deputy Vice-Chancellor, 1998); *b* 29 Feb. 1936; *s* of Ronald Horace Green and Josephine May Headley; *m* 1959, Helen Mary McIntyre; three *s* three *d*. *Educ:* Univ. of Tasmania (BSc Hons 1957; MSc 1959; DSc 1988); Univ. of Cambridge (PhD 1962). FAA 1974; Fellow, Aust. Inst. of Mining and Metallurgy, 1987. Geologist, Bureau of Mineral Resources, Geology and Geophysics, Canberra, 1957–59; Postgrad. Scholarship, Royal Commn for Exhibn of 1851, 1959–62; Research School of Earth Sciences, Australian National University: Res. Fellow, 1962–65; Fellow, 1965–68; Sen. Fellow, 1968–74; Professorial Fellow, 1974–76; Prof. of Geology, Univ. of Tasmania, 1977–93. Chief Science Advr, Dept of Arts, Sport, Envmt, Tourism and Territories, 1991–93. Hallimond Lect., Mineralogical Soc., 1996. Hon. Fellow: Eur. Union of Geoscis, 1985; Geol Soc. of America, 1986. Hon DLitt Tasmania, 1994. Edgeworth David Medal, Royal Soc., NSW, 1968; Stilwell Medal, Geol Soc. of Australia, 1977; Mawson Medal, 1982, Jaeger Medal, 1990, Aust. Acad. of Sci.; A. G. Werner Medaille, Deutsche Mineralogische Ges., 1998; Murchison Medal, Geol Soc., 2000. *Publications:* numerous articles in fields of experimental petrology and geochemistry, in learned jls. *Recreations:* tennis, music. *Address:* Research School of Earth Sciences, Australian National University, Canberra, ACT 0200, Australia. *T:* (2) 61252487, *Fax:* (2) 61250756.

GREEN, David John Mark; QC 2000; a Recorder, since 2000; *b* 8 March 1954; *s* of John Geoffrey Green and Margaret Rowena Green (*née* Millican); *m* 1980, Kate Sharkey; one *s* two *d*. *Educ:* Christ's Hosp., Horsham; St Catharine's Coll., Cambridge (MA Hons). Defence Intelligence Staff, MoD, 1975–78; called to the Bar, Inner Temple, 1979; practising barrister, 1979–. Liveryman, Co. of Gardeners, 2000–. *Recreations:* walking, gardening. *Address:* 18 Red Lion Court, EC4A 3EB. *T:* (020) 7520 6000. *Club:* Garrick.
See also G. S. Green.

GREEN, Prof. Dennis Howard, FBA 1992; Schröder Professor of German, University of Cambridge, 1979–89; Fellow of Trinity College, Cambridge, since 1949; *b* 26 June 1922; *s* of Herbert Maurice Green and Agnes Edith Green (*née* Fleming); *m* 1st, 1947, Dorothy Warren (marr. diss. 1972); one *d*; 2nd, 1972, Margaret Parry (*d* 1997); 3rd, 2001, Sarah Redpath. *Educ:* Latymer Upper Sch., London; Trinity Coll., Cambridge; Univ. of Basle. Univ. of Cambridge, 1940–41 and 1945–47; Univ. of Basle (Dr Phil.), 1947–49; Military service (RAC), 1941–45; Univ. Lecturer in German, St Andrews, 1949–50; Research Fellowship, Trinity Coll., Cambridge (first year held *in absentia*), 1949–52; Univ. Asst Lectr in German, Cambridge, 1950–54; Teaching Fellowship, Trinity Coll., Cambridge, 1952–66; Head of Dept of Other Languages, 1956–79, and Prof. of Modern Languages, Cambridge, 1966–79; Visiting Professor: Cornell Univ., 1965–66; Auckland Univ., 1966; Yale Univ., 1969; ANU, Canberra, 1971; UCLA, 1975; Univ. of Pennsylvania, 1975; Univ. of WA, 1976; Univ. of Freiburg, 1990; Vis. Fellow, Humanities Res. Centre, Canberra, 1978. Fellow, Netherlands Inst. for Advanced Study, Wassenaar, 1998. Pres., MHRA, 1997. *Publications:* The Carolingian Lord, 1965; The Millstätter Exodus: a crusading epic, 1966; (with Dr L. P. Johnson) Approaches to Wolfram von Eschenbach, 1978; Irony in the Medieval Romance, 1979; The Art of Recognition in Wolfram's Parzival, 1982; Medieval Listening and Reading, 1994; Language and History in the early Germanic World, 1998; reviews and articles in learned journals. *Recreations:* walking and foreign travel. *Address:* Trinity College, Cambridge CB2 1TQ. *T:* (01223) 339517.

GREEN, Prof. Diana Margaret, PhD; Vice-Chancellor, Sheffield Hallam University, since 1998; *b* 10 April 1943; *d* of Charles Edward Harris and Joan Harris (*née* Beresford); *m* 1967, Neville A. Green (marr. diss. 1979). *Educ:* South Park High Sch. for Girls, Lincoln; Reading Univ.; Queen Mary Coll., London (BSc Econ.); London Sch. of Econs (PhD Econ. 1976). HM CS, 1969–76; Lectr, Sen. Lectr and Actg Hd, Dept of Politics and Govt, City of London Poly., 1976–83; University of Central England: Hd of Dept, 1984–87; Asst Dir, 1987–92; Pro Vice-Chancellor, 1992–98. Consultant (part-time), DTI, 1976–81. Mem., Quality Assessment Cttee, HEFCE, 1992–96; Chm., SRHE, 1998–99. Member: Black Country Develt Corp., 1992–94; Alexandra NHS Healthcare Trust, 1996–98. Mem., W Midlands Regl Council, CBI, 1994–98. Founder Dir, Midlands Excellence, 1996–; Director: Phoenix Sports UK, 1997–2000; Sheffield TEC, 1998–2001; Sheffield Industrial Mus Trust, 1998–; Sheffield First for Investment, 1999–; Sheffield Galls and Museums Trust, 2000–; Sheffield One, 2000–. Mem. Council, All Party Parly Univ. Gp. FRSA. Freeman, City of London, 1998. *Publications:* articles, chapters, books and reports on industrial change and quality in higher education; contrib. to THES. *Recreations:* flying light aircraft, music, art, theatre. *Address:* Vice-Chancellor's Office, Sheffield Hallam University, Sheffield S1 1WB. *T:* (0114) 225 2050; *e-mail:* d.green@shu.ac.uk.

GREEN, Rev. Canon (Edward) Michael (Bankes); Archbishops' Adviser in Evangelism, since 1992; Senior Research Fellow, Wycliffe Hall, Oxford, since 1997; *b* 20 Aug. 1930; British; *m* 1957, Rosemary Wake (*née* Storr); two *s* two *d*. *Educ:* Clifton Coll.; Oxford and Cambridge Univs. BD Cantab 1966. Exeter Coll., Oxford, 1949–53 (1st cl. Lit. Hum.); Royal Artillery (Lieut, A/Adjt), 1953–55; Queens' Coll., Cambridge, 1955–57 (1st cl. Theol. Tripos Pt III; Carus Greek Testament Prize; Fencing Blue), and Ridley Hall Theol Coll., 1955–57; Curate, Holy Trinity, Eastbourne, 1957–60; Lectr, London Coll. of Divinity, 1960–69; Principal, St John's Coll., Nottingham (until July 1970, London Coll. of Divinity), 1969–75; Canon Theologian of Coventry, 1970–76, Canon Theologian Emeritus, 1978–; Rector of St Aldate's, Oxford, 1975–87 (with Holy Trinity, Oxford, 1975–82 and with St Matthew, 1982–87); Prof. of Evangelism at Regent Coll., Vancouver, Univ. of BC, 1987–92. Member: Doctrine Commission of the Church, 1968–77; Church Unity Commn, 1974–. Leader of missions, overseas and in UK. Hon. DD Toronto, 1992; DD Lambeth, 1996. *Publications:* Called to Serve, 1964; Choose Freedom, 1965; The Meaning of Salvation, 1965; Man Alive, 1967; Runaway World, 1968; Commentary on 2 Peter and Jude, 1968; Evangelism in the Early Church, 1970; Jesus Spells Freedom, 1972; New Life, New Lifestyle, 1973; I Believe in the Holy Spirit,

1975, new edn 1985; You Must Be Joking, 1976; (ed) The Truth of God Incarnate, 1977; Why Bother With Jesus?, 1979; Evangelism—Now and Then, 1979; What is Christianity?, 1981; I Believe in Satan's Downfall, 1981; The Day Death Died, 1982; To Corinth with Love, 1982; World on the Run, 1983; Freed to Serve, 1983; The Empty Cross of Jesus, 1984; Come Follow Me, 1984; Lift Off to Faith, 1985; Baptism, 1987; Matthew for Today, 1988; Ten Myths about Christianity, 1988; Evangelism Through the Local Church, 1990; Reflections from the Lions Den, 1990; Who is this Jesus?, 1991; My God, 1992; On Your Knees, 1992; Good News and How to Share It, 1993; Acts for Today, 1993; (with Alister McGrath) Springboard for Faith, 1993; (with Paul Stevens) New Testament Spirituality, 1994; How Can I Lead a Friend to Christ?, 1995; Critical Choices, 1995; Strange Intelligence, 1997; Evangelism for Amateurs, 1998; After Alpha, 1998; Bible Reading for Amateurs, 1999; Churchgoing for Amateurs, 2000; The Message of Matthew, 2000; Asian Tigers for Christ, 2001; contribs to various jls. *Recreations:* family, countryside pursuits, squash, fly fishing. *Address:* 7 Little Acreage, Old Marston, Oxford OX3 0PS. *T:* (01865) 248387, *Fax:* (01865) 792083.

GREEN, Dr Frank Alan, CEng; FIM; Principal, Charing Green Associates, since 1983; non-executive Director: 2 GC Ltd, since 2000; Somerset Health Authority, since 2001; *b* 29 Oct. 1931; *s* of Frank Green and Winifred Hilda (*née* Payne); *m* 1957, Pauline Eleanor Tayler; one *s* two *d.* *Educ:* Mercers Sch., London; Univ. of London (BScEng, PhD); Univ. of Exeter (MA 2001). CEng 1980; FIM 1978. UKAEA, 1956–57; various appts, Glacier Metal Co. Ltd (Associated Engrg Gp), 1957–65; Technical Dir, Alta Friccion SA, Mexico City, 1965–68; Manufg Dir, Stewart Warner Corp., 1968–72; Marketing Develt Manager, Calor Gp, 1972–74; Manufg Dir, 1974–77, Man. Dir, 1977–81, British Twin Disc Ltd, Rochester; Industrial Advr (Under-Sec.), DTI, 1981–84. Director: Gen. Technology Systems (Scandinavia), 1989–91; Gen. Technology Systems (Portuguesa), 1989–91; Principal Consultant, General Technology Systems Ltd, 1984–90. Dir, Anglo-Mexican Chamber of Commerce, Mexico City, 1966–68. Member of Council: Inst. of Metals, 1990–91; Inst. of Materials, 1992–94; Chm., W of England Metals and Materials Assoc., 1999–2000. *Publications:* contrib. technical, historical and managerial books and jls in UK and Mexico. *Recreations:* photography, military history, rough walking, wine. *Address:* Fernlea House, 49 Ditton Street, Ilminster, Som TA19 0BW. *Club:* Old Mercers.

GREEN, Geoffrey Hugh, CB 1977; Deputy Under-Secretary of State (Policy), Procurement Executive, Ministry of Defence, 1975–80; *b* 24 Sept. 1920; *o s* of late Duncan M. and Kate Green, Bristol; *m* 1948, Ruth Hazel Mercy; two *d.* *Educ:* Bristol Grammar Sch.; Worcester Coll., Oxford (Exhibr), 1939–41, 1945–47 (MA). Served with Royal Artillery (Ayrshire Yeomanry): N Africa and Italy, 1942–45 (Captain). Entered Min. of Defence, Oct. 1947; Principal, 1949; Asst Sec., 1960; Asst Under-Sec. of State, 1969; Dep. Under-Sec. of State, 1974. *Recreations:* travel, music, walking. *Address:* 47 Kent Avenue, Ealing, W13 8BE.

See also D. J. M. Green.

GREEN, Geoffrey Stephen; Senior Partner, Ashurst Morris Crisp, since 1998; *b* 3 Sept. 1949; *s* of John Geoffrey Green and Margaret Rowena Green (*née* Millican); *m* 1982, Sarah Charlton Chesshire; three *s.* *Educ:* St Catharine's Coll., Cambridge (MA). Admitted Solicitor, 1975. Solicitor, 1975–, Partner, 1983–, Ashurst Morris Crisp. *Recreations:* golf, tennis, riding. *Address:* (office) Broadwalk House, 5 Appold Street, EC2A 2HA. *T:* (020) 7638 1111.

See also D. J. M. Green.

GREEN, Gerard Nicholas Valentine; Chief Executive, Health Care Projects Ltd, since 1999 (Executive Director, 1997); *b* 6 Aug. 1950; *s* of James Arnold Green and Margarathe Ella Green; *m* 1977, Maralyn Ann Ranger; one *s* one *d.* *Educ:* Highgate Sch.; University Coll., London (BA); Univ. of Warwick (MA); Birkbeck Coll., London (MA). AHSM. Nat. admin. trainee, 1974–75; Dep. Hosp. Sec., St George's Hosp., SW17, 1975–77; Asst Sector Administrator, Cane Hill Hosp., Surrey, 1977–79; Sector Administrator, Farnborough Hosp., Kent, 1979–82; Administrator, KCH, 1982–84; Chief Exec. Officer, Tabuk Military Hosp., Saudi Arabia, 1984–87; Dist Gen. Man., Bromley HA, 1987–89; Regl Gen. Man., SE Thames RHA, 1989–94; Chief Exec., Royal Hosps NHS Trust, 1994–97. Non-exec. Dir, Meridian Hosp. Co. plc, 2000–. Mem., UKCC, 1993–98. FRSA 1989. *Recreations:* travel, reading. *Address:* Health Care Projects Ltd, 3 Cobden Court, Wimpole Close, Bromley, Kent BR2 9JF. *Club:* Reform.

GREEN, (Gregory) David, CMG 1999; Director-General, British Council, since 1999; *b* 2 Dec. 1948; *s* of Thomas Dixon Green and Mary Mabella Green (*née* Walley); *m* 1977, Corinne Butler; three *d.* *Educ:* Leys Sch., Cambridge; Keswick Hall Coll. of Educn, Norwich (Cert Ed); Trinity Hall, Cambridge (BEd). Volunteer, VSO, Pakistan, 1967–68; teaching, Conisborough and Rotherham, 1972–76; Dir, Children's Relief Internat., 1976–79; Save the Children Fund: Staff Develt and Trng Officer, 1979; Dep. Dir of Personnel, 1982; Dir of Personnel, 1983; Dir of Personnel and Admin., 1988–90; Dir, VSO, 1990–99. Dir and Council Mem., Council for Colony Holidays for Schoolchildren, 1970–80; Member Council: Assoc. of Active Learning, 1990–92; VSO, 2000–. Mem., Laurence Olivier Awards Panel, 1984–85. FRGS 1991; FRSA 1990. *Publication:* Chorus, 1977. *Recreations:* theatre, music, painting, woodworking. *Address:* British Council, 10 Spring Gardens, SW1A 2BN. *T:* (020) 7389 4977, *Fax:* (020) 7389 4984.

GREEN, Hon. Sir Guy (Stephen Montague), AC 1994; KBE 1982; CVO 2000; Governor of Tasmania, since 1995; *b* 26 July 1937; *s* of Clement Francis Montague Green and Beryl Margaret Jenour Green; *m* 1963, Rosslyn Mary Marshall; two *s* two *d.* *Educ:* Launceston Church Grammar Sch.; Univ. of Tasmania. Alfred Houston Schol. (Philosophy) 1958; LLB (Hons) 1960. Admitted to Bar of Tasmania, 1960; Partner, Ritchie & Parker Alfred Green & Co. (Launceston), 1963–71; Magistrate 1971–73; Chief Justice of Tasmania, 1973–95; University of Tasmania: Mem., Faculty of Law, 1974–85; Chancellor, 1985–95. Lieut-Gov., Tasmania, 1982–95. Pres., Tasmanian Bar Assoc., 1968–70; Chm., Council of Law Reporting, 1978–85. Dep. Chm., Australian Inst. of Judicial Admin, 1986–88. Chm., Tasmanian Cttee, Duke of Edinburgh's Award Scheme in Australia, 1975–80; Dir, Winston Churchill Meml Trust, 1975–85 (Dep. Nat. Chm., 1980–85; Chm. Tasmanian Regional Cttee, 1975–80). St John Ambulance, Australia: Pres., Tasmanian Council, 1984–92; Priory Exec. Officer, 1984–91; Chancellor, 1991–95; Dep. Prior, 1995–. Hon. LLD Tasmania, 1996. KStJ 1985. *Address:* Government House, Hobart, Tas 7001, Australia. *Club:* Tasmanian (Hobart).

GREEN, Rev. Humphrey Christian, (Father Benedict Green, CR); formerly Principal, College of the Resurrection, Mirfield; *b* 9 Jan. 1924; *s* of late Rev. Canon Frederick Wastie Green and Marjorie Susan Beltt Green (*née* Gosling). *Educ:* Dragon Sch., Oxford; Eton (King's Scholar); Merton Coll., Oxford (Postmaster). BA 1949, MA 1952. Served War, RNVR, 1943–46. Deacon 1951, priest 1952; Asst Curate of Northolt, 1951–56; Lectr in Theology, King's Coll., London, 1956–60. Professed in Community of the Resurrection (taking additional name of Benedict), 1962; Vice-Principal, Coll. of the Resurrection, 1965–75; Principal, 1975–84. Associate Lectr in Dept of Theology and Religious Studies, Univ. of Leeds, 1967–87. Mem., SNTS, 1989–. *Publications:* The Gospel according to Matthew (New Clarendon Bible), 1975; Lay Presidency at the Eucharist, 1994; Matthew: poet of the Beatitudes, 2001; contrib.: Towards a Church Architecture (ed P. Hammond), 1962; The Anglican Synthesis (ed W. R. F. Browning), 1964; Synoptic Studies (ed C. M. Tuckett), 1984; The Making of Orthodoxy (ed R. Williams), 1989; The Synoptic Gospels: source criticism and the new literary criticism (ed C. Focant), 1993; theological jls. *Recreations:* walking, music, synoptic criticism. *Address:* House of the Resurrection, Mirfield, W Yorks WF14 0BN. *T:* (01924) 483328, *Fax:* (01924) 490489.

GREEN, John Edward, PhD; FREng, FRAeS, FAIAA; Consultant and Chief Scientist to Aircraft Research Association Ltd, since 1995 (Chief Executive, 1988–95); *b* 26 Aug. 1937; *s* of John Green and Ellen Green (*née* O'Dowd); *m* 1959, Gillian (*née* Jackson); one *s* one *d.* *Educ:* Birkenhead Inst. Grammar Sch.; St John's Coll., Cambridge (Scholar; BA 1959; MA 1963; PhD 1966). CEng 1972; FRAeS 1978. Student Apprentice, Bristol Aircraft Ltd, 1956; De Havilland Engine Co., 1959–61; Royal Aircraft Establishment, 1964–81: Head of Transonic/Supersonic Wind Tunnel Div., 1971; Head of Propulsion Div., 1973; Head of Noise Div., 1974; Head of Aerodynamics Dept., 1978–81; Dir, Project Time and Cost Analysis, MoD (PE), 1981–84; Minister–Counsellor Defence Equipment, and Dep. Head of British Defence Staff, Washington, 1984–85; Dep. Dir (Aircraft), RAE, 1985–87. Vis. Prof., Cranfield Univ., 1996–. President: Internat. Council of the Aeronautical Scis, 1996–98 (Mem. Council, 1986–2000; Chm., Prog. Cttee, 1992–96); RAeS, 1996–97 (Mem. Council, 1986–2000; Vice Pres., 1992–95; Hon. Treas., 1992–96); Mem. Council, AIRTO, 1988–95. Mem. Court, Cranfield Univ. (formerly Cranfield Inst. of Technol.), 1988– (Mem. Council, 1995–). Goldstein Lectr, 1991, Busk Prize, 1992, de Havilland Lectr, 2000, RAeS. FREng (FEng 1994); FAIAA 1999. *Publications:* contribs to books and learned jls, chiefly on fluid mechanics and aerodynamics. *Recreations:* music, mountain walking (Munroist, 1994). *Address:* 1 Leighton Street, Woburn, Beds MK17 9PJ. *T:* (01525) 290631.

GREEN, John Louis, FCA; Chairman: Principal Investment Management, since 2000; Inventive Leisure plc; *b* 2 March 1945; *s* of Stanley and Rose Green; *m* 1972, Kathleen Whelan; three *s* one *d.* *Educ:* Merchant Taylors' Sch., Northwood; Oriel Coll., Oxford (MA). FCA 1970. Price Waterhouse & Co., 1966–69; Kleinwort Benson, 1969–70; McAnally Montgomery & Co., 1970–79; James Capel, 1979–92; HSBC Investment Bank, 1992–96, Man. Dir, HSBC-Capel UK, 1995–96; Chief Exec., James Capel Investment Mgt, 1996–98. Dir various cos. *Recreations:* golf, opera, reading. *Address:* Silver Trees, Park Lane, Ashtead, Surrey KT21 1EJ. *T:* (01372) 274976. *Clubs:* Royal Automobile, Institute of Directors; Wisley Golf.

GREEN, John Michael, CB 1976; Commissioner, 1971–85, Deputy Chairman, 1973–85, Board of Inland Revenue; *b* 5 Dec. 1924; *s* of late George and Faith Green; *m* 1951, Sylvia (*née* Crabb) (*d* 1999); one *s* one *d.* *Educ:* Merchant Taylors' Sch., Rickmansworth; Jesus Coll., Oxford (MA (Hons)). Served War, Army, RAC, 1943–46. Entered Inland Revenue as Asst Principal, 1948; served in HM Treasury, as Principal, 1956–57; Asst Sec., 1962; Under Sec., Bd of Inland Revenue, 1971. Mem., NW Surrey HA, 1989–95. *Recreation:* gardening. *Address:* 5 Bylands, White Rose Lane, Woking, Surrey GU22 7LA. *T:* (01483) 772599. *Club:* Reform.

GREEN, Dr John Timothy; Secretary, School of Medicine, Imperial College of Science, Technology and Medicine, London University, since 1998; *b* 1 Jan. 1944; *s* of Thomas Albert Green and Joan (*née* Chamberlain); *m* 1985, Susan Mary Shattock; one *s.* *Educ:* King Edward's Five Ways Sch., Birmingham; Queens' Coll., Cambridge (BA 1966; MA 1970, PhD Maths 1970). Queens' College, Cambridge: Bye Fellow, 1970–72; Fellow, 1972–93; Lectr in Maths, 1972–93; Dean of Coll., 1972–77; Tutor, 1977–80; Sen. Tutor, 1980–93; Life Fellow, 1993; Chief Exec., RSocMed, 1993–96; Dir, Historic Properties (London), English Heritage, 1997–98. Director: S Leics Garages Ltd, 1985–95; Pennant Hotels Ltd, 1987–95; RSM Press Ltd, 1993–96; Chadwyck-Healey Ltd, 1997–99; Kennedy Inst. of Rheumatology, 1999–; Ind. Dir, 3i plc, 1996–. Member: CBI Professions Wkg Gp, 1995–96; London First Medicine, 1995–96. Recruitment Advr, FCO, 1992–99. Trustee: Harpur Trust, Bedford, 1984–87; Project Hope, 1995– (Vice-Chm., 1998–). Governor: Hills Rd Sixth Form Coll., Cambridge, 1993–98; Perse Sch., Cambridge, 2001–. *Publications:* contrib. Jl Fluid Mechanics and others. *Recreations:* opera, music, fell-walking. *Address:* 40 Newton Road, Cambridge CB2 2AL. *T:* (01223) 353756.

GREEN, Sir Kenneth, Kt 1988; MA; Vice-Chancellor (formerly Director), Manchester Metropolitan University (formerly Manchester Polytechnic), 1981–97; *b* 7 March 1934; *s* of James William and Elsie May Green; *m* 1961, Glenda (*née* Williams); one *d.* *Educ:* Helsby Grammar Sch.; Univ. of Wales, Bangor (BA 1st Cl. Hons); Univ. of London (MA). 2nd Lieut, S Wales Borderers, 1955–57. Management Trainee, Dunlop Rubber Co., 1957–58; Teacher, Liverpool, 1958–60; Lecturer: Widnes Technical Coll., 1961–62; Stockport College of Technology, 1962–64; Sen. Lectr, Bolton College of Education, 1964–68; Head of Educn, City of Birmingham College of Education, 1968–72; Dean of Faculty, Manchester Polytechnic, 1973–81. Vice-Chm., Manchester TEC, 1989–93 (Mem. Bd, 1989–93); Member: Council, CNAA, 1985–93; UFC, 1989–93. Chm., Council of Mgt, Rathbone Soc., 1993–95; Jt Chm., Rathbone Community Industry Ltd, 1995–97. Member: Governing Body, The Heath Comprehensive Sch., Runcorn, 1988–92; Governing Body, Victoria Rd Co. Primary Sch., Runcorn, 1990– (Chm., 1993–). CIMgt 1996. Hon. Mem., Manchester Literary & Philosophical Soc.; Hon. MRNCM; Hon. Fellow, Bolton Inst. of Higher Educn, 1997. Hon. LLD Manchester, 1992; Hon. DLitt: Salford, 1997; Manchester Metropolitan, 1998. *Recreations:* Rugby football, beer tasting. *Address:* 40 Royden Avenue, Runcorn, Cheshire WA7 4SP. *T:* (01928) 575201.

GREEN, Rt Rev. Laurence Alexander; *see* Bradwell, Area Bishop of.

GREEN, Prof. Leslie Leonard, CBE 1989; PhD; FInstP; Professor of Experimental Physics, University of Liverpool, 1964–86, now Emeritus; Director, Daresbury Laboratory, 1981–88; *b* 30 March 1925; *s* of Leonard and Victoria Green; *m* 1952, Dr Helen Therese Morgan; one *s* one *d.* *Educ:* Alderman Newton's Sch., Leicester; King's Coll., Cambridge (MA, PhD). FInstP 1966. British Atomic Energy Proj., 1944–46; Univ. of Liverpool: Lectr, 1948–57; Sen. Lectr, 1957–62; Reader, 1962–64; Dean, Faculty of Sciences, 1969–72; Pro-Vice-Chancellor, 1978–81. Mem., SRC Nuclear Physics Bd, 1972–75 and 1979–82. *Publications:* articles on nuclear physics in scientific jls. *Address:* Oakwood House, Eastbury, Hungerford, Berks RG17 7JP.

GREEN, Lucinda Jane, MBE 1978; three-day event rider; *b* 7 Nov. 1953, *d* of late Maj. Gen. George Erroll Prior-Palmer, CB, DSO, and Lady Doreen Hersey Winifred Prior-Palmer; *m* 1981, David (marr. diss. 1992), *s* of Burrington Green, Brisbane; one *s* one *d.* *Educ:* St Mary's, Wantage; Idbury Manor, Oxon. Member of winning Junior European Team, 1971; Winner, 3 Day Events: Badminton Horse Trials Championships, 1973, 1976, 1977, 1979, 1983, 1984; Burghley, 1977, 1981; Individual European Championships, 1975, 1977; World Championship, 1982; Member: Olympic Team, Montreal, 1976, Los Angeles, 1984; European Championship Team: Luhmühlen, W Germany, 1975 (team Silver Medallist and individual Gold Medallist); Burghley, 1977 (team Gold Medallist),

1985 (team Gold Medallist), 1987 (team Gold Medallist); European Team, 1979, 1983 (team and individual Silver Medallist); Alternative Olympic Team, 1980; World Championship Team: Kentucky, 1978; Luhmühlen, W Germany, 1982 (team and individual Gold Medallist). Co-presenter, Horses, Channel 4, 1987; Commentator: BBC, Badminton, 1987–2000; BBC, Olympic Games, 1988; Channel 7, Australia, Olympic Games, 1992, 1996 and 2000; Presenter, Rural Rides, Meridian TV, 1997 and 1998. Editorial Consultant, Eventing, 1989–92. *Publications:* Up, Up and Away, 1978; Four Square, 1980; Regal Realm, 1983; Cross-Country Riding, 1986, 2nd edn 1995; The Young Rider, 1993. *Recreations:* driving, ski-ing, scuba diving, travelling abroad. *Address:* The Tree House, Appleshaw, Andover SP11 9BS.

GREEN, Prof. Malcolm, DM; FRCP; Vice Principal and Head of National Heart and Lung Institute, Imperial College School of Medicine, since 1997; Professor of Respiratory Medicine, Imperial College, since 1998; Consultant Physician, Royal Brompton Hospital (formerly Brompton Hospital), since 1975; *b* 25 Jan. 1942; *s* of James Bisdee Malcolm Green and Frances Marjorie Lois Green; *m* 1971, Julieta Caroline Preston; two *s* two *d* (and one *d* decd). *Educ:* Charterhouse Sch. (Foundn Scholar); Trinity Coll., Oxford (Exhibnr; BA 1963; BSc 1965; MA, BM, BCh 1967; DM 1978); St Thomas's Hosp. Med. Sch. (Scholar). FRCP 1980 (MRCP 1970). Jun. appts, St Thomas' and Brompton Hosps, 1968–71; Lectr, Dept of Medicine, St Thomas' Hosp., 1971–74; Radcliffe Travelling Fellow, Harvard University Med. Sch., 1971–73; Sen. Registrar, Westminster and Brompton Hosps, 1974–75; Consultant Physician and Physician i/c Chest Dept, St Bartholomew's Hosp. 1975–86; Dean, Nat. Heart and Lung Inst., 1988–90 (Mem., Cttee of Management, 1988–95); Dir, BPMF, 1991–96. Member: Supraregl Services Adv. Cttee, 1991–96; NHS Taskforce on Res. (Culyer Cttee), 1993–94; Health of the Nation Wider Health Wkg Gp, 1991–97; NHS Central R&D Cttee, 1995– (Chm., 1999); NHS Exec. Bd, 1999; Chm., NHS R&D Bd, 1999; acting Dir, R&D for NHS, 1999. Chm., Exec. Cttee and Nat. Council, British Lung Foundn, 1984–94 (Pres. and Chm., Council, 1994–); Chm. Acad. Steering Gp, BPMF, 1989–90; Member, Committees of Management, Institutes of Child Health, Psychiatry, Neurology, Ophthalmology, Cancer Research, Dental Surgery, and RPMS, 1991–96. Member: Bd of Govs, Nat. Heart and Chest Hosps, 1988–90; Senate, Imperial Coll., 1998– (Mem. Council, 1997–98). Chm., London Medicine, 1996–2000; Bd Mem., London First Centre, 1996–99, London First, 2000–. Non-exec. Dir, St Mary's NHS Trust, 1997–. Trustee: Heart Disease and Diabetes Res. Trust, 1988–; Fledgeling Charity Funds, 1993–98. Treasurer, 1977–85, Pres., 1992–, United Hosps Sailing Club. FMedSci 2000. *Publications:* chapters and articles in med, books and jls on gen. medicine, respiratory medicine and respiratory physiology. *Recreations:* sailing, ski-ing. *Address:* 38 Lansdowne Gardens, SW8 2EF. *T:* (020) 7622 8286. *Clubs:* Royal Thames Yacht; Itchenor Sailing; Imperial Poona Yacht (Hon. Sec.).

GREEN, Prof. Malcolm Leslie Hodder, PhD; FRS 1985; CChem, FRSC; Professor of Inorganic Chemistry, since 1989, and Head of Department, Inorganic Chemistry Laboratory, since 1988, University of Oxford; Fellow of St Catherine's College, Oxford, since 1988; *b* 16 April 1936; *s* of late Leslie Ernest Green, MD and Sheila Ethel (*née* Hodder); *m* 1965, Jennifer Clare Bilham; two *s* one *d. Educ:* Denstone Coll.; Acton Technical Coll. (BSc); Imperial Coll. of Science and Technol., London Univ. (DIC, PhD 1958); MA Cantab. CChem, FRSC 1981. Asst Lectr in Inorganic Chem., Univ. of Cambridge, 1960–63; Fellow of Corpus Christi Coll., Cambridge, 1961–63; University of Oxford: Septcentenary Fellow and Tutor in Inorganic Chem., Balliol Coll., 1963–88; Deptl Demonstrator, 1963; Lectr, 1965–88; British Gas Royal Soc. Sen Res. Fellow, 1979–86. A. P. Sloan Vis. Prof., Harvard Univ., 1973; Sherman Fairchild Vis. Scholar, CIT, 1981. Tilden Lectr and Prize, RSC, 1982; Debye Lectr, Cornell Univ., 1985; Sir Edward Frankland Prize Lectr, 1988; Ernest H. Swift Lectr, CIT, 1998. Dr *hc* Universidade Téchnico de Lisboa, 1996. Corday–Morgan Medal and Prize in Inorganic Chem., Chemical Soc., 1974; Medal for Transition Metal Chem., Chemical Soc., 1978; Award for Inorganic Chem., ACS, 1984; RSC Award for Organometallic Chem., 1986; Karl-Ziegler Prize, Ges. Deutscher Chemiker, 1992; Davy Medal, Royal Soc., 1995; Award for Organometallic Chem., ACS, 1997; Sir Geoffrey Wilkinson Medal, RSC, 1999. *Publications:* Organometallic Compounds: Vol. II, The Transition Elements, 1968; (with G. E. Coates, P. Powell and K. Wade) Principles of Organometallic Chemistry, 1968. *Address:* St Catherine's College, Oxford OX1 3UJ.

GREEN, Malcolm Robert, DPhil; Member, City of Glasgow Council, since 1995; Lecturer in Roman History, University of Glasgow, 1967–98; *b* 4 Jan. 1943; *m* 1971; one *s* two *d. Educ:* Wyggeston Boys' School, Leicester; Magdalen College, Oxford. MA, DPhil. Member: Glasgow Corp., 1973–75; Strathclyde Regional Council, 1975–96 (Chairman: Educn Cttee, 1982–90; Envmt Sub-Cttee, 1990–94; Racial Equality Sub Cttee, 1994–96); Chm., Educn Cttee, 1996–99, Business Manager, 1999–, City of Glasgow Council. Chairman: Educn Cttee, Convention of Scottish Local Authorities, 1978–90; Management Side, Scottish Jt Negotiating Cttees for Teaching Staff in Sch. and Further Educn, 1977–90; Nat. Cttee for In-Service Training of Teachers, 1977–86; Scottish Cttee for Staff Develt in Educn, 1987–91. Commissioner, Manpower Services Commn, 1983–85. *Recreation:* talking politics. *Address:* 46 Victoria Crescent Road, Glasgow G12 9DE. *T:* (0141) 339 2007.

GREEN, Margaret Beryl; *see* Clunies Ross, M. B.

GREEN, Rt Rev. Mark, MC 1945; an Assistant Bishop, Diocese of Chichester, since 1982; Hon. Assistant, St Mary, Eastbourne, since 1994; *b* 28 March 1917; *s* of late Rev. Ernest William Green, OBE, and Miranda Mary Green; unmarried. *Educ:* Rossall Sch.; Lincoln Coll., Oxford (MA). Curate, St Catherine's Gloucester, 1940; Royal Army Chaplains' Dept, 1943–46 (despatches, 1945); Dir of Service Ordination Candidates, 1947–48; Vicar of St John, Newland, Hull, 1948–53; Short Service Commn, Royal Army Chaplains' Dept, 1953–56; Vicar of South Bank, Teesside, 1956–58; Rector of Cottingham, Yorks, 1958–64; Vicar of Bishopthorpe and Acaster Malbis, York, 1964–72; Hon. Chaplain to Archbp of York, 1964–72; Rural Dean of Ainsty, 1964–68; Canon and Prebendary of York Minster, 1963–72; Bishop Suffragan of Aston, 1972–82; Hon. Asst, Christ Church, St Leonards-on-Sea, 1982–94. Chm. of Governing Body, Aston Training Scheme, 1977–83; Provost, Woodard Schs Southern Div., 1982–89. Hon. DSc Aston, 1980. *Publication:* Diary of Doubt and Faith, 1974. *Address:* Flat 27, Selwyn House, Selwyn Road, Eastbourne, E Sussex BN21 2LF. *T:* (01323) 642707.

GREEN, Dame Mary Georgina, DBE 1968; BA; Head Mistress, Kidbrooke School, SE3, 1954–73; Chairman, BBC London Local Radio Council, 1973–78; Chairman, General Optical Council, 1979–85 (Member, 1977–79); *b* 27 July 1913; *er d* of late Edwin George Green and Rose Margaret Green (*née* Gibbs). *Educ:* Wellingborough High Sch.; Westfield Coll., University of London (Hon. Fellow, 1976; Fellow, QMW, 1989; Hon. Fellow, QMW, 1995). Assistant Mistress: Clapham High Sch., 1936–38; Streatham Hill and Clapham High Sch., 1938–40; William Hulme's Sch., Manchester, 1940–45; Head Mistress, Colston's Girls' Sch., Bristol, 1946–53. Member: Central Advisory Council for Education (Eng.), 1956–63; Church of England Board of Education, 1958–65; Council King George's Jubilee Trust, 1963–68; Court of Governors, London Sch. of Economics and Political Science, 1964–83; Royal Commission on Trade Unions and Employers' Assocs, 1965–68; Council, City University, 1969–78; Cttee of Inquiry into Nurses' Pay, 1974; Press Council, 1976–79; Review Body on Doctors' and Dentists' Remuneration, 1976–79. Dep. Chm., E-SU, 1976–82 (Governor, 1974–82); a Governor: BBC, 1968–73; Royal Ballet Sch., 1969–72; Centre for Educnl Develt Overseas, 1970–74; Rachel McMillan Coll. of Educn, 1970–73; Ditchley Foundn, 1978–97. Hon. DSc: City, 1981; Bradford, 1986. Hon. MADO 1985; Hon. FBCO 1985. *Address:* 45 Winn Road, SE12 9EX. *T:* (020) 8857 1514.

GREEN, Matthew Roger; MP (Lib Dem) Ludlow, since 2001; *b* 12 April 1970; *s* of Roger Hector Green and Pamela Gillian Green; *m* 1999, Sarah Louise Henthorn. *Educ:* Birmingham Univ. (BA (Hons) Medieval Studies). Sales and Marketing Manager, Plaskit Ltd, 1991–96; self employed, working in timber products and PR sectors, 1996–. Contested (Lib Dem) Wolverhampton SW, 1997. *Recreations:* cricket, mountaineering. *Address:* House of Commons, SW1A 0AA. *T:* (020) 7219 8253. *Club:* Liberal.

GREEN, Michael; *see* Green, N. M.

GREEN, Rev. Canon Michael; *see* Green, Rev. Canon E. M. B.

GREEN, Prof. Michael Boris, FRS 1989; John Humphrey Plummer Professor of Theoretical Physics and Fellow of Clare Hall, University of Cambridge, since 1993; *b* 22 May 1946; *s* of Absalom and Genia Green. *Educ:* Cambridge Univ. (BA, PhD; Rayleigh Prize 1969). Res. Fellow, Inst. for Advanced Study, Princeton, NJ, 1970–72; Fellowships in Cambridge, 1972–77; SERC Advanced Fellow, Oxford, 1977–79; Lectr, Queen Mary Coll., London Univ., 1979–85; Prof. of Physics, QMC, later QMW, 1985–93. Vis. Associate, Caltech, Pasadena, for periods during 1981–85; Nuffield Science Fellowship, 1984–86; SERC Sen. Fellowship, 1986–91. Maxwell Medal and Prize, Inst. of Physics, 1987; Hopkins Prize, Cambridge Philosophical Soc., 1987; Dirac Medal, Internat. Centre for Theoretical Physics, Trieste, 1989. *Publications:* Superstring Theory, vols I and II (with J. H. Schwarz and E. Witten), 1987; many contribs to physics and mathematics jls. *Address:* Department of Applied Mathematics and Theoretical Physics, University of Cambridge, Cambridge CB3 0WA.

GREEN, Dr Michael Frederick; Consultant Physician, Department of Geriatric Medicine, Board of Health, Guernsey, since 1984; *b* 29 Aug. 1939; *s* of Frederick and Kathleen Green; *m* 1977, Janet Mary; seven *s* one *d. Educ:* Dulwich Coll.; Jesus Coll., Cambridge (MA); St Thomas' Hosp. (MB, BChir). FRCP 1980. Consultant, N Middlesex and St Ann's Hosps, 1969–71; Consultant, Dept of Geriatric Medicine, Royal Free Hospital, 1972–84. Mem., GMC, 1973–79. Medical Adviser, Royal Life Saving Soc., 1970–84; Post Grad. Tutor/Clinical Sec., Princess Elizabeth Hosp., St Martin, Guernsey, 1990–. Member various bodies mainly involved with the elderly, including: British Geriatrics Soc.; Cruse (Nat. Assoc. for Widows); British Soc. for Research on Ageing. Governor: Queen Elizabeth Schs, Barnet, 1973–79; Christchurch Sch., Hampstead, 1980–83. Founder Chm., Friends of Elizabeth Coll., Guernsey, 1989–90. Mem. Bd, Jl of Medical Ethics, 1980–84; Chm., Editl Bd, Geriatric Medicine, 1984– (Medical Editor, 1971–84). *Publications:* Health in Middle Age, 1978; co-author books and articles on medical admin, geriatric medicine, hypothermia, neurology, endocrinology, rehabilitation, pressure sores, psychiatry of old age. *Recreations:* family, gardening, swimming and lifesaving, magic, writing, broadcasting, lecturing and teaching. *Address:* c/o Princess Elizabeth Hospital, Le Vauquiedor, Guernsey GY4 6UU.

GREEN, Michael John; Controller, BBC Radio 4, 1986–96; Deputy Managing Director, BBC Network Radio, 1993–96; *b* 28 May 1941; *s* of David Green and Kathleen (*née* Swann); *m* 1965, Christine Margaret Constance Gibson; one *s* one *d. Educ:* Repton Sch.; Barnsley Grammar Sch.; New Coll., Oxford (BA Modern Langs). Swiss Broadcasting Corp., 1964–65; Sheffield Star, 1965–67; Producer, BBC Radio Sheffield, 1967–70; Documentary Producer, BBC Manchester, 1970–77; Editor, File on Four, 1977; Head of Network Radio, Manchester, 1978–86. Chm., Radio Acad., 1990–95. Mem., NCC, 1997–. *Recreations:* France, canals, cinema, collecting glass.

GREEN, Michael Philip; Chairman: Carlton Communications Plc, since 1983 (Chief Executive, 1983–91); Independent Television News Ltd, since 1993; ONdigital plc, since 1997; *b* 2 Dec. 1947; *s* of Cyril and Irene Green; *m* 1st, 1972, Hon. Janet Frances Wolfson (*see* Hon. J. F. W. de Botton) (marr. diss. 1989); two *d*; 2nd, 1990, Theresa Mary Buckmaster (*see* T. M. Green); three *s* one *d. Educ:* Haberdashers' Aske's School. Director and Co-Founder, Tangent Industries, 1968. Founder, Tangent Charitable Trust, 1984; Chm., Carlton Television Ltd, 1991–94; Director: GMTV Ltd, 1992–; Reuters Holdings PLC, 1992–99; Getty Communications plc, 1997–98. Chm., The Media Trust, 1997–. Hon. DLitt City, 1999. *Recreations:* reading, bridge, television. *Address:* Carlton Communications Plc, 25 Knightsbridge, SW1X 7RZ. *T:* (020) 7663 6363. *Club:* Portland.

GREEN, Prof. Mino, FIEE; Professor of Electrical Device Science, Electrical Engineering, 1983–92, now Emeritus, Senior Research Fellow, since 1992, Imperial College of Science and Technology; *b* 10 March 1927; *s* of Alexander and Elizabeth Green; *m* 1951, Diana Mary Allen; one *s* one *d. Educ:* Dulwich Coll.; University Coll., Durham Univ. (BSc, PhD, DSc). Group Leader: Solid State Res., Lincoln Laboratory, MIT, 1951–55; Res., Zenith Radio Corp., USA, 1956–60; Associate Dir, Electrochemistry Lab., Univ. of Pennsylvania, 1960–62; Man. Dir, Zenith Radio Research Corp. (UK) Ltd, 1962–72; Lectr, then Reader, Elec. Engrg Dept, Imperial Coll. of Science and Technology, 1972–83. *Publications:* Solid State Surface Science, vols I, II and III (ed), 1969–73; many pubns (and some patents) on various aspects of semiconductor and optical device science. *Recreations:* walking, art appreciation. *Address:* 55 Gerard Road, SW13 9QH. *T:* (020) 8748 8689. *Club:* Hurlingham.

GREEN, Nicholas Nigel, PhD; QC 1998; *b* 15 Oct. 1958; *s* of John Reginald Green and Pauline Barbara Green; *m* 1990, Fiona Clare Cramb; one *s* one *d. Educ:* King Edward's VI Sch., Camp Hill, Birmingham; Univ. of Leicester (LLB 1980); Univ. of Toronto (LLM 1981); Univ. of Southampton (PhD 1985). Lectr in Law, Univ. of Southampton, 1981–85; pt-time Lectr in Law, UCL, 1985–87; called to the Bar, Inner Temple, 1986; in practice at the Bar, 1986–. Chm., Bar European Gp, 1999–2001; Vice Chm., Internat. Relns Cttee, Bar Council of England and Wales, 2000–; UK Perm. Rep. of CCBE to European Court of Justice, Court of First Instance and EFTA Court. Vis. Prof. of Law, Univ. of Durham, 2000–. *Publications:* Commercial Agreements and Competition Law: practice and procedure in the UK and EEC, 1986, 2nd edn (jtly) 1997; (jtly) The Legal Foundations of the Single European Market, 1991; over 50 articles in legal jls worldwide. *Recreations:* family, swimming (former international, 1976–77), collecting Victorian watercolours. *Address:* Brick Court Chambers, 7–8 Essex Street, WC2R 3LD.

GREEN, Dr (Norman) Michael, FRS 1981; affiliated to Department of Mathematical Biology, National Institute for Medical Research, since 1992; *b* 6 April 1926; *s* of Ernest Green and Hilda Margaret Carter; *m* 1953, Iro Paulina Moschouti; two *s* one *d. Educ:*

Dragon Sch., Oxford; Clifton Coll., Bristol; Magdalen Coll., Oxford (BA; Athletics Blue, Cross Country Blue); UCH Med. Sch., London (PhD). Res. Student, Univ. of Washington, Seattle, 1951–53; Lectr in Biochemistry, Univ. of Sheffield, 1953–55; Res. Fellow and Lectr in Chem. Pathol., St Mary's Hosp. Med. Sch., London, 1956–62; Vis. Scientist, NIH, Maryland, 1962–64; Res. Staff, Divs of Biochem. and Protein Structure, NIMR, 1964–91. *Publications:* research papers on the structure of proteins and of membranes, in scientific jls. *Recreations:* mountain climbing, pyrotechnics. *Address:* 57 Hale Lane, Mill Hill, NW7 3PS.

GREEN, Sir Owen (Whitley), Kt 1984; Chairman, BTR plc, 1984–93 (Managing Director, 1967–86); *b* Stockton-on-Tees, 14 May 1925; *m* 1948, Doreen Margaret Spark; one *s* two *d*. FCA 1950. Served RNVR, 1942–46. BTR, 1956–93. Dir, The Spectator, 1988–93. Trustee, Natural History Mus., 1986–95. Businessman of the Year, 1982; BIM Gold Medal, 1984; Founding Societies' Centenary Award, ICA, 1985. *Recreation:* golf. *Address:* Edgehill, Succombs Hill, Warlingham, Surrey CR6 9JG.

GREEN, Patrick G.; *see* Grafton-Green.

GREEN, Pauline; Chief Executive, Co-operative Union Ltd, since 2000; *b* 8 Dec. 1948; *d* of late Bertram Wiltshire and of Lucy Wiltshire; *m* 1971, Paul Adam Green; one *s* one *d*. *Educ:* John Kelly Secondary Modern Sch. for Girls, Brent; Kilburn Poly.; Open Univ. (BA); London School of Economics (MSc). Sec., 1981, Chair, 1983, Chipping Barnet Labour Party. MEP (Lab): London N, 1989–99; London Reg., 1999; Leader: European PLP, 1993–94; Gp of Pty of Eur. Socialists, 1994–99. Contested (Lab) Arkley ward, Barnet Council elecns, 1986. Parly Asst, Co-operative Movement, 1986–89. Pres., Co-operative Congress, 1997; Vice Pres., Socialist International, 1994–. Mem., NEC, Labour Party, 1998–99. Mem., USDAW. *Recreations:* music, swimming. *Address:* (office) Holyoake House, Hanover Street, Manchester M60 0AS.

GREEN, Brig. Percy William Powlett, CBE 1960 (OBE 1956); DSO 1946; *b* 10 Sept. 1912; *er s* of late Brig.-Gen. W. G. K. Green, CB, CMG, DSO, Indian Army; *m* 1943, Phyllis Margery Fitz Gerald May (*d* 1995), *d* of late Lieut-Col A. H. May, OBE; one *s* one *d*. *Educ:* Wellington Coll.; RMC. Commnd Northamptonshire Regt, 1932; Op. NW Frontier, India, 1936–37; BEF 1939–40; Lt-Col Comdg 2nd W Yorks Regt, 1945–46; Burma, 1944–45; Lt-Col Comdg 1 Malay Regt, 1946–47; Comd 4th King's African Rifles, 1954–56; Op. against Mau Mau; Col, Gen. Staff, War Office, 1956–57; Chief of Staff (Brig.) E Africa Comd, 1957–60; DDMI, War Office, 1961–63; Chief of Staff, N Ireland Command, 1963–65; Dep. Comdr, Aldershot District, 1965–67; retired, 1967. ADC to the Queen, 1965–67. Dep. Colonel, Royal Anglian Regt, 1966–76. *Recreations:* field sports. *Address:* Grudds, South Warnborough, Hook, Hants RG29 1RW. *T:* (01256) 862472.

GREEN, Prof. Peter Morris; author and translator since 1953; Professor of Classics, University of Texas at Austin, 1972–97 (James R. Dougherty Jr Centennial Professor of Classics, 1982–84, 1985–97), now Emeritus; Adjunct Professor of Classics, University of Iowa, since 1998; *b* 22 Dec. 1924; *o c* of late Arthur Green, CBE, MC, LLB, and Olive Slaughter; *m* 1st, 1951, Lalage Isobel Pulvertaft (marr. diss.); two *s* one *d*; 2nd, 1975, Carin Margreta, *y d* of late G. N. Christensen, Saratoga, USA. *Educ:* Charterhouse; Trinity Coll., Cambridge. Served in RAFVR, 1943–47: overseas tour in Burma Comd, 1944–46. 1st Cl. Hons, Pts I and II, Classical Tripos, 1949–50; MA and PhD Cantab 1954; Craven Schol. and Student, 1950; Dir of Studies in Classics, 1951–52; Fiction Critic, London Daily Telegraph, 1953–63; Literary Adviser, The Bodley Head, 1957–58; Cons. Editor, Hodder and Stoughton, 1960–63; Television Critic, The Listener, 1961–63; Film Critic, John o'London's, 1961–63; Mem. Book Soc. Cttee, 1959–63. Former Mem. of selection cttees for literary prizes: Heinemann Award, John Llewellyn Rhys, W. H. Smith £1000 Award for Literature. Translator of numerous works from French and Italian, including books by Simone de Beauvoir, Fosco Maraini, Joseph Kessel. FRSL 1956; Mem. Council, Royal Society of Literature, 1958–63 (resigned on emigration). In 1963 resigned all positions and emigrated to Greece as full-time writer (1963–71). Vis. Prof. of Classics: Univ. of Texas, 1971–72; UCLA, 1976; Mellon Prof. of Humanities, Tulane Univ., 1986; Vis. Prof. of History, Univ. of Iowa, 1997–98; Sen. Fellow for independent study and res., National Endowment for the Humanities, 1983–84. Editor, Syllecta Classica, 1999–. *Publications:* The Expanding Eye, 1953; Achilles His Armour, 1955; Cat in Gloves (pseud. Denis Delaney), 1956; The Sword of Pleasure (W. H. Heinemann Award for Literature), 1957; Kenneth Grahame, 1859–1932: A Study of his Life, Work and Times, 1959; Essays in Antiquity, 1960; Habeas Corpus and other stories, 1962; Look at the Romans, 1963; The Laughter of Aphrodite, 1965, repr. 1993; Juvenal: The Sixteen Satires (trans.), 1967, 3rd edn 1998; Armada from Athens: The Failure of the Sicilian Expedition, 415–413 BC, 1970; Alexander the Great: a biography, 1970; The Year of Salamis, 480–479 BC, 1971, rev. as The Greco-Persian Wars, 1996; The Shadow of the Parthenon, 1972; The Parthenon, 1973; A Concise History of Ancient Greece, 1973; Alexander of Macedon 356–323 BC: a historical biography, 1974, repr. 1991; Ovid: The Erotic Poems (trans.), 1982; Beyond the Wild Wood: the world of Kenneth Grahame, 1982; Medium and Message Reconsidered: the changing functions of classical translation, 1986; Classical Bearings: interpreting ancient history and culture, 1989; Alexander to Actium: the historical evolution of the Hellenistic Age, 1990; (ed) Hellenistic History and Culture, 1993; Yannis Ritsos: The Fourth Dimension (trans.), 1993; Ovid: The Poems of Exile (trans.), 1994; Apollonios Rhodios: The Argonautika (trans. and commentary), 1997. *Recreations:* travel, swimming, spear-fishing, table-tennis, amateur archæology, avoiding urban life. *Address:* c/o Department of Classics, University of Iowa, 202 Schaeffer Hall, Iowa City, IA 52242, USA. *T:* (319) 3352323, *Fax:* (319) 3352326; *e-mail:* peter-green-1@uiowa.edu. *Club:* Savile.

GREEN, Robert James; Member (Lib Dem), Reading Borough Council, since 1995; Mayor of Reading, 2000–01; *b* 27 Jan. 1937; *er s* of Ronald Percy Green and Doris Rose (*née* Warman); *m* 1960, Jill Marianne Small; one *d* (one *s* decd). *Educ:* Kent College, Canterbury. Executive Officer, Board of Trade, 1957; Asst Principal, 1963, Principal, 1967, Min. of Housing and Local Govt; Secretary, Water Resources Board, 1972–74; Asst Secretary: Dept of the Environment, 1974; Dept of Transport, 1980; Under Sec., 1982; Regl Dir, Northern Reg., 1982–83, and Yorks and Humberside Reg., 1982–86; Dir of Rural Affairs, DoE, 1988–91; Dir, Local Govt, 1991–92; Prin. Estabt and Finance Officer, Office of the Rail Regulator, 1993–94. Non-exec. Dir, Butterley Bricks Ltd, 1988–90. Mem. (Lib Dem), Berks CC, 1995–98. *Recreation:* theatre, including amateur dramatics. *Address:* Runge's Cottage, 11 St Andrews Road, Caversham, Reading RG4 7PH.

GREEN, Maj.-Gen. Robert Leslie Stuart; *b* 1 July 1925; *s* of Leslie Stuart Green and Eliza Dorothea Andrew; *m* 1952, Nancy Isobel Collier; two *d*. *Educ:* Chorlton Sch. 2nd Bn Black Watch, India, 1944–46; 6 Airborne Div., Palestine, 1946; 2 Parachute Bde, UK and Germany, 1946–47; 1st Bn HLI, UK, ME and Cyprus, 1947–56; ptsc 1959; jssc 1962; 1st Bn Royal Highland Fusiliers, UK, Germany and Gibraltar, 1959–69, Comd 1967–69; staff apptmt 1970; Military Dir of Studies, RMCS, 1970–72; Sen. Military Officer, Royal Armament Res. and Develt Estabt, 1973–75; Vice-Pres., Ordnance Bd, 1976–78, Pres., March-June 1978. Col, The Royal Highland Fusiliers, 1979–91. Hon. Vice Pres., CARE, 1995– (Exec. Gov., 1980–90; Chm., 1991–95). Freeman, City of London, 1983. FIMgt. *Recreations:* fishing, music. *Address:* Royal Bank of Scotland, 43 Curzon Street, Mayfair, W1Y 7RF. *Club:* Naval and Military.

GREEN, Rodney Alan Rupert; Chief Executive, Leicester City Council, since 1996; *b* 7 Feb. 1953; *s* of Timothy Green and Mercy Green (*née* Mathison); *m* 1975, Helen Frances Benjamin; two *s*. *Educ:* Christ's Hosp., Horsham; Emmanuel Coll., Cambridge (MA 1974). Greater London Council: grad. trainee, Dir-Gen.'s Dept, 1974–76; Scientific Br. Admin. Officer, 1976–78; Surrey County Council: Head, Teaching Personnel Section, 1978–82; Principal: Schools, 1982–84; Special Needs, 1984–87; Asst Co. Educn Officer, 1987–91; Asst Chief Exec., W Glamorgan CC, 1991–96. Director: Leics TEC, 1998–2001; Nat. Space Centre, 1998– (Vice-Chm., Propco, 1999–2001); Leicester Regeneration Co., 2001–. *Recreations:* films, theatre, travel, Rugby, swimming, Biblical studies. *Address:* Leicester City Council, New Walk Centre, Welford Place, Leicester LE1 6ZG. *T:* (0116) 252 6000.

GREEN, Lt-Col Sir Simon (Lycett), 5th Bt *cr* 1886, of Wakefield, Yorkshire and Ken Hill, Norfolk; TD 1947; DL; Chairman, Green's Economiser Group plc, 1956–83; *b* 11 July 1912; *s* of Sir Edward Arthur Lycett Green, 3rd Bt and Elizabeth Green (*née* Williams); S brother, 1996; *m* 1st, 1935, Gladys (marr. diss. 1971), *d* of Arthur Ranicar; one *d*; 2nd, 1971, Mary, *d* of George Ramsden. *Educ:* Eton; Magdalene Coll., Cambridge (BA). Served War, 1939–45. Lt-Col comdg Queen's Own Yorkshire Dragoons Yeomanry, 1947–51. DL WR Yorks, 1952; JP Wakefield, 1959. *Recreations:* shooting, racing. *Heir: cousin* Edward Patrick Lycett Green [*b* 14 Oct. 1950; *m* 1st, 1971, Corden Sarah (marr. diss. 1975), *d* of C. B. Stretton Wilson; 2nd, 1977, Annette Patricia Josephine, *d* of O. P. J. Rochfort; two *d*]. *Address:* Cliff Bank, N Rigton, Leeds LS17 0BZ. *T:* (01423) 734582.

GREEN, Stephen Keith; Executive Director, Investment Banking and Markets, HSBC Holdings plc, since 1998; *b* 7 Nov. 1948; *s* of late Dudley Keith Green and of Dorothy Rosamund Mary Green; *m* 1971, Janian Joy; two *d*. *Educ:* Lancing Coll.; Exeter Coll., Oxford (BA PPE); MIT (MSc Pol Sci.). ODA, FCO, 1971–77; McKinsey & Co. Inc., 1977–82; HongKong & Shanghai Banking Corp. Ltd, 1982–92; HSBC Hldgs plc, 1993–. Member, Supervisory Bd: HSBC Trinkaus & Burkhardt KGaA, Germany, 1993–; Crédit Commercial de France, 2001–; Director: HSBC Bank plc, 1995–; PEC Concerts Ltd, 1999–. Dir, Poplar Housing and Regeneration Community Assoc., 2000–. Ordained deacon, 1987; priest, 1988; NSM, dio. of London. *Publication:* Serving God? Serving Mammon?, 1996. *Recreations:* opera, art, European literature, walking. *Address:* HSBC Holdings plc, Thames Exchange, 10 Queen Street Place, EC4R 1BQ. *T:* (020) 7336 3354. *Club:* Athenæum.

GREEN, Susan Valerie; District Judge (Magistrates' Courts), Inner London, since 2001; *b* 1 Nov. 1954; *d* of Nat Green and Ettie Green (*née* Blacker). *Educ:* Birmingham Univ. (LLB); Coll. of Law, Guildford. Admitted solicitor, 1981; J. P. Malnick and Co., subsequently Malnick & Rance: articled clerk, 1979–81; Asst Solicitor, 1981-82; Partner, 1982-98; Consultant, Traymans, 1998-2000. Formerly Sec. and Pres., NE London Law Soc.; Pres., London Criminal Courts Solicitors' Assoc., 1998-99. *Recreations:* sports, cookery, travel, all things Australasian. *Address:* c/o Camberwell Green Magistrates' Court, D'Eynsford Street, SE5 7UP. *Club:* Two Brydges.

GREEN, Terence Anthony; Chief Executive, Bhs Ltd, since 2000; *b* 9 Oct. 1951; *s* of Henry Green and Nora Green (*née* Sayers), *m* 1981, Geraldine A. Daniels (marr. diss. 1996); one *s* two *d*; one *d* by Vanessa Field. *Educ:* Liverpool Univ. (BSc Maths, Stats and Computer Sci.). Exec. Dir, Burton Gp plc, 1992–98; Chief Executive: Debenhams, 1992–98; Topshop and Top Man, 1995–98; Debenhams plc, 1998–2000; Debenhams demerged from Burton Gp, 1998. Non-exec. Dir, First Choice Holidays plc, 1997–. FRSA 1997. *Recreations:* theatre, food, opera, reading, collecting art and fine wines. *Address:* (office) Marylebone House, 129–137 Marylebone Road, NW1 5QD.

GREEN, Terence Arthur; Director and Deputy Group Chief Executive, National Westminster Bank, 1987–89; *b* 19 May 1934; *m* 1957, Leeta (*née* Beales); two *s* one *d*. *Educ:* South East Essex County Technical College; Harvard Business School (AMP 1980). ACIB. Joined Westminster Bank, 1950; Dep. Gen. Manager, Internat. Banking Div., Nat. Westminster Bank, 1982; Gen. Manager, Business Development Div., 1985. *Recreations:* golf, cricket, fishing.

GREEN, Theresa Mary; Chairman, Royal Marsden NHS Trust, since 1998; *b* 29 July 1964; *d* of Richard Buckmaster and Jacqueline Buckmaster (*née* Leche); *m* 1990, Michael Philip Green, *qv*; three *s* one *d*. *Educ:* Putney High Sch.; Lady Margaret Hall, Oxford (MA); City Univ. (LLB 1993). Called to the Bar, Middle Temple, 1994. Head of Corporate Communications, Carlton Communications Plc, 1986–90. Non-exec. Dir, Royal Berkshire and Battle Hosps NHS Trust, 1994–98. Member: Res. Ethics Cttee, Royal Marsden Hosp., 1994–98 (Chm., 1996); Council and Bd of Mgt, Inst. of Cancer Res., 1998–. Trustee, Nat. Portrait Gall., 1999–. *Address:* Royal Marsden Hospital NHS Trust, Fulham Road, SW3 6JJ.

GREEN, Thomas Charles, CB 1971; Chief Charity Commissioner, 1966–75; *b* 13 Oct. 1915; *s* of late Charles Harold Green and late Hilda Emma Green (*née* Thomas); *m* 1945, Beryl Eva Barber, *widow* of Lieut N. Barber; one *d* (and one step *d*). *Educ:* Eltham Coll.; Oriel Coll., Oxford. Entered Home Office, 1938. Served with RAF, 1940–45. Asst Secretary: Home Office, 1950–64; Charity Commn, 1964–65. UK representative on UN Commn on Narcotic Drugs, 1957–64. Nuffield Travelling Fellowship, 1959–60. *Recreations:* gardening, photography. *Address:* Coombe Bungalow, Coombe Lane, Compton Bishop, Somerset BS26 2HE.

GREEN, Rev. Vivian Hubert Howard, DD, FRHistS; Fellow and Tutor in History, 1951–83, Rector, 1983–87, Hon. Fellow, 1987, Lincoln College, Oxford; *b* 18 Nov. 1915; *s* of Hubert James and Edith Eleanor Playle Green; unmarried. *Educ:* Bradfield Coll., Berks; Trinity Hall, Cambridge (Scholar). Goldsmiths' Exhibnr; 1st Cl. Hist. Tripos, Parts I and II; Lightfoot Schol. in Ecclesiastical Hist.; Thirlwall Medal and Prize, 1941; MA 1941; MA Oxon by incorp., 1951; DD Cambridge, 1958; DD Oxon by incorp., 1958. Gladstone Research Studentship, St Deiniol's Library, Hawarden, 1937–38; Fellow of St Augustine's Coll., Canterbury, 1939–48; Chaplain, Exeter Sch. and St Luke's Training Coll., Exeter, 1940–42; Chaplain and Asst Master, Sherborne Sch., Dorset, 1942–51; Lincoln College, Oxford: Chaplain, 1951–69; Sen. Tutor, 1953–62 and 1974–77; Sub-Rector, 1970–83; acting Rector, 1972–73. Deacon, 1939; Priest, 1940. Select Preacher, Oxford, 1959–60, 1992. Vis. Prof. of History, Univ. of S Carolina, 1982. *Publications:* Bishop Reginald Pecock, 1945; The Hanoverians, 1948; From St Augustine to William Temple, 1948; Renaissance and Reformation, 1952; The Later Plantagenets, 1955; Oxford Common Room, 1957; The Young Mr Wesley, 1961; The Swiss Alps, 1961; Martin Luther and the Reformation, 1964; John Wesley, 1964; Religion at Oxford and Cambridge (historical survey), 1964; The Universities, 1969; Medieval Civilization in Western Europe, 1971; A History of Oxford University, 1974; The Commonwealth of

Lincoln College 1427–1977, 1979; Love in a Cool Climate: the letters of Mark Pattison and Meta Bradley 1879–1884, 1985; (ed) Memoirs of an Oxford Don: Mark Pattison, 1988; (with William Scoular) A Question of Guilt: the murder of Nancy Eaton, 1988; The Madness of Kings, 1993; A New History of Christianity, 1996; The European Reformation, 1998; contributor to: Dictionary of English Church History (ed Ollard, Crosse and Bond); The Oxford Dictionary of the Christian Church (ed Cross); European Writers, The Middle Ages and Renaissance (ed W. T. H. Jackson and G. Stade), vols I and II, 1983; The History of the University of Oxford, vol. V, The Eighteenth Century (ed L. S. Sutherland and L. G. Mitchell), 1986. *Address:* Lincoln College, Oxford OX1 3DR. *T:* (01865) 279830; Calendars, Burford, Oxford OX8 4LS. *T:* (01993) 823214.

GREEN-PRICE, Sir Robert (John), 5th Bt *cr* 1874; landowner; Assistant Professor of English, Chiba University of Commerce, 1982–97; *b* 22 Oct. 1940; *o s* of Sir John Green-Price, 4th Bt, and Irene Marion (*d* 1954), *d* of Major Sir (Ernest) Guy Lloyd, 1st Bt, DSO; *S* father, 1964. *Educ:* Shrewsbury. Army Officer, 1961–69; Captain, RCT, retd. ADC to Governor of Bermuda, 1969–72. Lectr in English, Teikyo Univ., 1975–82. Part-time Lecturer: Keio Univ., 1977–97; Waseda Univ., 1986–97; Guest Lectr, NHK Radio, 1978–83. *Heir: uncle* Powell Norman Dansey Green-Price [*b* 22 July 1926; *m* 1963, Ann Stella, *d* of late Brig. Harold George Howson, CBE, MC, TD; one *s* one *d*].

GREENALL, family name of **Baron Daresbury**.

GREENAWAY, Prof. David; Pro-Vice-Chancellor, since 1994, and Professor of Economics, since 1987, University of Nottingham; *b* 20 March 1952; *s* of David and Agnes Greenaway; *m* 1975, Susan Elizabeth Hallam; two *s*. *Educ:* Henry Mellish Grammar Sch.; London Univ. (BSc ext. 1974); Liverpool Univ. (MCom 1975); DLitt Nottingham 1997. Lectr in Econs, Leicester Poly., 1975–78; University of Buckingham: Lectr, 1978–83; Sen. Lectr, 1983–85; Reader, 1985–86; Prof. of Econs, 1986–87. Non-exec. Dir, Nottingham HA, 1994–98. Member: Council, 1990–97, Exec., 1991–97, REconS; Acad. Adv. Council, IEA, 1991–; Technology Foresight Steering Gp, 1994–95; Council, ESRC, 1997–; Armed Forces Pay Review Body, 1997–; Chair, Panel for Econs and Econometrics, RAE, HEFCE, 2001 (Vice Chair, 1996). Adviser: UNIDO, 1983; World Bank, 1986, 1988; GATT, 1986; DTI, 1994; UNECE, 1994; Commonwealth Secretariat, 1997; Asian Develt Bank, 1997; Caribbean Regl Negotiating Machinery, 2000. Gov., NIESR, 1995–. FRSA 1994; AcSS 2000. *Publications:* International Trade Policy, 1983; (jtly) Economics of Intra-Industry Trade, 1986; (jtly) Imperfect Competition and International Trade, 1986; Companion to Contemporary Economic Thought, 1991; (jtly) Evaluating Trade Policy in Developing Countries, 1993; (jtly) Economics of Commodity Markets, 1999; Globalisation and Labour Markets, 2000; papers in learned jls. *Recreations:* golf, tennis, football, wine, reading. *Address:* School of Economics, University of Nottingham, University Park, Nottingham NG7 2RD. *T:* (0115) 951 5469; 238 Ruddington Lane, Wilford, Nottingham NG11 7DQ.

GREENAWAY, Frank, MA, PhD; CChem, FRSC, FSA, FMA; Research Fellow, The Science Museum, 1980–91 (Hon. Fellow, 1992); Reader in the History of Science, Davy-Faraday Research Laboratory of the Royal Institution, 1970–85; *b* 9 July 1917; 3rd *s* of late Henry James Greenaway; *m* 1942, Margaret (Miranda), 2nd *d* of late R. G. Heegaard Warner and *widow* of John Raymond Brumfit; three *d* (one *s* decd), and one step *s*. *Educ:* Cardiff High Sch.; Jesus Coll., Oxford (Meyricke Exhibitioner); University Coll. London. MA Oxon, PhD London. Served War of 1939–45, RAOC, as Inspecting Ordnance Officer, 1940–41 (invalided). Science Master: Bournemouth Sch., 1941–42; Epsom Gram. Sch., 1942–43; Passport Control, 1943–44; Research Labs, Kodak Ltd, 1944–49; Asst Keeper, Science Museum, 1949; Dep. Keeper, 1959; Keeper, Dept of Chemistry, 1967–80. Regents' Fellow, Smithsonian Instn, Washington, DC, 1985. Member Council: Brit. Soc. for the Hist. of Science, 1958–68, 1974–78 (Vice-Pres. 1962–65); Museums Assoc., 1961–70, 1973–76 (Hon. Editor, 1965–70); Royal Instn, 1990–93 (Vice-Pres., 1992–93; Chm., Cttee of Visitors, 1964–65). Mem. Brit. Nat. Cttee of Internat. Council of Museums, 1956–58, 1962–71, 1977–83; Membre Correspondant de l'Académie Internationale d'Histoire des Sciences, 1963. Member: Council, Soc. for History of Alchemy and Chemistry, 1967–74 (Sec., 1967–74); History of Medicine Adv. Panel, The Wellcome Trust, 1968–74; Higher Educn Adv. Cttee, The Open Univ., 1970–73; British Nat. Cttee for Hist. of Sci., 1972–81; British Nat. Cttee, ICSU, 1972–77; Council, Internat. Union of the Hist. and Philos. of Science, 1972–81 (Sec., 1972–77); Council of Management, Royal Philharmonic Soc., 1980–84, 1986–89; President: Commonwealth Assoc. of Museums, 1979–83; Nonsuch Antiquarian Soc., 1990–97. Boerhaave Medal, Leyden Univ., 1968. *Publications:* Science Museums in Developing Countries, 1962; John Dalton and the Atom, 1966; (ed) Lavoisier's Essays Physical and Chemical, 1971; (ed with Roger French) Science in the Early Roman Empire, 1986; Science International: the history of the International Council of Scientific Unions, 1996; Editor, Royal Institution Archives, 1971; Official Publications of the Science Museum; Papers on history of chemistry and on museology. *Recreations:* music, travel. *Address:* 5 Lyefield Court, Emmer Green, Reading RG4 8AP. *T:* (0118) 946 4314. *Club:* Athenæum.

See also C. J. Brumfit.

GREENAWAY, Sir John (Michael Burdick), 3rd Bt *cr* 1933, of Coombe, Surrey; farmer, since 1980; *b* 9 Aug. 1944; *o s* of Sir Derek Burdick Greenaway, 2nd Bt, CBE, and of Sheila Beatrice Greenaway (*née* Lockett); *S* father, 1994; *m* 1982, Susan Margaret (*née* Birch); one *s* one *d*. *Educ:* Harrow Sch.; Grenoble Univ. The Life Guards, 1965–70. Dir, Daniel Greenaway & Sons Ltd, 1970–79. *Recreations:* ski-ing, tennis, riding. *Heir: s* Thomas Edward Burdick Greenaway, *b* 3 April 1985. *Address:* Lois Weedon House, Weedon Lois, Towcester, Northants NN12 8PJ. *T:* (01327) 860472.

GREENAWAY, Peter; film director, painter and writer; *b* April 1942; *m*; two *d*. *Educ:* Forest Sch.; Walthamstow Coll. of Art. Film Editor, Central Office of Information, 1965–76. Maker of short films, 1966–, of feature length films, 1978–. *Exhibitions:* Lord's Gall., 1964; The Physical Self, Rotterdam, 1991; 100 Objects to Represent the World, Acad. of Fine Arts, Vienna, 1992; Flying Out of this World, Louvre, 1992; Watching Water, Venice, 1993; Some Organising Principles, Swansea, 1993; The Audience of Macon, Cardiff, 1993; The Stairs, Geneva, 1994, Munich, 1995; Spellbound, London, 1996; Flying Over Water, Barcelona, 1997; *one-man shows:* Canterbury, 1989; Carcassone, Paris, 1989; NY, Melbourne, Liège, Tokyo, Fukoa, Munich, Copenhagen, Oddense, Brussels, 1990; Brentford, Dublin, 1991; Bremen, NY, 1992; Tempe, Ariz, and Salzburg, 1994; Biel-Bienne, Switzerland, New York, and Munich, 1995; Milan, Ghent, and Thessaloniki, 1996; Manchester, 1998; Edinburgh, 1999; *group shows* include: Freezeframe, Lamont Gall., 1996; The Director's Eye, Mus. of Modern Art, Oxford, 1996. *Films:* (writer and director): Train, 1966; Tree, 1966; Five Postcards from Capital Cities, 1967; Revolution, 1967; Intervals, 1969; Erosion, 1971; H is for House, 1973; Windows, 1975; Water Wrackets, 1975; Goole by Numbers, 1976; Dear Phone, 1977; 1–1Co, 1978; A Walk Through H, 1978; Vertical Features Remake, 1978; The Falls, 1980 (Special Award, BFI); Act of God, 1981 (Best short film, Melbourne Film Fest.); Zandra Rhodes, 1981; The Draughtsman's Contract, 1982; Four American Composers, 1983; Making a Splash, 1984; (jtly) A TV Dante-Canto V, 1984; Inside Rooms – The Bathroom, 1985; A Zed and Two Noughts, 1985; The Belly of an Architect, 1986; Fear of Drowning, 1988; Drowning by Numbers, 1988 (Prize for Best Artistic Contribution, Cannes Film Fest.); The Cook, the Thief, his Wife and her Lover, 1989; Prospero's Books, 1990; M is for Man, Music, Mozart, 1991; Rosa, 1992; Darwin, 1992; The Baby of Macon, 1993; The Stairs, Geneva, 1994; The Pillow Book, 1996; The Bridge, 1996; 8½ Women, 1999; *operas:* Rosa: a Horse Drama, 1994; Writing to Vermeer, 1999. Officier de l'Ordre des Arts et des Lettres (France), 1998. *Publications:* The Falls, 1993; filmscripts and exhibn catalogues. *Address:* c/o The Vue, 387b King Street, W6 9NJ.

GREENBERG, Joanna Elishever Gabrielle; QC 1994; a Recorder, since 1995; *b* 28 Nov. 1950; *d* of Ivan Marion Greenberg and Doris Rosalie Greenberg (*née* Sandground). *Educ:* Brondesbury and Kilburn High Sch. for Girls; King's Coll. London (LLB, AKC). Called to the Bar, Gray's Inn, 1972. An Asst Recorder, 1992–95. *Address:* 3 Temple Gardens, Temple, EC4Y 9AU. *T:* (020) 7583 1155.

GREENBURY, Sir Richard, Kt 1992; Chairman, 1991–99, and Chief Executive, 1988–99, Marks & Spencer plc; *b* 31 July 1936; *s* of Richard Oswald Greenbury and Dorothy (*née* Lewis); *m* 1st, 1959, Sian Eames Hughes (marr. diss.); two *s* two *d*; 2nd, 1985, Gabrielle Mary McManus (marr. diss. 1996); 3rd, 1996, Sian Eames (*née* Hughes). *Educ:* Ealing County Grammar Sch. Joined Marks & Spencer Ltd as Jun. Management Trainee, 1952; Alternate Dir, 1970; Full Dir, 1972; Jt Man. Dir, 1978–85; Chief Operating Officer, 1986–88. Non-executive Director: British Gas, 1976–87; MB Group (formerly Metal Box), 1985–89; ICI, 1992–93; Lloyds Bank, 1992–97; Zeneca, 1993–99; Electronics Boutique, 2000–; Mem. Supervisory Bd, Philips Electronics NV, 1998–. Mem., UK Adv. Bd, British American Chamber of Commerce, 1989–99. Trustee, Royal Acad., 1992–97. *Recreations:* tennis (Member Mddx County Team for 12 years, has also played for International Tennis Club of GB), reading, music. *Address:* c/o Electronics Boutique, Link House, Ellesfield Avenue, Bracknell RG12 8TB. *Clubs:* All England Lawn Tennis and Croquet, International Tennis Club of GB.

GREENE, family name of **Baron Greene of Harrow Weald**.

GREENE OF HARROW WEALD, Baron *cr* 1974 (Life Peer), of Harrow; **Sidney Francis Greene,** Kt 1970; CBE 1966; Director: Trades Union Unit Trust, 1970–80; RTZ Corporation, 1975–80; Times Newspapers Holdings Ltd, 1980–82 (Times Newspapers Ltd, 1975–80); *b* 12 Feb. 1910; *s* of Frank James Greene and Alice (*née* Kerrod); *m* 1936, Masel Elizabeth Carter; three *d*. *Educ:* elementary. Joined Railway Service, 1924; appointed Union Organiser, 1944, Asst Gen. Sec., 1954, Gen. Sec., Nat. Union of Railwaymen, 1957–75. Mem., TUC Gen. Council, 1957–75 (Chm., 1969–70); Chm., TUC Economic Cttee, 1968–75. Member: National Economic Development Council, 1962–75; Advisory Council, ECGD, 1967–70; part-time Member: Southern Electricity Board, 1964–77; Nat. Freight Corp., 1973–77; a Dir, Bank of England, 1970–78. JP London, 1941–65. FCIT. *Recreations:* reading, gardening. *Address:* 26 Kynaston Wood, Boxtree Road, Harrow Weald, Mddx HA3 6UA.

GREENE, Anthony Hamilton Millard K.; *see* Kirk-Greene.

GREENE, Graham Carleton, CBE 1986; Chairman of Trustees, British Museum, 1996–July 2002 (Trustee, since 1978); Chairman, London Merchant Securities plc, since 2000 (Director, since 1996); *b* 10 June 1936; *s* of Sir Hugh Carleton Greene, KCMG, OBE and Helga Mary Connolly; *m* 1957, Judith Margaret (marr. diss.), *d* of Rt Hon. Lord Gordon-Walker, CH, PC; *m* 1976, Sally Georgina Horton, *d* of Sidney Wilfred Eaton; one *s*, and one step *s* one step *d*. *Educ:* Eton; University Coll., Oxford (MA). Merchant Banking, Dublin, New York and London, 1957–58; Secker & Warburg Ltd, 1958–62; Jonathan Cape, 1962–90 (Man. Dir, 1966–88). Director: Chatto, Virago, Bodley Head & Jonathan Cape Ltd, 1969–88 (Chm., 1970–88); Jackdaw Publications Ltd (Chm. 1964–88); Cape Goliard Press Ltd, 1967–88; Guinness Mahon Holdings Ltd, 1968–79; Australasian Publishing Co. Pty Ltd, 1969–88 (Chm., 1978–88); Sprint Productions Ltd, 1971–80; Book Reps (New Zealand) Ltd, 1971–88 (Chm., 1984–88); CVBC Services Ltd (Chm. 1972–88); Guinness Peat Group PLC, 1973–87; Grantham Book Storage Ltd (Chm. 1974–88); Triad Paperbacks Ltd, 1975–88; Chatto, Virago, Bodley Head & Jonathan Cape Australia Pty Ltd (Chm., 1977–88); Greene, King PLC, 1979–; Statesman & Nation Publishing Co. Ltd, 1980–85 (Chm., 1981–85); Statesman Publishing Co. Ltd, 1980–85 (Chm., 1981–85); Nation Pty Co. Ltd (Chm., 1981–87); New Society Ltd (Chm., 1984–87); Random House Inc., 1987–88; Random House UK Ltd, 1988–90; British Museum Co. (formerly British Museum Publications) Ltd, 1988– (Chm., 1988–96); Merlin Internat. Green, subseq. Jupiter Internat. Green Investment Trust plc, 1989–; Henry Sotheran Ltd, 1990–; Ed Victor Ltd, 1991–; Rosemary Sandberg Ltd, 1991–; Libra KFT (Budapest), 1991–. Pres., Publishers Assoc., 1977–79 (Mem. Council, 1969–88; Trustee, 1995–97); Member: Book Develt Council, 1970–79 (Dep. Chm., 1972–73); Internat. Cttee, Internat. Publishers Assoc., 1977–88 (Exec. Cttee, 1981–88); Groupe des Editeurs de Livres de la CEE, (Fedn of European Publishers), 1977–86 (Pres., 1984–86); Arts Council Working Party Sub-Cttee on Public Lending Right, 1970; Paymaster General's Working Party on Public Lending Right, 1970–72; Board, British Council, 1977–88; Chairman: Nat. Book League, 1974–76 (Dep. Chm., 1971–74); Nat. Book Cttee, 1994–95; Museums and Galls Commn, 1991–96; Mem. Gen. Cttee, Royal Literary Fund, 1975. Chm., Friends of Musica nel Chiostro, 1993–; Dir, Garsington Opera Ltd, 1996– (Mem. Adv. Cttee, 1990–96); Mem., Adv. Bd, Mus. of Modern Art, Oxford, 1992–96. Trustee: George Bernard Shaw Estate, 1986–; Han Suyin Fund for Scientific Exchange, 1989–; Open Coll. of the Arts, 1990–97; Chm., BM Develt Trust, 1986–93 (Vice Chm., 1993–); Pres., BM Foundn Inc., 1989–90; Dir, American Friends of BM, 1990–. Vice-Pres., GB-China Centre, 1997– (Chm., 1986–97). Gov., Compton Verney House Trust, 1995–. Freeman, City of London, 1960; Liveryman, Fishmongers' Co., 1960–. Chevalier de l'Ordre des Arts et des Lettres, France, 1985. *Address:* 6 Bayley Street, Bedford Square, WC1B 3HB. *T:* (020) 7304 4101.

GREENE, Jenny, (Mrs Michael Boys-Greene); Editor, Country Life, 1986–93, retired; *b* 9 Feb. 1937; *d* of Captain James Wilson Greene and Mary Emily Greene; *m* 1971, John Gilbert (marr. diss. 1987); *m* 1994, Michael Boys-Greene. *Educ:* Rochelle Sch., Cork; Trinity Coll., Dublin; Univ. of Montpellier, France. Researcher, Campbell-Johnson Ltd, 1963–64; Account-Exec., Central News, 1964–65; Account-Exec., Pemberton Advertising, 1965–66; Publicity Exec., Revlon, 1966–71; Beauty Editor, Woman's Own, 1971–75; Features Writer and Theatre Critic, Manchester Evening News, 1975–77; Asst Editor, Woman's Own, 1977–78; Editor: Homes and Gardens, 1978–86; A La Carte, 1984–85; columnist, Today, 1985–87. Contrib., Country Life and Gardens Illustrated, 1998–. *Recreations:* gardening, cooking. *Address:* En Chau, 71520 Trivy, France.

GREENE, Sir (John) Brian M.; *see* Massy-Greene.

GREENER, Sir Anthony (Armitage), Kt 1999; Chairman, University for Industry Ltd, since 2000; Deputy Chairman, British Telecommunications plc, since 2001; *b* 26 May 1940; *s* of William and Diana Marianne Greener; *m* 1974, Min Ogilvie; one *s* one *d*. *Educ:* Marlborough Coll. FCMA. Marketing Manager, Thames Board Mills, 1969; Retail

Controller 1972, Dir 1974, Alfred Dunhill Ltd; Man. Dir, Alfred Dunhill Ltd, subseq. Dunhill Holdings plc, 1975; Man. Dir, United Distillers, 1987–92, Chm., 1996–97; Guinness PLC: Dir, 1986–97; Jt Man. Dir, 1989–91; Chief Exec., 1992–97; Chm., 1993–97; Jt Chm., 1997–98, Chm., 1998–2000, Diageo plc. Director: Louis Vuitton Moet Hennessy, 1989–97; Reed International, 1990–98; Reed Elsevier, 1993–98. *Recreations:* ski-ing, sailing. *Address:* Ufi Ltd, 5th Floor, 88 Kingsway, Holborn, WC2B 6AA. *Clubs:* Royal Ocean Racing; Royal Yacht Squadron (Cowes).

GREENFIELD, Baroness *cr* 2001 (Life Peer), of Ot Moor in the County of Oxfordshire; **Susan Adele Greenfield,** CBE 2000; DPhil; Professor of Pharmacology, Oxford University, since 1996; Fellow, since 1985 and Senior Research Fellow, since 1999, Lincoln College, Oxford; Hon. Research Fellow, St Hilda's College, Oxford, since 1999; Director, Royal Institution, since 1998; *b* 1 Oct. 1950; *d* of Reginald Myer Greenfield and Doris Margaret Winifred Greenfield; *m* 1991, Peter William Atkins, *qv. Educ:* Godolphin and Latymer Sch. for Girls; St Hilda's Coll., Oxford (BA Hons Exp. Psychol. 1973; MA 1978; DPhil 1977; Hon. Fellow, 1999). Dame Catherine Fulford Sen. Scholarship, St Hugh's Coll., Oxford, 1974; MRC Training Fellow, Univ. Lab of Physiol., Oxford, 1977–81; Collège de France, Paris; Royal Soc. Study Visit Award, 1978; MRC-INSERM French Exchange Fellow, 1979–80; Oxford University: Jun. Res. Fellow, Green Coll., 1981–84; Lectr in Synaptic Pharmacol., 1985–96. Co-founder, Synaptica Ltd, 1997. Gresham Prof. of Physic, Gresham Coll., 1995–; Vis. Fellow, Inst. of Neuroscience, La Jolla, USA, 1995; Vis. Dist. Scholar, Queen's Univ., Belfast, 1996. Mem., Nat. Adv. Cttee on Cultural and Creative Educn, 1998–; Pres., ASE, 2000; Vice-Pres., Assoc. of Women in Sci. and Engrg, 2001. Trustee, Science Mus., 1998–. Presenter, Brain Story, BBC 2, 2000. Dimbleby Lectr, 1999. Hon. Fellow, Cardiff Univ., 2000. Hon. FRCP 2000. Hon. DSc: Oxford Brookes, 1997; St Andrew's, Exeter, 1998; London, N London, Sheffield Hallam, 1999; Heriot-Watt, Brunel, Buckingham, Staffordshire, 2000; Leicester, Richmond American Internat., Leeds, Birmingham, Liverpool, 2001; DUniv Open, 2001. Michael Faraday Award, Royal Soc., 1998; Woman of Distinction, Jewish Care, 1998. *Publications:* (ed with C. B. Blakemore) Mindwaves, 1987; (with G. Ferry) Journey to the Centers of the Brain, 1994; Journey to the Centers of the Mind, 1995; (ed) The Human Mind Explained, 1996; The Human Brain: a guided tour, 1997; (ed) Brain Power, 2000; Private Life of the Brain, 2000; Brain Story, 2000; contribs to learned jls, press and media. *Recreations:* aerobics, travel. *Address:* Lincoln College, Oxford OX1 3DR. *T:* (01865) 271628.

GREENFIELD, Prof. (Archibald) David (Mant), CBE 1977; FRCP; Foundation Dean of the Medical School, 1966–81 and Professor of Physiology, 1966–82 in the University of Nottingham; now Professor Emeritus; *b* 31 May 1917; *s* of late A. W. M. Greenfield, MA, and Winifred (*née* Peck), Parkstone, Dorset; *m* 1943, Margaret (*née* Duane) (*d* 1999); one *s* one *d. Educ:* Poole Grammar Sch.; St Mary's Hospital Medical Sch. BSc London, 1st class Hons Physiology, 1937; MB, BS, 1940, MSc 1947, DSc 1953, London; FRCP, 1973. Dunville Prof. of Physiology in the Queen's Univ. of Belfast, 1948–64; Prof. of Physiology in the Univ. of London, at St Mary's Hosp. Med. Sch., 1964–67. Sometime Examr, Oxford, Cambridge and 21 other Univs, RCS and RCSI; Chm., Special Trustees, Nottingham Univ. Hosps, 1984–90. Member: Physiol. Systems Bd, MRC, 1976–77; UGC, 1977–82 (Chm. Med. and Dental Sub-Cttees, Assessor to MRC); UPGC, Hong Kong, 1984–89 (Mem. 1981–89 and Chm. 1985–89, Med. Sub-Cttee); GMC and GMC Educn Cttee, 1979–82; Med. Acad. Adv. Cttee, Chinese Univ., Hong Kong, 1976–80; Foundn Cttee, Sultan Qaboos Univ., Oman, 1981–86; Sheffield RHB, 1968–74; Nottingham Univ. HMC, 1969–74; Notts AHA(T), 1974–79. Pres., Sect. of Biomed. Scis, British Assoc. for Advancement of Sci., 1972; Mem., Biochemical and Medical Research Societies. Hon. Mem., Physiological Soc., 1987. Chm., Editorial Bd, Monographs of the Physiological Soc., 1975–79; Member, Editorial Board: Amer. Heart Jl, 1959–66; Clinical Science, 1960–65; Cardiovascular Research, 1966–79; Circulation Res., 1967–73. OStJ 1978. Hon. LLD Nottingham, 1977; Hon DSc QUB, 1978. Order of Sultan Qaboos of Oman, 2nd Class, 1986. *Publications:* papers on control of circulation of the blood, mainly in Lancet, Journal of Physiology, Clinical Science, and Journal of Applied Physiology. *Recreations:* sketching, bird watching, travel. *Address:* 25 Sutton Passeys Crescent, Nottingham NG8 1BX. *T:* (0115) 978 2424.

GREENFIELD, Edward Harry, OBE 1994; Chief Music Critic, The Guardian, 1977–93; *b* 30 July 1928; *s* of Percy Greenfield and Mabel (*née* Hall). *Educ:* Westcliff High Sch.; Trinity Hall, Univ. of Cambridge (MA). Joined staff of Manchester Guardian, 1953: Record Critic, 1955; Music Critic, 1964; succeeded Sir Neville Cardus as Chief Music Critic, 1977. Broadcaster on music and records for BBC radio, 1957–. Mem., critics' panel, Gramophone, 1960–. Pres., Fedn of Recorded Music Socs, 1997–. Master, Art Workers Guild, 2002. Hon. GSM 1991. Goldener Verdienstzeichen, Salzburg, 1981. *Publications:* Puccini: keeper of the seal, 1958; monographs on Joan Sutherland, 1972, and André Previn, 1973; (with Robert Layton, Ivan March and initially Denis Stevens) Stereo Record Guide, 9 vols, 1960–74; Penguin Stereo Record Guide, 5th edn 1986; (jtly) Penguin Guide to Compact Discs, Cassettes and LPs, 1986, 4th edn as Penguin Guide to Compact Discs, 1992, 12th edn 2001; Penguin Guide to Opera on Compact Discs, 1993. *Recreations:* work, living in Spitalfields. *Address:* 16 Folgate Street, E1 6BX. *T:* (020) 7377 7555. *Club:* Critics' Circle.

GREENFIELD, Howard; *see* Greenfield, R. H.

GREENFIELD, Dr Peter Rex; Senior Principal Medical Officer, Department of Health (formerly of Health and Social Security), 1983–91, retired; *b* 1 Dec. 1931; *s* of late Rex Youhill Greenfield and Elsie Mary Greenfield (*née* Douthwaite); *m* 1954, Faith Stella, *d* of George and Stella Gigg; eight *s* two *d. Educ:* Cheltenham College; Pembroke College, Cambridge (BA 1954; MB, BChir 1957; MA 1985); St George's Hosp. Med. Sch., London. DObst RCOG 1960. 2nd Lieut, R Signals, 1950–51; House appts, St George's Hosp., 1958; Gen. Med. Pract., Robertsbridge, Sussex, 1959–69; MO, Vinehall Sch., Robertsbridge, 1964–69; MO, Battle Hosp., 1964–69; joined DHSS, 1969; Chief Med. Advr (Social Security), 1983–86. Mem., Jt Formulary Cttee, British Nat. Formulary, 1978–82; Chm., Informal Working Gp on Effective Prescribing, 1981–82. Medical Mem., The Appeals Service, 1999–. Chm. of Trustees, Chaseley Home for Disabled Ex-Servicemen, Eastbourne, 1995–2001 (Trustee, 1983–2001). QHP 1987–90. Hon. Mem., BPA, 1991–96; Hon. FRCPCH 1996. Mem., Salehurst PCC, 1995–. *Publications:* contribs to med. jls on geriatric day care, hypothermia and DHSS Regional Med. Service. *Recreations:* golf, swimming, walking, music, pinball. *Address:* Lorne House, Bellhurst Road, Robertsbridge, East Sussex TN32 5DW. *T:* (01580) 880209.

GREENFIELD, (Robert) Howard, FCA; CIGasE; Project Director, Regional Organisation Review, British Gas plc, 1990, retired; *b* 4 Feb. 1927; *s* of James Oswald Greenfield and Doris Burt Greenfield; *m* 1951, Joyce Hedley Wells; one *s* one *d. Educ:* Rutherford Coll., Newcastle upon Tyne. FCA 1953; CIGasE 1982. Northern Gas Board, 1956–74, Regional Service Manager, 1968–74; Northern Gas: Dir of Customer Service, 1974; Dir of Marketing, 1976; Dep. Chm., 1977; Chm., N Eastern Reg., 1982–85; Regl Chm., British Gas, N Western, 1985–89. OStJ 1988. *Recreations:* salmon fishing, photography. *Address:* Manor Top, Chestnut Hill, Keswick, Cumbria CA12 4LT.

GREENGARD, Prof. Paul, PhD; Vincent Astor Professor and Head, Laboratory of Molecular and Cellular Neuroscience, Rockefeller University, New York, since 1983; *b* 11 Dec. 1925; *m* 1986, Ursula von Rydingsvard; two *s* one *d. Educ:* Hamilton Coll., NY (AB 1948); Univ. of Pennsylvania; Johns Hopkins Univ. (PhD Neurophysiol. 1953). Served USNR, 1943-46. Research posts at: Inst. of Psychiatry, Univ. of London, 1953-54; Molteno Inst., Univ. of Cambridge, 1954–55; NIMR, London, 1955–58; Lab. of Clinical Biochem., NIH, 1958–59; Dir, Dept. of Biochem., Geigy Res. Labs, NY, 1959-67; Prof. of Pharmacol. and Psychiatry, Yale Univ. Sch. of Medicine, 1968–83. Visiting Professor: Albert Einstein Coll. of Medicine, NY, 1968–70; Depts of Pharmacol. and Microbiol., Vanderbilt Univ. Sch. of Medicine, Nashville, 1968; Henry Bronson Prof. of Pharmacol., Yale Univ. Sch. of Medicine, 1981; Wellcome Vis. Prof. in Basic Med. Scis, Univ. of Iowa, 1986. Founder and Series Editor: Advances in Biochemical Psychopharmacol., 1968–; Advances in Cyclic Nucleotide and Protein Phosphorylation Res., 1971–; mem., numerous editl bds and editl adv. bds. Hon. MD Karolinska Inst., 1987. Hold numerous awards including: Award in the Neuroscis, NAS, 1991; Ralph W. Gerard Prize in Neurosci., Soc. For Neurosci., 1994; Charles A. Dana Award for Pioneering Achievements in Health, 1997; Nobel Prize in Physiol. or Medicine, 2000. *Publications:* Cyclic Nucleotides, Phosphorylated Proteins and Neuronal Function, 1978; (with E. J. Nestler) Protein Phosphorylation in the Nervous System, 1984; contrib. numerous chapters and reviews. *Address:* Laboratory of Molecular and Cellular Neuroscience, Rockefeller University, 1230 York Avenue, New York, NY 10021, USA. *T:* (212) 3278780.

GREENGROSS, family name of **Baroness Greengross**.

GREENGROSS, Baroness *cr* 2000 (Life Peer), of Notting Hill in the Royal Borough of Kensington and Chelsea; **Sally Greengross,** OBE 1993; Director General (formerly Director), Age Concern England, 1987–2000; Vice-President (Europe), International Federation on Ageing, since 1987 (Secretary General, 1982–87); Secretary General, Eurolink Age, since 1989; *b* 29 June 1935; *m* Sir Alan Greengross, *qv*; one *s* three *d. Educ:* Brighton and Hove High Sch.; LSE. Formerly linguist, executive in industry, lectr and researcher; Asst Dir, 1977–82, Dep. Dir, 1982–87, Age Concern England, Jt Chm. Bd, Age Concern Inst. of Gerontology, KCL, 1987–; Co-ordinator, Prog. for Elderly People within Second EEC Prog. to Combat Poverty, 1985–89; Vice Pres., Res. Inst. for Care of Elderly, 1987–; Member: Standing Adv. Cttee on Transport for Disabled and Elderly People, 1986–88; Adv. Cttee, Carnegie Inquiry into Third Age, 1992–93; Adv. Cttee on European Year of Older People, 1992–93; Adv. Council of European Movement, 1992–; Adv. Panel, Centre for Voluntary Orgns, LSE, 1991–; Adv. Cttee to the Sec. of State, DFEE (formely Dept of Employment), on Older Workers, 1993–97; Adv. Gp to Sec. of State, DoH, on Health of the Nation, 1991–97; Bd, World Orgn for Care in Home and Hospice, 1993–; BT Forum Develt Adv. Gp, 1994–; HEA Adv. Gp for Health Promotion and Older People, 1996–; EC Adv. Gp for Fifth Framework Prog. (R&D): Key Action on the Ageing Population, 1998–; Govt Task Gp on The Giving Age, 1999–; DTI Foresight Initiative; Exec. Bd, Campaign for Learning, 1998–; Exec. Bd, Britain in Europe, 1999–; Govt External Ref. Gp of Nat. Care Standards, 2000. Vice Pres., EXTEND, 1996–. Independent Member: UN Network on Ageing, 1983–; WHO Network on Ageing, 1983–. Former Member: Inner London Juvenile Court Panel; Management Bd, Hanover Housing Gp. Trustee: British Assoc. of Domiciliary Care Officers, 1989–; Telethon, 1992–95; One 20 Timebank, 1999–; Patron: Home Concern, 1993–; Action on Elder Abuse, 1999–; James Powell UK Trust, 1999–; Groundwork Foundn, 1999–; ESRC Connect, 1999–; Pennell Initiative, 1999–; Sheffield Inst. for Studies on Ageing, 1999–. Hon. Pres., Women for Europe, 1999–. Consultant, Jl of Educnl Gerontology, 1987–; Editl Advr, Home Care, 1993–. FRSH 1994; FRSA 1994. Hon. DLitt Ulster, 1994; DUniv Kingston, 1996. UK Woman of Europe Award, EC, 1990. *Publications:* (ed) Ageing: an adventure in living, 1985; (ed) The Law and Vulnerable Elderly People, 1986; (jtly) Living, Loving and Ageing, 1989; and others on ageing issues and social policy. *Recreations:* countryside, music. *Address:* 9 Dawson Place, W2 4TD. *T:* (020) 7229 1939. *Clubs:* Reform, Hurlingham.

GREENGROSS, Sir Alan (David), Kt 1986; DL; Managing Director, Indusmond (Diamond Tools) Ltd; Director, Blazy & Clement Ltd and associated companies; *b* 1929; *m* Sally (*see* Baroness Greengross); one *s* three *d. Educ:* University Coll. Sch.; Trinity Coll., Cambridge (Sen. Schol.; MA). Formerly Member Council, London Borough of Camden (past Alderman). Dep. Traffic Comr, 1968–70. GLC: Member (C), 1977–84; Leader, Planning and Communications Policy, 1979–81; Leader of the Opposition, 1983–84. Director: Port of London Authority, 1979–83; London First Centre, 1994–; Chm., London Regl Passengers Cttee, 1996–; Mem., Central Rail Users Consultative Cttee, 1996–. Chm., Bloomsbury and Islington HA, 1990–93. Vis Prof., City of London Polytechnic, 1988–. Dir, The Roundhouse Black Arts Centre, 1988–89. Chairman: Steering Gp, Inst. for Metropolitan Studies, 1989–; Policy Gp, Bartlett Sch. of the Built Envmt, UCL, 1993–; Dir, Built Envmt Res. Foundn, 1996–. Member, Governing Council: UCS, 1987–; UCL, 1991–. DL Greater London, 1986. *Address:* 9 Dawson Place, W2 4TD. *Clubs:* Hurlingham, Royal Society of Medicine.

GREENHALGH, Colin Ayton, OBE 1997; DL; MA; Principal, Hills Road Sixth Form College, Cambridge, since 1984; *b* 11 Aug. 1941; *s* of Robert Ayton Greenhalgh and Ethel Mary Henderson (*née* Cattermole); *m* 1966, Vivienne Christine Grocock; one *s* two *d. Educ:* Gateway Sch., Leicester; St John's Coll., Cambridge (MA); Univ. of Nottingham (PGCE). Teacher of Hist., Bradford Grammar Sch., 1964–70; Hd of Hist., Hd of Upper Sch. and Dep. Hd, Bulmershe Sch., Reading, 1970–76; Dep. Hd and Second Master, St Bartholomew's Sch., Newbury, 1976–84. Non-exec. Dir, Cambs HA, 2000–. Mem., Cambs LEA Inspectorate, 1991–92; Further Education Funding Council: Mem., Eastern Regl Cttee, 1993–98, Quality Assessment Cttee, 1997–2001; Bd Mem., Further Educn Develt Agency, 1999–2001; Mem. Appeals Panel, Oxford, Cambridge and RSA Exams Bd, 2000–. Board Member: Learning and Skills Develt Agency, 2001–; Further Educn Cttee, SHA, 1998–; Cambridgeshire Association of Secondary Heads: Sec., 1988–89; Chm., 1989–90. Mem., Stapleford Parish Council, 1996–. Governor, Stapleford Primary Sch., 1992–. Hon. Sen. Mem., Wolfson Coll., Cambridge, 1990–. Chm., Johnian Soc., St John's Coll., Cambridge, 1999– (Sec., 1992–99); Mem., Rotary Club, Cambridge. DL Cambs, 1998. *Recreations:* churches and country houses, cinema, collecting books, sport, travel, Venice. *Address:* Hills Road Sixth Form College, Cambridge CB2 2PE. *T:* (01223) 247251. *Clubs:* MCC; Hawks (Cambridge); Cambridge University Cricket, Leicestershire County Cricket.

GREENHALGH, Jack; Vice-Chairman, Cavenham Ltd, 1974–81; retired; *b* 25 July 1926; *s* of Herbert Greenhalgh and Alice May (*née* Clayton); *m* 1951, Kathleen Mary Hammond (*d* 1983); two *s* two *d. Educ:* Manchester Grammar Sch.; Trinity Coll., Cambridge (MA Hons). FIMgt. Marketing Dept, Procter & Gamble Ltd, Newcastle upon Tyne, 1950–59; Marketing Dir, Eskimo Foods Ltd, Cleethorpes, 1959–64; Dir of Continental Ops,

Compton Advertising Inc., NY, 1964–65; Cavenham Ltd, 1965–81: Man. Dir, 1968–79. *Recreations:* golf, sailing.

GREENHALGH, Paul; President, Nova Scotia College of Art and Design; *b* 21 Oct. 1955; *s* of William Greenhalgh and Marie Joan Greenhalgh; *m* 1981, Belinda Keith Hayes; two *s*. *Educ:* Bolton Smithills Grammar Sch.; Univ. of Reading (BA); Courtauld Inst., Univ. of London (MA). Lectr, Cardiff Inst., 1980–87; Dep. Curator of Ceramics and Glass, V&A Mus., 1988–92; Tutor in Art History, RCA, 1990–92; Head of Art History, Camberwell Coll. of Arts, 1992–94; Hd of Res. V&A Mus., 1994. Curator, Art Nouveau 1890–1914 exhibn, V&A and Nat. Gall. of Art, Washington, 2000, Metropolitan Mus., Tokyo, 2001. Art History Academic Editor, Manchester Univ. Press, 1989–. Mem., Crafts Council Educn Cttee, 1992–. *Publications:* Ephemeral Vistas: great exhibitions, expositions universelles and worlds fairs 1850–1939, 1988; (ed) Modernism in Design, 1990; Quotations and Sources on Design and the Decorative Arts 1800–1990, 1993; (ed) Art Nouveau 1890–1914, 2000; The Essential Art Nouveau, 2000. *Recreations:* running, soccer, hockey. *Address:* Nova Scotia College of Art and Design, 5163 Duke Street, Halifax, NS B3J 3J6, Canada. *T:* (902) 4948114.

GREENHALGH, Prof. Roger Malcolm, FRCS; Professor of Surgery and Head of Department of Vascular Surgery, Imperial College School of Medicine at Charing Cross Hospital, since 1997; Hon. Consultant Surgeon, Charing Cross Hospital, since 1976; *b* 6 Feb. 1941; *s* of John Greenhalgh and Phyllis Poynton; *m* 1964, Karin Maria Gross; one *s* one *d*. *Educ:* Clare Coll., Cambridge; St Thomas' Hosp., London. BA 1963, BChir 1966, MB, MA 1967, MChir 1974, MD 1983 (Cantab); FRCS 1971. Ho. Surg., 1967, Casualty Officer, 1968, St Thomas' Hosp.; Sen. Ho. Officer, Hammersmith Hosp., 1969; Registrar in Surgery, Essex County Hosp., Colchester, 1970–72; Lectr and Sen. Registrar in Surgery, St Bartholomew's Hosp., 1972–76; Sen. Lectr in Surgery, Charing Cross Hosp., 1976–81; Head of Dept of Surgery, 1981, Prof. of Surgery, 1982–97, Chm. of Dept of Surgery, 1989–97, Dean, 1993–97, Charing Cross Hosp. Med. Sch., later Charing Cross and Westminster Med. Sch.; Chm., Directorate of Surgery, Hammersmith Hosps NHS Trust, 1994–98. Chm., Europ. Examining Bd, Surgery Qualification, 1995–; Pres., Surgery sect., EU of Medical Specialities, 1998–. Sometime examiner, Univs of Cambridge, London, Edinburgh, Bristol, Leicester, UCD, Southampton, Birmingham, Hong Kong. Chairman: Liaison Cttee, Bioengrg Centre, Roehampton, London, 1985–88; Riverside Med. Council, 1992–93; Mem., Scientific Cttee on Tobacco and Health (formerly Ind. Scientific Enquiry into Smoking and Health), 1979–. Vice-President: Section of Surgery, RSM, 1986–89; BRCS, 1992–; Sec. Gen. and Chm. Exec. Cttee, Assoc. of Internat. Vascular Surgeons, 1982–; Chm. Dirs and Trustees, European Soc. for Vascular Surgery, 1987– (Mem. Council, 1987–93); Mem. Council, Assoc. of Surgeons of GB and Ireland, 1993–; Pres., Vascular Soc. of GB and Ire., 1999–. Corresponding Mem., Soc. for Vascular Surgery, 1991; Hon. FRCSE 1998; Hon. Member: Canadian Vascular Soc., 1991; Polish Surgical Soc., 1991; German Vascular Soc., 1992; Hellenic Surgical Soc., 1992; Brazilian Angiology Soc., 1994; Hellenic Vascular Surg. Soc., 1995; Austrian Vascular Soc., 1997. Moynihan Fellow of Assoc. of Surgeons, 1974; Hunterian Prof., RCS, 1980. Chm. Editl Bd, European Jl of Vascular Surgery, 1987–93; Ed., Vascular News, 1998–. *Publications:* Progress in Stroke Research, 1, 1979; Smoking and Arterial Disease, 1981; Hormones and Vascular Disease, 1981; Femoro-distal bypass, 1981; Extra-Anatomic and Secondary Arterial Reconstruction, 1982; Progress in Stroke Research, 2, 1983; Vascular Surgical Techniques, 1984, 2nd edn 1989, 3rd edn as Vascular and Endovascular Surgical Techniques, 1994; Diagnostic Techniques and Assessment Procedures in Vascular Surgery, 1985; Vascular Surgery: issues in current practice, 1986; Indications in Vascular Surgery, 1988; Limb Salvage and Amputations for Vascular Disease, 1988; The Cause and Management of Aneurysms, 1990; The Maintenance of Arterial Reconstruction, 1991; Vascular Surgical Emergencies, 1992; Surgery for Stroke, 1993; Vascular Imaging for Surgeons, 1995; Trials and Tribulations of Vascular Surgery, 1996; Clinical Surgery, 1996; Inflammatory and thrombotic problems in vascular surgery, 1997; Indications in Vascular and Endovascular Surgery, 1998; The Durability of Vascular and Endovascular Surgery, 1999; Vascular and Endovascular Opportunities, 2000. *Recreations:* tennis, ski-ing, swimming, music. *Address:* 271 Sheen Lane, East Sheen, SW14 8RN. *T:* (020) 8878 1110. *Club:* Athenæum.

GREENHILL, family name of **Baron Greenhill.**

GREENHILL, 3rd Baron *cr* 1950, of Townhead; **Malcolm Greenhill;** retired from Ministry of Defence; *b* 5 May 1924; *s* of 1st Baron Greenhill, OBE and Ida, *d* of late Mark Goodman; *S* brother, 1989. *Educ:* Kelvinside Acad., Glasgow; Glasgow Univ. (BSc). CPA. Ministries of Aircraft Production and Supply, 1944–54; UK Scientific Mission, Washington DC, USA, 1950–51; UKAEA, 1954–73; MoD, 1973–89. *Recreation:* gardening. *Address:* 28 Gorselands, Newbury, Berks RG14 6PX. *T:* (01635) 45651. *Club:* Civil Service.

GREENHILL, Dr Basil Jack, CB 1981; CMG 1967; FRHistS; FSA; author; Vice President, SS Great Britain Project, since 1992 (Chairman, 1982–92); Chairman, Centre for Maritime Historical Studies, University of Exeter, since 1991; Consultant, Chatham Publishing, since 1996; *b* 26 Feb. 1920; *o c* of B. J. and Edith Greenhill; *m* 1st, 1950, Gillian (*d* 1959), *e d* of Capt. Ralph Tyacke Stratton, MC; one *s*; 2nd, 1961, Ann, *d* of Walter Ernest Giffard; one *s*. *Educ:* Bristol Grammar Sch.; Bristol Univ. (T. H. Green Scholar; PhD 1980). Served War of 1939–45: Lieut RNVR (Air Br.). Diplomatic Service, 1946–66; served: Pakistan; UK Delegn, New York; Tokyo; UK Delegate to Conf. on Law of the Sea, Geneva; Dep. High Comr in Pakistan; Ottawa. Dir, Nat. Maritime Mus., Greenwich, 1967–83. Mem., Ancient Monuments Bd for England, 1972–84; Vice Chm. Bd, Trustees of the Royal Armouries, 1984–88; First Pres., Internat. Congress of Maritime Museums, 1975–81; President: Devonshire Assoc., 1984; Devon Hist. Soc., 1993–96; Trustee: Royal Naval Museum, Portsmouth, 1973–83; Mary Rose Trust, 1979–83; RAF Museum, 1987–96; Univ. of Hull Maritime Hist. Trust, 1997–. Governor, Dulwich Coll., 1974–88; Chairman: Dulwich Picture Gall., 1977–88; Nat. Museums' Directors' Conf., 1980–83; Govt Adv. Cttee on Historic Wreck Sites, 1986–96. Principal Advisor: BBC TV series: The Commanding Sea, 1980–82; Trade Winds, 1984–85; BBC Radio series: The British Seafarer, 1980–82; The Sea, The Sea, 1991. Hon. Fellow: Univ. of Exeter, 1985; Univ. of Hull, 2001. Hon. DLitt: Plymouth, 1996; Hull, 2002. Kt Comdr, Order of White Rose, Finland, 1980. *Publications:* The Merchant Schooners, Vol. I, 1951, Vol. II, 1957, rev. edns 1968, 1978, 1988; (ed and prefaced) W. J. Slade's Out of Appledore, 1959, rev. edns 1972, 1974, 1980; Sailing For A Living, 1962; (with Ann Giffard) Westcountrymen in Prince Edward's Isle, 1967, 3rd edn 1990 (Amer. Assoc. Award) (filmed 1975); (with Ann Giffard) The Merchant Sailing Ship: A Photographic History, 1970; (with Ann Giffard) Women under Sail, 1970; Captain Cook, 1970; Boats and Boatmen of Pakistan, 1971; (with Ann Giffard) Travelling by Sea in the Nineteenth Century, 1972; (with Rear-Adm. P. W. Brock) Sail and Steam, 1973; (with W. J. Slade) West Country Coasting Ketches, 1974; A Victorian Maritime Album, 1974; A Quayside Camera, 1975; (with L. Willis) The Coastal Trade: Sailing Craft of British Waters 900–1900, 1975; Archaeology of the Boat, 1976; (with Ann Giffard) Victorian and Edwardian Sailing Ships, 1976, rev. edns 1981, 1982, 1987; (with Ann Giffard) Victorian and Edwardian Ships and Harbours, 1978; (ed and prefaced) Georg Kåhrés The Last Tall Ships, 1978 (trans. Norwegian, 1980); (with Ann Giffard) Victorian and Edwardian Merchant Steamships, 1979; Schooners, 1980; The Life and Death of the Sailing Ship, 1980; (with Michael Mason) The British Seafarer, 1980; (with Denis Stonham) Seafaring Under Sail, 1981; Karlsson, 1982; The Woodshipbuilders, 1986; The Grain Races, 1986; (with Ann Giffard) The British Assault on Finland 1854–55, 1988; The Evolution of the Wooden Ship, 1988; (with John Hackman) The Herzogin Cecilie, 1991 (trans. Swedish, 1991, German, 1993); (ed jtly and contrib.) The New Maritime History of Devon, vol. 1, 1993, vol. 2, 1994; (ed and contrib.) The Advent of Steam, 1993; (ed and contrib.) The Last Century of Sail, 1993; (with Owain Roberts) The Årby Boat, 1993; (with Ann Giffard) Steam, Politics and Patronage, 1994; The Bertha L. Downs, 1995; The Archaeology of Boats and Ships: an introduction, 1995; (ed and prefaced) The Evolution of the Sailing Ship 1250–1580, 1995; (with Peter Allington) Paddle Wheel, Sail and Screw, 1996; (ed and contrib.) The Chatham Directory of Inshore Craft, 1997; numerous articles, reviews and broadcasts. *Recreations:* boating, travel, coarse gardening. *Address:* West Boetheric Farmhouse, St Dominic, Saltash, Cornwall PL12 6SZ. *Clubs:* Arts (Hon. Mem.); Karachi Yacht (Karachi); Åland Nautical (Mariehamn).

See also Sir C. S. R. Giffard.

GREENING, Rear-Adm. Sir Paul (Woollven), GCVO 1992 (KCVO 1985); Master of HM's Household, 1986–92; an Extra Equerry to the Queen, since 1983; *b* 4 June 1928; *s* of late Captain Charles W. Greening, DSO, DSC, RN, and Mrs Molly K. Greening (*née* Flowers); *m* 1951, Monica, *d* of late Mr and Mrs W. E. West, East Farndon, Market Harborough; one *s* one *d*. *Educ:* Mowden Sch., Brighton; Nautical Coll., Pangbourne. Entered RN, 1946; Midshipman, HMS Theseus, 1947–48; Sub-Lt and Lieut, HM Ships Zodiac, Neptune, Rifleman, Asheldham (CO), and Gamecock, 1950–58; Lt-Comdr, HM Ships Messina (CO), Loch Killisport, Urchin, and Collingwood, 1958–63; Comdr 1963; CO HMS Lewiston, and SO 2nd Minesweeping Sqdn, 1963–64; jssc 1964; Naval Plans, MoD (Navy), 1965–67; CO HMS Jaguar, 1967–68; Fleet Plans Officer, Far East Fleet, 1969–70; Captain 1969; CO HMS Aurora, 1970–71; Captain Naval Drafting, 1971–74; Sen. Officers War Course, 1974; Dir of Officers Appts (Seamen), MoD (Navy), 1974–76; Captain BRNC Dartmouth, 1976–78; Naval Secretary, 1978–80; Flag Officer, Royal Yachts, 1981–85; retired 1985. ADC to the Queen, 1978. Mem. Council, Mission to Seafarers (formerly Missions to Seamen), 1994–. Younger Brother of Trinity House, 1984–. Vice Pres., Assoc. of Royal Yachtsmen, 1999–. *Recreations:* golf, gardening, following cricket. *Clubs:* Army and Navy; Corhampton Golf.

GREENLAND, Dennis James, DPhil; FRS 1994; FIBiol; Visiting Professor, University of Reading, since 1987; *b* 13 June 1930; *s* of James John and Lily Florence Greenland; *m* 1955, Edith Mary Johnston; one *s* two *d*. *Educ:* Portsmouth Grammar Sch.; Christ Church, Oxford (MA, DPhil). Lecturer: Univ. of Ghana, 1955–59; Waite Agricl Res. Inst., Adelaide, 1959–63; Reader and Head of Soil Science, Waite Agricl Res. Inst., 1963–70; Professor and Head of Dept of Soil Science, Univ. of Reading, 1970–79; Director of Research, Internat. Inst. of Tropical Agriculture, Nigeria, 1974–76 (on secondment from Univ. of Reading); Dep. Dir Gen., Internat. Rice Res. Inst., Los Baños, Philippines, 1979–87; Scientific Dir, CAB Internat., 1987–92. Chm., Scientific Adv. Panel, Commonwealth Develt Corp., 1992–96. FIBiol 1974; FWA 1987. Hon. Member: Amer. Soc. of Soil Science, 1993; Amer. Soc. of Agronomy, 1993. Hon. DrAgSci Ghent, 1982. *Publications:* contributions: (jtly) The Soil Under Shifting Cultivation, 1960; (ed jtly) Soil Conservation and Management in the Humid Tropics, 1977; (ed jtly) Chemistry of Soil Constituents, 1978; (ed jtly) Soil Physical Properties and Crop Production in the Tropics, 1979; (ed) Characterisation of Soils in Relation to Their Classification and Management for Crop Production: some examples from the humid tropics, 1981; (ed jtly) The Chemistry of Soil Processes, 1981; (ed jtly) Soil Resilience and Sustainable Land Use, 1994; The Sustainability of Rice Farming, 1997; (ed jtly) Land Resources: on the edge of the Malthusian precipice, 1997; numerous scientific articles in learned jls. *Recreations:* golf, bridge, watching cricket. *Address:* Low Wood, The Street, South Stoke, Oxon RG8 0JS.

GREENOAK, Francesca; gardening and natural history writer, occasional broadcaster; *b* 6 Sept. 1946; *d* of Francis Buchanan Greenoak and Alice Lavinia (*née* Marston); *m* 1981, John Kilpatrick; one *s* one *d*. *Educ:* St Mary's Convent Grammar Sch., Woodford Green; Univ. of Essex (BA Hons). Book Club Associates, 1968; Editor: George Harrap, 1970; Penguin Educn, Penguin Books, 1972; Chameleon Publishing Co-operative, 1974; Gardening Correspondent: She mag., 1978–80; The Times, 1986–94; Gardens Ed., Good Housekeeping, 1993–96; Express Saturday, 1997–99; The European, 1997–99. Mem. Council, Garden History Soc., (Ed., Garden History Soc. News, 1999–; Chm., Educn and Publns Cttee, 2000–). Mem., Soc. of Teachers of the Alexander Technique, 1999–; Alexander Teacher, Arts Educn Sch., Tring, 2000–; Ed., Alexander Jl, 2001–. Leverhulme Res. Award, to study cultural and natural history of churchyards, 1995. *Publications:* Guide to Wildflowers, 1977; All The Birds of the Air, 1979, 2nd edn as British Birds: their folklore, names and literature, 1997; Forgotten Fruit, 1983; (with R. Mabey) Back to the Roots, 1983; God's Acre, 1985, 2nd edn as Wildlife in Churchyards, 1993; (ed) Journals of Gilbert White, 3 vols, 1989; Glorious Gardens, 1989; Fruit and Vegetable Gardens, 1990; Water in Small Gardens, 1996; Natural Style for Gardens, 1998. *Recreations:* literature, gardening, botany, music, education and science. *Address:* 4 Wood Row, Wigginton, Tring, Herts HP23 6HS.

GREENOCK, Lord; Alan George Cathcart; *b* 16 March 1986; *s* and *heir* of Earl Cathcart, *qv*.

GREENOUGH, Beverly, (Mrs P. B. Greenough); *see* Sills, B.

GREENSHIELDS, Robert McLaren; HM Diplomatic Service, retired; Counsellor, Foreign and Commonwealth Office, 1985–88; *b* 27 July 1933; *s* of late Brig. James Greenshields, MC, TD, and of Mrs J. J. Greenshields; *m* 1960, Jean Alison Anderson; one *s* two *d*. *Educ:* Edinburgh Academy; Lincoln Coll., Oxford (MA Hons). National Service, 2nd Lieut Highland Light Infantry, 1952–54. District Officer, Tanganyika, HMOCS, 1958–61; Asst Master and Housemaster, Gordonstoun Sch., 1962–68; HM Diplomatic Service, 1969–88. *Recreations:* ornithology, conservation, farming.

GREENSLADE, Roy; freelance journalist, broadcaster and author, since 1992; *b* 31 Dec. 1946; *s* of Ernest Frederick William Greenslade and Joan Olive (*née* Stocking); *m* 1984, Noreen Anna Taylor (*née* McElhone); one step *s* one step *d*. *Educ:* Dagenham County High Sch.; Sussex Univ. (BA (Hons) Politics, 1979). Trainee journalist, Barking Advertiser, 1962–66; Sub-Editor: Lancashire Evening Telegraph, 1966–67; Daily Mail, 1967–69; The Sun, 1969–71; researching and writing book, 1973–75; Daily Star, 1979–80; Daily Express, 1980–81; Daily Star, 1981; Asst Editor, The Sun, 1981–87; Man. Editor, Sunday Times, 1987–90; Editor, Daily Mirror, 1990–91; Consultant Editor, Today and Sunday Times, 1991. Columnist: Observer, 1996; Guardian, 1996–. Dir, Impact Books, 1993–98. Presenter: Mediumwave, Radio 4, 1995–96; Britain Talks Back, TV, 1996–97. Mem. Bd, British Journalism Review, 1994–. Hon. DLitt Brighton, 1999. *Publications:* Goodbye to the Working Class, 1975; Maxwell's Fall, 1992. *Recreations:* reading, snooker. *Address:* Ballyarr House, Ramelton, Co. Donegal, Ireland.

GREENSPAN, Alan; Chairman, Board of Governors of the Federal Reserve System, since 1987; *b* 6 March 1926; *o s* of late Herbert Greenspan and Rose (*née* Goldsmith); *m* 1997, Andrea Mitchell. *Educ:* New York Univ. (BS 1948; MA 1950; PhD 1977). Vice-Pres., 1954–58, Pres., 1958–74 and 1977–87, Townsend-Greenspan & Co., NY. Adjunct Prof., Graduate Sch. of Business Management, NY Univ., 1977–87. Director: Trans World Financial Co., 1962–74; Dreyfus Fund, 1970–74; Gen. Cable Corp., 1973–74, 1977–78; Sun Chemical Corp., 1973–74; Gen. Foods Corp., 1977–85; J. P. Morgan & Co., 1977–87; Mobil Corp., 1977–87; ALCOA, 1978–87. Consultant to Council of Economic Advisers, 1970–74, to US Treasury, 1971–74, to Fed. Reserve Board, 1971–74; Chairman: Council of Economic Advisers, 1974–77; Nat. Commn on Social Security Reform, 1981–83; Dir, Council on Foreign Relations; Member: President's Econ. Policy Adv. Board, 1981–87; President's Foreign Intell. Adv. Board, 1983–85. Jefferson Award, 1976; William Butler Meml Award, 1977. *Address:* Federal Reserve System, 20th Street & Constitution Avenue NW, Washington, DC 20551, USA.

GREENSTOCK, Sir Jeremy (Quentin), KCMG 1998 (CMG 1991); HM Diplomatic Service; British Permanent Representative to the United Nations, since 1998; *b* 27 July 1943; *s* of late John Wilfrid Greenstock and Ruth Margaret Logan; *m* 1969, Anne Derryn Ashford Hodges; one *s* two *d*. *Educ:* Harrow Sch.; Worcester Coll., Oxford (MA Lit. Hum.). Asst Master, Eton Coll., 1966–69; entered HM Diplomatic Service, 1969; MECAS, 1970–72; Dubai, 1972–74; Private Sec. to the Ambassador, Washington, 1974–78; FCO, 1978–83 (Planning Staff, Personnel Ops Dept, N East and N African Dept); Counsellor (Commercial), Jedda, 1983–85, Riyadh, 1985–86; Hd of Chancery, Paris, 1987–90; Asst Under-Sec. of State, FCO, 1990–93; Minister, Washington, 1994–95; Dep. Under Sec. of State, FCO, 1995; Pol Dir, FCO, 1996–98. *Recreations:* travel, music, golf, ski-ing. *Address:* Foreign and Commonwealth Office, Whitehall, SW1A 2AH. *Club:* Oxford and Cambridge.

GREENTREE, (William Wayne) Chris; Chairman (non-executive), Xxtra Oil Inc., 1993–97; *b* 6 April 1935; *s* of J. Murray and Grace M. Greentree; *m* 1st, 1956, Patricia Ann Hugo (marr. diss. 1990); four *d* (and one *d* decd); 2nd, 1990, Hilary J. Wilson; one *d*. *Educ:* Moose Jaw Technical High Sch., Saskatoon; Univ. of Alberta (BSc Hons, PEng). Joined Shell Canada, 1957: technical and managerial appts, onshore and offshore exploration; Ranger Oil London, 1972–79: Man. Dir, 1976; Mapco Inc. USA: Sen. Vice Pres. Exploration and Production, 1979–82; Chief Exec., LASMO Gp, 1982–93. Ordre National du Mérite (Gabon), 1987. *Recreations:* golf, ski-ing. *Address:* Quinta do Lago, Almancil, Portugal.

GREENWAY, family name of **Baron Greenway**.

GREENWAY, 4th Baron *cr* 1927; **Ambrose Charles Drexel Greenway;** Bt 1919; photographer and author; *b* 21 May 1941; *s* of 3rd Baron Greenway and of Cordelia Mary, *d* of late Major Humfrey Campbell Stephen; *S* father, 1975; *m* 1985, Mrs Rosalynne Schenk. *Educ:* Winchester. Chm., Marine Soc., 1994–2000. Elected Mem., H of L, 1999. *Publications:* Soviet Merchant Ships, 1976; Comecon Merchant Ships, 1978; A Century of Cross Channel Passenger Ferries, 1980; A Century of North Sea Passenger Steamers, 1986. *Recreations:* ocean racing and cruising, swimming. *Heir:* *b* Hon. Nigel Paul Greenway [*b* 12 Jan. 1944; *m* 1979, Gabrielle, *e d* of Walter Jean Duchardt; two *s*]. *Address:* c/o House of Lords, SW1A 0PW. *Club:* House of Lords Yacht.

GREENWAY, Prof. Diana Eleanor, PhD; FBA 2001; Professor of Medieval History, University of London, since 1998; *b* 21 Dec. 1937; *d* of Charles Greenway and Winifred Greenway (*née* Keene). *Educ:* Aylesbury Grammar Sch.; Girton Coll., Cambridge (BA Hist. 1959; MA 1963; PhD 1967). Asst Archivist, Lambeth Palace Liby, 1963–64; University of London: Ed., Fasti Ecclesiae Anglicanae 1066–1300 (7 vols, 1968–2001), at Inst. of Historical Res., 1964–; teaching hist. and palaeography, 1966–97; Reader in Medieval Hist., 1993–98. Founder and Chair, Univ. of London Palaeography and Diplomatic Teachers' Gp, 1993–98. Gen. Ed., Oxford Medieval Texts, 1974–97. Literary Dir, RHistS, 1982–87. Dir, Summer Insts in Palaeography, Newberry Liby, Chicago, 1985, 1990 and 1994. British Rep., Assembly of Repertorium Fontium Historiae Medii Aevi, 1993–. *Publications:* Charters of the Honour of Mowbray, 1107–91, 1972; (ed jtly) Early Yorkshire Families, 1973; (ed jtly) Richard fitzNigel: Dialogus de Scaccario, 1983; (ed jtly) Tradition and Change: Essays in honour of Marjorie Chibnall, 1985; (ed jtly) Handbook of British Chronology, 1986; (jtly) The Chronicle of Jocelin Brakeland, 1989; Henry, Archdeacon of Huntingdon: Historia Anglorum, 1996; (ed jtly) The Book of the Foundation of Walden Monastery, 1999; Saint Osmund, Bishop of Salisbury 1078 to 1099, 1999; Henry of Huntingdon: The History of the English People 1000–1154, 2002; contrib. articles to learned jls. *Recreation:* birdwatching. *Address:* Institute of Historical Research, University of London, Senate House, WC1E 7HU.

GREENWAY, Harry; *b* 4 Oct. 1934; *s* of John Kenneth Greenway and Violet Adelaide (*née* Bell); *m* 1969, Carol Elizabeth Helena, *e d* of late Major John Robert Thomas Hooper, barrister at law and Metropolitan Stipendiary Magistrate, and Dorinda Hooper (*née* de Courcy Ireland); one *s* two *d*. *Educ:* Warwick Sch.; College of St Mark and St John, London; Univ. of Caen, Normandy. Assistant Master, Millbank Sch., 1957–60; successively, Head of English Dept, Sen. Housemaster, Sen. Master, Acting Dep. Head, Sir William Collins Sch., 1960–72; Dep. Headmaster, Sedgehill Sch. (Comprehensive for 2,000 plus pupils), 1972–79. MP (C) Ealing North, 1979–97; contested (C) same seat, 1997. Vice-Chm., Greater London Cons. Members, 1981–97; Chairman: All Party Adult Educn Cttee, 1979–97; All Party Parly Friends of Cycling, 1987–95; Member: Parly Select Cttee on Educn, Science and the Arts, 1979–92; Parly Select Cttee on Employment, 1992–95, on Educn and Employment, 1995–97; Vice-Chairman: Cons. Parly Educn Cttee, 1983–87 (Sec., 1981); Cons. Parly Sports Cttee, 1990–97 (Sec., 1986–90); Parly Sec., Cons. National Adv. Cttee on Educn, 1981–94; Sec., Cons. Parly Arts and Heritage Cttee, 1986–87. Parly Sec., Cons. Nat. Educn Soc., 1995–97 (Dep. Pres., 1998–); Chm., Mauritius Parly Gp, 1983–97. Led All Party Parly Delegn to Sri Lanka, 1985, to Gibraltar, 1989. Pres., Cons. Trade Unionist Teachers, 1982–83; Chm., Atlantic Educn Cttee, 1981–85; Open University: Mem. Council, 1981–99; Audit Cttee, 1997–99; Grievance Cttee, 1998–99; Mem., Educn Cttee, NACRO, 1985–88. President: Nat. Equine Welfare Council, 1990–; Assoc. of British Riding Schs, 1993–; Spencer Hockey Club, 2000–; Mem. Council, British Horse Soc., 1973–97 (Trustee, 1998–); Mem. Bd of Govs, Horse Rangers Assoc., 2000–; Founder Trustee, The Greater London Equestrian Centres Trust Ltd; Trustee, Teenage Cancer Trust, 1991–. Chm., National Prayer Breakfast, 1995. Freeman, City of London, 1986; Liveryman, Farriers' Co., 1986–. DUniv Open, 2001. British Horse Soc. Award of Merit, 1980. Kt Comdr's Cross, Order of Merit (Poland), 1998. *Publications:* Adventure in the Saddle, 1971; (ed and compiled) Electing to Bat: tales of glory and disaster from the Palace of Westminster, 1996; regular contributor to educnl and equestrian jls. *Recreations:* riding (Asst Instructor, BHS, 1966), ski-ing, choral music, hockey (Vice-Pres., England Schoolboys' Hockey Assoc.; Founder, Lords and Commons Hockey Club), tennis, cricket, parliamentary parachutist. *Address:* 64 Cambridge Street, Westminster, SW1V 4QQ. *Clubs:* St Stephen's Constitutional, MCC, Ski Club of Gt Britain.

GREENWAY, John Robert; MP (C) Ryedale, since 1987; *b* 15 Feb. 1946; *s* of Thomas William and Kathleen Greenway; *m* 1974, Sylvia Ann Gant; two *s* one *d*. *Educ:* Sir John Deane's Grammar School, Northwich; London College of Law. Midland Bank, 1964; Metropolitan Police, 1965–69; Equitable Life Assurance Soc., 1970–71; National Provident Instn, 1971–72; own firm of insurance brokers, J. R. Greenway, subseq. Greenway Middleton, & Co. Ltd, York, then Greenway Smart and Cook Ltd, now Smart and Cook Ltd, 1972–. Treasurer, Ryedale Cons. Assoc., 1984–86; Mem., North Yorks CC, 1985–87; Vice-Chm., N Yorks Police Authy, 1986–87. PPS to Minister of State, MAFF, 1991–92; Opposition front bench spokesman on home affairs, 1997–2000, on sport and tourism, 2000–2001. Mem., Home Affairs Select Cttee, 1987–97. Sec., Cons. backbench Health Cttee, 1988–91; Vice-Chairman: Cons. backbench Agricl Cttee, 1989–97; All Party Football Cttee, 1989–; Chairman: All Party Racing and Bloodstock Cttee, 1993–97; All Party Insce and Financial Services Gp, 1992– (Sec., 1991–92); Jt Chm., All Party Opera Gp, 1994–. Chm., Fedn of Insce and Investment Intermediary Assocs, 1998–; Mem., Insce Brokers Registration Council, 1991–. *Recreations:* opera, football (Pres., York City FC), wine, travel, gardening. *Address:* 11 Oak Tree Close, Strensall, York YO3 5TE. *T:* (01904) 490535.

GREENWELL, (Arthur) Jeffrey, CBE 1991; DL; Chief Executive, Northamptonshire County Council, 1973–96; Independent Adjudicator, Department of the Environment, Transport and the Regions, since 1998; *b* 1 Aug. 1931; *s* of late George Greenwell and of Kate Mary Greenwell (*née* Fleming), Durham; *m* 1958, Margaret Rosemary, *d* of late Sidney David Barnard; one *s* two *d*. *Educ:* Durham Sch.; University Coll., Oxford (MA). FCIS. Solicitor (Hons). Nat. Service, RHA, 1950–51. Articled to Town Clerk, Newcastle upon Tyne, 1955–58; law tutor, Gibson & Weldon, 1958–59; Asst Solicitor, Birmingham Corp., 1959–61; Hants County Council: Asst Solicitor, 1961–64; Asst Clerk, 1964–67; Dep. Clerk of Council, Dep. Clerk of the Peace and Dep. Clerk, Hants River Authy, 1967–73; Clerk of Northants Lieutenancy, 1977–96. Chm., Assoc. of Co. Chief Execs, 1993–94 (Hon. Sec., 1980–84); Hon. Sec., SOLACE, 1984–88 (Pres., 1991–92); President: CIS, 1989; Northants Assoc. of Local Councils, 1974–96. Chm., Home Office Gp on Juvenile Crime, 1987. Vice-Pres., Internat. City Management Assoc., 1990–92; Chm., Northants ACRE, 1998–. Trustee, Central Festival Opera. Gov., UC, Northampton. DL Northants, 1996. *Recreations:* bridge, travel, local history, going to meetings. *Address:* 2 Hillside Way, Northampton NN3 3AW. *T:* (01604) 401858.

GREENWELL, Sir Edward (Bernard), 4th Bt *cr* 1906; DL; farmer, since 1975; *b* 10 June 1948; *s* of Sir Peter McClintock Greenwell, 3rd Bt, TD, and of Henrietta (who *m* 1985, Hugh Kenneth Haig), 2nd *d* of late Peter and Lady Alexandra Haig-Thomas; *S* father, 1978; *m* 1974, Sarah Louise Gore-Anley; one *s* three *d*. *Educ:* Eton; Nottingham University (BSc); Cranfield Institute of Technology (MBA). Dep. Pres., CLA, 1999–. DL Suffolk, 1988. *Heir:* *s* Alexander Bernard Peter Greenwell, *b* 11 May 1987. *Address:* Gedgrave Hall, Woodbridge, Suffolk IP12 2BX. *T:* (01394) 450440. *Club:* Turf.

GREENWELL, Jeffrey; *see* Greenwell, A. J.

GREENWOOD, family name of **Viscount Greenwood**.

GREENWOOD, 3rd Viscount *cr* 1937, of Holbourne, co. London; **Michael George Hamar Greenwood;** Baron Greenwood 1929; Bt 1915; *b* 5 May 1923; *yr s* of 1st Viscount Greenwood, PC, KC and Margery, DBE, 2nd *d* of Rev. Walter Spencer; *S* brother, 1998. *Educ:* Eton; Christ Church, Oxford; Webber-Douglas Sch. of Singing and Dramatic Art. Served War of 1939–45, RCS. With Cazenove & Co., 1944–47; actor, 1947–. *Theatre* incl. King of France in Joan of Arc at the Stake, 1947; *films:* The Big Money; House in the Woods; The Bank Raiders; Poor Cow; The Insomniac; *television* includes: The Appleyards, Emergency Ward 10, Falstaff, Great Expectations, Androcles and the Lion, Charlie Drake Show, Dixon of Dock Green, Rob Roy, Adam Adamant Lives, Honey Lane, Gnomes of Dulwich, Eric Sykes Show. *Heir:* none. *Address:* 63 Portsea Hall, Portsea Place, W2 2BY. *T:* (020) 7402 2975.

GREENWOOD, Alan Eliezer; His Honour Judge Greenwood; a Circuit Judge, since 2000; *b* 5 June 1947; *s* of Rabbi Hans Isaac Grunewald and Martha Grunewald; *m*, Naomi (*née* Ohayon); two *s* one *d*. *Educ:* University Coll., London (LLB Hons). Called to the Bar, Middle Temple, 1970; in practice at the Bar, 1971-2000. *Recreations:* travel, film, theatre, football, tennis, ski-ing, swimming, cycling, walking. *Address:* Luton Crown Court, 7 George Street, Luton LU1 2AA.

GREENWOOD, Allen Harold Claude, CBE 1974; JP; Deputy Chairman, British Aerospace, 1977–83 (Member, Organizing Committee, 1976–77); Chairman, British Aircraft Corporation, 1976 (Deputy Chairman, 1972–75); *b* 4 June 1917; *s* of Lt-Col Thomas Claude Greenwood and Hilda Letitia Greenwood (*née* Knight). *Educ:* Cheltenham Coll. Coll. of Aeronautical Engineering. Pilot's Licence, 1939. Joined Vickers-Armstrongs Ltd, 1940; served RNVR (Fleet Air Arm), 1942–52 (Lt-Cmdr); rejoined Vickers-Armstrongs Ltd, 1946, Dir, 1960; British Aircraft Corp., 1962, Dep. Man. Dir, 1969; Director: British Aircraft Corp. (Holdings), 1972; BAe Australia Ltd, 1977–83; Chm., BAe Inc., 1977–80. Director: SEPECAT SA, 1964; Europlane Ltd, 1974–83; Chairman: Panavia GmbH, 1969–72; Remploy Ltd, 1976–79 (Vice-Chm., 1973). Pres., Assoc. Européenne des Constructeurs de Material Aerospatial, 1974–76; Pres., 1970–72, Dep. Pres., 1981–82, SBAC; Vice-Pres., Engineering Employers' Fedn, 1982–83; Mem., National Def. Industry Council, 1970–72. Pres., Cheltenham Coll. Council, 1980–85; Member: Council, Cranfield Inst. of Technology, 1970–79; Council, CBI, 1970–77; Assoc. of Governing Bodies of Public Schools, 1982–85; Council, St John's Sch., Leatherhead, 1970–85 (Chm., 1979–85). JP Surrey 1962, Hampshire, 1975. Freeman, City of London. Liveryman, Company of Coachmakers, Guild of Air Pilots. General Comr for Income Tax, 1970–74. *Address:* 2 Rookcliff, Park Lane, Milford-on-Sea, Hants SO41 0SD. *T:* (01590) 642893. *Clubs:* White's, Royal Automobile; Royal Lymington Yacht.

GREENWOOD, Prof. Christopher John; QC 1999; Professor of International Law, London School of Economics, since 1996; *b* 12 May 1955; *o s* of Murray Guy Greenwood and Diana Maureen (*née* Barron); *m* 1978, Susan Anthea, *d* of late Geoffrey and of Patricia Longbotham; two *d*. *Educ:* Wellingborough Sch.; Magdalene Coll., Cambridge (MA, LLB; Whewell Schol. in Internat. Law 1977). Pres., Cambridge Union Soc., 1976. Called to the Bar, Middle Temple, 1978; Fellow, Magdalene Coll., Cambridge, 1978–96; Asst Lectr in Law, 1981–84, Lectr, 1984–96, Univ. of Cambridge. Mem., Panel of Arbitrators, Law of the Sea Convention, 1998–. Gov., Ditchley Foundn, 2001–. Jt Editor, International Law Reports, 1990–. *Publications:* contrib. articles in Brit. Year Book of Internat. Law, Internat. and Comparative Law Qly, Modern Law Rev. and other legal jls. *Recreations:* politics, walking. *Address:* Essex Court Chambers, 24 Lincoln's Inn Fields, WC2A 3EG. *T:* (020) 7813 8000; Law Department, London School of Economics, Houghton Street, WC2A 2AE. *T:* (020) 7955 7250. *Club:* Oxford and Cambridge.

GREENWOOD, David Ernest; Research Director, Centre for European Security Studies, Groningen; *b* 6 Feb. 1937; *s* of Ernest Greenwood and Doris (*née* Cowsill); *m* 1st,

1960, Helen Ramshaw (marr. diss.); two *s*; 2nd, 1986, Margaret McRobb (*née* Cruickshank). *Educ:* Manchester Grammar Sch.; Liverpool Univ. (BA, MA). Educn Officer, RAF, 1959–66; Economic Advr, MoD, 1966–67; University of Aberdeen: Lectr 1967, Sen. Lectr 1970, Reader 1975, in Higher Defence Studies; Dir, Centre for Defence Studies, 1976–97. Vis. Fellow, IISS, 1974–75; Visiting Professor: Nat. Defense Acad., Yokosuka, 1981–82; Univ. of Nat. and World Econ., Sofia, 1994–; Czech Mil. Acad., Brno, 1996–; Olin Prof., USAF Acad., Colorado Springs, 1991–92. Member: FCO Adv. Panel on Arms Control and Disarmament, 1974–; Honeywell Adv. Council, 1981–85; ACOST Study Gp on Defence R&D, 1987–88. Cons., EEC, 1980–85 and 1987–. *Publications:* Budgeting for Defence, 1972; (jtly) British Security Policy and the Atlantic Alliance: prospects for the 1990s, 1987; The European Defence Market, 1991; Resource Allocation and Resources Management in Defence, 1996; numerous monographs, res. reports, contribs to symposia, jl and newspaper articles. *Recreations:* cooking, golf, racing. *Address:* 7 Westhill Grange, Westhill AB32 6QJ. *T:* (01224) 741508; 31a Lutkenieuwstraat, 9712 AW Groningen, Netherlands. *T:* (50) 3132520. *Club:* Royal Air Force.

GREENWOOD, Duncan Joseph, CBE 1993; PhD, DSc; FRS 1985; CChem, FRSC; FIHort; Head of Soils and Crop Nutrition, 1966–92, Emeritus Fellow, since 1992, Horticulture Research International (formerly National Vegetable Research Station, then AFRC Institute of Horticultural Research), Wellesbourne, Warwick; *b* 16 Oct. 1932; *s* of Herbert James Greenwood and Alison Fairgrieve Greenwood. *Educ:* Hutton Grammar Sch., near Preston; Liverpool Univ. (BSc 1954); Aberdeen Univ. (PhD 1957; DSc 1972). CChem, FRSC 1977; FIHort 1986. Res. Fellow, Aberdeen Univ., 1957–59; Res. Leader, National Vegetable Res. Station, 1959–66. Vis. Prof. of Plant Scis, Leeds Univ., 1985–93; Hon. Prof. of Agricl Chem., Birmingham Univ., 1986–93. Chm., Agriculture Gp, Soc. of Chemical Industry, 1975–77; President: Internat. Cttee of Plant Nutrition, 1978–82; British Soc. of Soil Science, 1991–92. Lectures: Blackman, Univ. of Oxford, 1982; Distinguished Scholars, QUB, 1982; Hannaford, Univ. of Adelaide, 1985; Shell, Univ. of Kent, 1988; Amos, Wye Coll., 1989. Sir Gilbert Morgan Medal, Soc. of Chemical Industry, 1962; Res. Medal, RASE, 1979; Grower of the Year Award for Lifetime Achievement, 2000. *Publications:* over 160 scientific papers on soil science, crop nutrition and fertilizers. *Address:* 23 Shelley Road, Stratford-upon-Avon, Warwicks CV37 7JR. *T:* (01789) 204735.

GREENWOOD, Prof. Geoffrey Wilson, PhD, DMet; FRS 1992; FInstP; FIM; FREng; Professor of Metallurgy, University of Sheffield, 1966–94, now Emeritus; *b* 3 Feb. 1929; *s* of Richard Albert Greenwood and Martha Alice (*née* Wilson); *m* 1954, Nancy Cole; two *s* one *d*. *Educ:* Grange Grammar Sch., Bradford; Univ. of Sheffield (BSc, PhD, DMet). FInstP 1966; FIM 1966; FREng (FEng 1990). SO and SSO, UKAEA, Harwell, 1953–60; Head, Fuel Materials Section, Berkeley Nuclear Labs, CEGB, 1960–65; Res. Manager, Scis Div., Electricity Council Res. Centre, 1965–66. Pro-Vice-Chancellor, Univ. of Sheffield, 1979–83. L. B. Pfeil Prize, Inst. Metals and Iron and Steel Inst., 1972; Rosenhain Medal, Metals Soc., 1975; Griffith Medal, Inst. of Materials, 1995. *Publications:* contribs to Metallurgy, Materials Science, Physics and Engrg. *Recreations:* music (oboe and piano playing), travel, variety of outdoor activities. *Address:* Department of Engineering Materials, University of Sheffield, Sir Robert Hadfield Building, Mappin Street, Sheffield S1 3JD. *T:* (0114) 222 5517; 26 Stumperlowe Hall Road, Sheffield S10 3QS. *T:* (0114) 230 3565. *Club:* Hallam Rotary (Sheffield).

GREENWOOD, Jeffrey Michael; Senior Partner, Nabarro Nathanson, 1987–95; *b* 21 April 1935; *s* of Arthur Greenwood and Ada Greenwood (*née* Gordon); *m* 1964, Naomi Grahame; three *s* one *d*. *Educ:* Raine's Foundation Sch.; LSE; Downing Coll., Cambridge (MA, LLM). Admitted solicitor 1960; Partner, Nabarro Nathanson, 1963–95, Consultant, 1995–2001. Dir, Bank Leumi (UK), 1990–; Chairman: Wigmore Property Investment Trust, 1996–; Stow Securities, 1997–; Dep. Chm., Jewish Chronicle, 1994–. Chm., CCETSW, 1993–98. Chairman: Jewish Welfare Bd, 1986–90; Jewish Care, 1990; Council Member: Jewish Historical Soc. of England, 1993–; Hampstead Garden Suburb Trust (Law Soc. Appointee), 1984–87; Trustee, Policy Res. Inst. for Ageing and Ethnicity, Bradford Univ., 2000–. Founder Mem., Campaign Cttee, ProHelp. Liveryman, Glovers' Co. *Publications:* articles in learned jls. *Recreations:* conversing with grandchildren, swimming, ski-ing, literature, travel. *Address:* (office) 5 Spencer Walk, Hampstead High Street, NW3 1QZ. *T:* (020) 7794 5281, *Fax:* (020) 7794 0094; *e-mail:* jeffrey@thegreenwoods.org.

GREENWOOD, Dr Jeremy John Denis; Director, British Trust for Ornithology, since 1988; *b* 7 Sept. 1942; *s* of Denis Greenwood and Phyllis Marjorie Greenwood (*née* Leat); *m* 1971, Cynthia Anne Jones; two *d*. *Educ:* Royal Grammar Sch., Worcester; St Catherine's Coll., Oxford (BA 1964); Univ. of Manchester (PhD 1972). MIBiol 1990; MIEEM 1991. Dundee University: Asst Lectr in Zoology, 1967–70; Lectr in Biol. Scis, 1970–87; Hon. Lectr, 1988–; University of East Anglia: Hon. Lectr, 1994–98; Hon. Reader, 1998–. Vis. Prof. in Animal Ecology, Univ. of Khartoum, 1976. Natural Environment Research Council: Workshop on Grey Seal Population Biol., 1979–84; Special Cttee on Seals, 1986–96; Terrestrial Life Scis Cttee, 1988–91; Chm. Exec. Cttee, European Bird Census Council, 1992–98; Member: Council, RSPB, 1983–88; Adv. Cttee on Birds, NCC, 1988–91; Envtl Res. Cttee, British Agrochem. Assoc., 1988–93; Grants Cttee, Internat. Council for Bird Preservation, British Section, 1988–92; Council, British Ornith. Union, 1989–93; Sci. Adv. Cttee, Wildfowl & Wetlands Trust, 1989–92; Professional Affairs Cttee, Inst. of Ecology and Envmtl Management, 1991–93. Dir, West Palaearctic Birds Ltd, 1990–. Pres., Scottish Ornithologists' Club, 1987. Editor, Bird Study, 1984–87; Mem., Editl Bd, Heredity, 1988–92. *Publications:* (ed jtly) Joint Biological Expedition to North East Greenland 1974, 1978; (ed jtly) Birds as Monitors of Environmental Change, 1993; papers in learned jls; chapters in books. *Recreations:* birdwatching, walking, gardening. *Address:* National Centre for Ornithology, Thetford, Norfolk IP24 2PU. *T:* (01842) 750050.

GREENWOOD, Prof. Norman Neill, DSc Melbourne; PhD, ScD Cambridge; FRS 1987; CChem, FRSC; Professor of Inorganic and Structural Chemistry, University of Leeds, 1971–90, now Emeritus; *b* Melbourne, Vic., 19 Jan. 1925; *er s* of Prof. J. Neill Greenwood, DSc and Gladys, *d* of late Moritz and Bertha Uhland; *m* 1951, Kirsten Marie Rydland, Bergen, Norway; three *d*. *Educ:* University High School, Melbourne; University of Melbourne; Sidney Sussex Coll., Cambridge. Laboratory Cadet, CSIRO Div. of Tribophysics, Melbourne, 1942–44; BSc Melbourne 1945, MSc Melbourne 1948; DSc Melbourne 1966. Masson Memorial Medal, Royal Australian Chem. Institute, 1945. Resident Tutor and Lecturer in Chemistry, Trinity Coll., Melbourne, 1946–48. Exhibn of 1851, Overseas Student, 1948–51; PhD Cambridge 1951; ScD Cambridge 1961. Senior Harwell Research Fellow, 1951–53; Lectr, 1953–60 Senior Lectr, 1960–61, in Inorganic Chemistry, Univ. of Nottingham; Prof. of Inorganic Chemistry, Univ. of Newcastle upon Tyne, 1961–71. Visiting Professor: Univ. of Melbourne, 1966; Univ. of Western Australia, 1969; Univ. of Western Ontario, 1973; Univ. of Copenhagen, 1979; La Trobe Univ., Melbourne, 1985; Wuhan Univ., People's Republic of China, 1985; Toho Univ., Tokyo, 1991–93; National Science Foundation Distinguished Vis. Prof., Michigan State Univ., USA, 1967. International Union of Pure and Applied Chemistry: Mem., 1963–83; Vice-Pres., 1975–77, Pres., 1977–81, Inorganic Chemistry Div.; Chm., Internat. Commn on Atomic Weights, 1969–75. Chemical Society: Vice Pres., 1979–80; Pres., Dalton Div., 1979–81; Award in Main Group Chemistry, 1975. Vice-Pres., 1989–90, Pres., 1990–91, Section B, Chemistry, BAAS. Lectures: Tilden, Chemical Soc., 1966–67; Hofmann, Ges. Deutscher Chemiker, 1983; Liversidge , RSC, 1983; first Egon Wiberg, Munich Univ., 1989; Ludwig Mond, RSC, 1991; Humphrey Davy, Royal Soc., 2000. MRI 1998. For. Associate, Académie des Sciences, Institut de France, 1992. Dr *hc* de l'Université de Nancy I, 1977; DSc *hc* Toho Univ., Tokyo, 2000. *Publications:* Principles of Atomic Orbitals, 1964 (rev. edns 1968, 1973, 1980); Ionic Crystals, Lattice Defects, and Nonstoichiometry, 1968; (jointly) Spectroscopic Properties of Inorganic and Organometallic Compounds, vols I-IX, 1968–76; (with W. A. Campbell) Contemporary British Chemists, 1971; (with T. C. Gibb) Mössbauer Spectroscopy, 1971; Periodicity and Atomic Structure, 1971; (with B. P. Straughan and E. J. F. Ross) Index of Vibrational Spectra, vol. I, 1972, (with E. J. F. Ross) vol. II, 1975, vol. III, 1977; The Chemistry of Boron, 1973, rev. edn 1975; (with A. Earnshaw) Chemistry of the Elements, 1984, rev. edn 1997; numerous original papers and reviews in chemical jls and chapters in scientific monographs. *Recreations:* ski-ing, music, travel. *Address:* School of Chemistry, University of Leeds, Leeds LS2 9JT; *e-mail:* n.n.greenwood@chem.leeds.ac.uk.

GREENWOOD, His Honour Peter Bryan; a Circuit Judge, 1972–99. Called to the Bar, Gray's Inn, 1955; Dep. Chm., Essex QS, 1968–71. *Address:* c/o The Crown Court, PO Box 9, Chelmsford, Essex CM1 1EL.

GREENWOOD, Peter Gerard, CBE 1997; Member (Lab) Blackburn Unitary (formerly Borough) Council, since 1982 (Mayor, 1997–98); Chairman, Association of District Councils, 1995–97; *b* 20 Dec. 1939; *s* of James Greenwood and Mary Quinn; *m* 1961, Dorothy Edmundson; three *s*. *Educ:* Blackburn Coll. (Dip Mgt Services 1979); Ruskin Coll., Oxford (Dip Lab. Studies 1981). Apprentice Engineer, 1955–61; Engineer, 1961–79; Ruskin Coll., Oxford, 1979–81; various posts, 1981–86. Blackburn Borough Council: Chairman: Finance and Performance Wkg Gp, 1986–87; Mgt and Finance Sub-Cttee, 1987–89; Policy & Resources Cttee, 1989–94; Leader, 1989–94. Vice Chm., Blackburn Coll., 1982–92. Chairman: Chapterhouse (ADC) Ltd, 1993–; ADC (Properties) Ltd, 1996– (Dir, 1995–); Dir, ADC (Trustees) Ltd, 1994–. Vice Chm., Central Bodies Adv. Gp, 1996–97 (Mem., 1993–97). *Publications:* articles in local govt press. *Recreations:* politics, current affairs, reading. *Address:* 44 Rosewood Avenue, Blackburn, Lancs BB1 9SZ. *T:* (01254) 696039. *Club:* Queens Park Working Men's.

GREENWOOD, Ronald, CBE 1981; Manager, England Association Football Team, 1977–82, retired; *b* 11 Nov. 1921; *s* of Sam and Margaret Greenwood; *m* Lucy Joan Greenwood; one *s* one *d*. *Educ:* Alperton School. Apprenticed signwriter, 1937; joined Chelsea FC, 1940; served RAF, 1940–45; Bradford Park Avenue FC, 1945 (Captain); Brentford FC, 1949 (over 300 matches); rejoined Chelsea FC, 1952 (League Champions, 1954–55); Fulham FC, Feb. 1955; coached Oxford Univ. team, 3 years, Walthamstow Avenue FC, 2 years; Manager, Eastbourne United FC and England Youth team; Asst Manager, Arsenal FC, 1958; Team Manager, England Under-23, 1958–61; Manager and Coach, later Gen. Manager, West Ham United FC, 1961–77 (FA Cup, 1964 and 1975; European Cup Winners' Cup, 1965); a FIFA technical adviser, World Cup series, 1966 and 1970. *Publication:* Yours Sincerely, 1984. *Address:* 24 Cromwell Court, Cromwell Road, Hove, Sussex BN3 6NS.

GREER, Adrian; Cultural Counsellor and Director, Russia, British Council, since 2000; *b* 26 April 1957; *s* of David Smith Greer and Christine Greer (*née* Dawson); *m* 1985, (Mary) Diana Cuddy; one *s* three *d*. *Educ:* Queen Mary's Grammar Sch., Walsall; St Andrews Univ. (MA Eng. Lang. and Lit.). CPFA 1984. Auditor, Nat. Audit Office, 1979–84; joined British Council, 1984; Finance Develt Office, 1984–85; Finance Manager, Japan, 1985-88; Finance Project Manager, 1988-89, Chief Accountant, 1989-91, London; Director: Lesotho and Swaziland, 1991-93; Zambia, 1993-96; Europe (Develt and Trng Services), 1996–98; Asia and Americas (Develt and Trng Services), 1998–2000. *Recreations:* travel, sport, running. *Address:* c/o British Council, 10 Spring Garden, SW1A 2AA. *Club:* Bramhall Golf.

GREER, Prof. David Clive; Professor of Music, University of Durham, 1986–2001, now Emeritus (Chairman, Music Department, 1986–94); *b* 8 May 1937; *s* of William Mackay Greer and Barbara (*née* Avery); *m* 1961, Patricia Margaret Regan (*d* 1999); two *s* one *d*. *Educ:* Dulwich Coll.; Queen's Coll., Oxford (BA 1960; MA 1964); MusD TCD, 1991. Lectr in Music, Birmingham Univ., 1963–72; Hamilton Harty Prof. of Music, QUB, 1972–84; Prof. of Music, Univ. of Newcastle upon Tyne, 1984–86. Mellon Vis. Fellow, 1989, Mayers Foundn Fellow, 1991, Huntington Liby, Calif; Folger Vis. Fellow, Folger Shakespeare Liby, Washington, 1994 and 1998. Mem. Bd, Arts Council of NI, 1972–84. Chm., Mgt Cttee, and Guest Conductor, Ulster Orch., 1972–84; Mem. Council, Royal Musical Assoc., 1977–90. FRSA 1986. Editor, Proceedings, subseq. Jl, of Royal Musical Assoc, 1977–90. *Publications:* (ed) English Madrigal Verse, 1967; Hamilton Harty: his life and music, 1979, 2nd edn 1980; Hamilton Harty: early memories, 1979; (ed) Collected English Lutenist Partsongs, 2 vols, 1987–89, and other editions of 16th and 17th century music; A Numerous and Fashionable Audience: the story of Elsie Swinton, 1997; (ed) John Dowland, Ayres for four voices, 2000; Musicology and Sister Disciplines: past, present, future, 2000; articles in Music and Letters, Music Review, Musical Times, Shakespeare Qly, English Studies, Notes & Queries, Lute Soc. Jl. *Recreations:* reading, cinema, walking. *Address:* The Music School, Palace Green, Durham DH1 3RL. *T:* (0191) 374 3220; *e-mail:* d.c.greer@durham.ac.uk. *Club:* Athenæum.

GREER, Prof. Germaine, PhD; writer and broadcaster; Professor of English and Comparative Studies, Warwick University, since 1998; *b* Melbourne, 29 Jan. 1939. *Educ:* Melbourne Univ. (BA 1959); Sydney Univ. (MA 1962); Commonwealth Scholarship, 1964; Cambridge Univ. (PhD 1967). Sen. Tutor in English, Sydney Univ., 1963–64; Asst Lectr, then Lectr in English, Warwick Univ., 1967–72; Lectr, American Program Bureau, 1973–78; Prof. of Modern Letters, Univ. of Tulsa, 1980–83; Founder Dir, Tulsa Centre for Studies in Women's Literature, 1981; Special Lectr and Unofficial Fellow, Newnham Coll., Cambridge, 1989–98. Vis. Prof., Univ. of Tulsa, 1979. Proprietor, Stump Cross Books, 1988–. *Publications:* The Female Eunuch, 1970; The Obstacle Race: the fortunes of women painters and their work, 1979; Sex and Destiny: the politics of human fertility, 1984; Shakespeare, 1986; The Madwoman's Underclothes: selected journalism, 1986; (ed jtly) Kissing the Rod: an anthology of 17th century verse, 1988; Daddy, We Hardly Knew You, 1989 (J. R. Ackerly Prize; Premio Internazionale Mondello); (ed) The Uncollected Verse of Aphra Behn, 1989; The Change: women, ageing and the menopause, 1991; Slip-shod Sibyls: recognition, rejection and the woman poet, 1995; (ed jtly) The Surviving Works of Anne Wharton, 1997; The Whole Woman, 1999; contribs to Journalist. *Address:* c/o Gillon Aitken Associates Ltd, 29 Fernshaw Road, SW10 0TG.

GREER, Ian Bramwell; Chairman: Corporate and Government Relations International Ltd, since 1998; International Government Relations, since 1997; *b* 5 June 1933; *s* of Bramwell and Janet Greer. *Educ:* Cranbrook Coll., Essex; Victoria Sch., Glasgow.

Conservative Central Office and Party Agent, 1956–67; Nat. Dir, Mental Health Trust, 1967–70; Man. Dir, Russell Greer & Associates, 1970–82; Chm., Ian Greer Associates, 1982–96. *Publications:* Right to be Heard, 1985; One Man's Word, 1997. *Recreations:* antiques, walking, gardening, dogs. *Address:* 16 Catherine Place, SW1E 4HF. *Club:* Royal Automobile.

GREET, Rev. Dr Kenneth Gerald; Secretary of the Methodist Conference, 1971–84; President of the Methodist Conference, 1980–81; Moderator, Free Church Federal Council, 1982–83; Vice-President, World Disarmament Campaign, since 1994; *b* 17 Nov. 1918; *e s* of Walter and Renée Greet, Bristol; *m* 1947, Mary Eileen Edbrooke; one *s* two *d*. *Educ:* Cotham Grammar Sch., Bristol; Handsworth Coll., Birmingham. Minister: Cwm and Kingstone Methodist Church, 1940–42; Ogmore Vale Methodist Church, 1942–45; Tonypandy Central Hall, 1947–54; Sec. Dept of Christian Citizenship of Methodist Church, 1954–71; Member: BCC, 1955–84 (Chm. of Exec., 1977–81); World Methodist Council, 1957–2001 (Chm., Exec. Cttee, 1976–81); Chairman: Exec., Temperance Council of Christian Churches, 1961–71; World Christian Temperance Fedn, 1962–72. Pres., Methodist Peace Fellowship, 1999–. Rep. to Central Cttee, WCC, Addis Ababa, 1971, Nairobi, 1975. Beckly Lectr, 1962; Willson Lectr, Kansas City, 1966; Cato Lectr, Sydney, 1975. Chm. Govs, Southlands Coll., Wimbledon, 1987–97. Hon. DD Ohio, USA, 1968; DUniv Surrey, 1998. *Publications:* The Mutual Society, 1962; Man and Wife Together, 1962; Large Petitions, 1964; Guide to Loving, 1965; The Debate about Drink, 1969; The Sunday Question, 1970; The Art of Moral Judgement, 1970; When the Spirit Moves, 1975; A Lion from a Thicket, 1978; The Big Sin: Christianity and the arms race, 1983; What Shall I Cry?, 1986; Life of Jabez Bunting, 1995; Fully Connected (autobiog.), 1997. *Recreations:* reading, photography. *Address:* 89 Broadmark Lane, Rustington, Sussex BN16 2JA. *T:* (01903) 773326; *e-mail:* greet@skynow.net.

GREETHAM, (George) Colin; Headmaster, Bishop's Stortford College, 1971–84; *b* 22 April 1929; *s* of late George Cecil Greetham and of Gertrude Greetham (*née* Heavyside); *m* 1963, Rosemary (*née* Gardner); two *s* one *d*. *Educ:* York Minster Song Sch.; St Peter's Sch., York; (Choral Scholar) King's Coll., Cambridge. BA (Hons) History Tripos Cantab, Class II, Div. I, 1952; Certif. of Educn (Cantab), 1953. *Recreations:* music, choral training, horticulture, bowls. *Address:* Chapelhead Farm, Crossroads, Keith, Banffshire AB55 6LQ.

GREGG, Hubert Robert Harry; actor, composer, lyric writer, author, playwright and director; *b* London, 19 July 1914; *s* of Robert Joseph Gregg and Alice Maud (*née* Bessant); *m* 1st, 1943, Zoe Gail (marr. diss. 1950); one *d*; 2nd, 1956, Pat Kirkwood (marr. diss. 1979); 3rd, 1980, Carmel Lytton; one *s* one *d*. *Educ:* St Dunstan's Coll.; Webber-Douglas Sch. of Singing and Dramatic Art; BA Hons Open 1997. Served War, 1939–44: private, Lincs Regt, 1939; commnd 60th Rifles, 1940; transf. Intell.; with Polit. Warfare Exec., 1942 (duties included broadcasting in German). *Stage:* 1st London appearance, Julien in Martine, Ambassadors', 1933; Birmingham Rep., 1933–34; Shakespearean roles, Open Air Theatre, Regent's Park and at Old Vic, 1934, 1935; 1st New York appearance, Kit Neilan in French without Tears, 1937 (and London, 1938–39); London appearances include: Pip in The Convict, 1935; roles in classics (Orlando, Henry V, Hamlet), 1935–36; Frederick Hackett in Great Possessions, 1937; Peter Scott-Fowler in After the Dance, 1939; Polly in Men in Shadow, 1942; Michael Caraway in Acacia Avenue, 1944; Earl of Harpenden in While the Sun Shines, 1945, 1946; Tom D'Arcy in Off the Record, 1947; Gabriel Hathaway in Western Wind, 1949; (1st musical), John Blessington-Briggs in Chrysanthemum, 1958; Lionel Toope in Pools Paradise, 1961. *Chichester Festival Theatre:* Alexander MacColgie Gibbs in The Cocktail Party, Antonio in The Tempest, and Announcer in The Skin of our Teeth, 1968; Sir Lucius O'Trigger in The Rivals, Britannus in Caesar and Cleopatra, and Marcellin in Dear Antoine (also London), 1971. *Directed, London:* The Hollow (Agatha Christie's 1st stage success), 1951; re-staged To Dorothy - a Son, 1952 (subseq. toured in play, 1952–53); The Mousetrap (for 7 yrs from 1953); Speaking of Murder, 1958; The Unexpected Guest, 1958; From the French, 1959; Go Back for Murder, 1960; Rule of Three, 1962; re-staged The Secretary Bird, 1969 (subseq. toured in play, 1969–70). 1st solo performance, Leicester, 1970; subseq. performances in Britain and America (subjects include Shakespeare, Shaw, Jerome K. Jerome, the London Theatre, and the 20s, 30s and 40s); solo perf., Words by Elgar, Music by Shaw, Malvern Fest., 1978, Edinburgh Fest., 1979. *Films include:* In Which We Serve; Flying Fortress; Acacia Avenue (USA as The Facts of Love); The Root of all Evil; Vote for Huggett; Once upon a Dream; Robin Hood (Walt Disney); The Maggie (USA as High and Dry); Svengali; Doctor at Sea (also wrote music and lyrics); Simon and Laura; Speaking of Murder; The Third Visitor; Final Appointment; Room in the House; Stars in Your Eyes (also co-dir. and wrote music and lyrics). *Author of plays:* We Have Company (played in tour, 1953); Cheque Mate (dir. and appeared in); Villa Sleep Four (played in tour, 1965); From the French (written under pseudonym of Jean-Paul Marotte); Who's Been Sleeping . . . ? (also appeared in); The Rumpus (played in tour, 1967); Dear Somebody (perf. Germany as Geliebtes Traumbild, 1984); (screenplay) After the Ball (adapted from own television biog. of Vesta Tilley). *Songs:* Author of over 200, including: I'm going to get lit up; Maybe it's because I'm a Londoner. BBC broadcasts in drama, revue, poetry, etc, 1933–; announcer, BBC Empire Service, 1934–35; radio musical of Three Men in a Boat, 1962 (adapted, wrote music and words, and appeared in); weekly radio progs with accent on nostalgia, 1965– (A Square Deal, I Remember it Well, Now and Then, Thanks for the Memory); Chairman: BBC TV Brains Trust, 1955; Youth Wants to Know, ITV, 1957; 40 week radio series on London theatres, 1974–75; biog. series: I Call it Genius, 1980–81; I Call it Style, 1981–; Hubert Gregg Remembers, ITV solo series, 1982–; 50 Years of Broadcasting, BBC celebration prog. Maybe It's Because …), 1984 (Sony Radio Award, 1985); Hubert Gregg Remembers (series for BBC World Service), 1985–; (wrote book, music and lyrics, and appeared in) Sweet Liza (radio musical play), 1985; (wrote script, music and lyrics for, and presented) My London (radio), 1986; (wrote and presented) Sounds and Sweet Airs (celebration of 60 yrs at the microphone), 1993; (wrote music and lyrics for) Sherry, 1993; (wrote and presented) Hubert Gregg and the Forties (commemorating 50th anniversary of D-Day), 1994; (wrote and presented) Hubert Gregg and the Twenties, Hubert Gregg and the Thirties, (radio), 1995; Hubert Gregg and the Fifties, 1996. Has dir., lectured and adjudicated at Webber-Douglas Sch., Central Sch. of Speech Trng and RADA. Patron, Cinema Theatre Assoc., 1973–; President: Northern Boys' Book Club, 1975– (succeeded P. G. Wodehouse); Concert Artists Assoc., 1979–80. Freedom of City of London, 1981. Gold Badge of Merit, British Acad. of Composers, Authors and Song Writers, 1982. *Publications:* April Gentleman (novel), 1951; We Have Company (play), 1953; A Day's Loving (novel), 1974; Agatha Christie and all that Mousetrap, 1980; Thanks for the Memory (biographies collected from radio series I Call it Genius and I Call it Style), 1983; Geliebtes Traumbild (play), 1984; music and lyrics. *Recreation:* cinematography. *Address:* c/o Broadcasting House, W1A 1AA. *Club:* Garrick.

GREGG, Prof. Paul James, MD; FRCS; Professor of Orthopaedic Surgical Science, University of Durham, since 2000; Consultant Orthopaedic Surgeon, South Tees Acute Hospitals NHS Trust, since 2000; *b* 26 Nov. 1945; *s* of George Ernest Gregg and Hebe Elizabeth Gregg; *m* 1977, Jennifer Hall; one *d*. *Educ:* St Peter's Sch., York; Med. Sch., Univ. of Newcastle upon Tyne (MB BS 1969; MD 1977). FRCS 1974; FRCSE *ad hominem* 1998. House Physician and House Surgeon, Royal Victoria Infirmary, Newcastle upon Tyne, 1969–70; surgical trng, Newcastle upon Tyne hosps, 1971–74; University of Newcastle upon Tyne: Demonstrator in Anatomy, 1970–71; Sen. Res. Associate, MRC Decompression Sickness Res. Team, 1976–77; Lectr in Orthopaedic Surgery, 1979–83; Sen. Registrar in Orthopaedic Surgery, N Reg. Trng Prog., 1977–79; Clin. Res. Fellow, Massachusetts Gen. Hosp., 1982–83; Sen. Lectr in Orthopaedic Surgery, Univ. of Edinburgh, 1983–85; Foundation Prof. of Orthopaedic Surgery, Univ. of Leicester, 1985–97; Prof. of Trauma and Orthopaedic Surgery, Univ. of Newcastle upon Tyne, 1997–2000. *Publications:* Fractures and Dislocations: principles of management, 1995; contribs to books; more than 100 scientific papers. *Recreations:* walking, golf. *Address:* The Old Vicarage, Grinton, Richmond, N Yorks DL11 6HR.

GREGG, Paul Richard; Chairman, Apollo Leisure Group plc, since 1978; *b* 2 Oct. 1941; *m* 1970, Anita Kim, (Nita), Grehan; two *s* one *d*. *Educ:* Hull Nautical Coll. ABC Cinema Gp, 1961–65; Star Gp of Cinemas, 1965–67; Pressed Steel Fisher Ltd, 1967–70; Entertainment Dir, Rover Motor Co., 1968–70; Entertainment and Tourist Manager, Southport DC, 1970–77. Mem., Variety Club of GB (former Pres.; Chief Barker, 1991). *Recreation:* theatre. *Address:* Apollo Leisure Group plc, Grehan House, Garsington Road, Cowley, Oxford OX4 5NQ. *T:* (01865) 782900, *Fax:* (01865) 782910. *Club:* Carlton.

GREGORIADIS, Prof. Gregory, PhD; Professor and Head, Centre for Drug Delivery Research, School of Pharmacy, University of London, since 1990; *b* 27 Feb. 1934; *s* of late Christos Gregoriadis and Athina Sakellariou; *m* 1968, Susan Byron-Brown; one *s* one *d*. *Educ:* Univ. of Athens (BSc 1958); McGill Univ. (MSc 1966; PhD 1968). Research Fellow: Albert Einstein Coll. of Medicine, 1968–70; Royal Free Hosp. Sch. of Medicine, 1970–72; Sen. Scientist, MRC, 1972–93. Founder and Dir, Lipoxen Ltd, 1998–. Fellow, Amer. Assoc. of Pharmaceutical Scientists, 1998. 15 NATO Scientific Affairs Div. awards, 1980–98; Founder's Award, Controlled Release Soc., 1994; Bangham Award, Liposome Res. Days Inc., 1995. *Publications:* (ed) Drug Carriers in Biology and Medicine, 1979; (ed jtly) Liposomes in Biology and Medicine, 1980; (ed jtly) Targeting of Drugs, 1982, 10th edn 2000; (ed) Liposome Technology, 1984, 2nd edn 1993; (ed) Liposomes as Drug Carriers: recent trends and progress, 1988; (ed jtly) Vaccines, 1989, 5th edn 1997; over 300 papers on drug and vaccine targeting. *Recreations:* creative writing, history and philosophy of Ancient Greece, politics. *Address:* Centre for Drug Delivery Research, School of Pharmacy, University of London, 29–39 Brunswick Square, WC1N 1AX. *T:* (020) 7753 5822.

GREGORIOS, His Eminence The Most Rev. the Archbishop of Thyateira and Great Britain; *see* Theocharus, Archbishop Gregorios.

GREGOROWSKI, Rt Rev. Christopher John; a Bishop Suffragan of Cape Town (Bishop of Table Bay), since 1998; *b* 19 Feb. 1940; *s* of William Victor Gregorowski and Doris Alice Gregorowski (*née* Skinner); *m* 1964, Margaret Merle Perold; two *d* (and one *d* decd). *Educ:* Diocesan Coll., Rondebosch, S Africa; Univ. of Cape Town (BA, MA); Birmingham Univ. (DPS); Cuddesdon Coll., Oxford. Deacon 1963, priest 1964, Church of Province of S Africa; Rector: St Cuthbert's, Tsolo, 1968–74; St Thomas, Rondebosch, 1974–86; All Saints, Somerset West, 1986–98. *Publications:* Why a Donkey was Chosen, 1975; The Bible for Little Children, 1982; Fly, Eagle, Fly!, 1982, 2nd edn 2000. *Recreations:* marathon running, reading, walking, ornithology. *Address:* 15 Starke Road, Bergvliet, 7945, South Africa. *T:* (21) 7125136. *Clubs:* Western Province Cricket, Spartan Harriers Athletic (Cape Town).

GREGORY, Alan Thomas, CBE 1984; Director, Willis Corroon (formerly Willis Faber) plc, 1987–97; *b* 13 Oct. 1925; *s* of Lloyd Thomas Gregory and Florence Abbott; *m* 1st, 1952, Pamela Douglas Scott (*d* 1986); one *s* two *d*; 2nd, 1988, Mrs Marion Newth (*née* Nash), JP. *Educ:* Dulwich Coll.; St John's Coll., Cambridge (Classics). Directed into coal mining, coal face worker, 1944; Min. of Power, 1948; JSSC 1957; Chm., NATO Petroleum Planning Cttee, 1967–70; joined British Petroleum, 1971; Gen. Manager, BP Italiana, 1972–73; Dir, Govt and Public Affairs, 1975–85, and Dir, UK and Ireland Region, 1980–85, British Petroleum Co.; Chm., BP Oil Ltd, 1981–85; Director: BP Chemicals International Ltd, 1981–85; National Home Loans Corp., 1985–91. Governor, Queen Mary Coll., London Univ., 1981–87. President, Inst. of Petroleum, 1982–84. Univ. Comr, 1988–95. Churchwarden, St Mary's, Stoke D'Abernon, 1990–92. *Recreations:* books, gardening, theatre. *Address:* Red Oak, 31 Fairmile Avenue, Cobham, Surrey KT11 2JA. *T:* (01932) 864457. *Club:* Travellers.

GREGORY, Rear-Adm. Alexander Michael, OBE 1987; Chief Executive, Mechanical and Metal Trades Confederation, since 2000; *b* 15 Dec. 1945; *s* of Vice-Adm. Sir (George) David (Archibald) Gregory, KBE, CB, DSO and Florence Eve Patricia Gregory (*née* Hill); *m* 1970, Jean Charlotte Muir; four *d*. *Educ:* Marlborough; BRNC Dartmouth. Served HM Ships Albion, Aisne, Narwhale, Otter, Warspite, Courageous, Odin (Australia), Finwhale (i/c), Repulse 1965–80; Staff, US 3rd Fleet, Hawaii, 1980–82; HMS Renown (i/c), 1982–85; Comdr 10th SM Sqdn and HMS Resolution (i/c), 1985–86; Jt Services Defence Coll., 1987; Naval Warfare, MoD, 1987–88; HMS Cumberland (i/c), 1988–91; Captain, 10th Submarine Sqdn, 1991–93; Naval Staff Duties, MoD, 1993–94; Naval Attaché, Washington, 1994–97; Flag Officer, Scotland, Northern England and NI, 1997–2000. Mem., Queen's Body Guard for Scotland, Royal Company of Archers. *Recreations:* shooting, fishing, ski-ing, gardening.

GREGORY, Clifford; Chief Scientific Officer, Department of Health and Social Security, 1979–84, retired; *b* 16 Dec. 1924; *s* of Norman and Grace Gregory; *m* 1948, Wyn Aveyard; one *d* (one *s* decd). *Educ:* Royal Coll. of Science, London Univ. (2nd Cl. Hons Physics; ARCS). Served War, RN, 1943–46. Lectr, Mddx Hosp. Med. Sch., 1949; Sen. Physicist, Mount Vernon Hosp., 1954; Dep. Reg. Physicist, Sheffield, 1960; Sen. Principal Scientific Officer, Min. of Health, 1966; Dep. Chief Scientific Officer, DHSS, 1972. *Publications:* scientific papers in med. and scientific jls. *Recreations:* outdoor pursuits, natural history. *Address:* 22 Lansdown Road, Gloucester GL1 3JD.

GREGORY, Conal Robert; company director, wine consultant and financial journalist; Director, Jackson Prentice Ltd, since 1999; *b* 11 March 1947; *s* of Patrick George Murray Gregory and Marjorie Rose Gregory; *m* 1971, Helen Jennifer Craggs; one *s* one *d*. *Educ:* King's College Sch., Wimbledon; Univ. of Sheffield (BA Hons Mod. Hist. and Pol Theory and Instns, 1968). Master of Wine by examination, Vintners' Co., 1979. Manager, Saccone & Speed Vintage Cellar Club, 1971–73; Wine Buyer, Reckitt & Colman, 1973–77; Editor, Internat. Wine and Food Soc's Jl, 1980–83; Dir, Standard Fireworks Ltd, 1987–92; Chm., Internat. Wine and Spirit Competition Ltd, 1997–98. Contested Lakenham, Norwich City election, 1976; Norfolk County Councillor, Thorpe Div., 1977–81; Vice-Pres., Norwich Jun. Chamber of Commerce, 1975–76; Mem., E Anglia Tourist Bd, 1979–81. Chairman: Norwich N Cons. Assoc., 1980–82; Norwich CPC, 1978–81; Vice-Chm., Eastern Area CPC, 1980–83; Member: Cons. Eastern Area Agric. Cttee, 1975–79; Cons. Provincial Council, Eastern Area, 1978–82; Chm. and Founder, Bow Gp of E Anglia, 1975–82; Nat. Vice-Chm., Bow Gp, 1976–77. MP (C) York, 1983–92. Hon. Treas., British/Cyprus CPA Gp, 1987–92; Sec., UK-Manx Parly Gp, 1987–92; Chm., Cons. Parly Food and Drinks Industries Cttee, 1989–92 (Vice-Chm.,

1985–89); Vice-Chairman: Cons. Parly Tourism Cttee, 1985–92; Cons. Parly Transport Cttee, 1987–89 and 1990–92 (Sec., 1983–87); All Party Parly Hospice Gp, 1990–92; All Party Parly Tourism Cttee, 1991–92 (Sec., 1983–91); Mem., Cttee, British Atlantic Gp of Young Politicians, 1983–92 (Chm., 1988–89; Pres., 1989–92); Pres., York Young Conservatives, 1982–93; Vice-President: Nat. Soc. of Cons. and Unionist Agents, Yorks Br., 1983–92; York Br., UNA, 1983–92. Parliamentary Consultant: The Market Res. Soc., 1984–91; Consort Hotels Ltd, 1984–91; Consultant: Andry Montgomery Ltd, 1979–97; Smith & Taylor Ltd, 1992–2000; CC&C Research, 1993–96; Cash Centres Ltd, 1995–; Emphasis Research and Marketing, 1997–; Jackson Nugent Vintners Ltd, 1997–. Fellow, Industry and Parlt Trust, 1984–87. Private Member's Bills on consumer safety, 1985, on smoke alarms, 1991, on cheque fraud, 1992. Patron, Nat. Trust for Welfare of the Elderly, 1983–92; Founder Mem., Wymondham Br., CEMS, 1979; Member: Wymondham Abbey PCC, 1982–83; Humbleyard Deanery Synod, 1982–83; High Steward's Cttee, York Minster Fund, 1983–89; York Archaeol Trust, 1983–; York Georgian Soc., 1982–92; York Civic Trust, 1982–92; 20th Century British Art Fair Council, 1992–; ESU, 1994–. Governor, Heartsease Sch., Norwich, 1977–83; Mem., Court of Governors: Univ. of Sheffield, 1977–; Univ. of York, 1983–92; Univ. of Hull, 1983–92. Wine Corresp., Catering Times, 1979–83. *Publications:* (with W. Knock) Beers of Britain, 1975; (with R. A. Adley) A Policy for Tourism?, 1977; A Caterer's Guide to Drinks, 1979; (with M. Shersby and A. McCurley) Food for a Healthy Britain, 1987; The Cognac Companion, 1997; contribs to The Times, Scotsman, Sunday Telegraph, etc. *Address:* c/o Jackson Nugent Vintners Ltd, 60 High Street, Wimbledon Village, SW19 5EE.

GREGORY, Janice; Member (Lab) Ogmore, National Assembly for Wales, since 1999; *b* 1955. Asst to Sir Raymond Powell, MP. Member: Fabian Soc.; USDAW. *Address:* National Assembly for Wales, Cardiff Bay, Cardiff CF99 1NA.

GREGORY, John Peter; JP; CEng, FIMechE; Director, ASL Ltd, 1986–91; *b* 5 June 1925; *s* of Mr and Mrs P. Gregory; *m* 1949, Lilian Mary (*née* Jarvis); one *s* one *d*. *Educ:* Ernest Bailey Sch., Matlock; Trinity Hall, Cambridge (Scholar, MA). CEng, FIMechE 1970. Served War, RAF Pilot, 1943–47. Joined Cadbury Bros Ltd, 1949, Dir 1962; Vice Chm., Cadbury Ltd, 1969–70, Dir, Cadbury Schweppes, 1971–82 (Chm., Overseas Gp and Internat. Tech. Dir, 1973–80); Director: National Vulcan Engrg Ins. Group Ltd, 1970–79; Amalgamated Power Engrg Ltd, 1973–81; Chm., Data Recording Instruments Ltd, 1982–84. Gen. Comr of Income Tax, 1978–82. Chm. Trustees, Middlemore Homes, 1970–82. Liveryman, Worshipful Co. of Needlemakers. JP Birmingham, 1979. *Recreations:* music, bridge, country pursuits, sailing. *Address:* 5 Place Stables, Place Road, Fowey, Cornwall PL23 1DR. *Clubs:* Carlton; Royal Fowey Yacht.

GREGORY, Prof. Kenneth John, PhD, DSc; Warden, Goldsmiths' College, University of London, 1992–98, now Professor Emeritus and Hon. Fellow; *b* 23 March 1938; *s* of Frederick Arthur Gregory and Marion Gregory; *m* Margaret Christine Wilmot; one *s* two *d*. *Educ:* University College London (BSc Special 1959; PhD 1962; DSc 1982; Fellow 1999). University of Exeter: Lectr in Geography, 1962–72; Reader in Physical Geography, 1972–76; University of Southampton: Prof. of Geography, 1976–92; Head of Geography Dept, 1978–83; Dean of Science, 1984–87; Dep. Vice-Chancellor, 1988–92; Vis. Prof., 1998–. Hon. Res. Fellow, UCL, 1993–; Hon. Prof., Univ. of Birmingham, 1997–; Leverhulme Emeritus Fellow, 1998–2001. Vis. Lectr, Univ. of New England, NSW, 1975; Distinguished Visiting Professor, 1987: Univ. Kebangsaan; Arizona State Univ.; Snyder Lectr, Univ. of Toronto, 1990. Pres., Commn on Global Continental Palaeohydrology, Internat. Assoc. on Union for Quaternary Res., 1999– (Vice-Pres., 1992). Trustee, Horniman Mus. and Gardens, 1997–. Gov., Southampton Inst., 1998– (Vice Chm., Bd of Govs, 1999–). For. Mem., Polish Acad. of Arts and Scis, 1995. Freeman, City of London, 1997; Liveryman, Goldsmiths' Co., 1998– (Freeman, 1997; Mem., Educn Cttee, 1999–). Hon. Fellow, Goldsmiths' Coll., 1998. Hon. DSc: Southampton, 1997; Greenwich, 1997. Back Award, 1980, Founder's Medal, 1993, RGS; Linton Award, British Geomorphological Res. Gp, 1999; Scottish Geographical Medal, RSGS, 2000. *Publications:* (with A. H. Shorter and W. L. D. Ravenhill) Southwest England, 1969; (with D. E. Walling) Drainage Basin Form and Process, 1973; (jtly) An Advanced Geography of the British Isles, 1974; (with E. Derbyshire and J. R. Hails) Geomorphological Processes, 1979; The Yellow River, 1980; The Nature of Physical Geography, 1985 (trans. Russian and Portuguese); (ed jtly) The Encyclopedic Dictionary of Physical Geography, 1985; (ed) Energetics of Physical Environment, 1987; (ed jtly) Human Activity and Environmental Processes, 1987; (ed jtly) Palaeohydrology in Practice, 1987; (ed jtly) Horizons in Physical Geography, 1988; (ed) The Earth's Natural Forces, 1990; (ed) The Guinness Guide to the Restless Earth, 1991; (ed jtly) Temperate Palaeohydrology, 1991; (ed jtly) Global Continental Palaeohydrology, 1995; (ed jtly) Global Continental Changes: the context of palaeohydrology, 1996; (ed jtly) Evaluating Teacher Quality in High Education, 1996; (ed) Geological Conservation Review Fluvial Geomorphology of Great Britain, 1997; (ed jtly) Palaeohydrology and Environmental Change, 1998; The Changing Nature of Physical Geography, 2000. *Recreations:* travel, gardening, reading. *Address:* Woolmer View, Longmoor Road, Griggs Green, Liphook, Hants GU30 7PB; *e-mail:* Ken.Gregory@btinternet.com.

GREGORY, Leslie Howard James; former National Officer of EETPU; *b* 18 Jan. 1915; *s* of J. F. and R. E. Gregory; *m* 1949, D. M. Reynolds; one *s* one *d*. *Educ:* Junior Section, Ealing College (formerly Acton Coll.) and state schools. Mem. Exec. Council, ETU, 1938–54; full-time Nat. Officer, 1954–79, retired. Member: CSEU Nat. Sub-Cttees, for Shipbuilding, 1966–79, for Railway Workshops, 1968–78; Craft Training Cttees of Shipbuilding ITB, 1965–77, and Engineering ITB, 1965–68; EDC for Elec. Engrg, 1967–74; EDC for Shipbuilding, 1974–76; Org. Cttee, British Shipbuilders, 1976–77; Bd, British Shipbuilders (part-time), 1977–80.

GREGORY, Prof. Peter John, PhD; FIBiol; Professor of Soil Science, since 1994, and Pro-Vice-Chancellor (Research), since 1998, University of Reading; *b* 19 July 1951; *s* of Joseph Henry Gregory and June Rosamond Gregory; *m* 1973, Jane Sandra Crump; two *s*. *Educ:* Chatham House Grammar Sch.; Univ. of Reading (BSc Soil Sci.); Univ. of Nottingham (PhD Soil Sci. 1977). FIBiol 1994. Lectr, Univ. of Reading, 1980–89; Principal Res. Scientist, CSIRO Div. of Plant Industry, Australia, 1990–93. *Publications:* Root Development and Function, 1987; Soils in the Urban Environment, 1991; Crop Production on Duplex Soils, 1992; Land Resources: on the edge of the Malthusian precipice?, 1997; numerous scientific papers on soil/plant interactions in learned jls and books. *Recreations:* gardening, folk dancing, fishing. *Address:* University of Reading, PO Box 233, Whiteknights, Reading RG6 6DW.

GREGORY, Peter Roland; Director, Personnel, Management and Business Services, National Assembly for Wales, since 2000; *b* 7 Oct. 1946; *s* of Tom and Ruby Gregory; *m* 1978, Frances Margaret Hogan. *Educ:* Sexeys Grammar Sch., Blackford, Som.; University College Swansea (BA Hons 1968); Manchester Univ. (PhD 1972). Joined Welsh Office, 1971; Private Sec. to Perm. Sec., 1974–75; Principal, 1976; Asst Sec., 1982; Under Sec, Transport, Planning and Envmt Gp, 1990–94; Dir, Health Dept, 1994–99; Dir, NHS Wales, 1999–2000. *Recreations:* walking, theatre, music. *Address:* National Assembly for Wales, Cathays Park, Cardiff CF1 3NQ.

GREGORY, Philip William; Chairman, United Bristol Healthcare NHS Trust, since 1998; *b* 30 Sept. 1947; *s* of late Thomas Douglas Gregory and of Winifred (*née* Brooks); partner, Rosemary Clarke. *Educ:* Beaminster Comprehensive Sch., Dorset; Southampton Coll. of Technology (Dip. Municipal Admin). Regl Official, NALGO, 1974-82; SW Regl Sec., TUC, 1982-93. Member: Dorset AHA, 1974-79; Somerset AHA, 1979-91. Member Board: South West Electricity, 1985-89; Bristol Develt Corp., 1988-96; DTI Develt Bd for SW, 1988-97; SW Regl Chm., Nat. Training Awards, 1993-97; Chm., Community Foundn Network, 1995-2000; Member: Employment Tribunal, 1975-; Bristol Initiative, 1989-. Mem., Lockleaze Ward, Bristol CC, 1992-99. Treas., Lockleaze Neighbourhood Trust, 1996-. *Recreations:* golf, gardening, walking, watching cricket (Somerset). *Address:* 42 Station Road, Shirehampton, Bristol BS11 9TX. *T:* (0117) 982 9408. *Club:* City and Port of Bristol Sports and Social.

GREGORY, Richard John; Managing Director, Yorkshire Television, since 1997; *b* 18 Aug. 1954; *s* of John and Joan Gregory; *m* 1976, Elaine Matthews; two *d*. Trainee, Doncaster Gazette, 1972–75; gen. reporter, Doncaster Evening Post, 1976; labour corresp. and industrial corresp., Sheffield Morning Telegraph, 1977–79; News Ed., Granada TV, 1979–81; Yorkshire Television: News Ed., 1981–82; Producer, 1982–84; Ed., Calendar, 1984–89; Hd of News, 1989–92; Controller, 1992–93; Dir, Regl Progs, 1993–95; Dir of Broadcasting, 1995; Man. Dir, Broadcasting, Yorkshire Tyne Tees, 1996–97. Non-executive Director: Yorkshire Bank, 2000–; Clydesdale Bank, 2000–. Mem., Yorks and Humber Regl Develt Agency, subseq. Yorkshire Forward, 1998– (Dep. Chm., 1999–); Chm., Yorks Initiative, 1997–2001; Mem., Yorks Regl Cultural Consortium, 2000–. Chm., Sheffield Hallam Univ., 1999–. Hon. DLit Bradford, 1999. *Recreation:* Peak District. *Address:* Yorkshire Television, Leeds LS3 1JS. *T:* (0113) 222 7184.

GREGORY, Prof. Richard Langton, CBE 1989; DSc; FRS 1992; FRSE 1969; Professor of Neuropsychology and Director of Brain and Perception Laboratory, University of Bristol, 1970–88, now Professor Emeritus and Senior Research Fellow; *b* 24 July 1923; *s* of C. C. L. Gregory, astronomer, and Patricia (*née* Gibson); *m* 1st, 1953, Margaret Hope Pattison Muir (marr. diss. 1966); one *s* one *d*; 2nd, 1967, Freja Mary Balchin (marr. diss. 1976). *Educ:* King Alfred Sch., Hampstead; Downing Coll., Cambridge, 1947–50 (Hon. Fellow, 1999); DSc Bristol, 1983. Served in RAF (Signals), 1941–46; Research, MRC Applied Psychology Research Unit, Cambridge, 1950–53; Univ. Demonstrator, then Lecturer, Dept of Psychology, Cambridge, 1953–67; Fellow, Corpus Christi Coll., Cambridge, 1962–67 (Hon. Fellow, 1997); Professor of Bionics, Dept of Machine Intelligence and Perception, Univ. of Edinburgh, 1967–70 (Chm. of Dept, 1968–70). Founder and Chm. Trustees, 1983–91, Pres., 1991–, The Exploratory Hands-on Science Centre. President: Section J, British Assoc. for Advancement of Science, 1975, Section X, 1986, and Section Q, 1989 and 1990; Experimental Psychol. Soc., 1981–82. Member: Royal Soc. Cttee for Public Understanding of Sci., 1986–92; BBC Sci. Consultative Gp, 1988–93. Royal Institution: Manager, 1971–74; Mem. Council and Vice-Pres., 1991–94; Christmas Lectr, 1967–68. Medawar Lectr, Royal Soc., 2001. DUniv: Open, 1990; Stirling, 1990; Hon. LLD Bristol, 1993; Hon. DSc: E Anglia, 1996; Exeter, 1996; York, 1998; UMIST, 1998; Keele, 1999; Edinburgh, 2000. Craik Prize for Physiological Psychology, St John's Coll., Cambridge, 1958; CIBA Foundn Research Prize, 1959; Waverley Gold Medal, 1960; Capire Internat. Prize, Internat. Cttee for Promotion of Advanced Educnl Res., Italy; Primo Rovis Prize, Trieste Internat. Foundn for Scientific Progress and Freedom, Italy; Michael Faraday Medal, Royal Soc., 1993; Lord Crook Medal, Spectacle Makers' Co., 1996; Hughlings Jackson Medal, RSocMed, 2000. Founder Editor, Perception, 1972. *Publications:* Recovery from Early Blindness (with Jean Wallace), 1963; Eye and Brain, 1966, 5th edn 1998; The Intelligent Eye, 1970; Concepts and Mechanisms of Perception, 1974; (ed jtly) Illusion in Nature and Art, 1973; Mind in Science, 1981; Odd Perceptions (essays), 1986; (ed) Oxford Companion to the Mind, 1987; (ed jtly) Evolution of the Eye and Visual System, vol. 2 of Vision and Visual Dysfunction, 1991; Even Odder Perceptions (essays), 1994; The Artful Eye, 1995; Mirrors in Mind, 1996; articles in various scientific jls and patents for optical and recording instruments and a hearing aid; radio and television appearances. *Recreations:* punning and pondering. *Address:* 23 Royal York Crescent, Clifton, Bristol BS8 4JX. *Clubs:* Athenæum, Chelsea Arts.

GREGORY, Roger Michael; Deputy Receiver for the Metropolitan Police, 1989–94, retired; *b* 1 June 1939; *s* of Walter James Gregory and Catherine Emma Gregory (*née* Regan); *m* 1961, Johanna Margaret O'Rourke; five *s* two *d*. *Educ:* Gillingham (Kent) Grammar Sch. Joined Metropolitan Police Civil Staff, 1957; Hd of Operations, Police National Computer Unit, 1976; Dep. Dir of Finance, Metropolitan Police, 1981; Dir of Computing, Metropolitan Police, 1983. *Recreations:* cricket, bridge, gentle gardening. *Address:* 29 Milton Road, Harpenden, Herts AL5 5LA.

GREGORY, Ronald, CBE 1980; QPM 1971; DL; Chief Constable of West Yorkshire Metropolitan Police, 1974–83, retired; *b* 23 Oct. 1921; *s* of Charles Henry Gregory and Mary Gregory; *m* 1942, Grace Miller Ellison; two *s*. *Educ:* Harris College. Joined Police Service, Preston, 1941. RAFVR, 1942–44; RNVR(A), 1944–46. Dep. Chief Constable, Blackpool, 1962–65; Chief Constable, Plymouth, 1965–68; Dep. Chief Constable, Devon and Cornwall, 1968–69; Chief Constable, West Yorkshire Constabulary, 1969–74. DL West Yorks, 1977. *Recreations:* golf, sailing, ski-ing.

GREGORY-HOOD, Peter Charles Freeman; HM Diplomatic Service, retired; *b* 12 Dec. 1943; *s* of late Col A. M. H. Gregory-Hood, OBE, MC and Diana, *d* of Sir John Gilmour, 2nd Bt (she *m* 2nd, Sir John Beith, KCMG); *m* 1966, Camilla Bethell; three *d*. *Educ:* Summerfields, St Leonard's; Eton Coll.; Aix-en-Provence Univ., Trinity Coll., Cambridge (BA Econs and Sociol.). Joined FCO, 1965: Third Sec., Dakar, 1967–69; Third, later Second Sec., Tel Aviv, 1969–71; First Secretary: FCO, 1972–76; (Commercial), Paris, 1976–80; FCO, 1980–86; (Inf.), New Delhi, 1986–90; Counsellor and Consul-Gen., Casablanca, 1990–95; Dep. High Comr, Colombo, 1995–98. *Recreations:* tennis, golf, swimming, ski-ing, theatre. *Address:* Loxley Hall, Warwick CV35 9SP. *Clubs:* White's, Royal Over-Seas League.

GREGSON, family name of **Baron Gregson.**

GREGSON, Baron *cr* 1975 (Life Peer), of Stockport in Greater Manchester; **John Gregson,** AMCT, CIMgt; DL; Non-Executive Director, Fairey Group plc (formerly Fairey Holdings Ltd), 1989–94; with British Steel plc (formerly British Steel Corporation), 1976–94; *b* 29 Jan. 1924. Joined Stockport Base Subsidiary, 1939; Fairey R&D team working on science of nuclear power, 1946; appointed to Board, 1966. Non-executive Dir, Innvotec Ltd (formerly Electra Corporate Ventures Ltd), 1989–99; non-exec. Dir, OSC Process Engineering Ltd, 1995. Mem., NRA, 1992–95. Member: H of L Select Cttee on Sci. & Technol., 1980–99; H of L Select Cttee on Sustainable Develt, 1994–96; President: Parly and Scientific Cttee, 1986–89; Finance and Industry Gp of Labour Party. Vice Pres., Assoc. of Metropolitan Authorities, 1984. President: Defence Manufacturers

Assoc., 1984–2000; Envmtl Industries Commn, 1994–96. Chairman: Waste Mgt Industry Trng and Adv. Bd, 1985–2000; Onyx Envmtl Trust, 1997–. Chm. Adv. Council, RMCS Shrivenham, 1985–99; Member Court: UMIST, 1976–; Univ. of Manchester, 1995–97. Hon. Fellow, Manchester Polytechnic, 1983; Hon. FIProdE 1982; Hon. FREng (Hon. FEng 1986); Hon. FICE 1987; Hon. FIEE. DUniv Open, 1986; Hon. DSc: Aston, 1987; Cranfield; Hon. DTech Brunel, 1989; Hon. DSc RMCS, 1990. DL Greater Manchester, 1979. *Recreations:* mountaineering, ski-ing, sailing, gardening. *Address:* 12 Rosemont Road, Richmond-upon-Thames, Surrey TW10 6QL. *T:* (020) 8948 2244, *Fax:* (020) 8948 3388; The Spinney, Cragg Vale, Mytholmroyd, Hebden Bridge, West Yorks HX7 5SR; 407 Hawkins House, Dolphin Square, SW1V 3XL.

GREGSON, Prof. Edward; composer; Principal, Royal Northern College of Music, Manchester, since 1996; *b* 23 July 1945; *s* of Edward Gregson and May Elizabeth (*née* Eaves); *m* 1967, Susan Carole Smith; two *s*. *Educ:* Manchester Central Grammar Sch.; Royal Academy of Music (GRSM, LRAM's Hon. FRAM 1990); Goldsmiths' Coll., Univ. of London (BMus Hons). Lectr in Music, Rachel McMillan Coll., London, 1970–76; Sen. Lectr, 1976–89, Reader, 1989–94, and Prof. of Music, 1994–96, Goldsmiths' Coll., Univ. of London. Hon. Prof. of Music, Univ. of Manchester, 1996. Mem., Music Industry Forum, DCMS, 1998–. Vice-Chm., Composers' Guild, 1976–78; Chm., Assoc. of Professional Composers, 1989–91; Director: PRS, 1995–; Associated Bd of Royal Schs of Music, 1996–; Hallé Orch., 1998–. Gov., Chetham's Sch. of Music, 1996–. Trustee: Nat. Foundn for Youth Music, 1999–. Composer, RSC History Play Cycles: Plantagenets Trilogy, 1988–89; Henry IV Parts 1 and 2, 1990–91. Fellow, Dartington Coll. of Arts, 1997. FRSA. Hon. FLCM 1999; FRCM 2000. Hon. DMus Sunderland, 1996. *Compositions include:* Oboe Sonata, 1965; Brass Quintet, 1967; Music for Chamber Orchestra, 1968; Horn Concerto, 1971; Essay for Brass Band, 1971; Tuba Concerto, 1976; Music for the York Cycle of Mystery Plays, 1976 and 1980; Connotations for Brass Band, 1977; Metamorphoses, 1979; Trombone Concerto, 1979; Trumpet Concerto, 1983; Piano Sonata in one movement, 1983; Contrasts for orchestra, 1983; Dances and Arias, 1984; Festivo, 1985; Missa Brevis Pacem, 1988; Celebration, 1991; Of Men and Mountains, 1991; The Sword and the Crown, 1991; Blazon, 1992; Clarinet Concerto, 1994; Concerto for Piano and Wind, 1995; The Kings Go Forth, 1996; Stepping Out, 1996; A Welcome Ode, 1997; …And the Seven Trumpets, 1998; Three Matisse Impressions, 1998; The Dance, forever the Dance, 1999; Violin Concerto, 2000; The Trumpets of the Angels, 2000. *Publications:* music articles in professional jls. *Recreations:* walking, wine, watching sport. *Address:* Royal Northern College of Music, 124 Oxford Road, Manchester M13 9RD. *T:* (0161) 907 5273, *Fax:* (0161) 273 8188.

GREGSON, Sir Peter (Lewis), GCB 1996 (KCB 1988; CB 1983); Permanent Secretary, Department of Trade and Industry, 1989–96; Director, Scottish Power, since 1996; *b* 28 June 1936; *s* of late Walter Henry Gregson and Lillian Margaret Gregson. *Educ:* Nottingham High Sch.; Balliol Coll., Oxford. Classical Hon. Mods, class I; Lit. Hum. class I; BA 1959; MA 1962. Nat Service, 1959–61; 2nd Lieut RAEC, attached to Sherwood Foresters. Board of Trade: Asst Principal, 1961; Private Sec. to Minister of State, 1963–65; Principal, 1965; Resident Observer, CS Selection Bd, 1966; London Business Sch., 1967; Private Sec. to the Prime Minister, 1968–72 (Parly Affairs, 1968–70; Econ. and Home Affairs, 1970–72); Asst Sec., DTI, and Sec., Industrial Development Adv. Bd, 1972–74; Under Sec., DoI, and Sec., NEB, 1975–77; Under Sec., Dept of Trade, 1977–80, Dep. Sec. (Civil Aviation and Shipping), 1980–81; Dep. Sec., Cabinet Office, 1981–85; Perm. Under-Sec. of State, Dept of Energy, 1985–89. Chm., Woolwich Pension Fund Trust Co. Ltd, 1999–2000; Dir, Woolwich plc, 1998–2000. CIMgt (CBIM 1988; Mem., Bd of Companions, 1996– (Dep. Chm., 1999–)); FRSA 1999. *Recreations:* gardening, listening to music. *Address:* c/o Scottish Power plc, 1 Atlantic Quay, Glasgow G2 8SP. *T:* (0141) 248 8200.

GREIG, Geordie Carron; Editor, Tatler, since 1999; *b* 16 Dec. 1960; *s* of Sir (Henry Louis) Carron Greig, *qv*; *m* 1995, Kathryn Elizabeth Terry; one *s* twin *d*. *Educ:* Eton Coll.; St Peter's Coll., Oxford (MA English Lit. and Lang.). Reporter: South East London and Kentish Mercury, 1981–83; Daily Mail, 1984–85; Today, 1985–87; Sunday Times: Reporter, 1987–89; Arts Corresp., 1989–91; NY Corresp., 1991–95; Literary Editor, 1995–99. *Publication:* Louis and the Prince, 1999. *Address:* Vogue House, Hanover Square, W1R 0AD. *T:* (020) 7499 9080. *Clubs:* White's, Colony Rooms.

GREIG, Sir (Henry Louis) Carron, KCVO 1995 (CVO 1973); CBE 1986; DL; Chairman, Horace Clarkson PLC (formerly H. Clarkson (Holdings) plc), 1976–93; Director, James Purdey & Sons Ltd, since 1972; an Extra Gentleman Usher to the Queen, since 1995 (Gentleman Usher, 1961–95); *b* 21 Feb. 1925; *s* of late Group Captain Sir Louis Greig, KBE, CVO, DL; *m* 1955, Monica Kathleen, *d* of late Hon. J. J. Stourton, TD; three *s* one *d*. *Educ:* Eton. Scots Guards, 1943–47, Captain. Joined H. Clarkson & Co. Ltd, 1948; Dir, 1954; Man. Dir, 1962; Chairman: H. Clarkson & Co. Ltd, 1973–85; Baltic Exchange (formerly Baltic Mercantile and Shipping Exchange), 1983–85 (Dir, 1978–85); Director: Williams & Glyn's Bank, 1983–85; Royal Bank of Scotland, 1985–95; Charterhouse, 1990–93. Vice-Chm., Not Forgotten Assoc., 1979–96. Chm., Schoolmistresses and Governesses Benevolent Instn, 1992– (Dep. Chm., 1966–92). Governor, United World Coll. of the Atlantic, 1985–96. DL Hants, 1992. *Address:* Brook House, Fleet, Hants GU13 8RF; Binsness, Forres, Moray. *Clubs:* White's; Royal Findhorn Yacht.

See also G. C. Greig.

GREIG-SMITH, Peter William, DPhil; Chief Executive, Centre for Environment, Fisheries and Aquaculture Science, since 1997; *b* 17 May 1953; *s* of Peter Greig-Smith and Edna (*née* Gonzalez); *m* 1978, June Ann Fettes (marr. diss. 2000); one *s* one *d*; *m* 2001, Lindsay Ann Murray. *Educ:* Aberdeen Univ. (BSc Hons Zoology 1975); Sussex Univ. (DPhil Behavioural Ecology 1980). Joined MAFF, 1980; Res. Scientist, Agricl Sci. Service, 1980–86; Head of Envmtl Res., 1986–90, of Conservation and Envmt Protection, 1990–92, Central Sci. Lab.; Head of Aquatic Envmt Protection, 1992–94, Dir, 1994–97, Directorate of Fisheries Res. *Publications:* edited jointly: Field Margins, 1987; Field Methods for the Study of Environmental Effects of Pesticides, 1988; Pesticides, Cereal Farming and the Environment: the Boxworth project, 1992; Ecotoxicology of Earthworms, 1992; ECOtoxicology: ecological dimensions, 1996; numerous articles in sci. jls. *Recreations:* mountains, golf, DIY. *Address:* Centre for Environment, Fisheries and Aquaculture Science, Pakefield Road, Lowestoft, Suffolk NR33 0HT.

GREINER, Hon. Nicholas Frank, (Nick), AC 1994; Deputy Chairman, Stockland Trust Property Group, since 1992; *b* 27 April 1947; *s* of Nicholas and Clare Greiner; *m* 1970, Kathryn Callaghan (AO 2001); one *s* one *d*. *Educ:* St Ignatius Coll., Riverview; Sydney Univ. (BEc Hons); Harvard Univ. (MBA High Dist.). Asst Vice-Pres., Boise Cascade Corp., USA, 1970–71; NSW Dir and Chief Exec., White River Corp., 1972–80; Chm., Harper & Row (Australasia), 1977–83. Chairman: Baulderstone Hornibrook, 1993–; United Utilities Australia Pty Ltd (formerly North West Water), 1993–; Natwest Markets, 1994–98 (Dir, 1992–98); IAMA (formerly SBS-IAMA) Ltd, 1994–2000; W. D. & H. O. Wills, 1996–99 (Dir, 1995–99); British American Tobacco Australasia, 1999–; BMC Media, 1999–; Nuance Australia, 2001–; Co-Chair, Ausflag Ltd, 1996–2000; Dep. Chm., Coles Myer, 1995–96 (Dir, 1992–2000). Director: Brian McGuigan Wines, 1992–; QBE Insce Gp, 1992–; Consultant: Clayton Utz, 1992–; Salomon Smith Barney, 1998–; Deloitte Touche Tohmatsu, 1999–. Prof., Macquarie Grad. Sch. of Management, 1992–. MP (L) Ku-ring-gai, NSW, 1980–92; Shadow Minister for Urban Affairs, June 1981; Shadow Treasurer, and Shadow Minister for Housing and Co-operatives, Oct. 1981; Leader of State Opposition, 1983–88; Shadow Treasurer, and Shadow Minister for Ethnic Affairs, 1983; Premier, Treasurer, and Minister for Ethnic and Aboriginal Affairs, NSW Coalition Govt, 1988–92. Dir, Sydney Organising Cttee for Olympic Games, 1993–2000. Pres., Squash Australia, 1996–2000. *Recreations:* walking, ski-ing, theatre, opera, spectator sports. *Address:* Level 10, 139 Macquarie Street, Sydney, NSW 2000, Australia.

GRENFELL, family name of **Baron Grenfell**.

GRENFELL, 3rd Baron *cr* 1902; **Julian Pascoe Francis St Leger Grenfell;** Baron Grenfell of Kilvey (Life Peer) 2000; *b* 23 May 1935; *o s* of 2nd Baron Grenfell, CBE, TD, and of Elizabeth Sarah Polk, *o d* of late Captain Hon. Alfred Shaughnessy, Montreal, Canada; *S* father, 1976; *m* 1st, 1961, Loretta Maria Reali (marr. diss. 1970), Florence; one *d*; 2nd, 1970, Gabrielle Raab (marr. diss. 1987), Berlin; two *d*; 3rd, 1987, Mrs Elisabeth Porter (marr. diss. 1992), Washington, DC; 4th, 1993, Mrs Dagmar Langbehn Debreil, *yr d* of late Dr Carl Langbehn, Berlin. *Educ:* Eton; King's Coll., Cambridge. BA (Hons), President of the Union, Cambridge, 1959. 2 Lieut, KRRC (60th Rifles), 1954–56; Captain, Queen's Royal Rifles, TA, 1963; Programme Asst, ATV Ltd, 1960–61; frequent appearances and occasional scripts, for ATV religious broadcasting and current affairs series, 1960–64. Joined World Bank, Washington, DC, 1965; Chief of Information and Public Affairs for World Bank Group in Europe, 1970; Dep. Dir, European Office, 1973; Special rep. of World Bank to UN, 1974–81; Special Advr, 1983–87, Sen. Advr, 1987–90; Head of Ext. Affairs, European Office, 1990–95; Sen. Advr, European Office, 1995, retired. UK Delegn to Parly Assemblies of Council of Europe and WEU, 1997–99. Chm., Econ. and Financial Subcttee, H of L Select Cttee on EU, 1999 and 2001–. *Publication:* (novel) Margot, 1984. *Recreations:* walking, European history. *Heir: cousin* Francis Pascoe John Grenfell [*b* 28 Feb. 1938; *m* 1977, Elizabeth Katharine, *d* of Hugh Kenyon]. *Address:* c/o House of Lords, SW1A 0PW. *Club:* Royal Green Jackets.

GRENFELL, Andrée, (Mrs David Milman); Director, Milman International Australia, since 1990; *b* 14 Jan. 1940; *d* of Stephen Grenfell (writer) and Sybil Grenfell; *m* 1st, 1972, Roy Warden; two step *s*; 2nd, 1984, David Milman; two step *s*. *Educ:* privately. Graduate Diploma in Agric., Hawkesbury Agricl Coll., 1989. Man. Dir, Elizabeth Arden Ltd, UK, 1974–76; Pres., Glemby Internat., UK and Europe, 1976–80; Sen. Vice Pres., Glemby Internat., USA, 1976–80. Chm., Kelly Burrell & Jones, 1988–91; Director: Harvey Nichols Knightsbridge, 1972–74; Peter Robinson Ltd, 1968–72; Non-executive Director: NAAFI, 1981–83; Prince of Wales Res. Inst., Sydney, 1994–. Mem. Council, Inst. of Dirs, 1976; FIMgt (FBIM 1977). Mem., Cercle des Amis de la Veuve. Business Woman of the Year, FT, 1979. *Recreations:* riding, dressage, swimming, yoga. *Address:* 3/1 Rosemont Avenue, Woollahra, NSW 2025, Australia. *T:* (2) 93275964, *Fax:* (2) 93275964.

GRENFELL, (Jeremy) Gibson; QC 1994; a Recorder, since 1992; *b* 13 Dec. 1945; *s* of Edward Gerald James Grenfell and June (*née* Hunkin). *Educ:* Falmouth Grammar Sch.; Fitzwilliam Coll., Cambridge (Open Exhibnr, MA). Called to the Bar, Middle Temple, 1969 (Harmsworth Schol.). *Address:* 2 Pump Court, Temple, EC4Y 7AH. *T:* (020) 7353 5597.

GRENFELL, Simon Pascoe; His Honour Judge Grenfell; a Circuit Judge, since 1992; *b* 10 July 1942; *s* of late Osborne Pascoe Grenfell and Margaret Grenfell; *m* 1974, Ruth De Jersey Harvard; one *s* three *d*. *Educ:* Fettes College; Emmanuel College, Cambridge (MA). Called to the Bar, Gray's Inn, 1965; practice on NE Circuit; a Recorder, 1985–92; Designated Civil Judge: Bradford Group of Courts, 1998–2000; Leeds Group of Courts, 2000–. Chancellor, dio. of Ripon, 1992–. *Recreations:* music, sailing, coarse gardening.

GRENFELL-BAINES, Prof. Sir George, Kt 1978; OBE 1960; DL; FRIBA; FRTPI; consultant architect-planner; consultant to Building Design Partnership; *b* Preston, 30 April 1908; *s* of Ernest Charles Baines and Sarah Elizabeth (*née* Grenfell); *m* 1st, 1939, Dorothy Hodson (marr. diss. 1952); two *d*; 2nd, 1954, Milena Ruth Fleischmann; one *s* one *d*. *Educ:* Roebuck Street Council Sch.; Harris Coll., Preston; Manchester Univ. (DipTP). RIBA Dist Town Planning, 1963. Commenced architectural practice, 1937; founded: Grenfell Baines Gp, 1940; Building Design Partnership, a multi-disciplinary practice covering all aspects of built environment, 1959 (Partner/Chm.), retired 1974; The Design Teaching Practice, 1974, retired 1979. Prof. and Head of Dept of Architecture, Univ. of Sheffield, 1972–75, Emeritus, 1976. Lectr/Critic, 14 USA and Canadian univs, 1966; initiated own lecture tour USSR, visiting 19 cities, 1971; expert adviser: UNESCO Conf. Bldgs; Higher Educn, Chile, 1968; Conescal, Mexico City, 1973. RIBA: Mem. Council (nationally elected), 1952–70; Vice-Pres., 1967–69; Ext. Examr, 12 Schs of Architecture, 1953–70. Chm. of Cttees on Professional Practice, Town Planning, Gp Practice and Consortia; Architectural Competition Assessor 8 times; competition entrant, several awards: first place in 7 (one internat.); 18 premiums (four internat.). Hon. Fellow: Metrop. Univ. of Manchester (formerly Manchester Poly.), 1974; Univ. of Central Lancs (formerly Lancashire Poly.), 1985; Hon. Vice-Pres., N Lancs Soc. Architects, 1977. Hon. Fellow, Amer. Inst. of Architects, 1982. Broadcaster, UK and Canada. Hon. DLitt Sheffield, 1981. DL Lancs, 1982. *Publications:* contribs to tech. jls. *Recreations:* brooding: on economics and alternative medicine; walking: on hills and by sea-shore. *Address:* 56 & 60 West Cliff, Preston, Lancs PR1 8HU. *T:* (01772) 252131, 555824.

GRENIER, Rear-Adm. Peter Francis, (Frank), CB 1989; self-employed glass engraver; Defence Advisor, House of Commons Defence Committee, since 1991; *b* 27 Aug. 1934; *s* of late Dr F. W. H. Grenier and Mrs M. Grenier; *m* 1957, Jane Susan Bradshaw; two *s* one *d* (and one *s* decd). *Educ:* Montpelier School, Paignton; Blundell's School, Tiverton. Entered RN (Special Entry), 1952; Midshipman, Mediterranean Fleet, 1953; commissioned, 1955; joined Submarine service, 1956; 1st command (HMS Ambush), 1965; final command (HMS Liverpool), 1982; Chief of Staff to C-in-C Naval Home Command, 1985–87; FO Submarines, and Comdr Submarine Forces E Atlantic, 1987–89. Vice-Pres., Royal Naval FA, 1988–. Liveryman: Painter-Stainers' Co., 1984; Glass Sellers' Co., 1987. Chm. of Govs, Blundell's Sch., 1991–96 (Gov., 1986–96). AFGE. *Recreations:* family, sketching and painting, glass engraving, golf. *Clubs:* Army and Navy; West Wilts Golf.

GRENSIDE, Sir John (Peter), Kt 1983; CBE 1974; Senior Partner, Peat, Marwick, Mitchell & Co., Chartered Accountants, 1977–86; *b* 23 Jan. 1921; *s* of late Harold Cutcliffe Grenside and late Muriel Grenside; *m* 1946, Yvonne Thérèse Grau; one *s* one *d*. *Educ:* Rugby School. ACA 1948, FCA 1960. War Service, Royal Artillery, 1941–46 (Captain). Joined Peat, Marwick, Mitchell & Co., 1948, Partner, 1960, Senior Partner, 1977; Chm., Peat Marwick Internat., 1980–83. Inst. Chartered Accountants: Mem. Council, 1966–83; Chm. of Parliamentary and Law Cttee, 1972–73; Vice-Pres., 1973–74; Dep. Pres., 1974–75; Pres., 1975–76; Chm., Overseas Relations Cttee, 1976–78; UK

Rep. on Internat. Accounting Standards Cttee, 1976–80. Jt Vice-Pres., Groupe d'Etudes des Experts Comptables de la CEE, 1972–75; Chm., Review Bd for Govt Contracts, 1983–86; Mem. Panel of Judges for Accountants' Award for Company Accounts, 1973–77. Director: Allied-Lyons plc, 1986–93; Nomura Bank Internat. plc, 1987–96. Master, Worshipful Co. of Chartered Accountants in England and Wales, 1987–88. *Publications:* various articles for UK and US accountancy jls. *Recreations:* tennis, bridge. *Address:* 51 Cadogan Lane, SW1X 9DT. *T:* (020) 7235 3372. *Clubs:* Pilgrims, MCC, All England Lawn Tennis, Hurlingham.

GRENVILLE; *see* Freeman-Grenville, family name of Lady Kinloss.

GRENVILLE, Prof. John Ashley Soames; Professor of Modern History, 1969–94, Professorial Research Fellow, Institute of German Studies, since 1994, University of Birmingham; *b* Berlin, 11 Jan. 1928; *m* 1st, 1960, Betty Anne Rosenberg (*d* 1974), New York; three *s*; 2nd, 1975, Patricia Carnie; one *d* one step *d*. *Educ:* Mistley Place and Orwell Park Prep. Sch.; Cambridge Techn. Sch.; corresp. courses; Birkbeck Coll.; LSE; Yale Univ. BA, PhD London; FRHistS. Postgrad. Schol., London Univ., 1951–53; Asst Lectr, subseq. Lectr, Nottingham Univ., 1953–64; Commonwealth Fund Fellow, 1958–59; Postdoctoral Fellow, Yale Univ., 1960–63; Reader in Modern History, Nottingham Univ., 1964–65; Prof. of Internat. History, Leeds Univ., 1965–69. Vis. Prof., Queen's Coll., NY City Univ., 1964, etc; Guest Professor, Univ. of Hamburg, 1980, 1994. Chm., British Univs History Film Consortium, 1968–71; Mem. Council: RHistS, 1971–73; List and Index Soc., 1966–71; Baeck Inst., London, 1981–. Consultant, American and European Bibliographical Centre, Oxford and California and Clio Press, 1960–88; Dir of Film for the Historical Assoc., 1975–78; Historical Adviser, World History, ZDF, German Television, 1982–98. Editor: Fontana History of War and Society, 1969–78; Leo Baeck Year Book, 1992–. *Publications:* (with J. G. Fuller) The Coming of the Europeans, 1962; Lord Salisbury and Foreign Policy, 1964 (2nd edn 1970); (with G. B. Young) Politics, Strategy and American Diplomacy: studies in foreign policy 1873–1917, 1966 (2nd edn 1971); Documentary Films (with N. Pronay), The Munich Crisis, 1968; The End of Illusions: from Munich to Dunkirk, 1970; The Major International Treaties 1914–1973: a history and guide, 1974, enlarged edn (jtly) 1900–1999, 2000; Europe Reshaped 1848–78, 1975, enlarged edn, 2000; Nazi Germany, 1976; World History of the Twentieth Century I, 1900–1945, 1980; Collins World History of the Twentieth Century, 1994, 2nd edn 1998, enlarged, 2000; contrib. various learned jls. *Recreation:* listening to music. *Address:* University of Birmingham, Institute for German Studies, Birmingham B15 2TT. *Club:* Athenæum.

GRENVILLE-GREY, Wilfrid Ernest; journalist at United Nations, New York, since 1990; *b* 27 May 1930; *s* of late Col Cecil Grenville-Grey, CBE and of Monica Grenville-Grey (*née* Morrison-Bell); *m* 1963, Edith Sibongile Dlamini (marr. diss. 1989), *d* of Rev. Jonathan Dlamini, Johannesburg; two *s* one *d*. *Educ:* Eton; Worcester College, Oxford (scholar; MA); Yale University (Henry Fellow, 1953–54). 2nd Lieut, KRRC, 1949–50. Overseas Civil Service, Nyasaland, 1956–59; Booker McConnell Ltd, 1960–63; Mindolo Ecumenical Foundn, Zambia, 1963–71 (Dir, 1966–71); Sec., Univ. Study Project on Foreign Investments in S Africa, 1971–72; Dir, Centre for Internat. Briefing, Farnham Castle, 1973–77; Internat. Defence and Aid Fund for Southern Africa, London and UN, 1978–83; Sec. for Public Affairs to Archbishop of Canterbury, 1984–87; British Dir, Global Forum of Spiritual and Parly Leaders on Human Survival, 1987–88; Internat. Develt Dir, Icewalk, 1988–89. *Publications:* All in an African Lifetime, 1969; Sixty Marker Buoys for a Sixtieth Birthday (anthology), 1990; Sixty-Five Marker Buoys for a Sixty-Fifth Birthday (aphorisms), 1995; UN Jigsaw, 2000. *Recreations:* gardening, apophthegms. *Address:* Apartment 4A, 30 Eastchester Road, New Rochelle, NY 10801, USA. *Club:* Travellers.

GRESHAM, Prof. (Geoffrey) Austin, TD 1966; FRCPath, FRCPE; Professor of Morbid Anatomy and Histopathology, Cambridge, 1973–92; Fellow and President, Jesus College, Cambridge, since 1964; Home Office Pathologist, since 1968; *b* 1 Nov. 1924; *s* of Thomas Michael and Harriet Anne Gresham; *m* 1950, Gweneth Margery Leigh; three *s* two *d*. *Educ:* Grove Park Sch., Wrexham; Caius Coll., Cambridge (Tancred Student and Schol.; MA; ScD); King's Coll. Hosp., London (Burney Yeo Schol., Todd and Jelf Medallist; MB BChir, MD). FRCPath 1973; FRCPE 1994. Served RAMC, 1950–52, Lt-Col RAMC V, 1961. Cambridge University: Demonstrator and Lectr in Pathology, 1953–62; Univ. Morbid Anatomist, 1962–73; Sec., Faculty Bd of Medicine, 1956–61; Chm., MD Cttee, 1991–; Dep. to Regius Prof. of Physic, 1991–; Dep. to Vice Chancellor, 1993–. Consultant Mem., Cambridge Dist Management Team, 1974–84; Chairman: Cambridge Dist Medical Cttee, 1974–84; Medical Staff Leave Cttee, 1974–84; Cambridge Dist Ethical Cttee, 1974–84; Member: European Atherosclerosis Soc., 1959–; British Atherosclerosis Discussion Gp, 1965–. Roy Cameron Meml Lectr, RC Path, 1983. Mem. Bd of Governors, United Cambridge Hosps, 1972–74. Hon. Fellow, British Assoc. of Forensic Medicine, 1996. Scientific Medal, Univ. of Tokyo, 1985. *Publications:* Introduction to Comparative Pathology, 1962; Biological Aspects of Occlusive Vascular Disease, 1964; Colour Atlas of General Pathology, 1971, 2nd edn 1993; Primate Atherosclerosis, 1976; Colour Atlas of Forensic Pathology, 1977; Post Mortem Procedures, 1979; Reversing Atherosclerosis, 1980; Arterial Pollution, 1981; Wounds and Wounding, 1987; contrib. chapters, and papers in many jls, about pathology. *Recreations:* gardening, playing organ, wine, silver, talking. *Address:* 18 Rutherford Road, Cambridge CB2 2HH. *T:* (01223) 841326.

GRETTON, family name of **Baron Gretton**.

GRETTON, 4th Baron *cr* 1944, of Stapleford; **John Lysander Gretton;** *b* 17 April 1975; *s* of 3rd Baron Gretton and of Jennifer Ann, *o d* of Edmund Moore; *S* father, 1989. *Educ:* Shrewsbury; RAC Cirencester. *Heir:* none.

GRETTON, Vice Adm. Michael Peter, CB 1998; Director, Duke of Edinburgh's Award, since 1998; *b* 14 March 1946; *s* of Vice Adm. Sir Peter Gretton, KCB, DSO, OBE, DSC, MA and of Dorothy (*née* Du Vivier); *m* 1973, Stephanie O'Neill; one *s* three *d*. *Educ:* Ampleforth Coll.; BRNC Dartmouth; Trinity Coll., Oxford (BA PPE; MA). Joined RN, 1963; served HMS Torquay, Tiger, Rothesay, Ark Royal and Bacchante; commanded: HMS Bossington, 1972–73; HMS Ambuscade, 1977–80; RCDS, 1987; commanded: HMS Invincible, 1988–90; NATO Standing Naval Force Atlantic, 1990–91; Dir of Naval Staff Duties, MoD, 1991–93; comd UK Task Force and NATO Anti-Submarine Warfare Striking Force, 1993–94; Rep. of SACLANT in Europe, 1994–98. Governor: St Edward's Sch., Oxford, 1985–; Farleigh Sch., Red Rice, 1992–; St Mary's Sch., Shaftesbury, 1998–. Pres., RN RFU, 1993–95. FNI 1994. *Recreations:* sport, sightseeing, listening to music. *Address:* Duke of Edinburgh's Award, Gulliver House, Madeira Walk, Windsor, Berks SL4 1EU. *Clubs:* Naval; I Zingari.

GREVE, Prof. John; Hon. Senior Research Fellow, University of York, since 1988; Professor of Social Policy and Administration, University of Leeds, 1974–87, now Emeritus; *b* 23 Nov. 1927; *s* of Steffen A. and Ellen C. Greve; *m* (marr. diss. 1986); one *s* one *d*. *Educ:* elementary and secondary Schs in Cardiff; London Sch. of Economics (BSc(Econ)). Various jobs, incl. Merchant Navy, Youth Employment Service, and insurance, 1946–55; student, 1955–58; research work, then Univ. teaching, 1958–. Has worked in Norway at research institutes. Community Programmes Dept, Home Office, 1969–74; Prof. of Social Admin, Univ. of Southampton, 1969–74. Hon. Vis. Prof., Univ. of York, 1987–88. Chm., Care and Support Services Ltd, 1995–97. Mem., Royal Commn on Distribution of Income and Wealth, 1974–79; directed GLC Enquiry into Homelessness in London, 1985–86; Member: Bd, East Thames Housing Group (formerly Mem. Management Cttee, E London Housing Assoc.), 1988–98; York CHC, 1997–. *Publications:* The Housing Problem, 1961 (and 1969); London's Homeless, 1964; Private Landlords in England, 1965; (with others) Comparative Social Administration, 1969, 2nd edn 1972; Housing, Planning and Change in Norway, 1970; Voluntary Housing in Scandinavia, 1971; (with others) Homelessness in London, 1971; Low Incomes in Sweden, 1978; (jtly) Sheltered Housing for the Elderly, 1983; Homelessness in Britain, 1990, rev. edn 1991; Poland—the reform of housing, 1994; various articles and papers, mainly on social problems, policies and administration, a few short stories. *Recreations:* walking, painting, listening to music, writing, good company. *Address:* 9 Westfield Close, Wigginton, York YO32 2JG.

GREVILLE, family name of **Earl of Warwick**.

GREVILLE, Brig. Phillip Jamieson, CBE 1972; freelance writer on defence, foreign affairs and Australian history; Australian Director, International Institute for Prisoners of War, since 1992; *b* 12 Sept. 1925; *s* of Col S. J. Greville, OBE and Mrs D. M. Greville; *m* 1948, June Patricia Anne Martin; two *s* one *d* (and one *s* one *d* decd). *Educ:* RMC Duntroon; Sydney Univ. (BEng). 2/8 Field Co., 2nd AIF, New Guinea, 1945; 1 RAR Korea (POW), 1951–53; Senior Instructor SME Casula, 1953–55; CRE, RMC Duntroon, 1955–58; Staff Coll., Camberley and Transportation Trng UK, 1959–61; Dir of Transportation AHQ, 1962–65; GSO1 1st Div., 1966; CE Eastern Comd, 1969–71; Comdr 1st Australian Logistic Support Group, Vietnam, 1971; Actg Comdr 1st Australian Task Force, Vietnam, 1971–72 (CBE); Dir of Transport, 1973–74; Dir Gen., Logistics, 1975–76; Comdr, Fourth Mil. District, 1977–80, retired. Adelaide Advertiser: Defence Writer, 1980–86; Pacific Defence Reporter, 1987–. Dir, Dominant Australia Pty, 1982–86. Nat. Pres., RUSI of Aust., 1983–. FIE(Aust), FCIT. *Publications:* A Short History of Victoria Barracks Paddington, 1969; The Central Organisation for War and its Application to Movements, 1975, Sapper series (RE Officers in Australia); The Army Portion of the National Estate, 1977; Why Australia Should Not Ratify the New Law of War, 1989; vol. 4, History of the Royal Australian Engineers, 1999. *Recreation:* golf. *Address:* 3 River Downs Crescent, River Downs, Qld 4210, Australia. *Club:* United Services (Brisbane).

GREWAL, Harnam Singh, CBE 1990; ED 1976; Secretary for the Civil Service, Government Secretariat, Hong Kong, 1987–90, retired; *b* 5 Dec. 1937; *s* of late Joginder Singh Grewal and Ajaib Kaur; *m* 1973, Shiv Pal Kaur Chima; one *s* one *d*. *Educ:* Sir Ellis Kadoorie Sch.; King's Coll., Univ. of Hong Kong (BA Hons 1959; DipEd 1960); Pembroke Coll., Cambridge Univ. (BA 1962; MA 1974). Asst Educn Officer, Hong Kong, 1962; Admin Officer, 1964; Dist Officer, Tai Po, 1970; Dep. Dir of Urban Services, New Territories, 1976; Dep. Sec. for CS, 1980; Comr of Customs and Excise, 1984; Sec. for Transport, 1986. Royal Hong Kong Regt (The Volunteers), 1963–84, Major (retd); Hon. Col, 1987–90. *Recreations:* hockey, squash. *Address:* 3495 Cadboro Bay Road, Victoria, BC V8R 5K7, Canada.

GREY, family name of **Earl Grey**.

GREY; *see* De Grey.

GREY, 6th Earl *cr* 1806; **Richard Fleming George Charles Grey;** Bt 1746; Baron Grey, 1801; Viscount Howick, 1806; *b* 5 March 1939; *s* of late Albert Harry George Campbell Grey (Trooper, Canadian Army Tanks, who *d* on active service, 1942) and Vera Helen Louise Harding; *S* cousin, 1963; *m* 1st, 1966, Margaret Ann (marr. diss. 1974), *e d* of Henry Bradford, Ashburton; 2nd, 1974, Stephanie Caroline, *o d* of Donald Gaskell-Brown and formerly wife of Surg.-Comdr Neil Leicester Denham, RN. *Educ:* Hounslow Coll.; Hammersmith Coll. of Bldg (Quantity Surveying). Public relations consultant. Chairman: Academy Beverage Co. Ltd, 1990–; London Cremation Co., 1992–; Roper Catering Events, 1993–; Director: Countess Grey Collection, 1993–; Covent Garden Quality, 1993–. President: Assoc. of Cost and Executive Accountants, 1978; Cremation Soc. of GB, 1992–. Mem., Liberal Party. *Recreations:* golf, sailing. *Heir:* *b* Philip Kent Grey [*b* 11 May 1940; *m* 1968, Ann Catherine, *y d* of Cecil Applegate, Kingsbridge, Devon; one *s* one *d*].

GREY de WILTON, Viscount; Julian Francis Martin Grosvenor; *b* 8 June 1959; *s* of Earl of Wilton, *qv*; *m* 1987, Danielle (marr. diss. 1990), sixth *d* of Theo Rossi, Sydney, Australia.

GREY OF CODNOR, 6th Baron *cr* 1397 (in abeyance 1496–1989); **Richard Henry Cornwall-Legh;** *b* 14 May 1936; *s* of 5th Baron Grey of Codnor, CBE and Dorothy (*d* 1993), *er d* of J. W. Scott; *S* father, 1996; *m* 1974, Joanna Storm, 7th *d* of Sir Kenelm Cayley, 10th Bt; three *s* one *d*. *Educ:* Stowe. High Sheriff, 1993, DL 1995, Cheshire. *Heir:* *s* Hon. Richard Stephen Cayley Cornwall-Legh, *b* 24 March 1976. *Address:* High Legh House, Knutsford, Cheshire WA16 0QR. *Clubs:* Boodle's, MCC.

GREY, Alan Hartley, OBE 1999; HM Diplomatic Service, retired; Judge, Council of Europe Administrative Tribunal (formerly Member, Council of Europe Appeals Board), 1993–96; *b* 26 June 1925; *s* of William Hartley Grey and Gladys Grey; *m* 1950, Joan Robinson (*d* 1985); one *s* one *d*. *Educ:* Bootle Secondary Sch. for Boys. RAF, 1943–48; Foreign Service (Br. B), 1948; Tel Aviv, 1949; Tabriz and Khorramshahr, 1950–52; 3rd Sec., Belgrade, 1952–54; Vice-Consul, Dakar, 1954–57; Second Sec. (Commercial), Helsinki, 1958–61; FO, 1961–64; Second Sec. (Econ.), Paris, 1964–66; FO (later FCO), 1966–70; Consul (Commercial), Lille, 1970–74; FCO, 1974–82; Ambassador at Libreville, 1982–84; re-employed in FCO (as Staff Assessor), 1985–90. Vice Chm., Lambeth Horticl Soc, 1998–. *Recreation:* gardening.

GREY, Sir Anthony (Dysart), 7th Bt *cr* 1814; former Inspector, Department of Industrial Affairs, Government of Western Australia; *b* 19 Oct. 1949; *s* of Edward Elton Grey (*d* 1962) (*o s* of 6th Bt) and of Nancy, *d* of late Francis John Meagher, Perth, WA; *S* grandfather, 1974; *m* 1970 (marr. diss.); *m* 1993, Alison Turner; two *d*. *Educ:* Guildford Grammar School, WA. *Recreations:* fishing, painting. *Address:* 38 Kings Park Road, W Perth, WA 6005, Australia.

GREY, Dame Beryl (Elizabeth), DBE 1988 (CBE 1973); a Director, Royal Opera House, since 1999; Prima Ballerina, Sadler's Wells Ballet, now Royal Ballet, 1941–57; Artistic Director, London Festival Ballet, 1968–79; *b* London, 11 June 1927; *d* of late Arthur Ernest Groom; *m* 1950, Dr Sven Gustav Svenson; one *s*. *Educ:* Dame Alice Owens Girls' Sch., London. Professional training: Madeline Sharp Sch., Sadler's Wells Sch. (Schol.), de Vos Sch. Début Sadler's Wells Co., 1941, with Ballerina rôles following same year in Les Sylphides, The Gods Go A'Begging, Le Lac des Cygnes, Act II, Comus. First full-length ballet, Le Lac des Cygnes on 15th birthday, 1942. Has appeared since in leading rôles of many ballets including: Sleeping Beauty, Giselle, Sylvia, Checkmate, Ballet Imperial, Donald of the Burthens, Homage, Birthday Offering, The Lady and the Fool. Film: The Black Swan (3 Dimensional Ballet Film), 1952. Left Royal Ballet, Covent Garden, Spring 1957, to become free-lance ballerina. Regular guest appearances with Royal Ballet at Covent Garden and on European, African, American and Far Eastern Tours. Guest Artist, London's Festival Ballet in London and abroad, 1958–64. First Western ballerina to appear with Bolshoi Ballet: Moscow, Leningrad, Kiev, Tiflis, 1957–58; First Western ballerina to dance with Chinese Ballet Co. in Peking and Shanghai, 1964. Engagements and tours abroad include: Central and S America, Mexico, Rhodesia and S Africa, Canada, NZ, Lebanon, Germany, Norway, Sweden, Denmark, Finland, Belgium, Holland, France, Switzerland, Italy, Portugal, Austria, Czechoslovakia, Poland, Rumania; Producer: Sleeping Beauty, 1967; Swan Lake, 1972, London Fest. Ballet; Giselle, Western Australia Ballet, 1984; Sleeping Beauty, Royal Swedish Co., Stockholm, 1985. Regular television and broadcasts in England and abroad; concert narrator. Dir-Gen., Arts Educational Trust, 1966–68. President: Dance Council of Wales, 1981–; ISTD, 1991– (Mem. Council, 1966–91; Chm., 1984–91); Vice-Pres., Royal Acad. of Dancing, 1980– (Exec. Mem., 1982–89); Mem. Bd, BRB, 1995–99; Mem. Council, 1984–96, Mem. Exec., 1995–96, Council for Dance Educn and Training. Trustee: London City Ballet, 1978–92; Adeline Genée Theatre, 1982–90; Royal Ballet Benevolent Fund, 1982– (Chm. Trustees, 1992–); Discs, 1994–; Vice Chm., Dance Teachers Benevolent Fund, 1985– (Trustee, 1981–); President: Keep Fit Assoc., 1992–93; E Grinstead Operatic Soc., 1986–; Vice-President: Music Therapy Charity, 1980–; British Fedn of Music Festivals, 1985–; London Ballet Circle, 2001–. Governor: Dame Alice Owens Girls' Sch., London, 1960–77; Frances Mary Buss Foundn, 1963–72; Royal Ballet, 1993– (Vice Chm. Govs, 1995–). Patron: Benesh Inst. of Choreology, 1988–; Dancers Resettlement Trust, 1988–; Nature Cure Clinic, 1988–; Language of Dance Centre, 1990–; Friends of Sadler's Wells Theatre, 1991–; Pro-Dogs, 1991–; Osteopathic Centre for Children, 1992–; Furlong Research Foundn, 1993–; AMBER Trust, 1995–; Legat Foundn, 1998–; Sussex Opera Ballet Soc., 2001–. FISTD 1960. Hon. DMus: Leicester, 1970; Univ. of London, 1996; Hon. DLitt: City, 1974; Buckingham, 1993; Hon. DEd CNAA, 1989. Queen Elizabeth II Coronation Award, Royal Acad. of Dancing, 1995. *Publications:* Red Curtain Up, 1958; Through the Bamboo Curtain, 1965; My Favourite Ballet Stories, 1981. *Relevant publications:* biographical studies (by Gordon Anthony), 1952, (by Pigeon Crowle), 1952; Beryl Grey, Dancers of Today (by Hugh Fisher), 1955; Beryl Grey, a biography (by David Gillard), 1977. *Recreations:* music, painting, reading, swimming. *Address:* Fernhill, Priory Road, Forest Row, Sussex RH18 5JE. *T:* (01342) 822539.

GREY, John Egerton, CB 1980; Clerk Assistant and Clerk of Public Bills, House of Lords, 1974–88; *b* 8 Feb. 1929; *s* of late John and Nancy Grey; *m* 1961, Patricia Hanna; two adopted *s*. *Educ:* Dragon Sch., Oxford; Blundell's; Brasenose Coll., Oxford. MA, BCL. Called to Bar, Inner Temple, 1954; practised at Chancery Bar, 1954–59. Clerk in Parliament Office, House of Lords, 1959–88. Adviser, Colchester CAB, 1989–99. *Recreations:* gardening, boating. *Address:* 51 St Peters Road, West Mersea, Colchester, Essex CO5 8LL. *T:* (01206) 383007. *Clubs:* Arts; West Mersea Yacht.

GREY, Maj.-Gen. John St John, CB 1987; *b* 6 June 1934; *s* of late Major Donald John Grey, RM and Doris Mary Grey (*née* Beavan); *m* 1958, Elisabeth Ann (*née* Langley); one *s* one *d*. *Educ:* Christ's Hospital. rcds, ndc, psc(M), osc(US). Commissioned 2/Lt 1952; Commando service, Malta, Egypt, Cyprus, 1955–64; Cruiser HMS Lion as OC RM, 1964–65; Instructor, Army Sch. of Infantry, 1967–69; US Marine Corps, 1970–71; Commanded 45 Cdo Gp (incl. tours in N Ireland and Arctic Norway), 1976–78; Mil. Sec. and Col Ops/Plans, MoD, 1979–84; Maj.-Gen. RM Commando Forces, 1984–87; RM COS, 1987–88, retired. Clerk, Pewterers' Co., 1988–96. Col Comdt RM, 1995–98. Pres., SSAFA, Devon, 1993. Member, Council: Exeter and E Devon, ESU, 2000–; St John Ambulance, Devon. Trustee, Northcott Devon Foundn. *Recreation:* sailing. *Address:* c/o Lloyds TSB, 4 Regent Street, Teignmouth, S Devon TQ14 8SL. *Clubs:* Army and Navy; Royal Naval Sailing Association (Portsmouth); Royal Marines Sailing.

GREY, Robin Douglas; QC 1979; a Recorder of the Crown Court, 1979–99; *b* 23 May 1931; *s* of Dr Francis Temple Grey, MA, MB, and Eglantine Grey; *m* 1st, 1972, Berenice Anna Wheatley (marr. diss.); one *s* one *d*; 2nd, 1993, Mrs Annick Regnault. *Educ:* Summer Fields Prep. Sch., Oxford; Eastbourne Coll.; London Univ. (LLB Hons). Called to the Bar, Gray's Inn, 1957. Crown Counsel, Colonial Legal Service, Aden, 1959–63 (Actg Registrar Gen. and Actg Attorney Gen. for short periods); practising barrister, 1963–; Dep. Circuit Judge, 1977. FCO Consultant to Govt of Russian Fedn, 1993–; led FCO team to Moscow on Jury Trials, 1993. Chm., Home Office Police Appeals Tribunals, 1990–; Legal Assessor to GMC, 1995–. Member: Internat. Bar Assoc., 1994; Cttee, Criminal Bar Assoc., 1990–93 (Chm., Internat. Sub-Cttee, 1993); Cttee, European Criminal Bar Assoc., 1998–; British Acad. of Forensic Sciences. *Recreations:* tennis, golf, fishing. *Address:* Queen Elizabeth Building, Temple, EC4Y 9BS. *T:* (020) 7583 5766; Dun Cottage, The Marsh, Hungerford, Berks RG17 0SN. *T:* (01488) 683578. *Club:* Hurlingham.

GREY, Wilfrid Ernest G.; *see* Grenville-Grey.

GREY EGERTON, Sir (Philip) John (Caledon), 15th Bt *cr* 1617; *b* 19 Oct. 1920; *er s* of Sir Philip Grey Egerton, 14th Bt; *S* father, 1962; *m* 1st, 1952, Margaret Voase (*d* 1971) (who *m* 1941, Sqdn Ldr Robert A. Ullman, *d* 1943), *er d* of late Rowland Rank; 2nd, 1986, Frances Mary (who *m* 1941 Sqdn Ldr William Dudley Williams, DFC, *d* 1976), *y d* of late Col R. M. Rainey-Robinson. *Educ:* Eton. Served Welsh Guards, 1939–45. *Recreation:* fishing. *Heir: cousin* Maj.-Gen. D. B. Egerton, *qv*. *Address:* Meadow House, West Stafford, Dorchester, Dorset DT2 8AQ.

GREY-THOMPSON, Tanni Carys Davina, OBE 2000 (MBE 1993); wheelchair athlete; Development Officer, UK Athletics, since 1996; *b* 26 July 1969; *d* of Peter Alexander Harvey Grey and Sulwen Davina Grey (*née* Jones); *m* 1999, Dr (Robert) Ian George Thompson. *Educ:* Loughborough Univ. (BA Hons Politics & Admin 1991). Member Council: Sports Council for Wales, 1996–; UK Sport, 1998–; Dep. Chm., UK Lottery Sports Fund. Has represented GB at 100m-800m distances, 1987–: competitor: Paralympics, 1988, 1992, 1996 and 2000 (winner 14 medals, incl. 9 Gold Medals); Olympics, 1992 and 1996 (in exhibn 800m); World Championships (winner 11 medals, incl. 5 Gold Medals); has broken over 20 world records; winner, London Marathon, 1992, 1994, 1996, 1998, 2001. Hon. Fellow, UWCC, 1997. Hon. Dr Sport Staffordshire, 1998, 2001; Hon. DBA Southampton, 1998; Hon. MSc Manchester Metropolitan, 1998; Hon. MA Loughborough, 1994; DUniv Surrey, 2000. *Publication:* Seize the Day (autobiog.), 2001. *Address:* c/o Creating Excellence, 1st Floor, Equity House, Knight Street, South Woodham Ferrers, Chelmsford, Essex CM3 5ZL. *T:* (01245) 328303.

GREY-WILSON, Christopher, PhD; Editor: Alpine Garden Society, since 1990; The New Plantsman, since 2001; *b* 28 Sept. 1944; *s* of late Vyvyan William Grey-Wilson and Jean Grey-Wilson (*née* Parsley); *m* 1978, Christine Mary Dent; one *d*. *Educ:* Churston Ferrers Grammar Sch.; Wye Coll., Univ. of London (BSc Hort. 1967); Reading Univ. (PhD 1976). Botanist (PSO), Royal Botanic Gardens, Kew, 1968–90. Editor, Curtis's Botanical Magazine, incl. Kew Magazine, 1983–89. Botanical Scientific expeditions: Iran and Afghanistan, 1971; Nepal, 1973, 1978, 1989; Kenya and Tanzania, 1976, 1979; Sri Lanka, 1978; W China, 1987, 1994. *Publications:* The Alpine Flowers of Britain and Europe, 1979, 2nd edn 1995; Impatiens of Africa, 1980; (jtly) Bulbs, 1981; (jtly) Gardening on Walls, 1983; The Genus Cyclamen, 1988; The Genus Dionysia, 1989; The Illustrated Flora of Britain and Northern Europe, 1989; Poppies, 1993; Mediterranean Wild Flowers, 1993; The Alpine Garden, 1994; (jtly) Gardening with Climbers, 1997; Cyclamen, 1997; Clematis: the genus, 2000; How to Identify Wild Flowers, 2000; numerous scientific papers in Kew Bulletin, gen. papers in The Garden, Bull. of Alpine Garden Soc., Gardens News and New Plantsman. *Recreations:* gardening, walking, drawing, photography, listening to classical music. *Address:* Red Lion Barn, East Church Street, Kenninghall, Suffolk NR16 2EP.

GRIBBLE, Rev. Canon Arthur Stanley, MA; Canon Residentiary and Chancellor of Peterborough Cathedral, 1967–79; Canon Emeritus since 1979; *b* 18 Aug. 1904; *er s* of J. B. Gribble; *m* 1938, Edith Anne, *er d* of late Laurence Bailey; one *s*. *Educ:* Queens' Coll. and Westcott House, Cambridge (Burney Student, Univ. of Cambridge); Univ. of Heidelberg. Curate: St Mary, Windermere, 1930–33, Almondbury, 1933–36; Chaplain Sarum Theological Coll., 1936–38; Rector of Shepton Mallet, 1938–54. Examining Chaplain to Bp of Bath and Wells, 1947–54; Proctor in Convocation, diocese Bath and Wells, 1947–54; Rural Dean of Shepton Mallet, 1949–54; Prebendary of Wiveliscombe in Wells Cathedral, 1949–54; Principal, Queen's Coll., Birmingham, 1954–67; Recognised Lectr, Univ. of Birmingham, 1954–67. Hon. Canon, Birmingham Cathedral, 1954–67. Commissary for the Bishop of Kimberley and Kuruman, 1964–66. Examng Chaplain to Bishop of Peterborough, 1968–84. Visiting Lectr, Graduate Theological Union, Berkeley, USA, 1970. *Recreation:* mountaineering. *Address:* 2 Coylton Terrace, Bayford Hill, Wincanton, Somerset BA9 9LQ. *T:* (01963) 33678.

GRIBBON, Deborah, PhD; Director, J. Paul Getty Museum, since 2000; Vice President, J. Paul Getty Trust, since 2000; *b* 11 June 1948; *d* of Daniel M. and Jane Gribbon; *m* 1976, Dr Winston Alt; two *d*. *Educ:* Wellesley Coll., Mass (BA Art Hist.1970); Harvard Univ. (MA Fine Arts 1972; PhD 1982). Teaching Fellow, Dept of Fine Arts, Harvard Univ., 1972-74; Curator, Isabella Stewart Gardner Mus., 1976-84; Instructor, Extension Sch., Harvard Univ., 1982-84; J. Paul Getty Museum: Asst Dir, 1984-87; Associate Dir for Curatorial Affairs, 1987-91; Associate Dir and Chief Curator, 1991-98; Dep. Dir and Chief Curator, 1998-2000. Phi Beta Kappa, 1970. *Publications:* Sculpture in the Isabella Stewart Gardner Museum, 1978; (with J. Walsh) The J. Paul Getty Museum and its Collections: a museum for a new century, 1997; contrib. articles to Burlington Mag. and Connoisseur. *Recreations:* running, yoga, cooking, time with family.

GRIBBON, Edward John; Under Secretary, Board of Inland Revenue, 1991–2000; Director, Compliance Division, 1996–2000; *b* 10 July 1943; *s* of late Henry Derwent Gribbon and Dorothy Gribbon (*née* Boyd); *m* 1968, Margaret Nanette Flanagan; one *s* two *d*. *Educ:* Coleraine Academical Instn; Univ. of London (LLB). FCA. Qualified as Chartered Accountant, 1965; joined Inland Revenue as HM Inspector of Taxes, 1966; HM Principal Inspector of Taxes, 1981; Dep. Dir of Operations, 1989; Dir, Business Profits Div., 1991–98. *Recreations:* family, photography, local church, ornithology, philately. *Address:* 76 Whitney Drive, Stevenage, Herts SG1 4BJ.

GRIBBON, Maj.-Gen. Nigel St George, OBE 1960; Chairman, 1982–97, Vice President, 1997–2001, UK Falkland Islands Trust; *b* Feb. 1917; *s* of late Brig. W. H. Gribbon, CMG, CBE; *m* 1943, Rowan Mary MacLiesh; two *s* one *d*. *Educ:* Rugby Sch.; Sandhurst. King's Own, 1937–42; active service, Iraq (Habbaniya), 1941 (wounded), Western Desert, 1942; GSO3 10th Indian Div., 1942; Staff Coll. Quetta, 1943; G2 HQ 55 Inf. Div., 1944; Army Airborne Transport Develt Centre, 1945; Bde Major, 1st Parachute Bde, 1946; served Palestine, 1946, Trieste, 1947–48, Malaysia, 1948–50; RAF Staff Coll., 1947; OC 5 King's Own, 1958–60; AMS WO, 1960–62; Comdr 161 Bde, 1963–65; Canadian Nat. Defence Coll., 1965–66; DMC MoD, 1966–67; BGS (I) BAOR, 1967–69; ACOS (Intelligence), SHAPE, 1970–72. Managing Director: Partnerplan Public Affairs Ltd, 1973–75; Sallingbury Ltd, 1977–85 (Chm., 1975–77 and 1984–85); Sallingbury Casey Ltd, 1986–87; Director: Gatewood Engineers Ltd, 1976–83; Chancellor Insurance Co. Ltd, 1986–92; Operational Planning Consultant, Venice-Simplon Orient Express, 1980–84. Canada-UK Chamber of Commerce: Mem. Council, 1979–99; Chm., Trade Cttee, 1980; Pres., 1981; Chm., Jt Cttee, Canada-UK and Canadian Chambers of Commerce, 1982–91. Hd of Secretariat, European Channel Tunnel Gp and Public Affairs Cttee, 1980–85; Chairman: Forces Financial Services, 1983–85; SHAPE Assoc. (UK Chapter), 1984–; Member: Council, British Atlantic Cttee, 1975–93 (Mem. Exec. Cttee, 1983–88); Cttee, Amer. European Atlantic Cttee, 1985–92; Eur. Atlantic Gp, 1974–87; Council, Mouvement Européen Français (Londres), 1979–87; Council, Wyndham Place Trust, 1979–82; Canadian War Meml Foundn, 1988–94; Adv. Cttee, Shackleton Meml Fund, 1995–97. Vice-President: King's Own Affairs, 1974–88; Lancaster Mil. Heritage Group, 2000–. Radio commentator and lectr on public affairs; organiser of chamber music concerts, 1991–. Freeman, City of London; Liveryman, Worshipful Co. of Shipwrights. *Recreations:* sailing, ski-ing, swimming, watercolour sketching. *Address:* The Pump Cottage, Orford, Woodbridge, Suffolk IP12 2LZ. *T:* (01394) 450413. *Clubs:* Army and Navy (Mem., Gen. and Finance Cttees, 1989–92), Little Ship (Rear Commodore Training, 1978–80; Hon. Life Mem.).

GRICE, Paul Edward; Clerk and Chief Executive, Scottish Parliament, since 1999; *b* 13 Oct. 1961; *s* of Kenneth William Grice and Maureen (*née* Power); *m* 1987, Elaine Rosie; two *d*. *Educ:* Archbishop Holgate's Sch., York; York Coll. of Arts and Technol.; Univ. of Stirling (BSc Econs and Envmtl Sci.). Dept of Transport, 1985–87; DoE, 1987–92; Scottish Office, Edinburgh, 1992–99: Head of Housing and Urban Regeneration Br., 1992–95; Head of Mgt and Change Unit, 1995–97; Head of Division, Constitution Group: Referendum, Scotland Bill, 1997–98; Dir of Implementation, 1998–99. *Recreations:* squash, cycling, reading, theatre, ballet. *Address:* Scottish Parliament, The Mound, Edinburgh EH99 1SP. *T:* (0131) 348 5255.

GRIDLEY, family name of **Baron Gridley**.

GRIDLEY, 3rd Baron *cr* 1955; **Richard David Arnold Gridley;** Lecturer in Leisure and Tourism and Information Technology, South Downs College of Further Education, since 1995; *b* 22 Aug. 1956; *o s* of 2nd Baron Gridley and Edna Lesley, *e d* of Richard Wheen; *S* father, 1996; *m* 1st, 1979, Amanda Mackenzie (marr. diss.); 2nd, 1983, Suzanne Elizabeth Hughes; one *s* one *d*. *Educ:* Monckton Combe; Portsmouth Polytech.; Univ. of Brighton (BA). Project manager, construction industry, 1980–92. Patron, Care for the Wild Internat, 1996. *Heir:* *s* Carl Richard Gridley, *b* 5 Feb. 1981. *Address:* Southview Cottage, Park Street, Slinfold, Horsham, W Sussex RH13 7RU.

GRIERSON, Prof. Donald, OBE 2000; PhD, DSc; FRS 2000; FIBiol; Professor of Plant Physiology, since 1986, Head, School of Biosciences, since 2000, Nottingham University;

b 1 Oct. 1945; *s* of John Harvey Grierson and Margaret (*née* Head); *m* 1965, Elizabeth Carole Judson; two *s* two *d*. *Educ:* Univ. of E Anglia (BSc 1967); Univ. of Edinburgh (Ellis Prize in Physiol. 1970; PhD 1971); DSc Nottingham 1999. FIBiol 1985. Plant Physiologist, British Sugar Corp. Res. Lab., Norwich, 1967–68; University of Nottingham: Asst Lectr in Plant Physiol., 1971–74; Lectr, 1974–82; Nuffield Foundn Sci. Res. Fellow, 1981–82; Reader, 1982–86; Head: Dept of Physiol. and Envmtl Sci., 1988–91 and 1992–94; Plant Sci. Section, 1988–97; Plant Sci. Div., 1997–. EMBO Res. Fellow, Genetics Dept, Univ. of Tubingen, 1975–76. Chm., Sainsbury Lab. Council, 2000–. Hon. DSc l'Institut Nat. Polytechnique de Toulouse, 2000. Res. Medal, RASE, 1990. *Publications:* (with S. N. Covey) Plant Molecular Biology, 1984, 2nd edn 1988 (English, Mandarin Chinese and Spanish edns); edited: (with H. Smith) The Molecular Biology of Plant Development, 1982; (with H. Thomas) Developmental Mutants in Higher Plants, 1987; (with G. W. Lycett) Genetic Engineering of Crop Plants, 1990; (with G. W. Lycett and G. A. Tucker) Mechanisms and Applications of Gene Silencing, 1996; Plant Biotechnology, vol I, 1991, vol II, 1991, vol III, 1993; contrib. numerous refereed scientific papers and articles. *Recreations:* walking, gardening. *Address:* Plant Science Division, School of Biosciences, University of Nottingham, Sutton Bonington Campus, Loughborough LE12 5RD. *T:* (0115) 951 6333.

GRIERSON, Sir Michael (John Bewes), 12th Bt *cr* 1685 (NS), of Lag, Dumfriesshire; retired; *b* 24 July 1921; *s* of Lt-Col Alexander George William Grierson, RM retd (*d* 1951) (2nd *s* of 9th Bt) and Violet Ethel (*d* 1980), *d* of Lt-Col Arthur Edward Bewes, CMG; *S* cousin, 1987; *m* 1971, Valerie Anne, *d* of late Russell Wright, Gidea Park, Essex; one *d*. *Educ:* Warden House School, Deal; St Edmund's School, Canterbury. Served War, RAF, 1941–46; subsequent career in civil engineering and local government; retired, 1986. *Recreations:* gardening, motoring, plane spotting, woodwork, photography. *Heir:* none. *Address:* 40c Palace Road, Streatham Hill, SW2 3NJ.

GRIERSON, Prof. Philip, MA, LittD; FBA 1958; FSA; Fellow, since 1935, Librarian, 1944–69, and President, 1966–76, Gonville and Caius College, Cambridge; Professor of Numismatics, University of Cambridge, 1971–78, now Emeritus; Professor of Numismatics and the History of Coinage, University of Brussels, 1948–81; Hon. Keeper of the Coins, Fitzwilliam Museum, Cambridge, since 1949; Adviser in Byzantine Numismatics to the Dumbarton Oaks Library and Collections, Harvard University, at Washington, USA, 1955–98; *b* 15 Nov. 1910; *s* of Philip Henry Grierson and Roberta Ellen Jane Pope. *Educ:* Marlborough Coll.; Gonville and Caius Coll., Cambridge (MA 1936, LittD 1971). University Lectr in History, Cambridge, 1945–59; Reader in Medieval Numismatics, Cambridge, 1959–71. Literary Dir of Royal Historical Society, 1945–55; Ford's Lectr in History, University of Oxford, 1956–57. Pres. Royal Numismatic Society, 1961–66. Corresp. Fellow, Mediaeval Acad. of America, 1972; Corresp. Mem., Koninklijke Vlaamse Acad., 1955; Assoc. Mem., Acad. Royale de Belgique, 1968. Hon. LittD: Ghent, 1958; Leeds, 1978; Hon. LLD Cambridge, 1993. *Publications:* Les Annales de Saint-Pierre de Gand, 1937; Books on Soviet Russia, 1917–42, 1943; Sylloge of Coins of the British Isles, Vol. I (Fitzwilliam Museum: Early British and Anglo-Saxon Coins), 1958; Bibliographie numismatique, 1966, 2nd edn 1979; English Linear Measures: a study in origins, 1973; (with A. R. Bellinger) Catalogue of the Byzantine Coins in the Dumbarton Oaks Collection and in the Whittemore Collection, vols 1, 2, 3, 5, 1966–99; Numismatics, 1975; Monnaies du Moyen Age, 1976; The Origins of Money, 1977; Les monnaies, 1977; Dark Age Numismatics, 1979; Later Medieval Numismatics, 1979; Byzantine Coins, 1982; Medieval European Coinage, vol. 1 (with M. Blackburn) The Early Middle Ages, 1986, vol. 14 (with L. Travaini) Italy III, 1998; The Coins of Medieval Europe, 1991; Tarì, Follari e Denari, 1991; (with M. Mays) Catalogue of Late Roman Coins in the Dumbarton Oaks Collection and in the Whittemore Collection, 1992; trans. F. L. Ganshof, Feudalism, 1952; editor: C. W. Previté-Orton, The Shorter Cambridge Medieval History, 1952; H. E. Ives, The Venetian Gold Ducat and its Imitations, 1954; Studies in Italian History presented to Miss E. M. Jamison, 1956; (with U. Westermark) O. Mørkholm, Early Hellenistic Coins, 1991; Studies in Numismatic Method, presented to Philip Grierson (Festschrift), 1983. *Recreation:* science fiction. *Address:* Gonville and Caius College, Cambridge CB2 1TA. *T:* (01223) 332450.

GRIERSON, Sir Ronald (Hugh), Kt 1990; Vice-Chairman, General Electric Co., 1968–91; Chairman: Advisory Board, Blackstone Group, since 1989; Bain & Co. International, since 1988; Director, Chime Communications (Bell Pottinger), since 1998, and other cos; *b* Nürnberg, Bavaria, 1921; *s* of Mr and Mrs E. J. Griessmann (name changed by Deed Poll in 1943); *m* 1966, (Elizabeth) Heather, Viscountess Bearsted (*d* 1993), *er d* of Mr and Mrs G. Firmston-Williams; one *s*, and one step *d*. *Educ:* Realgymnasium, Nürnberg; Lycée Pasteur, Paris; Highgate Sch., London; Balliol Coll., Oxford. Served HM Forces 1940–46 (despatches); TA, 1948–54. Staff Mem., The Economist, 1947–48; S. G. Warburg & Co., 1948–86 (Dir, 1958–68 and 1980–86); Dep. Chm. and Man. Dir, IRC, 1966–67; Chm., Orion Bank, 1971–73; Dir-Gen., Industrial and Technological Affairs, EEC, 1973–74; Sen. Partner, Panmure Gordon & Co., 1974–76. Board Member: BAC, 1970–71; Internat. Computers, 1974–76; Davy Internat., 1969–73; Nat. Bus Co., 1984–86; RJR Nabisco Inc. (formerly R. J. Reynolds), 1977–89; Chrysler Corp., 1983–91; W. R. Grace & Co., 1987–94; Daily Mail & Gen. Trust, 1994–2001. Chairman: European Orgn for Cancer Treatment Res., 1976–2000; South Bank Bd, 1984–90. Mem., Bd of Trustees, Phillips Collection, Washington, 1980–98. Member: Atlantic Coll. Council, 1960–70; Harvard Coll. Faculty, 1964–65; CNAA, 1978–84; Arts Council of GB, 1984–88; Ernst von Siemens Foundn, 1977–98; Bd of Visitors, N Carolina Sch. of the Arts, 1984–90; European Arts Foundn, 1987–88; Trustee: Prince of Liechtenstein Foundn, 1991–; European Studies Foundn, Oxford Univ., 1991–. Hon. Dr of Law, Grove City Coll., USA, 1986. Comdr, Order of Merit of the Republic of Italy, 1980; Comdr's Cross, Order of Merit (Germany), 1993; Commandeur, Légion d'honneur (France), 1994. *Address:* 5–7 Carlton Gardens, SW1Y 5AD. *Clubs:* White's, Pratt's, Beefsteak.

GRIESE, Sister Carol, CHN; Religious Sister since 1970; *b* 26 Sept. 1945; *d* of Gwendoline and Donald Griese. *Educ:* Merrywood Grammar School, Bristol; King's College London (BA Hons English 1968); Clare Hall, Cambridge (Cert. Theol. 1970). Member, Community of the Holy Name, 1970–; Lay Rep. of Religious in General Synod, 1980–95. Mem., Crown Appointments Commn, 1990–92. *Recreations:* reading, walking. *Address:* Convent of the Holy Name, Morley Road, Oakwood, Derby DE2 4QZ. *T:* (01332) 671716.

GRIEVE, Hon. Lord; William Robertson Grieve, VRD 1958; a Senator of the College of Justice in Scotland, 1972–88; *b* 21 Oct. 1917; *o s* of late William Robertson Grieve (killed in action 1917) and late Mrs Grieve; *m* 1947, Lorna St John (*d* 1989), *y d* of late Engineer Rear-Adm. E. P. St J. Benn, CB; one *s* one *d*. *Educ:* Glasgow Academy; Sedbergh; Glasgow Univ. MA 1939, LLB 1946 (Glasgow); Pres. Glasgow Univ. Union, 1938–39. John Clark (Mile-end) Scholar, 1939. RNVR: Sub-Lt 1939; Lieut 1942; Lt-Comdr 1950; served with RN, 1939–46. Admitted Mem. of Faculty of Advocates, 1947; QC (Scot.) 1957. Junior Counsel in Scotland to Bd of Inland Revenue, 1952–57. Advocate-Depute (Home), 1962–64; Sheriff-Principal of Renfrew and Argyll, 1964–72; Procurator of the Church of Scotland, 1969–72; a Judge of the Courts of Appeal of Jersey and Guernsey, 1971. Independent Chm., Fish Farming Adv. Cttee, 1989. Chairman of Governors: Fettes Trust, 1978–86; St Columba's Hospice, 1981–99. *Recreations:* golf, painting. *Address:* 20 Belgrave Crescent, Edinburgh EH4 3AJ. *T:* (0131) 332 7500. *Clubs:* New (Edinburgh); Hon. Company of Edinburgh Golfers; West Sussex Golf; Queen's Park Rangers Football.

See also M. R. C. Grieve.

GRIEVE, Alan Thomas; Chairman, Jerwood Foundation, since 1991; *b* 22 Jan. 1928; *s* of late Lewis Miller Grieve and Doris Lilian (*née* Amner); *m* 1st, 1957, Anne, *d* of Dr Lawrence Dulake (marr. diss. 1971); two *s* one *d*; 2nd, 1971, Karen Louis, *d* of late Michael de Sirvac Dunn; one *s* one *d*. *Educ:* Aldenham; Trinity Hall, Cambridge (MA, LLM). Nat. Service, 2nd Lieut, 14/20 King's Hussars; Capt., City of London Yeo., TA. Admitted solicitor, 1953; Senior Partner: Taylor & Humbert, 1979–82; Taylor Garrett, 1982–88; Cons., Taylor Joynson Garrett, 1988–2001. Director: Baggeridge Brick plc, 1964; Wilson Bowden plc, 1993–96, and other cos; Chm., Reliance Resources Ltd, 1978–97. Royal College of Physicians: Member: F and GP Bd, 1986–92; Educnl Assets Bd, 1988–90. Chm., Racehorse Owners Award, 1978–99. Patron, Brendoncare for the Elderly, 1993–; Ambassador, Samaritans, 1999–. Trustee: Med. Insce Agency Charity, 1992–98; Hereford Mappa Mundi Trustee Co. Ltd, 1998–. *Publication:* Purchase Tax, 1958. *Recreations:* performing and visual arts, horse-racing, country life. *Address:* (office) 22 Fitzroy Square, W1P 5HJ. *T:* (020) 7388 6287, *Fax:* (020) 7388 6289; Stoke Lodge, Clee Downton, Ludlow, Salop SY8 3EG. *T:* (01584) 823413, *Fax:* (01584) 823419. *Clubs:* Boodle's; Hawks (Cambridge); Baur au Lac (Zurich).

See also Baron Harlech.

GRIEVE, Dominic Charles Roberts; MP (C) Beaconsfield, since 1997; barrister; *b* 24 May 1956; *s* of William Percival Grieve, QC; *m* 1990, Caroline Hutton; two *s* (and one *s* decd). *Educ:* Westminster Sch.; Magdalen Coll., Oxford (MA Modern History). Called to the Bar, Middle Temple, 1980. Mem., Hammersmith and Fulham LBC, 1982–86. Contested (C) Norwood, 1987. Opposition front bench spokesman: for Scotland and on constitutional affairs, 1999–2001; on home affairs, 2001–. Member: Jt Select Cttee on Statutory Instruments, 1997–; Select Cttee on Envmtl Audit, 1997–. Chm. Res. Cttee, Soc. of Cons. Lawyers, 1992–95. Member: Council, Justice, 1997–; Franco-British Soc., 1997–; Luxembourg Soc., 1997–. Mem., London Dio. Synod, C of E, 1995–. *Recreations:* mountaineering, ski-ing, fell walking, travel, architecture. *Address:* House of Commons, SW1A 0AA. *T:* (020) 7219 3000; 1 Temple Gardens, EC4Y 9BB. *T:* (020) 7353 0407. *Club:* Carlton.

GRIEVE, Michael Robertson Crichton; QC 1998; a Recorder, since 2000; *b* 12 Aug. 1951; *s* of Hon. Lord Grieve, *qv*; *m* 1983, Nadine Hilary Dyer, *d* of L. S. Dyer, Mill House, W Farleigh, Kent; one *s*. *Educ:* Edinburgh Acad.; Sedbergh Sch.; New Coll., Oxford (BA PPE 1st cl. Hons 1972). Called to the Bar, Middle Temple, 1975; in practice at the Bar, 1975–; an Asst Recorder, 1998–2000. *Recreations:* playing and watching football, tennis, music. *Address:* Doughty Street Chambers, 11 Doughty Street, WC1N 2PG. *T:* (020) 7404 1313. *Clubs:* Riverside Racquet, Queen's Park Rangers Football.

GRIEVE, William Robertson; *see* Grieve, Hon. Lord.

GRIEVES, David, CBE 1988; Vice Chairman, British Steel plc, 1991–94; Chairman, BSC Industry plc, since 1995–98 (Deputy Chairman, 1980–95); *b* 10 Jan. 1933; *s* of Joseph and Isabel Grieves; *m* 1960, Evelyn Muriel Attwater; two *s*. *Educ:* Durham Univ. BSc. PhD. Graduate apprentice, United Steel cos, 1957; Labour Manager, Appleby Frodingham Steel Co., 1962; British Steel Corporation: Manager, Industrial Relations, S Wales Group, 1967; Gen. Man., Stocksbridge and Tinsley Park Works, 1971; Personnel Dir, Special Steels Div., 1973; Dir, Indust. Relations, 1975; Man. Dir, Personnel and Social Policy, 1977; Dir, BSC, later British Steel plc, 1983. Chm., Avesta Sheffield, 1992–94. Mem. (non-exec), Post Office, 1990–98. Mem., Employment Appeal Tribunal, 1983–. *Address:* 4 Oak Way, West Common, Harpenden, Herts AL5 2NT. *T:* (01582) 767425, *Fax:* (01582) 761330.

GRIEVES, John Kerr; Senior Partner, Freshfields, 1990–96; *b* 7 Nov. 1935; *s* of Thomas and Nancy Grieves; *m* 1961, Ann Gorrell (*née* Harris); one *s* one *d*. *Educ:* King's Sch., Worcester; Keble Coll., Oxford (MA Law); Harvard Business Sch. (AMP). Articled clerk and asst solicitor, Pinsent & Co., Birmingham, 1958–61; joined Freshfields, 1963; Partner, 1964–96; Deptl Man. Partner, Company Dept, 1974–78; Man. Partner, 1979–85; Head, Corporate Finance Group, 1985–89. Director: British Invisibles, 1992–96; Northern Electric plc, 1996–97; Enterprise Oil plc, 1996–; Barclays Private Bank Ltd, 1997–; Hillsdown Holdings plc, 1997–98; New Look Group plc, 1998–2000; Chairman: First Leisure Corp. plc, 1998–2000; Esporta plc, 2000–; Advr, Apax Partners, 1996–99. Mem., Reporting Financial Review Panel, 1998–. Officer, Order of the Crown (Belgium), 1993. *Recreations:* the arts (especially music), sport. *Address:* 7 Putney Park Avenue, SW15 5QN. *T:* (020) 8876 1207. *Clubs:* Athenæum, Roehampton.

GRIEW, Prof. Stephen, PhD; Emeritus Professor and Senior Scholar, Atkinson College, York University, Toronto, since 1993; *b* 13 Sept. 1928; *e s* of late Harry and Sylvia Griew, London, England; *m* 1st, 1955, Jane le Geyt Johnson (marr. diss.); one *s* two *d* (and one *s* decd); 2nd, 1977, Eva Margareta Ursula, *d* of late Dr and Fru Johannes Ramberg, Stockholm, Sweden; one *d* and one step *s*. *Educ:* Univ. of London (BSc, Dip Psych); Univ. of Bristol (PhD). Vocational Officer, Min. of Labour, 1951–55; Univ. of Bristol: Research Worker, 1955–59; Lectr, 1959–63; Kenneth Craik Research Award, St John's Coll., Cambridge, 1960; Prof. of Psychology: Univ. of Otago, Dunedin, NZ, 1964–68 (Dean, Faculty of Science, 1967–68); Univ. of Dundee, 1968–72; Vice-Chancellor, Murdoch Univ., Perth, WA, 1972–77; Chm., Dept of Behavioural Science, Faculty of Medicine, Univ. of Toronto, 1977–80; Pres., 1980–85, University Prof., 1986–87, Athabasca Univ.; Dean, 1987–90, Prof. of Admin. Studies, 1990–93, Atkinson Coll., York Univ., Toronto; Pres., Senior Univ., Toronto, 1993–95; Adjunct Prof. of Psychol., 1993–, Dir, Inst. for Behavioural Res. in Health, 1996–97, Curtin Univ. of Technol., Perth, WA. Consultant, OECD, Paris, 1963–64; Expert, ILO, Geneva, 1966–67; Mem., Social Commn of Rehabilitation Internat., 1967–75; Consultant, Dept of Employment, 1970–72; Vis. Prof., Univ. of Western Ont., London, Canada, 1970 and 1971; Vis. Fellow, Wolfson Coll., Cambridge, 1985–86; Vis. Professorial Fellow, Curtin Univ. of Technol., Perth, 1993; Vis. Prof. of Gerontology, St Thomas Univ., Fredericton, Canada, 1998–99. Vice-Pres., Australian Council on the Ageing, 1975–76. FBPsS 1960; Fellow, Gerontological Soc. (USA), 1969. *Publications:* Beyond Permissiveness, 1992; handbooks and monographs on ageing and vocational rehabilitation, and articles in Jl of Gerontology and various psychological jls. *Recreations:* music, travel, writing. *Address:* Department of Gerontology, St Thomas University, Fredericton, NB E3B 5G1, Canada.

GRIFFEE, Andrew John; Controller, BBC English Regions, since 1999; *b* 25 Aug. 1961; *s* of John William Griffee and Kathleen Sandra Griffee; *m* 1988, Helen Caroline Emery; one *s* one *d*. *Educ:* Duke of York's Military Sch., Dover; Univ. of Manchester (BA 1st cl. Hons). Reporter: Poole and Dorset Herald, 1982–86; Northern Echo, 1986–87; Bath

Evening Chronicle, 1987–89; Asst News Editor, BBC Bristol, 1989–92; Editor, News and Current Affairs, 1992–96, Head of Regl and Local Progs, 1996–99, BBC South. *Address:* Tan House Farm, Aston Bank, Knighton on Teme, Worcs WR15 8LZ. *T:* (01584) 781798.

GRIFFIN, Major Sir (Arthur) John (Stewart), KCVO 1990 (CVO 1974; MVO 1967); Press Secretary to HM Queen Elizabeth the Queen Mother, 1956–91; *b* 1924; *s* of Arthur Wilfrid Michael Stewart Griffin and Florence May Griffin; *m* 1962, Henrietta Montagu Douglas Scott; two *s*. *Educ:* Harrow School. Regular Army Officer, The Queen's Bays, later The Queen's Dragoon Guards, 1942–58. *Recreations:* cricket, fishing, shooting. *Address:* Barton's Cottage, Bushy Park, Teddington, Middx TW11 0EA. *Club:* MCC.

GRIFFIN, Avril; *see* MacRory, A.

GRIFFIN, Sir (Charles) David, Kt 1974; CBE 1972; *b* 8 July 1915; *s* of Eric Furnival Griffin and Nellie Clarendon Griffin (*née* Devenish-Meares); *m* 1941, Jean Falconer Whyte; two *s*. *Educ:* Cranbrook Sch., Sydney; Univ. of Sydney (LLB and Golf Blue). 8th Aust. Div. 2nd AIF, 1940–45; POW Changi, Singapore, 1942–45. Associate to Sir Dudley Williams and Mem. Bar NSW, 1946–49; Solicitor, Sydney, 1949–64. Alderman, Sydney City Council, 1962–74, Chm. Finance Cttee, 1969–72; Lord Mayor of Sydney, 1972–73. Hon. Chm., Nabalco Pty Ltd, 1980–; Director: Lawpoint Pty Ltd, 1985–98 (Chm., 1985–88); OTC/Lawpoint, 1988–. Mem. Council, Royal Agricl Soc.; Mem. Nat. Council, Scout Assoc. of Australia (Life Councillor, NSW Br.); Dir, Nat. Seniors' Assoc. of Aust., 1991–. *Publications:* The Happiness Box (for children); The Will of the People; sundry speeches and short stories. *Recreations:* golf, fly-fishing. *Address:* c/o Lawpoint Pty, 9 Hunter Street, Sydney, NSW 2000, Australia. *Clubs:* Union (Sydney); Royal Sydney Golf, Pine Valley Golf (NJ, USA).

GRIFFIN, Prof. George Edward, PhD; FRCP, FRCPE, FRCPath, FMedSci; Chairman, Division of Infectious Diseases, and Professor of Infectious Diseases and Medicine, since 1992, and Chairman, Department of Internal Medicine, since 1994, St George's Hospital Medical School; *b* 27 Feb. 1947; *s* of Herbert Griffin and Enid Mary Griffin (*née* Borril); *m* 1972, Daphne Joan Haylor (*d* 1998), Romford; two *s* one *d*. *Educ:* Malet Lambert Grammar Sch., Kingston upon Hull; King's Coll., London (BSc); St George's Hosp. Med. Sch. (MB, BS); Univ. of Hull (PhD 1974); Harvard Univ. (Harkness Fellow). MRCP 1979, FRCP 1988; FRCPE 1994; FRCPath 1998. Registrar and Tutor in Medicine, RPMS, 1977–78; St George's Hospital Medical School: Lectr in Medicine, 1978–82; Wellcome Trust Sen. Lectr, 1982–90; Dir, Wellcome Trust Clinical Tropical Unit, 1994–; Hon. Cons. Physician, St George's Hosp., 1988–. Vis. Prof. of Medicine, Univ. of Michigan, 1992–. Mem., Adv. Cttee on Dangerous Pathogens, DoH, 1994–98. Wellcome Trust: Member: Infection and Immunity Panel, 1989–94; Tropical Interest Gp, 1991–94; Internat. Interest Gp, 1991–; Medical Research Council: Chm., Cttee for Develt and Implementation of Vaccines, 1994–; Member: Physiological Medicine and Infection Bd, 1994–; AIDS Vaccine Cttee, 1995–; HIV Virucidal Cttee, 1995–; Bd, PHLS, 1995–. Founder FMedSci 1998. *Publications:* scientific and clinical papers relating to pathogenesis of infection, vaccines. *Recreations:* walking, gardening, music. *Address:* 8 Buxton Drive, New Malden, Surrey KT3 3UZ. *T:* (020) 8949 4953. *Club:* Royal Automobile.

GRIFFIN, Prof. James Patrick, DPhil; White's Professor of Moral Philosophy, University of Oxford, 1996–2000; Fellow, Corpus Christi College, Oxford, 1996–2000, now Emeritus Fellow; *b* 8 July 1933; *s* of Gerald Joseph Griffin and Catherine Griffin (*née* Noonan); *m* 1966, Catherine Maulde von Halban (*d* 1993); one *s* one *d*. *Educ:* Choate Sch., Wallingford, Conn; Yale Univ. (BA 1955); Oxford Univ. (DPhil 1960; MA 1963). University of Oxford: Rhodes Schol., Corpus Christi Coll., 1955–58; Sen. Schol., St Antony's Coll., 1958–60; Lectr, Christ Church, 1960–66; Fellow and Tutor in Philosophy, Keble Coll., 1966–96 (Hon. Fellow, 1996); Lectr in Philosophy, 1964–90; Radcliffe Fellow, 1982–84; Reader, 1990–96. Visiting Professor: Univ. of Wisconsin, 1970, 1978; Univ. of Santiago de Compostela, 1988, 1995; Gtr Philadelphia Philosophy Consortium, 1989; ITAM, Mexico, 1994; UNAM, Mexico, 1995, etc. Medal, Nat. Educn Commn, Poland, 1992. Order of Diego de Lusada (Venezuela), 1999. *Publications:* Wittgenstein's Logical Atomism, 1964, repr. 1997; Well-Being: its meaning, measurement and moral importance, 1986; (jtly) Values, Conflict and the Environment, 1989, 2nd edn 1996; Value Judgement: improving our ethical beliefs, 1996; articles in philosophical jls. *Recreations:* eating, drinking. *Address:* 10 Northmoor Road, Oxford OX2 6UP. *T:* (01865) 554130. *Club:* Oxford and Cambridge.

GRIFFIN, Janet Mary, (Mrs Paul Griffin); *see* Turner, J. M.

GRIFFIN, Prof. Jasper, FBA 1986; Professor of Classical Literature, and Public Orator, Oxford University, since 1992; Fellow and Tutor in Classics, Balliol College, Oxford, since 1963; *b* 29 May 1937; *s* of Frederick William Griffin and Constance Irene Griffin (*née* Cordwell); *m* 1960, Miriam Tamara Dressler; three *d*. *Educ:* Christ's Hospital; Balliol College, Oxford (1st Cl. Hon. Mods 1958; 1st Cl. Lit. Hum. 1960; Hertford Scholar 1958; Ireland Scholar 1958). Jackson Fellow, Harvard Univ., 1960–61; Oxford University: Dyson Research Fellow, Balliol Coll., 1961–63; Reader in Classical Lit., 1990–92. T. S. Eliot Meml Lectr, Univ. of Kent at Canterbury, 1984. *Publications:* Homer on Life and Death, 1980; Homer, 1980; Snobs, 1982; Latin Poets and Roman Life, 1985; The Mirror of Myth, 1986; (ed with J. Boardman and O. Murray) The Oxford History of the Classical World, 1986; Virgil, 1986; Homer, The Odyssey, 1987; Homer, Iliad ix, 1995. *Address:* Balliol College, Oxford OX1 3BJ. *T:* (01865) 77782.

GRIFFIN, Sir John; *see* Griffin, Sir A. J. S.

GRIFFIN, Dr John Parry, BSc, PhD, MB, BS; FRCP, FRCPath, FFPM; Director, John Griffin Associates Ltd, since 1994; Hon. Consultant, Lister Hospital, Stevenage; *b* 21 May 1938; *o s* of late David J. Griffin and Phyllis M. Griffin; *m* 1962, Margaret, *o d* of late Frank Cooper and Catherine Cooper; one *s* two *d*. *Educ:* Howardian High Sch., Cardiff; London Hosp. Medical Coll. Lethby and Buxton Prizes, 1958; BSc (1st Cl. Hons) 1959; PhD 1961; George Riddoch Prize in Neurology, 1962; MB, BS 1964; LRCP, MRCS 1964; MRCP 1980, FRCP 1990; FRCPath 1986 (MRCPath 1982); FFPM 1989. Ho. Phys., London Hosp. Med. Unit, and Ho. Surg., London Hosp. Accident and Orthopaedic Dept, 1964–65; Lectr in Physiology, King's Coll., London, 1965–67; Head of Clinical Research, Riker Laboratories, 1967–71; SMO, Medicines Div., 1971–76; PMO, Medicines Div., and Medical Assessor, Cttee on Safety of Medicines, 1976–77; SPMO and Professional Head of Medicines Div., DHSS, 1977–84; Med. Assessor, Medicines Commn, 1977–84; Dir, Assoc. of the British Pharmaceutical Industry, 1984–94. Faculty Mem., Scripps Med. Res. Center, San Diego, 1997–98; Vis. Prof., Univ. of Surrey, 2000–. Mem., Jt Formulary Cttee for British Nat. Formulary, 1978–84; UK Rep., EEC Cttee on Proprietary Med. Products; Chm., Cttee on Prop. Med. Products Working Party on Safety Requirements, 1977–84. Mem. Bd, Faculty of Pharmaceutical Med., RCP, 1993– (Chm., Bd of Examiners, 1997–). FRSocMed. Thomas Young Lectr and Gold Medallist, St George's Hosp. Med. Sch., 1992. *Publications:* (jtly) Iatrogenic Diseases, 1972, 3rd edn 1985; (jtly) Manual of Adverse Drug Interactions, 1975, 5th edn 1997; (jtly) Drug Induced Emergencies, 1980; Medicines: research, regulation and risk, 1989, 2nd edn 1992; (jtly) International Medicines Regulations, 1989; (jtly) Textbook of Pharmaceutical Medicine, 1993, 4th edn 2001; numerous articles in sci. and med. jls, mainly on aspects of neurophysiology, clinical pharmacology, toxicology and pharmacoeconomics. *Recreations:* gardening, local history. *Address:* Quartermans, Digswell Lane, Digswell, Herts AL6 0SP.

GRIFFIN, Keith Broadwell, DPhil; Distinguished Professor of Economics, University of California, Riverside, since 1988 (Chairman, Department of Economics, 1988–93); *b* 6 Nov. 1938; *s* of Marcus Samuel Griffin and Elaine Ann Broadwell; *m* 1956, Dixie Beth Griffin; two *d*. *Educ:* Williams Coll., Williamstown, Mass (BA; Hon DLitt, 1980); Balliol Coll., Oxford (BPhil, DPhil). Fellow and Tutor in Econs, Magdalen Coll., Oxford, 1965–76, Fellow by special election, 1977–79; Warden, Queen Elizabeth House, Oxford, 1978–79 (Actg Warden, 1973 and 1977–78); Dir, Inst. of Commonwealth Studies, Oxford, 1978–79 (Actg Dir, 1973 and 1977–78); Pres., Magdalen Coll., Oxford, 1979–88. Chief, Rural and Urban Employment Policies Br., ILO, 1975–76; Vis. Prof., Inst. of Econs and Planning, Univ. of Chile, 1962–63 and 1964–65; Dist. Vis. Prof., Amer. Univ. in Cairo, 2001; Vis. Fellow, Oxford Centre for Islamic Studies, 1998. Consultant: ILO, 1974, 1982, 1994, 1996, 1997; Internat. Bank for Reconstruction and Develt, 1973; UN Res. Inst. for Social Develt, 1971–72; FAO, 1963–64, 1967, 1978; Inter-Amer. Cttee for Alliance for Progress, 1968; US Agency for Internat. Develt, 1966; UNDP, 1989, 1991–98. Res. Adviser, Pakistan Inst. of Develt Econs, 1965, 1970; Sen. Adviser, OECD Develt Centre, Paris, 1986–88; Economic Advr, Govt of Bolivia, 1989–91. Member: Council, UN Univ., 1986–92; UN Cttee for Develt Planning, 1987–94; Chm., UN Res. Inst. for Social Develt, 1988–95. Mem., World Commn on Culture and Develt, 1994–95. Pres., Develt Studies Assoc., 1978–80. FAAAS 1997. *Publications:* (with Ricardo ffrench-Davis) Comercio Internacional y Politicas de Desarrollo Economico, 1967; Underdevelopment in Spanish America, 1969; (with John Enos) Planning Development, 1970; (ed) Financing Development in Latin America, 1971; (ed with Azizur Rahman Khan) Growth and Inequality in Pakistan, 1972; The Political Economy of Agrarian Change, 1974, 2nd edn 1979; (ed with E. A. G. Robinson) The Economic Development of Bangladesh, 1974; Land Concentration and Rural Poverty, 1976, 2nd edn 1981; International Inequality and National Poverty, 1978; (with Ashwani Saith) Growth and Equality in Rural China, 1981; (with Jeffrey James) The Transition to Egalitarian Development, 1981; (ed) Institutional Reform and Economic Development in the Chinese Countryside, 1984; World Hunger and the World Economy, 1987; Alternative Strategies for Economic Development, 1989; (ed with John Knight) Human Development and the International Development Strategy for the 1990s, 1990; (ed) The Economy of Ethiopia, 1992; (ed with Zhao Renwei) The Distribution of Income in China, 1993; (with Terry McKinley) Implementing a Human Development Strategy, 1994; (ed) Poverty and the Transition to a Market Economy in Mongolia, 1995; Studies in Globalization and Economic Transitions, 1996; (ed) Social Policy and Economic Transformation in Uzbekistan, 1996; (ed) Economic Reform in Vietnam, 1998; Studies in Development Strategy and Systemic Transformation, 2000. *Recreation:* travel. *Address:* Department of Economics, University of California, Riverside, CA 92521, USA.

GRIFFIN, Kenneth James, OBE 1970; Deputy Chairman, Ugland International, 1993–97; *b* 1 Aug. 1928; *s* of late Albert Griffin and late Catherine (*née* Sullivan); *m* 1951, Doreen Cicely Simon (*d* 1992); one *s* one *d* (and one *s* decd). *Educ:* Dynevor Grammar Sch., Swansea; Swansea Technical College. Area Sec., ETU, 1960; Dist Sec., Confedn of Ship Building Engrg Unions, 1961; Sec., Craftsmen Cttee (Steel), 1961; Mem., Welsh Council, 1968; Mem., Crowther Commn on Constitution (Wales), 1969; Joint Sec., No 8 Joint Industrial Council Electrical Supply Industry, 1969; Industrial Adviser, DTI, 1971–72; Co-ordinator of Industrial Advisers, DTI, 1972–74; Special Adviser, Sec. of State for Industry, 1974; part-time Mem., NCB, 1973–82; a Dep. Chm., British Shipbuilders, 1977–83; Chm., Blackwall Engrg, 1983–85; Member: Suppl. Benefits Commn, 1968–80; Solicitors Disciplinary Tribunal, 1982–. Chm., Network Housing Assoc., 1991–97; Vice-Chm., UK Housing Trust, 1989–; Mem. Bd, Housing Corp., 1995–; Exec. Advr, Mobile Training, 1989–90. *Recreations:* golf, music, reading. *Address:* 214 Cyncoed Road, Cyncoed, Cardiff CF2 6RS. *T:* (029) 2075 2184. *Club:* Reform.

GRIFFIN, Paul, MBE 1961; MA Cantab; writer; *b* 2 March 1922; *s* of late John Edwin Herman Griffin; *m* 1946, Felicity Grace, *d* of late Canon Howard Dobson; one *s* one *d*. *Educ:* Framlingham Coll.; St Catharine's Coll., Cambridge. Served War in Gurkhas, India, Burma, Malaya, 1940–46; North-West Frontier, 1941–43; Chindits, 1943–44. Asst Master and Senior English Master, Uppingham Sch., 1949–55; Principal, English Sch. in Cyprus, 1956–60; Headmaster, Aldenham Sch., 1962–74; Principal, Anglo-World Language Centre, Cambridge, 1976–82; Treasurer, Corp. of Sons of the Clergy, 1978–86. *Publications:* Sing Jubilee, 1996; Nearly Funny Poems, 1996; Songs About Suffolk, 1997; Going Away, 1999; Lighthearted Lines, 2000; collaborated in: How to Become Ridiculously Well-Read in One Evening, 1985; How to Become Absurdly Well-Informed about the Famous and Infamous, 1987; The Dogsbody Papers, 1988; How to Be Tremendously Tuned-in to Opera, 1989; How to Be Well-Versed in Poetry, 1990; How to Be European, 1991; poems, humour, articles, broadcasts. *Recreation:* literary competitions. *Address:* 1 Crombie House, The Common, Southwold, Suffolk IP18 6AL. *T:* (01502) 723709. *Club:* Army and Navy.

GRIFFIN, Very Rev. Victor Gilbert Benjamin; Dean of St Patrick's Cathedral, Dublin, 1969–91; *b* 24 May 1924; *s* of Gilbert B. and Violet M. Griffin, Carnew, Co. Wicklow; *m* 1958, Daphne E. Mitchell; two *s*. *Educ:* Kilkenny Coll.; Mountjoy Sch., and Trinity Coll., Dublin. MA, 1st class Hons in Philosophy. Ordained, 1947; Curacy, St Augustine's, Londonderry, 1947–51; Curacy, Christ Church, Londonderry, 1951–57; Rector of Christ Church, Londonderry, 1957–69. Lecturer in Philosophy, Magee Univ. Coll., Londonderry, 1950–69. Hon. MRIAI 1992. Hon. DD TCD, 1992. *Publications:* Trends in Theology, 1870–1970, 1970; Anglican and Irish, 1976; Pluralism and Ecumenism, 1983; The Mark of Protest: experience of a Southern Protestant in Northern Ireland and the Republic, 1993; The Churches and Sectarianism in Ireland, 1995; Swift and His Hospital, 1995; Swift's Message to Ireland Today, 1996; contrib. to New Divinity. *Recreations:* music, golf. *Address:* 7 Tyler Road, Limavady, N Ireland BT49 0DW. *Clubs:* Friendly Brothers of St Patrick, Kildare Street and University (Dublin).

GRIFFINS, Roy Jason; Director-General, Civil Aviation, Department of the Environment, Transport and the Regions, since 1999; *b* 8 May 1946; *s* of Manuel Griffins and Betty Griffins; *m* 1984, Margaret Alison Redfern; one *d*. *Educ:* Blackpool Grammar Sch.; Bristol Univ. (BA). Barclays Bank Foreign Branches, 1967–68; Systems Analyst, Internat. Computers Ltd, 1968–70; Sen. Systems Analyst, with BBC, 1970–74; Copywriter, Krohn Advertising, Montreal, 1975–76; Principal, Wildlife Conservation, DoE, 1976–77; First Sec. (Envmt), UK Representation to EC, Brussels (on secondment), 1978–80; Sec. to Third London Airport Inquiry, DoE, 1981–83; Department of Transport: Principal (Aviation), then Head, Airports Policy, 1984–87; Principal Private Sec. to Sec. of State for Transport, 1987–89; Counsellor, Washington (on secondment), 1990–93; Asst Sec., Channel Tunnel Rail Link, Dept of Transport, 1993–96; Dir,

Railways, DETR, 1996–99. *Recreations:* tennis, France, films, food. *Address:* Department of the Environment, Transport and the Regions, Great Minster House, 76 Marsham Street, SW1P 4DR. *Club:* Reform.

GRIFFITH, Rev. (Arthur) Leonard; Lecturer in Homiletics, Wycliffe College, Toronto, 1977–87, retired; *b* 20 March 1920; *s* of Thomas Griffiths and Sarah Jane Taylor; *m* 1947, Anne Merelie Cayford; two *d. Educ:* Public and High Schs, Brockville, Ont; McGill Univ., Montreal (BA, McGill, 1942); United Theological Coll., Montreal (BD 1945; Hon. DD 1962); Mansfield Coll., Oxford, England, 1957–58. Ordained in The United Church of Canada, 1945; Minister: United Church, Arden, Ont, 1945–47; Trinity United Church, Grimsby, Ont, 1947–50; Chalmers United Church, Ottawa, Ont, 1950–60; The City Temple, London, 1960–66; Deer Park United Church, Toronto, 1966–75; ordained in Anglican Church 1976; Minister, St Paul's Church, Bloor St, Toronto, 1975–85. Hon. DD Wycliffe Coll., Toronto, 1985. *Publications:* The Roman Letter Today, 1959; God and His People, 1960; Beneath The Cross of Jesus, 1961; What is a Christian?, 1962; Barriers to Christian Belief, 1962; A Pilgrimage to the Holy Land, 1962; The Eternal Legacy, 1963; Pathways to Happiness, 1964; God's Time and Ours, 1964; The Crucial Encounter, 1965; This is Living!, 1966; God in Man's Experience, 1968; Illusions of our Culture, 1969; The Need to Preach, 1971; Hang on to the Lord's Prayer, 1973; We Have This Ministry, 1973; Ephesians: a positive affirmation, 1975; Gospel Characters, 1976; Reactions to God, 1979; Take Hold of the Treasure, 1980; From Sunday to Sunday, 1987. *Recreations:* music, drama, travelling, adult education. *Address:* 91 Old Mill Road, Etobicoke, ON M8X 1G9, Canada.

GRIFFITH, (Edward) Michael (Wynne), CBE 1986; Vice Lord-Lieutenant for the County of Clwyd, since 1986; Chairman, Countryside Council for Wales, 1991–2000; *b* 29 Aug. 1933; *e s* of Major H. W. Griffith, MBE; *m* Jill Grange, *d* of Major D. P. G. Moseley, Dorfold Cottage, Nantwich; one *s* (and two *s* decd). *Educ:* Eton; Royal Agricultural College. Regional Dir, National Westminster Bank Ltd, 1974–92; Mem. Welsh Bd, Nationwide Anglia Bldg Soc., 1986–89. High Sheriff of Denbighshire, 1969. Chairman: Clwyd HA, 1980–90; National Trust Cttee for Wales, 1984–91 (Mem., National Trust Exec. and Council, 1989–2000); Glan Clwyd Hosp. Trust, 1993–99; Denbighshire and Conway Hosp. Trust, 1999–; Council, Univ. of Wales Coll. of Medicine, 1997–; Dir, Land Authority Wales, 1989–90. Member: Countryside Commn Cttee for Wales, 1972–78; Min. of Agriculture Regional Panel, 1972–77; ARC, 1973–82; UFC (Wales), 1989–92; HEFCW, 1992–95; British Library Bd, 1992–95. Patron, The Prince's Trust Bro. FRSA 1993; FLS 1995. DL Clwyd, 1985. *Address:* Greenfield, Trefnant, Clwyd LL16 5UE. *T:* (01745) 730633. *Club:* Boodle's.

GRIFFITH, Prof. John Aneurin Grey, LLB London, LLM London; Hon. LLD Edinburgh 1982, York, Toronto, 1982, Manchester 1987; FBA 1977; Barrister-at-law; Chancellor of Manchester University, 1986–93; Emeritus Professor of Public Law, University of London; *b* 14 Oct. 1918; *s* of Rev. B. Grey Griffith and Bertha Griffith; *m* 1941, Barbara Eirene Garnet, *d* of W. Garnet Williams; two *s* one *d. Educ:* Taunton Sch.; LSE. British and Indian armies, 1940–46. Lectr in Law, UCW, Aberystwyth, 1946–48; Lectr in Law and Reader, LSE, 1948–59, Prof. of English Law, 1959–70, Prof. of Public Law, 1970–84. Vis. Professor of Law: Univ. of California at Berkeley, 1966; York Univ., 1985. Mem., Marlow UDC, 1950–55, and Bucks CC, 1955–61. Editor, Public Law, 1956–81. *Publications:* (with H. Street) A Casebook of Administrative Law, 1964; Central Departments and Local Authorities, 1966; (with H. Street) Principles of Administrative Law, 5th edn, 1973; Parliamentary Scrutiny of Government Bills, 1974; (with T. C. Hartley) Government and Law, 1975, 2nd edn 1981; (ed) From Policy to Administration, 1976; The Politics of the Judiciary, 1977, 5th edn 1997; Public Rights and Private Interests, 1981; (with M. T. Ryle) Parliament, 1989; Judicial Politics, since 1920: a chronicle, 1993; articles in English, Commonwealth and American jls of law, public administration and politics. *Recreations:* drinking beer, writing bad verse. *Address:* 2 The Close, Spinfield Lane, Marlow, Bucks SL7 2LA.

GRIFFITH, Kenneth; actor, writer and documentary film-maker; formed own film company, Breakaway Productions Ltd, 1982; *b* 12 Oct. 1921; *g s* of Ernest and Emily Griffith; three marriages dissolved; three *s* two *d. Educ:* council and grammar schs, Tenby, Pembrokeshire, SW Wales. Became a professional actor at Festival Theatre, Cambridge, 1937; films and television; served War, RAF; post war, associated with Tyrone Guthrie at Old Vic; unknown number of films, partic. for Boulting brothers; unknown number of television plays; rarely theatre; made first documentary film at invitation of David Attenborough and Huw Wheldon, 1964; best documentaries include: Life of Cecil Rhodes; Hang Up Your Brightest Colours (life of Michael Collins; suppressed by Lew Grade at behest of IBA for twenty years, until broadcast in 1993); The Public's Right to Know; The Sun's Bright Child (life of Edmund Kean); Black as Hell, Thick as Grass (the 24th Regt in Zulu War); The Most Valuable Englishman Ever (life of Thomas Paine for BBC TV); Clive of India (Channel Four); The Light (life of David Ben Gurion for Channel Four); But I Have Promises to Keep (life of Jawaharlal Nehru for Indian Govt), 1987; The Girl Who Didn't Run (on Zola Budd for BBC TV), 1989; Roger Casement, the Heart of Darkness (for BBC TV), 1992; The Untouchable (life of Dr Ambedkar for BBC TV), 1996; The Legend of George Rex (Channel 4), 1997; Against Empire (to commemorate 2nd Anglo-Boer War, for BBC), 1999; Dreyfus (BBC TV); *relevant film:* The Tenby Poisoner (film biography, BBC TV), 1993. *Publications:* Thank God we kept the Flag Flying, 1974; (with Timothy O'Grady) Curious Journey, 1981 (based on unshown TV documentary); The Discovery of Nehru, 1989; The Fool's Pardon (autobiog.), 1994. *Recreations:* talking; collecting British Empire military postal history (envelopes, post-cards), also ephemera connected with southern Africa. *Address:* 110 Englefield Road, Islington, N1 3LQ. *T:* (020) 7226 9013.

GRIFFITH, Rev. Leonard; *see* Griffith, Rev. A. L.

GRIFFITH, Michael; *see* Griffith, E. M. W.

GRIFFITH EDWARDS, James; *see* Edwards.

GRIFFITH-JONES, David Eric; QC 2000; FCIArb; a Recorder, since 1997; *b* Nairobi, 7 March 1953; *s* of Sir Eric Newton Griffith-Jones, KBE, CMG, QC and Mary Patricia Griffith-Jones; *m* 1st, 1978, Deborah Judith Laidlaw Mockeridge (marr. diss. 1983); 2nd, 1984, Virginia Ann Meredith Brown; two *s* one *d. Educ:* Marlborough Coll.; Bristol Univ. (LLB 1974). FCIArb 1991. Called to the Bar, Middle Temple, 1975; Asst Recorder, 1992–97. Asst Boundary Comr, 2000–. Mem., Sports Disputes Resolution Panel, 2000–. *Publication:* Law and the Business of Sport, 1997. *Recreations:* sport, country pursuits. *Address:* Devereux Chambers, Devereux Court, WC2R 3JJ. *T:* (020) 7353 7534; *e-mail:* griffith-jones@devchambers.co.uk. *Clubs:* Sevenoaks Rugby Football, Falconhurst Cricket (Kent).

GRIFFITH-JONES, Richard Haydn; His Honour Judge Griffith-Jones; a Circuit Judge, since 1999; *b* 29 June 1951; *s* of Wyn and Mary Griffith-Jones; *m* 1974, Susan Hale; three *s* one *d. Educ:* Solihull Sch.; Leeds Univ. (LLB Hons). Called to the Bar, Middle Temple, 1974; a Recorder, 1994–99. *Publication:* contrib. to Law Qly Rev. *Recreations:* poultry keeping, watching Association football. *Address:* 1 Fountain Court, Steelhouse Lane, Birmingham B4 6DR.

GRIFFITH-JONES, Rev. Robin Guthrie; Master of The Temple, Temple Church, since 1999; *b* 29 May 1956; *s* of Mervyn and Joan Griffith-Jones. *Educ:* Westminster; New Coll., Oxford (MA); Westcott House; Christ's Coll., Cambridge (MA). Christie's (English Drawings and Watercolours), 1978–84; ordained deacon, 1989; priest, 1990; Curate, St Jude, Cantril Farm and Stockbridge Village, Liverpool, 1989–92; Chaplain, Lincoln Coll., Oxford, 1992–99. *Publication:* The Four Witnesses, 2000. *Address:* Master's House, Temple, EC4Y 7BB. *T:* (020) 7353 8559. *Club:* Pratt's.

GRIFFITH WILLIAMS, John; QC 1985; **His Honour Judge Griffith Williams;** a Circuit Judge, since 2000; *b* 20 Dec. 1944; *s* of Griffith John Williams, TD and Alison Williams; *m* 1971, Mair Tasker Watkins, *d* of Rt Hon. Sir Tasker Watkins, *qv*; two *d. Educ:* King's School, Bruton; The Queen's College, Oxford (BA). Served 4th Bn, RWF (TA), 1965–68; Welsh Volunteers (TAVR), 1968–71 (Lieut). Called to the Bar, Gray's Inn, 1968, Bencher, 1994; a Recorder, 1984–2000; a Dep. High Court Judge, 1993–2000. Mem., Criminal Injuries Compensation Bd, 1999–2000. Mem., Bar Council, 1990–93; Leader, Wales and Chester Circuit, 1996–98 (Treas., 1993–95). Asst Comr, Boundary Commn for Wales, 1994–2000. Chancellor, dio. of Llandaff, 1999– (Dep. Chancellor, 1996–99). Fellow, Woodard Corp. (Western Div.), 1994–. *Recreation:* golf. *Address:* c/o The Crown Court, Cathays Park, Cardiff CF10 3PG. *Clubs:* Army and Navy; Cardiff and County (Cardiff); Royal Porthcawl Golf.

GRIFFITHS, family name of **Barons Griffiths** and **Griffiths of Fforestfach.**

GRIFFITHS, Baron *cr* 1985 (Life Peer), of Govilon in the County of Gwent; **William Hugh Griffiths,** Kt 1971; MC 1944; PC 1980; a Lord of Appeal in Ordinary, 1985–93; *b* 26 Sept. 1923; *s* of late Sir Hugh Griffiths, CBE, MS, FRCS; *m* 1949, Evelyn (*d* 1998), *d* of Col K. A. Krefting; one *s* three *d*; *m* 2000, Baroness Brigstocke, *qv*. *Educ:* Charterhouse; St John's Coll., Cambridge (Hon. Fellow, 1985). Commissioned in Welsh Guards, 1942; demobilised after war service, 1946. Cambridge, 1946–48. BA 1948. Called to the Bar, Inner Temple, 1949, Bencher, 1971; QC 1964; Treasurer of the Bar Council, 1968–69. Recorder of Margate, 1962–64, of Cambridge, 1964–70; a Judge of the High Court of Justice, Queen's Bench Division, 1971–80; a Lord Justice of Appeal, 1980–85. A Judge, National Industrial Relations Court, 1973–74. Chm., Security Commn, 1985–92; Mem., Adv. Council on Penal Reform, 1967–70; Chm., Tribunal of Inquiry on Ronan Point, 1968; Vice-Chm., Parole Bd, 1976–77; Mem., Chancellor's Law Reform Cttee, 1976–93; Pres., Senate of the Inns of Court and the Bar, 1982–84; Chm., Lord Chancellor's Adv. Cttee on Legal Educn and Conduct, 1991–93. Hon. Mem., Canadian Bar Assoc., 1981; Hon. Fellow: Amer. Inst. of Judicial Admin, 1985; Amer. Coll. of Trial Lawyers, 1988. Hon. LLD: Wales, 1987; De Montfort, 1993. *Recreations:* cricket, golf, fishing. *Address:* c/o House of Lords, SW1A 0PW. *Clubs:* Garrick, MCC (Pres., 1990–91); Hawks (Cambridge); Royal and Ancient (St Andrews) (Captain, 1993–94); Sunningdale Golf.

See also D. C. P. McDougall.

GRIFFITHS, Lady; *see* Brigstocke, Baroness.

GRIFFITHS OF FFORESTFACH, Baron *cr* 1991 (Life Peer), of Fforestfach in the county of West Glamorgan; **Brian Griffiths;** Vice Chairman, Goldman Sachs (Europe), since 1991; *b* 27 Dec. 1941; *s* of Ivor Winston Griffiths and Phyllis Mary Griffiths (*née* Morgan); *m* 1965, Rachel Jane Jones; one *s* two *d. Educ:* Dynevor Grammar School; London School of Economics, Univ. of London. (BSc (Econ), MSc (Econ)). Assistant Lecturer in Economics, LSE, 1965–68, Lecturer in Economics, 1968–76; City University: Prof. of Banking and Internat. Finance, 1977–85; Dir, Centre for Banking and Internat. Finance, 1977–82; Dean, Business Sch., 1982–85; Head of Prime Minister's Policy Unit, 1985–90. Vis. Prof., Univ. of Rochester, USA, 1972–73; Prof. of Ethics, Gresham Coll., 1984–87; Dir, Bank of England, 1984–86 (Mem., Panel of Academic Consultants, 1977–86). Director: Herman Miller, 1991–; Times Newspapers, 1991–; HTV (Wales), 1991–93; Servicemaster, 1992–; Telewest, 1994–98; English, Welsh and Scottish Railway, 1996–; Chairman: Trillium, 1998–; Westminster Health Care, 1999–. Chairman: Centre for Policy Studies, 1991–2000; Sch. Exams and Assessment Council, 1991–93; Trustees, Lambeth Fund, 1997–. Fellow, Trinity Coll., Carmarthen, 1997. Hon. DSc City, 1999. *Publications:* Is Revolution Change? (ed and contrib.) 1972; Mexican Monetary Policy and Economic Development, 1972; Invisible Barriers to Invisible Trade, 1975; Inflation: The Price of Prosperity, 1976; (ed with G. E. Wood) Monetary Targets, 1980; The Creation of Wealth, 1984; (ed with G. E. Wood) Monetarism in the United Kingdom, 1984; Morality and the Market Place, 1989. *Address:* c/o House of Lords, SW1A 0PW. *Club:* Garrick.

GRIFFITHS, (Albert) John; Member (Lab) Newport East, National Assembly for Wales, since 1999; *b* 19 Dec. 1956; *s* of Albert John Griffiths and Hannah Griffiths (*née* O'Connor); *m* 1978, Alison Kim Hopkins; two *s. Educ:* UC, Cardiff (LLB Hons Law); Dip. in Social Studies, 1996. Lectr in Further Educn and Higher Educn, 1988–89; Production Exec., 1989–90; solicitor, 1990–99. *Recreations:* cricket, tennis, running, circuit training, reading, travel. *Address:* National Assembly for Wales, Cardiff Bay, Cardiff CF99 1NA. *T:* (029) 2089 8307.

GRIFFITHS, Prof. Allen Phillips; Professor of Philosophy, University of Warwick, 1964–92, now Emeritus; Director, Royal Institute of Philosophy, 1979–94; *b* 11 June 1927; *s* of John Phillips Griffiths and Elsie Maud (*née* Jones); *m* 1st, 1948, Margaret Lock (*d* 1974); one *s* one *d*; 2nd, 1984, Vera Clare (marr. diss. 1990). *Educ:* University Coll., Cardiff (BA; Hon. Fellow 1984); University Coll., Oxford (BPhil). Sgt, Intell. Corps, 1945–48 (despatches). Asst Lectr, Univ. of Wales, 1955–57; Lectr, Birkbeck Coll., Univ. of London, 1957–64. Pro-Vice-Chancellor, Univ. of Warwick, 1970–77. Vis. Professor: Swarthmore Coll., Pa, 1963; Univ. of Calif, 1967; Univ. of Wisconsin, 1965 and 1970; Carleton Coll., Minnesota, 1985. Silver Jubilee Medal, 1977. *Publications:* (ed) Knowledge & Belief, 1967; (ed) Of Liberty, 1983; (ed) Philosophy and Literature, 1984; Philosophy and Practice, 1985; (ed) Contemporary French Philosophy, 1988; (ed) Key Themes in Philosophy, 1989; (ed) Wittgenstein Centenary Essays, 1990; (ed) A. J. Ayer Memorial Essays, 1992; (ed) The Impulse to Philosophise, 1993; articles in learned philosophical jls. *Address:* 6 Brockley Road, West Bridgford, Nottingham NG2 5JY. *T:* (0115) 878 0159; *e-mail:* allen@coolsite.net.

GRIFFITHS, Rt Rev. Ambrose; *see* Griffiths, Rt Rev. M. A.

GRIFFITHS, Antony Vaughan, FBA 2000; Keeper, Department of Prints and Drawings, British Museum, since 1991; *b* 28 July 1951; *s* of Richard Cerdin Griffiths and Pamela de Grave Griffiths (*née* Hetherington). *Educ:* Highgate Sch.; Christ Church, Oxford (BA); Courtauld Inst. of Art, London Univ. (MA). Joined Dept of Prints and Drawings, BM, 1976, as Asst Keeper; Dep. Keeper, 1981–91. *Publications:* Prints and

Printmaking, 1980, 2nd edn 1996; (with Reginald Williams) The Department of Prints and Drawings in the British Museum: a user's guide, 1987; British Museum exhibn catalogues; contribs to learned jls, esp. Print Qly. *Address:* 1 Highbury Hill, N5 1SU.

GRIFFITHS, Air Vice-Marshal Arthur, CB 1972; AFC 1964; *b* 22 Aug. 1922; *s* of late Edward and Elizabeth Griffiths; *m* 1950, Nancy Maud Sumpter; one *d*. *Educ:* Hawarden Grammar School. Joined RAF, 1940; war service with No 26 Fighter Reconnaissance Sqdn; post-war years as Flying Instructor mainly at CFS and Empire Flying Sch.; psc 1954; comd No 94 Fighter Sqdn Germany, 1955–56; Dirg Staff, RCAF Staff Coll., Toronto, 1956–59; HQ Bomber Comd, 1959–61; comd No 101 Bomber Sqdn, 1962–64; Gp Captain Ops, Bomber Comd, 1964–67; comd RAF Waddington, 1967–69; AOA and later Chief of Staff, Far East Air Force, 1969–71; Head of British Defence Liaison Staff, Canberra, 1972–74; Dir Gen., Security (RAF), 1976–77, and Comdt-Gen. RAF Regt, 1975–77. *Address:* Water Lane House, Castor, Peterborough PE5 7BJ. *T:* (01733) 380742. *Club:* Royal Air Force.

GRIFFITHS, Hon. Clive Edward, AO 1997; JP; Agent-General for Western Australia, since 1997; *b* Perth, WA, 20 Nov. 1928; *s* of T. E. Griffiths and D. M. Beattie; *m* 1st, 1949, Myrtle Holtham (marr. diss. 1995; she *d* 1996); one *d*; 2nd, 1995, Norma Marie Paonessa. *Educ:* Fremantle Boys' High Sch.; Kalgoorlie Sch. of Mines. Electrical Engineer and Contractor, 1953–66. City Councillor, S Perth, 1962–66; MLC (L), WA, 1965–97 (Pres., 1977–97); Parly Sec., Lib Party and Jt Govt Parties, 1974–77; Regl Rep. for Australia and Pacific Region, 1988–90, Chm., Exec. Cttee, 1990–93, Commonwealth Parly Assoc. JP W Australia, 1983. *Recreations:* sailing, football, cricket. *Address:* Government of Western Australia European Office, 5th Floor, Australia Centre, Corner of Strand & Melbourne Place, WC2B 4LG. *T:* (020) 7240 2881. *Clubs:* Royal Over-Seas League, East India; Shelley Sailing, South Perth Yacht.

GRIFFITHS, Courtenay Delsdue McVay; QC 1998; a Recorder, since 2000; *b* 10 Oct. 1955; *s* of Wrenford Dacosta Griffiths and Adelaide Tamonda Griffiths; *m* 1985, Angela Maria Hill; three *s*. *Educ:* Bablake Sch., Coventry; LSE, London Univ. (LLB Hons 1979). Called to the Bar, Gray's Inn, 1980; Legal Asst, GLC Police Cttee, 1980–84; Revson Fellow, Urban Legal Studies Prog., City Coll., CUNY, 1984–85; in practice at the Bar, 1985–; an Asst Recorder, 1999–2000. Hon. Lectr in Law, KCL, 1987–. *Recreations:* swimming, squash, music (reggae and soul), play piano, drawing and painting. *Address:* 2 Garden Court, Temple, EC4Y 9BL. *T:* (020) 7353 1633.

GRIFFITHS, David Howard, OBE 1982; Chairman, Eastern Region, British Gas Corporation, 1981–87; *b* 30 Oct. 1922; *s* of David Griffiths and Margaret (*née* Jones); *m* 1949, Dilys Watford John; two *d*. *Educ:* Monmouth Sch.; Sidney Sussex Coll., Cambridge (Exhibnr; BA 1941, MA 1946, LLB 1946). Admitted Solicitor of the Supreme Court, 1948. Asst Solicitor, Newport Corp., 1948; Wales Gas Board: Solicitor, 1949; Management Develt Officer, 1965; Dir of Develt, 1967; Wales Gas: Dir of Conversion, 1970; Sec., 1973; Dep. Chm., Eastern Gas, 1977. Vice Pres., Contemporary Arts Soc., Wales, 1977. *Recreations:* reading, golf, music. *Address:* 12 Fallows Green, Harpenden, Herts AL5 4HD.

See also R. St B. Methven.

GRIFFITHS, David Hubert; Clerk/Adviser, House of Commons European Scrutiny Committee (formerly Select Committee on European Legislation), since 1998; *b* 24 Dec. 1940; *s* of late Hubert Griffiths and of Margaret Joan Waldron; *m* Mary Abbott; one *s* one *d*. *Educ:* Kingswood School, Bath; St Catharine's College, Cambridge (MA). Joined Ministry of Agriculture, Fisheries and Food as Asst Principal, 1963; Principal, 1968; Asst Secretary, 1975; Under Secretary, 1982–97; Hd, European Communities Gp, 1982–83; Fisheries Sec., 1983–87; Hd, Food, Drink and Marketing Policy Gp, 1987–90; Dir of Establishments, 1990–94; Hd, Arable Crops and Horticulture Gp, 1995–97. Non-exec. Dir, ICI (Paints Div.), 1985–87. *Recreations:* golf, cooking, music. *Address:* (office) 7 Millbank, SW1P 3JA. *Club:* Richmond Golf.

GRIFFITHS, His Honour David John; a Circuit Judge, 1984–2000; Resident Judge, Maidstone Crown Court, 1995–2000; *b* 18 Feb. 1931; *m* Anita; three *s* one *d*. *Educ:* St Dunstan's Coll., Catford, SE6. Admitted to Roll of Solicitors, 1957; apptd Notary Public, 1969; Principal: D. J. Griffiths & Co., Bromley, 1960–84; Harveys, Lewisham, 1970–84. A Recorder, 1980–84. Mem., Scriveners Co., 1983. *Recreations:* riding, music (male voice choir). *Club:* Farmers'.

GRIFFITHS, David Laurence; His Honour Judge Griffiths; a Circuit Judge, since 1989; *b* 3 Aug. 1944; *s* of late Edward Laurence Griffiths and of Mary Middleton Pudge; *m* 1971, Sally Hollis; four *d*. *Educ:* Christ's Hospital; Jesus College, Oxford (MA). Called to the Bar, Lincoln's Inn, 1967; an Asst Recorder, 1981; Recorder, 1985. *Recreations:* walking, cycling, watching Rugby and cricket, opera, history, classical music. *Address:* Southampton Combined Court Centre, The Courts of Justice, London Road, Southampton SO9 5AF.

GRIFFITHS, Ven. Dr David Nigel, FSA; Archdeacon of Berkshire, 1987–92, now Emeritus; Chaplain to The Queen, 1977–97; *b* 29 Oct. 1927; *o s* of late William Cross Griffiths, LDS, and Doris May (*née* Rhodes); *m* 1953, Joan Fillingham; two *s* one *d*. *Educ:* King Edward's Sch., Bath; Cranbrook; Worcester Coll., Oxford (MA; Gladstone Meml Prize, Arnold Historical Essay Prize); Lincoln Theol Coll.; PhD Reading, 1991. An economist before ordination; Consultant at FAO, Rome, 1952–53. Curate, St Matthew, Northampton, 1958–61; Headquarters Staff, SPCK, 1961–67; Rector of Minster Parishes, Lincoln, 1967–73; Vice-Chancellor and Librarian, Lincoln Cathedral, 1967–73; Rector of Windsor, 1973–87; Rural Dean of Maidenhead, 1977–82 and 1985–87; Hon. Canon of Christ Church, Oxford, 1983–88, now Emeritus. Warden, St Anne's Bede Houses, Lincoln, 1993–98. Trustee, Lincolnshire Old Churches Trust, 1995–. Served TARO and RMFVR, 1946–50; Chaplain, RNR, 1963–77 (Reserve Decoration, 1977); OCF, Household Cavalry, 1973–87, 1st Bn Irish Guards, 1977–80. FSA 1973. Fredson Bowers Award, Bibliographical Soc. of America, 1996; Bibliographical Soc. Award (UK), 1997. *Publications:* articles on bibliography and church history. *Recreations:* walking, bibliomania. *Address:* 2 Middleton's Field, Lincoln LN2 1QP. *T:* (01522) 525753.

GRIFFITHS, Sir Eldon (Wylie), Kt 1985; National Chairman, World Affairs Councils of America; *b* 25 May 1925; *s* of Thomas H. W. Griffiths and Edith May; *m*; one *s* one *d*. *Educ:* Ashton Grammar Sch.; Emmanuel Coll., Cambridge (MA); MA Yale. Fellow, Saybrook Coll., Yale, 1948–49; Correspondent, Time and Life magazines, 1949–55; Foreign Editor, Newsweek, 1956–63; Columnist, Washington Post, 1962–63; Conservative Research Department, 1963–64. MP(C) Bury St Edmunds, May 1964–1992; Parly Sec., Min. of Housing and Local Govt, June-Oct. 1970; Parly Under-Sec. of State, DoE, and Minister for Sport, 1970–74; opposition spokesman on trade and industry, and Europe, 1974–76. Former Chairman: Anglo-Iranian Parly Gp; Anglo-Polish Parly Gp. Pres., Special Olympics (UK). Consultant/Adviser, Nat. Police Federation, to 1988; President: Assoc. of Public Health Inspectors, 1969–70; Friends of Gibraltar; World Affairs Council, Orange County, California. Regents' Prof., Univ. of California, Irvine. Dir, Center for Internat. Business, Chapman Univ., Orange, Calif. Dir, US and UK cos. Hon. Freeman, City of London; Hon. Citizen, Orange County, California. Medal of Honour, Republic of China, Taiwan. *Recreations:* reading, swimming, cricket. *Address:* 29091 Ridgeview, Laguna Niguel, CA 92691, USA. *Club:* Carlton.

GRIFFITHS, Harold Morris; Assistant Secretary, HM Treasury, 1978–86; *b* 17 March 1926; *s* of Rt Hon. James Griffiths, CH; *m* 1st, 1951, Gwyneth Lethby (*d* 1966); three *s* one *d*; 2nd, 1966, Elaine Burge (*née* Walsh); two *s*. *Educ:* Llanelly Grammar Sch.; London Sch. of Economics. Editorial Staff: Glasgow Herald, 1949–55; Guardian, 1955–67; Information Division, HM Treasury: Deputy Head, 1967–68, Head, 1968–72; Asst Sec., HM Treasury, 1972–75; Counsellor (Economic), Washington, 1975–78. *Address:* The Old Coach House, Park Road, Hampton Hill, Mddx TW12 1HR. *T:* (020) 8979 1214.

GRIFFITHS, Howard; Command Secretary, RAF Logistics Command, 1994–98; *b* 20 Sept. 1938; *s* of Bernard and Olive Griffiths; *m* 1963, Dorothy Foster (*née* Todd); one *s* one *d*. *Educ:* London School of Economics (BScEcon, MScEcon). Ministry of Defence: Research Officer, 1963–69; Principal, Army Dept, 1970–72; Central Staffs, 1972–76; Asst Secretary, Head of Civilian Faculty, National Defence Coll., 1976–78; Procurement Executive, 1978–80; Deputy and Counsellor (Defence), UK Delegn, Mutual and Balanced Force Reductions (Negotiations), Vienna, 1980–84; Asst Sec., Office of Management and Budget, 1984–86; Asst Sec. and Head of Defence Arms Control Unit, 1986–88; Asst Under Sec. of State (Policy), 1988–91; Fellow, Center for Internat. Affairs, Harvard Univ., 1991–92; Assistant Under Secretary of State: (Ordnance), 1992; (Supply and Orgn) (Air), 1993–94. *Address:* 95 Brands Hill Avenue, High Wycombe HP13 5PX.

See also L. Griffiths.

GRIFFITHS, Howard; Editor, Pulse, since 1979; Group Editor, The Practitioner, since 1994 (Editor, 1988–94); *b* 6 Aug. 1947; *m* 1977, Lynda Smith; three *d*. *Educ:* Cowbridge Grammar School; Merton College, Oxford (BA). Feature writer, Pulse, 1973. *Recreation:* family. *Address:* United Business Media International, City Reach, 5 Greenwich View Place, Millharbour, E14 9NN.

GRIFFITHS, Jane Patricia; MP (Lab) Reading East, since 1997; *b* 17 April 1954; *d* of late John Griffiths and of Patricia Griffiths (*née* Thomas); *m* 1st, 1975, Ralph Spearpoint (marr. diss. 1994); one *s* one *d*; 2nd, 1999, Andrew Tattersall. *Educ:* Univ. of Durham (BA Hons Russian). GCHQ linguist, 1977–84; Editor, BBC Monitoring, 1984–97. Mem. (Lab), Reading BC, 1989–99. *Publication:* (with John Newman) Bushido, 1988. *Recreation:* urban living. *Address:* House of Commons, SW1A 0AA. *T:* (020) 7219 4122.

GRIFFITHS, John; *see* Griffiths, A. J.

GRIFFITHS, John Calvert, CMG 1983; QC 1972; SC (Hong Kong) 1997; *b* 16 Jan. 1931; *s* of Oswald Hardy Griffiths and Christina Flora Griffiths; *m* 1958, Jessamy, *er d* of Prof. G. P. Crowden and Jean Crowden; three *d*; *m* 1999, Marie Charlotte Biddulph. *Educ:* St Peter's Sch., York (scholar); Emmanuel Coll., Cambridge (sen. exhibnr) (BA 1st Cl. Hons 1955; MA 1960). Called to Bar, Middle Temple, 1956 (Bencher, 1983), Hong Kong, 1979; a Recorder, 1972–90. Attorney-General of Hong Kong, 1979; Mem. Exec. and Legislative Councils, and Chm. Hong Kong Law Reform Commn, 1979–83. Member: Exec. Cttee, General Council of the Bar, 1967–71, 1983–89 (Treas., 1987); Senate of Inns of Court and the Bar, 1984–86 (Mem., Exec. Cttee, 1973–77); Council of Legal Educn, 1983–; Nat. Council of Social Service, 1974–79; Greater London CAB Exec. Cttee, 1978–79; (co-opted) Develt and Special Projects Cttee, 1977–79; Court, Hong Kong Univ., 1980–84; Exec. Cttee, Prince Philip Cambridge Scholarships, 1980–84. Lieutenant, RE, 1949–50 (Nat. Service). *Recreations:* fishing, reading, gardening. *Address:* Des Voeux Chambers, 10F Bank of East Asia Building, 10 Des Vœux Road Central, Hong Kong. *T:* 25263071; Brick Court, 7–8 Essex Street, WC2R 3LD. *T:* (020) 7379 3550. *Clubs:* Flyfishers', Hurlingham; Hong Kong, Hong Kong Jockey (Hong Kong).

GRIFFITHS, John Charles; JP; Chairman: Minerva Arts Channel, since 1989; Minerva Vision, since 1989; *b* 19 April 1934; *s* of Sir Percival Griffiths, KBE, CIE; *m* 1st, 1956, Ann Timms (marr. diss.); four *s*; 2nd, 1983, Carole Jane Mellor (marr. diss.); one *d*. *Educ:* Uppingham; Peterhouse, Cambridge (MA). Dep. General Manager, Press Association, 1968–70; PR adviser, British Gas, 1970–74; Chm., MSG Public Relations, 1974–78; Chm. and founder, The Arts Channel, 1983–89. Chairman: National League of Young Liberals, 1962–64 (Mem., Nat. Exec., 1964–66); Assoc. of Liberals in Small Business and Self Employed, 1980; Pres., Liberal Party, 1982–83. Contested (L): Ludlow, 1964; Wanstead and Woodford, 1966; Bedford, Feb. 1974, Oct. 1974. Develt Dir, Bardsey Island Trust, 1992–96. Chm. Govs, Llangynidr Sch., 1993–95. JP Cardiff, 1960. *Publications:* The Survivors, 1964; Afghanistan, 1967; Modern Iceland, 1969; Three Tomorrows, 1980; The Science of Winning Squash, 1981; Afghanistan: key to a Continent, 1981; The Queen of Spades, 1983; Flashpoint Afghanistan, 1986; The Third Man: the life and times of William Murdoch, 1992; Nimbus, 1994; Fathercare, 1997; Imperial Call, 1997. *Recreations:* conversation, reading, music, walking. *Address:* White Rocks House, Garway Hill, Hereford HR2 8RX.

GRIFFITHS, Sir John N.; *see* Norton-Griffiths.

GRIFFITHS, John Pankhurst, RIBA; Clerk to the Worshipful Company: of Chartered Architects, since 1995; of Tylers and Bricklayers, 1996–97; Vice-President, Upkeep, since 1993; *b* 27 Sept. 1930; *s* of late William Bramwell Griffiths and Ethel Doris Griffiths (*née* Pankhurst); *m* 1959, Helen Elizabeth (*née* Tasker); two *s* one *d*. *Educ:* Torquay Grammar School; King George V School, Southport; School of Architecture, Manchester Univ. Dip Arch. Resident architect, Northern Nigeria, for Maxwell Fry, 1956–58; staff architect, Granada Television, 1959; Founder and first Dir, Manchester Building Centre, 1959–65; Head of Tech. Inf., Min. of Public Buildings and Works, later DoE, 1965–77; formed Building Conservation Assoc. later Building Conservation Trust, subseq. Upkeep, 1977, Dir, 1979–93. Mem. Bd of Mgt, Surrey Historic Bldgs Trust, 1996–; Trustee, Tylers and Bricklayers Craft Trust, 1993–96. *Publications:* articles in tech. and prof. jls. *Recreations:* looking at buildings, writing, speaking, cooking. *Address:* 28 Palace Road, East Molesey, Surrey KT8 9DL. *T:* (020) 8224 9328.

GRIFFITHS, (John) Peter (Gwynne); QC 1995; a Recorder, since 1991; *b* 9 Dec. 1945; *m* 1st (marr. diss.); four *c*; *m* 2nd; two *c*. *Educ:* Bristol Univ. (Civil Engrg); UWIST (LLB Hons). Called to the Bar, Gray's Inn, 1970. *Recreations:* angling, sailing, ski-ing, the arts. *Address:* 2 Bedford Row, WC1R 4BU. *T:* (020) 7440 8888.

GRIFFITHS, Lawrence; a Recorder of the Crown Court, 1972–93; *b* 16 Aug. 1933; *s* of Bernard Griffiths and Olive Emily Griffiths (*née* Stokes); *m* 1959, Josephine Ann (*née* Cook); one *s* two *d*. *Educ:* Gowerton Grammar Sch.; Christ's Coll., Cambridge (MA). Called to Bar, Inner Temple, 1957; practised Swansea, 1958–99; Mem. Wales and Chester Circuit; Prosecuting Counsel to Inland Revenue for Wales and Chester Circuit, 1969–93; Standing Counsel to HM Customs and Excise for Wales and Chester Circuit, 1989–93. Mem., Mental Health Review Tribunal for Wales, 1970–91. *Recreations:* wine, walking,

travel by sea, snooker. *Address:* 26 Hillside Crescent, Uplands, Swansea SA2 0RD. *T:* (01792) 473513; (chambers) Iscoed Chambers, 86 St Helens Road, Swansea SA1 4BQ. *T:* (01792) 652988. *Club:* Bristol Channel Yacht (Swansea).
See also H. Griffiths.

GRIFFITHS, Rev. Dr Leslie John; Superintendent Minister, Wesley's Chapel, since 1996; President of the Methodist Conference, 1994–95; *b* 15 Feb. 1942; *s* of late Sidney and Olwen Griffiths; *m* 1969, Margaret, *d* of Alfred and Kathleen Rhodes; two *s* one *d*. *Educ:* Llanelli Grammar Sch.; Univ. of Wales (BA); Univ. of Cambridge (MA); Univ. of London (PhD). Junior Res. Fellow, University Coll. of S Wales and Monmouthshire, Cardiff, 1963; Asst Lectr in English, St David's Coll., Lampeter, 1964–67; trained for Methodist Ministry, Wesley Ho., Cambridge, 1967–70; Asst Minister, Wesley Church, Cambridge, 1969–70; Petit Goâve Circuit, Haïti, 1970–71; Port-au-Prince Circuit and Asst Headmaster, Nouveau Collège Bird, 1971–74; Minister, Reading Circuit, 1974–77; Superintendent Minister: Cap Haïtien Circuit, Haïti, 1977–80; Wanstead and Woodford Circuit, 1980–86; W London Mission, 1986–91; Finchley and Hendon Circuit, 1991–96. Hon. Canon, St Paul's Cathedral, 2000–. Trustee: Addiction Recovery Foundn, 1989–; Sir Halley Stewart Trust, 1999–; Art and Christian Enquiry, 1999–. Dir, Birnbeck Housing Assoc., 1992–96. Gov., Bd of Christian Aid, 1990–98 (Chm., Africa and ME Cttee, 1991–95); Chm., Bd of Govs, Southlands Coll., 1997–; Mem. Council, Univ. of Surrey Roehampton (formerly Roehampton Inst.), 1997–; Chairman: Methodist Church's European Reference Gp, 1996–99; Churches Adv. Council on Local Broadcasting, 1996–2000. Hon. Fellow, Sarum Coll., 2001. *Publications:* A History of Haïtian Methodism, 1991; Letters Home, 1995; The Aristide Factor, 1997; Touching the Pulse: worship and our diverse world, 1998. *Recreations:* fun and fellowship spiced with occasional moments of solitude. *Address:* Wesley's Chapel, 49 City Road, EC1Y 1AU. *T:* (020) 7253 2262. *Club:* Graduate Centre (Cambridge).

GRIFFITHS, Rt Rev. (Michael) Ambrose; *see* Hexham and Newcastle, Bishop of, (RC).

GRIFFITHS, Nigel; MP (Lab) Edinburgh South, since 1987; Parliamentary Under-Secretary of State (Minister for Small Business), Department of Trade and Industy, since 2001; *b* 20 May 1955; *s* of late Lionel and Elizabeth Griffiths; *m* 1979, Sally, *d* of Hugh and Sally McLaughlin. *Educ:* Hawick High Sch.; Edinburgh Univ. (MA 1977); Moray House Coll. of Education. Joined Labour Party, 1970; Pres., EU Labour Club, 1976–77; Sec., Lothian Devolution Campaign, 1978; Rights Adviser to Mental Handicap Pressure Group, 1979–87. City of Edinburgh: District Councillor, 1980–87 (Chm., 1986–87; Chm., Housing Cttee; Chm., Decentralisation Cttee); Member: Edinburgh Festival Council, 1984–87; Edinburgh Health Council, 1982–87; Exec., Edinburgh Council of Social Service, 1984–87; Wester Hailes Sch. Council, 1981. Opposition Whip, 1987–89; Opposition front bench spokesman on consumer affairs, 1989–97; Parly Under-Sec. of State, DTI, 1997–98. Exec. Mem. and Convenor, Finance Cttee, Scottish Constitutional Convention. Vice Pres., Inst. of Trading Standards Admin, 1994–. Member: War on Want, SEAD, Amnesty Internat., Anti-apartheid, Friends of the Earth, Nat. Trust, Ramblers' Assoc. *Publications:* Guide to Council Housing in Edinburgh, 1981; Council Housing on the Point of Collapse, 1982; Welfare Rights Survey, 1981; various welfare rights guides. *Recreations:* squash, travel, live entertainment, badminton, hill walking and rock climbing, architecture, reading, politics. *Address:* 30 McLaren Road, Edinburgh EH9 2BN. *T:* (0131) 667 1947; (office) 31 Minto Street, Edinburgh, EH9 2BT. *T:* (0131) 662 4520. *Address:* House of Commons, SW1A 0AA. *T:* (020) 7219 3442.

GRIFFITHS, Paul Anthony; writer; Music Critic of The New Yorker, 1992–96; *b* 24 Nov. 1947; *s* of Fred Griffiths and Jeanne Veronica (*née* George); *m* 1st, 1977 two *s*; 2nd, 1998, Anne Kathryn West. *Educ:* King Edward's Sch., Birmingham; Lincoln Coll., Oxford (BA, MSc). Area Editor for Grove's Dictionary of Music and Musicians, 6th edn, 1973–76; Asst Music Critic, 1979–82, Music Critic, 1982–92, The Times. *Publications:* A Concise History of Modern Music, 1978; Boulez, 1978; A Guide to Electronic Music, 1979; Modern Music, 1980; Cage, 1981; Igor Stravinsky: The Rake's Progress, 1982; Peter Maxwell Davies, 1982; The String Quartet, 1983; György Ligeti, 1983, 2nd edn 1997; Bartók, 1984; Olivier Messiaen, 1985; New Sounds, New Personalities, 1985; The Thames & Hudson Encyclopaedia of 20th-Century Music, 1986; Myself and Marco Polo (novel), 1989; The Lay of Sir Tristram (novel), 1991; The Jewel Box (libretto), 1991; Stravinsky, 1992; Modern Music and After, 1995; Marco Polo (libretto), 1996; What Next? (libretto), 1999. *Recreation:* swimming. *Address:* 416 East 83rd Street, New York, NY 10028, USA. *T:* (212) 7449532.

GRIFFITHS, Prof. Paul David, MD; Professor of Virology, Royal Free and University College Medical School (formerly Royal Free Hospital School of Medicine), since 1989; *b* 30 Jan. 1953; *s* of George Griffiths and Jean Beckett (formerly Griffiths, *née* Pring); *m* 1979, Brenda Louise Attenborough; three *s*. *Educ:* St Bartholomew's Hosp. Med. Coll., Univ. of London (BSc 1974; MB BS Hons 1977; MD 1982); DSc (Med) London, 1995. FRCPath 1996. Lawrence Postgrad. Res. Schol., 1979; Lectr, Bart's Med. Coll., 1979–82; Fogarty Internat. Scholar, NIH, USA, 1980–81; Royal Free Hospital School of Medicine, London University: Sen. Lectr in Virology, 1982–86; Reader, 1986–87; Chm., Univ. Div. of Pathology and Communicable Diseases, 1991–95. William Julius Mickle Fellow, London Univ., 1991. Member: UK med. socs; Amer. Soc. for Microbiol.; Internat. AIDS Soc. Editor, Reviews in Medical Virology, 1990–. Ian Howat Prize in Med. Microbiol., 1975, Wheelwright Prize for Paediatrics, 1977, St Bartholomew's Hosp. Med. Coll.; Wellcome Award, European Gp for Rapid Viral Diagnosis, 1988. *Publications:* papers on viruses, HIV/AIDS, herpes viruses and cytomegalovirus. *Recreations:* family, music, viruses, bridge. *Address:* Royal Free and University College Medical School, Royal Free Campus, Department of Virology, Rowland Hill Street, Hampsted NW3 2PF. *T:* (020) 7794 0500.

GRIFFITHS, Peter; *see* Griffiths, J. P. G.

GRIFFITHS, Peter Anthony; Executive Director, The Health Quality Service, since 1997; *b* 19 May 1945; *m* 1966, Margaret Harris; two *s*. *Educ:* Swansea Technical Coll. Regl admin. trainee, Welsh Hosp. Bd, Cardiff Royal Inf., 1963–66; nat. admin. trainee, Birmingham Reg./Nuffield Centre, Leeds, 1966–69; Dep. Hosp. Sec., E Birmingham HMC, 1969–71; Dep. Dist Administrator, Hosp. Sec., Southampton and SW Hampshire Health Dist (Teaching), 1971–76; Dist Administrator, Medway Health Dist, 1976–81; Actg Area Administrator, Kent AHA, 1981–82; Dist Administrator 1982–84, Dist Gen. Man. 1984–88, Lewisham and N Southwark HA; Regl Gen. Manager, SE Thames RHA, 1988–89; Dep. Chief Exec., NHS Management Exec., 1990–91; Chief Exec., Guy's and Lewisham NHS Trust, 1991–94; Dep. Chief Exec., King's Fund, 1994–97. *Recreation:* golf. *Address:* King's Fund, 11–13 Cavendish Square, W1M 0AN.

GRIFFITHS, Prof. Peter Denham, CBE 1990; MD, FRCPath, FRCPE; Professor of Biochemical Medicine 1968–89, and Dean, Faculty of Medicine and Dentistry, 1985–89, University of Dundee (Vice-Principal, 1979–85); Hon. Consultant Clinical Chemist, Tayside Health Board, 1966–89; *b* 16 June 1927; *s* of Bernard Millar Griffiths and Florence Marion Fletcher; *m* 1949, Joy Burgess; three *s* one *d*. *Educ:* King Edward VI Sch., Southampton; Guy's Hosp. Med. Sch., Univ. of London (BSc 1st Cl. Hons, MD). LRCP, MRCS; FRCPath 1978; FRCPE 1998. Served RN, 1946–49. Jun. Lectr in Physiol., Guy's Hosp. Med. Sch., 1957–58; Registrar, then Sen. Registrar in Clin. Path., Guy's and Lewisham Hosps, London, 1958–64; Consultant Pathologist, Harlow Gp of Hosps, Essex, 1964–66; Sen. Lectr in Clin. Chemistry, Univ. of St Andrews and subseq. Univ. of Dundee, 1966–68. Pres., Assoc. of Clin. Biochemists, UK, 1987–89 (Chm. Council, 1973–76); Member: Tayside Health Bd, 1977–85; GMC, 1986–93; various cttees of SHHD and DHSS, 1969–. Dir, Drug Development (Scotland), 1982–89. Dir, Dundee Rep. Theatre, 1977–90. FIMgt; FRSA. Consulting Editor, Clinica Chimica Acta, 1986–96 (Mem. Editl Bd, 1976; Jt Editor-in-Chief, 1979–85). *Publications:* contrib. scientific and med. jls (pathology, clin. chemistry, computing). *Recreations:* music, gardening, walking. *Address:* 52 Albany Road, West Ferry, Dundee DD5 1NW. *T:* (01382) 776772.

GRIFFITHS, Peter Harry Steve; *b* 24 May 1928; *s* of W. L. Griffiths, West Bromwich; *m* 1962, Jeannette Christine (*née* Rubery); one *s* one *d*. *Educ:* City of Leeds Training Coll. BSc (Econ.) Hons London, 1956; MEd Birmingham, 1963. Headmaster, Hall Green Road Sch., West Bromwich, 1962–64. Senior Lectr in Economic Hist., The Polytechnic, Portsmouth (formerly Portsmouth Coll. of Technology), 1967–79. Fulbright Exchange Prof. of Economics, Pierce Coll., Los Angeles, Calif, 1968–69. Councillor, Smethwick, 1955–64 (Chm., Education Cttee; Leader, Conservative Group of Councillors, 1960–64). MP (C): Smethwick, 1964–66; Portsmouth N, 1979–97; contested (C) Portsmouth N, Feb. 1974, and 1997. *Publication:* A Question of Colour?, 1966. *Recreations:* motoring, writing, computing. *Club:* Sloane.

GRIFFITHS, Peter John; higher education management consultant; *b* 19 April 1944; *s* of Ronald Hugh Griffiths and Emily Vera (*née* Cockshutt); *m* 1968, Lesley Florence (*née* Palmer) (marr. diss. 1993); two *d*. *Educ:* Battersea Grammar Sch.; Univ. of Leicester (BA Classics); McMaster Univ. (MA Classics). University of London: Asst to Principal, 1968–70; Asst Sec. to Cttee of Enquiry into governance of the university, 1970–72; Special Duties Officer, Vice-Chancellor's and Principal's Office, 1972–78; Dep. Head, Legal and Gen. Div., Court Dept, 1978–82; Asst Clerk of the Court, 1982–85; Dep. Clerk of the Court, 1985–87; Clerk of the Court, 1987–91; Dir of Resources and Planning, 1991–93; Sec. and Chief Admin. Officer, Charing Cross and Westminster Med. Sch., 1993–97; Dep. Sec., Imperial Coll. Sch. of Medicine, 1997–2000. *Recreation:* choral singing. *Address:* Upland House, Upland Road, Sutton, Surrey SM2 5HW. *T:* (020) 8643 3599.

GRIFFITHS, Phillip A., PhD; Director, Institute for Advanced Study, Princeton, since 1991; *b* 18 Oct. 1938; *s* of Phillip Griffiths and Jeanette (*née* Field); *m* 1st, 1958, Ann Lane Crittenden-Witt (marr. diss.); one *s* one *d*; 2nd, 1968, Marian Folsom Jones; two *d*. *Educ:* Wake Forest Univ. (BS 1959); Princeton Univ. (PhD 1962). University of California, Berkeley: Miller Fellow, 1962–64, 1975–76; Faculty Mem., 1964–67; Princeton University: Vis. Prof., 1967–68; Prof., 1968–72; Mem., Inst. for Advanced Study, 1968–70; Harvard University: Prof., 1972–83; Dwight Parker Robinson Prof. of Maths, 1983; Provost and James B. Duke Prof. of Maths, Duke Univ., 1983–91. Mem., US Nat. Sci. Bd, 1991–96. Member, Board of Directors: Bankers Trust New York Corp., 1994–99; Oppenheimer Funds, 1999–. Sec., Internat. Mathematical Union, 1999–2000; Chm., Sci. Insts Gp, NGO, 1999–. Mem., US Nat. Acad. of Scis, 1979–. Hon. DSc Wake Forest, 1973; De *hc* Angers, France, 1979; Hon. degree Peking, 1983. Leroy P. Steele Prize, Amer. Math. Soc., 1971; Dannie Heineman Prize, Acad. of Scis, Göttingen, 1979. *Publications:* (with J. Adams) Topics in Algebraic and Analytic Geometry, 1974; Entire Holomorphic Mappings in One and Several Complex Variables, 1976; (with J. Harris) Principles of Algebraic Geometry, 1978; An Introduction to the Theory of Special Divisors on Algebraic Curves, 1980; (jtly) Exterior Differential Systems, 1980; (jtly) Geometry of Algebraic Curves, Vol. I, 1985; Algebraic Curves, 1985; (with G. R. Jensen) Differential Systems and Isometric Embeddings, 1987; contrib. Annals of Math. Studies, Progress in Maths. *Recreation:* sailing. *Address:* Institute for Advanced Study, Einstein Drive, Princeton, NJ 08540, USA. *T:* (609) 7348200.

GRIFFITHS, Prof. Ralph Alan, PhD; DLitt; FRHistS; Professor of Medieval History, University of Wales, Swansea, since 1982; *b* 4 Nov. 1937; *er s* of Thomas Rowland Griffiths and Marion Lovin Griffiths (*née* Jones). *Educ:* Lewis Sch., Pengam, Gwent; Univ. of Bristol (BA 1959; PhD 1963; DLitt 1983). FRHistS 1966. Research Asst, Bd of Celtic Studies, Univ. of Wales, 1961–64; University of Wales, Swansea: Asst Lectr, 1964–66; Lectr, 1966–71; Sen. Lectr, 1971–78; Reader, 1978–82; Dean of Admissions, 1990–; Pro-Vice-Chancellor, 1998–. Visiting Professor: Dalhousie Univ., Canada, 1964; Ohio Univ., 1977, 1981; Haverford Coll., USA, 1977, 1981; Lectures: James Ford in English Hist., Univ. of Oxford, 1993; Sir John Rhys, British Acad., 2001; Stenton, Reading Univ., 2001. Member: Royal Commn on Ancient and Historical Monuments (Wales), 1990– (Chm., 1999–); Hist. and Archaeol Panel, Humanities Res. Bd, 1994–96; Adv. Council on Public Records, 1996–. Mem. Council, RHistS, 1987–91 (Vice-Pres., 1992–96). Hon. Sec., Glamorgan Co. History Trust, 1974–; Trustee, Glamorgan-Gwent Archaeol Trust, 1985–98; Pres., S Wales Record Soc., 1994–97. *Publications:* The Principality of Wales in the Later Middle Ages, I: South Wales 1277–1536, 1972; The Reign of King Henry VI, 1981, 2nd edn 1998; (with R. S. Thomas) The Making of the Tudor Dynasty, 1985, 2nd edn 1990; (with J. Cannon) The Oxford Illustrated History of the British Monarchy, 1988, 2nd edn 1998; King and Country: England and Wales in the Fifteenth Century, 1990; Sir Rhys ap Thomas and his Family, 1993; Conquerors and Conquered in Medieval Wales, 1994; (with J. Gillingham) Medieval Britain: a very short introduction, 2000; contrib. to books and learned jls. *Recreations:* music, travel, American writing, Shakespeare. *Address:* Department of History, University of Wales, Swansea SA2 8PP. *T:* (01792) 295226.

GRIFFITHS, Richard; actor; *b* Thornaby-on-Tees, 31 July 1947; *s* of Thomas Griffiths, steelworker, and Jane Griffiths (*née* Denmark); *m* Heather. *Educ:* St Bede's RC Boys' Secondary Modern Sch.; Stockton/Billingham Tech. Coll.; Northern Sch. of Music (Drama Dept); RCA, Manchester; Sch. of Theatre, Manchester Poly. (Dip. Speech and Drama (Hons); Dip. Associateship). *Stage* includes: Royal Shakespeare Company: Henry VIII, 1983; Once in a Lifetime; Volpone, 1983; Red Star, 1984; After Aida, 1988, Verdi's Messiah, Old Vic; Rules of the Game, 1992, The Life of Galileo, 1994, Almeida; Art, Wyndham's, 1997, 2001; Katherine Howard, 1998, The Man Who Came to Dinner, 1999, Chichester Fest. Th.; Luther, RNT, 2001; *films* include: Gandhi, 1982; Gorky Park, 1983; A Private Function, 1984; Greystoke, 1984; Whoops Apocalypse, 1986; Withnail and I, 1988; King Ralph, 1991; Naked Gun 2½, 1991; Funny Bones, 1995; Sleepy Hollow, 2000; Vatel, 2000; Harry Potter and the Philosopher's Stone, 2001; *television* includes: Bird of Prey, 1982; The Cleopatras, 1983; Merry Wives of Windsor, 1983; The Marksman, 1987; Ffizz, 1987; A Kind of Living, 1988; Pie in the Sky, 1994; In the Red, 1998; Gormenghast, 2000; Hope and Glory, 2000; numerous radio appearances. Awards include: Carlton Hobbs, BBC, 1970; Best Supporting Actor, Clarence Derwent, 1979; Best Newcomer, and Best Supporting Actor, Plays and Players, 1979; Gold (Best Actor),

1994, Silver, 1996, Sony Radio Awards; Gold, Assoc. of Colls, 2000. Hon. DLitt Durham, 1998. *Address:* c/o Michael Whitehall Ltd, 125 Gloucester Road, SW7 4TE.

GRIFFITHS, Richard Anthony; Senior Partner, Farrer & Co., 1993–2000; *b* 30 Oct. 1936; *s* of Howel Harris Griffiths and Rena Kelford Griffiths; *m* 1970, Sheila Mary Wallace; two *d*. *Educ:* Denstone Coll.; Trinity Coll., Cambridge (MA). Admitted Solicitor, 1963; Partner, Farrer & Co., 1966–2000. Life Trustee, Sir John Soane's Mus., 1994– (Chm., 1997–). Mem. Council, ICRF, 1997–. FRSA. *Recreations:* golf, theatre, travel. *Address:* Wyndham House, Wickham Market, Suffolk IP13 0QU. *Clubs:* Oxford and Cambridge; Royal Wimbledon Golf, Aldeburgh Golf.

GRIFFITHS, Robert; *see* Griffiths, W. R.

GRIFFITHS, Prof. Roderic Keith, CBE 2000; Professor of Public Health Practice, University of Birmingham, since 1990; Regional Director of Public Health, NHS Executive West Midlands (formerly West Midlands Regional Health Authority), since 1993; *b* 12 April 1945; *s* of Tom and Olwen Griffiths; *m* 1st, 1967, Margaret Ash (marr. diss. 1993); one *s* two *d*; 2nd, 1995, Lois Parker. *Educ:* Birmingham Univ. (BSc, MB ChB 1969). Lectr in Anatomy, 1970, in Social Medicine, 1978, Birmingham Univ; GP in Birmingham, 1975; Dir of Public Health, Central Birmingham HA, 1982. Mem., Birmingham Lunar Soc., 1992–. *Publications:* articles on stress in bones, and public health in UK. *Recreations:* ski-ing, pottery, sailing very occasionally. *Address:* Bartholomew House, 142 Hagley Road, Birmingham B16 9PA. *T:* (0121) 224 4682.

GRIFFITHS, Roger Noel Price, MA Cantab; Membership Secretary, The Headmasters' Conference, 1990–97 (Deputy Secretary, The Headmasters' Conference and Secondary Heads' Association, 1986–89); *b* 25 Dec. 1931; *er s* of late William Thomas and of Annie Evelyn Griffiths; *m* 1966, Diana, *y d* of late Capt. J. F. B. Brown, RN; three *d*. *Educ:* Lancing Coll.; King's Coll., Cambridge. Asst Master at Charterhouse, 1956–64; Headmaster, Hurstpierpoint Coll., 1964–86. Governor: Mill Hill Sch., 1987–92; Tormead Sch., 1987–94; Prebendal Sch., Chichester, 1987–; Worth Sch., 1990–99. Mem., Management Cttee, Pallant House Trust, Chichester, 1987–92. Asst to Court of Worshipful Co. of Wax Chandlers, 1985, Master, 1990. MA Oxon, by incorporation, 1960. JP Mid Sussex, 1976–86. *Recreations:* music, theatre, bowls. *Address:* Hanbury Cottage, Cocking, near Midhurst, West Sussex GU29 0HF. *T:* (01730) 813503. *Clubs:* East India, Devonshire, Sports and Public Schools; Sussex (Sussex).

GRIFFITHS, Samantha; *see* Heath, S.

GRIFFITHS, Siân Meryl, (Mrs Ian Wylie), OBE 2000; FFPHM, FRCP; Director of Public Health and Health Policy, Oxfordshire Health Authority, since 1994; *b* 20 March 1952; *d* of late John Daniel Griffiths, FRCS and of Rosemary Marjorie Griffiths (*née* Quick); *m* 1st, 1978, Anthony Chu; two *d*; 2nd, 1987, Ian Wylie; one *s*. *Educ:* Felixstowe College; N London Collegiate Sch.; New Hall, Cambridge (MB BChir 1977; MA). MSc London, 1981. DRCOG 1979; FFPHM 1991; FRCP 1998. Clinical MO, KCH, 1979–80; Res. Fellow, NY, 1981; Dist. MO, City and Hackney HA, 1985–87; Consultant in Public Health Medicine, Oxford RHA, 1988–90; Regl Dir of Public Health and Health Policy, SW Thames RHA, 1990–93. Hon. Sen. Clin. Lectr, Oxford Univ., 1997–; Vis. Prof., Oxford Brookes Univ., 1999–. Mem., Health Policy Forum, IPPR, 1998–2000; Advr, Democratic Health Network, 1999–2001. Co-Chair, Assoc. of Public Health, 1995–99; Member Board: NAHAT, 1995–98; FPHM, 1999– (Treas., 1995–99; Vice-Pres., 2000–01; Pres., 2001–); New Opportunities Fund, 1998–; Nat. Cancer Task Force, 2001–. Trustee, Thames Valley Partnership, 1999–2001. Mem. Adv. Cttee, Common Purpose, 1999–. *Publications:* Indicators for Mental Health, 1990; Creating a Common Profile, 1990; (ed jtly) Prevention of Suicide, 1993; (ed) Perspectives in Public Health, 1999; contribs to med. jls. *Recreations:* spending time with family, films, theatre. *Address:* 39 Leckford Road, Oxford OX2 6HY. *T:* (01865) 514855.

GRIFFITHS, Trevor; playwright; *b* 4 April 1935; *s* of Ernest Griffiths and Anne Connor. *Educ:* Manchester Univ. BA (Hons) Eng. Lang. and Lit. Teaching, 1957–65; Educn Officer, BBC, 1965–72. Writer's Award, BAFTA, 1981. *Publications:* Occupations, 1972, 3rd edn 1980; Sam Sam, 1972; The Party, 1974, 2nd edn 1978; Comedians, 1976, 2nd edn 1979; All Good Men, and Absolute Beginners, 1977; Through the Night, and Such Impossibilities, 1977; Thermidor and Apricots, 1977; (jtly) Deeds, 1978; (trans.) The Cherry Orchard, 1978; Country, 1981; Oi for England, 1982; Sons and Lovers (television version), 1982; Judgement Over the Dead (television screenplays of The Last Place on Earth), 1986; Fatherland (screenplay), and Real Dreams, 1987; Collected Plays for Television, 1988; Piano, 1990; The Gulf Between Us, 1992; Hope in the Year Two, 1994; Thatcher's Children, 1994; Who Shall Be Happy ...?, 1996; Collected Stage Plays, Vol. 1, 1996; Food for Ravens, 1998. *Address:* c/o Peters, Fraser & Dunlop, Drury House, 34–43 Russell Street, WC2B 5HA. *T:* (020) 7344 1000, *Fax:* (020) 7352 7356.

GRIFFITHS, William Arthur; Principal Inspector, Bucks Social Services, since 1995; *b* 25 May 1940; *s* of Glyndwr and Alice Rose Griffiths; *m* 1963, Margaret Joan Dodd (marr. diss. 1988); two *s* one *d*. *Educ:* Owen's Sch., London; Queens' Coll., Cambridge; Univ. of Manchester. VSO, 1959–60. Probation Officer, Southampton. 1965–71; Home Office, 1971–76; Chief Probation Officer, N Ireland, 1977–84; Dir, NCVO, 1985–86; mgt consultant, 1986–95. Official Visitor, Ministry of Community Develt, Singapore, 1982 and 1985. Mem., Westminster CC, 1990–94. *Recreations:* literature, travel, horseracing. *Address:* Mavis Bank, Church Road, Greatworth, Banbury OX17 2DU. *T:* (01295) 711983.

GRIFFITHS, (William) Robert; QC 1993; SC (NSW) 1999; *b* 24 Sept. 1948; *s* of late (William) John Griffiths and of Megan Marjorie Griffiths (*née* Green); *m* 1984, Angela May Crawford; one *s* two *d*. *Educ:* Haverfordwest Grammar Sch.; St Edmund Hall, Oxford (Open Schol.; BCL, MA). VSO, 1973. Called to the Bar, Middle Temple, 1974; Jun. Counsel to the Crown (Common Law), 1989–93; *ad hoc* admission to Bar of Brunei, 1997; admitted as Legal Practitioner, NSW, 1998. Chairman: Test Match Grounds Consortium, 1998–; First Class Forum Internet Working Party, 2000–. Marylebone Cricket Club: Member: Cttee, 2001–; Estates Sub-Cttee, 1996–; Cricket Cttee, 2000–; Indoor Sch. and Coaching Sub-Cttee, 2000–. Freeman, City of London, 1997. *Recreations:* reading, collecting modern first editions, Victorian and modern British paintings, 18th and 19th century furniture; cricket (Schoolboy Cricket Internat., Wales, 1966–68; rep. Glamorgan CCC (non first-class), 1967–68, OUCC and OUCC (Authentics), 1968–72), Rugby (Schoolboy Internat., Wales, 1965–66), travel. *Address:* 4/5 Gray's Inn Square, Gray's Inn, WC1R 5AY. *T:* (020) 7404 5252; Selborne Chambers, 174 Phillip Street, Sydney, NSW 2000, Australia. *T:* (2) 92334081. *Club:* MCC.

GRIFFITHS, Winston James; MP (Lab) Bridgend, since 1987; *b* 11 Feb. 1943; *s* of (Rachel) Elizabeth Griffiths and (Evan) George Griffiths; *m* 1966, (Elizabeth) Ceri Griffiths; one *s* one *d*. *Educ:* State schools in Brecon; University College of South Wales and Monmouthshire, Cardiff. BA, DipEd. Taught in Tanzania, Birmingham, Barry, Cowbridge. MEP (Lab) Wales South, 1979–89; a Vice Pres., 1984–87; formerly Chm., Parliamentarians Global Action for Disarmament, Develt and World Reform (formerly Parliamentarians for World Order); formerly Mem., delegn to S Asia; Hon. Life Mem., European Parlt, 1989. Opposition front bench spokesman on: envmtl protection, 1990–92, on education, 1992–94; on Welsh affairs, 1994–97; Parly Under-Sec. of State, Welsh Office, 1997–98. Member: Labour Movt for Europe; Labour Campaign for Electoral Reform. Member: Christian Socialist Movement; Amnesty International; Fabian Society; Anti-Apartheid Movement; Socialist Educn Assoc.; Socialist Health Assoc. President: Kenfig Hill and Dist Male Voice Choir, 1986–; Porthcawl Choral Soc., 1993–; Cefn Cribwr Boys' and Girls' (formerly Boys') Club, 1987–. Methodist local preacher, 1966–. *Address:* House of Commons, SW1A 0AA; Tŷ Llon, John Street, Y Graig, Cefn Cribwr, Mid Glamorgan CF32 0AB. *T:* (01656) 740526.

GRIGG, John (Edward Poynder), FRSL; writer; *b* 15 April 1924; *s* of late 1st Baron Altrincham and Joan Dickson-Poynder; *m* 1958, Patricia, *d* of late H. E. Campbell and Marion Wheeler; two *s*. *Educ:* Eton; New Coll., Oxford (Exhibitioner). MA, Modern History; Gladstone Memorial Prize. Grenadier Guards, 1943–45. Editor, National and English Review, 1954–60; Columnist for The Guardian, 1960–70; with The Times, 1986–93. Pres., The London Library, 1996– (Chm., 1985–91). Pres., Blackheath Soc. Contested (C) Oldham West, 1951 and 1955. *Publications:* Two Anglican Essays, 1958; The Young Lloyd George, 1973; Lloyd George: the People's Champion, 1978 (Whitbread Award); 1943: The Victory That Never Was, 1980; Nancy Astor: Portrait of a Pioneer, 1980; Lloyd George: From Peace to War 1912–1916, 1985 (Wolfson Literary Prize); The History of The Times, Vol. 6: the Thomson Years, 1993; contribs to other books, incl. DNB; articles and reviews. *Address:* 32 Dartmouth Row, SE10 8AW. *T:* (020) 8692 4973. *Clubs:* Garrick, Beefsteak.

See also Rt Hon. Sir W. A. Campbell.

GRIGG, Prof. Ronald Ernest; PhD; FRS 1999; Professor of Organic Chemistry, since 1989, and Director, Molecular Innovation Diversity and Automated Synthesis Centre, since 1995, University of Leeds. *Educ:* Univ. of Nottingham (PhD). Formerly Lectr, Dept of Chemistry, Univ. of Nottingham; Prof. of Organic Chemistry, QUB, 1974–89. Co-ordinator, Eur. Network on Cascade Combinatorial Chem., 1998–. Royal Society of Chemistry: Chm., Heterocyclic Gp, 1985–87; Heterocyclic Chemistry Medal, 1985; Tilden Medal and Lectr, 1986; Pedler Medal and Lectr, 1998. *Publications:* contribs to sci. jls. *Address:* School of Chemistry, University of Leeds, Leeds LS2 9JT.

GRIGGS, Rt Rev. Ian Macdonald; Bishop Suffragan of Ludlow, 1987–94; Hon. Assistant Bishop, Diocese of Carlisle, since 1994; *b* 17 May 1928; *s* of late Donald Nicholson Griggs and Agnes Elizabeth Griggs; *m* 1953, Patricia Margaret Vernon-Browne; two *s* three *d* (and one *s* decd). *Educ:* Brentwood School; Trinity Hall, Cambridge (MA); Westcott House, Cambridge. Curate, St Cuthbert, Copnor, dio. Portsmouth, 1954–59; Domestic Chaplain to Bishop of Sheffield, 1959–64; Diocesan Youth Chaplain (part-time), 1959–64; Vicar of St Cuthbert, Fir Vale, dio. Sheffield, 1964–71; Vicar of Kidderminster, 1971–83; Hon. Canon of Worcester Cathedral, 1977–83; Archdeacon of Ludlow, 1984–87; Priest-in-Charge, St Michael, Tenbury, 1984–88. Chm., Churches' Council for Health and Healing, 1990–99. Gov., Atlantic Coll., 1991–. *Recreations:* mountaineering, hill-walking. *Address:* Rookings, Patterdale, Penrith, Cumbria CA11 0NP. *T:* (01768) 482064.

GRIGGS, Jeremy David; His Honour Judge Griggs; a Circuit Judge, since 1995; *b* 5 Feb. 1945; *s* of Celadon Augustine Griggs and Ethel Mary Griggs (*née* Anderson); *m* 1st, 1971, Wendy Anne Russell (*née* Culham) (marr. diss. 1982); two *s* one *d*; 2nd, 1985, Patricia Maynard; two step *d*. *Educ:* St Edward's Sch., Oxford; Magdalene Coll., Cambridge (MA). Called to the Bar, Inner Temple, 1968; Mem., Western Circuit, 1968–; a Recorder, 1990–95. Bar Rep., CCBE, 1990–94. Chm., London Choral Soc., 1986–90. *Recreations:* playing the piano, walking on Dartmoor. *Address:* Exeter Combined Court Centre, The Castle, Exeter EX4 3TH. *Club:* Royal Western Yacht.

GRIGGS, Norman Edward, CBE 1976; Vice-President, The Building Societies Association, since 1981 (Secretary-General, 1963–81); *b* 27 May 1916; *s* of late Archibald Griggs and late Maud Griggs (*née* Hewing); *m* 1947, Livia Lavinia Jandolo; one *s* one step *s*. *Educ:* Newport Grammar Sch.; London Sch. of Econs and Polit. Science (BScEcon). FCIS. Accountancy Dept, County of London Electric Supply Co. Ltd, 1933–40; service in RE and RAPC, Middle East, 1940–46; Asst Sec., Glass Manufrs' Fedn, 1946–52; Sec., Plastics Inst., 1952–56; Asst Sec., Building Socs Assoc., 1956–61, Dep. Sec. 1961–63. Sec.-Gen., Internat. Union of Building Socs and Savings Assocs, 1972–77; Vice-Pres., Metropolitan Assoc. of Building Socs, 1981–89. *Publications:* poetry: Life in the Withered Shell, 1990; Sharp-Eyed and Wary, 1991; The Solitary Watcher, 1995; Life on the Brink, 1999. *Recreation:* print addict. *Address:* 5 Gledhow Gardens, SW5 0BL. *T:* (020) 7373 5128. *Club:* Hurlingham.

GRIGOR, (William Alexander) Murray; independent film maker and exhibition designer; Director: Viz Ltd, since 1972; Channel Four Television, 1995–99; *b* 20 June 1939; *s* of James McIntosh Grigor and Katharine Grigor (*née* Murray); *m* 1968, (Joan) Barbara Sternschein (*d* 1994); two *d*. *Educ:* Loretto Sch.; St Andrews Univ. (BSc). Film Editor, BBC, 1963–67; Dir, Edinburgh Internat. Film Fest., 1967–72. Mem. Production Bd, BFI, 1968–72; Hon. Chm., Edinburgh Internat. Fest., 1991–94. *Films* include: Mackintosh, 1968; Big Banana Feet, 1975; The Architecture of Frank Lloyd Wright, 1981; Eduardo Paolozzi—Sculptor, 1986 (Rodin Prize, Paris Biennale, 1992); Nineveh on the Clyde, (Priz Desjardins, Montreal), 2000; The Work of Angels, 2001; television series, Face of Russia, 1998. *Exhibitions:* Scotch Myths, Edinburgh Fest., 1981; Scotland Creates, McLellan, Glasgow, 1990; Seeds of Change, Royal Mus. of Scotland, 1992; The Sixties, Barbican, 1992; The Unknown Genius: Alexander Greek Thomson, Glasgow 1999; John Byrne at 60, Paisley Mus. and Art Galls, 2000. UK/US Bicentennial Fellow in the Arts, 1976; Hon. FRIAS 1994; Hon. FRIBA 1999. Reith Award, RTS, 1990. *Publication:* (with Richard Murphy) The Architects' Architect, 1993. *Recreations:* architectural and landscape forays, home and abroad. *Address:* (office) 4 Bank Street, Inverkeithing, Fife KY11 1LR. *T:* (01383) 412811. *Club:* Chelsea Arts.

GRIGSON, Hon. Sir Geoffrey (Douglas), Kt 2000; **Hon. Mr Justice Grigson;** a Judge of the High Court of Justice, Queen's Bench Division, since 2000; *b* 28 Oct. 1944; *s* of Frederic Walter Grigson and Nora Marion Grigson; *m* 1967, Jay Sibbring (marr. diss. 1998); two *s* one *d*. *Educ:* Denstone Coll.; Selwyn Coll., Cambridge (MA). Called to the Bar, Gray's Inn, 1968; Midland and Oxford Circuit; a Recorder, 1985–89; a Circuit Judge, 1989–2000; a Permanent Judge, CCC, 1993–2000. A Dep. Sen. Judge, Sovereign Base Area, Cyprus, 1997–2000. *Recreation:* reading newspapers. *Address:* Royal Courts of Justice, Strand, WC2A 2LL. *Club:* Achilles.

GRIGSON, Sophie; freelance food writer and broadcaster, since 1983; *b* 19 June 1959; *d* of late Geoffrey Edward Harvey Grigson and Jane Grigson; *m* 1992, William Black (marr. diss. 2001); one *s* one *d*. *Educ:* UMIST (BSc Hons Maths). Cookery Correspondent: Evening Standard, 1986–93; Independent, 1993–94; Sunday Times Magazine, 1994–96; Restaurant Reviewer, Independent on Sunday, 1997–98. Presenter: Grow Your Greens, and, Eat Your Greens, Channel 4, 1993; Travels à la Carte, 1994; Curious Cooks, Radio 4, 1994, 1995; Sophie's Meat Course, Channel 4, 1995; Taste of The Times, Channel 4, 1997; Sophie Grigson's Herbs, BBC2, 1999; Feasts for a Fiver, BBC2, 1999; Sophie's Sunshine Food, BBC2, 2000. Trustee, Jane Grigson Trust, 1991–. Food Writer of the Year, Restaurateurs' Assoc. of GB, 1992; Magazine Writer of the Year, Guild of Food Writers, 1998. *Publications:* Food For Friends, 1987; (with J. Molyneux) The Carved Angel Cookbook, 1990; Sophie's Table, 1990; Sophie Grigson's Ingredients Book, 1991; The Students' Cookbook, 1992; Eat Your Greens, 1993; (with William Black) Travels à la Carte, 1994; Sophie's Meat Course, 1995; Sophie Grigson's Taste of The Times, 1997; (with William Black) Fish, 1998; Sophie Grigson's Herbs, 1999; Feasts for a Fiver, 1999; Sunshine Food, 2000. *Recreations:* travel, reading, eating. *Address:* c/o Borra Garson, Deborah McKenna Ltd, Claridge House, 29 Barnes High Street, SW13 9LW. *T:* (020) 8876 0051.

GRILLET, Alain R.; *see* Robbe-Grillet.

GRILLS, Michael Geoffrey; a Recorder of the Crown Court, since 1982; a District Judge, since 1991; *b* 23 Feb. 1937; *s* of Frank and Bessie Grills; *m* 1969, Ann Margaret Irene (*née* Pyle); two *d. Educ:* Lancaster Royal Grammar Sch.; Merton Coll., Oxford (MA). Admitted Solicitor, 1961; Partner with Crombie Wilkinson & Robinson, York, 1965; County Court and District Registrar, York and Harrogate District Registries, 1973–90. *Recreations:* music, tennis, ski-ing. *Address:* Cobblestones, Skelton, York YO3 6XX. *T:* (01904) 470246.

GRIMA, Andrew Peter; Jeweller by appointment to HM the Queen; Managing Director, Andrew Grima Ltd, since 1966; *b* 31 May 1921; *s* of late John Grima and Leopolda Farnese; *m* 1st, 1947, Helène Marianne Haller (marr. diss. 1977); one *s* two *d*; 2nd, 1977, Joanne Jill, (Jojo), Maughan-Brown, *d* of late Captain Nigel Maughan-Brown, MC and of Mrs Graham Rawdon; one *d. Educ:* St Joseph's Coll., Beulah Hill; Nottingham Univ. Served War of 1939–45, REME, India and Burma, 1942–46 (despatches, 1945); commanded div. workshop. Director and jewellery designer. Exhibitions worldwide, designed and made prestige watch collection for Omega, "About Time", 1971; 40 year retrospective exhibn, Goldsmiths' Hall, 1991. Opened shops in Jermyn Street, 1966; Sydney and New York, 1970; Zürich, 1971; Tokyo, 1973; Lugano, 1987; Gstaad, 1992. Duke of Edinburgh Prize for Elegant Design, 1966; Queen's Award to Industry, 1966; 12 Diamond Internat. New York Awards, 1963–67. Freeman, City of London, 1964; Liveryman, Worshipful Co. of Goldsmiths, 1968. *Publications:* contribs to: International Diamond Annual, S Africa, 1970; 6 Meister Juweliere unserer Zeit, 1971; By Royal Command, 1999; Artists and Authors at War, 1999; *relevant publication:* Grima 1951–1991, by Johann Willsberger, 1991. *Recreations:* paintings, sculpture, food and wine. *Address:* Vieux Gstaad, 3780 Gstaad, Switzerland; Albany, Piccadilly, W1V 9RR.

GRIME, Prof. John Philip, PhD; FRS 1998; Director, Unit of Comparative Plant Ecology, since 1989, and Professor, since 1983, University of Sheffield; *b* 30 April 1935; *s* of Robert and Gertrude Grime; *m* 1966, Jean Carol Sorensen (marr. diss. 1982); one *s. Educ:* Middleton Grammar Sch., Lancs; Sheffield Univ. (BSc; PhD 1960). Postgrad. researcher, Univ. of Sheffield, 1960–63; Ecologist, Connecticut Agricl Expt Stn, 1963–65; University of Sheffield: Res. Ecologist, Nature Conservancy Grassland Res. Unit, 1965–71; Dep. Dir, NERC Unit of Comparative Ecol., 1971–89. Vice Pres., British Ecological Soc., 1989–91. Foreign Mem., Royal Netherlands Acad. Arts and Sci., 1991; Hon. Member: Lund Ecological Soc., 1992; Ecol Soc. of America, 1998. Hon. Dr Univ. of Nijmegen, Netherlands, 1998. Marsh Award for Ecol., British Ecol Soc., 1997. *Publications:* (with P. S. Lloyd) Ecological Atlas of Grassland Plants, 1973; Plant Strategies and Ecological Processes, 1979; (jtly) Comparative Plant Ecology: a functional approach to common British species, 1988; numerous contribs to scientific jls. *Recreation:* league and friendly cricket. *Address:* Unit of Comparative Plant Ecology, University of Sheffield, Sheffield S10 2TN; 63 Bramley Court, Ryegate Road, Sheffield, Yorks S10 5FB. *T:* (0114) 268 0996.

GRIME, Mark Stephen Eastburn; QC 1987; a Recorder, since 1990; *b* 16 March 1948; *s* of R. T. Grime, ChM, FRCS and late M. D. Grime; *m* 1973, Christine Emck; two *d. Educ:* Wrekin College; Trinity College, Oxford (Scholar; MA). FCIArb 1997. Called to the Bar, Middle Temple, 1970, Bencher, 1997; practising Northern Circuit, 1970–; Asst Recorder, 1988–90; Technol. and Construction Recorder, 1998–. Chairman: Disciplinary Appeal Tribunal, UMIST, 1980–; Northern Arbitration Assoc., 1994–98 (Mem. Council, 1990–94). *Recreations:* antiquarian horology, sailing. *Address:* Homestead Farm, Jackson's Edge, Disley, Cheshire SK12 2JR. *T:* (01663) 766976; Deans Court Chambers, 24 St John Street, Manchester M3 4DF. *T:* (0161) 214 6000.

GRIMLEY, Very Rev. Robert William; Dean of Bristol, since 1997; *b* 26 Sept. 1943; *s* of William Bracebridge Grimley and Gladys Mary (*née* Draper); *m* 1968, Joan Elizabeth Platt; two *s* one *d. Educ:* Derby Sch.; Christ's Coll., Cambridge (BA 1966; MA 1970); Wadham Coll., Oxford (BA 1968; Ellerton Theol Essay Prize, 1974; MA 1976); Ripon Hall, Oxford. Ordained deacon, 1968, priest, 1969; Asst Curate of Radlett, 1968–72; Chaplain, King Edward's Sch., Birmingham and Hon. Curate, St Mary, Moseley, 1972–84; Vicar, St George's, Edgbaston, 1984–97. Examining Chaplain to the Bishop of Birmingham, 1988–97; Bishops' Inspector of Theol Colls, 1998–. Chaplain to the High Sheriff of W Midlands, 1988–89. Governor: The Queen's Coll., Birmingham, 1974–97; The Foundn of the Schs of King Edward VI in Birmingham, 1991–97; Bristol Cathedral Sch., 1997–; Kingswood Sch., 1998–. *Recreations:* reading, Europe, languages, bread-making. *Address:* The Deanery, 20 Charlotte Street, Bristol BS1 5PZ. *T:* (0117) 926 2443, (Cathedral) (0117) 926 4879; *e-mail:* dean@bristol.anglican.org.

GRIMLEY EVANS, Sir John, Kt 1997; FRCP; Professor of Clinical Geratology (formerly Geriatric Medicine), University of Oxford, since 1985; Fellow of Green College, Oxford, since 1985; *b* 17 Sept. 1936; *s* of Harry Walter Grimley Evans and Violet Prenter Walker; *m* 1966, Corinne Jane Cavender; two *s* one *d. Educ:* King Edward's Sch., Birmingham (Foundn Scholar); St John's Coll., Cambridge (Rolleston Scholar; MA, MD); Balliol Coll., Oxford (DM); FFPHM. Res. Asst, Nuffield Dept of Clin. Med., Oxford, 1963–65; Vis. Scientist, Sch. of Public Health, Univ. of Michigan, 1966; Res. Fellow, Med. Unit, Wellington Hosp., NZ, 1966–69; Lectr in Epidemiology, LSHTM, 1970–71; Consultant Physician, Newcastle Gen. Hosp., 1971–73; Prof. of Medicine (Geriatrics), Univ. of Newcastle upon Tyne, 1973–84. Chairman: Specialist Adv. Cttee on Geriatric Medicine, Jt Cttee for Higher Med. Trng, 1979–86; RCP Geriatric Medicine Cttee, 1989–94; Member: WHO Expert Panel on Care of Elderly, 1984– (Rapporteur, 1987); MRC, 1992–95 (Chm., Health Services Res. Cttee, 1989–92; Chm., Health Service and Public Health Res. Bd, 1992–94); Cttee on Med. Aspects of Food Policy, DoH, 1992–2000 (Chm., 1999–2000); GMC, 1994–; Central R & D Cttee, DoH, 1997–. Chm., Examining Bd, Dip. in Geriatric Medicine, 1985–90. Royal College of Physicians: Pro-censor, 1990–91; Censor, 1991–92; Vice-Pres., 1993–95; Harveian Orator, 1997. Founder FMedSci 1998. Editor, Age and Ageing, 1988–95. *Publications:* Care of the Elderly, 1977; (jtly) Advanced Geriatric Medicine (series), 1981–; (jtly) Improving the Health of Older People: a world view, 1990; (jtly) The Oxford Textbook of Geriatric Medicine, 1992, 2nd edn 2000; papers on geriatric medicine and epidemiology of chronic disease. *Recreations:* fly-fishing, literature. *Address:* Donnington Farmhouse, Meadow Lane, Iffley, Oxford OX4 4ED. *Club:* Royal Society of Medicine.

GRIMMETT, Prof. Geoffrey Richard, DPhil; Professor of Mathematical Statistics, Cambridge University, since 1992 (Director of Statistical Laboratory, 1994–2000); Professorial Fellow of Churchill College, Cambridge, since 1999; *b* 20 Dec. 1950; *s* of Benjamin and Patricia Grimmett; *m* 1986, Rosine Bonay; one *s. Educ:* King Edward's Sch., Birmingham; Merton Coll., Oxford (BA 1971; MSc 1972; MA, DPhil 1974). Jun. Res. Fellow, New Coll., and IBM Res. Fellow, Oxford Univ., 1974–76; Bristol University: Lectr, 1976–85; Reader, 1985–89; Prof. of Maths, 1989–92. Vis. appts at Cornell Univ., Univ. of Arizona, Univ. of Rome II, Univ. of Utah, etc. Man. Ed., Probability Theory and Related Fields, 2000–. Mem., GB Fencing Team, 1973–77. Hon. FIA 1999. *Publications:* (with D. R. Stirzaker) Probability and Random Processes, 1982, 3rd edn 2001; (with D. J. A. Welsh) Probability: an introduction, 1986; Percolation, 1989, 2nd edn 1999; (with D. R. Stirzaker) One Thousand Exercises in Probability, 2001; contrib. to learned jls. *Recreations:* mountaineering, music. *Address:* Statistical Laboratory, University of Cambridge, Wilberforce Road, Cambridge CB3 0WB. *T:* (01223) 337957. *Clubs:* Alpine; Climbers'.

GRIMSBY, Bishop Suffragan of, since 2000; **Rt Rev. David Douglas James Rossdale;** *b* 22 May 1953; *m* 1982, Karen; two *s. Educ:*, KCL; Westminster Coll., Oxford (MA 1990); Roehampton Inst. (MSc 2000). Ordained deacon, 1981, priest, 1982; Curate, Upminster, 1981–86; Vicar: St Luke, Moulsham, 1986–90; Cookham, 1990–2000; Area Dean of Maidenhead, 1994–2000. Hon. Canon, Christ Church, Oxford, 1999–2000; Canon and Preb., Lincoln Cathedral, 2000–. *Recreations:* travel, cookery. *Address:* Bishop's House, Church Lane, Irby-upon-Humber, Grimsby DN37 7JR. *T:* (01472) 371715.

GRIMSEY, Colin Robert; JP; consultant; *b* Manchester, 24 Dec. 1943; *yr s* of Arthur and Joan Grimsey; *m* 1976, Elizabeth Sermon; one *s* one *d. Educ:* Dartford Grammar Sch.; King's Coll., London (BSc Hons Physics 1964). Asst Principal, MoT, 1968–72; Principal, DoE, 1972–75; CSSB, 1975; DoE, 1976–79; Asst Sec., Dept of Transport, 1979–89; Under Sec., seconded to LRT, 1989–91; Dir of Finance, 1991–93, Head of Railways Directorate, 1993–96, Dept of Transport. JP NW Surrey, 1997. *Recreations:* family, choral singing, opera and theatre going, walking.

GRIMSHAW, Maj.-Gen. Ewing Henry Wrigley, CB 1965; CBE 1957 (OBE 1954); DSO 1945; *b* 30 June 1911; *s* of Col E. W. Grimshaw; *m* 1943, Hilda Florence Agnes Allison (*d* 1993); two *s* one *d. Educ:* Brighton Coll. Joined Indian Army, 1931. Served War of 1939–45, Western Desert and Burma (despatches twice); Brig. 1944 (youngest on active service). Transferred to Royal Inniskilling Fusiliers, 1947; active service in Malaya, 1948 and 1950, Kenya, 1954, Suez, 1956 and Cyprus, 1958; GOC 44th Div. (TA) and Home Counties Dist, 1962–65. Col, The Royal Inniskilling Fusiliers, 1966–68; Dep. Col, The Royal Irish Rangers, 1968–73. Dep. Constable, Dover Castle, 1962–65.

GRIMSHAW, Nicholas Thomas, CBE 1993; RA 1994; Chairman, Nicholas Grimshaw & Partners Ltd, architects, planners and industrial designers, since 1980; *b* 9 Oct. 1939; *s* of Thomas Cecil Grimshaw and Hannah Joan Dearsley; *m* 1972, Lavinia, *d* of John Russell, *qv*; two *d. Educ:* Wellington College, Edinburgh College of Art; Architectural Assoc. Sch. AA Dip. Hons 1965; RIBA 1967; FCSD (FSIAD 1969); numerous prizes and scholarships. Major projects include: Channel Tunnel terminal, Waterloo (Mies van der Rohe Pavilion Award, 1994, RIBA Building of the Year Award, 1994); British Pavilion for Expo '92, Seville, Spain; Financial Times Printing Plant (Royal Fine Art Commn/Sunday Times Building of the Year Award, 1989); Pusan Internat. Rly Terminus, Korea, 1996; Zurich Airport Expansion, 1996; Regl HQ for Orange Telephones, Darlington, 1996; restoration of Paddington Stn, 1996; restoration of existing Spa and new building, Bath, 1997; Caixa Galicia Art Foundn, La Coruña, Spain, 1997; Berlin Stock Exchange and Communications Centre; British Airways Combined Operations Centre, Heathrow; HQ for Igus GmbH, Cologne; RAC Rescue Services HQ; Satellite and Piers, Heathrow Airport; Research Centre for Rank Xerox; BMW HQ, Bracknell; Herman Miller Factory, Bath; Oxford Ice Rink; Gillingham Business Park; J. Sainsbury Superstore, Camden; Head Office and Printing Press for Western Morning News; redevelopment of Terminal One, Manchester Airport, for MA plc; teaching and res. bldg, Univ. of Surrey; head office for Mabeg GmbH, Soest (RIBA Internat. Award), 1999; Eden Project, St Austell, 2000; Exhibn Hall, Frankfurt Fair, 2000; HQ and factory for Ffeiffer Vacuum, Dortmund, 2000; high-speed rly stn, Biljmer, Amsterdam, 2000. Pres. Council, AA, 1999–2001. Assessor for: British Construction Industry Awards; DoE; British Gas; Scottish Develt Agency. Hon. Mem., Bund Deutscher Architekten, 1997. Hon. FAIA 1995. Hon. DLitt South Bank, 1993. Awards and Commendations include: RIBA, 1975, 1978, 1980, 1983, 1986, 1989, 1990, 1991, 1994, 1995, 1996, 1999; Financial Times (for Industrial Architecture), 1977, 1980, 1995; Structural Steel Design, 1969, 1977, 1980, 1989, 1993, 1994, 1995, 2000; Civic Trust, 1978, 1982, 1989, 1990, 1991, 1996; British Construction Industry Awards, 1988, 1989, 1992, 1993, 1995, 1996; Royal Fine Art Commn/Sunday Times Bldg of the Year Award, 1989, 1993, 1995; Constructa Preis for Industrial Architecture in Europe, 1990; Quaternario Foundn Internat. Award for Innovative Technol. in Architecture, 1993; AIA/London UK Chapter Design Excellence Award, 1995; Nat. Heritage Arts Sponsorship Scheme Award, 1995; Design Innovation Award, 1996; British Council for Offices Award, 1996; Internat. Brunel Award, 1996. *Publications:* Nicholas Grimshaw & Partners: product and process, 1988; (jtly) Architecture, Industry and Innovation: the work of Nicholas Grimshaw & Partners 1966–88, 1995; (jtly) Structure, Space & Skin: the work of Nicholas Grimshaw & Partners 1988–93, 1993; Equilibrium: the work of Nicholas Grimshaw & Partners 1993–99, 2000; articles for RSA Jl. *Recreations:* sailing, tennis. *Address:* 1 Conway Street, Fitzroy Square, W1P 6LR. *T:* (020) 7291 4141.

See also T. Traeger.

GRIMSTON, family name of **Baron Grimston of Westbury** and of **Earl of Verulam.**

GRIMSTON, Viscount; James Walter Grimston; *b* 6 Jan. 1978; *s* and *heir* of Earl of Verulam, *qv. Educ:* Eton; St Edmund Hall, Oxford. *Recreations:* art, hill walking.

GRIMSTON OF WESTBURY, 2nd Baron *cr* 1964; **Robert Walter Sigismund Grimston;** Bt 1952; Director, Gray's Inn (Underwriting Agencies) Ltd, 1965–90, retired (Chairman, 1970–88); Director, River Clyde Holdings, 1986–88; *b* 14 June 1925; *s* of 1st Baron Grimston of Westbury and Sybil Edith Muriel Rose (*d* 1977), *d* of Sir Sigismund Neumann, 1st Bt; *S* father, 1979; *m* 1949, Hon. June Mary Ponsonby, *d* of 5th Baron de Mauley; two *s* one *d. Educ:* Eton. Served as Lt Scots Guards, 1943–47; NW Europe, 1944–45. Oil Industry, 1948–53; Sales Director, Ditchling Press, 1953–61; Dir, Hinton Hill & Coles Ltd, 1962–83. Freeman, City of London, 1981; Liveryman, Worshipful Co. of Gold and Silver Wyre Drawers, 1981. *Recreations:* tennis, shooting, golf, walking. *Heir: s* Hon. Robert John Sylvester Grimston [*b* 30 April 1951; *m* 1984, Emily Margaret, *d* of Major John Shirley; two *d. Educ:* Eton; Reading Univ. (BSc). Chartered Accountant.

Commnd The Royal Hussars (PWO), 1970–81, Captain 1976]. *Address:* The Old Rectory, Westwell, near Burford, Oxon OX18 4JT. *Club:* Boodle's.

GRIMTHORPE, 4th Baron *cr* 1886; **Christopher John Beckett,** Bt 1813; OBE 1958; DL; Deputy Commander, Malta and Libya, 1964–67; *b* 16 Sept. 1915; *e s* of 3rd Baron Grimthorpe, TD, and Mary Lady Grimthorpe (*d* 1962); *S* father, 1963; *m* 1954, Lady Elizabeth Lumley (*see* Lady Grimthorpe); two *s* one *d*. *Educ:* Eton. 2nd Lieut, 9 Lancers, 1936; Lt-Col, 9 Lancers, 1955–58; AAG, War Office, 1958–61; Brigadier, Royal Armoured Corps, HQ, Western Command, 1961–64. Col, 9/12 Royal Lancers, 1973–77. ADC to the Queen, 1964–67. Director: Standard Broadcasting Corp. of Canada (UK), 1972–86; Thirsk Racecourse Ltd, 1972–; Yorkshire Post Newspapers, 1973–86; Pres., London Metropolitan Region YMCA, 1972–86. Mem., Jockey Club. DL North Yorkshire, 1969. *Recreations:* travel, horse sports. *Heir: s* Hon. Edward John Beckett [*b* 20 Nov. 1954; *m* 1992, Mrs Carey Elisabeth McEwen, *d* of Robin Graham; one *s*]. *Address:* Westow Hall, York YO60 7NE. *T:* (01653) 618225. *Clubs:* Cavalry and Guards, Portland.

GRIMTHORPE, Lady; Elizabeth Beckett, DCVO 1995 (CVO 1983); Lady of the Bedchamber to HM Queen Elizabeth The Queen Mother, since 1973; *b* 22 July 1925; 2nd *d* of 11th Earl of Scarbrough, KG, GCVO, PC and Katharine Isabel, Countess of Scarbrough, DCVO, K-i-H Gold Medal; *m* 1954, 4th Baron Grimthorpe, *qv*; two *s* one *d*. *Address:* Westow Hall, York YO60 7NE. *T:* (01653) 618225.

GRIMWADE, Sir Andrew (Sheppard), Kt 1980; CBE 1977; Australian industrialist; *b* 26 Nov. 1930; *s* of late Frederick and Gwendolen Grimwade; *m* 1959, Barbara (*d* 1990), *d* of J. B. D. Kater; one *s*. *Educ:* Melbourne C of E Grammar Sch.; Trinity Coll., Melbourne Univ. (Exhib. Eng.; BSc); Oriel Coll., Oxford (swimming blue; MA). FRACI, FAIM. Vice-Chm., Nat. Mutual Life Assoc., 1988– (Dir, 1970–); Dep. Chm., NZ Ski Fields Ltd; Director: IBM (Aust.); Sony (Aust.) Pty Ltd; Nat. Aust. Bank, 1965–85; Commonwealth Ind. Gases, 1960–90. Mem., first Aust. Govt Trade Mission to China, 1973. Mem., Australian Govt Remuneration Tribunal, 1974–82. Pres., Walter and Eliza Hall Inst. of Med. Research, 1978– (Mem. Bd, 1963–). Chairman: Australian Art Exhibn Corp. (Chinese Exhibn), 1976–77; Australian Govt Official Estabts Trust, 1976–82; Trustee, Victorian Arts Centre, 1980–90; Emeritus Trustee, Nat. Gallery of Vic, 1990– (Trustee, 1964–90; Pres., 1976–90). Member: Council for Order of Australia, 1975–82; Felton Bequests' Cttee, 1973–. *Publication:* Involvement: The Portraits of Clifton Pugh and Mark Strizic, 1969. *Recreations:* skiing, cattle breeding, Australian art. *Address:* PO Box 134, E Melbourne, Vic 3002, Australia. *T:* (3) 98225990. *Clubs:* Melbourne, Australian (Melbourne).

GRIMWADE, Rev. Canon John Girling; Chaplain to the Queen, 1980–90; permission to officiate, dioceses of Gloucester and Oxford, since 1989; *b* 13 March 1920; *s* of Herbert Alfred and Edith Grimwade; *m* 1951, Adini Anne Carus-Wilson; one *s* one *d*. *Educ:* Colet Court; St Paul's Sch.; Keble Coll., Oxford; Cuddesdon Coll. MA Oxon. Friends' Ambulance Unit, 1940–45. Curate of Kingston-upon-Thames, 1950–53; Curate, University Church of St Mary-the-Virgin, Oxford, and Secretary of Oxford Univ. Student Christian Movement, 1953–56; Vicar of St Mark's, Smethwick, 1956–62; Rector of Caversham, 1962–81, and Priest-in-Charge of Mapledurham, 1968–81; Rector of Caversham and Mapledurham, 1981–83; Priest-in-Charge, Stonesfield, Oxford, 1983–89. Chm., House of Clergy, Oxford Diocesan Synod, 1976–82; Agenda Sec., Oxford Dio. Synod, 1983–88; Diocesan Press Officer, Oxford, 1983–89. Hon. Canon of Christ Church, Oxford, 1974–90, Hon. Canon Emeritus, 1990–. *Recreation:* gardening. *Address:* 88 Alexander Drive, Cirencester, Glos GL7 1UJ.

GRINDON, John Evelyn, CVO 1957; DSO 1945; AFC 1948; Group Captain, RAF retired; *b* 30 Sept. 1917; *s* of Thomas Edward Grindon (killed in action, Ypres, Oct. 1917), and Dora (*née* Eastlake), Corisande, East Pentire, Cornwall. *Educ:* Dulwich College. Flight Cadet at RAF College, Cranwell, 1935–37; served in Advanced Air Striking Force, BEF, France, 1939–40 (No 150 Sqdn) and in No 5 Group Bomber Command (Nos 106, 630 and 617 Sqdns) during War of 1939–45, as Flight and Sqdn Comdr; Chief Instructor, Long Range Transport Force, 1946–49; Commanded The Queen's Flight, 1953–56; V-bomber captain and Station Comdr, 1956–57; retired at own request 1959. Dir/Gen. Manager in printing/publishing, 1961–71; Metropolitan Police, New Scotland Yard, 1976–81. *Recreations:* opera, ocean surf, racing. *Club:* Royal Air Force.

GRINDROD, Helen Marjorie; QC 1982; a Recorder of the Crown Court, 1981–95; *b* 28 Feb. 1936; *d* of late Joseph and Marjorie Pritchard; *m* 1958, Robert Michael Grindrod; one *s*. *Educ:* Liverpool Inst. High Sch. for Girls; St Hilda's Coll., Oxford (MA; Hon. Fellow). Teacher, 1957–59. Called to the Bar, Lincoln's Inn, 1966, Bencher, 1990; Northern Circuit, 1966–. *Address:* 15–19 Devereux Court, WC2R 3JJ; 18 St John Street, Manchester M3 4EA.

GRINDROD, Most Rev. John Basil Rowland, KBE 1983; Archbishop of Brisbane and Metropolitan of Queensland, 1980–89; Primate of Australia, 1982–89; *b* 14 Dec. 1919; *s* of Edward Basil and Dorothy Gladys Grindrod; *m* 1949, Ailsa W. (*d* 1981), *d* of G. Newman; two *d*; *m* 1983, Mrs Dell Cornish, *d* of S. J. Caswell. *Educ:* Repton School; Queen's College, Oxford; Lincoln Theological College. BA 1949; MA 1954. Deacon, 1951; Priest, 1952, Manchester. Curate: St Michael's, Hulme, 1951–54; Bundaberg, Qld, 1954–56; Rector: All Souls, Ancoats, Manchester, 1956–60; Emerald, Qld, 1960–61; St Barnabas, N Rockhampton, Qld, 1961–65; Archdeacon of Rockhampton, Qld, 1960–65; Vicar, Christ Church, S Yarra, Vic, 1965–66; Bishop of Riverina, NSW, 1966–71; Bishop of Rockhampton, 1971–80. Hon. ThD, 1985. *Address:* 14B Thomas Street, Murwillumbah, NSW 2484, Australia.

GRINLING, Jasper Gibbons, CBE 1978; Chairman, London Jazz Radio plc, 1989–91, retired; *b* 29 Jan. 1924; *s* of late Lt-Col Antony Gibbons Grinling, MBE, MC, and Jean Dorothy Turing Grinling; *m* 1950, Jane Moulsdale; one *s* two *d*. *Educ:* Harrow (Scholar); King's Coll., Cambridge (Exhibnr, BA). CIMgt (FBIM 1969). Served War, 12th Lancers, 1942–46 (Captain). Joined W. & A. Gilbey Ltd, 1947, Dir 1952; Man. Dir, Gilbeys Ltd, 1964; Man. Dir, International Distillers & Vintners Ltd, 1967; Dir, North British Distillery Co. Ltd, 1968–86; Dir of Corporate Affairs, Grand Metropolitan, 1981–85, Dir of Trade Relations, 1985–86; Chm., The Apple & Pear Develt Council, 1986–89. Pres., EEC Confedn des Industries Agricoles et Alimentaires, 1976–80; Mem. Council, Scotch Whisky Assoc., 1968–86. Chevalier, Ordre National du Mérite, France, 1983. *Publication:* The Annual Report, 1986. *Recreations:* gardening, jazz drumming, painting, vineyard proprietor. *Address:* The Old Vicarage, Helions Bumpstead, near Haverhill, Suffolk CB9 7AS. *T:* (01440) 730316.

GRINSTEAD, Sir Stanley (Gordon), Kt 1986; FCA; CIMgt; Chairman and Director, Harmony Leisure Group, 1989–92; *b* 17 June 1924; *s* of Ephraim Grinstead and Lucy Grinstead (*née* Taylor); *m* 1955, Joyce Preston; two *d*. *Educ:* Strodes, Egham. Served Royal Navy, 1943–46 (Pilot, FAA). Franklin, Wild & Co., Chartered Accountants, 1946–56; Hotel York Ltd, 1957; Grand Metropolitan Ltd, 1957–62; Union Properties (London) Ltd, 1958–66; Grand Metropolitan Ltd, 1964–87: Dep. Chm. and Group Man. Dir, 1980–82; Gp Chief Exec., 1982–86; Chm., 1982–87; Chm., Reed Internat., 1988–89 (Dir, 1981–90). Trustee, FAA Museum. Vice-Pres., CGLI, 1986–90. Master, Brewers' Co., 1983–84. *Recreations:* gardening, cricket, racing, breeding of thoroughbred horses. *Clubs:* Army and Navy, MCC; Surrey County Cricket (Hon. Treas., 1987–94).

GRINYER, Prof. Peter Hugh; Emeritus Professor, University of St Andrews, since 1993; *b* 3 March 1935; *s* of Sidney George and Grace Elizabeth Grinyer; *m* 1958, Sylvia Joyce Boraston; two *s*. *Educ:* Balliol Coll., Oxford (BA, subseq. MA, PPE); LSE (PhD in Applied Economics). Unilever Sen. Managerial Trainee, 1957–59; PA to Man. Dir, E. R. Holloway Ltd, 1959–61; Lectr and Sen. Lectr, Hendon Coll. of Tech., 1961–64; Lectr, 1965–69, Sen. Lectr, 1969–72, City Univ.; Reader, 1972–74, Prof. of Business Strategy, 1974–79, City Univ. Business School; Esmée Fairbairn Prof. of Econs (Finance and Investment), Univ. of St Andrews, 1979–93 (Vice-Principal, 1985–87, Actg Principal). Chairman: St Andrews Management Inst., 1989–96; St Andrews Strategic Management Ltd, 1989–96. Vis. Prof., Stern Sch. of Business, New York Univ., 1992, 1996–98; Erskine Fellow, Univ. of Canterbury, NZ, 1994. Member: Business and Management Studies Sub-Cttee, UGC, 1979–85; Scottish Legal Aid Bd, 1992–2000; Appeal Tribunals Panel, Competition Commn, 2000–. Founding Dir, Glenrothes Enterprise Trust, 1983–86; Director: John Brown PLC, 1984–86; Don and Low (Hldgs) Ltd (formerly Don Bros Buist), 1985–91; Ellis and Goldstein (Hldgs) PLC, 1987–88; Chm., McIlroy Coates, 1991–95. *Publications:* Corporate Models Today (with J. Wooller), 1975, 2nd edn 1979; (with G. D. Vaughan and S. Birley) From Private to Public, 1977; (with J.-C. Spender) Turnaround: the fall and rise of Newton Chambers, 1979; (with D. G. Mayes and P. McKiernan) Sharpbenders, 1988; (with Dr Foo Check Teck) Organzing for Strategy: Sun Tzu business warcraft, 1994; some 55 papers in academic jls. *Recreations:* hill walking, golf. *Address:* 60 Buchanan Gardens, St Andrews, Fife KY16 9LX. *Club:* Royal & Ancient Golf (St Andrews).

GRISHAM, John; author; *b* 8 Feb. 1955; *m* Renée Jones; one *s* one *d*. *Educ:* Mississippi State Univ. (BS Accounting); Univ. of Mississippi (JD 1981). Mem., Miss. Bar, 1981; Law practice, Southaven, 1981–91; Mem. (Democrat), Miss. House of Reps, 1984–90. *Publications:* The Firm, 1991; The Pelican Brief, 1992; A Time to Kill, 1992; The Client, 1993; The Chamber, 1994; The Rainmaker, 1995; The Runaway Jury, 1996; The Partner, 1997; The Street Lawyer, 1998; The Testament, 1999; The Brethren, 2000; A Painted House, 2001. *Recreations:* reading, coaching baseball. *Address:* c/o Doubleday & Co. Inc., 1540 Broadway, New York, NY 10036, USA.

GRIST, Ian; Chairman, South Glamorgan Health Authority, 1992–96; *b* 5 Dec. 1938; *s* of late Basil William Grist, MBE and Leila Helen Grist; *m* 1966, Wendy Anne (*née* White), BSc; two *s*. *Educ:* Repton Sch.; Jesus Coll., Oxford (Schol.). Plebiscite Officer, Southern Cameroons, 1960–61; Stores Manager, United Africa Co., Nigeria, 1961–63; Wales Information Officer, Conservative Central Office, 1963–74; Conservative Research Dept, 1970–74. MP (C) Cardiff North, Feb. 1974–1983, Cardiff Central, 1983–92; contested (C) Cardiff Central, 1992. PPS to Secretary of State for Wales, 1979–81; Parly Under Sec. of State, Welsh Office, 1987–90. Mem., Select Cttee on: Violence in the Family, 1977–79; Welsh Affairs, 1981–83 and 1986–87; Register of Members' Interests, 1983–87. Chm., Cons. W African Cttee, 1977–87 and 1991–92. Vice-Chm., Assoc. of Conservative Clubs, 1978–82. *Recreations:* reading, listening to music. *Address:* 1 Heol Ifor, Rhiwbina, Cardiff CF14 1SZ. *T:* (029) 2062 7483.

GRIST, John Frank; broadcasting consultant; Supervisor of Parliamentary Broadcasting, 1991–93 (Supervisor of Broadcasting, House of Commons, 1989–91); *b* 10 May 1924; *s* of Austin Grist, OBE, MC, and Ada Mary Grist (*née* Ball); *m* Gilian, *d* of Roger Cranage and Helen Marjorie Rollett; one *s* two *d*. *Educ:* Ryde Sch., IoW; London Sch. of Economics and Political Science (BSc Econ); Univ. of Chicago. RAF Pilot, 1942–46. BBC External Services, 1951–53; seconded to Nigerian Broadcasting Service, 1953–56; BBC TV Talks and Current Affairs at Lime Grove, 1957–72, producer of political programmes and Editor of Gallery and of Panorama; Hd of Current Affairs Gp, 1967–72; Controller, English Regions BBC, 1972–77; US Rep., BBC, 1978–81; Man. Dir, Services Sound and Vision Corp., 1982–88. Specialist Advr to Select Cttee on Televising of Proceedings of H of C, 1988–89. Observer, Russian Election, 1993; Advr, Indep. Media Commn, S African Elections, 1994. BP Press Fellow, Wolfson Coll., Cambridge, 1988. Gov., Royal Star and Garter Home, 1986–94. FRTS 1986 (Mem. Council, 1984–88). *Address:* 4 Burlington House, Kings Road, Richmond, Surrey TW10 6NW. *T:* (020) 8940 6351. *Club:* Reform.

GRIST, Prof. Norman Roy, FRCPE; Professor of Infectious Diseases, University of Glasgow, 1965–83, now Emeritus; *b* 9 March 1918; *s* of Walter Reginald Grist and Florence Goodwin Grist (*née* Nadin); *m* 1943, Mary Stewart McAlister. *Educ:* Shawlands Acad., Glasgow; University of Glasgow (BSc 1939; MB, ChB (Commendation), 1942). MRCPE 1950, FRCPE 1958; Founder Mem., 1963, FRCPath 1967; MRCPGlas 1980, FRCPGlas 1983. Ho. Phys. Gartloch Hosp., 1942–43; RAMC, GDO 223 Fd Amb. and RMO 2/KSLI, 1943–46; Ho. Surg. Victoria Inf., Glasgow, 1946–47; Res. Phys, Ruchill Hosp., Glasgow, 1947–48; Research Asst, Glasgow Univ. Dept of Infectious Diseases, 1948–52; Lectr in Virus Disease, Glasgow Univ., 1952–62, and Regional Adviser in Virology to Scottish Western Reg. Hosp. Bd, 1960–74; Reader in Viral Epidemiology, Glasgow Univ., 1962–65. Mem., Expert Adv. Panel on Virus Diseases to WHO, 1967–. Pres., Glasgow Natural History Soc., 1993–96. Hon. Mem., Assoc. of Clin. Pathology, 1989. Bronze Medal, Helsinki Univ., 1973; Orden Civil de Sanidad, cat. Encomienda, Spain, 1974. *Publications:* Diagnostic Methods in Clinical Virology, 1966, 3rd edn, 1979; (with D. Reid and I. W. Pinkerton) Infections in Current Medical Practice, 1986; (with D. O. Ho-Yen, E. Walker and G. R. Williams) Diseases of Infection, 1987, 2nd edn 1993; numerous contribs. to British and international med. jls. *Recreations:* gardener's mate, natural history. *Address:* 5A Hyndland Court, 6A Sydenham Road, Glasgow G12 9NR. *T:* (0141) 339 5242. *Club:* Royal Scottish Automobile (Glasgow).

GRIST, Maj.-Gen. Robin Digby, CB 1994; OBE 1979; DL; Director, : Gloucestershire Enterprise Ltd, since 2001; Quality South West (QUEST) Ltd, since 2001; *b* 21 Oct. 1940; *s* of late Lt-Col and Mrs Digby Grist; *m* 1971, Louise Littlejohn; one *s* two *d*. *Educ:* Radley Coll.; Royal Military Acad., Sandhurst. Commnd, Gloucestershire Regt, 1960; seconded to Army Air Corps, 1965–69; active service, Aden and S Arabia, 1966–67 (despatches); CO 1st Bn Gloucestershire Regt, 1979–82; Comdr 6 Airmobile Bde, 1985–86; RCDS 1987; Mil. Attaché and Comdr Brit. Army Staff, Washington, USA, 1988–89; Dir, AAC, 1989–92; Dir Gen., AGC, 1992–94. Man. Dir, Business Link, Gloucestershire, 1997–98. Col, The Gloucestershire Regt, 1990–94, The Royal Gloucestershire, Berkshire and Wiltshire Regt, 1994–2001; Dir, Corporate Affairs, The Link Gp (Glos), 1998–2001. Chm., Glos Community Foundn, 2000–. DL Gloucestershire, 1995. *Publications:* Their Laurels are Green: a short history of The Royal Gloucestershire, Berkshire and Wiltshire Regiment, 1997; articles in mil. jls, particularly on airmobility. *Recreations:* fishing, gardening. *Address:* Regimental Headquarters, Royal Gloucestershire, Berkshire and Wiltshire Regiment, Custom House, Gloucester GL1 2HE. *Club:* Army and Navy.

GRISWOLD, Most Rev. Frank Tracy, III; Presiding Bishop, Episcopal Church in the United States of America, since 1998; *b* 18 Sept. 1937; *s* of Frank Tracy Griswold Jr and Luisa Johnson (*née* Whitney); *m* 1965, Phoebe Wetzel; two *d. Educ:* Harvard Univ. (BA 1959); Gen. Theol Seminary (Cert. 1960); Oriel Coll., Oxford (MA 1966). Ordained deacon, 1962, priest, 1963; Curate, Church of the Redeemer, Bryn Mawr, Penn, 1963–67; Rector: St Andrew's, Yardley, Penn, 1967–74; St Martin-in-the-Fields, Philadelphia, 1974–85; Bishop Coadjutor of Chicago, 1985–87; Bishop of Chicago, 1987–97. Hon. DD: Gen. Theol Seminary, 1985; Seabury-Western Theol Seminary, 1985; Nashotah House, Wisconsin, 2000; Univ. of the South, 2001. *Address:* Episcopal Church Center, 815 Second Avenue, New York, NY 10017, USA.

GROBEL, Peter Denis Alan Christian Joseph; His Honour Judge Grobel; a Circuit Judge, since 2001; *b* 11 Aug. 1944; *s* of Cyril Peter Grobel and Kathleen (*née* Donaghy); *m* 1975, Susan Twemlow, LRAM; three *s* one *d. Educ:* Mt St Mary's Coll.; University Coll. London (LLB Hons). Called to the Bar, Lincoln's Inn, 1967; in practice at common law bar, 1971–2001; a Recorder, SE Circuit, 1991–2001. Chm., Special Educnl Needs Tribunal, 1994–2001. *Recreation:* parish politics. *Address:* c/o Inner London Crown Court, SE1 6AZ.

GROBLER, Richard Victor, CBE 1996; Deputy Secretary of Commissions, Lord Chancellor's Department, 1984–96; *b* Umtali, S Rhodesia, 27 May 1936; *m* 1961, Julienne Nora de la Cour (*née* Sheath); one *s* three *d. Educ:* Bishop's, Capetown; Univ. of Cape Town (BA). Called to the Bar, Gray's Inn, 1961; joined staff of Clerk of the Court, Central Criminal Court, 1961; Dep. Clerk of the Court, 1970; Dep. Courts Administrator, 1972; Courts Administrator, Inner London Crown Court, 1974; Sec., Lord Chancellor's Adv. Cttee on Justices of the Peace for Inner London and Jt Hon. Sec., Inner London Br. of Magistrates' Assoc., 1974–77; Courts Administrator, Central Criminal Court, and Co-ordinator, Crown Courts Taxations, SE Circuit, 1977–79; Dep. Circuit Administrator, S Eastern Circuit, 1979–83. Dir, Housing Solutions Ltd, 2000–. Gov., Furze Platt Sen. Sch., 1997–. Liveryman, Worshipful Company of Gold and Silver Wyre Drawers. *Recreations:* gardening, swimming, golf. *Address:* Bradgate, 269 Courthouse Road, Maidenhead, Berks SL6 6HF. *T:* (01628) 624280.

GROCOCK, Dr (Catherine) Anne; Executive Director, The Royal Society of Medicine, since 1997; *b* 7 March 1947; *d* of late Arthur Raymond Grocock and Alice Grace Grocock. *Educ:* Westonbirt Sch.; St Anne's Coll., Oxford (BA Zool. 1968; MA, DPhil 1973). University of Oxford: Deptl Demonstrator in Human Anatomy, 1973–79; Deptl Res. Asst, 1979–80 and 1982–85, and ICRF Res. Fellow, 1985–89, Dept of Human Anatomy; Lectr in Anatomy, Merton Coll., Oxford, 1977–80 and 1985–89; Bursar and Official Fellow, St Antony's Coll., Oxford, 1990–97. Chm., Reproduction Res. Inf. Services Ltd, 1988–93. Mem. Cttee of Mgt, Royal Medical Benevolent Fund, 1998–. Trustee, Nat. Mus. Sci. and Industry, 1996– (Chm. Audit Cttee, 1997–). Mem. Council, Taunton Sch., 1990–2001; Gov., Westonbirt Sch., 1991–97. Mem. Exec. Cttee, Oxford Soc., 1995–; Pres., ASM, St Anne's Coll., Oxford, 1997–2000. FRSA 2000. *Publications:* contribs to learned jls in reproductive physiology. *Recreations:* opera, sculpture. *Address:* The Royal Society of Medicine, 1 Wimpole Street, W1M 8AE. *T:* (020) 7290 2900. *Club:* Reform.

GROCOTT, family name of **Baron Grocott.**

GROCOTT, Baron *cr* 2001 (Life Peer), of Telford in the County of Shropshire; **Bruce Joseph Grocott;** a Lord-in-Waiting (Government Whip), since 2001; *b* 1 Nov. 1940; *s* of Reginald Grocott and Helen Grocott (*née* Stewart); *m* 1965, Sally Barbara Kay Ridgway; two *s. Educ:* Hemel Hempstead Grammar Sch.; Leicester and Manchester Univs. BA(Pol), MA(Econ). Admin. Officer, LCC, 1963–64; Lectr in Politics, Manchester Univ., Birmingham Polytechnic, and N Staffs Polytechnic, 1964–74. Television presenter and producer, 1979–87. Chm., Finance Cttee, Bromsgrove UDC, 1972–74. Contested (Lab): Lichfield and Tamworth, 1979; The Wrekin, 1983. MP (Lab): Lichfield and Tamworth, Oct. 1974–1979; The Wrekin, 1987–97; Telford, 1997–2001. Parliamentary Private Secretary: to Minister for Local Govt and Planning, 1975–76; to Minister of Agriculture, 1976–78; Dep. Shadow Leader, H of C, 1987–92; Opposition front bench spokesman on foreign affairs, 1992–93; PPS to Leader of the Opposition, 1994–97, to Prime Minister, 1997–2001. Mem., Select Cttee on Nat. Heritage, 1994–95. *Recreations:* sport, fiction writing, steam railways. *Address:* House of Lords, SW1A 0PW. *Club:* Trench Labour.

GROGAN, John Timothy; MP (Lab) Selby, since 1997; *b* 24 Feb. 1961; *s* of John Martin Grogan and late Maureen Grogan (*née* Jennings). *Educ:* St Michael's Coll., Leeds; St John's Coll., Oxford (BA Hons 1982; Pres., Student Union, 1982). Asst to Leader, Wolverhampton Council, 1985–87; Communications Dir, Leeds CC, 1987–94; Press Officer, Eur. Parly Lab. Party, 1994–95; Conf. Organiser, Yorks, 1995–97. Contested (Lab): Selby, 1987, 1992; York, EP elecn, 1989. *Recreations:* running, football, keen supporter of Bradford City FC and Yorks CCC. *Address:* House of Commons, SW1A 0AA; (office) 58 Gowthorpe, Selby, North Yorks YO8 0ET. *T:* (01757) 291152. *Club:* Yorks CC.

GRONOW, David Gwilym Colin, MSc, PhD; Member, Electricity Council, 1985–90, retired; *b* Leigh-on-Sea, 13 Jan. 1929; *s* of David Morgan Gronow and Harriet Hannah Gronow; *m* 1st, 1953, Joan Andrew Bowen Jones (marr. diss. 1970); one *s* one *d*; 2nd, 1970, Rosemary Freda Iris Keys. *Educ:* North Street Elem. Sch., Leigh-on-Sea; Grammar Sch., Swansea; University Coll. London (MSc, PhD). Institute of Aviation Medicine, RAF Farnborough, Hants: Jun. Technician, 1951–53; Sci. Officer, then Sen. Sci. Officer, 1953–57; Sen. Sci. Officer, UKAEA, Capenhurst, Cheshire, 1957; Second Asst Engr, then Sen. Asst Engr, CEGB, HQ Operations Dept, London, 1957–64; Asst Commercial Officer/Asst Chief Commercial Officer/Chief Commercial Officer, SSEB, Glasgow, 1964–78; Marketing Advr, 1978–80, Commercial Advr, 1980–85, Electricity Council, London. *Recreations:* travel, bird watching, theatre, horse racing. *Address:* 8 Arundel Way, Highcliffe, Christchurch, Dorset BH23 5DX.

GROOM, Brian William Alfred; Political Editor, Financial Times, since 2000; *b* 26 April 1955; *s* of Fred and Muriel Groom; *m* 1980, Carola May Withington; one *s* one *d. Educ:* Manchester Grammar Sch.; Balliol Coll., Oxford (BA Hons). Journalist: Goole Times, 1976–78; Financial Times, 1978–88; Dep. Editor, 1988–94, Editor, 1994–97, Scotland on Sunday; British and Regl Affairs Ed., FT, 1997–2000. *Recreations:* reading, cinema, cricket, walking. *Address:* Press Gallery, House of Commons, SW1A 0AA. *T:* (020) 7219 4380.

GROOM, Maj.-Gen. John Patrick, CB 1984; CBE 1975 (MBE 1963); Director General, Guide Dogs for the Blind Association, 1983–89; *b* Hagley, Worcs, 9 March 1929; *s* of Samuel Douglas Groom and Gertrude Groom (*née* Clinton); *m* 1951, Jane Mary Miskelly; three *d. Educ:* King Charles I Sch., Kidderminster; Royal Military Academy, Sandhurst. Enlisted as Sapper, Dec. 1946; commnd into RE, 1949; regimental service, N Africa, Egypt, Singapore, Malaya, UK, 1949–59; sc Camberley, 1960; War Office, 1961–63; regimental service, UK, Aden, 1963–65 (despatches); Directing Staff, Staff Coll., 1965–68; Regimental Comdr, BAOR, 1968–70; MoD, Military Operations, 1970–71; Dep. Sec., Chiefs of Staff Cttee, 1971–73; HQ Near East Land Forces, Cyprus, 1973–75; RCDS 1976; Comdr, Corps of Royal Engineers, BAOR (Brig.), 1976–79; Chief Engineer, HQ BAOR, 1979–82; Head of Army Trng Rev. Team, MoD (Army), 1982–83. Col Comdt, 1983–91, Rep. Col Comdt, 1986, RE. Chairman: GDBA (Trading Co.) Ltd, 1984–89; GDBA (Recreational Services) Co. Ltd, 1986–89; (non-exec.) BKP Environmental Services Ltd, 1992–99; Dir, GDBA (Pension Fund Trustees) Ltd, 1985–89; Hon Vice-Pres., Internat. Fedn of Guide Dog Schs, 1989–. Chm., Reach Foundn, 1993–96; Member: Adv. Bd, Talking Newspapers, 1988; Council, Oakhaven Hospice, 1992–96. Governor: Gordon's Sch., Woking, 1982–88; Sandle Manor Sch., Fordingbridge, 1984–88. Vice-Chm., Solent Protection Soc., 1994–99; Chm., Adv. Bd, Yarmouth Harbour Comrs, 1997–; Member: RYA, 1982–; ASA, 1982–. FIMgt (FBIM 1979); FIPlantE 1976; Fellow, RSPB 1975. Freeman, City of London, 1978; Liveryman, Worshipful Co. of Plumbers, 1978–92. *Recreations:* ocean sailing, country pursuits, the environment. *Address:* Bridge End Cottage, Walhampton, Lymington, Hants SO41 5RD. *T:* (01590) 675710. *Clubs:* Royal Ocean Racing; Royal Engineer Yacht; Royal Lymington Yacht; British Kiel Yacht (Germany) (Life Mem.); Kieler Yacht (Germany) (Hon. Mem.).

GROOM, Michael John, FCA; President, Institute of Chartered Accountants in England and Wales, 2001–June 2002 (Deputy President, 2000–01); *b* 18 July 1942; *s* of Thomas Rowland Groom and Eliza Groom; *m* 1966, Sheila Mary Cartwright; two *d. Educ:* St Chad's Grammar Sch., Wolverhampton; Cotton Coll., N Staffs. FCA 1964. Articled, Plevey & Co., Chartered Accountants, 1958–63; Sen. Clerk, Dixon Hopkinson, Chartered Accountants, 1963–65; Sec. and Dir, Thorneville Properties Ltd/Aldridge Builders Ltd, 1965–67; Manager/Partner, Camp Ravenscroft & Co., Chartered Accountants, 1967–71; in practice as chartered accountant, 1971–76, 1981–89; Partner, Tansley Witt/Binder Hamlyn, Chartered Accountants, 1976–81. Non-exec. Dir of public cos; lectr and consultant on strategy formulation in the medium-sized business, the rôle of the non-exec. director, mgt and financial advice, professional practice mgt. Mem., Ct of Assistants, Chartered Accountants' Co. *Publications:* The Chartac Administration Manual, 1975; Financial Management in the Professional Office, 1977; (jtly) Cash Control in the Smaller Business, 1978; (jtly) Current Cost Accounting the Easy Way, 1980; Budgeting and Cash Management, 1981; joint author and series editor, 1975–81: The Chartac Accounting Manual; The Chartac Auditing Manual; The Chartac Taxation Manual; The Chartac Accounting and Auditing Model File. *Recreations:* ballet, theatre, music, photography, travel, food and wine. *Address:* 14 High Meadows, Compton, Wolverhampton WV6 8PH. *T:* and *Fax:* (01902) 759894. *Clubs:* Wolverhampton Lawn Tennis and Squash, Albert Lawn Tennis (Wolverhampton).

GROOM, Hon. Raymond John; MHA (L) for Denison, Tasmania, since 1986; Shadow Minister for Industrial Relations and for Workplace Standards, since 1998, for Public Sector Management, since 1999, for Consumer Affairs, for Justice and Shadow Attorney-General, since 2001; *b* 3 Sept. 1944; *s* of Raymond James Groom and Eileen Margaret (*née* Waters); *m* 1967, Gillian M. Crisp; four *s* two *d. Educ:* Burnie High Sch., Tasmania; Univ. of Melbourne (LLB 1967). Barrister and Solicitor, Supreme Court, Victoria, 1968, Tasmania, 1970; practised: Melbourne, 1968–69; Burnie, 1969–76; Partner, Hudson and Mann, Tasmania, 1969–76. Sec., Law Liby Cttee, NW Tasmania Law Soc., 1969–75; Mem. Council, Bar Assoc., Tasmania, 1974–75. MHR, Braddon, Tasmania, 1975–84; Federal Minister for: Envmt, Housing, Community Develt, 1977–78; Housing and Construction, 1978–80; Mem., Parly Delegn to Bangladesh, India, Sri Lanka, 1978; Leader, Australian Delegn to ESCAP UN Meeting, Manila (Chm., First Session), 1979; Chm., S Pacific Commonwealth and State Housing Ministers Conf., NZ, 1980; Tasmania: Minister for Forests, Sea Fisheries and Mines, and Minister Assisting the Premier, 1986–89; Dep. Premier, 1988; Dep. Leader, Liberal Party, 1986–91; Shadow Attorney-General and Shadow Minister for Deregulation, 1989–91; Leader of Opposition, Shadow Treas. and Shadow Minister for Commonwealth and State Relns, 1991–92; Premier of Tasmania, 1992–96; Treas. and Minister for Economic Develt, 1992–93; Minister for State Develt and Resources, for Forests, and for Mines, 1993–96; Attorney-General, Minister for Justice, Minister for Tourism and for Workplace Standards, 1996–98; Shadow Minister: for Justice and for Tourism, 1998–99; for Educn and Trng, 1999–2001. Chm., Australian Construction Industry Council, 1979–80. *Recreations:* family, painting, golf, football. *Address:* 25 Cromwell Street, Battery Point, Tas 7004, Australia. *T:* (3) 62248181; Parliament House, Hobart, Tas 7000, Australia. *T:* (3) 62332448. *Clubs:* Melbourne Cricket; Royal Hobart Golf; Royal Yacht (Tasmania).

GROOTENHUIS, Prof. Peter, FREng, FIMechE; Professor of Mechanical Engineering Science, Imperial College of Science, Technology and Medicine, 1972–89, now Emeritus Professor and Senior Research Fellow; *b* 31 July 1924; *yr s* of Johannes C. Grootenhuis and Anna C. (*née* van den Bergh); *m* 1954, Sara J. Winchester, *o c* of late Major Charles C. Winchester, MC, The Royal Scots (The Royal Regt), and Margaret I. (*née* de Havilland); one *d* one *s. Educ:* Nederlands Lyceum, The Hague; City and Guilds College. BSc MechEng 1944, PhD, DIC, DSc London Univ.; Apprenticeship and Design Office, Bristol Aero Engine Co., 1944–46; Lectr 1949, Reader 1959, Mech. Eng. Dept, Imperial College, research in heat transfer and in dynamics; Dir, Derritron Electronics, 1969–82; Partner, Grootenhuis Allaway Associates, consultants in noise and vibration, 1970–93; Associate Mem., Ordnance Board, 1965–70; Mem. Governing Body, Imperial College, 1974–79. FCGI 1976, Mem., Inst. of Acoustics; Fellow, Soc. of Environmental Engineers (Pres., 1964–67); FREng (FEng 1982). *Publications:* technical papers to learned jls, and patents. *Recreations:* sailing, gardening. *Club:* Athenæum.

GROSBERG, Prof. Percy, PhD; CEng, MIMechE, FTI; Research Professor of Textile Engineering, 1961–90, and Head of Department of Textile Industries, 1975–83 and 1987–89, University of Leeds, now Emeritus Professor; Marcus Sieff Professor of Textile Technology, Shenkar College of Engineering and Design (formerly of Textile Technology and Fashion), Ramat Gan, Israel, since 1991; *b* 5 April 1925; *s* of late Rev. and Mrs Gershon Grosberg, Tel-Aviv; *m* 1951, Queenie Fisch; one *s* one *d* (and one *s* decd). *Educ:* Parktown Boys' High Sch., Johannesburg; Univ. of the Witwatersrand; University of Leeds. BScEng, MScEng, PhD Witwatersrand; CEng, MIMechE 1965; FTI 1966 (Hon. FTI 1988). Sen. Res. Officer S African Wool Textile Res. Inst., 1949–55; University of Leeds: ICI Res. Fellow, 1955; Lectr in Textile Engrg, 1955–61. Hon. Fellow, Shenkar Coll. of Textile Technology and Fashion, Israel, 1993. Warner Memorial Medal, 1968; Textile Inst. Medal, 1972; Distinguished Service Award, Indian Inst. of Technol., Delhi, 1985. *Publications:* An Introduction to Textile Mechanisms, 1968; Structural Mechanics of Fibres, Yarns and Fabrics, 1969; Yarn Production: theoretical aspects, 1999; papers on rheology of fibrous assemblies, mechan. processing of fibres, and other res. topics in Jl of Textile Inst., Textile Res. Jl, and other sci. jls. *Recreations:* music, travel. *Address:* Apartment 25, 55 Shlomo Hamelech Street, Netanya 42267, Israel. *T:* (9) 8628652.

GROSE, Vice-Adm. Sir Alan, KBE 1989; Group Executive, Security, De Beers Consolidated Mines Ltd, 1993–2000; *b* 24 Sept. 1937; *s* of George William Stanley Grose and Ann May Grose (*née* Stanford); *m* 1961, Gillian Ann (*née* Dryden-Dymond); two *s* one *d*. *Educ:* Strodes School; Britannia Royal Naval College, Dartmouth. Served: Mediterranean and S Atlantic, 1957–63; sub-specialised in Navigation, 1964; RAN, 1964–66; Home, W Indies, Med., 1966–72; Comd, HMS Eskimo, 1973–75; Staff of C-in-C, Naval Home Command, 1975–77; MoD, 1977–79; RCDS 1980; Comd, HMS Bristol, 1981–82; RN Presentation Team, 1983–84; Comd, HMS Illustrious, 1984–86; Flag Officer, Sept. 1986; ACDS, Operational Requirements (Sea Systems), MoD, 1986–88; Flag Officer Flotilla Three and Comdr, Anti-Submarine Warfare Striking Force, 1988–90; Flag Officer Plymouth, Naval Base Comdr Devonport, Comdr Central Sub Area Eastern Atlantic, and Comdr Plymouth Sub Area Channel, 1990–92, retired. *Recreations:* genealogy, game-viewing. *Address:* c/o Barclays Bank, Princess Street, Plymouth PL1 2HA; *e-mail:* sagrose@mweb.co.za. *Club:* Kimberley.

GROSS, John Jacob; writer and editor; theatre critic, Sunday Telegraph, since 1989; *b* 12 March 1935; *s* of late Abraham Gross and Muriel Gross; *m* 1965, Miriam May (*see* M. M. Gross) (marr. diss. 1988); one *s* one *d*. *Educ:* City of London Sch.; Wadham Coll., Oxford. Editor, Victor Gollancz Ltd, 1956–58; Asst Lectr, Queen Mary Coll., Univ. of London, 1959–62; Fellow, King's Coll., Cambridge, 1962–65; Literary Editor, New Statesman, 1973; Editor, TLS, 1974–81; editorial consultant, Weidenfeld (Publishers) Ltd, 1982; on staff of New York Times, 1983–88; Dir, Times Newspapers Holdings, 1982. A Trustee, National Portrait Gall., 1977–84. Hon. DHL Adelphi Univ., 1995. *Publications:* The Rise and Fall of the Man of Letters (1969 Duff Cooper Memorial Prize), 1969; Joyce, 1971; (ed) The Oxford Book of Aphorisms, 1983; (ed) The Oxford Book of Essays, 1991; Shylock, 1992; (ed) The Modern Movement, 1992; (ed) The Oxford Book of Comic Verse, 1994; (ed) The New Oxford Book of English Prose, 1998; A Double Thread, 2001. *Address:* 74 Princess Court, Queensway, W2 4RE. *Club:* Beefsteak.

GROSS, Miriam Marianna, (Lady Owen); Literary Editor, Sunday Telegraph, since 1991; *b* 12 May 1939; *d* of late Kurt May and of Wera May; *m* 1st, 1965, John Gross (marr. diss. 1988); one *s* one *d*; 2nd, 1993, Sir Geoffrey Owen, *qv*. *Educ:* Dartington Hall Sch.; St Anne's Coll., Oxford (MA). Observer: Dep. Lit. Editor, 1969–81; Woman's Editor, 1981–84; Arts Editor, Daily Telegraph, 1986–91. Editor, Book Choice, Channel Four TV, 1986–91. *Publications:* (ed) The World of George Orwell, 1971; (ed) The World of Raymond Chandler, 1976. *Recreations:* painting, upholstering. *Address:* 24A St Petersburgh Place, W2 4LB. *T:* (020) 7538 7191.

GROSS, Hon. Sir Peter Henry, Kt 2001; **Hon. Mr Justice Gross;** a Judge of the High Court, Queen's Bench Division, since 2001; *b* 13 Feb. 1952; *s* of late Sam Lewis Gross and of Fanny Alice Gross; *m* 1985, Ruth Mary Cullen; two *s*. *Educ:* Herzlia Sch., Cape Town; Univ. of Cape Town (BBusSc, MBusSc); Oriel Coll., Oxford (Rhodes Scholar, MA, BCL, Eldon Scholar). Called to the Bar, Gray's Inn, 1977, Bencher, 2000; admitted to the Bar of NSW, 1986; QC 1992; a Recorder, 1995–2001. Chairman: London Common Law and Commercial Bar Assoc., 1995–97; Bar Educn and Trng Cttee, 1998–2000; Bar Internat. Relations Cttee, 2001. *Publication:* Legal Aid and its Management, 1976. *Recreations:* jogging, cricket, sailing. *Address:* Royal Courts of Justice, Strand, WC2A 2LL. *Club:* Oxford and Cambridge.

GROSS, Solomon Joseph, CMG 1966; *b* 3 Sept. 1920; *s* of late Abraham Gross; *m* 1948, Doris Evelyn Barker (*d* 2000); two *d*. *Educ:* Hackney Downs Sch.; University Coll., London. RAF, Burma, India. Ministry of Supply, 1947; OEEC, Paris, 1948–51; British Embassy, Washington, 1951–53; Board of Trade, 1954–57; British Trade Commr, Pretoria, SA, 1958–62; Principal British Trade Commr, Ghana, 1963–66; British Deputy High Commr, Ghana, 1966–67; Board of Trade, 1967–69; Minister, British Embassy, Pretoria, 1969–73; Chargé d'Affaires at various times in Ghana and S Africa; Under-Sec., Dept of Industry, 1974–80; Dir for Regional Affairs, British Technology Gp, 1983–84. Bd Mem., BSC, later British Steel plc, 1978–90; Dir, Technical Audit Group Ltd, 1986–90. Mem., Overseas Cttee, CBI, 1987–90; Mem., External Relations Cttee and Chm., USA Wkg Pty, UNICE, Brussels, 1987–90. *Recreations:* gardening, history, do-it-yourself. *Address:* 38 Barnes Court, Station Road, New Barnet, Herts EN5 1QY. *T:* (020) 8449 2710. *Club:* Royal Automobile.

GROSSART, Sir Angus (McFarlane McLeod), Kt 1997; CBE 1990; DL; Managing Director, since 1969, and Chairman, Noble Grossart Ltd, Merchant Bankers, Edinburgh, since 1990; Chairman, Scottish Investment Trust PLC, since 1975; merchant banker; *b* 6 April 1937; 3rd *s* of William John White Grossart and Mary Hay Gardiner; *m* 1978, Mrs Gay Thomson; one *d*. *Educ:* Glasgow Acad.; Glasgow Univ. (MA 1958, LLB 1960). CA 1962; Mem., Faculty of Advocates, 1963. Practised at Scottish Bar, 1963–69. Major directorships include: Edinburgh US Tracker Trust, 1973–; Royal Bank of Scotland plc, 1982– (Vice Chm., 1996–); Scottish Financial Enterprise, 1987–; British Petroleum Scottish Bd, 1990–; Trinity Mirror (formerly Mirror Gp) PLC, 1998–; Scottish & Newcastle plc, 1998–; Chm., Scotland Internat., 1997–; Dep. Chm., Edinburgh Fund Managers PLC, 1991– (Chm., 1983–91). Mem., Scottish Develt Agency, 1974–78; Dir, St Andrews Management Inst., 1990–97 (Chm. Adv. Council, 1994–97). Chm., Bd of Trustees, National Galleries of Scotland, 1988–97 (Trustee, 1986–97); Trustee and Dep. Chm., Nat. Heritage Meml Fund, 1999–; Vice Pres., Scottish Opera, 1986–93; Director: Edinburgh Internat. Film Festival, 1994–96; Friends of Royal Scottish Acad., 1989–97; Chm., Fine Art Soc., 1998–. Formerly: Trustee, Scottish Civic Trust; Dir, Scottish Nat. Orch.; Mem., Scottish Industrial Develt Adv. Bd. FRSE 1998. DL Edinburgh, 1996. Livingstone Captain of Industry Award, 1990. Hon. LLD Glasgow, 1985; Hon. DBA Strathclyde, 1998. Lord Provost of Glasgow Award for public service, 1994. Formerly, Scottish Editor, British Tax Encyc., and British Tax Rev. *Recreations:* golfing (runner-up, British Youths' Golf Championship, 1957; Captain, Scottish Youths Internat., 1956 and 1957), the applied and decorative arts, Scottish castle restoration. *Address:* 48 Queen Street, Edinburgh EH2 3NR. *T:* (0131) 226 7011. *Clubs:* New, Honourable Company of Edinburgh Golfers (Edinburgh); Royal and Ancient (St Andrews).

GROSSMAN, Loyd Daniel Gilman; broadcaster, writer; Chairman, Campaign for Museums, since 1995; *b* Boston, Mass, 16 Sept. 1950; *s* of late David K. Grossman and Helen Katherine Grossman (*née* Gilman); *m* 1985, Hon. Deborah Jane, *d* of Baron Puttnam, *qv*; two *d*. *Educ:* Marblehead High Sch.; Boston Univ. (BA *cum laude*); London School of Economics (MSc Econ.). Design Editor, Harpers and Queen, 1981–84; Contributing Editor, The Sunday Times, 1984–86. *Television* includes: deviser or writer or presenter: Through the Keyhole, 1983–; Behind the Headlines; Masterchef, 1990–2000 (Glenfiddich Award, 1996); The Dog's Tale, 1993; Junior Masterchef, 1995–99; Off Your Trolley, 1995; Conspicuous Consumption, 1996; The World on a Plate, 1997; Loyd on Location, 2000–. Member: Museums and Galleries Commn, 1996–2000; Bd, mda (formerly Museum Documentation Assoc.), 1998–2001; Re:source (formerly Museums, Libraries and Archives Council), 1999–; Commissioner: English Heritage, 1997– (Chairman: Mus and Collections Adv. Cttee. 1997–2001; Chm., Nat. Blue Plaques Panel; Mus and Archives Panel, 2001–; Mem., Archives, Libraries and Info. Adv. Cttee; Mem., Urban Panel); Royal Commn on Histl Monuments of England, 1999–; Chm., Museums and Galleries Month 2000; Co-Chm., Mus and Galls Month 2001; Chairman: Public Monuments and Sculpture Assoc., 2001–; The 24 Hour Mus., 2001–. Member: Cttee, British Liby of Pol and Econ. Sci.; NW Regl Cultural Consortium, 2000–. Trustee, Mus. of Sci. and Industry in Manchester. Mem., Court of Govs, LSE, 1996–. Chm., Conservation Awards, 1998–. Vice-Pres., Sick Children's Trust; Patron: Nat. Canine Defence League (Hon. Life Mem.); Scuba Trust; Latymer Disabled Sub Aqua Club; Nat. Eczema Soc.; Assoc. for Heritage Interpretation. FRSA; FSAScot. *Publications:* The Social History of Rock Music, 1975; Harpers and Queen Guide to London's 100 Best Restaurants, 1987; The Dog's Tale, 1993; Loyd Grossman's Italian Journey, 1994; (ed) Courvoisier's Book of the Best, 1994–96; The World on a Plate, 1997; The 125 Best Recipes Ever, 1998; articles on architecture, design and food in newspapers and magazines. *Recreations:* fishing, scuba diving, looking at buildings, tennis, chess, the Boston Red Sox. *Address:* Campaign for Museums, 35–37 Grosvenor Gardens, SW1W 0BX. *T:* (020) 7233 9796, *Fax:* (020) 7233 6770. *Clubs:* Flyfishers', Hurlingham, Chelsea Arts.

GROSVELD, Prof. Franklin Gerardus, (Frank), PhD; FRS 1991; Professor and Head of Department of Cell Biology and Genetics, Erasmus University, Rotterdam, since 1993; *b* 18 Aug. 1948; *m*; two *s*. *Educ:* Univ. of Amsterdam (MSc); McGill Univ. (PhD). Sen. Scientist, NIMR, 1982–93. *Publications:* papers on human globin genes. *Address:* Department of Cell Biology and Genetics, Faculty of Medicine, Erasmus University, Rotterdam, PO Box 1738, 3000 DR Rotterdam, The Netherlands.

GROSVENOR, family name of **Earl of Wilton** and of **Duke of Westminster**.

GROSVENOR, Earl; Hugh Richard Louis Grosvenor; *b* 29 Jan. 1991; *o s* and *heir* of Duke of Westminster, *qv*.

GROSZ, Stephen Ernest; Partner, Bindman & Partners, solicitors, since 1981; *b* 14 April 1953; *s* of Emil, (Joe), Grosz and Therese Grosz (*née* Baer); *m* 1981, Judith Beale (marr. diss. 1995). *Educ:* William Ellis Sch.; Clare Coll., Cambridge (BA 1974); Université Libre de Bruxelles (licencié special en droit européen 1976). Joined Bindman & Partners, 1976. Significant cases include: Marshall *v* Southampton & SW Hants AHA, instrumental in changing UK law on equal rights for retirement age and for compensation for discrimination; R *v* Sec. of State for Foreign & Commonwealth Affairs ex parte World Develt Movt, in which the High Court declared unlawful aid for construction of the Pergau Dam in Malaysia; R *v* Lord Chancellor ex parte Witham, quashing changes to court fees as contrary to constitutional rights of access to the courts; R *v* MoD ex parte Lustig-Prean and Lustig-Prean & others *v* UK, concerning the rights of homosexuals & lesbians to serve in the armed forces; Abdulaziz & others *v* UK, instrumental in removing sex discrimination from the immigration rules; Silver & others *v* UK, instrumental in removing restrictions on prisoners' rights to respect for correspondence; Sutherland *v* UK, in which the European Commission of Human Rights ruled unlawful discrimination in the age of consent for gay men; R *v* Sec. of State for Home Dept, ex parte Amnesty Internat. & others, concerning disclosure of med. reports relating to extradition of Augusto Pinochet. Gov., British Inst. of Human Rights, 1992–; Member: Mgt Cttee, Public Law Project, 1991–; Council, Justice, 1997–; Council, Liberty, 2001–; Member Advisory Board: Judicial Review Qly, 1996–; Educn, Public Law and the Individual, 1996–. Mem., Editl Bd, Civil Procedure. *Publications:* (jtly) Human Rights: the 1998 Act and the European Convention, 2000; *contributions to:* Public Interest Law, 1986; Atkin's Court Forms, 1987; Public Interest Perspectives in Environmental Law, 1995; articles and reviews in newspapers and legal jls. *Recreations:* cycling, walking, choral singing, eating and drinking, trying to make people laugh. *Address:* (office) 275 Gray's Inn Road, WC1X 8QF. *T:* (020) 7833 4433.

GROTRIAN, Sir Philip Christian Brent, 3rd Bt *cr* 1934; *b* 26 March 1935; *s* of Robert Philip Brent Grotrian (*d* on active service, 1945) (*y s* of 1st Bt), and Elizabeth Mary, *d* of Major Herbert Hardy-Wrigley; *S* uncle, 1984; *m* 1st, 1960, Anne Isabel, *d* of Robert Sieger Whyte, Toronto; one *s*; 2nd, 1979, Sarah Frances, *d* of Reginald Harry Gale, Montreal; one *s* one *d*. *Educ:* Eton; Trinity Coll., Toronto. *Heir: s* Philip Timothy Adam Brent Grotrian, *b* 9 April 1962. *Address:* RR3, Mansfield, ON LON 1MO, Canada; Calle Ample 2, Regencós, Gerona, Spain.

GROUES, Henri Antoine; *see* Pierre, Abbé.

GROUND, (Reginald) Patrick; QC 1981; *b* 9 Aug. 1932; *s* of late Reginald Ground and Ivy Elizabeth Grace Ground (*née* Irving); *m* 1964, Caroline Dugdale; three *s* one *d*. *Educ:* Beckenham and Penge County Grammar Sch.; Lycée Gay Lussac, Limoges, France; Selwyn Coll., Cambridge (Open Exhibnr; MA Mod. Langs, French and Spanish); Magdalen Coll., Oxford (MLitt, Mod. History). Inner Temple Studentship and Foster Boulton Prize, 1958; called to the Bar, Inner Temple, 1960, Bencher, 1987. National Service, RN, 1954–56: Sub-Lt RNVR; served in Mediterranean Fleet and on staff of C-in-C Mediterranean; rep. RN at hockey and lawn tennis; Lt-Comdr RNR. Worked for FO on staff of Wilton Park European Conf. Centre, 1958–60. Councillor, London Bor. of Hammersmith, 1968–71 (Chm., Cttees responsible for health and social services, 1969–71). Contested (C): Hounslow, Feltham and Heston, Feb. and Oct. 1974, and 1979; Feltham and Heston, 1992 and 1997. MP (C) Feltham and Heston, 1983–92. PPS to the Solicitor General, 1987–92. Treasurer and Pres., Oxford Univ. Cons. Assoc., 1958; Chm., Fulham Soc., 1975–96. *Publications:* articles on housing, security of tenure and paying for justice. *Recreations:* lawn tennis, theatre, sailing, travel, forestry. *Address:* 13 Ranelagh Avenue, SW6 3PJ. *T:* (020) 7736 0131. *Clubs:* Brooks's, Carlton.

GROVE, Dr Andrew Steven; Chairman, Intel Corporation, since 1998 (President, since 1979, Chief Executive Officer, 1987–98); *b* Budapest, 2 Sept. 1936; *m* 1958, Eva; two *d*. *Educ:* City Coll. of NY (BSc Chem. Engrg); Univ. of Calif, Berkeley (PhD Chem. Engrg). FIEEE. Asst Dir of R&D, Fairchild Semiconductor, 1967–68; joined Intel, 1968. Mem., Nat. Acad. of Engrg. Fellow, Amer. Acad. of Arts & Scis, 1994. Hon. DEng Worcester. Engrg Leadership Recognition Award, 1987; Heinz Foundn Award for Technol. and the Econ., 1995; Time Man of the Year, 1997; IEEE 2000 Medal of Honour, 1998. *Publications:* Physics and Technology of Semiconductor Devices, 1967; High Output Management, 1983; One-on-One With Andy Grove, 1987; Only the Paranoid Survive, 1996. *Address:* Intel Corporation, 2200 Mission College Boulevard, Santa Clara, CA 95052–8119, USA.

GROVE, Sir Charles Gerald, 5th Bt *cr* 1874; *b* 10 Dec. 1929; *s* of Walter Peel Grove (*d* 1944) (3rd *s* of 2nd Bt) and Elena Rebecca, *d* of late Felipe Crosthwaite; *S* brother, 1974. *Heir: b* Harold Thomas Grove, *b* 6 Dec. 1930.

GROVE, Maj.-Gen. David Anthony, OBE 1985; DL; retired, 1993; *b* 26 Aug. 1941; *s* of Lancelot Townley Grove and Joan Blanche Grove (*née* Hill); *m* 1971, Olivia Mary Crook; one *s* one *d*. *Educ:* Charterhouse Sch.; Univ. of Alberta (BSc Hons Physics). psc† 1974, RCDS 1988. Commissioned Royal Engineers, 1965; served BAOR, 1965–68; UKLF, 1969–70; Instructor, RSME, 1971–72; Staff College; DAA&QMG, 24 Airportable Bde, 1975–76; BAOR, 1977–78; Instructor, Staff College, 1983; MA to VCGS, 1983–84; ASD, 1985; Comdt, RSME, 1986–87; Dep. Mil. Sec. (A), 1989–90;

DGPS (Army), 1991–92; led Study into Future Career Structures for Army Officers and Soldiers, 1992–93. Col Comdt, RE, 1995–. Chm., RE Assoc., 1997–2000. Trustee, Haig Homes, 1998–. Comr, Duke of York's Royal Mil. Sch., 1998– (Chm. of Comrs, 2000–). Chm., Stelling Minnis Parish Council, 1999–. Churchwarden, St Mary's, Stelling, 1999–. DL Kent, 2001. *Recreations:* golf, gardening, ski-ing. *Club:* Army and Navy.

GROVE, Dennis; *see* Grove, W. D.

GROVE, Sir Edmund (Frank), KCVO 1982 (CVO 1974; LVO 1963; MVO 1953); Chief Accountant of the Privy Purse, 1967–82, and Serjeant-at-Arms, 1975–82, retired; *b* 20 July 1920; *s* of Edmund Grove and Sarah Caroline (*née* Hunt); *m* 1945, Grete Elisabet, *d* of Martinus Skou, Denmark; two *d.* Served War, RASC, ME, 1940–46 (C-in-C's Commendation). Entered the Household of King George VI, 1946 and of Queen Elizabeth II, 1952. Chevalier: Order of the Dannebrog, Denmark, 1974; Légion d'Honneur, France, 1976; Officer, Order of the Polar Star, Sweden, 1975. *Recreation:* gardening. *Address:* Chapel Cottage, West Newton, King's Lynn, Norfolk PE31 6AU.

GROVE, Rear-Adm. John Scott, CB 1984; OBE 1964; RN retired, 1985; nuclear engineering consultant to Ministry of Defence, 1985–99; *b* 7 July 1927; *s* of late William George Grove and Frances Margaret Scott Grove; *m* 1950, Betty Anne (*née* Robinson); one *s* (one *d* decd). *Educ:* Dundee High Sch.; St Andrews Univ. University Coll., 1944–47 (BScEng 1st Cl. Hons). National Service, Royal Engineers, 1947–48; Instructor Br., Royal Navy, 1948–50; Electrical Engrg Br., RN, 1950, qualified in Submarines, 1953; post graduate trng in Nuclear Engrg, Imperial Coll., London, 1958–59; sea service in HMS Forth and HM Submarines Tally-Ho, Turpin (FO Subs' Commendation, special op., 1955), Porpoise, Dreadnought (1st Sen. Engrg Officer, RN first nuclear sub., 1960–64); service in Ship Dept, 1964–67; staff of Flag Officer Submarines, 1967–70; Naval Asst to Controller of the Navy, 1970–73; staff of Flag Officer Submarines, 1975–77; commanded HMS Fisgard, 1977–79; Chief Strategic Systems Exec. (formerly Chief Polaris Exec.), 1980–85; Chief Naval Engr Officer, 1983–85. Comdr 1963; Captain 1970; Rear-Adm. 1980. Dir, Devonport Mgt Ltd, Devonport Royal Dockyard, 1987–91; engrng consultant 1991–98. Gov., British Maritime Technol. (Quality Assurance), 1990–94. Chm., Friends of RN Mus. and HMS Victory, 1995–99. Master, Engineers' Co., 1994–95 (Sen. Warden, 1993–94). *Recreations:* walking, gardening. *Address:* Maryfield, South Close, Wade Court, Havant, Hants PO9 2TD. *T:* (023) 9247 5116. *Club:* Army and Navy.

GROVE, Trevor Charles; JP; editorial consultant and writer; *b* 1 Jan. 1945; *s* of Ronald and Lesley Grove; *m* 1975, Valerie Jenkins (*see* V. Grove); one *s* three *d. Educ:* St George's, Buenos Aires; Radley; St Edmund Hall, Oxford. Editorial Staff, Spectator, 1967–70; Leader Writer, then Features Editor, Evening Standard, 1970–78; Asst Editor, Sunday Telegraph, 1978–80; Sen. Asst Editor, Observer, 1980–83; Editor, Observer Magazine, 1983–86; Asst Editor, Daily Telegraph, 1986–89; Editor, Sunday Telegraph, 1989–92; Gp Exec. Ed. and Dep. Ed., Daily Telegraph, 1992–94. Launch Editor, El Periódico de Tucumán, Argentina, 1994. JP Haringey, 1999. *Publications:* (co-ed) Singlehanded, 1984; (ed) The Queen Observed, 1986; The Juryman's Tale, 1998. *Recreations:* tennis, feeding the family, walking the dog. *Address:* 14 Avenue Road, Highgate, N6 5DW. *T:* (020) 8348 2621.

GROVE, Valerie; feature writer, The Times, since 1992; *b* 11 May 1946; *d* of Doug Smith, cartoonist; *m* 1st, 1968, David Brynmor Jenkins (marr. diss. 1975); 2nd, 1975, Trevor Charles Grove, *qv*; one *s* three *d. Educ:* South Shields Grammar Sch.; Kingsbury County Grammar Sch.; Girton Coll., Cambridge (MA 1969). Evening Standard, 1968–87; Sunday Times, 1987–92. *Publications:* (as Valerie Jenkins) Where I Was Young, 1976; (as Valerie Grove): The Compleat Woman, 1987; Dear Dodie: the life of Dodie Smith, 1996; Laurie Lee: the well-loved stranger, 1999. *Recreations:* tennis, archives, walking Dalmatian. *Address:* 14 Avenue Road, Highgate, N6 5DW. *T:* (020) 8348 2621; *e-mail:* vgrove@dircon.co.uk.

GROVE, (William) Dennis; Chairman, North West Water Group, 1989–93; *b* 23 July 1927; *s* of late William Grove and Elizabeth Charlotte Grove (*née* Bradley); *m* 1953, Audrey Irma Saxel; one *s* one *d. Educ:* Gowerton School; King's College, London (BSc). Joined Dunlop Group, 1951, subseq. Overseas Gen. Manager, to 1970; Chm. and Chief Exec., TPT, 1970–85; Vice-Pres., Sonoco International, 1978–85; Chm., NW Water Authy, 1985–89. *Recreations:* sports bystander, travel, golf. *Address:* Alderley Edge, Cheshire SK9 7XD. *Club:* Bramall Park Golf.

GROVE-WHITE, Prof. Robin Bernard; Professor of Environment and Society, since 2000, and Director of Centre for Study of Environmental Change, since 1991, Lancaster University; *b* 17 Feb. 1941; *s* of Charles William Grove-White and Cecile Mary Rabbidge; *m* 1st, 1970, Virginia Harriet Ironside (marr. diss.); one *s*; 2nd, 1979, Helen Elizabeth Smith; two *s* one *d. Educ:* Uppingham Sch.; Worcester Coll., Oxford (BA). Freelance writer for TV, radio, press and advertising in UK, Canada and US, 1963–70; McCann-Erickson Ltd, London, 1970; Asst Secretary, 1972–80, Dir, 1981–87, CPRE; Res. Fellow, Centre for Envmtl Technol., Imperial Coll., London, 1987–89; Sen. Res. Fellow, Lancaster Univ., 1989–91. Member: Forestry Commn, 1991–98; Agric. and Envmt Biotechnology Commn, 2000–. Chm., Greenpeace UK, 1997–. *Publications:* (contrib.) Politics of Physical Resources, 1975; (contrib.) Future Landscapes, 1976; (with Michael Flood) Nuclear Prospects, 1976; contribs to New Scientist, Nature, Times, Independent, etc. *Recreations:* walking, cricket. *Address:* Conder Mill Cottage, Quernmore, Lancaster LA2 9EE. *T:* (01524) 382501.

GROVER, Derek James Langlands, CB 1999; Director, Adult Learning Group (formerly Skills and Lifelong Learning), Department for Education and Skills (formerly Department for Education and Employment), since 1998; *b* 26 Jan. 1949; *s* of Donald James Grover and late Mary Barbara Grover; *m* 1972, Mary Katherine Morgan; one *s. Educ:* Hove County Grammar Sch. for Boys; Clare Coll., Cambridge (Foundn Schol. 1970; BA Eng. Lit. 1971, MA 1975; Grene Prize 1971). Various positions, Dept. of Employment, 1971–78; Cabinet Office, 1978–80; MSC, 1980–87; Training Agency: Head of Personnel, 1987–89; Dir of Youth Training, 1989; Dir of Systems and Strategy, 1989; Dir of Trng Strategy and Standards, later of Trng Strategy and Infrastructure, 1990–94; Dep. Chief Exec. and Sen. Dir of Operations, Employment Service, 1994–97; Dir of Employment and Adult Trg, DFEE, 1997–98. FRSA 1991. MIPD (MIPM 1993). *Recreations:* music, reading, walking, watching cricket. *Address:* c/o Department for Education and Skills, Moorfoot, Sheffield S1 4PQ. *T:* (0114) 259 3969.

GROVES, John Dudley, CB 1981; OBE 1964; Director-General, Central Office of Information, 1979–82; Head of Profession for Government Information Officer Group, 1981–82; *b* 12 Aug. 1922; *y s* of late Walter Groves; *m* 1943, Pamela Joy Holliday; one *s* two *d. Educ:* St Paul's Sch. Reporter, Richmond Herald, 1940–41; Queen's Royal Regt, 1941–42; commnd in 43rd Reconnaissance Regt, 1942; served in NW Europe, 1944–45 (despatches); Observer Officer, Berlin, 1945; Press Association (Press Gallery), 1947–51; Times (Press Gallery and Lobby), 1951–58; Head of Press Sect., Treasury, 1958–62; Dep. Public Relations Adviser to Prime Minister, 1962–64 (Actg Adviser, 1964); Chief Information Officer, DEA, 1964–68; Chief of Public Relations, MoD, 1968–77; Dir of Information, DHSS, 1977–78. Mem., Working Party on Censorship, 1983. *Publication:* (with R. Gill) Club Route, 1945. *Recreations:* walking, painting. *Address:* Mortimers, Manningford Bohune, Pewsey, Wilts SN9 5PG.

GROVES, His Honour Richard Bebb, TD 1966; RD 1979; a Circuit Judge, 1985–2000; *b* 4 Oct. 1933; *s* of George Thomas Groves and Margaret Anne (*née* Bebb); *m* 1958, Eileen Patricia (*née* Farley); one *s* one *d. Educ:* Bancroft's Sch., Woodford Green, Essex. Admitted Solicitor of the Supreme Court, 1960. Partner, H. J. Smith & Co. and Richard Groves & Co., 1962–85. Dep. Circuit Judge, 1978–80; a Recorder, 1980–85. Nijmegen Medal, Royal Netherlands League for Physical Culture, 1965 and 1966. *Recreations:* Royal Naval Reserve, tennis, philately, walking, reading. *Clubs:* Royal Automobile; Chelmsford (Chelmsford).

GROVES, Ronald Edward, CBE 1972; Chairman, 1982–87, and Managing Director, 1984–86, Meyer International plc (following merger of International Timber with Montague L. Meyer in 1982); *b* 2 March 1920; *s* of Joseph Rupert and Eva Lilian Groves; *m* 1940, Beryl Doris Lydia Collins (*d* 2000); two *s* one *d. Educ:* Watford Grammar School. Joined J. Gliksten & Son Ltd; served War of 1939–45, Flt-Lt RAF, subseq. Captain with BOAC; re-joined J. Gliksten & Son Ltd, 1946: Gen. Works Man. 1947; Dir 1954; Jt Man. Dir 1964; Vice-Chm. 1967; Dir, Gliksten (West Africa) Ltd, 1949; Vice-Chm., International Timber Corp. Ltd, 1970 (name of J. Gliksten & Son Ltd changed to International Timber Corp. Ltd, 1970 following merger with Horsley Smith & Jewson Ltd); Chief Exec., 1973, Chm., 1976, Internat. Timber. Dir, Nat. Building Agency, 1978–82; Mem., EDC for Building, 1982–86; President: National Council of Building Material Producers, 1987–90 (Mem., Cttee of Management, 1982–94); Timber Trade Fedn of UK, 1969–71; London and District Sawmill Owners Assoc., 1954–56; Timber Res. and Develt Assoc., 1990–; Chm., Nat. Sawmilling Assoc., 1966–67; Mem., London and Regional Affairs Cttee, 1980–95, and Mem. Council, 1982–95, London Chamber of Commerce and Industry; Mem., London Regl Council, CBI, 1983–87; Dir, Business in the Community, 1984–87. Chairman: Rickmansworth UDC, 1957–58, 1964–65 and 1971–72 (Mem., 1951–74); W Herts Main Drainage Authority, 1970–74; Three Rivers District Council, 1977–78 (Mem., 1974–96); Mem., Herts CC, 1964–74. Pres., SW Herts Conservative Assoc., 2000–. Chairman of Governors: Watford Grammar Sch. for Girls, 1980–98; Watford Grammar Sch. for Boys, 1980–98. *Recreations:* visiting theatre and opera; local community work. *Address:* 8 Pembroke Road, Moor Park, Northwood, Mddx HA6 2HR. *T:* (01923) 823187.

GRUBB, Prof. Andrew, LLD; Professor of Medical Law, since 1998, and Head of Department, since 1999, Cardiff Law School, Cardiff University; *b* 24 March 1958; *s* of late Graham Grubb and of Valerie Grubb; *m* 1988, Helga Anne Moore; two *s* one *d. Educ:* Brynmawr Comprehensive Sch.; Selwyn Coll., Cambridge (BA 1st Cl. Hons 1979; MA 1983); LLD London 1998. Called to the Bar, Inner Temple, 1980 (Scarman Schol., 1980; Certificate of Honour 1980). Cambridge University: Law Fellow, Fitzwilliam Coll., 1981–90; Asst Univ. Lectr, 1984–89, Univ. Lectr, 1989–90, in Law; King's College, London: Sen. Lectr in Law, 1990–92; Reader in Med. Law, 1992–94; Prof. of Health Care Law, 1994–98; acting Dir, 1992–93, Dir, 1993–97, Centre of Med. Law and Ethics. Visiting Professor of Law: Boston Univ. Sch. of Law, 1989; Univ. of New Mexico Sch. of Law, 1989. Member: Ethical Cttee, RCP, 1994–; HFEA, 1997–; pt-time Immigration Adjudicator, 1996–; pt-time Special Adjudicator, 1997–; Chm., Indep. Review Panel (NHS Complaints), Wales, 1998–99. Vice Pres., Wales Medico-Legal Soc., 2000–. Founder FMedSci 1998. Editor, Medical Law Review, 1993–. *Publications:* (with I. Kennedy) Medical Law: cases and materials, 1989, rev. edn, Medical Law: text with materials, 1994, 3rd edn 2000; (with D. Pearl) Blood Testing, AIDS and DNA Profiling: law and policy, 1990; (jtly) Doctors' Views on the Management and Care of Patients in Persistent Vegetative State: a UK study, 1997; (ed with I. Kennedy) Principles of Medical Law, 1998. *Recreations:* music and music trivia, theatre, science fiction, the Welsh countryside, Welsh Rugby. *Address:* Cardiff Law School, Cardiff University, PO Box 427, Cardiff CF10 3XJ. *T:* (029) 2087 4177.

GRUBB, Prof. Peter John, PhD, ScD; Professor of Investigative Plant Ecology, Cambridge University, 2000–01, now Emeritus; Fellow, Magdalene College, Cambridge, 1960–2001 now Emeritus (President, 1991–96); *b* 9 Aug. 1935; *s* of Harold Amos Grubb and Phyllis Gertrude (*née* Hook); *m* 1965, Elizabeth Adelaide Anne, *d* of Charles Edward and Adelaide Gertrude Hall; one *s* one *d. Educ:* Royal Liberty Sch.; Magdalene Coll., Cambridge (Schol.; BA 1957; PhD 1962; ScD 1995). Magdalene College, Cambridge: John Stothert Bye Fellow, 1958–60; Res. Fellow, 1960; Tutor, 1963–74; Jt Dir of Studies in Natural Scis, 1980–96; Cambridge University: Demonstrator in Botany, 1961–64; Lectr, 1964–92; Reader, 1992–2000. Nuffield-Royal Soc. Bursar, Univ. of Adelaide, 1963; Hon. Res. Fellow, ANU, 1970–71; Vis. Prof., Cornell Univ., 1982, 1987; Sen. Vis. Researcher, CSIRO Tropical Forest Res. Centre, Atherton, 1992–2000; Vis. Prof., ICSTM, 1999–. Editor: Jl of Ecology, 1972–77; Biol Flora of British Isles, 1978–87. Jt Leader, Cambridge Expedn to Colombian Cordillera Oriental, 1957; Leader, Oxford Univ. Expedn to Ecuador, 1960. President: Brit. Ecol Soc., 1990–91; Cambridge Philosophical Soc., 1990–91. Frank Smart Prize in Botany, Cambridge Univ., 1956; Rolleston Meml Essay Prize, Oxford Univ., 1963. *Publications:* (with P. F. Stevens) Forests of Mt Kerigomna, Papua New Guinea, 1985; (ed with J. B. Whittaker) Toward a More Exact Ecology, 1989; papers in ecol and botanical jls. *Recreations:* history of buildings and landscape, biographies. *Address:* Magdalene College, Cambridge CB3 0AG. *T:* (01223) 332109.

GRUDER, Jeffrey Nigel; QC 1997; *b* 18 Sept. 1954; *s* of late Bernard Gruder and of Lily Gruder; *m* 1979, Gillian Vera Hyman; one *s* two *d. Educ:* City of London Sch.; Trinity Hall, Cambridge (MA). Called to the Bar, Middle Temple, 1977; in practice at the Bar, 1978–. *Recreations:* reading, theatre, tennis. *Address:* Essex Court Chambers, 24 Lincoln's Inn Fields, WC2A 3ED. *T:* (020) 7813 8000.

GRUENBERG, Prof. Karl Walter; Professor of Pure Mathematics in the University of London, at Queen Mary and Westfield (formerly Queen Mary) College, 1967–93, Emeritus since 1993; *b* 3 June 1928; *s* of late Paul Gruenberg and Anna Gruenberg; *m* 1973, Margaret Semple; one *s* one *d. Educ:* Shaftesbury Grammar Sch.; Kilburn Grammar Sch.; Cambridge Univ. BA 1950, PhD 1954. Asst Lectr, Queen Mary Coll., 1953–55; Commonwealth Fund Fellowship, 1955–57 (at Harvard Univ., 1955–56; at Inst. for Advanced Studies, Princeton, 1956–57). Queen Mary College: Lectr, 1957–61; Reader, 1961–67. Visiting Professor: Univ. of Michigan, 1961–62, 1978; Cornell Univ., 1966–67; Univ. of Illinois, 1972; Australian Nat. Univ., 1979 and 1987. Mem., Maths Cttee, SERC, 1983–86. *Publications:* Cohomological Topics in Group Theory, 1970; Relation Modules of Finite Groups, 1976; Linear Geometry (jtly with A. J. Weir), 2nd edn 1977; articles on algebra in various learned jls. *Address:* School of Mathematical Sciences, Queen Mary and Westfield College (University of London), Mile End Road, E1 4NS. *T:* (020) 8980 4811.

GRUFFYDD, Prof. (Robert) Geraint, FBA 1991; Director, University of Wales Centre for Advanced Welsh and Celtic Studies, Aberystwyth, 1985–93; *b* 9 June 1928; *s* of Moses and Ceridwen Griffith; *m* 1953, Elizabeth Eluned Roberts; two *s* one *d*. *Educ:* University Coll. of N Wales, Bangor (BA; Hon. Fellow, 1993); Jesus Coll., Oxford (DPhil; Hon. Fellow, 1992). Asst Editor, Geiriadur Prifysgol Cymru, 1953–55; Lectr, Dept of Welsh, UCNW, 1955–70; Prof. of Welsh Language and Literature, UCW, Aberystwyth, 1970–79; Librarian, Nat. Library of Wales, 1980–85. Vice-Pres., Univ. of Wales, Aberystwyth, 1996–2001. Chairman: Welsh Books Council, 1980–85; Welsh Language Section, Welsh Acad., 1986–90; Bd of Celtic Studies, Univ. of Wales, 1991–93. President: Cambrian Archæol Assoc., 1991–92; Internat. Congress of Celtic Studies, 1995–. Hon. DLitt Wales, 1997. *Publications:* (ed) Meistri'r Canrifoedd, 1973; (ed) Cerddi '73, 1973; (ed) Bardos, 1982; (ed) Cerddi Saunders Lewis, 1986; Dafydd ap Gwilym, 1987; (ed) Y Gair ar Waith, 1988; Llenyddiaeth y Cymry, ii, 1989; (gen. editor) Cyfres Beirdd y Tywgsogion (Poets of the Princes series), 7 vols, 1991–96; (co-ed) Hispano-Gallo-Brittonica, 1995; (ed) A Guide to Welsh Literature, Vol. 3, 1997; (co-ed) Gwaith Einion Offeiriad a Dafydd Ddu o Hiraddug, 1997; articles, etc, on Welsh literary and religious history in various collaborative vols and learned jls. *Recreations:* reading, walking, travel. *Address:* Eirianfa, Caradog Road, Aberystwyth, Ceredigion SY23 2JY. *T:* (01970) 623396.

GRUFFYDD JONES, Daniel; *see* Jones.

GRUGEON, Sir John (Drury), Kt 1980; DL; Chairman, Kent Police Authority, 1992–98; *b* 20 Sept. 1928; *s* of Drury Grugeon and Sophie (*née* Pratt); *m* 1st, 1955, Mary Patricia (*née* Rickards) (marr. diss. 1986); one *s* one *d*; 2nd, 1989, Pauline Lois, *widow* of Dr Roland Phillips. *Educ:* Epsom Grammar Sch.; RMA, Sandhurst. Commissioned, The Buffs, Dec. 1948; served 1st Bn in Middle and Far East and Germany; Regimental Adjt, 1953–55; Adjt 5th Bn, 1956–58; left Army, 1960. Joined Save and Prosper Group, 1960. Kent County Council: Mem., 1967–2001; Leader, 1973–82; Vice-Chm., 1987–89; Chm., 1989–91, 1997–99; Chairman: Superannuation Fund, 1982–87; Fire and Public Protection Cttee, 1984–87. Chm., Policy Cttee, Assoc. of County Councils, 1978–81 (Chm., Finance Cttee, 1976–79); Vice Chm., Assoc. of Police Authorities, 1997–98 (Chm., Finance Gp, 1997–98). Dir, Internat. Garden Fest. '84, Liverpool, 1982–83. Chm., Tunbridge Wells HA, 1984–92. Member: SE Economic Planning Council, 1971–74; Medway Ports Authority, 1977–93; Dep. Chm., Medway (Chatham) Dock Co., 1983–92. Vice-Chm., Cons. Nat. Adv. Cttee for Local Govt, 1975–82. Liveryman, Ironmongers' Co., 1977–. DL Kent, 1986. *Recreations:* cricket, shooting, local govt. *Address:* 3 Eastgate Road, Tenterden, Kent TN30 7AH. *T:* (01580) 763494. *Clubs:* Carlton, MCC; Kent County CC.

GRUNDY, David Stanley, CB 1997; Commissioner for Policy and Resources, Forestry Commission, 1992–97; *b* 10 April 1943; *s* of Walter Grundy and Anne Grundy (*née* Pomfret); *m* 1965, Elizabeth Jenny Schadla Hall; one *s*. *Educ:* De La Salle Coll., Manchester; Jesus Coll., Cambridge (MA); Jesus Coll., Oxford (MPhil). Asst Principal, MOP, 1967–70; Asst Private Sec. to Minister, Min. of Technology, 1970–71; Principal, DTI, 1971–73; Economic Adviser: FCO, 1976–78; DoE, 1978–79; Chief Economic Advr, Govt of Vanuatu, 1979–81; Forestry Commission: Chief Economist, 1982–90; Comr for Finance and Admin, 1990–92. Member: Scottish Ornithological Club; Scottish Wildlife Trust. *Recreations:* angling, bird watching, gardening, tennis. *Address:* 9 Ann Street, Edinburgh EH4 1PL. *Club:* Dean Tennis (Edinburgh).

GRUNDY, (James) Milton; Founder and Chairman, The Milton Grundy Foundation (formerly Warwick Arts Trust), since 1978; *b* 13 June 1926. *Educ:* Sedbergh Sch.; Gonville and Caius Coll., Cambridge (MA). Called to the Bar, Inner Temple, 1954. Founder and Chm., Gemini Trust for the Arts, 1959–66; Founder Mem. and Pres., Internat. Tax Planning Assoc., 1975–; Charter Mem., Peggy Guggenheim Collection, 1980–89; Chm., Internat. Management Trust, 1986–96; Trustee: Nat. Museums and Galls of Merseyside, 1987–96; New End Theatre, Hampstead, 1994–96. *Publications:* Tax and the Family Company, 1956, 3rd edn 1966; Tax Havens, 1968, 7th edn (as Offshore Business Centres) 1997; Venice, 1971, 5th edn 1998; The World of International Tax Planning, 1984; (jtly) Asset Protection Trusts, 1990, 3rd edn 1997; (with V. I. Atroshenko) Mediterranean Vernacular, 1991. *Recreation:* conversation. *Address:* Gray's Inn Tax Chambers, Gray's Inn, WC1R 5JA. *T:* (020) 7242 2642.

GRUNDY, Ven. Malcolm Leslie; Archdeacon of Craven, since 1994; *b* 22 March 1944; *s* of Arthur James Grundy and Gertrude Alice Grundy; *m* 1972, Wendy Elizabeth Gibson; one *s*. *Educ:* Sandye Place Sch., Beds; Mander Coll., Bedford; King's Coll., London (AKC 1968); Open Univ. (BA 1976). Ordained deacon, 1969, priest, 1970; Curate, St George's, Doncaster, 1969–72; Chaplain and Sen. Chaplain, Sheffield Industrial Mission, 1972–80; Dir of Educn, dio. of London, 1980–86; Team Rector of Huntingdon, 1986–91; Dir, Avec, 1991–94; Hon. Canon of Ely, 1988–94. *Publications:* Light in the City, 1990; An Unholy Conspiracy, 1992; Community Work, 1995; (ed) The Parchmore Partnership, 1995; Management and Ministry, 1996; Understanding Congregations, 1998; (contrib.) Managing, Leading, Ministering, 1999; (jtly) Faith on the Way, 2000. *Recreations:* classic cars, gardening, writing. *Address:* The Vicarage, Gisburn, Clitheroe, Lancs BB7 4HR.

GRUNDY, Stephanie Christine; Legal Adviser, Treasury Solicitor's Department, since 1992; *b* 11 Dec. 1958; *d* of Harry Grundy and June (*née* Hazell). *Educ:* Grange Sch., Oldham; Hertford Coll., Oxford (Schol.; Gibbs Prize; MA, BCL). Called to the Bar, Middle Temple, 1983. Research Asst, Law Commn, 1985; Asst Parly Counsel, 1985–92; on secondment to Law Commn, 1988–90. *Recreations:* running, mountaineering, architecture. *Address:* HM Treasury, Parliament Street, SW1P 3AG.

GRUNSELL, Prof. Charles Stuart Grant, CBE 1976; PhD; Professor of Veterinary Medicine, University of Bristol, 1957–80, now Emeritus; *b* 6 Jan. 1915; *s* of Stuart and Edith Grunsell; *m* 1939, Marjorie Prunella Wright; one *s* two *d*. *Educ:* Shanghai Public Sch.; Bristol Grammar Sch. Qualified as MRCVS at The Royal (Dick) Veterinary Coll., Edinburgh, 1937; FRCVS 1971. In general practice at Glastonbury, Som., 1939–48. PhD Edinburgh, 1952. Senior Lecturer in Veterinary Hygiene and Preventive Medicine, University of Edinburgh, 1952. Pro-Vice-Chancellor, Univ. of Bristol, 1974–77. Chm., Veterinary Products Cttee, 1970–80. Mem., General Synod of C of E, 1980–85; a Diocesan Reader. Defence Medal 1946. *Publications:* papers on the Erythron of Ruminants, on Vital Statistics in Veterinary Medicine, on Preventive Medicine, and on veterinary education. *Recreation:* gardening. *Address:* Greenleaves, Mead Lane, Sandford, Bristol BS19 5RG. *T:* (01934) 822461.

GRUNWALD, Henry Cyril; QC 1999; *b* 15 Aug. 1949; *s* of Eugen Grunwald and Hetty Grunwald (*née* Steppel); *m* 1976, Alison Appleton; two *s* two *d*. *Educ:* City of London Sch.; University Coll. London (LLB Hons). Called to the Bar, Gray's Inn, 1972. Vice-Pres., Bd of Deputies of British Jews, 1997–; Warden, Hampstead Synagogue, 1997–. Trustee, Relate N London, 1996–. *Recreations:* family, friends, theatre, reading, travel. *Address:* 2 Tudor Street, EC4Y 0AA. *T:* (020) 7797 7111. *Club:* Royal Automobile.

GUAY, Richard; Delegate General for Quebec in Brussels, since 1999; *b* Montreal, 15 Nov. 1943; *s* of late Maurice Guay and Irène (*née* Brassard); *m* 1980, Marie-France Fortier; one *s* one *d*. *Educ:* Coll. Jean de Brébeuf, Montreal; Univ. of Montreal (law degree). Radio Canada: journalist, Montreal, 1966–69; Corresp., UN and NY, 1969–71; Lectr, Sch. of Journalism, Dakar Univ., 1971–73; Co-ordinator of Intergovtl Relns, Min. of Communications, Quebec, 1973–75; Counsellor to Dep. Minister, Min. of Culture, 1975–76. National Assembly, Quebec: Mem. for Taschereau, 1976–85; Parly Asst, Min. of Communications, 1976–79, Min. of Housing, 1979–82; Dep. Leader of Govt, 1982–83; Speaker, 1983–85. Mem. Bd, Internat. Assoc. of French-speaking Parliamentarians, 1983–85 (Grand Officier, Ordre de la Pléiade, 1991); Canadian Rep., Internat. Exec., CPA, 1983–85; Lawyer, specialising in arbitration, Montreal, 1986–95; Agent Gen., then Deleg. Gen., for Quebec in London, 1995–99. *Recreations:* music, reading, ski-ing. *Address:* Avenue des Arts 46, 1000 Brussels, Belgium. *T:* (2) 5120036.

GUAZZELLI, Rt Rev. Victor; Emeritus Auxiliary Bishop of Westminster, (RC); Titular Bishop of Lindisfarne, since 1970; *b* 19 March 1920; *s* of Cesare Guazzelli and Maria (*née* Frepoli). *Educ:* Parochial Schools, Tower Hamlets; English Coll., Lisbon. Priest, 1945. Asst, St Patrick's, Soho Square, 1945–48; Bursar and Prof. at English Coll., Lisbon, 1948–58; Westminster Cathedral: Chaplain, 1958–64; Hon. Canon, 1964; Sub-Administrator, 1964–67; Parish Priest of St Thomas', Fulham, 1967–70; Vicar General of Westminster, 1970; Aux. Bishop of Westminster (Bishop in E London), 1970–97. President: Pax Christi, 1975–; Apostleship of the Sea, 1993–; Chm., Cttee, Faith and Cultures. *Address:* Westminster Cathedral Clergy House, 42 Francis Street, SW1P 1QW. *T:* (020) 7987 4663.

GUBBAY, Hon. Anthony Roy; Chief Justice of Zimbabwe, 1990–2001; *b* 26 April 1932; *s* of Henry and Gracia Gubbay; *m* 1962, Alice Wilma Sanger; two *s*. *Educ:* Univ. of Witwatersrand, SA (BA); Jesus Coll., Cambridge Univ. (MA, LLM; Hon. Fellow, 1992). Admitted to practice, 1957; emigrated to S Rhodesia, 1958; in private practice as advocate, Bulawayo; SC 1974; Judge: of the High Court, 1977–83; of the Supreme Court, 1983–90. Pres., Valuations Bd, 1974–77; National President: Special Court for Income Tax Appeals, 1974–77; Fiscal Court, 1974–77; Patents Tribunal, 1974–77. Chairman: Legal Practitioners' Disciplinary Tribunal, 1981–87; Law Develt Commn, 1990–2001; Judicial Service Commn, 1990–2001. Mem., Perm. Court of Arbitration, 1993–. Mem., Commonwealth Reference Gp on the promotion of human rights of women and the girl child through the Judiciary, 1996–. Patron, Commonwealth Magistrates' and Judges' Assoc., 1994–2001. Pres., Oxford and Cambridge Soc. of Zimbabwe. Hon. Bencher, Lincoln's Inn, 1997. DU Essex, 1994. Great Cross, Order of Rio Branco (Brazil), 1999. *Recreations:* classical music, philately, tennis. *Club:* Harare.

GUBBAY, Raymond Jonathan, CBE 2001; Managing Director, Raymond Gubbay Ltd, since 1966; *b* 2 April 1946; *s* of David and late Ida Gubbay; *m* 1972, Johanna Quirke (marr. diss. 1988); two *d*. *Educ:* University Coll. Sch., Hampstead. Concert promoter, 1966–: regular series of concerts at major London concert halls, including: Royal Festival Hall; Royal Albert Hall; The Barbican (*c* 1,200 concerts, 1982–), also major regl arenas and concert venues; has presented many of the world's greatest artists in concert; The Ratepayers Iolanthe, South Bank and Phoenix Theatre, 1984; The Metropolitan Mikado, South Bank, 1985; also Royal Opera prodn of Turandot, Wembley Arena, 1991; Royal Albert Hall: Centenary prodn of La Bohème, 1996; Carmen, 1997; Swan Lake, 1997; Madam Butterfly, 1998; Romeo and Juliet, 1998; Tosca, 1999; Sleeping Beauty, 2000; Aida, 2001; D'Oyly Carte Opera Co., RFH, 1998 and 1999, Queen's Th., 1998–99, and Savoy Th., 2000; Ute Lemper, Queen's Th., 1999. Founder, City of London Antiques and Fine Art Fair, Barbican Exhibn Halls, 1987–92. Hon. FRAM 1988; Hon FTCL 2000. *Recreations:* living in Paris having four grandchildren. *Address:* Knight House, 29–31 East Barnet Road, New Barnet, Herts EN4 8RN. *T:* (020) 8216 3000, *Fax:* (020) 8216 3001; 51 rue Monsieur Le Prince, Paris, France.

GUBBINS, Prof. David, PhD; FRS 1996; CPhys, FInstP; Professor of Geophysics, School of Earth Sciences, University of Leeds, since 1989; *b* 31 May 1947; *s* of late Albert Edmund Gubbins and of Joyce Lucy Gubbins; *m* 1972, (Margaret) Stella McCloy; one *s* two *d*. *Educ:* King Edward VI Grammar Sch., Southampton; Trinity Coll., Cambridge (BA, PhD). CPhys, FInstP 1996. Vis. Res. Fellow, Univ. of Colorado, 1972–73; Instructor in Applied Maths, MIT, 1973–74; Asst Prof., Inst. of Geophysics and Planetary Physics, UCLA, 1974–76; Cambridge University: Res. Assistant and Sen. Assistant in Res., Dept of Geodesy and Geophysics, 1976–81; Asst Dir of Res., Dept of Earth Scis, 1981–89; Fellow of Churchill Coll., 1978–90. Fellow, Amer. Geophys. Union, 1985. *Publications:* Seismology and Plate Tectonics, 1990; scientific papers. *Recreations:* sailing, swimming. *Address:* School of Earth Sciences, University of Leeds, Leeds LS2 9JT. *T:* (0113) 233 5255. *Club:* Wigtown Bay Sailing.

GUCKIAN, Dr Noel Joseph, OBE 2001; HM Diplomatic Service; Deputy Head of Mission and HM Consul-General, Tripoli, since 1999 (Head of British Interests Section, 1998–99, then Chargé d'Affaires *ai* on restoration of diplomatic relations, 1999); *b* 6 March 1955; *s* of William Joseph Guckian and Mary Patricia Joan Guckian (*née* Kelly); *m* 1990, Lorna Ruth Warren; one *s* two *d*. *Educ:* Notre Dame Internat. Sch., Rome; New Univ. of Ulster (BA Hons History 1976); UCW, Aberystwyth (MSc Econ, Internat. Politics 1977; PhD Internat. Politics 1985). FCO 1980; Arabic at SOAS, 1983–84; Jedda, 1984–87; 1st Sec., Financial, Paris, 1988; Head, British Interest Section, Tripoli, 1990; Head, Political Section, Kuwait, 1991–92; Counsellor and Dep. Head of Mission, Muscat, 1994–98. *Recreations:* fly-fishing, diving, sailing. *Address:* c/o Foreign and Commonwealth Office, SW1A 2AH. *Clubs:* Royal Commonwealth Society, Royal Over-Seas League; Salisbury and District Angling.

GUDERLEY, Daisy Deborah, (Mrs C. Guderley); *see* Hyams, D. D.

GUÉGUINOU, Jean, Hon. GCVO 1996; Chevalier de la Légion d'Honneur, 1991; Officier de l'Ordre du Mérite, 1995 (Chevalier, 1979); Ambassador of France to the Holy See, since 1998; *b* 17 Oct. 1941. *Educ:* Ecole Nationale d'Administration. Press and Inf. Dept, Min. of Foreign Affairs, Paris, 1967–69; Second Sec., London, 1969–71; Chargé de Mission, Private Office of Ministre d'Etat, Minister of Nat. Defence, 1971–73; Asst Private Sec., then Special Advr to Minister of Foreign Affairs, 1973–76; Principal Private Sec. to Minister of State resp. to Prime Minister, 1976–77; Head of Southern Africa and Indian Ocean Dept, Min. of Foreign Affairs, 1977–82; Consul Gen., Jerusalem, 1982–86; Dir of Press and Inf. Dept, Min. of Foreign Affairs, and Ministry Spokesman, 1986–90; French Ambassador: in Prague, 1990–93 (Czechoslavakia, 1990–92; Czech Republic, 1993); to UK, 1993–98. Mem. Governing Body, Agence France Presse, 1986–90. KSG 1976. *Address:* French Embassy to the Holy See, via Piave 23, 00187 Rome, Italy. *T:* (6) 4883841. *Clubs:* Brooks's; Cercle Foch (Paris); Golf de St Germain en Laye.

GUERITZ, Rear-Adm. Edward Findlay, CB 1971; OBE 1957; DSC 1942, and Bar, 1944; *b* 8 Sept. 1919; *s* of Elton and Valentine Gueritz; *m* 1947, Pamela Amanda Bernhardina Britton, *d* of Commander L. H. Jeans, and *widow* of Lt-Comdr E. M. Britton, RN; one *s* one *d*. *Educ:* Cheltenham Coll. Entered Navy, 1937; Midshipman, 1938; served

War of 1939–45 (wounded; DSC and Bar): HMS Jersey, 5th Flotilla, 1940–41; Combined Ops (Indian Ocean, Normandy), 1941–44; HMS Saumarez (Corfu Channel incident), 1946; Army Staff Coll., Camberley, 1948; Staff of C-in-C S Atlantic and Junior Naval Liaison Officer to UK High Comr, S Africa, 1954–56; Near East Operations, 1956 (OBE); Dep. Dir, RN Staff Coll., 1959–61; Naval Staff, Admty, 1961–63; idc 1964; Captain of Fleet, Far East Fleet, 1965–66; Dir of Defence Plans (Navy), 1967; Dir, Jt Warfare Staff, MoD, 1968; Admiral-President, Royal Naval Coll., 1968–70 (concurrently first Pres., RN Staff Coll.); Comdt, Jt Warfare Estabt, 1970–72. Lt-Comdr 1949; Comdr 1953; Captain 1959; Rear-Adm. 1969; retd 1973. Dep. Dir and Editor, 1976–79, Dir and Editor-in-Chief, 1979–81, RUSI. Specialist Adviser, House of Commons Select Cttee on Defence, 1975–95. Chief Hon. Steward, Westminster Abbey, 1975–85. President: Soc. for Nautical Res., 1974–90 (Hon. Vice Pres., 1990); J and K Class Destroyer Assoc., 1990–99; Vice-Pres., RN Commando Assoc., 1993–; Vice Chairman: Council for Christian Approaches to Defence and Disarmament, 1974–80; Victoria League, 1985–88; Marine Soc., 1988–93 (Vice Pres., 1991); Member Council: Fairbridge-Drake Soc., 1981–90; British Atlantic Cttee, 1977–89; HOST (Hosting for Overseas Students Trust), 1987–90 (founding Governor). Mem., Bd of War Studies, Univ. of London, 1969–85. *Publications:* (jtly) The Third World War, 1978; (ed jtly) Ten Years of Terrorism, 1979; (ed jtly) Will the Wells Run Dry, 1979; (ed jtly) Nuclear Attack: Civil Defence, 1982; editor, RUSI Brassey's Defence Year Book, 1977–78, 1978–79, 1980, 1981. *Recreations:* history, gardening. *Address:* Hemyngsby, 56 The Close, Salisbury, Wilts SP1 2EL. *Clubs:* Army and Navy, Royal Commonwealth Society.

GUERNSEY, Lord; Charles Heneage Finch-Knightley; Vice Lord-Lieutenant for West Midlands, since 1990; *b* 27 March 1947; *s* and *heir* of 11th Earl of Aylesford, *qv*; *m* 1971, Penelope Anstice, *y d* of Kenneth A. G. Crawley; one *s* four *d* (incl. twin *d*). *Educ:* Oundle, Trinity Coll., Cambridge. DL West Midlands, 1986. *Recreations:* shooting, fishing, Real tennis, cricket. *Heir: s* Hon. Heneage James Daniel Finch-Knightley, *b* 29 April 1985. *Address:* Packington Hall, Meriden, Coventry CV7 7HF. *T:* (01676) 522274.

GUERNSEY, Dean of; *see* Trickey, Very Rev. F. M.

GUEST, family name of **Viscount Wimborne**.

GUEST; *see* Haden-Guest.

GUEST, Prof. Anthony Gordon, CBE 1989; QC 1987; FBA 1993; FCIArb; Barrister-at-Law; Professor of English Law, King's College, University of London, 1966–97; *b* 8 Feb. 1930; *o s* of late Gordon Walter Leslie Guest and Marjorie (*née* Hooper), Maidencombe, Devon; unmarried. *Educ:* Colston's Sch., Bristol; St John's Coll., Oxford (MA). Exhibr and Casberd Schol., Oxford, 1950–54; 1st cl. Final Hon. Sch. of Jurisprudence, 1954. Bacon Schol., Gray's Inn, 1955; Barstow Law Schol., 1955; called to Bar, Gray's Inn, 1956, Bencher, 1978. University Coll., Oxford: Lectr, 1954–55; Fellow and Prælector in Jurisprudence, 1955–65; Dean, 1963–64; Reader in Common Law to Council of Legal Educn (Inns of Court), 1967–80. Travelling Fellowship to S Africa, 1957; Mem., Lord Chancellor's Law Reform Cttee, 1963–84; Mem., Adv. Cttee on establishment of Law Faculty in University of Hong Kong, 1965; UK Deleg. to UN Commn on Internat. Trade Law, NY, Geneva and Vienna, 1968–84 and 1986–87, to UN Conf. on Limitation of Actions, 1974; Mem., Board of Athlone Press, 1968–73; Mem. Governing Body, Rugby Sch., 1968–88. FKC 1982; FCIArb 1984. Served Army and TA, 1948–50 (Lieut RA). *Publications:* (ed) Anson's Principles of the Law of Contract, 21st to 26th edns, 1959–84; Chitty on Contracts: (Asst Editor) 22nd edn 1961 and 28th edn 1999, (Gen. Editor) 23rd to 27th edns, 1968–94; (ed) Oxford Essays in Jurisprudence, 1961; The Law of Hire-Purchase, 1966; (Gen. Editor) Benjamin's Sale of Goods, 1st to 5th edns, 1974–97; (ed jtly) Encylopedia of Consumer Credit, 1975; (jtly) Introduction to the Law of Credit and Security, 1978; (ed) Chalmers and Guest on Bills of Exchange, 14th edn 1991, 15th edn 1998; Only Remember Me (anthology), 1993; articles in legal jls. *Address:* 28 Caroline Terrace, SW1W 8JT. *T:* (020) 7730 2799. *Club:* Garrick.

GUEST, Christopher; *see* Haden-Guest, 5th Baron.

GUEST, George Howell, CBE 1987; MA, MusB (Cantab); MusD (Lambeth), 1977; FRCO 1942; FRSCM 1973; Hon. RAM 1984; Organist of St John's College, Cambridge, 1951–91 (Fellow, since 1956); University Organist, Cambridge University, 1974–91; *b* 9 Feb. 1924; *s* of late Ernest Joseph Guest and late Gwendolen (*née* Brown); *m* 1959, Nancy Mary, *o d* of late W. P. Talbot; one *s* one *d*. *Educ:* Friars Sch., Bangor; King's Sch., Chester; St John's Coll., Cambridge. Chorister: Bangor Cath., 1933–35; Chester Cath., 1935–39. Served in RAF, 1942–46. Sub-Organist, Chester Cath., 1946–47; Organ Student, St John's Coll., Cambridge, 1947–51; John Stewart of Rannoch Scholar in Sacred Music, 1948; University Asst Lectr in Music, Cambridge, 1953–56, Univ. Lectr, 1956–82; Prof. of Harmony and Counterpoint, RAM, London, 1960–61. Director: Berkshire Boy Choir, USA, 1967, 1970; Arts Theatre, Cambridge, 1977–90. Concerts with St John's Coll. Choir in USA, Canada, Japan, Aust., Brazil, Hong Kong, most countries in W Europe; concerts and choral seminars in the Philippines and in S Africa; concerts with Community of Jesus Choir, USA, in Hungary, Yugoslavia and USSR; fests adjudicator in GB, Ire., Hong Kong and Patagonia. Mem. Council: RCO, 1964– (Pres., 1978–80); RSCM, 1983–. Examiner to Associated Bd of Royal Schs of Music, 1959–92. Aelod er Anrhydedd, Gorsedd y Beirdd, Eisteddfod Genedlaethol Cymru, 1977; Dir, Côr Cenedlaethol Ieuenctid Cymru, 1984; Artistic Dir, Llandaf Festival, 1985. President: Cathedral Organists' Assoc., 1980–82; IAO, 1987–89. Hon. FRCCO 1991; Hon. Fellow: UCNW, 1989; Univ. of Wales, Aberystwyth, 1999; Hon. FWCMD 1992. Hon. DMus Wales, 1989. John Edwards Meml Award, Guild for Promotion of Welsh Music, 1986. *Publication:* A Guest at Cambridge, 1994. *Recreation:* the Welsh language. *Address:* 9 Gurney Way, Cambridge CB4 2ED. *T:* (01223) 354932.

GUEST, Ivor Forbes, FRAD 1982; Chairman, 1969–93, Member, 1965–93, Executive Committee, a Vice-President, since 1993, Royal Academy of Dancing; Solicitor; *b* 14 April 1920; *s* of Cecil Marmaduke Guest and Christian Forbes Guest (*née* Tweedie); *m* 1962, Ann Hutchinson; no *c*. *Educ:* Lancing Coll.; Trinity Coll., Cambridge (MA). Admitted a Solicitor, 1949; Partner, A. F. & R. W. Tweedie, 1951–83, Tweedie & Prideaux, 1983–85. Organised National Book League exhibn of books on ballet, 1957–58; Mem. Cttee, Soc. for Theatre Research, 1955–72; Chm., Exec. Cttee, Soc. for Dance Research, 1982–97 (Pres., 1998–); Jt Pres., Dolmetsch Early Dance Soc., 1990–; Member: Exec. Cttee, British Theatre Museum, 1957–77 (Vice-Chm., 1966–77); Cttee, The Theatre Museum, 1984–89 (Mem., Adv. Council, 1974–83). Editorial Adviser to the Dancing Times, 1963–; Trustee: Calvert Trust, 1976–; Cecchetti Soc. Trust, 1978–; Radcliffe Trust, 1997– (Sec., 1966–96). DUniv Surrey, 1997. Queen Elizabeth II Coronation Award for services to ballet, 1992; Lifetime Achievement Award, Congress on Res. in Dance, 2000. Chevalier, Ordre des Arts et des Lettres (France), 1998. *Publications:* Napoleon III in England, 1952; The Ballet of the Second Empire, 1953–55; The Romantic Ballet in England, 1954; Fanny Cerrito, 1956; Victorian Ballet Girl, 1957; Adeline Genée, 1958; The Alhambra Ballet, 1959; La Fille mal gardée, 1960; The Dancer's Heritage, 1960; The Empire Ballet, 1962; A Gallery of Romantic Ballet, 1963; The Romantic Ballet in Paris, 1966; Carlotta Zambelli, 1969; Dandies and Dancers, 1969; Two Coppélias, 1970; Fanny Elssler, 1970; The Pas de Quatre, 1970; Le Ballet de l'Opéra de Paris, 1976; The Divine Virginia, 1977; Adeline Genée: a pictorial record, 1978; Lettres d'un Maître de ballet, 1978; contrib. Costume and the 19th Century Dancer, in Designing for the Dancer, 1981; Adventures of a Ballet Historian, 1982; Jules Perrot, 1984; Gautier on Dance, 1986; Gautier on Spanish Dancing, 1987; Dr John Radcliffe and his Trust, 1991; Ballet in Leicester Square, 1992; (contrib.) Musica in Scena, 1995; The Ballet of the Enlightenment, 1996; Ballet Under Napoleon, 2001. *Address:* 17 Holland Park, W11 3TD. *T:* (020) 7229 3780. *Clubs:* Garrick, MCC.

GUEST, Prof. John Rodney, FRS 1986; Professor of Microbiology, Sheffield University, since 1981; *b* 27 Dec. 1935; *s* of Sidney Ramsey Guest and Dorothy Kathleen Guest (*née* Walker); *m* 1962, Barbara Margaret (*née* Dearsley); one *s* two *d*. *Educ:* Campbell College, Belfast; Leeds Univ. (BSc); Trinity Coll., Oxford Univ. (DPhil). Guinness Fellow, Oxford, 1960–62, 1965; Fulbright Scholar and Research Associate, Stanford, 1963, 1964; Sheffield University: Lectr, Sen. Lectr, Reader in Microbiology, 1965–81. SERC Special Res. Fellow, 1981–86. Marjory Stephenson Prize Lectr, Soc. Gen. Microbiol., 1992; Leeuwenhoek Lectr, Royal Soc., 1995. *Publications:* contribs to Jl of Gen. Microbiol., Biochem. Jl, Microbiol., Molec. Microbiol. *Recreations:* walking in the Peak District, squash, beekeeping, polyfilling. *Address:* Department of Molecular Biology and Biotechnology, Sheffield University, Western Bank, Sheffield S10 2TN. *T:* (0114) 222 4406.

GUEST, Melville Richard John; Chief Executive, Asia House, since 1996; *b* 18 Nov. 1943; *s* of late Ernest Melville Charles Guest and Katherine Mary Guest; *m* 1970, Beatriz Eugenia, (Jenny), Lopez Colombres de Velasco; four *s*. *Educ:* Rugby Sch.; Magdalen Coll., Oxford (MA Jurisprudence). HM Diplomatic Service, 1966–96: Third, later Second, Sec., Tokyo, 1967–72; Pvte Sec. to Parly Under-Sec. of State, FCO, 1973–75; First Sec., Paris, 1975–79; FCO, 1979–80; Prés.-Dir Gén., Soc. Française des Industries Lucas, 1980–85; Dir, Thomson-Lucas SA, 1980–85; Director: Franco-British Chamber of Commerce, 1980–85; Channel Tunnel Gp, 1985–86; Counsellor (Commercial), Tokyo, 1986–89; Counsellor (Political) and Consul General, Stockholm, 1990–93; Head, S Pacific Dept, 1993–94, SE Asian Dept, 1994–96, FCO. Mem., Bd of Govs, Ampleforth Coll., 1989–96. *Address:* Asia House, 105 Piccadilly, W1V 9FN. *Club:* Hurlingham.

GUETERBOCK, family name of **Baron Berkeley**.

GUGGENHEIM, Anna Maeve; QC 2001; *b* 2 Sept. 1959; *d* of Peter Francis Guggenheim and Maura Teresa Guggenheim (*née* McCarthy); *m* 1987, Mark Eban; one *s* one *d*. *Educ:* King Edward VI High Sch. for Girls, Edgbaston; Somerville Coll., Oxford (BA Juris 1981). Called to the Bar, Gray's Inn, 1982; barrister, 1982–. *Recreation:* sailing. *Address:* Crown Office Chambers, 1 Paper Buildings, Temple, EC4Y 7EP. *T:* (020) 7797 8100.

GUILD, Ivor Reginald, CBE 1985; FRSE; Partner in Shepherd and Wedderburn, WS, 1951–94; *b* 2 April 1924; 2nd *s* of Col Arthur Marjoribanks Guild, DSO, TD, DL, and Phyllis Eliza Cox. *Educ:* Cargilfield; Rugby; New Coll., Oxford (MA); Edinburgh Univ. (LLB). FRSE 1990. WS 1950. Procurator Fiscal of the Lyon Court, 1960–94; Bailie of Holyrood House, 1980–95; Registrar, Episcopal Synod of Episc. Church in Scotland, 1967–; Chancellor, diocese of: Edinburgh, 1985–95; St Andrews, 1985–98. Chairman: Edinburgh Investment Trust Ltd, 1974–94 (Dir, 1972–94); Dunedin Income Growth Investment Trust plc (formerly First Scottish American Investment Trust plc), 1973–94 (Dir, 1964–94); Dunedin Worldwide Investment Trust plc (formerly Northern American Investment Trust plc), 1973–94 (Dir, 1964–94); Scottish Oriental Smaller Companies Trust PLC, 1995–; Dir, New Fulcrum Investment Trust, 1986–. Member: Council on Tribunals, 1976–85; Interception of Communications Tribunal, 1985–96; Immigration Appeal Adjudicator, 1988–95. Chm., Nat. Mus. of Antiquities of Scotland, 1981–85. Editor, Scottish Genealogist, 1959–94. *Recreations:* genealogy, golf. *Club:* New (Edinburgh).

GUILD, Rear-Adm. Nigel Charles Forbes, PhD; Controller of the Navy, and Executive Director 4, Defence Procurement Agency, Ministry of Defence, since 2000; *b* 9 Feb. 1949; *s* of Surg. Capt. William John Forbes Guild and Joan Elizabeth Guild (*née* Innes); *m* 1971, Felicity Jean Wilson; two *s*. *Educ:* Fernden Sch.; Bryanston Sch.; BRNC Dartmouth; Trinity Coll., Cambridge (BA); Univ. of Bristol (PhD 1979). MIEE 1980; MIMA 1980. Joined Royal Navy, 1966; HMS Hermes, 1972–75; Weapons Trials, 1976–78; British Underwater Test and Evaluation Centre Project, 1979–82; HMS Euryalus, 1982–84 and 1986–87; Future Projects (Naval), 1984–85; HMS Beaver, 1987–88; Staff Weapons Engr Officer to FO Sea Trng, 1988–90; MA to Chief of Defence Procurement, 1991–92; CSO (E) Surface Flotilla, 1993–95; Project Dir, PE, MoD, 1996–99. *Publications:* contrib. papers on Fuzzy Logic. *Recreations:* rowing, village pantomime, steam boating. *Address:* Defence Procurement Agency, Maple 2c Mailpoint 1, MoD Abbey Wood, Bristol BS34 8JH. *Club:* Leander (Henley on Thames).

GUILDFORD, Bishop of, since 1994; **Rt. Rev. John Warren Gladwin;** *b* 30 May 1942; *s* of Thomas Valentine and Muriel Joan Gladwin; *m* 1981, Lydia Elizabeth Adam. *Educ:* Hertford Grammar School; Churchill Coll., Cambridge (BA History and Theology, MA 1969); St John's Coll., Durham (Dip. Theol). Asst Curate, St John the Baptist Parish Church, Kirkheaton, Huddersfield, 1967–71; Tutor, St John's Coll., Durham and Hon. Chaplain to Students, St Nicholas Church, Durham, 1971–77; Director, Shaftesbury Project on Christian Involvement in Society, 1977–82; Secretary, Gen. Synod Board for Social Responsibility, 1982–88; Prebendary, St Paul's Cathedral, 1984–88; Provost of Sheffield, 1988–94. Mem., Gen Synod of C of E, 1990–. Jt Pres., Church Nat. Housing Coalition, 1997–; Chm. Bd, Christian Aid, 1998–. *Publications:* God's People in God's World, 1979; The Good of the People, 1988; Love and Liberty, 1998. *Recreations:* gardening, travel. *Address:* Willow Grange, Woking Road, Guildford GU4 7QS. *T:* (01483) 590500, *Fax:* (01483) 590501.

GUILDFORD, Dean of; *no new appointment at time of going to press.*

GUILFORD, 10th Earl of, *cr* 1752; **Piers Edward Brownlow North;** Baron Guilford 1683; *b* 9 March 1971; *s* of 9th Earl of Guilford and Osyth Vere Napier, *d* of Cyril Napier Leeston Smith; *S* father, 1999; *m* 1994, Michèle Desvaux de Marigny; one *d*. *Heir: great uncle* Hon. Charles Evelyn North [; *b* 18 March 1918; *m* 1st, 1942, Maureen O'Callaghan (marr. diss. 1957), *d* of Maj. F. C. B. Baldwin; one *s* one *d*; 2nd, 1959, Joan Aston, *d* of Maj. F. B. Booker]. *Address:* Waldershare Park, Dover, Kent CT15 5BA. *T:* (01304) 820245.

GUILFOYLE, Dame Margaret (Georgina Constance), DBE 1980; Chair, Judicial Remuneration Tribunal, 1995–2001; Deputy Chair, Infertility Authority, 1995–2001; *b* 15 May 1926; *d* of William and Elizabeth McCartney; *m* 1952, Stanley M. L. Guilfoyle; one *s* two *d*. *Educ:* ANU (LLB 1990). FCIS; FCPA. Accountant, 1947. Senator for Victoria, 1971–87; Minister: for Education, Commonwealth of Australia, 1975; for Social

Security, 1975–80; for Finance, 1980–83. Dep. Chm., Mental Health Res. Inst., 1988–2001; Dir, Aust. Children's TV Foundn, 1989–July 2002. *Recreations:* reading, gardening. *Address:* 21 Howard Street, Kew, Vic 3101, Australia. *Club:* Lyceum (Melbourne).

GUILLE, Ven. John Arthur; Archdeacon of Winchester, since 2000; Canon Residentiary of Winchester Cathedral, since 1999; *b* 21 May 1949; *s* of Arthur Leonard Guille and Winifred Maud Guille (*née* Lane); *m* 1976, Susan Stallard; one *s* two *d*. *Educ:* Guernsey GS for Boys; Christ Church Coll., Canterbury (CertEd London 1970); Salisbury and Wells Theol Coll.; BTh Southampton 1979. Teacher of Religious Studies: Stockbridge Co. Secondary Sch., 1970–72; St Sampson's Secondary Sch., 1972–73; ordained deacon, 1976, priest, 1977; Curate, Chandler's Ford, 1976–80; Priest i/c, St John, Surrey Road, Bournemouth, 1980–84, Vicar, St John with St Michael, 1984–89; Rector, St André de la Pommeraye, Guernsey, 1989–99; Vice Dean, Guernsey, 1996–99; Archdeacon of Basingstoke, 1999–2000. *Recreations:* walking, gardening. *Address:* 6 The Close, Winchester, Hants SO23 9LS. *T:* (01962) 863603, *Fax:* (01962) 857242; *e-mail:* john.guille@winchester-cathedral.org.uk.

GUILLEBAUD, (Jette) Margaret; Chairman, South West Arts, 1991–97; Member, Arts Council of England, 1994–97; *b* 24 March 1948; *d* of Justin Brooke and Kirsten (*née* Møller-Larsen); *m* 1st, 1971, Robin Simon, *qv* (marr. diss. 1978); one *s* one *d*; 2nd, 1984, Hugh Guillebaud. *Educ:* Wycombe Abbey Sch. (Head Girl); Exeter Univ. (BA Hons Eng.). Tutor, Oxford Sch. of English, Verona, Italy, 1971–72; Examr, Oxford Exams Bd, 1972–75; Tutor, Open Univ., 1973–75; Man. Dir, Jobline Employment Agency, 1989–91; Chm., English Regl Arts Bds, 1993–94. Chm., Glos Ambulance NHS Trust, 1991–93. Director: Cheltenham Festivals Ltd, 1991–96; at Bristol (formerly Bristol 2000), 1995–; Harbourside Centre, Bristol, 1995–2000; South West Film Commn, 1997–. Trustee, Holburne Mus., Bath, 1997–. Governor, Bath Spa UC (formerly Bath Coll. of Higher Educn), 1996–98. JP S Glos, 1988–98. FRSA 1992. Hon. MA UWE, 1998. *Recreations:* opera, theatre, visual arts, fishing, travel. *Address:* Wellington Lodge, Wellington Square, Cheltenham, Glos GL50 4JU. *T:* (01242) 244408.

GUILLEM, Sylvie; ballet dancer; *b* Paris, 23 Feb. 1965. *Educ:* Ecole de Danse, Paris Opera. With Paris Opera, 1981–89, Etoile, 1984; with Royal Ballet Co., 1989–; guest artist with other cos, 1989–. Lead roles in: Giselle; Swan Lake; La Bayadère; Cinderella; Sleeping Beauty; Romeo and Juliet; Raymonda; Manon; Don Quixote; Marguerite and Armand; Lilac Garden. Title role created for her in Sissi, Rudra Béjart Co.; other created roles in: In the Middle, somewhat Elevated; Le Martyre de Saint-Sebastien; Firstext. Prod Giselle for Nat. Ballet of Finland, 1999. Comdr des Arts et des Lettres (France), 1988. *Address:* c/o Royal Ballet Company, Royal Opera House, Covent Garden, WC2E 9DD.

GUILLEMIN, Prof. Roger Charles Louis, MD, PhD; Distinguished Professor, Salk Institute, La Jolla, since 1997; *b* Dijon, France, 11 Jan. 1924 (naturalized US Citizen, 1963); *s* of Raymond Guillemin and Blanche (*née* Rigollot); *m* 1951, Lucienne Jeanne Billard; one *s* five *d*. *Educ:* Univ. of Dijon (BA 1941, BSc 1942); Faculty of Medicine, Lyons (MD 1949); Univ. of Montreal (PhD 1953). Resident Intern, univ. hosps, Dijon, 1949–51; Associate Dir, then Asst Prof., Inst. of Exper. Medicine and Surgery, Univ. of Montreal, 1951–53; Associate Dir, Dept of Exper. Endocrinol., Coll. de France, Paris, 1960–63; Prof. of Physiol., Baylor Coll. of Med., Houston, 1953–70; Adjunct Prof. of Physiol., Baylor Coll. of Med., 1970–; Resident Fellow and Res. Prof., Salk Inst. for Biol Studies, 1970–89; Dist. Scientist, Whittier Inst. for Diabetes and Endocrinology, La Jolla, 1989–97 (Dir, 1993–94). Adjunct Prof. of Medicine, UCSD, 1970–94. Chm., Labs for Endocrinology, Salk Inst., 1970–89. Member: Nat. Acad. of Sciences, USA; Amer. Acad. Arts and Scis; Amer. Physiol Soc.; Endocrine Soc. (Pres., 1986); Soc. of Exptl Biol. and Medicine; Internat. Brain Res. Orgn; Internat. Soc. Res. Biol Reprodn. Foreign Associate: Acad. des Sciences, France; Acad. Nat. de Médecine, Paris; Hon. Mem., Swedish Soc. of Med. Scis; Foreign Mem., Acad. Royale de Médecine de Belgique. Mem. Club of Rome. Hon. DSc: Rochester, NY, 1976; Chicago, 1977; Manitoba, 1984; Kyung Hee Univ., Seoul, Korea, 1986; Univ. de Paris VII, 1986; Madrid, 1988; Univ. Claude Bernard, Lyon, 1989; Laval Univ., Quebec, 1990; Sherbrooke Univ., Quebec, 1997. Hon. MD: Ulm, 1978; Montreal, 1979; Univ. Libre de Bruxelles, Belgium, 1979; Turin, 1985; Barcelona, 1988; Univ. Claude Bernard, Lyon I, 1989; Laval Univ., Quebec, 1996; Hon. LMed Baylor Coll. of Med., 1978. Gairdner Internat. Award, 1974; Lasker Award, USA, 1975; Dickson Prize in Medicine, Univ. of Pittsburgh, 1976; Passano Award in Med. Sci., Passano Foundn, Inc., 1976; Schmitt Medal in Neuroscience, Neurosciences Res. Prog., MIT, 1977; National Medal of Science, USA, 1977; (jtly) Nobel Prize in Physiology or Medicine, 1977; Barren Gold Medal, USA, 1979; Dale Medal (Soc. for Endocrinology), UK, 1980; Ellen Browning Scripps Soc. Medal, Scripps Meml Hosps Foundn, San Diego, 1988; Dist. Scientist Award, Nat. Diabetes Res. Coalition, 1996. Légion d'Honneur, France, 1974. *Publications:* scientific pubns in learned jls. *Recreation:* computer art (one-man shows, Milan, 1991, Houston, 1996). *Address:* The Salk Institute, 10010 N Torrey Pines Road, La Jolla, CA 92037–1099, USA.

GUILLERY, Prof. Rainer Walter, PhD; FRS 1983; Visiting Professor, Department of Anatomy, University of Wisconsin, since 1996; Dr Lee's Professor of Anatomy, and Fellow of Hertford College, University of Oxford, 1984–96; *b* 28 Aug. 1929; *s* of Hermann Guillery and Eva (*née* Hackel); *m* 1954, Margot Cunningham Pepper (marr. diss. 2000); three *s* one *d*. *Educ:* University Coll. London (BSc, PhD; Fellow, 1987). Asst Lectr, subseq. Reader, Anatomy Dept, UCL, 1953–64; Associate Prof., subseq. Prof., Anatomy Dept, Univ. of Wisconsin, Madison, USA, 1964–77; Prof., Dept of Pharmacol and Physiol Sciences, Univ. of Chicago, 1977–84. Pres., Anatomical Soc. of GB&I, 1994–96. Editor-in-chief, European Jl of Neuroscience, 1988–92. *Publications:* (jtly) Exploring the Thalamus, 2001; contrib. Jl of Anat., Jl of Comp. Neurol., Jl of Neuroscience, and Brain Res. *Address:* c/o Department of Anatomy, University of Wisconsin, 1300 University Avenue, Madison, WI 53706, USA.

GUILLOU, Prof. Pierre John, MD; FRCS, FMedSci; Professor of Surgery, St James's University Hospital, Leeds, since 1993; Dean of the School of Medicine, University of Leeds, since 1998; *b* 30 Oct. 1945; *s* of Sarah Anne Guillou (*née* Greenfield) and Yves Guillou; *m* 1974, Elizabeth Anne Sowden; one *s* one *d*. *Educ:* Normanton Grammar Sch.; Univ. of Leeds (BSc; MB ChB 1970; MD 1975). Leeds Gen. Infirmary and St James's Univ. Hosp., 1970–73; S Manchester Univ. Hosp., 1973–74; Surgical Registrar, Leeds Gen. Infirmary, 1974–76; Lectr in Surgery, Univ. of Leeds, 1976–79; MRC Fellow in Immunology, Hôpital Necker, Paris, 1979–80; Sen. Lectr in Surgery, Univ. of Leeds, 1980–88; Prof. of Surgery, Imperial Coll. of Sci., Technology and Medicine and Dir, Academic Surgical Unit, St Mary's Hosp., London, 1988–93. Visiting Professor: Aust. Surgical Res. Soc., 1989, 1992; Univ. of Richmond, Va, 1992; S African Surgical Res. Soc., 1993; Ethicon, Malaysia, 1995; Sir Arthur Sims Commonwealth Prof., 1996; Lectures: Crookshank, Royal Soc. of Radiologists, 1990; Smith, Univ. of WA, 1991; A. B. Mitchell, QUB, 1991; jt meeting of Royal Colls of Surgeons of India and Glasgow, Madras, 1992; G. B. Ong, also Wilson T. S. Wang Internat. Surgical Symposium on Surgical Oncology, Chinese Univ. of Hong Kong, 1992, 1994; Annual Scientific Meeting of the Royal Coll. of Surgeons of Thailand, 1993; Stanford Cade, RCS, 1994; Marjorie Budd, Univ. of Bristol, 1995; 12th Asia Pacific Cancer Conf., Singapore, 1995. Member: James IV Assoc. of Surgeons, 1992–; Eur. Surgical Assoc., 1994–. Founder FMedSci 1998. Mem. Bd, British Jl of Surgery, 1994–. *Publications:* (ed) Surgical Oncology, 1991; Clinical Surgery, 1992; numerous papers on immunology, cell biology and surgery in treatment of cancer. *Recreations:* work, golf, fishing, work. *Address:* Academic Surgical Unit, Clinical Sciences Building, St James's University Hospital, Beckett Street, Leeds LS9 7TF. *T:* and *Fax:* (0113) 244 9618. *Club:* Royal Society of Medicine.

GUINERY, Paul Trevor; broadcaster; *b* 19 Jan. 1957; *s* of Dennis William Prickett and Eileen Grace Guinery. *Educ:* St Paul's Sch.; Royal Coll. of Music (ARCM 1975); Queen's Coll., Oxford (BA 1979). Joined BBC, 1980: studio manager, 1980–85; announcer and newsreader: World Service, 1985–89; Radio 3, 1989–; Presenter: Your Concert Choice, 1990–92; Concert Hall, 1992–98; Sacred and Profane, 1993–98; Choral Voices, 1998; Sounding the Millennium, 1999; Choirworks, 1999–. Vice-Chm., Delius Soc., 2001–. *Recreations:* playing the piano, theatre, collecting sheet music. *Address:* c/o BBC Radio 3, Broadcasting House, W1A 1AA.

GUINNESS, family name of **Earl of Iveagh** and **Baron Moyne**.

GUINNESS, Hon. Desmond (Walter); writer; *b* 8 Sept. 1931; *yr s* of 2nd Baron Moyne and of Hon. Diana Mitford (now Hon. Lady Mosley); *m* 1st, 1954, Marie-Gabrielle von Urach (marr. diss. 1981; she *d* 1989); one *s* one *d*; 2nd, Penelope, *d* of Graham and Teresa Cuthbertson. *Educ:* Gordonstoun; Christ Church, Oxford (MA). Founder, 1958, and Chm., 1958–91, Irish Georgian Society to work for the study of, and protection of, buildings of architectural merit in Ireland, particularly of the Georgian period. Hon. LLD TCD, 1980. *Publications:* Portrait of Dublin, 1967; Irish Houses and Castles, 1971; Mr Jefferson, Architect, 1973; Palladio, 1976; Georgian Dublin, 1980; The White House: an architectural history, 1981; Newport Preserv'd, 1982; (with Jacqueline O'Brien) Great Irish Houses and Castles, 1992; (with Jacqueline O'Brien) Dublin: a Grand Tour, 1994. *Clubs:* Chelsea Arts; Kildare Street and University, Friendly Brothers of St Patrick (Dublin).

GUINNESS, Sir Howard (Christian Sheldon), Kt 1981; VRD 1953; *b* 3 June 1932; *s* of late Edward Douglas Guinness, CBE and Martha Letière (*née* Sheldon); *m* 1958, Evadne Jane Gibbs; two *s* one *d*. *Educ:* King's Mead, Seaford, Sussex; Eton Coll. National Service, RN (midshipman); Lt-Comdr RNR. Union Discount Co. of London Ltd, 1953; Guinness Mahon & Co. Ltd, 1953–55; S. G. Warburg & Co. Ltd, 1955–85 (Exec. Dir, 1970–85). Dir, Harris & Sheldon Gp Ltd, 1960–81; Dir and Dep. Chm., Youghal Carpets (Holdings) Ltd, 1972–80. Director: Quality Milk Producers Ltd, 1988–2000; Riyad Bank Europe, 1993–99. Chm., N Hampshire Conservative Assoc., 1971–74; Vice-Chm. 1974, Chm. 1975–78, and Treasurer 1978–81, Wessex Area, Cons. Assoc. Mem. Council, English Guernsey Cattle Soc., 1963–72, 1996–99. *Recreations:* skiing, tennis. *Address:* The Manor House, Glanvilles Wootton, Sherborne, Dorset DT9 5QF. *T:* (01963) 210217. *Club:* White's.

See also Sir J. R. S. Guinness.

GUINNESS, James Edward Alexander Rundell, CBE 1986; Director, Guinness Peat Group, 1973–87 (Joint Chairman, 1973–77; Deputy Chairman, 1977–84); Deputy Chairman, Provident Mutual Life Assurance Association, 1983–89; *b* 23 Sept. 1924; *s* of late Sir Arthur Guinness, KCMG and Frances Patience Guinness, MBE (*née* Wright); *m* 1953, Pauline Mander; one *s* four *d*. *Educ:* Eton; Oxford. Served in RNVR, 1943–46. Joined family banking firm of Guinness Mahon & Co., 1946, Partner 1953; Chm., Guinness Mahon Hldgs Ltd, 1968–72. Chm., Public Works Loan Bd, 1979–90 (Comr, 1960–90). *Recreations:* shooting, fishing. *Address:* Coldpiece Farm, Hound Green, Hook, Hants RG27 8LQ. *T:* (01734) 326292. *Clubs:* Brooks's, Pratt's; Royal Yacht Squadron (Cowes).

GUINNESS, Sir John (Ralph Sidney), Kt 1999; CB 1985; Chairman, Trinity Group Finance Ltd, since 1999; *b* 23 Dec. 1935; *s* of late Edward Douglas Guinness and Martha Letière (*née* Sheldon); *m* 1967, Valerie Susan North; one *s* one *d* (and one *s* decd). *Educ:* Rugby Sch.; Trinity Hall, Cambridge (BA Hons History, MA Hons). Union Discount Co. Ltd, 1960–61; Overseas Develt Inst., 1961–62; joined FO, 1962; Econ. Relations Dept, 1962–63; Third Sec., UK Mission to UN, New York, 1963–64; seconded to UN Secretariat as Special Asst to Dep. Under-Sec. and later Under-Sec. for Econ. and Social Affairs, 1964–66; FCO, 1967–69; First Sec. (Econ.), Brit. High Commn, Ottawa, 1969–72; seconded to Central Policy Rev. Staff, Cabinet Office, 1972–75; Counsellor, 1974; Alternate UK Rep. to Law of the Sea Conf., 1975–77; seconded to CPRS, 1977–79; transferred to Home Civil Service, 1980; Under-Sec., 1980–83, Dep. Sec., 1983–91, Permanent Sec., 1991–92, Dept of Energy. Chm., British Nuclear Fuels, 1992–99; Director: Guinness Mahon Hldgs, 1993–99; Ocean Gp, 1993–2000; Mithras Investment Trust, 1994–. Governor, Oxford Energy Inst., 1984–92. Chm., Reviewing Cttee on Export of Works of Art, 1995–. Member: E Anglia Regl Cttee, NT, 1989–94; Develt Cttee, Nat. Portrait Gall., 1994–99; Council, BITC, 1992–99; Pres. Cttee, CBI, 1997–99 (Mem. Council, 1993–97); Dir, UK-Japan 2000 Gp, 1995–99. Mem., Adv. Council, Business Div., Prince's Trust, 1999–; Trustee: Prince's Youth Business Trust, 1992–99; Royal Collection Trust, 2001–. Gov., Compton Verney House Trust, 2000–. Hon. Freeman, Co. of Fuellers, 1999. Hon. Fellow: Mgt Sch., Lancaster Univ., 1997; Univ. of Central Lancashire, 1998. *Recreation:* iconography. *Clubs:* Brooks's, Beefsteak.

See also Sir H. C. S. Guinness.

GUINNESS, Sir Kenelm (Ernest Lee), 4th Bt *cr* 1867; formerly independent engineering consultant; *b* 13 Dec. 1928; *s* of late Kenelm Edward Lee Guinness and Mrs Josephine Lee Guinness; *S* uncle, 1954; *m* 1961, Mrs Jane Nevin Dickson; two *s*. *Educ:* Eton Coll.; Massachusetts Institute of Technology, USA. Late Lieut, Royal Horse Guards. With IBRD, Washington, 1954–75. *Heir: s* Kenelm Edward Lee Guinness, *b* 30 Jan. 1962. *Address:* (home) Rich Neck, Claiborne, MD 21624, USA. *T:* (410) 7455079. *Clubs:* Cavalry and Guards; Household Division Yacht; Cruising of America.

GUISE, Sir John (Grant), 7th Bt *cr* 1783; Jockey Club Official, 1968; *b* 15 Dec. 1927; *s* of Sir Anselm William Edward Guise, 6th Bt and Nina Margaret Sophie (*d* 1991), *d* of Sir James Augustus Grant, 1st Bt; *S* father, 1970; *m* 1992, Sally, *d* of late Cdre H. G. C. Stevens, RN. *Educ:* Winchester; RMA, Sandhurst. Regular officer, 3rd The King's Own Hussars, 1948–61. *Recreations:* hunting, shooting. *Heir: b* Christopher James Guise [*b* 10 July 1930; *m* 1969, Mrs Carole Hoskins Benson, *e d* of Jack Master; one *s* one *d*]. *Address:* Elmore Court, Gloucester GL2 3NT. *T:* (01452) 720293.

GULL, Prof. Keith, PhD; Professor of Molecular Biology, University of Manchester, since 1989; *b* 29 May 1948; *s* of David Gull and Doris Gull (*née* Manging); *m* 1972, Dianne Hilary Leonora Elgar; one *s* one *d*. *Educ:* Queen Elizabeth Coll., Univ. of London (BSc Hons 1969, PhD 1972, Microbiology). University of Kent: Lectr, 1972–82; Sen. Lectr, 1982–84; Reader, 1984–86; Prof. of Cell Biology, 1986–89. Vis. Sen. Scientist, Sandoz Inst., Vienna, 1978; Vis. Prof., McArdle Lab. for Cancer Res., Univ. of Wisconsin, 1982.

Darwin Lectr, BAAS, 1983; Marjory Stephenson Lectr, Soc. for Gen. Microbiology, 1996. FMedSci 1999. *Publications:* numerous contribs to books and scientific jls. *Recreations:* fly fishing, painting. *Address:* School of Biological Sciences, University of Manchester, Stopford Building, Oxford Road, Manchester M13 9PT. *T:* (0161) 275 5108.

GULL, Sir Rupert (William Cameron), 5th Bt *cr* 1872, of Brook Street; company director; *b* 14 July 1954; *s* of Sir Michael Swinnerton Cameron Gull, 4th Bt and Yvonne (*d* 1975), *o d* of Dr Albert Oliver Macarius Heslop, Cape Town; *S* father, 1989; *m* 1980, Gillian Lee, *d* of Robert MacFarlaine; three *d. Educ:* Diocesan Coll., Cape Town; Cape Town Univ. *Heir: cousin* Angus William John Gull [*b* 24 Dec. 1963; *m* 1988, Jacqueline Mary, *d* of Gerald Edgar Ford]. *Address:* 2 Harcourt Road, Claremont, Cape Town, South Africa.

GULLICK, Stephen John; His Honour Judge Gullick; a Circuit Judge, since 1998; *b* 22 Feb. 1948; *s* of David and Evelyn Gullick; *m* 1973, Lesley Steadman; two *s. Educ:* Taunton Sch.; Birmingham Univ. (LLB 1970). Called to the Bar, Gray's Inn, 1971; in practice at the Bar, 1971–98; a Recorder, 1990–98; Standing Counsel, HM Customs and Excise, 1991–98; North Eastern Circuit. *Recreations:* campanology, watching sport. *Address:* Leeds Combined Court Centre, 1 Oxford Row, Leeds LS1 3BG.

GULLY, family name of **Viscount Selby**.

GUMBEL, Elizabeth-Anne, (Mrs Michael Wainwright); QC 1999; *b* 17 Oct. 1953; *d* of Walter and Muriel Gumbel; *m* 1984, Michael Wainwright; one *s* one *d. Educ:* St Paul's Girls' Sch.; Wycombe Abbey Sch.; Lady Margaret Hall, Oxford (MA). Called to the Bar, Inner Temple, 1974. *Address:* 199 Strand, WC2R 1DR.

GUMBS, Hon. Sir Emile (Rudolph), Kt 1994; Chief Minister, Anguilla, 1977–80 and 1984–94; *b* 18 March 1928; *s* of Johnson Emile Gumbs and Inez Beatrice Gumbs (*née* Carty); *m* 1st, 1964, Janice Anne Bradley; one *s* one *d*; 2nd, 1993, Louisa Josephine DeRoche. *Educ:* St Kitts/Nevis Grammar Sch. Captain, Schooner Warspite, 1955–64; Manager, Anguilla Road Salt Co., 1964–77 and 1980–84. Elected Rep., Road N Anguilla, 1968–94; Minister of Govt, 1976–80 and 1984–94. *Recreations:* sailing, fishing, bird watching. *Address:* Sandy Ground, PO Box 70, Anguilla, British West Indies. *T:* 4972711, *Fax:* 4973292.

GUMLEY-MASON, Frances Jane, MA; broadcaster and journalist; Headmistress, St Augustine's Priory, Ealing, since 1995; *b* 28 Jan. 1955; *o d* of late Franc Stewart Gumley and Helen Teresa (*née* McNicholas); name changed to Gumley-Mason by statutory declaration, 1995; *m* 1988, Andrew Samuel Mason (now Gumley-Mason); one *s* one *d. Educ:* St Augustine's Priory, Ealing; St Benedict's Sch., Ealing (Greek only); Newnham Coll., Cambridge (MA). Parly research, 1974; Braille transcriber, 1975; Catholic Herald: Editorial Assistant and Assistant Literary Editor, Dec. 1975; Literary Editor and Staff Reporter, 1976–79; Editor, 1979–81; RC Asst to Head of Religious Broadcasting, and sen. producer, religious progs, radio, and producer, religious television, 1981–88; Series Editor, Religious Programmes, C4, 1988–89; guest producer, scriptwriter and presenter, BBC World Service and Radio 4, 1989–94. Mistress of The Keys, Guild of Catholic Writers, 1983–88. *Publications:* (as F. J. Gumley, with Brian Redhead): The Good Book, 1987; The Christian Centuries, 1989; The Pillars of Islam, 1990; Protestors for Paradise, 1993; (jtly) Discovering Turkey, 1995. *Recreation:* playing with her children's toys. *Address:* St Augustine's Priory, Hillcrest Road, Ealing, W5 2JL.

GUMMER, family name of **Baron Chadlington**.

GUMMER, Rt Hon. John Selwyn; PC 1985; MP (C) Suffolk Coastal, since 1983 (Eye, Suffolk, 1979–83); *b* 26 Nov. 1939; *s* of late Canon Selwyn Gummer and Sybille (*née* Mason); *m* 1977, Penelope Jane, *yr d* of John P. Gardner; two *s* two *d. Educ:* King's Sch., Rochester; Selwyn Coll., Cambridge (Exhibr). BA Hons History 1961; MA 1971; Chm., Cambridge Univ. Conservative Assoc., 1961; Pres., Cambridge Union, 1962; Chm., Fedn of Conservative Students, 1962. Editor, Business Publications, 1962–64; Editor-in-Chief, Max Parrish & Oldbourne Press, 1964–66; BPC Publishing: Special Asst to Chm., 1967; Publisher, Special Projects, 1967–69; Editorial Coordinator, 1969–70. Mem., ILEA Educn Cttee, 1967–70; Dir, Shandwick Publishing Co., 1966–81; Man. Dir, EP Gp of Cos, 1975–81; Chairman: Selwyn Shandwick Internat., 1976–81, Siemssen Hunter Ltd, 1979–80 (Dir, 1973–80). Contested (C) Greenwich, 1964 and 1966; MP (C) Lewisham W, 1970–Feb. 1974; PPS to Minister of Agriculture, 1972; an additional Vice-Chm., Conservative Party, 1972–74; an Asst Govt Whip, 1981; a Lord Comr of HM Treasury, 1981–83; Parly Under-Sec. of State for Employment, Jan.–Oct. 1983; Minister of State, Dept of Employment, 1983–84; Paymaster-Gen., 1984–85; Chm., Cons. Party, 1983–85; Minister of State: MAFF, 1985–88; DoE, 1988–89; Minister of Agric., Fisheries and Food, 1989–93; Sec. of State for the Envmnt, 1993–97. Chairman: Cons. Gp for Europe, 1997–; Marine Stewardship Council, 1998–. Chairman: Sancroft Internat. Ltd, 1997–; Valpak Ltd, 1998–; Director: General Utilities Ltd, 1997–; Ambio Ltd, 1997–. Mem., Gen. Synod of the Church of England, 1979–92. *Publications:* (jtly) When the Coloured People Come, 1966; The Permissive Society, 1971; (with L. W. Cowie) The Christian Calendar, 1974; (contrib.) To Church with Enthusiasm, 1969; (contrib.) Faith In Politics, 1987; Christianity and Conservatism, 1990. *Address:* House of Commons, SW1A 0AA.
See also Baron Chadlington.

GUMMOW, Hon. William Montague Charles, AC 1997; **Hon. Justice Gummow;** Justice, High Court of Australia, since 1995; *b* 9 Oct. 1942; *s* of W. C. R. Gummow and A. C. Gummow (*née* Benson). *Educ:* Sydney Grammar Sch.; Univ. of Sydney (BA 1962; LLB 1965; LLM 1970). Admitted Solicitor, Supreme Court of NSW, 1966; Partner, Allen, Allen & Hemsley, 1969–76; admitted to NSW Bar, 1976; in practice at the Bar, 1976–86; QC (NSW) 1986; Judge, Federal Court of Australia, 1986–95. Clarendon Law Lectr, Oxford Univ., 1999. Mem., Amer. Law Inst., 1997. Hon. LLD Sydney, 1992. *Publications:* Jacobs' Law of Trusts in Australia, 3rd edn 1971 to 6th edn (jtly) 1997; Equity: doctrines and remedies, 1975, 3rd edn (jtly) 1992; Cases and Materials on Equity and Trusts, 1975, 4th edn 1993. *Address:* Judges' Chambers, High Court of Australia, PO Box E435, Kingston, ACT 2604, Australia. *T:* (2) 62706955. *Club:* Australian (Sydney).

GUN-MUNRO, Sir Sydney Douglas, GCMG 1979; Kt 1977; MBE 1957; FRCS; Governor-General of St Vincent and the Grenadines, 1979–85, retired (Governor, 1977–79); *b* 29 Nov. 1916; *s* of Barclay Justin Gun-Munro and Marie Josephine Gun-Munro; *m* 1943, Joan Estelle Benjamin; two *s* one *d. Educ:* Grenada Boys' Secondary Sch.; King's Coll. Hosp., London (MB, BS Hons 1943); Moorfields Hosp., London (DO 1952). MRCS, LRCP 1943; FRCS 1985. House Surg., EMS Hosp., Horton, 1943; MO, Lewisham Hosp., 1943–46; Dist MO, Grenada, 1946–49; Surg., Gen. Hosp., St Vincent, 1949–71; Dist MO, Bequia, St Vincent, 1972–76. *Recreations:* tennis, boating. *Address:* PO Box 51, Bequia, St Vincent and the Grenadines, West Indies. *T:* 83261.

GUNAWARDENA, Jeremy Harin Charles, PhD; Director, Basic Research Institute in the Mathematical Sciences, Hewlett-Packard Laboratories, since 1998; *b* 12 Nov. 1955; *s* of Charles Gunawardena and Yvonne Gunawardena (*née* Weerakoon). *Educ:* Imperial Coll., London (BSc); Trinity Coll., Cambridge (MA; PhD 1983). L. E. Dickson Instr, Dept of Mathematics, Univ. of Chicago, 1981–83; Res. Fellow in Mathematics, Trinity Coll., Cambridge, 1983–87; Mem., Technical Staff, Hewlett-Packard Labs, 1987–. Vis. Schol., Dept of Computer Sci., Stanford Univ., 1992–94; Vis. Res. Fellow, Trinity Coll., Cambridge, 1995; Prof. Invitée, Ecole Normale Supérieure, Paris, 2000. Mem., EPSRC, 1999–. *Publication:* (ed) Idempotency, 1998. *Recreations:* tennis, cricket, classical music, flying aeroplanes. *Address:* Basic Research Institute in the Mathematical Sciences, Hewlett-Packard Laboratories, Filton Road, Stoke Gifford, Bristol BS34 8QZ. *T:* (0117) 312 8216.

GUNN, John Angus Livingston; Head of Heritage and Tourism Group, Department of National Heritage, 1992; *b* 20 Nov. 1934; *s* of late Alistair L. Gunn, FRCOG, and Mrs Sybil Gunn, JP; *m* 1959, Jane, *d* of Robert Cameron; one *s* one *d. Educ:* Fettes Coll., Edinburgh (Foundationer); Christ Church, Oxford (Scholar; BA 1st Cl. Hons in Classical Hon. Mod., 1955, and in final sch. of Psychology, Philosophy and Physiology, 1957; Passmore-Edwards Prizeman, 1956; MA). National Service, commnd in S Wales Borderers (24th Regt), 1957–59. Entered Min. of Transport, 1959; Principal Private Sec. to Ministers of Transport, 1967–68; Asst Sec., MoT, DoE and Civil Service Dept, 1969–75; Under-Sec., DoE, 1976–92; Greater London Housing and Planning Directorate, 1976; Water Directorate, 1981; Water Privatisation Directorate, 1987; Heritage and Royal Estate Directorate, 1990.

GUNN, Prof. John Charles, CBE 1994; MD; FMedSci, FRCPsych; Professor of Forensic Psychiatry, Institute of Psychiatry, since 1978; *b* 6 June 1937; *s* of Albert Charles Gunn and late Lily Hilda Edwards; *m* 1st, 1959, Celia Willis (marr. diss. 1986, she *d* 1989); one *s* one *d*; 2nd, 1989, Pamela Taylor, *qv. Educ:* Brighton, Hove and Sussex Grammar Sch.; Reigate Grammar Sch.; Birmingham Univ. (MB ChB 1961; Acad. DPM 1966; MD 1969). MRCPsych 1971, FRCPsych 1980. Queen Elizabeth Hosp., Birmingham, 1961–63; Maudsley Hosp., 1963–67; Institute of Psychiatry: Res. Worker, 1967–69; Lectr, 1969–71; Sen. Lectr, 1971–75; Dir, Special Hosps Res. Unit, 1975–78. H. B. Williams Vis. Prof. to Aust. and NZ, 1985. Advisor, H of C Select Cttees on Violence in Marriage, 1975, on Prison Med. Service, 1986; Member: Home Sec's Adv. Bd on Restricted Patients, 1982–91; Royal Commn on Criminal Justice, 1991–93. WHO Specialist Advisor in Forensic Psychiatry to China, 1987; Consultant, Eur. Cttee for Prevention of Torture, 1993–. Royal College of Psychiatrists: Chm., Res. Cttee, 1976–80; Dep. Chief Examr, 1993–95; Mem., Council, 1977–83, 1997–; Mem., Exec. Cttee, 1998–. Founder FMedSci 1998. Editor, Criminal Behaviour and Mental Health, 1991–. *Publications:* Epileptics in Prison, 1977; Psychiatric Aspects of Imprisonment, 1978; Current Research in Forensic Psychiatry and Psychology, vols 1–3, 1982–85; Violence in Human Society, 1983; (ed with P. J. Taylor) Forensic Psychiatry: clinical, legal and ethical issues, 1993. *Recreations:* theatre, opera, cinema, photography, walking, living with Pamela. *Address:* Department of Forensic Psychiatry, Institute of Psychiatry, De Crespigny Park, Denmark Hill, SE5 8AF. *T:* (020) 7701 7063; *e-mail:* j.gunn@iop.kcl.ac.uk. *Clubs:* Athenæum, Royal Society of Medicine.

GUNN, Prof. Sir John (Currie), Kt 1982; CBE 1976; MA (Glasgow and Cambridge); FRSE, FIMA; FInstP; Cargill Professor of Natural Philosophy, 1949–82 and Head of Department, 1973–82, Dean of Faculties, 1989–91, University of Glasgow; *b* 13 Sept. 1916; *s* of Richard Robertson Gunn and Jane Blair Currie; *m* 1944, Betty Russum (OBE 1984); one *s. Educ:* Glasgow Acad.; Glasgow Univ.; St John's Coll., Cambridge. Engaged in Admiralty scientific service, first at Admiralty Research Laboratory, later at Mine Design Dept, 1939–45; Research Fellow of St John's Coll., Cambridge, 1944; Lecturer in Applied Mathematics: Manchester Univ., 1945–46; University Coll., London, 1946–49. Member: SRC, 1968–72; UGC, 1974–81. Hon. DSc: Heriot-Watt, 1981; Loughborough, 1983; DUniv Open, 1989. *Publications:* papers on mathematical physics in various scientific journals. *Recreations:* golf, music, chess. *Address:* 32 Beaconsfield Road, Glasgow G12 0NY. *T:* (0141) 357 2001.

GUNN, John Humphrey; company director and corporate development adviser; Director, Scheidegg Ltd, since 1997; *b* 15 Jan. 1942; *s* of Francis (Bob) Gunn and Doris Gunn; *m* 1965, Renate Sigrid (*née* Boehme); three *d. Educ:* Sir John Deane's Grammar School, Northwich; Univ. of Nottingham (BA Hons 1964). Barclays Bank, 1964–68; Astley & Pearce, 1968–85; Chief Executive: Exco International, 1979–85; British & Commonwealth Holdings, 1986–87 and 1990 (Chm., 1987–90). Hon. LLD Nottingham, 1989. *Recreations:* golf, ski-ing, mountain walking, classical music, opera. *Address:* 2nd Floor, 25 Watling Street, EC4M 9BR. *T:* (020) 7236 6236. *Club:* MCC.

GUNN, Marion Ballantyne; Head of Fire Service and Emergency Planning Division, Scottish Executive Justice Department (formerly Scottish Office Home and Health, then Home, Department), 1992–2001; *b* 31 Oct. 1947; *d* of Dr Allan Christie Tait and Jean Ballantyne Hay; *m* 1985, Donald Hugh Gunn; one step *s. Educ:* Jordanhill College School; Dumfries Academy; Univ. of Edinburgh (MA Hons 1969); Open Univ. (BA 1975). Management trainee, Lewis's, Bristol, 1969–70; joined Scottish Office, 1970; posts in Scottish Educn Dept and Scottish Develt Dept, 1970–90; Asst Sec., 1984; Head of Roads Policy and Programme Div., 1987; Head of Water Policy Div., 1990. Research Fellow, Univ. of Glasgow, 1983–84. *Recreations:* gardening, badminton. *Address:* 32 Warriston Avenue, Edinburgh EH3 5NB. *T:* (0131) 552 4476.

GUNN, Pamela Jane; *see* Taylor, P. J.

GUNN, Sir Robert (Norman), Kt 1995; DL; Chairman, Further Education Funding Council for England, 1992–97; Chairman, 1985–90, Chief Executive, 1983–87 and Director, 1976–90, The Boots Company PLC; *b* 16 Dec. 1925; *s* of late Donald Macfie Gunn and Margaret (*née* Pallister); *m* 1956, Joan Parry, JP; one *d. Educ:* Royal High Sch., Edinburgh; Worcester Coll., Oxford (MA). Served RAC, 1944–47 (Lieut). Joined Boots, 1951; Merchandise Buyer, 1962–70; Head of Warehousing and Distribn, 1971–73; Dir of Property, 1973–78; Dir, Industrial Div., 1979–83 (Man. Dir 1980–83); Vice-Chm., 1983–85. Director: Foseco plc (formerly Foseco Minsep), 1984–91; East Midlands Electricity, 1990–95; Nottingham Building Soc., 1990–97. Member: Bd of Management, Assoc. of British Pharmaceutical Industry, 1981–84 (Vice-Pres., 1983–84); Council, CBI, 1985–90; PCFC, 1989–93; HEFCE, 1992–94. CIMgt (CBIM 1983); FInstD 1985; FRSA. DL Notts, 1995. Hon. LLD Nottingham, 1993. *Recreations:* gardening, travel. *Address:* Tor House, Pinfold Lane, Elston, near Newark, Notts NG23 5PD.

GUNN, Thomson William, (Thom); poet; Senior Lecturer, English Department, University of California (Berkeley), 1990–99; *b* 29 Aug. 1929; *s* of Herbert Smith Gunn, and Ann Charlotte Gunn (*née* Thomson); unmarried. *Educ:* University Coll. Sch., Hampstead; Trinity Coll., Cambridge. British Army (National Service), 1948–50; lived in Paris six months, 1950; Cambridge, 1950–53; lived in Rome, 1953–54; has lived in California since 1954. Lectr, later Associate Prof., English Dept, University of Calif (Berkeley), 1958–66, Vis. Lectr, 1975–90. *Publications:* Poetry from Cambridge, 1953; Fighting Terms, 1954; The Sense of Movement, 1957; My Sad Captains, 1961; Selected Poems (with Ted Hughes), 1962; Five American Poets (ed with Ted Hughes), 1962;

Positives (with Ander Gunn), 1966; Touch, 1967; Poems 1950–1966: a selection, 1969; Moly, 1971; Jack Straw's Castle and other poems, 1976; Selected Poems, 1979; The Passages of Joy, 1982; The Occasions of Poetry (ed Clive Wilmer), 1982; The Man with Night Sweats, 1992; Collected Poems, 1993; Shelf Life, 1993; Boss Cupid, 2000. *Recreations:* cheap thrills. *Address:* 1216 Cole Street, San Francisco, CA 94117, USA.

GUNN, Sir William (Archer), AC 1990; KBE 1961; CMG 1955; JP; Australian grazier and company director; Chairman, International Wool Secretariat, 1961–73; *b* Goondiwindi, Qld, 1 Feb. 1914; *s* of late Walter and Doris Isabel Gunn, Goondiwindi; *m* 1939, Mary (Phillipa), *d* of F. B. Haydon, Murrurundi, NSW; one *s* two *d*. *Educ:* The King's Sch., Parramatta, NSW. Director: Rothmans of Pall Mall (Australia) Ltd; Grazcos Co-op. Ltd; Clausen Steamship Co. (Australia) Pty Ltd; Walter Reid and Co. Ltd; Gunn Rural Management Pty Ltd; Chairman and Managing Director: Moline Pastoral Co. Pty Ltd; Roper Valley Pty Ltd; Coolibah Pty Ltd; Mataranba Pty Ltd; Unibeef Australia Pty Ltd; Gunn Development Pty Ltd; Chairman: Australian Wool Bd, 1963–72; Qld Adv. Bd, Develt Finance Corp., 1962–72; Member: Commonwealth Bank Bd, 1952–59; Qld Bd, Nat. Mutual Life Assoc., 1955–67; Reserve Bank Bd, 1959–; Aust. Meat Bd, 1953–66; Aust. Wool Bureau, 1951–63 (Chm. 1958–63); Aust. Wool Growers Council, 1947–60 (Chm. 1955–58); Graziers Federal Council of Aust., 1950–60 (Pres. 1951–54); Aust. Wool Growers and Graziers Council, 1960–65; Export Develt Council, 1962–65; Australian Wool Corp., 1973; Faculty of Veterinary Science, University of Qld, 1953–; Exec. Council, United Graziers Assoc. of Qld, 1944–69 (Pres., 1951–59; Vice-Pres., 1947–51); Aust. Wool Testing Authority, 1958–63; Council, NFU of Aust., 1951–54; CSIRO State Cttee, 1951–68; Chairman: The Wool Bureau Inc., New York, 1962–69; Trustee: Qld Cancer Fund; Australian Pastoral Research Trust, 1959–71. Coronation Medal, 1953; Golden Fleece Achievement Award (Bd of Dirs of Nat. Assoc. of Wool Manufrs of America), 1962; Award of Golden Ram (Natal Woolgrowers Assoc. of SA), 1973. *Address:* Goondiwindi, Qld 4390, Australia. *Clubs:* Queensland, Tattersalls, Queensland Turf (Brisbane); Union (Sydney); Australian (Melbourne).

GUNNELL, Sally Jane Janet, OBE 1998 (MBE 1993); athlete, retired 1997; television presenter; *b* 29 July 1966; *m* 1992, Jonathan Bigg; two *s*. *Educ:* Chigwell High School. Life Member, Essex Ladies' Club, 1978; GB Team Captain, 1992–97; 400 m hurdles wins include: Olympic Champion, 1992; World Champion, 1993; World Record Holder, 1993; European Champion, 1994; Commonwealth Champion, 1994; also Commonwealth Champion, 100 m hurdles, 1986, 1990. *Publications:* Running Tall, 1994; Be Your Best, 2001. *Address:* Old School Cottage, School Lane, Pyecombe, W Sussex BN45 7FQ.

GUNNELL, (William) John; *b* 1 Oct. 1933; *s* of late William Henry and Norah Gunnell; *m* 1955, Jean Louise, *d* of late Frank and Harriet Louise Lacey; three *s* one *d*. *Educ:* King Edward's Sch., Birmingham; Univ. of Leeds (BSc Hons). Hospital porter, St Bartholomew's, London, 1955–57; Teacher, Leeds Modern Sch., 1959–62; Head of Science, United Nations International Sch., New York, 1962–70; Lectr, Centre for Studies in Science and Mathematics Education, Univ. of Leeds, 1970–88. Chm., Crown Point Foods, 1988–90. County Councillor for Hunslet, 1977–86; Leader of Opposition, 1979–81, Leader, 1981–86, W Yorks MCC; Mem. for Hunslet, Leeds MDC, 1986–92 (Chm., Social Services Cttee, 1990–92). MP (Lab) Leeds South and Morley, 1992–97, Morley and Rothwell, 1997–2001. Chm., Educn and Employment Deptl Cttee, 1997–99. Chairman: Yorkshire Enterprise Ltd (formerly W Yorks Enterprise Bd), 1982–90 and 1994–96 (Vice-Chm., 1990–94); Yorkshire Fund Management Ltd, 1989–97 (non-exec. Dir, 1989–). Chairman: Yorks and Humberside Develt Assoc., 1981–93 (Hon. Pres., 1993–97); Leeds/Bradford Airport jt cttee, 1981–83; N of England Regional Consortium, 1984–92 (Hon. Pres., 1992–97); Member: Audit Commn, 1983–90; Leeds Develt Corp., 1988–92; Leeds Eastern AHA, later Leeds Health Care, 1990–92. Advr to Conseil des Régions d'Europe, subseq. Assembly of Regions of Europe, 1986– (Mem. Bureau, 1985–86). Hon. Pres., RETI, 1985–87. Spokesman for MCCs in their campaign against abolition, 1983–85. Mem., Fabian Soc., 1972–. Director: Opera North, 1982–; Leeds Theatre Trust, 1986–93. *Publications:* Selected Experiments in Advanced Level Chemistry, 1975, and other texts (all with E. W. Jenkins); (contrib.) Local Economic Policy, 1990. *Recreations:* music, opera, watching cricket and soccer. *Clubs:* Warwickshire CC; Yorkshire CC.

GUNNING, Prof. Brian Edgar Scourse, FRS 1980; FAA 1979; Professor of Plant Cell Biology, Australian National University, 1974–97, now Emeritus; *b* 29 Nov. 1934; *s* of William Gunning and Margaret Gunning (*née* Scourse); *m* 1964, Marion Sylvia Forsyth; two *s*. *Educ:* Methodist Coll., Belfast; Queen's Univ., Belfast (BSc (Hons), MSc, PhD); DSc ANU. Lecturer in Botany, 1957–65, Reader in Botany, 1965–74, Queen's Univ., Belfast. Hon. MRIA 1999. *Publications:* Ultrastructure and the Biology of Plant Cells (with Dr M. Steer), 1975; Intercellular Communication in Plants: studies on plasmodesmata (with Dr A. Robards), 1976; (with M. Steer) Plant Cell Biology, 1996; contribs to research jls. *Recreations:* hill walking, photography. *Address:* 29 Millen Street, Hughes, ACT 2605, Australia. *T:* (2) 62812879.

GUNNING, Sir Charles Theodore, 9th Bt *cr* 1778, of Eltham, Kent; CD 1964; RCN retired; engineering consultant, Promaxis Systems Inc., Ottawa; *b* 19 June 1935; *s* of Sir Robert Gunning, 8th Bt and of Helen Nancy, *d* of Vice-Adm. Sir Theodore John Hallett, KBE, CB; *S* father, 1989; *m* 1st, 1969, Sarah (marr. diss. 1982), *d* of Col Patrick Arthur Easton; one *d*; 2nd, 1989, Linda Martin (*née* Kachmar). *Educ:* Canadian Mil. Coll.; RNEC Plymouth; Tech. Univ. of NS. PEng; MCIMarE. Chm., Nat. Council in Canada, Royal Commonwealth Soc., 1990–93 (Pres., Ottawa Br.; a Nat. Vice-Chm.). Silver Jubilee Medal, 1977. *Heir: b* John Robert Gunning [*b* 17 Sept. 1944; *m* 1969, Alina Tylicki (marr. diss. 1995); two *s* one *d*]. *Address:* 2940 McCarthy Road, Ottawa, ON K1V 8K6, Canada.

GUNSTON, Sir John (Wellesley), 3rd Bt *cr* 1938, of Wickwar, Co. Gloucester; company director; *b* 25 July 1962; *s* of Sir Richard Gunston, 2nd Bt and of Mrs Joan Elizabeth Marie Gunston; *S* father, 1991; *m* 1990, Rosalind (marr. diss. 1998), *y d* of Edward Gordon Eliott; one *s*. *Educ:* Harrow; RMA Sandhurst. BSAP Reserve, Rhodesia, 1979–80. Commnd 1st Bn Irish Guards, 1981. Since 1983 has covered wars, revolutions and foreign travel assignments in: Afghanistan, Albania, Brazil, Burma, Colombia, Egypt, Eritrea, Israel (West Bank and Gaza), Lebanon, Liberia, South Africa, Sudan, Uganda, Ulster (esp. Derry) and also in North America, Eastern Europe and South East Asia. Dir, North-West Frontier Productions, 1995–; Man. Dir, Hard News Ltd, 1998–. Chm., Rory Peck Trust and Award, 1995–97. Fellow: Soc. of Authors, 1994; RSAA, 1995; FRGS 1988; FRAS 1998. *Recreations:* books, biking and ballistics. *Heir: s* Richard St George Gunston, *b* 3 July 1992. *Address:* c/o 127 Piccadilly, W1E 6YZ. *Clubs:* Cavalry and Guards, Special Forces.

GUNTER, John Forsyth; freelance theatre and opera designer; Associate Designer, Royal National Theatre, since 1991 (Head of Design, 1989–91); *b* 31 Oct. 1938; *s* of late Herbert and Charlotte Gunter; *m* 1969, Micheline McKnight; two *d*. *Educ:* Bryanston Public Sch.; Central Sch. of Art and Design (Dip. with distinction). Started career in rep. theatre in GB; Resident Designer: English Stage Co., 1965–66 (subseq. designed 28 prodns for co.); Zürich Schauspielhaus, 1970–73; freelance design work for West End, NT, RSC, Old Vic and for Broadway, New York, 1973–, incl. Peter Hall Co. season, Piccadilly Th., 1998; designer of operas: for cos in GB, Italy, Germany, Austria, Australia and USA; Glyndebourne Fest. Op., 1985–; Royal Opera House, Covent Gdn, 1997–; La Scala, Milan, 1988. Head, Theatre Dept, Central Sch. of Art and Design, 1974–82. FRSA 1982. Many awards for design of Guys and Dolls, NT, 1982, incl. SWET Award for Best Design 1982, Drama Magazine Best Design Award 1982, Plays and Players Award for Best Design 1983; Plays and Players and Olivier Awards for Best Design 1984, for design of Wild Honey, NT, 1984; Emmy Award, 1994, for set design of Porgy and Bess. *Recreations:* getting out into the countryside, tennis. *Address:* c/o Peter Murphy, Curtis Brown, 4th Floor, Haymarket House, 28–29 Haymarket, SW1Y 4SP.

GUNTON, Rev. Prof. Colin Ewart, DPhil, DD; Professor of Christian Doctrine, King's College, University of London, since 1984; *b* 19 Jan. 1941; *s* of Herbert Ewart Gunton and Mabel Priscilla Gunton; *m* 1964, Jennifer Mary Osgathorpe; two *s* two *d*. *Educ:* Nottingham High Sch.; Hertford Coll., Oxford (Schol; BA Lit. Hum. 1964); Mansfield Coll., Oxford (BA Theol. 1966; MA 1967; DPhil 1973); DD London 1993. Ordained Minister, United Reformed Ch., 1972; Associate Minister, Brentwood URC, 1975–. King's College, London: Lectr in Philosophy of Religion, 1969–80; Lectr in Systematic Theol., 1980–83; Sen. Lectr, 1983–84; Dean, Faculty of Theol. and Religious Studies, 1988–90; Head, Dept of Theol. and Religious Studies, 1993–96. Bampton Lectr, Univ. of Oxford, 1992; Warfield Lectr, Princeton Theol Seminary, 1993. Pres., Soc. for Study of Theol., 1993–94. Jt Editor, Internat. Jl of Systematic Theology, 1999–. Hon. DD Aberdeen, 1999. *Publications:* Becoming and Being: the doctrine of God in Charles Hartshorne and Karl Barth, 1978; Yesterday and Today: a study of continuities in Christology, 1983, 2nd edn 1997; Enlightenment and Alienation: an essay towards a Trinitarian Theology, 1985; The Actuality of Atonement: a study of metaphor, rationality and the Christian Tradition, 1989; (ed with D. W. Hardy) On Being the Church: essays on the Christian Community, 1989; The Promise of Trinitarian Theology, 1991, 2nd edn 1997; (ed with C. Schwoebel) Persons, Divine and Human: King's College essays in theological anthropology, 1992; Christ and Creation: the 1990 Didsbury Lectures, 1993; The One, the Three and the Many: God, Creation and the Culture of Modernity (Bampton Lectures), 1993; A Brief Theology of Revelation (Warfield Lectures), 1995; (ed) God and Freedom: essays in historical and systematic theology, 1995; Theology through the Theologians, 1996; (ed) Cambridge Companion to Christian Doctrine, 1997; (ed) The Doctrine of Creation: essays in dogmatics, history and philosophy, 1997; The Triune Creator: a historical and systematic study, 1998; Intellect and Action, 2000; (ed) Trinity, Time and Church: a response to the theology of Robert W. Jenson, 2000; Theology through Preaching: sermons for Brentwood, 2001; The Christian Faith: an introduction to Christian doctrine, 2001; contrib. to Scottish Jl of Theol., Jl of Theol Studies, Religious Studies, Mod. Theol., Theol., Expository Times, Theol. Today, Neue Zeitschrift für Systematische Theologie und Religionsphilosophie, Internat. Jl of Systematic Theol. *Recreations:* music, gardening, walking. *Address:* Department of Theology and Religious Studies, King's College, Strand, WC2R 2LS. *T:* (020) 7848 2459; 7 Oxford Court, Brentwood, Essex CM14 5EU. *T:* (01277) 221585.

GURDON, family name of **Baron Cranworth**.

GURDON, Sir John (Bertrand), Kt 1995; DPhil; FRS 1971; Master, Magdalene College, Cambridge, 1995–Sept. 2002; John Humphrey Plummer Professor of Cell Biology, University of Cambridge, 1983–2001; Chairman, Wellcome Cancer Research Campaign Institute, Cambridge, 1991–2001; *b* 2 Oct. 1933, *s* of late W. N. Gurdon, DCM, formerly of Assington, Suffolk, and Elsie Marjorie (*née* Byass); *m* 1964, Jean Elizabeth Margaret Curtis; one *s* one *d*. *Educ:* Edgeborough; Eton (Fellow, 1978–93); Christ Church, Oxford; BA 1956; DPhil 1960. Beit Memorial Fellow, 1958–61; Gosney Research Fellow, Calif. Inst. Technol., 1962; Departmental Demonstrator, Dept of Zool., Oxford, 1963–64; Vis. Research Fellow, Carnegie Instn, Baltimore, 1965; Lectr, Dept of Zoology, Oxford, 1965–72; Research Student, Christ Church, 1962–72; Mem. Staff, MRC Lab. of Molecular Biology, Cambridge, 1972–83 (Hd, Cell Biology Div., 1979–83); Fellow, Churchill Coll., Cambridge, 1973–94. Fullerian Prof. of Physiology and Comparative Anatomy, Royal Instn, 1985–91. Lectures: Harvey Soc., NY, 1973; Dunham, Harvard, 1974; Croonian, Royal Soc., 1976; Carter-Wallace, Princeton, 1978; Woodhull, Royal Instn, 1980; Florey, Aust., 1988; Fischberg Meml, Geneva, 1989; Rutherford, Royal Soc., 1996; Rodney Porter Meml, Oxford, 1999. Pres., Internat. Soc. Develt Biol., 1989–93. Gov., The Wellcome Trust, 1995–2000. Chm., Co. of Biologists, 2001–. Hon. Foreign Member: Amer. Acad. of Arts and Scis, 1978; Foreign Associate: Nat. Acad. of Sciences, USA, 1980; Belgian Royal Acad. of Scis, Letters and Fine Arts, 1984; Foreign Member: Amer. Philos. Soc., 1983; Lombardy Acad. Sci., Italy, 1989; Acad. Les Sciences, France, 1990. Hon. Student, Christ Church, Oxford, 1985. Hon. DSc: Chicago, 1978; René Descartes, Paris, 1982; Oxford, 1988; Hull, 1998; Glasgow, 2000. Albert Brachet Prize (Belgian Royal Academy), 1968; Scientific Medal of Zoological Soc., 1968; Feldberg Foundn Award, 1975; Paul Ehrlich Award, 1977; Nessim Habif Prize, Univ. of Geneva, 1979; CIBA Medal, Biochem. Soc., 1980; Comfort Crookshank Award for Cancer Research, 1983; William Bate Hardy Prize, Cambridge Philos. Soc., 1984; Prix Charles Léopold Mayer, Acad. des Scis, France, 1984; Ross Harrison Prize, Internat. Soc. Develt Biol., 1985; Royal Medal, Royal Soc., 1985; Emperor Hirohito Internat. Prize for Biology, Japan Acad., 1987; Wolf Prize in Medicine, Israel, 1989; Jan Waldenstram Medal, Swedish Oncol. Soc., 1991; Dist. Service Award, Miami, 1992; Edridge Green Medal, RCOphth, 1997; Jean Brachet Meml Prize, Internat. Soc. Diffn, 2000; Conklin Medal, Soc. Develt. Biol., 2001. *Publications:* Control of Gene Expression in Animal Development, 1974; articles in scientific jls, especially on nuclear transplantation. *Recreations:* skiing, tennis, horticulture, Lepidoptera. *Address:* (until Sept. 2002) The Master's Lodge, Magdalene College, Cambridge CB3 0AG; (from Sept. 2002) Whittlesford Grove, Whittlesford, Cambridge CB2 4AZ. *Club:* Eagle Ski.

GURNEY, Nicholas Bruce Jonathan; Chief Executive (formerly City Manager), Portsmouth City Council, since 1994; *b* 20 Jan. 1945; *s* of Bruce William George Gurney and Cynthia Joan Watkins Mason (*née* Winn); *m* 1st, 1970, Patricia Wendy Tulip (marr. diss. 1987); two *s* one *d*; 2nd, 1989, Caroline Mary (*née* Bentley). *Educ:* Wimbledon College; Christ's College, Cambridge. BA 1966, MA 1969. Lectr in English, Belize Teachers' Training College, Belize, as part of British Volunteer Programme, 1966–67; MoD 1967; Asst Private Sec., Minister of State for Defence, 1970–72; Civil Service Dept, 1972–74; Private Sec. to Lord Privy Seal and Leader of House of Lords, 1974–77; Civil Service Dept and Management Personnel Office, 1978–83; Grade 3, Cabinet Office, and CS Comr, 1983–88; Dept of Health, 1988–90; Chief Exec., Wokingham DC, 1990–93. *Address:* Civic Offices, Guildhall Square, Portsmouth PO1 2AL.

GURR, Dr Michael Ian; Maypole Scientific Services, private nutrition consultancy, 1990–99; Partner, Isles of Scilly Specialist Crops, since 1999; *b* 10 April 1939; *s* of Henry Ormonde Gurr and Hilda Ruth Gurr; *m* 1963, Elizabeth Anne Mayers; two *s* one *d*. *Educ:* Dunstable Grammar Sch.; Univ. of Birmingham (BSc, PhD). Postdoctoral Fellowship, Harvard Univ., 1964–66; Unilever European Fellowship of Biochem. Soc., State Univ. of

Utrecht, 1966–67; Res. Scientist, Unilever Res. Lab., Sharnbrook, Bedford, 1967–78; Hd, Department of Nutrition, Nat. Inst. for Res. in Dairying, Shinfield, Reading, 1978–85; Dir, Reading Lab. of AFRC Inst. of Food Res., 1985–86; Nutrition Consultant and Hd of Nutrition Dept, MMB, 1986–90. Visiting Professor: Univ. of Reading, 1986–99; Oxford Poly., later Oxford Brookes Univ., 1990–99. Chairman: Editl Bd, British Jl of Nutrition, 1988–90; Editl Adv. Bd, British Nutrition Foundn, 1994–; Man. Ed., Nutrition Research Reviews, 1991–99. *Publications:* Lipid Biochemistry: an introduction (jtly), 1971, 5th edn 2001; Role of Fats in Food and Nutrition, 1984, 2nd edn 1992; numerous original pubns and reviews. *Recreations:* sailing, walking, gardening, piano playing, choral singing. *Address:* Vale View Cottage, Maypole, St Mary's, Isles of Scilly TR21 0NU. *T:* (01720) 422224.

GUSTERSON, Prof. Barry Austin, PhD; FRCPath; Professor of Pathology, University of Glasgow, since 2000; *b* Colchester, 24 Oct. 1946; *s* of Joseph Austin Gusterson and Doris Edith (*née* Fairweather); *m* 1972, Ann Josephine Davies; one *s* two *d*. *Educ:* St Bartholomew's Hosp., London (BSc Physiol. 1967; MB BS 1976); Royal Dental Hosp. (BDS 1972); Inst. Cancer Res. (PhD 1980). FRCPath 1995. Sen. Clinical Scientist and Cons., Ludwig Inst. Cancer Res., London, 1983–86; Cons. in Histopathol., Royal Marsden Hosp., 1984–; Prof. of Histopathol., and Chm., Sect. of Cell Biol and Exptl Pathol., Inst. of Cancer Res., London Univ., 1986–2000. Founding Dir, Toby Robins Breast Cancer Res. Centre, London, 1998–. Dir, Pathology, Internat. Breast Cancer Study Gp, Berne, 1995–. Oakley Lectr, Pathological Soc. of GB and Ire., 1986. Chm., Pathology Gp, Orgn Eur. Cancer Insts, Geneva, 1992–96 (Mem., Faculty Bd, 1992–96); Mem., Faculty Bd, Eur. Soc. Mastoogy, Milan, 1994–. Mem., Brit. Soc. Cell Biol. *Publications:* contrib. chapters in books and numerous articles to professional jls. *Recreations:* antique English glass and furniture, gardening, walking, reading. *Address:* Department of Pathology, Western Infirmary, Glasgow G11 6NT. *T:* (0141) 211 2233.

GUTCH, Richard Evelyn; Director for England, Community Fund, since 2001; *b* 17 Nov. 1946; *s* of Sir John Gutch, KCMG, OBE, and of Diana Mary Gutch (*née* Worsley); *m* 1971, Rosemary Anne Capel Pike; two *s*. *Educ:* Winchester Coll.; Gonville and Caius Coll., Cambridge (BA); University Coll. London (MPhil). Town planning posts in Camden and S Yorks, 1970–76; Sen. Lectr, Planning Unit, PCL, 1976–80; Asst to Chief Exec., Brent LBC, 1980–85; Asst Dir, NCVO, 1985–92; Chief Exec., Arthritis Care, 1992–2001. FRSA 1992. *Publications:* reports and booklets. *Recreations:* the arts, Venice, the Isle of Wight, walking, carpentry, gardening. *Address:* 2 Whitehall Gardens, Chiswick, W4 3LT. *T:* (020) 8995 7292.

GUTERRES, António Manuel de Oliveira; Deputy (Socialist), Portuguese Parliament, 1976–83 and since 1985; Prime Minister of Portugal, since 1995; *b* 30 April 1949; *m* (wife decd); one *s* one *d*. *Educ:* Technical Univ. of Lisbon. Electrical engr; Asst Prof., Technical Univ. of Lisbon, 1973–75; Chief of Staff to Sec. of State for Industry, 1974–75. Mem., Commn for European Integration, 1976–79; Pres., Parly Commn for Economy and Finance, 1977–79, for Territory Admin, Local Power and Envmt, 1985–88; Strategic Develt Dir, State Investment and Participation Agency, 1984–85. Mem., Parly Assembly, Council of Europe, 1981–83. Mem., Municipal Assembly of Fundão, 1979– (Pres.). Portuguese Socialist Party: joined 1974; Mem., Nat. Secretariat, 1986–88; Pres., Parly Gp, 1988–91; Sec.-Gen., 1992–; Vice Pres., Socialist Internat., 1992–. Founder and Vice Pres., Portuguese Assoc. for Consumer Protection, 1973–74; Mem., Assoc. for Economic and Social Develt, 1970–96. *Publications:* articles in jls. *Address:* Office of the Prime Minister, Presidencia do Conselho de Ministros, Rua da Imprensa à Estrela 2, 1200 Lisbon, Portugal. *Fax:* (1) 3951616.

GUTFREUND, Prof. Herbert, FRS 1981; Professor of Physical Biochemistry, University of Bristol, 1972–86, now Emeritus; Scientific Member (external), Max-Planck-Institut für medizinische Forschung, Heidelberg, since 1987; *b* 21 Oct. 1921; *s* of late Paul Peter Gutfreund and Clara Angela (*née* Pisko); *m* 1958, Mary Kathelen, *er d* of late Mr and Mrs L. J. Davies, Rugby; two *s* one *d*. *Educ:* Vienna; Univ. of Cambridge (PhD). Research appts at Cambridge Univ., 1947–57; Rockefeller Fellow, Yale Univ., 1951–52; part-time Research Associate, Yale Univ., 1953–58; Principal Scientific Officer, National Inst. for Research in Dairying, Univ. of Reading, 1957–65; Visiting Professor: Univ. of California, 1965; Max Planck Inst., Göttingen, 1966–67; Reader in Biochemistry and Director of Molecular Enzymology Laboratory, Univ. of Bristol, 1967–72. Visiting appointments: Univ. of Leuven, 1972; Univ. of Adelaide, 1979; Univ. of Alberta, 1983. Part-time Scholar in Residence, NIH, Bethesda, 1986–89. Hon. Member: British Biophysical Soc., 1990; Amer. Soc. for Biochem. and Molecular Biol., 1993; Biochemical Soc., 1996. *Publications:* An Introduction to the Study of Enzymes, 1966; Enzymes: Physical Principles, 1972; (ed) Chemistry of Macromolecules, 1974; (ed) Biochemical Evolution, 1981; Biothermodynamics, 1983; Kinetics for the Life Sciences, 1995; papers and reviews on many aspects of physical biochemistry. *Recreations:* mountain walking in Austria, gardening, reading general literature and philosophy of science, listening to music and all other good things in life. *Address:* Somerset House, Chilton Road, Upton, Oxon OX11 9JL. *T:* (01235) 851468; *e-mail:* h.gutfreund@bristol.ac.uk. *Club:* Oxford and Cambridge.

GUTFREUND, John Halle; President, Gutfreund & Co. Inc., since 1993; *b* 14 Sept. 1929; *s* of B. Manuel Gutfreund and Mary Halle Gutfreund; *m* 1st, 1958, Joyce L. Gutfreund; three *s*; 2nd, 1981, Susan K. Gutfreund; one *s*. *Educ:* Oberlin College, Ohio (BA 1951). Served in Army, 1951–53; Salomon Brothers, 1953–91: Exec. Partner, 1966; Managing Partner, 1978; Chm. and Chief Exec., 1981–91; Chm., Pres. and Chief Exec., Salomon Inc, 1986–91. Vice-Chm., NY Stock Exchange, 1985–87; formerly: Mem., Bd of Dirs, Securities Industry Assoc.; Mem., Bd of Govs and Pres., Bond Club of NY; Chm., Downtown-Lower Manhattan Assoc.; Chm., Wall Street Cttee for Lincoln Center's 1986–87 Corporate Fund Campaign. Member: Council on Foreign Relations; Brookings Instn; past Mem., Tri-Lateral Commn. Director: Nutrition 21 Inc. (formerly Ambi Inc.); Ascent Assurance Inc.; Evercel Inc.; Baldwin Piano & Organ Co.; LCA-Vision Inc.; Universal Bond Fund; AccuWeather Inc.; Arch Wireless; Maxicare Health Plans Inc. Dir, Montefiore Medical Center Corp. (Mem. Exec. Cttee, Bd of Trustees; Mem., Financial and Real Estate Cttees); Mem., Bd of Trustees and Finance and Nominating Cttees, NY Public Library (Vice-Chm., Corporate Congress). Chm. Bd Trustees, Aperture Foundn; Hon. Trustee, Oberlin Coll. Hon. DH Oberlin Coll., 1987. *Address:* 712 Fifth Avenue, 38th Floor, New York, NY 10019, USA. *T:* (212) 9561190.

GUTHARDT, Rev. Dame Phyllis (Myra), DBE 1993; PhD; retired Methodist minister; *b* 1 Aug. 1929; *d* of Johan Detlef Guthardt and Amelia Guthardt. *Educ:* Auckland Univ. (BA 1957), Canterbury Univ. (MA 1959), Univ. of NZ; Newnham Coll., Cambridge (PhD 1963). Primary school teacher, 1950–53; Methodist theol trng, 1954–56; ordained, 1959 (first woman ordained in NZ); active ministry in Methodist and Presbyterian parishes, incl. hosp. and univ. chaplaincy, 1957–90. Pres., Methodist Ch. of NZ, 1985–86; Mem. Praesidium, World Methodist Council, 1986–91. Chancellor, Univ. of Canterbury, 1999– (Mem. Council, 1981–; Pro-Chancellor, 1992–99). Hon. Dr Waikato, 1986. *Publications:* contrib. theol jls. *Recreations:* music, reading, restoring house, gardening. *Address:* 5 Cholmondeley Lane, Governors Bay, RD1 Lyttelton, New Zealand. *T:* (3) 3299675.

GUTHRIE, family name of **Baron Guthrie of Craigiebank.**

GUTHRIE OF CRAIGIEBANK, Baron *cr* 2001 (Life Peer), of Craigiebank in the City of Dundee; **Gen. Charles Ronald Llewelyn Guthrie,** GCB 1994 (KCB 1990); LVO 1977; OBE 1980; Chief of the Defence Staff, 1997–2001; Aide-de-Camp General to the Queen, 1993–2001; *b* 17 Nov. 1938; *s* of late Ronald Guthrie and Nina (*née* Llewelyn); *m* 1971, Catherine, *er d* of late Lt Col Claude Worrall, MVO, OBE, Coldstream Guards; two *s*. *Educ:* Harrow; RMA Sandhurst. Commnd Welsh Guards, 1959; served: BAOR, Aden; 22 SAS Regt, 1965–69; psc 1972; MA (GSO2) to CGS, MoD, 1973–74; Brigade Major, Household Div., 1976–77; Comdg 1st Bn Welsh Guards, Berlin and N Ireland, 1977–80; Col GS Military Ops, MoD, 1980–82; Commander: British Forces New Hebrides, 1980; 4th Armoured Brigade, 1982–84; Chief of Staff 1st (BR) Corps, 1984–86; GOC NE Dist and Comdr 2nd Infantry Div., 1986–87; ACGS, MoD, 1987–89; Comdr 1 (BR) Corps, 1989–91; Comdr Northern Army Gp, 1992–93; C-in-C BAOR, 1992–94; CGS, 1994–97. Dir, N. M. Rothschild & Sons, 2001–. Col Comdt, Intelligence Corps, 1986–95; Col, The Life Guards, 1999–; Gold Stick to the Queen, 1999–; Col Comdt, SAS Regt. President: Army Saddle Club, 1991–96; Army LTA, 1991–99; Fedn of London Youth Clubs, 2001; Army Benevolent Fund, 2002. Freeman, City of London, 1988; Liveryman, Painter Stainers' Co., 1989. Kt, SMO Malta, 1999. Comdr, Legion of Merit (USA). *Recreations:* tennis, opera, travel. *Address:* PO Box 25439, SW1P 1AG. *Clubs:* White's, Beefsteak, All England Lawn Tennis and Croquet, Queen's.

See also J. D. Guthrie.

GUTHRIE, Rev. Donald Angus; Rector, Holy Spirit Episcopal Church, Missoula, Montana, 1979–93; *b* 18 Jan. 1931; *s* of Frederick Charles and Alison Guthrie; *m* 1st, 1959, Joyce Adeline Blunsden (*d* 1976); two *s* one *d*; 2nd, 1977, Lesley Josephine Boardman (marr. diss. 1983); 3rd, 1984, Carolyn Wallop Alderson. *Educ:* Marlborough Coll.; Trinity Coll., Oxford (MA). Rector, St John's Church, Selkirk, 1963–69; Vice-Principal, Episcopal Theological Coll., Edinburgh, 1969–74; Priest-in-Charge, Whitburn Parish Church, Tyne and Wear, 1974–76; Provost, St Paul's Cathedral, Dundee, 1976–77; Episcopal Chaplain to Univ. of Montana, 1977–79. *Recreations:* walking, reading. *Address:* 5115 Clearview Way, Missoula, MT 59803, USA.

GUTHRIE, (Garth) Michael; Chairman: Casual Dining Ltd, since 1999; Welcome Break Holdings Ltd, since 2000 (Director, since 1997); *b* 30 April 1941; *s* of Harry and Ann Guthrie; *m* 1963, Joyce Fox; one *s* two *d*. *Educ:* Blackpool Catering Coll. (FHCIMA). Joined Mecca Leisure, 1961; Man. Dir, 1980; Chm., 1981–90; Chief Exec., 1985–90; Founder Dir, 1990, Chm. and Chief Exec., 1991–96, BrightReasons Gp; Chm. and CEO, Pavilion Services Gp, 1991–94; Jt Dep. Chm., Queensborough Hldgs, 1997–2000. Dep. Chm., Tomorrow's People Trust, 1996–2000. Hon. Fellow, Oxford Brookes Univ. 1995. *Recreations:* ski-ing, swimming, gardening. *Address:* (office) 2 Vantage Court, Tickford Street, Newport Pagnell, Bucks MK16 9EZ. *T:* (01908) 299700, *Fax:* (01908) 299887.

GUTHRIE, James Dalglish; QC 1993; a Recorder, since 1999; *b* 21 Feb. 1950; *s* of late Ronald Guthrie and Nina Guthrie (*née* Llewelyn); *m* 1981, Lucille Gay Page-Roberts; one *s* one *d*. *Educ:* Harrow; Worcester Coll., Oxford (BA Modern History). Called to the Bar, Inner Temple, 1975, Bencher, 2000; admitted as barrister: Turks and Caicos Is, 1995; St Lucia, 1997; St Vincent and The Grenadines, 1998; Trinidad and Tobago, 2000. *Recreations:* fishing, painting, travel. *Address:* 3 Hare Court, Temple, EC4Y 7BJ. *T:* (020) 7415 7800. *Club:* Turf.

See also Gen. Sir C. R. L. Guthrie.

GUTHRIE, Sir Malcolm (Connop), 3rd Bt *cr* 1936; *b* 16 Dec. 1942; *s* of Sir Giles Connop McEacharn Guthrie, 2nd Bt, OBE, DSC, and of Rhona, *d* of late Frederic Stileman; *S* father, 1979; *m* 1967, Victoria, *o d* of late Brian Willcock; one *s* one *d*. *Educ:* Millfield. *Heir: s* Giles Malcolm Welcome Guthrie [*b* 16 Oct. 1972; *m* 2000, Susan, *e d* of Bill and Sheila Thompson]. *Address:* Brent Eleigh, Belbroughton, Stourbridge, Worcestershire DY9 0DW.

GUTHRIE, Michael; *see* Guthrie, G. M.

GUTHRIE, Robert Isles Loftus, (Robin); Director of Social and Economic Affairs, Council of Europe, 1992–98; *b* 27 June 1937; *s* of late Prof. W. K. C. Guthrie, FBA and of Adele Marion Ogilvy, MA; *m* 1963, Sarah Julia Weltman; two *s* one *d*. *Educ:* Clifton Coll.; Trinity Coll., Cambridge (MA); Liverpool Univ. (CertEd); LSE (MScEcon). Head of Cambridge House (Univ. settlement in S London), 1962–69; teacher, ILEA, 1964–66; Social Develt Officer, Peterborough Develt Corp., 1969–75; Asst Dir, Social Work Service, DHSS, 1975–79; Dir, Joseph Rowntree Meml Trust, 1979–88; Chief Charity Comr for England and Wales, 1988–92. Mem., expedns in Anatolia, British Inst. of Archaeol. at Ankara, 1958–62. Member: Arts Council of GB, 1979–81 and 1987–88 (Regional Cttee, 1976–81); Council, Policy Studies Institute, 1979–88; Council, York Univ., 1982–94; Chairman: Yorkshire Arts Assoc., 1984–88; Council of Regional Arts Assocs, 1985–88; York Early Music Foundn, 1995–; Jessie's Fund, 1998–2001; Yorkshire Regl Arts Bd, 2000–; Trustee: Rodolfus Choir, 1998–; Thalidomide Trust, 1999–. FRSA. Hon. DLitt Bradford, 1991. *Publications:* (ed) Outlook, 1963; (ed) Outlook Two, 1965; various articles, speeches and lectures. *Recreations:* music, mountains, travel, sheep. *Address:* Braeside, Acomb, York YO24 4EZ.

GUTHRIE, Roy David, (Gus), AM 1996; PhD, DSc; FTSE, FRSC, FRACI; FAIM; Director, Gus Guthrie Consulting Pty Ltd, since 1996; Chairman, Queensland Innovation Council, since 1999; *b* 29 March 1934; *s* of David Ephraim Guthrie and Ethel (*née* Kimmins); *m* 1st, 1956, Ann Hoad (marr. diss. 1981); three *s*; 2nd, 1982, Lyn Fielding. *Educ:* Dorking Grammar Sch.; King's Coll., Univ. of London (BSc, PhD, DSc). Shirley Inst., Manchester, 1958–60; Asst Lectr, then Lectr, Univ. of Leicester, 1960–63; Lectr, then Reader, Univ. of Sussex, 1963–73; Griffith University, Brisbane: Foundation Prof. of Chemistry, 1973–81; Inaugural Chm., School of Science, 1973–78; Pro-Vice-Chancellor, 1980–81; Professor Emeritus, 1982; Sec. Gen., Royal Soc. of Chemistry, 1982–85; Pres., NSW Inst. of Technol., 1986–87, Vice-Chancellor and Pres., Univ. of Technol., Sydney, 1988–96. DUniv: Griffith, 1981; UTS, 1996. *Publications:* An Introduction to the Chemistry of Carbohydrates (with J. Honeyman), 2nd edn 1964, 3rd edn 1968, 4th edn 1974; over 130 scientific papers. *Recreations:* theatre, music, tai chi, croquet. *Address:* PO Box 369, Buderim, Qld 4556, Australia.

GUTTERIDGE, Prof. William Frank, MBE (mil.) 1946; Director, Research Institute for the Study of Conflict and Terrorism, 1994–2001; *b* 21 Sept. 1919; *s* of Frank Leonard Gutteridge and Nora Conwy (*née* Tighe); *m* 1944, Margaret McCallum Parker; three *d*. *Educ:* Stamford Sch., Lincs; Hertford Coll., Oxford (MA Mod. Hist., DipEd). Served War, 1939–46: commnd Manchester Regt; India/Burma, 1942/45: Staff Officer, 33 Indian Corps, finally DAAG 2nd British Div. Sen. Lectr in Commonwealth Hist. and Govt, RMA Sandhurst, 1949–63; Nuffield Foundn/Home CS Travelling Fellow studying rôle of Armed Forces in Commonwealth Africa, 1960–61; Hd, Langs and Mod. Studies Dept, Lanchester Poly., Coventry, 1963–71; Aston University: Dir, Complementary Studies, 1971–80; Prof. of Internat. Studies, 1976–82; Hd, Pol and Econ. Studies Dept, 1980–82; Prof. Emeritus, 1982; Editl Cons., Inst. for Study of Conflict, 1982–89; Exec. and Editl Dir, Res. Inst. for Study of Conflict and Terrorism, 1989–94. Sec., Brit. Pugwash Gp for Sci. and World Affairs, 1965–86. Chm., CNAA Cttee for Arts and Social Studies, 1978–84. *Publications:* Armed Forces in New States, 1962; Military Institutions and Power in New States, 1965; The Military in African Politics, 1969; Military Regimes in Africa, 1975; The New Terrorism, 1986; South Africa from Apartheid to National Unity 1981–94, 1995; South Africa's Defence and Security Forces into the 21st Century, 1996; (with J. E. Spence) Violence in Southern Africa, 1997; Latin America and the Caribbean: prospects for democracy, 1997; South Africa: potential of Mbeki's presidency, 1999. *Recreations:* research, writing. *Address:* 26 St Mark's Road, Leamington Spa, Warwickshire CV32 6DL. *T:* (01926) 425276, *Fax:* (01926) 833307.

GUY, Frances Mary; HM Diplomatic Service; Ambassador to the Yemen, since 2001; *b* 1 Feb. 1959; *d* of David Guy and Elizabeth Guy (*née* Hendry); *m* 1989, Guy Raybaudo; one *s* two *d. Educ:* Aberdeen Univ. (MA Hons); Johns Hopkins Univ., Bologna (Dip.); Carleton Univ., Ottawa (MA Internat. Relns). Entered FCO, 1985: lang. trng, 1987; Second Sec. (Chancery), Khartoum, 1988–91; First Secretary: FCO, 1991–95; and Hd, Pol Section, Bangkok, 1995–96; Dep. Hd of Mission, Addis Ababa, 1997–2001. *Recreations:* swimming, tennis. *Address:* c/o Foreign and Commonwealth Office, King Charles Street, SW1A 2AH; British Embassy, Sana'a, Republic of Yemen. *Club:* Royal Commonwealth Society.

GUY, Geoffrey Colin, CMG 1964; CVO 1966; OBE 1962 (MBE 1957); Governor and Commander in Chief, St Helena and its Dependencies, 1976–81, retired; first elected Speaker of the Legislative Council, St Helena, 1989; *b* 4 Nov. 1921; *s* of late E. Guy, 14 Woodland Park Road, Headingley, Leeds, and of Constance Reed Guy (*née* Taylor); *m* 1946, Joan Elfreda Smith; one *s. Educ:* Chatham House Sch., Ramsgate; Brasenose Coll., Oxford. Served RAF, 1941–46: reconnaissance pilot Spitfires and Hurricanes, Middle East and Burma, 1943–45; Special Force 136, 1945 (Flight Lieut). Asst Ed., Courtaulds Works Mag., 1948; management staff, Scribbans-Kemp Ltd, 1948–51; Colonial Administrative Service, Sierra Leone: Cadet, 1951; Asst Sec. Chief Comr Protectorate, 1953–54; District Comr, Tonkolili Dist, 1955; Administrator, Turks and Caicos Islands, and Chm. and Man. Dir, Turks Island Salt Co., 1958–65; Administrator, Dominica, 1965–67, Governor, March-Nov. 1967; Asst Sec., Soil Assoc., 1968; Sec., Forces Help Soc. and Lord Roberts' Workshops, 1970–73; Administrator, Ascension Island, 1973–76. *Recreations:* reading, walking, swimming. *Address:* Tamarisk Cottage, Kirk Hammerton, York YO26 8DA. *Clubs:* Royal Air Force, Victory Services.

GUY, John Westgarth, OBE 1986; HM Diplomatic Service, retired; Consul General, St Petersburg, 1995–2000; *b* 17 July 1941; *s* of late John Westgarth Guy and Stella (*née* Sanderson); *m* 1961, Sylvia Kathleen Stokes; one *s* one *d. Educ:* Queen Mary's Sch. for Boys, Basingstoke. CRO, 1960; Karachi, 1961–63; Calcutta, 1964–67; Vice Consul, New York, 1968–70; FCO, 1970–72; Third Secretary: Moscow, 1972–73; Jakarta, 1974; Second Sec., São Paulo, 1975–77; FCO, 1977–79; DTI, 1979–80; First Secretary: Yaoundé, 1981–84; Maputo, 1984–87; FCO, 1987–91; High Comr, PNG, 1991–94; RCDS, 1995. *Recreations:* squash, golf, sailing. *Address:* 15 Bow Field, Hook, Hants RG27 9SA.

GUY, (Leslie) George; Assistant Secretary, Craft Sector, Amalgamated Union of Engineering Workers/Technical Administrative and Supervisory Section, 1983–84, retired; *b* 1 Sept. 1918; *s* of Albert and Annie Guy; *m* 1940, Audrey Doreen (*née* Symonds); two *d. Educ:* secondary modern school. National Union of Sheet Metal Workers: shop steward; Member: Branch and District Cttees; Nat. Executive Cttee; National President, June 1972–74; Asst General Secretary, 1974–77; Gen. Sec., Nat. Union of Sheet Metal Workers, Coppersmiths, Heating and Domestic Engrs, 1977–83, when Union transferred its engagements to AEUW/TASS. Member: General Council, TUC, 1977–83; Exec., CSEU, 1977–84; Engrg Industry Trng Bd, 1979–84; Council, Marine Training Assoc., 1983–. *Recreations:* work and politics.

GUY, Captain Robert Lincoln, LVO 1980; RN; Executive Director, Japan Society, since 1998; *b* 4 Sept. 1947; *s* of late John Guy and Susan Guy; *m* 1981, Rosemary Ann Walker; two *d. Educ:* Radley Coll. Entered BRNC Dartmouth, 1966; ADC to Governor and Commander-in-Chief, Gibraltar, 1973; commanded: HMS Ashton, 1974; HMS Kedleston, 1975; HMS Sirius, 1984–85. Equerry to the Queen, 1977–80; First Lieut, HMS Antelope, 1981–82. Lieut 1971; Lt-Comdr 1979; Comdr 1983; Captain 1991. *Recreations:* polo, skiing, shooting. *Address:* Stable House, South Warnborough, Hook, Hants RG29 1RQ. *T:* (01256) 862254. *Club:* White's.

GUY, Gen. Sir Roland (Kelvin), GCB 1987 (KCB 1981); CBE 1978 (MBE 1955); DSO 1972; Governor, Royal Hospital, Chelsea, 1987–93; *b* 25 June 1928; *s* of Lt-Col Norman Greenwood Guy and Mrs Edna Guy; *m* 1957, Dierdre, *d* of Brig. P. H. Graves Morris, DSO, MC, and Mrs Auriol Graves-Morris; two *d. Educ:* Wellington Coll.; RMA Sandhurst. Commnd KRRC, 1948; 1950–71: Signals Officer, Germany; Adjt Kenya Regt, and 2 KRRC; Weapon Trng Officer 1 KRRC; Staff Coll., Camberley; MoD; Co. Comdr 2 RGJ; DS Staff Coll.; Bn 2 i/c; Mil. Asst to Adjt Gen.; CO 1 RGJ; Col GS HQ Near East Land Forces, 1971; Comd 24 Airportable Bde, 1972; RCDS, 1975; Principal SO to CDS, 1976–78; Chief of Staff, HQ BAOR, 1978–80; Mil. Sec., 1980–83; Adjt Gen., 1984–86; ADC Gen. to the Queen, 1984–87; served in Kenya, Libya, British Guiana, Cyprus, Malaysia, W Germany and Berlin. Colonel Commandant: 1st Bn Royal Green Jackets, 1981–86 (Rep. Col Comdt, 1985–86); Small Arms School Corps, 1981–87; Kenya Regt Assoc., 1988–. Chairman: Army Benevolent Fund, 1987–93; Royal Cambridge Home for Soldiers' Widows, 1987–93; Mem. Council of Management, PDSA, 1987– (Chm. Council of Mgt, 1994–98). Governor: Wellington Coll., 1987–98 (Vice Pres., 1990–98); Milton Abbey Sch., 1987–2000. *Recreations:* music, travel, painting. *Address:* c/o NatWest Bank, 25 Market Place, Blandford Forum, Dorset DT11 7AQ. *Clubs:* Army and Navy, MCC.

GUYATT, Richard Gerald Talbot, CBE 1969; Rector, Royal College of Art, 1978–81 (Pro-Rector, 1974–78; Professor of Graphic Arts, 1948–78); *b* 8 May 1914; *s* of Thomas Guyatt, sometime HM Consul, Vigo, Spain and Cecil Guyatt; *m* 1941, Elizabeth Mary Corsellis; one step *d. Educ:* Charterhouse. Freelance designer: posters for Shell-Mex and BP, 1935. War Service: Regional Camouflage Officer for Scotland, Min. of Home Security. Dir and Chief Designer, Cockade Ltd, 1946–48; Co-designer of Lion and Unicorn Pavilion, Festival of Britain, 1951; Consultant Designer to: Josiah Wedgwood & Sons, 1952–55, 1967–70; Central Electricity Generating Bd, 1964–68; British Sugar Bureau, 1965–68; W. H. Smith, 1970–87. Vis. Prof., Yale Univ., 1955 and 1962. Ceramic Designs for Min. of Works (for British Embassies), King's Coll. Cambridge, Goldsmiths' Co. and Wedgwood commem. mugs for Coronation, 1953, Investiture, 1969, Royal Silver Wedding, 1973, Millennium, 2000 and Golden Jubilee, 2002. Designed: silver medal for Royal Mint, Mint Dirs Conf., 1972; 700th Anniv. of Parlt stamp, 1965; Postal Order forms, 1964 for Post Office; Silver Jubilee stamps, 1977; commem. crown piece for 80th birthday of HM Queen Elizabeth The Queen Mother, 1980. Member: Stamp Adv. Cttee, 1963–74; Internat. Jury, Warsaw Poster Biennale, 1968; Bank of England Design Adv. Cttee, 1968–75; Adv. Council, Victoria and Albert Mus., 1978–81. Chm., Guyatt/Jenkins Design Group. Governor, Imperial Coll. of Sci. and Technol., 1979–81. FSIA; Hon. ARCA. Misha Black Meml Medal, for distinguished services to design educn, SIAD, 2000. *Address:* Forge Cottage, Ham, Marlborough, Wilts SN8 3RB. *T:* (01488) 668270.

GUYTON, Marjorie A.; *see* Allthorpe-Guyton.

GUZ, Prof. Abraham, MD; FRCP; Professor of Medicine, Charing Cross and Westminster Medical School, University of London, 1981–94, now Emeritus; *b* 12 Aug. 1929; *s* of Akiwa Guz and Esther Guz; *m* 1957, Nita (*née* Florenz); three *d. Educ:* Grocers' Co. Sch.; Charing Cross Hosp. Med. Sch., Univ. of London (MB BS 1952; MD 1967). MRCP 1954, FRCP 1969. Hosp. appts, Charing Cross Hosp., 1952–53; Asst Lectr in Pharmacol., Charing Cross Hosp. Med. Sch., 1953–54; RAMC 1954–56; Hosp. appts, RPMS, Hammersmith Hosp., 1956–57; Research Fellow: Harvard Med. Sch., 1957–59; Cardiovascular Res. Inst., Univ. of California, 1959–61; Lectr in Medicine, 1961, later Sen. Lectr and Reader, Charing Cross Hosp. Med Sch. Pro-Censor and Censor, RCP, 1979–87. Visiting Scientist, Univ. Lab. of Physiology, Oxford, 1994–. Fellow, Imperial Coll. Sch. of Medicine, 2000–. Pres., British Assoc. of Lung Res., 1998–. *Publications:* Dyspnoea, 1984; articles on mechanisms underlying breathlessness, mechanisms resp. for ventilatory response to exercise, measurement of performance of left ventricle. *Recreations:* family, violin in quartet, Jewish culture study. *Address:* 3 Littleton Road, Harrow, Middx HA1 3SY. *T:* (020) 8422 2786; (office) Charing Cross Hospital, Fulham Palace Road, W6 8RF. *T:* (020) 8846 7337, *Fax:* (020) 8846 7326; *e-mail:* a.guz@ic.ac.uk.

GWILLIAM, John Albert, MA Cantab; Headmaster of Birkenhead School, 1963–88; *b* 28 Feb. 1923; *s* of Thomas Albert and Adela Audrey Gwilliam; *m* 1949, Pegi Lloyd George; three *s* two *d. Educ:* Monmouth Sch.; Trinity Coll., Cambridge. Assistant Master: Trinity Coll., Glenalmond, 1949–52; Bromsgrove Sch., 1952–56; Head of Lower Sch., Dulwich Coll., 1956–63. *Address:* Araulfan, 13 The Close, Llanfairfechan, Gwynedd LL33 0AG.

GWILLIAM, Kenneth Mason; Economic Adviser, Transport (formerly Principal Transport Economist), World Bank, Washington, since 1993; *b* 27 June 1937; *s* of John and Marjorie Gwilliam; *m* 1987, Sandra Wilson; two *s* by former *m. Educ:* Magdalen Coll., Oxford (BA 1st Cl. Hons PPE). Res. Asst, Fisons Ltd, 1960–61; Lecturer: Univ. of Nottingham, 1961–65; Univ. of E Anglia, 1965–67; Prof. of Transport Economics, Univ. of Leeds, 1967–89; Prof. of Econs of Transport and Logistics, Erasmus Univ., Rotterdam, 1989. Director: Nat. Bus Co., 1978–82; Yorkshire Rider, 1986–88. Editor, Jl of Transport Economics and Policy, 1977–87. *Publications:* Transport and Public Policy, 1964; Economics and Transport Policy, 1975; (jtly) Deregulating the Bus Industry, 1984. *Recreations:* walking, golf. *Address:* World Bank, 1818 H Street NW, Washington, DC 20433, USA. *T:* (202) 4733743, *Fax:* (202) 5223223.

GWILLIAM, Michael Colin; Planning and Transport Director, South East England Regional Assembly, since 2001; *b* 4 Jan. 1948; *s* of Alfred Gwilliam and late Grace Gwilliam; *m* 1st, 1970, Mary (marr. diss. 1995); two *d*; 2nd, 1996, Janice; two step *d. Educ:* Keble Coll., Oxford (MA Hist.); University Coll. London (DipTP); De Montfort Univ., Leicester (DMS). Chief Planner, Leics CC, 1985–88; Co. Planning Officer, Bedfordshire CC, 1988–96; Dir, The Civic Trust, 1996–2000. Vice-Pres., County Planning Officers Soc., 1995–96. FRSA 1989. Hon. RICS 1999. *Publications:* Sustainable Renewal of Suburban Areas, 1999; Small Town Vitality, 2000. *Recreations:* hill-walking, gardening, bonsai, music. *Address:* 32A Ropery Street, E3 4QG. *T:* (020) 8980 1209.

GWILLIAM, Robert John; Senior Associate Solicitor, British Telecommunications PLC, 1990–96; *b* 6 Jan. 1943; *s* of Benjamin Harold Gwilliam and Dora Gwilliam; *m* 1966, Linda Mary Ellway; two *s. Educ:* Lydney Grammar Sch.; Nottingham Univ. (BA Hons Law); Cambridge Univ. (Dip. Criminology); College of Law. Admitted Solicitor, 1969; practised in Local Govt Prosecuting Depts, 1969–83; Chief Prosecuting Solicitor for Hampshire, 1983–86; Chief Crown Prosecutor, Crown Prosecution Service: London South/Surrey Area, 1986; Inner London Area, 1987; London and SE Regl Dir, Grade 3, 1987–89. *Recreations:* criminology, amateur music making, supporting Rugby, walking in Purbeck, golf. *Address:* 11 Steepways, Peverill Road, Swanage, Dorset BH19 2DF.

GWILT, George David, FFA; General Manager, 1979–84, Managing Director and Actuary, 1984–88, Standard Life Assurance Company; *b* 11 Nov. 1927; *s* of Richard Lloyd Gwilt and Marjory Gwilt (*née* Mair); *m* 1956, Ann Dalton Sylvester; three *s. Educ:* Sedbergh Sch.; St John's Coll., Cambridge (MA). FFA 1952; FBCS. Joined Standard Life Assurance Co., 1949: Asst Official, 1956; Asst Actuary, 1957; Statistician, 1962; Mechanisation Manager, 1964; Systems Manager, 1969; Dep. Pensions Manager, 1972; Pensions Actuary, 1973; Asst General Manager and Pensions Manager, 1977; Asst Gen. Man. (Finance), 1978. Dep. Chm., Associated Scottish Life Offices, 1986–88. Special Advr in Scotland, Citicorp, 1989–91; Director: Hammerson Property Investment and Develt Corp., 1979–94; Scottish Mortgage and Trust, 1983–98; European Assets Trust NV, 1979–2000; Hodgson Martin, 1989–2000. Trustee, TSB of South of Scotland, 1966–83. Member: Younger Cttee on Privacy, 1970–72; Monopolies and Mergers Commn, 1983–87. Pres., Faculty of Actuaries, 1981–83. Convener, Scottish Poetry Library, 1988–2001. *Recreation:* flute playing. *Address:* 39 Oxgangs Road, Edinburgh EH10 7BE. *T:* (0131) 445 1266. *Clubs:* Royal Air Force; New (Edinburgh).

GWILT, Michael Peter; Group Managing Director, Onlyfair Denmark ApS, since 1999; *b* 29 April 1957; *s* of Geoffrey and Joy Gwilt; *m* 1984, Cheryl Harrison; one *s. Educ:* Bishop Perowne C of E Sch., Worcester; King's Sch., Worcester. Family business, R. & G. Gwilt Engineering, 1975–82; Uniweld Ltd, 1983–84; joined Interleasing (UK) Ltd, 1984: Sales and Mktg Dir, 1988–94; Managing Director: Interleasing North, 1994–97; Cowie Interleasing, 1997; Gp Man. Dir, Arriva plc, 1998. *Recreations:* swimming, travelling, theatre, ballet, reading, cycling.

GWYER, Ven. Judith; *see* Rose, Ven. K. J.

GWYNEDD, Viscount; David Richard Owen Lloyd George; *b* 22 Jan. 1951; *s* and *heir* of 3rd Earl Lloyd George of Dwyfor, *qv*; *m* 1985, Pamela, *o d* of late Alexander Kleyff; two *s. Educ:* Eton. *Heir: s* Hon. William Alexander Lloyd George, *b* 16 May 1986.

GWYNN, Dominic Leigh Denys; Partner, Martin Goetze and Dominic Gwynn, Organ Builders, since 1979; *b* 18 Aug. 1953; *s* of Kenneth Leigh Maxwell Gwynn and Elisabeth (*née* Molenaar); *m* 1976, Antonia Rosamund Cordy; two *d. Educ:* Christ's Hosp.; St John's Coll., Oxford (BA Hons; MA). Major projects include: reconstructions: 1716 Handel organ, St Lawrence Whitchurch, Little Stanmore, 1994; 1743 organ, St Helen Bishopsgate, London, 1995; new organs: Handel House Mus., 1998; Magdalene Coll., Cambridge, 2000. *Publications:* (contrib.) Performing Purcell's Music, 1995; contribs to Jl British Inst. of Organ Studies, Organ Yearbook and Organists Review. *Recreations:* choral singing; early modern church, social and cultural history. *Address:* Gardens House, Welbeck, Worksop, Notts S80 3LW. *T:* (home) (01909) 486144; (office) (01909) 485635.

GWYNN, Edward Harold, CB 1961; Deputy Under-Secretary of State, Ministry of Defence, 1966–72; retired 1972; *b* 23 Aug. 1912; *y s* of late Dr E. J. Gwynn, Provost of Trinity Coll., Dublin, and late Olive Ponsonby; *m* 1937, Dorothy, *d* of late Geoffrey S. Phillpotts, Foxrock, Co. Dublin; one *s* two *d* (and two *d* decd). *Educ:* Sedbergh School; TCD. Entered Home Office, 1936; Assistant Secretary, 1947; Assistant Under-Secretary of State, 1956; Principal Finance Officer (Under-Secretary), Ministry of Agriculture, 1961–62; Deputy Under-Secretary of State, Home Office, 1963–66. *Recreations:* gardening, the countryside. *Address:* The Chestnuts, Minchinhampton, Glos GL6 9AR. *T:* (01453) 832863.

GWYNN-JONES, Peter Llewellyn, CVO 1998 (LVO 1994); Garter Principal King of Arms, since 1995; Genealogist, Order of the Bath, Order of St Michael and St George, and Order of St John, since 1995; *b* 12 March 1940; *s* of late Major Jack Llewellyn Gwynn-Jones, Cape Town, and late Mary Muriel Daphne, *d* of Col Arthur Patrick Bird Harrison, and step *s* of late Lt-Col Gavin David Young, Long Burton, Dorset. *Educ:* Wellington Coll.; Trinity Coll., Cambridge (MA). Assistant to Garter King of Arms, 1970; Bluemantle Pursuivant of Arms, 1973; Secretary, Harleian Society, 1981–94; House Comptroller of College of Arms, 1982–95; Lancaster Herald of Arms, 1982–95. Inspector of Regtl Colours, 1995–, of RAF Badges, 1996–. Freeman and Liveryman: Painter Stainers' Co., 1997; Scriveners' Co., 1997. Hon. Citizen, State of Tennessee, 1991. FSA 1997. KStJ 1995. *Publications:* Heraldry, 1993; The Art of Heraldry, 1998. *Recreations:* tropical forests, wild life conservation, fishing. *Address:* College of Arms, Queen Victoria Street, EC4V 4BT. *T:* (020) 7248 0911; 79 Harcourt Terrace, SW10. *T:* (020) 7373 5859.

GWYNNE JONES, family name of **Baron Chalfont**.

GWYTHER, Christine; Member (Lab) Carmarthen West and South Pembrokeshire, National Assembly for Wales, since 1999; *b* 9 Aug. 1959; *d* of Ivor George Gwyther and Marjorie Gwyther (*née* Doidge). *Educ:* Pembroke Sch.; UC, Cardiff. Milford Haven Waterway Enterprise Zone, 1986; local govt officer, S Pembrokeshire DC, 1987–96, Pembrokeshire CC, 1996–99. Sec. for Agric. and Rural Develt, Nat. Assembly for Wales, 1999–2000. Mem., Pembrokeshire Business Club. Mem., RSPB. *Address:* National Assembly for Wales, Cardiff Bay, Cardiff CF99 1NA.

GYLLENHAMMAR, Dr Pehr Gustaf; Chairman: CGNU (formerly CGU) plc, since 1998; Lazard AB, since 1999; Managing Director, Lazard Frères & Co., since 2000 (Senior Adviser, 1996–99); *b* 28 April 1935; *s* of Pehr Gustaf Victor Gyllenhammar and Aina Dagny Kaplan; *m* 1959, Eva Christina, *d* of Gunnar Ludvig Engellau; one *s* three *d*. *Educ:* University of Lund. LLB. Mannheimer & Zetterlöf, solicitors, 1959; Haight, Gardner, Poor & Havens, NY, 1960; Amphion Insurance Co., Gothenburg, 1961–64; Skandia Insurance Co., 1965, Exec. Vice-Pres., 1968, Pres. and Chief Exec. Officer, 1970; AB Volvo, Gothenburg, 1970, Man. Dir and Chief Exec. Officer, 1971; Chm. and Chief Exec. Officer, 1983–90, Exec. Chm. Bd of Dirs, 1990–93, Volvo; Dep. Chm., Commercial Union plc, 1997–98. Chm., MC European Capital (Holdings), SA, 1994–96; Dir of companies in Sweden, Netherlands, UK and USA. Member: Internat. Adv. Cttee, Chase Manhattan Bank, NA, NY, 1972–95; Bd, Cttee of Common Market Automobile Constructors, 1977–91; Bd, Assoc. des Constructeurs Européens d'Automobiles, 1991–93; Bd, Fedn of Swedish Industries, 1979–93; Roundtable of European Industrialists, 1982–93; Bd Trustees, Rockefeller Univ., NY, 1991–96. Lethaby Prof., Royal Coll. of Art, London, 1977; Mem., Royal Swedish Acad. of Engineering Scis, 1974. Hon. DM Gothenburg Univ., 1981; Hon. DTech Brunel, 1987; Hon. DEng Technical Univ., NS, 1988; Hon. DSocSc Helsinki, 1990. Golden Award, City of Gothenburg, 1981. Officer, Royal Order of Vasa, 1973; King's Medal, with Ribbon of Order of Seraphim, 1981; Commander: Order of Lion of Finland, 1977 (Comdr 1st Class 1986); Ordre National du Mérite, France, 1980; St Olav's Order, Norway, 1984; Légion d'honneur, France, 1987; Order of Leopold, Belgium, 1989; Kt Grand Officer, Order of Merit, Italy, 1987. *Publications:* Mot sekelskiftet på måfå (Toward the Turn of the Century, at Random), 1970; Jag tror på Sverige (I Believe in Sweden), 1973; People at Work (US), 1977; En industripolitik för människan (Industrial policy for human beings), 1979; Fortsättning följer . . . (To Be Continued . . .), 2000. *Recreations:* tennis, sailing, skiing, riding. *Address:* CGNU plc, St Helen's, 1 Undershaft, EC3P 3DQ.

H

HAAN, Christopher Francis; Partner, Hammond Suddards, solicitors, since 1995. LLB. Admitted solicitor, 1968. Partner: Herbert & Gowers, 1969–71; Linklaters & Paines, 1974–81; S. J. Berwin & Co., 1982–92 (Sen. Partner, 1988–92); Coudert Brothers, 1992–94. *Address:* 7 Devonshire Square, Cutlers Gardens, EC2M 4YH. *T:* (020) 7655 1000.

HAAVISTO, Heikki Johannes; Chairman Board of Directors, Raisio Group, since 1997 (Chairman, Administrative Council, 1977–96); *b* Turku, Finland, 20 Aug. 1935; *s* of Urho and Alli Haavisto; *m* 1964, Maija Rihko; three *s. Educ:* Univ. of Helsinki (MSc, LLM). Hd of Dept, Oy Vehnä Ab, 1963–66; Sec.-Gen., Central Union of Agricl Producers and Forest Owners, 1966–75 (Pres., 1976–94); Member, Administrative Council: Osuuskunta Metsäliitto, Helsinki, 1976–93 (Vice-Chm. and Pres., 1976–93); Central Union Co-op. Banks, Helsinki, 1985–93; Minister of For. Affairs, Finland, 1993–95. Chm., Delegn, Finnish Co-operative Pellervo, Helsinki, 1979–. Mem., Internat. Policy Council on Agric. and Trade, Washington, 1988–. Mem., Centre Party, Finland. Hon. PhD Turku; Hon. Dr Agr. & For., Hon. DVM Helsinki, 1995. *Address:* Hintsa, 21200 Raisio, Finland.

HABAKKUK, Sir John (Hrothgar), Kt 1976; FBA 1965; FRHistS; Fellow, All Souls College, Oxford, 1950–67 and since 1988; Principal of Jesus College, Oxford, 1967–84, Hon. Fellow, 1984; *b* 13 May 1915; *s* of Evan Guest and Anne Habakkuk; *m* 1948, Mary Richards; one *s* three *d. Educ:* Barry County Sch.; St John's Coll., Cambridge (scholar and Strathcona student), Hon. Fellow 1971. Historical Tripos: Part I, First Class, 1935; Part II, First Class (with distinction), 1936. Fellow, Pembroke Coll., Cambridge, 1938–50, Hon. Fellow 1973; Director of Studies in History and Librarian, 1946–50; Temporary Civil Servant: Foreign Office, 1940–42, Board of Trade, 1942–46; University Lecturer in Faculty of Economics, Cambridge, 1946–50; Chichele Prof. of Economic History, Oxford, 1950–67; Vice-Chancellor, Oxford Univ., 1973–77, a Pro Vice-Chancellor, 1977–83; Pres, UC Swansea, 1975–84 (Hon. Fellow, 1991). Visiting Lecturer, Harvard University, 1954–55; Ford Research Professor, University of California, Berkeley, 1962–63; Ford Lecturer, 1984–85. Member: Grigg Cttee on Departmental Records, 1952–54; Advisory Council on Public Records, 1958–70; SSRC, 1967–71; Nat. Libraries Cttee, 1968–69; Royal Commn on Historic Manuscripts, 1978–90; Admin. Bd, Internat. Assoc. of Univs, 1975–85. Chairman: Cttee of Vice Chancellors and Principals of Univs of UK, 1976–77; Adv. Gp on London Health Servs, 1980–81; Oxfordshire DHA, 1981–84. Pres., RHistS, 1976–80. Foreign Member: Amer. Phil. Soc.; Amer. Acad. of Arts and Sciences. Hon. DLitt: Wales, 1971; Cambridge, 1973; Pennsylvania, 1975; Kent, 1978; Ulster, 1988. *Publications:* American and British Technology in the Nineteenth Century, 1962; Population Growth and Economic Development since 1750, 1971; Landowners: marriage, debt and the estates system 1650–1950, 1994; articles and reviews. *Address:* 28 Cunliffe Close, Oxford OX2 7BL. *T:* (01865) 556583.

HABERFELD, Dame Gwyneth; *see* Jones, Dame G.

HABGOOD, family name of **Baron Habgood**.

HABGOOD, Baron *cr* 1995 (Life Peer), of Calverton in the county of Buckinghamshire; **Rt Rev. and Rt Hon. John Stapylton Habgood;** PC 1983; MA, PhD; Archbishop of York, 1983–95; *b* 23 June 1927; *s* of Arthur Henry Habgood, DSO, MB, BCh, and Vera (*née* Chetwynd-Stapylton); *m* 1961, Rosalie Mary Anne Boston; two *s* two *d. Educ:* Eton; King's Coll., Cambridge (Hon. Fellow, 1986); Cuddesdon Coll., Oxford. Univ. Demonstrator in Pharmacology, Cambridge, 1950–53; Fellow of King's Coll., Cambridge, 1952–55; Curate of St Mary Abbots, Kensington, 1954–56; Vice-Principal of Westcott House, Cambridge, 1956–62; Rector of St John's Church, Jedburgh, 1962–67; Principal of Queen's College, Birmingham, 1967–73; Bishop of Durham, 1973–83. Hulsean Preacher, Cambridge Univ., 1987–88; first Athenæum Lectr, 1998; Bampton Lectr, Oxford Univ., 1999; Gifford Lectr, Aberdeen Univ., 2000. Moderator, Church and Society Sub-Unit, WCC, 1983–91. Pro-Chancellor, Univ. of York, 1985–90. Chm., UK Xenotransplantation Interim Regulatory Authy, 1997–. Hon. DD: Durham, 1975; Cambridge, 1984; Aberdeen, 1988; Huron, 1990; Hull, 1991; Oxford, Manchester, and York, 1996. *Publications:* Religion and Science, 1964; A Working Faith, 1980; Church and Nation in a Secular Age, 1983; Confessions of a Conservative Liberal, 1988; Making Sense, 1993; Faith and Uncertainty, 1997; Being a Person, 1998; Varieties of Unbelief, 2000. *Recreations:* painting, DIY. *Address:* 18 The Mount, Malton, N Yorks YO17 7ND. *Club:* Athenæum.

HABGOOD, Anthony John; Chairman, Bunzl plc, since 1996 (Chief Executive, 1991–96); *b* 8 Nov. 1946; *s* of John Michael Habgood and Margaret Diana Middleton Habgood (*née* Dalby); *m* 1974, Nancy Atkinson; two *s* one *d. Educ:* Gonville and Caius Coll., Cambridge (MA Econ 1971); Carnegie Mellon Univ., Pittsburgh (MS Indust. Admin 1970). Boston Consulting Gp, 1970–86: Director, 1976; Management Cttee, 1979; Exec. Cttee, 1981; Tootal Group, 1986–91: Director, 1986; Chief Exec., 1991. Director: Geest, 1988–93; Power Gen, 1993–2001; Schroder Ventures Internat. Investment Trust, 1995–; NatWest Gp, 1998–2000. *Recreations:* country pursuits. *Address:* Bunzl plc, 110 Park Street, W1Y 3RB. *Club:* Royal Norfolk and Suffolk Yacht.

HACKER, Alan Ray, OBE 1988; clarinettist and conductor; *b* 30 Sept. 1938; *s* of Kenneth and Sybil Hacker; *m* 1st, 1959, Anna Maria Sroka; two *d*; 2nd, 1977, Karen Evans (marr. diss. 1994); one *s*; 3rd, 1995, Margaret Lee. *Educ:* Dulwich Coll.; Royal Academy of Music. FRAM. Joined LPO, 1958; Prof., RAM, 1960–76; Lectr, 1976–84, Sen. Lectr in Music, 1984–87, Univ of York. Founded: Pierrot Players (with S. Pruslin and H. Birtwistle), 1965; Matrix, 1971; Music Party for authentic performance of classical music, 1972; Classical Orch., 1977; Guest Cond., Orchestra la Fenice, Venice, 1981–; operatic cond. début, Den Bergtagna, Sweden, 1986, York Fest., 1988; conducted 1st major British prodn of Mozart's La Finta Giardiniera, 1989; German operatic début, Don Giovanni, Così fan Tutte, Stuttgart, 1991, Julius Caesar, Halle, Ulisse, Stuttgart, 1992; La Cenerentola, Barcelona, 1993; King Arthur, Stuttgart, 1995; Xerxes, Cologne, 1996; Alcina, Stuttgart, 1998; Saul, Berlin, 1999. Orchestral work with: Südwestfunk and Berlin Radio Orch., 1992; Orchestre Nat. de Lille, 1996; Gürzenich Orchester, Cologne, 1996. First modern "authentic" perfs, 1977–, incl: Mozart's Symphonies 39, 40; Beethoven's Symphonies 2, 3, 7, 9 and Egmont; Haydn's Harmonie and Creation Masses, Symphony 104 and Trumpet Concerto. Revived basset clarinet and restored orig. text, Mozart's concerto and quintet, 1967; revived baroque clarinet (hitherto unplayed), 1975. Premieres of music by Birtwistle, Boulez, Morton Feldman, Goehr, Maxwell Davies, Stockhausen, Blake, Mellers, Salvatore Sciarrino and Judith Weir; cond 5 staged perfs of Bach's St John Passion for European Music Year, 1984. Sir Robert Mayer Lectr, Leeds Univ., 1972–73. Mem. Fires of London, 1970–76; Dir, York Early Music Festival. Teacher, lectr and conductor, Banff Centre, Canada, 1986–. Many recordings. *Publications:* Scores of Mozart Concerto and Quintet, 1972; 1st edn of reconstructed Mozart Concerto, 1973; Schumann's Soirėestucke, 1985. *Recreation:* cookery. *Address:* Hindlea, Broughton, Malton, N Yorks YO17 6QJ.

HACKER, Rt Rev. George Lanyon; Hon. Assistant Bishop, diocese of Carlisle, since 1994; Bishop Suffragan of Penrith, 1979–94; *b* 27 Dec. 1928; *s* of Edward Sidney Hacker and Carla Lanyon; *m* 1969, June Margaret Erica Smart; one *s* one *d. Educ:* Kelly College, Tavistock; Exeter College, Oxford (BA 1952, MA 1956); Cuddesdon College, Oxford. Deacon 1954, priest 1955, Bristol; Curate of St Mary Redcliffe, Bristol, 1954–59; Chaplain, King's College London at St Boniface Coll., Warminster, 1959–64; Perpetual Curate, Church of the Good Shepherd, Bishopwearmouth, 1964–71; Rector of Tilehurst, Reading, 1971–79. Pres., Rural Theol. Assoc., 1989–94; Pres., Age Concern Cumbria, 1991– (Chm., 1987–91); Chm., Age Concern Eden, 1994–2000; Episcopal Advr, Anglican Young People's Assoc., 1987–94. Editor, Chrism, 1996–. *Publication:* The Healing Stream: Catholic insights into the ministry of healing, 1998. *Recreations:* gardening, book binding, writing poetry. *Address:* Keld House, Milburn, Penrith, Cumbria CA10 1TW. *T:* (01768) 361506; *e-mail:* bishhack@talk21.com.

HACKER, Peter Michael Stephen, DPhil; Fellow and Tutor in Philosophy, since 1966, and Librarian, since 1986, St John's College, Oxford; *b* 15 July 1939; *s* of Emeric Hacker and Thea Hacker (*née* Mendel); *m* 1963, Sylvia Dolores Imhoff; two *s* one *d. Educ:* Queen's Coll., Oxford (MA); St Antony's Coll., Oxford (DPhil). Jun. Res. Fellow, Balliol Coll., Oxford, 1965–66; British Acad. Res. Reader, 1985–87; Leverhulme Res. Fellow, 1991–94. Visiting Professor: Swarthmore Coll., Pa, 1973, 1986; Univ. of Michigan, Ann Arbor, 1974; Queen's Univ., Ont, 1985. *Publications:* Insight and Illusion, 1972, 2nd edn 1986; Appearance and Reality, 1987; (ed) The Renaissance of Gravure: the art of S. W. Hayter, 1988; Wittgenstein: meaning and mind, 1990; (ed) Gravure and Grace: the engravings of Roger Vieillard, 1993; Wittgenstein: mind and will, 1996; Wittgenstein's Place in Twentieth Century Analytic Philosophy, 1996; Wittgenstein: connections and controversies, 2001; with G. P. Baker: Wittgenstein: understanding and meaning, 1980; Frege: logical excavations, 1984; Language, Sense and Nonsense, 1984; Scepticism, Rules and Language, 1984; Wittgenstein: rules, grammar and necessity, 1985. *Recreations:* art history, music. *Address:* St John's College, Oxford OX1 3JP.

HACKER, Richard Daniel; QC 1998; *b* 26 March 1954; *s* of Samuel Hacker and Lilli Hacker (*née* Eick); *m* 1988, Sarah Anne, *d* of R. J. Millar, Bath; one *d. Educ:* Haberdashers' Aske's Sch.; Downing Coll., Cambridge (Wiener Anspach Schol., 1976; BA Law 1976; MA 1979); Univ. Libre de Bruxelles (Licence Spéciale en Droit Européen (Distinction) 1978). Called to the Bar, Lincoln's Inn, 1977 (Hardwicke Schol.; Student of the Year Prize), *ad eundem* Gray's Inn, 1989; in practice at the Bar, 1979–. Asst Parly Boundary Comr, 2000–; Chm., Inquiry into Herts Parly Constituency Boundaries, 2000. *Recreations:* travel, food, opera, family life. *Address:* 3–4 South Square, Gray's Inn, WC1R 5HP. *T:* (020) 7696 9900, *Fax:* (020) 7696 9911; *e-mail:* hackerqc@mail.com.

HACKETT, Dennis William; journalist; publishing and communications consultant; Director, Media Search & Selection Ltd, since 1988; *b* 5 Feb. 1929; *s* of James Joseph Hackett and Sarah Ellen Hackett (*née* Bedford); *m* 1st, 1953, Agnes Mary Collins; two *s* one *d*; 2nd, 1974, Jacqueline Margaret Totterdell; one *d. Educ:* De La Salle College, Sheffield. Served with RN, 1947–49. Sheffield Telegraph, 1945–47 and 1949–54; Daily Herald, 1954; Odhams Press, 1954; Deputy Editor, Illustrated, 1955–58; Daily Express, 1958–60; Daily Mail, 1960; Art Editor, Observer, 1961–62; Deputy Editor, 1962, Editor, 1964–65, Queen; Editor, Nova, 1965–69; Publisher, Twentieth Century Magazine, 1965–72; Editorial Dir, George Newnes Ltd, 1966–69; Dir, IPC Newspapers, 1969–71; Associate Editor, Daily Express, 1973–74; TV critic: The Times, 1981–85; Tablet, 1984–92; Editorial Consultant, You, The Mail on Sunday magazine, 1982–86; Exec. Editor, 1986–87, Editor-in-chief, 1987, Today; Editor-in-Chief, M, The Observer Magazine, 1987–88; Editor, Management Today, 1992–94. Chm., Design and Art Directors' Assoc., 1967–68. *Publications:* The History of the Future: Bemrose Corporation 1826–1976, 1976; The Big Idea: the story of Ford in Europe, 1978. *Recreations:* reading, walking. *Address:* Wessington House, Station Road, Blockley, Moreton-in-Marsh, Glos GL56 9DZ. *Club:* Royal Automobile.

HACKETT, John Charles Thomas, FIMgt; Director General, Federation of Civil Engineering Contractors, 1992–96; *b* 4 Feb. 1939; *s* of late Thomas John Hackett and Doris Hackett; *m* 1958, Patricia Margaret, *d* of late Eric Ronald Clifford and Margaret Tubb. *Educ:* Glyn Grammar Sch., Epsom, Surrey; London Univ. (LLB Hons, external). Prodn Planning Manager, Rowntree Gp, 1960–64; Prodn Controller, Johnson's Wax, 1964; Commercial Sec., Heating and Ventilating Contractors' Assoc., 1964–70; Sec., Cttee of Assocs of Specialist Engrg Contractors, 1968–79; Dep. Dir, 1970–79, Dir,

1980–84, British Constructional Steelwork Assoc.; Dir Gen., BIBA, subseq. BIIBA, 1985–91. Member: Council, CBI, 1980–88 and 1992–96; CBI Gp of Chief Execs of Major Sector Assocs, 1980–84 and 1992–96. FIMgt (FBIM 1981). *Publication:* BCSA Members' Contractual Handbook, 1972, 2nd edn 1979. *Recreations:* music, reading, walking, motoring. *Address:* 15 Downsway Close, Tadworth, Surrey KT20 5DR. *T:* (01737) 813024.

HACKETT, John Wilkings, CMG 1989; Director, Financial, Fiscal and Enterprise Affairs, Organisation for Economic Co-operation and Development, Paris, 1979–89; *b* 21 Jan. 1924; *s* of Albert and Bertha Hackett; *m* 1952, Anne-Marie Le Brun. *Educ:* LSE (BSc(Econ) 1950); Institut d'Etudes Politiques, Paris (Diplôme 1952); Univ. of Paris (Dr d'état ès sciences economiques 1957). Served RN, 1942–46. Economic research, 1952–57; OECD, 1958–89. FRSA 1986. *Publications:* Economic Planning in France (with A.-M. Hackett), 1963; L'Economie Britannique—problèmes et perspectives, 1966; (with A.-M. Hackett) The British Economy, 1967; articles on economic subjects in British and French economic jls. *Recreations:* music, painting, reading. *Address:* 48 rue de la Bienfaisance, 75008 Paris, France. *Club:* Cercle de l'Union Interalliée (Paris).

HACKETT, Peter, OBE 1990; DL; PhD; FREng; Director, 1993–94, and Principal, 1970–94, Camborne School of Mines (first Fellow, 1990); Adviser on Cornwall, Exeter University, 1994–98; *b* 1 Nov. 1933; *s* of Christopher and Evelyn Hackett; *m* 1958, Esmé Doreen (*née* Lloyd); one *s* one *d*. *Educ:* Mundella Grammar Sch.; Nottingham Univ. (BSc 1st Cl. Hons Mining Engrg; PhD). FIMM 1971, Hon. FIMM 1993; FREng (FEng 1983). Lecturer, Nottingham Univ., 1958–70; Vis. Lectr, Univ. of Minnesota, 1969; Vis. Professor, Univ. of California at Berkeley, 1979. Pres., IMM, 1989–90. Chm., Port of Falmouth Sailing Assoc., 1998–. DL Cornwall, 1993. *Publications:* contribs to learned jls on geotechnical subjects and mining engrg educn. *Recreations:* sailing, classic vehicles. *Club:* Royal Cornwall Yacht (Falmouth).

HACKING, family name of **Baron Hacking**.

HACKING, 3rd Baron *cr* 1945, of Chorley; **Douglas David Hacking;** Bt 1938; International Arbitrator; Solicitor of Supreme Court of England and Wales, since 1977; Attorney and Counselor-at-Law of State of New York, since 1975; Barrister-at-law, 1963–76 and since 1999; Chartered Arbitrator, since 1999; *b* 17 April 1938; *er s* of 2nd Baron Hacking, and Daphne Violet (*d* 1998), *e d* of late R. L. Finnis; *S* father, 1971; *m* 1st, 1965, Rosemary Anne, *e d* of late Francis P. Forrest, FRCSE; two *s* one *d*; 2nd, 1982, Dr Tessa M. Hunt, MB, MRCP, FRCA, *er d* of Roland C. C. Hunt, CMG; three *s*. *Educ:* Aldro School, Shackleford; Charterhouse School; Clare College, Cambridge (BA 1961, MA 1968). Called to the Bar, Middle Temple, Nov. 1963 (Astbury and Harmsworth Scholarships). Served in RN, 1956–58; Ordinary Seaman, 1956; Midshipman, 1957; served in HMS Ark Royal (N Atlantic), 1957; HMS Hardy (Portland) and HMS Brocklesby (Portland and Gibraltar), 1958; transferred RNR as Sub-Lt, 1958, on completion of National Service; transf. List 3 RNR, HMS President, 1961; Lieut 1962; retired RNR, 1964. With Simpson, Thacher and Bartlett, NYC, 1975–76; with Lovell, White and King, 1976–79; Partner: Richards Butler, 1981–94; Sonnenscheins, 1994–99. Mem., H of L Select Cttee on the European Community, 1989–93, 1995–99. Chm. Steering Cttee, London Internat. Arbitration Trust, 1980–81. Trustee, Carthusian Trust, 1971–. Gov., Charlotte Sharman Sch., Southwark, 1996–97. Member: Amer. Bar Assoc.; Bar Assoc. of City of New York. Pres., Assoc. of Lancastrians in London, 1971–72, 1998. Apprenticed to Merchant Taylors' Co., 1955, admitted to Freedom, 1962; Freedom, City of London, 1962. FCIArb 1979. *Recreations:* running, walking. *Heir: s* Hon. Douglas Francis Hacking, *b* 8 Aug. 1968. *Address:* 27 West Square, Kennington, SE11 4SP. *T:* (020) 7735 4400; *e-mail:* ddhacking@aol.com. *Clubs:* Reform, MCC; Century (NY).

HACKING, Anthony Stephen; QC 1983; a Recorder, since 1985; a Deputy High Court Judge (Queen's Bench Division), since 1993; *b* 12 Jan. 1941; *s* of late John and Joan Hacking, Warwick; *m* 1969, Carin, *d* of Dr Svante and Brita Holmdahl, Gothenburg; one *d* three *s*. *Educ:* Warwick Sch.; Lincoln Coll., Oxford (MA). Called to the Bar, Inner Temple, 1965, Bencher, 1993. *Address:* 1 King's Bench Walk, Temple, EC4Y 7DB. *T:* (020) 7936 1500, *Fax:* (020) 7936 1590.

HACKLAND, Sarah Ann; *see* Spencer, S. A.

HACKNEY, Archdeacon of; *see* Dennen, Ven. Lyle.

HACKNEY, Arthur, RWS 1957 (VPRWS 1974–77); RE 1960 (Hon. RE 1982); ARCA 1949; artist; Principal Lecturer (formerly Deputy Head), Fine Art Department, West Surrey College of Art and Design (Farnham Centre) (formerly Farnham School of Art), 1979–85, retired; *b* 13 March 1925; *s* of late J. T. Hackney; *m* 1955, Mary Baker, ARCA; two *d*. *Educ:* Burslem Sch. of Art; Royal Coll. of Art, London. Served in Royal Navy, Western Approaches, 1942–46. Travelling scholarship, Royal College of Art, 1949; part-time Painting Instructor, Farnham Sch. of Art, 1950, Lecturer, 1962; Head of Dept: Graphic, 1963–68; Printmaking, 1968–79. Work represented in Public Collections, including Bradford City Art Gallery, Victoria and Albert Museum, Guildhall Art Gall., Ashmolean Museum, Wellington Art Gallery (NZ), Nottingham Art Gallery, Keighley Art Gallery (Yorks), Wakefield City Art Gallery, Graves Art Gallery, Sheffield, Preston Art Gallery, City of Stoke-on-Trent Art Gall., Kent Educn Cttee, Staffordshire Educn Cttee, RCA. Mem., Fine Art Bd, CNAA, 1975–78. Work reproduced in 20th Century Painters and Sculptors, by Francis Spalding, 1990. *Address:* Woodhatches, Spoil Lane, Tongham, Farnham, Surrey GU10 1BP. *T:* (01252) 23919. *Club:* Chelsea Arts.

HACKNEY, Roderick Peter, PhD; PPRIBA; Managing Director, Rod Hackney & Associates, since 1972; *b* 3 March 1942; *s* of William Hackney and Rose (*née* Morris); *m* 1964, Christine Thornton; one *s*. *Educ:* John Bright's Grammar School, Llandudno; Sch. of Architecture, Manchester Univ. (BAArch 1966, MA 1969, PhD 1979). ARIBA 1969; FCIArb 1977; ASAI; FFB 1987; MCIOB 1987. Job Architect, EXPO '67, Montreal, for Monorail Stations; Housing Architect, Libyan Govt, Tripoli, 1967–68; Asst to Arne Jacobsen, Copenhagen, working on Kuwait Central Bank, 1968–71. Established Castward Ltd, building and develt firm, 1983 (Sec., 1983–92). Royal Institute of British Architects: Pres., 1987–89; Mem. Council, 1978–84 (Vice-Pres., Public Affairs, and Overseas Affairs, 1981–83), and 1991–99 (Vice-Pres., Internat. Affairs, 1992–94); Hon. Librarian, 1998–99; Dir, RIBAC Cos, 1996–2001. Mem. Council, Internat. Union of Architects, 1981–85, and 1991–, First Vice-Pres., 1985–87, Pres., 1987–90. Vis. Prof., Paris, 1984; Special Prof., Nottingham Univ., 1987–90; Vis. Prof., Xian Univ., China, 1999; has lectured in Europe, N and S America, Asia, Middle East, Australia and Africa. Chm., Times/RIBA Community Enterprise Scheme, 1985–89; Mem. Council, Nat. Historical Bldg Crafts Inst., 1989–; Advr on regeneration and inner city problems in Sweden, Italy, Brazil, USA, Russia and Germany, 1990–; Internat. Advr, Centre for Internat. Archl Studies, Univ. of Manchester Sch. of Architecture, 1992–; Jury Mem., overseas housing develts; Juror for internat. competitions in Netherlands and China, 1992–; deleg., UK and overseas confs. Chairman: Trustees, Inner City Trust, 1986–97; British Architectl Liby Trust, 1999–2001. President: Snowdonia (formerly Snowdonia Nat. Park) Soc., 1987–; N Wales Centre, NT, 1990–. Patron: Llandudno Mus. and Art Gall, 1988–; Dome Project, Buxton, 2000–. Hon. FAIA 1988; Hon. FRAIC 1990; Hon. Fellow: United Architects of Philippines, 1988; Fedn of Colls of Architects, Mexico, 1988; Indian Inst. of Architecture, 1990; Hon. Mem., Superior Council of Colls of Architects of Spain, 1987. Hon. DLitt Keele, 1989. Awards and prizes include: DoE Award for Good Design in Housing (1st Prize), 1975; 1st Prize, St Ann's Hospice Arch. Comp., 1976; RICS Conservation Award, 1980; Sir Robert Matthew Prize, IUA, 1981; PA Consulting Gp Award for Innovation in Bldg Design and Construction (for Colquhoun St, Stirling), 1988; Award for work and leader of Community Arch. Movt, Charleston, USA, 1989; The Times, BITC, and Housing and Homeless Award, 1993. *Television:* Build Yourself a House, 1974; Community Architecture, 1977; BBC Omnibus, 1987; consultant, Europe by Design, BBC, 1991; *radio:* The Listener, 1986; Third Ear, 1990; Call to Account, 1992; Woman's Hour, 1992; Common Ground, 1996. Consultant, World Architecture Review Agency, China, 1992; Advr, Habitat Center News Jl, India, 1992–. *Publications:* Highfield Hall: a community project, 1982; The Good the Bad and the Ugly, 1990; Good Golly Miss Molly (music play), 1991; articles in UK and foreign architectural jls. *Recreations:* outdoor pursuits, walking, photography, travelling, looking at buildings, speaking at conferences. *Address:* St Peter's House, Windmill Street, Macclesfield, Cheshire SK11 7HS. *T:* (01625) 431792; *e-mail:* rod@stpeter.demon.co.uk. *Club:* Royal Commonwealth Society.

HACKSTON, Fiona C.; *see* Clarke-Hackston.

HADDACKS, Vice-Adm. Sir Paul (Kenneth), KCB 2000; Director, NATO International Military Staff, since 2001; *b* 27 Oct. 1946; *s* of Kenneth Alexander Haddacks and Edith Lillian Haddacks (*née* Peardon); *m* 1970, Penny Anne Robertson; one *s*. *Educ:* Plymouth Coll.; Kingswood Sch., Bath; BRNC; RN Staff Coll., RCDS. Joined RN 1964; commanded HM Ships: Scimitar, 1971–72; Cleopatra, 1981–82; Naiad, 1982–83; Intrepid, 1986–88; US Naval Acad., 1979–80; Asst Dir, Navy Plans, 1984–86; Dep. Dir, Naval Warfare, 1988–89; Comdr, RN Task Force, Gulf, 1990; Captain of the Fleet, 1991–94; Asst CoS (Policy) to SACEUR, 1994–97; UK Mil. Rep., HQ NATO, 1997–2000. *Recreations:* family, travel. *Address:* c/o Naval Secretary, Victory Building, HM Naval Base, Portsmouth PO1 3LR. *Clubs:* Army and Navy; Royal Naval Sailing Association.

HADDAOUI, Khalil; Moroccan Ambassador to the Court of St James's, 1991–99; *b* 21 April 1937; *m*; three *c*. *Educ:* School of Higher Business Studies, Paris; Inst. of Internat. Relations, Paris. Joined Ministry of Foreign Affairs, 1966; served Rome, London, Algiers, Madrid; Adviser to Moroccan Minister for Foreign Affairs, 1976; Ambassador to Liberia and Sierra Leone, 1982, to UN, 1985; Dir of Internat. Orgn, 1986, of European and American Affairs, 1990, Min. for Foreign Affairs. *Address:* c/o Moroccan Embassy, 49 Queen's Gate Garden, SW7 5NE.

HADDINGTON, 13th Earl of, *cr* 1619; **John George Baillie-Hamilton;** Lord Binning, 1613; Lord Binning and Byres, 1619; *b* 21 Dec. 1941; *o s* of 12th Earl of Haddington, KT, MC, TD, and Sarah (*d* 1995), *y d* of G. W. Cook, Montreal; *S* father, 1986; *m* 1st, 1975, Prudence Elizabeth (marr. diss. 1981), *d* of A. Rutherford Hayles; 2nd, 1984, Susan Jane Antonia, 2nd *d* of John Heyworth; one *s* two *d*. *Educ:* Ampleforth. *Heir: s* Lord Binning, *qv*. *Address:* Mellerstain, Gordon, Berwickshire TD3 6LG; Tyninghame, Dunbar, East Lothian. *Clubs:* Turf, Chelsea Arts; New (Edinburgh).

HADDO, Earl of; Alexander George Gordon; DL; *b* 31 March 1955; *s* and *heir* of 6th Marquess of Aberdeen and Temair, *qv*; *m* 1981, Joanna Clodagh Houldsworth; three *s* one *d*. *Educ:* Cothill House, Abingdon; Harrow School; Polytechnic of Central London (DipBE). ARICS 1979–95. With Gardiner and Theobald, Chartered Quantity Surveyors, 1976–82; Speyhawk plc, Property Developers, 1982–86; London & Edinburgh Trust plc, Property Developers, 1986–94; Managing Director: Letinvest, 1989–94; Kellie Estates Ltd, 1995–; Gordon Land Ltd, 2000–; non-executive Director: Mobile Cardiovascular Science plc, 1992–99; Gordon Enterprise Trust, 1998–. DL Aberdeenshire, 1998. *Recreations:* golf, music, theatre. *Heir: s* Viscount Formartine, *qv*. *Address:* House of Formartine, Methlick, Ellon, Aberdeenshire AB41 7EQ. *T:* (01651) 851664. *Clubs:* MCC; Royal Aberdeen Golf.

HADDON, Kenneth William, FCA; Chairman, Axa Reinsurance UK plc, 1994–99 (Chief Executive Officer, 1987–98); *b* 30 April 1938; *s* of William Percy Haddon and Constance Margaret Haddon; *m* 1966, Jarmaine (*née* Cook); one *s* one *d*. *Educ:* Minchenden Grammar Sch. FCA 1960. Nat. Service, RAF, 1960–62. Chartered Accountant, Thomson McLintock, 1962–64; London Reinsurance Co., later Netherlands Reinsurance Gp, then NRG London Reinsurance Co.: Sec. and Accountant, 1964; various posts, 1964–82; Gen. Manager, 1983–87. Chairman: London Underwriting Centre, 1995–98, and 1999–; London Processing Centre, 1997–99; London Internat. Insce and Reinsce Mkt Assoc., 1997–98. *Recreations:* golf, running, gardening. *Address:* Greenacres, Staines Green, near Hertford, Herts SG14 2LN. *T:* (01992) 583965. *Clubs:* City of London, Royal Society of Arts, Langbourn Ward; Brookmans Park Golf.

HADDON-CAVE, Charles Anthony; QC 1999; a Recorder, since 2000; *b* 20 March 1956; *s* of Sir (Charles) Philip Haddon-Cave, KBE, CMG; *m* 1980, Amanda Charlotte Law; two *d*. *Educ:* King's Sch., Canterbury; Pembroke Coll., Cambridge (MA). Called to the Bar, Gray's Inn, 1978; in practice as barrister, London and Hong Kong, 1980–. *Recreations:* art, music, running. *Address:* 4 Essex Court, Temple, EC4Y 9AJ. *T:* (020) 7653 5653. *Club:* Royal Automobile.

HADDRILL, Stephen Howard; Director of Employment Relations, Department of Trade and Industry, since 2000; *b* 12 Jan. 1956; *s* of Albert George and Pauline Haddrill; *m* 1983, Joanne Foakes; two *s*. *Educ:* Trinity Sch., Croydon; New Coll., Oxford (BA Modern Hist. and Econs). Joined Department of Energy, 1978: Private Sec. to Sec. of State, 1987–89; Asst Sec., Nuclear Power Policy, 1989–90; Mem., Governor's Central Policy Unit, Hong Kong Govt, 1991–94; Department of Trade and Industry, 1994–: Dep. Dir, Competitiveness Unit, 1994–98; Dir, Consumer Affairs, 1998–2000. *Recreations:* gardening, sailing. *Address:* Department of Trade and Industry, 1 Victoria Street, SW1H 0ET. *T:* (020) 7215 5000.

HADEN-GUEST, family name of **Baron Haden-Guest**.

HADEN-GUEST, 5th Baron *cr* 1950, of Saling, Essex; **Christopher Haden-Guest;** film director, writer, actor and musician (as Christopher Guest); *b* 5 Feb. 1948; *s* of 4th Baron Haden-Guest and of Jean Haden-Guest (*née* Hindes); *S* father, 1996; *m* 1984, Jamie Lee Curtis; one *s* one *d* (both adopted). *Educ:* The Stockbridge Sch.; New York Univ. *Films:* (writer, dir and actor): Waiting for Guffman, 1997; Best in Show, 2000; (writer and dir) The Big Picture; (writer and actor) This is Spinal Tap, 1984; (dir) Almost Heroes, 1998. Scriptwriter for TV and radio progs. *Recreations:* fly-fishing, ski-ing. *Heir: b* Hon. Nicholas Haden-Guest [*b* 5 May 1951; *m* 1st, 1980, Jill Denby (marr. diss. 1988); one *d*; 2nd, 1989, Pamela Rack; one *d*]. *Address:* 253A 26th Street #300, Santa Monica, CA 90402, USA.

HADFIELD, Antony; Senior Partner, Hadfield Associates, since 1997; *b* 9 Sept. 1936; *s* of Thomas Henry Hadfield and Edna (*née* Cooke); *m* 1959, Dorothy Fay Osman; one *s*. *Educ:* Sheffield; Brighton; Middx Poly. (BA). CEng; FIEE. Design engr, Plessey, 1958–62; design and project engr, Metal Industries Gp, 1962–65; design engr, CEGB, 1965–67; Sen. Engr and Manager, Eastern Electricity, 1967–77; Area Manager, Yorks Electricity, 1977–79; Dir of Engrg, Midlands Electricity, 1979–85; Chief Exec. and Dep. Chm., NI Electricity, 1985–91; Man. Dir, 1991–94, Chief Exec., 1994–97, Northern Electric plc; Chief Exec., Teesside Power Ltd, 1998–2000 (Dir, 1991–97). Chairman: Northern Inf. Systems Ltd, 1994–97; NEDL Ltd, 1994–97; Northern Utility Services Ltd, 1994–97; Sovereign Exploration Ltd, 1996–97; Dep. Chm., BCN Data Systems Ltd, 1998–2000. Associate PB Power Ltd, 1997–. Mem., Competition (formerly Monopolies and Mergers) Commn, 1998–. Chm., Power Div., IEE, 1992–93. Chm., BITC, Tyneside, 1993–97. CIMgt; FRSA. *Recreations:* mountaineering, sailing.

HADFIELD, (Geoffrey) John, CBE 1980; TD 1963; MS, FRCS; Surgeon, Stoke Mandeville Hospital, 1960–88, retired; Hon. Tutor in Surgery, University College Hospital Medical School, 1968–88; *b* 19 April 1923; *s* of late Prof. Geoffrey Hadfield, MD, and Eileen D'Arcy Irvine; *m* 1960, Beryl, *d* of late Hubert Sleigh, Manchester; three *d*. *Educ:* Merchant Taylors' Sch.; St Bartholomew's Hosp., London Univ. MB BS 1947, MS 1954, London; MRCS LRCP 1946, FRCS 1948. Ho. Officer Appts, Demonstr. of Anatomy, Registrar and Sen. Lectr in Surgery, St Bart's Hosp.; Fellow in Surgery, Memorial Hosp., New York; served RAMC, Far East, 1948–50; TAVR, 1950–73; Lt-Col, RAMC RARO, Hon. Col 219 Gen. Hosp., TAVR. Royal College of Surgeons of England: Arris and Gale Lectr, 1954; Hunterian Prof., 1959; Erasmus Wilson Demonstr., 1969; Arnott Demonstr., 1972; Stamford Cade Meml Lectr, 1978; Mem., Council, 1971–83, Vice-Pres., 1982–83; Mem., Court of Examiners, Final FRCS, 1972–78 (Chm., 1977–78); Mem., Ct of Examiners, Primary FRCS, 1982–85. Examiner in Surgery for Univs of Liverpool, Bristol and Leeds, and Vis. Examiner to univs in Middle and Far East. Fellow, 1955, Sen. Fellow, 1988, Assoc. of Surgs of GB and Ireland; Senior Member: Brit. Assoc. of Urol Surgs (Mem. Council, 1979–82); Brit. Assoc. of Surg. Oncology (Mem., Nat. Cttee, 1972–75); Brit. Assoc. of Clin. Anatomists (Mem. Council, 1976–80). Hon. FCPS (Pak) (Liaison Officer), 1991. SPk 2000. *Publications:* (with M. Hobsley) Current Surgical Practice, vol. 1, 1976, vol. 2, 1978, vol. 3, 1981, vol. 4, 1986, vol. 5, 1990; (with M. Hobsley and B. C. Morson) Pathology in Surgical Practice, 1985; (jtly) Imaging in Surgical Practice, 1989; articles in jls and chapters in books on diseases of the breast, cancer, urology, trauma, varicose veins and med. educn. *Recreations:* ocean racing and cruising, travel, walking, golf. *Address:* Milverton House, 6 St John's Close, Bishopsteignton, near Teignmouth, Devon TQ14 9RT. *T:* (01626) 779537. *Clubs:* Army and Navy; Teign Corinthian Yacht.

See also J. I. H. Hadfield.

HADFIELD, James Irvine Havelock, FRCS, FRCSE; Anatomy Supervisor, Jesus College, and Demonstrator, Department of Anatomy, University of Cambridge, since 1995; Consultant Surgeon (Urologist), Bedford General Hospital, 1965–95; *b* 12 July 1930; *s* of Prof. G. Hadfield and S. V. E. Hadfield (*née* Irvine); *m* 1957, Ann Pickernell Milner; one *s* two *d*. *Educ:* Radley College; Brasenose College, Oxford (MA, BM, BCh 1955, MCh Pt I 1960); St Thomas's Hosp. Med. Sch. FRCS 1960, FRCSE 1960; FICS 1990. House Surgeon, St Thomas' Hosp., 1955; Lectr in Anatomy, St Thomas's Hosp. Med. Sch., 1956–57; RSO, Leicester Royal Inf., 1960–62; Surgical Tutor, Oxford Univ., 1962–66; Med. Dir, Bedford Hosp. NHS Trust, 1990–95. Arris and Gale Lectr, RCS, 1967; Examnr in Surgery, Univ. of Cambridge, 1976–82; Examnr in MRCS, LRCP, 1974–80; Examnr, FRCSE, 1989–95. *Publications:* Topics in Core Clinical Anatomy, 1999; articles in surgical jls on Metabolic Response to Trauma, Urology, and Surgical Anatomy of the Veins of the Legs. *Recreations:* watching rowing, shooting, unwilling gardener, trying to catch unwilling salmon in South West Wales. *Address:* Baker's Barn, Stagsden West End, near Bedford MK43 8SZ. *T:* (01234) 824514. *Clubs:* Vincent's (Oxford); Leander, London Rowing.

See also G. J. Hadfield.

HADFIELD, John; *see* Hadfield, G. J.

HADFIELD, Sir Ronald, Kt 1995; QPM 1989; DL; Police Advisor to North Wales Tribunal into Child Abuse, 1996–98; Chief Constable, West Midlands, 1990–96; *b* 15 July 1939; *s* of George and Phyllis Marjorie Hadfield; *m* 1961, Anne Phyllisia Worrall; one *s* one *d*. *Educ:* Chadderton Grammar School. Joined Oldham Borough Police Force, 1958; served in Lancashire and Greater Manchester Police Forces; Asst Chief Constable, Derbyshire Constabulary, 1981; Dep. Chief Constable, 1986, Chief Constable, 1987, Nottinghamshire Constabulary. DL W Midlands, 1994. Advr in communications and law to cos in Midlands. *Recreations:* golf, fishing.

HADID, Zaha Mohammad; architectural designer; *b* Baghdad, 31 Oct. 1950. *Educ:* Sch. of Architecture, Architectural Assoc., London (Diploma Prize). Lectr, AA, 1977, 1980; Vis. Design Critic, Harvard Grad. Sch. of Design, 1986; Vis. Prof., 1987, Kenzo Tange Prof., 1994, Columbia Univ., NY; Sullivan Prof., Univ. of Illinois, 1997; Guest Prof., Hochschule für Bildende Kunst, Hamburg, 1997. *Projects* include: 59 Eaton Place, SW1, 1980 (RIBA, Gold Medal, 1982); Hamburg Docklands Bauforum 1, 1985, Bauforum 2, 1989; Tomigaya and Azabu-Jyuban, Tokyo, 1987; Monsoon Restaurant, Sapporo, Japan, 1989 (completed 1990); Bordeaux Docklands, 1989; Osaka Folly, 1989 (completed 1990); Vitra Fire Station, Weil am Rhein, 1990 (completed 1993); Hotel Billie Strauss, Stuttgart, 1992–95; Kunst und Medienzentrum Rheinhafen, Düsseldorf, 1993; Cardiff Bay Opera House, 1994–96 (Opera House Trust First Prize, 1994; Special Award, Royal Acad. Summer Exhibn, 1995); Spittelau Viaduct Mixed Use Project, Vienna, 1994–97; Contemporary Arts Center, Cincinnati, 1998; Contemporary Arts Centre, Rome; Science Centre, Wolfsburg; Bridge Structure, Abu Dhabi; Tram station, Strasbourg. Has exhibited in Europe, Japan, and USA; has lectured in Europe, USA, Australia, Brazil, Canada, China, Hong Kong, Jordan, Lebanon, Mexico, Taiwan, Thailand, and UAE. *Publications:* articles in newspapers, magazines and architectl and design jls. *Address:* (office) Studio 9, 10 Bowling Green Lane, EC1R 0BD. *T:* (020) 7253 5147, *Fax:* (020) 7251 8322.

HADINGHAM, Reginald Edward Hawke, CBE 1988 (OBE 1971); MC 1943 and Bar 1943; TD 1946; Life President, Sparks, the sportsman's charity, 1995 (Chairman, 1968–94); *b* 6 Dec. 1915; *s* of Edward Wallace Hadingham and Ethel Irene Penelope Gwynne-Evans; *m* 1940, Lois Pope, *d* of Edward and Nora Pope; two *d*. *Educ:* Rokeby Preparatory, Wimbledon; St Paul's. Joined Slazengers, 1933, European Sales Manager, 1936. Joined TA, 57th Anti-Tank Regt, 1938, commnd into 67th Anti-Tank Regt 1938; served War of 1939–45 with 67th Anti-Tank Regt, RA; commanded 302 Battery, 1942–45 (MC Salerno 1943 and Bar, Garigliano 1943); CO 67 Regt, 1945 until disbanded, Oct. 1945. Returned to Slazengers as Asst Export Manager, Jan. 1946; Export Manager, 1949; Gen. Sales Manager, 1951; Sales Dir, 1952; Man. Dir, 1969; Chm. and Man. Dir, 1973; Chm. (Non-Exec.), 1976–83. All England Lawn Tennis Club: Mem. Cttee, 1976–84; Chm. of Club, and of Cttee of Management, The Championships, Wimbledon, 1984–89; Vice-Pres., 1990–; Pres., Internat. Lawn Tennis Club of GB, 1991–. Thrice Pres., Sette of Odd Volumes (Treasurer, 1953–). *Recreations:* reading, writing verse. *Address:* 3 Boleyn Lodge, 2 Marryat Road, Wimbledon, SW19 5BD. *T:* (020) 8946 9611. *Clubs:* Queen's, All England Lawn Tennis, Hurlingham, International Lawn Tennis of GB; Fitzwilliam Lawn Tennis (Dublin).

HADLEE, Sir Richard (John), Kt 1990; MBE 1980; New Zealand cricketer, retired; *b* 3 July 1951; *s* of Walter Hadlee, CBE; *m* 1973, Karen Ann Marsh; two *s*; *m* 1999, Dianne Taylor. *Educ:* Christchurch Boys' High Sch. Played for: Canterbury, 1972–89; Nottinghamshire (UK), 1978–87 (made 1000 runs and took 100 wickets in English season, 1984); Tasmania, 1979–80; Test début for NZ, 1973; toured: Australia, 1972–73, 1973–74, 1980–81, 1985–86; England, 1973, 1978, 1983, 1986, 1990; India, 1976, 1988; Pakistan, 1976; Sri Lanka, 1983–84, 1987; West Indies, 1984–85. Holder of world record of 431 Test wickets, 1990 (passed previous record of 373 in 1988). *Publication:* Rhythm and Swing (autobiog.), 1989. *Address:* Box 29186, Christchurch, New Zealand. *Club:* MCC (Hon. Life Mem.).

HADLEY, David Allen, CB 1991; Deputy Secretary (Agricultural Commodities, Trade and Food Production), Ministry of Agriculture, Fisheries and Food, 1993–96; *b* 18 Feb. 1936; *s* of Sydney and Gwendoline Hadley; *m* 1965, Veronica Ann Hopkins; one *s*. *Educ:* Wyggeston Grammar Sch., Leicester; Merton Coll., Oxford. MA. Joined MAFF, 1959; Asst Sec., 1971; HM Treas., 1975–78; Under Sec., 1981–87, Dep. Sec., 1987–89, MAFF; Dep. Sec., Cabinet Office, 1989–93. *Recreations:* gardening, music. *Address:* Old Mousers, Dormansland, Lingfield, Surrey RH7 6PP.

HADLEY, Gareth Morgan; Director of Personnel, HM Prison Service, since 1999; *b* 22 April 1951; *s* of Ronald Hadley and Gweneth Doreen Hadley (*née* Morgan). *Educ:* Harrow Weald Grammar Sch.; University Coll. London (BSc); Henley Mgt Coll. (MA). FCIPD. Greater London Council, 1972–86: Asst to Hd of Industrial Relns, 1980–81; Head: Central Recruitment, 1981–83; craft, operative manual and fire service employee relns, 1983–86; Asst Dir of Personnel, ILEA, 1986–89; British Railways Board, 1989–97: Gp Employee Relns Manager, 1989–94; Director: Employee Relns, 1994–97; Human Resources, N and W Passenger Ops, 1994–97; Principal, Gareth Hadley Associates, 1997–99. Chairman: British Transport Police Pension Fund, 1992–97; ScotRail Railways Ltd, 1996–97. *Recreations:* opera, food and drink. *Address:* HM Prison Service Headquarters, Cleland House, Page Street, SW1P 4LN. *T:* (020) 7217 2944; *e-mail:* prisons-dop@prisons-dop.demon.co.uk. *Club:* Savile.

HADLEY, Graham Hunter; energy and business management consultant; Senior Adviser, National Economic Research Associates, since 1996; *b* 12 April 1944; *s* of late Dr A. L. Hadley and Mrs L. E. Hadley; *m* 1971, Lesley Ann Smith; one *s*. *Educ:* Eltham Coll., London; Jesus Coll., Cambridge (BA Hons Mod. Hist.). Entered Civil Service (Min. of Aviation), 1966; Dept of Energy, 1974; seconded to: Civil Service Commn, 1976–77; British Aerospace, 1980–81; Under-Sec., Dept of Energy, 1983; Sec., CEGB, 1983–90; Exec. Dir, 1990–95, and Man. Dir, Internat. Business Develt, 1992–95, National Power. Mem., Competition (formerly Monopolies and Mergers) Commn, 1998–. Dir, de Havilland Aircraft Mus. Trust, 1990–. *Recreations:* include cricket, golf, theatre, architecture, aviation. *Address:* Sundance House, Cold Aston, Cheltenham GL54 3BN.

HADRILL, Andrew Frederic W.; *see* Wallace Hadrill.

HAENDEL, Ida, CBE 1991; violinist; *b* Poland, 15 Dec. 1928; Polish parentage. Began to play at age of 3½; amazing gift discovered when she picked up her sister's violin and started to play. Her father, a great connoisseur of music, recognised her unusual talent and abandoned his own career as an artist (painter) to devote himself to his daughter; studied at Warsaw Conservatoire and gained gold medal at age of seven; also studied with such masters as Carl Flesch and Georges Enesco. British début, Queen's Hall, with Sir Henry Wood, playing Brahms' Violin Concerto. Gave concerts for British and US troops and in factories, War of 1939–45; after War, career developed to take in North and South America, USSR and Far East, as well as Europe; has accompanied British orchestras such as London Philharmonic, BBC Symphony and English Chamber on foreign tours including Hong Kong, China, Australia and Mexico; performs with major orchestras worldwide, incl. Berlin Philharmonic, Boston Symphony, and Concertgebouw. Has performed with conductors such as Beecham, Klemperer, Szell, Celibidache, Mata, Pritchard, Rattle, Haitink, Ashkenazy; performances include appearances at BBC Prom. A major interpreter of Sibelius, Brahms and Beethoven. Concerts, Edinburgh Fest., masterclasses. Huberman Prize; Sibelius Medal, Sibelius Soc. of Finland, 1982. *Publication:* Woman with Violin (autobiog.), 1970. *Address:* c/o Askonas Holt Ltd, 27 Chancery Lane, WC2A 1PF.

HAGARD, Dr Spencer, FFPHM; Senior Lecturer, Health Promotion Research Unit, and Course Organiser, MSc (Health Promotion Sciences), London School of Hygiene and Tropical Medicine; *b* 25 Oct. 1942; *s* of Maurice (Bozzie) Markham (killed in action, 11 June 1944) and Eva Markham (*née* Mearns, subseq. Hagard) and, by adoption, of late Noel Hagard; *m* 1968, Michele Dominique, *d* of late Stanislas and Madeleine Aquarone; two *s* one *d*. *Educ:* Varndean Grammar Sch., Brighton; Univ. of St Andrews (MB ChB 1968); Univ. of Glasgow (PhD 1977); MA Cantab 1977. DPH 1972; FFPHM (FFCM 1981). Jun. med. appts, Arbroath, London and Dorking; MO and Med. Supt, Kawolo Hosp., Lugazi, Uganda, 1971–72; MO, Health Dept, Glasgow, 1972–74; Trainee in Community Med., Greater Glasgow Health Bd, 1974–77; Specialist in Comm. Med., Cambs AHA, 1977–82; Dist MO, Cambridge HA, 1982–87; Chief Exec., HEA, 1987–94. Associate Lectr, Univ. of Cambridge Sch. of Clinical Med., 1977–87; Visiting Professor: LSHTM, 1993–95, 1996–99; Univ. of Bergen, 2001–. Hon. Consultant, Camden and Islington Community Health Services Trust, 1996–; Consultant: WHO, 1991–; DFID, 1999–; World Bank, 2000–; Health Policy Advr, Hungarian Govt, 1996–2000. National Association for the Education of Sick Children: Mem. Council, 1995–; Trustee, 1997–; Chm. of Trustees, 2000–. Sec., Eur. Cttee for Health Promotion Develt, 1995–; Pres., Internat. Union for Health Promotion and Educn, 1996–2001. FRSA 1997. *Publications:* Health, Society and Medicine (with Roy Acheson), 1984; papers in BMJ and other learned jls. *Recreations:* marriage, family, studying human beings, politics, gardening, reading, photography, appreciation of art, music, sporting new dawns (Brighton & Hove Albion, Sussex CCC). *Address:* 396 Milton Road, Cambridge CB4 1SU. *T:* (01223) 563774, *Fax:* (01223) 423970.

HAGART-ALEXANDER, Sir Claud; *see* Alexander.

HAGERTY, William John Gell; writer and broadcaster; media columnist, New Statesman, since 2000; *b* 23 April 1939; *s* of William (Steve) Hagerty and Doris Hagerty (*née* Gell); *m* 1st, 1965, Lynda Beresford (marr. diss. 1990); one *s* one *d* (and one *d* decd); 2nd, 1991, Elizabeth Vercoe (*née* Latta); one *s*. *Educ:* Beal Grammar Sch., Ilford. Local newspapers, East London, 1955–58; RAF Nat. Service, 1958–60; local newspapers, Sunday Citizen, Daily Sketch, 1960–67; Daily Mirror, 1967–81; Sunday Mirror and Sunday People, 1981–85; Managing Editor (Features), Today, 1986; Editor, Sunday Today, 1987; Deputy Editor: Sunday Mirror, 1988–90; Daily Mirror, 1990–91; Editor,

The People, 1991–92; Theatre Critic, 1993–95, Film Critic, 1994–95, Today; Theatre Critic, News of the World, 1996–2000; Punch 2001–. Consultant, Tribune, 1993–. Press Guy, Variety Club of GB, 1994–. *Publication:* Flash, Bang, Wallop! (with Kent Gavin), 1978. *Recreations:* musical theatre, watching cricket, lunch with Keith Waterhouse. *Address:* Bull Cottage, 10/11 Strand-on-the-Green, Chiswick, W4 3PQ. *Clubs:* Royal Automobile, Gerry's.

HAGESTADT, John Valentine; adviser on inward investment, since 1998; *b* 11 Oct. 1938; *s* of late Leonard and Constance Hagestadt; *m* 1963, Betty Tebbs; three *d. Educ:* Dulwich Coll.; Worcester Coll., Oxford (BA). Asst Principal, Min. of Aviation, 1963; Principal, BoT, 1967; Nuffield Travelling Fellow, 1973–74; Asst Sec., Vehicles Div., Dept of Industry, 1976; Asst Sec., Overseas Trade Div. (Middle East and Latin America), Dept of Trade, 1980; Dir, British Trade Develt Office, NY 1982; Dir, Invest in Britain Bureau, NY, 1984–87; Head, N Amer. Br., DTI, 1987–93; Dir, Govt Office for London, 1994; Dir, Invest in Britain Bureau, DTI, 1995–96; Advr, Internat. Investment, OECD, 1997–98. *Address:* 14 Carlisle Mansions, Carlisle Place, SW1P 1HX. *T:* and *Fax:* (020) 7828 0042; *e-mail:* jhagestadt@aol.com.

HAGGARD, Prof. Mark Peregrine, CBE 2001; PhD; FMedSci; Medical Research Council External Staff, Cambridge; founder Director, Medical Research Council Institute of Hearing Research, 1977–2001; *b* 26 Dec. 1942; *m* 1962, Liz (*née* Houston); two *s. Educ:* Edinburgh Univ. (MA Psych, 1st cl. hons); Corpus Christi Coll., Cambridge (PhD Psych 1967). Univ. Demonstrator in Experimental Psychology, Univ. of Cambridge, 1967–71; Prof. of Psychology and Head of Dept, QUB, 1971–76; sabbatical, 1975–76; Special Prof. in Audiological Scis, Nottingham Univ., 1980–. Founder FMedSci 1998. *Publications:* Screening Children's Hearing, 1991; Research in the Development of Effective Services for Hearing-impaired People, 1993; contribs to learned jls. *Recreations:* ski-ing, choral music. *Address:* MRC Institute of Hearing Research, University Park, Nottingham NG7 2RD. *T:* (0115) 922 3431. *Club:* Royal Society of Medicine.

HAGGART, Mary Elizabeth; *see* Scholes, M. E.

HAGGERSTON GADSDEN, Sir Peter Drury; *see* Gadsden.

HAGGETT, Prof. Peter, CBE 1993; FBA 1992; Professor of Urban and Regional Geography, 1966–98, now Emeritus Professor, and Acting Vice-Chancellor, 1984–85, University of Bristol; *b* 24 Jan. 1933; *s* of Charles and Elizabeth Haggett, Pawlett, Somerset; *m* 1956, Brenda Woodley; two *s* two *d. Educ:* Dr Morgan's Sch., Bridgwater; St Catharine's Coll., Cambridge (Exhib. and Scholar; MA 1958; PhD 1970; ScD 1985). Asst Lectr, University Coll. London, 1955–57; Demonstrator and University Lectr, Cambridge, 1957–66, and Fellow, Fitzwilliam Coll., 1963–66 (Hon. Fellow, 1994). Leverhulme Research Fellow (Brazil), 1959; Canada Council Fellow, 1977; Erskine Fellow (NZ), 1979; Res. Fellow, Res. Sch. of Pacific Studies, ANU, 1983. Visiting Professor: Berkeley; Monash; Pennsylvania State; Toronto; Western Ontario; Wisconsin; Hill Prof., Minnesota, 1994. Member, SW Economic Planning Council, 1967–72. Governor, Centre for Environmental Studies, 1975–78; Member: Council, RGS, 1972–73, 1977–80; UGC, 1985–89; Nat. Radiological Protection Bd, 1986–93; Chm., Hist. of Med. Grants Panel, Wellcome Trust, 1994–2000. Vice-Pres., British Acad., 1995–97. Hon. Fellow, Bristol Univ., 1998. Hon. DSc: York, Canada, 1983; Durham, 1989; Copenhagen, 1999; Hon. LLD Bristol, 1986. Cullum Medal of American Geographical Soc., 1969; Meritorious Contribution Award, Assoc. of American Geographers, 1973; Patron's Medal, RGS, 1986; Prix Internationale de Géographie, 1991; Lauréat d'Honneur, IGU, 1992; Scottish Medal, RSGS, 1993; Anders Retzius Gold Medal, Sweden, 1994. *Publications:* Locational Analysis in Human Geography, 1965; Geography: a modern synthesis, 1972, 4th edn, 1983; The Geographer's Art, 1990; Geographical Structure of Epidemics, 2000; Geography: a global synthesis, 2001; *jointly:* (with R. J. Chorley): Models in Geography, 1967; Network Analysis in Geography, 1969; (with M. D. I. Chisholm) Regional Forecasting, 1971; (with A. D. Cliff and others): Elements of Spatial Structure, 1975; Spatial Diffusion, 1981; Spatial Aspects of Influenza Epidemics, 1986; Atlas of Disease Distributions, 1988; Atlas of AIDS, 1992; Measles: an historical geography, 1993; Deciphering Global Epidemics, 1998; Island Epidemics, 2000; research papers on related geographical topics. *Recreations:* natural history, cricket. *Address:* 5 Tun Bridge Close, Chew Magna, Somerset BS40 8SU. *Club:* Oxford and Cambridge.

HAGGETT, Stuart John, MA; Headmaster, Birkenhead School, since 1988; *b* 11 April 1947; *s* of William Francis and Doreen Ada Haggett; *m* 1971, Hilary Joy Hammond; two *d. Educ:* Dauntsey's Sch., West Lavington, Wilts; Downing Coll., Cambridge (MA 1972); PGCE London (ext.), 1970. Canford Sch., Wimborne, Dorset, 1970–83: Head of Modern Languages, 1973–83; Housemaster, 1975–83; Second Master, King's Sch., Rochester, 1983–88. *Recreations:* France (travel and culture), sport, theatre, architecture, cooking. *Address:* Birkenhead School, 58 Beresford Road, Birkenhead, Merseyside CH43 2JD. *T:* (0151) 652 4014.

HAGGIE, Dr Paul; HM Diplomatic Service; Foreign and Commonwealth Office, since 2001; *b* 30 Aug. 1949; *s* of George Henry Haggie and Eva Haggie (*née* Hawke); *m* 1979, Rev. Deborah (marr. diss. 2000), *d* of Douglas Graham Frazer, CBE; one *s* one *d. Educ:* Royal Grammar Sch., Newcastle upon Tyne; Manchester Univ. (BA; PhD 1974). Joined HM Diplomatic Service, 1974: Second, later First Sec., Bangkok, 1976–80; First Secretary: FCO, 1980–82; Islamabad, 1982–86; FCO, 1986–89; Pretoria, 1989–93; Counsellor, FCO, 1993–94; on secondment to Cabinet Office as Sec., Requirements and Resources, 1994–96; FCO, 1996–98; Counsellor and UK Perm. Rep. to ESCAP, Bangkok, 1998–2001. *Publications:* Britannia at Bay: the defence of the British Empire against Japan 1931–1941, 1981; contrib. various articles to historical jls. *Recreations:* Rugby, riding, swimming, scuba, music, history (esp. maritime). *Address:* c/o Foreign and Commonwealth Office, King Charles Street, SW1A 2AH; 2 Marc Brunel Way, Historic Dockyard, Chatham, Kent ME4 4BH. *Clubs:* Royal Automobile; Royal Bangkok Sports (Thailand).

HAGUE, Prof. Clifford Bertram; Professor, School of Planning and Housing, Edinburgh College of Art, Heriot-Watt University, since 1995; *b* 22 Aug. 1944; *s* of Bertram Hague and Kathleen Mary Hague; *m* 1966, Irene Williamson; one *s* three *d. Educ:* Magdalene Coll., Cambridge (MA); Univ. of Manchester (DipTP). MRTPI 1973. Planning Asst, Glasgow Corp., 1968–69; Edinburgh College of Art, Heriot-Watt University: Lectr, 1969–73; Sen. Lectr, 1973–90; Head, Sch. of Planning and Housing, 1990–95. Mem. Jury, Internat. Urban Planning and Design Competition for the banks of Huangpu River, 2001–. President: RTPI, 1996–97; Commonwealth Assoc. of Planners, 2000–. AcSS; Mem., Inst. for Learning and Teaching. FRSA. Centenary Medal, Technical Univ. of Brno, 2000. *Publications:* The Development of Planning Thought: a critical perspective, 1984; articles in Town Planning Rev., Town and Country Planning, Planning, etc. *Recreations:* Manchester United, cricket, theatre. *Address:* 14 Dalhousie Terrace, Edinburgh EH10 5NE. *T:* (0131) 447 5265.

HAGUE, Prof. Sir Douglas (Chalmers), Kt 1982; CBE 1978; Chairman, Oxford Strategy Network, since 1984; Associate Fellow, Templeton College, Oxford, since 1983; *b* Leeds, 20 Oct. 1926; *s* of Laurence and Marion Hague; *m* 1947, Brenda Elizabeth Fereday (marr. diss. 1986); two *d*; *m* 1986, Janet Mary Leach. *Educ:* Moseley Grammar Sch.; King Edward VI High Sch., Birmingham; University of Birmingham. Assistant Tutor, Faculty of Commerce, Birmingham Univ., 1946; Assistant Lecturer, University College, London, 1947, Lecturer, 1950; Reader in Political Economy in University of London, 1957; Newton Chambers Professor of Economics, University of Sheffield, 1957–63. Visiting Professor of Economics, Duke Univ., USA, 1960–61; Head of Department of Business Studies, University of Sheffield, 1962–63; Professor of Applied Economics, University of Manchester, 1963–65; Prof. of Managerial Economics, Manchester Business Sch., 1965–81, Dep. Dir, 1978–81, Vis. Prof., 1981–; Vis. Prof., Imperial Coll. of Science and Technol., London, 1988–92. Chairman: Metapraxis Ltd, 1984–90; Doctus Consulting Europe, 1991–94; Wire Ltd, 1999–2000; Director: Economic Models Ltd, 1970–78; The Laird Gp, 1976–79; CRT Gp, 1990–96 (Chm., 1992–93). Rapporteur to International Economic Association, 1953–78, Editor General, 1981–86; Chm., ESRC, 1983–87; Member Working Party of National Advisory Council on Education for Industry and Commerce, 1962–63; Consultant to Secretariat of NEDC, 1962–63; Member: Treasury Working Party on Management Training in the Civil Service, 1965–67; EDC for Paper and Board, 1967–70; (part-time) N Western Gas Board, 1966–72; Working Party, Local Govt Training Bd, 1969–70; Price Commn, 1973–78 (Dep. Chm., 1977); Director: Manchester School of Management and Administration, 1964–65; Centre for Business Research, Manchester, 1964–66. Member Council, Manchester Business School, 1964–81; Chairman, Manchester Industrial Relations Society, 1964–66; President, NW Operational Research Group, 1967–69; British Chm., Carnegie Project on Accountability, 1968–72; Jt Chm., Conf. of Univ. Management Schools, 1971–73; Chairman: DoI Working Party, Kirkby Manufacturing and Engineering Co., 1978; Professional Develt Cttee, Inst. of Dirs, 1993–96; Planning Cttee, Oxford Risk Inst., 1998–99. Trustee, Demos, 1996–. Economic adviser to Mrs Thatcher, Gen. Election campaign, 1979; Adviser to PM's Policy Unit, 10 Downing St, 1979–83. Industrial Consultant. Hon. LittD Sheffield, 1987. *Publications:* Costs in Alternative Locations: The Clothing Industry (with P. K. Newman), 1952; (with A. W. Stonier) A Textbook of Economic Theory, 1953, 4th edn 1973; (with A. W. Stonier) The Essentials of Economics, 1955; The Economics of Man-Made Fibres, 1957; (ed) Stability and Progress in the World Economy, 1958; (ed) The Theory of Capital, 1961; (ed) Inflation, 1962; (ed with Sir Roy Harrod) International Trade Theory in a Developing World, 1965; (ed) Price Formation in Various Economies, 1967; Managerial Economics, 1969; (ed with Bruce L. R. Smith) The Dilemma of Accountability in Modern Government, 1970; Pricing in Business, 1971; (with M. E. Beesley) Britain in the Common Market: a new business opportunity, 1973; (with W. E. F. Oakeshott and A. A. Strain) Devaluation and Pricing Decisions: a case study approach, 1974; (with W. J. M. Mackenzie and A. Barker) Public Policy and Private Interests: the institutions of compromise, 1975; (with Geoffrey Wilkinson) The IRC: an experiment in industrial intervention, 1983; (with Peter Hennessy) How Adolf Hitler reformed Whitehall, 1985; (ed) The Management of Science, 1991; Beyond Universities: a new republic of the intellect, 1991; Transforming the Dinosaurs, 1993; (with Kate Oakley) Spin-offs and Start-ups in UK Universities, 2000; articles in economic, financial and management journals. *Recreations:* church organs, watching Manchester United. *Address:* Templeton College, Oxford OX1 5NY. *T:* (01865) 422500. *Club:* Athenæum.

HAGUE, Ffion Llywelyn; Director, Leonard Hull International Plc, since 2000; *b* 21 Feb. 1968; *d* of (John) Emyr Jenkins, *qv*, and Myra (*née* Samuel); *m* 1997, William Jefferson Hague, *qv*. *Educ:* Jesus Coll., Oxford (BA English Lit. 1989); UCW, Aberystwyth (MPhil Welsh Lit. 1993). Joined CS, 1991; Asst Private Sec. to Sec. of State for Wales, 1994–97; Dir of Policy and Planning, Arts & Business (formerly Dir of Ops, ABSA), 1997–2000. Mem. Bd, British Council, 1999–. Dir, Voices Foundn, 1998–. *Address:* (office) 46–47 Mount Street, W1K 2SA.

HAGUE, Rt Hon. William (Jefferson); PC 1995; MP (C) Richmond, Yorks, since Feb. 1989; *b* 26 March 1961; *s* of Timothy Nigel Hague and Stella Hague; *m* 1997, Ffion Llywelyn Jenkins (*see* F. L. Hague). *Educ:* Wath-upon-Dearne Comprehensive School; Magdalen College, Oxford (MA); Insead (MBA). Pres., Oxford Union, 1981; Pres., Oxford Univ. Cons. Assoc., 1981. Management Consultant, McKinsey & Co., 1983–88. Political Adviser, HM Treasury, 1983. Contested (C) Wentworth, S Yorks, 1987. PPS to Chancellor of the Exchequer, 1990–93; Parly Under-Sec. of State, DSS, 1993–94; Minister for Social Security and Disabled People, DSS, 1994–95; Sec. of State for Wales, 1995–97; Leader, Cons. Party and Leader of the Opposition, 1997–2001. *Address:* House of Commons, SW1A 0AA. *T:* (020) 7219 3000, (020) 7222 9000. *Clubs:* Beefsteak, Carlton, Buck's, Pratt's, Budokwai.

HAHN, Carl Horst, Dr rer. pol.; German business executive; *b* 1 July 1926; *m* 1960, Marisa Traina; three *s* one *d*. Chm. Bd, Continental Gummi-Werke AG, 1973–81; Chm. Mgt Bd, Volkswagen AG, 1981–92. Chm. Supervisory Bd, Gerling-Konzern Speziale Kreditversicherungs-AG, Cologne; Member, Supervisory Board: Hanseatisches Wein- und Sekt-Kontor, Hamburg; Sachsenring AG, Zwickau; Perot Systems, Dallas; Maincontrol, Vienna, Va; Member, International Advisory Board: Instituto de Empresa, Madrid; Timken Co., Canton, Ohio; Textron Inc., Providence; TRW Inc., Cleveland; Board Member: Mayo Clinic Stiftung, Frankfurt; Lauder-Inst. Wharton Sch., Philadelphia; Mem. Internat. Adv. Cttee, Salk Inst., La Jolla, Calif. Advr to Pres. of Republic of Kyrgyzstan. Chm., Bd of Trustees, Kunstmuseum, Wolfsburg. *Address:* Porschestrasse 53, 38440 Wolfsburg, Germany. *T:* (5361) 26680, *Fax:* (5361) 266815.

HAHN, Prof. Frank Horace, FBA 1975; Professor of Economics, University of Cambridge, 1972–92, now Emeritus; Fellow of Churchill College, Cambridge, since 1960; *b* 26 April 1925; *s* of Dr Arnold Hahn and Maria Hahn; *m* 1946, Dorothy Salter; no *c. Educ:* Bournemouth Grammar School; London School of Economics (Hon. Fellow, 1989). PhD London, MA Cantab. Univ. of Birmingham, 1948–60, Reader in Mathematical Economics, 1958–60; Univ. Lectr in Econs, Cambridge, 1960–67; Prof. of Economics, LSE, 1967–72; Frank W. Taussig Res. Prof., Harvard, 1975–76. Visiting Professor: MIT, 1956–57; Univ. of California, Berkeley, 1959–60; Schumpeter Prof., Vienna Univ. of Econs and Business Admin, 1984; Prof. Ordinario, Univ. of Siena, 1992–2000. Fellow, Inst. of Advanced Studies in Behavioural Sciences, Stanford, 1966–67. Mem. Council for Scientific Policy, later Adv. Bd of Res. Councils, 1972–75. Fellow, Econometric Soc., 1962; Vice-Pres., 1967–68; Pres., 1968–69; Pres., Royal Economic Soc., 1986–89. Managing Editor, Review of Economic Studies, 1965–68. Foreign Hon. Mem., Amer. Acad. of Arts and Sciences, 1974; Hon. Mem., Amer. Economic Assoc., 1986; For. Associate, US Nat. Acad. of Scis, 1988; Mem., Academia Europaea, 1989. Hon. DSocSci Birmingham, 1981; Hon DLitt: East Anglia, 1984; Leicester, 1993; Dr Econ *hc* Strasbourg, 1984; Hon. DSc(Econ) London, 1985; DUniv York, 1991; Hon. PhD Athens, 1993; Dr *hc* Paris X (Nanterre), 1999. Palacky Gold Medal, Czechoslovak Acad. of Scis, 1991. *Publications:* (with K. J. Arrow) General Competitive Analysis, 1971; The Share of Wages in the National Income, 1972; Money and Inflation, 1982; Equilibrium and Macro-Economics, 1984; Money, Growth and Stability, 1985; (ed and contrib.) The Economics of Missing Markets, Information and Games, 1989; (with Robert Solow) A Critical Essay on Modern Macroeconomic Theory, 1995; articles in learned journals. *Address:* 16 Adams Road, Cambridge CB3 9AD. *T:* (01223) 352560.

HAIDAR, Salman; High Commissioner for India in the United Kingdom, 1998; *b* 17 June 1938; *s* of Mohammed Haidar and Mumtaz Abdullah; *m* Kusum; one *s* one *d. Educ:* St Stephen's Coll.; Delhi Univ. (Hons English); Magdalene Coll., Cambridge (BA Hons English). Joined Indian Foreign Service, 1960; Cairo, 1961–63; UK, 1963–66; First Sec., Kabul, 1970–72; Counsellor and Minister, and Dep. Permt Rep., Permt Mission of India, NY, 1977–80; Ambassador to Bhutan, 1980–83; Dep. and acting High Comr, UK, 1987–91; Ambassador to China, 1991–92; Sec. (East), responsible for Africa, Asia, Latin America, ME and Central Asia, 1992; Foreign Sec., 1995–97. *Recreation:* tennis. *Clubs:* Travellers, Garrick; Delhi Gymkhana, Delhi Golf.

HAIG, family name of **Earl Haig**.

HAIG, 2nd Earl *cr* 1919; **George Alexander Eugene Douglas Haig,** OBE 1966; ARSA 1988; Viscount Dawick, *cr* 1919; Baron Haig and 30th Laird of Bemersyde; is a painter; Member, Queen's Body Guard for Scotland; *b* March 1918; *o s* of 1st Earl and Hon. Dorothy Vivian (*d* 1939) (Author of A Scottish Tour, 1935), *d* of 3rd Lord Vivian; *S* father, 1928; *m* 1st, 1956, Adrienne Thérèse, *d* of Derrick Morley; one *s* two *d*; 2nd, 1981, Donna Geroloma Lopez y Royo di Taurisano. *Educ:* Stowe; Christ Church, Oxford. MA Oxon. 2nd Lieut Royal Scots Greys, 1938; retired on account of disability, 1951, rank of Captain; Hon. Major on disbandment of HG 1958; studied painting Camberwell School of Art; paintings in collections of Arts Council and Scottish Nat. Gallery of Modern Art. War of 1939–45 (prisoner). Member: Royal Fine Art Commission for Scotland, 1958–61; Council and Executive Cttee, Earl Haig Fund, Scotland, 1950–65 and 1966– (Pres., 1980–86); Scottish Arts Council, 1969–75; President, Scottish Craft Centre, 1950–75. Member Council, Commonwealth Ex-Services League, 1960–96; President: Officers' Association (Scottish Branch), 1987–95 (Chm., 1977–87); Nat. Ex-Prisoner of War Assoc., 1998–; Vice-President: Friends of St George's Meml Church, Ypres, 1955–; Scottish National Institution for War Blinded; Royal Blind Asylum and School; President Border Area British Legion, 1955–61; Chairman SE Scotland Disablement Advisory Cttee, 1960–73; Vice-Chairman, British Legion, Scotland, 1960, Chairman, 1962–65, Pres., 1980–86; Chm., Bd of Trustees, Scottish National War Memorial, 1983–95 (Trustee, 1961–95); Trustee, National Gallery of Scotland, 1962–72; Chairman: Berwickshire Civic Soc., 1971–73; Friends of DeMarco Gall., 1968–71. Berwickshire: DL 1953; Vice-Lieutenant, 1967–70; DL Ettrick and Lauderdale (and Roxburghshire), 1977–93. KStJ 1977. FRSA 1951. *Publication:* My Father's Son (autobiog.), 2000. *Heir: s* Viscount Dawick, *qv. Address:* Bemersyde, Melrose, Scotland TD6 9DP. *T:* (01835) 822762. *Clubs:* Cavalry and Guards, Beefsteak; New (Edinburgh).

See also Baron Astor of Hever, Baron Dacre of Glanton.

HAIG, General Alexander Meigs, Jr; Chairman and President, Worldwide Associates, Inc., since 1984; *b* 2 Dec. 1924; *m* 1950, Patricia Fox; two *s* one *d. Educ:* schs in Pennsylvania; Univ. of Notre Dame; US Mil. Acad., West Point (BS); Univs of Columbia and Georgetown (MA); Ground Gen. Sch., Fort Riley; Armor Sch., Fort Knox; Naval and Army War Colls. 2nd Lieut 1947; Far East and Korea, 1948–51; Europe, 1956–59; Vietnam, 1966–67; CO 3rd Regt, subseq. Dep. Comdt, West Point, 1967–69; Sen. Mil. Adviser to Asst to Pres. for Nat. Security Affairs, 1969–70; Dep. Asst to Pres. for Nat. Security Affairs, 1970–73; Vice-Chief of Staff, US Army, Jan.–July 1973, retd; Chief of White House Staff, 1973–74 when recalled to active duty; Supreme Allied Commander Europe, 1974–79, and Commander-in-Chief, US European Command, 1974–79. President and Chief Operating Officer, United Technologies, 1979–81. Secretary of State, USA, 1981–82. Sen. Fellow, Hudson Inst. for Policy Research, 1982–84. Director: MGM Mirage Inc.; Metro-Goldwyn-Mayer Inc.; Interneuron Pharmaceuticals, Inc.; CompuServe Interactive Services Inc. Member: Presidential Cttee on Strategic Forces, 1983–; Presidential Commn on Chemical Warfare Review, 1985; Bd of Special Advisers, President's Commn on Physical Fitness and Sports, 1984–. Hosts own weekly television prog., World Business Review. Hon. LLD: Niagara; Utah; hon. degrees: Syracuse, Fairfield, Hillsdale Coll., 1981. Awarded numerous US medals, badges and decorations; also Vietnamese orders and Cross of Gallantry; Medal of King Abd el-Aziz (Saudi Arabia). *Publications:* Caveat: realism, Reagan and foreign policy, 1984; Inner Circles, 1992. *Recreations:* tennis, golf. *Address:* (office) 1155 15th Street NW (Suite 800), Washington, DC 20005, USA; *e-mail:* ahaig@aol.com.

HAIG, Ian Maurice, AM 1988; Public Affairs Consultant, Burke-Gosling & Co., since 1990; Senior Counsel, Global Agenda, since 1996; *b* 13 Dec. 1936; *s* of P. K. Haig; *m* 1959, Beverley, *d* of J. A. Dunning, OBE; two *s* one *d. Educ:* Pulteney Grammar School, Adelaide; University of Adelaide. Private Sec. to Pres. of Senate, Canberra, 1958–59; Asst Sec., Commonwealth Parly Conf., London, 1960; Public Relations Officer, Shell Co. of Australia, 1962; British Foreign Office School of Middle East Studies, 1963; Asst Trade Comr and Trade Comr, Los Angeles, 1966–68; Trade Comr, Beirut, 1969–73; Ambassador at large, Middle East, 1973; Ambassador to Saudi Arabia, Kuwait and United Arab Emirates, 1974–76; Australian Comr, Hong Kong, 1976–79; Dir of Administration, A.C.I. Ltd, 1979–81; Man. Dir, A.C.I. Fibreglass (Aust.), 1982; Agent Gen. for Victoria in London, 1983–85 and 1988–90; Chm., Immigration Panel, 1987; Dir, Aust. Wheat Bd, 1985–88; Chief Exec., Monash-ANZ Centre for Internat. Briefing, 1990–96. *Publications:* Arab Oil Politics, 1978; Oil and Alternative Sources of Energy, 1978; Australia and the Middle East, 1983. *Recreations:* cricket, golf. *Address:* 3 Chastleton Avenue, Toorak, Vic 3142, Australia. *Clubs:* MCC; Melbourne, Australian (Melbourne); Royal Melbourne Golf.

HAIG, Dame Mary Alison G.; *see* Glen Haig.

HAIGH, Brian Roger; Lecturer for Hawksmere plc, since 1993; *b* 19 Feb. 1931; *s* of Herbert Haigh and Ruth Haigh (*née* Lockwood); *m* 1953, Sheila Carter; one *s* one *d. Educ:* Hillhouse Central School, Huddersfield. Min. of Supply, 1949; National Service, RAF, 1949–51. Min. of Supply/Min. of Aviation, 1951–62; NATO Bullpup Production Orgn, 1962–67 (Head of Contracts, Finance and Admin, 1965–67); Min. of Technology, Aviation Supply, Defence (Defence Sales Orgn), 1968–73 (Asst Dir, Sales, 1971–73); Nat. Defence Coll., 1973–74; Ministry of Defence: Asst Dir, Contracts, 1974; Dir of Contracts (Weapons), Dec. 1974; Principal Dir of Navy Contracts, 1978; Under Secretary, 1980; Dir-Gen., Defence Contracts, 1980–86. Dir of Professional Educn and Trng, Lion Worldwide Div., Keiser Enterprises Inc., 1986–91. *Recreations:* family, music, opera, bridge. *Address:* c/o Barclays Bank plc, Kingston Business Centre, 9 Clarence Road, Kingston-upon-Thames KT1 1NY.

HAIGH, (Christopher) Nigel (Austin), OBE 1992; Member, Management Board, European Environment Agency (nominated by European Parliament), since 2000; *b* 23 Feb. 1938; *s* of Anthony Haigh, CMG and Gertrude, (Pippa), Haigh (*née* Dodd); *m* 1971, Carola Pickering; two *d. Educ:* Eton; King's Coll., Cambridge (MA Mech. Scis). Nat. Service, 2nd Lieut, RB, 1956–58. Tech Assistant, F. B. Dehn and Co., Chartered Patent Agents, 1962–68; Co. Patent Agent, Tracked Hovercraft Ltd, 1968–70; Sen. Patent Agent, BSC, 1970–72; Asst Sec., Anti-Concorde Project, 1972–73; Civic Trust, 1973–80; Institute for European Environmental Policy, London: Hd of London Office, 1980–89; Dir, 1990–98. Non-exec. Dir, Merlin, subseq. Jupiter, Internat. Green Investment Trust, 1989–94. Mem., Envmt Agency, 1995–2000; Vice-Pres., European Envmtl Bureau, 1975–79; Chm., Green Alliance, 1989–97. Specialist Advr, H of L Select Cttee on EC, 1982–93. Hon. Res. Fellow, Faculty of Laws, UCL, 1990–; Vis. Res. Fellow, Imperial Coll. Centre for Envmtl Tech., 1991–. Member, Editorial Board: Jl of Envmtl Law, 1989–; Internat. Envmtl Affairs, 1989–99. *Publications:* EEC Environmental Policy and Britain, 1984, 2nd edn 1987; (ed) Manual of Environmental Policy: the EU and Britain (looseleaf), 1992. *Recreations:* painting, looking at paintings, looking at towns. *Address:* 50 Grove Lane, Camberwell, SE5 8ST. *T:* (020) 7703 2719.

HAIGH, Edward; Assistant General Secretary, Transport and General Workers' Union, 1985–91; *b* 7 Nov. 1935; *s* of Edward and Sarah Ellen Haigh; *m* 1st, 1958, Patricia (marr. diss. 1982); one *s* two *d*; 2nd, 1982, Margaret; two step *d. Educ:* St Patrick's RC Sch., Birstall; St Mary's RC Sch., Batley, W Yorks. Carpet weaver, 1956–69; shop steward, 1960–69; National Union of Dyers, Bleachers and Textile Workers: Dist Organiser, 1969–73; Dist Sec., 1973–77; Nat. Organiser/Negotiator, 1977–79; Asst Gen. Sec., 1979–82; Nat. Sec., Textile Gp, TGWU, 1982–85. Mem., Labour Party NEC, 1982–91. JP Batley, W Yorks, 1971–85. *Recreations:* politics (Labour Party), Rugby League football, cricket. *Club:* Birstall Irish Democratic League (W Yorks).

HAIGH, Maurice Francis; a Recorder of the Crown Court, 1981–96; a Chairman of Tribunals, 1984–2001; *b* 6 Sept. 1929; *s* of William and Ceridwen Francis Haigh. *Educ:* Repton. Asst cameraman in film production; worked for Leslie Laurence Productions Ltd, London, Manchester Film Studios, and finally for Anglo-Scottish Pictures Ltd at London Film Studios, Shepperton, 1946–49; in commerce, 1950–52. Called to the Bar, Gray's Inn, 1955. *Recreations:* reading, cycling, fell and mountain walking. *Address:* c/o Kenworthy's Buildings, 83 Bridge Street, Manchester M3 2RF. *T:* (0161) 832 4036. *Club:* English-Speaking Union.

HAIGH, Nigel; *see* Haigh, C. N. A.

HAILEY, Arthur; author; *b* 5 April 1920; *s* of George Wellington Hailey and Elsie Mary Wright; *m* 1st, 1944, Joan Fishwick (marr. diss. 1950); three *s*; 2nd, 1951, Sheila Dunlop; one *s* two *d. Educ:* English elem. schs. Pilot, RAF, 1939–47; Air Ministry staff officer, 1945–47; first ed. aircrew trng mag., Air Clues (Flt-Lt; AE); RCAF (R) (Flt-Lt 1951). Emigrated to Canada, 1947; became Canadian citizen, with dual nationality, 1952; various positions in industry and sales until becoming free-lance writer, 1956. Member: Authors League of America; (Life), Writers Guild of America; (Hon. Life), Alliance of Canadian Cinema, Television and Radio Artists; (Life), Writers Guild, Canada. *Films:* Time Lock, 1957; The Young Doctors, 1961. *Publications:* (in 40 countries and 38 languages): Flight into Danger (with John Castle) (also a play, and filmed 1956 as Zero Hour), 1958, US edn, as Runway Zero-Eight; The Final Diagnosis, 1959; Close-Up (collected plays), 1960; In High Places, 1962; Hotel, 1965 (filmed, 1966, also television series); Airport, 1968 (filmed, 1970); Wheels, 1971 (filmed 1978); The Moneychangers, 1975 (filmed, 1976); Overload, 1979; Strong Medicine, 1984 (filmed, 1986); The Evening News, 1990; Detective, 1997. *Address:* (home) Lyford Cay, PO Box N7776, Nassau, Bahamas; (office) Nancy Stauffer Associates, PO Box 1203, Darien, CT 06820, USA. *Club:* Lyford Cay (Life Mem.) (Bahamas).

HAILSHAM, 2nd Viscount, *cr* 1929, of Hailsham; Baron, *cr* 1928 [disclaimed his peerages for life, 20 Nov. 1963]; *see under* Baron Hailsham of St Marylebone.

HAILSHAM OF SAINT MARYLEBONE, Baron *cr* 1970 (Life Peer), of Herstmonceux; **Quintin McGarel Hogg;** PC 1956; KG 1988; CH 1974; FRS 1973; Editor, Halsbury's Laws of England, 4th edition, 1972–98; *b* 9 Oct. 1907; *er s* of 1st Viscount Hailsham, PC, KC, and Elizabeth (*d* 1925), *d* of Judge Trimble Brown, Nashville, Tennessee, USA, and *widow* of Hon. A. J. Marjoribanks; *S* father, 1950, as 2nd Viscount Hailsham, but disclaimed his peerages for life, 20 Nov. 1963 (Baron *cr* 1928, Viscount *cr* 1929); *m* 1944, Mary Evelyn (*d* 1978), *d* of late Richard Martin of Ross; two *s* three *d*; *m* 1986, Deirdre Shannon (*d* 1998). *Educ:* Eton (Schol., Newcastle Schol.); Christ Church, Oxford (Scholar; Hon. Student, 1962). First Class Hon. Mods, 1928; First Class Lit. Hum., 1930; Pres., Oxford Union Soc., 1929. Served War of 1939–45: commissioned Rifle Bde Sept. 1939; served Middle East Forces, Western Desert, 1941 (wounded); Egypt, Palestine, Syria, 1942; Temp. Major, 1942. Fellow of All Souls Coll., Oxford, 1931–38, 1961–; Barrister, Lincoln's Inn, 1932; a Bencher of Lincoln's Inn, 1956, Treasurer, 1975; QC 1953. MP (C) Oxford City, 1938–50, St Marylebone, (Dec.) 1963–70; Jt Parly Under-Sec. of State for Air, 1945; First Lord of the Admiralty, 1956–57; Minister of Education, 1957; Dep. Leader of the House of Lords, 1957–60; Leader of the House of Lords, 1960–63; Lord Privy Seal, 1959–60; Lord Pres. of the Council, 1957–59 and 1960–64; Minister for Science and Technology, 1959–64; Minister with special responsibility for: Sport, 1962–64; dealing with unemployment in the North-East, 1963–64; higher education, Dec. 1963–Feb. 1964; Sec. of State for Education and Science, April–Oct. 1964; Lord High Chancellor of GB, 1970–74 and 1979–87. Chm. of the Conservative Party Organization, Sept. 1957–Oct. 1959. Rector of Glasgow Univ., 1959–62; Chancellor, Univ. of Buckingham, 1983–92. Pres. Classical Assoc., 1960–61. Lectures: John Findley Green Foundation, 1960; Richard Dimbleby, 1976; Hamlyn, 1983; Granada, 1987; Warburton, 1987, F. A. Mann, 1988, Lincoln's Inn. Hon. Bencher, Inn of Court of NI, 1981; Hon. FICE 1963; Hon. FIEE 1972; Hon. FIStructE 1960. Hon. Freeman, Merchant Taylors' Co., 1971. Hon. DCL: Westminster Coll., Fulton, Missouri, USA, 1960; Newcastle, 1964; Oxon, 1974; Hon. LLD: Cambridge, 1963; Delhi, 1972; St Andrews, 1979; Leeds, 1982; Hon. DLitt Ulster, 1988. *Publications:* The Law of Arbitration, 1935; One Year's Work, 1944; The Law and Employers' Liability, 1944; The Times We Live In, 1944; Making Peace, 1945; The Left was never Right, 1945; The Purpose of Parliament, 1946; Case for Conservatism, 1947; The Law of Monopolies, Restrictive Practices and Resale Price Maintenance, 1956; The Conservative Case, 1959; Interdependence, 1961; Science and Politics, 1963; The Devil's Own Song, 1968; The Door Wherein I Went, 1975; Elective Dictatorship, 1976; The Dilemma of Democracy, 1978; Hamlyn Revisited: the British legal system (Hamlyn Lectures), 1983; A Sparrow's Flight (autobiog.), 1990; On The Constitution, 1992; Values: collapse and cure, 1994. *Heir:* (*to disclaimed viscountcy*): *s* Rt Hon. Douglas Martin Hogg, *qv. Address:* House of Lords, SW1A 0PW. *Clubs:* Carlton, Alpine, MCC.

See also Baroness Hogg and Hon. Dame M. C. Hogg.

HAIN, Rt Hon. Peter (Gerald); PC 2001; MP (Lab) Neath, since April 1991; Minister of State, Foreign and Commonwealth Office, 1999–2000 and since 2001; *b* 16 Feb. 1950; *s* of Walter and Adelaine Hain; *m* 1975, Patricia Western; two *s. Educ:* Queen Mary College, London (BSc Econ 1st cl. hons); Univ. of Sussex (MPhil). Brought up in S Africa, until family forced to leave in 1966, due to anti-apartheid activity, since when lived in UK.

Union of Communication Workers: Asst Research Officer, 1976–87; Head of Research, 1987–91. Chm., Stop the Seventy Tour campaign, 1969–70; Nat. Chm., Young Liberals, 1971–73; Press Officer, Anti-Nazi League, 1977–80. Contested (Lab) Putney, 1983, 1987. An Opposition Whip, 1995–96; an Opposition Spokesman on employment, 1996–97; Parly Under-Sec. of State, Welsh Office, 1997–99; Minister of State, DTI, Jan.–June 2001. *Publications:* Don't Play with Apartheid, 1971; Community Politics, 1976; Mistaken Identity, 1976; (ed) Policing the Police, vol. I, 1978, vol. II, 1980; Neighbourhood Participation, 1980; Crisis and Future of the Left, 1980; Political Trials in Britain, 1984; Political Strikes, 1986; A Putney Plot?, 1987; The Peking Connection (novel), 1995; Ayes to the Left, 1995; Sing the Beloved Country, 1996. *Recreations:* soccer, cricket, Rugby player, fan of Chelsea FC and Neath RFC, rock and folk music fan. *Address:* House of Commons, SW1A 0AA. *T:* (020) 7219 3000; 14 The Parade, Neath SA11 1RA. *T:* (01639) 630152. *Clubs:* Neath Workingmen's; Resolven Rugby, Resolven Royal British Legion Institute.

HAINES, Prof. Andrew Paul, MD; FRCP, FRCGP, FFPHM; Dean, and Professor of Public and Primary Care, London School of Hygiene and Tropical Medicine, University of London, since 2001; *b* 26 Feb. 1947; *s* of Charles George Thomas Haines and Lilian Emily Haines; *m* 1st, 1982, June Marie Power (marr. diss. 1987); 2nd; 1998, Dr Anita Berlin; two *s. Educ:* King's Coll., London (MB BS 1969; MD Epidemiology 1985). MRCP 1971, FRCP 1993; MRCGP 1976, FRCGP 1993; MFCM 1987, FFPHM 1992. Mem. Scientific Staff, MRC Epidemiology and Med. Care Unit, 1974–87; part-time Sen. Lectr in General Practice, Middlesex Hosp. Med. Sch., 1980–84, St Mary's Hosp. Med. Sch., 1984–87; on secondment as Dir, R&D, NE Thames RHA, subseq. N Thames Reg., NHS Exec., 1993–96; Prof. of Primary Health Care, UCL, 1987–2000; Head, Dept of Primary Care and Population Scis, Royal Free and UC Med. Sch., 1998–2000. Mem., MRC, 1996–98; Chm., Health Services and Public Health Bd, 1996–98. Consultant, WHO, 1998. Founder FMedSci 1998. *Publications:* (ed jtly) Climate Change and Human Health, 1996; (ed jtly) Evidence Based Practice in Primary Care, 1998; (ed jtly) Getting Research Findings into Practice, 1998; numerous articles in medical and scientific jls. *Recreations:* travel, environmental issues. *Address:* London School of Hygiene and Tropical Medicine, Keppel Street, WC1E 7HT. *T:* (020) 7927 2278; 36 Mackeson Road, NW3 2LT.

HAINES, Christopher John Minton; Chairman, Sterling Publishing Group, since 1996; *b* 14 April 1939; *m* 1967, Christine Cobbold; two *s* two *d. Educ:* Stowe. The Rifle Brigade, 1959–68; sugar trade, 1968–89; Chm., James Budgett & Son, 1984–89. Non-executive Director: Devonshire Arms (Bolton Abbey), 1995–; Harlequin FC, 1998–; Cardinal Management Ltd (formerly Custodial Asset Management), 1999–. Chief Exec., The Jockey Club, 1989–93. *Recreations:* music, gardening, racing. *Club:* Turf.
See also M. Haines.

HAINES, Joseph Thomas William; Assistant Editor, The Daily Mirror, 1984–90; Group Political Editor, Mirror Group Newspapers, 1984–90; *b* 29 Jan. 1928; *s* of Joseph and Elizabeth Haines; *m* 1955, Irene Betty Lambert; no *c. Educ:* Elementary Schools, Rotherhithe, SE16. Parly Correspondent, The Bulletin (Glasgow) 1954–58, Political Correspondent, 1958–60; Political Correspondent: Scottish Daily Mail, 1960–64; The Sun, 1964–68; Dep. Press Sec. to Prime Minister, Jan.-June 1969; Chief Press Sec. to Prime Minister, 1969–70 and 1974–76, and to Leader of the Opposition, 1970–74; Feature Writer, 1977–78, Chief Leader Writer, 1978–90, The Daily Mirror. Political Columnist, Today, 1994–95. Director: Mirror Gp Newspapers (1986) Ltd, 1986–92; Scottish Daily Record & Sunday Mail Ltd, 1986–92. Mem. Tonbridge UDC, 1963–69, 1971–74. Mem., Royal Commn on Legal Services, 1976–79. *Publications:* The Politics of Power, 1977; (co-editor) Malice In Wonderland, 1986; Maxwell, 1988. *Recreations:* heresy and watching football. *Address:* 1 South Frith, London Road, Southborough, Tunbridge Wells, Kent TN4 0UQ. *T:* (01732) 365919.

HAINES, Miranda, (Mrs Luke Taylor); Executive Editor, Geographical magazine (Editor, 1999–2000); *b* 15 Oct. 1968; *d* of Christopher Haines, *qv*; *m* 1998, Luke Taylor. *Educ:* Manchester Coll., Oxford (BA Hons English Lit.). International Herald Tribune, 1993–96; freelance writer, London, 1996–97; Editor, Traveller magazine, 1997–98. *Publications:* (ed jtly) The Traveller's Handbook, 1998; (ed jtly) The Traveller's Health Book, 1998. *Recreation:* travelling. *Address:* (office) 47c Kensington Court, W8 5DA; 49 Avonmore Road, W14 8RT.

HAINES, Ronald William Terence, FICE, FIStructE; Director of Construction Services, HM Prison Service, 1993–96; *b* 19 Dec. 1937; *s* of John William Haines and Mary Agnes Power; *m* 1957, Linda, *d* of Sidney and Lilian Hampton; one *s* two *d. Educ:* South East London Tech. Coll.; Regent Street Poly.; City Univ. MCIWEM. Design Engineer: William Harbrow & Co., 1954–56; Liverpool Reinforced Concrete Co., 1956–58; Civil and Structl Engr, Min. of Works and MPBW, 1958–67; Chief Civil and Structl Engr, Home Office, 1967–87; Dep. Dir of Works, HM Prison Service, Home Office, 1987–93. *Recreations:* organic farming, walking, theatre. *Address:* Barklye Farm, Swife Lane, Broad Oak, Heathfield, E Sussex TN21 8UR.

HAINING, Thomas Nivison, CMG 1983; HM Diplomatic Service, retired; writer and lecturer on international affairs and Mongolian history; Hon. Research Fellow, Department of History, University of Aberdeen, since 1991 (Hon. Research Associate, 1988–90); *b* 15 March 1927; *m* 1955, Dorothy Patricia Robson; one *s. Educ:* Edinburgh Univ.; Göttingen Univ. Foreign Office, 1952; served Vienna, Moscow, Rome and New York; Counsellor, FCO, 1972–79; Ambassador and Consul-Gen. to the Mongolian People's Republic, 1979–82. Hon. Pres., Chinese Studies Gp, Aberdeen Univ, 1989–. FRAS 1993. *Publications:* (contrib.) Mongolia Today, 1989; (trans. and ed) Ratchnevsky, Genghis Khan: his life and legacy, 1991; (contrib.) Legacy of the Mongol Empire, 1993; (contrib.) The Mongols of the 13th century through the eyes of early European travellers, 1995. *Address:* Carseview, 7 The Banks, Brechin, Angus DD9 6JD. *T:* (01356) 622584. *Clubs:* Royal Automobile; Royal Northern and University (Aberdeen).

HAINSWORTH, Gordon, MA; public sector consultant, since 1992; Chief Executive, Manchester, 1988–92; *b* 4 Nov. 1934; *s* of Harry and Constance Hainsworth; *m* 1962, Diane (*née* Thubron); one *s* one *d. Educ:* Leeds Modern Sch.; Trinity Coll., Cambridge (MA). Teaching, Leeds, Birmingham and West Riding, 1958–65; Admin. Assistant, Leeds, 1965–69; Asst Education Officer, Manchester, 1969–74; Under-Secretary (Education), Assoc. of Metropolitan Authorities, 1974–76; Dep. Educn Officer, Manchester, 1976–80; Director of Education, Gateshead, 1980–83; Chief Educn Officer, Manchester, 1983–88. Registered Inspector (Schs), OFSTED, 1992–99; Schs Adjudicator, 1999–. *Recreations:* family, golf, bridge, walking. *Address:* 14 Oldham Road, Denshaw, Oldham OL3 5SL. *T:* (01457) 820398.

HAINWORTH, Henry Charles, CMG 1961; HM Diplomatic Service, retired; *b* 12 Sept. 1914; *o s* of late Charles S. and Emily G. I. Hainworth; *m* 1944, Mary, *yr d* of late Felix B. and Lilian Ady; two *d. Educ:* Blundell's Sch.; Sidney Sussex Coll., Cambridge. Entered HM Consular Service, 1939; HM Embassy, Tokyo, 1940–42; seconded to Ministry of Information (Far Eastern Bureau, New Delhi), 1942–46; HM Embassy, Tokyo, 1946–51; Foreign Office, 1951–53; HM Legation, Bucharest, 1953–55; NATO Defence Coll., Paris, 1956; Political Office, Middle East Forces (Nicosia), 1956; Foreign Office, 1957–61 (Head of Atomic Energy and Disarmament Dept, 1958–61); Counsellor, United Kingdom Delegation to the Brussels Conference, 1961–63; HM Minister and Consul-Gen. at British Embassy, Vienna, 1963–68; Ambassador to Indonesia, 1968–70; Ambassador and Perm. UK Rep. to Disarm. Conf., Geneva, 1971–74. Chm., Anglo-Indonesian Soc., 1992–99. *Publication:* A Collector's Dictionary, 1980. *Recreations:* reading, fishing. *Address:* 23 Rivermead Court, Ranelagh Gardens, SW6 3RU.

HAIRD, Susan Margaret, (Mrs D. L. Simpson); Director, Export Control and Non-Proliferation, Department of Trade and Industry, since 2000; *b* 10 Oct. 1952; *d* of Douglas and Myrah Haird; *m* 1979, David Lee Simpson; one *s* one *d. Educ:* Dollar Acad.; St Andrews Univ. (MA Hons Hist. and Econs); Coll. of Europe, Bruges (Cert. and Dip. in Advanced Eur. Studies). Stage at EC, 1976; joined Department of Trade and Industry, 1976: Private Secretary: to Perm. Sec., 1978; to Parly Under-Sec., 1979; Commercial Relns and Exports Div., 1980–84; Personnel Div. 1985–89; Industrial Materials Div., 1989; Equal Opportunities Div., Cabinet Office (on loan), 1989–92; Atomic Energy Div., 1992–96; Office of Manpower Econs, 1996–99; Dir, Export Control, 1999–2000. *Recreations:* family, travel, swimming. *Address:* Department of Trade and Industry, 4 Abbey Orchard Street, SW1P 2HT. *T:* (020) 7215 0720.

HAITINK, Bernard, Hon. KBE 1977; Commander, Order of Orange Nassau, 1988; Music Director, Royal Opera House, Covent Garden, 1987–Sept. 2002; Music Director designate, Dresden Staatskapelle; *b* Amsterdam, 4 March 1929. *Educ:* Amsterdam Conservatory. Studied conducting under Felix Hupke, but started his career as a violinist with the Netherlands Radio Philharmonic; in 1954 and 1955 attended annual conductors' course (org. by Netherlands Radio Union) under Ferdinand Leitner; became 2nd Conductor with Radio Union at Hilversum with co-responsibility for 4 radio orchs and conducted the Radio Philharmonic in public during the Holland Fest., in The Hague, 1956; conducted the Concertgebouw Orch., Oct. 1956; then followed guest engagements with this and other orchs in the Netherlands and elsewhere. Debut in USA, with Los Angeles Symph. Orch., 1958; 5 week season with Concertgebouw Orch., 1958–59, and toured Britain with it, 1959; apptd (with Eugen Jochum) as the Orchestra's permanent conductor, Sept. 1961; sole artistic dir and permanent conductor of the orch., 1964–88; toured Japan, USSR, USA and Europe; 1974; début at Royal Opera House, Covent Garden, 1977. London Philharmonic Orchestra: Principal Conductor, Artistic Dir, 1967–79, Pres., 1990; toured: Japan, 1969; USA, 1970, 1971, 1976; Berlin, 1972; Holland, Germany, Austria, 1973; USSR, 1975. Musical Dir, Glyndebourne Opera, 1978–88; conducted Figaro for rebuilt opera house of Glyndebourne (60th anniversary), 1994; Music Dir, EU Youth Orch., 1994–99; Principal Guest Conductor, Boston Symph. Orch., 1995–. Appearances at BBC Promenade Concerts and at Tanglewood, Salzburg and Edinburgh Festivals. Hon. RAM 1973; Hon. FRCM 1984. Hon. DMus: Oxford, 1988; Leeds, 1988. Bruckner Medal of Honour, 1970; Gold Medal, Internat. Gustav Mahler Soc., 1971; Erasmus Prize, Netherlands, 1991. Chevalier de L'Ordre des Arts et des Lettres, 1972; Officer, Order of the Crown (Belgium), 1977. *Address:* c/o Askonas Holt Ltd, Lonsdale Chambers, 27 Chancery Lane, WC2A 1PF.

HAJDUCKI, Andrew Michael; QC (Scot.) 1994; FSAScot; *b* London, 12 Nov. 1952; *s* of Henryk Hajducki, civil engineer, and Catherine Maxwell Moore, teacher; *m* 1980, Gayle Shepherd; two *s* one *d* (and one *s* decd). *Educ:* Dulwich Coll.; Downing Coll., Cambridge (BA 1975; MA 1979). FSAScot 1990. Called to the Bar, Gray's Inn, 1976; Advocate at Scots Bar, 1979–; Tutor, Edinburgh Univ., 1979–81; reporter, Session Cases, 1980; temp. Sheriff, 1987–99. Safeguarder: Lothian Reg. Children's Panel, 1987–96; Edinburgh and E Lothian Children's Panels, 1996–98; Reporter, Scottish Legal Aid Bd, 1999–; Arbitrator, Motor Insurers' Bureau (Untraced Drivers) scheme, 2000–. Contested (Scottish L), local govt elections, 1979–84. *Publications:* The North Berwick & Gullane Branch Lines, 1992; Scottish Civic Government Licensing Law, 1994, 2nd edn 1997; The Haddington, Macmerry & Gifford Branch Lines, 1994; The Lauder Light Railway, 1996; Civil Jury Trials, 1998; (contrib.) Scottish Licensing Handbook, 1999; (contrib.) Renton & Brown's Statutory Offences, 1999; articles in Scots Law Times and other legal, local history and railway jls. *Recreations:* reading, travel, local history and topography, marathon running. *Address:* Advocates' Library, Parliament House, Edinburgh EH1 1RF. *T:* (0131) 226 2881.

HAJI-IOANNOU, Stelios; Founder, and Chairman, easyGroup; *b* 14 Feb. 1967; *s* of Loucas Haji-Ioannou. *Educ:* LSE; City of London Business Sch. (Masters). Joined Troodos Maritime, 1988; Founder: Stelmar Tankers, based in Athens and London, 1992; easyJet Airline Co. Ltd, 1995; easyEverything (internet cafés), 1999. *Recreation:* yachting. *Address:* easyJet, easyLand, Luton Airport, Beds LU2 9LS. *T:* (01582) 443333.

HAJNAL, John, FBA 1966; Professor of Statistics, London School of Economics, 1975–86 (Reader, 1966–75); *b* 26 Nov. 1924; *s* of late Kálmán and Eva Hajnal-Kónyi; *m* 1950, Nina Lande; one *s* three *d. Educ:* University Coll. Sch., London; Balliol Coll., Oxford. Employed by: Royal Commission on Population, 1944–48; UN, New York, 1948–51; Office of Population Research, Princeton Univ., 1951–53; Manchester Univ., 1953–57; London Sch. of Economics, 1957–. Vis. Fellow Commoner, Trinity Coll., Cambridge, 1974–75; Vis. Prof., Rockefeller Univ., NY, 1981. Mem. Internat. Statistical Institute. *Publications:* The Student Trap, 1972; papers on demography, statistics, mathematics, etc. *Address:* 95 Hodford Road, NW11 8EH. *T:* (020) 8455 7044.

HAKIM, Prof. Nadey, MD, PhD; Consultant Surgeon, since 1995, and Surgical Director, Transplant Unit, since 1996, St Mary's Hospital, London; *b* 9 April 1958; *s* of Subhy Elias A. Hakim and Katy Hakim (*née* Namur); *m* 1992, Nicole Abounader; one *s* three *d. Educ:* René Descartes Univ., Paris (MD 1983); University Coll. London (PhD 1991). Fellow in Surgery: Mayo Clinic, Rochester, Minn, 1987–89; Univ. of Minnesota, 1993–95. Hon. Consultant Paediatric Transplant Surgeon, Gt Ormond St Hosp., 1996–; Hon. Consultant Transplant Surgeon: Royal Free Hosp., 1996–; Hammersmith Hosp., 1998–; Harefield Hosp., 2000–. Hon. Prof. of Surgery, Univ. of São Paulo, 1999. Ed.-in-Chief, Internat. Surgery, 2001–. First Vice-Pres., Internat. Coll. Surgeons, 2000–. KStJ 1998. Hon. Dr Charles Univ., Prague, 1998. Laureate, Faculty of Medicine, Paris, 1994; Prize of Excellence in Medicine, Makhzoum Foundn, 1998. *Publications:* Enteric Physiology of Transplanted Intestine, 1994; Introduction to Organ Transplantation, 1997; British Symposium Pancreas Transplantation, 1998; Transplantation Surgery, 2001; Access Surgery, 2001. *Recreations:* sculpture, clarinet, languages. *Address:* 34 Holcroft Road, NW2 2BL.
See also N. S. Hakim.

HAKIM, Naji Subhy; organist and composer; Professor of Musical Analysis, Conservatoire National de Boulogne-Billancourt, since 1988; Organist, Eglise de la Trinité, Paris, since 1993; *b* Beirut, 11 Nov. 1955; *s* of Subhy Elias A. Hakim and Katy Hakim; *m* 1980, Marie-Bernadette Dufourcet; one *s* one *d. Educ:* Ecole Nationale Supérieure des Télécommunications, Paris (Ingénieur); Conservatoire National Supérieur de Musique, Paris. Organist, Basilique du Sacré-Coeur, Paris, 1985–93. Vis. Prof., RAM, 1993–. Mem., Consociatio Internat. Musicae Sacrae, Rome. Prix André Caplet, Académie des Beaux-Arts, 1991; first prizes at internat. organ, improvisation and composition competitions. *Compositions* include: works for organ, violin, flute, guitar, trumpet, Fantasy for Piano and Orchestra, two concertos for organ, an oratorio, symphony, Les Noces de l'Agneau, and a symphonic poem, Hymne de l'Univers; three Masses. *Publications:* Guide Pratique d'Analyse Musicale, 1991, 5th edn 1999; Anthologie Musicale pour l'Analyse de la Forme, 1995; The Improvisation Companion, 2000. *Address:* Conservatoire de Boulogne-Billancourt, 22 Rue de la Belle Feuille, 92100 Boulogne-Billancourt, France.

HAKTANIR, Korkmaz; Ambassador of Turkey to the Court of St James's, since 2000; *b* 24 Jan. 1943; *m* Handan; one *s* one *d*. *Educ:* Ankara Univ. Joined Ministry of Foreign Affairs, Turkey, 1965; Dep. Hd of Mission, Perm. Delegn to UN, 1984–88; Dep. and Directorate Gen. for Bilateral Political Affairs, 1988–91; Ambassador: to Iran, 1991–94; to Poland, 1994–96; Dep. and Under-Sec., Min. of Foreign Affairs, 1996–2000. *Address:* Turkish Embassy, 43 Belgrave Square, SW1X 8PA. *T:* (020) 7393 0202. *Clubs:* Cavalry and Guards, Travellers.

HALABY, Najeeb Elias; President, Halaby International Corporation, since 1973; Chairman, National Center for Atmospheric Research Foundation, since 1985; *b* 19 Nov. 1915; *s* of late Najeeb Elias Halaby and of Laura Wilkins Halaby; *m* 1st, 1946, Doris Carlquist (marr. diss. 1976); one *s* two *d*; 2nd, 1980, Jane Allison Coates (*d* 1996); *m* 1997, Libby Anderson Cater. *Educ:* Stanford Univ. (AB); Yale Univ. (LLB); Bonar Law Coll., Ashridge, (Summer) 1939. Called to the Bar: California, 1940; District of Columbia, 1948; NY, 1973. Practised law in Los Angeles, Calif, 1940–42, 1958–61; Air Corps Flight Instructor, 1940; Test pilot for Lockheed Aircraft Corp., 1942–43; Naval aviator, established Navy Test Pilot Sch., 1943; formerly Chief of Intelligence Coordination Div., State Dept; Foreign Affairs Advisor to Sec. of Defense; Chm., NATO Military Production and Supply Board, 1950; Asst Administrator, Mutual Security Economic Cooperation Administration, 1950–51; Asst Sec. of Defense for Internat. Security, 1952–54; Vice-Chm., White House Advisory Group whose report led to formation of Federal Aviation Agency, 1955–56, Administrator of the Agency, 1961–65; Pan American World Airways: Director, 1966–72; President, 1968–71; Chief Executive, 1969–72; Chairman, 1970–72; Associate of Laurance and Nelson Rockefeller, 1954–57; Past Exec. Vice-Pres. and Dir, Servomechanisms Inc.; Sec.-Treas., Aerospace Corp., 1959–61; Pres., American Technology Corp.; Chm., Dulles Access Rapid Transit Inc., 1985–98. Founder-Chm., US-Japan Econ. Council, 1971–73; Trustee: Aspen Inst., Aspen, Colo.; Eisenhower Exchange Fellowships, Inc.; Wolf Trap Foundn; Amer. Univ. of Beirut; Coll. of William and Mary; Governor, Flight Safety Foundn. Member: Smithson Soc.; Brookings Council; Madison Council. Chm., SCF, 1992–. Fellow, Amer. Inst. of Aeronautics and Astronautics. Hon. LLB: Allegheny Coll., Pa, 1967; Loyola Coll., LA, 1968. Monsanto Safety Award; FAA Exceptional Service Medal; G. L. Cabot Medal, Aero Club of New England, 1964; Gilbert Award, Air Traffic Controllers' Assoc., 1989. *Publications:* Crosswinds (memoir), 1979; First Forty Years of Jet Aviation, 1979. *Recreations:* golf, skiing, flying. *Address:* 175 Chain Bridge Road, McLean, VA 22101–1907, USA. *Clubs:* Alibi, Metropolitan, Chevy Chase (Washington); Bohemian (California); Tower (Virginia).

HALBERG, Sir Murray (Gordon), Kt 1988, MBE 1961; *b* 7 July 1933; *s* of Raymond Halberg; *m* 1959, Phyllis, *d* of Alex Korff; two *s* one *d*. *Educ:* Avondale College. Started internat. distance running, Commonwealth Games, 1954; Commonwealth Gold Medals, 3 miles, 1958, 1962; Olympic Gold Medal, 5,000 metres, Rome, 1960; world records at 2 miles and 3 miles, 1961, participant in 4×1 mile record. Founder, Halberg Trust (to honour sporting excellence and to support children with disabilities).

HALBERT, Derek Rowland; His Honour Judge Halbert; a Circuit Judge, since 1995; *b* 25 March 1948; *s* of Ronald Halbert and Freda Mabel Halbert (*née* Impett); *m* 1972, Heather Rose Ashe; two *d*. *Educ:* King's Sch., Chester; Selwyn Coll., Cambridge (MA Law 1974); Open Univ. (BA Technol. 1984). Called to the Bar, Inner Temple, 1971; Mem., Wales and Chester Circuit, 1971–; a Recorder, 1991–95. *Recreations:* walking, ice skating, tennis. *Address:* The Crown Court, The Castle, Chester CH1 2AN. *Club:* Leander (Henley).

HALDANE, Prof. Frederick Duncan Michael, PhD; FRS 1996; Eugene Higgins Professor of Physics, Princeton University, since 1990; *b* 14 Sept. 1951; *s* of Frederick Paterson Haldane and Ljudmila Haldane (*née* Renko); *m* 1981, Odile Marie Elisabeth Belmont; one *s* one *d*. *Educ:* St Paul's Sch.; Christ's Coll., Cambridge (BA 1973; MA; PhD 1978). FInstP. Physicist, Inst. Laue-Langevin, Grenoble, 1977–81; Asst Prof., Univ. of Southern California, 1981–85; Mem. Technical Staff, AT&T Bell Labs, 1985–87; Prof. of Physics, Univ. of California, San Diego, 1987–90. Fellow: Amer. Phys. Soc. (Oliver E. Buckley Prize in Condensed-Matter Physics, 1993); Amer. Acad. of Arts and Scis. *Publications:* contribs to Jl of Physics, Physical Review and other learned jls. *Address:* 74 Maclean Circle, Princeton, NJ 08540, USA. *T:* (609) 9211531.

HALE, Rt Hon. Dame Brenda (Marjorie), DBE 1994; PC 1999; **Rt Hon. Lady Justice Hale;** a Lord Justice of Appeal, since 1999; *b* 31 Jan. 1945; *d* of Cecil Frederick Hale and Marjorie Hale (*née* Godfrey); *m* 1st, 1968, Anthony John Christopher Hoggett, *qv* (marr. diss. 1992); one *d*; 2nd, 1992, Julian Thomas Farrand, *qv*. *Educ:* Richmond High School for Girls, Yorks; Girton College, Cambridge (MA; Hon. Fellow, 1996). Called to the Bar, Gray's Inn, 1969; University of Manchester: Asst Lectr in Law, 1966; Lectr, 1968; Sen. Lectr, 1976; Reader, 1981; Prof., 1986–89. Vis. Prof., KCL, 1990–; Vis. Fellow, Nuffield Coll., Oxford, 1997–. Barrister, Northern Circuit, 1969–72; Law Comr, 1984–93. QC 1989; a Recorder, 1989–94; a Judge of the High Court, Family Div., 1994–99; Family Div. Liaison Judge for London, 1997–99. Legal Mem., Mental Health Review Tribunal for NW Region, 1979–80; Member: Council on Tribunals, 1980–84; Civil and Family Cttee, Judicial Studies Bd, 1990–94; Human Fertilisation and Embryology Authy, 1990–93. Man. Trustee, Nuffield Foundn, 1987–; Governor, Centre for Policy on Ageing, 1990–93. Pres., Nat. Family Mediation, 1994– (Chm., Nat. Family Conciliation Council, then Nat. Assoc. of Family Mediation and Conciliation Services, 1989–93). Editor, Jl of Social Welfare Law, 1978–84. Hon. LLD: Sheffield, 1989; London Guildhall, 1996; Manchester, 1997. *Publications:* Mental Health Law, 1976, 4th edn 1996; Parents and Children, 1977, 4th edn 1993; (with D. S. Pearl) The Family Law and Society: Cases and Materials, 1983, 4th edn 1996; (with S. Atkins) Women and the Law, 1984; Mental Health Law, in Halsbury's Laws of England, 4th edn 1992; From the Test Tube to the Coffin: choice and regulation in private life (Hamlyn Lectures), 1996; contribs to legal periodicals and other texts. *Recreations:* domesticity, drama, duplicate bridge. *Address:* Royal Courts of Justice, Strand, WC2A 2LL.

HALE, David John; His Honour Judge Hale; a Circuit Judge, since 1994; *b* 18 June 1948; *s* of John and Kathleen Hale; *m* 1st, 1974, Lynn Thomas (*d* 1998); 2nd, 1999, Mrs Eileen Rafferty (*née* Hawthornthwaite). *Educ:* Calday Grange GS, West Kirby; Liverpool Univ. (LLB (Hons)). Called to the Bar, Gray's Inn, 1970; in practice, 1970–94; Wales and Chester Circuit. *Address:* Warrington Crown Court, Legh Street, Warrington WA1 1UR. *T:* (01925) 256700.

HALE, Prof. Geoffrey, PhD; Research Lecturer, Sir William Dunn School of Pathology, University of Oxford, and Research Director, Therapeutic Antibody Centre, since 1995; Professor of Therapeutic Immunology, University of Oxford, since 2000; *b* 2 Sept. 1953; *s* of Harold and Christine Hale; *m* 1977, Gillian Hutson; one *s* two *d*. *Educ:* Fitzwilliam Coll., Cambridge (MA; PhD 1977). University of Cambridge: Research Asst, Dept of Biochem., 1977–80; Sen. Res. Associate, Dept of Pathology, 1980–95; Reader in Therapeutic Immunol., Oxford Univ., 1998–2000. *Publications:* numerous contribs on protein chemistry and therapeutic uses of monoclonal antibodies in various jls. *Recreations:* playing the piano, watching the garden grow. *Address:* 64 Arlington Drive, Marston, Oxford OX3 0SJ. *T:* (01865) 248260.

HALE, John Hampton; Director: Pearson plc, 1983–93 (Managing Director, 1983–86); Pearson Inc. (USA), 1983–93 (Chairman, 1983–86); *b* 8 July 1924; *s* of Dr John Hale and Elsie (Coles) Hale; *m* 2nd, 1980, Nancy Ryrie Birks; one *s* two *d* by former marriage. *Educ:* Eton College (King's Scholar); Magdalene Coll., Cambridge (Mech. Scis Tripos, BA, MA); Harvard Grad. Sch. of Business Admin (Henry Fellow, 1948). RAF and Fleet Air Arm Pilot, 1943–46. Alcan Aluminium Ltd, Montreal, NY and London, 1949–83; Exec. Vice-Pres., Finance, 1970–82, Dir, Alcan Aluminium, 1970–85; Dir, Aluminium Co. of Canada, 1970–85 (Chm., 1979–83). Director: Nippon Light Metal Co., Japan, Indian Aluminium Co. and Alcan Australia, 1970–83; Canadian Adv. Bd, Allendale Mutual Insurance Co., 1977–83; Scovill Inc. (USA), 1978–85; Ritz-Carlton Hotel, Montreal, 1981–83; Concordia Univ. Business Sch., 1981–83; Bank of Montreal, 1985–95 (Mem., Internat Adv. Council, 1986–89); The Economist Newspaper, 1984–95; SSMC Inc. (USA), 1986–89; Chm., Fairey Holdings, 1983–87. Member: Lloyds, 1960–91; Exec. Cttee, British-North American Cttee, 1980–90; Council, Industry for Management Educn, 1983–87; Lay Mem., Stock Exchange Council, London, 1987–91. Chairman: Chambly County Protestant Central Sch. Bd, 1957–60; Business Graduates Assoc., 1967–70; Mem., Accounting Research Adv. Bd, Canadian Inst. of Chartered Accountants, 1975–81 (Chm., 1978–81). Director: Mont St Hilaire Nature Conservation Assoc., 1977–83 (Pres., 1980–83); Foundn for Canadian Studies, 1988–98; Governor, Stratford Festival, Ontario, 1981–83. Trustee, Royal Armouries, 1992–95. Mem., Court of Assts, Armourers' & Brasiers' Co., 1985– (Master, 1990 and 1998). *Recreations:* ski-ing, sailing, fishing, shooting, old Canadian books. *Address:* 71 Eaton Terrace, SW1W 8TN. *T:* (020) 7730 2929. *Clubs:* Royal Thames Yacht; Mount Royal (Montreal); Toronto.

HALE, Norman Morgan, CB 1992; Under Secretary, Department of Health (formerly of Health and Social Security), 1975–93; *b* 28 June 1933; *s* of late Thomas Norman Hale and Ada Emily Hale, Evesham, Worcs; *m* 1965, Sybil Jean (*née* Maton); one *s* one *d*. *Educ:* Prince Henry's Grammar Sch., Evesham; St John's Coll., Oxford (MA). Min. of Pensions and National Insurance, 1955; Asst Sec., Nat. Assistance Bd, 1966; Min. of Social Security, 1966; CSD, 1970–72. Consultant: MoD, 1994; Medicines Control Agency, 1994–; National Trust, 1995–97. Churchwarden Emeritus, St Mary the Virgin, Ewell (Churchwarden, 1993–97). Chm. of Govs, Ewell Grove Infant Sch., 1998–. *Recreations:* gardening, historical geography. *Address:* 64 Castle Avenue, Ewell, Epsom, Surrey KT17 2PH. *T:* (020) 8393 3507. *Club:* Oxford and Cambridge.

HALE, Raymond, CPFA; County Treasurer, Leicestershire County Council, 1977–97; *b* 4 July 1936; *s* of Tom Raymond Hale and Mary Jane (*née* Higgin); *m* 1959, Ann Elvidge; one *s*. *Educ:* Baines Grammar Sch., Poulton-le-Fylde. Lancashire CC, 1952–54; served Royal Air Force, 1954–56; Lancashire CC, 1956–61; Nottinghamshire CC, 1961–65; Leicestershire CC, 1965–97. Treasurer: Leics Police Authy, 1977–97; Leicester Univ. Med. Sch. and Associated Leics Teaching Hosps Jt Trust (Medisearch), 1988–; Access Cttee for England, 1997–99; Chm., Hind Sisters Homes Charity, 1993–; Treas. and Co. Sec., Leics Guild of Disabled, 1999– (Vice-Chm., 1990–97). *Recreations:* Rugby, cricket, gardening. *Address:* The Stables, Main Street, Nailstone, Nuneaton, Warwicks CV13 0QB. *T:* (01530) 264174.

HALES, Antony John; Director, 1989–99, Chief Executive, 1991–99, Allied Domecq (formerly Allied-Lyons) PLC; *b* 25 May 1948; *s* of Sidney Alfred Hales and Margaret Joan (*née* Wood); *m* 1975, Linda Churchlow; three *s* one *d*. *Educ:* Repton; Bristol Univ. (BSc Chem). With Cadbury Schweppes, 1969–79; Mkting Dir, Joshua Tetley & Son, 1979–83; Managing Director: Halls Oxford & West Brewery Co., 1983–85; Ind Coope-Taylor Walker, 1985–87; Retail Dir, Allied Breweries, 1987; Man. Dir, Ansells, 1987–89; Chief Exec., J. Lyons & Co., 1989–91; Chairman: Allied Domecq Spirits & Wine Ltd (formerly Hiram Walker Gp), 1992–99; Allied Domecq (formerly Allied Lyons) Retail, 1992–99. Director: Hyder PLC (formerly Welsh Water), 1993–97; Aston Villa plc, 1997–; non-executive Director: HSBC (formerly Midland) Bank, 1994–2001; David Halsall Internat., 2000–; Tempo Hldgs, 2000–; Reliance Security Gp, 2001–. Chm., Nat. Manufg Council, CBI, 1993–95.

HALES, Prof. (Charles) Nicholas, PhD, MD; FRCPath, FRCP, FMedSci; FRS 1992; Professor of Clinical Biochemistry, and Head of Department of Clinical Biochemistry, University of Cambridge, 1977–Sept. 2002; Fellow, Downing College, Cambridge, 1964–70 and 1977–Sept. 2002; *b* 25 April 1935; *s* of late Walter Bryan Hales and Phyllis Marjory Hales; *m* 1st, 1959, Janet May Moss; two *s*; 2nd, 1978, Margaret Griffiths; one *d*. *Educ:* King Edward VI Grammar Sch., Stafford; Univ. of Cambridge (BA 1956, MB, BChir, MA 1959, PhD 1964, MD 1971). MRCPath 1971, FRCPath 1980; MRCP 1971, FRCP 1976. House Surgeon, UCH, 1959, House Physician, 1960; Stothert Res. Fellow, Royal Soc., 1963–64; Lectr, Dept of Biochem., Univ. of Cambridge, 1964–70; Clinical Asst, Addenbrooke's Hosp., Cambridge, 1961–68, Hon. Consultant in Clin. Biochem., 1968–70; Prof. of Med. Biochem., Welsh National Sch. of Medicine, Cardiff, and Hon. Consultant in Med. Biochem., University Hosp. of Wales, Cardiff, 1970–77. Consultant in Med. Biochem., South Glam Health Authority (T). Mem., MRC, 1988–90. Founder FMedSci 1998. Lectures: Banting Meml, British Diabetic Assoc., 1991; Croonian, RCP, 1992; Kroc, Center for Diabetes Res., Univ. of Uppsala, 1992; Dale, Nat. Inst. for Biol Standards & Control, 1992; Kettle, RCPath, 1993; W. H. S. George Meml, 1993. Medal, Soc., for Endocrinology, 1981; Foundn Award, Assoc. of Clin. Biochemists, 1991; Zeneca Award in Analytical Biochem., Biochemical Soc., 1994. *Recreations:* music, fishing. *Address:* Department of Clinical Biochemistry, Addenbrooke's Hospital, Hills Road, Cambridge CB2 2QR. *T:* (01223) 336787.

HALES, Prof. Frederick David, FREng, FIMechE, FIMA; Professor of Surface Transport, Loughborough University of Technology, 1968–93, now Professor Emeritus; *b* 19 Dec. 1930; *s* of Christina Frances and Frederick David Hales; *m* 1955, Pamela Hilary Warner; one *s* one *d* (and one *d* decd). *Educ:* Kingswood Grammar Sch.; Bristol Univ. (BSc Hons Maths, PhD). Sigma Xi. Asst Chief Aerodynamicist, Bristol Aircraft, 1953–60; Group Research Head, MIRA, 1960–67; Vis. Scientist, Stevens Inst., Hoboken, 1967–68; Loughborough University: Hd of Dept of Transport Technology, 1982–89; Pro-Vice-Chancellor, 1984–85, Sen. Pro-Vice-Chancellor, 1985–87; acting Vice-Chancellor, 1987–88; Dean of Engrg, 1989–92. Mem., Tech. Adv. Council to Ford Motor Co.,

1985–93; Scientific Visitor to Dept of Transport, 1986–90. FREng (FEng 1990). Hon. DSc Loughborough, 2000. *Publications:* papers on dynamics and vehicle control and stability. *Recreations:* sailing, photography, wine, wood carving, painting. *Address:* 14 Kenilworth Avenue, Loughborough, Leics LE11 4SL. *T:* (01509) 261767. *Clubs:* Rutland Sailing, Clyde Cruising.

HALES, Prof. Nicholas; *see* Hales, Prof. C. N.

HALEY, Prof. Keith Brian, PhD; CMath, FIMA; FOR; Professor of Operational Research, Birmingham University, 1968–99, now Emeritus; *b* 17 Nov. 1933; *s* of Arthur Leslie Haley and Gladys Mary Haley; *m* 1960, Diana Elizabeth Mason; one *s. Educ:* King Edward VI, Five Ways, Birmingham; Birmingham Univ. (BSc, PhD). FIMA 1970; FOR 1976; CompOR 1997. OR Scientist, NCB, 1957–59; Birmingham University: Lectr, 1959–63; Sen. Lectr, 1963–68; Head, Dept of Engrg Prodn, 1981–89; Head, Centre for Ergonomics and OR, 1990–91; Dir, Centre of Applied Gerontology, 1991–95; Hd, Sch. of Manufg and Mech. Engrg, 1994–96. President: ORS, 1982–83; IFORS, 1992–94 (Vice-Pres., 1983–86); Editor, Jl of ORS, 1972–80. Governor, Bromsgrove Sch., 1968–. *Publications:* Mathematical Programming for Business and Industry, 1966; Operational Research '75, 1976; Operational Research '78, 1979; Search Theory and Applications, 1980; Applied Operations Research in Fishing, 1981; many articles. *Recreations:* squash, bridge. *Address:* 22 Eymore Close, Selly Oak, Birmingham B29 4LB. *T:* (0121) 475 3331.

HALFORD, Alison Monica; Member (Lab) Delyn, National Assembly for Wales, since 1999; *b* 8 May 1940; *d* of William Charles Halford and Yvonne (*née* Bastien). *Educ:* Notre Dame Grammar Sch., Norwich. Metropolitan Police, 1962–83; Asst Chief Constable (most senior post for woman in UK), Merseyside Police, 1983–92. Mem. (Lab) Flintshire CC, 1995–99. Police Long Service and Good Conduct Medal, 1984. Following police tapping her telephone in sex discrimination case, brought action in which Court of Human Rights ruled, 1997, that statutory warning required. *Publication:* No Way up the Greasy Pole (autobiog.), 1993. *Recreations:* work, serving the community, golf, painting, bridge, music. *Address:* (constituency office) Greenfield Business Centre, Greenfield, Holywell, Flintshire CH8 7QB. *T:* (01352) 716574.

HALFPENNY, Ven. Brian Norman, CB 1990; Team Rector of the Parish of the Ridge, Redditch, 1991–2001; *b* 7 June 1936; *s* of Alfred Ernest Halfpenny and Fanny Doris Halfpenny (*née* Harman); *m* 1961, Hazel Beatrice Cross; three *d. Educ:* George Dixon Grammar Sch., Birmingham; St John's Coll., Oxford (BA 1960; MA 1964); Wells Theol Coll. Curate, Melksham, 1962–65; Chaplain, RAF, 1965–91; served RAF Stations Cosford, Wildenrath, Leeming, Hong Kong, Brize Norton, Halton, Akrotiri; RAF Coll., Cranwell, 1982–83; Asst Chaplain-in-Chief, Support Comd, 1983–85, Strike Comd, 1985–88; QHC 1985–91; Chaplain-in-Chief and Archdeacon, RAF, 1988–91; Priest i/c St Clement Danes, 1988–91. Canon and Prebendary, Lincoln Cathedral, 1989–91. Co. Chaplain, RBL, Worcs, 1994–2001. Mem., Gen. Synod of C of E, 1988–91. Vice-Pres., Clergy Orphan Corp., 1988–91. Mem. Council, RAF Benevolent Fund, 1988–91; Visitor, Soldiers' and Airmen's Scripture Readers Assoc., 1988–91. *Recreations:* music, theatre, running. *Address:* 80 Roman Way, Bourton-on-the-Water, Cheltenham, Glos GL54 2EW. *T:* (01451) 821589. *Clubs:* Royal Air Force; Oxford Union Society.

HALIFAX, 3rd Earl of, *cr* 1944; **Charles Edward Peter Neil Wood;** Bt 1784; Viscount Halifax, 1866; Baron Irwin, 1925; JP; Vice Lord-Lieutenant, East Riding of Yorkshire, since 1996; *b* 14 March 1944; *s* of 2nd Earl of Halifax and Ruth (*d* 1989), *d* of late Captain Rt Hon. Neil James Archibald Primrose, MC, sometime MP; *S* father, 1980; *m* 1976, Camilla, *d* of late C. F. J. Younger, DSO, TD; one *s* one *d. Educ:* Eton; Christ Church, Oxford. Contested (C) Dearne Valley, Feb. and Oct. 1974. High Steward of York Minster, 1988–. JP Wilton Beacon, 1986; DL Humberside, 1983–96. *Heir: s* Lord Irwin, *qv. Address:* Garrowby, York YO41 1QD. *Clubs:* White's, Pratt's.

HALIFAX (NS), Archbishop of, (RC), since 1991; **Most Rev. Austin-Emile Burke;** *b* 1922. Ordained priest, 1950; Suffragan Bishop of Yarmouth, 1968–91. *Address:* Chancery Office, PO Box 1527, 1531 Grafton Street, Halifax, NS B3J 2Y3, Canada. *Fax:* 423–5201.

HALIFAX, Archdeacon of; *see* Inwood, Ven. R. N.

HALL, Prof. Alan, PhD; FRS 1999; Professor of Cell and Molecular Biology, Department of Biochemistry and Molecular Biology, University College London. *Educ:* Oxford Univ. (BA 1974); Harvard Univ. (PhD 1977). Post-doctoral Fellow, Univ. of Edinburgh, 1977–79, Zürich Univ., 1979–80; Inst. for Cancer. Res., 1980–92; UCL, 1992–. *Publications:* contribs to jls. *Address:* MRC Laboratory for Molecular Cell Biology, University College London, Gower Street, WC1E 6BT.

HALL, Rt Rev. (Albert) Peter; Bishop Suffragan, then Area Bishop, of Woolwich, 1984–96; Hon. Assistant Bishop, diocese of Birmingham, since 1997; *b* 2 Sept. 1930; *s* of William Conrad Hall and Bertha Gladys Hall; *m* 1957, Valerie Jill Page; two *s. Educ:* Queen Elizabeth Grammar School, Blackburn; St John's Coll., Cambridge (MA Mod. Langs); Ridley College, Cambridge. Deacon 1955, priest 1956; Curate: St Martin, Birmingham, 1955–60; St Mary Magdalene, Avondale, Zimbabwe, 1960; Rector of Avondale, Zimbabwe, 1963–70; Rector of Birmingham, 1970–84. *Recreation:* mountain walking. *Address:* 27 Jacey Road, Birmingham B16 0LL.

HALL, Alfred Charles, CBE 1977 (OBE 1966); HM Diplomatic Service, retired; *b* 2 Aug. 1917; *s* of Alfred Hall and Florence Mary Hall; *m* 1945, Clara Georgievna Strunina, Moscow; five *s* one *d. Educ:* Oratory Sch.; Open Univ. (BA); Univ. of Kent (MA 1995). Served War, RA and Intell. Corps, 1939–43. LCC, 1934–39 and 1946–49; FO, with service in Saudi Arabia, Algeria, Egypt, Iran and USSR, 1943–46; FCO (formerly CRO and CO), with service in Pakistan, India, Nigeria, Canada and Australia, 1949–75; Dep. High Comr in Southern India, 1975–77. Grants Officer, SCF, 1979–82. *Publications:* papers on foreign and Commonwealth relations. *Recreations:* music, politics. *Address:* 10A Castle Avenue, Dover CT16 1EZ; White Cliff, St Margaret's Bay, Kent CT15 6HR. *Club:* Royal Commonwealth Society.

HALL, Prof. Alfred Rupert, LittD; FBA 1978; Professor of the History of Science and Technology, Imperial College of Science and Technology, University of London, 1963–80; *b* 26 July 1920; *s* of Alfred Dawson Hall and Margaret Ritchie; *m* 1st, 1942, Annie Shore Hughes; two *d*; 2nd, 1959, Marie Boas (*see* M. B. Hall). *Educ:* Alderman Newton's Boy's Sch., Leicester; Christ's Coll., Cambridge (scholar). LittD Cantab 1975. Served in Royal Corps of Signals, 1940–45. 1st cl. Historical Tripos Part II, 1946; Allen Scholar, 1948; Fellow, Christ's Coll., 1949–59, Steward, 1955–59; Curator, Whipple Science Mus., Cambridge and University Lectr, 1950–59. Medical Research Historian, University of Calif, Los Angeles, 1959–60, Prof. of Philosophy, 1960–61; Prof. of History and Logic of Science, Indiana Univ., 1961–63. Royal Society Lectures: Wilkins, 1973; Leeuwenhoek, 1988. FRHistS. Pres., British Soc. for History of Science, 1966–68; Pres., Internat. Acad. of the History of Science, 1977–81; Wellcome Trust: Chm., Adv. Panel on History of Medicine, 1974–80; Co-ordinator, History of Medicine, 1981–85. Co-editor, A History of Technology, 1951–58. Corresp. Mem., Soc. for the History of Technology, 1970. Hon. Laureate, Univ. of Bologna, 1999. Silver Medal, RSA, 1974; (jtly) Sarton Medal, History of Science Soc., 1981. *Publications:* Ballistics in the Seventeenth Century, 1952; The Scientific Revolution, 1954; From Galileo to Newton, 1963; The Cambridge Philosophical Society: a history, 1819–1969, 1969; Philosophers at War, 1980; Short History of the Imperial College, 1982; The Revolution in Science 1500–1750, 1983; Henry More: Magic, Religion and Experiment, 1990; with Marie Boas Hall: Unpublished Scientific Papers of Isaac Newton, 1962; Correspondence of Henry Oldenburg, 1965–86; (with Laura Tilling) Correspondence of Isaac Newton, vols 5–7, 1974–77; (ed with Norman Smith) History of Technology, 1976–83; (with B. A. Bembridge) Physic and Philanthropy: a history of the Wellcome Trust, 1986; Isaac Newton: Adventurer in Thought, 1992; Newton, his Friends and his Foes, 1993; All was Light, 1993; Essays on the History of Science and Technology, 1994; Isaac Newton: Eighteenth Century perspectives, 1998; contributor to Isis, Annals of Science, etc. *Address:* 14 Ball Lane, Tackley, Oxford OX5 3AG. *T:* (01869) 331257.

HALL, Anthony Stewart, (Tony); Director, Central Council for Education and Training in Social Work, 1986–97; *b* 26 Oct. 1945; *s* of Dora Rose Ellen Hall (*née* Rundle) and Albert Hall; *m* 1968, Phoebe Katharine Souster; one *s* one *d. Educ:* Gillingham Grammar School; London Sch. of Economics (BScSoc). Research Student, LSE, 1968–71; Lectr in Management and Organisation Studies, Nat. Inst. for Social Work, 1971–73; Lectr in Social Admin, Univ. of Bristol, 1973–78; Dir, Assoc. of British Adoption and Fostering Agencies, 1978–80; Dir and Sec., British Agencies for Adoption and Fostering, 1980–86; Dep. Man. Dir, Retirement Security Ltd, 1997. *Publications:* A Management Game for the Social Service (with J. Algie), 1974; The Point of Entry: a study of client reception in the social services, 1975; (ed) Access to Birth Records: the impact of S.26 of the Children Act 1975, 1980; (with Phoebe Hall) Part-time Social Work, 1980; (series editor) Child Care Policy and Practice, 1982–86; chapters in books and articles in professional and learned jls. *Recreations:* photography, genealogy, watching sport and old films, music, stamps, computers. *Address:* 115 Babington Road, Streatham, SW16 6AN. *T:* (020) 8480 9045; *e-mail:* tonyhall@tinyworld.co.uk.

HALL, Anthony William, (Tony); Executive Director, Royal Opera House, since 2001; *b* 3 March 1951; *s* of late Donald William Hall and of Mary Joyce Hall; *m* 1977, Cynthia Lesley Hall (*née* Davis); one *s* one *d. Educ:* King Edward's Sch., Birmingham; Birkenhead Sch., Merseyside; Keble Coll., Oxford (Exhibnr; MA). Joined BBC as News trainee, 1973; Producer: World Tonight, 1976; New York (Radio), 1977; Sen. Producer, World at One, 1978; Output Editor, Newsnight, 1980; Sen. Producer, Six O'Clock News, 1984; Asst Editor, Nine O'Clock News, 1985; Editor: News and Election '87, 1987; News and Current Affairs, BBC TV, 1988–90; Dir, 1990–93, Man. Dir, 1993–96, News and Current Affairs, BBC; Chief Exec., BBC News, 1996–2001. Mem., King's Healthcare Expert Reference Gp, 1995–96. Mem., Steering Cttee, Regeneration through Heritage, BITC, 1999–. Dir, Theatre Royal, Stratford, 1999–. Hon. Vis. Fellow, City Univ., 1999–. Mem. Council, Brunel Univ., 1999–. Patron, Newsworld, 1999; Gov. for Media, World Econ. Forum, 2000. Mem. Cttee, Race for Opportunity, 1999–2001 (as Race Champion led BBC's campaign on diversity and race issues). Liveryman, Painter Stainers' Co., 1989–. FRTS 1994 (Chm., 1998–); FRSA 1997. *Publications:* King Coal: a history of the miners, 1981; Nuclear Politics, 1984; articles in various periodicals. *Recreations:* church architecture, opera, walking. *Address:* c/o Royal Opera House, Covent Garden, WC2E 9DD. *T:* (020) 7212 9111.

HALL, Arthur Herbert; Librarian and Curator, Guildhall Library and Museum, and Director of Guildhall Art Gallery, 1956–66; retired; *b* 30 Aug. 1901; *y s* of Henry and Eliza Jane Hall, Islington, London; *m* 1927, Dorothy Maud (*née* Barton); two *s* one *d. Educ:* Mercers' Sch., Holborn, London. Entered Guildhall Library as junior asst, 1918; Dep. Librarian, 1943–56. Hon. Librarian, Clockmakers' and Gardeners' Companies, 1956–66. Served with RAOC, 1942–46. Chm. Council, London and Middlesex Archæological Soc., 1957–64, Vice-Pres., 1962–; Member: Council of London Topographical Soc., 1960–67; Exec. Cttee, Friends of Nat. Libraries, 1965–69. Hon. Sec., Middlesex Victoria County History Council, 1966–78; Enfield Archaeological Soc. (Hon. Sec., 1966–71); Master, 1974–75, Hon. Clerk, 1965–74, Asst Hon. Clerk, 1975–86, Civic Guild of Old Mercers. Liveryman of the Clockmakers Co. Pres., Upper Norwood Athenæum, 1993–96. FLA 1930; FSA 1963.

HALL, Sir Basil (Brodribb), KCB 1977 (CB 1974); MC 1945; TD 1952; Member, European Commission of Human Rights, 1985–93; Legal Adviser, Broadcasting Complaints Commission, 1981–93; *b* 2 Jan. 1918; *s* of late Alfred Brodribb Hall and of Elsie Hilda Hall, Woking, Surrey; *m* 1955, Jean Stafford Gowland; two *s* one *d. Educ:* Merchant Taylors' Sch. Articled Clerk with Gibson & Weldon, Solicitors, 1935–39; admitted Solicitor, 1942. Served War of 1939–45: Trooper, Inns of Court Regt, 1939; 2nd Lieut, 12th Royal Lancers, 1940; Captain, 27th Lancers, 1941; Major, 27th Lancers, 1942. Legal Asst, Treasury Solicitor's Dept, 1946; Sen. Legal Asst, 1951; Asst Treasury Solicitor, 1958; Principal Asst Solicitor, 1968; Dep. Treasury Solicitor, 1972; HM Procurator Gen. and Treasury Solicitor, 1975–80. Chm., Civil Service Appeal Bd, 1981–84 (Dep. Chm., 1980–81). Mem. Council, Nat. Army Museum, 1981–92. *Recreations:* military history, travel. *Address:* Woodlands, 16 Danes Way, Oxshott, Surrey KT22 0LX. *T:* (01372) 842032. *Club:* Athenæum.

HALL, Very Rev. Bernard, SJ; Superior, Jesuit House of Writers, Rome, since 1994; *b* 17 Oct. 1921. *Educ:* St Michael's Coll., Leeds; Heythrop Coll., Oxford. LicPhil, STL. Captain RA, 1941–46. Entered Society of Jesus, 1946; ordained priest, 1955; Provincial of the English Province, Society of Jesus, 1970–76; Rector, Collegio San Roberto Bellarmino, Rome, 1976–82 and 1989–94; English Asst to Father General, SJ, Rome, 1982–88. *Address:* Casa degli Scrittori, via dei Penitenzieri 20, 00193 Rome, Italy.

HALL, Betty, CBE 1977; Regional Nursing Officer, West Midlands Regional Health Authority, 1974–81; *b* 6 June 1921; *d* of John Hall and Jane (*née* Massey), Eagley, Lancs. *Educ:* Bolton Sch.; Royal Infirm., Edinburgh (RGN); Radcliffe Infirm., Oxford and St Mary's Hosp., Manchester (SCM); Royal Coll. of Nursing (RNT). Nursed tuberculous patients from concentration camps, Rollier Clinic, Leysin, 1948–49; Ward Sister, Salford Royal Hosp., 1949–51; Sister Tutor, Royal Masonic Hosp., London, 1952–54; Principal Tutor, St Luke's Hosp., Bradford, 1954–61 (Mem. Leeds Area Nurse Trng Cttee); King Edward's Hosp. Fund Admin. Staff Coll., 1961–62; Work Study Officer to United Bristol Hosps, 1961–64; Asst Nursing Officer to Birmingham Regional Hosp. Bd, 1964–65, Regional Nursing Officer, 1966–81. Mem., Exec. Cttee, Grange-over-Sands Abbeyfield Soc., 1982–93. Hon. Sec., Grange-over-Sands RUKBA, 1987–2001. *Recreations:* reading, tapestry making, cricket. *Address:* Chailey, Ash Mount Road, Grange-over-Sands, Cumbria LA11 6BX. *Club:* Naval and Military.

HALL, Brian; *see* Hall, F. B.

HALL, Prof. Bronwyn Hughes, PhD; Professor of Economics, University of California at Berkeley; Professor of Economics, and Fellow of Nuffield College, Oxford University,

1996–2001; *b* 1 March 1945; *d* of Richard Roberts Hughes and Elizabeth Flandreau Hughes; *m* 1966, Robert Ernest Hall (marr. diss. 1983); one *s* one *d*. *Educ:* Wellesley Coll., Mass (BA 1966); Stanford Univ. (PhD 1988); MA Oxon 1997. Programmer: Lawrence Berkeley Lab., Berkeley, Calif, 1963–66; Lyman Lab. of Physics, Harvard Univ., 1966–67; Lawrence Berkeley Lab., 1967–70; Sen. Programmer, Harvard Inst. of Econ. Res., 1971–77; National Bureau of Economic Research, Cambridge, Massachusetts: Research Economist, 1977–88; Res. Associate, 1988–; Asst. Prof., 1987–94, Assoc. Prof., 1994–99, Univ. of Calif, Berkeley; Internat. Res. Associate, Inst. for Fiscal Studies, London, 1995–. Mem., Sci. Technol. and Econ. Policy Bd, Nat. Res. Council, Washington. Sloan Dissertation Fellow, 1985–86; Hoover Instn Nat. Fellow, 1992–93. Owner and Chief Exec. Officer, TSP Internat., Palo Alto, Calif, 1977–. Mem., Sigma Xi Soc., 1966. Associate Editor, Econs of Innovation and New Technol., 1994– (Mem. Edtl Bd, 1989–94); Mem. Adv. Bd, Internat. Finance jl, 1997–. Mem. Internat. Adv. Bd, New Econ. Sch., Moscow, 1997–. *Publications:* TSP 4.3 User's Manual, 1977, rev. edn, version 4.5, 1999; TSP 4.3 Reference Manual, 1977, rev. edn, version 4.5, 1999; contrib. articles to Amer. Econ. Rev., Econometrica, Jl Industrial Econs, Jl Econometrics, Brookings Papers on Econ, Activity, Econs of Innovation and New Technol. *Recreations:* travel, walking, opera, painting. *Address:* Department of Economics, University of California at Berkeley, Berkeley, CA 94720, USA. *T:* (510) 6423878.

HALL, Christopher Myles; Editor of The Countryman, 1981–96; *b* 21 July 1932; *s* of Gilbert and Muriel Hall; *m* 1957, Jennifer Bevan Keech (marr. diss. 1980); one *s* one *d*; lives with Kate Ashbrook, *qv*. *Educ:* Berkhamsted Sch.; New Coll., Oxford (2nd cl. Hons PPE); Kellogg Coll., Oxford (MSt English Local History, with distinction, 1996). Reporter and Feature-writer, Daily Express, 1955–58; Sub-editor and Leader-writer, Daily Mirror, 1958–61; Feature-writer and Leader-writer, Daily Herald/Sun, 1961–65; Special Asst (Information): to Minister of Overseas Develt, 1965–66; to Minister of Transport, 1966–68; Chief Information Officer, MoT, 1968; Ramblers' Association: Sec., 1969–74; Mem. Exec. Cttee, 1982–84; Vice-Chm., 1984–87; Chm., 1987–90; Pres., 1990–93; Vice-Pres., 1993–; Chm., Oxfordshire Area, 1984–87, 1994–97, Footpaths and Publicity Sec., 1997–98; Dir, Council for Protection of Rural England, 1974–80. Pres., The Holiday Fellowship, 1974–77; Vice-Chm., S Reg. Council of Sport and Recreation, 1976–82; Member: DoT Cttee of Inquiry into Operators' Licensing, 1977–79; Common Land Forum, 1984–86; Hon. Sec., Chiltern Soc., 1965–68; Chm., Oxfordshire Local Hist. Assoc., 2001–. Columnist, Rambling Today, 1993–96; Editor, Oxfordshire Local History, 1997–. *Publications:* How to Run a Pressure Group, 1974; (jtly) The Countryside We Want, 1988; The Countryman's Yesterday, 1989; Scenes from The Countryman, 1992; contributions to: Motorways in London, 1969; No Through Road, 1975; The Countryman's Britain, 1976; Book of British Villages, 1980; Sunday Times Book of the Countryside, 1981; Walker's Britain, 1982; Britain on Backroads, 1985; Making Tracks, 1985; (with John Tookey) The Cotswolds, 1990; pamphlets; contrib. to Vole, The Countryman, New Statesman, New Scientist, The Geographical Magazine, Country Living, The Guardian and various jls. *Recreation:* walking in the countryside. *Address:* Telfer's Cottage, Turville, Henley-on-Thames RG9 6QL. *T:* (01491) 638396. *Club:* Oxford and Cambridge.

HALL, David, CBE 1983; QPM 1977; consultant in security and personnel management; Chief Constable of Humberside Police, 1976–91; *b* 29 Dec. 1930; *s* of Arthur Thomas Hall and Dorothy May Charman; *m* 1952, Molly Patricia Knight; two *s*. *Educ:* Richmond and East Sheen Grammar School for Boys. Joined Metropolitan Police and rose through ranks from PC to Chief Supt, 1950–68; Staff Officer to Chief Inspector of Constabulary, Col Sir Eric St Johnson, 1968; Asst Chief Constable, 1970, Dep. Chief Constable, 1976, Staffordshire Police. Vice-Pres., Assoc. of Chief Police Officers of England, Wales and NI, 1982–83, Pres. 1983–84. CIMgt (CBIM 1988). Freeman, City of London, 1987. OStJ 1980. *Recreations:* gardening, walking, playing the piano. *Address:* Fairlands, 1 Copper Beech Close, West Leys Park, Kemp Road, Swanland, North Ferriby HU14 3LR.

HALL, David John, CMG 2001; Deputy Chief Executive and Director, Central Services Group, British Trade International, since 1999; *b* 15 July 1942; *s* of late Alexander G. Hall and Molly Hall, Aberdeen; *m* 1965, Elizabeth Adams; one *s* two *d*. *Educ:* Trinity Coll., Glenalmond; Pembroke Coll., Oxford (BA Mod. Langs). FO, 1964–67; Bahrain, 1967–69; Dubai, 1969–70; FCO, 1970–74; Bonn, 1974–76; joined Dept of Trade, later DTI, 1976; Asst Sec., 1982; Counsellor (Trade and Envmt), Washington, 1988; Under-Sec., 1991; Dir, Projects Export Promotion, 1991–97; Dep. Dir-Gen., Export Promotion, DTI, and Dir, Overseas Trade, FCO, 1997–99. *Recreations:* music, gardening, dogs. *Address:* c/o Department of Trade and Industry, Kingsgate House, 66–74 Victoria Street, SW1E 6SW. *T:* (020) 7215 8600.

HALL, Prof. David Michael Baldock, FRCP, FRCPCH; Professor of Community Paediatrics, University of Sheffield, since 1993; President, Royal College of Paediatrics and Child Health, since 2000; *b* 4 Aug. 1945; *s* of Ronald Hall and Ethel Gwen Hall (*née* Baldock); *m* 1966, Susan M. Luck; two *d*. *Educ:* Reigate Grammar Sch.; St George's Hosp., London Univ. (MB, BS; BSc; Univ. Gold Medal). FRCP 1986; FRCPCH 1996. SMO, Baragwanath Hosp., Johannesburg, 1973–76; Sen. Registrar, Charing Cross Hosp., 1976–78; Consultant Paediatrician, St George's Hosp., 1978–93. Hon FFPHM 1999. *Publications:* Health for All Children, 1989, 3rd edn 1996; Child with a Disability, 1996; contrib. numerous papers to jls, etc. *Recreations:* horses, plumbing. *Address:* Storrs House Farm, Storrs Lane, Stannington, Sheffield S6 6GY.

HALL, Col David Stevenson, CBE 1993; TD 1971; Chairman: Meadowcroft Management Ltd, since 1985; NHS Logistics, since 2000; *b* 29 March 1938; *s* of late Robert Hall and Maude Hall; *m* 1962, Marion Esmé Blundstone; one *s* one *d*. *Educ:* Scarborough Coll. Nat. Service, RAOC, 1956–58. Man. Dir, UDS Tailoring Ltd, 1979–81; Chm. and Man. Dir, Collier Holdings plc, 1982–85. Non-executive Director: Sharp and Law plc, 1989–90; Toye plc, 1994–95. Chairman: United Leeds Teaching Hosps NHS Trust, 1995–98; NHS Supplies, 1998–2000. Trustee, RAOC Charitable Trust, 1993–2000. RAOC (TA), 1958–93; Col, 1985–89; ADC, 1986–91; TA Col Logistics MoD/UKLF, 1989–93; Hon. Col, RAOC Specialist Units, 1991–93; Combat Services Support Group, RLC(V), 1995–2000. Freeman, City of London, 1993. *Recreations:* cricket, reading. *Address:* Meadowcroft, Elmwood Lane, Barwick in Elmet, Leeds LS15 4JX. *T:* (0113) 281 3587. *Clubs:* Army and Navy, MCC.

HALL, Denis C.; *see* Clarke Hall.

HALL, Denis Whitfield, CMG 1962; late Provincial Commissioner, Kenya; *b* 26 Aug. 1913; *s* of late H. R. Hall, Haslemere, Surrey; *m* 1940, Barbara Carman; two *s*. *Educ:* Dover College; Wadham Coll., Oxford. Dist Officer, Kenya, 1936; Personal Asst to Chief Native Comr, 1948; Senior Dist Comr, 1955; Provincial Comr, Coast Province, 1959. Dep. Chm., Sussex Church Campaign, 1964–73. *Recreations:* sailing, tennis, walking, motoring. *Address:* Martins, Priory Close, Boxgrove, West Sussex PO18 0EA. *Clubs:* Oxford Union; Oxford University Yacht.

HALL, Sir Douglas (Basil), 14th Bt *cr* 1687; KCMG 1959 (CMG 1958); *b* 1 Feb. 1909; *s* of late Capt. Lionel Erskine Hall and late Jane Augusta Hall (*née* Reynolds); *S* brother, Sir Neville Hall, 13th Bt, 1978; *m* 1933, Rachel Marion Gartside-Tippinge (*d* 1990); one *s* two *d* (and one *s* decd). *Educ:* Radley Coll.; Keble Coll., Oxford (MA). Joined Colonial Admin. Service, 1930; posted to N Rhodesia as Cadet; District Officer, 1932; Senior District Officer, 1950; Provincial Commr, 1953; Administrative Sec., 1954; Sec. for Native Affairs to Government of Northern Rhodesia, 1956–59, Acting Chief Sec. for a period during 1958; Governor and C-in-C, Somaliland Protectorate, 1959–60. JP Co. Devon, 1964, Chm., Kingsbridge Petty Sessional Div., 1971–79. *Publications:* various technical articles. *Recreation:* vintage cars. *Heir:* *s* John Douglas Hoste Hall [*b* 7 Jan. 1945; *m* 1972, Angela Margaret, *d* of George Keys; two *s*]. *Address:* Little Barnford, Orchard Farm, Parwich, Ashbourne, Derbys DE6 1QB. *T:* (01335) 390436.

HALL, Duncan; Managing Director, Duncan Hall Associates Ltd, since 1998; *b* 2 Sept. 1947; *s* of Leslie and Joan Elizabeth Hall; *m* 1970, Jane Elizabeth Menzies; two *s* one *d*. *Educ:* Acklam Hall Grammar Sch. LLB Hons. Articled Clerk and Senior Legal Assistant, Wellingborough UDC, 1970–74; Corby District Council: PA to Chief Exec., 1974–75; Asst Chief Exec., 1975–78; Housing and Property Controller, 1978–79; Chief Exec., 1980–87; Chief Exec., Teesside Develt Corp., 1987–98. CIMgt; FRSA. *Recreations:* reading, travel, music, theatre, shooting. *Address:* Duncan Hall Associates Ltd, The Old Chapel, South Green, Staindrop, Darlington, Co. Durham DL2 3LD. *T:* (01833) 660077, *Fax:* (01833) 660088.

HALL, Sir Ernest, Kt 1993; OBE 1986; DL; pianist and composer, since 1954; property developer, since 1971; Chairman, Dean Clough Business, Arts and Education Centre, since 1983; *b* 19 March 1930; *s* of Ernest and Mary Elizabeth Hall; *m* 1st, 1951, June (*née* Annable) (*d* 1994); two *s* two *d*; 2nd, 1975, Sarah (*née* Wellby); one *s*. *Educ:* Bolton County Grammar Sch.; Royal Manchester Coll. of Music (ARMCM (teacher and performer) 1950–51; Royal Patron's Fund Prize for Composition, 1951). Textile manufr, 1961–71. Dep. Chm., Eureka! Children's Museum, 1989–2000; Mem., Arts Council of England (formerly of GB), 1990–97; Chm., Yorks and Humberside Arts Bd, 1991–97; Pres., Yorks Business in the Arts, 1990–; Vice-Pres., RSA, 1994–99. Trustee: Yorkshire Sculpture Park, 1989–; Henry Moore Foundn., 1999–. DL W Yorks, 1991. Chancellor, Univ. of Huddersfield, 1996–. Hon. Fellow: Huddersfield Polytechnic, 1989; Leeds Polytechnic, 1991; Bolton Inst., 1994. DUniv: York, 1986; Leeds Metropolitan, 1996; Hon. DLitt Bradford, 1990; Hon. DArt Bristol Poly, 1991; Hon. LLD Leeds, 1996. Envmt Award, Business and Industry Panel, RSA, 1988; Guildhall Helping Hand, Nat. Fedn of Self-Employed and Small Businesses, 1989; Special Free Enterprise Award, Aims of Industry, 1989; Best Practice Award, BURA, 1992; Lifetime Achievement Award, Inst. for Social Inventions, 1992; Albert Medal, RSA, 1994; Montblanc de la Culture UK Award, Fondation d'Enterprise, France, 1996; Goodman Award, ABSA, 1997. *Recreations:* equestrianism, gardening, art collecting, theatre, languages. *Address:* Dean Clough, Halifax HX3 5AX. *T:* (01422) 255257, *Fax:* (01422) 255250.

HALL, (Frederick) Brian; Master (Care and Protection), Supreme Court of Judicature of Northern Ireland, since 1986; *b* 2 Oct. 1934; *s* of Frederick Hall and late Mary Hall (*née* Kernahan); *m* 1965, Isobel Frances Deirdre Boyce; two *d*. *Educ:* Coleraine Academical Inst.; Queen's Univ. Belfast (LLB). Admitted Solicitor, NI, 1958; Legal Adviser, Min. of Home Affairs, 1972; Asst Solicitor, NI Office, 1973; Dep. Dir, NI Court Service, 1979; Official Solicitor to Supreme Court, NI, 1982. Mem., Sec. of State's Cttee on County Courts and Magistrates' Courts, 1974. *Recreations:* golf, travel, reading. *Address:* Royal Courts of Justice, PO Box 410, Chichester Street, Belfast BT1 3JF. *T:* (028) 9023 5111. *Club:* Royal Belfast Golf.

HALL, Sir (Frederick) John (Frank), 3rd Bt *cr* 1923; *b* 14 Aug. 1931; *er s* of Sir Frederick Henry Hall, 2nd Bt, and Olwen Irene (*d* 1993), *yr d* of late Alderman Frank Collis, Stokeville, Stoke-on-Trent, and Deganwy, Llandudno; *S* father, 1949; *m* 1st, 1956, Felicity Anne (marr. diss. 1960), *d* of late Edward Rivers-Fletcher, Norwich, and of Mrs L. R. Galloway; 2nd, 1961, Patricia Ann Atkinson (marr. diss. 1967); two *d*; re-married, 1967, 1st wife, Felicity Anne Hall; two *d*. *Educ:* Bryanston Sch. Personnel Manager, Universal Pattern & Precision Engineering Co. Ltd, 1955–59; Personnel Officer, The Nestlé Co. Ltd, 1959–63; Personnel Man., Johnson Wax Ltd, 1963–65; UK Head Office Trng and Mgt Develt Man., The Nestlé Co. Ltd, 1965–67; Gp Personnel Man., Findus Ltd, 1967–69; Sen. Man., McLintock Mann & Whinney Murray, 1969–76; Dir, Thomson McLintock Associates, 1976–87; founder Chm., KPMG Career Consultancy Services, 1983–93; Partner, KPMG Peat Marwick, 1987–93, retd. Dir, Roffey Park Inst., 1978–90 (Vice Chm., 1983–85; Chm., 1985–87). *Recreations:* music, collecting antique gramophone records, magic (Mem., The Magic Circle). *Heir:* *b* David Christopher Hall [*b* 30 Dec. 1937; *m* 1st, 1962, Irene (marr. diss. 1987), *d* of William Duncan, Aberdeen; one *s* one *d*; 2nd, 1991, Annie Madelaine Renée Olivier, adopted *d* of late Bottemanne Raould]. *Address:* Carradale, 29 Embercourt Road, Thames Ditton, Surrey KT7 0LH. *T:* (020) 8398 2801.

HALL, Rear-Adm. Geoffrey Penrose Dickinson, CB 1973; DSC 1943; DL; Hydrographer of the Navy 1971–75; retired; *b* 19 July 1916; *er s* of late Major A. K. D. Hall and late Mrs P. M. Hall; *m* 1945, Mary Ogilvie Carlisle; two *s* one *d*. *Educ:* Haileybury. Served in American waters, 1935–37 and on Nyon Patrol during Spanish Civil War; joined surveying service, 1938, served in Indian Ocean until 1939 when transf. to minesweeping in Far East; hydrographic duties, home waters, Iceland, W Africa; navigational and minesweeping duties, Icelandic waters; transf. to Combined Ops, SE Asia; subseq. comd frigate, British Pacific Fleet; from 1947, hydrographic work: with RNZN, 1949–51; subseq. five comds i/c surveys at home and abroad; served ashore and in Atlantic, Indian Ocean, Antarctic waters (Cuthbert Peek Grant, RGS, for work in furtherance of oceanographical exploration); twice Asst Hydrographer; surveyed between S Africa and Iceland, 1965–67; Asst Dir (Naval), Hydrographic Dept, Taunton, 1970. Cadet 1934; Midshipman 1935; Sub-Lt 1938; Lieut 1939; Lt-Comdr 1945; Comdr 1953; Captain 1961; Rear-Adm. 1971. Pres., Hydrographic Soc., 1975. DL Lincs, 1982. *Publications:* Sailor's Luck (autobiog.), 1999; contribs to Nature, Deep Sea Research, Internat. Hydrographic Review, Navy International. *Recreation:* country pursuits. *Address:* Manby House, Manby, Louth, Lincs LN11 8UF. *T:* (01507) 327777. *Clubs:* Naval and Military, Royal Navy.

HALL, Prof. George Martin, PhD, DSc; FRCA; Foundation Professor of Anaesthesia, St George's Hospital Medical School, since 1992; *b* 14 May 1944; *s* of George Vincent Hall and Dora Hortensia Hall; *m* 1964, Marion Edith Burgin; one *d*. *Educ:* University Coll. Hosp. Med. Sch. (MB BS 1967; PhD 1976); DSc London, 1999. FRCA 1971. Royal Postgraduate Medical School: Sen. Lectr in Anaesthesia, 1977–85; Reader, 1985–89; Prof. of Clinical Anaesthesia, 1989–92. Hunterian Prof., RCS, 1983–89. *Publications:* How to Write a Paper, 1994, 2nd edn 1998; How to Survive in Anaesthesia, 1997; Short Practice of Anaesthesia, 1997; Diabetes: emergency and hospital management, 1999; Perioperative Care of the Eye Patient, 2000; How to Present at Meetings, 2001; res. papers on anaesthesia and physiology. *Recreations:* running, dog walking, supporting Staffordshire.

Address: Department of Anaesthesia and Intensive Care Medicine, St George's Hospital Medical School, SW17 0RE. *T:* (020) 8725 2615. *Club:* Farmers'.

HALL, Rev. Canon George Rumney, LVO 1999; Rector of the Sandringham Group of Parishes, since 1987; Domestic Chaplain, since 1987, Chaplain to The Queen, since 1989; *b* 7 Nov. 1937; *s* of John Hall; *m* 1965, Diana Lesley Brunning; one *s* one *d. Educ:* Brasted Place, Kent; Westcott House, Cambridge. Deacon 1962, priest 1963; Assistant Curate: St Philip's, Camberwell, 1962–65; Holy Trinity, Waltham Cross, 1965–67; Rector of Buckenham, Hassingham, Strumpshaw, dio. Norwich, 1967–74; Chaplain: St Andrew's Psychiatric Hosp., Norwich, 1967–72; HM Prison, Norwich, 1972–74; Vicar of Wymondham, 1974–87; RD of Humbleyard, 1986–87; Hon. Canon, Norwich Cathedral, 1987–; RD of Heacham and Rising, 1989–2001. Founder Mem., Wymondham Branch of Mind Day Centre; Mem. Bd, Cotman Housing Assoc., Norwich. *Recreations:* walking, reading, theatre, music. *Address:* The Rectory, Sandringham, Norfolk PE35 6EH. *T:* (01485) 540587.

HALL, Graham Joseph, CEng, FIEE; Chairman, Regional Development Agency for Yorkshire and the Humber (Yorkshire Forward), since 1998; *b* 12 Oct. 1943; *s* of Herbert and Phyllis Hall; *m* 1963, Pamela Wilmot; one *s* one *d. Educ:* Doncaster Technical Coll.; Rotherham Coll. of Tech. (DipEE 1967); Blackburn Coll. of Tech. CEng 1977; FIEE 1988. Commercial Dir, 1984–89, Divl Dir, Energy Supply, 1989–91, Yorkshire Electricity Bd; Gp Exec. Dir, 1991–97, Gp Ops Dir, 1997, Chief Exec., 1998–2001, Yorkshire Electricity Gp plc. Mem. Ct Dirs, Bank of England, 2001–. Chm., Yorks and the Humber Regl Council, CBI, 1997–99. FIMgt 1987. Hon. DEng Bradford, 1999. *Recreations:* gardening, golf. *Address:* Yorkshire Forward, Victoria House, 2 Victoria Place, Leeds LS11 5AE.

HALL, Harold Percival, CMG 1963; MBE 1947; Director of Studies, Royal Institute of Public Administration, 1974–85; *b* 9 Sept. 1913; *s* of late Major George Charles Hall; *m* 1939, Margery Hall, *d* of late Joseph Dickson; three *s* (including twin *s*). *Educ:* Portsmouth Grammar Sch.; Royal Military College, Sandhurst (Prize Cadet; King's India Cadet; Hockey Blue Cricket Cap). Commissioned Indian Army, 1933. Indian Political Service, 1937–47. Private Sec. to Resident, Central India States, 1937; Magistrate and Collector, Meerut, 1938–39. Military Service, 1938–43 (Major). Staff Coll., Quetta, 1941. Asst Political Agent, Loralai, 1943, Nasirabad, 1944; Dir, Food and Civil Supplies, and Dep. Sec., Revenue, Baluchistan, 1945–46; Principal, Colonial Office, 1947; Asst Sec. (Head of Pacific and Indian Ocean Dept), Colonial Office, 1955–62; Sec., Commonwealth Royal Comn on Fedn of Malaya's independence, 1956; Seconded to Office of UK Comr-Gen. for SE Asia, 1962–63; British Dep. High Comr for Eastern Malaysia, Kuching, Sarawak, 1963–64; Asst Sec., Colonial Office, 1965–66; Assistant Under-Secretary of State: Commonwealth Office, 1966–68; MoD, 1968–73. Mem. Governing Body, Sch. of Oriental and African Studies, 1971–74. *Recreation:* gardening. *Address:* Robina, The Chase, Ringwood, Dorset BH24 2AN. *T:* (01425) 479880.

HALL, Prof. Henry Edgar, FRS 1982; Emeritus Professor of Physics, University of Manchester, since 1995; *b* 1928; *s* of John Ainger Hall; *m* 1962, Patricia Anne Broadbent; two *s* one *d. Educ:* Latymer Upper Sch., Hammersmith; Emmanuel Coll., Cambridge. BA 1952; PhD 1956. At Royal Society Mond Laboratory, Cambridge, 1952–58; Senior Student, Royal Commission for the Exhibition of 1851, 1955–57; Research Fellow of Emmanuel Coll., 1955–58; Lecturer in Physics, 1958–61, Prof. of Physics, 1961–95, Univ. of Manchester. Simon Memorial Prize (with W. F. Vinen), 1963. Visiting Professor: Univ. of Western Australia, 1964; Univ. of Oregon, 1967–68; Cornell Univ., 1974, 1982–83; Univ. of Tokyo, 1985. *Publications:* Solid State Physics, 1974; papers in scientific journals. *Recreation:* mountain walking. *Address:* The Schuster Laboratory, The University, Manchester M13 9PL.

HALL, Air Vice-Marshal Hubert Desmond, CB 1979; CBE 1972; AFC 1963; FRAeS; RAF retd; *b* 3 June 1925; *s* of Charles William and Violet Victoria Kate Hall; *m* 1951, Mavis Dorothea (*née* Hopkins). *Educ:* Portsmouth Municipal Coll. Commissioned RAF, 1945; RAF Coll., Cranwell QFI, 1951–55; Flt Comdr, 9 Sqdn, 1955–56; 232 OCU Gaydon, Sqdn Ldr, Medium Bomber Force; Instructor, Wing Comdr 1962; 3 Group Headquarters (Training), 1963–65; Air Warfare Coll., 1965; commanded No 57 Sqdn (Victors), 1966–68; Gp Captain Nuclear Operations SHAPE HQ, 1968–71; comd RAF Waddington, 1971–73; Overseas Coll. of Defence Studies India, 1974; MoD: Director (Air Cdre) of Establishments, RAF, 1975–77; Air Comdr Malta, 1977–79; Air Vice-Marshal 1979; Defence Advr, Canberra, 1980–82. Pres., ACT, Australian-Britain Soc., 1993–. Mem., St John Council, ACT, 1983–. KStJ 1992. Queen's Commendation, 1957. *Recreations:* gardening, reading. *Address:* 7 Richardson Street, Garran, ACT 2605, Australia. *Club:* Royal Air Force.

HALL, Prof. James Snowdon, CBE 1976; Professor of Agriculture, Glasgow University, and Principal, West of Scotland Agricultural College, 1966–80; *b* 28 Jan. 1919; *s* of Thomas Blackburn Hall and Mary Milburn Hall; *m* 1942, Mary Smith; one *s* one *d. Educ:* Univ. of Durham (BSc Hons). FRAgS, FIBiol. Asst Technical Adviser, Northumberland War Agric. Exec. Commn, 1941–44; Lectr in Agriculture, Univ. of Newcastle upon Tyne, 1944–54; Principal, Cumbria Coll. of Agriculture and Forestry, 1954–66. *Address:* 26 Earls Way, Doonfoot, Ayr KA7 4HE. *T:* (01292) 441162.

HALL, Janice Elizabeth, (Jan), OBE 1996; Partner, Spencer Stuart, since 1997; *b* 1 June 1957; *d* of John Brian Hall and Jean Hall; *m* 1996, Dr David Costain; one *s. Educ:* St Anne's Coll., Oxford (MA Hons). Mktg Manager, ICI, 1979–83; Chm. and Chief Exec., Coley Porter Bell, 1983–93; Eur. Chief Exec., GGT Gp, 1994–97. Senior non-executive Director: First Choice Holidays, 1994–; Veos, 1998–. Advr on CS Appointments. Hon. Prof., Warwick Business Sch., 1995– (Mem., Bd, 1993–). Mem. Council, IoD, 1991–. *Address:* 37 St John's Wood Road, NW8 8RA. *T:* (020) 7286 5740.

HALL, Her Honour Jean Graham, LLM (London); a Circuit Judge (formerly Deputy Chairman, South-East London Quarter Sessions), 1971–89; *b* 26 March 1917; *d* of Robert Hall and Alison (*née* Graham). *Educ:* Inverkeithing Sch., Fife; St Anne's Coll., Sanderstead; London Sch. of Economics. Gold Medal (Elocution and Dramatic Art), Incorporated London Acad. of Music, 1935; Teacher's Dipl., Guildhall Sch. of Music, 1937; Social Science Cert., London Sch. of Economics, 1937; LLB (Hons), London, 1950. FCIArb 1990. Club Leader and subseq. Sub-Warden, Birmingham Univ. Settlement, 1937–41; Sec., Eighteen Plus (an experiment in youth work), 1941–44; Probation Officer, Hants, subseq. Croydon, 1945–51. Called to Bar, Gray's Inn, 1951. Metropolitan Stipendiary Magistrate, 1965–71. Pres., Gray's Inn Debating Soc., 1953; Hon. Sec., Soc. of Labour Lawyers, 1954–64; Pres., British Soc. of Criminology, 1971–74. Chm. Departmental Cttee on Statutory Maintenance Limits, 1966–68. Contested (Lab) East Surrey, 1955. FRSA 1994; Mem., Academy of Experts, 1991. Hon. LLD Lincoln, USA, 1979. *Publications:* Towards a Family Court, 1971; (jtly) Child Abuse: procedure and evidence, 1978, 3rd edn 1993; (jtly) The Expert Witness, 1992, 3rd edn 2001; (jtly) Crimes Against Children, 1992; (jtly) Haldane: statesman, lawyer, philosopher, 1996; (jtly) A Perfect Judge, 1999; (jtly) Oscar Wilde: the tragedy of being earnest, 2001. *Recreations:* travel, congenial debate, writing. *Club:* University Women's.

HALL, Jean Morag; *see* Rankine, J. M.

HALL, Joan Valerie, CBE 1990; Member, Central Transport Consultative Committee, 1981–86; *b* 31 Aug. 1935; *d* of late Robert Percy Hall and Winifred Emily Umbers. *Educ:* Queen Margaret's Sch., Escrick, York; Ashridge House of Citizenship. Contested (C) Barnsley, 1964 and 1966. MP (C) Keighley, 1970–Feb. 1974; PPS to Minister of State for Agriculture, Fisheries and Food, 1972–74. Vice-Chm., Greater London Young Conservatives, 1964. Chm., Sudan Studies Soc. of UK, 1989–92. Mem. Council, Univ. of Buckingham (formerly University Coll. Buckingham), 1977–. *Address:* 7 Greenland, High Hoyland, Barnsley, South Yorks S75 4AZ. *T:* (01226) 380117.

HALL, Sir John; *see* Hall, Sir F. J. F.

HALL, John; *see* Hall, W. J.

HALL, Sir John, Kt 1991; Chairman: Cameron Hall Developments Ltd, 1973–93; Newcastle United Football Club, 1992–97; a Director, Bank of England, 1996–98; *b* 21 March 1933; *m* Mae; one *s* one *d. Educ:* Bedlington Grammar Sch. Chartered surveyor. Developed MetroCentre (shopping and leisure complex), Gateshead, 1985. Mem., Millennium Commn, 1994–2000. Gordon Grand Fellow, Yale Univ., 1991. Hon. DCL: Newcastle upon Tyne, 1988; Durham, 1995. NE Business Man of the Year, 1987. *Address:* Wynyard Hall, Billingham, Cleveland TS22 5NF.

HALL, John Anthony Sanderson, DFC 1943; QC 1967; FCIArb 1982; *b* 25 Dec. 1921; *s* of late Rt Hon. W. Glenvil Hall, PC, MP, and late Rachel Ida Hall (*née* Sanderson); *m* 1st, Nora Ella Hall (*née* Crowe) (marr. diss. 1974); one *s* two *d*; 2nd, Elizabeth Mary, widow of Alan Riley Maynard. *Educ:* Leighton Park Sch.; Trinity Hall, Cambridge (MA). Served RAF, 1940–46, 85 Squadron and 488 (NZ) Squadron (Squadron Leader; DFC and Bar). Called to Bar, Inner Temple, 1948, Master of the Bench, 1975; Western Circuit; Dep. Chm., Hants Quarter Sessions, 1967; Recorder of Swindon, 1971; a Recorder of the Crown Court, 1972–78. Member: Gen. Council of the Bar, 1964–68, 1970–74; Senate of the Four Inns of Court, 1966–68, 1970–74; Council of Legal Educn, 1970–74. Mem., 1972–79, Chm., 1978–79, UK Deleg. to Consultative Cttee, Bars and Law Socs of EEC; Mem., Foreign Compensation Commn, 1983–91. Dir Gen., Internat. Fedn of Producers of Phonograms and Videograms, 1979–81; Dir, City Disputes Panel, 1994–99. Governor, St Catherine's Sch., Bramley, 1967–88. *Recreation:* fly fishing. *Address:* 2 Dr Johnson's Buildings, Temple, EC4Y 7AY; Swallows, Blewbury, Oxon. *Club:* Royal Air Force.

HALL, Ven. John Barrie; Archdeacon of Salop, since 1998; *b* 27 May 1941; *s* of Arthur Cyril Hall and Beatrice Hall (*née* Clark); *m* 1963, Kay Deakin; three *s. Educ:* Salisbury and Wells Theol Coll. Self-employed in garage and caravan sales until 1982; ordained deacon, 1984, priest, 1985; Curate, St Edward, Cheddleton, 1984–88; Vicar, Rocester, then Rocester and Croxden with Hollington, 1988–98. Hon. Canon of Lichfield Cathedral, 1999. Chm., Shropshire Historical Churches Trust, 1998–. *Recreations:* reading, a little walking, most sports (now watching only). *Address:* Tong Vicarage, Shifnal, Shropshire TF11 8PW. *T:* (01902) 372622.

HALL, Sir John (Bernard), 3rd Bt *cr* 1919; Chairman, The Nikko Bank (UK) plc, 1992–95 (Managing Director, 1990–92); *b* 20 March 1932; *s* of Lieut-Col Sir Douglas Montgomery Bernard Hall, DSO, 2nd Bt, and Ina Nancie Walton (Nancie Lady Hall), *d* of late Col John Edward Mellor, CB (she *m* 2nd, 1962, Col Peter J. Bradford, DSO, MC, TD, who *d* 1990; she *d* 1998); *S* father, 1962; *m* 1957, Delia Mary (*d* 1997), *d* of late Lieut-Col J. A. Innes, DSO; one *s* two *d*; *m* 1998, Diana Joan Tower, *d* of late Surg.-Comdr E. R. Sorley and *widow* of Peter Ravenshear. *Educ:* Eton; Trinity Coll., Oxford (MA). FCIB 1976. Lieut, Royal Fusiliers (RARO). J. Henry Schroder Wagg & Co. Ltd, formerly J. Henry Schröder & Co., 1955–73 (Dir, 1967–73); Director: The Antofagasta (Chili) and Bolivia Rly Co. Ltd, 1967–73; Bank of America International, 1974–82; Man. Dir, European Brazilian Bank, subseq. Eurobraz, 1983–89 (Dir, 1976–89); a Vice-Pres., Bank of America NT & SA, 1982–90; Chm., Assoc. of British Consortium Banks, 1985–86. Chm., Anglo-Colombian Soc., 1978–81. Member: St Alban's Diocesan Synod and Bd of Finance, 1992–2000; Bishop's Stortford Deanery Synod, 1991–2000; Albury PCC, 1990–2000. FRGS 1988; FRSA 1989. Mem., Lord Mayor of London's No 1 Cttee, 1993–95; Liveryman, Clothworkers' Co., 1957 (Mem., Court of Assts, 1987–; Master, 1999–2000). Mem. Court, Univ. of Leeds, 1994–2000. *Recreations:* travel, fishing. *Heir: s* David Bernard Hall, *b* 12 May 1961. *Address:* Deanery Lodge, Church Walk, Hadleigh, Ipswich, Suffolk IP7 5ED. *T:* (01473) 828966. *Clubs:* Boodle's, Lansdowne, City of London.

HALL, John Peirs; Managing Director, Brewin Dolphin Holdings plc, since 1987; *b* 26 June 1940; *s* of Robert Noel Hall and Doreen Cecelia Hall (*née* Russell); *m* 1965, Sarah Gillian Page; four *s. Educ:* Stowe. Reid Hurst-Brown, Stockbrokers, 1959–65; joined Wontner Renwick & Francis, 1965, which became Wontner Dolphin & Francis, 1970, then Brewin Dolphin, 1974; Partner, 1967; Chm., Mgt Cttee, 1980. Freeman, City of London, 1970; Mem., Ct of Assts, Co. of Merchant Taylors, 1993–. *Recreations:* sailing, golf, breeding British White cattle. *Address:* Chalkhouse Green Farm, Kidmore End, near Reading RG4 9AZ. *T:* (0118) 972 3631. *Clubs:* City of London; Royal Yacht Squadron, Island Sailing; Huntercombe Golf.

HALL, Rev. Canon John Robert; General Secretary, Church of England Board of Education and National Society for Promoting Religious Education, since 1998; *b* 13 March 1949; *e s* of Ronald John Hall, FCIB, FCIS and late Katie Margaret Brock Hall (*née* Walker). *Educ:* St Dunstan's Coll.; St Chad's Coll., Durham (BA Hons Theol.); Cuddesdon Theol Coll. Head of RE, Malet Lambert High Sch., Hull, 1971–73; ordained deacon, 1975, priest, 1976; Curate, St John the Divine, Kennington, 1975–78; Priest-in-charge, All Saints', S Wimbledon, 1978–84; Vicar, St Peter's, Streatham, 1984–92; Dir of Educn, Dio. Blackburn, 1992–98; Residentiary Canon, Blackburn Cathedral, 1994–98, Canon Emeritus, 2000 (Hon. Canon, 1992–94, 1998–2000); Examng Chaplain to Bp of Southwark, 1988–92. Member: Gen. Synod of C of E, 1984–92; C of E Bd of Educn, 1991–92; Lancs Educn Cttee, 1992–98; Council, National Soc., 1997–98; Gen. Teaching Council, 2000–. Chm., Fedn of Catholic Priests, 1991–94. Mem. Council, Sch. of St Mary and St Anne, Abbots Bromley, 1992–; Member, Governing Body: Urban Learning Foundn, 1998–; Canterbury Christ Church UC, 1999–. Trustee, St Gabriel's Trust, 1998–. Fellow, Midland Div., Woodard Corp., 1992–. *Publications:* (contrib.) Distinctiveness in Church Schools, 1998; contrib. Church Times, TES, Parly Brief, Guardian, C of E Newspaper. *Recreations:* music, British political history. *Address:* 25 Goodenough Road, Wimbledon, SW19 3QW. *T:* (020) 8543 7428; (office) Church House, Great Smith Street, Westminster, SW1P 3NZ. *T:* (020) 7898 1500. *Club:* Athenæum.

HALL, Dr John Tristan Dalton; University Librarian, University of Durham, since 1989; *b* 28 Oct. 1945; *m* 1970, Inge Lise Lindqvist; one *s* two *d. Educ:* Lady Lumley's Sch.,

Pickering; Univ. of Manchester (BA 1968; PhD 1977); MA Cantab 1989. Asst Librarian, John Rylands Univ. Library of Manchester, 1971–78; Sub-Librarian (Special Collections), Edinburgh Univ. Library, 1978–86; Dep. Librarian, Cambridge Univ. Library, 1986–89; Fellow, Darwin Coll., Cambridge, 1987–89. *Publications:* Manuscript Treasures in Edinburgh University Library: an album of illustrations, 1980; The Tounis College: an anthology of Edinburgh University student journals 1823–1923, 1985; articles and reviews in learned jls. *Recreations:* music, pottery, gardening. *Address:* 8 Springfield Park, Durham DH1 4LS.

HALL, Jonathan David D.; *see* Durham Hall.

HALL, Maj.-Gen. Jonathan Michael Francis Cooper, CB 1998; OBE 1987; Lieutenant Governor, Royal Hospital, Chelsea, since 1997; Member, HM Body Guard of Honourable Corps of Gentlemen-at-Arms, since 1999; *b* 10 Aug. 1944; *s* of Charles Richard Hall and Rosemary Hall (*née* Beckwith); *m* 1968, Sarah Linda Hudson; two *d*. *Educ:* Taunton Sch.; RMA Sandhurst. Commissioned 3rd Carabiniers, 1965; Staff Coll., 1977; commanded Royal Scots Dragoon Guards, 1984–86 and 12th Armd Bde, 1988–90; Higher Command and Staff Course, 1988; Mem., RCDS, 1991; Dep. Mil. Sec., MoD(A), 1992–93; DRAC, 1994; GOC Scotland, and Gov., Edinburgh Castle, 1995–97. Colonel Commandant: RAVC, 1995–2001; Scottish Div., 1995–97; Col, Royal Scots Dragoon Guards, 1998–. FIMgt 1996. Hon. Associate Mem., BVA, 1996. OStJ 1997. *Recreations:* country, music, tennis, travel. *Address:* Home HQ, Royal Scots Dragoon Guards, The Castle, Edinburgh EH1 2YT. *T:* (0131) 310 5100/5101. *Clubs:* Cavalry and Guards (Mem., Gen. Cttee), MCC; Caledonian, Royal Scots (Edinburgh); Woodroffe's.

HALL, Judith Myfanwy Sarah, (Mrs A. Becker); Editor, BBC Homes & Antiques magazine, since 1994; Editor-in-Chief, BBC Good Homes magazine, since 1997; *b* 23 July 1947; *d* of late Norman Alfred Hall and of Vera May Hall (*née* Harris); *m* 1984, Andrew Becker; one *s*. *Educ:* Eltham Hill Grammar Sch. for Girls; Warwick Univ. Editl Asst, Everyman's Liby, 1968–71; Asst Fiction Ed., Woman's Weekly, 1971–74; Fiction Ed., 1974–76, Features Ed., 1976–80, Woman's Jl; Deputy Ed., Woman's World, 1980–82; Dep. Ed., 1982–84, Ed., 1984–87, Woman's Realm; Editor, Woman's Weekly, 1987–92; freelance journalist and TV script editor, 1992–94. Editor of Year, Specialist Interest Magazines, BSME, 1995. *Recreations:* family, theatre, reading, cinema, gardening. *Address:* BBC Worldwide, 80 Wood Lane, W12 0TT. *T:* (020) 8433 3483. *Club:* Academy.

HALL, Julian; His Honour Judge Julian Hall; a Circuit Judge, since 1986; Resident Judge, Northampton Combined Court Centre, since 2000; *b* 13 Jan. 1939; *s* of late Dr Stephen Hall, FRCP and Dr Mary Hall, Boarstall Tower, Bucks; *m* 1st, 1968, M. Rosalind Perry (marr. diss. 1988); one *s* one *d*; 2nd, 1989, Ingrid Cecilia, *er d* of late Rev. Canon Ronald Lunt, MC. *Educ:* Eton (Scholar); Christ Church, Oxford (Scholar; MA); Trinity Coll., Dublin (LLB). ARCM (flute). Industrial Chemist, Shell Internat. Chemical Co., 1961–63. Called to the Bar, Gray's Inn, 1966; in practice in Common Law Chambers on Northern Circuit, Manchester, 1966–86; Standing Prosecuting Counsel to Inland Revenue, Northern Circuit, 1985–86; a Recorder, 1982–86. Tutor judge, Judicial Studies Bd, 1989–93. Chm., Northants Family Mediation Service, 1995–2000; Pres., Mental Health Rev. Tribunals, 1997–. *Recreation:* making music, in orchestras, choirs and at home. *Address:* c/o Crown and County Courts, 85–87 Lady's Lane, Northampton NN1 3HQ. *T:* (01604) 470400.

See also C. E. Henderson.

HALL, Prof. Laurance David, PhD; FRS(Can) 1982; CChem, FRSC, FCIC; (first) Herchel Smith Professor of Medicinal Chemistry, University of Cambridge, since 1984, and Professorial Fellow, Emmanuel College, since 1987; *b* 18 March 1938; *s* of Daniel William Hall and Elsie Ivy Hall; *m* 1962, Winifred Margaret (*née* Golding); twin *s* two *d*. *Educ:* Leyton County High Sch.; Bristol Univ. (BSc 1959; PhD 1962); MA Cantab 1990. FCIC 1973; FRSC 1985. Post-doctoral Fellow, Ottawa Univ., 1962–63; Dept of Chemistry, Univ. of British Columbia: Instr II, 1963–64; Asst Prof., 1964–69; Associate Prof., 1969–73; Prof., 1973–84. Alfred P. Sloan Foundn Res. Fellow, 1971–73; Canada Council Killam Res. Fellow, 1982–84. Lederle Prof., RSM, 1984; Vis. Professor: Univ. of NSW, 1967; Univ. of Cape Town, 1974; Northwestern Univ., Evanston, Ill, 1982. Lectures include: Van Cleave, Univ. of Saskatchewan, Regina, 1983; Cecil Green, Galveston Univ., Texas, 1983; Brotherton, Leeds Univ., 1985; Philip Morris, Richmond Univ., Va, 1985; Scott, Cambridge Univ., 1986; Larmor, Cambridge Philosophical Soc., 1986; C. B. Purves, McGill Univ., 1987; Eduard Faber Med. Physics, Univ. of Chicago, 1990; Friday Evening Discourse, Royal Instn, London, 1991, 1997; Merck Frosst, Montreal, 1994; public, 1995, Henderson Trust, 1996, RSChem; Horizon, Cleveland Clinic Foundn, Ohio, 1995; Harry Hallam Meml, Swansea, 1998. Fellow, Cambridge Philosophical Soc. Hon. DSc Bristol, 2000. Jacob Bielly Faculty Res. Prize, Univ. of BC, 1974; Tate and Lyle Award for Carbohydrate Chemistry, Chemical Soc., 1974; Merck, Sharpe and Dohme Lecture Award, Chemical Inst. of Canada, 1975; Corday Morgan Medal and Prize, Chemical Soc., 1976; Barringer Award, Spectroscopy Soc. of Canada, 1981; Interdisciplinary Award, RSC, 1988; Chemical Analysis and Instrumentation Award, RSC, 1990. *Publications:* over 500 research pubns. *Recreations:* music, travel, research. *Address:* Herchel Smith Laboratory for Medicinal Chemistry, Robinson Way, Cambridge CB2 2PZ. *T:* (01223) 336805, *Fax:* (01223) 336748.

HALL, Sir Laurence Charles B.; *see* Brodie-Hall.

HALL, Lee; dramatist; *b* 20 Sept. 1966; *s* of Peter and Sylvia Hall. *Educ:* Benfield Comprehensive Sch., Newcastle; Fitzwilliam Coll., Cambridge (BA English Lit.). Writer in Residence: Live Th., Newcastle upon Tyne, 1997–98; RSC, 1998–99. *Plays:* I Luv You Jimmy Spud (radio), 1995 (Sony Award); Spoonface Steinberg (radio), 1996; The Student Prince (TV), 1996; Mr Puntila and his Man Matti (trans.), Almeida, 1997; Cooking with Elvis, Live Th., transf. Whitehall, 2000; A Servant to Two Masters, RSC at Young Vic, 2000; *films:* Billy Elliot, 2000; Gabriel and Me, 2001. *Publications:* Spoonface Steinberg and other plays, 1996; Cooking with Elvis, 1999; A Servant to Two Masters (new adaptation), 2000; Pinocchio (new adaptation), 2000; Billy Elliot (screenplay), 2001. *Recreations:* cooking, reading, sleeping. *Address:* c/o Rod Hall Agency, 7 Goodge Place, W1T 4SF.

HALL, Margaret Dorothy, OBE 1973; RDI 1974; Head of Design, British Museum, 1964–2001; *b* 22 Jan. 1936; *d* of Thomas Robson Hall and Millicent (*née* Britton). *Educ:* Bromley County Grammar Sch.; Bromley College of Art; Royal College of Art (DesRCA). Design Assistant: Casson, Condor & Partners, 1960–61; Westwood Piet & Partners, 1961–63; Dennis Lennon & Partners, 1963–64; British Museum, 1964–2001: exhibitions designed include: Masterpieces of Glass, 1968; Museum of Mankind, 1970; Treasures of Tutankhamun, 1972; Nomad and City, 1976; Captain Cook in the South Seas, 1979. Designer, Manuscripts and Men, National Portrait Gallery, 1969. Chm., Gp of Designers/Interpreters in Museums, 1978–81; Mem. Council, RSA, 1984–89. FCSD (FSIAD 1975–90; MSIAD 1968) (Chm., SIAD Salaried Designers Cttee, 1979–81). Chm., Wynkyn de Worde Soc., 1982. Governor, Ravensbourne College of Art, 1973–78. FRSA 1974; FMA 1983. *Publication:* On Display: a grammar of museum exhibition design, 1987. *Club:* Double Crown (Pres., 1998).

HALL, Dr Marie Boas, FBA 1994; Reader in History of Science and Technology, University of London, 1964–80, Reader Emeritus, since 1980; *b* 18 Oct. 1919; *d* of Ralph Philip Boas and Louise (*née* Schutz); *m* 1959, Alfred Rupert Hall, *qv*. *Educ:* Radcliffe Coll. (AB 1940; MA 1942); Cornell Univ. (PhD 1949). Assistant Professor of History: Univ. of Mass, 1949–52; Brandeis Univ., 1952–57; Associate Prof., UCLA, 1957–61; Prof. of Hist. and Logic of Sci., Indiana Univ., 1961–63; Sen. Lectr, Imperial Coll., Univ. of London, 1963–64. Guggenheim Fellow, 1955–56. Mem., Liby Cttee, Royal Soc., 1983–93. Fellow, Amer. Acad. of Arts and Scis, 1955–63. Mem., Académie internat. d'histoire des sciences, 1960; Sec., Hist. of Science Soc., 1953–57. Pfizer Award, 1959, (jtly) Sarton Medal, 1981, Hist. of Science Soc. *Publications:* The Establishment of the Mechanical Philosophy, 1952, 2nd edn 1981; Robert Boyle and Seventeenth Century Chemistry, 1958; The Scientific Renaissance 1450–1630, 1962, repr. 1994; Robert Boyle on Natural Philosophy, 1965; All Scientists Now: the Royal Society in the Nineteenth Century, 1984; Promoting Experimental Learning: experiment and the Royal Society 1660–1727, 1991; The Library and Archives of the Royal Society, 1992; with A. R. Hall: Unpublished Scientific Papers of Isaac Newton, 1962; A Brief History of Science, 1962, 2nd edn 1988; The Correspondence of Henry Oldenburg, 13 vols, 1965–86; contribs to major history of science jls. *Address:* 14 Ball Lane, Tackley, via Kidlington, Oxon OX5 3AG. *T:* (01869) 331257.

HALL, Dr Michael George, FRS 1993; scientific consultant, since 1991; *b* 16 Oct. 1931; *s* of George Albert Victor Hall and Mabel Hall (*née* Gittins); *m* 1964, Merete Blatz; one *s* one *d*. *Educ:* Sydney Grammar Sch.; Univ. of Sydney (BSc, BE, MEngSc, PhD). Research in Fluid Dynamics at Aerodynamics Dept, RAE, 1958–91, retired 1991; sabbatical at Dept of Mechanics, Johns Hopkins Univ., 1966–67. Founder-Director, Hall C. F. D. Ltd, 1991–. *Publications:* contribs on fluid dynamics to sci. and tech. jls. *Recreations:* ski-ing, walking, do-it-yourself. *Address:* 8 Dene Lane, Farnham, Surrey GU10 3PW. *T:* (01252) 793283.

HALL, Michael Kilgour H.; *see* Harrison-Hall.

HALL, Prof. Michael Robert Pritchard, FRCP, FRCPE; Professor of Geriatric Medicine, University of Southampton, 1970–87, now Emeritus; Hon. Consultant Physician, Southampton University Hospitals, 1970–87; *b* 13 May 1922; *s* of Augustus Henry Hall, MC and Elizabeth Jane Lord; *m* 1947, Joan Jardine, (Eileen), *d* of Dr John McCartney; two *d*. *Educ:* Shrewsbury Sch.; Worcester Coll., Oxford (MA, BM, BCh). FRCP 1970; FRCPE 1971. Served War, Indian Army, 1941–46 (Temp. Captain). Consultant Physician, Newcastle upon Tyne Gen. Hosp., 1962–70; Hon. Lecturer in Medicine: Univ. of Durham, 1962–63; Univ. of Newcastle upon Tyne, 1963–70. Auckland Savings Bank Vis. Prof., Univ. of Auckland, NZ, 1974; Vis. Lecturer: Dalhousie Univ., NS, 1979; (Tayside Health Bd), Univ. of Dundee, 1981; Examr, Dip. of Geriatric Medicine, RCP, 1985–91. Chairman: British Soc. for Res. on Ageing, 1976–79; Assoc. of Professors of Geriatric Medicine, 1985–86; European Cttee, Sandoz Foundn of Gerontological Research, 1986–90 (Mem., 1990–92); Member: DHSS Cttee for Review of Medicines, 1976–82; Fitness and Health Adv. Gp to Sports Council, 1977–90; Southampton and SW Hants CHC, 1997–2001 (Chm., 1999–2001); Governing Body and Exec. Cttee, Age Concern (England), 1975–77 and 1980–83; Council, Internat. Assoc. of Gerontology, 1981–85; President, Tissue Viability Soc., 1983–84; Bath Res. Inst. for Care of the Elderly, 1987–94; Chm., Age Concern (Hants), 1992–95; Life Vice-Pres., Northumberland Cheshire Home, 1970; Vice-Pres., Research into Ageing (formerly British Foundn for Age Res.), 1998– (Trustee and Gov., 1979–97); Member: NEC, Abbeyfield Soc., 1989–93 (Chm., Extra Care Cttee, 1989–90; Chm., Care and Develt Cttee, 1990–93); Council, RSAS, 1989–96; BMA, 1953–; British Geriatrics Soc., 1963– (President's Medal, 1992); Trustee: McCarthy Foundn, 1987–96; Brendoncare Foundn, 1999– (Vice-Chm., 1986–99). FRSocMed 1991. *Publications:* Medical Care of the Elderly, 1978, 3rd edn 1993; chapters and contribs to various books on aspects of ageing and geriatric medicine; articles and papers in med. jls. *Recreations:* fly-fishing, golf, gardening. *Address:* Peartree Cottage, Emery Down, Lyndhurst, Hants SO43 7FH. *T:* (023) 8028 2541. *Club:* MCC.

HALL, Michael Thomas; MP (Lab) Weaver Vale, since 1997 (Warrington South, 1992–97); *b* 20 Sept. 1952; *s* of late Thomas and Veronica Hall; *m* 1975, Lesley Evelyn Gosling; one *s*. *Educ:* Padgate Coll. of Higher Educn (Teachers' Cert. 1977); N Cheshire Coll., Victoria Univ., Manchester (BEd Hons 1987). Scientific Asst, ICI Ltd, 1969–73; teaching history and physical educn, Bolton, 1977–85; support teacher, Halton Community Assessment Team, 1985–92. Councillor, Warrington Borough Council, 1979–93: Chairman: Envmtl Health Cttee, 1981–84; Finance Sub-Cttee, 1984–85; Policy and Resources Cttee, 1985–92; Dep. Leader of Council, 1984–85, Leader 1985–92. Member, Parish Council: Great Sankey, 1979–83; Birchwood and Croft, 1983–87; Poulton with Fearnhead, 1987–93. PPS to Ldr of the House of Commons and Pres. of the Council, 1997–98; an Asst Govt Whip, 1998–2001; PPS to Sec. of State for Health, 2001–. Member: Modernisation Select Cttee, 1997–98; Public Accounts Cttee, 1992–97; Chm., Labour Party Back Bench Educn Cttee, 1996–97. *Recreations:* tennis, reading, cooking. *Address:* House of Commons, SW1A 0AA.

HALL, Patrick; MP (Lab) Bedford, since 1997; *b* 20 Oct. 1951. *Educ:* Bedford Modern Sch.; Birmingham Univ.; Oxford Poly. Local Govt Planning Officer; Bedford Town Centre Co-ordinator. Mem., Bedfordshire CC, 1989–97. Contested (Lab) Bedfordshire N, 1992. *Address:* House of Commons, SW1A 0AA; 5 Mill Street, Bedford MK40 3EX.

HALL, Rt Rev. Peter; *see* Hall, Rt Rev. A. P.

HALL, Peter Dalton, CB 1986; Under Secretary, Solicitor's Office, Board of Inland Revenue, 1979–86; *b* 1 Aug. 1924; *s* of Edward and Kathleen Hall; *m* 1952, Stella Iris Breen; four *s* two *d*. *Educ:* Rishworth Sch.; St Catharine's Coll., Cambridge (exhibnr; MA, LLB). Served War of 1939–45, Intelligence Corps; seconded to AIF and served with US Forces in New Guinea and Philippines; GOC Commendation; Major. Called to the Bar, Middle Temple, 1951; entered Inland Revenue Solicitor's Office, 1952. Mem., Bar Council 1967–70; Clerk to City of London Comrs, 1988–99. Parish Councillor, 1967–. Non-exec. Dir, Milton Keynes HA, 1992–93. Freeman, City of London, 1993. *Recreations:* gardening, music, conservation. *Address:* Apple Tree Cottage, Woughton-on-the-Green, Bucks MK6 3BE. *T:* and *Fax:* (01908) 679504.

HALL, Sir Peter (Edward), KBE 1993; CMG 1987; HM Diplomatic Service, retired; *b* 26 July 1938; *s* of late Bernard Hall and Monica Hall (*née* Blackbourn); *m* 1972, Marnie Kay; one *s* one *d*. *Educ:* Portsmouth Grammar Sch.; HM Services (Jt Services Sch. for Linguists); Pembroke Coll., Cambridge (Scholar; 1st Cl. parts I and II, Mediaeval and Modern Langs Tripos). Foreign Office, 1961–63; 3rd Sec., Warsaw, 1963–66; 2nd Sec., New Delhi, 1966–69; FCO (European Integration Dept), 1969–72; 1st Sec., UK Permanent Representation to EEC, 1972–76; Asst Head, Financial Relations Dept, FCO,

1976–77; Counsellor, Caracas, 1977–78; Hd of British Information Services, NY, 1978–83 and Counsellor, British Embassy, Washington, 1981–83; Dir of Res., FCO, 1983–86; Under Sec., Cabinet Office, 1986–88; Vis. Schol., Stanford Univ., 1988–89; Ambassador to Yugoslavia, 1989–92; Advr to Lord Carrington, 1992, Lord Owen, 1992–93, Peace Conf. on Yugoslavia; Ambassador to Argentina, 1993–97. *Recreations:* reading (A. Powell, Byron), music (Rolling Stones, Mozart). *Address:* 13 Raby Place, Bathwick, Bath BA2 4EH.

HALL, Prof. Peter Gavin, DPhil; FRS 2000; Professor of Statistics, Australian National University, since 1988; *b* 20 Nov. 1951; *s* of William Holman Hall and Ruby Violet (*née* Payne-Scott); *m* 1977, Jeannie Jean Chien Loh. *Educ:* Univ. of Sydney (BSc 1st Cl. Hons); Australian Nat. Univ. (MSc 1976); Brasenose Coll., Oxford (DPhil 1976). Lectr in Stats, Univ. of Melbourne, 1976–78; Australian National University: Lectr in Stats, 1978–82; Sen. Lectr, 1983–85; Reader, 1986–88. FIMS 1984; FAA 1987; Fellow, Amer. Statistical Assoc., 1996. Dr *hc* Univ. Catholique de Louvain, 1997. Medal, Australian Mathematical Soc., 1986; Rollo Davison Prize, Cambridge Univ., 1986; Lyle Medal, 1989, Hannan Medal, 1995, Australian Acad. of Sci.; Pitman Medal, Statistical Soc. of Australia, 1990. *Publications:* (with C. C. Heyde) Martingale Limit Theory and its Applications, 1980; Rates of Convergence in the Central Limit Theorem, 1982; Introduction to the Theory of Coverage Processes, 1988; The Bootstrap and Edgeworth Expansion, 1992; contrib. numerous papers. *Recreations:* photography, interests in railway and aviation. *Address:* Centre for Mathematics and its Applications, John Dedman Mathematical Sciences Building # 27, Australian National University, Canberra, ACT 0200, Australia.

HALL, Sir Peter (Geoffrey), Kt 1998; FBA 1983; Professor of Planning, 1992–99, and Director, School of Public Policy, 1995–99, University College London, now Professor Emeritus; *b* 19 March 1932; *s* of Arthur Vickers Hall and Bertha Hall (*née* Keefe); *m* 1st, 1962, Carla Maria Wartenberg (marr. diss. 1966); 2nd, 1967, Magdalena Mróz; no *c*. *Educ:* Blackpool Grammar Sch.; St Catharine's Coll., Cambridge Univ. (MA, PhD; Hon. Fellow, 1988). Asst Lectr, 1957, Lectr, 1960, Birkbeck Coll., Univ. of London; Reader in Geography with ref. to Regional Planning, London Sch. of Economics and Political Science, 1966; University of Reading: Prof. of Geography, 1968–89, now Prof. Emeritus; Head, Dept of Geog., 1968–80; Chm., Sch. of Planning Studies, 1971–77 and 1983–86; Dean of Urban and Regional Studies, 1975–78; Prof. of City and Regl Planning, 1980–92, and Dir, Inst. of Urban and Regl Develt, 1989–92, Univ. of Calif, Berkeley, now Prof. Emeritus. Member: SE Regional Planning Council, 1966–79; Nature Conservancy, 1968–72; Transport and Road Research Laboratory Adv. Cttee on Transport, 1973–78; Environmental Bd, 1975–79; SSRC, 1975–80 (Chm., Planning Cttee); EEC Expert Gp on New Tendencies of Social and Economic Develt, 1975–77; Standing Adv. Cttee on Trunk Road Assessment, 1978–80; DETR Urban Task Force, 1998–99; Exec. Cttee, Regional Studies Assoc., 1967–78 (Hon. Jl Editor, 1967–78); Exec. Cttee, Fabian Soc., 1964–80 (Chm. 1971–72); Chm., Town and Country Planning Assoc., 1995–99. Special Advr, Sec. of State for Environment, 1991–94. Governor, Centre for Environmental Studies, 1975–80. Chm., Tawney Soc., 1983–85 (Vice-Chm., 1982–83). FRGS; Hon. RTPI, 1975. Hon. DSS Birmingham, 1989; Hon. PhD Lund Univ., Sweden, 1992; Hon. LittD: Sheffield, 1995; Newcastle, 1995; Hon. DEng Technical Univ. of Nova Scotia, 1996; Hon. DArts Oxford Brookes, 1997; Hon. LLD Reading, 1999. Editor, Built Environment, 1977–. *Publications:* The Industries of London, 1962; London 2000, 1963 (reprint, 1969); Labour's New Frontiers, 1964; (ed) Land Values, 1965; The World Cities, 1966, 3rd edn 1984; Containment of Urban England, 1973; Urban and Regional Planning, 1974, 2nd edn 1982; Europe 2000, 1977; Great Planning Disasters, 1980; Growth Centres in the European Urban System, 1980; The Inner City in Context, 1981; Silicon Landscapes, 1985; Can Rail Save the City?, 1985; High Tech America, 1986; Cities of Tomorrow, 1988; London 2001, 1989; The Rise of the Gunbelt, 1991; Technoples of the World, 1994; Sociable Cities, 1998; Cities in Civilization, 1998; Urban Future 21, 2000. *Recreations:* writing, reading, talking. *Address:* Bartlett School, University College London, Wates House, 22 Gordon Street, WC1H 0QB; 12 Queens Road, W5 2SA. *Club:* Athenæum.

HALL, Peter George; (part-time) Chairman, Snamprogetti Ltd, 1988–97; *b* 10 Dec. 1924; *s* of Charles and Rosina Hall; *m* 1949, Margaret Gladys (*née* Adams); two *s* two *d*. *Educ:* Sandown, IoW, Grammar Sch.; Southampton Univ. (BScEng). FInstPet. Anglo-Iranian Oil Co., 1946–51; Esso Petroleum Co. Ltd: various positions at Fawley Refinery, 1951–63; Manager, Milford Haven Refinery, 1963–66; Employee Relations Manager, 1966–70; Vice-Pres., General Sekiyu Seisei, Tokyo, 1971–74; Asst Gen. Man., Refining, Imperial Oil Ltd, Toronto, 1974–76; Refining Man., Exxon Corp., New York, 1976–77; Director, Esso Petroleum Co. Ltd, London, 1977–78; Vice-Pres., Esso Europe Inc. London, 1979–81; Man. Dir, Esso Petroleum Co., 1982–84; Pres., Esso Norge, 1984–87. *Recreations:* opera, classical music, walking, gardening. *Address:* Oakley, Mill Lawn, Burley, Ringwood, Hants BH24 4HP.

HALL, Sir Peter (Reginald Frederick), Kt 1977; CBE 1963; director of plays, films and operas; own producing company, Peter Hall Co., formed 1988; Artistic Director, Old Vic, 1997; *b* Bury St Edmunds, Suffolk, 22 Nov. 1930; *s* of late Reginald Edward Arthur Hall and Grace Pamment; *m* 1956, Leslie Caron (marr. diss. 1965); one *s* one *d*; *m* 1965, Jacqueline Taylor (marr. diss. 1981); one *s* one *d*; *m* 1982, Maria Ewing, *qv* (marr. diss. 1990); one *d*; *m* 1990, Nicola Frei; one *d*. *Educ:* Perse Sch., Cambridge; St Catharine's Coll., Cambridge (MA Hons; Hon. Fellow, 1964). Professional début directing The Letter, Th. Royal, Windsor, 1953; Director: Oxford Playhouse, 1954–55; Arts Theatre, London, 1955–57 (directed several plays incl. first productions of Waiting for Godot (new prodn, Old Vic, 1997), South, Waltz of the Toreadors); formed own producing company, International Playwrights' Theatre, 1957, and directed their first production, Camino Real; at Sadler's Wells, directed his first opera, The Moon and Sixpence, 1957. First productions at Stratford: Love's Labour's Lost, 1956; Cymbeline, 1957; first prod. on Broadway, The Rope Dancers, Nov. 1957. Plays in London, 1956–58: Summertime, Gigi, Cat on a Hot Tin Roof, Brouhaha, Shadow of Heroes; Madame de . . ., Traveller Without Luggage, A Midsummer Night's Dream and Coriolanus (Stratford), The Wrong Side of the Park, 1959; apptd Dir of Royal Shakespeare Theatre, Jan. 1960, responsible for founding RSC as a permanent ensemble, and its move to Aldwych Theatre, 1960; Man. Dir at Stratford-on-Avon and Aldwych Theatre, London, 1960–68; Associate Dir, RSC, 1968–73; Dir, Nat. Theatre, 1973–88; Artistic Dir, Glyndebourne Fest., 1984–90. Plays produced/directed for *Royal Shakespeare Company:* Two Gentlemen of Verona, Twelfth Night, Troilus and Cressida, 1960; Ondine, Becket, Romeo and Juliet, 1961; The Collection, Troilus and Cressida, A Midsummer Night's Dream, 1962; The Wars of the Roses (adaptation of Henry VI Parts 1, 2 and 3, and Richard III), 1963 (televised for BBC, 1965); Sequence of Shakespeare's histories for Shakespeare's 400th anniversary at Stratford: Richard II, Henry IV Parts 1 & 2, Henry V, Henry VI, Edward IV, Richard III, 1964; The Homecoming, Hamlet, 1965; The Government Inspector, Staircase, 1966; The Homecoming (NY) (Tony Award for Best Dir), 1966; Macbeth, 1967; A Delicate Balance, Silence, Landscape, 1969; The Battle of the Shrivings, 1970; Old Times, 1971 (NY, 1971, Vienna, 1972); All Over, Via Galactica (NY), 1972; Julius Caesar, 1995; plays produced/directed for *National Theatre:* The Tempest, 1973; John Gabriel Borkman, Happy Days, 1974; No Man's Land, Hamlet, 1975; Tamburlaine the Great, 1976; No Man's Land (NY), Volpone, Bedroom Farce, The Country Wife, 1977; The Cherry Orchard, Macbeth, Betrayal, 1978; Amadeus, 1979, NY 1981 (Tony Award for Best Director); Othello, 1980; Family Voices, The Oresteia, 1981, 1986 (Evening Standard Award for Best Director, 1981); Importance of Being Earnest, 1982; Other Places, 1982; Jean Seberg, 1983; Animal Farm, Coriolanus, 1984; Martine, Yonadab, 1985; The Petition, Coming into Land, 1986; Antony and Cleopatra (Evening Standard Award for Best Director), Entertaining Strangers, 1987; The Tempest, Cymbeline, Winter's Tale, 1988; The Oedipus Plays, 1996; plays produced/directed for *Peter Hall Company:* Orpheus Descending, NY, 1988; Merchant of Venice, 1989; The Wild Duck, Phoenix, 1990; The Homecoming, Comedy, 1990; Twelfth Night, The Rose Tattoo, Tartuffe, Playhouse, 1991; Four Baboons Adoring the Sun, NY, 1992; Sienna Red, 1992; All's Well That Ends Well, RSC, 1992; An Ideal Husband, Globe, 1992, Haymarket, Old Vic, 1996; The Gift of the Gorgon, Wyndham's, 1993; Separate Tables, Albery, 1993; Lysistrata, Old Vic and Wyndhams, 1993; She Stoops to Conquer, Queen's, 1993; Piaf, Piccadilly, 1993; An Absolute Turkey, Globe, 1994; On Approval, Playhouse, 1994; Hamlet, Gielgud, 1994; The Master Builder, 1995, Mind Millie for Me, 1996, A Streetcar Named Desire, 1997, Haymarket; Waste, The Seagull, King Lear, Waiting for Godot, Old Vic, 1997; The Misanthrope, Major Barbara, Filumena, Kafka's Dick, Piccadilly, 1998; *other productions:* Amadeus, Old Vic, 1998; Lenny, Queen's, 1999; Cuckoos, Gate, Notting Hill, 2000; Japes, The Royal Family, Th. Royal, Haymarket, 2001; Tantalus, Denver, 2000, UK tour and Barbican, 2001. *Films:* Work is a Four Letter Word, 1968; A Midsummer Night's Dream, Three into Two Won't Go, 1969; Perfect Friday, 1971; The Homecoming, 1973; Akenfield, 1974; She's Been Away, 1989; Orpheus Descending, 1991; Final Passage, 1996. *Opera:* at Covent Garden: Moses and Aaron, 1965; The Magic Flute, 1966; The Knot Garden, 1970; Eugene Onegin, Tristan and Isolde, 1971; Salome, 1988; Albert Herring, 1989; at Glyndebourne: La Calisto, 1970; Il Ritorno d'Ulisse in Patria, 1972; The Marriage of Figaro, 1973, 1989; Don Giovanni, 1977; Così Fan Tutte, 1978, 1988; Fidelio, 1979; A Midsummer Night's Dream, 1981, 2001; Orfeo ed Euridice, 1982; L'Incoronazione di Poppea, 1984, 1986; Carmen, 1985; Albert Herring, 1985, 1986; Simon Boccanegra, 1986, 1998; La Traviata, 1987; Falstaff, 1988; Otello, 2001; at Metropolitan Opera, NY: Macbeth, 1982; Carmen, 1986; at Bayreuth: The Ring, 1983; at Geneva: Figaro, 1983; at Los Angeles: Salome, 1986; Così Fan Tutte, 1988; The Magic Flute, 1992; at Chicago: Figaro, 1987; Salome, 1988; at Houston: New Year (world première), 1989. *Television:* Presenter, Aquarius (LWT), 1975–77; Carmen, 1985; Oresteia (C4), L'Incoronazione di Poppea, Albert Herring, 1986; La Traviata, 1987; The Marriage of Figaro, 1989; (series) The Camomile Lawn (C4), 1992. Associate Prof. of Drama, Warwick Univ., 1966–. Mem., Arts Council, 1969–73; Founder Mem., Theatre Dirs' Guild of GB, 1983–. Wortham Prof. of Performing Arts, Houston Univ., 1999–; Chancellor, Kingston Univ., 2000–. DUniv York, 1966; Hon. DLitt Reading, 1973; Hon. LittD: Liverpool, 1974; Leicester, 1977. Hamburg Univ. Shakespeare Prize, 1967; Standard Special Award, 1979; Standard Award for outstanding achievement in Opera, 1981; Lifetime Achievement Award, South Bank Show, 1998; Olivier Special Award for Lifetime Achievement, 1999. Chevalier de l'Ordre des Arts et des Lettres, 1965. *Publications:* (with John Barton) The Wars of the Roses, 1970; (with Inga-Stina Ewbank) John Gabriel Borkman, an English version, 1975; Peter Hall's Diaries (ed John Goodwin), 1983; Animal Farm, a stage adaptation, 1986; (with Inga-Stina Ewbank) The Wild Duck, an English adaptation, 1990; Making an Exhibition of Myself (autobiog.), 1993; (with Nicki Frei) trans. Feydeau, An Absolute Turkey, 1994; (with Inga-Stina Ewbank) The Master Builder, an English version, 1995; The Necessary Theatre, 1999; Exposed by the Mask, 2000. *Recreation:* music. *Club:* Garrick.

HALL, Philip David; Editor-in-chief, Hello! magazine, since 2001; *b* 8 Jan. 1955; *s* of Norman Philip Hall and Olive Jean Hall; *m* 1997, Marina Thomson, patent attorney; one *d*. *Educ:* Beal Grammar Sch., Ilford. Reporter: Dagenham Post, 1974–77; Ilford Recorder, 1977–80; Sub-editor: Newham Recorder, 1980–84; Weekend Magazine, 1984–85; The People: Reporter, 1985–86; Chief Reporter, 1986–89; News Editor, 1989–92; News Editor, Sunday Express, 1992–93; News of the World: Asst Editor (Features), 1993–94; Dep. Editor, 1994–95; Editor, 1995–2000; with Max Clifford Associates, 2000. Mem., Press Complaints Commn, 1998–2000. Mem., Guild of Editors. *Recreations:* golf, cinema, theatre. *Address:* (office) Wellington House, 69–71 Upper Ground, SE1 9PQ. *Clubs:* London Press; Wentworth (Virginia Water); Loch Lomond Golf.

HALL, Raymond Walter, CBE 1993; FREng; Chief Executive, Magnox Electric plc, 1996–98; *b* 24 Sept. 1933; *s* of Alfred Henry Hall and Elsie Frieda Hall; *m* 1955, Diane Batten; one *s* three *d*. *Educ:* Portsmouth, Grays Thurrock, and Gravesend Colls of Technology. FIMechE 1981; FIEE 1983; FINucE 1983; FREng (FEng 1993). Engineering and managerial positions, CEGB, 1975–89: Station Manager: Trawsfynydd Nuclear Power Station, 1975–77; Hinkley Point A & B Nuclear Power Stations, 1978–82; Corporate Trng Manager, 1983–85; Corporate Dir of Personnel, 1986–87; Divl Dir of Generation, 1988–89; Exec. Dir, Operations, Nuclear Electric plc, 1990–95. World Association of Nuclear Operators: Gov., Main Bd, 1993–97; Chm., Paris Centre, 1993–97; Chairman: Orgn Producteurs d'Energie Nucléaire, 1994–97; British Nuclear Industry Forum, 1997– (Mem. Bd, 1996–). Trustee, Bristol Exploratory, 1992–2000. FRSA 1980; FIMgt 1980; FIPD 1988. Freeman: City of London, 1996; Worshipful Co. of Engrs, 1996 (Liveryman, 1997–). *Publications:* contribs to learned jls on nuclear engrg matters. *Recreations:* music, gardening, walking, squash. *Address:* Kingsthorn, Staplehay, Taunton, Somerset TA3 7HA. *T:* (01823) 252325, *Fax:* (01823) 327689.

HALL, Sir Robert de Zouche, KCMG 1953 (CMG 1952); MA; resident in New Zealand; *b* 27 April 1904; *s* of late Arthur William Hall, Liverpool; *m* 1932, Lorna Dorothy (*née* Markham); one *s* one *d*. *Educ:* Willaston Sch.; Gonville and Caius Coll., Cambridge. MA, 1932. Colonial Administrative Service, Tanganyika, 1926; Provincial Comr, 1947; Senior Provincial Comr, 1950; Mem. for Local Government, Tanganyika, 1950–53. Governor, Comdr-in-Chief, and Vice-Adm., Sierra Leone, 1953–56. Hon. Sec. Vernacular Architecture Group, 1959–72, Pres., 1972–73; Chm. Governing Body, Somerset County Museum, 1961–73; Mem. Gisborne Museum Staff, NZ, 1974–80. *Publication:* (ed) A Bibliography on Vernacular Architecture, 1973.

HALL, Ruth, FRCP, FRCPCH, FFPHM; Chief Medical Officer, National Assembly for Wales (formerly Welsh Office), since 1997; *b* 8 Feb. 1948; *d* of Robert and Molly Dobson; *m* 1971, William Hall; two *s* two *d*. *Educ:* Sch. of St Helen and St Katherine, Abingdon; King's Coll. Hosp. Med. Sch., London (MB BS 1970). LRCP, MRCS 1970; FFPHM 1994; FRCPCH 1997; FRCP 2000. Posts in London, 1970–71, Chester, 1971–73, and N Wales, 1973–97; Dir of Public Health, N Wales HA, 1995–97. *Address:* National Assembly for Wales, Cathays Park, Cardiff CF10 3NQ.

HALL, Sasha; *see* Wass, S.

HALL, Simon Robert Dawson, MA; Warden of Glenalmond College, 1987–91; *b* 24 April 1938; *s* of late Wilfrid Dawson Hall and Elizabeth Helen Hall (*née* Wheeler); *m* 1961, Jennifer Harverson; two *s*. *Educ:* Tonbridge School; University College, Oxford. 2nd

Lieut, 7th Royal Tank Regt, 1956–58. Asst Master, Gordonstoun School, 1961–65; Joint Headmaster, Dunrobin School, 1965–68; Haileybury: Asst Master, 1969–79; Senior Modern Languages Master, 1970–76; Housemaster, Lawrence, 1972–79; Second Master, 1976–79; Headmaster, Milton Abbey School, 1979–87. 21st SAS Regt (TA), 1958–61; Intelligence Corps (V), 1968–71. *Recreations:* reading, music, motoring, sailing, hill-walking. *Address:* Whitemere, Wigginton, Banbury, Oxon OX15 4JU.

HALL, Prof. the Rev. Stuart George; Priest-in-Charge, St Michael's, Elie, and St John's, Pittenweem, 1990–98; Professor of Ecclesiastical History, King's College, University of London, 1978–90; *b* 7 June 1928; *s* of George Edward Hall and May Catherine Hall; *m* 1953, Brenda Mary Henderson; two *s* two *d*. *Educ:* University Coll. Sch., Hampstead; New Coll., and Ripon Hall, Oxford (BA 1952, MA 1955, BD 1973). National Service, Army, 1947–48. Deacon 1954, priest 1955; Asst Curate, Newark-on-Trent Parish Church, 1954–58; Tutor, Queen's Coll., Birmingham, 1958–62; Lectr in Theology, Univ. of Nottingham, 1962–73, Sen. Lectr, 1973–78. Editor for early church material, Theologische Realenzyklopädie. *Publications:* Melito of Sardis On Pascha and fragments: (ed) texts and translations, 1979; Doctrine and Practice in the Early Church, 1991; (ed) Gregory of Nyssa, Homilies on Ecclesiastes, 1993; (ed with Averil Cameron) Eusebius, Life of Constantine, 1999; contrib. to Cambridge Ancient History, Expository Times, Heythrop Jl, Jl of Eccles. History, Jl of Theol Studies, Religious Studies, Studia Evangelica, Studia Patristica, Theology and Theologische Realenzyklopädie. *Recreations:* gardening, choral music. *Address:* 15 High Street, Elie, Leven, Fife KY9 1BY. *T:* (01333) 330216.

HALL, Prof. Stuart McPhail; Professor of Sociology, The Open University, 1979–98, now Emeritus; Visiting Professor, Goldsmiths College, London University; *b* 3 Feb. 1932; *s* of Herman and Jessie Hall; *m* 1964, Catherine Mary Barrett; one *s* one *d*. *Educ:* Jamaica Coll.; Merton Coll., Oxford (MA; Rhodes Scholar, 1951). Editor, New Left Review, 1957–61; Lectr, Film and Mass Media Studies, Chelsea Coll., London Univ., 1961–64; Centre for Cultural Studies, Univ. of Birmingham: Res. Fellow, 1964–68; Actg Dir, 1968–72; Dir, 1972–79. Hon. Fellow, Portsmouth Polytechnic, 1988; Centenary Fellow, Thames Polytechnic, 1990. Hon DLitt: Massachusetts, 1989; City, Kingston, Oxford Brookes, 1993; Sussex, 1994; Leeds, Middlesex, Keele, 1995; East London, London, 1998; W Indies, 1999; Birmingham, 2000; Teesside; Hon. DCL Durham. *Publications:* (jtly) The Popular Arts, 1964; (ed jtly) Resistance Through Rituals, 1974; (jtly) Policing The Crisis, 1978; Culture, Media, Language, 1980; (ed jtly) The Politics of Thatcherism, 1983; State and Society in Contemporary Britain, 1984; Politics and Ideology, 1986; The Hard Road to Renewal, 1988; (jtly) Questions of Cultural Identity, 1996; Critical Dialogues in Cultural Studies, 1996; Representations, 1997; *festschrift:* Without Guarantees, 2000. *Address:* 21 Ulysses Road, NW6 1ED.

HALL, Col Thomas Armitage, CVO 1998; OBE 1966; Lieutenant, HM Body Guard of Honourable Corps of Gentlemen at Arms, 1994–98; *b* 13 April 1928; *s* of Athelstan Argyle Hall and Nancy Armitage Hall (*née* Dyson); *m* 1954, Mariette Hornby; two *s* four *d*. *Educ:* Heatherdown Sch.; Eton Coll. Commissioned, 11th Hussars, 1947, Berlin; ADC to CIGS, 1952–53; Adjutant, 11 H Malayan Emergency, 1953–56 (despatches); Army Staff Coll., 1960–61; Sqdn Leader 11 H, Aden, Gulf, Kenya, Kuwait, 1961–62; Instr, RN Staff Coll., Greenwich, 1962–64; CO 11 H, Germany, 1965–66; Equerry to King of Thailand, 1966; Regtl Col, Royal Hussars, 1974–83; Advr to Crown Prince of Japan, 1983–85. Regl Dir, Lloyds Bank, 1983–85. Chm., Internat. Lang. Centres, 1971–88. High Sheriff, Oxon, 1981–82. FRSA. *Recreations:* ski-ing, shooting, travel, architecture. *Address:* Marylands Farm, Chiselhampton, Oxford OX44 7XD. *T:* (01865) 890350. *Club:* Cavalry and Guards (Chm., 1990–96).

HALL, Thomas William; Under-Secretary, Department of Transport, 1976–79 and 1981–87; retired; *b* 8 April 1931; *s* of Thomas William and Euphemia Jane Hall; *m* 1961, Anne Rosemary Hellier Davis; two *d*. *Educ:* Hitchin Grammar Sch.; St John's Coll., Oxford (MA); King's Coll., London (MA). Asst Principal, Min. of Supply, 1954; Principal: War Office, Min. of Public Building and Works, Cabinet Office, 1958–68; Asst Sec., Min. of Public Building and Works, later DoE, 1968–76; Under Sec., Depts of Environment and Transport, 1979–81. Member: Road Traffic Law Review, 1985–88; Transport Tribunal, 1990–99. *Recreations:* music, literature, gardening, walking. *Address:* 43 Bridge Road, Epsom, Surrey KT17 4AN. *T:* (01372) 725900.

HALL, Victor Edwin; His Honour Judge Victor Hall; a Circuit Judge, since 1994; *b* 2 March 1948; *s* of Robert Arthur Victor James Hall and Gwladys (*née* Fukes); *m* 1974, Rosemarie Berdina Jenkinson; two *s*. *Educ:* Univ. of Hull (LLB 1969). Lectr in Law, Kettering Tech. Coll., 1969–71; called to the Bar, Inner Temple, 1971; an Asst Recorder, 1983–88; a Recorder, 1988. Asst Parly Boundary Comr, 1991–93. Deacon in Free Church. *Recreations:* walking, ski-ing, cookery. *Address:* Leicester Crown and County Courts, Wellington Street, Leicester LE1 6ZZ.

HALL, (Wallace) John; Regional Director, DTI East (Cambridge), Department of Trade and Industry, 1989–94; *b* 5 Oct. 1934; *s* of Claude Corbett Hall and Dulcie Hall (*née* Brinkworth); *m* 1962, Janet Bowen; three *d*. *Educ:* Crypt Sch., Gloucester; Hertford Grammar Sch.; Downing Coll., Cambridge (MA Classics). National Service, RAF, 1953–55. Pirelli-General Cable Works Ltd, 1958–62; Sales Manager, D. Meredew Ltd, 1962–67; Principal, Min. of Technology, 1967–70; Dept of Trade and Industry, Civil Aviation Policy, 1970–72; Consul (Commercial), São Paulo, Brazil, 1972–76; Asst Secretary, Dept of Trade, Shipping Policy, 1976–79; Counsellor (Economic), Brasilia, 1979–81; Consul-Gen., São Paulo, 1981–83; Assistant Secretary, DTI: Internat. Trade Policy, 1983–85; Overseas Trade (E Asia), 1985–89. *Recreations:* bridge, tennis and other sports, daughters. *Address:* 27 Wilbury Road, Letchworth, Herts SG6 4JW.

HALL, Prof. Wendy, (Mrs Peter Chandler), CBE 2000; PhD; FREng; Professor of Computer Science, University of Southampton, since 1994; *b* 25 Oct. 1952; *d* of Kenneth D. Hall and Elizabeth Hall; *m* 1980, Dr Peter E. Chandler. *Educ:* Ealing Grammar Sch. for Girls; Univ. of Southampton (BSc Maths 1974; PhD 1977); City Univ. (MSc Computer Sci. 1986). CEng 1990; FIEE 1998. Lecturer: in Engrg, Oxford Poly., 1977–78; La Sainte Union Coll. of Higher Educn, 1978–84; Lectr, 1984–90, Sen. Lectr, 1990–94, Dept of Electronics and Computer Sci., Univ. of Southampton. Mem., EPSRC, 1997– (Sen. Fellow, 1996–2001). FBCS 1996 (Vice Pres., 1998–); FREng 2000. *Publications:* (jtly) Rethinking Hypermedia: the microcosm approach, 1996; (jtly) Hypermedia and the Web: an engineering approach, 1999; articles in jls, conf. proceedings. *Recreations:* rapidly becoming a keep-fit fanatic as middle-age approaches, spending many hours in the local gym and swimming pool; walking with my husband, particularly in the New Forest; fine wines and dining, travelling, theatre; favourite form of relaxation is reading a good book on a sunny beach. *Address:* Department of Electronics and Computer Science, University of Southampton, Southampton SO17 1BJ. *T:* (023) 8059 2388.

HALL, William, CBE 1991; DFC 1944, FRICS; Member of the Lands Tribunal for Scotland, 1971–91, and for England and Wales, 1979–91; *b* 25 July 1919; *s* of Archibald and Helen Hall; *m* 1945, Margaret Semple (*née* Gibson); one *s* three *d*. *Educ:* Paisley Grammar Sch. FRICS 1948. Served War, RAF (pilot) 1939–45 (despatches, 1945). Sen. Partner, R. & W. Hall, Chartered Surveyors, 1949–79. Chm., Scottish Br., RICS, 1971; Member: Valuation Adv. Council, 1970–80; Erskine Hosp. Exec., 1976–99. Hon. Sheriff, Paisley, 1974–. *Recreation:* golf. *Address:* Windyridge, Brediland Road, Paisley, Renfrewshire PA2 9HF. *T:* (01505) 813614. *Club:* Royal Air Force.

HALL, Prof. William Bateman, FREng; Professor of Nuclear Engineering, University of Manchester, 1959–86, now Emeritus; *b* 28 May 1923; *s* of Sidney Bateman Hall and Doris Hall; *m* 1950, Helen Mary Dennis; four *d*. *Educ:* Urmston Grammar Sch.; College of Technology, Manchester. Engineering apprenticeship, 1939–44; Royal Aircraft Establishment, 1944–46; United Kingdom Atomic Energy Authority (formerly Dept of Atomic Energy, Min. of Supply), 1946–59: Technical Engineer, 1946–52; Principal Scientific Officer, 1952–56; Senior Principal Scientific Officer, 1956–58; Dep. Chief Scientific Officer, 1958. Mem., Adv. Cttee on Safety of Nuclear Installations, 1972–83. Pro-Vice-Chancellor, Univ. of Manchester, 1979–82. FREng (FEng 1986). *Publications:* Reactor Heat Transfer, 1958; papers to scientific and professional institutions. *Recreations:* music, designing and making steam engines. *Address:* High Raise, Eskdale, Holmrook, Cumbria CA19 1UA. *T:* (01946) 723275.

HALL, William Joseph; JP; Lord-Lieutenant of Co. Down, since 1996; *b* 1 Aug. 1934; *s* of late Capt. Roger Hall and Marie Hall; *m* 1964, Jennifer Mary Corbett; one *s* one *d*. *Educ:* Ampleforth Coll., York. SSC, Irish Guards, 1952–56. With W. C. Pitfield & Hugh McKay, investment mgt co., then with Shell Oil, Canada, 1956–62; dir of own wine wholesale business, also sheep farmer and commercial narcissus bulb grower, 1962–90, retired. Mem., Lord Chancellor's Adv. Cttee on JPs, 1975– (Chm., Ards Div., 1996–). County Down: JP 1973; DL 1975–93; High Sheriff, 1983; Vice Lord Lieutenant, 1993–96. NI ACF, 1967–79 (Hon. Major, 1980; Pres., NI ACFA, 1999–); Pres., RFCA NI, 2000–; Chm., Ulster Br., Irish Guards Assoc., 1979–. CStJ 1997. *Recreations:* field sports in general, bridge, travel abroad when time allows! *Address:* Narrow Water Castle, Warrenpoint, Co. Down, Northern Ireland BT34 3LE. *T:* (028) 4175 4904, *Fax:* (028) 4175 4990. *Club:* Down Hunt (Downpatrick).

HALL, Willis; writer; *b* 6 April 1929; *s* of Walter and Gladys Hall; *m* 1973, Valerie Shute; one *s* (and three *s* by previous marriages). *Educ:* Cockburn High Sch., Leeds. Member: The Magic Circle; Internat. Brotherhood of Magicians; Soc. of Amer. Magicians; Malta Magicians Soc. TV plays include: The Villa Maroc; They Don't all Open Men's Boutiques; Song at Twilight; The Road to 1984; TV series: The Fuzz, 1977; The Danedyke Mystery, 1979; Stan's Last Game, 1983; The Bright Side, 1985; The Return of the Antelope, 1986; The Reluctant Dragon, 1988; (with Keith Waterhouse): The Upper Crusts, 1973; Billy Liar, 1974; Worzel Gummidge, 1979 (adapted as stage musical, 1981). *Publications:* (with Michael Parkinson) The A-Z of Soccer, 1970; Football Report, 1973; Football Classified, 1974; My Sporting Life, Football Final, 1975; *children's books:* The Royal Astrologer, 1960; The Gentle Knight, 1967; The Incredible Kidnapping, 1975; The Summer of the Dinosaur, 1977; The Last Vampire, 1982; The Inflatable Shop, 1984; The Return of the Antelope, 1985; Spooky Rhymes, 1987; The Antelope Company at Large, 1987; Dr Jekyll and Mr Hollins, 1988; Henry Hollins and the Dinosaur, 1988; The Vampire's Holiday, 1991; The Vampire's Revenge, 1993; The Vampire's Christmas, 1994; The Vampire Vanishes, 1995; Vampire Park, 1996; The Vampire Hunt, 1998; Vampire Island, 1999, *plays:* The Long and the Short and the Tall, 1959; A Glimpse of the Sea, 1969; Kidnapped at Christmas, 1975; Walk on, Walk on, 1975; Stag Night, 1976; Christmas Crackers, 1976; A Right Christmas Caper, 1977; (with Keith Waterhouse): Billy Liar, 1960; Celebration, 1961; All Things Bright and Beautiful, 1962; England Our England, 1962; Squat Betty and The Sponge Room, 1963; Say Who You Are, 1965; Whoops-a-Daisy, 1968; Children's Day, 1969; Who's Who, 1972; *adaptations:* (with Keith Waterhouse) de Filippo, Saturday, Sunday, Monday, 1973; (with Keith Waterhouse) de Filippo, Filumena, 1977; (with Denis King) A. A. Milne, The Wind in the Willows (musical), 1985; (with John Cooper) Charles Kingsley, The Water Babies (musical), 1987; Charlotte Brontë, Jane Eyre, 1992; Jane Austen, Mansfield Park, 1993; Alexandre Dumas, The Three Musketeers, 1994; *musicals:* (with Keith Waterhouse): The Card, 1973; Budgie, 1989; (with Denis King) Treasure Island, 1985; (with George Stiles and Anthony Drewe) J. M. Barrie, Peter Pan, 2000. *Recreation:* magic. *Address:* c/o Alexandra Cann representation, 12 Abingdon Road, W8 6AF. *Clubs:* Garrick, Royal Over-Seas League, Lansdowne.

HALL-MATTHEWS, Rt Rev. Anthony Francis Berners; Bishop Resident in Mareeba, Diocese of North Queensland, since 1999; *b* 14 Nov. 1940; *s* of Rev. Cecil Berners Hall and Barbara (who *m* 1944, Rt Rev. Seering John Matthews); *m* 1966, Valerie Joan Cecil; two *s* three *d*. *Educ:* Sanctuary School, Walsingham, Norfolk; Southport School, Queensland; St Francis Theol Coll., Milton, Brisbane. ThL Aust. Coll. of Theology, 1962; Graduate Dip. of Arts, James Cook Univ. of N Qld, 1997. Asst Curate at Darwin, 1963–66; Chaplain, Carpentaria Aerial Mission, 1966–84, and Rector of Normanton, 1966–76; Hon. Canon of Carpentaria, 1970–76; Archdeacon of Cape York Peninsula, 1976–84; Priest-in-charge of Cooktown, Dio. Carpentaria, 1976–84; Bishop of Carpentaria, 1984–96. Principal, Carpentaria Consulting Services, 1997–99. *Recreations:* flying, reading, composting. *Address:* 5 Wattle Close, Yungaburra, Queensland 4872, Australia. *T:* (7) 40953188.

HALL WILLIAMS; *see* Williams.

HALLAM, Bishop of, (RC), since 1997; **Rt Rev. John Rawsthorne;** *b* Crosby, Merseyside, 12 Nov. 1936. Priest, 1962; Titular Bishop of Rotdon and an Auxiliary Bishop of Liverpool, 1981–97. Pres., St Joseph's Coll., 1982–97; Adminr, St Mary's, Highfield, 1982. *Address:* Quarters, Carsick Hill Way, Sheffield S10 3LY. *T:* (0114) 230 9101.

HALLAM, David John Alfred; Director of Communications, Birmingham Heartlands and Solihull NHS Trust, since 2000; *b* 13 June 1948; *s* of Arthur Ernest Hallam and Marjorie Ethel Hallam (*née* Gibbs); *m* 1988, Claire Vanstone; two *s* one *d*. *Educ:* Upton House Secondary Modern Sch., London; Univ. of Sussex (BA). Res. Asst, Sussex CC, 1971–73; Information Officer, Birmingham Social Services Dept, 1973–80; Public Relations Officer, Nat. Children's Home, 1984–89. Mem., Sandwell BC, W Midlands, 1976–79. MEP (Lab) Hereford and Shropshire, 1994–99; contested (Lab) W Midlands Reg., 1999. Mem., Agricl Cttee, 1994–99, Substitute Mem., Budget Cttee, 1997–99, Europ. Parlt; Mem., Slovak Delegn, 1995–99; Substitute Mem. of Israel Delegn and to EU African, Caribbean and Pacific Parly Assembly, 1994–99. Contested (Lab): Shropshire and Staffordshire, European parly elections, 1984, 1989; Hereford, 2001. MCIM; MIPR. Methodist local preacher. Editor, The Potter, newspaper, 1982–94.

HALLATT, Rt Rev. David Marrison; an Assistant Bishop, Diocese of Sheffield, since 2001; *b* 15 July 1937; *s* of John Vincent Hallatt and Edith Elliott Hallatt; *m* 1967, Margaret Smitton; two *s*. *Educ:* Birkenhead School; Southampton Univ. (BA Hons Geography 1959); St Catherine's Coll., Oxford (BA Theology 1962; MA 1966). Curate, St Andrew's, Maghull, Liverpool, 1963–67; Vicar, All Saints, Totley, dio. Sheffield, 1967–75; Team

Rector, St James & Emmanuel, Didsbury, Manchester, 1975–89; Archdeacon of Halifax, 1989–94; Bishop Suffragan of Shrewsbury, 1994–2001. *Recreations:* walking, birdwatching, music, crosswords. *Address:* 1 Merbeck Grove, High Green, Sheffield S35 4HE. *T:* (0114) 284 4440.

HALLCHURCH, David Thomas, TD 1965; Chief Justice, Turks and Caicos Islands, West Indies, 1996–98; *b* 4 April 1929; *s* of Walter William Hallchurch and Marjorie Pretoria Mary Hallchurch (*née* Cooper); *m* 1st, 1954, Gillian Mary Jagger (marr. diss. 1972); three *s*; 2nd, 1972, Susan Kathryn Mather Brennan; one step *s* one step *d*. *Educ:* Bromsgrove Sch.; Trinity Coll., Oxford (MA Hons). Called to the Bar, Gray's Inn, 1953; Whitehead Travelling Scholarship, Canada and USA, 1953–54; practised as barrister-at-law on Midland and Oxford Circuit, 1954–60 and 1964–96; a Recorder, 1980–97. Puisne Judge, Botswana, 1986–88; Actg Chief Justice, Turks and Caicos Is, 1993. Pt-time Immigration Adjudicator, 1990–96; Asst Comr, Parly Boundary Commn for England, 1992. Legal Mem., Mental Health Review Tribunal for the West Midlands, 1979–86. Major, Staffs Yeomanry (Queen's Own Royal Regiment), TA, 1953–66. *Recreations:* cricket, drawing (cartoons). *Address:* Neachley House, Tong, Shifnal, Shropshire TF11 8PH. *Club:* Vincent's (Oxford).

HALLETT, Anthony Philip; Chairman, Richmond Football Club, 1991–95 and since 1999 (Chief Executive, 1998–99); *b* 11 Feb. 1945; *s* of late Maurice George Hallett and Ann Halliwell Bailey; *m* 1972, Faith Mary Holland-Martin; three *s*. *Educ:* Ipswich Sch.; Britannia RN Coll. Joined RN 1963; served in HM Ships Victorious and Hermes; Flag Lieut, Hong Kong; HMS Eskimo; RNC Greenwich; BRNC, 1975–77; MoD, 1978–79; HMS Invincible, 1979–81; served C-in-C Fleet, 1982–83; HMS Illustrious, 1983–85; MoD, 1986–90; RNSC Greenwich, 1990–91; Sec. to Chief of Fleet Support, 1992–94; Captain, RN, retd 1995. Rugby Football: Navy Captain, 1969; 11 caps; played for US Portsmouth, Banbury, Blackheath, Richmond, Oxfordshire, S Counties, Combined Services, Hong Kong v England 1971. Rugby Football Union: Mem., 1979–97; Privilege Mem., 1997–; Chm., Ground Cttee, 1979–95; Chm., Redevelt Twickenham, 1991–95; Sec., 1995–97; Chief Exec., 1997; Selector and Chm., RN RU, 1985–94. Man. Dir, Parallel Media Rugby Ltd, 1999–2001. *Recreations:* plantsman and garden design (Mem., Nat. Gardens Scheme), paintings, all sports. *Address:* 26 Nassau Road, Barnes, SW13 9QE. *Clubs:* Army and Navy, East India, Lord's Taverners.

HALLETT, Hon. Dame Heather (Carol), DBE 1999; **Hon. Mrs Justice Hallett;** a Judge of the High Court of Justice, Queen's Bench Division, since 1999; Presiding Judge, Western Circuit, since 2001; *b* 16 Dec. 1949; *d* of late Hugh Hallett, QPM and of Doris Hallett; *m* 1974, Nigel Wilkinson, *qv*; two *s*. *Educ:* St Hugh's Coll., Oxford (MA; Hon. Fellow, 1999). Called to the Bar, Inner Temple, 1972, Bencher, 1993; QC 1989; a Recorder, 1989–99; a Dep. High Court Judge, 1995–99. Leader, S Eastern Circuit, 1995–97. Chm., Gen. Council of the Bar, 1998 (Vice Chm., 1997). Hon. LLD Derby, 2000. *Recreations:* theatre, music, games. *Address:* Royal Courts of Justice, Strand, WC2A 2LL.

HALLETT, James Windham John H.; *see* Hughes-Hallett.

HALLETT, Victor George Henry; Deputy Social Security Commissioner and Deputy Child Support Commissioner, 1993–95; *b* 11 Feb. 1921; *s* of Dr Denys Bouhier Imbert Hallett; *m* 1947, Margaret Hamlyn. *Educ:* Westminster; Queen's Coll., Oxford (MA). Served War, 1939–45 (wounded 1945, despatches 1946). Called to Bar, Inner Temple, 1949. Mem., Land Registration Rules Cttee, 1971–76; Conveyancing Counsel of the Court, 1971–76; Nat. Insce, subseq. Social Security, Comr, 1976–93. *Publications:* Key and Elphinstone's Conveyancing Precedents (ed jtly), 15th edn, 1952; Prideaux's Precedents in Conveyancing (ed jtly), 25th edn, 1953; Hallett's Conveyancing Precedents, 1965; (with Nicholas Warren) Settlements, Wills and Capital Transfer Tax, 1979. *Address:* 20 Ashley Court, Ashley Road, Epsom, Surrey KT18 5AJ.

HALLEY, Laurence; *see* O'Keeffe, P. L.

HALLGARTEN, Anthony Bernard Richard; QC 1978; **His Honour Judge Hallgarten;** a Circuit Judge, since 1993; Business List Judge, Central London County Court, since 1994; *b* 16 June 1937; *s* of late Fritz and Friedel Hallgarten; *m* 1962, Katherine Borchard (marr. diss. 1996); one *s* three *d*; *m* 1998, Theresa Carlson. *Educ:* Merchant Taylors' Sch., Northwood; Downing Coll., Cambridge (BA). Called to the Bar, Middle Temple, 1961 (Barstow Scholar, Inns of Court, 1961); Bencher, 1987; a Recorder, 1990–93. Chm., Bar/Inns' Councils Jt Regulations Cttee, 1990–93. Chair, Management Cttee, Camden Victim Support, 1989–93. *Recreations:* ski-ing, SW France, cycling. *Clubs:* Garrick, MCC.

HALLIBURTON, Rev. Canon Robert John; Canon Residentiary and Chancellor of St Paul's Cathedral, since 1989; *b* 23 March 1935; *s* of Robert Halliburton and Katherine Margery Halliburton (*née* Robinson); *m* 1968, Jennifer Ormsby Turner; one *s* two *d* (and one *s* one *d* decd). *Educ:* Tonbridge Sch.; Selwyn Coll., Cambridge (MA); Keble Coll., Oxford (DPhil); St Stephen's House, Oxford. Curate, St Dunstan and All Saints, Stepney, 1961; Tutor, St Stephen's House, Oxford, 1967; Vice-Principal, St Stephen's House, 1971; Lectr, Lincoln Coll., Oxford, 1973; Principal of Chichester Theol Coll., 1975–82, Canon and Prebend of Chichester Cathedral, 1976–82, Canon Emeritus, 1982–88, Canon and Preb. of Wightring and Theol Lectr, 1988–90; Priest in Charge, All Souls, St Margaret's-on-Thames, 1982–89. Lecturer: Southwark Ordination Course, 1984–89; Missionary Inst., Mill Hill, 1984–89. Select Preacher, Oxford Univ., 1976–77. Consultant, Anglican-Roman Catholic Internat. Commn, 1971–81; Mem., Doctrinal Commn of C of E, 1978–86. Examining Chaplain to Bishop of Kensington, 1983–. Chm., Anglo-Catholic Ordination Candidates' Fund, 1996–. Pres., Sion Coll., 1998–99. *Publications:* The Authority of a Bishop, 1986; Educating Rachel, 1987; contribs to: The Eucharist Today, ed R. C. D. Jasper, 1974; The Study of Liturgy, ed C. P. M. Jones, 1978; Confession and Absolution, ed G. Rowell and M. Dudley, 1990; The Oil of Gladness, ed G. Rowell and M. Dudley, 1992; reports of C of E Doctrinal Commission, Believing in the Church, 1982, We believe in God, 1987; articles in Studia Patristica, La Revue des Etudes Augustiniennes, Faith and Unity. *Recreations:* music, gardening. *Address:* 1 Amen Court, EC4M 7BU. *T:* (020) 7248 1817. *Club:* Athenæum.

HALLIDAY, Prof. Alexander Norman, PhD; FRS 2000; Professor, Eidgenössische Technische Hochschule, Zürich, since 1998; *b* 11 Aug. 1952; *s* of Ronald James Rivers Halliday and Kathleen Elizabeth Halliday; *m* 1986, Christine Craig Young; two *s*. *Educ:* Univ. of Newcastle upon Tyne (BSc Hons Geology, PhD Physics). Postdoctoral Fellow, 1976–81, Lectr, 1981–86, Scottish Univs Res. and Reactor Centre, E Kilbride; Department of Geological Sciences, University of Michigan: Associate Prof., 1986–91; Prof., 1991–98; Adjunct Prof., 1998–2000. Pres., Geochemical Soc., 1995–97. Fellow, Amer. Geophysical Union, 2000 (Bowen Award, 1998). *Publications:* over 200 articles in sci. jls. *Recreation:* cycling. *Address:* Department of Earth Sciences, Institute for Isotope Geology and Mineral Resources, ETH Zentrum, NO, 8092 Zürich, Switzerland. *T:* (1) 6327525.

HALLIDAY, Charlotte Mary Irvine, NEAC 1961; RWS 1976 (ARWS 1971); topographical artist; Keeper, New English Art Club, since 1989; *b* 5 Sept. 1935; *d* of late Edward Halliday, CBE, RP, RBA and Dorothy Halliday. *Educ:* Francis Holland Sch.; Royal Academy Sch. *Commissions* include: construction of the Shell Centre, 1957–59; head offices of many City banks and insurance cos, incl. Willis Faber, Nat West Tower; clubs, colleges, major ecclesiastical buildings, incl. St Paul's and Salisbury Cathedrals; numerous stately and private homes. *Publications:* (illus.) A. Stuart Gray, Edwardian Architecture, 1985; (with A. Stuart Gray) Fanlights, a visual architectural history, 1990. *Recreations:* London Orpheus Choir, walking in the Downs, cats. *Address:* 36A Abercorn Place, St John's Wood, NW8 9XP. *T:* (020) 7289 1924; St Magnus Cottage, Houghton, near Arundel, W Sussex.

HALLIDAY, Prof. Fred; Professor of International Relations, London School of Economics and Political Science, since 1985; *b* 22 Feb. 1946; *s* of Arthur Halliday and Rita (*née* Finigan); *m* Dr Maxine Molyneux; one *s*. *Educ:* Ampleforth Coll.; Univ. of Oxford (BA 1st Cl.); School of Oriental and African Studies (MSc); London School of Economics (PhD 1985). Dept. of Internat. Relations, LSE, 1983–. Associate Fellow, Inst. for Policy Studies, Washington, 1990–; Fellow, Transnational Inst., Amsterdam and Washington, 1973–85. Sen. Fellow, 21st Century Trust; Mem., Adv. Council, The Foreign Policy Centre, 1999–; Gov., LSE, 1994–98. Contributing Ed., Middle East Reports, 1978–; Mem. Editl Bd, New Left Rev., 1969–83. *Publications:* Arabia without Sultans, 1974; Iran: dictatorship and development, 1978; (with Maxine Molyneux) The Ethiopian Revolution, 1981; Threat from the East?, 1982; The Making of the Second Cold War, 1983, 2nd edn 1986; Cold War, Third World, 1989; Revolution and Foreign Policy: the case of South Yemen 1967–1987, 1990; Arabs in Exile: the Yemen communities in Britain, 1992; Rethinking International Relations, 1994; Islam and the Myth of Confrontation, 1996; Revolution and World Politics: the rise and fall of the sixth great power, 1999; Nation and Religion in the Middle East, 2000; The World at 2000, 2000. *Recreations:* languages, travel, lunch, Le Monde. *Address:* D510 London School of Economics and Political Science, Houghton Street, WC2A 2AE. *T:* (020) 7955 7389, *Fax:* (020) 7955 7446.

HALLIDAY, Ian Francis, FCA; Finance Director, Lowndes Lambert Group Ltd, 1981–87; *b* 16 Nov. 1927; *s* of Michael and Jean Halliday; *m* 1952, Mary Busfield; one *s* two *d*. *Educ:* Wintringham Grammar Sch., Grimsby; Lincoln Coll., Oxford (MA Mathematics). Armitage & Norton, Chartered Accountants, 1951–69; qual. as Chartered Accountant, 1954; Partner, 1957; Finance Dir, Allied Textile Co. Ltd, 1970–74; on secondment as Dep. Director of Industrial Development Unit, Dept of Industry, 1974–77; Finance Dir, Leslie & Godwin (Holdings) Ltd, internat. insce and re-insce Lloyd's Brokers, 1977–80; Chief Exec., NEB, 1980. Mem., PLA, 1984–97. *Recreation:* gardening. *Address:* Blackmore Farm, Broadway, Bourn, Cambs CB3 7TA.

HALLIDAY, Prof. Ian Gibson, PhD; Chief Executive, Particle Physics and Astronomy Research Council, since 1998; Professor of Physics and Head of Department, University of Wales, Swansea (formerly University College, Swansea), since 1992 (on leave of absence) (Dean of Graduate School, 1993–96); *b* 5 Feb. 1940; *s* of John Alexander Halliday and Gladys (*née* Taylor); *m* 1965, Ellenor Gardiner Hervey Wilson; one *s* one *d*. *Educ:* Kelso High Sch.; Perth Acad.; Edinburgh Univ. (MA 1961; MSc 1962); Clare Coll., Cambridge (PhD 1964). Instructor, Princeton Univ., 1964–66; Fellow, Christ's Coll., Cambridge, 1966–67; Imperial College, University of London: Lectr, 1967–75; Reader, 1975–90; Prof., 1990–92. Chm., Prior Options Review of Royal Observatories, 1995. Mem., PPARC, 1994–98. *Publications:* numerous papers on theoretical particle physics in Nuclear Physics, Physics Letters. *Recreations:* sewin fishing, golf, tennis. *Address:* 65 Owls Lodge Lane, Mayals, Swansea SA3 5DP. *T:* (office) (01793) 442067.

HALLIDAY, John Frederick, CB 1994; Deputy Under Secretary of State, Home Office, 1990–2001; *b* 19 Sept. 1942; *s* of E. Halliday; *m* 1970, Alison Burgess; four *s*. *Educ:* Whitgift School, Croydon; St John's College, Cambridge (MA). Teacher, under VSO, Aitchison College, Lahore, 1964–66; Home Office, 1966; Principal Private Sec. to Home Sec., 1980; Asst Under-Sec. of State, Home Office, 1983–87; Under Sec., DHSS, then Dept of Health, 1987–90, on secondment. *Recreations:* music, squash, theatre.

HALLIDAY, Prof. Michael Alexander Kirkwood; Professor of Linguistics in the University of Sydney, 1976–87, Emeritus Professor since 1988; *b* 13 April 1925; *s* of late Wilfrid J. Halliday and Winifred Halliday (*née* Kirkwood). *Educ:* Rugby School; University of London. BA London; MA, PhD, Cambridge. Served Army, 1944–47. Asst Lectr in Chinese, Cambridge Univ., 1954–58; Lectr in General Linguistics, Edinburgh Univ., 1958–60; Reader in General Linguistics, Edinburgh Univ., 1960–63; Dir, Communication Res. Centre, UCL, 1963–65; Linguistic Soc. of America Prof., Indiana Univ., 1964; Prof. of General Linguistics, UCL, 1965–71; Fellow, Center for Advanced Study in the Behavioral Sciences, Stanford, Calif., 1972–73; Prof. of Linguistics, Univ. of Illinois, 1973–74; Prof. of Language and Linguistics, Essex Univ., 1974–75. Visiting Professor of Linguistics: Yale, 1967; Brown, 1971; Nairobi, 1972; Nat. Univ. of Singapore, 1990–91; Internat. Christian Univ., Tokyo, 1992; Lee Kuan Yew Distinguished Visitor, Nat. Univ. of Singapore, 1986; Hon. Sen. Res. Fellow, Birmingham Univ., 1991. FAHA 1979. Corresp. FBA 1989; For. Mem., Academia Europaea, 1994. Guest Prof., Peking Univ., 1995. Hon. Fellow: Univ. of Wales, Cardiff, 1998; Central Inst. of English and For. Langs, Hyderabad, India, 1999. Dr *hc* Nancy, 1968; Hon. DLitt: Birmingham, 1987; York (Canada), 1988; Athens, 1995; Macquarie, 1996; Lingnan, Hong Kong, 1999. *Publications:* The Language of the Chinese 'Secret History of the Mongols', 1959; (with A. McIntosh and P. Strevens) The Linguistic Sciences and Language Teaching, 1964; (with A. McIntosh) Patterns of Language, 1966; Intonation and Grammar in British English, 1967; A Course in Spoken English: Intonation, 1970; Explorations in the Functions of Language, 1973; Learning How To Mean, 1975; (with R. Hasan) Cohesion in English, 1976; System and Function in Language, ed G. Kress, 1976; Language as Social Semiotic, 1978; An Introduction to Functional Grammar, 1985; Spoken and Written Language, 1985; (with J. Martin) Writing Science, 1993; (with C. Matthiessen) Construing Experience as Meaning, 1999; articles in Jl of Linguistics, Word, Trans of Philological Soc., Functions of Lang., etc. *Address:* PO Box 42, Urunga, NSW 2455, Australia.

HALLIDAY, Norman Pryde; Consultant Adviser to Minister of Health, Saudi Arabia, since 1996; *b* 28 March 1932; *s* of late James and Jessie Thomson Hunter Halliday; *m* 1953, Eleanor Smith; three *s* one *d*. *Educ:* Woodside, Glasgow; King's Coll., London; King's Coll. Hosp. Med. Sch. SRN 1955; MB, BS, MRCS, LRCP 1964; DCH RCPGlas 1969; MBA: Warwick, 1991; Open Univ., 1992. Various posts in clinical medicine, incl. Registrar (Paediatrics), KCH, London; SMO, DHSS, 1972; SPMO (Under Sec.), DHSS, later DoH, 1977–92. Gen. Man., Eur. Dialysis and Transplant Assoc., 1994–95. Tutor: Open Univ., 1992–; Warwick Univ., 1992–. QHP 1990–93. *Publications:* articles on medical subjects in professional journals. *Recreations:* photography, sub aqua diving, fashion, DIY, cross-bow shooting. *Address:* Gurrs Farm, Crowborough Hill, Crowborough, E Sussex TN6 2SD. *T:* (01892) 669132.

HALLIDAY, Rt Rev. Robert Taylor; Bishop of Brechin, 1990–96; *b* 7 May 1932; *s* of James Halliday and Agnes Logan Halliday (*née* Scott); *m* 1960, Georgina Mabel, (Gena) (*née* Chadwin); one *d*. *Educ:* High Sch. of Glasgow; Univ. of Glasgow (MA, BD); Episcopal Theol Coll., Edinburgh. Deacon 1957; priest 1958. Assistant Curate: St Andrew's, St Andrews, 1957–60; St Margaret's, Newlands, Glasgow, 1960–63; Rector, Church of the Holy Cross, Davidson's Mains, Edinburgh, 1963–83; External Lectr in New Testament, Episcopal Theol Coll., Edin., 1963–74; Canon of St Mary's Cathedral, Edinburgh, 1973–83; Rector of St Andrew's, St Andrews, 1983–90; Tutor in Biblical Studies, Univ. of St Andrews, 1984–90; warrant, dio. of Edinburgh, 1997–. Hon. Canon, Trinity Cathedral, Davenport, Iowa, 1990. *Recreations:* walking, reading, gardening, uniting the Church. *Address:* 28 Forbes Road, Edinburgh EH10 4ED. *T:* (0131) 221 1490.

HALLIDAY, Vice-Adm. Sir Roy (William), KBE 1980; DSC 1944; Director General of Intelligence, Ministry of Defence, 1981–84; *b* 27 June 1923; *m* 1945, Dorothy Joan Meech. *Educ:* William Ellis Sch.; University College Sch. Joined Royal Navy, 1941; served in Fleet Air Arm (fighter pilot) in World War II, in HMS Chaser, HMSs Victorious and Illustrious; test pilot, Boscombe Down, 1947–48; Comdg Officer 813 Sqdn (Wyverns, HMS Eagle), 1954; Army Staff Coll., Camberley; Comdr, 1958; Exec. Officer Coastal Forces Base (HMS Diligence), 1959; Sen. Officer 104th Minesweeping Sqdn, Far East Flt, in comd (HMS Houghton), 1961–62; Naval Asst to Chief of Naval Information, 1962–64; comdr (Air) HMS Albion, 1964–66; Captain, 1966; Dep. Dir Naval Air Warfare, 1966–70; HMS Euryalus in comd and as Captain D3 Far East Fleet and D6 Western Fleet, 1970–71; Commodore, 1971; Cdre Amphibious Warfare, 1971–73; Cdre Intelligence, Defence Intelligence Staff, 1973–75; Comdr British Navy Staff, Washington, Naval Attaché, and UK Nat. Liaison Rep. to SACLANT, 1975–78; Dep. Chief of Defence Staff (Intelligence), 1978–81. ADC to the Queen, 1975. *Recreations:* gardening, walking. *Address:* Willow Cottage, Bank, Lyndhurst, Hants SO43 7FD. *Club:* Naval.

HALLIDAY, S. F. P.; *see* Halliday, F.

HALLIDAY, Sandra Pauline, CEng; Founder and Principal, Gaia Research, since 1996; *b* 14 April 1957; *d* of late Bernard Derek Arthur Halliday and of Joyce Heaton Halliday (*née* Atkin); *m* 1995, Howard Liddell. *Educ:* Warwick Univ. (BSc Hons Engrg Design and Appropriate Technology); Reading Univ. (MPhil 1999). MCIBSE 1994. Research: Univ. of Bath, 1986–89 (Res. Officer, 1986; Sen. Res. Officer, 1987); Univ. of Reading, 1989–91 (Vis. Res. Officer, 1991); Res. Engr to Prin. Res. Engr, and Head of Centre for Construction Ecology, BSRIA, 1990–95. Current research projects incl. active and passive solar design, innovative building membranes, roundpole construction, daylighting, low allergy housing, research and guidance in sustainable construction. FRSA. *Publications:* Green Guide to the Architects' Job Book, 2000; papers, articles, technical reports and conf. proceedings. *Recreations:* squash, Go, walking, cycling, ecology. *Address:* (office) The Monastery, Hart Street Lane, Edinburgh EH1 3RG.

HALLIDAY, Prof. Timothy Richard, DPhil; Professor in Biology, The Open University, since 1991; *b* 11 Sept. 1945; *s* of Jack and Edna Halliday; *m* 1970, Carolyn Bridget Wheeler; one *s* two *d*. *Educ:* Marlborough Coll.; New Coll., Oxford (MA, DPhil); King's Coll., Cambridge (CertEd). Lectr, Sen. Lectr and Reader, 1977–91, Open Univ. Internat. Dir, IUCN/SSC Declining Amphibian Populations Task Force, 1994. Chm., Conservation and Consultancy Bd, Zool Soc. of London, 1993–96. *Publications:* Vanishing Birds, 1978; Sexual Strategy, 1980; (with K. Adler) The Encyclopedia of Reptiles and Amphibians, 1986 (numerous foreign language edns); (ed) Animal Behavior, 1994. *Recreations:* biological illustration, gardening, travel. *Address:* 21 Farndon Road, Oxford OX2 6RT. *T:* (01865) 512163; Department of Biological Sciences, The Open University, Milton Keynes MK7 6AA. *T:* (01908) 653831.

HALLINAN, Mary Alethea, (Lady Hallinan); *see* Parry Evans, M.A.

HALLIWELL, Prof. Richard Edward Winter; William Dick Professor of Veterinary Clinical Studies, Royal (Dick) School of Veterinary Studies, University of Edinburgh, since 1988 (Dean, Faculty of Veterinary Medicine, 1990–94); *b* 16 June 1937; *s* of Arthur Clare Halliwell and Winifred Dorothea Goode; *m* 1963, Jenifer Helen Roper; two *d*. *Educ:* St Edward's Sch., Oxford; Gonville and Caius Coll., Cambridge (MA, VetMB, PhD); MRCVS. Jun. Fellow in Vet. Surgery, Univ. of Bristol, 1961–63; private vet. practice, London, 1963–68; Vis. Fellow in Dermatology, Univ. of Pennsylvania Sch. of Vet. Med., 1968–70; Wellcome Vet. Fellowship Univ. of Cambridge, 1970–73; Asst Prof. of Dermatology, Univ. of Pennsylvania Sch. of Vet. Med., 1973–77; Prof. and Chm., Dept of Med. Scis, Univ. of Florida Coll. of Vet. Med., 1977–88; Prof., Dept of Med. Microbiol., Univ. of Florida Coll. of Med., 1977–88. UK Rep., EC Adv. Cttee on Vet. Trng, 1994–. President: Amer. Acad. of Veterinary Allergy, 1978–80; Amer. Assoc. of Veterinary Immunologists, 1984; Amer. Coll. of Veterinary Dermatology, 1984–86; Eur. Assoc. of Estabs for Vet. Educn, 1994–98; Eur. Coll. of Vet. Dermatology, 1996–98; World Congress of Vet. Dermatology Assoc., 1999–. FMedSci 1999. *Publications:* (with N. T. Gorman) Veterinary Clinical Immunology, 1989; (with C. von Tscharner) Advances in Veterinary Dermatology, 1990; numerous pubns in area of clin. immunology and vet. dermatology. *Recreations:* hill walking, surfing. *Address:* 2A Ainslie Place, Edinburgh EH3 6AR. *T:* (0131) 225 8765.

HALLON, Gayle, (Mrs J. A. Hodgson); Her Honour Judge Hallon; a Circuit Judge, South Eastern Circuit, since 1992; *b* 10 Aug. 1946; *d* of late Douglas Hallon, VRD, FRCS and Enid (*née* Bailey); *m* 1971, John Arnold Hodgson. *Educ:* Cheltenham Ladies' Coll.; St Hugh's Coll., Oxford (MA). Called to the Bar, Inner Temple, 1968; practised at the Bar, 1969–92; Recorder, 1987–92. *Recreations:* gardening, acting. *Address:* The Court House, College Road, Bromley, Kent BR1 3PX. *T:* (020) 8464 9727.

HALLSWORTH, Prof. Ernest Gordon, DSc, FRSC, FTSE; scientific consultant and author; Chairman of Directors, Hallsworth and Associates; *b* 1913; *s* of Ernest and Beatrice Hallsworth, Ashton-under-Lyne, Lancs; *m* 1st, 1943, Elaine Gertrude Seddon (*d* 1970), *d* of R. C. Weatherill, Waverley, NSW; two *s* one *d* and one step *s*; 2nd, 1976, Merrily Ramly; one step *d*. *Educ:* Ashton Grammar Sch., Ashton-under-Lyne, Lancs; Univ. of Leeds. University of Leeds: First Cl. Hons in Agric. Chem., Sir Swire Smith Fellow, 1936; Asst Lectr in Agric. Chem., 1936; PhD 1939; DSc 1964. Lectr in Agric. Chem., Univ. of Sydney, 1940–51; Prof. of Soil Science, Univ. of West Australia, 1960–61; Prof. of Agric. Chem. and Head Dept Agric. Sci., Univ. Nottingham, 1951–64 (Dean, Faculty of Agric. and Hort., 1951–60); Chief of Div. of Soils, CSIRO, 1964–73; Chm., Land Resources Labs, CSIRO, 1973–78; Hon. Professorial Fellow, Science Policy Res. Unit, Sussex Univ., 1979–85. Pres. Lecturers' Assoc., Sydney Univ., 1946–49. Treas., Aust. Assoc. of Scientific Workers, 1943; Member: Science Advisory Panel, Australian Broadcasting Commn, 1949–51; Pasture Improvement Cttee, Australian Dairy Produce Bd (NSW), 1948–51; Chm. Insecticides and Fungicides Cttee, Australian Standards Inst., 1949–51. President: Internat. Soc. of Soil Science, 1964–68; Sect. 13, Aust. and NZ Assoc. for the Advancement of Science, 1976. Mem. Council, Flinders Univ., 1967–79; Chief Scientific Liaison Officer (Aust.), London, 1971. Fellow: Aust. Acad. of Technol Scis and Engrg, 1976–; World Acad. of Art and Science, 1989–; Mem., Académie d'Agriculture de France, 1983–; Hon. Member: Aust. Soc. of Soil Sci., 1984; Internat. Soc. of Soil Sci., 1990. Prescott Medal, Aust. Soc. Soil Science, 1984; Dokuchaev Medal, All-Union Soc. of Soil Sci., 1990. *Publications:* (Ed) Nutrition of the Legumes, 1958; (ed with D. V. Crawford) Experimental Pedology, 1964; (with others) Handbook of Australian Soils, 1968; (with others) Principles of a Balanced Land Use Policy for Australia, 1976; Where Shall We Build Our New Cities?, 1978; Land and Water Resources of Australia, 1979; Socio-economic Effects and Restraints in Tropical Forest Management, 1982; The Anatomy, Physiology and Psychology of Erosion, 1987; contributions to: Aust. Jl Science, Jl Soc. Chem. Indust., Experimental Agric., Jl Agric. Science, Aust. Medical Jl, Jl Soil Science. *Recreations:* talking, pedology. *Address:* 8 Old Belair Road, Mitcham, SA 5062, Australia. *T:* (8) 82716423; 1 Bellevue Cottages, Blackboys, near Uckfield, Sussex. *T:* (01825) 890606. *Club:* Farmers'.

HALLWARD, Bertrand Leslie, MA; *b* 24 May 1901; *er s* of late N. L. Hallward, Indian Educational Service, and Evelyn A. Gurdon; *m* 1926, Catherine Margaret (*d* 1991), 2nd *d* of late Canon A. J. Tait, DD; four *d*. *Educ:* Haileybury Coll. (Scholar); King's Coll., Cambridge (Scholar). Fellow of Peterhouse, 1923–39 (Hon. Fellow, 1956), and Univ. Lectr, 1926–39, Cambridge; Headmaster of Clifton Coll., 1939–48; Vice-Chancellor, Nottingham Univ., 1948–65 (Hallward Library named at Nottingham Univ., 1989). Editor, Classical Qly, 1935–39. Hon. LLD: Chattanooga, USA, 1958; Sheffield, 1964; Nottingham, 1965. *Publications:* Chapters II, III, IV, and part of VII (the Second and Third Punic Wars) in Cambridge Ancient History, Vol. VIII, 1930; *relevant publication:* Bertrand Hallward, by Derek Winterbottom, 1996. *Address:* 5 High Street, Chesterton, Cambridge CB4 1NQ.

See also W. O. Chadwick, G. C. H. Spafford.

HALNAN, His Honour Patrick John; a Circuit Judge, 1986–97; *b* 7 March 1925; *s* of E. T. and A. B. Halnan; *m* 1955, Judith Mary (*née* Humberstone); four *c*. *Educ:* Perse Sch., Cambridge; Trinity Coll., Cambridge (MA). Army, 1943–47; TA, 1951–58. Solicitor. Asst Solicitor, Hants CC, 1954–58; Clerk to the Justices, Cambs, 1958–78; Metropolitan Stipendiary Magistrate, 1978–86; a Recorder, 1983–86; SE Circuit. Sec., Justices' Clerks' Soc., 1972–76, Pres., 1978. Chm., Road Traffic Cttee, Magistrates' Assoc., 1981–87. *Publications:* (ed with Prof. R. M. Jackson) Leo Page, Justice of the Peace, 3rd edn 1967; (ed) Wilkinson's Road Traffic Offences, 7th edn 1973 to 14th edn 1989; (with David Latham) Drink/Driving Offences, 1979; Road Traffic, 1981; Drink/Drive: the new law, 1984. *Recreations:* Freemasonry, travelling, bridge, postal history. *Club:* Oxford and Cambridge.

HALONEN, Tarja Kaarina; President of Finland, since 2000; *b* Helsinki, 24 Dec. 1943; *m* (marr. diss.); one *d*; *m* 2000, Pentti Arajarvi. *Educ:* Univ. of Helsinki (ML). Lawyer, Lainvalvonta Oy, 1967–68; Social Welfare Officer and Organizing Sec., Nat. Union of Finnish Students, 1969–70; Lawyer, Cultural Orgn of Finnish Trade Unions, 1970–74; lawyer, 1975–79. Parly Sec. to Prime Minister, 1974–75; Mem., Helsinki CC, 1977–96. MP (SDP), Finland, 1979–2000; Chm., Parly Social Affairs Cttee, 1984–87; Minister, Min. of Social Affairs and Health, 1987–90; Minister: for Nordic Co-operation, 1989–91; of Justice, 1990–91; for Foreign Affairs, 1995–2000. *Address:* Office of the President, 00170 Helsinki, Finland.

HALPERN, Prof. Jack, FRS 1974; Louis Block Distinguished Service Professor of Chemistry, University of Chicago, since 1984; *b* Poland, 19 Jan. 1925 (moved to Canada, 1929; USA 1962); *s* of Philip Halpern and Anna Sass; *m* 1949, Helen Peritz; two *d*. *Educ:* McGill Univ., Montreal. BSc 1946, PhD 1949. NRC Postdoc. Fellow, Univ. of Manchester, 1949–50; Prof. of Chem., Univ. of Brit. Columbia, 1950–62 (Nuffield Foundn Travelling Fellow, Cambridge Univ., 1959–60); Prof. of Chem., Univ. of Chicago, 1962–71, Louis Block Prof., 1971–84. Visiting Prof.: Univ. of Minnesota, 1962; Harvard Univ., 1966–67; CIT, 1969; Princeton Univ., 1970–71; Copenhagen Univ., 1978; Firth Vis. Prof., Sheffield, 1982; Sherman Fairchild Dist. Scholar, CIT, 1979; Guest Scholar, Kyoto Univ., 1981; Phi Beta Kappa Vis. Scholar, 1990; R. B. Woodward Vis. Prof., Harvard Univ., 1991; External Sci. Mem., Max Planck Institut für Kohlenforschung, Mulheim, 1983–; Lectureships: 3M, Univ. of Minnesota, 1968; FMC, Princeton Univ., 1969; Du Pont, Univ. of Calif., Berkeley, 1970; Frontier of Chemistry, Case Western Reserve Univ., 1971, 1989; Venable, Univ. of N Carolina, 1973; Ritter Meml, Miami Univ., 1980; University, Univ. of Western Ontario, F. J. Toole, Univ. of New Brunswick, 1981; Werner, Univ. of Kansas, Lansdowne, Univ. of Victoria, 1982; Welch, Univ. of Texas, 1983; Kilpatrick, Illinois Inst. of Tech., 1984; Dow, Univ. of Ottawa, Boomer, Univ. of Alberta, 1985; Bailar, Univ. of Illinois, 1986; Priestley, Penn State Univ., 1987; Taube, Stanford Univ., 1988; Res. Schol., Drew Univ., Liebig. Univ. of Colorado, 1989; Kennedy, Washington Univ., Karcher, Univ. of Oklahoma, Nieuland, Notre Dame, Swift, CIT, Hutchison, Univ. of Rochester, 1992; Rhone-Poulenc, Scripps Res. Inst., Basolo, Northwestern Univ., 1993; Patrick, Kansas State Univ., Jonassen, Tulane Univ., 1995. Associate Editor: Jl of Amer. Chem. Soc.; Inorganica Chimica Acta; Mem. Editorial Bds: Accounts of Chemical Research; Jl of Catalysis; Catalysis Reviews; Jl of Coordination Chem.; Inorganic Syntheses; Jl of Molecular Catalysis; Jl of Organometallic Chemistry; Amer. Chem. Soc. Advances in Chemistry series; Gazzetta Chimica Italiana; Organometallics; Catalysis Letters; Reaction Kinetics and Catalysis Letters; Co-editor, OUP International Series of Monographs in Chemistry; Sen. Contributing Editor, Proceedings of Nat. Acad. of Scis. Member: Nat. Sci. Foundn Chemistry Adv. Panel, 1967–70; MIT Chemistry Vis. Cttee, 1968–70; Argonne Nat. Lab. Chemistry Vis. Cttee, 1970–73; Amer. Chem. Soc. Petroleum Res. Fund Adv. Bd, 1972–74; NIH Medicinal Chem. Study Sect., 1975–78 (Chm., 1976–78); Princeton Univ. Chem. Adv. Council, 1982–; Chemistry Adv. Cttee, CIT, 1991–; Encyclopaedia Britannica Univ. Adv. Cttee, 1985–. Mem., Bd of Trustees and Council, Gordon Research Confs, 1968–70; Chm., Gordon Conf. on Inorganic Chem., 1969; Chm., Amer. Chemical Soc. Div. of Inorganic Chem., 1971; Mem., 1985–, Mem., Council, 1990–, Chm., Chem. Sect., Vice-Pres., 1993–, Nat. Acad. of Scis (For. Mem., 1984–85). Chm., German–Amer. Acad. Council, 1993–96, Chm. Bd of Trustees, 1996–. Member: Bd of Dirs, Renaissance Soc., 1984–; Bd of Govs, Smart Mus., Univ. of Chicago, 1988–; Adv. Bd, Court Theatre, Univ. of Chicago, 1989–; Dir, Amer. Friends of Royal Soc., 2000–. Fellow, Amer. Acad. of Arts and Sciences, 1967; Sci. Mem., Max Planck Soc., 1983. Hon. FRSC 1987. Hon. DSc: Univ. of British Columbia, 1986; McGill Univ., 1997. Holds numerous honours and awards, including: Amer. Chem. Soc. Award in Inorganic Chem., 1968; Chem. Soc. Award, 1976; Humboldt Award, 1977; Kokes Award, Johns Hopkins Univ., 1978; Amer. Chem. Soc. Award for Distinguished Service in the Advancement of Inorganic Chemistry, 1985; Willard Gibbs Medal, 1986; Bailar Medal, Univ. of Illinois, 1986; Hoffman Medal, German Chem. Soc., 1988; Chemical Pioneer Award, Amer. Inst. of Chemists, 1991; Paracelsus Prize, Swiss Chem. Soc., 1992; Basolo Medal, Northwestern Univ., 1993; Robert A. Welch Award in Chemistry, 1994; Amer. Chem. Soc. Award in Organometallic Chemistry, 1995. Cross of Merit (Germany), 1996. *Publications:* Editor (with F. Basolo and J. Bunnett) Collected Accounts of Transition Metal Chemistry, vol. I, 1973, vol. II, 1977; contrib. articles on Catalysis and on Coordination Compounds to Encyclopaedia Britannica; numerous articles to Jl of Amer. Chemical Soc. and other scientific jls. *Recreations:* art, music, theatre. *Address:* Department of Chemistry, University of Chicago, 5735 South Ellis Avenue, Chicago, IL 60637, USA. *T:* (773) 7027095. *Club:* Quadrangle (Chicago).

HALPERN, Sir Ralph (Mark), Kt 1986; Chairman, Halpern Associates, since 1994; Chairman, 1981–90, and Chief Executive, 1978–90, Burton Group plc (Managing Director, 1978); *b* 1938; *m* (marr. diss.); one *d*; one *s*. *Educ:* St Christopher School, Letchworth. Started career as trainee, Selfridges; joined Burton Group, 1961; founder, Top Shop, 1970. Member: President's Cttee, CBI, 1984–90; President's Cttee, Business in the Community, 1991–92; Adv. Council, Prince's Youth Business Trust, 1991–. Chm., British Fashion Council, 1990–94. Local Councillor, Surrey; Chm., E Surrey Rural Police and Community Partnership Gp. FInstD; CIMgt. *Club:* Reform.

HALSALL, Hazel Anne; *see* Blears, H. A.

HALSBURY, 4th Earl of; *see* Giffard, A. E.

HALSEY, Prof. Albert Henry, FBA 1995; Professor of Social and Administrative Studies, University of Oxford, 1978–90, now Emeritus; Professorial Fellow of Nuffield College, Oxford, 1962–90, now Emeritus; *b* 13 April 1923; *m* 1949, Gertrude Margaret Littler; three *s* two *d*. *Educ:* Kettering Grammar Sch.; London Sch. of Econs (BSc (Econ); PhD; Hon. Fellow, 1993); MA Oxon. RAF, 1942–47; student LSE, 1947–52; Research Worker, Liverpool Univ., 1952–54; Lectr in Sociology, Birmingham Univ., 1954–62; Dir, Dept of Social and Admin. Studies, Oxford Univ., 1962–78. Fellow, Center for Advanced Study of Behavioral Sciences, Palo Alto, Calif, 1956–57; Vis. Prof. of Sociology, Univ. of Chicago, 1959–60. Adviser to Sec. of State for Educn, 1965–68; Chm. of CERI at OECD, Paris, 1968–70. Reith Lectr, 1977. MAE 1992; Foreign Associate, Amer. Acad. of Educn.; Foreign Mem., Amer. Acad. of Arts and Scis, 1988. Hon. Fellow: Goldsmiths' Coll., 1992; Westminster Coll., 1996; Royal Statistical Soc., 1999. Hon. DSocSc Birmingham, 1987; DUniv Open, 1990; Hon. DLitt: Glamorgan, 1994; Leicester, 1995; Warwick, 1995. *Publications:* (jtly) Social Class and Educational Opportunity, 1956; (jtly) Technical Change and Industrial Relations, 1956; (with J. E. Floud) The Sociology of Education, Current Sociology VII, 1958; (jtly) Education, Economy and Society, 1961; Ability and Educational Opportunity, 1962; (with G. N. Ostergaard) Power in Co-operatives, 1965; (with Ivor Crewe) Social Survey of the Civil Service, 1969; (with Martin Trow) The British Academics, 1971; (ed) Trends in British Society since 1900, 1972; (ed) Educational Priority, 1972; Traditions of Social Policy, 1976; Heredity and Environment, 1977; Change in British Society, 1978, 4th edn 1995; (jtly) Origins and Destinations, 1980; (with Norman Dennis) English Ethical Socialism, 1988; Decline of Donnish Dominion, 1992, 2nd edn 1995; No Discouragement, 1996; (jtly) Education, Culture, Economy, Society, 1997; (ed) British Social Trends: the twentieth century, 2000; numerous articles and reviews. *Address:* 28 Upland Park Road, Oxford OX2 7RU. *T:* (01865) 558625.

HALSEY, Rt Rev. (Henry) David; Bishop of Carlisle, 1972–89; *b* 27 Jan. 1919; *s* of George Halsey, MBE and Gladys W. Halsey, DSc; *m* 1947, Rachel Margaret Neil Smith; four *d*. *Educ:* King's Coll. Sch., Wimbledon; King's Coll., London (BA); Wells Theol College. Curate, Petersfield, 1942–45; Chaplain, RNVR, 1946–47; Curate, St Andrew, Plymouth, 1947–50; Vicar of: Netheravon, 1950–53; St Stephen, Chatham, 1953–62; Bromley, and Chaplain, Bromley Hosp., 1962–68; Rural Dean of Bromley, 1965–66; Archdeacon of Bromley, 1966–68; Bishop Suffragan of Tonbridge, 1968–72. Entered House of Lords, 1976. *Recreations:* cricket, sailing, reading, gardening, walking. *Address:* Bramblecross, Gully Road, Seaview, Isle of Wight PO34 5BY.
See also D. French.

HALSEY, Rev. John Walter Brooke, 4th Bt *cr* 1920 (but uses designation Brother John Halsey); *b* 26 Dec. 1933; *s* of Sir Thomas Edgar Halsey, 3rd Bt, DSO, and of Jean Margaret Palmer, *d* of late Bertram Willes Dayrell Brooke; *S* father, 1970. *Educ:* Eton; Magdalene College, Cambridge (BA 1957). Deacon, 1961, priest, 1962, Diocese of York; Curate of Stocksbridge, 1961–65; Brother in Community of the Transfiguration, 1965–. *Heir: cousin* Nicholas Guy Halsey, TD [*b* 14 June 1948; *m* 1976, Viola Georgina Juliet, *d* of Maj. George Thorne, MC, DL; one *s*]. *Address:* The Hermitage, 23 Manse Road, Roslin, Midlothian EH25 9LF.

HALSEY, Philip Hugh, CB 1986; LVO 1972; Deputy Secretary, Department of Education and Science, 1982–88; *b* 9 May 1928; *s* of Sidney Robert Halsey and Edith Mary Halsey; *m* 1956, Hilda Mary Biggerstaff; two *s*. *Educ:* University Coll. London (BSc; Fellow, 1992). Headmaster, Hampstead Sch., 1961; Principal, DES, 1966; Under-Sec., 1977. Chm. and Chief Exec., Sch. Exams and Assessment Council, 1988–91; Mem., Sch. Teachers' Review Body, 1991–96.

HALSEY, Simon Patrick; Chorus Director, City of Birmingham Symphony Orchestra, since 1982; Chief Conductor, Berlin Rundfunk Chor, since 2000; *b* 8 March 1958; *s* of Louis Arthur Owen Halsey and Evelyn Elisabeth (*née* Calder); *m* 1986, Lucy Jane Lunt; one *s* one *d*. *Educ:* chorister, New Coll., Oxford; Winchester Coll.; King's Coll., Cambridge (Choral Schol.; BA 1979; MA 1983); Royal Coll. Music (Schol.). Conductor, Scottish Opera (Opera-Go-Round), 1979; Dir of Music, Univ. of Warwick, 1980–88; Principal Conductor, City of Birmingham Touring Opera, 1987–2000; Chorus Dir, De Vlaamse Opera, Antwerp, 1991–94; Artistic Dir, BBC Nat. Chorus of Wales, 1995–2000. Chief Guest Conductor: Netherlands Radio Choir, 1995–; Sydney Philharmonia Choirs, 1997–; frequent Guest Conductor of choruses, Châtelet Th., Paris, 1996–, and Salzburg Fest., 1998–; Chorus Dir, Sydney Olympic Games, 2000. Consultant Ed., Faber Music, 1994–. Hon. Dr UCE, 2000. Recording awards include: Gramophone Record of Year, Gramophone Magazine, 1988; Deutsche Schallplatten Kritiek Preis, 1993. *Publications:* Ed., 30 vols of choral music, 1995–. *Recreations:* reading, walking. *Address:* Granby House, 279 High Street, Henley-in-Arden, Warwickshire B95 5BG. *T:* (01564) 794873.

HALSTEAD, Sir Ronald, Kt 1985; CBE 1976; Deputy Chairman, British Steel plc (formerly British Steel Corporation), 1986–94; *b* 17 May 1927; *s* of Richard and Bessie Harrison Halstead; *m* 1968, Yvonne Cecile de Monchaux (*d* 1978); two *s*. *Educ:* Lancaster Royal Grammar Sch.; Queens' Coll., Cambridge (Hon. Fellow, 1985). MA, FRSC. Research Chemist, H. P. Bulmer & Co, 1948–53; Manufg Manager, Macleans Ltd, 1954–55; Factory Manager, Beecham Products Inc. (USA), 1955–60; Asst Managing Dir, Beecham Research Labs, 1960–62; Vice-Pres. (Marketing), Beecham Products Inc. (USA), 1962–64; Pres., Beecham Research Labs Inc. (USA), 1962–64; Chairman: Food and Drink Div., Beecham Group Ltd, 1964–67; Beecham Products, 1967–84; Man. Dir (Consumer Products) Beecham Gp, 1973–84; Chm. and Chief Exec., Beecham Gp, 1984–85. Dir, Otis Elevator Co. Ltd (UK), 1978–83; Non-Exec. Director: BSC, later British Steel, 1979–94; The Burmah Oil PLC, 1983–89; Amer. Cyanamid Co. (USA), 1986–94; Davy Corp. plc, 1986–91; Gestetner Holdings PLC, 1986–95; Laurentian Financial Gp, 1991–95. Mem. Egg Re-organisation Commn, 1967–68; Pres., Incorp. Soc. of Brit. Advertisers, 1971–73; Chairman: British Nutrition Foundn, 1970–73; Knitting Sector Gp (formerly Knitting Sector Working Party), NEDO, 1978–90; Bd for Food Studies, Reading Univ., 1983–86; Garment and Textile Sector Gp, NEDO, 1991–93; CAB Internat., 1995–98; Cons. Foreign and Commonwealth Council, 1995–. Vice-Chairman: Proprietary Assoc. of GB, 1968–77; Advertising Assoc., 1973–81; Food and Drink Industries Council, 1973–76; Member: Council and Exec. Cttee, Food Manufrs' Fedn Inc., 1966–85 (Pres., 1974–76); Council, British Nutrition Foundn, 1967–79; Cambridge Univ. Appts Bd, 1969–73; Council, CBI, 1970–86; Council, BIM, 1972–77; Council, Univ. of Buckingham (formerly University Coll. at Buckingham), 1973–95; Council, Nat. Coll. of Food Technol., 1977–78 (Chm. Bd, 1978–83); Council, Univ. of Reading, 1978–98; AFRC, 1978–84; Council, Trade Policy Res. Centre, 1985–89; Monopolies and Mergers Commn, 1993–99 (Mem., Newspaper Panel, 1980–92); Industrial Develt Adv. Bd, 1984–93 (Chm., 1985–93); Council and Exec. Cttee, Imperial Soc. of Knights Bachelor, 1986–. Dir and Hon. Treas., Centre for Policy Studies, 1984–93. Trustee, Inst. of Economic Affairs, 1980–93. Governor, Ashridge Management Coll., 1970– (Vice-Chm., 1977–); President: Nat. Advertising Benevolent Soc., 1978–80; Inst. of Packaging, 1981–82 (a Vice-Pres., 1979–81). Fellow, Marketing Soc., 1981; FIMgt; FInstM; FIGD; FRSA; FRSC. Hon. Fellow, Inst. of Food Sci. and Technol., 1983–84. Hon. DSc: Reading, 1982; Lancaster, 1987. *Recreations:* sailing, squash racquets, ski-ing. *Address:* 37 Edwardes Square, W8 6HH. *T:* (020) 7603 9010. *Clubs:* Athenæum, Brooks's, Hurlingham, Carlton, Lansdowne, Royal Thames Yacht.

HALVERSON, Hon. Robert George, OBE 1978; Ambassador for Australia to Ireland and the Holy See, since 1999; *b* 22 Oct. 1937; *m* 1958, Margaret Charlton; three *s* one *d*. *Educ:* Swinburne Tech. Coll.; Canberra Coll. of Advanced Education. Joined RAAF, 1956; commnd, 1957; retired in rank of Gp Capt., 1981; with Robertson Thompson Partners, 1981–84. MP (L) Casey, Victoria, 1984–98; Chief Opposition Whip, 1994–96; Speaker, House of Reps, Australia, 1996–98. *Address:* Australian Embassy Dublin, Locked Bag 40, Kingston, ACT 2604, Australia.

HALWARD, Robin Paul; Director General, Northern Ireland Prison Service, since 1998; *b* 10 June 1951; *s* of Raymond Silburn Halward and Joan Margaret Halward (*née* Whittles); *m* 1974, Valerie Jean Taylor; one *s* one *d*. *Educ:* Royal Grammar Sch., Guildford; Trinity Coll., Cambridge (MA). Housemaster, Gaynes Hall Borstal, 1973–77; Assistant Gov., Gartree Prison, 1977–80; Tutor, Prison Service Coll., Wakefield, 1980–84; Dep. Gov., Manchester Prison, 1984–88; Asst Dir, Prison Service N Reg., 1988–90; Governor: Leeds Prison, 1990–92; Manchester Prison, 1992–95; Prison Service Area Manager, Mersey and Manchester, 1996–97; Sec., Metropolitan Police Cttee, 1997–98. *Recreations:* city life in Manchester, squash, hill-walking. *Address:* Prison Service Headquarters, Dundonald House, Upper Newtownards Road, Belfast BT4 3SU. *T:* (028) 9052 5219.

HAM, Prof. Christopher John, PhD; Policy Analyst, Strategy Unit, Department of Health, since 2000 (on secondment); Professor of Health Policy and Management and Director, Health Services Management Centre, University of Birmingham, since 1992; *b* 15 May 1951; *s* of Raymond Percival Thomas Ham and Agnes Anne Ham (*née* Evans); *m* 1980, Ioanna Burnell; two *s* one *d*. *Educ:* Cardiff High Sch.; Univ. of Kent (BA MPhil); Univ. of Bristol (PhD 1983). Research Asst, Univ. of Leeds, 1975–77; Lectr in Health Policy, Univ. of Bristol, 1977–86; Fellow, King's Fund Coll. and King's Fund Inst., 1986–92. Advr to World Bank, WHO, Audit Commn, NAO, BMA, RCP, etc. FRSocMed; Founder FMedSci 1998. *Publications:* Policy Making in the NHS, 1981; Health Policy in Britain, 1982, 4th edn 1999; (with M. J. Hill) The Policy Process in the Modern Capitalist State, 1984; Managing Health Services, 1986; (jtly) Health Check: health care reforms in an international context, 1990; The New NHS: organisation and management, 1991; (jtly) Priority Setting Processes for Healthcare, 1995; Public, Private or Community: what next for the NHS?, 1996; Management and Competition in the NHS, 1994, 2nd edn 1997; (ed) Health Care Reform, 1997; (with S. Pickard) Tragic Choices in Health Care: the case of Child B, 1998; (with A. Coulter) The Global Challenge of Health Care Rationing, 2000; The Politics of NHS Reform 1988–1997, 2000. *Recreations:* sport, music, theatre, reading, travel. *Address:* Health Services Management Centre, University of Birmingham, Birmingham B15 2RT. *T:* (0121) 414 6214.

HAM, David Kenneth R.; *see* Rowe-Ham.

HÄMÄLÄINEN-LINDFORS, Sirkka Aune-Marjatta, DSc; Member, Executive Board, European Central Bank, since 1998; *b* 8 May 1939; *m* Bo Lindfors; two *c*. *Educ:* Helsinki Sch. of Econs and Business Admin (BSc Econs 1961; MSc Econs 1964; Licentiate of Sci. (Econs) 1979; DSc 1981). Economics Department, Bank of Finland: Economist, 1961–72; Head of Office, 1972–79; acting Head of Econs Dept, 1979–81; Dir, Econs Dept, Finnish Min. of Finance, 1981–82; Bank of Finland: Dir resp. for macroeconomic analysis and monetary and exchange rate policy, 1982–91; Mem. of Bd, 1991–92; Gov. and Chm. of Bd, 1992–98. Docent and Adjacent Prof. in Econs, Helsinki Sch. of Econs and Business Admin, 1991–. Member: Council, European Monetary Inst., 1992–98; Economic Council of Finland, 1992–98; Nat. Bd of Economic Defence, 1992–98; Internat. Adv. Council, CEPS, 1993–98; Trilateral Commn (Europe), 1995–; Bd, Foundn for Economic Educn, 1996–; Central Bank Governance Steering Cttee, BIS, 1996–; Develt Prog. of Nat. Strategy, 1996–98; Finnish Public R&D Financing Evaluation Gp, 1998; Chm., Bd of Financial Supervision Authy, 1996–97. Member: Bd, Finnish Nat. Theatre, 1992–98; Supervisory Bd, Finnish Cultural Foundn, 1996–; Bd, The Raging Roses, theatre gp (Chm., 1997–99). Hon. Dr Turku Sch. of Econs and Business Admin, 1995. Comdr, 1st Cl., Order of White Rose (Finland); Merit Medal, 1st Cl., Order of White Star (Estonia). *Publications:* numerous articles on economics and monetary policy. *Address:* European Central Bank, Kaiserstrasse 29, 60311 Frankfurt, Germany. *T:* (69) 13440, *Fax:* (69) 13446000.

HAMANN, Paul; Creative Director, Factual Programmes, Shine Ltd, since 2001; Chairman, Reprieve, since 2000; *b* 9 Nov. 1948; *s* of Leonard Hamann and Anita Davies; *m* 1st, 1971, Kay Allen (marr. diss. 1981); (one *d* decd); 2nd, 1981, Marilyn Wheatcroft (marr. diss. 1999); one *s* one *d*. Dir and Prod., over 50 documentaries for BBC TV, 1976–88: incl. Your Life in Their Files, Sister Genevieve, Pushers At the Edge of the Union, A Company, Africa's Last Colony, Transmit and be Damned, Phantom, Lest We Forget, The Duty Men (Best Factual Series Award, BAFTA, 1987), Fourteen Days in May (Grierson Award, BFI, 1988); Editor, BBC 1 Documentaries, 1989–93: series incl. Inside Story, Rough Justice, Children's Hospital; Head of Documentaries, 1994–97, Head of Documentaries and Hist. and of Community Prog. Unit, 1997–2000, BBC TV. Chm., Factual Bd, 1996–99; Mem. Council, BAFTA, 1993–96. *Publications:* (with Peter Gillman) The Duty Men, 1987; contrib. professional jls. *Recreations:* my children, popular culture, opera, Italy. *Address:* c/o Reprieve, PO Box 31941, W2 6XY; *e-mail:* paul@hamann.co.uk.

HAMBIDGE, Most Rev. Douglas Walter, DD; Principal, St Mark's Theological College, and Assistant Bishop, Dar es Salaam, 1993–95; *b* London, England, 6 March 1927; *s* of Douglas Hambidge and Florence (*née* Driscoll); *m* 1956, Denise Colvill Lown; two *s* one *d*. *Educ:* London Univ.; London Coll. of Divinity. BD, ALCD; DD, Anglican Theol. Coll. of BC, 1970. Asst Curate, St Mark's, Dalston, 1953–56; Rector: All Saints,

Cassiar, BC, 1956–58; St James, Smithers, BC, 1958–64; Vicar, St Martin, Fort St John, BC, 1964–69; Canon, St Andrew's Cathedral, Caledonia, 1965–69; Bishop of Caledonia, 1969–80; Bishop of New Westminster, 1980; Archbishop of New Westminster and Metropolitan of Province of BC, 1981–93. Mem., ACC, 1990–93 (Mem., Standing Cttee, 1990–93). Pres., Missions to Seamen, 1980–93. Chancellor, Vancouver Sch. of Theology, 1999– (Mem. Bd of Governors, 1980–85). *Address:* 1621 Golf Club Drive, Delta, BC V4M 4E6, Canada; *e-mail:* hambidge@vst.edu.

HAMBLEDEN, 4th Viscount *cr* 1891; **William Herbert Smith;** *b* 2 April 1930; *e s* of 3rd Viscount and Patricia, GCVO (*d* 1994), *d* of 15th Earl of Pembroke, MVO; *S* father, 1948; *m* 1st, 1955, Donna Maria Carmela Attolico di Adelfia (marr. diss. 1988), *d* of late Count Bernardo Attolico and of Contessa Eleonora Attolico di Adelfia, Via Porta Latina, Rome; five *s*; 2nd, 1988, Mrs Lesley Watson. *Educ:* Eton. *Heir: s* Hon. William Henry Bernard Smith [*b* 18 Nov. 1955; *m* 1983, Sarah Suzanne, *d* of Joseph F. Anlauf and Mrs Suzanne K. Anlauf; two *d*]. *Address:* The Estate Office, Hambleden, Henley-on-Thames, Oxon. *T:* (01491) 571252.

HAMBLEN, Prof. David Lawrence, CBE 2001; FRCSE, FRCS, FRCSGlas; Professor of Orthopaedic Surgery, University of Glasgow, 1972–99, now Emeritus; Hon. Consultant Orthopaedic Surgeon, since 1972, and Chairman, since 1997, Greater Glasgow Health Board; *b* 31 Aug. 1934; *s* of Reginald John Hamblen and Bessie Hamblen (*née* Williams); *m* 1968, Gillian Frances Bradley; one *s* two *d*. *Educ:* Roan Sch., Greenwich; Univ. of London (MB BS 1957); PhD Edinburgh 1975. FRCSE 1962; FRCS 1963; FRCSGlas 1976. Fellowships at Harvard Med. Sch. and Massachusetts Gen. Hosp., 1966–67; Lectr in Orthopaedics, Nuffield Orthopaedic Centre, Univ. of Oxford, 1967–68; Sen. Lectr in Orthopaedic Surgery, Univ. of Edinburgh and Hon. Consultant Orthopaedic Surgeon to SE Regl Hosp. Bd, Scotland, 1968–72. Hon. Consultant in Orthopaedic Surgery to the Army in Scotland, 1976–99. Vis. Prof., Univ. of Strathclyde (Nat. Centre for Trng and Educn in Prosthetics and Orthotics), 1981–. Non-exec. Dir, W Glasgow Hosps Univ. NHS Trust, 1994–97. Chm. Council, Jl of Bone and Joint Surgery, 1995–. Member: British Orthopaedic Assoc. (Pres., 1990–91); British Hip Soc. (Pres., 2001–02); European Hip Soc. *Publications:* (ed with J. C. Adams): Outline of Fractures, 10th edn 1992, 11th edn 1999; Outline of Orthopaedics, 11th edn, 1990, 12th edn, 1995, 13th edn, 2001. *Recreations:* golf, music, reading. *Address:* Greater Glasgow Health Board, Dalian House, 350 St Vincent Street, Glasgow G3 8YZ. *T:* (0141) 201 4600, *Fax:* (0141) 201 4630. *Club:* Royal Society of Medicine.

HAMBLEN, Derek Ivens Archibald, CB 1978; OBE 1956; *b* 28 Oct. 1917; *s* of late Leonard Tom Hamblen and Ruth Mary Hamblen, *d* of Sir William Frederick Alphonse Archibald; *m* 1950, Pauline Alison, *d* of late Gen. Sir William Morgan, GCB, DSO, MC; one *s* one *d*. *Educ:* St Lawrence Coll., Ramsgate; St John's Coll., Oxford (Casberd Exhibn); Portuguese Essay Prize, 1938; BA Hons (Mod. Langs) 1940, MA 1949. Served War, 1940–46: 1st Army, N Africa, 1942–43; Major, GS, AFHQ, N Africa and Italy, and Adv. Mission to British Mil. HQ, Greece, 1944–45; GSO1, Allied Commn for Austria, 1945–46; Lt-Col, 1946. War Office, later Ministry of Defence, 1946–77: seconded HQ British Troops, Egypt, 1946–47; Asst Sec., Office of UK High Commn in Australia, 1951–55; seconded Foreign Office, 1957–60; Asst Sec., 1964–68; a Special Advr to NATO and SHAPE, 1968–74; Under Sec., 1974–77, retired. Mem. Bd of Governors, St Lawrence Coll., 1977–91 (Vice-Pres., 1991–). FRSA 1987. Medal of Merit, 1st cl. (Czechoslovakia), 1946. *Recreations:* cricket, hockey (represented Oxford v Cambridge, 1940), golf, music, reading. *Address:* c/o Lloyds TSB, East Grinstead, West Sussex RH19 1AH. *Clubs:* MCC; Vincent's (Oxford).
See also N. A. Hamblen.

HAMBLEN, Nicholas Archibald; QC 1997; a Recorder, since 2000; *b* 23 Sept. 1957; *s* of Derek Ivens Archibald Hamblen, *qv*; *m* 1985, Kate Hayden; one *s* one *d*. *Educ:* Westminster Sch.; St John's Coll., Oxford (MA); Harvard Law Sch. (LLM). Called to the Bar, Lincoln's Inn, 1981; specialist in commercial law; an Asst Recorder, 1999–2000. *Address:* 20 Essex Street, WC2R 3AL. *Clubs:* MCC, Hurlingham; Vincent's (Oxford).

HAMBLETON, Prof. Kenneth George, FREng; Professor of Defence Engineering, University College London, since 1991; *b* 15 Jan. 1937; *s* of George William Hambleton and Gertrude Nellie Hambleton (*née* Brighouse); *m* 1959, Glenys Patricia Smith; one *s* one *d*. *Educ:* Chesterfield Grammar Sch.; Queens' Coll., Cambridge (MA). CEng, FIEE; FRAeS; FREng (FEng 1994). Services Electronics Res. Lab., Baldock, 1958–73; ASWE, Portsdown, 1973–81; a Dep. Dir, ASWE, 1981–82; Dir, Strategic Electronics-Radar, MoD PE, 1982–85; Asst Chief Scientific Advr (Projects and Res.), MoD, 1985–86; Dir Gen., Air Weapons and Electronic Systems, 1986–90, Air 3, 1990–91, MoD. *Publications:* numerous articles and letters in nat. and internat. physics and electronic jls. *Recreations:* chess, bridge, golf, music—especially jazz. *Address:* c/o University College London, 66–72 Gower Street, WC1E 6BT.

HAMBLIN, Jeffrey John, OBE 1999; Chief Executive, British Tourist Authority, since 1999; *b* 11 April 1945; *s* of late John Birkbeck Hamblin and Florence Hamblin; *m* 1968, Valerie Whitehead. *Educ:* Northern Counties Coll.; Univ. of Newcastle upon Tyne. Geography teacher, Newcastle, 1966–72; Devel Officer, Northumbria Tourist Bd, 1972–78; Dir, E Midlands Tourist Bd, 1978–85; British Tourist Authority: Manager, Canada, 1985–88; General Manager: Northern Europe, 1988–91; Europe, 1991–93; The Americas, 1993–98. *Recreations:* golf, philately, gardening, reading. *Address:* British Tourist Authority, Thames Tower, Black's Road, Hammersmith, W6 9EL. *T:* (020) 8563 3031.

HAMBLING, Sir (Herbert) Hugh, 3rd Bt *cr* 1924; *b* 3 Aug. 1919; *s* of Sir (Herbert) Guy (Musgrave) Hambling, 2nd Bt; *S* father, 1966; *m* 1st, 1950, Anne Page Oswald (*d* 1990), Spokane, Washington, USA; one *s*; 2nd, 1991, Helen, *widow* of David Gavin. *Educ:* Wixenford Preparatory Sch.; Eton Coll. British Airways Ltd, 1937–39. RAF Training and Atlantic Ferry Command, 1939–46. British Overseas Airways: Montreal, 1948; Seattle, 1950; Manager, Sir Guy Hambling & Son, 1956; BOAC Representative, Douglas, Los Angeles, and Boeing Co., Seattle, 1957–75; Royal Brunei Airlines Rep., Boeing Co., Seattle, 1975. *Heir: s* (Herbert) Peter Hugh Hambling [*b* 6 Sept. 1953; *m* 1991, Lorayn Louise, *d* of late Frank Koson; two *s*]. *Address:* 1219 Evergreen Point Road, Medina, WA 98039, USA. *T:* (425) 4540905, *Fax:* (425) 4542048; Rookery Park, Yoxford, Suffolk IP17 3HQ, England. *T:* (01728) 668310.

HAMBLING, Maggi, OBE 1995; artist; *b* 23 Oct. 1945; *d* of late Harry Hambling and Marjorie Hambling (*née* Harris). *Educ:* Hadleigh Hall Sch., Suffolk; Amberfield Sch., Suffolk; Ipswich Sch. of Art; Camberwell Sch. of Art (DipAD 1967); Slade Sch. of Fine Art (HDFA 1969). Boise Travel Award, NY, 1969; first Artist in Residence, Nat. Gall., London, 1980–81; Tutor in Painting and Drawing, Morley Coll. *One-man exhibitions include:* Paintings and Drawings, Morley Gall., London, 1973; New Oil Paintings, Warehouse Gall., London, 1977; Drawings and Paintings on View, Nat. Gall., 1981; Pictures of Max Wall, Nat. Portrait Gall., 1983 (and tour); Maggi Hambling, Serpentine Gall., 1987 (and tour); An Eye Through a Decade, Yale Center for British Art, Newhaven, Conn, 1991; Towards Laughter, Northern Centre for Contemporary Art, 1993–94 (and tour); Maggi Hambling, Marlborough Fine Art, London, 1996; A Matter of Life and Death, Yorkshire Sculpture Park, 1997; also exhibn, A Statue for Oscar Wilde, Nat. Portrait Gall., and Hugh Lane Gall. of Modern Art, Dublin, 1997; statue, A Conversation with Oscar Wilde, bronze and granite, Adelaide Street, London, 1998; Good Friday paintings, drawings and sculpture, Gainsborough's House, Sudbury, Suffolk, 2000, LMH, Oxford, 2001; Henrietta Moraes, Marlborough Fine Art, London, 2001; Father, Morley Gall., London, 2001; *public collections include:* Arts Council; Australian Nat. Gall.; Birmingham City Art Gall.; British Council; BM; Contemporary Art Soc.; Gulbenkian Foundn, Lisbon; Harris Mus. and Art Gall., Preston; Imperial War Mus.; Nat. Gall.; Nat. Portrait Gall.; Rugby Collection; Scottish Nat. Gall. of Modern Art, Edinburgh; Scottish Nat. Portrait Gall., Edinburgh; Southampton Art Gall.; Swindon Art Gall.; Tate Gall.; V&A Mus.; Wakefield Art Gall.; Whitworth Art Gall.; Yale Center for British Art. *Publication:* (with John Berger) Maggi & Henrietta, 2001. *Recreation:* tennis. *Address:* Morley College, Westminster Bridge Road, SE1 7HT. *Club:* Chelsea Arts.

HAMBRO, family name of **Baron Hambro.**

HAMBRO, Baron *cr* 1994 (Life Peer), of Dixton and Dumbleton, in the County of Gloucester; **Charles Eric Alexander Hambro;** Chairman: Hambros PLC, 1983–97; Guardian Royal Exchange Assurance, 1988–99 (Director, 1968–99; Deputy Chairman, 1974–88); *b* 24 July 1930; *s* of late Sir Charles Hambro, KBE, MC, and Pamela Cobbold; *m* 1st, 1954, Rose Evelyn (marr. diss. 1976), *d* of Sir Richard Cotterell, 5th Bt, CBE; two *s* one *d*; 2nd, 1976, Cherry Felicity, *d* of Sir John Huggins, GCMG, MC. *Educ:* Eton. Served Coldstream Guards, 1949–51; joined Hambros Bank Ltd, 1952: Man. Dir, 1957; Dep. Chm., 1965; Chm., 1972–83; Director: P&OSN Co., 1987–; Taylor Woodrow, 1962–97; NHS-Nuova Holding Sanpaolo SpA (formerly Istituto Bancario San Paolo di Torino, then San Paolo Bank Hldgs), 1989–98. Chm., Royal National Pension Fund for Nurses, 1968–2000. Trustee, British Museum, 1984–94. *Recreations:* shooting, farming, forestry. *Address:* Dixton Manor, Gotherington, Cheltenham, Glos GL52 9RB. *T:* (01242) 672011. *Clubs:* White's, MCC.

HAMBRO, James Daryl; Chairman, J. O. Hambro Capital Management Ltd, since 1994; *b* 22 March 1949; *s* of late Jocelyn Hambro, MC and Ann Silvia Hambro (*née* Muir); *m* 1981, Diana Cherry; three *d*. *Educ:* Eton College; Harvard Business Sch. Hambros Bank, 1970–85 (Exec. Dir, 1982–85); J. O. Hambro & Co., subseq. J. O. Hambro Ltd, 1986–99. Chairman: Ashtenne Hldgs, 1997–; Singer & Friedlander AIM VCT, 2000–; Director: Wilton's (St James's) Ltd, 1992–; Primary Health Properties, 1996–; Capital Opportunities Trust, 1997–; Enterprise Capital Trust, 1997–. Dep. Chm., Peabody Trust, 1998–; Trustee, Henry Smith's Charity; Chm., Internat. Students' Trust. *Recreations:* shooting, golf, farming. *Address:* J. O. Hambro Capital Management Ltd, Ryder Court, 14 Ryder Street, SW1Y 6QB; 15 Elm Park Road, SW3 6BP. *T:* (020) 7352 0526; Manor Farm, Kimberley, Wymondham, Norfolk NR9 4DT. *T:* (01603) 759329. *Clubs:* White's, Pratt's; Royal West Norfolk.
See also R. A. Hambro, R. N. Hambro.

HAMBRO, Richard Alexander; Chairman, J. O. Hambro Investment Management Ltd, since 1986; *b* 1 Oct. 1946; 2nd *s* of late Jocelyn Olaf Hambro, MC; *m* 1st, 1973, Hon. Charlotte Soames (marr. diss. 1982); one *d*; 2nd, 1984, Juliet Mary Elizabeth Grana (*née* Harvey) (marr. diss. 1992); 3rd, 1993, Mary James (*née* Briggs). *Educ:* Eton; Univ. of Munich. Joined Hambros Bank, 1966, Director, 1979; Pres., Hambro America Inc., 1977–82; Chairman: I. Hennig & Co., 1982–; Hattron, 1992–; Director: Wilton's (St James's), 1982–; Lynton Group Inc., 1986– (Chm., 1986–97); Edinburgh Japan plc, 1996–; Anglo American Gold Investment Co., 1997–; J. O. Hambro Mansford Ltd, 1998–. Chairman: Macmillan Cancer Relief (formerly Cancer Relief Macmillan Fund), 1991–2001; Jt British Cancer Charities, 1995–; Colon Cancer Concern, 1995–. Mem., Jockey Club, 1997–. *Recreations:* golf, horse breeding. *Address:* Waverton House, Sezincote, Moreton-in-Marsh, Glos GL56 9TB. *T:* (01386) 700700; 4 Egerton Place, SW3 2EF. *T:* (020) 7589 7483. *Clubs:* Pratt's, White's; The Brook (New York) (Gov.).
See also J. D. Hambro, R. N. Hambro.

HAMBRO, Rupert Nicholas; Chairman, J. O. Hambro Ltd, since 1986 (Group Managing Director, 1986–94); *b* 27 June 1943; *s* of late Jocelyn Olaf Hambro, MC and Ann Silvia (*née* Muir); *m* 1970, Mary Robinson Boyer; one *s* one *d*. *Educ:* Eton; Aix-en-Provence. Peat Marwick Mitchell & Co., 1962–64; joined Hambros Bank, 1964, Director, 1969, Dep. Chm., 1980, Chm., 1983–86; Chairman: J. O. Hambro Magan Ltd, 1988–96; J. O. Hambro Mansford Ltd, 1998–; Rupert Hambro & Partners Ltd. Director: Anglo American Corporation of South Africa, 1981–97; Racecourse Hldgs Trust Ltd, 1985–94; Telegraph Group Ltd (formerly Daily Telegraph PLC, then The Telegraph plc), 1986–; Sedgwick Group plc, 1987–92; Triton Europe plc, 1987–90; Pioneer Concrete Hldgs PLC, 1989–99; Hamleys plc, 1988–96 (Chm., 1989–94); Peel Hunt plc, 2000–; Abel Hadden & Co. Ltd; Chatsworth House Trust Ltd; Mem. Supervisory Bd, Bank Gutmann AG; Chairman: Wilton's (St James's) Ltd, 1987–; Mayflower Corp. Plc, 1988–; Internat. Adv. Bd, Montana AG, Vienna, 1988–2000; Fenchurch plc, 1993–97; CTR Group plc, 1990–97; Longshot Ltd, 1996–; Woburn Golf & Country Club Ltd, 1998–; Longshot Health & Fitness Ltd, 1999–; Longshot Hotels Ltd; Roland Berger & Partners Ltd, 2000–; Walpole Cttee Ltd; Jermyn Street Assoc. Ltd. Chairman: Assoc. of International Bond Dealers, 1979–82; Soc. of Merchants Trading to the Continent, 1995–. Member: SE Econ. Planning Council, 1971–74; Internat. Council, US Information Agency, 1988–. Treas., NACF, 1991–; Chairman: Patrons, RBS, 1997–; Govs, Mus. of London, 1998–. Vice-Chm., NABC, 1991–96; Chairman: Trustees, Boys' Club Trust, 1991–2000; Silver Trust, 1987–; Partners of the World, 1990–97. Dep. Pres., Anglo-Danish Soc., 1987–. Liveryman: Fishmongers' Co., 1996– (Freeman, 1969–); Goldsmiths' Co., 1994– (Mem. Ct of Assts 1998–). Hon. Fellow, Univ. of Bath, 1998. Knight of the Falcon (Iceland), 1986. *Recreations:* Tuscany, golf, shooting, walking. *Address:* Rupert Hambro & Partners Ltd, 8th Floor, 54 Jermyn Street, SW1Y 6LX. *T:* (020) 7292 3777. *Clubs:* White's, Pratt's, Walbrook; Jupiter Island (Florida).
See also J. D. Hambro, R. A. Hambro.

HAMBURGER, Michael Peter Leopold, OBE 1992; MA (Oxon); *b* Berlin, 22 March 1924; *e s* of late Prof. Richard Hamburger and Mrs L. Hamburger (*née* Hamburg); *m* 1951, Anne Ellen File; one *s* two *d*. *Educ:* Westminster Sch.; Christ Church, Oxford. Army Service, 1943–47; Freelance Writer, 1948–52; Asst Lectr in German, UCL, 1952–55; Lectr, then Reader in German, Univ. of Reading, 1955–64. Florence Purington Lectr, Mount Holyoke Coll., Mass, 1966–67; Visiting Professor, State Univ. of NY: at Buffalo, 1969; at Stony Brook, 1971; Vis. Fellow, Center for Humanities, Wesleyan Univ., Conn, 1970; Vis. Prof. Univ. of S Carolina, 1973; Regent's Lectr, Univ. of California, San Diego, 1973; Vis. Prof., Boston Univ., 1975–77; part-time Prof., Univ. of Essex, 1978. Bollingen Foundn Fellow, 1959–61, 1965–66. FRSL 1972–86. Corresp. Mem., Deutsche Akademie für Sprache und Dichtung, Darmstadt, 1973. Hon. LittD UEA, 1988; Hon. Dr Phil Technische Univ., Berlin, 1995. Translation Prizes: Deutsche Akademie für Sprache und Dichtung, Darmstadt, 1964; Arts Prize, Inter Nationes, Bonn, 1976; Medal, Inst. of Linguists, 1977; Schlegel-Tieck Prize, London, 1978, 1981; Wilhelm-Heinse Prize (medallion), Mainz, 1978; Goethe Medal, 1986; Austrian State Prize for Literary Translation, 1988. *Publications: poetry:* Flowering Cactus, 1950; Poems 1950–1951, 1952; The Dual Site, 1958; Weather and Season, 1963; Feeding the Chickadees, 1968; Penguin Modern Poets (with A. Brownjohn and C. Tomlinson), 1969; Travelling, 1969; Travelling, I-V, 1973; Ownerless Earth, 1973; Travelling VI, 1975; Real Estate, 1977; Moralities, 1977; Variations, 1981; Collected Poems, 1984; Trees, 1988; Selected Poems, 1988; Roots in the Air, 1991; Collected Poems 1941–1994, 1995; Late, 1997; Intersections, 2000; *translations:* Poems of Hölderlin, 1943, rev. edn as Hölderlin: Poems, 1952; C. Baudelaire, Twenty Prose Poems, 1946, repr. 1968 and 1988; L. van Beethoven, Letters, Journals and Conversations, 1951, repr. 1967 and 1984; J. C. F. Hölderlin, Selected Verse, 1961, repr. 1986; G. Trakl, Decline, 1952; A. Goes, The Burnt Offering, 1956; (with others) H. von Hofmannsthal, Poems and Verse Plays, 1961; B. Brecht, Tales from the Calendar, 1961; (with C. Middleton) Modern German Poetry 1910–1960, 1962; (with others) H. von Hofmannsthal, Selected Plays and Libretti, 1964; G. Büchner, Lenz, 1966; H. M. Enzensberger, Poems, 1966; (with C. Middleton) G. Grass, Selected Poems, 1966; J. C. F. Hölderlin, Poems and Fragments, 1967 (Arts Council trans. prize, 1969), new enlarged edn 1994; (with J. Rothenberg and the author) H. M. Enzensberger, The Poems of Hans Magnus Enzensberger, 1968; H. M. Enzensberger, Poems For People Who Don't Read Poems, 1968; (with C. Middleton), G. Grass, The Poems of Günter Grass, 1969; P. Bichsel, And Really Frau Blum Would Very Much Like To Meet The Milkman, 1968; G. Eich, Journeys, 1968; N. Sachs, Selected Poems, 1968; Peter Bichsel, Stories for Children, 1971; Paul Celan, Poems, 1972, new enlarged edn, as Poems of Paul Celan, 1988 (European Translation Prize, 1990), 3rd edn 1995; (ed) East German Poetry, 1972; Peter Huchel, Selected Poems, 1974; German Poetry 1910–1975, 1977; Helmut Heissenbüttel, Texts, 1977; Franco Fortini, Poems, 1978; An Unofficial Rilke, 1981; Peter Huchel, The Garden of Theophrastus, 1983; Goethe, Poems and Epigrams, 1983; Günter Eich, Pigeons and Moles, 1991; H. M. Enzensberger, Selected Poems, 1994; G. Grass, Novemberland, 1996; Goethe, Roman Elegies and other Poems and Epigrams, 1996; H. M. Enzensberger, Kiosk (poetry), 1997; Ernst Jandl, Thingsure (poetry), 1997; Friedrich Hölderlin, Selected Poems and Fragments, 1998; G. Grass, Selected Poems 1956 to 1993, 1999; *prose:* Testimonies, selected shorter prose 1950–1987, 1989; Michael Hamburger in Conversation with Peter Dale (interview), 1998; *criticism:* Reason and Energy, 1957; From Prophecy to Exorcism, 1965; The Truth of Poetry, 1970, new edn 1996; Hugo von Hofmannsthal, 1973; Art as Second Nature, 1975; A Proliferation of Prophets, 1983; After the Second Flood: essays in modern German Literature, 1986; *memoirs:* A Mug's Game, 1973, rev. edn as String of Beginnings, 1991. *Recreations:* gardening, walking. *Address:* c/o John Johnson Ltd, Clerkenwell House, 45/47 Clerkenwell Green, EC1R 0HT.

HAMEED, A. C. Shahul; MP (United Nat. Party) Harispattuwa, Sri Lanka, since 1960; Minister of Foreign Affairs, Sri Lanka, 1977–89 and 1993–94; *b* 10 April 1929; *m*; two *s* one *d*. Former Dep. Chm., Public Accounts Cttee; has been concerned with foreign affairs, public finance and higher education; Minister of Higher Educn, Science and Technology, 1989–90; Minister of Justice and of Higher Educn, 1990–93. Chm., United Nat. Party, Sri Lanka, 1995. Leader of delegns to internat. confs, incl. UN; Chm., Ministerial Conf. of Non-Aligned Countries, 1977–79; Mem., Conf. of UN Cttee on Disarmament, 1989–93. Governor, Univ. of Sri Lanka. *Publications:* In Pursuit of Peace: on non-alignment and regional cooperation, 1983; Owl and the Lotus, 1986; Disarmament—a multilateral approach, 1988; Foreign Policy Perspectives of Sri Lanka, 1988; short stories and poems. *Address:* United National Party, 400 Kotte Road, Pitakotte, Sri Lanka.

HAMER, Hon. Sir Rupert (James), AC 1992; KCMG 1982; ED; LLM (Melb.); FAIM; Premier of Victoria, Australia, and Treasurer, 1972–81; *b* 29 July 1916; *s* of H. R. Hamer; *m* 1944, April F., *d* of N. R. Mackintosh; two *s* two *d*. *Educ:* Melbourne Grammar and Geelong Grammar Schs; Trinity Coll., Univ. of Melbourne (LLM; Fellow, 1982). Solicitor, admitted 1940. Served War of 1939–45: 5½ years, AIF, Tobruk, Alamein, NG, Normandy. MLC (L) E Yarra, 1958–71; MLA (L) Kew, Vic, 1971–81; Minister for: Immigration, 1962–64; Local Govt, 1964–71; Chief Sec. and Dep. Premier, Victoria, 1971–72; Minister for: the Arts, 1972–79; State Develt, Decentralization and Tourism, 1979–81. Chairman: Vic. State Opera, 1982–; Friends of Royal Botanic Gdns, Melbourne, 1992–. Vice-Chm., Cttee of Management, Werribee Park; Nat. Pres., Save the Children Fund (Australia), 1989–; President: Vic. Coll. of the Arts, 1982–; Melbourne Internat. Chamber Music Festival, 1989–; Greenhouse Action, Australia, 1989–; Melbourne Foundn Day Cttee, 1992–; Consultative Council on Cancer & Heart Disease, 1994–; Nat. Heritage Foundn, 1997–. Mem., Melbourne Scots Council, 1981–. Chieftain, Vic. Pipe Bands Assoc., 1976–; Trustee: Yarra Bend Park, 1974–; Melbourne Cricket Ground, 1976–. CO, Vic. Scottish Regt, CMF, 1954–58. Hon. LLD Univ. of Melbourne, 1982; DUniv Swinburne, 1995. *Recreations:* tennis, Australian Rules football, walking, music. *Address:* 35 Heather Grove, Kew, Victoria 3101, Australia.

HAMILTON, family name of **Duke of Abercorn,** of **Lord Belhaven,** and of **Barons Hamilton of Dalzell** and **HolmPatrick.**

HAMILTON; *see* Baillie-Hamilton, family name of Earl of Haddington.

HAMILTON; *see* Dalrymple Hamilton and Dalrymple-Hamilton.

HAMILTON; *see* Douglas-Hamilton.

HAMILTON, 15th Duke of, *cr* 1643, Scotland, **AND BRANDON,** 12th Duke of, *cr* 1711, Great Britain; **Angus Alan Douglas Douglas-Hamilton;** Premier Peer of Scotland; Hereditary Keeper of Palace of Holyroodhouse; *b* 13 Sept. 1938; *e s* of 14th Duke of Hamilton and Brandon, PC, KT, GCVO, AFC, and of Lady Elizabeth Percy, OBE, DL, *er d* of 8th Duke of Northumberland, KG; *S* father, 1973; *m* 1972, Sarah (marr. diss. 1987; she *d* 1994), *d* of Sir Walter Scott, 4th Bt; two *s* two *d*; *m* 1988, Jillian (marr. diss. 1995), *d* of late Noel Robertson; *m* 1998, Kay Carmichael, *d* of Norman Dutch. *Educ:* Eton; Balliol Coll., Oxford BA(Engrg) 1960; MA 1982. CEng, MIMechE; FBIS. Flt Lieut RAF; invalided, 1967. Flying Instructor, 1965; Sen. Commercial Pilot's Licence, 1967; Test Pilot, Scottish Aviation, 1971–72. Mem. Council, CRC, 1978–. Mem., Queen's Body Guard for Scotland, 1975–. Hon. Mem., Royal Scottish Pipers Soc., 1977; Mem., Piobaireachd Soc., 1979. Hon. Air Cdre, No 2 (City of Edinburgh) Maritime HQ Unit, RAuxAF, 1982–93. KStJ 1975 (Prior, Order of St John in Scotland, 1975–82). *Publication:* Maria R, 1991. *Heir: s* Marquess of Douglas and Clydesdale, *qv*. *Address:* Lennoxlove, Haddington, E Lothian EH41 4NZ. *T:* (0162082) 3720. *Clubs:* Royal Air Force; New (Edinburgh).

See also Baron Selkirk of Douglas.

HAMILTON, Marquess of; James Harold Charles Hamilton; *b* 19 Aug. 1969; *s* and *heir* of Duke of Abercorn, *qv*. A Page of Honour to the Queen, 1982–84. *Address:* Barons Court, Omagh, Co. Tyrone BT78 4EZ.

HAMILTON OF DALZELL, 4th Baron *cr* 1886; **James Leslie Hamilton;** DL; *b* 11 Feb. 1938; *s* of 3rd Baron Hamilton of Dalzell, GCVO, MC and Rosemary Olive (*d* 1993), *d* of Maj. Hon. Sir John Coke, KCVO; *S* father, 1990; *m* 1967, Corinna, *yr d* of Sir Pierson Dixon, GCMG, CB; four *s* (incl. twins). *Educ:* Eton. Served Coldstream Guards, 1956–58. Mem., Stock Exchange, 1967–80. Dir, Rowton Hotels plc, 1978–84; Chm., Queen Elizabeth's Foundn for the Disabled, 1989–. DL Surrey, 1993. *Heir: s* Hon. Gavin Goulburn Hamilton [*b* 8 Oct. 1968; *m* 1997, Harriet, *yr d* of Thomas Roskill; twin *d*]. *Address:* Stockton House, Stockton, Norton Shifnal, Salop TF11 9EF; Betchworth House, Betchworth, Surrey RH3 7AE.

See also Rt Hon. Sir A. G. Hamilton.

HAMILTON, Hon. Lord; Arthur Campbell Hamilton; a Senator of the College of Justice in Scotland, since 1995; *b* 10 June 1942; *s* of James Whitehead Hamilton and Isobel Walker Hamilton (*née* McConnell); *m* 1970, Christine Ann Croll; one *d*. *Educ:* The High School of Glasgow; Glasgow Univ.; Worcester Coll., Oxford (BA); Edinburgh Univ. (LLB). Admitted member, Faculty of Advocates, 1968; QC (Scot.) 1982; Standing Junior Counsel: to Scottish Development Dept, 1975–78; to Board of Inland Revenue (Scotland), 1978–82; Advocate Depute, 1982–85; Judge, Courts of Appeal, Jersey and Guernsey, 1988–95; Pres., Pensions Appeal Tribunals for Scotland, 1992–95. *Recreations:* hill walking, music, history. *Address:* 8 Heriot Row, Edinburgh EH3 6HU. *T:* (0131) 556 4663. *Club:* New (Edinburgh).

HAMILTON (NZ), Bishop of, (RC), since 1994; **Rt Rev. Denis George Browne,** CNZM 2001; *b* 21 Sept. 1937; *s* of Neville John Browne and Catherine Anne Browne (*née* Moroney). *Educ:* Holy Name Seminary, Christchurch, NZ; Holy Cross College, Mosgiel, NZ. Assistant Priest: Gisborne, 1963–67; Papatoetoe, 1968–71; Remuera, 1972–74; Missionary in Tonga, 1975–77; Bishop of Rarotonga, 1977–83; Bishop of Auckland, 1983–94. Hon. DD. *Recreation:* golf. *Address:* Chanel Centre, PO Box 4353, Hamilton East, New Zealand.

HAMILTON, Adrian Walter; QC 1973; a Recorder of the Crown Court, 1974–95; *b* 11 March 1923; *er s* of late W. G. M. Hamilton, banker, Fletching, Sussex and of late Mrs S. E. Hamilton; *m* 1966, Jill, *d* of S. R. Brimblecombe, Eastbourne; two *d*. *Educ:* Highgate Sch.; Balliol Coll., Oxford (BA 1st cl. Jurisprudence 1948; MA 1954; Jenkyns Law Prize; Paton Meml Student, 1948–49). Served with RN, 1942–46: Ord. Seaman, 1942; Sub-Lt RNVR, 1943, Lieut 1946. Cassel Scholar, Lincoln's Inn, 1949; called to Bar, Lincoln's Inn, 1949 (Bencher 1979), Middle Temple and Inner Temple; Dep. High Court Judge, 1982–95. Mem., Senate of Inns of Court and the Bar, 1976–82, Treas., 1979–82; Mem. Council, Inns of Court, 1987–91. Mem., Council of Legal Educn, 1977–87. Chairman: Appellate Cttee for Exam. Irregularities, London Univ., 1985–; Mental Health Review Tribunals, 1986–95; Lautro Disciplinary Cttees, 1991–94. Inspector, Peek Foods Ltd, 1977. *Recreations:* family, golf, sailing, gardening. *Address:* 7 King's Bench Walk, Temple, EC4Y 7DS. *T:* (020) 7583 0404. *Clubs:* Garrick; Piltdown Golf.

HAMILTON, Adrianne Pauline U.; *see* Uziell-Hamilton.

HAMILTON, Rt Rev. Alexander Kenneth, MA; Hon. Assistant Bishop, Diocese of Bath and Wells, since 1988; *b* 11 May 1915; *s* of Cuthbert Arthur Hamilton and Agnes Maud Hamilton; unmarried. *Educ:* Malvern Coll.; Trinity Hall, Cambridge (MA 1941); Westcott House, Cambridge. Asst Curate of Birstall, Leicester, 1939–41; Asst Curate of Whitworth with Spennymoor, 1941–45; Chaplain, RNVR, 1945–47; Vicar of S Francis, Ashton Gate, Bristol, 1947–58; Vicar of S John the Baptist, Newcastle upon Tyne, 1958–65; Rural Dean of Central Newcastle, 1962–65; Bishop Suffragan of Jarrow, 1965–80. *Publication:* Personal Prayers, 1963. *Recreations:* golf, trout fishing. *Address:* 3 Ash Tree Road, Burnham-on-Sea, Somerset TA8 2LB. *Clubs:* Naval; Burnham and Berrow Golf.

HAMILTON, Alexander Macdonald, CBE 1979; Senior Partner, 1977–90, Consultant, 1990–94, McGrigor Donald, Solicitors, Glasgow; *b* 11 May 1925; *s* of John Archibald Hamilton and Thomasina Macdonald or Hamilton; *m* 1953, Catherine Gray; two *s* one *d*. *Educ:* Hamilton Acad. (Dux, 1943); Glasgow Univ. (MA 1948, LLB 1951). Solicitor. Served War, RNVR, 1943–46. Dir, Royal Bank of Scotland, 1978–96 (Vice Chm., 1990–96). Law Soc. of Scotland: Mem. Council, 1970–82; Vice-Pres., 1975–76; Pres., 1977–78. Pres., Glasgow Juridical Soc., 1955–56. Vice-Pres. and Chm., Greater Glasgow Scout Council, 1978–85; Cttee Chm., Scottish Council, Scout Assoc., 1986–92. Sec., Cambuslang Old Parish Church, 1991– (Session Clerk, 1969–91); Vice-Chm., Cambuslang Community Council, 1978–94. *Recreations:* golf, sailing. *Address:* 30 Wellshot Drive, Cambuslang, Glasgow G72 8BT. *T:* (0141) 641 1445. *Clubs:* Royal Scottish Automobile (Glasgow); Royal Northern & Clyde Yacht.

HAMILTON, Sir Andrew Caradoc, 10th Bt *cr* 1646, of Silverton Hill, Lanarkshire; *b* 23 Sept. 1953; *s* of Sir Richard Hamilton, 9th Bt and Elizabeth Vidal Barton; *S* father, 2001; *m* 1984, Anthea Jane Huntingford; three *d*. *Educ:* Charterhouse; St Peter's Coll., Oxford (MA). *Heir: cousin* Paul Howden Hamilton [*b* 24 Dec. 1951; *m* 1980, Elizabeth Anne Harrison; two *d*].

HAMILTON, Andrew Ninian Roberts; His Honour Judge Andrew Hamilton; a Circuit Judge, Midland Circuit, since 2001; *b* 7 Jan. 1947; *s* of Robert Bousfield Hamilton and Margery Wensley Iowerth Hamilton (*née* Roberts); *m* 1982, Isobel Louise Goode; one *s* one *d*. *Educ:* Cheltenham Coll.; Birmingham Univ. (LLB). Called to the Bar, Gray's Inn, 1970; in practice, Midland and Oxford Circuit; Asst Recorder, 1993–99; a Recorder, 1999–2001. Mem. (C) Nottingham CC, 1973–91 (Chairman: Transport Cttee, 1976; Archaeology Cttee, 1987–91; Vice-Chm., Leisure Services Cttee, 1987–88; Hon. Alderman, 1991). Chairman: Nottingham Civic Soc., 1978–83 (Vice-Pres., 1983–); Nottingham Civic Soc. Sales Ltd, 1988–2001; Nottingham Park Conservation Trust, 1992–2001; Dir, Nottingham and Notts United Services Club, 1994–2001. Chm., Nottingham Bar Mess, 1995–2001. External examiner, BVC, Nottingham Trent Univ., 1997–2000. Contested (C) Ilkeston, Oct. 1974. *Publications:* Nottingham's Royal Castle and Ducal Palace, 1976, 5th edn 1999; Nottingham, City of Caves, 1978, 2nd edn 1985; Historic Walks in Nottingham, 1978, 2nd edn 1985. *Recreations:* tennis, walking, local history. *Address:* The Court Service, Midland Circuit, The Priory Courts, 33 Bull Street, Birmingham B4 6DW. *Club:* Nottingham and Notts United Services.

HAMILTON, Rt Hon. Sir Archibald (Gavin), Kt 1994; PC 1991; *b* 30 Dec. 1941; *yr s* of 3rd Baron Hamilton of Dalzell, GCVO, MC; *m* 1968, Anne Catharine Napier; three *d*. *Educ:* Eton Coll. Borough Councillor, Kensington and Chelsea, 1968–71. Contested (C) Dagenham, Feb. and Oct., 1974. MP (C) Epsom and Ewell, April 1978–2001; PPS to Sec. of State for Energy, 1979–81, to Sec. of State for Transport, 1981–82; an Asst Govt Whip, 1982–84; a Lord Comr of HM Treasury (Govt Whip), 1984–86; Parly Under-Sec. of State for Defence Procurement, MoD, 1986–87; PPS to Prime Minister, 1987–88; Minister of State, MoD, 1988–93. Member: Intelligence and Security Cttee, 1994–97; Select Cttee on Standards in Public Life, 1995; Select Cttee on Members' Interests, 1995.

Chm., 1922 Cttee, 1997–2001 (Exec. Mem., 1995–97). Gov., Westminster Foundn for Democracy, 1993–99. *Club:* White's.

HAMILTON, Arthur Campbell; *see* Hamilton, Hon. Lord.

HAMILTON, Arthur Richard C.; *see* Cole-Hamilton.

HAMILTON, David; MP (Lab) Midlothian, since 2001; *b* 24 Oct. 1950; *s* of Agnes and David Hamilton; *m* 1969, Jean Macrae; two *d. Educ:* Dalkeith High Sch. Coalminer, 1965–85; Landscape Supervisor, Midlothian Council, 1987–89; Training Officer and Placement Officer, Craigmillar Fest. Soc., 1989–92; Chief Exec., Craigmillar Opportunities Trust, 1992–2000. Mem., Midlothian Council, 1995–2001. *Recreations:* films, current affairs. *Address:* (constituency office) 95 High Street, Dalkeith, Midlothian EH22 1AX.

HAMILTON, David Stewart; Solicitor to Commissioner of Police of the Metropolis, since 1995; *b* 1 April 1946; *s* of Ralph James Hamilton and Jean Isabel Hamilton; *m* 1975, Maureen Underwood; two *d. Educ:* Highgate Sch.; Coll. of Law, Lancaster Gate. Articled Clerk, 1965–70, Asst Solicitor, 1970–71, Partner, 1971–78, D. Miles Griffiths Piercy & Co.; Asst Solicitor, 1978–79, Partner, 1979–80, Gaitskell Dodgson & Bleasdale; joined Solicitor's Dept, Metropolitan Police, 1980: Sen. Legal Asst, 1981–85; Asst Solicitor, 1985–95. Member: Law Soc., 1970–; Assoc. of Police Lawyers, 1995–; Commonwealth Law Assoc., 1996–; ACPO. *Recreations:* walking large hairy dog, fair weather cycling, steam railways. *Address:* c/o Solicitor's Department, New Scotland Yard, Victoria, SW1H 0BG. *T:* (020) 7230 7353.

HAMILTON, Donald Rankin Douglas; His Honour Judge Donald Hamilton; a Circuit Judge, since 1994; *b* 15 June 1946; *s* of Allister McNicoll Hamilton and Mary Glen Hamilton (*née* Rankin); *m* 1974, (Margaret) Ruth Perrens; one *s* one *d. Educ:* Rugby Sch.; Balliol Coll., Oxford (BA). Called to the Bar, Gray's Inn, 1969 (Atkin Schol. 1970); pupillage in Birmingham, 1970–71; practised in Birmingham, 1971–94; Designated Family Judge, Birmingham CC, 1996–. Mem., Council of Mgt, CBSO, 1974–80; Dir, CBSO Soc. Ltd, 1984–99; Trustee, City of Birmingham Orchestral Endowment Fund. *Recreation:* music. *Address:* Birmingham County Court, The Priory Courts, 33 Bull Street, Birmingham B4 6DS.

HAMILTON, Douglas Owens; Senior Partner, Norton Rose (formerly Norton, Rose, Botterell & Roche), 1982–94; *b* 20 April 1931; *s* of Oswald Hamilton and Edith Hamilton; *m* 1962, Judith Mary Wood; three *s. Educ:* John Fisher Sch., Purley, Surrey; Univ. of London (LLB). Admitted Solicitor, 1953; joined Botterell & Roche, 1955, Partner, 1959; Exec. Partner, Norton, Rose, Botterell & Roche, 1976–82. Mem., Chancellor's Court of Benefactors, Oxford Univ., 1990–94. Chm., Thames Nautical Trng Trust Ltd, 1995–98; Vice-Chm., Marine Soc., 1993–99; Hon. Treasurer: British Maritime Charitable Foundn, 1987–97; British Polish Legal Assoc., 1989–93. *Recreation:* travelling. *Address:* Boarsney, Salehurst, East Sussex TN32 5SR.

HAMILTON, Duncan Graeme; Member (SNP) Highlands and Islands, Scottish Parliament, since 1999; *b* 3 Oct. 1973; *s* of David Gentles Hamilton and Elsa Catherine Hamilton (*née* Nicolson). *Educ:* Glasgow Univ. (MA 1st Cl. Hons Hist.); Edinburgh Univ. (LLB Scots Law); Kennedy Sch. of Govt, Harvard Univ. (Kennedy Schol.). Asst Brand Manager, Proctor & Gamble, 1995; Aide and advr to Alex Salmond, MP, 1997–99. Mem., Health and Community Care Cttee, 1999–2000, Enterprise and Life Long Learning Cttee, 2000–, Scottish Parlt. Mem., SNP, 1994–; Asst to SNP Chief Exec., 1998–99. *Recreations:* football, reading, friends. *Address:* Scottish Parliament, Edinburgh EH99 1SP. *T:* (0131) 348 5700.

HAMILTON, Dundas; *see* Hamilton, J. D.

HAMILTON, Eben William; QC 1981; *b* 12 June 1937; *s* of late Rev. John Edmund Hamilton, MC and Hon. Lilias Hamilton (*née* Maclay); *m* 1st, 1973, Catherine Harvey (marr. diss. 1977); 2nd, 1985, Themy Rusi Bilimoria, *y d* of late Brig. Rusi Bilimoria. *Educ:* Winchester; Trinity Coll., Cambridge. Nat. Service: 4/7 Royal Dragoon Guards, 1955–57; Fife and Forfar Yeomanry/Scottish Horse, TA, 1958–66. Called to the Bar, Inner Temple, 1962, Bencher, 1985. Jt DTI Inspector, Atlantic Computers plc, 1990–94. FRSA 1988. *Address:* 1 New Square, Lincoln's Inn, WC2A 3SA. *T:* (020) 7405 0884. *Club:* Garrick.

See also Martha Hamilton.

HAMILTON, Sir Edward (Sydney), 7th and 5th Bt, *cr* 1776 and 1819; *b* 14 April 1925; *s* of Sir (Thomas) Sydney (Percival) Hamilton, 6th and 4th Bt, and Bertha Muriel, *d* of James Russell King, Singleton Park, Kendal; *S* father, 1966. *Educ:* Canford Sch. Served Royal Engineers, 1943–47; 1st Royal Sussex Home Guard, 1953–56. *Recreations:* Spiritual matters, music. *Heir:* none. *Address:* The Cottage, Fordwater Road, East Lavant, Chichester, West Sussex PO18 0AL. *T:* (01243) 527414.

HAMILTON, Eleanor Warwick, (Mrs T. King); QC 1999; a Recorder, since 2000; *b* 13 Sept. 1957; *d* of Selby William Guy Hamilton and Dr Margaret Hamilton; *m* 1981, Thomas King; four *d. Educ:* Queen Margaret's Sch., Escrick; Hull Univ. (LLB). Called to the Bar, Inner Temple, 1979; Asst Recorder, 1996–2000. Mem., Full Stop Cttee, W Yorks NSPCC. Chm. Governors, Queen Margaret's Sch., 1992–; Mem. Council and Chapter, York Univ. *Recreations:* walking, cycling, veteran gymnastics. *Address:* 6 Park Square, Leeds LS1 2LW. *T:* (0113) 245 9763.

HAMILTON, Fabian; MP (Lab) Leeds North East, since 1997; *b* 12 April 1955; *s* of late Mario Uziell-Hamilton and of Adrianne Uziell-Hamilton, *qv*; *m* 1980, Rosemary Ratcliffe; one *s* two *d. Educ:* Brentwood Sch., Essex; Univ. of York (BA Hons). Graphic designer (own company), 1979–94; computer systems consultant, 1994–97. Leeds City Council: Mem. (Lab), 1987–97; Chm., Employment and Econ. Develt Cttee, 1994–96; Chm., Educn Cttee, 1996–97. Mem., Select Cttee on Foreign Affairs, 2001–. Contested (Lab) Leeds NE, 1992. Trustee, Nat. Heart Res. Fund, 1999–. *Recreations:* film, theatre, opera, photography, cycling. *Address:* House of Commons, SW1A 0AA. *T:* (020) 7219 3493.

HAMILTON, Prof. George Heard; Director, Sterling and Francine Clark Art Institute, 1966–77, now Emeritus; Professor of Art, Williams College, Williamstown, Massachusetts, 1966–75, now Emeritus; Director of Graduate Studies in Art History, Williams College, 1971–75; *b* 23 June 1910; *s* of Frank A. Hamilton and Georgia Neale Heard; *m* 1945, Polly Wiggin; one *s* one *d. Educ:* Yale Univ. BA 1932; MA 1934; PhD 1942. Research Asst, Walters Art Gallery, Baltimore, 1934–36; Mem. Art History Faculty, Yale Univ., 1936–66 (Prof., 1956–66); Robert Sterling Clark Prof. of Art, Williams Coll., 1963–64. Slade Prof. of Fine Art, Cambridge Univ., 1971–72; Kress Prof. in Residence, Nat. Gall of Art, Washington, DC, 1978–79. FRSA 1973; Fellow, Amer. Acad. of Arts and Science, 1979. Hon. LittD Williams Coll., 1977; Wilbur Lucius Cross Medal, Yale Grad. Sch., 1977; Amer. Art Dealers' Assoc. award for excellence in art hist., 1978. *Publications:* (with D. V. Thompson, Jr) De Arte Illuminandi, 1933; Manet and His Critics, 1954; The Art and Architecture of Russia, 1954; Monet's Paintings of Rouen Cathedral, 1960; European Painting and Sculpture, 1880–1940, 1967; (with W. C. Agee) Raymond Duchamp-Villon, 1967; 19th and 20th Century Art: Painting, Sculpture, Architecture, 1970; Articles in Burlington Magazine, Gazette des Beaux-Arts, Art Bulletin, etc. *Recreations:* music, gardening. *Address:* 121 Gale Road, Williamstown, MA 01267, USA. *T:* (413) 4588626. *Clubs:* Century Association (New York); Elizabethan (New Haven); Edgartown Yacht (Mass).

HAMILTON, Brig. Hugh Gray Wybrants, CBE 1964 (MBE 1945); DL; Chairman, Forces Help Society and Lord Roberts Workshops, 1976–91; *b* 16 May 1918; *s* of Lt-Col H. W. Hamilton, late 5th Dragoon Guards; *m* 1944, Claire Buxton; two *d. Educ:* Wellington Coll., Berks; Peterhouse, Cambridge; Royal Mil. Academy. Commissioned with Royal Engineers, 1938. War Service in BEF, BNAF, BLA, 1939–45. Post War Service in Australia, BAOR, France and UK. Instructor, Army Staff Coll., Camberley, 1954–56; Student, IDC, 1965; retired, 1968. Gen. Manager, Corby Develt Corp., 1968–80. DL Northants, 1977. *Recreations:* riding, sailing, DIY. *Address:* Cherwell House, Hogg End, Chipping Warden, Banbury OX17 1LY. *T:* (01295) 660656.

HAMILTON, Iain McCormick; His Honour Judge Iain Hamilton; a Circuit Judge, since 2000; *b* 11 Nov. 1948; *s* of James Hamilton and Mary Isabella Hamilton; *m* 1975, Marilyn Tomlinson; one *s* two *d. Educ:* Heversham Grammar Sch.; Manchester Poly. (BA Hons Law). Admitted solicitor, 1974; Walls, Johnston & Co., Stockport, 1974–94; Jones Maidment Wilson, Manchester, 1994–2000; Asst Recorder, 1992–96; Recorder, 1996–2000. Pres., Stockport Law Soc., 1990–91. Chm., Child Concern, 1992–93 and 1996–99. *Recreations:* music, reading, cooking. *Address:* Manchester Crown Court, Minshull Street, Manchester M1 3FS. *T:* (0161) 954 7500.

HAMILTON, Ian; poet; *b* 24 March 1938; *s* of Robert Tough Hamilton and Daisy McKay; *m* 1st, 1963, Gisela Dietzel; one *s*; 2nd, 1981, Ahdaf Soueif; two *s. Educ:* Darlington Grammar Sch.; Keble Coll., Oxford (BA Hons). Editor, Review, 1962–72; Poetry and Fiction Editor, Times Literary Supplement, 1965–73; Lectr in Poetry, Univ. of Hull, 1972–73; Editor, The New Review, 1974–79. Presenter, Bookmark (BBC TV series), 1984–87. E. C. Gregory Award, 1963; Malta Cultural Award, 1974. *Publications:* (ed) The Poetry of War 1939–45, 1965; (ed) Alun Lewis: poetry and prose, 1966; (ed) The Modern Poet, 1968; The Visit (poems), 1970; A Poetry Chronicle, 1973; (ed) Robert Frost: selected poems, 1973; The Little Magazines, 1976; Returning (poems), 1976; Robert Lowell: a biography, 1983; (ed) Yorkshire in Verse, 1984; (ed) The New Review Anthology, 1985; Fifty Poems, 1988; In Search of J. D. Salinger, 1988; (ed) Soho Square, 1989; Writers in Hollywood, 1990; (ed) The Faber Book of Soccer, 1992; Keepers of the Flame: literary estates and the rise of biography, 1992; (ed) The Oxford Companion to Twentieth Century Poetry in English, 1994; Walking Possession: essays and reviews, 1994; Gazza Italia, 1994; Steps (poems), 1997; A Gift Imprisoned: the poetic life of Matthew Arnold, 1998; The Trouble with Money, and other essays, 1998; Sixty Poems, 1999; (ed) The Penguin Book of Twentieth Century Essays, 1999. *Address:* c/o Gillon Aitken Associates, 29 Fernshaw Road, SW10 0TG.

HAMILTON, Ian Lethame; Chief Executive, St George's Healthcare NHS Trust, since 1999; *b* 24 July 1951; *s* of Robert Hamilton and Margaret Henderson (*née* McKay). *Educ:* Larkhall Acad.; Glasgow Coll. of Technol. CIPFA 1974. Supervisory accountant, 1975–78, Asst Chief Accountant, 1978–81, Strathclyde Regl Council; Regl Finance Officer, Housing Corp., 1981–83; Dep. Dir of Finance, Wandsworth HA, 1983–88; Project Manager, King's Fund Centre for Health Services Develt, 1988–89 (on secondment); Resource Mgt Project Manager, Wandsworth HA, 1989–91; Dir of Service Develt, 1991–98, Dep. Chief Exec., 1998–99, St George's Healthcare NHS Trust. *Recreations:* gardening, reading, country walks. *Address:* St George's Hospital, Blackshaw Road, Tooting, SW17 0QT. *T:* (020) 8725 1635.

HAMILTON, Ian Robertson; QC (Scot.) 1980; *b* Paisley, Scotland, 13 Sept. 1925; *s* of John Harris Hamilton and Martha Robertson; *m* 1974, Jeannette Patricia Mari Stewart, Connel, Argyll; one *s* (one *s* two *d* by former *m*). *Educ:* John Neilson Sch., Paisley; Allan Glens Sch., Glasgow; Glasgow and Edinburgh Univs (BL). Served RAFVR, 1944–48. Called to the Scottish Bar, 1954 and to the Albertan Bar, 1982. Advocate Depute, 1962; Dir of Civil Litigation, Republic of Zambia, 1964–66; Hon. Sheriff of Lanarks, 1967; retd from practice to work for National Trust for Scotland and later to farm in Argyll, 1969; returned to practice, 1974; Sheriff of Glasgow and Strathkelvin, May-Dec. 1984; resigned commn Dec. 1984; returned to practice. Founder, Castle Wynd Printers, Edinburgh, 1955 (published four paper-back vols of Hugh MacDiarmid's poetry, 1955–56). Founder and first Chm., The Whichway Trust, to provide adventure training for young offenders, 1988. Chief Pilot, Scottish Parachute Club, 1978–80. Student Pres., Heriot-Watt Univ., 1990–96; Rector, Aberdeen Univ., 1994–96. Hon. LLD Aberdeen, 1997. *Publications:* No Stone Unturned, 1952 (also New York); The Tinkers of the World, 1957 (Foyle award-winning play); The Taking of the Stone of Destiny, 1991; *autobiography:* A Touch of Treason, 1990; A Touch More Treason, 1994; contrib. various jls. *Recreations:* motor biking, poker. *Address:* Lochnabeithe, North Connel, Oban, Argyll PA37 1QX. *T:* (01631) 710427.

HAMILTON, James, CBE 1979; *b* 11 March 1918; *s* of George Hamilton and Margaret Carey; *m* 1945, Agnes McGhee; one *s* three *d* (and one *s* decd). *Educ:* St Bridget's, Baillieston; St Mary's, High Whifflet. District Councillor, 6th Lanarks, 1955–58; Lanarks County Council, 1958–64. National Executive Mem., Constructional Engrg Union, 1958–71, Pres., 1968–69; Chm., Trade Union Group, Parly Labour Party, 1969–70. MP (Lab): Bothwell, 1964–83; Motherwell N, 1983–87. Asst Govt Whip, 1969–70; an Opposition Whip, 1970–74; a Lord Comr of the Treasury and Vice-Chamberlain of the Household, 1974–78; Comptroller of HM Household, 1978–79. *Recreations:* tennis, badminton, golf. *Address:* 12 Rosegreen Crescent, North Road, Bellshill, Lanarks ML4 1NT. *T:* (01698) 842071.

HAMILTON, Sir James (Arnot), KCB 1978 (CB 1972); MBE 1952; FRSE; FREng; Permanent Under-Secretary of State, Department of Education and Science, 1976–83; *b* 2 May 1923; *m* 1947, Christine Mary McKean (marr. diss.); three *s. Educ:* University of Edinburgh (BSc). Marine Aircraft Experimental Estab., 1943: Head of Flight Research, 1948; Royal Aircraft Estab., 1952; Head of Projects Div., 1964; Dir, Anglo-French Combat Aircraft, Min. of Aviation, 1965; Dir-Gen. Concorde, Min. of Technology, 1966–70; Deputy Secretary: (Aerospace), DTI, 1971–73; Cabinet Office, 1973–76. Dir, Hawker Siddeley Gp, 1983–91; Mem. Adv. Bd, Brown & Root (UK) Ltd, 1983–97; Chm., Brown & Root (UK) Ltd (later Brown & Root Ltd), 1998–2000; Director: Smiths Industries plc, 1984–93; Devonport Royal Dockyard, 1987–97. Trustee, British Museum (Natural Hist.), 1984–88. President: Assoc. for Science Educn, 1984–85; NFER in England and Wales, 1984–98. Vice-Pres., Council, Reading Univ., 1983–95; Vice-Chm. Council, UCL, 1985–98. FREng (FEng 1981). DUniv Heriot-Watt, 1983; Hon. LLD CNAA, 1983. *Publications:* papers in Reports and Memoranda series of Aeronautical

Research Council, Jl RAeS, and technical press. *Address:* Pentlands, 9 Cedar Road, Farnborough, Hants GU14 7AF. *T:* (01252) 543254. *Club:* Athenæum.

HAMILTON, (James) Dundas, CBE 1985; Chairman: Wates City of London Properties plc, 1984–94; LWT Pension Trustees Ltd, 1992–94; *b* 11 June 1919; *o s* of late Arthur Douglas Hamilton and Jean Scott Hamilton; *m* 1954, Linda Jean, *d* of late Sinclair Frank Ditcham and Helen Fraser Ditcham; two *d.* *Educ:* Rugby; Clare Coll., Cambridge. Served War, Army (Lt-Col RA), 1939–46. Member, Stock Exchange, 1948, Mem. Council, 1972–78 (Dep. Chm., 1973–76). Partner, 1951–86, Sen. Partner, 1977–85, Fielding, Newson-Smith & Co. Chairman: TSB Commercial Holdings (formerly UDT Holdings), 1985–90 (Dir, 1983–90); United Dominions Trust Ltd, 1985–89; Director: Richard Clay plc, 1971–84 (Vice-Chm., 1981–84); LWT (Holdings) plc, 1981–91; Datastream Hldgs Ltd, 1982–86; TSB Gp plc, 1985–90; TSB Investment Management Ltd, 1986–88; Archival Facsimiles Ltd, 1986–89; WIB Publications Ltd, 1987–98 (Chm., 1990–98); Camp Hopson & Co., 1991–. Dep. Chm., British Invisible Exports Council, 1976–86; Member: Exec. Cttee, City Communications Centre, 1976–88; City and Industrial Liaison Council, 1987–98 (Chm., 1970–73 and 1991–95). Governor, Pasold Res. Fund, 1976–90 (Chm., 1978–86). Member: Council of Industrial Soc., 1959–78 (Exec. Cttee, 1963–68; Life Mem., 1978); Adv. Bd, RCDS, 1980–87. Contested (C) East Ham North, 1951. FRSA 1988. *Publications:* The Erl King (radio play), 1949; Lorenzo Smiles on Fortune (novel), 1953; Three on a Honeymoon (TV series), 1956; Six Months Grace (play, jointly with Robert Morley), 1957; Stockbroking Today, 1968, 2nd edn 1979; Stockbroking Tomorrow, 1986; 21 Years to Christmas (short stories and verse), 1994. *Recreations:* writing, photography, swimming, golf, watching tennis. *Address:* 45 Melbury Court, W8 6NH. *T:* (020) 7602 3157. *Clubs:* City of London, Hurlingham, All England Lawn Tennis and Croquet; Royal and Ancient Golf (St Andrews); Hankley Common; Worplesdon; Kandahar Ski.

HAMILTON, John; His Honour Judge John Hamilton; a Circuit Judge, since 1987; *b* 27 Jan. 1941; *s* of late John Ian Hamilton and Mrs Margaret Walker; *m* 1965, Patricia Ann Hamilton (*née* Henman); two *s* one *d.* *Educ:* Durlston Court Prep. Sch., New Milton, Hants; Harrow (schol.); Hertford Coll., Oxford (schol.). MA Jurisp. Oxon. Called to Bar, Gray's Inn, 1965; a Recorder, 1985. KStJ 1982. *Recreations:* jogging, golf, bridge. *Address:* Red Stack, Anstey, near Buntingford, Herts SG9 0BN. *T:* (01763) 848536.

HAMILTON, Kirstie Louise, (Mrs Charles Stewart-Smith); City Editor, Sunday Times, since 1997; *b* 5 April 1963; *d* of Elizabeth Kate Marie Hamilton and Mark Robert Hamilton; *m* 1998, Charles Stewart-Smith; one *s.* *Educ:* Hillcrest High Sch., Hamilton, NZ. Columnist, National Business Review, NZ, 1988–89; Business Correspondent, Evening Standard, 1989–92; Business Correspondent, 1992–95, Dep. City Editor, 1995–96, Sunday Times; City Editor, The Express and Sunday Express, 1996–97. *Recreations:* riding, ski-ing. *Address:* (office) 1 Pennington Street, E1 9XW.

HAMILTON, Loudon Pearson, CB 1987; Chairman: Hanover (Scotland) Housing Association, since 1998; Scottish Food Quality Certification Co., since 1995; *b* 12 Jan. 1932; *s* of Vernon Hamilton and Jean Mair Hood; *m* 1st, 1956, Anna Mackinnon Young (*d* 1993); two *s*; 2nd, 1997, Rosemary Hutton (*née* Griffiths). *Educ:* Hutchesons' Grammar Sch., Glasgow; Glasgow Univ. (MA Hons Hist.). National Service, 2nd Lieut RA, 1953–55. Inspector of Taxes, Inland Revenue, 1956–60; Asst Principal, Dept of Agriculture and Fisheries for Scotland, 1960; Private Sec. to Parly Under-Secretary of State for Scotland, 1963–64; First Secretary, Agriculture, British Embassy, Copenhagen and The Hague, 1966–70; Asst Secretary, Dept of Agriculture and Fisheries for Scotland, 1973–79; Principal Estabt Officer, Scottish Office, 1979–84; Sec., Scottish Office Agric. and Fisheries Dept, 1984–92. Mem., AFRC, 1984–92; Chairman: Scottish Agricl and Rural Develt Centre, 1992–; Scottish Seed Potato Develt Council, 1996–97. *Address:* 8A Dick Place, Edinburgh EH9 2JL. *T:* (0131) 667 5908.

HAMILTON, Sir Malcolm William Bruce S.; *see* Stirling-Hamilton.

HAMILTON, Martha, (Mrs R. R. Steedman), OBE 1988; Headmistress, St Leonards School, St Andrews, 1970–88; *d* of Rev. John Edmund Hamilton and Hon. Lilias Maclay; *m* 1977, Robert Russell Steedman, *qv.* *Educ:* Roedean Sch.; St Andrews Univ. (MA Hons Hist.); Cambridge Univ. (DipEd); Edinburgh Univ. (Dip. Adult Educn). Principal, Paljor Namgyal Girls' High School, Gangtok, Sikkim, 1959–66. Mem., Task Force to examine under-achievement in schs in Scotland, 1996. Member: Assoc. for Protection of Rural Scotland Award Panel, 1989–92; Fife Health Bd, 1991–98 (Vice Chm., 1994–98); Court of Dirs, Edinburgh Acad., 1992–2000. Convenor, Assoc. for Applied Arts, 1992–98. Gov., New Sch., Butterstone, 1997–. Awarded Pema Dorji (for services to education), Sikkim, 1966. *Recreations:* ski-ing, photography. *Address:* Muir of Blebo, Blebo Craigs, by Cupar, Fife KY15 5UG.
See also E. W. Hamilton.

HAMILTON, Mary Margaret; *see* Kaye, M. M.

HAMILTON, (Mostyn) Neil; *b* 9 March 1949; *s* of Ronald and Norma Hamilton; *m* 1983, (Mary) Christine Holman. *Educ:* Amman Valley Grammar School; University College of Wales, Aberystwyth (BSc Econ, MSc Econ); Corpus Christi College, Cambridge (LLB). Called to the Bar, Middle Temple, 1979. MP (C) Tatton, 1983–97; contested (C) same seat, 1997. PPS to Minister of State for Transport, 1986–87; an Asst Govt Whip, 1990–92; Parly Under-Sec. of State, DTI, 1992–94. Mem., Select Cttee on Treasury and Civil Service, 1987–90; Vice-Chm., Conservative backbench Trade and Industry Cttee, 1984–90 (Sec., 1983 and 1994–97); Secretary: Cons. backbench Finance Cttee, 1987–90 and 1995–97; UK–ANZAC Parly Gp, 1984–97; Chm., All Party Anglo-Togo Parly Gp, 1988–97; Vice-Pres., Small Business Bureau, 1985–97. Vice-Pres., Cheshire Agricl Soc., 1986–. *Publications:* UK/US Double Taxation, 1980; The European Community—a Policy for Reform, 1983; (ed) Land Development Encyclopaedia, 1981–; (jtly) No Turning Back, 1985; Great Political Eccentrics, 1999; pamphlets on state industry, schools and the NHS. *Recreations:* gardening, opera, the arts, architecture and conservation, country pursuits, silence. *Address:* The Old Rectory, Nether Alderley, Macclesfield, Cheshire SK10 4TW.

HAMILTON, Myer Alan Barry K.; *see* King-Hamilton.

HAMILTON, Neil; *see* Hamilton, M. N.

HAMILTON, Nigel; Permanent Secretary, Department of Education, Northern Ireland, since 1998; *b* 19 March 1948; *s* of James and Jean Hamilton; *m* 1974, Lorna Woods; two *s.* *Educ:* Queen's Univ., Belfast (BSc Hons); Henley Mgt Coll.; Federal Exec. Inst., Virginia; Univ. of Ulster (Dip. Co. Dirn 1994). Joined NICS, 1970; posts in phys. develt areas, incl. roads, water and housing; Asst Sec., Housing and Local Govt Div., 1975; Under Sec., Central Community Relns, Urban Regeneration, 1990. *Recreations:* Rugby (Pres., Ulster Referees Soc., 1996–97), golf. *Address:* Department of Education, Rathgael House, Bangor, Co. Down BT19 7PR. *T:* (028) 9127 9309.

HAMILTON, Nigel John Mawdesley; QC 1981; *b* 13 Jan. 1938; *s* of late Archibald Dearman Hamilton and Joan Worsley Hamilton (*née* Mawdesley); *m* 1963, Leone Morag Elizabeth Gordon; two *s.* *Educ:* St Edward's Sch., Oxford; Queens' Coll., Cambridge. Nat. Service, 2nd Lieut, RE, Survey Dept, 1956–58. Assistant Master: St Edward's Sch., Oxford, 1962–63; King's Sch., Canterbury, 1963–65. Called to the Bar, Inner Temple, 1965, Bencher, 1989. Mem., Gen. Council of the Bar, 1989–94. Mem. (C) for Chew Valley, Avon CC, 1989–93. *Recreation:* fishing. *Address:* St John's Chambers, Small Street, Bristol BS1 1DW. *Club:* Flyfishers'.

HAMILTON, Peter Bryan, MA; Head Master of King Edward VI School, Southampton, 1996–April 2002; Head Master of Haberdashers' Aske's School, from April 2002; *b* 28 Aug. 1956; *s* of Brian George Hamilton and Clara Hamilton (*née* Marchi); *m* 1st, 1981, Danièle Lahaye (marr. diss. 1987); one *d*; 2nd, 1993, Sylvie (*née* Vulliet); one *d.* *Educ:* King Edward VI Grammar Sch., Southampton; Christ Church, Oxford (1st Cl. Hons Modern Languages 1979; MA). Head of French, Radley Coll., 1981–89; Head of Modern Langs and Housemaster of Wren's, Westminster Sch., 1989–96. Examnr in French, Oxford and Cambridge Schs Exam. Bd, 1992–. Governor: Stroud Sch., 1997–; Princes' Mead, 1997–; Durlston Court Sch., 1999–. *Recreations:* canoeing, hill walking, karate, sailing, ski-ing, squash, wind surfing, comparative literature, French and German cinema, opera, classical music. *Address:* (until April 2002) King Edward VI School, Kellett Road, Southampton SO15 7UQ; (from April 2002) Haberdashers' Aske's School, Butterfly Lane, Elstree, Borehamwood, Herts WD6 3AF.

HAMILTON, Richard, CH 2000; painter; *b* 24 Feb. 1922; *s* of Peter and Constance Hamilton; *m* 1st, 1947, Terry O'Reilly (*d* 1962); one *s* one *d*; 2nd, 1991, Rita Donagh. *Educ:* elementary; Royal Academy Schs; Slade Sch. of Art. Jig and Tool draughtsman, 1940–45. Lectr, Fine Art Dept, King's Coll., Univ. of Durham (later Univ. of Newcastle upon Tyne), 1953–66. *Devised exhibitions:* Growth and Form, 1951; Man, Machine and Motion, 1955. *Collaborated on:* This is Tomorrow, 1956; 'an Exhibit', 1957; exhibn with D. Roth, ICA New Gall., 1977. *One man art exhibitions:* Gimpel Fils, 1951; Hanover Gall., 1955, 1964; Robert Fraser Gall., 1966, 1967, 1969; Whitworth Gall, 1972; Nigel Greenwood Inc., 1972; Serpentine Gall., 1975; Stedelijk Mus., Amsterdam, 1976; Waddington Gall., 1980, 1982, 1984; Anthony d'Offay Gall., 1980, 1991, 1995; Charles Cowles Gall., NY, 1980; Galérie Maeght, Paris, 1981; Tate Gall., 1983–84; Thorden and Wetterling, Stockholm, 1984; DAAD Gall., Berlin, 1985; Fruitmarket Gall., Edinburgh, 1988; Moderna Museet, Stockholm, 1989; Venice Biennale, 1993; San Francisco Mus. of Modern Art, 1996; other exhibitions abroad include: Kassel, 1967, 1997 (Arnold Bode Prize); New York, 1967; Milan, 1967, 1968, 1969, 1971, 1972, 1974, 1990; Hamburg, 1969; Berlin, 1970, 1971, 1973; Bremen, 1998; *retrospective exhibitions:* Tate Gallery, 1970 (also shown in Eindhoven and Bern), 1992; Guggenheim Museum, New York, 1973 (also shown in Cincinnati, Munich, Tübingen, Berlin); Musée Grenoble, 1977; Kunsthalle Bielefeld, 1978; Kunstmus., Winterthur, 1990 (also shown in Hannover and Valencia); Tate Gall., 1992; Irish Mus. of Modern Art, Dublin, 1992. William and Noma Copley award, 1960; John Moores prize, 1969; Talens Prize International, 1970; Golden Lion of Venice, 1993. *Publication:* Collected Words 1953–1982, 1982. *Address:* c/o Tate Gallery, Millbank, SW1P 4RG.

HAMILTON, His Honour Richard Graham; a Circuit Judge, 1986–97; Chancellor, Diocese of Liverpool, 1976–Aug. 2002; *b* 26 Aug. 1932; *s* of late Henry Augustus Rupert Hamilton and Frances Mary Graham Hamilton; *m* 1960, Patricia Craghill Hamilton (*née* Ashburner); one *s* one *d.* *Educ:* Charterhouse; University Coll., Oxford (MA); MA Screenwriting, Liverpool John Moores Univ., 1999. Called to Bar, Middle Temple, 1956; a Recorder, 1974–86. Regular broadcasting work for Radio Merseyside, inc. scripts: Van Gogh in England, 1981; Voices from Babylon, 1983; A Longing for Dynamite, 1984; Dark Night, 1988 (winner of first prize for a short religious play, RADIUS); Murder Court productions (dramatised trials), Liverpool: The Maybrick Case, 1989; The Veronica Mutiny, 1990. *Publications:* Foul Bills and Dagger Money, 1979; All Jangle and Riot, 1986; A Good Wigging, 1988. *Recreations:* reading, walking, films. *Club:* Athenæum (Liverpool).

HAMILTON, Susan, (Mrs Eric Kelly); QC 1993; **Her Honour Judge Susan Hamilton;** a Circuit Judge, since 1998; *m* 1977, Dr Eric Peter Kelly; two *s.* *Educ:* Hove Grammar Sch. for Girls. Called to the Bar, Middle Temple, 1975; a Recorder, 1996–98. *Publications:* The Modern Law of Highways, 1981; (contrib.) Halsbury's Laws of England, vol. 21, 4th edn, 1995, vol. 39(1), 4th edn, 1998; (contrib.) Encyclopaedia of Forms and Precedents, 5th edn, 1986. *Recreations:* sailing, gardening, tapestry, travelling. *Address:* Maidstone Group of Courts, Maidstone, Kent ME16 8EQ. *Club:* Royal Southern Yacht.

HAMILTON-DALRYMPLE, Sir Hew; *see* Dalrymple.

HAMILTON FRASER, Donald; *see* Fraser.

HAMILTON-RUSSELL, family name of **Viscount Boyne**.

HAMILTON-SMITH, family name of **Baron Colwyn**.

HAMLEY, Donald Alfred, CBE 1985; HM Diplomatic Service, retired; *b* 19 Aug. 1931; *s* of Alfred Hamley and Amy (*née* Brimacombe); *m* 1958, Daphne Griffith; two *d.* *Educ:* Devonport High Sch., Plymouth. Joined HM Foreign (subseq. Diplomatic) Service, 1949; Nat. Service, 1950–52; returned to FO; served in: Kuwait, 1955–57; Libya, 1958–61; FO, 1961–63; Jedda, 1963–65 and 1969–72; Rome, 1965–69; seconded to DTI, 1972–73; Commercial Counsellor, Caracas, 1973–77; seconded to Dept of Trade, 1977–80; Consul-Gen., Jerusalem, 1980–84; retired, 1984. *Address:* 1 Forge Close, Hayes, Bromley BR2 7LP. *T:* (020) 8462 6696. *Club:* Royal Automobile.

HAMLIN, Prof. Michael John, CBE 1994; FICE, FIWEM, FREng; FRSE; consulting water engineer, since 1984; Principal and Vice Chancellor of the University of Dundee, 1987–94; *b* 11 May 1930; *s* of late Dr Ernest John Hamlin and Dorothy Janet Hamlin; *m* 1951, Augusta Louise, *d* of late William Thomas Tippins and Rose Louise Tippins; three *s.* *Educ:* St John's Coll., Johannesburg; Dauntsey's Sch.; Bristol Univ. (BSc); Imperial Coll. of Science and Technol., London (DIC). FIWEM (FIWES 1973); FICE 1981; FREng (FEng 1985); FRSE 1990. Asst Engineer, Lemon & Blizard, Southampton, 1951–53; Engineer: Anglo-American Corp., Johannesburg, 1954–55; Stewart, Sviridov & Oliver, Johannesburg, 1955; Partner, Rowe & Hamlin, Johannesburg, 1956–58; Univ. of Witwatersrand, 1959–60; University of Birmingham, 1961–87: Prof. of Water Engrg, 1970–87; Hd of Dept of Civil Engrg, 1980–87; Pro Vice-Chancellor, 1985–87; Vice-Principal, 1987. Chm., Aquatic and Atmospheric Phys. Scis Grants Cttee, NERC, 1975–79; Member: Severn Trent Water Authority, 1974–79; British National Cttee for Geodesy and Geophysics, 1979–84 (Chm., Hydrology Sub-Cttee, 1979–84); Scottish Econ. Council, 1989–93; Internat. Relns Cttee, 1992–95, Scientific Unions Cttee, 1995–99, Royal Soc. President: Internat. Commn on Water Resource Systems of the Internat. Assoc. of Hydrological Scis (IAHS), 1983–87; British Hydrological Soc., 1995–97. Chm., Scottish Centre for Children with Motor Impairment, 1991–94. Hon. Life Mem., Guild of Students, Birmingham Univ., 1980; Hon. Mem., Students' Assoc.,

Dundee Univ., 1994–. FRCPS (Glas) 1992; Hon. FRCGP 1993. Dist. Fellow, Internat. Med. Univ., Kuala Lumpur, 1999. Hon. LLD: St Andrews, 1989; Dundee, 1996; Hon. DEng: Birmingham, 1995; Bristol, 2000. President's Premium, IWES, 1972. OStJ 1991. *Publications:* contribs on public health engrg and water resources engrg in learned jls. *Recreations:* walking, gardening. *Address:* The Coombes, near Ludlow, Shropshire SY8 3AQ.

HAMLISCH, Marvin; composer, conductor, pianist, entertainer; *b* 2 June 1944; *s* of Max and Lilly Hamlisch; *m* 1989, Terre Blair. *Educ:* Professional Children's Sch.; Queen's Coll., NY; Juilliard Sch., NY. Début as a pianist, Minnesota Orch., 1975; solo concert tours; conductor of various orchestras throughout USA; Musical Dir and Conductor, Barbra Streisand tour, 1994 (Emmy Awards for Outstanding Individual Achievement in Music and Lyrics and in Music Direction, 1995); Principal Pops Conductor: Pittsburgh SO, 1995–; Baltimore SO, 1996–2000; National SO, Washington, 2000–. Mem., ASCAP. *Compositions* include: *film scores:* The Swimmer, 1968; Bananas, 1971; The Way We Were (Acad. and Grammy Awards for Best Original Score, and for Best Song of the Year for title song), 1974; Starting Over, 1979; Ordinary People, 1980; Sophie's Choice, 1982; *film themes:* Three Men and a Baby, 1987; January Man, 1988; The Experts, 1989; *songs:* Sunshine Lollipops and Rainbows; Good Morning America; Nobody Does it Better; One Song (for Barcelona Olympics), 1992; *musicals:* A Chorus Line, 1975 (Pulitzer Prize); They're Playing Our Song, 1979; The Goodbye Girl, 1993; Sweet Smell of Success, 2000; *symphony in one movement,* Anatomy of Peace, 1991. Acad. Award for best adaptation, for The Sting, 1974; Grammy Awards: Best New Artist, 1974; Best Pop Instrumental, for The Entertainer, 1974. *Publication:* The Way I Was (autobiog.), 1992. *Recreation:* loves to travel. *Address:* c/o Nancy Shear Arts Services, 180 West End Avenue, #28N, New York, NY 10023, USA. *T:* (212) 4969418, *Fax:* (212) 7878174.

HAMLYN, Prof. David Walter; Professor of Philosophy and Head of Philosophy Department, Birkbeck College, University of London, 1964–88, now Professor Emeritus (Head of Classics Department, 1981–86); Vice-Master, Birkbeck College, 1983–88, Fellow, 1988; *b* 1 Oct. 1924; *s* of late Hugh Parker Hamlyn and late Gertrude Isabel Hamlyn; *m* 1949, Eileen Carlyle Litt; one *s* one *d*. *Educ:* Plymouth Coll.; Exeter Coll., Oxford. BA (Oxon) 1948, MA 1949 (1st cl. Lit. Hum., 1st cl. Philosophy and Psychology, 1950). War Service, RAC and IAC, Hodson's Horse (Lieutenant), 1943–46. Research Fellow, Corpus Christi Coll., Oxford, 1950–53; Lecturer: Jesus Coll., Oxford, 1953–54; Birkbeck Coll., London, 1954–63, Reader, 1963–64. Pres., Aristotelian Soc., 1977–78. Member: Council, Royal Inst. of Philosophy, 1968– (Vice-Chm., 1991–95; Mem. Exec., 1971–97); Nat. Cttee for Philosophy, 1986–92 (Hon. Vice-Pres., 1992–). Mem., London Univ. Senate, 1981–87 (Mem. several cttees; Chm., Academic Council Standing Sub-cttee in Theology, Arts and Music, 1984–87); Governor: Birkbeck Coll., 1965–69; City Lit., 1982–86 (Vice-Chm., 1985–86); Central London Adult Educn Inst., 1987–90; Chm. Governors, Heythrop Coll., 1971–78, Mem., 1984–95, Fellow, 1978. Mem., Wissenschaftliche Leitung der Schopenhauerges., 1992–. Editor of Mind, 1972–84; Consulting Editor, Jl of Medical Ethics, 1981–90. *Publications:* The Psychology of Perception, 1957 (repr. with additional material, 1969); Sensation and Perception, 1961; Aristotle's *De Anima*, Books II and III, 1968; The Theory of Knowledge, 1970 (USA), 1971 (GB); Experience and the Growth of Understanding, 1978 (Spanish trans., 1981; Korean trans., 1990); Schopenhauer, 1980; Perception, Learning and the Self, 1983; Metaphysics, 1984; History of Western Philosophy, 1987 (Dutch trans., 1988; Portuguese trans., 1990; Swedish trans., 1995); In and Out of the Black Box, 1990; Being a Philosopher, 1992; Understanding Perception, 1996; contrib. to several other books and to many philosophical, psychological and classical jls. *Recreations:* playing and listening to music, reading, gardening. *Address:* 38 Smithy Knoll Road, Calver, Hope Valley, Derbyshire S32 3XW. *T:* (01433) 631326.

HAMLYN, Peter John, MD; FRCS; Consultant Neurological and Spinal Surgeon: St Bartholomew's Hospital, since 1990; The Royal London Hospital, since 1996; *b* 10 Aug. 1957; *s* of David William Hamlyn and Paula Anne Hamlyn (*née* Bowker); *m* 1994, Geraldine Marie Frances Shepherd; three *s*. *Educ:* N Cestrian Grammar Sch.; Solihull Sixth Form Coll.; University Coll. London (BSc 1st Cl. Hons Neurosci. 1979; MB BS 1982; MD 1994 (Rogers Prize)). FRCS 1986; FISM 1995. Corresp. in sports medicine, Daily Telegraph, 1993–. Founder, and Vice-Chm., 1997–, British Brain and Spine Foundn. *Publication:* Neurovascular Compression of the Cranial Nerves in Neurological and Systematic Disease, 1999. *Recreation:* sculpture. *Address:* Department of Neurosurgery, Royal London Hospital, E1 1BB. *T:* (020) 7377 7209.

HAMMARSKJÖLD, Knut (Olof Hjalmar Åkesson); Director, since 1948, and Chairman, 1987–94, now Emeritus Chairman, Sydsvenska Dagbladet AB, Newspaper Group, Malmö; Minister Plenipotentiary, since 1966; *b* Geneva, 16 Jan. 1922; Swedish; *m*; four *s*. *Educ:* Stockholm Univ. Entered Swedish Foreign Service, 1946; served in Paris, Vienna, Moscow, Bucharest, Kabul, Sofia, 1947–55; 1st Sec., Foreign Office, 1955–57; Head of Foreign Relations Dept, Royal Bd of Civil Aviation, Stockholm, 1957–59; Dep. Head of Swedish Delegn to OEEC, Paris, 1959–60; Dep. Sec.-Gen., EFTA, Geneva, 1960–66; International Air Transport Association (IATA): Dir Gen., 1966–84; Chm. Exec. Cttee, 1981–84; Internat. Affairs Counsel, 1985–86; Mem., Inst. of Transport, London; Dir, Inst. of Air Transport, Paris, 1974–; Dir.-Gen., Atwater Inst. Inf./Communications, Montreal, 1985–98; Mem., Internat. Aviation Management Training Inst., Montreal; Director: Prisma Transport Consultants Ltd, Geneva/Brussels, 1987–; Blenheim Aviation Services Ltd, 1992–. Chm., I-L Consult Baltic, Suders/Hamra, Gotland, 1994–. Chm., Ind. Commn for Reform of UNESCO, 1989–93; Sen. Special Advr to Dir Gen. of UNESCO, 1993–; Hon. Ambassador, UNESCO, 1991. Hon. Fellow, Canadian Aeronautics and Space Inst., Ottawa; Hon. Academician, Mexican Acad. of Internat. Law; Hon. FCIT (London). Edward Warner Award, ICAO, 1983. Comdr (1st cl.), Order of North Star (Sweden); NOR (Sweden); Légion d'Honneur (France); Grand Cross Order of Civil Merit (Spain); Grand Officer, Order of Al-Istiqlal (Jordan); Commander: Order of Lion (Finland); Oranje Nassau (Netherlands); Order of Falcon (1st cl.) (Iceland); Order of Black Star (Benin). *Publications:* articles on political, economic and aviation topics. *Recreations:* music, painting, ski-ing. *Address:* Rue St Germain 11, 1204 Geneva, Switzerland.

HAMMER, James Dominic George, CB 1983; Chairman, Certification Management Council, Zurich (formerly Eagle Star) Certification Ltd, since 1996; *b* 21 April 1929; *s* of E. A. G. and E. L. G. Hammer; *m* 1955, Margaret Eileen Halse; two *s* one *d*. *Educ:* Dulwich Coll.; Corpus Christi Coll., Cambridge. BA Hons Mod. Langs. Joined HM Factory Inspectorate, 1953; Chief Inspector of Factories, 1975–84; Dep. Dir Gen., HSE, 1985–89. Dir, UK SKILLS, 1990–2000. Pres., Internat. Assoc. of Labour Inspection, 1984–93; Chairman: Nat. Certification Scheme for In-Service Inspection Bodies, 1990–92; Nat. Steering Cttee, Eur. Year of Safety, Health and Hygiene at Work 1992, 1991–93; NACCB, 1992–95; Nat. Exam. Bd in Occupational Safety and Health, 1992–95. Vice Chm., Camberwell HA, 1982–91; Associate Mem., King's Healthcare, 1992–97. FRSA 1984; FIOSH 1992. *Address:* 10 Allison Grove, Dulwich, SE21 7ER. *T:* (020) 8693 2977.

HAMMERBECK, Brig. Christopher John Anthony, CB 1991; Executive Director, British Chamber of Commerce in Hong Kong, since 1994; *b* 14 March 1943; *s* of Sqn Leader O. R. W. Hammerbeck and I. M. Hammerbeck; *m* 1974, Alison Mary Felice (marr. diss. 1996); one *s* two *d*. *Educ:* Mayfield Coll., Sussex. Commnd, 1965; 2nd RTR, 1965–70; Air Adjt, Parachute Sqn, RAC, 1970–72; GSO3 (Ops), HQ 20 Armoured Bde, 1972–74; psc, 1975; DAA&QMG, HQ 12 Mechanised Bde, 1976–78; Sqn Comdr, 4th RTR, 1978–80; DAAG(O), MoD, 1980–82; Directing Staff, Army Staff Coll., 1982–84; CO, 2nd RTR, 1984–87; Col, Tactical Doctrine/Op. Requirement 1 (BR) Corps, 1987–88; RCDS, 1989; Comdr, 4th Armoured Brigade, 1990–92; Dep. Comdr, British Forces Hong Kong, 1992–94. President: Hong Kong Br., RBL, 1995–; HK Ex-Servicemen's Assoc., 1995–. MIMgt. *Recreations:* sailing, golf, ski-ing, bobsleigh, reading, travel. *Address:* British Chamber of Commerce in Hong Kong, Emperor Group Centre, 288 Hennessy Road, Wanchai, Hong Kong. *Clubs:* Army and Navy, Royal Over-Seas League; Shek O (Hong Kong).

HAMMERSLEY, Dr John Michael, FRS 1976; Reader in Mathematical Statistics, University of Oxford, and Professorial Fellow, Trinity College, Oxford, 1969–87, now Emeritus Fellow; part-time Consultant, Oxford Centre for Industrial and Applied Mathematics, since 1987; *b* 21 March 1920; *s* of late Guy Hugh Hammersley and Marguerite (*née* Whitehead); *m* 1951, Shirley Gwendolene (*née* Bakewell); two *s*. *Educ:* Sedbergh Sch.; Emmanuel Coll., Cambridge. MA, ScD (Cantab); MA, DSc (Oxon). War service in Royal Artillery, Major, 1940–45. Graduate Asst, Design and Analysis of Scientific Experiment, Univ. of Oxford, 1948–55; Principal Scientific Officer, AERE, Harwell, 1955–59; Sen. Research Officer, Inst. of Economics and Statistics, Univ. of Oxford, 1959–69; Sen. Research Fellow, Trinity Coll., Oxford, 1961–69. FIMS 1959; FIMA 1964; Fulbright Fellow, Princeton, 1955; Erskine Fellow, 1978; Rouse Ball lectr, Univ. of Cambridge, 1980. Mem., ISI, 1961. Von Neumann Medal for Applied Maths, Brussels, 1966; IMA Gold Medal, 1984; Pólya Prize, London Math. Soc., 1997. *Publications:* (with D. C. Handscomb) Monte Carlo Methods, 1964, rev. edn 1966, 5th edn 1984, trans. as Les Méthodes de Monte Carlo, 1967; papers in scientific jls. *Address:* 11 Eynsham Road, Oxford OX2 9BS. *T:* (01865) 862181.

HAMMERSLEY, Rear-Adm. Peter Gerald, CB 1982; OBE 1965; *b* 18 May 1928; *s* of late Robert Stevens Hammersley and Norah Hammersley (*née* Kirkham); *m* 1959, Audrey Cynthia Henderson Bolton; one *s* one *d*. *Educ:* Denstone Coll.; RNEC Manadon; Imperial Coll., London (DIC). Served RN, 1946–82; Long Engrg Course, RNEC Manadon, 1946–50; HMS Liverpool, 1950–51; Advanced Marine Engrg Course, RNC Greenwich, 1951–53; HMS Ocean, 1953–54; joined Submarine Service, 1954; HMS Alaric, HMS Tiptoe, 1954–58; Nuclear Engrg Course, Imperial Coll., 1958–59; First Marine Engineer Officer, first RN Nuclear Submarine, HMS Dreadnought, 1960–64; DG Ships Staff, 1965–68; Base Engineer Officer, Clyde Submarine Base, 1968–70; Naval Staff, 1970–72; Asst Director, S/M Project Team, DG Ships, 1973–76; CO, HMS Defiance, 1976–78; Captain, RNEC Manadon, 1978–80; CSO (engrg) to C-in-C Fleet, 1980–82. Comdr 1964; Captain 1971; Rear-Adm. 1980; Chief Exec., British Internal Combustion Engine Manufacturers' Assoc., 1982–85; Dir, British Marine Equipment Council, 1985–92. Fellow, Woodard Schs Corp., 1992–98. Gov., Denstone Coll., 1986–98 (Chm., 1994–98). Master, Engineers' Co., 1988–89. *Recreations:* walking, gardening, golf. *Address:* Wistaria Cottage, Linersh Wood, Bramley, near Guildford GU5 0EE. *Club:* Army and Navy.

HAMMERSLEY, Philip Tom, CBE 2000 (OBE 1989), CEng; Chairman, University Hospitals of Leicester NHS Trust, since 2000; *b* 10 Feb. 1931; *s* of Tom Andrew Hammersley and Winifred Hammersley (*née* Moyns); *m* 1954, Lesley Ann Millage; two *s* one *d*. *Educ:* Bancroft's Sch.; Imperial Coll., Univ. of London (BSc Eng.). CEng 1965; MIMechE 1965. Tech. Officer, ICI Plastics Div., 1954–65; Clarks Ltd: Chief Engr, 1965–68; Prodn Services Manager, 1968–71; Dir, Children's Div., 1971–79; Pres., Striderite Footwear, Boston, Mass, 1979–81; British Shoe Corporation, Leicester: Factories Dir, 1981–87; Man. Dir, Freeman, Hardy & Willis, 1987–89; Commercial Dir, 1989–90; non-exec. Dir, BSS Gp PLC, 1991–99 (Dep. Chm., 1995; Chm., 1995–99). Vice-Chm., Leics HA, 1990–92; Chm., Leicester Royal Infirmary NHS Trust, 1992–97; Regl Chm., Trent, NHS Exec., DoH, 1997–99. Chm. Council, Shoe & Allied Trades Res. Assoc., 1983–86; Pres., Brit. Footwear Manufacturers Fedn, 1986–87; Chm., E Midlands Regl Council, CBI, 1988–90. Trustee, Nat. Space Sci. Centre, 1997–. Mem. Council, Univ. of Leicester, 1991–. Freeman, City of London, 1983; Mem., Patten Makers' Co., 1983–. Hon. DBA De Montfort, 1999. *Recreations:* golf, theatre, music. *Address:* The Hollies, Wibtoft, near Lutterworth, Leics LE17 5BB. *T:* (01455) 220363. *Clubs:* East India, MCC; Leicestershire Golf.

HAMMERTON, His Honour Rolf Eric; a Circuit Judge, 1972–94; *b* 18 June 1926; *s* of Eric Maurice Hammerton and Dora Alice Hammerton (*née* Zander); *m* 1953, Thelma Celestine Hammerton (*née* Appleyard); one *s* three *d*. *Educ:* Brighton, Hove and Sussex Grammar Sch.; Peterhouse, Cambridge (MA, LLB). Philip Teichman Prize, 1952; called to Bar, Inner Temple, 1952; Sussex County Courts: Designated Judge, Children's Cases, 1990–94; Principal Judge, Civil Matters, 1992–94. Contributing Editor, Butterworth's County Court Precedents and Pleadings, 1985–2000. Liveryman, Cooks' Co., 1979– (Mem. Court, 1996–). *Recreation:* cooking.

HAMMICK, Sir Stephen (George), 5th Bt *cr* 1834; DL; *b* 27 Dec. 1926; *s* of Sir George Hammick, 4th Bt; *S* father, 1964; *m* 1953, Gillian Elizabeth Inchbald; two *s* one *d*. *Educ:* Stowe. Royal Navy as Rating (hostilities only), 1944–48; RAC Coll., Cirencester, 1949–50; MFH Cattistock Hunt, 1961 and 1962. Mem. (C), Dorset CC, 1958– (Vice-Chm., 1985–88; Chm., 1988–93). High Sheriff, Dorset, 1981–82, DL Dorset, 1989. Farmer, with 450 acres. *Recreations:* hunting, fishing, sailing. *Heir:* *s* Paul St Vincent Hammick [*b* 1 Jan. 1955; *m* 1984, Judith Mary, *d* of Ralph Ernest Reynolds]. *Address:* Badgers, Wraxall, Dorchester DT2 0HN. *T:* (01935) 83343.

HAMMOND, Sir Anthony (Hilgrove), KCB 2000 (CB 1992); Standing Counsel to General Synod of the Church of England, since 2000; Legal Counsel to Hakluyt & Co. Ltd, since 2001; *b* 27 July 1940; *s* of late Colonel Charles William Hilgrove Hammond and Jessie Eugenia Hammond (*née* Francis); *m* 1988, Avril Collinson. *Educ:* Malvern Coll.; Emmanuel Coll., Cambridge (BA, LLB). Admitted Solicitor of Supreme Court, 1965. Articled with LCC, 1962; Solicitor, GLC, 1965–68; Home Office: Legal Assistant, 1968; Sen. Legal Assistant, 1970; Asst Legal Advr, 1974; Principal Asst Legal Advr, 1980–88, Legal Advr, 1988–92, Home Office and NI Office; Solicitor and Dep. Sec., then Dir Gen. Legal Services, DTI, 1992–97; HM Procurator Gen., Treasury Solicitor and Queen's Proctor, 1997–2000. Mem. Bd, Inst. of Advanced Legal Studies, 1997–. Fellow, Soc. of Advanced Legal Studies, 1997. Freeman, City of London, 1991; Liveryman, Glass Sellers' Co., 1991– (Mem., Ct of Assistants, 2000–). Hon. QC 1997. *Recreations:* bridge, music, opera, walking, birdwatching. *Address:* General Synod, Church House, Great Smith Street, SW1P 3NZ.

HAMMOND, Eric Albert Barratt, OBE 1977; General Secretary, Electrical, Electronic, Telecommunication and Plumbing Union, 1984–92; *b* 17 July 1929; *s* of Arthur Edgar

Hammond and Gertrude May Hammond; *m* 1953, Brenda Mary Edgeler; two *s*. *Educ:* Corner Brook Public Sch. Shop Steward, 1953–63; Branch Sec., 1958–63, Exec. Councillor, 1963–, EETPU. Borough and Urban District Councillor, 1958–63. Mem., TUC Gen. Council, 1983–88. Member: Electronics EDC, 1967–92; Industrial Development Adv. Bd, 1977–87; Adv. Council on Energy Conservation, 1974–77; (part-time) Monopolies and Mergers Commn, 1978–84; Engrg Council, 1984–90; ACARD, 1985–87; NEDC, 1989–92; Lord Chancellor's Adv. Cttee on Legal Educn and Conduct, 1991–; Employment Appeal Tribunal, 1992–; Chm., Electronic Components and Technology Sector Gp (formerly Electronic Components Sector Working Party), 1975–92. Mem. Bd, Kent Thame-side, Groundwork, 1991–95. Gov., Gravesend Grammar Sch. for Boys, 1987– (Vice-Chm., 1989–94, Chm., 1994–); Chm., Support Kent Schools, 1998–. *Publication:* Maverick: the life of a union rebel, 1992. *Recreations:* gardening, photography. *Address:* 9 Dene Holm Road, Northfleet, Kent DA11 8LF. *Club:* Gravesend Rugby.

HAMMOND, Prof. Gerald, PhD; FBA 1998; John Edward Taylor Professor of English Literature, University of Manchester, since 1993; *b* 3 Nov. 1945; *s* of Frank George Hammond and Ruth Hammond (*née* Wallen); *m* 1971, Patsy Talat Naheed Khaliq; one *s* one *d*. *Educ:* University Coll. London (BA 1968; PhD 1974). University of Manchester: Lectr, 1971–83, Sen. Lectr, 1983–90, Reader, 1990–93, in English; Dean, Faculty of Arts, 1999–. Distinguished Vis. Humanities Prof., Auburn Univ., Alabama, 1987; Nat. Sci. Council of Taiwan Res. Fellow, 1997–98. Chatterton Lecture, 1985, Warton Lecture, 1995, British Acad. *Publications:* (ed) The Metaphysical Poets, 1974; (ed) John Skelton: poems, 1980; The Reader and Shakespeare's Young Man Sonnets, 1981; The Making of the English Bible, 1984; (ed) Sir Walter Ralegh, 1984; (ed) Elizabethan Poetry, Lyrical and Narrative, 1984; (ed) Richard Lovelace: poems, 1987; Fleeting Things: English poets and poems 1616–1660, 1990; Horseracing: a book of words, 1992; articles in learned jls, reviews. *Recreation:* horseracing. *Address:* 29 Belfield Road, Manchester M20 6BJ. *T:* (0161) 445 2399; *e-mail:* gerald.hammond@man.ac.uk.

HAMMOND, James Anthony; His Honour Judge Hammond; a Circuit Judge, since 1986; *b* 25 July 1936; *s* of James Hammond and Phyllis Eileen Hammond; *m* 1963, Sheila Mary Hammond, JP (*née* Stafford); three *d*. *Educ:* Wigan Grammar Sch.; St Catherine's Coll., Oxford (MA). Called to Bar, Lincoln's Inn, 1959; National Service, 1959–61; a Recorder, 1980–86. Councillor: Up Holland UDC, 1962–66; Skelmersdale and Holland UDC, 1970–72. Chairman: NW Branch, Society of Labour Lawyers, 1975–86; W Lancs CAB, 1982–86; Pres., NW Branch, Inst. for Study and Treatment of Delinquency, 1987–. *Recreations:* hockey, walking, sailing. *Clubs:* Wigan Hockey (Vice Pres., 1983–); Orrell Rugby Union Football.

HAMMOND, (John) Martin; Headmaster, Tonbridge School, since 1990; *b* 15 Nov. 1944; *s* of Thomas Chatterton Hammond and Joan Cruse; *m* 1974, Meredith Jane Shier; one *s* one *d*. *Educ:* Winchester Coll. (Scholar); Balliol Coll., Oxford (Domus Scholar). Oxford University: Hertford Scholar and (1st) de Paravicini Scholar, (2nd) Craven Scholar, 1st Cl. Hons Mods, 1963; Chancellor's Latin Prose Prize, Chancellor's Latin Verse Prize, Ireland Scholar, 1964; Gaisford Greek Prose Prize, Gaisford Greek Verse Prize (jtly), 1965; 2nd Cl. Lit. Hum. 1966. Asst Master, St Paul's Sch., 1966–71; Teacher, Anargyrios Sch., Spetsai, Greece, 1972–73; Asst Master, Harrow Sch., 1973–74; Head of Classics, 1974–80, and Master in College, 1980–84, Eton Coll.; Headmaster, City of London Sch., 1984–90. Mem., Gen. Adv. Council of BBC, 1987–91. *Publications:* Homer, The Iliad (trans.), 1987; Homer, The Odyssey (trans.), 2000. *Address:* The Headmaster's House, Tonbridge School, Tonbridge, Kent TN9 1JP. *T:* (01732) 365555.

HAMMOND, Julia Jessica; *see* Eccleshare, J. J.

HAMMOND, Martin; *see* Hammond, J. M.

HAMMOND, Michael Harry Frank, CBE 1990; DL; Chief Executive and Town Clerk, Nottingham City Council, 1974–90; *b* 5 June 1933; *s* of late Edward Cecil Hammond and Kate Hammond; *m* 1965, Jenny Campbell; two *s* one *d*. *Educ:* Leatherhead; Law Society Sch. of Law; Nottingham Univ. (LLM Internat. Law 1996). Admitted solicitor, 1958; Asst Sol. in Town Clerk's office, Nottingham, 1961–63; Prosecuting Sol., 1963–66; Asst Town Clerk, 1966–69; Dep. Town Clerk, Newport, Mon, 1969–71; Dep. Town Clerk, Nottingham, 1971–74. Hon. Secretary: Major City Councils Gp, 1977–88; Notts County Br., Assoc. of District Councils, 1974–88; Chairman: Assoc. of Local Authority Chief Execs, 1984–85; E Midlands Br., Soc. of Local Authority Chief Execs, 1988–90; Pres., Notts Law Soc., 1989–90 (Vice-Pres., 1988–89). Mem., Nat. Forest Adv. Bd, 1991–95. Member: Midlands Regl Cttee, N British Housing Assoc., 1992–97; Develt Steering Gp, St John's Coll., Nottingham, 1995–2000; URC E Midlands Province Listed Bldgs Adv. Cttee, 1995–2000; Notts Valuation Tribunal, 1998–. Trustee, Hillsborough Disaster Appeal Fund, 1989–96; Chm., E Midlands Chair in Stroke Medicine Appeal, 1991–92. British Red Cross Society: Pres., 1995–, Chm. Council, 1998–, Notts Br. (Trustee, 1992–97; Dep. Pres., 1994); Nat. Trustee, 1998–2000; Mem., Midlands Reg. Council, 1998–; Trustee, Nottingham Almshouse and Nottingham Annuity Charities, 1994–. Governor, Nottingham High Sch., 1990–. An Elections Supervisor, Rhodesia/Zimbabwe Independence Elections, 1980. Mem., Magdala Debating Soc., 1990–94. Mem., RAI, 1993. DL Notts, 1990. Rhodesia Medal, 1980; Zimbabwe Independence Medal, 1980. *Recreations:* bowls, gardening, travel. *Address:* 41 Burlington Road, Sherwood, Nottingham NG5 2GR. *T:* (0115) 960 2000. *Clubs:* Nottingham and Notts United Services (Nottingham); Queen Anne Bowling Green (Pres., 1999–2000); Nottingham Rugby (Mem. Cttee, 1994–97).

HAMMOND, Prof. Norman David Curle, FSA, FBA; Archaeology Correspondent, The Times, since 1967; Professor of Archaeology, Boston University, and Associate in Maya Archaeology, Peabody Museum, Harvard University, since 1988; *b* 10 July 1944; *er s* of late William Hammond and Kathleen Jessie Hammond (*née* Howes); *m* 1972, Jean, *er d* of late A. H. Wilson and Beryl Wilson; one *s* one *d*. *Educ:* Varndean GS; Peterhouse, Cambridge (Trevelyan Schol.; BA 1966; Dip. Classical Archaeol. 1967; MA 1970; PhD 1972; ScD 1987). FSA 1974 (Mem. Council, 1996–99). Centre of Latin American Studies, Cambridge: Res. Fellow, 1967–71; Leverhulme Res. Fellow, 1972–75; Res. Fellow, Fitzwilliam Coll., Cambridge, 1973–75; Sen. Lectr, Univ. of Bradford, 1975–77; Rutgers University: Vis. Prof., 1977–78; Associate Prof., 1978–84; Prof. of Archaeol., 1984–88; Irvine Chair of Anthropol., Calif. Acad. of Scis, 1984–85; Fellow in Pre-Columbian Studies, Dumbarton Oaks, Washington, 1988. Rockefeller Foundn Scholar, Bellagio, 1997. Visiting Professor: Univ. of California, Berkeley, 1977; Jilin Univ., Changchun, 1981; Univ. of Paris, Sorbonne, 1987; Univ. of Bonn, 1994; Visiting Fellow: Worcester Coll., Oxford, 1989; Peterhouse, Cambridge, 1991, 1996–97; McDonald Inst., Cambridge Univ., 1997. Lectures: Curl, RAI, 1985; Bushnell, Cambridge Univ., 1997; Willey, Harvard Univ., 2000; Brunswick Distinguished, MMA, 2001. Acad. Trustee, Archaeol. Inst. of America, 1990–93 (Stone Lect., 1998; Brush Lect., 2001). Hon. Mem., Phi Beta Kappa, 1989. Corresp. FBA 1998. Mem. editl bds, archaeol. jls, USA, UK, 1984–; editor, Afghan Studies, 1976–79; Consulting Editor, Liby of Congress, 1977–89; archaeol. consultant, Scientific American, 1979–95. Excavations and surveys: Libya and Tunisia, 1964; Afghanistan, 1966; Belize, 1970–2000 (Lubaantun, Nohmul, Cuello, La Milpa); Ecuador, 1972–84. Hon. DSc Bradford, 1999. Press Award, British Archaeol Awards, 1994, (jtly) 1998; Soc. of Antiquaries Medal, 2001. *Publications:* (ed) South Asian Archaeology, 1973; (ed) Mesoamerican Archaeology, 1974; Lubaantun: a Classic Maya realm, 1975; (ed) Social Process in Maya Prehistory, 1977; (ed with F. R. Allchin) The Archaeology of Afghanistan, 1978; (ed with G. R. Willey) Maya Archaeology and Ethnohistory, 1979; Ancient Maya Civilisation, 1982, 5th edn 1994; (gen. editor) Archaeology Procs, 44th Congress of Americanists, 1982–84; (ed) Nohmul: excavations 1973–83, 1985; (ed) Cuello: an early Maya community in Belize, 1991; The Maya, 2000; contribs to learned and unlearned jls. *Recreations:* heraldry, genealogy, serendipity. *Address:* Wholeway, Harlton, Cambridge CB3 7ET. *T:* (01223) 262376; 83 Ivy Street, Apt 32, Brookline, MA 02446, USA. *T:* (617) 7399077. *Clubs:* Athenæum; Tavern (Boston).

HAMMOND, Prof. Paul Francis; Professor of Seventeenth-Century English Literature, University of Leeds, since 1996; *b* 8 Oct. 1953; *s* of Ronald Francis Hammond and Maureen Margaret Hammond (*née* Butler). *Educ:* Peter Symonds' Sch., Winchester; Trinity Coll., Cambridge (BA, MA; PhD 1979; LittD 1996). Fellow, Trinity Coll., Cambridge, 1978–82; University of Leeds: Lectr in English, 1978–89; Sen. Lectr, 1989–95; Reader in Seventeenth-Century Literature, 1995–96. An Associate Ed., New DNB, 1998–. *Publications:* John Oldham and the Renewal of Classical Culture, 1983; (ed) Selected Prose of Alexander Pope, 1987; John Dryden: a literary life, 1991; (ed) The Poems of John Dryden: Vol. 1: 1649–1681, 1995; Vol. 2: 1682–1685, 1995; Vol. 3 (jtly): 1686–1693, 2000; Vol. 4 (jtly): 1693–1696, 2000; Love Between Men in English Literature, 1996; Dryden and the Traces of Classical Rome, 1999; (ed jtly) John Dryden: Tercentenary Essays, 2000; articles on seventeenth century English literature in scholarly jls. *Recreations:* Classical and French culture, theatre, music, swimming. *Address:* School of English, University of Leeds, Leeds LS2 9JT. *T:* (0113) 233 4739.

HAMMOND, Philip; MP (C) Runnymede and Weybridge, since 1997; *b* 4 Dec. 1955; *s* of Bernard Lawrence Hammond and Doris Rose Hammond; *m* 1991, Susan Carolyn, *d* of E. Williams-Walker; one *s* two *d*. *Educ:* Shenfield Sch., Brentwood; University Coll., Oxford (Open Scholar, 1st cl. PPE, MA). Various posts, Speywood Labs Ltd, 1977–81; Dir, Speywood Medical Ltd, 1981–83; established and ran medical equipment distribution co., and dir, medical equipment manufg cos, 1983–94; Partner, CMA Consultants, 1993–95; Director: Castlemead Ltd, 1984–; Castlemead Homes Ltd, 1994–. Consultant, Govt of Malawi, 1995–97. Contested (C) Newham NE, June 1994. Opposition spokesman on health and social services, 1998–2001. Mem., Select Cttee on Envmt, Transport and the Regions, 1997–98. Sec., Cons. Parly Health Cttee, 1997–98. *Recreations:* reading, cinema, walking. *Address:* House of Commons, SW1A 0AA. *T:* (020) 7219 4055. *Clubs:* Carlton; Weybridge Conservative.

HAMMOND, Roy John William; Director, City of Birmingham Polytechnic, 1979–84; *b* 3 Oct. 1928; *s* of John James Hammond and Edith May Hammond; *m* 1st, 1949, Audrey Cecilia Dagmar Avello (*d* 1988); three *d*; 2nd, 1990, Dorothy Forder. *Educ:* East Ham Grammar Sch.; University College of the South West, Exeter; Sorbonne, Paris. BA Hons, 1st Cl. French and Latin, London. Royal Air Force Education Branch, 1952–56; Asst Lectr, Blackburn Municipal Technical Coll. and School of Art, 1956–59; Head of Department: Herefordshire Technical Coll., 1960–66; Leeds Polytechnic, 1966–71; Asst Dir, City of Birmingham Polytechnic, 1971–79. Hon. Fellow, Univ. of Central England in Birmingham (formerly City of Birmingham Poly.), 1985. FRSA. *Recreations:* cricket, theatre, music, walking, flying.

HAMMOND, Simon Tristram; His Honour Judge Simon Hammond; a Circuit Judge, since 1993; *b* 5 Jan. 1944; *s* of Philip J. Hammond and Sylvia D. (*née* Sillem); *m* 1976, Louise (*née* Weir); one *s* two *d*. *Educ:* Eastbourne Coll.; Coll. of Law. Articled to Philip J. Hammond, Leicester; admitted Solicitor, 1967; Solicitor, later Partner, Victor J. Lissack, London, 1968–76; Partner, Philip J. Hammond & Sons, Leicester, 1977–93. An Asst Recorder, 1985–90; a Recorder, 1990–93. Asst Comr to Parly Boundary Commn for England, 1992. Member: Law Soc's Standing Cttee on Criminal Law, 1982–91; Crown Court Rules Cttee, 1988–93; Enforcement Sub-cttee, Home Office Rev. of Magistrates Court Procedure, 1989–90. Churchwarden, 1990–. *Recreations:* horses, hunting, ski-ing, vegetable gardening. *Address:* c/o Circuit Administrator's Office, Midland and Oxford Circuit, 2 Newton Street, Birmingham B4 6NE.

HAMMOND-CHAMBERS, (Robert) Alexander; Chairman, Ivory & Sime, 1985–91; Chairman, Edinburgh Green Belt Trust, since 1991; *b* 20 Oct. 1942; *s* of late Robert Rupert Hammond-Chambers and of Leonie Elise Noble (*née* Andrews); *m* 1968, Sarah Louisa Madeline (*née* Fanshawe); two *s* one *d*. *Educ:* Wellington College; Magdalene College, Cambridge (Hons Economics). Ivory & Sime: joined 1964; Partner, 1969; Director, 1975, upon incorporation; Dep. Chm., 1982. Chairman: American Opportunity Trust plc, 1993–; Dobbies Garden Centres plc, 1994–; Fidelity Special Values plc, 1994–; Fidelity Japanese Values plc, 1997– (Dir, 1994–); Ivory & Sime Optimum Income Trust plc, 1997–; Director: Internat. Biotechnology Trust plc, and other cos. Overseas Governor, Nat. Assoc. of Securities Dealers Inc., 1984–87. *Recreations:* tennis, sailing, photography, golf. *Address:* The Old White House, 144 Liberton Drive, Edinburgh EH16 6TQ. *T:* (0131) 672 1697. *Club:* New (Edinburgh).

HAMMOND-STROUD, Derek, OBE 1987; concert and opera baritone; Professor of Singing, Royal Academy of Music, 1974–90; *b* 10 Jan. 1926; *s* of Herbert William Stroud and Ethel Louise Elliott. *Educ:* Salvatorian Coll., Harrow, Mddx; Trinity Coll. of Music, London; in Vienna and Munich with Elena Gerhardt and Gerhard Hüsch. Glyndebourne Festival Opera, 1959; Sadler's Wells Opera (later ENO), 1961; Royal Opera, Covent Garden, 1971; Houston Grand Opera, USA, 1975; Netherlands Opera, 1976; Metropolitan Opera, NY, 1977; Teatro Colón, Buenos Aires, 1981; Munich State Opera, 1983. Concerts and Lieder recitals at Edinburgh, Aldeburgh, Munich and Vienna Festivals, and in Spain, Iceland and Denmark. BBC Promenade Concerts, 1968–. Pres., Univ. of London Opera Gp, 1971. Freeman, City of London, 1952; Hon. RAM 1976; Hon. FTCL, 1982. Sir Charles Santley Meml Gift, Worshipful Co. of Musicians, 1988. Recordings include: The Ring (Goodall); Der Rosenkavalier (de Waart). *Recreations:* chess, study of philosophy. *Address:* 18 Sutton Road, Muswell Hill, N10 1HE. *T:* (020) 8883 2120.

HAMNETT, Prof. Andrew, DPhil; CChem, FRSC; Principal and Vice-Chancellor, University of Strathclyde, since 2001; *b* 12 Nov. 1947; *s* of Albert Edward Hamnett and Dorothy Grace Hamnett (*née* Stewart); *m* 1976, Suzanne Marie Parkin; three *d*. *Educ:* William Hulme's Grammar Sch., Manchester; University Coll., Oxford (Open Schol.; BA Hons Chem. 1970); St John's Coll., Oxford (Sen. Schol.; DPhil 1973). CChem, FRSC 1991. Jun. Res. Fellow in Chemistry, Queen's Coll., Oxford, 1972–77; Deptl Res. Asst, then Lectr in Inorganic Chemistry, Oxford Univ., 1977–89; Fellow by Special Election, then Tutorial Fellow, St Catherine's Coll., Oxford, 1980–89; University of Newcastle upon Tyne: Prof. of Physical Chemistry, 1989–2000; Pro-Vice-Chancellor, 1993–2000. Killam Fellow, Univ. of BC, 1974–76. *Publications:* (with P. A. Christensen) Techniques and Mechanism in Electrochemistry, 1994; (ed with R. G. Compton) Novel Methods of

Studying the Electrode-Electrolyte Interface, 1989; (jtly) Electrochemistry, 1998; numerous papers and review articles on physical and inorganic chemistry. *Recreations:* music, languages, philately. *Address:* University of Strathclyde, 16 Richmond Street, Glasgow G1 1XQ. *T:* (0141) 548 2000. *Clubs:* Athenæum, Caledonian.

HAMNETT, Katharine; fashion designer; *b* 16 Aug. 1947; *d* of Gp Capt. James Appleton. *Educ:* Cheltenham Ladies' Coll.; St Martin's Sch. of Art. Set up Tuttabankem (with Anne Buck), 1969–75; freelance designer in London, Paris, Milan, New York and Hong Kong, 1975–79; established Katharine Hamnett Ltd, 1979, and subseq. launched men's and women's collections, Asia, Europe, USA; transf. production to Italy, 1989, moving from manufacturing to licensing base. Vis. Prof., London Inst., 1997–. Numerous awards include British Fashion Designer of the Year, 1984. *Publications:* contribs to fashion magazines and newspapers. *Recreations:* gardening, agriculture, photography, archaeology, travel. *Address:* Katharine Hamnett Ltd, 202 New North Road, N1 7BJ. *T:* (020) 7354 4400.

HAMNETT, Thomas Orlando; Chairman, Greater Manchester Council, 1975–1976, Vice-Chairman, 1976; *b* 28 Sept. 1930; *s* of John and Elizabeth Hamnett; *m* 1954, Kathleen Ridgway; one *s* five *d*. *Educ:* Stockport Jun. Techn. Sch. Sheetmetal craftsman, 1946. Member, Manchester City Council, 1963 until re-organisation (Vice-Chm., Health Cttee, Chm. sub cttee on Staff on Cleansing Cttee, Mem. Policy and Finance Cttees), and 1978–92 (Member: Direct works, Markets, and Personnel Cttees; Transportation, Education, and Recreation and Arts Cttees, Greater Manchester Council; Chm., Environmental Services Cttee, City Council, Manchester, 1982). *Recreations:* football, cricket, table tennis. *Club:* Gorton Trades and Labour (Chm.).

HAMON, Francis Charles, OBE 2000; Deputy Bailiff, Jersey, 1995–2000; Commissioner, Jersey Financial Services Commission, since 2000; Chairman, Channel Television, since 2000; *b* 30 July 1939; *s* of Clifford Charles Hamon and Lily Kathleen (*née* Le Gentil); *m* 1963, Sonia Muriel Parslow; one *s* one *d*. *Educ:* Victoria Coll., Jersey. First staff announcer, Channel TV, 1962–64; Asst Land Officer, States of Jersey, 1964–66; called to the Bar: Middle Temple, 1966; Jersey, 1968; in private practice in Jersey, 1968–87; Sen. Partner, Crill, Cubitt-Sowden & Tomes, 1985–87; Comr (Judge), Royal Court, Jersey, 1988–95. Director: Royal Bank of Scotland (Jersey) Ltd, 1982–95 (Dep. Chm., 1986–95); Media Hldgs Ltd, 2000–. Chm., Jersey Arts Trust, 1992–95. Founder Member: Good Theatre Co.; Jersey Fencing Club; Jersey Rugby Fives Assoc. Gov., Victoria Coll., 1987–97. *Recreations:* theatre, bird-watching, travel, Rugby fives, reading. *Address:* La Maison du Sud, Trinity, Jersey JE3 5HW. *T:* (01534) 863199.

HAMPDEN; *see* Hobart-Hampden.

HAMPDEN, 6th Viscount *cr* 1884; **Anthony David Brand;** DL; land agent; *b* 7 May 1937; *s* of 5th Viscount Hampden and Imogen Alice Rhys, *d* of 7th Baron Dynevor; *S* father, 1975; *m* 1969, Cara Fiona (marr. diss. 1988), *e d* of Claud Proby; two *s* one *d*; *m* 1993, Mrs Sally Snow, *d* of Sir Charles Hambro, KBE, MC. *Educ:* Eton. Chairman: Sussex CLA, 1985–88; Governing Body, Emanuel Sch., 1985–. DL E Sussex, 1986. *Publications:* Henry and Eliza, 1980; A Glimpse of Glynde, 1997. *Heir:* *s* Hon. Francis Anthony Brand, *b* 17 Sept. 1970. *Address:* Glynde Place, Glynde, Lewes, Sussex BN8 6SX. *Club:* White's.

HAMPEL, Sir Ronald (Claus), Kt 1995; Chairman, ICI plc, 1995–99; United Business Media (formerly United News & Media), since 1999; *b* 31 May 1932; *s* of Karl Victor Hugo Hampel and Rutgard Emil Klothilde Hauck; *m* 1957, Jane Bristed Hewson; three *s* one *d*. *Educ:* Canford Sch., Wimborne; Corpus Christi Coll., Cambridge (MA Mod. Lang. and Law; Hon. Fellow, 1996). Nat. service, 2nd Lt, 3rd RHA, 1951–52. Joined ICI, 1955; Vice-Pres., ICI US, 1973–77; Gen. Manager, Commercial, 1977–80; Chairman: ICI Paints, 1980–83; ICI Agrochemicals, 1983–85; Dir, ICI, 1985–99; Chief Operating Officer, 1991–93, Dep. Chm. and Chief Exec., 1993–95, ICI plc. Non-executive Director: Powell Duffryn, 1984–88; Commercial Union, 1988–95; BAE Systems (formerly British Aerospace), 1989–; ALCOA (USA), 1995–. Dir, Amer. Chamber of Commerce, 1986–91; Chm., Cttee on Corporate Governance, 1995–98; Member: Listed Cos Adv. Cttee, Stock Exchange, 1996–99; Nomination Cttee, NY Stock Exchange, 1996–98. Mem. Exec. Cttee, British North America Cttee, 1989–95. Mem., European Round Table, 1995–99. CIMgt (CBIM 1985); FRSA 1992. *Recreations:* tennis, golf, ski-ing, music (opera/ballet). *Clubs:* MCC, All England Lawn Tennis; Royal & Ancient.

HAMPSHIRE, Margaret Grace, MA; JP; Principal of Cheltenham Ladies' College, 1964–79; *b* 7 Sept. 1918; *o d* of Dr C. H. Hampshire, CMG, MB, BS, BSc, sometime Sec. of British Pharmacopœia Commission, and Grace Mary Hampshire. *Educ:* Malvern Girls' Coll.; Girton Coll., Cambridge. BA 1941; MA 1945. Entered Civil Service, Board of Trade, 1941. Joined Staff of Courtaulds, 1951. Head of Government Relations Department, 1959–64. Member: Board of Governors, University Coll. Hosp., 1961–64; Marylebone Borough Council, 1962–64; SW Regional Hosp. Board, 1967–70; Midlands Electricity Consultative Council, 1973–80; Vice-Pres., Intensive Care Trust, Cheltenham Hosp., 1985– (Chm., 1982–85). Reader, Painswick, Sheepscombe and Cranham, dio. of Gloucester, 1987–. County Sec., Gloucestershire Girl Guides, 1980–85; Governor, Alice Ottley Sch., Worcester, 1979–92. JP Cheltenham, 1970. *Recreations:* music, reading, foreign travel. *Address:* Ringwood, 9 The Croft, Painswick, Glos GL6 6QP.

HAMPSHIRE, Prof. Michael John, CBE 1987; CPhys, CEng; Research Professor of Electronic Information Technology, University of Salford, since 1990 (Professor, 1985–90); *b* 13 Oct. 1939; *s* of Jack and Hilda May Hampshire; *m* 1962, Mavis (*née* Oakes); one *d*. *Educ:* Heckmondwike Grammar Sch.; Univ. of Birmingham (BSc Physics, PhD Elec. Engrg). FIEE, FInstP. University of Salford: Lectr, 1964; Sen. Lectr, 1972; Prof. of Solid State Electronics, 1977; Chm., Dept of Electronic and Electrical Engrg, 1981–89; Asst Man. Dir, 1989–95, Dir, 1989–98, Salford Univ. Business Services Ltd. Consultant: Ferranti, 1970–74; Volex Gp, 1977–99 (Chm., R&D Cttee, 1987–92); Thorn EMI Flow Measurement, 1980–88. Founder and Chm., Vertec (Electronics), 1982–92 (Dir, 1992–98). Commendation EPIC Award, 1982; Academic Enterprise Award, 1982; Techmart Technology Transfer Trophy, 1984. Hon. MIED 1982. *Publications:* Electron Physics and Devices, 1969; 80 pubns and patents on solid state electronics and electronic systems, vehicle multiplexing, innovation. *Recreations:* music, golf. *Address:* 3 Brookfield, Upper Hopton, Mirfield, West Yorks WF14 8HL.

HAMPSHIRE, Nancy Lynn Delaney, (Lady Hampshire); *see* Cartwright, N. L. D.

HAMPSHIRE, Sir Stuart (Newton), Kt 1979; FBA 1960; Warden of Wadham College, Oxford University, 1970–84; *b* 1 Oct. 1914; *s* of G. N. Hampshire and Marie West; *m* 1st, 1961, Renee Ayer (*d* 1980); 2nd, 1985, Nancy Lynn Delaney Cartwright, *qv*; two *d*. *Educ:* Repton; Balliol Coll., Oxford. 1st Cl. Lit Hum, Oxford, 1936. Fellow of All Souls Coll., and Lectr in Philosophy, Oxford, 1936–40. Service in Army, 1940–45. Personal Asst to Minister of State, Foreign Office, 1945; Lectr in Philosophy, University Coll., London, 1947–50; Fellow of New Coll., Oxford, 1950–55; Domestic Bursar and Research Fellow, All Souls Coll., 1955–60; Grote Prof. of Philosophy of Mind and Logic, Univ. of London, 1960–63; Prof. of Philosophy, Princeton Univ., 1963–70; Prof., Stanford Univ., 1985–91. Fellow, Amer. Acad. of Arts and Sciences, 1968. Hon. DLitt Glasgow, 1973. *Publications:* Spinoza, 1951; Thought and Action, 1959; Freedom of the Individual, 1965; Modern Writers and other essays, 1969; Freedom of Mind and other essays, 1971; (ed jtly) The Socialist Idea, 1975; Two Theories of Morality, 1977; (ed) Public and Private Morality, 1978; Morality and Conflict, 1983; Innocence and Experience, 1989; Justice is Conflict, 1999; articles in philosophical journals. *Address:* 7 Beaumont Road, The Quarry, Headington, Oxford OX3 8JN. *T:* (01865) 761688.

HAMPSHIRE, Susan, OBE 1995; actress; *b* 12 May 1942; *d* of George Kenneth Hampshire and June Hampshire; *m* 1st, 1967, Pierre Granier-Deferre (marr. diss. 1974); one *s* (one *d* decd); 2nd, 1981, Sir Eddie Kulukundis, *qv*. *Educ:* Hampshire Sch., Knightsbridge. *Stage:* Expresso Bongo, Saville, tour, 1959; 'that girl' in Follow That Girl, Vaudeville, 1960; Fairy Tales of New York, Comedy, 1961; Marion Dangerfield in Ginger Man, Royal Court, 1963; Past Imperfect, St Martin's and Savoy, 1964; Kate Hardcastle in She Stoops to Conquer, tour, 1966; On Approval, tour, 1966; Mary in The Sleeping Prince, St Martin's, tour, 1968; Nora in A Doll's House, Greenwich, 1972; Katharina in The Taming of the Shrew, Shaw, 1974; Peter in Peter Pan, Coliseum, 1974; Jeannette in Romeo and Jeannette, tour, 1975; Rosalind in As You Like It, Shaw, 1975; title rôle in Miss Julie, Greenwich, 1975; Elizabeth in The Circle, Haymarket, 1976; Ann Whitefield in Man and Superman, Savoy, 1978; Siri Von Essen in Tribades, Hampstead, 1978; Victorine in An Audience Called Edouard, Greenwich, 1978; Irene in The Crucifer of Blood, Haymarket, 1979; Ruth Carson in Night and Day, Phoenix, 1979; Elizabeth in The Revolt, New End, 1980; Stella Drury in House Guest, Savoy, 1981; Elvira in Blithe Spirit, Vaudeville, 1986; Marie Stopes in Married Love, Wyndhams, 1988; Countess in A Little Night Music, Piccadilly, 1989; Mrs Anna in The King and I, Sadler's Wells, 1990; Gertrude Lawrence in Noel and Gertie, Duke of York's, 1991; Dowager Countess of Marshwood in Relative Values, Savoy, 1993; Suzanna in Suzanna Andler, Battersea, 1995; Alicia in Black Chiffon (tour), 1996; *TV Serials:* Katy in What Katy Did; Andromeda (title rôle), Fleur Forsyte in The Forsyte Saga (Emmy Award for Best Actress, 1970), Becky Sharp in Vanity Fair (Emmy Award for Best Actress, 1973), Sarah Churchill, Duchess of Marlborough, in The First Churchills (Emmy Award for Best Actress, 1971), Glencora Palliser in The Pallisers; Lady Melfont in Dick Turpin; Signora Neroni in The Barchester Chronicles; Martha in Leaving, 2 series; Going to Pot, 3 series; Don't tell Father; Esme Harkness in The Grand, 2 series; Coming Home; Monarch of the Glen, 3 series. *Films include:* During One Night, The Three Lives of Thomasina, Night Must Fall, Wonderful Life, Paris in August, The Fighting Prince of Donegal, Monte Carlo or Bust, Rogan, David Copperfield, Living Free, A Time for Loving, Malpertius (E. Poe Prizes du Film Fantastique, Best Actress, 1972), Neither the Sea Nor the Sand, Roses and Green Peppers, Bang. Dir, Conservation Foundn, 1995–; Mem. Exec. Cttee, Population Concern; Pres., Dyslexia Inst.; Vice-Pres., Internat. Tree Foundn. Hon. DLitt: London, 1981; City, 1984; St Andrews, 1986; Hon. DEd Kingston, 1994; Hon. DArts Pine Manor Coll., Boston, USA, 1994. *Publications:* Susan's Story, 1981; The Maternal Instinct, 1984; Lucy Jane at the Ballet, 1989; Lucy Jane on Television, 1989; Trouble Free Gardening, 1989; Every Letter Counts, 1990; Lucy Jane and the Dancing Competition, 1991; Easy Gardening, 1991; Lucy Jane and the Russian Ballet, 1993; Rosie's First Ballet Lesson, 1996. *Recreations:* gardening, music, the study of antique furniture. *Address:* c/o Chatto & Linnit Ltd, 123A King's Road, SW3 4PL. *T:* (020) 7352 7722, *Fax:* (020) 7352 3450.

HAMPSON, Caroline; *see* St John-Brooks, C.

HAMPSON, Christopher, CBE 1994; Chairman: RMC Group, 1996–April 2002; British Biotech plc, since 1998; *b* 6 Sept. 1931; *s* of Harold Ralph Hampson and Geraldine Mary Hampson; *m* 1954 Joan Margaret Cassils Evans; two *s* three *d*. *Educ:* McGill Univ. (BEng Chem 1952). Vice-Pres., 1956–78 and Sen. Vice-Pres., 1982–84, Canadian Industries, Canada; Imperial Chemical Industries: Gen. Manager, Planning, 1978–82; Man. Dir and Chief Exec. Officer, ICI Australia, 1984–87; Exec. Dir, ICI, 1987–94; Chm., Yorkshire Electricity Gp, 1994–97. Non-executive Director: SNC-Lavalin Group, 1992–; TransAlta Corp., 1993–; BG plc, 1997–2000; Lattice Gp plc, 2000–. Mem. Bd, 1996–99, Dep. Chm., 1999–2000, Environment Agency. *Recreations:* tennis, ski-ing. *Address:* 77 Kensington Court, W8 5DT. *Clubs:* Boodle's, Hurlingham; York (Toronto).

HAMPSON, Dr Keith; *b* 14 Aug. 1943; *s* of Bertie Hampson and Mary Elizabeth Noble; *m* 1st, 1975, Frances Pauline (*d* 1975), *d* of Mr and Mrs Mathieu Donald Einhorn; 2nd, 1979, Susan, *d* of Mr and Mrs John Wilkie Cameron. *Educ:* King James I Grammar Sch., Bishop Auckland, Co. Durham; Univ. of Bristol; Harvard Univ. BA, CertEd, PhD. Personal Asst to Edward Heath, 1966 and 1970 Gen. Elections and in his House of Commons office, 1968; Lectr in American History, Edinburgh Univ., 1968–74. Mem., Gen. Adv. Council, IBA, 1980–88. MP (C) Ripon, Feb. 1974–1983, Leeds North West, 1983–97; contested (C) Leeds North West, 1997. PPS: to Minister for Local Govt, 1979–83; to Sec. of State for Environment, 1983; to Sec. of State for Defence, 1983–84. Member: Select Cttee on Trade and Industry, 1987–97; Public Accounts Commn, 1992–97; Vice Chairman: Cons. Parly Educn Cttee, 1975–79; Cons. Parly Defence Cttee, 1988–89 (Sec., 1984–88). Mem., Educn Adv. Cttee of UK Commn for UNESCO, 1980–84. Vice President: WEA, 1978–97; Assoc. of Business Executives, 1979–; Vice-Chm., Youthaid, 1979–83. *Recreations:* DIY, music. *Club:* Carlton.

HAMPSON, Prof. Norman, FBA 1980; Professor of History, University of York, 1974–89; *b* 8 April 1922; *s* of Frank Hampson and Elizabeth Jane Fazackerley; *m* 1948, Jacqueline Gardin; two *d*. *Educ:* Manchester Grammar Sch.; University Coll., Oxford (MA); Dr de l'Univ. Paris. Service in Royal Navy, 1941–45. Manchester Univ., 1948–67: Lectr and Sen. Lectr; Prof. of Modern History, Univ. of Newcastle, 1967–74. Hon. DLitt Edinburgh, 1989. *Publications:* La Marine de l'an II, 1959; A Social History of the French Revolution, 1963; The Enlightenment, 1968; The First European Revolution, 1969; The Life and Opinions of Maximilien Robespierre, 1974; A Concise History of the French Revolution, 1975; Danton, 1978; Will and Circumstance: Montesquieu, Rousseau and the French Revolution, 1983; Prelude to Terror, 1988; Saint-Just, 1991; The Perfidy of Albion, 1998; Not Really What You'd Call a War, 2001. *Address:* 305 Hull Road, York YO10 3LU. *T:* (01904) 412661.

HAMPSON, Peter, QPM 1998; Chief Constable, West Mercia Constabulary, since 1999; *b* 8 Jan. 1947; *s* of Maj. Ronald Hampson, MBE and Edith Hampson; *m* 1971, Pamela Mary Cotes; one *s* two *d*. *Educ:* Sandford Orleigh Sch., Newton Abbot; King's Coll. London (LLB 1982; AKC). Joined Metropolitan Police Service, 1967: Constable, 1967–71; Chief Superintendent, 1991–94; Asst Chief Constable, Surrey Police, 1994–96; Asst Inspector of Constabulary, Home Office, 1996–99. FRSA 1992. OStJ 1998. *Recreations:* family and friends, reading, theatre, cycling, music, St John Ambulance Brigade, National Trust. *Address:* West Mercia Constabulary, PO Box 55, Hindlip Hall, Worcester WR3 8SP. *T:* (01905) 723000.

HAMPSON, Stephen Fazackerley; Under Secretary, Scottish Executive (formerly Scottish Office), since 1993; Head of Enterprise and Industrial Affairs Group, Scottish Executive Enterprise and Lifelong Learning Department, since 2000; *b* 27 Oct. 1945; *s* of

Frank Hampson and Helen (*née* Ellis); *m* 1970, Gunilla Brunk; one *s* one *d*. *Educ:* University Coll., Oxford (BPhil; MA). Lectr, Aberdeen Univ., 1969–71; Economist, NEDO, 1971–75; various posts, Scottish Office, 1975–78, and at Scottish Office, then Scottish Executive, 1981– (Hd, Envmt Gp, 1993–2000); First Sec., FCO, New Delhi, 1978–81. Mem. Bd, British Trade Internat., 2000–. Hon. FCIWEM 1998. *Address:* Glenelg, Park Road, Kilmacolm PA13 4EE. *T:* (01505) 872615.

HAMPSON, Sir Stuart, Kt 1998; Chairman, John Lewis Partnership, since 1993; *b* 7 Jan. 1947; *s* of Kenneth and Mary Hampson; *m* 1973, Angela McLaren; one *s* one *d*. *Educ:* Royal Masonic Sch., Bushey; St John's Coll., Oxford (BA Mod. Langs, MA). Board of Trade, 1969–72; FCO UKMIS to UN, Geneva, 1972–74; Dept of Prices and Consumer Protection, 1974–79; Dept of Trade, 1979–82; John Lewis Partnership, 1982–: Dir of Research and Expansion, 1986; Dep. Chm., 1989. Dep. Chm., London First, 1992–97; Chm., Centre for Tomorrow's Company, 1998–99. Chm., RSA, 1999–2001 (Treas., 1997–98; Dep. Chm., 1998–99). Hon. DBA Kingston, 1998. *Address:* John Lewis Partnership, 171 Victoria Street, SW1E 5NN. *T:* (020) 7828 1000.

HAMPSON, (Walter) Thomas; singer; *b* Elkhart, Indiana, 28 June 1955; *s* of Walter Hampson and Ruthye Hampson; one *d*. *Educ:* Eastern Washington Univ. (BA Govt); Fort Wright Coll.; Music Acad. of West. Début in Hansel and Gretel, 1974; with Düsseldorf Ensemble, 1981–84; title rôle in Der Prinz von Homburg, Darmstadt, 1982; débuts: Cologne, Munich, Santa Fé, 1982–84; Metropolitan Opera, NY, Vienna Staatsoper, Covent Garden, 1986; La Scala Milan, Deutsche Oper, Berlin, 1989; Carnegie Hall, San Francisco Opera, 1990; rôles include: Marcello in La Bohème; Gugliemo in Così fan tutte; Figaro in Il Barbiere di Siviglia; Count in Le Nozze di Figaro; Ulisse in Il Ritorno d'Ulisse in Patria; Lescaut in Manon; Count in La Traviata; Vicomte de Valmont in Dangerous Liaisons (world première); Marquis de Posa in Don Carlos; Riccardo in I Puritani; Wolfram in Tannhäuser; Oreste in Iphigénie en Tauride; Amfortas in Parsifal; title rôles: Don Giovanni; Der Prinz von Homburg; Billy Budd; Hamlet; Eugene Onegin; William Tell; Werther (seldom-performed baritone version); Doktor Faust. Has performed with Wiener Philharmoniker, NY Philharmonic, LPO and Chicago Symphony orchs. Recital repertoire includes Schumann, Mahler and American Art Song. Has made numerous recordings. Hon. RAM 1996. Hon. Dr: San Francisco Conservatory of Music; Whitworth Coll., USA. Awards include: Gold Medal, Internat. Mahler Soc.; Lotte Lehman Medal, Music Acad. of West, 1979; Edison Prize, Netherlands, 1990 and 1992; Grand Prix du Disque, 1990, 1996, Echo Klassik, 1995, Deutsche Schallplattenpreis; Cannes Classical Award, 1994; Citation of Merit, Nat. Arts Club, 1997; Vienna Kammersänger, 1999. *Publications:* (ed jtly) Mahler Songs: critical edition, 1993; (ed jtly) Schumann/Heine 20 Lieder und Gesänge: critical edition. *Address:* c/o IMG Artists Europe, 616 Chiswick High Road, W4 5RX.

HAMPSTEAD, Archdeacon of; *see* Lawson, Ven. M. C.

HAMPTON, 6th Baron *cr* 1874; **Richard Humphrey Russell Pakington;** Bt 1846; *b* 25 May 1925; *s* of 5th Baron Hampton, OBE, and Grace Dykes (*d* 1959), 3rd *d* of Rt Hon. Sir Albert Spicer, 1st Bt; *S* father, 1974; *m* 1958, Jane Elizabeth Farquharson, *er d* of late T. F. Arnott, OBE, TD, MB, ChB; one *s* two *d*. *Educ:* Eton; Balliol Coll., Oxford. RNVR, 1944–47. Varied employment, with advertising agencies, 1949–58; Worcestershire Branch, CPRE, 1958–71. Liberal Party Spokesman on NI, H of L, 1977–87. President: S Worcs Liberal Assoc., 1978–88; Upton-on-Severn Civic Soc., 1986–93. A Liberal Democrat. *Publication:* (written with his father, Humphrey Pakington) The Pakingtons of Westwood, 1975. *Heir: s* Hon. John Humphrey Arnott Pakington [*b* 24 Dec. 1964; *m* 1996, Siena, *yr d* of Remo Caldato].

HAMPTON, Antony Barmore, TD 1954; DL; President, Record Marples Tools Ltd (formerly Bahco Record Tools), since 1981 (Chairman, 1958–81); President, Engineering Employers Federation, 1980–82; *b* 6 March 1919; *s* of Charles William Hampton and Winifred Elizabeth Hampton; *m* 1948, Helen Patricia Lockwood; five *s*. *Educ:* Rydal Sch.; Christ's Coll., Cambridge, 1938–40 (MA). Indian Army 1941–46 (despatches). C. and J. Hampton Ltd, 1947, until merger with Ridgway, 1972 (Chm. of both, 1958–81); Lloyds Bank Ltd: Chm., Yorkshire Board, 1972–84 (Mem., 1961–85); Director, UK Board, 1972–85. Dir, Black Horse Agencies Ltd, 1983–85; Mem., Engrg Industry Trng Bd, 1979–82; Master Cutler of Hallamshire, 1966–67. Chm., Crucible Theatre Trust, Sheffield, 1970–82. DL S Yorkshire (previously W Riding) 1972. *Recreations:* sailing, fishing. *Address:* Tideway, 20 Wittering Road, Hayling Island, Hants PO11 9SP. *T:* (023) 9246 4361. *Club:* Little Ship (Hon. Life Mem., 1998).

HAMPTON, Bryan; Head of Exports to the Americas, Department of Trade and Industry, 1992–95; *b* 4 Dec. 1938; *s* of William Douglas Hampton and Elizabeth Cardwell; *m* 1964, Marilyn Joseph; five *d*. *Educ:* Harrow County Grammar Sch. for Boys. Board of Trade: Exec. Officer, 1957; Asst Private Sec. to Parly Sec., 1961; Private Sec. to Minister of State (Lords), 1963; Asst Principal, 1965; Second Sec., UK Delegn to EFTA/GATT, Geneva, 1966; Principal, DTI, 1969; Asst Sec., Dept of Energy, 1974; Counsellor (Energy), Washington, 1981–86; Head, Br. 1, Atomic Energy Div., 1986–89, Dir, Personnel, 1989–92, Dept of Energy. Gov., Chenies Sch., 1996–2000. *Recreations:* music, golf. *Address:* Orchard House, Berks Hill, Chorleywood, Herts WD3 5AG. *T:* (01923) 282311. *Club:* Northwood Golf (Chm., 1999–).

HAMPTON, Christopher James, CBE 1999; FRSL; playwright; *b* 26 Jan. 1946; *s* of Bernard Patrick Hampton and Dorothy Patience Hampton (*née* Herrington); *m* 1971, Laura Margaret de Holesch; two *d*. *Educ:* Lancing Coll.; New Coll., Oxford (MA; Hon. Fellow, 1997). First play: When Did You Last See My Mother?, 1964 (perf. Royal Court Theatre, 1966; transf. Comedy Theatre; prod. at Sheridan Square Playhouse, New York, 1967). Resident Dramatist, Royal Court Theatre, Aug. 1968–70. FRSL 1976 (Mem. Council, 1984–90). Officier, l'Ordre des Arts et des Lettres (France), 1997. *Plays:* Total Eclipse, Prod. Royal Court, 1968; The Philanthropist, Royal Court and Mayfair, 1970 (Evening Standard Best Comedy Award, 1970; Plays & Players London Theatre Critics Best Play, 1970), Ethel Barrymore Theatre, New York, 1971, Chichester, 1985; Savages, Royal Court, 1973, Comedy, 1973, Mark Taper Forum Theatre, Los Angeles, 1974 (Plays & Players London Theatre Critics Best Play, Jt Winner, 1973; Los Angeles Drama Critics Circle Award for Distinguished Playwriting, 1974); Treats, Royal Court, 1976, Mayfair, 1976; Able's Will, BBC TV, 1977; After Mercer, Nat. Theatre, 1980; The History Man (from Malcolm Bradbury) BBC TV, 1981; Total Eclipse (rev. version) Lyric, Hammersmith, 1981; The Portage to San Cristobal of A. H. (from George Steiner), Mermaid, 1982; Tales from Hollywood, Mark Taper Forum Theatre, Los Angeles, 1982, NT 1983 (Standard Best Comedy Award, 1983); Les Liaisons Dangereuses (from Laclos), RSC, 1985, transf. Ambassadors Th., 1986, NY, 1987 (Plays & Players London Theatre Critics Best Play, Jt Winner, 1985; Time Out Best Production Award, 1986; London Standard Best Play Award, 1986; Laurence Olivier Best Play Award, 1986; NY Drama Critics' Circle Best For. Play Award, 1987); Hotel du Lac (from Anita Brookner), BBC TV, 1986 (BAFTA Best TV Film Award, 1987); The Ginger Tree (from Oswald Wynd), BBC TV, 1989; White Chameleon, Nat. Theatre, 1991; Alice's Adventures Under Ground, Nat. Theatre, 1994; *musical:* Sunset Boulevard (book and lyrics with Don Black), Adelphi, and Shubert Theatre, LA, 1993, Minskoff Theatre, NY, 1994 (Tony Award: Best Original Score, 1995; Best Book of a Musical, 1995); *translations:* Marya, by Isaac Babel, Royal Court, 1967; Uncle Vanya, by Chekhov, Royal Court, 1970; Hedda Gabler, by Ibsen, Fest. Theatre, Stratford, Ont, 1970, Almeida, Islington, 1984, rev. version, NT, 1989; A Doll's House, by Ibsen, Playhouse Theatre, New York, 1971, Criterion, London, 1973, Vivian Beaumont Theatre, New York, 1975; Don Juan, by Molière, Bristol Old Vic, 1972; Tales from the Vienna Woods, by Horváth, National Theatre, 1977; Don Juan Comes Back from the War, by Horváth, Nat. Theatre, 1978; Ghosts, by Ibsen, Actors' Co., 1978; The Wild Duck, by Ibsen, Nat. Theatre, 1979; The Prague Trial, by Chereau and Mnouchkine, Paris Studio, 1980; Tartuffe, by Molière, RSC, 1983; Faith, Hope and Charity, by Horváth, Lyric, Hammersmith, 1989; Art, by Yasmina Reza, Wyndhams, 1996 (Standard Best Comedy Award and Laurence Olivier Best Comedy Award, 1997), NY (Tony Award, Best Play), 1998; An Enemy of the People, by Ibsen, RNT, 1997; The Unexpected Man, by Yasmina Reza, RSC, 1998; Conversations After a Burial, by Yasmina Reza, Almeida, 2000; Life x 3, by Yasmina Reza, RNT, 2000; *screenplays:* A Doll's House, 1973; Tales From the Vienna Woods, 1979; The Honorary Consul, 1983; The Good Father, 1986 (Prix Italia 1988); Wolf at the Door, 1986; Dangerous Liaisons, 1988 (Academy Award, and Writers Guild of America Award, for best adapted screenplay; Critics' Circle Award for best screenplay, 1989; BAFTA best screenplay award, 1990); Total Eclipse, 1995; Mary Reilly, 1996; (*also directed*): Carrington, 1995 (Special Jury Prize, Cannes Fest., 1995); The Secret Agent, 1996. *Publications:* When Did You Last See My Mother?, 1967; Total Eclipse, 1969, rev. version, 1981; The Philanthropist, 1970, 2nd edn 1985, The Philanthropist and other plays, 1991; Savages, 1974; Treats, 1976; Able's Will, 1979; Tales from Hollywood, 1983; The Portage to San Cristobal of A. H. (George Steiner), 1983; Les Liaisons Dangereuses, 1985; Dangerous Liaisons: the film, 1989; The Ginger Tree, 1989; White Chameleon, 1991; (with Don Black) Sunset Boulevard, 1993; Alice's Adventures Under Ground, 1995; Carrington, 1995; Total Eclipse: the film, 1996; Plays One, 1997; The Secret Agent and Nostromo (Conrad), 1997; *translations:* Isaac Babel, Marya, 1969; Chekhov, Uncle Vanya, 1971; Ibsen, Hedda Gabler, 1972, rev. version 1989; Ibsen, A Doll's House, 1972, 2nd edn 1989; Molière, Don Juan, 1972; Horváth, Tales from the Vienna Woods, 1977; Horváth, Don Juan Comes Back from the War, 1978; Ibsen, The Wild Duck, 1980; Ibsen, Ghosts, 1983; Molière, Tartuffe, 1984, 2nd edn 1991; Horváth, Faith, Hope and Charity, 1989; Yasmina Reza, Art (Scott Moncrieff Trans. Prize, Translators' Assoc.), 1997; Ibsen, An Enemy of the People, 1997; Yasmina Reza, The Unexpected Man, 1998; Yasmina Reza, Conversations After a Burial, 2000; Yasmina Reza, Life x 3, 2000. *Recreations:* travel, cinema. *Address:* 2 Kensington Park Gardens, W11 3HB. *Club:* Dramatists'.

HAMPTON, Sir Geoffrey; *see* Hampton, Sir L. G.

HAMPTON, John; a Recorder of the Crown Court, 1983–98; *b* 13 Nov. 1926; *e s* of late Thomas Victor Hampton and Alice Maud (*née* Sturgeon), Oulton Broad; *m* 1954, Laura Jessie, *d* of Ronald Mylne Ford and Margaret Jessie Ford (*née* Coghill), Newcastle-under-Lyme; three *d*. *Educ:* Bradford Grammar School; University College London (LLB). Served Royal Navy, 1945–47. Called to the Bar, Inner Temple, 1952; NE Circuit; Solicitor General and Attorney General; Dep. Circuit Judge, 1975–82. Dep. Chm., Agricultural Land Tribunal, Yorks and Lancs Area, 1980–82, Yorks and Humberside Area, 1982–99; Dep. Traffic Comr, NE Traffic Area, 1988–94. *Recreations:* mountaineering, sailing. *Address:* c/o 37 Park Square, Leeds LS1 2NY. *T:* (0113) 243 9422; *e-mail:* chambers@no37.co.uk.

HAMPTON, Sir (Leslie) Geoffrey, Kt 1998; Director, Leadership Centre, and Dean, School of Education, University of Wolverhampton, since 1999; *b* 2 Aug. 1952; *s* of Leslie and Irene Hampton; *m* 1975, Christine Joyce Bickley; two *s*. *Educ:* King Alfred's Coll., Winchester (Cert Ed); Southampton Univ. (BEd); Birmingham Univ. (MEd). Teacher of Technology, Pensnett Sch., Dudley, W Midlands, 1973–86 (Dep. Head, 1985–86); Dep. Head, Buckpool Sch., Dudley, 1986–93; Headteacher, Northicote Sch., Wolverhampton, 1993–99. Co-Dir, Nat. ICT Res. Centre, 2001–. *Publications:* (contrib.) Developing Quality Systems in Education, ed G. Doherty, 1994; (jtly) Transforming Northicote, 2000. *Recreations:* DIY, cycling, gardening. *Address:* University of Wolverhampton, Walsall Campus, Gorway Road, Walsall WS1 3BD.

HAMPTON, Surgeon Rear-Adm. Trevor Richard Walker, CB 1988; FRCPE; Surgeon Rear-Admiral (Operational Medical Services), 1987–89; *b* 6 June 1930; *s* of Violet and Percy Hampton; *m* 1st, 1952, Rosemary (*née* Day); three *d*; 2nd, 1976, Jennifer (*née* Bootle). *Educ:* King Edward VII Grammar School, King's Lynn; Edinburgh University. MB, ChB 1954; MRCPE 1964. Resident House Officer, Edinburgh Royal Infirmary, 1954–55; joined RN as Surgeon Lieut, 1955; served in HM Ships Ganges, Harrier and Victorious, 1955–62; Clinical Asst, Dept of Medicine, Edinburgh Univ., 1964; RN Hosp., Gibraltar, 1965–68; Consultant Physician, RN Hospitals, Plymouth, 1969–74, Haslar, 1975–79; MO i/c, RN Hosp., Gibraltar, 1980–82, RN Hosp., Plymouth, 1982–84; Surgeon Rear-Adm., Support Medical Services, 1984–87. QHP 1983–89. OStJ 1983. *Publications:* contribs to Jl of RN Med. Service. *Recreations:* reading, writing, resting.

HAMWEE, Baroness *cr* 1991 (Life Peer), of Richmond upon Thames; **Sally Rachel Hamwee;** Member (Lib Dem), since 2000 and Chairman, since 2001, London Assembly, Greater London Authority (Deputy Chairman, 2000–01); Partner, Clintons, solicitors; *b* 12 Jan. 1947; *d* of late Alec Hamwee and Dorothy (*née* Saunders). *Educ:* Manchester High Sch. for Girls; Girton Coll., Cambridge (MA). Admitted as solicitor, 1972. Councillor, London Borough of Richmond upon Thames, 1978– (Chm., Planning Cttee, 1983–87; Vice Chm., Policy and Resources Cttee, 1987–92); Chair, London Planning Adv. Cttee, 1986–94; Chm., Members' Policy Gp, London and SE Regl Planning Conf., 1989–91. Vice Chm., Assoc. of Liberal Democrat Councillors, 1988–99; Member: Nat. Exec., Liberal Party, 1987–88; Federal Exec., Liberal Democrats, 1989–91; Lib Dem spokesman on envmt (local govt, 1991–, planning and housing, 1993–), H of L. Member: Adv. Council, London First, 1996–98 (Dir, 1993–96); Council, Parents for Children, 1977–86; Council of Mgt, Refuge (formerly Chiswick Family Rescue), 1991–; Joseph Rowntree Foundn Inquiry, Planning for Housing, 1992–94; Council, Family Policies Study Centre, 1994–2000. Legal Advr, Simon Community, 1980–; Dir, In Harmony, 1994–98; Chm., Xfm Ltd, 1996–98. Pres., Town and Country Planning Assoc. *Address:* 101A Mortlake High Street, SW14 8HQ. *T:* (020) 8878 1380.

HAMYLTON JONES, Keith, CMG 1979; HM Diplomatic Service, retired; HM Ambassador, to Costa Rica, 1974–79, to Honduras, 1975–78, and to Nicaragua, 1976–79; *b* 12 Oct. 1924; *m* 1953, Eira Morgan; one *d*. *Educ:* St Paul's Sch.; Balliol Coll., Oxford (Domus Scholar in Classics, 1943); BA 1948; MA 1950. Welsh Guards, 1943; Italy, 1944 (Lieut); S France, 1946 (Staff Captain). HM Foreign Service, 1949; 3rd Sec., Warsaw, 1950; 2nd Sec., Lisbon, 1953; 1st Sec., Manila, 1957; Head of Chancery and HM Consul, Montevideo, 1962; Head of Chancery, Rangoon, 1967; Asst Head of SE Asia Dept, FCO, 1968; Consul-General, Lubumbashi, 1970–72; Counsellor, FCO, 1973–74. Operation Raleigh: Chm. for Devon and Cornwall, 1983–85; led internat. expedn to Costa Rica,

Feb-May 1985. Chairman: Anglo-Costa Rican Soc., 1983–88; Anglo-Central American Soc., 1988–91. *Publication:* (as Peter Myllent) The Ideal World, 1972. *Recreations:* reading, writing, walking. *Address:* Morval House, Morval, near Looe, Cornwall PL13 1PN.

HAN Suyin, (Dr Elizabeth Comber); doctor and author; (*née* Elizabeth Kuanghu Chow); *b* 12 Sept. 1917; *d* of Y. T. Chow (Zhou) (Chinese) and M. Denis (Belgian); *m* 1st, 1938, General P. H. Tang (*d* 1947); one *d*; 2nd, 1952, L. F. Comber (marr. diss. 1968); 3rd, 1971, Vincent Ruthnaswamy. *Educ:* Yenching Univ., Peking, China; Brussels Univ., Brussels, Belgium; London Univ., London, England. Graduated MB, BS, London (Hons) in 1948, a practising doctor until 1964. *Publications: as Han Suyin:* Destination Chungking, 1942; A Many Splendoured Thing, 1952; And the Rain My Drink, 1956; The Mountain Is Young, 1958; Cast but One Shadow and Winter Love, 1962; The Four Faces, 1963; China in the Year 2001, 1967; The Morning Deluge, 1972; Wind in the Tower, 1976; Lhasa, the Open City, 1977; Les Cent Fleurs: La Peinture Chinoise, 1978; La Chine aux Mille Visages, 1980; Chine: Terre Eau et Hommes, 1981; Till Morning Comes, 1982; The Enchantress, 1985; A Share of Loving, 1987; Han Suyin's China, 1988; Fleur de Soleil, 1988; Tigers and Butterflies, 1990; Les Yeux de Demain, 1992; Eldest Son: Zhou Enlai and the making of modern China (1898–1976), 1994; *autobiography:* China: autobiography, biography, history (6 vols): The Crippled Tree, 1965; A Mortal Flower, 1966; Birdless Summer, 1968; My House Has Two Doors, 1980; Phoenix Harvest, 1980; Wind in my Sleeve, 1992. *Recreations:* economics studies, lecturing, founding exchanges in science. *Address:* 37 Montoie, Lausanne 1007, Switzerland.

HANAN, Dame Elizabeth (Ann), DNZM 1998; Deputy Mayor, Dunedin City, since 1998 (City Councillor, since 1986); Chair, Otago Museum Trust Board, 1987–99 (Member, since 1986); *b* 21 Aug. 1937; *d* of Sir John Walsh, *qv*; *m* 1966, John Murray Hanan; one *s* two *d*. *Educ:* Columba Coll.; Otago Girls' High Sch.; Otago Univ. (BSc 1961; Dip. Recreation and Sport 1983). Secondary School Teacher, Christchurch, London and Dunedin, 1960–66, 1984–88; Supervisor and Demonstrator, Chemistry, Univ. of Otago, 1975–86; Tutor, Otago Poly., 1982–85. Member: NZ Council, 1986–88, Bd, 1989–98, Consumers' Inst. of NZ; Electrical Workers' Registration Bd, 1993–98 (Presiding Mem., 1993–97). Member: Otago Br., Fedn of Univ. Women, 1961– (Pres., 1990–92); Otago Theatre Trust, 1986–; Bd of Mgt, Fortune Theatre, 1995–; Discovery World, 1989–98; Chair, Assoc. of Science and Technology Centres, 1994–96; Pres., Internat. Science Fest., Dunedin, 1996–. Commemoration Medal, 1990, Suffrage Centennial Medal, 1993, NZ. *Publication:* Playgrounds and Play, 1981 (trans. Japanese 1993). *Recreations:* walking, reading, computers, geneaology, theatre, gardening. *Address:* 159 Highgate, Dunedin, New Zealand. *T:* and *Fax:* (3) 4774388; *e-mail:* ehanan@dcc.govt.nz. *Club:* University (Dunedin).

HANBURY-TENISON, (Airling) Robin, OBE 1981; MA, FLS, FRGS; farmer; President, Survival International (Chairman since 1969); *b* 7 May 1936; *s* of late Major Gerald Evan Farquhar Tenison, Lough Bawn, Co. Monaghan, Ireland, and Ruth, *o* surv. *c* of late John Capel Hanbury, JP, DL, Pontypool Park, Monmouthshire; *m* 1st, 1959, Marika Hopkinson (*d* 1982); one *s* one *d*; 2nd, 1983, Mrs Louella Edwards, *d* of Lt Col G. T. G. Williams, DL, and Mrs Williams, Menkee, St Mabyn, Cornwall; one *s*. *Educ:* Eton; Magdalen Coll., Oxford (MA). Made first land crossing of South America at its widest point, 1958 (Mrs Patrick Ness Award, RGS, 1961); explored Tassili N'Ajjer, Tibesti and Aïr mountains in Southern Sahara, 1962 66; crossed S America in a small boat from the Orinoco to Buenos Aires, 1964–65; Geographical Magazine Amazonas Expedn, by Hovercraft, 1968; Trans-African Hovercraft Expedn (Dep. Leader), 1969; visited 33 Indian tribes as guest of Brazilian Govt, 1971; Winston Churchill Memorial Fellow, 1971; British Trans Americas Expedn, 1972; explored Outer Islands of Indonesia, 1973; Eastern Sulawesi, 1974; Sabah, Brunei, Sarawak, 1976; RGS Mulu (Sarawak) Expedn (Leader), 1977–78; expedns to Ecuador, Brazil and Venezuela, 1980–81; rode across France, 1984; rode along Great Wall of China, 1986; rode through New Zealand, 1988; led mission for IUCN, Friends of the Earth and Survival Internat. to Malaysia to investigate imprisonment of envmtl protesters, 1988; rode as pilgrim to Santiago de Compostela, 1989; rode across Spain driving 300 cattle on Trans Humance, 1991; visited tribal peoples of E Siberia for Survival Internat., 1992 and 1994; rode route of proposed Pennine Bridleway, 1994; visited: tribal people of Arunachal Pradesh, NE India, 1995; Innu of Labrador, 1997; Tuareg of Ténére desert, S Sahara, 1999; Mulu (film for C4), 1999. Chief Executive: BFSS, 1995–97; Countryside Alliance (BFSS, Countryside Business Gp and Countryside Movt), 1997–98; organised Countryside Rally, 1997, Countryside March, 1998. Comr of Income Tax, 1965–95; Mem., SW Regl Panel, MAFF, 1993–96; Mem. of Lloyd's, 1976–95. Mem., Invest in Britain (formerly Think British) Campaign, 1987–; Trustee, Ecological Foundn, 1988–; Pres., Cornwall Wildlife Trust, 1988–95; Patron, Cornwall Heritage Trust, 1994–. Mem. Council, RGS, 1968–70, 1971–76, 1979–82, 1995– (Vice-Pres., 1982–86); Patron's Medal, RGS, 1979; Krug Award of Excellence, 1980; Farmers Club Cup, 1998; Personality of the Year, Internat. Council for Game and Wildlife Conservation, 1998; Contribution to Countryside Award, CLA, 2000; Medal of Italian Chamber of Deputies, Pio Manzù Centre, 2000; Mungo Park Medal, RSGS, 2001. Dr *hc* Mons-Hainaut, 1992. *Publications:* The Rough and the Smooth, 1969; Report of a Visit to the Indians of Brazil, 1971; A Question of Survival, 1973; A Pattern of Peoples, 1975; Mulu: the rain forest, 1980; Aborigines of the Amazon Rain Forest: the Yanomami, 1982; Worlds Apart (autobiog.), 1984; White Horses Over France, 1985; A Ride along the Great Wall, 1987; Fragile Eden: a ride through New Zealand, 1989; Spanish Pilgrimage: a canter to St James, 1990; (ed) The Oxford Book of Exploration, 1993; *for children:* Jake's Escape, 1996; Jake's Treasure, 1998; Jake's Safari, 1998; articles in: The Times, Spectator, Daily Mail, Sunday Express, etc; articles and reviews in Geographical Magazine (numerous), Geographical Jl, Ecologist, Traveller, etc. *Recreations:* travelling, riding across countries. *Address:* Cabilla Manor, Cardinham, Bodmin, Cornwall PL30 4DW. *T:* (01208) 821224; *e-mail:* robin@cabilla.co.uk. *Clubs:* Pratt's, Groucho, Geographical; Kildare Street and University (Dublin).

See also Sir R. Hanbury-Tenison.

HANBURY-TENISON, Sir Richard, KCVO 1995; JP; Lord-Lieutenant of Gwent, 1979–2000; *b* 3 Jan. 1925; *e s* of late Major G. E. F. Tenison, Lough Bawn, Co. Monaghan, Ireland, and Ruth, *o c* of late J. C. Hanbury, JP, DL, Pontypool Park, Monmouthshire; *m* 1955, Euphan Mary, *er d* of late Major A. B. Wardlaw-Ramsay, 21st of Whitehill, Midlothian; three *s* two *d*. *Educ:* Eton; Magdalen Coll., Oxford. Served Irish Guards, 1943–47 (Captain, wounded). Entered HM Foreign Service, 1949: 1st Sec., Vienna, 1956–58; 1st Sec. (and sometime Chargé d'Affaires), Phnom Penh, 1961–63, and Bucharest, 1966–68; Counsellor, Bonn, 1968–70; Head of Aviation and Telecommunications Dept, FCO, 1970–71; Counsellor, Brussels, 1971–75; retired from Diplomatic Service, 1975. South Wales Regional Dir, Lloyds Bank, 1980–91 (Chm., 1987–91). Dir, Gwent TEC, 1991–99. Mem. Court and Council, Nat. Museum of Wales, 1980– (Chm., Art Cttee, 1986–90). President: Gwent Assoc. of Vol. Orgns (formerly Monmouthshire Rural Community Council), 1959–; Internat. Tree Foundn, Wales; St David's Assoc. Hospice Care, 1998–; Gwent Local Hist. Council, 1979–; Gwent County History Assoc., 1998–; Gwent County Scout Council, 1979–2000. President: TA&VRA for Wales, 1985–90; S Wales Regl Cttee, TA&VRA, 1990–2000. Hon. Col, 3rd (V) Bn, The Royal Regt of Wales, 1982–90. DL 1973, High Sheriff 1977, JP 1979, Gwent. Hon. Fellow, UCW, Newport, 1997. KStJ 1990 (CStJ 1980). Dulverton Flagon, Timber Growers (UK), 1990. *Publication:* The Hanburys of Monmouthshire, 1995. *Recreations:* shooting, fishing, forestry. *Address:* Clytha Park, Abergavenny NP7 9BW; Lough Bawn, Co. Monaghan, Eire. *Clubs:* Boodle's; Cardiff and County; Kildare Street and University (Dublin).

See also A. R. Hanbury-Tenison.

HANBURY-TENISON, Robin; *see* Hanbury-Tenison, A. R.

HANBURY-TRACY, family name of **Baron Sudeley**.

HANCOCK, Brian John; Member (Plaid Cymru) Islwyn, National Assembly for Wales, since 1999; *b* 8 Aug. 1950; *s* of John and Joan Hancock; *m* 1972, Elizabeth Kalynka; one *s* one *d*. *Educ:* Poly. of Wales (BSc Chem. Engrg 1974); Aston Univ. (Post Grad. Dip. Occupnl Safety and Health, 1986). Registered Safety Practitioner, 1994; MIOSH 1992; AMIChemE. Chemical Project Engr, Monsanto Ltd, 1974–76; Shift Prodn Supervisor, 1976–80, Asst Plant Manager, 1980–85, ReChem International Ltd; Chemical Specialist Inspector of Factories, Health and Safety Inspectorate, 1985–88; Health, Safety and Envmt Supt, BP Chemicals, 1988–92; health, safety and envmt consultant and advr, and Dir of own consultancy, 1992–. Gov., primary and secondary schs, 1985–. *Recreations:* running and athletics (Chair, Newport Harriers AC), Rugby, DIY. *Address:* National Assembly for Wales, Cardiff Bay, Cardiff CF99 1NA. *T:* (029) 2089 8292; (home) (01633) 853622; *e-mail:* Brian.Hancock@Wales.gov.uk. *Clubs:* Newport Harriers Athletic, Celtic Manor Sports and Fitness.

HANCOCK, Christine; President, International Council of Nurses, since 2001. *Educ:* London School of Economics (BScEcons). RGN. Formerly: Chief Nursing Officer, Bloomsbury Health Authority; General Manager, Waltham Forest Health Authority; Gen. Sec., RCN, 1989–2001. *Address:* International Council of Nurses, 3 Place Jean-Marteau, 1201 Geneva, Switzerland.

HANCOCK, Christopher Patrick; QC 2000; *b* 7 June 1960; *s* of Alan Hancock and Dr R. Ann Turner; *m* 1985, Diane Galloway; two *s*. *Educ:* Perse Sch. for Boys, Cambridge; Trinity Coll., Cambridge (MA Hons); Harvard Law Sch. (LLM). Called to the Bar, Middle Temple, 1983; in practice at the Bar, 1985–. *Recreations:* golf, music, watching football, family. *Address:* 20 Essex Street, WC2R 3AL. *T:* (020) 7583 9294.

HANCOCK, Sir David (John Stowell), KCB 1985; Chairman, CLP Envirogas Ltd, since 2001; Senior Adviser, Newcourt Capital, since 1999; *b* 27 March 1934; *s* of late Alfred George Hancock and Florence Hancock (*née* Barrow); *m* 1966, Sheila Gillian Finlay; one *s* one *d*. *Educ:* Whitgift Sch.; Balliol Coll., Oxford. 2nd Lieut, RTR, 1953–54. Asst Principal, Bd of Trade, 1957; transf. to HM Treasury, 1959; Principal, 1962; Harkness Fellow, 1965–66; Private Sec. to Chancellor of the Exchequer, 1968–70; Asst Sec., 1970; Financial and Economic Counsellor, Office of UK Permanent Rep. to European Communities, 1972–74; Under Sec., 1975–80; Dep. Sec., 1980–82; Dep. Sec., Cabinet Office, 1982–83; Perm. Sec., DES, 1983–89; Exec. Dir, Hambros Bank Ltd, 1989–98; Dir, Hambros PLC, 1989–98; Sen. Advr, S. G. Hambros, 1998–99. Dir, European Investment Bank, 1980–82. Chairman: Dyvell (Hldgs) Ltd, 1990–94; MRC Pension Trust Ltd, 1991–; Combined Landfill Projects Ltd, 1993–2001. Dir, AXA Equity & Law plc, 1992–95. Chm., NFHA Inquiry into Governance of Housing Assocs, 1994–95. Chairman: British Selection Cttee of Harkness Fellowships, 1988–92 (Mem., 1984–92); Foundn for Young Musicians, 1990–99; Member: E London Partnership, 1991–98; Royal Nat. Theatre Bd, 1996–; South Bank Bd, 2000–; Court, Luton Univ., 1998–; Gov., City Lit. Inst., 2000–01. Trustee, St Catharine's Foundn, Cumberland Lodge, 1989–; Chm., St Katharine and Shadwell Trust, 1990–99. Pres., Old Whitgiftian Assoc., 2000–01. Freeman, City of London, 1989. FRSA 1986; CIMgt (CBIM 1987). Hon. LLD Poly. of E London, 1990. *Recreations:* walking, reading, gardening, theatre, opera. *Clubs:* Athenæum, Civil Service.

HANCOCK, Elisabeth Joy; Head, Old Palace School, Croydon, since 2000; *b* 2 Dec. 1947; *d* of Reginald Arthur Lord and Evelyn Maud Mary Lord; *m* 1970, Barry Steuart Hancock; one *d*. *Educ:* Queen's Coll., Harley Street; Nottingham Univ. (BA Hons); Univ. of Sussex (PGCE). GB East Europe Centre, 1969; Nevill Sch., Hove, 1969–72; Brighton and Hove High Sch. (GPDST), 1972–89, Dep. Hd, 1986–89; Head, Bromley High Sch. (GDST), 1989–2000. FRSA 1988; MInstD. *Publication:* Teaching History, 1970. *Recreations:* theatre, opera, watching cricket. *Address:* Old Palace School, Old Palace Road, Croydon CR0 1AX. *T:* (020) 8688 2027. *Clubs:* Royal Over-Seas League, St James'.

HANCOCK, Group Captain Ethnea Mary, RRC 1990; Director and Matron-in-Chief, Princess Mary's Royal Air Force Nursing Service, and Deputy Director, Defence Nursing Services (Organisation), 1991–94; *b* 5 April 1937; *d* of late Sydney Ludwig Hancock and Catherine Teresa Hancock (*née* O'Dea). *Educ:* Convent of the Cross, Boscombe; University Coll. Hosp., London; RGN 1958; Southlands Hosp., Shoreham; Whittington Hosp., London; RM 1960. Joined PMRAFNS, 1961–65; Columbia Presbyterian Medical Center, NY, 1966–67; rejoined PMRAFNS, 1967; served RAF Hosps and Units, UK, N Africa, Cyprus, Singapore, Germany; appts include Sen. Matron, RAF Hosp., Ely, 1985–87; MoD, 1987–88; Principal Nursing Officer, PMRAFNS, 1988–91. QHNS, 1991–94. *Recreations:* home and garden, music, travelling, ski-ing, golf. *Address:* First Direct, PO Box HK16, Millshaw Park Lane, Leeds LS11 0YF. *Club:* Royal Air Force.

HANCOCK, Geoffrey Francis, CMG 1977; HM Diplomatic Service, retired; Foreign and Commonwealth Office, 1979–82; *b* 20 June 1926; *s* of Lt-Col Sir Cyril Hancock, KCIE, OBE, MC; *m* 1960, Amelia Juana Aragon; one *s* one *d*. *Educ:* Wellington; Trinity Coll., Oxford. MA 1951. Third Sec., Mexico City, 1953; Second Sec., Montevideo, 1956; Foreign Office, 1958; Madrid, 1958; FO, 1960; MECAS, 1962; First Sec., Baghdad, 1964–67 and 1968–69; FCO, 1969–73; Counsellor, Beirut, 1973–78. Founder, Middle East Consultants, 1983. Dir, mizg, 1996–. *Recreations:* music, sailing. *Address:* c/o Lloyds TSB, 8/10 Waterloo Place, SW1Y 4BE. *Clubs:* Athenæum, Royal Air Force.

HANCOCK, Janet Catherine, FRGS; HM Diplomatic Service; Deputy Head of Mission, Tunis, since 2000; *b* 1 Jan. 1949; *d* of Joseph Paul Knox and Alice Cecælia (*née* Ouzman); *m* 1973, Roger Arnold Hancock (marr. diss. 1976); partner, David Kemp. *Educ:* Convent of Jesus and Mary, Felixstowe and Ipswich; St Anne's Coll., Oxford (MA); Birkbeck Coll., London (MA). Entered FCO, 1971: res. analyst, 1971–94; Beirut, 1985, 1986, 1987; Hd, ME and N Africa Res. Gp, 1994–2000; Dep. Head of Mission, Jerusalem, 1998. FRGS 1998. *Publications:* contrib. articles to Mediterranean Politics, Jl Royal Soc. for Asian Affairs, etc. *Recreations:* riding, natural history, dalmatians. *Address:* c/o Foreign and Commonwealth Office, King Charles Street, SW1A 2AH.

HANCOCK, Prof. Keith Jackson, AO 1987; Vice-Chancellor, The Flinders University of South Australia, 1980–87; Senior Deputy President, Australian Industrial Relations Commission (formerly Australian Conciliation and Arbitration Commission), 1992–97

(Deputy President, 1987–92); *b* 4 Jan. 1935; *s* of late A. S. Hancock and Mrs R. D. Hancock; three *s* one *d*. *Educ:* Univ. of Melbourne (BA); Univ. of London (PhD). Tutor in Economic History, Univ. of Melbourne, 1956–57; Lectr in Economics, Univ. of Adelaide, 1959–63; Professor of Economics, 1964–87, now Emeritus, and Pro-Vice-Chancellor, 1975–79, Flinders Univ. of SA. Hon. Vis. Prof., Univ. of Adelaide, 1998–. Chairman: Cttee of Inquiry into S Australian Racing Industry, 1972–74; Nat. Superannuation Cttee of Inquiry, 1973–77; Cttee of Review of Aust. Industrial Relns Law and Systems, 1983–85; Mem., Review Gp on Aust. Financial Instns, 1983. Pres., Acad. of Social Sciences in Australia, 1981–84. FASSA 1968. Hon. Fellow, LSE, 1982. Hon. DLitt Flinders, 1987. *Publications:* The National Income and Social Welfare, 1965; (with P. A. Samuelson and R. H. Wallace) Economics (Australian edn), 1969, 2nd edn 1975; (ed jtly) Applied Economics: readings for Australian students, 1975; Incomes Policy in Australia, 1981; (ed jtly) Japanese and Australian Labour Markets: a comparative study, 1983; (ed) Australian Society, 1989; contrib. to various racing industry, superannuation, and financial and industrial law systems reports in Australia; articles in Economic Jl, Economica, Amer. Econ. Rev. and other jls. *Recreations:* bridge, sailing, music. *Address:* 6 Maturin Road, Glenelg, SA 5045, Australia. *T:* (8) 82948667. *Clubs:* Adelaide (Adelaide); Royal South Australian Yacht Squadron.

HANCOCK, Maj.-Gen. Michael Stephen, CB 1972; MBE 1953; retired 1972; Planning Inspector, Department of the Environment, 1972–87; *b* 19 July 1917; *s* of late Rev. W. H. M. Hancock and late Mrs C. C. Hancock (*née* Sherbrooke); *m* 1941, Constance Geraldine Margaret Ovens (*d* 1999), *y d* of late Brig.-Gen. R. M. Ovens, CMG; one *s* one *d*; *m* 2001, Margaret Alicia Griffin, *d* of Lt-Col F. E Walter, DSO and *widow* of Maj. J. R. Griffin. *Educ:* Marlborough Coll.; RMA, Woolwich. Commnd into Royal Signals, 1937; Comdr, Corps Royal Signals, 1st British Corps, 1963–66; Sec., Mil. Cttee, NATO, 1967–68; Chief of Staff, FARELF, 1968–70; VQMG, MoD, 1970–72. Col Comdt, Royal Signals, 1970–77. Chm., CCF Assoc., 1972–82, Vice Pres., 1982–96; Chm., NE Surrey Dist Scouts, 1979–82, Pres., 1982–. CEng; FIEE. *Publication:* Lucky Signaller, 1998. *Recreation:* chess.

HANCOCK, Michael Thomas, CBE 1992; MP (Lib Dem) Portsmouth South, since 1997; *b* 9 April 1946; *m* 1967, Jacqueline, *d* of Sidney and Gwen Elliott; one *s* one *d*. *Educ:* well. Member: Portsmouth City Council, 1971– (for Fratton Ward, 1973–; Leader, Lib Dem Gp, 1989–97; Chm., Planning and Econ. Develt Cttee, 1991–94); Hampshire County Council, 1973–97 (Leader of the Opposition, 1977–81, 1989–93; Leader, Lib Dem Gp, 1989–97; Leader of Council, 1993–97). Joined SDP, 1981 (Mem., Nat. Cttee, 1984); contested Portsmouth S (SDP) 1983, (SDP/Alliance) 1987. MP (SDP) Portsmouth S, June 1984–87. Lib Dem parly spokesman on defence, 1997–2001. Member: Public Admin Cttee, 1997–99; Select Cttee on Defence, 1998–; Panel of Chairmen, 2000–. Contested (Lib Dem) Wight and Hampshire South, Eur. Parly elecns, 1994. Dist Officer for Hants, IoW and CI, Mencap, 1989–97. Vice Chairman: Portsmouth Operating Co., 1992–; Portsmouth Docks, 1992–. Dir, Daytime Club, BBC, 1987–90. Bd of Dirs, Drug Rehabilitation Unit, Alpha Drug Clinic, Alpha House, Droxford, 1971–; Chm., Southern Br., NSPCC, 1989–. Trustee, Royal Marine Museum, 1993. Hon. Alderman, Hants, 1997. Hon. award for contrib. to Anglo-German relations, Homborn, W Germany, 1981. *Publications:* contribs to various jls. *Recreations:* people, living life to the full. *Address:* (office) 1A Albert Road, Southsea PO5 2SE; House of Commons, SW1A 0AA. *T:* (home) (01329) 287340. *Clubs:* too many to mention.

HANCOCK, Norman, CB 1976; CEng, FRINA; RCNC; Director of Warship Design, and Project Director, Invincible and Broadsword, Ministry of Defence, 1969–76; *b* 6 March 1916; *o s* of Louis Everard Hancock, Plymouth; *m* 1940, Marie E., *d* of William E. Bow; two *s*. *Educ:* Plymouth Grammar Sch.; RNC Greenwich. Asst Constructor, AEW, Haslar, 1940; Constructor, Naval Construction Dept, 1944; British Services Observer (Constructor Comdr), Bikini, 1946. HM Dockyard, Singapore, 1949; Frigate design, Naval Construction Dept, 1952; Chief Constructor in charge of R&D, 1954; Prof. of Naval Architecture, RNC, Greenwich, 1957–62; Asst Dir of Naval Construction, in charge of Submarine Design and Construction, 1963–69. Liveryman, Worshipful Co. of Shipwrights; past Mem. Council, RINA. *Recreations:* organ music, cabinet making, travel. *Address:* 41 Cranwells Park, Bath, Somerset BA1 2YE. *T:* (01225) 426045.

HANCOCK, P(ercy) E(llis) Thompson, FRCP; former Hon. Consultant Physician: The Royal Free Hospital; The Royal Marsden Hospital; Potters Bar and District Hospital; National Temperance Hospital; Bishop's Stortford and District Hospital; *b* 4 Feb. 1904; *s* of Frank Hancock; *m* 1932, Dorothy Barnes (*d* 1953); two *d*; *m* 1955, Laurie Newton Sharp (*d* 1999). *Educ:* Wellington Coll., Berks; Caius Coll., Cambridge; St Bartholomew's Hospital. MB 1937, BCh 1930, Cantab; FRCP 1944. Formerly: Senior Examiner in Medicine, Univ. of London; Dir of Dept of Clinical Res., Royal Marsden Hosp. and Inst. of Cancer Res. Member: Council, Imperial Cancer Res. Fund; Grand Council, Cancer Research Campaign; Mem. Exec. Cttee, Action on Smoking and Health; Sen. Mem., Assoc. of Physicians, GB and Ireland. Hosp. Visitor, King Edward's Hosp. Fund for London. FRSocMed (Pres., Section of Oncology, 1974–75); Fellow, Assoc. Européene de Médecine Interne d'Ensemble. Corresp. Mem., Società Italiana de Cancerologia. Hon. Member: American Gastroscopic Soc., 1958; Sociedad Chilena de Cancerología; Sociedad Chilena de Hematología; Sociedad Médica de Valparaíso; Medal, Societa Medica Chirurgica di Bologna, 1964. *Publications:* (joint) Cancer in General Practice; The Use of Bone Marrow Transfusion with massive Chemotherapy, 1960; (joint) Treatment of Early Hodgkin's Disease, 1967. *Recreations:* dining and wining. *Address:* 23 Wigmore Place, W1H 9DD. *T:* (020) 7631 4679.

HANCOCK, Ven. Peter; Archdeacon of The Meon, since 1999; *b* 26 July 1955; *s* of Kenneth and Jean Hancock; *m* 1979, Elizabeth Jane Sindall; two *s* two *d*. *Educ:* Price's Sch., Fareham; Selwyn Coll., Cambridge (BA 1976; MA 1979); Oak Hill Theol Coll. (BA 1980). Ordained deacon, 1980, priest, 1981; Curate: Christ Church, Portsdown, 1980–83; Radipole and Melcombe Regis Team Ministry, 1983–87; Vicar, St Wilfrid, Cowplain, 1987–99; RD of Havant, 1993–98. Hon. Canon, Portsmouth Cathedral, 1997–99. *Recreations:* walking, reading, swimming, travel, golf. *Address:* Victoria Lodge, 36 Osborn Road, Fareham, Hants PO16 7DS. *T:* (01329) 280101.

HANCOCK, Ronald John; business consultant; Director: Insituform Ltd, 1987–94; Travelines, 1991–94; Permaline, 1991–94; *b* 11 Feb. 1934; *s* of George and Elsie Hancock; *m* 1970, Valerie Hancock; two *d*. *Educ:* Dudley Grammar Sch., Dudley. FCMA. Served HM Forces, 1952–61. Schweppes Ltd, 1962–63; Mullard Ltd, 1963–66; Valor Group, 1966–68; BL Ltd, 1968–85. Chairman: Leyland Vehicles, 1981–85; Leyland Vehicles Exports Ltd, 1981–85; Bus Manufacturers Limited, 1981–85; Bus Manufacturers (Holdings) Ltd, 1981–85; Eastern Coachworks Ltd, 1981–85; Bristol Commercial Vehicles Ltd, 1981–85; Self-Changing Gears Ltd, 1981–85; Bedfordshire Chamber of Training Ltd, 1990–; Director: BL Staff Trustees Ltd, 1981–85; Leyland Nigeria Ltd, 1981–85; BL International Ltd, 1981–85; Land Rover-Leyland International Holdings Ltd (formerly BLIH), 1982–85; Land Rover-Leyland Ltd, 1983–85; Chloride Gp plc, 1985–87; Man. Dir, AWD Ltd, 1987–90. *Recreations:* travel, reading. *Address:* 5 Shardeloes, Amersham, Bucks HP7 0RL.

HANCOCK, Sheila, OBE 1974; actress and director; *d* of late Enrico Hancock and late Ivy Woodward; *m* 1st, 1955, Alexander Ross (*d* 1971); one *d*; 2nd, 1973, John Thaw, *qv*; one *d*. *Educ:* Dartford County Grammar Sch.; Royal Academy of Dramatic Art. Acted in Repertory, Theatre Workshop, Stratford East, for 8 years. Associate Dir, Cambridge Theatre Co., 1980–82; Artistic Dir, RSC Regional Tour, 1983–84; acted and directed, NT, 1985–86. Dir, The Actors Centre, 1978–. West End starring roles in: Rattle of a Simple Man, 1962; The Anniversary, 1966; A Delicate Balance (RSC), 1969; So What About Love?, 1969; Absurd Person Singular, 1973; Déjà Revue, 1974; The Bed Before Yesterday, 1976; Annie, 1978; Sweeney Todd, 1980; The Winter's Tale, RSC, Stratford 1981, Barbican 1982; Peter Pan, Barbican, 1982–83; The Cherry Orchard, The Duchess of Malfi, National, 1985–86; Greenland, Royal Court, 1988; Prin, Lyric, Hammersmith, 1989, Lyric, Shaftesbury Avenue, 1990; A Judgement in Stone, The Way of the World, Lyric, Hammersmith, 1992; Harry and Me, Royal Court, 1996; Lock Up Your Daughters, Chichester, 1996; Then Again…, Lyric, Hammersmith, 1997; Vassa, Albery, 1999; Under the Blue Sky, Royal Court, 2000; In Extremis, RNT, 2000. Has starred in several successful revues; appeared on Broadway in Entertaining Mr Sloane. Directed: The Soldier's Fortune, Lyric, Hammersmith, 1981; A Midsummer Night's Dream, RSC, 1983; The Critic, National, 1986. *Films:* The Love Child, 1987; Making Waves, 1987; Hawks, 1988; Buster, 1988; Three Men and a Little Lady, 1990; Hold Back the Night, 1999. *Television:* many successes, including Jumping the Queue, The Rivals, and several comedy series, incl. Gone to the Dogs, 1991, Gone to Seed, 1992, Brighton Belles, 1993; other appearances include: The Buccaneers, 1994; Dangerous Lady, 1994; Close Relations, 1998; Eastenders, Love or Money, The Russian Bride, Bedtime, 2001; wrote and acted in Royal Enclosure, 1990. Awards: Variety Club, London Critics, Whitbread Trophy (for best Actress on Broadway). *Publication:* Ramblings of an Actress, 1987. *Recreations:* reading, music. *Address:* c/o ICM, 76 Oxford Street, W1N 0AX.

HAND, Rt Rev. Geoffrey David, KBE 1984 (CBE 1975); *b* 11 May 1918; *s* of Rev. W. T. Hand. *Educ:* Oriel College, Oxford; Cuddesdon Theological Coll., BA 1941, MA 1946. Deacon, 1942; Priest, 1943. Curate of Heckmondwike, 1942–46; Missioner, Diocese of New Guinea, 1946–50; Priest in charge: Sefoa, 1947–48; Sangara, 1948–50; Archdeacon, North New Guinea, 1950–65; Bishop Coadjutor of New Guinea, 1950–63; Bishop of New Guinea (later Papua New Guinea), 1963–77; Archbishop of Papua New Guinea, 1977–83; Bishop of Port Moresby, 1977–83; Priest-in-charge, East with West Rudham, Houghton next Harpley, Syderstone, Tatterford and Tattersett, dio. Norwich, 1983–85. *Address:* PO Box 28, N Waigani, NCD, Papua New Guinea. *T:* 3260317.

HAND, Prof. Geoffrey Joseph Philip, DPhil; Barber Professor of Jurisprudence in the University of Birmingham, 1980–92, now Professor Emeritus; *b* 25 June 1931; *s* of Joseph and Mary Macaulay Hand. *Educ:* Blackrock Coll.; University Coll., Dublin (MA); New Coll., Oxford (DPhil); King's Inns, Dublin. Called to Irish Bar, 1961. Lecturer: Univ. of Edinburgh, 1960; Univ. of Southampton, 1961; University Coll., Dublin, 1965; Professor: University Coll., Dublin, 1972–76; European University Inst., Fiesole, 1976–80; Dean of Faculty of Law, University Coll., Dublin, 1970–75. Chairman: Arts Council of Ireland, 1974–75; Irish Manuscripts Commn, 1998–. Mem. Council, RIA, 1994–98 (Vice Pres., 1996–97). *Publications:* English Law in Ireland 1290–1324, 1967; Report of the Irish Boundary Commission 1925, 1969; (with Lord Cross of Chelsea) Radcliffe and Cross's English Legal System, 5th edn 1971, 6th edn 1977; (with J. Georgel, C. Sasse) European Election Systems Handbook, 1979; Towards a Uniform System of Direct Elections, 1981; (ed with J. McBride) Droit sans Frontières, 1991; numerous periodicals. *Recreations:* listening to classical music, playing chess. *Address:* 72 Granitefield, Dun Laoghaire, Republic of Ireland. *Clubs:* Oxford and Cambridge; Royal Irish Yacht (Dun Laoghaire); Kildare Street and University (Dublin); Casino Maltese (Valletta).

HAND, Graham Stewart; HM Diplomatic Service; *b* 3 Nov. 1948; *s* of Ronald Charles Hand and Mary Fraser Hand (*née* Stewart); *m* 1973, Anne Mary Seton Campbell; one *s* one *d* (and one *s* decd). *Educ:* RMA Sandhurst; St John's Coll., Cambridge (MA 1979). Regular Army, 1969–80; FCO, 1980; served UN Dept, 1980–82; Dakar, 1982–84; News Dept, FCO, 1984–87; Head of Chancery, Helsinki, 1987–90; Aid Policy Dept, ODA, 1991–92; Head of Human Rights Policy Dept, FCO, 1992–94; Dep. High Comr, Nigeria, 1994–96; RCDS, 1997; Ambassador to Bosnia and Herzegovina, 1998–2001. *Recreations:* opera, choral singing, sailing, golf, cooking. *Address:* c/o Foreign and Commonwealth Office, SW1A 2AH.

HAND, Jessica Mary; *see* Pearce, J. M.

HAND, John Lester; QC 1988; a Recorder, since 1991; *b* 16 June 1947; *s* of John James and Violet Hand; *m* 1st, 1972, Helen Andrea McWatt (marr. diss.); 2nd, 1990, Lynda Ray Ferrigno; one *d*. *Educ:* Huddersfield New College; Univ. of Nottingham (LLB 1969). Called to the Bar, Gray's Inn, 1972, Bencher, 1996; Northern Circuit, 1972. Legal Assessor, GMC and GDC, 1990–. *Recreations:* computers, travel. *Address:* 9 St John Street, Manchester M3 4DN. *T:* (0161) 955 9000; Old Square Chambers, 1 Verulam Buildings, Gray's Inn, WC1R 5QL. *T:* (020) 7269 0300; *e-mail:* JohnHand@cwcom.net.

HANDCOCK, family name of **Baron Castlemaine**.

HANDFORD, Rt Rev. (George) Clive; *see* Cyprus and the Gulf, Bishop in.

HANDLEY, Ven. Anthony Michael; Archdeacon of Norfolk, since 1993; *b* 3 June 1936; *s* of Eric Harvey Handley and Janet Handley; *m* 1962, Christine May Adlington; two *s* one *d*. *Educ:* Spalding Grammar School; Selwyn Coll., Cambridge (MA Hons); Chichester Theological Coll. Asst Curate, Thorpe St Andrew, 1962–66; Anglican Priest on Fairstead Estate, 1966–72; Vicar of Hellesdon, 1972–81; RD of Norwich North, 1979–81; Archdeacon of Norwich, 1981–93. Proctor in Convocation, 1980–85; Mem., General Synod, 1990–95. Research Project, The Use of Colour, Shape, and Line Drawings as Experiential Training Resources, 1976. County Scout Chaplain for Norfolk. *Publication:* A Parish Prayer Card, 1980. *Recreations:* climbing mountains, painting, bird watching. *Address:* 40 Heigham Road, Norwich NR2 3AU. *T:* (01603) 611808, *Fax:* (01603) 618954.

HANDLEY, Mrs Carol Margaret; Headmistress, Camden School for Girls, 1971–85; *b* 17 Oct. 1929; *d* of Claude Hilary Taylor and Margaret Eleanor Taylor (*née* Peebles); *m* 1952, Eric Walter Handley, *qv*. *Educ:* St Paul's Girls' Sch.; University Coll., London (BA), Fellow 1977. Asst Classics Mistress: North Foreland Lodge Sch., 1952; Queen's Gate Sch., 1952; Head of Classics Dept, Camden Sch. for Girls, 1956; Deputy Headmistress, Camden Sch. for Girls, 1964. Sen. Mem., Wolfson Coll., Cambridge, 1989–. Member Council: RHC, then RHBNC, 1977–95; Middx Hosp. Med. Sch., 1980–84; Mem. Governors and Council, Bedford Coll., 1981–85. Pres., Classical Assoc., 1996–97. *Publications:* articles and book reviews for classical jls. *Recreation:* gardening. *Address:* Colt House, 44 High Street, Little Eversden, Cambs CB3 7HE.

HANDLEY, Sir David John D.; *see* Davenport-Handley.

HANDLEY, David Thomas, CMG 2000; HM Diplomatic Service, retired; Director, Market Relations, BAE SYSTEMS, since 2000; *b* 31 Aug. 1945; *s* of late Leslie Thomas Handley and Frances Handley (*née* Harrison); *m* 1st, 1967, Lilian Duff (marr. diss. 1977); one *s* one *d*; 2nd, 1978, Susan Elizabeth Beal; two *s* one *d* (and one *d* decd). *Educ:* Univ. of Newcastle upon Tyne (BA Jt Hons Politics and Econs). British Leyland Motor Corp., 1967–72; joined FCO, 1972: language studies, MECAS, Lebanon, 1974–76; First Sec., Budapest, 1978–81; Hd of British Interests Sect. and Chargé d'Affaires, Guatemala City, 1984–87; Counsellor: Cairo, 1990–93; FCO, 1993–2000. *Recreations:* family, friends, fitness (physical and mental), fun. *Address:* The Red House, Froxfield, Hants GU23 1BB. *T:* (01730) 827039.

HANDLEY, Prof. Eric Walter, CBE 1983; FBA 1969; Professor of Ancient Literature, Royal Academy, since 1990; Fellow, Trinity College, Cambridge, since 1984; *b* 12 Nov. 1926; *s* of late Alfred W. Handley and A. Doris Cox; *m* 1952, Carol Margaret Taylor (*see* C. M. Handley). *Educ:* King Edward's Sch., Birmingham; Trinity Coll., Cambridge. Stewart of Rannoch Schol. and Browne Medal, 1945. University College London: Asst Lectr in Latin and Greek, 1946; Lectr, 1949; Reader, 1961; Prof. of Latin and Greek, 1967–68; Prof. and Head of Dept of Greek, 1968–84; Hon. Fellow, 1989; Dir, 1967–84, Sen. Res. Fellow, 1995–, Inst. of Classical Studies, Univ. of London; Regius Prof. of Greek, Cambridge Univ., 1984–94. Vis. Lectr on the Classics, Harvard, 1966; Vis. Mem., Inst. for Advanced Study, Princeton, 1971; Visiting Professor: Stanford Univ., 1977; Melbourne Univ., 1978; Vis. Senior Fellow, Council of the Humanities, Princeton, 1981. Sec. Council Univ. Classical Depts, 1969–70, Chm., 1975–78. President: Classical Assoc., 1984–85; Hellenic Soc., 1993–96; Foreign Sec., British Academy, 1979–88. Union Académique Internationale: Mem., Commn des Affaires Internes, 1984–91; Mem. du Bureau, 1991–2000; Vice-Pres., 1995–97, 1999–2000; Mem., Comité Scientifique, Fondation Hardt, Geneva, 1978–99 (Conseil, 1995–99). Member: Academia Europaea, 1988; Norwegian Acad. of Science and Letters, 1996. Foreign Mem., Societas Scientiarum Fennica, 1984; Hon. Mem., Hungarian Acad. of Scis, 1993; Corresp. Mem., Acad. of Athens, 1995. Chm., Gilbert Murray Trust, 1988–. Hon. RA 1990. Dr *hc* Athens, 1995. (Jtly) Cromer Greek Prize, 1958. *Publications:* (with John Rea) The Telephus of Euripides, 1957; The Dyskolos of Menander, 1965; (contrib.) Cambridge History of Classical Literature, 1985; (with André Hurst) Relire Ménandre, 1990; (jtly) The Oxyrhynchus Papyri LIX, 1992; (with J.-M. Bremer) Aristophane, 1993; (with J. R. Green) Images of the Greek Theatre, 1995; (jtly) The Oxyrhynchus Papyri LXIV, 1997; papers in class. jls, etc. *Recreations:* walking, travel. *Address:* Trinity College, Cambridge CB2 1TQ. *Club:* Oxford and Cambridge.

HANDLEY, Paul; Editor, Church Times, since 1995; *b* 29 May 1958; *s* of Arnold Terence Handley and Margaret Hardy; *m* 1980, Terence MacMath; two *s* two *d*. *Educ:* Colchester Royal Grammar Sch.; Goldsmiths Coll., Univ. of London (BA English 1980). News Editor, Church of England Newspaper, 1981–85; freelance publisher, writer, 1986–88; Reporter, Church Times, 1988–90; Press Sec. to Archbishop of Canterbury, 1990–92; freelance writer, 1992–94; News Editor, Church Times, 1994. *Address:* c/o Church Times, 33 Upper Street, N1 0PN. *T:* (020) 7359 4570; *e-mail:* editor@churchtimes.co.uk.

HANDLEY, Vernon George, FRCM 1972; Principal Guest Conductor, Royal Liverpool Philharmonic Orchestra, 1989–95, now Conductor Laureate; Associate Conductor, Royal Philharmonic Orchestra, since 1994 (Guest Conductor, 1961–94); Chief Conductor, West Australian Symphony Orchestra, since 1993; *b* 11 Nov. 1930; 2nd *s* of Vernon Douglas Handley and Claudia Lilian Handley, Enfield; *m* 1st, 1954, Barbara (marr. diss.), *e d* of Kilner Newman Black and Joan Elfriede Black, Stoke Gabriel, Devon; one *s* one *d* (and one *s* decd); 2nd, 1977, Victoria (marr. diss.), *d* of Vaughan and Nona Parry-Jones, Guildford, Surrey; one *s* one *d*; 3rd, 1987, Catherine, *e d* of Kenneth and Joan Newby, Harrogate, Yorks; one *s*. *Educ:* Enfield Sch.; Balliol Coll., Oxford (BA; Hon. Fellow, 1999); Guildhall Sch. of Music. Conductor: Oxford Univ. Musical Club and Union, 1953–54; OUDS, 1953–54; Tonbridge Philharmonic Soc., 1958–61; Hatfield Sch. of Music and Drama, 1959–61; Proteus Choir, 1962–81; Musical Dir and Conductor, Guildford Corp., and Conductor, Guildford Philharmonic Orch. and Choir, 1962–83, Conductor Emeritus, Guildford Philharmonic Orch., 1984; Prof. at RCM: for Orchestra and Conducting, 1966–72; for Choral Class, 1969–72. Principal Conductor: Ulster Orch., 1985–89; Malmö SO, 1985–88. Guest Conductor from 1961: Bournemouth Symph. Orch.; Birmingham Symph. Orch.; BBC Welsh Orch.; BBC Northern Symph. Orch.; Royal Liverpool Philharmonic Orch.; Ulster Orch.; Scottish Nat. Orch.; Philharmonia Orch.; Strasbourg Philharmonic Orch., 1982–; Helsinki Philharmonic, 1984–; Amsterdam Philharmonic, 1985; Guest Conductor, 1961–83, Principal Guest Conductor, 1983–85, BBC Scottish Symphony Orch.; Guest Conductor, 1961–83, Associate Conductor, 1983–86, London Philharmonic Orch.; Chief Guest Conductor, Melbourne SO, 1992–95; conducted London Symphony Orch. in internat. series, London, 1971; toured: Germany, 1966, 1980; S Africa, 1974; Holland, 1980; Sweden, 1980, 1981; Germany, Sweden, Holland and France, 1982–83; Australia, 1986; Japan, 1988; Australia, 1989; Artistic Dir, Norwich and Norfolk Triennial Fest., 1985. Regular broadcaster and has made many records. Vice-President: Delius Soc., 1983–; Elgar Soc., 1984–; Fellow Goldsmiths' Coll. 1987; Hon. Mem., Royal Philharmonic Soc., 1989. Hon. RCM, 1970; FRCM 1972. Arnold Bax Meml Medal for Conducting, 1962; Conductor of the Year, British Composers' Guild, 1974; Hi-Fi News Audio Award, 1982; BPI Classical Award, 1986, 1988; Gramophone Record of the Year, 1986, 1989; Classic CD Magazine Record of the Year (Contemporary), 1995. DUniv Surrey, 1980; Hon. DMus Liverpool, 1993. *Recreations:* bird photography, old-fashioned roses. *Address:* Cwm Cottage, Bettws, Abergavenny, Monmouthshire NP7 7LG. *T:* (01873) 890135.

HANDLEY-TAYLOR, Geoffrey, FRSL 1950; writer; Hon. Home and Overseas Information Correspondent, John Masefield Research and Studies, 1958–93; *b* 25 April 1920; 2nd *s* of Walter Edward Taylor and Nellie Hadwin (*née* Taylor), Horsforth. *Educ:* widely. Served War of 1939–45: Duke of Wellington's Regt and War Office. Literary and ballet lecture tours, UK and overseas, 1946–57. Chairman, British Poetry-Drama Guild, 1948–52; Vice-Pres., Leeds Univ. Tudor Players, 1948–50; Publisher, Leeds University Poetry, 1949; featured in NBC-TV (USA) People series, 1955; Founder, Winifred Holtby Meml Collection, Fisk Univ., Nashville, 1955; Hon. Gen. Sec., Dumas Assoc., 1955–57; Donor, Sir Ralph Perring City of London Collection, Fisk Univ., 1962–65; Pres., St Paul's Literary Soc., Covent Garden, 1966–68; Chm., General Council, Poetry Society, 1967–68; served on PCC, St Paul's, Covent Garden, 1967–68; Mem. Gen. Council, National Book League, 1968; Pres., Lancashire Authors' Assoc., 1969–72; a Trustee, Gladstone Meml Library, London, 1974–78; Jt Literary Trustee, Estate of Vera Brittain, 1979–90; (with Corliss Lamont) Hon. Founder Mem., John Masefield Soc., 1993–97. Several Foreign decorations and awards. *Publications:* Mona Inglesby, Ballerina and Choreographer, 1947; Italian Ballet Today, 1949; (foreword to) Stars of the Opera, ed Frank Granville Barker, 1949; New Hyperion, 1950; Literary, Debating and Dialect Societies of GB, Ireland and France, 5 pts, 1950–54; A Selected Bibliography of Literature Relating to Nursery Rhyme Reform, 1952; Winifred Holtby Bibliography and Letters, 1955; (with Frank Granville Barker) John Gay and the Ballad Opera, 1956; (with Thomas Rae) The Book of the Private Press, 1958; John Masefield, OM, The Queen's Poet Laureate, 1960; (with Vera Brittain) Selected Letters of Winifred Holtby and Vera Brittain 1920–1935, 1961, 2nd edn 1970; Bibliography of Monaco, 1961, 2nd edn 1968; Bibliography of Iran, 1964, 5th edn 1969; (with Timothy d'Arch Smith) C. Day Lewis, Poet Laureate, 1968; ed, County Authors Today Series, 9 vols, 1971–1973; Pogg (a satire), 1980; (with John Malcolm Dockeray) Vera Brittain, Occasional Papers, 1983; also contribs to: Encycl. Britannica, Hinrichsen Music Book, 1949–1958; Airs from The Beggar's Opera, arr. Edith Bathurst, 1953; The Beggar's Opera, ed Edward J. Dent, 1954; Kathleen: the life of Kathleen Ferrier 1912–1953, ed Maurice Leonard, 1988; (foreword to) John Masefield: a bibliographical description of his first, limited, signed and special editions, ed Crocker Wight, 1992; Markova: the legend, ed Maurice Leonard, 1995.

HANDLIN, Prof. Oscar; Carl M. Loeb University Professor, Harvard University, since 1984; Director, Harvard University Library, 1979–84; *b* 29 Sept. 1915; *m* 1st, 1937, Mary Flug; one *s* two *d*; 2nd, 1977, Lilian Bombach. *Educ:* Brooklyn Coll. (AB); Harvard (MA, PhD). Instructor, Brooklyn Coll., 1938–39; Harvard Univ.: Instructor, 1939–44; Asst Prof., 1944–48; Associate Prof., 1948–54; Prof. of History, 1954–65; Charles Warren Prof. of Amer. Hist., and Dir, Charles Warren Center for Studies in Amer. Hist., 1965–72; Carl H. Pforzheimer Univ. Prof., 1972–84; Harmsworth Prof. of Amer. History, Oxford Univ., 1972–73. Dir, Center for Study of History of Liberty in America, 1958–67; Chm., US Bd of Foreign Scholarships, 1965–66 (Vice-Chm. 1962–65). Hon. Fellow, Brandeis Univ., 1965. Hon. LLD: Colby Coll., 1962; Harvard, 1993; Hon. LHD: Hebrew Union Coll., 1967; Northern Michigan, 1969; Seton Hall Univ., 1972; Hon. HumD Oakland, 1968; Hon. LittD Brooklyn Coll., 1972; Hon. DHL: Boston Coll., 1975; Lowell, 1980; Cincinnati, 1981; Massachusetts, 1982; Clark Univ., Mass, 1989. *Publications:* Boston's Immigrants, 1790–1865, 1941; (with M. F. Handlin) Commonwealth, 1947; Danger in Discord, 1948; (ed) This Was America, 1949; Uprooted, 1951, 2nd edn 1972; Adventure in Freedom, 1954; American People in the Twentieth Century, 1954 (rev. edn 1963); (ed jtly) Harvard Guide to American History, 1954; Chance or Destiny, 1955; (ed) Readings in American History, 1957; Race and Nationality in American Life, 1957; Al Smith and his America, 1958; (ed) Immigration as a Factor in American History, 1959; John Dewey's Challenge to Education, 1959; (ed) G. M. Capers, Stephen A. Douglas, Defender of the Union, 1959; Newcomers, 1960; (ed jtly) G. Mittleberger, Journey to Pennsylvania, 1960; (ed) American Principles and Issues, 1961; (with M. F. Handlin) The Dimensions of Liberty, 1961; The Americans, 1963; (with J. E. Burchard) The Historian and the City, 1963; Firebell in the Night, 1964; A Continuing Task, 1964; (ed) Children of the Uprooted, 1966; The History of the United States, vol. 1, 1967, vol. 2, 1968; America: a History, 1968; (with M. F. Handlin) The Popular Sources of Political Authority, 1967; The American College and American Culture, 1970; Facing Life: Youth and the Family in American History, 1971; A Pictorial History of Immigration, 1972; (with M. F. Handlin) The Wealth of the American People, 1975; Truth in History, 1979, 2nd edn 1997; The Distortion of America, 1981, 2nd edn 1997; with L. Handlin: Abraham Lincoln and the Union, 1980; A Restless People, 1982; Liberty and Power, 1986; Liberty in Expansion, 1989; Liberty in Peril, 1992; Liberty and Equality, 1994; From the Outer World, 1997. *Address:* 18 Agassiz Street, Cambridge, MA 02140, USA. *Clubs:* St Botolph (Boston); Faculty (Cambridge, Mass).

HANDOVER, Richard Gordon; Group Chief Executive, W H Smith PLC (formerly W H Smith Group plc), since 1997; *b* 13 April 1946; *s* of Gordon Handover and Hilda Handover (*née* Dyke); *m* 1972, Veronica Joan Woodhead; one *s* two *d*. *Educ:* Blundell's Sch. Joined W H Smith, 1964: various jun. managerial appts, 1964–74; sen. mgt appts, 1974–89; Man. Dir, Our Price Music, 1989–95; joined main co. bd, 1995; Man. Dir, W H Smith News, 1995–97. Non-exec. Dir, Nationwide Bldg Soc., 2000–. Chm., Age Concern Enterprises Ltd, 1992–99; Dir, BITC, 1999–. *Recreations:* tennis, golf, horses, painting. *Address:* W H Smith PLC, Nations House, 103 Wigmore Street, W1U 1WH. *T:* (020) 7409 3222, *Fax:* (020) 7629 3600.

HANDS, Guy; Founder and Managing Director, Principal Finance Group, Nomura International plc, since 1994; *b* 27 Aug. 1959; *s* of Christopher and Sally Hands; *m* 1984, Julia Caroline Ablethorpe; two *s* two *d*. *Educ:* Judd Sch., Tonbridge; Mansfield Coll., Oxford (BA Hons PPE). Hd of Eurobond Trading, Goldman Sachs, 1982–94 (Trading, 1986; Hd, Global Asset Structuring Gp, 1990). *Recreations:* films, wine, fine art. *Address:* Nomura House, 1 St Martin's-le-Grand, EC1A 4NP. *T:* (020) 7521 2000.

HANDS, Terence David, (Terry); theatre and opera director; Director, Clwyd Theatr Cymru (formerly Theatr Clwyd), since 1997 (Artistic Consultant, 1996–97); *b* 9 Jan. 1941; *s* of Joseph Ronald Hands and Luise Berthe Kohler; *m* 1st, 1964, Josephine Barstow (marr. diss. 1967); 2nd, 1974, Ludmila Mikael (marr. diss. 1980); one *d*; partner, 1988, Julia Lintott; two *s*. *Educ:* Woking Grammar Sch.; Birmingham Univ. (BA Hons Eng. Lang. and Lit.); RADA (Hons Dip.). Founder-Artistic Dir, Liverpool Everyman Theatre, 1964–66 (Hon. Dir, 1996); Artistic Dir, RSC Theatregoround, 1966–67; Associate Dir, 1967–77, Jt Artistic Dir, 1978–86, Chief Exec. and Artistic Dir, 1986–91, Director Emeritus, 1991, RSC; Consultant Dir, Comédie Française, 1975–80. Associate Mem., RADA; Hon. Fellow, Shakespeare Inst. Pres., Arvon Foundn, 1990–. Hon. DLitt Birmingham, 1988; Hon. Dr Middlesex, 1997. Chevalier des Arts et des Lettres, 1973. *Director* (for Liverpool Everyman Theatre, 1964–66): The Importance of Being Earnest; Look Back in Anger; Richard III; The Four Seasons; Fando and Lis; *Artistic Director* (for RSC Theatregoround): The Proposal, 1966; The Second Shepherds' Play, 1966; The Dumb Waiter, 1967; Under Milk Wood, 1967; *directed for RSC:* The Criminals, 1967; Pleasure and Repentance, 1967; The Latent Heterosexual, 1968; The Merry Wives of Windsor, 1968, Japan tour, 1970; Bartholomew Fair, 1969; Pericles, 1969; Women Beware Women, 1969; Richard III, 1970, 1980; Balcony, 1971, 1987; Man of Mode, 1971; The Merchant of Venice, 1971; Murder in the Cathedral, 1972; Cries from Casement, 1973; Romeo and Juliet, 1973, 1989; The Bewitched, 1974; The Actor, 1974; Henry IV, Parts 1 and 2, 1975; Henry V, 1975, USA and European Tour, 1976; Old World, 1976; Henry VI parts 1, 2 and 3 (SWET Award, Dir of the Year, Plays and Players, Best Production, 1978), Coriolanus, 1977, European tour, 1979; The Changeling, 1978; Twelfth Night, The Children of the Sun, 1979; As You Like It, Richard II, 1980; Troilus and Cressida, 1981; Arden of Faversham, Much Ado About Nothing, 1982 (European tour and Broadway, 1984), Poppy, 1982; Cyrano de Bergerac, 1983 (SWET Best Dir award), Broadway, 1984 (televised, 1984); Red Noses, 1985; Othello, 1985; The Winter's Tale, 1986; Scenes from a Marriage, 1986; Julius Caesar, 1987; Carrie (Stratford and Broadway), 1988; (with John Barton) Coriolanus, 1989; Romeo and Juliet, 1989; Singer, 1989; Love's Labours Lost, 1990; The Seagull, 1990; Tamburlaine the Great, 1992 (Evening Standard Award, London Drama Critics Award, 1993); *directed for Royal Nat. Theatre:* The Merry Wives of Windsor, 1995; *directed for Chichester Festival Theatre:* Hadrian VII, 1995; The Visit, 1995; *directed for Birmingham Rep.:* The Importance of Being Earnest, 1995 (transf. Old Vic, 1995); *directed for Theatr Clwyd/Clwyd Theatr Cymru:* The Importance of Being Earnest, (also Birmingham and Toronto), Equus, A Christmas Carol, 1997; The Journey of Mary Kelly, The Norman Conquests, 1998; Twelfth Night, Macbeth, Under Milk Wood, 1999; Private Lives, 2000; King Lear, 2001; *directed for*

Comédie Française: Richard III, 1972 (Meilleur Spectacle de l'Année award); Pericles, 1974; Twelfth Night, 1976 (Meilleur Spectacle de l'Année award); Le Cid, 1977; Murder in the Cathedral, 1978; *directed for Paris Opéra:* Verdi's Otello, 1976 (televised 1978); *directed for Burg Theatre, Vienna:* Troilus and Cressida, 1977; As You Like It, 1979; *directed for Royal Opera:* Parsifal, 1979; *directed for Teatro Stabile di Genova, Italy:* Women Beware Women, 1981; *directed for Schauspielhaus, Zürich:* Arden of Faversham, 1992; *directed for Recklinghausen:* Buffalo Bill, 1992; *directed for Bremen:* Simon Boccanegra, 1992; *directed for National Theatre, Oslo:* Merry Wives of Windsor, 1995; The Pretenders, 1996; The Seagull, 1998; Sag Mir Wo Die Blumen Sind, Berlin, 1993; Hamlet, Marigny Theatre, Paris, 1994; Royal Hunt of the Sun, Tokyo, 1996; *recording:* Murder in the Cathedral, 1976; *television:* Cyrano de Bergerac, 1984. *Publications:* trans. (with Barbara Wright) Genet, The Balcony, 1971; Pleasure and Repentance, 1976; (ed Sally Beauman) Henry V, 1976; Hamlet (French trans.), 1994; contribs to Theatre 72, Playback. *Address:* c/o Clwyd Theatr Cymru, Mold, Flintshire CH7 1YA.

HANDY, Charles Brian, CBE 2000; author; *b* 25 July 1932; *s* of Archdeacon Brian Leslie Handy and Joan Kathleen Herbert Handy (*née* Scott); *m* 1962, Elizabeth Ann Hill; one *s* one *d*. *Educ:* Oriel Coll., Oxford (BA 1956; MA 1966; Hon. Fellow, 1998); MIT (SM 1967). Shell Internat. Petroleum Co., 1956–65; Charter Consolidated Ltd, 1965–66; Sloan Sch. of Management, MIT (Internat. Faculty Fellow), 1967–68; London Business School, 1968–94; Prof., 1972–77; Vis. Prof., 1977–94; Fellow, 1994; Warden, St George's House, Windsor Castle, 1977–81. Chm., Royal Soc. for Encouragement of Arts, Manufactures and Commerce, 1987–89. FCGI 2000. Hon. Fellow: Inst. of Educn, London Univ., 1999; St Mary's Coll., Twickenham, 1999. Hon. DLitt: Bristol Poly., 1988; Open Univ., 1989; UEA, 1993; QUB, 1998; Middlesex, 1998; Exeter, 1999; Essex, Hull, Durham, 2000. *Publications:* Understanding Organizations, 1976, 4th edn 1999; Gods of Management, 1978, 2nd edn 1991; Future of Work, 1982; Understanding Schools as Organizations, 1986; Understanding Voluntary Organizations, 1988; The Age of Unreason, 1989; Inside Organizations, 1990; Waiting for the Mountain to Move, 1991; The Empty Raincoat, 1994; Beyond Certainty (essays), 1995; The Hungry Spirit, 1997; The New Alchemists, 1999; Thoughts for the Day, 1999; The Elephant and the Flea, 2001. *Address:* 1 Fairhaven, 73 Putney Hill, SW15 3NT. *T:* (020) 8788 1610; Old Hall Cottages, Bressingham, Diss, Norfolk IP22 2AG. *T:* (01379) 687546.

HANDY, Prof. Nicholas Charles, ScD; FRS 1990; Professor of Quantum Chemistry, Cambridge University, since 1991; Fellow, St Catharine's College, Cambridge, since 1965; *b* 17 June 1941; *s* of late Kenneth George Edwards Handy and of Ada Mary Handy (*née* Rumming); *m* 1967, Elizabeth Carole Gates; two *s*. *Educ:* Clayesmore Sch., Dorset; St Catharine's College, Cambridge (MA, PhD); ScD Cantab 1996. Cambridge University: Salters' Fellow, 1967–68; Demonstrator, 1972–77; Lectr, 1977–89; Reader in Quantum Chemistry, 1989–91; Steward, 1971–88, Pres., 1994–97, St Catharine's Coll. Harkness Fellow, Johns Hopkins Univ., 1968–69; Vis. Prof., Berkeley, Bologna, Sydney, Georgia. Lennard-Jones Lectr, RSC, 1983. Mem., Internat. Acad. of Quantum Molecular Science, 1988–. Dr *hc* Univ. de Marne-la-Vallée, France, 2000. Prize in Theoretical Chem., RSC, 1987; Schrodinger Medal, World Assoc. of Theoretically Oriented Chemists, 1997. *Publications:* papers in learned jls of chem. phys. *Recreations:* gardening, bridge, philately, travel. *Address:* Department of Chemistry, Lensfield Road, Cambridge CB2 1EW. *T:* (01223) 336373.

HANGARTNER, John Robert Wilfred; Principal Director, Brett Cook Consulting Ltd, since 2001; *b* 5 Feb. 1955; *s* of John Hangartner and Ita Patricia (*née* Brett); *m* 1980, Jillian Mary Ansell; one *s* one *d*. *Educ:* Merchant Taylors' Sch., Northwood; Guy's Hosp. Med. Sch., Univ. of London (BSc Hons 1976; MB, BS 1979); Open Univ. (MBA 1995). MRCS, LRCP 1979; MRCPath 1988, FRCPath 1997. Clin. Lectr in Histopathology, St George's Hosp. Med. Sch., 1983–88; Department of Health: SMO, 1988–91; Temp. PMO, 1991–93; PMO, 1993; Under Sec., and SPMO, 1993–97; CMO, Guardian Health Ltd, 1997–2000; Sen. Med. Advr, PPP healthcare, 1999–2000. Chm., Hosp. Jun. Staff Cttee, BMA, 1984–85. FRSocMed; FRSA 1994. *Recreations:* photography, singing. *Address:* Brett Cook Consulting Ltd, 11 Annesley Road, Blackheath, SE3 0JX. *T:* (020) 8319 3164, *Fax:* (020) 8319 8775.

HANHAM, family name of **Baroness Hanham**.

HANHAM, Baroness *cr* 1999 (Life Peer), of Kensington in the Royal Borough of Kensington and Chelsea; **Joan Brownlow Hanham,** CBE 1997; JP; Chairman, St Mary's Hospital NHS Trust, since 2000; *b* 23 Sept. 1939; *d* of Alfred Spark and Mary (*née* Mitchell); *m* 1964, Dr Iain William Ferguson Hanham; one *s* one *d*. *Educ:* Hillcourt Sch., Dublin. Royal Borough of Kensington and Chelsea: Mem. (C), 1970–; Mayor, 1983–84; Leader of Council, 1989–2000; Chairman: Town Planning Cttee, 1984–86; Social Services Cttee, 1987–89; Policy and Resources Cttee, 1989–. Chm., Policy Cttee, London Boroughs Assoc., 1991–95. An Opposition Whip, H of L, 2000–. Mem., Mental Health Act Commn, 1983–90; non-exec. Mem., NW Thames RHA, 1983–94; non-exec. Dir, Chelsea and Westminster Health Care NHS Trust, 1994–. Vice-Pres., Commonwealth Inst. JP City of London Commn 1984, and Inner London Family Proceedings Court, 1992. Freeman, City of London, 1984. *Recreations:* music, travel. *Address:* c/o The Town Hall, Hornton Street, W8 7NX. *Club:* Hurlingham.

HANHAM, Prof. Harold John; Vice-Chancellor, University of Lancaster, 1985–95; *b* Auckland, New Zealand, 16 June 1928; *s* of John Newman Hanham and Ellie Malone; *m* 1973, Ruth Soulé Arnon, *d* of Prof. Daniel I. Arnon, Univ. of Calif, Berkeley. *Educ:* Mount Albert Grammar Sch.; Auckland UC (now Univ. of Auckland); Univ. of New Zealand (BA 1948, MA 1950); Selwyn Coll, Cambridge (PhD 1954). FRHistS 1960; FAAAS 1974. Asst Lectr to Sen. Lectr, in Govt, Univ. of Manchester, 1954–63; Prof. and Head of Dept of Politics, Univ. of Edinburgh, 1963–68; Prof. of History, 1968–73 and Fellow of Lowell House, 1970–73, Harvard Univ.; Prof. of History and Political Science, 1972–85 and Dean, Sch. of Humanities and Social Sci., 1973–84, MIT; Hon. Prof. of History, Univ. of Lancaster, 1985–. Mem., ESRC, 1986. Guggenheim Fellow, 1972–73. Hon. AM Harvard, 1968. John H. Jenkins Prize for Bibliography, Union Coll., 1978. *Publications:* Elections and Party Management, 1969, 2nd edn 1978; The Nineteenth-Century Constitution, 1969; Scottish Nationalism, 1969; Bibliography of British History 1851–1914, 1976. *Recreations:* discovering Canada, squash. *Address:* Long Barn, Cross Howe Lane, Clapham, Lancaster LA2 8DL. *Clubs:* Oxford and Cambridge, Royal Commonwealth Society; St Botolph (Boston).

HANHAM, Sir Michael (William), 12th Bt *cr* 1667; DFC 1945; RAFVR; *b* 31 Oct. 1922; *s* of Patrick John Hanham (*d* 1965) and Dulcie (*d* 1979), *yr d* of William George Daffarn and *widow* of Lynn Hartley; *S* kinsman, Sir Henry Phelips Hanham, 11th Bt, 1973; *m* 1954, Margaret Jane, *d* of W/Cdr Harold Thomas, RAF retd, and Joy (*née* MacGeorge); one *s* one *d*. *Educ:* Winchester. Joined RAF 1942, as Aircrew Cadet; served No 8 (Pathfinder) Gp, Bomber Command, 1944–45; FO 1945. At end of war, retrained as Flying Control Officer; served UK and India, 1945–46; demobilised, 1946. Joined BOAC, 1947, Traffic Branch; qualified as Flight Operations Officer, 1954; served in Africa until 1961; resigned, 1961. Settled at Trillinghurst Farmhouse, Kent and started garden and cottage furniture making business, 1963; moved to Wimborne, 1974; now engaged with upkeep of family house and estate. Governor of Minster and of Dumpton School. *Recreations:* conservation (Vice-Chm. Weald of Kent Preservation Soc., 1972–74, 1976–2000; Mem. Cttee, Wimborne Civic Soc., 1977–), preservation of steam railways, painting. *Heir:* *s* William John Edward Hanham [*b* 4 Sept. 1957; *m* 1st, 1982, Elizabeth Anne Keyworth (marr. diss. 1988), *yr d* of Paul Keyworth, Farnham and Mrs Keith Thomas, Petersfield; 2nd, 1996, Jennifer, *o d* of Harold Sebag-Montefiore, *qv*]. *Club:* Royal Air Force.

HANKES-DRIELSMA, Claude Dunbar; strategist and financial adviser; *b* 8 March 1949. *Educ:* Grey. With Manufacturers Hanover, 1968–72; Robert Fleming & Co. Ltd, 1972–77, Director 1974–77; Chairman: Management Cttee, Price Waterhouse and Partners, 1983–89; Action Resource Centre, 1986–91 (Mem., 1983–86); Mem., Governing Council, 1986–91, Pres's Cttee, 1988–91, Business in the Community (Chm., Target Team on Voluntary Sector Initiatives, 1987–90). Advr to Bd, (Corange) Boehringer Mannheim, 1988–94; Dep. Chm., Leutwiler and Partners Ltd, 1992–96. Assisted Dr Fritz Leutwiler in his role as independent mediator between South African govt and foreign banks, 1985–86; initiated attempt to secure Thyssen Collection for Britain, 1988; Chm., Adv. Cttee to Kingdom of Jordan on Strategic Economic Policy Issues, 1993–94. Mem., Deanery Synod, 1984–93. Trustee, Windsor Leadership Trust, 1998– (Chm., 2000–); Fellow and Advr, St George's House, Windsor Castle, 2000–. Hon. Fellow, Corpus Christi Coll., Oxford. *Publications:* The Dangers of the Banking System: funding country deficits, 1975; Nobel Industrier indep. report, Stockholm, 1991. *Recreations:* gardening, walking, ski-ing, reading, ancient art. *Address:* Stanford Place, Faringdon, Oxon SN7 8EX. *T:* (01367) 240547, *Fax:* (01367) 242853. *Club:* Turf.

HANKEY, family name of **Baron Hankey**.

HANKEY, 3rd Baron *cr* 1939, of The Chart, Surrey; **Donald Robin Alers Hankey;** *b* 12 June 1938; *s* of 2nd Baron Hankey, KCMG, KCVO and Frances Bevyl Stuart-Monteth (*d* 1957); *S* father, 1996; *m* 1st, 1963, Margaretha Thorndahl (marr. diss. 1974); 2nd, 1974, Eileen Désirée (marr. diss. 1994), *yr d* of Maj.-Gen. Stuart Battye, CB; two *d*; 3rd, 1994, June, *d* of late Dr Leonard Taboroff. *Educ:* Rugby; University Coll. London (DipArch). RIBA. Founder and Chm., Gilmore Hankey Kirke Ltd, architects, planners and conservation specialists (part of the GHK Group of cos incl. engrg, econs and mgt), 1987; Vice Chm., ICOMOS (UK), 1997–. Founder and former Chm., All Party Gp on Architecture and Planning. Consultant to: World Bank; ODA; UN Develt Prog.; Council of Europe; British govt depts; owners of historic and private houses. FRSA. *Recreations:* piano, the arts, cultural anthropology, tennis, ski-ing. *Heir:* *b* Hon. Alexander Maurice Alers Hankey, PhD [*b* 18 Aug. 1947; *m* 1970, Deborah Benson (marr. diss. 1990)]. *Address:* 8 Sunset Road, SE5 8EA.

HANKINS, (Frederick) Geoffrey; Chairman, Fitch Lovell plc, 1983–90 (Chief Executive, 1982–89); Director, Booker plc, 1990–97; *b* 9 Dec. 1926; *s* of Frederick Aubrey Hankins and Elizabeth (*née* Stockton); *m* 1951, Iris Esther Perkins; two *d*. *Educ:* St Dunstan's College. Commissioned Army, 1946–48; J. Sainsbury management trainee, 1949–51, manufacturing management, 1951–55; Production/Gen. Manager, Allied Suppliers, 1955–62; Production Dir, Brains Food Products, 1962–69; Kraft Foods, 1966–69; Gen. Man., Millers, Poole, 1970–72, Man. Dir, 1972–82, Chm., 1975–86; Fitch Lovell: Dir, 1975–90; Chm., Manufacturing Div., 1975–84; Chairman: Robirch, 1975–84; Jus Rol, 1976–85; Blue Cap Frozen Food Services, 1975–84; Newforge Foods, 1979–84; Bells Bacon (Evesham), 1980–83; L. Noel, 1982–84; Dir, Salaison Le Vexin, 1980–90. Liveryman, Poulters' Co., 1982–. *Recreations:* genealogy, antiques, practical pursuits. *Address:* 51 Elms Avenue, Parkstone, Poole, Dorset BH14 8EE.

HANKINS, Prof. Harold Charles Arthur, CBE 1996; PhD; FREng, FIEE; Principal, 1984–95, Vice-Chancellor, 1994–95, University of Manchester Institute of Science and Technology; *b* 18 Oct. 1930; *s* of Harold Arthur Hankins and Hilda Hankins; *m* 1955, Kathleen Higginbottom; three *s* one *d*. *Educ:* Crewe Grammar Sch.; Univ. of Manchester Inst. of Science and Technol. (BSc Tech, 1st Cl. Hons Elec. Engrg, 1955; PhD 1971). CEng, FREng (FEng 1993); FIEE 1975; AMCT 1952. Engrg Apprentice, British Rail, 1947–52; Electronic Engr, subseq. Asst Chief Engr, Metropolitan Vickers Electrical Co. Ltd, 1955–68; Univ. of Manchester Inst. of Science and Technology: Lectr in Elec. Engrg, 1968–71; Sen. Lectr in Elec. Engrg, 1971–74; Prof. of Communication Engrg, and Dir of Med. Engrg Unit, 1974–84; Vice Principal, 1979–81; Dep. Principal, 1981–82; Actg Principal, 1982–84. Non-executive Director: THORN EMI Lighting Ltd, 1979–85; Bodycote International, 1992–97; Dir, Inward, 1992–95; Mem. Bd, Trafford Park Develt Corp., 1996–98; Chairman: Trafford Park Manufacturing Inst., 1997–; Elliott Absorbant Products, 1999–. Instn of Electrical Engineers: Mem., NW Centre Cttee, 1969–77, Chm. 1977–78; Chm., M2 Exec. Cttee, 1979–82; Mem., Management and Design Div. Bd, 1980–82. Chm., Chemical Engrg, Instrumentation, Systems Engrg Bd, CNAA, 1975–81; Member: Cttee for Science and Technol., CNAA, 1975–81; Cttee of Vice-Chancellors and Principals, 1984–95; Parly Scientific Cttee, 1985–95; Engrg Council, 1993–95; Bd of Govs, Manchester Polytechnic, 1989– (Hon. Fellow, 1984); Bd of Govs, South Cheshire Coll., 1990–96; Pres., Cheadle Hulme Sch., 1996–. Hon. DSc Manchester, 1995; DUniv Open, 1996; Hon. DEng UMIST, 1996. Reginald Mitchell Gold Medal, Assoc. of Engrs, 1990. *Publications:* 75 papers in learned jls; 10 patents for research into computer visual display systems. *Recreations:* military history, hill walking, music, choral work. *Address:* Rosebank, Kidd Road, Glossop, Derbyshire SK13 9PN. *T:* (01457) 853895.

HANKS, Patrick Wyndham; Director of Lexicography, LingoMotors, Boston, USA, since 2000; *b* 24 March 1940; *s* of Wyndham George Hanks and Elizabeth Mary (*née* Rudd); *m* 1st, 1961, Helga Gertrud Ingeborg Lietz (marr. diss. 1968); one *s* one *d*; 2nd, 1979, Julie Eyre (marr. diss. 1996); two *d*. *Educ:* Ardingly Coll., Sussex; University Coll., Oxford (BA, MA). Editor, Dictionaries and Reference Books, Hamlyn Group, 1964–70; Man. Dir, Laurence Urdang Associates, 1970–79; Dir, Surnames Res. Project, Univ. of Essex, 1980–83; Project Manager, Cobuild, Univ. of Birmingham, 1983–87; Chief Editor, Collins English Dictionaries, 1987–90; Manager, then Chief Editor, Current English Dictionaries, OUP, 1990–2000. Vis. Scientist (corpus lexicography), AT&T Bell Labs, 1988–90; Chief Investigator, Hector project in corpus analysis, Systems Res. Centre, Digital Equipment Corp., Palo Alto, 1992–93. *Publications:* (ed) Hamlyn World Dictionary, 1971; (ed) Collins English Dictionary, 1979, 2nd edn 1986; (with J. Corbett) Business Listening Tasks, 1986; (managing editor) Collins Cobuild English Language Dictionary, 1987; (with F. Hodges) Dictionary of Surnames, 1988; (with F. Hodges) Dictionary of First Names, 1990; (ed jtly) Oxford Concise Dictionary of First Names, 1992, 2nd edn 1997; (ed jtly) New Oxford Dictionary of English, 1998; (ed) New Oxford Thesaurus of English, 2000; articles in Computational Linguistics, Corpus Linguistics, Computing and the Humanities, Internat. Jl of Lexicography, Onoma, Names, and other jls. *Recreations:* onomastics, bridge, hiking, punting. *Address:* LingoMotors, 585 Massachusetts Avenue, Cambridge, MA 02139, USA.

HANKS, Tom; actor; *b* 9 July 1956; *s* of Amos Hanks and Janet; *m* 1st, 1978, Samantha Lewes (marr. diss. 1985); one *s* one *d*; 2nd, 1988, Rita Wilson; two *s*. *Educ:* Calif State

Univ. *Films* include: Splash, 1984; Bachelor Party, 1984; The Money Pit, 1986; Dragnet, 1987; Big, 1988; Punchline, 1988; Turner and Hooch, 1989; The Bonfire of the Vanities, 1990; A League of their Own, 1992; Sleepless in Seattle, 1993; Philadelphia, 1994 (Best Actor Award, Berlin Film Fest.; Acad. Award for Best Actor); Forrest Gump, 1995 (Acad. Award for Best Actor); Apollo 13, 1995; (also writer and dir) That Thing You Do!, 1997; Saving Private Ryan, 1998; You've Got Mail, 1999; The Green Mile, 2000; Cast Away, 2001; *television* includes: Bosom Buddies, 1980–82; co-prod., Band of Brothers, 2001. *Address:* c/o Creative Artists Agency, 9830 Wilshire Boulevard, Beverly Hills, CA 90212, USA.

HANLEY, Rt Hon. Sir Jeremy (James), KCMG 1997; PC 1994; chartered accountant, company director, lecturer and broadcaster; *b* 17 Nov. 1945; *s* of late Jimmy Hanley and of Dinah Sheridan; *m* 1973, Verna, Viscountess Villiers (*née* Stott); one *s*, one step *d*, and one *s* by previous marriage. *Educ:* Rugby. FCA 1969; FCCA 1980; FCIS 1980. Peat Marwick Mitchell & Co., 1963–66; Lectr in law, taxation and accountancy, Anderson Thomas Frankel, 1969, Dir 1969; Man. Dir, ATF (Jersey and Ireland), 1970–73; Dep. Chm., The Financial Training Co. Ltd, 1973–90; Sec., Park Place PLC, 1977–83; Chm., Fraser Green Ltd, 1986–90. Non-executive Director: ITE Gp, 1997–; Brass Tacks Publishing, 1997–2000; GTECH Hldgs Corp.; Eur. Adv. Bd, Credit Lyonnais, 2000–; Chairman: Internat. Trade and Investment Missions, 1997–; AdVal Gp plc, 1998–; Braingames Network plc, 2000–; Falcon Fund Mgt Ltd, 2000–. Dir, Arab-British Chamber of Commerce, 1998–. Parly Advr to ICA, 1986–90. Contested (C) Lambeth Central, April 1978, 1979. MP (C) Richmond and Barnes, 1983–97; contested (C) Richmond Park, 1997. PPS to Minister of State, Privy Council Office (Minister for CS and the Arts), 1987–90, to Sec. of State for Envmt, 1990; Parly Under-Sec. of State, NI Office, 1990–93 (Minister for Health, Social Security and Agric., 1990–92, for Pol Develt, Community Relns and Educn, 1992–93); Minister of State for the Armed Forces, MoD, 1993–94; Chm. of Cons. Party and Minister without Portfolio, 1994–95; Minister of State, FCO, 1995–97. Mem., H of C Select Cttee on Home Affairs, 1983–87 (Mem., Subcttee on Race Relns and Immigration, 1983–87); Jt Vice-Chm., Cons. Back-bench Trade and Industry Cttee, 1983–87. Member: British-American Parly Gp, 1983–97; Anglo-French Parly Gp, 1983–97; British-Irish Interparly Body, 1990; Life Member: CPA, 1983; IPU, 1983; Chm., Cons Candidates Assoc., 1982–83. Member: Bow Gp, 1974– (Chm., Home Affairs Cttee); European Movt, 1974–97; Mensa, 1968–. Chm., British-Iranian Chamber of Commerce, 2000–. Freeman, City of London, 1989; Liveryman, Chartered Accountants' Co., 1993– (Mem., Ct of Assts, 1996–). *Recreations:* cookery, chess, cricket, languages, theatre, cinema, music, golf. *Address:* 6 Butts Mead, Northwood, Middlesex HA6 2TL. *T:* (01923) 826675. *Clubs:* Garrick, Pilgrims, Lord's Taverners.

HANMER, Sir John (Wyndham Edward), 8th Bt *cr* 1774; JP; DL; *b* 27 Sept. 1928; *s* of Sir (Griffin Wyndham) Edward Hanmer, 7th Bt, and Aileen Mary (*d* 1967), *er d* of Captain J. E. Rogerson; *S* father, 1977; *m* 1954, Audrey Melissa, *d* of Major A. C. J. Congreve; two *s*. *Educ:* Eton. Captain (retired), The Royal Dragoons. Director: Chester Race Co., 1978–; Ludlow Race Club, 1980–; Bangor-on-Dee Races, 1980–. JP Flintshire, 1971; High Sheriff of Clwyd, 1977; DL Clwyd, 1978. *Recreations:* horseracing, shooting. *Heir: s* (Wyndham Richard) Guy Hanmer [*b* 27 Nov. 1955; *m* 1986, Elizabeth A., *yr d* of Neil Taylor; two *s* one *d*]. *Address:* The Mere House, Hanmer, Whitchurch, Shropshire SY13 3DG. *T:* (01948) 830383. *Club:* Army and Navy.

See also Sir James Wilson, Bt.

HANN, Air Vice-Marshal Derek William; Director-General RAF Personal Services, Ministry of Defence, 1987–89, retired; *b* 22 Aug. 1935; *s* of Claude and Ernestine Hann; *m* 1st, 1958, Jill Symonds (marr. diss. 1987); one *s* one *d*; 2nd, 1987, Sylvia Jean Holder. *Educ:* Dauntsey's Sch., Devizes. Joined RAF, 1954; served in Fighter (65 Sqdn) and Coastal (201 and 203 Sqdns) Commands and at HQ Far East Air Force, 1956–68; MoD, 1969–72 and 1975–77; Comd No 42 Sqdn, RAF St Mawgan, 1972–74; Comd RAF St Mawgan, 1977–79; RCDS 1980; Dir of Operational Requirements 2, MoD, 1981–84; C of S, HQ No 18 Gp, 1984–87. Membership Sec., Hawk and Owl Trust, 1995–. *Recreations:* theatre, music, horology, campanology. *Address:* 12 Westbourne Gardens, Hove BN3 5PP. *T:* (01626) 334864.

HANN, Sir James, Kt 1996; CBE 1977; Chairman: Hickson International, 1994–99; Bath Press Group, 1997–99; *b* 18 Jan. 1933; *s* of Harry Frank and Bessie Gladys Hann; *m* 1958, Jill Margaret Howe (*d* 1999); one *s* one *d*. *Educ:* Peter Symonds Sch., Winchester; IMEDE, Lausanne, Switzerland. FCIM, FInstPet, CIMgt. James Hann & Sons, 1950–52; Royal Artillery, 1952–54; United Dairies, 1954–65; IMEDE, 1965–66; Managing Director: Hanson Dairies, Liverpool, 1966–72; Seaforth Maritime, Aberdeen, 1972–86; Chairman: Bauteil Engineering, Glasgow, 1986–88; Exacta Holdings, Selkirk, 1986–90; Associated Fresh Foods, Leeds 1987–89; Strathclyde Inst., Glasgow, 1987–90; Scottish Nuclear, 1990–95; Eurotherm plc, 1996–98; Dep. Chm., Scottish Transport Gp, 1987–90. Director: William Baird, 1991–2001; NFU Mutual and Avon Gp, 1993–98. Comr, Northern Lighthouse Bd, 1990–95 (Chm., 1993–94). Member: Offshore Energy Technology Bd, 1982–85; Offshore Tech. Adv. Gp, 1983–86; Nationalised Industries Chairman's Gp, 1990–95. Life Mem., Beaver Club, Montreal, 1981 (for services to Canadian offshore industry). Burgess of Guild, Aberdeen, 1982–. Hon. FINucE 1993; Hon. Fellow European Nuclear Soc., 1994. *Recreations:* sailing, reading, music. *Address:* Wrington, N Somerset.

HANNA, Brian Petrie, CBE 2000; Chief Executive, Belfast City Council, since 1994; *b* 15 Dec. 1941; *m* 1968, Sylvia Campbell; one *d*. *Educ:* Royal Belfast Academical Instn; Belfast Coll. of Technol.; Ulster Coll., NI Poly. (DMS). FCIEH. Belfast Corporation: Clerical Asst, City Treasurer's Dept, 1959; Health Department: Clerical Officer, 1960–61; Pupil Public Health Inspector, 1961–65; Public Health Inspector, 1965–73; Sen. Trng Advr, Food and Drink ITB, 1974–75; Principal Public Health Inspector, Eastern Gp Public Health Cttee, Castlereagh BC, 1975–77; Belfast City Council: Dep. Dir, 1978–84, Dir, 1984–92, Envmtl Health Services; Dir, Health and Envmtl Services, 1992–94. Mem., UK Sustainable Develt Commn. Gov., Royal Belfast Academical Instn. CIMgt. Hon. DSc (Econ) QUB. *Recreations:* apart from my family, the sport of hockey (Past Pres., Irish Hockey Union). *Address:* Belfast City Council, City Hall, Belfast BT1 5GS. *T:* (028) 9032 0202.

HANNA, Carmel; Member (SDLP) South Belfast, Northern Ireland Assembly, since 1998; *b* 26 April 1946; *d* of John and Mary McAleenan; *m* 1973, Eamon Hanna; one *s* three *d*. *Educ:* Our Lady's Grammar Sch., Newry; Belfast City Hosp. (SRN); Royal Maternity Hosp. (SCM). Staff nurse in hosps in Belfast (Accident and Emergency), Guernsey, and Dublin, 1967–73; Staff Nurse, Musgrave Park Hosp., 1984–93; Social Worker, South and East Belfast HSS Trust, 1993–98. Mem. (SDLP) Belfast CC, 1997–. *Publication:* (ed) Abolishing Past Dissensions: essays to mark the bicentenary of the United Irishmen, 1998. *Recreations:* aromatherapy, reflexology, gardening, travel, Irish history, cooking. *Address:* 12 Bawnmore Road, Belfast BT9 6LA. *T:* (028) 9066 7577, 9068 3535.

HANNA, Prof. David Colin, PhD; FRS 1998; Professor of Physics, since 1988, and Deputy Director, Optoelectronics Research Centre, since 1989, University of Southampton; *b* 10 April 1941; *s* of James Morgan Hanna and Vera Elizabeth Hanna (*née* Hopkins); *m* 1968, Sarah Veronica Jane Heigham; two *s*. *Educ:* Nottingham High Sch.; Jesus Coll., Cambridge (BA 1962); Southampton Univ. (PhD 1967). University of Southampton: Lectr, Dept of Electronics, 1967–78; Sen. Lectr, 1978–84; Reader, Dept of Physics, 1984–88. Consiglio Nazionale della Ricerca Vis. Fellow, Politecnico di Milano, 1971; Alexander von Humboldt Fellow, Univ. of Munich, 1978–79. Dir-at-Large, 1996, Fellow, 1998, Optical Soc. of America. Max Born Medal and Prize, German Physical Soc., 1993; Quantum Electronics and Optics Prize, Eur. Physical Soc., 2000; Alexander von Humboldt Res. Award, Alexander von Humboldt Foundn, 2000. *Publications:* Nonlinear Optics of Free Atoms and Molecules, 1979; more than 250 papers in learned jls on lasers and nonlinear optics. *Recreations:* walking, climbing, gardening, cooking, sailing, music, theatre, travel. *Address:* Optoelectronics Research Centre, University of Southampton, Southampton SO17 1BJ. *T:* (023) 8059 2150.

HANNAH, Prof. Leslie; Chief Executive, Ashridge Management College, since 2000; *b* 15 June 1947; *s* of Arthur Hannah and Marie (*née* Lancashire); *m* 1984, Nuala Barbara Zahedieh (*née* Hockton) (marr. diss. 1998), *e d* of Thomas and Deirdre Hockton; one *s* two step *d*. *Educ:* Manchester Grammar Sch.; St John's and Nuffield Colleges, Oxford. MA, PhD, DPhil. Research Fellow, St John's Coll., Oxford, 1969–73; Lectr in economics, Univ. of Essex, 1973–75; Lectr in recent British economic and social history, Univ. of Cambridge, and Fellow and Financial Tutor, Emmanuel Coll., Cambridge, 1976–78; London School of Economics: Dir, Business History Unit, 1978–88; Prof. of Business Hist., 1982–97; Pro-Dir, 1995–97; Acting Dir, 1996–97; Dean, City Univ. Business Sch., 1997–2000, Vis. Prof., 2000–. Vis. Prof., Harvard Univ., 1984–85. Director: NRG London Reinsurance, 1986–93; London Econs Ltd, 1991–2000. *Publications:* Rise of the Corporate Economy, 1976, 2nd edn 1983; (ed) Management Strategy and Business Development, 1976; (with J. A. Kay) Concentration in Modern Industry, 1977; Electricity before Nationalisation, 1979; Engineers, Managers and Politicians, 1982; Entrepreneurs and the Social Sciences, 1983; Inventing Retirement, 1986; contribs to jls. *Recreation:* Scotland. *Address:* Ashridge Management College, Berkhamsted, Herts HP4 1NS. *T:* (01442) 841001. *Club:* Institute of Directors.

HANNAH, His Honour William; a Circuit Judge, 1988–95; *b* 31 March 1929; *s* of William Bond Hannah and Elizabeth Alexandra Hannah; *m* 1950, Alma June Marshall; one *s* one *d*. *Educ:* Everton School, Notts. Called to the Bar, Gray's Inn, 1970. RAF 1947–52; Police Officer, 1952–77. *Recreations:* golf, swimming, walking, theatre. *Address:* c/o New Court Chambers, 3 Broad Chare, Newcastle upon Tyne NE1 3DQ. *Club:* South Shields Golf.

HANNAM, Sir John (Gordon), Kt 1992; *b* 2 Aug. 1929; *s* of Thomas William and Selina Hannam; *m* 1st, 1956, Wendy Macartney; two *d*; 2nd, 1983, Mrs Vanessa Wauchope (*née* Anson). *Educ:* Yeovil Grammar Sch. Studied Agriculture, 1945–46. Served in: Royal Tank Regt (commissioned), 1947–48; Somerset LI (TA), 1949–51. Studied Hotel industry, 1950–52; Managing Dir, Hotels and Restaurant Co., 1952–61; Developed Motels, 1961–70; Chm., British Motels Fedn, 1967–74, Pres. 1974–80; Mem. Council, BTA, 1968–69; Mem. Economic Research Council, 1967–85. MP (C) Exeter, 1970–97. PPS to: Minister for Industry, 1972–74; Chief Sec., Treasury, 1974. Mem., Select Cttee on Procedure, 1993–97; Secretary: Cons. Parly Trade Cttee, 1971–72; All-Party Disablement Gp, 1974–92 (Co-Chm., 1992–97); 1922 Cttee, 1987–97; Mem., Govt Adv. Cttee on Transport for Disabled, 1983–97; Chairman: Anglo-Swiss Parly Gp, 1987–97; West Country Cons. Cttee, 1973–74, 1979–81; Cons. Party Energy Cttee, 1979–92; Arts and Leisure Standing Cttee, Bow Group, 1975–84; Vice-Chairman: Arts and Heritage Cttee, 1974–79; British Cttee of Internat. Rehabilitation, 1979–92. Captain: Lords and Commons Tennis Club, 1975–97; Lords and Commons Ski Club, 1977–82; Cdre, House of Commons Yacht Club, 1975. Mem., Snowdon Working Party on the Disabled, 1975–76; Chm. Trustees, Snowdon Awards Scheme, 1997–. Vice-President: Disablement Income Gp; Council, Action Research for Crippling Diseases; Disabled Motorists Gp; Bd Mem., Rehabilitation UK, 1995–. Member: Bd, Nat. Theatre, 1979–92; Glyndebourne Festival Soc.; Council, British Youth Opera, 1989– (Chm., 1997–). Hon. MA Open, 1986. *Recreations:* music (opera), theatre, sailing (anything), ski-ing (fast), Cresta tobogganing (foolish), gardening; county tennis and hockey (Somerset tennis champion, 1953). *Address:* 85 Bromfelde Road, SW4 6PP. *Clubs:* Royal Yacht Squadron, All England Lawn Tennis, International Lawn Tennis.

HANNAM, Michael Patrick Vivian, CBE 1980; HM Diplomatic Service, retired; Consul General, Jerusalem, 1976–80; *b* 13 Feb. 1920; *s* of Rev. Wilfrid L. Hannam, BD, and Dorothy (*née* Parker); *m* 1947, Sybil Huggins; one *s* one *d*. *Educ:* Westminster Sch. LMS Railway, 1937–40. Served in Army, 1940–46 (Major, RE). LMS Railway, 1946–50; Malayan Railway, 1950–60. FO, 1960–62; First Sec., British Embassy, Cairo, 1962–65; Principal British Trade Comr, Hong Kong, 1965–69 (and Consul, Macao, 1968–69); Counsellor, Tripoli, 1969–72; Counsellor (Economic and Commercial), Nairobi, 1972–73, Dep. High Commissioner, Nairobi, 1973–76. Mem. Exec. Cttee, Palestine Exploration Fund, 1982–92 (Keeper of Written Archive, 1989–92). Chm. Governors, Rose Hill Sch., Tunbridge Wells, 1980–85; Chm. Council, British Sch. of Archaeology in Jerusalem, 1983–90. *Recreations:* music, research into 19th century Jerusalem, translating Homer. *Address:* Little Oaklands, Langton Green, Kent TN3 0HP. *T:* (01892) 862163. *Club:* Army and Navy.

HANNAN, Daniel John; Member (C) South East Region, England, European Parliament, since 1999; *b* 1 Sept. 1971; *s* of late Hugh R. Hannan and of Lavinia M. Hannan (*née* Moffat); *m* 2000, Sara Maynard. *Educ:* Marlborough; Oriel Coll., Oxford (MA). Leader writer, Daily Telegraph, 1996–. Dir, European Res. Gp, 1994–99. *Publications:* Time for a Fresh Start in Europe, 1993; Britain in a Multi-Speed Europe, 1994; The Challenge of the East, 1996; A Guide to the Amsterdam Treaty, 1997. *Recreation:* English poetry. *Address:* Conservative Central Office, 32 Smith Square, SW1P 3HH. *T:* (020) 7984 8238. *Club:* Carlton.

HANNAN, Menna; *see* Richards, M.

HANNAY, family name of **Baron Hannay of Chiswick.**

HANNAY OF CHISWICK, Baron *cr* 2001 (Life Peer), of Bedford Park in the London Borough of Ealing; **David Hugh Alexander Hannay,** GCMG 1995 (KCMG 1986; CMG 1981); British Government Special Representative for Cyprus, since 1996; *b* 28 Sept. 1935; *s* of late Julian Hannay; *m* 1961, Gillian Rex; four *s*. *Educ:* Winchester; New Coll., Oxford. Foreign Office, 1959–60; Tehran, 1960–61; 3rd Sec., Kabul, 1961–63; 2nd Sec., FO, 1963–65; 2nd, later 1st Sec., UK Delegn to European Communities, Brussels, 1965–70; 1st Sec., UK Negotiating Team with European Communities, 1970–72; Chef de Cabinet to Sir Christopher Soames, Vice President of EEC, 1973–77; Head of Energy, Science and Space Dept, FCO, 1977–79; Head of Middle East Dept, FCO, 1979; Asst Under-Sec. of State (European Community), FCO, 1979–84; Minister, Washington,

1984–85; Ambassador and UK Permanent Rep. to Eur. Communities, Brussels, 1985–90; British Perm. Rep. to UN, 1990–95; retd from Diplomatic Service, 1995. Prime Minister's Personal Envoy to Turkey, 1998; EU Presidency Special Rep. for Cyprus, 1998. Non-executive Director: Chime Communications, 1996–; Aegis, 2000–. Mem., Council of Britain in Europe, 1999–. Mem. Court and Council, 1998–, Pro-Chancellor, 2001–, Birmingham Univ. *Recreations:* travel, gardening, photography. *Address:* 3 The Orchard, W4 1JZ. *Club:* Travellers.

HANNAY, Elizabeth Anne Scott, MA; Head Mistress, Godolphin School, Salisbury, 1980–89; *b* 28 Dec. 1942; *d* of Thomas Scott Hannay and Doreen Hewitt Hannay. *Educ:* Heathfield Sch., Ascot; St Hugh's Coll., Oxford (MA). Assistant Mistress: St Mary's Sch., Calne, 1966–70; Moreton Hall Sch., Shropshire, 1970–72; S Michael's, Burton Park, Petworth, 1973–75; Dep. Headmistress, St George's Sch., Ascot, 1975–80. *Address:* Downend Cottage, Tichborne, near Alresford, Hants SO24 0NA.

HANNEN, Rt Rev. John Edward; Bishop of Caledonia, 1981–2001; *b* 19 Nov. 1937; *s* of Charles Scott Hannen and Mary Bowman Hannen (*née* Lynds); *m* 1977, Alana Susan Long; two *d. Educ:* McGill Univ. (BA); College of the Resurrection, Mirfield (GOE). Asst Curate, St Alphege's, Solihull, Warwicks, 1961–64; Priest in Charge, Mission to the Hart Highway, Diocese of Caledonia, BC, 1965–67; Priest, St Andrew's, Greenville, BC, 1967–68; Priest in Charge, Church of Christ the King, Port Edward, BC, 1969–71; Rector, Christ Church, Kincolith, BC, 1971–81; Regional Dean of Metlakatla, 1972–78; Acting Metropolitan, Ecclesiastical Province of BC and Yukon, 1993–94. Chm., Council of the North, Gen. Synod, Anglican Ch of Canada, 1993–95. Hon. DD Manitoba, 1997. *Recreation:* music. *Address:* c/o Diocese of Caledonia, PO Box 278, Prince Rupert, BC V8J 3P6, Canada.

HANNIGAN, James Edgar, CB 1981; Deputy Secretary, Department of Transport, 1980–88; *b* 12 March 1928; *s* of late James Henry and Kathleen Hannigan; *m* 1955, Shirley Jean Bell (decd); two *d. Educ:* Eastbourne Grammar Sch.; Sidney Sussex Coll., Cambridge (BA). Civil Service, 1951; Asst Sec., Housing Div., Min. of Housing and Local Govt, 1966–70; Asst Sec., Local Govt Div., DoE, 1970–72. Under Sec. 1972; Regional Dir for West Midlands, DoE, 1972–75; Chm., West Midlands Economic Planning Bd, 1972–75; Dir of Housing 'B', DoE, 1975–78; Dep. Sec., 1978; NI Office, 1978–80. Mem., Internat. Exec. Cttee, PIARC, 1985–90. Trustee, Clapham Junction Disaster Fund, 1989–90.

HANNINGFIELD, Baron *cr* 1998 (Life Peer), of Chelmsford in the co. of Essex; **Paul Edward Winston White;** DL; farmer; Member (C), since 1970, and Leader, Conservative Group, since 1992, Essex County Council; *b* 16 Sept. 1940; *s* of Edward Ernest William White and Irene Joyce Gertrude White (*née* Williamson). *Educ:* King Edward VI Grammar Sch., Chelmsford (Nuffield Scholarship). Chm., 1989–92, Leader, 1998–99, Essex CC. Chairman: Council, Local Educn Authorities, 1990–92; Eastern Area, FEFC, 1992–97. Dep. Chm., LGA, 1997–. Mem., EU Cttee of the Regions (Vice Pres., European People's Party, 1998–; Vice Pres., Transport and Information Soc. Commn, 1998–). Mem. Ct, Essex Univ., 1980–. DL Essex, 1991. *Publications:* many contribs to local govt jls. *Recreations:* gardening, wine and food, travel, walking the dog. *Address:* Pippins Place, Helmons Lane, West Hanningfield, Chelmsford, Essex CM2 8UW. *T:* (01245) 400229.

HANNON, Rt Rev. Brian Desmond Anthony; Bishop of Clogher, 1986–2001; *b* 5 Oct. 1936; *s* of late Ven. Arthur Gordon Hannon and of Hilda Catherine Stewart-Moore Hannon (*née* Denny); *m* 1964, Maeve Geraldine Audley (*née* Butler); three *s. Educ:* Mourne Grange Prep. School, Co. Down; St Columba's Coll., Co. Dublin; Trinity Coll., Dublin (BA Hons 1959, 1st Class Divinity Testimonium 1961). Deacon 1961, priest 1962; Diocese of Derry: Curate-Assistant, All Saints, Clooney, Londonderry, 1961–64; Rector of Desertmartin, 1964–69; Rector of Christ Church, Londonderry, 1969–82; RD of Londonderry, 1977–82; Diocese of Clogher: Rector of St Macartin's Cathedral, Enniskillen, 1982–86; Canon of Cathedral Chapter, 1983; Dean of Clogher, 1985. Chm., Council for Mission in Ireland, C of I, 1987–99. Pres., CMS (Ireland), 1990–96; Chm., Irish Council of Churches, 1992–94; Co-Chm., Irish Inter-Church Meeting, 1992–94; Mem., WCC Central Cttee, 1983–92. Chm. of Western (NI) Education and Library Bd, 1985–87 and 1989–91 (Vice-Chm., 1987–89 and 1991–93). Hon. MA TCD, 1962. *Publication:* (editor/author) Christ Church, Londonderry—1830 to 1980—Milestones, Ministers, Memories, 1980. *Recreations:* walking, music, travel, sport. *Address:* Drumconnis Top, 202 Mullaghmeen Road, Ballinamallard, Co. Fermanagh, N Ireland BT94 2HE. *T:* (028) 6638 8557, *Fax:* (028) 6638 8086; *e-mail:* bdah@btinternet.com.

HANNON, Richard Michael; racehorse trainer; *b* 30 May 1945; *m* 1966, Josephine Ann McCarthy; two *s* four *d* (of whom two *s* one *d* are triplets). First trainer's licence, 1970; wins include: 2000 Guineas, 1973 (Mon Fils), 1987 (Don't Forget Me), 1990 (Tirol); Irish 2000 Guineas, 1987 (Don' Forget Me), 1990 (Tirol); leading trainer, 1992; trained record number of winners (182), 1993 season. *Address:* East Everleigh Stables, Marlborough, Wilts SN8 3EY.

HANON, Bernard; Officier, Ordre National du Mérite, 1980; Managing Director, Hanon Associés, since 1986; *b* 7 Jan. 1932; *s* of Max Hanon and Anne Smulevicz; *m* 1965, Ghislaine de Bragelongne; two *s. Educ:* HEC 1955; Columbia Univ. (MBA 1956; PhD 1962). Dir of Marketing, Renault Inc., USA, 1959–63; Asst Prof. of Management Sci., Grad. Sch. of Business, NY Univ., 1963–66; Head, Dept of Economic Studies and Programming, 1966–69, Dir of Corporate Planning and Inf. Systems, 1970–75, Régie Nat. des Usines Renault; Dir, Renault Automotive Ops, 1976; Executive Vice President: i/c Automobile Div., 1976–81; Renault Gp, 1981; Chm. and Pres., Régie Nationale des Usines Renault, 1981–85. *Address:* Hanon Associés, 31 rue François 1er, 75008 Paris, France. *Clubs:* Racing Club de France, Automobile Club de France (Paris); Golf de St Germain.

HANRAHAN, Brian; Diplomatic Editor, BBC Television, since 1997; *b* 22 March 1949; *s* of Thomas Hanrahan and Kathleen McInerney; *m* 1986, Honor Wilson; one *d. Educ:* Essex University (BA). BBC, 1971–: Far East correspondent, 1983–85; Moscow correspondent, 1986–89; Diplomatic correspondent, 1989–97. DU Essex, 1990. *Publication:* (with Robert Fox) I Counted Them All Out and I Counted Them All Back, 1982. *Address:* c/o Foreign News Department, BBC TV Centre, Wood Lane, W12 7RD.

HANROTT, Francis George Vivian, CBE 1981; Chief Officer, Technician Education Council, 1973–82; *b* 1 July 1921; *s* of late Howard Granville Hanrott and Phyllis Sarah Hanrott; *m* 1953, Eileen Winifred Appleton; three *d. Educ:* Westminster Sch.; King's Coll., Univ. of London (BA Hons). Served War, RN (Air Br.), 1940–45; Lieut (A) RNVR. Asst Master, St Marylebone Grammar Sch., 1948–50; Lectr, E Berks Coll. of Further Educn, 1950–53; Asst Educn Officer, Wilts, 1953–56; Staff Manager, GEC Applied Electronics Labs, 1956–59; Asst Educn Officer, Herts, 1959–66; Registrar and Sec., CNAA, 1966–73. Hon. MA Open Univ., 1977. *Recreations:* music, angling. *Address:* Coombe Down House, Salcombe Road, Malborough, Kingsbridge, Devon TQ7 3BX. *T:* (01548) 842721.

HÄNSCH, Dr Klaus; Member (SPD), European Parliament, since 1979 (President, 1994–97); *b* Sprottau, Silesia, 15 Dec. 1938; *s* of Willi Hänsch and Erna (*née* Sander); *m* 1969, Ilse Hoof. *Educ:* Univ. of Cologne (degree in Pol Sci. 1965); Univ. of Paris; Univ. of Berlin (PhD 1969). Escaped from Silesia to Schleswig-Holstein, 1945. Mil. Service, 1959–60. Res. Asst, Otto Suhr Inst., Free Univ. of Berlin, 1966–68; Ed., Dokumente, 1968–69; Advr to Rep. of FRG under Franco-German Treaty, 1969–70; Press Officer, 1970–79 and expert advr, 1977–79, to Minister for Sci. and Res., N Rhine/Westphalia; Lectr, Duisburg Univ., 1976– (Hon. Prof., 1994). European Parliament: Member: Foreign Affairs and Security and other cttees, 1979–94; For. Affairs, Human Rights, Common Security and Defence Policy Cttee, 1997–; Vice-Chm., Party of Eur. Socialists Gp, 1997–; Adv. Mem., Bundestag Cttee on EC issues, 1985–95; Chm., Delgn for relns with US, 1987–89. Member: SPD, 1964–; ÖTV (Union of Tspt and Public Service Workers). *Publications:* pamphlets, contribs to books, and many articles on politics and society in France and on issues relating to unification of Europe and European security policy. *Address:* European Parliament, Rue Wiertz, 1047 Brussels, Belgium; Europabüro, Kavelleriestrasse 16, 40213 Düsseldorf, Germany. *T:* (211) 13622254.

HANSEN, Alan David; football commentator, BBC, since 1992; *b* 13 June 1955; *s* of John and Anne Hansen; *m* 1980, Janette Rhymes; one *s* one *d. Educ:* Lornshill Acad. Professional footballer, Liverpool FC, 1977–91: League Champions, 1979, 1980, 1982, 1983, 1984, 1986, 1988, 1990; Capt., FA Cup winning team, 1986, 1988; winners: European Cup, 1978, 1981, 1984; League Cup, 1981, 1982, 1983, 1984. *Publications:* Tall, Dark and Hansen, 1988; Matter of Opinion, 1999. *Clubs:* Hillside Golf; Southport and Birkdale Cricket.

HANSEN, Prof. Jean-Pierre, DèS; Professor of Theoretical Chemistry, and Fellow of Corpus Christi College, University of Cambridge, since 1997; *b* 10 May 1942; *s* of late Georges Hansen and Simone Flohr; *m* 1971, Martine Bechet; one *d. Educ:* Athénée Grand-Ducal de Luxembourg; Univ. de Liège (Licence en Sciences Physiques, 1964); Univ. de Paris (DèS 1969). CChem, FRSC 1998. Chargé de recherche, CNRS, France, 1967–73; Prof. of Physics, Univ. Pierre et Marie Curie, Paris, 1973–87; Directeur Adjoint, 1987–93, Prof. and Hd of Dept of Physics, 1987–97, Ecole Normale Supérieure, Lyons. Miller Prof., Univ. of Calif at Berkeley, 1992. Mem., Inst. Universitaire de France, 1992–97. Grand Prix de l'Etat, Académie des Sciences, Paris, 1990; Prix Spécial, Soc. Française de Physique, 1998. Chevalier de l'Ordre de la Couronne de Chêne (Luxembourg), 1997. *Publications:* (jtly) Theory of Simple Liquids, 1976, 2nd edn 1986; (ed jtly) Liquids, Freezing and the Glass Transition, 1991; papers in internat. jls. *Recreations:* history of art, classical music, hill walking. *Address:* Department of Chemistry, Lensfield Road, Cambridge CB2 1EW. *T:* (01223) 336376.

HANSENNE, Michel; Member (Christian Social Party), European Parliament, since 1999; *b* 23 March 1940; *s* of Henri and Charlier Georgette Hansenne; *m* 1978, Mme Gabrielle Vanlandschoot; one *s* one *d. Educ:* Liège Univ. (Dr Law 1962; degree in Econs and Finance, 1967). Research work, Univ. of Liège, 1962–72. Mem. Belgian Parliament, 1974–89; Minister: for French Culture, 1979–81; for Employment and Labour, 1981–88; for Civil Service, 1988–89; Dir-Gen., ILO, 1989–99. Mem., EPP Gp, EP, 1999–. *Publications:* Emploi, les scénarios du possible, 1985; Un garde-fou pour la mondialisation: le BIT dans l'après-guerre froide, 1999; articles in national and international jls. *Address:* 28 rue des Deux Eglises, 4120 Neupre, Belgium.

HANSFORD, John Edgar, CB 1982; Under-Secretary, Defence Policy and Matériel Group, HM Treasury, 1976–82, retired; *b* 1 May 1922; *s* of Samuel George Hansford, ISO, MBE, and Winifred Louise Hansford; *m* 1947, Evelyn Agnes Whitehorn; one *s. Educ:* Whitgift Middle Sch., Croydon. Clerical Officer, Treasury, 1939. Served War of 1939–45: Private, Royal Sussex Regt, 1940; Lieutenant, Royal Fusiliers, 1943; served in: Africa, Mauritius, Ceylon, India, Burma, on secondment to King's African Rifles; demobilised, 1946. Exec. Officer, Treasury, 1946–50; Higher Exec. Officer, Regional Bd for Industry, Leeds, 1950–52; Exchange Control, Treasury, 1952–54; Agricultural Policy, Treasury, 1954–57; Sen. Exec. Officer, and Principal, Defence Div., Treasury, 1957–61; Principal, Social Security Div., Treasury, 1961–66; Public Enterprises Div., 1966–67; Overseas Develt Div., 1967–70; Asst Sec., Defence Policy and Matériel Div., Treasury, 1970–76; Under-Sec. in charge of Gp, 1976. *Recreations:* gardening, motoring.

HANSON, family name of **Baron Hanson**.

HANSON, Baron *cr* 1983 (Life Peer), of Edgerton in the County of West Yorkshire; **James Edward Hanson,** Kt 1976; Chairman, Hanson PLC, 1965–97, Chairman Emeritus, 1998; Director: Hanson Transport Group Ltd, since 1946 (Chairman, 1965–96); Hanson Capital Ltd, since 2000; *b* 20 Jan. 1922; *s* of late Robert Hanson, CBE and late Louisa Ann (Cis) (*née* Rodgers); *m* 1959, Geraldine (*née* Kaelin); two *s*, and one step *d.* War Service 1939–46. Mem., Ct of Patrons, RCS, 1991–; Trustee, Hanson Fellowship of Surgery, Oxford; Fellow, Cancer Res. Campaign. Life Mem., Royal Dublin Soc., 1948. Freeman, City of London, 1964; Hon. Liveryman, Worshipful Co. of Saddlers. FRSA; CIMgt. Hon. FRCR 1998. Hon. Fellow, St Peter's Coll., Oxford, 1996. Hon. LLD Leeds, 1984; Hon. DBA Huddersfield, 1991. *Address:* 28 Old Brompton Road, (Box 164), SW7 3SS. *T:* (020) 7245 6996. *Clubs:* Brooks's; Huddersfield Borough; The Brook (NY); Toronto.

HANSON, Dr Bertram Speakman, CMG 1963; DSO 1942; OBE 1941; ED; *b* 6 Jan. 1905; *s* of William Speakman Hanson and Maggie Aitken Hanson; *m* 1932, Mayne, *d* of T. J. Gilpin; three *s* one *d. Educ:* St Peter's Coll., Adelaide; University of Adelaide (MB, BS). War Service: Comd 2/8 Aust. Field Amb., 1940–43; ADMS, 9 Aust. Div., 1943–44. Pres., SA Branch of BMA, 1952–53; Pres. College of Radiologists of Australasia, 1961–62 (Gold Medal, 1990); Mem., Radiation Health Cttee of Nat. Health and Med. Research Coun., 1963–67; Hon. Radiotherapist, Royal Adelaide Hospital, 1952–64; Pres., The Australian Cancer Soc., 1964–67 (Gold Medal, 1979); Chairman: Exec. Board, Anti-Cancer Foundation, University of Adelaide, 1955–74; Anti-Cancer Foundation, Universities of South Aust., 1980–86; Mem. Council, International Union Against Cancer, 1962–74. Pres., Nat. Trust of South Aust., 1979–82. FFR (Hon.) 1964; FAMA 1967; FRCR (Hon.) 1975. DUniv Adelaide, 1985. *Publications:* sundry addresses and papers in Med. Jl of Australia. *Recreation:* gardening. *Address:* 10 Rugby Street, Kingswood, SA 5062, Australia. *Club:* Adelaide.

HANSON, Brian John Taylor, CBE 1996; Director of Legal Services to the Archbishops' Council, 1999–2001; Registrar and Legal Adviser to General Synod of Church of England, 1975–2001; Joint Principal Registrar, Provinces of Canterbury and York, 1980–2001; Registrar, Convocation of Canterbury, 1982–2001; *b* 23 Jan. 1939; *o s* of Benjamin John Hanson and Gwendoline Ada Hanson (*née* Taylor); *m* 1972, Deborah Mary Hazel, *yr d* of Lt-Col R. S. P. Dawson, OBE; two *s* three *d. Educ:* Hounslow Coll.; Law Society's Coll. of Law; Univ. of Wales (LLM 1994). Solicitor (admitted 1963) and ecclesiastical notary; in private practice, Wilson Houlder & Co., 1963–65; Solicitor with Church Comrs, 1965–99; Asst Legal Advr to General Synod, 1970–75. Member: Legal Adv. Commn of General Synod, 1980–2001 (Sec., 1970–86); Gen. Council, Ecclesiastical Law Soc., 1987–. Guardian, Nat. Shrine of Our Lady of Walsingham, 1984–; Fellow,

Corp. of SS Mary and Nicholas (Woodard Schools), 1987–; Member Council: St Luke's Hosp. for the Clergy, 1985–2001 (Archbishop's Nominee, St Luke's Res. Foundn, 1998–); Chichester Cath., 2000–. Governor: St Michael's Sch., Burton Park, 1987–94; Pusey House, Oxford, 1993–; Quainton Hall Sch., 1994–. Chm., Chichester Diocesan Bd of Patronage, 1998–. Freeman, City of London, 1991; Liveryman, Co. of Glaziers and Painters of Glass, 1992–. FRSA 1996; FInstD 1998. *Publications:* (ed) The Canons of the Church of England, 2nd edn 1975, 5th edn 1993; (ed) The Opinions of the Legal Advisory Commission, 6th edn 1985; (ed) Atkin's Court Forms, ecclesiastical vol., 1992, 2nd edn 1996; (jtly) Moore's Introduction to English Canon Law, 3rd edn 1992. *Recreations:* the family, gardening, genealogy. *Address:* Dalton's Farm, Bolney, West Sussex RH17 5PG. *T:* (01444) 881890.

HANSON, Sir (Charles) Rupert (Patrick), 4th Bt *cr* 1918, of Fowey, Cornwall; Revenue Assistant, HM Inspector of Taxes, since 1993; *b* 25 June 1945; *s* of Sir Charles John Hanson, 3rd Bt and of Patricia Helen (*née* Brind; now Mrs Miéville); *S* father, 1996; *m* 1977, Wanda Julia, *d* of Don Arturo Larrain, Santiago, Chile; one *s*. *Educ:* Eton Coll.; Polytech. of Central London. BA (CNAA) Modern Langs; Dip. in Technical and Specialised Trans. Technical, legal and commercial translator, 1977–83; TEFL (part-time), 1981–83; voluntary charity worker, 1984–85; Inland Revenue, 1986–. *Recreations:* classical music, writing poetry, tennis, walking. *Heir: s* Alexis Charles Hanson, *b* 25 March 1978. *Address:* 125 Ditchling Road, Brighton, Sussex BN1 4SE. *T:* (01273) 697882.

HANSON, David George; MP (Lab) Delyn, since 1992; *b* 5 July 1957; *s* of Brian George Hanson and Glenda Doreen (*née* Jones); *m* 1986, Margaret Rose Mitchell; one *s* two *d*. *Educ:* Verdin Comprehensive, Winsford, Ches.; Hull Univ. (BA Hons, PGCE). Vice-Pres., Hull Univ. Students' Union, 1978–79. Management trainee, Co-op. Union/Plymouth Co-op. Soc., 1980–82; with Spastics Soc., 1982–89; Dir, RE-SOLV (Soc. for Prevention of Solvent Abuse), 1989–92. Councillor: Vale Royal BC, 1983–91 (Leader, Lab Gp, 1989–91); Northwich Town Council, 1987–91. Contested (Lab): Eddisbury, 1983; Delyn, 1987; Cheshire W (European Parlt), 1984. PPS to Chief Sec. to HM Treasury, 1997–98; an Asst Govt Whip, 1998–99; Parly Under-Sec. of State, Wales Office, 1999–2001; PPS to the Prime Minister, 2001–. *Recreations:* football, family, cinema. *Address:* House of Commons, SW1A 0AA. *T:* (020) 7219 5064; (constituency office) 64 Chester Street, Flint, Clwyd CH6 5DH. *T:* (01352) 763159.

HANSON, Derrick George; financial consultant; writer, director of companies; Chairman: Moneyguide Ltd, since 1978; Albany Investment Trust plc, since 2000 (Director, since 1980); Barrister; *b* 9 Feb. 1927; *s* of late John Henry Hanson and of Frances Elsie Hanson; *m* 1st, 1951, Daphne Elizabeth (*née* Marks) (*d* 1971); one *s* two *d*; 2nd, 1974, Hazel Mary (*née* Buckley) (*d* 1984); 3rd, 1986, Patricia (*née* Skillicorn). *Educ:* Waterloo Grammar Sch.; London Univ. (LLB (Hons)); Liverpool Univ. (LLM); Lancaster Univ. (MPhil). Called to Bar, Lincoln's Inn, 1952. Joined Martins Bank Ltd, 1943; Chief Trustee Manager, Martins Bank Ltd, 1963; Dir and Gen. Manager, Martins Bank Trust Co. Ltd, 1968; Dir and Gen. Manager, Barclays Bank Trust Co. Ltd, 1969–76; Chairman: Barclays Unicorn Ltd, 1972–76; Barclays Life Assce Co. Ltd, 1972–76; City of London & European Property Co. Ltd, 1980–86; Key Fund Managers Ltd, 1984–87; Birmingham Midshires Bldg Soc., 1988–90 (Dir, 1982–90); British Leather Co. Ltd, 1993–94 (Dir, 1983–94); A. C. Morrell Employees' Trust, 1983–95; Director: Barclaytrust Property Management Ltd, 1971–76; Barclays Bank plc, Manchester Bd, 1976–77; Toye & Co. plc, 1981–92; James Beattie PLC, 1984–97; Sen. Adviser (UK), Manufacturers Hanover Trust Co., 1977–79; Adviser, Phillips Gp, Fine Art Auctioneers, 1977–82. Assessor, Cameron Tribunal, 1962; Dir, Oxford Univ. Business Summer Sch., 1971. Chm., Southport and Formby DHA, 1986–89; Member: NW Industrialists' Council, 1977–83; South Sefton Health Authority, 1979–82; Mersey RHA, 1982–86. Pres., Assoc. of Banking Teachers, 1979–88. Mem. Council, Liverpool Univ., 1980–84; Chm., Christian Arts Trust, 1980–86, 1997–. Mem., NW Regl Cttee, NT, 1990–96. Hon. FCIB 1987. Hon. Fellow, City Univ., 1977–86. *Publications:* Within These Walls: a century of Methodism in Formby, 1974; Service Banking, 1979; Moneyguide: The Handbook of Personal Finance, 1981; Dictionary of Banking and Finance, 1985; God and the Profits, 1999. *Recreations:* golf, gardening, hill-walking. *Address:* Tower House, Grange Lane, Formby, Merseyside L37 7BR. *Clubs:* Royal Automobile; Formby Golf (Formby, Lancs).

HANSON, James Donald; Chairman, Northern Leisure plc, since 1999; *b* 4 Jan. 1935; *s* of late Mary and Leslie Hanson; *m* 1st, 1959, Patricia Margaret Talent (marr. diss. 1977); two *s*; 2nd, 1978, Anne Barbara Asquith. *Educ:* Heath Grammar School, Halifax. ACA 1956, FCA 1966. Joined Arthur Andersen & Co., Chartered Accountants, 1958; established north west practice, 1966, Managing Partner, North West, 1968–82; Sen. Partner, UK, 1982–89; Man. Partner, Strategic Affairs and Communications, Andersen Worldwide, 1989–97. Member: Internat. Operating Cttee, 1982–97; Internat. Board of Partners, 1985–97; Manchester Soc. of Chartered Accountants, 1967–81 (Pres., 1979); Council, CBI, 1982–97. Mem., Council and Court, Manchester Univ., 1982–; Chm., Manchester Univ. Superannuation Scheme. *Recreations:* ski-ing, tennis. *Address:* 18 Thurloe Place, SW7 2SP. *T:* (020) 7814 7776.

HANSON, Sir John (Gilbert), KCMG 1995; CBE 1979; Warden, Green College, Oxford, since 1998; *b* 16 Nov. 1938; *s* of Gilbert Fretwell Hanson and Gladys Margaret (*née* Kay); *m* 1962, Margaret Clark; three *s*. *Educ:* Manchester Grammar Sch.; Wadham Coll., Oxford (BA Lit. Hum. 1961, MA 1964; Hon. Fellow, 1997). Asst Principal, WO, 1961–63; British Council: Madras, India, 1963–66; ME Centre for Arab Studies, Lebanon, 1966–68; Rep., Bahrain, 1968–72; Dep. Controller, Educn and Science Div., 1972–75; Representative, Iran, and Counsellor (Cultural) British Embassy, Tehran, 1975–79; Controller, Finance Div., 1979–82; RCDS, 1983; Head, British Council Div. and Minister (Cultural Affairs), British High Commn, New Delhi, 1984–88; Dep. Dir-Gen., 1988–92; Dir-Gen., 1992–98. Patron, GAP, 1989–98. Member: Franco-British Council, 1992–98; UK-Japan 2000 Gp, 1993–98; Council, VSO, 1993–98; Chm., Bahrain-British Foundn, 1997–. Pres., British Skin Foundn, 1997–. Member Governing Council: Soc. for S Asian Studies, 1989–93; SOAS, 1991–99; Univ. of London, 1996–99. Trustee, Charles Wallace (India) Trust, 1998–2000. FRSA 1993; CIMgt 1993. Hon. Fellow, St Edmund's Coll., Cambridge, 1998. Hon. DLitt Oxford Brookes, 1995; Hon. Dr: Humberside, 1996; Greenwich, 1996. *Recreations:* books, music, sport, travel. *Address:* Warden's Lodgings, Green College, Oxford OX2 6HG. *Clubs:* Athenæum, MCC; Gymkhana (Madras).

HANSON, Neil; Under Secretary, and Controller, Newcastle upon Tyne Central Office, Department of Health and Social Security, 1981–83; *b* 21 March 1923; *s* of late Reginald William Hanson and Lillian Hanson (*née* Benson); *m* 1st, 1950, Eileen Ashworth (*d* 1976); two *s*; 2nd, 1977, Margaret Brown-Smelt. *Educ:* City of Leeds Sch. Served War, 1942–46, N Africa, Sicily, Italy. Jun. Clerk, Leeds Social Welfare Cttee, 1939; Clerical Officer, 1948–50, Exec. Officer, 1950–56, Nat. Assistance Bd; Manager, Suez and Hungarian Refugee Hostels, 1956–59; Higher Exec. Officer, 1959–62, Sen. Exec. Officer, 1963–66, Nat. Assistance Bd; Principal, Min. of Social Security, 1967–73; Sen. Principal, 1973–76, Asst Sec., 1976–80, DHSS. *Recreations:* bowls, bridge, music, walking. *Address:* 4 Woodbourne, Leeds LS8 2JW. *T:* (0113) 265 3452.

HANSON, Sir Rupert; *see* Hanson, Sir C. R. P.

HANWORTH, 3rd Viscount *cr* 1936, of Hanworth, co. Middlesex; **David Stephen Geoffrey Pollock;** Bt 1922; Baron Hanworth 1926; Reader in Econometrics, Queen Mary and Westfield College, University of London, since 1992; *b* 16 Feb. 1946; *er s* of 2nd Viscount Hanworth and of Isolda Rosamond, *yr d* of Geoffrey Parker; *S* father, 1996; *m* 1968, Elizabeth Liberty, *e d* of Lawrence Vambe, MBE; two *d*. *Educ:* Wellington Coll.; Guildford Tech. Coll.; Sussex Univ. (BA); Univ. of Southampton (MSc); Univ. of Amsterdam (DEcon). Lectr, Dept of Economics, QMC, later QMW, 1971–92. *Heir: b* Hon. Richard Charles Standish Pollock [*b* 6 Feb. 1951; *m* 1982, Annette Louise, *d* of Peter Lockhart; twin *s*].

HAPGOOD, Mark Bernard; QC 1994; *b* 2 April 1951; *m* 1978, Linda Fieldsend; two *d*. *Educ:* Nottingham Univ. (LLB). Called to the Bar, Gray's Inn, 1979. *Publications:* (ed) Paget's Law of Banking, 10th edn, 1989, 11th edn, 1996; (contrib.) Halsbury's Laws of England, vol. 3 (1): Banking, reissue, 1989; Bills of Exchange, vol. 4 (1), reissue, 1992. *Recreations:* running, roller-skating, 16th/17th century financial documents. *Address:* Brick Court Chambers, 7–8 Essex Street, WC2R 3LD. *Clubs:* St Enedoc Golf; Rock Sailing.

HARARE (formerly SALISBURY), Archbishop of, (RC), since 1976; **Most Rev. Patrick Fani Chakaipa;** *b* 25 June 1932; *s* of Chakaipa and Chokutaura. *Educ:* Chishawasha Minor and Regional Major Seminary, nr Harare; Kutama Teachers' Coll. Ecclesiastic qualifications in Philosophy and Theology; Teacher Training Cert. Asst priest, Makumbi Mission, 1967–69; Priest-in-Charge, All Souls Mission, Mutoko, 1969–73; Episcopal Vicar, Mutoko-Mrewa Area, 1970–73; Auxiliary Bishop of Salisbury, 1973–76. Pres., Inter-Regl Meeting of Bishops of Southern Africa, 1992–95. Chancellor, Catholic Univ. in Zimbabwe, 1998–. *Publications:* Karikoga, 1958; Pfumo reRopa, 1961; Rudo Ibofu, 1961; Garandichauya, 1963; Dzasukwa, 1967. *Recreation:* chess. *Address:* PO Box Cy 330, Causeway, Harare, Zimbabwe. *T:* 792125.

HARBERTON, 10th Viscount *cr* 1791; **Thomas de Vautort Pomeroy;** Baron Harberton 1783; *b* 19 Oct. 1910; *s* of 8th Viscount Harberton, OBE, and Mary Katherine (*d* 1971), *d* of A. W. Leatham; *S* brother, 1980; *m* 1978, Vilma (*d* 2000), *widow* of Sir Alfred Butt, 1st Bt. *Educ:* Eton. Joined Welsh Guards, 1932; transferred to RAOC, 1939; served BEF, then in India; retired, 1952. *Heir: nephew* Henry Robert Pomeroy [*b* 23 April 1958; *m* 1990, Caroline Mary, *d* of Jeremy Grindle; two *s*]. *Club:* Cavalry and Guards.

HARBIDGE, Ven. Adrian Guy; Archdeacon of Bournemouth, since 2000; *b* 10 Nov. 1948; *s* of John and Pat Harbidge; *m* 1975, Bridget West-Watson; one *s* one *d*. *Educ:* Marling Sch., Stroud; St John's Coll., Durham (BA); Cuddesdon Coll., Oxford. Purser, Mercantile Marine, 1970–73. Deacon 1975, priest 1976; Curate, Romsey Abbey, 1975–80; Vicar: St Andrew's, Bennett Road, Bournemouth, 1980–86; Chandler's Ford, 1986–99; RD of Eastleigh, 1993–99; Archdeacon of Winchester, 1999–2000. Hon. Canon, St Peter's Cathedral, Tororo, Uganda, 2000. *Publication:* Those whom DDO hath joined together . . . . . , 1996. *Recreations:* landscape gardening, walking, raising the Titanic. *Address:* Glebe House, 22 Bellflower Way, Chandler's Ford, Hants SO53 4HN. *T:* (02380) 260955.

HARBISON, Dr Samuel Alexander, CB 1998; HM Chief Inspector of Nuclear Installations, Health and Safety Executive, 1991–98; *b* 9 May 1941; *s* of Adam Harbison and Maude Harbison (*née* Adams); *m* 1st, 1964, Joyce Margaret Buick (marr. diss. 1991); three *d*; 2nd, 1991, Margaret Gail (*née* Vale). *Educ:* Queen's Univ., Belfast (Hons BSc); Univ. of California, Los Angeles (MSc); Univ. of London (PhD). Reactor Physicist, UKAEA, Windscale, 1962–64; Research and Teaching Asst, UCLA, 1964–66; Research at Rutherford High Energy Lab., Harwell, 1966–69; Sen. Lectr, Royal Naval Coll., Greenwich, 1969–74; Nuclear Installations Inspectorate, HSE, 1974–98. Chm., Defence Nuclear Safety Cttee, 2001–. *Publications:* An Introduction to Radiation Protection (with A. Martin), 1972, 4th edn 1996; numerous sci. and tech. papers in learned jls. *Recreations:* gardening, music, walking. *Address:* 41 New Road, Meopham, Kent DA13 0LS.

HARBISON, Air Vice-Marshal William, CB 1977; CBE 1965; AFC 1956; RAF, retired; Vice-President, British Aerospace Inc., Washington, DC, 1979–92; *b* 11 April 1922; *s* of W. Harbison; *m* 1950, Helen, *d* of late William B. Geneva, Bloomington, Illinois; two *s*. *Educ:* Ballymena Academy, N Ireland. Joined RAF, 1941; 118 Sqdn Fighter Comd, 1943–46; 263, 257 and 64 Sqdns, 1946–48; Exchange Officer with 1st Fighter Group USAF, 1948–50; Central Fighter Estabt, 1950–51; 4th Fighter Group USAF, Korea, 1952; 2nd ATAF Germany: comd No 67 Sqdn, 1952–55; HQ No 2 Group, 1955; psc 1956; Air Min. and All Weather OCU, 1957; comd No 29 All Weather Sqdn Fighter Comd, Acklington and Leuchars, 1958–59; British Defence Staffs, Washington, 1959–62; jssc 1962; comd RAF Leuchars Fighter Comd, 1963–65; ndc 1965–66; Gp Capt. Ops: HQ Fighter Comd, 1967–68; No 11 Group Strike Comd, 1968; Dir of Control (Ops), NATCS, 1968–72; Comdr RAF Staff, and Air Attaché, Washington, 1972–75; AOC 11 Group, RAF, 1975–77. *Recreations:* flying, motoring. *Address:* 3292 Annandale Road, Falls Church, VA 22042, USA.

HARBORD-HAMOND, family name of **Baron Suffield**.

HARBORNE, Prof. Jeffrey Barry, PhD, DSc; FRS 1995; Emeritus Professor of Botany, University of Reading, since 1993; *b* 1 Sept. 1928; *s* of late Frank Percy Harborne, Bristol, and Phyllis Maud (*née* Sherriff); *m* 1953, Jean Charlotte, *d* of late Dr John Buchanan; two *s*. *Educ:* Wycliffe Coll., Stonehouse, Glos; Univ. of Bristol (BSc; PhD 1953; DSc 1966). Biochemist, John Innes Inst., 1955–65; Res. Fellow, Univ. of Liverpool, 1965–68; University of Reading: Reader, 1968–76; Prof. of Botany, 1976–93. Visiting Professor: Univ. of Texas, 1976; Univ. of Calif, 1977; Plenary Lectr, IUPAC Nat. Prods Symposium, 1976. Editor-in-Chief, Jl Phytochemistry, 1972–98. Member: RSC, 1956; Biochemical Soc., 1957. FLS 1986; FIBiol 1994. Gold Medal in Botany, Linnean Soc., 1985; Silver Medal: Phytochemical Soc. of Europe, 1986; Internat. Soc. of Chemical Ecology, 1993. *Publications:* Biochemistry of Phenolic Compounds, 1964; Comparative Biochemistry of the Flavonoids, 1967; Phytochemical Phylogeny, 1970; Phytochemical Ecology, 1972; Phytochemical Methods, 1973, 3rd edn 1998; Introduction to Ecological Biochemistry, 1977, 4th edn 1993; Phytochemical Aspects of Plant and Animal Coevolution, 1978; Plant Chemosystematics, 1984; Phytochemical Dictionary, 1993, 2nd edn 1999; The Flavonoids: advances in research since 1986, 1994; Dictionary of Plant Toxins, 1996. *Recreations:* rambling, classical music. *Address:* Department of Botany, Plant Science Laboratories, University of Reading, Reading RG6 6AS. *T:* (0118) 931 8162.

HARBORNE, Peter Gale; HM Diplomatic Service; High Commissioner, Trinidad and Tobago, since 1999; *b* 29 June 1945; *s* of late Leslie Herbert and Marie Mildred Edith Harborne; *m* 1976, Tessa Elizabeth Henri; two *s*. *Educ:* King Edward's Sch., Birmingham; Birmingham Univ. (BCom). Dept of Health, 1966–72; FCO, 1972–74; 1st Sec., Ottawa, 1974–75; 1st Sec. Commercial, Mexico City, 1975–78; Lloyd's Bank Internat., 1979–81; FCO, 1981–83; Head of Chancery, Helsinki, 1983–87; Dep. Head of Mission, Budapest, 1988–91; Counsellor, FCO, 1991–95; Ambassador, Slovak Republic, 1995–98.

Recreations: watching cricket, playing tennis, the arts, cross-country ski-ing. *Address:* c/o Foreign and Commonwealth Office, King Charles Street, SW1A 2AH. *Club:* MCC.

HARBOTTLE, Rev. Anthony Hall Harrison, LVO 1979; Priest-in-charge of East Dean with Friston and Jevington, 1995–96 (Rector, 1981–95); Chaplain to the Queen, 1968–95; *b* 3 Sept. 1925; *y s* of Alfred Charles Harbottle, ARIBA, and Ellen Muriel, *o d* of William Popham Harrison; *m* 1955, Gillian Mary, *o d* of Hugh Goodenough; three *s* one *d*. *Educ:* Sherborne Sch.; Christ's Coll., Cambridge (MA); Wycliffe Hall, Oxford. Served War in Royal Marines, 1944–46. Deacon 1952, priest 1953; Asst Curacies: Boxley, 1952–54; St Peter-in-Thanet, 1954–60; Rector of Sandhurst with Newenden, 1960–68; Chaplain of the Royal Chapel, Windsor Great Park, 1968–81. Founder Mem., Kent Trust for Nature Conservation, 1954; Mem., Green Alliance, 1984. County Chaplain, Royal British Legion (Sussex), 1982–2002. Special Life Mem., British Entomol and Natural Hist. Soc., 1998. FRES 1971. *Publications:* contribs to entomological jls, on lepidoptera. *Recreations:* butterflies and moths, nature conservancy, entomology, ornithology, philately, coins, Treasury and bank notes, painting, cooking, lobstering. *Address:* 44 Summerdown Road, Eastbourne BN20 8DQ.

HARBOTTLE, (George) Laurence; Consultant, Harbottle & Lewis, Solicitors (Senior Partner, 1955–95); *b* 11 April 1924; *s* of George Harbottle and Winifred Ellen Benson Harbottle. *Educ:* The Leys Sch., Cambridge; Emmanuel Coll., Cambridge (MA). Solicitor 1952. Served War: commnd RA, 1942; Burma and India; Temp. Captain; Adjt 9th Fd Regt, 1945–47. Theatre Companies: Chairman: Theatre Centre, 1959–88; Prospect, 1966–77; Royal Exchange (69), 1968–83; Cambridge, 1969–92; Director: The Watermill, 1970–75; The Bush (Alternative), 1975–77. Arts Council: Mem., 1976–77–78; Mem., Drama Panel, 1974–78; Chairman: Housing the Arts, 1977–78; Trng Cttee, 1977–78; Chm. of Govs, Central Sch. of Speech and Drama, 1982–99 (Vice Chm., 1977–82); Chm., ICA, 1986–90 (Dep. Chm., 1977–86). Hon. Solicitor: Soc. for Theatre Res.; Nat. Council for Drama Trng. Pres., Theatrical Management Assoc., 1979–85 (Hon. Vice-Pres., 1992–); Vice-President: Music Users Council, 1985–; Theatres Adv. Council, 1986–88; Theatres Nat. Cttee, 1986–91. Member: Justice Cttee on Privacy, 1970; Theatres Trust, 1980–99 (Chm., 1992–99). Gov., City Literary Inst., 1990–94; Trustee: Equity Trust Fund, 1989–94; Olivier Foundn, 1990–; Peggy Ramsay Foundn, 1992–. *Recreations:* works of art, gardening, tennis. *Address:* c/o Harbottle & Lewis, Hanover House, 14 Hanover Square, W1R 0BE. *Club:* Savile.

HARBOUR, Malcolm; Member (C) West Midlands, European Parliament, since 1999; *b* 19 Feb. 1947; *s* of John and Bobby Harbour; *m* 1969, Penny Johnson; two *d*. *Educ:* Bedford Sch.; Trinity Coll., Cambridge (MA Mech Eng); Aston Univ. Business Sch. (Dip. Mgt Studies). CEng, MIMechE, 1975; FIMI 1984. Engr Apprentice, BMC Longbridge, 1967–69; Design and Develt Engr, BMC, 1969–72; Product Planning Manager, Rover-Triumph, 1972–76; Project Manager, Medium Cars, BL Cars, 1976–80; Austin-Rover: Director: Business Planning, 1980–82; Mkting, 1982–84; Sales, UK and Ireland, 1984–86; Overseas Sales, 1986–89; Founder Partner, Harbour Wade Brown, motor industry consultants, 1989–99; Founder Dir, Internat. Car Distrib. Prog., 1993–; Project Dir, 3 Day Car Prog., 1998–99. European Parliament: Cons. spokesman on internal market, 1999–; Member: Cttee for legal affairs and internal market, 1999–; Cttee for industry, external trade, res. and energy, 1999–; Cons. Delegn Bureau, 1999–; Delegn to Japan, 1999. Rapporteur, Eur. Commn Reform, 2000. *Publications:* reports on the car industry for DTI, OECD, etc. *Recreations:* choral singing, motor sport, travel, cooking. *Address:* Manor Cottage, Manor Road, Solihull, W Midlands B91 2BL. *T:* (0121) 711 3158; European Parliament, Rue Wiertz, 1047 Brussels, Belgium. *T:* (2) 2845132; *e-mail:* mharbour@europarl.eu.int.

HARCOURT; *see* Vernon-Harcourt, family name of Baron Vernon.

HARCOURT, Prof. Geoffrey Colin, AO 1994; PhD, LittD; FASSA; Fellow and College Lecturer in Economics, Jesus College, Cambridge, 1982–98, now Emeritus Fellow (President, 1988–89 and 1990–92); Reader (*ad hominem*) in the History of Economic Theory, Cambridge University, 1990–98, now Emeritus; *b* 27 June 1931; *s* of Kenneth Kopel Harcourt and Marjorie Rahel (*neé* Gans); *m* 1955, Joan Margaret Bartrop; two *s* two *d*. *Educ:* Malvern Grammar Sch.; Wesley Coll., Melbourne; Queen's Coll., Univ. of Melbourne (BCom (Hons) 1954; MCom 1956; Hon. Fellow, 1998); King's Coll., Cambridge. PhD 1960, LittD 1988, Cantab. University of Adelaide: Lectr in Econs, 1958–62; Sen. Lectr, 1963–65; Reader, 1965–67; Prof. of Econs (Personal Chair), 1967–85, Prof. Emeritus 1988; Cambridge University: Lectr in Econs and Politics, 1964–66, 1982–90; Fellow and Dir of Studies in Econs, Trinity Hall, 1964–66. Leverhulme Exchange Fellow, Keio Univ., Tokyo, 1969–70; Visiting Fellow: Clare Hall, Cambridge, 1972–73; ANU, 1997; Vis. Prof., Scarborough Coll., Univ. of Toronto, 1977, 1980; Hon. Prof., Univ. of NSW, 1997, 1999. Howard League for Penal Reform, SA Branch: Sec., 1959–63; Vice-Pres., 1967–74; Pres., 1974–80. Mem., Exec. Cttee, Campaign for Peace in Vietnam, 1967–75 (Chm., 1970–72). Mem., Aust. Labor Party Nat. Cttee of Enquiry, 1978–79. Pres., Econ. Soc. of Aust. and NZ, 1974–77; Mem. Council, Roy. Econ. Soc., 1990–95. FASSA 1971 (Exec. Cttee Mem., 1974–77). Lectures: Wellington-Burnham, Tufts Univ., USA, 1975; Edward Shann Meml, Univ. of WA, 1975; Newcastle, in Pol Economy, Univ. of Newcastle, NSW, 1977; Academy, Acad. of Social Scis in Aust., 1978; G. L. Wood Meml, Univ. of Melbourne, 1982; John Curtin Meml, ANU, 1982; Special Lectr in Econs, Manchester Univ., 1983–84; Nobel Conf., Minnesota, USA, 1986; Laws, Univ. of Tennessee at Knoxville, USA, 1991; Second Donald Horne Address, Melbourne, 1992; Sir Halford Cook, Queen's Coll., Melbourne, 1995; Kingsley Martin Meml, Cambridge, 1996; Annual Colin Clark, Univ. of Qld, 1997. Distinguished Fellow, Economic Soc. of Australia, 1996. Hon. LittD De Montfort, 1997. *Publications:* (with P. H. Karmel and R. H. Wallace) Economic Activity, 1967 (trans. Italian, 1969); (ed jtly) Readings in the Concept and Measurement of Income, 1969, 2nd edn 1986; (ed with N. F. Laing) Capital and Growth: Selected Readings, 1971 (trans. Spanish, 1977); Some Cambridge Controversies in the Theory of Capital, 1972 (trans. Italian, 1973, Polish and Spanish, 1975, Japanese 1980); Theoretical Controversy and Social Significance: an evaluation of the Cambridge controversies (Edward Shann Meml Lecture), 1975; (ed) The Microeconomic Foundations of Macroeconomics, 1977; The Social Science Imperialists: selected essays (ed Prue Kerr), 1982; (ed) Keynes and his Contemporaries, 1985; (ed with Jon Cohen) International Monetary Problems and Supply-Side Economics: Essays in Honour of Lorie Tarshis, 1986; Controversies in Political Economy (selected essays, ed O. F. Hamouda), 1986; On Political Economists and Modern Political Economy (selected essays, ed C. Sardoni), 1992; Markets, Madness and a Middle Way (Second Annual Donald Horne Address), 1992; Post-Keynesian Essays in Biography: portraits of Twentieth Century political economists, 1993; (ed jtly) The Dynamics of the Wealth of Nations, Growth, Distribution and Structural Change: essays in honour of Luigi Pasinetti, 1993; (ed jtly) Income and Employment in Theory and Practice, 1994; Capitalism, Socialism and Post-Keynesianism: selected essays, 1995; (ed with P. A. Riach) A 'Second Edition' of The General Theory, 2 vols, 1997; 50 Years a Keynesian and other essays, 2001; Selected Essays on Economic Policy, 2001; many articles in learned jls and chapters in edited books. *Recreations:* cricket, Australian rules football, running (not jogging), bike riding, reading, politics. *Address:* Jesus College, Cambridge CB5 8BL. *T:* (01223) 339436; 43 New Square, Cambridge CB1 1EZ. *T:* (01223) 360833. *Clubs:* Melbourne Cricket, South Australian Cricket Association.

HARCOURT, Geoffrey David, RDI 1978; DesRCA, FCSD; freelance consultant designer, since 1962; *b* 9 Aug. 1935; *s* of William and Barbara Harcourt; *m* 1965, Jean Mary Vaughan Pryce-Jones; one *s* one *d*. *Educ:* High Wycombe Sch. of Art; Royal Coll. of Art; DesRCA, Silver Medal 1960. FSIAD 1968. Designer: Latham, Tyler, Jensen, Chicago, 1960–61; Jacob Jensen, Copenhagen, 1961; Andrew Pegram Ltd, London, 1961–62; consultant, Artifort, Holland, 1962–95 (domestic and business furniture designer; models still in prodn include chaise longue, 1970 and Michigan chair, 1978); two chairs submitted for DesRCA diploma, 1960, in commercial prodn, 2001. Visiting Lecturer: High Wycombe Coll. of Art and Design, 1963–74; Leicester Polytechnic, 1982–93; Ext. Assessor for BA Hons degrees, Kingston Polytechnic, 1974–77, Loughborough Coll. of Art and Design, 1978–81, Belfast Polytechnic, 1977–81 and Buckinghamshire Coll. of Higher Educn, 1982–85; Ext. Examnr, RCA, 1996–98. Chair design for Artifort awarded first prize for creativity, Brussels, 1978; Member: Design Awards Cttee, Design Council, 1979–80; Furniture Design Wkg Party, EDC, 1986–87; Chm., RSA Bursaries Cttee (Furniture Design Section, 1982–86, Ceramics Section, 1989–91, Woven Textiles, 1992–94, Footwear, 1996–97); approved consultant, Design Council 'Support for Design' initiative. Work exhibited: permanent collection, Steidlijk Mus., Amsterdam, 1967; Prague Mus. of Decorative Arts, 1972; Science Mus., London, 1972; Design Council, London and Glasgow, 1976 and 1981; Eye for Industry Exhibn, V&A, 1987; Nederlands Textielmuseum, 1988; Manchester Prize exhibn, City Art Gall., 1988; St George's Hall, Windsor Exhibn, Architecture Foundn, London, 1993; RCA Centennial Exhibn, 1996. Chm., Adv. Panel to Lord Lieutenant of Oxfordshire, 1998–2000. FRSA 1979. Freeman, City of London; Liveryman, Worshipful Co. of Furniture Makers (Chm., Design Awards Cttee, 1994–97). JP Thame and Henley, 1981–2000 (Chm., Youth Court Panel, 1993–95; Chm. Bench, 1996–98). *Recreations:* making things, cooking, golf. *Address:* The Old Vicarage, Benson, Oxfordshire OX10 6SF. *Club:* Goring and Streatley Golf.

HARCOURT, Michael Franklin; Senior Associate, Sustainable Development Research Institute, University of British Columbia, since 1996; Premier of British Columbia, 1991–96; *b* Edmonton, Alta, 6 Jan. 1943; *e s* of Frank and Stella Louise Harcourt; *m* 1971, Beckie Salo; one *s*. *Educ:* Sir Winston Churchill High Sch., Vancouver; University of British Columbia (LLB 1968). Lawyer, Vancouver, 1968–72. Alderman, 1972–80, Mayor, 1980–86, City of Vancouver. MLA (NDP) Vancouver Centre, 1986–91, Vancouver-Mt Pleasant, 1991–96; Leader of the Opposition, BC, 1987–92. *Recreations:* tennis, golf, ski-ing, watching basketball and football. *Address:* 4707 Trafalgar Street, Vancouver, BC V6L 2M8, Canada.

HARCOURT-SMITH, Air Chief Marshal Sir David, GBE 1989; KCB 1984; DFC 1957; aviation consultant; Chairman, Chelworth Defence Ltd, since 1991; Controller Aircraft, Ministry of Defence, Procurement Executive, 1986–89, retired; *b* 14 Oct. 1931; *s* of late Air Vice-Marshal G. Harcourt-Smith, CB, CBE, MVO, and of M. Harcourt-Smith; *m* 1957, Mary (*née* Entwistle); two *s* one *d*. *Educ:* Felsted Sch.; RAF College. Commnd 1952; flying appts with Nos 11, 8 and 54 Squadrons; Staff Coll., 1962; OC No 54 Squadron, 1963–65; PSO to AOC-in-C, Tech. Training Comd, 1965–67; Defence Planning Staff, 1967–68; OC No 6 Squadron, 1969–70; Central Tactics and Trials Organisation, 1970–72; OC RAF Brüggen, 1972–74; Dir of Op. Requirements, 1974–76; RCDS, 1977; Comdt, RAF Coll., Cranwell, 1978–80; Asst Chief of Air Staff (Op. Reqs), 1980–84; AOC-in-C, RAF Support Command, 1984–85. Dir, DESC, 1991–. Gov., Downe House, 1993–. *Recreations:* walking, golf. *Address:* c/o Barclays Bank, 13 High Street, Shaftesbury, Dorset SP7 8JD. *Club:* Royal Air Force.

HARDAKER, Rev. Canon Ian Alexander; Clergy Appointments Adviser, 1985–98; Chaplain to the Queen, 1994–May 2002; *b* 14 May 1932; *s* of Joseph Alexander Hardaker and Edna Mary (*née* Theede); *m* 1963, Susan Mary Wade Bottom; two *s* two *d*. *Educ:* Kingston Grammar Sch.; Royal Military Acad., Sandhurst; King's Coll., London (BD, AKC). Commnd East Surrey Regt, 1952. Curate, Beckenham Parish Ch., 1960–65; Vicar of Eynsford and Rector of Lullingstone, 1965–70; Vicar of St Stephen's, Chatham, 1970–85; Rural Dean of Rochester, 1978–85. St Augustine's Medal, 1998. *Recreations:* walking, photography, family, gardening. *Address:* The Old Post Office, Huish Champflower, Wiveliscombe, Taunton, Somerset TA4 2EY. *Club:* Royal Commonwealth Society.

HARDCASTLE, Sir Alan (John), Kt 1992; FCA; Chairman, Board of Banking Supervision, since 1998 (Member, since 1986); Chief Accountancy Adviser to HM Treasury and Head of Government Accountancy Service, 1989–93; *b* 10 Aug. 1933; *s* of late William and of Catherine Hardcastle; *m* 1st, 1958, Dinah (*née* Beattie) (marr. diss. 1983); two *s*; 2nd, 1983, Ione Marguerite (*née* Cooney); two step *d*. *Educ:* Haileybury Coll. Articled to B. W. Brixey, 1951–56; qualified, 1956; Nat. Service as Sub-Lieut RNVR, 1956–58. Joined Peat, Marwick, Mitchell & Co. (later Peat Marwick McLintock, then KPMG), 1958; Partner 1967; Gen. Partner 1972–88. DoT Inspector into affairs of St Piran Ltd (reported 1981). Non-exec. Dir, Chelsfield, 1994–. Inst. of Chartered Accountants in England and Wales: Mem. Council, 1974–94; Pres., 1983–85; Pres., Chartered Accountants Students' Soc. of London, 1976–80. Chm., Regulatory Bd and Dep. Chm. of Council, Lloyd's, 1993–97 (Mem. Council, 1987–88). Master, Co. of Chartered Accountants in England and Wales, 1978–79. Hon. Treas., Berkeley Square Charitable Trust; Trustee, Thalidomide Trust, 1997–. Life Gov. and Mem. Council, Haileybury Coll., 1995–; Chm. Govs, Lambrook Haileybury Sch., 1998–. Speaker and author of papers on accountancy topics. *Recreations:* music, theatre, fishing, the company of family and friends. *Address:* 53 Wynnstay Gardens, Allen Street, W8 6UU. *Clubs:* Athenæum, Naval.

HARDCASTLE, Prof. Jack Donald, CBE 1998; MChir (Cantab); FRCP, FRCS; Lead Clinician, Mid Trent Cancer Network, since 1998; Professor of Surgery, University of Nottingham, 1970–98, then Emeritus; *b* 3 April 1933; *s* of Albert Hardcastle and Bertha (*née* Ellison); *m* 1965, Rosemary Hay-Shunker; one *s* one *d*. *Educ:* St Bartholomew's Grammar Sch., Newbury; Emmanuel Coll., Cambridge (Senior Scholar 1954; BA, MA; Windsor Postgrad. Schol.); London Hospital (Open Scholarship 1955; MB, BChir, MChir (Distinction)). MRCP 1961; FRCS 1962; FRCP 1984. House Phys./Surg., Resident Accoucheur, London Hosp., 1959–60; Ho. Surg. to Prof. Aird, Hammersmith Postgraduate Hosp., 1961–62; London Hospital: Research Asst, 1962; Lectr in Surgery, 1963; Registrar in Surgery, 1964; Registrar in Surgery, Thoracic Unit, 1965; Sen. Registrar in Surgery, 1965; Sen. Registrar, St Mark's Hosp., London, 1968; Sen. Lectr in Surgery, London Hosp., 1968. Sir Arthur Sims Commonwealth Travelling Prof., RCS, 1985; Mayne Vis. Prof., Univ. of Brisbane, 1987. Member Council: RCS, 1987– (Dir, Raven Dept of Educn, 1994–; Vice-Pres., 1995–97); Med. Protection Soc., 1995–. Founder FMedSci 1998. Hon. FRCSGlas. *Publications:* Isolated Organ Perfusion (with H.

D. Ritchie), 1973; various scientific papers. *Recreations:* ski-ing, walking. *Address:* Goverton Heights, Goverton, Bleasby, Nottingham NG14 7FN. *T:* (01636) 830316.

HARDCASTLE, (Jesse) Leslie, OBE 1974; exhibition and museum consultant, since 1996; *b* 8 Dec. 1926; *s* of Francis Ernest Hardcastle and Dorothy Schofield; *m* 1968, Vivienne Mansel Richards; two *s*. *Educ:* St Joseph's College, Croydon. British Lion Film Productions, 1943–44; Royal Navy, 1944–47. British Film Inst., 1947–94; Telekinema Festival of Britain, 1951; London Film Fest. admin, 1958–91; Controller, NFT, 1968–91; Museum of the Moving Image: originator, 1981–88; Curator, 1988–94. Sec., Projected Picture Trust. Vice Pres., The Soho Soc.; Dep. Chm., Soho Housing Assoc. *Recreations:* community work, theatre, music, cinema. *Address:* 37c Great Pulteney Street, W1R 3DE.

HARDENBERGER, (Ulf) Håkan; musician; international trumpet soloist; *b* 27 Oct. 1961; *s* of Åke and Mona Hardenberger; *m* 1986, Heidi Thomassen; two *s*. *Educ:* Paris Conservatory. Hon. RAM 1992. *Address:* c/o Svensk Konsertdirektion AB, Box 5076, 412 68 Göteborg, Sweden.

HARDIE, family name of **Baron Hardie**.

HARDIE, Baron *cr* 1997 (Life Peer), of Blackford in the City of Edinburgh; **Andrew Rutherford Hardie;** PC 1997; a Senator of the College of Justice in Scotland and Lord of Session, since 2000; *b* 8 Jan. 1946; *s* of Andrew Rutherford Hardie and Elizabeth Currie Lowe; *m* 1971, Catherine Storrar Elgin; two *s* one *d*. *Educ:* St Mungo's Primary Sch., Alloa; St Modan's High Sch., Stirling; Edinburgh Univ. (MA, LLB Hons). Enrolled Solicitor, 1971; Mem., Faculty of Advocates, 1973; Advocate Depute, 1979–83; QC (Scot.) 1985; Lord Advocate, UK, 1997–99, Scotland, 1999–2000. Treasurer, 1989–94, Dean, 1994–97, Faculty of Advocates. Hon. Bencher, Lincoln's Inn, 1998. *Address:* 4 Oswald Road, Edinburgh EH9 2HF. *T:* (0131) 667 7542. *Clubs:* Caledonian, Murrayfield Golf (Edinburgh).

HARDIE, Dr Alexander, OBE 1990; Fellow and Bursar, Oriel College, Oxford, 2001; *b* 5 March 1947; *s* of Alexander Merrie Hardie and Phyllis A. I. Hardie; *m* 1971, Jillian Hester Rowlands; one *s* two *d*. *Educ:* Aberdeen Grammar Sch.; Bristol Grammar Sch.; Univ. of Edinburgh (MA); Corpus Christi Coll., Oxford (DPhil). Jun. Research Fellow, Univ. of Bristol, 1972–73; HM Diplomatic Service, 1973–2001: FCO, 1973–77; First Secretary: Budapest, 1977–78; Bucharest, 1979–81; FCO, 1981–86; Lusaka, 1986–90; FCO, 1990–93; Counsellor, Pretoria, 1993–97; FCO, 1997–2001. Hon. Res. Associate in Classics, Royal Holloway, London Univ., 1998–2001. *Publication:* Statius and the Silvae, 1983. *Recreations:* classical studies, golf. *Address:* Oriel College, Oxford OX1 4EW.

HARDIE, (Charles) Jeremy (Mawdesley), CBE 1983; Research Associate, Centre for Philosophy of Natural and Social Sciences, London School of Economics and Political Science, since 1999; Chairman, W. H. Smith Group, 1994–99 (Director, 1988–99; Deputy Chairman, 1992–94); *b* 9 June 1938; *s* of Sir Charles Hardie, CBE; *m* 1st, 1962, Susan Chamberlain (marr. diss. 1976); two *d* two *s*; 2nd, 1978, Xandra, Countess of Gowrie (marr. diss. 1994), *d* of late Col R. A. G. Bingley, CVO, DSO, OBE; one *d*; 3rd, 1994, Kirsteen Margaret Tait. *Educ:* Winchester Coll.; New Coll., Oxford (2nd Cl. Hon. Mods, 1st Cl. Lit. Hum.); Nuffield Coll., Oxford (BPhil Econs). ACA 1965, Peat, Marwick, Mitchell & Co.; Nuffield Coll., Oxford, 1966–67; Jun. Res. Fellow, Trinity Coll., Oxford, 1967–68; Fellow and Tutor in Econs, Keble Coll., Oxford, 1968–75 (Hon. Fellow, 1998). Partner, Dixon Wilson & Co., 1975–82. Chairman: Nat. Provident Instn, 1980–89 (Dir, 1972–89, Dep. Chm., 1977); Alexander Syndicate Management Ltd, 1982–95; Radio Broadland Ltd, 1983–85 (Dir, 1983–90); D. P. Mann Underwriting Agency Ltd, 1983–99; Loch Fyne Restaurants Ltd, 2000–. Director: Alexanders Discount Co. Ltd, 1978–87 (Dep. Chm., 1981–84; Chm., 1984–86); John Swire & Sons Ltd, 1982–98; Amdahl (UK) Ltd, 1983–86; Mercantile House Holdings Ltd, 1984–87; Additional Underwriting Agencies (No 3) Ltd, 1985–; Alexanders Laing & Cruickshank Gilts Ltd, 1986–87 (Chm., 1986); Northdoor Hldgs, 1989–93. Chm., Centre for Economic Policy Res., 1984–89; Treas., REconS, 1987–93; Dep. Chm., NAAFI, 1986–92 (Dir, 1981–). Member: Monopolies and Mergers Commn, 1976–83 (Dep. Chm., 1980–83); Council, Oxford Centre for Management Studies, 1978–85; Hammersmith Health Authority, 1982–83; Arts Council of GB, 1984–86; Peacock Cttee on Financing of BBC, 1985–86. Mem. Council, King's Coll., 1992– (Dep. Chm., 1997–). Contested Norwich South, (SDP) 1983, (SDP/Alliance) 1987. Trustee: Esmée Fairbairn Charitable Trust, 1972–; Butler Trust, 1985–87. *Recreations:* sailing, skiing. *Address:* 13 Ainger Road, NW3 3AR. *T:* (020) 7722 6916.

HARDIE, Brig. Donald David Graeme, TD 1968; JP; FIM; Lord-Lieutenant, Dunbartonshire (formerly Strathclyde Region, Districts of Dumbarton, Clydebank, Bearsden and Milngavie, Strathkelvin, Cumbernauld and Kilsyth), since 1990; Keeper of Dunbarton Castle, since 1996; Chairman, J. & G. Hardie & Co. Ltd, since 1999; *b* 23 Jan. 1936; *m* 1st, 1961, Rosalind Allan Ker (marr. diss. 1998); two *s*; 2nd, 1999, Sheena Roome. *Educ:* Larchfield, Blairmore and Merchiston Castle Schools. U.T.R. Management Trainee, 1956–59; F. W. Allen & Ker, 1960–61; J. & G. Hardie & Co., 1961–; Gilbert Plastics, 1973–76; Man. Dir, Hardie Mgt Consultants, 2001–; Director: Hardie Polymers, 1976–2001; Hardie Polymers (England), 1989–2001; Ronaash, 1988–2000; Preston Associates Ltd, 1999–; Lullaby Products Ltd, 1999–. Commissioned 41st Field Regt RA, 1955; Battery Comdr, 277 (Argyll & Sutherland Highlanders) Regt, RA TA, 1966; CO GSV OTC, 1973; TA Colonel: Lowlands, 1976; DES, 1980; Scotland, 1985; Hon. Colonel: Glasgow and Lanarks Bn, ACF, 1990–2000; 105 Air Defence Regt, RA(V), 1992–99; ACF Brig. Scotland, 1987; Chm., RA Council for Scotland, 1996–2001. President: Dunbartonshire Scouts, and Girl Guides, 1994–; Boys Bde, Argyll and Lennox, 1999–. Trustee, Tullochan Trust, 1996; Patron, Cornerstone, 1999–. Chieftain, Loch Lomond Games, 1996–. JP Dumbarton, 1990. KStJ 1996. *Recreations:* ski-ing, sailing, shooting, fishing. *Address:* Boturich, by Alexandria, Dunbartonshire G83 8LX. *T:* (01389) 830241. *Clubs:* Royal Scots (Edinburgh); Royal Northern and Clyde Yacht.

HARDIE, Sir Douglas (Fleming), Kt 1990; CBE 1979; JP; non-executive Chairman, DDS Medicines Research Ltd, since 1997; Chairman, Edward Parker & Co. Ltd, 1960–98 (Managing Director, 1960–90); *b* 26 May 1923; *s* of late James Dunbar Hardie, JP, and of Frances Mary (*née* Fleming); *m* 1945, Dorothy Alice Warner; two *s* one *d*. *Educ:* Arnhall & Seafield House Prep. Schs; Trinity Coll., Glenalmond, Perthshire. Trooper, 58 Trng Regt, RAC, Bovington, 1941; commnd RMA, Sandhurst, 1942; 1st Fife and Forfar Yeomanry, NW Europe, 1942–46 (despatches); demobilised rank of Major. Dir 1961–84, Chm. 1984–85, H. & A. Scott (Holdings) Ltd; Chairman: A. G. Scott (Textiles) Ltd, 1985–88; Grampian TV, 1989–93 (Dir, 1984–93); Director: Dayco Rubber (UK) Ltd, 1956–86; Clydesdale Bank, 1981–92; Alliance Trust, 1982–93; Second Alliance Trust, 1982–93. Dep. Chm., SDA, 1978–91. Chm., CBI Scotland, 1976–78; Bd Mem., N of Scotland Hydro Elec. Bd, 1977–83; Mem., Scottish Econ. Council, 1977–91; Vice Chm., Prince's Scottish Youth Business Trust, 1987–. Mem. Council, Winston Churchill Meml Trust, 1985–. Deacon Convener, Nine Incorporated Trades (Dundee), 1951–54. FRSA 1988; CIMgt (CBIM 1990). JP Dundee, 1970. Hon. LLD Dundee, 1992. *Recreations:* golf, fishing. *Address:* The Anchorage, 8 Bingham, Dundee DD4 7HH. *T:* (01382) 456772. *Clubs:* Caledonian; Royal & Ancient Golf (St Andrews); Blairgowrie Golf; Panmure Golf (Barry).

HARDIE, Jeremy; *see* Hardie, C. J. M.

HARDIE, Michael John, OBE 1989; HM Diplomatic Service, retired; *b* 14 July 1938; *s* of John Thomas Hardie and Annie Smethurst; *m* 1st, 1967, Patricia Louisa Hulme (marr. diss. 1986); two *s* one *d*; 2nd, 1990, Jean Fish; one step *s* one step *d*. *Educ:* St Ambrose Coll., Hale Barns, Cheshire; De La Salle Coll., Salford. HM Forces (Intelligence Corps), 1957–59; FO 1959; served Bahrain, Elisabethville, Bathurst, Sofia, Vienna, Munich and Cape Town, to 1979; First Secretary, 1979; BMG Berlin, 1979–81; Malta, 1981–83; FCO, 1983–86; Lagos, 1986–89; Counsellor, 1988; New Delhi, 1990–93; High Comr, Gambia, 1994–95. *Recreations:* golf, music. *Address:* 17 Dunham Lawn, Bradgate Road, Altrincham, Cheshire WA14 4QJ.

HARDIE, Miles Clayton, OBE 1988; Director General, International Hospital Federation, 1975–87; *b* 27 Feb. 1924; *s* of late Frederick Hardie and Estelle (*née* Clarke); *m* 1st, 1949, Pauline (marr. diss. 1974), *d* of late Sir Wilfrid Le Gros Clark, FRS; two *s*; 2nd, 1974, Melissa (marr. diss. 1984), *d* of late James Witcher, Houston, Texas; 3rd, 1985, Elizabeth, *d* of late Dudley Ash, *widow* of H. Spencer Smith. *Educ:* Charterhouse; Oriel Coll., Oxford (MA). Served War, RAF, 1943–46. Admin. Asst, Hosp. for Sick Children, London, 1949–51; Sec., Victoria Hosp. for Children, 1951–55; Sec., Bahrain Govt Med. Dept, 1956–58; joined staff of King Edward's Hosp. Fund for London, 1958, Dep. Dir, King's Fund Centre, 1963–66, Dir, 1966–75. Hon. Sec., British Hosps Export Council, later Assoc. of British Health-Care Industries, 1964–67, Mem. Council, 1967–75, 1987–; Mem. Council, Nat. Assoc. of Leagues of Hosp. Friends, 1970–75; Member: Adv. Council, Nat. Corp. Care of Old People, 1973–76; Council of Management, MIND/Nat. Assoc. for Mental Health, 1967–86; Man. Cttee of Spinal Injuries Assoc., 1975–79; Bd of Governors, Volunteer Centre, 1977–80; Council, Appropriate Health Resources and Technologies Action Gp, 1977–89. Adviser to WHO, 1978– (WHO Health for All by the year 2000 Medal, 1987). Hon. Member: Amer. Hosp. Assoc., 1983–; Polish Hosp. Assoc., 1985–. Mem., Ct of Assistants, Salters' Co., 1969–79. *Recreations:* gardening, walking. *Address:* Tallow Cottage, Fishers Lane, Charlbury, Oxford OX7 3RX. *T:* (01608) 810088.

See also P. R. Hardie.

HARDIE, Dr Philip Russell, FBA 2000; Reader in Latin Literature, University of Cambridge, since 1998; Fellow, New Hall, Cambridge, since 1990; *b* 13 July 1952; *s* of Miles Clayton Hardie, *qv* and Pauline Le Gros (*née* Clark); partner, Susan Elizabeth Griffith; two *s*. *Educ:* St Paul's Sch., London; Corpus Christi Coll., Oxford (MA); MPhil London; PhD Cantab 1990. Editl Asst, Oxford Dictionaries, 1977–80; P. S. Allen Jun. Res. Fellow, Corpus Christi Coll., Oxford, 1980–84; Guest Faculty appt in Classical Hist., Sarah Lawrence Coll., NY, 1984–85; Fellow and Coll. Lectr in Classics, Magdalene Coll., Cambridge, 1986–90. *Publications:* Virgil's Aeneid: cosmos and imperium, 1986; The Epic Successors of Virgil, 1993; (ed) Virgil Aeneid 9, 1994; Virgil, 1998. *Recreations:* walking, music. *Address:* New Hall, Cambridge CB3 0DF. *T:* (01223) 762100.

HARDIE BOYS, Rt Hon. Sir Michael, GNZM 1996; GCMG 1996; PC 1989; Governor General of New Zealand, 1996–2001; *b* Wellington, 6 Oct. 1931; *s* of Hon. Mr Justice Reginald Hardie Boys and Edith May (*née* Bennett); *m* 1957, Edith Mary Zohrab; two *s* two *d*. *Educ:* Wellington Coll.; Victoria Univ. (BA, LLB). Admitted Barrister and Solicitor, 1954; Partner, Scott Hardie Boys & Morrison, 1955–80; Chm., Legal Aid Bd, 1978–80; Judge of NZ High Court, 1980–89; Judge of the Court of Appeal, NZ, 1989–96. Pres., Wellington Dist Law Soc., 1979; Treas., NZ Law Soc., 1980. Hon. Bencher, Gray's Inn, 1994. Hon. Fellow, Wolfson Coll., Cambridge, 1995. Hon. LLD Victoria Univ. of Wellington, 1997. *Address:* 340A Ngarara Road, Kapiti Coast, New Zealand.

HARDING, family name of **Baron Harding of Petherton**.

HARDING OF PETHERTON, 2nd Baron *cr* 1958, of Nether Compton; **John Charles Harding;** farmer, 1968–90; *b* 12 Feb. 1928; *s* of Field Marshal 1st Baron Harding of Petherton, GCB, CBE, DSO, MC, and Mary Gertrude Mabel (*d* 1983), *er d* of late Joseph Wilson Rooke, JP; *S* father, 1989; *m* 1966, Harriet, *d* of Maj.-Gen. James Francis Hare, CB, DSO; two *s* one *d*. *Educ:* Marlborough College; Worcester Coll., Oxford (BA). National Service, 1945–48; 2nd Lieut, 11th Hussars (PAO), 1947; demobilised, 1948; Oxford Univ., 1948–51; Regular Commn, 11th Hussars (PAO), 1953; retired from Army, 1968. *Recreations:* hunting, racing. *Heir:* *s* Hon. William Allan John Harding [*b* 5 July 1969; *m* 2000, Susannah, *od* of Richard Ratcliff]. *Address:* Myrtle Cottage, Lamyatt, near Shepton Mallet, Somerset BA4 6NP. *T:* (01749) 812292.

HARDING, Prof. Anthony Filmer, PhD; FBA 2001; FSA; Professor of Archaeology, University of Durham, since 1990; *b* 20 Nov. 1946; *s* of Edward Filmer Harding and Enid (*née* Price); *m* 1976, Lesley Eleanor Forbes; two *s*. *Educ:* Corpus Christi Coll., Cambridge (MA, PhD 1973). FSA 1983. Lectr in Archaeol., 1973–88, Sen. Lectr, 1988–90, Univ. of Durham. *Publications:* (with J. M. Coles) The Bronze Age in Europe, 1979; The Mycenaeans and Europe, 1984; Henge Monuments and Related Sites of Great Britain, 1987; Die Schwerter im ehemaligen Jugoslawien, 1995; European Societies in the Bronze Age, 2000. *Recreations:* music, gardening, walking. *Address:* Department of Archaeology, University of Durham, South Road, Durham DH1 3LE. *T:* (0191) 374 1123.

HARDING, Prof. Dennis William, MA, DPhil; FRSE; Abercromby Professor of Archaeology, University of Edinburgh, since 1977; *b* 11 April 1940; *s* of Charles Royston Harding and Marjorie Doris Harding. *Educ:* Keble Coll., Oxford (BA, MA, DPhil). Assistant Keeper, Dept of Antiquities, Ashmolean Museum, Oxford, 1965–66; Lecturer in Celtic Archaeology, 1966, Sen. Lectr, 1975–77, Univ. of Durham; University of Edinburgh: Dean, Faculty of Arts, 1983–86; Vice-Principal, 1988–91. Member: Board of Trustees, National Museum of Antiquities of Scotland, 1977–85; Ancient Monuments Board for Scotland, 1979–83; Scottish Postgrad. Studentships Awards Cttee, 1981– (Chm., 1997–). FRSE 1986. *Publications:* The Iron Age in the Upper Thames Basin, 1972; The Iron Age in Lowland Britain, 1974; (with A. J. Challis) Later Prehistory from the Trent to the Tyne, 1975; ed and contrib., Archaeology in the North: Report of the Northern Archaeological Survey, 1976; ed and contrib., Hillforts: later prehistoric earthworks in Britain and Ireland, 1976; Prehistoric Europe, 1978; (with I. M. Blake and P. J. Reynolds) An Iron Age Settlement in Dorset: excavation and reconstruction, 1993; (with T. N. Dixon) Dun Bharabhat, Cnip: an Iron Age settlement in West Lewis, 2000, (with S. M. D. Gilmour) The Iron Age Settlement at Beirgh, Riof, Isle of Lewis, 2000. *Address:* Department of Archaeology, The Old High School, Infirmary Street, Edinburgh EH1 1LT. *T:* (0131) 650 2364.

HARDING, Derek William; Executive Secretary, Royal Statistical Society, 1986–95; *b* 16 Dec. 1930; *o s* of late William Arthur Harding; *m* 1954, Daphne Sheila, *yr d* of late Reginald Ernest Cooke; one *s* one *d*. *Educ:* Glendale Grammar Sch., London; Univ. of

Bristol (BSc). FInstP, CPhys, FIM, CEng. Develt Engr, Pye Ltd, 1954–56; Sen. Physics Master, Thornbury Grammar Sch., Bristol, 1956–60; Sen. Lectr in Physical Science, St Paul's Coll., Cheltenham, 1960–64; Asst Organiser, Nuffield Foundn Science Teaching Project, 1964–67; joined staff of Instn Metallurgists, 1967, Registrar-Sec., 1969–76. Sec.-Gen., British Computer Soc., 1976–86. Pres., Rotary Club of Enfield, 2000–01. *Recreation:* off-shore sailing. *Address:* 16 Exeter Road, N14 5JY. *T:* (020) 8368 1463. *Clubs:* Athenæum, Cruising Association.

HARDING, Sir (George) William, KCMG 1983 (CMG 1977); CVO 1972; HM Diplomatic Service, retired; *b* 18 Jan. 1927; *s* of late Lt Col G. R. Harding, DSO, MBE, and Grace Henley (*née* Darby); *m* 1955, Sheila Margaret Ormond Riddel; four *s*. *Educ:* Aldenham; St John's College, Cambridge. Royal Marines, 1945–48. Entered HM Foreign Service, 1950; served (other than in London) in Singapore, 1951–52; Burma, 1952–55; Paris, 1956–59; Santo Domingo, 1960–63; Mexico City, 1967–70; Paris, 1970–74; Ambassador to Peru, 1977–79; Asst Under-Sec. of State, FCO, 1979–81; Ambassador to Brazil, 1981–84; Dep. Under-Sec. of State, FCO, 1984–86. Mem., Trilateral Commn, 1988–93. Vis. Fellow, Harvard Centre for Internat. Affairs, 1986. Chairman: First Spanish Investment Trust, 1987–96; Thai-Euro Fund, 1988–97; British Thai Business Gp, 1995–97; Dir, Lloyds Bank Plc, 1988–93. Chairman: Margaret Mee Amazon Trust, 1988–94; Anglo-Peruvian Soc., 1987–89; Brazilian Chamber of Commerce in Britain, 1988–91. Vice-Pres., RGS, 1991–93; Mem. Council, RIIA, 1988–94. *Address:* La Dreyrie, 24510 Pezuls, France. *Clubs:* Beefsteak; Leander.

HARDING, James Owen Glyn; Director and Chief Executive, National Society for the Prevention of Cruelty to Children, 1995–2000; *b* 18 Oct. 1942; *s* of Walter James Harding and Elizabeth May Harding; *m* 1965, Sally Goldie; one *s* two *d*. *Educ:* Pinner Grammar Sch.; Univ. of Sussex (BA); Univ. of Exeter (Home Office Letter of Recognition in Child Care). Royal Borough of Kensington and Chelsea: Child Care Officer and Sen. Child Care Officer, Children's Dept, 1968–71; Area Officer and Asst Dir, Social Services Dept, 1971–85; National Society for the Prevention of Cruelty to Children: Dir, Child Care, 1986–89; Dep. Chief Exec. and Dir of Children's Services, 1989–95. Mem., Commn of Inquiry on death of Kimberley Carlisle, 1987. *Publications:* (jtly) A Child in Mind, 1987; The Parentalk Guide to Being a Grandparent, 2001; contrib. to various jls on social work and children's issues. *Recreations:* writing, literature, walking, sport, the theatre. *Address:* c/o NSPCC, 42 Curtain Road, EC2A 3NH.

HARDING, Keith; Member (C) Mid Scotland and Fife, Scottish Parliament, since 1999. *b* 21 Nov. 1938; *s* of late Cyril Dennis Harding and Ella Evelyn Harding; *m* 1974, Elizabeth Anne Fowler; one *s* one *d*. *Educ:* Chipping Norton GS; Oxford Coll. of Further Educn. Newsagent and banker. Mem (C) Stirling DC, then Stirling Council, 1986–99 (Leader, 1993–96; Opposition Leader, 1996–99). *Address:* Scottish Parliament, Edinburgh EH99 1SP; 4 Stirling Road, Dunblane FK15 9EP.

HARDING, Rt Rev. Malcolm Alfred Warden; Bishop of Brandon, 1992–2001; *b* 28 June 1936; *s* of Henry Warden Harding and Grace (*née* Walker); *m* 1962, Marylou (*née* Richards); one *s* two *d*. *Educ:* Univ. of Western Ontario (BA 1959); Huron Coll. (LTh 1962); Univ. of Manitoba (BSW 1964, MSW 1966). Ordained deacon, 1962; i/c of five rural parishes, dio. of Fredericton, 1962–63; Child Welfare Worker, Children's Aid Soc., Ont., 1963–64; Social Worker, 1966–68, Supervisor, 1968–73, Manitoba Dept of Health and Social Develt; ordained priest, 1973; Priest-in-charge, Birtle, Solsgirth, 1973–78; Rector, St George's, Brandon, 1978–92; Archdeacon of Brandon, 1986–92; Diocesan Administrator, Brandon, 1992. Hon. DD Huron, 1993. *Recreations:* model railroad, fishing, reading, railway enthusiast. *Address:* 17 Durum Drive, Brandon, MB R7B 3M3, Canada.

HARDING, Air Vice-Marshal Peter John, CB 1993; CVO 1998; CBE 1985; AFC 1974; FRAeS; Defence Services Secretary to the Queen, Director General of Reserve Forces and Cadets, and Assistant Chief of Defence Staff (Personnel), 1994–98; *b* 1 June 1940; *s* of John Fitz Harding and Marjorie Clare; *m* 1966, Morwenna Jacquiline St John Grey; two *s*. *Educ:* Solihull School. Joined RAF, 1960; Pilot, 249 Sqn, Cyprus, 1962–65; RAF Coll., 1965–70; Cyprus, 1971–72; Waddington, 1972–74; RNC, 1974; RAF Germany, 1974–76; OC Pilot Buccaneers Sqns, 1977–80; Directing Staff, RAF Staff Coll., 1981; Station Comdr, Honington, 1982–84; RCDS 1985; Dir Nuclear Systems, MoD, 1986–88; Dep. C-in-C, RAF Germany, 1989–91; Dep. COS (Ops), HQ AAFCE, 1991–94. ADC to the Queen, 1982–84. Dep. Chm. Govs, Taunton Sch., 2001. Legion of Merit (USA), 1998. *Recreations:* cricket, golf, gardening, family, philately, hobby farming, classic cars. *Clubs:* Royal Air Force, Innominate, Pilgrims; Royal Cinque Ports (Deal).

HARDING, Marshal of the Royal Air Force Sir Peter (Robin), GCB 1988 (KCB 1983; CB 1980); FRAeS; CIMgt; Deputy Chairman, GEC Marconi Ltd, 1995–98; *b* 2 Dec. 1933; *s* of late Peter Harding and Elizabeth Clear; *m* 1955, Sheila Rosemary May; three *s* one *d*. *Educ:* Chingford High Sch. Joined RAF, 1952; Pilot, 12 Sqdn, 1954–57; QFI and Flt Comdr, RAF Coll., Cranwell, 1957–60; Pilot, 1 Sqdn, RAAF, 1960–62; sc 1963; Air Secretary's Dept, MoD, 1964–66; OC, 18 Sqdn, Gutersloh and Acklington, 1966–69; jssc, Latimer, 1969–70; Defence Policy Staff, MoD, 1970–71; Director, Air Staff, Briefing, MoD, 1971–74; Station Comdr, RAF Brüggen, 1974–76; ADC to the Queen, 1975; Dir of Defence Policy, MoD, 1976–78; Asst Chief of Staff (Plans and Policy), SHAPE, 1978–80; AOC No 11 Group, 1981–82; VCAS, 1982–84; VCDS, 1985; AOC-in-C, RAF Strike Comd, and C-in-C, UK Air Forces, 1985–88; Chief of Air Staff, 1988–92; Chief of the Defence Staff, 1992–94. Chm. and Chief Exec., Merlyn Internat. Associates Ltd, 1997–; Chm., Thorlock Internat. Ltd, 1999–2000. FRAeS 1983, Hon. CRAeS 1989; CIMgt (CBIM 1984); FRSA 1988. Liveryman, GAPAN, 1989. Member: Council, Winston Churchill Meml Trust, 1990–; Leonard Cheshire Conflict Recovery Centre, 1998–. Vice Pres., Guild of Aviation Artists, 1994–. Hon. DSc Cranfield, 1990. Legion of Merit (USA), 1992. *Publications:* articles for professional jls, magazines and books. *Recreations:* pianoforte, bridge, birdwatching, shooting, fishing. *Clubs:* Beefsteak, Garrick.

HARDING, Roger John, CMG 1986; Chairman: Sujanara Ltd, since 1991; Bill Hill & Partners Ltd, since 1996; Director, ITT Defence Ltd, since 1993; *b* 7 April 1935; *s* of Charles William Harding and Lilian Mabel (*née* Trowbridge); *m* 1960, June Elizabeth Tidy; four *d*. *Educ:* Price's Sch., Fareham, Hants; Southern Grammar Sch., Portsmouth, Hants. Board of Trade, 1954–74; War Office, then Min. of Defence, 1974–91: Head of Defence Secretariat 8, 1979–82; Counsellor, Defence Supply, 1982–86, Minister, Defence Material, 1986–88, Washington; Dir Gen., Marketing, MoD, 1988–91. *Recreations:* soccer, cricket, golf, following fortunes of Portsmouth FC. *Club:* St John's Village (Woking).

HARDING, Sir Roy (Pollard), Kt 1985; CBE 1978; *b* 3 Jan. 1924; *s* of W. F. N. Harding, BEM and P. E. Harding; *m* 1948, Audrey Beryl Larkin, JP; two *s* one *d*. *Educ:* Liskeard Grammar Sch.; King's Coll., Univ. of London (BSc; AKC; DPA). CMath, FIMA; FZS. Ballistics research, schools and college teaching, to 1950; Educn Admin, Wilts, Bucks, Herts, Leics, to 1960; Dep. Chief Educn Officer, 1960–66, Chief Educn Officer, 1966–84, Bucks. Adviser: County Councils Assoc., 1972–74; Assoc. of County Councils, 1973–84 (incl. Finance, 1978–81, Policy, 1981–84); Council of Local Educn Authorities, 1975–84. Member: Printing and Publishing Ind. Trng Bd, 1970–72; BBC Further Educn Adv. Council, 1970–75; Burnham Cttee, 1972–77; Sec. of State's Vis. Cttee, Cranfield Inst. of Technology, 1976–81; DES/Local Authority Expenditure Steering Gp, Educn, 1976–84; Councils and Educnl Press (Longmans) Editorial Adv. Panel, 1977–86; Teaching of Mathematics in Schools (Cockcroft) Cttee, 1978–82; Educn Management Inf. Exchange, 1981–89; Board, Nat. Adv. Body for Higher Educn, 1982–84; A Level (Higginson) Cttee, 1987–88; Assoc. of Educn Cttees Trust, 1989–; CBI Educn Foundn, 1990–94; Educn Cttee, Royal Soc., 1991–96 (Vice-Chm., 1995–96); various univ. cttees, incl. Open Univ. Council, 1985–96; Chairman: County Educn Officers' Soc., 1978–79 (Sec., 1973–76); Educn Policy Interchange Cttee, 1979–89; Open Univ. INSET Sector Programme Bd, 1983–87; Governing Body, Staff Coll. (formerly Further Educn Staff Coll.), 1986–95; EMIS Ltd, 1988–91; FEFCE Tariff Adv. Cttee, 1993–98; Vice-Chm., Secondary Exams Council, 1983–86. President: Soc. of Educn Officers, 1977–78 (Mem. Exec., 1974–79; Chm. Internat. Cttee, 1980–83; Gen. Sec., 1984–89); British Educnl Equipment Assoc., 1980–83; Educn Sect., BAAS, 1986–87; Nat. Inst. Adult Continuing Educn, 1988–94; IMA, 1990, 1991 (Council, 1983–88, 1990–97). Centenary Fellow, Thames Polytechnic, 1990. DUniv Open, 1985; Hon. LLD Leicester, 1995. Wappenteller, Rheinland/Pfalz, Germany, 1978. Gold Cross of Merit, Polish Govt in Exile, 1984. *Recreations:* travel, music. *Address:* 27 King Edward Avenue, Aylesbury, Bucks HP21 7JE. *T:* (01296) 423006.

HARDING, Wilfrid Gerald, CBE 1978; FRCP, FFCM, DPH; Area Medical Officer, Camden and Islington Area Health Authority (Teaching), 1974–79; Hon. Consultant in Community Medicine, University College Hospital, London, 1971–79; *b* 17 March 1915; *s* of late Dr *hc* Ludwig Ernst Emil Hoffmann and Marie Minna Eugenie (*née* Weisbach); *m* 1st, 1938, Britta Charlotta Haraldsdotter, Malmberg (marr. diss. 1970); three *s*; 2nd, 1973, Hilary Maxwell. *Educ:* Französisches Gymnasium, Berlin; Süddeutsches Landerziehungsheim, Schondorf, Bavaria; Woodbrooke Coll., Selly Oak, Birmingham; University Coll. London; University Coll. Hosp. Med. Sch. (interned twice in 1939 and 1940). MRCS, LRCP 1941; DPH London 1949; MRCP 1968; FFCM 1972; Hon. FFCM 1986; FRCP 1972. Ho. Phys. and Ho. Surg., UCH, 1941–42; Asst MOH, City of Oxford, 1942–43; RAMC, 1943–47, Field Units in NW Europe, 1 Corps Staff and Mil. Govt, Lt-Col (Hygiene Specialist). In charge of health services, Ruhr Dist of Germany, CCG, 1947–48; LSHTM, 1948–49; career posts in London public health service, 1949–64; MOH, London Bor. of Camden, and Principal Sch. MO, ILEA, 1965–74. Hon. Lectr, Dept of Sociol., Bedford Coll., London Univ., 1969–77; Civil Consultant in Community Medicine to RAF, 1974–78. Chm. of Council, Soc. of MOH, 1966–71 (Pres. 1971–72); Chm., Prov. Bd of FCM, Royal Colls of Physicians of UK, 1971–72 (Vice-Pres., 1972–75, Pres., 1975–78). Member: Central Health Services Council and Standing Med. Adv. Cttee, 1966–71 and 1975–78; Standing Mental Health Adv. Cttee, 1966–71; Bd of Studies in Preventive Med. and Public Health, Univ. of London, 1963–79; Council, UCH Med. Sch., 1965–78; Bd of Management, LSHTM, 1968–82; Council for Educn and Trng of Health Visitors, 1965–77; Council, ASH, 1970–73 and 1978–82; Public Health Laboratory Service Bd, 1972–83. Armed Services Med. Adv. Bd, 1975–78; GMC, 1979–84; Vice-Chm., Dartford and Gravesham CHC, 1984–89. Chm., DHSS Working Gp on Primary Health Team, 1978–80 (reported 1981). Hon. Advr, Office of Health Econs, 1977–. Councillor, Sevenoaks DC, 1979– (Vice-Chm., 1996–97; Chm., 1997–98); Chm., Farningham Parish Council, 1983–89. Chm., Farningham Woods Nature Reserve, 1983–. Broadcasts on public health and community medicine. *Publications:* papers on public health and community med. in medical books and jls; Parkes Centenary Meml Lecture (Community, Health and Service), 1976. *Recreations:* watching river birds, music, wine. *Address:* Bridge Cottage, High Street, Farningham, Dartford DA4 0DW. *T:* (01322) 862733. *Club:* Athenæum.

HARDING, Sir William; *see* Harding, Sir G. W.

HARDINGE, family name of **Viscount Hardinge** and **Baron Hardinge of Penshurst**.

HARDINGE, 6th Viscount *cr* 1846, of Lahore and of King's Newton, Derbyshire; **Charles Henry Nicholas Hardinge;** Bt 1801; Senior Manager, Global Private Banking, Royal Bank of Canada Europe Ltd; *b* 25 Aug. 1956; *s* of 5th Viscount Hardinge and of Zoë Anne, *d* of Hon. Hartland de Montarville Molson, OBE, Montreal; *S* father, 1984; *m* 1985, Julie Therese Sillett, *d* of Joan Sillett of Sydney, Australia; two *d* one step *s*. *Heir:* *b* Hon. Andrew Hartland Hardinge [*b* 7 Jan. 1960; *m* 1990, Sophia Mary, *e d* of Capt. W. D. A. Bagnell; two *s* one *d*]. *Address:* Broadmere House, Broadmere, Farleigh Wallop, Basingstoke, Hants RG25 2JA.

HARDINGE OF PENSHURST, 4th Baron *cr* 1910; **Julian Alexander Hardinge;** Director: Book Tokens Ltd, since 1984; Batch.co.uk, since 1998; *b* 23 Aug. 1945; *s* of 3rd Baron Hardinge of Penshurst and Janet Christine Goschen (*d* 1970), *d* of late Lt-Col Francis Cecil Campbell Balfour, CIE, CVO, CBE, MC; *S* father, 1997. *Educ:* Eton; Trinity Coll., Cambridge. A Page of Honour to HM the Queen, 1959–62. Booksellers' Association: Chairman: Coll. and Univ. Booksellers Gp, 1985–87; Export Booksellers Gp, 1993–95. Dir, John Smith & Son, Booksellers, 1998–. Chm., Mind Sports Olympiad, 1998–. *Heir:* *b* Hon. Hugh Francis Hardinge, *b* 9 April 1948. *Address:* Flat 1/R, 50 Leven Street, Pollokshields, Glasgow G41 2JE.

HARDMAN, Ven. Christine Elizabeth; Archdeacon of Lewisham, since 2001; *b* 27 Aug. 1951; *d* of Wynford Atkins and Margaret Elizabeth Atkins; *m* 1971, Roger John Hardman; two *d*. *Educ:* Queen Elizabeth's Girls' Grammar Sch., Barnet; Univ. of London (BScEcon (ext.) 1973); Westminster Coll., Oxford (MTh 1994). Ordained deaconess, 1984, deacon, 1987, priest, 1994; Deaconess, Markyate Street, 1984–88; Course Dir, St Albans MTS, later St Albans and Oxford Ministry Course, 1988–96; Vicar, Holy Trinity, Stevenage, 1996–2001; RD Stevenage, 1999–2001. *Recreations:* cycling, running, cinema, theatre. *Address:* 129a Honor Oak Park, SE23 3LD.

HARDMAN, John Nimrod, FCA; Chairman: ASDA Group PLC (formerly ASDA-MFI), 1988–91 (Deputy Chairman, 1986–87; Director, 1984–91); Dewhurst Butchers, since 1996; *b* 8 Oct. 1939; *s* of late Harry John Hardman and of Florence Gladys Sybil Anne Hardman (*née* Dolby); *m* 1966, Joan McHugh; one *s* one *d*. *Educ:* Quarry Bank High Sch., Liverpool; Liverpool Univ. (BComm Hons). FIGD. Duncan Watson & Short, Chartered Accts, 1962–66; RCA Corp., 1967–69; Finance Dir, Thorn Colour Tubes Ltd, 1969–75; Dir, Europe, Africa and Far East, RCA Corp. Picture Tube Div., 1976–80; Finance Director: Oriel Foods, 1981; ASDA Stores, 1981–84 (Man. Dir, 1984–89); Director: Maples Stores plc, 1995–98; Adderley and Featherstone plc, 1991–. Director: Leeds Develt Corp, 1988–92; Yorks Electricity Bd, 1989–97. CIMgt. *Recreations:* golf, tennis, shooting, cricket. *Address:* Hillside, Spofforth Hill, Wetherby, Yorks LS22 4SF. *Clubs:* Lord's Taverners'; Liverpool Artists, Royal Liverpool Golf, Liverpool Racquets (Liverpool); Pannal Golf (Harrogate).

HARDMAN, Richard Frederick Paynter, CBE 1998; CGeol, FGS; Exploration Director, Amerada Hess Ltd, 1989–98; Director and Vice-President, Exploration Amerada Hess International Ltd, since 1998; *b* 2 May 1936; *s* of late Dr Charles Ramsay Hardman and of Mary Hardman (*née* Barnsley); *m* 1st, 1960, Janet Quintrell Treloar (marr. diss.); two *s* two *d*; 2nd, 1982, Marilyn Merryweather (marr. diss.); one *d*; 3rd, 1995, Elizabeth Jane Atkinson. *Educ:* Arnold Sch., Blackpool; Corpus Christi Coll., Oxford (MA). FGS 1959; CGeol 1991. Nat. Service, RN, 1954–56. Geologist with BP, in UK, Libya, Kuwait, Colombia, 1959–69; Exploration Manager with Amoco, Superior Oil and Amerada Hess, based in London and Norway, 1969–88; Vice-Pres., NW Europe, Amerada Hess Internat. Ltd, 1996–98. Dir, DENERCO OIL A/S, 1997–. Mem., Programme Bd, Brit. Geol Survey, 1993–95. Mem., NERC, 1998–. Geological Society: Chm., Petroleum Gp, 1987–90; Pres., 1996–98. Chm., Petroleum Exploration Soc. of GB, 1985–86; Pres., Earth Sci. Teachers Assoc., 1993–95; Mem. Adv. Council, Amer. Assoc. of Petroleum Geologists, 2000– (Pres., Eur. Chapter, June 2002–). *Publications:* (ed jtly) Tectonic Events Responsible for Britain's Oil and Gas Reserves, 1990; (ed) Exploration Britain: geological insights for the next decade, 1992; papers on chalk as an oil and gas reservoir. *Recreations:* geology, jam making, theatre, music, ski-ing, wide open spaces. *Address:* c/o Amerada Hess Ltd, 33 Grosvenor Place, SW1X 7HY. *T:* (020) 7887 2600. *Club:* Athenæum.

HARDMAN MOORE, John Halstead; *see* Moore, J. H. H.

HARDSTAFF, Veronica Mary; *b* 23 Oct. 1941; *d* of Rev. Ernest Tutt and Mary Tutt; *m* 1964 (marr. diss. 1977); one *s* one *d*. *Educ:* Manchester Univ. (BA Hons German); Cologne Univ. Teacher of German and French: High Storrs Girls' GS, Sheffield, 1963–66; St Peter's Sec. Mod. Sch., Sheffield, 1969–70; Knottingley High Sch., 1977–79; Frecheville Sch., Sheffield, 1979–86; Birley Sch., Sheffield, 1986–94. Mem. (Lab), Sheffield CC, 1971–78. MEP (Lab) Lincs and Humberside S, 1994–99; contested (Lab) Yorks and Humber Reg., 1999. Vice-Chm., Jt Parly Cttee, EP-Poland, 1995–99. *Recreations:* reading, walking, classical music, playing flute. *Address:* 64 Linaker Road, Sheffield S6 5DT. *T:* (0114) 233 5414. *Club:* Sheffield Trades and Labour.

HARDWICK, Christopher, MD, FRCP; Physician Emeritus, Guy's Hospital, since 1976; *b* 13 Jan. 1911; *s* of Thomas Mold Hardwick and Harriet Taylor; *m* 1938, Joan Dorothy Plummer; two *s*. *Educ:* Berkhamsted Sch.; Trinity Hall, Cambridge; Middlesex Hospital. MRCS, LRCP 1935; MA (Cambridge) 1937; MD (Cambridge) 1940; FRCP 1947. House Physician, House Surgeon and Med. Registrar, Middlesex Hosp., 1935 and 1938–41; House physician and Registrar, Hosp. for Sick Children, Gt Ormond Street, 1936–38. Wing Comdr, Medical Specialist, RAF Med. Service, 1941–46. Physician, Guy's Hosp., 1946–76. Hon. Vis. Phys., Johns Hopkins Hosp., Baltimore, 1954. Mem. Council, RCP, 1965–68; Mem. Board of Governors, Guy's Hospital, 1967–74. Chm., British Diabetic Assoc., 1974–80. *Publications:* contribs to medical literature. *Recreations:* gardening, reading. *Address:* 8 Sondes Farm, Glebe Road, Dorking, Surrey RH4 3EF.

HARDWICK, Donald, CBE 1980; PhD; Director, Johnson & Firth Brown plc, 1973–89 (Chairman, Steel Division, 1975–85); *b* 1926; *m* 1950, Dorothy Mary Hardwick; two *s*. *Educ:* Tadcaster Grammar Sch.; Sheffield Univ. (BMet 1st Cl. Hons 1947, Mappin Medal; PhD 1954). FIM. After appointments with English Electric Co., BISRA, and BSA Gp Research Centre, became first C. H. Desch Res. Fellow, Sheffield Univ. Joined Brown Firth Res. Laboratories, 1959; Man. Dir, Firth Brown Ltd, 1974–78; Mem. Bd, Johnson & Firth Brown, on amalgamation with Richard Johnson & Nephew, 1973. Director: Mitchell Somers Gp, 1974–89; Eagle Trust plc, 1987–89. Pres., BISPA, 1977–79. *Recreations:* fell walking, gardening. *Address:* 43 Dore Road, Dore, Sheffield S17 3NA.

HARDWICK, Prof. James Leslie, MSc, PhD, DDS; FDSRCS; Professor of Preventive Dentistry, University of Manchester, 1960–78, now Emeritus; *b* 27 March 1913; *o s* of George Hardwicke Hardwick and Mary Ann Hardwick; *m* 1954, Eileen Margaret Isobel Gibson; two *s* two *d*. *Educ:* Rugby Sch.; Birmingham Univ. MDS 1948, PhD 1950, DDS 1984, Birmingham; FDSRCS 1954; MSc 1964. Private and hospital dental practice, 1935–39. Served War of 1939–45, Army Dental Corps. University of Birmingham: Lecturer, 1945–48, Sen. Lecturer in Operative Dental Surgery, 1948–52; Reader in Dental Surgery, 1952–60. *Publications:* editor of and contributor to dental and other scientific journals and textbooks. *Address:* 167 Stanley Road, Cheadle Hulme, Cheshire SK8 6RF. *T:* (0161) 437 3555.

HARDWICK, Mary, (Mollie); author; *b* Manchester; *d* of Joseph Greenhalgh and Anne Frances Atkinson; *m* 1961, Michael John Drinkrow Hardwick (*d* 1991); one *s*. *Educ:* Manchester High Sch. for Girls. Announcer, BBC (Radio) N Region, 1940–45; BBC (Radio) Drama Dept, 1946–62; freelance, 1963–. FRSA 1966. *Publications:* Stories from Dickens, 1968; Emma, Lady Hamilton, 1969; Mrs Dizzy, 1972; Upstairs Downstairs: Sarah's Story, 1973, The Years of Change, 1974, The War to end Wars, 1975, Mrs Bridges' Story, 1975, The World of Upstairs Downstairs, 1976; Alice in Wonderland (play), 1975; Beauty's Daughter, 1976 (Elizabeth Goudge Award for best historical romantic novel of year); The Duchess of Duke Street: The Way Up, 1976, The Golden Years, 1976, The World Keeps Turning, 1977; Charlie is my Darling, 1977; The Atkinson Heritage, 1978; Thomas and Sarah, 1978; Thomas and Sarah: Two for a Spin, 1979; Lovers Meeting, 1979; Sisters in Love, 1979; Dove's Nest, 1980; Willowwood, 1980; Juliet Bravo 1, 1980; Juliet Bravo 2, 1980; Monday's Child, 1981; Calling Juliet Bravo: New Arrivals, 1981; I Remember Love, 1982; The Shakespeare Girl, 1983; By the Sword Divided, 1983; The Merrymaid, 1984; Girl with a Crystal Dove, 1985; Malice Domestic, 1986; Parson's Pleasure, 1987; Uneaseful Death, 1988; Blood Royal, 1988; The Bandersnatch, 1989; Perish in July, 1989; The Dreaming Damozel, 1990; Come away Death, 1997; *with Michael Hardwick:* The Jolly Toper, 1961; The Sherlock Holmes Companion, 1962; Sherlock Holmes Investigates, 1963; The Man Who Was Sherlock Holmes, 1964; Four Sherlock Holmes plays, 1964; The Charles Dickens Companion, 1965; The World's Greatest Sea Mysteries, 1967; Writers' Houses: a literary journey in England, 1968; Alfred Deller: A Singularity of Voice, 1968, rev. edn 1980; Charles Dickens As They Saw Him, 1969; The Game's Afoot (Sherlock Holmes Plays), 1969; Plays from Dickens, 1970; Dickens's England, 1970; The Private Life of Sherlock Holmes, 1970; Four More Sherlock Holmes Plays, 1973; The Charles Dickens Encyclopedia, 1973; The Bernard Shaw Companion, 1973; The Charles Dickens Quiz Book, 1974; The Upstairs Downstairs Omnibus, 1975; The Gaslight Boy, 1976; The Hound of the Baskervilles and Other Sherlock Holmes Plays, 1982; numerous plays and scripts for radio and TV; contribs to women's magazines.

HARDWICK, Nicholas Lionel; Chief Executive, British Refugee Council, since 1995; *b* 19 July 1957; *s* of Lionel and Nancy Hardwick; one *d*; *m* 1985, Susan Heaven; one *s*. *Educ:* Epsom Coll.; Hull Univ. (BA Hons English Lit. 1979). Youth Training Manager, NACRO, 1980–85; Dep. Chief Exec., Soc. Voluntary Associates, 1986; Chief Exec., Centrepoint, 1986–95. Special Advr, Rough Sleeping, DoE, 1991. Chm., European Council for Refugees and Exiles, 1999–. Chm., Gtr London Radio Adv. Council, 1993–95; Mem., BBC SE Regl Adv. Cttee, 1993–95. Mem., Social Security Adv. Cttee, 1994–99. Bd Mem., Stonebridge HAT, 1994–97. FRSA 1995. *Recreations:* walking, Spain. *Address:* British Refugee Council, 3 Bondway, SW8 1SJ.

HARDWICKE, 10th Earl of, *cr* 1754; **Joseph Philip Sebastian Yorke;** Baron Hardwicke 1733; Viscount Royston 1754; *b* 3 Feb. 1971; *s* of Philip Simon Prospero Rupert Lindley, Viscount Royston (*d* 1973) and Virginia Anne (*d* 1988), *d* of Geoffrey Lyon; *S* grandfather, 1974. *Heir: cousin* Charles Edward Yorke, *b* 18 March 1951.

HARDY; *see* Gathorne-Hardy, family name of Earl of Cranbrook.

HARDY, family name of **Baron Hardy of Wath.**

HARDY OF WATH, Baron *cr* 1997 (Life Peer), of Wath upon Dearne in the co. of South Yorkshire; **Peter Hardy;** DL; *b* 17 July 1931; *s* of Lawrence Hardy and of Mrs I. Hardy, Wath upon Dearne; *m* 1954, Margaret Anne Brookes; two *s*. *Educ:* Wath upon Dearne Grammar Sch.; Westminster Coll., London (Teacher's Cert., London Univ.); Sheffield Univ. (DipEd). LCP. RAF, 1949–51. Schoolmaster in S Yorkshire, 1953–70. Member: Wath upon Dearne UDC, 1960–70 (Chm. Council, 1968–69); Governing Body of Wath Grammar Sch., 1960–71 (Chm. of Governors, 1969–70). Pres., Wath upon Dearne Labour Party, 1960–68. Contested (Lab): Scarborough and Whitby, 1964; Sheffield, Hallam, 1966. MP (Lab) Rother Valley, 1970–83, Wentworth, 1983–97. PPS to Sec. of State for the Environment, 1974–76; PPS to Foreign Sec., 1976–79. Hon. Sec., All-Party Gp for Energy Studies, 1992–97; Vice-Chm., All-Party Conservation Cttee, 1972–97; Chm., PLP Energy Cttee, 1974–92; Parly attachment to RAF, 1992–93. Member: CSCE Assembly, 1992–97; UK delegn, 1976–97, and Lab. delegn (Leader, 1983–95) to Council of Europe and WEU; Chm., Cttee on Environment, Council of Europe, 1986–89 (Chm., Sub Cttee on Natural Envmt, 1978–86 and 1990–94; Vice-Chm., Socialist Gp, 1983–96); Chm., All Pty Conservation Gp, 2000–. Member: Council, RSPB, 1984–89; Central Exec. Cttee, NSPCC, 1985–94; Bd, Landscape Foundn, 1996–2000. Vice-Pres., S Yorks Foundn, 1993; Patron, Yorkshire Wildlife Trust. President: Peak Dist and S Yorks Br., CPRE; Rotherham ATC. DL S Yorks, 1997. *Publications:* A Lifetime of Badgers, 1975; various articles on educational and other subjects. *Recreation:* watching wild life, judging dogs. *Address:* 2 Gorse Close, Brampton, Bierlow, Rotherham, South Yorkshire S63 6HW. *T:* (01709) 874590. *Club:* Kennel (Hon. Mem.).

HARDY, Alan; Member (C) for Brent North, Greater London Council, 1967–86 (Chairman, Finance and Establishment Committee, 1977–81); *b* 24 March 1932; *s* of late John Robert Hardy and Emily Hardy; *m* 1972, Betty Howe, *d* of late Walter and Hilda Howe. *Educ:* Hookergate Grammar Sch.; Univ. of Manchester; Inst. of Historical Res., Univ. of London (MA). Res. Asst to Sir Lewis Namier, History of Parliament Trust, 1955–56; Res. Officer and Dep. Dir, London Municipal Soc., 1956–63; Mem. British Secretariat, Council of European Municipalities, 1963–64. Lectures on British Monarchy. Member: Local Authorities' Conditions of Service Adv. Bd, 1977–81; Nat. Jt Council for Local Authorities' Services (Manual Workers), 1977–81. Mem. Bd, Harlow Develt Corp., 1968–80. Hon. Life Pres., Brent North Conservative Assoc., 1986. Contested (C) Islington SW, 1966. *Publications:* Queen Victoria Was Amused, 1976; The Kings' Mistresses, 1980. *Recreation:* admiring old things. *Address:* 20 Meadowside, Cambridge Park, Twickenham, Middx TW1 2JQ. *T:* (020) 8892 7968.

HARDY, Anna Gwenllian; *see* Somers Cocks, A. G.

HARDY, Prof. Barbara Gladys; Professor of English Literature, Birkbeck College, University of London, 1970–89, now Emeritus; teacher and author; *b* 27 June 1924; *d* of Maurice and Gladys Nathan; *m* Ernest Dawson Hardy (decd); two *d*. *Educ:* Swansea High Sch. for Girls; University Coll. London (BA, MA). FRSL 1997. Subsequently on staff of English Dept of Birkbeck Coll., London; Prof. of English, Royal Holloway Coll., Univ. of London, 1965–70. Dir, Yeats Summer School, 1990–91. Pres., Dickens Soc., 1987–88; Vice-President: Thomas Hardy Soc., 1991–; George Eliot Fellowship, 1992–. Mem. Welsh Acad. Hon. Mem., MLA. Hon. Prof. of English, UC Swansea, 1991. Hon. Fellow: Birkbeck Coll., London, 1991; RHBNC, 1992; Univ. of Wales, Swansea, 1998. DUniv Open, 1981. *Publications:* The Novels of George Eliot, 1959 (Rose Mary Crawshay Prize); The Appropriate Form, 1964; (ed) George Eliot: Daniel Deronda, 1967; (ed) Middlemarch: Critical Approaches to the Novel, 1967; The Moral Art of Dickens, 1970; (ed) Critical Essays on George Eliot, 1970; The Exposure of Luxury: radical themes in Thackeray, 1972; (ed) Thomas Hardy: The Trumpet-Major, 1974; Tellers and Listeners: the narrative imagination, 1975; (ed) Thomas Hardy: A Laodicean, 1975; A Reading of Jane Austen, 1975; The Advantage of Lyric, 1977; Particularities: readings in George Eliot, 1982; Forms of Feeling in Victorian Fiction, 1985; Narrators and Novelists: collected essays, 1987; Swansea Girl, 1993; London Lovers (novel), 1996 (Sagittarius Prize, 1997); Henry James: the later writing, 1996; Shakespeare's Storytellers, 1997; Thomas Hardy: imagining imagination, 2000; Dylan Thomas: an original language, 2000; Severn Bridge (poems), 2001. *Address:* c/o Birkbeck College, Malet Street, WC1E 7HX.

HARDY, Rev. Canon Brian Albert; Rector, All Saints, St Andrews, 1991–96; *b* 3 July 1931; *s* of Albert Charles Hardy and Edith Maude Sarah Mabe. *Educ:* City Boys' School, Leicester; St John's Coll., Oxford (MA, DipTheol); Westcott House, Cambridge. Curate, Rugeley, Staffs, 1957–62; Chaplain, Downing Coll., Cambridge, 1962–66; Livingston (West Lothian) Ecumenical Team Ministry, 1966–74; Churches' Planning Officer for Telford, Salop, 1974–78; Chaplain, Coates Hall Theological Coll., Edinburgh, 1978–82; Rector, St Columba's by the Castle Episcopal Church, Edinburgh, 1982–91; Episcopalian Chaplain, Royal Infirmary of Edinburgh and Royal Edinburgh Hosp., 1982–86; Dean of the dio. of Edinburgh, 1986–91. Hon. Canon, Edinburgh Cathedral, 1991. *Recreations:* music, especially choral and piano; cycling. *Address:* 3/3 Starbank Road, Newhaven, Edinburgh EH5 3BN. *T:* (0131) 551 6783.

HARDY, Rev. Prof. Daniel Wayne; Director, Center of Theological Inquiry, Princeton, New Jersey, 1990–95; *b* 9 Nov. 1930; *s* of John Alexander Hardy and Barbara Wyndham Harrison; *m* 1958, Kate Perrin Enyart; two *s* two *d*. *Educ:* Phillips Exeter Acad., Exeter, NH; Haverford Coll., Haverford, Penn (BA); Gen. Theological Seminary, NY (STB, STM); St John's Coll., Univ. of Oxford. Deacon 1955, priest 1956; Asst Minister, Christ Ch, Greenwich, Conn, 1955–59; Vicar, St Barnabas Ch, Greenwich, 1956–59; Instr, Rosemary Hall, Greenwich, 1957–59; Fellow and Tutor, Gen. Theol Seminary, NY, 1959–61; Lectr in Modern Theol Thought, 1965–76, Sen. Lectr, 1976–86, Univ. of Birmingham; Van Mildert Prof. of Divinity, Univ. of Durham, and Residentiary Canon, Durham Cathedral, 1986–90 (Hon. Fellow, Durham Univ., 1991). Hon. Mem. and Advr, Centre for Advanced Religious and Theol Studies, Cambridge Univ., 1996–. Moderator, Gen. Ministerial Exam., C of E, 1983–89. Pres., Soc. for the Study of Theology, 1987–88. Editor, Cambridge Studies in Christian Doctrine, 1991–. *Publications:* (with D. F. Ford) Jubilate: theology in praise, 1984; (with D. F. Ford) Praising and Knowing God, 1985; Education for the Church's Ministry, 1986; God's Ways with the World, 1996; Finding the Church, 2001; *contributor to:* Schleiermacher and Barth: beyond the impasse, 1987; Keeping the Faith, 1987; The Modern Theologians, 1989, 2nd edn 1997; (and ed jtly) On Being the Church, 1989; (and ed jtly) The Weight of Glory: essays in honour of Peter

Baelz, 1991; Christ and Context, 1993; Worship and Ethics: Lutherans and Anglicans in dialogue, 1996; Essentials of Christian Community: essays in honour of Daniel W. Hardy, 1996; The Doctrine of Creation, 1997; Spirituality and Theology, 1998; Science Meets Faith: theology and science in conversation, 1998; Where Shall Wisdom Be Found?, 1999; Seeing Beyond the Word: visual arts and the Calvinist tradition, 1999; articles in Theology, Expository Times, Anglican Theol Rev., etc; *festschrift:* Essentials of Christian Community: essays in honour of Daniel W. Hardy, 1996. *Recreations:* swimming, ski-ing, music, photography. *Address:* 101 Millington Lane, Newnham, Cambridge CB3 9HA.

See also D. F. Ford.

HARDY, David Ian Brooker; Managing Director, Open Learning Company, since 2000; President, Open Learning Foundation, since 2000; *b* 28 Sept. 1950; *s* of Leslie Hardy and Ruth Eveline Hardy (*née* Brooker); *m* 1979, Christine Mary Wilson; two *d*. *Educ:* Bradford Grammar Sch.; Univ. of London (BSc Hons); Univ. of Leeds (Grad. Cert Ed). FIPD. Dept of Educn, Leeds City Council, 1979–85; Department of Education and Science: Yorks and Humberside, 1985–86; Nat. Manager, Post Experience Vocational Educn, 1986–90; Asst Sec., 1990; Chief Exec., Open Poly., then Open Learning Foundn, 1990–2000. Moderator, BTEC, 1982–85; Member, CNAA, 1991–92; Pres., Eur. Assoc. Distance Teaching Univs, 1999–; Vice Pres. (Europe), Internat. Council for Open and Distance Educn, 1999–; Mem., Eur. Open and Distance Learning Liaison Cttee, 1999–. Mem. Council, Bradford Chamber of Commerce, 1982–86. *Publications:* (jtly) Onchocerciasis in Zaire, 1977; articles in learned jls. *Recreations:* swimming, fell walking, keeping fit. *Address:* Open Learning Company, 3 Devonshire Street, W1W 5BA. *T:* (020) 7323 0466.

HARDY, David Malcolm; Chief Executive, The London Clearing House, since 1987; *b* 16 July 1955; *s* of Roy Hardy and late Mary (*née* Ebsworth); *m* 1981 (marr. diss. 1995); one *s* one *d*; *m* 1995, Marion Dorothy Brazier. *Educ:* Westcliff High Sch. ACIB; FCT. Barclays Bank, 1973–81; Barclays Merchant Bank, 1981–85; London Clearing House, 1985–. Director: London Commodity Exchange (1986) Ltd, 1991–96; Internat. Petroleum Exchange of London Ltd, 1993–99; Futures and Options Assoc., 1993–. Freeman, City of London, 1994. *Recreations:* golf, photography. *Address:* London Clearing House, Aldgate House, 33 Aldgate High Street, EC3N 1EA. *T:* (020) 7426 7000. *Clubs:* Pyrford Golf; Westcliff Hockey.

HARDY, Sir David (William), Kt 1992; Chairman, Transport Research Laboratory, since 1996; Chairman of Trustees, National Maritime Museum, since 1995 (Trustee, since 1992); *b* 14 July 1930; 3rd *s* of late Brig. John H. Hardy, CBE, MC; *m* 1957, Rosemary, *d* of late Sir Godfrey F. S. Collins, KCIE, CSI, OBE; one *s* one *d*. *Educ:* Wellington Coll.; Harvard Business School (AMP). Chartered Accountant. Served 2nd RHA, 2/Lt, 1953–54. Funch Edye & Co. Inc., NY, New Orleans and Norfolk, Va, 1954–64 (Dir, 1960); Vice Pres. Finance and Admin., Imperial Tobacco, USA, 1964–70; HM Govt Co-ordinator of Industrial Advrs, 1970–72; Gp Finance Dir, Tate & Lyle Ltd, 1972–77; Dir, Ocean Transport & Trading PLC, 1977–83; Chairman: Ocean Inchcape, 1980–83; London Park Hotels, 1983–87; Globe Investment Trust, 1983–90 (Dir, 1976–90); Docklands Light Railway, 1984–87; Swan Hunter, 1986–88; MGM Assurance, 1986–2000 (Dep. Chm., 1985–86; Dir, 1985–2000); Europa Minerals, 1991–94; Bankers Trust Investment Management, 1992–94; Burmine Ltd, 1992–96; Y. J. Lovell, 1994–99; 100 Group Chartered Accountants, 1986–88; LDDC, 1988–92 (Dep. Chm., 1988); Deputy Chairman: LRT, 1984–87; Agricultural Mortgage Corp., 1985–92 (Dir, 1973–); Director: Sturge Holdings PLC, 1985–95; Waterford Wedgwood plc (formerly Waterford Glass), 1984–90; Paragon Group, 1985–88; Aberfoyle Holdings, 1986–91; Chelsea Harbour Ltd, 1986–90; Electra Kingsway Managers Hldgs Ltd, 1990–91; Tootal Gp, 1990–91; CIBA-GEIGY, 1991–96; Hanson, 1991–2001; J. A. Devenish, 1991–93; Stirling-Lloyd Holdings, 1992–; James Fisher & Sons, 1993–; Milner Estates (formerly Conrad Ritblat) plc, 1996–99; Imperial Tobacco Gp, 1996–2001; Sons of Gwalia, 1996–99; Milner Consultancies, 2000–; Adv. Dir, HSBC Investment Banking, 1995–97. Chm., Engrg Marketing Adv. Cttee, DTI, 1989–90; Member: NEDC Cttee for Agriculture, 1970–72; Export Credit Guarantees Adv. Council, 1973–78; Industrial Develt Adv. Bd, DTI, 1992–96; Co-opted Council of Inst. of Chartered Accountants, 1974–78; Economic and Fiscal Policy Cttee, CBI, 1981–88; Council, BIM, 1974–78 (CIMgt (CBIM 1975)). Mem., Develt Cttee, NACF, 1988–98; Vice Chm., St Katherine and Shadwell Trust, 2000 (Mem., 1990–); Founder Mem., Royal Albert Dock Trust, 1992–; Dir, Greenwich Millennium Trust, 1996–2001. President: Poplar, Blackwall and Dist Rowing Club, 1992–; Pitlochry Angling Club, 1994–. Gov., Chelsea Open Air Nursery Sch., 1992– (Dep. Chm., 1994–). Hon. British Consul, Norfolk, Va, 1960–62. Member: Co. of Chartered Accountants, 1976; Co. of Shipwrights, 1990. Younger Brother, Trinity House, 1996. FCIT 1988. *Address:* National Maritime Museum, Greenwich SE10 9NF. *T:* (020) 8312 6630. *Clubs:* Brooks's, MCC, Flyfishers', HAC.

HARDY, Herbert Charles; non-executive Director: Accord Holdings, since 2000; Press Holdings, since 1999 (Deputy Chairman and Chief Executive, 1995–99); Deputy Chairman, The Scotsman Publications Ltd, 1995–99; *b* 13 Dec. 1928; *s* of Charles John Hardy and Margaret Elizabeth (*née* Burniston); *m* 1959, Irene Burrows (marr. diss. 1992); one *d*; *m* 1999, Janet Goldsmith. *Educ:* RMA, Sandhurst. Chief Exec., Associated Newspapers Ltd, 1989–94; Chm., Evening Standard Co. Ltd, 1989–94; Chief Exec., The European, 1995–98; Director: Associated Newspaper Hldgs, 1986–94; Channel 4 Television Corp., 1992–98 (Dep. Chm., 1997–98); Channel One TV, 1994–95; Teletext Holdings, 1995–96. *Recreations:* golf, horse racing.

HARDY, Sir James (Gilbert), Kt 1981; OBE 1975; Director, BRL Hardy Ltd, since 1992; Chairman of Directors: Thomas Hardy & Sons Pty Ltd, 1981–92; Houghton Wines Pty Ltd, 1981–92; Director/Trustee, HM Bark Endeavour Foundation, since 1996; *b* 20 Nov. 1932; *s* of Tom Mayfield Hardy and Eileen C. Hardy; *m* 1st, 1956, Anne Christine Jackson (marr. diss. 1991); two *s*; 2nd, 1991, Joan Margaret McInnes. *Educ:* St Peter's Coll., Adelaide, SA; S Australian Sch. of Mines; S Australian Inst. of Technol. (Dip. in Accountancy). FCPA; FAICD. National Service, 13th Field Artillery Regt, Adelaide, 1951. Elder Smith & Co. Ltd, 1951; J. C. Correll & Co., 1952; Thomas Hardy & Sons Pty Ltd, Winemakers, Adelaide, 1953–92: Shipping Clerk, Sales Rep., Sales Supervisor and Lab. Asst, 1953–62; Dir and Manager, Sydney Br., 1962–77; Regional Dir, Eastern Australia, 1977–81. Director: S Australian Film Corp., 1981–87; America's Cup Challenge 1983 Ltd, 1981–85; Advertiser Newspapers Ltd, 1983–88; Lorna Hodgkinson Sunshine Home Ltd, 1993–. Dep. Chm., Racing Rules Cttee, Yachting Fedn, 1969–81; Dir of Sailing/Captain, S Australian Challenge for the Defence of America's Cup 1984–87. Vice Pres., Internat. 12 Metre Assoc., 1986–. Treasurer, Liquor Trade Supervisory Council of NSW, 1965–70; Fellow, Catering Inst. of Australia, 1972; Pres., Wine and Brandy Assoc. of NSW, 1980–83. NSW Chm., Aust. National Travel Assoc., 1976; Vice Pres., Royal Blind Soc. of NSW, 1980–88 (Mem. Council, 1967–91); Pres., NSW Aust. Football League and Sydney Football League, 1982–83; Pres., "One and All" Sailing Ship Assoc. of SA Inc., 1981–90; Chm., Adelaide 1998 Commonwealth Games Bid, 1990–92; Mem., Bd of Advice, Rothmans Nat. Sport Foundn, 1985–87; Trustee: Rothmans Foundn, 1987–93; Sydney Cricket and Sports Ground Trust, 1990–95; Mem., Council, Australian Nat. Maritime Mus., 1992–97. Chairman: Adv. Cttee, Life Educn Centre of SA, 1988–91; Landcare Australia Ltd Foundn, 1994–98; Adv. Cttee, Natural Heritage Trust, 1998–. Member: Exec. Cttee, Neurosurgical Res. Foundn of SA, 1988–; Adv. Bd, John Curtin Sch. of Medical Res., ANU, Canberra, 1982–87. Dep. Grand Master, United Grand Lodge of NSW, 1977–80. Australian Yachtsman of the Year, 1981. *Recreation:* yachting (skipper or helmsman in America's Cup and Admiral's Cup races). *Address:* BRL Hardy Wine Co., 27 Myrtle Street, Pagewood, NSW 2019, Australia. *T:* (2) 96665855, *Fax:* (2) 93169738. *Clubs:* Royal Ocean Racing; Australian, Tattersalls, Royal Sydney Yacht Squadron (Sydney); Cruising Yacht of Australia (NSW); Royal Perth Yacht; Fort Worth Boat (Texas, USA); New York Yacht.

HARDY, Maj.-Gen. John Campbell, CB 1985; LVO 1978; Administrator, Sion College, 1993–2000; *b* 13 Oct. 1933; *s* of late General Sir Campbell Hardy, KCB, CBE, DSO; *m* 1961, Jennifer Mary Kempton; one *s* one *d*. *Educ:* Sherborne School. Joined Royal Marines, 1952; 45 Commando, 1954; HMS Superb, 1956; Instructor, NCOs' School, Plymouth, 1957; 42 Commando, 1959; 43 Commando, 1962; Adjt, Jt Service Amphibious Warfare Centre, 1964; Company Comdr, 45 Commando, 1965; sc Bracknell, 1966; Instr, RNC Greenwich, 1967; Extra Equerry to Prince Philip, 1968–69; SO, Dept of CGRM, 1969; Rifle Company Comdr, 41 Commando, 1971; ndc Latimer, 1972; Staff of Chief of Defence Staff, 1973; Staff Officer HQ Commando Forces, 1975; CO RM Poole, 1977; CofS and Asst Defence Attaché, British Defence Staff Washington, 1979; ADC to the Queen, 1981–82; Chief of Staff to Comdt Gen. RM, 1982–84; DCS (Support) to C-in-C Allied Forces N Europe, 1984–87. Col Comdt, RM, 1990–94. Dir, British Digestive Foundn, 1987–92. *Address:* c/o National Westminster Bank plc, 31 High Street, Deal, Kent CT14 6EW. *Club:* Army and Navy.

HARDY, Michael James Langley; Director for Telecommunications Policy and Postal Services, Directorate-General for Information Technologies and Industries, and Telecommunications, Commission of the European Communities, 1992–93; *b* 30 Jan. 1933; *s* of James Hardy and Rosina (*née* Langley); *m* 1959, Dr Swana Metger; one *s* two *d*. *Educ:* Beckenham Grammar Sch.; Magdalen Coll., Oxford (Exhibnr; BA 1956; MA 1959); Magdalene Coll., Cambridge (LLB 1957; LLM 1963); Exeter Sch. of Art and Design (BA (Fine Art) Plymouth, 1996). Called to the Bar, Gray's Inn, 1957. Asst Lecturer, Law Faculty: Manchester Univ., 1958–59; KCL, 1959–60; Legal Officer, later Sen. Legal Officer, Legal Service, UN, 1960–73; Legal Adviser, Govt of Nepal, 1968–69 (on leave of absence from UN); Commn of the European Communities, 1973–93: Legal Adviser, Legal Service, 1973–77; Head of Div., Japan, Australia and NZ, Directorate-General for External Relations, 1978–82; Head of Commn Delegn, New York, 1982–87; Dir for Gen. Affairs, Directorate-Gen. for Telecommunications, Information Industries and Innovation, 1987–92. *Publications:* Blood Feuds and the Payment of Blood Money in the Middle East, 1963; Modern Diplomatic Law, 1968; articles in legal and political science jls. *Recreations:* walking, talking. *Address:* Castle House, Gidleigh, Devon TQ13 8HR. *T:* (01647) 433567.

HARDY, Sir Richard (Charles Chandos), 5th Bt *cr* 1876, of Dunstall Hall, co. Stafford; *b* 6 Feb. 1945; *o s* of Sir Rupert Hardy, 4th Bt and of Hon. Diana Joan Allsopp, *er d* of 3rd Baron Hindlip; *S* father, 1997; *m* 1972, Venetia, *d* of late Simon Wingfield Digby, TD; four *d*. *Educ:* Eton. *Heir: cousin* Gerald Alan Hardy [*b* 4 April 1926; *m* 1953, Carolyn, *d* of Maj.-Gen. Arthur Charles Tarver Evanson, CB, MC; two *d*]. *Address:* Springfield House, Gillingham, Dorset SP8 5RD.

HARDY, Robert; *see* Hardy, T. S. R.

HARDY, His Honour Robert James; a Circuit Judge, 1979–94; *b* 12 July 1924; *s* of James Frederick and Ann Hardy; *m* 1951, Maureen Scott; one *s* one *d*. *Educ:* Mostyn House Sch.; Wrekin Coll.; University Coll., London (LLB). Served, 1942–46, Royal Navy, as Pilot, Fleet Air Arm. Called to Bar, 1950; a Recorder of the Crown Court, 1972–79. *Recreation:* sailing. *Address:* Smithy House, Sandlebridge, Little Warford, Cheshire SK9 7TY. *T:* (01565) 872535; Betlem, Mallorca.

HARDY, Rt Rev. Robert Maynard, CBE 2001; Bishop of Lincoln, 1986–2001; *b* 5 Oct. 1936; *s* of Harold and Monica Mavie Hardy; *m* 1970, Isobel Mary, *d* of Charles and Ella Burch; two *s* one *d*. *Educ:* Queen Elizabeth Grammar School, Wakefield; Clare College, Cambridge (MA). Deacon 1962, priest 1963; Assistant Curate, All Saints and Martyrs, Langley, Manchester, 1962; Fellow and Chaplain, Selwyn College, Cambridge, 1965 (Hon. Fellow, 1986); Vicar of All Saints, Borehamwood, 1972; Priest-in-charge, Aspley Guise, 1975; Course Director, St Albans Diocese Ministerial Training Scheme, 1975; Incumbent of United Benefice of Aspley Guise with Husborne Crawley and Ridgmont, 1980; Bishop Suffragan of Maidstone, 1980–86; Bishop to HM Prisons, 1985–2001. Hon. DD Hull, 1992. *Recreations:* walking, gardening, reading. *Address:* Carleton House, Back Lane, Langwathby, Penrith, Cumbria CA10 1NB. *T:* (01768) 881210.

HARDY, (Timothy Sydney) Robert, CBE 1981; FSA; actor and writer; *b* 29 Oct. 1925; *s* of late Major Henry Harrison Hardy, CBE, and Edith Jocelyn Dugdale; *m* 1st, 1952, Elizabeth (marr. diss.), *d* of late Sir Lionel Fox and Lady Fox; one *s*; 2nd, 1961, Sally (marr. diss. 1986), *d* of Sir Neville Pearson, 2nd Bt, and Dame Gladys Cooper, DBE; two *d*. *Educ:* Rugby Sch.; Magdalen Coll., Oxford (Hons degree, Eng. Lit.). *Stage:* Shakespeare Meml Theatre, 1949–51; London, West End, 1951–53; Old Vic Theatre, 1953–54; USA, 1954 and 1956–58 (plays incl. Hamlet and Henry V); Shakespeare Meml 1959 Centenary Season; Rosmersholm, Comedy, 1960; The Rehearsal, Globe, 1961; A Severed Head, Criterion, 1963; The Constant Couple, New, 1967; I've Seen You Cut Lemons, Fortune, 1969; Habeas Corpus, Lyric, 1974; Dear Liar, Mermaid, 1982; Winnie, Victoria Palace, 1988; Body and Soul, Albery, 1992; Churchill, in Celui qui a dit non, Paris, 1999; *films include:* The Far Pavilions, 1983; The Shooting Party, 1985; Jenny's War, 1985; Paris by Night, 1988; War and Remembrance, 1988; Mary Shelley's Frankenstein, 1994; A Feast at Midnight, 1995; Sense and Sensibility, 1996; Mrs Dalloway, 1997; The Tichborne Claimant, 1998; The Barber of Siberia, 1998; My Life So Far, 1998; An Ideal Husband, 1999; *television:* David Copperfield; Age of Kings, 1960; Trouble-shooters, 1966–67; Elizabeth R, 1970; Manhunt, 1970; Edward VII, 1973; All Creatures Great and Small, 1978–80, 1983, 1985, 1987–90; Speed King; Fothergill; Winston Churchill—The Wilderness Years, 1981; Paying Guests, 1986; Make and Break, 1986; Churchill in the USA, 1986; Hot Metal, 1987, 1988; Northanger Abbey, 1987; Marcus Welby in Paris (film), 1988; Sherlock Holmes, 1991; Inspector Morse, 1992; Middlemarch, 1993; Castle Ghosts, 1995, 1996 and 1997; Gulliver's Travels (film), Bramwell, 1996; Nancherro, 1998; Midsomer Murders, Tenth Kingdom, 1999; Justice in Wonderland, 2000. Author of TV documentaries: Picardy Affair, 1962; The Longbow, 1972; Horses in our Blood, 1977; Gordon of Khartoum, 1982. Consultant, Mary Rose Trust, 1979– (Trustee, 1991–); Trustee, WWF (UK), 1983–89; Mem., Bd of Trustees of the Royal Armouries, 1984–95; Chm., Berkshire, Buckinghamshire and Oxfordshire Naturalists' Trust Appeal, 1984–90. FSA 1996. Master, Court of Worshipful Co. of Bowyers, 1988–90. Hon. DLitt: Reading, 1990; Durham, 1997. *Publication:* Longbow, 1976, 2nd edn 1992. *Recreations:* archery, horsemanship, bowyery. *Address:* c/o Chatto & Linnit, 123A King's Road, SW3 4PL. *Clubs:* Buck's, Royal Toxophilite, British Longbow.

HARDYMAN, Norman Trenchard, CB 1984; Secretary, Universities Funding Council, 1988–90 (University Grants Committee, 1982–89); *b* 5 Jan. 1930; *s* of late Rev. Arnold Victor Hardyman and late Laura Hardyman; *m* 1961, Carol Rebecca Turner; one *s* one *d*. *Educ:* Clifton Coll.; Christ Church, Oxford. Asst Principal, Min. of Educn, 1955; Principal 1960; Private Sec. to Sec. of State for Educn and Science, 1966–68; Asst Sec. 1968–75, Under-Sec., 1975–79, DES; Under-Sec., DHSS, 1979–81. Mem., UGC for Univ. of S Pacific, 1990–. Treasurer, Univ. of Exeter, 1991–2001. *Recreations:* walking, gardening, reading, photography. *Address:* Sherwell, The Drive, Dawlish, Devon EX7 9JB. *T:* (01626) 866091.

HARE, family name of **Viscount Blakenham** and **Earl of Listowel**.

HARE, Sir David, Kt 1998; FRSL 1985; playwright; *b* 5 June 1947; *s* of Clifford Theodore Rippon Hare and Agnes Cockburn Hare; *m* 1st, 1970, Margaret Matheson (marr. diss. 1980); two *s* one *d*; 2nd, 1992, Nicole Farhi, *qv*. *Educ:* Lancing Coll.; Jesus Coll., Cambridge (MA Hons). Founded Portable Theatre, 1968; Literary Manager and Resident Dramatist, Royal Court, 1969–71; Resident Dramatist, Nottingham Playhouse, 1973; founded Joint Stock Theatre Group, 1975; US/UK Bicentennial Fellowship, 1997; founded Greenpoint Films, 1982; Associate Dir, Nat. Theatre, 1984–88, 1989–97. Officier, l'Ordre des Arts et des Lettres (France), 1997. *Author of plays:* Slag, Hampstead, 1970 (Evening Standard Drama Award, 1970), Royal Court, 1971, NY, 1991; The Great Exhibition, Hampstead, 1972; Knuckle (televised, 1989), Comedy, 1974 (John Llewellyn Rhys Award, 1974); Fanshen, Joint Stock, 1975, NT 1992; The Secret Rapture, NT, 1988 (Drama Award, best play of the year; London Critics Poll, Best Play), NY, 1989 (dir, NY only); Racing Demon, NT, 1990 (Olivier Award, Plays and Players Award, for best play of the year; Critics' Circle Best Play of the Year; Time Out Award, 1990), NY, 1995; Murmuring Judges, NT, 1991; The Absence of War, NT, 1993 (televised, 1996); Skylight, RNT, 1995 (Olivier Award, Best Play, 1996; NY Critics Circle Best Play, 1997), NY and Wyndhams, 1996, Vaudeville, 1997; Amy's View, RNT, transf. Aldwych, 1997, NY 1999; The Judas Kiss, Playhouse, then NY, 1998; Via Dolorosa, Royal Court (Time Out Outstanding Achievement Award), 1998 (also actor), NY (NY Critics Circle, Outer Circle, Drama League, Drama Desk, and Joan Cullman Awards) 1999; *author and director of plays:* Brassneck (with Howard Brenton), Nottingham Playhouse, 1973; Teeth 'n' Smiles, Royal Court, 1975, Wyndhams, 1976; Plenty, NT, 1978, NY, 1983 (NY Critics' Circle Award), Albery (dir. J. Kent), 1999; A Map of the World, Adelaide Fest., 1982, NT, 1983, NY, 1985 (Dramalogue Award); (with Howard Brenton) Pravda, NT, 1985 (London Standard Award; Plays and Players Award; City Limits Award); The Bay at Nice, and Wrecked Eggs, NT, 1986; My Zinc Bed, Royal Court, 2000; *opera libretto:* The Knife, NY Shakespeare Fest., 1987 (also directed); *TV plays:* Man Above Men, 1973; Licking Hitler, 1978 (BAFTA award, 1978) (also directed); Dreams of Leaving, 1980 (also directed); Saigon—Year of the Cat, 1983; Heading Home, 1991. *Directed:* The Party, NT, 1974; Weapons of Happiness, NT, 1976; Total Eclipse, Lyric, Hammersmith, 1981; King Lear, NT, 1986; The Designated Mourner, RNT, 1996; Heartbreak House, Almeida, 1997. *Adapted:* Pirandello, The Rules of the Game, NT, 1971, Almeida, 1992; Brecht, Life of Galileo, Almeida, 1994; Brecht, Mother Courage and her Children, RNT, 1995; Chekhov, Ivanov, Almeida, 1997; Schnitzler (La Ronde), The Blue Room, Donmar Warehouse, 1998, NY 1999, Th. Royal, Haymarket, 2000; Chekhov, Platonov, Almeida, 2001. *Films:* wrote and directed: Wetherby, 1985 (Golden Bear award, 1985); Paris by Night, 1988; Strapless, 1989; (screenplay) Plenty, 1985; Damage (adapted from novel by Josephine Hart), 1992; The Secret Rapture, 1994; dir., The Designated Mourner, 1997; wrote and acted, Via Dolorosa, 2000; (screenplay) The Hours (adapted from novel by Michael Cunningham), 2001; *Publications:* Slag, 1970; The Great Exhibition, 1972; Knuckle, 1974; Brassneck, 1974; Fanshen, 1976; Teeth 'n' Smiles, 1976; Plenty, 1978; Licking Hitler, 1978; Dreams of Leaving, 1980; A Map of the World, 1982; Saigon, 1983; Pravda, 1985; Wetherby, 1985; The Bay at Nice and Wrecked Eggs, 1986; The Secret Rapture, 1988; Paris By Night, 1989; Strapless, 1990; Racing Demon, 1990; Writing Lefthanded, 1991; Heading Home, 1991; Murmuring Judges, 1991; The Absence of War, 1993; Asking Around, 1993; Rules of the Game, 1994; Skylight, 1995; Mother Courage, 1995; Plays One, 1996; Plays Two, 1996; Amy's View, 1997; Ivanov, 1997; The Judas Kiss, 1998; The Blue Room, 1998; Via Dolorosa, 1998; Acting Up, 1999; My Zinc Bed, 2000; Platonov, 2001; The Hours, 2002.

HARE, Ewan Nigel Christian, (Nick); Deputy Secretary-General (Development Co-operation) of the Commonwealth, 1993–99; *b* 11 May 1939; *m* 1985, Raina Ho; one *s* two *d*. *Educ:* Earlham Coll. (BA); Carleton Univ. (DPA). First Sec., Canadian High Commn, Accra, 1969–72; Canadian International Development Agency: Regl Dir, Asia SE, 1972–76; Regl Dir, Central and S Africa, 1976–78; Dir-Gen., Resources Br., 1978–80; Dir-Gen., UN Progs, 1980–84; Ambassador of Canada to Zaire, Rwanda, Burundi and Congo, 1984–87; Dir, Africa Trade Div., Dept of Foreign Affairs, Ottawa, 1987–88; Dir-Gen., Industrial Co-operation Prog., Canadian Internat. Develt Agency, 1988–91; Canadian High Comr to Nigeria and Ambassador to Benin, 1991–93. *Recreations:* ski-ing, canoeing, jogging, sailing. *Address:* 1239 Donald Munro Drive, Carp, ON KOA 1L0, Canada. *Club:* Little Ship.

HARE, Prof. (Frederick) Kenneth, CC 1987 (OC 1978); OOnt 1989; PhD; FRSC 1968; Professor of Geography and Physics, 1969–84, and Director, Institute for Environmental Studies, 1974–79, now University Professor Emeritus in Geography, University of Toronto; *b* Wylye, Wilts, 5 Feb. 1919; *s* of Frederick Eli Hare and Irene Smith; *m* 1st, 1941, Suzanne Alice Bates (marr. diss. 1952); one *s*; 2nd, 1953, Helen Neilson Morrill; one *s* one *d*. *Educ:* Windsor Grammar Sch.; King's Coll., University of London (BSc); Univ. of Montreal (PhD). Lectr in Geography, Univ. of Manchester, 1940–41; War service in Air Min., Meteorological Office, 1941–45; McGill University: Asst and Assoc. Prof. of Geography, 1945–52; Prof. of Geography and Meteorology, 1952–64; Chm. of Dept, 1950–62; Dean of Faculty of Arts and Science, 1962–64; Prof. of Geography, Univ. of London (King's Coll.), 1964–66; Master of Birkbeck Coll., Univ. of London, 1966–68; Pres., Univ. of British Columbia, 1968–69; Provost, Trinity Coll., Toronto, 1979–86; Chancellor, Trent Univ., 1988–95; Chm., Adv. Bd on Internat. Progs, Univ. of Toronto, 1990–94. Vis. Centenary Prof., Univ. of Adelaide, 1974. FKC 1967. Sci. Advr, Dept of the Environment, Canada, 1972–74. Mem. Nat. Research Council of Canada, 1962–64; Chm. of Bd, Arctic Inst. of N America, 1963; Mem., NERC, 1965–68; Dir, Resources for the Future, 1968–80; Member: SSRC, Canada, 1974–76; Adv. Council, Electric Power Res. Inst., 1978–80. Chairman: Adv. Cttee on Canadian Demonstration Projects, 1974–75, for 1976 UN Conf. on Human Settlements; Special Prog. Panel on Ecoscis, NATO, 1975; Federal Study Gp on Nuclear Waste Disposal, 1977; Climate Programme Planning Bd, Govt of Canada, 1979–90; Commn on Lead in the Environment, RSC, 1984–86; Section W, AAAS, 1985–86; Technical Adv. Panel on Nuclear Safety, Ontario Hydro, 1990–94 (Mem., 1994–99); Comr, Ontario Nuclear Safety Review, 1987–88. President: Canadian Assoc. of Geographers, 1963–64; RMetS, 1967–68 (Vice-Pres., 1968–70); Sigma Xi, 1986–87; Hon. Pres., Assoc. of Amer. Geographers, 1964. Fellow, Amer. Meteorological Soc., 1969 (Emeritus Fellow, 1994); Hon. Fellow: Amer. Geographical Soc., 1963; Royal Canadian Geographical Soc., 1997. Hon. Life Mem., Birkbeck Coll., 1969; Hon. Fellow, Trinity Coll., Toronto, 1990. Hon. LLD: Queen's (Canada) Univ., 1964; Univ. of W Ontario, 1968; Trent Univ., 1979; Memorial Univ., 1985; Toronto, 1987; Hon. DSc: McGill, 1969; York (Canada), 1978; Windsor, 1988; Guelph, Ontario, 1996; DSc *ad eund.* Adelaide, 1974; Hon. DSLitt Thorneloe Coll., Sudbury (Canada), 1984. Hon. Cert. Graduation, Nat. Defence Coll., Kingston, Canada, 1986. Meritorious Achievement Citation, Assoc. Amer. Geographers, 1961; President's Prize, RMetS (Can.), 1961, 1962; Patterson Medal, Can. Met. Service, 1973; Massey Medal, Royal Can. Geographical Soc., 1974; Patron's Medal, RGS, 1977; Award for Scholarly Distinction, Canadian Assoc. of Geographers, 1979; Univ. of Toronto Alumni Assoc. Faculty Award, 1982; Sir William Dawson Medal, RSC, 1987; Cullum Medal, Amer. Geographical Soc., 1987; Internat. Meteorol Orgn Prize, 1988. *Publications:* The Restless Atmosphere, 1953; On University Freedom, 1968; (with M. K. Thomas) Climate Canada, 1974, 2nd edn 1979; numerous articles in Quarterly Jl Royal Meteorological Soc., Geography, and other learned jls. *Recreation:* music. *Address:* 301 Lakeshore Road West, Oakville, ON L6K 1G2, Canada. *Clubs:* McGill Faculty (Montreal) (Hon. Life Mem.); Toronto Faculty, York (Toronto).

HARE, Kenneth; *see* Hare, F. K.

HARE, Prof. Lisa Anne; *see* Jardine, L. A.

HARE, Margaret Flora, (Mrs David Hare); *see* Spittle, M. F.

HARE, Sir Nicholas (Patrick), 7th Bt *cr* 1818, of Stow Hall, Norfolk; *b* 27 Aug. 1955; *o s* of Sir Philip Hare, 6th Bt and of Anne Lisle Hare (*née* Nicholson); *S* father, 2000; *m* 1982, Caroline Keith, *d* of T. P. K. Allan; two *s*. *Educ:* Bryanston. *Heir: s* Thomas Hare, *b* 7 Aug. 1986. *Address:* Marsh Barn, Ashley, Tetbury, Glos GL8 8SX.

HARE, Nick; *see* Hare, E. N. C.

HARE, Nicole, (Lady Hare); *see* Farhi, N.

HARE, Paul Webster, LVO 1985; HM Diplomatic Service; Ambassador to the Republic of Cuba, since 2001; *b* 20 July 1951; *s* of Maurice Leslie Hare and Anne Dorothy Hare (*née* Webster); *m* 1978, Lynda Carol Henderson, *d* of Ian Stuart McWalter Henderson, CBE, GM, KPM and Marie Beatrice Henderson (*née* Green); three *s* three *d*. *Educ:* Leeds Grammar Sch. (Foundn Schol.); Trinity Coll., Oxford (Open Schol., MA 1st Cl. Hons PPE 1972). Qualified as solicitor, with Herbert Smith & Co., London, 1973–75; TEFL, Biella and Genoa, Italy, 1976; Corporate Finance Dept, J. Henry Schroder Wagg & Co., London, 1976–78; entered HM Diplomatic Service, 1978: Private Sec. to Ambassador to EC, Brussels, 1979–80; First Sec. and Hd of Chancery, Lisbon, 1981–85; FCO, 1985–88; Consul and Dep. Dir, Investment, USA, NY, 1988–94; Dep. Hd of Mission and Counsellor (Commercial and Economic), Caracas, 1994–97; Hd, Non-Proliferation Dept, FCO, 1997–2001. Pres., Baseball Softball UK, 2000–. Order of Prince Henry the Navigator (Portugal), 1985; Order of 5 May 1810, Barinas (Venezuela), 1995. *Recreations:* family, music (piano, lieder), sport (squash, baseball, tennis), writing novels. *Address:* c/o Foreign and Commonwealth Office, King Charles Street, SW1A 2AH. *Clubs:* Rocky Point (Old Greenwich, Conn); Caracas Sports.

HARE, Rt Rev. Richard; *see* Hare, Rt Rev. Thomas Richard.

HARE, Prof. Richard Mervyn, FBA 1964; White's Professor of Moral Philosophy, University of Oxford, and Fellow of Corpus Christi College, Oxford, 1966–83 (Hon. Fellow, 1983); *b* 21 March 1919; *s* of late Charles Francis Aubone Hare and late Louise Kathleen (*née* Simonds); *m* 1947, Catherine, *d* of Sir Harry Verney, 4th Bt, DSO; one *s* three *d*. *Educ:* Rugby (Schol.); Balliol Coll., Oxford (Schol.). Commissioned Royal Artillery, 1940; Lieut, Indian Mountain Artillery, 1941; Prisoner of War, Singapore and Siam, 1942–45. 1st Lit. Hum. 1947. Fellow and Tutor in Philosophy, Balliol Coll., Oxford, 1947–66, Hon. Fellow, 1974; Wilde Lectr in Natural Religion, Oxford, 1963–66. Graduate Res. Prof. of Phil., Univ. of Florida at Gainesville, 1983–94. Visiting Fellow: Princeton, 1957; ANU, 1966; Center for Advanced Study in Behavioral Sciences, Stanford, 1980; Visiting Professor: Univ. of Michigan, 1968; Univ. of Delaware, 1974. Pres., Aristotelian Soc., 1972–73. Member: Nat. Road Safety Advisory Council, 1966–68; C of E Working Parties on Medical Questions, 1964–75. Hon. Fellow, Inst. of Life Scis, Hastings Center, 1974; For. Hon. Mem., American Acad. of Arts and Sciences, 1975. Hon. PhD Lund, 1991. Tanner Award, 1979. *Publications:* The Language of Morals, 1952; Freedom and Reason, 1963; Essays on Philosophical Method, 1971; Practical Inferences, 1971; Essays on the Moral Concepts, 1972; Applications of Moral Philosophy, 1972; Moral Thinking, 1981; Plato, 1982; Hare and Critics, 1988; Essays in Ethical Theory, 1989; Essays on Political Morality, 1989; Essays on Religion and Education, 1992; Essays on Bioethics, 1993; Zum Moralischen Denken, 1994; Sorting Out Ethics, 1997; Objective Prescriptions and Other Essays, 1999. *Recreations:* music, gardening. *Address:* Bywater, The Street, Ewelme, near Wallingford, Oxon OX10 6HQ.

HARE, Rt Rev. (Thomas) Richard; Suffragan Bishop of Pontefract, 1971–92; *b* 29 Aug. 1922; *m* 1963, Sara (*d* 1999), *d* of Lt-Col J. E. Spedding, OBE; one *s* two *d*. *Educ:* Marlborough; Trinity Coll., Oxford; Westcott House, Cambridge. RAF, 1942–45. Curate of Haltwhistle, 1950–52; Domestic Chaplain to Bishop of Manchester, 1952–59; Canon Residentiary of Carlisle Cathedral, 1959–65; Archdeacon of Westmorland and Furness, 1965–71; Vicar of St George with St Luke, Barrow-in-Furness, 1965–69; Vicar of Winster, 1969–71. *Address:* Wood Cottage, Mirehouse, Keswick, Cumbria CA12 4QE. *T:* (017687) 72996.

HARE DUKE, Rt Rev. Michael Geoffrey; Bishop of St Andrews, Dunkeld and Dunblane, 1969–94; *b* 28 Nov. 1925; *s* of late A. R. A. Hare Duke, Civil Engineer; *m* 1949, Grace Lydia Frances McKean Dodd; one *s* three *d*. *Educ:* Bradfield Coll.; Trinity Coll., Oxford. BA 1949, MA 1951. Sub-Lt, RNVR, 1944–46. Deacon, 1952; Priest, 1953; Curate, St John's Wood Church, 1952–56; Vicar, St Mark's, Bury, 1956–62; Pastoral Dir, Clin. Theol. Assoc., 1962–64; Vicar, St Paul's, Daybrook, and Pastoral Consultant to Clin. Theol. Assoc., 1964–69; OCF, E Midland Dist HQ, 1968–69. Chairman: Scottish Assoc. for Mental Health, 1978–85; Age Concern Scotland, 1994–2000. Mem. Editorial Bd, Contact Magazine, 1962–79. Hon. DD St Andrews, 1994. *Publications:* (jtly) The Caring Church, 1963; (jtly) First Aid in Counselling, 1968; Understanding the Adolescent, 1969; The Break of Glory, 1970; Freud, 1972; Good News, 1976; Stories, Signs and Sacraments in the Emerging Church, 1982; (ed) Praying for Peace, 1991; Hearing the Stranger, 1994; contributor to: Expository Times, Blackfriars, New Christian, Church Quarterly Review, Church Times, Contact. *Address:* 2 Balhousie Avenue, Perth PH1 5HN. *T:* and *Fax:* (01738) 622642; *e-mail:* bishmick@aol.com.

HAREN, Dr Patrick Hugh, FREng, FIEE; Group Chief Executive, Viridian Group PLC, and Chairman, Northern Ireland Electricity plc, since 1998; *b* 4 Aug. 1950; *s* of

James Joseph Haren and Sarah Haren; *m* 1971, Anne Elizabeth McNally; two *s*. *Educ:* Queen's Univ. Belfast (BSc 1971; PhD 1976); University Coll., Dublin (MBA 1986). FIEE 1990; FREng (FEng 1998). Power Systems Engrg, Electricity Supply Bd, Dublin, 1971–73; Engr, Superconducting Magnet Prog., CERN, Geneva, 1976–78; Electricity Supply Board, Dublin: engrg appts, 1978–84; Divl Manager, Strategic Planning, 1985–87; Regl Accountant, 1987–88; Manager, Business Ventures, 1988–89; Dir, 1989–92; Dir, Hoermann Electronics Ltd, 1990–91; Chief Exec., NI Electricity, 1992–98. Mem. Study Cttee, Power System Operation and Control, CIGRE, 1982–86. *Publications:* technical papers in power system operation and computer control. *Recreations:* ski-ing, walking, languages. *Address:* Viridian Group PLC, Danesfort House, 120 Malone Road, Belfast BT9 5HT. *T:* (028) 9066 8416.

HARES, Phillip Douglas George, CBE 1985; Chairman and Chief Executive, 1986–87, and Board Member for Finance, 1981–86, British Shipbuilders (Deputy Chief Executive, 1983–86); *b* 31 Dec. 1926; *s* of Edgar Sidney George and Edith Winifred Frances Hares; *m* 1955, Violet May Myers; one *s* one *d*. *Educ:* Richmond and East Sheen Grammar Sch. Involved with management sciences and computing in various commercial, industrial, and consulting organisations, 1952–69, dating from early application of computers in 1952 with J. Lyons & Co. Ltd; Asst Man. Dir (Ops), British Mail Order Corp. Ltd (Great Universal Stores), 1969–77; Man. Dir (Finance), British Shipbuilders, 1978–81, Corporate Man. Dir, 1982–83; Chairman: Falmouth Shiprepair Ltd, 1983–85; Vosper Shiprepairers Ltd, 1983–85; Dir, Iron Trades Insce Gp, 1985–97. Member Council: CBI, 1983–87 (Mem., Economic Situation Cttee, 1983–87); Amer. Bureau of Shipping, 1986–87. FRSA 1987–91. Freeman, City of London, 1983; Liveryman, Worshipful Co. of Shipwrights, 1984–94. *Recreations:* reading, music, genealogy. *Address:* Leverets, 8 Downside Close, Charmouth, Dorset DT6 6BH. *T:* (01297) 560042; *e-mail:* phillipshares@clara.net.

HAREWOOD, 7th Earl of, *cr* 1812; **George Henry Hubert Lascelles,** KBE 1986; Baron Harewood, 1796; Viscount Lascelles, 1812; President, British Board of Film Classification, 1985–97; *b* 7 Feb. 1923; *er s* of 6th Earl of Harewood, KG, GCVO, DSO, and HRH Princess Mary (Princess Royal; who *d* 28 March 1965); *S* father, 1947; *m* 1st, 1949, Maria Donata (marr. diss. 1967; she *m* 1973, Rt Hon. (John) Jeremy Thorpe), *d* of late Erwin Stein; three *s*; 2nd, 1967, Patricia Elizabeth, *d* of Charles Tuckwell, Australia; one *s* and one step *s*. *Educ:* Eton; King's Coll., Cambridge (MA; Hon. Fellow, 1984). Served War of 1939–45, Capt. Grenadier Guards (wounded and prisoner, 1944, released May 1945); ADC to Earl of Athlone, 1945–46, Canada. Editor of magazine "Opera" 1950–53; Royal Opera House, Covent Garden: a Dir, 1951–53; on staff, 1953–60; a Dir, 1969–72; Chm. Bd, ENO (formerly Sadler's Wells Opera), 1986–95 (Man. Dir, 1972–85); Artistic Director: Edinburgh Internat. Festival, 1961–65; Leeds Festival, 1958–74; Adelaide Festival 1988; Artistic Adviser: New Philharmonia Orch., London, 1966–76; Buxton Fest., 1993–98; Man. Dir, English Nat. Opera North, 1978–81. Governor of BBC, 1985–87. Chm., Music Advisory Cttee of British Council, 1956–66; Chancellor of the Univ. of York, 1963–67; Member: Arts Council, 1966–72; Gen. Adv. Council of BBC, 1969–77. President: English Football Assoc., 1963–72; Leeds United Football Club, 1962–. Hon. RAM, 1983; Hon. LLD: Leeds, 1959; Aberdeen, 1966; Hon. DMus Hull, 1962; DUniv York, 1982. Janáček Medal, 1978. *Publications:* (ed) Kobbé's Complete Opera Book, 1953, 4th edn 1997; The Tongs and the Bones (autobiog.), 1981; Kobbé's Illustrated Opera Book, 1989; Pocket Kobbé, 1994. *Heir: s* Viscount Lascelles, *qv*. *Address:* Harewood House, Leeds LS17 9LG.

See also Barry Tuckwell.

HARFORD, Sir (John) Timothy, 3rd Bt *cr* 1934; Vice-Chairman, 1985–87, Deputy Chairman, 1987–93, Chairman, 1993–99, Wesleyan and General, then Wesleyan Assurance Society; *b* 6 July 1932; *s* of Sir George Arthur Harford, 2nd Bt and Anstice Marion (*d* 1993), *d* of Sir Alfred Tritton, 2nd Bt; *S* father, 1967; *m* 1962, Carolyn Jane Mullens; two *s* one *d*. *Educ:* Harrow Sch.; Oxford Univ.; Harvard Business Sch. Philip Hill Higginson Erlangers Ltd, 1960–63; Director: Birmingham Industrial Trust Ltd, 1963–67; Singer & Friedlander Ltd, 1970–88 (Local Dir, 1967–69); Dep. Chm., Wolseley-Hughes Gp, then Wolseley Gp, 1983–97; Chm., 1990–94, Dep. Chm., 1994–97, Kwik Save Gp; Dep. Chm., Wagon Industrial Holdings, 1991–98. *Recreations:* wine and food, travel. *Heir: s* Mark John Harford [*b* 6 Aug. 1964; *m* 1999, Louise, *d* of Robert Langford]. *Address:* South House, South Littleton, Evesham, Worcs WR11 5TJ. *T:* (01386) 830478. *Club:* Boodle's.

HARGREAVES, Andrew Raikes; UK Chairman, European Aeronautics Defence and Space Company, since 2000; *b* 15 May 1955; *s* of Col and Mrs D. W. Hargreaves; *m* 1978, Fiona Susan, *o d* of G. W. Dottridge; two *s*. *Educ:* Eton; St Edmund Hall, Oxford (MA Hons). Auctioneer and valuation expert, Christies, 1977–81; executive, Hill Samuel & Co. Ltd, 1981–83; Asst Dir, Sanwa Internat. Ltd, 1983–85; Asst Dir J. Henry Schroder Wagg & Co. Ltd, 1985–87; Consultant: Schroders plc, 1987–92; Midlands Electricity plc, 1989–97; UK Man. Dir, Daimler-Benz, subseq. DaimlerChrysler, Aerospace AG, 1997–2000. Non-exec. Dir, EADS Defence Systems and Electronics (UK) Ltd, 2001–. Contested (C) Blyth Valley, 1983. MP (C) Birmingham, Hall Green, 1987–97; contested (C) same seat, 1997. PPS to Ministers of State, FCO, 1992–97. Member: Select Cttee on Information, 1992–97; Select Cttee for Parly Comr for Admin, 1993–97; Secretary: back bench Urban and Inner Cities Cttee, 1987–91 (Chm., 1992–94); back bench Defence Cttee, 1992–94 (Vice-Chm., 1994–97). Mem., Bow Gp. *Recreations:* fishing, gardening, walking, antiques, art. *Address:* EADS (UK) Ltd, The Economist Building, 25 St James's Street, SW1A 1HA. *Club:* Boodle's.

HARGREAVES, David Harold, PhD; Chief Executive, Qualifications and Curriculum Authority, 2000–01; Fellow, Wolfson College, Cambridge, since 1988; *b* 31 Aug. 1939; *s* of Clifford and Marion Hargreaves. *Educ:* Bolton School; Christ's College, Cambridge (MA, PhD). Asst Master, Hull Grammar Sch., 1961–64; Research Associate, Dept. of Sociology and Social Anthropology, Univ. of Manchester, 1964–65; Lectr, Senior Lectr then Reader, Dept. of Education, Univ. of Manchester, 1965–79; Reader in Education and Fellow of Jesus College, Oxford, 1979–84; Chief Inspector, ILEA, 1984–88; University of Cambridge: Prof. of Educn, 1988–2000; Member: Gen. Bd of the Faculties, 1989–92; Local Exams Syndicate, 1990–92; Bd of Grad. Studies, 1990–92; Chairman: Council, Sch. of Humanities and Soc. Scis, 1990–92; Cttee on the Training and Develt of Univ. Teachers, 1990–92; Needs Cttee, 1991–92. Member: Educn Res. Bd, SSRC, 1979–82; Educn Adv. Council, Royal Opera House, Covent Garden, 1985–90; Educn Adv. Council, IBA, 1988–90; ESRC, 1991–95; Res. Cttee, Teacher Trng Agency, 1995–97; Educn Cttee, Nat. Endowment for Sci., Technol. and the Arts, 1999–; Nat. Educnl Res. Forum, 1999–; Bd, British Educnl Communications and Technol. Agency, 1999–2000; Jt Vice-Chm., Sec. of State for Educn and Employment's Standards Task Force, 1997–. Chairman: Eastern Arts Bd, 1991–94; Res. Centres Bd, 1992–94; Internat. Adv. Council on Quality of Educn, NSW, 1993–95. Non-exec. Dir, W Suffolk Hosps NHS Trust, 1998–2000. FRSA 1984; Founding Academician, Acad. of Social Scis, 1999. *Publications:* Social Relations in a Secondary School, 1967; Interpersonal Relations and Education, 1972; (jtly) Deviance in Classrooms, 1975; The Challenge for the Comprehensive School, 1982; (jtly) Planning for School Development, 1990; (jtly) The Empowered School, 1991; The Mosaic of Learning, 1994; (jtly) On-the-Job Training for Surgeons, 1997; (jtly) On-the-Job Training for Physicians, 1997; Creative Professionalism, 1998. *Recreation:* the arts. *Address:* Wolfson College, Cambridge CB3 9BB. *Club:* Athenæum.

HARGREAVES, Prof. Ian Richard; Professor of Journalism, University of Wales, Cardiff, since 1998; *b* 18 June 1951; *s* of Ronald and Edna Hargreaves; *m* 1st, 1972, Elizabeth Anne Crago (marr. diss. 1991); one *s* one *d*; 2nd, 1993, Adele Esther Blakebrough, *d* of Rev. E. and M. Blakebrough; two *d*. *Educ:* Burnley Grammar Sch.; Altrincham Grammar Sch.; Queens' Coll., Cambridge (MA). Community worker, Kaleidescope Project, 1972–73; Reporter, Keighley News, 1973–74; Journalist, Bradford Telegraph & Argus, 1974–76; Financial Times, 1976–87: Industrial Corresp.; Transport Corresp.; New York Corresp.; Social Affairs Ed.; Resources Ed.; Features Ed.; Man. Ed., 1987–88, Controller, 1988–89, Dir, 1989–90, News and Current Affairs, BBC; Dep. Editor, The Financial Times, 1990–94; Editor: Independent, 1994–96; New Statesman & Soc., then New Statesman, 1996–98. Mem. Bd, S London and Maudsley NHS Trust, 2000–. Chm., Demos, 1997–; Member Board: New Statesman, 1996–; Greenpeace UK, 1997–; Presentable. *Publications:* Sharper Vision: the BBC and the communications revolution, 1993; (with Ian Christie) Tomorrow's Politics: the third way and beyond, 1998; Who's Misunderstanding Whom?: science and the media, 2000. *Recreations:* football, fell-walking, tennis. *Address:* Centre for Journalism Studies, Bute Building, King Edward VII Avenue, Cardiff CF1 3NB. *T:* (029) 2087 5420.

HARGREAVES, Prof. John Desmond; Professor of History, University of Aberdeen, 1962–85; *b* 25 Jan. 1924; *s* of Arthur Swire Hargreaves and Margaret Hilda (*née* Duckworth); *m* 1950, Sheila Elizabeth (*née* Wilks); one *s* two *d*. *Educ:* Skipton Grammar Sch.; Bootham; Manchester Univ. War service, 1943–46. Asst Princ., War Office, 1948; Lectr in History: Manchester Univ., 1948–52; Fourah Bay Coll., Sierra Leone, 1952–54; Aberdeen Univ., 1954–62. Vis. Prof., Union Coll. Schenectady, New York, 1960–61; Univ. of Ibadan, 1970–71. Mem., Kidd Cttee on Sheriff Court Records, 1966. Pres., African Studies Assoc. (UK), 1972–73. Hon. DLitt Sierra Leone, 1984. *Publications:* Life of Sir Samuel Lewis, 1958; Prelude to the Partition of West Africa, 1963; West Africa: the Former French States, 1967; France and West Africa, 1969; West Africa Partitioned: Vol. I, The Loaded Pause, 1974, Vol. II, The Elephants and the Grass, 1985; The End of Colonial Rule in West Africa, 1979; Aberdeenshire to Africa, 1981; Decolonization in Africa, 1988, 2nd edn 1996; (ed) Aberdeen University 1945–81, 1989; Tensions and Trust (Crathes Castle Community Play), 1992; Academe and Empire, 1994. *Recreations:* hill-walking, theatre. *Address:* Balcluain, Raemoir Road, Banchory, Kincardine AB31 5UJ. *T:* (01330) 825588.

HARGREAVES, (Joseph) Kenneth; Secretary, Association of Conservative Clubs, 1995–99; *b* 1 March 1939; *s* of James and Mary Hargreaves. *Educ:* St Mary's Coll., Blackburn; Manchester Coll. of Commerce. ACIS. Standard Cost/Wages Clerk, NCB, 1957–61; Audit Asst, Treasurer's Dept, Lancs CC, 1961–63; Office Manager, Shopfitters (Lancashire) Ltd, Oswaldtwistle, 1963–83. MP (C) Hyndburn, 1983–92; contested (C) Hyndburn, 1992. Nat. Chm., Right to Life, 2000–; Pres., Accrington and Dist Blind Soc., 1999–. ACIS, 1962; FFA, 1989. Fellow, Inst. of Financial Accountants. *Recreations:* Gilbert and Sullivan, classical music, travel. *Address:* 31 Park Lane, Oswaldtwistle, Accrington, Lancs BB5 3AF. *T:* (01254) 230401.

HARGROVES, Brig. Sir (Robert) Louis, Kt 1987; CBE 1965; DL; *b* 10 Dec. 1917; *s* of William Robert and Mabel Mary Hargroves (*née* Lalonde); *m* 1940, Eileen Elizabeth Anderson; four *d*. *Educ:* St John's College, Southsea. Commissioned South Staffordshire Regt, 1938; served War of 1939–45; CO 1 Staffords, 1959–61; GSO1, RMA Sandhurst, 1962–63; Brig. 1964; comd Aden Bde, 1964–66; MoD, 1966–69; N Command, 1969–72; retired, 1972. Col. Staffordshire Regt, 1971–77. DL Staffs 1974. *Recreations:* field sports. *Address:* Hyde Cottage, Temple Guiting, Cheltenham, Glos GL54 5RT. *T:* (01451) 850242.

HARINGTON, Gen. Sir Charles (Henry Pepys), GCB 1969 (KCB 1964; CB 1961); CBE 1957 (OBE 1953); DSO 1944; MC 1940; ADC (General) to the Queen, 1969–71; *b* 5 May 1910; *s* of Lt-Col H. H. Harington and Dorothy Pepys; *m* 1942, Victoire Marion Williams-Freeman (*d* 2000); one *s* two *d*. *Educ:* Malvern; Sandhurst. Commissioned into 22nd (Cheshire) Regt, 1930. Served War of 1939–45: France and Belgium (incl. Dunkirk), 2nd Bn Cheshire Regt, 1939–40; CO, 1st Bn Manchester Regt and GSO1, 53 (Welch) Div., NW Europe, 1944–45. DS Staff Coll., 1946; GSO1 Mil. Mission Greece, 1948; CO 1st Bn The Parachute Regt, 1949; Mil. Asst to CIGS, 1951; SHAPE, 1953; Comdr 49 Inf. Bde in Kenya, 1955; idc 1957; Comdt Sch. of Infantry, 1958; GOC 3rd Div., 1959; Comdt, Staff Coll., Camberley, 1961; C-in-C Unified Command Middle East, 1963; DCGS, 1966; Chief of Personnel and Logistics, to the three Services, 1968–71, retired; Col The Cheshire Regt, 1962–68. Col Comdt, Small Arms Sch. Corps, 1964–70; Col Comdt, The Prince of Wales Div., 1968–71. President: Combined Cadet Force Assoc., 1971–80; Milocarian (Tri-Service) Athletic Club, 1966–99. Chm. Governors, Royal Star and Garter Home, 1972–80. Commissioner: Royal Hosp., Chelsea, 1970–79; Duke of York's Royal Military Sch., 1971–89. Vice-President: Royal Star and Garter Home, 1980–; Dogs' Home, Battersea, 1993–. Knight Officer with swords, Order of Orange Nassau (Netherlands), 1945. *Clubs:* Army and Navy, Hurlingham (Pres.), 1979–2000.

HARINGTON, Kenneth Douglas Evelyn Herbert; Metropolitan Magistrate, 1967–84; *b* 30 Sept. 1911; *yr s* of late His Honour Edward Harington; *m* 1st, 1939, Lady Cecilia Bowes-Lyon (*d* 1947), *er d* of 15th Earl of Strathmore; 2nd, 1950, Maureen Helen McCalmont (*d* 1992), *d* of Brig.-Gen. Sir Robert McCalmont, KCVO, CBE, DSO; two *s*. *Educ:* Stowe. War of 1939–45: Served NW Europe (Major, Coldstream Guards). Hon. Attaché, British Legation, Stockholm, 1930–32; Barrister, Inner Temple, 1952; Acting Deputy Chm., Inner London and NE London Quarter Sessions, 1966–67. *Recreations:* shooting, fishing. *Address:* Baker's Cottage, Great Rissington, Cheltenham, Glos GL54 2LP. *T:* (01451) 820858.

See also M. K. Harington.

HARINGTON, Michael Kenneth; His Honour Judge Harington; a Circuit Judge, since 2000; *b* 9 Aug. 1951; *s* of Kenneth Douglas Evelyn Herbert Harington, *qv*, and late Maureen Helen (*née* McCalmont); *m* 1984, Deirdre Christine Kehoe; one *s* two *d*. *Educ:* Eton Coll.; Christ Church, Oxford (MA). Called to the Bar, Inner Temple, 1974; a Recorder, 1998. *Recreations:* golf, shooting. *Address:* Southampton Crown Court, Courts of Justice, London Road, Southampton, Hants SO15 2XQ. *Club:* MCC.

HARINGTON, Sir Nicholas (John), 14th Bt *cr* 1611; Legal Adviser, Export Credits Guarantee Department, since 1988; *b* 14 May 1942; *s* of His Honour John Charles Dundas Harington, QC (*d* 1980) (*yr s* of 12th Bt) and Lavender Cecilia Harington (*d* 1982), *d* of late Major E. W. Denny, Garboldisham Manor, Diss; *S* uncle, 1981. *Educ:* Eton; Christ Church, Oxford (MA Jurisprudence). Called to the Bar, 1969. Employed in Persian Gulf, 1971–72. Joined Civil Service, 1972. *Recreations:* numerous. *Heir: b* David Richard

Harington [*b* 27 June 1944; *m* 1983, Deborah (*née* Catesby); two *s*]. *Address:* The Ring o'Bells, Whitbourne, Worcester WR6 5RT. *T:* (01886) 821819.

HARKER, (Ronald) David; Chief Executive, National Association of Citizens Advice Bureaux, since 1997; *b* 2 March 1951; *s* of Stanley Harker and Mary Harker (*née* Macaulay); *m* 1980, Diane Summers; one *s*. *Educ:* Queen Elizabeth Grammar Sch., Darlington; Univ. of E Anglia (BA Social Studies); Univ. of Essex (MA Sociol.); London Business Sch. (MBA). Dep. Gen. Sec., Voluntary Action Lewisham, 1974–78; Res. and Press Asst, COHSE, 1978–79; Policy Analyst, London Borough of Camden, 1979–80; Dir, Lady Margaret Hall Settlement, 1980–84; Director: CAG Consultants, 1985–89; Nat. Deafblind and Rubella Assoc. (Sense), 1989–97. Non-exec. Dir, PIRC Ltd. *Recreations:* sailing, cycling, ski-ing, walking. *Address:* National Association of Citizens Advice Bureaux, Myddelton House, 115/123 Pentonville Road, N1 9LZ. *T:* (020) 7833 7038, *Fax:* (020) 7833 4371; *e-mail:* david.harker@nacab.org.uk. *Club:* Southwold Sailing.

HARKINS, His Honour Gerard Francis Robert; a Circuit Judge, 1986–2001; *b* 13 July 1936; *o s* of Francis Murphy Harkins and Katherine Harkins (*née* Hunt). *Educ:* Mount St Mary's College, Spinkhill, near Sheffield; King's College in University of Durham (now Univ. of Newcastle upon Tyne). LDS Dunelm 1961. Dental surgeon in general practice, Yorks, 1961–70; called to the Bar, Middle Temple, 1969; practised NE Circuit, 1970–86. Mem., Northumbria Probation Cttee, 1993–97. Pres., Mount Assoc., 1991–92. Governor, Mount St Mary's, 1990–93. *Address:* 34 Wyncote Court, Jesmond Park East, Newcastle upon Tyne NE7 7BG. *Club:* Lansdowne.

HARKNESS, Very Rev. James, CB 1993; OBE 1978; Moderator of the General Assemby of The Church of Scotland, 1995–96; a Chaplain to the Queen in Scotland, since 1996 (an Extra Chaplain, 1995–96); Dean of the Chapel Royal in Scotland, since 1996; *b* 20 Oct. 1935; *s* of James and Jane Harkness; *m* 1960, Elizabeth Anne Tolmie; one *s* one *d*. *Educ:* Univ. of Edinburgh (MA). Asst Minister, North Morningside Parish Church, Edinburgh, 1959–61; joined RAChD, 1961: Chaplain: 1 KOSB, 1961–65; 1 Queen's Own Highlanders, 1965–69; Singapore, 1969–70; Dep. Warden, RAChD Centre, 1970–74; Senior Chaplain: N Ireland, 1974–75; 4th Div., 1975–78; Asst Chaplain Gen., Scotland, 1980–81; Senior Chaplain: 1st British Corps, 1981–82; BAOR, 1982–84; Dep. Chaplain Gen. to the Forces, 1985–86, Chaplain Gen., 1987–95. QHC 1982–95. Chaplain, BLESMA, 1995–; Nat. Chaplain, 1995–, Pres., 2001–, RBL, Scotland. Chm., Bd of Dirs, Carberry, 1998–2001. Mem., Pensions Appeal Tribunals, Scotland, 1999–. Member: Scot. Adv. Cttee, ICRF, 1995–2000; Exec. Cttee, Anglo-Israel Assoc., 1995–; Pres., Soc. of Friends, St Andrew's, Jerusalem, 1998–. Pres., ACFA, Scotland, 1996–. Trustee: Nat. Prayer Breakfast for Scotland, 1996–; Liberating Scots Trust, 1998–; Gen. Trustee, Church of Scotland, 1996–. Gov., Fettes Coll., 1999–. Patron, St Mary's Music Sch., Edinburgh, 1995. FRSA 1992. Hon. DD Aberdeen, 2000. ChStJ 1999 (OStJ 1988). *Recreations:* general pursuits. *Address:* 13 Saxe Coburg Place, Edinburgh EH3 5BR. *Club:* New (Edinburgh).

HARKNESS, Rear-Adm. James Percy Knowles, CB 1971; *b* 28 Nov. 1916; *s* of Captain P. Y. Harkness, West Yorkshire Regt, and Gladys Dundas Harkness (*née* Knowles); *m* 1949, Joan, *d* of late Vice-Adm. N. A. Sulivan, CVO; two *d*. Dir-Gen., Naval Manpower, 1970; retired 1972. *Recreation:* sailing.

HARLAND, Bryce; *see* Harland, W. B.

HARLAND, Rt Rev. Ian; an Assistant Bishop, Diocese in Europe, since 2000; *b* 19 Dec. 1932; *s* of late Canon Samuel James Harland and of Brenda Gwendolyn Harland; *m* 1967, Susan Hinman; one *s* three *d*. *Educ:* Dragon School, Oxford; Haileybury; Peterhouse, Cambridge (MA); Wycliffe Hall, Oxford. Teaching at Sunningdale School, 1956–58; Curate, Melton Mowbray, 1960–63; Vicar, Oughtibridge, Sheffield, 1963–72; Member, Wortley RDC, 1969–73; Vicar, St Cuthbert, Fir Vale, Sheffield, 1972–75; Priest-in-charge, All Saints, Brightside, 1973–75; RD of Ecclesfield, 1973–75; Vicar of Rotherham, 1975–79; RD of Rotherham, 1976–79; Archdeacon of Doncaster, 1979–85; Bishop Suffragan of Lancaster, 1985–89; Bishop of Carlisle, 1989–2000. Proctor in Convocation, 1975–85. Hon. Treas., The Middle Way, 1998–2000. Pres., Abbotsholme Sch., 1999–. Entered H of L, 1996. *Recreations:* politics, sport. *Address:* White House, 11 South Street, Gargrave, Skipton BD23 3RT. *T:* (01756) 748623.

HARLAND, Air Marshal Sir Reginald (Edward Wynyard), KBE 1974; CB 1972; AE 1945; engineering and management consultant; *b* 30 May 1920; *s* of Charles Cecil Harland and Ida Maud (*née* Bellhouse); *m* 1942, Doreen Rosalind, *d* of late W. H. C. Romanis; two *s* two *d* (and one *s* decd). *Educ:* Summer Fields, Oxford; Stowe; Trinity Coll., Cambridge (MA). Served War of 1939–45: RAE Farnborough, 1941–42; N Africa, Italy and S France, 1942–45. Techn. trng, techn. plans and manning depts, Air Min., 1946–49; pilot trng, 1949–50; Chief Engrg Instructor, RAF Coll., Cranwell, 1950–52; Guided Weapon trng, RMCS Shrivenham, 1952–53; Thunderbird Project Officer: RAE Farnborough, 1953–55; Min. of Supply, 1955–56; psa 1957; Ballistic Missile Liaison Officer, (BJSM) Los Angeles, 1958–60; CO, Central Servicing Develt Estab., Swanton Morley, 1960–62; STSO, HQ No 3 (Bomber) Gp, Mildenhall, 1962–64; AO i/c Engrg, HQ Far East Air Force, Singapore, 1964–66; Harrier Project Dir, HQ Min. of Technology, 1967–68; idc 1969; AOC No 24 Group, RAF, 1970–72; AO Engineering, Air Support Command, 1972; AOC-in-C, RAF Support Command, 1973–77. Technical Dir, W. S. Atkins & Partners, 1977–82; Consultant to Short Brothers Ltd, 1983–88. Mem. Council, IMgt (formerly BIM), 1973–78, 1980–86, 1987–90, 1992–98; President: Soc. Environmental Engrs, 1974–78 (Fellow, 1977); IIExE, 1997–99 (Fellow, 1997); Vice-Chm., CEI, 1983–84. Chairman: Suffolk Preservation Soc., 1988–91; Suffolk Professional Engrs, 1991–97; Suffolk Br., Cambridge Soc., 1998–; Gov., ESU, 1993–; President: East Reg., ESU, 1992–; Old Stoic Soc., 1999–2000. Contested Bury St Edmunds, (SDP) 1983, (SDP/Alliance) 1987. Sen. Academic Fellow, Leicester Poly. (now De Montfort Univ.), 1989. CEng 1966; FIMechE 1967; FIEE 1964; FRAeS 1967; CIMgt (FBIM 1974; Verulam Medal, 1991); FAPM 1988. FRSA 1993. *Publications:* occasional articles in engrg and management jls. *Recreations:* better management, better government. *Address:* 49 Crown Street, Bury St Edmunds, Suffolk IP33 1QX. *T:* (01284) 763078; *e-mail:* rewharland@aol.com. *Club:* Royal Air Force.

HARLAND, (William) Bryce, QSO 1992; Director, New Zealand Institute of International Affairs, since 1997; High Commissioner for New Zealand in the United Kingdom 1985–91; *b* 11 Dec. 1931; *s* of Edward Dugard Harland and Annie McDonald Harland (*née* Gordon); *m* 1st, 1957, Rosemary Anne Gordon (marr. diss. 1977); two *s* (and one *s* decd); 2nd, 1979, (Margaret) Anne Blackburn; one *s*. *Educ:* Victoria Univ., Wellington, NZ (MA Hons); Fletcher School of Law and Diplomacy, Boston, Mass, USA (AM). Joined NZ Dept of External Affairs, 1953; diplomatic postings: Singapore, 1956; Bangkok, 1957; NY, 1959; Wellington, 1962; Washington, 1965; Wellington, 1969; First NZ Ambassador to China, 1973–75; Ministry of Foreign Affairs, Wellington: Head of African and European Divs, 1976–77; Asst Sec., 1977–82; Perm. Rep. of NZ to the UN, NY, 1982–85 (Chm., Economic and Financial Cttee, Gen. Assembly, 1984). Vis. Fellow, All Souls Coll., Oxford, 1991. KStJ 1985. Hon. Freeman, City of London, 1987. *Publications:* On Our Own: New Zealand in the emerging tripolar world, 1992; Asia—What Next?, 1992; Collision Course: America and East Asia in the past and the future, 1996; sundry articles. *Recreations:* reading history, walking. *Address:* 9 Tinakori Road, Wellington, New Zealand. *Clubs:* Royal Over-Seas League (Vice Pres.); Wellington.

HARLE, James Coffin, DPhil, DLitt; Keeper, Department of Eastern Art, Ashmolean Museum, Oxford, 1967–87; Student of Christ Church, Oxford, 1970–87, now Emeritus; *b* 5 April 1920; *s* of James Wyly Harle and Elfrieda Frances (*née* Baumann); *m* 1st, 1949, Jacqueline Thérèse Ruch (marr. diss. 1966, she *d* 1968); 2nd, 1967, Mrs Carola Sybil Mary Fleming (*d* 1971); 3rd, 1973, Lady (Betty) Hulbert. *Educ:* St George's Sch., Newport, RI; Princeton Univ. (BA 1942, Phi Beta Kappa); Oxford Univ. (BA 1st cl. Sanskrit and Pali, 1956; DPhil 1959; DLitt 1989). Served War, 1942–46, USNR (Aviation Br.), retd as Lieut; DFC (US). Asst to Dean of the College, Princeton, 1947; Part-time instructor in English, Princeton, 1948–49; Fulbright Lectr, Philippines, 1953–54; Ashmolean Museum: Asst Keeper, 1960; Sen. Asst Keeper, 1962. Pres., Soc. for S Asian Studies (British Acad.), 1990–95. *Publications:* Tower Gateways in South India, 1963; Gupta Sculpture, 1974; The Art and Architecture of the Indian Subcontinent, 1986; articles in periodicals on Indian Art. *Address:* Hawkswell, 34 Portland Road, Oxford OX2 7EY. *T:* (01865) 515236. *Club:* Princeton (New York).

HARLE, John Crofton, FGSM; saxophonist, composer, conductor; *b* 20 Sept. 1956; *s* of Jack Harle and Joyce Harle (*née* Crofton); *m* 1985, Julia Jane Eisner; two *s*. *Educ:* Newcastle Royal Grammar Sch.; Royal Coll. of Music (Foundn Schol.; ARCM (Hons) 1978); private study in Paris, 1981–82. FGSM 1990. Leader of Myrha Saxophone Quartet, 1977–82; formed duo with pianist John Lenehan, 1979; saxophone soloist, 1980–, with major internat. orchs, incl. LSO, English Chamber Orch., LPO, Amsterdam Concertgebouw, New World Symphony; Principal Saxophone, London Sinfonietta, 1987–97; Prof. of Saxophone, GSMD, 1988–. Formed: Berliner Band, 1983; John Harle Band, 1988. Compositions for several ensembles, 1983–, incl. London Brass and LSO. Frequent composer and soloist on TV (incl. BBC series, Silent Witness, and History of Britain) and feature films; regular broadcaster on BBC Radio; featured in One Man and his Sax, BBC2 TV, 1988. Has made many recordings. Major works written for him by Dominic Muldowney, Ned Rorem, Richard Rodney Bennett, Luciano Berio, Michael Nyman, Gavin Bryars, Mike Westbrook, Stanley Myers, Harrison Birtwistle, Michael Torke, John Tavener, Sally Beamish. Dannreuther Concerto Prize, Royal Coll. of Music, 1980; GLAA Young Musician, 1979, 1980. *Publication:* John Harle's Saxophone Album, 1986. *Recreations:* family life, cooking. *Address:* IMG Artists, 616 Chiswick High Road, W4 5RX. *T:* (020) 8233 5800.

HARLECH, 6th Baron *cr* 1876; **Francis David Ormsby Gore;** *b* 13 March 1954; *s* of 5th Baron Harlech, KCMG, PC, and Sylvia (*d* 1967), *d* of Hugh Lloyd Thomas, CMG, CVO; *S* father, 1985; *m* 1986, Amanda Jane (marr. diss. 1998), *d* of Alan T. Grieve, *qv*; one *s* one *d*. *Educ:* Worth. *Heir: s* Hon. Jasset David Cody Ormsby Gore, *b* 1 July 1986. *Address:* The Mount, Racecourse Road, Oswestry, Shropshire SY10 7PH. *Club:* Brooks's.

HARLECH, Pamela, Lady; journalist and producer; *b* 18 Dec. 1934; *d* of Ralph Frederick Colin and Georgia Talmey; *m* 1969, 5th Baron Harlech, KCMG, PC (*d* 1985); one *d*. *Educ:* Smith Coll., Northampton, Mass, Finch Coll. (BA). London Editor, (American) Vogue, 1964–69; Food Editor, (British) Vogue, 1971–82; freelance journalist, 1972–; prodn work for special events, 1986–87; Commissioning Editor, Thames and Hudson, Publishers, 1987–89. Chairman: Women's Playhouse Trust, 1984–94; V&A Enterprises, 1987–94; English Nat. Ballet, 1990–2000; Council, British Amer. Arts Assoc., 1990–92; Trustee, V&A Mus., 1986–94; Member: Welsh Arts Council, 1981–85; Arts Council of GB, 1986–90; South Bank Bd, 1986–94; Council, Managing Bd, Cruisaid, 1987–96; Council, ABSA, 1988–95 (Chm., Judging Panel for Awards, 1989–90). Pres., Bath Cancer Support, 1998–. *Publications:* Feast without Fuss, 1976; Pamela Harlech's Complete Guide to Cooking, Entertainment and Household Management, 1981; Vogue Book of Menus, 1985. *Recreations:* music, cooking, laughing. *Address:* Hinton Field, Hinton Charterhouse, Bath BA2 7SR. *T:* (020) 7581 1245.

HARLEN, Prof. Wynne, OBE 1991; PhD; Director, Scottish Council for Research in Education, 1990–99; *b* 12 Jan. 1937; *d* of Arthur Mitchell and Edith (*née* Radcliffe); *m* 1958, Frank Harlen (*d* 1987); one *s* one *d*. *Educ:* St Hilda's Coll., Oxford (BA 1958; MA 1961); Univ. of Bristol (PhD 1974). Asst teacher, Cheltenham Ladies' Coll., 1959–60; Lectr, St Mary's Coll. of Educn and Glos Coll. of Art, 1960–66; Research Fellow: Univ. of Bristol, 1966–73; Univ. of Reading, 1973–77; Sen. Res. Fellow, KCL, 1977–84; Sidney Jones Prof. of Science Educn, Univ. of Liverpool, 1985–90. Visiting Professor: Univ. of Liverpool, 1990–2001; Bristol Univ., 2000–. Bernard Osher Fellow, Exploratorium, San Francisco, 1995. Chair, Sci. Expert Gp, OECD Student Assessment Project, 1998–. FRSA 1990; FEIS 1999. Editor, Primary Sci. Rev., 1999–. *Publications include:* Science 5/13: a formative evaluation, 1977; Guides to Assessment: Science, 1983; New Trends in Primary Science Education, 1983; Teaching and Learning Primary Science, 1985, 2nd edn 1994; Primary Science: taking the plunge, 1985; The Teaching of Science, 1992, 3rd edn 2000; Enhancing Quality in Assessment, 1994; Developing Primary Science, 1997; Effective Teaching of Science: a review of research, 1999; Teaching, Learning and Assessing Science: 5–12, 2000; numerous articles in jls incl. Internat. Jl Sci. Educn, Studies in Educnl Evaluation, Cambridge Jl Educn, Curriculum Jl, Brit. Educnl Res. Jl, Res. Papers in Educn, Jl Curriculum Studies, Assessment in Educn, Studies in Sci. Educn. *Recreations:* opera, orchestral music, hill-walking, gardening. *Address:* 26 Torphin Road, Edinburgh EH13 0HW. *T:* (0131) 441 6130.

HARLEY, Gen. Sir Alexander (George Hamilton), KBE 1996 (OBE 1981); CB 1991; Master Gunner, St James's Park, since 2001; Chairman, Purple International, since 2001; *b* India, 3 May 1941; *s* of late Lt-Col William Hamilton Coughtrie Harley, 1st Punjab Regt and later Royal Indian Engineers, and of Eleanor Blanche (*née* Jarvis); *m* 1967, Christina Valentine, *d* of late Edmund Noel Butler-Cole and Kathleen Mary (*née* Thompson); two *s*. *Educ:* Caterham Sch.; RMA Sandhurst. Commissioned RA 1962; 1962–73: 7 Para Regt RHA; Staff Capt. MoD; Adjutant; Canadian Staff Coll.; Mil. Asst, MoD, 1974–75; Battery Comdr, 1975–78 (despatches); Directing Staff, Staff Coll., 1978–79; CO 19 Field Regt RA, 1979–82; Col Defence Staff, and Operations Centre, Falklands War, MoD, 1983–85; Comdr 33 Armd Brigade, 1985–87; Chief of Ops, Northern Army Group, 1988–90; Asst Chief Jt Ops, Overseas and Gulf War, MoD, 1990–93; Administrator, Sovereign Base Areas, and Comdr British Forces Cyprus, 1993–95; DCDS Commitments, and Dir Jt Ops, MoD, 1995–97. Adjt Gen., 1997–2000; ADC Gen. to the Queen, 1998–2000. Col Comdt, HAC, RHA. Pres., Combined Services Hockey, 1995–2000 (Hon. Vice-Pres.); Patron, The Nordics Hockey Club, 1992–. Hon. Vice Pres., Raleigh Internat. FIMgt (FBIM 1982). *Recreations:* country pursuits, hockey. *Address:* PO Box 30999, SE1 5UJ. *Club:* Naval and Military.

HARLEY, Ian, FCA, FCIB; Chief Executive, Abbey National plc, since 1998; *b* 30 April 1950; *s* of Michael Harley and Mary Harley (*née* Looker); *m* 1975, Rosalind Caroline Smith; three *s*. *Educ:* Falkirk High Sch.; Edinburgh Univ. (MA 1972). FCA 1982; FCIB 1998. Articled Clerk, Touche Ross, 1972–76; Corporate Planning Team, Morgan

Crucible, 1976; joined Abbey National, 1977. Dir, Dah Sing Financial Hldgs, Hong Kong, 1998–; non-exec. Dir, Rentokil Initial plc, 1999–. Chm., Assoc. for Payment Clearing Services, 1998–. Dep. Pres., CIB, 2001–. *Recreations:* reading, walking, cycling. *Address:* Abbey National plc, Abbey House, Baker Street, NW1 6XL. *T:* (020) 7612 4129. *Club:* Oriental.

HARLING, Christopher Charles, FRCP, FFOM, FFPHM; Consultant Occupational Physician, Bristol Royal Infirmary, since 1988; *b* 12 Jan. 1951; *s* of Robert and Dorothy Harling; *m* 1976, Philippa Ann Capper; two *s*. *Educ:* Leeds GS; Manchester GS; Keble Coll., Oxford (MA); University Coll. Hosp. Med. Sch. (MB BS). DAvMed 1988; FFOM 1991; FRCP 1995; FFPHM 1999. Res. Fellow and Hon. Registrar, Inst. Envmtl and Offshore Medicine, Univ. of Aberdeen, 1979–80; Area MO, NCB, 1981–84; Consultant Occupational Physician, Sheffield HA, 1984–88; Sen. Lectr in Occupl Medicine, Univ. of Bristol, 1988–. Civilian Consultant Advr in Occupational Medicine to RN, 1993–. MO, RNR, 1988–96 (PMO, HMS Flying Fox, 1995–96). Hon. Sec., Specialist Trng Authy of Med. Royal Colls, 1999– (Vice-Chm., 1998–99); Sec., 1987–90, Chm., 1990–93, Assoc. NHS Occupational Physicians; Mem. Council, 1982–84, Mem., NHS Work Gp, 1985–87, SOM; Faculty of Occupational Medicine, Royal College of Physicians: Examr, 1990–, Dep. Chief Examr, 1993–94; NHS Liaison Officer, 1992; Vice-Dean, 1994–96; Dean, later Pres., 1996–99. *Publications:* papers on occupational medicine and health care workers. *Recreations:* sailing, flying. *Address:* 8 Burlington Road, Bristol BS6 6TL. *T:* (0117) 973 4023. *Club:* Naval.

HARLOE, Prof. Michael Howard, PhD; Vice-Chancellor, University of Salford, since 1997; *b* 11 Oct. 1943; *s* of Maurice Edward and May Cecilia Harloe; *m* 1976, Judy Rosilyn Philip; one *s* two *d*. *Educ:* Watford Boys' GS; Worcester Coll., Oxford (MA 1970); PhD Essex 1984. Res. Asst, Borough of Swindon, 1967–69; Res. Officer, LSE, 1969–72; PSO, Centre for Envmtl Studies, London, 1972–80; University of Essex: Lectr, 1980–84, Sen. Lectr, 1984–87, Reader, 1987–90, Prof., 1990–97, Dept of Sociology; Dean of Social Scis, 1988–91; Pro-Vice-Chancellor, 1992–97. AcSS. *Publications:* (jtly) The Organisation of Housing: public and private enterprise in London, 1974; Swindon, A Town in Transition: a study in urban development and overspill policy, 1975; (ed) Captive Cities: studies in the political economy of cities and regions, 1977; (ed) New Perspectives in Urban Change and Conflict, 1981; (ed with E. Lebas) City, Class and Capital, 1981 (US edn 1982); Private Rented Housing in the United States and Europe, 1985; (jtly) Housing and Social Change in Europe and the USA, 1988; (ed and contrib.) Place, Policy and Politics, 1990; (with M. Martens) New Ideas for Housing: the experience of three countries, 1990; (ed jtly) Divided Cities: New York and London in the contemporary world, 1992; The People's Home: social rented housing in Europe and America, 1995; (ed) Sociology of Urban Communities, Vols I–III, 1996; (ed jtly) Cities After Socialism: urban and regional change and conflict in post-Socialist societies, 1996. *Recreations:* gardening, travel, reading, sociology. *Address:* University of Salford, Salford M5 4WT. *T:* (0161) 295 5477. *Club:* Oxford and Cambridge.

HARLOW, Archdeacon of; *see* Taylor, Ven. P. F.

HARLOW, Prof. Carol R., PhD; FBA 1999; Professor of Public Law, London School of Economics, University of London, since 1989; *b* 28 Aug. 1935; *d* of late Prof. Charles Harold Williams and Clare Williams (*née* Pollak); *m* 1958, Michael Harlow; one *s* one *d*. *Educ:* King's Coll., London (LLB 1956; LLM 1970); LSE (PhD 1980). Lectr, Kingston Poly., 1972–76; Lectr, 1976–86, Reader, 1986–89, LSE. Jean Monnet Prof., European Univ. Inst., 1995, 1996. Hon. QC 1996. *Publications:* Compensation and Government Torts, 1982; (jtly) Law and Administration, 1984, 2nd edn 1997; Understanding Tort Law, 1986, 2nd edn 1995; (jtly) Pressure Through Law, 1992. *Recreations:* theatre, gardening, walking, painting. *Address:* Law Department, London School of Economics, Houghton Street, WC2A 2AE. *T:* (020) 7955 7248.

HARMAN, Rt Hon. Harriet; PC 1997; QC 2001; MP (Lab) Camberwell and Peckham, since 1997 (Peckham, Oct. 1982–1997); Solicitor-General since 2001; *b* 30 July 1950; *d* of late John Bishop Harman, FRCS, FRCP, and of Anna Charlotte Harman; *m* 1982, Jack Dromey; two *s* one *d*. *Educ:* St Paul's Girls' Sch.; York Univ. Brent Community Law Centre, 1975–78; Legal Officer, NCCL, 1978–82. Opposition Chief Sec. to the Treasury, 1992–94; opposition front bench spokesman: on employment, 1994–95; on health, 1995–96; on social security, 1996–97; Sec. of State for Social Security, 1997–98. Mem., NEC, Labour Party, 1993–. *Publications:* Sex Discrimination in Schools, 1977; Justice Deserted: the subversion of the jury, 1979; The Century Gap, 1993. *Address:* House of Commons, SW1A 0AA.

HARMAN, Gen. Sir Jack (Wentworth), GCB 1978 (KCB 1974); OBE 1962; MC 1943; Deputy Supreme Allied Commander, Europe, 1978–81, retired; *b* 20 July 1920; *s* of late Lt-Gen. Sir Wentworth Harman, KCB, DSO, and late Dorothy Harman; *m* 1947, Gwladys May Murphy (*d* 1996), *d* of Sir Idwal Lloyd and *widow* of Lt-Col R. J. Murphy; one *d*, and two step *d*; *m* 2001, Sheila Florence Perkins (*née* Gurdon), *widow* of Maj. Christopher Perkins, Hampshire Regt. *Educ:* Wellington Coll.; RMC Sandhurst. Commissioned into The Queen's Bays, 1940, Bt Lt-Col, 1958; Commanding Officer, 1st The Queen's Dragoon Guards, 1960–62; commanded 11 Infantry Bde, 1965–66; attended IDC, 1967; BGS, HQ Army Strategic Command, 1968–69; GOC, 1st Div., 1970–72; Commandant, RMA, Sandhurst, 1972–73; GOC 1 (British) Corps, 1974–76; Adjutant-General, 1976–78. ADC Gen. to the Queen, 1977–80. Col, 1st The Queen's Dragoon Guards, 1975–80; Col Comdt, RAC, 1977–80. Dir, Wilsons Hogg Robinson (formerly Wilsons (Insurance Brokers)), 1982–88. Vice-Chairman: Nat. Army Museum, 1980–87; AA, 1986–89 (Mem. Cttee, 1981–85). *Address:* Sandhills House, Dinton, near Salisbury, Wilts SP3 5ER. *T:* (01722) 716288. *Club:* Cavalry and Guards.

HARMAN, Sir Jeremiah (LeRoy), Kt 1982; a Justice of the High Court, Chancery Division, 1982–98; *b* 13 April 1930; *er s* of late Rt Hon. Sir Charles Eustace Harman, PC; *m* 1960, Erica Jane (marr diss. 1986), *e d* of late Hon. Sir Maurice Richard Bridgeman, KBE; two *s* one *d*; *m* 1987, Katharine Frances Goddard, *d* of late Rt Hon. Sir Eric Sachs and *widow* of George Pulay. *Educ:* Horris Hill Sch.; Eton Coll. Served Coldstream Guards and Parachute Regt, 1948–51; Parachute Regt (TA), 1951–55. Called to the Bar, Lincoln's Inn, 1954, Bencher, 1977, Treas., 2000; QC 1968; called to Hong Kong Bar, 1978, Singapore Bar, 1980; Mem., Bar Council, 1963–67. Dir, Dunford & Elliott Ltd, 1972–79. *Recreations:* fishing, watching birds, reading. *Address:* c/o Treasury Office, Lincoln's Inn, WC2A 3TL.

HARMAN, Sir John (Andrew), Kt 1997; Chairman, Environment Agency, since 2000 (Member of Board, since 1995); *b* 30 July 1950; *s* of John E. Harman and Patricia J. Harman (*née* Mullins); *m* 1971, Susan Elizabeth Crowther; one *s* three *d*. *Educ:* St George's Coll., Weybridge; Manchester Univ. (BSc Hons Maths); Huddersfield Coll. of Educn (Technical) (PGCE). Maths teacher, Greenhead Coll., Huddersfield, 1973–79; Head of Maths, Barnsley 6th Form Coll., 1979–90; Sen. Lectr in Maths, Barnsley Coll., 1990–97. Joined Labour Party, 1977: various posts, incl. Br. Sec., Co-ordinating Cttee Chm. and Constituency Vice-Chm.; Mem., Policy Commns on Envmt, 1995–96, and Local Govt, 1995–. Member (Lab): W Yorks CC, 1981–86 (Vice-Chm. 1982–85, Chm. 1985–86, Finance Cttee); Kirklees MDC, 1986–2000 (Leader, Council, and Labour Gp, 1986–99). Dep. Chm. 1988–92, Vice-Chm. 1992–97, AMA; Local Government Association: Dep. Leader, Labour Gp, 1997–2000; Chm., Urban Commn, 1997–2000. Mem., Sec. of State's New Deal Task Force, 1997–; Member, UK Delegation to: Earth Summit, Rio de Janeiro, 1992; UN Commn on Sustainable Develt. Chm., Kirklees Stadium Develt Ltd, 1993–. Dir, Energy Saving Trust, 1996–. Contested (Lab) Colne Valley, 1987, 1992. FRSA 1994. Hon. FICE 2000. Hon. DCL Huddersfield, 2000. *Recreations:* music, reading, gardening, Huddersfield Town AFC. *Address:* 82A New North Road, Huddersfield HD1 5NE; (office) 25th Floor, Millbank Tower, 21–24 Millbank, SW1P 4XL. *T:* (020) 7863 8720.

HARMAN, Robert Donald; QC 1974; a Recorder of the Crown Court, 1972–97; a Judge of the Courts of Appeal of Jersey, 1986–98, and of Guernsey, 1986–99; *b* 26 Sept. 1928; *o s* of late Herbert Donald Harman, MC and Dorothy (*née* Fleming); *m* 1st, 1960, Sarah Elizabeth (*d* 1965), *o d* of late G. C. Cleverly; two *s*; 2nd, 1968, Rosamond Geraldine, JP, 2nd *d* of late Comdr G. T. A. Scott, RN; two *d*. *Educ:* privately; St Paul's Sch.; Magdalen Coll., Oxford. Called to Bar, Gray's Inn, 1954, Bencher, 1984; South-Eastern Circuit; a Junior Prosecuting Counsel to the Crown at Central Criminal Court, 1967–72; a Senior Treasury Counsel, 1972–74. Mem., Senate of the Inns of Court and the Bar, 1985–87. Appeal Steward, BBB of C, 1981–98. Liveryman, Goldsmiths' Co. *Address:* 2 Harcourt Buildings, Temple, EC4Y 9DA. *T:* (020) 7353 2112; The Clock House, near Sparsholt, Winchester, Hants SO21 2LX. *T:* (01962) 776461. *Clubs:* Garrick, Beefsteak, Pratt's; Swinley Forest Golf.

HARMER, David John; Chief Executive, John Grooms Housing Association, since 1988; *b* 14 May 1940; *s* of Stanley James Arthur Harmer and Eileen Joan (*née* Callaghan); *m* 1971, Janet Arnott Dodds; one *s* one *d*; one *s* one *d* from previous *m*. *Educ:* Dulwich Coll.; Spurgeon's Coll. Surveyor, Portman Family Settled Estates, 1957–61; Ministerial Assistant, W Ham Central Mission, 1961–62; Church Pastor, Shaftesbury Soc., 1964–71; Founder, 1971, Dep. Dir, 1971–88, Shaftesbury Soc. Housing Assoc. Member: Exec., Christian Alliance Housing Assoc., 1987–90; Regl Exec., Nat. Housing Fedn, 1987–95 (Chm., 1990–93); Chm., Nat. Wheelchair Housing Assoc. Gp, 1992–95. Shaftesbury Society: Mem. Council, 1995–; Mem., Urban Action Cttee, 1995– (Chm., 1997–99). WHam Central Mission Wkg Gp, 2000. *Recreations:* housing and disability issues, Church and Christian activities, exhibition budgerigars (Sec., Croydon Budgerigar Soc., 2000–), fuchsias. *Address:* John Grooms Housing Association, 50 Scrutton Street, EC2A 4XQ. *T:* (020) 7452 2000.

HARMSWORTH, family name of **Viscount Rothermere** and **Baron Harmsworth.**

HARMSWORTH, 3rd Baron *cr* 1939, of Egham; **Thomas Harold Raymond Harmsworth;** publisher; *b* 20 July 1939; *s* of Hon. Eric Beauchamp Northcliffe Harmsworth (*d* 1988) and Hélène Marie (*d* 1962), *d* of Col Jules Raymond Dehove; *S* uncle, 1990; *m* 1971, Patricia Palmer, *d* of late M. P. Horsley; two *s* three *d*. *Educ:* Eton; Christ Church, Oxford (MA). Nat. Service, Royal Horse Guards (The Blues), 1957–59 (2nd Lieut). Stockbroker, 1962–74; DHSS, 1974–88. Chm., Dr Johnson's House Trust. *Recreations:* sundry, including music. *Heir:* *s* Hon. Dominic Michael Eric Harmsworth, [*b* 18 Sept. 1973; *m* 1999, Veronica Patricia, *d* of Luis and Veronica Ausset, San Fernando, Chile; one *d*]. *Address:* The Old Rectory, Stoke Abbott, Beaminster, Dorset DT8 3JT. *T:* (01308) 868139.

HARMSWORTH, Sir Hildebrand Harold, 3rd Bt *cr* 1922; gardening writer; *b* 5 June 1931; *s* of Sir Hildebrand Alfred Beresford Harmsworth, 2nd Bt, and Elen, *d* of Nicolaj Billenstein, Randers, Denmark; *S* father, 1977; *m* 1960, Gillian Andrea, *o d* of William John Lewis; one *s* two *d*. *Educ:* Harrow; Trinity College, Dublin. *Heir:* *s* Hildebrand Esmond Miles Harmsworth [*b* 1 Sept. 1964; *m* 1988, Ruth Denise, *d* of Dennis Miles; one *s* two *d*]. *Address:* Ewlyn Villa, 42 Leckhampton Road, Cheltenham GL53 0BB.

HARNDEN, Arthur Baker, CB 1969; TD; BSc; CEng, FIEE; FIMgt; Chairman, Appeals Tribunals, Supplementary Benefits Commission, 1970–82; *b* 6 Jan. 1909; *s* of Cecil Henry Harnden and Susan (*née* Baker); *m* 1st, 1935, Maisie Elizabeth Annie (*d* 1970), *d* of A. H. Winterburn, LRIBA; one *s*; 2nd, 1971, Jean Kathleen (*d* 2000) *d* of H. F. Wheeler and *widow* of Eric J. Dedman; one step *s*. *Educ:* various state schools; Northampton Inst. (BSc London Univ. 1937). Exec. Engr, GPO, 1933; Royal Corps of Signals, 1939–45; Lt-Col GSO1, WO, 1942; DCSO Antwerp, 1944, Hamburg 1945. Dir, London Telecommunications Region, GPO, 1962; Senior Dir, Operations, PO (Telecommunications), 1967–69. Principal, Comrie House Sch., Finchley, 1971–72. *Recreations:* painting and potting. *Address:* 6 Haddenhurst Court, Terrace Road South, Binfield, Bracknell, Berks RG42 4BQ.

HARNDEN, Prof. David Gilbert, PhD; FRCPath; FRSE 1982; FIBiol; Chairman, South Manchester University Hospitals NHS Trust, since 1997; *b* 22 June 1932; *s* of William Alfred Harnden and Anne McKenzie Wilson; *m* 1955, Thora Margaret Seatter; three *s*. *Educ:* George Heriot's School, Edinburgh; University of Edinburgh. BSc. Lectr, Univ. of Edinburgh, 1956–57; Sci. Mem., Radiobiology Unit, MRC, Harwell, 1957–59; Sci. Mem., Clinical and Population Cytogenetics Unit, MRC, Edinburgh, 1959–69; Prof. of Cancer Studies, Univ. of Birmingham, 1969–83; Dir, Paterson Labs, later Paterson Inst. for Cancer Res., Christie Hosp. and Holt Radium Inst., later Christie Hosp. NHS Trust, 1983–97; Hon. Prof. of Experimental Oncology, 1983–97, Prof. Emeritus, 1998–, Univ. of Manchester; Emeritus Fellow, CRC, 1997. Chairman: Educn Cttee, Cancer Res. Campaign, 1987–92; NW Regl Adv. Cttee on Oncology Services, 1991–95. Dir, Christie Hosp. (NHS) Trust, 1991–97. Trustee: New Heart/New Start, Wythenshawe Hosp. Transplant Fund, 1998–; Gray Lab. Cancer Res. Trust, 2000–; Chm., Trustees, Friends of Rosie, Children's Cancer Res. Fund, 1999–. Hon. MRCP 1987. Chm., Editorial Bd, British Jl of Cancer, 1983–98. Mem., NRPB, 1995–99. *Publications:* papers on cancer research and human genetics in learned jls. *Recreation:* sketching people and places. *Address:* South Manchester University Hospitals NHS Trust, Wythenshawe Hospital, Southmoor Road, Wythenshawe, Manchester M23 9LT. *T:* (0161) 291 2020, *Fax:* (0161) 291 2037.

HARNEY, Mary; TD (Prog. Dem.) Dublin SW; Tánaiste and Minister for Enterprise, Trade and Employment, since 1997; Leader, Progressive Democrats, since 1993; *b* March 1953. *Educ:* Convent of Mercy, Inchicore, Dublin; Presentation Convent, Clondalkin, Co. Dublin; Trinity Coll., Dublin (BA). Contested (FF) Dublin SE, 1977. Mem. Dublin CC, 1979–91. Senator, 1977–81; TD Dublin SW: FF, 1981–85; Prog. Dem., 1985–; Minister of Envmtl Protection, 1989–92. Progressive Democrats: Co-Founder, 1985; Dep. Leader, and Spokesperson on Justice, Equality and Law Reform, 1993. *Address:* 11 Serpentine Terrace, Ballsbridge, Dublin 4, Ireland.

HARPER, Donald John; Chief Scientist, Royal Air Force, 1980–83; *b* 6 Aug. 1923; *s* of Harry Tonkin and Caroline Irene Harper; *m* 1947, Joyce Beryl Kite-Powell; two *d*. *Educ:* Purley County Grammar Sch. for Boys; Queen Mary Coll., London. 1st cl. BSc (Eng) 1943; CEng, FRAeS. Joined Aero Dept, RAE Farnborough, 1943; Scientific Officer,

Spinning Tunnel, 1947–49; High Speed and Transonic Tunnel, 1950–59; Sen. Scientific Officer; Principal Scientific Officer, 1955; Dep. Head of Tunnel, 1958–59; Space Dept RAE, Satellite Launching Vehicles, 1960–62; Senior Principal Scientific Officer, MoD, Central Staff, 1963–65; Head of Assessment Div., Weapons Dept, RAE, 1966–68; Dir of Project Time and Cost Analysis, MoD (PE), 1968–71; Dir-Gen., Performance and Cost Analysis, MoD (PE), 1972–77; Dir-Gen. Research C, MoD (PE), 1978–83. Mem. Council, RAeS, 1990–92. *Publications:* contrib. Aeronautical Res. Council reports and memoranda and techn. press. *Recreations:* music, especially choral singing; gardening, home improvement, family history research, fell-walking.

HARPER, Dame Elizabeth (Margaret Way), DBE 1995; farmer, retired; New Zealand President, Save the Children, 1990–93, retired; *b* 20 June 1937; *d* of Jack Horsford Horrell and Margaret Faith Horrell (*née* Rickard); *m* 1956, Charles John Harper; two *s* (one *d* decd). *Educ:* Lagmhor Sch., Mid-Canterbury, NZ; Ashburton High Sch.; Craighead Diocesan Sch., Timaru. Save the Children: Br. Sec., 1970–84; Pres., Ashburton Br., 1984–87; S Island Vice-Pres., 1987–89. Red Cross volunteer, Dist Nursing Service, 1984–; night sitter volunteer for terminally ill, 1987–. Ashburton Benevolent Trust Bd, 1998–. Save the Children Award for Dist. and Meritorious Service, 1994. *Recreations:* golf, sewing, knitting. *Address:* Ashburton, New Zealand.

HARPER, Prof. Fred, PhD; educational consultant, Central and Eastern Europe; Dean, Seale-Hayne Faculty of Agriculture, Food and Land Use, University of Plymouth (formerly Plymouth Polytechnic), 1989–97, now Emeritus Professor of Agriculture; *b* 7 June 1947; *s* of Frederick and Queenie Elizabeth Harper; *m* 1971, Moyna Carole Hunter (marr. diss. 1996); one *d*. *Educ:* Univ. of Nottingham (BSc Hons Agric., PhD). Lecturer: Writtle Agricl Coll., Chelmsford, 1971–75; and Dir of Studies, Univ. of Edinburgh, 1975–82; Vice-Principal and Dir of Studies, Harper Adams Agricl Coll., Shropshire, 1983–88; Principal, Seale-Hayne Coll., Devon, 1988–89. ARAgS, 1993. *Publications:* The Principles of Arable Crop Production, 1983; numerous pubns on crop physiology and production, agricl educn and overseas agriculture. *Recreations:* walking, travel, observing wildlife, watching sport. *Address:* Kolora Park, Dunsford, Exeter EX6 7JU. *T:* (01647) 252258.

HARPER, Heather Mary, (Mrs E. J. Benarroch), CBE 1965; soprano; Professor of Singing and Consultant, Royal College of Music, 1985–93; Director of Singing Studies, Britten-Pears School, Aldeburgh, since 1986; *b* 8 May 1930; *d* of late Hugh Harper, Belfast; *m* 1973, Eduardo J. Benarroch. *Educ:* Trinity Coll. of Music, London. Has sung many principal roles incl. Arabella, Ariadne, Marschallin, Chrysothemis, Elsa and Kaiserin, at Covent Garden, Glyndebourne, Sadler's Wells, Bayreuth, Teatro Colon (Buenos Aires), Edinburgh Fest., La Scala, NY Met, San Francisco, Deutsche Oper (Berlin), Frankfurt, Netherlands Opera, Canadian Opera Co., Toronto, and sang at every Promenade Concert season, 1957–90; created the soprano role in Benjamin Britten's War Requiem in Coventry Cathedral in 1962; soloist at opening concerts: Maltings, Snape, 1967; Queen Elizabeth Hall, 1967. Toured USA, 1965, and USSR, 1967, with BBC SO; toured USA annually, 1967–91, and appeared regularly at European music fests; toured: Japan and S Korea as Principal Soloist Soprano with Royal Opera Co., 1979; Australia and Hong Kong with BBC Symph. Orch., 1982; has also sung in Asia, Middle East, Australia and S America; Principal Soloist Soprano with Royal Opera House Co., visit to Los Angeles Olympic Games, 1984; Principal Soloist with BBC Philharmonic Orch.'s first South American tour, 1989. Has made many recordings, incl. works of Britten, Beethoven, Berg, Mahler, Mozart, Strauss and Verdi; broadcasts frequently throughout the world, and appears frequently on TV; Masterclasses for advanced students and young professionals, Britten-Pears Sch.; retired from operatic stage, 1984, from concert stage, 1991. Member: BBC Music Panel, 1989; RSA Music Panel, 1989. FTCL; FRCM 1988; Hon. RAM, 1972. Hon. DMus Queen's Univ., Belfast, 1966; Hon. DLitt Ulster, 1992. Edison Award, 1971; Grammy Nomination, 1973; Grammy Award, 1979, 1984, 1991; Best vocal performance for Ravel's Scheherezade; Grand Prix du Disque, 1979. *Recreations:* gardening, cooking.

HARPER, James Norman; barrister; a Recorder of the Crown Court, 1980–84; *b* 30 Dec. 1932; *s* of late His Honour Judge Norman Harper and Iris Irene Harper; *m* 1956, Blanka Miroslava Eva Sigmund (*d* 1999); one *s* one *d*. *Educ:* Marlborough Coll.; Magdalen Coll., Oxford (BA Hons). Called to the Bar, Gray's Inn, 1957; Attorney Gen. of NE Circuit, 1992–96. Pres., Northumberland County Hockey Assoc., 1982–. *Recreations:* cricket, hockey, painting. *Address:* 33 Broad Chare, Newcastle upon Tyne NE1 3DQ. *T:* (0191) 232 0541. *Club:* MCC.

HARPER, Prof. John Lander, CBE 1989; DPhil; FRS 1978; Emeritus Professor of Botany, University of Wales, since 1982: Head, Unit of Plant Population Biology, School of Plant Biology, Bangor, 1982–90; *b* 27 May 1925; *s* of John Hindley Harper and Harriett Mary (*née* Archer); *m* 1954, Borgny Lerø; one *s* two *d*. *Educ:* Lawrence Sheriff Sch., Rugby; Magdalen Coll., Oxford (BA, MA, DPhil). Demonstr, Dept of Agriculture, Univ. of Oxford, 1951, Lectr 1953; Rockefeller Foundn Fellow, Univ. of Calif, 1960–61; Prof. of Agricultural Botany, 1960, Prof. of Botany, 1977–82 and Head of Sch. of Plant Biology, 1967–82, University Coll. of North Wales, Bangor. Member: NERC, 1971–81; AFRC, 1980–90; Jt Nature Conservation Cttee, 1991–94. Trustee, Natural Hist. Mus., 1993–97. For. Assoc., US Nat. Acad. of Sciences, 1984. Hon. DSc Sussex, 1984; Dr (*hc*) Univ. Nacional Autónoma de México, 1997. *Publications:* Biology of Weeds, 1960; Population Biology of Plants, 1977; (with M. Begon and C. Townsend) Ecology: organisms, populations and communities, 1985, 3rd edn 1997; Fundamentals of Ecology, 2000; papers in Jl of Ecol., New Phytologist, Annals of Applied Biol., Evolution, and Proc. Royal Soc. (Editor, Series B, 1993–98). *Recreation:* gardening. *Address:* The Lodge, Chapel Road, Brampford Speke, Exeter EX5 5HG. *T:* (01392) 841929. *Club:* Farmers'.

HARPER, John Mansfield; Managing Director, Seaford Head Advisers, since 1995; *b* 17 July 1930; *s* of late T. J. Harper and May (*née* Charlton); *m* 1956, Berenice Honorine, *d* of Harold Haydon; one *s* one *d*. *Educ:* Merchant Taylors' Sch.; St John's Coll., Oxford. 2nd Lieut Royal Corps of Signals, 1948–49. Asst Principal, Post Office, 1953; Private Sec. to Dir-Gen., 1956–58; Principal, 1958–66; Asst Sec., Reorganization Dept, 1966–69; Dir, North-Eastern Telecommunications Region, 1969–71; Dir, Purchasing and Supply, 1972–75; Sen. Dir, Planning and Provisioning, 1975–77; Asst Man. Dir, Telecommunications, 1978–79; Dep. Man. Dir, British Telecommunications (Post Office), 1979–81; Man. Dir, Inland Division, BT, 1981–83, retired. Sen. Partner, Lullington Gp, 1993–96. Advr to Bd, NEC (UK) Ltd, 1985–92; Advr, BICC Ltd, 1994–96; Specialist Advr, Parly Select Cttee on Trade and Industry, 1994 and 1997. Vis. Fellow, Sci. Policy Res. Unit, Univ. of Sussex, 1992–93. Chm., Infrastructure Policy Gp, Electronic Engrg Assoc., 1989–90. CompIEE; CIMgt. *Publications:* Telecommunications and Computing: the uncompleted revolution, 1986; Telecommunications Policy and Management, 1989; The Third Way: telecommunications and the environment, 1990; A 21st Century Structure for UK Telecoms, 1991; Monopoly and Competition in British Telecommunications, 1997. *Recreations:* music, gardening, amateur radio. *Address:* 4 Friston Downs, Friston, Eastbourne, E Sussex BN20 0ET. *Club:* National Liberal.

HARPER, Prof. John Martin, PhD; FRCO(CHM); Director General, Royal School of Church Music, since 1998; *b* 11 July 1947; *s* of Geoffrey Martin and Kathleen Harper; *m* 1970, Cynthia Margaret Dean (marr. diss.); three *s*; *m* 1991, Sally Elizabeth Roper. *Educ:* King's Coll. Sch., Cambridge (Chorister); Clifton Coll., Bristol (Music Scholar); Selwyn Coll., Cambridge (Organ Scholar; MA); Birmingham Univ. (PhD); MA Oxon. Music Tutor, West Bromwich Residential Arts Centre, 1970–71; Dir, Edington Music Fest., 1971–78; Dir of Music, St Chad's Cathedral, Birmingham, 1972–78; Lectr in Music, Birmingham Univ., 1974–75, 1976–81; Asst Dir of Music, King Edward's Sch., Birmingham, 1975–76; Fellow, Organist, Informator Choristarum and Tutor in Music, Magdalen Coll., and Univ. Lectr in Music, Oxford, 1981–90; University College of North Wales, then Univ. of Wales, Bangor: Prof. of Music, 1991–98; RSCM Res. Prof. in Christian Music and Liturgy, 1998–. Leverhulme Fellow, 1997–98. Dir, Centre for Advanced Welsh Music Studies, 1994–. Founder Editor, Welsh Music History, 1996–99; Jt Ed., Plainsong and Medieval Music, 1999–. Member Council: UCNW, 1991–94; Plainsong and Mediaeval Music Soc., 1994– (Chm., 1998–); Guild of Church Musicians, 1995– (Hon. Fellow, 1996); Secretary: Cathedral Organists' Assoc., 1998–; Cathedral Music Working Party, 1998–; Trustee, Early English Organ Project, 1999– (Chm., 2000–). Advr, Panel of Monastic Musicians, 1976–. Recordings, 1974–, incl. The English Anthem (5 vols), with Magdalen Coll. Choir. Benemerenti Papal award, 1978. *Publications:* choral compositions, 1974–; (ed) Orlando Gibbons: consort music, 1982; The Forms and Orders of Western Liturgy, 1991; (ed) Hymns for Prayer and Praise, 1996; (ed) Music for Common Worship (3 vols), 2000; contribs to: New Grove Dictionary of Music and Musicians, 1980, 2000; Frescobaldi Studies, 1987; Die Musik in Geschichte und Gegenwart, 1994; Blackwell History of Music in Britain, Vol. 2, 1995; articles and reviews in music jls and papers. *Recreations:* walking, church architecture. *Address:* Royal School of Church Music, Cleveland Lodge, Westhumble, Dorking, Surrey RH5 6BW. *T:* (01306) 872800; Bethania, Llangoed, Beaumaris, Anglesey LL58 8PH. *Club:* Athenæum.

HARPER, Prof. (John) Ross, CBE 1986; Senior Partner: Ross Harper & Murphy, Solicitors, since 1961; Harper Macleod, since 1991; Professor of Law, Strathclyde University, since 1986; *b* 20 March 1935; *s* of late Rev. Thomas Harper, BD, STM, PhD and Margaret Simpson Harper (later Clarkson); *m* 1963, Ursula Helga Renate Gathman; two *s* one *d*. *Educ:* Hutchesons' Boys' Grammar School; Glasgow Univ. (MA, LLB), Pres., Students Rep. Council, 1955. Pres., Scottish Union of Students, 1956–58; Chm.,, Internat. Students' Conf., 1958. Asst Solicitor, McGettigan & Co., Glasgow, 1959; founded Ross Harper & Murphy, 1961, as two Partner firm (now 23 Partners), specialised in Criminal Law, later developing into Commercial Law. Temp. Sheriff, 1979–89; a Parly Comr, 1992–. Pres., Law Soc. of Scotland, 1988–89 (Vice-Pres., 1987–88). Pres., Glasgow Bar Assoc., 1975–78; International Bar Association: Chm., Criminal Law Div., 1983–87; Chm., Gen. Practice Section, 1990–92 (Sec. and Treas., 1988–90); Vice-Pres., 1992–94; Pres., 1994–96. Chairman: Mining (Scotland), 1997– (Jt Chm., 1993–95); Scottish Coal, 1997–; Alarm Protection Ltd, 2000–; Africa Holdings (SA) (Pty) Ltd, 2001–. Chm., Finance Cttee, Greater Glasgow Health Board, 1984–87; Non-Exec. Dir, Scottish Prison Service, 1993–96. Trustee: Nat. Galls of Scotland, 1996–99; Strathclyde Univ. Foundn Bd, 1997–. Contested (C): Hamilton, 1970; W Renfrewshire, Feb. and Oct. 1974. Founder Chm., Soc. of Scottish Cons. Lawyers, 1982–86; Pres., Scottish Cons. & Unionist Assoc., 1989 (Hon. Sec., 1986–89). *Publications:* A Practitioner's Guide to the Criminal Courts, 1985; Glasgow Rape Case, 1985; Fingertip Criminal Law, 1986; pamphlets on devolution, referendums, etc. *Recreations:* bridge, angling. *Address:* 23 Clabon Mews, Cadogan Square, SW1X 0EG. *Club:* Caledonian.

HARPER, Joseph Charles; QC 1992; *b* 21 March 1939; *e s* of Frederick Charles Harper and Kitty (*née* Judah); *m* 1984, Sylvia Helen Turner (marr. diss. 1994); two *d*. *Educ:* Charterhouse; LSE (BA, LLB, LLM). ARCM 1960. Lectr, later Hd, Dept of Law, Kingston Poly., 1965–70; called to the Bar: Gray's Inn, 1970 (Bencher, 2000); Antigua, 1985. Mem. Council, Justice, 1979–91. *Publications:* (Specialist Editor) Hill and Redman, Law of Landlord and Tenant (looseleaf), 17th edn 1982, 18th edn 1988–; (ed and contrib.) Halsbury's Laws of England, vol. 8(I) Compulsory Acquisition of Land, rev. 4th edn, 1996. *Recreations:* music (especially playing the French horn), bibliomania. *Address:* 4 Breams Buildings, EC4A 1AQ. *T:* (020) 7353 5835. *Club:* Garrick.

HARPER, Malcolm Charles, CMG 2000; Director, United Nations Association, since 1982; *b* 21 June 1939; *s* of Leonard Robert Harper and Enid Harper (*née* Redman); *m* 1966, Ann Patricia Broad; one *s* two *d*. *Educ:* Marlborough Coll.; Trinity Hall, Cambridge (MA Hons Hist. and Theol.). Lay Personal Asst to Anglican Archbp of Cape Town, 1961–62; with OXFAM, 1963–81: served in E Africa, 1968–71; Emergencies Officer, 1972–75; Communications Dir, 1975–81; in Cambodia, 1979–80. Mem. Exec. Cttee, World Fedn of UNAs, Geneva, 1981– (Chm., 1995–2000). Mem., RIIA, 1999–. FRSA 1998. Albert Einstein Gold Medal, UNESCO, 1995; Soka Gakkai Internat. Medal (Japan), 1999. *Publications:* contrib. chapters to several UN-orientated books. *Recreations:* cricket, long-distance walking, jogging, photography, theatre. *Address:* The Cottages, Church Lane, Charlbury, Oxon OX7 3PX. *T:* and *Fax:* (01608) 810464. *Clubs:* MCC, Cricketers'; Charlbury Cricket (Oxon), Nonnunquam Cricket.

HARPER, Richard Saul; District Judge, Principal Registry of the Family Division, since 1994; *b* 19 June 1953; *s* of Alfred and Netta Harper; *m* 1988, Amanda Louise Price; two *s* one *d*. *Educ:* Magdalen Coll., Oxford (MA). Called to the Bar, Gray's Inn, 1975; practising barrister, 1976–94. *Publications:* Child Care Law: a basic guide for practitioners, 1991; Medical Treatment and the Law: the protection of adults and minors in the Family Division, 1999. *Recreations:* international affairs, reading, sport. music. *Address:* Principal Registry of the Family Division, First Avenue House, 42–49 High Holborn, WC1V 6NP. *T:* (020) 7947 6943.

HARPER, Robin Charles Moreton; Member (Green) Lothians, Scottish Parliament, since 1999; *b* 4 Aug. 1940; *s* of Comdr C. H. A. Harper, OBE, RN and late Jessicca Harper; *m* 1994, Jennifer Helen Carter (*née* Brown); one step *s*. *Educ:* Aberdeen Univ. (MA); Heriot Watt Univ. (Dip. Guidance & Curriculum). Teacher: Braehead Sch., Fife, 1964–68, 1970–71; Kolanya Sch., Kenya, 1968; Amukura Sch., Kenya, 1969; actor and stage manager, Ayr Civic Theatre, 1971; teacher: English, Newbattle High Sch., 1971–72; Modern Studies, Boroughmuir High Sch., 1972–99. Rector, Edinburgh Univ., 2000–. FEIS; FRSA. *Recreations:* hill walking, music, photography. *Address:* Scottish Parliament, George IV Bridge, Edinburgh EH99 1SP. *T:* (0131) 348 5000.

HARPER, William Ronald; water industry consultant, since 1998; *b* 5 June 1944; *s* of William and Dorothy Harper; *m* 1969, Susan Penelope (*née* Rider); two *s* two *d*. *Educ:* Barton Peveril Grammar Sch., Eastleigh, Hants. IPFA 1965. Hampshire CC, 1960–64; Eastbourne CBC, 1964–68; Chartered Inst. of Public Finance and Accountancy, 1968–70; Greenwich London BC, 1970–74; Thames Water Authority: joined 1974; Dir of Finance, 1982; Dir of Corporate Strategy, 1984; Man. Dir, 1986; Dep. Chm., Thames Water Utilities, 1989; Thames Water PLC: Bd Mem., 1989–97; Gp Dir, Corporate Activities, 1992; Divl Dir, Products, 1994; Strategy Dir, 1996–97. Chm., Foundn for Water Res., 1989–94. Member: Council, Water Services Assoc., 1990–94; Bd of Management, Water

Training, 1991–99 (Chm., 1993–99). CEN Rapporteur–Water, 1998–. Chm., Churches in Reading Drop-in Centre, 1998–. Trustee, Berks Young Musicians Trust, 1998–. *Address:* 37 Kidmore End Road, Reading, Berks RG4 8SN. *T:* (0118) 947 4476.

HARPUM, Charles; barrister; Fellow, Downing College, Cambridge, 1977–2001, now Emeritus; *b* 29 March 1953; *s* of Dr John Richard Harpum and Beatrice Doreen Harpum (*née* Harper). *Educ:* Queen Elizabeth Grammar Sch., Penrith; Cheltenham Grammar Sch.; Downing Coll., Cambridge (BA 1st Cl. Hons with Dist. 1975; LLB 1st Cl. Hons with Dist. 1977; Chancellor's Medal; MA 1979). Called to the Bar, Lincoln's Inn, 1976, Bencher, 2001. Asst Lectr in Law, 1979–84, Lectr, 1984–98, Cambridge Univ.; a Law Comr, 1994–2001. Vis. Schol., Sch. of Law, Univ. of Va, Charlottesville, USA, 1991. *Publications:* (contrib.) Megarry and Wade's Law of Real Property, 6th edn 1998; numerous articles on property law in learned jls. *Recreations:* travelling, listening to classical music, designing gardens, drinking single island malts. *Address:* Falcon Chambers, Falcon Court, EC4Y 1AA. *T:* (020) 7353 2484.

HARRAP, Prof. Kenneth Reginald, CBE 1998; PhD, DSc; CChem, FRSC; Partner, Weston & Harrap Consulting, since 1997; Professor of Biochemical Pharmacology, Institute of Cancer Research, 1984–97, now Emeritus; *b* 20 Nov. 1931; *s* of George Ernest Harrap and Lilian Florence Olive Harrap (*née* Critchley); *m* 1st, 1954, Kathleen Ann Gotts (marr. diss. 1980); two *d*; 2nd, 1983, Beverley Jane Weston. *Educ:* George Green Sch.; London Univ. (BSc 1955; PhD 1961; DCC 1963; DSc 1977). CChem 1975; FRSC 1980. Institute of Cancer Research, Royal Marsden Hospital: Lectr, subseq. Sen. Lectr, in Chemistry, 1954–64; Head, Leukaemia Biochemistry Gp, 1964–70; Head of Department: Applied Biochemistry, 1970–77; Biochemical Pharmacology, 1977–82; Chm., Drug Develt Section, 1982–94; Dir, CRC Centre for Cancer Therapeutics, 1994–97; Friend and Vis. Scientist, 1997–. Emeritus Fellow, and Award of Distinction, CRC, 1998. Bruce F. Cain Meml Award, Amer. Assoc. of Cancer Res., 1995, NZ Cancer Soc., 1996; Barnett Rosenberg Award, Internat. Symposium on Platinum Compounds in Cancer Chemotherapy, 1995. *Publications:* 400 papers in learned jls, contribs to books, reviews etc. *Recreations:* yachting and off-shore cruising, wildlife, concert music, opera. *Address:* Little Orchard, Wonham Way, Peaslake, Surrey GU5 9PA. *Clubs:* Sussex Yacht, Island Sailing, Cowes Corinthian Yacht.

HARREL, David Terence Digby; Senior Partner, S. J. Berwin & Co., Solicitors, since 1992; *b* 23 June 1948; *s* of Capt. H. T. Harrel; *m* 1974, Julia Mary Reeves; two *s* one *d*. *Educ:* Marlborough Coll.; Bristol Univ. (LLB). William Charles Crocker: articled clerk, 1971–74; Asst Solicitor, 1974–77; Partner, 1977–79; Partner: Burton & Ramsden, 1979–81; S. J. Berwin & Co., 1982–. *Recreations:* golf, tennis, fishing, shooting, walking, reading. *Address:* 33 Ursula Street, SW11 3DW. *T:* (020) 7223 0637. *Club:* Royal St George's Golf (Sandwich).

HARRELL, Lynn Morris; 'cellist; Principal, Royal Academy of Music, 1993–95; *b* 30 Jan. 1944; *s* of Mack Harrell, Metropolitan Opera baritone and Marjorie Harrell (*née* Fulton), violinist; *m* 1976, Linda Blandford; one *s* one *d* (twins). *Educ:* Julliard Sch. of Music; Curtis Inst. of Music. Principal 'Cellist, Cleveland Orch., 1963–71; Professor: College Conservatory of Music, Cincinatti, 1971–77; Juilliard Sch. of Music, 1977–86; International Chair of 'Cello Studies, RAM, 1987–93; Piatigorsky Chair, Sch. of Music, USC, 1987–93; Artistic Dir, Los Angeles Philharmonic Inst., 1988–92. Numerous recording awards. *Recreations:* fishing, music. *Address:* c/o IMG Europe, 616 Chiswick High Road, W4 5RX.

HARRER, Prof. Heinrich; author and explorer; awarded title of Professor by President of Austrian Republic, 1964; *b* Hüttenberg, 6 July 1912; *m*; one *s*; *m* 1953, Margaretha Truxa (marr. diss. 1958); *m* 1962, Katharina Haarhaus. *Educ:* University of Graz, Austria (graduated in Geography, 1938). First ascent, Eiger North Wall, 1938; Himalayan Expedition, 1939; interned in India, 1939–44; Tibet, 1944–51; Himalayan Expedition, 1951; expeditions: to the Andes, 1953; to Alaska, 1954; to Ruwenzori (Mountains of the Moon), Africa, 1957; to West New Guinea, 1961–62; to Nepal, 1965; to Xingu Red Indians in Mato Grosso, Brazil; to Bush Negroes of Surinam (Surinam Expedn with King Leopold of Belgium), 1966; to the Sudan, 1970; to North Borneo (Sabah) (with King Leopold of Belgium), 1971; N-S crossing of Borneo, 1972; Valley of Flowers (Alaknanda), 1974; Andaman Islands, 1975; Zangkar-Ladakh, 1976. Inauguration of Heinrich Harrer Mus., Hüttenberg, 1992; inauguration of Lingkor (Tibetan pilgrim path), Hüttenberg, 1995. Mem., Austrian Acad. of Scis, 1995. Hon. Mem., Humboldt Soc. for Sci., Art and Educn. 35 short films on expeditions. Prize for best documentary book, Donanland, 1982; Golden medal, Humboldt Soc., 1985; Medal, Explorers' Club, NY, 1991; Internat. Prize for Literature, Italy, 1998. Hon. Citizen, Hüttenberg, 1983; Orders from Germany, Austria, Carinthia, Styria, 70th birthday, 1982; highest orders from Carinthia, Styria, 80th birthday, 1992. Austrian National Amateur Golf Champion, 1958; Austrian National Seniors Golf Champion, 1970. Hon. Pres., Austrian Golf Association, 1964 (Pres., 1949–64). *Publications:* Seven Years in Tibet, 1953 (Great Britain, and numerous other countries; filmed, 1997); Meine Tibet-Bilder, 1953 (Germany); The White Spider, History of the North Face of the Eiger, 1958; Tibet is My Country: biography of Thubten Jigme Norbu, *e b* of Dalai Lama, 1960 (Eng.); I Come from the Stone Age, 1964 (London); The Last 500, 1975; The Last Caravan, 1976; Return to Tibet, 1984; Meine Forschungsreisen, 1986; Das Buch vom Eiger, 1988; Borneo, 1988; Bhutan, 1989; Lost Lhasa, 1992. *Address:* Barbarasiedlung 15, 9376 Knappenberg, Austria. *Clubs:* Alpine (Hon. Mem.); Explorers' (New York) (Hon. Mem.), Royal and Ancient (St Andrews); PEN (Liechtenstein).

HARRHY, Eiddwen Mair; soprano; Professor of Singing, Royal College of Music, since 2001; *b* 14 April 1949; *d* of David and Emily Harrhy; *m* Greg Strange, journalist and broadcaster; one *d*. *Educ:* St Winefride's Convent, Swansea; Royal Manchester College of Music (Gold Medal Opera Prize); Paris (Miriam Licette Prize). Welsh Nat. Opera Chorus, 1970–71; Glyndebourne Festival Opera Chorus, 1971–73; début at Royal Opera House, Covent Garden, Wagner Ring Cycle, 1974; début, ENO, 1975; performances: Welsh Nat. Opera; La Scala Milan; Teatro Colon Buenos Aires; ENO; Glyndebourne; Opera North; Scottish Opera; UK and overseas orchestras; BBC promenade concerts; Australia, NZ, Hong Kong, S America, Europe, Scandinavia, USA; numerous recordings. Vocal Tutor, WCMD, 1996–2001. Founder: Trust for Young Musicians, 1992; Crisis Messiah, 1992. *Recreations:* chamber music, ski-ing, golf. *Address:* c/o Phoenix Artists Management, 4th Floor, 6 Windmill Street, W1P 1HF.

HARRIES, Prof. John Edward, PhD; CPhys, FInstP; FRMetS; Professor of Earth Observation, Imperial College of Science, Technology and Medicine, since 1994; *b* 26 March 1946; *s* of Brynmor and Marion Harries; *m* 1968, Sheila Margaret Basford; two *s* one *d*. *Educ:* Univ. of Birmingham (BSc Hons Physics 1967); King's Coll., London (PhD Physics 1971). Nat. Physical Lab., 1967–80; SO, later SSO, then PSO; Hd, Envmtl Standards Gp, 1976–80; Rutherford Appleton Laboratory, 1980–93; SPSO and Hd, Geophysics and Radio Div., 1980–84; DCSO, 1984; Associate Dir and Hd of Space Science Dept, 1984–93. Mem., NERC, 1995–97. President: Internat. Radiation Commn, 1992–96; RMetS, 1994–96. *Publications:* Earthwatch: the climate from space, 1991; more than 100 articles in books, jls and magazines. *Recreations:* walking, reading, music, supporting Welsh Rugby. *Address:* Blackett Laboratory, Imperial College, Prince Consort Road, SW7 2BZ. *T:* (020) 7594 7670; *e-mail:* j.harries@ic.ac.uk.

HARRIES, Rt Rev. Richard Douglas; *see* Oxford, Bishop of.

HARRINGTON, 11th Earl of, *cr* 1742; **William Henry Leicester Stanhope;** Viscount Stanhope of Mahon and Baron Stanhope of Elvaston, Co. Derby, 1717; Baron Harrington, 1729; Viscount Petersham, 1742; late Captain 15th/19th Hussars; *b* 24 Aug. 1922; *o s* of 10th Earl and Margaret Trelawney (Susan) (*d* 1952), *d* of Major H. H. D. Seaton; *S* father, 1929; *m* 1st, 1942, Eileen (from whom he obtained a divorce, 1946; she *d* 1999), *o d* of late Sir John Grey, Enville Hall, Stourbridge; one *s* one *d* (and one *d* decd); 2nd, 1947, Anne Theodora (from whom he obtained a divorce, 1962), *o d* of late Major Richard Arenbourg Blennerhassett Chute; one *s* two *d*; 3rd, 1964, Priscilla Margaret, *d* of Hon. A. E. Cubitt and Mrs Ronald Dawnay; one *s* one *d*. *Educ:* Eton; RMC, Sandhurst. Served War of 1939–45, demobilised 1946. Owns about 700 acres. Became Irish Citizen, 1965. *Heir: s* Viscount Petersham, *qv*. *Address:* The Glen, Ballingarry, Co. Limerick, Eire.
See also Baron Ashcombe, Earl Cawdor.

HARRINGTON, Dr Albert Blair, CB 1979; Head of Civil Service Department Medical Advisory Service, 1976–79; *b* 26 April 1914; *s* of late Albert Timothy Harrington and Lily Harrington; *m* 1939, Valerie White (*d* 1996); one *d*. *Educ:* Brisbane Grammar Sch., Qld; Aberdeen Univ. MB, ChB 1938, MD 1944. House Phys., Woodend Hosp., Aberdeen, 1938–39; service in RAMC (Field Amb., Blood Transfusion Phys., Neurologist), 1940–45; MO (Head Injuries) and Dep. Supt, Stoke Mandeville Hosp., 1946–48; Med. Supt, Dunston Hill Hosp., Gateshead, 1948–50; SMO (Pensions), Cleveleys, 1950–53; Med. Supt, Queen Mary's Hosp., Roehampton, 1954–56; SMO, Dept of Health (Hosp. Bldg and later Regional Liaison Duties), 1956–68; PMO (Hosp. Bldg), 1968–73; SPMO (Under-Sec.), DHSS, 1973–76. Chm., CS Med. Appts Bds, 1979–86. FFCM (Foundn Fellow) 1972. *Publications:* articles on Sjögren's Disease, paralytic poliomyelitis, and hospital planning, medical care and the work of the Medical Advisory Service. *Recreations:* gardening, country life; formerly tennis. *Address:* 59 Lauderdale Drive, Petersham, Richmond, Surrey TW10 7BS. *T:* (020) 8940 1345. *Club:* Athenæum.

HARRINGTON, Illtyd; JP; DL; *b* 14 July 1931; *s* of Timothy Harrington and Sarah (*née* Burchell); unmarried. *Educ:* St Illtyd's RC Sch., Dowlais; Merthyr County Sch.; Trinity Coll., Caermarthen. Member: Paddington Borough Council, 1959–64; Westminster City Council, 1964–68 and 1971–78, Leader, Lab. Gp, 1972–74; GLC, 1964–67 and for Brent S, 1973–86: Alderman, 1970–73; Chairman, Policy and Resources Cttee, 1973–77, Special Cttee, 1985–86; Dep. Leader, 1973–77, 1981–84; Dep. Leader of the Opposition, 1977–81; Chm. of the Council, 1984–85. Special Advr to Chm. and Leader of ILEA, 1988–90; Waterways Advr to Mayor of London, 2001. JP Willesden 1968. First Chairman, Inland Waterways Amenity Adv. Council, 1968–71; Chm., London Canals Consultative Cttee, 1965–67, 1981–; Vice Pres., IWA, 1990–; Member: British Waterways Bd, 1974–82; BTA, 1976–80. Member: Bd, Theatre Royal, Stratford E, 1978–; Bd, Wiltons Music Hall, 1979–; Nat. Theatre Bd, 1975–77; Bd, National Youth Theatre, 1976–; Globe Theatre Trust, 1986–; Chm., Half Moon Theatre, 1978–90; Director: Soho Poly Theatre, 1981–; The Young Vic, 1981–. Chm., Nat. Millennium Maritime Fest., 1997–; Mem., London Dockland Mgt Adv. Gp, 1997–. President: Grand Union Canal Soc., 1974–; Islington Boat Club, 1985–; SE Region, IWA, 1986–; Immunity (Legal aid facility for AIDS victims), 1986–; Chairman: Kilburn Skills, 1977–; Battersea Park Peace Pagoda, 1984–; Limehouse Basin Users Gp, 1986–; Vice Pres., Coventry Canal Soc., 1970–. Patron, Westminster Cathedral Appeal, 1977–. Gov., London Marathon, 1980–91. Trustee: Kew Bridge Pumping Mus., 1976–; Queen's Jubilee Walkway, 1977–; Chiswick Family Rescue, 1978–; Arthur Koestler Awards for Prisoners, 1987–; CARE, 1987–; Dominica Overseas Student Fund, 1987–; Mem., Montgomery Canal Trust, 1988–; Managing Trustee, Mutual Municipal Insurance Co., 1985–96. Governor, Brunel Univ., 1981–87. DL Greater London, 1986. Contributor, The Guardian, 1982–; Books Ed., Camden Jl gp of papers, 1995–. *Recreations:* defender of local government; laughing, singing and incredulity. *Address:* 16 Lea House, Salisbury Street, NW8 8BJ. *T:* (020) 7402 6356. *Club:* Savile.

HARRINGTON, Prof. (John) Malcolm, CBE 1992; MD; FRCP, FFOM, FFOMI, FMedSci; Foundation Professor of Occupational Health, and Director, Institute of Occupational Health, University of Birmingham, 1981–2000; *b* 6 April 1942; *s* of John Roy Harrington and Veda Naomi Harrington; *m* 1967, Madeline Mary Davies; one *d*. *Educ:* King's Coll., London (BSc, MSc); Westminster Hosp. Med. Sch. MD 1976; FFOM 1981; FRCP 1982; FFOMI 1994; MFPHM 1996. Hospital appointments, 1966–69; Lectr in Occupational Medicine, LSHTM, 1969–75; Vis. Scientist, Centers for Disease Control, Atlanta, US Public Health Service, 1975–77; Sen. Lectr in Occupational Medicine, LSHTM, 1977–80. Chm., Ind. Injuries Adv. Council, 1982–96. Founder FMedSci 1998. *Publications:* (ed jtly) Occupational Hygiene, 1980, 2nd edn 1995; (with F. S. Gill) Occupational Health, 1983, 4th edn 1998; (ed) Recent Advances in Occupational Health, Vol. 2 1984, Vol. 3 1987; (ed jtly) Hunter's Diseases of Occupation, 9th edn 2000; papers in scientific professional jls. *Recreations:* music, gardening, cricket, reading biographies, theatre. *Club:* Athenæum.

HARRINGTON, Patrick John; QC 1993; a Recorder, since 1991; *b* 23 June 1949; *s* of late Murtagh Joseph Harrington and of Eileen Mary Harrington (*née* Kelly); *m* 1975, Susan Jane, BSc, *o c* of Captain K. W. Bradley, RN; one *s* one *d*. *Educ:* Ebbw Vale Grammar Sch.; Birmingham Coll. of Commerce. LLB Hons London. Called to the Bar, Gray's Inn, 1973; Leader, Wales and Chester Circuit, 2000–. Chm., Gwent Health Research Ethics Cttee, 1993–97. *Recreations:* playing and listening to music, squash, tennis, ski-ing, classic motoring, horse racing. *Address:* Farrar's Building, Temple, EC4Y 7BD; Broom House, Raglan, Monmouthshire NP15 2HW. *Clubs:* Cardiff and County; Ebbw Vale Rugby Football; Glamorgan CC.

HARRIS, family name of **Barons Harris, Harris of Haringey, Harris of High Cross, Harris of Peckham** and of **Earl of Malmesbury**.

HARRIS, 8th Baron *cr* 1815, of Seringapatan and Mysore and of Belmont, Kent; **Anthony Harris;** *b* 8 March 1942; *s* of 7th Baron Harris and of Laura Cecilia (*née* McCausland); *S* father, 1996; *m* 1966, Anstice, *d* of Alfred Winter; two *d*. *Heir: cousin* Comdr Antony John Temple Harris, OBE, RN [*b* 5 Aug. 1915; *m* 1940, Doris, *o c* of F. D. Drake; two *s*].

HARRIS OF HARINGEY, Baron *cr* 1998 (Life Peer), of Hornsey in the London Borough of Haringey; **Jonathan Toby Harris;** (Leader, Labour Group, since 2000); Chairman, Metropolitan Police Authority, since 2000; Member (Lab) Brent and Harrow, London Assembly, Greater London Authority, since 2000; *b* 11 Oct. 1953; *s* of Prof. Harry Harris, FRS and of Muriel Hargest; *m* 1979, Ann Sarah Herbert; two *s* one *d*. *Educ:* Haberdashers' Aske's Sch., Elstree; Trinity Coll., Cambridge (BA Hons NatScis and Econ). Chair, Cambridge Univ. Labour Club, 1973; Pres., Cambridge Union Soc., 1974. Economics Div., Bank of England, 1975–79; Electricity Consumers' Council, 1979–86,

Dep. Dir, 1983; Dir, Assoc. of CHCs for England and Wales, 1987–98. Non-exec. Dir, London Ambulance Service NHS Trust, 1998–. Consultant Advr, KPMG, 1999–; Trng Advr, Infolog Ltd, 1998–; Sen. Associate, King's Fund, 1999–. Mem., Haringey BC, 1978– (Chair, Social Services Cttee, 1982–87; Leader, 1987–99); Mem., Adv Cabinet, Mayor of London, 2000–. Dep. Chair, AMA, 1991–96 (Chair, Social Services Cttee, 1986–93); Chair: Assoc. of London Authorities, 1993–95 (Dep. Chair, 1990–93; Chair, Social Services Cttee, 1984–88); Assoc. of London Govt, 1995–2000; LBTC-Training for Care, 1986–94; Local Govt Anti-Poverty Unit, 1994–97; Local Government Association: Chairman: Labour Gp, 1996–; Community Safety Panel, 1997–98; Mem., Exec., 1999–. Nat. Chair, Young Fabian Gp, 1976–77; Chair, Hornsey Labour Party, 1978, 1979, 1980; Mem., Labour Party Nat. Policy Forum, 1992–; Co-opted Mem., Lab. Party Local Govt Cttee, 1993–. Dep. Chair, Nat. Fuel Poverty Forum, 1981–86; Member: London Drug Policy Forum, 1990–98; Jt London Adv. Panel, 1996–97. Jt Chair: London Pride Partnership, 1995–98; London Waste Action, 1997–2000; Member: King's Fund Orgnl Audit Adv. Council, 1991–98; Exec. Cttee, RADAR, 1991–93; Nat. Nursery Exam. Bd, 1992–94; Home Office Adv. Council on Race Relations, 1992–97; Bd, London First, 1993–; Exec. Council, RNIB, 1993–94; Cttee of Regns of EU, 1994–; NHS Charter Advisor's Gp, 1997–98; London Pension Funds Authority, 1998–2000; Metropolitan Police Cttee, 1998–2000; Bd, London Develt Partnership, 1998–2000. Chair, English Nat. Stadium Trust, 1997–. Trustee: Evening Standard Blitz Meml Appeal, 1995–99; Help for Health Trust, 1995–97; The Learning Agency, 1996–98. Mem. Court, Middx Univ., 1995–. Governor: Nat. Inst. for Social Work, 1986–94; Sch. of St David and St Katherine, 1978–96; St Mary's Schs, Hornsey, 1978–96. FRSA 1993. Freeman, City of London, 1998. *Publications:* (with Nick Butler and Neil Kinnock) Why Vote Labour?, 1979; (contrib.) Economics of Prosperity, 1980; (ed with Jonathan Bradshaw) Energy and Social Policy, 1983; (contrib.) Rationing in Action, 1993; (contrib.) Whistleblowing in the Health Service: accountability, law, and professional practice, 1994. *Recreations:* reading, walking. *Address:* House of Lords, SW1A 0PW.

HARRIS OF HIGH CROSS, Baron *cr* 1979 (Life Peer), of Tottenham in Greater London; **Ralph Harris;** Founder President, Institute of Economic Affairs, since 1990 (General Director, 1957–87, Chairman, 1987–89); *b* 10 Dec. 1924; *m* 1949, Jose Pauline Jeffery; one *d* (two *s* decd). *Educ:* Tottenham Grammar Sch.; Queens' Coll., Cambridge (Exhibr, Foundn Schol.). 1st Cl. Hons Econs, MA Cantab. Lectr in Polit. Economy, St Andrews Univ., 1949–56. Contested (C): Kirkcaldy, 1951; Edinburgh Central, 1955. Leader-writer, Glasgow Herald, 1956. Trustee: Wincott Foundn; Ross McWhirter Foundn.; Inst. for Study of Civil Soc., 2000–. Chairman: Bruges Gp, 1989–91; FOREST, 1989–; Jt Chm., Internat. Centre for Res. into Economic Transformation, Moscow, 1990–95. Mem. Council, Univ. of Buckingham, 1980–95; Dir, (Independent National) Times Newspapers Hldgs Ltd, 1988–. Chm., Birling Gap Cliff Protection Assoc., 1997–. Free Enterprise Award, 1976. Hon. DSc Buckingham, 1984. *Publications:* Politics without Prejudice, a biography of R. A. Butler, 1956; Hire Purchase in a Free Society, 1958, 3rd edn 1961; (with Arthur Seldon) Advertising in a Free Society, 1959; Advertising in Action, 1962; Advertising and the Public, 1962; (with A. P. Herbert) Libraries: Free for All?, 1962; Choice in Welfare, 1963; Essays in Rebirth of Britain, 1964; Choice in Welfare, 1965; Right Turn, 1970; Choice in Welfare, 1970; Down with the Poor, 1971; (with Brendan Sewill) British Economic Policy 1970–74, 1975; Crisis '75, 1975; Catch '76, 1976, Freedom of Choice: consumers or conscripts, 1976; (with Arthur Seldon) Pricing or Taxing, 1976; Not from Benevolence, 1977; (ed with Arthur Seldon) The Coming Confrontation, 1978; (with Arthur Seldon) Over-ruled on Welfare, 1979; End of Government, 1980; Challenge of a Radical Reactionary, 1981; No, Minister!, 1985; What Price Democracy?, 1985; The Enemies of Progress, 1986; (with Arthur Seldon) Welfare Without the State, 1987; Beyond the Welfare State, 1988; Murder a Cigarette, 1998; columnist in Truth, Statist, etc. *Recreations:* reading, writing, talking, swimming. *Address:* 5 Cattley Close, Wood Street, Barnet, Herts EN5 4SN. *Clubs:* Political Economy, Mont Pelerin Society.

HARRIS OF PECKHAM, Baron *cr* 1995 (Life Peer), of Peckham in the London Borough of Southwark; **Philip Charles Harris,** Kt 1985; Chairman: Harris Ventures Ltd, since 1988; Carpetright plc, since 1993; *b* 15 Sept. 1942; *s* of Charles William Harris, MC and Ruth Ellen (*née* Ward); *m* 1960, Pauline Norma (*née* Chumley); three *s* one *d*. *Educ:* Streatham Grammar School. Chm., 1964–88, Chief Exec., 1987–88, Harris Queensway Plc; Chm., C. W. Harris Properties Ltd, 1988–97. Dir, Harveys Hldgs, 1986–2000; non-executive Director: Great Universal Stores, 1986–; Fisons Plc, 1986–94; Molyneux Estates, 1990–95. Mem., British Show Jumping Assoc., 1974–. Chm., Guy's and Lewisham NHS Trust, 1991–93; Vice-Chm., Lewisham Hospital NHS Trust, 1993–97; Member: Council of Governors, UMDS of Guy's and St Thomas's Hosps, 1984– (Hon. Fellow, 1992); Court of Patrons, RCOG, 1984–; Chm., Generation Trust, 1984–. Dep. Chm., Cons. Party Bd of Treasurers, 1993–97. Dep. Chm., Nat. Appeal Bd, NSPCC, 1998–. Trustee, RA, 1998–. Freeman, City of London, 1992. Hon. Fellow, Oriel Coll., Oxford, 1989; FGCL 1995; Hon. FRCR 1993. Hon. DEc Richmond Coll., London, 1996; Hon. LLD South Bank, 1998. Hambro Business Man of the Year, 1983. *Recreations:* football, cricket, show jumping, tennis. *Address:* Carpetright plc, Amberley House, New Road, Rainham, Essex RM13 8QN.

HARRIS OF RICHMOND, Baroness *cr* 1999 (Life Peer), of Richmond in the county of North Yorkshire; **Angela Felicity Harris;** DL; *b* 4 Jan. 1944; *d* of late Rev. George Henry Hamilton Richards and Eva Richards; *m* 1st, 1965, Philip Martin Bowles (marr. diss. 1975); one *s*; 2nd, 1976, John Philip Roger Harris. *Educ:* Canon Slade Grammar Sch., Bolton, Lancs. Air Stewardess, 1963–65; Careers Advr and Employment Asst, 1974–76. Member (L, then Lib Dem): Richmond Town Council, 1978–81 and 1991–99; Richmondshire DC, 1978–89; N Yorks CC, 1981–. Chm., N Yorks Police Authy, 1995–. Dep. Chm., Assoc. of Police Authorities, 1997–. DL N Yorks, 1994. *Address:* House of Lords, SW1A 0PW.

HARRIS, Prof. Adrian Llewellyn, FRCP; Imperial Cancer Research Fund Professor of Clinical Oncology, Oxford University, since 1988; *b* 10 Aug. 1950; *s* of Luke and Julia Harris; *m* 1975, Margaret Susan Denman; one *s* one *d*. *Educ:* Univ. of Liverpool (BSc Hons Biochem. 1970; MB ChB Hons 1973); DPhil Oxon 1978. MRCP 1975, FRCP 1985. Hosp. appts, Liverpool, 1973–74; Clinical Scientist, MRC Clinical Pharmacology Unit, Radcliffe Infirmary, Oxford and Nuffield Dept of Medicine, 1975–78; Registrar in Academic Unit, Royal Free Hosp., 1978–80; Lectr and Sen. Registrar, Inst. for Cancer Res., Royal Marsden Hosp., 1980–82; Vis. Researcher, Imp. Cancer Res. Fund Mutagenesis Lab., London, 1982–83; Prof. of Clinical Oncology, Newcastle upon Tyne Univ., 1983–88. *Publications:* papers on growth factors in cancer, mechanisms by which cancers become resistant to treatment, hormone and drug treatment of cancer. *Recreations:* swimming, modern dance, science fiction. *Address:* Imperial Cancer Research Fund Clinical Oncology Unit, Churchill Hospital, Headington, Oxford OX3 7LJ. *T:* (01865) 64841.

HARRIS, Anne Macintosh, (Mrs H. J. L. Harris), CBE 1985; National Chairman, National Federation of Women's Institutes, 1981–85; *b* 17 April 1925; *d* of Montague Macintosh Williams and Marguerite Anne Williams (*née* Barrington); *m* 1950, Henry John Leshley Harris (*d* 2001); one *s* three *d*. *Educ:* Battle Abbey Sch.; Swanley Horticultural Coll. and Wye Coll. (Swanley Dip. in Horticulture, 1946). Owned and ran nursery/market garden and shop, 1946–53. Mem., WI, 1947–; Mem., NFWI Exec. Cttee, 1973–85 (Vice-Chm., 1979–81); Chm., NFWI Markets Sub-Cttee, 1972–79; WI representative: on Women's National Commn, 1982–85; on Advertising Adv. Cttee, IBA, 1984–87. Mem. Council Nat. Trust, 1981–85. Trustee, Help the Aged, 1985–. Chm., Tunbridge Wells East District Local Assoc. Girl Guides, 1963–79; Vice-Chm., Brenchley PCC, 1978–82. FRSA 1986. *Recreations:* gardening, walking, reading, music. *Club:* Agricola Club and Swanley Guild (Wye).

HARRIS, Anthony David, CMG 1995; LVO 1979; HM Diplomatic Service, retired; Director, Robert Fleming and Co. Ltd, since 1999; *b* 13 Oct. 1941; *s* of Reginald William Harris and Kathleen Mary Harris (*née* Daw); *m* 1st, 1970, Patricia Ann Over (marr. diss. 1988); one *s*; 2nd, 1988, Sophie Kisling; two *s* one *d*. *Educ:* Plymouth College; Exeter College, Oxford (BA, 2nd cl. Hons Lit. Hum.). Third Sec., Commonwealth Relations Office, 1964; Middle East Centre for Arab Studies, Lebanon, 1965; Third, later Second Sec., and Vice-Consul, Jedda, 1967; Second Sec. (Inf.), Khartoum, 1969; First Sec., FCO, 1972; First Sec., Head of Chancery and Consul, Abu Dhabi, 1975; First Sec., UK Mission to UN, Geneva, 1979; Counsellor, FCO, 1982; seconded to MoD as Regl Marketing Dir 1 (Arabian Peninsula and Pakistan), 1983; Dep. Head of Mission, Cairo, 1986; Head of Information Dept, FCO, 1990–93; Scrutiny of Security in FCO, 1993–94; Ambassador to UAE, 1994–98. Mem. Council, RSAA, 1999–. Dep. Chm. (Gulf Affairs), Next Century Foundn, 1999–. *Recreations:* shooting (HM the Queen's Prize, Bisley, 1964; British team to Canada, 1974), ski-ing, climbing, diving. *Address:* c/o Robert Fleming and Co. Ltd, 25 Copthall Avenue, EC2R 7DR. *Clubs:* Reform; Commonwealth Rifle (Bisley).

HARRIS, Anthony Geoffrey S.; *see* Stoughton-Harris.

HARRIS, Anthony George, OBE 1991; Principal, Harper Adams Agricultural College, 1977–94, retired; *b* 29 July 1929; *s* of John and Emily Kate Harris; *m* 1955, Sylvia Pyle; one *s* one *d* (and two *s* decd). *Educ:* Seale-Hayne Agricl Coll. (NDA, CDA Hons). FIBiol, FRAgS. Lectr in Agric., Dorset Coll. of Agric., 1953–55; Lectr in Crop Production, Harper Adams Agricl Coll., 1955–58; Vice-Principal, Walford Coll. of Agric., 1958–66; Principal, Merrist Wood Agric. Coll., 1967–77. Hon. FRASE 1999. DUniv Open 1996. *Publications:* Crop Husbandry, 1961; Farm Machinery, 1965, 2nd edn 1974. *Recreations:* walking, reading. *Club:* Farmers'.

HARRIS, Rt Rev. Mgr Anthony John, SCA; priest, Our Lady of the Visitation, Greenford, since 1994; *b* 6 May 1940; *s* of Philip John Harris and Eileen (*née* Kelly). *Educ:* St Patrick's Seminary, Thurles, Co. Tipperary (graduated in Phil. and Theol.). Ordained as Pallottine Priest, 1965; Dean of Discipline, 1965; Assistant Priest: Clerkenwell, 1965–68; Hastings, 1968–73; joined Chaplains' Br., RAF, 1973; served in UK, Germany, Cyprus and Ascension Island; Asst Principal Chaplain, 1986–92; Prin. RC Chaplain to RAF, 1992–94; VG, RAF, 1992–94. Prelate of Honour, 1992. *Recreations:* walking, swimming. *Address:* Our Lady of the Visitation, Greenford Road, Greenford, Middx UB6 9AN. *Clubs:* Royal Air Force; Essex.

HARRIS, Prof. Anthony Leonard, CGeol; FRSE, FGS; Professor of Geology, University of Liverpool, 1987–2001, now Emeritus (Dean, Faculty of Science, 1994–2000); *b* 11 May 1935; *s* of Thomas Haydn Harris and Dora Harris (*née* Wilkinson), *m* 1959, Noreen Jones; one *s* one *d*. *Educ:* Cardiff High Sch.; University College of Wales, Aberystwyth (BSc, PhD). Geologist and Principal Geologist, British Geol Survey, 1959–71; Liverpool University: Lectr, Sen. Lectr, then Reader, 1971–87; Head, Dept of Earth Scis, 1987–94. Pres., Geolog. Soc., 1990–92. Major John Coke Medal, Geolog. Soc., 1985; C. T. Clough Meml Medal, Geolog. Soc. of Edinburgh, 1989. *Publications:* (ed and contrib.) Caledonides of the British Isles, 1979; The Caledonian-Appalachian Orogen, 1988; papers in learned jls. *Recreations:* music, ornithology. *Address:* Department of Earth Sciences, University of Liverpool, PO Box 147, Liverpool L69 3BX; 12 Aigburth Hall Road, Liverpool L19 9DQ.

HARRIS, Rt Rev. Augustine; Bishop (RC) of Middlesbrough, 1978–92, now Bishop Emeritus; *b* 27 Oct. 1917; *s* of Augustine Harris and Louisa Beatrice (*née* Rycroft). *Educ:* St Francis Xavier's Coll., Liverpool; Upholland Coll., Lancs. Ordained, 1942; Curate at: St Oswald's, Liverpool, 1942–43; St Elizabeth's, Litherland, Lancs, 1943–52; Prison Chaplain, HM Prison, Liverpool, 1952–65; Sen. RC Priest, Prison Dept, 1957–66; English Rep. to Internat. Council of Sen. Prison Chaplains (RC), 1957–66; Titular Bishop of Socia and Auxiliary Bishop of Liverpool, 1965–78. Mem. Vatican Delegn to UN Quinquennial Congress on Crime, London, 1960 and Stockholm, 1965; Liaison between English and Welsh Hierarchy (RC) and Home Office, 1966–92; Episcopal Moderator to Fédération Internationale des Associations Médicales Catholiques, 1967–76; Episcopal Pres., Commn for Social Welfare (England and Wales), 1972–83; Chm., Dept for Social Responsibility, Bishops Conf. of Eng. and Wales, 1984–92. Mem., Central Religious Advisory Council to BBC and IBA, 1974–78. *Publications:* articles for criminological works. *Address:* 17 Old Town Lane, Formby, Merseyside L37 3HJ.

HARRIS, Basil Vivian, CEng, MIEE; Chief Engineer, Communications Division, Foreign and Commonwealth Office, 1979–81, retired; *b* 11 July 1921; *s* of late Henry William and Sarah May Harris; *m* 1943, Myra Winifred Mildred Newport (*d* 1997). *Educ:* Watford Grammar School. GPO Engineering Dept (Research), 1939; served RAF, 1943–46; GPO Engineering Dept (Radio Branch), 1946; Diplomatic Wireless Service, FCO, 1963; Dep. Chief Engineer, Communications Division, FCO, 1971. *Publications:* contribs to technical jls on communications. *Recreations:* golf, photography, travel. *Address:* 13 Decoy Drive, Eastbourne, Sussex BN22 0AB. *T:* (01323) 505819. *Club:* Royal Eastbourne Golf.

HARRIS, Ven. Brian; *see* Harris, Ven. R. B.

HARRIS, Brian Nicholas, FRICS; Consultant, Insignia Richard Ellis (formerly Richard Ellis, then Richard Ellis St Quintin), Chartered Surveyors and International Property Consultants, since 1996 (Chairman of Partnership, 1984–93; Partner, 1961–96); *b* 12 Dec. 1931; *s* of Claude Harris and Dorothy (*née* Harris); *m* 1961, Rosalyn Marion Caines; two *d*. *Educ:* King Alfred's Sch., Wantage; College of Estate Management. Chartered Surveyor. Chm., City of London Br. of RICS, 1984–85; Member of Council: London Chamber of Commerce, 1985– (Dep. Chm., 1990–92; Pres., 1992–94; Bd Mem., 1989–96); ABCC, 1992–98 (Mem. Bd, 1994–98; Chm., Southern Reg., 1994–96); Australian British Chamber of Commerce (UK), 1988–2000; Mem., Aust. and NZ Trade Adv. Cttee, 1991–98. Chm., Priority Sites Ltd, 2001–. Chm., Heathrow Airport Support Gp, 1993–99; Bd Mem., London First, 1993–94. Hon. Property Advr, Order of St John, 1996–. Chairman: London Chamber of Commerce Educnl Trust, 2000–; Britain Australia Soc., 2002–. Gov., Woldingham Sch., 1986–93 (Dep. Chm., 1991–93). FRSA 1987. Mem., Court of Common Council, City of London, 1996–; Sheriff, City of London, 1998–99; Member: Ct of Assistants, Co. of Glaziers and Painters of Glass, 1990–; Guild of

Freemen of City of London; Liveryman, Co. of World Traders. *Recreations:* flyfishing, gardening, golf. *Address:* Grants Paddock, Grants Lane, Limpsfield, Surrey RH8 0RQ. *T:* (01883) 723215. *Clubs:* Carlton, City of London, Flyfishers'; Tandridge Golf.

HARRIS, Brian Thomas, OBE 1983; QC 1982; *b* 14 Aug. 1932; *s* of Thomas and Eleanor Harris; *m* 1957, Janet Rosina Harris (*née* Hodgson); one *s* one *d*. *Educ:* Henry Thornton Grammar Sch.; King's Coll., Univ. of London. LLB (Hons). Called to the Bar, Gray's Inn, 1960; joined London Magistrates' Courts, 1963; Clerk to the Justices, Poole, 1967–85; Dir, Professional Conduct Dept, 1985–94, Sec., Exec. Cttee, Jt Disciplinary Scheme, 1986–94, ICAEW. Member: Juvenile Courts Committee, Magistrates' Assoc., 1973–85; NACRO Juvenile Crime Adv. Cttee, 1982–85; former member: CCETSW working party on legal trng of social workers (report, 1974); NACRO cttee on diversion (Zander report, 1975); HO/DHSS working party on operation of Children and Young Persons' Act 1969 (report, 1978); ABAFA working party on care proceedings (report, 1979). Chairman: Membership and Disciplinary Tribunal, PIA, 1994–; Disciplinary Tribunal, SFA, 1994–; Appeals Tribunal, Assoc. of Accounting Technicians, 1996–. Pres., Justices' Clerks Soc., 1981–82. Editor: Justice of the Peace Review, 1982–85 (Legal Editor, 1973; Jt Editor, 1978); The Regulator and Professional Conduct Qly, 1994–98. *Publications:* Criminal Jurisdiction of Magistrates, 1969, 11th edn 1988; Warrants of Search and Entry, 1973; The Courts, the Press and the Public, 1976; The Rehabilitation of Offenders, 1976, 3rd edn 1999; New Law of Family Proceedings in Magistrates' Courts, 1979; (ed jtly) Clarke Hall and Morrison on Children, 1985; The Law and Practice of Disciplinary and Regulatory Proceedings, 1995, 2nd edn 1999; The Tribunal Member, 1995; The Literature of the Law, 1998; (ed) entry on Magistrates in Halsbury's Laws of England, 4th edn 1979. *Recreation:* the contemplation of verse. *Address:* Church Barn, High Street, Yardley Hastings, Northants NN7 1ER. *T:* (01604) 696071.

HARRIS, Cecil Rhodes, FCIS, FSCA; Deputy Chairman, Trade Indemnity PLC, 1986–93; Chief Executive, Commercial Union Assurance Company Ltd, 1982–85; *b* 4 May 1923; *s* of Frederick William Harris and Dorothy Violet Plum; *m* 1946, Gwenyth Evans; one *s* two *d*. *Educ:* private schools. FCIS 1950; FSCA 1951. Joined Employers Liability Assurance, 1949, Asst Sec., 1961–64, Overseas Manager, Northern & Employers, 1965–68; Commercial Union Assurance Co. Ltd: Asst Gen. Man., 1969–73; Dep. Gen. Man., 1974; Dir and Sec., 1975–78; Exec. Dir, 1979; Dep. Chief Gen. Man., 1980–82. *Recreations:* tennis, study of the Scriptures. *Address:* Ashley, 35a Plough Lane, Purley, Surrey CR8 3QJ. *T:* (020) 8668 2820.

HARRIS, Charles; *see* Harris, G. C. W.

HARRIS, Christopher H.; *see* Heaton-Harris.

HARRIS, Prof. Christopher John, DPhil; Professor of Mathematical Economics, University of Cambridge and Fellow, King's College, Cambridge, since 1995; *b* 22 Sept. 1960; *s* of Colin Christopher Harris and Barbara Kay (*née* Hall); *m* 1993, Qun Li. *Educ:* Oundle Sch.; Corpus Christi Coll., Oxford (BA Maths 1981); Nuffield Coll., Oxford (MPhil Econ 1983; DPhil Econ 1984). Prize Research Fellow, Nuffield Coll., Oxford, 1983–84; Univ. Lectr in Econs, Univ. of Oxford and Fellow of Nuffield Coll., 1984–94. Vis. Prof., MIT, 1990–91. *Publications:* articles on dynamic games and theory of industrial organisation in Econometrica, Rev. of Econ. Studies, Jl of Econ. Theory, etc. *Recreations:* walking, running, swimming. *Address:* Faculty of Economics and Politics, Austin Robinson Building, Sidgwick Avenue, Cambridge CB3 9DD.

HARRIS, Prof. Christopher John, PhD; FIMA, FREng, FIEE; Professor of Computational Intelligence (formerly Lucas Professor of Aerospace Systems Engineering), since 1987, and Head of Department of Electronics and Computer Science, since 1999, Southampton University; *b* 23 Dec. 1945; *s* of George Harris and Hilda Harris; *m* 1965, Ruth Joy Harris; one *s* two *d*. *Educ:* Univ. of Leicester (BSc); MA Oxon; Univ. of Southampton (PhD 1972). FIMA 1979; CEng 1979; FIEE 1991; FREng (FEng 1996). Lecturer: Hull Univ., 1967–72; UMIST, 1972–76; Oxford Univ., 1976–80; Fellow, St Edmund Hall, Oxford, 1976–80; Dep. Chief Scientist, MoD, 1980–84; Prof., Cranfield Inst. of Technol., 1984–86. Hon. Professor: Univ. Hong Kong, 1991; Huazhong Univ., China, 1991. Achievement Medal, 1998, Faraday Medal, 2001, IEE. *Publications:* (with J. F. Miles) Stability of Linear Systems, 1980, 2nd edn 1985; (with J. M. Valenca) Stability of Input-output Dynamic Systems, 1983, 2nd edn 1987; (ed) Applications of Artificial Intelligence to C^2 Systems, 1988; (jtly) Intelligent Control: aspects of fuzzy logic and neural nets, 1993; (with M. Brown) Neurofuzzy Adaptive Modelling and Control, 1994; (jtly) Advanced Adaptive Control, 1995; Adaptive Neural Network Control of Robotic Manipulators, 1998. *Recreations:* scuba diving, gardening, fly fishing. *Address:* 14 Beechwood Rise, West End, Southampton, Hants SO18 3PW. *T:* (023) 8047 2363.

HARRIS, David; Director, Commission of the European Communities, Directorate for Social and Demographic Statistics, 1973–87; *b* 28 Dec. 1922; *s* of David and Margaret Jane Harris; *m* 1946, Mildred Alice Watson; two *d*. *Educ:* Bootle Grammar Sch.; LSE (BScEcon). FSS. Statistician, BoT, 1960; Statistician 1966 and Chief Statistician 1968, HM Treasury; Chief Statistician, Central Statistical Office, Cabinet Office, 1969. *Recreations:* tennis, swimming, economics. *Address:* 64 Rue de Rodenbourg, 6950 Olingen, Luxembourg.

HARRIS, David Anthony; *b* 1 Nov. 1937; *s* of late E. C. Harris and Betty Harris; *m* 1st, 1962, Diana Joan Hansford (*d* 1996); one *s* one *d*; 2nd, 1998, Mrs Alison Bunker. *Educ:* Mount Radford Sch., Exeter. Jun. Reporter, Express and Echo, Exeter, 1954–58. Nat. Service, commnd Devonshire and Dorset Regt, 1958; Staff Captain (Public Relns) GHQ, MELF, 1959. Reporter, Western Morning News, 1960–61; joined Daily Telegraph, Westminster Staff, 1961; Political Correspondent, Daily Telegraph, 1976–79; MEP (C) Cornwall and Plymouth, 1979–84. Chm., Parly Lobby Journalists, 1977–78. Mem. (C) Bromley, and Bromley, Ravensbourne, GLC, 1968–77; Chm. Thamesmead Cttee, 1971–73. Contested (C) Mitcham and Morden, Feb. 1974. MP (C) St Ives, 1983–97. PPS to Minister of State for Foreign and Commonwealth Affairs, 1987–88, to Sec. of State for Foreign and Commonwealth Affairs, 1988–89, to Dep. Prime Minister and Leader of Commons, 1989–90. Member, Select Committee: on Agriculture, 1983–87; on Broadcasting, 1988–97; on Foreign Affairs, 1991–97; on Social Security, 1991–92. Chairman: Cons. Fisheries Cttee, 1987–97; W Country Cons. MPs, 1991–92. Leading Cons. spokesman for Cornwall, 1997–. President: Sea Safety Gp UK, 1992–; Lizard Lifeboat, 1990–. Mem. Council, Royal Nat. Mission to Deep Sea Fishermen, 1993–. *Recreations:* gardening, reading obituaries. *Address:* Trewedna Farm, Perranwell Station, near Truro, Cornwall TR3 7PQ.

HARRIS, David John, CMG 1999; PhD; Professor of Public International Law, University of Nottingham, since 1981; *b* 3 July 1938; *s* of Sidney and May Harris; *m* 1963, Sandra Jean Nelson; two *s*. *Educ:* Sutton High Sch., Plymouth; KCL (LLB 1959); LSE (LLM 1961). Asst Lectr, QUB, 1962–63; University of Nottingham: Asst Lectr, 1963–64; Lectr, 1964–73; Sen. Lectr in Law, 1973–81; Head, Law Dept, 1987–90. Mem., Cttee of Indep. Experts, European Social Charter, 1990–96. *Publications:* Cases and Materials on Public International Law, 1973, 5th edn 1998; The European Social Charter, 1984, 2nd edn 2001; (with M. O'Boyle and C. Warbrick) The Law and Practice of the European Convention on Human Rights, 1995. *Recreations:* travelling, walking. *Address:* School of Law, The University, Nottingham NG7 2RD. *T:* (0115) 951 5701.

HARRIS, (David) Kenneth, CBE 1992; journalist, author and broadcaster; Chairman, George Outram & Co. Ltd, later Caledonian Newspaper Publishing, 1981–92; Director, The Observer Ltd, 1978–93; *b* 11 Nov. 1919; *s* of David and Kathleen Harris; *m* 1st, 1949, Doris Young-Smith (*d* 1970); 2nd, 1987, Jocelyn Rymer. *Educ:* Trowbridge High Sch.; Wadham Coll., Oxford. Served War, RA, 1940–45. Sheffield Telegraph, 1948–50; The Observer: Washington Corresp., 1950–53; Editl Staff, 1953–76; Associate Editor, 1976–84. Freelance TV and radio broadcaster, BBC and ITV, 1957–85. Debating tour for Oxford Union, USA, 1947; Founder, Observer Mace Debating Tournaments, 1953; Chm., ESU Overseas Debating Selection Cttee, 1960–95. *Publications:* Travelling Tongues, 1949; About Britain, 1967; Conversations, 1967; Talking To …, 1971; Attlee (authorised biog.), 1982; David Owen Personally Speaking, 1987; Thatcher, 1988; The Queen, 1994. *Recreations:* walking, horse racing, fishing, reading. *Address:* 45 Molyneux Street, W1H 5JD. *T:* (020) 7262 6172. *Club:* Athenæum.

HARRIS, David Michael; QC 1989; **His Honour Judge Harris;** a Circuit Judge, since 2001; *b* 7 Feb. 1943; *s* of Maurice and Doris Harris; *m* 1970, Emma Lucia Calma; two *s* one *d*. *Educ:* Liverpool Institute High School for Boys; Lincoln Coll., Oxford (BA 1964; MA 1967); Trinity Hall, Cambridge (PhD 1969). Asst Lectr in Law, Manchester Univ., 1967–69. Called to the Bar, Middle Temple, 1969; Bencher, 1997; Asst Recorder, 1984–88; a Recorder, 1988–2001; a Dep. High Ct Judge, 1993–. *Publications:* (ed jtly) Winfield and Jolowicz on Tort, 9th edn, 1971; (ed jtly) Supplement to Bingham's Modern Cases on Negligence, 3rd edn, 1985. *Recreations:* the Arts, travel, sport. *Address:* c/o Courts of Justice, Crown Square, Manchester M60 9DJ. *T:* (0151) 243 6000.

HARRIS, Prof. David Russell, FSA; Professor of Human Environment, Institute of Archaeology, University College London, 1979–98, now Professor Emeritus (Director, 1989–96); *b* 14 Dec. 1930; *s* of Dr Herbert Melville Harris and Norah Mary Harris; *m* 1957, Helen Margaret Wilson; four *d*. *Educ:* St Christopher Sch., Letchworth; Oxford Univ. (MA, BLitt); Univ. of California, Berkeley (PhD). Nat. Service, RAF, 1949–50. Teaching Asst and Instructor, Univ. of California, 1956–58; Lectr, QMC, London, 1958–64; Lectr and Reader, UCL, 1964–79. Member: Mus. of London Archaeol. Cttee, 1984–91; English Heritage Sci. and Conservation Panel, 1985–99; Chm., Sci.-based Archaeol. Cttee, SERC, 1989–92. President: Prehistoric Soc., 1990–94; UK Chapter, Soc. for Economic Botany, 1995–97; Anthropol. and Archaeol. Sect., BAAS, 2000. Hon. Fellow, UCL, 2000. *Publications:* Plants, Animals and Man in the Outer Leeward Islands, 1965; (with B. W. Hodder) Africa in Transition, 1967; Human Ecology in Savanna Environments, 1980; (with G. C. Hillman) Foraging and Farming, 1989; Settling Down and Breaking Ground: rethinking the neolithic revolution, 1990; (with K. D. Thomas) Modelling Ecological Change, 1991; The Archaeology of V. Gordon Childe, 1994; The Origins and Spread of Agriculture and Pastoralism in Eurasia, 1996; (jtly) Plants for Food and Medicine, 1998. *Recreations:* mountain walking, archaeological-ecological travel. *Address:* Institute of Archaeology, University College London, 31–34 Gordon Square, WC1H 0PY. *T:* (020) 7679 7495. *Club:* Athenæum.

HARRIS, Evan; MP (Lib Dem) Oxford West and Abingdon, since 1997; *b* 21 Oct. 1965; *s* of Prof. Frank Harris, *qv*. *Educ:* Blue Coat Sch., Liverpool; Wadham Coll., Oxford (BA Hons Physiol.); Oxford Univ. Med. Sch. (BM BCh 1991). House Officer, John Radcliffe Hosp. and Royal Liverpool Univ. Hosp., 1991–92; Sen. House Officer (Medicine), Central Oxford Hosps, 1992–94; Hon. Registrar in Public Health, and Regl Task Force MO, Oxford Regl Postgrad. Dept of Med. Educn and Oxfordshire HA, 1994–97. Mem. Council, BMA, 1994–97 (Mem., Med. Ethics Cttee, 1999–). Parly Lib Dem spokesman on: NHS, med. staff and trng, 1997–99; higher educn, 1999–2001; science and women's issues, 1999–; health, 2001–. Chm., All Party Kidney Gp, 1999–; Officer, All Party Gp on Refugees, and on AIDS, 1997–. *Publications:* contribs to med. jls. *Recreations:* chess, bridge, football, television. *Address:* 32A North Hinksey Village, Oxford OX2 0NA. *T:* (01865) 250424, (office) (01865) 245584; House of Commons, SW1A 0AA. *Clubs:* National Liberal; Oxford Rotary.

HARRIS, Frank; *see* Harris, W. F.

HARRIS, Prof. Frank, CBE 1996; FMedSci; Dean, Faculty of Medicine and Biological Sciences (formerly of Medicine) and Professor of Paediatrics, University of Leicester, 1990–2000, now Professor Emeritus; Hon. Consultant Paediatrician, Leicester Royal Infirmary, 1990–2000; *b* 6 Oct. 1934; *s* of David and Miriam Harris; *m* 1963, Brenda van Embden; two *s*. *Educ:* Univ. of Cape Town (MB ChB 1957; MMed (Paed), 1963; MD 1964). FRCPE 1975; FRCP 1982; FRCPCH 1997 (Hon. FRCPCH 2000). Groote Schuur and Red Cross War Memorial Children's Hosp., Cape Town; CSIR Res. Fellow, Dept of Medicine, Univ. of Cape Town; Lectr and Sen. Lectr in Child Health, Univ. of Sheffield, 1965–74; University of Liverpool: Prof. of Child Health and Dir, Inst. of Child Health, 1974–89; Pro-Vice-Chancellor, 1981–84; Dean, Faculty of Medicine, 1985–89; Hon. Cons. Paediatrician to Royal Liverpool Children's Hosps at Myrtle Street and Alderhey. Exec. Sec., Council of Deans of UK Med. Schs and Faculties, 1992–96. Member: Liverpool AHA and DHA, 1977–84; Mersey RHA, 1983–89; Trent RHA, 1990; Vice-Chm., Leics HA, 1993–97, 1998–2000 (non-exec. Dir, 1990–). Member: Cttee on Review of Medicines, 1981–90; Cttee on Safety of Medicines, 1990–92; Joint Planning Adv. Cttee, DoH, 1990–94; GMC, 1990–99 (Overseas Review Bd, 1992–96; Educn Cttee, 1994–99; Preliminary Proceedings Cttee, 1994–99; Registration Cttee, 1997–99; Overseas Cttee, 1997–98); NAHAT Wkg Gp on Teaching, Res. and Audit, 1992–93. Exec., Univ. Hosps Assoc., 1991–98; Exec. Cttee, Assoc. of Med. Schs in Europe, 1993–99; Adv. Cttee on Med. Trng, EC, 1994–2001 (Chm., 1999–2001). Examr for RCP and Univs, UK and overseas. Founder FMedSci 1998. *Publications:* Paediatric Fluid Therapy, 1973; chapters in med. books; contribs to med. jls. *Recreations:* bridge, reading, travel. *Address:* 39 Frenchay Road, Oxford OX2 6TG.
See also E. Harris.

HARRIS, (Geoffrey) Charles (Wesson); QC 1989; **His Honour Judge Charles Harris;** a Circuit Judge, since 1993; *b* 17 Jan. 1945; *s* of late G. Hardy Harris and M. J. P. Harris (*née* Wesson); *m* 1970, Carol Ann Alston; two *s* one *d*. *Educ:* Repton; Univ. of Birmingham (LLB). Called to the Bar, Inner Temple, 1967; practice on Midland and Oxford Circuit and in London, 1967–93; a Recorder, 1990–93; Designated Civil Judge: Oxford and Northampton, 1998–2001; Oxford/Thames Valley, 2001–. Member: Parole Bd, 1995–; Crown Court Rule Cttee, 1997–. Contested (C) Penistone, Yorks, Oct. 1974. *Publications:* contrib. to Halsbury's Laws of England, 4th edn 1976, and other legal publications; magazine articles on stalking and ballooning. *Recreations:* history, architecture, fireworks, stalking, ski-ing. *Address:* c/o Oxford Crown Court, St Aldates, Oxford. *Club:* Kandahar.

HARRIS, Sir Henry, Kt 1993; FRCP; FRCPath; FRS 1968; Regius Professor of Medicine, University of Oxford, 1979–92; Head of the Sir William Dunn School of Pathology, 1963–94; Hon. Director, Cancer Research Campaign, Cell Biology Unit, 1963–92; Fellow of Lincoln College, Oxford, 1963–79, Hon. Fellow 1980; Student of Christ Church, Oxford, 1979–92, Emeritus Student, 1992; *b* 28 Jan. 1925; *s* of late Sam and late Ann Harris; *m* 1950, Alexandra Fanny Brodsky; one *s* two *d*. *Educ:* Sydney Boys' High Sch. and University of Sydney, Australia; Lincoln Coll., Oxford. Public Exhibnr, University of Sydney, 1942; BA Mod. Langs, 1944; MB BS 1950; Travelling Schol. of Austr. Nat. Univ. at Univ. of Oxford, 1952; MA; DPhil (Oxon), 1954, DM 1979. Dir of Research, Brit. Empire Cancer Campaign, at Sir William Dunn Sch. of Pathology, Oxford, 1954–59; Visiting Scientist, Nat. Institutes of Health, USA, 1959–60; Head of Dept of Cell Biology, John Innes Inst., 1960–63; Prof. of Pathology, Univ. of Oxford, 1963–79. Vis. Prof., Vanderbilt Univ., 1968; Walker-Ames Prof., University of Washington, 1968; Foreign Prof., Collège de France, 1974. Non-Exec. Mem., Oxford RHA, 1990–92; Hon. Consulting Pathologist, Oxford HA, 1992. Member: ARC, 1968–78 (Chm., Animals Res. Bd, 1976–78); Council, European Molecular Biology Organization, 1974–76; Council, Royal Society, 1971–72; Scientific Adv. Cttee, CRC, 1961–85; Governor, European Cell Biology Organization, 1973–75. Lectures: Almroth Wright, 1968; Harvey, Harvey Soc. NY, 1969; Dunham, Harvard, 1969; Jenner Meml, 1970; Croonian, Royal Soc., 1971; Nat. Insts of Health, USA, 1971; Foundation, RCPath, 1973; Woodhull, Royal Instn, 1975; Rotherham, Lincoln Coll., Oxford, 1979; Herbert Spencer, Oxford Univ., 1979, 1992; Opening Plenary, Internat. Congress of Cell Biology, 1980; First Distinguished, in Experimental Pathology, Pittsburgh Univ., 1982; Louis Gross Meml, NY, 1983; Claude Bernard, Acad. des Sciences, Paris, 1984; Jean Brachet Meml, Vancouver, 1990; Kettle, RCPath, 1991; Romanes, Oxford Univ., 1993. Foreign Hon. Mem., Amer. Acad. Arts and Sciences; Foreign Mem., Max-Planck Soc.; Hon. Member: Amer. Assoc. of Pathologists; German Soc. of Cell Biology; Corresp. Member: Amer. Assoc. for Cancer Res.; Aust. Acad. of Science. Foreign Correspondent, Waterford Striped Bass Derby Assoc.; Hon. Fellow, Cambridge Philosophical Soc. Hon. FRCPA. Hon. DSc Edinburgh, 1976; Hon. MD: Geneva, 1982; Sydney, 1983. Feldberg Foundn Award, Ivison Macadam Meml Prize, RCSE; Prix de la Fondation Isabelle Decazes de Noüe for cancer research; Madonnina Prize for medical scis (City of Milan), 1979; Royal Medal, Royal Soc., 1980; Osler Medal, RCP, 1984; Katherine Berkan Judd Award, Sloan-Kettering Inst., NY, 1991. *Publications:* Nucleus and Cytoplasm, 1968, 3rd edn, 1974; Cell Fusion, 1970; La Fusion cellulaire, 1974; The Balance of Improbabilities, 1987; The Cells of the Body: a history of somatic cell genetics, 1995; The Birth of the Cell, 1999; Things Come to Life, 2001; papers on cellular physiology and biochemistry, in scientific books and jls, and some fiction. *Recreation:* history. *Address:* c/o Sir William Dunn School of Pathology, South Parks Road, Oxford OX1 3RE. *T:* (01865) 275500.

HARRIS, Hugh Christopher Emlyn; Director, Global Network, London First, since 1999 (Director of Operations, 1995–99); Director, African and Caribbean Westminster Initiative, since 2000; *b* 25 March 1936; *s* of Thomas Emlyn Harris and Martha Anne (*née* Davies); *m* 1968, Pamela Susan Woollard; one *s* one *d*. *Educ:* The Leys Sch., Cambridge; Trinity Coll., Cambridge (BA 1959; MA). ACIB 1963; FCIPD (FIPM 1990, FIPD). Bank of England, 1959–94: Chief of Corporate Services, 1984–88; Associate Dir, 1988–94; Comr, 1995, Dep. Chm., 1996–2000, CRE. Director: BE Services Ltd, 1984–94; BE Museum Ltd, 1989–94; BE Property Holdings Ltd, 1989–94; Securities Management Trust Ltd, 1987–94; Solefield School Educational Trust Ltd, Sevenoaks, 1986–; Global Cultural Diversity Congress Ltd, 1998–2000. Dir, London Film Commn, 1996–2000. Member: Governing Council, BITC, 1986–94; Business Leaders Team, BITC Race for Opportunity Campaign, 1994–98; Windsor Fellowship Adv. Council, 1988–94; Council, London Civic Forum, 2001–. FRSA. *Recreations:* tennis, watching Rugby, theatre, opera. *Address:* London First, 1 Hobhouse Court, Suffolk Street, SW1Y 4HH. *T:* (020) 7665 1570; *e-mail:* hharris@london–first.co.uk.

HARRIS, Air Cdre Irene Joyce, (Joy), CB 1984; RRC 1976; SRN, SCM; Director, Nursing Services (RAF), and Matron-in-Chief, Princess Mary's Royal Air Force Nursing Service, 1981–84; *b* 26 Sept. 1926; *d* of late Robert John Harris and Annie Martha Harris (*née* Breed). *Educ:* Southgate County Sch.; Charing Cross Hosp.; The London Hosp.; Queen Mary's Maternity Home, Hampstead. SRN 1947, SCM 1950. Joined Princess Mary's RAF Nursing Service, 1950; gen. nursing and midwifery duties in UK, Singapore, Germany and Cyprus; Dep. Matron, 1970; Sen. Matron, 1975; Principal Matron, 1978; Dep. Dir, Nursing Services (RAF), 1981. QHNS 1981–84. *Recreations:* travel, ornithology, music, archaeology, gardening. *Address:* 51 Station Road, Haddenham, Ely, Cambs CB6 3XD. *Club:* Royal Air Force.

HARRIS, Sir Jack Wolfred Ashford, 2nd Bt *cr* 1932; Chairman, Bing Harris & Co. Ltd, Wellington, NZ, 1935–78 (Director until 1982), retired; *b* 23 July 1906; *er s* of Rt Hon. Sir Percy Harris, 1st Bt, PC, and Frieda Bloxam (*d* 1962); *S* father, 1952; *m* 1933, Patricia, *o d* of A. P. Penman, Wahroonga, Sydney, NSW; two *s* one *d*. *Educ:* Shrewsbury Sch.; Trinity Hall, Cambridge. BA (Cantab) History; then one year's study in Europe. Joined family business in New Zealand, 1929, and became director shortly afterwards. Past Pres. Wellington Chamber of Commerce. Served during War of 1939–45, for three years in NZ Home Forces. *Recreations:* gardening, fishing, swimming. *Heir: s* Christopher John Ashford Harris [*b* 26 Aug. 1934; *m* 1957, Anna, *d* of F. de Malmanche, Auckland, NZ; one *s* two *d*]. *Address:* Flat 2602, Peninsula Tower, 37 Glen Street, Milson's Point, Sydney, NSW 2061, Australia. *Clubs:* Union (Sydney); Wellington (Wellington, NZ).

HARRIS, Prof. James William, DCL, PhD; FBA 2001; Professor of Law, Oxford University, since 1996; Fellow, Keble College, Oxford, since 1973; *b* 17 March 1940; *s* of James Harris and Jessica (*née* Wentworth); *m* 1968, Jose Ferial Chambers (*see* J. F. Harris); one *s*. *Educ:* Worcester Coll.; Wadham Coll., Oxford (MA; PhD 1973; DCL 2001). Admitted solicitor, 1965; Lectr, LSE, 1966–73. Mellon Res. Fellow, Princeton Univ., 1985; Allen, Allen & Hemsley Vis. Prof., Univ. of Sydney, 1987; Dist. Vis. Prof., Univ. of Hong Kong, 1994. *Publications:* Variation of Trusts, 1975; Law and Legal Science, 1979; Legal Philosophies, 1980, 2nd edn 1997; (with Sir Rupert Cross) Precedent in English Law, 4th edn 1991; Property and Justice, 1996; Property Problems: from genes to pension funds, 1997; contrib. articles to Oxford Jl Legal Studies, Cambridge Law Jl, Law Qly Rev., Ratio Juris. *Recreations:* walking, Shakespeare, Wagner. *Address:* Keble College, Oxford OX1 3PG. *T:* (01865) 272748.

HARRIS, Jeffery Francis, FCA; Chairman, Alliance UniChem plc, since 2001; *b* 8 April 1948; *s* of Ernest and Kathleen Veronica Harris; *m* 1976, Elizabeth Helen Hancock; two *s*. *Educ:* Rendcomb Coll., Cirencester; Southampton Univ. (BSc Hons 1970). FCA 1979. Trainee chartered accountant, 1970; with Barton Mayhew & Co., later Ernst & Young, 1980–85; UniChem, subseq. Alliance UniChem, 1985–: Gp Chief Accountant, 1985–86; Finance Dir, 1986–91; Dep. Chief Exec., 1991–92; Chief Exec., 1992–2001. Chairman: Internat. Pharmaceutical Services Orgn, 1995–98; British Assoc. of Pharmaceutical Wholesalers, 1996–98. *Recreations:* walking, ski-ing, cycling, gardening, opera. *Address:* Alliance House, 2 Heath Road, Weybridge, Surrey KT13 8AP. *T:* (01932) 870581.

HARRIS, Jeremy Michael; Archbishop of Canterbury's Secretary for Public Affairs and Deputy Chief of Staff, Lambeth Palace, since 1999; *b* 31 Oct. 1950; *s* of David Arnold Harris and Beryl May Harris (*née* Howe); *m* 1983, Susan Lynn Roberts; one *s* one *d*. *Educ:* Sevenoaks Sch., Kent; Clare Coll., Cambridge (BA Hons); Nottingham Univ. (PGCE 1972). BBC News: Reporter, BBC Radio News, 1978–82; Madrid Corresp., 1982–86; Moscow Corresp., 1986–89; Foreign Affairs Corresp., 1989–90; Washington Corresp., 1990–95; Radio Presenter, BBC Current Affairs Progs incl. World Tonight, and Today, 1995–99. *Recreations:* theatre, maps, walking. *Address:* 26 Ellingham Road, W12 9PR. *T:* (020) 7898 1200. *Club:* Arts.

HARRIS, Very Rev. John; Dean of Brecon, and Vicar of Brecon St Mary with Battle and Llanddew, 1993–98; *b* 12 March 1932; *s* of Richard and Ivy Harris; *m* 1956, Beryl June Roberts; two *s* one *d*. *Educ:* St David's Coll., Lampeter (BA 1955); Salisbury Theol Coll. Ordained deacon, 1957, priest, 1958; Curate: Pontnewynydd, 1957–60; Bassaleg, 1960–63; Vicar: Penmaen, 1963–69; St Paul, Newport, 1969–84; Maindee, 1984–93; RD of Newport, 1977–93. Canon, St Woolos Cath., 1984–93. *Recreations:* classical archæology, music, ballet, natural history. *Address:* 40 Mounton Drive, Chepstow, Monmouthshire NP16 5EH.

HARRIS, Prof. John Buchanan, PhD; CBiol, FIBiol; Professor of Experimental Neurology, Newcastle upon Tyne University, since 1980; *b* 18 Jan. 1940; *s* of John Benjamin Sargent Harris and Mary Isobel Harris; *m* 1965, Christine Margaret Holt; one *s* one *d* (and one *s* decd). *Educ:* Tiffin Sch.; Bradford Inst. of Technol.; Univ. of Bradford (PhD 1967); BPharm (London ext. 1963). MRPharmS 1964; FIBiol 1981; CBiol 1990. Research Asst, Univ. of Bradford, 1963–67; Newcastle upon Tyne University: Sen. Res. Associate, 1967–72; Principal Res. Associate, 1972–74; Sen. Lectr, 1974–80. Wellcome Fellow, Univ. of Lund, Sweden, 1970–71; MRC/NIH Fellow, UCLA, 1977–78; Wellcome/Ramaciotti Fellow, Monash Univ., Melbourne, 1980. *Publications:* (ed) Muscular Dystrophy and Other Inherited Diseases of Skeletal Muscle in Animals, 1979; (ed jtly) Natural Toxins: animal, plant and microbial, 1986; (ed jtly) Muscle Metabolism, Vol. 4 (3) of Baillière's Endocrinology and Metabolism, 1990; (ed jtly) Medical Neurotoxicology, 1999. *Address:* School of Neurosciences and Psychiatry, Faculty of Medicine, University of Newcastle upon Tyne, Framlington Place, Newcastle upon Tyne NE2 4HH. *T:* (0191) 222 6648, *Fax:* (0191) 222 5772; *e-mail:* J.B.HARRIS@ncl.ac.uk.

HARRIS, John Charles; solicitor; International Management and Legal Consultant, John Harris Consultancy, since 1986; Executive Director: Solace International (1992) Ltd, 1992–2000; Solace International Southern Africa Pty Ltd, since 1993; Chairman, Coal Authority, since 1999; *b* 25 April 1936; *s* of Sir Charles Joseph William Harris, KBE; *m* 1961, Alison Beryl Sturley; one *s* one *d*. *Educ:* Dulwich College; Clare College, Cambridge. MA, LLM. 2nd Lieut, Intelligence Corps, 1954–56. UKAEA (seconded to OECD), 1959–63; articled to Town Clerk, Poole, 1963–66; Asst Sol., then Senior Asst Sol., Poole BC, 1966–67; Asst Sol., then Principal Asst to Chief Exec. and Town Clerk, 1967–71, Dep. Town Clerk, 1972–73, County Borough of Bournemouth; County Sec., 1973–83, Chief Exec. and County Clerk, 1983–86, S Yorks CC; Dir, S Yorks Passenger Transport Exec., 1984–86; Sec. to Yorkshire and Humberside County Councils Assoc., 1984–86; Advr and Dir, S Yorks Residuary Body, 1985–86; Clerk to Lord Lieutenant of S Yorks, 1984–86; Public Sector Adviser/Associate Consultant: PA Consulting Gp, 1986–91; Daniel Bates Partnership, 1991–95. Adviser to AMA Police and Fire Cttee, 1976–86; Member: Home Office Tripartite Working Party on Police Act 1964, 1983–86; Rampton SHSA Cttee, 1989–96; Arts Council Touring Bd, 1989–92; Pontefract HA, 1990–93; Council, Local Govt Internat. Bureau, 1993–96. Board Member: Northern Counties Housing Assoc. Ltd, 1990– (Chm., 1994–2000); Northern Counties Specialised Housing Assoc. Ltd, 1990– (Chm., 1994–); Dir, Trustee, and Mem. Bd, Homeless Internat. Ltd, 1998–2000; Dir, South Africa Housing Network Trust Ltd, 1998–2001. Chm., Soc. of County Secretaries, 1983–84; Mem. Exec. Council, Solace, 1984–86; Mem., Law Society. Independent Member: W Yorks Police Authy, 1994–99; Police Cttee, AMA, 1995. Hon. PR Officer, S Yorks and Humberside Region, Riding for Disabled Assoc., 1983–92 (Mem., Publications Cttee, 1987–90); Trustee: S Yorks Charity Inf. Service, 1977–87; Housing Assocs Charitable Trust, 1994–96; Founder Mem./Sec., Barnsley Rockley Rotary Club, 1976–79 (Hon. Sec.); Vice-Chm. and Sec., Friends of Opera North, 1979–86; Member: Council/Co., and Develt Cttee, Opera North, 1980–95; Guild of Freemen, City of London, 1967; Justice; European Movement; Charter 88; Actsa. Governor, Felkirk (formerly Ackworth Moor Top) Community Special Sch., Wakefield, 1996– (Chm., 1998–). DL S Yorks, 1986. FRSA 1984. *Publications:* correspondent on public affairs. *Recreations:* being with family and friends, competitive trail riding, riding Welsh cobs, opera, foreign travel, visiting South Africa, supporting community development in Ivory Park Township, Midrand. *Address:* Long Lane Close, High Ackworth, Pontefract, Yorks WF7 7EY. *T:* (01977) 795450, *Fax:* (01977) 795470; *e-mail:* jcharris@lineone.net.

HARRIS, Dr John Edwin, MBE 1981; FRS 1988; FREng; Editor, Interdisciplinary Science Reviews, since 1996; *b* 2 June 1932; *s* of late John Frederick Harris and Emily Margaret (*née* Prosser); *m* 1956, Ann Foote; two *s* two *d*. *Educ:* Larkfield Grammar Sch., Chepstow; Dept of Metallurgy, Univ. of Birmingham (BSc 1953, PhD 1956, DSc 1973). FIM 1974; FREng (FEng 1987); FInstP 1992. Joined Associated Electrical Industries, 1956; CEGB, 1959–89; seconded to Sheffield Univ., 1959–61; Berkeley Nuclear Labs, 1961–89, Sect. Head, 1966–89; Univ. Liaison Manager, Nuclear Electric plc, 1989–90. Visiting Professor: Nuclear Engrg, Manchester Univ., 1991–; Corrosion Sci., UMIST, 1992–; Materials and Manufacture, Univ. of Plymouth (formerly Plymouth Poly.), 1992–; Visiting Lecturer: Bristol Univ., 1992–; Oxford Univ., 1992–. Member: Bd, British Nuclear Energy Soc., 1974–88; Watt Cttee Wkg Party on Atmospheric Attack on Inorganic Materials, 1987; Home Office Wkg Party on Adjudications in HM Prisons, 1974; Chm., Leyhill Prison Bd of Visitors, 1973–74. Mem., Assoc. of British Science Writers. Public Lectr, Tate Gall., 1984; Molecule Club Lectr, 1985 and 1987; Friday Evening Discourse, Royal Instn, 1998. Member, Editorial Board: Material Science and Technology, 1985–; Euro Materials, 1994–. FRSA 1989. Internat. Metallographic Soc. Award, 1976; Esso Gold Medal, Royal Soc., 1979; Interdisciplinary Award, RSC, 1987. *Publications:* (ed) Physical Metallurgy of Reactor Fuel Elements, 1975; Vacancies '76, 1977; (jtly) Metals and the Royal Society, 1999; scientific papers on nuclear metallurgy, deformation and corrosion; articles in New Scientist and The Guardian. *Recreations:* writing popular science articles, studying decay of buildings. *Address:* Church Farm House, 28 Hopton Road, Upper Cam, Dursley, Glos GL11 5PB. *T:* (01453) 543165. *Club:* Cam Bowling (non-playing member).

HARRIS, John Frederick, OBE 1986; FSA; Curator, British Architectural Library's Drawing Collection and Heinz Gallery, 1960–86; Consultant: to Collection, Canadian Centre for Architecture, 1986–88 (Member Advisory Board, 1983–88); Heinz Architectural Center, Carnegie, 1991–94; Victoria and Albert Museum Primary Galleries Project, since 1996; *b* 13 Aug. 1931; *s* of Frederick Harris and Maud (*née* Sellwood); *m* 1960, Eileen Spiegel, New York; one *s* one *d*. *Educ:* Cowley C of E School. Itinerant before 1956; Library of Royal Inst. of Architects, 1956. Mem., Mr Paul Mellon's Adv. Bd,

1966–78; Trustee, Amer. Mus. in Britain, 1974–88; Chm., Colnaghi & Co., 1982–92. President: Internat. Confedn on Architectural Museums, 1981–84 (Chm., 1979–81; Hon. Life Pres., 1984); Marylebone Soc., 1978–80; Twentieth Century Soc. (formerly Thirties Soc.), 1986– (Mem. Cttee, 1979–); Member: Council, Drawing Soc. of America, 1962–68; Council, Victorian Soc., 1974–; Nat. Council, Internat. Council of Monuments and Sites, 1976–83; Soc. of Dilettanti, 1977–; Member Committee: Soc. of Architectural Historians of GB, 1958–66; Georgian Gp, 1970–74, 1986–89; Save Britain's Heritage, 1970–; Stowe Landscape, 1980– (Patron, Stowe Gardens Buildings Trust, 1986–92); Bldg Museum Proj., 1980–86; Garden History, 1980–84; Jl of Garden History, 1980–89. Member: Adv. Council, Drawings Center, NY, 1983–89; Management Cttee, Courtauld Inst. of Art, 1983–87; Somerset House Building Cttee, 1986–89; Council, Royal Archaeol. Inst., 1984–86; Adv. Cttees, Historic Bldgs and Monuments Commn, 1984–88; Ashton Meml Steering Gp, 1984–86; GLC Historic Buildings Panel, 1984–86; Ambrose Congreve Award, 1980–82; Ashmole Archive Cttee, 1985–87; Adv. Bd, Irish Architectural Archive, 1988–91; Appeal Cttee, Painshill Park Trust, 1988–89; Spencer House Restoration Cttee, 1986–95; Nat. Trust Arts Panel, 1996–; Trustee: Architecture Foundn, 1991–94; Save Europe's Heritage, 1996–; Holborne Mus., Bath, 2000–. Andrew W. Mellon Lectr in Fine Arts, Nat. Gall., Washington, 1981; Slade Prof. of Fine Art, Univ. of Oxford, 1982–83. Exhibitions Organizer: The King's Arcadia, 1973; The Destruction of the Country House (with Marcus Binney), 1974; The Garden, 1979; Dir, British Country House Exhibn, Nat. Gall., Washington, 1982–83; many exhibns in Heinz Gall.; travelling exhibns and catalogues: Italian Architectural Drawings, 1966; Sir Christopher Wren, 1970; Designs of the British Country House, 1985. FSA 1968; FRSA 1975; Hon. FRIBA 1972; Hon. MA Oxon, 1982; Hon. Brother Art Workers' Guild, 1972. Harris Testimonial Medal, 1999. Editor, Studies in Architecture, 1976–. *Publications:* English Decorative Ironwork, 1960; Regency Furniture Designs, 1961; (ed), The Prideaux Collection of Topographical Drawings, 1963; (jtly) Lincolnshire, 1964; (contrib.) The Making of Stamford, 1965; (jtly) Illustrated Glossary of Architecture, 1966, 2nd edn 1969; (jtly) Buckingham Palace, 1968; Georgian Country Houses, 1968; (contrib.), Concerning Architecture, 1968; Sir William Chambers, Knight of the Polar Star, 1970 (Hitchcock Medallion 1971); (ed), The Rise and Progress of the Present State of Planting, 1970; (ed jtly) The Country Seat, 1970; Catalogue of British Drawings for Architecture, Decoration, Sculpture and Landscape Gardening in American Collections, 1971; A Country House Index, 1971, 2nd edn 1979; Catalogue of the Drawings Collection RIBA: Inigo Jones and John Webb, 1972; contrib., Guide to Vitruvius Britannicus, 1972; (jtly) The King's Arcadia: Inigo Jones and The Stuart Court, 1973; Catalogue of the Drawings Collection RIBA: Colin Campbell, 1973; Headfort House and Robert Adam, 1973; (jtly) The Destruction of the Country House, 1974; Gardens of Delight, The Art of Thomas Robins, 1976; Gardens of Delight, The Rococo English Landscape of Thomas Robins, 1978; (jtly) Catalogue of Drawings by Inigo Jones, John Webb and Isaac de Caus in Worcester College, Oxford, 1979; A Garden Alphabet, 1979; (ed), The Garden Show, 1979; The Artist and the Country House, 1979 (Sir Banister Fletcher prize, 1979), 2nd edn 1986; (contrib.), Village England, 1980; (contrib.) Lost Houses of Scotland, 1980; The English Garden 1530–1840: a contemporary view, 1981; (contrib.), John Claudius Loudon and the Early Nineteenth Century in Great Britain, Washington, 1980; (jtly) Interiors, 1981; The Palladians, 1981; Die Hauser der Lords und Gentlemen, 1982; William Talman, Maverick Architect, 1982; (contrib.) SAVE Gibraltar's Heritage, 1982; Architectural Drawings in the Cooper Hewitt Museum, New York, 1982; (contrib.) Vanishing Houses of England, 1982; (contrib.) Macmillan Encyclopedia of Architecture, 1982; (contrib.) Great Drawings from the Collection of Royal Institute of British Architects, 1983; (jtly) Britannia Illustrata Knyff & Kip, 1984; The Design of the British Country House, 1985; (jtly) Inigo Jones—Complete Architectural Drawings, 1989; (contrib.) In Honor of Paul Mellon, Collector and Benefactor, 1986; (contrib.) Canadian Centre for Architecture Building and Gardens, 1989; (contrib.) The Fashioning and Functioning of the British Country House, 1989; (jtly) Jamaica's Heritage: an untapped resource, 1991; (contrib.) Writers and their Houses, 1993; The Palladian Revival: Lord Burlington, his villa and garden at Chiswick, 1994; The Artist and the Country House, 1995; (ed jtly and contrib.) Sir William Chambers: architect to George III, 1996; (contrib.) Chambers and Adelcranz, 1997; No Voice from the Hall: early memories of a country house snooper, 1998; articles in Apollo, and other jls. *Recreations:* grand hotels, history of World War I and flinting.

HARRIS, John Frederick, CEng, FIEE; Chairman, Telefax Holdings Ltd, since 1995; *b* 9 Dec. 1938; *s* of Jack Harris and Lily Harris; *m* 1960, Diana Joyce Brown; one *s* two *d.* *Educ:* Central Grammar School, Birmingham. Technical posts, Midlands Electricity, 1955–70; managerial posts, Southern Electricity, 1970–78; Chief Engineer, NW Electricity Board, 1978–79, Dep. Chm., 1979–82; Chm., E Midlands Electricity Bd, then E Midlands Electricity plc, 1982–94. Dir, Nottingham Develt Enterprise, 1992–95. Gov., Nottingham Trent Univ., 1993–95; Trustee, Djanogly City Tech. Coll., 1990–. Pres., Nottingham VSO, 1984–. CIMgt. Hon. DTech. *Recreation:* golf. *Club:* Reform.

HARRIS, Air Marshal Sir John (Hulme), (Win), KCB 1992 (CB 1991); CBE 1982; Air Officer Commanding No 18 Group (RAF Strike Command) and Commander Maritime Air Eastern Atlantic and Allied Forces Northwestern Europe (formerly Channel), 1992–96; *b* 3 June 1938; *s* of late George W. H. Harris and Dorothy Harris (*née* Hulme); *m* 1962, Williamina (*née* Murray); two *s.* *Educ:* English Sch., Cairo; King Edward VII Sch., King's Lynn. No 224 Sqn, RAF, 1960–62; RAF Leeming, Flying Instructor, 1963–67; Exchange Officer, US Navy Air Test and Evaluation Sqn, Florida, 1968–70; Central Tactics and Trials Organisation, 1970–73; OC No 201 Sqn, 1973–75; Nat. Defence Coll., 1975–76; OPCON (CCIS) Project Team, Northwood, 1976–78; SASO, RAF Pitreavie Castle, 1979; OC RAF Kinloss, 1979–81; Internat. Mil. Staff, Brussels, 1982–83; RCDS, 1984; Dir Training (Flying), RAF, 1985–87; Comdt Gen., RAF Regiment and Dir Gen. of Security (RAF), 1987–89; ACDS (Logistics), 1990–91; COS, HQ No 18 Gp (RAF Strike Comd), 1991–92. ADC to the Queen, 1979–81. *Recreations:* fly fishing for salmon, trout and navigators, gardening, travel. *Address:* c/o Lloyds TSB, Cox's and King's Branch, 7 Pall Mall, SW1Y 5NA. *Club:* Royal Air Force.

HARRIS, Prof. John Morley, DPhil; Sir David Alliance Professor of Bioethics, University of Manchester, since 1997; *b* 21 Aug. 1945; *s* of Albert Harris and Ruth Harris; *m* 1978, Sita Williams; one *s.* *Educ:* University of Kent at Canterbury (BA 1966); Balliol Coll., Oxford (DPhil 1976). Lectr in Philosophy, 1974–77, Sen. Lectr, 1977–79, City of Birmingham Poly.; Associate Lectr in Philosophy, Brunel Univ., 1977–79; University of Manchester: Lectr in Philosophy, 1979–84, Sen. Lectr, 1984–88, Dept of Educn; Res. Dir, Centre for Social Ethics and Policy, 1986–; Reader in Applied Philosophy, Sch. of Educn, 1988–90; Prof. of Bioethics and Applied Philosophy, 1990–97; Dir, Inst. of Medicine, Law and Bioethics, 1996–. Series Ed., Social Ethics and Policy, 1985–; Founder and a Gen. Ed., Issues in Biomedical Ethics series, 1994–. Member: Adv. Cttee on Genetic Testing, 1997–99; Human Genetics Commn, 1999–; Ethics Cttee, BMA, 1991–97 and 1999–. Chm., Values and Attitudes Wkg Party, Age Concern, 1996–99. Mem., Romanian Acad. Med. Scis, 1994–. *Publications:* Violence and Responsibility, 1980; The Value of Life, 1985; (ed with S. Hirsch) Consent and the Incompetent Patient, 1988; (ed with A. Dyson) Experiments on Embryos, 1990; Wonderwoman and Superman: ethics and human biotechnology, 1992; (ed with A. Dyson) Ethics and Biotechnology, 1994; Clones, Genes and Immortality, 1998; (ed jtly) AIDS: ethics, justice and European policy, 1998; (ed with S. Holm) The Future of Human Reproduction, 1998; (ed jtly) A Companion to Genethics: philosophy and the genetic revolution, 2001; (ed.) Bioethics, 2001; The Safety of the People, 2002. *Recreations:* cooking, walking, arguing, Italy. *Address:* School of Law, University of Manchester, Oxford Road, Manchester M13 9PL. *T:* (0161) 275 3473.

HARRIS, His Honour John Percival, DSC 1945; QC 1974; a Circuit Judge, 1980–95; *b* 16 Feb. 1925; *o s* of late Thomas Percival Harris and Nora May Harris; *m* 1959, Janet Valerie Douglas; one *s* two *d.* *Educ:* Wells Cathedral Sch.; Pembroke Coll., Cambridge. BA 1947. Served in RN, 1943–46: Midshipman, RNVR, 1944, Sub-Lt 1945. Called to Bar, Middle Temple, 1949, Bencher 1970. A Recorder of the Crown Court, 1972–80; Dep. Sen. Judge, Sovereign Base Areas, Cyprus, 1983–2000 (Acting Sen. Judge, 1995). *Recreations:* golf, reading, Victorian pictures. *Address:* Tudor Court, Fairmile Park Road, Cobham, Surrey KT11 2PP. *T:* (01932) 864756. *Clubs:* Royal St George's Golf (Sandwich); Woking Golf, Rye Golf.

HARRIS, John Robert, FRIBA; architect; Founder and Senior Partner, John R. Harris Architects, London, 1949–98 (also Founder and Senior Partner of associated firms in Brunei, Qatar, Dubai, Hong Kong), now Consultant; Partner, CDH Architectes, Paris, since 1978; *b* 5 June 1919; *s* of late Major Alfred Harris, CBE, DSO and Rosa Alfreda Alderson; *m* 1950, Gillian, *d* of Col C. W. D. Rowe, CB, MBE, TD, DL, JP; one *s* one *d.* *Educ:* Harrow Sch.; Architectural Assoc. Sch. of Architecture (AA Dipl. Hons). FRIBA 1949; HKIA 1982; Membre de l'Ordre des Architectes Français, 1978. Served War, TA and Active Service, 1939–45 (TEM 1945); Lieut RE, Hong Kong, 1940–41; POW of Japanese, 1941–45; Mem., British Army Aid Gp, China, 1943–45; Hong Kong Resistance, 1942–45. Projects won in internat. competition: State Hosp., Qatar, 1953; New Dubai Hosp., 1976; Corniche and Traffic Intersection, Dubai, 1978; HQ for Min. of Social Affairs and Labour, Oman, 1979; Tuen Mun Hosp., Hong Kong, 1981 (internat. assessment); Ruler's Office, Dubai, 1985. Architects and planners for Zhuhai New Town, Economic Zone, People's Republic of China, 1984; Q-Tel HQ, Qatar, 1991; Deira Sea Corniche masterplan, Dubai, 1993. Major works in UK include: hospitals: Royal Northern, London, 1973; Ealing, 1976; RAF Upper Heyford, 1982; RAF Bentwaters, 1982; Stoke Mandeville, 1983; Wellesley House and St Peter's Court School, 1975; apartments, Hyde Park, 1983; dept stores in Barnstaple, Basildon, Cwmbran, Eltham, Harlow, Hammersmith, Sutton Coldfield and Worthing; refurbishment, Natural Hist. Mus., 1982–89; redevelt, Dorchester Hotel, 1989; develt, Gloucester Road Station site; redevelt, Sheraton Grand Hotel, Edinburgh, 1993; Royal residence adjoining Windsor Park, 1998. Major works overseas include: National Bank of Dubai HQ Bldg, 1968; Sulaibikhat Hosp., Kuwait, 1968; Grindlay's Bank, Muscat, 1969; Rashid Hosp., Dubai, 1973; dept stores in Antwerp, Brussels, Lille, Paris and Strasbourg, 1973–83; shopping centres, Oman, 1978 and 1984; Internat. Trade Centre, Dubai, 1979; British Embassy, Chancery Offices and Ambassador's Residence, Abu Dhabi, 1982; University Teaching Hosp., Maiduguri, Nigeria, 1982; Caritas Hosp., Hong Kong, 1983; Women's Hosp., Doha, 1984; Shell Recreation Centre, Brunei, 1984; Wafi Shopping Mall, Dubai, 1991 and 1998; British Bank of ME HQ, Dubai, 1993; 3,000 seat Conf. Centre, Doha, 1997; Equine Hosp., Dubai, 1997; Harrow Internat. Sch., Bangkok, 1997; Internat. Hotel Develt, Armenia, 1998; Palace Develt, Bahrain, 1998. FRSA 1982. Cert., Internat. Hosp. Fedn, 1993; Structural Steel Design Award, London Docklands, 1993. Silver Jubilee Medal, 1977. *Publications:* (jtly) John R. Harris Architects, 1984; contrib. to books and architectural and technical jls. *Recreations:* architecture, sailing, travel. *Address:* 24 Devonshire Place, W1G 6BX. *T:* (020) 7935 9353. *Clubs:* Special Forces, Royal Thames Yacht.

See also R. M. Harris.

HARRIS, (John Robert) William, FRCP, FRCPI; Consultant in Genito-Urinary Medicine, since 1976, and Medical Director, since 1991, St Mary's Hospital NHS Trust; *b* 25 Sept. 1943; *s* of William James Smyth Harris and Anne (*née* Glass); *m* 1st, 1968, Mary Elizabeth Keating (marr. diss. 1992; remarried 1994); one *s* one *d.* *Educ:* Ballymena Acad.; Queen's Univ., Belfast (MB). FRCP 1985; FRCPI 1996. Postgrad. trng, Royal Victoria Hosp., Belfast and Liverpool Sch. of Tropical Medicine, 1968–72; Consultant and Hon. Sen. Lectr, Sheffield Royal Infirmary, 1972–74; Consultant, King's Coll. Hosp., 1974–75. Lock Lectr, RCPSG, 1993. Internat. Health Award, 1973; Scott-Heron Medal, Royal Victoria Hosp., Belfast, 1985. *Publications:* Recent Advances in Sexually Transmitted Diseases, 1975, 4th edn 1991; papers on sexually transmitted diseases, AIDS and sexual dysfunction. *Recreations:* walking, cinema, travel. *Address:* 77 Harley Street, W1N 1DE. *T:* (020) 7486 4166. *Club:* Athenæum.

HARRIS, Jonathan David, OBE 1993; FRICS; President, Royal Institution of Chartered Surveyors, 2000–01; *b* 28 Sept. 1941; *s* of Wilfred Harris and Ann Harris (*née* Godel); *m* 1964, Jeniffer Cecilia Fass; one *s* three *d.* *Educ:* Haberdashers' Aske's Sch. FRICS 1964. Pepper Angliss & Yarwood, Chartered Surveyors, 1959–94 (Sen. Partner, 1974–94); Dir, Carlisle Gp, 1987–99. Board Member: Plymouth Develt Corp., 1993–96; Real Estate Adv. Gp, UN, 2001–. Committee Member: Sackville Property Unit Trust, 1974–99; Langbourn Income Growth & Property Unit Trust, 1984–. Mem., Property Forum, Bank of England, 1988–. Founder and Pres., Continuing Professional Develt Foundn, 1980–; launched Inst. of Continuing Professional Develt, 1997. Treas., Prison Reform Trust, 1998–. Trustee: Understanding Industry, 1997– (Chm., 1997–99); LPO, 1996–. Gov., Univ. of Westminster (formerly Poly. of Central London), 1988–99. Liveryman: Co. of Chartered Surveyors, 1977; Co. of Basketmakers, 1962. Hon. DLitt Westminster, 1998. *Recreations:* golf, grandchildren, charitable works. *Address:* 24 Hays Mews, W1J 5PY. *T:* (020) 7495 3132.

HARRIS, Prof. Jose Ferial, PhD; FBA 1993; Professor of Modern History, University of Oxford, since 1996; Fellow, St Catherine's College, Oxford, since 1978; *d* of Leonard Cecil Chambers and Freda Ellen Chambers (*née* Brown); *m* 1968, James William Harris, *qv*; one *s.* *Educ:* Dame Alice Harpur Sch., Bedford; Newnham Coll., Cambridge (MA, PhD). Res. Fellow, Nuffield Coll., Oxford, 1966–69; Lectr, 1969–74, Sen. Lectr, 1974–78, Dept of Social Sci. and Admin, LSE; Reader in Modern History, Oxford Univ., 1990–96. Vis. Res. Fellow, Princeton, 1985–86. Ford Lectr in English History, Oxford Univ., 1996–97; Leverhulme Res. Prof., Oxford Univ., 1998–. *Publications:* Unemployment and Politics: a study in English social policy, 1972, 2nd edn 1984; William Beveridge: a biography, 1977, 2nd edn 1997; Private Lives, Public Spirit: a social history of Britain 1870–1914, 1993, 2nd edn 1994; Ferdinand Tönnies: community and civil society, 2001. *Recreations:* the lesser arts, walking, river boats, solitude, family life. *Address:* 5 Belbroughton Road, Oxford OX2 6UZ.

HARRIS, Joseph Hugh; JP; Vice Lord-Lieutenant of Cumbria, since 1994; *b* 3 June 1932; *s* of late John Frederick Harris and of Gwendolen Arden Harris; *m* 1957, Anne, *d* of Brig. Leslie Harrison McRobert, CBE. *Educ:* Aysgarth Sch.; Harrow; Royal Agric. Coll. (MRAC). Lieut, 11th Hussars, PAO. Chairman: Cumbrian Newspapers Ltd, 1987–;

Grasmere Sports (Dir, 1977). Member: Northern Regl Panel, MAFF, 1977–83; Rural Develt Commn, 1989–. Royal Agricultural Society: Sen. Steward, 1960–77; Dep. Pres., 1987; Trustee, 1992–; Hon. Dir, Royal Show, 1978–82. High Sheriff of Cumbria, 1976–77; DL 1984, JP 1971, Cumbria. Chm., Penrith and Alston Bench, 1991–95. Chm. of Govs, Aysgarth Sch., 1975–78; Gov., RAC, Cirencester, 1987–90. Liveryman, Farmers' Co., 1973–. *Recreations:* shooting, country sports, conservation. *Address:* Brackenburgh, Calthwaite, Penrith, Cumbria CA11 9PW. *T:* (01768) 885253, *Fax:* (01768) 885020.

HARRIS, Air Cdre Joy; *see* Harris, I. J.

HARRIS, Dr Keith Murray, CBiol, FIBiol, FRES; Director, International (formerly Commonwealth) Institute of Entomology, 1985–92; *b* 26 Nov. 1932; *s* of Clifford Murray Harris and Doris (*née* Cottam); *m* 1957, Elizabeth Harrison; one *s* one *d. Educ:* Lewis Sch., Pengam; Univ. of Wales, Aberystwyth (BSc, DSc); Selwyn Coll., Cambridge (DipAgricSci); Imperial Coll. of Tropical Agric., Trinidad (DipTA). FRES 1960; FIBiol 1985. Entomologist, then Sen. Entomologist, Federal Dept of Agricl Res., Nigeria, 1955–62; Sen. Res. Fellow, BM (Natural History), 1962–66; Entomologist and Sen. Scientist, RHS, Wisley, 1966–74; Principal Taxonomist, Commonwealth Inst. of Entomology, 1974–85. *Publications:* (jtly) Collins Guide to the Pests, Diseases and Disorders of Garden Plants, 1981, 2nd edn as Collins Photoguide to the Pests, Diseases and Disorders of Garden Plants, 1998; scientific research papers and articles on pests of cultivated plants, esp. pests of African cereal crops, and on taxonomy and biol. of gall midges. *Recreations:* walking, cycling, gardening, music. *Address:* 81 Linden Way, Ripley, Woking, Surrey GU23 6LP. *T:* (01483) 224963.

HARRIS, Kenneth; *see* Harris, D. K.

HARRIS, Leonard John; Commissioner, and Director, VAT Policy (formerly Internal Taxes), Customs and Excise, 1991–96; *b* 4 July 1941; *s* of Leonard and May Harris; *m* 1st, 1965, Jill Christine Tompkins (marr. diss.); one *s* two *d*; 2nd, 1986, Jennifer Dilys Biddiscombe (*née* Barker). *Educ:* Westminster City Sch.; St John's Coll., Cambridge. BA 1964 (Eng. Lit.), MA 1967. HM Customs and Excise: Asst Principal, 1964; Private Sec. to Chairman, 1966–68; Principal, 1969; CS Selection Bd, 1970; HM Customs and Excise, 1971; Cabinet Office, 1971–74; First Sec., UK Rep. to EEC, 1974–76, Counsellor, 1976–77; Asst Sec., HM Customs and Excise, 1977–80, Cabinet Office, 1980–83; Under Sec., 1983; Comr of Customs and Excise, 1983–87; Under Sec., MPO, 1987; Under Sec., HM Treasury, 1987–91. *Recreations:* cooking, music, naturism. *Address:* French Oak, Sires Hill, North Moreton, Oxon OX11 9BG. *Clubs:* Oxford Naturist (Oxford).

HARRIS, Lyndon Goodwin, RI 1958; RSW 1952; RWA 1947; artist in oil, water-colour, stained glass, and etching; *b* 25 July 1928; *s* of late S. E. Harris, ACIS and late Mary Elsie Harris. *Educ:* Halesowen Grammar Sch. Studied Art at: Birmingham Coll. of Art; Slade Sch. of Fine Art, 1946–50; University of London Inst. of Education, 1950–51; Courtauld Inst.; Central Sch. of Art and Crafts, London. Leverhulme Schol., Pilkington Schol., Slade Schol., and Slade Anatomy Prizeman; Dip. Fine Art (London) 1949; Courtauld Certificate, 1950; ATD 1951. *Works exhibited:* Paris Salon (Gold Medal, Oil Painting; Honourable Mention, Etching); RA (first exhibited at age of 13), RSA, RI, RSW, NEAC, RBA, RGI, RWA, and principal provincial galleries. *Works in permanent collections:* Govt Art Collection; University Coll., London; Birmingham and Midland Inst.; City of Worcester; (stained glass) Gorsty Hill Methodist Church, Halesowen. *Recreation:* music (organ and pianoforte).

HARRIS, Mark; Assistant Treasury Solicitor, Department for Education (formerly Education and Science), 1988–94; *b* 23 Feb. 1943; *s* of late Solomon Harris and Eva (*née* Lazarus); *m* 1972, Sharon Frances Colin; one *d. Educ:* Central Foundation Boys' Grammar Sch., London; London School of Economics and Political Science, London Univ. (LLB Hons). Solicitor of the Supreme Court, 1967. Entered Solicitor's Office, Dept of Employment, as Legal Asst, 1968; Sen. Legal Asst, 1973; Asst Solicitor, 1978; Legal Advr, 1987–88. Vol. mem. mgt cttee and journalist, Essex Jewish News. *Publications:* several short stories, magazine and newspaper articles. *Recreations:* travel, walking, short-story writing, theatre, London Jewish Male Choir (first tenor). *Address:* 17 Marlands Road, Clayhall, Ilford, Essex IG5 0JL.

HARRIS, Mark Philip Allen; Chief Executive, National Lottery Commission, since 1999; *b* 29 July 1961; *s* of Roy Allen Harris and Vivienne Harris; *m* 1993, Patricia Mary Allen; one *s* one *d. Educ:* Bishop's Stortford Coll.; Nottingham Univ. (LLB Hons). CPFA 1987. Audit Examr, 1983–88, Manager, 1988–91, Sen. Manager, 1991–94, District Audit; Associate Controller, Audit Commn, 1994–97; Exec. Consultant, Hammersmith Hosps NHS Trust, 1997–98; Associate Dir (Strategic Develt), Audit Commn, 1998–99. *Recreations:* family, hill walking, mountaineering literature, ski-ing. *Address:* National Lottery Commission, 2 Monck Street, SW1P 2BQ. *T:* (020) 7227 2011.

HARRIS, Prof. Sir Martin (Best), Kt 2000; CBE 1992; DL; Vice-Chancellor, Manchester University, since 1992; *b* 28 June 1944; *s* of William Best Harris and Betty Evelyn (*née* Martin); *m* 1966, Barbara Mary (*née* Daniels); two *s. Educ:* Devonport High Sch. for Boys, Plymouth; Queens' Coll., Cambridge (BA, MA; Hon. Fellow, 1992); Sch. of Oriental and African Studies, London (PhD). Lecturer in French Linguistics, Univ. of Leicester, 1967; University of Salford: Sen. Lectr in French Linguistics, 1974; Prof. of Romance Ling., 1976–87; Dean of Social Sciences and Arts, 1978–81; Pro-Vice-Chancellor, 1981–87; Vice-Chancellor, Essex Univ., 1987–92. Chairman: CVCP, 1997–99 (Vice-Chm., 1995–97); NW Univs Assoc., 1999–2000. Member: Internat. Cttee for Historical Linguistics, 1979–86; UGC, 1984–87; HEFCE Review of Univ. Libraries, 1992–93; Chairman: NI Sub Cttee, UFC (formerly UGC), 1985–91; Nat. Curriculum Wkg Gp for Modern Foreign Langs, 1989–90; HEFCE/CVCP Review of Postgrad. Educn, 1995–96; Clinical Standards Adv. Gp, 1996–99; DfEE Careers Review, 2000. Mem., Commn for Health Improvement, 1999–. Mem. Council, Philological Soc., 1979–86, 1988–92. Chm. of Govs, Centre for Inf. on Lang. Teaching, 1990–96; Vice Chm. of Governors, Parrs Wood High Sch., 1982–86; Gov., Colchester Sixth Form Coll., 1988–92; Member Governing Body: Anglia Polytechnic Univ. (formerly Anglia Poly.), 1989–93; SOAS, London Univ., 1990–93; Mem. High Council, Eur. Univ. Inst., 1992–96. Mem. Editorial Board: Journal Linguistics, 1982 91; Diachronica, 1983–92; French Studies, 1987–93; Jt Gen. Editor, Longman Linguistics Library, 1982–96. MAE 1991; AcSS 2001. DL Greater Manchester, 1998. Hon. Fellow: Bolton Inst., 1996; Univ. of Central Lancashire, 1999; Hon. RMCM 1996. Hon. LLD QUB, 1992; DUniv Essex, 1993; Hon. DLitt: Salford, 1995; Manchester Metropolitan. *Publications:* (ed) Romance Syntax: synchronic and diachronic perspectives, 1976; The Evolution of French Syntax: a comparative approach, 1978; (ed with N. Vincent) Studies in the Romance Verb, 1982; (ed with P. Ramat) Historical Development of Auxiliaries, 1987; (ed with N. Vincent) The Romance Languages, 1988; about 35 articles in appropriate jls and collections. *Recreations:* gardening, travel, wine. *Address:* University of Manchester, Oxford Road, Manchester M13 9PL. *T:* (0161) 275 7399, *Fax:* (0161) 272 6313.

HARRIS, Maurice Kingston, CB 1976; Secretary, Northern Ireland Ministry of Home Affairs, 1973, seconded to Northern Ireland Office, 1974–76; *b* 5 Oct. 1916; *s* of Albert Kingston Harris and Annie Rebecca Harris; *m* 1948, Margaret, *d* of Roderick Fraser and Gertrude McGregor; one *s* three *d. Educ:* The Perse Sch.; London Univ. 1st cl. Hons Mod. Langs, 1939. Served in Indian Army, 8th Punjab Regt, 1942–46. Colonial Office, 1946–47. Entered Northern Ireland Civil Service, 1947, and served in various Ministries; retired 1976. *Recreations:* music, walking. *Address:* 27 Strangford Avenue, Belfast BT9 6PG. *T:* (028) 9068 1409.

HARRIS, Mervyn Leslie Richard; a District Judge (Magistrates' Courts) (formerly Stipendiary Magistrate), Nottinghamshire, since 1991; *b* 9 Aug. 1942; *s* of Albert Leslie Harris and Gladys Mary (*née* Plummer); *m* 1967, Marcia Jane Tomblin; one *s* one *d. Educ:* King Henry VIII Sch., Coventry; University Coll. London (LLB 1964). Admitted solicitor, 1969; Partner, Hughes & Masser, solicitors, Coventry, 1969–91. Chm. (part-time), Social Security Appeals Tribunal, 1985–91; Actg Stipendiary Magistrate, 1987–91. Clerk to local charities in Coventry and Atherstone. *Recreations:* walking, railways, railway history, watching football, Rugby and cricket.

HARRIS, Michael David, FRCO; Organist and Master of the Music, St Giles' Cathedral, Edinburgh, since 1996; organ recitalist, conductor and adjudicator; *b* 29 Dec. 1958; *s* of David John Harris and Muriel Harris (*née* Pearson); *m* 1987, Brigitte Johanne Hannelore Schröder; one *d. Educ:* King's Sch., Gloucester; Reading Sch.; St Peter's Coll., Oxford (MA); Royal Coll. of Music (ARCM); FRCO 1980. Sub Organist, Leeds Parish Church, 1982–86; Asst Dir of Music, Leeds Grammar Sch., 1982–86; Asst Organist, Canterbury Cathedral, 1986–96; Organist, King's Sch., Canterbury, 1986–96; Lectr in Music, Napier Univ., Edinburgh, 1996–; Dir, Scottish Chamber Choir, 1997–. *Recreations:* railways, cooking. *Address:* St Giles' Cathedral, Edinburgh EH1 1RE.

HARRIS, Hon. Michael Deane; MPP (PC) for Nipissing, Ontario, since 1981; Premier of Ontario, since 1995; *b* 23 Jan 1945; *s* of Sidney Deane Harris and Hope Gooding Harris (*née* Robinson); *m* Janet Ina Harrison; two *s. Educ:* East Algonguin High Sch.; North Bay Teachers' Coll. Formerly: teacher; worked for family-owned tourist and ski resorts; Parly Asst to Minister of the Envmt; Minister of Natural Resources and Minister of Energy, 1985. House Leader, 1986–89, Leader, 1990–, Ontario Progressive Conservative Party. Trustee, 1975–81, Chm., 1977–81, Nipissing Bd of Educn. *Address:* Legislative Building, Queen's Park, Toronto, Ont M7A 1A1, Canada.

HARRIS, Michael Frank; His Honour Judge Michael Harris; a Circuit Judge, since 1992; *b* 11 Jan. 1942; *s* of Joseph Frank Harris and Edna Harris; *m* 1969, Veronica Brend; one *s* one *d. Educ:* St Bartholomew's Grammar Sch., Newbury; Merton Coll., Oxford (BA). Called to the Bar, Middle Temple, 1965; a Recorder, 1990–92. Chief Social Security Comr and Chief Child Support Comr, 2001–. President: Social Security, Medical, Disability and Child Support Appeal Tribunals, 1998–99; The Appeals Service, 1999–. *Recreations:* piano playing, amateur dramatics, walking, music, theatre, travel, reading. *Address:* c/o South Eastern Circuit Office, New Cavendish House, 18 Maltravers Street, WC2R 3EU.

HARRIS, Rear-Adm. Michael George Temple; Clerk to the Clothworkers' Co. of the City of London and Secretary to the Clothworkers' Foundation, 1992–2001; *b* 5 July 1941; *s* of Comdr Antony John Temple Harris, OBE, RN and Doris Drake Harris; *m* 1970, Katrina Chichester; three *d. Educ:* Pangbourne Coll.; RNC, Dartmouth. FRGS 1978; FNI 1988. Qualified Submarines, 1963, TAS 1968; commanded HM Submarines: Osiris, 1970–72; Sovereign, 1975–77 (N Pole, 1976); 3rd Submarine Sqn, 1982–85; commanded HM Ships: Cardiff, 1980–82 (Falkland Is, 1982); Ark Royal, 1987–89; ACDS (NATO/UK), 1989–92. Exchange service with USN, 3rd Fleet Staff, 1972–75. Younger Brother of Trinity House, 1989–. Mem., Ancient Soc. of Coll. Youths, 1995–. Liveryman, Clothworkers' Co., 1997– (Mem., Ct of Assistants, 2001–). Gov., Pangbourne Coll., 1997–. *Recreations:* riding, fishing, bell-ringing, monumental brasses, reading. *Club:* Naval and Military.

HARRIS, Michael John; Vice Chairman, Egg plc, since 2000; *b* 10 March 1949; *s* of John Melton and Ivy May Harris; *m* 1971, Susan Cooper; one *s* one *d. Educ:* Dudley Grammar Sch.; University Coll. London (BSc Chemistry). Variety of positions in IT, incl. Head of Systems Develt for Retail Bank, Midland Bank, 1972–86; Dir, Space-Time Systems, 1986–88; Chief Executive: Firstdirect, 1988–91; Mercury Communications Ltd, 1991–95; Prudential Banking, then Egg, 1995–2000. *Recreations:* tennis, walking, theatre, photography, watching Aston Villa. *Address:* Egg plc, 1 Waterhouse Square North, 138–142 Holborn Bars, EC1N 2NA. *T:* (020) 7526 2613.

HARRIS, Miriam Janine; Project Director, Whitehall II Stress-Health Study, Department of Epidemiology and Public Health, University College London, since 2000; *b* 22 June 1945; *d* of late Frank Lesser and Mira Lesser; *m* 1968, John Harris. *Educ:* Liverpool Univ. (BA Hons Psychol.). Res. assistant, Tavistock Inst. of Human Relns, 1966–69; SO, then SSO, SSRC, 1969–78; Social Science Grants Officer, Nuffield Foundn, 1979–80; Sen. Res. Fellow, Goldsmiths' Coll., Univ. of London, 1980–82; Sec., Nuffield Foundn Pharmacy Inquiry, 1983–85; Res. Advr, ABRC, 1986–87; Exec. Dir, Clore Foundn, 1988–97; Practice Res. Manager, RPSGB, 1998–2000. *Address:* Department of Epidemiology and Public Health, University College London, 1–19 Torrington Place, WC1E 6BT. *T:* (020) 7679 5937; *e-mail:* miriam.harris@ucl.ac.uk.

HARRIS, Patricia Ann, (Mrs J. N. K. Harris); Central President, The Mothers' Union, 1989–94 (Vice-President, 1986–88); *b* 29 May 1939; *m* 1963, Rev. James Nigel Kingsley Harris, BA; one *s* one *d. Educ:* Trinity Coll., Carmarthen (Hon. Fellow, 1995). Teaching Dip. Teacher, 1959–63; pt-time special needs teacher, 1963–88; vol. teacher, Gloucester Prison, 1978–85. Member: Glos Dio. Synod, 1980–2001; C of E General Synod, 1985–2000 (Mem. Exec., 1991–2001, Vice Chm., 1996–2001, Chm., Trust Funds, 1996–2001, Bd of Mission); Bishops' Council, 1985–2001; Cttee, Partnership for World Mission, 1993–2000; Women's Nat. Commn, 1994–96; USPG Council, 1994–96; Cttee, Black Anglican Concerns, 1995–96; Council, 1996–, Publications Cttee, 1997–, Bible Reading Fellowship. Mothers' Union: Young Wives Leader, 1963–65; Enrolling Mem., 1967–76; Presiding Mem., 1969–74; Diocesan Social Concern Chm., 1974–80; Pres., Glos dio., 1980–85; Worldwide Council 1995–. Hon. Lay Canon, Gloucester Cathedral, 2001 . Mem., Archbishops' Bd of Examiners, 1996–99. Paul Harris Fellow, Rotary Internat., 1995. Cross of St Augustine, 1995. *Recreations:* swimming, watching Rugby, cooking, craft work. *Address:* The Vicarage, Elm Road, Stonehouse, Glos GL10 2NP. *T:* (01453) 822332.

HARRIS, Rt Rev. Patrick Burnet; Assistant Bishop, dioceses of Lincoln and of Europe, since 1999; *b* 30 Sept. 1934; *s* of Edward James Burnet Harris and Astrid Kendall; *m* 1968, Valerie Margaret Pilbrow; two *s* one *d. Educ:* St Albans School; Keble Coll., Oxford (MA). Asst Curate, St Ebbe's, Oxford, 1960–63; Missionary with S American Missionary Soc., 1963–73; Archdeacon of Salta, Argentina, 1969–73; Diocesan Bishop of Northern Argentina, 1973–80; Rector of Kirkheaton and Asst Bishop, Dio. Wakefield, 1981–85;

Sec., Partnership for World Mission, 1986–88; Asst Bishop, Dio. Oxford, 1986–88; Bishop of Southwell, 1988–99. Mem., South Atlantic Council, 1986–. Chairman: Bible Reading Fellowship, 1995–98; Council, Ridley Hall, 1994–; Pres., S Amer. Mission Soc.; Vice-Pres., TEAR Fund. Took his seat in H of L, 1996. *Recreations:* ornithology, S American Indian culture, music, harvesting. *Address:* Meadow Cottage, 17 Dykes End, Collingham, Newark, Notts NG23 7LD.

HARRIS, Prof. Paul Lansley, DPhil; FBA 1998; Professor, Harvard University, since 2001; *b* 14 May 1946; *s* of Joseph and Betty Harris; *m* Pascale Torracinta; three *s*. *Educ:* Chippenham Grammar Sch.; Sussex Univ. (BA Psychol.); Linacre Coll., Oxford (DPhil Psychol. 1971). Research Fellow: Center for Cognitive Studies, Harvard Univ., 1971–72; in Exptl Psychol., Oxford Univ., 1972–73; Lectr, Dept of Psychol., Lancaster Univ., 1973–76; Reader, Free Univ., Amsterdam, 1976–79; Lectr, Dept of Social Psychology, LSE, 1979–81; Oxford University: Lectr in Exptl Psychol., 1981–96; Reader, 1996–98; Prof. of Develtl Psychol., 1998–2001; Fellow, St John's Coll., 1981–2001, now Emeritus. Fellow, Center for Advanced Study in Behavioral Scis, Stanford, USA, 1992–93. *Publications:* Children and Emotion, 1989; The Work of the Imagination, 2000; articles in learned jls, incl. Child Development, and Developmental Psychology. *Recreations:* cooking, writing. *Address:* Harvard Graduate School of Education, Cambridge, MA 02138, USA.

HARRIS, Prof. Peter Charles, MD, PhD; FRCP; Simon Marks Professor of Cardiology, University of London, 1966–88, now Emeritus; Consultant Physician, National Heart and Chest Hospitals; *b* 26 May 1923; *s* of late David Jonathan Valentine and Nellie Dean Harris; *m* 1st, 1952, Felicity Margaret Hartridge (marr. diss. 1982); two *d*; 2nd, 1989, Frances Monkarsh. *Educ:* St Olave's Grammar Sch.; Univ. of London. MB, BS (London) 1946; MRCP 1950; MD (Univ. medal) 1951; PhD 1955; FRCP 1965. House appts at King's Coll. Hospital, and elsewhere, 1946–55; Nuffield Fellow, Columbia Univ., New York, 1955–57; Lectr, Sen. Lectr and Reader in Medicine, Univ. of Birmingham, 1957–66; Dir, Inst. of Cardiology, Univ. of London, 1966–73. Pres., Internat. Soc. for Heart Research, 1981–83. Mem., Instituto Veneto, 1994. Hon. FACC, 1976. Editor, Cardioscience, 1990–96. *Publications:* The Human Pulmonary Circulation (with D. Heath), 1962, 3rd edn 1986; articles to jls, etc, on cardio-pulmonary physiology and biochemistry. *Recreation:* chamber music. *Address:* 42 Great Percy Street, WC1X 9QR. *T:* (020) 7278 2911; 2089 Gulf of Mexico Drive #209, Longboat Key, FL 34228, USA. *T:* (941) 3831067.

HARRIS, Group Captain Peter Langridge, CBE 1988; AE 1961 (Clasp 1971); CEng, FIEE; ADC to the Queen, 1984–88; Inspector, Royal Auxiliary Air Force, 1983–88; *b* 6 Sept. 1929; *s* of Arthur Langridge Harris and Doris Mabel (*née* Offen); *m* 1955, (Yvonne) Patricia Stone; two *d*. *Educ:* St Edward's Sch., Oxford; Univ. of Birmingham (BSc). CEng, FIEE 1976. Served: RAF, 1947–49; RAFVR, 1949–60; RAuxAF, 1960–78 and 1982–88; commanded 1 (Co. Hertford) Maritime HQ Unit, 1973–77; Air Force Mem., 1978–94, Vice-Chm. (Air), 1988–94, TA&VRA for Greater London; Gp Captain 1983. Elliott Bros (London) Ltd, 1952–55; Decca Navigator Co. Ltd, 1955–59; GEC plc, 1959–89; retired. Mem. Bd, Milton Keynes Business Venture, 1983–89. Mem. Bd of Management, Princess Marina House, Rustington, 1990–. Chm., Hatfield Dist IEE, 1979–80. Mem., Council, Reserve Forces Assoc., 1989–95. Pres., 1 Maritime HQ Unit Old Comrades Assoc., 1990–. Freeman, GAPAN, 1987–. DL Greater London, 1986–98. CMJ 1998 (Chevalier, OSMTH, 1994). *Recreation:* travel. *Address:* 10 Dolphin Court, St Helens Parade, Southsea, Hants PO4 0QL. *T:* (023) 9281 7602. *Clubs:* Royal Air Force; Royal Naval and Royal Albert Yacht (Portsmouth).

HARRIS, Peter Michael; Official Solicitor to the Supreme Court, 1993–99; *b* 13 April 1937; *s* of Benjamin Warren Harris and Ethel Evelyn Harris (*née* Mabbutt); *m* 1963, Bridget Burke; one *s* two *d*. *Educ:* Cirencester Grammar School; Britannia Royal Naval College, Dartmouth. Cadet, RN, 1953; Lieut Comdr 1967; retired from RN 1972. Called to the Bar, Gray's Inn, 1971; Lord Chancellor's Department: Legal Asst, 1974; Dep. Circuit Administrator, Midland and Oxford Circuit, 1980; Head of Property and Family Law Div., 1982; Head of Civil Courts Div., 1985; Circuit Administrator, Northern Circuit, 1986–93. Associate Sen. Res. Fellow, Inst. of Advanced Legal Studies, London Univ., 1999–. Chm., Nat. Council for Family Proceedings, 1999–2000. Trustee: Sieff foundn, 1999–; Grandparents' Fedn, Professional Adv. Gp, Nat. Youth Advocacy Service, 1999–. Asst Ed., Atkin's Court Forms, 1997–. *Publications:* The Children Act 1989: a procedural handbook, 1991; The Expert Witness Pack, 1997. *Recreations:* reading, walking, swimming, gardening. *Address:* 23 Rook Wood Way, Little Kingshill, Great Missenden, Bucks HP16 0DF.

HARRIS, Philip; Principal, Monopolies and Mergers Commission, 1977–85, retired; *b* Manchester, 15 Dec. 1915; *er s* of S. D. Harris and Sarah Chazan; *m* 1939, Sarah Henriques Valentine (*d* 1996); three *d*. *Educ:* Manchester Grammar Sch.; Trinity Hall, Cambridge (Open Scholarship, BA 1st Cl (with dist.), Historical Tripos, MA 1970). Asst Principal, Board of Trade, 1938–40. Served War, 1940–45; Anti-Aircraft Command and Western Europe; 2nd Lieut RA, 1941; Lieut, 2/8th Lancs Fusiliers, 1944; Capt., 6th Royal Welch Fusiliers, 1945. Principal, Board of Trade, 1946; Asst Sec., Board of Trade, 1948–64; Asst Registrar, Office of the Registrar of Restrictive Trading Agreements, 1964–66, Principal Asst Registrar, 1966–73; Principal Asst Registrar, Fair Trading Div. I, DTI, 1973; Dir, Restrictive Trade Practices Div., Office of Fair Trading, 1973–76. Nuffield Travelling Fellowship, 1956–57 (study of Indian Industrial Development). UK Mem., EEC Adv. Cttee on Cartels and Monopolies, 1973–76; Mem., Labour Finance and Industry Gp, 1990–. Leader, UK Delgn to Internat. Cotton Advisory Cttee, 1960, 1963. Lectr, Univ. of the Third Age, London, 1995–. *Publications:* various articles on monopolies and restrictive trade practices policy and current developments in UK competition law and administration. *Recreation:* history. *Address:* 23 Court House Gardens, Finchley, N3 1PU. *T:* (020) 8346 3138.

HARRIS, Phillip, FRCSE, FRCPE, FRCSGlas; FRSE; former Consultant Neurosurgeon; formerly Deputy Director, Department of Surgical Neurology, Royal Infirmary and Western General Hospital, Edinburgh; Senior Lecturer, Edinburgh University, 1955–87; Member, MRC Brain Metabolism Unit, University of Edinburgh, 1952–80; Editor, Paraplegia, later Spinal Chord, 1980–97, now Emeritus Editor; *b* Edinburgh, 28 March 1922; *s* of late Simon Harris, Edinburgh; *m* 1949, Sheelagh Shèna (*née* Coutts); one *s* one *d*. *Educ:* Royal High Sch., Edinburgh; Edinburgh Univ.; Sch. of Med. of Royal Colls, Edinburgh. Medallist in Anatomy, Physiol., Physics, Materia Medica and Therapeutics, Med., Midwifery and Gynaec., and Surgery. LRCP and LRCSE, LRCPSGlas 1944; FRCSE 1948; MRCPE 1954; FRCPE 1959; FRCSGlas 1964 (*ad eundem*). Capt., RAMC, 1945–48. Past Chm., Sch. of Occupational Therapy, Edinburgh. Sometime Vis. Prof./Guest Chief in Neurosurg., USA, Canada, Europe, S America, Far East, Middle East and Russia; Lectures: Sydney Watson-Smith, RCPE, 1967; Honeymoon-Gillespie, Edinburgh Univ., 1968. Mem., WHO Cttee for Prevention of Neurotrauma, 1985. Past Chm., Professional and Linguistics Assessments Bd, GMC. World Federation of Neurosurgical Societies: Sen. UK Deleg. in Neurosurg. and Hon. Vice-Pres., 1977–94; Dep. Chm., Neurotraumatol. Cttee; Founder, Internat. Conf. of Recent Advances in Neurotraumatol.; Founder and Past Chairman: Epilepsy Soc., SE Scotland; Scottish Assoc. of Neurol Scis; Scottish Sports Assoc. for Disabled (Hon. Pres.); Past Member of Council: Soc. of British Neurolog. Surgs; Neurol Sect., RSocMed; Past Pres., British Cervical Spine Soc. Past Director, Epilepsy Internat.; Dir and Trustee, Scottish Trust for Physically Disabled; Mem. Council, Thistle Foundn. President: Royal High Sch. FP Club, 1978; Edinburgh Rotary Club, 1991–92. Inventor of neurosurg. instruments and apparatus. Medal, Internat. Med. Soc. of Paraplegia, 1985; Dr A. S. Lakshumpathi Medal and Prize, Madras, 1986. *Publications:* (ed jtly) Epilepsy, 1971; (ed jtly) Head Injuries, 1971; chapters in books on neurological surgery; over 100 papers in scientific jls on various neurosurgical topics. *Recreations:* sport, music, travel. *Address:* 4/5 Fettes Rise, Edinburgh EH4 1QH. *T:* (0131) 552 8900. *Clubs:* New (Edinburgh); Royal Scottish Automobile (Glasgow).

HARRIS, Ven. (Reginald) Brian; Archdeacon of Manchester, 1980–98; a Residentiary Canon of Manchester Cathedral, 1980–98, Sub-Dean 1986–98; *b* 14 Aug. 1934; *s* of Reginald and Ruby Harris; *m* 1959, Anne Patricia Hughes; one *s* one *d*. *Educ:* Eltham College; Christ's College, Cambridge (MA); Ridley Hall, Cambridge. Curate of Wednesbury, 1959–61; Curate of Uttoxeter, 1961–64; Vicar of St Peter, Bury, 1964–70; Vicar of Walmsley, Bolton, 1970–80; RD of Walmsley, 1970–80. *Recreations:* walking, painting, music. *Address:* 9 Cote Lane, Hayfield, High Peak SK22 2HL. *T:* (01663) 746321.

HARRIS, Richard Reader; *b* 4 June 1913; *s* of Richard Reader Harris; *m* 1940, Pamela Rosemary Merrick Stephens; three *d*. *Educ:* St Lawrence Coll., Ramsgate. Called to the Bar, 1941. Fire Service, 1939–45. MP (C) Heston and Isleworth, 1950–70. *Recreations:* squash, tennis.

HARRIS, Richard Travis; Director, Burton Group plc, 1984–92; *b* 15 April 1919; 2nd *s* of Douglas Harris and Emmeline Harris (*née* Travis); *m* 1st, 1941, June Constance Rundle (marr. diss. 1953); two *d*; 2nd, 1953, Margaret Sophia Nye (*née* Aron); one *s* one *d*. *Educ:* Charterhouse; RMA Woolwich. Served War of 1939–45, France, Western Desert, Tunisia, Italy (despatches twice); BAOR, 1945–46; Sudan Defence Force Signal Regt, 1947–50 (CO, 1948–50); retired from Royal Signals, 1950, Lt-Col. Man. Dir, Rediffusion (Nigeria) Ltd and Gen. Manager, Rediffusion in Africa, 1951–54; Dep. Gen. Manager, Associated-Rediffusion Ltd, 1954–57; Man. Dir, Coates & Co. (Plymouth) Ltd, 1957–64 (Dir, 1957–68); Man. Dir, 1964–78, Chm., 1970–78, Dollond & Aitchison Ltd; Chm., Dollond & Aitchison Group Ltd (formerly TWW Enterprises Ltd), 1970–78 (Dir, 1968–85); Director: Gallaher Ltd, 1970–87 (Dep. Chm., 1978–84); Dollond International Ltd, 1973–83; Filotechnica Salmoiraghi SpA, 1974–83; Istituto Ottico Vigano SpA, 1974–83; Saunders Valve Co. Ltd, 1978–84; Mono Pumps Ltd, 1978–84; Formatura Iniezione Polimeri SpA, 1978–84; Tobacco Kiosks Ltd, 1978–84; Gallaher Pensions Ltd, 1975–84. Chairman: Fedn of Optical Corporate Bodies, 1970–82; Fedn of Ophthalmic & Dispensing Opticians, 1985–87 (Vice-Pres., 1987–97); Vice-Pres., Inst. of Dirs, 1985–89 (Chm. Council, 1982–85); Mem. Exec. Cttee, Wider Share Ownership Council, 1987–91; Mem. Council, Univ. of Birmingham, 1978–93, Life Mem., Court, 1981. Governor, Royal Shakespeare Theatre, 1980–94. Master, Coachmakers' and Coach Harness Makers Co., 1963–64. *Recreation:* fishing. *Address:* Hunters Care Centre, Cherry Tree Lane, Cirencester GL7 5DT.

HARRIS, Robert Dennis; writer; *b* 7 March 1957; *s* of late Dennis Harris and Audrey (*née* Hardy); *m* 1988, Gillian, *d* of Sir Derek Hornby, *qv* and Margaret (*née* Withers); two *s* two *d*. *Educ:* King Edward VII Sch., Melton Mowbray; Selwyn Coll., Cambridge (BA Hons English). Pres., Cambridge Union, 1978. Joined BBC TV Current Affairs Dept, 1978; Reporter, Newsnight, 1981–85, Panorama, 1985–87; Political Editor, Observer, 1987–89; Political Columnist, Sunday Times, 1989–92, 1996–97. FRSL 1996. *Publications:* (with Jeremy Paxman) A Higher Form of Killing: the history of gas and germ warfare, 1982; Gotcha! the media, the government and the Falklands crisis, 1983; The Making of Neil Kinnock, 1984; Selling Hitler: the story of the Hitler diaries, 1986 (televised, 1991); Good and Faithful Servant: the unauthorized biography of Bernard Ingham, 1990; Fatherland (novel), 1992 (filmed, 1994); The Media Trilogy, 1994; Enigma (novel), 1995 (filmed, 2001); Archangel (novel), 1998. *Recreations:* collecting books, walking. *Address:* The Old Vicarage, Kintbury, Berks RG17 9TR. *T:* (01488) 658073.

HARRIS, Robert Malcolm; HM Diplomatic Service, retired; Governor of Anguilla, 1997–2000 (Acting Governor, 1996–97); *b* 9 Feb. 1941; *m* 1984, Mary Lavinia Allmark (*née* Taggart). Joined Foreign Office, 1960, Archives Clerk, 1960–62; Istanbul, 1962–63; Cento, Ankara, 1963–65; Blantyre, 1965–69; FCO, 1969; Moscow, 1970–72; FCO, 1972–75; Second Sec., Dublin, 1975–79; Nat. Defence Coll., Latimer, 1979–80; First Sec., FCO, 1980–84; Hd of Chancery, Brunei, 1984–89; Consul, Lyon, 1989–90; First Sec., FCO, 1990–92; Chargé d'Affaires, Almaty, 1992–93; First Sec., FCO, 1993–96. *Recreations:* golf, music, gardening. *Address:* Le Bourg, 46500 Miers, France. *Club:* Royal Over-Seas League.

HARRIS, Robin (David Ronald), CBE 1988; Advisor to Baroness Thatcher, since 1990; *b* 22 June 1952; *s* of Ronald Desmond Harris and Isabella Jamieson Harris. *Educ:* Canford Sch.; Exeter Coll., Oxford (Stapeldon Schol., MA History, DPhil). Desk Officer, Conservative Res. Dept, 1978–81; Special Adviser: to Financial Sec. to the Treasury, 1981–83; to Home Secretary, 1983–85; Dir, Conservative Res. Dept, 1985–89; Mem., Prime Minister's Policy Unit, 1989–90. *Recreations:* reading, travel. *Club:* Oxford and Cambridge.

HARRIS, Rolf, AM 1989; OBE 1978 (MBE 1968); entertainer; *b* 30 March 1930; *s* of C. G. Harris and A. M. Harris (*née* Robbins); *m* 1958, Alwen Hughes, sculptress; one *d*. *Educ:* Bassendean State Sch.; Perth Modern Sch.; Univ. of WA; Claremont Teachers' Coll. Jun. backstroke champion, Australia, 1946; teacher, Perth; paintings exhibited, RA, London, 1954, 1955; *television series* include: Rolf Harris Show, 1967–71; Cartoon Time, 1984–89; Rolf's Cartoon Club, 1989–93; Animal Hospital, 1994–; Rolf's Amazing Animals, 1997–; *recordings* include: Tie Me Kangaroo Down Sport, 1960; Sun Arise, 1962; Two Little Boys, 1969. *Publications:* Write Your Own Pop Song, 1968; Rolf Goes Bush, 1975; Picture Book of Cats, 1978; Looking at Pictures, 1978; Instant Music, 1980; Your Cartoon Time, 1986; Catalogue of Comic Verse, 1988; Every Picture Tells a Story, 1989; Win or Die: the making of a King, 1989; Your Animation Time, 1991; Personality Cats, 1992; Me and You and Poems Too, 1993. *Address:* c/o Billy Marsh and Associates, 174–178 North Gower Street, NW1 2NB. *T:* (020) 7388 6858.

HARRIS, Rosemary Jeanne; author; *b* 1923; *yr d* of Marshal of the RAF Sir Arthur Harris, 1st Bt, GCB, OBE, AFC, LLD, and of Barbara Kyrle Money. *Educ:* privately; Thorneloe Sch., Weymouth; St Martin's, Central and Chelsea Schs of Art. Red Cross Nursing Auxiliary, London, Westminster Div., from 1941. Student, 1945–48; picture restorer, 1949; student at Courtauld Inst. (Dept of Technology), 1950; Reader, MGM, 1951–52; subseq. full-time writer. Reviewer of children's books for The Times, 1970–73. Television plays: Peronik, 1976; The Unknown Enchantment, 1981. *Publications:* The

Summer-House, 1956; Voyage to Cythera, 1958; Venus with Sparrows, 1961; All My Enemies, 1967; The Nice Girl's Story, 1968; A Wicked Pack of Cards, 1969; The Double Snare, 1975; Three Candles for the Dark, 1976; *for children:* The Moon in the Cloud, 1968 (Carnegie Medal); The Shadow on the Sun, 1970; The Seal-Singing, 1971; The Child in the Bamboo Grove, 1971; The Bright and Morning Star, 1972; The King's White Elephant, 1973; The Lotus and the Grail, 1974; The Flying Ship, 1974; The Little Dog of Fo, 1976; I Want to be a Fish, 1977; A Quest for Orion, 1978; Beauty and the Beast, 1979; Greenfinger House, 1979; Tower of the Stars, 1980; The Enchanted Horse, 1981; Janni's Stork, 1982; Zed, 1982; (adapted) Heidi, by Johanna Spyri, 1983; Summers of the Wild Rose, 1987; (ed) Poetry Anthology: Love and the Merry-Go-Round, 1988; Colm of the Islands, 1989; Ticket to Freedom, 1991; The Wildcat Strike, 1995; The Haunting of Joey M'basa, 1996. *Recreations:* music, theatre.

HARRIS, Rosina Mary; Consultant, Taylor Joynson Garrett, 1989–95; Partner, Joynson-Hicks, Solicitors, 1954–89 (Senior Partner, 1977–86); *b* 30 May 1921; *d* of late Alfred Harris, CBE, DSO, and Rosa Alfreda Harris. *Educ:* St Swithun's Sch., Winchester; Oxford Univ. (BA 1946, MA; BCL 1947). Joined American Ambulance of GB, 1940. Member, Whitford Committee (a Cttee set up under the Chairmanship of Hon. Mr Justice Whitford to enquire into and report as to copyright law), 1973. Silver Jubilee Medal, 1977. *Recreations:* theatre, riding. *Address:* 23 Devonshire Place, W1G 6JB.

See also J. R. Harris.

HARRIS, Prof. Roy, MA, DPhil, PhD; FRSA; Professor of General Linguistics, University of Oxford, 1978–88, now Emeritus; Fellow of Worcester College, Oxford, 1978–88; *b* 24 Feb. 1931; *s* of Harry and Emmie J. Harris; *m* 1955, Rita Doreen Shulman; one *d*. *Educ:* Queen Elizabeth's Hospital, Bristol; St Edmund Hall, Oxford (MA, DPhil; Hon. Fellow 1987); SOAS, London (PhD). Lecteur, Ecole Normale Supérieure, Paris, 1956–57; Asst Lectr, 1957–58, Lectr, 1958–60, Univ. of Leicester; Exeter Coll., Oxford, 1960–76; Keble Coll., Oxford, 1960–67; Magdalen Coll., Oxford, 1960–76; New Coll., Oxford, 1960–67; Faculty of Medieval and Modern Languages, Oxford, 1961–76; Fellow and Tutor in Romance Philology, Keble Coll., Oxford, 1967–76; Prof. of the Romance Langs, Oxford Univ., and Fellow of Trinity Coll., 1976–77; Prof. of English Language, Univ. of Hong Kong, 1988–91; Dir d'études associé, Ecole Pratique des Hautes Etudes, Paris, 1991–92; Fellow, Univ. Professors, Boston, 1993–95. Visiting Professor: Jawaharlal Nehru Univ., New Delhi, 1986; State Univ. of NY, 1987; Overseas Res. Fellow, Univ. of Cape Town, 1996; Dist. Vis. Schol., Univ. of Adelaide, 1997, 1999. Council Member, Philological Soc., 1978–82. Editor, Language & Communication, 1980–. Scott Moncrieff prize, Translators' Assoc. (Soc. of Authors), 1984. *Publications:* Synonymy and Linguistic Analysis, 1973; Communication and Language, 1978; The Language-Makers, 1980; The Language Myth, 1981; (trans.) F. de Saussure: Course in General Linguistics, 1983; (ed) Approaches to Language, 1983; (ed) Developmental Mechanisms of Language, 1985; The Origin of Writing, 1986; Reading Saussure, 1987; Language, Saussure and Wittgenstein, 1988; (ed) Linguistic Thought in England 1914–1945, 1988; (with T. J. Taylor) Landmarks in Linguistic Thought: the Western tradition from Socrates to Saussure, 1989, 2nd edn 1997; La sémiologie de l'écriture, 1993; Signs of Writing, 1995; The Language Connection, 1996; Signs, Language and Communication, 1996; Introduction to Integrational Linguistics, 1998; Rethinking Writing, 2000; Saussure and his Interpreters, 2001; contribs to Analysis, Behavioral and Brain Sciences, Encounter, Essays in Criticism, French Studies, History and Philosophy of Logic, International Jl of Moral and Social Studies, Jl of Linguistics, Language Sciences, Linguistics, Medium Ævum, Mind, Revue de linguistique romane, Semiotica, Studies in Eighteenth-Century Culture, Theoria, TLS, Zeitschrift für romanische Philologie. *Recreations:* cricket, modern art and design. *Address:* 2 Paddox Close, Oxford OX2 7LR. *T:* (01865) 554256.

HARRIS, Terence Victor; Keeper of Japanese Antiquities, British Museum, since 1997; *b* 3 Aug. 1942; *s* of William Victor Clayton Harris and Theresa Harris (*née* Bingham); *m* 1974, Kazuko Yanagawa; one *s*. *Educ:* Bancroft's Sch., Essex (Drapers' Co. Schol.); Birmingham Univ. (BSc Mech. Engrg). Lectr, Komazawa Univ., Tokyo, 1968–71; self-employed, Japanese Engineering Translation and Consultancy, 1971–78; British Museum: Res. Asst, Dept of Oriental Antiquities, 1978–87; Asst Keeper of Japanese Antiquities, 1987–97. Mem., HAC. *Publications:* A Book of Five Rings, 1974 (trans. several languages); Swords of the Samurai, 1990; Kamakura: the renaissance of Japanese sculpture, 1991; Japanese Imperial Craftsmen, 1994; Netsuke: the Hull Grundy collection, 1987; (jtly) Masterpieces of Japanese Art, 1991. *Recreation:* Kendo-Japanese sword-fencing. *Address:* British Museum, Great Russell Street, WC1B 3DG.

HARRIS, (Theodore) Wilson, CCH 1991; *b* 24 March 1921; *m* 1st, 1945, Cecily Carew; 2nd, 1959, Margaret Whitaker (*née* Burns). *Educ:* Queen's Coll., Georgetown, British Guiana. Studied land surveying, British Guiana, 1939, and subseq. qualified to practise; led many survey parties (mapping and geomorphological research) in the interior; Senior Surveyor, Projects, for Govt of British Guiana, 1955–58. Came to live in London, 1959. Writer in Residence, Univ. of West Indies and Univ. of Toronto, 1970; Commonwealth Fellow, Leeds Univ., 1971; Vis. Prof., Univ. of Texas at Austin, 1972; Guggenheim Fellow, 1973; Henfield Fellow, UEA, 1974; Southern Arts Writer's Fellowship, 1976; Guest Lectr, Univ. of Mysore, 1978; Vis. Lectr, Yale Univ., 1979; Writer in Residence: Univ. of Newcastle, Australia, 1979; Univ. of Qld, Australia, 1986; Vis. Prof., Univ. of Texas at Austin, 1981–82; Regents' Lectr, Univ. of California, 1983. Hon. DLit Univ. of West Indies, 1984; Hon. DLitt: Kent at Canterbury, 1988; Essex, 1996; Macerata (Italy), 1999; Liège, 2001. Guyana Prize for Fiction, 1985–87; Premio Mondello dei Cinque Continenti, 1992. *Publications:* Eternity to Season (poems, privately printed), 1954; Palace of the Peacock, 1960, 4th edn 1998; The Far Journey of Oudin, 1961; The Whole Armour, 1962; The Secret Ladder, 1963; Heartland, 1964; The Eye of the Scarecrow, 1965; The Waiting Room, 1967; Tradition, the Writer and Society: Critical Essays, 1967; Tumatumari, 1968; Ascent to Omai, 1970; The Sleepers of Roraima (a Carib Trilogy), 1970; The Age of the Rainmakers, 1971; Black Marsden, 1972; Companions of the Day and Night, 1975; Da Silva da Silva's Cultivated Wilderness (filmed, 1987), and Genesis of the Clowns, 1977; The Tree of the Sun, 1978; Explorations (essays), 1981; The Angel at the Gate, 1982; The Womb of Space: the cross-cultural imagination, 1983; Carnival, 1985; The Infinite Rehearsal, 1987; The Four Banks of the River of Space, 1990; The Radical Imagination (essays), 1992; Resurrection at Sorrow Hill, 1993; Jonestown, 1996; Selected Essays, 1999; The Dark Jester, 2001. *Address:* c/o Faber and Faber, 3 Queen Square, WC1N 3AU.

HARRIS, Thomas, (Tom); MP (Lab) Glasgow, Cathcart, since 2001; *b* 20 Feb. 1964; *s* of Tom Harris and Rita Harris (*née* Ralston); *m* 1998, Carolyn Moffat; one *s* by previous marriage. *Educ:* Garnock Acad., Kilbirnie, Ayrshire; Napier Coll., Edinburgh (SHND Journalism). Trainee Reporter, E Kilbride News, 1986–88; Reporter, Paisley Daily Express, 1988–90; Press Officer: Labour Party in Scotland, 1990–92; Strathclyde Regl Council, 1993–96; Sen. Media Officer, Glasgow CC, 1996; PR Manager, E Ayrshire Council, 1996–98; Chief PR and Marketing Officer, Strathclyde PTE, 1998–2001. *Recreations:* badminton, astronomy, hill walking, cinema. *Address:* House of Commons, SW1A 0AA. *T:* (020) 7219 8237. *Club:* Cathcart Labour Party Social (Glasgow).

HARRIS, Thomas George, CMG 1995; HM Diplomatic Service; Director-General, Trade and Investment in the US, and Consul-General, New York, since 1999; *b* 6 Feb. 1945; *s* of late Kenneth James Harris and of Dorothy Harris; *m* 1967, Mei-Ling Hwang; three *s*. *Educ:* Haberdashers' Aske's School; Gonville and Caius College, Cambridge. MA. Board of Trade, 1966–x69; British Embassy, Tokyo, 1969–71; Asst Private Sec. to Minister for Aerospace, 1971–72; Dept of Trade, 1972–76; Cabinet Office, 1976–78; Principal Private Sec. to Sec. of State for Trade, 1978–79; Asst Sec., Dept of Trade, 1979–83; Counsellor (Commercial), British Embassy, Washington, 1983–88; Head of Chancery, Lagos, 1988–90; Dep. High Comr, Nigeria, 1990–91; Head, East African Dept, 1991–92, African Dept (Equatorial), 1992–94, FCO; Ambassador, Repub. of Korea, 1994–97; Dir-Gen., Export Promotion, DTI, 1997–99 (on secondment). *Address:* c/o Foreign and Commonwealth Office, SW1A 2AH. *Club:* Oxford and Cambridge.

HARRIS, (Walter) Frank; retired 1982; *b* 19 May 1920; *m* Esther Blanche Hill; two *s* two *d*. *Educ:* King Edward's Sch., Birmingham; University of Nottingham (BCom (Hons) 1949); BSc (1st cl. Hons) Open Univ., 1994. Served Royal Air Force, 1939–46. University, 1946–49. Ford Motor Company, 1950–65; Principal City Officer and Town Clerk, Newcastle upon Tyne, 1965–69. Comptroller and Dir, Admin, Massey-Ferguson (UK), 1969–71; Finance Dir, Dunlop SA Ltd, 1972–79; Business Planning Exec., Dunlop Ltd (UK Tyre Gp), 1979–81. *Recreations:* astrophysics, fell walking, DIY, gardening. *Address:* Acomb High House, Northumberland NE46 4PH. *T:* (01434) 602844.

HARRIS, William; *see* Harris, J. R. W.

HARRIS, Prof. William Anthony, PhD; Professor of Anatomy, Cambridge University, since 1997; Fellow, Clare College, Cambridge, since 1997; *b* 26 Nov. 1950; *s* of Louis Jacob Harris and Helen Gallendar Harris; *m* 1983, Christine Elizabeth Holt; one *s* one *d*. *Educ:* Univ. of Calif, Berkeley (BA); California Inst. Technol. (PhD 1976). Jun. Fellow, Harvard Univ., 1977–80; Faculty Mem., Univ. of Calif, San Diego, 1980–97; engaged in res. on genetic and molecular basis of neural develt. *Publications:* Genetic Neurobiology, 1982; Development of the Nervous System, 2000. *Recreations:* ice-hockey, painting. *Address:* Department of Anatomy, Cambridge University, Downing Street, Cambridge CB2 3DY. *T:* (01223) 766137.

HARRIS, Sir William (Gordon), KBE 1969; CB 1963; MA (Cantab); FREng, FICE; Director-General, Highways, Ministry of Transport, later Department of the Environment, 1965–73; *b* 10 June 1912; *s* of late Capt. James Whyte Harris, Royal Naval Reserve, and Margaret Roberta Buchanan Forsyth; *m* 1st, 1938, Margaret Emily Harvie (*d* 1991); three *s* one *d*; 2nd, 1992, Mrs Rachel Bishop (*née* Goucher). *Educ:* Liverpool Coll.; Sidney Sussex Coll., Cambridge (Mechanical Sciences Tripos and BA 1932; MA 1937). London Midland & Scottish Railway, 1932–35; Sudan Irrigation Dept, 1935–37; joined Civil Engineer in Chief's Dept, Admiralty, 1937; Asst Civil Engineer in Chief, 1950; Deputy Civil Engineer in Chief, 1955; Civil Engineer in Chief, 1959; Dir-Gen., Navy Works, 1960–63; Dir-Gen. of Works, MPBW, 1963–65. Partner, Peter Fraenkel & Partners, 1973–78; Chm., B & CE Holiday Management Co. & Benefit Trust Co., 1978–87. Dir, British Sch. of Osteopathy, 1982–92 (Chm., 1990–92). Chief British Delegate to: Perm. Internat. Assoc. of Navigation Congresses, 1969–85 (Vice-Pres., 1976–79); Perm. Internat. Assoc. of Road Congresses, 1970–73; Mem., Dover Harbour Bd, 1959–82 (Dep. Chm., 1975–79; Chm., 1980–82); Chm., Construction Industry Manpower Bd, 1976–79. Commonwealth Fund (of New York) Fellowship, 1950–51. A Vice-Pres., Instn Civil Engineers, 1971–74, Pres. 1974–75. FREng (FEng 1977). Mem., Smeatonian Soc. of Civil Engineers, 1966– (Pres., 1984). Hon. DSc City, 1977. Hon. Seabee, US Navy, 1961. Decoration for Distinguished Civilian Service to US Army, 1985. *Recreations:* gardening, 16 grandchildren, two great-grandchildren. *Address:* Ninesprings, 10 Church Lane, East Carlton, Market Harborough, Leics LE16 8YA. *T:* (01536) 771307.

HARRIS, Wilson; *see* Harris, T. W.

HARRISON; *see* Graham-Harrison.

HARRISON, family name of **Baron Harrison**.

HARRISON, Baron *cr* 1999 (Life Peer), of Chester in the county of Cheshire; **Lyndon Henry Arthur Harrison;** *b* 28 Sept. 1947; *s* of late Charles William Harrison and Edith (*née* Johnson); *m* 1980, Hilary Anne Plank; one *s* one *d*. *Educ:* Oxford Sch.; Univ. of Warwick (BA Hons 1970); Univ. of Sussex (MA 1971); Univ. of Keele (MA 1978). Part time Lectr, N Staffs Polytechnic, 1973–75; Research Officer, Students' Union, UMIST, 1975–78; Union Manager, NE Wales Inst. of Higher Educn, Wrexham, 1978–89. Cheshire County Councillor, 1981–90 (Chairman: Libraries and Countryside Cttee, 1982, 1984–89; Further Educn, 1984–89; Tourism, 1985–89). Dep. Chm., NW Tourist Bd, 1987–89. MEP (Lab) Cheshire W, 1989–94, Cheshire W and Wirral, 1994–99. European Parliament: Lab spokesman on monetary union, and on ASEAN and Korea, 1994–99; Vice-President: Tourism Intergp, 1995–99; Small and Med. Size Enterprises Intergp, 1995–99. Vice Chm., ACC, 1990–. Liaison Peer, NI Office, 2000–; Mem., H of L Cttee on Common Foreign and Security Policy, 2000–. *Recreations:* chess, bridge, the arts, sport. *Address:* House of Lords, SW1A 0PW.

HARRISON, (Alastair) Brian (Clarke); DL; *b* 3 Oct. 1921; *s* of late Brig. E. F. Harrison, Melbourne; *m* 1952, Elizabeth Hood Hardie, Oaklands, NSW, Aust.; one *s* one *d*. *Educ:* Geelong Grammar Sch.; Trinity Coll., Cambridge. Capt. AIF. MP (C) Maldon, Essex, 1955–Feb. 1974; Parliamentary Private Secretary to: Minister of State, Colonial Office, 1955–56; Sec. of State for War, 1956–58; Minister of Agriculture, Fisheries and Food, 1958–60. Mem. Victoria Promotion Cttee (London); Mem. One Nation Gp which published The Responsible Society, and One Europe; toured USA on ESU Ford Foundation Fellowship, 1959; Commonwealth Parliamentary Assoc. Delegations: Kenya and Horn of Africa, 1960; Gilbert and Ellice Islands, New Hebrides and British Solomon Islands Protectorate. Chm., Standing Conf. of Eastern Sport and Physical Recreation, 1974–. Organizer (with Univ. of WA), expedns to Nepal studying human physiol., 1979–87. High Sheriff, 1979, DL 1980, Essex. *Publications:* (jtly) The cumulative effect of High Altitude on Motor Performance: a comparison between caucasian visitors and native highlanders, 1985; (jtly) Entrainment of respiratory frequency to exercise rhythm during hypoxia, 1987. *Recreations:* photography, gardening. *Address:* Green Farm House, Copford, Colchester, Essex CO6 1DA. *Clubs:* Pratt's; Melbourne (Melbourne); Weld (Perth).

HARRISON, Dr (Anne) Victoria; Executive Secretary, Wolfson Foundation, since 1997; *d* of Lawrence Greggain and Amy Isabel Greggain (*née* Briggs); *m* 1967, Brian Howard Harrison, *qv*. *Educ:* Workington GS; Milham Ford Sch., Oxford; St Anne's Coll., Oxford (BA 1st Cl. Hons Animal Physiology 1965; Theodore Williams Schol. 1965; MA 1970; DPhil 1970). Exec. Editor, Internat. Abstracts of Biological Scis, 1971–72; MRC HQ Office, 1972–83, PSO, 1974; seconded to Science and Technology Secretariat, Cabinet Office, 1983–85, Dep. to Chief Scientific Advr, 1984–85; Head of Secretariat, MRC, 1985–89; Head of Policy Div., AFRC, 1989–94; Dir of Policy and Assessment,

BBSRC, 1994–97. FRSocMed 1986. *Recreations:* phoning friends from the bath, walking on Hinksey Hill. *Address:* Wolfson Foundation, 8 Queen Anne Street, W1G 9LD. *T:* (020) 7323 5730.

HARRISON, Air Vice-Marshal Anthony John, CB 1997; CBE 1992 (OBE 1986); Executive Vice-President and General Manager, Singapore, BAE SYSTEMS (formerly British Aerospace) plc, since 1998; *b* 9 Nov. 1943; *s* of Jack and Jean Harrison; *m* 1965, Glynn Dene Hyland-Smith; one *s* one *d. Educ:* Woodbridge Sch., Suffolk. Commnd RAF, 1963; Commanding Officer: 617 Sqdn (The Dambusters), 1982–85; RAF Bruggen, 1989–92; Dir, Jt Warfare, MoD, 1992–94; ACDS (Ops), MoD, 1994–97. Upper Freeman, GAPAN, 1985. Pres., Woodbridge RAF Assoc., 1994. FRAeS. *Recreations:* golf, tennis, aviation history. *Address:* BAE SYSTEMS plc, 435 Orchard Road #21–04, Wisma Atria, Singapore 238877. *Club:* Royal Air Force.

HARRISON, Brian; *see* Harrison, A. B. C.

HARRISON, Brian; *see* Harrison, F. B.

HARRISON, Prof. Brian Howard, DPhil; FRHistS; Editor, New Dictionary of National Biography, since 2000; Titular Professor of Modern History, University of Oxford, since 1996; Fellow of Corpus Christi College, Oxford, since 1967; *b* 9 July 1937; *s* of Howard Harrison and Mary Elizabeth (*née* Savill); *m* 1967, Anne Victoria Greggain (*see* A. V. Harrison). *Educ:* Merchant Taylors' Sch., Northwood; St John's Coll., Oxford (BA 1st Cl. Hons Mod. Hist. 1961; MA 1966; DPhil 1966). FRHistS 1973. Nat. Service, 2nd Lieut, Malta Signal Sqdn, 1956–58. Oxford University: Sen. Schol., St Antony's Coll., 1961–64; Jun. Res. Fellow, Nuffield Coll., 1964–67; Tutor in Modern Hist. and Pols, 1967–2000, Sen. Tutor, 1984–86 and 1988–90, Vice-Pres., 1992, 1993 and 1996–98, Corpus Christi Coll.; Univ. Reader in Modern British History, 1990–2000. Visiting Professor: Univ. of Michigan (Ann Arbor), 1970–71; Harvard Univ., 1973–74; Visiting Fellow: Melbourne Univ., 1975; ANU, 1995. *Publications:* Drink and the Victorians, 1971, 2nd edn 1994; Separate Spheres: the opposition to women's suffrage in Britain, 1978; (ed with P. Hollis) Robert Lowery: Chartist and lecturer, 1979; Peaceable Kingdom: stability and change in modern Britain, 1982; (with C. Ford) A Hundred Years Ago: Britain in the 1880s in words and photographs, 1983; Prudent Revolutionaries: portraits of British feminists between the wars, 1987; (ed and contrib.) The History of the University of Oxford, Vol. 8: The Twentieth Century, 1994; (ed) Corpuscles: a history of Corpus Christi College, Oxford, 1994; The Transformation of British Politics 1860–1995, 1996. *Recreations:* looking at architecture, listening to classical music. *Address:* Corpus Christi College, Oxford OX1 4JF. *T:* (01865) 276700.

HARRISON, Prof. Bryan Desmond, CBE 1990; PhD; FRS 1987; FRSE; Professor of Plant Virology, University of Dundee, 1991–96, now Professor Emeritus; *b* 16 June 1931; *s* of John William and Norah Harrison; *m* 1968, Elizabeth Ann Latham-Warde; two *s* one *d. Educ:* Whitgift Sch., Croydon; Reading Univ. (BSc Hons Agric. Bot. 1952); London Univ. (PhD 1955). FRSE 1979. Postgraduate student, ARC, 1952; Scottish Hort. Res. Inst., Dundee, 1954; Rothamsted Exp. Station, 1957; Head, Virology Section, 1966, Dep. Dir, 1979, Scottish Hort. Res. Inst.; Head, Virology Dept, Scottish Crop Res. Inst., 1981–91. Visiting Professor: Japan Soc. for Promotion of Science, 1970; Organization of American States, Venezuela, 1973; Hon. Prof., Univ. of St Andrews, 1986–; Hon. Vis. Prof., Univ. of Dundee, 1988–91. Pres., Assoc. of Applied Biologists, 1980–81. Life Mem., Internat. Cttee for Taxonomy of Viruses, 1997. Hon. Member: Assoc. of Applied Biologists, 1989; Soc. for Gen. Microbiol., 1990; Phytopathological Soc. of Japan, 1992; For. Associate, US Nat. Acad. of Scis, 1998. Hon. DAgrFor Univ. of Helsinki, 1990. *Publications:* Plant Virology: the principles (with A. J. Gibbs), 1976 (trans Russian and Chinese); research papers and reviews on plant viruses and virus diseases. *Recreations:* growing garden crops, foreign travel. *Address:* Scottish Crop Research Institute, Invergowrie, Dundee DD2 5DA. *T:* (01382) 562731, *Fax:* (01382) 562426.

HARRISON, Bryan James; Special Adviser, Workforce and Development, NHS Executive, since 1999; *b* 30 Oct. 1947; *s* of late James Harrison and of Doris (*née* Burnham); *m* 1st, 1973 (marr. diss. 1988); two *d*; 2nd, 1990, Valerie Mayo; one *d. Educ:* Southmoor Sch., Sunderland; Exeter Univ. (BA Politics). DHSS, 1971–81; seconded to Camden and Islington AHA, 1981–82; Dist Administrator, Islington HA, 1982–84; District General Manager: Islington HA, 1984–88; Bloomsbury HA, 1988–90; Bloomsbury and Islington HA, 1990–92; Regl Gen. Manager, NE Thames RHA, 1992–94; Chief Exec., Forest Healthcare NHS Trust, 1995–99. *Recreations:* reading, music, history, soccer. *Address:* 33 Millman Street, WC1N 3EJ. *T:* (020) 7692 3307.

HARRISON, Cameron Elias; Director of Educational Policy, Open Society Institute, Budapest, since 1998; *b* 27 Aug. 1945; *s* of Elias Harrison and Herries Harrison; *m* 1968, Pearl Leimon; one *s* one *d. Educ:* Cumnock Acad.; Strathclyde Univ. (BSc Hons Physics); Stirling Univ. (MEd). Physics Teacher, Greenock Acad., 1968–71; Head of Physics, Graeme High Sch., 1971–79; Depute Rector, Kirkcudbright Acad., 1979–82; Rector, The Gordon Schools, 1982–91; Chief Exec., Scottish Consultative Council on the Curriculum, 1991–98. Sec.-Gen., Consortium of Instns for Develt & Res. in Educn in Europe, 1993–. FRSA. *Publication:* Managing Change, 1989. *Recreations:* Rugby, walking, singing, talking, listening, teaching, learning. *Address:* Educational Policy Institute, Nador Utca 11, Budapest 1051, Hungary; Woodfield, Priormuir, St Andrews, Fife KY16 8LP; *e-mail:* ⟨harrison@osi.hu⟩.

HARRISON, Claude William, RP 1961; artist; portrait painter and painter of conversation pieces, imaginative landscapes and murals, etc; *b* Leyland, Lancs, 31 March 1922; *s* of Harold Harrison and Florence Mildred Ireton; *m* 1947, Audrey Johnson; one *s. Educ:* Hutton Grammar Sch., Lancs. Served in RAF, 1942–46. Royal Coll. of Art, 1947–49; Studio in Ambleside, 1949–52. Exhibited since 1950 at: RA; RSA; Royal Society Portrait Painters; New English Art Club, etc. Hon. RP 1990. *Publication:* The Portrait Painter's handbook, 1968. *Recreation:* painting. *Address:* Barrow Wife, Cartmel Fell, near Grange over Sands, Cumbria LA11 6NZ. *T:* (01539) 531323.

HARRISON, Sir Colin; *see* Harrison, Sir R. C.

HARRISON, Rev. Fr Crispin; *see* Harrison, Rev. Fr M. B. C.

HARRISON, Sir David, Kt 1997; CBE 1990; FREng; Fellow, since 1957, and Master, 1994–2000, Selwyn College, Cambridge; *b* 3 May 1930; *s* of Harold David Harrison and Lavinia Wilson; *m* 1962, Sheila Rachel Debes; one *s* one *d* (and one *s* decd). *Educ:* Bede Sch., Sunderland; Clacton County High Sch.; Selwyn Coll., Cambridge (1st Cl. Pts I and II Natural Sciences Tripos, BA 1953, PhD 1956, MA 1957, ScD 1979). CEng, FREng (FEng 1987); FRSC (FRIC 1961), FIChemE 1968. 2nd Lieut, REME, 1949. Cambridge University: Research student, Dept of Physical Chemistry, 1953–56; Univ. Asst Lectr in Chem. Engrg, 1956–61; Univ. Lectr, 1961–79; Sen. Tutor, Selwyn Coll., 1967–79; Mem., Council of the Senate, 1967–75; Mem., Univ. Council, 1995–2000; Dep. Vice-Chancellor, 1995–2000; Pro-Vice-Chancellor, 1997; Chm., Faculty Bd of Educn, 1976–78, of Engrg, 1994–2001; Vice-Chancellor: Univ. of Keele, 1979–84; Univ. of Exeter, 1984–94. Visiting Professor of Chemical Engineering: Univ. of Delaware, USA, 1967; Univ. of Sydney, 1976. Chm., Adv. Cttee on Safety in Nuclear Installations, 1993–99; Mem., Engineering Council, 1994–96. Hon. Editor, Trans Instn of Chemical Engrs, 1972–78; Member Council: Lancing Coll., 1970–82; Haileybury, 1974–84; St Edward's, Oxford, 1977–89; Bolton Girls' Sch., 1981–84; Shrewsbury Sch., 1983– (Chm., 1989–); Taunton Sch., 1986–89; Fellow, Woodard Corporation of Schools, 1972–94; Chairman: Bd of Trustees, Homerton Coll., Cambridge, 1979–; UCCA, 1984–91; Voluntary Sector Consultative Council, 1984–88; Southern Univs Jt Bd, 1986–88; Church and Associated Colls Adv. Cttee, PCFC, 1988–91; CVCP, 1991–93; Bd of Management, Northcott Theatre, 1984–94; Eastern Arts Bd, 1994–98 (Mem., Arts Council of England, 1996–98); Council, RSCM, 1996–; Ely Cathedral Council, 2000–. Pres., IChemE, 1991–92 (Vice-Pres., 1989–91); Dir, Salters' Inst. of Industrial Chemistry, 1993–. Mem., Marshall Aid Commemoration Commn, 1982–89. FRSA 1985; CIMgt (CBIM 1990). Freeman, City of London, 1998; Liveryman, Salters' Co., 1998. DUniv Keele, 1992; Hon. DSc Exeter, 1995. George E. Davis Medal, IChemE, 2001. *Publications:* (with J. F. Davidson) Fluidised Particles, 1963; (also with J. F. Davidson) Fluidization, 1971, rev. edn (with J. F. Davidson and R. Clift) 1985; numerous articles in scientific and technological jls. *Recreations:* music, tennis, hill walking, good food. *Address:* 7 Gough Way, Cambridge CB3 9LN. *T:* (01223) 359315. *Clubs:* Athenæum, Oxford and Cambridge; Federation House (Stoke-on-Trent).

HARRISON, Denis Byrne; Town Clerk and Chief Executive Officer, Sheffield, 1966–74; *b* 11 July 1917; *y s* of late Arthur and Priscilla Harrison; *m* 1956, Alice Marion Vickers (*d* 1989), *e d* of late Hedley Vickers. *Educ:* Birkenhead Sch.; Liverpool Univ. (LLM). Legal Associate Mem. RTPI, 1949. Articled to E. W. Tame, OBE (Town Clerk of Birkenhead); admitted Solicitor, 1939; Asst Solicitor to Birkenhead Corp., 1939. Served War, 1939–46: 75th Shropshire Yeo. (Medium Regt) RA, Combined Ops Bombardment Unit; Staff Captain at HQ of OC, Cyprus. First Asst Solicitor, Wolverhampton Co. Borough, 1946–49; Dep. Town Clerk of Co. Boroughs: Warrington, 1949–57; Bolton, 1957–63; Sheffield, 1963–66; Local Govt Ombudsman, 1974–81, and Vice-Chm., Commn for Local Admin, 1975–81. Member: Advisory Council on Noise, 1970–79; Cttee on the use of values in the public service, 1972–73. Mem. Council, 1975–82, Pro-Chancellor, 1980–82, Univ. of Sheffield. JP City of London, 1976–86. *Recreations:* reading, walking. *Address:* 2 Leicester Close, Henley-on-Thames, Oxon RG9 2LD. *T:* (01491) 572782.

HARRISON, (Desmond) Roger (Wingate); Chairman, Toynbee Hall, since 1990; Deputy Chairman, Capital Radio, 1991–2000 (Director, 1975–2000); *b* 9 April 1933; *s* of late Maj.-Gen. Desmond Harrison, CB, DSO and Kathleen Harrison (*née* Hazley); *m* 1965, Victoria Lee-Barber, MVO, *d* of Rear-Adm. John Lee-Barber, CB, DSO; three *d* (and one *s* one *d* decd). *Educ:* Rugby School; Worcester College, Oxford (MA); Harvard Univ. Business Sch. Writing freelance, principally for The Times, 1951–57; joined staff of The Times, 1957–67; The Observer: joined 1967; Dir, 1970–92; Jt Managing Dir, 1977–84; Chief Exec., 1984–87. Dir, The Oak Foundn, 1987–89. Chairman: Greater Manchester Cablevision, 1990–93; Sterling Publishing, 1993–96; Director: LWT and LWT (Holdings), 1976–94; Sableknight, 1981–; Trinity International Holdings, 1991–. Mem. Council, NPA, 1967–87. Chairman: Asylum Aid, 1991–98; Royal Acad. of Dancing, 1993–. Governor, Sadler's Wells, 1984–95. *Recreations:* theatre, country pursuits, tennis. *Address:* 35 Argyll Road, W8 7DA. *Clubs:* Beefsteak, Flyfishers', Queen's.

HARRISON, Sir Donald (Frederick Norris), Kt 1990; MD, MS, PhD; FRCS; Professor of Laryngology and Otology (University of London), 1963–90, and Dean, 1989–90, Institute of Laryngology and Otology, Gray's Inn Road, WC1, Emeritus Professor, 1990; Emeritus Surgeon, Moorfields Eye Hospital, 1991; Surgeon, Royal National Throat, Nose and Ear Hospital, 1962–90; Civilian Consultant on ENT to RN; *b* 9 March 1925; *s* of Frederick William Rees Harrison, OBE, JP, and Florence, *d* of Robert Norris, Portsmouth, Hants; *m* 1949, Audrey, *o d* of Percival Clubb, Penarth, Glam; two *d. Educ:* Newport High Sch., Mon; Guy's Hosp. MD (London) 1960; MS (London) 1959; PhD (London) 1983; FRCS 1955; FRCOphth 1993. Ho. Surg., Guy's Hosp. and Royal Gwent Hospital, Newport; Surg. Registrar, Shrewsbury Eye and Ear Hosp.; Senior Registrar, Throat and Ear Dept, Guy's Hosp.; University Reader in Laryngology, Inst. of Laryngol. and Otol. Hunterian Prof., RCS, 1962; Eramus Wilson Demonstrator, RCS, 1971. Lectures: Chevalier Jackson, 1964; Yearsley, 1972; Wilde, 1972; Litchfield, 1973; Semon, 1974; Colles, RCSI, 1977; Jobson Horne, BMA, 1979; Conacher, Toronto, 1978; Harris, USA, 1984; Putney, USA, 1985; Baker, USA, 1986; Bryce, Toronto, 1987; McBride, Edinburgh, 1987; Douglas J. Guthrie, Edinburgh, 1988; Bob Owen (first), Cardiff, 1988; Ogura, USA, 1990; Som, USA, 1991; Stirk Adams, Birmingham, 1992; Watson-Williams, Bristol, 1994. Wellcome Prof., S Africa, 1988. Master, British Acad. Conf. on ENT, 1991. W. J. Harrison Prize, RSM, 1978; Medal of Paris, 1988; Gold medal, Internat. Fedn of Oto Rhino Laryngological Socs, 1985; Gold Medal, NY Eye & Ear Alumni Assoc., 1988; Gold Medal, Joshi Meml Lecture, Indian ENT Soc., 1990; Holmgren Medal, Sweden, 1993. Mem. of Court of Examiners, RCS; Examr, NUI; External Examr, Univs of Melbourne, Southampton, Sydney, Manchester, Liverpool, Glasgow, Hong Kong, Belfast, Oxford and Cambridge; Scientific Fellow, Royal Zoological Soc. of London; FRSM (Pres., 1994–96; Pres., Sect. of Laryngology, 1984 (former Vice-Pres.); Mem. Council, Sect. of Oncology; Hon. Sec., 1987–93). Mem. Council: Brit. Assoc. of Otolaryngologists; Brit. Assoc. of Head and Neck Oncologists (Pres.). Former Chairman: Special Adv. Cttee on Human Communication; Bd Postgrad. Med. Studies, London Univ.; Pres., World Congress Laryngeal Cancer, 1994; Chm., Centennial Conf., Laryngeal Cancer, 1974; Asst Sec., Collegium Oto-Rhino-Laryngologium; Sen. Mem., Anatomical Soc. of Great Britain; Member: Cttee of Management, Institute of Cancer Research; Internat. Cttee for Cancer of Larynx; Chm., NE Thames Region Postgrad. Cttee. Editorial Board: Acta Otolaryngologica; Practica Oto-Rhino-Laryngologica; Annals of Oto-Rhino-Laryngology; Excerpta Medica (Sect. II); Otolaryngological Digest. Hon. Fellow: Acad. ENT, America, 1976; Triol. Soc., USA, 1977; Amer. Laryngol Assoc., 1979; Hon. FRACS 1977; Hon. FRCSE 1981; Hon. FCSSA 1988; Hon. FACS 1990; Hon. FRSocMed 1991; Hon. FRCSI 1991; Hon. FACR 1995. Hon. Member: NZ ENT Soc.; Jamaican ENT Soc.; Polish ENT Soc.; Egyptian ENT Soc.; Otolaryngological Soc., Australia; Yugoslavian ENT Soc.; Spanish ENT Soc.; Philippine ENT Soc.; Hong Kong ENT Soc.; For. Mem., Internat. Broncho-œsophagological Soc.; Corresp. Member: Amer. Head and Neck Soc.; Soc. Française d'Otorhinolaryngologie; Otolaryngological Soc., Denmark; Amer. Acad. of Facial Plastic Reconstr. Surgery; Pacific Coast Oto-Ophthalmological Soc.; Amer. Laryngological Soc.; Yeoman, Soc. of Apothecaries. *Publications:* (ed jtly) Scientific Basis of Otolaryngology, 1976; Dilemmas in ENT, 1990; Neoplasms of the Upper Jaw, 1993; Comparative Anatomy of Mammalian Larynx, 1995; Sir Felix Semon: Victorian laryngologist (1849–1921), 2000; articles on familial hæmorrhagic telangiectases, meatal oseomata, cancer chemotherapy, head and neck surgery in learned jls; chapters in text books on ent. and gen. surgery. *Recreations:* heraldry, radio control models. *Address:* Springfield, 6 Fisher's Farm, Horley, Surrey RH6 9DQ. *T:* (01293) 784307.

HARRISON, Edward Peter Graham, (Ted), PhD; broadcaster, television producer, writer and cartoonist; *b* 14 April 1948; *s* of Rev. Peter Harrison and Joan Harrison; *m* 1968, Helen Grace Waters; one *s* one *d. Educ:* Grenville Coll., Bideford, Devon; University of Kent at Canterbury (PhD 1998). Graduate trainee, Kent Messenger, 1968–72; Reporter: Morgan-Grampian Magazines, 1972; Southern Television, 1970–73; BBC World Service, Radio 4 You and Yours, 1972–80; BBC Radio 4 Sunday, 1972–; BBC TV Scotland Current Account, 1981–83; Presenter and Reporter, BBC Radio Scotland News and Current Affairs, 1980–85; Reporter: BBC Radio 4 World Tonight, 1981–83; BBC Radio 4 World at One and PM, 1983–87; Presenter: Radio 4 Opinions, 1986–87; Radio 4 Sunday, 1986–88 and Soundings, 1985–88; ITV series The Human Factor, 1986–92; Channel 4 series on Lambeth Conf., 1988; BBC Religious Affairs Corresp., 1988–89; presenter, Does He Take Sugar?, Radio 4, 1991–95. Director: Pilgrim Productions, 1992–; UnstAnimation Studio, 2000–. Contested (L) gen. elections: Bexley, 1970; Maidstone, Feb. 1974. London exhibition of caricatures, 1977; exhibition of watercolours, Oxford, Canterbury, 1981. *Publications:* Modern Elizabethans, 1977; (jtly) McIndoe's Army, 1978; Marks of the Cross, 1981; Commissioner Catherine, 1983; Much Beloved Daughter, 1984; The Durham Phenomenon, 1985; Living with kidney failure, 1990; Kriss Akabusi — on track, 1991; The Elvis People, 1992; Members Only, 1994; Stigmata: a medieval mystery for a modern age, 1994; Letters to a friend I never knew, 1995; Disability: rights and wrongs, 1995; Tanni, 1996; Defender of the Faith, 1996; Diana: icon and sacrifice, 1998; Beyond Dying, 2000. *Recreation:* drawing caricatures of friends and foes. *Club:* Athenæum.

HARRISON, Sir Ernest (Thomas), Kt 1981; OBE 1972; FCA; Chairman, Racal Electronics Plc, 1966–2000 (Chief Executive, 1966–92); Director, Camelot Group plc, 1993–2000; *b* 11 May 1926; *s* of late Ernest Horace Harrison and Gertrude Rebecca Gibbons Harrison; *m* 1960, Phyllis Brenda Knight (Janie); three *s* two *d. Educ:* Trinity Grammar Sch., Wood Green, London. Qualified as Chartered Accountant, 1950; served Articles with Harker Holloway & Co.; joined Racal Electronics as Secretary and Chief Accountant, when company commenced manufacturing, 1951; Director, 1958, Dep. Man. Dir, 1961. Chairman: Racal Telecom, then Vodafone Gp, Plc, 1988–98; Chubb Security, 1992–97. Active in National Savings movement, 1964–76, for which services awarded OBE. Chm., Ronald Raven Chair in Clinical Oncology Trust, 1991–. Mem., Jockey Club, 1990–. Mem., RSA. Liveryman, Scriveners' Co. CompIERE 1975; CIMgt (CBIM 1976); CompIEE 1978. Sch. Fellowship, Royal Free Hosp. Sch. of Medicine, 1995. Hon. FCGI 1990; Hon. FREng (Hon. FEng 1997). Hon. DSc: Cranfield, 1981; City, 1982; DUniv: Surrey, 1981; Edinburgh, 1983. Businessman of the Year, 1981; Founding Society's Centenary Award, ICA, 1990; Mountbatten Medal, Nat. Electronic Council, 1992. *Recreations:* horse racing (owner), gardening, wild life, sport, espec. soccer.

HARRISON, Sir Francis Alexander Lyle, (Sir Frank), Kt 1974; MBE 1943; DL; QC (NI); President, Lands Tribunal for Northern Ireland, 1964–83; District Electoral Areas Commissioner, 1984; *b* 19 March 1910; *s* of Rev. Alexander Lyle Harrison and Mary Luise (*née* Henderson), Rostrevor, Co. Down; *m* 1940, Norah Patricia (*née* Rea) (*d* 1999); two *d. Educ:* Campbell Coll., Belfast; Trinity Coll., Dublin. BA (Moderator in Legal Sci.), LLB (Hons). Called to Bar of NI, 1937, Bencher, 1961. Served War: commissioned Gen. List, Oct. 1939; ADC to GOC, NI, 1939–40; Major, Dep. Asst Adjt-Gen., HQ, NI, 1941–45 (MBE). Apptd to determine Industrial Assurance disputes in NI, 1946–62; Counsel to Attorney-Gen., NI, 1946–48; KC 1948. Legal Adviser to Min. of Home Affairs, 1949–61, Sen. Crown Prosecutor, Co. Fermanagh, 1948–54; subseq. for Counties Tyrone, Londonderry and Antrim, 1954–64; Chm., Mental Health Review Tribunal, 1948–64; Counsel to the Speakers of House of Commons and Senate of NI, 1953–64; Mem. Statute Law Cttee, NI, 1953–64; Chm., Advisory Cttee under Civil Authorities Special Powers Acts (NI), 1957–62; Chm., Shaftesbury Sq. HMC, 1964–73; Founder Mem., NI Assoc. of Mental Health, 1959. Boundary Comr under Local Govt (Boundaries) Act (NI), 1971 and 1982–84. DL Co. Down, 1973. *Publications:* Report of Working Party on Drug Dependence, 1968; Recommendations as to Local Government Boundaries and Wards in Northern Ireland, 1972, 1984; Recommendations as to District Electoral Areas in Northern Ireland, 1985. *Recreations:* hybridisation of narcissi, country pursuits, social service. *Address:* Ballydorn Hill, Killinchy, Newtownards, Co. Down, Northern Ireland BT23 6QB. *T:* (028) 9754 1250.

HARRISON, Francis Anthony Kitchener; *b* 28 Aug. 1914; *s* of late Fred Harrison, Headmaster of Newcastle High Sch., Staffs, and Mrs M. M. Harrison (*née* Mitchell); *m* 1955, Sheila Noëlle, *d* of late Lt-Col N. D. Stevenson and of Lady Nye; three *s* one *d. Educ:* Winchester; New Coll., Oxford. Asst Principal, India Office, Nov. 1937; 1st Sec., UK High Commn, New Delhi, 1949–51; Commonwealth Relations Office, 1951–56; Asst Sec., 1954; Dep. High Comr for the UK at Peshawar, 1956–59; Asst Sec., CRO, 1959–61; British Dep. High Comr, New Zealand, 1961–64; Asst Sec., Cabinet Office, 1965–67; Asst Dir, Civil Service Selection Bd, 1967–79. *Recreations:* reading, writing. *Address:* Lea Farm, Bramley, near Guildford, Surrey GU5 0LR. *T:* (01483) 893138.

HARRISON, Sir Frank; *see* Harrison, Sir Francis A. L.

HARRISON, (Fred) Brian, CBE 1982; FCA; *b* 6 March 1927; *s* of Fred Harrison and Annie Harrison; *m* 1950, Margaret Owen (*d* 1995); two *s. Educ:* Burnley Grammar Sch. FCA 1960 (ACA 1950). East Midlands Div., NCB, 1953–67 (Chief Accountant, No 1 Area, 1962–67); Chief Accountant, N Derbyshire Area, NCB, 1967–68; Finance Dir, Coal Products Div., NCB, 1968–71; Dep. Man. Dir, Coal Products Div., NCB, subseq. Dep. Chief Exec., NCB (Coal Products) Ltd, 1971–76, Chm., 1978–83. Mem., NCB, 1976–85. Chm., British Investment Trust, 1978–85. Master, Chartered Accountants' Co., 1994–95; Mem., Ct of Assistants, Fuellers' Co., 1996– (Master, 2000–01). *Recreations:* music, theatre. *Address:* 11 Hillcrest, King Harry Lane, St Albans, Herts AL3 4AT. *T:* (01727) 46938.

HARRISON, George, MBE 1965; musician, composer, film producer; *b* 25 Feb. 1943; *s* of Harold and Louise Harrison; *m* 1966, Patricia Ann Boyd (marr. diss. 1977); *m* 1978, Olivia Arias; one *s.* Member: The Rebels, 1956–58; The Quarrymen, 1958–60; The Beatles, 1960–70; Traveling Wilburys, 1987–90; solo performer, 1970–; *songs* composed include: (Beatles songs): Blue Jay Way; I Want To Tell You; Taxman; Here Comes the Sun; Something; Within You Without You; (solo): My Sweet Lord; Give Me Love (Give Me Peace On Earth); Bangladesh; Dark Horse; Living in the Material World; All Those Years Ago; Mind Set On You; *films* (performer, with The Beatles): A Hard Day's Night, 1964; Help!, 1965; Magical Mystery Tour (TV film), 1967; Yellow Submarine, 1968; Let It Be, 1970. Jt Founder, Handmade Films; *films* produced include: Life of Brian, 1979; Time Bandits, 1981; The Missionary, 1982; Privates on Parade, 1984; A Private Function, 1985; Mona Lisa, 1986; Withnail and I, 1987. *Publications:* (ed) Raga Mala: the autobiography of Ravi Shankar, 1999; (with Sir Paul McCartney and Ringo Starr) The Beatles Anthology, 2000. *Address:* Harrisongs Ltd, PO Box 16115, SW3 1ZL.

HARRISON, (George) Michael (Antony), CBE 1980; Chief Education Officer, City of Sheffield, 1967–85; *b* 7 April 1925; *s* of George and Kathleen Harrison; *m* 1951, Pauline (*née* Roberts); two *s* one *d. Educ:* Manchester Grammar Sch.; Brasenose Coll., Oxford. MA (LitHum); DipEd. Military service, Lieut, Parachute Regt, 1947. Asst Master, Bedford Modern Sch., 1951–53; Admin. Asst, W Riding CC, Education Dept, 1953–55; Asst Educn Officer, Cumberland CC Educn Dept, 1955–64; Dep. Educn Officer, Sheffield, 1965–67. Advr, Educn and NVQ Programmes, Dept of Employment, 1985–96. Hon. Research Fellow, Leeds Univ., 1985–89; Associate Prof., Sheffield Univ., 1991–95. Member various cttees, incl.: Taylor Cttee of Enquiry on Govt in Schools, 1975–77; UK Nat. Commn for Unesco Educn Adv. Cttee, 1977–83; Yorkshire and Humberside Econ. Planning Council, 1978–79; Technician Educn Council, 1979–83; Engineering Council, 1982–87; Board, Nat. Adv. Body on Local Authority Higher Educn, 1981–83. Pres., Soc. of Educn Officers, 1976; Vice-Pres., Standing Conf. on Schools' Science and Technology, 1980– (Chm. 1975–79). Vice-Pres., St William's Foundn, York, 1998–. Hon. LLD Sheffield, 1988. *Recreation:* foreign travel. *Address:* Keeper's Cottage, Rigmaden Court, Mansergh, Carnforth, Lancs LA6 2ET. *T:* (015242) 76335.

HARRISON, Maj.-Gen. Ian Stewart, CB 1970; Captain of Deal Castle, since 1980; *b* 25 May 1919; *s* of Leslie George Harrison and Evelyn Simpson Christie; *m* 1942, Winifred Raikes Stavert; one *s* one *d. Educ:* St Albans Sch. Commissioned, Royal Marines, 1937; service at sea, in Norway, Middle East, Sicily, BAOR, 1939–45; Staff Coll., Camberley (student), 1948; HQ 3rd Commando Bde, 1949–51 (despatches); Staff of Comdt-Gen., RM, 1951–52; Staff Coll., Camberley (Directing Staff), 1953–55; Commandant, RM Signal Sch., 1956–58; Joint Services Staff Coll. (Student), 1958; CO 40 Commando, RM, 1959–61; Dir, Royal Marines Reserves, 1962; Staff of Comdt-Gen., RM, 1963–64; Joint Warfare Estabt, 1965–67; British Defence Staff, Washington, DC, 1967–68; Chief of Staff to Comdt-Gen., RM, 1968–70, retired. ADC to HM the Queen, 1967–68. Representative Col Comdt, Royal Marines, 1981–82. Dir-Gen. British Food Export Council, 1970–77; Dir, British Consultants Bureau, 1977–87. Chm., Chichester Festivities, 1979–89. Governor, E. Hayes Dashwood Foundn, 1977–99. *Recreations:* sailing, real tennis, golf. *Address:* Manor Cottage, Runcton, Chichester, W Sussex PO20 6PU. *T:* (01243) 785480. *Clubs:* Army and Navy; Royal Yacht Squadron, Royal Naval Sailing Association, Royal Marines Sailing (Commodore, 1968–70); Royal St George's Golf.

HARRISON, Jessel Anidjah; President, Slimma Group Holdings Ltd, retired 1989; *b* 28 May 1923; *s* of Samuel Harrison and Esta (*née* Romain); *m* 1st, 1943, Irene (*née* Olsberg) (marr. diss. 1956); one *s* one *d*; 2nd, 1961, Doreen Leigh. *Educ:* Vernon House Preparatory Sch.; Brondesbury Coll.; Macauley Coll., Cuckfield, Sussex. Chairman: Slimma Ltd, 1964; Slimma (Wales) Ltd, 1971; Emu Wool Industries, later Slimma Gp Hldgs, 1973; Dir, Tootals Clothing Div., 1977–89. Member: European Trade Cttee, 1975–; Clothing Industry Productivity Resources Agency, 1978–85; British Overseas Trade Adv. Council, 1978–85. Vice Pres., Clothing Export Council of Great Britain, 1977 (Chm., 1973); Chm., British Overseas Trade Group for Israel, 1978–83, Vice-Pres., 1987–. Pres., Clothing Institute, 1978. *Recreations:* golf, walking. *Address:* 113 Abbotsbury Road, W14 8EP. *T:* (020) 7603 7468. *Club:* Royal Automobile.

HARRISON, Surgeon Vice-Adm. Sir John (Albert Bews), KBE 1982; FRCP, FRCR; Medical Director General (Naval), 1980–83; *b* 20 May 1921; *s* of late Albert William Harrison and Lilian Eda Bews, Dover, Kent; *m* 1943, Jane (*née* Harris) (*d* 1988); two *s. Educ:* Queens' Coll., Cambridge; St Bartholomew's Hosp. RN 1947–83: served: RM Infirmary, Deal, 1948; HMS Sparrow, Amer. WI stn, 1949; RN Hosp., Plymouth, 1951; HMS Ganges, 1952; Admiralty Med. Bd and St Bartholomew's Hosp., 1953; RN Hosps, Hong Kong, 1955, Chatham, 1958, Haslar, 1959; St Bart's and Middlesex Hosps, 1961; RN Hosps Malta, 1962, Haslar, 1964–75; Adviser in Radiol., 1967–79; Dep. Med. Dir Gen. and Dir Med. Personnel and Logistics, 1975–77; Dean of Naval Medicine and Surgeon Rear-Adm., Inst. of Naval Medicine, 1977–80. Mem., Council for Med. Postgrad. Educn of Eng. and Wales, 1977–79. Pres., Section of Radiology, RSM, 1984–85. Fellow: RSM; MedSocLond (Pres. 1985–86). CStJ 1983. QHP 1976–83. *Publications:* Hyperbaric Osteonecrosis et al, 1975; articles in med. press on sarcoidosis, tomography, middle ear disease, and dysbaric osteonecrosis. *Recreations:* fishing, cricket, countryman. *Address:* Alexandra Cottage, Swanmore, Hampshire SO3 2PB. *Club:* MCC.

HARRISON, John Clive, LVO 1971; HM Diplomatic Service, retired; High Commissioner, Mauritius, 1993–97; *b* 12 July 1937; *s* of Sir Geoffrey Harrison, GCMG, KCVO; *m* 1967, Jennifer Heather Burston; one *s* two *d. Educ:* Winchester Coll.; Jesus Coll., Oxford. BA. Entered Foreign Office, 1960; Rangoon, 1961; Vientiane, 1964; FO, 1964; Second, later First, Sec. (Information), Addis Ababa, 1967; Ankara, 1971; seconded to Cabinet Office, 1973; First Sec., FCO, 1976; First Sec., Head of Chancery and Consul, Luxembourg, 1978; Counsellor and Head of Chancery, Lagos, 1981–84; Counsellor, attached to Protocol Dept, FCO, 1984; Hd of Consular Dept, FCO, 1985–89; Dep. High Comr, Islamabad, 1989–93. *Recreations:* gardening, tennis, golf, family holidays. *Address:* Wymering, Sheet Common, Petersfield, Hants GU31 5AT. *Clubs:* Royal Over-Seas League; Petersfield Golf.

HARRISON, Prof. John Fletcher Clews, PhD; Emeritus Professor of History, University of Sussex, since 1985 (Professor of History, 1970–82; Hon. Professor of History, 1982–85); *b* 28 Feb. 1921; *s* of William Harrison and Mary (*née* Fletcher); *m* 1945, Margaret Ruth Marsh; one *s* one *d. Educ:* City Boys' Sch., Leicester; Selwyn Coll., Cambridge (Schol. and Prizeman; Goldsmiths' Open Exhibnr in History, BA 1st Cl. Hons 1942, MA 1946); PhD Leeds. Served Army, 1941–45 (overseas 1942–45): commnd, Leics Regt and seconded to KAR, 1942; Captain and Adjt, 17th Bn, KAR, 1943–44; Staff Captain, GSOIII, E Africa Comd, 1944–45. Lectr, Dept of Adult Educn and Extra-Mural Studies, Univ. of Leeds, 1947–58; Dep. Dir, Extra-Mural Studies and Dep. Head of Dept, Univ. of Leeds, 1958–61; Prof. of History, Univ. of Wisconsin, USA, 1961–70. Research and teaching (Fulbright Award), Univ. of Wisconsin, 1957–58; Faculty Res. Fellow, SSRC, USA, 1963–64; Vis. Professorial Res. Fellow, ANU, 1968–69 and 1977; Res. Fellow, Harvard Univ., 1972–73; Social Sci. Res. Fellow, Nuffield Foundn, 1975; Vice-Chancellor's Cttee Visitor, NZ, 1977; Herbert F. Johnson Res. Prof., Univ. of Wisconsin, 1977–78; Hon. Prof. of History, Warwick Univ., 1987–92. Vice-Pres., Soc. for Study of Labour History, 1984– (Sec., 1960–61; Chm., 1974–81); Mem., Adv. and Editorial Bds, Victorian Studies, 1963–. Hon. Mem., Phi Beta Kappa, Wisconsin, 1978. *Publications:* A History of the Working Men's College 1854–1954, 1954; Social Reform in Victorian Leeds: The Work of James Hole 1820–1895, 1954; Learning and Living 1790–1960: A Study in the History of the English Adult Education Movement, 1961, Toronto 1961; ed, Society and Politics in England 1780 1960, NY 1965; ed, Utopianism and Education: Robert Owen and the Owenites, NY 1968; Quest for the New Moral World: Robert Owen and the Owenites in Britain and America, 1969, NY 1969 (Walter D. Love Meml Prize, USA, 1969); The Early Victorians 1832–1851, 1971, NY 1971; The Birth and Growth of Industrial England 1714–1867, 1973; ed, Eminently Victorian, BBC 1974; (with Dorothy Thompson) Bibliography of the Chartist Movement 1837–1976, 1978; The Second Coming: Popular Millenarianism 1780–1850, 1979, NJ 1979; The Common People, 1984; Late Victorian Britain 1875–1901, 1990; Scholarship Boy: a personal history of the mid-twentieth century, 1995; *festschriften:* New Views of Co-operation, ed S. Yeo, 1988; Living and Learning, ed I. Dyck and M. Chase, 1996; articles and reviews in

Victorian Studies, TLS and usual academic history jls. *Recreations:* walking, gardening, book collecting. *Address:* Mill Cottage, Sandford Mill Close, Cheltenham, Glos GL53 7QZ. *T:* (01242) 510205.

HARRISON, Hon. Sir (John) Richard, Kt 1980; ED; grape grower; *b* 23 May 1921; *s* of William Harrison and Jean (*née* Bell); *m* 1948, Margaret Kelly; three *s* one *d*. *Educ:* Wanganui Collegiate Sch.; Canterbury University Coll. (BA). CO, Hawke's Bay Regt, 1956–59. MP (Nat) for Hawke's Bay, 1963–84; Govt Whip, 1970–71; Opposition Whip, 1974–75; Chm. of Cttees, 1972, 1976–77; Speaker, House of Representatives, 1978–84. Pres., Commonwealth Parly Assoc., 1978–79. Pres., Nat. Soc. on Alcoholism and Drug Dependence, 1986–89; Patron, Prison Fellowship, NZ, 1988–. *Recreations:* gardening, classical music. *Address:* Springfield, RD2, Takapau, New Zealand.

HARRISON, Kenneth Cecil, OBE 1980 (MBE mil. 1946); FLA; City Librarian, Westminster, 1961–80, retired; Consultant Librarian, Ranfurly Library Service, 1983–90; *b* 29 April 1915; *s* of Thomas and Annie Harrison; *m* 1941, Doris Taylor; two *s*. *Educ:* Grammar Sch., Hyde. Asst, Hyde Public Library, 1931–37; Branch Librarian, Coulsdon and Purley Public Libraries, 1937–39; Borough Librarian: Hyde, 1939–47; Hove (also Curator), 1947–50; Eastbourne, 1950–58; Hendon, 1958–61. HM Forces, 1940–46; commnd RMC Sandhurst, 1942; served with E Yorks Regt in Middle East, Sicily and NW Europe (wounded, 1944; Major 1944–46). President: Library Assoc., 1973; Commonwealth Library Assoc., 1972–75 (Exec. Sec., 1980–83); Vice-President: Internat. Assoc. Metropolitan Libraries; Westminster Arts Council (Hon. Sec. 1965–80). Member: IFLA Public Libraries Cttee, 1969–81; Central Music Library Council, 1961–80; Library Assoc. Council, 1953–79; MCC Arts and Library Cttee, 1973–89; Westminster Abbey Liby Cttee, 1973–80; Chm. Jt Organising Cttee for Nat. Library Week, 1964–69. British Council: Cultural Exchange Scholar to Romania, 1971; Mem., Library Adv. Panel, 1974–80; Consultant to Sri Lanka, 1974, to India, 1981. UNESCO Consultant to the Seychelles and Mauritius, 1977–78; Commonwealth Relations Trust Consultant to Ghana, Sierra Leone and The Gambia, 1979; Library Consultant, Bermuda, 1983. Sec., Assoc. of Past Rotarians, 1996–99; Pres., Past Rotarians Club of Eastbourne, 2000–01. Commonwealth Foundn Scholar, E and Central Africa, 1975. C. C. Williamson Meml Lectr, Nashville, Tenn, 1969. Governor, Westminster College, 1962–80. Editor, The Library World, 1961–71. Knight, First Class, Order of the Lion (Finland), 1976. *Publications:* First Steps in Librarianship, 1950, 5th edn 1980; Libraries in Scandinavia, 1961, 2nd edn 1969; The Library and the Community, 1963, 3rd edn 1977; Public Libraries Today, 1963; Facts at your Fingertips, 1964, 2nd edn 1966; British Public Library Buildings (with S. G. Berriman), 1966; Libraries in Britain, 1968; Public Relations for Librarians, 1973, 2nd edn 1982; International Librarianship, 1989; A Librarian's Odyssey, 2000; *edited:* Prospects for British Librarianship, 1976; Public Library Policy, 1981; Public Library Buildings 1975–83, 1987; Library Buildings 1984–89, 1990; contribs to many British and foreign jls and encyclopædias. *Recreations:* reading, writing, travel, wine, cricket, crosswords. *Address:* 5 Tavistock, Devonshire Place, Eastbourne, E Sussex BN21 4AG. *T:* (01323) 726747; *e-mail:* kch@mistral.co.uk. *Clubs:* Royal Commonwealth Society, MCC.

HARRISON, Michael; *see* Harrison, G. M. A.

HARRISON, Dr Michael; JP; Chairman and Medical Director, Midlands Health Consultancy Network Ltd, since 1996; *b* 1 March 1939; *s* of Frank Harrison and Ruby Wilhelmina (*née* Proctor); *m* 1962, Ann Haiser; two *d*. *Educ:* Leamington Coll.; Univ. of London (St Mary's Hosp.) (MB BS, BA). LRCP, MRCS, DPH, FFPHM, MHSM, FRSH. Hosp. med. appts, 1964–66; health MO appts, 1966–70; Birmingham RHB, 1971–74; specialist in community medicine, W Midlands RHA, 1974–76; Area MO, Sandwell AHA, 1976–83; Dist MO, 1983–88, Dist Gen. Manager, 1985–88, Sandwell HA; Sen. Clinical Lectr, Univ. of Birmingham, 1988; Regl Dir of Public Health and Regl MO, 1988–93, Exec. Dir, 1990–94, Dep. Chief Exec., 1993–94, West Midlands RHA. Cons. Advr, WHO, 1989. Pres., Assoc. for Industrial Archaeology, 1998. Pres., Droitwich Spa Saltway Rotary Club. FIMgt. SBStJ. JP Birmingham, 1980. *Recreations:* sailing, photography, industrial archaeology. *Address:* 19 Sandles Close, Droitwich Spa, Worcs WR9 8RB. *T:* (01905) 798308.

HARRISON, Michael Anthony; Director, Kettle's Yard, University of Cambridge, since 1992; *b* 30 April 1947; *s* of William Harrison and Gweneth Harrison (*née* Cooke); *m* 1973, Marie-Claude Bouquet; three *s* one *d*. *Educ:* Newcastle Royal GS; Aylesbury GS; Oxford Coll. of Tech.; Univ. of Nottingham (BA Hons Fine Art/Art Hist.). Arts Council: Regl Art Officer, 1971–73; Exhibn Organiser, 1973–77; Asst Dir for Regl Exhibns, Arts Council, 1977–88, South Bank Centre, 1988–90; Head of Fine Art, Winchester Sch. of Art, 1990–92. *Publications:* numerous exhibn catalogues. *Recreations:* books, cinema, music, more art. *Address:* Kettle's Yard, Castle Street, Cambridge CB3 0AQ. *T:* (01223) 352124.

HARRISON, Rev. Fr (Michael Burt) Crispin, CR; Superior of the Community of the Resurrection, Mirfield, since 1998; *b* 26 April 1936. *Educ:* Univ. of Leeds (BA Phil. with Hist. 1959); Trinity Coll., Oxford (BA Theol. 1962; MA 1966); Coll. of the Resurrection, Mirfield. Ordained deacon, 1963; priest, 1964; Curate: St Aidan, W Hartlepool, 1963–64; All Saints, Middlesbrough, 1964–66; licensed to officiate, Dio. Wakefield, 1966–69, 1978–87 and 1998–; professed, CR, 1968; Tutor, St Peter's Coll. and Lectr, Federal Theol Seminary, S Africa, 1970–77; Tutor, Coll. of the Resurrection, 1978–84, Vice-Principal, 1984–87; Provincial and Prior, St Peter's Priory, Johannesburg, 1987–97; Canon Theologian, Dio. of Christ the King, S Africa, 1990–97. *Address:* House of the Resurrection, Mirfield, W Yorks WF14 0BN. *T:* (01924) 483301.

HARRISON, Hon. Sir Michael (Guy Vicat), Kt 1993; **Hon. Mr Justice Harrison;** a Judge of the High Court of Justice, Queen's Bench Division, since 1993; *b* 28 Sept. 1939; *s* of late Hugh Francis Guy Harrison and Elizabeth Alban Harrison (*née* Jones); *m* 1966, Judith (*née* Gist); one *s* one *d*. *Educ:* Charterhouse; Trinity Hall, Cambridge (MA). Called to the Bar, Gray's Inn, 1965, Bencher, 1993; QC 1983; a Recorder, 1989–93. Dep. Chm., Parly Boundary Commn for England, 1996– (Asst Comr, 1981–93). Chm., Panel for Examination of Structure Plans, Somerset, 1981, Isles of Scilly, 1982, W Sussex, 1986. *Recreations:* tennis, sailing, fishing. *Address:* Royal Courts of Justice, Strand, WC2A 2LL.

HARRISON, Prof. Michael Jackson; Vice-Chancellor, University of Wolverhampton, 1992–98 (Director, Wolverhampton Polytechnic (formerly The Polytechnic, Wolverhampton), 1985–92); *b* 18 Dec. 1941; *s* of Jackson Harrison and Norah (*née* Lees); *m* 1974, Marie Ghislaine Félix. *Educ:* Guildford Tech. Coll.; Univ. of Leicester (BA, MA). Lecturer in Sociology: Enfield Coll. of Technol., 1966–67; Univ. of Leeds, 1967–68; Sen. Lectr, Enfield Coll. of Technol., 1968–72; Principal Lectr, Sheffield City Polytechnic, 1972–76; Head of Dept, Hull Coll. of Higher Educn, 1976–81; Asst Dir, 1982–84, Dep. Dir, 1985, The Polytechnic, Wolverhampton. Vis. Lectr, Univ. of Oregon, 1971. Governor: Bilston Community Coll.; Thomas Telford CTC. FIMgt (FBIM 1983). *Publications:* (jtly) A Sociology of Industrialisation, 1978; contribs to learned jls. *Recreations:* cinema, travelling, music. *Address:* 34 Mount Road, Penn, Wolverhampton WV4 5SW. *T:* (01902) 338807.

HARRISON, Sir Michael James Harwood, 2nd Bt *cr* 1961, of Bugbrooke; JP; Director of private companies; *b* 28 March 1936; *s* of Sir (James) Harwood Harrison, 1st Bt, TD, MP (C) Eye, Suffolk 1951–79, and Peggy Alberta Mary (*d* 1993), *d* of late Lt-Col V. D. Stenhouse, TD; *S* father, 1980; *m* 1967, Rosamund Louise, *d* of Edward Clive; two *s* two *d*. *Educ:* Rugby. Served with 17th/21st Lancers, 1955–56. Member of Lloyd's. Mem. Council, Sail Training Assoc.; Vice-Pres., Assoc. of Combined Youth Clubs. Patron and Lord of the Manor, Bugbrooke, Northampton, 1980–. Master, Mercers' Co., 1986–87; Freeman of the City of London. JP London, 1993. *Recreations:* sailing, ski-ing, riding (horse and bicycle), Daily Telegraph crossword. *Heir:* *s* Edwin Michael Harwood Harrison, *b* 29 May 1981. *Address:* 35 Paultons Square, SW3 5DT. *T:* (020) 7352 1760. *Clubs:* Boodle's, MCC; Aldeburgh Yacht.

HARRISON, Mrs Molly, MBE 1967; Curator, Geffrye Museum, 1941–69; *b* Stevenage, 23 Sept. 1909; *d* of late Ethel and late Ernest Charles Hodgett; *m* 1940, Gordon Frederick Harrison; three *d*. *Educ:* Friends Sch., Saffron Walden; Convent in Belgium; Sorbonne. Teaching in various schs, 1934–39; Asst to Curator, Geffrye Museum, 1939–41. FMA 1952; Member: Council Museums Assoc., 1953–56; Council of Industrial Design, 1958–61; Cttee of Management, Society of Authors, 1967. Lectr on varied educational topics. FRSA 1968. Editor, Local Search Series, 1969–77. *Publications:* Museum Adventure, 1950; Picture Source Books for Social History, 1951, 1953, 1955, 1957, 1958, 1960 and 1966; Furniture, 1953; Learning out of School, 1954; Food, 1954; Homes, 1960; Children in History, 1958, 1959, 1960, 1961; Your Book of Furniture, 1960; Shops and Shopping, 1963; How They Lived, 1963; Changing Museums, 1967; Hairstyles and Hairdressing, 1968; The English Home, 1969; People and Furniture, 1971; The Kitchen in History, 1972; Homes, 1973; Museums and Galleries, 1973; On Location: Museums, 1974; People and Shopping, 1975; Home Inventions, 1975; Homes in Britain, 1975; Markets and Shops, 1979; Growing Up in Victorian Times, 1980; Homes in History, 1983; The Story of Travelling (4 vols), 1983, 1984; numerous articles and reviews. *Recreations:* reading, gardening. *Address:* New Place, High Street, Whitchurch-on-Thames, Oxon RG8 7ET. *T:* (0118) 984 3736.

HARRISON, Patricia Mary, DCNZM 2001; QSO 1987; Member, Otago Regional Council, since 1996; *b* 6 Sept. 1932; *d* of Hugh and Catherine Thomson; *m* 1957, Arthur Keith Harrison; one *s* two *d*. *Educ:* Otago Girls' High Sch.; Dunedin Teachers' Coll.; Otago Univ. (MA Hons Philosophy; James Clark Meml Prize in Philosophy 1955). Hd of English, Burnside High Sch., 1973–75; Principal, Queen's High Sch., Dunedin, 1975–94. Chm., Otago Youth Wellness Trust, 1996–. Chm., Otago Regl Access Employment Council, 1985–87. Mem. Council, Univ. of Otago, 1985–96. Board Member: YWCA, 1970–80; Southern Th. Trust, 1987–90. Commemoration Medal (NZ), 1990; Suffrage Medal (NZ), 1993. *Publication:* Magic, Myth and Legends: a supplementary English text, 1974. *Recreations:* gardening, bridge, walking. *Address:* 31 Gladstone Road, Dalmore, Dunedin North, New Zealand. *T:* (3) 4738606.

HARRISON, Patrick Kennard, CBE 1982; Director, Building Museum Project, 1990–97; *b* 8 July 1928; *e s* of late Richard Harrison and Sheila Griffin; *m* 1955, Mary Wilson, *y d* of late Captain G. C. C. Damant, CBE, RN; one *d*. *Educ:* Lord Williams's Sch., Thame; Downing Coll., Cambridge (Exhbnr in English). Asst Principal, Dept of Health for Scotland, 1953; Private Sec. to Deptl Sec. and to Parly Secs, Scottish Office, 1958–60; Principal, Scottish Develt Dept and Regional Develt Div., Scottish Office, 1960–68; Sec., RIBA, 1968–87. Hon. Mem., Amer. Inst. of Architects, 1978. Hon. FRIAS, 1987; Hon. FRIBA, 1988. *Address:* 28B Moray Place, Edinburgh EH3 6BX. *T:* (0131) 225 5342; Upper Stewarton, Eddleston, Peebles EH45 8PP. *T:* (01721) 730602. *Clubs:* Reform; New (Edinburgh).

HARRISON, Prof. Paul Jeffrey; Professor of Psychiatry, University of Oxford, since 2000; Fellow, Wolfson College, Oxford, since 1997; *b* 18 Oct. 1960; *s* of Walford John Harrison and Bridget Ann Harrison; *m* 1984, Sandra Hallett; three *d*. *Educ:* City of London Sch.; Balliol Coll., Oxford (BA 1982; BM BCh 1985; MA 1987); DM Oxon 1991; MRCPsych 1989. MRC Teaching Fellow, St Mary's Hosp. Med. Sch., 1988; University of Oxford: Clinical Lectr in Psychiatry, 1991; Wellcome Trust Sen. Res. Fellow, 1995; Clinical Reader in Psychiatry, 1997–2000. Collegium Internationale Neuropsychopharmacologium Schizophrenia Award, 1998. *Publications:* Lecture Notes on Psychiatry, 8th edn, 1998; The Neuropathology of Schizophrenia, 2000; articles on schizophrenia, depression and Alzheimer's disease. *Recreations:* sport, music. *Address:* University Department of Psychiatry, Warneford Hospital, Oxford OX3 7JX. *T:* (01865) 223730.

HARRISON, Ven. Peter Reginald Wallace; Archdeacon of the East Riding, since 1999; *b* 22 June 1939; *s* of Gilbert V. W. Harrison and Mary L. W. Harrison (*née* Blair); *m* 1970, Elizabeth Mary Byzia; one *s* one *d*. *Educ:* Charterhouse; Selwyn Coll., Cambridge (BA Theol 1962); Ridley Hall, Cambridge. Ordained deacon, 1964, priest, 1965; Curate, St Luke's, Barton Hill, Bristol, 1964–69; Youth Worker and Chaplain, Greenhouse Trust, London, 1969–77; Dir, Northorpe Hall Trust, Mirfield, 1977–84; Team Rector, Drypool Team Ministry, Hull, 1984–98. *Recreation:* various sports. *Address:* Brimley Lodge, Molescroft Road, Beverley HU17 7DX. *T:* (01482) 881659.

HARRISON, Philippa Mary; Chairman, Little, Brown & Co. (UK), since 2000; *b* 25 Nov. 1942; *d* of Charles Kershaw Whitfield and Alexina Margaret Whitfield; *m* 1968 (marr. diss. 1976). *Educ:* Walthamstow Hall; Bristol Univ. (BA Hons); Courtauld Inst. Promotions Organiser, Associated Book Publishers, 1963–66; reader and editor, Jonathan Cape, 1967–73; Editl Dir, Hutchinson, 1974–78; Jt Editor-in-Chief, Penguin, 1979–80; Editl Dir, Michael Joseph, 1980–85; Man. Dir and Publisher, Macmillan London, 1986–88; Managing Director: V&A Enterprises, 1990–91; Macdonald & Co., subseq. Little, Brown & Co. (UK), 1991–96; Chief Exec. and Publisher, Little, Brown & Co. (UK), 1996–2000. Member: Freedom to Publish Cttee, 1985–88; Bd, Book Marketing Council, 1983–88; Booker Mgt Cttee, 1987–89; Literature Panel, Arts Council, 1988–92; Adv. Cttee, Centre for the Book, British Liby, 1996–; Dir, Royal Acad. of Arts Enterprise Bd, 1999–. Mem. Council, Publishers' Assoc., 1995– (Pres., 1998–99). Dir, Book Tokens Ltd, 1996–. Trustee, Eric & Salome Estorick Foundn, 1996–99. CIMgt 1987 (Mem. Bd, 1999–); FRSA 1992. *Recreations:* walking, gardening, theatre, politics, looking at pictures, friends. *Address:* Little, Brown & Co. (UK), Brettenham House, Lancaster Place, WC2E 7EN. *T:* (020) 7911 8002. *Club:* Groucho.

HARRISON, Hon. Sir Richard; *see* Harrison, Hon. Sir J. R.

HARRISON, Sir (Robert) Colin, 4th Bt *cr* 1922; *b* 25 May 1938; *s* of Sir John Fowler Harrison, 2nd Bt, and Kathleen (*d* 1993), *yr d* of late Robert Livingston, The Gables, Eaglescliffe, Co. Durham; *S* brother, 1955; *m* 1963, Maureen, *er d* of late E. Leonard Chiverton, Garth Corner, Kirkbymoorside, York; one *s* two *d*. *Educ:* St Peter's Coll., Radley; St John's Coll., Cambridge. Commissioned with Fifth Royal Northumberland Fusiliers (National Service), 1957–59. Chm., John Harrison (Stockton) Ltd. Chm., Young Master Printers Nat. Cttee, 1972–73. *Heir:* *s* John Wyndham Fowler Harrison, *b* 14 Dec. 1972. *Address:* Stearsby Hall, Stearsby, York YO61 4SA. *T:* (01347) 888226.

HARRISON, Robert Michael; QC 1987; a Recorder, since 1985; *b* 3 Nov. 1945; *s* of Robert William and Bertha Harrison; *m* 1974, Jennifer Armstrong; one *s*. *Educ:* Heckmondwike Grammar School; Hull Univ. (LLB). Called to the Bar, Gray's Inn, 1969. *Address:* Park Court Chambers, 16 Park Place, Leeds LS1 2SJ. *T:* (0113) 243 3277.

HARRISON, Roger; *see* Harrison, D. R. W.

HARRISON, Prof. Roy Michael, PhD, DSc; FRSC, FRMetS; Queen Elizabeth II Birmingham Centenary Professor of Environmental Health, since 1991, and Head, Division of Environmental Health & Risk Management, since 1999, University of Birmingham; *b* 14 Oct. 1948; *s* of Wilfred Harrison and Rosa (*née* Cotton); *m* 1st, 1981, Angela Copeman (marr. diss.); one *s* one *d*; 2nd, 1989, Susan Sturt; one *s*. *Educ:* Henley Grammar Sch.; Univ. of Birmingham (BSc; PhD 1972; DSc 1988). FRMetS 1982; FRSC 1988. Res. Asst, Imperial Coll., Univ. of London, 1972–74; Lectr, Lancaster Univ., 1974–84; Reader, Univ. of Essex, 1984–91. Margary Lectr, RMetS, 1994; John Jeyes Lectr, RSC, 1995. Department of the Environment: Mem., Photochem. Oxidants Rev. Gp, 1986–97; Chm., Quality of Urban Air Rev. Gp, 1991–97; Member: Expert Panel on Air Quality Standards, 1992–; Adv. Cttee on Hazardous Substances, 2001–; Chm., Airborne Particles Expert Gp, 1997–99; Department of Health: Member: Cttee on Med. Effects of Air Pollution, 1993–; Health Adv. Gp on Chem. Contamination Incidents, 1994–. Hon. Consulting Envmtl Toxicologist, Nat. Poisons Inf. Service, Birmingham Centre and W Midlands Poisons Unit, 1994–99. Mem., HEFCE Panel, 2001 RAE. Chm., Envmt Gp, RSC, 1990–91. Hon. FFOM 1998; Hon. MFPHM 1997. *Publications:* (with D. P. H. Laxen) Lead Pollution: causes and control, 1981; Pollution: causes, effects and control, 1983, 4th edn 2001; (with R. Perry) Handbook of Air Pollution Analysis, 2nd edn 1986; (jtly) Acid Rain: scientific and technical advances, 1987; (with S. Rapsomanikis) Environmental Analysis using Chromatography Interfaced with Atomic Spectroscopy, 1989; (jtly) Introductory Chemistry for the Environmental Sciences, 1991, 2nd edn (with S. J. de Mora) 1996; (with R. S. Hamilton) Highway Pollution, 1991; (jtly) Handbook for Urban Air Improvement, 1992; Understanding Our Environment: an introduction to environmental chemistry and pollution, 1992, 3rd edn 1999; (with M. Radojevic) Atmospheric Acidity: sources, consequences and abatement, 1992; (with F. E. Warner) Radioecology after Chernobyl: biogeochemical pathways of artificial radionuclides, SCOPE 50, 1993; (jtly) Urban Air Quality in the United Kingdom, 1993; (jtly) Diesel Vehicle Emissions and Urban Air Quality, 1993; (jtly) Airborne Particulate Matter in the United Kingdom, 1996; (with R. Van Grieken) Atmospheric Particles, 1998; (jtly) Source Apportionment of Airborne Particulate Matter in the United Kingdom, 1999; many papers to learned jls. *Recreations:* mowing and other outdoor pursuits. *Address:* Division of Environmental Health & Risk Management, University of Birmingham, Edgbaston, Birmingham B15 2TT. *T:* (0121) 414 3494.

HARRISON, Ted; *see* Harrison, E. P. G.

HARRISON, Sir Terence, Kt 1995; DL; FREng; FIMechE, FIMarE; Chairman, Alfred McAlpine plc, since 1996 (Director, since 1995); *b* 7 April 1933; *s* of late Roland Harrison and of Doris (*née* Wardle); *m* 1956, June (*née* Forster); two *s*. *Educ:* A. J. Dawson Grammar Sch., Co. Durham; West Hartlepool and Sunderland Tech. Colls. BSc(Eng) Durham. CEng 1964; FIMechE 1984; FIMarE 1973; FREng (FEng 1988). Marine engrg apprenticeship, Richardson's Westgarth, Hartlepool, 1949–53; commnd REME, service in Nigeria, 1955–57; Clarke Chapman, Gateshead (Marine Division): Res. Engr, 1957; Chief Mechanical Engr, 1967; Man. Dir, 1969; Man. Dir, Clarke Chapman Ltd, Gateshead, 1976; Northern Engineering Industries plc: Dir, 1977; Man. Dir, UK Ops, 1980–83; Chief Exec., 1983–86; Exec. Chm., 1986–93; Rolls-Royce: Dir, 1989; Chief Exec., 1992–96. Director: Barclays Bank (Regl Bd), 1986–98; T&N, 1995–98. Member: ACOST, 1987; Engrg Council, 1990–93. Pres., BEAMA, 1989–90. Pres., NEC Inst., 1988. DL Tyne and Wear, 1989. Hon. DEng Newcastle, 1991; Hon. DTech Sunderland, 1995; Hon. DSc Durham, 1996. *Publications:* technical papers to mechanical, marine and mining societies. *Recreations:* golf, fell walking. *Address:* 2 The Garden Houses, Whalton, Northumberland NE61 3HB. *T:* (01670) 775400; (office) Alfred McAlpine, 8–10 Suffolk Street, SW1Y 4HG. *T:* (020) 7930 6255.

HARRISON, Tony, FRSL; poet; *b* 30 April 1937; *s* of Harry Ashton Harrison and Florrie (*née* Wilkinson-Horner); *m* 1st, 1960, Rosemarie Crossfield (*née* Dietzsch); one *s* one *d*; 2nd, 1984, Teresa Stratas. *Educ:* Cross Flatts County Primary Sch.; Leeds Grammar Sch.; Univ. of Leeds (BA, Dip.Linguistics). Lecturer in English: Ahmadu Bello Univ., Zaria, N Nigeria, 1962–66; Charles Univ., Prague, 1966–67; Northern Arts Fellow in Poetry, Univs of Newcastle and Durham, 1967–68 and 1976–77; UNESCO Fellow in Poetry, Cuba, Brazil, Senegal, Gambia, 1969; Gregynog Arts Fellow, Univ. of Wales, 1973–74; Resident Dramatist, National Th., 1977–79; UK/US Bi-Centennial Fellow, New York, 1979–80. Pres., Classical Assoc., 1987–88. FRSL 1984. *Publications:* Earthworks, 1964; Aikin Mata, 1966; Newcastle is Peru, 1969; The Loiners (Geoffrey Faber Meml Prize), 1970; The Misanthrope, 1973; Phaedra Britannica, 1975; Palladas: poems, 1975; The Passion, 1977; Bow Down, 1977; From The School of Eloquence and other poems, 1978; The Bartered Bride, 1978; Continuous, 1981; A Kumquat for John Keats, 1981; US Martial, 1981; The Oresteia, 1981; Selected Poems, 1984, expanded edn 1987; The Mysteries, 1985; Dramatic Verse 1973–85, 1985; v., 1985; The Fire-Gap, 1985; Theatre Works 1973–85, 1986; The Trackers of Oxyrhynchus, 1990; v. and other poems, 1990; A Cold Coming: Gulf War poems, 1991; The Common Chorus, 1992; The Gaze of the Gorgon (Whitbread Award for Poetry), 1992; Square Rounds, 1992; Black Daisies for the Bride, 1993; Poetry or Bust, 1993; A Maybe Day in Kazakhstan, 1994; The Shadow of Hiroshima, 1995; Permanently Bard, 1995; Plays Three: The Kaisers of Carnuntum, The Labourers of Herakles, Poetry or Bust, 1996; The Prince's Play, 1996; Prometheus, 1998 (also Dir, film, 1999); Plays One: The Mysteries, 1999; Laureate's Block and Other Poems, 2000; Plays Two: The Oresteia, The Common Chorus, The Trojan Women, 2001; Plays Four: The Misanthrope, Phaedra Britannica, The Prince's Play, 2001. *Address:* c/o Gordon Dickerson, 2 Crescent Grove, SW4 7AH.

HARRISON, Valerie, (Mrs D. M. Harrison); *see* Caton, V.

HARRISON, Victoria; *see* Harrison, A. V.

HARRISON, Rt Hon. Walter; PC 1977; JP; public affairs consultant, since 1987; *b* 2 Jan. 1921; *s* of Henry and Ada Harrison; *m* 1948, Enid Mary (*née* Coleman) (*d* 1990); one *s* one *d*; *m* 1991, Jane Marguerite Richards (*d* 2000). *Educ:* Dewsbury Technical and Art Coll. Served RAF, 1940–45. Electrical Inspector and Electrical Foreman, Electricity Supply Industry, 1937–64; Welfare Personnel Officer, Civil and Engrg Industry, 1945–48. MP (Lab) Wakefield, 1964–87. Asst Govt Whip, 1966–68; a Lord Comr of the Treasury, 1968–70; Dep. Chief Opposition Whip, 1970–74 and 1979–83; Treasurer of HM Household and Dep. Chief Govt Whip, 1974–79. Held several positions in the Trade Union and Labour movements. West Riding CC, 1958–64; Alderman, Castleford Borough Council, 1959–66 (Councillor, 1952–59); JP West Riding Yorks, 1962. *Address:* 1 Milnthorpe Drive, Sandal, Wakefield WF2 7HU. *T:* (01924) 255550.

HARRISON, William Alistair, CVO 1996; HM Diplomatic Service; Head of Chancery and Political Counsellor, UK Mission to United Nations, New York, since 2000; *b* 14 Nov. 1954; *s* of William Kent Harrison and Alice Rita Harrison; *m* 1st, 1981, Theresa Mary Morrison (marr. diss. 1991); 2nd, 1996, Sarah Judith Wood; one *d*. *Educ:* Newcastle Royal Grammar Sch.; University Coll., Oxford (BA 1977; MA 1980); Birkbeck Coll., London (DipEcon 1995). Joined FCO, 1977: Third, later Second Sec., Warsaw, 1979–82; First Sec., FCO, 1982–84; Private Sec. to Parly Under-Sec., FCO, 1984–86; First Sec., UK Mission to UN, NY, 1987–92; Deputy Head: ME Dept, FCO, 1992–95; of Mission, Warsaw, 1995–98; Foreign Policy Advr to Dir-Gen. for External Relations, EC, Brussels, 1998–2000. *Recreations:* music, mathematics. *Address:* c/o Foreign and Commonwealth Office, King Charles Street, SW1A 2AH. *T:* (020) 7270 3000.

HARRISON, William Robert; Harrison Lovegrove, since 1999; *b* 5 Oct. 1948; *s* of William Harrison and Catherine Harrison; *m* 1970, Jacqueline Ann Brown; one *s* one *d*. *Educ:* London Sch. of Econs (BSc Econ, MSc Econ). Associate Dir, Mfrs Hanover Ltd, London, 1971–75; Sen. Finance Dir, BNOC, 1975–78; Dep. Man. Dir, Lehman Bros Kuhn Loeb, NY and London, 1978–81; Gp Treas., and Hd, Corporate Finance, Tricentrol Oil Corp., 1981–83; Dir, Corporate Finance, J. Henry Schroder Wagg & Co. Ltd, 1983–86; Lehman Brothers, London: Man. Dir, 1986–93; Vice Chm. and Head, European Investment Banking, Lehman Bros Internat. Ltd, 1986–93; Robert Fleming, London: Chief Exec., Global Investment Banking, 1993–96; Mem., Gp Exec. and Gp Hldg Bd, 1993–96; Chief Exec., BZW, 1996–97; Dir, Barclays Bank, 1996–97; Vice-Chm., Global Corporates and Instns, Deutsche Morgan Grenfell, then Deutsche Bank, 1998–99. Non-exec. Dir, Pilkington plc, 1998–. Mem., Adv. Council, Herbert Smith & Co. High Sheriff, Gtr London, 1997–98. Hon. Trustee, Foundn & Friends, Royal Botanic Gdns, Kew, 1996–. *Recreations:* sport, travel, gardening.

HARRISON-HALL, His Honour Michael Kilgour; DL; a Circuit Judge, 1972–97; *b* 20 Dec. 1925; *s* of late Arthur Harrison-Hall, Oxford; *m* 1951, Jessie Margaret (*d* 2000), *d* of late Rev. Arthur William Brown, Collingbourne Ducis, Wilts; two *s* two *d*. *Educ:* Rugby; Trinity College, Oxford. Called to Bar, Inner Temple, 1949. Dep. Chm., Warwickshire QS, 1968–71; a Recorder of the Crown Court, 1972. DL Warwicks, 1985. *Address:* Ivy House, Church Street, Barford, Warwick CV35 8EN. *T:* (01926) 624272. *Clubs:* Oxford and Cambridge; Leander.

HARRISS, Gerald Leslie, DPhil; FBA 1986; Fellow and Tutor, Magdalen College, Oxford, 1967–92, Emeritus Fellow, since 1992; Reader in Modern History, Oxford University, 1990–92; *b* 22 May 1925; *s* of Walter and Mabel Harriss; *m* 1959, Margaret Anne Sidaway; two *s* three *d*. *Educ:* Chigwell Sch.; Magdalen Coll., Oxford (BA 1st Cl. History, MA, DPhil). Service in RNVR, 1944–46. Research Fellow, Durham Univ., 1953–55; Asst Lectr, Manchester Univ., 1955–56; Lectr 1956, Sen. Lectr 1965, Reader 1965–67, Durham Univ. *Publications:* King, Parliament and Public Finance in Medieval England, 1975; (ed) Henry V: the practice of kingship, 1985; Cardinal Beaufort, 1988; (cd) K. B. McFarlane, Letters to Friends, 1997; numerous articles on late medieval English history. *Address:* Fairings, 2 Queen Street, Yetminster, Dorset DT9 6LL.

HARROD, Dominick Roy; journalist and broadcaster; Programme Director, St George's House, Windsor Castle, 1994–98; President, Institute of Journalists, 1994–95; *b* 21 Aug. 1940; *s* of Sir Roy Forbes Harrod, FBA and of Wilhelmine Harrod (*née* Cresswell), OBE; *m* 1974, Christina Hobhouse (*d* 1996); one *s*. *Educ:* Westminster School; Christ Church, Oxford (MA Modern Greats). Sunday Telegraph, 1962–66; Daily Telegraph: Washington corresp., 1966–69; Economics corresp., 1969–71; BBC Economics corresp., 1971–78; Dir of Information, Dunlop Ltd, 1979; Economics Editor, BBC Radio, 1979–93; City Editor, The Yorkshire Post, 1993–94. Member: Council, SCF, 1988–96; Bd for Social Responsibility, C of E, 1996–. Founder Mem., Norfolk Churches Trust, 1973. FJI 1990; FRSA 1992. *Publications:* The Politics of Economics, 1978; Making Sense of the Economy, 1983; War, Ice and Piracy, 2000. *Recreations:* reading, sailing. *Address:* 4 Duke's Avenue, W4 2AE. *Club:* Garrick.

HARROLD, Roy Mealham; farmer, 1947–91; *b* 13 Aug. 1928; *s* of John Frederick Harrold and Ellen Selena Harrold (*née* Mealham); *m* 1968, Barbara Mary, *yr d* of William and Florence Andrews; one *s* one *d*. *Educ:* Stoke Holy Cross Primary Sch.; Bracondale Sch., Norwich. County Chm., Norfolk Fedn of Young Farmers' Clubs, 1956–57; Mem., Nat. Council of Young Farmers, 1957–60; Mem. Council, Royal Norfolk Agric. Assoc., 1972–75, 1980–83, 1987–89; Mem., Press Council, 1976–83. Mem., UK Shareholders Assoc., 1993–. Lay Chm., Norwich East Deanery Synod, 1970–79; Member: Norwich Dio. Synod, 1970–96; Norwich Dio. Bd of Patronage, 1970–82; Norwich Dio. Bd of Finance, 1983–96; Pastoral Asst, St Peter Mancroft, Norwich, 1991– (Church Warden, 1978–82, 1988–92). *Recreations:* music, opera, ballet. *Address:* Salamanca Farm, Stoke Holy Cross, 118 Norwich Road, Norwich NR14 8QJ. *T:* (01508) 492322.

HARROP, Sir Peter (John), KCB 1984 (CB 1980); Second Permanent Secretary, Department of the Environment, 1981–86; *b* 18 March 1926; *s* of late Gilbert Harrop, OBE; *m* 1975, Margaret Joan, *d* of E. U. E. Elliott-Binns, CB; two *s*. *Educ:* King Edward VII Sch., Lytham, Lancs; Peterhouse, Cambridge. MA (Hist. Tripos). Served RNVR, 1945–47 (Sub-Lt). Min. of Town and Country Planning, 1949; Min. of Housing and Local Govt, 1951; Dept of the Environment, 1970 (Chm., Yorks and Humberside Economic Planning Bd, and Regional Dir, 1971–73); Under Sec., HM Treasury, 1973–76; Deputy Secretary: DoE, 1977–79, 1980–81; Cabinet Office, 1979–80. Mem. Bd, 1987–91, Chm., 1988–91, National Bus Co.; non-executive Director: Nat. Home Loans Hldgs (formerly Corp.) plc, 1987–92; Municipal Mutual Insurance Ltd, 1988–2001; Thames Water plc, 1989–95 (Mem., Thames Water Authority, 1986–89). Chm., UK Cttee, European Year of the Environment, 1987–88. Chm. of Govs., Richmond upon Thames Coll., 1993–96. Hon. Trustee, British Mus., 1987–97. *Recreations:* golf, sailing. *Address:* 19 Berwyn Road, Richmond, Surrey TW10 5BP. *Clubs:* Oxford and Cambridge, Roehampton; Ski of Great Britain; Island Cruising (Salcombe).

HARROWBY, 7th Earl of, *cr* 1809; **Dudley Danvers Granville Coutts Ryder,** TD; Baron Harrowby, 1776; Viscount Sandon, 1809; *b* 20 Dec. 1922; *er s* of 6th Earl of Harrowby and Lady Helena Blanche Coventry (*d* 1974), *e d* of late Viscount Deerhurst; *S* father, 1987; *m* 1949, Jeannette Rosalthé (*d* 1997), *yr d* of late Captain Peter Johnston-Saint; one *s* one *d*. *Educ:* Eton. Lt-Col RA; OC 254 (City of London) Field Regt, RA (TA), 56 Armoured Div., 1962–64. Served War of 1939–45: 59 Inf. Div., in NW Europe (wounded); 5 Para. Bde, India and Java (political offr), 1941–45. Man. Dir, 1949–89, Dep. Chm., 1970–89, Coutts & Co.; Director: Dinorwic Slate Quarries Co., 1951–69; United Kingdom Provident Institution, 1955–86 (Dep. Chm., 1956–64); National Provincial Bank, 1964–69; National Westminster Bank Plc, 1968–87 (Dep. Chm., 1971–87); Olympia Group, 1968–73 (Chm., 1971–73); Sheepbridge Engrg Ltd, 1977–79; Saudi Internat. Bank, 1980–82, 1985–87; Powell Duffryn Trustees Ltd, 1981–86; Orion Pacific Ltd, 1980–81; Orion Pension Trustee Co. Ltd, 1980–81; Chairman: International Westminster Bank Plc, 1977–87; Powell Duffryn Gp, 1981–86 (Dir, 1976–86); National Westminster Unit Trust Managers, 1979–83; Orion Bank Ltd, 1979–81; Bentley Engineering Co. Ltd, 1983–86; NatWest Investment Bank, 1986–87; Dowty Group,

1986–91 (Dir, 1986–91); The Private Bank & Trust Co., 1989–92; Private Financial Hldgs, 1992–94. Chm., Nat. Biol Standards Bd, 1973–88. Mem. Kensington Borough Council, 1950–65 (Chm., Gen. Purposes Cttee, 1957–59), Kensington and Chelsea BC, 1965–71 (Chm., Finance Cttee, 1968–71); Mem. Exec. Cttee, London area Cons. Assoc., 1949–50; Hon. Treasurer, S Kensington Cons. Assoc., 1953–56; Pres., Wolverhampton SW Cons. Assoc., 1959–68. Pres., Historical and Civic Soc. Hon. Treasurer: Family Welfare Assoc., 1951–65; Central Council for the Care of Cripples, 1953–60. General Commissioner for Income Tax, 1954–71; Member: Lord Chancellor's Adv. Investment Cttees, for Court of Protection, 1965–77, for Public Trustee, 1974–77; Inst. Internat. d'Etudes Bancaires, 1977–87; Trilateral Commn, 1980–94. Manager, Fulham and Kensington Hosp. Group, 1953–56; Member: Cttee of Management, Inst. of Psychiatry, 1953–73 (Chm. 1965–73); Board of Governors, Bethlem Royal and Maudsley (Postgraduate Teaching) Hosps, 1955–73 (Chm. 1965–73); Dep. Chm., London Postgraduate Cttee, Teaching Hosps Assoc., 1968–69; Trustee, Psychiatry Research Trust, 1982–; Mem. Bd of Govs, Univ. of Keele, 1956–68. Pres., Staffordshire Soc., 1957–59 (Hon. Treas., 1947–51). Dep. Pres., Staffs Army Cadet League. Mem., Ct of Assts, Goldsmiths' Co., 1972–77. Governor, Atlantic Inst. for Internat. Affairs, 1983–88. Hon. FRCPsych. Hon. DSc Keele, 1996. *Heir: s* Viscount Sandon, *qv. Address:* Apt 20, Albert Bridge House, 127 Albert Bridge Road, SW11 4PL. *T:* (020) 7223 7535; Sandon Hall, Stafford ST18 0BZ. *T:* (01889) 508338. *Address:* Burnt Norton, Chipping Campden, Glos GL55 6PR. *T:* (01386) 841488.

HARROWER, Rt Rev. John Douglas; *see* Tasmania, Bishop of.

HARSTON, Julian John Robert Clive; HM Diplomatic Service, retired; Deputy Special Representative of UN Secretary-General to Bosnia and Hercegovina, since 1999; *b* 20 Oct. 1942; *s* of late Col Clive Harston, ERD, and of Kathleen Harston; *m* 1966, Karen Howard Oake (*née* Longfield) (marr. diss. 2000); one *s. Educ:* King's Sch., Canterbury; Univ. of London (BSc). British Tourist Authority, 1965–70; FCO, 1970; Consul, Hanoi, 1973; 1st Secretary: Blantyre, 1975; Lisbon, 1982; Counsellor, Harare, 1984–88; FCO, 1988–91; Counsellor, UK Mission, Geneva, 1991–95. Head, Political and Civil Affairs, UN Peace Forces, Zagreb, former Yugoslavia, 1995–96; Dir, UN Liaison Office, Belgrade, Fed. Repub. of Yugoslavia, 1996; Rep. of Sec.-Gen. and Hd of Mission, UN Civilian Police Mission, Haiti, 1998. *Recreations:* photography, travel. *Clubs:* East India, Royal Automobile; Gremio Literario (Lisbon); Harare (Zimbabwe).

HART, Alan; broadcasting consultant, since 1991; Director, Global AMG, 1995–2000; Executive Director, Eurosport Consortium, since 1997; *b* 17 April 1935; *s* of late Reginald Thomas Hart and Lillian Hart; *m* 1961, Celia Mary Vine; two *s* one *d. Educ:* Pinnerwood Primary Sch.; University College Sch., Hampstead. Reporter: Willesden Chronicle and Kilburn Times, 1952–58; Newcastle Evening Chronicle, 1958; London Evening News, 1958–59; Editorial Asst, BBC Sportsview, 1959–61; Television Sports Producer, BBC Manchester, 1962–64; Asst Editor, Sportsview, 1964–65; Editor, Sportsview, 1965–68; Editor, Grandstand, 1968–77; Head of Sport, BBC Television, 1977–81; Controller, BBC1 Television, 1981–84; Special Asst to Dir Gen., BBC, 1985; Controller, Internat. Relations, BBC, 1986–91. Dir, Eurosport, 1991–97 (Chm., 1989–91); Chm., British Eurosport, 1997–99. Advr on management of E European broadcasting services, EBU, 1991–93. FRTS 1983. Vice-Pres., Watford FC, 1995–. *Recreations:* sport, music, walking. *Address:* Cutwellwalls, Avonwick, near South Brent, Devon TQ10 9HA.

HART, Alan Edward; Chief Executive, Equal Opportunities Commission, 1985–89; *b* 28 July 1935; *m* 1961, Ann Derbyshire; one *s* one *d. Educ:* Varndean County Grammar Sch., Brighton; Lincoln Coll., Univ. of Oxford (MA). Solicitor. Dep. Town Clerk, City of Salford, 1970–73; Dir of Admin, 1973–75, Chief Exec., 1975–85, Wigan MBC.

HART, Alexander Hendry; QC (Canada) 1969; Agent General for British Columbia in the United Kingdom and Europe, 1981–87; *b* Regina, Sask., 17 July 1916; *s* of Alexander Hart and Mary (*née* Davidson); *m* 1948, Janet MacMillan Mackay; three *s* one *d. Educ:* Dalhousie Law School (LLB). Served War, Royal Canadian Artillery, 1939–45; retired with rank of Major. Read law with McInnis, Mcquarrie and Cooper; called to Bar of Nova Scotia, 1947. Vice-Pres., Marketing, 1967–71; Sen. Vice-Pres., Canadian Nat. Rlwys, 1971–81. Dep. Internat. Pres., Pacific Basin Economic Council, 1980–81; Pres., Canada-UK Chamber of Commerce, 1983; Past Pres., Vancouver Board of Trade; Past Chm., Western Transportation Adv. Council; Past Mem., University Council of British Columbia; Past Pres., Canada Japan Soc. of Vancouver. *Recreation:* golf. *Address:* 1515 Dorcas Point Road, Nanoose Bay, BC V0R 2R0, Canada. *Clubs:* Royal & Ancient Golf (St Andrews); Vancouver, Men's Canadian, Shaughnessy Golf and Country (Vancouver).

HART, Anelay Colton Wright; Partner in Appleby, Hope & Matthews, 1963–95; *b* 6 March 1934; *s* of Anelay Thomas Bayston Hart and Phyllis Marian Hart; *m* 1979, Margaret Gardner (*née* Dewing). *Educ:* Stamford Sch.; King's Coll., London (LLB). Solicitor, retd. Advisory Director, World Society for the Protection of Animals, 1982–; RSPCA: Mem. Council, 1969–95; Hon. Treasurer, 1974–81; Chm. of Council, 1981–83, 1985–86, 1988–90; Vice-Chm. Council, 1983–84, 1986–88; Queen Victoria Silver Medal, 1984. President, Rotary Club of South Bank and Eston, 1972–73. *Recreation:* walking. *Club:* Royal Over-Seas League.

HART, Anthony; *see* Hart, T. A. A.

HART, Anthony John, OBE 1995; DSC 1945; JP; Chairman, Cunningham Hart & Co. Ltd, 1985–87 (Senior Partner, 1972–85), retired; *b* 27 Dec. 1923; *s* of Cecil Victor Hart and Kate Winifred Hart (*née* Boncey); *m* 1947, E. Penelope Morris; one *s* one *d. Educ:* King's College Sch., Wimbledon; Dauntsey's Sch. ACII, FCILA. RN, 1942–46 (Ordinary Seaman to Lieut). Joined Hart & Co., 1946, Partner 1952, Senior Partner 1969; on merger name changed to Cunningham Hart & Co. Mem. Council, CILA, 1964, Pres., 1970–71. Chm., Medic Alert Foundn in UK, 1971–83; Governor, Dauntsey's Sch., 1982–93; Mem. Council, Mansfield House University Settlement, 1975–90. Liveryman, 1960, Master, 1976–77, Broderers' Co.; Liveryman, 1979, Mem. Court, 1986, Insurers' Co. Alderman, Ward of Cheap, City of London, 1977–84. FRSA. JP City of London, 1977 (Vice-Chm. of Bench, 1991–93). *Recreation:* golf. *Address:* Merrington Place, Rolvenden, Cranbrook, Kent TN17 4PJ. *T:* (01580) 241428. *Clubs:* City Livery; Littlestone Golf.

HART, Anthony Ronald; QC (NI) 1983; **His Honour Judge Hart;** a County Court Judge, Northern Ireland, since 1985; Recorder of Belfast, since 1997; Chancellor, Diocese of Clogher, Church of Ireland, since 1990; *b* 30 April 1946; *s* of Basil and Hazel Hart; *m* 1971, Mary Morehan; two *s* two *d. Educ:* Portora Royal Sch., Enniskillen; Trinity Coll., Dublin (BA Mod.); Queen's Univ., Belfast. Called to the Bar of NI, 1969, Bencher 1995; called to the Bar, Gray's Inn, 1975. Jun. Crown Counsel for Co. Londonderry, 1973–75 and for Co. Down, 1975–79; Asst Boundary Comr, 1980–81; part-time Chm. of Industrial Tribunals, 1980–83; Dep. County Court Judge, 1983–85; Recorder of Londonderry, 1985–90. Member: Council of Legal Educn (NI), 1977–83; Review Cttee on Professional Legal Educn in NI, 1984–85; Standing Adv. Commn on Human Rights, 1984–85; Judicial Studies Bd for NI, 1993–97; Criminal Justice Issues (formerly Criminal Justice Consultative) Gp for NI, 1993–; Civil Justice Reform Gp, 1998–99; Chairman: Council of HM Co. Court Judges in NI, 1995–98 (Hon. Sec., 1989–95); County Court Rules Cttee (NI), 1997–. Pres., Irish Legal History Soc., 1991–94. *Publications:* A History of the King's Serjeants at Law in Ireland: honour rather than advantage?, 2000; (Consultant Ed.) Valentine on Criminal Procedure in Northern Ireland, 1989; (contrib.) Brehons, Serjeants and Attorneys: studies in the history of the Irish legal profession, 1990; (contrib.) Explorations in Law and History: Irish legal history society discourses 1989–1994, 1995. *Recreations:* gardening, reading. *Address:* c/o Northern Ireland Court Service, Windsor House, Bedford Street, Belfast BT2 7LT.

HART, David Michael, OBE 1988; General Secretary, National Association of Head Teachers, since 1978; *b* 27 Aug. 1940; *s* of Edwin Henry Hart and Freda Muriel Hart; *m* 1st (marr. diss.); two *s*; 2nd, 1996, Frances Katrina Morton. *Educ:* Hurstpierpoint Coll., Sussex. Solicitor 1963, Herbert Ruse Prizeman. Editor, Heads' Legal Guide, 1984. Hon. FCollP 1986; FRSA 1990. Hon. Dr UCE, 1999. *Recreations:* tennis, walking, riding. *Address:* Whinby Cottage, Haltcliffe, Hesket Newmarket, Wigton, Cumbria CA7 8JT. *T:* (01697) 478318. *Club:* Wig and Pen.

HART, Most Rev. Denis James; *see* Melbourne, Archbishop of, (RC).

HART, His Honour Donald; QC 1978; a Circuit Judge, 1989–98; President, Mental Health Review Tribunals (restricted patients), 1983–2000; *b* 6 Jan. 1933; *s* of Frank and Frances Hart; *m* 1st, 1958, Glenys Thomas (marr. diss. 1990); two *s* two *d*; 2nd, 1990, Joan Turton. *Educ:* Altrincham Grammar Sch.; Magdalen Coll., Oxford. MA. Macaskie Scholar, Arden and Atkin Prize, Lee Essay Prize (Gray's Inn), 1956. Called to the Bar, Gray's Inn, 1956; Northern Circuit, 1956; a Recorder, 1978–89; Designated Family Judge for Liverpool, 1992–98. *Recreations:* garden, travel, opera, cuisine. *Address:* 217 Knutsford Road, Grappenhall, Cheshire WA4 2TX. *T:* (01925) 604228.

HART, Edwina, MBE 1998; Member (Lab) Gower, National Assembly for Wales, since 1999; Minister (formerly Secretary) for Finance, Local Government and Communities, since 2000; *b* 26 April 1957; *d* of Eric G. Thomas and Hannah J. Thomas; *m* 1976, Robert B. Hart; one *d.* Member: Employment Appeal Tribunal, 1992–99; Broadcasting Council for Wales, 1995–99; Adv. Cttee Wales, EOC, 1998–99. Nat. Pres., BIFU, 1992–94; Chair, Wales TUC, 1997–98. National Assembly for Wales: Finance Sec., 1999–2000. Chm., Equal Opportunity Cttee, 2000–; Mem., SW Wales Regl Cttee, 1999–. Non-executive Director: Chwarae Teg, 1994–99; Wales Millennium Centre, 1997–99. Mem., Council, 1998–99, Ct of Govs, 2000, Univ. of Wales, Swansea. *Recreations:* reading, music, cookery. *Address:* National Assembly for Wales, Crickhowell House, Cardiff CF99 1NA. *T:* (029) 2089 8400.

HART, Dr (Everard) Peter, CChem, FRSC; Rector, Sunderland Polytechnic, 1981–90; *b* 16 Sept. 1925; *s* of Robert Daniel Hart and Margaret Stokes; *m* Enid Mary Scott; three *s* one *d. Educ:* Wyggeston Grammar Sch., Leicester; Loughborough Coll.; London Univ. (BSc, PhD). Asst Lectr, Lectr and Sen. Lectr, Nottingham and Dist Technical Coll., 1951–57; Sunderland Technical College, later Sunderland Polytechnic: Head of Dept of Chemistry and Biology, 1958–69; Vice-Principal, 1963–69; Dep. Rector, 1969–80. Member: Cttee for Sci. and Technol., CNAA, 1974–77; Gen. Council, Northern Arts, 1982–90. Royal Institute of Chemistry: Mem. Council, 1963–65, 1970–73; Vice-Pres., 1973–75. FRSA 1985. Hon. DCL Sunderland, 1994. *Recreations:* music, opera, theatre, travel. *Address:* Redesdale, The Oval, North End, Durham City DH1 4NE. *T:* (0191) 384 8305.

HART, F(rancis) Dudley, MD; FRCP; Physician, and Physician-in-charge Rheumatism Unit, Westminster Hospital, SW1, 1946–74; Emeritus Physician: Hospital of St John and St Elizabeth, London; Westminster Hospital; lately Consulting Rheumatologist, The Star and Garter Home for Disabled Sailors, Soldiers and Airmen, Richmond; lately Hon. Consulting Physician (Civilian) to the Army; *b* 4 Oct. 1909; *s* of Canon C. Dudley Hart and Kate Evelyn Bowden; *m* 1944, Mary Josephine, *d* of late Luke Tully, Carrigaline, Co. Cork; one *s* two *d. Educ:* Grosvenor Sch., Nottingham; Edinburgh Univ. MB, ChB Edinburgh 1933, MD 1939; MRCP 1937, FRCP 1949. House physician and clinical asst, Brompton Hosp., 1937; Med. Registrar, Royal Northern Hosp., 1935–37; Med. Registrar, Westminster Hosp., 1939–42; Med. Specialist and Officer i/c Med. Div., RAMC, 1942–46. Mem., Cttee on Review of Medicines, 1975–82. Ex-Pres. Heberden Soc.; Member: BMA; Med. Soc. of London. Arris and Gale Lectr, RCS, 1955; Ellman Lectr, RCP, 1969; Stanley Davidson Lectr, Univ. of Aberdeen, 1970; Bradshaw Lectr, RCP, 1975; Alexander Brown Meml Lectr, Univ. of Ibadan, Nigeria, 1979; Bernadine Becker Lectr, NY, 1984. Exec. Mem. and Vice-Pres., Arthritis Res. Campaign (formerly Arthritis and Rheumatism Council); Hon. FRSocMed. Hon. Member: British Soc. for Rheumatology; Ligue Française contre le Rheumatisme; La Societa di Rheumatologia Italia; American Rheumatism Association; Australian Rheumatism Association. *Publications:* (co-author) Drugs: actions, uses and dosage, 1963; (ed) French's Differential Diagnosis, 10th edn, 1973, 12th edn, 1985; (ed) The Treatment of Chronic Pain, 1974; Joint Disease: all the arthropathies, 1975, 4th edn 1987; (ed) Drug Treatment of the Rheumatic Diseases, 1978, 3rd edn 1987; (ed) Clinical Rheumatology Illustrated, 1987; (ed) Diagnostic Features of Disease, 1987; Colour Atlas of Rheumatology, 1987; (jtly) Clinical Problems in Rheumatology, 1993; contributions to: Pye's Surgical Handicraft, 1939–72; Cortisone and ACTH, 1953; Miller's Modern Medical Treatment, 1962; Copeman's Textbook of the Rheumatic Diseases (ed J. T. Scott), 3rd edn 1964, 5th edn 1978; Encyclopedia of General Practice, 1964; Chambers's Encyclopædia, 1964; Drug Treatment, 1976; Butterworth's Medical Dictionary (all rheumatological sections), 1978; Overcoming Arthritis, 1981; articles and broadcasts on general medicine and rheumatism. *Recreations:* multi-track recording, travelling. *Address:* 19 Ranulf Road, Hampstead, NW2 2BT. *T:* (020) 7794 2525.

HART, (Frank) Donald; *see* Hart, Donald.

HART, Frank Thomas; JP; BA; *b* London, 9 Nov. 1911; *s* of late Samuel Black and Ada Frances Laura Hart; *m* 1938, Eveline Brenda Deakin (*d* 1993), Leek, Staffs; three *s. Educ:* Gravesend and Sheerness Junior Technical Schs. DPA (London); Diploma of Economics (London); BA Open, 1982. Asst Sec., Buchanan Hospital, St Leonards-on-Sea, 1931–34; Sec., 1934–42; Sec., Central London Eye Hospital, 1942–44; Sec.-Superintendent, Princess Louise Hospital, 1944–48; Superintendent, Royal Infirmary, Sheffield, 1948–52; House Governor and Sec. to the Bd, Charing Cross Hospital, 1952–73; Hospital Manager, Zambia Medical Aid Soc., 1973–75. Mem. Tribunal set up by President of Zambia to hear applications for release from political detainees. Life Pres., League of Friends, Charing Cross Hosp., 1985–; Past Pres., Assoc. of Hosp. Secretaries; Past Pres. of the Hospital Officers' Club. JP: Co. Middx, 1955–65; Co. Surrey, 1965–77; East Sussex, 1978–81. Freeman, City of London, 1959; Mem., Worshipful Soc. of Apothecaries. *Publications:* (jointly) A Study of Hospital Administration, 1948; Roots of Service (A History of Charing Cross Hospital), 1985. *Recreations:* all games, walking, reading. *Address:* 124 Marine Court, St Leonards on Sea, East Sussex TN38 0DY.

HART, Sir Graham (Allan), KCB 1996 (CB 1987); Chairman, King's Fund, since 1998; *b* 13 March 1940; *s* of Frederick and Winifred Hart; *m* 1964, Margaret Aline Powell; two *s*. *Educ:* Brentwood Sch.; Pembroke Coll., Oxford (Hon. Fellow 1997). Assistant Principal, 1962, Principal, 1967, Ministry of Health; Asst Registrar, General Medical Council, 1969–71; Principal Private Sec. to Secretary of State for Social Services, 1972–74; Asst Sec., 1974, Under Sec., 1979, DHSS; Under Sec., Central Policy Review Staff, 1982–83; Dep. Sec., DHSS, then DoH, 1984–89; Sec., Home and Health Dept, Scottish Office, 1990–92; Perm. Sec., DoH, 1992–97. Chairman: NACAB, 1999– (Chm., Governance Rev. Gp, 1998–99); Pharmacy Res. Trust, 1999–; Mem., Audit Commn, 1999–. *Address:* New Belmont, 1 Oaklands Road, Bromley BR1 3SJ. *T:* (020) 8464 9456.

HART, Guy William Pulbrook, OBE 1985; HM Diplomatic Service, retired; *b* 24 Dec. 1931; *s* of late Ernest Guy Hart and Muriel Hart (*née* Walkington); *m* 1954, Elizabeth Marjorie (*née* Bennett); one *s* two *d*. *Educ:* Cranleigh School. Commissioned, Intelligence Corps, 1951–60. British Cellophane Ltd, 1960–62; CRO, 1962; Consular Officer, Kuala Lumpur, 1963–67; Hungarian Language Course, 1967; Second Sec. (Inf.), Budapest, 1968–71; News Dept, FCO, 1971–74; Second Sec. (Econ.), later First Sec. (Inf.), British Mil. Govt, Berlin, 1974–78; First Sec. (Comm.), Port of Spain, 1978–82, Budapest, 1982–85; Asst Head, Inf. Dept, FCO, 1986; Ambassador to the Mongolian People's Republic, 1987–89; High Comr to Seychelles, 1989–91; Head of British delegn, EC monitor mission, Zagreb, 1993–94; Mem., UN Observer mission, SA election; CSCE observer, election in former Yugoslav republic of Macedonia, 1994. *Publication:* White Month's Return: Mongolia comes of age, 1993. *Recreations:* Alpine sports, shooting, painting. *Address:* 1 Marsh Mill, Wargrave Road, Henley on Thames, Oxon RG9 3JD.

HART, Dr James Maurice, QPM 1999; Assistant Commissioner, City of London Police, since 1998; *b* 10 Sept. 1947; *s* of late Lewis Hart and Beatrice Withington; *m* 1993, Julie Anne Russell; two *s*. *Educ:* Wayneflete Sch., Esher; Kingston Coll.; City Univ. (BSc Hons Systems and Mgt; PhD 1995). Joined Surrey Police, 1966; transf. to Metropolitan Police, as Chief Inspector, 1983; posts at Heathrow Airport, New Scotland Yard and Notting Hill; Chief Superintendent, 1989; Divl Comdr, Wandsworth, 1990–94; Hd, Diplomatic Protection Br., 1994; Asst Chief Constable, Surrey Police, 1994–98: Head: Support Services, 1994–95; Territorial Policing, 1995–96; Specialist Ops, 1997–98; City of London Police: Dep. to Comr and Operational Hd, 1998–99; Head, Support Services, 2000–01. Association of Chief Police Officers: Chm., Firearms Licensing Cttee, 1999–; Mem. Cabinet (Dep. Chief Officers' Rep.), 2001. FIMgt 1998. *Publication:* (jtly) Neighbourhood Policing: theoretical basis for community sector policing, 1981. *Recreations:* ski-ing, creating home and garden, walking, cooking and eating. *Address:* City of London Police, 26 Old Jewry, EC2R 8DJ. *T:* (020) 7601 2002.

HART, Michael, CBE 1990; MA; FRSA; Education Consultant, European Commission, 1990–93; *b* 1 May 1928; *yr s* of late Dr F. C. Hardt; *m* 1956, Lida Dabney Adams, PhD (Wisconsin Univ.). *Educ:* Collège Français, Berlin; Landerziehungsheim Schondorf; Keble Coll., Oxford (Exhib.). 1st Cl. Hons History, 1951. Administrative Asst, UNRRA, 1945–47; Asst Master and Head of History, Sherborne Sch., 1951–56; Head of History, 1956–61, and Housemaster of School House, 1961–67, Shrewsbury Sch.; Headmaster of Mill Hill Sch., 1967–74; HM Inspector of Schs, DES, 1974–76; Headmaster, European Sch., Mol, Belgium, 1976–80; Headmaster, European Sch., Luxembourg, 1980–89; Dir, European Classes, Alden Biesen, Belgium, 1989–92. Commandeur de l'Ordre de Mérite (Luxembourg), 1989. *Publications:* The EEC and Secondary Education in the UK, 1974; The European Dimension in Primary and Secondary Education, 1992; contrib. to Reader's Digest World Atlas and Atlas of British Isles. *Recreations:* dogs, history, music, bridge. *Address:* 21 Cranborne Avenue, Eastbourne BN20 7TS.

HART, Prof. Michael, CBE 1993; FRS 1982; CPhys, FInstP; Professor of Physics, University of Manchester, 1984–93, now Emeritus; Chairman, National Synchrotron Light Source, Brookhaven National Laboratory, 1995–2000; *b* 4 Nov. 1938; *s* of Reuben Harold Victor Hart and Phyllis Mary (*née* White); *m* 1963, Susan Margaret (*née* Powell); three *d*. *Educ:* Cotham Grammar Sch., Bristol; Bristol Univ. (BSc, PhD, DSc). FInstP 1971. Research Associate: Dept of Materials Science and Engrg, Cornell Univ., 1963–65; Dept of Physics, Bristol Univ., 1965–67; Lectr in Physics, 1967–72, Reader in Physics, 1972–76, Bristol Univ.; Sen. Resident Res. Associate of Nat. Research Council, Nat. Aeronautics and Space Admin Electronics Research Center, Boston, Mass, 1969–70; Special Advisor, Central Policy Review Staff, Cabinet Office, 1975–77; Wheatstone Prof. of Physics and Head of Physics Dept, KCL, 1976–84; Science Pogramme Co-ordinator (part-time, on secondment), Daresbury Lab., SERC, 1985–88. Prof. of Applied Physics, De Montfort Univ., 1993–98; Hon. Prof. in Engrg, Warwick Univ., 1993–98; Vis. Prof. in Physics, Bristol Univ., 2000–. Amer. Crystallographic Assoc.'s Bertram Eugene Warren Award for Diffraction Physics (jtly with Dr U. Bonse), 1970; Charles Vernon Boys Prize of Inst. of Physics, 1971. *Publications:* numerous contribs to learned jls on x-ray optics, defects in crystals and synchrotron radiation. *Recreations:* weaving, flying kites. *Address:* 2 Challoner Court, Merchants Landing, Bristol BS1 4RG. *T:* (0117) 921 5291; *e-mail:* m.hart@bristol.ac.uk.

HART, Michael, FCII; non-executive Chairman, Flemings European Fledgeling Investment Trust plc, since 1998; *b* 28 Sept. 1937; *s* of William and Kathleen Hart; *m* (separated); two *s* two *d*. FCII 1971. Man. Dir, 1987–94, Chm., 1994–95, Provincial Insurance plc; Chief Exec., Sun Life and Provincial (Hldgs) plc, 1995–97, retired. Director: Inter American Insurance Ltd, 1998–; Active Languages Ltd, 1999–; Furness Building Soc., 2000–. Mem. Council, Lancaster Univ., 1998–. Chm. Trustees, Brewery Arts Centre, 1997–. *Recreations:* walking, wine. *Address:* Holly Tree Barn, Mewith, High Bentham LA2 7AY. *T:* (015242) 62568.

HART, Hon. Sir Michael (Christopher Campbell), Kt 1998; **Hon. Mr Justice Hart;** a Judge of the High Court of Justice, Chancery Division, since 1998; *b* 7 May 1948; *s* of Raymond David Campbell Hart and Penelope Mary Hart (*née* Ellis); *m* 1st, 1972, Melanie Jane Sandiford (marr. diss. 1996); two *d*; 2nd, 1996, Sara Jane Hargreaves; one *s*. *Educ:* Winchester College; Magdalen College, Oxford (MA, BCL). Called to the Bar, Gray's Inn, 1970, Bencher, 1995; QC 1987; QC (NI) 1994. Fellow, All Souls College, Oxford, 1970–77, 1979–86, 1993–95, 2001–. *Address:* c/o Royal Courts of Justice, Strand, WC2A 2LL.

HART, Prof. Oliver Simon D'Arcy, PhD; Professor of Economics, since 1993, and Andrew E. Furer Professor, since 1997, Harvard University; *b* 9 Oct. 1948; *s* of Philip Montagu D'Arcy Hart, *qv* and Ruth Hart; *m* 1974, Rita Goldberg (who retains maiden name); two *s*. *Educ:* University Coll. Sch.; Univ. of Cambridge (BA 1969); Univ. of Warwick (MA 1972); Princeton Univ. (PhD 1974). Lectr in Econs, Univ. of Essex, 1974–75; Asst Lectr in Econs, subseq. Lectr, Univ. of Cambridge, 1975–81; Fellow of Churchill Coll., Cambridge, 1975–81; Prof. of Economics, LSE, 1982–85; Prog. Dir, Centre for Economic Policy Res., 1983–84; Prof. of Economics, MIT, 1985–93. Centennial Vis. Prof., LSE, 1997–. Fellow: Econometric Soc., 1979 (Mem. Council, 1982–); Amer. Acad. of Arts and Scis, 1988. Corresp. FBA 2000. Editor, Review of Economic Studies, 1979–83. Dr *hc*: Free Univ. of Brussels, 1992; Univ. of Basel, 1994. *Publications:* Firms, Contracts, and Financial Structure, 1995; articles on economic theory in Econometrica, Rev. of Econ. Studies, Jl of Pol Economy. *Recreations:* playing and watching tennis. *Address:* Department of Economics, Harvard University, Cambridge, MA 02138, USA.

HART, Peter; *see* Hart, E. P.

HART, P(hilip) M(ontagu) D'Arcy, CBE 1956; MA, MD (Cambridge); FRCP; Medical Research Council grant holder, National Institute for Medical Research, 1965–93, now Visiting Scientist (Director, Tuberculosis Research Unit, Medical Research Council, 1948–65); *b* 25 June 1900; *s* of late Henry D'Arcy Hart and late Hon. Ethel Montagu; *m* 1941, Ruth, *d* of late Herbert Meyer and late Grete Meyer-Larsen; one *s*. *Educ:* Clifton Coll.; Gonville and Caius Coll., Cambridge; University Coll. Hospital. Dorothy Temple Cross Fellowship to USA, 1934–35; Consultant Physician, UCH, 1934–37; Mem. Scientific Staff, MRC, 1937–48; Mem. Expert Cttee on Tuberculosis, WHO, 1947–64. Hon. FMedSci 1999. Goldsmith Entrance Exhibnr, Filliter Exhibnr, Magrath Scholarship, Tuke Medals, UCH Medical Sch., 1922–25; Horton Smith MD Prize, Cambridge, 1930; Royal College of Physicians: Milroy Lecture, 1937; Mitchell Lecture, 1946; Weber-Parkes Prize, 1951; Marc Daniels Lecture, 1967; Stewart Prize, BMA, 1964; British Thoracic Soc. Medal, 1996. *Publications:* scientific papers on respiratory disease, epidemiology and cell biology. *Address:* 37 Belsize Court, NW3 5QN. *T:* (020) 7435 4048. *Club:* Athenæum.

See also O. S. D'A. Hart.

HART, Roger Dudley, CMG 1998; HM Diplomatic Service; Ambassador to Peru, since 1999; *b* 29 Dec. 1943; *s* of Alfred John Hart and Emma Jane Hart; *m* 1968, Maria de Los Angeles (Angela) de Santiago Jimenez; two *s*. *Educ:* St Olave's Grammar Sch., London; Univ. of Birmingham (BA 1965). FO 1965; served British Mil. Govt W Berlin, Bahrain and FCO, to 1975; First Sec. (Aid), Nairobi, 1975–78; First Sec. (Commercial), Lisbon, 1978–83; FCO, 1983–85; RCDS 1985; BNSC, 1986; Consul-Gen., Rio de Janeiro, 1986–90; Dep. Hd of Mission, Mexico City, 1990–93; Head of Nationality, Treaty and Claims Dept, FCO, 1993–95; Ambassador to Angola, and (non-resident) to São Tomé and Príncipe, 1995–98. Citizen, 1989, Pedro Ernesto Medal, 1990, Rio de Janeiro. *Recreations:* travel, classical music, watching football and cricket. *Address:* c/o Foreign and Commonwealth Office, King Charles Street, SW1A 2AH. *Club:* Royal Over-Seas League.

HART, (Thomas) Anthony (Alfred), MA; Headmaster, Cranleigh School, 1984–97; *b* 4 March 1940; *er s* of Rev. Arthur Reginald Hart and Florence Ivy Hart; *m* 1971, Daintre Margaret Withiel (*née* Thomas); one *s* one *d*. *Educ:* City of Bath Sch.; New Coll., Oxford (2nd Cl. Hons PPE; MA); Pres., Oxford Union, 1963. Served with VSO, Mzuzu Secondary Sch., Nyasaland, 1959–60. Asst Principal and Principal, Min. of Transport, 1964–69; seconded to Govt of Malaŵi as Transport Adviser, 1969–70; Principal, DoE and CSD, 1970–73; Head, Voluntary Services Unit, Home Office, 1973–75; Asst Sec., CSD and HM Treasury, 1975–84. *Recreations:* lotus-eating, catching up, learning Greek. *Address:* PO Box 59340, Pissouri, 4607, Cyprus. *T:* (5) 222802, *Fax:* (5) 222801.

HART-DAVIS, Dr Adam John; freelance photographer, writer and broadcaster, since 1994; *b* 4 July 1943; *yr s* of Sir Rupert Hart-Davis; *m* 1965, Adrienne Alpin (marr. diss. 1995); two *s*. *Educ:* Eton; Merton Coll., Oxford (BA 1st Cl. Hons Chemistry 1966); York Univ. (DPhil 1968). Post-doctoral Research: Univ. of Alberta, Edmonton, 1969–71; Univ. of Oxford, 1971; College Science Editor, Clarendon Press (OUP), 1971–77; Researcher, 1977–83, Producer, 1983–94, Yorkshire Television. Presenter: TV series: Local Heroes, 1992–2000; Hart-Davis on History, 1998, 1999; Secret City, 2000; What the Romans Did for Us, 2000; What the Victorians Did for Us, 2001; Science Shack, 2001; radio series, Inventors Imperfect, 1999–. *Publications:* Don't Just Sit There!, 1980; (with Hilary Lawson) Where There's Life …, 1982; Scientific Eye, 1986; Mathematical Eye, 1989; World's Weirdest "True" Ghost Stories, 1991; (with Susan Blackmore) Test Your Psychic Powers, 1995; Thunder, Flush and Thomas Crapper, 1997; Science Tricks, 1997; (with Paul Bader) The Local Heroes Book of British Ingenuity, 1997; (with Paul Bader) More Local Heroes, 1998; Amazing Math Puzzles, 1998; Eurekaaargh!, 1999; (with Paul Bader) The Local Heroes Book of DIY Science, 2000; Chain Reactions, 2000; What the Victorians Did for Us, 2001. *Recreations:* cycling, ping pong, photography, drinking wine. *Address:* 31 Berkeley Road, Bishopston, Bristol BS7 8HF. *T:* (0117) 944 6022.

HART-DAVIS, (Peter) Duff; author and journalist; *b* 3 June 1936; *er s* of Sir Rupert Hart-Davis; *m* 1961, Phyllida Barstow; one *s* one *d*. *Educ:* Eton; Worcester Coll., Oxford (BA 1960). Nat. Service, Coldstream Guards, 1955–57. Joined Sunday Telegraph, 1961; Editor, News Background page, 1966–70; feature writer, 1971–75; Literary Editor, 1975–76; Asst Editor, 1976–78. Country Columnist, Independent, 1986–. *Publications:* Ascension, 1972; Peter Fleming, 1974; Monarchs of the Glen, 1978; Hitler's Games, 1986; (ed) The Letters and Journals of Sir Alan Lascelles: Vol. 1, End of an Era, 1986; Vol. 2, In Royal Service, 1989; Armada, 1988; Country Matters, 1989; The House the Berrys Built, 1990; Wildings: the secret garden of Eileen Soper, 1991; Further Country Matters, 1992; When the Country Went to Town, 1997; Raoul Millais, 1998; *fiction:* The Megacull, 1968; The Gold of St Matthew, 1970; Spider in the Morning, 1972; The Heights of Rimring, 1980; Level Five, 1982; Fire Falcon, 1983; The Man-eater of Jassapur, 1985; Horses of War, 1991. *Recreations:* opera, wine, cutting and splitting firewood, deer. *Address:* Owlpen Farm, Uley, Glos GL11 5BZ. *T:* (01453) 860239. *Club:* Garrick.

See also A. J. Hart-Davis.

HART DYKE, Captain David, CBE 1990; LVO 1980; RN; Clerk to Worshipful Company of Skinners, since 1990; *b* 3 Oct. 1938; *s* of Comdr Rev. Eric Hart Dyke and Mary Hart Dyke; *m* 1967, Diana Margaret, *d* of Sir William Luce, GBE, KCMG; two *d*. *Educ:* St Lawrence College, Ramsgate; BRNC Dartmouth. RN 1958; served Far East and Middle East; navigation specialist; Exec. Officer, HMS Hampshire, 1974–76; Staff, RN Staff Coll., 1976–78; Comdr, HM Yacht Britannia, 1978–80; Captain HMS Coventry; action in Falklands, 1982; ACOS to C-in-C Fleet, 1982–84; Asst Naval Attaché, Washington, 1985–87; Dir, Naval Recruiting, 1987–89. ADC to the Queen, 1988–89. *Publications:* articles on Falklands campaign for professional jls, incl. Naval Review. *Recreations:* painting, garden design, reading, military history. *Address:* Hambledon House, Hambledon, Hants PO7 4RU. *T:* (023) 9263 2380. *Club:* Naval and Military.

HART DYKE, Sir David (William), 10th Bt *cr* 1677, of Horeham, Sussex; journalist; *b* 5 Jan. 1955; *s* of Sir Derek William Hart Dyke, 9th Bt and Dorothy Moses; *S* father, 1987. *Educ:* Ryerson Polytechnical Institute (BA). *Recreations:* portage camping, ice hockey, reading. *Heir:* *uncle* (Oliver) Guy Hart Dyke [*b* 9 Feb. 1928; *m* 1974, Sarah Alexander, *d* of late Rev. Eric Hart Dyke; one *s* one *d*]. *Address:* 28 King Street West, Apt 14B, Stoney Creek, ON L8G 1H4, Canada.

HART-LEVERTON, Colin Allen; QC 1979; a Recorder of the Crown Court, since 1979; *b* 10 May 1936; *s* of Monty Hart-Leverton and Betty (*née* Simmonds); one *s*; *m* 1990,

Kathi Jo, *d* of Hal and Jan Davidson. *Educ:* Stowe; self-taught thereafter. Mem., Inst. of Taxation, 1957 (youngest to have ever qualified); called to the Bar, Middle Temple, 1957 (youngest to have ever qual.). Contested (L): Bristol West, 1959 (youngest cand.); Walthamstow West, 1964. Prosecuting Counsel, Central Criminal Court, 1974–79; Dep. Circuit Judge, 1975; Attorney-at-Law, Turks and Caicos Islands, Caribbean, 1976. Occasional television and radio broadcasts. *Recreations:* table-tennis, jazz. *Address:* 8 King's Bench Walk, Temple, EC4Y 7DU. *T:* (020) 7797 8888.

HARTE, Julia Kathleen; *see* McKenzie, J. K.

HARTE, Dr Michael John; consultant in information technology, since 1995; Director General Information Technology Systems, Ministry of Defence, 1994–95; *b* 15 Aug. 1936; *s* of late Harold Edward Harte and Marjorie Irene Harte; *m* 1st, 1962, Diana Hayes (marr. diss. 1971); 2nd, 1975, Mary Claire Preston; four step *d. Educ:* Charterhouse; Trinity Coll., Cambridge (BA); University Coll., London (PhD; Dip. in Biochem. Engrg). Sen. Scientific Officer, Micro-biol Res. Estab., MoD, 1963; Principal, MoD, 1967; Private Sec. to Minister of State for Def., 1972; Asst Sec., Central Policy Rev. Staff, 1973; Asst Sec., MoD, 1975–77; Counsellor, Budget and Infrastructure, UK Delegn to NATO, 1977–81; Chm., NATO Civil and Mil. Budget Cttees, 1981–83; Asst Sec., MoD, 1983–85; Assistant Under Secretary of State: (Dockyard Planning Team), MoD, 1985–87; (Personnel) (Air), MoD, 1987–90; (Resources), MoD, 1990–93. Non-exec. Dir, GlaxoChem., 1988–91. FRSA 1995. *Recreation:* growing and cooking vegetables. *Address:* Greenman Farm, Wadhurst, E Sussex TN5 6LE. *T:* (01892) 783292.

HARTER, Caryl, (Mrs David Harter); *see* Churchill, C.

HARTHAN, John Plant, MA; FLA; Keeper of the Library, Victoria and Albert Museum, 1962–76; *b* 15 April 1916; *y s* of late Dr George Ezra Harthan, Evesham, Worcs, and Winifred May Slater. *Educ:* Bryanston; Jesus Coll., Cambridge; University Coll., London. Asst-Librarian, Southampton Univ., 1940–43; Royal Society of Medicine Library, 1943–44; Asst Under-Librarian, Cambridge Univ. Library, 1944–48; Asst-Keeper of the Library, Victoria and Albert Museum, 1948. FLA 1939. *Publications:* Bookbindings in the Victoria and Albert Museum, 1950, 3rd edn 1985; (ed jtly) F.D. Klingender, Animals in Art and Thought, 1971; Books of Hours, 1977, 3rd edn 1988; The History of the Illustrated Book, 1981; Introduction to Illuminated Manuscripts, 1983. *Recreations:* history of religion, royalty, music, botany, writing. *Address:* The Cotswold Home, Woodside Drive, Bradwell Grove, Burford, Oxon OX18 4XA.

HARTILL, Edward Theodore, FRICS; City Surveyor, Corporation of London, since 1985; *b* 23 Jan. 1943; *s* of Clement Augustus Hartill and late Florence Margarita Hartill; *m* 1975, Gillian Ruth (*née* Todd); two *s*, and two *s* from previous marr. *Educ:* Priory Sch. for Boys, Shrewsbury; Coll. of Estate Management, London Univ. BSc (Estate Management); FRICS 1978. Joined Messrs Burd and Evans, Land Agents, Shrewsbury, 1963; Estates Dept, Legal and Gen. Assce Soc., 1964–73; Property Investment Dept, Guardian Royal Exchange Assce Gp, 1973–85 (Hd Office Manager, 1980–85). Vis. Lectr in Law of Town Planning and Compulsory Purchase, Hammersmith and W London Coll. of Advanced Business Studies, 1968–78. Royal Institution of Chartered Surveyors: Member: Gen. Practice Divl Council, 1989–97 (Pres., 1992–93); Gen. Council, 1990–; Hon. Treas., 2000–. Mem., Assoc. of Chief Estates Surveyors and Property Managers in Local Govt (formerly Local Authority Valuers Assoc.), 1985– (Mem., Nat. Council, 1988–; Pres., 1996–97); Mem. Steering Gp, 1992–99, and Chm., Property Services Sub-Gp, 1992–99, Construction Industry Standing Conf.; Founder Mem. and Chm., Property Services NTO, 1999–. Hon. Mem., Investment Property Forum, 1995. Hon. Associate, Czech Chamber of Appraisers, 1992. Mem., British Schs Exploring Soc. FRSA 1993. Liveryman, Worshipful Co. of Chartered Surveyors, 1985– (Mem., Court of Assistants, 1991–; Chm. Organising Cttee, UK Property Marketing Awards, 1999). *Publications:* occasional lectures and articles on professional topics. *Recreations:* films, hill walking, travel. *Address:* 215 Sheen Lane, East Sheen, SW14 8LE. *T:* (020) 8878 4494.
See also R. J. Hartill.

HARTILL, Rosemary Jane; independent broadcaster and writer; Religious Affairs Correspondent, BBC, 1982–88; *b* 11 Aug. 1949; *d* of Clement Augustus Hartill and late Florence Margarita Ford. *Educ:* Wellington Girls' High Sch., Salop; Bristol Univ. (BA (Hons) English). Editor: Tom Stacey (Publishing) Ltd, 1970–73; David and Charles Ltd, 1973–75; Sen. Non-Fiction Editor, Hamish Hamilton Children's Books Ltd, 1975–76; freelance journalist and broadcaster, 1976–82; freelance book and ballet reviewer, TES, 1976–80; Religious Affairs Reporter, BBC, 1979–82; Reporter: BBC Everyman Prog., 1987; ITV Human Factor series, 1989–92; Presenter: BBC Woman's Hour (NE edns), 1989–90; Meridian Books (BBC World Service), and numerous other progs. Founder, Rosemary Hartill & Associates, 1996; Co-Founder, Voyager TV Ltd, 1997; non-executive Director: Shared Interest, 1996–; Ethical Investment Res. and Inf. Service, 1997–2001. Bd Mem., Northumbrian Probation Service, 2000–. Trustee, Alternatives to Violence Project, 1997–2000. Mem., Soc. of Friends (Mem., Former Yugoslavia Project Mgt Gp, 2000–). Hon. DLitt: Hull, 1995; Bristol, 2000. Sandford St Martin Trust personal award for outstanding contrib. to religious broadcasting, 1994, and other awards. *Publications:* (ed) Emily Brontë: poems, 1973; Wild Animals, 1978; In Perspective, 1988; Writers Revealed, 1989; Were You There?, 1995; (ed) Florence Nightingale, 1996. *Recreations:* wildlife, walking, theatre, gardening, art exhibitions, being in Northumberland. *Address:* Old Post Office, Eglingham, Alnwick, Northumberland NE66 2TX.
See also E. T. Hartill.

HARTING, Henry Maria Robert Egmont M.; *see* Mayr-Harting.

HARTINGTON, Marquess of; Peregrine Andrew Morny Cavendish, CBE 1997; Her Majesty's Representative, Ascot, since 1998; *b* 27 April 1944; *s* of 11th Duke of Devonshire, *qv* and of Duchess of Devonshire, *qv*; *m* 1967, Amanda Carmen, *d* of late Comdr E. G. Heywood-Lonsdale, RN, and of Mrs Heywood-Lonsdale; one *s* two *d. Educ:* Eton; Exeter Coll., Oxford. Sen. Steward, Jockey Club, 1989–94; Chm., British Horseracing Bd, 1993–96. Dep. Chm., Sotheby's Holdings Inc., 1996– (Dir, 1994–). *Heir: s* Earl of Burlington, *qv*. *Address:* Beamsley Hall, Bolton Abbey, Skipton, N Yorks BD23 6HD.

HARTLAND, Michael; *see* James, M. L.

HARTLAND-SWANN, Julian Dana Nimmo, CMG 1992; HM Diplomatic Service, retired; Thai-Europe business consultant, since 1997; *b* 18 Feb. 1936; *s* of late Prof. J. J. Hartland-Swann and of Mrs Kenlis Hartland-Swann (*née* Taylour); *m* 1960, Ann Deirdre Green (*d* 2000); one *s* one *d. Educ:* Stowe; Lincoln Coll., Oxford (History). HM Forces, 1955–57. Entered HM Diplomatic Service, 1960; 3rd Sec., Brit. Embassy, Bangkok, 1961–65; 2nd, later 1st Sec., FO, 1965–68; 1st Sec., Berlin, 1968–71; 1st Sec. and Head of Chancery, Vienna, 1971–74; FCO, 1975–77; Counsellor, 1977; Ambassador to Mongolian People's Republic, 1977–79; Counsellor and Dep. Head of Mission, Brussels, 1979–83; Head of SE Asian Dept, FCO, 1983–85; Consul Gen., Frankfurt, 1986–90; Ambassador to Burma (Myanmar), 1990–95; Exec. Dir, Eur. Business Inf. Centre, Delegn of the EC to Thailand, 1995–97. *Recreations:* French food, sailing, restoring ruins. *Address:* Résidence Hof Ten Berg, Clos Hof Ten Berg 30, 1200 Brussels, Belgium.

HARTLEY, Prof. Brian Selby, PhD; FRS 1971; Chairman, Agrol Ltd, 1993–2000; Professor of Biochemistry, Imperial College, University of London, 1974–91, Emeritus Professor, 1991; Senior Research Fellow, Centre for Biotechnology, 1991–94 (Director, 1982–91); *b* 16 April 1926; *s* of Norman and Hilda Hartley; *m* 1949, Kathleen Maude Vaughan; three *s* one *d. Educ:* Queens' Coll., Cambridge; Univ. of Leeds. BA 1947, MA 1952, Cantab; PhD 1952, Leeds. ICI Fellow, Univ. of Cambridge, 1952; Helen Hay Whitney Fellow, Univ. of Washington, Seattle, USA, 1958; Fellow and Lectr in Biochemistry, Trinity Coll., Cambridge, 1964; Scientific Staff, MRC Laboratory of Molecular Biology, 1961–74. Mem. Council: EMBO (European Centre for Molecular Biology), 1978–84; Royal Soc., 1982–84. Hon. Mem., Amer. Soc. of Biological Chemists, 1977. British Drug Houses Medal for Analytical Biochemistry, 1969. *Publications:* papers and articles in scientific jls and books. *Recreations:* fishing, gardening. *Address:* Grove Cottage, Smith Street, Elsworth, Cambridge CB3 8HY.

HARTLEY, David Fielding, PhD; CEng; FBCS; Executive Director, Cambridge Crystallographic Data Centre, since 1997; Fellow of Clare College, Cambridge, since 1987; *b* 14 Sept. 1937; *s* of late Robert M. Hartley and Sheila E. Hartley, LRAM; *m* 1960, Joanna Mary (*d* 1998), *d* of late Stanley and of Constance Bolton; one *s* two *d. Educ:* Rydal Sch.; Clare Coll., Cambridge (MA, PhD). University of Cambridge: Sen. Asst in Research, Mathematical Lab., 1964–65; Asst Dir of Research, 1966–67; Univ. Lectr, 1967–70; Dir, Univ. Computing Service, 1970–94; Jun. Research Fellow, Churchill Coll., Cambridge, 1964–67; Fellow, Darwin Coll., Cambridge, 1969–86; Chief Exec., UK Educn and Res. Networking Assoc., 1994–97. British Computer Society: Mem. Council, 1970–73, 1977–80, 1985–90, 1998–; Vice Pres. (Technical), 1985–87, (External Relns), 1987–90; Dep. Pres., 1998–99; Pres., 1999–2000. Chm., Inter-University Cttee on Computing, 1972–74; Mem., Computer Board for Univs and Research Councils, 1979–83; Mem. Council of Management, Numerical Algorithms Gp Ltd, 1979– (Chm., 1986–97); adviser to Prime Minister, Information Technology Adv. Panel, 1981–86; DTI Hon. Adviser in Information Technology (on sabbatical leave), 1983; Mem. various Govt, Res. Council and Industry cttees and consultancies. Mem., BBC Science Consultative Gp, 1984–87. Dir, CADCentre Ltd, 1983–94. Governor, Rydal Sch., 1982–88. Medal of Merits, Nicholas Copernicus Univ., Poland, 1984. *Publications:* papers in scientific jls on operating systems, programming languages, computing service management. *Address:* CCDC, 12 Union Road, Cambridge CB2 1EZ. *T:* (01223) 336409.

HARTLEY, Prof. Frank Robinson, CChem, FRSC; Vice-Chancellor, Cranfield University (formerly Cranfield Institute of Technology), since 1989; *b* 29 Jan. 1942; *s* of Sir Frank Hartley, CBE; *m* 1964, Valerie Peel; three *d. Educ:* King's College Sch., Wimbledon (Sambrooke Schol.); Magdalen Coll., Oxford (Demy; BA, MA, DPhil, DSc). FRAeS 1996. Post-doctoral Fellow, Commonwealth Scientific and Industrial Research Organisation, Div. of Protein Chemistry, Melbourne, Aust., 1966–69; Imperial Chemical Industries Research Fellow and Tutor in Physical Chemistry, University Coll. London, 1969–70; Lectr in Inorganic Chemistry, Univ. of Southampton, 1970–75; Professor of Chemistry and Head of Dept of Chemistry and Metallurgy, 1975–82, Acting Dean, 1982–84, Principal and Dean, 1984–89, RMCS, Shrivenham. Chm., Cranfield IT Inst., 1989–90 (Dir, 1986–89); Man. Dir, CIT (Holdings) Ltd, 1993– (Dir, 1989–93); Chm., CIM Inst., 1990–; Dir, Cranfield Ventures Ltd, 1990– (Man. Dir, 2000–); non-executive Director: T & N, 1989–98; Eastern Regl Adv. Bd, National Westminster Bank, 1990–92; Kalon, 1994–99; Kenwood, 1995–99; Hunting-BRAE Ltd, 1999–; Bedfordshire TEC, 1994–96. Sen. Travelling Fellow, ACU, 1986. Special Advr to Prime Minister on defence systems, 1988–91; Special Advr to H of L Select Cttee on Sci. and Technol., 1994–95; Mem., Parly Scientific Cttee, 1986– (Mem. Council and Gen. Purposes Cttee, 1992–98; Vice-Pres., 1995–98). Member: Internat. Adv. Bd, Kanagawa Acad. of Sci. and Technol., Japan, 1989–; Bd, Internat. Foundn for Artificial Intelligence, 1990–. Chm., Lorch Foundn, 1995–; Dir, Shuttleworth Trust, 1994–97. Gov., Welbeck Coll., 1984–89; Mem. Court, Bath Univ., 1982–89. Mem., Oxford Union. FRSA 1988. Editor-in-Chief, Brassey's New Battlefield Weapons Systems and Technology series, 1988–. *Publications:* The Chemistry of Platinum and Palladium (Applied Science), 1973; Elements of Organometallic Chemistry (Chemical Soc.), 1974, Japanese edn 1981, Chinese edn 1989; (with C. Burgess and R. M. Alcock) Solution Equilibria, 1980, Russian edn 1983; (with S. Patai) The Chemistry of the Metal—Carbon Bond, vol. 1 1983, vol. 2 1984, vol. 3 1985, vol. 4 1987, vol. 5 1989; Supported Metal Complexes, 1985, Russian edn 1987; The Chemistry of Organophosphorus Compounds, vol. 1, 1990, vol. 2, 1992, vol. 3, 1994, vol. 4, 1996; Chemistry of the Platinum Group Metals, 1991; papers in inorganic, coordination and organometallic chemistry in major English, Amer. and Aust. chemical jls. *Recreations:* gardening, swimming, cliff walking, reading. *Address:* Cayley Lodge, Prince Philip Avenue, Wharley End, Cranfield, Bedford MK43 0SX. *Clubs:* Institute of Directors; Shrivenham.

HARTLEY, His Honour Gilbert Hillard; retired; a Circuit Judge (formerly Judge of County Courts), 1967–82; *b* 11 Aug. 1917; *s* of late Percy Neave Hartley and late Nellie Bond Hartley (*née* Hillard); *m* 1948, Jeanne, *d* of late C. W. Gall, Leeds; one *s* two *d. Educ:* Ashville, Harrogate; Exeter Coll., Oxford. Called to Bar, Middle Temple, 1939. Served with Army, 1940–46. Recorder of Rotherham, 1965–67; Dep. Chm., WR of Yorkshire QS, 1965–71. *Address:* Nidd Rise, Main Street, Moor Monkton, York YO26 8JA.

HARTLEY, Prof. Keith, PhD; Professor of Economics, since 1987, and Director, Centre for Defence Economics, since 1990, University of York; *b* 14 July 1940; *s* of Walter and Ivy Hartley; *m* 1966, Winifred Kealy; one *s* two *d. Educ:* Univ. of Hull (BSc Econs; PhD 1974). Dir, Inst. for Res. in Social Scis, Univ. of York, 1982–94. NATO Res. Fellow, 1977–79 and 1986–87. *Publications:* Economics of Defence Policy, 1991; (with T. Sandler) Economics of Defense, 1995; Political Economy of NATO, 1999. *Recreations:* walking, angling, football, reading. *Address:* Centre for Defence Economics, University of York, York YO1 5DD. *T:* (01904) 433680.

HARTLEY, Richard Leslie Clifford; QC 1976; *b* 31 May 1932; *s* of late Arthur Clifford Hartley, CBE and late Nina Hartley. *Educ:* Marlborough Coll.; Sidney Sussex Coll., Cambridge (MA). Called to the Bar, Gray's Inn, 1956, Bencher, 1986. *Recreations:* golf, tennis, horse racing. *Address:* 15 Chesham Street, SW1X 8ND. *T:* (020) 7235 2420. *Clubs:* Garrick, MCC; Woking Golf; Rye Golf; St Enodoc Golf; New Zealand Golf (Weybridge).

HARTMANN, Dr Peter, Hon. KBE 1992; Ambassador of Germany to France, since 1998; *b* 9 Oct. 1935; *m* Baroness Lonny von Blomberg-Hartmann. *Educ:* Frankfurt; Papal Univ., Rome (LPH); Cologne; Fribourg Univ. (DPhil). Foreign Service, 1965; Washington, 1966; Karachi, 1968; EC Brussels, 1971; Buenos Aires, 1978; Head, Foreign Relations Office, CDU, 1981–84; Federal Chancellery: Head, European Policy, 1984–87; Asst Under-Sec., Foreign, Security and Develt Policy, 1987–90; Dep Under-Sec., Foreign

Security Policy, and Advr to Federal Chancellor, 1991–93; Ambassador to UK, 1993–95; Under Sec. of State, Foreign Min., Germany, 1995–98. *Address:* 78 rue de Lille, 75007 Paris, France.

HARTNACK, Paul Richard Samuel, CB 1999; Comptroller General and Chief Executive, The Patent Office, 1990–99; *b* 17 Nov. 1942; *s* of Carl Samuel and Maud Godden Hartnack; *m* 1966, Marion Quirk; two *s*. *Educ:* Hastings Grammar Sch. Clerical and Exec. posts, BoT, 1961–67; Asst Sec., Cttee of Enquiry into Civil Air Transport, 1967–68; Second Sec., British Embassy, Paris, 1969–71; Exec. posts, DTI, 1972–78; Asst Sec., NEB, 1978–80; Sec., Brit. Technology Gp, 1981–85; Asst Sec., Finance and Resource Management Div., DTI, 1985–89. *Recreation:* gardening. *Address:* 24 Benslow Rise, Hitchin, Herts SG4 9QX. *T:* (01462) 457312.

HARTNETT, David Anthony; Commissioner, Board of Inland Revenue, since 2000; *b* 25 Feb. 1951; *s* of George Peter Hartnett and Mary Christine Hartnett (*née* O'Donoghue); *m* 1977, Aileen Patricia Mary O'Dempsey; two *s* one *d*. *Educ:* Hampton Sch.; Birmingham Univ. (BA Hons Latin). Inland Revenue, 1976–: Inspector of Taxes, 1976–86; Investigation Manager, 1986–91; Dir, Financial Intermediaries and Claims Office, 1991–96; Asst Dir, Personal Tax Div., 1996–98; Dir, Savings and Investment and Capital and Valuation Divs, 1998–99; Dir, Capital and Savings Div., 1999–2000. *Recreations:* food, wine, Marcus Tullius Cicero. *Address:* Inland Revenue, Somerset House, Strand, WC2R 1LB. *T:* (020) 7438 6789.

HARTNOLL, Mary Charmian, CBE 1990; Director of Social Work, Glasgow City Council, 1995–98; *b* 31 May 1939; *d* of Rev. Sydney W. Hartnoll and Margaret Hartnoll. *Educ:* Colston's Girls' Grammar Sch., Bristol; Bedford Coll., Univ. of London (BA Hons); Univ. of Liverpool (HO Cert. in Child Care). Child Care Officer, Dorset CC, 1961–63; various posts, County Borough of Reading, 1963–74; Asst Dir, Berks CC, 1974–75; Divl Officer, Reading, 1975–77; Dir of Social Work: Grampian Regl Council, 1978–93; Strathclyde Regl Council, 1993–95. Chm., E Park, Glasgow, 2000–. Hon. LLD Robert Gordon Univ., 1993. *Recreations:* natural history, walking, music, theatre going.

HARTOG, Harold Samuel Arnold; Knight, Order of the Netherlands Lion; KBE (Hon.) 1970; Advisory Director, Unilever NV, 1971–75; *b* Nijmegen, Holland, 21 Dec. 1910; *m* 1963, Ingeborg Luise Krahn. *Educ:* Wiedemann Coll., Geneva. Joined Unilever, 1931. After service with Dutch forces during War of 1939–45 he joined management of Unilever interests in France, and subseq. took charge of Unilever cos in the Netherlands; elected to Bds of Unilever, 1948; Mem. Rotterdam Group Management and responsible for Unilever activities in Germany, Austria and Belgium, 1952–60; subseq. Mem. Cttee for Unilever's overseas interests, in London; became, there, one of the two world co-ordinators of Unilever's foods interests, 1962; Chm., Unilever NV, 1966–71. *Recreations:* history of art, collecting Chinese pottery and porcelain. *Address:* Kösterbergstrasse 40B, 22587 Hamburg, Germany. *Clubs:* Dutch; Ubersee (Hamburg); Golf (Falkenstein).

HARTOP, Barry; Chairman, Locum Group Ltd, since 1997; Chief Executive, Nextra (UK) Ltd, since 2001; *b* 15 Aug. 1942; *s* of Philip William Hartop and Constance Winifred (*née* Drew); *m* 1966, Sandra Swan; one *s* one *d*. *Educ:* Durham Univ. (BSc Hons Chem. Engrg). Prodn and technical mgt, Lever Bros Ltd, 1965–72; Unilever PLC: Chm., Cost Reduction and R&D, 1977–80; Man. Dir, European Business Centre, 1980–83; Chm. and Man. Dir, Lever Industrial Ltd, 1983–89; Man. Dir, Gestetner Hldgs, 1989–92; Chief Executive: WDA, 1994–96; Millennium Exhibn, 1996; Man. Dir, Norsk Data, 1997–2001. Chm., Hammicks Bookshops Ltd, 1994–98. Gov., Royal Grammar Sch., Guildford, 1991–. *Recreations:* squash, tennis, keep fit, sitting in the sun, gardening. *Address:* Field Cottage, The Ridgeway, Guildford, Surrey GU1 2DG. *T:* (01483) 577617.

HARTRIDGE, David Charles, CMG 2001; Special Adviser to Director-General, World Trade Organization; *b* 22 April 1939; *s* of Sidney George Hartridge and Mabel Kate (*née* Hunt); *m* 1965, Dorothy Ann Ling (marr. diss. 1997); two *d*. *Educ:* Windsor Grammar Sch.; Oriel Coll., Oxford (MA). BoT, 1961–71; First Sec., UK Mission, Geneva, 1971–75; Asst Sec., DTI, 1977–79; Counsellor, UK Repn to EEC, Brussels, 1979–80; Chef de Cabinet, GATT, 1980–85; Dir, GATT and WTO, 1985–2001, Dir, Services Div., 1993–2001, Dir-in-Charge, May–Sept. 1999. *Recreations:* bird watching, music, history. *Address:* 23 Route de Sauverny, Grilly 01220, France. *T:* (4) 50201993.

HARTWELL, Sir Anthony; *see* Hartwell, Sir F. A. C. P.

HARTWELL, Sir (Francis) Anthony (Charles Peter), 6th Bt *cr* 1805, of Dale Hall, Essex; marine consultant; *b* 1 June 1940; *o s* of Sir Brodrick William Charles Elwin Hartwell, 5th Bt and of his 1st wife, Marie Josephine Hartwell, *d* of S. P. Mullins; *S* father, 1993; *m* 1968, Barbara Phyllis Rae (marr. diss. 1989), *d* of H. Rae Green; one *s*. *Educ:* Thames Nautical Coll., HMS Worcester. Cadet, RNR. Master's Foreign Going (Cl. 1) Cert. MNI, MRIN. Captain (Master Mariner), 1972. Sea Service Navigating Officer, Asst Nautical Inspector, then Cargo Supt (Overseas Containers Ltd) London, P&O Group, 1958–71; Chief Officer/Master, North Sea ops, Ocean Inchcape Ltd, 1972–73; P&O Cadet Trng Officer, 1973–75; overseas port management, Nigeria, Papua New Guinea and Saudia Arabia, 1975–87; Branch Manager, Lloyds Agency, Dammam, Saudi Arabia, 1987–89; marine surveyor and nautical consultant, Saudi Arabia, The Maldives, Nigeria, Cyprus, 1989–93. *Recreations:* ocean sailing, scuba diving, photography. *Heir: s* Timothy Peter Michael Charles Hartwell, *b* 8 July 1970. *Clubs:* Cachalots-Southampton Master Mariners'; Old Worcester's Association.

HARTY, Bernard Peter, CBE 1998; Chairman: London Pension Fund Authority, since 1999; English China Clay Pension Fund, since 2000; London Processing Centre Pension Fund, since 2001; *b* 1 May 1943; *s* of William Harty and Eileen Nora (*née* Canavan); *m* 1965, Glenys Elaine Simpson; one *d*. *Educ:* St Richards Coll., Droitwich; Ullathorne Grammar Sch., Coventry. CPFA 1966; FBCS 1996. Accountant, Coventry CBC, 1961–69; Forward Budget Planning Officer, Derbyshire CC, 1969–72; Chief Accountant, Bradford CBC, 1972–74; Chief Finance Officer, Bradford MDC, 1973–76; County Treasurer, Oxfordshire CC, 1976–83; Chamberlain, 1983–99, and Town Clerk, 1996–99, City of London Corp.; Man. Dir, Barbican Centre, 1994–95. Chm. 1994–2000, Chm., London Br. Adv. Bd, 2000–, Dexia Public Finance Bank. Mem. Nat. Cttee, Information Technol. Year 1982 (IT82); Chm., IT82 Local Govt Cttee, 1982. Chm., Foundn for IT in Local Govt, 1988 91. Chm., Treasury Management Panel, 1991–94, Superannuation Investments Panel, 1994–95, CIPFA; Member: Local Govt Sub Gp, Financial Law Panel, 1993–95; HM Treasury Cttee on Local Authy Borrowing, 1994–95. Mem., Bd, Gloucestershire Everyman Theatre, 1998–. Freeman, City of London, 1983; Liveryman, Worshipful Co. of Tallow Chandlers, 1984; Founder Mem., Co. of Information Technologists (Hon. Liveryman, 1997). Hon. DPhil London Guildhall Univ., 1997. Commander, Nat. Order of Merit (France), 1996. *Publications:* papers in professional jls. *Recreations:* theatre, music, National Trust, sport. *Address:* London Pension Fund Authority, Dexter House, 2 Royal Mint Court, EC3N 4LP.

HARUNA, Alhaji; *see* Gwandu, Emir of.

HARVEY, family name of **Baron Harvey of Tasburgh.**

HARVEY OF TASBURGH, 2nd Baron *cr* 1954, of Tasburgh, Norfolk; **Peter Charles Oliver Harvey;** Bt 1868; FCA; *b* 28 Jan. 1921; *er s* of 1st Baron Harvey of Tasburgh, GCMG, GCVO, CB, and Maud Annora (*d* 1970), *d* of late Arthur Watkin Williams-Wynn; *S* father, 1968; *m* 1957, Penelope Anne (*d* 1995), *d* of Lt-Col Sir William Makins, 3rd Bt; two *d*. *Educ:* Eton; Trinity College, Cambridge. Served 1941–46 with Royal Artillery, Tunisia, Italy. Bank of England, 1948–56; Binder Hamlyn & Co., 1956–61; Lloyds Bank International Ltd (formerly Bank of London and South America), 1961–75; English Transcontinental Ltd, 1975–78; Brown, Shipley & Co., 1978–81. *Recreations:* sailing, music. *Heir: nephew* Charles John Giuseppe Harvey, *b* 4 Feb. 1951. *Address:* Crownick Woods, Restronguet, Mylor, Falmouth, Cornwall TR11 5ST. *Clubs:* Brooks's; Royal Cornwall Yacht.

HARVEY, Alan Frederick Ronald, OBE 1970; HM Diplomatic Service, retired; *b* 15 Dec. 1919; *s* of Edward Frederick and Alice Sophia Harvey; *m* 1946, Joan Barbara (*née* Tuckey); one *s*. *Educ:* Tottenham Grammar Sch. Air Ministry, 1936–40 (Civil Service appt). Served War, RAF, 1940–46. Air Min., 1946–49; Foreign Office, 1949–52 (on transfer to Diplomatic Service); HM Vice-Consul, Turin, 1953–55; Second Sec.: Rome, 1956; Tokyo, 1957–59; HM Consul (Information): Chicago, 1959–62; FO, 1963–65; First Sec. (Commercial): Belgrade, 1965–67; Tokyo, 1967–72; Commercial Counsellor: Milan, 1973–74; Rome, 1975–76; Consul-General in Perth, 1976–78. *Recreations:* gardening, golf. *Address:* Tresibbett, Altarnun, near Launceston, Cornwall PL15 7RF. *Clubs:* Royal Commonwealth Society, Civil Service.

HARVEY, Alan James, (Tim), RDI 1991; production designer, film and television; *b* 14 Oct. 1936; *s* of Ernest Harvey and Ida Harvey; *m* 1958, Sheila Todd; one *s* one *d*. *Educ:* Hampton Grammar Sch.; Manchester Univ. (BA Hons Architecture). Designer: BBC TV N Region, 1960–64; Telefis Eireann, 1964–66; BBC Scotland, 1966–69; BBC London, 1969–88; freelance film designer, 1988–; *films* include: Henry V, 1989; Much Ado About Nothing, 1993; Mary Shelley's Frankenstein, 1994; Othello, 1995; Hamlet, 1996. US Emmy Award, 1974, 1976; BAFTA Design Awards, 1976, 1985, 1987; Design Award, RTS, 1982. *Recreations:* football, Italian language and culture, family. *Address:* 2 Cambridge Court, Clevedon Road, Twickenham, Middx TW1 2HT. *T:* (020) 8892 3969.

HARVEY, Prof. Andrew Charles, FBA 1999; Professor of Econometrics, University of Cambridge, since 1996; Fellow, Corpus Christi College, Cambridge, since 1996; *b* 10 Sept. 1947; *s* of Richard Arthur Harvey and Margaret Frances Harvey (*née* Clark); *m* 1969, Lavinia Mary Young; one *s* one *d*. *Educ:* Leeds Modern Sch.; Univ. of York (BA); LSE (MSc). Economist and statistician, Central Bureau of Stats, Nairobi, 1969–71; Lectr, Univ. of Kent at Canterbury, 1971–77; Vis. Prof., Univ. of British Columbia, 1977–78; London School of Economics: Sen. Lectr, 1978–81; Reader, 1981–84; Prof. of Econometrics, 1984–96. Fellow, Econometric Soc., 1990. *Publications:* The Econometric Analysis of Time Series, 1981, 2nd edn 1990; Time Series Models, 1981, 2nd edn 1993; Forecasting, Structural Time Series Models and the Kalman Filter, 1989. *Recreations:* football, opera. *Address:* Faculty of Economics and Politics, Sidgwick Avenue, Cambridge CB3 9DD.

HARVEY, Anne Caroline Ballingall, (Mrs John Harvey); *see* McIntosh, A. C. B.

HARVEY, Rev. Canon Anthony Ernest, DD; Canon of Westminster, 1982–99, and Sub-Dean, 1987–99, Canon Emeritus, 1999; *b* 1 May 1930, *s* of Cyril Harvey, QC, and Nina (*née* Darley); *m* 1957, Julian Elizabeth McMaster; four *d*. *Educ:* Dragon Sch., Oxford; Eton Coll.; Worcester Coll., Oxford (BA, MA, DD 1983); Westcott House, Cambridge. Curate, Christ Church, Chelsea, 1958–62; Research Student, Christ Church, Oxford, 1962–69; Warden, St Augustine's Coll., Canterbury, 1969–76; Univ. Lectr in Theology and Fellow of Wolfson Coll., Oxford, 1976–82; Chaplain, The Queen's Coll., 1977–82; Librarian, Westminster Abbey, 1983–98. Examining Chaplain to Archbishop of Canterbury, 1975; Six Preacher, Canterbury Cathedral, 1977; Bampton Lectr, 1980. Member: Gen. Synod Doctrine Commn, 1977–86; Archbishop's Commn on Urban Priority Areas, 1983–85. *Publications:* Companion to the New Testament (New English Bible), 1970, 2nd edn 1980; Priest or President?, 1975; Jesus on Trial, 1976; Something Overheard, 1977; (ed) God Incarnate: story and belief, 1981; Jesus and the Constraints of History, 1982; Believing and Belonging, 1984; (ed) Alternative Approaches to New Testament Study, 1985; (ed) Theology in the City, 1989; Strenuous Commands, 1990, 2nd edn 1996; Retaliation, 1992; Promise or Pretence?: a Christian's guide to sexual morals, 1994; (ed) The Funeral Effigies of Westminster Abbey, 1994; Renewal through Suffering: a study of 2 Corinthians, 1996; Marriage, Divorce and the Church, 1997; Demanding Peace: Christian responses to war and violence, 1999; By What Authority?: the churches and social concern, 2001; articles in classical and theological jls. *Recreations:* music, walking. *Address:* Mendelssohn Cottage, Broadway Road, Willersey, Broadway, Worcs WR12 7PH. *T:* (01386) 859260.

HARVEY, Anthony Peter; Chairman: The Broad Oak Consultancy, since 1991; Heathfield Partnership, 1997–99; *b* 21 May 1940; *s* of Frederick William Henry Harvey and late Fanny Evelyn Harvey (*née* Dixon); *m* 1963, Margaret Hayward; three *s* one *d*. *Educ:* Hertford Grammar Sch. MIInfS. Dept of Oriental Printed Books, British Museum, 1958–60; British Museum (Natural History): Dept of Palaeontology, 1960–75; Librarian, 1963–75; Head, Dept of Library Services, 1981–88; Co-ordinator of Planning and Development, 1985–88; Head of Marketing and Develt, 1988–91. Dir, Natural History Mus. Develt Trust, 1990–91. Chm., Geology Inf. Gp, 1975–78, Liby Cttee, 1981–84, Geolog. Soc.; Member: Printing Hist. Soc., 1965–; Garden Hist. Soc., 1988–; Soc. for Hist. of Natural Hist., 1963– (Treas., 1964–). Trustee, Britain Australia Bicentennial Trust, 1988–. Freeman, City of London, 1985; Liveryman, Co. of Marketors, 1991. *Publications:* (ed) Secrets of the Earth, 1967; (ed) Directory of Scientific Directories, 1969, 4th edn 1986; Prehistoric Man, 1972; Guide to World Science, vol. 1, 1974; (ed) Encyclopedia of Prehistoric Life, 1979; European Sources of Scientific and Technical Information, 1981, 7th edn 1986; numerous contribs to learned jls, ref. works and periodicals. *Recreations:* garden history and design, transport history. *Address:* Oak Cottage, 23 High Street, Welshpool, Powys SY21 7JP. *T:* (01938) 559087.

HARVEY, Arthur Douglas; Assistant Under-Secretary of State, Ministry of Defence, 1969–76; *b* 16 July 1916; *o s* of late William Arthur Harvey and Edith Alice; *m* 1940, Doris Irene Lodge (*d* 1997); one *s* (and one *s* decd). *Educ:* Westcliff High Sch.; St Catharine's Coll., Cambridge. Wrangler, Maths Tripos, 1938. Entered War Office, 1938; served in Army, 1940–45; Princ. 1945; Registrar, Royal Military College of Science, 1951–54; Asst Sec. 1954; Under-Sec. 1969. *Address:* 36b Lovelace Road, Long Ditton, Surrey KT6 6ND. *T:* (020) 8399 0587.

HARVEY, Barbara Fitzgerald, CBE 1997; FSA 1964; FBA 1982; Fellow of Somerville College, Oxford, 1956–93, now Emeritus Fellow; Reader (*ad hominem*) in Medieval History, Oxford University, 1990–93; *b* 21 Jan. 1928; *d* of Richard Henry Harvey and Anne Fitzgerald (*née* Julian). *Educ:* Teignmouth Grammar Sch.; Bishop Blackall Sch.,

Exeter; Somerville Coll., Oxford (Schol.). First Cl. Final Honour Sch. of Modern History, Oxford, 1949; Bryce Student, Oxford Univ., 1950–51; BLitt Oxon 1953. Assistant, Dept of Scottish History, Edinburgh Univ., 1951–52; Asst Lectr, subseq. Lectr, Queen Mary Coll., London Univ., 1952–55; Tutor, Somerville Coll., Oxford, 1955–93; Vice-Principal, 1976–79, 1981–83. Assessor, Oxford Univ., 1968–69. Ford's Lectr, Oxford, 1989. Mem., Royal Commn on Historical MSS, 1991–97. A Vice-Pres., RHistS, 1986–90. Gen. Editor, Oxford Medieval Texts, 1987–99. *Publications:* Documents Illustrating the Rule of Walter de Wenlok, Abbot of Westminster 1283–1307, 1965; Westminster Abbey and its Estates in the Middle Ages, 1977; (ed with L. C. Hector) The Westminster Chronicle 1381–94, 1982; Living and Dying in England 1100–1540: the monastic experience, (jtly, Wolfson Foundn History Prize), 1993; (ed) The Twelfth and Thirteenth Centuries, 2001; contribs to Economic History Rev., Trans Royal Historical Soc., Bulletin of Inst. of Historical Research, etc. *Address:* 66 Cranham Street, Oxford OX2 6DD. *T:* (01865) 554766.

HARVEY, Prof. Brian Wilberforce; Professor of Law, University of Birmingham, 1973–98, now Emeritus; *b* 17 March 1936; *s* of Gerald and Noelle Harvey. *Educ:* Clifton Coll., Bristol; St John's Coll., Cambridge (Choral Schol., MA, LLM). Solicitor, 1961. Lectr, Birmingham Univ., 1962–63; Sen. Lectr, Nigerian Law Sch., 1965–67; Lectr, Sen. Lectr and Prof. of Law, QUB, 1967–73; University of Birmingham: Dir, Legal Studies, 1973–76; Dean, Faculty of Law, 1982–85; Pro-Vice-Chancellor, 1986–91; Founding Dir, Legal Office, 1990–98. Vis. Prof., Univ. of Singapore, 1985–86. Chairman: Gtr Birmingham Social Security Appeal Tribunals, 1982–; Medical Appeals Tribunals, 1985–; Disability Appeal Tribunals, 1992–. Member: Statute Law Cttee (NI), 1972–73; Cttee on Legal Educn (NI), 1972–73; Adviser, Council of Legal Educn (NI), 1976–79. Mem., British Hallmarking Council, 1989–91. *Publications:* Law of Probate Wills and Succession in Nigeria, 1968; (jtly) Survey of Northern Ireland Land Law, 1970; Settlements of Land, 1973; (ed) Vocational Legal Training in UK and Commonwealth, 1975; (ed) The Lawyer and Justice, 1978; The Law of Consumer Protection and Fair Trading, 1978, 5th edn 1996; (jtly) Consumer and Trading Law Cases and Materials, 1985, 2nd edn 1998; (jtly) Law and Practice of Auctions, 1985, 2nd edn 1995; (jtly) The Law and Practice of Marketing Goods and Services, 1990; Violin Fraud: deception, forgery, theft and the law, 1992, 2nd edn (jtly) 1997; The Violin Family and its Makers in the British Isles: an illustrated history and directory, 1995; Buying and Selling Art and Antiques—The Law, 1998. *Recreations:* performing and listening to music. *Address:* c/o Department of Law, The University, Birmingham B15 2TT.
See also J. D. Harvey.

HARVEY, Bryan Hugh, CBE 1978; Adviser, Ministry of Defence, 1985–94; Chairman, Advisory Committee on Major Hazards, 1974–83; *b* 17 Oct. 1914; *y s* of late Oliver Harvey and Ellen Harvey (*née* Munn); *m* 1st, 1941, Margaret (*d* 1986), 2nd *d* of late E. G. Palmer; one *d;* 2nd, 1989, Christiane, *widow* of Maj. John Walton. *Educ:* KES Birmingham; Bristol Grammar Sch.; Corpus Christi Coll., Oxford; Harvard Univ. BA 1936; MA 1945; MSc 1953 (Industrial Hygiene). RAFVR, 1943–45. Printing industry until 1938, when joined Inspectorate of Factories; Dep. Chief Inspector, 1965; Chief Inspector, 1971–74; Dep. Dir Gen. (Dep. Sec.), Health and Safety Exec., 1975–76. Advr to Employment Cttee, H of C, 1980–83. Rockefeller Foundn Fellow, 1952–53; Hon. Lectr, Dept of Occupational Health, Univ. of Manchester, 1954–59; Vis. Prof., Univ. of Aston in Birmingham, 1972–79; External Examiner, Loughborough Univ. of Technology, 1984–89. Hon. Mem., British Occupational Hygiene Soc. (Pres. 1976–77). FSA 1964; Hon. Fellow, Instn of Occupational Safety and Health. *Publications:* (with R. Murray) Industrial Health Technology, 1958; (ed) Handbook of Occupational Hygiene, 1980; many articles in jls on industrial safety and hygiene, and industrial archaeology. *Recreations:* industrial archaeology, Georgian architecture, cabinet making. *Address:* 2 Surley Row, Caversham, Reading, Berks RG4 8LY. *T:* (0118) 947 9453. *Clubs:* Leander, Phyllis Court (Henley-on-Thames).

HARVEY, Caroline; *see* Trollope, Joanna.

HARVEY, Prof. Charles Richard Musgrave, (3rd Bt *cr* 1933, but does not use the title); *b* 7 April 1937; *s* of Sir Richard Musgrave Harvey, 2nd Bt, and Frances Estelle (*d* 1986), *er d* of late Lindsay Crompton Lawford, Montreal; *S* father, 1978; *m* 1967, Celia Vivien, *d* of late George Henry Hodson; one *s* one *d. Educ:* Marlborough; Pembroke Coll., Cambridge (BA 1960, MA 1964). Professorial Fellow, Institute of Development Studies, Sussex (on leave of absence); Sen. Res. Fellow, Botswana Institute for Development Policy Analysis, Gaborone, 1996–. *Heir: s* Paul Richard Harvey, *b* 1971.

HARVEY, (Christopher) Paul (Duncan); HM Diplomatic Service; Deputy High Commissioner, Kenya, since 2000; *b* 21 July 1956; *s* of late Prof. William John Harvey and of Margaret Anne Harvey; *m* 1989, Anasaini Kamakorewa; one *s* one *d. Educ:* Royal Belfast Academical Instn; University Coll., Oxford (MA); Downing Coll., Cambridge. Joined FCO, 1986: 2nd Sec., Suva, 1988–90; 1st Sec., Brussels, 1990–94; FCO, 1995–98; UK Rep. to Sierra Leone Peace Talks, Lome, 1999; UK Special Rep. for Peace in Sierra Leone, 1999–2000. *Recreations:* golf, organic gardening. *Address:* c/o Foreign and Commonwealth Office, King Charles Street, SW1A 2AH. *Club:* Muthaiga (Nairobi).

HARVEY, Prof. David Robert, FRCP, FRCPCH; Professor of Paediatrics and Neonatal Medicine, Imperial College School of Medicine (formerly Royal Postgraduate Medical School) at Hammersmith Hospital, since 1995; Consultant Paediatrician, Queen Charlotte's and Chelsea (formerly Queen Charlotte's Maternity) Hospital, since 1970; *b* 7 Dec. 1936; *s* of Cyril Francis Harvey and Margarita Harvey (*née* Cardew Smith); partner 1970, Teck Ong. *Educ:* Dulwich Coll.; Guy's Hosp. Med. Sch. (MB BS 1960). MRCP 1963, FRCP 1976; FRCPCH 1997. House Officer: Guy's Hosp., 1960–61; Central Middx Hosp., 1961–62; Amer. Hosp., Paris, 1963; Neonatal House Officer, 1964, Neate Res. Fellow, 1964–65, Hammersmith Hosp.; House Officer, Hosp. for Sick Children, Gt Ormond St, 1966; Paediatric Registrar, Hammersmith and Hillingdon Hosps, 1966–68; Nuffield Res. Fellow, Oxford, 1968–69; Paediatric Sen. Registrar, Hammersmith Hosp., 1969–70; Consultant Paediatrician: St Charles' Hosp., London, 1970–87; St Mary's Hosp., London, 1987–92; Sen. Lectr, RPMS, 1992–95. Hon. Secretary: Neonatal Soc., 1975–79; BPA, 1979–84. Handcock Prize, RCS, 1960. *Publications:* (ed jtly) Biology of Play, 1977; (jtly) The Sick Newborn Baby, 1981; (ed jtly) Child Health, 1985; (ed) New Parents, 1988; (ed jtly) The Baby under 1000 grams, 1989; (ed jtly) The Stress of Multiple Births, 1991; (jtly) Colour Guide: Neonatology, 1991; (ed jtly) Community Child Health and Paediatrics, 1995; contrib. to professional jls. *Recreations:* listening to opera, learning Chinese. *Address:* Department of Paediatrics and Neonatal Medicine, Imperial College School of Medicine, Hammersmith Hospital, Du Cane Road, W12 0NN. *T:* (020) 8383 1134, *Fax:* (020) 8748 2378.

HARVEY, Prof. David William; Professor of Geography, Department of Geography and Environmental Engineering, Johns Hopkins University, since 1993; *b* 31 Oct. 1935; *s* of Frederick and Doris Harvey. *Educ:* St John's Coll., Cambridge (BA (Hons), MA, PhD). Lectr, Univ. of Bristol, 1961–69; Prof. of Geography, Johns Hopkins Univ., 1969–86; Halford Mackinder Prof. of Geography, 1987–93, and Fellow, St Peter's Coll., 1987–93, Sen. Res. Fellow, 1993–, Oxford Univ. Guggenheim Meml Fellow, 1976–77. Corresp. FBA 1998. Dr (*hc*) Buenos Aires, 1997. Outstanding Contributor Award, Assoc. of Amer. Geographers, 1980; Gill Meml Award, RGS, 1982; Anders Retzius Gold Medal, Swedish Soc. for Anthropology and Geography, 1989; Patron's Medal, RGS, 1995; Vautrin Lud Internat. Prize in Geography, 1995. *Publications:* Explanation in Geography, 1969, 4th edn 1978; Social Justice and the City, 1973, 3rd edn 1989; The Limits to Capital, 1982, 2nd edn 1984; The Urbanisation of Capital, 1985; Consciousness and the Urban Experience, 1985; The Urban Experience, 1989; The Condition of Postmodernity, 1989; Justice, Nature and the Geography of Difference, 1996. *Address:* Department of Geography and Environmental Engineering, Johns Hopkins University, Baltimore, MD 21218, USA.

HARVEY, DeAnne; *see* Julius, D.

HARVEY, Rt Rev. Donald Frederick; *see* Newfoundland, Eastern, and Labrador, Bishop of.

HARVEY, Estella Jacqueline, (Mrs J. G. Harvey); *see* Hindley, E. J.

HARVEY, Dr Helen Lesley; Headmistress, St Swithun's School, since 1995; *b* 7 April 1950; *d* of George Frederick Cox and Olive Cox; *m* 1975, Dr H. Hale Harvey (marr. diss. 1999); one *s* one *d. Educ:* Lordswood Sch., Birmingham; Bedford Coll., Univ. of London (BSc); Chester Beatty Cancer Res. Inst., Surrey (PhD). Asst Mistress, Greylands Coll., IoW, 1975–76; Asst Mistress, 1976–89, Dep. Headmistress, 1989–90, Headmistress, 1990–94, Upper Chine Sch., Shanklin, IoW. *Recreations:* sailing, walking. *Address:* The Cottage, 154 Alresford Road, Winchester, Hants SO21 1HB.

HARVEY, Jack; *see* Rankin, I. J.

HARVEY, John Edgar, CBE 1994; Director, Burmah Oil Trading Ltd and subsidiary companies in Burmah Oil Group, 1974–80; *b* 24 April 1920; *s* of John Watt Harvey and Charlotte Elizabeth Harvey; *m* 1945, Mary Joyce Lane, BA, JP; one *s. Educ:* Xaverian Coll., Bruges, Belgium; Lyme Regis Grammar Sch. Radio Officer, in the Merchant Navy, 1939–45. Contested (C): St Pancras North, 1950; Walthamstow East, 1951; Mem. Nat. Exec. Cttee., Conservative Party, 1950–55; Chm., Woodford Conservative Assoc., 1954–56. MP (C) Walthamstow East, 1955–66. Founder Chm., Cttee of Greater London Cons. MPs, 1963–66. Mem., Speaker's Conf. on Electoral Reform, 1965–66. Regular broadcaster on parly affairs, BBC French Service, 1957–63. Pres., Wanstead & Woodford Conservative Assoc., 1986–93. A Founding Mem., Internat. Churchill Socs' Churchill Center, Washington, 1996. Mem., NSPCC Central Executive Cttee, 1963–68. Governor, Forest Sch., 1966–78. Verderer of Epping Forest, 1970–98; Reeve of Forest, Parish of Loughton, 1998–. Freeman, State of Texas, 1957. Freeman, City of London, 1966; Past Master, Guild of Freemen of City of London; Liveryman, Basketmakers' Co. *Recreations:* various in moderation. *Address:* 43 Traps Hill, Loughton, Essex IG10 1TB. *T:* (020) 8508 8753. *Clubs:* City of London, City Livery.

HARVEY, Prof. Jonathan Dean; composer; Professor of Music, Stanford University, since 1995; *b* 3 May 1939; *s* of Gerald and Noelle Harvey; *m* 1960, Rosaleen Marie Barry; one *s* one *d. Educ:* St Michael's Coll., Tenbury; Repton; St John's Coll., Cambridge (MA, DMus); Glasgow Univ. (PhD). Lectr, Southampton Univ., 1964–77; Sussex University: Reader, 1977–80; Prof. of Music, 1980–95; Hon. Prof., 1995. Bloch Prof., Univ. of California, Berkeley, 1995; Vis. Prof., Imperial Coll., London, 1999–. Harkness Fellow, Princeton Univ., 1969–70. Composer in association with: Sinfonia 21, 1996–; Ictus Ensemble, 1997–. Works performed at many festivals and international centres. Mem., Academia Europaea, 1989. FRCM 1995; FRSCM 2000. Hon. DMus: Southampton, 1990; Bristol, 1994; Sussex, 2000. *Publications:* The Music of Stockhausen, 1975; Music and Inspiration, 1999; In Quest of Spirit, 1999; *compositions:* Persephone Dream, for orch., 1972; Inner Light (trilogy), for performers and tape, 1973–77; Smiling Immortal, for chamber orch., 1977; String Quartet, 1977; Magnificat and Nunc Dimittis, for choir and organ, 1978; Album, for wind quintet, 1978; Hymn, for choir and orch., 1979; Be(com)ing, for clarinet and piano, 1979; Concelebration, instrumental, 1979, rev. 1981; Mortuos Plango, Vivos Voco, for tape, 1980; Passion and Resurrection, church opera, 1981; Resurrection, for double chorus and organ, 1981; Whom Ye Adore, for orch., 1981; Bhakti, for 15 insts and tape, 1982; Easter Orisons, for chamber orch., 1983; The Path of Devotion, for choir and orch., 1983; Nachtlied, for soprano, piano and tape, 1984; Gong-Ring, for ensemble with electronics, 1984; Song Offerings, for soprano and players, 1985 (Britten Award for Composition, 1993); Madonna of Winter and Spring, for orch., synthesizers and electronics, 1986; Lightness and Weight, for tuba and orch., 1986; Forms of Emptiness, for choir, 1986; Tendril, for ensemble, 1987; Timepieces, for orch., 1987; From Silence for soprano and players with electronics, 1988; Valley of Aosta for 13 players, 1988; String Quartet No 2, 1989; Ritual Melodies for tape, 1990; Cello Concerto, 1990; Serenade in Homage to Mozart, for wind, 1991; Inquest of Love (opera), 1992; Lotuses, 1992; Scena, 1992; The Riot, for trio, 1993; One Evening, for 2 singers, instruments and electronics, 1994; String Quartet No 3, 1996; Percussion Concerto, 1997; Ashes Dance Back, for choir with electronics, 1997; Wheel of Emptiness, for ensemble, 1997; Calling Across Time, for chamber orch., 1998; Tranquil Abiding, for orch., 1998; White as Jasmine, for soprano and orch., 1999; Mothers Shall Not Cry, for voices, orch. and electronics, 2000; Bird Concerto with Pianosong, 2001. *Recreations:* tennis, walking, meditation. *Address:* c/o Faber Music, 3 Queen Square, WC1N 3AU. *T:* (020) 7833 7911.
See also B. W. Harvey.

HARVEY, Kenneth George, CEng, FIEE; Chairman, Pennon Group (formerly South West Water) plc, since 1997; *b* 22 July 1940; *s* of George Harvey and Nellie Harvey (*née* Gilmore); *m* 1st, 1963, Wendy Youldon (*d* 1982); one *s* one *d;* 2nd, 1990, Anne Model. *Educ:* Urmston Grammar Sch., Manchester; City Univ. (BSc, 1st Cl. Hons Elec. Eng). Student Apprentice, Westinghouse, 1958–63; Southern and London Electricity Boards, 1963–81; London Electricity Board: Engineering Dir, 1981–84; Dep. Chm., 1984–89; Chm. and Chief Exec., NORWEB plc (formerly North Western Electricity Bd), 1989–95. Chairman: Greater Manchester Buses South Ltd, 1993–95; Intercare Gp plc, 1996–; Comax plc, 1997–99; Beaufort Group plc, 1998–; non-exec. Dir, Lattice Gp, 2000–. Pres., Electricity Assoc., 1992–93. Chm., Royal Exchange Theatre Co., Manchester, 1994–98. *Recreations:* sport, gardening, DIY, theatre. *Address:* c/o Pennon Group plc, Peninsula House, Rydon Lane, Exeter EX2 7HR.

HARVEY, Prof. Leonard Patrick; Fellow, Oxford Centre for Islamic Studies, since 1994; Cervantes Professor of Spanish, King's College, University of London, 1973–84, now Professor Emeritus; *b* 25 Feb. 1929; *s* of Francis Thomas Harvey and Eva Harvey; *m* 1954, June Rawcliffe; two *s. Educ:* Alleyn's Sch., Dulwich; Magdalen Coll., Oxford. 1st cl. hons BA Mod. Langs 1952; 2nd cl. Oriental Studies 1954; MA 1956; DPhil 1958. Lectr in Spanish, Univ. of Oxford, 1957–58; Univ. of Southampton, 1958–60; Queen Mary Coll., Univ. of London: Lectr, 1960–63; Reader and Head of Dept, 1963; Prof. of Spanish, 1967–73; Dean of Faculty of Arts, 1970–73; Dean of Faculty of Arts, KCL, 1979–81; FKC 1992. Vis. Prof., Univ. of Victoria, BC, 1966; Vis. Fellow, Oxford Centre for Islamic Studies, 1993–94. Mem. UGC, 1979–83. Chm., Educn Cttee, Hispanic and Luso-Brazilian Council, 1984–87. *Publications:* Islamic Spain 1250–1500, 1990; articles in Al-Andalus, Bulletin of Hispanic Studies, Nueva Revista de Filología Española, Al-Masāq, Al-Qantara, etc. *Address:* Oxford Centre for Islamic Studies, George Street, Oxford OX1 2AR. *T:* (01865) 278730.

HARVEY, Mary Frances Clare, (Mrs D. R. Feaver), MA; Headmistress, St Mary's Hall, Brighton, 1981–88; *b* 24 Aug. 1927; *e d* of late Rev. Oliver Douglas Harvey and Frances Hilda Harvey (*née* Howes); *m* 1988, Rt Rev. Douglas Russell Feaver (*d* 1997). *Educ:* St Mary's Sch., Colchester; St Hugh's Coll., Oxford (BA, Final Honour Sch. of Mod. Hist., 1950; Diploma in Educn, 1951; MA 1954). History Mistress, St Albans High Sch., 1951; Head of History Dept, Portsmouth High Sch., GPDST, 1956; Headmistress: Sch. of St Clare, Penzance, 1962–69; Badminton Sch., Westbury on Trym, Bristol, 1969–81. Governor, Bristol Cathedral Sch., 1978–81; Foundn Gov. and Trustee, Sexey's Sch., Bruton, 1994–95. *Recreations:* music, travel, reading, needlework. *Address:* Blackman House, Canon Lane, Chichester, West Sussex PO19 1PX.

HARVEY, Michael, MBE 2001; freelance lettering designer, since 1955; *b* 11 Nov. 1931; *s* of Leslie Arthur Harvey and Betty Eileen Harvey; *m* 1956, Patricia Evelyn Hills; three *d*. *Educ:* Ewell Castle Sch. Engrg draughtsman, 1947–55; Asst to Reynolds Stone, inscription carving, 1955–61. Pt-time Lectr, Bournemouth & Poole Coll. of Art & Design, 1961–80; Vis. Lectr, Dept of Typography & Graphic Communication, Univ. of Reading, 1993–2001. Co-Founder, Fine Fonts, 2000. *Work* includes: inscription carving, book jacket design, type design (Monotype, Adobe, Dutch Type Library); collaboration with Ian Hamilton Finlay on carved poetry, sundials, graphic works; design and carving of inscriptions, Sainsbury Wing, Nat. Gall., London, 1990. Mem., Royal Mint Adv. Cttee, 1991–. Gov., Arts Inst. at Bournemouth, 1998–. *Publications:* Lettering Design, 1975; Creative Lettering: drawing & design, 1985; Carving Letters in Stone & Wood, 1987; Calligraphy in the Graphic Arts, 1988; Reynolds Stone: engraved lettering in wood, 1992; Creative Lettering Today, 1996. *Recreations:* reading, listening to jazz, photography, cycling. *Address:* 4 Valley Road, Bridport, Dorset DT6 4JR. *T:* (01308) 422777; *e-mail:* perdido@dircon.co.uk. *Clubs:* Double Crown, Ronnie Scott's.

HARVEY, Michael Llewellyn Tucker; QC 1982; a Recorder, since 1986; *b* 22 May 1943; *s* of Rev. Victor Llewellyn Tucker Harvey and Pauline Harvey (*née* Wybrow); *m* 1972, Denise Madeleine Neary; one *s* one *d*. *Educ:* St John's Sch., Leatherhead; Christ's Coll., Cambridge (BA Hons Law, LLB, MA). Called to the Bar, Gray's Inn, 1966 (Uthwatt Schol. 1965, James Mould Schol. 1966; Bencher, 1991). *Publication:* joint contributor of title 'Damages' in Halsbury's Laws of England, 4th edn 1975. *Recreations:* shooting, golf. *Address:* 2 Crown Office Row, Temple, EC4Y 7HJ. *T:* (020) 7797 8100. *Clubs:* Athenæum; Hawks (Cambridge).

HARVEY, Neil; Head of Business Statistics Division, Central Statistical Office, 1989–93; *b* 10 Feb. 1938; *s* of Edward Felters and Lucy Felters (*née* Graves; she *m* 2nd, Frederick Harvey); *m* 1963, Clare Elizabeth Joscelyne; two *s*. *Educ:* Eton House Sch., Essex; LSE. BSc(Econ). Economist/Statistician, Kuwait Oil Co., 1959–62; Statistician, Midland Bank Economics Dept, 1962–65; Asst Statistician/Statistician, DEA, 1965–69; Statistician, HM Treasury, 1969–73; Chief Statistician, Inland Revenue, 1973–77; Controller, Statistical Office, HM Customs and Excise, 1977–84; Under Sec., Statistics Div. 1, DTI, 1984–89. *Recreation:* reading.

HARVEY, Nicholas Barton; MP (Lib Dem) North Devon, since 1992; *b* 3 Aug. 1961; *s* of Frederick Barton Harvey and Christine Diana Rosalind (*née* Gildea). *Educ:* Queen's Coll., Taunton; Middlesex Poly. (BA Hons). Communications and Marketing Consultant: Profile Public Relns, 1984–86; Dewe Rogerson Ltd, 1986–91; Westminster Consortium, 1991–92. Lib Dem spokesman: on transport, 1992–94; on trade and industry, 1994–97; on regions, 1997–99; on health, 1999–2001; on culture, media and sport, 2001–; Chair, Campaigns and Communications, 1994–99. *Recreations:* travelling, walking, playing piano, soccer enthusiast. *Address:* House of Commons, SW1A 0AA. *T:* (020) 7219 6232. *Club:* National Liberal.

HARVEY, Paul; *see* Harvey, C. P. D.

HARVEY, Prof. Paul Dean Adshead, FSA, FRHistS; Professor Emeritus, University of Durham, since 1985; *b* 7 May 1930; *s* of John Dean Monroe Harvey and Gwendolen Mabel Darlington (*née* Adshead); *m* 1968, Yvonne Crossman. *Educ:* Bishop Feild Coll., St John's, Newfoundland; Warwick Sch.; St John's Coll., Oxford (BA 1953; MA; DPhil 1960); FRHistS 1961, FSA 1963. Asst Archivist, Warwick County Record Office, 1954–56; Asst Keeper, Dept of Manuscripts, British Museum, 1957–66; Lectr, 1966–70, Sen. Lectr, 1970–78, Dept of History, Univ. of Southampton; Prof. of Mediaeval Hist., Univ. of Durham, 1978–85. Mem., Adv. Council on Public Records, 1984–89. Vice-Pres., Surtees Soc., 1978–; Chm., British Records Assoc., 1995–2000. Hon. Fellow, Portsmouth Polytechnic, 1987. Jt Gen. Editor, Southampton Records Series, 1966–78; Gen. Editor, Portsmouth Record Series, 1969–. *Publications:* The printed maps of Warwickshire 1576–1900 (with H. Thorpe), 1959; A Medieval Oxfordshire Village: Cuxham 1240–1400, 1965; (ed with W. Albert) Portsmouth and Sheet Turnpike Commissioners' minute book 1711–1754, 1973; Manorial records of Cuxham, Oxfordshire, circa 1200–1359, 1976; The history of topographical maps: symbols, pictures and surveys, 1980; (ed) The peasant land market in medieval England, 1984; Manorial records, 1984; (ed with R. A. Skelton) Local maps and plans from medieval England, 1986; Medieval Maps, 1991; Maps in Tudor England, 1993; (with A. McGuinness) A guide to British medieval seals, 1996; Editing Historical Records, 2001; contribs to: The Victoria History of the County of Oxford, vol. 10, 1972; History of Cartography, vol. 1, 1987; Agrarian History of England and Wales, vol. 3, 1991; articles in learned jls and periodicals. *Recreations:* British topography and topographical writings. *Address:* Lyndhurst, Farnley Hey Road, Durham DH1 4EA. *T:* (0191) 3869396. *Club:* Athenæum.

HARVEY, Prof. Paul H., DPhil, DSc; FRS 1992; Professor in Zoology, and Fellow of Jesus College, since 1996, Head of Department of Zoology, since 1998, Oxford University; *b* 19 Jan. 1947; *s* of Edward Walter Harvey and Eileen Joan (*née* Pagett); *m*; two *s*. *Educ:* Queen Elizabeth's Grammar Sch., Hartlebury; Univ. of York (BA 1st Cl. Hons, DPhil); Univ. of Oxford (MA, DSc). Lectr in Biology, Univ. of Wales, Swansea, 1971–73; University of Sussex: Lectr in Biology, 1973–84; Reader, 1984–85; Oxford University: Lectr in Zoology, 1985–89; Reader, 1989–96; Fellow, Merton Coll., 1985–96. Vis. Lectr in Biology, Harvard Univ., 1978–79; Visiting Professor: Harvard Univ., 1980; Univ. of Washington, Seattle, 1982; Princeton Univ., 1984–85. Sec., Zoological Soc. of London, 2000–; Mem. Council, Royal Soc., 2000–. Scientific Medal, Zool Soc., 1986; J. Murray Luck Award, Nat. Acad. of Scis, USA, 1997. *Publications:* The Comparative Method in Evolutionary Biology, 1991; edited books; scientific papers. *Recreations:* walking, aggressive gardening. *Address:* Department of Zoology, University of Oxford, South Parks Road, Oxford OX1 3PS. *T:* (01865) 271260.

HARVEY, Peter, CB 1980; Consultant, Solicitor's Office, Department of Trade and Industry, 1994–96 and 1997–99; *b* 23 April 1922; *o s* of Rev. George Leonard Hunton Harvey and Helen Mary (*née* Williams); *m* 1950, Mary Vivienne, *d* of John Osborne Goss and Elsie Lilian (*née* Bishop); one *s* one *d*. *Educ:* King Edward VI High Sch., Birmingham; St John's Coll., Oxford (MA, BCL). RAF, 1942–45. Called to the Bar, Lincoln's Inn, 1948. Entered the Home Office as a Legal Assistant, 1948; Principal Asst Legal Advr, 1971–77; Legal Advr, DES, 1977–83; Consultant, Legal Advr's Br., Home Office, 1983–86; Asst Counsel to the Speaker, H of C, 1986–94. Mem., Legal Affairs Cttee, Inst. for Citizenship Studies, 1992–94. *Publications:* contributor to Halsbury's Laws of England (3rd and 4th edns). *Recreations:* history, genealogy, walking. *Address:* Mannamead, Old Avenue, Weybridge, Surrey KT13 0PS. *T:* (01932) 845133.

HARVEY, Peter Kent; DL; Chairman: Poole Hospital NHS Trust, since 2001; Dorset Health Trust, since 2000; Clerk to Dorset Police Authority, since 1995; *b* 1 Feb. 1946; *s* of John Alan Harvey and late Joan Harvey; *m* 1976, Wendy Anne; one *d*. *Educ:* Bishop Wordsworth's Sch., Salisbury; Liverpool Univ. (LLB Hons). Articled Clerk, 1968–71, Asst Solicitor, 1971, IoW CC; Asst Solicitor, Bournemouth BC, 1971–73; Dorset County Council: Sen. Asst Solicitor, 1973; Actg Asst Clerk, 1973–74; Dep. County Solicitor, 1974–85; County Solicitor and Dep. Chief Exec., 1985–91; Chief Exec., and Clerk to the Dorset Lieutenancy, 1991–99. Clerk to Dorset Fire Authy, 1997–99. Director: Dorset TEC, 1991–99; Dorset Business Link, 1997–99; Chairman: Dorset Strategic Bd of Young Enterprise, 1996–99; Poole Bay Primary Care Trust 2001–01. Trustee and Sec., Police Partnership Trust, 1997–. DL Dorset, 1999. *Recreations:* golf, sailing. *Address:* Dorset Police Authority, Force Headquarters, Winfrith, Dorchester, Dorset DT2 8DZ.

HARVEY, Rt Rev. Philip James Benedict, OBE 1973; retired Auxiliary Bishop of Westminster (RC) (Bishop in North London, 1977–91); Titular Bishop of Bahanna; *b* 6 March 1915; *s* of William Nathaniel and Elizabeth Harvey. *Educ:* Cardinal Vaughan Sch., Kensington; St Edmund's Coll., Ware, Herts. Ordained Priest, Westminster, 1939; Assistant Priest: Cricklewood, 1939–45; Kentish Town, 1945–46; Fulham, 1946–53; Asst Administrator, Crusade of Rescue, 1953–63, Administrator 1963–77. *Address:* Flat 1, 8 Morpeth Terrace, SW1P 1EQ. *T:* (020) 7798 9018.

HARVEY, Richard John, FIA; Group Chief Executive, CGNU, since 2001 (Deputy Group Chief Executive, 2000–01); *b* 11 July 1950; *s* of Lester Harvey and Jean Rose Harvey; *m* 1971, Karen Vowles; one *s* two *d*. *Educ:* Univ. of Manchester (BSc Hons Maths). FIA 1975. Personal Pensions Manager, Phoenix Assurance, 1983–85; Mkting Manager, Sun Alliance, 1985–87; Gen. Manager, Sun Alliance Life (NZ), 1987–92; Chief Exec., Norwich Union Hldgs (NZ), 1992–93; Norwich Union: Gen. Manager (Finance), 1993–94; Actuary, 1994; Gp Finance Dir, 1995–97; Dep. Gp Chief Exec., 1997; Gp Chief Exec., 1998–2000. *Recreations:* theatre, ski-ing, squash. *Address:* CGNU, St Helen's, 1 Undershaft, EC3P 3DQ.

HARVEY, Robert Lambart; author and journalist; *b* 21 Aug. 1953; *s* of Hon. John and Elena Harvey; *m* 1981, Jane Roper; one *s*. *Educ:* Eton; Christ Church, Oxford (BA 1974, MA 1978). Staff Correspondent, The Economist, 1974–81, Asst Editor, 1981–83; Columnist and Leader Writer, Daily Telegraph, 1987–91. MP (C) SW Clwyd, 1983–87. Mem., House of Commons Select Cttee on Foreign Affairs, 1984–87. Mem., Wilton Park Council, 1984–88; For. Sec.'s Rep., Adv. Bd for Woodrow Wilson Chair of Internat. Politics, 1985–92. *Publications:* Portugal: birth of a democracy, 1978; Fire Down Below: a study of Latin America, 1988; (ed) Blueprint 2000, 1989; The Undefeated: a study of modern Japan, 1994; The Return of the Strong: the drift to global disorder, 1995; Clive: the life and death of a British Emperor, 1998; Liberators: Latin America's struggle for independence 1810–1830, 2000; Cochrane: the life and exploits of a fighting captain, 2000. *Recreations:* the arts, films, music, swimming, walking. *Clubs:* Brooks's, Lansdowne.

HARVEY, Tim; *see* Harvey A. J.

HARVEY, William Graeme; naturalist; *b* 15 Jan. 1947; *s* of Jack Harvey and late Grace (*née* Wilson); *m* 1999, Pauline Maria Hayes; one *s* two *d* by former marriage. *Educ:* Simon Langton Grammar Sch., Canterbury; University Coll., Oxford (BA Geography; MA). British Council, 1969–2000: Tanzania, 1970–73; Indonesia, 1974–76; Personnel, 1976–80; Madras, 1980–83; Educnl Contracts, 1983–86; Rep., Bangladesh, 1986–90; Gen. Manager, Tech. Co-operation Trng, 1990–92; Regl Dir, Eastern and Central Africa, and Dir, Kenya, 1993–98; Dir, Internat. Partnerships, 1998–2000. MBOU. *Publications:* Birds in Bangladesh, 1990; contrib. UK, African and Asian ornithol and conservation jls and books. *Recreations:* bird watching, conservation, gardening, poetry, pop music, Coronation Street. *Address:* c/o Foreign and Commonwealth Office (New Delhi), SW1A 2AH; Pound Farm, Blackham, Tunbridge Wells TN3 9TY. *Club:* Madras (Chennai).

HARVEY-JONES, Sir John (Henry), Kt 1985; MBE 1952; Chairman: Parallax Enterprises, 1987–96; Imperial Chemical Industries PLC, 1982–87; business executive; *b* London, 16 April 1924; *s* of Mervyn Harvey-Jones, OBE, and Eileen Harvey-Jones; *m* 1947, Mary Evelyn Bignell; one *d*. *Educ:* Tormore Sch., Deal, Kent; RNC, Dartmouth, Devon. Served RN, 1937–56: specialised in submarines; qual. as Russian interpreter, 1946, and subseq. as German interpreter; appts in Naval Intell. (MBE); resigned, 1956, Lt-Comdr. Joined ICI as Work Study Officer, Wilton, 1956; commercial appts at Wilton and Heavy Organic Chemicals Div. until apptd Techno-Commercial Dir, 1967; Dep. Chm., HOC Div., 1968; Chm., ICI Petrochemicals Div., 1970–73; Main Bd, ICI, 1973, Dep. Chm., 1978–82. Chairman: Phillips-Imperial Petroleum, 1973–75; Burns Anderson, 1987–90 (non-exec. Dir, 1987–91); The Economist, 1989–94 (Dir, 1987–94); Trendroute Ltd, 1988–91; Didacticus Video Productions Ltd, 1989–97; Deputy Chairman: GPA Ltd, 1989–93 (Dir, 1987–93); Director: ICI Americas Inc., 1975–76; Fiber Industries Inc., 1975–78; Carrington Viyella Ltd, 1981–82 (non-exec. Dir, 1974–79); Grand Metropolitan PLC, 1983–94 (Dep. Chm., 1987–91); non-exec. Dir, Reed International PLC, 1975–84. Vice Pres., Indust. Participation Assoc., 1983–; Hon. Vice-Pres., Inst. of Marketing, 1982–89. Member: Welsh Develt Internat., 1989–93; Foundn Bd, Internat. Management Inst., Geneva, 1984–87; Internat. Council, Eur. Inst. of Business Admin, 1984–87; Adv. Council, Prince's Youth Business Trust, 1986–97; Soc. of Chem. Industry, 1978–; Hon. Consultant, RUSI, 1987–. Chancellor, Bradford Univ., 1986–91; Chm. Council, St James's and the Abbey Sch., Malvern, 1987–93; Vice-President: Book Trust Appeal Fund, 1987–; Hearing & Speech Trust, 1985–; Heaton Woods Trust, 1986–; Fellow, Smallpeice Trust, 1988–; Trustee: Conf. Bd, 1984–86; Multiple Sclerosis Res. Charitable Trust, 1999–; Hon. Trust Mem., Andrea Adams Trust, 2000–. Chm. Council, Wildfowl Trust, 1987–94. Hon. President: Univ. of Bradford MBA Alumni Assoc., 1989; Friends of Brecon Jazz, 1989–. Patron: MSC Nat. Trng Awards, 1987; Steer Orgn, 1988–; Nat. Canine Defence League, 1990–; Kingwood Trust, 1996–; Royal Nat. Submarine Mus. Centennial Appeal, 1999–; Modem, 2000–; Amor Foundn for Street Children in El Salvador, 2000–; Vice-Patron, British Polio Fellowship, 1988–. Gov., E-SU, 1987–91. Chm. Judges, Teaching Awards, 1999–2000. Hon. FRSC 1985; Hon. FIChemE 1985; Hon. Mem. CGLI, 1988; FRSA 1979 (Vice-Pres., 1988–92). Sen. Ind. Fellow, Leicester Polytechnic, 1990; Hon. Fellow, Polytechnic of Wales. Hon. LLD: Manchester, 1985; Liverpool, 1986; London, 1987; Cambridge, 1987; DUniv

Surrey, 1985; Hon. DSc: Bradford, 1986; Leicester, 1986; Keele, 1989; Exeter, 1989; Hon. DCL Newcastle, 1988; Hon. DBA Internat. Management Centre, 1990; Hon. DTech Loughborough, 1991. Gold Medal, BIM, 1985; Centenary Medal, SCI, 1986; J. O. Hambro British Businessman of the Year, 1986; Award of Excellence in Communication, Internat. Assoc. of Business Communicators, 1987; Radar Man of the Year, 1987; CGIA in Technol. (*hc*), 1987. Comdr's Cross, Order of Merit, Germany. Television: Troubleshooter (series), 1990; Troubleshooter Specials – Eastern Europe, 1991; Troubleshooter 2, 1992; Troubleshooter Returns, 1995; Troubleshooter: Back in Business, 2000. *Publications:* Making it Happen: reflections on leadership, 1987; Troubleshooter, 1990; Getting it Together, 1991; Troubleshooter 2, 1992; Managing to Survive, 1993; All Together Now, 1994; Troubleshooter Returns, 1995. *Recreations:* ocean sailing, swimming, the countryside, cooking, contemporary literature. *Address:* c/o PO Box 18, Ross-on-Wye, Herefordshire HR9 7PH. *T:* (01989) 567171, *Fax:* (01989) 567173. *Clubs:* Athenæum, Garrick, Groucho.

HARVIE, Sir John (Smith), (Sir Jack), Kt 1997; CBE 1992; Senior Partner, J. S. Harvie & Co., since 1993; *b* 9 Aug. 1936; *s* of Alexander Wood Harvie and Margaret Isabella Smith Harvie; *m* 1958, Elizabeth Maxwell; one *s* two *d.* *Educ:* Ibrox Secondary Sch., Glasgow. Served HLI, 1954–57; Founder, J. S. Harvie & Co., 1959; Chairman: Central Building Contractors (CBC) Ltd, 1971–; Hugh Muirhead & Son Ltd, 1972–; T. W. Scott Ltd, 1974–; City Link Developments (Glasgow) Ltd, 1984–. *Recreations:* travel, reading. *Address:* Auchencraig, Mugdock, Milngavie, Glasgow G62 8EJ.

HARVIE, Jonathan Alexander; QC 1992; a Recorder, since 2000; *b* 21 March 1950; *s* of late Anthony Bedford Harvie and of Winifred Jean Harvie (*née* Treliving); *m* 1981, Antonia Mary Lea, *d* of Rev. His Honour Christopher Gerald Lea, *qv*; two *s* one *d.* *Educ:* King's Sch., Canterbury; Brasenose Coll., Oxford (BA Jurisprudence). Called to the Bar, Middle Temple, 1973. Asst Recorder, 1994–2000. Mem., Internat. Soc. of Dendrologists. *Recreations:* gardening, racing, golf, music. *Address:* Blackstone Chambers, Blackstone House, Temple, EC4Y 9BW. *T:* (020) 7583 1770; Windmills, Hurstbourne Tarrant, Hants SP11 0DQ. *T:* (01264) 736547. *Clubs:* White's; Swinley Forest Golf; Vincent's (Oxford).

HARVIE-WATT, Sir James, 2nd Bt *cr* 1945, of Bathgate, Co. Lothian; FCA; company director; *b* 25 Aug. 1940; *s* of Sir George Harvie-Watt, 1st Bt, QC, TD and of Bettie, *o d* of late Paymaster-Capt. Archibald Taylor, OBE, RN; *S* father, 1989; *m* 1966, Roseline, *d* of late Baron Louis de Chollet, Fribourg, Switzerland, and Frances Tate, Royal Oak, Maryland, USA; one *s* one *d.* *Educ:* Eton; Christ Church, Oxford (MA). FCA 1975 (ACA 1965). Lieut London Scottish (TA), 1959–67. With Coopers & Lybrand, 1962–70; Executive, British Electric Traction Co. Ltd, and Director of subsid. companies, 1970–78; Man. Dir, Wembley Stadium Ltd, 1973–78; Chairman: Cannons Sports & Leisure Ltd, 1990–93; A H Ball Gp, then Langley & Johnson, now Medi@Invest, 1995–; Oliver & Saunders Gp, 1997–; HiLife Hldgs, 2000–. Director: Lake & Elliot Industries Ltd, 1988–93; Penna Holdings plc, 1995–; US Smaller Companies Investment Trust PLC, 1998–2000; Wellington Mgt Portfolios (Ire.), 2000–, and other cos. Mem. Executive Cttee, London Tourist Board, 1977–80; Member: Sports Council, 1980–88 (Vice-Chm., 1985–88; Mem. Sports Council enquiries into: Financing of Athletics in UK, 1983; Karate, 1986); Indoor Tennis Initiative Bd, 1986–89. Chm., Crystal Palace Nat. Sports Centre, 1984–88; Dir, National Centres Bd, 1987–88. Member Management Cttee: Nat. Coaching Foundn, 1984–88; Holme Pierrepont Nat. Water Sports Centre, 1985–88; Mem., Stella Artois Tournament Cttee, 1988–95; Dir, Internat. Tennis Hall of Fame, 1996– (Mem., Internat. Council, 1995–96; Mem., Exec. Cttee, 1997–). Mem. Council, NPFA, 1985–90. FRSA 1978. OStJ 1964, and Mem. London Council of the Order, 1975–84. *Heir:* *s* Mark Louis Harvie-Watt [*b* 19 Aug. 1969; *m* 1996, Miranda, *d* of Martin Thompson]. *Recreations:* shooting, tennis, golf, photography. *Address:* 15 Somerset Square, Addison Road, W14 8EE. *T:* (020) 7602 6944. *Clubs:* White's, Pratt's, Queen's (Vice-Chm., 1987–90; Chm., 1990–93; Dir, 1987–); Sunningdale Golf; Swinley Forest Golf.

HARWOOD, John Warwick; Chief Executive, Learning and Skills Council, since 2000; *b* 10 Dec. 1946; *s* of Dennis G. and Mrs W. G. Harwood, West Camel, Somerset; *m* 1967, Diana, *d* of late Harford Thomas; one *s* one *d.* *Educ:* Univ. of Kent at Canterbury (BA Hons); Univ. of London (MA). Admin. Officer, GLC, 1968–73; Private Sec. to Leader of ILEA, 1973–77; Head of Chief Exec.'s Office, London Bor. of Hammersmith and Fulham, 1977–79; Asst Chief Exec., London Bor. of Hammersmith and Fulham, 1979–82; Chief Exec., London Bor. of Lewisham, 1982–89; Hon. Clerk, S London Consortium, 1983–89; Chief Exec., Oxfordshire CC, 1989–2000; Clerk, Lieutenancy for Oxfordshire, 1989–2001. Director: N Oxfordshire Business Venture Ltd, 1989–98; Thames Business Advice Centre Ltd, 1989–99; Heart of England TEC, 1990–2001 (Chm., 2000–); South East Regional Investment Ltd, 1998–2000. Member: Commn on Future of Voluntary Sector, 1995–96; Business Link Accreditation Adv. Bd, 1996–2000. Chair, Local Authorities Race Relations Information Exchange, 1990–2000; Mem. Exec. Cttee, TCPA, 1981–89. Chm., Parrott & Lee Foundn, 1998–; Trustee: Oxfordshire Community Foundn, 1996–; Oxfordshire Victoria County History Trust Appeal, 1997–. Mem. Ct, Oxford Brookes Univ., 1999–. Hon. MA Kent, 1995. *Publications:* (contrib.) The Renaissance of Local Government, 1995; (contrib.) Understanding British Institutions, 1998. *Recreations:* walking, cooking, gardening. *Address:* (office) Cheylesmore House, Quinton Road, Coventry CV1 2WT. *T:* (024) 7686 3192.

HARWOOD, Ronald, CBE 1999; FRSL; writer; *b* 9 Nov. 1934; *s* of late Isaac Horwitz and late Isobel Pepper; *m* 1959, Natasha Riehle; one *s* two *d.* *Educ:* Sea Point Boys' High Sch., Cape Town; RADA. FRSL 1974. Actor, 1953–60. Artistic Dir, Cheltenham Festival of Literature, 1975; Presenter: Kaleidoscope, BBC, 1973; Read All About It, BBC TV, 1978–79. Visitor in Theatre, Balliol Coll., Oxford, 1986. TV plays include: The Barber of Stamford Hill, 1960; (with Casper Wrede) Private Potter, 1961; The Guests, 1972; Breakthrough at Reykjavik, 1987; Countdown to War, 1989; adapted several of Roald Dahl's Tales of the Unexpected for TV, 1979–80; TV series, All the World's a Stage, 1984; screenplays include: A High Wind in Jamaica, 1965; One Day in the Life of Ivan Denisovich, 1971; Evita Perón, 1981; The Dresser, 1983; Mandela, 1987; The Browning Version, 1994; Cry, The Beloved Country, 1995. Directed: The Odd Couple, 1989, Poison Pen, 1993, Royal Exchange, Manchester; Another Time, Steppenwolf Theatre, Chicago, 1991. Chairman: Writers Guild of GB, 1969; Council, RSL, 2001– (Mem., 1998–2001); Member: Lit. Panel, Arts Council of GB, 1973–78; Cttee, Royal Literary Fund, 1995–; Cttee, English PEN, 1987–93 (Pres., 1989–93); Pres., Internat. PEN, 1993–97. Gov., Central Sch. of Speech and Drama, 1993–98. Stefan Mitrov Ljubiša Prize, 2000. Chevalier, Nat. Order of Arts and Letters (France), 1996. *Publications: novels:* All the Same Shadows, 1961; The Guilt Merchants, 1963; The Girl in Melanie Klein, 1969; Articles of Faith, 1973; The Genoa Ferry, 1976; Cesar and Augusta, 1978; Home, 1993 (Jewish Qly prize for fiction, 1994); *short stories:* One. Interior. Day.—adventures in the film trade, 1978; (co-ed) New Stories 3, 1978; *biography:* Sir Donald Wolfit, CBE—his life and work in the unfashionable theatre, 1971; (ed) The Ages of Gielgud, 1984; (ed) Dear Alec: Guinness at seventy-five, 1989; *essays:* (ed) A Night at the Theatre, 1983; (ed) The Faber Book of Theatre, 1993; *plays:* Country Matters, 1969; The Ordeal of Gilbert Pinfold (from Evelyn Waugh), 1977; A Family, 1978; The Dresser, 1980 (New Standard Drama Award; Drama Critics Award); After the Lions, 1982; Tramway Road, 1984; The Deliberate Death of a Polish Priest, 1985; Interpreters, 1985; J. J. Farr, 1987; Ivanov (from Chekhov), 1989; Another Time, 1989; Reflected Glory, 1992; Poison Pen, 1993; The Collected Plays of Ronald Harwood, 1993; Ronald Harwood: Plays 2, 1995; Taking Sides, 1995; The Handyman, 1996; Goodbye Kiss, 1997; Equally Divided, 1998; Quartet, 1999; *musical libretto:* The Good Companions, 1974; *historical:* All the World's a Stage, 1983. *Recreation:* watching cricket. *Address:* c/o Judy Daish Associates, 2 St Charles Place, W10 6EG. *T:* (020) 8964 8811. *Clubs:* Garrick, MCC.

HASAN, Wajid Shamsul; Adviser to Hon. Benazir Bhutto, 1997; *b* 5 Jan. 1941; *s* of late Shamsul Hasan and Amir Begum; *m* Zarina Wajid Hasan; one *s.* *Educ:* Karachi Univ. (LLB 1964); Master in Internat. Relations 1962. Freelance journalist, 1960; joined Jang Group of Newspapers, 1962; Editor, The News (English lang. daily), 1969; Founding Editor, MAG (English Weekly), 1981. Chm., Nat. Press Trust, 1989–90. Press Adviser to Hon. Benazir Bhutto, 1991–94; High Comr for Pakistan in London, 1994–97. Mem., RSAA. *Recreation:* reading. *Address:* Flat 2, 122 Finchley Road NW3 5HT. *Clubs:* Royal Over-Seas League, Travellers.

HASELDEN, Prof. Geoffrey Gordon; Brotherton Professor of Chemical Engineering, University of Leeds, 1960–86, now Emeritus; *b* 4 Aug. 1924; *s* of George A. Haselden and Rose E. (*née* Pleasants); *m* 1945, Eileen Doris Francis; three *d.* *Educ:* Sir Walter St John's Sch.; Imperial Coll. of Science and Technology. BScChemEng London 1944; FCGI; PhD (Eng) Chem Eng London, 1947; DScEng London, 1962; DIC; CEng; FIMechE; FIChemE; MInstR. Mem. Gas Research Bd, 1946–48; Lectr in Low Temperature Technology, Chemical Engrg Dept, 1948–57, Senior Lectr in Chemical Engrg, 1957–60, Imperial Coll. Chm., British Cryogenics Council, 1967–71. President: Commn A3, Internat. Inst. of Refrigeration, 1971–79; Inst. of Refrigeration, 1981–84; Vice-Pres., IChemE, 1984–85. Gen. Editor, Internat. Jl of Refrigeration, 1978–88. *Publications:* Cyrogenic Fundamentals, 1971; research papers in Trans Inst. Chem. Eng., etc. *Recreation:* Methodist lay preacher. *Address:* 12 High Ash Drive, Wigton Lane, Leeds LS17 8RA. *T:* (0113) 268 7047, *Fax:* (0113) 268 8206; *e-mail:* gghaselden@leeds178.fsnet.co.uk.

HASELER, Dr Stephen Michael Alan; author; Professor of Government, London Guildhall University (formerly City of London Polytechnic), since 1986; *b* 9 Jan. 1942; *m* 1967, Roberta Alexander. *Educ:* London School of Economics. BSc(Econ), PhD. Contested (Lab): Saffron Walden, 1966; Maldon, 1970. Chm., Labour Political Studies Centre, 1973–78. Mem. GLC, 1973–77, Chm. General Purposes Cttee, 1973–75. Founder Mem., SDP, 1981. Visiting Professor: Georgetown Univ., Washington DC, 1978; Johns Hopkins Univ., 1984; Maryland Univ., 1984–. Founder and Co-Chm., Radical Soc., 1988–; Chm., Republic, 1992–; Dir, Euro Res. Forum, 1997–. MInstD 1987. *Publications:* The Gaitskellites, 1969; Social-Democracy—Beyond Revisionism, 1971; The Death of British Democracy, 1976; Eurocommunism: implications for East and West, 1978; The Tragedy of Labour, 1980; Anti-Americanism, 1985; Battle for Britain: Thatcher and the New Liberals, 1989; The Politics of Giving, 1992; The End of the House of Windsor: Birth of a British Republic, 1993; The English Tribe: identity, nation and Europe, 1996; The Super-Rich: the unequal world of global capitalism, 2000. *Recreations:* cricket, American politics. *Address:* 2 Thackeray House, Ansdell Street, W8 5HA. *T:* (020) 7937 3976, (020) 7320 1152.

HASELGROVE, Dennis Cliff, CB 1963; MA; FSA; Under Secretary, Department of the Environment, 1970–75; *b* 18 Aug. 1914; *s* of late H. Cliff Haselgrove, LLB, Chingford; *m* 1941, Evelyn Hope Johnston, MA, *d* of late R. Johnston, Edinburgh; one *s.* *Educ:* Uppingham Sch.; King's Coll., Cambridge. 1st Class, Classical Tripos, Parts I and II. Entered Ministry of Transport, Oct. 1937; Private Sec. to Permanent Sec., and Asst Priv. Sec. to Minister, 1941. Served in Intelligence Corps and 10th Baluch Regt, IA, 1941–45. Min. of Transport: Asst Sec., 1948; Under-Sec., 1957–70. Govt Delegate to: ILO Asian Maritime Conf., 1953; Internat. Conf. on Oil Pollution of the Sea, 1954, 1962; Internat. Lab. Conf. (Maritime Session), 1958; Internat. Conf. on Safety of Life at Sea, 1960. Imperial Defence Coll., 1955. *Recreations:* archæology, travel, philately. *Address:* 10 Church Gate, SW6 3LD. *T:* (020) 7736 5213.

HASELHURST, Rt Hon. Sir Alan (Gordon Barraclough), Kt 1995; PC 1999; MP (C) Saffron Walden, since July 1977; Chairman of Ways and Means and Deputy Speaker, since 1997; *b* 23 June 1937; *s* of late John Haselhurst and Alyse (*née* Barraclough); *m* 1977, Angela (*née* Bailey); two *s* one *d.* *Educ:* King Edward VI Sch., Birmingham; Cheltenham Coll.; Oriel Coll., Oxford. Pres., Oxford Univ. Conservative Assoc., 1958; Sec., Treas. and Librarian, Oxford Union Soc., 1959–60; Nat. Chm., Young Conservatives, 1966–68. MP (C) Middleton and Prestwich, 1970–Feb. 1974. PPS to Sec. of State for Educn, 1979–82. Mem., H of C Select Cttee on European Legislation, 1982–97, on Catering, 1991–97, on Transport, 1992–97; Hon. Sec., All Party Parly Cricket Gp, 1993–. Chm., Rights of Way Review Cttee, 1983–93. Chairman: Manchester Youth and Community Service, 1974–77; Commonwealth Youth Exchange Council, 1978–81; Chm. Trustees, Community Development (formerly Projects) Foundn, 1986–97. *Publications:* Occasionally Cricket, 1999; Eventually Cricket, 2001. *Recreations:* gardening, theatre, music, watching cricket. *Address:* House of Commons, SW1A 0AA. *Clubs:* MCC; Essex CC (Mem., Exec. Cttee, 1996–).

HASELOCK, Rev. Canon Jeremy Matthew; Residentiary Canon and Precentor, Norwich Cathedral, since 1998; *b* 20 Sept. 1951; *s* of Kenneth Pool Haselock and Pamela Haselock (*née* Bolus). *Educ:* Univ. of York (BA Hons History 1973); Univ. of York Centre for Mediaeval Studies (BPhil 1974); St Stephen's House, Oxford (BA Theol. 1982, MA 1985). Deacon 1983, priest 1984; Asst Curate, St Gabriel, Pimlico, 1983–86; Asst Priest, St John, Lafayette Sq., Washington, 1985; Asst Curate, St James, Paddington, 1986–88; Domestic Chaplain to Bp of Chichester, 1988–91; Vicar of Boxgrove, 1991–98; Chichester Dio. Liturgical Advr, 1991–98; Preb. of Fittleworth and Canon of Chichester Cathedral, 1994–2000. Proctor in Convocation and Mem., Gen. Synod, 1995–. Chm., Norwich Dio. Liturgical Cttee, 1998–; Member: C of E Liturgical Commn, 1996–; C of E Liturgical Publishing Gp, 2001–; Chichester DAC for Care of Churches, 1991–98; Norwich DAC for Care of Churches, 1998–; Pubns Cttee, 1988–93, Archaeol Working Party, 1997–99, Council for Care of Churches. Chm. of Govs, Boxgrove Sch., 1991–98; Gov., Norwich Sch., 1998–. Dep. Chaplain Gen., Order of St Lazarus of Jerusalem, 1998–. *Publications:* (with Roger Greenacre) The Sacrament of Easter, 1989, 3rd edn 1995; chapters in works on history, art and architecture of English cathedrals; articles, reviews and papers on liturgical and artistic matters. *Recreations:* foreign travel, collecting Oriental porcelain, music and theatre, especially opera, reading, church crawling, conversation, cooking and entertaining, wine. *Address:* 34 The Close, Norwich NR1 4DZ. *T:* (01603) 619169. *Clubs:* Athenæum; Norfolk (Norwich).

HASHIMOTO, Ryutaro; MHR (LDP) Okayama, District 2, 1963–96, District 4, since 1996; Prime Minister of Japan, 1996–98; *b* 29 July 1937; *s* of Ryogo Hashimoto and Masa Hashimoto; *m* 1966, Kumiko Nakamura; two *s* three *d.* *Educ:* Dept of Law, Keio Univ. (BSc). Vice-Minister of Health and Welfare, 1970–71; Dir, Social Affairs Div., 1972–74,

Dep. Chm., 1974–76, Policy Res. Council, LDP; Chm., Standing Cttee on Social and Labor Affairs, House of Reps, 1976–78; Minister of Health and Welfare, 1978–79; Policy Research Council, Liberal Democratic Party: Chairman, Research Commission on: Public Admin and Finances, 1980–86; Fundamental Policies for Medical Care, 1984–86; Minister of Transport, 1986–87; Actg Sec.-Gen., 1987–89, Sec.-Gen., 1989, LDP; Minister of Finance, 1989–91; Liberal Democratic Party: Chairman: Res. Commn on Fundamental Policies for Envmtl Issues, 1993; Policy Res. Council, 1993–94; Pres., 1995–; Minister of Internat. Trade and Industry, 1994–96; Dep. Prime Minister, 1995–96; Minister for Admin. Reform, 2000–01. Grand-Croix: Ordre de la Couronne (Belgium), 1996; Ordre National de Mérite (France), 1996; Das Grosskreuz (Germany), 1997. *Publication:* Vision of Japan, 1993. *Recreations:* mountain climbing, photography, Kendo (Japanese fencing). *Address:* 1-11-23 Nagata-cho, Chiyoda-ku, Tokyo 100, Japan.

HASHMI, Dr Farrukh Siyar, OBE 1974; FRCPsych; Consultant Psychiatrist: All Saints' Hospital, Birmingham, 1969–92; Woodbourne Priory Hospital (formerly Woodbourne Clinic), Edgbaston, since 1992; Psychotherapist, HM Prison, Stafford, 1973–92; *b* Gujrat, Pakistan, 12 Sept. 1927; *s* of Dr Ziaullah Qureshi and Majida Qureshi; *m* 1972, Shahnaz; one *s* two *d*. *Educ:* King Edward Med. Coll., Lahore (Punjab Univ.). MB, BS; MRCPsych; DPM; FRCPsych 1979. Mayo Hosp. and King Edward Med. Coll., Lahore, March–Sept. 1953; New End Hosp., Hampstead, 1954; Children's Hosp., Birkenhead, 1954–55; Sen. House Officer, Brook Gen. Hosp., Woolwich, 1955–56; Snowdon Road Hosp., Bristol, 1956; Asst MOH, Co. Berwicks, 1957; Scholar, Volkart Foundn, Switzerland, 1958–60; psychiatric medicine: Registrar, Uffculme Clinic and All Saints Hosp., Birmingham, 1960–63, Sen. Registrar, 1966–69; Research Fellow, Dept of Psychiatry, Birmingham Univ., 1963–66. Chairman: Psychiatric Div., West Birmingham Health Dist., 1977–83 and 1988–92; Woodbourne Clinic Hosp. Management Team, 1989–; Member: Race Relations Bd, W Midlands Conciliation Cttee, 1968–81; Community Relations Working Party, NAYC, 1968–81; Home Secretary's Adv. Cttee on Race, 1976–81 (formerly Mem., HO Adv. Cttee on Race Relations Research); CRE, 1980–86; Working Party on Community and Race Relations Trng, HO Police Trng Council, 1982–83; Wkg Gp on Ethnic Minorities, W Midlands RHA, 1982–92; Mental Health Services Cttee, RHA, 1976–92; Council, Mind (NAMH), 1976–81; UK Cttee, World Fedn for Mental Health, 1978–81; Health and Welfare Adv. Panel, NCCI, 1966–81; Cttee of Inquiry into Educn of Children from Ethnic Minority Gps (Swann Cttee), 1982–85; Warley Area Social Services Sub-Cttee, 1973–81; Central DHA, Birmingham, 1982–90; BBC Regl Adv. Council, 1970–77; GMC, 1979–84 (GMC Mem., Tribunal on Misuse of Drugs, 1983–84); Parole Board, 1981–85; Alternate Mem., Economic Social Cttee, EEC, 1985; Advisory Consultant, C of E Bd for Social Responsibility, 1984–87; consultant psychiatrist in eating disorders, St Michael's Hosp., Warwick, 1994–98. President: Pakistan Med. Soc., UK, 1974–76; Overseas Doctors Assoc., UK, 1975–79; Founder and Chm., Iqbal Acad., Coventry Cathedral, 1972–86. Member Editorial Board: New Community, 1972–82; Medicos, 1977–81. Involved in clinical trials and psycho-pharmacological studies, *eg* assessing effects of drugs in anxiety states and neurotic illness, incl. antidepressants. *Publications:* Pakistan Family in Britain, 1965; Mores, Migration and Mental Illness, 1966; Psychology of Racial Prejudice, 1966; Community Psychiatric Problems among Birmingham Immigrants, 1968; In a Strange Land, 1970; Measuring Psychological Disturbance in Asian Immigrants to Britain, 1977. *Recreations:* writing, reading, music. *Address:* Shahnaz, 5 Woodbourne Road, Edgbaston, Birmingham B15 3QJ. *Club:* Edgbaston Priory (Birmingham).

HASKARD, Sir Cosmo (Dugal Patrick Thomas), KCMG 1965 (CMG 1960); MBE 1945; *b* 25 Nov. 1916; *o c* of late Brig.-Gen. J. McD. Haskard, CMG, DSO and Alicia, *d* of S. N. Hutchins, Ardnagashel, Bantry, Co. Cork; *m* 1957, Phillada, *o c* of late Sir Robert Stanley, KBE, CMG and Lady Stanley (*née* Ursula Cracknell); one *s*. *Educ:* Cheltenham; RMC Sandhurst; Pembroke Coll., Cambridge (MA). Served War of 1939–45 (MBE); 2nd Lieut, TA (Gen. List), 1938; emergency Commn, Royal Irish Fusiliers, 1939; seconded KAR, 1941; served 2nd Bn, E Africa, Ceylon, Burma; Major 1944. Apptd Colonial Service cadet, Tanganyika, 1940, but due to war service did not take up duties until 1946 in which yr transf. to Nyasaland; Dist Comr, 1948; served on Nyasaland-Mozambique Boundary Commn, 1951–52; Provincial Commissioner, 1955; acting Secretary for African Affairs, 1957–58; Sec. successively for Labour and Social Development, for Local Government, and for Natural Resources, 1961–64; Governor and C-in-C, Falkland Islands, and High Comr for the British Antarctic Territory, 1964–70. Trustee, Beit Trust, 1976–. *Address:* Tragariff, Bantry, Co. Cork, Ireland.

HASKARD, Prof. Dorian Oliver, DM; FRCP; Sir John McMichael Professor of Cardiovascular Medicine, and Professor of Rheumatology, National Heart and Lung Institute, Imperial College School of Medicine (formerly Royal Postgraduate Medical School) at Hammersmith Hospital, since 1995; *b* 8 July 1951; *s* of Oliver Patrick Miller Haskard and Anna Caroline (*née* Worthington); *m* 1980, Kathleen Ann Keitzman; three *s*. *Educ:* Eton Coll.; St Edmund Hall, Oxford (MA; DM 1989); Middlesex Hosp. Med. Sch. FRCP 1994. Res. Fellow, Southwestern Med. Sch., Dallas, 1984–86; Wellcome Trust Sen. Res. Fellow in Clinical Sci., UMDS, Guy's Hosp., 1987–90; Royal Postgraduate Medical School, Hammersmith Hospital: Sen. Lectr in Rheumatology, 1990–94; Reader, 1994. *Publications:* papers on rôle of blood vessels in inflammation. *Recreation:* gardening. *Address:* National Heart and Lung Institute, Imperial College School of Medicine, Hammersmith Hospital, Du Cane Road, W12 0NN. *T:* (020) 8383 3064.

HASKEL; family name of Baron Haskel.

HASKEL, Baron *cr* 1993 (Life Peer), of Higher Broughton in the Metropolitan County of Greater Manchester; **Simon Haskel;** *b* Kaunas, Lithuania, 9 Oct. 1934; *s* of late Isaac and Julia Haskel; *m* 1962, Carole Lewis, New York, USA; one *s* one *d*. *Educ:* Salford Coll. of Advanced Technol. (BSc Textile Technol.). ATI. Nat Service commn, RA, 1959. Joined Perrotts Ltd, 1961; Chm., Perrotts Gp and associated cos, 1973–97. An opposition whip, H of L, 1994–97; an opposition spokesman on trade and industry, 1995–97; a Lord in Waiting (Govt Whip), 1997–98; front bench spokesman on trade and industry, on treasury, and on social security, 1997–98. Mem., Select Cttee on Sci. and Technol., 1995–97, 1999–. Labour Party: Sec., 1972 Industry Gp, 1976–81; Sec., 1981–90, Chm., 1990–96, Finance and Industry Gp. Chm., Thames Concerts Soc., 1982–90; Vice Chm., Exec. Cttee, Inst. of Jewish Policy Res. (formerly Inst. of Jewish Affairs), 1991–. FRSA 1979. *Recreations:* music, cycling. *Address:* House of Lords, SW1A 0PW. *T:* (020) 7219 4076. *Club:* Reform.

HASKELL, (Donald) Keith, CMG 1991; CVO 1979; international affairs consultant; HM Diplomatic Service, retired; *b* 9 May 1939; *s* of Donald Eric Haskell and Beatrice Mary Haskell (*née* Blair); *m* 1966, Maria Luisa Soeiro Tito de Morais; two *s* two *d* (and one *s* one *d* decd). *Educ:* Portsmouth Grammar Sch.; St Catharine's Coll., Cambridge (BA 1961, MA 1964). Joined HM Foreign Service, 1961; served in: London, Lebanon, Iraq, Libya; HM Consul, Benghazi, 1969–70; First Sec., Tripoli, 1970–72; Foreign and Commonwealth Office, 1972–75; Chargé d'Affaires and Consul-Gen., Santiago, 1975–78; Counsellor and Consul-Gen., Dubai, 1978–81; Hd, Nuclear Energy Dept, FCO, 1981–83; Hd, Middle East Dept, FCO, 1983–84; Hd of Chancery, Bonn, 1985–88; on secondment as an advr to industry, 1988–89; Ambassador: to Peru, 1990–95; to Brazil, 1995–99. Dr *hc* Univ. of Iquitos, Peru, 1992. Foundation Medal, Soka Univ. of Japan, 1975. Grand Cross, Order of Rio Branco (Brazil), 1997. *Recreations:* rifle shooting (captained Cambridge Univ. Rifle Assoc., 1960–61; represented England and GB in shooting competitions on various occasions), squash, tennis, wine and food. *Address:* Barn Cottage, Brightstone Lane, Farringdon, Alton, Hants GU34 3DP. *Club:* Hawks (Cambridge).

HASKELL, Keith; *see* Haskell, D. K.

HASKELL, Peter Thomas, CMG 1975; PhD, CBiol, FIBiol; Research Consultant, School of Pure and Applied Biology, University of Wales College of Cardiff, 1992–94, Fellow, 1994, retired; *b* 21 Feb. 1923; *s* of late Herbert James and Mary Anne Haskell; *m* 1st, 1946; one *s*; 2nd, 1979, Aileen Kirkley. *Educ:* Portsmouth Grammar Sch.; Imperial Coll., London. BSc, ARCS, PhD. Asst Lectr, Zoology Dept, Imperial Coll., London, 1951–53; Lectr, 1953–55; Sen. Sci. Officer, Anti-Locust Research Centre, Colonial Office, 1955–57; Principal Sci. Officer, 1957–59; Dep. Dir, 1959–62; Dir, Anti-Locust Research Centre, ODM, 1962–71; Dir, Centre for Overseas Pest Res. and Chief Advr on Pest Control, ODA, 1971–83; Dir, Cleppa Park Field Res. Stn, UC Cardiff, later Univ. of Wales Coll. of Cardiff, 1984–91. Consultant: FAO, UN, 1962–; UNDP, 1970–; WHO, 1973–91; OECD, 1975–; UNEP, 1976–91; Agricl and Vet. Adv. Cttee, British Council, 1976–90; Plants and Soils Res. Cttee, AFRC, later Plants and Envnt Res. Cttee, 1988–91; IFAD, 1995–; Mem., UNDP/FAO Special Adv. Cttee on Desert Locust, 1990–. Vice-Pres., Inst. of Biology, 1982. Professorial Res. Fellow, University Coll., Cardiff, 1971–83. Mem., Bd of Governors, Internat. Centre for Insect Physiology and Ecology, Kenya, 1972– (Vice-Chm., 1978; Chm., 1979–). Vis. Prof., Univ. of Newcastle, 1977. Thamisk Lectr, Royal Swedish Acad. of Scis, 1979. Van Den Brande Internat. Prize, 1982. Chief Editor, Tropical Pest Management, 1985–92; Mem., Editorial Bd, Review of Applied Entomol., 1988–91. *Publications:* Insect Sounds, 1962; The Language of Insects, 1962; Pesticide Application: principles and practice, 1985; Ecotoxicology: pesticides and beneficial organisms, 1998; many papers and articles in scientific and literary jls. *Recreations:* gardening, reading. *Address:* 2 Chapel Heights, Bolnore Road, Haywards Heath, West Sussex RH16 4AN; La Payrastrié, Montredon-Labessonnié, 81360 Tarn, France.

HASKINS, family name of **Baron Haskins**.

HASKINS, Baron *cr* 1998 (Life Peer), of Skidby in the co. of the East Riding of Yorkshire; **Christopher Robin Haskins;** Chairman: Northern Foods, 1986–May 2002; Express Dairies plc, 1998–May 2002; *b* 30 May 1937; *s* of Robin and Margaret Haskins; *m* 1959, Gilda Horsley; three *s* two *d*. *Educ:* Trinity Coll., Dublin (BA Mod). Ford Motor Co., Dagenham, 1960–62; Northern Foods, formerly Northern Dairies, 1962–. Chm., Better Regulation Task Force, 1997–March 2002; Mem., New Deal Task Force, 1997–2001. Mem. Bd, Yorks and Humber Regl Develt Agency, 1998–. Member: Culliton Irish Industrial Policy Review Gp, 1991–92; Commn for Social Justice, 1992–94; UK Round Table on Sustainable Develt, 1995–98; Hampel Cttee on Corporate Governance, 1996–97. Mem. Adv. Bd, NACAB, 2000–. Dir, Nat. Children's Trust for Ire., 2001–; Trustee: Runnymede Trust, 1989–98; Demos, 1993–2000; Civil Liberties Trust, 1997–99; Legal Assistance Trust, 1998–; Lawes Agricl Trust, 1999–. Hon. LLD: Hull; Dublin; DLitt Leeds Metropolitan; Essex; Hon. DSc Cranfield. *Recreations:* writing, week-end farm relief-man, cricket. *Address:* Quarryside Farm, Main Street, Skidby, near Cottingham, East Yorks HU16 5TG. *T:* (01482) 842692.

HASKINS, Sam, (Samuel Joseph); photographic designer; *b* 11 Nov. 1926; *s* of Benjamin G. Haskins and Anna E. Oelofse; *m* 1952, Alida Elzabé van Heerden; two *s*. *Educ:* Helpmekaar Sch.; Witwatersrand Technical Coll.; Bolt Court Sch. of Photography. Freelance work: Johannesburg, 1953–68; London, 1968–. One-man Exhibitions: Johannesburg, 1953, 1960; Tokyo, 1970, 1973, 1976, 1981, 1985, 1987–88, 1990, 1992, 1993, 1996, 1999; London, 1972, 1976, 1978, 1980, 1987, 1999; Paris, 1973; Amsterdam, 1974; NY, 1981; San Francisco, 1982; Toronto, 1982; Bologna, 1982; Auckland, 1991; Sydney, 1991; Hong Kong, 1991; Taipei, 1991; Singapore, 1991; Osaka, 1990, 1992, 1993, 1997, 2000; Prague, 1993; Palermo, 1993; Glasgow, 1997; Berlin, 2000. *Publications:* Five Girls, 1962; Cowboy Kate and other stories, 1964 (Prix Nadar, France, 1964); November Girl, 1966; African Image, 1967 (Silver Award, Internat. Art Book Contest, 1969); Haskins Posters, 1972 (Gold Medal, New York Art Directors Club, 1974); Photo-Graphics, 1980 (Kodak Book Award); portfolios in most major internat. photographic magazines. *Recreations:* sculpting, books, music. *Address:* 9A Calonne Road, SW19 5HH. *T:* (020) 8946 9660; *e-mail:* sam@haskins.com.

HASLAM, family name of **Baron Haslam**.

HASLAM, Baron *cr* 1990 (Life Peer), of Bolton in the County of Greater Manchester; **Robert Haslam,** Kt 1985; CEng, FInstME; Chairman, Wasserstein Perella & Co. Ltd, 1991–99; *b* 4 Feb. 1923; *s* of Percy and Mary Haslam; *m* 1st, 1947, Joyce Quin (*d* 1995); two *s*; 2nd, 1996, Elizabeth, *widow* of Hon. Michael Sieff, CBE. *Educ:* Bolton Sch.; Birmingham Univ. (BSc Coal Mining, 1st Cl.). Joined Manchester Collieries Ltd, 1944; National Coal Board, Jan. 1947; Mining Engr, Oct. 1947, Personnel Director, 1960, ICI Nobel Division; Director, 1963, Dep. Chm., 1966, ICI Plastics Div.; Dep. Chm., 1969, Chm., 1971, ICI Fibres Div.; Dir, ICI Ltd, 1974–83; Chairman: ICI Americas Inc., 1978–81; Dep. Chm., ICI plc, 1980–83; Chairman: British Steel Corporation, 1983–86; Tate & Lyle plc, 1983–86 (non-exec. Dep. Chm., 1982; Dir, 1978–86); British Coal, 1986–90 (Non-exec. Dep. Chm., 1985–86; Dep. Chm., 1986); Bechtel Ltd, 1991–94; Director: Fibre Industries, Inc., 1971–75; Imperial Metal Industries, 1975–77; AECI Ltd, 1978–79; Carrington Viyella, 1982–83; Cable and Wireless, 1982–83; Bank of England, 1985–93; Adv. Dir, Unilever, 1986–93. Chairman: Man-Made Fibres Producers Cttee, 1972–74; Nationalized Industries Chairmen's Group, 1985–86 (Mem., 1983–90); British Occupl Health Res. Foundn, 1991–2000; Member: BOTB, 1981–85 (Chm., N America Adv. Gp, 1982–85); NEDC, 1985–89. Pres., IMinE, 1989–90. Chairman: Michael Sieff Foundn, 1995–; Council, Manchester Business Sch., 1985–90; Governors, Bolton Sch., 1990–97; Mem. Council, RHBNC, 1992–96. Freeman, City of London, 1985. Hon. FIMinE 1987. Hon. DTech Brunel, 1987; Hon. DEng Birmingham, 1987. *Recreations:* golf, travel. *Address:* c/o House of Lords, SW1A 0PW. *Club:* Wentworth.

HASLAM, Christopher Peter de Landre; HM Diplomatic Service; Ambassador (non-resident) to Marshall Islands, Micronesia and Palau, since 2000; Deputy High Commissioner to Fiji Islands, Tuvalu, Kiribati and Nauru, since 2000; *b* 22 March 1943; *s* of late Jack Harold Haslam and Molly Patricia Haslam; *m* 1969, Lana Whitley; two *s*. *Educ:* Ashley Co. Secondary Modern, Hants. Admiralty, 1960–66; joined HM Diplomatic Service, 1966: Jakarta, 1969–72; Attaché, Sofia, 1972–74; FCO, 1974–78; Canberra, 1978–82; Second Sec. (Commercial), Lagos, 1982–86; FCO, 1986–89; First Sec. (Commercial), Copenhagen, 1989–93; FCO Inspectorate, 1993–96; First Sec. (Commercial and Econ.), Colombo, 1996–99. *Recreations:* reading, table tennis, tennis, amateur novelist. *Address:* c/o Foreign and Commonwealth Office, SW1A 2AH. *Club:* Rotary (Suva).

HASLAM, Rear Adm. Sir David William, KBE 1984 (OBE 1964); CB 1979; President, Directing Committee, International Hydrographic Bureau, Monaco, 1987–92; *b* 26 June 1923; *s* of Gerald Haigh Haslam and Gladys Haslam (*née* Finley). *Educ:* Ashe Prep. Sch., Etwall; Bromsgrove Sch., Worcs. FRGS, FRIN, FRICS. Special Entry Cadet, RN, 1941; HMS Birmingham, HMAS Quickmatch, HMS Resolution (in Indian Ocean), 1942–43; specialised in hydrographic surveying, 1944; HMS White Bear (surveying in Burma and Malaya), 1944–46; comd Survey Motor Launch 325, 1947; RAN, 1947–49; HMS Scott, 1949–51; HMS Dalrymple, 1951–53; i/c RN Survey Trng Unit, Chatham, 1953–56; HMS Vidal, 1956–57; comd, HMS Dalrymple, 1958; comd, HMS Dampier, 1958–60; Admty, 1960–62; comd, HMS Owen, 1962–64; Exec. Officer, RN Barracks, Chatham, 1964–65; Hydrographer, RAN, 1965–67; comd, HMS Hecla, 1968–70; Asst Hydrographer, MoD, 1970–72; comd, HMS Hydra, 1972–73; Asst Dir (Naval) to Hydrographer, 1974–75; sowc 1975; Hydrographer of the Navy, 1975–85. Acting Conservator, River Mersey, 1985–87; Advr on Port Appts, Dept of Transport, 1986–87. Underwriting Mem., Lloyd's, 1986–93. Pres., Hydrographic Soc., 1977–79. Vice-Pres., Bromsgrove Sch., 1997– (Gov., 1977–97). President: English Schs Basketball Assoc., 1973–96; Derbyshire CCC, 1991–92. Liveryman, Chartered Surveyors' Co., 1983–. FRSA. *Address:* 146 Worcester Road, Bromsgrove, Worcs B61 7AS. *T:* (01527) 574068.

HASLAM, Geoffrey; *see* Haslam, W. G.

HASLAM, Rev. John Gordon; part-time Chairman of Industrial Tribunals, since 1996; non-stipendiary Church of England priest; a Chaplain to the Queen, since 1989; *b* 15 July 1932; *s* of Ernest Henry Haslam and Constance Mabel (*née* Moore); *m* 1st, 1957, Margaret Anne Couse (*d* 1985); two *s* one *d*; 2nd, 1987, Marian Kidson Clarke. *Educ:* King Edward's Sch., Birmingham; Birmingham Univ. (LLB); Queen's Coll., Birmingham. National Service, RA, 1956–58 (2nd Lieut). Solicitor's Articled Clerk, Johnson & Co., Birmingham, 1953–56; Asst Solicitor, 1958–62, Partner, 1962–75, Pinsent & Co., Solicitors, Birmingham; a Chm. of Industrial Tribunals, 1976–92, Regl Chm., 1992–96. Ordained deacon and priest, Birmingham dio., 1977; Hon. Curate: St Michael's, Bartley Green, Birmingham, 1977–79; St Mary's, Moseley, Birmingham, 1980–96; Hon. Hosp. Chaplain, 1980–88; temp. service as priest in many Birmingham parishes, 1983–96; licensed to officiate, Hereford dio., 1996–. *Recreations:* gardening, steam railways, fell walking. *Address:* 16 Mill Street, Ludlow, Salop SY8 1BE. *T:* (01584) 876663.

HASLAM, Jonathan, CBE 1997; Director of Corporate Affairs, London Metal Exchange, since 1997; *b* 2 Oct. 1952; *s* of Arthur and Irene Florence; *m* 1982, Dawn Rachel Saunders; two *s*. *Educ:* Cowbridge Grammar Sch., Glam; Plymouth Poly. (BSc Hons Geog. 1975); Croydon Coll. of Art and Technol. (HNC Business Studies). Mgt Trainee, National Westminster Bank, 1975–79; Information Officer: COI, 1979–82; Dept of Industry, 1982–84; Sen. Inf. Officer, Home Office, 1984–86; Chief Press Officer, then Dep. Hd of Inf., Dept of Employment, 1986–89; Dep. Dir of Inf, Home Office, 1989–91; Dep. Press Sec. to Prime Minister, 1991–95; Head of Inf. and Press Sec. to Minister, Min. of Agriculture, 1995–96; Chief Press Sec. to Prime Minister, 1996–97; Dir of Communications, DFEE, 1997. *Recreations:* golf, music (especially Pink Floyd and Vivaldi), cinema, Concept rowing machines. *Address:* London Metal Exchange, 56 Leadenhall Street, EC3A 2DX.

HASLAM, Dr Michael Trevor, FRCPG, FRCPsych; retired consultant psychiatrist and medical director; *b* 7 Feb. 1934; *s* of Gerald Haslam and Edna Beatrice Haslam (*née* Oldfield); *m* 1959, Shirley Dunstan Jefferies; one *s* two *d*. *Educ:* Sedbergh Sch.; St John's Coll., Cambridge (MA, MD); St Bartholomew's Hosp. Captain, RAMC, 1960–62; hosp. posts, York, 1962–64, Newcastle upon Tyne, 1964–67; Consultant Psychiatrist: Doncaster, 1967–70; York, 1970–89; Medical Director: Harrogate Clinic, 1989–91; SW Durham Mental Health NHS Trust, 1993–96; S Durham Health Care NHS Trust, 1996–98. Chm., Soc. of Clinical Psychiatrists; former Cttee Chm., RCP. FRSocMed. Membership Sec., Guild of Freemen; Freeman, City of London, 1973; Liveryman, Soc. of Apothecaries, 1973. *Publications:* Psychiatric Illness in Adolescence, 1975; Sexual Disorders, 1978 (trans. Spanish, 1980); Psychosexual Disorders, 1979; Psychiatry Made Simple, 1982, 2nd edn 1990 (trans. Polish, 1997); Transvestism, 1993; Clifton Hospital: an era, 1997; articles in learned jls. *Recreations:* writing, music, fives, squash, croquet, travel. *Address:* Chapel Garth, Crayke, York YO61 4TE. *T:* (01347) 823042.

HASLAM, Richard Michael, FSA; writer on architecture; buildings consultant; painter; *b* 27 Sept. 1944; *s* of Cecil Henry Cobden Haslam and Sylvia Lois Haslam (*née* Assheton); *m* 1980, Charlotte Sophia Dorrien Smith (*d* 1997); two *s* one *d*. *Educ:* Eton Coll. (Oppidan Schol.); New Coll., Oxford (BA 1966, MA 1967); Courtauld Inst. of Art (MA 1969). FSA 1987. Res. Asst to Sir Nikolaus Pevsner, 1969–71; Statistician, Lloyd's, 1971–72; set up consultancy on the use, repair, and commissioning of buildings, 1982. Curator, Clough Williams-Ellis exhibn, Heinz Gall., RIBA, 1997. Member: Architectl Panel, 1979–, Cttee for Wales, 1980–88, Properties Cttee, 1985–, NT; Historic Buildings Council for Wales, 1980–98; Royal Commn on Ancient and Historical Monuments of Wales, 1986–98; Friends' Cttee, Centro Internazionale di Studi di Architettura 'A. Palladio', 1995–; Prize Jury, Premio Dedalo+Minosse for commng a building, 1998–. Trustee, Venice in Peril Fund, 1992–. *Publications:* The Buildings of Wales: Powys, 1979; From Decay to Splendour: the repair of church treasures, 1985; Clough Williams-Ellis's Drawings, 1996; articles in Country Life, Arte Lombarda, Perspectives on Architecture and other jls. *Recreations:* walking, ski-ing, having people to stay. *Address:* Bramley Grange, Bramley, Tadley, Hants RG26 5DJ. *T:* (01256) 881245; Parc, Llanfrothen, Gwynedd LL48 6SP. *T:* (01766) 770573.

HASLAM, (William) Geoffrey, OBE 1985; DFC 1944; Director, Prudential Corporation PLC, 1980–87 (Deputy Chairman, 1980–84); *b* 11 Oct. 1914; *yr s* of late William John Haslam and late Hilda Irene Haslam; *m* 1941, Valda Patricia Adamson; two *s* one *d*. *Educ:* New Coll. and Ashville Coll., Harrogate. War Service with RAF, No 25 Sqdn (night fighters), 1940–46. Joined Prudential Assurance Co. Ltd, 1933: Dep. Gen. Manager, 1963; Gen. Manager, 1969; Chief Gen. Manager, 1974–78; Chief Exec., 1979; Dep. Chm., 1980–84. Chairman: Industrial Life Offices Assoc., 1972–74; British Insurance Assoc., 1977–78. Chm., St Teresa's Hospital, Wimbledon, 1983–87; Vice Pres., NABC, 1983–. *Recreation:* golf. *Address:* 6 Ashbourne Road, W5 3ED. *T:* (020) 8997 8164. *Clubs:* Royal Air Force, MCC.

HASLETT, Prof. Christopher, FRCP, FRCPE, FMedSci; FRSE; Professor of Respiratory Medicine and Director, Rayne Laboratories, University of Edinburgh, since 1990; Hon. Consultant Physician, Lothian Acute Hospitals Trust, since 1990; *b* 2 April 1953; *s* of James and Elizabeth Haslett; *m* 1973, Jean Margaret Hale; one *s* one *d*. *Educ:* Wirral Grammar Sch.; Univ. of Edinburgh Med. Sch. (BSc 1st Cl. Hons Pathology 1974; MB ChB Hons 1974; Ettles Schol.; Leslie Gold Medal for most distinguished grad. 1977). MRCP 1979, FRCP 1991; FRCPE 1988. Jun. med. posts, Edinburgh, 1977–79; Rotating Med. Registrar, Ealing Hosp. and Hammersmith Hosp., 1980–82; MRC Travelling Fellow, Nat. Jewish Hosp., Denver, 1982–85; MRC Sen. Clin. Fellow and Sen. Lectr, Dept of Medicine, RPMS, Hammersmith Hosp., 1986–90; Associate Dean (Res.), 1996–, and Head, Div. of Clin. Sci. and Community Health, 1998–, Univ. of Edinburgh. Vice-Chairman: Res. Cttee, Nat. Asthma Campaign, 1990–94; MRC Molecular and Cellular Medicine Bd, 1994–98; Mem., MRC Systems A Grants Cttee, 1990–92; Chairman: Lung Injury Section, European Respiratory Soc., 1994–98 (Sec., 1991–94); MRC ROPA Infection and Immunity Panel, 1995, 1996. Medal and Prize for Sci., Saltire Soc., 1996; Gilston Lecture and Medal, Intensive Care Soc., 1998; numerous lectures in UK and abroad. FMedSci 1998. *Publications:* (Sen. Ed.) Davidson's Textbook of Medicine, 17th edn 1995, 18th edn 1999; (ed jtly) ARDS—Acute Respiratory Distress Syndrome in Adults, 1997; numerous articles in learned jls concerning inflammatory cell biology and inflammatory lung disease. *Recreations:* Rugby Union (spectating only, these days), contemporary fiction, cooking, eating and drinking (not necessarily in that order). *Address:* Department of Medical and Radiological Sciences, Royal Infirmary, Lauriston Place, Edinburgh EH3 9YW. *T:* (0131) 536 2263; *e-mail:* C.Haslett@ed.ac.uk.

HASSALL, Prof. Cedric Herbert, FRS 1985; CChem, FRSC; Hon. Visiting Professor, University of North London, since 1999; *b* 6 Dec. 1919; *s* of late H. Hassall, Auckland, NZ; *m* 1st, 1946, H. E. Cotti (marr. diss. 1982); one *d* (and one *s* decd); 2nd, 1984, J. A. Mitchelmore. *Educ:* Auckland Grammar Sch., NZ; Auckland Univ. (MSc); Univ. of Cambridge (PhD, ScD). Lectr, Univ. of Otago, NZ, 1943–45; Sen. studentship, Royal Commn for 1851, Cambridge, 1946–48; Foundn Prof. of Chem., Univ. of WI, 1948–56; Carnegie and Rockefeller Fellowships in USA, 1950, 1956; Head, Dept of Chemistry, Univ. Coll., of Swansea, UCW, 1957–71; Dir of Research, Roche Products Ltd, 1971–84. Comr, Royal Univ. of Malta, 1964–71; Planning Adviser: Univ. of Jordan, 1965–71; Univ. of Aleppo, 1965; Abdul Aziz Univ., Jedda, 1966, 1968. Visiting Professor: Univ. of Kuwait, 1969, 1979, 1997; Aligarh Univ., India (Royal Soc.), 1969–70; Univ. of Liverpool, 1971–79; UCL, 1979–85; Warwick Univ., 1985–95; Hon. Visiting Professor: UC, Cardiff, 1985–92; Imperial Coll., London, 1989–97. Pres., Chem. Section of British Assoc., 1987; Member: various cttees of Royal Soc. Chem., 1959– (Pres., Perkin Div., 1985–87); Council, British Technol. Gp, 1986–92; various Govt cttees relating to sci. affairs; Co-ordinator, Molecular Recognition Initiative, SERC, 1987–90; ODA Advr on science, technology and educn in India, China and Indonesia, 1989–. Chm., Steering Cttee, Oxford Centre for Molecular Scis, 1988–92. Chm., Mother and Child Foundn, 1995–2001; Dir, IMET 2000, 2001–. Hon. Fellow, UC of Swansea, 1986. Hon. DSc West Indies, 1975. *Publications:* papers on aspects of organic chemistry, largely in Jl of Chemical Soc. *Recreation:* travel. *Address:* 2 Chestnut Close, Westoning, Beds MK45 5LR. *T:* (01525) 712909, *Fax:* (01525) 752550; *e-mail:* CHhassall@aol.com.

HASSALL, Eric Ronald, CBE 1999; FIMM, FRICS, FGS; Deputy Chairman, Coal Authority, 1997–2000; Chairman, British Geological Survey Board, 1994–2001; *b* 16 Nov. 1930; *s* of George Arthur Hassall and Margaret Hassall; *m* 1953, Joan Wilson; two *s* three *d*. *Educ:* Leigh Grammar Sch.; Wigan Mining Coll.; Coll. of Estates Management, Manchester Business Sch. CEng. National Coal Bd, 1947–72; Wardell Armstrong: Partner, 1972–81; Sen. Partner, 1981–91; Chairman, 1991–94. Crown Mineral Agent, 1988–92. Mem., NERC, 1993–98. Mem., Keele Univ. Council, 1995–. Pres., IMinE, 1997–99. Hon. DSc Staffordshire, 1995. *Publications:* contribs on mining technology. *Recreations:* golf, sport, reading, engineering, science, painting, family. *Address:* 33 Sneyd Avenue, Newcastle under Lyme, Staffs ST5 2PZ. *T:* (01782) 619835; *e-mail:* Eric.Hassall@UKgateway.net. *Clubs:* Lancashire County Cricket; Newcastle under Lyme Golf; Little Aston Golf.

HASSALL, Tom Grafton, OBE 1999; FSA; archaeological consultant; Secretary and Chief Executive, Royal Commission on Historical Monuments of England, 1986–99; Fellow, St Cross College, Oxford, since 1974; *b* 3 Dec. 1943; *s* of late William Owen Hassall and Averil Grafton Beaves; *m* 1967, Angela Rosaleen Goldsmith; three *s*. *Educ:* Dragon Sch., Oxford; Lord Williams's Grammar Sch., Thame; Corpus Christi Coll., Oxford (BA History). FSA 1971. Assistant local editor, Victoria County History of Oxford, 1966–67; Director, Oxford Archaeological Excavation Cttee, 1967–73; Dir, Oxfordshire (now Oxford) Archaeological Unit, 1973–85; Associate Staff Tutor, Oxford Univ. Dept for External Studies, 1978–85. Vis. Fellow, Kellogg Coll., Oxford, 1999–. Trustee, Oxford Preservation Trust, 1973–; Chairman: Standing Conf. of Archaeol Unit Managers, 1980–83; British Archaeological Awards, 1983–88; Internat. Council on Monuments and Sites, UK, 1997–; Victoria History of Oxfordshire Trust, 1997–; Kelmscott Mgt Cttee, 2000–; President: Council for British Archaeology, 1983–86; Oxfordshire Architectural and Historical Soc., 1984–92; Mem., Ancient Monuments Adv. Cttee, Historic Buildings and Monuments Commn, 1984–93. Guest Lectr, Swan Hellenic Cruises, 1981–. Crew mem., Athenian Trireme, 1987. Hon. MIFA 1999. *Publications:* Oxford: the city beneath your feet, 1972; specialist articles on archaeology. *Recreation:* boating. *Address:* Durham House, 42 Rewley Road, Oxford OX1 2RQ. *T:* (01865) 205266. *Club:* Athenæum.

HASSAN, Mamoun Hamid; independent producer/director; Director of Editing, International Film and Television School, Cuba, since 1998; *b* Jedda, 12 Dec. 1937; *s* of late Dr Hamid Hassan and of Fatma Hassan (*née* Sadat); *m* 1966, Moya Jacqueline Gillespie, MA Oxon; two *s*. Formerly script writer, editor and director; Head of Production Board, British Film Inst., 1971–74; Head of Films Branch, UNRWA, Lebanon, 1974–76; Bd Mem., 1978–84, Man. Dir, 1979–84, Nat. Film Finance Corp. Member: Cinematograph Films Council, 1977–78; Scottish Film Production Fund, 1983–87; Advr, European Script Fund, 1989–90; Sen. Consultant for UNESCO, Harare, Zimbabwe, 1991–93; Hd of Editing, Nat. Film and Television Sch., 1993–97 (Gov., 1983–92). Visiting Lecturer: UCLA; California Inst. of the Arts; Europ. Film Coll.; Satyajit Ray Inst. of Film & Television, Calcutta. Films produced include: No Surrender, 1985. Producer and presenter, Movie Masterclass, C4 series, 1988, 2nd series, 1990. *Publications:* articles in THES. *Address:* High Ridge, 9 High Street, Deddington, Oxford OX15 0SJ.

HASSELL, Barry Frank; Chief Executive, Independent Healthcare Association, since 1992; *b* 26 Sept. 1944; *s* of late Edgar Frank Hassell and of Rosetta Ethel Hassell (*née* Townsend); *m* 1971, Sylvia Booth; two step *s*. *Educ:* Swanscombe County Secondary Sch. (Head Boy); London Business Sch. (London Exec. Prog.). FIM. Accounting, marketing and directors appts, UK, Scandinavia, Africa, 1959–73; Management Consultant, 1973–85; Special Projects Exec., Spastics Soc., 1980–85; Chief Exec., Tadworth Court Trust, 1983–92. Dir, Project Bombay, 1983–88. Vice Pres., Union of European Private Hosps, 1997, 2000 (Hon. Sec., 1993–97). Gov., Nat. Inst. for Social Work, 1998–. FRGS. *Publications:* articles on health and social care issues. *Recreations:* travel, photography, ski-ing. *Address:* Independent Health Care Association, Westminster Tower, 3 Albert Embankment, SE1 7SP. *T:* (020) 7793 4620, *Fax:* (020) 7820 3738.

HASSELL, Prof. Michael Patrick, FRS 1987; Professor of Insect Ecology, since 1979, and Head of Department of Biology, since 1993, Imperial College of Science, Technology and Medicine; Director, Silwood Park, since 1988; *b* 2 Aug. 1942; *s* of Albert Marmaduke Hassell and Gertrude Hassell (*née* Loeser); *m* 1st, 1966, Glynis Mary Everett (marr. diss.

locomotives. *Address:* St Dunstan's House, 133–137 Fetter Lane, EC4A 1HD. *T:* (020) 7947 6022. *Clubs:* Athenæum, Garrick, Hurlingham.

HAVILLAND; *see* de Havilland.

HAWARDEN, 9th Viscount (Ire.), *cr* 1793; **Robert Connan Wyndham Leslie Maude;** Bt 1705; Baron de Montalt 1785; *b* 23 May 1961; *s* of 8th Viscount and of Susannah Caroline Hyde, *d* of late Maj. Charles Phillips Gardner; *S* father, 1991; *m* 1995, Judith Anne, *y d* of John Bates; one *s* one *d. Educ:* St Edmund's Sch., Canterbury; RAC Cirencester. *Heir: s* Hon. Varian John Connan Eustace Maude, *b* 1 Sept. 1997. *Address:* Great Bossington Farm House, Bossington, Adisham, near Canterbury, Kent CT3 3LN.

HAWES, Ven. Arthur John; Archdeacon of Lincoln, and Canon and Prebendary of Lincoln Cathedral, since 1995; *b* 31 Aug. 1943; *s* of John and Sylvia Hawes; *m* 1969, Melanie Harris; one *s* one *d. Educ:* City of Oxford High Sch. for Boys; Chichester Theol Coll.; Univ. of Birmingham (Dip. in Pastoral Studies, 1972; Dip. in Liturgy and Architecture, 1975); Univ. of E Anglia (BA Hons 1986). Ordained deacon, 1968, priest, 1969; Asst Curate, St John the Baptist, Kidderminster, 1968–72; Priest-in-charge, St Richard's, Droitwich, 1972–76; Rector: Alderford with Attlebridge and Swannington, 1976–92; St Faith's, Gaywood, King's Lynn, 1992–95. Chaplain, Hellesdon and David Rice Hosps, Yare Clinic, 1976–92; Rural Dean of Sparham, 1981–91; Hon. Canon of Norwich Cathedral, 1988–95. Chm., Norwich Diocesan Bd for Social Responsibility, 1990–95. Comr, NHS Mental Health Act, 1986–94. Patron, MIND, 1995–. *Publications:* (ed jtly) The Ann French Memorial Lectures, 1996; contribs to theol jls. *Recreations:* golf, theatre, music. *Address:* Archdeacon's House, Northfield Road, Quarrington, Lincs NG34 8RT. *T:* (01529) 304348, *Fax:* (01529) 304354; *e-mail:* ad.oflincoln@virgin.net. *Club:* Sleaford Golf.

HAWKE, family name of **Baron Hawke**.

HAWKE, 11th Baron *cr* 1776, of Towton; **Edward George Hawke,** TD; FRICS; *b* 25 Jan. 1950; *s* of 10th Baron and of his 2nd wife, Georgette Margaret, *d* of George S. Davidson; *S* father, 1992; *m* 1993, Bronwen, *d* of William James, MRCVS; one *s* one *d. Educ:* Eton. 2nd Lt, 1st Bn Coldstream Guards, 1970–73; Territorial Army, Queen's Own Yeomanry, 1973–93 (Major). Hon. Col, Cheshire Yeomanry, 1998–. *Heir: s* William Martin Theodore Hawke, *b* 23 June 1995.

HAWKE, Hon. Robert James Lee, AC 1979; business consultant; Adjunct Professor, Research School of Pacific Studies and Social Sciences, Australian National University, 1992–95; Prime Minister of Australia, 1983–91; *b* 9 Dec. 1929; *m* 1st, 1956, Hazel Masterson (marr. diss. 1995); one *s* two *d* (and one *s* decd); 2nd, 1995, Blanche d'Alpuget. *Educ:* Univ. of Western Australia (LLB, BA(Econ)); Oxford Univ. (BLitt; Hon. Fellow, University Coll., 1984). Research Officer and Advocate for Aust. Council of Trade Unions, 1958–69. Pres., ACTU, 1970–80. MP (Lab) Wills, Melbourne, 1980–92; Australian Labor Party: Mem., Nat. Exec., 1971–91; Pres., 1973–78; Leader, 1983–91. Leader of the Opposition, Feb.–March 1983. Member: Governing Body of Internat. Labour Office, 1972–80; Board, Reserve Bank of Australia, 1973–80; Aust. Population and Immigration Council, 1976–80; Aust. Manufacturing Council, 1977–80. Chm., Cttee of Experts on Membership of Educn Internat. 1993–, Hon. Vis. Prof., Univ. of Sydney, 1992–97. Mem. Adv. Bd, Inst. for Internat. Studies, Stanford Univ. Hon. DLitt W Australia, 1984; Hon. Dr Nanjing, 1986; Hon. DPhil Hebrew Univ. of Jerusalem, 1987; Hon. LLD Univ. of NSW, 1987. *Publication:* The Hawke Memoirs, 1994. *Recreations:* tennis, cricket, reading, golf, horse racing, snooker. *Address:* c/o GPO Box 36, Sydney, NSW 2001, Australia.

HAWKEN, Lewis Dudley, CB 1983; a Deputy Chairman of the Board of Customs and Excise, 1980–87; *b* 23 Aug. 1931; *s* of late Richard and Doris May Evelyn Hawken; *m* 1954, Bridget Mary Gamble (*d* 1989); two *s* one *d. Educ:* Harrow County Sch. for Boys; Lincoln Coll., Oxford (MA). Comr of Customs and Excise, 1975. *Recreations:* collecting Victorian books, tennis. *Address:* 19 Eastcote Road, Ruislip, Mddx HA4 8BE. *T:* (01895) 632405. *Clubs:* Oxford and Cambridge, MCC.

HAWKER, Ven. Alan Fort; Archdeacon of Malmesbury, since 1999; *b* 23 March 1944; *s* of Albert Hawker and Florence Lilian Hawker (*née* Fort); *m* 1968, Jeanette Dorothy Law; one *s* three *d. Educ:* Buckhurst Hill County High Sch.; Hull Univ. (BA Hons Soc. Studies 1965); Clifton Theol Coll. (DipTh 1968). PACTA 1973. Asst Curate, St Leonard and St Mary, Bootle, 1968–71; Asst Curate (with charge), St Paul, Fazakerley, 1971–73; Vicar, St Paul, Goose Green, 1973–81; Team Rector, St Mary, Southgate (Crawley), 1981–98; Canon and Prebendary, Chichester Cathedral, 1991–98; Proctor in Convocation, 1990–; RD of E Grinstead, 1993–98; Archdeacon of Swindon, 1998–99. Chm., Gen. Synod Working Party on Clergy Discipline and Reform of Ecclesiastical Courts, 1994–; Mem., Gen. Synod Standing Cttee, 1995–98. CEDR Accredited Mediator, 1996–. *Publication:* Under Authority, 1996. *Recreations:* walking, railways, theatre, reading, music. *Address:* Church Paddock, Church Lane, Kington Langley, Chippenham, Wilts SN15 5NR. *T:* (01249) 750085, *Fax:* (01249) 750086; *e-mail:* alan@venjen.fsnet.co.uk.

HAWKER, Rt Rev. Dennis Gascoyne; Hon. Assistant Bishop, diocese of Norwich, since 1993; *b* 8 Feb. 1921; *o s* of late Robert Stephen and Amelia Caroline Hawker; *m* 1944, Margaret Hamilton, *d* of late Robert and Daisy Henderson; one *s* one *d. Educ:* Addey and Stanhope Grammar Sch.; Queens' Coll., Cambridge (MA); Cuddesdon Theological Coll., Oxford. Lloyds Bank, 1939–40. Served War, Commissioned Officer, Royal Marines, 1940–46 (War Substantive Major). Deacon, 1950; Priest, 1951; Asst Curate, St Mary and St Eanswythe, Folkestone, 1950–55; Vicar, St Mark, South Norwood, 1955–60; St Hugh's Missioner, Dio. Lincoln, 1960–65; Vicar, St Mary and St James, Gt Grimsby, 1965–72; Bishop Suffragan of Grantham, 1972–87. Canon and Prebendary of Clifton, in Lincoln Cath., 1964–87; Proctor in Convocation, 1964–74. Hon. Chaplain, RNR, 1979–. *Address:* Pickwick Cottage, Hall Close, Heacham, Kings Lynn, Norfolk PE31 7JT. *T:* (01485) 570450. *Club:* Army and Navy.

HAWKER, Graham Alfred, CBE 1999; DL; Chief Executive, Welsh Development Agency, since 2000 (Deputy Chairman, 1998–2000); *b* 12 May 1947; *s* of Alfred Hawker and Sarah Rebecca (*née* Bowen); *m* 1967, Sandra Ann Evans; one *s* one *d. Educ:* Bedwelty Grammar Sch. CIPFA 1969; FCCA 1981. Trainee Acctnt, Caerphilly DC, 1964–66; Abercarn District Council: Acctnt, 1966–67; Chief Acctnt, 1967–68, Dep. Treas., 1968–70; Chief Auditor, Taf Fechan Water Bd, 1970–74; Welsh Water Authority: Audit Manager, 1974–78; Div. Finance Manager, 1978–84; Chief Acctnt, 1984–86; Dir, Planning and Develt, 1986–87; Dir, Finance, 1987–89; Welsh Water, later Hyder, PLC: Dir, Finance, 1989–91; Gp Man. Dir, 1991–93; Chief Exec., 1993–2000. A Dir, Bank of England, 1998–2000. Chairman: Dwr Cymru Ltd, 1993–2000; Hyder Consulting (formerly Acer), 1993–2000; Swalec, 1996–2000. Chm., BITC (Wales), 1994–2000. CIMgt; FRSA. DL Gwent, 1998. *Recreations:* family, walking, wine, career. *Address:* Welsh Development Agency, Principality House, The Friary, Cardiff CF10 3FE. *Clubs:* Cardiff and County (Cardiff); Abergavenny Rugby Club (Pres.).

HAWKES, David, MA, DPhil; Research Fellow, All Souls College, Oxford, 1973–83, now Emeritus; *b* 6 July 1923; *s* of Ewart Hawkes and Dorothy May Hawkes (*née* Davis); *m* 1950, Sylvia Jean Perkins; one *s* three *d. Educ:* Bancroft's Sch. Open Scholarship in Classics, Christ Church, Oxford, 1941; Chinese Hons Sch., Oxford, 1945–47; Research Student, National Peking Univ., 1948–51. Formerly University Lecturer in Chinese, Oxford; Prof. of Chinese, Oxford Univ., 1959–71. *Publications:* Ch'u Tz'ŭ, Songs of the South, 1959, rev. edn as The Songs of the South: an Ancient Chinese Anthology of Poems by Qu Yuan and Other Poets, 1985; A Little Primer of Tu Fu, 1967, repr. 1987; The Story of the Stone, vol. 1, 1973, vol. 2, 1977, vol. 3, 1980; Classical, Modern and Humane: essays in Chinese Literature (ed J. Minford and Siu-kit Wong), 1989.

HAWKES, (John) Garry, CBE 1999; Chief Executive, Gardner Merchant, 1978–98; Director, Trusthouse Forte, 1983–1993; *b* 26 Aug. 1939; *s* of John and Joyce Hawkes; *m* 1963, Peggy Lee; one *d. Educ:* Rowlinson Sch., Sheffield; Huddersfield Coll. of Technology. Joined Gardner Merchant, 1963; Regl Dir, 1972–76; European Man. Dir, 1976; Man. Dir, Gardner Merchant Ltd, 1977–95. Directeur Général, Sodexho SA, 1995–98. Chairman: Nat. Council, NTO, 1997–; British Trng Internat., 1997–2001; ARAMARK UK, 2000–. FHCIMA 1982. Hon. Fellow: Huddersfield Univ., 1996; Oxford Brookes Univ., 1997. *Recreations:* theatre, modern design, travel. *Address:* Coalpit, Rookery Way, Haywards Heath, W Sussex RH16 4RE; Penthouse 1220 The White House, 9 Belvedere Road, SE1 8YN. *T:* (020) 7928 4441.

HAWKES, Prof. John Gregory, OBE 1994; Mason Professor of Botany and Head of Plant Biology Department, University of Birmingham, 1967–82, now Emeritus; *b* 27 June 1915; *s* of C. W. and G. M. Hawkes; *m* 1941, Ellen Barbara Leather; two *s* two *d. Educ:* Univ. of Cambridge. BA, MA, PhD, ScD. Botanist, Potato Res. Station of Commonwealth Agricultural Bureaux, 1939–48, 1951–52; Dir of Potato Research Project, Min. of Ag., Colombia, S America, 1948–51; Birmingham University: Lectr and Sen. Lectr in Taxonomic Botany, 1952–61; Prof. of Taxonomic Botany (Personal Chair), 1961–67. Pres., Linnean Soc. of London, 1991–94. Linnean Soc. Gold Medal, 1984. *Publications:* (with J. P. Hjerting) The Potatoes of Argentina, Brazil, Paraguay, and Uruguay, 1969; (with D. A. Cadbury and R. C. Readett) A Computer-Mapped Flora, 1971; (with O. H. Frankel) Crop Genetic Resources for Today and Tomorrow, 1975; Conservation and Agriculture, 1978; (with R. N. Lester and A. D. Skelding) The Biology and Taxonomy of the Solanaceae, 1979; The Diversity of Crop Plants, 1983; (with J. P. Hjerting) The Potatoes of Bolivia, 1989; The Potato: evolution, biodiversity and genetic resources, 1990; (with J. M. M. Engels and M. Worede) Plant Genetic Resources of Ethiopia, 1991; Genetic Conservation of World Crop Plants, 1991; (jtly) Solanaceae III – taxonomy, chemistry, evolution, 1991; (jtly) Plant Genetic Conservation: the *in situ* approach, 1996; (jtly) The *Ex Situ* Conservation of Plant Genetic Resources, 2000; contribs to various botanical and plant breeding jls. *Recreations:* walking, gardening, travel, art, archaeology. *Address:* 66 Lordswood Road, Birmingham B17 9BY. *T:* (0121) 427 2944. *Club:* Athenæum.

HAWKES, Michael John; Deputy Chairman, Kleinwort, Benson Group plc, 1988–90; *b* 7 May 1929; *s* of Wilfred Arthur Hawkes and Anne Maria Hawkes; *m* 1st, 1957, Gillian Mary Watts; two *s* two *d*; 2nd, 1973, Elizabeth Anne Gurton. *Educ:* Bedford School; New College, Oxford (Exhibnr; MA); Gray's Inn. Kleinwort Sons & Co. Ltd, 1954; Kleinwort, Benson Ltd: Director, 1967; Vice Chm., 1974; Dep. Chm., 1982; Chm., 1983–87; Director, Kleinwort Benson Lonsdale plc, 1974–88; Chairman: Sharps Pixley Ltd, 1971–89; Kleinwort Benson Investment Trust, 1984–89. Mem., Management Bd Sovereign (formerly W Berks) Housing Assoc., 1988–97. Gov., The Willink Sch., 1988–96. *Recreations:* long distance walking, golf, gardening. *Address:* Brookfield House, Burghfield Common, Berks RG7 3BD. *T:* (0118) 983 2912; White Bays, Daymer Lane, Trebetherick, N Cornwall PL27 6SA. *T:* (01208) 862280. *Club:* Leander (Henley on Thames).

HAWKES, Nigel John Mytton, CBE 1999; Health Editor, The Times, since 2000; *b* 1 Sept. 1943; *s* of R. W. Hawkes, MBE and K. M. Hawkes; *m* 1971, Jo Beresford; two *s* one *d. Educ:* Sedbergh Sch.; St Catherine's Coll., Oxford (MA). Mem., editl staff, Nature, 1966–69; Sci. Editor, Science Jl, 1969–70; Associate Editor, Telegraph Mag., 1970–72; The Observer: Sci. Corresp., 1972–81; Foreign News Editor, 1981–83; Diplomatic Corresp., 1983–87; Diplomatic Editor, 1987–90; Science Editor, The Times, 1990–2000. Gov., British Nutrition Foundn, 1999– (British Nutrition Foundn Award, 1992). *Publications:* The Computer Revolution, 1971; Early Scientific Instruments, 1978; (ed and contrib.) Tearing Down the Curtain, 1989; Structures, 1991; Man on the Move, 1992; numerous science and technology titles for children and teenagers. *Recreations:* walking, opera. *Address:* Well House, Front Road, Woodchurch, Kent TN26 3QE. *T:* (01233) 860518.

HAWKES, Raymond; Deputy Director, Naval Ship Production, 1977–78, retired; *b* 28 April 1920; *s* of Ernest Hawkes; *m* 1951, Joyce Barbara King; one *s* one *d. Educ:* RNC Greenwich. 1st cl. Naval Architecture, RCNC; CEng; FRINA. Ship design, Bath, 1942–45 and 1954–56; aircraft carrier research at RAE Farnborough, 1945–49; hydrodynamic research at A.E.W. (Admiralty Experiment Works) Haslar, 1949–54; Principal Admty Overseer, Birkenhead, 1956–58; ship prodn, Bath, 1958–62; Chief Cons. Design, assault ships, survey fleet, small ships and auxiliaries, 1962–69; Senior Officers War Course 1966; Asst Dir Warship Design and Project Man. for Through Deck Cruiser, 1969–72; Dep. Dir, Warship Design, 1972–77. *Recreation:* golf. *Address:* Wood Meadow, Beechwood Road, Combe Down, Bath BA2 5JS. *T:* (01225) 832885.

HAWKESBURY, Viscount; Luke Marmaduke Peter Savile Foljambe; with Property Vision, since 1999; *b* 25 March 1972; *s* and *heir* of 5th Earl of Liverpool, *qv. Educ:* Ampleforth; Roehampton Inst. *Recreations:* golf, field sports, sailing, sub-aqua. *Clubs:* Turf; Old Amplefordian Golf Soc.

HAWKESWORTH, Gareth; *see* Hawkesworth, W. G.

HAWKESWORTH, John Stanley; film and television producer and dramatist; *b* 7 Dec. 1920; *s* of Lt-Gen. Sir John Hawkesworth, KBE, CB, DSO, and Lady (Helen Jane) Hawkesworth; *m* 1943, Hyacinthe Gregson-Ellis; one *s. Educ:* Rugby Sch.; Oxford Univ. (BA war degree). Joined Grenadier Guards, 1940; commnd 1941; demobilised 1946 (Captain). Entered film industry as Designer: The Third Man, The Man Who Never Was, The Prisoner, Father Brown; became Producer/Dramatist, Tiger Bay; TV creations include: Upstairs, Downstairs; The Duchess of Duke Street; Danger UXB; The Flame Trees of Thika; The Tale of Beatrix Potter; By the Sword Divided; Oscar; Sherlock Holmes, The Return of Sherlock Holmes and The Sign of Four; Campion; Chelworth; screenplay: Mrs 'Arris Goes to Paris, 1992. One man show (paintings), The Studio, Glebe Place, London, 1989, 1995, 1997 and 1999; exhibn, film designs, Austin/Desmond Fine Art, London, 1991; exhibn, paintings of Pembrokeshire, Newport, 1994. Many television awards, incl. Peabody Award, Univ. of Georgia, 1977. *Publications:* Upstairs, Downstairs, 1972; In My Lady's Chamber, 1973. *Recreations:* golf, gardening. *Address:* Fishponds House, Knossington, Oakham, Rutland LE15 8LX. *T:* (01664) 454339.

HAWKESWORTH, (Thomas) Simon (Ashwell); QC 1982; **His Honour Judge Hawkesworth;** a Circuit Judge, since 1999; *b* 15 Nov. 1943; *s* of late Charles Peter Elmhirst Hawkesworth and of Felicity Hawkesworth; *m* 1st, 1970, Jennifer Lewis (marr. diss. 1989); two *s*; 2nd, 1990, Dr May Bamber, MD, MRCP; twin *s*. *Educ:* Rugby Sch.; The Queen's Coll., Oxford (MA). Called to the Bar, Gray's Inn, 1967, Bencher 1990; a Recorder, 1982–99. *Address:* Combined Court Centre, Leeds LS1 3BG.
See also W. G. Hawkesworth.

HAWKESWORTH, (Walter) Gareth; His Honour Judge Gareth Hawkesworth; a Circuit Judge, since 1999; *b* 29 Dec. 1949; *s* of late Charles Peter Elmhirst Hawkesworth and of Felicity Hawkesworth (*née* Ashwell); *m* 1982, Barbara Joyce Tapper; one *s* one *d*, and one step *d*. *Educ:* Rugby Sch.; Magdalene Coll., Cambridge (Schol.; BA 2nd Cl. Hons Law, MA); Council of Legal Educn. Called to the Bar, Gray's Inn, 1972; joined Fenners Chambers, Cambridge, 1974; a Recorder, 1995–99. *Recreations:* gardening, theatre, travel.
See also T. S. A. Hawkesworth.

HAWKING, Prof. Stephen William, CH 1989; CBE 1982; FRS 1974; Fellow of Gonville and Caius College, Cambridge; Lucasian Professor of Mathematics, Cambridge University, since 1979; *b* 8 Jan. 1942; *s* of Dr F. and Mrs E. I. Hawking; *m* 1st, 1965, Jane Wilde (marr. diss. 1995); two *s* one *d*; 2nd, 1995, Elaine Mason. *Educ:* St Albans Sch.; University Coll., Oxford (BA), Hon. Fellow 1977; Trinity Hall, Cambridge (PhD), Hon. Fellow 1984. Research Fellow, Gonville and Caius Coll., 1965–69; Fellow for distinction in science, 1969–; Mem. Inst. of Theoretical Astronomy, Cambridge, 1968–72; Research Asst, Inst. of Astronomy, Cambridge, 1972–73; Cambridge University: Research Asst, Dept of Applied Maths and Theoretical Physics, 1973–75; Reader in Gravitational Physics, 1975–77, Professor, 1977–79. Fairchild Distinguished Schol., Calif Inst. of Technol., 1974–75. Mem., Pontifical Acad. of Scis, 1986–; Foreign Member: Amer. Acad. of Arts and Scis, 1984; Amer. Philosophical Soc., 1985. Hon. Mem., RAS (Can), 1985. Hon. DSc: Oxon, 1978; Newcastle, Leeds, 1987; Cambridge, 1989; hon. degrees: Chicago, 1981; Leicester, New York, Notre Dame, Princeton, 1982. (Jtly) Eddington Medal, RAS, 1975; Pius XI Gold Medal, Pontifical Acad. of Scis, 1975; Dannie Heinemann Prize for Math. Phys., Amer. Phys. Soc. and Amer. Inst. of Physics, 1976; William Hopkins Prize, Cambridge Philosoph. Soc., 1976; Maxwell Medal, Inst. of Physics, 1976; Hughes Medal, Royal Soc., 1976; Albert Einstein Award, 1978; Albert Einstein Medal, Albert Einstein Soc., Berne, 1979; Franklin Medal, Franklin Inst., USA, 1981; Gold Medal, RAS, 1985; Paul Dirac Medal and Prize, Inst. of Physics, 1987; (jtly) Wolf Foundn Prize for Physics, 1988; Britannica Award, 1989. *Publications:* (with G. F. R. Ellis) The Large Scale Structure of Space-Time, 1973; (ed W. W. Israel) General Relativity: an Einstein centenary survey, 1979; (ed with M. Roček) Superspace and Supergravity, 1981; (ed jtly) The Very Early Universe, 1983; (with W. Israel) 300 Years of Gravitation, 1987; A Brief History of Time, 1988; Black Holes and Baby Universes, 1993; The Universe in a Nutshell, 2001. *Address:* Department of Applied Mathematics and Theoretical Physics, Centre for Mathematical Sciences, Wilberforce Road, Cambridge CB3 0WA. *T:* (01223) 337843.

HAWKINS, Prof. Anthony Donald, CBE 2000; PhD; FRSE; Director, Fisheries Research Services, Scottish Executive (formerly Director of Fisheries Research, Scottish Office Agriculture and Fisheries Department), since 1987; Hon. Research Professor, Aberdeen University, since 1987; *b* 25 March 1942; *s* of Kenneth St David Hawkins and Marjorie Lillian Hawkins; *m* 1966, Susan Mary Fulker; one *s*. *Educ:* Poole Grammar Sch.; Bristol Univ. (BSc 1st Cl. Hons Zoology, 1963; PhD 1968). Dept of Agriculture and Fisheries for Scotland: Scientific Officer, Marine Lab., Aberdeen, 1965, Chief Scientific Officer, 1987. Consultant to FAO, Peru, 1975; Hon. Lectr, Univ. of St Andrews, 1983. FRSE 1988. A. B. Wood Medal and Prize, Inst. of Acoustics, 1978. *Publications:* (ed and contrib.) Sound Reception in Fish, 1976; (ed and contrib.) Aquarium Systems, 1981; pubns on marine science, fish physiology and salmon biology. *Recreations:* angling, riding, whippet breeding. *Address:* Kincraig, Blairs, Aberdeen AB12 5YT. *T:* (01224) 868984; *e-mail:* hawkinsad@marlab.ac.uk.

HAWKINS, Catherine Eileen, CBE 1992; World Health Organisation Consultant to Middle Eastern Sector, since 1993; debt consultant; *b* 16 Jan. 1939; *d* of Stanley Richard Hawkins and Mary-Kate Hawkins. *Educ:* La Retraite High Sch., Clifton. SRN, CMB (Pt 1), HVCert, DN London, Queen's Inst. of Nursing Cert, IRCert. General nursing, student, 1956–59; Staff Nursing, Charing Cross Hosp., SRN, 1960–61; Pt 1 midwifery, St Thomas' Hosp., 1961; Health Visitor Student, LCC, RCN, 1961–62; LCC Health Visitor, 1962–63; Bristol CC HV, 1963–64; Project Leader, Bahrain Public Health Service, 1964–66; Field Work Teacher, HV, 1966–68; Health Centre Administrator, 1968–71; Administrator, Res. Div., Health Educn Council, 1971–72; Sen. Nursing Officer, Community Services, 1972–74; Area Nurse Service Capital Planning, Avon AHA, 1974–79; Dist Nursing Officer, Bristol and Weston DHA, 1979–82; Chief Nursing Officer, Southmead DHA, 1982–84; Regional Nursing Officer, 1984, Regl Gen. Manager, 1984–93, SW RHA. Non-exec. Dir, N Bristol NHS Trust, 1999–. *Address:* 20 Gordano Gardens, Easton-in-Gordano, Bristol BS20 0PD.

HAWKINS, Christopher James; Deputy Chairman, Black Country Development Corporation, 1992–98; non-executive chairman of a number of cos, 1988–99; *b* 26 Nov. 1937; *s* of Alec Desmond Hawkins and Christina Barbara; *m* Susan Ann Hawkins; two *d*. *Educ:* Bristol Grammar Sch.; Bristol Univ. BA (Hons) Economics. Joined Courtaulds Ltd, Head Office Economics Dept, 1959; seconded to UK aid financed industrial and economic survey of Northern Nigeria, 1960; similar mission to Tunisia to work on 5 year plan, 1961; Research Div. Economist, Courtaulds Ltd, 1961–66, Building Develt Manager, 1965–66; Lectr in Economics, 1966, Sen. Lectr, 1973–83, Univ. of Southampton. MP (C) High Peak, 1983–92. *Publications:* Capital Investment Appraisal, 1971; Theory of the Firm, 1973; The British Economy: what will our children think?, 1982; Britain's Economic Future: an immediate programme for revival, 1983; articles in Jl of Industrial Economics, Amer. Economic Review. *Recreations:* reading, music, sailing. *Address:* 18 Daniell's Walk, Lymington, Hants SO41 3PN.

HAWKINS, Air Vice-Marshal David Richard; *see* Hawkins-Leth.

HAWKINS, Air Vice-Marshal Desmond Ernest, CB 1971; CBE 1967; DFC and Bar, 1942; *b* 27 Dec. 1919; *s* of Ernest and Lilian Hawkins; *m* 1947, Joan Audrey (*née* Munro); one *s*, and one step *s*. *Educ:* Bancroft Sch. Commissioned in RAF, 1938. Served War of 1939–45: Coastal Command and Far East, commanding 36, 230 and 240 Sqdns, 1940–46 (despatches). Commanded RAF Pembroke Dock, 1946–47 (despatches). Staff appts, 1947–50; RAF Staff Coll., 1950; Staff appts, 1951–55; commanded 38 Sqdn, OC Flg, RAF Luqa, 1955–57; jssc, 1957; Staff appts, 1958–61; SASO 19 Gp, 1961–63; commanded RAF Tengah, 1963–66; idc 1967; commanded RAF Lyneham, 1968; SASO, HQ, RAF Strike Command, 1969–71; Dir-Gen., Personal Services (RAF), MoD, 1971–74; Dep. Man. Dir, Services Kinema Corp., 1974–80. *Recreation:* sailing. *Clubs:* Royal Air Force, Cruising Association, Royal Cruising; Royal Lymington Yacht.

HAWKINS, Prof. Eric William, CBE 1973; Director, Language Teaching Centre, University of York, 1965–79, now Professor Emeritus; *b* 8 Jan. 1915; *s* of James Edward Hawkins and Agnes Thompson (*née* Clarie); *m* 1938, Ellen Marie Thygesen, Copenhagen; one *s* one *d*. *Educ:* Liverpool Inst. High Sch.; Trinity Hall, Cambridge (Open Exhibn). MA, CertEd, FIL. War Service, 1st Bn The Loyal Regt, 1940–46 (despatches 1945); wounded N Africa, 1943; Major 1945. Asst Master, Liverpool Coll., 1946–49; Headmaster: Oldershaw Grammar Sch., Wallasey, 1949–53; Calday Grange Grammar Sch., Ches, 1953–65. Member: Central Adv. Council for Educn (England) (Plowden Cttee), 1963–66; Rampton Cttee (educn of ethnic minorities), 1979–81. Hon. Prof., University Coll. of Wales, Aberystwyth, 1979–89. Comenius Fellow, Centre for Inf. on Lang. Teaching, 2000. Hon. DLitt Southampton, 1997. Gold Medal, Inst. Linguists, 1971. Comdr, Ordre des Palmes Académiques (France), 1986. *Publications:* (ed) Modern Languages in the Grammar School, 1961; (ed) New Patterns in Sixth Form Modern Language Studies, 1970; A Time for Growing, 1971; Le français pour tout le monde, vols 1–5, 1974–79; Modern Languages in the Curriculum, 1981; Awareness of Language: an Introduction, 1984; (ed) Intensive Language Teaching and Learning, 1988; (ed) 30 Years of Language Teaching, 1996; Listening to Lorca, 1999. *Recreation:* walking.
See also M. R. Jackson.

HAWKINS, Dr John, OBE 2001; Project Manager, Knowledge and Learning Centres, British Council, since 2001; *b* 13 Oct. 1944; *s* of Maurice and Anna Hawkins; *m* 1968, Pamela June Donnelly; one *s* one *d*. *Educ:* Reading Univ. (BSc Physical Properties of Materials; PhD); Univ. of East Anglia (MA Develt Studies, 1994). Joined British Council, 1971; served Lahore, Islamabad, Bogotá, and Buenos Aires; Budget Department: Management Accountant, 1980–85; Dir, 1985–92; Manager, HQ Relocation Project, 1991–92; Head, Accommodation Services, 1992–93; Regl Dir, W Africa, 1994–97; Dir, Africa and S Asia, 1997–2000; Acting Dir of Finance, 2000; Special Projects, 2000–01. *Recreations:* running, tennis, walking, history. *Address:* British Council, 10 Spring Gardens, SW1A 2BN.

HAWKINS, Prof. John David, FBA 1993; Professor of Ancient Anatolian Languages, School of Oriental and African Studies, University of London, since 1993; *b* 11 Sept. 1940; *s* of John and Audrey Hawkins. *Educ:* Bradfield Coll.; University Coll., Oxford (BA 1962; MA 1965); Inst. of Archaeol., Univ. of London (Postgrad. Dip. 1964). School of Oriental and African Studies, University of London: Res. Fellow, 1964–67; Lectr, then Sen. Lectr, 1967–93. *Publication:* The Hieroglyphic Inscription of the Sacred Pool Complex at Boğazköy-Hattusa, 1995. *Recreations:* gardening, political cartoons, caricature. *Address:* School of Oriental and African Studies, University of London, Thornhaugh Street, WC1H 0XG. *T:* (020) 7323 6291.

HAWKINS, Nicholas John; MP (C) Surrey Heath, since 1997 (Blackpool South, 1992–97); *b* 27 March 1957; *s* of Arthur Ernest Hawkins, PhD, FInstP, CPhys and Patricia Jean Hawkins, BSc, BA (*née* Papworth); *m* 1979, Angela Margaret Turner, MA Oxon, CPFA (marr. diss. 1999); two *s* one *d*; *m* 2001, Mrs Jenny Cassar. *Educ:* Bedford Modern Sch.; Lincoln Coll., Oxford (MA); Inns of Court Sch. of Law. ACIArb. Called to the Bar, Middle Temple, 1979 (Harmsworth Sen. Scholar). Practised from chambers in Birmingham and Northampton, 1979–86. Company Legal Advr, Access, 1987–89; Gp Legal Advr, Lloyds Abbey Life, 1989–92. Mem., Bar Council, 1988–95; Chm., Bar Assoc. for Commerce, Finance and Industry, 1994–95. Contested (C) Huddersfield, 1987. PPS to Ministers of State, MoD, 1995–96, to Sec. of State for Nat. Heritage, 1996–97; opposition frontbench spokesman: on legal affairs, 1999–2001; on home affairs, 2000–2001. Mem., Transport Select Cttee, 1993–95, Home Affairs Select Cttee, 1998–99; Sec., Cons. backbench Educn Cttee, 1993–95; Vice Chairman: Cons. backbench Culture, Media and Sport (formerly Nat. Heritage) Cttee, 1997–; Cons. backbench Home Affairs Cttee, 1997–; Chm., Cons. backbench Sports Cttee, 1994–; Vice-Chairman: All-Party Sports Cttee, 1997–; All-Party Gp on Insurance and Financial Services, 1995–. Chm., W Lancs Support Gp, Marie Curie Cancer Care, 1992–96. *Publications:* booklets and articles on Conservative policy, transport hist., sport, and legal and employment matters. *Recreations:* cricket, music, theatre, transport history, Rugby, soccer, swimming. *Address:* House of Commons, SW1A 0AA. *T:* (020) 7219 6329. *Clubs:* MCC; Surrey Conservative and Unionist; Surrey CC; Lord's Taverners.

HAWKINS, Sir Paul (Lancelot), Kt 1982; TD 1945; FRICS; *b* 7 Aug. 1912; *s* of L. G. Hawkins and of Mrs Hawkins (*née* Peile); *m* 1st, 1937, E. Joan Snow (*d* 1984); two *s* one *d*; 2nd, 1985, Tina Daniels. *Educ:* Cheltenham Coll. Joined Family Firm, 1930; Chartered Surveyor, 1933. Served in TA, Royal Norfolk Regt, 1933–45; POW Germany, 1940–45. MP (C) SW Norfolk, 1964–87. An Asst Govt Whip, 1970–71; a Lord Comr of the Treasury, 1971–73; Vice-Chamberlain of HM Household, 1973–74. Mem., H of C (Services) Select Cttee, 1976–87. Mem., Delegn to Council of Europe and WEU, 1976–87; Chm., Agricl Cttee, Council of Europe, 1985–87. Dir (non-exec.), Gorham Bateson (Agriculture) Seed Specialists, 1989–. CC Norfolk, 1949–70, Alderman, 1968–70. *Recreations:* walking, gardening, travel. *Address:* Stables, Downham Market, Norfolk PE38 9NL.

HAWKINS, Sir Richard Caesar, 9th Bt *cr* 1778, of Kelston, Somerset; *b* 29 Dec. 1958; *yr s* of Sir Humphry Hawkins, 7th Bt and of Anita, *d* of C. H. Funkey; *S* brother, 1999; *m* 1992, Ernestine Ehrensperger; one *s*. *Educ:* Hilton Coll., Natal; Witwatersrand Univ. *Heir: s* Jonathan Caesar Hawkins, *b* 23 June 1992. *Address:* PO Box 410838, Craighall, 2024, South Africa.

HAWKINS, Richard Graeme; QC 1984; **His Honour Judge Hawkins;** a Circuit Judge, since 1989; *b* 23 Feb 1941; *s* of late Denis William Hawkins and Norah Mary (*née* Beckingsale); *m* 1969, Anne Elizabeth, *d* of late Dr and Mrs Glyn Edwards, The Boltons, Bournemouth; one *s* one *d*. *Educ:* Hendon County Sch.; University College London (LLB Hons 1962). Called to the Bar, Gray's Inn, 1963. A Recorder, 1985–89. Mem., Hon. Soc. of Gray's Inn, 1959–. Liveryman, Curriers' Co., 1995–. *Recreation:* sailing. *Address:* Central Criminal Court, EC4M 7EH. *T:* (020) 7248 3277. *Club:* Royal Thames Yacht.

HAWKINS, Rt Rev. Richard Stephen; *see* Crediton, Bishop Suffragan of.

HAWKINS-LETH, Air Vice-Marshal David Richard, CB 1992; MBE 1975; DL; Co-Founder and Chairman, Hawkins Environmental Ltd, since 1999; Gentleman Usher to the Queen, since 1994; *b* 5 April 1937; 2nd *s* of late Gp Capt. Charles Richard John Hawkins, OBE, AFC and Norah (*née* Terry); *m* 1st, 1965, Wendy Elizabeth Harris (marr. diss. 1981); one *s* one *d*; 2nd, 1982, Elaine Kay Nelson (marr. diss. 1997); 3rd, 1998, Dr Karen Hansen-d'Leth. *Educ:* Worth; Downside Sch.; RMA Sandhurst. Commnd RAF Regt, 1959; Flt Comdr Cyprus and Singapore, 1960–62; ADC to CAS, Air Chief Marshal Sir Charles Elworthy, 1963–65; jun. RAF Regt instructor, RAF Coll., Cranwell, 1965–68; 2nd i/c 63 Sqdn, Singapore, 1968–69; Sqdn Ldr, 1969; Jt Thai/US Mil. R&D Centre as airfield defence specialist, Bangkok, 1969–71; CO, 37 Sqdn, UK, NI and Belize, 1971–74; CO, Queen's Colour Sqdn of RAF, 1974–76; Wing Comdr, on staff of Comdt-Gen., RAF Regt, MoD, 1976–79; Chief, Survivability Br., HQ AAFCE, 1979–82; Sen. Comd RAF Regt Officer, HQ Strike Comd/HQ UK Air, 1982–86; Gp Capt., 1982;

CO, RAF Catterick, RAF Regt Depot, 1986–88; NATO Defence Coll., Rome, 1988–89; Dir, RAF Personal Services 1, MoD, 1989–90; Air Cdre, 1989; Dir, RAF Regt, MoD, 1990–91; Comdt-Gen., RAF Regt, and Dir-Gen., RAF Security, 1991–93; Yeoman Usher of the Black Rod and Dep. Serjeant-at-Arms, H of L, 1994–99. Parachute Wings: UK, 1969; Thai Army (Master), 1970; Thai Police (Master), 1970; US Army (1st class), 1971. Vice-Chm. (Air), TA&VRA, Gtr London, 1994–. Trustee, Battle of Britain Meml Trust, 1998–. Freeman, City of London, 1992. FIMgt; FITD; MInstD. DL Gtr London, 1994. *Recreations:* golf, ski-ing, walking, shooting. *Club:* Royal Air Force.

HAWKSLEY, (Philip) Warren; Director, Society for the Prevention of Solvent and Volatile Substance Abuse, since 1998; *b* 10 March 1943; *s* of late Bradshaw Warren Hawksley and Monica Augusta Hawksley; *m* 1999, Kathleen Margaret (*née* Lloyd). *Educ:* Denstone Coll., Uttoxeter. Employed by Lloyd's Bank after leaving school. Dir, Edderton Hall, 1989–97. Member: Salop County Council, 1970–81; West Mercia Police Authority, 1977–81. MP (C) The Wrekin, 1979–87; contested (C) same seat, 1987; MP (C) Halesowen and Stourbridge, 1992–97; contested (C) Stourbridge, 1997. Member: Select Cttee on Employment, 1986–87 and 1994–97; Home Affairs Select Cttee, 1996–97; Jt Sec., Cons. Back bench Cttee for New Town and Urban Affairs, 1984–87; Sec., W Midlands Cons. Party Gp, 1992–97. Hon. Pres., Catering Industries Liaison Council, 1992–98. *Recreations:* collecting political memorabilia, shooting, good food and wines.

HAWKSWORTH, Prof. David Leslie, CBE 1996; DSc; FIBiol, FLS; consultant mycologist and environmental biologist; Director, MycoNova, since 1998; *b* Sheffield, 5 June 1946; *e s* of late Leslie Hawksworth and Freda Mary (*née* Dolamore); *m* 1st, 1968, Madeleine Una Ford (marr. diss. 1998); one *s* one *d*; 2nd, 1999, Patricia Ann Taylor (*née* Ford). *Educ:* Herbert Strutt Grammar Sch., Belper; Univ. of Leicester (BSc 1967; PhD 1970; DSc 1980). FIBiol 1982; FLS 1969. Mycologist, Commonwealth Mycological Inst., Kew, 1969–81; sci. asst to Exec. Dir, CAB, 1981–83; Dir, Internat. Mycol Inst., CAB Internat., 1983–97. Visiting Professor: Univ. of Riyadh, 1978; Univ. of Reading, 1984–; Univ. of Assiut, 1985; Univ. of Kent 1990–; Univ. of London, 1992–; Univ. Complutense, Madrid, 2000–01. Mem. Council, English Nature, 1996–99. President: British Lichen Soc., 1986–87 (Hon. Mem., 1997); Eur. Congress of Mycologists, 1989; Br. Mycol Soc., 1990 (Centenary Fellow, 1996); Internat. Mycol Assoc., 1990–94 (Sec.-Gen., 1977–90; Hon. Pres., 1994–); Internat. Union of Biol Sci., 1994–97; Vice-Pres., Linnean Soc., 1985–88; Treasurer and Editor-in-Chief, Systematics Assoc., 1972–86; Treas., Internat. Congress of Systematic and Evolutionary Biol., 1989–96; Chairman: Internat Commn on Taxonomy of Fungi, 1982–; Ruislip-Northwood Woods Adv. Working Party, 1979–82; Internat. Cttee on Bionomenclature, 1994–; Chief Rapp., CAB Internat. Review Confs, 1985, 1990, 1993, 1996. FRSA 1997. Hon. Member: Soc. Lichenologica Italiana, 1989; Ukranian Botanical Soc., 1992; Mycol Soc. of America, 1994; Assoc. Latinoamericana de Micología, 1996. FD *hc* Umeå, 1996. First Bicent. Medal, Linnean Soc., 1978. Editor: The Lichenologist, 1970–90; Systema Ascomycetum, 1986–98; Mycosystema, 1987–; Exec. Editor, Mycological Research, 2000–. *Publications:* (jtly) Dictionary of the Fungi, 6th edn 1971 to 8th edn 1995; (ed jtly) Air Pollution and Lichens, 1973; Mycologist's Handbook, 1974; (ed) The Changing Flora and Fauna of Britain, 1974; (jtly) Lichens as Pollution Monitors, 1976; (ed jtly) Lichenology: progress and problems, 1976; (jtly) Lichenology in the British Isles 1568–1975, 1977; (jtly) Key Works to the Fauna and Flora of the British Isles and Northwestern Europe, 4th edn 1978, 5th edn 1988; (ed) Advancing Agricultural Production in Africa, 1984; (jtly) The Lichen-Forming Fungi, 1984; (jtly) The British Ascomycotina, 1985; (ed jtly) Coevolution and Systematics, 1986; (ed jtly) Coevolution of Fungi with Plants and Animals, 1988; (ed jtly) Living Resources for Biotechnology, 1988; (ed) Prospects in Systematics, 1988; (jtly) International Mycological Directory, 1990; (ed) Frontiers in Mycology, 1991; (ed) Improving the Stability of Names, 1991; (ed) The Biodiversity of Microorganisms and Invertebrates: their role in sustainable agriculture, 1991; (jtly) Lichen Flora of Great Britain and Ireland, 1992; (jtly) Biodiversity and Biosystematic Priorities: microorganisms and invertebrates, 1993; (jtly) IMI: retrospect and prospect, 1993; (ed) Identification and Characterization of Pest Organisms, 1994; Glossary of Terms Used in Bionomenclature, 1994; (ed) Ascomycete Systematics: problems and perspectives in the nineties, 1994; (jtly) The Biodiversity of Microorganisms and the Role of Microbial Resource Centres, 1994; (ed jtly) Microbial Diversity and Ecosystem Function, 1995; (ed jtly) Biodiversity Information: needs and options, 1997; (ed) The Changing Wildlife of Great Britain and Ireland, 2001; numerous papers on biodiversity, biol nomenclature, fungi (including lichens). *Recreations:* lichenology, bionomenclature, second-hand books. *Address:* MycoNova, 114 Finchley Lane, Hendon NW4 1DG.

HAWLEY, Sir Donald (Frederick), KCMG 1978 (CMG 1970); MBE 1955; HM Diplomatic Service, retired; British High Commissioner in Malaysia, 1977–81; Barrister-at-law; consultant in Middle Eastern and South East Asian affairs; *b* 22 May 1921; *s* of late Mr and Mrs F. G. Hawley, Little Gaddesden, Herts; *m* 1964, Ruth Morwenna Graham Howes, DL, *d* of late Rev. P. G. Howes and of Mrs Howes, Charmouth, Dorset; one *s* three *d*. *Educ:* Radley; New Coll., Oxford (MA). Served in HM Forces, 1941. Sudan Political Service, 1944; joined Sudan Judiciary, 1947. Called to Bar, Inner Temple, 1951. Chief Registrar, Sudan Judiciary, and Registrar-Gen. of Marriages, 1951; resigned from Sudan Service, 1955; joined HM Foreign Service, 1955; FO, 1956: Political Agent, Trucial States, in Dubai, 1958; Head of Chancery, British Embassy, Cairo, 1962; Counsellor and Head of Chancery, British High Commission, Lagos, 1965; Vis. Fellow, Dept of Geography, Durham Univ., 1967; Counsellor (Commercial), Baghdad, 1968; HM Consul-General, Muscat, 1971; HM Ambassador to Oman, 1971–75; Asst Under Sec. of State, FCO, 1975–77. Mem., London Adv. Cttee, Hongkong and Shanghai Banking Corp.; Chairman: Ewbank Preece Gp, 1982–86, Special Advr, 1986–; Centre for British Teachers, 1987–91. Pres. Council, Reading Univ., 1987–94; Vice-Pres., Anglo-Omani Soc., 1981–; Chairman: British Malaysian Soc., 1983–95 (Vice Pres., 1993–); Sudan Pensioners Assoc., 1992–; Royal Soc. for Asian Affairs, 1994. Gov., ESU, 1989–95. Pres., Sudan Defence Force Dinner Club. Hon. DLitt Reading, 1994; Hon. DCL Durham, 1997. *Publications:* Handbook for Registrars of Marriage and Ministers of Religion, 1963 (Sudan Govt pubn); Courtesies in the Trucial States, 1965; The Trucial States, 1971; Oman and its Renaissance, 1977, rev. edn 1995; Courtesies in the Gulf Area, 1978; Manners and Correct Form in the Middle East, 1984, 2nd edn 1996; Sandtracks in the Sudan, 1995; (ed) Sudan Canterbury Tales, 1999; Desert Wind and Tropic Storm (autobiog.), 2000; (ed) Khartoum Perspectives 1940s, 2001. *Recreations:* tennis, travel, gardening. *Address:* Little Cheverell House, near Devizes, Wilts SN10 4JJ. *T:* (01380) 813322. *Clubs:* Travellers, Beefsteak.

HAWLEY, Henry Nicholas, (8th Bt *cr* 1795). *S* father, 1988, but does not use the title and his name is not on the Official Roll of Baronets.

HAWLEY, James Appleton, TD 1969; Lord-Lieutenant of Staffordshire, since 1993; *b* 28 March 1937; *s* of late John J. Hawley and Mary Hawley, JP; *m* 1961, Susan, *d* of Alan Stott, JP, DL; one *s* two *d*. *Educ:* Uppingham; St Edmund Hall, Oxford (MA Jurisp.). Called to the Bar, Middle Temple, 1961. Nat. Service, 2nd Lieut South Staffs Regt, Cyprus; Lieut to Major, Staffs Yeomanry Regt (QORR). Chairman: John James Hawley (Speciality Works) Ltd, 1961–98; J. W. Wilkinson & Co., 1970–98; Dir, Stafford Railway Building Soc., 1985–. Past Pres., Made-Up Textiles Assoc.; Past Chm., Camping Trade Assoc. Patron, Staffs Young Enterprises. President: RFCA West Midlands; Staffs Scouts; St John Council for Staffs; CPRE (Staffs); Vice President: Nat. Meml Arboretum; Walsall Soc. for the Blind (Chm., 1977–92); Chm. Council, Lichfield Cathedral, 2000–; also Pres., Vice-Pres., and Patron, other organisations and charities in Staffs. Mem. Court, Keele Univ. Freeman, City of London; Liveryman, Saddlers' Co. JP Staffs 1969; High Sheriff, Staffs, 1976–77; DL Staffs 1978. KStJ 1993. *Recreations:* family, Staffordshire, outdoor pursuits. *Address:* Lieutenancy Office, Martin Street, Stafford ST16 2LH. *T:* (01785) 276805, *Fax:* (01785) 276115. *Club:* Oxford and Cambridge.

HAWLEY, Dr Robert, CBE 1997; FREng, FIEE, FIMechE, FInstP; FRSE; Chairman: Engineering Council, since 1999; Particle Physics and Astronomy Research Council, since 1999; *b* 23 July 1936; *s* of William and Eva Hawley; *m* Valerie (*née* Clarke); one *s* one *d*; *m* Pamela (*née* Neesham). *Educ:* Wallasey Grammar Sch.; Wallasey Technical Coll.; Birkenhead Technical Coll.; Durham Univ. (BSc 1959; PhD 1963); Newcastle upon Tyne Univ. (DSc 1976). FIEE 1970; FREng (FEng 1979); FIMechE 1987; FInstP 1971. FRSE 1997. Student apprentice, BICC, Prescot, 1952–55; C. A. Parsons & Co. Ltd: Head of Res. Team, 1961–64; Chief Elec. Engr, 1970–74; Dir of Prodn and Engrg, 1974–76; Man. Dir, NEI Parsons Ltd, 1976–84; NEI plc: Man. Dir, Power Engrg Gp, 1984–89; Man. Dir, 1989–92; Chm., NEI ABB Gas Turbines Ltd, 1990–92; Chief Executive: Nuclear Electric plc, 1992–96; British Energy plc, 1996–97. Mem. Bd, Rolls-Royce plc, 1989–92. Non-executive Chairman: Rotork plc, 1997–98; INBIS Group plc, 1997–2000; ERAtech Ltd, 1997–99; Taylor Woodrow plc, 1999–; non-executive Director: W. S. Atkins Ltd, 1994–97; Tricorder Technology, 1997–; Colt Telecom Gp, 1998–; Consultant, ABB Ltd, 1993–97; Adviser: SEMA Gp, 1995–97; HSBC Investment Bank, 1998–. Member: NE Indust. Develt Bd, DTI, 1989–92; Bd, Northern Develt Co., 1989–92; Industrial Develt Adv. Bd, DTI, 1994–2000; Pres., Partnership Korea, DTI, 1995–. Chairman: Hawley Cttee on Corporate Governance Information Management, 1993–98; Hawley Gp on Engrg Profession, DTI and Engrg Council, 1999–2001. Mem., Annual Review Sub-group, and Chm., Energy Wkg Pty, 1986–87, ACARD; Member: DFEE Women's Issues Wkg Gp, 1996–97; Mgt and Leadership in the Professions, DFEE, 2000–. Institution of Electrical Engineers: Vice Pres., 1991–95; Dep. Pres., 1995–96; Pres., 1996–97. Member Council: Fellowship of Engrg, 1981–84; Foundn for Sci. and Technol., 1999–; Royal Instn, 2000–; Mem., Council for Industry and Higher Educn, 2000–. Pres., Energy Industries Club, 1989–91. Mem., Boat and Shoreworks Cttee, RNLI, 1992–95. Trustee, Daphne Jackson Trust, 2000–. Lectures include: C. A. Parsons Meml, IEE and Royal Soc., 1977; Hunter Meml, IEE, 1990; Blackadder, NEC Inst., 1992; Wilson Campbell Meml, Univ. of Newcastle upon Tyne, 1994; Bowden, UMIST, 1994; J. G. Collier Meml, Univ. of Brunel, 1997. Member: Court, Univ. of Newcastle upon Tyne, 1979–; Bd of Advrs, Elec. Engrg, Univ. of London, 1982–86; Chm., Council, Univ. of Durham, 1997–. Freeman, City of London, 1985. Mem., Nat. Acad. of Engrg of Korea, 2001. FRSE 1997. Hon. FINucE 1994. Hon. DSc: Durham, 1996; City, 1998; Hon. DEng: South Bank, 1997; West of England, 1997; Hon. DTech Staffordshire. Waverley Gold Medal, RSA, 1960; Achievement Medal, for outstanding contribs to power engrg, IEE, 1989. Premio Vicente Lecuna Medal, Venezuela, 1997; Order of Diplomatic Service Kwongda Medal, Korea, 1999. *Publications:* (with A. Maitland) Vacuum as an Insulator, 1967; (with A. A. Zaky): Dielectric Solids, 1970; Conduction and Breakdown in Mineral Oil, 1973; Fundamentals of Electromagnetic Field Theory, 1974; technical papers on electrical breakdown in vacuum, liquids and solids, electrical machine design and power generation. *Recreations:* gardening, philately. *Address:* Summerfield, Rendcomb, nr Cirencester, Glos GL7 7HB. *T:* (01285) 831610, *Fax:* (01285) 831801. *Clubs:* Athenæum; New (Edinburgh).

HAWORTH, Rev. Betsy Ellen; Non-Stipendiary Minister, St Paul, Astley Bridge, Bolton, Diocese of Manchester, 1989–99; *b* 23 July 1924; *d* of Ambrose and Annie Kenyon; *m* 1953, Rev. Fred Haworth (*d* 1981); one *s* two *d*. *Educ:* William Temple Coll. IDC (C of E). Licensed as lay worker, dio. Manchester, 1952, dio. Blackburn, 1965; elected Mem., Church Assembly, 1965–70, Gen. Synod, 1970–75, 1975–80, 1980–85, Ex-officio Mem., 1985–88. Advr for Women's Ministry, dio. Manchester, 1971–81. Third Church Estates Comr, 1981–88. Deaconess 1980; ordained Deacon, 1989. Examining Chaplain to Bishop of Manchester, 1981–94. *Address:* 14 Sharples Hall Fold, Sharples, Bolton, Lancs BL1 7EH.

HAWORTH, John Liegh W.; *see* Walker-Haworth.

HAWORTH, Jonathan Mayo; His Honour Judge Jonathan Haworth; a Circuit Judge, since 1996; *b* 5 Oct. 1948; *s* of George Henry Haworth and Elsa Sophia Haworth; *m* 1973, Brigitte Ilse Müller; one *s* one *d*. *Educ:* King Edward VII Grammar Sch., Sheffield; King's Coll., London (LLB Hons). Called to the Bar, Middle Temple, 1971; practised from Fenners Chambers, Cambridge, 1973–96. *Recreations:* reading, computers, music, cricket. *Address:* c/o Cambridge Crown Court, 10 Downing Street, Cambridge CB2 3DS.

HAWORTH, Sir Philip, 3rd Bt *cr* 1911, of Dunham Massey, Co. Chester; farmer; *b* 17 Jan. 1927; *s* of Sir Arthur Geoffrey Haworth, 2nd Bt, and Emily Dorothea, (Dorothy) (*d* 1980), *er d* of H. E. Gaddum; *S* father, 1987; *m* 1951, Joan Helen, *d* of late S. P. Clark, Ipswich; four *s* one *d*. *Educ:* Dauntsey's; Reading Univ. BSc (Agric.) 1948. *Recreations:* music, art, ornithology. *Heir:* *s* Christopher Haworth [*b* 6 Nov. 1951; *m* 1994, Susan Rachel, *d* of David Ives and *widow* of Jonathan Dent; one *s* one *d*, and two step *s*]. *Address:* Free Green Farm, Over Peover, Knutsford, Cheshire WA16 9QX. *Club:* Farmers'.

HAWORTH, Richard James; His Honour Judge Haworth; a Circuit Judge, since 1993; *b* 1 Dec. 1943; *s* of late Richard Arthur Haworth and Lily Haworth; *m* 1974, Jane Seren, *y d* of His Honour John Glyn Burrell, QC and of Dorothy Burrell. *Educ:* Ampleforth. Called to the Bar, Inner Temple, 1970; practised on SE Circuit, 1970–93; a Recorder, 1990–93. Mem., Inner Temple Bar Liaison Cttee, 1987–93. *Recreations:* music, English naive paintings, carpentry, walking. *Address:* The Crown Court, 6–8 Penrhyn Road, Kingston-upon-Thames, Surrey KT1 2BB. *T:* (020) 8240 2500.

HAWTHORN, Ven. Christopher John; Archdeacon of Cleveland, 1991–2001; *b* 29 April 1936; *s* of late Rev. John Christopher Hawthorn and Susan Mary Hawthorn; *m* 1964, Elizabeth Margaret Lowe; three *s* one *d*. *Educ:* Marlborough Coll.; Queens' Coll., Cambridge (MA Hons); Ripon Hall, Oxford. Deacon 1962, priest 1963; Asst Curate, Sutton-in-Holderness, 1962–66; Vicar: St Nicholas, Hull, 1966–72; Christ Church, Coatham, 1972–79; St Martin's-on-the-Hill, Scarborough, 1979–91; RD Scarborough, 1982–91. Proctor in Convocation, 1987–90; Canon of York, 1987–2001. *Recreations:* gardening, fell walking, sport. *Address:* 43 Barley Rise, Strensall, York YO32 5AB. *T:* (01904) 492060.

HAWTHORN, Prof. Geoffrey Patrick; Professor of International Politics, University of Cambridge, since 1998; Fellow, Clare Hall, Cambridge, since 1982; *b* 28 Feb. 1941; *s* of Kathleen Mary Hawthorn (*née* Candy); *m* 1st, 1969, Ruth Legg (marr. diss. 1986); two *s*; 2nd, 1987, Gloria Carnevali; one *s*. *Educ:* Jesus Coll., Oxford (BA); London Sch. of

Economics. Lectr in Sociology, Univ. of Essex, 1964–70; University of Cambridge: Lectr in Sociology, 1970–85; Reader in Sociology and Politics, 1985–98; Fellow, Churchill Coll., 1970–76. Vis. Prof. of Sociology, Harvard Univ., 1973–74, 1989–90; Vis. Mem., IAS, Princeton, 1989–90. *Publications:* The Sociology of Fertility, 1970; Enlightenment and Despair, 1976, 2nd edn 1987; (ed) Population and Development, 1977; (ed) The Standard of Living, 1987; Plausible Worlds, 1991; The Future of Asia and the Pacific, 1998; articles and reviews in learned jls and other periodicals. *Recreations:* ornithology, music. *Address:* Faculty of Social and Political Sciences, University of Cambridge, 8–9 Jesus Lane, Cambridge CB5 8BA. *T:* (01223) 740076.

HAWTHORNE, James Burns, CBE 1982; management consultant; Partner, James Hawthorne Associates, since 1993 (Director, 1987–92); *b* 27 March 1930; *s* of Thomas Hawthorne and Florence Hawthorne (*née* Burns); *m* 1958, Patricia King; one *s* two *d.* *Educ:* Methodist Coll.; Queen's Univ., Belfast (BA); Stranmillis Coll. of Educn. Master at Sullivan Upper Sch., Holywood, 1951–60; joined Educn Dept, BBC, 1960; Schools Producer in charge, N Ireland, 1967; Chief Asst, N Ireland, 1969–70; seconded to Hong Kong Govt, as Controller Television, 1970; Dir of Broadcasting, Hong Kong, 1972–77 (resigned from BBC staff, 1976, *ie* seconded status ended; rejoined BBC, Jan. 1978); Controller, BBC NI, 1978–87. Member: NI Council for Educn Develt, 1980–85; Fair Employment Agency, 1988–89; Accreditation Panel, Hong Kong Acad. for the Performing Arts, 1988. Chairman: Ulster History Circle, 1987–89; NI Health Promotion Agency (formerly Unit), 1988–97; Cultural Traditions Gp, 1989–90; NI Community Relations Council, 1990–96; Prison Arts Foundn, 1997–. Comr, Commn for Racial Equality, NI, 1997–2000. Vis. Prof., Media Studies, Univ. of Ulster, 1993–99. Chm., Lecale Histl Soc., 2000–. JP Hong Kong, 1972–77. Queen's Univ. New Ireland Soc. award for community relations work, 1967; Winston Churchill Fellowship, 1968; FRTS 1988 (Cyril Bennett Award, 1986). Hon. LLD QUB, 1988. *Publications:* (ed) Two Centuries of Irish History, 1966, repr. 1967, 1969, rev. edn 1974; Reporting Violence: lessons from Northern Ireland, 1981. *Recreations:* angling, music. *Address:* The Long Mill, Lissara, 67 Kilmore Road, Crossgar, N Ireland BT30 9HJ. *Club:* BBC.

HAWTHORNE, Sir Nigel (Barnard), Kt 1999; CBE 1987; DL; self-employed actor and writer; *b* Coventry, 5 April 1929; *s* of Charles Barnard Hawthorne and Agnes Rosemary (*née* Rice). *Educ:* Christian Brothers' Coll., Cape Town, S Africa. Entered theatre professionally, 1950; returned to England, 1951, where he has worked ever since, with the exception of a small number of engagements abroad. *Stage:* Otherwise Engaged, 1976; Privates on Parade, 1978 (Best Supporting Actor, SWET and Clarence Derwent awards); Peer Gynt, and Tartuffe, with RSC, 1983–84 (Tartuffe televised 1985); Across from the Garden of Allah, 1986; Jacobowski and the Colonel, NT, 1986; The Magistrate, NT, 1986; Hapgood, Aldwych, 1988; Shadowlands, Queen's, 1989, Broadway, 1990–91 (Tony Award for Best Actor, 1991); The Madness of George III, NT, 1992 (Olivier Award for Best Actor, 1992; Evening Standard Best Actor Award, 1992), American tour, 1993, European tour, 1994; The Clandestine Marriage (also dir), Queen's, 1994; King Lear, RSC, and Japan, 1999; *television:* Marie Curie, 1977; Destiny, 1978; Edward and Mrs Simpson, 1978; The Knowledge, 1979; Yes Minister (series), annually 1980–83, 1985–86, Yes, Prime Minister (series), 1986, 1987 (Broadcasting Press Guild Award, 1980; BAFTA Best Light Entertainment Performance, 1981, 1982, 1986, 1987); The Critic, 1982; The Barchester Chronicles, 1982; Mapp and Lucia, 1984–86; The Miser, 1988; The Shawl, 1989; Relatively Speaking, 1989; The Trials of Oz, 1991; Flea-Bites, 1992; Late-Flowering Lust, 1994; The Fragile Heart, 1996 (BAFTA Best TV Actor, 1997); Forbidden Territory, 1997; Victoria and Albert, 2001; Call Me Claus, 2001; *films:* Firefox, Gandhi, Golda, 1981; John Paul II, 1983; The House, 1984; The Chain, 1985; Demolition Man, 1993; The Madness of King George, 1994; Richard III, Inside, Twelfth Night, 1996; Murder in Mind, Amistad, Madeline, The Object of My Affection, 1997; At Sachem Farm, The Clandestine Marriage, A Reasonable Man, The Big Brass Ring, 1998; The Winslow Boy, 1999. DL Herts, 1999. Hon. MA: Sheffield, 1987; Leicester, 1994; Hon. DLitt: Hertfordshire, 1992; Keele, 1999. *Recreations:* swimming, gardening, painting.

HAWTHORNE, Prof. Sir William (Rede), Kt 1970; CBE 1959; MA; ScD; FRS 1955; FREng, FIMechE; Master of Churchill College, Cambridge, 1968–83; Hopkinson and ICI Professor of Applied Thermodynamics, University of Cambridge, 1951–80; Head of Department of Engineering, 1968–73; *b* 22 May 1913; *s* of William Hawthorne, MInstCE, and Elizabeth C. Hawthorne; *m* 1939, Barbara Runkle (*d* 1992), Cambridge, Massachusetts, USA; one *s* two *d.* *Educ:* Westminster Sch.; Trinity Coll., Cambridge (Hon. Fellow, 1995); Massachusetts Institute of Technology, USA. Development Engineer, Babcock & Wilcox Ltd, 1937–39; Scientific Officer, Royal Aircraft Establishment, 1940–44; seconded to Sir Frank Whittle, 1940–41; British Air Commission, Washington, 1944; Dep. Dir Engine Research, Min. of Supply, 1945; Massachusetts Institute of Technology: Associate Prof. of Mechanical Engineering, 1946; George Westinghouse Prof. of Mechanical Engineering, 1948–51; Jerome C. Hunsaker Prof. of Aeronautical Engineering, 1955–56; Vis. Inst. Prof., 1962–69; Mem. Corporation, 1969–74. Chairman: Home Office Scientific Adv. Council, 1967–76; Defence Scientific Adv. Council, 1969–71; Adv. Council for Energy Conservation, 1974–79; Member: Energy Commn, 1977–79; Standing Commn on Energy and the Environment, 1978–81. Director: Dracone Developments Ltd, 1958–87; Cummins Engine Co. Inc., 1974–86. Governor, Westminster Sch., 1956–76. A Vice-Pres., Royal Soc., 1969–70 and 1979–81; Mem. Council, 1968–70, 1979–81 (Royal Medal, 1982). Foreign Associate: US Nat. Acad. of Sciences, 1965; US Nat. Acad. of Engrg, 1976. Fellow, Imperial Coll., London Univ., 1983. Hon. FAIAA; Hon. FRAeS; Hon. FASME; Hon. FRSE 1983. Hon. DEng: Sheffield, 1976; Liverpool 1982; Hon. DSc: Salford, 1980; Strathclyde, 1981; Bath, 1981; Oxon, 1982; Sussex, 1984. Medal of Freedom (US), 1947. *Publications:* papers in mechanical and aeronautical journals. *Address:* Churchill College, Cambridge CB3 0DS. *Club:* Athenæum.

See also J. O'Beirne Ranelagh.

HAWTIN, Brian Richard, CB 1997; Director General, International Security Policy, Ministry of Defence, since 1999; *b* 31 May 1946; *s* of late Dick Hawtin and Jean (*née* Middleton); *m* 1969, Anthea Fry; two *d.* *Educ:* Portsmouth Grammar Sch.; Christ Church, Oxford (MA). Ministry of Defence, 1967–: Asst Private Sec. to Permt Under Sec. of State, 1970; seconded to FCO as First Sec., UK Delegn to NATO, Brussels, 1978–80; Asst Sec., 1981; RCDS 1987; Private Sec. to Sec. of State for Defence, 1987–89; Asst Under Sec. of State (material/naval), 1989–92, (Progs), 1992–94, (Home and Overseas), 1994–96, (Policy), 1997–99; Fellow, Center for Internat. Affairs, Harvard Univ., 1996–97. *Recreations:* walking, ceramics. *Address:* c/o Ministry of Defence, Main Building, Whitehall, SW1A 2HB.

HAWTIN, Rt Rev. David Christopher; *see* Repton, Bishop Suffragan of.

HAWTIN, Michael Victor; Director, Underwriting Group, Export Credits Guarantee Department, 1992–95; *b* 7 Sept. 1942; *s* of Guy and Constance Hawtin; *m* 1966, Judith Mary Eeley; one *s* one *d.* *Educ:* Bournemouth Sch.; St John's Coll., Cambridge (MA); Univ. of Calif, Berkeley (MA). Asst Principal, 1964–69, Principal, 1969–77, HM Treasury; seconded to Barclays Bank, 1969–71; Asst Sec., HM Treasury, 1977–83, Under Sec. (Principal Finance Officer), PSA, 1983–86; Under Sec., HM Treasury, 1986–88; Dir, Resource Management Gp and Principal Establishment and Finance Officer, ECGD, 1988–92. *Recreations:* music, travel.

HAWTON, Prof. Keith Edward, DSc, DM; FRCPsych; Consultant Psychiatrist, Oxfordshire Mental Healthcare NHS Trust (formerly Oxfordshire Mental Healthcare Unit), since 1984; Professor of Psychiatry, Oxford University, since 1996; *b* 23 Dec. 1942; *s* of Leslie William Hawton and Eliza Hawton; *m* 1978, Joan Kirk; two *d.* *Educ:* Balliol Coll., and Med. Sch., Oxford (MB 2001; BChir 1969; DM 1980; DSc 2001); St John's Coll., Cambridge (MA 1970). FRCPsych 1990. Trng in psychiatry, 1970–73; Res. Psychiatrist, Clin. Lectr and Clin. Tutor in Psychiatry, Dept of Psychiatry, Oxford Univ., 1974–84. Boerhaave Vis. Prof., Leiden Univ., 1990–91. Stengel Res. Award, Internat. Assoc. for Suicide Prevention, 1995; Dublin Award, Amer. Assoc. Suicidology, 2001. *Publications:* Attempted Suicide: a practical guide, 1982, 2nd edn 1987; Sex Therapy: a practical guide, 1985; Cognitive Behaviour Therapy for Psychiatric Problems, 1989; Suicide and Stress in Farmers, 1998; The International Handbook of Suicide and Attempted Suicide, 2000. *Recreations:* fishing, cricket, wines, golf. *Address:* Centre for Suicide Research, University Department of Psychiatry, Warneford Hospital, Oxford OX3 7JX. *T:* (01865) 226258.

HAWTREY, John Havilland Procter, CBE 1958; FICE; *b* 16 Feb. 1905; *e s* of late Edmond Charles Hawtrey and late Helen Mary Hawtrey (*née* Durand); *m* 1947, Kathleen Mary (*d* 1992), *d* of late Captain M. T. Daniel, RN, Henley-on-Thames; one *s* one *d.* *Educ:* Eton; City and Guilds Engineering Coll., London (BSc 1927). Asst Engineer, later Dist Engineer, Burma Railways, 1927–47. Served War of 1939–45: with RE, 1940–46; Major 1942, in India and Burma, 1942–46 (despatches). Entered office of Crown Agents for Oversea Govts and Administrations, 1948: Chief Civil Engineer, 1956; Crown Agent and Engineer-in-Chief, 1965; retired, 1969. *Address:* 76 Makins Road, Henley-on-Thames, Oxon RG9 1PR. *T:* (01491) 574896.

HAXBY, Donald Leslie, CBE 1988; principal of veterinary practice, Southwell, 1979–93; *b* 4 Aug. 1928; *s* of Leslie Norman Haxby and Ruth Blount; *m* 1953, Barbara Mary Smith (marr. diss. 1986); one *s* two *d.* *Educ:* Queen Elizabeth Grammar Sch., Barnet; Royal Veterinary Coll., London. MRCVS 1953. Army Service, Queen's Royal Regt, RAEC, Sudan Defence Force, 1946–48 (Warrant Officer I). Practice in Leics and Shropshire, 1953–55; research, Boots Pure Drug Co., 1955–57 (clinical pathologist); vet. practice, Southwell, 1957–93. Lecturer: Animal Husbandry, Nottingham Coll. of Agriculture, 1969–93; Poultry Production and Public Health, London and Glasgow Univs, 1978–93; External Examiner: Vet. Medicine, Glasgow Univ., 1980–85; Animal Husbandry, Bristol Univ., 1987–93. Official Vet. Surgeon, Newark DC, 1979–85; Consultant to: W. & J. B. Eastwood, 1972–78; Hillsdown Holdings, 1982–90; Smith Kline Beecham Animal Health, 1982–89; Cyanamid GB, 1982–85; Duphar-Philips Solvay, 1982–93; I. M. C. & Cambridge-Naremco Products, USA, 1985–90. Mem., Parly and Sci. Cttee, H of C, 1979–86; Sci. Advr to Agric. Select Cttee, H of C, 1989–93. Mem. Council, 1983–84, Hon. Lectr, 1984–91, Royal Vet. Coll.; President: E Midlands Vet. Assoc. (and Treasurer), 1973–75; BVA, 1977–78 (Mem. Council, 1958–); RCVS, 1983–84 (Mem. Council, 1971–99); Mem., Animal Health and Tech. Cttee, British Poultry Fedn, 1974–90; Chm., World Vet. Poultry Assoc., 1985–89. Mem., Farm Animal Welfare Council, 1981–92; Trustee and Treasurer, Gordon Meml Trust, 1982–93; Governor, Houghton Poultry Res. Station, 1983–90. Man. Dir, Don Haxby Associates, 1993–96. *Recreations:* work, reading, golf, gardening, cycling. *Address:* Candant House, Main Street, Upton, Newark, Notts NG23 5ST. *T:* and. *Fax:* (01636) 812020. *Clubs:* Farmers', Savile.

HAY, family name of **Earls of Erroll** and **Kinnoull,** and of **Marquis of Tweeddale.**

HAY, Lord; Harry Thomas William Hay; *b* 8 Aug. 1984; *s* and *heir* of Earl of Erroll, *qv.*

HAY, Prof. Allan Stuart, PhD; FRS 1981; Tomlinson Professor of Chemistry, McGill University, Montreal, since 1997 (Professor of Polymer Chemistry, 1987–97); *b* 23 July 1929; *s* of Stuart Lumsden and Verna Emila Hay; *m* 1956, Janet Mary Keck; two *s* two *d.* *Educ:* Univ. of Alberta (BSc Hon, MSc); Univ. of Illinois (PhD). General Electric Research and Development Center, Schenectady, NY: Research Associate, 1955; Manager, Chemical Laboratory, 1968; Research and Develt Manager, Chemical Labs, 1980–87. Adjunct Professor, Polymer Science and Engineering Dept, Univ. of Massachusetts, 1975. Hon. DSc Alberta, 1987. Soc. of Plastics Engrs Internat. award in Plastics Science and Engineering, 1975; Achievement award, Industrial Res. Inst., 1984; Chemical Pioneer, Amer. Inst. of Chemists, 1985; Carothers Award, ACS, 1985; Macromolecular Sci. and Engrg Award, Canadian Inst. of Chem., 1998. *Publications:* numerous papers and contribs to learned jls. *Recreations:* philately, reading, swimming. *Address:* 5015 Glencairn Avenue, Montreal, QC H3W 2B3, Canada.

HAY, Barbara Logan, CMG 1998; MBE 1991; HM Diplomatic Service; Consul-General, St Petersburg, since 2000; *b* 20 Jan 1953; *d* of late Alfred Hay and of Isa Hay (*née* Burgon). *Educ:* Boroughmuir Sen. Secondary Sch., Edinburgh. Joined Diplomatic Service, 1971; Russian language training, 1974–75; served Moscow and Johannesburg; Asst Private Sec. to Perm. Under-Sec. and Head of Diplomatic Service, 1981–83; FCO and Montreal; First Sec. (Inf.), Moscow, 1988–91; Consul-Gen., St Petersburg, 1991–92; Jt Assistance Unit (Central Europe), FCO, 1992–94; Ambassador, Republic of Uzbekistan and (non-res.), Republic of Tajikistan, 1995–99; Counsellor, FCO, 1999–2000. FRSA. *Recreations:* theatre, travel, Scottish country dancing, music, keeping in touch with friends. *Address:* c/o Foreign and Commonwealth Office, SW1A 2AH. *Club:* University Women's.

HAY, Sir David (Osborne), Kt 1979; CBE 1962; DSO 1945; retired public servant; *b* 29 Nov. 1916; 2nd *s* of late H. A. Hay, Barwon Heads, Victoria; *m* 1944, Alison Marion Parker Adams; two *s.* *Educ:* Geelong Grammar Sch.; Brasenose Coll., Oxford; Melbourne Univ. Joined Commonwealth Public Service, 1939. Australian Imperial Force, 1940–46: Major, 2nd Sixth Infantry Bn; served in Western Desert, Greece, New Guinea. Rejoined External Affairs Dept, 1947; Imp. Def. Coll., 1954; Minister (later Ambassador) to Thailand, 1955–57; High Comr in Canada, 1961–64; Ambassador to UN, New York, 1964–65; First Asst Secretary, External Affairs, 1966; Administrator of Papua and New Guinea, 1967–70; Sec., Dept of External Territories, Canberra, 1970–73; Defence Force Ombudsman, 1974–76; Sec., Dept of Aboriginal Affairs, 1977–79. *Publications:* The Delivery of Services financed by the Department of Aboriginal Affairs, 1976; Nothing Over Us: the story of the 2nd Sixth Australian Infantry Battalion, 1985; The Life and Times of William Hay of Boomanoomana 1816–1908, 1990. *Address:* Boomanoomana Homestead, via Mulwala, NSW 2647, Australia. *Clubs:* Australian, Melbourne (Melbourne).

HAY, Sir David (Russell), Kt 1991; CBE 1981; FRCP; FRACP; (first) Medical Director, National Heart Foundation of New Zealand, 1977–92; Cardiologist, Canterbury Hospital (formerly North Canterbury Hospital) Board, 1964–89; Hon. Consulting Physician, Canterbury Area Health Board, since 1990; *b* 8 Dec. 1927; twin *s* of Sir James Lawrence Hay, OBE, and Lady (Davidina Mertel) Hay; *m* 1958, Dr Jocelyn Valerie Bell; two *d*. *Educ:* St Andrew's Coll., Christchurch; Otago Univ., Univ. of New Zealand (MB, ChB; MD). FRACP 1965; FRCP 1971. Resident appts, Christchurch, Royal South Hants, Hammersmith, Brompton and National Heart Hosps, 1951–55; Sen. Registrar, Dunedin and Christchurch Hosps, 1956–59; Physician, N Canterbury Hosp. Bd, 1959–64; Head of Dept of Cardiology, 1969–78; Chm. of Medical Services and Hd of Dept of Medicine, 1978–84. Chm., Christchurch Hosps Med. Staff Assoc., 1983–85; Clin. Lectr, Christchurch Clinical Sch., Univ. of Otago, 1973–80; Clin. Reader, 1980–88. Pres., Nat. Heart Foundn of NZ, 1996–99 (Councillor, 1968–92, 1996–99; Mem. Scientific Cttee, 1968–92); Vice-Pres., RACP, 1988–92 (Councillor, 1964–66, 1987–88; Examiner, 1974–75; Censor, 1975–79, and 1990–92); Mem. Specialist Adv. Cttee on Cardiology, 1980–90; Chm., Central Specialists Cttee of BMA, 1967–68; Pres., Canterbury Div. of BMA, 1972. Chm., NZ Region of Cardiac Soc. of Australia and NZ, and Councillor, 1977–81. Overseas Regl Advr, 1987–2000, Emeritus Internat. Advr, 2000, RCP. Member: Resuscitation Cttee of Nat. Cttee on Emergency Care, 1979–87; Health Promotion Forum of NZ, 1984–91; NZ Govt Adv. Cttee on Prevention of Cardiovascular Disease, 1985–86; NZ Govt Adv. Cttee on Smoking and Health, 1974–88; Ethics Cttee, Southern Regl HA, Canterbury, 1994–97; WHO Expert Adv. Panel on Tobacco or Health, 1977–; WHO Working Gp on Tobacco or Health in Western Pacific Reg., Manila, 1994; Hypertension Task Force, 1988–89; Life Member: Nat. Heart Foundn, 1992; ANZ Cardiac Soc., 1992. Speaker: World Conf. on Smoking and Health, Stockholm, 1979; Internat. Soc. and Fedn of Cardiology Workshop, Jakarta, 1982; Internat. Congress on Preventive Cardiology, Washington, 1989; World Congress of Cardiology, Manila, 1990. Nat. Heart Foundn Lecture, 1992; Charles Burns Oration, 1992. Trustee: J. L. Hay Charitable Trust; W. H. Nicholls Charitable Trust; Edna and Winifred White-Parsons Charitable Trust; Keith Laugesen Charitable Trust. College Medal, RACP, 1993; WHO Tobacco or Health Medal, 1995. Commemoration Medal, NZ, 1990. *Publications:* (ed) Coronary Heart Disease: prevention and control in NZ, 1983; 97 sci. papers in various med. jls, mostly on smoking and health and preventive cardiology. *Recreations:* golf, writing. *Address:* 20 Greers Road, Christchurch 4, New Zealand. *T:* 3585482. *Club:* Christchurch Golf.

See also Sir Hamish Hay, Dame M. L. Salas.

HAY, Rt Rev. Mgr George Adam; Canon, Plymouth Cathedral Chapter, since 1994; Parish Priest, Church of Our Lady and St Denis, St Marychurch, Torquay, since 1997; *b* 14 Nov. 1930; *s* of late Sir William Rupert Hay, KCMG, KCIE, CSI, and late Sybil Ethel, *d* of Sir Stewart Abram. *Educ:* Ampleforth College, York; New Coll., Oxford (BA History, MA); Venerable English Coll., Rome (STL). National Service as Midshipman RNVR, 1949–50; student, Oxford, 1950–53; Venerable English Coll., Rome, 1953–60. Ordained priest at Rome, 1959; Curate, Sacred Heart Church, Exeter, and part-time RC Chaplain to students at Exeter Univ., 1960; Chaplain to students at Exeter Univ. and Priest-in-charge, Crediton, 1966–78; Rector, Venerable English Coll., Rome, 1978–84; Parish Priest: St John the Baptist, Dartmouth, 1984; Sacred Heart and St Teresa, Paignton, 1984–91; St Boniface, Okehampton and Holy Family, Chagford, 1991–97. *Recreations:* fly fishing, mountain walking. *Address:* The Presbytery, Priory Road, St Marychurch, Torquay TQ1 4NY.

HAY, Sir Hamish (Grenfell), Kt 1982; JP; Mayor of Christchurch, New Zealand, 1974–89; Director: Canterbury Development Corporation, 1983–96; Christchurch International Airport Ltd, 1988–96; *b* 8 Dec. 1927; twin *s* of Sir James Lawrence Hay, OBE, and Lady (Davidina) Hay; *m* 1955, Judith Leicester Gill (QSO 1987; CNZM 1998); one *s* four *d*. *Educ:* St Andrew's Coll., Christchurch; Univ. of Canterbury, NZ (BCom). FCA(NZ). Councillor: Christchurch City Council, 1959–74; Canterbury Regl Council, 1995– (Dep. Chm., 1998–2001). Member: Victory Park Bd, 1974–89; Lyttelton Harbour Bd, 1983–89. Chairman: Christchurch Town Hall Board of Management, 1962–92; Canterbury Museum Trust Bd, 1981–84; Canterbury United Council, 1983–86; Museum of New Zealand, Wellington, 1992–98 (Chm., 1992–94). President: Christchurch Aged People's Welfare Council, 1974–89; Christchurch Civic Music Council, 1974–89; Christchurch Symphony Orchestra, 1982–88; Chm., Christchurch Arts Festival, 1965–74; past Mem., Queen Elizabeth II Arts Council. Chm., New Zealand Soc. of Accountants (Canterbury Br.), 1958; Dep. Man. Dir, Haywrights Ltd, 1962–74. Mem. Council, Univ. of Canterbury, 1974–89; Chm. of Governors, McLean Inst., 1974–89; Governor, St Andrew's Coll., 1986–92. Vice-Pres., Municipal Assoc. of NZ, 1974–88. Trustee, Canterbury Savings Bank, 1962–88 (Pres., 1974–75); Dir, Trust Bank Canterbury Ltd, 1988–95. Mem., Charles Upham Trust, 1986– (Dep. Chm., 1990–); Trustee: J. L. Hay Charitable Trust, 1959–; Trust Bank Canterbury Community Trust, 1988–96; Christchurch City Mission Foundn, 1999–. Paul Harris Fellow, Rotary Internat., 1997. JP New Zealand, 1990. Silver Jubilee Medal, 1977; Commemoration Medal, NZ, 1990; Order of the Rising Sun (with Gold Rays), Japan, 1990. *Publication:* Hay Days (autobiog.), 1989. *Recreations:* gardening, listening to good music. *Address:* 70 Heaton Street, Merivale, Christchurch 5, New Zealand. *T:* 3557244; Rue Balguerie, Akaroa, New Zealand. *Club:* Christchurch Rotary (New Zealand).

See also Sir D. R. Hay, Dame M. L. Salas.

HAY, Lady (Helen) Olga; *see* Maitland, Lady H. O.

HAY, Sir James Brian D.; *see* Dalrymple-Hay.

HAY, John Anthony; Vice-Chancellor, University of Queensland, since 1996; *b* 21 Sept. 1942; *s* of J. E. and N. M. E. Hay; *m* 1965, Barbara McKenna; three *s* one *d*. *Educ:* Perth Modern Sch.; Univ. Western Australia (BA Hons 1964; PhD 1976); Pembroke Coll., Cambridge (BA 1966; MA 1969). University of Western Australia: Lectr, Sen. Lectr and Prof. of English, 1967–87; Dep. Chm., Acad. Bd, 1985; Monash University: Dean, Faculty of Arts, 1987–88; Dep. Vice-Chancellor, 1988–91; Vice-Chancellor and Pres., Deakin Univ., 1992–95. Editor, Aumla, Jl of Australasian Univs Lang. and Lit. Assoc., 1985–92. Hon. LittD Deakin, 1995. *Publications:* Spectrum I, II & III, 1971–79; Directions in Australian Secondary English, 1975; Western Australian Literature: a bibliography, 1975; Testing English Comprehension, 1979; K. S. Pritchard, 1984; European Relations, 1985; The Early Imprints at New Norcia, 1986; Australian Studies in Tertiary Institutions, 1987; Western Australian Writing, 1989; Narrative Issues, 1990; Bibliography of Australian Literature, I & II, 1995. *Recreations:* walking, cinema. *Address:* Vice-Chancellor's Office, University of Queensland, Brisbane, Qld 4072, Australia. *T:* (7) 33651300.

HAY, Prof. John Duncan, MA, MD, FRCP; Professor of Child Health, University of Liverpool, 1957–74, now Professor Emeritus; *b* 6 Feb. 1909; *s* of late Prof. John Hay; *m* 1936, Jannett Ceridwen Evans; one *s* two *d*. *Educ:* Liverpool Coll.; Sidney Sussex Coll., Cambridge; Liverpool Univ. MB, ChB, 1st Cl. Hons, Liverpool, 1933; MA 1934, MB 1935, Cambridge; MD Liverpool, 1936; DCH London, MRCP 1939; FRCP 1951. Holt Fellowship in Pathology, Liverpool, 1935; Cons. Pædiatrician to: Royal Liverpool Children's Hospital, 1939–74; Royal Liverpool Babies' Hospital, 1939–61; Birkenhead Children's Hosp., 1937–54; Liverpool Maternity Hosp. 1946–74; Lancashire County Hosp., Whiston, 1942–51; Liverpool Open-Air Hospital, Leasowe, and Mill Road Maternity Hosp., 1947–74; Alder Hey Children's Hosp., 1957–74; Liverpool Education Cttee, 1951–72. Demonstrator in Pathology, University of Liverpool, 1935 and 1938; Asst Lectr in Clinical Pædiatrics, University of Liverpool, 1948–57. Brit. Paediatric Association: Treasurer, 1964–71; Pres., 1972–73; Hon. Mem., 1973; President: Liverpool Med. Instn, 1972–73; Liverpool Paediatric Club, 1975–; Hon. Mem. Assoc. European Paediatric Cardiologists, 1975–. RAMC (Major and Lieut-Col), 1942–46. *Publications:* contribs to Archives of Disease in Childhood, British Heart Journal, BMJ, Lancet, Practitioner, Brit. Encyclopædia of Medical Practice, Medical Progress, 1957, Cardiovascular Diseases in Childhood. *Recreations:* music, fell walking. *Address:* c/o The Croft, Packhorse Lane, Marcham, Abingdon, Oxon OX13 6NT. *T:* (01865) 391216.

HAY, Sir John (Erroll Audley), 11th Bt *cr* 1663 (NS) of Park, Wigtownshire; *b* 3 Dec. 1935; *o s* of Sir Arthur Thomas Erroll Hay, 10th Bt, ISO, ARIBA and his 1st wife, Hertha Hedwig Paula Louise (*d* 1994), *d* of Ludwig Stölzle, Nagelberg, Austria; *S* father, 1993. *Educ:* Gordonstoun; St Andrews Univ. (MA). *Heir:* none.

HAY, Rev. Richard, CMG 1992; Vicar, St Paul's, Addlestone, since 1999; *b* 4 May 1942; *s* of Prof. Denys Hay, FBA, FRSE and Sarah Gwyneth Morley; *m* 1969, Miriam Marguerite Alvin England; two *s*. *Educ:* George Watson's Coll., Edinburgh; Edinburgh Univ.; Balliol Coll., Oxford (BA Hons, Mod. Hist.); Cranmer Hall, Durham. Assistant Principal, HM Treasury, 1963–68; Secretary, West Midlands Economic Planning Council, 1966–67; Private Sec. to Financial Sec., Treasury, 1967–68; Principal, Treasury, 1968–73; European Commission: Member, Cabinet of Sir Christopher (later Lord) Soames, Vice-Pres., 1973–75; Dep. Chef de Cabinet, 1975–77; Chef de Cabinet to Mr Christopher (now Lord) Tugendhat, Member, 1977–79; Dir, Economic Structures and Community Interventions, Directorate-Gen. for Economic and Financial Affairs, 1979–81; Dep. Dir-Gen., 1981–86, Dir-Gen., 1986–91, Directorate-General for Personnel and Admin, EC; Special Advr, EC, 1991. Consultant, Sharing of Ministries Abroad, 1992–94. Ordained deacon, 1996, priest, 1997; Curate, St Clement and All Saints, Hastings, 1996–99. *Address:* 140 Church Road, Addlestone, Surrey KT15 1SJ.

HAY, Robert Colquhoun, CBE 1988; WS; Sheriff Principal of North Strathclyde, 1989–98; *b* 22 Sept. 1933; *s* of late J. B. Hay, dental surgeon, Stirling and Mrs J. Y. Hay; *m* 1958, Olive Black; two *s* two *d*. *Educ:* Univ. of Edinburgh (MA, LLB). Legal practice, 1957–63, 1968–76; Depute Procurator Fiscal, Edinburgh, 1963–68; Temp. Sheriff, 1984–89; Chm., 1976–81, Pres., 1981–89, Industrial Tribunals for Scotland. Mem., Sheriff Court Rules Council, 1989–95 (Chm., 1993–95). Comr, Northern Lighthouse Bd, 1989–98 (Vice-Chm., 1991–92; Chm., 1992–93). Hon. Sheriff, Dumbarton, 1999. Comr for Clan Hay, 1995–. *Publication:* contrib. Laws of Scotland: Stair Memorial Encyclopedia, 1988. *Recreations:* walking, sailing. *Address:* Rocklee, Cove, Argyll & Bute G84 0NN. *T:* (01436) 842269. *Club:* Royal Highland Yacht (Oban).

HAY, Robin William Patrick Hamilton; Recorder, since 1985; barrister; *b* 1 Nov. 1939; *s* of William R. Hay and Dora Hay; *m* 1969, Lady Olga Maitland, *qv*; two *s* one *d*. *Educ:* Eltham; Selwyn Coll., Cambridge (MA, LLB). Called to the Bar, Inner Temple, 1964. Chm., Nat. Musicians Symphony Orchestra, 1990–. *Recreations:* church tasting, gastronomy, choral singing. *Address:* Goldsmith Building, Temple EC4Y 7BL. *Club:* Garrick.

HAY, Prof. Roderick James, DM; FRCP, FRCPath; Mary Dunhill Professor of Cutaneous Medicine, London University, since 1990, and Dean for External Affairs, Guy's, King's and St Thomas' Hospitals' Medical and Dental School of King's College London, since 1998; Hon. Consultant Dermatologist, since 1979, and Dean, since 1993, St John's Institute of Dermatology; *b* 13 April 1947; *s* of Kenneth Stuart Hay and Margery Geidt (*née* Winterbotham); *m* 1973, Delyth Price; two *d*. *Educ:* Wellington Coll.; Merton Coll., Oxford (BA 1968; BM BCh 1971; MA 1979; DM 1980); Guy's Hosp. Med. Sch. MRCP 1974, FRCP 1981; MRCPath 1981, FRCPath 1992. House physician and surgeon, SHO and Dermatol. Registrar, Guy's Hosp., 1971–75; London School of Hygiene and Tropical Medicine: Wellcome Res. Fellow, 1975–77; Lectr, 1977–79; Sen. Lectr, 1979–83; Reader in Clinical Mycology, 1983–89; Prof., UMDS, later Guy's, King's and St Thomas' Hosps' Med. Sch. of KCL, 1989–; Clinical Dir, Dermatology, Guy's and St Thomas' NHS Trust, 1996–. Mem. Bd, Internat. Foundn of Dermatol., 1996–. *Publications:* Clinicians Guide to Fungal Disease, 1981; Medical Mycology, 1996; contribs to med. and scientific jls on immunology and treatment of fungal infections and epidemiology of skin disease. *Recreations:* gardening, music. *Address:* St John's Institute of Dermatology, St Thomas' Hospital, SE1 7EH. *T:* (020) 7960 5802; Hill House, Wootton, Woodstock, Oxon OX20 1DX.

HAY, Sir Ronald Frederick Hamilton, 12th Bt *cr* 1703, of Alderston; *b* 1941; *s* of Sir Ronald Nelson Hay, 11th Bt and of Rita, *d* of John Munyard; *S* father, 1988; *m* 1978, Kathleen, *d* of John Thake; two *s* one *d*. *Heir:* *s* Alexander James Hay; *b* 1979.

HAY, William; Member (DemU) Foyle, Northern Ireland Assembly, since 1998; *b* 16 April 1950; *m* (marr. diss.); three *s* two *d*. *Educ:* Newbuildings Primary Sch.; Faughen Valley High Sch. Mem. (DemU), Derry CC, 1981–. Contested (DemU) Foyle, 2001. *Address:* 9 Ebrington Terrace, Waterside, Londonderry BT47 1JS.

HAY-CAMPBELL, (Thomas) Ian, LVO 1994; HM Diplomatic Service; Deputy Head of Mission, Oslo, since 2001; *b* 19 May 1945; *s* of Thomas Neil Hay-Campbell and Anthea Joan Hay-Campbell (*née* Carey); *m* 1970, Margaret Lorraine (*née* Hoadley); four *s*. *Educ:* Wanganui Collegiate Sch., NZ; Victoria Univ. of Wellington (BA Hons History). Radio Journalist, NZBC, Wellington, 1969–72; Radio Producer, subseq. Editor, BBC World Service, 1972–84; joined FCO, 1984; First Sec., FCO, 1984–87; Dep. Head of Mission, Kinshasa, 1987–90; FCO, 1990–94; Head of Press and Public Affairs Section, Moscow, 1994–97; Dep. High Comr, Harare, 1998–2001. *Recreations:* modern history, reading, tennis, trams. *Address:* c/o Foreign and Commonwealth Office, King Charles Street, SW1A 2AH. *Club:* Royal Over-Seas League.

HAY DAVISON, Ian Frederic; *see* Davison.

HAY-PLUMB, Paula Maria; Chief Executive, English Partnerships, since 1999; *b* 18 March 1960; *d* of Henry Sephton Green and Eileen Green (*née* Milburn); *m* 1984, Martin Hay-Plumb; one *s* one *d*. *Educ:* Univ. of Exeter (BSc Hons 1980). ACA 1983; MCT 1989. Qualified as chartered accountant with Peat, Marwick, Mitchell; Marks and Spencer plc, 1984–88; Olympia & York Canary Wharf Ltd, 1989–93, Gp Financial Controller; Finance Dir, 1994–96, Man. Dir (Ops), 1996–99, English Partnerships. Chm., DETR Coalfields Task Force, 1997–98 (reported 1998). *Recreations:* music, theatre. *Address:* English Partnerships, 110 Buckingham Palace Road, SW1W 9SB.

HAYASHI, Sadayuki, Hon. GCVO 1998; Ambassador of Japan to the Court of St James's, 1997–2001; *b* 10 Nov. 1937; *s* of Tomohiko and Ayako Hayashi; *m* 1969, Chieko

Kumazawa; three *d. Educ:* Univ. of Tokyo (BA 1960); St John's Coll., Oxford (BA 1962). Entered Ministry of Foreign Affairs, Japan, 1960; Attaché, London, 1962–64; First Secretary: Kuala Lumpur, 1970–72; Washington, 1972–74; Private Sec. to Chief Cabinet Sec., Prime Minister's Office, 1976; Dep. Consul-Gen., Hong Kong, 1978–81; Counsellor, Permt Mission of Japan to UN, NY, 1981–84; Dir, Financial Affairs Div., Minister's Secretariat, 1984–86; Dep. Dir-Gen., UN Bureau, 1986; Minister, Permt Mission of Japan to Internat. Orgns, and concurrently Consul-Gen., Geneva, 1987–89; Director-General: Econ. Affairs Bureau, 1989–92; for Inspection (rank of ambassador), 1992; Dep. Vice-Minister, 1992–94; Dep. Minister, 1994, Vice Minister, 1995–97, for Foreign Affairs. *Recreations:* trekking, walking, collecting classic cameras. *Address:* c/o Embassy of Japan, 101–104 Piccadilly, W1J 7JT. *T:* (020) 7465 6500.

HAYCRAFT, Anna Margaret, FRSL; writer; *b* 9 Sept. 1932; *d* of John and Alexandra Lindholm; *m* 1956, Colin Haycraft (*d* 1994); four *s* one *d* (and one *s* one *d* decd). *Educ:* Bangor County Grammar School for Girls; Liverpool School of Art. Fiction editor, Gerald Duckworth & Co., 1970; Columnist: The Spectator, 1985–89; The Universe, 1989–91; The Catholic Herald, 1991–96, 1998–; The Oldie, 1996–. FRSL 1999. *Publications: as Anna Haycraft:* Natural Baby Food, 1977; (with Caroline Blackwood) Darling, You Shouldn't Have Gone to So Much Trouble, 1980; *as Alice Thomas Ellis:* The Sin Eater, 1977; The Birds of the Air, 1980; The Twenty-Seventh Kingdom, 1982; The Other Side of the Fire, 1983; Unexplained Laughter, 1985 (Yorkshire Post Novel of the Year, 1985); (with Tom Pitt-Aikens) Secrets of Strangers, 1986; Home Life, 1986; More Home Life, 1987; The Clothes in the Wardrobe, 1987, The Skeleton in the Cupboard, 1988, The Fly in the Ointment, 1989, trilogy; Home Life Three, 1988; (with Tom Pitt-Aikens) The Loss of the Good Authority, 1989; (ed) Wales: an anthology, 1989; Home Life Four, 1989; A Welsh Childhood (autobiog.), 1990; The Inn at the Edge of the World, 1990 (Writers' Guild Award, 1990); Pillars of Gold, 1992; The Serpent on the Rock, 1994; The Evening of Adam, 1994; Cat Among the Pigeons: collection of 'Catholic Herald' essays, 1994; Fairy Tale, 1996; (ed) Valentine's Day, 2000. *Address:* c/o Peters Fraser & Dunlop, Drury House, 34–43 Russell Street, W2B 5HA.

HAYDAR, Dr Loutof Allah; Syrian Ambassador to the People's Republic of China, since 1990; *b* 22 March 1940; *s* of Haydar and Mary; *m* 1968, Hayat Hassan; one *s* three *d. Educ:* Damascus Univ. (BA English Literature 1964); Moscow State Univ. (PhD 1976). Joined Foreign Office, 1965; served at Syrian Embassy: London, 1965–67; Bonn, 1967–68; Moscow, 1970–75; served with Syrian Delegation to UN, New York, 1978–82; Syrian Ambassador to UK, 1982–86. *Publication:* The Ancient History of Palestine and the Middle East (PhD Thesis), 1976; The Grand Spring: a collection of literary short stories, 1997. *Address:* Syrian Embassy, 6 Dong Si Jie, San Li Tun, Beijing 100600, China.

HAYDAY, Anthony Victor; HM Diplomatic Service, retired; Ambassador to Madagascar, 1987–90; *b* 1 June 1930; *s* of Charles Leslie Victor Hayday and Catherine (*née* McCarthy); *m* 1966, Anne Heather Moffat (*d* 1995); one *s* one *d. Educ:* Beckenham and Penge Grammar School. Royal Air Force, 1949–50; HM Foreign (later Diplomatic) Service, 1950; Brazzaville, 1953; British Information Services, New York, 1955; FO, 1958; Vice Consul, Houston, 1961; 2nd Secretary, Algiers, 1962; FO (later FCO), 1966; 1st Secretary, New Delhi, 1969; Head of Chancery, Freetown, 1973; on secondment to Commonwealth Secretariat, 1976–80; Dep. High Comr, Calcutta, 1981–85; Consul-Gen., Cleveland, 1985–87. *Recreations:* birdwatching, athletics. *Address:* Meadow Cottage, Swillbrook, Minety, Malmesbury, Wilts SN16 9QA. *Clubs:* Blackheath Harriers; Bengal (Calcutta).

HAYDEN, Hon. William George, AC 1989; cattle farmer, Brisbane Valley; Governor-General of Australia, 1989–96; *b* Brisbane, 23 Jan. 1933; *s* of G. Hayden, Oakland, Calif, USA; *m* 1960, Dallas, *d* of W. Broadfoot; one *s* two *d. Educ:* Brisbane State High Sch. BEcon, Univ. of Qld. Public Service, Qld, 1950–52; Police Constable in Queensland, 1953–61. MHR (Lab) for Oxley, Qld, 1961–88. Parly Spokesman on Health and Welfare, 1969–72; Minister for Social Security, Australian Govt, 1972–75; Federal Treasurer, June–Nov. 1975; Leader of Australian Labor Party and the Opposition, 1977–83; spokesman on defence, 1976–77 and on economic management, 1976–83; Minister for Foreign Affairs, 1983–87, and for Trade, 1987–88. Adjunct Prof., Qld Univ. of Technol., Brisbane, 1996. Chm., Editl Cttee, Quadrant Jl, 1998–. Hon. FRACP 1995. Hon. Dr: Griffith Univ., 1990; Univ. of Central Qld, 1992; Hon. LLD Univ. of Qld, 1990; Hon. DLitt Univ. of S Qld, 1997. Australian Humanist of the Year, 1996. Kt, Order of St John in Australia, 1989. Gwangha Medal, Order of Diplomatic Merit, Korea. *Publication:* Hayden: an autobiography, 1996. *Recreations:* reading, music, golf, horse riding, cross-country ski-ing, bushwalking. *Address:* PO Box 7829, Waterfront Place, Brisbane, Qld 4001, Australia. *T:* (7) 32293500, *Fax:* (7) 32293499.

HAYDEN, William Joseph, CBE 1976; Chairman and Chief Executive, Jaguar plc, 1990–92; *b* 19 Jan. 1929; *s* of George Hayden and Mary Ann Hayden (*née* Overhead); *m* 1954, Mavis Ballard; two *s* two *d. Educ:* Romford Tech. College. Served Army, 1947–49. Ford Motor Co.: Briggs Motor Bodies, Dagenham, 1950–57; financial staff, Dagenham, 1957–63; Div. Controller, Ford Chassis, Transmission and Engine Div., Dagenham, 1963–67; Gen. Ops Manager, Transmission, Chassis and Truck Mfg Ops, 1967–71; Vice-President: Truck Mfg Ops, 1971; Power Train Ops, 1972; Mfg Ford of Europe, Inc., 1974–90. Director (non-executive): Hawtell Whiting, 1992–96; Trans Tec. 1993–96. *Recreations:* golf, gardening, soccer. *Address:* Buckley Green Farm, Buckley Green, Henley in Arden, Warwickshire B95 5QF. *Clubs:* Thorndon Park Golf; Royal Porthcawl Golf; Stratford on Avon Golf.

HAYDON, Francis Edmund Walter; HM Diplomatic Service, retired; *b* 23 Dec. 1928; *s* of late Surgeon Captain Walter T. Haydon, RN and Maria Christina Haydon (*née* Delahoyde); *m* 1959, Isabel Dorothy Kitchin; two *s* two *d. Educ:* Downside School; Magdalen College, Oxford. BA (1st cl. Modern History) 1949. Asst London correspondent, Agence France-Presse, 1951–52; Asst diplomatic correspondent, Reuters, 1952–55; joined Foreign Office, 1955; Second Sec., Benghazi, 1959, Beirut, 1962; First Sec., Blantyre, 1969, Ankara, 1978; Counsellor, FCO, 1981–87. *Recreations:* lawn tennis, cricket, bridge, travel, enjoying the countryside. *Address:* Le Picachon, La Rue des Bouillons, Trinity, Jersey JE3 5BB. *T:* (01534) 863155.

HAYE, Colvyn Hugh, CBE 1983; Commissioner for Hong Kong, 1984–87; *b* 7 Dec. 1925; 3rd *s* of Colvyn Hugh Haye and Avis Rose Kelly; *m* 1949, Gloria Mary Stansbury; two *d. Educ:* Sherwood Coll.; Univ. of Melbourne (BA, Teachers' Cert.); Christchurch Coll., Oxford (Overseas Service Trng Course). Served War, RNVR, Midshipman and Sub-Lt, 1944–46. Victorian State Educn Service, 1947–52; joined Colonial Service, now HMOCS, Hong Kong Government: Educn Officer, 1953; Sen. Educn Officer, 1962 (world tour, educnl estabs, and trng at Centre for Educnl Television Overseas, London, 1964); Asst Dir and Head of Educnl Television Service, 1969; Dep. Dir, 1975; Dir of Educn and Official Mem., Legislative Council, 1980; Sec., Administrative Service and Comr, London Office, 1984. Jardine Educn Foundn Visitor, Univs of Oxford and Cambridge, 1990–97. Mem. Council, Overseas Service Pensioners' Assoc., 1988–97. JP Hong Kong, 1971–87. *Recreations:* reading, writing, talking, walking. *Address:* Balmenoch, Gwydyr Road, Crieff, Perthshire PH7 4BS. *T:* and *Fax:* (01764) 656626. *Club:* Hong Kong (Hong Kong).

HAYES, Sir Brian, Kt 1998; CBE 1992; QPM 1985; Special Adviser on Security to the Football Association, since 1998; Deputy Commissioner of Metropolitan Police, 1995–98; *b* 25 Jan. 1940; 2nd *s* of James and Jessie Hayes; *m* 1960, Priscilla Rose Bishop; one *s* three *d. Educ:* Plaistow County Grammar Sch.; Sheffield Univ. (BA Hons 1st Cl. Mod. Langs). Metropolitan Police, 1959–77; seconded Northern Ireland, 1971–72; Police Adviser, Mexico, 1975 and 1976, Colombia, 1977 and 1993; British Police representative, EEC, 1976–77; Asst Chief Constable, Surrey Constabulary, 1977–81; Dep. Chief Constable, Wiltshire Constabulary, 1981–82; Chief Constable, Surrey Constabulary, 1982–91; Inspector of Constabulary for SE England, 1991–95. Vice-Pres., ACPO, 1990–91. Chm., Police Athletic Assoc., 1989–91 (Nat. Sec., 1984–88); Pres., Union Sportive des Polices d'Europe, 1990–92. Security Consultant, TRI-MEX Internat. Ltd, 1999–. Freeman, City of London, 1998. OStJ 1987. Police Long Service and Good Conduct Medal, 1981; Cruz al Merito Policial (Spain), 1998. *Recreations:* martial arts, running, sailing, golf. *Address:* c/o New Scotland Yard, Broadway, SW1H 0BG. *T:* (020) 7230 1212, *Telex:* 893421 Metpol Ldn.

HAYES, Sir Brian (David), GCB 1988 (KCB 1980 CB 1976); Permanent Secretary, Department of Trade and Industry, 1985–89, retired (Joint Permanent Secretary, 1983–85); *b* 5 May 1929; *s* of late Charles and Flora Hayes, Bramerton, Norfolk; *m* 1958, Audrey Jenkins; one *s* one *d. Educ:* Norwich Sch.; Corpus Christi Coll., Cambridge. BA (Hist.) 1952, PhD (Cambridge) 1956. RASC, 1947–49. Joined Min. of Agriculture, Fisheries and Food, 1956; Asst Private Sec. to the Minister, 1958; Asst Sec., 1967; Under-Sec., Milk and Poultry Gp, 1970–73; Dep. Sec., 1973–78; Permanent Sec., 1979–83. Director: Guardian Royal Exchange, 1989–99; Tate & Lyle, 1989–98; Adv. Dir, Unilever plc, 1990–99. Chm., CBI Educn Foundn, 1991–96. Dir, SANE, 1990–. Lloyd's Members' Ombudsman, 1994–. *Recreations:* reading, television, opera.

HAYES, Colin Graham Frederick, MA; RA 1970 (ARA 1963); painter; *b* 17 Nov. 1919; *s* of Gerald Hayes and Winifred (*née* Yule); *m* 1st, 1949, Jean Westbrook Law (*d* 1988); three *d*; 2nd, 1992, Marjorie Christensen. *Educ:* Westminster Sch.; Christ Church, Oxford. Served Royal Engineers, 1940–45 (Middle East) (Capt.). Ruskin Sch. of Drawing, 1946–47. Tutor, Sen. Tutor and Reader, Royal College of Art, 1949–84; Hon. ARCA, 1960; Fellow, RCA, 1960–84 (Hon. Fellow, 1984). Pres., Royal Soc. of British Artists, 1993–98. Work in Collections: Arts Council; British Council; Carlisle Museum, etc. *Publications include:* Renoir, 1961; Stanley Spencer, 1963; Rembrandt, 1969; many articles on painting in jls. *Address:* 2 Annandale Road, W4 2HF. *T:* (020) 8994 8762.

HAYES, Most Rev. James Martin; Archbishop (RC) of Halifax (NS), 1967–90, now Archbishop Emeritus; *b* 27 May 1924; *s* of late L. J. Hayes. *Educ:* St Mary's Univ., Halifax; Holy Heart Seminary, Halifax; Angelicum Univ., Rome. Asst, St Mary's Basilica, 1947–54; Chancellor and Sec. of Archdiocese of Halifax, 1957–65; Rector, St Mary's Basilica, 1963–65; Auxil. Bp of Halifax, 1965–66; Apostolic Administrator of Archdiocese of Halifax, 1966–67. Pres., Canadian Conf. of Catholic Bishops, 1987–89. Hon. DLitt St Anne's Coll., Church Point, NS, 1966; Hon. DTh King's Coll., Halifax, NS, 1967; Hon. DHL Mount St Vincent Univ., Halifax, 1985; Hon. LLD: St Mary's Univ., Halifax, 1985; St Thomas Univ., 1989; Hon. DD Atlantic Sch. of Theol., Halifax, 1986. *Address:* Catholic Pastoral Centre, Archdiocese of Halifax, PO Box 1527, 1531 Grafton Street, Halifax, NS B3J 2Y3, Canada.

HAYES, Jeremy Joseph James; barrister; freelance journalist and broadcaster; political editor, Punch magazine; *b* 20 April 1953; *s* of Peter and Daye Hayes; *m* 1979, Alison Gail Mansfield; one *s* one *d. Educ:* Oratory Sch.; Chelmer Inst. LLB London. Called to the Bar, Middle Temple, 1977. MP (C) Harlow, 1983–97; contested (C) same seat, 1997. PPS to Minister of State, NI Office, 1992–94, DoE, 1994–97. Member, Select Committee: on Social Services, 1987–90; on Health, 1990–91; on National Heritage, 1996–97; formerly: Member: All Party Parly Gp on Human Rights; All Party Parly Gp on Race Relations; Vice Chm., All Party AIDS Cttee; Chm., All Party ASH Gp. Promoter: Parents' Aid (No 2) Bill; Sexual Offences Bill; Sponsor: Video Recordings Act; Protection of Children against Tobacco Act; Freedom of Information (Medical Records) Act. Member: FRAME; Amnesty Internat. Fellow, Industry and Parliament Trust. Hon. Dir, State Legislative Leaders Foundn, USA. Gov., Oratory Sch.; Vice Pres., Wendens Ambo Cricket Club. Freeman, City of London; Liveryman, Fletchers' Co.; Freeman, Co. of Watermen and Lightermen. *Recreations:* playing biffing games with my son, practising the violin with my daughter, and slumping in front of the TV with my wife. *Clubs:* Carlton, Savile; Essex.

HAYES, John Henry; MP (C) South Holland and The Deepings, since 1997; *b* 23 June 1958; *s* of Henry John Hayes and late Lily Hayes; *m* 1997, Susan Jane Hopewell; one *s. Educ:* Colfe's Grammar Sch., London; Univ. of Nottingham (BA Hons, PGCE). Dir, Data Base Ltd, 1983–99. Mem., Nottinghamshire CC, 1985–98. Contested (C) Derbyshire NE, 1987, 1992. Opposition front-bench spokesman on educn and employment, 2000–01; an Opposition Whip, 2001–. A Vice-Chm., Cons. Party, 1999–2000. *Recreations:* the arts, good food and wine, many sports, antiques, history, gardening. *Address:* House of Commons, SW1A 0AA. *T:* (020) 7219 3453.

HAYES, John Trevor, CBE 1986; MA Oxon, PhD London; FSA; Director of the National Portrait Gallery, London, 1974–94; *b* 21 Jan. 1929; *er s* of late Leslie Thomas Hayes and late Gwendoline (*née* Griffiths), London. *Educ:* Ardingly; Keble Coll. Oxford (Open Exhibr; Hon. Fellow, 1984); Courtauld Inst. of Art, London; Inst. of Fine Arts, New York. Asst Keeper, London Museum, 1954–70, Dir, 1970–74; Commonwealth Fund Fellow, 1958–59 (NY Univ.); Vis. Prof. in History of Art, Yale Univ., 1969. Chm., Walpole Soc., 1981–96. *Publications:* London: a pictorial history, 1969; The Drawings of Thomas Gainsborough, 1970; Catalogue of Oil Paintings in the London Museum, 1970, 2nd edn (with Mireille Galinou), 1996; Gainsborough as Printmaker, 1971; Rowlandson: Watercolours and Drawings, 1972; Gainsborough: Paintings and Drawings, 1975; The Art of Graham Sutherland, 1980; The Landscape Paintings of Thomas Gainsborough, 1982; The Art of Thomas Rowlandson, 1990; The Portrait in British Art, 1991; Catalogue of the British Paintings in the National Gallery of Art, Washington, 1992; Gainsborough and Rowlandson: a New York private collection, 1998; The Letters of Thomas Gainsborough, 2001; various London Museum and Nat. Portrait Gall. pubns; catalogues of Gainsborough exhibns for Tate Gall., Grand Palais and Ferrara Arte; numerous articles in The Burlington Magazine, Apollo and other jls. *Recreations:* ballet, opera, European travel. *Address:* 61 Grantham Road, Chiswick, W4 2RT. *T:* (020) 8747 9768. *Club:* Garrick.

HAYES, John William, CBE 1995; Chairman, Disciplinary Appeals Committee, Chartered Institute of Public Finance Accountants, since 2001; *b* 10 Feb. 1945; *s* of late Dick Hayes and of Bridget Isobel Hayes; *m* 1970, Jennifer Hayes (*née* Harvey); two *s* one *d. Educ:* Nottingham High Sch.; Morecambe Grammar Sch.; Victoria Univ. of Manchester (LLB). Solicitor. Articled Thomas Foord, 1966–69; Worthing Borough Council, 1966–69; Nottingham County Borough Council, 1969–71; Somerset CC, 1971–74; Asst, Dep. Clerk and Dep. Chief Exec., Notts CC, 1974–80; Clerk and Chief

Exec., Warwicks CC, 1980–86; Sec.-Gen., Law Soc., 1987–96; Chm., OPRA, 1996–2001. Chm., Local Govt Gp, Law Soc., 1981–82; Sec., Warwicks Probation Cttee, 1983–86; Clerk to Warwicks Magistrates' Courts' Cttee, 1983–86; Clerk to Lord Lieut of Warwicks, 1980–86. Chm., Ind. Inquiry into River Vessel Safety, 1992. Chm., Coventry Dio. Church Urban Fund, 1989–91; Member: Council, Warwick Univ., 1980–90; Bishop of Coventry's Board of Social Responsibility, 1981–86; Inner Cities' Task Force, 1985–86. Occasional Chm., Consultants Appts Panels, Guy's and St Thomas' Hosp., 1998–; Legal Assessor, British Council of Osteopathy, 1998–. Gov., Kingsley School, 1986–92. Hon. LLD De Montfort, 1996. *Recreations:* cricket, music, idleness. *Club:* Sussex CC.

HAYES, Dr William; President, St John's College, University of Oxford, 1987–2001; Senior Research Fellow, Clarendon Laboratory, Oxford University, since 1987; Pro-Vice-Chancellor, University of Oxford, 1990–2001; *b* 12 Nov. 1930; *s* of Robert Hayes and Eileen Tobin; *m* 1962, Joan Ferriss (*d* 1996); two *s* one *d*. *Educ:* University Coll., Dublin (MSc, PhD); Oxford Univ. (MA, DPhil). St John's College, Oxford: 1851 Overseas Schol., 1955–57; Official Fellow and Tutor, 1960–87; Principal Bursar, 1977–87; University Lectr, Oxford Univ., 1962–87; Dir and Head of Clarendon Lab., Oxford, 1985–87. Oxford University: Mem., Gen. Bd of the Faculties, 1985–88; Mem., Hebdomadal Council, 1989–2000; Chm., Curators of Univ. Chest, 1992–2000; Delegate, OUP, 1991–2001. Temporary research appointments at: Argonne Nat. Lab., 1957–58; Purdue Univ., 1963–64; RCA Labs, Princeton, 1968; Univ. of Illinois, 1971; Bell Labs, 1974. Mem., Physics Cttee, SERC, 1982–85. Hon. MRIA 1998. Hon. DSc: NUI, 1988; Purdue Univ., 1996. *Publications:* (ed) Crystals with the Fluorite Structure, 1974; (with R. Loudon) Scattering of Light by Crystals, 1978; (with A. M. Stoneham) Defects and Defect Processes in non-metallic Solids, 1985; contribs to Procs of Royal Soc., Jl of Physics, Physical Rev., etc. *Recreations:* walking, reading, listening to music. *Address:* St John's College, Oxford OX1 3JP. *T:* (01865) 277300.

HAYES, William; General Secretary, Communication Workers Union, since 2001; *b* 8 June 1953; *s* of William and Margaret Hayes; *m* 1995, Dian Lee; one *s*. *Educ:* St Swithin's Secondary Modern; Univ. of Liverpool (Dip. Trade Union Studies). Fitter-welder, 1968–71; factory worker, 1971–73; unemployed, 1973–74; joined Post Office, 1974, Postman; Lay Official, Union of Post Office Workers, subseq. UCW, then CWU, 1992; Nat. Official, CWU, 1992–2001. *Recreations:* films, music, books, Liverpool FC. *Address:* Communication Workers Union, 150 The Broadway, Wimbledon, SW19 1RX.

HAYHOE, family name of **Baron Hayhoe**.

HAYHOE, Baron *cr* 1992 (Life Peer), of Isleworth in the London Borough of Hounslow; **Bernard John Hayhoe, (Barney),** Kt 1987; PC 1985; CEng, FIMechE; Chairman, Guy's and St Thomas' NHS Trust, 1993–95; *b* 8 Aug. 1925; *s* of late Frank Stanley and Catherine Hayhoe; *m* 1962, Anne Gascoigne Thornton, *o d* of Bernard William and Hilda Thornton; two *s* one *d*. *Educ:* State schools; Borough Polytechnic. Tool Room Apprentice, 1941–44; Armaments Design Dept, Ministry of Supply, 1944–54; Inspectorate of Armaments, 1954–63; Conservative Research Dept, 1965–70. Heston and Isleworth, 1970–74, MP (C) Brentford and Isleworth, 1974–92; PPS to Lord President and Leader of House of Commons, 1972–74; an additional Opposition Spokesman on Employment, 1974–79; Parly Under Sec. of State for Defence for the Army, 1979–81; Minister of State: CSD, 1981; HM Treasury, 1981–85; (Minister for Health) DHSS, 1985–86. Member: Select Cttee on Race Relations and Immigration, 1971–73; Select Cttee on Defence, 1987–92; H of C Commn, 1987–92; Public Accounts Commn, 1987–92; H of L Select Cttee on Public Service, 1997–98; Hon. Sec., 1970–71, Vice-Chm., 1974, Cons. Parly Employment Cttee; Jt Hon. Sec., 1970–73, Vice-Chm., 1973–76, Cons. Gp for Europe; Vice-Chm., Cons. Party Internat. Office, 1973–79. Mem., Trilateral Commn, 1977–79. Chm., Hansard Soc., 1990–94. Governor, Birkbeck Coll., 1976–79. Pres., Help the Hospices, 1992–98; Trustee: British Brain and Spine Foundn, 1992–; Liver Res. Trust, 1994–. *Address:* 20 Wool Road, SW20 0HW. *T:* (020) 8947 0037. *Club:* Garrick.

See also F. G. J. Hayhoe.

HAYHOE, Prof. Frank George James, MD, FRCP, FRCPath; Leukaemia Research Fund Professor of Haematological Medicine, University of Cambridge, 1968–88; Fellow, Darwin College, Cambridge, since 1964, Vice-Master, 1964–74; *b* 25 Oct. 1920; *s* of late Frank Stanley and Catherine Hayhoe; *m* 1945, Jacqueline Marie Marguerite (*née* Dierkx); two *s*. *Educ:* Selhurst Grammar Sch.; Trinity Hall, Cambridge; St Thomas's Hospital Medical Sch. BA Cantab 1942; MRCS, LRCP 1944; MB, BChir Cantab 1945; MRCP 1949; MA Cantab 1949; MD Cantab 1951; FRCP 1965; FRCPath 1971. Captain RAMC, 1945–47. Registrar, St Thomas' Hosp., 1947–49. Elmore Research Student, Cambridge Univ., 1949–51; Royal Soc. Exchange Res. Schol., USSR, 1962–63; Lectr in Medicine, Cambridge Univ., 1951–68; Mem. Council of Senate, 1967–71. Member: Bd of Governors, United Cambridge Hospitals, 1971–74; Cambs AHA, 1974–75; GMC, 1982–88. Lectures: Langdon Brown, RCP, 1971; Cudlip Meml, Ann Arbor, 1967; vis. lectr at med. schs in N and S America, Europe, Middle East, Africa, India. Hon. MD: L'Aquila, 1992; Montpellier, 1993. G. F. Götz Foundn Prize, Zürich Univ., 1974; Suniti Rana Panja Gold Medal, Calcutta Sch. of Trop. Med., 1979. *Publications:* (ed) Lectures in Haematology, 1960; Leukaemia: Research and Clinical Practice, 1960; (jtly) Cytology and Cytochemistry of Acute Leukaemia, 1964; (ed) Current Research in Leukaemia, 1965; (with R. J. Flemans) An Atlas of Haematological Cytology, 1969, 3rd edn 1992; (with J. C. Cawley) Ultrastructure of Haemic Cells, 1973; (jtly) Leukaemia, Lymphomas and Allied Disorders, 1976; (jtly) Hairy Cell Leukaemia, 1980; (with D. Quaglino) Haematological Cytochemistry, 1980, 3rd edn 1994; (ed with D. Quaglino) The Cytobiology of Leukaemias and Lymphomas, 1985; (with D. Quaglino) Haematological Oncology, 1992; contribs to med. and scientific jls, on haematological topics, especially leukaemia. *Address:* 20 Queen Edith's Way, Cambridge CB1 7PN. *T:* (01223) 248381.

See also Baron Hayhoe.

HAYMAN, family name of **Baroness Hayman**.

HAYMAN, Baroness *cr* 1995 (Life Peer), of Dartmouth Park in the London Borough of Camden; **Helene Valerie Hayman,** PC 2001; *b* 26 March 1949; *d* of late Maurice Middleweek and Maude Middleweek; *m* 1974, Martin Hayman; four *s*. *Educ:* Wolverhampton Girls' High Sch.; Newnham Coll., Cambridge (MA). Pres., Cambridge Union, 1969. Worked with Shelter, Nat. Campaign for the Homeless, 1969; Camden Council Social Services Dept, 1971; Dep. Dir, Nat. Council for One Parent Families, 1974. Vice-Chairman: Bloomsbury HA, 1988–90 (Mem., 1985–90); Bloomsbury and Islington HA, 1991–92 (Mem., 1990–91); Chm., Whittington Hosp. NHS Trust, 1992–97. Contested (Lab) Wolverhampton SW, Feb. 1974; MP (Lab) Welwyn and Hatfield, Oct. 1974–1979. Parliamentary Under-Secretary of State: DETR, 1997–98; DoH, 1998–99; Minister of State, MAFF, 1999–2001. Member: RCOG Ethics Cttee, 1982–96; UCL/UCH Cttee on Ethics of Clinical Investigation, 1987–96 (Vice-Chm., 1990–96); Council, UCL, 1992–97.

HAYMAN, (Anne) Carolyn; Chief Executive, The Foyer Federation, since 1996; Member, Commonwealth Development Corporation, 1994–99; *b* 23 April 1951; *d* of Walter Kurt Hayman, *qv* and late Margaret Riley Crann; *m* 1980, Peter John Bury; two *d*. *Educ:* Putney High Sch. for Girls; Newnham Coll., Cambridge (BA Classics and Philosophy); Sch. of Oriental and African Studies (MSc Econ). Admin Trainee, ODM, 1975–78; Advr, Central Policy Review Staff, 1978–80; Senior Consultant, Office Automation: EOSYS, 1980–82; Coopers & Lybrand, 1982–83; Jt Man. Dir, Korda & Co., 1983–95; Exec. Dir, Rutherford Ventures, 1995–96. Chairman: Cambridge Animation Systems, 1990–96; Atraverda, 1992–97. Dir, Technology & Law, 1982–85. Member: Council, Pitcom, 1981–83; Council for Industry and Higher Educn, 1992–97; Board, Industrial Res. and Tech. Unit, 1995–97. Editor, Work and Society, 1984–86. *Recreations:* children, music, languages, long distance travel. *Address:* 36 Lawford Road, NW5 2LN. *T:* (020) 7916 2689; (office) 146–148 Clerkenwell Road, EC1R 5DG. *T:* (020) 7833 8616.

HAYMAN, His Honour John David Woodburn; a Circuit Judge, 1976–92; *b* 24 Aug. 1918; *m* Jane (*née* Davison); two *s* four *d*. *Educ:* King Edward VII Sch., Johannesburg; St John's Coll., Cambridge (MA, LLM). Served with S African Forces, 1940–42. Called to the Bar, Middle Temple, 1945. Sometime Lecturer in Law: University Coll. of Wales, Aberystwyth; Leeds Univ.; Cambridge Univ.

HAYMAN, Prof. Walter Kurt, MA; ScD (Cambridge); FRS 1956; FIC; Professor of Pure Mathematics, University of York, 1985–93, now Emeritus; Senior Research Fellow, Imperial College, London, since 1995; *b* 6 Jan. 1926; *s* of late Franz Samuel Haymann and Ruth Therese (*née* Hensel); *m* 1st, 1947, Margaret Riley Crann (*d* 1994), MA Cantab, *d* of Thomas Crann, New Earswick, York; three *d*; 2nd, 1995, Dr Waficka Katifi. *Educ:* Gordonstoun Sch.; St John's Coll., Cambridge. Lecturer at King's Coll., Newcastle upon Tyne, 1947, and Fellow of St John's Coll., Cambridge, 1947–50; Lecturer, 1947, and Reader, 1953–56, Exeter; Prof. of Pure Maths, 1956–85, and Dean of RCS, 1978–81, Imperial Coll., London (FIC 1989). 1st Smiths prize, 1948, shared Adams Prize, 1949, Junior Berwick Prize, 1955; Senior Berwick Prize, 1964. Visiting Lecturer at Brown Univ., USA, 1949–50, at Stanford Univ., USA (summer) 1950 and 1955, and to the American Mathematical Soc., 1961. Co-founder with Mrs Hayman of British Mathematical Olympiad; Vice-Pres., London Mathematical Soc., 1982–84. Foreign Member: Finnish Acad. of Science and Letters; Accademia Nazionale dei Lincei, Rome; Corresp. Mem., Bavarian Acad. of Science. Hon. DSc: Exeter, 1981; Birmingham, 1985; NUI, 1997; Hon. Dr rer. nat. Giessen, 1992; Hon. DPhil Uppsala, 1992. de Morgan Medal, London Mathematical Soc., 1995. *Publications:* Multivalent Functions (Cambridge, 1958, 2nd edn 1994) Meromorphic Functions (Oxford, 1964); Research Problems in Function Theory (London, 1967); Subharmonic Functions, vol. I, 1976, vol. II, 1989; papers in various mathematical journals. *Recreations:* music, travel. *Address:* Department of Mathematics, Imperial College, Huxley Building, 180 Queen's Gate, SW7 2BZ; 104 Cranford Lane, Harlington, Middx UB3 5HB.

See also A. C. Hayman.

HAYMAN-JOYCE, Lt-Gen. Sir Robert (John), KCB 1996 CBE 1989 (OBE 1979); DL; Chairman, Raytheon Systems Ltd, since 2000; *b* 16 Oct. 1940; *s* of late Major T. F. Hayman-Joyce and B. C. Bruford; *m* 1968, Diana Livingstone-Bussell; two *s*. *Educ:* Radley Coll.; Magdalene Coll., Cambridge (MA). Commnd 11th Hussars (PAO), 1963; CO Royal Hussars (PWO), 1980–82; Comdr RAC, 1 (BR) Corps, 1983–85; Dir, UK Tank Programme, 1988; Dir Gen., Fighting Vehicles and Engr Equipment, later Land Fighting Systems, MoD (PE), 1989–92; Dir, RAC, 1992–94; Military Sec., MoD, 1994–95; MGO, 1995–98, and Dep. Chief of Defence Procurement (Ops), 1996–98. Non-exec. Dir, Alvis plc, 1999–. Col Comdt RAC, 1995–99. Chm. Trustees, Tank Mus., 1995–. DL Gwent, 1997. Hon. DSc Cranfield, 1998. *Recreations:* ski-ing, horses. *Address:* Raytheon Systems Ltd, 80 Park Lane, W1K 7TR; c/o Barclays Bank, 5 High Street, Andover, Hants SP10 1LN. *Clubs:* Cavalry and Guards; Leander (Henley-on-Thames).

HAYNES, Ernest Anthony, (Tony), CIGasE; Regional Chairman, British Gas plc, East Midlands, 1983–87; *b* 8 May 1922; *s* of Joseph Ernest Haynes and Ethel Rose (*née* Toomer); *m* 1946, Sheila Theresa (*née* Blane); two *s* two *d*. *Educ:* King Edward VI Grammar Sch., Totnes, S Devon. Joined Devonshire Regt, 1940; RMC Sandhurst, 1941; commnd Hampshire Regt, 1941; served in N Africa, Italy and NW Europe; Captain, 1946. Joined Torquay and Paignton Gas Co., 1947; appts with: West Midlands and Northern Gas Boards; Gas Council; Eastern; Dep. Chm., North Eastern, 1977–78; Dep. Chm., North Thames Gas, 1979–82. Vice-Pres., Internat. Colloquium about Gas Marketing, 1983–84. Silver Medal, IGasE, for paper, Energy Conservation—a marketing opportunity. *Recreations:* golf, flyfishing.

HAYNES, John Harold, OBE 1995; Chairman, Haynes Publishing Group plc; *b* 25 March 1938; *s* of Harold and Violet Haynes; *m* 1963, Annette Constance Coleman-Brown; three *s*. *Educ:* Sutton Valence Sch. Nat. Service, Flt Lieut, RAF, 1957. Wrote first car manual, Building an Austin 750 Special, at age of 16; founded J. Haynes & Co., 1960; Haynes Publishing Group plc, floated on London Stock Exchange, 1979. Founder, Haynes Motor Mus., Sparkford. Mem., Guild of Motoring Writers, 1974. *Publications:* numerous books on motors and motoring, incl. Haynes Owners Workshop Manuals. *Recreations:* reading, walking, motor car rallying, Haynes Motor Museum, opened 1985. *Address:* Haynes Publishing Group plc, Sparkford, near Yeovil, Som BA22 7JJ. *T:* (01963) 440635. *Club:* Royal Automobile.

HAYNES, Lawrence John; Chief Executive, 186k Ltd, since 2000; *b* 6 Dec. 1952; *s* of Donald H. Haynes and Irene E. Haynes (*née* Langford); *m* 1978, Carol Anne Nelson; one *d*, and two step *d*. *Educ:* Heriot-Watt Univ. (BA Hons Business Law 1983). FIHT 1995; FCIT 1996. RAF technician, 1969–78; Head of Contracts, British Aerospace (Space Systems), 1983–89; Legal Dir, 1989–90, Man. Dir, 1990–91, Microtel Communications; Man. Dir, British Aerospace Communications, 1991–92; Project Dir, British Aerospace, 1992–94; Chief Exec., Highways Agency, 1994–99; Partner and Hd of Ops, Eur. BPO, PricewaterhouseCoopers, 1999–2000. FRSA 1994. *Recreation:* sailing. *Address:* (office) The Spectrum, Queens Road, Reading RG1 4BQ.

HAYNES, Very Rev. Peter; Dean of Hereford, 1982–92, now Dean Emeritus; Vicar, St John Baptist, Hereford, 1983–92; *b* 24 April 1925; *s* of Francis Harold Stanley Haynes and Winifred Annie Haynes; *m* 1952, Ruth, *d* of late Dr Charles Edward Stainthorpe, MRCS, LRCP, Brunton Park, Newcastle upon Tyne; two *s*. *Educ:* St Brendan's Coll., Clifton; Selwyn Coll., Cambridge (MA); Cuddesdon Theol Coll., Oxford. Staff of Barclays Bank, 1941–43; RAF, 1943–47. Deacon 1952, Priest 1953. Asst Curate, Stokesley, 1952–54; Hessle, 1954–58; Vicar, St John's Drypool, Hull, 1958–63; Bishop's Chaplain for Youth and Asst Dir of Religious Educn, Dio. Bath and Wells, 1963–70; Vicar of Glastonbury, 1970–74 (with Godney from 1972); Archdeacon of Wells, Canon Residentiary and Prebendary of Huish and Brent in Wells Cathedral, 1974–82. Proctor in Convocation, 1976–82. Mem., Dioceses Commn, 1978–86. *Recreations:* sailing, model engineering. *Address:* 23 Conway Crescent, Burnham-on-Sea, Somerset TA8 2SL. *T:* (01278) 789048.

HAYTER, 3rd Baron *cr* 1927 of Chislehurst, Kent; **George Charles Hayter Chubb,** KCVO 1977; CBE 1976; Bt 1900; a Deputy Chairman, House of Lords, 1981–95; Managing Director, 1941–71, Chairman, 1957–81, Chubb & Son's Lock & Safe Co. Ltd; *b* 25 April 1911; *e s* of 2nd Baron Hayter and Mary (*d* 1948), *d* of J. F. Haworth; *S* father, 1967; *m* 1940, Elizabeth Anne Rumbold, MBE 1975; three *s* one *d. Educ:* Leys Sch., Cambridge; Trinity Coll., Cambridge (MA). Chairman: Royal Society of Arts, 1965–66; Management Cttee, King Edward's Hospital Fund for London, 1965–82; Executives Assoc. of GB, 1960; Duke of Edinburgh's Countryside in 1970 Cttee. President: Canada-United Kingdom Chamber of Commerce, 1966–67; Royal Warrant Holders Association, 1967; Business Equipment Trades Association, 1954–55. Mem., CoID, 1964–71; Chairman: EDC International Freight Movement, 1972–79; British Security Industry Assoc., 1973–77. Worshipful Company of Weavers': Liveryman, 1934–; Upper Bailiff, 1961–62. *Publication:* Security offered by Locks and Safes (Lecture, RSA), 1962. *Heir: s* Hon. (George) William (Michael) Chubb [*b* 9 Oct. 1943; *m* 1983, Waltraud, *yr d* of J. Flackl, Sydney, Australia; one *s*]. *Address:* Ashtead House, Ashtead, Surrey KT21 1LU. *T:* (01372) 273476.

HAYTER, Dianne; Chief Executive, Pelican Centre, since 1999; *b* 7 Sept. 1949; *d* of late Alec Hayter and late Nancy Hayter; *m* 1994, Prof. (Anthony) David Caplin. *Educ:* Trevelyan Coll., Durham Univ. (BA Hons Sociology and Social Admin). Research Assistant: General and Municipal Workers Union, 1970–72; European Trade Union Confedn (ETUC), Brussels, 1973; Research Officer, Trade Union Adv. Cttee to OECD (TUAC-OECD), Paris, 1973–74; Fabian Society: Asst Gen. Sec., 1974–76; Gen. Sec., 1976–82; Mem. Exec. Cttee, 1986–95; Chm., 1992–93; Journalist, A Week in Politics, Channel Four, 1982–84; Dir, Alcohol Concern, 1984–90; Chief Exec., European PLP, 1990–96; Dir of Corporate Affairs, Wellcome Trust, 1996–99. Member: Royal Commn on Criminal Procedure, 1978–80; Consumer Panel, FSA, 2001–. Chair, Camden Alcoholics Support Assoc., 1996–. Member: Exec. Cttee, London Labour Party, 1977–83; Nat. Constitution Cttee, Labour Party, 1987–98; Labour Party NEC, 1998–; Chm., Holborn & St Pancras Lab Party, 1990–93. Member: Labour Party; 300 Group; Soc. of Labour Lawyers; Socialist Health Assoc.; GMB; Poale Zion; Co-op. Party; Socialist Educn Assoc. JP Inner London, 1976–90. *Publications:* The Labour Party: crisis and prospects (Fabian Soc.), 1977; (contrib.) Labour in the Eighties, 1980. *Recreations:* reading, politics. *Address:* Pelican Centre, North Hampshire Hospital, Aldermaston Road, Basingstoke RG24 9NA. *T:* (01256) 314746, *Fax:* (home) (020) 7428 7526; *e-mail:* d.hayter@btinternet.com.

HAYTER, Paul David Grenville, LVO 1992; Clerk Assistant, since 1997, and Clerk of Legislation (formerly Principal Clerk of Public Bills), since 1994, House of Lords; *b* 4 Nov. 1942; *s* of Rev. Canon Michael George Hayter and Katherine Patricia Hayter (*née* Schofield); *m* 1973, Hon. Deborah Gervaise, *d* of Baron Maude of Stratford-upon-Avon, TD, PC; two *s* one *d. Educ:* Eton (King's Scholar); Christ Church, Oxford (MA). Clerk, Parlt Office, House of Lords, 1964; seconded as Private Sec. to Leader of House and Chief Whip, House of Lords, 1974–77; Clerk of Cttees, 1977; Principal Clerk of Cttees, 1985–90; Prin. Finance Officer, 1991–94; Reading Clerk, 1991–97. Sec., Assoc. of Lord-Lieutenants, 1977–91. *Recreations:* music, gardening, botanising, archery, painting. *Address:* Walnut House, Charlton, Banbury OX17 3DR.

HAYTHORNE, John; *see* Parsons, Sir R. E. C. F.

HAYTHORNTHWAITE, Richard Neil; Chief Executive, Invensys plc, since 2001; *b* 17 Dec. 1956; *s* of Christopher Scott Haythornthwaite and Angela Mary Haythornthwaite (*née* Painter); *m* 1979, Janeen Marie Dennis; one *s* one *d. Educ:* Colston's Sch., Bristol; Queen's Coll., Oxford (MA Geol.); Massachusetts Inst. of Technol. (SM Mgt). With BP, 1978–95, Pres., BP Venezuela, 1993–95; Commercial Dir, Premier Oil, 1995–97; Blue Circle Industries: Chief Exec., Heavy Bldgs Materials, Europe and Asia, 1997–99; Gp CEO, 1999–2001. Non-executive Director: Cookson Gp plc, 1999–; ICI plc, 2001–; Lafarge SA, 2001–. Chm., Centre for Creative Communities, 1996–. *Recreations:* tennis, ski-ing, travel, visual arts. *Address:* Invensys plc, Invensys House, Carlisle Place, SW1P 1BX. *Club:* Royal Automobile.

HAYTON, Prof. David John; Professor of Law, King's College London, since 1987; *b* 13 July 1944; *s* of Arthur Hayton and Beatrice (*née* Thompson); *m* 1979, Linda Patricia Rae; one *s. Educ:* Newcastle Royal GS; Univ. of Newcastle upon Tyne (LLB 1st Cl. Hons 1966; LLD 1980). Called to the Bar, Inner Temple, 1968, and Lincoln's Inn *aeg.* Lectr, Sheffield Univ., 1966–69; private practice, Lincoln's Inn, 1970–; Lectr, QMC, London, 1970–73; Lectr, Univ. of Cambridge and Fellow of Jesus Coll., 1973–87; Dean, Law Faculty, KCL, 1988–90; Chm., London Univ. Bd of Studies in Law, 1992–95. Vis. Lectr, Inns of Court Sch. of Law, 1971–84, Hon. Reader, 1984–96. A Recorder, 1992–2000; Actg Justice, Supreme Ct, Bahamas, 2000. Chm., Council, Pension Trustees Forum, 1992–95. Hon. Sec., SPTL, 1996–. Head of UK Delegns to The Hague Confs on Private Internat. Law, 1984, 1988. *Publications:* Registered Land, 1973, 3rd edn 1981; Law of Trusts, 1989, 3rd edn 1998; Hayton & Marshall: Cases & Commentary on Trusts, 6th edn 1975 to 10th edn 1996; Underhill & Hayton: Law of Trusts and Trustees, 13th edn 1979 to 15th edn 1995; Hayton Report on Financial Services and Trust Law, 1990; (ed) European Succession Laws, 1991, 2nd edn 1998; contribs to chapters in books on trusts, tax and estate planning; articles in learned jls. *Recreations:* working out in gym, watching Rugby and cricket, reading novels, wine tasting. *Address:* Law School, King's College, Strand, WC2R 2LS. *T:* (020) 7873 2452. *Clubs:* Athenæum, Royal Commonwealth Society, MCC.

HAYWARD, Sir Anthony (William Byrd), Kt 1978; *b* 29 June 1927; *s* of Eric and Barbara Hayward; *m* 1955, Jenifer Susan McCay; two *s* two *d. Educ:* Stowe Sch., Buckingham; Christ Church, Oxford. Served RNVR, 1945–48. With family business in Calcutta, 1948–57; Shaw Wallace & Co. Ltd, India, 1957–78; Man. Dir, Guthrie Berhad, Singapore, 1978–81; Pres. and Chief Exec. Officer, Private Investment Co. for Asia (PICA) SA, 1982–84. Pres., Associated Chambers of Commerce and Industry of India, 1977–78. *Recreations:* golf, photography, reading. *Address:* Manwood House, Sandwich, Kent CT13 9HX. *T:* (01304) 612244. *Clubs:* Oriental; Royal St George's Golf.
See also Ven. J. D. R. Hayward.

HAYWARD, Ven. Derek; *see* Hayward, Ven. J. D. R.

HAYWARD, Gerald William; HM Diplomatic Service, retired; *b* 18 Nov. 1927; *s* of late Frederick William Hayward and Annie Louise (*née* Glasscock); *m* 1956, Patricia Rhonwen (*née* Foster Hall); one *s* three *d. Educ:* Tottenham Grammar School; London and Hong Kong Univs. HM Forces, 1946–57. Joined HM Foreign (subseq. HM Diplomatic) Service, 1957; served Bangkok, Hong Kong, Copenhagen, Kuala Lumpur; FCO, 1980–82; (part-time), Cabinet Office,1984–92. *Address:* Fosters, 9 Ashley Road, Sevenoaks, Kent TN13 3AW. *T:* (01732) 451227.

HAYWARD, Sir Jack (Arnold), Kt 1986; OBE 1968; Chairman, Grand Bahama Development Co. Ltd and Freeport Commercial and Industrial Ltd, since 1976; *b* Wolverhampton, 14 June 1923; *s* of late Sir Charles Hayward, CBE and Hilda, *d* of John and Alexandra Arnold; *m* 1948, Jean Mary Forder; two *s* one *d. Educ:* Northaw Prep Sch.; Stowe Sch., Buckingham. Joined RAF, 1941; flying training in Clewiston, Florida, USA; active service as officer pilot in SE Asia Comd, demobilised as Flt-Lt, 1946. Joined Rotary Hoes Ltd, 1947; served S Africa branch until 1950. Founded USA operations Firth Cleveland Gp of Companies, 1951; joined Grand Bahama Port Authority Ltd, Freeport, Grand Bahama Island, 1956. President: Lundy Field Soc.; Wolverhampton Wanderers FC; Vice-Pres., SS Great Britain project; Hon. Life Vice-Pres., Maritime Trust, 1971. Paul Harris Fellow (Rotary), 1983. FRGS 1989. Hon. LLD Exeter, 1971; Hon. DBA Wolverhampton, 1994. William Booth Award, Salvation Army, 1987. *Recreations:* promoting British endeavours, mainly in sport; watching cricket; amateur dramatics; preserving the British landscape, keeping all things bright, beautiful and British. *Address:* Seashell Lane (PO Box F-40099), Freeport, Grand Bahama Island, Bahamas. *T:* (242) 3525165. *Clubs:* MCC (Hon. Life Mem.), Pratt's, Royal Air Force, Royal Automobile (Sen. One Hundred); Surrey CC (Hon. Life Mem.).

HAYWARD, Prof. Jack Ernest Shalom, FBA 1990; Research Professor of Politics, University of Hull, since 1999; *b* 18 Aug. 1931; *s* of Menahem and Stella Hayward; *m* 1965, Margaret Joy Glenn; one *s* one *d. Educ:* LSE (BSc Econ 1952; PhD 1958). Asst Lectr and Lectr, Univ. of Sheffield, 1959–63; Lectr and Sen. Lectr, Univ. of Keele, 1963–73; Prof. of Politics, Univ. of Hull, 1973–92; Prof. of Politics and Dir, European Studies Inst. and Centre for European Politics, Econs and Soc., Univ. of Oxford, and Fellow, St Antony's Coll., Oxford, 1993–98, now Prof. and Fellow Emeritus. Sen. Res. Fellow, Nuffield Coll., Oxford, 1968–69; Vis. Prof., Univ. of Paris III, 1979–80; Elie Halévy Vis. Prof., Inst. d'Etudes Politiques, Paris, 1990–91. Political Studies Association: Chm., 1975–77; Pres., 1979–81; Vice-Pres., 1981–. Editor, Political Studies, 1987–93. Chevalier de l'Ordre National du Mérite (France), 1980; Chevalier de la Légion d'Honneur (France), 1996. *Publications:* Private Interests and Public Policy, 1966; The One and Indivisible French Republic, 1973; The State and the Market Economy, 1986; After the French Revolution, 1991; De Gaulle to Mitterrand, 1993; Industrial Enterprise and European Integration, 1995; Governing the New Europe, 1995; The Crisis of Representation in Europe, 1995; Elitism, Populism and European Politics, 1996; The British Study of Politics in the Twentieth Century, 1999. *Recreations:* music, reading, walking. *Address:* Hurstwood, 17 Church Lane, Kirk Ella, Hull HU10 7TA. *Club:* Royal Commonwealth Society.

HAYWARD, Ven. (John) Derek (Risdon), OBE 2000; Vicar of Isleworth, 1964–94; General Secretary, Diocese of London, 1975–93; Archdeacon of Middlesex, 1974–75, now Archdeacon Emeritus; *b* 13 Dec. 1923; *s* of late Eric Hayward and of Barbara Olive Hayward; *m* 1965, Teresa Jane Kaye; one *d* (one *s* decd). *Educ:* Stowe; Trinity Coll., Cambridge (BA 1956, MA 1964). Served War of 1939–45, Lieut 27th Lancers, Middle East and Italy, 1943–45 (twice wounded). Man. Dir, Hayward Waldie & Co., Calcutta (and associated cos), 1946–53. Trinity Coll., Cambridge, 1953–56, Westcott House, Cambridge, 1956–57. Asst Curate, St Mary's Bramall Lane, Sheffield, 1957–58; Vicar, St Silas, Sheffield, 1959–63. Mem., General Synod, 1975–90. Chm., SCM Press, 1992–98 (Dir, 1985–99); Trustee: Church Urban Fund, 1987–94; Bath Preservation Trust, 1996–. Chm., Herschel Mus., Bath, 1996–. Chm. Council, St Luke's Hosp. for the Clergy, 1991–. Bronze Star (US) 1945. *Recreations:* walking, ski-ing, looking after my dog. *Address:* 5 Sion Hill Place, Bath BA1 5SJ. *T:* (01225) 336305, *Fax:* (01225) 421862.
See also Sir Anthony Hayward.

HAYWARD, Richard Michael; His Honour Judge Hayward; a Circuit Judge, since 1996; *b* 12 July 1946; *s* of George Michael Hayward and Esmé Mary Florence Hayward (*née* Howard); *m* 1969, Laura Louise Buchan; two *s* one *d. Educ:* Highgate Sch.; Inns of Court Sch. of Law. Called to the Bar, Middle Temple, 1969; in practice at the Bar, 1970–96; Asst Recorder, 1990–94; Recorder, 1994–96. *Recreations:* golf, painting, horses, gardening. *Club:* Rye Golf.

HAYWARD, Robert Antony, OBE 1991; Chief Executive, Brewers and Licensed Retailers Association, since 1999; *b* 11 March 1949; *s* of late Ralph and of Mary Hayward. *Educ:* Abingdon Sch.; Maidenhead Grammar Sch.; University Coll. of Rhodesia; BSc Econ Hons London (external). Personnel Officer, Esso Petroleum, 1971–75; Personnel Manager: Coca Cola Bottlers (S & N) Ltd, 1975–79; GEC Large Machines, 1979–82; Dir Gen., British Soft Drinks Assoc., 1993–99. MP (C) Kingswood, 1983–92; contested (C): Kingswood, 1992, Christchurch, July 1993. PPS to Minister for Corporate and Consumer Affairs, 1985–87, to Minister for Industry, 1986–87, to Sec. of State for Transport, 1987–89. Mem., Commons Select Cttee on Energy, 1983–85. Dir, Stonewall Gp, 1997–. *Recreations:* Rugby, psephology. *Address:* (office) 42 Portman Square, W1H 0BB. *T:* (020) 7486 4831; 11 Grosvenor Park, SE5 0NQ.

HAYWARD ELLEN, Patricia Mae; *see* Lavers, P. M.

HAYWARD SMITH, Rodger; QC 1988; a Recorder, since 1986; *b* 25 Feb. 1943; *s* of Frederick Ernest Smith and late Heather Hayward (*née* Rodgers); *m* 1975, Gillian Sheila (*née* Johnson); one *s* one *d. Educ:* Brentwood Sch.; St Edmund Hall, Oxford (MA). Called to the Bar, Gray's Inn, 1967; a Deputy High Ct Judge, 1990–. A Legal Assessor, GMC, 2000–. Ed. and contrib., Child Law Bulletin, 1994–2001; contrib., Solicitors Law Jl, 2001–. *Publication:* (ed jtly and contrib.) Jackson's Matrimonial Finance and Taxation, 5th edn 1992, 7th edn 2001. *Address:* 1 King's Bench Walk, Temple, EC4Y 7DB. *Club:* Toppesfield Ramblers.

HAYWOOD, Sir Harold, KCVO 1988; OBE 1974; DL; Chairman, BBC/ITC Central Appeals Advisory Committee, 1989–93; Chairman, YMCA, 1989–93; *b* 30 Sept. 1923; *s* of Harold Haywood and Lilian (*née* Barrett); *m* 1944, Amy (*née* Richardson); three *s. Educ:* Guild Central Sch., Burton-on-Trent; Westhill Coll. of Educn, Selly Oak, Birmingham (Certificate of Educn, 1948). Organiser, St John's Clubland, Sheffield, 1948–51; Tutor, Westhill Coll. of Educn, 1951–53; Regional Organiser, Methodist Youth Dept, 1954–55; Dir of Education and Trng, 1955–66, Dir of Youth Work, 1966–74, NAYC; Gen. Sec., Educnl Interchange Council, 1974–77; Dir, Royal Jubilee and Prince's Trusts, 1977–88. Chm., Assoc. of Charitable Foundns, 1989–92; Trustee, Charities Aid Foundn, 1988–98 (Chm., Grants Council, 1989–97); Patron, Kids Internat. UK, 1994–; Vice-President: Commonwealth Youth Exchange Council, 1988–; Derbys Community Foundn, 1998–; Chm., Multi-Faith Campaign, Univ. of Derby, 1999–; Pres., RBL, Oakwood, Derbys, 2000–. DL Greater London, 1983. FRSA. *Recreations:* the garden, books, theatre. *Address:* Thatched House, 2 Smalley Drive, Oakwood, Derbyshire DE21 2SF. *T:* (01332) 281948. *Clubs:* Athenæum, Civil Service, Penn.

HAYWOOD, Nigel Robert; HM Diplomatic Service; Assistant Director (Personnel), Foreign and Commonwealth Office, since 2000; *b* 17 March 1955; *yr s* of late Leslie Haywood and of Peggy (*née* Webb, now Sewell); *m* 1979, Mary Louise Smith; three *s. Educ:* Truro Sch.; New Coll., Oxford (MA, MPhil). MIL 1988. Lt, RAEC, 1977–80. Joined HM Diplomatic Service, 1983: Second, later First, Sec., Budapest, 1985–89; FCO, 1989–92; Dep. Consul-Gen., Johannesburg, 1992–96; Counsellor and Dep. Head, UK

the H Bomb, 1960; Labour Britain and the World, 1963; Healey's Eye, 1980; Labour and a World Society, 1985; Beyond Nuclear Deterrence, 1986; The Time of My Life (autobiog.), 1989; When Shrimps Learn to Whistle (essays), 1990; My Secret Planet, 1992; Denis Healey's Yorkshire Dales, 1995; Healey's World, 2002. *Recreations:* travel, photography, music, painting. *Address:* Pingles Place, Alfriston, East Sussex BN26 5TT.

HEALEY, Lady; Edna May Healey; writer; *b* 14 June 1918; *d* of Rose and Edward Edmunds; *m* 1945, Baron Healey, *qv*: one *s* two *d*. *Educ:* Bell's Grammar School, Coleford, Glos; St Hugh's College, Oxford (BA, Dip Ed). Taught English and History: Keighley Girls' Grammar School, 1940–44; Bromley Girls' High Sch., 1944–47; freelance lecturer, England and America; television writer and presenter; radio writer and broadcaster. *Publications:* Lady Unknown: life of Angela Burdett-Coutts, 1978; Wives of Fame, 1986; Coutts & Co. 1692–1992: the portrait of a private bank, 1992; The Queen's House: a history of Buckingham Palace, 1997; Emma Darwin, 2001. *Recreations:* gardening, listening to music. *Address:* Pingles Place, Alfriston, East Sussex BN26 5TT.

HEALEY, Sir Charles Edward C.; *see* Chadwyck-Healey.

HEALEY, Deryck John, FRSA 1978; FCSD; artist, sculptor; *b* 30 Jan. 1937; *s* of Leonard Melvon Healey and Irene Isabella Healey (*née* Ferguson); *m* 1962, Mary Elizabeth Pitt Booth (decd); two *s*. *Educ:* Northlands High Sch., Natal, SA (Victoria League Empire Scholar; DipAD, SA, 1955; Golden Jubilee Cert. of Merit, 1957); Manchester Polytechnic (DipAd 1958, Textile Design Prize, 1957, 1958; Design Travel Bursary, 1958; Royal Manch. Inst. Cert. of Merit, 1958; Calico Printers' Assoc. Fellow, 1961–62). Design Man., Good Hope Textiles, SA, 1959–66; Chairman: Deryck Healey Associates, London, 1966–85; Deryck Healey International, 1969–85; Dreamshire, 1985–87; Design Man., WPM London (Wallpaper mfrs), 1966–68; ICI Design Studio Manager, Asst to Elsbeth Juda, 1968–80; Consultant, D. H. I. Interiors Ltd, 1983–85; Design Consultant, Wedgwood, 1984–88. Chm., CNAA Textile and Fashion Bd, 1971–81; Member: CNAA Art and Design Cttee, 1971–81; Design Council Textile Design Selection Cttee, 1978–87; Craft Council Bd, 1983–85 (Textile Panel, 1980; Finance and Gen. Purposes Cttee, 1983–85; Chairman: Textile Develt Group, 1982–84; Projects and Organisations Cttee, 1983–85). RSA: Annual Sponsor, D. Healey Fashion and Colour Bursaries, 1978–85; Mem. Bursary Bd, 1982–88. Patron, New Art Tate Gall., 1983–. Member: Contemp. Art Soc., 1982–; ICA, 1970–; Chelsea Arts Club, 1982–88; Friend of RA, 1980–. SIAD: Mem., British Design Export Gp, 1980; Chm., Textile and Fashion Gp, 1966–67. External Examiner, Textile and Fashion courses: CNAA BA and MA; Liverpool, BA, 1978–80; Manchester, MA, 1976–79; Kingston, BA, 1978–80; St Martin's, BA, 1978–80; Glasgow, BA, 1979–82; RCA, Textiles, 1980; Adviser and External Examiner, Middx Polytechnic, BA, 1982–86; External Examiner: London Coll. of Furniture, BTEC, 1985–86; BA Fashion, St Martin's Sch. of Art, 1985–87. Vis Prof., RCA. Exhibitions: Salama-Caro Gall., London, 1990, 1991, 1994; Frankfurt Internat. Art Fair, 1990; Venice, 1990; Internat. Art Fairs, Cologne and Chicago, 1990; Phoenix Univ., Arizona, 1991; Fosbury, UK, 1991; Santa Fé, Mexico, 1992; Galerie Langer Fain, Paris, 1992; Koplin Gall., LA, 1993; Art of Concern, Base, London, 1994; Deaf, Edinburgh, 1996; Behind Walls, RSA, 1997; Back to Front, Natal Soc. of Art Gall., Durban, 1998; Blue Gall., London, 1998; Fragments, Natal Soc. of Art Gall., Durban, 2001; Words, Les Livres Gall., Colchester, 2001. Installation, Seamen's Mission, Glasgow, 1992; special commn sculpture, Manchester Internat. Concert Hall, 1996. FCSD (FSIAD 1964). Hon. FRCA 2000. CoID Design Award, 1964; Queen's Award to Industry for Export, 1974; RSA Bicentenary Medal, 1981; Textile Institute Design Medal, 1982. *Publications:* Colour, 1980 (Mem. Editorial Bd and contrib.); Living with Colour, 1982; The New Art of Flower Design, 1986; Big Names, 1991; Open Studio, 1994; Our Island Garden Project, 1995. *Address:* Ballast Quay House, Ballast Quay Road, Wivenhoe CO7 9JT. *Clubs:* various.

HEALEY, Edna May; *see* Lady Healey.

HEALEY, John; MP (Lab) Wentworth, since 1997; Parliamentary Under-Secretary of State, Department for Education and Skills, since 2001; *b* 13 Feb. 1960; *s* of Aidan Healey, OBE and Jean Healey; *m* 1993, Jackie Bate; one *s*. *Educ:* Christ's Coll., Cambridge (schol., BA 1982). Charity campaigner, 1984–90; Campaigns Manager, Issue Communications, 1990–92; Head of Communications, MSF, 1992–94; Campaigns Dir, TUC, 1994–97. PPS to Chancellor of the Exchequer, 1999–2001. Contested (Lab) Ryedale, 1992. *Address:* House of Commons, SW1A 0AA; *e-mail:* healeyj@parliament.uk.

HEALY, Bernadine P., (Mrs F. Loop), MD; Dean, College of Medicine, Ohio State University, since 1995; *b* 2 Aug. 1944; *d* of Michael J. Healy and Violet (*née* McGrath); *m* 1985, Floyd Loop; two *d*. *Educ:* Vassar Coll. (AB *summa cum laude* 1965); Harvard Med. Sch. (MD *cum laude* 1970). Intern in medicine, 1970–71, asst resident, 1971–72, Johns Hopkins Hosp., Balt.; Staff Fellow, Sect. Pathology, Nat. Heart, Lung and Blood Inst., NIH, 1972–74; Johns Hopkins University School of Medicine: Fellow, Cardiovascular Div., Dept of Medicine, 1974–76; Fellow, Dept of Pathology, 1975–76; Asst Prof. of Medicine and Pathology, 1976–81; Associate Prof. of Medicine, 1977–82; Asst Dean for Postdoctoral Programs and Faculty Develt, 1979–84; Associate Prof. of Pathology, 1981–84; Prof. of Medicine, 1982–84; Active Staff, Medicine and Pathology, 1976, Dir, Coronary Care Unit, 1977–84, Johns Hopkins Hosp.; Dep. Dir, Office of Sci. and Technol. Policy, Exec. Office of Pres., White House, Washington, 1984–85; Chm., Res. Inst., Cleveland Clinic Foundn, 1985–91; Dir, NIH, 1991–93; Sen. Policy Advr, Page Center for Health and Science Policy, Cleveland Clinic Foundn, 1993–95. *Address:* Ohio State University, 254 Meiling Hall, 370 West 9th, Columbus, OH 43210, USA.

HEALY, Prof. John Francis, MA, PhD; Professor of Classics, London University, 1966–90, now Professor Emeritus; Chairman of Department, Royal Holloway and Bedford New College, 1985–88 (Head of Department, Royal Holloway College, 1966–85); *b* 27 Aug. 1926; *s* of late John Healy and Iris Maud (*née* Cutland); *m* 1st, 1957, Carol Ann McEvoy; one *s*; 2nd, 1985, Barbara Edith Henshall. *Educ:* Trinity Coll., Cambridge (Open Exhbn in Classics 1943; Classical Prelim. Cl. 1 1944; Classical Tripos: 1st Cl. Pt I 1949, 1st Cl. Pt II 1950 (dist. Cl. Archaeol.); Sen. Schol. 1950; BA 1950, MA 1952, PhD 1955). War service, 1944–48. Captain, Intelligence Corps, 1946–48. Walston student, Brit. Sch. of Archaeol., Athens, 1950; G. C. Winter Warr Schol., Cambridge, 1951; Manchester University: Asst Lectr in Classics, 1953–56; Lectr in Classics and Class. Archaeol., 1956–61; London University: Reader in Greek, Bedford Coll., 1961–66; Chm., Bd of Studies in Classics, 1979–81; Dean of Faculty of Arts, Royal Holloway Coll., 1978–81. Chm. Finance Cttee, Inst. of Classical Studies, London, 1967–88. FRNS 1950; FRSA 1971; MRI 1979. *Publications:* contrib. (A. Rowe) Cyrenaican Expeditions of the University of Manchester, 1955–57; Mining and Metallurgy in the Greek and Roman World, 1978, rev. and trans. edn, Miniere e Metallurgia nel Mondo Greco e Romano, 1993; Sylloge Nummorum Graecorum, vol. VII, The Raby and Güterbock collections in Manchester University Museum, 1986; Pliny the Elder, Natural History, 1991; Pliny the Elder, On Science and Technology, 1999; articles and reviews in Jl of Hellenic St., Numismatic Chron., Nature, Amer. Num. Soc.'s Mus. Notes, Jl of Metals, Class. Rev., Gnomon. *Recreations:* travel, music, creative gardening. *Club:* Cambridge Union Society.

HEALY, Maurice Eugene, OBE 2001; Director, National Consumer Council, 1987–91; *b* 27 Nov. 1933; *s* of late Thomas Healy and Emily Healy (*née* O'Mahoney); *m* 1958, Jose Barbara Speller Dewdney; two *d* (and one *d* decd). *Educ:* Downside School; Peterhouse, Cambridge (BA Classics). Nat. service, Royal Artillery, 1954–56. BoT, 1956–60; Consumers' Assoc., working on Which?, 1960–76; Head of Editl Dept and Editor of Which?, 1973–76; Nat. Consumer Council, 1977–91. Chairman, Consumer Policy Committee: BSI, 1993–98; ISO, 1996–98; Member: Council, Bureau Européen des Unions de Consommateurs, 1977–91; Council, Insurance Ombudsman Bureau, 1991– (Chm., 1996–); Code of Banking Practice Review Cttee, 1991–99; Indep. Management Cttee, Optical Consumer Complaints Service, 1992–99; Bd, Jazz Services Ltd, 1992–; Consumer Panel, PIA, 1993–98; Assessor to Auld Cttee on reform of shop hours, 1984. Chm., Patients' Assoc., 1991–93. Trustee, European Res. Inst. for Consumer Affairs, 1990–. Hon. Vice-Pres., NFCG. Chm. of Governors, Highgate Wood School, 1983–86. FRSA. Hon. Mem., Inst. of Consumer Affairs; Assoc. Mem., UK Ombudsman Assoc. *Publications:* contribs to Which? and Nat. Consumer Council and other jls and conf. papers. *Recreations:* jazz, Irish music, Shona sculpture. *Address:* 15 Onslow Gardens, Muswell Hill, N10 3JT. *T:* (020) 8883 8955. *Clubs:* Ronnie Scott's, Burmese Cat.

HEALY, Prof. Thomas Edward John, MD; FRCA; consultant anaesthetist, since 1997; Professor of Anaesthesia, University of Manchester, 1981–97, now Emeritus; *b* 11 Dec. 1935; *s* of late Thomas Healy and Gladys May Healy; *m* 1966, Lesley Edwina Sheppard; one *s* three *d*. *Educ:* Guy's Hosp. Med. Sch., London Univ. (BSc 1st Cl. Hons 1961; MB BS 1964; DA 1967; MD 1975; Hon. MSc 1982); Cardiff Univ. (LLM 1999). LRCP 1963; MRCS 1963; FRCA (FFARCS 1968). Consultant Anaesthetist i/c Intensive Care, Gen. Hosp., then Queen's Med. Centre, Nottingham, 1971–81. Mem., Med. Adv. Bd, Med. Litigation, 2000–. Editor-in-Chief, European Jl Anaesthesiology, 1994–99; Mem. Editl Bd, Jl Evaluation in Clinical Practice, 1995–99. Mem., S Manchester HA, 1981–89. Mem. and Chm., tribunal and appeals cttees. Royal College of Anaesthetists: examr for Fellowship exam, 1976–89; Mem. Council, 1989–97; Chm., Professional Standards Cttee, 1994–97; Section of Anaesthesia, Royal Society of Medicine: Mem. Council, 1985–; Hon. Sec., 1986–88; Pres., 1996–97; Member Council: Assoc. Anaesthetists GB and Ireland, 1973–76; Anaesthetic Res. Soc., 1978–81; Postgrad. Med. Fellowship, 1991–94; Academician, 1980, Mem., Senate and Exec. Cttee, 1984–, European Acad. Anaesthesiology. Special Visitor, Shanghai Med. Coll., 1994–. Gov., Linacre Centre for Health Care Ethics, 1999–. Hon. Mem., Romanian Soc. Anaesthesiology, 1995. Chm., Fundraising Cttee, ReachOut, 1998–. *Publications:* Aids to Anaesthesia 1: the basic sciences, 1980 (trans. Spanish), 3rd edn 1991; Aids to Anaesthesia 2: clinical practice, 1984, 2nd edn 1999; (ed) Anaesthesia for Day Case Surgery, 1990; (ed) Wylie and Churchill-Davidson's A Practice of Anaesthesia, 6th edn 1995; numerous scientific papers. *Recreations:* walking, reading, keep fit, sleeping. *Address:* Department of Anaesthesia, Manchester Royal Infirmary, Oxford Road, Manchester M13 9WL.

HEALY, Tim T.; *see* Traverse-Healy.

HEANEY, Seamus Justin, FBA; Member of Irish Academy of Letters; Professor of Poetry, Oxford University, 1989–94; Boylston Professor of Rhetoric and Oratory at Harvard University (formerly Visiting Professor), 1985–97; Ralph Waldo Emerson Poet in Residence, Harvard University, since 1998; *b* 13 April 1939; *s* of Patrick and Margaret Heaney; *m* 1965, Marie Devlin; two *s* one *d*. *Educ:* St Columb's College, Derry; Queen's University, Belfast (BA first cl. 1961). Teacher, St Thomas's Secondary Sch., Belfast, 1962–63; Lectr, St Joseph's Coll. of Educn, Belfast, 1963–66; Lectr, Queen's Univ., Belfast, 1966–72; free-lance writer, 1972–75; Lectr, Carysfort Coll., 1975–81. Corresp. FBA, 1999. Hon. DLitt Oxon, 1997. Bennett Award, 1982; Nobel Prize for Literature, 1995. *Publications:* Preoccupations: Selected Prose 1968–1978, 1980; The Government of the Tongue, 1988; The Cure at Troy (a version of Sophocles' Philoctetes), 1990; The Redress of Poetry, 1995; (jtly) Homage to Robert Frost, 1998; *poetry:* Eleven Poems, 1965; Death of a Naturalist, 1966 (Somerset Maugham Award, 1967; Cholmondeley Award, 1968); Door into the Dark, 1969; Wintering Out, 1972; North, 1975 (W. H. Smith Award; Duff Cooper Prize); Field Work, 1979; Selected Poems, 1965–1975, 1980; (ed with Ted Hughes) The Rattle Bag, 1982; Sweeney Astray, 1984, rev. edn as Sweeney's Flight, (with photographs by Rachel Giese), 1992; Station Island, 1984; The Haw Lantern, 1987 (Whitbread Award, 1987); New Selected Poems 1966–1987, 1990; Seeing Things, 1991; The Spirit Level (Whitbread Book of the Year), 1996; (ed with Ted Hughes) The School Bag, 1997; Opened Ground: poems 1966–1996, 1998; trans., Beowulf (Whitbread Book of the Year), 1999; Electric Light, 2000. *Address:* c/o Faber & Faber, 3 Queen Square, WC1N 3RU.

HEANLEY, Charles Laurence, TD 1950; FRCS; Consulting Surgeon; *b* 28 Feb. 1907; *e s* of Dr C. M. Heanley; *m* 1935; three *s*. *Educ:* Epsom Coll.; Downing Coll., Cambridge (Exhib., Schol.); London Hosp. BA Cambridge (Nat. Sci. Tripos) 1929, MA 1934; MRCS, LRCP 1932; MB, BCh Cambridge 1934; FRCS 1933; MRCP 1935. London Hosp., 1929; Surg. First Asst, 1936. Served War of 1939–45; France, Surgical Specialist, 17th Gen. Hosp., 1939–40; Surgeon Specialist, RAMC Park Prewitt Plastic Unit, 1941–42; India, OC No 3 British Maxillo-Facial Surgical Unit and Lieut-Col OC Surgical Div., 1942–45; Surg. in charge of Dept of Plastic Surg., London Hosp. (now Royal London Hosp.), 1946–64. Cons. Surg. Worthing Hosp., Bethnal Green Hosp., and Plastic Unit Queen Victoria Hosp., East Grinstead, 1945; Plastic Surg. London Hosp.; Hon. Cons. Plastic Surg. Royal National and Golden Square Hosps, 1969. *Publications:* varied medical articles. *Recreations:* swimming, archæology. *Address:* Vainona, St George, Woodmancote, Henfield, West Sussex BN5 9ST. *T:* (01273) 492947.

HEAP, Sir Brian; *see* Heap, Sir R. B.

HEAP, Dr John Arnfield, CMG 1991; Director, 1992–97, Executive Director, 1998, Scott Polar Research Institute, Cambridge University; *b* 5 Feb. 1932; *s* of late David and Ann Heap; *m* 1960, Margaret Grace Gillespie (*née* Spicer); one *s* two *d*. *Educ:* Leighton Park Sch.; Edinburgh Univ. (MA 1955); Clare Coll., Cambridge (PhD 1962). Falkland Islands Dependencies Survey, 1955–62; Res. Fellow, Dept of Geology, 1962–63, Great Lakes Res. Div., 1963–64, Univ. of Michigan; Polar Regions Section, FCO, 1964–92: Head of Section, 1975–92; Adminr, British Antarctic Territory, 1989–92. Mem., UK Delegns to Antarctic Treaty Consultative Meetings, 1966–92; UK Comr, Commn for Conservation of Antarctic Marine Living Resources, 1982–92. Treas., Internat. Glaciological Soc., 1980–; Chairman: UK Antarctic Heritage Trust, 1996–; Trans-Antarctic Assoc., 1998–. Mem. (Lib Dem), S Cambs DC, 1999–. Editor, Handbook of the Antarctic Treaty System, 1977–94. *Publication:* Sea Ice in the Antarctic, 1963. *Address:* The Old House, 25 High Street, Harston, Cambridge CB2 5PX. *T:* (01223) 870288; Acharonich, Ulva Ferry, Isle of Mull PA73 6LY. *T:* (01688) 500219.

HEAP, Sir Peter (William), KCMG 1995 (CMG 1987); HM Diplomatic Service, retired; *b* 13 April 1935; *s* of Roger and Dora Heap; *m* 1st, Helen Wilmerding; two *s* two *d*; 2nd, Dorrit Breitenstein; 3rd, 1986, Ann Johnson; one step *s* one step *d*. *Educ:* Bristol Cathedral Sch.; Merton Coll., Oxford. 2nd Lt Glos Regt and RWAFF, 1954–56. Joined Diplomatic Service, 1959; Third Sec., Dublin, 1960; Second Sec., Ottawa, 1960; First

Sec., Colombo, 1963–66; seconded to MoD, 1966–68; FO, 1968–71; Dep. Dir-Gen., British Information Services, New York, 1971–76; Counsellor, Caracas, 1976–80; Head of Energy, Science and Space Dept, FCO, 1980–83; High Comr to the Bahamas, 1983–86; Minister and Dep. High Comr, Lagos, 1986–89; British Trade Comr, Hong Kong, and Consul-Gen., Macau, 1989–92; Ambassador to Brazil, 1992–95. Advisor: to Bd, HSBC Investment Bank, 1995–98; BOC Gp, 1997–2001; Consultant: Amerada Hess plc, 1996–; non-exec. Dir, D. S. Wolf Internat., 1998–99. Chairman: Brazilian Chamber of Commerce in GB, 1996–; British Business Adv. Forum for Brazil, 1998–; Mem., Internat. Cttee, CBI, 1997–. *Address:* (home) 6 Carlisle Mansions, Carlisle Place, SW1P 1HX.

HEAP, Sir (Robert) Brian, Kt 2001; CBE 1994; FRS 1989; FRSC; FIBiol; Master, St Edmund's College, Cambridge, since 1996; *b* 27 Feb. 1935; *s* of late Bertram Heap and Eva Mary Heap (*née* Melling); *m* 1961, Marion Patricia Grant; two *s* one *d*. *Educ:* New Mills Grammar Sch.; Univ. of Nottingham (BSc, PhD); King's Coll., Cambridge (MA, ScD). Univ. Demonstrator, Cambridge, 1960; Lalor Res. Fellow, ARC Babraham, Cambridge, 1963; Staff Mem., AFRC Babraham, 1964–95: Hd, Dept of Physiology, 1976; Hd, Cambridge Res. Station, 1986; Dir, Inst. of Animal Physiol. and Genetics Res., Cambridge and Edinburgh, 1989–93; Dir of Science, AFRC, 1991–94; Dir, AFRC Babraham Inst., 1993–94. Vis. Prof., Univ. of Nairobi, 1974; Vis. Res. Fellow, Murdoch Univ., 1976; Special Prof., Univ. of Nottingham, 1988–; Vis. Prof., Univ. of Guelph, 1990; Vis. Sen. Fellow, Sch. of Clin. Medicine, Univ. of Cambridge, 1994–2001. Mem., Scientific Adv. Bd, Merck, Sharp and Dohme, 1990–98. UK Rep. NATO Sci. Cttee, Brussels, 1998–. Member: Exec. Council, ESF, 1994–97; Council, Royal Soc., 1994– (Foreign Sec. and Vice-Pres., 1996–2001); Nuffield Council on Bioethics, 1997–2001; Member Committee: Soc. for Study of Fertility, 1967–72; Jls of Reproduction and Fertility Ltd; Bibliography of Reproduction, 1967–70; Soc. and Jl of Endocrinology, 1980–84; Placenta; Oxford Reviews of Reproductive Biology, 1981–94. Consultant: WHO, Geneva, 1975–82; China, 1981–85. Chairman: Ciba Foundn Symposium, 1978; Harden Conf., 1984. Pres., Inst. of Biol., 1996–98. Lectures: Hammond, Soc. for Study of Fertility, 1986; Linacre, Oxford Univ., 1993; Annual, RASE, 1995; Robinson Meml, Univ. of Nottingham, 1997; Rutherford Meml, South Africa, 1999. Hon. Foreign Fellow, Korean Acad. of Sci. and Technol., 1998. Hon. Fellow, Green Coll., Oxford, 1997. Hon. DSc: Nottingham, 1994; York, 2001. Research Medallist, RASE, 1976; Inventor's Award, AFRC, 1980. *Publications:* sci. papers on reproductive biology, endocrinology, and biotechnology, in various biol and med. jls. *Recreations:* music, hiking, kite flying. *Address:* St Edmund's College, Cambridge CB3 0BN.

HEAPS, Jeremy David P.; *see* Pickett-Heaps.

HEAPS, John Edward; Chief Executive, Britannia Building Society, 1993–99; *b* 24 Feb. 1939; *m* 1985, Shirley (*née* Jones); two *d*; one *s* one *d* from previous marr. *Educ:* Caldy Grange Grammar Sch., W Kirby; Oldershaw Grammar Sch., Wallasey. FCIB (FCBSI 1992). Colne Building Society: Sec., 1972; Chief Exec., 1972–80; Chief Exec. and Dir, 1980–83; Britannia Building Society: Dep. Gen. Manager, 1983–87; Gen. Manager, 1987–91; Inf. Systems Dir, 1991; Dep. Man. Dir, 1991–93. Chm., BSA, 1998–99 (Mem. Council, 1994; Dep. Chm., 1996–98); Dir, Bldg Socs Trust, 1997–99. Dir, Staffs TEC, 1996–99. Trustee, Keele Develt Trust, 1996–. Mem. Court, Univ. of Keele, 1994–. MIMgt. *Recreations:* family pursuits. *Address:* Top House Farm, Dodsleigh, Stoke on Trent, Staffs ST10 4QA.

HEARD, Peter Graham, CB 1987; FRICS; IRRV; Deputy Chief Valuer, Valuation Office, Board of Inland Revenue, 1983–89; *b* 22 Dec. 1929; *s* of late Sidney Horwood Heard and Doris Winifred Heard, MBE; *m* 1953, Ethne Jean Thomas; two *d*. *Educ:* Exmouth Grammar School. Articled to W. W. Needham, 1946; joined Valuation Office, 1950; served in Exeter, Kidderminster, Dudley, Leeds; District Valuer, Croydon, 1971; Superintending Valuer, Chief Valuer's Office, 1973; Asst Sec., Bd of Inland Revenue, 1975; Superintending Valuer, Midlands, 1977; Asst Chief Valuer, 1978. *Recreations:* cricket, golf, countryside, walking the dog, theatre. *Address:* Romany Cottage, High Street, Lindfield, Sussex RH16 2HR. *T:* (01444) 482095. *Clubs:* MCC, Civil Service.

HEARN, Barry Maurice William, FCA; Chairman, Matchroom Ltd, since 1982; *b* 19 June 1948; *s* of George Sydney and Barbara Winifred Hearn; *m* 1970, Susan Clark; one *s* one *d*. *Educ:* Buckhurst Hill Grammar School. Owner and Chm., Leyton Orient FC, 1995–. Chm., Professional Darts Corp., 2001–. *Publication:* The Business, 1990. *Recreations:* cricket, fishing, snooker, golf. *Address:* Matchroom Ltd, 10 Western Road, Romford, Essex RM1 3JT. *T:* (01708) 782200.

HEARN, David Anthony; General Secretary, Broadcasting Entertainment Cinematograph Theatre Union, 1991–93 (General Secretary, 1987–90, Joint General Secretary, 1984–87, Broadcasting and Entertainment Trades Alliance); Chairman, Litho and Digital Impressions Ltd, since 1997; *b* 4 March 1929; *s* of James Wilfrid Laurier Hearn and Clara (*née* Barlow); *m* 1952, Anne Beveridge; two *s*. *Educ:* Trinity Coll., Oxford (MA). Asst to Gen. Sec., Assoc. of Broadcasting Staff, 1955; subseq. Asst Gen. Sec., then Dep. Gen. Sec.; Gen. Sec., Assoc. of Broadcasting and Allied Staffs, 1972–84. Dir, Nat. Campaign for the Arts Ltd, 1986–93. Chm., Film and Electronic Media Cttee, Fedn of Entertainment Unions, 1991–93; Mem., British Screen Adv. Council, 1987; President: Internat. Fedn of Audio Visual Unions, 1991–93 (Gen. Sec., W European Sect., 1984–91); Eur. Cttee of Trade Unions in Arts, Mass Media and Entertainment, 1992–93. Sen. Res. Fellow, Nuffield Coll., Oxford, 1970–71. *Address:* 4 Stocks Tree Close, Yarnton, Kidlington, Oxon OX5 1LU. *T:* (01865) 374613.

HEARN, Donald Peter; Bursar and Fellow of Clare College, Cambridge, since 2001; *b* 2 Nov. 1947; *s* of late Peter James Hearn and Anita Margaret Hearn; *m* 1973, Rachel Mary Arnold; two *d*. *Educ:* Clifton College; Selwyn College, Cambridge (MA). FCA. Ernst & Whinney, 1969–79; Group Financial Controller, Saga Holidays, 1979–83; Chief Financial Officer, Lee Valley Water Co., 1983–86; Finance Dir, 1986–2001, Sec., 1989–2001, RHS. Gen. Comr for Taxes, 1990–. Mem., F and GP Cttee, RPMS, Univ. of London, 1991–97; Imperial College: Chm., Audit Cttee, 1996–; Mem. Court, 1998–; Mem., House Cttee, 1998–; Gov., 2001–; Mem., Selwyn Coll. Assoc. Cttee, 1997–2001; Governor, Woldingham Sch., 1990–93. *Recreations:* gardening, running. *Address:* Clare College, Cambridge CB2 1TL. *T:* (01223) 333222.

HEARN, Rt Rev. George Arthur; Bishop of Rockhampton, 1981–96; Vicar of Canterbury, diocese of Melbourne, 1996–2001; *b* 17 Nov. 1935; *s* of Albert Frederick and Edith Maxham Hearn; *m* 1957, Adele Taylor; two *s* one *d*. *Educ:* Northcote High School; University High School; Latrobe Univ., Melbourne. BA, ThL 1965, DipRE, ThSchol Aust. Coll. of Theology; MACE. Deacon 1964, priest 1965, Diocese of Gippsland; Curate of Traralgon, 1964–66; Vicar of Omeo, 1966–69; Rector of Wonthaggi, 1969–73; Rector of Kyabram, dio. Bendigo, 1973–77; Field Officer, Dept of Christian Education, Diocese of Melbourne, 1977–79; Dir, Gen. Bd of Religious Education, 1978–81. *Recreations:* gardening, reading, golf, music. *Address:* 2 Arthur Street, Doncaster, Vic 3108, Australia.

HEARN, Prof. John Patrick, PhD; Deputy Vice-Chancellor (Research), Australian National University, since 2001; *b* Limbdi, India, 24 Feb. 1943; *s* of Lt-Col Hugh Patrick Hearn, Barrister, and Cynthia Ellen (*née* Nicholson); *m* 1967, Margaret Ruth Patricia McNair; four *s* one *d*. *Educ:* Crusaders' Sch., Headley, Hants; St Mary's Sch., Nairobi, Kenya; University Coll., Dublin (BSc, MSc); ANU, Canberra (PhD). Lectr in Zool., 1967–69, and Dean of Science, 1968–69, Strathmore Coll., Nairobi; Res. Scholar, ANU, 1969–72; scientist, MRC Reproductive Biology Unit, Edinburgh, 1972–79; Consultant Scientist, WHO Special Prog. of Res. in Human Reproduction, Geneva, 1978–79; Zoological Society of London: Dir, Wellcome Labs of Comparative Physiology, 1979–80; Dir of Science and Dir, Inst. of Zool., 1980–87; Dep. Sec., AFRC, 1987–90; Dir, MRC/AFRC Comparative Physiology Res. Gp, 1983–89; Dir, Wisconsin Regl Primate Res. Center and Prof. in Physiol., Med. Sch., Univ. of Wisconsin-Madison, 1989–96; Consultant Scientist, WHO Res. Prog. in Family and Reproductive Health, Geneva, 1996–98; Dir, Res. Sch. of Biol Scis, ANU, 1998–2001. Vis. Prof. in Biology (formerly in Zoology), UCL, 1979–93; Vis. Prof., New England Primate Res. Center, Harvard Univ. Med. Sch., 1989–91; Hon. Res. Fellow, CSIRO Wildlife and Ecology, 1999–. Pres., Internat. Primatological Soc., 1984–88; Chm., Soc. for Reproductive Biology, 2000–. Scientific Medal, Zool Soc. London, 1983; Osman Hill Medal, Primate Soc. of GB, 1986. *Publications:* (ed with H. Rothe and H. Wolters) The Biology and Behaviour of Marmosets, 1978; (ed) Immunological Aspects of Reproduction and Fertility Control, 1980; (ed) Reproduction in New World Primates, 1982; (ed) Advances in Animal Conservation, 1985; (ed) Reproduction and Disease in Captive and Wild Animals, 1988; (ed) Conservation of Primate Species studied in Biomedical Research, 1994; papers on develtl and reproductive physiol. in scientific jls. *Recreations:* wildlife, running, swimming. *Address:* Australian National University, Canberra, ACT 0200, Australia. *T:* (2) 61253841, *Fax:* (2) 61250758; *e-mail:* john.hearn@anu.edu.au. *Club:* Athenæum.

HEARNDEN, Dr Arthur George, OBE 1990; education consultant; General Secretary, Independent Schools Joint Council, 1985–97; *b* 15 Dec. 1931; *s* of Hugh and Violet Hearnden; *m* 1962, Josephine McNeill; one *s* two *d*. *Educ:* Methodist Coll., Belfast; Christ's Coll., Cambridge (MA); Wadham Coll., Oxford (DPhil). 2nd Lieut, Royal Signals, 1955–57; teacher, various schs, incl. Aldenham (1959–67), and in exchange posts, Lycée d'Aix-les-Bains and Bunsengymnasium, Heidelberg, 1957–68; Res. Officer, Oxford Univ., 1969–71; Lectr in Comparative Education, Inst. of Education, Univ. of London, 1972–74; Sec., Standing Conf. on Univ. Entrance, 1975–84. Member: Sch. Exams and Assessment Council, 1988–91; Funding Agency for Schs, 1994–98 (Chm. of Finance, 1997–98); Press Complaints Commn, 1999–. Pres., Ind. Schs Assoc., 1997–; Hon. Vice Pres., Council of British Indep. Schs in EC, 1997–; Chm., HSBC Bursary Fund, 1998–; Trustee: Hall Sch. Charitable Trust, 1988– (Chm, 1998–); Youth for Britain-Worldwide Volunteering, 1993–2000 (Chm., 1995–2000). Governor: Wychwood Sch., 1983–90; Abbotsholme, 1985–92; Oxford High Sch., 1985–92; Abingdon Sch., 1988–99; Dunottar Sch, 1990–92; Newton Prep. Sch., 1992–. *Publications:* Paths to University, 1973; Bildungspolitik in der BRD und DDR, 1973 (trans. Education in the Two Germanies, 1974); Education, Culture and Politics in West Germany, 1974; (ed) The British in Germany, 1978; (ed) From School to University, 1980; Red Robert, a Life of Robert Birley, 1984; reports and articles in learned jls. *Recreations:* family, hill walking, gardens, theatre. *Address:* Hethe House, Hethe, Bicester, Oxon OX27 8ES. *T:* (01869) 277985, *Fax:* (01869) 278445. *Clubs:* Athenæum; Radley Golf.

HEARNE, Sir Graham (James), Kt 1998; CBE 1990; Chairman, Enterprise Oil plc, since 1991 (Chief Executive, 1984–96); *b* 23 Nov. 1937; *s* of Frank Hearne and Emily (*née* Shakespeare); *m* 1961, Carol Jean (*née* Brown); one *s* two *d* (and one *d* decd). *Educ:* George Dixon Grammar Sch., Birmingham. Admitted solicitor, 1959: Pinsent & Co., Solicitors, 1959–63; Fried, Frank, Harris, Shriver & Jacobson, Attorneys, NYC, 1963–66; Herbert Smith & Co., Solicitors, 1966–67; IRC, 1967–68; N. M. Rothschild & Sons Ltd, 1968–77; Finance Dir, Courtaulds Ltd, 1977–81; Chief Exec., Tricentrol, 1981–83; Gp Man. Dir, Carless, Capel and Leonard, 1983–84. Non-executive Director: N. M. Rothschild & Sons Ltd, 1970–; Northern Foods, Ltd, 1976–82; BPB Industries, 1982–91; Reckitt & Colman, 1990–97; Courtaulds, 1991–98; Wellcome, 1991–95; The Wellcome Foundn, 1991–95; Gallaher Ltd, 1997– (Dep. Chm., 1997–); BTR plc, 1998–99; Invensys (formerly BTR Siebe) plc, 1999–; Novar (formerly Caradon) plc, 1999– (Chm., 1999–); Seascope Shipping Hldgs plc, 1999–; part-time Member: British National Oil Corp., 1975–78; Dover Harbour Bd, 1976–78. Chm., Brindex (Assoc. of British Indep. Oil Exploration Cos), 1986–88. Trustee: Philharmonia Orch. Trust, 1982–; Chichester Fest. Theatre Trust, 1988–98; Hayward Foundn, 1992–. High Sheriff, Greater London, 1995. *Address:* 5 Crescent Place, SW3 2EA. *Clubs:* Reform, Brooks's, MCC.

HEARNE, Peter Ambrose, FREng; Chairman, GEC Avionics, 1992–94; *b* 14 Nov. 1927; *e s* of late Arthur Ambrose Hearne, MD, and Helen Mackay Hearne; *m* 1952, Georgina Gordon Guthrie; three *s*. *Educ:* Sherborne Sch., Dorset; Loughborough Coll. of Technol. (DLC); Cranfield Inst. of Technol. (MSc); MIT. Design Engr, Saunders Roe, 1946–47; Ops Develt Engr, BOAC, 1949–54; Helicopter Proj. Engr, BEA, 1954–58; Marketing Manager, British Oxygen, 1958–59; Divl Man., Guided Weapons, Elliott Flt Automation, 1959; Asst Gen. Man., 1960, Dir and Gen. Man., 1966–87, Marconi (later GEC) Avionics; Asst Man. Dir, 1987–90, Pres., US Ops, 1990–92, GEC Marconi. Vis. Prof., Cranfield Inst. of Technol., 1981–82. Chm., Cranfield Soc., 1965–67, Pres., 1981–88; Pres., Royal Aeronautical Society, 1980–81 (Vice-Pres., 1976–79; Hon FRAeS 1990; Wright Bros Lectr, 1991); Vice Chm., 1997–99, Vice Pres., 1999–, British Gliding Assoc. FREng (FEng 1984); FRIN 2000. John Curtis Sword, Aviation Week, 1982; Diamond C badge, 1988. *Publications:* papers in Jl of RAeS and NATO Agard series. *Recreations:* flying with and without engines, sailing, model railways. *Address:* The Limes, Wateringbury, Kent ME18 5NY. *Clubs:* Surrey and Hants Gliding; Southwold Sailing; Aero Alpin (Gap).

HEARST, Stephen, CBE 1980; FRSA; independent television producer and consultant, since 1986; *b* Vienna, Austria, 6 Oct. 1919; *m* 1948, Lisbeth Edith Neumann; one *s* one *d*. *Educ:* Vienna Univ.; Reading Univ. (Dip. Hort.); Brasenose Coll., Oxford (MA). Free lance writer, 1949–52; joined BBC as producer trainee, 1952; Documentary television: script writer, 1953–55; writer producer, 1955–65; Exec. Producer, Arts Programmes Television, 1965–67; Head of Arts Features, Television, 1967–71; Controller, Radio 3, 1972–78; Controller, Future Policy Gp, 1978–82; Special Adviser to Dir-Gen., BBC, 1982–86. Vis. Fellow, Inst. for Advanced Studies, Edinburgh Univ., 1988. FRSA 1980. *Publications:* Two Thousand Million Poor, 1965; Artistic Heritage and its Treatment by Television, 1982; (contrib.) The Third Age of Broadcasting (ed Wenham), 1982; (contrib.) Television and the Public Interest (ed Jay G. Blumler), 1991; (contrib.) Literacy is not enough (ed Brian Cox), 1998. *Recreations:* gardening, swimming, reading, listening to music. *Address:* c/o British Academy of Film and Television Arts, 195 Piccadilly, W1V 9LG.

HEARTH, John Dennis Miles, CBE 1983; Chief Executive, Royal Agricultural Society of England, 1972–89 and 1991–92; *b* 8 April 1929; *s* of late Cyril Howard Hearth, MC, and Dr Pauline Kathleen Hearth, MB, BCh; *m* 1959, Pamela Anne (*née* Bryant); two *s* (one *d* decd). *Educ:* The King's Sch., Canterbury; Brasenose Coll., Oxford (MA). Called to the Bar, Gray's Inn, 1962. Administrative Officer, HM Overseas Civil Service, 1953–61; Editor, Fairplay Shipping Journal, Fairplay Publications Ltd, 1961–66; Cunard Steam-Ship Co. Ltd, 1966–71 (various appts and Main Board Joint Ventures Director, 1969–71). Mem., Gen. Adv. Council, BBC, 1990–95; Chairman: Rural and Agricl Affairs Cttee, BBC, 1990–96; Nat. Rural Enterprise Centre, RASE, 1988–94; British Food and Farming Ltd, 1989–; Management Cttee, Nat. Fedn of Young Farmers' Clubs, 1989–95. Pres., British Pig Assoc., 1990–93. Mem. Council, Conservation Foundn, 1987–94; Dep. Chm., Rural Housing Trust (formerly NAC Rural Trust), 1992– (Trustee, 1987–); Chm., English Villages Housing Assoc., 1995–97 (Mem., 1990–; Chm. Finance Cttee, 1990–97); Chm., English Rural Housing Assoc., 1999– (Mem. Cttee, 1993–); Mem., Rural Adv. Gp, Housing Corp., 1999–. Governor, RAC, Cirencester, 1975–92; Mem., 1985–98, Treasurer, 1989–98, Warwick Univ. Council; Director: Univ. of Warwick Science Park Ltd, 1990–98; Warwick Univ. Trng Ltd, 1998–; Warwick Univ. Services Ltd, 1998–; Trustee, Univ. of Warwick Foundn, 2001–. CIMgt (CBIM 1980); FRSA 1989. Hon. FRASE 1989. Hon. LLD Warwick, 1999. *Recreations:* travel, history, theatre, photography, golf. *Address:* Bayard's, Fenny Compton, Southam, Warwicks CV47 2XY. *T:* (01295) 770849. *Club:* Royal Anglo-Belgian.

HEASLIP, Rear-Adm. Richard George, CB 1987; Director-General, English-Speaking Union, 1987–90; *b* 30 April 1932; *s* of Eric Arthur Heaslip and Vera Margaret (*née* Bailey); *m* 1959, Lorna Jean Grayston, Halifax, NS, Canada; three *s* one *d* (incl. twin *s* and *d*). *Educ:* Royal Naval Coll., Dartmouth. CO HMS Sea Devil, 1961–62; Exec. Officer, HMS Dreadnought (1st British nuclear submarine), 1965–66; CO HMS Conqueror (nuclear submarine), 1971–72; CO Second Submarine Sqdn, 1975–77; Staff, SACLANT, 1980–82; Staff, CDS, 1982–84; Dep. Asst COS (Ops), Staff of SACEUR, 1984; Flag Officer Submarines, and Comdr Submarine Forces Eastern Atlantic, 1984–87. ADC 1984–85. Member: European Atlantic Gp Cttee, 1988–89; Bureau, Standing Conf. of Atlantic Orgns, 1988–89. Chm., RN Football Assoc., 1976–84; Pres., London Submarine Old Comrades Assoc., 1987–. *Recreations:* walking, music, gardening. *Address:* South Winds, Wallis Road, Waterlooville, Hants PO7 7RX; *e-mail:* richardheaslip@netscape.net.

HEATH, Angela; *see* Heath, L. A.

HEATH, Prof. Anthony Francis, PhD; FBA 1992; Professor of Sociology, University of Oxford, since 1996; Fellow of Nuffield College, Oxford, since 1987; *b* 15 Dec. 1942; *s* of Ronald John Heath and Cicely Florence (*née* Roberts); *m* 1983, Dr Mary-Jane Pearce, MRCGP, FRCPsych; two *s* one *d*. *Educ:* Merchant Taylors', Crosby; Trinity Coll., Cambridge (BA 1st cl. Classics pt I, 1st cl. Econs pt II; PhD 1971). Asst Principal, HM Treasury, 1965–66; Fellow of Churchill Coll., 1967–70, Asst Lectr, Faculty of Econs, 1968–70, Cambridge Univ.; Univ. Lectr and Fellow of Jesus Coll., Oxford, 1970–86. Dir, 1983, 1987, 1992 and 1997 British Election Studies, and Co-Dir, Centre for Res. into Elections and Social Trends, 1994–, ESRC. *Publications:* Rational Choice and Social Change, 1976; (jtly) Origins and Destinations, 1980; Social Mobility, 1981; (jtly) How Britain Votes, 1985; (jtly) Understanding Political Change, 1991; (jtly) Labour's Last Chance, 1994; (jtly) The Rise of New Labour, 2001; contribs to Jl of Royal Stat. Soc., Amer. Jl of Sociol., Eur. Sociol Rev., Eur. Jl of Sociol., Eur. Jl of Pol Res., Sociology, British Jl of Pol. Sci.; Electoral Studies, Acta Sociologica, Oxford Rev. of Educn. *Recreations:* piano playing, cross-country running. *Address:* 72 Lonsdale Road, Oxford OX2 7EP. *T:* (01865) 553512. *Clubs:* Achilles; Hawks (Cambridge).

HEATH, Bernard Oliver, OBE 1980; CEng, FRAeS; Professor of Aeronautical Engineering (British Aerospace Integrated Chair), Salford University, 1983–89; *b* 8 March 1925; *s* of Bernard Ernest Heath and Ethel May Heath; *m* 1948, Ethel Riley; one *s*. *Educ:* Derby Sch.; Bemrose Sch., Derby; University Coll. of Nottingham (BSc Univ. of London 1944); Imperial Coll. of Science and Technology (DIC 1945). CEng 1966; FRAeS 1978; HMIED 1975. English Electric Co.: Stressman (loading and stressing of Canberra), 1945; Aerodynamicist, Lightning, 1948; Aerostructures Gp Leader (Lightning loading and aeroelasticity), 1951; Chief Proj. Engr, 1957; Asst Chief Engr, Canberra and TSR2, 1959; British Aircraft Corporation: TSR2 Proj. Manager (Develt), 1963; Special Dir, 1965; Leader, Jaguar Technical Team, 1965; Proj. Manager, AFVG, 1966; Panavia: Dir, Systems Engrg (Warton), 1969–81; Dir, MRCA, 1970; Dir of Engrg, 1974; British Aerospace: Technical Dir, Warton Div., 1978–81; Divisional Dir of Advanced Engrg, 1981–84. Chm., SBAC Technical Bd, 1980–82. RAeS Silver Medal (for outstanding work over many yrs on design and develt of mil. aircraft), 1977; (jtly) Internat. Council of Aeronautical Sciences Von Karman Award (for successful internat. co-operation on Tornado), 1982; Corresp. Mem., Deutsche Ges. für Luft und Raumfahrt, 1993. *Publications:* papers to AGARD, Internat. Council of Aeronautical Sciences Congresses; contrib. RAeS Jl, Flight, The Times, R & D Mgt, RAF Histl Soc. and Aircraft Engrg. *Recreation:* history of transport. *Address:* c/o Company Secretary, BAE Systems, Warton Aerodrome, Preston, Lancs PR4 1AX.

HEATH, David William St John, CBE 1989; MP (Lib Dem) Somerton and Frome, since 1997; *b* 16 March 1954; *s* of Eric Heath and Pamela Heath; *m* 1987, Caroline Netherton; one *s* one *d*. *Educ:* Millfield Sch.; St John's Coll., Oxford (MA Physiological Scis); City Univ. FADO 1979. In practice as optician, 1979–86. Somerset County Council: Councillor (Lib Dem), 1985–97; Leader, 1985–89; Chm., Educn Cttee, 1996–97. Vice Chm., Assoc. of County Councils, 1993–97. Chm., Avon & Somerset Police Authy, 1993–96; Vice Chm., Cttee of Local Police Authorities, 1993–97. Mem., Audit Commn, 1995–97. Contested (Lib Dem) Somerton and Frome, 1992. Lib Dem spokesman on European affairs, 1997–98, on foreign affairs, 1999–2001, on work, family and pensions, 2001–. Mem., Witham Friary Friendly Soc., 1984–. FRSA 1995. *Recreations:* cricket, Rugby football, pig breeding until recently. *Address:* The Yard, Witham Friary, near Frome, Somerset BA11 5HF. *T:* (01749) 850458. *Club:* National Liberal.

HEATH, (Edward) Peter, OBE 1946; *b* 6 June 1914; a Deputy Chairman, Inchcape & Co. Ltd, 1976–79; *m* 1953, Eleanor Christian Peck; one *s* three *d*. *Educ:* St Lawrence Coll., Ramsgate. Joined Borneo Co. Ltd, 1934; interned in Thailand, 1941–45. Gen. Manager, Borneo Co. Ltd, 1953–63; a Man. Dir, 1963–67; a Man. Dir, Inchcape & Co. Ltd, 1967–75. Director: Mann Egerton & Co. Ltd, 1973–79; Dodwell & Co. Ltd, 1974–79; Inchcape Far East Ltd, 1972–79; Chairman: Toyota GB and Pride & Clark, 1978–79; Anglo-Thai Corp. Ltd, 1978–79; Dep. Chm., Bewac Motor Corp., 1970–79. Consultant, Matheson & Co. Ltd, 1980–83; Director: Matheson Motor Hldgs, 1981–83; Lancaster Gp Hldgs, 1981–83. Dep. Chairman: Hong Kong Assoc., 1975–79; Anglo Thai Soc., 1975–85. Order of White Elephant (5th Cl.) (Thailand); Officer, Order of Orange Nassau (Netherlands). *Recreations:* hunting, gardening, motoring. *Address:* Cooks Place, Albury, Guildford, Surrey GU5 9BJ. *T:* (01483) 202698.

HEATH, Rt Hon. Sir Edward (Richard George), KG 1992; MBE 1946; PC 1955; Member, Public Review Board, Arthur Andersen & Co., 1978–98; *b* Broadstairs, Kent, 9 July 1916; *s* of late William George and Edith Anne Heath. *Educ:* Chatham House Sch., Ramsgate; Balliol Coll., Oxford (Scholar; Hon. Fellow, 1969). Scholar, Gray's Inn, 1938 (Hon. Bencher, 1972). Pres. Oxford Univ. Conservative Assoc., 1937; Chm. Federation of Univ. Conservative Assocs, 1938; Pres. Oxford Union, 1939; Oxford Union debating tour of American Univs, 1939–40; Pres. Federation of University Conservative and Unionist Associations, 1959–77, Hon. Life Patron, 1977. Served War of 1939–45 (despatches, MBE); in Army, 1940–46, in France, Belgium, Holland and Germany; gunner in RA, 1940; Major 1945. Lieut-Col comdg 2nd Regt HAC, TA, April 1947–Aug. 1951; Master Gunner within the Tower of London, 1951–54. Administrative Civil Service, 1946–47 resigning to become prospective candidate for Bexley. MP (C): Bexley, 1950–74; Bexley, Sidcup, 1974–83; Old Bexley and Sidcup, 1983–2001; Asst Conservative Whip, Feb. 1951; Lord Commissioner of the Treasury, Nov. 1951, and Joint Deputy Govt Chief Whip, 1952, and Dep. Govt Chief Whip, 1953–55; Parliamentary Sec. to the Treasury, and Government Chief Whip, Dec. 1955–Oct. 1959; Minister of Labour, Oct. 1959–July 1960; Lord Privy Seal, with Foreign Office responsibilities, 1960–63; Sec. of State for Industry, Trade, Regional Development and Pres. of the Board of Trade, Oct. 1963–Oct. 1964; Leader of the Opposition, 1965–70; Prime Minister and First Lord of the Treasury, 1970–74; Leader of the Opposition, 1974–75; Father of the H of C, 1992–2001. Chm., Commonwealth Parly Assoc., 1970–74. Mem., Indep. Commn on Internat. Development Issues, 1977–79. Mem. Council, Royal College of Music, 1961–70; Chm., London Symphony Orchestra Trust, 1963–70; Vice-Pres., Bach Choir, 1970–; Pres., European Community Youth Orchestra, 1977–80; Hon. Mem., LSO, 1974–; has made orchestral recordings. Smith-Mundt Fellowship, USA, 1953; Vis. Fellow, Nuffield Coll., Oxford, 1962–70, Hon. Fellow, 1970; Chubb Fellow, Yale, 1975; Montgomery Fellow, Dartmouth Coll., 1980. Lectures: Cyril Foster Meml, Oxford, 1965; Godkin, Harvard, 1966; Montagu Burton, Leeds, 1976; Edge, Princeton, 1976; Romanes, Oxford, 1976; Ishizaka, Japan, 1979; Felix Neubergh, Gothenburg, 1979, 10th STC Communication, London, 1980, Noel Buxton, Univ. of Essex, 1980; Alastair Buchan Meml, London, 1980; Hoover, Univ. of Strathclyde, 1980; Stanton Griffis Disting., Cornell Univ., 1981; Edwin Stevens, RSM, 1981; William Temple, York, 1981; City of London, Chartered Insce Inst., 1982; John Findley Green, Westminster Coll., Missouri, 1982; Mizuno, Tokyo, 1982; ITT European, Brussels, 1982; Bruce Meml, Keele Univ., 1982; Gaitskell, Univ. of Nottingham, 1983; Trinity Univ., San Antonio, 1983; lect. to mark opening Michael Fowler Centre, Wellington, NZ, 1983; Bridge Meml, Guildhall, 1984; David R. Calhoun Jr Meml, Washington Univ., St Louis, 1984; Corbishley Meml, RSA, 1984; John Rogers Meml, Llandudno, 1985; George Woodcock, Univ. of Leicester, 1985; RIIA, 1985; John F. Kennedy Meml, Oxford, 1986; Edward Boyle Meml, RSA, 1988. Deroy Prof., Univ. of Michigan, 1990. Liveryman, Goldsmiths' Co., 1966; Hon. Freeman, Musicians' Co., 1973. Hon. FRCM; Hon. FRCO; Hon. Fellow, Royal Canadian Coll. of Organists. Hon. DCL: Oxon, 1971; Kent, 1985; Hon. DTech Bradford, 1971; Hon. LLD: Westminster Coll., Salt Lake City, 1975; Greenwich, 2001; Dr *hc* Univ. of Paris, Sorbonne, 1976; Hon. Dr of Public Admin, Wesleyan Coll., Macon, Ga, 1981; Hon. DL Westminster Coll., Fulton, Missouri, 1982; Hon. HLD Bellarmine Coll., Kentucky, 1994; DUniv Open, 1997. Charlemagne Prize, 1963; Estes J. Kefauver Prize 1971; Stresseman Gold Medal, 1971; Freiherr Von Stein Foundn Prize, 1972; Gold Medal of City of Paris, 1978; World Humanity Award, 1980; Gold Medal, European Parlt, 1981; Gold Medal, Fondation du Mérite Européen, 1994; Gold Medal, Jean Monnet Foundn, 1999. Grand Cross, Order of Merit (Germany), 1993; Grand Cross, Order of Liberty and Unity (Latin America), 1994; Order of the Aztec Eagle (Mexico), 1994; Grand Cordon, Order of the Rising Sun (Japan), 1998. Winner, Sydney to Hobart Ocean Race, 1969; Captain: Britain's Admiral's Cup Team, 1971, 1979; Britain's Sardinia Cup Team, 1980. *Publications:* (joint) One Nation—a Tory approach to social problems, 1950; Old World, New Horizons (Godkin Lectures), 1970; Sailing: a course of my life, 1975; Music: a joy for life, 1976, 2nd edn 1996; Travels: people and places in my life, 1977; Carols: the joy of Christmas, 1977; The Course of My Life (autobiog.), 1998. *Recreations:* sailing, music. *Clubs:* Buck's, Carlton, St Stephen's Constitutional (Jt Pres., 1979–88); Royal Yacht Squadron.

HEATH, Henry Wylde Edwards, CMG 1963; QPM; Commissioner of Police, Hong Kong, 1959–67, retired; *b* 18 March 1912; *s* of late Dr W. G. Heath and late Mrs L. B. Heath; *m* 1945, Joan Mildred Critchett; two *s* one *d*. *Educ:* Dean Close Sch.; HMS Conway. Probationer Sub-Inspector of Police, Leeward Islands, 1931; Asst Supt, Hong Kong, 1934; Superintendent, 1944; Asst Commissioner, 1950. Colonial Police Medal, 1953; QPM, 1957. *Recreations:* golf, ski-ing. *Address:* Quintynes Cottage, 4 Firle Drive, Seaford, Sussex BN25 2HT. *Clubs:* Seaford Golf; Kandahar Ski.

HEATH, Prof. John Baldwin; management consultant; Secretary General, International Council for Peace, Reconciliation and Recovery, 1996–99; *b* 25 Sept. 1924; *s* of late Thomas Arthur Heath and late Dorothy Meallin; *m* 1953, Wendy Julia Betts (marr. diss. 1995); two *s* one *d*. *Educ:* Merchant Taylors' Sch.; St Andrews Univ.; Cambridge Univ. RNVR, 1942–46. Spicers Ltd, 1946–50; Lecturer in Economics, Univ. of Manchester, 1956–64; Rockefeller Foundation Fellowship, 1961–62; Dir, Economic Research Unit, Bd of Trade, 1964–67; Dir, Economic Services Div., BoT, 1967–70; Prof. of Economics, London Business Sch., 1970–86; Dir, London Sloan Fellowship Programme, 1983–86. Chm., EXE Ltd, 1982–93; Dir, Health Policy Unit, 1994–95. Member: Mechanical Engrg EDC, 1971–76; British Airports Authy, 1980–86; Economic Adviser, CAA, 1972–78. *Publications:* Public Enterprise at the Crossroads, 1990; Revitalizing Socialist Enterprise, 1993; articles in many learned jls on competition and monopoly, productivity, cost-benefit analysis. *Recreations:* music, walking. *Address:* 27 Chalcot Square, NW1 8YA. *T:* (020) 7722 4301, *Fax:* (020) 7483 0369.

HEATH, John Moore, CMG 1976; HM Diplomatic Service, retired; *b* 9 May 1922; *s* of late Philip George and Olga Heath; *m* 1952, Patricia Mary Bibby; one *s* one *d*. *Educ:* Shrewsbury Sch.; Merton Coll., Oxford (MA). Served War of 1939–45, France, Belgium and Germany: commnd Inns of Court Regt, 1942; Capt. GSO3 11th Armoured Div., 1944–45 (despatches). Merton Coll., 1940–42, 1946–47. Entered Foreign Service, 1950; 2nd Sec., Comr-Gen.'s Office, Singapore, 1950–52; 1st Sec. (Commercial), Jedda, 1952–56; 1st Sec., FO, 1956–58; Nat. Def. Coll., Kingston, Ont., 1958–59; Head of Chancery and HM Consul, Brit. Embassy, Mexico City, 1959–62; Head of Chancery, Brit. Embassy, Kabul, Afghanistan, 1963–65; Counsellor and Head of Establishment and Organisation Dept, FCO (formerly DSAO), 1966–69; Counsellor (Commercial), Brit. Embassy, Bonn, 1969–74; Overseas Trade Advr, Assoc. of British Chambers of Commerce, on secondment, 1974; Consul-Gen., Chicago, 1975–79; Ambassador to Chile, 1980–82. Dir Gen., Canning House (Hispanic and Luso-Brazilian Council), 1982–87. Chm., Anglo-Chilean Soc., 1987–89. FRPSL 1999. Orden al Merito por Servicios Distinguidos, Peru, 1984; Orden al Merito, Gran Oficial, Chile, 1991. *Publications:* The British Postal Agencies in Mexico 1825–1876, 1969; The Heath family engravers 1779–1878, 1993; Mexican Maritime Mail from Colonial Times to the Twentieth Century, 1997. *Recreations:* book collecting, Mexican philately, walking. *Address:* 6 Cavendish Crescent, Bath, Avon BA1 2UG. *Club:* Naval and Military.

HEATH, (Lettyce) Angela; JP; non-executive Director, The North West London Hospitals (formerly Northwick Park and St Mark's) NHS Trust, since 1996; *b* 27 May 1944; *d* of late Frank Buchanan Ryde and Emily Rose Ryde (*née* Davies); *m* 1st, 1966, Gareth Thomas (marr. diss. 1975); 2nd, 1985, Roger Heath; two step *d*. *Educ:* Birmingham Univ. (BA 1966; MA 1968); Birbeck Coll., London (MSc 1999). Department of the Environment, 1971–96: Admin. Trainee, 1971; Private Sec. to Minister of Housing, 1979; Asst Sec., 1983; Central Policy Planning Unit, 1983–85; Local Govt Div., 1985–87; Personnel Management, 1987–90; Housing Corp. Finance, 1990–91; Under-Sec., 1992; Regl Dir for London, 1992–94; Dir, Regeneration Progs, Govt Office for London, 1994–95; Dir, Local Govt, 1995–96. Vis. Sen. Fellow, Sch. of Public Policy, Univ. of Birmingham, 1997–99. JP Middlesex, 1997. FRSA 1995. *Address:* 6 High View, Pinner, Middx HA5 3PA.

HEATH, Sir Mark, KCVO 1980; CMG 1980; Minister, then Ambassador, to the Holy See, 1980–85; *b* 22 May 1927; *m* 1954, Margaret Alice Bragg; two *s* one *d*. *Educ:* Marlborough; Queens' Coll., Cambridge. RNVR, 1945–48. HM Foreign (subseq. Diplomatic) Service, 1950–85; served in Indonesia, Denmark, Bulgaria, Canada; with OECD; with Hong Kong Government, 1985–88. Chm., Friends of Anglican Centre, Rome, 1984–90. *Address:* St Lawrence, Lansdown Road, Bath BA1 5TD.

HEATH, Michael John, MBE 2001; freelance cartoonist, since 1956; Cartoons Editor, The Spectator, since 1989; *b* 13 Oct. 1935; *s* of George Heath and Alice (Queenie) Stewert Morrison Bremner; *m* 1959, Hanne Sternkopf (marr. diss. 1992); two *d*; partner, Martha Swift; two *d*. *Educ:* no education to speak of (Devon, Hampstead and Brighton); Brighton Art Coll. Trained as animator, Rank Screen Services, 1955; started placing cartoons in Melody Maker, 1955; contributed to: Lilliput; Tatler; John Bull; Man about Town; Men Only; Honey; Punch, 1958–89; Spectator, 1958–; Private Eye, 1964– (strips include The Gays, The Regulars, Great Bores of Today, Baby); Sunday Times, 1967–; London Standard, 1976–86, 1995–96; Mail on Sunday, 1985–; The Independent, 1986–97 (Political Cartoonist, 1991–96); London Daily News, 1987. Pocket Cartoonist of the Year, Cartoonist Club of GB, 1977; Glen Grant Cartoonist of the Year, 1978; What the Papers Say Cartoonist of the Year, 1982. *Publications:* Private Eye Cartoon Library, 1973, 2nd edn 1975; The Punch Cartoons of Michael Heath, 1976; Book of Bores, No 1, 1976, No 2, Star Bores, 1979, No 3, Bores Three, 1983; Love All, 1982; Best of Heath (foreword by Malcolm Muggeridge), 1984; Welcome to America, 1985; Heath's Nineties, 1997. *Recreations:* listening to Charlie Parker and Thelonious Monk, walking. *Address:* 1 Bassett Chambers, 27 Bedfordbury, Covent Garden, WC2N 4BJ. *T:* (020) 7379 0087. *Club:* Colony Room.

HEATH, Michael John; His Honour Judge Heath; a Circuit Judge, since 1995; Resident Judge: Grimsby Crown Court, since 1999; Lincoln Combined Court Centre, since 2000; *b* Grimsby, 12 June 1948; *s* of Norman Heath and late Dorothy Heath; *m* 1972, Heather, *d* of late Christopher Croft and of Mrs D. Croft, Hetton-le-Hole; two *s*. *Educ:* Barcroft County Sch., Wintringham; Grammar Sch., Grimsby; Leeds Univ. (LLB). FCIArb. Asst Solicitor, R. A. C. Symes and Co., Scunthorpe, 1975, Partner, 1977; Dep. Dist Judge, 1987–95; a Recorder, 1993–95; Solicitor Advocate (All Courts), 1994. Chm., Humberside Area Criminal Justice Strategy Cttee, 2000–. Hon. Recorder, City of Lincoln, 2001. *Recreations:* soccer, cricket, keeping a low profile. *Address:* Lincoln Combined Court Centre, 360 High Street, Lincoln LN5 7RL. *T:* (01522) 883000.

HEATH, Maj.-Gen. Michael Stuart, CB 1994; CBE 1991; CEng, FIEE; Director of Corporate Strategy, NXT plc, since 1999; *b* 7 Sept. 1940; *s* of late Bernard Stuart Heath and of Blanche Dorothy Ellen Heath (*née* Fairey); *m* 1965, Frances Wood; one *s* one *d*. *Educ:* St Albans Sch.; Welbeck Coll.; Royal Military Coll. of Science (BSc Eng Upper 2nd cl. Hons London). Commissioned REME, 1961; served Malaya, BAOR, Edinburgh, to 1971; RMCS and Staff Coll., 1972–73; Armour Sch., Bovington, 1974–75; Comd 7 Field Workshop, BAOR, 1976–77; Nat. Defence Coll., 1978; Berlin Field Force, 1978–80; Comd Maint., HQ 2 Armd Div., BAOR, 1981–82; MoD, 1982–85; RCDS, 1986; Dir, Support Planning (Army), MoD, 1987–89; Comd Maint., HQ BAOR, 1990–91; Dir Gen., Electrical and Mechanical Engrg. subseq. Equipment Support (Army), MoD, 1991–93; Team Leader, Army Costs Study Team, 1994. Dir Gen., Engrg Council, 1995–98. FIMgt. *Recreations:* walking, music, photography, restoring antique furniture. *Address:* c/o Barclays Bank, 167 High Street, Bromley, Kent BR1 1NL. *Club:* Army and Navy.

HEATH, Peter; *see* Heath, E. P.

HEATH, Samantha; Member (Lab), London Assembly, Greater London Authority, since 2000; *b* 6 June 1960; *d* of Harvey and Gillian Heath; *m* 1991, Robert Griffiths; one *s*. *Educ:* Heriot-Watt Univ. (BSc Hons); Univ. of Greenwich (PGCE 1999). Civil engineer, Sir Robert McAlpine & Sons Ltd, 1982–92; Sen. Lectr in Construction, Univ. of Greenwich, 1992–2000. *Address:* Greater London Authority, Romney House, 43 Marsham Street, SW1P 3PY. *T:* (020) 7983 4000.

HEATH-BROWN, Prof. David Rodney, (Roger), PhD; FRS 1993; Professor of Pure Mathematics, and Fellow of Worcester College, University of Oxford, since 1999; *b* 12 Oct. 1952; *s* of Basil Heath-Brown and Phyllis Joan (*née* Watson); *m* 1992, Ann Louise Sharpley; two *d*. *Educ:* Welwyn Garden City Grammar Sch.; Trinity Coll., Cambridge (BA, MA, PhD). Jun. Res. Fellow, Trinity Coll., Cambridge, 1977–79; Oxford University: Fellow and Tutor in Pure Maths, Magdalen Coll., 1979–98, Emeritus Fellow, 1999; Reader in Pure Maths, 1990–98. Corresp. Mem., Akad. der Wissenschaften, Göttingen, 1999. Jun. Berwick Prize, 1981, Sen. Berwick Prize, 1996, London Math. Soc. *Publications:* numerous mathematical papers in learned jls. *Recreations:* field botany, nature conservation, gardening. *Address:* Mathematical Institute, 24–29 St Giles', Oxford OX1 3LB. *T:* (01865) 273535.

HEATH-STUBBS, John (Francis Alexander), OBE 1989; poet; Lecturer in English Literature, College of St Mark and St John, Chelsea, 1963–73; *b* 9 July 1918; *s* of Francis Heath Stubbs and Edith Louise Sara (*née* Marr). *Educ:* Bembridge School; Worcester Coll. for the Blind, and privately; Queen's Coll., Oxford. English Master, Hall Sch., Hampstead, 1944–45; Editorial Asst, Hutchinson's, 1945–46; Gregory Fellow in Poetry, Leeds Univ., 1952–55; Vis. Prof. of English: University of Alexandria, 1955–58; University of Michigan, 1960–61. Pres., Poetry Soc., 1993–. FRSL 1953. Queen's Gold Medal for Poetry, 1973; Oscar Williams/Jean Durwood Award, 1977; Cholmondeley Award, 1989; Commonwealth Poetry Prize, 1989; Howard Sargeant Award, 1989. *Publications: verse:* Wounded Thammuz, 1942; Beauty and the Beast, 1943; The Divided Ways, 1946; The Swarming of the Bees, 1950; A Charm against the Toothache, 1954; The Triumph of the Muse, 1958; The Blue Fly in his Head, 1962; Selected Poems, 1965; Satires and Epigrams, 1968; Artorius, 1973; A Parliament of Birds, 1975; The Watchman's Flute, 1978; Mouse, the Bird and the Sausage, 1978; Birds Reconvened, 1980; Buzz Buzz, 1981; Naming the Beasts, 1982; The Immolation of Aleph, 1985; Cats' Parnassus, 1987; Time Pieces, 1988; Collected Poems, 1988; A Partridge in a Pear Tree, 1988; A Ninefold of Charms, 1989; Selected Poems, 1990; The Parson's Cat, 1992; Sweetapple Earth, 1993; Chimeras, 1994; Galileo's Salad, 1996; The Torriano Sequences, 1997; The Sound of Light, 1999; *drama:* Helen in Egypt, 1958; *criticism:* The Darkling Plain, 1950; Charles Williams, 1955; The Pastoral, 1969; The Ode, 1969; The Verse Satire, 1969; Literary Essays, 1998; *translations:* (with Peter Avery) Hafiz of Shiraz, 1952; (with Iris Origo) Leopardi, Selected Prose and Poetry, 1966; (with Carol A. Whiteside) The Poems of Anyte, 1974; (with Peter Avery) The Rubaiyat of Omar Khayyam, 1979; The Eight Poems of Sulpicia, 2000; *edited:* Selected Poems of Jonathan Swift, 1948; Selected Poems of P. B. Shelley, 1948; Selected Poems of Tennyson, 1948; Selected Poems of Alexander Pope, 1964; (with David Wright) The Forsaken Garden, 1950; Images of Tomorrow, 1953; (with David Wright) Faber Book of Twentieth Century Verse, 1953; (with Martin Green) Homage to George Barker on his Sixtieth Birthday, 1973; Selected Poems of Thomas Gray, 1983; (with Phillips Salman) Poems of Science, 1984; David Gray, In the Shadows, 1991; *autobiography:* Hindsights, 1993. *Recreation:* taxonomy. *Address:* 22 Artesian Road, W2 5AR. *T:* (020) 7229 6367.

HEATHCOAT-AMORY, Rt Hon. David (Philip); PC 1996; FCA; MP (C) Wells, since 1983; *b* 21 March 1949; *s* of late Roderick and Sonia Heathcoat-Amory; *m* 1978, Linda Adams; one *s* one *d* (and one *s* decd). *Educ:* Eton Coll.; Oxford Univ. (MA PPE). Qual. as Chartered Accountant with Price Waterhouse & Co., 1974; FCA 1980. Worked in industry, becoming Asst Finance Dir of British Technology Gp, until 1983 when resigned to fight Gen. Election. PPS to the Financial Sec. to the Treasury, 1985–87, to the Home Secretary, 1987–88; an Asst Govt Whip, 1988–89; a Lord Comr of HM Treasury, 1989; Parly Under Sec. of State, DoE, 1989–90, Dept. of Energy, 1990–92; Dep. Govt Chief Whip and Treasurer, HM Household, 1992–93; Minister of State, FCO, 1993–94; HM Paymaster General, 1994–96; Shadow Chief Sec. to HM Treasury, 1997–2000. *Recreations:* fishing, shooting, music, growing trees. *Address:* 12 Lower Addison Gardens, W14 8BQ. *T:* (020) 7603 3083. *Clubs:* Avalon (Glastonbury); Wells Conservative.

HEATHCOAT AMORY, Sir Ian, 6th Bt *cr* 1874; DL; *b* 3 Feb. 1942; *s* of Sir William Heathcoat Amory, 5th Bt, DSO, and Margaret Isabel Dorothy Evelyn (*d* 1997), *yr d* of Sir Arthur Havelock James Doyle, 4th Bt; *S* father, 1982; *m* 1972, Frances Louise, *d* of J. F. B. Pomeroy; four *s*. *Educ:* Eton. Chairman: Lowman Manufacturing Co. Ltd, 1976–; DevonAir Radio Ltd, 1983–90; Dir, Watts Blake Bearne & Co. PLC, 1984–88. Mem., Devon CC, 1973–85. JP Devon, 1980–93; DL Devon, 1981. *Heir: s* William Francis Heathcoat Amory, *b* 19 July 1975. *Address:* Calverleigh Court, Tiverton, Devon EX16 8BB.

HEATHCOTE, Dr (Frederic) Roger; Chief Executive, Employment Tribunals Service, since 2000; *b* 19 March 1944; *s* of late Frederic William Trevor Heathcote and Kathleen Annie Heathcote; *m* 1st, 1970, Geraldine Nixon (marr. diss. 1986); 2nd, 1986, Mary Campbell Syme Dickson; one *s* one step *d*. *Educ:* Bromsgrove Sch.; Birmingham Univ. (BSc (Hons) Physics, PhD). Res. Associate, Birmingham Univ., 1969–70; joined CS as Asst Principal, Min. of Technology (later DTI), 1970; Private Secretary to: Secretary (Industrial Develt), 1973; Permanent Under Sec. of State, Dept of Energy, 1974; Department of Energy: Principal, 1974; Asst Sec., 1978; Dir of Resource Management (Grade 4), 1988; Under Sec., Coal Div., 1989–91; Prin. Estabt and Finance Officer, 1991–92; Hd of Services Mgt Div., DTI, 1992–96; Dir, Export Control and Non-Proliferation, DTI, 1996–2000; UK Gov., IAEA, and UK Rep., Exec. Council of Orgn for the Prohibition of Chemical Weapons, 1996–2000. Non-exec. Dir, Trafalgar House Property Ltd, 1988–94. *Recreations:* reading, gardening, painting. *Address:* c/o Employment Tribunals Service, 7th Floor, 19–29 Woburn Place, WC1H 0LU.

HEATHCOTE, Brig. Sir Gilbert (Simon), 9th Bt *cr* 1733; CBE 1964 (MBE 1941); *b* 21 Sept. 1913; *s* of Col R. E. M. Heathcote, DSO (*d* 1970), Manton Hall, Rutland and Millicent Heathcote (*d* 1977), *d* of William Walton, Horsley Priory, Nailsworth, Glos; *S* to baronetcy of 3rd Earl of Ancaster, KCVO, 1983; *m* lst, 1939, Patricia Margaret (*née* Leslie) (marr. diss. 1984); one *s* one *d*; 2nd, 1984, Ann, *widow* of Brig. J. F. C. Mellor, DSO, OBE. *Educ:* Eton; RMA Woolwich. Commnd RA, 1933, War Service in Europe, 1939–44; Comdr RA, 1960–62; Chief of Staff, Middle East Comd, 1962–64; retd. Vice-Pres., Royal Star and Garter Home, Richmond, 1990–. *Recreations:* writing, travel. *Heir: s* Mark Simon Robert Heathcote, OBE [*b* 1 March 1941; *m* 1975, Susan, *d* of late Lt-Col George Ashley; two *s*]. *Address:* The Coach House, Tillington, near Petworth, Sussex GU28 0RA. *Clubs:* Garrick, Army and Navy.

HEATHCOTE, Sir Michael Perryman, 11th Bt *cr* 1733; *b* 7 Aug. 1927; *s* of Sir Leonard Vyvyan Heathcote, 10th Bt, and Joyce Kathleen Heathcote (*d* 1967); *S* father, 1963; *m* 1956, Victoria Wilford, *e d* of Comdr J. E. R. Wilford, RN, retd; two *s* one *d*. *Educ:* Winchester Coll.; Clare Coll., Cambridge. Started farming in England, 1951, in Scotland, 1961. Is in remainder to Earldom of Macclesfield. *Recreations:* fishing, shooting, farming. *Heir: s* Timothy Gilbert Heathcote, *b* 25 May 1957. *Address:* Warborne Farm, Boldre, Lymington, Hants SO41 5QD. *T:* (01590) 673478.

HEATHCOTE, Roger; *see* Heathcote, F. R.

HEATHCOTE-DRUMMOND-WILLOUGHBY, family name of **Baroness Willoughby de Eresby**.

HEATHCOTE-SMITH, Clifford Bertram Bruce, CBE 1963; HM Diplomatic Service, 1936–72; acting Senior Clerk, Department of Clerk of House of Commons, 1973–77; *b* 2 Sept. 1912; *s* of late Sir Clifford E. Heathcote-Smith, KBE, CMG; *m* 1940, Thelma Joyce Engström; two *s*. *Educ:* Malvern; Pembroke Coll., Cambridge. Entered Consular Service, 1936; served in China, 1937–44; Foreign Office, 1944–47; Political Adviser, Hong-Kong, 1947–50, Montevideo, 1951–56; Commercial Counsellor: Ankara, 1956–60; Copenhagen, 1960–64; Washington, 1964–65; Dep. High Comr, Madras, 1965–68; a Diplomatic Service Inspector, 1969–72. *Address:* 4 Britts Farm Road, Buxted, E Sussex TN22 4LZ. *T:* (01825) 733635.

HEATHER, Stanley Frank, CBE 1980; Comptroller and City Solicitor, City of London Corporation, 1974–80; Attorney and General Counsel, City of London (Arizona) Corporation, 1974–81; *b* 8 Jan. 1917; *s* of Charles and Jessie Heather; *m* 1946, Janet Roxburgh Adams (*d* 1989), Perth; one *s* one *d*. *Educ:* Downhills Sch.; London Univ. Commnd Reconnaissance Corps, RAC, 1941; India/Burma Campaign, 1942–45. Admitted Solicitor, 1959. Asst Solicitor, City of London, 1963; Dep. Comptroller and City Solicitor, 1968. Captain, Sussex Professional Golfers' Union, 1985–86; Patron, Southern Reg., PGA. FRSA 1981. *Recreations:* golf, fishing. *Address:* 11 Farebrothers, Church Street, Warnham, W Sussex RH12 3DZ. *T:* (01403) 267724. *Clubs:* City Livery, Guildhall.

HEATLEY, Brian Antony; Mathematics teacher, Graveney School, Tooting, since 1997; *b* 20 April 1947; *s* of Thomas Russell Heatley and Margaret Ross (*née* Deacon); *m*; one *d*. *Educ:* Sheen Grammar Sch.; St John's Coll., Cambridge (BA); Balliol Coll., Oxford; Warwick Univ. (MPhil). Volunteer teacher, Ethiopia, 1969–71; Department of Trade and Industry, 1974–89: appts include Financial Services, Consumer Protection and Radio

Communications; Head, Small Firms and Enterprise Br., 1989–90, Head, Resource Planning Br., 1990–93, Dept of Employment; Head of Adults and Trng Strategy, Dept of Employment, then DFEE, 1993–96. Student teacher, Sheffield Univ., 1996–97. *Recreations:* running, walking, history, photography, food. *Address:* 141 Larkhall Lane, SW4 6RG.

HEATLY, Sir Peter, Kt 1990; CBE 1971; DL; Director, Peter Heatly & Co. Ltd, 1958–96; Chairman, Commonwealth Games Federation, 1982–90; *b* 9 June 1924; *s* of Robert Heatly and Margaret Ann Heatly; *m* 1st, 1948, Jean Robertha Hermiston (*d* 1979); two *s* two *d*; 2nd, 1984, Mae Calder Cochrane. *Educ:* Leith Academy; Edinburgh Univ. (BSc). CEng, FICE. Chm., Scottish Sports Council, 1975–87. DL City of Edinburgh, 1984. Dr *hc* Edinburgh, 1992; Hon. DLitt Queen Margaret Coll., 1994; DUniv Stirling, 1998. *Recreations:* swimming, golf, gardening. *Address:* Lanrig, Balerno, Edinburgh EH14 7AJ. *T:* (0131) 449 3998. *Club:* New (Edinburgh).

HEATON, David, OBE 1993; Consultant, Museums and Galleries Commission, 1984–93; *b* 22 Sept. 1923; *s* of late Dr T. B. Heaton, OBE, MD; *m* 1961, Joan, *d* of Group Captain E. J. Lainé, CBE, DFC; two *s* one *d*. *Educ:* Rugby Sch. Served RNVR, 1942–46. Ghana, 1948–58; Cabinet Office, 1961–69; Home Office, 1969–83; Under Sec. of State, 1976–83. *Address:* 53 Murray Road, SW19 4PF. *T:* (020) 8947 0375.

HEATON, Frances Anne; Director, Lazard Brothers & Co. Ltd, since 1987; *b* 11 Aug. 1944; *d* of John Ferris Whidborne and Marjorie Annie (*née* Maltby); *m* 1969, Martin Heaton; two *s*. *Educ:* Queen Anne's, Caversham; Trinity Coll., Dublin (BA, LLB). Called to the Bar, Inner Temple, 1967. Dept. of Econ. Affairs, 1967–70; HM Treasury, 1970–80; seconded to S. G. Warburg & Co. Ltd, 1977–79; Lazard Brothers & Co. Ltd, 1980–; seconded as Dir Gen., Panel on Takeovers and Mergers, 1992–94. Director: W. S. Atkins, 1990– (Dep. Chm., 1996–); Bank of England, 1993–2001; Elementis plc (formerly Harrisons & Crosfield), 1994–99; Commercial Union, 1994–98; BUPA, 1998–2001. Mem., Cttee on Standards in Public Life, 1997–. *Recreations:* riding, gardening, bridge. *Address:* Lazard, 21 Moorfields, EC2P 2HT.

HEATON, (William) John; Chief Executive, Horserace Totalisator Board, since 1997; *b* 12 Jan. 1954; *s* of Ronald and Hilda Heaton; *m* 1986, Judith Ann Hatcher; one *s* one *d*. *Educ:* Wigan Grammar Sch.; Sheffield Univ. (LLB); Admitted Solicitor, 1975. Principal Solicitor, Manchester CC, 1976–83; Co. Sec. and Solicitor, Horserace Totalisator Bd, 1983–96. *Recreations:* Rugby, golf, horseracing. *Address:* Tote House, 74 Upper Richmond Road, SW15 2SU. *Clubs:* Richmond Rugby; Royal Mid Surrey Golf.

HEATON, Sir Yvo (Robert) Henniker-, 4th Bt *cr* 1912; *b* 24 April 1954; *s* of Sir (John Victor) Peregrine Henniker-Heaton, 3rd Bt, and of Margaret Patricia, *d* of late Lieut Percy Wright, Canadian Mounted Rifles; *S* father, 1971; *m* 1978, Freda, *d* of B. Jones; one *s* one *d*. Mem., North West Leics DC, 1987–95. Chm., Kegworth Cons. Assoc., 1988–94. Gov., Ashby Willesley Sch., 1996–. *Publication:* Corporate Computer Insurance, 1990. *Heir:* *s* Alastair (John) Henniker-Heaton, *b* 4 May 1990. *Address:* 7 Brendon Way, Ashby de la Zouch, Leics LE65 1EY.

HEATON-HARRIS, Christopher; Member (C) East Midlands, European Parliament, since 1999; *b* 28 Nov. 1967; *s* of David Barry Heaton-Harris and Ann Geraldine Heaton-Harris; *m* 1990, Jayne Yvonne Carlow; two *d*. *Educ:* Tiffin Grammar Sch. for Boys, Kingston upon Thames. Dir, What 4 Ltd (wholesale fruit and vegetable co.), 1995–. Contested (C) Leicester South, 1997. *Recreation:* class 1 soccer referee. *Address:* (office) Manor Farm, Adwincle, Kettering, Northants NN14 3EL. *T:* and *Fax:* (01832) 720098.

HEATON-WARD, Dr William Alan, FRCPsych; Lord Chancellor's Medical Visitor, 1978–89; *b* 19 Dec. 1919; *s* of Ralph Heaton-Ward, MA, and Mabel Orton; *m* 1945, Christine Edith Fraser; two *d*. *Educ:* Sefton Park Jun. Sch.; Queen Elizabeth's Hosp., Bristol; Univ. of Bristol Med. Sch. MB, ChB, 1944; DPM 1948; FRCPsych 1971. Jun. Clerk, Messrs W. D. & H. O. Wills, 1936–38; House Phys., Bristol Royal Inf., 1944–45; MO, Littlemore Mental Hosp., 1945–46; served RNVR, 1946–48: Surg. Lt-Comdr; Neuropsychiatrist, Nore Comd; Sen. Registrar, St James Hosp., Portsmouth, 1948–50; Dep. Med. Supt, Hortham Brentry Gp, 1950–54; Stoke Park Hosp. Group: Consultant Psych., 1954–78, Hon. Consultant Psych., 1978–; Med. Supt, 1954–61; Cons. Psych. i/c, 1963–74; Clinical Teacher in Mental Health, Univ. of Bristol, 1954–78; Cons. Psych., Glos Royal Hosp., 1962–67. Mem., SW Mental Health Review Tribunal, 1960–78, 1985–92. Hon. Cons. Adviser: NAMH, 1966–73; CARE, 1970–78; British Council Vis. Lectr, Portugal, 1971. Royal Coll. of Psychiatrists: Vice Pres., 1976–78; Blake Marsh Lectr, 1976; Burden Res. Gold Medal and Prize Winner, 1978. Pres., Brit. Soc. for Study of Mental Subnormality, 1978–79; Vice-President: Fortune Centre of Riding Therapy, 1980–; RESCARE, Nat. Soc. for Mentally Handicapped People in Residential Care, 1995–; Avon Riding Centre for the Disabled, 1997–; Mem. Council, Inst. of Mental Subnormality, 1972–76; Hon. Mem., Amer. Assoc. of Physician Analysts, 1976–. Mem., Adv. Council, Radio Bristol, 1985–88. *Publications:* Notes on Mental Deficiency (jtly), 1952, 3rd edn 1955; Mental Subnormality, 1960, 5th edn, (jtly) as Mental Handicap, 1984; Left Behind, 1977; papers on all aspects of care and treatment of mentally handicapped people and on gen. psychiatric topics; book revs. *Recreations:* following all forms of outdoor sport, gardening, seeking the sun, philately, asking Why? *Address:* Bala Netty, 27 Withey Close West, Westbury on Trym, Bristol BS9 3SX. *T:* (0117) 968 1940. *Club:* Savages (Bristol).

HEAVEN, Derick; High Commissioner for Jamaica in London, 1994–99, and Ambassador (non-resident) to Scandinavia, Spain and Portugal; *b* 19 Dec. 1940; *m* 1966, Thyra Reid; two *s* one *d*. *Educ:* Cornwall Coll.; Jamaica Sch. of Agriculture. Mem., St Catherine Parish Council, 1974–76; MP for South St Catherine, 1976–80; Parly Sec., Min. of Foreign Affairs, then Minister of Trade and Commerce, 1980; involved in farming and business interests, 1980–89; Consul-General, New York, 1989–92; Ambassador to Japan and (non-resident) to People's Republic of China and Republic of Korea, 1992–94. Chm., Commonwealth Fund for Tech. Co-operation, 1996–99. *Recreations:* reading, travelling, sports. *Address:* c/o Jamaican High Commission, 1–2 Prince Consort Road, SW7 2BZ. *T:* (020) 7823 9911, *Fax:* (020) 7589 5154.

HEAVENER, Rt Rev. Robert William; Bishop of Clogher, 1973–80, retired; *b* 28 Feb. 1905; *s* of Joseph and Maria Heavener; *m* 1936, Ada Marjorie, *d* of Rev. Chancellor Thomas Dagg; one *s* one *d*. *Educ:* Trinity Coll., Dublin (MA). Ordained, 1929; Curate, Clones; Diocesan Curate, 1930; Curate-in-charge, Lack, 1933–38; Rector, Derryvullen N, 1938–46; Rector, Monaghan, 1946–73; Rural Dean, 1946. Examining Chaplain and Canon of Clogher, 1951–62; Canon of St Patrick's Cathedral, Dublin, 1962–68; Archdeacon of Clogher, 1968–73. OCF, 1938–43; Member of Staff of Command Welfare Officer, NI District, 1938–43. *Publications:* Co. Fermanagh, 1940 (a short topographical and historical account of NI); Diskos, 1970 (a collection of material for Adult Education); (as Robert Cielou) Spare My Tortured People, 1983 (an attempt to understand the Ulster situation today); Credo, 1993 (local history viewed in context of past and present). *Recreations:* tennis, rare book collecting. *Address:* 12 Church Avenue, Newtownabbey, Co. Antrim BT37 0PJ. *T:* (028) 9086 3242. *Club:* Friendly Brother House (Dublin).

HEBBLETHWAITE, Rev. Canon Brian Leslie; University Lecturer in Divinity, Cambridge, 1977–99, and Life Fellow of Queens' College, since 1994; *b* 3 Jan. 1939; *s* of Alderman Cyril Hebblethwaite and Sarah Anne Hebblethwaite; *m* 1991, Emma Sian, *d* of John Ivor Disley, *qv*; one *d*. *Educ:* Clifton Coll.; Magdalen Coll., Oxford (BA LitHum 1961; MA 1967); Magdalene Coll., Cambridge (BA Theol 1963; MA 1968; BD 1984); Westcott House, Cambridge; Univ. of Heidelberg. Curate, All Saints', Elton, Bury, 1965–68; Cambridge University: Bye-Fellow and Chaplain, 1968, Fellow and Dean of Chapel, 1969–94, Queens' Coll.; Univ. Asst Lectr in Divinity, 1973–77; Sen. Proctor, 1998–99; Examng Chaplain to Bishop of Manchester, 1977–98; Canon Theologian, Leicester Cathedral, 1982–. Pres., Soc. for Study of Theology, 1989–91. Editor for Ethics, Theologische Realenzyklopädie, 1980–. *Publications:* Evil, Suffering and Religion, 1976; The Problems of Theology, 1980; (ed jtly) Christianity and Other Religions, 1980; The Adequacy of Christian Ethics, 1981; (ed jtly) The Philosophical Frontiers of Christian Theology, 1982; The Christian Hope, 1984; Preaching Through the Christian Year 10, 1985; The Incarnation, 1987; The Ocean of Truth, 1988; (ed jtly) Divine Action, 1990; The Essence of Christianity, 1996; Ethics and Religion in a Pluralistic Age, 1997. *Recreations:* fell-walking, opera, cathedral and church architecture, books. *Address:* The Old Barn, 32 High Street, Stretham, Ely, Cambs CB6 3JQ. *T:* (01353) 648279. *Club:* Athenæum.

HEBDITCH, Maxwell Graham, CBE 1994; Chairman, Cultural Heritage National Training Organisation (formerly Museum Training Institute), since 1997 (Board Member, since 1990); *b* 22 Aug. 1937; *s* of late Harold Hebditch, motor engr, Yeovil, and Lily (*née* Bartle); *m* 1963, Felicity Davies; two *s* one *d*. *Educ:* Yeovil Sch.; Magdalene Coll., Cambridge. MA, FSA, FMA. Field Archaeologist, Leicester Museums, 1961–64; Asst Curator in Archaeology, later Curator in Agricultural and Social History, City Museum, Bristol, 1965–71; Dir, Guildhall Mus., London, 1971–74; Dep. Dir, 1974–77, Dir, 1977–97, Mus. of London. Co-Dir, Mus. Leadership Prog., UEA, 1994–. Mem., EC Cttee of Cultural Consultants, 1990–92. Chm., UK Nat. Cttee, ICOM, 1981–87; Pres., Museums Assoc., 1990–92 (Vice-Pres., 1988–90). Hon. Curator, Lyme Regis Mus., 2000–. Hon. DLitt City, 1992. *Publications:* contribs to archaeological and museological jls and books. *Recreation:* archaeology. *Address:* The Garden House, Fons George Road, Taunton TA1 3JU; Cultural Heritage National Training Organisation, Glyde House, Glydegate, Bradford BD5 0UP. *T:* (01274) 391056.

HEBER-PERCY, Algernon Eustace Hugh; Lord-Lieutenant for Shropshire, since 1996 (Vice Lord-Lieutenant, 1990–96); *b* 2 Jan. 1944; *s* of Brig. A. G. W. Heber-Percy, DSO and Daphne Wilma Kenyon (*née* Parker Bowles); *m* 1966, Hon. Margaret Jane Lever, *y d* of 3rd Viscount Leverhulme, *qv*; one *s* three *d*. *Educ:* Harrow; Mons OTC. Lieut Grenadier Guards, 1962–66. Farmer and landowner. Chm., Mercia Regional Cttee, Nat. Trust, 1990–99; Trustee, Nat. Gardens Scheme, 1990–. Pres., Shropshire and Mid Wales Hospice, 1988–; Chm., Walker Trust Cttee, 1990– (Mem., 1990–). Hon. Colonel: 5th Bn, Shropshire and Herefordshire LI (Vol.), 1998–99; W Midlands Regt, 1999–. DL Shropshire, 1986; High Sheriff of Shropshire, 1987. *Recreations:* gardening, country sports. *Address:* Hodnet Hall, Hodnet, Market Drayton, Shropshire TF9 3NN. *T:* (01630) 685202. *Club:* Cavalry and Guards.

HECKMAN, Prof. James Joseph, PhD; Henry Schultz Distinguished Service Professor, University of Chicago, since 1974; *b* 19 April 1944; *s* of John Jacob Heckman and Bernice Irene Medley Heckman; *m* 1st, 1964, Sally Lentz (marr. diss. 1971); 2nd, 1979, Lynne Pettler; one *s* one *d*. *Educ:* Colorado Coll. (BA Math 1965); Princeton (MA Econ 1968; PhD Econ 1971). Instructor-Associate Prof., Columbia Univ., 1970–74: Associate Prof., 1973–77, Prof. of Econs, 1977–, Univ. of Chicago; Yale Univ. (on leave), 1988–90. Guggenheim Fellow, 1977–78; Fellow, Center for Advanced Study in Behavioral Sci., 1977–78. Member: Amer. Acad., 1985–; NAS, 1992–; Fellow, Econometric Soc., 1980. Mem., Chicago Council on Foreign Relations. Hon. MA Yale, 1989; Hon. PhD Colorado Coll., 2001. John Bates Clark Medal, American Econ. Soc., 1983; Nobel Prize for Economics, 2000. *Publications:* Longitudinal Analysis of Labor Market Data, 1985; The Economic Approach to Social Program Evaluation, 2001; other smaller books and over 200 articles. *Recreations:* hiking, bicycling, reading. *Address:* 4807 S Greenwood, Chicago, IL 60615, USA. *T:* (773) 2684597; (office) Dept of Economics, University of Chicago, 1126 E 59th Street, Chicago, IL 60637, USA.

HECTOR, Alistair Gordon; Headmaster, George Heriot's School, Edinburgh, since 1998; *b* 5 Oct. 1955; *s* of Gordon Matthews Hector, CMG, CBE; *m* 1980, Rosemary Ann Craig; two *s* one *d*. *Educ:* Edinburgh Acad.; Univ. of St Andrews (MA); Univ. of Erlangen, Germany. Lektor in English, Univ. of Erlangen, 1978–80; Head of German, Merchiston Castle Sch., Edinburgh, 1980–85; Head of Dept, German, 1986–89, Modern Langs, 1989–95, King Edward's Sch., Bath; Dep. Headmaster, Warwick Sch., 1995–97. *Recreations:* sport, walking, music, travel, family. *Address:* George Heriot's School, Lauriston Place, Edinburgh EH3 9EQ. *T:* (0131) 229 7263.

HEDDY, Brian Huleatt; HM Diplomatic Service, retired; Regional Co-ordinator and Resettlement Officer, British Refugee Council, 1979–82; *b* 8 June 1916; *o s* of late Dr William Reginald Huleatt Heddy, Barrister-at-Law, and Ruby Norton-Taylor; *m* 1st, 1940, Barbara Ellen Williams (*d* 1965); two *s* one *d*; 2nd, 1966, Ruth Mackarness (*née* Hogan) (*d* 1967); (one step *s* two step *d*); 3rd, 1969, Horatia Clare Kennedy. *Educ:* St Paul's Sch.; Pembroke Coll., Oxford. Commissioned in 75th (Highland) Field Regt, Royal Artillery, Nov. 1939; served in France 1940; WA, 1943; War Office and France, 1944–45; Mem. of Gray's Inn. Entered Foreign Service, 1945. Appointed to Brussels, 1946; Denver, 1948; Foreign Office, 1952; Tel Aviv, 1953; UK Delegation to ECSC, Luxembourg, 1955; Foreign Office, 1959; promoted Counsellor, 1963; Consul-Gen. at Lourenço Marques, 1963–65; Head of Nationality and Consular Dept, Commonwealth Office, 1966–67; Head of Migration and Visa Dept, FCO, 1968–71; Consul-Gen. in Durban, 1971–76. *Recreations:* travel, reading. *Address:* Abbots Litten Cottage, Long Street, Sherborne, Dorset DT9 3BU. *T:* (01935) 813335. *Clubs:* East India, Devonshire, Sports and Public Schools, MCC.

HEDGECOE, Prof. John, Dr RCA; FCSD; Professor of Photography, Royal College of Art, London, 1975–94, now Emeritus; Pro Rector, 1981–93, Acting Rector, 1983–84; *b* 24 March 1937; *s* of William Hedgecoe and Kathleen Don; *m* 1960, Julia Mardon (marr. diss. 1995); two *s* one *d*. *Educ:* Gulval Village Sch., Cornwall; Guildford Sch. of Art. Staff Photographer, Queen Magazine, 1957–72; Freelance: Sunday Times and Observer, 1960–70; most internat. magazines, 1958–; Portrait, HM the Queen, for British and Australian postage stamps, 1966; photographed The Arts Multi-Projection, British Exhibn, Expo Japan Show, 1970. Royal College of Art: started Photography Sch., 1965: Head of Dept and Reader in Photography, 1965–74; Fellow, 1973; awarded Chair of Photography, 1975; started Audio/Visual Dept, 1980; started Holography Unit, 1982; Managing Trustee, 1983; Sen. Fellow, 1992. Vis. Prof., Norwegian Nat. Television Sch., Oslo, 1985. Man. Dir, Lion & Unicorn Press Ltd, 1986–94; Director: John Hedgecoe Ltd,

1965–95; Perennial Pictures Ltd, 1980, 1991. Mem. Photographic Bd, CNAA, 1976–78; Gov., W Surrey Coll. of Art (and Mem. Acad. Adv. Bd), 1975–; Acad. Gov., Richmond Coll., London; Trustee, The Minories Victor Batte-Lay Trust, 1985–88. Consultant, English Heritage, 1995– (Head of External Pubns). Has illustrated numerous books, 1958–; has contributed to numerous radio broadcasts. Television: Tonight, Aust. TV, 1967; Folio, Anglia, 1980; 8 progs on Photography, Channel Four, 1983, repeated 1984; Winners, Channel Four, 1984; Light and Form, US Cable TV, 1985. Exhibitions: London, Sydney, Toronto, Edinburgh, Venice, Prague; one-man exhibitions: RCA, 2000; Nat. Portrait Gall., 2000; Sainsbury Centre for Visual Arts, UEA, 2000; Westcliffe Gall., Sheringham, 2000; Guild House Gall., Guildford, 2001; collections: V&A Museum; Art Gall. of Ontario; Nat. Portrait Gall., London; Citibank, London; Henry Moore Foundn; Museum of Modern Art, NY; Leeds City Art Gall.; Ministry of Culture, Morocco. FRSA. Hon. FIIPC. Laureate and Medal for contribution to photography, Govt of Czechoslovakia, 1989. *Publications:* Henry Moore, 1968 (prize best art book, world-wide, 1969); (jtly) Kevin Crossley-Holland book of Norfolk Poems, 1970; Sculptures of Picasso, 1970; (jtly) Photography, Material and Methods, 1971–74 edns; Henry Moore, Energy in Space, 1973; The Book of Photography, 1976; Handbook of Photographic Techniques, 1977, 3rd edn 1992; The Art of Colour Photography, 1978 (Kodak Photobuchpreis Stuttgart 1979; Grand Prix Technique de la Photographie, Musée Français de la Photographie, Paris 1980); Possessions, 1978; The Pocket Book of Photography, 1979; Introductory Photography Course, 1979; Master Classes in Photography: Children and Child Portraiture, 1980; (illus.) Poems of Thomas Hardy, 1981; (illus.) Poems of Robert Burns, 1981; The Book of Advanced Photography, 1982; What a Picture!, 1983; The Photographer's Work Book, 1983, new edn 1997; Aesthetics of Nude Photography, 1984; The Workbook of Photo Techniques, 1984, 2nd edn 1997; The Workbook of Darkroom Techniques, 1984, 2nd edn 1997; Pocket Book of Travel and Holiday Photography, 1986; Henry Moore: his ideas, inspirations and life as an artist, 1986, new edn 1999; The Three Dimensional Pop-up Photography Book, 1986; (with A. L. Rowse) Shakespeare's Land, 1986; Photographer's Manual of Creative Ideas, 1986, new edn 1999; (with A. L. Rowse) Rowse's Cornwall, 1987; Practical Portrait Photography, 1987, new edn 2000; Practical Book of Landscape Photography, 1988, new edn 2000; Hedgecoe on Video, 1988; Hedgecoe on Photography, 1988; Complete Photography Guide, 1990; Video Photographer's Handbook, 1992; Zillij, 1992; John Hedgecoe's Complete Guide to Video, 1992; (jtly) The Art of Moroccan Ceramics, 1993; John Hedgecoe's Basic Photography, 1993; The New Book of Photography, 1994; Black and White Photography, 1994; Camcorder Basics, 1995; John Hedgecoe—a Complete Introductory Guide to Video, 1995; Breakfast with Dolly (novel), 1996; Figure and Form, 1996; John Hedgecoe's New Introductory Photography Course, 1996; The Spirit of the Garden, 1997; England's World Heritage, 1997; A Monumental Vision: the sculpture of Henry Moore, 1998; The Art of Colour Photography, 1998; Photography Sourcebook of Creative Ideas, 1998; John Hedgecoe's 35mm Photography, 1999; Portraits by John Hedgecoe, 2000; Photographing your Children, 2000; How to Take Great Photographs, 2001. *Recreations:* sculpture, building, gardening. *Address:* c/o Collins & Brown, London House, Parkgate Road, SW11 4NQ. *Club:* Arts.

HEDGELAND, Air Vice-Marshal Philip Michael Sweatman, CB 1978 OBE 1957 (MBE 1948); CEng, FIEE; *b* 24 Nov. 1922; *s* of Philip and Margaret Hedgeland, Maidstone, Kent; *m* 1946, Jean Riddle Brinkworth, *d* of Leonard and Anne Brinkworth, Darlington, Co. Durham; two *s*. *Educ:* Maidstone Grammar Sch.; City and Guilds Coll., Imperial Coll. of Science and Technology, London. BSc(Eng), ACGI (Siemens Medallist). Served War: commnd into Technical Br., RAF, 1942; despatches, 1943; Radar Officer, Pathfinder Force and at TRE, Malvern. Radar Develt Officer, Central Bomber Estabt, 1945–48; Radio Introd. Unit Project Officer for V-Bomber Navigation and Bombing System, 1952–57; Wing Comdr Radio (Air) at HQ Bomber Comd, 1957–60; jssc 1960; Air Ministry Technical Planning, 1961–62; aws 1963; Dir of Signals (Far East), Singapore, 1963–65; commanded RAF Stanbridge (Central Communications Centre), 1966–67; SASO, HQ Signals Comd/90 Gp, 1968–69; IDC, 1970; MoD Procurement Exec., Project Dir for Airborne Radar, 1971–74; Vice-Pres., Ordnance Bd, 1975–77, Pres., 1977–78. FCGI 1977. Pres., Pathfinder Assoc., 1985–87. *Recreations:* audio engineering, horticulture, amateur radio. *Club:* Royal Air Force.

HEDGER, Eric Frank, CB 1979; OBE 1960; Under Secretary, Director General of Defence Contracts, Ministry of Defence, 1969–80; *b* 15 Sept. 1919; *s* of late Albert Frank Hedger and Ellen Agnes Hedger (*née* Laffey); *m* 1945, Joan Kathleen Bernas; two *s* one *d*. *Educ:* St Luke's, Southsea. War Service, 1939–46 (despatches 1945): Adjutant, 10 Air Formation Signals; Adjutant, then 2nd i/c, 7 Indian Air Formation Signals. Secretary, Admiralty Awards Council, 1946–49; Admin. Staff Coll., 1958; Dir of Navy Contracts, 1968. Mem. of Council and Bd of Management, Inst. of Purchasing and Supply, 1974–75. Advr, Defence Manufacturers Assoc., 1983–88. FInstPS. *Recreations:* music, reading, gardening. *Address:* Helere House, Ridgeway Mead, Sidmouth, Devon EX10 9DT. *T:* (01395) 577741.

HEDGER, John Clive, CB 1998; education consultant; *b* 17 Dec. 1942; *s* of late Leslie John Keith Hedger and of Iris Hedger (*née* Friedlos); *m* 1966, Jean Ann Felstead; two *s* one *d*. *Educ:* Quirister Sch., Winchester; Victoria Coll., Jersey; Univ. of Sussex (BA 1965; MA 1966). Dept of Educn and Science, 1966; Asst Private Sec., 1970; Sec., Cttee of Enquiry on Educn of Handicapped, 1974–76; Under Sec., DES, 1988–92; Dep. Sec., Dept for Educn, 1992–95; Dir of Ops, DFEE, 1995–2000. Associate, Finance and Education Services Ltd. Trustee, Rathbone CI. Mem. Council, Radley Coll.; Gov., Technology Coll., Kingshurst. *Recreations:* coarse acting, walking, coarse sailing, growing things. *Address:* Poultons, Cookham, Berks SL6 9HW. *T:* (01628) 524146. *Club:* Odney (Cookham).

HEDGES, Anthony (John); Reader in Composition, University of Hull, 1978–95; *b* 5 March 1931; *s* of late S. G. Hedges; *m* 1957, Delia Joy Marsden; two *s* two *d*. *Educ:* Bicester Grammar Sch.; Keble Coll., Oxford. MA, BMus, LRAM. National Service as solo pianist and arranger Royal Signals Band, 1955–57. Teacher and Lecturer, Royal Scottish Academy of Music, 1957–63. During this period became a regular contributor to Scotsman, Glasgow Herald, Guardian, Musical Times, etc. Lecturer in Music, Univ. of Hull, 1963, Sen. Lectr, 1968. The Composers' Guild of Great Britain: Chm., Northern Br., 1966–67; Mem. Exec. Cttee of Guild, 1969–73, 1977–81, 1982–87; Chm. of Guild, 1972, Jt Chm., 1973. Member: Council, Central Music Library, Westminster, 1970; Council, Soc. for Promotion of New Music, 1974–81; Music Bd, CNAA, 1974–77; Music Panel, Yorks Arts Assoc., 1974–75, Lincs and Humberside Arts Assoc., 1975–78; Founder-conductor, The Humberside Sinfonia, 1978–81. Hon. DMus Hull, 1997. Wrote regularly for Yorkshire Post, 1963–78, and contributed to many jls, incl. Composer, Current Musicology, etc, and also broadcast on musical subjects. *Publications include: (works): orchestral:* Comedy Overture, 1962 (rev. 1967); Overture, October '62, 1962 (rev. 1968); Sinfonia Semplice, 1963; Expressions for Orchestra, 1964; Prelude, Romance and Rondo, strings, 1965; Concertante Music, 1965; Four Miniature Dances, 1967; A Holiday Overture, 1968; Variations on a theme of Rameau, 1969; Kingston Sketches, 1969; An Ayrshire Serenade, 1969; Four Diversions, strings, 1971; Celebrations, 1973; Symphony no 1, 1972–73; Festival Dances, 1976; Overture, Heigham Sound, 1978; Four Breton Sketches, 1980; Sinfonia Concertante, 1980; Scenes from the Humber, 1981; A Cleveland Overture, 1984; Concertino for Horn and String Orchestra, 1987; Sinfonia Giovanile, 1992; Showpiece, 1995; Symphony no 2, 1997; Trumpet Concerto, 2000; Fidlers Green, 2001; *choral:* Gloria, unaccompanied, 1965; Epithalamium, chorus and orch. (Spencer), 1969; To Music, chorus and orch. (various texts), 1972; Psalm 104, 1973; A Manchester Mass, chorus, orch. and brass band, 1974; A Humberside Cantata, 1976; Songs of David, 1978; The Temple of Solomon, 1979; I Sing the Birth: canticles for Christmas, 1985; I'll make me a world, 1990; *chamber music:* Five Preludes, piano, 1959; Four Pieces, piano, 1966; Rondo Concertante, violin, clarinet, horn, violoncello, 1967; Sonata for violin and harpsichord, 1967; Three Songs of Love, soprano, piano (from Song of Songs), 1968; String Quartet, 1970; Rhapsody, violin, piano, 1971, revd 1988; piano sonata, 1974; Song Cycle, 1977; Piano Trio, 1977; Fantasy for Violin and Piano, 1981; Sonatinas for Flute, Viola, Cello, 1982; Wind Quintet, 1984; Flute Trios, 1985, 1989; Fantasy Sonata for bassoon and piano, 1986; Clarinet Quintet, 1987; Flute Sonata, 1988; Five Aphorisms, piano, 1990; In such a night, string quartet, 1990; Bassoon Quintet, 1991; Piano Quartet, 1992; Trombone Sonata, 1994; Two Song Cycles, 1997; *opera:* Shadows in the Sun (lib. Jim Hawkins), 1976; *musical:* Minotaur (lib. Jim Hawkins), 1978; *miscellaneous:* many anthems, partsongs, albums of music for children; music for television, film and stage. *Recreations:* reading, crosswords, walking. *Address:* Malt Shovel Cottage, 76 Walkergate, Beverley, HU17 9ER. *T:* (01482) 860580.

HEDGES, Michael Irving Ian, QPM 1995; Chief Constable, South Yorkshire Police, since 1998; *b* 27 Jan. 1948; *s* of Arthur and Helen Hedges; *m* 1968, Beryl Janet Smith; one *s*. *Educ:* Holyrood Sch., Chard, Som.; King's College, London (LLB). Constable, Somerset and Bath Police, 1967–72; transf. to Metropolitan Police, 1972–87; Chief Superintendent, Thames Valley Police, 1987–88; Asst Chief Constable, Avon and Somerset Police, 1988–93; Dep. Chief Constable, South Yorkshire Police, 1993–98. RHS Medal for Gallantry, 1968. *Recreations:* swimming, reading, golf, fly fishing, gardening; an active Rotarian. *Address:* South Yorkshire Police HQ, Snig Hill, Sheffield S3 8LY. *T:* (0114) 252 3400; *e-mail:* mike.hedges@southyorks.pnn.police.uk.

HEDLEY, Prof. Anthony Johnson; JP; MD; FRCPE, FRCPGlas, FRCP, FFPHM; Professor of Community Medicine, University of Hong Kong, since 1988; *b* 8 April 1941; *s* of Thomas Johnson Hedley and Winifred Duncan; *m* 1st, 1967, Elizabeth-Anne Walsh (marr. diss. 1992); 2nd, 1996, Andrea Marilyn Miller. *Educ:* Rydal Sch.; Aberdeen Univ. (MB, ChB 1965; MD 1972); Edinburgh Univ. (Dip. Soc. Med. 1973). MRCP 1973; FRCPE 1981; FRCPGlas, 1985; FRCP 1987; FFPHM (FFCM 1981; MFCM 1975). Lectr in Community Medicine, Univ. of Aberdeen, 1974–76; Sen. Lectr in Community Health, Univ. of Nottingham, 1976–83; Prof.-Designate in Community Medicine, 1983–84, Henry Mechan Prof. of Public Health, 1984–88, Univ. of Glasgow. Med. Adviser (Thailand), ODA, 1977–. Chm., HK Council on Smoking and Health, 1997–. JP Hong Kong, 1998. Hon. MD Khon Kaen Univ., 1983. Bronze Bauhinia Star, HKSAR, 2000. *Publications:* papers and chapters on endocrine disease, surveillance of chronic disease, tobacco control and on med. educn. *Recreations:* long-distance running, photography, rifle shooting, flying (private pilot's licence, 1992). *Address:* Flat B6, Block 2, Tam Towers, 25 Sha Wan Drive, Victoria Road, Pok fu Lam, Hong Kong. *T:* 28194708, *Fax:* 28559014. *Clubs:* Rydal Veterans (Colwyn Bay); Hong Kong Aviation (Hong Kong).

HEDLEY, Rev. Charles John Wykeham, PhD; Rector of St James's, Piccadilly, since 1999; *b* 26 June 1947; *s* of Harry and Elisabeth Hedley. *Educ:* Christ's Hospital, Horsham; Royal Holloway Coll., Univ. of London (BSc; PhD 1973); Fitzwilliam Coll., Cambridge (MA); Westcott House, Cambridge. Deacon 1976, priest 1977; Asst Curate, St Anne's, Chingford, 1976–79; Curate, St Martin-in-the-Fields, 1979–86; Chaplain, Christ's Coll., Cambridge, 1986–90; Team Rector of Gleadless, Sheffield, 1990–99. *Recreations:* walking, squash, classical music. *Address:* St James's Rectory, 197 Piccadilly, W1V 0LL. *T:* (020) 7734 4511, *Fax:* (020) 7734 7449.

HEDLEY, Hon. Sir Mark, Kt 2002; **Hon. Mr Justice Hedley;** a Judge of the High Court, Family Division, since 2002; *b* 23 Aug. 1946; *s* of late Peter and of Eve Hedley; *m* 1973, Erica Britton; three *s* one *d*. *Educ:* Framlingham College; Univ. of Liverpool (LLB Hons). Called to the Bar, Gray's Inn, 1969; VSO, Sudan, 1969–70; practice at Liverpool Bar, 1971–92; Head of Chambers, 1983–92; a Recorder, 1988–92; a Circuit Judge, 1992–2001. *Recreations:* cricket, railways. *Address:* Royal Courts of Justice, Strand, WC2A 2LL.

HEDLEY, Prof. Ronald; Director, Trent Polytechnic, Nottingham, 1970–80 (now Nottingham Trent University), Emeritus Professor, 1980; *b* 12 Sept. 1917; *s* of Francis Hedley, Hebburn, Co. Durham; *m* 1942; one *s* one *d*. *Educ:* Jarrow Grammar Sch.; Durham Univ. (MA, DipEd); Ecole Normale d'Instituteurs, Evreux. Various appts in teaching and educational administration, 1947–64; Dep. Dir of Education, Nottingham, 1964–70. Chm., Regional Acad. Bd, Regional Adv. Council for Further Educn in E Midlands, 1972–76; Member: Central Council for Educn and Trng in Social Work, 1971–77; Nat. Adv. Council for Educn for Ind. and Commerce, 1973–77; Central Council for Educn and Trng of Health Visitors, 1972–77; Cttee for Arts and Social Studies, CNAA, 1974–76; Personal Social Services Council, 1974–78; Cttee on Recreation Management Training, 1977–80; Local Govt Trng Bd, 1978–81; Adv. Cttee for Supply and Educn of Teachers, 1980–81, Chm., Local Cttee for Teacher Educn, King Alfred's Coll., Winchester, 1986–89. FRSA 1970. Hon. Fellow: Trent Polytechnic, 1980; Nottingham Trent, 1992. Hon. Senator, Fachhochschule, Karlsruhe, Germany, 1980. Hon. LLD Nottingham, 1981; DUniv Nottingham Trent, 1993. *Address:* Evergreen, Haydn Close, Kings Worthy, Hants SO23 7RD. *T:* (01962) 884142.

HEDLEY, Ronald Henderson, CB 1986; DSc, PhD; FIBiol; Director, British Museum (Natural History), 1976–88; *b* 2 Nov. 1928; *s* of Henry Armstrong Hedley and Margaret Hopper; *m* 1957, Valmai Mary Griffith, New Zealand; one *s*. *Educ:* Durham Johnston Sch.; King's Coll., Univ. of Durham. Commissioned in Royal Regt of Artillery, 1953–55. Sen. Scientific Officer, British Museum (Natural History), 1955–61; New Zealand Nat. Research Fellow, 1960–61; Principal Scientific Officer, 1961–64; Dep. Keeper of Zoology, 1964–71; Dep. Dir, 1971–76. Vis. Lectr in Microbiology, Univ. of Surrey, 1968–75. Mem. Council, Fresh Water Biological Assoc., 1972–76; Trustee, Percy Sladen Meml Fund, 1972–77; Pres., British Section, Soc. of Protozoology, 1975–78; Member Council: Marine Biolog. Assoc., 1976–79, 1981–92; Zoological Soc., London, 1981–85 (Hon. Sec., 1977–80; Vice-Pres., 1980–85); Mem., Internat. Trust for Zoological Nomenclature, 1977–90. Member: Council, Royal Albert Hall, 1982–88; National Trust, 1985–88. *Publications:* (ed with C. G. Adams) Foraminifera, vols 1–3, 1974, 1976, 1978; (with C. G. Ogden) Atlas of Testate Amoebae, 1980; technical papers, mainly on biology, cytology and systematics of protozoa, 1956–. *Recreations:* horology, horticulture, humour. *Club:* Civil Service.

HEDLEY-MILLER, Dame Mary (Elizabeth), DCVO 1989; CB 1983; Ceremonial Officer, Cabinet Office, 1983–88; *b* 5 Sept. 1923; *d* of late J. W. Ashe; *m* 1950, Roger

Latham Hedley-Miller; one *s* two *d*. *Educ:* Queen's Sch., Chester; St Hugh's Coll., Oxford (MA). Joined HM Treasury, 1945; served in UK Treasury Delegn, Washington DC, 1947–49; Under-Sec., HM Treasury, 1973–83. Alternate Dir, Monetary Cttee, EEC, and Alternate Exec. Dir, European Investment Bank, 1977–83. *Recreations:* family, including family music; reading. *Address:* 108 Higher Drive, Purley, Surrey CR8 2HL. *T:* (020) 8660 1837. *Club:* Oxford and Cambridge.

HEDWORTH, (Alan) Toby; QC 1996; a Recorder, since 1995; *b* 23 April 1952; *s* of late John William Swaddle Hedworth and of Margaret Ena Hedworth (*née* Dodds); *m* 1987, Kathleen Mary (*née* Luke); two *d*. *Educ:* Kings Sch., Tynemouth; Royal Grammar Sch., Newcastle upon Tyne; St Catharine's Coll., Cambridge (MA). Called to the Bar, Inner Temple, 1975; Head, Trinity Chambers, Newcastle upon Tyne, 1999–. Vice Chm., Northumberland and Newcastle Soc, 1997–. *Recreations:* Newcastle United, the English Lake District, motoring, the built environment. *Address:* Trinity Chambers, 9–12 Trinity Chare, Quayside, Newcastle upon Tyne NE1 3DF. *T:* (0191) 232 1927. *Club:* Northern Counties (Newcastle upon Tyne).

HEFFER, Simon James; columnist, Daily Mail, 1993–94 and since 1995; *b* 18 July 1960; *er s* of late James Heffer and of Joyce Mary Heffer (*née* Clements); *m* 1987, Diana Caroline, *d* of Sqdn Ldr P. A. Clee; two *s*. *Educ:* King Edward VI Sch., Chelmsford; Corpus Christi Coll., Cambridge (BA 1982; MA 1986). Medical journalist, 1983–86; Leader Writer and Parly Sketch Writer, Daily Telegraph, 1986–91; Dep. Ed. and Political Corresp., Spectator, 1991–94; Dep. Ed., Daily Telegraph, 1994–95. *Publications:* Moral Desperado: a life of Thomas Carlyle, 1995; Power and Place: the political consequences of King Edward VII, 1998; Like the Roman: the life of Enoch Powell, 1998; Nor Shall My Sword: the reinvention of England, 1999; Vaughan Williams, 2000. *Recreations:* cricket, music, bibliophily, my family. *Address:* The Daily Mail, 2 Derry Street, W8 5TT. *T:* (020) 7938 6000. *Clubs:* Beefsteak, Garrick, MCC.

HEGARTY, Frances; *see* Fyfield, Frances.

HEGARTY, John Kevin; Creative Director, since 1982, and Chairman, since 1991, Bartle Bogle Hegarty Ltd; *b* 20 May 1944; *s* of Matthew and Anne Hegarty; *m* (separated); one *s* one *d*. *Educ:* Challoner Grammar Sch.; Hornsey Sch. of Art; London Coll. of Printing. Junior Art Dir, Benton & Bowles, 1965–66; Art Director: John Collings and Partners, 1966–67; Cramer Saatchi, 1967–70; Saatchi & Saatchi: Founding Shareholder, 1970; Dep. Creative Dir, 1971–73; Founding Partner and Creative Dir, TBWA, London, 1973–82. FRSA 1992. *Recreations:* tennis, ski-ing. *Address:* (office) 60 Kingly Street, W1R 6DS. *Club:* Groucho.

HEGARTY, Most Rev. Séamus; *see* Derry, Bishop of, (RC).

HEGARTY, Dr Seamus; Director, National Foundation for Educational Research, since 1994; *b* 19 Oct. 1945; *s* of James Hegarty and Mary Hegarty; *m* 1972, Carol Halls; two *s* one *d*. *Educ:* St Colman's Coll., Fermoy; University Coll., Dublin (BSc, HDipEd); Univ. of London Inst. of Educn (PhD 1975). Mgt trng, 1969–70; teaching, 1970–75; research, 1975–94. Visiting Professor: Reading Univ., 1996; London Univ. Inst. of Educn, 1996–. MInstD 1994. Ed., Educnl Res., 1983–; Founder Ed., European Jl Special Needs Educn, 1986–. *Publications:* Able to Learn?: the pursuit of culture-fair assessment, 1978; Educating Pupils with Special Needs in the Ordinary School, 1981; Integration in Action, 1982; Recent Curriculum Development in Special Education, 1982; The Making of a Profession, 1983; Training for Management in Schools, 1983; Research and Evaluation Methods in Special Education, 1985; Meeting Special Needs in Ordinary Schools, 1987, 2nd edn 1993; Developing Expertise: INSET for special educational needs, 1988; Review of the Present Situation of Special Education, 1988; Boosting Educational Achievement, 1989; Educating Children and Young People with Disabilities: principles and the review of practice, 1993; New Perspectives in Special Education: a six-country study of integration, 1994; Review of the Present Situation in Special Needs Education, 1995; The Role of Research in Mature Education Systems, 1997. Hon. Dr Free Univ. of Brussels, 1997; DUniv York, 1999. *Recreations:* contemporary fiction, music, board games, golf. *Address:* National Foundation for Educational Research, The Mere, Upton Park, Slough SL1 2DQ. *T:* (01753) 574123. *Club:* West Middlesex Golf.

HEGARTY, Thomas Brendan; QC 1992; **His Honour Judge Hegarty;** a Circuit Judge, since 1996; *b* 6 June 1943; *s* of Thomas Hegarty and Louise (*née* Conlan); *m* 1972, Irene Letitia Hall; one *s* one *d*. *Educ:* St Joseph's Coll., Dumfries; St John's Coll., Cambridge (BA 1964; LLB 1965; MA 1970). Called to the Bar, Middle Temple, 1970; a Recorder, 1988–96. *Address:* 8 King Street, Manchester M2 6AQ. *Club:* Manchester Tennis and Racquet.

HEGGESSEY, Lorraine Sylvia; Controller, BBC1, since 2000; *b* 16 Nov. 1956; *d* of Sam and Doris Heggessey; *m* 1985, Ronald de Jong, musician and composer; two *d*. *Educ:* Durham Univ. (BA Hons English Lit.). BBC: News Trainee and Sub Editor, 1979–83; Producer: Panorama, 1983–86; This Week, 1986–91; Editor, Biteback, 1991–92; Series Producer, The Underworld, 1992–94; Exec. Producer, BBC Science (QED, Animal Hospital, The Human Body, Minders), 1994–97; Head of Children's Programmes, 1997–2000; Jt Dir, Factual and Learning Progs, 2000. *Recreations:* ski-ing, tennis, gym, my children, having fun and laughing. *Address:* c/o BBC TV Centre, Wood Lane, W12 7RJ. *T:* (020) 8576 1622.

HEGGS, Geoffrey Ellis; Chairman of Industrial Tribunals, 1977–97, Regional Chairman, London North, 1990–97; a Recorder of the Crown Court, 1983–97; *b* 23 Oct. 1928; *s* of George Heggs, MBE and Winifred Grace Heggs; *m* 1953, Renée Fanny Madeleine Calderan (*see* R. F. M. Heggs); two *s* one *d*. *Educ:* Elizabeth Coll., Guernsey; LLB London. Admitted Solicitor, 1952. Rotary Foundn Fellow, Yale Univ., 1953–54; LLM Yale; Asst Sec., Law Soc., 1956–58; practised as solicitor in London, 1958–77. Mem., City of London Solicitors' Company. *Recreations:* military history, music, painting, sailing. *Address:* 12 Audley Road, Ealing, W5 3ET. *T:* (020) 8997 0305.

HEGGS, Renée Fanny Madeleine, (Miguette); a Social Security Commissioner, since 1981; a Child Support Commissioner, since 1993; *b* 29 Nov. 1929; *d* of E. and G. Calderan; *m* 1953, Geoffrey Ellis Heggs, *qv*; two *s* one *d*. *Educ:* Notting Hill and Ealing High Sch., GPDST; LLB (London) 1952. Admitted Solicitor, 1955; practising Solicitor, 1955–81. Chm., Nat. Insce Local Tribunal, 1976–81; pt-time Chm. of Industrial Tribunals, 1978–81; Pres., Appeal Tribunal under London Building Acts, 1979–81; Legal Mem., 1985–2000, Dep. Regl Chm., 1995–2000, Mental Health Review Tribunal. *Recreations:* music, travelling. *Address:* (office) Harp House, 83 Farringdon Street, EC4A 4DH. *T:* (020) 7353 5145.

HEGINBOTHAM, Christopher John; Chairman and Chief Executive, Eastern Region Specialised Commissioning Group, since 2000; *b* 25 March 1948; *s* of Joseph William and Marjorie Heginbotham; *m* 1988, Barbara Joyce, *d* of Charles and Lois-Ella Gill, Cincinnati, Ohio; two *d*. *Educ:* Univ. of Birmingham (BSc Hons); Univ. of Essex (MSc); MA Wales 1989. Area Manager, Circle Thirty Three Housing Trust, 1977–80; Assistant Borough Housing Officer, London Borough of Haringey, 1980–82; Nat. Dir, MIND (Nat. Assoc. for Mental Health), 1982–88; Fellow in Health Services Management, King's Fund Coll., London, 1989–93; Chief Executive: Riverside Mental Health NHS Trust, 1993–96; E and N Herts HA, 1996–2000. Member: Hampstead DHA, 1981–87; Waltham Forest DHA, 1989–92 (Vice-Chm., 1991–92); Chm., Redbridge and Waltham Forest FHSA, 1992–93. Member: Nat. Adv. Council on Employment of Disabled People, 1983–90; Bd, World Fedn for Mental Health, 1985–89 (rep., UN Commn on Human Rights, 1985–91); Bd, Internat. Acad. of Law and Mental Health, 1987–89. Vis. Res. Fellow, Univ. of Glasgow Inst. of Law and Ethics in Medicine, 1987–91; Vis. Sen. Fellow, Health Services Mgt Centre, Univ. of Birmingham, 1994–. *Publications:* Housing Projects for Mentally Handicapped People, 1981; Promoting Residential Services for Mentally Handicapped People, 1982; Webs and Mazes: approaches to community care, 1984; The Rights of Mentally Ill People, 1987; Return to Community, 1990; (with T. Campbell) Mental Illness: prejudice, discrimination and the law, 1990; (with C. Ham) Purchasing Dilemmas, 1992; Philosophy, Psychiatry and Psychopathy, 2000. *Recreations:* creative writing, walking. *Address:* TWI, Building 13, Granta Park, Great Abington, Cambridge CB1 6AL. *T:* (01223) 892106.

HEGINBOTHAM, Prof. Wilfred Brooks, OBE 1978; FREng; Director General, Production Engineering Research Association of Great Britain (PERA), Melton Mowbray, 1979–84; *b* 9 April 1924; *s* of Fred and Alice Heginbotham; *m* 1957, Marjorie Pixton; three *d*. *Educ:* Manchester Univ. (UMIST). BScTech 1949; MScTech 1950; PhD (Manchester) 1956; DSc (Manchester) 1979. FIProdE; MIMechE; FREng (FEng 1985); FRSA. Started in industry as wood pattern maker; part-time courses to HNC, 1938–46; Walter Preston Schol., Manchester Coll. of Tech., 1946; joined staff, 1951; Lectr in Production Engineering subjects, UMIST, 1951–58; industrial experience for 10 years; Nottingham University: Sen. Lectr, 1958; started first BSc course in Prod. Engrg in UK, 1961; Head of Dept of Prod. Engrg and Prod. Management, 1961–63; Cripps Prof., 1963–79; Dean, Faculty of Applied Science, 1967–71; Special Prof. of Prodn Engrg, 1983–86; Prof. Emeritus, 1990. Hon. Prof., Dept of Engrg, Univ. of Warwick, 1984–89; Vis. Prof., Univ. of RI, USA, 1987; Vis. Sen. Res. Fellow, Dept of Mech. Engrg, Univ. of Birmingham, 1989–. Developed group to study Automatic Assembly Systems and Industrial Robot devices, including computer vision and tactile sense, and co-operated with industry in development of advanced automation equipment. Chm. Org. Cttee for establishment of Brit. Robot Assoc., 1977, Chm. of Council, 1977–80, Pres., 1980–84. Editor-in-Chief: The Industrial Robot; Assembly Automation; Advanced Manufacturing Technology Journal. Hon. DTech Scis Eindhoven, 1981; Hon. DSc Aston, 1983. Engelberger Award, Robot Inst. of America, 1983. *Publications:* Programmable Assembly, 1984; (ed with D. T. Pham) Robot Grippers, 1986; contribs to Encyc. Brit. on Robot Devices and to prof. pubns on metal cutting, automated assembly, industrial robots, artificial intelligence and production processes. *Recreations:* gliding, model aircraft construction and operation (radio controlled). *Address:* 7 Paddocks View, Eaton Grange, Long Eaton, Notts NG10 3QF. *T:* (0115) 946 3250.

HEGLAND, David Leroy, DFC 1944; Director: Kemtron Ltd; Galena; Massey-Ferguson Holdings (Australia) Ltd; Carlton and United Breweries Holdings Ltd; Plessey Pacific Pty Ltd; cattle grazier; *b* 12 June 1919; *s* of Lee and Jennie Hegland; *m* 1944, Dagmar Cooke; two *s* one *d*. *Educ:* Whitman Coll., Washington, USA (BA). Served War, 1942–45; USN aircraft pilot in Pacific Ocean areas; Lt Comdr USNR, 1945. Managing Director: GM International, Copenhagen, 1956–58, GM South African, Port Elizabeth, 1958–61; GM Holden's Pty Ltd, Melbourne, 1962–65; Chm. and Man. Dir, Vauxhall Motors Ltd, Luton, 1966–70; Dir, General Motors Ltd, London, 1966–70; Chm., GKN Australia Ltd, and Dir, Ajax GKN Holdings Pty Ltd, and Guest, Keen & Nettlefolds (Overseas) Ltd, 1972–80. Member: Albury-Wodonga Develt Corp., 1980–81; Industry Forum, Aust. Acad. of Science, 1972; Aust. Inst. of Dirs; Delta Sigma Rho. FIMI. Richard Kirby medal for production engrg, 1964. *Recreations:* flying, tennis, riding. *Address:* 300 Hot Springs Road #A30, Santa Barbara, CA 93108–2038, USA. *Clubs:* Royal & Ancient Golf (St Andrews); Melbourne, Victoria Racing (Melbourne); Albury (Albury, NSW).

HEIGL, Peter Richard; HM Diplomatic Service; High Commissioner to the Bahamas, since 1999; *b* 21 Feb. 1943; *s* of late Joseph William Heigl and Violet Heigl (*née* Gatti); *m* 1965, Sally Lupton; three *s* one *d*. *Educ:* Worthing Technical High Sch. Min. of Power, 1963–66; Min. of Technology, 1966–70; DTI, 1970–74; FCO, 1974; served: Kuala Lumpur, 1974–78; Accra, 1978–81; FCO, 1981–84; 1st Sec., Riyadh, 1984–86; Consul (Commercial), Jedda, 1986–89; FCO, 1989–91; Dep. Head of Mission, Khartoum, 1991–93; Chargé, Phnom Penh, 1994; Dep. Head of Mission, Kathmandu, 1994–99. *Recreations:* family, travel, swimming, reading, local history. *Address:* c/o Foreign and Commonwealth Office, SW1A 2AH; Ashfold House, Buckland Dene, Lymington, Hants SO41 9DT.

HEILBRON, Hilary Nora Burstein; QC 1987; *b* 2 Jan. 1949; *d* of Dr Nathaniel Burstein and Dame Rose Heilbron, *qv*. *Educ:* Huyton College; Lady Margaret Hall, Oxford (MA). Called to the Bar, Gray's Inn, 1971; Bencher, 1995; Mem., 1996, SC 1997, Bar of NSW. DTI Inspector into Blue Arrow plc, 1989–91. Chairman: London Common Law and Commercial Bar Assoc., 1992–93; Jt Gen. Council of Bar and Law Soc. indep. working party into civil justice, 1993. Dir, The City Disputes Panel Ltd, 1994–. Vice-Chm., Marshall Aid Commemoration Commn, 1998–; Member: Adv. Council, Centre for Dispute Resolution, 1996–; Civil Justice Council, 1998–. *Recreations:* travel, gardening. *Address:* Brick Court Chambers, 7–8 Essex Street, WC2R 3LD. *T:* (020) 7379 3550.

HEILBRON, Dame Rose, DBE 1974; a Judge of the High Court of Justice, Family Division, 1974–88; *b* 19 Aug. 1914; *d* of late Max and Nellie Heilbron; *m* 1945, Dr Nathaniel Burstein; one *d*. *Educ:* Belvedere Sch., GPDST; Liverpool University, LLB 1st Class Hons, 1935; Lord Justice Holker Scholar, Gray's Inn, 1936; LLM 1937. Called to Bar, Gray's Inn, 1939, Bencher, 1968, Treasurer, 1985; joined Northern Circuit, Leader, 1973–74, Presiding Judge, 1979–82; QC 1949; Recorder of Burnley, 1956–71, a Recorder, and Hon. Recorder of Burnley, 1972–74. Mem., Bar Council, 1973–74. Chm., Home Sec's Adv. Gp on Law of Rape, 1975–. Hon. Fellow: Lady Margaret Hall, Oxford, 1976; UMIST, 1986; Hon. LLD: Liverpool, 1975; Warwick, 1978; Manchester, 1980; CNAA, 1988. Formerly Hon. Col, WRAC(TA).

See also H. N. B. Heilbron.

HEIM, Most Rev. Bruno Bernard, PhD, JCD; Apostolic Nuncio to the Court of St James's, 1982–85 (Apostolic Delegate, 1973–82); *b* Olten, Switzerland, 5 March 1911; *s* of Bernard and Elisabeth Heim-Studer. *Educ:* Olten, Engelberg and Schwyz; St Thomas of Aquino Univ.; Gregorian Univ.; Univ. of Fribourg; Papal Acad. of Diplomacy. Priest 1938; Vicar in Basle and Arbon, 1938–42; Chief Chaplain for Italian and Polish Internees in Switzerland, 1943–45; Sec., Papal Nunciature in Paris; Auditor at Nunciature in Vienna; Counsellor and Chargé d'affaires at Nunciature in Germany; titular Archbp of Xanthos, 1961; Apostolic Delegate to Scandinavia, 1961–69; Apost. Nuncio (Ambassador): to Finland, 1966–69; to Egypt, 1969–73; President of Caritas Egypt, 1969–73. Lauréat, French Acad.; Corresp. Mem., Real Academia de la Historia, Madrid,

1950; Mem. Council, Internat. Heraldic Acad.; Patron, Cambridge Univ. Heraldic and Genealogical Soc. Grand Cross: Order of Malta, 1950; Teutonic Order, 1961; Order of Finnish Lion, 1969; Order of St Maurice and Lazarus, 1973; (1st Class) Order of the Republic, Egypt, 1975; Bailiff Grand Cross and Grand Prior, Constantinian Order of St George; Sub-Prelate, Order of St John; Comdr, Order of Isabel la Catolica; Gr. Officer Order of Holy Sepulchre; Orders of Merit: Germany, Italy, Austria; Officier Légion d'honneur, etc. *Publications:* Die Freundschaft nach Thomas von Aquin, 1934; Wappenbrauch und Wappenrecht in der Kirche, 1947; Coutumes et droit héraldiques de l'Eglise, 1949; L'oeuvre héraldique de Paul Boesch, 1973; Heraldry in the Catholic Church, 1978, rev. and enlarged edn 1981; Armorial Liber Amicorum, 1981; Or and Argent, 1994; contrib. Adler, Zeitschrift f. Heraldik und Genealogie, Heraldisk Tidskrift. *Recreations:* heraldry, heraldic painting, cooking, gardening. *Address:* Zehnderweg 31, 4600 Olten, Switzerland.

HEIM, Paul Emil, CMG 1988; a Chairman: Financial Services Tribunal, since 1988; Value Added Tax Tribunal, since 1989; President, FIMBRA Appeal Tribunals, since 1990; a Deputy Chairman, PIA Appeal Tribunal, since 1994; Visiting Professor, Leicester University, since 1988; *b* 23 May 1932; *s* of George Heim and Hedy Heim (*née* Herz); *m* 1962, Elizabeth, *er d* of late Lt-Col G. M. Allen, MBE; one *s* two *d*. *Educ:* Prince of Wales School, Nairobi; King's Coll., Univ. of Durham (LLB). Called to the Bar, Lincoln's Inn, 1955, Bencher, 1986. Dep. Registrar, Supreme Court of Kenya, then Sen. Dep. Registrar, Magistrate and Acting Registrar (HMOCS), 1954–65; admitted Advocate, Supreme Court, 1959; Administrator, European Court of Human Rights, Strasbourg, 1965, European Commn of Human Rights, Strasbourg, 1966; Principal Administrator, Political Directorate, Council of Europe, 1967, Dep. Head, Private Office, 1969; Head of Div., then Dir, European Parlt, 1973–81; Registrar, European Court of Justice, 1982–88; Pres., Heads of Admin of EC Instns, 1986–88; Special Advr, European Court of Justice, 1988–89. Hon. Res. Fellow, Univ. of Exeter, 1988–. Chm., George Heim Meml Trust, 1998–; Dep. Chm., Luxembourg Soc., 1999–. Grand Officer, Order of Merit (Luxembourg), 1998. *Address:* Wearne Wych, Langport, Somerset TA10 9AA.

HEIN, Prof. Jotun John; Professor of Bioinformatics, University of Oxford, and Fellow of University College, Oxford, since 2001; *b* Denmark, 19 July 1956; *s* of Piet Hein and Gerd Erikson; *m* 2001, Anne-Mette Pederse; two *d*. *Educ:* Aarhus Univ. (Licentiate in Sci. 1990). Asst Prof., 1990–94, Associate Prof., Aarhus Univ., 1994–2001. *Recreations:* reading, golf, tennis, badminton. *Address:* Peter Medawar Building for Pathogen Research, South Parks Road, Oxford OX1 3SY. *T:* (01865) 281541.

HEINE, Prof. Volker, FRS 1974; Professor of Theoretical Physics, University of Cambridge, 1976–97; Fellow of Clare College, Cambridge, since 1960; *b* 19 Sept. 1930; *m* 1955, M. Daphne Hines; one *s* two *d*. *Educ:* Otago Univ. (MSc, DipHons); Cambridge Univ. (PhD). FInstP. Demonstrator, Cambridge Univ., 1958–63, Lectr 1963–70; Reader in Theoretical Physics, 1970–76. Vis. Prof., Univ. of Chicago, 1965–66; Vis. Scientist, Bell Labs, USA, 1970–71. For. Mem., Max-Planck Inst., Stuttgart, 1980–. Fellow, Amer. Phys. Soc., 1987. Royal Medal, Royal Soc., 1993; Paul Dirac Medal, Inst. of Physics, 1993; Max Born Medal, Inst. of Physics and German Physical Soc., 2001. *Publications:* Group Theory in Quantum Mechanics, 1960; (jtly) Solid State Physics Vol. 24, 1970, Vol. 35, 1980; articles in Proc. Royal Soc., Jl Physics, Physical Review, etc. *Address:* Cavendish Laboratory, Madingley Road, Cambridge CB3 0HE.

HEISBOURG, François; Professor, Institut d'Etudes Politiques, Paris; *b* 24 June 1949; *s* of Georges Heisbourg, *qv*; *m* 1989, Elyette, *d* of Georges Levy; two *s*. *Educ:* Landon School, Bethesda, Maryland; Collège Stanislas, Paris; Inst. d'Etudes Politiques, Paris; Ecole Nationale d'Administration, Paris. French Foreign Ministry: Asst to Head of Economics Dept, 1978; Mem., Policy Planning Staff, 1979; 1st Sec., French Mission to UN, NY, 1979–81; Diplomatic Adviser to Minister of Defence, 1981–84. Vice-Pres., Thomson SA, Paris, 1984–87; Dir, IISS, 1987–92; Sen. Vice-Pres., Matra Défense-Espace, Paris, 1992–98; Hd, French Interministerial gp on study of internat. relations and strategic affairs, 1999–2000. Chairman: Exec. Cttee, IISS, 1997–; Geneva Centre for Security Policy, 1998–. Numerous foreign orders. *Publications:* Emiliano Zapata et la Révolution mexicaine, 1978; (with P. Boniface) La Puce, les Hommes et la Bombe, 1986; (contrib.) The Conventional Defence of Europe, 1986; (contrib.) Conventional Arms Control and East-West Security, 1989; (ed) The Changing Strategic Landscape, 1989; (ed) The Strategic Implications of Change in the Soviet Union, 1990; (contrib.) The Shape of the New Europe, 1992; (contrib.) Western Europe and the Gulf War, 1992; Les Volontaires de l'An 2000, 1995; Warfare, 1997; European Defence: making it work, 2000; contribs to internat. jls. *Recreations:* hiking, old atlas collecting. *Club:* Travellers (Paris).

HEISBOURG, Georges; Ambassador of Luxembourg, retired; *b* 19 April 1918; *s* of Nicolas Heisbourg and Berthe (*née* Ernsterhoff); *m* 1945, Hélène Pinet; two *s* one *d*. *Educ:* Athénée, Luxembourg; Univs of Grenoble, Innsbruck and Paris. Head of Govt Press and Information Office, Luxembourg, 1944–45; Attaché 1945–48, Sec. 1948–51, of Legation, London; Head of Internat. Organisations Section, Dir of Political Affairs, Min. of For. Affairs, Luxembourg, 1951–58; Luxembourg Ambassador to USA, Canada and Mexico, 1958–64; Perm. Rep. to UN, 1958–61; Luxembourg Ambassador: to Netherlands, 1964–67; to France, 1967–70; Perm. Rep. to OECD, 1967–70; Sec. Gen., WEU, 1971–74; Ambassador to USSR, Finland, Poland and Outer Mongolia, 1974–77; Perm. Rep. to Council of Europe, 1978–79; Ambassador to Fed. Rep. of Germany and to Denmark, 1979–83. Médaille de l'Ordre de la Résistance, Grand Officer, Nat. Order of Crown of Oak, 1980 (Chevalier, 1958), Comdr, Order of Adolphe de Nassau, 1963, and Grand Officer, Order of Merit, 1976, Luxembourg; also holds decorations from Austria, Belgium, France, Germany, Italy, Mexico, and the Netherlands. *Publication:* Le Gouvernement Luxembourgeois en exil 1940, Vol. I, 1986, Vol. II, 1987, Vol. III, 1989, Vol. IV, 1991. *Recreation:* swimming. *Address:* 9A Boulevard Joseph II, 1840 Luxembourg.
See also F. Heisbourg.

HEISER, Sir Terence Michael, (Sir Terry), GCB 1992 (KCB 1987; CB 1984); Permanent Secretary, Department of the Environment, 1985–92; *b* 24 May 1932; *s* of David and Daisy Heiser; *m* 1957, Kathleen Mary Waddle; one *s* two *d*. *Educ:* Grafton Road Primary Sch., Dagenham; London Evacuee Sch., Sunninghill, Berks; Windsor County Boy's Sch., Berks; Birkbeck Coll., Univ. of London; BA (Hons English). Served in RAF, 1950–52; joined Civil Service 1949, served with Colonial Office, Min. of Works, Min. of Housing and Local Govt; Principal Private Sec. to Sec. of State for the Environment, 1975–76; Under Secretary: Housing Directorate, 1976–79; Local Govt Finance Directorate, 1979–81; Dep. Sec., DoE, 1981–85. Non-exec. Director: Abbey National plc, 1992–; Sainsbury plc, 1992–2000; Wessex Water plc, 1993–98. Mem. Bd, PIA, 1994–2000. Chm., Gen. Adv. Council, BBC, 1992–96. Adv. Panel on Spoliation, DCMS. Mem. Exec. Cttee, Nat. Trust, 1993–; Trustee: V&A Mus., 1993–; Prince of Wales Phoenix Trust, 1996–. Governor, Birkbeck Coll., London, 1990–; Mem. Council, Sussex Univ., 1999–. Freeman, City of London, 1990. Hon. Fellow, Birkbeck Coll., London, 1988. Hon. DLitt Bradford, 1988. *Recreations:* reading, walking, talking. *Club:* Garrick.

HEISKELL, Andrew; Chairman Emeritus, New York Public Library (Chairman, 1981–90; Director, since 1978); Chairman of the Board, 1960–80, and Chief Executive Officer, 1969–80, Time Inc., retired; *b* Naples, 13 Sept. 1915; *s* of Morgan Heiskell and Ann Heiskell (*née* Hubbard); *m* 1937, Cornelia Scott (marr. diss.); one *s* one *d*; *m* 1950, Madeleine Carroll (marr. diss.); *m* 1965, Marian, *d* of Arthur Hays Sulzberger, and *widow* of Orvil E. Dryfoos. *Educ:* Switzerland; France; University of Paris. Science teacher, Ecole du Montcel, Paris, 1935. Life Magazine: Science and Medicine Editor, 1937–39; Asst Gen. Manager, 1939–42; Gen. Manager, 1942–46; Publisher, 1946–60; Vice-Pres., Time, Inc., 1949–60. Overseer, Harvard Univ., 1973–79 (Pres., Bd of Overseers, 1977); Fellow, Harvard Coll., 1979–89. Chm., President's Cttee on Arts and Humanities, 1982–90; Vice-Chm., Vivian Beaumont Theater; Director: Enterprise Foundn; Bryant Park Restoration Corp.; Mem. Bd of Visitors, Graduate Sch. and University Center, City Univ. of New York; Chairman, Executive Committee: People for the American Way; Amer. Acad. in Rome; Inst. of Internat. Educn; eponymous Andrew Heiskell Library for Blind and Physically Handicapped, opened 1991. Gold Medal Award of Merit, Wharton Sch. Alumni Soc., Univ. of Pennsylvania, 1968; John W. Gardner Leadership Award. Hon. LLD: Shaw Univ., 1968; Lake Erie Coll., 1969; Hofstra Univ., 1972; Hobart and William Smith Colls, 1973; Harvard, 1989; Hon. DLitt Lafayette Coll., 1969. *Address:* Time and Life Building, Rockefeller Center, New York, NY 10020; 870 United Nations Plaza, New York, NY 10017; Darien, CT, USA.

HELAISSI, Sheikh Abdulrahman Al-, Hon. GCVO; retired; Saudi Arabian Ambassador to the Court of St James's, 1966–76; *b* 24 July 1922. *Educ:* Universities of Cairo and London. Secretary to Embassy, London, 1947–54; Under-Sec., Min. of Agriculture, 1954–57; Head of Delegn to FAO, 1955–61; Ambassador to Sudan, 1957–60; Representative to UN, and to various confs concerned with health and agriculture; Delegate to Conf. of Non-aligned Nations, Belgrade, 1961; Ambassador: Italy and Austria, 1961–66; UK and Denmark (concurrently), 1966–76. Versed in Islamic Religious Law. *Publication:* The Rehabilitation of the Bedouins, 1959. *Address:* PO Box No 8062, Riyadh-11482, Saudi Arabia.

HELE, Desmond George K.; *see* King-Hele.

HELE, James Warwick, CBE 1986; High Master of St Paul's School 1973–86; *b* 24 July 1926; *s* of John Warwick Hele, Carlisle; *m* 1948, Audrey Whalley; four *d*. *Educ:* Sedbergh Sch.; Hertford Coll., Oxford; Trinity Hall, Cambridge (Schol., MA). 1st cl. hons History Tripos 1951. 5th Royal Inniskilling Dragoon Guards, 1946–48. Asst Master, Kings College Sch., Wimbledon, 1951–55; Rugby School: Asst Master, 1955–73; Housemaster, Kilbracken, 1965–73; 2nd Master, 1970–73. Chairman: Headmasters' Conference, 1982 (Chm., Acad. Cttee, 1979–81); Indep. Schs Adv. Cttee, 1983–88; Member: Secondary Exams Council, 1986–88; Exec. Cttee, GBA, 1988–97. Chairman: Westminster Centre for Educn, 1991–97; Combined Trusts Scholarship Trust, 1986–. Mem., Dorset FHSA, 1990–92. Trustee, Brathay Hall, 1977–91. Governor: Rossall Sch., 1985–90; Uppingham Sch., 1986–92; Port Regis Sch., Shaftesbury, 1986–2001; Sherborne Sch., 1986–96 (Chm. Govs, 1990–96); Chm., Clouds House, East Knoyle, 1992–2000. *Recreations:* Rugby football (Oxford Univ. XV 1944), hill walking. *Address:* Hillside, Hawkesdene Lane, Shaftesbury, Dorset SP7 8EX. *T:* (01747) 854205. *Club:* East India, Devonshire, Sports and Public Schools.

HELEY, (Neil) Patrick; a District Judge (Magistrates' Courts) (formerly Stipendiary Magistrate), Norfolk, since 1994; *b* 25 April 1949; *s* of John William Heley and late Hilary Heley (*née* Stretton); *m* 1975, Jane Louise Holliday-Rhodes; one *s* one *d*. *Educ:* Leeds Univ. (LLB). Qualified as solicitor, 1973; Asst Solicitor, W Yorks County Prosecuting Solicitor's Office, 1974–82; Partner, Green Williamson & Way, Wakefield, 1984–93. Member: Bd of Visitors, Wakefield Prison, 1984–91; Duty Solicitor Cttee, Legal Aid Bd, 1992–94. *Recreations:* opera, music, literature, the countryside, small French restaurants. *Address:* The Magistrates' Court, Bishopgate, Norwich NR3 1UP. *T:* (01603) 679500.

HELLAWELL, Keith, QPM 1990; UK Anti-Drugs Co-ordinator, 1998–2001; *b* 18 May 1942; *s* of Douglas Hellawell and Ada Alice Hellawell (*née* Battye); *m* 1963, Brenda Hey; one *s* two *d*. *Educ:* Kirkburton Sec. Mod. Sch.; Dewsbury Tech. Coll.; Barnsley Coll. of Mining; London Univ. (LLB 1972); Cranfield Inst. of Tech. (MSc 1982); Police Staff Coll. Huddersfield Borough Police, 1962; seconded to Home Office, 1975–78, incl. service in NI; Asst Chief Constable, W Yorks Police, 1983; Dep. Chief Constable, Humberside Police, 1985; Chief Constable: Cleveland Police, 1990; W Yorks Police, 1993–98. Advr, Crimestoppers Trust, 1994–. Member: Adv. Council on Misuse of Drugs, 1994–; Bd, Northern Counties Housing Assoc. Ltd, 1996–; St John's Council, W Yorks, 1983–85 and 1993–; Council, NSPCC (Trustee, 1993–2000; Chm., Services to Children's Cttee, 1996–). Mem., Editl Bd, Forensic Medicine Jl, 1996–. Hon. LLD Bradford, 1998; Hon. DSSc Leeds, 1998; Hon. DCL Huddersfield, 1998. OStJ 1996. *Recreations:* design, gardening, reading, sport.

HELLIER, Maj.-Gen. Eric James, CBE 1977 (OBE 1970, MBE 1967); Regional Manager, International Military Services, 1981–92; *b* 23 July 1927; *s* of Harry and Elizabeth Hellier; *m* 1952, Margaret Elizabeth Leadeham; one *s* one *d* (and one *s* decd). *Educ:* Hugh Saxons Sch.; Cardiff Univ. Served, 1945–66: Exec. Officer, RNVR; regtl duty, Royal Signals; Staff Coll. and Jt Services Staff Coll; GSO2 WO; DAA&QMG 39 Inf. Bde; CO, 24 Signals Regt, 1967–69; GSO1 Plans (Operational Requirements) MoD, 1970; Col A/Q HQ 4 Div, 1971–72; Comd Bde Royal Signals and Catterick Garrison, 1973–74; RCDS, 1975; Brig A/Q HQ 1(BR), Corps, 1976–79; Maj. Gen. Admin, UKLF, 1979–81. Col Comdt, 1981–87, Rep. Col Comdt, 1983, Royal Corps of Signals. Chairman: Gen. Purposes Cttee, Regular Forces Employment Assoc., 1983–91; Royal Signals Instn, 1984–89; Fund Raising Cttee, Nat. Mus. of Army Communications, 1991–97; Trustee, Royal Signals Mus., 1998–. *Recreations:* golf, squash, ski-ing, sailing. *Address:* Goddards, 27 Church Street, Wherwell, Hants SP11 7JJ. *T:* (01264) 860710.

HELLINGA, Dr Lotte, FBA 1990; Secretary, Consortium of European Research Libraries, since 1994; a Deputy Keeper, Humanities and Social Sciences, British Library, 1986–95; *b* 9 Sept. 1932; *d* of Arie Querido and Catharina Geertruida Querido (*née* Nagtegaal); *m* Wytze Hellinga (*d* 1985); one *s*. *Educ:* Univ. of Amsterdam. Lectr, then Sen. Lectr, Univ. of Amsterdam, 1967–76; Asst Keeper, British Liby, 1976–86. Vice Pres., Bibliographical Soc., 1996–. Correspondent, Royal Netherlands Acad. of Scis, 1989–. Gutenberg Preis, Mainz, 1989. *Publications:* The Fifteenth Century Printing Types of the Low Countries, 1966; Caxton in Focus, 1982; (ed jtly) The Cambridge History of the Book in Britain, vol. III, 1999; numerous articles in learned jls. *Address:* 40A Canonbury Square, N1 2AW. *T:* (020) 7359 2083.

HELLIWELL, Prof. John Richard, DPhil, DSc; FInstP, FRSC, FIBiol; Professor of Structural Chemistry, Manchester University, since 1989; *b* 19 Sept. 1953; *s* of Henry Smith Helliwell and Amy (*née* Southam); *m* 1978, Madeleine Berry; two *s* one *d*. *Educ:* Ossett Sch.; Univ. of York (BSc 1st cl. Hons Physics 1974; DSc 1996); Balliol Coll., Univ. of Oxford (DPhil Molecular Biophysics 1978). CPhys, FInstP 1986; CChem, FRSC 1995; CBiol, FIBiol 1998. MRC Res. Asst and Jun. Res. Fellow, Linacre Coll., Oxford, 1978;

Lectr in Biophysics, Keele Univ., jtly with SERC Daresbury Lab., 1979–83; SSO, then PSO, SERC Daresbury Lab., 1983–85; Lectr in Physics, York Univ., 1985–88; jtly with SERC Daresbury Lab., 1985–93; jtly with CLRC Daresbury Lab., 2001–. Vis. Res. Scholar, Cornell Univ., 1994; Vis. Prof., Univ. of Chicago, 1994. Member: Nat. Cttee, British Biophysical Soc., 1996–; UK Delegn, Council of Eur. Synchrotron Radiation Facility, Grenoble, 1997–2000; Neutron Beam Scientific Priorities Cttee, Institut Laue Langevin, Grenoble, 1998–2001 (Chm., 1999–2001); Leader, UK Delegn, World Congress of Biophysics, New Delhi, 1999. Conference Lectures: Yugoslav-Italian Crystallographic Assoc., 1989; Soc. of Crystallographers of Australia, 1994 (1987 Fellow (Hon.), 1994); British Crystallographic Assoc., 1995; 2nd Internat. Conf. on Life Science, Japan, 1996; other Lectures: Ilyas Haneef Meml, Univ. of Leeds, 1993; Herzenberg Symposium, Yale Univ., 1995; Chem. Dept Dedication, Univ. of Toledo, 1998; K. Banerjee Meml, and Silver Medal, Indian Assoc. for Cultivation of Sci., Calcutta, 2000; 150th Anniv. W. L. Bragg, Univ. of Manchester. Transactions Symposium Orgnr, Amer. Crystallographic Assoc., 1999. Mem. Court, UMIST, 1996–. Hon. Mem., Nat. Inst. of Chem., Slovenia, 1997–. Editor-in-Chief, Internat. Union of Crystallography's Jls, 1996–. *Publications:* Macromolecular Crystallography with Synchrotron Radiation, 1992; (ed jtly) Time-resolved Macromolecular Crystallography, 1992; (ed jtly) Synchrotron Radiation in the Biosciences, 1994; (ed jtly) Time-resolved Diffraction, 1997; original res. papers and reviews in scientific jls. *Recreations:* family, squash, walking the dog. *Address:* Department of Chemistry, University of Manchester, Manchester M13 9PL. *T:* (0161) 275 4694, *Fax:* (0161) 275 4734; *e-mail:* John.Helliwell@man.ac.uk.

HELLYER, Hon. Paul Theodore; PC (Canada) 1957; FRSA 1973; Syndicated Columnist, Toronto Sun, 1974–84; *b* Waterford, Ont, Canada, 6 Aug. 1923; *s* of A. S. Hellyer and Lulla M. Anderson; *m* 1945, Ellen Jean, *d* of Henry Ralph, Toronto, Ont; two *s* one *d*. *Educ:* Waterford High Sch., Ont; Curtiss-Wright Techn. Inst. of Aeronautics, Glendale, Calif; University of Toronto (BA). Fleet Aircraft Mfg Co., Fort Erie, Ont. Wartime service, RCAF and Cdn Army. Propr Mari-Jane Fashions, Toronto, 1945–56; Treas., Curran Hall Ltd, Toronto, 1950 (Pres., 1951–62). Elected to House of Commons, 1949; re-elected, 1953; Parly Asst to Hon. Ralph Campney, Minister of Nat. Defence, 1956; Associate Minister of Nat. Defence, 1957; defeated in gen. elections of June 1957 and March 1958; re-elected to House of Commons in by-election Dec. 1958 and again re-elected June 1962, April 1963, Nov. 1965, June 1968, and Oct. 1972; defeated gen. election July 1974; Minister of National Defence, 1963–67; Minister of Transport, 1967–69, and Minister i/c Housing, 1968–69; resigned 1969 on question of principle relating to housing. Chm., Federal Task Force on Housing and Urban Develt, 1968. Served as a Parly Rep. to NATO under both L and C administrations. Joined Parly Press Gallery, Oct. 1974. Distinguished visitor, York Univ., 1969–70. Founder and Leader, Action Canada party, 1971; joined Progressive Cons. Party, 1972; Candidate for leadership of Progressive Cons. Party, Feb. 1976; re-joined Liberal Party, Nov. 1982, resigned Dec. 1996; Leader, Canadian Action Party, 1997–. Exec. Dir, The Canada Uni Assoc., 1991–. *Publications:* Agenda: a Plan for Action, 1971; Exit Inflation, 1981; Jobs for All—Capitalism on Trial, 1984; Canada at the Crossroads, 1990; Damn the Torpedoes, 1990; Funny Money: a common sense alternative to mainline economics, 1994; Surviving the Global Financial Crisis: the economics of hope for Generation X, 1996; Arundel Lodge: a little bit of old Muskoka, 1996; The Evil Empire: globalization's darker side, 1997; Stop: think, 1999; Goodbye Canada, 2001. *Recreations:* philately, music. *Address:* Suite 506, 65 Harbour Square, Toronto, ON M5J 2L4, Canada. *Club:* Ontario.

HELM, Marie Theresa C.; *see* Conte-Helm.

HELMER, Roger; Member (C) East Midlands, European Parliament, since 1999; *b* 25 Jan. 1944; *s* of Charles Henry Helmer and Nellie Ethel Helmer; *m* 1st, 1967, Veronica Logan (marr. diss. 1984); one *s* one *d*; 2nd, 1987, Sara Thomas (*née* Winterbottom). *Educ:* King Edward VI Sch., Southampton; Churchill Coll., Cambridge (BA, MA). Various mkting and gen. mgt posts with major multinationals, Procter & Gamble, Readers' Digest, and Guinness Plc, UK and overseas, especially E and SE Asia, 1965–98. *Recreation:* walking the dog. *Address:* c/o Blaby Conservative Office, 35 Lutterworth Road, Blaby, Leicester LE8 4DW. *T:* (0116) 277 9992.

HELMORE, Roy Lionel, CBE 1980; Principal, Cambridgeshire College of Arts and Technology, 1977–86; Fellow of Hughes Hall, Cambridge, 1982–94, now Emeritus Fellow; *b* 8 June 1926; *s* of Lionel Helmore and Ellen Helmore (*née* Gibbins); *m* 1969, Margaret Lilian Martin. *Educ:* Montrose Academy; Edinburgh Univ. (BScEng); MA (Cantab). FIEE. Crompton Parkinson Ltd, 1947–49; Asst Lectr, Peterborough Techn. Coll., 1949–53; Lectr, subseq. Sen. Lectr, Shrewsbury Techn. Coll., 1953–57; Head of Electrical Engrg and Science, Exeter Techn. Coll., 1957–61; Principal, St Albans Coll. of Further Education, 1961–77. Association of Principals of Colleges: Hon. Sec., 1968–71; Pres., 1972–73; Hon. Treasurer, 1983–86; Chm., of Council, Assoc. of Colls of Further and Higher Educn, 1987–88. Member: BBC Further Educn Adv. Council, 1967–73; Air Transport and Travel ITB, 1967–73; Technician Educn Council, 1973–79 (Vice-Chm.); Manpower Services Commn, 1974–82; RAF Trng and Educn Adv. Cttee, 1976–79; Chm., Trng and Further Educn Cons. Gp, 1977–82. JP St Albans, 1964–78. *Publication:* CCAT—a brief history, 1989. *Recreations:* gardening, watercolours, bowls. *Address:* 5 Beck Road, Saffron Walden, Essex CB11 4EH. *T:* (01799) 523981.

HELTAY, Laszlo Istvan; Founder and Music Director, Academy of St Martin in the Fields Chorus, 1975–99; Director, Chorus of Radio Televisión Española SA (RTVE), Madrid, since 1998; *b* Budapest, 5 Jan. 1930; *s* of Laszlo Heltay and Gizella Somogy; *m* 1964, Hilary Nicholson. *Educ:* Franz Liszt Acad. of Music, Budapest (MA); Merton Coll., Oxford (MLitt; Hon. Fellow, 1997). Associate Conductor, NZBC Symphony Orchestra and Dir, NZ Opera Co., 1964–67; Conductor, Phoenix Opera Co., 1970–73; Founder and Music Dir, Brighton Fest. Chorus, 1968–95; Dir of Music, Royal Choral Soc., 1985–95. Has conducted major orchestras including: Philharmonia, Royal Philharmonic, London Philharmonic, Dresden Philharmonic, Dallas Symphony, Budapest Philharmonic; also radio orchestras and choirs. Choral music for film, Amadeus, 1984. Has made recordings. Hon. DMus Sussex, 1995. Internat. Kodaly Medal, 1982. *Recreations:* chess, tennis, swimming.

HELY-HUTCHINSON, family name of **Earl of Donoughmore**.

HELY HUTCHINSON, Hon. Timothy Mark; Group Chief Executive, Hodder Headline Ltd, since 1993; *b* 26 Oct. 1953; *s* of Earl of Donoughmore, *qv* and late Sheila (*née* Parsons). *Educ:* Eton Coll. (Oppidan Schol.); Magdalen Coll., Oxford (William Doncaster Schol.; MA Mod. Langs and Phil.). Various appts, Macmillan Publishers, 1975–82; Managing Director: Macdonald & Co. (Publishers) Ltd, 1982–86; Headline Book Publishing PLC, 1986–93. Director: WH Smith plc, 1999–; Inflexion plc, 2000–. Venturer of the Year Award, Brit. Venture Capital Assoc., 1990. *Recreations:* opera, horse-racing, bridge. *Address:* Hodder Headline Ltd, 338 Euston Road, NW1 3BH. *Club:* Groucho.

HEMANS, Simon Nicholas Peter, CMG 1992; CVO 1983; HM Diplomatic Service, retired; Partner, Cranmore Co., since 1997; *b* 19 Sept. 1940; *s* of late Brig. Peter Rupert Hemans, CBE, and Margaret Estelle Hemans (*née* Melsome); *m* 1970, Ursula Martha Naef; three *s* one *d*. *Educ:* Sherborne; London School of Economics (BScEcon). Joined Foreign Office, 1964; British Embassy, Moscow, 1966–68; FO, 1968–69; Dep. Commissioner, Anguilla, March-Oct. 1969; FO, 1969–71; UK Mission to UN, New York, 1971–75; British Embassy, Budapest, 1975–79; FO, 1979–81; Dep. High Comr, Nairobi, 1981–84; Head of Chancery, Moscow, 1985–87; Head of Soviet Dept, FCO, 1987–90; Asst Under-Sec. of State (Africa), FCO, 1990–92; Ambassador, Ukraine, 1992–95; High Comr to Kenya, 1995–97. *Publication:* trans., Savchuk, The Streets of Kiev, 1996. *Recreation:* travel. *Address:* 73 Cranmore Lane, Aldershot, Hants GU11 3AP.

HEMERY, David Peter, MBE 1969; President, UK Athletics, since 1998; Senior Partner, Performance Consultants, since 1989; *b* 18 July 1944; *s* of Peter Ronald Bentley Hemery and Eileen Beatrice Price; *m* 1981, Vivian Mary Bruford; two *s*. *Educ:* Boston Univ. (BSc Internat. Business 1968; DEd Social Psychology 1984); St Catherine's Coll., Oxford (CertEd 1970); Harvard Univ. (MEd 1972). Commonwealth Games: Gold Medal, 110m Hurdles, 1966, 1970; Captain, England Team, 1970; Olympic Games: Gold Medal, 400m Hurdles, 1968 (World Record); Bronze Medal, 400m Hurdles, 1972; Silver Medal, 4×400m, 1972. Teacher, Coach and Housemaster, Millfield Sch., 1970–71 and 1972–73; Dir, Sobell Sports Centre, 1973–75; Teacher and Coach, Boston Univ., 1976–83; coaching course for Nat. Coaching Foundn, 1983–85; mgt trng. Mem., Nat. Cttee, and Exec., BOA. Coach and Advr, sch. to internat. level. *Publications:* Another Hurdle (autobiog.), 1975; The Pursuit of Sporting Excellence, 1986, 2nd edn as Sporting Excellence: what makes a champion, 1991; Athletics in Action, 1987; Winning without Drugs, 1989. *Recreations:* family, human potential and purpose, sport, walking and running. *Address:* White Acre, Fyfield, Marlborough, Wilts SN8 1PX. *T:* (01672) 861645.

HEMINGFORD, 3rd Baron *cr* 1943, of Watford; **Dennis Nicholas Herbert;** Deputy Chief Executive, Westminster Press, 1992–95 (Editorial Director, 1974–92); *b* 25 July 1934; *s* of 2nd Baron Hemingford and Elizabeth McClare (*d* 1979), *d* of Col J. M. Clark, Haltwhistle, Northumberland; *S* father, 1982; known professionally as Nicholas Herbert; *m* 1958, Jennifer Mary Toresen Bailey (OBE 1997), DL, *d* of F. W. Bailey, Harrogate; one *s* three *d*. *Educ:* Oundle Sch.; Clare Coll., Cambridge (MA). Reuters Ltd, 1956–61; The Times: Asst Washington Corresp., 1961–65; Middle East Corresp., 1965–68; Dep. Features Editor, 1968–70; Editor, Cambridge Evening News, 1970–74. Vice-Pres., Guild of British Newspaper Editors, 1979, Pres., 1980–81. Mem. Bd, Assoc. of British Editors (Hon. Sec., 1985–95), 1985–95. Member: Council, Europa Nostra, 1999–; Culture Cttee, UK Commn, UNESCO, 2000–; Chm., East Anglia Regl Cttee, Nat. Trust, 1990–2000. Pres., Huntingdonshire Family History Soc., 1985–. Trustee, Bell Educnl Trust, 1985–90. *Heir:* *s* Hon. Christopher Dennis Charles Herbert, *b* 4 July 1973. *Address:* Old Rectory, Hemingford Abbots, Huntingdon PE18 9AN. *T:* (01480) 466234. *Club:* Royal Commonwealth Society.

See also Hon. Lady Goodhart, H. T. Moggridge.

HEMINGWAY, Peter, FCA; Director and Chief General Manager, Leeds Permanent Building Society, 1982–87; *b* 19 Jan. 1926; *s* of William Edward and Florence Hemingway; *m* 1952, June Maureen, *d* of Maurice and Lilian A. Senior. *Educ:* Leeds College of Commerce. With John Gordon, Walton & Co., Chartered Accountants, Leeds, 1941–62, Partner 1959–62; Director, Provincial Registrars Ltd, 1955–62; joined Leeds Permanent Bldg Soc. as Secretary, 1962. Local Dir (Leeds), Royal Insurance (UK) Ltd, 1983–93; Dir, Homeowners Friendly Soc., 1983–86. Hon. Sec. 1970–82, Vice-Chm. 1982–84, Chm. 1984–86, Yorkshire and North Western Assoc. of Building Societies; Vice Pres., Northern Assoc. of Building Socs, 1988–96; Mem. Council: Building Societies Assoc., 1981–87; Chartered Building Societies Inst., 1982–87. *Recreations:* travel, motor racing, music, gardening. *Address:* Old Barn Cottage, Kearby, near Wetherby, Yorks LS22 4BU. *T:* (0113) 288 6380.

HEMINSLEY, Stephen John; Director of National Services, Board of Inland Revenue, since 2001; *b* 19 Dec. 1951; *s* of John and Joyce Margaret Heminsley; *m* 1980, Yvonne Lesley Stephenson; one *s* one *d*. *Educ:* Joseph Leckie Sch., Walsall. CIPFA 1986. Department of Health and Social Security, later Department of Social Security: Office Supervisor, 1972–77; Internal Auditor, 1977–88; Project Manager, DSS Financial Systems Strategy, 1988–90; Director of: Finance (Contributions Agency), 1990–95; Business Planning (CSA), 1995–97; Strategy and Planning (Benefits Agency), 1997–2000; Pensions, subseq. Children and Pensioners, 2000–01. *Recreations:* walking, Rugby Union, family, member of a rock band. *Address:* Board of Inland Revenue, Benton Park View, Benton Park Road, Longbenton, Newcastle upon Tyne NE98 1ZZ. *Club:* Handsworth Rugby Union Football.

HEMM, Amanda Jane; *see* Roocroft, A. J.

HEMMING, Air Commodore Idris George Selvin, CB 1968 CBE 1959 (OBE 1954); retired; *b* 11 Dec. 1911; *s* of late George Hemming, Liverpool; *m* 1939, Phyllis, *d* of Francis Payne, Drogheda, Eire; two *s*. *Educ:* Chalford, Glos.; Wallasey, Cheshire. Joined RAF, 1928; served War of 1939–45, UK, India and Burma; Gp Capt. 1957; Air Cdre 1962; Dir of Equipment (Pol.) (RAF), MoD, 1962–66; Dir of Equipment (1) (RAF), MoD, Harrogate, 1966–68. *Recreations:* cricket, golf. *Address:* Ash House, St Chloe Green, Amberley, near Stroud, Glos GL5 5AP. *T:* (01453) 873581. *Club:* Royal Air Force.

HEMMING, John Henry, CMG 1994; DLitt; FSA; Joint Chairman: Hemming Publishing Ltd (formerly Municipal Journal Ltd), since 1976 (Director, since 1962; Deputy Chairman, 1967–76); Hemming Group Ltd (formerly Municipal Publications Ltd), since 1976; Director and Secretary, Royal Geographical Society, 1975–96; *b* 5 Jan. 1935; *s* of late Henry Harold Hemming, OBE, MC, and Alice Louisa Weaver, OBE; *m* 1979, Sukie, *d* of late M. J. Babington Smith, CBE; one *s* one *d*. *Educ:* Eton College; McGill University; Oxford University (DLitt 1981). FSA 1998. Chairman: Brintex Ltd, 1979– (Man. Dir, 1963–70, Dep. Chm. 1976–78); Newman Books, 1979–. Member, Iriri River Expedition, Brazil, 1961; Leader, Maracá Rainforest Project, Brazil, 1987–88; Co-Chm., Jordan Badia R&D Prog. Member Bd, British Council, 1993–; Chm., Anglo-Peruvian Soc., 1996–; Member Council: Anglo-Brazilian Soc., 1963–71, 1974–; Pro Natura Internat., 1991–; Hakluyt Soc., 1996–. Corres. Mem., Academia Nacional de la Historia, Venezuela. Dep. Chm., Lepra, 1998–; Sponsor, Survival International; Trustee: L. S. B. Leakey Trust, 1986–; Gilchrist Educnl Trust, 1988–; Rainforest Foundn, 1997–; John Ellerman Foundn, 1998–; Global Diversity Foundn, 1999–; Cusichaca Trust, 1999–; Chairman: Empire and Commonwealth Mus. Trust, 1990–99; Rainforest Club, 1997–; Greencard Trust, 1997– (Mem. Council, 1989–); Patron, Earth Love Fund, 1996–. Hon. DLitt Warwick, 1989; DUniv Stirling, 1991. Mungo Park Medal, RSGS, 1988; Founder's Medal, RGS, 1990; Washburn Medal, Boston Mus. of Sci., 1990; Citation of Merit, Explorers' Club, NY, 1997; Special Award, Instituto Nacional de Cultura, Peru, 1997. Orden al Mérito (Peru), 1986; Order of Cruzeiro do Sul (Brazil), 1998. *Publications:* The Conquest of the Incas, 1970 (Robert Pitman Literary Prize, 1970, Christopher Award, NY, 1971); (jt) Tribes of the Amazon Basin in Brazil, 1972; Red Gold: The Conquest of the Brazilian Indians, 1978; The Search for El Dorado, 1978; Machu Picchu, 1981; Monuments of the Incas, 1982; The New Incas, 1983; (ed) Change in the Amazon Basin (2 vols), 1985; Amazon Frontier: the defeat of the Brazilian Indians, 1987; Maracá, 1988; Roraima: Brazil's northernmost frontier, 1990; Maracá Rainforest Island, 1993; (ed) The Rainforest Edge, 1994; The Golden Age of Discovery, 1998. *Recreations:* writing, travel. *Address:* 10 Edwardes Square, W8 6HE. *T:* (020) 7602 6697. *Clubs:* Boodle's, Beefsteak, Geographical.

See also L. A. Service.

HEMMING, Martin John; Legal Adviser, Ministry of Defence, since 1998; *b* 29 May 1949; *s* of Albert Reuben Hemming and Constance Rosaline Hemming; *m* 1976, Kathleen Siân Davies; one *s* one *d. Educ:* Tudor Grange Grammar Sch., Solihull; Fitzwilliam Coll., Cambridge (BA 1971); London School of Economics and Political Science (LLM 1973). Called to the Bar, Gray's Inn, 1972; practising barrister, 1974–82; Sen. Legal Asst, Treasury Solicitor's Dept, 1982–85; Legal Advr (Grade 6), MoD, 1985–88; Asst Treasury Solicitor, 1988–98. *Address:* Ministry of Defence, Metropole Building, Northumberland Avenue, WC2N 5BL. *T:* (020) 7218 0723.

HEMMINGS, David Leslie Edward; actor, director and producer; engaged in entertainment industry since 1949; watercolour painter; *b* 18 Nov. 1941; *m* 1st, 1960, Genista Ouvry; one *d*; 2nd, 1969, Gayle Hunnicutt (marr. diss. 1975); one *s*; 3rd, 1976, Prudence J. de Casembroot (marr. diss.); two *s*; *m* Lucy Williams; two *c. Educ:* Glyn Coll., Epsom, Surrey. Miles, in The Turn of the Screw, English Opera Group, 1954; Five Clues to Fortune, 1957; Saint Joan, 1957; The Heart Within, 1957; Men of Tomorrow, 1958; In the Wake of a Stranger, 1958; No Trees in the Street, 1959; Some People, 1962; Play it Cool, 1962; Live it Up, 1963; Two Left Feet, 1963; The System, 1964; Be my Guest, 1965; Eye of the Devil, 1966; Blow Up, 1966; Camelot, 1967; Barbarella, 1967; Only When I Larf, 1968; The Charge of the Light Brigade, 1968; The Long Day's Dying, 1968; The Best House in London, 1968; Alfred the Great, 1969; Fragment of Fear, 1970; The Walking Stick, 1970; Unman, Wittering & Zigo, 1971; The Love Machine, 1971; Voices, 1973; Don't Worry Momma, 1973; Juggernaut, 1974; Quilp, 1974; Profundo Rosso, 1975; Islands in the Stream, 1975; The Squeeze, 1976; Jeeves (musical), Her Majesty's, 1975; Power Play, 1978; Thirst, 1979; Beyond Reasonable Doubt, 1980; Jekyll and Hyde, 1980; Harlequin, 1980. BBC TV, Scott Fitzgerald, 1975; ITV, The Rime of the Ancient Mariner, 1978; ITV, Charlie Muffin, 1979. Directed: Running Scared, 1972; The 14, 1973 (Silver Bear Award, Berlin Film Festival, 1973); Disappearance, 1977; Power Play, 1977; Just a Gigolo, 1978; David Bowie Stage, 1979; Murder By Decree, 1979; Survivor, 1979; Race to the Yankee Zephyr, 1980; also in Australia, NZ etc. Produced: Strange Behaviour, 1981; Turkey Shoot, 1981. Director: International Home Video FGH Pty Ltd (Melbourne); Film and General Holdings Inc. (California). *Recreation:* painting. *Clubs:* Chelsea Arts, Magic Circle.

HEMP, Prof. William Spooner, MA, FRAeS; Stewarts and Lloyds Professor of Structural Engineering, Oxford University, 1965–83; Emeritus Fellow of Keble College, Oxford, since 1984 (Professorial Fellow, 1965–83); *b* 21 March 1916; *s* of late Rev. William James Hemp and Daisy Lilian Hemp; *m* 1938, Dilys Ruth Davies; one *s. Educ:* Paston Grammar Sch., North Walsham; Jesus Coll., Cambridge (Scholar, MA). Aeronautical Engineer, Bristol Aeroplane Co., 1938–46. Coll. of Aeronautics: Senior Lecturer, 1946–50; Prof. of Aircraft Structures and Aeroelasticity, 1950–65; Head of Dept of Aircraft Design, 1951–65; Dep. Principal, 1957–65. Mem. of various cttees of Aeronautical Research Council since 1948. Visiting Prof., Stanford Univ., Calif, 1960–61. *Publications:* Optimum Structures, 1973; research papers in the Theory of Structures, Solid Mechanics and Applied Mathematics. *Recreations:* mountain walking, music. *Address:* Duffryn House, Church Lane, Horton-cum-Studley, Oxford OX33 1AW.

HEMPHILL, 5th Baron *cr* 1906, of Rathkenny and Cashel; **Peter Patrick Fitzroy Martyn Martyn-Hemphill;** *b* 5 Sept. 1928; *o s* of 4th Baron Hemphill and Emily, *d* of F. Irving Sears, Webster, Mass; *S* father, 1957; *m* 1952, Olivia Anne, *er d* of Major Robert Francis Ruttledge, MC, Cloonee, Ballinrobe, County Mayo; one *s* two *d*; assumed surname of Martyn in addition to Hemphill, 1959. *Educ:* Downside; Brasenose Coll., Oxford (MA Jurisp.). Sen. Steward, Irish Turf Club, 1985–88; Steward, Irish Nat. Hunt Steeplechase Cttee, 1973–76 and 1978–81. *Heir: s* Hon. Charles Andrew Martyn Martyn-Hemphill [*b* 8 Oct. 1954; *m* 1985, Sarah J. F., *e d* of Richard Lumley; two *s* three *d*]. *Address:* Raford, Kiltulla, Co. Galway, Eire. *Clubs:* White's; Royal Irish Automobile (Dublin); Irish Cruising.

HEMPLEMAN-ADAMS, David, OBE 1998 (MBE 1994); explorer and mountaineer; company director; *b* 10 Oct. 1956; *m* Claire; three *d. Educ:* Manchester Univ. Ascents: Mt McKinley, Alaska Range, 1980; Kilimanjaro, Tanzania, 1981; Mt Everest, Himalayas, 1993; Vinson Massif, Antarctica, 1994; Aconcagua, Andes, 1994; Mt Carstenz, Indonesia, 1995. Arctic/Antarctic expeditions: first solo unsupported expedition to magnetic North Pole, 1984; leader of first unsupported gp expedition to geomagnetic North Pole, 1992; first Briton to walk solo and unsupported to South Pole, 1996; first person to climb highest peaks of all seven continents and trek to magnetic and geographic North and South Poles. Hot-air balloon flights: first to cross Andes, 1998; first to cross North-West Passage, 1999; first to fly to North Pole, 2000; first to fly solo across Arctic Ocean, 2000. Livingstone Medal, RSGS, 1997. *Publications:* Race Against Time: North Geomagnetic Pole expedition, 1993; Walking on Thin Ice, 1998.

HEMPSALL, Dr David Stuart, MA; Headmaster, Queen Elizabeth's Grammar School, Blackburn, since 1995; *b* 4 Jan. 1947; *s* of Harold and Freda Hempsall; *m* 1969, Patricia Land; one *s* one *d. Educ:* Manchester GS; Sidney Sussex Coll., Cambridge (MA); Univ. of Kent (PhD). Assistant Master: Sir William Nottidge Sch., Whitstable, 1971–72; Rugby Sch., 1973–85 (Head of History, 1977–85); Headmaster, Scarborough Coll., 1985–95. FRSA. *Publications:* articles in hist. and educnl learned jls. *Recreations:* do-it-yourself, hill-walking, music, sport, reading. *Address:* Queen Elizabeth's Grammar School, West Park Road, Blackburn BB2 6DF. *T:* (01254) 686300.

HEMSLEY, Thomas Jeffrey, CBE 2000; free-lance opera and concert singer; Professor: Guildhall School of Music and Drama, since 1987; Trinity College of Music, 1988–93; *b* 12 April 1927; *s* of Sydney William Hemsley and Kathleen Annie Hemsley (*née* Deacon); *m* 1960, Hon. Gwenllian Ellen James, *d* of 4th Baron Northbourne; three *s. Educ:* Ashby de la Zouch Grammar Sch.; Brasenose Coll., Oxford (MA). Vicar Choral, St Paul's Cathedral, 1950–51; Prin. Baritone, Stadttheater, Aachen, 1953–56; Deutsche Oper am Rhein, 1957–63; Opernhaus, Zurich, 1963–67; Glyndebourne, Bayreuth, Edinburgh Festivals, etc. Vis. Prof., RCM, 1986; Guest Prof., Royal Danish Acad. of Music, 1990–91. Mem., Roy. Philharmonic Soc., 1968–. FGSM 1996; Hon. RAM 1974; Hon. FTCL 1988. FRSA 1991. *Publication:* Singing & Imagination, 1998. *Address:* 10 Denewood Road, N6 4AJ. *T:* (020) 8348 3397. *Club:* Garrick.

HENAO, Rev. Sir Ravu, Kt 1982; OBE 1975; Executive Secretary, Bible Society of Papua New Guinea, 1980–87; retired; *b* 27 March 1927; *s* of Boga Henao and Gaba Asi; *m* 1944, Lahui Peri; four *s* five *d. Educ:* Port Moresby (completed standard 5); Lawes Theol Coll., Fife Bay, Milne Bay Province. Primary sch. teacher, various schs in Central Dist, 1944–66 (pastor as well as teacher, 1946); Chm. (full-time), Papua Ekalesia (national church related to London Missionary Soc.), 1967; Bishop of United Church for Papua Mainland Region, 1968–80. Hon. DTech PNG Univ. of Technology, 1987. *Publications:* (with Raymond Perry) Let's Discuss These Things, 1966; (with Alan Dunstan) Paul's Letter to the Galatians, 1974. *Recreations:* fishing, hunting, gardening. *Address:* c/o PO Box 1224, Port Moresby, Papua New Guinea. *T:* 217893.

HENBEST, Harold Bernard; *see* Herbert, H. B.

HENDER, John Derrik, CBE 1986; DL; public sector consultant; Chief Executive, West Midlands Metropolitan County Council, 1973–86; *b* 15 Nov. 1926; *s* of late Jessie Peter and late Jennie Hender; *m* 1949, Kathleen Nora Brown; one *d. Educ:* Great Yarmouth Grammar School. IPFA, FCA, FIMgt. Deputy Borough Treasurer: Newcastle-under-Lyme, 1957–61; Wolverhampton County Borough, 1961–64; City Treas. 1965–69, Chief Exec. and Town Clerk 1969–73, Coventry County Borough. DL West Midlands, 1975. *Publications:* numerous articles relating to various aspects of local govt and related matters. *Recreation:* gardening. *Address:* Endwood, South Avenue, Thorpe St Andrew, Norwich NR7 0EZ.

HENDERSON, family name of **Baron Faringdon**.

HENDERSON, Barry; *see* Henderson, J. S. B.

HENDERSON, Bernard Vere, CBE 1987; Chairman: Anglian Water, 1981–94; British Waterways Board, 1994–99; *b* 8 July 1928; *s* of late Percy Cecil and Ruth Elizabeth Henderson; *m* 1952, Valerie Jane Cairns; two *s* one *d. Educ:* Ampleforth Coll.; Harvard Business Sch. Served Army, RE, 1946–48. P. C. Henderson Group, 1949–80 (Man. Dir, 1958–80). Chm., Water Services Assoc., 1990–91. Chm., Australia and NZ Trade Adv. Cttee, 1994–95. *Recreations:* countryside, narrow boat cruising.

HENDERSON, Charles Edward, CB 1992; FIA; Chairman: Totalfinaelf Holding UK, since 1998; Totalfinaelf Exploration UK, since 1998; *b* 19 Sept. 1939; *s* of late David Henderson and of Giorgiana Leggatt Henderson; *m* 1966, Rachel Hilary Hall, *d* of late Dr Stephen Hall, FRCP and Dr Mary Hall; one *d* one *s. Educ:* Charterhouse; Pembroke Coll., Cambridge (MA). FIA 1965. Actuarial Trainee, subseq. Asst Investment Sec., Equity & Law Life Assurance Soc., 1960–70; ECGD, 1971–73; DTI, 1973–74; Dept of Energy, 1974–88: Asst Sec., 1975; Under Sec., 1982; Atomic Energy Div., 1982; Oil Div., 1985; Prin. Estabt and Finance Officer, 1986–88; Head, Office of Arts and Libraries, 1989–92; Dep. Sec., DTI, 1992–96. Mem., Competition (formerly Monopolies and Mergers) Commn, 1998–. Dir, Aluminium Corp. Ltd, 1981–84. Sen. Associate, Cambridge Energy Res. Associates, 1998–. President: Soc. for Underwater Technology, 1999–; Inst. of Petroleum, 2000–. *Recreations:* making and listening to music, mountaineering, golf. *Address:* 17 Sydney House, Woodstock Road, W4 1DP. *T:* (020) 8994 1345.

See also Julian Hall.

HENDERSON, Rt Rev. Charles Joseph; Auxiliary Bishop in Southwark, (RC), since 1972; Titular Bishop of Tricala, since 1972; Area Bishop with responsibility for South East Metropolitan London, since 1980; *b* 14 April 1924; *s* of Charles Stuart Henderson and Hanora Henderson (*née* Walsh). *Educ:* Mount Sion Sch., Waterford; St John's Seminary, Waterford. Priest, 1948; Curate, St Stephen's, Welling, Kent, 1948–55; English Martyrs, Streatham, SW16, 1955–58; Chancellor, RC Diocese of Southwark, 1958–70; Vicar General, RC Diocese of Arundel and Brighton, 1965–66; Episcopal Vicar for Religious, Southwark, 1968–73; Vicar General, RC Archdiocese of Southwark, 1969; Parish Priest, St Mary's, Blackheath, 1969–82; Canon of Cathedral Chapter, 1972; Provost of Cathedral Chapter, 1973–2001. Member: Ecumenical Commn for England and Wales, 1976–92; Nat. Catholic Commn for Racial Justice, 1978–81; English Anglican/RC Cttee, 1982–, Co. Chm. 1983–92; Methodist/RC Nat. Ecumenical Cttee, 1983 and Co. Chm. 1984–92; Chairman: RC Cttee for Dialogue with Other Faiths, 1984–; RC Nat. Cttee for Catholic–Jewish Relations, 1992; RC Consultant-Observer, BCC, 1982–86; Exec. Cttee, inter-faith network for UK, 1987–; Member: Pontifical Council for Inter-religious Dialogue, 1990–2000; Exec. Cttee, CCJ, 1992–. Papal Chamberlain, 1960; Prelate of Papal Household, 1965. Freeman, City of Waterford, 1973. Kt Comdr with Star of Equestrian Order of Holy Sepulchre, Jerusalem, 1973 (Prior, Southwark Sect., 1994–); Silver Palm of Jerusalem, 1998; Gold Medallion Award, Internat. CCJ, 2001. *Recreation:* special interest in sport. *Address:* Park House, 6A Cresswell Park, Blackheath, SE3 9RD. *T:* (020) 8318 1094.

HENDERSON, David; *see* Henderson, P. D.

HENDERSON, Sir Denys (Hartley), Kt 1989; Chairman: The Rank Group Plc (formerly Rank Organisation), 1995–2001; Imperial Chemical Industries PLC, 1987–95; ZENECA Group plc, 1993–95; First Crown Estate Commissioner, 1995–Sept. 2002; *b* 11 Oct. 1932; *s* of John Hartley Henderson and Nellie Henderson (*née* Gordon); *m* 1957, Doreen Mathewson Glashan, *o d* of Robert and Mary Glashan; two *d. Educ:* Aberdeen Grammar School; Univ. of Aberdeen (MA, LLB). Solicitor; Mem., Law Soc. of Scotland. Joined ICI as lawyer in Secretary's Dept, London, 1957; Chm., ICI Paints Div., 1977; ICI Main Bd Dir, 1980; Dep. Chm., 1986–87. Non-executive Director: Dalgety plc, 1981–87 and 1996–98 (Chm., 1997–98); Barclays Bank, 1983–97; Barclays, 1985–97; Barclays International, 1985–87; RTZ Corp., 1990–96; MORI, 1995–; Schlumberger Ltd, 1995–2001. Member: CBI President's Cttee, 1987–96; Adv. Council, Prince's Youth Business Trust, 1986–99; Adv. Cttee on Business Appointments, 1994–; Greenbury Cttee on Directors' Remuneration, 1994–95. Mem., European Round Table, 1992–94. Pres., Soc. of Business Economists, 1990–94. Pres. and Chm. Bd, British Quality Foundn, 1993–97. Trustee, Natural Hist. Mus., 1989–98. Chancellor, Bath Univ., 1993–98; Mem. Court of Governors, Henley Management Coll., 1986–96 (Chm., 1989–96); Chm., Univ. of Aberdeen Quincentenary Appeal Cttee, 1993–96. Hon. Vice-Pres., Chartered Inst. of Marketing, 1989–95. CIMgt (CBIM 1981); FInstM 1987. Hon. FCGI 1990. DUniv: Brunel, 1987; Strathclyde, 1993; Hon. LLD: Aberdeen, 1987; Nottingham, 1990; Manchester, 1991; Bath, 1993; Hon. DSc: Cranfield Inst. of Technol., 1989; Teesside, 1993. Centenary Medal, SCI, 1993. *Recreations:* family life, swimming, reading, travel, minimal gardening, unskilled but enjoyable golf. *Address:* The Crown Estate, 16 Carlton House Terrace, SW1Y 5AH. *Clubs:* Athenæum, Royal Automobile.

HENDERSON, Derek, FDSRCS; Senior Consultant Oral and Maxillo-facial Surgeon, St Thomas' Hospital, 1975–93; Consultant, St George's Hospital, 1975–86; Emeritus Consultant in Oral and Maxillo-facial Surgery, Guy's and St Thomas' Hospital NHS Trust, since 1993; *b* 9 April 1935; *s* of Robert Henderson and Dorothy Edith Henderson; *m* 1961, Jennifer Jill Anderson; one *s* one *d. Educ:* Dulwich Coll.; London Univ. (BDS Hons 1956, MB, BS Hons 1963). FDSRCS (Eng) 1960 (LDS 1956); MRCS, LRCP 1963. Dental and med. trng, KCH, London, 1952–56 and 1959–63 (Prizeman); house surg. appts, KCH and Royal Dental Hosp., 1956–59; King's Coll. Hospital: Lectr in Dental Materials, 1958–65; ENT House Officer, and Casualty Off., 1964; Registrar in

Oral Surg., Queen Mary's Hosp., Roehampton, and Westminster Hosp., 1965; Sen. Registrar in Oral Surg., United Cardiff Hosps, 1965–67; Consultant Oral Surgeon to Eastern Reg. Hosp. Bd, Scotland, and Dundee Dental Hosp., 1967–69 (Hon. Sen. Lectr, Univ. of Dundee); Consultant i/c Reg. Maxillo-facial Service to Glasgow and West of Scotland, based on Canniesburn Plastic and Oral Surg. Unit, Glasgow, 1969–75 (Hon. Clinical Teacher, Glasgow Univ.); Consultant, Royal Dental Hosp., 1975–85. Recognised Teacher, London Univ., 1977–93; Hon. Consultant, Charing Cross Hosp., 1977–93; Hon. Civilian Consultant: Queen Elizabeth Mil. Hosp., Woolwich (formerly Queen Alexandra Mil. Hosp., Millbank), 1976–81; in Oral Surgery, RN, 1971–93, Army, 1981–93; Hon. Sen. Lectr in Oral Surg., Royal Dental Sch., London, 1977–85. Vis. Prof. and Lectr, Brazil, Argentina, Chile, USA, Spain, Venezuela, Australia, Holland, Saudi Arabia, Uruguay, Italy, SA, NZ. Mem. Senate, Royal Surgical Colls of GB and Ire., 1993–96; Royal College of Surgeons: Hunterian Prof., 1975–76; Mem. Council, 1984–86 (Collyer Gold Medal, 1995); Kelsey Fry Adviser in Postgraduate Educnl Trng, 1975–80, Mem. Bd, 1978–86, Mem. Exec. Cttee, 1983–86, and Vice-Dean, 1984–85, Faculty of Dental Surgery (also Examr, FDSRCS). Member: Central Cttee for Hospital Dental Services, 1978–85 (Mem. Exec. Cttee, 1980–85); Central Cttee for Univ. Dental Teachers and Research Workers, 1978–81; Negotiating Subcttee, CCHMS, 1980–85; European Assoc. for Maxillo-Facial Surg.; BMA; Craniofacial Soc. (Mem. Council, 1973–77); Oral Surgery Club GB (Pres., 1992–93). Fellow: BAOMS (Pres., 1994–95; Mem. Council, 1974–76, 1977–80, 1984–86; Downs Prize, 1992). Internat. Assoc. of Oral Surgeons. Hon. Mem., Amer. Assoc. of Oral Surgeons in Europe; Hon. Associate Life Mem., Soc. of Maxillo-facial and Oral Surgeons of SA; Hon. Pres., Inst. of Maxillo-Facial Technol., 1977–78. *Publications:* An Atlas and Textbook of Orthognathic Surgery, 1985 (Astra Prize, Soc. of Authors, 1986); contribs on general oral surgery to British Jl of Oral Surgery and British Dental Jl, and especially on surgery of facial and jaw deformity to Brit. Jl of Oral Surg. and Brit. Jl of Plastic Surg. *Recreation:* fly fishing. *Address:* La Soleille, Route de Beaulieu, Beynat 19190, France. *Club:* Royal Navy Medical.

HENDERSON, Dr Derek Scott, FRSSAf; Principal and Vice-Chancellor, Rhodes University, Grahamstown, South Africa, 1975–96; *b* 28 Oct. 1929; *s* of late Ian Scott and Kathleen Elizabeth Henderson (*née* White); *m* 1958, Thelma Muriel, *d* of W. E. B. Mullins; two *d. Educ:* St John's Coll., Johannesburg; Rhodes University Coll. (BSc); Oxford Univ. (MA); Cambridge Univ. (MA); Harvard Univ. (PhD). FRSSAf 1995. Exec. Trainee, Anglo American Corp. of S Africa, 1953–56; Engr, Advanced Systems Develt, IBM Corp., Poughkeepsie, NY, 1960–62; Univ. of the Witwatersrand: Dir of Computer Centre, 1964–69; Prof. of Computer Science, 1967–75; Dean of Science Faculty, 1974–75. Chm., J. L. B. Smith Inst. of Ichthyology, 1976–96; Mem. Council, CSIR, 1982–87; Mem., Scientific Adv. Council, 1988–93; Mem. Bd, SABC, 1990–93; Vice-Chm., Leather Res. Inst., 1976–96; Mem. Council, Grahamstown (formerly 1820) Foundn (Vice-Chm., 1976–89); Pres., SA Council of Automation and Computation, 1974. Chairman: Hillbrow Br., Progressive Party, 1964–65; Johannesburg Br., Kolbe Assoc. of Catholic Graduates, 1964; Mem. Council, St Andrew's Coll., 1986–; Trustee, SA Foundn, 1976–96; Patron, All Saints Coll., Bisho, 1986–96. Dir, Sabinet, 1983–88. Fellow, Computer Soc. of SA, 1974. Hon. LLD Rhodes, 1997. *Recreation:* golf. *Address:* 1 Ross Street, Grahamstown, 6139, S Africa. *T:* (46) 6223908. *Club:* Port Elizabeth (Port Elizabeth, S Africa).

HENDERSON, Douglas John; MP (Lab) Newcastle upon Tyne North, since 1987; *b* 9 June 1949; *s* of John and Joy Henderson; *m* 1974, Janet Margaret Graham (marr. diss.); one *s*; partner, Geraldine Daly; one *d. Educ:* Waid Academy, Anstruther, Fife; Central Coll., Glasgow; Univ. of Strathclyde. Apprentice, Rolls Royce, 1966–68; Clerk, British Rail, 1969; Research Officer, GMWU, 1973–75; Regional Organiser, GMWU, then GMB, 1975–87. Mem. Exec., Scottish Council, Labour Party, 1979–87 (Chm., 1984–85). Opposition spokesman on trade and industry, 1988–92, on local govt, 1992–94, on public service, 1994–95, on home affairs, 1995–97; Minister of State: (Europe), FCO, 1997–98; (Minister for the Armed Forces), MoD, 1998–99. Sec., GMB Parly Gp, 1987–97; Chm., Northern Gp of Lab MPs, 2000–. *Recreations:* athletics, mountaineering. *Address:* House of Commons, SW1A 0AA. *T:* (constituency office) (0191) 286 2024. *Clubs:* Elswick Harriers, Lemington Labour, Newburn Memorial, Dinnington, Union Jack (Newcastle).

HENDERSON, Douglas Mackay, CBE 1985; FRSE 1966; FLS; HM Botanist in Scotland, since 1987; *b* 30 Aug. 1927; *s* of Captain Frank Henderson and Adine C. Mackay; *m* 1952, Julia Margaret Brown; one *s* two *d. Educ:* Blairgowrie High Sch.; Edinburgh Univ. (BSc). Scientific Officer, Dept of Agriculture and Fisheries for Scotland, 1948–51. Royal Botanic Garden, Edinburgh, 1951–87, Regius Keeper, 1970–87; Adminr, Inverewe, Nat. Trust for Scotland, 1987–92. Hon. Prof., Edinburgh Univ., 1983–. Sec., Internat. Assoc. of Botanical Gardens, 1969–81. Curator of Library and Museum, Royal Soc. of Edinburgh, 1978–87. Mem. Council, Nat. Trust for Scotland, 1992–; Sec., Highland Cttee, Help the Aged, 1995–. VMH, 1985. *Publications:* British Rust Fungi (with M. Wilson), 1966; (with J. H. Dickson) A Naturalist in the Highlands: the life and travels of James Robertson in Scotland 1767–1771, 1993; many papers on taxonomy of cryptogams. *Recreations:* music, hill walking, cooking, painting, sailing. *Address:* Larachan, 54 Lonemore, Gairloch, W Ross IV22 2DB. *T:* (01445) 712391; 38E Cramond Vale, Edinburgh EH4 6RB. *T:* (0131) 312 8432.

HENDERSON, Gavin Douglas; Principal, Trinity College of Music, since 1994; *b* 3 Feb. 1948; *s* of Magnus Reg Henderson and Sybil (*née* Horton); *m* 1st, 1973, Jane Williams (marr. diss. 1977); 2nd, 1983, Carole Becker (marr. diss. 1992); two *s*; 3rd, 1992, Mary Jane Walsh. *Educ:* Brighton Coll.; Brighton Coll. of Art; Kingston Art Coll.; University Coll. London; Slade Sch. of Fine Art. Leader and Dir, Henderson Brass Consort, 1968–75; Principal Trumpet, Worthing Municipal and Concert Orchs, 1969–70; Dep. Front of House and Publicity Manager, Victoria Theatre, Stoke-on-Trent, 1970–71; Founder and Dir, Crawley Fest., 1971–73; Artistic Director: York Fest. Mystery Plays, 1972–76; Portsmouth Fest., 1974–76; Chief Exec., New Philharmonia and Philharmonia Orchs, 1975–78; Dir, S Hill Park Arts Centre and Founder, Wilde Theatre, Bracknell, 1979–84; Artistic Director: Brighton Internat. Fest., 1983–94; Dartington Internat. Summer Sch., 1985–; London Contemporary Dance Trust, 1986–87; Court in the Act, Royal Acad. of Arts, 1993; Pres. and Artistic Advr, Bournemouth Fest., 1996– (Artistic Dir, 1994–96). Chairman: Clarion Concert Agency, 1972–75; Palindrome Prodns Ltd, 1994–; World Circuit Arts, 1995–; Youth Music Trust, 1998–. Writer and presenter, A View of …, BBC TV Series, 1983. Member: Music Panel and Opera Cttee, 1973–75, Regl Cttee, 1981–84, Arts Council of GB; Arts Council of England, 1994–98 (Chm., Music Panel, 1994–); Arts Cttee, RSA, 1991–94; Chm., British Arts Fests Assoc., 1994– (Dep. Chm., 1987–94); Member: Exec. Cttee, SE Arts Assoc., 1982–89 (Chm., Festival Panel, 1986–89); Exec. Bd, European Fests Assoc., 1988–94 (Vice Pres., 1994–); Southern Arts Bd, 1990–93; Arts Initiative in Mgt Cttee, Gulbenkian Foundn, 1982–83. Trustee, Electro-Acoustic Music Soc., 1984–90. Judge: Prudential Awards, 1992; Audi Young Musician of the Year, 1993; Barclays New Stages, 1994; British Gas Working for Cities, 1995. Pres., Nat. Piers Soc., 1986–. One-man exhibitions: Gall. 185, Brighton, 1968; Mulberry Gall., Lancaster, 1969. Governor: Brighton Univ. (formerly Poly.), 1987–; Chetham's Sch., Manchester, 1994–. Hon. Fellow: Univ. of Sussex, 1991; Univ. of Brighton, 1993. Hon. MA Sussex, 1992. Europe Award, E Sussex CC, 1992. *Publications:* Picasso and the Theatre, 1982; articles for Classical Music, Tempo, Musical Times, Stage, and Listener. *Recreations:* seaside pierage, cooking seafood, vintage motor-racing. *Address:* Trinity College of Music, Mandeville Place, W1M 6AQ. *T:* (020) 7935 5773. *Clubs:* Garrick, Savile.

HENDERSON, Prof. George David Smith, FSA; Professor of Medieval Art, Cambridge, 1986–96, then Emeritus; Fellow of Downing College, Cambridge, 1974–94; *b* 7 May 1931; *yr s* of late Very Rev. Prof. George David Henderson, DLitt, DTh, DD and Jenny Holmes McCulloch Henderson (*née* Smith); *m* 1957, Isabel Bisset Murray; one *s* one *d. Educ:* Aberdeen Grammar Sch.; Univ. of Aberdeen (MA 1953); Courtauld Inst., Univ. of London (BA 1956); Trinity Coll., Cambridge (MA, PhD 1961). Research Fellow, Barber Inst. of Art, Univ. of Birmingham, 1959–60; Graham Robertson Research Fellow, Downing Coll., Cambridge, 1960–63; University of Manchester: Asst Lectr in History of Art, 1962–64; Lectr, 1964–66; University of Edinburgh: Lectr in Fine Arts, 1966–71; Reader in Fine Arts, 1971–73; University of Cambridge: Lectr in History of Art, 1974–79; Head of Dept, 1974–88; Reader in Medieval Art, 1979–86; a Syndic, Fitzwilliam Museum, 1974–98. Mem., Ely Cathedral Fabric Adv. Cttee, 1990–98. FRSA 1997. *Publications:* Gothic, 1967; Chartres, 1968; Early Medieval, 1972, repr. 1993; (ed with Giles Robertson) Studies in Memory of David Talbot Rice, 1975; Bede and the Visual Arts (Jarrow Lect.), 1980; Losses and Lacunae in Early Insular Art (Garmonsway Lect.), 1982; Studies in English Bible Illustration, 1985; From Durrow to Kells, 1987; (contrib.) The Eadwine Psalter, 1992; (contrib.) Emulation and Innovation in Carolingian Culture, 1993; Vision and Image in Early Christian England, 1999; articles in UK and Amer. jls and papers in procs of internat. confs. *Recreations:* listening to Wagner, porphyrology, looking for agates. *Address:* The Old Manse, Nigg by Tain, Ross and Cromarty IV19 1QR. *Club:* Oxford and Cambridge.

HENDERSON, Prof. George Patrick, FRSE 1980; Professor of Philosophy in the University of Dundee (formerly Queen's College, Dundee), 1959–80, Dean, Faculty of Arts and Social Sciences, 1973–76; *b* 22 April 1915; *e s* of Rev. George Aitchison Henderson, MA, and Violet Margaret Mackenzie; *m* 1939, Hester Lowry Douglas McWilliam, BSc (*d* 1978), *d* of Rev. John Morell McWilliam, BA. *Educ:* Elgin Academy; St Andrews Univ. (Harkness Scholar); Balliol Coll., Oxford. 1st Class Hons in Philosophy, University of St Andrews, 1936; Miller Prize and Ramsay Scholarship; MA 1936; Ferguson Scholarship in Philosophy, 1936; 2nd Class Lit Hum, University of Oxford, 1938; BA 1938. Asst in Logic and Metaphysics, University of St Andrews, 1938; Shaw Fellow in Mental Philosophy, University of Edinburgh, 1938. MA Oxon, 1943. Army Service, 1940–46; Royal Artillery (commissioned 1940, Adjutant 1942–43) and Gen. Staff (GSO 3 1945); served in UK, Italy and Greece. Lecturer in Logic and Metaphysics, University of St Andrews, 1945; Senior Lecturer, 1953. Corresp. Member: Acad. of Athens, 1973; Ionian Acad., 1975. Editor of the Philosophical Quarterly, 1962–72. *Publications:* The Revival of Greek Thought 1620–1830, 1970 (trans. Greek, 1994); The Ionian Academy (trans. Greek), 1980; E. P. Papanoutsos, 1983; The Ionian Academy, 1988 (2nd edn, trans. Greek, 1994); numerous articles and reviews in learned jls. *Recreations:* modern Greek studies, gardening.

HENDERSON, Giles Ian, CBE 1992; Master, Pembroke College, Oxford, since 2001; *b* 20 April 1942; *s* of late Charles David Henderson and Joan K. Firmin; *m* 1971, Lynne Fyfield; two *s* one *d. Educ:* Michaelhouse, Natal; Univ. of Witwatersrand (BA); Magdalen Coll., Oxford (Sen. Mackinnon Scholar; MA, BCL). Fulbright Award, 1966–67. Associate in Law, Univ. of California at Berkeley, 1966–67; joined Slaughter and May, 1968; admitted Solicitor, 1970; Partner, Slaughter and May, 1975, Sen. Partner, 1993–2001. Member: Hampel Cttee on Corporate Governance, 1995–98; Financial Reporting Council, 1998–2001; UK—China Forum, 1999–. Non-exec. Dir, Land Securities plc, 2000–. Trustee, Burghley House Preservation Trust, 2001–. *Recreations:* sport, opera, ballet. *Address:* The Master's Lodging, Pembroke College, Oxford OX1 1DW. *T:* (01865) 276403. *Clubs:* City Law; Wildernesse Golf.

HENDERSON, Rear Adm. Iain Robert, CB 2001; CBE 1991; Chief Executive, Sue Ryder Care, since 2001; Gentleman Usher of the Scarlet Rod, Order of the Bath, since 2001; *b* 1 April 1948; *s* of John and Christina Henderson; *m* 1976, Rosalind Margaret Arkell; two *s* two *d. Educ:* Epsom Coll. BRNC 1965; qualified as: rotary wing pilot, 1971; fixed wing pilot, 1974; Exec. Officer, HMS Plymouth, 1980–82; CO, HMS Ariadne, 1984–85, HMS Charybdis, 1985; Trng Comdr, BRNC, 1986–87; Directorate of Naval Officer Appointments (Seaman) (Air), 1988–90; CO, HMS London, 1990–91; AD Warfare Directorate of Naval Plans, 1991–93; CO, RNAS Yeovilton, 1993–96; Comdr, Naval Base, Portsmouth, 1996–98; FONA, 1998–2000; AOC No 3 Gp and FOMA, 2000–01. ADC to the Queen, 1996–98. Freeman, City of London, 1992; Liveryman, Co. of Upholders, 1996–; Mem., Ct of Assts, Guild of Freemen, City of London, 1997. *Recreations:* equestrian and country pursuits. *Address:* Sue Ryder Care, 114–118 Southampton Row, WC1B 5AA.

HENDERSON, Ian James, CBE 2001; FRICS; Chief Executive, Land Securities PLC, since 1997; *b* 18 July 1943; *s* of Robert and Sheila Henderson; *m* 1972, Sheila Sturrock; one *s* one *d. Educ:* BSc (Estate Mgt). FRICS 1978. Joined Land Securities, 1971. Dir, London First. Vice Chm., Bd of Mgt, Central and Cecil Housing Trust. Vice-Pres., British Property Fedn. *Address:* (office) 5 Strand, WC2N 5AF. *T:* (020) 7413 9000.

HENDERSON, Ivan John; MP (Lab) Harwich, since 1997; *b* 7 June 1958; *s* of Margaret Bloice and step *s* of late Michael Bloice; *m* 1992, Jo'anne Atkinson; one *s* one *d* by a previous marriage. *Educ:* Sir Anthony Deane Comprehensive Sch., Harwich. British Rail, Sealink, 1975–97: dock operative; Union Orgnr, Docks, and Exec. Officer, RMT, 1991–94. Member (Lab): Harwich Town Council, 1986–97; Tendring DC, 1995–97. PPS to Minister of State, Home Office, 2001–. *Recreations:* football, golf, sailing. *Address:* (office) Kingsway House, 21 Kingsway, Harwich, Essex CO12 3AB. *T:* (01255) 552859. *Clubs:* Harwich and Parkeston Football; Harwich and Dovercourt Cricket (Vice Pres., 1997).

HENDERSON, Dr James Ewart, CVO 1988; DSc; President, Mastiff Electronic Systems Ltd, since 1995 (Managing Director, 1982–90; Chairman, 1985–95); *b* 29 May 1923; *s* of late Rev. James Ewart Henderson, MA, BD and Agnes Mary (*née* Crawford); *m* 1st, 1949, Alice Joan Hewlitt (*d* 1999); one *d*; 2nd, 1966, Nancy Maude Dominy; two *s. Educ:* private sch.; Glasgow Univ. (MA); Edinburgh Univ. Operational research on air rockets and guns, MAP, 1943–44; hon. commn in RAFVR, 1944–46; operational assessment of air attacks in Belgium, Holland and Germany, 2TAF, 1944–45; exper. research on fighter and bomber capability, and on the use of radar and radio aids: RAF APC Germany, 1945–46, Fighter Comd, 1946–49 and CFE, 1949–52; research on weapons effects and capability: Air Min., 1952–54, AWRE 1955, Air Min., 1955–58; Asst Scientific Adviser (Ops), Air Min., 1958–63; Dep. Chief Scientist (RAF), MoD, 1963–69; Chief Scientist (RAF) and Mem., Air Force Bd, 1969–73. Aviation Consultant, Hawker Siddeley Aviation Ltd, 1973–77; Financial Consultant, Charles Stapleton & Co. Ltd, 1973–78; freelance Operational Res. and Management Consultant, 1975–78; Scientific Advr, BAe, 1978–82; Director: Lewis Security Systems Ltd, 1976–77; Mastiff Security

Systems Ltd, 1977–82; Pres. and Chief Exec., Mastiff Systems US Inc., 1982–88; Chm., TIB Netherlands, 1982–86. Life Vice-Pres., Air League, 1994 (Mem. Council, 1979–80; Chm., 1981–87; Pres., 1987–94); Chm., Air League Educational Trust, 1983–87. FInstD 1978. *Publications:* technical papers on operational capability of aircraft and weapons; UK manual on Blast Effects of Nuclear Weapons. *Recreations:* sailing, golf, opera, photography. *Clubs:* Naval and Military; Royal Scottish Automobile (Glasgow); Moor Park Golf; New Zealand Golf; Royal Western Yacht.

HENDERSON, (James Stewart) Barry; management consultant; *b* 29 April 1936; *s* of James Henderson, CBE and Jane Stewart Henderson (*née* McLaren); *m* 1961, Janet Helen Sprot Todd; two *s*. *Educ:* Lathallan Sch.; Stowe Sch. Nat. Service, Scots Guards, 1954–56; electronics and computer industries, 1957–65; Scottish Conservative Central Office, 1966–70; computer industry, 1971–74; management consultant, 1975–86; paper industry, 1987–90; Dir, British Paper and Board Industry Fedn, 1990–92; Partner, Henderson Consulting, 1993–. Contested (C): E Edinburgh, 1966; E Dunbartonshire, 1970; Fife NE, 1987. MP (C): East Dunbartonshire, Feb.–Sept. 1974; E Fife, 1979–83; Fife NE, 1983–87. PPS to Economic Sec. to HM Treasury, 1984–87. Member: Select Cttee on Scottish Affairs, 1979–87; H of C Chairmen's Panel, 1981–83; Chm., Scottish Cons. Back Bench Cttee, 1983–84; Vice-Chm., PITCOM, 1986–87. Member: project review team, Right to Manage, DETR, 2001–02; Extra Parly Panel, 2001–. Comr, Strathclyde Tram Public Inquiry, 1996. Trustee, St Andrews Links Trust, 1979–87. Comr, Gen. Assembly of Church of Scotland, 1986. Sec., 1997–2000, Vice-Chm., 2000–, Pimlico Village Housing Co-op. *Publications:* various pamphlets on Scottish, European and environmental issues. *Address:* 33 Longleat House, 18 Rampayne Street, SW1V 2TG. *T:* and *Fax:* (020) 7828 0056.

HENDERSON, Dame Joan; *see* Kelleher, Dame J.

HENDERSON, Sir (John) Nicholas, GCMG 1977 (KCMG 1972; CMG 1965); KCVO 1991; HM Diplomatic Service, retired; re-appointed, Ambassador to Washington, 1979–82; author and company director; *b* 1 April 1919; *s* of Prof. Sir Hubert Henderson; *m* 1951, Mary Barber (*née* Cawadias) (OBE 1988); one *d*. *Educ:* Stowe Sch.; Hertford Coll., Oxford (Hon. Fellow 1975). Mem. HM Diplomatic Service. Served Minister of State's Office, Cairo, 1942–43; Asst Private Sec. to the Foreign Sec., 1944–47; HM Embassy, Washington, 1947–49; Athens, 1949–50; Permanent Under Secretary's Dept, FO, 1950–53; HM Embassy, Vienna, 1953–56; Santiago, 1956–59; Northern Dept, FO, 1959–62; Permanent Under Secretary's Dept, 1962–63; Head of Northern Dept, Foreign Office, 1963; Private Sec. to the Sec. of State for Foreign Affairs, 1963–65; Minister in Madrid, 1965–69; Ambassador to Poland, 1969–72, to Federal Republic of Germany, 1972–75, to France, 1975–79. Lord Warden of the Stannaries, Keeper of the Privy Seal of the Duke of Cornwall, and Mem. of Prince's Council, 1985–90. Mem., BBC General Adv. Council, 1983–87; Chm., Channel Tunnel Gp, 1985–86; Director: Foreign & Colonial Investment Trust, 1982–88; M&G Reinsurance, 1982–90; Hambros, 1983–89; Tarmac, 1983–89; F&C Eurotrust, 1984–; Eurotunnel, 1986–88; Supervisory Bd, Fuel-Tech NV, 1987–; Sotheby's, 1989–. Trustee, Nat. Gallery, 1985–89. Pres., Hertford Soc., 1984–89. Romanes Lectr, 1986. Hon. DCL Oxford, 1987. *Publications:* Prince Eugen of Savoy (biography), 1964; The Birth of Nato, 1982; The Private Office, 1984; Channels and Tunnels, 1987; Mandarin: the diaries of Nicholas Henderson, 1994; Old Friends and Modern Instances (memoirs), 2000; various stories and articles in Penguin New Writing, Horizon, Apollo, Country Life, The Economist and History Today. *Recreations:* tennis, gardening. *Address:* 6 Fairholt Street, SW7 1EG. *T:* (020) 7589 4291. *Clubs:* Brooks's, Pratt's.

See also Earl of Drogheda.

HENDERSON, John Ronald, CVO 1985 OBE 1985 (MBE 1945); Lord-Lieutenant of Berkshire, 1989–95; Chairman, Henderson Administration (Group), 1983–90; *b* 6 May 1920; *s* of Major R. H. W. Henderson and Mrs Marjorie Henderson (*née* Garrard); *m* 1st, 1949, Sarah Katherine Beckwith-Smith (*d* 1972); two *s* one *d*; 2nd, 1976, Catherine Christian; one step *s* two step *d*. *Educ:* Eton; Cambridge Univ. Served War: ADC to Field Marshal Montgomery, 1942–46; retd Major, 12th Royal Lancers, 1946. Trustee, Winston Churchill Meml Trust, 1985–. Vice Lord-Lieutenant, Berks, 1979–89. KStJ 1989. *Recreations:* racing, shooting, golf, tennis. *Address:* Bennetts Farm, West Woodhay, Newbury, Berks RG20 0BL. *T:* (01488) 668271. *Club:* White's.

HENDERSON, Hon. Launcelot Dinadan James; QC 1995; *b* 20 Nov. 1951; *er s* of Baron Henderson of Brompton, KCB; *m* 1989, Elaine Elizabeth Webb; two *s* one *d*. *Educ:* Westminster Sch.; Balliol Coll., Oxford (MA). Fellow of All Souls Coll., Oxford, 1974–81 and 1982–89; called to the Bar, Lincoln's Inn, 1977; practised as Barrister (Chancery), 1978–; Standing Junior Counsel: to Inland Revenue (Chancery), 1987–91; to Inland Revenue, 1991–95. *Recreations:* botany, art, music. *Address:* 5 Stone Buildings, Lincoln's Inn, WC2A 3XT. *T:* (020) 7242 6201.

See also Bishop of Tuam, Killala and Achonry.

HENDERSON, Leslie Edwin, CBE 1982; Director of Contracts, Property Services Agency, 1978–82, retired; *b* 16 Dec. 1922; *s* of Thomas Edwin and Mabel Mary Henderson; *m* 1946, Marjorie (*née* Austin); two *s*. *Educ:* Ealing County Sch., London. Entered Civil Service (BoT) as Clerical Officer, 1939; Min. of Shipping, 1939; served in RAF, 1941–46; Min. of War Transport, 1946; subsequently in: Min. of Transport and Civil Aviation, MoT, DoE; Head of Contracts, Highways, Dept of Transport, 1968–78. *Recreations:* gardening, do-it-yourself. *Address:* 61 Greenacres Avenue, Ickenham, Mddx UB10 8HH. *T:* (01895) 672536.

HENDERSON, Mark; lighting designer, since 1981; *b* 26 Sept. 1957; *s* of Gordon Henderson and Margaret Henderson (*née* Moakes); two *s*. *Educ:* Sherwood Hall Tech. Grammar Sch., Mansfield. Chief electrician for Kent Opera, English Music Th., London Contemporary Dance, Sadler's Wells and Opera North, 1978–; lighting designs for: *theatre:* numerous West End productions including: Grease, Follies, Carmen Jones, Rowan Atkinson in Revue, Home, Design for Living; Passion, 1996; West Side Story, 1998; Spend, Spend, Spend, 1999; The Real Thing, 2000; Sunset Boulevard, 2001; RNT productions include: Cat on a Hot Tin Roof (also Broadway), 1988; Hamlet, 1989; The Oedipus Plays, 1996; Amy's View, Copenhagen, Antony and Cleopatra, 1998; Battle Royal, 1999; All My Sons, 2001; RSC productions include: Macbeth, Kiss Me Kate, The Lion, the Witch and the Wardrobe; Almeida Theatre productions include: Phèdre, The Ice Man Cometh, 1998; Vassa, Plenty, 1999; Richard II, Coriolanus, 2000; Lulu, 2001; *opera* productions include: The Flying Dutchman (Royal Opera); Anna Karenina, The Silver Tassie, 2000, ENO; Otello, Glyndebourne, 2001; *dance* productions include: Agora, Shadows in the Sun (London Contemp. Dance Th.); Quicksilver (Rambert Dance Co.); Tales of Beatrix Potter, The Judas Tree, Daphnis and Chloë (Royal Ballet); The Nutcracker, 1999; *films* include: The Tall Guy, 1988; Under Milk Wood, 1992. Olivier Awards: Lighting Designer of the Year, 1992; Best Lighting Designer, 1995, and 2000. *Address:* 34 Indigo Mews, Carysfort Road, N16 9AE.

HENDERSON, Michael John Glidden, FCA; Director: Ronar Services Ltd, since 1991; Cyril Sweett Ltd, since 1998; ECO-BAT Technologies plc, since 1999; *b* 19 Aug. 1938; *s* of William Glidden Henderson and Aileen Judith Henderson (*née* Malloy); *m* 1965, Stephanie Maria Henderson; four *s*. *Educ:* St Benedict's Sch., Ealing. FCA 1971. Took articles with William Dyson Jones & Co., 1956; qual. as chartered accountant, 1961; Whinney Smith & Whinney & Co., 1963; Goodlass Wall & Lead Industries, later Cookson Group plc, 1965; Cookson Group: Dir, 1975; Man. Dir, 1979; Chief Exec., 1984–90; Chm. and Chief Exec., 1990. Chm., Henderson Crosthwaite Hldgs Ltd, 1995–2000; Dir, Tioxide Gp, 1987–90; non-executive Director: Guinness Mahon Holdings, 1988–2000; Three Counties Ltd, 1991–. Mem., Innovation Adv. Bd, DTI, 1988–93. Trustee, Natural History Mus. Develt Trust, 1990–2000. FRSA 1989. Governor: St George's Coll., Weybridge, 1990–; Cranmore Sch., W Horsley, 1992–. *Recreations:* tennis, golf, watching all sports. *Address:* Langdale, Woodland Drive, East Horsley, Surrey KT24 5AN. *T:* (01483) 283844; (office) 21 Woodstock Street, W1C 2AP. *T:* (020) 7495 5994, *Fax:* (020) 7495 5993. *Clubs:* MCC, Queen's; Wisley Golf.

HENDERSON, Sir Nicholas; *see* Henderson, Sir J. N.

HENDERSON, (Patrick) David, CMG 1992; economist, author and consultant; *b* 10 April 1927; *s* of late David Thomson Henderson and late Eleanor Henderson; *m* 1960, Marcella Kodicek; one *s* one *d*. *Educ.* Ellesmere Coll., Shropshire; Corpus Christi Coll., Oxford. Fellow and Tutor in Economics, Lincoln Coll., Oxford, 1948–65 (Hon. Fellow, 1991); Univ. Lectr in Economics, Oxford, 1950–65; Commonwealth Fund Fellow (Harvard), 1952–53; Junior Proctor, Oxford Univ., 1955–56; Economic Adviser, HM Treasury, 1957–58; Chief Economist, Min. of Aviation, 1965–67; Adviser Harvard Development Advisory Service (Athens and Kuala Lumpur), 1967–68; Vis. Lectr, World Bank, 1968–69; Economist, World Bank, 1969–75, Dir of Economics Dept 1971–72; Prof. of Political Economy, UCL, 1975–83; Hd of Econs and Stats Dept, OECD, 1984–92. Mem., Commn on Environmental Pollution, 1977–80; Special Adviser, Sec. of State for Wales, 1978–79; Member: Nat. Ports Council, 1979–81; Bd, Commonwealth Develt Corp., 1980–83. Formerly Visiting Fellow or Professor: OECD Develt Centre, Paris; Centre for Eur. Policy Studies, Brussels; Fondation Nationale des Sciences Politiques, Paris; Monash Univ., Melb.; Univ. of Melb.; NZ Business Roundtable; Melb. Business Sch. Reith Lectr, BBC, 1985; Copland Meml Address, 1989; Shapiro Lectr, LSE, 1993; Downing Oration, Melbourne Univ., 1995; Hibberd Lectr, Melb. Business Sch., 1997; Wincott Lecture, 2000. *Publications:* India: the energy sector, 1975; Innocence and Design: the influence of economic ideas on policy, 1986; The Changing Fortunes of Economic Liberalism, 1998; (jointly) Nyasaland: The Economics of Federation, 1960; ed and contrib.: Economic Growth in Britain, 1965; contrib: The British Economy in the 1950's, 1962; Public Enterprise, 1968; Public Economics, 1969; Unfashionable Economics, 1970; The World Bank, Multilateral Aid and the 1970's, 1973; The Economic Development of Yugoslavia, 1975; Contemporary Problems of Economic Policy, 1983; Protectionism and Growth, 1985; Economic Policies for the 1990s, 1991; (ed jtly) Trade Blocs: the future of regional integration, 1994; articles in economic and other jls.

HENDERSON, Prof. Paul, DPhil; Director of Science, Natural History Museum, since 1995; *b* 7 Nov. 1940; *s* of Thomas William Henderson and Dorothy Violet (*née* Marriner); *m* 1966, Elizabeth Kathryn Ankerson; one *s* one *d*. *Educ:* King's Coll. Sch., Wimbledon; Univ. of London (BSc 1963); Univ. of Oxford (DPhil 1966). FGS 1990; CGeol 1990. Asst Lectr in Chemistry, Glasgow Univ., 1967–68; Lectr in Geochem., Chelsea Coll., Univ. of London, 1968–76; British Museum (Natural History), subseq. Natural History Museum: PSO, 1977, Grade 6, 1984, Dep. Keeper, 1987, Keeper, 1989–95, Dept of Mineralogy; Associate Dir, Earth Scis, 1992–95. Visiting Professor: Univ. of Bern, Switzerland, 1989; UCL, 1990–98 (Hon. Prof., 1999–); Vis. Res. Fellow, Univ. of Alberta, Canada, 1976; Hon. Research Fellow: Chelsea Coll., Univ. of London, 1979–85; RHBNC, Univ. of London, 1985–86. Pres., Mineralogical Soc., 1989–91 (Mem. Council, 1974–76 and 1986–89); Member Council: Eur. Assoc. for Geochem., 1986–94; Internat. Mineralog. Assoc., 1989–94. Member: Sci. Adv. Bd, Museum für Naturkunde, Berlin, 1994–99; Sci. Adv. Cttee, Muséum Nat. d'Histoire Naturelle, Paris, 2000–01. Fourmarier Medal, Belgian Geol Soc., 1989. *Publications:* Inorganic Geochemistry, 1982; (ed) Rare Earth Element Geochemistry, 1984; contribs to jls on geochem. and mineral chem. *Recreations:* music, Paris, wine. *Address:* Science Directorate, Natural History Museum, Cromwell Road, SW7 5BD. *T:* (020) 7942 5299, *Fax:* (020) 7942 5765; *e-mail:* P.Henderson@nhm.ac.uk.

HENDERSON, Air Vice-Marshal Peter William, CB 2000; MBE 1982; CEng, FRAeS; aerospace consultant; *b* 5 Nov. 1945. *Educ:* RAF Coll. Cranwell (BSc CNAA). Inspectorate of Flight Safety, 1975; RAF Germany, 1978; RAF Staff Coll., 1982; RAF Abingdon, 1982–84; Dept of Air Mem. for Supply and Orgn, 1984–87; Mem., Ordnance Bd, 1987; Stn Comdr, Abingdon, 1990–92; Logistic Comd Project Sponsor, HQ RAF Support Comd, 1992–95; Dir 1995–97, Dir Gen., 1997–99, RAF Support Mgt; Dir Gen., Equipment Support (Air), Mem., Defence Logistics Mgt Bd, and Mem., Air Force Bd, Defence Council, 1999–2000, retd. *Recreations:* golf, garden design, music. *Clubs:* Royal Air Force; Truro Golf.

HENDERSON, Dr Richard, FRS 1983; Director, Medical Research Council Laboratory of Molecular Biology, Cambridge, since 1996; Fellow of Darwin College, Cambridge, since 1981; *b* 19 July 1945; *s* of John and Grace Henderson; *m* 1st, 1969, Penelope FitzGerald (marr. diss. 1988); one *s* one *d* (and one *d* decd); 2nd, 1995, Jade Li. *Educ:* Hawick High Sch.; Boroughmuir Secondary Sch.; Edinburgh Univ. (BSc); Cambridge Univ. (PhD). Helen Hay Whitney Fellow, Yale, 1970–73; Mem. Scientific Staff, MRC Lab. of Molecular Biol., 1973–. Founder FMedSci 1998. Foreign Associate, Acad. of Sci., USA, 1998. William Bate Hardy Prize, Cambridge Phil Soc., 1978; Ernst Ruska Prize for Electron Microscopy, Ernst Ruska Foundn, 1981; Lewis S. Rosenstiel Award, Brandeis Univ., 1991; Louis Jeantet Award, Jeantet Foundn, Geneva, 1993; Gregori Aminoff Prize, Royal Swedish Acad. of Scis, 1999. *Publications:* research pubns and reviews in scientific jls. *Recreations:* canoeing, wine-tasting. *Address:* MRC Laboratory of Molecular Biology, Hills Road, Cambridge CB2 2QH. *T:* (01223) 248011.

HENDERSON, Rt Rev. Richard Crosbie Aitken; *see* Tuam, Killala and Achonry, Bishop of.

HENDERSON, Major Richard Yates, TD 1966; JP; Lord-Lieutenant of Ayrshire and Arran, since 1991; *b* 7 July 1931; *s* of late John Wishart Henderson and Dorothy (*née* Yates); *m* 1957, Frances Elizabeth Chrystal; two *s* one *d* (and one *s* decd). *Educ:* Rugby; Hertford Coll., Oxford (BA); Glasgow Univ. (LLB). Served Royal Scots Greys, 1950–52; Ayrshire Yeomanry TA, 1953–69. Partner, Mitchells Robertson, Solicitors, Glasgow, 1958–90; Trustee, TSB, Glasgow, 1966–74; Dir, West of Scotland TSB, 1974–83. Hon. Sheriff, S Strathclyde, Dumfries and Galloway at Ayr, 1997. Brig., Royal Company of Archers, Queen's Body Guard for Scotland. Hon. Col, Ayrshire Yeo. Sqn, Scottish Yeo., 1992–97; Pres., Lowlands TAVRA, 1996–2000. DL Ayrshire, 1970–90. *Recreations:* shooting, tennis, golf. *Address:* Blairston, by Ayr KA7 4EF. *T:* (01292) 441601. *Club:* Western (Glasgow).

HENDERSON, Robert Brumwell, CBE 1979; Managing Director, 1959–83, Chairman, 1983–91, Ulster TV; *b* 28 July 1929; *s* of late Comdr Oscar Henderson, CVO, CBE, DSO, RN, and of Mrs Henderson; *m* 1st, 1953, Joy Frances Duncan (marr. diss. 1969); two *d*; 2nd, 1970, Patricia Ann Davison. *Educ:* Brackenber House Sch., Belfast; Bradfield Coll., Berks; Trinity Coll., Dublin. BA (Hons) 1951, MA 1959. Journalism: London, Liverpool, Glasgow and Belfast, 1951–59. Director: ITN, 1964–68; Independent Television Publications, 1969–86. Dep. Chm., Powerscreen Internat., 1989–92; Director: Ulster Cablevision, 1985–93; Laganside Corp., 1988–92; Airtronics Internat., 1990–95, etc. Chm., Publicity Assoc. of NI, 1959–60; Vice-Pres., Co-operation North, 1984–; President: Radio Industries Club of NI, 1963–70, 1972–80; NI Chamber of Commerce and Industry, 1980–81; NI Chartered Inst. of Marketing, 1984–92; Assoc. of Ulster Drama Festivals, 1984–; Chm., NI Millenium Bid Cttee, 1994–; Member: Exec. Council, Cinema and Television Benevolent Fund, 1980–84; Council for Continuing Educn, 1975–85; NI Council for Educnl Develt, 1980–; Cttee to Review Higher Educn in NI, 1964; various cttees of Trinity Coll. Dublin, Univ. of Ulster; Senate, Queen's Univ. of Belfast, 1980–; Council, Inst. of Dirs, 1973–93 (Chm., NI Br., 1973–79); Design Council (NI), 1980–92; Governor, Ulster Polytechnic, 1979–84. FRTS 1977 (Mem. Council, 1981–84, Chm., 1982–84, Vice Pres., 1986–91). Hon. DLitt Ulster, 1982. *Publications:* Midnight Oil, 1961; A Television First, 1977; Amusing, 1984. *Recreations:* reading, theatre and cinema, golf. *Address:* 8 Crabtree Road, Ballynahinch, Co. Down, N Ireland BT24 8RH. *Clubs:* Royal County Down Golf; Malone Golf.

HENDERSON, Robert Ewart; QC (Scot.) 1982; *b* 29 March 1937; *s* of William Ewart Henderson and Agnes Ker Henderson; *m* 1st, 1958, Olga Sunter (marr. diss. 1978); one *s* two *d*; 2nd, 1982, Carol Black (marr. diss. 1988); one *s*; 3rd, 1995, Carolyn Gell. *Educ:* Larchfield Sch., Helensburgh; Morrison's Acad., Crieff; Glasgow Univ. (BL 1962). Admitted to Faculty of Advocates, 1963. National Service, 2nd Lieut RA, 1956–58. Hon. Sheriff-Substitute, Stirling, Dunbarton and Clackmannan, 1968; Standing Jun. Counsel in Scotland, DTI, 1970–74, Dept of Trade, 1974–77; Temp. Sheriff, 1978. Pres., Glasgow Univ. Law Soc., 1961–62; Chairman: NHS Appeal Tribunal, 1972; Medical Appeal Tribunal (Scotland), 1985–93; War Pensions Appeal Tribunal, 1986–. Contested (C) Inverness-shire, Feb. and Oct. 1974. *Recreations:* golf, sailing. *Address:* The Old Schoolhouse, Gullane, East Lothian EH31 2AF. *T:* (01620) 842012. *Clubs:* New (Edinburgh); Hon. Company of Edinburgh Golfers (Muirfield); Royal St George's Golf (Sandwich).

HENDERSON, Roger Anthony; QC 1980; a Recorder of the Crown Court, since 1983; a Deputy High Court Judge, since 1987; *b* 21 April 1943; *s* of late Dr Peter Wallace Henderson and of Dr Stella Dolores Henderson; *m* 1968, Catherine Margaret Williams; three *d* (and one *d* decd). *Educ:* Radley Coll.; St Catharine's Coll., Cambridge (Scholar; 1st Cl. Hons degree in Law, MA; Adderley Prize for Law, 1964). Inner Temple: Duke of Edinburgh Award, 1962; Major Scholarship, 1964; called to the Bar, 1964; Bencher, 1985. Counsel to King's Cross Inquiry, 1988. Mem., Bar Council, 1988–91; Chm., Public Affairs Cttee of Bar, 1989–90. Chm., Civil Service Arbitration Tribunal, 1994–; Member: Exec. Council, British Acad. of Forensic Sciences, 1977–90 (Pres., 1986–87); Council of Legal Educn, 1983–90. Gov., London Hosp. Med. Coll., 1989–96 (Chm., Council, 1993–96); Chm., Special Cttee, St Peter's Hosps, 1989–92; Mem. Council, QMW, 1993–. FRSA 1994. *Recreations:* fly-fishing, gardening, shooting. *Address:* 2 Harcourt Buildings, Temple, EC4Y 9DB. *T:* (020) 7583 9020, 9 Brunswick Gardens, W8 4AS. *Address:* Holbury Mill, Lockerley, Romsey, Hants SO52 0JR. *T:* (01794) 340583; Upper Round Road, St John's Parish, Nevis, West Indies. *Club:* Boodle's.

HENDERSON, Victor Joseph, CMG 2000; HM Diplomatic Service, retired; Ambassador to the Yemen, 1997–2001; *b* 10 Jan. 1941; *s* of Frederick Ilwyn Henderson and Mary Elizabeth Henderson; *m* 1966, Heather Winifred Steed; one *s* one *d*. *Educ:* Rhondda Co. Grammar Sch. for Boys; King's Coll., London (BA Hons Spanish 1961). Joined HM Diplomatic Service, 1966: MECAS, Lebanon, 1967–69; Third Sec. (Commercial), Jedda, 1969–72; Second Sec. (Commercial), Bahrain, 1972–75; FCO, 1975–78; Second, later First Sec., Caracas, 1978–82; Consul, Jerusalem, 1982–87; FCO, 1987–90; First Sec. (Political, later Commercial), Helsinki, 1990–94; Dep. Head, Jt Export Promotion Directorate, FCO/DTI, 1995–97. *Recreations:* watching cricket, reading, listening to music (especially jazz). *Address:* c/o Foreign and Commonwealth Office, King Charles Street, SW1A 2AH.

HENDERSON-STEWART, Sir David (James), 2nd Bt *cr* 1957; *b* 3 July 1941; *s* of Sir James Henderson-Stewart, 1st Bt, MP, and of Anna Margaret (*née* Greenwell); *S* father, 1961; *m* 1972, Anne, *d* of Count Serge de Pahlen; three *s* one *d*. *Educ:* Eton Coll.; Trinity Coll., Oxford. *Heir: s* David Henderson-Stewart, *b* 2 Feb. 1973. *Address:* 90 Oxford Gardens, W10 5UW. *T:* (020) 8960 1278.

HENDON, David Anthony, FIEE; Chief Executive, Radiocommunications Agency, since 1998; *b* 19 Oct. 1949; *s* of Anthony Leonard Hendon and Constance Audrey Hendon (*née* Clayton); *m* 1976, Gillian Anne Iles; one *s* two *d*. *Educ:* Royal Grammar Sch., Guildford; Southampton Univ. (BSc Eng 1972). FIEE 2000. MoD, 1973–84 (Principal, 1981–84); Asst Dir (Engrg), Home Office, 1984–88; Dep. Dir, 1988–92, Dir, 1992–98, Technol., Policy, Communications and Inf., Industries Directorate, DTI. Chm. Bd, Eur. Telecommunications Standards Inst., 1995–99. Chm., Radio Spectrum Internat. Consulting Ltd, 1998–. Spastics Society, later Scope: Mem. Council, 1987–96; Vice-Chm., 1991–93; Chm., Audit Cttee, 1993–. Chm., White Lodge Centre, Chertsey, 1980–85. Gov., Guildford Co. Sch., 1994–98. *Recreations:* reading, red wine, the Internet. *Address:* Radiocommunications Agency, 189 Marsh Wall, E14 9SX. *T:* (020) 721 0570.

HENDRICK, Mark Phillip, CEng; MP (Lab and Co-op) Preston, since Nov. 2000; *b* 2 Nov. 1958; *s* of Brian Francis Hendrick and Jennifer (*née* Chapman). *Educ:* Liverpool Poly. (BSc Hons Electrical and Electronic Engrg); Univ. of Manchester (MSc Computer Sci.; Cert Ed). CEng 1987; MIEE 1987. Trainee Technician, Signal and Telecommunications, BR, 1975–78; Student Engr, 1979–81; RSRE Malvern, MoD, 1979; Special Systems Unit, STC plc, 1980; AEG Telefunken, Seligenstadt, Germany, 1981; Design Engr, Daresbury Lab., SERC, 1982–84 and 1985–88; Lectr, Stockport Coll., 1989–94. MEP (Lab and Co-op) Lancashire Central, 1994–99; contested (Lab) NW Reg., 1999. *Recreations:* football supporter (Manchester City and Preston North End), travel, chess, German and French. *Address:* c/o House of Commons, SW1A 0AA; 24 Farcham Close, Preston, Lancs PR2 8FH. *T:* (01772) 795157. *Clubs:* Deepdale Labour; Penwortham Sports and Social (Preston).

HENDRICKS, Barbara; American soprano; *b* 20 Nov. 1948; *d* of Rev. M. L. Hendricks and Della Hendricks; *m*; one *s* one *d*. *Educ:* Univ. of Nebraska (BS Chem. and Math. 1969); Juilliard Sch. of Music, NY (Schol.); studied under Jennie Tourel. Début, l'Incoronazione di Poppea, San Francisco Opera, 1976; has appeared with opera cos of Berlin, Boston, Florence, Glyndebourne, Hamburg, La Scala, Milan, LA, Royal Opera, Covent Garden, etc; concert performances with major orchestras; numerous recordings. Goodwill Ambassador, UN High Commn for Refugees, 1987. Hon. Dr Juilliard, NY, 2000. Commandeur des Arts et des Lettres (France), 1986. *Address:* PO Box 224, 1815 Clarens, Switzerland.

HENDRICKSE, Prof. Ralph George, MD; FRCP, FRCPE; Professor and Head of Department of Tropical Paediatrics, 1974–91, and Dean, 1988–91, Liverpool School of Tropical Medicine, now Professor Emeritus; *b* 5 Nov. 1926; *s* of William George Hendrickse and Johana Theresa Hendrickse (*née* Dennis); m 1948, Begum Johanara Abdurahman; one *s* four *d*. *Educ:* Livingstone High Sch.; Univ. of Cape Town (MD). FMCPaed (Hon. Foundn Fellow). Res. MO, McCord Zulu Hosp., Durban, 1949–54, incl. secondment to Willis F. Pierce Meml Hosp., S Rhodesia, as MO i/c, 1951; postgrad. studies, Glasgow and Edinburgh, 1955; Sen. Registrar, UCH, Ibadan, Nigeria, 1955–57; Sen. Lectr, Univ. of Ibadan, 1957–62, and Hon. Consultant Paediatrician, UCH, 1957–69; Prof. and Head of Paediatrics, Univ. of Ibadan, 1962–69. Dir, Inst. of Child Health, 1964–69; Sen. Lectr, Liverpool Univ. Sch. of Trop. Med., 1969–74. Mem., Standing Panel of Experts in Public Health Medicine, Univ. of London, 1990–. Hon. Vis. Prof., Santo Tomas Univ., Philippines. Hon. Founder FRCPCH 1996; Hon. Member: BPA, 1995; Philippines Paed. Soc. Founder and Editor-in-Chief, Annals of Tropical Paediatrics, 1981–. Hon. DSc (Med.) Cape Town, 1998. Frederick Murgatroyd Prize, RCP, 1970. *Publications:* Paediatrics in the Tropics: current review, 1981; (ed and contrib.) Paediatrics in the Tropics, 1991; papers in learned jls. *Recreations:* photography, sketching, theatre, swimming, travel. *Address:* Beresford House, 25 Riverbank Road, Heswall, Wirral, Merseyside L60 4SQ. *T:* (0151) 342 5510.

HENDRIE, Dr Gerald Mills; Professor of Music, The Open University, 1969–90; *b* 28 Oct. 1935; *s* of James Harold Hendrie and Florence Mary MacPherson; *m* 1st, 1962, Dinah Florence Barsham, BMus, PhD (*d* 1985); two *s*; 2nd, 1986, Dr Lynette Anne Maddern, MB, BS. *Educ:* Framlingham Coll., Suffolk; Royal Coll. of Music; Selwyn Coll., Cambridge (MA, MusB, PhD). FRCO, ARCM. Director of Music, Homerton Coll., Cambridge, 1962–63; Lectr in the History of Music, Univ. of Manchester, 1963–67; Prof. and Chm., Dept of Music, Univ. of Victoria, BC, Canada, 1967–69; Reader in Music, subseq. Prof., The Open Univ., 1969–90; Dir of Studies in Music, St John's Coll., Cambridge, 1981–84, Supervisor, 1977–84. Vis. Fellow in Music, Univ. of WA, 1985. *Publications:* Musica Britannica XX, Orlando Gibbons: Keyboard Music, 1962, 2nd rev. edn, 1967; G. F. Handel: Anthems für Cannons, 3 vols, 1985, 1987, 1991; Anthems für die Chapel Royal, 1992; Utrecht Te Deum und Jubilate, 1998; articles for Die Musik in Geschichte und Gegenwart; musical compositions include: Five Bagatelles for piano, 1980; Four Excursions for piano, 1983; Three Pieces for flute and piano, 1985; Specula Petro for organ, 1988; Quintet for Brass, 1988; Choral: Hommage à César Franck for organ, 1990; Le Tombeau de Marcel Dupré (for organ): Toccata and Fugue, 1991; Prelude and Fugue, 1991; Prelude and Fugue on the name BACH, 1992; Two Sketches on the name BACH, 1993; In Praise of St Asaph, 1994; Sonata: In Praise of Reconciliation, for organ, 1998, for piano, 1998; Requiem, for soprano, chorus, organ, 1998; Premier Livre d'Orgue, 1999; Deuxième Livre d'Orgue, 2000; much church music. *Recreations:* walking, gardening. *Address:* Au Village, 32190 Caillavet, France. *T:* 562644104.

HENDRIE, Robert Andrew Michie; HM Diplomatic Service, retired; Ambassador to Uruguay, 1994–98; *b* 4 May 1938; *s* of John Hendrie, Edinburgh and Effie Campbell (*née* Mackay); *m* 1964, Consuelo Liaño Solórzano; two *d*. *Educ:* Bradford Grammar Sch.; Trinity Hall, Cambridge (BA, MA). Joined HM Diplomatic Service, 1961; MECAS, Beirut, 1961–62; Political Residency, Bahrain, 1962–65; Tehran, 1965–68; Tripoli, 1968–69; Latin America Dept, FCO, 1969–73; Lima, 1973–75; Buenos Aires, 1975–80; Asst Hd, Central Africa Dept, ME Dept and Inf. Dept, FCO, 1980–86; Consul-General: Lille, 1986–90; Dubai, UAE, 1990–94. MIL 1987. MIMgt 1979. *Recreations:* reading, walking, watching Rugby, languages. *Address:* c/o Foreign and Commonwealth Office, King Charles Street, SW1A 2AH. *Club:* Roehampton.

HENDRON, Joseph Gerard; Member (SDLP) Belfast West, Northern Ireland Assembly, since 1998; *b* 12 Nov. 1932; *m* 1974, Sally (*née* Lennon); three *s* one *d*. *Educ:* St Malachy's Coll.; Queen's Univ., Belfast (MB 1957). FRCGP 1987. GP, W Belfast. Mem. (SDLP) Belfast CC, 1981–93. MP (SDLP) Belfast W, 1992–97; contested (SDLP) same seat, 1983, 1987, 1997. Chm., Health, Social Services and Public Safety Cttee, NI Assembly. *Address:* Stormont Castle, Belfast BT4 3ST.

HENDRY, Prof. Arnold William; Professor of Civil Engineering, University of Edinburgh, 1964–88, now Emeritus; *b* 10 Sept. 1921; *s* of late Dr George Hendry, MB, ChB, Buckie, Scotland; *m* 1st, 1946, Sheila Mary Cameron Roberts (*d* 1966), Glasgow; one *s* one *d* (and one *s* decd); 2nd, 1968, Elizabeth Lois Alice Inglis, Edinburgh. *Educ:* Buckie High Sch.; Aberdeen Univ. Civil engineer with Sir William Arrol & Co. Ltd, Bridge builders and Engineers, Glasgow, 1941–43; Asst in Engineering, University of Aberdeen, 1943–46; Lecturer in Civil Engineering, 1946–49; Reader in Civil Engineering, Univ. of London, King's Coll., 1949–51; Prof. of Civil Engrg and Dean of Fac. of Engrg, Univ. of Khartoum, 1951–57; Prof. of Building Science, University of Liverpool, 1957–63. *Publications:* An Introduction to Photo-Elastic Analysis, 1948; (with L. G. Jaeger) The Analysis of Grid Frameworks, 1958; The Elements of Experimental Stress Analysis, 1964, 2nd edn 1977; Structural Brickwork, 1981; An Introduction to the Design of Load Bearing Brickwork, 1981; Structural Masonry, 1990, 2nd edn 1998; (ed) Reinforced and Prestressed Masonry, 1991; (with B. P. Sinha and S. R. Davies) Design of Masonry Structures, 1997; Masonry Wall Construction, 2000; (with F. M. Kalaf) A Career in Ivory Towers, 2001; over 150 papers and articles in professional and technical jls. *Recreations:* walking, travel, reading. *Address:* 146/6 Whitehouse Loan, Edinburgh EH9 2AN.

HENDRY, Charles; MP (C) Wealden, since 2001; Chairman, Agenda Group Ltd, since 2001 (Director and Chief Executive, 1999–2001); *b* 6 May 1959; *s* of late Charles William Righton Hendry and of Margaret Anne Hendry; *m* 1995, Mrs Sallie A. Moores; two *s*, and one step *s* one step *d*. *Educ:* Rugby Sch.; Univ. of Edinburgh (BCom Hons 1981). Account Dir, Ogilvy and Mather PR, 1983–86; Burson-Marsteller: Associate Dir (PR), 1986–88; Sen. Counsellor, Public Affairs, 1990–92. Special Adviser to: Rt Hon. John Moore, 1988; Rt Hon. Anthony Newton, 1988–89; Chief of Staff to Leader of Cons. Party, 1997; Hd of Business Liaison, Cons. Party, 1997–99. Vice-Chm., Battersea Cons. Assoc., 1981–83. Contested (C): Clackmannan, 1983; Mansfield, 1987; MP (C) High Peak, 1992–97; contested (C) same seat, 1997. PPS to Sec. of State for Educn and Employment, 1995; a Vice Chm., Cons. Party, 1995–97; an Opposition Whip, 2001–. Mem. Select Cttee on Procedure, 1992–94, on NI Affairs, 1994–97. Secretary: Conservative Back bench Social Services Cttee, 1992–94; Cons. Back bench Home Improvement Sub-Cttee, 1993–94; Cons. Back bench Urban Affairs Cttee, 1994; Jt Chm., All-Party Party Gp on Homelessness, 1992–96. Sec., E Midlands Area Cons. MPs, 1992–97. Pres., British Youth Council, 1992–97; Trustee: Drive for Youth, 1989–99; Friends of NACAB, 1992–95; Big Issue Foundn, 1995–97 (Patron, 1997–). *Recreations:* tennis, ski-ing, theatre. *Address:* House of Commons, SW1A 0AA.

HENDRY, Prof. David Forbes, PhD; FBA 1987; Professor of Economics, University of Oxford, since 1982; Fellow, Nuffield College, Oxford, since 1982; *b* 6 March 1944; *s* of

Robert Ernest Hendry and Catherine Helen (*née* Mackenzie); *m* 1966, Evelyn Rosemary (*née* Vass); one *d*. *Educ:* Aberdeen Univ. (MA 1st Cl. Hons); LSE (MSc Distinction, PhD). Fellow, Econometric Soc., 1975. Lectr, LSE, 1969, Reader, 1973, Prof. of Econometrics, 1977. Vis. Professor: Yale Univ., 1975; Univ. of Calif, Berkeley, 1976; Catholic Univ. of Louvain, 1980; Univ. of Calif, San Diego, 1981, 1989–90; Vis. Research Prof., Duke Univ., 1987–91. Chm., Res. Assessment Panel in Econs, HEFC, 1996. Pres., Royal Economic Soc., 1992–95 (Hon. Vice Pres., 1995–). Hon. Foreign Member: Amer. Economic Assoc., 1991; Amer. Acad. of Arts and Scis, 1994. Hon. LLD Aberdeen, 1987; Hon. DSc Nottingham, 1998. Guy Medal in Bronze, Royal Statistical Soc., 1986. Editor: Rev. of Econ. Studies, 1971–75; Econ. Jl, 1976–80; Oxford Bulletin of Economics and Statistics, 1983–. *Publications:* (ed with K. F. Wallis) Econometrics and Quantitative Economics, 1984; PC-GIVE, 1989; (with A. J. Neale and N. R. Ericsson) PC-NAIVE, 1991; Econometrics: alchemy or science?, 1993; (jtly) Cointegration, Error Correction and the Econometric Analysis of Non-stationary Data, 1993; Dynamic Econometrics, 1995; (ed with M. S. Morgan) The Foundations of Econometric Analysis, 1995; (with J. A. Doornik) Empirical Econometric Modelling, 1996; (with J. A. Doornik) An Interface to Empirical Modelling, 1996; (with J. A. Doornik) Modelling Dynamic Systems using PcFiml, 1997; (with M. P. Clements) Forecasting Economic Time Series, 1998; (with M. P. Clements) Forecasting Non-Stationary Economic Time Series, 1999; papers in econometrics, statistics and economics jls. *Recreation:* golf. *Address:* Nuffield College, Oxford OX1 1NF; 26 Northmoor Road, Oxford OX2 6UR. *T:* (01865) 515588.

HENDRY, Ian Duncan, CMG 1996; HM Diplomatic Service; Deputy Legal Adviser, Foreign and Commonwealth Office, since 1999; *b* 2 April 1948; *s* of Duncan William Hendry and Edna Beatrice Hendry (*née* Woodley); *m* 1st, 1973, Elizabeth Anne Southall (marr. diss.); one *s* one *d*; 2nd, 1991, Sally Annabel Hill. *Educ:* Uppingham Sch.; King's Coll., London (LLB, LLM). Called to the Bar, Gray's Inn, 1971; Asst Legal Advr, FCO, 1971–82 and 1985–86; Legal Advr, BMG, Berlin, 1982–85; Legal Counsellor: FCO, 1986–91; UK Perm. Representation to EC, 1991–95; FCO, 1995–99. *Publications:* (with M. C. Wood) The Legal Status of Berlin, 1986; (jtly) The External Relations of the European Communities, 1996; articles in Internat. and Comparative Law Qly and German Yearbook of Internat. Law. *Recreations:* travel, cricket, percussion, the exotic. *Address:* Woodlands Cottage, Sturmer, Haverhill, Suffolk CB9 7UW.

HENDRY, Stephen Gordon, MBE 1993; professional snooker player, since 1986; *b* 13 Jan. 1969; *s* of Gordon John Hendry and Irene Agnes (*née* Anthony); *m* 1995, Amanda Elizabeth Theresa Tart; one *s*. *Educ:* Inverkeithing High Sch. Embassy World Champion, 1990, 1992, 1993, 1994, 1995, 1996, 1999 (record number of wins); Benson & Hedges Masters Champion, 1989, 1990, 1991, 1992, 1993, 1996; UK Professional Champion, 1989, 1990, 1994, 1995, 1996; World Doubles Champion, 1987. *Publication:* Remember My Name, 1989. *Recreations:* golf, music, cars. *Address:* Stephen Hendry Snooker Ltd, Kerse Road, Stirling FK7 7SG. *T:* (01786) 462634, *Fax:* (01786) 450068. *Club:* Lord's Taverners (Scotland).

HENDY, John Giles; QC 1987; *b* 11 April 1948; *s* of late Jack and of Mary Hendy; *m*; one *d*. *Educ:* Ealing Technical College (LLB); Queen's Univ., Belfast (DipLL, LLM). Called to the Bar, Gray's Inn, 1972; Bencher, 1995. Dir, Newham Rights Centre, 1973–76; Lectr, Middlesex Polytechnic, 1976–77; Barrister, 1977–. Vis. Prof., Sch. of Law, KCL, 1999–. Chm., Inst. of Employment Rights, 1989–. Member, Editorial Committee: Encyc. of Employment Law, 1990–; The Litigator, 1996–. *Publications:* (jointly): Personal Injury Practice, 2nd edn 1993, 3rd edn 1999; Redgrave's Health and Safety, 2nd edn 1994, 3rd edn 1998; Munkman on Employer's Liability, 12th edn 1995, 13th edn 2001. *Address:* Old Square Chambers, 1 Verulam Buildings, Gray's Inn, WC1R 5LQ. *T:* (020) 7269 0331, *Fax:* (020) 7405 1387.

HENES, John Derek; Head, UK Delegation to UK/French Channel Tunnel Intergovernmental Commission, since 1997; *b* 8 June 1937; *s* of Frederick William Kingaby Henes and Joan Elizabeth Henes (*née* Colbourne); *m* 1981, Virginia Elizabeth Evans; one *s* one *d*. *Educ:* Christ's Hospital; Gonville and Caius College, Cambridge (MA). Ministry of Aviation, 1963; Dept of Trade, 1971; Private Sec. to Christopher Chataway, 1973–74, to Lord Beswick, 1974–75; Asst Sec., 1975; Dept of Transport, 1983–96; Under Sec., 1989. *Recreations:* reading, music. *Address:* Department of Transport, Local Government and the Regions, 76 Marsham Street, SW1P 4DR.

HENHAM, His Honour John Alfred; a Circuit Judge, 1983–95; *b* 8 Sept. 1924; *s* of Alfred and Daisy Henham; *m* 1946, Suzanne Jeanne Octavie Ghislaine Pinchart (*d* 1972); two *s*. Stipendiary Magistrate for S Yorks, 1975–82; a Recorder of the Crown Court, 1979–82. *Address:* c/o The Law Courts, 50 West Bar, Sheffield S3 8PH.

HENIG, Prof. Stanley; Professor of European Politics, 1982–97 and Head of Department of European Studies, 1990–97, University of Central Lancashire (formerly Preston, then Lancashire, Polytechnic); *b* 7 July 1939; *s* of Sir Mark Henig and Grace (*née* Cohen); *m* 1966, Ruth Beatrice Munzer (marr. diss.); two *s*. *Educ:* Wyggeston Grammar Sch.; Corpus Christi Coll., Oxford. BA 1st Cl. Hons, 1961; MA 1965 Oxon. Teaching Asst, Dept of Politics, Univ. of Minnesota, 1961; Research Student, Nuffield Coll., 1962; Lecturer in Politics, Lancaster Univ., 1964–66; MP (Lab) Lancaster, 1966–70; Lectr in Politics, Warwick Univ., 1970–71; Lectr, Civil Service Coll., 1972–75; Preston, subseq. Lancashire, Polytechnic: Head of Div. of Social Admin, later Sch. of Social Studies, 1976–82; Dean, Faculty of Social Studies, 1985–90. Sen. Res. Fellow, Federal Trust, 2001–. Mem., Lancaster CC, 1981–99 (Leader, 1991–99); Dep. Ldr, Lab. Gp, ADC, 1995–97; Sec., Lab. Gp, LGA, 1997–99. Governor, British Inst. of Recorded Sound, 1975–80. Secretary: Historic Masters Ltd, 1983–; Historic Singers Trust, 1985–. Chm., Court, RNCM, 1986–89. Asst Editor, Jl of Common Market Studies, 1964–72, Editor, 1973–76. *Publications:* (ed) European Political Parties, 1969; External Relations of the European Community, 1971; (ed) Political Parties in the European Community, 1979; Power and Decision in Europe, 1980; Uniting of Europe, 1997; (jtly) Enrico Caruso—Recollections and Retrospective, 1999; (ed) The Kosovo Crisis, 2001. *Recreation:* collector of old gramophone records. *Address:* 10 Yealand Drive, Lancaster LA1 4EW. *T:* (01524) 69624.

HENLEY, 8th Baron *cr* 1799 (Ire.); **Oliver Michael Robert Eden;** Baron Northington (UK) 1885; *b* 22 Nov. 1953; *er s* of 7th Baron Henley and of Nancy Mary, *d* of Stanley Walton, Gilsland, Cumbria; *S* father, 1977; *m* 1984, Caroline Patricia, *d* of A. G. Sharp, Mackney, Oxon; three *s* one *d*. *Educ:* Clifton; Durham Univ. (BA 1975). Called to the Bar, Middle Temple, 1977. A Lord in Waiting (Govt Whip), 1989; Parliamentary Under-Secretary of State: DSS, 1989–93; Dept of Employment, 1993–94; MoD, 1994–95; Minister of State, DFEE, 1995–97; Opposition spokesman on home affairs, 1997–98; Opposition Chief Whip, H of L, 1998–2001; elected Mem., H of L, 1999. Mem., Cumbria CC, 1986–89. Chm., Penrith and the Border Conservative Assoc., 1987–89. Pres., Cumbria Assoc. of Local Councils, 1981–89. Pres., Cumbria Trust for Nature Conservation, 1988–89. *Heir: s* Hon. John Michael Oliver Eden, *b* 30 June 1988. *Address:* Scaleby Castle, Carlisle, Cumbria CA6 4LN. *Clubs:* Brooks's; Pratt's.

HENLEY, Sir Douglas (Owen), KCB 1973 (CB 1970); Comptroller and Auditor General, 1976–81; *b* 5 April 1919; *m* 1942, June Muriel Ibbetson; four *d*. *Educ:* Beckenham County Sch.; London Sch. of Economics (Hon. Fellow, 1974). BSc (Econ.), 1939; Gerstenberg Studentship and Leverhulme Res. Studentship (not taken up). Served Army, 1939–46; Queen's Own Royal West Kent Regt and HQ 12th Inf. Bde (despatches twice, Italy, 1945). Treasury, 1946; Treas. rep. (Financial Counsellor) in Tokyo and Singapore, 1956–59; Asst Under-Sec. of State, DEA, 1964–69, Dep. Under-Sec. of State, 1969; Second Permanent Sec., HM Treasury, 1972–76. Mem. Council, GDST (formerly GPDST), 1982–2000 (Hon. Vice Pres., 2000–). Hon. LLD Bath, 1981. *Address:* Walwood House, Park Road, Banstead, Surrey SM7 3ER. *T:* (01737) 352626.

HENLEY, Rt Rev. Michael Harry George; *see* St Andrews, Dunkeld and Dunblane, Bishop of.

HENN, Charles Herbert; Assistant Under Secretary of State, Ministry of Defence, 1979–88; *b* 11 July 1931; *s* of Herbert George Henn and Ellen Anne Henn; *m* 1955, Ann Turner; one *s* one *d*. *Educ:* King's Coll. Sch., Wimbledon; Queen's Coll., Oxford (BA). National Service, REME, 1952–54 (2/Lieut). Scientific Officer, WO, 1954; Sen. Scientific Officer, 1957; Principal, 1964; Private Sec. to Minister of State for Defence, 1969; Asst Sec., 1972. *Recreations:* walking, running, listening to music.

HENNESSY, family name of **Baron Windlesham.**

HENNESSY, Christopher; journalist; Chairman, Associated Catholic Newspapers (1912) Ltd, 1970–79; Trustee, The Universe, 1979–87 (Editor, 1954–72); *b* 29 Dec. 1909; *e s* of Daniel and Anne Hennessy; *m* 1942, Kathleen Margaret Cadley, Liverpool. *Educ:* St Edward's Coll., Liverpool. Served War of 1939–45 as Commissioned Officer in British and Indian Armies; commanded a Territorial Army Unit in the North-West, 1950–55. KCSG 1975. *Recreation:* travel. *Address:* Flat 49, The Metropole, The Leas, Folkestone, Kent CT20 2LU.

HENNESSY, Sir James (Patrick Ivan), KBE 1982 (OBE 1968; MBE 1959); CMG 1975; HM Diplomatic Service, retired; *b* 26 Sept. 1923; *s* of late Richard George Hennessy, DSO, MC; *m* 1947, Patricia, *o d* of late Wing Comdr F. H. Unwin, OBE; five *d* (one *s* decd). *Educ:* Bedford Sch.; King's Coll., Newcastle; Sidney Sussex Coll., Cambridge; LSE. Served RA, 1942–44; seconded IA, 1944–46, Adjt and Battery Comdr, 6th Indian Field Regt. Apptd to HM Overseas Service, Basutoland, District Officer, 1948; Judicial Comr, 1953; Dist Comr, 1954–56; Jt Sec., Constitutional Commn, 1957–59; Supervisor of Elections, 1959; Sec. to Exec. Council, 1960; seconded to Office of High Comr, Cape Town/Pretoria, 1961–63; Perm. Sec. for local govt, 1964; MLC, 1965; Sec. for External Affairs, Defence and Internal Security, 1967; Prime Minister's Office, 1968. Retired, later apptd to HM Diplomatic Service; FO, 1968–70; Chargé d'Affaires, Montevideo, 1971–72; High Comr to Uganda and Ambassador (non-resident), Rwanda, 1973–76; Consul-Gen., Cape Town, 1977–80; Governor and C-in-C, Belize, 1980–81; HM Chief Inspector of Prisons for England and Wales, 1982–87. Mem., Parole Bd, 1988–91. Trustee, Butler Trust, 1988–98. *Clubs:* Naval and Military, Royal Commonwealth Society.

HENNESSY, Brig. Mary Brigid Teresa, (Rita), CBE 1988 (MBE 1967); RRC 1982; Matron-in-Chief, Queen Alexandra's Royal Army Nursing Corps, 1985–89 and Director of Defence Nursing Service, 1986–89; *b* 27 Jan. 1933; *d* of late Bartholomew and Nora Agnes Hennessy. *Educ:* Convent of Mercy, Ennis, Co. Clare; Whittington Hosp., Highgate, London; Victoria Maternity Hosp., Barnet. SRN; SCM. Joined QARANC, 1959; service in Britain, Singapore, Malaya, Germany; various hosp. appts, 1959–74; seconded to office of Chargé d'affaires, Peking, 1965–67; Dep. Matron, Hongkong, 1976; Lt-Col 1979; Col 1982; Brig., Matron-in-Chief and Dir of Army Nursing Services, 1985. QHNS 1985–89. *Recreations:* music, theatre, gardening.

HENNESSY, Prof. Peter John, FRHistS; AcSS; Attlee Professor of Contemporary British History, Queen Mary, University of London, since 2001; *b* 28 March 1947; *s* of William Gerald and Edith Hennessy; *m* 1969, Enid Mary Candler; two *d*. *Educ:* Marling Sch., Stroud; St John's Coll., Cambridge (BA 1969), PhD Cantab 1990; LSE (Hon. Fellow, 2000); Harvard, 1971–72 (Kennedy Meml Scholar). FRHistS 1993. Reporter, THES, 1972–74, The Times, 1974–76; Lobby corresp., Financial Times, 1976; Whitehall corresp., The Times, 1976–82; journalist, The Economist, 1982; home leader writer and columnist, The Times, 1982–84; columnist: New Statesman, 1986–87; The Independent, 1987–91; Director, 1989–93; Prof. of Contemporary History, QMW, Univ. of London, 1992–2000; Chm., Kennedy Meml Trust, 1995–2000. Co-Founder and Co-Dir, 1986–89, Mem. Bd, 1989–98, Inst. of Contemporary British Hist. (Hon. Fellow, 1995). Vis. Prof. of Govt, Strathclyde Univ., 1989–; Gresham Prof. of Rhetoric, 1994–97; Vis. Lectr, Dept of Politics, Univ. of Strathclyde, 1983–84 (Hon. Res. Fellow, 1985–89); Visiting Fellow: Policy Studies Inst., 1986–91 (Sen. Fellow, 1984–85; Council Mem., 1991–97); Univ. Depts of Politics, Reading 1988–94, Nottingham 1989–95; RIPA, 1989–92; Hon. Res. Fellow, Dept of Politics and Sociology, Birkbeck Coll., London, 1990–91; Vis. Scholar, Centre for Australian Public Sector Management, Griffith Univ., Brisbane, 1991. Mem., Steering Gp, Sharman Review of Audit and Accountability for Central Govt, 2000–01. Vice-President: Politics Assoc., 1985–90; RHistS, 1996–2000; Pres., Johnian Soc., 1995. Trustee, Attlee Foundn, 1985–98 (Patron, 1998–). Partner, Intellectual R and D, 1990–. Mem. Bd, Inst. of Histl Res., 1992–97; Mem. Council, Gresham Coll., 1996–97 (Fellow, 1997). FRSA 1992. Founding AcSS, 1999. Presenter: Under Fire, TV, 1985–87; Radio 4 Analysis programme, 1986–92; writer and presenter, What Has Become of Us, TV, 1994; numerous other radio and TV productions. Hon. DLitt: Univ. of W England, 1995; Univ. of Westminster, 1996; Kingston, 1998. *Publications:* (with Keith Jeffery) States of Emergency, 1983; (with Michael Cockerell and David Walker) Sources Close to the Prime Minister, 1984; What the Papers Never Said, 1985; Cabinet, 1986; (ed with Anthony Seldon) Ruling Performance, 1987; Whitehall, 1989, rev. edn 2001; Never Again: Britain, 1945–51, 1992 (Duff Cooper Prize, 1993; NCR Book Award for Non-Fiction, 1993); The Hidden Wiring: unearthing the British Constitution, 1995; Muddling Through: power, politics and the quality of government in postwar Britain, 1996; The Prime Minister: the office and its holders since 1945, 2000. *Recreations:* reading, listening to music, searching for the British Constitution, watching West Ham. *Address:* Department of History, Queen Mary, Mile End Road, E1 4NS. *T:* (020) 7882 5016. *Clubs:* Savile; Attlee Memorial Runners.

HENNESSY, Richard Patrick, FCA; Chief Financial Officer, HSBC (formerly Midland) Bank plc, since 1996; *b* 16 Nov. 1953; *s* of Graham Harold Hennessy and Dolores Hennessy (*née* Ellul); *m* 1979, Angela Carthew; one *s* one *d*. *Educ:* Newcastle Univ. (BA Hons Econs and Accounting). FCA 1979; Associate, Hong Kong Soc. of Accountants 1980. Manager, Peat Marwick Mitchell, London, 1976–80; Sen. Manager, Peat Marwick Mitchell & Co., Hong Kong, 1980–82; Gp Financial Accountant, Hongkong & Shanghai Banking Corp. Ltd, 1982–84; Financial Controller, Saudi British Bank, 1984–88; Sen. Gp Financial Accountant, Hongkong & Shanghai Banking Corp. Ltd, 1988–92; Gp Chief Accountant, HSBC Holdings plc, 1992–95. Mem. Banking Sub-Cttee, ICAEW, 1993–.

Recreations: family, motor sport, music, walking, swimming. *Address:* c/o HSBC Bank plc, Poultry, EC2P 2BX. *T:* (020) 7260 8241.

HENNIG, Dr Georg, Hon. LVO 1969; Ambassador to the UK, 1993–96; retired, 1999; *b* 3 Sept. 1937; *s* of late Max Hennig and Eva (*née* Weinberger); *m* 1968, Ilona Esterhazy; one *s*. *Educ:* Schottengymnasium, Vienna; Univ. of Vienna (Dr jur 1960); Bologna Centre, Sch. of Advanced Internat. Studies, Johns Hopkins Univ. (Dip.). Protocol Div., Legal Dept, Federal Min. for Foreign Affairs, Vienna, 1961–63; Perm. Mission to UN, NY, 1963–66; Personal Asst to Foreign Minister, 1966–70; First Sec., Madrid, 1970–71; Sen. Dir, Office of Sec.-Gen. of UN, 1972–75; Minister, Hd of Office of Sec.-Gen. for Foreign Affairs, Vienna, 1976–79; Ambassador to: India, and accredited to Bangladesh, Sri Lanka and Nepal, 1979–83; Japan, and accredited to Republic of Korea, 1983–86; Special Advr to Federal Pres. of Austria, 1987–92; Ambassador at Federal Min. for Foreign Affairs, Vienna, 1992–93. Dir Gen., Office of Federal Pres., Austria, 1996–99. Grand Decoration of Honour in Gold (Austria), 1992. *Recreations:* reading, shooting. *Address:* Akademiestrasse 2, 1010 Vienna, Austria. *Club:* St Johann's (Vienna).

HENNIKER, 8th Baron *cr* 1800; **John Patrick Edward Chandos Henniker-Major,** KCMG 1965 (CMG 1956); CVO 1960; MC 1945; Bt 1765; Baron Hartismere (UK) 1866; DL; Director, Wates Foundation, 1972–78; *b* 19 Feb. 1916; *s* of 7th Baron Henniker, and Molly (*d* 1953), *d* of Sir Robert Burnet, KCVO; *S* father, 1980; *m* 1946, Margaret Osla Benning (*d* 1974); two *s* one *d*; *m* 1976, Julia Marshall Poland (*née* Mason). *Educ:* Stowe; Trinity Coll., Cambridge. HM Foreign Service, 1938; served 1940–45, Army (Major, The Rifle Brigade). HM Embassy Belgrade, 1945–46; Asst Private Secretary to Secretary of State for Foreign Affairs, 1946–48; Foreign Office, 1948–50; HM Embassy, Buenos Aires, 1950–52; Foreign Office, 1952–60 (Counsellor and Head of Personnel Dept, 1953); HM Ambassador to Jordan, 1960–62; to Denmark, 1962–66; Civil Service Commission, 1966–67; Asst Under-Secretary of State, FO, 1967–68. Dir-Gen., British Council, 1968–72. Lay Mem., Mental Health Review Tribunal (Broadmoor), 1975–81; Member: Parole Bd, 1979–83; Council, Univ. of E Anglia, Norwich, 1979–86; Council, Toynbee Hall, 1978–90, Dep. Chm., 1982–86; Chm., Intermediate Treatment Fund, Rainer Foundn, 1985–90. Chairman: Suffolk Community Alcohol Services, 1983–93; Suffolk Rural Housing Assoc., 1984–; Pres., Suffolk Agricl Assoc., 1989. Trustee: City Parochial Foundn, 1973–90; London Festival Ballet, 1975–85. Governor: Cripplegate Foundn, 1979–90; Stowe Sch., 1982–90. Hon. (Lay) Canon of St Edmundsbury Cathedral, 1986–92. DL Suffolk, 1988. Hon. DCL UEA, 1989; Hon. LLD New England Coll., NH, 1993. *Recreations:* gardening, ornithology. *Heir:* *s* Hon. Mark Ian Philip Chandos Henniker-Major [*b* 29 Sept. 1947; *m* 1973, Lesley Antoinette Masterton-Smith (marr. diss. 1995); two *s* three *d*; *m* 1996, Bente Toft]. *Address:* Red House, Thornham Magna, Eye, Suffolk IP23 8HH. *Club:* Special Forces.

HENNIKER, Sir Adrian Chandos, 9th Bt *cr* 1813, of Newton Hall, Essex; *b* 18 Oct. 1946; *s* of Brig. Sir Mark Chandos Auberon Henniker, 8th Bt, CBE, DSO, MC and Kathleen Denys (*d* 1998), *d* of John Anderson; *S* father, 1991; *m* 1971, Ann, *d* of Stuart Britton; twin *d*. *Educ:* Marlborough. *Heir:* none. *Address:* The Coach House, Llwyndu, Abergavenny, Gwent NP7 7HG.

HENNIKER HEATON, Sir Yvo Robert, *see* Heaton.

HENNIKER-MAJOR, family name of **Baron Henniker**.

HENREY, Mrs Robert; authoress; *b* Paris, 13 Aug. 1906; maiden name Madeleine Gal; *m* 1928, Robert Selby Henrey (*d* 1982), *o s* of Rev. Thomas Selby Henrey, Vicar of Old Brentford, Mddx, and Euphemia, *d* of Sir Coutts and Lady Lindsay of Balcarres; one *s*. *Educ:* Protestant Girls' Sch., Clichy; Convent of The Holy Family, Tooting, SW. *Publications:* autobiographical sequence in the following chronological order: The Little Madeleine, 1951, New York, 1953; An Exile in Soho, 1952; Julia, 1971; A Girl at Twenty, 1974; Madeleine Grown Up, 1952, New York 1953; Green Leaves, 1976; Madeleine Young Wife, New York 1954, London 1960; London under Fire 1940–45, 1969; A Month in Paris, 1954; Milou's Daughter, 1955, New York 1956; Her April Days, 1963; Wednesday at Four, 1964; Winter Wild, 1966; She Who Pays, 1969; The Golden Visit, 1979 (read in the above order these volumes make one consecutive narrative); *other books:* A Farm in Normandy, 1941; A Village in Piccadilly, 1943; The Incredible City, 1944; The Foolish Decade, 1945; The King of Brentford, 1946; The Siege of London, 1946; The Return to the Farm, 1947; London (with illustrations by Phyllis Ginger RWS) 1948, New York, 1949; A Film Star in Belgrave Square, 1948; A Journey to Vienna, 1950; Matilda and the Chickens, 1950; Paloma, 1951, New York, 1955; A Farm in Normandy and the Return, 1952; Madeleine's Journal, 1953; This Feminine World, 1956; A Daughter for a Fortnight, 1957; The Virgin of Aldermanbury (illustrations by Phyllis Ginger), 1958; Mistress of Myself, 1959; The Dream Makers, 1961; Spring in a Soho Street, 1962. *Recreations:* most feminine occupations: sewing, knitting, ironing, gardening. *Address:* c/o J, M. Dent & Sons, Aldine House, 33 Welbeck Street, W1M 8LX; Ferme Robert Henrey, 14640 Villers-sur-Mer, Calvados, France. *T:* Calvados 31870388.

HENRIQUES, Hon. Sir Richard (Henry Quixano), Kt 2000; **Hon. Mr Justice Henriques;** a Judge of the High Court of Justice, Queen's Bench Division, since 2000; Presiding Judge, North Eastern Circuit, since 2001; *b* 27 Oct. 1943; *s* of late Cecil Quixano Henriques and Doreen Mary Henriques; *m* Joan Hilary, (Toni), (*née* Senior); one *s* and one step *s*. *Educ:* Bradfield Coll., Berks; Worcester Coll., Oxford (BA). Called to the Bar, Inner Temple, 1967; Bencher, 1994. A Recorder, 1983–2000; QC 1986; Mem., Northern Circuit (Leader, 1995–98). Member: Gen. Council of the Bar, 1993–98; Criminal Justice Liaison Cttee, 1993–95; Northern Circuit Exec. Cttee, 1993–98. Council Mem., Rossall Sch., 1985–95. *Recreations:* bridge, golf. *Address:* Royal Courts of Justice, Strand, WC2A 2LL. *Club:* North Shore Golf (Blackpool).

HENRY, David; Senior Director, Postal Services, 1978–82, retired; *b* 19 April 1925; *s* of Thomas Glanffrwd Henry and Hylda Frances Henry. *Educ:* Midhurst Grammar Sch.; St John's Coll., Cambridge (MA Hons). Assistant Postal Controller, 1950; Head Postmaster, Norwich, 1961; Postal Controller, 1966; Controller Operations, 1968; Director, Midlands Postal Region, 1969; Chairman, Midlands Postal Board, 1974; Dir, London Postal Region, 1977. Freeman, City of London, 1978. JP Birmingham, 1972–77. *Recreations:* Rugby football, cricket.

HENRY, Rt Hon. Sir Denis (Robert Maurice), Kt 1986; PC 1993; a Lord Justice of Appeal, 1993–2002; *b* 19 April 1931; *o s* of late Brig. Maurice Henry and Mary Catherine (*née* Irving); *m* 1963, Linda Gabriel Arthur; one *s* one *d* (and one *d* decd). *Educ:* Shrewsbury; Balliol Coll., Oxford (MA). 2nd Lieut, KORR, 1950–51. Called to the Bar, Inner Temple, 1955, Bencher, 1985; QC 1977; a Recorder, 1979–86; a Judge of the High Court, QBD, 1986–93. Chm., Judicial Studies Bd, 1994–99. Part-time Tutor, New Coll., Oxford, 1985–90. Mem., Civil Justice Council, 1998–99. *Recreation:* golf. *Address:* c/o Royal Courts of Justice, Strand, WC2A 2LL.

HENRY, Prof. (Diana) Kristin, (Mrs G. G. Blakey), FRCP, FRCPath; Professor of Histopathology, Imperial College School of Medicine (formerly Charing Cross and Westminster Medical School), London University, 1987–98, now Emeritus Professor; Hon. Consultant Pathologist, Charing Cross Hospital, since 1984; *b* 13 Dec. 1934; *d* of late Colin Neil Thorburn Henry and of Vera (*née* Christensen); *m* 1st, 1960, Charles Michael Yates (marr. diss.); 2nd, 1967, George Gavin Blakey; one *s* one *d*. *Educ:* Malvern Girls' Coll.; St Thomas's Hosp. (MB BS). MRCP 1963, FRCP 1982; MRCPath 1965, FRCPath 1977. Junior appts at Lambeth Hosp., Chelsea Hosp. for Women and Brompton Hosp., 1956–64; Res. Registrar, Bd of Governors, Hosp. of Diseases of the Chest, 1964–66; MRC Fellow in Immunology, Middx Hosp., 1966–69; Reader, 1974–82, Prof. of Histopathology, 1982–84, Westminster Med. Sch., London Univ.; Prof. of Histopathology, Charing Cross & Westminster Med. Sch., 1984–87; Jt COS for Histopathology, Hammersmith Hosps NHS Trust, 1995–98. Mem., Editl Bd, Histopathology, 1975–; Ed., Current Diagnostic Pathology, 1993–. External Examiner in Final Examination in Pathology to: Leicester Univ., 1987–89; UMDS, 1990–92; RCSI Med. Sch., 1993–96; Birmingham Univ. Med. Sch., 1996–99; Sen. Examr, Charing Cross & Westminster Med. Sch., 1993–99. Sec. and Dep. Co-ordinator, Subject Panel of Pathology, London Univ., 1994–. British Council Lectr and Foundn Lectr to Coll. of Pathologists, Sri Lanka, 1987; First Cooray Meml Oration and Gold Medal, Sri Lanka, 1987; First Daphne Attegale Meml Oration and Gold Medal, Sri Lanka, 1998. Member: Thymic Tumour Panel, MRC, 1974–79; Pathology Panel, Brit. Nat. Lymphoma Investigation, MRC, 1975–87 (Expert Pathologist representing BNLI in Nat. Cancer Inst. (USA) study of lymphomas, 1976–81 (report pubd 1982)). Mem., Kettering Prize Award Cttee, Gen. Motors Cancer Res. Foundn, 1981–82. Founder Member: British Lymphoma Pathology Gp, 1974–; Eur. Bone Marrow Pathology Gp, 1992–; Member: Eur. Assoc. Haematopathology, 1986–; Melanoma Study Gp, 1989–. Treas., 1981–94, Pres., 1994–96, Cunningham Gold Medal, British Div., Internat. Acad. of Pathology; Vice-Pres. for Europe, Internat. Acad. of Pathology, 1999–. *Publications:* (contrib.) Pathology of Myasthenia Gravis, 1969; Systematic Pathology, vol. 7: 2nd edn, The Thymus Gland (contrib.), 1978; 3rd edn, The Thymus, Lymph Nodes, Spleen and Lymphatics (ed with W. St C. Symmers and contrib.), 1992; (with G. Farrer-Brown) A Colour Atlas of Thymus and Lymph Node Pathology with Ultrastructure, 1981; (contrib.) The Human Thymus in Disease, 1981; (contrib.) Ultrastructure of the Small Intestine, 1982; (contrib.) Bone Marrow Transplantation in Mucopolysaccharidoses, 1984; contrib. to: Recent Advances in Pathology, 9th edn 1975, 10th edn 1978; Recent Results in Cancer Research, 1978; numerous contribs to learned jls in field of haematopathology (incl. Lymphoma Study Gp pubns), and oncology. *Recreations:* painting, driving, animal welfare. *Address:* Imperial College School of Medicine at Charing Cross Hospital, Fulham Palace Road, W6 8RF. *T:* (020) 8846 7133; Quorn House, Hingham, Norfolk NR9 4AF. *T:* (01953) 851475. *Club:* Royal Over-Seas League.

HENRY, Sir Geoffrey (Arama), KBE 1992; Prime Minister, Cook Islands, 1983, and 1989–99; *b* Aitutaki, Cook Is, 16 Nov. 1940; *s* of Arama Henry and Mata Uritaua; *m* 1965, Louisa Olga Hoff; four *s* two *d*. *Educ:* St George's Prep. Sch., Wanganui, NZ; Wanganui Collegiate Sch.; Victoria Univ., Wellington, NZ (BA English and Educn). School Teacher, 1965–67; entered politics, 1965–68; public service, 1970–72; returned to politics, and Cabinet Minister, 1972–78; Leader of Opposition, 1978–83, 1983–84; Dep. Prime Minister in Coalition Govt, 1984; Leader of Opposition, 1985–89. Chm., Standing Cttee, Pacific Is Develt Prog. (EWC), 1989; Organiser, Jt Commercial Commn, USA and Pacific Is, 1990; Chm., Econ. Summit of Small Island States, 1992. Chancellor, Univ. of S Pacific, 1992. Chambellan de l'Ordre des Coteaux de Champagne, 1991. Silver Jubilee Medal, 1977; NZ Commemoration Medal, 1990. *Recreations:* golf, Rugby, Rugby league, other sports, reading, music. *Address:* PO Box 281, Rarotonga, Cook Islands. *Clubs:* Rarotonga Golf, Rarotonga Bowling, Rarotonga Fishing, Lions, Rarotonga (Cook Islands).

HENRY, Hugh; Member (Lab) Paisley South, Scottish Parliament, since 1999; *b* 12 Feb. 1952; *s* of Joseph and Mary Henry; *m* Jacqueline (*née* Muldoon); one *s* two *d*. *Educ:* Glasgow Univ. (BAcc). Worked in accountancy, teaching and social work. Member (Lab): Renfrew DC, 1985–96; Renfrewshire Council, 1995–99 (Leader, 1995–99). Convenor, European Cttee, Scottish Parlt, 1999–. Mem., Cttee of the Regions, EU. *Address:* Scottish Parliament, Edinburgh EH99 1SP; 1 Parksail, Erskine PA8 7HT.

HENRY, John Philip; Chairman: Holst Birthplace Trust, since 1999; Cheltenham Civic Society; *b* 8 Oct. 1946; *s* of late L. Henry, MD, FRCS and P. M. Henry, MB, ChB; *m* 1992, Gillian Mary Richardson; one *s* one *d*. *Educ:* Cheltenham Coll.; Queen's Coll., Oxford (MA). Psychologist, Road Research Lab., 1968; Admin Trainee, DoE, 1972; Principal, 1976; Private Sec., Minister for Housing and Construction, 1981–83; Asst Sec., 1983–89; Regl Dir, Yorks and Humberside Regl Office, Depts of the Envmt and Transport, 1990–94; Prin. Finance Officer, Property Hldgs, DoE, 1994–95; Hd of Agencies Gp, OPS, Cabinet Office, 1995–96. Non-exec. Dir, E Glos NHS Trust. *Recreations:* arts, architecture, children. *Address:* 71 Hatherley Road, Cheltenham, Glos GL51 6EG.

HENRY, Rt Hon. John (Steele), DCNZM 2001; PC (NZ) 1996; Judge, Court of Appeal, New Zealand, 1995–2000; *b* 3 July 1932; *s* of Hon. Sir Trevor Ernest Henry, *qv*; *m* 1957, Jennefer Lynne Stevenson; one *s* two *d*. *Educ:* King's Coll., Auckland; Auckland Univ. (LLB 1955). QC (NZ) 1980; High Court Judge, 1984–95. Commemoration Medal (NZ), 1990. *Recreations:* fishing, tramping. *Address:* 310 Riddell Road, Auckland, New Zealand. *T:* (9) 5758526. *Club:* Northern (Auckland).

HENRY, Keith Nicholas, FREng; Group Executive Vice-President and Chief Executive, Engineering and Construction, Kvaerner E&C PLC, since 2000; *b* 3 March 1945; *s* of Kenneth G. Henry and Barbara Henry; *m* 1974, Susan Mary Horsburgh; two *d*. *Educ:* Bedford Sch.; London Univ. (BSc Hons Civil Engrg (ext.) 1967); Birmingham Univ. (MSc Foundn Engrg 1969). With Internat. Mgt and Engrg Gp Ltd, 1969–71; Project Engr, then Manager, Brown & Root, 1971–77; Engrg Manager, Brown & Root Far East, 1977–80; Brown & Root (UK) Ltd: Engrg Manager, 1980–84; Commercial Dir, 1984–85; Technical Dir and Chief Engr, 1985–88; Managing Director: Brown & Root Vickers Ltd, 1987–89; Brown & Root Marine, 1989; Chief Executive: Brown & Root Ltd, 1990–95; Nat. Power plc, 1995–99. Non-exec. Dir, Enterprise Oil, 1995–. FREng (FEng 1988). *Recreations:* shooting, sailing. *Address:* (office) 20 Eastbourne Terrace, W2 6LE. *Club:* Royal Automobile.

HENRY, Kristin; *see* Henry, D. K.

HENRY, Lenworth George, (Lenny), CBE 1999; stand-up comedian, since 1975; actor; *b* 29 Aug. 1958; *s* of Winston Henry and Winifred Henry; *m* 1984, Dawn R. French; one adopted *d*. *Educ:* Bluecoat Secondary Mod. Sch.; W. R. Tewson Sch.; Preston Coll. Trustee, Comic Relief, 1987–. Won New Faces Talent Show, 1975; *TV appearances* include: Fosters, 1976–77; Tiswas, 1978–81; 3 of a Kind, 1981–84; Lenny Henry Show, 1984, 1985, 1987, 1988, 1995; Lenny Henry Tonight, 1986; Xmas Specials, 1987, 1988, 1994, 1995; Chef, 1992, 1994, 1996; Lenny's Big Amazon Adventure, 1997;

Lenny Goes to Town, 1998; Hope and Glory, 1999, 2000; Lenny's Big Atlantic Adventure, 2000; *films:* Coast to Coast, 1984; Work Experience, 1989; Alive and Kicking, 1990; True Identity, 1990. *Publications:* Quest for the Big Woof; Charlie and the Big Chill, 1995; (jtly) Charlie, Queen of the Desert, 1996. *Recreations:* funkateer, reading quality graphic novels, going to nursery, books, pretending to be a soul singer, being with friends and family, cooking. *Address:* c/o PBJ Management Ltd, 7 Soho Street, W1D 3DQ. *T:* (020) 7287 1112. *Clubs:* Groucho, Soho House.

HENRY, Sir Patrick (Denis), 3rd Bt *cr* 1923, of Cahore, co. Londonderry; businessman; *b* 20 Dec. 1957; *s* of Denis Valentine Henry (*d* 1983), *yr s* of 1st Bt, and of Elizabeth Henry (*née* Walker); *S* uncle, 1997; *m* 1997, Georgina Ravenscroft. *Educ:* Corpus Christi Coll., Oxford (BA (Hons) Modern History 1978). *Address:* The Mount, Cleavesty Lane, East Keswick, Leeds LS17 9EZ. *Club:* Blackburn Rovers.

HENRY, Hon. Sir Trevor (Ernest), Kt 1970; Judge, Fiji Court of Appeal, 1974–85; *b* 9 May 1902; *s* of John Henry and Edith Anna (*née* Eaton); *m* 1930, Audrey Kate Sheriff; one *s* one *d. Educ:* Rotorua District High Sch.; Univ. of New Zealand (Auckland). LLB 1925, LLM Hons 1926, NZ. Solicitor of Supreme Court of NZ, 1923, Barrister, 1925. Judge of the Supreme Court of NZ, 1955–77. *Recreation:* fishing. *Address:* 25 Ngaroma Road, Epsom, Auckland, New Zealand. *Club:* Northern (Auckland).
See also Rt Hon. J. S. Henry.

HENRY, Wendy Ann; Editor-in-Chief, Successful Slimming, since 1997; Editorial Director, New Publications, Globe Communications, since 1997; *d* of Bernard and Elsa Henry; *m* 1980, Tim Miles; one *d. Educ:* Queen Mary School, Lytham. Reporter, Daily Mail, Manchester, 1975, News of the World, 1976; Features Editor, Woman Magazine, 1979; Asst Editor, The Sun, 1981; Editor: Sunday Magazine, 1986; The News of the World, 1987–88; Dep. Editor, The Sun, 1988; Editor: The People, 1989; The Globe, Florida, 1990; Daily News, weekend section, NY, 1997. Mem., Weight Watchers. *Recreation:* sleeping. *Address:* c/o Globe Communications, 5401 NW Broken Sound Boulevard, Boca Raton, FL 33431, USA.

HENSCHEL, Ruth Mary; *see* Ashton, R. M.

HENSHALL, Rt Rev. Michael; Bishop Suffragan of Warrington, 1976–96; an Assistant Bishop, diocese of York, since 1999; *b* 29 Feb. 1928; *m* Ann Elizabeth (*née* Stephenson); two *s* one *d. Educ:* Manchester Grammar Sch.; St Chad's Coll., Durham (BA 1954, DipTh 1956). Deacon 1956, priest 1957, dio. York; Curate of Holy Trinity, Bridlington and of Sewerby, 1956–59; Priest-in-charge, All Saints, Conventional District of Micklehurst, 1959–62; Vicar, 1962–63; Vicar of Altrincham, 1963–75; Proctor in Convocation, 1964–75; Mem., Terms of Ministry Cttee, General Synod, 1970–75; Hon. Canon of Chester, 1972–75; Secretary, Chester Diocesan Advisory Board for Ministry, 1968–75; Canon Emeritus of Chester Cathedral, 1979. Chairman: Northern Ordination Course Council, 1985–96; Churches Gp NW, Industry Year, 1985–90; Council, St Chad's Coll., Univ. of Durham, 1992–2000; Vice-Chm., National Soc., 1994–96; Mem. Council, Coll. of Preachers, 1989– (Ed., Journal, 1998–). *Publication:* Dear Nicholas, 1989. *Recreations:* military history, old battlefields, etc. *Address:* 28 Hermitage Way, Sleights, Whitby, N Yorks YO22 5HG. *T:* (01947) 811233.

HENSHAW, David George; Chief Executive, Liverpool City Council, since 1999; *b* 7 March 1949; *s* of George Ronald Henshaw and Irene Henshaw; *m* 1st 1978, Rosemary St C. Herbert (marr. diss. 2000); two *s*; 2nd, 2000, Alison Joy Jones. *Educ:* Sheffield Poly. (BA Public Admin 1973); Univ. of Birmingham (MScSoc 1975). Corporate Planning Officer, S Yorks MCC, 1974–84; Prin. Asst County Clerk, then Asst Chief Exec., Essex CC, 1984–89; Chief Exec., Knowsley MBC, 1989–99. Clerk to Merseyside Police Authy, 1989–2000. Dir and Dep. Chm., Mersey Partnership, 1993–. Dep. Chm., Nat. Task Force on Crime Reduction, 2000–; Mem., Independent Rev. of Higher Educn Pay and Conditions, 1999. Pres., SOLACE, 2000–01. Fellow, Liverpool Univ., 1998; Vis. Fellow, Royal Inst. of Technol., Melbourne, Aust., 1997. *Recreations:* golf, opera, walking. *Address:* Municipal Buildings, Dale Street, Liverpool L69 2DH. *T:* (0151) 225 2334. *Clubs:* Athenæum (Liverpool); Royal St Davids Golf (Harlech).

HENSHAW, Prof. Denis Lee, PhD; Professor of Physics, University of Bristol, since 1995; *b* 4 May 1946; *s* of late Frederick Henshaw and Evelyne May (*née* Fox); *m* 1994, Wassana. *Educ:* Westfield Coll., Univ. of London (BSc 1969); Univ. of Nottingham (PhD 1974). Teacher, Mundella GS, 1969–70; University of Bristol: Res. Associate, 1973–82; Res. Fellow, 1982–90; Sen. Res. Fellow, 1990–95. Dir, Track Analysis Systems Ltd, Bristol, 1984–. Member, Editorial Board: Physics in Medicine and Biol., 1994–97; Internat. Jl Radiation Biol., 1995–. *Publications:* numerous scientific papers in learned jls. *Recreations:* hot-air ballooning, Italian language and culture. *Address:* H. H. Wills Physics Laboratory, University of Bristol, Tyndall Avenue, Bristol BS8 1TL. *T:* (0117) 926 0353.

HENSHAW, Frank Charles, CBE 1993; DL; FRICS; General Manager, Milton Keynes Development Corporation, 1980–92; *b* 28 Aug. 1930; *s* of Frank and Edith Annie Henshaw; *m* 1966, Patricia Jane McDonald; one *s* one *d. Educ:* Towcester Grammar Sch.; Coll. of Estate Management. FRICS 1959. Nat. service, RAF, 1948–50. Quantity Surveyor: Northants CC, 1947–53; Coventry City Council, 1953–63; Prin. Quantity Surveyor, Midlands Housing Consortium, 1963–65; Chief Quantity Surveyor: Runcorn Develt Corp., 1965–70; Sheffield City Council, 1970–71; Milton Keynes Development Corporation: Chief Quantity Surveyor, 1971–74; Exec. Dir, 1974–78; Dep. Gen. Manager, 1978–80. Chm., Milton Keynes Housing Assoc., 1985–88; Dep. Chm., Central Milton Keynes Shopping Man. Co., 1978–89. Pres., Milton Keynes and N Bucks TEC, 1992–95 (Dir, 1990–92). DL Bucks, 1995. Hon. Fellow, De Montfort Univ., 1993. DUniv Open, 1994. OON 1989. *Recreations:* golf, travel. *Club:* Woburn Golf and Country.

HENSLEY, John; *b* 28 Feb. 1910; *s* of late Edward Hutton and Marion Hensley; *m* 1st, 1940, Dorothy Betty (*d* 1969), *d* of Percy George and Dorothy Coppard; one *s*; 2nd, 1971, Elizabeth, *widow* of Charles Cross and *d* of Harold and Jessie Coppard. *Educ:* Malvern; Trinity Coll., Cambridge (Chancellor's Classical Medal, MA). Entered Min. of Agriculture and Fisheries, 1933; Priv. Sec. to Chancellor of Duchy of Lancaster and Minister of Food, 1939; Priv. Sec. to Minister of Agriculture and Fisheries, 1945; Asst Sec., 1946; Under Sec., 1957. Member: Agricultural Research Council, 1957–59; Council, Nat. Inst. of Agricultural Botany, 1970–73; Sec., Cttee of Inquiry into Veterinary Profession, 1971–75; retired 1975. *Recreations:* theatre, opera, genealogy. *Address:* 109 Markfield, Courtwood Lane, Croydon CR0 9HP. *T:* (020) 8657 6319.

HENSON, Marguerite Ann, (Mrs Nicky Henson); *see* Porter, M. A.

HENSON, Nicholas Victor Leslie, (Nicky); actor; *b* 12 May 1945; *s* of Leslie Henson and Billie Collins; *m* 1st, 1968, Una Stubbs (marr. diss.); two *s*; 2nd, 1986, Marguerite Porter, *qv*; one *s. Educ:* St Bede's, Eastbourne; Charterhouse. Formerly popular song writer; Founder Mem., Young Vic; first stage appearance, 1962; *London stage:* All Square, Vandeville, 1963; Camelot, Drury Lane, 1964; Passion Flower Hotel, Prince of Wales, 1965; Canterbury Tales, Phoenix, 1968; Ride Across Lake Constance, Mayfair, 1973; Hamlet, Greenwich, 1973; Midsummer Night's Dream, Regent's Park, 1973; Cinderella, Casino, 1973; Mardi Gras, Prince of Wales, 1976; Rookery Nook, Her Majesty's, 1980; Noises Off, Savoy, 1982; The Relapse, Lyric, 1983; Sufficient Carbohydrate, Albery, 1984; Journey's End, Whitehall, 1986; The Three Sisters, Royal Court, 1990; Matador, Queen's, 1991; Reflected Glory, Vaudeville, 1992; An Ideal Husband, Globe, 1993, NY, 1996, Australia, 1997; Rage, Bush, 1994; Alarms and Excursions, Gielgud, 1998; Passion Play, Comedy, 2000; *Young Vic:* Scapino, Waiting for Godot, She Stoops to Conquer, Taming of the Shrew, Measure for Measure, Soldier's Tale, Oedipus, Romeo and Juliet, The Maids, Look Back in Anger, Rosencrantz and Guildenstern are Dead, Charley's Aunt; *National Theatre:* Cherry Orchard, Macbeth, The Woman, The Double Dealer, A Fair Quarrel, Browning Version, Provok'd Wife, Elephant Man, Mandragola; *Royal Shakespeare Co.:* Man and Superman, Merry Wives of Windsor, As You Like It; *television series:* Life of Balzac, 1976; Seagull Island, 1981; Happy Apple, 1983; Thin Air, 1988; The Green Man, 1990; The Healer, 1994; Preston Front, 1994; Shine on Harvey Moon, 1994; 30 films. *Recreation:* music. *Address:* c/o Richard Stone, 2 Henrietta Street, WC2E 8PS. *T:* (020) 7497 0849.

HENTON, (Margaret) Patricia, FCIWEM; CGeol, FGS; Chief Executive, Scottish Environment Protection Agency, since 2000 (Director, Environmental Strategy, 1995–2000); *b* 30 Oct. 1949; *d* of Robert Stuart Sanderson and Lois Lindsay Sanderson; *m* 1971, Richard George Henton; one *s* one *d. Educ:* George Watson's Coll., Edinburgh; Univ. of Manchester (BSc Hons Geol./Geog. 1970). FGS 1974; FCIWEM 1979; MInstWM, 1981; CGeol 1990. Geologist, Associated Portland Cement Manufacturers, 1970–71; Hydrogeologist, Clyde River Purification Bd, 1972–75; Geologist, NCB Opencast Exec., 1975; Inspector, 1975–79, Hydrologist, 1979–83, Forth River Purification Bd; Associate, 1983–85, Sen. Associate, 1985–90, Dir, Scotland and NI, 1990–95, Aspinwall & Co. Ltd. Dir, Scotland and NI Forum for Envmtl Res., 1996–. Mem., Sec. of State for Scotland's Adv. Gp on Sustainable Develt, 1993–98. Mem. Council, NERC, 1999–2001; Additional Mem., Water Panel, Competition Commn, 1998–2000. Pres., CIWEM, 1995–96; *Recreations:* travel, ornithology, the Levant, hill-walking, gardens. *Address:* Scottish Environment Protection Agency, Erskine House, Castle Business Park, Stirling FK9 4TR. *T:* (01786) 457701.

HENTY, Jonathan Maurice; Commissioner of Social Security and Child Support, since 1993; *b* 22 Dec. 1933; *s* of Richard Iltid Henty and Lettice Ellen (*née* Moore Gwyn); *m* 1st, 1956, Margaret Louise Sadler (*d* 1972); one *s* one *d* (and one *s* decd); 2nd, 1977, Veronica Mary Francis Miller; two *d. Educ:* Eton; New Coll., Oxford (MA). Called to the Bar, Lincoln's Inn, 1957, Bencher, 1989. Chancellor, Dio. Hereford, 1977–2000; Deputy Chancellor: Dio. Lincoln, 1994–98; Dio. Chelmsford, 1997–2000; Dio. London, 1997–2000. *Recreations:* fishing, art and architecture. *Address:* Fisher Hill House, Northchapel, Petworth, W Sussex GU28 9EJ. *Club:* Athenæum.

HENWOOD, John Philip, MBE 1998; Chairman, Byerley Ltd, since 2000; Director, ComProp Ltd (formerly Channel Television Group) (Chief Executive and Managing Director, 1987–2000); *b* 27 Aug. 1945; *s* of late Snowdon William Henwood and Amy Doris Henwood (*née* Stickley); *m* 1970, Sheila Patricia Renault (marr. diss. 1994). *Educ:* St Lawrence Sch.; Victoria Coll., Jersey. Joined Channel Television Ltd, later Channel Television Group, 1962: ops trainee, 1962–64; cameraman, 1964–65; Hd of Studio, 1965–66; Dep. Ops Manager, 1966–70; Producer/Dir (setting up commercial prodn unit), 1970–77; Hd, News and Features, 1977–83; Programme Controller, 1983–86; Dir of Progs, 1986–87. Mem., States of Jersey Review Panel of Machinery of Govt, 1999–2001. Sen. Steward, CI Racing and Hunt Club, 1998; Pres., Jersey Race Club, 1998–2001. Pres. Jersey Br., CIM; Chm., Jersey IoD, 2001–. *Recreations:* horse racing, the thoroughbred, writing, ski-ing, old motor cars. *Address:* Les Carrières, St John, Jersey, Channel Islands JE3 4DN. *Clubs:* Victoria (Jersey), MG Owners.

HENZE, Hans Werner; composer; Professor of Composition, Royal Academy of Music, 1987–91; *b* 1 July 1926; *s* of Franz Gebhard Henze and Margarete Geldmacher. *Educ:* Bünde i/W; Bielefeld i/W; Braunschweig. Studying music in Heidelberg, 1945; First Work performed (Chamber Concerto), at Darmstadt-Kranichstein, 1946; Artistic Dir of Ballet, Hessian States Theatre, Wiesbaden, 1950; Prof. of Composition, Acad. Mozarteum, Salzburg, 1962–67. Definite departure for Italy; Artistic Director: Internat. Art Workshop, Montepulciano, Tuscany, 1976–80, 1989–; Philharmonic Acad., Rome, 1981–82; Munich Biennale, Internat. Fest. of New Music Theatre, 1988, 1990, 1992, 1994, 1996; Prof. of Composition, Hochschule für Musik, Cologne, 1980–91; Composer-in-Residence, Berlin Philharmonic Orchestra, 1991–92. Member: German Acad. of Arts, Berlin; Philharmonic Acad., Rome; Acad. Scientiarum et Artium Europaea, Salzburg, 1992. Hon. Member: Deutsche Oper, Berlin, 1982; AAIL, 1982; Internat. Soc. for New Music, 1991; Nat. Acad. of Santa Cecilia, Rome, 1995. Hon. FRNCM 1998. Hon. DMus: Edinburgh, 1970; Univ. of Osnabrück, 1996. Robert Schumann Prize, 1951; Prix d'Italia, 1953; Nordrhein-Westfalen Award, 1957; Berlin Prize of Artists, 1959; Great Prize for Artists, Hanover, 1961; Louis Spohr Prize, Brunswick, 1976; Bach Prize, Hamburg, 1983; Siemens Prize, 1990; Duisburg Music Award, Köhler Osbahr Foundn, 1995; Special Cultural Award, Munich, 1996; Annette von Droste Hülshoff Prize, Landschaftsverband Westfalen-Lippe, 1996; Hans von Bülow Medal, Berlin Philharmonic Orch., 1997; Bavarian Order of Maximilian for Science and Art, 1998. Grand Cross, Order of Merit (Germany), 1991. *Compositions:* 9 symphonies; 13 full length operas, 3 one-act operas, 1 children's opera, 2 radio-operas; ballets; chamber music; choral works; concerti for piano, violin, viola, violoncello, double bass, oboe, clarinet, trumpet, guitar and harp; various symphonic works; song cycle; music theatre works incl. The Magic Theatre, Boulevard Solitude, The Prince of Homburg, Elegy for Young Lovers, The Bassarids, The Young Lord, Natascha Ungeheuer, Moralities, La Cubana, The Ocean Betrayed, Venus and Adonis. *Publications:* Undine, Diary of a Ballet, 1959; Essays, 1964; (with H. Enzenberger) El Cimarrón: ein Werkstattbericht, 1971; Musik und Politik, 1975, 1984; Neue Aspekte der musikalischen Ästhetik: vol. I, Zwischen den Kulturen, 1979; vol. II, Die Zeichen, 1981; vol. III, Lehrgänge, 1986; vol. IV, Chiffren, 1990; vol. V, Musik und Mythos, 1997; The English Cat, 1983; Reiselieder mit böhmischen Quinten (autobiog.), 1996 (trans. English as Bohemian Fifths, 1998); Komponieren in der Schule, 1998. *Address:* Schott Musik International, Weihergarten 5, 55116 Mainz, Germany.

HEPBURN, Sir John Alastair Trant Kidd B.; *see* Buchan-Hepburn.

HEPBURN, John William; Director of Establishments, Ministry of Agriculture, Fisheries and Food, 1996–98; *b* 8 Sept. 1938; *s* of late Dugald S. Hepburn and Margarita R. Hepburn; *m* 1972, Isla Marchbank; one *s. Educ:* Hutchesons' Grammar Sch.; Glasgow Univ. (MA); Brasenose Coll., Oxford. Assistant Principal, 1961, Principal, 1966, MAFF; First Secretary, UK Delegn to European Communities, Brussels, 1969–71; Private Sec. to Minister of Agriculture, Fisheries and Food, 1971–73; Asst Sec., 1973–81, Under Sec., 1982–96, MAFF. *Recreation:* golf.

HEPBURN, Katharine; actress; *b* 12 May 1907; *d* of late Dr Thomas N. Hepburn and Katharine Houghton; *m* Ludlow Ogden Smith (marr. diss.). *Educ:* Hartford; Bryn Mawr

College. First professional appearance on stage, Baltimore, 1928, in Czarina; first New York appearance, 1928, in Night Hostess (under name Katherine Burns), The Millionairess, New Theatre, London, 1952. Entered films, 1932; notable films: A Bill of Divorcement; Morning Glory; Little Women; The Little Minister; Mary of Scotland; Quality Street; Stage Door; The Philadelphia Story; Keeper of the Flame; Dragon Seed; Woman of the Year; Under-current; Without Love; Sea of Grass; Song of Love; State of the Union; Adam's Rib; The African Queen; Pat and Mike; Summer Madness; The Iron Petticoat; The Rainmaker; His Other Woman; Suddenly, Last Summer; Long Day's Journey into Night; Guess Who's Coming to Dinner; The Madwoman of Chaillot; The Lion in Winter; The Trojan Women; A Delicate Balance; Rooster Cogburn; On Golden Pond. *Stage:* Warrior's Husband; The Philadelphia Story; Without Love; As You Like It; Taming of the Shrew; Merchant of Venice; Measure for Measure, Australia, 1955; Coco, 1970; A Matter of Gravity, NY, 1976, tour, 1977; The West Side Waltz, NY, 1981. Academy Awards for performances in Morning Glory, Guess Who's Coming to Dinner, The Lion in Winter, On Golden Pond. *Publications:* The Making of The African Queen, 1987; Me: stories of my life, 1991.

HEPBURN, Prof. Ronald William; Professor of Moral Philosophy, University of Edinburgh, 1975–96 (Professor of Philosophy, 1964–75), now Professor Emeritus; *b* 16 March 1927; *s* of late W. G. Hepburn, Aberdeen; *m* 1953, Agnes Forbes Anderson; two *s* one *d*. *Educ:* Aberdeen Grammar Sch.; University of Aberdeen. MA 1951, PhD 1955 (Aberdeen). National service in Army, 1944–48. Asst, 1952–55, Lecturer, 1955–60, Dept of Moral Philosophy, University of Aberdeen; Visiting Associate Prof., New York University, 1959–60; Prof. of Philosophy, University of Nottingham, 1960–64. Stanton Lecturer in the Philosophy of Religion, Cambridge, 1965–68. *Publications:* (jointly) Metaphysical Beliefs, 1957; Christianity and Paradox, 1958; Wonder and Other Essays: eight studies in aesthetics and neighbouring fields, 1984; The Reach of the Aesthetic: collected essays, 2001; contrib. to learned journals; broadcasts. *Address:* 8 Albert Terrace, Edinburgh EH10 5EA.

HEPBURN, Stephen; MP (Lab) Jarrow, since 1997; *b* 6 Dec. 1959; *s* of Peter and Margaret Hepburn. *Educ:* Springfield Comprehensive Sch., Jarrow; Newcastle Univ. Former Res. Asst to Donald Dixon, MP. Mem. (Lab) S Tyneside MBC, 1985– (Chair: Finance Cttee, 1989–90; Tyne & Wear Pensions, 1989–97; Dep. Leader, 1990–97). Mem., Defence Select Cttee, 1999–. President: Bilton Hall Boxing Club; Jarrovians RFC; Jarrow FC. *Recreation:* sports. *Address:* House of Commons, SW1A 0AA. *T:* (constituency office) (0191) 420 0648. *Clubs:* Neon (Jarrow); Iona (Hebburn).

HEPBURNE-SCOTT, family name of **Lord Polwarth**.

HEPHER, Michael Leslie; Chairman, since 2000 and Chief Executive, since 2001, Telecity plc; *b* 17 Jan. 1944; *s* of Leslie and Edna Hepher; *m* 1971, Janice Morton; one *s* two *d*. *Educ:* Kingston Grammar School. FIA; Associate, Soc. of Actuaries; FLIA. Provident Life Assoc., UK, 1961–67; Commercial Life Assurance, Canada, 1967–70; Maritime Life Assurance Co., Canada, 1970–79; Chm. and Man. Dir, Abbey Life Group, UK, subseq. Lloyds Abbey Life, 1980–91; Gp Man. Dir, BT, 1991–95; Chief Exec., 1996–98 and Chm., 1997–98, Charterhouse plc. Non-exec. Chm., HambroFraserSmith, 1999–2000; non-executive Director: Kingfisher, 1997–; Canada Life Assurance Co., 1999–. *Recreations:* reading, golf. *Address:* (office) 61 Jermyn Street, SW1Y 6LX. *T:* (020) 7292 3792, *Fax:* (0870) 124 7245.

HEPPEL, Peter John Merrick; QC 1992; **His Honour Judge Heppel;** a Circuit Judge, since 1998; *b* 31 March 1948; *s* of late John Edward Thomas and Ida Florence Heppel, Romford, Essex; *m* 1980, Janice Coulton (marr. diss. 1995); two *s* two *d*. *Educ:* Royal Liberty Sch., Romford; Univ. of Hull (LLB Hons); University Coll. London (LLM). Called to the Bar, Middle Temple, 1970 (Harmsworth Scholar); in practice, NE Circuit, 1972–98; a Recorder, 1988–98. Designated Civil Judge: Hull Combined Court Centre, 2000–; Grimsby Combined Court Centre, 2000–; Magistrates' Liaison Judge, Hull Combined Court Centre, 1999–. Fellow, Soc. for Advanced Legal Studies. Mem. Court, Univ. of Hull. *Recreations:* music, cricket. *Address:* Warriston, Parkfield Avenue, North Ferriby, Humberside HU14 3AL; Hull Combined Court Centre, Lowgate, Hull HU1 2EZ. *T:* (01482) 586161. *Club:* Sloane.

HEPPELL, John; MP (Lab) Nottingham East, since 1992; a Lord Commissioner of HM Treasury (Government Whip), since 2001; *b* 3 Nov. 1948; *m* 1974, Eileen Golding; two *s* one *d*. *Educ:* Rutherford Grammar Sch.; SE Northumberland Technical Coll.; Ashington Technical Coll. Fitter: NCB, 1964–70; various cos, 1970–75; diesel fitter, 1975–78, workshop supervisor, 1978–89, British Rail. Mem. (Lab) Nottinghamshire CC, 1981–93. PPS to Leader of House of Lords, 1997–98; PPS to Dep. Prime Minister and Sec. of State for Envmt, Transport and the Regions, 1998–2001. *Address:* House of Commons, SW1A 0AA.

HEPPELL, (Thomas) Strachan, CB 1986; Consultant, Department of Health, 1995–2000; Chairman, Management Board, European Medicines Evaluation Agency, 1994–2000; *b* 15 Aug. 1935; *s* of late Leslie Thomas Davidson Heppell and Doris Abbey Heppell (*née* Potts); *m* 1963, Felicity Ann Rice; two *s*. *Educ:* Acklam Hall Grammar Sch., Middlesbrough; The Queen's Coll., Oxford. National Assistance Board, Ministry of Social Security/DHSS: Asst Principal, 1958; Principal, 1963–73 (seconded to Cabinet Office, 1967–69); Asst Director of Social Welfare, Hong Kong, 1971–73; Asst Sec., DHSS, 1973–78 (Social Security Adviser, Hong Kong Govt, 1977); Under Sec., DHSS, 1979–83; Dep. Sec., DHSS, later DoH, 1983–95. Chm., Family Fund Trust, 1997–; Mem., Broadcasting Standards Commn, 1996–. Vis. Fellow, LSE, 1997–. *Publications:* contribs on health, social welfare and regulatory affairs. *Recreations:* gardening, travelling.

HEPPLE, Prof. Bob Alexander; Master of Clare College, Cambridge, since 1993; Professor of Law, University of Cambridge, 1995–2001, now Emeritus; *b* 11 Aug. 1934; *s* of late Alexander Hepple and Josephine Zwarenstein; *m* 1st, 1960, Shirley Goldsmith; one *s* one *d*; 2nd, 1994, Mary Coussey. *Educ:* Univ. of Witwatersrand (BA 1954, LLB *cum laude* 1957); Univ. of Cambridge (LLB 1966; MA 1969; LLD 1993). Attorney, S Africa, 1958; Lectr in Law, Univ. of Witwatersrand, 1959–62; Advocate, S Africa, 1962–63. Left S Africa after detention without trial for anti-apartheid activities, 1963. Called to Bar, Gray's Inn, 1966, Bencher, 1996; Lectr in Law, Nottingham Univ., 1966–68; Fellow of Clare Coll., Cambridge and Univ. Lectr in Law, 1968–76; Prof. of Comparative Social and Labour Law, Univ. of Kent, 1976–77 (Hon. Prof., 1978–83); Prof. of English Law, 1982–93, Dean of Faculty of Laws and Head of Dept of Laws, 1989–93, UCL; Chm., Cttee of Heads of Univ. Law Schs, 1992–93. Chairman: Industrial Tribunals (England and Wales), pt-time 1975–77 and 1982–93, full-time 1977–82; Cttee, Justice Report on Industrial Tribunals, 1987. Member: Judicial Studies Bd (Tribunals Cttee), 1988–93; Lord Chancellor's Adv. Cttee on Legal Educn and Conduct, 1994–99; Commn on Future of Multi-Ethnic Britain, 1998–2000; Legal Services Consultative Panel, 2000–01; Mem., Nuffield Council on Bioethics and Chm., Wkg Pty on Genetics and Human Behaviour, 2000–. Mem., CRE, 1986–90. Chairman: Univ. of Cambridge Local Exams Syndicate, 1994–98; Septemviri, Univ. of Cambridge, 1995–98; Managers, Smuts Fund, Cambridge, 1995–. Expert consultant to EC Commn, 1974–, and to ILO, 1990–; Advr to Russian Fedn, 1992, to S African Govt, 1994–96. Hon. QC 1996. Hon. Prof., Univ. of Cape Town, 1999. Hon. LLD Witwatersrand, 1996. *Publications:* (with M. Coussey) Independent Review of Enforcement of UK Anti-Discrimination Legislation, 2000; various books and articles on labour law, race relations, law of tort, etc; Founding Editor, Industrial Law Jl, 1972–77; Gen. Ed (jtly) Encyclopedia of Labour Relations Law, 1972–90; Chief Editor, International Encyclopedia of Comparative Law, Vol. XV, Labour Law, 1979–. *Address:* The Master's Lodge, Clare College, Cambridge CB2 1TL. *Club:* Reform.

HEPPLEWHITE, Rosalind Mary Joy, (Ros); Chief Executive and Registrar, General Dental Council, 1996–2000; *b* 20 Dec. 1952; *d* of Anne and Anthony Phillips; *m* 1971, Julian Hepplewhite; one *s* one *d*. *Educ:* University College London (BA Hons). Asst House Governor, 1980–83, and Hosp. Sec., 1983–84, Bethlem Royal and Maudsley Hosps; Unit Administrator (Mental Health), Hammersmith and Fulham HA, 1984–85; Unit Gen. Manager (Mental Health and Mental Handicap), 1985–88, Dir, Corporate Develt, 1988–89, Brighton HA; Nat. Dir, MIND (Nat. Assoc. of Mental Health), 1989–91; Chief Exec., CSA, 1992–94. Mem., Leics and Rutland Probation Bd, 2001–. *Recreation:* home and family. *Address:* The Old Rectory, Burton Overy, Leics LE8 9DR. *T:* (020) 7887 3810.

HEPWORTH, Rear-Adm. David, CB 1976; retired from RN, 1976; *b* 6 June 1923; *s* of Alfred Ernest Hepworth and Minnie Louisa Catherine Bennet Tanner (*née* Bowden); *m* 1st, 1946, Brenda June Case (marr. diss. 1974); one *s* one *d*; 2nd, 1975, Eileen Mary Macgillivray (*née* Robson). *Educ:* Banbury Grammar School. Boy Telegraphist, RN, 1939; HMS Ganges, 1939–40; served in Atlantic, Mediterranean and E Indies Fleets; commnd 1944; submarines and midget submarines, 1945–50; Home, Australian and Far East Stns, 1951–58; Sen. Officer Submarines Londonderry, 1959–61; CO HMS Ashanti, 1961–64; jssc 1964; Dep. Dir Undersea Warfare, MoD, 1964–66; idc 1967; CO HMS Ajax and Captain (D) 2nd Far East Destroyer Sqdn, 1968–69; Dir RN Tactical Sch. and Maritime Tactical Sch., 1969–71; Dir Naval Warfare, MoD, 1971–73; Staff of Vice-Chief of Naval Staff, 1973–76. Lt-Comdr 1952; Comdr 1958; Captain 1964; Rear-Adm. 1974. Naval Advr to Internat. Military Services Ltd, 1977–83. *Recreations:* home and garden. *Address:* Darville House, Lower Heyford, Oxon OX25 3PD. *T:* (01869) 347460.

HEPWORTH, Noel Peers, OBE 1980; Chairman, Institute of Public Finance Ltd, since 1996; Director, Chartered Institute of Public Finance and Accountancy, 1980–96; *b* 22 Dec. 1934; *m* 1963, Jean Margaret Aldcroft; one *s* three *d*. *Educ:* Crewe County Grammar Sch.; London Univ. CPFA (IPFA 1958); DPA 1963. Nat. Service, RAF, 1953–55. NW Gas Bd, 1951–58; Asst City Treasurer, Manchester, 1965–72; Dir of Finance, Croydon, 1972–80. Financial Advr to London Boroughs Assoc. and AMA, 1972–80; Mem., London Treasurers' Adv. Body, 1972–80; Member: Dept of Envmt Property Adv. Group, 1980–88; Audit Commn, 1983–91; Adv. Bd, Treasury Solicitor Agency, 1996–. Pres., Internat. Consortium on Governmental Financial Management, 1987–92; Proj. Dir, Eur. Fedn of Accountants single Eur. currency project, 1996–. Chm., FEE Public Sector Cttee, 1988–. FRSA 1985. Freeman, City of London, 1991. Hon. DSc (Econ) Hull; Hon. LLD Brighton; Hon. DSc City. *Publications:* Finance of Local Government, 1970, 7th edn 1984, Japanese edn 1983; Housing Rents, Costs and Subsidies, 1978, 2nd edn 1981; contribs to technical and financial jls, local govt press and nat. and internat press. *Recreations:* gardening, walking. *T:* (020) 8667 1144; *e-mail:* Noel.Hepworth@ipf.co.uk.

HERALD, John Pearson; Sheriff of North Strathclyde, since 1992; *b* 12 July 1946; *s* of Andrew James Herald and Martha Wilson or Herald; *m* 1969, Catriona McDougall Anderson; one *d*. *Educ:* Hillhead High Sch., Glasgow; Univ. of Glasgow (LLB). Partner, Carlton Gilruth, Dundee, 1971–91; Dir, William Halley & Sons, Dundee, 1988–91. Depute Town Clerk, Newport-on-Tay, 1970–75; Temp. Sheriff, 1984–91; Chm., Industrial Tribunals, 1984–91. Sec., Angus Legal Aid Cttee, 1979–87; Mem., Legal Aid Central Cttee, 1981–87; Chm., Dundee CAB, 1972–79 and 1982–91. *Recreations:* reading, golf, soccer. *Address:* Sheriff's Chambers, Sheriff Court House, 1 Nelson Street, Greenock PA15 1TR. *T:* (01475) 787073.

HERAT, (James Edward) Harold; MP (United National Party) Puttalam District, Sri Lanka, 1989–94; Minister of Justice, 1993–94; State Minister of Finance, 1989–94; *b* 10 Nov. 1930; *s* of Dr Albert Edward Herat and Enid Evangeline Henrietta Dagmar Herat; *m* 1965, Gwendoline; one *s* two *d*. *Educ:* Maris Stella Coll., Negombo; St Joseph's Coll., Colombo. Attorney-at-Law. MP (UNP) Nattandiya, NW Province, 1977; Minister of Coconut Industries, 1978, and concurrently Dep. Minister, Janatha Estates Develt, 1980; Minister of Foreign Affairs, 1990–93. Mem., Court of Univ. of Sri Lanka, 1980, 1981, 1982. JP and Unofficial Magistrate, 1968. *Recreations:* tennis, riding, swimming. *Address:* Mudukatuwa Estate, Marawila, Sri Lanka. *Clubs:* Sri Lanka Tennis Association (Vice-Patron), Marawila Sports (Patron).

HERBECQ, Sir John (Edward), KCB 1977; a Church Commissioner, 1982–96; *b* 29 May 1922; *s* of late Joseph Edward and Rosina Elizabeth Herbecq; *m* 1947, Pamela Filby; one *d*. *Educ:* High Sch. for Boys, Chichester. Clerical Officer, Colonial Office, 1939; Asst Principal, Treasury, 1950; Private Sec. to Chm., UK Atomic Energy Authority, 1960–62; Asst Sec., Treasury, 1964; Asst Sec., 1968, Under Sec., 1970, Dep. Sec., 1973, Second Permanent Sec., 1975–81, CSD. Dep. Chm., Review Body for Nursing Staff, Midwives, Health Visitors and Professions Allied to Medicine, 1986–91 (Mem., 1983–91); Chm., Malaŵi Civil Service Review Commn, 1984–85. Member: C of E Pensions Bd, 1985–89; Chichester Diocesan Bd of Finance, 1983–97 (Chm., 1989–97). *Recreations:* Scottish country dancing (ISTD Supreme Award with Hons), walking, watching cricket. *Address:* Maryland, Ledgers Meadow, Cuckfield, Haywards Heath, West Sussex RH17 5EW. *T:* (01444) 413387.

HERBERT, family name of **Earls of Carnarvon, Pembroke,** and **Powis,** and **Baron Hemingford**.

HERBERT, Lord; William Alexander Sidney Herbert; *b* 18 May 1978; *s* and *heir* of Earl of Pembroke and Montgomery, *qv*. *Educ:* Bryanston Sch.; Sheffield Univ. *Recreations:* scuba diving, ski-ing.

HERBERT, Alfred James; British Council Representative, Portugal, 1980–84, retired; *b* 16 Oct. 1924; *s* of Allen Corbyn Herbert and Betty Herbert; *m* 1st, 1958, Helga Elberling (*d* 1981); two *s*; 2nd, 1982, Dr Wanda Wolska. *Educ:* Royal Masonic Schs; University Coll. London (BA 1950, MA 1952). Guest Prof. of English Lit., Univs of Yokohama and Tokyo, 1958–60; Lectr, English Dept, Birmingham Univ., 1960–62; joined British Council, 1962: Sierra Leone, 1962–65; Brazil, 1965–68; Representative: Somalia, 1968–70; Pakistan, 1974–77; Poland, 1977–80. *Publications:* Modern English Novelists, (Japan), 1960; Structure of Technical English, 1965. *Recreations:* travelling, reading. *Address:* Quinta do Val do Riso, São Simão, Azeitão, 2900 Setubal, Portugal.

HERBERT, Brian Douglas; Director of Performance Review, East Anglian Regional Health Authority, 1989–91; *b* 29 May 1930; *s* of Stanley and Kathleen Herbert; *m* 1st, 1952, Linda (marr. diss.); two *s* one *d*; 2nd, 1973, Lila; one *d*. *Educ:* Ipswich School. IPFA. Local Govt Finance, 1946–63; Health Service: Asst Treasurer, NW Metropolitan RHB, 1963; Group Treasurer, SW Middlesex HMC, 1967; Area Treasurer, Ealing, Hammersmith and Hounslow AHA(T), 1973; Regional Treasurer, 1981, Dir of Finance and Administration, 1985, E Anglian RHA. *Address:* 3 Dane Drive, Cambridge CB3 9LP. *T:* (01223) 574305.

HERBERT, Rt Rev. Christopher William; *see* St Albans, Bishop of.

HERBERT, (Elizabeth) Jane; Chief Executive, South Manchester University Hospitals NHS Trust, since 1998; *b* 17 July 1956; *d* of Reginald John Herbert and Elsa Herbert (*née* Drake). *Educ:* Durham Univ. (BSc 1977); Bath Univ. (MBA 1991). Factory Manager, Clarks Shoes, 1986–91; Unit Gen. Manager, Greater Glasgow Health Bd, 1991–92; Chief Exec., W Glasgow Hosps Univ. NHS Trust, 1993–98. *Recreations:* sailing, ornithology, music. *Address:* (office) Tower Block, Wythenshawe Hospital, Southmoor Road, Wythenshawe, Manchester M23 9LT. *T:* (0161) 291 2023.

HERBERT, Frederick William; Emeritus Fellow in Industrial Relations, International Management Centre, Buckingham, 1985–92; Chairman, NALGO Insurance Association Ltd, 1981–93; *b* London, 18 Dec. 1922; *s* of late William Herbert and Alice Herbert; *m* 1948, Nina Oesterman; two *d*. *Educ:* Ealing Boys' Grammar Sch. Served RAFVR, 1942–46. Local Govt Finance, Mddx CC, 1939–65; Greater London Council: Local Govt Finance, 1965–72; Personnel Management, Estabt Officer, 1972–77; Asst Dir of Personnel, 1977–80; Head of Industrial Relations, 1980–82; Controller of Personnel, 1982–84. Parly Correspondent, Eurotunnel (UK), 1986–87. FRSA 1986. *Recreations:* cricket, music (classical and jazz), theatre, Antient Society of Cogers (debating). *Address:* 20 Priory Hill, Wembley, Mddx HA0 2QF. *T:* (020) 8904 8634. *Clubs:* Royal Over-Seas League, MCC.

HERBERT, Prof. Harold Bernard; consultant, holistic learning; *b* 10 March 1924; *s* of late A. Bernard Henbest and Edith Winifred Henbest (*née* Herbert); *m* 1948, Rosalind Eve Skone James; two *s* one *d*. *Educ:* Barking Abbey Sch.; Imperial Coll. of Science, London. Beit Research Fellow, 1947–48; Lectr, University of Manchester, 1948–56; Research Fellow, Harvard Univ., 1953–54; Vis. Prof., UCLA, 1954; Reader, KCL, 1956–57; Prof of Organic Chemistry, QUB, 1958–73. Founder, The Learning Soc., 1988. *Publications:* Organic Chemistry (with M. F. Grundon), 1968; contribs to Jl of Chemical Soc. *Address:* 5 Witley Court, Coram Street, WC1N 1HD. *T:* (020) 7278 0888.

HERBERT, James; author; *b* 8 April 1943; *s* of Herbert Herbert and Catherine (*née* Riley); *m* 1967, Eileen O'Donnell; three *d*. *Educ:* Our Lady of Assumption Sch., Bethnal Green; St Aloysius Coll., Highgate; Hornsey Coll. of Art. Typographer, paste-up artist, general dogsbody for John Collings Advertising, 1962–65; Art director, later group head and associate dir, Charles Barker Advertising, 1965–77. Mem., Lloyd's, 1983–89. Avoriaz Grand Prize for Literature Fantastique, 1977. *Publications:* The Rats, 1974 (filmed, 1982); The Fog, 1975; The Survivor, 1976 (filmed, 1986); Fluke, 1977 (filmed, 1995); The Spear, 1978; Lair, 1979; The Dark, 1980; The Jonah, 1981; Shrine, 1983; Domain, 1984; Moon, 1985; The Magic Cottage, 1986; Sepulchre, 1987; Haunted, 1988 (filmed, 1995); Creed, 1990; Portent, 1992; James Herbert: haunted by horror (ed S. Jones), 1992; James Herbert's Dark Places, 1993; The City, 1993; The Ghosts of Sleath, 1993; '48, 1996; Others, 1999; Once, 2001. *Recreations:* playing guitar, piano, painting, sketching, photography, study of unnatural phenomena and the paranormal, swimming, reading, films, people. *Address:* c/o Bruce Hunter, David Higham Associates, 5–8 Lower John Street, Golden Square, W1R 4HA. *T:* (020) 7437 7888.

HERBERT, Jane; *see* Herbert, E. J.

HERBERT, Jeffrey William, FREng, FIMechE; EurIng; engineer and industrialist; Chief Executive, 1990–96, Chairman, 1996–2001, Charter plc; *b* 21 July 1942; *s* of Alexander William John Herbert and Amy (*née* Whitwell); *m* 1965, Sheila Heane; one *s* two *d*. *Educ:* Loughborough Univ. (DLC, BEng Mech. and Prodn Engrg; Hon. DTech 1999). MIEE 1968; FIMechE 1992; CEng, FREng (FEng 1993). Managing Director: Rover-Triumph Cars Ltd, 1976–81; GEC Diesels Ltd, 1981–85; Exec. Dir, Industry, Charter Consolidated PLC, 1985–89. Chairman: Cape plc, 1985–96; Anderson Gp plc, 1987–95; Esab AB, 1994–2001; British South Africa Co., 1996–2001; Howden Gp plc, 1997–2001; Howden Africa Hldgs Ltd, 1997–2001; Claverham Ltd, 1998–2000; Concentric Gp plc, 1999–; Dep. Chm., Vickers plc, 1997–2000 (non-exec. Dir, 1991–); non-exec. Dir, M & G Investment Trust, 1992–. Mem. Council, 1995–, Hon. Treas., 1997–, Royal Acad. of Engrg. CIMgt; FRSA 1993. Freeman, City of London, 1993; Liveryman, Wheelwrights' Co., 1993. *Recreations:* shooting, walking, wine, veteran and classic cars. *Address:* Baytrees, Long Road West, Dedham, Colchester, Essex CO7 6EL.

HERBERT, Jocelyn, Hon. ARCA 1964; RDI 1971; designer; *b* 22 Feb. 1917; *d* of Sir Alan Patrick Herbert, CH, and Gwendolen (*née* Quilter); *m* 1937, Anthony Lousada (marr. diss. 1960); one *s* three *d*. *Educ:* St Paul's Girls' Sch.; Paris and Vienna; London Theatre Studio; Slade School of Art. Started painting at André L'Hote's Sch., Paris, 1932–33; studied drawing and painting with Leon Underwood, 1934; trained as theatre designer with Michel St Denis and George Devine, London Th. Studio, 1936–37; joined staff of English Stage Co., Royal Court Th., 1956; became freelance designer, 1958, centred largely on Royal Court. Hon. FRA, 1991. *Plays designed*, 1957–: *Royal Court Theatre:* Ionesco: The Chairs, The Lesson, Exit the King; W. B. Yeats: Purgatory; Ann Jellico: Sport of My Mad Mother; Samuel Beckett: Krapp's Last Tape, Happy Days, Not I, Footfalls, That Time; Arnold Wesker: Roots, The Kitchen, I'm Talking about Jerusalem, Chips with Everything; Arden: Serjeant Musgrave's Dance; Christopher Logue: Trials by Logue, Antigone, The Trial of Cob and Leach; Middleton: The Changeling; Shakespeare: Midsummer Night's Dream, Julius Caesar; John Osborne: Luther, A Patriot for Me, Inadmissible Evidence; Barry Reckford: Skyvers; W. Solvonka: The Lion and the Jewel; O'Neil and Seabrook: Life Price; Donald Howarth: Three Months Gone; David Storey: Home, The Changing Room, Cromwell, Life Class; Christopher Hampton: Savages, The Portage to San Cristobal of A. H.; Joe Orton: What the Butler Saw; David Hare: Teeth 'n' Smiles; Mustapha Matura: Rum and Coca Cola; *RSC:* Richard III; Ibsen's Ghosts; *Phoenix:* Brecht's Baal; Ronald Harwood's J. J. Fahr; *National Theatre:* Othello; Brecht's Mother Courage and Life of Galileo; A Woman Killed with Kindness; Adrian Mitchell's Tyger; Aeschylus' The Oresteia; Tony Harrison: The Trackers of Oxyrhynchus; Square Rounds; David Storey: Early Days; The March on Russia; Stages; *Queen's:* The Seagull; Brecht's Joan of the Stockyard; *Round House:* Hamlet; *Albery:* Pygmalion; *Aldwych:* Saratoga; (New York) Wesker's The Merchant; *Haymarket:* Heartbreak House; *Lyric, Hammersmith:* The Devil and the Good Lord; *Lyric, Shaftesbury Ave:* Gigi; *Haymarket, Leicester:* Timon of Athens; Julius Caesar; Sophocles' Creon; also Tony Harrison: The Kaisers of Carnuntum, Austria, 1995; The Labourers of Herakles, Delphi, 1995. *Opera*, 1967, and 1975–: Sadler's Wells: Gluck's Orpheus and Euridice; Paris Opera: Verdi's The Force of Destiny, 1975; Metropolitan, NY: Alban Berg's Lulu, 1977; Mozart's The Abduction, 1979; Brecht and Weil's Rise and Fall of the City of Mahagonny, 1979; Coliseum: Birtwistle's The Mask of Orpheus, 1986. *Films:* Tony Richardson: (colour cons. and costumes) Tom Jones, 1961, (prodn designer) Hamlet, 1969, Ned Kelly, 1970, Hotel New Hampshire, 1983; Karel Reiss: (prodn designer) Isadora, 1968; Lindsay Anderson: (prodn designer) If . . . , 1969, O Lucky Man!, 1972; Whales of August, 1987; Tony Harrison: (prodn designer) Prometheus, 1999. Retrospective exhibn of theatre work, Royal Nat. Theatre, 1993. *Relevant publication:* Jocelyn Herbert: a theatre workbook, ed Cathy Courtney, 1993. *Recreations:* the country, painting. *Address:* 45 Pottery Lane, W11 4LY. *T:* (020) 7727 1104.

HERBERT, Mark Jeremy; QC 1995; *b* 12 Nov. 1948; *yr s* of late Kenneth Falkner Herbert and of Kathleen Ellis Herbert; *m* 1977, Shiranikha Pullenayegum. *Educ:* Lancing Coll,; King's Coll., London (BA). Called to the Bar, Lincoln's Inn, 1974; in practice at Chancery Bar, 1975–. *Publications:* (contrib.) Whiteman on Capital Gains Tax, 4th edn 1988; Drafting and Variation of Wills, 1989. *Recreations:* bell-ringing, theatre, travel. *Address:* 5 Stone Buildings, Lincoln's Inn, WC2A 3XT. *T:* (020) 7242 6201.

HERBERT, Nicholas; *see* Hemingford, 3rd Baron.

HERBERT, Adm. Sir Peter (Geoffrey Marshall), KCB 1983; OBE 1969; Non-Executive Director, Radamec Group plc, since 1985; consultant; *b* 28 Feb. 1929; *s* of A. G. S. Herbert and P. K. M. Herbert; *m* 1953, Ann Maureen (*née* McKeown); one *s* one *d*. *Educ:* Dunchurch Hall; RN Coll., Dartmouth. Specialised in submarines, 1949; served in submarines, 1950–68: Comd HM Submarines Scythian, Porpoise and Excalibur, 1956–60; Submarine Staff, 1960–62; Comd nuclear submarine, HMS Valiant, 1963–68; Comd HMS Venus, 1964; Dep. Dir, Naval Equipment, 1969; Comd 10th (Polaris) Submarine Squadron, 1970–72; COS to Flag Officer Submarines, 1972–74; Comd HMS Blake, 1974–75; Dep. Chief, Polaris Exec., 1976–78; Flag Officer Carriers and Amphibious Ships, 1978–79; Dir Gen., Naval Manpower and Training, 1980–81; Flag Officer Submarines and Comdr Submarines Eastern Atlantic, 1981–83; VCDS (Personnel and Logistics), 1983–85. Chm., SSAFA, 1985–93. President: Glos Br., King George's Fund for Sailors, 1990–; North Cotswold RNLI, 1990–. Governor: Cheam School, 1987–2000 (Chm., 1992–2000); Cheltenham Ladies' Coll., 1993–. Chm., Royal Soc. of St George, 1995–97. CIMgt; MINucE. *Recreations:* woodwork, gardening. *Club:* Army and Navy.

HERBERT, Prof. Robert Louis, PhD; Alumnae Foundation Professor of Art, 1990–96, Andrew W. Mellon Professor of Humanities, 1996–97, now Emeritus, Mount Holyoke College, Mass; *b* 21 April 1929; *s* of John Newman Herbert and Rosalia Harr Herbert; *m* 1953, Eugenia Randall Warren; one *s* two *d*. *Educ:* Wesleyan Univ., Middletown, Conn (BA 1951); Yale Univ. (MA 1954, PhD 1957). Fulbright Scholar, Paris, 1951–52; Faculty, Yale Univ., 1956–90: Associate Prof., 1963; Prof., 1966; Departmental Chm., 1965–68; Robert Lehman Prof. of Hist. of Art, 1974–90. Guggenheim Fellow, 1971–72; Slade Prof. of Fine Art, Oxford, 1978. Organizer of exhibitions: Barbizon Revisited, Boston Museum of Fine Arts and others, 1962–63; Neo-Impressionism, Solomon R. Guggenheim Mus., 1968; J. F. Millet, Musées Nationaux, Paris, and Arts Council, London, 1975–76; Léger's Le Grand Déjeuner, Minneapolis Inst. of Arts and Detroit Inst. of Arts, 1980; Seurat, Musées Nationaux, Paris and Metropolitan Mus., NY, 1991; Peasants and 'Primitivism': French prints from Millet to Gauguin, Mount Holyoke Coll., RI Sch. of Design, and Univ. of Chicago, 1995–96. Fellow, Amer. Acad. of Arts and Sciences, 1978; Mem., Amer. Philosophical Soc., 1993. Chevalier, 1976, Officier, 1990, Ordre des Arts et des Lettres. *Publications:* Barbizon Revisited, 1962–63; Seurat's Drawings, 1963; The Art Criticism of John Ruskin, 1964; Modern Artists on Art, 1964, rev. edn 2000; Neo-Impressionism, 1968; David, Voltaire, 'Brutus' and the French Revolution, 1972; J. F. Millet, 1975; (ed jtly) Société Anonyme and Dreier Bequest at Yale University: a catalogue raisonné, 1984; Impressionism: art, leisure and Parisian society, 1988; Monet on the Normandy Coast, 1994; Nature's Workshop: Renoir's writings on the decorative arts, 2000; from Millet to Léger, 2002; articles in learned jls.

HERBERT, Robin Arthur Elidyr, CBE 1994; DL; JP; Chairman, Leopold Joseph Holdings PLC, since 1978; *b* 5 March 1934; *s* of late Sir John Arthur Herbert, GCIE and Lady Mary Herbert; *m* 1st, 1960, Margaret Griswold Lewis (marr. diss. 1988); two *s* two *d*; 2nd, 1988, Philippa Harriet King. *Educ:* Eton; Christ Church, Oxford (MA); Harvard Business School (MBA). ARICS. 2nd Lieut Royal Horse Guards, 1953–54; Captain Royal Monmouthshire RE, 1962–68. Chairman: Union Discount Co. of London, later Union PLC, 1990–96 (Director, 1989–96); Lands Improvement Holdings PLC; Foreign & Colonial Income Growth Investment Trust, 1994–; Director: Nat. Westminster Bank, 1972–92; Agricl Mortgage Corp., 1985–93; Marks & Spencer, 1986–91; Consolidated Gold Fields, 1986–89 (Dep. Chm., 1988–89); F&C Smaller Companies Investment Trust, 1985–; Federated Aggregates, 1991–95; SWOAC Holdings, 1990–98. Financial Advisor: Water Superannuation Fund, 1986–89; Nat. Rivers Authy, 1989–96. Mem. Council, BBA, 1992–98. Dep. Chm., Countryside Commn, 1971–80; Member: Council, National Trust, 1969–87 (Mem., Exec. Cttee, 1969–84; Chm. Cttee for Wales, 1969–84); Nat. Water Council, 1980–83; Welsh Develt Agency, 1980–86; Darwin Initiative Adv. Cttee, 1993–99; Royal Parks Agency Adv. Gp, 1993–2000. Royal Horticultural Society: Mem. Council, 1971–74 and 1979–94; Pres. and Chm. Council, 1984–94; Pres. Emeritus, 1994–. Trustee, Royal Botanic Gardens, Kew, 1987–97 (Chm., 1991–97). DL 1968, JP 1964, High Sheriff 1972, Monmouthshire. *Recreations:* dendrology, walking. *Address:* Newadd, Llanbedr, Crickhowell, Powys NP8 1SP. *T:* (01873) 812164. *Clubs:* Brooks's, Pratt's.

HERBERT, Sir Walter William, (Sir Wally), Kt 2000; Polar explorer; *b* 24 Oct. 1934; *s* of Captain W. W. J. Herbert and Helen (*née* Manton); *m* 1969, Marie, *d* of Prof. C. A. McGaughey; one *d* (and one *d* decd). Trained as surveyor in RE; Egypt, 1953–54, demob. 1955; travelled in Middle East, 1955; Surveyor with Falkland Is Dependencies Survey; Hope Bay, Antarctica, 1955–58; travelled in S America, 1958–59; Mem. expedn to Lapland and Spitzbergen, 1960; travelled in Greenland, 1960; Surveyor, NZ Antarctic Expedn, 1960–62; leader Southern Party; mapped 26,000 sq. miles of Queen Maud Range and descended Amundsen's route to Pole on 50th anniv.; led expedn to NW Greenland, 1966–67; dog-sledged 1,400 miles Greenland to Canada in trng for trans-Arctic crossing; led British Trans-Arctic Expedn, 1968–69, which made 3,800–mile first surface crossing of Arctic Ocean from Alaska via North Pole to Spitzbergen; led Ultima Thule expedn (filming Eskimos, Thule District), 1971–73; led expedn to Lapland, 1975; led expedn to Greenland, 1978–82 (attempting first circumnavigation by dog sledge and skin boat); led filming expedn to NW Greenland, Ellesmere Island and North Pole, 1987. One-man exhibitions: QE-2, 1994; Explorers Club, NY, 1994; Jamestown Coll., NY, 1994; Australian Geographic Soc., 1994; Travellers' Club, London, 1997; Atlas Gallery, 1999. Hon. Mem., British Schools Exploring Soc.; Jt Hon. Pres., World Expeditionary Assoc. FRGS. Hon. Fellow, New World Acad., 1993. Polar Medal 1962, and clasp 1969; Livingstone Gold Medal, RSGS, 1969; Founder's Gold Medal, RGS, 1970; City of Paris Medal, 1983; French Geog. Soc. Medal, 1983; Explorers' Medal, Explorers' Club, 1985; Finn Ronne Award, 1985. *Publications:* A World of Men, 1968; Across the Top of the

World, 1969; (contrib.) World Atlas of Mountaineering, 1969; The Last Great Journey on Earth, 1971; Polar Deserts, 1971; Eskimos, 1976 (Jugendbuchpreis, 1977); North Pole, 1978; (contrib.) Expeditions the Expert's Way, 1977; (contrib.) Bell House Book, 1978; Hunters of the Polar North, 1982; The Noose of Laurels, 1989; The Third Pole, 2002. *Recreation:* painting. *Address:* Catlodge, Laggan, Inverness-shire PH20 1AH. *T:* and *Fax:* (01528) 544396. *Clubs:* Lansdowne; Explorers (NY).

HERBERT, William Penry Millwarden; Member, Cardiff City Council, 1970–96; Lord Mayor of Cardiff, 1988–89; *b* 31 March 1921; *s* of William John Herbert and Esabella Marinda Francis; *m* 1945, Ellen Vera McCarthy; two *d* (one *s* decd). *Educ:* Argoed Elementary Sch., Blackwood, Monmouthshire. Cert. of Professional Competence, Transport, 1977. Miner, 1934–37; Railwayman, 1937–45. Served RE, 1945–47. 1947–78: Guest Keen Iron and Steel Works; Guest Keen and Baldwins British Steel Corp.; Plant Supervisor, Traffic Foreman, Transport Manager. *Recreations:* dancing, gardening, reading, travel. *Address:* 27 Wellwood, Llanedeyrn, Cardiff, South Glamorgan CF3 7JP. *Club:* City Social (Cathays, Cardiff).

HERBERT-JONES, Hugh Jarrett, (Hugo), CMG 1973; OBE 1963; HM Diplomatic Service, retired; company director; *b* 11 March 1922; *s* of late Dora Herbert-Jones (*née* Rowlands), MBE and Captain Herbert-Jones; *m* 1954, Margaret (*d* 1996), *d* of Rev. J. P. Veall; one *s* two *d*. *Educ:* Bryanston; Worcester Coll., Oxford. History Scholar. Commnd Welsh Guards, 1941; served NW Europe and Middle East; wounded 1944; demobilised 1946 (Major). Entered Foreign (later Diplomatic) Service, 1947; served: Hamburg, 1947; Berlin, 1949; Hong Kong, 1951; Phnom Penh, 1955; Saigon, 1956; Nairobi, 1959; Pretoria/Cape Town, 1963; FCO, 1966; Paris, 1973; FCO, 1975–79; Internat. Affairs Dir, CBI, 1979–87. Pres., Aldeburgh Soc., 1997–99. *Recreations:* sailing, golf, shooting, music, spectator sports. *Address:* Prior's Hill, 48 Park Road, Aldeburgh, Suffolk IP15 5ET. *T:* and *Fax:* (01728) 453335; *e-mail:* hugo@herbertjones.fsnet.co.uk. *Clubs:* Garrick, MCC; London Welsh Rugby Football; Aldeburgh Yacht.

HERBISON, Dame Jean (Marjory), DBE 1985; CMG 1976; Associate Director, Christchurch Polytechnic, New Zealand, 1975–84, retired; *b* 29 April 1923; *d* of William Herbison and Sarah Jane Herbison (*née* McKendry). *Educ:* Univ. of Canterbury (BA); Auckland Teachers' Coll. (Dip Teaching); Univ. of Northern Iowa (MA); Inst. of Education, Univ. of London. AIE 1974. Teaching, Avonside Girls' High School, Christchurch, 1952–59; Dean, 1960–68, Vice-Principal, 1968–74, Christchurch Teachers' Coll.; Assoc. Dir, Christchurch Polytechnic, 1975–84; Mem. Council, 1970–84, Chancellor, 1979–84, Univ. of Canterbury. Chairperson, NZ Council for Educnl Research, 1986–88 (Mem., 1977–88); Member: UGC, 1985–90; Ministerial Cttee of Inquiry into Curriculum, Assessment and Qualifications in the Senior Secondary Sch., 1985–87; Commonwealth Council for Educnl Admin, 1970– (Vice-Pres., 1982–86); NZ Vice-Chancellors' Cttee, Univ. Review Panel, 1987. Fellow: Commonwealth Council for Educnl Admin., 1986; NZ Educnl Admin. Soc., 1990; Hon. Fellow: NZ Educnl Inst.; NZ Inst. of Management. Hon. DLitt Canterbury, 1987. Queen's Silver Jubilee Medal, 1977. *Recreations:* gardening, walking, reading. *Address:* 2/172 Soleares Avenue, Christchurch 8008, New Zealand. *T:* (3) 3849086.

HERBISON-ARGENTA, Nancy Maureen; soprano; Visiting Professor Guildhall School of Music and Drama, since 1997; *b* Nelson, Canada, 17 Jan. 1957; *d* of Hugh and Agnes Herbison. *Educ:* Vancouver Community Coll.; Univ. of Western Ontario (Artist Dip. in Performance). Début, Hippolyte and Aricie, Fest. d'Aix en Provence, 1983; has performed in Australia, Europe, Japan, N America, S America, with major orchestras and companies, including Australian Chamber Orch., LPO, Monteverdi Choir and Orch., Philharmonia Orch., St Louis SO. *Recreations:* walking, gardening, cycling, woodwork. *Address:* c/o Askonas Holt Ltd, 27 Chancery Lane, WC2A 1PF. *T:* (020) 7400 1700.

HERCUS, Hon. Dame (Margaret) Ann, DCMG 1988; international consultant; *b* 24 Feb. 1942; *d* of Horace Sayers and Mary (*née* Ryan); *m* John Hercus; two *s*. *Educ:* Victoria Univ. of Wellington; Univs. of Auckland (BA) and Canterbury (LLB). Lawyer and Staff Training Officer, Beath & Co., Christchurch, 1969–70; Mem., Price Tribunal and Trade Practices Commn, 1973–75; Dep. Chm., Commerce Commn, 1975–78; Chm., Consumer Rights Campaign, 1975; MP (Lab) Lyttleton, 1978–87; in opposition, 1978–84; Minister of Social Welfare, Police and Women's Affairs, 1984–87; Ambassador to UN, 1988–90; internat. consultant, 1991–98; Chief of Mission, UN Force in Cyprus, 1998–99. *Address:* 82A Park Terrace, Christchurch 8001, New Zealand.

HERD, Frederick Charles; Assistant Under-Secretary of State (Civilian Management, General), Ministry of Defence, 1970–75; *b* 27 April 1915. *Educ:* Strode's Sch., Egham; Sidney Sussex Coll., Cambridge. Asst Principal, Admiralty, 1937; Principal, 1941; Asst. Sec., 1950; Asst Under-Sec. of State, 1964. *Recreations:* music, country walking, bridge. *Address:* 11 Bloemfontein Avenue, W12 7BJ.

HERDAN, Bernard Laurence, CEng; Chief Executive, UK Passport Agency and Criminal Records Bureau, since 1999; *b* 23 Nov. 1947; *s* of Dr Gustav Herdan and Estelle Muriel Innes Herdan (*née* Jackson); *m* 1971, Janet Elizabeth Hughes; one *d* (and one *d* decd). *Educ:* Bristol Grammar Sch.; Churchill Coll., Cambridge (BA Hons 1969, MA); Bath Univ. (DMS 1972). CEng, MIEE 1971. Systems Designer, BAe, 1969–73; Prog. Manager, ESA, 1973–84; Managing Consultant, BIS Mackintosh, 1984–85; Man. Dir, Defence Technology Enterprises, 1985–89; Commercial Dir, Meteorological Office, 1990–95; Chief Exec., Driving Standards Agency, 1995–99. MInstD 1986. Editor-in-Chief, Space Communication and Broadcasting, 1982–86. *Publications:* papers in professional jls. *Recreations:* horse riding, ski-ing, foreign travel, theatre, the arts. *Address:* UK Passport Agency, Clive House, Petty France, SW1H 9HD. *T:* (020) 7271 8881.

HERDMAN, (John) Mark (Ambrose), CBE 1990; LVO 1979; HM Diplomatic Service, retired; *b* 26 April 1932; *s* of late Comdr Claudius Alexander Herdman, DL, RN, and Joan Dalrymple Herdman (*née* Tennant); *m* 1963, Elizabeth Anne Dillon; one *s* two *d*. *Educ:* St Edward's Sch., Oxford; Trinity Coll., Dublin (BA, MA); Queen's Coll., Oxford (postgrad.). HMOCS, Kenya, 1954–64; joined HM Diplomatic Service, 1964; Second, later First Sec., CRO, 1964–65; ODM, 1965; MECAS, 1965–66; Amman, 1966–68; FCO, 1969–71; Lusaka, 1971–74; Hd of Chancery, Jedda, 1974–76; FCO, 1976–78; Lilongwe, 1978–81; FCO, 1981–83; Dep. Governor, Bermuda, 1983–86; Gov., British Virgin Is, 1986–91; Hd of British Delegn to EC Monitoring Mission in Yugoslavia, 1991–92. *Recreations:* fishing, watching cricket, philately. *Address:* Tullywhisker House, Berry Lane, Fox Corner, Worplesdon, Surrey GU3 3PU. *T:* (01483) 232900. *Clubs:* Ebury Court; Surrey CC.

HERDON, Christopher de Lancy, OBE 1971; HM Diplomatic Service, retired; freelance journalist, since 1983; news editor, The Tablet, since 1986; *b* 24 May 1928; *s* of late Wilfrid Herdon and Clotilde (*née* Parsons); *m* 1953, Virginia Grace; two *s* two *d* (and one *s* decd). *Educ:* Ampleforth; Magdalen Coll., Oxford. Foreign Office, 1951; Vienna, 1953; 2nd Sec., Baghdad, 1957; Beirut, 1961; 1st Sec., Amman, 1962; FO, 1965; Aden, 1967; FCO, 1970; Counsellor: Rome, 1973; FCO, 1977; retired 1983. RC Observer, BCC, 1984–90; Mem., Assembly of Council of Churches for Britain and Ireland, 1990–94. *Recreations:* painting, music, sailing, long-distance walking. *Address:* Moses Farm, Lurgashall, Petworth, W Sussex GU28 9EP. *T:* (01428) 707323. *Club:* Reform.

HEREFORD, 18th Viscount *cr* 1550; **Robert Milo Leicester Devereux;** Bt 1611; Premier Viscount of England; *b* 4 Nov. 1932; *o s* of Hon. Robert Godfrey de Bohun Devereux (*d* 1934) and Audrey Maureen Leslie, DStJ 1963 (*d* 1978) (she *m* 2nd 1961, 7th Earl of Lisburne; who *d* 1965), *y d* of late James Meakin, Westwood Manor, Staffs and of late Countess Sondes; *S* grandfather, 1952; *m* 1969, Susan Mary (marr. diss. 1982), *o c* of Major Maurice Godley, Ide Hill, Sevenoaks, Kent, and of Mrs Glen Godley, Ascott, Shipston-on-Stour, Warwicks; two *s*. *Educ:* Eton. Served Royal Horse Guards (The Blues), 1960–63. Member: Royal Philharmonic Soc.; Royal Philharmonic Orchestra Assoc. OStJ. *Heir:* *s* Hon. Charles Robin de Bohun Devereux, *b* 11 Aug. 1975.

HEREFORD, Bishop of, since 1990; **Rt Rev. John Keith Oliver;** *b* 14 April 1935; *s* of Walter Keith and Ivy Oliver; *m* 1961, Meriel Moore; two *s* one *d*. *Educ:* Westminster School; Gonville and Caius Coll., Cambridge (MA, MLitt); Westcott House. Asst Curate, Hilborough Group of Parishes, Norfolk, 1964–68; Chaplain and Asst Master, Eton College, 1968–72; Team Rector: South Molton Group of Parishes, Devon, 1973–82; Parish of Central Exeter, 1982–85; Archdeacon of Sherborne, 1985–90. Chm., ABM, 1993–98. *Publications:* The Church and Social Order, 1968; contribs to Theology, Crucible. *Recreations:* railways, music, architecture, motorcycling. *Address:* Bishop's House, The Palace, Hereford HR4 9BN. *Clubs:* United Oxford & Cambridge; Worcester CC.

HEREFORD, Dean of; *no new appointment at time of going to press.*

HEREFORD, Archdeacon of; *see* Hooper, Ven. M. W.

HERFT, Rt Rev. Roger Adrian; *see* Newcastle, NSW, Bishop of.

HERITAGE, John Langdon, CB 1991; Director, Chesham Building Society, 1989–2001 (Chairman, 1992–97); *b* 31 Dec. 1931; *s* of Frank and Elizabeth Heritage; *m* 1956, Elizabeth Faulkner, *d* of Charles and Ethel Robertson; two *s* one *d*. *Educ:* Berkhamsted Sch., Exeter Coll., Oxford (MA). Called to the Bar, Middle Temple, 1956. National Service, Royal Hampshire Regt and Royal W African Frontier Force. Legal Asst, Treasury Solicitor's Office, 1957, Sen. Legal Asst 1964; Asst Solicitor, Lord Chancellor's Dept, 1973; Sec., Royal Commn on Legal Services, 1976–79; Under Sec., 1983; Circuit Administrator, South Eastern Circuit, 1983–88; Hd of Judicial Appts, Lord Chancellor's Dept, 1989–92. *Publications:* articles in legal jls. *Recreation:* making things. *Address:* Hurdle House, 1 Chestnut Lane, Amersham, Bucks HP6 6EN. *Club:* Oxford and Cambridge.

HERITAGE, Robert, CBE 1980; RDI 1963; DesRCA, FCSD; Professor, School of Furniture Design, Royal College of Art, 1974–85; *b* 2 Nov. 1927; *m* Dorothy; two *s* one *d*. *Educ:* Royal College of Art, RCA, 1950; freelance designer, 1961. *Recreations:* tennis, fishing. *Address:* 12 Jay Mews, Kensington Gore, SW7 2EP.

HERLIE, Eileen; actress; *b* Glasgow, 8 March 1920; *d* of Patrick Herlihy (Irish) and Isobel Cowden (Scottish); *m* 1st, 1940, Philip Barrett (marr. diss.); 2nd, 1951, Witold Kuncewicz (marr. diss.). *Educ:* Shawlands Academy, Glasgow. First stage appearance, Lyric, Glasgow, 1938; first London appearance, as Mrs de Winter in Rebecca, Ambassadors', 1942; varied repertoire with own company, 1942–44; Old Vic Co., Playhouse, Liverpool, 1944–45, including: Lady Sneerwell in The School for Scandal, Doll Common in The Alchemist; Lyric, Hammersmith, 1945–46, including: Andromache in The Trojan Women, Alcestis in Thracian Horses, Queen in The Eagle Has Two Heads; title rôle in Medea, Globe, 1948; Paula in The Second Mrs Tanqueray, Haymarket, 1950; Mrs Marwood in The Way of the World, Belvidera in Venice Preserv'd, Lyric, Hammersmith, 1953; Irene in A Sense of Guilt, King's, Glasgow, 1953; Mrs Molloy in The Matchmaker, Haymarket, 1954, transf. NY, 1955; Emilia Marty in The Makropoulos Secret, NY, 1957; Paulina in The Winter's Tale, Beatrice in Much Ado About Nothing, Stratford, Ont, 1958; Ruth Gray in Epitaph for George Dillon, NY, 1958; Lily in Take Me Along (musical), NY, 1959; Elizabeth Hawkes-Bullock in All American (musical), NY, 1962; Stella in Photo Finish, NY, 1963; Queen Gertrude in Hamlet, NY, 1964; Lady Fitzbuttress in Halfway up the Tree, NY, 1967; Martha in Who's Afraid of Virginia Woolf?, Chicago, 1971; Countess Matilda Spina in Emperor Henry IV, 1973; Queen Mary in Crown Matrimonial, NY, 1973. *Films:* Hungry Hill, 1947; Hamlet, 1948; Angel with the Trumpet, 1949; Gilbert and Sullivan, 1952; Isn't Life Wonderful?, 1952; She Didn't Say No!, 1958; Freud, 1962; The Seagull, 1968. *Television:* Myrtle Fargate in All My Children, ABC TV, 1976–. *Recreations:* riding, reading, music. *Address:* Apt 13P, 405 East 54th Street, New York, NY 10022, USA.

HERMAN, David Joseph; Vice President, Russia and New Independent States, GM Moscow, since 1998; *b* 14 Jan. 1946; *m* Isabel Roehrenbach; two *d*. *Educ:* New York Univ. (BA Govt Affairs 1967); LSE; Harvard Univ. Grad. Sch. (JD 1971). Attorney, Legal Staff, General Motors, NY, 1973; Manager, Sales Devélt (USSR), GM Internat. Ops, 1976; Special Asst to Man. Dir, GM España, 1979–82; Managing Director: GM Chile, Santiago, 1982; GM Colombia, 1984–86; GM Continental, Antwerp, 1986–88; Exec. Dir, Europ. Parts & Accessories, GM Europe, 1988–89; Pres. and Chief Exec. Officer, SAAB Automobile, 1989–92; Chm. and Man. Dir, Adam Opel AG, 1992–98. Vice Pres., Gen. Motors Corp., 1992–. *Recreations:* golf, opera, bridge. *Address:* General Motors CIS, Gogolevsky Blvd 11, 9th Floor, 121019 Moscow, Russia.

HERMANN, Alexander Henry Baxter; HM Diplomatic Service, retired; *b* 28 Dec. 1917; *m* Rita Rosalind Fernandes. Joined Foreign Service, 1939; served 1942–55; Peking, Ahwaz, Chengtu, Chungking, Shanghai, Quito, Panama, Tamsui; Foreign Office, 1956; Commercial Counsellor and Consul-General, Rangoon, 1957–61; HM Consul-General at Marseilles, also to Monaco, 1961–65; Diplomatic Service Inspector, 1965–66; Counsellor, Hong Kong Affairs, Washington, 1967–70, 1974–77; Consul-General, Osaka, 1971–73. *Address:* Old Place, Aldwick, Sussex.

HERMER, Julius; solicitor; Consultant with: Howard Palser Grossman Hermer & Partners, 1996–99; Robertsons, since 1999; Lord Mayor of Cardiff, 1987–88; *b* 18 Nov. 1933; *s* of Saul and Cissie Hermer; *m* 1960, Gloria Cohen; three *s* one *d*. *Educ:* St Illtyd's Coll., Cardiff; Peterhouse, Cambridge (BA, MA). Partner, 1959–95, Grossman & Hermer, subseq. Crowley, Grossman & Hermer, Grossman, Hermer & McCarthy, and Grossman, Hermer Seligman. Member: Cardiff City Council, 1964–88, 1991–96 (Chm., Planning Cttee, 1980–84; Dep. Lord Mayor of Cardiff, 1979–80, 1986–87); S Glam CC, 1974–96 (Vice-Chm. of Council and Dep. Leader of Cons. Party, 1977–78). Pres., Cardiff W Cons. Assoc., 1999– (Dep. Chm., 1985). Chm., S Glam Appeal, Sir Geraint Evans Wales Heart Res. Inst., 1991–97. *Recreations:* Freemasonry, sport, wine, food, travel, politics. *Address:* 28 Palace Road, Llandaff, Cardiff CF5 2AF. *T:* (029) 2056 6198.

HERMITAGE, Peter Andrew, QPM 1996; Director, National Police Training (with rank of Chief Constable), 1996–99; Chairman, East Kent Hospitals NHS Trust, since

2000; *b* 26 Sept. 1948; *s* of late Thomas Henry Hermitage and Freda Helen Hermitage; *m* 1971, Brenda Howard; one *s* one *d*. *Educ:* Chatham House GS, Ramsgate. Joined Kent Constabulary, 1968: numerous operational, investigative and organisational roles, incl. Dir, Jun. Comd Course, Police Staff Coll., Bramshill, 1986–87; Asst Chief Constable, Kent, 1990–94; Asst Inspector of Constabulary, Home Office, 1994–96. Ed., Police Jl, 1997–99. Vice-Pres., Police Mutual Assce Soc., 1997–99. Gov., Christchurch UC, Canterbury, 1999–. MRSH 1992; FIPD 1997; MInstD 1999. *Recreations:* Rugby, painting water colours, family. *Address:* 4 Ealham Close, Canterbury, Kent CT4 7BW.

HERMON, Sir John (Charles), Kt 1982; OBE 1975; QPM 1988; Chief Constable, Royal Ulster Constabulary, 1980–89; *b* 23 Nov. 1928; *s* of late William Rowan Hermon and Agnes Hermon; *m* 1954, Jean Webb (*d* 1986); one *s* one *d*; *m* 1988, Sylvia Paisley (*see* Sylvia Hermon); two *s*. *Educ:* Larne Grammar Sch. Accountancy training and business, 1946–50; joined RUC, 1950. Pres., Internat. Professional Security Assoc., 1993–96. CStJ 1984. *Publication:* Holding the Line: an autobiography, 1997. *Recreations:* boating, reading, walking. *Club:* Donaghadee Golf.

HERMON, Peter Michael Robert; Head of Information Systems, CL-Alexanders Laing and Cruickshank Holdings Ltd, 1989–90; *b* 13 Nov. 1928; British; *m* 1954, Norma Stuart Brealey; two *s* two *d*. *Educ:* Nottingham High Sch.; St John's and Merton Colls, Oxford. 1st cl. hons Maths Oxon. Leo Computers Ltd, 1955–59; Manager, Management and Computer Divs, Dunlop Co., 1959–65; Information Handling Dir, BOAC, 1965–68; Management Services Dir, BOAC, and Mem. Bd of Management, 1968–72; Mem. of Board, BOAC, 1972; British Airways: Gp Management Services Dir, 1972–78; Board Mem., 1978–83; Management Services Dir, 1978–82; Man. Dir, European Services Div., 1982–83. Man. Dir, Tandem Computers Ltd, 1983–84; Dir, Tandem UK, 1983–85; Head of Systems and Communications, Lloyd's of London, 1984–86; Informations Systems Dir, Harris Queensway, 1986–88. Mem. Bd of Dirs, Internat. Aeradio Ltd, 1966–83, Chm., 1982–83; Chm., Internat. Aeradio (Caribbean) Ltd, 1967–83; Mem. Bd, SITA, 1972–83, Chm., 1981–83. *Publications:* Hill Walking in Wales, 1991; (jtly) User-Driven Innovation: the world's first business computer, 1996. *Recreations:* hill walking, music, cats. *Address:* White Flints, Quentin Way, Wentworth, Virginia Water, Surrey GU25 4PS.

HERMON, Sylvia, (Lady Hermon); MP (UU) Down North, since 2001; *b* 11 Aug. 1955; *d* of Robert and Mary Paisley; *m* 1988, Sir John (Charles) Hermon, *qv*; two *s*. *Educ:* UCW, Aberystwyth (LLB 1st Cl. Hons); Coll. of Law, Chester. Lectr in Law, QUB, 1978–88; PR Consultant, 1993–96. Chm., N Down Unionist Assoc., 2001–. *Publication:* A Guide to EEC Law in Northern Ireland, 1986. *Recreations:* swimming, fitness-training, proof reading, ornithology. *Address:* House of Commons, SW1A 0AA.

HERMON-TAYLOR, Prof. John, FRCS; Professor of Surgery, St George's Hospital Medical School, since 1976; *b* 16 Oct. 1936; *s* of late Hermon Taylor, FRCS; *m* 1971, Eleanor Ann Pheteplace, of Davenport, Iowa; one *s* one *d*. *Educ:* Harrow Sch. (Shepherd-Churchill Open Major Entrance Schol.); St John's Coll., Cambridge (travelling schol., 1955; BA 1957, MB BChir 1960, MChir 1968); London Hosp. Med Coll. (Open Entrance Schol., 1957, prizes in Med., Path., and Obst.). FRCS 1963 (Hallett Prize, 1962). Training in surgery, 1962–68; MRC Travelling Fellow to Mayo Clinic, USA, 1968–69 (Vis. Prof., 1980, 1985); Senior Lectr, 1970, Reader in Surgery, 1971–76, London Hosp. Med. Coll. Pearce-Gould Vis. Prof., Middlesex Hosp., 1982; Vis. Prof., Pakistan Inst. of Med. Scis, Islamabad, 1989. Hon. Consultant in Gen. Surgery to RN, 1989–. Mem. Council, Assoc. of Surgeons of GB and Ireland, 1981–84; Dir, James IV Assoc. of Surgeons, 1983–86. Member: Council, Action Research, 1988–97; Scientific Cttee, British Digestive Foundn, 1991–95; Medical Adv. Cttee, British Liver Trust, 1995–96; Health Services Res. and Clin. Epidemiol. Adv. Cttee, Wellcome Trust, 1996–2001 (Mem., Clinical Panel, 1985–88); wking gp on Crohn's disease and paratuberculosis, Scientific Cttee on Animal Health and Animal Welfare, EC, 1998–2000. Dir, BioScience Internat. Inc., 1987–. Mem., numerous professional bodies, UK and overseas. Innovator of the Year award, Times Newspaper/Barclays Bank, 1988. *Publications:* scientific papers on purification and biochem. of enteropeptidase, diseases of pancreas, peptide chem., enzymeactivation in gastric disorders, on causation and specific treatment of Crohn's disease, mycobacterial genetics, epidemiology of breast cancer, biolog. res. on common solid tumours. *Recreations:* fishing, sailing, shooting, growing soft fruit and vegetables. *Address:* 11 Parkside Avenue, Wimbledon, SW19 5ES. *T:* (020) 8767 7631.

HERN, Jane Carolyn; Registrar, Royal College of Veterinary Surgeons, since 1997; *b* 22 Sept. 1954; *d* of George Kenneth Hern and Elizabeth Ellen Hern (*née* Byford). *Educ:* Girton Coll., Cambridge (BA Hons Law 1976; MA). Articles with Lovell, White & King, 1977–79; admitted as solicitor, 1979; LCD, 1979–87, Law Commn, 1981–86; Law Soc., 1987–96: Asst Sec.-Gen., 1992–95; Dir, Management and Planning Directorate, 1995–96; Actg Sec.-Gen., 1996. *Recreations:* eating, drinking, reading crime thrillers, visiting places of historic interest. *Address:* (office) Belgravia House, 62–64 Horseferry Road, SW1P 2AF. *T:* (020) 7222 2001.

HERN, Major William Richard, (Dick), CVO 1980; CBE 1998; racehorse trainer; *b* Holford, Somerset, 20 Jan. 1921; *m* 1956, Sheilah Joan Davis (*d* 1998). Served War of 1939–45, North Irish Horse. Asst Trainer to Major M. B. Pope, MC, 1952–57; licence to train under Jockey Club rules, 1957–97; leading trainer, 1962, 1972, 1980, 1983. Races won include: Derby, 1979, 1980, 1989 (Troy, Henbit, Nashwan); 2,000 Guineas, 1971, 1989 (Brigadier Gerard, Nashwan); 1,000 Guineas, 1974, 1995 (Highclere, Harayir); St Leger, 1962, 1965, 1974, 1977, 1981, 1983 (Hethersett, Provoke, Bustino, Dunfermline, Cut Above, Sun Princess); Epsom Oaks, 1977, 1980, 1983 (Dunfermline, Bireme, Sun Princess); King George VI and Queen Elizabeth Diamond Stakes, 1972, 1979, 1980, 1985, 1989 (Brigadier Gerard, Troy, Ela-Mana-Mou, Petoski, Nashwan); Champion Stakes, 1971, 1972 (Brigadier Gerard); Eclipse Stakes, 1972, 1980, 1989, 1990 (Brigadier Gerard, Ela-Mana-Mou, Nashwan, Elmaamul); Coronation Cup, 1974, 1975 (Buoy, Bustino). Leading Trainer, Flat Seasons, 1962, 1972, 1980, 1983. *Address:* The Old Rectory, West Ilsley, Newbury, Berks RG20 7AR. *T:* (01635) 281251.

HERON, Sir Conrad (Frederick), KCB 1974 (CB 1969); OBE 1953; Permanent Secretary, Department of Employment, 1973–76; *b* 21 Feb. 1916; *s* of Richard Foster Heron and Ida Fredrika Heron; *m* 1948, Envye Linnéa Gustafsson; two *d*. *Educ:* South Shields High Sch.; Trinity Hall, Cambridge. Entered Ministry of Labour, 1938; Principal Private Secretary to Minister of Labour, 1953–56; Under-Secretary, Industrial Relations Dept, 1963–64 and 1965–68, Overseas Dept, 1964–65; Dep. Under-Sec. of State, Dept of Employment, 1968–71; Dep. Chm., Commn on Industrial Relations, 1971–72; Second Permanent Sec., Dept of Employment, 1973. *Address:* Old Orchards, West Lydford, Somerton, Somerset TA11 7DG. *T:* (01963) 240387.

HERON, Sir Michael (Gilbert), Kt 1996; Chairman, Post Office, 1993–97; *b* 22 Oct. 1934; *s* of Gilbert Thwaites Heron and Olive Lilian (*née* Steele); *m* 1958, Celia Veronica Mary Hunter; two *s* one *d* (and one *d* decd). *Educ:* St Joseph's Acad., Blackheath; New Coll., Oxford (MA Hist.). Lieut RA, 1953–55. Dir, BOCM Silcock, 1971–76; Chm., Batchelors Foods, 1976–82; Dep. Co-ordinator, Food & Drinks Co-ordination, Unilever, 1982–86; Dir, Unilever, 1986–92. Food and Drink Federation: Mem. Cttee, 1986–92; Mem. Council, 1986–92; Chm., Food Policy Res. Cttee, 1987–92. Mem., Armed Forces Pay Rev. Bd, 1981–82. Dep. Chm. and Mem. Bd, BITC, 1991–95; Member: Policy Steering Bd, BESO, 1992–93; CBI Council, 1992–95; Dep. Chm., NACETT, 1993–95; Chairman: NCVQ, 1994–97; Council for Industry and Higher Educn, 1999–. Chm., N London, Prince's Trust Business Div. formerly PYBT), 1999–. Chm. Council, St George's Hosp. Med. Sch., 1992–98; Mem., Governing Body, Douai Abbey, 1991–97. *Recreation:* avid Rugby football watcher. *Address:* 43 Albion Gate, Albion Street, W2 2LG. *T:* (020) 7262 8091.

HERON, Raymond, CBE 1984; retired; Deputy Director, Propellants, Explosives and Rocket Motor Establishment, Ministry of Defence (Procurement Executive), 1977–84; *b* 10 April 1924; *s* of Lewis and Doris Heron; *m* 1948, Elizabeth MacGathan; one *s* one *d*. *Educ:* Heath Grammar Sch., Halifax; Queen's Coll., Oxford (BA Physics). Shell Refining and Marketing Co., 1944–47; RN, Instructor Branch, 1947–52; Rocket Propulsion Estabt, Min. of Supply (later Min. of Technology), 1952–67; Cabinet Office, 1967; Asst Dir, Min. of Technology, 1967–73; Dep. Dir, Explosives Research and Development Estabt, MoD, 1973; Special Asst to Sec. (Procurement Exec.), MoD, 1973–74; Head of Rocket Motor Exec. and Dep. Dir/2, Rocket Propulsion Estabt, MoD (PE), 1974–76. *Publications:* articles in scientific and technical jls. *Recreations:* music, hill walking, golf. *Address:* 9 Grange Gardens, Wendover, Aylesbury, Bucks HP22 6HB. *T:* (01296) 622921. *Club:* Ashridge Golf.

HERON, Robert, CVO 1988; MA; Director, Duke of Edinburgh's Award Scheme, 1978–87; *b* 12 Oct. 1927; *s* of James Riddick Heron and Sophie Leathem; *m* 1953, Patricia Mary Pennell; two *s* one *d*. *Educ:* King Edward's Sch., Birmingham; St Catharine's Coll., Cambridge. Housemaster: Strathallan, Perthshire, 1952–59; Christ Coll., Brecon, 1959–62; Headmaster, King James I Sch., IOW, 1962–66. Head of Educational Broadcasting, ATV Network Ltd, 1966–69, responsible for production of TV programme series in the scis, langs, soc. documentary, leisure interests, music, drama; Deleg., EBU study gps on educnl broadcasting, 1967–69; Programme Dir, The Electronic Video Recording Partnership (CBS Inc. USA/ICI/Ciba-Geigy UK), 1970–77; Managing Dir, EVR Ltd, 1974–77, and of EVR Enterprises Ltd, 1975–77. Freeman, City of London, 1981. Formerly 6/7th Bn, The Black Watch (RHR) TA. *Recreations:* travel, sport. *Address:* Well Cottage, Cove, Tiverton, Devon EX16 7RT. *Clubs:* Rugby; Hawks (Cambridge); Achilles.

HERON-MAXWELL, Sir Nigel (Mellor), 10th Bt *cr* 1683; *b* 30 Jan. 1944; *s* of Sir Patrick Ivor Heron-Maxwell, 9th Bt and of D. Geraldine E., *yr d* of late Claud Paget Mellor; *S* father, 1982; *m* 1972, Mary Elizabeth Angela, *o d* of late W. Ewing, Co. Donegal; one *s* one *d*. *Educ:* Milton Abbey. *Heir: s* David Mellor Heron-Maxwell, *b* 22 May 1975. *Address:* 50 Watlington Road, Old Harlow, Essex CM17 0DY.

HERRIDGE, Michael Eric James; HM Diplomatic Service; Deputy High Commissioner, Chennai, since 1999; *b* 23 Sept. 1946; *s* of late Robert James Herridge and Mary Herridge (*née* Beckitt); *m* 1968, Margaret Elizabeth Bramble; one *d*. *Educ:* Ashley Sch., Hampshire; Bournemouth Coll. Joined HM Diplomatic Service, 1966; Prague, 1969–72; Nairobi, 1972–75; FCO, 1975–79; Second Sec., Lagos, 1979–82; Second, then First, Sec., UKMIS NY, 1982–86; FCO, 1986–90; First Sec., Madrid, 1990–95; FCO, 1995–99. *Recreations:* genealogy, home computing, gardening, horse riding. *Address:* c/o Foreign and Commonwealth Office, King Charles Street, SW1A 2AH. *Club:* Madras (Chennai).

HERRIES OF TERREGLES, Lady (14th in line, of the Lordship *cr* 1490); **Anne Elizabeth Fitzalan-Howard;** *b* 12 June 1938; *e d* of 16th Duke of Norfolk, KG, GCVO, GBE, TD, PC, and Lavinia Duchess of Norfolk, LG, CBE (*d* 1995); *S* to lordship upon death of father, 1975; *m* 1985, Colin Cowdrey (Baron Cowdrey of Tonbridge, CBE; *d* 2000). Racehorse trainer. *Recreations:* riding, golf, breeding spaniels. *Heir: sister* Lady Mary Katharine Mumford, *qv*. *Address:* Angmering Park, Littlehampton, West Sussex BN16 4EX. *T:* (01903) 871421.

HERRING, Cyril Alfred; management consultant; Senior Partner, Cyril Herring & Associates, since 1978; Chairman and Managing Director, Southern Airways Ltd, since 1978; *b* Dulwich, 17 Jan. 1915; *s* of Alfred James Herring and Minnie Herring (*née* Padfield); *m* 1939, Helen (*née* Warnes); three *s*. *Educ:* Alleyn's Sch.; London School of Economics. BSc(Econ); FCMA; JDipMA; IPFA; FCIT; FILT. Chief Accountant, Straight Corporation Ltd, 1936–46; joined BEA, 1946; Chief Accountant, 1951–57; Personnel Director, 1957–65; Financial Director, 1965–71; Executive Board Member, 1971–74; Mem., British Airways Bd, 1972–78; Chief Executive, British Airways Regional Div., 1972–74; Finance Dir, 1975–78; Chm. and Man. Dir, British Air Services Ltd, 1969–76; Chairman: Northeast Airlines Ltd, 1969–76; Cambrian Airways Ltd, 1973–76; London Rail Adv. Cttee, 1976–80; CIPFA Public Corporations Finance Group, 1976–78. Member Council: Chartered Inst. of Transport, 1971–74; Inst. of Cost and Management Accountants, 1967–77 (Vice-Pres., 1971–73, Pres., 1973–74); CBI, 1975–78 (Mem. Financial Policy Cttee, 1975–78, Finance and General Purposes Cttee, 1977–78). Freeman, City of London; Liveryman, GAPAN. *Recreations:* flying, motoring, boating. *Address:* Cuddenbeake, St Germans, Cornwall PL12 5LY. *Club:* Reform.

HERRINGTON, Air Vice-Marshal Walter John, CB 1982; Royal Air Force, retired; *b* 18 May 1928; *s* of Major H. Herrington, MBE, MM and Daisy Restal Gardiner; *m* 1958, Joyce Maureen Cherryman; two *s*. *Educ:* Woking Grammar Sch.; RAF Coll., Cranwell. Commnd RAF, 1949, Pilot; 1950–69: Long Range Transp. Sqdns 24, 53, 99; ADC to C-in-C Bomber Comd; Reconnaissance Sqdns; RAF Staff Coll.; Exchange Officer, USAF Acad., Colo; Comd 100 Sqdn; Jt Services Staff Coll.; Air Sec.'s Dept; Stn Comdr RAF Honnington, 1969–71; Ops Dept, MoD, 1971–73; RCDS (student) 1974; Defence Attaché, Paris, 1975–77. Hon. ADC to the Queen, 1971–74; Senior RAF Mem., Directing Staff, RCDS, 1978–80; Dir of Service Intelligence, 1980–82. Aviation Advr, Internat. Mil. Services, 1982–89; aviation and security consultant, 1989–95. Member: European Security Study Gp, 1982–83; Central Council, TA&VRA, 1984–90; Council, Officers Pensions Soc., 1983–89. *Publications:* The Future for the Defence Industry, 1991; text books for courses on air power for USAF Academy. *Recreations:* reading, international affairs, sport. *Club:* Royal Air Force.

HERRMANN, Georgina, DPhil; FBA 1999; Reader in the Archaeology of Western Asia, University College London, 1993–Sept. 2002; *b* 20 Oct. 1937; *d* of John Walker Thompson and Gladys Elaine Thompson; *m* 1965, Prof. Luke John Herrmann; two *s*. *Educ:* Inst. of Archaeology, Univ. of London (post-grad. dip. 1963); St Hugh's Coll., Oxford (DPhil 1966). FSA 1968. Sec., Foreign Office, 1956–61; J. R. MacIver Jun. Res. Fellow, Oxford, 1966–68; Calouste Gulbenkian Fellow, Cambridge, 1974–76; Regents' Prof., Univ. of Calif at Berkeley, 1986; Leverhulme Res. Fellow, 1989–91; part-time Lecturer: Inst. of Archaeology, London Univ., 1985–91; in Mesopotamian Archaeology, UCL, 1991–93. Dir, excavations at Merv, Turkmenistan, 1992–2001. Hon. Foreign

Mem., Amer. Inst. of Archaeology, 1997. Editor, Iran (jl of British Inst. of Persian Studies), 1966–81. Laureate, Rolex Award for Enterprise, 1996. *Publications:* Ivories from Nimrud, III (with M. Mallowan), 1974, IV, 1986, V, 1992; The Iranian Revival, 1977; Iranische Denkmaler (recording Sasanian rock reliefs), 8–11, 1977–83, and 13, 1989; (ed) Furniture of Western Asia, Ancient and Traditional, 1996; Monuments of Merv I, 1999. *Recreations:* planting trees, walking. *Address:* The Coombes, Sibbertoft, Market Harborough, Leics LE16 9TZ. *T:* (01858) 880872.

HERROD, His Honour Donald; QC 1972; a Circuit Judge, 1978–95; *b* 7 Aug. 1930; *o s* of Wilfred and Phyllis Herrod, Doncaster; *m* 1959, Kathleen Elaine Merrington, MB, ChB; two *d.* *Educ:* grammar schs, Doncaster and Leeds. Called to the Bar, 1956. A Recorder of the Crown Court, 1972–78. Member: Parole Bd, 1978–81; Judicial Studies Bd, 1982–86. *Recreation:* golf.

HERRON, Very Rev. Andrew; Clerk to the Presbytery of Glasgow, 1959–81; Editor, Church of Scotland Year Book, 1961–92; *b* 29 Sept. 1909; *s* of John Todd Herron and Mary Skinner Hunter; *m* 1935, Joanna Fraser Neill; four *d.* *Educ:* Glasgow Univ. (MA, BD, LLB). ATCL 1930. Minister: at Linwood, 1936–40, at Houston and Killellan, 1940–59; Clerk to the Presbytery of Paisley, 1953–59; Moderator of General Assembly of Church of Scotland, 1971–72. Convener: Dept of Publicity and Publications, 1959–68; Gen. Admin Cttee; Business Cttee, Gen. Assembly, 1972–76, 1978; Gen. Trustee, Church of Scotland. Barclay Trust Lectr, 1989. Hon. DD: St Andrews, 1975; Glasgow, 1989. Hon. LLD Strathclyde, 1983. *Publications:* Record Apart, 1974; Guide to the General Assembly of the Church of Scotland, 1976; Guide to Congregational Affairs, 1978; Guide to Presbytery, 1983; Kirk by Divine Right (Baird lectures), 1985; A Guide to the Ministry, 1987; A Guide to Ministerial Income, 1987; Minority Report, 1990; Houston and Killellan: a handful of yesterdays, 1993; The Law and Practice of the Kirk: a guide and commentary, 1995; Inter Alia, 1995; Kirk Lore, 1999; Laughing Matters, 2000.

HERSCHBACH, Prof. Dudley Robert; Baird Professor of Science, Harvard University, since 1976; *b* 18 June 1932; *s* of Robert D. Herschbach and Dorothy E. Herschbach; *m* 1964, Georgene L. Botyos; two *d.* *Educ:* Campbell High School; Stanford Univ. (BS Math 1954, MS Chem 1955); Harvard Univ. (AM Physics 1956, PhD Chem Phys 1958). Junior Fellow, Soc. of Fellows, Harvard, 1957–59; Asst Prof., 1959–61, Associate Prof., 1961–63, Univ. of California, Berkeley; Prof. of Chemistry, Harvard Univ., 1963–76. Hon. DSc: Univ. of Toronto, 1977; Dartmouth Coll., 1992; Charles Univ., Prague, 1993; Wheaton Coll., 1995; Franklin & Marshall Coll., 1998. (Jtly) Nobel Prize for Chemistry, 1986; US Nat. Medal of Sci., 1991; Heyrovský Medal, Czech Acad. of Scis, 1992; Walker Prize, Boston Mus. of Sci., 1994. *Publications:* over 350 research papers, chiefly on quantum mechanics, chemical kinetics, reaction dynamics, molecular spectroscopy, collision theory, in Jl of Chemical Physics. *Recreations:* hiking, canoeing, chess, poetry, viola. *Address:* 116 Conant Road, Lincoln, MA 01773, USA. *T:* (home) (781) 2591386; (office) (617) 4953218.

HERSCHELL, family name of **Baron Herschell**.

HERSCHELL, 3rd Baron *cr* 1886; **Rognvald Richard Farrer Herschell;** late Captain Coldstream Guards; *b* 13 Sept. 1923; *o s* of 2nd Baron and Vera (*d* 1961), *d* of Sir Arthur Nicolson, 10th Bt, of that Ilk and Lasswade; *S* father, 1929; *m* 1940, Lady Heather, *d* of 8th Earl of Dartmouth, CVO, DSO; one *d.* *Educ:* Eton. Page of Honour to the King, 1935–40. Served World War II, 1942–45. *Heir:* none. *Address:* Westfield House, Ardington, Wantage, Oxon OX12 8PN. *T:* (01235) 833224.
See also J. P. Kiszely.

HERSEY, David Kenneth; lighting designer; founder Chairman, DHA Lighting, since 1972; *b* 30 Nov. 1939; *s* of Ella Morgan Decker and C. Kenneth Hersey; *m* Demetra Maraslis; one *s* two *d.* *Educ:* Oberlin Coll., Ohio. Left NY for London, 1968; lighting designer for theatre, opera and ballet cos, incl. Royal Opera House, ENO, Glyndebourne, Ballet Rambert, London Contemporary Dance, Scottish Ballet; lighting consultant to Nat. Theatre, 1974–84; many productions for RSC. Chm., Assoc. of Lighting Designers, 1984–86. *Designs include:* Evita, 1978 (Tony award, 1980); Nicholas Nickleby, 1980; Cats, 1981 (Tony and Drama Desk awards, 1983); Song and Dance, 1982; Guys and Dolls, 1982; Starlight Express, 1984; Les Misérables, 1985 (Tony award, 1987); Porgy and Bess, 1986; Chess, 1986; Miss Saigon, 1989 (Drama Desk award, 1991); Oliver, 1995; Martin Guerre, Jesus Christ Superstar, 1996; My Fair Lady, 2001. Olivier Award for best lighting designer, 1995. *Recreation:* sailing (Millennium Odyssey Round the World Yacht Rally, 1998–2000). *Address:* DHA Lighting Ltd, 284–302 Waterloo Road, SE1 8RQ.

HERTFORD, 9th Marquess of, *cr* 1793; **Henry Jocelyn Seymour;** Baron Conway of Ragley 1703; Baron Conway of Killultagh 1712; Earl of Hertford, Viscount Beauchamp 1750; Earl of Yarmouth 1793; *b* 6 July 1958; *s* of 8th Marquess of Hertford and of Comtesse Louise de Caraman Chimay; *S* father, 1997; *m* 1990, Beatriz, *d* of Jorge Karam; two *s* two *d.* Heir: s Earl of Yarmouth, *qv.*

HERTFORD, Bishop Suffragan of, since 2001; **Rt Rev. Christopher Richard James Foster;** *b* 7 Nov. 1953; *s* of Joseph James Frederick Foster and Elizabeth Foster (*née* Gibbs); *m* 1982, Julia Marie Jones (*d* 2001); one *s* one *d.* *Educ:* University Coll., Univ. of Durham (BA 1975); Univ. of Manchester (MA (Econ.) 1977); Trinity Hall, Cambridge (BA 1979, MA 1983); Westcott House, Cambridge. Lectr in Economics, Univ. of Durham, 1976–77; ordained deacon, 1980, priest, 1981; Asst Curate, Tettenhall Regis, Wolverhampton, 1980–82; Chaplain, Wadham Coll., Oxford and Asst Priest, Univ. Church of St Mary, with St Cross and St Peter in the East, Oxford, 1982–86; Vicar, Christ Church, Southgate, London, 1986–94; CME Dir, Edmonton Episcopal Area, 1988–94; Sub Dean and Canon Residentiary, Cathedral and Abbey Church of St Alban, 1994–2001. *Address:* Hertford House, Abbey Mill Lane, St Albans, Herts AL3 4HE. *T:* (01727) 866420.

HERTFORD, Archdeacon of; *see* Jones, Ven. T. P.

HERTRICH, Rainer; President and Chief Executive Officer, DaimlerChrysler Aerospace AG, since 2000; Co-Chief Executive Officer, European Aeronautic Defence and Space Company, since 2000; *b* 6 Dec. 1949. *Educ:* apprenticeship and business training, Siemens AG; Technical Univ. of Berlin; Univ. of Nuremberg (Bachelor of Commerce). Messerschmitt-Bölkow-Blohm GmbH: Information Processing Supervisor, Controlling Dept, Mil. Aircraft Div. 1977; Hd, Controlling Dept, 1978, CFO, 1983, Service Div. (Ottobrunn); Hd, Controlling and Finance Dept, Dynamics Div. 1984; CFO and Mem. Div. Mgt, Marine and Special Products Div. 1987; DaimlerBenz Aerospace: Hd of Divl Controlling, Central Controlling Section, Deutsche Aerospace AG, 1990; Sen. Vice Pres., Corporate Controlling, 1991; Hd, Aeroengines business unit, 1996; Mem., Exec. Cttee, 1996–; President and CEO, Motorentund Turbinen Union München GmbH, 1996. *Address:* European Aeronautic Defence and Space Company NV, Drentastraat 24, 1083 HK Amsterdam, Netherlands.

HERVEY, family name of **Marquess of Bristol**.

HERVEY, Rear Adm. John Bethell, CB 1982; OBE 1970; independent naval consultant; *b* 14 May 1928; *s* of late Captain Maurice William Bethell Hervey, RN, and Mrs Joan Hervey (*née* Hanbury); *m* 1950, (Audrey) Elizabeth Mote; two *s* one *d.* *Educ:* Marlborough Coll., Wilts. Joined RN, 1946; specialised in submarines, 1950, nuclear submarines, 1968; command appointments: HMS Miner VI, 1956; HMS Aeneas, 1956–57; HMS Ambush, 1959–62; HMS Oracle, 1962–64; Sixth Submarine Div., 1964–66; HMS Cavalier, 1966–67; HMS Warspite, 1968–69; Second Submarine Sqdn, 1973–75; HMS Kent, 1975–76; staff appointments: Course Officer, Royal Naval Petty Officers Leadership Sch., 1957–59; Submarine Staff Officer to Canadian Maritime Comdr, Halifax, NS, 1964–66; Ops Officer to Flag Officer Submarines, 1970–71; Def. Op. Requirements Staff, 1971–73; Dep. Chief of Allied Staff to C-in-C Channel and C-in-C Eastern Atlantic (as Cdre), 1976–80; Comdr British Navy Staff, and British Naval Attaché, Washington, and UK Nat. Liaison Rep. to SACLANT, 1980–82, retired. Comdr 1964, Captain 1970, Rear Adm. 1980. Marketing Vice-Pres., Western Hemisphere, MEL, 1982–86. Pres., HMS Cavalier Assoc., 1995–; Chm., Friends of RN Submarine Mus., 1995–99. FIMgt (FBIM 1983). *Publication:* Submarines, 1994. *Recreations:* walking, talking, reading. *Address:* c/o National Westminster Bank, 208 Piccadilly, W1A 2DG. *Clubs:* Army and Navy, Royal Navy of 1765 and 1785, Anchorites (Pres., 1988).

HERVEY, Sir Roger Blaise Ramsay, KCVO 1991; CMG 1980; HM Diplomatic Service; Ambassador to Mexico, 1992–94; *b* 3 Oct. 1934. HM Forces, 1953–55. Joined Diplomatic Service, 1958; Bonn, 1958; FO, 1961; Prague, 1963; First Sec., FO, 1965; Office of Political Advr, Singapore, 1968; FCO, 1970; First Sec. and Head of Chancery, Bogotá, 1974; Counsellor, FCO, 1976; Counsellor, The Hague, 1979; Minister, Madrid, 1982; Asst Under Sec. of State (Protocol) and Vice Marshal of Diplomatic Corps, 1986. *Address:* c/o Foreign and Commonwealth Office, SW1A 2AH.

HERVEY-BATHURST, Sir Frederick John Charles Gordon; *see* Bathurst.

HERZBERG, Charles Francis; consultant; Chairman, Unique Business Services Ltd (formerly Newcastle upon Tyne Polytechnic Products Ltd), 1988–95; *b* 26 Jan. 1924; *s* of Dr Franz Moritz Herzberg and Mrs Marie Louise Palache; *m* 1956, Ann Linette Hoare; one *s* two *d.* *Educ:* Fettes Coll., Edinburgh; Sidney Sussex Coll., Cambridge (MA). CEng, FIMechE, MIGasE. Alfred Herbert Ltd, 1947–51; Chief Engr and Dir, Hornflowa Ltd, Maryport, 1951–55; Chief Engr, Commercial Plastics Gp of Cos, and Dir, Commercial Plastics Engrg Co. at Wallsend on Tyne, North Shields, and Cramlington, Northumberland, 1955–66; Corporate Planning Dir, Appliance Div., United Gas Industries, and Works Dir, Robinson Willey Ltd, Liverpool, 1966–70; Man. Dir and Chief Exec., Churchill Gear Machines Ltd, Blaydon on Tyne, 1970–72; Regional Industrial Director, Dept of Industry, N Region, 1972–75; Dir of Corporate Develt, Clarke Chapman Ltd, 1975–77; Gp Industrial Planning Adviser, 1977–84, Dir Industrial Planning, 1984–88, Northern Engineering Industries plc; Dir, Northern Investors Co. Ltd, 1984–89; Pres., Tyne & Wear Chamber of Commerce and Industry, 1989–90 (Vice-Pres., 1986–89). Gov., Univ. of Northumbria (formerly Newcastle upon Tyne Poly.), 1986–96 (Hon. Fellow, 1991). *Recreation:* shooting. *Address:* 3 Furzefield Road, Gosforth, Newcastle upon Tyne NE3 4EA. *T:* (0191) 285 5202. *Club:* East India, Devonshire, Sports and Public Schools.

HERZOG, Roman, Hon. GCB 1998; President of the Federal Republic of Germany, 1994–99; *b* 5 April 1934; *m* 1958, Christiane Krauss; two *s.* *Educ:* Munich, Berlin and Tübingen Univs. DJur. Lecturer: in Law, Munich Univ., 1958–66; in Law and Politics, Free Univ. of Berlin, 1966–69 (Dean, Faculty of Law, 1967–68); Prof. of Politics, 1969–73, Rector, 1971–73, Postgrad. Sch. of Admin. Scis, Speyer. Rep. of Rhineland-Palatinate, Bundestag, 1973–78; Minister for Culture and Sport, 1978–80, for the Interior, 1980–83, Baden-Württemberg; Vice-Pres, 1983–87, Pres., 1987–94, Federal Constitutional Court. Mem. Federal Cttee, CDU, 1979–83. DCL Oxon, 1997. *Publications:* (jtly) Kommentar zur Grundgesetz, 1966, 3rd edn 1987; Allgemeine Staatslehre, 1971; Staaten der Frühzeit, 1988; Ursprünge und Herr-schaftsformen, 1988; Staat und Recht im Wandel, 1993; Preventing the Clash of Civilizations: a peace strategy for the 21st century, 1999; vols of collected speeches. *Address:* (office) Prinzregentenstrasse 89, 81675 Munich, Germany.

HESELTINE, family name of **Baron Heseltine**.

HESELTINE, Baron *cr* 2001 (Life Peer), of Thenford in the County of Northamptonshire; **Michael Ray Dibdin Heseltine,** CH 1997; PC 1979; *b* 21 March 1933; *s* of late Col R. D. Heseltine, Swansea, Glamorgan; *m* 1962, Anne Harding Williams; one *s* two *d.* *Educ:* Shrewsbury Sch.; Pembroke Coll., Oxford (BA PPE; Hon. Fellow 1986). Pres. Oxford Union, 1954. National Service (commissioned), Welsh Guards, 1959. Director of Bow Publications, 1961–65; Chm., Haymarket Press, 1966–70; Dir, Haymarket Publishing Gp, 1997–. Contested (C): Gower, 1959; Coventry North, 1964. MP (C): Tavistock, 1966–74; Henley, 1974–2001. Vice-Chm., Cons. Parly Transport Cttee, 1968; Opposition Spokesman on Transport, 1969; Parly Sec., Min. of Transport, June-Oct. 1970; Parly Under-Sec. of State, DoE, 1970–72; Minister for Aerospace and Shipping, DTI, 1972–74; Opposition Spokesman on: Industry, 1974–76; Environment, 1976–79; Sec. of State for the Environment, 1979–83 and 1990–92, for Defence, 1983–86; Pres., BoT, 1992–95; First Sec. of State and Dep. Prime Minister, 1995–97. Chairman: Cons. Mainstream, 1998–; Anglo-China Forum, 1998–. Mem., Millennium Fund Commn, 1995–. Pres., Assoc. of Conservative Clubs, 1978; Vice-Pres., 1978, Pres., 1982–84, Nat. Young Conservatives; Pres., Conservative Gp for Europe, 2001. Mem. Council, Zoological Soc. of London, 1987–90. Patron, Nat. Centre for Competitiveness, Univ. of Luton, 2001. Hon. Fellow: Leeds Polytechnic, 1988; Univ. of Wales, Swansea, 2001. Hon. FRIBA 1991; Hon. FCIM 1998. Hon. LLD Liverpool, 1990. *Publications:* Reviving the Inner Cities, 1983; Where There's a Will, 1987; The Challenge of Europe, 1989; Life in the Jungle (memoirs), 2000. *Address:* c/o House of Lords, SW1A 0PW. *Club:* Carlton.

HESELTINE, Rt Hon. Sir William (Frederick Payne), GCB 1990 (KCB 1986; CB 1978); GCVO 1988 (KCVO 1982; CVO 1969; MVO 1961); AC 1988; QSO 1990; PC 1986; Deputy Chairman, P & O Australia Ltd, since 1998 (Director, since 1990); *b* E Fremantle, W Australia, 17 July 1930; *s* of late H. W. Heseltine; *m* 1st, Ann Elizabeth (*d* 1957), *d* of late L. F. Turner, Melbourne; 2nd, Audrey Margaret, *d* of late S. Nolan, Sydney; one *s* one *d.* *Educ:* Christ Church Grammar Sch., Claremont, WA; University of Western Australia (1st class hons, History). Prime Minister's dept, Canberra, 1951–62; Private Secretary to Prime Minister, 1955–59; Asst Information Officer to The Queen, 1960–61; Acting Official Secretary to Governor-General of Australia, 1962; Asst Federal Director of Liberal Party of Australia, 1962–64; attached to Household of Princess Marina for visit to Australia, 1964; attached to Melbourne Age, 1964; Asst Press Secretary to the Queen, 1965–67, Press Secretary, 1968–72; Assistant Private Secretary to the Queen, 1972–77, Dep. Private Secretary, 1977–86, Private Sec., and Keeper of the Queen's Archives, 1986–90. Chm., NZI Insurance Australia Ltd, 1992–98 (Dep. Chm., 1991–92); Director: West Coast Telecasters Ltd, 1991–96; NZI Insurance NZ, 1996–98. Pres., Royal Western Australian Histl Soc., 1998–2000. *Address:* PO Box 35, York, WA 6302, Australia. *Club:* Weld (Perth).

HESFORD, Stephen; MP (Lab) Wirral West, since 1997; *b* 27 May 1957; *s* of Bernard and Nellie Hesford; *m* 1984, Elizabeth Anne Henshall; two *s*. *Educ:* Univ. of Bradford (BScSoc Econs/Politics 1978); Poly. of Central London (Post-grad. Dip. in Law 1980). Called to the Bar, Gray's Inn, 1981. Contested (Lab) S Suffolk, 1992. Founder and Sec., All-Party Parly Gp on Primary Care and Public Health, 1998–; Mem., Health Select Cttee., 1999–. Mem. Bd, Mind, 1998. FRIPHH 1998; Fellow, Soc. of Public Health. Mem., IoD, 2001–. *Recreations:* watching sons play football, reading. *Address:* House of Commons, SW1A 0AA. *T:* (020) 7219 6227. *Club:* Lancashire County Cricket (Life Mem.).

HESKETH, 3rd Baron *cr* 1935, of Hesketh; **Thomas Alexander Fermor-Hesketh,** KBE 1997; PC 1991; Bt 1761; Chairman, British Mediterranean Airways, since 1994; *b* 28 Oct. 1950; *s* of 2nd Baron and Christian Mary, OBE 1984, *o d* of Sir John McEwen, 1st Bt of Marchmont, DL, JP; *S* father, 1955; *m* 1977, Hon. Claire, *e d* of 3rd Baron Manton, *qv*; one *s* two *d*. *Educ:* Ampleforth. A Lord in Waiting (Govt Whip), 1986–89; Parly Under-Sec. of State, DoE, 1989–90; Minister of State, DTI, 1990–91; Capt. of Gentlemen-at-Arms (Govt Chief Whip in H of L), 1991–93. Non-exec. Dep. Chm., Babcock Internat., 1993–; non-exec. Dir, British Aerospace, 1993–. Pres., British Racing Drivers' Club, 1994–99. Hon. FSE. *Heir: s* Hon. Frederick Hatton Fermor-Hesketh, *b* 13 Oct. 1988. *Address:* Easton Neston, Towcester, Northamptonshire NN12 7HS. *T:* (01327) 350445. *Clubs:* White's, Turf.

HESLAM, (Mary) Noelle, (Mrs David Heslam); *see* Walsh, M. N.

HESLOP, David Thomas, OBE 1987; CompIGasE; Regional Chairman, British Gas plc Southern, 1989–94; *b* 16 Sept. 1932; *s* of late John Heslop and Frances Mary (*née* Brooks); *m* 1952, Barbara Mary Seddon; one *s* one *d*. *Educ:* Henley Management Coll. (GMC 1974); Harvard Business Sch. (AMP 1981). CompIGasE 1990. Commercial Sales Officer, Scottish Gas, 1960; Marketing Develt Man., West Midlands Gas, 1965; Sales Man., South Eastern Gas, 1972; Dir of Sales, North Western Gas, 1976; HQ Dir of Sales, British Gas, 1982. Pres., Internat. Gas Marketing Colloquium, 1986–89. FCIM 1977; CIMgt (CBIM 1990). *Recreations:* chess, choral singing, walking, Rugby. *Address:* Prestolee, Rhinefield Road, Brockenhurst, Hants SO42 7SR.

HESLOP, Martin Sydney; QC 1995; Senior Treasury Counsel, since 1993; a Recorder of the Crown Court, since 1993; *b* 6 Aug. 1948; *s* of late Sydney Heslop and of Patricia (*née* Day); *m* 1994, Aurea Jane (*née* Boyle). *Educ:* St George's Coll., Weybridge; Bristol Univ. LLB Hons 1971. Called to the Bar, Lincoln's Inn, 1972; Jun. Treasury Counsel, 1987; First Jun. Treasury Counsel, 1992–93. Asst Recorder, 1989–93. *Recreations:* sailing, travel, photography. *Address:* 1 Hare Court, Temple, EC4Y 7BE. *T:* (020) 7353 5324. *Clubs:* Royal London Yacht, Bar Yacht.

HESLOP, Philip Linnell; QC 1985; *b* 24 April 1948; *s* of late Richard Norman Heslop and of Ina Winifred Heslop, Merstham, Surrey. *Educ:* Haileybury; Christ's Coll., Cambridge (schol.; BA Hons (Law Tripos) 1970; LLM 1971). Called to the Bar, Lincoln's Inn, 1970, Bencher, 1993; Jt Jun. Counsel (Chancery), DTI, 1979–85. Called to Bars of Hong Kong, Bermuda and Gibraltar for specific cases. Dep. Chm., Membership Tribunal, IMRO, 1988–; DTI Inspector, Consolidated Goldfields PLC. Chm., CU Cons. Assoc., 1969; Pres., Cambridge Union Soc., 1971; Chm., Coningsby Club, 1976; contested (C) Lambeth Vauxhall, 1979. *Publication:* (ed jtly) Crew on Meetings, 1975. *Recreations:* travel, sailing, ski-ing, history. *Address:* 4 Stone Buildings, Lincoln's Inn, WC2A 3XT. *T:* (020) 7242 5524.

HESSAYON, Dr David Gerald; gardening author; Chairman: Expert Publications Ltd, since 1988; Hessayon Books, since 1993; *b* 13 Feb. 1928; *s* of Jack and Lena Hessayon; *m* 1951, Joan Parker Gray (*d* 2001); two *d*. *Educ:* Salford Grammar Sch.; Leeds Univ. (BSc 1950); Manchester Univ. (PhD 1954). FRMS 1960; FRES 1960; FRSA 1970; FIBiol 1971; FIMgt (FBIM 1972); FIHort 1986. Res. Fellow, UC of Gold Coast, 1953. Pan Britannica Industries Ltd: Technical Man., 1955–60; Tech. Dir, 1960–64; Man. Dir, 1964–91; Chm., 1972–93; Chm., Turbair Ltd, 1972–93. Chm., British Agrochemicals Assoc., 1980–81. Vice-Patron, Royal Nat. Rose Soc., 1987–; Patron, Essex Gardens Trust, 1996–. Mem., Guild of Freemen, City of London, 1977–; Liveryman, Gardeners' Co., 1985. Hon. DSc: Manchester, 1990; Hertfordshire, 1994. Lifetime Achievement Trophy, Nat. British Book Awards, 1992; Veitch Gold Meml Medal, RHS, 1992. *Publications:* Be Your Own Gardening Expert, 1959, rev. edn 1977; Be Your Own House Plant Expert, 1960; Potato Growers Handbook, 1961; Silage Makers Handbook, 1961; Be Your Own Lawn Expert, 1962, rev. edn 1979; Be Your Own Rose Expert, 1964, rev. edn 1977; (with J. P. Hessayon) The Garden Book of Europe, 1973; Vegetable Plotter, 1976; Be Your Own House Plant Spotter, 1977; Be Your Own Vegetable Doctor, 1978; Be Your Own Garden Doctor, 1978; The House Plant Expert, 1980, rev. edn 1991; The Rose Expert, 1981, rev. edn 1996; The Lawn Expert, 1982, rev. edn 1997; The Cereal Disease Expert, 1982; The Tree and Shrub Expert, 1983; The Armchair Book of the Garden, 1983; The Flower Expert, 1984, rev. edn 1999; The Vegetable Expert, 1985; The Indoor Plant Spotter, 1985; The Garden Expert, 1986; The Gold Plated House Plant Expert, 1987; The Home Expert, 1987; Vegetable Jotter, 1989; Rose Jotter, 1989; House Plant Jotter, 1989; The Fruit Expert, 1990; Be Your Own Greenhouse Expert, 1990; The Bio Friendly Gardening Guide, 1990; The Bedding Plant Expert, 1991, rev. edn 1996; The Garden DIY Expert, 1992; The Rock and Water Garden Expert, 1993; The Flowering Shrub Expert, 1994; The Greenhouse Expert, 1994; The Flower Arranging Expert, 1994; The Container Expert, 1995; The Bulb Expert, 1995; The Easy-care Gardening Expert, 1995; The New Vegetable & Herb Expert, 1997; The Evergreen Expert, 1998; The Pocket Flower Expert, 2001; The Pocket Tree & Shrub Expert, 2001; The Pocket Garden Troubles Expert, 2001. *Recreations:* American folk music, cartophily, thinking about the book I should be writing. *Address:* c/o Transworld Publishers, 61–63 Uxbridge Road, W5 5SA.

HESSE, Prof. Joachim Jens, PhD; Founding Director, European Centre for Comparative Government and Public Policy, Berlin, since 1997; *b* 20 Nov. 1942; *s* of Joachim Hesse and Frieda Hesse (*née* Madrowski); *m* 1981, Irmgart Wethmar-von Hagen; one *s* one *d*. *Educ:* Schadow Gymnasium, Berlin; Univ. of Goettingen; Univ. of Kiel; Univ. of Berlin (Dipl. Volkswirt. 1967); Univ. of Cologne (PhD Econs 1972). Res. Associate, German Inst. of Urbanism, Berlin, 1968–73; Professor of: Pol and Admin. Scis, Univ. of Constance, 1973–77; Pol Sci. and Comparative Govt, Duisburg, 1978–83; Exec. Dir, Rhine–Ruhr Inst. for Social Res. and Public Policy Studies, 1980–84; Prof. of Pol and Admin. Scis, German Post-Grad. Sch. of Admin. Scis, Speyer, 1984–90; Prof. of Eur. Politics and Comparative Govt, and Fellow of Nuffield College, Oxford Univ., 1991–97. Vis. Prof., Coll. of Europe, Bruges, 1987–90; Visiting Scholar: Harvard Univ., 1984–85; Oxford Univ., 1988–89. Consultant: OECD, UN, EEC, ILO, World Bank, 1972–. Man. Editor, Staatswissenschaften und Staatspraxis, 1990–; Internat. Editor, Public Admin, 1992–95; General Editor: Jahrbuch zur Staatswissenschaft und Staatspraxis, 1987–; European Yearbook on Comparative Govt and Public Admin., 1994–. *Publications:* include: (ed) Local Government and Urban Affairs in International Perspective, 1991; Das Regierungssystem der Bundesrepublik Deutschland, 7th edn, 1992, 8th edn, 1997; Administrative Transformation in Central and Eastern Europe, 1993; Constitutional Policy and Change in Europe, 1995; Regions in Europe, 3 vols, 1996–; Der überforderte Staat, 1997. *Address:* European Centre for Comparative Government and Public Policy, Rheinbabenallee 49, 14199 Berlin, Germany; Nuffield College, Oxford OX1 1NF.

HESSE, Mary Brenda, MA, MSc, PhD; FBA 1971; Professor of Philosophy of Science, University of Cambridge, 1975–85; Fellow of Wolfson College (formerly University College), Cambridge, 1965–92, subseq. Hon. Fellow; *b* 15 Oct. 1924; *d* of Ethelbert Thomas Hesse and Brenda Nellie Hesse (*née* Pelling). *Educ:* Imperial Coll., London; University Coll., London. MSc, PhD (London); DIC; MA (Cantab). Lecturer: in Mathematics, Univ. of Leeds, 1951–55; in Hist. and Philosophy of Science, UCL, 1955–59; in Philosophy of Science, Univ. of Cambridge, 1960–68; Reader in Philosophy of Sci., Cambridge Univ., 1968–75; Vice-Pres., Wolfson Coll., 1976–80. Member: Council, British Acad., 1979–82; UGC, 1980–85. Visiting Professor: Yale Univ., 1961; Univ. of Minnesota, 1966; Univ. of Chicago, 1968. Stanton Lectr, Cambridge, 1977–80; Joint Gifford Lectr, Edinburgh, 1983. Pres., Cambridge Antiquarian Soc., 1996–98. Mem., Academia Europaea, 1989. Hon. DSc: Hull, 1984; Guelph, Ontario, 1987. Editor, Brit. Jl for the Philosophy of Science, 1965–69. *Publications:* Science and the Human Imagination, 1954; Forces and Fields, 1961; Models and Analogies in Science, 1963; The Structure of Scientific Inference, 1974; Revolutions and Reconstructions in the Philosophy of Science, 1980; (jtly) The Construction of Reality, 1987; articles in jls of philosophy and of the history and philosophy of science. *Recreations:* walking, landscape history and archaeology. *Address:* Wolfson College, Cambridge CB3 9BB. *Club:* Royal Commonwealth Society.

HESSELL TILTMAN, John, LVO 1997; Director of Property Services, HM Household, since 1996 (Deputy Director, 1991–96); *b* 27 Aug. 1942; *s* of Henry Hessell Tiltman and Rita Florence Hessell Tiltman; *m* 1969, Monique Yvonne Françoise Louge; one *s* one *d*. *Educ:* Brighton Coll.; Brighton Coll. of Art (DipArch 1965). ARIBA 1968. Project Architect, GLC, 1965–68; Property Services Agency, Department of the Environment, 1969–90: Project Architect, 1969–76; Project Manager: PO and BT works, 1976–82; RN works, 1982–85; Chief Architect, work in RN Trng Estabts, 1985–88; Hd of Royal Palaces Gp, 1988–90; Project Dir, reconstruction of fire-damaged areas of Windsor Castle, 1993–97. *Recreations:* performing and visual arts, oil painting, bridge, travel. *Address:* Apartment 4A, Clock Court, Kensington Palace, W8 4PU.

HESTER, Rev. Canon John Frear; Canon Residentiary and Precentor of Chichester Cathedral, 1985–97, Canon Emeritus 1997; Chaplain to the Queen, 1984–97; *b* 21 Jan. 1927; *s* of William and Frances Mary Hester; *m* 1959, Elizabeth Margaret, *d* of Sir Eric Riches, MC, MS, FRCS; three *s*. *Educ:* West Hartlepool Grammar School; St Edmund Hall, Oxford (MA); Cuddesdon Coll., Oxford. Captain RAEC, 1949–50. Personal Asst to Bishop of Gibraltar, 1950; Deacon, 1952; Priest, 1953; Assistant Curate: St George's, Southall, 1952–55; Holy Redeemer, Clerkenwell, 1955–58; Sec., Actors' Church Union, 1958–63; Chaplain, Soc. of the Sisters of Bethany, Lloyd Sq., 1959–62; Dep. Minor Canon of St Paul's Cathedral, 1962–75; Rector of Soho, 1963–75; Priest-in-charge of St Paul's, Covent Garden, 1969–75; Senior Chaplain, Actors' Church Union, 1970–75; Chaplain to Lord Mayor of Westminster, 1970–71; in residence at St George's Coll. and the Ecumenical Inst., Tantur, Jerusalem, 1973; Chm., Covent Garden Conservation Area Adv. Cttee, 1971–75; Vicar of Brighton, 1975–85; Canon and Prebendary of Chichester Cathedral, 1976–85; RD of Brighton, 1976–85; Commissary of the Bishop of Nakuru, 1991–2000. Chm., Chichester Diocesan Overseas Council, 1985–94. Editor, Christian Drama, 1957–59. Lectr and preacher, US, 1961–; Leader of Pilgrimages to the Holy Land, Turkey, etc, 1962–. Mem., Worshipful Co. of Parish Clerks, 1970–86; Mem., Oving Parish Council, 1999–. Chaplain, Brighton and Hove Albion FC, 1979–97; Vice-Pres., Actors' Church Union, 2000– (Southern Area Chaplain,1992–2000); Vice-Pres., 1979– and Hon. Chaplain, 1975–79 and 1988–, Royal Theatrical Fund (formerly Royal Gen. Theatrical Fund Assoc.). Chm. of Trustees, Chichester Centre of Arts, 1989–98; Chm., Chichester Arts Liaison Gp, 1990–95; Trustee, Chichester Fest. Theatre, 1990–; Pres., Forum Soc., 1985–2000; Vice-Pres., Sussex Guild (formerly Guild of Sussex Craftsmen), 1991–; Governor: Lavant House Sch., 1993–95; Lavant House Rosemead, 1995– (Chm. Govs, 1995–99). Hon. Life Mem., British Actors' Equity Assoc. Chichester Civic Award, 1996. *Publication:* Soho Is My Parish, 1970. *Recreations:* sitting down; pulling legs; watching soccer and other drama; Middle Eastern studies. *Address:* The Hovel, Oving, Chichester PO20 6DE. *T:* (01243) 782071; *e-mail:* thehovel@bigfoot.com.

HESTER, Prof. Ronald Ernest, DSc, PhD; CChem, FRSC; Professor of Chemistry, University of York, since 1983; *b* 8 March 1936; *s* of Ernest and Rhoda Hester; *m* 1958, Bridget Ann Maddin; two *s* two *d*. *Educ:* Royal Grammar Sch., High Wycombe; London Univ. (BSc; DSc 1979); Cornell Univ. (PhD 1962). CChem 1975; FRSC 1971. Res. Fellow, Cambridge Univ., 1962–63; Asst Prof., Cornell Univ., 1963–65; University of York: Lectr, 1965–71; Sen. Lectr, 1971–76; Reader, 1976–83. Science and Engineering Research Council: Chm., Chemistry Cttee, 1988–90; Mem., Science Bd, 1988–90; Mem., Council, 1990–94. Chm., Envmt Group, RSC, 1982–85. European Editor, BioSpectroscopy, 1994–. *Publications:* (jtly) Inorganic Chemistry, 1965; (ed with R. J. H. Clark) Advances in Infrared and Raman Spectroscopy, 12 vols, 1975–85; (ed with R. J. H. Clark) Advances in Spectroscopy, 14 vols, 1986–98; (ed with R. M. Harrison) Issues in Environmental Science and Technology, 16 vols, 1994–2001; 350 research papers. *Recreations:* tennis, squash, golf, ski-ing, paragliding, travel. *Address:* Department of Chemistry, University of York, York YO10 5DD. *T:* (01904) 432557.

HESTON, Charlton; actor (films, stage and television), USA; *b* Evanston, Ill, 4 Oct. 1924; *s* of Russell Whitford Carter and Lilla Carter (*née* Charlton); *m* 1944, Lydia Marie Clarke (actress), Two Rivers, Wisconsin; one *s* one *d*. *Educ:* New Trier High Sch., Ill; Sch. of Speech, Northwestern Univ., 1941–43. Served War of 1939–45, with 11th Army Air Forces in the Aleutians. Co-Dir (with wife), also both acting, Thomas Wolfe Memorial Theatre, Asheville, NC (plays: the State of the Union, The Glass Menagerie, etc). In Antony and Cleopatra, Martin Beck Theatre, New York, 1947; also acting on Broadway, 1949 and 1950, etc; London stage début (also dir.), The Caine Mutiny Court Martial, Queen's, 1985 (filmed, 1988); A Man for All Seasons, Savoy, 1987, tour 1988; (with wife) Love Letters, UK tour, 1997. *Films:* (1950–) include: Dark City, Ruby Gentry, The Greatest Show on Earth, Arrowhead, Bad For Each Other, The Savage, Pony Express, The President's Lady, Secret of the Incas, The Naked Jungle, The Far Horizons, The Private War of Major Benson, The Ten Commandments (Moses), The Big Country, Ben Hur (Acad. Award for best actor, 1959), The Wreck of the Mary Deare, El Cid, 55 Days at Peking, The Greatest Story Ever Told, Major Dundee, The Agony and the Ecstacy, Khartoum, Will Penny, Planet of the Apes, Soylent Green, The Three Musketeers, Earthquake, Airport 1975, The Four Musketeers, The Last Hard Men, Battle of Midway, Two-Minute Warning, Gray Lady Down, Crossed Swords, The Mountain Men, The Awakening, Mother Lode, Music Box, Treasure Island, Solar Crisis, True Lies, Alaska, Hamlet, Any Given Sunday. TV appearances, esp. in Shakespeare. Mem., Screen Actors' Guild (Pres., 1966–69); Mem., Nat. Council on the Arts, 1967–; Chm., Amer. Film Inst., 1961–; Chm., Center Theatre Group, LA, 1963; Chm. on the Arts for Presidential Task

Force on the Arts and Humanities, 1981–. Is interested in Shakespearian roles. Hon. Dr: Jacksonville Univ., Fla; Abilene Christian Univ., Texas. Academy Award, 1978; Jean Hersholt Humanitarian Award, 1978. *Publications:* (ed Hollis Alpert) The Actor's Life: Journals 1956–1976, 1979; Beijing Diary, 1990; In the Arena (autobiog.), 1995. *Club:* All England Lawn Tennis.

HETHERINGTON, Sir Arthur (Ford), Kt 1974; DSC 1944; FREng; Chairman, British Gas Corporation, 1973–76 (Member 1961, Deputy Chairman 1967–72, Chairman 1972, Gas Council); *b* 12 July 1911; *s* of late Sir Roger Hetherington and Lady Hetherington; *m* 1937, Margaret Lacey; one *s* one *d*. *Educ:* Highgate Sch.; Trinity Coll., Cambridge (BA). Joined staff of Gas Light & Coke Company, 1935. Served War, RNVR, 1941–45. North Thames Gas Board, 1945–55; joined staff of Southern Gas Board, 1955; Deputy Chairman, 1956; Chairman 1961–64; Chairman, E Midlands Gas Board, 1964–66. FREng (FEng 1976). Hon. FIGasE. Hon. DSc London, 1974. *Address:* 32 Connaught Square, W2 2HL. *T:* (020) 7723 3128. *Club:* Athenæum.

HETHERINGTON, Stephen; Director, Hetherington Seelig, since 1981; *b* 20 May 1949; *s* of Jack Hetherington and Constance Alice, (Billie), Hetherington (*née* Harper); three *d*. *Educ:* Northern Sch. of Music; Royal Acad. of Music. Freelance trumpeter, with symphony orchs, incl. LSO, Philharmonia, CBSO, ENO and London Festival Ballet, 1969–75. Formed Hetherington Seelig (with J. Seelig), 1981: co. presented opera, ballet, theatre and music worldwide, and manages theatres, incl. Wycombe Swan Th.; consultant to govts and cultural instns; formed business plans for Lowry Project (Nat. Landmark Millennium Project for the Arts), 1995, Chief Exec., 1996–2000; currently working on major urban regeneration projects, and leading Birmingham CC's bid to become Eur. Capital of Culture, 2008. *Recreations:* sailing, flying. *Address: e-mail:* old.gaffer@virgin.net.

HETHERINGTON, Sir Thomas Chalmers, (Tony), KCB 1979; CBE 1970; TD; QC 1978; Director of Public Prosecutions, 1977–87; Head of the Crown Prosecution Service, 1986–87; *b* 18 Sept. 1926; *er s* of William and Alice Hetherington; *m* 1953, June Margaret Ann Catliff; four *d*. *Educ:* Rugby Sch.; Christ Church, Oxford. Served in Royal Artillery, Middle East, 1945–48; Territorial Army, 1948–67. Called to Bar, Inner Temple, 1952; Bencher, 1978. Legal Dept, Min. of Pensions and Nat. Insce, 1953; Law Officers' Dept, 1962, Legal Sec., 1966–75; Dep. Treasury Solicitor, 1975–77. Jt Head, War Crimes Inquiry, 1988–89. Trustee, Maxwell Pension Trust, 1995–97. Pres., Old Rugbeians Soc., 1988–90. *Publication:* Prosecution and the Public Interest, 1989. *Address:* Rosemount, Mount Pleasant Road, Lingfield, Surrey RH7 6BH. *T:* (01342) 833923.

HETZEL, Phyllis Bertha Mabel, (Mrs R. D. Hetzel, jr); Registrar of the Roll, and Bye-Fellow, Newnham College, Cambridge, 1993–98; President, Lucy Cavendish College, Cambridge, 1979–84; *b* 10 June 1918; *d* of Stanley Ernest and Bertha Myson; *m* 1st, 1941, John Henry Lewis James (*d* 1962); one *d*; 2nd, 1974, Baron Bowden (marr. diss. 1983, he *d* 1989); 3rd, 1985, Ralph Dorn Hetzel (*d* 1994). *Educ:* Wimbledon High Sch.; Newnham Coll., Cambridge (MA). Commonwealth (now Harkness) Fellow, 1957–58. BoT, 1941; Principal 1947; Asst Sec., 1960; DEA, 1964–69; Min. of Technology, 1969–70; Dept of Trade and Industry, 1970–75; Asst Under-Sec. of State 1972; Regional Dir, NW Region, DTI, subseq. DoI, 1972–75. Member: Monopolies and Mergers Commn, 1975–78; Local Govt Boundary Commn for England, 1977–81; W Midlands Cttee, National Trust, 1970–81. Chm., Manchester, Marriage Guidance Council, 1976–79. Member: Court, Manchester Univ., 1976–83; Court and Council, UMIST, 1978–80; Council of Senate, Cambridge Univ., 1983–84; Bd, American Friends of Cambridge University Inc., 1985–98. Vice-Pres., Oxford and Cambridge Club of Los Angeles, 1986–92. *Publications:* The Concept of Growth Centres, 1968; Gardens through the Ages, 1971; Regional Policy in Action, 1980; contrib. Public Administration, Cambridge Review, Encycl. Britannica. *Recreations:* landscape architecture, conservation, writing, piano, family. *Address:* 18 Trafalgar Road, Cambridge CB4 1EU. *T:* (01223) 369878; Newnham College, Cambridge CB3 9DF.

HEWARD, Edmund Rawlings, CB 1984; Chief Master of the Supreme Court (Chancery Division), 1980–85 (Master, 1959–79); *b* 19 Aug. 1912; *s* of late Rev. Thomas Brown Heward and Kathleen Amy Rachel Rawlings; *m* 1945, Constance Mary Sandiford, *d* of late George Bertram Crossley, OBE. *Educ:* Repton; Trinity Coll., Cambridge. Admitted a solicitor, 1937. Enlisted Royal Artillery as a Gunner, 1940; released as Major, DAAG, 1946. Partner in Rose, Johnson and Hicks, 9 Suffolk St, SW1, 1946. LLM 1960. *Publications:* Guide to Chancery Practice, 1962 (5th edn 1979); Matthew Hale, 1972; (ed) Part 2, Tristram and Coote's Probate Practice, 24th edn, 1973, 26th edn, 1983; (ed) Judgments and Orders in Halsbury's Laws of England, 4th edn; Lord Mansfield, 1979, paperback 1985; Chancery Practice, 1983, 2nd edn 1990; Chancery Orders, 1986; Lord Denning—A Biography, 1990, 2nd edn 1997; Masters in Ordinary, 1991; The Great and the Good—a life of Lord Radcliffe, 1995; A Victorian Law Reformer—a life of Lord Selborne, 1998; Lives of the Judges: Jessel, Cairns, Bowen and Bramwell, 2001. *Address:* 36a Dartmouth Row, Greenwich, SE10 8AW. *T:* (020) 8692 3525. *Clubs:* Oxford and Cambridge, Travellers.

HEWES, Robin Anthony Charles; Chief Executive, New Millennium Experience Co., 2001 (Finance Director, 2000–01); *b* 15 April 1945; *s* of late Leslie Augustus Hewes and Lily Violet Hewes (*née* Norfolk); *m* 1967, Christine Diane Stonebridge; one *s* two *d*. *Educ:* Colchester Royal Grammar School; Bristol Univ. (LLB Hons 1966). Inspector of Taxes, 1966; Department of Industry, 1974; Cabinet Office (Management and Personnel Office), 1985–87; Dir, Enterprise and Deregulation Unit, DTI, 1987–88; Lloyd's of London: Head, later Dir, Regulatory Services, 1988–94 (nominated Member, Council of Lloyd's and Lloyd's Regulatory Bd, 1993–94); Dir, Finance and Mem., Lloyd's Mkt Bd, 1994–2000. Non-exec. Dir, Comforto-Vickers (formerly Vickers Business Equipment Div.), 1984–88. Lloyd's Silver Medal, 1996. *Address:* 38 Plovers Mead, Wyatts Green, Brentwood, Essex CM15 0PS. *T:* (01277) 822891.

HEWETSON, Ven. Christopher; Archdeacon of Chester, 1994–Aug. 2002; *b* 1 June 1937; *s* of Edward and Mary Hewetson; *m* 1963, Alison Mary Croft; four *d*. *Educ:* Shrewsbury Sch.; Trinity Coll., Oxford (MA); Chichester Theol Coll. Assistant Master: Dragon Sch., Oxford, 1960–64 and 1966–67; The Craig, Windermere, 1964–66. Ordained deacon, 1969, priest, 1970; Assistant Curate: SS Peter and Paul, Leckhampton, 1969–71; All Saints, Wokingham, 1971–73; Vicar, St Peter's, Didcot, 1973–82; Rector, All Saints, Ascot Heath, 1982–90; Chaplain, St George's Sch., Ascot, 1985–88; RD, Bracknell, 1986–90; Priest i/c, Holy Trinity, Headington Quarry, 1990–94; Hon. Canon, Christ Church, Oxford, 1992–94; RD, Cowley, 1994. Chester Cath. Chapter, 2001. *Recreations:* fell walking, old houses, opera. *Address:* 8 Queens Park Road, Chester CH4 7AD. *T:* (01244) 675417.

HEWETSON, Sir Christopher (Raynor), Kt 1984; TD 1967; DL; Partner, Lace Mawer (formerly Laces), Solicitors, Liverpool, 1961–95; President, Law Society, 1983–84; *b* 26 Dec. 1929; *s* of Harry Raynor Hewetson and Emma Hewetson; *m* 1962, Alison May Downie, *d* of late Prof. A. W. Downie, FRCP, FRS; two *s* one *d*. *Educ:* Sedbergh Sch.; Peterhouse, Cambridge (MA). National Service, 2nd Lieut 4th RHA, 1951–53; Territorial Service, 1953–68: Lt-Col commanding 359 Medium Regt, RA, TA, 1965–68. Qualified as solicitor, 1956. Mem. Council, Law Society, 1966–87; Vice-Pres., 1982–83; President, Liverpool Law Society, 1976. Gov., Coll. of Law, 1969–94 (Chm., 1977–82). Hon. Col, 33 Signal Regt (V), 1992–94. DL Merseyside, 1986, High Sheriff, Merseyside, 1998. *Recreations:* golf, walking, music. *Address:* 24c Westcliffe Road, Birkdale, Southport, Merseyside PR8 2BU. *T:* (01704) 567179. *Clubs:* Army and Navy; Athenæum (Pres., 1997–98) (Liverpool); Royal Birkdale Golf (Capt., 1993–94) (Southport).

HEWETT, Sir Richard Mark John, 7th Bt *cr* 1813, of Nether Seale, Leicestershire; Western Geco, since 2000; *b* 15 Nov. 1958; *er s* of Sir Peter John Smithson Hewett, 6th Bt, MM and of Jennifer Ann Cooper Hewett; *S* father, 2001. *Educ:* Bradfield Coll.; Jesus Coll., Cambridge (BA Nat. Scis 1980). Career in geophysical software develt; Seismograph Service Ltd, 1980–91; Schlumberger Geco Prakla, 1991–2000; Western Geco, 2000–. *Recreations:* filk music, SF, choral singing, folk harp, astronomy. *Heir: b* David Patrick John Hewett [*b* 24 June 1968; *m* 1997, Kate Elizabeth Ormand; one *s* one *d*]. *Address:* 118 Lovibonds Avenue, Orpington, Kent BR6 8EN. *T:* (01689) 851472.

HEWETT, Major Richard William; Senior Vice President and Director, International Operations, Reader's Digest Association Inc., 1986–88; *b* 22 Oct. 1923; *s* of late Brig. W. G. Hewett, OBE, MC, and Louise S. Hewett (*née* Wolfe); *m* 1954, Rosemary Cridland; two *d*. *Educ:* Wellington Coll., Berks. Enlisted RA, 1941; commnd RA, 1943; regular commn 1944: served Normandy, India, UK, Malaya; regtl duty, flying duties Air OP, Instr, OCTU, Mons, 1954; sc 1955; Staff and regtl duties, Germany, 1956–59; Mil. Mission, USA, 1959–61. Joined Reader's Digest Assoc. Ltd, 1962; Dir 1976; Man. Dir, 1981–84; Chm. and Man. Dir, 1984–86. *Recreations:* tennis, fishing, travelling.

HEWISH, Prof. Antony, MA, PhD; FRS 1968; FInstP; Professor of Radioastronomy, University of Cambridge, 1971–89, now Emeritus (Reader, 1969–71); Fellow of Churchill College since 1962; *b* 11 May 1924; *s* of late Ernest William Hewish and Frances Grace Lanyon Pinch; *m* 1950, Marjorie Elizabeth Catherine Richards; one *s* one *d*. *Educ:* King's Coll., Taunton; Gonville and Caius Coll., Cambridge (BA 1948, MA 1950, PhD 1952; Hamilton Prize, Isaac Newton Student, 1952; Hon. Fellow, 1976). FInstP 1998. RAE Farnborough, 1943–46; Research Fellow, Gonville and Caius Coll., 1952–54; Asst Dir of Research, 1954–62; Fellow, Gonville and Caius Coll., 1955–62; Lectr in Physics, Univ. of Cambridge, 1962–69. Dir, Mullard Radio Astronomy Observatory, Cambridge, 1982–87. Visiting Prof. in Astronomy, Yale, 1963; Prof. of the Royal Instn, 1977; Vikram Sarabhai Prof., Physical Res. Lab., Ahmedabad, India, 1988. Lectures: Karl Schwarzschild, Bonn, 1971; Lindsay Meml, Maryland, 1972; Larmor, Cambridge, 1973; Harland, Exeter, 1974; Kelvin, IEE, 1975; Halley, Oxford, 1979; Selby, Cardiff, 1983; Krishnan Meml, New Delhi, 1989; Gold, Cornell, 1992; Saha Meml, Calcutta, 1993; Birla Meml, Hyderabad, 1993; Waynick Meml, Penn State, 2000. Foreign Mem., Belgian Royal Acad., 1990; Foreign Hon. Mem., Amer. Acad. of Arts and Sciences; Foreign Fellow, Indian Nat. Sci. Acad., 1982; Hon. Fellow, Instn of Electronics and Telecommunication Engrs, India, 1985. Hon. DSc: Leicester, 1976; Exeter, 1977; Manchester, 1989; Santa Maria, Brazil, 1989; Univ. Teknologi Malaysia, 1997; Hon. ScD Cambridge, 1996. Eddington Medal, Royal Astronomical Soc., 1969; Charles Vernon Boys Prize, Inst. of Physics and Physical Soc., 1970; Dellinger Gold Medal, Internat. Union of Radio Science, 1972; Michelson Medal, Franklin Inst., 1973; Hopkins Prize, Cambridge Phil Soc., 1973; Holweck Medal and Prize, Soc. Française de Physique, 1974; Nobel Prize for Physics (jtly), 1974; Hughes Medal, Royal Soc., 1977; Vainu Bappu Prize, Indian Nat. Sci. Acad., 1996. *Publications:* Papers in Proc. Royal Society, Phys. Soc., Mon. Not. Royal Astr. Soc., etc. *Recreations:* music, gardening, cliff-walking. *Address:* Pryor's Cottage, Kingston, Cambridge CB3 7NQ. *T:* (01223) 262657; *e-mail:* ah120@mrao.cam.ac.uk.

HEWISON, Prof. Robert Alwyn Petrie, DLitt; cultural historian; Theatre Critic, Sunday Times, since 1981; Slade Professor of Fine Art, Oxford University, 1999–2000; *b* 2 June 1943; *s* of Robert John Petrie Hewison and Nancy Courtenay (*née* Henderson); *m* 1st, 1981, Jackie Staples (marr. diss. 1986); one *d*; 2nd, 1986, Erica Jane Bolton; two *d*. *Educ:* Bedford Sch.; Ravensbourne Coll. of Art and Design; Brasenose Coll., Oxford (BA 1965; MA 1970; MLitt 1972; DLitt 1989). Grad. trainee, Southern Television, 1966; independent writer and critic, 1967–. Guest Curator: J. B. Speed Art Mus., Louisville, Ky, 1978; Museo Correr, Venice, 1983; Ashmolean Mus., Oxford, 1996; Tate Gall., London, 2000. Vis. Prof., De Montfort Univ., 1993–95; Prof. in Literary and Cultural Studies, 1995–2000, Prof., Dept of English, 2001–, Univ. of Lancaster. Mem., Writers' Guild of GB, 1968–. *Publications:* John Ruskin: the argument of the eye, 1976; Under Siege: literary life in London 1939–45, 1977, rev. edn 1988; Ruskin and Venice, 1978; Irreverence, Scurrility, Profanity, Vilification and Licentious Abuse: Monty Python, the case against, 1981, 2nd edn 1990; (ed) New Approaches to Ruskin: 13 essays, 1981; In Anger: culture in the Cold War 1945–60, 1981, rev. edn 1988; (ed) The Ruskin Art Collection at Oxford: the rudimentary series, 1984; Footlights!: a hundred years of Cambridge comedy, 1986; The Heritage Industry: Britain in a climate of decline, 1987; Too Much: art and society in the Sixties 1960–75, 1988; Future Tense: a new art for the Nineties, 1990; Culture and Consensus: England, art and politics since 1940, 1995, rev. edn 1997; Ruskin and Oxford: the art of education, 1996; (ed) Ruskin's Artists: studies in the Victorian visual economy, 2000; (jtly) Ruskin, Turner and the Pre-Raphaelites, 2000; Ruskin's Venice, 2000. *Recreation:* gardening. *Address:* c/o Peters, Fraser & Dunlop, Drury House, 34–43 Russell Street, WC2B 5HA.

HEWISON, William Coltman; freelance illustrator, caricaturist and writer, since 1950; *b* 15 May 1925; *s* of Ralph Hewison and Mary Hewison; *m* 1950, Elsie Hammond; one *s* one *d*. *Educ:* S Shields High Sch.; S Shields Art Sch. (Bd of Educn Drawing Cert.); Regent St Poly. Art Sch. (Nat. Dip. in Painting); London Univ. (Art Teachers' Dip.). Enlisted in RAC, 1943; Gunner/Wireless Operator in 1st RTR, Normandy to Holland, 1944; casualty, Nov. 1944, evacuated to UK hosp.; GHQ Egypt, 1945–47. Part-time art teacher, 1950–57; Punch: contributor, 1950–92; Dep. Art Editor, 1957–60; Art Editor, 1960–84; Art Critic, 1984–87; contributor, The Times, 1992–; drawings in collections: V&A Mus., 1976; British Museum, 1991; Karikatur & Cartoon Mus., Basel, 1994; Graphic Arts Collection, Princeton Univ., 1997. *Publications:* Types Behind the Print, 1963; Mindfire (novel), 1973; The Cartoon Connection, 1977; (with Ross Thomson) How to Draw & Sell Cartoons, 1985; ed and introduced twenty-two Punch cartoon collections, 1979–90. *Recreations:* open air drawing. *Address:* 5 Southdown Drive, Wimbledon, SW20 8EZ.

HEWITT, family name of **Viscount Lifford**.

HEWITT, Prof. (Brian) George, PhD; FBA 1997; Professor of Caucasian Languages, School of Oriental and African Studies, London University, since 1996; *b* 11 Nov. 1949; *s* of late Thomas Douglas Hewitt and Joan (*née* Cousins); *m* 1976, Zaira Kiazimovna Khiba; two *d*. *Educ:* Doncaster Grammar Sch. for Boys; St John's Coll., Cambridge (BA 1972; Dip. in Linguistics 1973; MA 1975; PhD 1982). Open Henry Arthur Thomas Schol. in Classics, 1969–72; John Stewart of Rannoch Univ. Schol. and Coll. Graves Prize, 1971; Warr Classical Student, 1972–73; British Council Exchange Postgrad. Student, Tbilisi, Georgia, 1975–76, 1979–80; Marjory Wardrop Scholar for Georgian Studies, 1978–81. Lectr in Linguistics, Hull Univ., 1981–88; Lectr in Linguistics and Caucasian Langs,

1988–92, Reader in Caucasian Langs, 1992–96, SOAS. Member, Editorial Board: Revue des Etudes Géorgiennes et Caucasiennes, 1985–; Central Asian Survey, 1993–. Mem. Council, Philological Soc., 1985–90; First Pres., Societas Caucasologica Europaea, 1986–88 and 1988–90. Hon. Rep. for Republic of Abkhazia in UK, 1993–. Hon. Member: Internat. Cherkess Acad. of Scis, 1997–; Abkhazian Acad. of Scis, 1997. Mem. Bd of Managers, Marjory Wardrop Fund, Oxford, 1983–. *Publications:* Lingua Descriptive Studies 2: Abkhaz, 1979; Typology of Subordination in Georgian and Abkhaz, 1987; (ed and contrib.) Indigenous Languages of the Caucasus 2: North West Caucasus, 1989; (ed and contrib.) Caucasian Perspectives, 1992; (ed and contrib. jtly) Subject, Voice and Ergativity: selected essays, 1995; Georgian: a learner's grammar, 1995; Georgian: a structural reference grammar, 1995; A Georgian Reader, 1996; (with Zaira Khiba) Abkhaz Newspaper Reader (with supplements), 1998; (ed and contrib.) The Abkhazians: a handbook, 1998; The Languages of the Caucasus: scope for study and survival (inaugural lecture), 1998; articles on Caucasian langs and politics in encycs, Central Asian Survey, Bedi Kartlisa, Revue des Etudes Géorgiennes et Caucasiennes. *Recreations:* classical music, growing fuchsias. *Address:* Department of Near and Middle East, School of Oriental and African Studies, Thornhaugh Street, Russell Square, WC1H 0XG. *T:* (020) 7898 4332; *e-mail:* gh2@soas.ac.uk.

HEWITT, Prof. (Charles) Nicholas, PhD; FRMetS; CChem; Professor of Atmospheric Chemistry, Lancaster University, since 1993; *b* 23 Sept. 1953; *s* of Peter Hewitt and Amanda Hewitt (*née* Rodwell); *m*; one *s* one *d*. *Educ:* Queen Elizabeth's Grammar Sch. for Boys, Barnet; Lancaster Univ. (BA 1976; PhD 1985). FRMetS 1985; CChem 1985; MRSC 1985. Lancaster University: New-Blood Lectr, 1985–91; Sen. Lectr, 1991–93. Vis. Fellow and Fulbright Schol., Univ. of Colo, Boulder, 1988–89; Vis. Scientist, Nat. Center for Atmospheric Res., Boulder, Colo, 1994–95. Member: Photochemical Oxidant Rev. Gp, DoE, 1991–99; Scientific Steering Cttee, Eurotrac-2 (a Eureka project), 1996–. Chm., Envmtl Chemistry Gp, RSC, 1996–98. *Publications:* Instrumental Analysis of Pollutants, 1991; Methods of Environmental Data Analysis, 1992; (with W. T. Sturges) Global Atmospheric Chemical Change, 1993; (with G. Davison) Air Pollution in the United Kingdom, 1997; Reactive Hydrocarbons in the Atmosphere, 1998; numerous articles in learned jls. *Recreation:* mountaineering in its widest sense. *Address:* Institute of Environmental and Natural Sciences, Lancaster University, Lancaster LA1 4YQ. *T:* (01524) 593931.

HEWITT, Sir (Cyrus) Lenox (Simson), Kt 1971; OBE 1963; company chairman and director; *b* 7 May 1917; *s* of Cyrus Lenox Hewitt and Ella Louise Hewitt; *m* 1943, Alison Hope (*née* Tillyard); one *s* two *d* (and one *d* decd). *Educ:* Scotch Coll., Melbourne; Melbourne Univ. (BCom). FASA, FCIS, CPA. Broken Hill Proprietary Co. Ltd, 1933–46; Asst Sec., Commonwealth Prices Br., Canberra, 1939–46; Economist, Dept of Post War Reconstruction, 1946–49; Official Sec. and Actg Dep. High Comr, London, 1950–53; Commonwealth Treasury: Asst Sec., 1953–55; 1st Asst Sec., 1955–62; Dep. Sec., 1962–66; Chm., Australian Univs Commn, 1967; Secretary to: Prime Minister's Dept, 1968–71; Dept of the Environment, Aborigines and the Arts, 1971–72; Dept of Minerals and Energy, 1972–75. Lectr, Econs and Cost Accountancy, Canberra UC, 1940–49, 1954. Acting Chairman: Pipeline Authority, 1973–75; Petroleum and Minerals Authority, 1974–75; Chairman: Qantas Airways Ltd, 1975–80 (Dir, 1973–80); Qantas Wentworth Hldgs Ltd, 1975–80; QH Tours Ltd, 1975–80 (Dir, 1974–80); Petroleum and Minerals Co. of Aust. Pty Ltd, 1975; Austmark Internat. Ltd, 1983–88; Northern Mining Corp. NL, 1984–85; State Rail Authority of NSW, 1985–88; Director: East/Aust. Pipeline Corp. Ltd, 1974–75; Mary Kathleen Uranium Ltd, 1975–80; Aust. Industry Develt Corp., 1975; Santos Ltd, 1981–82; Pontello Constructions Ltd, 1980–82; Aberfoyle Ltd, 1981–89; Endeavour Resources Ltd, 1982–86; Ansett Transport Industries Ltd, 1982–88; Short Brothers (Australia) Ltd, 1981–91; Airship Industries PLC, 1984–88; Qintex Australia Ltd, 1985–90; British Midland Airways (Australia) Pty Ltd, 1985–; Universal Telecasters Securities Ltd, 1986–90; Mirage Management Ltd, 1986–91; Qintex Ltd, 1987–90; Qintex America Ltd, 1987–90; Fortis Pacific Aviation Ltd, 1987–; Fortis Aviation Group Ltd, 1988–; Hope Downs Ltd, 1993–; Hancock Minerals Ltd, 1993–. Dep. Chm., Aust. Atomic Energy Commn, 1972–77; Chairman: Exec. Cttee, IATA, 1976–77 (Mem., 1975–80); Orient Airlines Assoc., 1977; State Rail Authority of NSW, 1985–88; Mem., Judicial Commn of NSW, 1986–89. *Recreation:* farming. *Address:* 9 Torres Street, Red Hill, Canberra, ACT 2603, Australia. *T:* (2) 62952446; (office) 3, 70 Pitt Street, Sydney, NSW 2000, Australia. *T:* (2) 92313233. *Clubs:* Brooks's; Melbourne (Melbourne); Union (Sydney).

See also Rt Hon. P. H. Hewitt.

HEWITT, Eric John, PhD, DSc; FRS 1982; Head of Biochemistry Group in Plant Sciences Division, Long Ashton Research Station, and Reader in Plant Physiology, University of Bristol, 1967–84, retired; *b* London, 27 Feb. 1919; *s* of Harry Edward Hewitt, OBE, MD, DPH, and Blanche (*née* Du Roveray); *m* 1943, Hannah Eluned (*née* Williams); one *s*. *Educ:* Whitgift Sch., S Croydon; King's Coll., Univ. of London, 1936–40 (BSc 1st Cl., AKC; DipEd); PhD, DSc Bristol; FIBiol. Asst Chemist/Chemist, MoS, 1940–42; Long Ashton Research Station: ARC Res. Grant Research Asst, 1942–45; Sen. Plant Physiologist, 1945–84; seconded to ARC Unit of Plant Nutrition (Micronutrients), 1952–59; SPSO (merit promotion), 1967. *Publications:* Sand and Water Culture Methods Used in the Study of Plant Nutrition, 1952, 2nd edn 1966; (with T. A. Smith) Plant Mineral Nutrition, 1975; (ed, with C. V. Cutting): (sympos.) Nitrogen Metabolism in Plants, 1968; (sympos.) Nitrogen Assimilation of Plants, 1979; approx. 150 research contribs to jls. *Recreations:* gardening, reading, news and records. *Address:* Langdales, 63 Ridgeway Road, Long Ashton, Bristol BS41 9EZ. *T:* (01275) 392274.

HEWITT, Francis Anthony; Chief Executive, Northern Ireland Growth Challenge, since 1996; *b* 1 July 1943; *s* of Joseph and Mary Hewitt; *m* 1968, Carol Burch; two *d*. *Educ:* Queen's Univ., Belfast (BScEcon). FCIM. NI Min. of Agriculture, 1961–63; HM Customs and Excise, 1963–72; NI Min. of Commerce Rep. in W Germany, 1973–78; NI Dept of Commerce, 1978–82; HM Consulate-Gen., LA, 1982–84; Industrial Development Board for Northern Ireland: Exec. Dir, Marketing, 1984–88; Dep. Chief Exec., 1988–96. *Recreations:* music, walking.

HEWITT, Gavin Wallace, CMG 1995; HM Diplomatic Service; Ambassador to Belgium, since 2001; *b* 19 Oct. 1944; *s* of George Burrill and Elisabeth Murray Hewitt; *m* 1973, Heather Mary Clayton; two *s* two *d*. *Educ:* George Watson's Boys' Coll., Edinburgh; Edinburgh Univ. (MA). Min. of Transport, 1967–70; on secondment from MoT as Third, later Second, Sec. to UK Delegn, EEC, Brussels, 1970–72; FCO, 1972–73; First Sec., British High Commn, Canberra, 1973–78; FCO, 1978–81; First Sec. and Head of Chancery, HM Embassy, Belgrade, 1981–84; Mem., Jt FCO/BBC Review Gp, BBC External Services, 1984; Counsellor on loan to Home Civil Service, 1984–87; Counsellor, Head of Chancery and Dep. Perm. Rep., UK Mission to UN, Geneva, 1987–91; Head, SE Asia Dept, FCO, 1992–94; Ambassador to Croatia, 1994–97; Ambassador to Finland, 1997–2000. Mem., Bd of Geneva English Sch., 1989–91 (Vice-Chm., 1990–91). *Recreations:* music, tinkering, walking. *Address:* c/o Foreign and Commonwealth Office, SW1A 2AH.

HEWITT, Prof. Geoffrey Frederick, FRS 1989; FREng; Courtaulds Professor of Chemical Engineering, 1993–99, now Emeritus, and Senior Research Fellow, since 1999, Imperial College of Science, Technology and Medicine (Professor of Chemical Engineering, 1985–93); *b* 3 Jan. 1934; *s* of Frederick and Elaine Hewitt; *m* 1956, Shirley Foulds; two *d*. *Educ:* Boteler Grammar School, Warrington; UMIST (BScTech, PhD). CEng, FREng (FEng 1984); FIMechE, FIChemE, CChem, FRSC. Scientist, Group Leader, Div. Head, Harwell Lab., specialising in heat transfer and fluid flow in multiphase systems, 1957–90. Pres., IChemE, 1989–90. Foreign Associate, US Nat. Acad. Engrg, 1998. FCGI. Hon. DSc Louvain, 1988; Hon. DEng: Heriot-Watt, 1995; UMIST, 1998. Max Jakob Award, ASME, 1995; Nusselt-Reynolds Prize, Assembly of World Conf. on Expertl Heat Transfer, Fluid Mechs and Thermodyns, 1997. *Publications:* (with N. S. Hall Taylor) Annular Two Phase Flow, 1970; (co-author) Two Phase Flow, 1973; Measurement of Two Phase Flow Parameters, 1978; (with J. G. Collier) Introduction to Nuclear Power, 1986; (jtly) Process Heat Transfer, 1994; (ed) International Encyclopedia of Heat and Mass Transfer, 1997; contribs to books, numerous papers. *Recreations:* bridge, music. *Address:* Department of Chemical Engineering and Chemical Technology, Imperial College of Science, Technology and Medicine, Prince Consort Road, SW7 2BY. *T:* (020) 7589 5111.

HEWITT, George; *see* Hewitt, B. G.

HEWITT, His Honour Harold; a Circuit Judge, 1980–90; *b* 14 March 1917; *s* of George Trueman Hewitt and Bertha Lilian Hewitt; *m* 1946, Doris Mary Smith; two *s*. *Educ:* King James I Grammar Sch., Bishop Auckland. Admitted solicitor (Hons), 1938; HM Coroner, S Durham, 1948–80; a Recorder of the Crown Court, 1974–80. Chairman (part-time): Industrial Tribunal, 1975–80; Milk and Dairies Tribunal, Northern Region, 1975–80. Member Council, Law Society, 1976–80. Pres., NE Region, YMCA, 1981–. *Recreations:* music, gardening, French literature. *Address:* Longmeadows, Etherley, Bishop Auckland, Co. Durham DL14 0HD. *T:* (01388) 832386. *Club:* Carlton.

HEWITT, Harry Ronald, FREng; Chairman, Johnson Matthey PLC, 1983–84; retired; *b* 12 April 1920; *s* of Charles William Hewitt and Florence Hewitt; *m* 1954, Rosemary Olive, *d* of Walter George Hiscock and Olive Mary Hiscock; two *s* one *d*. *Educ:* City of Leeds High Sch,; Leeds Coll. of Technol. (BSc London 1941). FREng (FEng 1982); MIChemE 1949; MRSC 1944; CBIM 1983 (MBIM 1947). Jun. Chemist, Joseph Watson & Sons, soap manufrs, Leeds, 1936–41; Chemist, Royal Ordnance Factories (explosive manuf.), 1941–45; Control Officer, Chemical Br., Control Commn, Germany, 1945–47; Works Manager, Consolidated Zinc Corp., Avonmouth and Widnes, 1947–58; Johnson Matthey: Gen. Man., 1958–62; Exec. Dir, 1962–76; Gp Man. Dir, 1976–83. Freeman, City of London, 1979; Liveryman, Worshipful Co. of Clockmakers, 1979. FRSA. *Recreations:* golf, tennis, skiing, music. *Address:* 6 Loom Lane, Radlett, Herts WD7 8AD. *T:* (01923) 5243.

HEWITT, Sir Lenox; *see* Hewitt, Sir C. L. S.

HEWITT, Michael Earling; Resident Adviser, Egyptian Capital Market Authority, 2000–April 2002; *b* 28 March 1936; *s* of late Herbert Erland Hewitt and Dorothy Amelia Hewitt; *m* 1961, Elizabeth Mary Hughes Batchelor (marr. diss. 2000); one *s* one *d*. *Educ:* Christ's Hospital; Merton College, Oxford (Chancellor's Prize for Latin Prose, 1958; MA (Modern Hist.)); BSc Econ London. Bank of England, 1961–94: Economic Adviser, Govt of Bermuda, 1970–74; Financial Forecaster, 1976–78; Adviser, Financial Instns, 1981–83; Head of Financial Supervision, Gen. Div., 1984–87; Head of Finance and Industry Area, 1987–88; Senior Advr, Finance and Industry, 1988–90; Dir of Central Banking Studies, 1990–94; Project Manager (IMF), EC Technical Assistance for CIS Trng Prog. for Central Bank of Russian Fedn, 1994–99, and Nat. Bank of Ukraine, 1997–98. Chm., OECD Gp of Experts on Systemic Risks in Securities Markets, 1988–90. *Recreations:* chess, wine, travel. *Address:* c/o FCO Cairo, Foreign and Commonwealth Office, King Charles Street, SW1A 2AH. *T:* (home) (2) 761 3438; (office) (2) 578 3727.

HEWITT, Nicholas; *see* Hewitt, C. N.

HEWITT, Sir Nicholas Charles Joseph, 3rd Bt *cr* 1921; *b* 12 Nov. 1947; *s* of Sir Joseph Hewitt, 2nd Bt and Marguerite, *yr d* of Charles Burgess; *S* father, 1973; *m* 1969, Pamela Margaret, *o d* of Geoffrey J. M. Hunt, TD; two *s* one *d*. *Heir: s* Charles Edward James Hewitt [*b* 15 Nov. 1970; *m* 2001, Alison, *d* of Peter Brown, Hobart, Tas]. *Address:* Colswayn House, Huttons Ambo, Yorks YO6 7HJ. *T:* (01653) 696557.

HEWITT, Rt Hon. Patricia Hope, PC 2001; MP (Lab) Leicester West, since 1997; Secretary of State for Trade and Industry, since 2001; Minister for Women, since 2001; *b* 2 Dec. 1948; *d* of Sir (Cyrus) Lenox (Simson) Hewitt, *qv*, and Alison Hope Hewitt; *m* 1981, William Birtles; one *s* one *d*. *Educ:* C of E Girls' Grammar Sch., Canberra; Australian Nat. Univ.; Newnham Coll., Cambridge (MA). MA Oxon; AMusA (piano). Public Relations Officer, Age Concern (Nat. Old People's Welfare Council), 1971–73; Women's Rights Officer, Nat. Council for Civil Liberties, 1973–74, Gen. Secretary 1974–83; Press and Broadcasting Sec., 1983–88, Policy Co-ordinator, 1988–89, to Leader of Opposition; Sen. Res. Fellow, 1989, Dep. Dir, 1989–94, Inst. for Public Policy Res.; Head, then Dir, of Research, Andersen Consulting, 1994–97. Associate, Newnham Coll., Cambridge, 1984–97; Vis. Fellow, Nuffield Coll., Oxford, 1992–. Trustee: Cobden Trust, 1974–83; Areopagitica Trust, 1981–84; Member: Sec. of State's Adv. Cttee on Employment of Women, 1977–84; Unofficial Cttee of Enquiry into Southall, 23 April 1979; National Labour Women's Cttee, 1979–83; Labour Party Enquiry into Security Services, 1980–81; Council, Campaign for Freedom of Information, 1983–89; Bd, Internat. League for Human Rights, 1984–97; Exec. Cttee, Fabian Soc., 1988–93; Co-Chm., Human Rights Network, 1979–81; Dep. Chair, Commn on Social Justice, 1993–95; Vice-Chairman: Healthcare 2000, 1995–96; British Council, 1997–98. Contested (Lab) Leicester East, 1983. Economic Sec., HM Treasury, 1998–99; Minister of State, DTI, 1999–2001. Mem., Select Cttee on Social Security, 1997–98. Mem. Council, Inst. for Fiscal Studies, 1996–98. Mem., Editorial Adv. Panel, New Socialist, 1980–90. FRSA 1992. *Publications:* Your Rights (Age Concern), 1973; Rights for Women (NCCL), 1975; Civil Liberties, the NCCL Guide (co-ed 3rd edn), 1977; The Privacy Report (NCCL), 1977; Your Rights at Work (NCCL), 1978, 2nd edn 1981; The Abuse of Power, 1981; (jtly) Your Second Baby, 1990; About Time: the revolution in work and family life, 1993. *Recreations:* reading, theatre, music, politics, gardening. *Address:* 75 Ashleigh Road, Leicester LE3 0FD. *T:* (0116) 251 6160.

HEWITT, Penelope Ann; Senior District Judge (Chief Magistrate), since 2000; *b* 4 May 1932; *d* of late William Mottershead, JP, MB ChB and Eileen Mottershead; *m* 1954, Peter Nisbet Hewitt; one *s* two *d*. *Educ:* Howell's Sch., Denbigh; BA Open Univ., 1975. Called to the Bar, Gray's Inn, 1978; in practice, Liverpool, 1978–90; Mem., Northern Circuit; District Judge (Magistrates' Courts) (formerly Stipendiary Magistrate), Leeds, 1990–2000. Lay Chm., Bolton Deanery Synod, 1984–90. Member: British Acad. of Forensic Scis, 1979; Magisterial Cttee, Judicial Studies Bd, 1993–98. JP Bolton, 1968–90. *Recreations:*

music, reading, opera, embroidery. *Address:* Bow Street Magistrates' Court, Bow Street, WC2E 7AS.

HEWITT, Peter John; Chief Executive, Arts Council of England, since 1998; *b* 17 Nov. 1951; *m* 1977, Joan Coventry; three *d*. *Educ:* Barnard Castle Sch.; Leeds Univ. (BA, MA). Inter-action, Kentish Town, 1976; Arts Officer, N Tyneside MBC, 1977–82; Northern Arts, 1982–97 (Chief Exec., 1992–97); Corporate Affairs Dir, Tees HA, 1997–98. *Recreations:* arts, walking, Middlesbrough FC. *Address:* (office) 14 Great Peter Street, SW1P 3NQ. *T:* (020) 7973 6575.

HEWITT, Peter McGregor, OBE 1967; Regional Director, East Midlands, Departments of the Environment and Transport, 1984–89; *b* 6 Oct. 1929; *e s* of late Douglas McGregor Hewitt and Audrey Vera Hewitt; *m* 1962, Joyce Marie Gavin; three *d*. *Educ:* De Aston Sch., Market Rasen, Lincs; Keble Coll., Oxford (MA). National Service (Army), 1947–49. HM Overseas Civil Service, 1952–64: served in Malaya and N Borneo; HM Diplomatic Service, 1964–71: served in FO, Shanghai and Canberra; Home Civil Service: Principal, 1971–77; Asst Sec., 1977–83; Grade 4, 1984. *Recreations:* cricket, music, gardening. *Address:* 14 Dovedale Road, West Bridgford, Nottingham NG2 6JA. *Club:* Royal Commonwealth Society.

HEWITT, Sheila Iffat; JP; Member: Radio Authority, since 1998; Legal Services Commission (formerly Legal Aid Board), since 1998; *b* Pakistan, 6 Oct. 1952; *m* 1973, Anthony Hewitt; two *s*. *Educ:* London Sch. of Econs and Pol Sci. (BSc Econ). ACIB 1975. Regl Chm., Eastern and Southern Areas, Legal Services Commn (formerly Legal Aid Bd), 1998–; Member: London Rent Assessment Panel, 1985–; Immigration Appeals Tribunal, 1992–. Non-exec. Bd Mem., Mid Surrey HA, 1992–95; Chm., Surrey Heartlands NHS Trust, 1995–98. JP Surrey, 1987. *Recreations:* mountain trekking, tennis. *Address:* Calderwood, Wilmerhatch Lane, Epsom, Surrey KT18 7EH. *T:* (01372) 273730, *Fax:* (01372) 271762. *Club:* Royal Automobile.

HEWITT, Stephen Geoffrey; Director of Business Design, Jobcentre Plus, Department for Work and Pensions, since 2001; *b* 9 March 1950; *s* of late Geoffrey Gordon Hewitt and Doreen Brinsdon Hewitt; *m* 1992, Jill Elizabeth Harris. *Educ:* Weymouth Grammar Sch.; Dulwich Coll.; Sussex Univ. (BSc Chem. 1971; MSc Hist. of Science 1972). Admin trainee, N Ireland Office, 1975; Private Sec. to Ray Carter, MP, 1977–78; transf. to Dept of Social Security, 1990; Dir of Personnel, 1993–98; Dir for People of Working Age, subseq. Dir of Working Age Change, 1998–2001. *Address:* c/o Department for Work and Pensions, Adelphi Building, 1–11 John Adam Street, WC2N 6HT. *T:* (020) 7962 8361.

HEWLETT, Stephen Edward; Director of Programmes, Carlton Television, since 1998; Managing Director, Carlton Productions, since 2001; *b* 8 Aug. 1958; *s* of Lawrence Edward Hewlett and Vera Mary Hewlett; partner, Karole Anne Lange; three *s*. *Educ:* Harold Malley Grammar Sch. for Boys, Solihull; Solihull Sixth Form Coll.; Univ. of Manchester (BSc Hons Liberal Studies in Sci. 1981). Researcher, Panorama, Nationwide and Watchdog, BBC, 1981–82; Producer and Dir, Diverse Reports and The Friday Alternative, Channel 4, 1982–87; BBC: Producer: Brass Tacks, 1987–88; Taking Liberties, 1988–90; Inside Story, 1990–92; Exec. Producer, Children's Hosp., The Skipper, Rough Justice, States of Terror, The Diamond Empire, 25 Bloody Years and The Dead (Best Single Documentary Award, RTS, 1994), 1992–94; Ed., Inside Story, 1992–94 (Best Single Documentary Award, BAFTA, 1994); Ed., Panorama and Exec. Ed., Special Projects, 1995–97; Hd, Factual Programmes, Channel 4, 1997–98. Hon. MA Salford, 1999. Interview of Year and Journalist of Year Awards, RTS, 1995. *Recreations:* cricket, swimming, sailing (occasionally). *Address:* Carlton Television, 35–38 Portman Square, W1H 0NU. *T:* (020) 7486 6688; *e-mail:* steve.hewlett@carltontv.co.uk.

HEWLETT-DAVIES, Mrs Janet Mary; journalist; public affairs consultant; *b* 13 May 1938; *d* of Frederick Charles and Margaret Ellen Hewlett; *m* 1964, Barry Davies. *Educ:* King Edward VI High School for Girls, Birmingham. Journalist, West Midlands 1956–59; BBC, 1959–65; Films Division, Central Office of Information, 1966–67; Press Officer: Prime Minister's Office, 1967–72; HM Customs and Excise, 1972–73; Principal Information Officer, Dept of Trade and Industry, 1973–74; Dep. Press Secretary to Prime Minister, 1974–76; Head of Information, Dept of Transport, 1976–79; Director of Information: DoE, 1979–82; DHSS, 1982–86; Dir of Public Affairs, Pergamon, BPCC and Mirror Gp of Cos, 1986–87. Vice-Chm., WHO Working Gp on Information and Health, 1983. *Recreations:* acting, Shakespeare's Globe, Brighton. *Address:* 44 Sussex Square, Brighton BN2 1GE. *T:* (01273) 693792, *Fax:* (01273) 628875; *e-mail:* shelley44@amserve.net. *Club:* Reform.

HEWSON, John Robert, AM 2001; PhD; investment banker and company director; Member, Advisory Board, ABN AMRO Australia Ltd, since 1998 (Chairman, 1996–98); *b* 28 Oct. 1946; *s* of Donald Hewson and late Eileen Isabella Hewson (*née* Tippett); *m* 1st, Margaret; two *s* one *d*; 2nd, 1988, Carolyn Somerville; one *d*. *Educ:* Univ. of Sydney (BEc Hons); Univ. of Saskatchewan (MA 1969); Johns Hopkins Univ. (MA, PhD 1971). Economist, IMF, 1971–74; Res. Economist, Reserve Bank of Australia, 1976; Economic Advr to Fed. Treas., 1976–82; University of New South Wales: Prof. of Econs, 1978–87; Head, Sch. of Econs, 1983–86; Dir, Japanese Econs Management Studies Centre, 1984–87. Dir, Macquarie Bank, 1985–87. MP (L) Wentworth, NSW, 1987–95; Shadow Minister for Finance, 1988–89; Shadow Treas., 1989–90; Leader of the Opposition, Australian Parlt, 1990–94; Shadow Minister for Industry, Commerce, Infrastructure and Customs, 1994–95. Chairman: Leadership Foundn Pty Ltd, 1998–; Australian Bus Manufg Co. Pty Ltd, 1999–; Universal Bus Co. Pty Ltd, 2000–; Global Renewables Ltd, 2000–; Belle Property, 2000– Strategic Capital Mgt Pty Ltd, 2000–; Vice-Chm., Qingdao Bus Co., 2001–; Director: Moran Health Care Group, 1998–; Moran Health Care (UK) Ltd, 1998–; IT&T Services Pty Ltd, 1996–; Gold and Resources Ltd, 2000– (Chm., 1996–98); Thorlock Internat. Ltd, 2000–; G. R. D. Kirfield, 2001–. Pres., Arthritis Foundn, 1997–. Columnist, Australian Financial Review. *Publications:* Liquidity Creation and Distribution in the Eurocurrency Market, 1975; (jtly) The Eurocurrency Markets and their Implications, 1975; Offshore Banking in Australia, 1981. *Recreations:* jazz, sport, cars, theatre, motor sports. *Address:* Level 29, ABN AMRO Tower, 88 Phillip Street, Sydney, NSW 2000, Australia. *T:* (2) 8259 6204, *Fax:* (2) 8259 5430; *e-mail:* john.hewson@au.abramro.com. *Clubs:* Australian, Union (Sydney); Australian Golf, Royal Sydney Golf.

HEXHAM AND NEWCASTLE, Bishop of, (RC), since 1992; **Rt Rev. (Michael) Ambrose Griffiths,** OSB; *b* 4 Dec. 1928; *s* of Henry and Hilda Griffiths. *Educ:* Ampleforth Coll.; Balliol Coll., Oxford (MA, BSc Chemistry). Entered monastery at Ampleforth, 1950; theological studies at S Anselmo, Rome, 1953–56; ordained priest, 1957; Prof. of Theology at Ampleforth, 1963; Sen. Science Master, Ampleforth Coll., 1967; Inspector of Accounts for English Benedictine Congregation, 1971 and 1985–92; Procurator (Bursar) at Ampleforth, 1972; Abbot of Ampleforth, 1976–84; Parish Priest, St Mary's, Leyland, Preston, 1984–92. Mem. Public School Bursars' Assoc. Cttee, 1975. *Recreation:* walking. *Address:* Bishop's House, East Denton Hall, 800 West Road, Newcastle upon Tyne NE5 2BJ.

HEXHAM AND NEWCASTLE, Auxiliary Bishop of, (RC); *see* Swindlehurst, Rt Rev. O. F.

HEY, Air Vice-Marshal Ernest, CB 1967 CBE 1963 (OBE 1954); CEng; Air Member for Technical Services, Department of Air, Canberra, 1960–72, retired; *b* Plymouth, Devon, 29 Nov. 1912; *s* of Ernest Hey, Terrigal, NSW; *m* 1936, Lorna, *d* of Sqdn Ldr A. Bennett, Melbourne; one *s* one *d*. *Educ:* Sydney Technical High Sch.; Sydney University. RAAF cadet, 1934; served War of 1939–45; Dir Technical Services, 1947–54; AOC Maintenance Comd, 1956–57; Imp. Defence Coll., 1957; Liaison Air Materiel Comd, USAF, 1958–59.

HEY, Prof. John Denis; Professor of Economics and Statistics, University of York, since 1984, part-time since 1998; Professore Ordinario, University of Bari, Italy, since 1998; *b* 26 Sept. 1944; *s* of George Brian Hey and Elizabeth Hamilton Hey (*née* Burns); *m* 1968, Margaret Robertson Bissett (marr. diss. 1998); one *s* two *d*. *Educ:* Manchester Grammar Sch.; Cambridge Univ. (MA); Edinburgh Univ. (MSc). Econometrician, Hoare & Co., 1968–69; Lectr in Economics, Univ. of Durham, 1969–73, Univ. of St Andrews, 1974–75; Lectr in Social and Economic Statistics, Univ. of York, 1975–81, Sen. Lectr, 1981–84. Co-Dir, Centre for Experimental Economics, Univ. of York, 1986–. Economic Consultant, Wise Speke & Co., 1972–87. Editor: Bulletin of Economic Research, 1984–86; Economic Journal, 1986–96. *Publications:* Statistics in Economics, 1974; Uncertainty in Microeconomics, 1979; Britain in Context, 1979; Economics in Disequilibrium, 1981; Data in Doubt, 1983; (ed jtly) Surveys in the Economics of Uncertainty, 1987; (ed) Current Issues in Microeconomics, 1989; (ed jtly) A Century of Economics, 1990; Experiments in Economics, 1991; (ed) The Future of Economics, 1992; (ed jtly) Recent Developments in Experimental Economics, 1993; (ed) The Economics of Uncertainty, 1997; articles in academic economics jls. *Recreations:* squash, walking, opera. *Address:* Department of Economics and Related Studies, University of York, Heslington, York YO1 5DD. *T:* (01904) 433786; Università degli Studi di Bari, via Camillo Rosalba 53, 70124 Bari, Italy.

HEYERDAHL, Thor; author and anthropologist, since 1938; *b* Larvik, Norway 6 Oct. 1914; *s* of Thor Heyerdahl and Alison Heyerdahl (*née* Lyng); *m* 1st, 1936, Liv Coucheron Torp (*d* 1969); two *s*; 2nd, 1949, Yvonne Dedekam-Simonsen; three *d*; 3rd, 1995, Jacqueline Beer. *Educ:* University of Oslo, 1933–36. Researches in the Marquesas Islands (Pacific), 1937–38; Researches among Coast Indians of Brit. Columbia, 1939–40. Active service Free Norwegian Army-Air Force parachute unit, 1942–45. Organised and led Kon-Tiki expedition, 1947. Continued research in USA and Europe, with authorship, 1948–. Organised and led Norwegian Archæological Expedition to the Galapagos Islands, 1952; experiments revealing tacking principles of balsa raft in Ecuador, 1953; field research, Bolivia, Peru, Colombia, 1954. Organised and led Norwegian Archæological Expedition to Easter Island and the East Pacific, 1955–56. Continued research, 1957–59. Made crossing from Safi, Morocco, to W Indies in papyrus boat, Ra II, 1970; sailed from Qurna, Iraq, to Djibouti in reed boat, Tigris, 1977–78; organised and led two archaeol expedns to Maldive Islands, 1982–84; leader, organiser jt Norwegian/Chilean archaeol expedn, Easter Island, 1986–88; organiser Kon-Tiki Mus.—Museo Brüning archaeol project, Tucume, Peru, 1988–; organiser, archaeol project, Tenerife, Canary Is, 1990–. Participation in Internat. Congress of Americanists, 1952–; Pacific Science Congresses, 1961–, all with lectures subseq. publ. in Proc. Congress. Vice-President: World Assoc. of World Federalists, 1966–; Foundn for Exploration and Research on Cultural Origins, 1990–; Trustee, Internat. Bd, World Wildlife Fund, 1977–; Internat. Patron, United World Colls, 1980. Mem., Royal Norwegian Acad. of Science, 1958; Fellow: New York Acad. of Sciences, 1960; Amer. Anthropological Assoc., 1966. Hon. Prof., Inst. Politecnico Nacional, Mexico, 1972. Hon. Dir, Explorers' Club, NY, 1982. Hon. Mem. Geog. Soc.: Peru, 1953; Norway, 1953; Brazil, 1954; USSR, 1964. Hon. Doctor: Oslo, 1961; USSR Acad. of Scis, 1980; Lima, 1990; Havana, 1992; Univ. of Maine, 1998; Univ. of Hartford, 1998; Latvian Acad. of Scis, 1998. Retzius Medal, Swedish Soc. for Anthropology and Geography, 1950; Mungo Park Medal, Royal Scottish Geographical Society, 1951; Prix Bonaparte-Wyse from Société de Géographie, Paris, 1951; Elish Kent Kane Gold Medal, Geog. Soc. of Philadelphia, 1952; Vega Medal, Swedish Soc. of Anthropology and Geography, 1962; Lomonosov Medal, Moscow Univ., 1962; Royal Gold Medal, Royal Geog. Society, London, 1964; Officer of El Orden por Méritos Distinguidos, Peru, 1953; Gold Medal City of Lima; Gr.-Officer, Order Al Merito della Repubblica Italiana, Italy, 1965; Comdr, Knights of Malta, 1970; Comdr with Star, Order of St Olav, Norway, 1970; Order of Merit, Egypt, 1971; Grand Officer, Royal Alaouites Order, Morocco, 1971; Hon. Citizen, Larvik, Norway, 1971; Kiril i Metodi Order, Bulgaria, 1972; Internat. Pahlavi Environment Prize, UN, 1978; Order of Golden Ark, Netherlands, 1980; Bradford Washburn Award, Boston Mus. of Science, USA, 1982; Internat. Prize, Spanish Geog. Soc., 1998. *Films:* The Kon-Tiki Expedition (Oscar award for camera achievement, Nat. Acad. Motion Picture Arts and Scis, 1951); Galapagos Expedition; Aku-Aku, The Secret of Easter Island; The Ra Expeditions; The Tigris Expedition; The Maldive Mystery. *Publications:* Paa Jakt efter Paradiset, 1938; The Kon-Tiki Expedition, 1948; American Indians in the Pacific: the theory behind the Kon-Tiki expedition, 1952; (with A. Skjolsvold) Archæological Evidence of Pre-Spanish Visits to the Galapagos Islands, 1956; Aku-Aku: The Secrets of Easter Island, 1957; Co-editor (with E. N. Ferdon, Jr) Reports of the Norwegian Archæological Expedition to Easter Island and the East Pacific, Vol. I: The Archæology of Easter Island, 1961, vol. II: Miscellaneous Papers, 1965; Navel of the World (Chapter XIV) in Vanished Civilizations, 1963; Indianer und Alt-Asiaten im Pazifik: Das Abenteuer einer Theorie, 1965 (Vienna); Sea Routes to Polynesia, 1968; The Ra Expeditions, 1970; Chapters in Quest for America, 1971; Fatu-Hiva Back to Nature, 1974; Art of Easter Island, 1975; Zwischen den Kontinenten, 1975; Early Man and the Ocean, 1978; The Tigris Expedition, 1980; The Maldive Mystery, 1986; Easter Island: the mystery solved, 1989; (jtly) Pyramids of Tucume, 1995; Green was the Earth on the Seventh Day, 1996; I Adams Fotspor (autobiog), 1998; contrib. National Geographical Magazine, Royal Geographical Journal, The Geographical Magazine, Archiv für Völkerkunde, Ymer, Swedish Geogr. Year-book, South-western Journal of Anthropology, Russian Academy of Sciences Yearbook, American Antiquity, Antiquity (Cambridge); works trans. into numerous languages; *relevant publications:* Senor Kon-Tiki, by Arnold Jacoby, 1965; The Kon-Tiki Man, by Christopher Ralling, 1990; Thor Heyerdahl the Explorer, by Snorre Evensberget, 1994. *Recreations:* outdoor life, travelling. *Address:* Kon-Tiki Museum, Bygdøynesveien 36, 0286 Oslo, Norway.

HEYES, David Alan; MP (Lab) Ashton under Lyne, since 2001; *b* 2 April 1946; *s* of Harold and Lilian Heyes; *m* 1968, Judith Gallagher; one *s* one *d*. *Educ:* Open Univ. (BA). Local govt manager, Manchester, 1962–86; trade union organiser, 1986–87; local govt manager, Oldham, 1987–90; self employed, computer graphics business, 1990–95; manager, CAB, Manchester, 1995–2001. *Address:* House of Commons, SW1A 0AA.

HEYGATE, Sir Richard John Gage, 6th Bt *cr* 1831, of Southend, Essex; Chief Executive, Sophron Partners Ltd, since 1998; *b* 30 Jan. 1940; *s* of Sir John Edward Nourse Heygate, 4th Bt and his 2nd wife, Gwyneth Eliot (*d* 1994), 2nd *d* of J. E. H. Lloyd; *S* brother, 1991; *m* 1st, 1968, Carol Rosemary (marr. diss. 1972), *d* of Comdr Richard

Michell; 2nd, 1974, Jong Ja (marr. diss. 1988), *d* of In Suk, Seoul; one *d*; 3rd, 1988, Susan Fiona, *d* of late Robert Buckley; two *s*. *Educ:* Repton; Balliol Coll., Oxford. IBM (UK) Ltd, 1967–70; McKinsey & Company Inc., 1970–77; Director: Olaf Foods, 1977–85; Index Gp, 1985–87; Principal, McKinsey and Co. Inc., 1987–98. Mem., Finance Cttee, Cancer Res., 1992–. *Heir: s* Frederick Carysfort Gage Heygate, *b* 28 June 1988. *Address:* 29 Rossetti Gardens Mansions, Flood Street, SW3 5QX.

HEYHOE, David Charles Ross, CB 1998; Director, Greenwich Hospital, since 1998; *b* 29 June 1938; *s* of late Cecil Ross Heyhoe and Clara Beatrice (*née* Woodard Knight); *m* 1972, Pauline Susan (*née* Morgan); one *s* one *d*. *Educ:* Beckenham and Penge Grammar Sch.; Worcester Coll., Oxford (Schol.; MA LitHum). Served HM Forces, RAEC, 1957–59. Asst Principal, War Office, 1963; Asst Private Sec. to Minister (Army), 1966; Principal, MoD, 1967; Asst Sec., 1975; Res. Associate, Inst. for Strategic Studies, 1975–76; Private Sec. to Leader of H of C, 1981–84; Asst Under Sec. of State, MoD, 1986–97. Mem., Royal Patriotic Fund Corp., 1998–. *Recreations:* books, sports, antiques. *Address:* c/o Greenwich Hospital, 40 Queen Anne's Gate, SW1H 9AP. *Clubs:* Oxford and Cambridge, Roehampton, Rosslyn Park FC.

HEYHOE FLINT, Rachael, MBE 1972; DL; public relations and sports marketing consultant; journalist, broadcaster, public speaker, sportswoman; *b* 11 June 1939; *d* of Geoffrey Heyhoe and Roma (*née* Crocker); *m* 1971, Derrick Flint, BSc; one *s* and one step *s* two step *d*. *Educ:* Wolverhampton High Sch. for Girls; Dartford Coll. of Physical Educn (Dip. in Phys. *Address:* Educn). Head of Phys. Education: Wolverhampton Municipal Grammar Sch., 1960–62; Northicote Sch., 1962–64; US Field Hockey Assoc. Coach, 1964 and 1965; Journalist, Wolverhampton Express & Star, 1965–72; Sports Editor, Wolverhampton Chronicle, 1969–71; first woman Sports Reporter, ITV, 1972; Daily Telegraph Sports Writer, 1967–; Vice-Chm., 1981–86, and Public Relations Officer, 1982–86, Women's Cricket Assoc.; Promotions Consultant, La Manga Club, Southern Spain, 1983–; PR Exec., Wolverhampton Wanderers Football Club, 1990– (Dir, 1997–); Chm., MG/Rover Dealer Share Trust, 2000–. Mem., Faldo Junior Series Adv. Panel, 1998–; Dep. Chm., United Charities Unit Trust Adv. Bd, 1993–; Mem. Cttee of Management, Family Assurance Soc., 1992–. Mem., Sportswriters Assoc., 1967. England Hockey rep., 1964 (goalkeeper); Mem., England Women's Cricket team, 1960–83, Captain, 1966–77. Hit first 6 in Women's Test Cricket 1963 (England *v* Australia, Oval); scored highest test score by England player in this country, 1976 (highest in world, 1976, now fourth highest) (179 runs for England *v* Australia, Oval). Pres., Lady Taverners Charity, 2000–. DL W Midlands, 1997. Best After Dinner Speakers Award, Guild of Professional Toastmasters, 1972. *Publications:* Just for Kicks, (Guide to hockey goalkeeping), 1966; Women's Hockey, 1975; (with Netta Rheinberg) Fair Play, The Story of Women's Cricket, 1976; (autobiog.) "Heyhoe!", 1978. *Recreations:* golf, cricket; former county squash player (Staffs). *Address:* Danescroft, Wergs Road, Tettenhall, Wolverhampton, West Midlands WV6 9BN. *Clubs:* MCC (Hon. Life Mem., 1999), Lord's Taverners, Cricketers'; Patshull Park Golf; South Staffs Golf; La Manga (Spain).

HEYMAN, Prof. Jacques, MA, PhD; FICE; FSA; FREng; Professor of Engineering, 1971–92, and Head of Department of Engineering, 1983–92, University of Cambridge, now Emeritus Professor; Fellow of Peterhouse, 1949–51, and 1955–92, now Emeritus Fellow; *b* 8 March 1925; *m* 1958, Eva Orlans (*d* 1982); three *d*. *Educ:* Whitgift Sch.; Peterhouse, Cambridge. Senior Bursar, Peterhouse, 1962–64; University Demonstrator, Engineering Dept, Cambridge Univ., 1951, University Lectr, 1954, Reader, 1968. Vis. Professor: Brown Univ., USA, 1957–58; Harvard Univ., 1966. Consultant Engineer: Ely Cathedral, 1972–; St Albans Cathedral, 1978–; Lichfield Cathedral, 1986–91; Worcester Cathedral, 1986–90; Gloucester Cathedral, 1989–90. Member: Architectural Adv. Panel, Westminster Abbey, 1973–98; Cathedrals Fabric Commn (formerly Cathedrals Adv. Commn) for England, 1981–2001; Council, ICE, 1960–63 and 1975–78; Smeatonian Soc. of Civil Engrs, 1982–. Hon FRIBA 1998. Hon. DSc Sussex, 1975. James Watt Medal, 1973. *Publications:* The Steel Skeleton, vol. 2 (with Lord Baker, M. R. Horne), 1956; Plastic Design of Portal Frames, 1957; Beams and Framed Structures, 1964, 2nd edn 1974; Plastic Design of Frames, vol. 1, 1969 (paperback 1980), vol. 2, 1971; Coulomb's Memoir on Statics, 1972, reprinted 1997 (trans. Italian, 1999); Equilibrium of Shell Structures, 1977; Elements of Stress Analysis, 1982; The Masonry Arch, 1982; Estructuras de Fábrica (collection of papers on masonry construction, trans. Spanish), 1995; The Stone Skeleton, 1995 (trans. Spanish, 1999); Elements of the Theory of Structures, 1996; Arches, Vaults and Buttresses, 1996; Structural Analysis, a Historical Approach, 1998; The Science of Structural Engineering, 1999; articles on plastic design, masonry construction and general structural theory. *Address:* 3 Banhams Close, Cambridge CB4 1HX. *T:* (01223) 357360.

HEYMANN, Prof. Franz Ferdinand, PhD; CPhys, FInstP; Quain Professor of Physics, and Head of Department of Physics and Astronomy, University College, University of London, 1975–87, now Professor Emeritus; *b* 17 Aug. 1924; *s* of Paul Gerhard Heymann and Magdalena Petronella Heymann; *m* 1950, Marie Powell. *Educ:* Univ. of Cape Town (BScEng with Distinction, 1944); Univ. of London (PhD 1953). FInstP 1966. Engr, Cape Town, 1944–45; Jun. Lectr in Engrg, Univ. of Cape Town, 1945–47; Special Trainee, Metropolitan Vickers, Manchester, 1947–50; University Coll. London: Asst Lectr in Physics, 1950–52; Lectr, 1952–60; Reader, 1960–66; Prof. of Physics, 1966–75; Fellow, 1987. *Publications:* scientific papers on res. done mainly in fields of particle accelerators and elementary particle physics. *Recreations:* music, philately, gardening. *Address:* Sunnybank, Gayle, Hawes, N Yorks DL8 3RS.

HEYTESBURY, 6th Baron *cr* 1828; **Francis William Holmes à Court;** Bt 1795; *b* 8 Nov. 1931; *s* of 5th Baron Heytesbury and Beryl (*d* 1968), *y d* of late A. E. B. Crawford, LLD, DCL, Aston Clinton House, Bucks; *S* father, 1971; *m* 1962, Alison, *e d* of Michael Graham Balfour, CBE; one *s* one *d*. *Educ:* Bryanston; Pembroke College, Cambridge (BA 1954). *Heir: s* Hon. James William Holmes à Court [*b* 30 July 1967; *m* 1995, Polly Jane, *d* of A. G. Kendrick].

HEYWARD, Rt Rev. Oliver Spencer; Bishop of Bendigo, 1975–91; Assistant to Primate of Anglican Church of Australia, 1991–95; *b* Launceston, Tasmania, 16 March 1926; *s* of Harold and Vera Heyward; *m* 1952, Peggy Butcher; four *s*. *Educ:* Church Gram. Sch., Launceston; Univ. of Tasmania (BA Hons 1949); Oriel Coll., Univ. of Oxford (BA 1953, MA 1956); Cuddesdon Coll., Oxford. RAAF, 1944–46. Rhodes Scholar, 1949. Deacon 1953, priest 1954, dio. Chichester; Asst Curate, St Peter's, Brighton, 1953–56; Rector of Sorell, Tasmania, 1956–60; Rector of Richmond, Tasmania, 1960–62; Precentor, St David's Cathedral, Hobart, 1962–63; Warden, Christ Coll., Univ. of Tasmania, 1963–74. Chm., Brotherhood of St Laurence, 1993–96. Pres., Bendigo Coll. of Advanced Educn, 1976–86; Comr, Victorian Post-Secondary Educn Commn, 1982–93. *Recreation:* gardening. *Address:* 7 Waltham Street, Richmond, Vic 3121, Australia.

HEYWOOD, Barry; *see* Heywood, R. B.

HEYWOOD, David George, CBE 1999; Chairman, Nestor Healthcare Group plc, since 1994; *b* 21 Aug. 1935; *s* of Samuel George Heywood and Hilda Kathleen Heywood (*née* Lamey); *m* 1960, Pamela Moore; two *s* one *d*. *Educ:* Kingswood Sch., Bath; Magdalene Coll., Cambridge (BA). ACCA 1964. With British American Tobacco Co. plc, 1960–91 (Dep. Chm., 1988–91); Chairman: G. S. Hldgs plc, 1993–99; Remploy Ltd, 1994–2000. Non-exec. Dir, Rentokil Initial plc, 1991–98. *Recreations:* golf, foreign travel. *Address:* Logie, Cedar Road, Woking, Surrey GU22 0JH. *T:* (01483) 773188. *Clubs:* Worplesdon Golf (Woking); Royal North Devon Golf (Westward Ho!).

HEYWOOD, Geoffrey, MBE (mil.) 1945; JP; Consulting Actuary; *b* 7 April 1916; *s* of Edgar Heywood and Annie (*née* Dawson), Blackpool; *m* 1941, Joan Corinna Lumley; one *s* one *d*. *Educ:* Arnold Sch., Blackpool; Open Univ. (BA Hons). Served War, 1940–46: Royal Artillery, N Africa, Italy, Greece; commissioned, 1941, Major, 1944; despatches, 1945. Refuge Assce Co. Ltd, 1933–40; Duncan C. Fraser & Co. (Consulting Actuaries), 1946–86 (Sen. Partner, 1952–86). Pres., Manchester Actuarial Soc., 1951–53; Chm., Assoc. of Consulting Actuaries, 1959–62; Founder Chm., Internat. Assoc. of Consulting Actuaries, 1968–72; Pres., Inst. of Actuaries, 1972–74 (Vice-Pres., 1964–67). Mem. Page Cttee to Review National Savings. Dep. Chm., Mersey Docks & Harbour Co., 1975–85; Mem., Nat. Bus Co., 1978–85. Chm., Merseyside Cable Vision, 1982–90; Director: Barclays Bank Trust Co., 1967–86; Liverpool Bd Barclays Bank, 1972–86; Barclays Unicorn Gp, 1977–85; Universities Superannuation Scheme, 1974–86. Corresp. Mem., Assoc. des Actuaires Suisses, 1973. FFA 1939; FIA 1946; FRAS 1982; FRSA 1986. Founder Master, Actuaries Co., 1979; Liveryman, Clockmakers' Co. JP Liverpool 1962. *Publications:* contribs to Jl Inst. Actuaries. *Recreation:* antiquarian horology. *Address:* Drayton, Croft Drive East, Caldy, Wirral, Merseyside CH48 1LS. *T:* (0151) 625 6707. *Clubs:* Army and Navy, Royal Automobile.

HEYWOOD, Jeremy John; Principal Private Secretary to the Prime Minister, since 1999 (Private Secretary, 1997–99); *b* 31 Dec. 1961; *s* of Peter Andrew Heywood and Brenda Heywood (*née* Swinbank); *m* 1997, Dr Suzanne Elizabeth Cook. *Educ:* Bootham Sch., York; Hertford Coll., Oxford (BA Hons Modern Hist. and Econs); London Sch. of Econs (MSc Econ); Harvard Business Sch. (PMD 1994). Econ. Asst, HSE, 1983–84; HM Treasury: Econ. Asst, 1984–85; Private Sec. to Financial Sec., 1986–88; Asst to UK Dir, IMF, Washington, 1988–90 (on secondment); HM Treasury: Private Sec. to Chief Sec., 1990–91; Principal Private Sec. to Chancellor of the Exchequer, 1991–94; Head, Corporate and Mgt Change, 1994–95; Head, Securities and Markets Policy, 1995–97. *Recreations:* travel, modern art, contemporary cinema, Manchester United.

HEYWOOD, Patricia Ann; World Wide President, Mothers' Union, since 2001; *b* 8 Feb. 1943; *d* of George and Joan Robinson; *m* 1965, David Main Heywood (*d* 1999); two *s*. *Educ:* Kendal High Sch.; Whitelands Coll., London. Teacher, 1964–68 and 1975–81. Joined, Mothers' Union, 1973; Diocesan Pres., St Andrew's, Dunkeld and Dunblane, and Mem., Central Executive, 1992–95; Provincial Pres. for Scotland and Mem., Trustee Bd, 1995–2000. *Recreations:* reading, gardening, walking, crafts. *Address:* c/o Mothers' Union, Mary Sumner House, 24 Tufton Street, SW1P 3RB.

HEYWOOD, Sir Peter, 6th Bt *cr* 1838, of Claremont, Lancashire; company director; *b* 10 Dec. 1947; *s* of Sir Oliver Kerr Heywood, 5th Bt and Denise Wymondham, 2nd *d* of late Jocelyn William Godefroi; *S* father, 1992; *m* 1970, Jacqueline Anne, *d* of Sir Robert Hunt, *qv*; two *d*. *Educ:* Bryanston Sch.; Keble Coll., Oxford (BA Hons). *Heir:* twin *b* Michael Heywood [*b* 10 Dec. 1947; *m* 1972, Caroline Awdry Greig; one *s* one *d*]. *Address:* 64 Newbridge Road, Bath, Avon BA1 3LA. *T:* (01225) 421581.

HEYWOOD, Dr (Ronald) Barry; Director, British Antarctic Survey, 1994–97; *b* 28 Sept. 1937; *s* of Ronald Heywood and Edith Henrietta Heywood (*née* Bradbury); *m* 1965, Josephine Despina Panagopoulos; two *d*. *Educ:* Ashby Grammar Sch., Leics; Birmingham Univ. (BSc 1959; MSc 1961); Queen Mary Coll., London Univ. (PhD 1970). MIBiol 1967. British Antarctic Survey: Biologist, 1961–68; Hd, Freshwater Res., 1968–83; Chief Scientist, Offshore Biol Prog., 1978–86; Hd, Marine Life Scis Div., 1986–87; Dep. Dir, 1988–94. UK Delegate: IOC Regl Cttee for Southern Ocean, 1987–97; SCAR, 1995–97 (Mem., Wkg Gp on Human Biol and Medicine, 1995–97); Council of Managers of Nat. Antarctic Progs, 1994–97. Chairman: Eur. Bd for Polar Sci., 1995–97; Jt Exec., Eur. Bds for Marine and Polar Sci., 1995–97; Mem., British Nat. Cttee Antarctic Res., 1994–97. Hon. Associate, RHC, 1981. Polar Medal, 1967 and Clasp, 1986. *Publications:* University Research in Antarctica, 1993; papers on freshwater and marine physics and biol. *Recreations:* walking, music. *Address:* Magdalene House, Glapthorn Road, Oundle, Peterborough PE8 4JA. *Club:* Antarctic.

HEYWOOD, Prof. Vernon Hilton; Emeritus Professor, University of Reading, since 1988; *b* 24 Dec. 1927; *s* of Vernon William and Marjorie Elizabeth Heywood; *m* 1st, 1952, María de la Concepción Salcedo Manrique; four *s*; 2nd, 1980, Christine Anne Brighton. *Educ:* George Heriot's Sch., Edinburgh; Edinburgh Univ. (BSc, DSc); Pembroke Coll., Cambridge (PhD). Lecturer 1955–60, Sen. Lectr 1960–63, Reader 1963–64, Professor 1964–68, Dept of Botany, Univ. of Liverpool; University of Reading: Prof. of Botany and Hd of Dept of Botany, 1968–88; Dean, Faculty of Science, 1978–81. Dir, 1987–92, Consultant Dir, 1993, Botanic Gardens Conservation Internat.; Chief Scientist (Plant Conservation), IUCN, 1988–92; Exec. Editor, Global Biodiversity Assessment, UNEP, 1993–98. Hon. Professor: Botanical Inst., Nanjing, 1989–; Univ. Juan Agustín Maza, Mendoza, Argentina, 1997–; Hon. Fellow, Royal Botanic Garden, Edinburgh, 1995–. Storer Lectr, Univ. of California, Davis, 1990; Regents' Lectr, Univ. of Calif, Riverside, 1998. Chm., European Plants Specialist Gp, Species Survival Commn of IUCN, 1984–87; Pres., Internat. Council on Medicinal and Aromatic Plants, 1994–; Member of Board: Genetic Resources Communications Systems Inc., 1990–94; Yves Rocher Foundn, 1991–; Conservatoire Botanique National, Porquerolles, 1991–, Bailleul, 1993–, Nancy, 1996–. Trustee: Royal Botanic Gardens, Kew, 1983–87; IUCN, UK, 1993–. Corresponding Mem., Botanical Soc. of Amer., 1987–. Hon. FLS 1999. Councillor of Honour, Consejo Superior de Investigaciones Científicas, Spain, 1970. Linnean Medal, Linnean Soc. of London, 1987; Hutchinson Medal, Chicago Hortl Soc., 1989. Order of the Silver Dog (Gran Canaria), 1989. *Publications:* Principles of Angiosperm Taxonomy (with P. H. Davis), 1963, 2nd edn 1965; (ed jtly) Flora Europaea: vol. 1 1964 (2nd edn 1993), vol. 2 1968, vol. 3 1972, vol. 4 1976, vol. 5 1980; Plant Taxonomy, 1967, 2nd edn 1976; Flowering Plants of the World, 1978, 2nd edn 1985; (jtly) Our Green and Living World, 1984; Las Plantas con Flores, 1985; (jtly) Botanic Gardens and the World Conservation Strategy, 1987; The Botanic Gardens Conservation Strategy, 1989; (jtly) International Directory of Botanic Gardens V, 1990; (jtly) Conservation of Medicinal Plants, 1991; (jtly) Conservation Techniques in Botanic Gardens, 1991; (jtly) Tropical Botanic Gardens: their role in conservation and development, 1991; (jtly) Proceedings of the International Symposium on Botanical Gardens, 1991; (jtly) Conservation des ressources végétales, 1991; (jtly) Centres of Plant Diversity: a guide and strategy for their conservation: vol. 1 1994, vol. 2 1995, vol. 3 1996; (ed) Global Biodiversity Assessment, 1995; Les Plantes à Fleurs, 1996; (jtly) Conservation of the Wild Relatives of Cultivated Plants Native to Europe, 1997; Use and Potential of Wild Plants in Farm Households,

1998; over 500 papers in sci. jls. *Recreations:* cooking, travel, music, writing. *Address:* White Mead, 22 Wiltshire Road, Wokingham RG40 1TP. *T:* (0118) 978 0185.

HEYWOOD-LONSDALE, Lt-Col Robert Henry, MBE 1952; MC 1945; Vice Lord-Lieutenant for Oxfordshire, 1989–96; *b* 18 Dec. 1919; *s* of Col John Pemberton Heywood-Lonsdale, DSO, OBE, TD and Hon. Helen Annesley; *m* 1952, Hon. Jean Helen Rollo, *d* of 12th Lord Rollo; one *s* three *d*. *Educ:* Eton. Grenadier Guards, 1938–56; Royal Wilts Yeo., 1961–67. Farmer. Co. Comr for Scouts, Oxfordshire, 1981–86. High Sheriff, Wilts, 1975; DL Wilts, 1972, Oxon, 1983. *Recreation:* country pursuits. *Address:* Mount Farm, Churchill, Oxon OX7 6NP. *T:* (01608) 658316. *Club:* Boodle's.

HEZLET, Vice-Admiral Sir Arthur Richard, KBE 1964; CB 1961; DSO 1944 (Bar 1945); DSC 1941; *b* 7 April 1914; *s* of late Maj.-Gen. R. K. Hezlet, CB, CBE, DSO; *m* 1948, Anne Joan Patricia, *e d* of late G. W. N. Clark, Carnabane, Upperlands, Co. Derry; two adopted *d*. *Educ:* RN College, Dartmouth. Comd HM Submarines: H44, Ursula, Trident, Thrasher and Trenchant, 1941–45; comd HMS Scorpion, 1949–50; Chief Staff Officer to Flag Officer (Submarines), 1953–54; Capt. (D), 6th Destroyer Squadron 1955–56; Dir, RN Staff Coll., Greenwich, 1956–57; comd HMS Newfoundland, 1958–59; Rear-Adm. 1959; Flag Officer (Submarines), 1959–61; Flag Officer, Scotland, 1961–62; Vice-Adm. 1962; Flag Officer, Scotland and Northern Ireland, 1963–64; retired 1964. Legion of Merit (Degree of Commander) (US), 1945. *Publications:* The Submarine and Sea Power, 1967; Aircraft and Sea Power, 1970; The 'B' Specials, 1972; Electron and Sea Power, 1975. *Address:* Bovagh House, Mullaghinch Road, Aghadowey, Co. Londonderry, N Ireland. *T:* (01265) 868206. *Clubs:* Army and Navy, Royal Ocean Racing.

HIBBARD, Prof. Bryan Montague, MD, PhD; FRCOG; Professor of Obstetrics and Gynaecology, University of Wales College of Medicine (formerly Welsh National School of Medicine), 1973–91, now Emeritus Professor; *b* 24 April 1926; *s* of Montague Reginald and Muriel Irene Hibbard; *m* 1955, Elizabeth Donald Grassie. *Educ:* Queen Elizabeth's Sch., Barnet; St Bartholomew's Hosp. Med. Coll., London (MD); PhD (Liverpool). MRCS 1950; FRCOG 1965. Formerly: Sen. Lectr, Liverpool Univ.; Consultant Obstetrician and Gynaecologist, Liverpool RHB, and Univ. Hosp. of Wales. Chairman, Joint Standing Committee: Obstetric Anaesthesia, RCOG/RCAnaes, 1988–91; RCOG/RCM, 1988–91; Member: Cttee on Safety of Medicines, 1979–83; Maternity Services Adv. Cttee, 1981–85; Council, RCOG, 1982–88, 1989–92; S Glam HA, 1983–88; Medicines Commn, 1986–89. President: Welsh Obst. and Gynaecol Soc., 1985–86; History of Medicine Soc. of Wales, 1995–96. Hon. Curator of Museum, RCOG, 1986–2000 (Hon. Librarian, 1992–94). Mem. Editl Bd, Confidential Enquiries into Maternal Deaths, 1985–96 (Chm., Clinical Sub-Group, 1990–96). Hon. FRANZCOG 1997. *Publications:* Principles of Obstetrics, 1988; The Obstetric Forceps, 1988; The Obstetrician's Armamentarium, 2000; numerous contribs to world medical literature. *Recreations:* collecting 18th century drinking glasses, fell walking, coarse gardening. *Address:* The Clock House, Cathedral Close, Llandaff, Cardiff CF5 2ED. *T:* (029) 2056 6636.

HIBBERT; *see* Holland-Hibbert, family name of Viscount Knutsford.

HIBBERT, Rev. Barrie Edward; Interim Minister, Flinders Street Baptist Church, Adelaide, since 2000; *b* 9 June 1935; *s* of Joseph and Eva Hibbert, Gisborne, NZ; *m* 1957, Ellen Judith Eade; one *s* two *d*. *Educ:* Victoria Univ. of Wellington, NZ (BA); Melbourne Coll. of Divinity, Vic, Australia (LTh); NZ Baptist Theol Coll. Minister: Baptist churches in Gore, Tawa and Dunedin, NZ, 1962–79; Flinders St Baptist Church, Adelaide, SA, 1979–87; Bloomsbury Central Baptist Church, London, 1987–99. *Address:* 1/9 Elizabeth Avenue, Plympton, SA 5038, Australia. *T:* (8) 82978558.

HIBBERT, Christopher, MC 1945; author; *b* 5 March 1924; *s* of late Canon H. V. Hibbert; *m* 1948, Susan Piggford; two *s* one *d*. *Educ:* Radley; Oriel Coll., Oxford (MA). Served in Italy, 1944–45; Capt., London Irish Rifles. Partner in firm of land agents, auctioneers and surveyors, 1948–59. Fellow, Chartered Auctioneers' and Estate Agents' Inst., 1948–59. Pres., Johnson Soc., 1980. FRSL, FRGS. Hon. DLitt Leicester, 1996. Heinemann Award for Literature, 1962; McColvin Medal, LA, 1989. *Publications:* The Road to Tyburn, 1957; King Mob, 1958; Wolfe at Quebec, 1959; The Destruction of Lord Raglan, 1961; Corunna, 1961; Benito Mussolini, 1962; The Battle of Arnhem, 1962; The Roots of Evil, 1963; The Court at Windsor, 1964; Agincourt, 1964; (ed) The Wheatley Diary, 1964; Garibaldi and His Enemies, 1965; The Making of Charles Dickens, 1967; (ed) Waterloo: Napoleon's Last Campaign, 1967; (ed) An American in Regency England: The Journal of Louis Simond, 1968; Charles I, 1968; The Grand Tour, 1969; London: Biography of a City, 1969; The Search for King Arthur, 1970; (ed) The Recollections of Rifleman Harris, 1970; Anzio: the bid for Rome, 1970; The Dragon Wakes: China and the West, 1793–1911, 1970; The Personal History of Samuel Johnson, 1971; (ed) Twilight of Princes, 1971; George IV, Prince of Wales, 1762–1811, 1972; George IV, Regent and King, 1812–1830, 1973; The Rise and Fall of the House of Medici, 1974; (ed) A Soldier of the Seventy-First, 1975; Edward VII: a portrait, 1976; The Great Mutiny: India 1857, 1978; Disraeli and His World, 1978; The Court of St James's, 1979; (ed) Boswell's Life of Johnson, 1979; The French Revolution, 1981; (ed) Greville's England, 1981; Africa Explored: Europeans in the Dark Continent, 1769–1889, 1982; (ed with Ben Weinreb) The London Encyclopaedia, 1983; Queen Victoria in Her Letters and Journals, 1984; Rome, Biography of a City, 1985; Cities and Civilizations, 1986; The English: A Social History 1066–1945, 1987; A Guide to Royal London, 1987; The Grand Tour, 1987; London's Churches, 1988; (ed) The Encyclopaedia of Oxford, 1988; Venice: biography of a city, 1988; Redcoats and Rebels: the war for America 1770–1781, 1990; The Virgin Queen: the personal history of Elizabeth I, 1990; (ed) Captain Gronow: his reminiscences of Regency and Victorian Life 1810–60, 1991; The Story of England, 1992; Cavaliers and Roundheads: the English at war 1642–1649, 1993; Florence: biography of a city, 1993; Nelson: a personal history, 1994; No Ordinary Place: Radley College and the public school system, 1997; Wellington: a personal history, 1997; George III: a personal history, 1998; Queen Victoria: a personal history, 2000; The Marlboroughs: John and Sarah Churchill 1650–1744, 2001. *Recreations:* gardening, travel, cooking, crosswords. *Address:* 6 Albion Place, West Street, Henley-on-Thames, Oxon RG9 2DT. *Clubs:* Garrick, Army and Navy.

HIBBERT, Sir Jack, KCB 1990; Director, Central Statistical Office, and Head of Government Statistical Service, 1985–92; *b* 14 Feb. 1932; *s* of late William Collier Hibbert and Ivy Annie (*née* Wigglesworth); *m* 1957, Joan Clarkson; two *s* one *d*. *Educ:* Leeds Grammar Sch.; London Sch. of Economics (BScEcon). Served Royal Air Force, 1950–52. Exchequer and Audit Dept, 1952–60; Central Statistical Office, 1960–65; LSE, 1965–66; CSO, 1966; Chief Statistician, 1970; Asst Dir, 1977; Under Sec., DTI, 1982–85. OECD and EUROSTAT Consultant, 1981 and 1993. *Publications:* Measuring the Effects of Inflation on Income, Saving and Wealth (OECD), 1983; articles in economic and statistical pubns. *Recreations:* golf, bridge. *Club:* Reform.

HIBBERT, Sir Reginald (Alfred), GCMG 1982 (KCMG 1979; CMG 1966); HM Diplomatic Service, retired; *b* 21 Feb. 1922; *s* of late Alfred Hibbert, MBE, Sawbridgeworth, Herts; *m* 1949, Ann Alun Pugh, *d* of late Sir Alun Pugh; two *s* one *d*. *Educ:* Queen Elizabeth's Sch., Barnet; Worcester Coll., Oxford (Hon. Fellow, 1991). Served with SOE and 4th Hussars in Albania and Italy, 1943–45. Entered Foreign Service, 1946; served in Bucharest, Vienna, Guatemala, Ankara, Brussels; Chargé d'Affaires, Ulan Bator, 1964–66; Research Fellow, Leeds Univ., 1966–67; Political Adviser's Office, Singapore, 1967–69; Political Adviser to C-in-C Far East, 1970–71; Minister, Bonn, 1972–75; Asst Under-Sec. of State, FCO, 1975–76; Dep. Under-Sec. of State, FCO, 1976–79; Ambassador to France, 1979–82; Dir, Ditchley Foundn, 1982–87. Vis. Fellow, Nuffield Coll., Oxford, 1984–88; Hon. Res. Fellow, UC, Swansea, 1988–. Chm., Franco-British Soc., 1990–95; President: Fédn Britannique des Alliances Françaises, 1997–99; Albania Soc. of Britain, 1996–2000. Commandeur, Légion d'Honneur (France), 1995. *Publication:* The Albanian National Liberation Struggle: the bitter victory, 1991. *Address:* Frondeg, Pennal, Machynlleth, Powys SY20 9JX. *T:* (01654) 791220. *Club:* Reform.

HICHENS, Antony Peverell, RD 1969; Chairman, David S. Smith (Holdings) plc, since 1999; *b* 10 Sept. 1936; *s* of late Lt-Comdr R. P. Hichens, DSO (and Bar), DSC (and 2 Bars), RNVR, and Catherine Gilbert Enys; *m* 1963, Szerina Neomi Hobday; one *d*. *Educ:* Stowe; Magdalen Coll., Oxford (MA Law); Univ. of Pennsylvania, Wharton Sch. (MBA). Midshipman, RNVR, 1954–56. Called to Bar, Inner Temple, 1960. Rio Tinto-Zinc Corp., 1960–72; Financial Dir, Redland, 1972–81; Man. Dir and Chief Financial Officer, Consolidated Gold Fields, 1981–89; Chairman: Y. J. Lovell (Holdings), 1990–94; Caradon, 1990–98; Lasmo plc, 2000–01; Dep. Chm., Candover Investments, 1989–. Mem. (non-exec.), British Coal Corp., 1992–97. Waynflete Fellow, Magdalen Coll., Oxford, 1997–. *Recreations:* travel, wine, shooting. *Address:* Slape Manor, Netherbury, near Bridport, Dorset DT6 5HL. *T:* (01308) 488232. *Clubs:* Brooks's, Naval.

HICK, Prof. John Harwood; Danforth Professor, 1979–92, and Director of Blaisdell Programs in World Religions and Cultures, 1983–92, Claremont Graduate School, California, now Professor Emeritus, Claremont Graduate University; *b* 20 Jan. 1922; *s* of Mark Day Hick and Mary Aileen (Hirst); *m* 1953, (Joan) Hazel, *d* of F. G. Bowers, CB, CBE, and Frances Bowers; two *s* one *d* (and one *s* decd). *Educ:* Bootham Sch., York; Edinburgh Univ. (MA 1948 (1st cl. hons Philos); DLitt 1974); Oriel Coll., Oxford (Campbell-Fraser schol.; DPhil 1950); Westminster Coll., Cambridge. Friends' Ambulance Unit, 1942–45. Ordained, Presb. C of E, 1953; Minister, Belford Presb. Church, Northumberland, 1953–56; Asst Prof. of Philosophy, Cornell Univ., 1956–59; Stuart Prof. of Christian Philosophy, Princeton Theolog. Seminary, 1959–64; S. A. Cook Bye-Fellow, Gonville and Caius Coll., Cambridge, 1963–64; PhD by incorporation; Lectr in Divinity, Cambridge Univ., 1964–67; H. G. Wood Prof. of Theology, Univ. of Birmingham, 1967–82, now Emeritus. Guggenheim Fellow, 1963–64, and 1985–86; Leverhulme Res. Fellow, 1976; Scholar-in-residence, Rockefeller Foundn Research Center, Bellagio, Italy, 1986; Fellow, Inst. for Advanced Res. in Arts and Social Scis (formerly the Humanities), Birmingham Univ., 1988–; Hon. Prof., Univ. of Wales, Lampeter, 1995–. Lectures: Mead-Swing, Oberlin Coll., USA, 1962–63; Mary Farnum Brown, Haverford Coll., USA 1964–65; James W. Richard, Univ. of Virginia, 1969; Distinguished Vis., Univ. of Oregon, 1969; Arthur Stanley Eddington Meml, 1972; Stanton, Cambridge Univ., 1974–77; Teape, Delhi and Madras, 1975; Ingersoll, Harvard, 1977; Hope, Stirling, 1977; Younghusband, London, 1977; Mackintosh, East Anglia, 1978; Riddell, Newcastle, 1978–79; Berkeley, TCD, 1979; Greenhoe, Louisville Pres. Sem., 1979; Potter, Washington State Univ., 1980; Montefiore, London, 1980; Brooks, Univ. of S California, 1982; Mars and Shaffer, Northwestern Univ., 1983; Niebuhr, Elmhurst Coll., 1986; Gifford, Edinburgh, 1986–87; Kegley, Calif State Univ.; Bakersfield, 1988; Suarez, Spring Hill Coll., 1988; Gates, Grinnell Coll., 1989; Birks, McGill Univ., 1989; Fritz Marti, Univ. of Southern Illinois, 1989; Brooke Anderson, Brown Univ., 1990; Eliot, Reed Coll., 1990; Resler, Ohio State Univ., 1991; Showers, Univ. of Indianapolis, 1993; McMartin, Ottawa Univ., 1993; Auburn, Union Theol Seminary, NY, 1994; Lily Montagu, London Soc. of Jews and Christians, London, 1994; Killeen, St Norbert Coll., Wis, 1995; Anne Spencer, Bristol Univ., 1996; Whyte, Oxford, 1998. Visiting Professor: Banares Hindu Univ., 1971; Visva Bharati Univ., 1971; Punjabi Univ., Patiala, 1971; Goa Univ., 1990; Visiting Fellow: British Acad. Overseas, 1974 and 1990; Univ. of Ceylon, 1974. Hulsean Preacher, Cambridge Univ., 1969; Select Preacher, Oxford Univ., 1970. Chairman: Religious and Cultural Panel, Birmingham Community Relations Cttee, 1969–74; Coordinating Working Party, Statutory Conf. for Revision of Agreed Syllabus of Religious Educn, Birmingham, 1971–74; Birmingham Inter-Faiths Council, 1975; President: Soc. for the Study of Theology, 1975–76; All Faiths for One Race, 1980–85 (Chm., 1972–73, 1978–80); Vice-President: World Congress of Faiths, 1993–; British Soc. for Philosophy of Religion, 1995–; Member: Amer. Acad. of Religion, 1980–94; Internat. Bd, Global Ethics and Religion Forum, Calif, 1998–; Member Emeritus: Amer. Soc. for the Study of Religion, 1992 (Mem., 1983); Amer. Philosophical Assoc., 1992 (Mem., 1980). Internat. Consultant, Internat. Interfaith Centre, Oxford, 1996–. Mem. Council, Selly Oak Colls, 1967–80; Governor, Queen's Coll., Birmingham, 1972–80. Member Editorial Board: The Encyclopedia of Philosophy; Religious Studies. Hon. Teol. Dr Uppsala, 1977. Louisville Grawemeyer Award in Religion, Univ. of Louisville and Louisville Theol Seminary, 1991. *Publications:* Faith and Knowledge, 1957, 2nd edn 1966; Philosophy of Religion, 1963, 4th edn 1990 (also Spanish, Portuguese, Chinese, Japanese, Korean, Finnish, Polish and Swedish edns); (ed) Faith and the Philosophers, 1963; (ed) The Existence of God, 1963; (ed) Classical and Contemporary Readings in the Philosophy of Religion, 1963, 3rd edn 1990; Evil and the God of Love, 1966, 2nd edn 1977; (ed) The Many-Faced Argument, 1967; Christianity at the Centre, 1968, 2nd edn as The Centre of Christianity, 1977 (trans. Dutch, Korean and Chinese); Arguments for the Existence of God, 1971 (trans. Polish); Biology and the Soul, 1972; God and the Universe of Faiths, 1973; (ed) Truth and Dialogue, 1974; Death and Eternal Life, 1976 (trans. Dutch); (ed) The Myth of God Incarnate, 1977 (trans. German and Arabic); God has Many Names, 1980 (trans. German, Japanese); (ed with Brian Hebblethwaite) Christianity and Other Religions, 1980; The Second Christianity, 1983 (trans. Japanese); (with Michael Goulder) Why Believe in God?, 1983; Problems of Religious Pluralism, 1985 (trans. Japanese); (ed with Hasan Askari) The Experience of Religious Diversity, 1985; An Interpretation of Religion, 1989 (trans. German, Chinese); (ed with Edmund Meltzer) Three Faiths—One God, 1989; (ed with Lamont Hempel) Gandhi's Significance for Today, 1989; (ed with Paul Knitter) The Myth of Christian Uniqueness, 1992 (trans. Japanese, Italian); Disputed Questions in Theology and the Philosophy of Religion, 1993; The Metaphor of God Incarnate, 1993 (trans. Japanese, Korean); The Rainbow of Faiths, 1995 (trans. Japanese, Chinese); The Fifth Dimension, 1999 (trans. Chinese, Japanese, Danish); Dialogues in the Philosophy of Religion, 2001. *Address:* 144 Oak Tree Lane, Selly Oak, Birmingham B29 6HU.

HICKEY, Most Rev. Barry James; *see* Perth (Australia), Archbishop of, (RC).

HICKEY, Sir Justin, Kt 1979; Chairman and Managing Director, Hickey Group; *b* 5 April 1920; *s* of Hon. Simon Hickey, Speaker, New South Wales Parliament, and Hilda

Ellen Hickey (*née* Dacey); *m* 1964, Barbara Standish Thayer; one *s* four *d*. *Educ:* De La Salle College, Sydney. Chairman: Australian Family Trust, 1965; Thayer Foundation (US), 1972; Director: Biocom Internat. Ltd (Bermuda), 1987–; Chemical Fuels Corp. (Atlanta, Ga), 1987–. Mem., Lloyd's of London, 1979. FRSA 1978. JP 1950. *Publication:* Just-In Business, 1998. *Recreations:* yachting, art collection. *Address:* 36 Cypress Drive, Broadbeach Waters, Qld 4217, Australia.

HICKEY, Dr Stephen Harald Frederick; Corporate Services Director, Department for Work and Pensions (formerly Department of Social Security), since 2000 (Principal Finance Officer, since 1998); *b* 10 July 1949; *s* of late Rev. Dr James Peter Hickinbotham and Ingeborg Hickinbotham; name changed by Deed Poll to Hickey, 1976; *m* 1976, Dr Janet Elizabeth Hunter; three *s*. *Educ:* St Lawrence Coll., Ramsgate; Corpus Christi Coll., Oxford (BA, MA); St Antony's Coll., Oxford (DPhil). Joined DHSS, 1974; Asst Sec., DHSS, later DSS, 1985–94; seconded to Rank Xerox (UK), 1989–90; Chief Exec., Civil Service Coll., 1994–98. *Publication:* Workers in Imperial Germany: the miners of the Ruhr, 1985. *Recreations:* music, tennis, walking, history. *Address:* Department for Work and Pensions, Richmond House, 79 Whitehall, SW1A 2NS.

HICKFORD, Very Rev. Michael Francis; Dean of Moray, Ross and Caithness, since 1998; Priest-in-charge, St James the Great, Dingwall with St Anne, Strathpeffer, since 1995; *b* 7 Oct. 1953; *s* of Frank Hickford and Cherryl Wendy Rosalind (*née* Mitchell). *Educ:* Gravesend Grammar Sch.; Edinburgh Theological Coll. Chaplain, St John's Cathedral, Oban, 1986–89; Rector, St Mungo, Alexandria, Dunbartonshire, 1989–95. *Recreations:* hill-walking, music, cookery, theatre. *Address:* The Parsonage, 4 Castle Street, Dingwall, Ross-shire IV15 9HU. *T:* (01349) 862204.

HICKINBOTTOM, Gary Robert, FCIArb; **His Honour Judge Hickinbottom;** a Circuit Judge, since 2000; *b* 22 Dec. 1955; *s* of Samuel Geoffrey Hickinbottom and Jean Irene Hickinbottom (*née* Greaney); *m* 1982, Paula Jayne Hughes; two *s* two *d*. *Educ:* Queen Mary's Grammar Sch., Walsall; University Coll., Oxford (MA); DipICArb. FCIArb 1995. Lectr, Poly. of Central London, 1980–81; admitted Solicitor, 1981; Partner, McKenna & Co., subseq. Cameron McKenna, 1986–2000; Lectr, University Coll., Oxford, 1987–89; Registered Mediator, 1991; Parking Adjudicator, Parking Appeals Service and Nat. Parking Adjudication Service, 1994–2000; Asst Recorder, 1994–98; Recorder, 1998–2000; Solicitor Advocate (all Courts), 1997. Asst Comr, Boundary Commn of England, 2000. Member: Gen. Council of Bar and Law Soc. Jt Wkg Party on Civil Courts, 1992–93; Law Soc. Wkg Party on Gp Actions, 1994–2000. *Publications:* various articles on law and legal procedure. *Recreations:* choral singing, opera, ballet, sport, Alpine walking. *Address:* c/o Swansea Civil Justice Centre, Caravella House, Quay West, Quay Parade, Swansea SA1 1SP. *T:* (01792) 510351. *Club:* London Welsh.

HICKLING, Rev. Canon Colin John Anderson; Canon Theologian, Leicester Cathedral, 1982–96, Canon Emeritus, since 1998; Hon. Lecturer in Biblical Studies, University of Sheffield, since 1986; Hon. Assistant Priest, St Mary's, Sprotbrough, since 1999; *b* 10 July 1931; *s* of late Charles Frederick Hickling, CMG, ScD, and late Marjorie Ellerington, *d* of late Henry Blamey. *Educ:* Taunton Sch.; Epsom Coll.; King's Coll., Cambridge (BA 1953, MA 1957); Chichester Theol Coll. Deacon 1957, priest 1958; Asst Curate, St Luke's, Pallion, Sunderland, 1957–61; Asst Tutor, Chichester Theol Coll., 1961–65; Asst Priest Vicar, Chichester Cath., 1964–65; Asst Lectr in New Testament Studies, King's Coll., Univ. of London, 1965–68, Lectr, 1968–84; Dep. Minor Canon, St Paul's Cath., 1969–78; Hon. Asst Priest, St John's, E Dulwich, 1970–84; Dep. Priest in Ordinary to the Queen, 1971–74; Priest in Ordinary to the Queen, 1974–84; Subwarden of King's Coll. Hall, 1969–78; Warden of King's Coll. Hostel, 1978–81; Tutor in Biblical Studies, Queen's Coll., Birmingham, 1984–85; E. W. Benson Fellow, Lincoln Theol Coll., 1985–86; Vicar of All Saints, Arksey, Sheffield, 1986–98. Mem., Liturgical Commn, 1981–86. Boyle Lectr, 1973–76; Select Preacher: Univ. of Cambridge, 1979; Univ. of Oxford, 1983. *Publications:* contributed to: Church without Walls, 1968; Catholic Anglicans Today, 1968; Bible Bibliography 1967–73, 1974; (also ed jtly) What About the New Testament?, 1975; St Paul: Teacher and Traveller, 1975; L'Evangile de Jean, 1977; Les Actes des Apôtres, 1979; The Ministry of the Word, 1979; This is the Word of the Lord, 1980; Studia Biblica 1978, Vol. III, 1980; Logia: the sayings of Jesus, 1982; Studia Evangelica, Vol. VII, 1982; A Dictionary of Biblical Interpretation, 1990; The Bible in Three Dimensions, 1990; Memorial Volume for J. Anastasiou, 1992; Resurrection, 1994; The Corinthian Correspondence, 1996; reviews and articles. *Recreation:* music. *Address:* 5 Chestnut Grove, Sprotbrough, Doncaster, S Yorks DN5 7RW. *T:* (01302) 852542.

HICKLING, Reginald Hugh, CMG 1968; PhD (London); QC (Gibraltar) 1970; *b* 2 Aug. 1920; *er s* of late Frederick Hugh Hickling and Elsie May Hickling, Malvern, Worcs; *m* 1945, Beryl Iris (*née* Dennett); two *s* one *d* (and one *s* decd). *Educ:* Buxton Coll.; Nottingham Univ. RNVR, 1941–46. Dep. Solicitor, Evening Standard, London, 1946–50; Asst Attorney-Gen., Sarawak, 1950–55; Legal Adviser, Johore, 1956; Legal Draftsman, Malaya, 1957; Parly Draftsman, Malaya, 1959; Comr of Law Revision, Malaya, 1961; Commonwealth Office, 1964; Legal Adviser to High Comr, Aden and Protectorate of S Arabia, 1964–67; Maritime Law Adviser: Thailand, 1968–69; Malaysia, 1969; Sri Lanka, 1970; Yemen Arab Republic, 1984, 1986; Attorney-General, Gibraltar, 1970–72. Lectr in SE Asian Law, SOAS, 1976–78, 1981–82; Visiting Professor, Faculty of Law: Univ. of Singapore, 1974–76 and 1978–80; Univ. of Malaya, 1983–84, 1986–88; Nat. Univ. of Malaysia, 1988–94; Adjunct Prof. of Law, Centre of Southeast Asian Law, Northern Territory Univ., 1995–. Advr on consumer law, Fiji, 1990, 1992, on legislative drafting, Fiji, 1996, 1998. Hon. JMN (Malaya), 1960. *Publications:* The Furious Evangelist, 1950; The English Flotilla, 1954 (US as Falconer's Voyage, 1956); Sarawak and Its Government, 1955; Festival of Hungry Ghosts, 1957; (ed) Malayan Constitutional Documents, 1958; An Introduction to the Federal Constitution, 1960; Lieutenant Okino, 1968; A Prince of Borneo, 1985; The Ghost of Orchard Road and other stories, 1985; Malaysian Law, 1987; Essays in Malaysian Law, 1991; Essays in Singapore Law, 1992; So Lucky and Other Stories, 1992; The Dog Satyricon, 1994; Finding Hobbes, 1994; (with Min Aun Wu) Conflict of Laws in Malaysia, 1995; Malaysian Public Law, 1997; The Lotus-eaters, 1997; Ikhlas in England, 2000; Memoir of a Wayward Lawyer, 2000. *Recreation:* not watching TV. *Address:* 1 Highfield Road, Malvern, Worcs WR14 1HR. *T:* (01684) 573477.

HICKMAN, Sir Glenn; *see* Hickman, Sir R. G.

HICKMAN, Sir (Richard) Glenn, 4th Bt *cr* 1903; *b* 12 April 1949; *s* of Sir Alfred Howard Whitby Hickman, 3rd Bt, and of Margaret Doris (*d* 1996), *o d* of Leonard Kempson; *S* father, 1979; *m* 1981, Heather Mary Elizabeth, *er d* of late Dr James Moffett, Swindon, and late Dr Gwendoline Moffett; two *s* one *d*. *Educ:* Eton. *Heir: s* Charles Patrick Alfred Hickman, *b* 5 May 1983. *Address:* Manor Farm House, Liddington, Wilts SN4 0HD. *Club:* Turf.

HICKMAN, Richard Michael; Chief Inquiry Reporter, Scottish Executive (formerly Scottish Office), since 1997; *b* 30 April 1942; *m* 1st, 1964, Lorna Dixon (marr. diss. 1992); two *s*; 2nd, 1993, Sandie Jane Randall; one step *s* one step *d*. *Educ:* Kingswood Sch., Bath; LSE (BA Hons Geog.); Regent St Polytechnic (DipTP); Univ. of British Columbia (MA Community and Regional Planning). MRTPI 1966. Planning Depts of LCC, 1963–65, of GLC, 1965–67; Scottish Develt Dept, 1969–78; Scottish Office Inquiry Reporters' Unit, 1979–. Vis. Fellow, Edinburgh Coll. of Art, 1994. *Recreations:* walking, sailing, travel. *Address:* Scottish Executive Inquiry Reporters' Unit, 2 Greenside Lane, Edinburgh EH1 3AG. *T:* (0131) 244 5644, *Fax:* (0131) 244 5680.

HICKMET, Richard Saladin; barrister-at-law; *b* 1 Dec. 1947; *s* of Ferid and Elizabeth Hickmet; *m* 1973, Susan (*née* Ludwig); three *d*. *Educ:* Millfield Sch.; Sorbonne; Hull Univ. (BA). Called to the Bar, Inner Temple, 1974. Mem., Wandsworth Borough Council, 1978–83 (Chm., Leisure and Amenities Cttee, 1980–83; privatised street cleansing, refuse collection, parks maintenance). Contested (C): Glanford and Scunthorpe, 1987; Eastbourne, Oct. 1990. MP (C) Glanford and Scunthorpe, 1983–87. *Recreations:* squash, hunting. *Address:* 12 Middle Street, Taunton TA1 1SH. *T:* (01823) 331919.

HICKOX, Richard Sidney; FRCO(CHM); conductor; Music Director: City of London Sinfonia, since 1971; City of London Sinfonia (formerly Richard Hickox) Singers, since 1971; London Symphony Chorus, since 1976; Associate Conductor, London Symphony Orchestra, since 1985; *b* Stokenchurch, Bucks, 5 March 1948; *m* 1976, Frances Ina Sheldon-Williams (marr. diss.); one *s*; *m* 1995, Pamela Helen Stephen; one *s* one *d*. *Educ:* in organ, piano and composition, Royal Acad. of Music (LRAM); Organ Scholar, Queens' Coll., Cambridge (MA). Début as professional conductor, St John's Smith Square, 1971; Organist and Master of the Music, St Margaret's, Westminster, 1972–82; Prom début, 1973. Artistic Director: Wooburn Fest., 1967–89; St Endellion Fest., 1974–; Christ Church Spitalfields Fest., 1978–94; Truro Fest., 1981–; Chester Summer Fest., 1989–; Northern Sinfonia, 1982–90 (Conductor Emeritus, 1996–); City of London Fest., 1994; Music Dir, Bradford Festival Choral Soc., 1978–98; Principal Guest Conductor: Dutch Radio Orch., 1980–84; Associate Conductor, San Diego Symphony Orch., 1983–84; also regularly conducts Philharmonia, RPO, Bournemouth Symphony Orch. and Sinfonietta, Royal Liverpool Phil. Orch., BBC Symphony, Concert, Scottish and Welsh Orchs, BBC Singers, Hallé Orch.; San Francisco Symphony Orch.; Detroit Symphony Orch.; Houston Symphony Orch.; National Symphony Orch., Washington; Rotterdam Philharmonic; Oslo Philharmonic; Turku Philharmonia; Salzburg Mozarteum; Suisse Romande; Stockholm Philharmonic. Conducted: ENO, 1979, 1996, 2000; Opera North, 1982, 1986, 1995; Scottish Opera, 1985, 1987; Royal Opera, 1985, 1999, 2001; has appeared at many music festivals incl. Proms, Flanders, Bath and Cheltenham. Co-founder, Opera Stage, 1985. Many recordings of choral and orchestral music. *Address:* 35 Ellington Street, N7 8PN.

HICKS; *see* Joynson-Hicks.

HICKS, Dr Brendan Hamilton, FRCP; Regional Postgraduate Dean Director, NHS South East Region, since 2001; *b* 22 Feb. 1942; *s* of Bryan Hamilton Hicks and Winifrede (*née* O'Leary); *m* 1966, Jackie Ann Box; one *s* one *d*. *Educ:* St Brendan's Coll., Bristol; Guy's Hosp. Med. Sch., Univ. of London (BSc 1962; MB BS 1965; MD 1976). FRCP 1982. Jun. med. posts, Guy's Hosp., RPMS and Brompton Hosp., 1965–67; Governors' Res. Schol. and Lectr in Medicine, Guy's Hosp. Med. Sch., 1967–72; NIH Internat. Fellow (US Public Health Service/MRC), Univ. of Michigan, Ann Arbor, 1972–73; Sen. Lectr in Medicine, Undergrad. Tutor and Hon. Consultant Physician, Guy's Hosp. and Med. Sch., 1974–80; Sen. Lectr in Medicine, UMDS of Guy's and St Thomas' Hosps, and Consultant Physician to Guy's and St Thomas' and Lewisham Hosps, 1981–95; Postgrad. Dean and Trust Dir, Postgrad. Med. and Dental Educn, Guy's and St Thomas' Hosp., 1985–95; Regl Postgrad. Dean Dir, NHS S Thames, and Univ. of London, 1996–2001. *Publications:* contrib. chapter in: A Short Textbook of Medicine, ed jtly, biennially, 1978–92; Principles of Clinical Medicine, ed Rees and Williams, 1995; contrib. papers in Metabolism, Diabetic Medicine, Clin. Endocrinol., etc. *Recreations:* books, theatre, music, narrow-boating, sailing, Cocker Spaniels. *Address:* 60 Greenwich Park Street, SE10 9LT. *T:* (020) 8858 7363; KSS Postgraduate Deanery, 20 Guilford Street, WC1N 1DZ. *T:* (020) 7692 3142; *e-mail:* bhicks@kssdeanery.ac.uk.

HICKS, Dr Colin Peter, CChm, FRSC; Director General, British National Space Centre, since 1999; *b* 1 May 1946; *s* of George Stephen Frederick Hicks and Irene Maud (*née* Hargrave); *m* 1967, Elizabeth Joan Payne; two *d*. *Educ:* Rutlish Grammar Sch., Merton; Univ. of Bristol (BSc, PhD). Lectr in Chemistry, Univ. of W Indies, Jamaica, 1970–73; ICI Res. Fellow, Univ. of Exeter, 1973–75; DTI, 1975–; NPL, 1975–80; Laboratory of Govt Chemist, 1984–87; Sec., Ind. Develt Adv. Bd, 1988–90; Hd, Res. and Technol. Policy Div., 1990–94; Hd of Envmt and Energy Technologies Div., 1994–96; Dir, Envmt, 1996–99. *Address:* British National Space Centre, 151 Buckingham Palace Road, SW1W 9SS.

HICKS, Gp Captain David; *see* Hicks, Gp Captain H. D.

HICKS, Group Captain (Harry) David, MBE 1967; Director General, English-Speaking Union, 1990–91 (Deputy Director General, 1985–90); *b* 13 July 1923; *s* of Walter Hicks and Clara Ann (*née* Jagger); *m* 1948, Jane Irene Mary Tibbs; one *s* one *d*. *Educ:* Grange Grammar Sch., Bradford; London Univ. (BA Hons 1947); Nottingham Univ. (PGCE 1948). Served War, 1942–45, as Pilot, 149 Sqdn, Bomber Comd. Schoolmaster, Surbiton Grammar Sch., 1948–49; Royal Air Force: Educn Br., 1950–54; Admin. Br., 1954–76, finally as Dep. Dir, Recruiting; Dir of Educn, E-SU, 1976–85; Gen. Dir, Internat. Shakespeare Globe Centre, 1991–92. Special Consultant to BBC English, 1991–95; German Language Consultant to Callon Sch., 1992–. Pres., Windsor and S Bucks Br., ESU, 1991–94; Consultant on public speaking and presentations, Bucks Red Cross, 1995–97; speaker, Bucks Fedn of WI Panels. *Recreations:* golf, tennis, playing piano. *Clubs:* Royal Air Force, English-Speaking Union.

HICKS, His Honour John Charles; QC 1980; a Judge of the Technology and Construction Court of the High Court (formerly the Official Referees' Courts), 1993–2000; a Circuit Judge, 1988–2000; *b* 4 March 1928; *s* of late Charles Hicks and late Marjorie Jane Hicks; *m* 1957, Elizabeth Mary, *o d* of late Rev. J. B. Jennings; one *d* (one *s* decd). *Educ:* King Edward VI Grammar Schs, Chelmsford and Totnes; London Univ. LLM 1954. Served RA (National Service), 1946–48. Admitted solicitor, 1952; called to the Bar, Middle Temple, 1966; a Recorder, 1978–88. Legal Dept, Thomas Tilling Ltd, 1953–54; Partner in Messrs Burchells, solicitors, 1955–65; Methodist Missionary Soc., Caribbean, 1965–66. Jl Sec., Methodist Conf., 1989–97. *Publications:* (ed jtly) The Constitution and Discipline of the Methodist Church in the Caribbean and the Americas, 1967, with annual supplements to 1987; (ed) The Constitutional Practice and Discipline of the Methodist Church, 6th edn 1974, 7th edn 1988, with annual supplements, 1974–97; articles in Mod. Law Rev., Cambridge Law Jl, Conveyancer, and Epworth Rev. *Recreations:* squash rackets, music, theatre, opera, the Methodist Constitution. *Address:* Flat 3, 17 Montagu Square, W1H 2LE. *T:* (020) 7935 6008.

HICKS, Maureen Patricia; Director of Fundraising and Marketing, Myton Hamlet Hospice, Warwick, since 1997; *b* 23 Feb. 1948; *d* of Ron and Nora Cutler; *m* 1973, Keith

Hicks; one *s* one *d*. *Educ:* Ashley Secondary School; Brockenhurst Grammar School; Furzedown College of Education. Teacher's Cert. Secondary Teacher, Drama and English, 1969–70; Marks & Spencer Management, 1970–74; Asst Area Educn Officer, 1974–76; Dir, Motor Museum, 1976–82; Project Dir, Stratford-upon-Avon Visitor Mgt Nat. Pilot Project, 1992–96. Mem., Stratford DC, 1979–84. MP (C) Wolverhampton North East, 1987–92; contested (C) Wolverhampton NE, 1992. PPS to Minister of State and Parly Under-Sec. of State, FCO, 1991–92; Sec., H of C Tourism Cttee, 1987–92. Non-executive Director: David Clarke Associates, 1992–96; S Warwicks Combined Care (formerly Mental Health Services) NHS Trust, 1994–. Mem., Women In Management Assoc. Hon. Fellow, Wolverhampton Univ., 1992. *Recreations:* amateur dramatics, music, golf, travel.

HICKS, Maj.-Gen. Michael; *see* Hicks, Maj.-Gen. W. M. E.

HICKS, Sir Robert, Kt 1996; Chairman, Westcountry Enterprises Ltd, since 1997; *b* 18 Jan. 1938; *s* of W. H. Hicks; *m* 1st, 1962, Maria Elizabeth Ann Gwyther (marr. diss. 1988); two *d*; 2nd, 1991, Mrs Glenys Foote. *Educ:* Queen Elizabeth Grammar Sch., Crediton; University Coll., London; Univ. of Exeter. Taught at St Austell Grammar Sch., 1961–64; Lecturer in Regional Geography, Weston-super-Mare Technical Coll., 1964–70. MP(C): Bodmin, 1970–Feb. 1974, Oct. 1974–1983; Cornwall SE, 1983–97. An Asst Govt Whip, 1973–74; Member: Select Cttee of House of Commons, European Legislation, 1973, 1976–97; Speaker's Panel, 1992–97; Vice-Chm., Cons. Parly European Affairs Cttee, 1979–81; Chairman: Cons. Parly Agric. Cttee, 1988–90 (Vice-Chm., 1972–73 (Chm., Horticultural Sub-Cttee), and 1974–82); Westcountry Gp of Cons. MPs, 1976–77; UK Gp, Parly Assoc. for Euro-Arab Co-operation, 1982–97; Vice-Chm., Cons. Party ME Council, 1992–97 (Treasurer, 1980–92); Parly Adviser to British Hotels, Restaurants and Caterers Assoc., 1974–97, to Milk Marketing Bd, 1985–97. Pres., Plymouth Albion RFC, 1991–96. Chm., Silvanus Trust, 1999–. *Recreations:* cricket, gardening, golf. *Address:* Burndoo, Luckett, Callington, Cornwall PL17 8NH. *Clubs:* Farmers', MCC.

HICKS, Robin Edgcumbe; Director, Expocentric.com, since 1999; *b* 6 Dec. 1942; *s* of late Ronald Eric Edgcumbe Hicks and Fredrica Hicks; *m* 1970, Sue (*née* Dalton); one *s* one *d*. *Educ:* Bancrofts' Sch.; Seale Hayne Coll. (NDA; Dip. Farm Management); Univ. of Reading (DipAgric Extension). ARAgS 1995. Farm worker, 1961–63; Agricl Advr, MAFF, 1967–69; Producer/Presenter, BBC Farming Today, 1969–71; Churchill Fellow, 1973; various production posts, radio and television, 1971–77; Hd of Marketing and Develt, RASE, 1977–79; Hd of Network Radio, BBC South and West, 1979–88; Chief Exec., RASE, 1989–91; Dir, Royal Smithfield Show, 1992–98; Chief Exec., Consortium of Rural TECs, 1998–99. Consultant: Royal Smithfield Show; Landscape '99. Mem., Bristol and Weston HA, 1986–88; Vice-Chm., Radio Acad., 1986–88; Trustee: St George's Music Trust, 1981–88; Rural Housing Trust, 1990–92; Member: Exec. Cttee, SW Arts, 1981–85; SW Concerts Bd, 1981–88; Trustee, Head Injury Recovery Trust, 1986–94. Freeman, City of London, 1977; Liveryman, Drapers' Co, 1981. *Recreations:* family, boating, gardening, theatre. *Address:* Collenshayne, Hemyock, Devon EX15 3QZ. *Club:* Farmers'.

HICKS, Thomas; *see* Steele, Tommy.

HICKS, William David Anthony; QC 1995; *b* 11 June 1951; *s* of Maj.-Gen. William Michael Ellis Hicks, *qv*; *m* 1982, Jennifer Caroline Ross; one *s* two *d*. *Educ:* Eton Coll.; Magdalene Coll., Cambridge (MA Econs). Called to the Bar, Inner Temple, 1975. *Recreations:* fishing, tennis, ski-ing. *Address:* 1 Serjeants' Inn, EC4Y 1NH. *T:* (020) 7583 1355. *Club:* Vanderbilt Racquets.

HICKS, Maj.-Gen. (William) Michael (Ellis), CB 1982; OBE 1967; Secretary, Royal College of Defence Studies, 1983–93; *b* 2 June 1928; *s* of late Group Captain William Charles Hicks, AFC, and Nellie Kilbourne (*née* Kay); *m* 1950, Jean Hilary Duncan; three *s*. *Educ:* Eton Coll.; RMA Sandhurst. Commnd 2 Lieut Coldstream Guards, 1948; served, 1948–67: regtl service, UK, Tripoli and Canal Zone; Instr, Sch. of Inf. (Captain); Staff Coll. (Major); GSO2 (Ops) HQ 4 Div.; regtl service, BAOR, UK and Kenya; JSSC; GSO (DS) Staff Coll.; GSO1 MO1, MoD, 1967–70 (Lt-Col); CO 1st Bn Coldstream Guards, 1970–72; RCDS, 1973 (Col); comd 4th Guards Armoured Bde, 1974–76 (Brig.); BGS Trng HQ UKLF, 1977–79; BGS (Author) attached to DMO, MoD, 1979; GOC NW Dist, 1980–83, retd. *Recreation:* gardening. *Address:* c/o Lloyds TSB, Cox's & King's, PO Box 1190, 7 Pall Mall, SW1Y 5NA.

HICKS BEACH, family name of **Earl St Aldwyn**.

HIDDEN, Hon. Sir Anthony Brian, Kt 1989; **Hon. Mr Justice Hidden;** a Judge of the High Court of Justice, Queen's Bench Division, since 1989; *b* 7 March 1936; *s* of late James Evelyn Harold Hidden, GM and Gladys Bessie (*née* Brooks); *m* 1982, Mary Elise Torriano Pritchard, *d* of R. C. Pritchard of Barton Abbotts, Tetbury, Glos; three *s* one *d*. *Educ:* Reigate Grammar Sch.; Emmanuel Coll., Cambridge (BA Hons 1957, MA 1960). 2nd Lieut, 1st Royal Tank Regt, Far East Land Forces, Hong Kong, 1958–59. Called to the Bar, Inner Temple, 1961, Bencher, 1985; Mem., Hon. Soc. of Inner Temple, 1956–, and of Lincoln's Inn (*ad eundem*), 1973–. QC 1976; a Recorder, 1977–89; Leader, SE Circuit, 1986–89. *Recreations:* reading, playing bad golf. *Address:* Royal Courts of Justice, Strand, WC2A 2LL.

HIDE, Prof. Raymond, CBE 1990; FRS 1971; Senior Research Investigator, Department of Mathematics, Imperial College, University of London, since 2000; Emeritus Professor of Physics, Oxford University, since 1994 (Research Professor, Departments of Physics and Earth Sciences, 1992–94); *b* 17 May 1929; *s* of late Stephen Hide and Rose Edna (*née* Cartlidge); *m* 1958, (Phyllis) Ann Licence; one *s* two *d*. *Educ:* Percy Jackson Grammar Sch., near Doncaster; Manchester Univ. (BSc 1st cl. hons Physics, 1950); Caius Coll., Cambridge (PhD 1953, ScD 1969). CPhys, FInstP, 1998. Res. Assoc. in Astrophysics, Univ. of Chicago, 1953–54; Sen. Res. Fellow, AERE Harwell, 1954–57; Lectr in Physics, Univ. of Durham (King's Coll., Newcastle), 1957–61; Prof. of Geophysics and Physics, MIT, 1961–67; Hd of Geophysical Fluid Dynamics Lab., Met. Office, 1967–90 (CSO 1975); Fellow, Jesus Coll., Oxford, 1983–96 (Hon. Fellow, 1997); Dir, Robert Hooke Inst. and Vis. Prof., Dept of Physics, Oxford Univ., 1990–92. Short-term vis. appts at Princeton Inst. for Advanced Study, 1954, MIT and UCLA, 1960, CIT, 1993 (Fairchild Schol.); Visiting Professor: UCL, 1967 84; Reading Univ., 1976–91; Leeds Univ., 1986–91; Gresham Prof. of Astronomy, Gresham Coll., City of London, 1985–90; Adrian Fellow, Univ. of Leicester, 1980–83. Distinguished Vis. Scientist, Jet Propulsion Lab., CIT, 1985–97; Hon. Sen. Res. Fellow, Inst. of Oceanographic Scis Deacon Lab., 1990–; Hon. Scientist, Rutherford Appleton Lab., 1992–. Member Council: RAS, 1969–72 and 1983–86 (Pres., 1983–85); Royal Meteorological Soc., 1969–72 and 1974–77 (Pres., 1974–76; Hon. Mem., 1989); NERC, 1972–75; Eur. Geophysical Soc., 1981–85 (Pres., 1982–84, Hon. Mem., 1988); Royal Soc., 1988–90. Lectures: Symons Meml, RMetS, 1970; R. A. Fisher Meml, 1977; Halley, Oxford, 1980; Jeffreys, RAS, 1981; Union, Internat. Union of Geodesy and Geophysics, Hamburg, 1983; Scott, Cambridge, 1984; Thompson, Toronto, 1984; Lindsay, NASA, 1988; Courtauld, Manchester Lit. & Phil Soc., 1996; Schuster, Manchester Univ., 1998; Starr, MIT, 2001. Mem., Pontifical Acad. of Scis, 1996; Fellow: Amer. Acad. of Arts and Sciences, 1964; Amer. Geophys. Union, 1967; Academia Europaea, 1988. Hon. DSc: Leicester, 1985; UMIST, 1994; Paris, 1995. Charles Chree Medal, Inst. Physics, 1975; Holweck Medal, Soc. Franç. de Physique, 1982; Gold Medal, RAS, 1989; William Bowie Medal, Amer. Geophysical Union, 1997; Hughes Medal, Royal Soc., 1998; Richardson Medal, European Geophys. Soc., 1999. *Publications:* papers in scientific jls. *Address:* Department of Mathematics, Imperial College, 180 Queen's Gate, SW7 2RH.

HIDER, David James; Director, Internal Communications Project, British Gas, 1994–95; *b* 5 Nov. 1934; *s* of Edward James Hider and Marguerite Noel Hider (*née* James); *m* 1963, Margaret Gilbert Macdonald Watson; two *s* one *d*. *Educ:* Roan Sch., Greenwich; King Edward VII Nautical Coll., Poplar. Master Mariner; DMS; CIGasE. Merchant Navy, 1952–67 (to Chief Officer); South Eastern Gas: Commercial Asst, 1967; Conversion Unit Manager, 1969; Area Service Manager, Sussex, 1973; Regl Service Manager, 1976; Dir of Marketing, 1981; British Gas: Dir of Service, 1983; Dir of Domestic Marketing, 1990; Regl Chm., British Gas S Western, 1990–94. Mem., SW IDB, 1997–99; Vice Chm., Bristol Regeneration Partnership, 2000–. Chm., Avon Youth Assoc., 1996–. Chm. and Man. Dir, St Peter's Hospice Enterprises, 2000–; Trustee, CLIC, 2000–. Gov., UWE, 1993–. *Publications:* contribs to Jl IGasE. *Recreations:* squash, swimming, walking, cooking, flying.

HIDER, Prof. Robert Charles, PhD; CChem, FRSC; Professor of Medicinal Chemistry, since 1987, Head, Department of Pharmacy, since 2000, King's College, London; *b* 14 Aug. 1943; *s* of Charles Thomas Hider and Josephine Mary (*née* Breitbach); *m* 1967, Shirley Christine Nickels; one *s* one *d*. *Educ:* King's Coll., London (BSc Chem. and Physics 1964; PhD Chem. 1967; FKC 1997). Wellcome Res. Fellow, St Thomas' Hosp., 1967–70; Lectr, then Reader, Dept of Chem., Essex Univ., 1970–87; Head, Sch. of Life, Basic Med. and Health Scis, then of Health & Life Scis, KCL, 1994–2000. Associated with develt of medicines for thalassaemia, anaemia, and renal failure. Vis. Prof., Dept of Biochem., Univ, of Calif, Berkeley, 1977 and 1980. Hon. MRPharmS, 1995. Member, Editorial Board: Toxicon, 1986–98; Biometals, 1990–; Biochem. Jl, 1996–. *Publications:* contrib. articles on pharmaceutically active peptides and metal chelating agents to pharmaceutical, biochem. and chem. jls. *Recreations:* arachnology, natural history, Australian philately. *Address:* 257 Point Clear Road, St Osyth, Essex C016 8JL. *T:* (01255) 821335.

HIELSCHER, Sir Leo (Arthur), Kt 1987; Chairman, Queensland Treasury Corporation, since 1988; *b* 1 Oct. 1926; *s* of Leslie Charles Hielscher and Elizabeth Jane Petersen; *m* 1948, Mary Ellen Pelgrave; one *s* one *d* (and one *s* decd). *Educ:* Brisbane State High Sch.; Univ. of Queensland (BComm, AAUQ). FCPA; FAIM. Queensland Public Service, 1942; RAAF, 1945–47; Asst Under Sec. (Budget), Qld Treasury, 1964, Dep. Under Treasurer, 1969–74; Under Treas. of Qld (CS Hd of Treasury Dept of Qld Govt), 1974–88. Eisenhower Exchange Fellow, 1973. Dir, Epic (Qld) Ltd; Chairman: Gladstone Special Steel Corp.; Autsafe Ltd; Sugar North. *Recreations:* golf, fishing, boating, theatre. *Address:* 8 Silverash Court, Capalaba, Brisbane, Qld 4157, Australia. *T:* (home) (7) 32060104, *Fax:* (7) 32064241, (business) (7) 38424620, *Fax:* (7) 32100262. *Clubs:* Brisbane, Queensland, Gailes Golf, Tattersalls (Brisbane).

HIGGINBOTHAM, Prof. James Taylor, PhD; FBA 1995; Professor of Philosophy and Linguistics, University of Southern California, since 2000; *b* 17 Aug. 1941; *s* of William Rufus Higginbotham and Eunice Taylor Higginbotham; *m* 1st, 1972, Jenni W. Caldwell (marr. diss. 1988); two *s*; 2nd, 1988, Nancy L. Roberts; two *s* two *d*. *Educ:* Columbia Univ., NY (BS 1967; PhD 1973). Columbia University, New York: Instructor in Philosophy, 1970–73; Asst Prof., 1973–80; Fellow in Humanities, 1975–77 and 1979–80; Massachusetts Institute of Technology: Vis. Associate Prof. of Philosophy, 1980–82; Associate Prof., 1982–87; Prof. of Philosophy and Linguistics, 1987–93; Prof. of Gen. Linguistics, Univ. of Oxford, 1993–2000; Fellow, Somerville Coll., Oxford, 1993–2000. *Publications:* articles in Jl Philosophy, Linguistic Inquiry, Mind and Language, Linguistics and Philosophy; contribs to several collections in linguistics and in philosophy. *Recreations:* chess, music. *Address:* Department of Philosophy, University of Southern California, 3709 Trousdale Parkway, Los Angeles, CA 90089-0451, USA. *T:* (213) 7404624.

HIGGINBOTTOM, Donald Noble; HM Diplomatic Service, retired; Counsellor, Foreign and Commonwealth Office, 1976–79; *b* 19 Dec. 1925; *s* of late Harold Higginbottom and Dorothy (*née* Needham); *m* 1950, Sarah Godwin. *Educ:* Calday Grange Grammar Sch., Cheshire; King's Coll., Cambridge (1st Cl. Hons Hist.); Yale Univ., USA (MA Hist.). Lectr in Humanities, Univ. of Chicago, 1951. Entered Foreign Office, 1953; Buenos Aires, 1955; Peking, 1958; Saigon, 1960; Phnom Penh, 1962; Singapore, 1964; Bangkok, 1971; Buenos Aires, 1974. *Recreations:* electronic clocks, power boating. *Address:* Apartado 54, 12580 Benicarló, Castellón, Spain. *Clubs:* Athenæum; Yacht Club Olivos (Buenos Aires).

HIGGINS; *see* Longuet-Higgins.

HIGGINS, family name of **Baron Higgins**.

HIGGINS, Baron *cr* 1997 (Life Peer), of Worthing, in the co. of West Sussex; **Terence Langley Higgins,** KBE 1993; PC 1979; DL; *b* 18 Jan. 1928; *s* of late Reginald and Rose Higgins, Dulwich; *m* 1961, Dame Rosalyn Higgins, *qv*; one *s* one *d*. *Educ:* Alleyn's Sch., Dulwich; Gonville and Caius Coll., Cambridge (BA (Hons) 1958; MA 1963; Pres. Cambridge Union Soc., 1958). Brit. Olympic Team (athletics) 1948, 1952. NZ Shipping Co., 1948–55; Lectr in Economic Principles, Dept of Economics, Yale Univ., 1958–59; Economist with Unilever, 1959–64. Dir, 1980–92, Consultant, 1992–, Lex Service Group (Chm., Lex Pension Fund Trustees, 1994–); Dir, First Choice Holidays (formerly Owners Abroad), 1992–97. MP (C) Worthing, 1964–97. Opposition Spokesman on Treasury and Economic Affairs, 1966–70; Minister of State, Treasury, 1970–72; Financial Sec. to Treasury, 1972–74; Opposition Spokesman: on Treasury and Econ. Affairs, 1974; for Trade, 1974–76; Principal Opposition Spokesman on social security, H of L, 1997–. Chairman: Select Cttee on Procedure, 1980–83; Select Cttee on Treasury and CS, 1983–92 (Mem., 1980–92); House of Commons Liaison Cttee, 1984–97; Sec., Cons. Parly Finance Cttee, 1965–66; Chm., Cons. Parly Cttee on Sport, 1979–81, on Transport, 1979–91; Member: Public Accounts Commn, 1984–97 (Chm., 1996–97); Exec. Cttee, 1922 Cttee, 1980–97. Mem., Claims Resolution Tribunal for Dormant Accounts in Switzerland. Member: Council, RIIA, 1979–85; Council, IAM, 1979–98. Governor: NIESR, 1989–; Dulwich Coll., 1980–95; Alleyn's Sch., 1995–99. Special Fellow, PSI, 1986 (Mem. Council, 1989–95); Trustee, Industry and Parlt Trust, 1985–91; Hon. Mem., Keynes College, Univ. of Kent, 1976–. DL W Sussex, 1989. *Address:* House of Lords, SW1A 0AA. *Clubs:* Reform, Yale; Hawks (Cambridge); Royal Blackheath Golf, Worthing Golf, Koninklijke Haagsche Golf.

HIGGINS, Andrew James, PhD; MRCVS; Scientific Director and Chief Executive, Animal Health Trust, Newmarket, 1988–99; *b* 7 Dec. 1948; *s* of late Edward James

Higgins and of Gabrielle Joy, *d* of late Sir John Kelland; *m* 1981, Nicola, *d* of late Peter Eliot and of Jenifer Eliot; one *s* three *d*. *Educ*: St Michael's Coll., Leeds; Royal Veterinary Coll., Univ. of London (BVetMed 1973; PhD 1985); Centre for Tropical Med., Univ. of Edinburgh (MSc 1977). CBiol 1993; FIBiol 1993. Commnd RAVC 1973. Vet. Officer to Sultan of Oman, 1975–76; Vet. Advr, ME and N Africa, Wellcome Foundn, 1977–82; Cons., FAO 1981–. Mem., Lord Chancellor's Adv. Sub-cttee for W Suffolk, 1999–. Member: Council, Soc. for Protection of Animals in N Africa, 1985–98 (Vice-Chm., 1986–89; Mem., Vet. Cttee, 1985–); Conservation and Welfare Cttee, 1987–96, Ethics Cttee, 1994–, Welfare Cttee, 1998–, Zool Soc. of London; Vet. Res. Club, 1989–; Vet. Panel, BEF, 1993–; Adv. Cttee on Quarantine, 1997–98; Trustee: Internat. League for the Protection of Horses, 1999–; Nat. Canine Defence League, 1999–; Consultant to Bd, British Horse Industry Confedn, 1998–. Hon. Vet. Advr to Jockey Club, 1988–99 (Mem. Vet. Cttee, 1992–99); Fédération Equestre Internationale: Hon. Scientific Advr, 1990–; Mem., Medication Sub-Cttee, Ethics Cttee, and Vet. Cttee, 1990–. Editor, The Vet. Jl (formerly British Vet. Jl), 1991– (Dep. Ed., 1990–91). Gov., St Edmunds Hosp. and Nursing Home, Bury St Edmunds, 1993–97. Scientific Fellow, Zool Soc.; MRSocMed 1994. Univ. of London Laurel, 1971; Ciba-Geigy Prize for Res. in Animal Health, 1985; Equine Veterinary Jl Open Award and medal, 1986; Centenary Prize, Central Vet. Soc., 1986; George Fleming Prize, British Vet. Jl, 1987; President's Award, Vet. Mktg Assoc., 1997. *Publications:* (contrib.) An Anatomy of Veterinary Europe, 1972; (ed and contrib.) The Camel in Health and Disease, 1986; (ed) The Equine Manual, 1995; papers in sci. and gen. pubns and communications to learned socs. *Recreations:* ski-ing, riding, opera, camels. *Address:* PO Box 274, Bury St Edmunds, Suffolk IP29 5LW. *T:* and *Fax:* (01284) 725463; *e-mail:* ajhvet@globalnet.co.uk. *Club:* Buck's.

HIGGINS, Prof. Christopher Francis, PhD; FRSE, FMedSci; Director, MRC Clinical Sciences Centre, and Professor, Imperial College School of Medicine, since 1998; *b* 24 June 1955; *s* of Prof. Philip John Higgins and Betty Ann Higgins (*née* Edmonds); *m* 1st, 1978, Elizabeth Mary Joy (marr. diss. 1994); two *d*; 2nd, 1994, Suzanne Wilson Higgins; three *d*. *Educ:* Univ. of Durham (BSc 1st Cl. Hons Botany 1976; PhD 1979). FRSE 1989. NATO-SERC postdoctoral Fellow, Univ. of California, Berkeley, 1979–81; University of Dundee: Lectr, 1981–87; Reader and Prof. of Molecular Genetics, 1987–89; Lister Inst. Res. Fellow, 1983–89; Oxford University: Principal Scientist, ICRF, and Dep. Dir, ICRF Labs, Inst. of Molecular Medicine, 1989–93; Fellow, Keble Coll., 1989–93; Nuffield Prof. of Clin. Biochemistry, and Fellow, Hertford Coll., 1993–97. Howard Hughes Internat. Res. Scholar; Fellow, EMBO, 1988. Mem., BBSRC, 1997–2000; Mem., Governing Council, John Innes Centre, 1994–2000. Charity Trustee: Future Harvest; 2 Higher Ground. Founding Editor and Editor-in-Chief, Molecular Microbiology, 1987–; Mem. Editl Bd, Cell, EMBO Jl. Founder FMedSci 1998 (Mem., Council, 2000–). Hugh Bean Prize, RCM, 1970; Fleming Medal, Soc. for Gen. Microbiol., 1987; CIBA Medal and Prize, Biochemical Soc., 1995. *Publications:* numerous research papers in learned jls. *Recreations:* my five daughters, classical music, playing the violin. *Address:* MRC Clinical Sciences Centre, Imperial College School of Medicine, Hammersmith Hospital Campus, Du Cane Road, W12 0NN. *T:* (020) 8383 8335, *Fax:* (020) 8383 8337; *e-mail:* christopher.higgins@csc.mrc.ac.uk.

HIGGINS, Clare Frances Elizabeth; actress; *d* of James Stephen Higgins and Paula Cecilia (*née* Murphy). *Educ:* St Philomena's Convent Sch., Derbys; Ecclesbourne Sch., Derbys; LAMDA. *Theatre includes:* A View from the Bridge, Harrogate; The White Devil, Oxford Playhouse; Beethoven's Tenth, Vaudeville; Jenkin's Ear, Royal Court; Ride Down Mount Morgan, Wyndhams; A Letter of Resignation, Comedy, 1997; Heartbreak House, 2000, The Secret Rapture, 2001, Chichester; Royal Exchange, Manchester: Measure for Measure; Rollo; Blood Black and Gold; The Deep Man; Greenwich: Time and the Conways; The Rivals; A Street Car Named Desire; Royal Shakespeare Company: A Midsummer Night's Dream, 1989; Hamlet, 1989; Antony and Cleopatra, 1992; Royal National Theatre: The Futurists, 1986; The Secret Rapture, 1988; Richard III, 1990; King Lear, 1990; Napoli Millionaria, 1991; The Absence of War, 1993 (televised, 1996); The Children's Hour, 1994 (Critics' Circle Award, 1995); Sweet Bird of Youth, 1995 (Olivier Award, 1995; Critics' Circle Award, 1995); The Walls, 2001; West Yorkshire Playhouse: The Seagull, 1998; Present Laughter, 1998; Private Lives, 1998; The Tempest, 1999. *Television includes:* Pride and Prejudice; Unity; Byron; The Concubine; Mitch; The Citadel; Cover Her Face; Foreign Body; Beautiful Lies; After the War; Downtown Lagos; Circle of Deceit; Man of the Month. *Films include:* 1919; Hellraiser; Hellbound; The Fruit Machine; Bad Behaviour, 1993; Let it Come Down, 1995; Easter House, 1995; Small Faces, 1996; House of Mirth, 1999. *Address:* c/o Conway van Gelder Ltd, 18–21 Jermyn Street, SW1Y 6HP.

HIGGINS, Colin Kirk; Sheriff for North Strathclyde at Paisley, since 1990; *b* 9 Nov. 1945; *s* of late William Higgins and Janet Currie (*née* Lenney); *m* 1971, Anne McMahon; one *s* two *d*. *Educ:* St Patrick's High Sch., Coatbridge; Glasgow Univ. (LLB). Apprenticed to Town Clerk, Coatbridge, 1967–69, Legal Asst, 1969–70; Assistant, 1970–73, Partner, 1974–90, James Bell & Sons, later Bell, Russell & Co. Dean, Airdrie Soc. of Solicitors, 1989–90. *Recreations:* walking, travel, theatre, racquet sports. *Address:* Paisley Sheriff Court, St James' Street, Paisley, Strathclyde PA3 2HW. *T:* (0141) 887 5291.

HIGGINS, Daniel John P.; *see* Pearce-Higgins.

HIGGINS, Jack; *see* Patterson, Harry.

HIGGINS, Prof. James, PhD; FBA 1999; Professor of Latin American Literature, University of Liverpool, since 1988; *b* 28 May 1939; *s* of Peter and Annie Higgins; *m* 1962, Kirstine Anne Atwell; two *s*. *Educ:* Our Lady's High Sch., Motherwell; Univ. of Glasgow (MA); Univ. of Lyons (LèsL); PhD Liverpool 1968. Department of Hispanic Studies, Liverpool University: Asst Lectr, 1964–67; Lectr, 1967–73; Sen. Lectr, 1973–83; Reader, 1983–88; Head of Dept, 1988–97. Visiting Professor: Univ. of Pittsburgh, 1968; Univ. of Waterloo, Ont, 1974; Univ. of West Indies, Trinidad, 1979; Univ. of Wisconsin-Madison, 1990; Hon. Prof., Univ. of San Marcos, Lima, 1984. Comdr, Order of Merit (Peru), 1988. *Publications:* Visión del hombre y de la vida en las últimas obras poéticas de César Vallejo, 1970; César Vallejo: an anthology of his poetry, 1970; The Poet in Peru, 1982; A History of Peruvian Literature, 1987; César Vallejo: a selection of his poetry (with trans), 1987; César Vallejo en su poesía, 1990; Cambio social y constantes humanas: la narrative corta de J. R. Ribeyro, 1991; Hitos de la poesía peruana, 1993; Myths of the Emergent: social mobility in contemporary Peruvian fiction, 1994; numerous articles. *Recreations:* reading, gardening, walking, football, whisky. *Address:* Department of Hispanic Studies, School of Modern Languages, University of Liverpool, Liverpool L69 3BX. *T:* (0151) 794 2775.

HIGGINS, John Andrew; Assistant Auditor General, National Audit Office, 1989–99; *b* 19 Feb. 1940; *s* of George Henry and Mildred Maud Higgins; *m* 1965, Susan Jennifer Mathis; one *s*. *Educ:* Hendon County Sch.; Hastings Grammar Sch. ARCO. Exchequer and Audit Department: Asst Auditor, 1958; Auditor, 1968; Sen. Auditor, 1971; Chief Auditor, 1977; Dep. Dir, 1981; Office of Auditor Gen. of Canada, 1983–84; Dir, Nat. Audit Office, 1984. CPFA. Treas., Crawley and Horsham Dist Organists' Assoc., 1994–; Mem. Mgt Cttee, Crawley Open House and Resources Centre, 1999–. *Recreations:* classical organ playing, golf, bridge, gardening, supporting Crystal Palace. *Address:* Zaria, 65 Milton Mount Avenue, Pound Hill, Crawley, Sussex RH10 3DP. *T:* (01293) 417075. *Club:* Ifield Golf and Country.

HIGGINS, Prof. John Christopher, FIEE; Director of Management Centre, University of Bradford, and Professor of Management Sciences, 1972–89, Emeritus Professor, since 1992; *b* 9 July 1932; *s* of Sidney James Higgins and Margaret Eileen Higgins (*née* Dealtrey); *m* 1960, Margaret Edna Howells; three *s*. *Educ:* Gonville and Caius Coll., Cambridge (MA); Univ. of London (BSc, MSc); PhD Bradford. Short service commission, RAF, 1953–56; 1956–70: Electronics Industry; Dept of Chief Scientist (RAF) in MoD; management consultancy; Director of Economic Planning and Research for IPC Newspapers Ltd. Member: Final Selection Bd for Civil Service Commn, 1976–91; Defence Scientific Adv. Council's Assessments Bd, 1976–83 (Chm. of its Cttee on Operational Analysis, 1980–83); UGC Sub-Cttee on Management and Business Studies, 1979–85; Yorks, Humberside and Midlands Industrial Develt Bd, 1988–91; Chm., Social Sciences Res. Council's Accountancy Steering Cttee and Member of its Management and Industrial Relns Cttee, 1976–80. Vis. Fellow, Wolfson Coll., Cambridge, 1985; Vis. Prof., Open Business School, Open Univ., 1991–97. *Publications:* Information Systems for Planning and Control: concepts and cases, 1976, new edn as Computer-Based Planning Systems, 1985; Strategic and Operational Planning Systems: Principles and Practice, 1980; numerous papers and articles on corporate planning, information systems and management educn. *Recreations:* violin/viola (ex National Youth Orchestra of Great Britain), cricket, fell-walking. *Address:* Woodfield, 36 Station Road, Baildon, West Yorkshire BD17 5NW. *T:* (01274) 592836.

HIGGINS, Dame Julia Stretton, DBE 2001 (CBE 1996); DPhil; FRS 1995; FREng; Professor of Polymer Science, Imperial College of Science, Technology and Medicine, University of London, since 1989 (Dean, City and Guilds College, 1993–97); *b* 1 July 1942; *d* of George Stretton Downes, *qv* and late Sheilah D. M. Downes (*née* Gavigan). *Educ:* Somerville Coll., Oxford (MA, DPhil 1968; Hon. Fellow, 1996). CChem 1991, FRSC 1991; CEng 1994, FREng 1999; FIM 1994; FCGI 1994; FInstP 1996; FIChemE 1997. Physics teacher, Mexborough Grammar Sch., 1966–68; Dept of Chemistry, Univ. of Manchester, 1968–72; Res. Fellow, Centre de Recherche sur les Macromolecules, Strasbourg, 1972–73; physicist, Inst Laue-Langevin, Grenoble, 1973–76; Dept of Chem. Engrg, Imperial Coll., Univ. of London, 1976–. Vis. Academic, Institut für Makromoleculare Chemie, Freiburg, 1988. Science and Engineering Research Council: Member: Neutron Beam Res. Cttee, 1979–83 and 1988–91; Polymers and Composites Cttee, 1989–94 (Chm., 1991–94); Materials Commn, 1991–94; Facilities Commn, 1993–94; Member: EPSRC, 1994–2000; Council for Central Lab. of the Res. Councils, 1995–2000; Sci. and Engrg Cttee, British Council, 1993–98; Council for Sci. and Technol., 1998–. Foreign Associate, Nat. Acad. Engrg, USA, 1999. Hon. DSc Nottingham, 1999; Hon. DEng Heriot-Watt, 2000. *Publications:* (with H. Benoît) Polymers and Neutron Scattering, 1994; contrib. articles on polymer science to learned jls. *Address:* Department of Chemical Engineering, Imperial College of Science, Technology and Medicine, Prince Consort Road, SW7 2BY. *T:* (020) 7594 5565.

See also G. P. S. Downes.

HIGGINS, Hon. Sir Malachy (Joseph), Kt 1993; **Hon. Mr Justice Higgins;** Judge of the High Court of Justice in Northern Ireland, since 1993 (Family Division, since 1996); *b* 30 Oct. 1944; *er s* of late James and May Higgins; *m* 1980, Dorothy Ann, *d* of Dr Leslie Grech, Malta; three *d*. *Educ:* St MacNissi's Coll., Garron Tower; Queen's Univ., Belfast (LLB); Middle Temple (BL). Called to NI Bar, 1969 (Bencher, 1993), to Irish Bar, 1978; QC (NI), 1985; County Court Judge, 1988–93; Recorder of Londonderry, 1990–93; County Court Judge for Co. Armagh, 1993. Judge in Residence, QUB, 1999–. Chm., Children Order Adv. Cttee, 1996–. *Recreations:* gardening, golf, sailing, walking. *Address:* Royal Courts of Justice, Belfast BT1 3JF; Ashdene, Comber, Co. Down. *Clubs:* Royal Ulster Yacht, Royal Belfast Golf.

HIGGINS, Michael Anthony, (Tony); Chief Executive, Universities and Colleges Admissions Service, since 1993; *b* 24 June 1944; *s* of Walter Higgins and Marjorie (*née* Dandy); *m* 1st, 1969, Hilary Patricia Noble (marr. diss. 1978); one *s* one *d*; 2nd, 1978, Janet Iris Dutnall Sadow (*née* Foreman) (marr. diss. 1998). *Educ:* Wyggeston Boys' Sch., Leicester; Univ. of Newcastle upon Tyne (BA). Admin. Asst, then Asst Registrar, Univ. of Leicester, 1967–78; seconded, part-time, to BAAS, 1970–72; Sen. Asst Registrar, Loughborough Univ. of Technol., 1979–84; Chief Exec., Polytechnics Central Admissions System, 1984–93. Chairman: Conf. of Univ. Administrators, 1982–84; Higher Educn Inf. Services Trust, 1991–93; Member: PCFC and HEFCE Cttees on Performance Indicators, 1989–94; FEFC Widening Participation Cttee, 1994–97; Bd, Nat. Adv. Cttee on Careers Educn and Guidance, 1998–; Council of Europe Develt Project on Access to Higher Educn, 1993–96. Chief Officer, Higher Educn Business Enterprises Ltd, 1995–2001; Member: Bd, ECCTIS 2000 Ltd, 1990–98; Local Govt Commn on sch. year, 1999–2000; Bd, HERO, 2000–. Res. Associate, Univ. of Oxford, 1998–. Overseas consultancies to govts and univs of Sweden, Uganda, BC, Slovenia, Taiwan, S Africa and Czech Republic. Chm., BBC Radio Leicester Adv. Council, 1980–84; Mem., BBC Midlands and E Adv. Council, 1992–95; Chm., Leicester Haymarket Theatre, 1986–91; Vice-Chm., Glos Everyman Theatre, 1991–93; Chm., Develt Cttee, Cheltenham Internat. Fests of Music, Literature and Jazz, 1988–2000. Vice-Chm., Governing Body, Glos Coll. of Arts and Technol., 1993–2000; Mem. Council, Cheltenham Coll., 1997–2000. FIMgt 1986; FRSA 1995. Hon. Fellow, Cheltenham and Glos Coll. of Higher Educn, 1998. Hon. DEd West of England, 1993. *Publications:* Young People's Knowledge of Higher Education, 1990; Getting into Polytechnic, 1991; How to Complete your UCCA/PCAS Form, 1991, 1992; Higher Education: the student experience, 1992; Adults' Knowledge of Higher Education, 1992; How to Complete your UCAS Form, annually 1993–; (ed) Student Mobility in the European Community, 1993; Clearing the Way, annually 1994–; Higher Education Sans Frontières: policy practice and the European student market, 1994; The Careers Adviser/Higher Education Interface, 1994; Higher Education: the international student experience, 1995; Practical Progression: matching advanced GNVQs to higher education programmes, 1995; chapters and articles in books, jls and newspapers. *Recreations:* golf, cooking, Rugby Union. *Address:* Rosehill, New Barn Lane, Cheltenham, Glos GL52 3LZ.

HIGGINS, Very Rev. Michael John; Dean of Ely, since 1991; *b* 31 Dec. 1935; *s* of Claud John and Elsie Higgins; *m* 1976, Bevyl Margaret Stringer; one *d*. *Educ:* Whitchurch Grammar Sch., Cardiff; Univ. of Birmingham (LLB 1957); Gonville and Caius Coll., Cambridge (LLB 1959, PhD 1962); Harvard Univ.; Ridley Hall, Cambridge. Lectr in English Law, Univ. of Birmingham, 1961–63. Ordained, 1965; Curate, Ormskirk Parish Church, dio. of Liverpool, 1965–68; Selection Sec., ACCM, 1968–74; Vicar, Frome and Priest-in-charge of Woodlands, dio. of Bath and Wells, 1974–80; Rector of Preston, and Leader of Preston Town Centre Team Ministry, dio. of Blackburn, 1980–91. *Publication:* The Vicar's House, 1988. *Recreations:* music, walking, travel. *Address:* The Deanery, Ely, Cambridgeshire CB7 4DN. *T:* (01353) 662432.

HIGGINS, Prof. Peter Matthew, OBE 1987; Bernard Sunley Professor and Chairman of Department of General Practice, United Medical Schools of Guy's and St Thomas' Hospitals (formerly Guy's Hospital Medical School), University of London, 1974–88, now Emeritus Professor; *b* 18 June 1923; *s* of Peter Joseph Higgins and Margaret Higgins; *m* 1952, Jean Margaret Lindsay Currie; three *s* one *d*. *Educ:* St Ignatius' Coll., London; UCH, London. MB, BS; FRCP, FRCGP. House Phys., Medical Unit, UCH, 1947; RAMC, 1948–49; House Phys., UCH, St Pancras, 1950; Resident MO, UCH, 1951–52; Asst Med. Registrar, UCH, 1953; Gen. Practice, Rugeley, Staffs, 1954–66, and Castle Vale, Birmingham, 1966–68; Sen. Lectr, Guy's Hosp. Med. Sch., 1968–74. Regl Advr in General Practice, SE Thames, 1970–88; Vice-Chm., SE Thames RHA, 1976–92; Chm., Kent FHSA, 1990–92. Mem., Attendance Allowance Bd, 1971–74; Chairman: Inquiry into A&E Dept, KCH, 1992; Review of Arrangements for Emergency Admissions, Ealing Hosp., 1994. Mem., National Council, 1985–95, Nat. Exec. Cttee, 1991–95, Family Service Units. Vice Chm. Governors, Linacre Centre for the Study of Medical Ethics, 1983–86; Mem. Court, Kent Univ., 1984–98. Hon. DSc Greenwich, 1998. *Publications:* articles in Lancet, BMJ, Jl RCGP, Epidemiology and Infection, British Jl of Psychiatry. *Address:* Wallings, Heathfield Lane, Chislehurst, Kent BR7 6AH. *T:* (020) 8467 2756.

HIGGINS, Phillip John; Corporate Manager, Cardiff County Council, since 1999; *b* 9 May 1946; *s* of Eugene Oswald Higgins and Dorothy Mary Higgins; *m* 1969, Anne Elizabeth Watkin; one *s* two *d*. *Educ:* Stand Grammar Sch., Manchester; Coll. of Commerce, Manchester. CIPFA (IMTA 1972). Halifax CBC, 1972–74; West Yorks CC, 1974–76; Gtr Manchester Council, 1976–85; Asst Co. Treas., S Glamorgan CC, 1985–88; Dir of Finance, Cardiff Bay Develt Corp., 1988–99. Treas., S Wales Magistrates' Courts Cttee, 1999–. FIMgt 1996. *Recreations:* reading political history, the countryside. *Address:* Wisteria Cottage, Llantrithyd, Cowbridge, Vale of Glamorgan CF71 7UB. *T:* (01446) 781676.

HIGGINS, Dame Rosalyn, DBE 1995; JSD; FBA 1995; QC 1986; a Judge of the International Court of Justice, since 1995; *b* 2 June 1937; *d* of Lewis Cohen and Fay Inberg; *m* 1961, Terence Langley Higgins (*see* Baron Higgins); one *s* one *d*. *Educ:* Burlington Grammar Sch., London; Girton Coll., Cambridge (Scholar; BA 1958, 1st Cl. Law Qualifying 1, 1st Cl. Tripos Pt II; 1st Cl. LLB 1959); Yale Law Sch., (JSD 1962). UK Intern, Office of Legal Affairs, UN, 1958; Commonwealth Fund Fellow, 1959; Vis. Fellow, Brookings Instn, Washington, DC, 1960; Jun. Fellow in Internat. Studies, LSE, 1961–63; Staff Specialist in Internat. Law, RIIA, 1963–74; Vis. Fellow, LSE, 1974–78; Professor of International Law: Univ. of Kent at Canterbury, 1978–81; LSE, London Univ., 1981–95. Gen. course, Hague Acad. of Internat. Law, 1991. Visiting Professor of International Law: Stanford Univ., 1975; Yale Univ., 1977. Bencher, Inner Temple, 1989. Mem., UN Cttee on Human Rights, 1985–. Hague Lectures on Internat. Law, 1982. Vice Pres., Amer. Soc. of Internat. Law, 1972–74 (Certif. of Merit, 1971, 1995). Membre de l'Institut de Droit International, 1993 (Associé, 1987). Dr *hc* Univ. of Paris XI, 1980. Manley Hudson Medal, 1998. Membre de l'Ordre des Palmes Académiques (France), 1988. *Publications:* The Development of International Law through the Political Organs of the United Nations, 1963; Conflict of Interests: international law in a divided world, 1965; The Administration of the United Kingdom Foreign Policy through the United Nations, 1966; (ed with James Fawcett) Law in Movement—essays in memory of John McMahon, 1974; UN Peacekeeping: documents and commentary: Vol. I, Middle East, 1969; Vol. II, Asia, 1971, Vol. III, Africa, 1980; Vol. IV, Europe, 1981; Problems and Process, 1994; articles for law jls and jls of internat. relations. *Recreations:* golf, cooking, eating. *Address:* International Court of Justice, Carnegieplein 2, 2517 KJ The Hague, Netherlands. *T:* (70) 3022323.

HIGGINS, Tony; *see* Higgins, M. A.

HIGGINS, Rear-Adm. William Alleyne, CB 1985; CBE 1980; *b* 18 May 1928; *s* of Comdr H. G. Higgins, DSO, RN, and Mrs L. A. Higgins; *m* 1963, Wiltraud Hiebaum; two *s* one *d*. *Educ:* Wellington College. Joined Royal Navy, 1945; Commander 1965; Captain 1973; Commodore, HMS Drake, 1980–82; Flag Officer Medway and Port Adm. Chatham, 1982–83; Dir. Gen. Naval Personal Services, 1983–86; Chief Naval Supply and Secretariat Officer, 1983–86. Sec., Defence, Press and Broadcasting Cttee, 1986–92. *Recreations:* skiing, mountaineering, Austin Sevening. *Club:* Royal Naval and Royal Marines Mountaineering.

HIGGINSON, Sir Gordon (Robert), Kt 1992; DL; PhD; FREng; Vice-Chancellor, 1985–94, Emeritus Professor of Engineering, 1994, University of Southampton; *b* 8 Nov. 1929; *s* of Frederick John and Letitia Higginson; *m* 1954, Marjorie Forbes Rannie (*d* 1996); three *s* two *d*. *Educ:* Leeds Univ. BSc, PhD. FICE; FIMechE; FREng (FEng 1991). Scientific Officer, then Sen. Scientific Officer, Min. of Supply, 1953–56; Lectr, Leeds Univ., 1956–62; Associate Prof., RMCS, Shrivenham, 1962–65; Durham University: Prof. of Engrg, 1965–85; Dean of Faculty of Science, 1972–75. Non-executive Director: Rolls-Royce, 1988–99; Pirelli General, 1995–; Pirelli UK Tyres, 1997–. DL Hants, 1994. Hon. FRCP 1992. Hon. DSc: Durham, 1991; Southampton, 1995; Bournemouth, 1997; Hon DSc (Eng) London, 1997; Hon. DEng Portsmouth, 1993; Hon. LLD Leeds, 1994. IMechE James Clayton Fund Prize, 1963 and 1979; Gold Medal, Brit. Soc. of Rheology, 1969. *Publications:* Elastohydrodynamic Lubrication (with D. Dowson), 1966, 2nd edn 1977; Foundations of Engineering Mechanics, 1974; papers on mechanics in various jls. *Address:* 61 Albany Park Court, Westwood Road, Southampton SO17 1LA.

HIGGS, Air Vice-Marshal Barry, CBE 1981; Assistant Chief of Defence Staff (Overseas), 1985–87; *b* 22 Aug. 1934; *s* of late Percy Harold Higgs and of Ethel Eliza Higgs; *m* 1957, Sylvia May Wilks; two *s*. *Educ:* Finchley County Secondary Grammar Sch. Served with Nos 207, 115, 138, 49 and 51 Sqdns, 1955–70; sc 1968; Forward Policy (RAF), 1971–73; ndc 1974; Comd No 39 (PR) Sqdn, 1975–77; Asst Dir Defence Policy, 1978–79; Comd RAF Finningley, 1979–81; RCDS 1982; Dep. Dir of Intelligence, 1983–85. Dir Gen., Fertiliser Manufacturers Assoc., 1987–98. ARAgS 1998. Francis New Meml Medal, Internat. Fertiliser Soc., 1999. *Recreations:* cruising, bridge, gardening, the outdoors, theatre. *Address:* 33 Parsonage Street, Cambridge CB5 8DN. *T:* (01223) 369062. *Club:* Royal Air Force.

HIGGS, Brian James; QC 1974; a Recorder of the Crown Court, 1974–98; Barrister-at-Law; *b* 24 Feb. 1930; *s* of James Percival Higgs and Kathleen Anne Higgs; *m* 1st, 1953, Jean Cameron DuMerton; two *s* three *d*; 2nd, 1980, Vivienne Mary Johnson; one *s*. *Educ:* Wrekin Coll.; London Univ. Served RA, 1948–50 (2nd Lieut). Called to Bar, Gray's Inn, 1955, Bencher, 1986; Mem., Hon. Soc. of Inner Temple (*ad eundem*), 1987. Contested (C) Romford, 1966. *Recreations:* gardening, golf, wine, chess, bridge. *Address:* 5 King's Bench Walk, Temple, EC4Y 7DN. *T:* (020) 7353 5638.

HIGGS, Derek Alan, FCA; Chairman, Partnerships UK plc, since 2000; Senior Adviser in the UK, UBS Warburg, since 2001; *b* 3 April 1944; *s* of Alan Edward Higgs and Freda Gwendoline Higgs (*née* Hope); *m* 1970, Julia Mary Arguile; two *s* one *d*. *Educ:* Solihull Sch.; Univ. of Bristol (BA 1965). FCA 1978. Chartered Accountant, Price Waterhouse & Co., 1965–69; Corp. Finance Exec., Baring Brothers & Co., Ltd, 1969–72; S. G. Warburg & Co. Ltd: Corp. Finance Exec., 1972–86; Head of Corp. Finance, 1986–94; Chm., 1994–96; Chm., Prudential Portfolio Managers Ltd, 1996–2000. Director: S. G. Warburg Gp plc, 1987–96; Prudential Corp. plc, 1996–2000; Jones Lang LaSalle Inc., 1999–; London Regl Transport, 1999–; Egg plc, 2000–; The British Land Co. PLC, 2000–(Dep. Chm., 2001–); Allied Irish Banks, 2000–. Dep. Chm., BITC, 1999–; Chm., Business in the Envmt, 1999–. Member: Adv. Cttee on Business and the Envmt, 1993–99; Financial Reporting Council, 1996–; Adv. Council, Envmtl Change Inst.; FTSE 4 Good Adv. Cttee; Dep. Chm., Fund Managers Assoc., 1998–2000. Dir, Coventry City Football Club (Hldgs) Ltd, 1996–. Dep. Chm., City of London Fest., 1998–2001 (Dir, 1995–2001). Mem. Council, Univ. of Bristol, 1994–97. Trustee, Architecture Foundn, 1998–. CIMgt. FRSA 1992. *Address:* 41 Upper Addison Gardens, W14 8AJ. *T:* (020) 7603 7874.

HIGGS, Prof. Peter Ware, PhD; FRS 1983; FRSE; Professor of Theoretical Physics, University of Edinburgh, 1980–96, now Emeritus; *b* 29 May 1929; *s* of Thomas Ware Higgs and Gertrude Maud (*née* Coghill); *m* 1963, Jo Ann, *d* of Jo C. and Meryl Williamson, Urbana, Ill; two *s*. *Educ:* Cotham Grammar Sch., Bristol; King's Coll., Univ. of London (BSc, MSc; PhD 1954; FKC 1998). FRSE 1974. Royal Commn for Exhibn of 1851 Sen. Student, KCL, 1953–54 and Univ. of Edinburgh, 1954–55; Sen. Res. Fellow, Univ. of Edinburgh, 1955–56; ICI Res. Fellow, UCL, 1956–57 and Imperial Coll., 1957–58; Lectr in Maths, UCL, 1958–60; Lectr in Mathematical Physics, 1960–70, and Reader in Math. Physics, 1970–80, Univ. of Edinburgh. Hon. FInstP 1998. Hon. DSc: Bristol, 1997; Edinburgh, 1998. Hughes Medal, Royal Soc., 1981; Rutherford Medal, 1984, Paul Dirac Medal, 1997, Inst. of Physics; James Scott Prize, RSE, 1993. *Publications:* papers on molecular vibrations and spectra, classical and quantum field theories, and on spontaneous breaking of gauge symmetries in theories of elementary particles. *Recreations:* walking, swimming, listening to music. *Address:* 2 Darnaway Street, Edinburgh EH3 6BG. *T:* (0131) 225 7060.

HIGHAM, Catherine Mary; *see* Ennis, C. M.

HIGHAM, Prof. Charles Franklin Wandesforde, PhD, ScD; FRSNZ; FRAS; FSA; FBA; Professor of Anthropology, University of Otago, New Zealand, since 1968; *b* 19 Oct. 1939; *s* of Ernest Harry Hamilton Higham and Eileen Florence Emily Higham (*née* Woodhead); *m* 1964, Pauline Askew; two *s* two *d*. *Educ:* Raynes Park Co. Grammar Sch.; St Catharine's Coll., Cambridge (Rugby blue, 1961–62; BA, MA; PhD 1966; ScD 1991). FSA 1984; FRAS 1986. Lectr in Prehist., Univ. of Otago, 1967–68. Vis. Prof., Univ. of London, 1978; Benians Fellow, St John's Coll., Cambridge, 1991–92. Mortimer Wheeler Lectr, 1983, Reckitt Lectr, 2002, British Acad. FRSNZ 1992; Corresp. FBA 2000. Mem. editl bds various learned jls. *Publications:* The Archaeology of Mainland Southeast Asia, 1989; (with R. Bannanurag) The Excavation of Khok Phanom Di: Vol. I, The Excavation, Chronology and Human Burials, 1990; The Bronze Age of Southeast Asia, 1996; The Civilisation of Angkor, 2001; with R. Thosarat: Khok Phanom Di: prehistoric adaptation to the world's richest habitat, 1994; (ed) The Excavation of Nong Nor, a Prehistoric Site in Central Thailand, 1998; Prehistoric Thailand: from first settlement to Sukhothai, 1998; contrib. to British Archaeol Reports. *Recreations:* brick-laying, jogging. *Address:* Department of Anthropology, PO Box 56, Dunedin, New Zealand. *T:* (3) 4798750; 1 Newbury Street, Company Bay, Dunedin, New Zealand. *T:* (3) 4761056. *Club:* Hawks (Cambridge).

HIGHAM, Geoffrey Arthur; Chairman, Rugby Group PLC, 1986–96 (Director, 1979–96); Director and Trustee, Building Centre Group, 1982–2001(Chairman, 1984–88); *b* 17 April 1927; *s* of Arthur Higham and Elsie Higham (*née* Vickerman); *m* 1951, Audrey Hill; one *s* and *d*. *Educ:* King William Coll., IOM; St Catharine's Coll., Cambridge (MA MechScis). Served RE, 1945–48. Metal Box Co., 1950–64; Montague Burton, 1964–65; Cape Industries, 1965–85: Man. Dir, 1971–80; Chm., 1980–85; Industrial Dir, Charter Consolidated, 1980–87; Director: Pirelli UK, 1987–; Travers Morgan, 1988–91; Try Gp, 1989–99; Vale Housing Assoc., 1998–. Chm., BIM Foundn, 1981–83; Vice Chm., Council, BIM, 1984–88; Mem. Council, CBI, 1994–96; Mem. Council, 1978–88, Chm., 1980–82, UK S Africa Trade Assoc. Trustee, Mansfield Coll., Oxford, 1988–95. CIMgt (CBIM 1975); FRSA 1989. *Recreations:* music, cricket, gardening. *Address:* 32 East St Helen Street, Abingdon, Oxfordshire OX14 5EB. *Clubs:* Army and Navy, Middlesex CC.

HIGHAM, John Arthur; QC 1992; Partner, Stephenson Harwood, solicitors, since 2000 (Consultant, 1999–2000); a Recorder, since 2000; *b* 11 Aug. 1952; *s* of late Frank Greenhouse Higham and of Muriel (*née* King); *m* 1st, 1982, Francesca Mary Antonietta Ronan (decd); one *s* two *d*; 2nd, 1988, Catherine Mary Ennis, *qv*; two *s* one *d*. *Educ:* Shrewsbury Sch.; Churchill Coll., Cambridge (MA, LLM). Called to the Bar, Lincoln's Inn, 1976; an Asst Recorder, Midland and Oxford Circuit, 1998–2000; admitted solicitor and authorised as solicitor advocate, 1999. *Publications:* (ed jtly) Loose on Liquidators, 2nd edn 1981; (ed jtly) Corporate Administrations and Rescue Procedures, 2nd edn 2001. *Recreations:* opera, cricket, gardening, children. *Address:* Stephenson Harwood, One St Paul's Churchyard, EC4M 8SH. *T:* (020) 7329 4422, *Fax:* (020) 7606 0822; *e-mail:* john.higham@shlegal.com.

HIGHAM, John Drew, CMG 1956; *b* 28 Nov. 1914; *s* of Richard and Margaret Higham, Pendleton, Lancs; *m* 1st, 1936, Mary Constance Bromage (*d* 1974); three *d*; 2nd, 1976, Katharine Byard Pailing, FRTPI. *Educ:* Manchester Grammar Sch.; Gonville and Caius Coll., Cambridge (Scholar). Asst Principal, Admiralty, 1936; Asst Private Sec. to First Lord, 1939; Private Sec. to Parliamentary Sec. and Parliamentary Clerk, 1940; Principal, Admiralty, 1941; transferred to Colonial Office, 1946; Asst Sec. Colonial Office, 1948; seconded to Singapore as Under Sec., 1953, and as Dir of Personnel, 1955–57 (acted on various occasions as Chief Sec.); Asst Sec., Min. of Housing and Local Govt, 1965; Head of Development Control Div., DoE, 1970–74. Vice-Chm., Bredon Parish Council, 1985–87. Chevalier 1st Cl. Order of St Olaf (Norway), 1948. *Address:* 17 Bannister Close, Oxford OX4 1SH. *T:* (01865) 251311. *Club:* National Liberal.

HIGHAM, Comdr Michael Bernard Shepley, CVO 1999; RN; Grand Secretary, United Grand Lodge of England, 1980–98; Secretary, Grand Charity, 1981–98; *b* 7 June 1936; *s* of late Anthony Richard Charles Higham, TD, FRCS and Mary Higham (*née* Shepley); *m* 1st, 1970, Caroline Verena Wells (marr. diss. 1996); one *s* one *d*; 2nd, 1997, Andrea Svedberg, *d* of late Elias Svedberg and Astrid Svedberg. *Educ:* Epsom Coll. Joined RN, 1954; served: HM Ships Triumph (twice), Eagle, Cavendish and Chichester; in offices of: C-in-C Portsmouth and C-in-C Plymouth; Flag Officers Plymouth, Scotland and NI; Adm. Comdg Reserves; on staff of C-in-C Fleet; retd RN, 1977. Called to the Bar, Middle Temple, 1968. Grand Secretary's Office, 1977–98; Dep. Grand Sec., 1978–80; Past Jun. Grand Warden, 1986–. Mem., RNSA. *Publication:* Freemasonry from Craft to tolerance, 1985. *Recreation:* sailing. *Address:* 13 Tite Street, SW3 4JR; Oyster Shell, Restronguet Passage, Mylor, Falmouth, Cornwall TR11 5ST. *Clubs:* Little Ship; Royal Cornwall Yacht (Falmouth).

HIGHAM, Norman, OBE 1984; Librarian, University of Bristol, 1966–89; *b* 14 June 1924; *s* of John Henry Higham, MM, and Edith Fanny (*née* Hubbard); *m* 1954, Jean

Elizabeth, *d* of Frederick William and Isabel Traylen; one *s* one *d*. *Educ:* Firth Park Grammar Sch., Sheffield; Univ. of Sheffield (BA 1st Cl. Hons English, Philos., Spanish); MA Leeds 1961. ALA 1956. Served RNVR, 1942–46 (Lieut Coastal Forces). Assistant Librarian: Univ. of Sheffield, 1953–57; Univ. of Leeds, 1957–62; Librarian, Loughborough Coll. of Advanced Technology, 1962–63; Dep. Librarian, Univ. of Leeds, 1963–66. Mem. Council, Standing Conf. on Nat. and Univ. Libraries, 1972–75 and 1979–86 (Chm., 1976–79); Pres., LA, 1983 (Mem. Council, 1975–86, Chm., 1978–81 and 1985–87); Member: UGC Steering Gp on Liby Res., 1977–83; Brit. Liby Bd, 1986–89 (Adv. Council, 1976–79, and 1990–94); Liby and Inf. Services Council (England), 1977–83; Sci. Inf. Cttee, Royal Soc., 1982–91; Standing Cttee on Libraries, CVCP, 1982–89; Nat. Cttee on Regl Liby Co-operation, 1985–89; Council, Liby and Inf. Co-operation Council, 1989– (Chm., 1989–92). Mem. Council and Trustee, Oxfam, 1973–79 and 1980–86. Hon. DLitt Bristol, 1989. *Publications:* A Very Scientific Gentleman: the major achievements of Henry Clifton Sorby, 1963; Computer Needs for University Library Operations, 1973; The Library in the University: observations on a service, 1980; articles and reviews in librarianship and history of science. *Recreations:* literature and the arts, music. *Address:* 30 York Gardens, Clifton, Bristol BS8 4LN. *T:* (0117) 973 6264. *Club:* Royal Commonwealth Society.

HIGHAM, Rear-Adm. Philip Roger Canning, CB 1972; *b* 9 June 1920; *s* of Edward Higham, Stoke Bishop, Bristol; *m* 1942, Pamela Bracton Edwards (*d* 2001), *er d* of Gerald Edwards, Southport, Lancs; two *s*. *Educ:* RNC Dartmouth. Cadet, 1937; Midshipman, 1938; Sub-Lt 1940; Lieut 1942; qual. Gunnery Officer, 1944; Second Gunnery Off., HMS Vanguard, Royal Tour of S Africa, 1947; psc 1948; Exper. Dept, HMS Excellent, 1951–52; Comdr, Devonport Gunnery Sch., 1953; Trials Comdr, RAE Aberporth, 1954–55; jssc 1956; Exper. Comdr, HMS Excellent, 1957–59; Admty (DTWP), 1960–61; Naval Attaché, Middle East, 1962–64; idc 1965; Dep. Chief Polaris Exec., 1966–68; Cdre i/c Hong Kong, 1968–70; Asst Chief of Naval Staff (Op. Requirements), 1970–72; retired list 1973; Dir, HMS Belfast Trust, 1973–78; Keeper, HMS Belfast, Imperial War Mus., 1978–83. Trustee, Portsmouth Naval Base Property Trust, 1985–92. *Address:* 1 John King Shipyard, King Street, Emsworth, Hants PO10 7AY. *T:* (01243) 372195.

HIGHFIELD, Ashley Gilroy Mark, CEng; Director, New Media and Technology, BBC, since 2000; *b* 3 Oct. 1965; *s* of Roy Highfield and Sheila Highfield. *Educ:* Elizabeth Coll., Guernsey; Royal Grammar Sch., High Wycombe; City Univeristy, London (BSc (Hons) Business Computing Systems). MBCS. Mgt Consultant, Coopers and Lybrand, 1988–94; Hd of IT and New Media, NBC Europe, 1994–95; Man. Dir, Flextech Interactive, Flextech Television, 1996–2000. Non-executive Director, 1999–2000: Xrefer.com Ltd; Multimap.com Ltd; Improveline.com Ltd; WayAheadGroup (ticketing) Ltd. *Recreations:* motor racing, reading, architecture, music, film. *Address:* BBC, Bush House, Aldwych, WC2B 4PH. *Club:* Soho House.

HIGHTON, David Peter; Chief Executive, Oxford Radcliffe Hospitals NHS Trust, since 2000; *b* 22 May 1954; *s* of Allan Peter Highton and May Comrie Highton (*née* Doughty); partner, Wendy Ann Attree; one *d*. *Educ:* Borden Grammar Sch., Sittingbourne; Univ. of Bristol (BSc Hons Econs 1975). ACA 1978, FCA 1989. Chartered Accountant, Turquands Barton Mayhew, 1975–79; Financial Accountant, Tunnel Avebe Starches Ltd, 1979–81; Financial Controller: R. P. Martin plc, 1981–83; Grand Metropolitan Brewing, 1983–87; Regl Finance Dir, Prudential Property Services, 1987–90; Dir of Finance and Chief Exec., Ealing HA, 1990–92; Dir of Finance, Riverside Hosps, 1992–94; Chief Exec., Chelsea and Westminster Hosp., 1994–2000. Non-exec. Dir, 2000–, Chm., 2001–, Healthwork UK. *Publications:* contribs to health mgt jls. *Recreations:* Rugby (semi-retired), books, films, good food. *Address:* John Radcliffe Hospital, Headley Way, Headington, Oxford OX3 9DU. *T:* (01865) 221610. *Clubs:* Sittingbourne Rugby (Pres.), Imperial Medicals Rugby (Vice Pres.).

HIGMAN, Prof. Graham, MA, DPhil; FRS 1958; Waynflete Professor of Pure Mathematics, Oxford University, and Fellow of Magdalen College, Oxford, 1960–84, now Professor Emeritus; *b* 1917; 2nd *s* of Rev. Joseph Higman; *m* 1941, Ivah May Treleaven (*d* 1981); five *s* one *d*. *Educ:* Sutton Secondary Sch., Plymouth; Balliol Coll., Oxford (Hon. Fellow 1984). Meteorological Office, 1940–46; Lecturer, University of Manchester, 1946–55; Reader in Mathematics at Oxford Univ., 1955–60; Senior Research Fellow, Balliol Coll., Oxford, 1958–60. George A. Miller Vis. Prof., Univ. of Illinois, 1984–86. Hon. DSc: Exeter, 1979; NUI, 1992. De Morgan Medal, London Mathematical Soc., 1974; Sylvester Medal, Royal Soc., 1979. *Publications:* papers in Proc. London Math. Soc., and other technical jls. *Address:* 64 Sandfield Road, Oxford OX3 7RL.

HIGNETT, John Mulock, FCA; Chairman, Schroder Income Growth Fund plc, since 1995; non-executive Director, Smiths Group plc, since 2000; *b* 9 March 1934; *s* of late Reginald and Marjorie Hignett; *m* 1961, Marijke Inge de Boer; one *s* one *d*. *Educ:* Harrow Sch.; Magdalene Coll., Cambridge (MA). Kemp Chatteris & Co., 1958–61; Deloitte & Co., 1961–63; joined Lazard Brothers & Co. Ltd, 1963; Manager, Issues Dept, 1971; Dir, 1972; Head of Corporate Finance Div., 1980; Man. Dir, 1984–88; Glaxo Holdings plc: Finance Dir, 1988–92; Man. Dir, Corporate Funds, 1992–94. Non-executive Director: TI Group plc, 1989–2000; Sedgwick Group plc, 1993–99; Alfred McAlpine plc, 1994–98. Director-General: Panel on Take-Overs and Mergers, 1981–83; Council for the Securities Industry, 1983. Dep. Chm., Internat. Shakespeare Globe Centre Ltd, 1990–. *Address:* Flat 5, 3 Belgrave Place, SW1X 8BU. *Clubs:* Royal Thames Yacht, MCC; Hawks (Cambridge).

HIGNETT, Peter George; Regional Veterinary Officer, People's Dispensary for Sick Animals, 1982–90, retired; *b* 3 June 1925; *s* of Harry Sutton Hignett and Annie Hignett; *m* 1st, 1948, Patricia Bishop (marr. diss. 1988); two *s* one *d*; 2nd, 1997, Janet McCully. *Educ:* Pontesbury C of E Sch.; King Edward VI Sch., Birmingham; Univ. of Liverpool (MRCVS). General practice, 1947–49; Wellcome Veterinary Res. Station, 1949–54; Reader in Veterinary Reproduction, Univ. of Glasgow, 1954–76; Gen. Man., Hampshire Cattle Breeders' Soc., 1976–82. Mem. Council, RCVS, 1972–96, Pres., 1981–82; President: Soc. for Study of Animal Breeding, 1966–68; Southern Counties Veterinary Soc., 1983–84; Secretary: Associated AI Centres, 1977–82; Edgar Meml Trust, 1977–82; Member: Trehane Cttee, 1979–82; Scientific Adv. Cttee, Animal Health Trust, 1983–85; Banner Cttee on Ethics of Emerging Technologies in Animal Breeding, 1993–95. Gov., Berks Coll. of Agric., 1990–93. Hon. FRCVS 1998. *Publications:* scientific papers on fertility in domestic animals. *Recreations:* gardening, sailing, music. *Address:* 70 Stonerock Cottages, Chilgrove, Chichester, W Sussex PO18 9NA. *T:* (01243) 535330. *Club:* Farmers'.

HIGTON, Dennis John, CEng, FIMechE, FRAeS; aeronautical mechanical engineer, retired; *b* 15 July 1921; *s* of John William and Lillian Harriett Higton; *m* 1945, Joy Merrifield Pickett; one *s* one *d*. *Educ:* Guildford Technical Sch.; RAE Farnborough Technical Sch. Mid-Wessex Water Co., 1937–38. RAE Engineering Apprentice, 1938–42; RAE Aerodynamics Dept (Aero Flight), 1942–52; learned to fly at No 1 EFTS RAF Panshangar, 1946; A&AEE Boscombe Down, Head of Naval Test and Supt of Performance, 1953–66; British Defence Staff, Washington DC, USA, 1966–70; MoD(PE) Anglo-French Helicopter Production, 1970–72; Director Aircraft Production, 1972–75; Under-Sec. and Dir-Gen. of Mil. Aircraft Projects, MoD, 1976–79, of Aircraft 4, 1979–80, of Aircraft 3, 1980–81; Hd, Engrg Profession, Air Systems Controllerate, MoD, 1976–81; aeronautical consultant and company dir, 1981–93. Chm., Technology Div., CS Commn, 1984–89. Mem., Fleet Air Arm Officers Assoc., 1960–. Chm., S Wilts and Salisbury Br., NSPCC, 1982–96. Mem., Exec. Cttee, Salisbury Gp of Artists, 1987–92. *Publications:* research and memoranda papers mainly on aerodynamic flight testing. *Recreations:* ski-ing, sailing, gardening, walking on Salisbury Plain, shooting, painting (Diploma in Fine Art, Southampton Inst. of Higher Educn, 1994). *Address:* Jasmine Cottage, Rollestone Road, Shrewton, Salisbury, Wiltshire SP3 4HG. *T:* (01980) 620276.

HILBORN, Rev. Dr David Henry; Theological Adviser, Evangelical Alliance (UK), since 1999; Minister, Queen's Park United Reformed Church, since 2000; *b* 4 Jan. 1964; *s* of Edwin Henry and Constance May Hilborn; *m* 1988, Mia Alison Kyte (*see* Rev. M. A. K. Hilborn); one *s* one *d*. *Educ:* Langley Park Sch. for Boys; Nottingham Univ. (BA English; PhD); Mansfield Coll., Oxford (MA Theol.). Ordinand, Mansfield Coll., Oxford, 1985–89; Minister, Keyworth URC, 1989–92; research and teaching, Nottingham Univ., 1992–94; Minister, City Temple URC, 1994–99 (Jt Minister, 1997–99). Theol Sec., Evangelical Alliance, 1997–99. *Publications:* Picking Up the Pieces: can Evangelicals adapt to contemporary culture?, 1997; (ed) Faith, Hope and Homosexuality, 1998; (ed) The Nature of Hell, 2000; articles in theological books and jls. *Recreations:* cricket, poetry. *Address:* Evangelical Alliance, Whitefield House, 186 Kennington Park Road, SE11 4BT. *T:* (020) 7207 2100; 1a Third Avenue, W10 4RQ. *e-mail:* acute@eauk.org.

HILBORN, Rev. Mia Alison Kyte; Head of Spiritual Care and Chaplaincy Team Leader, Guy's and St Thomas' Hospital NHS Trust, since 2001; Associate Minister, Queen's Park United Reformed Church, since 2000; *b* 7 March 1963; *d* of late Harry Stephen Broadbelt and Jean Margaret Broadbelt; *m* 1988, Rev. David Henry Hilborn, *qv*; one *s* one *d*. *Educ:* City Univ. (BSc (Hons) Econs and Psychol.); Mansfield Coll., Oxford (MA Theol.). Ordination, URC, 1989; Minister, Friary URC, West Bridgford, Nottingham, 1989–94; City Temple URC, 1994–2000, Jt Minister, 1997–99; Free Church Chaplain, St Bart's Hosp., and Children's Chaplain, Bart's and The London NHS Trust, 1997–2001. *Recreations:* reading, theatre, knitting, Internet. *Address:* 1a Third Avenue, W10 4RQ.

HILD, Maj.-Gen. (John) Henry, MBE 1969; CEng, FIEE; FIMgt; Director: Siemens (UK) plc, 1984–97; Siemens Plessey Electronic Systems Ltd, 1989–95; consultant, since 1984; *b* 28 March 1931; *m* 1954, Janet Macdonald Brown; one *s* one *d*. *Educ:* Blackfriars, Laxton; Sandhurst. Joined Army, 1949; commissioned, 1952; Korea, 1952–53; sc 1961; MoD, DAQMG, 1962–64; Borneo, 1965; Hong Kong, 1966–67; 1 (BR) Corps, DAQMG, 1968–69; CO 18 Sig. Regt, 1969–71; DS, Staff Coll., 1972–73; Comd 1 Sig. Gp, 1974–76; Comdt, Sch. of Sigs, 1976–78; RCDS 1979; HQ BAOR, DQMG and CSO, 1980–84. Col Comdt, RCS, 1984–90. Dir, RCS Assoc. Trustee Ltd, 1989–97. Mem., Caravan Club Council, 1985–95. Princess Mary Medal, Royal Signals Inst., 1996. *Recreations:* entertaining friends, travel, sport. *Address:* c/o Lloyds TSB, 5 The Square, Petersfield, Hants GU32 3HL. *Clubs:* Army and Navy; Royal Signals Yacht (Adm., 1984–89).

HILDITCH, David William; Member (DemU) Antrim East, Northern Ireland Assembly, since 1998; *b* 23 July 1963; *s* of David and Agnes Hilditch; *m* 1987, Wilma McCalmont; two *s*. *Educ:* Carrickfergus Grammar Sch. Carrickfergus Borough Council: Mem. (DemU), 1991–; Dep. Mayor, 1994–96; Mayor, 1997–98. Dist Master, Carrickfergus, Loyal Orange Instn, 1993–. *Address:* 130 Salia Avenue, Carrickfergus, Co. Antrim BT38 8NE. *T:* (028) 9335 1090.

HILDRETH, (Henry) Jan (Hamilton Crossley); independent consultant; Chairman: South West London and St George's Mental Health (formerly Pathfinder) NHS Trust, since 1994; High Performance Sports Ltd, since 1995; *b* 1 Dec. 1932; *s* of Maj.-Gen. Sir (Harold) John (Crossley) Hildreth, KBE, and late Mrs Joan Elise Hallett (*née* Hamilton); *m* 1958, Wendy Moira Marjorie, *d* of late Arthur Harold Clough, CMG, OBE; two *s* one *d*. *Educ:* Wellington Coll.; The Queen's Coll., Oxford. National Service in RA, BAOR, 1952–53; 44 Parachute Bde (TA), 1953–58. Oxford, Hon. Mods (Nat. Sci.), BA (PPE) 1956, MA. Baltic Exchange, 1956; Royal Dutch Shell Group, 1957: served Philippines (marketing) and London (finance); Kleinwort, Benson Ltd, 1963; NEDO, 1965; Member of Economic Development Cttees for the Clothing, the Hosiery and Knitwear, and the Wool Textile industries; Mem., London Transport Bd, subseq. LTE, 1968–72: main responsibilities Finance, Marketing, Corp. Plan, Data Processing, and Estates; Asst Chief Exec., John Laing & Son Ltd, 1972–74; Dir-Gen., Inst. of Directors, 1975–78. Director: Minster Trust Ltd, 1979–94; Monument Oil and Gas plc, 1984–88; non-exec. dir of several cos, 1983–96; Chairman: Carroll Securities Ltd, 1986–91; Sea Catch PLC, 1987–94; Scallop Kings PLC, 1987–97. Member: Cttee, GBA, 1978–86 and 1997–2000; Council, ISIS, 1979–82; Exec. Cttee, Industrial Soc., 1973–84 (Hon. Life Mem., 1984); Council, British Exec. Service Overseas, 1975–91; Council, SCOPE (formerly Spastic Soc.), 1980–83, 1985– (Chm. Audit Cttee, 1990–92; Hon. Treas., 1992–97); Review Body for Nursing and Midwifery Staff and Professions Allied to Medicine, 1989–95; Council, St George's Hosp. Med. Sch., 1995–; Dir, Contact A Family, 1980–89. Constituency Chm., 1986–89, Pres., 1989–92, Wimbledon Cons. Assoc. Governor: Wellington Coll., 1974–; Eagle House Sch., 1986–. FCIT. FRSA. *Recreations:* cross-country, mountain and road running, photography, water mills, and others. *Address:* 50 Ridgway Place, Wimbledon, SW19 4SW. *Clubs:* Athenæum; Vincent's (Oxford); Thames Hare and Hounds.

HILDREW, Bryan, CBE 1977; FREng; Managing Director, Lloyds Register of Shipping, 1977–85; *b* 19 March 1920; *s* of Alexander William Hildrew and Sarah Jane (*née* Clark); *m* 1950, Megan Kathleen Lewis; two *s* one *d*. *Educ:* Bede Collegiate Sch., Sunderland; Technical Coll., Sunderland; City and Guilds, Imperial Coll., London (MSc, DIC). FIMechE, FIMarE; FREng (FEng 1976). Engineer Officer, RN, 1941–46. Lloyds Register of Shipping: Research Surveyor, 1948–67 (Admiralty Nuclear Submarine Project, 1956–61); Chief Engineer Surveyor, 1967–70; Technical Dir, 1970–77. Chm., Abbeyfield, Orpington, 1985–. President: IMechE, 1980–81; IMarE, 1983–85; Chm., CEI, 1981–82. FCGI 1990. Hon. DEng Newcastle, 1987; DUniv Surrey, 1994. *Recreations:* orienteering, walking. *Address:* 8 Westholme, Orpington, Kent BR6 0AN. *T:* (01689) 825451.

HILDYARD, Robert Henry Thoroton; QC 1994; *b* 10 Oct. 1952; *s* of Sir David (Henry Thoroton) Hildyard, KCMG, DFC and Millicent Hildyard, *d* of Sir Edward Baron; *m* 1980, Isabella Jane Rennie; two *d* (and one *d* decd). *Educ:* Eton Coll.; Christ Church, Oxford (BA Hons Hist.). Called to the Bar, Inner Temple, 1977; Jun. Counsel to Crown (Chancery), 1992–94. *Recreations:* family, tennis, shooting, opera, writing doggerel. *Address:* 4 Stone Buildings, Lincoln's Inn, WC2A 3XT. *T:* (020) 7242 5524. *Club:* Hurlingham.

HILL, family name of **Marquess of Downshire** and **Baron Sandys.**

HILL; *see* Clegg-Hill, family name of Viscount Hill.

HILL; *see* Erskine-Hill.

HILL, 8th Viscount *cr* 1842; **Antony Rowland Clegg-Hill;** Bt 1726–27; Baron Hill 1814; *b* 19 March 1931; *s* of 7th Viscount Hill and Elisabeth Flora (*d* 1967), *d* of Brig.-Gen. George Nowell Thomas Smyth-Osbourne, CB, CMG, DSO; *S* father, 1974; *m* 1st, 1963, Juanita Phyllis (marr. diss. 1976), *d* of John W. Pertwee, Salfords, Surrey; 2nd, 1989, Elizabeth Harriett, *d* of Ronald L. Offer, Salisbury, Wilts. *Educ:* Kelly Coll.; RMA, Sandhurst. Formerly Captain, RA. Freeman of Shrewsbury, 1957. *Heir: cousin* Peter David Raymond Charles Clegg-Hill [*b* 17 Oct. 1945; *m* 1973, Sharon Ruth Deane, Kaikohe, NZ; two *s* five *d*].

HILL, Prof. Alan Geoffrey, MA; FBA 1994; Professor of English Language and Literature in the University of London at Royal Holloway and Bedford New College (formerly Royal Holloway College), 1981–96, now Emeritus; *b* 12 Dec. 1931; *yr s* of Thomas Murton Hill and Alice Marion Hill (*née* Nunn); *m* 1960, Margaret Vincent Rutherford, MA; three *d*. *Educ:* Dulwich Coll. (Sen. Foundn Schol.); St Andrews Univ. (MA 1st Cl. Hons English Lang. and Lit.); Merton Coll., Oxford (BLitt). Asst Lectr/Lectr in English, Exeter Univ., 1958–62; Lectr in English, St Andrews Univ., 1962–68; Sen. Lectr in English, Dundee Univ., 1968–80. Vis. Professor of English, Univ. of Saskatchewan, 1973–74; British Acad./Royal Soc. of Canada Vis. Lectr, Canadian univs, 1997; Hon. Fellow, Inst. for Advanced Res. in Humanities, Birmingham Univ., 1996–. External Examiner in English: Univ. of Buckingham, 1986–90; Nat. Univ. of Singapore, 1996–98. Lectures: Crowsley, Charles Lamb Soc., 1981; Warton, British Acad., 1986; Newman Centenary, Univ. of Malta, 1990; Lambeth Palace Library, 1992; Tewkesbury Abbey, 2000. Founded Centre for Study of Victorian Art, RHC, 1981. Trustee, Dove Cottage Trust, 1969–; General Editor, The Letters of William and Dorothy Wordsworth, 1979–. Member: Editl Bd, Forum for Modern Language Studies, 1964–69; Publications Bd, Tennyson Res. Bulletin, 1993–2000. *Publications:* The Letters of William and Dorothy Wordsworth, vol. III, The Middle Years, Part 2, 1812–1820, 2nd edn (rev. and ed with Mary Moorman), 1970; vol. IV, The Later Years, Part 1, 1821–1828, 2nd edn (rev. and ed), 1978; vol. V, The Later Years, Part 2, 1829–1834, 2nd edn (rev. and ed), 1979; vol. VI, The Later Years, Part 3, 1835–1839, 2nd edn (rev. and ed), 1982; vol. VII, The Later Years, Part 4, 1840–1853, 2nd edn (rev. and ed), 1988; vol. VIII, A Supplement of New Letters, 1993; (ed) Selected Letters of Dorothy Wordsworth, 1981; (ed) Selected Letters of William Wordsworth, 1984; (ed) John Henry Newman, Loss and Gain, 1986; Wordsworth's Grand Design, 1987; (ed with Ian Ker) Newman After A Hundred Years, 1990; (ed) Ford Madox Ford, The Soul of London, 1995; Tennyson, Wordsworth, and the 'Forms' of Religion, 1997; Newman's Idea of a University, Revisited, 1998; Lyrical Ballads (1800): a bicentenary celebration, 2000; (ed) Newman, Callista, 2001; contrib. DNB, articles and reviews in literary, historical and theological jls. *Recreations:* music, fine arts, ecclesiology, travel. *Address:* The Pleck, British Camp, Malvern, Worcs WR13 6HR. *T:* (01684) 540513. *Club:* Savile.

HILL, Alastair Malcolm, OBE 2000; QC 1982; *b* 12 May 1936; *s* of Prof. Sir Ian George Wilson Hill, CBE, LLD, FRCP, FRSE and Lady (Audrey) Hill; *m* 1969, Elizabeth Maria Innes; one *s* one *d*. *Educ:* Trinity Coll., Glenalmond; Keble Coll., Oxford (Stevenson-Chatterton Schol.; BA Hons Jurisp. 1959). Nat. Service, RHA, 1954–56. Called to the Bar, Gray's Inn, 1961; South Eastern Circuit; a Recorder, 1982. *Recreations:* collecting prints and watercolours, opera, fly-fishing. *Address:* New Court Chambers, 5 Verulam Buildings, Gray's Inn, WC1R 5LY. *T:* (020) 7831 9500.

HILL, Allen; *see* Hill, H. A. O.

HILL, Antony James de Villiers; Headmaster, St Mark's School, Southborough, Mass, since 1994; *b* 1 Aug. 1940; *s* of James Kenneth Hill and Hon. Yvonne Aletta Hill, *d* of 2nd Baron de Villiers; *m* 1974, Gunilla Els-Charlotte Emilie (Elsa) Nilsson; one *d*. *Educ:* Sydney Grammar School; Sydney Univ. (BA Hons); Boston Univ. (MEd). Law Clerk, 1962–64; Antarctic Expedition, 1964–65; Master, Canberra Grammar Sch., 1965–66; Instructor, Himalayan Mountaineering Inst., Darjeeling, 1967–68; Master, Sydney C of E Grammar Sch., 1967–72, 1977; Mem. Faculty: Phillips Acad., Andover, Mass, 1972–74; Boston Univ., 1974–76; Senior Master, King's Sch., Parramatta, 1977–81; Headmaster: Christ Church Grammar Sch., WA, 1982–87; Melbourne C of E Grammar Sch., later Melbourne Grammar Sch., 1988–94. *Recreations:* running, climbing, sailing, theatre, music, reading. *Address:* St Mark's School, 25 Marlborough Road, PO Box 9105, Southborough, MA 01772, USA. *T:* (508) 7866104, *Fax:* (508) 7866109; *e-mail:* antonyhill@stmarksschool.org. *Clubs:* Weld (Perth, WA); Savage (Melbourne).

HILL, Sir Arthur (Alfred), Kt 1989, CBE 1980; Chairman, Walsall District Health Authority, 1982–92; *b* 14 May 1920; *s* of Arthur James Hill and Phoebe Mary Hill (*née* Prees); *m* 1947, Alma M. E. Bate (CBE 1981); one *s* two *d*. *Educ:* Langley High Sch.; Halesowen Technical Coll. Served RAFVR, 1939–45. Joint Company Director: Arthur Brook Cars Ltd, 1948–68; Abro Finance Ltd, 1950–65; Cradley Heath Motor Co. Ltd, 1956–65. Trainer/Man., Dudley Council Voluntary Services, 1980–82. Chm., CPC, 1969–72; Treas., 1973–76, Chm., 1976–79, Pres., 1985–88, W Midlands Area Cons. Council; Mem., Cons. Nat. Union, 1966–80; Chairman: Kidderminster Cons. Assoc., 1964–67; Walsall S Cons. Assoc., 1981–84. Mem., Rowley Regis BC, 1948–57. Chm., Bd of Govs, Rowley Regis Grammar Sch., 1961–64. *Recreations:* travelling, golf. *Address:* Lichfield, 1 Mellish Road, Walsall, West Midlands WS4 2DQ. *T:* (01922) 634949.

HILL, Sir Brian (John), Kt 1989; FRICS; FCIOB; President, Higgs and Hill plc, 1993–97; *b* 19 Dec. 1932; *s* of Doris Winifred Hill and Gerald Aubrey Hill, OBE; *m* 1959, Janet J. Newman; two *s* one *d*. *Educ:* Stowe School; Emmanuel College, Cambridge. BA (Land Economy); MA. Managing Director, Higgs and Hill Building Ltd, 1966–78; Higgs and Hill plc: Group Managing Dir, 1972–83; Chm. and Chief Exec., 1983–89; Exec. Chm., 1989–91; non-exec. Chm., 1991–92. Director: Etonbrook Properties, 1991–93; Southern Reg. Nat. Westminster Bank, 1990–92; Chairman: Goldsborough Healthcare plc, 1993–97; Sackville Property Unit Trust, 1999–. President: London Region, Nat. Fedn of Building Trades Employers, 1981–82; CIOB, 1987–88; Building Employers Confedn, 1992–95; Chairman: Vauxhall Coll. of Building and Further Educn, 1976–86; Nat. Contractors Group, 1983–84; Director: Building Centre, 1977–85; LDDC, 1994–98. Property Services Agency: Mem. Adv. Bd, 1981–86; Mem. Bd, 1986–88. Mem. Cttee, Lazard Property Unit Trust, 1982–98. Dir (formerly Gov.), 1985–97 (Chm., 1992–97), and Special Trustee, 1990–2000. Great Ormond Street Hosp. for Sick Children; Chm., Children's Trust, Tadworth, 1998–; Trustee, Falkland Is Meml Trust, 1997–. Governor: Aberdour Sch., 1988–; Pangbourne Coll., 2000–. Hon. FIStructE; Hon. FCGI; Hon. Fellow, Inst. of Child Health, 1996. Hon. DSc Westminster, 1994; Hon. LLD South Bank, 1995. *Recreations:* travelling, tennis, gardening, amateur dramatics. *Address:* Corner Oak, 5 Glen Close, Kingswood, Surrey KT20 6NT. *T:* (01737) 832424. *Club:* Royal Automobile.

HILL, Charles; *see* Hill, R. C.

HILL, Christopher; *see* Hill, J. E. C.

HILL, Rt Rev. Christopher John; *see* Stafford, Bishop Suffragan of.

HILL, Prof. Christopher John, DPhil; Montague Burton Professor of International Relations, London School of Economics and Political Science, since 1991; *b* 20 Nov. 1948; *s* of Peter Alan Hill and Sylvia Dawn Hill; *m* 1970, Maria McKay; one *s* one *d*. *Educ:* Merton Coll., Oxford (BA 1st Cl. Hons Modern History 1970); Nuffield Coll., Oxford (DPhil 1979). London School of Economics and Political Science: Noel Buxton Student in Internat. Relns, 1973–74; Lectr, 1974–90, Sen. Lectr, 1990–91, in Internat. Relns; Convenor, Dept of Internat. Relns, 1994–97; Vice Chm., Academic Bd, 1999–. Vis. Prof., Dartmouth Coll., NH, 1985; Visiting Fellow: RIIA, 1980–81; Woodrow Wilson International Centre for Scholars, Washington, 1984; European University Inst., Florence, 1992–93, 1998. *Publications:* (ed) National Foreign Policies and European Political Co-operation, 1983; Cabinet Decisions in Foreign Policy, 1991; (ed jtly) Two Worlds of International Relations, 1994; (ed) The Actors in Europe's Foreign Policy, 1996;(ed jtly) European Foreign Policy: key documents, 2000; many articles in learned jls and contribs to books. *Recreations:* Wolverhampton Wanderers FC, the visual arts. *Address:* Department of International Relations, London School of Economics and Political Science, Houghton Street, WC2A 2AE. *T:* (020) 7955 7390.

HILL, Rev. Canon Colin Arnold Clifford, OBE 1996; Vicar of Croydon and Chaplain to Archbishop Whitgift Foundation, 1973–94; Chaplain to the Queen, 1990–99; *b* 13 Feb. 1929; *s* of William and May Hill; *m* 1st, 1957, Shirley (*d* 1961); one *s*; 2nd, 1971, Irene Chamberlain; one step *s*. *Educ:* Reading Sch.; Bristol Univ.; Ripon Hall Theol Coll., Oxford. Ordained deacon, Sheffield Cathedral, 1957, priest, 1958; Rotherham Parish Church; Vicar of Brightside, 1960; Rector of Easthampstead, Bracknell, 1964; Chaplain, RAF Staff Coll., Bracknell, 1968. Hon. Canon, Canterbury, 1975, Canon Emeritus, 1984; Hon. Canon, Southwark, 1984, Canon Emeritus, 1994. Proctor in Convocation and General Synod, Dio. Oxford, 1970–73, Dios of Canterbury and Southwark, 1980–84. Religious Advr, London Borough of Croydon, 1973–94; Chairman: Church Tenements Trust, 1973–94; Croydon Industrial Mission, 1975–94. Chm., Croydon Crime Prevention Initiative, 1989–94; Vice Chm., Croydon Police Consultative Cttee, 1985–94. Founder, Bracknell Samaritans, 1968; Founder Chm., Croydon Youth Counselling Agency, 1974–94. *Recreations:* boating, walking, reading. *Address:* Silver Birches, 70 Preston Crowmarsh, Wallingford, Oxon OX10 6SL. *T:* (01491) 836102. *Club:* Leander.

HILL, Damon Graham Devereux, OBE 1997; motor racing driver, retired; Chairman: Damon Hill BMW, Warwick, since 2001; P1 International Ltd; *b* 17 Sept. 1960; *s* of late Graham Hill, OBE and of Bette Hill; *m* 1988, Georgie Hill; two *s* two *d*. *Educ:* Haberdashers' Aske's Sch. Began motorcycle racing, 1979; Formula 3, 1986; Formula 3000, 1988; Formula 1, 1992–99: Brabham team, 1992; with Williams Team, 1991–96: test driver, 1991; driver, 1993–96; Grand Prix wins: 3 in 1993, 6 in 1994, 4 in 1995, 8 in 1996 (Argentina, Australia, Brazil, Canada, France, Germany, Japan, San Marino), 1 in 1998; Drivers' World Championship, 1996; with Arrows team, 1997; with Jordan team, 1998–99. Numerous awards incl. BBC Sports Personality of the Year, 1994 and 1996. *Publications:* Grand Prix Year, 1994; Championship Year, 1996. *Address:* c/o Clyde & Co., 51 Eastcheap, EC3M 1JP.

HILL, Prof. David Keynes, ScD; FRS 1972; Professor of Biophysics, Royal Postgraduate Medical School, University of London, 1975–82, now Professor Emeritus; *b* 23 July 1915; *s* of late Prof. Archibald Vivian Hill, CH, OBE, ScD, FRS, and Margaret Neville, *d* of late Dr J. N. Keynes; *m* 1949, Stella Mary Humphrey; four *d*. *Educ:* Highgate Sch.; Trinity Coll., Cambridge. ScD Cantab 1965. Fellow, Trinity Coll., Cambridge, 1940–48; Physiologist on staff of Marine Biological Assoc., Plymouth, 1948–49; Sen. Lectr, 1949–62, Reader in Biophysics, 1962–75, Vice-Dean, 1969–74, Royal Postgrad. Med. Sch., London Univ. Physiological Society: Editor of Journal, 1969–76; Chm., Bd of Monographs, 1979–81. *Publications:* Scientific papers in Jl Physiology. *Address:* Ivy Cottage, Winksley, Ripon, N Yorks HG4 3NR. *T:* (01765) 658562.
See also Polly Hill.

HILL, David Neil, MA, FRCO; Organist and Master of Music, Winchester Cathedral, 1988–July 2002; *b* 13 May 1957; *s* of James Brian Greatrex Hill and Jean Hill; *m* 1st, 1979, Hilary Llystyn Jones (marr. diss.); one *s* one *d*; 2nd, 1994, Alice Mary Wills; one *s* one *d*. *Educ:* Chetham's School of Music, Manchester; St John's College, Cambridge (organ student; toured Aust. 1977, USA and Canada, 1978, Japan, 1979; MA). Sub-Organist, Durham Cathedral, 1980–82; Organist and Master of Music, Westminster Cathedral, 1982–88. Conductor: Alexandra Choir, 1979–87; Waynflete Singers, Winchester, 1988–; Associate Chorus Master, 1987–98, Artistic Dir, 1992–98, Philharmonia Chorus; Musical Dir, Bach Choir, 1998–. Mem. Council, RCO, 1984–. Recordings with Westminster Cathedral Choir (Gramophone award, 1985); concerts and tours abroad, including tours as organist or with Cathedral Choir to Australia, USA and Philippines. *Recreations:* food, wine, cricket, golf, cars. *Address:* (until July 2002) 1 The Close, Winchester, Hants SO23 9LS. *T:* (01962) 857200, *Fax:* (01962) 857201. *Club:* Athenæum.

HILL, David Rowland; Director, Good Relations, since 1998; Managing Director, Keith McDowall Associates, since 2000; *b* 1 Feb. 1948; *s* of Rowland Foster Hill and Rita Maud Hill; *m* 1974, Janet Gibson (marr. diss. 1992); one *s* one *d*. *Educ:* King Edward VI Sch., Birmingham; Brasenose Coll., Oxford Univ. (BA PPE). Unigate Ltd, 1970–72; Asst to Rt Hon. Roy Hattersley, MP, 1972–76; Political Advr, Dept of Prices and Consumer Protection, 1976–79; Head of Staff: Rt Hon. Roy Hattersley, 1979–83; Dep. Leader of Labour Party's Office, 1983–91; Dir of Campaigns and Communications, Lab Party, 1991–93; Chief Spokesperson for Labour Party, 1993–98. *Recreations:* cinema, watching sport, foreign travel. *Address:* 1 Rectory Road, Walthamstow, E17 3BG. *T:* (020) 8520 8753.

HILL, Rev. Mgr Edward Peter; Officiating Chaplain (RC), RAF Brize Norton, since 2000; *b* 8 Aug. 1943; *s* of Leslie John Hill and Constance Irene Hill. *Educ:* Holy Family RC Primary Sch., Morden; John Fisher Independent Sch., Purley; St Joseph's Jun. Seminary, Mark Cross, Sussex; St John's Seminary, Wonersh. Ordained priest, 1968; Assistant Priest: St Saviour, Lewisham, 1968–72; St Thomas of Canterbury, Wandsworth, 1972–78; St Peter, Woolwich, 1978–82; served as RAF Chaplain, 1982–2000: Cranwell, Wildenrath, Brampton, Brize Norton, Rheindahlen; Asst Principal Chaplain, Support Command, Brampton, and Personnel and Trng Comd, Innsworth; Prin. RC Chaplain and Dir, Chaplaincy Services 2, RAF, 1997–2000; held rank of Gp Captain; QHC 1997–2000. Prelate of Honour to the Pope, 1997. *Recreations:* most sports (interest in, only now, as spectator and studier). *Club:* Royal Air Force.

HILL, (Eliot) Michael; QC 1979; QC (NSW) 1991; *b* 22 May 1935; *s* of Cecil Charles Hill and Rebecca Betty Hill; *m* 1965, Kathleen Irene (*née* Hordern); one *s* two *d*. *Educ:*

Bancroft's Sch., Essex; Brasenose Coll., Oxford (MA). Called to the Bar, Gray's Inn, 1958, Bencher, 1986; Member: Senate of the Inns of Court and the Bar, 1976–79 and 1982–86; Bar Council, 1986–87 and 1989–90. South-Eastern Circuit. Prosecuting Counsel to Crown, Inner London Sessions, 1969–74; Jun. Pros. Counsel to Crown, Central Criminal Court, 1974–77; a Sen. Pros. Counsel to Crown, 1977–79; a Recorder, 1977–97. Chairman: Criminal Bar Assoc., 1982–86 (Sec., 1973–75; Vice-Chm., 1979–82); Inns of Court Advocacy Training Cttee, 1995–99; Member: Council of Legal Educn, 1977–86; Criminal Law Revision Cttee, 1983–; Bd of Dirs, Internat. Soc. for Reform of Criminal Law, 1988– (Chm., Management Cttee, 1991–95; Pres., 1999–). Dir, Bar Mutual Indemnity Fund Ltd, 1987– (Chm., Investment Cttee, 1991–). *Recreations:* family, friends, riding, fishing and just living. *Address:* (chambers) 23 Essex Street, WC2R 3AS. *T:* (020) 7413 0353, (020) 8287 9005, *Fax:* (020) 7413 0374, (020) 8287 9005; *e-mail:* michaelhill@23essexstreet.co.uk; michaelhillqc@cs.com. *Club:* Garrick.

HILL, Air Cdre Dame Felicity (Barbara), DBE 1966 (OBE 1954); Director of the Women's Royal Air Force, 1966–69; *b* 12 Dec. 1915; *d* of late Edwin Frederick Hill and late Mrs Frances Ada Barbara Hill (*née* Cocke). *Educ:* St Margaret's Sch., Folkestone. Joined WAAF, 1939; commnd, 1940; served in: UK, 1939–46; Germany, 1946–47; Far East Air Force, 1949–51; other appts included Inspector of WRAF, 1956–59; OC, RAF Hawkinge, 1959–60; OC, RAF Spitalgate, 1960–62; Dep. Dir, 1962–65. Hon. ADC to the Queen, 1966–69. *Address:* Worcester Cottage, Mews Lane, Winchester, Hants SO22 4PS. *Club:* Royal Air Force.

HILL, Prof. Geoffrey (William), FRSL; University Professor, and Professor of Literature and Religion, Boston University, since 1988; founding Co-Director, Editorial Institute, Boston University, since 1998; *b* 18 June 1932; *s* of William George Hill and Hilda Beatrice Hill (*née* Hands); *m* 1st, 1956, Nancy Whittaker (marr. diss. 1983); three *s* one *d*; 2nd, 1987, Alice Goodman; one *d*. *Educ:* County High Sch., Bromsgrove; Keble Coll., Oxford (BA 1953, MA 1959; Hon. Fellow, 1981). Mem., academic staff, Univ. of Leeds, 1954–80 (Prof. of Eng. Lit., 1976–80); Univ. Lectr in English and Fellow of Emmanuel College, Cambridge, 1981–88. Churchill Fellow, Univ. of Bristol, 1980. Lectures: Clark, Trinity Coll., Cambridge, 1986; Tanner, Brasenose Coll., Oxford, 2000; Ward-Phillips, Univ. of Notre Dame, 2000. English version of Ibsen's Brand produced at National Theatre, London, 1978. FRSL 1972; Fellow, Amer. Acad. of Arts and Scis, 1996. Hon. Fellow, Emmanuel Coll., Cambridge, 1990. Whitbread Award, 1971; RSL Award (W. H. Heinemann Bequest), 1971; Loines Award, Amer. Acad. and Inst. of Arts and Letters, 1983; Ingram Merrill Foundn Award in Literature, 1985. Hon. DLitt Leeds, 1988. *Publications: poetry:* For the Unfallen, 1959 (Gregory Award, 1961); King Log, 1968 (Hawthornden Prize, 1969; Geoffrey Faber Meml Prize, 1970); Mercian Hymns, 1971 (Alice Hunt Bartlett Award, 1971); Somewhere is Such a Kingdom: Poems 1952–1971, 1975; Tenebrae, 1978 (Duff Cooper Meml Prize, 1979); The Mystery of the Charity of Charles Péguy, 1983; Collected Poems, 1985; New and Collected Poems 1952–1992, 1994; Canaan, 1996; The Triumph of Love, 1998 (Cholmondeley Award, 1999; Heinemann Award, 2000; T. S. Eliot Prize, 2000); Speech! Speech!, 2000; *poetic drama:* Henrik Ibsen, Brand: a version for the English Stage, 1978, 3rd edn 1996; *criticism:* The Lords of Limit, 1984; The Enemy's Country, 1991. *Address:* Editorial Institute, Boston University, 725 Commonwealth Avenue, Boston, MA 02215, USA.

HILL, George Raymond, FCA, FCIT; FHCIMA; Director, Ashford International Hotel PLC, 1987–99; *b* 25 Sept. 1925; *s* of George Mark and Jill Hill; *m* 1948, Sophie (*née* Gilbert); two *d*. *Educ:* St Dunstan's Coll., London. Royal Marines, 1943–46 (Lieut). Distillers Co. Ltd (Industrial Group), 1952–66; BP Chemicals Ltd, 1967–69; British Transport Hotels Ltd: Chief Exec., 1970–76; Chm., 1974–76; Dir, Bass PLC, 1976–84 (Mem. Exec. Cttee); Chm., Bass UK Ltd, 1978–80; Chairman: Howard Machinery PLC (later H. M. Holdings PLC), 1984–85; Sims Catering Butchers plc, 1985–87; Director: Prince of Wales Hotels PLC, 1985–86; Chester Internat. Hotel, 1987–92; Regal Hotel Gp, 1989–92 (non-exec. Chm.). Member Boards: British Railways (Scottish), and British Rail Hovercraft Ltd, 1972–76; British Tourist Auth., 1981–89 (Chm., Marketing Cttee, 1985–89); Chairman: Liquor Licensing Working Party, 1985–; Channel Tunnel Nat. Tourism Working Pty, 1986–89. Member: Hotel and Catering Industry Trng Bd, 1973–80; Civil Service Final Selection Bd, 1973–80; Cttee of Inquiry on Motorway Service Areas, 1978; BHRCA (Bd Chm., 1979–80; Nat. Council Chm., 1985–86; Fellow, BHA); Pres., Licensed Victuallers Schs, 1982–83. Mem., HAC. FRSA 1980. *Publication:* Figuring For Fun: a ladder of opportunity, 1999. *Recreations:* music, theatre, works of art, country life. *Address:* 23 Sheffield Terrace, W8 7NQ. *T:* (020) 7727 3986.

HILL, Graham Chadwick, FRSC; Headmaster, Dr Challoner's Grammar School, Amersham, since 1993; *b* 11 Jan. 1942; *s* of Harold Hill and Harriet (*née* Chadwick); *m* 1964, Elizabeth Wadsworth; three *d*. *Educ:* Bacup and Rawtenstall Grammar Sch.; Trinity Coll., Cambridge (BA, MA, PGCE Dist, AdvDipEd). FRSC 1985. Asst Science Master, Marlborough Coll., 1965–70; Sen. Chemistry Master, 1970–75, Sen. Science Master, 1975–78, Bristol Grammar Sch.; Dep. Headmaster, Dr Challoner's Grammar Sch., 1978–86, 1989–93; Sen. Fellow, Univ. of York, 1986–87. Chm., 1987–89, Trustee, 1991–93, ASE. FRSA 1993. Guinness Award for Sci. Teachers, 1968; Bronze Medallion, RSC, 1986. *Publications:* Chemistry in Context, 1978, 5th edn 2000; Chemistry in Context Laboratory Manual and Study Guide, 1982; Chemistry Counts, 1986; Letts Revise Science, 1990; Science Scene (booklets, books and teachers' guides), 1990–92; Materials, 1992; Science for GCSE, 1998, 2nd edn 2001; Foundation Science for GCSE, 2001; contribs to learned jls. *Recreations:* walking, gardening, theatre. *Address:* Dr Challoner's Grammar School, Chesham Road, Amersham, Bucks HP6 5HA. *T:* (01494) 721685.

HILL, Graham Starforth; Resident Consultant, office in Rome 1992–94, and in Milan, 1990–94, Frere Cholmeley, later Frere Cholmeley Bischoff, solicitors; Consultant: to Monaco office, Frere Cholmeley, later Frere Cholmeley Bischoff, solicitors, 1984–94; to Rodyk and Davidson, solicitors, Singapore, 1985–96; *b* 22 June 1927; *s* of late Harold Victor John Hill and Helen Dora (*née* Starforth); *m* 1952, Margaret Elise Ambler (marr. diss.); one *s* one *d*. *Educ:* Dragon Sch., Oxford; Winchester Coll.; St John's Coll., Oxford (MA Hons). Called to the Bar, Grays Inn, 1951; admitted solicitor, 1961; also admitted solicitor Malaysia, Singapore and Hong Kong; Notary Public and Comr for Oaths, Singapore. Flying Officer, RAF, 1948–50. Crown Counsel, Colonial Legal Service, Singapore, 1953–56; Partner, subseq. Sen. Partner, Rodyk and Davidson, Advocates and Solicitors, Singapore, 1957–76. Chm., Guinness Mahon & Co. Ltd, 1979–83 (Dir, 1977–79); non-exec. Dir, Phelan, Lewis and Peat Ltd, 1984–86. Mem., Malayan Bd of Income Tax, 1957–60. Formerly (all Singapore): Hon. Legal Adviser to High Commn; Law Reform Comr; dir of numerous cos; Member: Univ. Faculty of Law; Constitutional Commn; Council, Law Soc. (Pres., 1970–74, Hon. Mem. 1978); Courts Martial Mil. Ct of Appeal; Council, Internat. Bar Assoc.; Discip. Cttee and Appeal Cttee, ICA, 1980–86. Trustee: Southwark Cathedral Develt Trust Fund, 1980–85; Royal Opera House Trust, 1982–85. FRSA. Cavaliere dell'Ordine della Stella della Solidarieta, and Commendatore dell'Ordine al Merito, Italy. *Publications:* co-editor, The Laws of Singapore, revised edition 1970; report of Constitutional Commission of Singapore. *Recreations:* music, Italy. *Address:* 36 Terrazze del Porto, CP 24, 07020 Porto Cervo, Sardegna, Italy. *T:* (0789) 92626; 10 St Thomas Street, Winchester, Hants SO23 9HE. *T:* (01962) 854146; *e-mail:* gshill@bigfoot.com. *Club:* Garrick.

See also I. S. Hill.

HILL, Rt Rev. Henry Gordon; Co-Chairman, Anglican-Orthodox Joint Doctrinal Commission, 1980–90; *b* 14 Dec. 1921; *s* of Henry Knox Hill and Kathleen Elizabeth (*née* Cunningham); unmarried. *Educ:* Queen's Univ., Kingston, Ont. (BA 1945); Trinity Coll., Toronto (LTh 1948); St John's Coll., Cambridge (MA 1952). Deacon, Dio. Ont., 1948; Priest (Bp of Ely for Ontario), 1949; Curate, Belleville, Ont., 1950; Rector of Adolphustown, Ont., 1951; Chaplain, St John's Coll., Cambridge, Eng., 1952; Curate, Wisbech, Cambs, 1955; Rector, St Thomas, Reddendale, Ont., 1957; Asst Prof., Canterbury Coll., Assumption Univ., Windsor, 1962–68; (Vice-Principal, 1965–68); Associate Prof. of History, Univ. of Windsor, Ont., 1968–74; Bishop of Ontario, 1975–81; Asst Bishop of Montreal, 1981–83. Warden, Sisters of St John the Divine, 1978–88; Vice-Pres., Fellowship of St Alban and St Sergius, 1980. Episcopal Consultant for the Eastern and Oriental Orthodox Churches, Lambeth Conf., 1988; formerly on staff of Primate of Canada, episcopal liaison with non-Chalcedonian orthodox church; estabd Scholarship of St Basil the Great, 1995 (for student exchanges between Anglican Ch of Canada, Oriental Orthodox Chs and Ch of the East). Hon. DD: Trinity Coll., Toronto, 1976; Montreal Dio. Theol Coll., 1976; Hon. LLD Univ. of Windsor, 1976; Hon. Dr, Theological Inst., Bucharest, 1977. KLJ 1980. Patriarchal Cross of Romanian Orthodox Church, 1969. *Publications:* Contemplation and Ecumenism (Monastic Studies No 15), 1984; Light Out of the East: chapters on the life and worship of the ancient orthodox churches, 1988; Engolpion, HH Ignatius Zakka Ivas, Syrian Orthodox Patriarch of Damascus, 1988; (ed and contrib.) Light from the East, 1988; (contrib.) Dictionary of the Ecumenical Movement, 1991; articles in Cdn Jl of Theology, Sobornost, Jl Fellowship of St Alban and St Sergius. *Recreations:* walking, reading. *Address:* St John's Convent, 1 Botham Road, Willowdale, ON M2N 2J5, Canada.

HILL, Prof. (Hugh) Allen (Oliver), FRS 1990; CChem, FRSC; Professor of Bioinorganic Chemistry, Oxford, since 1992; Fellow and Praelector, The Queen's College, Oxford, since 1965; *b* 23 May 1937; *s* of Hugh Rankin Stewart Hill and Elizabeth Hill (*née* Burns); *m* 1967, Boglárka Anna Pinter; two *s* one *d*. *Educ:* Royal Belfast Academical Institution; QUB (BSc 1959; PhD 1962); Univ. of Oxford (MA 1964; DSc 1986). Research Fellowships, 1962–65; Oxford University: Deptl Demonstrator, 1965–67, Lectr, 1967–90, in Inorganic Chemistry; Reader in Bioinorganic Chemistry, 1990–92; Sen. Proctor, 1976–77. Vis. appts, Harvard, Univ. of Sydney, Univ. of California, 1970–82; Vis. Prof., Harvard Med. Sch., 1996–2001; Pacific Coast Lects, 1981; Robinson Lectr, RSC, 1994. Chm., Davy Faraday Cttee, 1996–98; Mem. Council, Royal Instn, 1995–98. Hon. DSc QUB, 1996. Interdisciplinary Award, RSC, 1987; Chemistry and Electrochemistry of Transition Metals Award, RSC, 1990; Mullard Award, Royal Soc., 1993; Breyer Medal, RACI, 1994. *Publications:* Physical Methods in Advanced Inorganic Chemistry (with P. Day), 1968; papers in professional jls. *Recreations:* gardening, music. *Address:* The Queen's College, Oxford OX1 4AW. *T:* (01865) 279177; *e-mail:* allen.hill@queens.ox.ac.uk.

HILL, Ian Macdonald, MS, FRCS; Consulting Cardiothoracic Surgeon, St Bartholomew's Hospital, since 1984 (Consultant Cardio-thoracic Surgeon, 1950–84); Hon. Consultant Thoracic Surgeon, SE Thames Regional Health Authority, since 1984 (Consultant Thoracic Surgeon, 1950–84); *b* 8 June 1919; British; *m* 1944, Agnes Mary Paice; three *s* one *d*. *Educ:* Stationers' Company Sch.; St Bartholomew's Hosp. Medical Coll. Undergrad. schols and medals, 1937–41; MB, BS (Hons) London, 1942; MRCS, LRCP 1942; FRCS 1944; MS London 1945. Demonstrator of Anatomy, St Bartholomew's, 1943; Surgical Chief Asst, St Bart's Hosp., 1944; RAF Medical Branch, 1946; Wing Comdr i/c Surg. Div. No 1 RAF Gen. Hosp., 1947; Senior Registrar, Thoracic Surg. Unit, Guy's Hosp., 1948; Surgical Chief Asst, Brompton Hosp. and Inst. of Diseases of the Chest, 1950. Sub-Dean, St Bart's Hosp. Med. Coll., 1964–73. FRSocMed. Member: Soc. of Apothecaries; Soc. of Thoracic Surgeons; Thoracic and Cardiac Socs. Governor, St Bartholomew's Hosp. Med. Coll., 1985–97. Freeman of City of London. *Publications:* articles in professional jls, mainly relating to lung and cardiac surgery, 1942–61. *Recreations:* old cars, furniture, keyboard instruments; gardening and house care. *Address:* Bracken Wood, Church Lane, Fernham, Faringdon, Oxon SN7 7PB. *T:* (01367) 820475.

HILL, His Honour (Ian) Starforth; QC 1969; a Circuit Judge, 1974–94; Resident Judge, Winchester Combined Court Centre, 1992–94; *b* 30 Sept. 1921; *s* of late Harold Victor John Hill; *m* 1st, 1950, Bridget Mary Footner; one *s* two *d*; 2nd, 1982, Greta Grimshaw; 3rd, 1986, Wendy Elizabeth Stavert. *Educ:* Shrewsbury Sch.; Brasenose Coll., Oxford (MA). 11th Sikh Regt, Indian Army, 1940–45, India, Africa, Italy (despatches). Called to Bar, Gray's Inn, 1949; Dep. Chm., Isle of Wight QS, 1968–71; Western Circuit; a Recorder of the Crown Court, 1972–74. Mem., Parole Bd, 1983–84. *Address:* Ladywell House, Ladywell Lane, Alresford, Hants SO24 9DF. *T:* (01962) 732131.

See also G. S. Hill.

HILL, Brig. James; *see* Hill, Brig. S. J. L.

HILL, Sir James Frederick, 4th Bt *cr* 1917; OBE 2000; DL; Chairman, Sir James Hill (Wool) Ltd, since 1991; *b* 5 Dec. 1943; *s* of Sir James Hill, 3rd Bt and of Marjory, *d* of late Frank Croft; *S* father, 1976; *m* 1966, Sandra Elizabeth, *o d* of J. C. Ingram; one *s* three *d*. Dir, Yorkshire Bldg Soc., 1972–96. Chm., British Wool Fedn, 1987–90. Chm., Black Dyke Band, 1999–. DL West Yorks, 1994. DUniv Bradford, 1997. *Heir: s* James Laurence Ingram Hill, *b* 22 Sept. 1973. *Address:* Roseville, Moor Lane, Menston, Ilkley, West Yorks LS29 6AP. *T:* (01943) 874624. *Clubs:* Royal Automobile; Bradford (Yorks); Ilkley Golf.

HILL, James William Thomas, (Jimmy), OBE 1995; Chairman, Jimmy Hill Ltd, since 1972; Presenter, The Last Word, Sky Sports, since 1998; *m* 1st, 1950, Gloria Mary (marr. diss. 1961); two *s* one *d*; 2nd, 1962, Heather Christine (marr. diss. 1982); one *s* one *d*; 3rd, 1991, Bryony Ruth Jarvis. *Educ:* Henry Thornton School, Clapham. Player, Brentford FC, 1949–52, Fulham FC, 1952–61; Gen. Manager, Coventry City FC, 1961–67, Managing Director, 1975–83, Chm., 1980–83; Chm., Fulham Football Club (1987) Ltd, 1987–97. London Weekend Television: Head of Sport, 1967–72; Controller of Press, Promotion and Publicity, 1971–72; Deputy Controller, Programmes, 1972–73; Soccer analyst, BBC, 1973–98. Mem., Sports Council, 1971–76. Hon. Chm., The Professional Footballers Assoc., 1957–61. *Publications:* Striking for Soccer, 1961; Improve your Soccer, 1964; Football Crazy, 1985; The Jimmy Hill Story (autobiog.), 1998. *Recreations:* golf, riding, tennis, bridge. *Address:* c/o Sky Sports, 6 Centaurs Business Park, Grant Way, Isleworth, Middx TW7 5QD. *Clubs:* Wig and Pen, All England Lawn Tennis and Croquet; The Berkshire.

HILL, Jimmy; *see* Hill, J. W. T.

HILL, John; *b* 28 April 1922; *s* of William Hallett Hill and Emily Hill (*née* Massey); *m* 1952, Hilda Mary Barratt; one *s*. *Educ:* Merchant Taylors' Sch., Crosby; Liverpool Univ. (BCom); Inst. of Public Finance and Accountancy, 1954. City Treasurer of Liverpool, 1974–82. Mem., Merseyside Residuary Body, 1985–88. Hon. Sen. Res. Fellow, Inst. of Local Govt Studies, Birmingham Univ., 1982–93. *Recreation:* music. *Address:* 325 Northway, Lydiate, Merseyside L31 0BW. *T:* (0151) 526 3699.

HILL, Sir John Alfred Rowley, 11th Bt *cr* 1779, of Brook Hall, Londonderry; *b* 29 Feb. 1940; *s* of Sir George Alfred Rowley Hill, 9th Bt and his 2nd wife, Jessie Anne (*née* Roberts; *d* 1995); *S* half-brother, 1992; *m* 1966, Diana Anne Walker (marr. diss. 1981); one adopted *s* one adopted *d*. *Heir: kinsman* Allan Claude Hill [*b* 10 Feb. 1936; *m* 1970, Rachel St Just (marr. diss. 1978); one *s* one *d*]. *Address:* 12 Ledbury Close, Oadby Grange, Leicester LE2 4SR.

HILL, John Andrew Patrick, CMG 2001; CBE 1978; Chairman, British Arab Commercial Bank, since 1996; *b* 8 Feb. 1936; *s* of Henry Wilfred Hill and Beatrice Rose Hill; *m* 1960, Barbara Anne Knifton; two *s* one *d*. *Educ:* Ealing Tech. Coll.; MECAS. Exec. (posts in India and ME), 1957–72, Area Manager, Saudi Arabia, 1972–77, British Bank of Middle East; Man. Dir, Saudi British Bank, 1978–79; Asst Gen. Manager, 1979–82, CEO, 1982–86, Gen. Manager, 1986–90, Hongkong and Shanghai Banking Corp. Director: HSBC Bank ME, 1980–; HSBC Republic Bank (Cyprus), 1986–; Arabian Gulf Investments (FE) Ltd, 1986–; Cyprus Popular Bank, 1986–; Jabah Investments Ltd, 1987–; Arab British Chamber of Commerce, 1996. FInstD 1996. Chm., Eric Thompson Charitable Trust, 1993–; Dir, Jerusalem and East Mission Trust, 1996–. *Recreations:* family, music, travel. *Address:* Hawkwood Manor, Sible Hedingham, Essex CO9 3RG. *T:* (01787) 460613. *Clubs:* Oriental, London Capital.

HILL, John Cameron, TD 1959; FRICS; Member, Lands Tribunal, 1987–99; *b* 8 April 1927; *s* of Raymond Cameron Hill and Margaret (*née* Chadwick); *m* 1954, Jane Edna Austin; one *s* one *d*. *Educ:* Trinity Coll., Oxford; College of Estate Management, London Univ. (BSc EstMan). Hillier Parker May & Rowden, 1953–88, Partner, 1962–88. Served TA (Major), 1949–73; Metropolitan Special Constabulary (Comdt), 1973–86. Liveryman, Co. of Chartered Surveyors, 1992. *Publication:* (jtly) Valuations: Principles into Practice, 1980, 4th edn 1993. *Recreations:* shooting, DIY. *Address:* Hastoe House, Hastoe, Tring, Herts HP23 6LS. *T:* (01442) 822084. *Clubs:* Army and Navy, Honourable Artillery Company.

HILL, John Edward Bernard; farming in Suffolk since 1946; *b* 13 Nov. 1912; *o s* of late Capt. Robert William Hill, Cambs Regt, and Marjorie Jane Lloyd-Jones, *d* of Edward Scott Miller; *m* 1944, Edith Luard (*d* 1995), *widow* of Comdr R. A. E. Luard, RNVR, and 5th *d* of late John Maxwell, Cove, Dunbartonshire; one adopted *d*. *Educ:* Charterhouse; Merton Coll., Oxford (MA). Various journeys; Middle East, Far East, India, USA, 1935–37; Far East, 1956–57; USA, 1958. Called to Bar, Inner Temple (Certificate of Honour), 1938. RA (TA), 1939; Air Observation Post Pilot, 1942; War Office, 1942; 651 (Air OP) RAF, Tunisia, 1942; wounded, 1943; invalided out, 1945. MP (C) South Norfolk, Jan. 1955–Feb. 1974; Mem. Parliamentary delegns: W Germany and Berlin, 1959; Ghana, 1965; IPU Conf., Teheran, 1966; CPA Conf., Uganda, 1967; Bulgaria, 1970; Council of Europe and WEU, 1970–72; Mem., European Parlt, 1973–74; Chm., Cons. Educn Cttee, 1971–73; Member: Select Cttee on Agriculture, 1967–69; Select Cttee on Procedure, 1970–71; Asst Govt Whip, 1959–60; a Lord Comr of the Treasury, 1960–64. Mem. East Suffolk and Norfolk River Board, 1952–62. Mem. Exec. Cttee, CLA, 1957–59, 1977–82. Member: Governing Body, Charterhouse Sch., 1958–90; Langley Sch., Norfolk, 1962–77; Governing Body, Sutton's Hosp., Charterhouse, 1966–97; GBA Cttee, 1966–79, 1980–83; Council, Univ. of East Anglia, 1975–82. *Recreations:* shooting, concerts, picture galleries. *Club:* Garrick.

HILL, (John Edward) Christopher, DLitt; FBA 1966; Master of Balliol College, Oxford, 1965–78; *b* 6 Feb. 1912; *m* 1st, 1944, Inez Waugh; (one *d* decd); 2nd, 1956, Bridget Irene Sutton; one *s* one *d* (and one *d* decd). *Educ:* St Peter's Sch., York; Balliol Coll., Oxford. BA 1931, DLitt 1965. Fellow of All Souls Coll., Oxford, 1934; Asst Lectr, University Coll., Cardiff, 1936; Fellow and Tutor in Modern History, Balliol Coll., Oxford, 1938. Private in Field Security Police, commissioned Oxford and Bucks Light Inf., 1940, Major; seconded to Foreign Office, 1943. Returned to Balliol, 1945; University Lectr in 16th- and 17th-century history, 1959; Ford's Lectr, 1962. Vis. Prof., Open Univ., 1978–80. Hon. Fellow, Lancs Polytechnic, 1988. Hon. DLitt: Hull, 1966; E Anglia, 1968; Glasgow, 1976; Exeter, 1979; Wales, 1979; Leicester, 1996; King Alfred's Coll., Winchester, 1996; Hon. LittD Sheffield, 1967; Hon. LLD Bristol, 1976; DUniv York, 1978; Hon. Dr Sorbonne Nouvelle, 1979; DUniv Open, 1982. Foreign Hon. Member: Amer. Acad. of Sciences, 1973; Hungarian Acad. of Sciences, 1982; Acad. of Sciences, GDR, 1988. *Publications:* The English Revolution 1640, 1940; (under name K. E. Holme) Two Commonwealths, 1945; Lenin and the Russian Revolution, 1947; The Good Old Cause (ed jointly with E. Dell), 1949; Economic Problems of the Church, 1956; Puritanism and Revolution, 1958; Oliver Cromwell, 1958; The Century of Revolution, 1961; Society and Puritanism in Pre-Revolutionary England, 1964; Intellectual Origins of the English Revolution, 1965; Reformation to Industrial Revolution, 1967; God's Englishman, 1970; Antichrist in 17th Century England, 1971; The World Turned Upside Down, 1972; ed, G. Winstanley, The Law of Freedom and other writings, 1973; Change and Continuity in Seventeenth Century England, 1975; Milton and the English Revolution, 1978 (Heinemann award; Milton Soc. of America award); Some Intellectual Consequences of the English Revolution, 1980; (with B. Reay and W. M. Lamont) The World of the Muggletonians, 1983; The Experience of Defeat: Milton and some contemporaries, 1984; Collected Essays Vol. I: Writing and Revolution in 17th Century England, 1985, Vol. II: Religion and Politics in 17th Century England, 1986, Vol. III: People and Ideas in 17th Century England, 1986; A Turbulent, Seditious, and Factious People: John Bunyan and his Church, 1988 (W. H. Smith Literary Award, 1989); A Nation of Change and Novelty: radical politics, religion and literature in 17th century England, 1990; The English Bible and the 17th Century Revolution, 1993; Liberty Against the Law, 1996; The Origins of the English Revolution Revisited, 1997; articles in learned journals, etc. *Address:* Woodway House, Sibford Ferris, Banbury, Oxon OX15 5RA.

HILL, John Lawrence; Chairman, Britannia Building Society, 1990–94; Chief Executive, Loss Prevention Council, 1986–96; *b* 21 July 1934; *s* of late Sidney Hill and Hilda Wardle Hill; *m* 1960, Elizabeth Godfrey; one *s* three *d*. *Educ:* Abbotsholme Sch.; Sidney Sussex Coll., Cambridge (MA). CEng, FIMechE; CIMgt. National Service, Royal Corps of Signals, 1953–55. Royal Dutch Shell Group, 1959–67; PA Consulting Group, 1967–86; Director: Britannia Building Soc., 1984–94; Britannia Life, 1989–94. Director: Loss Prevention Certification Bd, 1986–96; Nat. Approval Council for Security Systems, 1990–96. Governor, Inst. of Risk Management, 1987–93. *Recreations:* golf, bridge, music. *Address:* Warwick Lodge, Warwicks Bench, Guildford, Surrey GU1 3TG. *T:* (01483) 566413. *Clubs:* Hawks (Cambridge); Royal & Ancient Golf, Worplesdon Golf.

HILL, Sir John McGregor, Kt 1969; BSc, PhD; FRS 1981; FREng, FInstP, FInstE; Chairman: Rea Brothers Group, 1987–95; British Nuclear Fuels PLC, 1971–83; Amersham International PLC, 1975–88; Aurora Holdings PLC, 1984–88; *b* 21 Feb. 1921; *s* of late John Campbell Hill and Margaret Elizabeth Park; *m* 1947, Nora Eileen Hellett; two *s* one *d*. *Educ:* King's Coll., London; St John's Coll., Cambridge. Flt Lieut, RAF, 1941. Cavendish Laboratory, Cambridge, 1946; Lecturer, London Univ., 1948. Joined UKAEA, 1950, Mem. for Production, 1964–67, Chm., 1967–81. Member: Advisory Council on Technology, 1968–70; Nuclear Power Adv. Bd, 1973–81; Energy Commn, 1977–79. Pres., British Nuclear Forum, 1984–92. FREng (FEng 1982). Hon. FIChemE 1977; Hon. FIEE 1981; Foreign Associate, US Nat. Acad. of Engineering, 1976. Hon. DSc Bradford, 1981. Melchett Medal, Inst. of Energy, 1974; Sylvanus Thompson Medal, Inst. of Radiology, 1978. *Recreation:* golf. *Address:* Dominic House, Sudbrook Lane, Richmond, Surrey TW10 7AT. *T:* (020) 8940 7221. *Club:* East India.

HILL, Sir John (Maxwell), Kt 1974; CBE 1969; DFC 1945; QPM; Chief Inspector of Constabulary, Home Office, 1972–75; *b* 25 March 1914; *s* of late L. S. M. Hill, Civil Servant, Plymouth; *m* 1939, Marjorie Louisa (*d* 1992), *d* of late John Oliver Reynolds, Aylesbury, Bucks; one *s* one *d*. *Educ:* Plymouth Coll. Metropolitan Police Coll., Hendon, 1938–39; joined Metropolitan Police, 1933. Served with RAF, 1942–45. Dep. Comdr, New Scotland Yard, 1959; Metropolitan Police: Comdr, No 3 District, 1963, Comdr, No 1 District, 1964; HM Inspector of Constabulary, 1965; Asst Comr (Administration and Operations), 1966–68; Asst Comr (Personnel and Training), 1968–71; Dep. Comr, 1971–72. *Recreations:* walking, golf. *Address:* 7 Killasser Court, Tadworth, Surrey KT20 5AN. *Clubs:* Royal Automobile, Royal Air Force.

HILL, Rear-Adm. John Richard; Editor, The Naval Review, since 1983; *b* 25 March 1929; *s* of Stanley Hill and May Hill (*née* Henshaw); *m* 1956, Patricia Anne Sales; one *s* two *d*. *Educ:* Royal Naval College, Dartmouth. China Station as midshipman, 1946–47; Sub-Lieut's Courses, 1948–49; Lieut, HM Ships: Gambia, 1950; Chevron, 1950–52; Tintagel Castle, 1952–54; Dryad (Navigation Specialist), 1954; Cardigan Bay, 1954–56; Albion, 1956–58; Roebuck, 1958–59; Lt-Comdr, Pembroke Dock, 1959–60; HMS Duchess, 1960–62; Comdr, MoD, 1963–65 and 1967–69; IDC 1965–67; HMS Dryad, 1969–71; Captain, MoD, 1973–75; Defence and Naval Attaché, The Hague, 1975–77; Cdre, MoD, 1977–80; Rear-Adm. 1981; Flag Officer, Admiralty Interview Bd, 1981–83. Under-Treas., Middle Temple, 1984–94 (Hon. Bencher, 1994); Sec., Council of Inns of Court, 1987–93; Member: Bd of War Studies, London Univ., 1986–94; Council, Foundn for Internat. Security, 1987–; Council, Navy Records Soc., 1993–2001 (Vice Pres., 1997–2001); Council, Soc. for Nautical Res., 1993–99 (Chm., 1994–99). Defence Fellow, University of London King's College, 1972. *Publications:* The Royal Navy Today and Tomorrow, 1981; Anti-Submarine Warfare, 1984; British Sea Power in the 1980s, 1985; Maritime Strategy for Medium Powers, 1986; Air Defence at Sea, 1988; Arms Control at Sea, 1988; (Gen. Ed.) Oxford Illustrated History of the Royal Navy, 1995; The Prizes of War, 1998; War at Sea in the Ironclad Age, 2000; Lewin of Greenwich, 2000; articles in Survival, Navy International, Brassey's Annual, NATO's 15 Nations, Naval Review, Naval Forces, DNB. *Recreations:* bridge, travel, gardening. *Address:* Cornhill House, The Hangers, Bishop's Waltham, Southampton SO32 1EF.

HILL, Jonathan Hopkin, CBE 1995; Founding Director, Quiller Consultants, since 1998; *b* 24 July 1960, *s* of Rowland Louis Hill and Paddy Marguerite (*née* Henwood); *m* 1988, Alexandra Jane Nettelfield; one *s* two *d*. *Educ:* Highgate Sch.; Trinity Coll., Cambridge (MA). RIT & Northern, 1983; Hamish Hamilton, 1984–85; Conservative Research Dept, 1985–86; Special Advr to Rt Hon. Kenneth Clarke at Dept of Employment, DTI and DoH, 1986–89; Lowe Bell Communications, 1989–91; No 10 Policy Unit, 1991–92; Political Sec. to Prime Minister, 1992–94; Sen. Consultant, Bell Pottinger Consultants, 1994–98. Mem. Council, Nat. Literacy Trust, 1995–; Bd Mem., Crime Concern, 1996–; Mem. Steering Gp, Mus. of British History, 1997–. Gov., Highgate Sch., 1995–. *Publication:* (with Baroness Hogg) Too Close to Call, 1995. *Recreations:* reading, gardening, walking on Exmoor. *Address:* (office) 11–12 Buckingham Gate, SW1E 6LB.

HILL, Keith; *see* Hill, T. K.

HILL, Len; *see* Hill, R. K. L.

HILL, Leslie Francis; Chairman, ITV, since 1994 (Director, since 1987); Director, Carlton Communications PLC, since 1994; *b* 2 Sept. 1936; *s* of late Elizabeth May and Francis Alfred Hill; *m* 1972, Christine Susan (*née* Bush); two *s*. *Educ:* Cotham Grammar School. FCA. Qualified as Chartered Accountant; with Ware, Ward (now Ernst & Young), 1952–62, Peat, Marwick, Mitchell, 1962–65; IPC Group, 1965–70, finally Finance Director, Music for Pleasure, continuing as such with EMI Group to 1971; EMI Group: Exec. Dir, 1972–73; Man. Dir, EMI NZ, 1973–74; Asst Dir, Group Music, 1975–76; Managing Director: EMI Records (UK), 1976–78; EMI Music, Europe, 1979–80; Jt Man. Dir, HAT Group plc, 1980–86; Dir, ITN, 1987–95; Man. Dir, 1987–91, Chm. and Chief Exec., 1991–95, Central Independent Television. *Recreations:* listening to music, reading, playing and watching cricket. *Address:* ITV Network Ltd, 200 Gray's Inn Road, WC1X 8HF. *T:* (020) 7843 8000.

HILL, Martyn Geoffrey; tenor singer; *b* 14 Sept. 1944; *s* of Norman S. L. Hill and Gwendoline A. M. Hill (*née* Andrews); three *s* one *d*. *Educ:* Sir Joseph Williamson's Mathematical School, Rochester, Kent; King's College, Cambridge; Royal College of Music (ARCM); vocal studies with Audrey Langford. On teaching staff, Trinity Coll. of Music, 1997–. Concert, oratorio, recital and operatic appearances throughout the world with major orchestras, conductors and choirs; numerous radio, TV and gramophone recordings. *Address:* c/o Owen/White Management, Top Floor, 59 Lansdowne Place, Hove, E Sussex BN3 1FL.

HILL, Michael; *see* Hill, E. M.

HILL, Rt Rev. Michael Arthur; *see* Buckingham, Area Bishop of.

HILL, Michael Thomas; HM Diplomatic Service; High Commissioner, Vanuatu, since 2000; *b* 2 Jan. 1945; *s* of late Roland Hill and Anne Hill (*née* McIlwraith); *m* 1977, Elizabeth Louise, *d* of Derrick Charles Carden, *qv*; three *s* one *d*. *Educ:* Bathgate Acad. Joined Foreign Office, 1963; served UKMIS NY, Vientiane, Kaduna, Sana'a; Dep. Hd of Mission, Ulan Bator, 1978–81; Consul, Port of Spain, 1981–85; FCO, 1985–88; Asst to Dep. Governor, Gibraltar, 1988–93; First Sec. and Hd of Aid Sect., Nairobi, 1993–2000. *Recreations:* golf, gardening, walking. *Address:* c/o Foreign and Commonwealth Office, King Charles Street, SW1A 2AH.

HILL, Michael William; President, Fédération Internationale d'Information et de Documentation, 1985–90; *b* 1928; *o s* of late Geoffrey William Hill, Ross on Wye and Torquay; *m* 1st, 1957, Elma Jack Forrest (*d* 1967); one *s* one *d*; 2nd, 1969, Barbara Joy Youngman. *Educ:* King Henry VIII Sch., Coventry; Nottingham High Sch.; Lincoln Coll., Oxford (MA, MSc). MRIC 1953; CChem; FIInfSc 1982. Research Chemist, Laporte Chemicals Ltd, 1953–56; Morgan Crucible Group: Laboratory Head, 1956; Asst Process Control Manager, 1958; Group Technical Editor, 1963; Asst Keeper, British

Museum, 1964; Dep. Librarian, Patent Office Library, 1965; Keeper, Nat. Ref. Library of Science and Invention, BM, 1968–73; British Library: Dir, Science Ref. Library, 1973–86; Associate Dir, Sci. Technology and Industry, 1986–88. Member: Exec. Cttee, Nat. Central Library, 1971–74; EEC/CIDST Working Parties on Patent documentation, 1973–80, and on Information for Industry, 1976–80; Board, UK Chemical Inf. Service, 1974–77; Adv. Cttee for Scottish Science Reference Library, 1983–87; Chairman: Circle of State Librarians, 1977–79; Council, Aslib, 1979–81; Vice Pres., IATUL, 1976–81; Founder, Western European Round Table on Information and Documentation, subseq. European Council of Information Assocs, 1980. Series Editor (with I. McIlwaine), Guides to Information Sources. *Publications:* Patent Documentation (with Wittmann and Schiffels), 1979; Michael Hill on Science, Technology and Information (ed by P. Ward), 1988; National Information Policies and Strategies, 1994; The Impact of Information on Society, 1998; papers on librarianship, documentation and information science in jls and conf. proceedings. *Address:* 137 Burdon Lane, Cheam, Surrey SM2 7DB. *T:* (020) 8642 2418. *Club:* Oxford and Cambridge.

HILL, Peter Whitehead; Editor, Daily Star, since 1998; *b* 6 April 1945; *s* of Becket and Edith Hill; *m* 1984, Vera Marshall (marr. diss. 1998); one *d*; partner, Marjorie Francis; one *s*. *Educ:* Hulme Grammar Sch., Oldham; Manchester Univ. Reporter, Colne Valley Guardian, 1961–62; sub-editor: Huddersfield Examr, 1962–63; Manchester Evening News, 1963–65; leader writer, Oldham Evening Chronicle, 1965–67; sub-ed., Daily Telegraph, 1967–74; sub-ed., Daily Mirror, 1974–78; Chief Sub-Ed., Sunday People, 1970–80; Chief Sub-Ed., Night Ed., Associate Ed., and Dep. Ed., Daily Star, 1978–98. *Recreations:* sailing, tennis, ski-ing, conversation, making mischief. *Address:* Daily Star, Ludgate House, 245 Blackfriars Road, SE1 9UX. *T:* (020) 7922 7474. *Clubs:* Harbour; Hollowshore Sailing (Faversham).

HILL, Dr Polly; Fellow, Clare Hall, Cambridge, 1965–81, now Emeritus; *b* 10 June 1914; *d* of Prof. A. V. Hill, CH, OBE, FRS, and Margaret, *d* of Dr J. N. Keynes and F. A. Keynes; *m* 1953, Kenneth Humphreys (marr. diss. 1961; he *d* 1985); one *d*. *Educ:* Newnham Coll., Cambridge; PhD Cantab 1967. Editorial Asst, REconS, 1936–38; research, Fabian Soc., 1938–39; temp. civil servant, 1940–51; editorial staff, West Africa (weekly), 1951–53; Res. Fellow, then Sen. Res. Fellow, Econs Dept, followed by Inst. of African Studies, Univ. of Ghana, 1954–65; financed by Center for Research on Econ. Develt, Univ. of Mich, Ann Arbor, mainly working in Cambridge and northern Nigeria, 1965–70, and by SSRC, mainly working in northern Nigeria, 1970–72; Smuts Reader in Commonwealth Studies, Cambridge Univ., 1973–79; fieldwork in villages in Karnataka, S India, 1977–78, and (as Leverhulme Emeritus Fellow) in Kerala, S India, 1981–82. Hon. Fellow, SOAS, 1998. *Publications:* The Unemployment Services, 1940; The Gold Coast Cocoa Farmer, 1956; The Migrant Cocoa-Farmers of Southern Ghana, 1963, 3rd edn 1977, repr. 1997; Rural Capitalism in West Africa, 1970, 2nd edn 1976; Rural Hausa, 1972; Population, Prosperity and Poverty: rural Kano, 1900 and 1970, 1977 (Amaury Talbot prize for African anthropology, 1977); Dry Grain Farming Families, 1982; Development Economics on Trial, 1986, 6th edn 1995; (ed with R. Keynes) Lydia and Maynard: letters between Lydia Lopokova and J. M. Keynes, 1989; Who were the Fen People? (Proc. Cambridge Antiquarian Soc.), 1993; articles on rural W Africa, India, and the earliest Cambridge women students, in learned jls; monographs and chapters in books. *Recreation:* poetry writing.

See also D. K. Hill.

HILL, (Robert) Charles; QC (NI) 1974; Member, Standing Advisory Commission on Human Rights under Northern Ireland Constitution Act 1973, 1991–96 (Chairman, 1992–95); *b* 22 March 1936; *s* of Benjamin Morrison Hill and Mary A. Hill (*née* Roche); *m* 1961, Kathleen Allen; three *s* one *d*. *Educ:* St Malachy's Coll., Belfast; Queen's Univ. Belfast (LLB); Trinity Coll., Dublin (MA). Called to the Bar: Inn of Court, NI, 1959, Bencher, 1988; Gray's Inn, 1971; King's Inns, Dublin, 1986; Sen. Counsel, Ireland, 1987. Official Referee under Finance Acts, 1976; Dep. County Court Judge, 1979–80. Chairman: Statutory Body, Pharmaceutical Soc. of NI, 1977–92; Poison Bd of NI, 1982–92. *Recreations:* history of art, forestry, shooting. *Address:* The Bar Library, Royal Courts of Justice, Chichester Street, Belfast BT1 3JP. *T:* (028) 9024 1523. *Club:* Kildare Street and University (Dublin).

HILL, Sir Robert (Charles Finch), KBE 1991; FREng, FIMechE, FIMarE; reliability consultant; President, Institute of Marine Engineers, 1995–96; *b* 1 May 1937; *s* of Frances Margaret Hill (*née* Lumsden) and Ronald Finch Hill; *m* 1971, Deborah Mary (*née* Windle); one *s* one *d*. *Educ:* Nautical Coll., Pangbourne; RNEC Manadon. BSc(Eng); CEng, FREng (FEng 1992). HMS Thermopylae, 1964–65; HMS Repulse, 1967–71; MoD (PE), 1971–74; RNEC Manadon, 1975–77; HMS Cleopatra, 1977–78; Nuclear Power Manager, Chatham, 1979–80; MoD (PE), 1980–84; RCDS 1985; HMS Raleigh in Comd, 1986–87; CSO (Engrg) to C-in-C Fleet, 1987–89; Chief Abovewater Systems Exec., 1989–91; Dep. Controller of the Navy (Vice-Adm.), 1989–93; Dir Gen. Submarines, 1991–93; retd. Independent Director: British Energy plc, 1999–; SEA (Group) Ltd, 1999–. *Recreations:* rhythm guitar, theatre, sailing. *Club:* Royal Over-Seas League.

HILL, Robert Williamson, (Robin), CEng, FIGasE; Regional Chairman, British Gas, North Western, 1990–93; *b* 8 Dec. 1936; *s* of William Hill and Mary Duncanson (*née* Williamson); *m* 1961, Janette Margaret (*née* Bald); one *s* two *d*. *Educ:* Dumbarton Acad.; Strathclyde Univ. (BSc 1st Cl. Hons). CEng, FIGasE 1958. Scottish Gas Board: various appts, 1958–70; Area Service Manager, subseq. Regional Service Manager, 1970–73; British Gas Corporation: Service Ops Manager, 1973–75; Asst Service Dir, 1975–76; Service Dir, 1977–82; Regl Chm., Scotland, 1982–89. Local Govt Staff Comr, 1994–97; Local Govt Property Comr, 1995–97. Pres., Assoc. for Sci. Educn, Scotland, 1985–86. Pres., IGasE, 1989–90 (Vice-Pres., 1987–89). Mem. Court, Heriot-Watt Univ., 1987–93. Hon. Mem., CGLI, 1981. *Recreation:* golf. *Address:* 5 Grange View, Linlithgow, W Lothian EH49 7HY. *T:* (01506) 671173.

HILL, Rodney, FRS 1961; PhD; ScD; Professor of Mechanics of Solids, University of Cambridge, 1972–79 (Reader, 1969–72); Fellow, Gonville and Caius College, since 1972; *b* 11 June 1921; *o s* of Harold Harrison Hill, Leeds; *m* 1946, Jeanne Kathlyn, *yr d* of C. P. Wickens, Gidea Park; one *d*. *Educ:* Leeds Grammar Sch.; Pembroke Coll., Cambridge. MA, PhD, ScD Cambridge. Armament Research Dept, 1943–46; Cavendish Laboratory, Cambridge, 1946–48; British Iron and Steel Research Assoc., 1948–50; University of Bristol: Research Fellow, 1950–53, Reader, 1953; Univ. of Nottingham: Prof. of Applied Mathematics, 1953–62; Professorial Research Fellow, 1962–63; Berkeley Bye-Fellow, Gonville and Caius Coll., Cambridge, 1963–69. Hon. DSc: Manchester, 1976; Bath, 1978. Von Karman Medal, ASCE, 1978; Gold Medal and Internat. Modesto Panetti Prize, Accademia delle Scienze di Torino, 1988; Royal Medal, Royal Soc., 1993. Editor, Jl of Mechanics and Physics of Solids, 1952–68. *Publications:* Mathematical Theory of Plasticity, 1950; Principles of Dynamics, 1964.

HILL, Rev. Roger Anthony John; Rector of Newark, since 1988; Chaplain to the Queen, since 2001; *b* 23 March 1945; *s* of Arthur and Gladys Hill; *m* 1972, Joanna Reading; three *s*. *Educ:* Univ. of Liverpool; Linacre Coll., Oxford (BA 1969; MA); Ripon Hall, Oxford. Ordained deacon, 1970, priest, 1971; Curate: St Peter, St Helier, Southwark, 1970–74; Dawley Parva, 1974–76; Team Vicar, 1976–81, Rector, 1981–88, Central Telford. RD Newark, 1990–95; Hon Canon, Southwell Minster, 1998–. *Recreations:* walking, travel. *Address:* The Rectory, Bede House Lane, Newark NG24 1PY. *T:* (01636) 704513. *Club:* Spire (Newark).

HILL, Roy Kenneth Leonard, (Len), CBE 1983; JP; Chairman, South West Water Authority, 1977–87; *b* 28 May 1924; *m* 1944, Barbara May Kendall. Mem., ASLEF; Plymouth City Councillor, 1961–68, 1970–74 (formerly Dep. Lord Mayor); County Councillor, Devon, 1974 (formerly Leader of Labour Gp). Chm., Water Authorities Assoc., 1983–86. Mem., SW Econ. Planning Council. Chm. Council, Coll. of St Mark and St John, Plymouth; Governor, Plymouth Polytechnic; Mem. Bd of Visitors, Dartmoor Prison. JP Plymouth, 1968. *Address:* 5 Revell Park Road, Plympton, Plymouth PL7 4EH. *T:* (01752) 339125.

HILL, Brig. (Stanley) James (Ledger), DSO 1942, and Bars, 1944, 1945; MC 1940; Vice-Chairman, Powell Duffryn Ltd, 1970–76 (Director, 1961–76); Chairman, Pauls & Whites Ltd, 1973–76 (Director, since 1970); Director: Lloyds Bank, 1972–79; Lloyds Bank UK Management Committee Ltd, 1979–81; *b* 14 March 1911; *s* of late Maj.-Gen. Walter Pitts Hendy Hill, CB, CMG, DSO, West Amesbury House, Wilts; *m* 1st, 1937, Denys, *d* of late E. Hubert Gunter-Jones, MC, JP, Gloucester House, Ledbury; one *d*; 2nd, 1986, Joan Patricia Haywood. *Educ:* Marlborough; RMC Sandhurst (Sword of Honour). 2nd Bn, Royal Fusiliers, 1931–35; 2nd Bn, RF, BEF, 1939; DAAG, GHQ, BEF, 1940; comd 1st Bn, Parachute Regt, N Africa landing, 1942; comd 3rd Parachute Bde, 1943–45; took part in Normandy and Rhine crossing (wounded thrice); comdr 4th Parachute Bde (TA), 1947–48. Apptd to Bd of Associated Coal & Wharf Cos Ltd, 1948; Pres., Powell Duffryn Group of Cos in Canada, 1952–58. Legion of Honour (France), 1942 (Grand Officier, 2000); Silver Star (USA), 1945; King Haakon VII Liberty Cross (Norway), 1945. *Recreation:* birdwatching. *Address:* Hidden House, Guilden Road, Chichester PO19 4LA. *T:* (01243) 789083. *Clubs:* Army and Navy; Island Sailing (IoW).

HILL, Starforth; *see* Hill, Ian S.

HILL, Stephen Guy; Chief Executive, Financial Times Group Ltd, since 1998; *b* 19 July 1960; *s* of Michael Lawrence Hill and Joan Florence Hill (*née* Luce). *Educ:* King Edward VII Sch., Lytham; St John's Coll., Cambridge (MA 1st Cl. Hons Law 1982); Harvard Business Sch. (PMD 1991). Consultant, Boston Consulting Gp, 1982–85; Exec. Asst to Chm., Guinness plc, 1985–87; Dir of Strategy, Pearson plc, 1987–92; Managing Director: Watford Observer Newspapers, 1992–93; Oxford & County Newspapers Ltd, 1993–95; Chief Exec., Westminster Press Ltd, 1995–96; Man. Dir, Financial Times Newspaper, 1996–99. Chm., Data Broadcasting Inc., 2000–; Mem., Mgt Bd, Pearson plc, 1999–; Dir, Marketwatch.com Inc., 2000–; non-exec. Dir, Royal & Sun Alliance Gp plc, 2000–. Mem. Council, Whitechapel Art Gall., 2000–. *Recreations:* triathlon, opera, cycling, ski-ing, scuba diving, theatre, travel. *Address:* c/o Financial Times, One Southwark Bridge, SE1 9HL. *T:* (020) 7873 3000.

HILL, Stephen Russell, OBE 1982; Chief Executive, Defence Aviation Repair Agency, since 1999; *b* 27 March 1942; *s* of late Henry Rowland Hill and Kathleen Bertha Hill; m 1964, Muriel Chisholm; one *s* one *d*. *Educ:* St Philip's Grammar Sch., Birmingham; Hendon CAT; BA Open Univ. 1980; Dip. Accounting and Finance 1988. CEng 1975; FIMechE 1985; FRAeS 1986. Marine Engr, BP Tanker Co., 1958–65; Civil Engrg projects, BP Refinery, Grangemouth, 1965–66; RAF, 1966–91: appts incl. Chief Engr, RAF Coningsby, 1981–84; Air Cdre, Dir of Support Mgt, 1989–91; Business Develt, BAe, 1991–95; Projects and Technical Dir, Serco Defence, 1995–96; Chief Exec., Naval Aircraft Repair Orgn, 1996–99. FIMgt 1987. *Recreation:* hill walking. *Address:* Defence Aviation Repair Agency, St Athan, Barry, Vale of Glamorgan CF62 4WA.

HILL, Dr Stuart John; Managing Director, AEA Technology Environment, since 2000; *b* 23 March 1950; *s* of late Maurice William Hill and of Dorothy Alice Hill (*née* Raynor); *m* 1st, 1972 (marr. diss. 1991); one *s* one *d*; 2nd, 1994, Frances Irene Susan Entwistle; one step *s*. *Educ:* Ecclesbourne GS, Duffield, Derbys; Peterhouse, Cambridge (schol.; BA Hons 1st cl. Engrg; Baker Prize; PhD 1975). BR Research Dept, 1975–77; GKN Technology Ltd, 1977–89; Business Develt Exec., GKN Automotive Div., 1989–90; Develt Dir, GKN Powder Metallurgy Div., 1990–91; Dir, Tech. Strategy, BRB, 1991–93; Man. Dir, BR Production Services, 1993–96; Chief Land Registrar and Chief Exec., HM Land Registry, 1996–99; Chief Exec., Housebuilders' Fedn, 1999–2000. FRSA 1996. *Publications:* (trans.) F. Schmelz *et al*, Universal Joints and Driveshafts, 1992; ed and contrib. books and learned jls on driveline components and engrg mgt. *Recreations:* organising conferences, Macintosh computers. *Address:* (office) AEA Technology Environment, Culham, Abingdon, Oxfordshire OX14 3ED. *T:* (01235) 463196. *Club:* Royal Over-Seas League.

HILL, Susan Elizabeth, (Mrs Stanley Wells); novelist and playwright; *b* 5 Feb. 1942; *d* of late R. H. and Doris Hill; *m* 1975, Prof. Stanley W. Wells, *qv*; two *d* (and one *d* decd). *Educ:* grammar schs in Scarborough and Coventry; King's Coll., Univ. of London. BA Hons English 1963; Fellow, 1978. FRSL 1972. Literary critic, various jls, 1963–; numerous plays for BBC, 1970–; Presenter, Bookshelf, Radio 4, 1986–87. Founder and Publisher, Long Barn Books, 1996; Founder Publisher and Ed., Books and Company, qly mag. *Publications:* The Enclosure, 1961; Do me a Favour, 1963; Gentleman and Ladies, 1969; A Change for the Better, 1969; I'm the King of the Castle, 1970; The Albatross, 1971; Strange Meeting, 1971; The Bird of Night, 1972; A Bit of Singing and Dancing, 1973; In the Springtime of the Year, 1974; The Cold Country and Other Plays for Radio, 1975; (ed) The Distracted Preacher and other stories by Thomas Hardy, 1979; The Magic Apple Tree, 1982; The Woman in Black: a ghost story, 1983 (adapted for stage, 1989); (ed) Ghost Stories, 1983; (ed) People, an anthology, 1983; Through the Kitchen Window, 1984; Through the Garden Gate, 1986; The Lighting of the Lamps, 1987; Lanterns Across the Snow, 1987; Shakespeare Country, 1987; The Spirit of the Cotswolds, 1988; Family (autobiog.), 1989; Air and Angels, 1991; The Mist in the Mirror: a ghost story, 1992; Mrs de Winter, 1993; (ed) Contemporary Women's Short Stories, 1995; (with Rory Stuart) Reflections from a Garden, 1995; Listening to the Orchestra (short stories), 1996; (ed) The Second Penguin Book of Women's Short Stories, 1997; The Service of Clouds, 1998; Felix Derby, 2002; *for children:* One Night at a Time, 1984; Mother's Magic, 1986; Can it be True?, 1988; Susie's Shoes, 1989; Stories from Codling Village, 1990; I've Forgotten Edward, 1990; I Won't Go There Again, 1990; (ed) The Walker Book of Ghost Stories, 1990; Pirate Poll, 1991; The Glass Angels, 1991; Beware, Beware!, 1993; King of King's, 1993; *play:* The Ramshackle Company, 1981. *Address:* Longmoor Farmhouse, Ebrington, Chipping Campden, Glos GL55 6NW. *T:* (01386) 593352, *Fax:* (01386) 593443.

HILL, (Trevor) Keith; MP (Lab) Streatham, since 1992; Treasurer of HM Household (Deputy Chief Whip), since 2001; *b* 28 July 1943; *s* of George Ernest Hill and Ena Ida (*née* Dakin); *m* 1972, Lesley Ann Sheppard. *Educ:* Corpus Christi Coll., Oxford (BA, MA); UCW, Aberystwyth (DipEd). Res. Asst in Politics, Univ. of Leicester, 1966–68; Belgian Govt Scholar, Brussels, 1968–69; Lectr in Politics, Univ. of Strathclyde, 1969–73; Res.

Officer, Labour Party Internat. Dept, 1974–76; Political Liaison Officer, NUR, subseq. Nat. Union of Rail, Maritime and Tspt Workers, 1976–92. An Asst Govt Whip, 1998–99; Parly Under-Sec. of State, DETR, 1999–2001. *Publications:* (contrib.) European Political Parties, 1969; (contrib.) Electoral Behaviour, 1974. *Recreations:* walks, books, films. *Address:* 110 Wavertree Road, Streatham Hill, SW2 3ST. *T:* (020) 8674 0434.

HILL, Prof. William George, FRS 1985; FRSE 1979; Professor of Animal Genetics, University of Edinburgh, since 1983; *b* 7 Aug. 1940; *s* of late William Hill and Margaret Paterson Hill (*née* Hamilton); *m* 1971, Christine Rosemary Austin; one *s* two *d. Educ:* St Albans School; Wye Coll., Univ. of London (BSc 1961); Univ. of California, Davis (MS 1963); Iowa State Univ.; Univ. of Edinburgh (PhD 1965; DSc 1976). University of Edinburgh: Asst Lectr, 1965–67, Lectr, 1967–74, Reader, 1974–83, in Genetics; Hd, Dept of Genetics, 1989–90; Hd, Inst. of Cell, Animal and Population Biol., 1990–93; Hd, Div. of Biol Scis, 1993–98; Dean and Provost, Faculty of Sci. and Engrg, 1999–. Visiting Professor/Research Associate: Univ. of Minnesota, 1966; Iowa State Univ., 1967–78; N Carolina State Univ., 1979, 1985, 1992–. Consultant Geneticist: Cotswold Pig Develt Co., 1965–99; British Friesian Cattle Soc., 1978–88; Holstein Friesian Soc., 1988–98. Chm., Org Cttee, 4th World Congress, 1990, Pres., 5th World Congress, Genetics Applied to Livestock Prodn; Pres., British Soc. Animal Sci., 1999–2000 (Vice-Pres., 1997–99). Member: Scientific Study Group, Meat and Livestock Commn, 1969–72; Cattle Res. Consultative Cttee, 1985–86; AFRC Animals Res. Grant Bd, 1986–92; Dir's Adv. Gp, AFRC Animal Breeding Res. Orgn, 1983–86; Tech. Cttee, 1992–99 (Chm., 1995–97), Develt Cttee, 1992–98, Animal Data Centre; Inst. Animal Physiology and Genetics Res., 1986–93; Bd Govs, Roslin Inst., 1994–; Council, Royal Soc., 1993–94; Commonwealth Scholarship Commn, 1998–. Editor: Animal Prodn, 1971–78; Genetics, 1993–94; Livestock Prodn Sci., 1994–95; Genetical Res., 1996–. *Publications:* (ed) Benchmark Papers in Quantitative Genetics, 1984; (ed) Evolution and Animal Breeding, 1989; numerous papers on quantitative and population genetics, biometrics and animal breeding, in sci. jls. *Recreations:* farming, bridge. *Address:* 4 Gordon Terrace, Edinburgh EH16 5QH. *T:* (0131) 667 3680. *Club:* Farmers'.

HILL-NORTON, family name of **Baron Hill-Norton**.

HILL-NORTON, Baron *cr* 1979 (Life Peer), of South Nutfield, Surrey; **Admiral of the Fleet Peter John Hill-Norton,** GCB 1970 (KCB 1967; CB 1964); Chairman, Military Committee of NATO, 1974–77; *b* 8 Feb. 1915; *s* of Capt. M. J. Norton and Mrs M. B. Norton; *m* 1936, Margaret Eileen Linstow; one *s* one *d. Educ:* RNC Dartmouth. Went to sea, 1932; commnd, 1936; specialised in Gunnery, 1939; War of 1939–45: Arctic Convoys; NW Approaches; Admiralty Naval Staff. Comdr 1948; Capt. 1952; Naval Attaché, Argentine, Uruguay, Paraguay, 1953–55; comd HMS Decoy, 1956–57; comd HMS Ark Royal, 1959–61; Asst Chief of Naval Staff, 1962–64; Flag Officer, Second-in-Command, Far East Fleet, 1964–66; Dep. Chief of the Defence Staff (Personnel and Logistics), 1966; Second Sea Lord and Chief of Naval Personnel, Jan.-Aug. 1967; Vice-Chief of Naval Staff, 1967–68; C-in-C Far East, 1969–70; Chief of the Naval Staff and First Sea Lord, 1970–71; Chief of the Defence Staff, 1971–73. President: Sea Cadets Assoc., 1977–84; Defence Manufacturers' Assoc., 1980–84; British Maritime League, 1982–85; Vice-Pres., RUSI, 1977–90. Liveryman, Shipwrights' Co., 1973, Mem. Court, 1979; Freeman, City of London, 1973. *Publications:* No Soft Options, 1978; Sea Power, 1982. *Recreations:* gardening, foreign travel. *Address:* Cass Cottage, Hyde, Fordingbridge, Hants SP6 2QH. *Clubs:* Army and Navy; Royal Navy of 1765.

See also Vice-Adm. Hon. Sir N. J. Hill-Norton.

HILL-NORTON, Vice-Adm. Hon. Sir Nicholas (John), KCB 1991; Chairman, British Greyhound Racing Board, since 2000; *b* 13 July 1939; *s* of Admiral of the Fleet Baron Hill-Norton, *qv*; *m* 1966, Ann Jennifer, *d* of Vice-Adm. D. H. Mason, CB, CVO; two *s* one *d. Educ:* Marlborough Coll.; RNC, Dartmouth; US Naval War Coll., Newport, RI. Royal Navy, 1957–95; Flag Officer, Gibraltar, 1987–90; Flag Officer Surface Flotilla and Comdr, Anti-Submarine Warfare Striking Force, 1990–92; DCDS, 1992–95. Defence Adviser: GEC-Marconi, 1995–99; BAE SYSTEMS, 1999–2000; Director: Matra Marconi Space, 1996–99; Marconi N America, 1997–2000; Lear Astronics (USA), 1996–99. Vice Pres., RUSI. *Recreations:* greyhound racing, travel, cooking, country sports, woodland management, being idle. *Clubs:* Farmers', Royal Navy of 1765 and 1785.

HILL-SMITH, His Honour Derek Edward, VRD 1958; FCIArb; a Circuit Judge, 1972–87, a Deputy Circuit Judge, 1987–96; *b* 21 Oct. 1922; *s* of Charles Hill-Smith and Ivy (*née* Downs); *m* 1950, Marjorie Joanna, *d* of His Honour Montague Berryman, QC; one *s* one *d. Educ:* Sherborne; Trinity Coll., Oxford (MA). RNVR, 1942–46; Lt-Comdr RNR. Trinity Coll., Oxford, 1941–42 and 1946–47 (MA, Classics and Modern Greats); BEA, 1947–48; business, 1948–50; teaching, 1950–54; called to Bar, Inner Temple, 1954; Dep. Chm., Kent QS, 1970; Recorder, 1972. Chm., Mental Health Review Tribunals, 1987–95. FCIArb 1994 (ACIArb 1993). *Publications:* contrib. Law Guardian. *Recreations:* the theatre, food and wine, collecting and restoring Old Masters and New Mistresses, the study of mediaeval church frescoes in Cyprus and Asia Minor. *Address:* c/o National Westminster Bank, North Street, Bishop's Stortford, Herts. *Clubs:* Garrick, Hurlingham; Bar Yacht.

HILL-TREVOR, family name of **Baron Trevor**.

HILL-WOOD, Sir David (Basil), 3rd Bt *cr* 1921; Consultant, Investec, since 1998; *b* 12 Nov. 1926; *s* of Sir Basil Samuel Hill Hill-Wood, 2nd Bt, and Hon. Joan Louisa Brand (*d* 1996), *e d* of 3rd Viscount Hampden; *S* father, 1954; *m* 1970, Jennifer, 2nd *d* of late Peter McKenzie Strang, Adelaide; two *s* one *d. Educ:* Eton. Served in Army (Grenadier Guards), 1945–48. Morgan Grenfell & Co. Ltd, 1948–55; Myers & Co., Stockbrokers, 1955–71, Sen. Partner, 1971–74; Director: Capel-Cure Myers Ltd, 1974–77; Guinness Mahon & Co. Ltd (Bankers), 1977–98. Aust. Rep., FA Council, 1978–. Chm., Royal Merchant Navy Foundn, 1975–. High Sheriff Berks, 1982. *Recreations:* soccer, golf. *Heir: s* Samuel Thomas Hill-Wood, *b* 24 Aug. 1971. *Address:* Dacre Farm, Farley Hill, Reading, Berks RG7 1XJ. *T:* (01734) 733185. *Clubs:* White's; Melbourne (Australia).

HILLARY, Sir Edmund (Percival), KG 1995; ONZ 1987; KBE 1953; author; lecturer; mountaineer; *b* 20 July 1919; *s* of Percival Augustus Hillary and Gertrude Hillary (*née* Clark); *m* 1st, 1953, Louise Mary Rose (*d* 1975), *d* of J. H. Rose; one *s* one *d* (and one *d* decd); 2nd, 1989, June Mulgrew, *widow* of Peter Mulgrew. *Educ:* Auckland Grammar Sch., Auckland, New Zealand. Apiarist, 1936–43. RNZAF, navigator on Catalina flying boats in Pacific Area, 1944–45. Apiarist (in partnership with brother W. F. Hillary), 1951–70. NZ High Comr to India, Nepal and Bangladesh, 1985–88. Himalayan Expeditions: NZ Gawhal Expedition, 1951; British Everest Reconnaissance, 1951; British Cho Oyu Expedition, 1952; Everest Expedition, 1953; with Sherpa Tenzing reached summit of Mount Everest, May 1953 (KBE). Leader of NZ Alpine Club Expedition to Barun Valley, East of Everest, 1954. Appointed, 1955, leader of New Zealand Transantarctic Expedition; completed overland journey to South Pole, Jan. 1958. Expeditions in Everest region, 1960–61, 1963, 1964, 1965, 1981; led expedition to Antarctic for geological and mountaineering purposes incl. first ascent of Mt Herschel, 1967; expedition to E Nepal (explored Himalayan rivers with two jet boats; first ascent of 180 miles of Sun Kosi river from Indian border to Katmandu), 1968; jet boat expedition up the Ganges, 1977. Built first hosp. for Sherpas in Everest area, with public subscription and NZ doctor, 1966; latterly Everest region has 25 schools, 2 hosps, 12 med. clinics, bridges, difficult access paths, fresh water pipelines; also re-afforestation prog. in Sagarmatha (Everest) Nat. Park. Internat. Dir, WWF; UNICEF Special Rep., Children of the Himalayas, 1991–. Consultant to Sears Roebuck & Co., Chicago, on camping and outdoor equipment. Hon. LLD: Univ. of Victoria, BC, Canada, 1969; Victoria Univ., Wellington, NZ, 1970. Hubbard Medal (US), 1954; Star of Nepal 1st Class; US Gold Cullum Geographical Medal, 1954; Founder's Gold Medal, Royal Geographical Society, 1958; Polar Medal, 1958. *Publications:* High Adventure, 1955; East of Everest, 1956 (with George Lowe); The Crossing of Antarctica, 1958 (with Sir Vivian Fuchs); No Latitude for Error, 1961; High in the Thin Cold Air, 1963 (with Desmond Doig); School House in the Clouds, 1965; Nothing Venture, Nothing Win (autobiog.), 1975; From the Ocean to the Sky: jet boating up the Ganges, 1979; (with Peter Hillary) Two Generations, 1983; Sagarmatha; View From the Summit (autobiog.), 1999. *Recreations:* mountaineering, ski-ing, camping. *Address:* 278A Remuera Road, Auckland 5, New Zealand. *Clubs:* New Zealand Alpine (Hon. Mem.; Pres. 1965–67); Explorers (New York) (Hon. Pres); Hon. Mem. of many other NZ and US clubs.

HILLEL, Mira B.; *see* Bar-Hillel.

HILLER, Dame Wendy, DBE 1975 (OBE 1971); actress; *b* 15 Aug. 1912; *d* of Frank Watkin and Marie Hiller, Bramhall, Cheshire; *m* 1937, Ronald Gow (*d* 1993); one *s* one *d. Educ:* Winceby House, Bexhill. Manchester Repertory Theatre; Sir Barry Jackson's tour of Evensong; Sally Hardcastle in Love on the Dole, London and New York; leading parts in Saint Joan and Pygmalion at Malvern Festival, 1936. *Plays include:* Twelfth Night (war factory tour); Cradle Song (Apollo); The First Gentleman (Savoy); Tess of the d'Urbervilles (Piccadilly); The Heiress (Biltmore, NY, and Haymarket, London); Ann Veronica (Piccadilly); Waters of the Moon (Haymarket), 1951–53; The Night of the Ball (New), 1955; Old Vic Season, 1955–56; Moon for the Misbegotten (NY), 1957; Flowering Cherry (Haymarket), 1958; Toys in the Attic (Piccadilly), 1960; Aspern Papers (NY), 1962; The Wings of the Dove (Lyric), 1963; The Sacred Flame (Duke of York's), 1967; When We Dead Awaken (Edinburgh Festival), 1968; The Battle of Shrivings (Lyric), 1970; Crown Matrimonial (Haymarket), 1972; John Gabriel Borkman (National), 1975; Lies! (Albery), 1975; Waters of the Moon (Chichester), 1977, (Haymarket) 1978; The Old Jest, 1980; The Importance of Being Earnest (Watford), 1981, (Royalty), 1987; The Aspern Papers (Haymarket), 1984; Driving Miss Daisy (Apollo), 1988. *Films:* Pygmalion; Major Barbara; I Know Where I'm Going; Outcast of the Islands; Separate Tables (Academy Award); Sons and Lovers; Toys in the Attic; A Man for All Seasons; David Copperfield; Murder on the Orient Express; The Elephant Man; The Lonely Passion of Judith Hearne, etc. *TV:* When We Dead Awaken, 1968; Peer Gynt, 1972; Clochemerle, 1973; Last Wishes, 1978; Richard II, 1979; Miss Morison's Ghosts, 1981; The Kingfisher, Witness for the Prosecution, Attracta, 1982; The Comedy of Errors, 1983; Death of the Heart, 1985; Darley's Folly, All Passion Spent, The Importance of Being Earnest, 1986; Ending Up, 1989; The Best of Friends, 1991; The Countess Alice, 1992. Hon. LLD Manchester, 1984. *Address:* c/o Chatto & Linnit, 123A King's Road, SW3 4PL.

HILLERY, Dr Patrick John; Uachtarán na hÉireann (President of Ireland), 1976–90; *b* Miltown Malbay, Co. Clare, 2 May 1923; *s* of Dr Michael Joseph Hillery and Ellen (*née* McMahon); *m* 1955, Dr Mary Beatrice Finnegan; one *s* one *d. Educ:* Miltown Malbay National Sch.; Rockwell Coll.; University Coll., Dublin. BSc; MB BCh, BAO, DPH. Mem. Health Council, 1955–57; MO, Miltown Malbay, 1957–59; Coroner for West Clare, 1958–59; TD (Mem. Dáil Eireann), Clare, 1951–73; Minister: for Educn, 1959–65; for Industry and Commerce, 1965–66; for Labour, 1966–69; of Foreign Affairs, 1969–72 (negotiated Ireland's accession to European Communities); Comr for Social Affairs and a Vice-Pres., Commn of the European Communities, 1973–76. MRIA 1963; Life Fellow, Irish Management Inst., 1981. Hon. FRCSI 1977; Hon. FFDRCSI 1977; Hon. FRCPI 1978; Hon. FRCGP 1982; Hon. FFCM RCSI, 1986; Hon. Fellow: Pharmaceutical Soc. of Ireland, 1984; All-India Inst. of Medical Sciences, 1978. Hon. LLD: NUI, 1962; Univ. of Dublin, 1977; Univ. of Melbourne, 1985; Hon. DPh Pontifical Univ. of Maynooth, 1988. Robert Schuman Gold Medal (France), 1986. Grand Cross and Grand Cordon, Order of Merit (Italy), 1986; Grand Cross of the Netherlands Lion, 1986; Grand Cross of the Legion of Honour (France), 1988; Collar of the Pian Order (Vatican State), 1989. *Address:* Grasmere, Greenfield Road, Sutton, Dublin 13, Ireland.

HILLHOUSE, Sir (Robert) Russell, KCB 1991; FRSE; Director, Scottish Provident Institution, since 1999; *b* 23 April 1938; *s* of Robert Hillhouse and Jean Russell; *m* 1966, Alison Janet Fraser; two *d. Educ:* Hutchesons' Grammar Sch., Glasgow; Glasgow Univ. (MA). FRSE 1995: Scottish Education Dept, 1962; HM Treasury, 1971; Asst Secretary, Scottish Office, 1974; Scottish Home and Health Dept, 1977; Under Sec. (Principal Finance Officer), Scottish Office, 1980; Under Sec., 1985–87, Sec., 1987–88, Scottish Educn Dept; Permanent Under-Sec. of State, Scottish Office, 1988–98. Dir, Bank of Scotland, 1998–2000. Chm., Scottish Consortium on Crime and Criminal Justice, 1999–. Chm., Hebrides Ensemble, 1999–; Mem. Adv. Council, Venture Scotland, 1989–; Chm., Upper Deeside Access Trust, 1998–. Foundn Patron, Develt Campaign, Queen Margaret UC, 1999–. Gov., RSAMD, 2000–. DUniv Glasgow, 1999; Hon. LLD Aberdeen, 1999; Hon. DLitt Napier, 1999. CIMgt (CBIM 1990). FRSA 1992. *Recreations:* making music, enjoying the countryside. *Address:* 19 Regent Terrace, Edinburgh EH7 5BS. *T:* (0131) 558 1680. *Club:* New (Edinburgh).

HILLIER, Bevis; author, art historian, journalist; *b* 28 March 1940; *s* of late Jack Ronald Hillier and of Mary Louise Hillier (*née* Palmer). *Educ:* Reigate Grammar Sch.; Magdalen Coll., Oxford (demy). Gladstone Memorial Prize, 1961. Editorial staff, The Times, 1963–68 (trainee, Home News Reporter, Sale Room Correspondent); Editor, British Museum Society Bulletin, 1968–70; Guest Curator, Minneapolis Inst. of Arts, USA, 1971; Editor, The Connoisseur, 1973–76; Antiques Correspondent, 1970–84, Dep. Literary Editor, 1980–82, The Times; Editor, The Times Saturday Review, 1982; Features Editor, 1982–83, Exec. Editor, 1983–84, Telegraph Sunday Magazine; Associate Editor, Los Angeles Times, 1984–88, Editor, Sotheby's Preview, 1990–93. Co-founder and first Chm., Thirties Soc., 1979; Vice-Pres., Betjeman Soc., 1988. Commendatore, Order of Merit (Italy), 1976. FRSA 1967; FRSL 1997. *Publications:* Master Potters of the Industrial Revolution: The Turners of Lane End, 1965; Pottery and Porcelain 1700–1914, 1968; Art Deco of the 1920s and 1930s, 1968; Posters, 1969; Cartoons and Caricatures, 1970; The World of Art Deco, 1971; 100 Years of Posters, 1972; Travel Posters, 1973; Victorian Studio Photographs, 1974; (jtly) Façade, 1974; Austerity/Binge, 1975; Punorama, 1975; Dead Funny, 1975; (ed with Mary Banham) A Tonic to the Nation: The Festival of Britain 1951, 1976; The New Antiques, 1977; Fougasse, 1978; Ealing Film Posters, 1981; Bevis Hillier's Pocket Guide to Antiques, 1981; Greetings from Christmas Past, 1982; The Style of the Century 1900–1980, 1983; John Betjeman: a life in pictures, 1984; Mickey Mouse Memorabilia, 1986; Young Betjeman, 1988; Early English Porcelain, 1992; (jtly) Art Deco

Style, 1997; contributor to books, and periodicals incl. The Connoisseur, Apollo, Trans English Ceramic Circle, Proc. Wedgwood Soc., etc. *Recreations:* piano, collecting. *Address:* c/o The Maggie Noach Literary Agency, 21 Redan Street, W14 0AB. *Club:* Garrick.

HILLIER, Malcolm Dudley; designer and author; *b* 1 Aug. 1936. *Educ:* St Paul's School; Guildhall School of Music (LGSM). Advertising career, Colman Prentis and Varley; later Dir of Television, S. H. Benson, 1958–74; started garden design co. (with Colin Hilton), and opened flower shop, specialising in dried flowers, 1974; formed design partnership, 1992; writer since 1985. *Publications:* Complete Book of Dried Flowers, 1986; Malcolm Hillier's Guide to Arranging Dried Flowers, 1987; Flowers, 1988; Container Gardening, 1991; Roses, 1991; Pot Pourri, 1991; Malcolm Hillier's Christmas, 1992; Little Scented Library, 1992; Garlands, 1994; Container Gardening throughout the Year, 1995; Good Food Fast, 1995; Malcolm Hillier's Colour Garden, 1995; Entertaining, 1997; Cat's Christmas, 1998. *Recreations:* poetry, pottery. *Address:* 101 Cheyne Walk, SW10 0DQ. *T:* (020) 7352 9031. *Club:* PEN.

HILLIER, Meg; Member (Lab) North East, London Assembly, Greater London Authority, since 2000; *b* 14 Feb. 1969; *d* of Richard and Anne Hillier; *m* 1997, Joe Simpson; one *s*. *Educ:* Portsmouth High Sch.; St Hilda's Coll., Oxford (BA Hons PPE); City Univ. (Dip. Newspaper Journalism). Reporter, S Yorks Times, 1991; Petty Officer, P & O European Ferries, 1992; PR Officer, Newlon Housing Gp, 1993; reporter, 1994–95, features editor, 1995–98, Housing Today; freelance, 1998–2000. Mem. (Lab) Islington BC, 1994– (Chair, Neighbourhood Services Cttee, 1995–97); Mayor, Islington, 1998–99. *Recreations:* gardening, local history. *Address:* Greater London Authority, Romney House, 43 Marsham Street, SW1P 3PY. *T:* (020) 7983 4400.

HILLIER, Prof. Paul Douglas; singer; Professor of Music and Director, Early Music Institute, Indiana University, Bloomington, since 1996; *b* 9 Feb. 1949; *s* of Douglas and Felicity Hillier; *m* 1977, Lena-Liis Kiesel; two *d*. *Educ:* Guildhall School of Music and Drama, London (AGSM). Vicar-Choral, St Paul's Cathedral, 1974–76; Musical Dir, Hilliard Ensemble, 1974–90; Prof. of Music, Univ. of Calif., Davis, 1990–96. Conductor: Western Wind Chamber Choir, 1985–89; Klemetti Inst. Chamber Choir, Finland, 1989–93; Dir, Theatre of Voices, 1989–. Gen. Editor, Fazer Editions of Early Music, Helsinki, 1992–. Edison Prize (Holland), 1989. *Publications:* 300 Years of English Partsongs, 1983; Romantic English Partsongs, 1986; The Catch Book, 1987; The Music of Arvo Pärt, 1997. *Recreations:* reading, walking. *Address:* School of Music, Indiana University, Bloomington, IN 47405, USA.

HILLIER, William Edward, CEng, FIEE; Visiting Industrial Fellow, Engineering Department, Cambridge University, 1996–98 and since 1999; *b* 11 April 1936; *s* of William Edward and Ivy Hillier; *m* 1958, Barbara Mary Thorpe; one *s* one *d*. *Educ:* Acton Grammar School; Open Univ. (BA). FIEE 1990. Missile Electronics Engineer, De Havilland Propellers, 1958–60; Semiconductor Test Equipment Design and Production Manager, 1960–64, Semiconductor Production Manager, 1965–70, Texas Instruments; Computer Aided Engineering Services Manager, up to Tech. Dir, CAD, Racal Redac, 1970–85 (Dep. Man. Dir, 1982–85); Dir, Application of Computers and Manufg Engrg Directorate, 1985–94, and Hd of IT, 1991–94, SERC; Corporate Industrial Marketing, EPSRC, 1994–96. Chairman: Computing and Control Div., IEE, 1993–94; Indust. Adv. Bd, Sch. of Manufg and Mech. Engrg, Birmingham Univ., 1997–. FIMgt. *Publications:* articles in professional papers. *Recreation:* railway preservation (company secretary to standard gauge railway operating company, Gloucestershire Warwickshire Steam Railway plc). *Address:* 19 Simon de Montfort Drive, Evesham, Worcs WR11 4NR. *T:* (01386) 443449.

HILLIER-FRY, (William) Norman, CMG 1982; HM Diplomatic Service, retired; High Commissioner in Uganda, 1980–83; *b* 12 Aug. 1923; *o s* of William Henry and Emily Hillier Fry; *m* 1948, Elizabeth Adèle Misbah; two *s* two *d*. *Educ:* Colfe's Grammar School, Lewisham; St Edmund Hall, Oxford (BA 1946). Served Army, 1942–45; commissioned, Loyal Regt, 1942. HM Foreign Service, 1946; served: Iran, 1947–52; Strasbourg (Delegation to Council of Europe), 1955–56; Turkey, 1956–59; Czechoslovakia, 1961–63; Counsellor, UK Disarmament Delegn, Geneva, 1968–71; Hd of ME Dept, ODA, 1971–74; Consul-Gen., Hamburg, 1974–79; Ambassador to Afghanistan, 1979–80. *Recreations:* music, theatre. *Address:* 127 Coombe Lane West, Kingston-upon-Thames, Surrey KT2 7HF.

HILLMAN, David, RDI 1997; FCSD; Director, Pentagram Design, since 1978; *b* 12 Feb. 1943; *s* of late Leslie Hillman and Marjorie Joan Hillman (*née* Nash); *m* 1st, 1963, Eileen Margaret Griffin (marr. diss. 1968); one *s* one *d*; 2nd, 1983, Jennie Diana Burns; two *s*. *Educ:* Aristotle Central Sch.; London Sch. of Printing and Graphic Art (NDD Graphic Design 1962). FCSD 1979. Design Asst, Sunday Times mag., 1962–65; Art Editor, London Life, 1965–66; Designer/Editor, Design for Living section, Sunday Times mag., 1966–68; Art Dir and Dep. Editor, Nova, 1968–75; freelance practice, 1975–78. Mem., Alliance Graphique Internat., 1977– (UK Pres., 1996–2000; Internat. Pres., 2000–). *Publications:* (ed jtly) Ideas on Design, 1986; Puzzlegrams, 1989; Pentagames, 1992; (ed jtly) Nova, 1993; (ed jtly) The Compendium, 1993; (jtly) Puzzlegrams Too, 1994; (ed jtly) Pentagram, Book 5, 1999; (jtly) Century Makers, 1999; (jtly) Terence Donovan, The Photographs. *Recreations:* ski-ing, modern jazz. *Address:* Asley Cottage, Inchbrook Hill, Nailsworth GL5 5HD. *T:* (01453) 836804.

HILLMAN, Prof. John Richard, PhD; FRSE; FLS, FIBiol, FIHort; Director, Scottish Crop Research Institute, since 1986; *b* 21 July 1944; *s* of late Robert Hillman and of Emily Irene (*née* Barrett); *m* 1967, Sandra Kathleen Palmer; two *s*. *Educ:* Chislehurst and Sidcup Grammar Sch. for Boys; University Coll. of Wales, Aberystwyth (BSc; PhD 1968). FRSE, FIBiol 1985; FLS 1982; FIHort 1997. Univ. of Nottingham: Asst Lectr in Physiology and Environmental Studies, 1968; Lectr, 1969; Univ. of Glasgow: Lectr in Botany, 1971; Sen. Lectr, 1977; Reader, 1980; Prof. of Botany, 1982. Visiting Professor: Univ. of Dundee, 1986–; Univ. of Strathclyde, 1986–; Univ. of Edinburgh, 1988–; Univ. of Glasgow, 1991–. Bawden Lectr, Brighton, 1993. Chm., Agric., Hort. and Forestry Sector Panel, UK Technology Foresight Prog., 1995–97 (Chm., Agric., Nat. Resources and Envmt Sector Panel, 1994–95); Dep. Chm., Mylnefield Research Services Ltd, 1993–. Pres., Agriculture & Food Sect., BAAS, 2000–. Member: Bd, BioIndustry Assoc., 1998–; Court, Univ. of Abertay Dundee, 1998–. FIMgt (FBIM 1987); FRSA 1997. Hon. DSc: Strathclyde, 1994; Abertay Dundee, 1996. British Potato Industry Award, 1999; Internat. Potato Industry Award, 2000. *Publications:* (ed) Isolation of Plant Growth Substances, 1978; (ed with A. Crozier) The Biosynthesis and Metabolism of Plant Hormones, 1984; (ed with C. T. Brett) Biochemistry of Plant Cell Walls, 1985; papers on plant physiol. and biotechnol. in learned jls. *Recreations:* landscaping, building renovations, horology, economics. *Address:* Scottish Crop Research Institute, Invergowrie, Dundee DD2 5DA. *T:* (01382) 562731. *Club:* Farmers'.

HILLS, Andrew Worth; Director, BBC Monitoring, since 1996; *b* 1 Sept. 1949; *s* of late Roland Frederick Hills and of Margaret Eunice (*née* Johnson); *m* 1st, 1974, Frances Mary Ralston (marr. diss. 1992); three *s*; 2nd, 1992, Mary Sandra Caraffi. *Educ:* Abingdon Sch.; Corpus Christi Coll., Cambridge (BA 1971; MA 1975). United Kingdom Atomic Energy Authority, 1971–96: Gen. Sec., AEE Winfrith, 1981–84; Principal Finance and Programmes Officer, 1984–86; Authority Personnel Officer, 1986–89; Exec. Dir, Finance and Personnel, 1989–91; Mem., UKAEA, 1991–94; Managing Director: Sites and Personnel, 1991–92; Corporate Services, 1992–94; Services Div., 1994–95; Dir, Special Projects, 1995–96. *Recreations:* church-crawling, music, reading. *Address:* BBC Monitoring, Caversham Park, Reading RG4 8TZ.

HILLS, Barrington William; racehorse trainer, since 1969; *b* 2 April 1937; *s* of William George Hills and Phyllis (*née* Biddle); *m* 1st, 1959, Maureen (marr. diss. 1977), *d* of late Patrick Newson; three *s*; 2nd, 1977, Penelope Elizabeth May, *d* of John Richard Woodhouse; two *s*. *Educ:* Robston Hall, Gloucester; St Mary's Convent, Newmarket; Mr Whittaker's, Worcester. National Service, King's Troop, RHA. Major race winners include: Prix de l'Arc de Triomphe, 1973 (Rheingold); 1,000 Guineas, 1978 (Enstone Spark); 2,000 Guineas, 1979 (Tap on Wood); Irish Derby, 1987 (Sir Harry Lewis); Irish 1,000 Guineas, 1993 (Nicer), 1999 (Hula Angel); St Leger, 1994 (Moonax); Irish Oaks, 1994 (Bolas); Prix Royal-Oak, 1994 (Moonax). *Recreations:* hunting, shooting, golf. *Address:* B. W. Hills Southbank Ltd, Southbank, Lambourn, Newbury, Berks RG17 7LL. *T:* (01488) 71548; *e-mail:* info@barryhills.com. *Club:* Turf.

HILLS, Air Vice-Marshal David Graeme Muspratt, CB 1985; OBE 1965; Director, Medical Policy and Plans, Ministry of Defence, 1983–85; *b* 28 Feb. 1925; *s* of late Arthur Ernest Hills and Muriel Steinman Hills (*née* Fisher); *m* 1960, Hilary Enid Mary, *d* of Rev. Raymond Morgan Jones and Mary Jones (*née* Ritson); two *s* one *d*. *Educ:* Salisbury Cathedral School; Epsom College; Middlesex Hosp. Medical School. MB BS 1949; MFCM, DPH, AFOM. Commissioned RAF Med. Branch, 1950; served UK, Korea (Casualty Evacuation and MO to 77 Sqn, RAAF; despatches), A&AEE, RAF Stanmore Park, RAF Tengah and MoD, 1951–68; OC RAF Hosp., Muharraq Bahrain, 1968–70; SMO RAF Cranwell, 1970–72; Dep. Dir Medical Personnel, RAF, 1972–75; PMO RAF Germany, 1975–78; Dep. Dir Gen., RAF Medical Services, 1979–83. QHS, 1980–85. Chm. of Council, Coll. of St. Barnabas, Lingfield, 1996–2000. CStJ. *Recreations:* music, painting, gardening, golf. *Club:* Royal Air Force.

HILLS, David Henry, CBE 1993; Director-General of Intelligence, Ministry of Defence, 1988–93; *b* 9 July 1933; *s* of Henry Stanford Hills and Marjorie Vera Lily Hills; *m* 1957, Jean Helen Nichols; one *s* two *d*. *Educ:* Varndean Sch., Brighton; Univ. of Nottingham (BA Econs). Served Army Intell. Corps, 1954–56. Entered MoD, 1956; other appointments include: NBPI, 1967–70; National Indust. Relations Court, 1971–73; Dir of Marketing, Defence Sales Orgn, MoD, 1979–82; Dir of Economic and Logistic Intell., MoD, 1982–88. *Recreations:* gardening, music.

HILLS, Air Vice-Marshal (Eric) Donald, CB 1973; CBE 1968 (MBE 1941); SASO Maintenance Command, 1971–73, retired; *b* 26 Jan. 1917; *s* of late Henry James Hills; *m* 1st, 1945, Pamela Mary (*d* 1989), *d* of late Col A. P. Sandeman, Cape Town; one *s* one *d*; 2nd, 1991, Lady Cynthia Way (*d* 2001). *Educ:* Maidstone Grammar Sch. Joined RAF 1939; Group Captain 1962; Dir of Equipment 3 (RAF), 1968–69; Air Cdre 1969; Dir of Equipment (Policy) (RAF), MoD, 1969–71; Air Vice-Marshal 1971. *Recreations:* gardening, sport as spectator. *Club:* Royal Air Force.

HILLS, Sir Graham (John), Kt 1988; PhD, DSc; FRSE, CChem, FRSC; Principal and Vice-Chancellor of the University of Strathclyde, 1980–91; Scottish Governor of the BBC, 1989–94; *b* 9 April 1926; *s* of Albert Victor Hills and Marjorie Hills (*née* Harper); *m* 1st, 1950, Brenda Stubbington (*d* 1974); one *s* three *d*; 2nd, 1980, Mary Jane McNaughton. *Educ:* Birkbeck Coll., London Univ. (BSc 1946, PhD 1950, DSc 1962; Hon. Fellow 1984). Lecturer in Physical Chemistry, Imperial College, 1949–62; Professor of Physical Chemistry, Univ. of Southampton, 1962–80; Visiting Professor: Univ. of Western Ontario, 1968; Case Western Reserve Univ., 1969; Univ. of Buenos Aires, 1977. President: Internat. Soc. of Electrochemistry, 1983–85; Soc. of Chemical Industry, 1991–93; Design Industries Assoc., 1992–96. Member: ACOST, 1987–93; Council, RSC, 1983–86; Council, CNAA, 1988–93; Design Council, 1989–90; Scottish Enterprise, 1991–93. Non-Executive Director: Scottish Post Office Bd, 1986–99; Scottish Develt Agency, 1988–90; Glasgow Action, 1986–90; Britoil, 1988–90. Chm. Council, Quarrier's Homes, 1992–97. Hon. FRSAMD 1988; Hon. Fellow, Polytechnic of E London, 1991; Hon. FRCPSGlas 1992; Hon. FCSD 1996. Hon. ScD Technical Univ. of Łodz, Poland, 1984; Hon. DSc: Southampton, 1984; Lisbon, 1994; Hon. LLD: Glasgow, 1985; Waterloo, Canada, 1991; Strathclyde, 1991; DUniv Paisley, 1993; Hon. DEd Abertay Dundee, 1999. Hon. Medal, Univ. of Pavia, 1988. Commander: Polish Order of Merit, 1984; Royal Norwegian Order of Merit, 1986. *Publications:* Reference Electrodes, 1961; Polarography, 1964; contrib. Faraday Transactions, on physical chemistry, espec. electrochemistry. *Recreations:* country life, European political history, rocking the boat. *Address:* 2 Holm Burn Place, Inverness IV2 6WT. *Club:* Athenæum.

HILLS, Jacqueline Sukie; *see* Binns, J. S.

HILLS, Prof. John Robert, CBE 1999; Professor of Social Policy, and Director, ESRC Research Centre for Analysis of Social Exclusion, London School of Economics, since 1997; *b* 29 July 1954; *s* of Derrick Walter Hills and Valerie Jean Hills (*née* Gribble); *m* 1989, Anne Elizabeth Power. *Educ:* Nottingham High Sch.; Abingdon Sch.; St John's Coll., Cambridge (BA 1976, MA); Birmingham Univ. (MSocSc 1980). Min. of Finance, Botswana, 1976–78; DoE, 1979–80; Treasury Cttee, H of C, 1980–82; Inst. for Fiscal Studies, 1982–84; Commn of Inquiry into Taxation, Zimbabwe, 1984–86; Welfare State Prog., LSE, 1986–97. *Publications:* (ed) The State of Welfare: the welfare state in Britain since 1974, 1990, 2nd edn (jtly), 1998; Unravelling Housing Finance: subsidies, benefits and taxation, 1991; The Future of Welfare, 1993, 2nd edn 1997; (ed jtly) The Dynamic of Welfare, 1995; (ed) New Inequalities: the changing distribution of income and wealth in the UK, 1996; (jtly) Paying for Health, Education and Housing, 2000. *Recreation:* fell walking. *Address:* Centre for Analysis of Social Exclusion, London School of Economics, Houghton Street, WC2A 2AE.

HILLS, Prof. Richard Edwin; Professor of Radio Astronomy, since 1990, and Deputy Head, Department of Physics, since 1999, University of Cambridge; Fellow of St Edmund's College, Cambridge, since 1993; *b* 30 Sept. 1945; *s* of Ronald Hills and Betty Dorothy Hills (*née* Davies); *m* 1973, Beverly Bevis; two *s*. *Educ:* Bedford Sch.; Queen's Coll., Cambridge (BA Physics); Univ. of California, Berkeley (PhD Astronomy). Research Scientist, Max Planck Inst. for Radio Astronomy, Bonn, 1972–74; Research Associate, 1974–84, Asst Dir of Research, 1984–90, Cavendish Lab., Cambridge; Project Scientist, James Clerk Maxwell Telescope, 1975–87. FRAS. Jackson-Gwilt Medal, RAS, 1989; MacRobert Award, Fellowship of Engineers, 1990. *Publications:* contribs to professional jls. *Recreations:* travel, DIY, music. *Address:* Cavendish Laboratory, Madingley Road, Cambridge CB3 0HE. *T:* (01223) 337300.

HILLSBOROUGH, Earl of; Arthur Francis Nicholas Wills Hill; company director and landowner; *b* 4 Feb. 1959; *s* and *heir* of Marquess of Downshire, *qv*; *m* 1990, Janey, *d* of Gerald Bunting; one *s* three *d*. *Educ:* Eton College; Royal Agricultural Coll., Cirencester; Central London Polytechnic. ACA 1985. Touche Ross & Co., 1981–87; Finance Controller, 1988–89, Finance Dir, 1989, Scheduling Technol. Gp Ltd. *Recreations:* country pursuits, sport. *Heir: s* Viscount Kilwarlin, *qv*. *Club:* White's.

HILSON, Malcolm Geoffrey, OBE 2001; HM Diplomatic Service, retired; High Commissioner, Vanuatu, 1997–2000; *b* 28 Sept. 1942; *s* of Geoffrey Norman and Mildred Alice Hilson; *m* 1965, Marian Joan Freeman; two *s*. *Educ:* Bedford Modern School. Entered Foreign Office, 1961; served Jakarta, Singapore, Bombay, Kuala Lumpur and FCO; First Sec., Kaduna, 1982–86; FCO, 1986–90; New Delhi, 1990–93; FCO, 1993–97. *Recreations:* gardening, cricket, tennis, photography, travel. *Address:* 268B Manchester Road, E14 3HW.

HILSUM, Prof. Cyril, CBE 1990; PhD; FRS 1979; FREng, FInstP, FIEE; Visiting Professor, University College London, since 1988; *b* 17 May 1925; *s* of Benjamin and Ada Hilsum; *m* 1947, Betty Cooper (*d* 1987); one *d* (and one *d* decd). *Educ:* Raines Sch., London; University Coll., London (BSc, PhD). FIEE 1967; FREng (FEng 1978); FIEEE 1984; FInstP 1960. Joined Royal Naval Scientific Service, 1945; Admiralty Res. Lab., 1947–50, and Services Electronics Res. Lab., 1950–64, working first on infra-red res., then on semiconductors; Royal Signals and Radar Estab., 1964–83, working first on compound semiconductors, later on flat panel electronic displays; CSO, 1974–83; Chief Scientist, Gen. Electric Co. Res. Labs, 1983–85; Dir of Res., GEC plc, 1985–93. Mem., SERC, 1984–88. Pres., Inst. of Physics, 1988–90. Foreign Associate, US National Acad. of Engrg, 1983. Hon. FInstP 2001. Hon. DEng: Sheffield, 1992; Nottingham Trent, 1997. Max Born Medal and Prize, 1987, Glazebrook Medal and Prize, 1997, Inst. of Physics; Faraday Medal, IEE, 1988; Braun Prize, Soc. for Inf. Display, 1998. *Publications:* Semiconducting III-V Compounds, 1961; over 100 scientific and technical papers. *Recreations:* ballroom dancing, tennis. *Address:* 12 Eastglade, Moss Lane, Pinner, Middx HA5 3AN. *T:* (020) 8866 8323, *Fax:* (020) 8933 6114.

HILTON OF EGGARDON, Baroness *cr* 1991 (Life Peer), of Eggardon in the County of Dorset; **Jennifer Hilton,** QPM 1989; *b* 12 Jan. 1936; *d* of John Robert Hilton, CMG. *Educ:* Bedales Sch.; Manchester Univ. (BA Hons Psychology 1970; MA (Research) 1971); London Univ. (Dip. Criminology 1972; Dip. History of Art 1982). Joined Metropolitan Police, 1956; Univ. Scholarship, 1967; Police Staff Coll. (Directing Staff), 1973–74; Met. Police Management Services Dept, 1975–76; Supt then Chief Supt, Heathrow Airport, Battersea, Chiswick, 1977–83; New Scotland Yard (Traffic, Courts, Obscene Publications, Planning, Neighbourhood Policing), 1983–87; Comdr, 1984; Head of Training, Metropolitan Police, 1988–90. House of Lords: Opposition Whip, 1991–95; opposition spokesperson on the envmt, 1991–97; Member: EC Sub-Cttee on Envmt, 1991–95 (Chm., 1995–98); Science and Technol. Cttee, 1993–95; EC Sub-Cttee on Defence and Foreign Affairs, 2000–, Chm., Adv. Panel on Works of Art, 1998–. *Publications:* The Gentle Arm of the Law, 1967, 2nd edn 1973; (with Sonya Hunt) Individual Development and Social Experience, 1975, 2nd edn 1981; articles in Police Jl, Police Review, etc. *Recreations:* gardening, history, art, travel. *Address:* House of Lords, SW1A 0PW.

HILTON, (Alan) John Howard; QC 1990; a Recorder, since 1986; *b* 21 Aug. 1942; *s* of Alan Howard Hilton and Barbara Mary Campbell Hilton; *m* 1st, 1968, Jasmina Laila Hamzavi; 2nd, 1978, Nicola Mary Bayley, *qv*; one *s*. *Educ:* Haileybury and Imperial Service Coll.; Manchester Univ. (LLB Hons). Called to the Bar, Middle Temple, 1964. *Recreations:* opera, cooking, magic, 19th century paintings of ladies, enjoying adjournments. *Address:* Queen Elizabeth Building, Temple, EC4Y 9BS. *T:* (020) 7583 5766. *Clubs:* Garrick, Les Six.

HILTON, Anthony Victor; City Editor, Evening Standard, 1984–89 and since 1996 (Managing Director, 1989–95); *b* 26 Aug. 1946; *s* of Raymond Walwork Hilton and Miriam Eileen Norah Hilton (*née* Kydd); *m* 1st, 1969, Patricia Moore; one *s*; 2nd, 1989, Cynthia June Miles; two *s* one *d*. *Educ:* Univ. of Aberdeen (MA Hons Econs 1968). Financial columnist: Guardian, 1968; Observer, 1969; Daily Mail, 1971; Sunday Express, 1972; Editor, Accountancy Age, 1974–79; NY corresp., Sunday Times, 1979–82; City Editor, The Times, 1982–83; Dir, Associated Newspapers, 1989–95. Dir, London Forum, 1993–94; Mem. Council, London First, 1996–98 (Dir, 1993–96). Mem. Cttee, St John's Ambulance Charity Appeal, 1992–94. Vice Pres., Children's Film Unit, 1993–96. *Publications:* How to communicate financial information to employees, 1979; City within a state: a portrait of the City of London, 1987. *Recreations:* canal cruising, cycling, bonfires. *Address:* Priory Farm, Hadleigh, Suffolk IP7 5AZ. *T:* (01473) 823185. *Clubs:* Reform, Lansdowne.

HILTON, Brian James George, CB 1992; non-executive director of public companies; Deputy Secretary, Department of Trade and Industry, 1994–99; *b* 21 April 1940; *s* of Percival William Hilton and late Gladys Hilton (*née* Haylett); *m* 1965, Mary Margaret Kirkpatrick; one *s* two *d*. *Educ:* St Marylebone Grammar Sch., London. Export Credits Guarantee Dept, 1958–68; Board of Trade, 1968–71; Foreign and Commonwealth Office, 1971–74: First Secretary to UK Delegn to OECD, Paris; Asst Sec., Dept of Industry, 1976–84; RCDS 1981; Hd, Financial Services Div., DTI, 1984–87; Hd, Central Unit (Under Sec.), DTI, 1987–89; Dep. Sec., MAFF, 1989–91; Dir, Citizen's Charter Unit, Cabinet Office, 1991–94. Foundation Governor, Hampden Gurney Primary Sch., London W1, 1976–. *Recreations:* cricket, Rugby, music, opera, gardening, fly fishing. *Address:* c/o National Westminster Bank, PO Box 3038, 57 Victoria Street, SW1H 0HN.

HILTON, John Howard; *see* Hilton, A. J. H.

HILTON, Rear-Adm. John Millard Thomas, FIMechE, FIEE; consulting engineer; *b* 24 Dec. 1934; *s* of late Edward Thomas Hilton and Margaret Norah Attrill (*née* Millard); *m* 1st, 1958, Patricia Anne Kirby (marr. diss. 1979); one *s* one *d*; 2nd, 1985, Cynthia Mary Caroline Seddon-Brown (*née* Hargreave); one step *d*. *Educ:* Wyggeston Grammar Sch. for Boys, Leicester; County High Sch., Clacton; RNC Dartmouth; RNEC Manadon; RNC Greenwich; City Univ. (MSc 1968); Imperial Coll. of Science and Technology (DIC 1973). Joined RN 1951; various sea and shore appts, 1951–80; Dep. Chief Naval Signal Officer, MoD, London, 1980–83; Project Dir, ARE Portsdown, 1984–87; Vice-Pres. (Navy), Ordnance Bd, 1987–88; Pres., Ordnance Bd, 1988–90. Dir, Christian Engineers in Develt, 1997– (Chm., 2000). Hon. DSc City, 2000. ADC to the Queen, 1985–88. Master, Scientific Instrument Makers' Co., 2000–Oct. 2001. *Publications:* professional papers. *Recreations:* gardening, personal computing, photography, Christian apologetics, family life. *Address:* Pennyfold, Church Road, Steep, near Petersfield, Hants GU32 2DF.

HILTON, Nicola Mary; *see* Bayley, N. M.

HILTON, Prof. Peter John, MA, DPhil Oxon, PhD Cantab; Distinguished Professor of Mathematics, State University of New York at Binghamton, 1982–93, Emeritus since 1993; *b* 7 April 1923; *s* of late Dr Mortimer Hilton and Mrs Elizabeth Hilton; *m* 1949, Margaret (*née* Mostyn); two *s*. *Educ:* St Paul's Sch.; Queen's Coll., Oxford. Asst Lectr, Manchester Univ., 1948–51, Lectr, 1951–52; Lectr, Cambridge Univ., 1952–55; Senior Lecturer, Manchester Univ., 1956–58; Mason Prof. of Pure Mathematics, University of Birmingham, 1958–62; Prof. of Mathematics, Cornell Univ., 1962–71, Washington Univ., 1971–73; Beaumont Univ. Prof., Case Western Reserve Univ., 1972–82. Distinguished Prof. of Maths, Univ. of Central Florida, 1994–. Visiting Professor: Cornell Univ., USA, 1958–59; Eidgenössische Techn. Hochschule, Zürich, 1966–67, 1981–82, 1988–89; Courant Inst., NY Univ., 1967–68; Univ. Aut. de Barcelona, 1989; Erskine Fellow, Univ. of Canterbury, NZ, 2001. Mahler Lectr, Australian Math. Soc., 1997. Mathematician-in-residence, Battelle Research Center, Seattle, 1970–82. Chairman: US Commn on Mathematical Instruction, 1971–74; NRC Cttee on Applied Maths Trng, 1977–; First Vice-Pres., Math. Assoc. of Amer., 1978–80. Corresp. Mem., Brazilian Acad. of Scis, 1979; Hon. Mem. Belgian Mathematical Soc., 1955. Hon. DHum N Michigan, 1977; Hon. DSc: Meml Univ. of Newfoundland, 1983; Univ. Aut. de Barcelona, 1989. Silver Medal, Univ. of Helsinki, 1975; Centenary Medal, John Carroll Univ., 1985. *Publications:* Introduction to Homotopy Theory, 1953; Differential Calculus, 1958; Homology Theory (with S. Wylie), 1960; Partial Derivatives, 1960; Homotopy Theory and Duality, 1965; (with H. B. Griffiths) Classical Mathematics, 1970; General Cohomology Theory and K- Theory, 1971; (with U. Stammbach) Course in Homological Algebra, 1971, 2nd edn 1996; (with Y.-C. Wu) Course in Modern Algebra, 1974; (with G. Mislin and J. Roitberg) Localization of Nilpotent Groups and Spaces, 1975; (with J. Pedersen) Fear No More, 1983; Nilpotente Gruppen und Nilpotente Räume, 1984; (with J. Pedersen) Build Your Own Polyhedra, 1987; (ed) Miscellanea Mathematica, 1991; (with D. Holton and J. Pedersen) Mathematical Reflections, 1996; numerous research articles on algebraic topology, homological algebra and category theory in British and foreign mathematical journals. *Recreations:* travel, sport, reading, theatre, chess, bridge, broadcasting. *Address:* Department of Mathematical Sciences, State University of New York, Binghamton, NY 13902–6000, USA.

HILTON, Prof. Rodney Howard, FBA 1977; Professor of Medieval Social History, University of Birmingham, 1963–82, now Emeritus; *b* 1916; *s* of John James Hilton and Anne Hilton. *Educ:* Manchester Grammar Sch.; Balliol Coll. and Merton Coll., Oxford (BA, DPhil). Army, 1940–46; Lectr and Reader in Medieval History, 1946–63, Dir, Inst. for Advanced Res. in the Humanities, 1984–87, Univ. of Birmingham. *Publications:* The Economic Development of Some Leicestershire Estates in the 14th and 15th Centuries, 1947; (with H. Fagan) The English Rising of 1381, 1950; (ed) Ministers' Accounts of the Warwickshire Estates of the Duke of Clarence, 1952; (ed) The Stoneleigh Leger Book, 1960; A Medieval Society, 1966, rev. edn 1983; The Decline of Serfdom in Medieval England, 1969, rev. edn 1983; Bondmen Made Free, 1973; The English Peasantry in the Later Middle Ages, 1975; (ed) Peasants, Knights and Heretics, 1976; (ed) The Transition from Feudalism to Capitalism, 1976; (ed with T. H. Aston) The English Rising of 1381, 1984; Class Conflict and the Crisis of Feudalism, 1985; English and French Towns in Feudal Society 1992; articles and reviews in Past and Present, English Historical Review, Economic History Review, etc. *Address:* School of History, University of Birmingham, Birmingham B15 2TT. *T:* (0121) 414 5736.

HILTON, Tessa, (Mrs G. Ball); *b* 18 Feb. 1951; *d* of Michael and Phyllis Hilton; *m* 1976, Graham Ball; two *s* one *d*. *Educ:* St Mary's Sch., Gerrards Cross. Trainee reporter, Mirror Gp Trng Scheme, Devon, 1970–74; Reporter, Sunday Mirror, 1974–78; freelance writer, 1978–85; Editor, Mother mag., 1985–87; Features Editor, then Asst Editor, Today, 1987–91; Femail Editor, Daily Mail, 1991–94; Asst Editor, Sun, 1994; Editor, Sunday Mirror, 1994–96; Dep. Editor, The Express, then Editor, Express on Sunday Magazine, 1996–99. *Publication:* Great Ormond Street Book of Child Health, 1990. *Recreation:* family life.

HIME, Martin, CBE 1987; HM Diplomatic Service, retired; *b* 18 Feb. 1928; *s* of Percy Joseph Hime and Esther Greta (*née* Howe); *m* 1st, 1960, Henrietta Fehling (marr. diss.); one *s* three *d*; 2nd, 1971, Janina Christine Majcher; one *d*. *Educ:* King's Coll. Sch., Wimbledon; Trinity Hall, Cambridge (MA). Served RA, 1946–48. Called to the Bar, Inner Temple, 1951; Marks and Spencer Ltd, 1952–58; joined HM Diplomatic Service, 1960; served in Tokyo, Kobe, Frankfurt and Buenos Aires, 1960–69; 2nd Sec., FCO, 1970–72; Consul, Johannesburg, 1972–74; 1st Sec. (Econ.), Pretoria, 1974–76; Asst Head, S Pacific Dept, FCO, 1976–79; Dep. High Comr in Bangladesh, 1979–82; Consul-General: Cleveland, Ohio, 1982–85; Houston, Texas, 1985–88; Personnel Assessor, FCO, 1988–93. Administrator, NHS Network, 1996–98. Gov., Granard Sch., Putney, 1995–. *Recreations:* golf, lawn tennis, books, table games. *Address:* Field House, 248 Dover House Road, Roehampton, SW15 5DA. *Clubs:* All England Lawn Tennis; Hawks (Cambridge); Royal Wimbledon Golf.

HIMSWORTH, Prof. Richard Lawrence, MD; FRCP; Professor of Health Research and Development, since 1993, and Director, Institute of Public Health, since 1999, Cambridge University; Fellow, Girton College, Cambridge, since 1995; *b* 14 June 1937; *s* of Sir Harold Himsworth, KCB, FRS; *m* 1966, Sara Margaret Tattersall; two *s* one *d*. *Educ:* Westminster Sch.; Trinity Coll., Cambridge (MD 1971); University Coll. Hosp. Med. Sch. FRCP 1977; FRCPE 1988; FRCPGlas 1990. Lectr in Medicine, UCH Med. Sch., 1967–71; MRC Travelling Fellow, New York, 1969–70; MRC Scientific Staff, Clinical Res. Centre, 1971–85: Asst Dir, 1978–82; Head, Endocrinology Res. Gp, 1979–85; Consultant Physician, Northwick Park Hosp., 1972–85; Regius Prof. of Medicine, Univ. of Aberdeen, and Hon. Consultant Physician, Aberdeen Royal Infirmary, 1985–93. Hon. Prof., UEA, 1994. Associate Dir, R&D, Anglia and Oxford RHA, 1994–; Dir, R&D, Eastern (formerly Anglia and Oxford) Region, NHS Exec., DoH, 1998–. Member: NW Thames RHA, 1982–85; Scottish Nat. Med. Adv. Cttee, 1990–92; Gen. Council, King Edward's Hosp. Fund for London, 1980– (Mem. London Commns, 1990–92, 1995–97). Liveryman, 1976–, Mem. Ct of Assts, 1995–, Goldsmiths' Co. *Publications:* scientific and medical papers. *Address:* Park House, 39 High Street, Balsham, Cambridge CB1 6DJ. *T:* (01223) 893975.

HINCE, Dr Trevor Anthony; Deputy Director General, since 1998, and Scientific Director, since 1996, Cancer Research Campaign; *b* 17 Aug. 1949; *s* of late Gerald Arthur Hince and Beryl Doris Hince (*née* Franklin); *m* 1st, 1972, Carol Jean Tarabella (marr. diss. 1996); 2nd, 1996, Sarah Elizabeth Verrall. *Educ:* Forest Grammar Sch., Winnersh; University Coll. London (BSc Hons 1971); Middlesex Hosp. Med. Sch. (PhD 1976); Brunel Univ./Henley Mgt Coll. (MSc 1988). Middlesex Hospital Medical School: Research Asst, 1971–76; Temp. Lectr in Pathology, 1976–79; Cancer Research Campaign: Asst Scientific Sec., 1980–86; Scientific Sec., 1986–89; Dep. Dir, Scientific Dept, 1989–96. Member: Gray Lab. Cancer Res. Trust Bd, 1995–; Council, Inst. of Cancer Res., 1996–; Council, Paterson Inst. for Cancer Res., Manchester, 1996–; Bd of Mgt, LSHTM, 1996–; Gov., Beatson Inst. for Cancer Res., Glasgow, 1996–. *Publications:* papers in scientific jls. *Recreations:* riding, walking, gardening, music. *Address:* (office) 10 Cambridge Terrace, NW1 4JL. *T:* (020) 7224 1333.

HINCH, Prof. Edward John, PhD; FRS 1997; Professor of Fluid Mechanics, since 1998, and Fellow of Trinity College, since 1971, University of Cambridge; *b* 4 March 1947; *s* of

Joseph Edward Hinch and Mary Grace Hinch (*née* Chandler); *m* 1969, Christine Bridges; one *s* one *d*. *Educ:* Edmonton County Grammar Sch.; Trinity Coll., Cambridge (BA 1968; PhD 1973). Asst Lectr, 1972–75, Lectr, 1975–94, Reader, 1994–98, Univ. of Cambridge. Chevalier de l'ordre national du Mérite (France), 1997. *Publications:* Perturbation Methods, 1991; papers on fluid mechanics and its applications in scientific jls. *Address:* Trinity College, Cambridge CB2 1TQ. *T:* (01223) 338427.

HINCHCLIFFE, Peter Robert Mossom, CMG 1988; CVO 1979; HM Diplomatic Service, retired; Ambassador to Jordan, 1993–97; *b* 9 April 1937; *s* of Herbert Peter and Jeannie Hinchcliffe; *m* 1965, Archbold Harriet Siddall; three *d*. *Educ:* Elm Park, Killylea, Co. Armagh, Prep. Sch.; Radley Coll.; Trinity Coll., Dublin (BA (Hons), MA). Military service, short service commission, W Yorks Regt, 1955–57; TCD, Dublin Univ., 1957–61; HMOCS: West Aden Protectorate, South Arabian Fedn, 1961–67; Admin. Asst, Birmingham Univ., 1968–69; FCO: 1st Sec., Near Eastern Dept, 1969–70; 1st Sec., UK Mission to UN, 1971–74; 1st Sec. and Head of Chancery, Kuwait, 1974–76; Asst Head of Science and Technology and Central and Southern African Depts, FCO, 1976–78; Dep. High Comr, Dar es Salaam, 1978–81; Consul-Gen., Dubai, 1981–85; Hd of Information Dept, FCO, 1985–87; Ambassador to Kuwait, 1987–90; High Comr to Zambia, 1990–93. Sen. Hon. Res. Fellow, QUB, 1997; Hon. Fellow, Edin. Univ., 1997. *Publications:* Time to Kill Sparrows (poetry anthology), 1999; (with B. Milton-Edwards): Jordan: a Hashemite Legacy, 2001; Conflicts in the Middle East since 1945, 2001. *Recreations:* golf, tennis, writing poetry. *Address:* Antrim House, Kirk Lane, Hutton, Berwick-upon-Tweed TD15 1TJ. *Clubs:* East India, Devonshire, Sports and Public Schools; Hirsel Golf; Royal Co. Down Golf (Newcastle, Co. Down).

HINCHINGBROOKE, Viscount; Luke Timothy Charles Montagu; *b* 5 Dec. 1969; *er s* and *heir* of Earl of Sandwich, *qv*. Director: Wide Multimedia, 1997–; Wide Learning, 1997–. *Address:* Mapperton House, Beaminster, Dorset DT8 3NR; *e-mail:* luke@widelearning.com.

HINCHLIFF, Stephen, CBE 1976; Chairman and Managing Director, Dexion Group, 1976–91, retired; *b* 11 July 1926; *s* of Gordon Henry and Winifred Hinchliff; *m* 1987, Anne Fiona Maudsly; one *d* and one *s* one *d* from a previous marriage. *Educ:* Almondbury Grammar Sch., Huddersfield; Boulevard Nautical Coll., Hull; Huddersfield Coll. of Technology; Cranfield Inst. of Technology (MSc). FIMechE, FIEE. Production Engr, Dowty Auto Units Ltd, 1953–54; Dowty Seals Ltd: Chief Prodn Engr, 1953–54; Works Manager, 1954–56; Dir, 1956–76; Dep. Man. Dir, 1966–67; Man. Dir, 1967–76; Dep. Chm., Dowty Gp Ltd, 1973–76; Man. Dir, Dowty Gp Industrial Div., 1973–76. CIMgt; FRSA. *Recreation:* walking. *Address:* Cedar House, Little Gaddesden, Berkhamsted, Herts HP4 1PE. *T:* (01442) 843728.

HINCHLIFFE, David Martin; MP (Lab) Wakefield, since 1987; *b* 14 Oct. 1948; *s* of late Robert Victor Hinchliffe and Muriel Hinchliffe; *m* 1982, Julia (*née* North); one *s* one *d*. *Educ:* Lawefield Lane Primary Sch., Wakefield; Cathedral C of E Secondary Modern Sch., Wakefield; Leeds Polytechnic (Cert. in Social Work); Bradford Univ. (MA Social Work and Community Work); Huddersfield Polytechnic (Cert Ed). Social Work with Leeds Social Services, 1968–79; Social Work Tutor, Kirklees Metropolitan Borough Council, 1980–87. An opposition front bench spokesman on personal social services and community care, 1992–95. Chm., Health Select Cttee, 1997–. *Publication:* Rugby's Class War, 2000. *Recreation:* Rugby League—supporter of Wakefield Trinity RLFC. *Address:* 6 Rishworth Street, Wakefield WF1 2BY. *T:* (01924) 290590. *Club:* Wakefield Labour.

HIND, Rt Rev. John William; *see* Chichester, Bishop of.

HIND, Kenneth Harvard, CBE 1995; barrister; *b* 15 Sept. 1949; *s* of George Edward and Brenda Hind; *m* 1977, Patricia Anne (*née* Millar); one *s* one *d*. *Educ:* Woodhouse Grove Sch., Bradford; Leeds Univ. (LLB 1971); Inns of Court Sch. of Law. Pres., Leeds Univ. Union, 1971–72. Called to the Bar, Gray's Inn, 1973; practised North Eastern circuit, 1973–83. MP (C) West Lancashire, 1983–92; contested (C): W Lancashire, 1992; Selby, 1997. PPS to Minister of State: for Defence Procurement, 1986–87; for Employment, 1987–89; for Northern Ireland, 1989–90; PPS to Sec. of State for Northern Ireland, 1990–92. Officer, Conservative Candidates Assoc., 1995–97. Member: Soc. of Conservative Lawyers, 1983–; Justice, Internat. Commn of Jurists, 1983–. Hon. Vice-Pres., Central and West Lancs Chamber of Industry and Commerce, 1983–. *Recreations:* music, sailing Enterprise, cricket. *Address:* 3 Temple Gardens, Temple, EC4Y 9AU; Spinneys, Hudnall Common, Little Gaddesden, Herts HP4 1QW; Haburn Hill Farm, Crockey Hill, York. *Club:* Selby Conservative.

HINDE, Prof. Robert Aubrey, CBE 1988; FRS 1974; Master of St John's College, Cambridge, 1989–94 (Fellow, 1951–54, 1958–89 and since 1994); *b* 26 Oct. 1923; *s* of late Dr and Mrs E. B. Hinde, Norwich; *m* 1st, 1948, Hester Cecily (marr. diss. 1971), *d* of late C. R. V. Coutts; two *s* two *d*; 2nd, 1971, Joan Gladys, *d* of F. J. Stevenson; two *d*. *Educ:* Oundle Sch.; St John's Coll., Cambridge; Balliol Coll., Oxford (Hon. Fellow, 1986). Served Coastal Comd, RAF, Flt-Lt, 1941–45. Research Asst, Edward Grey Inst., Univ. of Oxford, 1948–50; Curator, Ornithological Field Station (now sub-Dept of Animal Behaviour), Madingley, Cambridge, 1950–65; St John's Coll., Cambridge: Steward, 1956–58; Tutor, 1958–63; Royal Soc. Res. Prof., Cambridge Univ., 1963–89. Hon. Dir, MRC Unit on Develt and Integration of Behaviour, 1970–89. Hitchcock Prof., Univ. of California, 1979; Green Vis. Scholar, Univ. of Texas, 1983. Mem. Council, Royal Soc., 1985–87. Croonian Lect., Royal Soc., 1990. Mem., Academia Europaea, 1990. Hon. Member: Assoc. for the Study of Animal Behaviour, 1987; Deutsche Ornithologische Ges., 1988; For. Hon. Mem., Amer. Acad. of Arts and Sciences, 1974; For. Associate, Nat. Acad. of Scis, USA, 1978; Hon. Fellow, Amer. Ornithologists' Union, 1977; Hon FBPsS 1981; Hon. FRCPsych 1988; Hon. FTCD, 1990. Hon. ScD: Univ. Libre, Brussels, 1974; Paris (Nanterre), 1979; Stirling, 1991; Göteborg, 1991; Edinburgh, 1992; Western Ontario, 1996; Oxford, 1998. Scientific Medal, Zoological Soc., 1961; Leonard Cammer Medal in Psychiatry, Columbia Coll., NY, 1980; Osman Hill Award, Primate Soc. of GB, 1980; Albert Einstein Award for Psychiatry, Albert Einstein Coll. of Medicine, NY, 1987; Huxley Medal, RAI, 1990; Distinguished Scientists Award, Soc. for Res. in Child Develt, 1991; Distinguished Career Award, Internat. Soc. for Study of Personal Relationships, 1992; Frink Medal, Zool Soc., 1992; G. Stanley Hall Medal, Amer. Psychol Assoc., 1993; Royal Medal, Royal Soc., 1996; Society's Medal, Assoc. for Study of Animal Behaviour, 1997. *Publications:* Animal Behaviour: a synthesis of Ethology and Comparative Psychology, 1966; (ed) Bird Vocalizations: their relations to current problems in biology and psychology, 1969; (ed jtly) Short Term Changes in Neural Activity and Behaviour, 1970; (ed) Non-Verbal Communication, 1972; (ed jtly) Constraints on Learning, 1973; Biological Bases of Human Social Behaviour, 1974; (ed jtly) Growing Points in Ethology, 1976; Towards Understanding Relationships, 1979; Ethology: its nature and relations with other sciences, 1982; (jtly) Defended to Death, 1982; (ed and contrib.) Primate Social Relationships: an integrated approach, 1983; (ed jtly) Social Relationships and Cognitive Development, 1985; Individuals, Relationships and Culture, 1987; (ed jtly) Relationships within Families, 1988; (ed jtly) Aggression and War, 1989; (ed jtly) Education for Peace, 1989; (ed and contrib) The Institution of War, 1991; (ed jtly) Co-operation and Prosocial Behaviour, 1991; (ed jtly) War: a necessary evil? 1994; Relationships: a dialectical perspective, 1997; Why Gods Persist, 1999; sundry papers in biological and psychological journals. *Address:* St John's College, Cambridge CB2 1TP. *T:* (01223) 339356; Park Lane, Madingley, Cambridge CB3 8AL. *T:* (01954) 211816.

HINDE, Thomas; *see* Chitty, Sir Thomas Willes.

HINDLEY, Prof. Colin Boothman; Director of Centre for Study of Human Development, 1967–88, and Professor of Child Development, 1972–84, now Professor Emeritus, Institute of Education, London; *b* Bolton, 1923; *m* 1945; two *s*. *Educ:* Bolton Sch.; Manchester Univ.; University Coll., London. MB, ChB Manchester 1946; BSc London 1949 (1st cl. Psychol.). Asst Med. Officer, Hope Hosp., Salford; Res. Psychologist and subseq. Sen. Lectr, London Univ. Inst. of Educn, 1949–72; Head of Adolescent Development Dip. Course, 1968–72. Psychol. Adviser, Internat. Children's Centre Growth Studies, Paris, 1954–84; Editor, Jl of Child Psychol. and Psychiat., 1959–69; Mem. Council, Brit. Psychol. Soc., 1970–73; Mem. Cttee, Internat. Soc. for Study Behavioural Develt, 1969–75; Mem. Assoc. Child Psychol. and Psychiat. (Chm. 1967–68). FBPsS. *Publications:* Conceptual and Methodological Issues in the Study of Child Development, 1980; chapters in Child Development: International Method of Study, ed Falkner, 1960; Learning Theory and Personality Development, in Psychosomatic Aspects of Paediatrics, ed Mackeith and Sandler, 1961; The Place of Longitudinal Methods in the Study of Development, in Determinants of Behavioural Development, ed Mönks, Hartup and de Wit, 1972; (jt ed. and contrib.) Development in Adolescence, 1983; contribs to jls. *Recreations:* jazz, literature, gardening, walking, travel, cinema, modern art, science, philosophy. *Address:* Institute of Education, 20 Bedford Way, WC1H 0AL. *T:* (020) 7636 1500.

HINDLEY, Estella Jacqueline; QC 1992; **Her Honour Judge Hindley;** a Circuit Judge, since 1997; *b* 11 Oct. 1948; *d* of Arthur John Hindley and Olive Maud (*née* Stanley); *m* 1980, John Gilbert Harvey; one *s*. *Educ:* Univ. of Hull (LLB Hons). Called to the Bar, Gray's Inn, 1971; a Recorder, 1989–97. Mem., Parole Bd. Chm., Birmingham Children's Hosp. NHS Trust, 2000–. Pres., Birmingham Medico-Legal Soc., 1999–. *Recreations:* book collecting, music, theatre. *Address:* The Priory Courts, 33 Bull Street, Birmingham B4 6DW. *T:* (0121) 681 3000.

HINDLEY, Michael John; *b* 11 April 1947; *s* of John and Edna Hindley; *m* 1980, Ewa Agnieszka (*née* Leszczyc-Grabianka); one *d*. *Educ:* Clitheroe Royal Grammar School; London University (BA Hons); Lancaster University (MA); Free University of West Berlin. Labour Councillor, Hyndburn District Council, 1979–84 (Leader, 1981–84); contested (Lab) Blackpool North, 1983. MEP (Lab) Lancashire E, 1984–94, Lancashire S, 1994–99. *Recreations:* swimming, walking, reading, music, travel. *Address:* 27 Commercial Road, Great Harwood, Lancs BB6 7HX. *T:* (01254) 887017. *Clubs:* Reform, Royal Commonwealth Society.

HINDLIP, 6th Baron *cr* 1886; **Charles Henry Allsopp;** Bt 1880; Chairman, Christie's International, since 1996 (Director, since 1986); *b* 5 Aug. 1940; *e s* of 5th Baron Hindlip and Cecily Valentine Jane, *o d* of Lt-Col Malcolm Borwick, DSO; *S* father, 1993; *m* 1968, Fiona Victoria Jean Atherley, *d* of late Hon. William Johnston McGowan, 2nd *s* of 1st Baron McGowan, KBE; one *s* three *d*. *Educ:* Eton. Coldstream Guards, 1959–62; joined Christie's, 1962; Gen. Manager, Christie's New York, 1965–70; Christie, Manson & Woods: Dir, 1970; Dep. Chm., 1985; Chm., 1986–96. Trustee, Chatham Historic Dockyard, 1989–. *Recreations:* painting, shooting, ski-ing. *Heir: s* Hon. Henry William Allsopp, *b* 8 June 1973. *Address:* Christie's International, 8 King Street, St James's, SW1Y 6QT. *T:* (020) 7839 9060. *Clubs:* White's, Pratt's.

HINDMARSH, Frederick Bell; Under-Secretary, Department of Health and Social Security, 1973–79, retired; *b* 31 Jan. 1919; *yr s* of Frederick Hindmarsh and Margaret May Hindmarsh; *m* 1947, Mary Torrance Coubrough; one *d*. *Educ:* County Grammar Sch., Acton. Clerical Officer, Min. of Health, 1936; Exec. Officer, 1937. Served war, Army, 1939–46. Min. of Pensions and Nat. Insurance and Min. of Social Security: Higher Exec. Officer, 1946; Sen. Exec. Officer, 1947; Chief Exec. Officer, 1951; Sen. Chief Exec. Officer, 1959; Prin. Exec. Officer, 1964; Asst Sec., DHSS, 1969. *Recreation:* music.

HINDMARSH, Irene, JP, MA; Principal, St Aidan's College, University of Durham, 1970–88; Second Pro-Vice-Chancellor, University of Durham, 1982–85; *b* 22 Oct. 1923; *d* of Albert Hindmarsh and Elizabeth (*née* White). *Educ:* Heaton High Sch.; Lady Margaret Hall, Oxford (MA Hons French); King's Coll., Univ. of Durham (PGCE). Taught at St Paul's Girls' Sch., London, 1947–49, Rutherford High Sch., Newcastle upon Tyne, 1949–59; Interchange Teacher, Lycée de Jeunes Filles, Dax, Landes, France, 1954–55; Lectr in Educn and French, King's Coll., Durham, 1959–64; Headmistress, Birkenhead High Sch., GPDST, 1964–70. Vis. Prof., New York State Univ., Syracuse, Cornell, Harvard, 1962; Delegate of Internat. Fedn of Univ. Women to UNO, NY, to Commns on Human Rights and Status of Women, 1962; Vis. Professor: Fu-Dan Univ., Shanghai, 1979, and again, 1980; SW China Teachers' Univ., Beibei, Sichuan, and Fu-Dan Univ., Shanghai, 1986. Delegate/Translator to internat. confs of FIPESO, 1963–70; Chairman: Internat. Cttee of Headmistresses' Assoc., 1966–70; Internat. Panel of Joint Four, 1967–70. Editor, Internat. Bull. of AHM, 1966–70. JP Birkenhead 1966, Durham 1974. FRSA 1989. *Publications:* various articles on educnl topics in AGM papers of Assoc. of Head Mistresses; contribs to prelim. papers of FIPESO meetings; seminar papers to symposia on lit. topics, Sèvres, under auspices of Council of Europe; contrib. re St Aidan's to Durham History from the Air. *Recreations:* travel, music, theatre, films, art, architecture. *Address:* 8 Dickens Wynd, Merryoaks, Elvet Moor, Durham DH1 3QR. *T:* (0191) 386 1881.

HINDSON, William Stanley, CMG 1962; BScEng, MIM, FIMechE; engineering and metallurgical consultant, 1974–94; *b* 11 Jan. 1920; *s* of late W. A. L. Hindson, Darlington; *m* 1944, Mary Sturdy (*d* 1961); one *s* one *d*; *m* 1965, Catherine Leikine, Paris, France; one *s*. *Educ:* Darlington Grammar Sch.; Coatham Sch., Redcar. With Dorman Long (Steel) Ltd, Middlesbrough, 1937–55; Metallurgical Equipment Export Co. Ltd and Indian Steelworks Construction Co. Ltd, 1956–62; Wellman Engineering Corp. Ltd, 1963–69; Cementation Co. Ltd, 1970–71; Humphreys & Glasgow, 1971–74. *Recreations:* chess, philately. *Address:* 36 Eresby House, Rutland Gate, SW7 1BG. *T:* (020) 7589 3194.

HINDUJA, Gopichand Parmanand; President, Hinduja Group of Companies, since 1962; *b* 29 Feb. 1940; *s* of Parmanand Deepchand Hinduja and Jamuna Parmanand Hinduja; *m* 1963, Sunita Gurnani; two *s* one *d*. *Educ:* Jai Hind Coll., Bombay, India. Joined family business, 1958; Head, Hinduja Gp's ops in Iran, 1958–78; resident in UK, 1982–; jtly (with brother) initiated diversification and expansion of Hinduja Gp. Pres., Hinduja Foundn, 1962–. Member: Adv. Council, Hinduja Cambridge Trust, 1991–; Adv. Cttee, Prince's Trust, 1991–; Duke of Edinburgh's Award Fellowship, 1987–. Patron: Balaji Temple, UK; Swaminarayan Hindu Mission, London. Chm., Gurnanak Trust, Teheran. MInstD. Hon. LLD Westminster, 1996; Hon. DEc Richmond Coll., 1997.

Recreations: Indian music, travel, sailing, yoga. *Address:* Hinduja Group of Companies, New Zealand House, 80 Haymarket, SW1Y 4TE. *T:* (020) 7839 4661. *Clubs:* Royal Automobile, Annabel's.
See also S. P. Hinduja.

HINDUJA, Srichand Parmanand; Chairman, Hinduja Group of Companies, since 1962; *b* 28 Nov. 1935; *s* of Hinduja Parmanand Deepchand and Hinduja Jamuna Parmanand Bajaj; *m* 1963, Madhu Srichand Menda; two *d. Educ:* National Coll., Bombay, India; Davar Coll. of Commerce, Mumbai. Joined family business; jtly (with brother) initiated diversification and expansion of Hinduja Gp. Chm., Hinduja Foundn, 1962–. Global Co-ordinator, IndusInd, 1962; Pres., IndusInd Internat. Fedn, 1996. Member, Advisory Council: Dharam Indic Res. Centres, Columbia, USA and Cambridge, UK; Hinduja Cambridge Trust, 1991–; Judge Inst. of Mgt, Cambridge, 1997. Mem., Duke of Edinburgh's Award Fellowship. Patron, Centre of India/US Educn, USA. Mem. Corp., Massachusetts Gen. Hosp. Hon. LLD Westminster, 1996; Hon. DEc Richmond Coll., 1997. *Publications:* Indic Research and Contemporary Crisis, 1995; The Essence of Vedic Marriage for Success and Happiness, 1996. *Recreations:* sports in general, but particularly tennis, volleyball and cricket, Indian classical music. *Address:* Hinduja Group of Companies, New Zealand House, 80 Haymarket, SW1Y 4TE. *T:* (020) 7839 4661. *Clubs:* Royal Over-Seas League, Les Ambassadeurs.
See also G. P. Hinduja.

HINE, Dame Deirdre (Joan), DBE 1997; FRCP, FFPHM; Chairman, Commission for Health Improvement, since 1999; Chief Medical Officer, Welsh Office, 1990–97; *b* 16 Sept. 1937; *d* of late David Alban Curran and of Noreen Mary Curran (*née* Cliffe); *m* 1963, Raymond Hine; two *s. Educ:* Heathfield House, Cardiff; Charlton Park, Cheltenham; Welsh Nat. Sch. of Medicine (MB BCh). DPH 1964; FFPHM 1978; FRCP 1993. Asst MO, Glamorgan CC, 1963–74; Specialist in Community Medicine, S Glam HA, 1974–82; Sen. Lectr in Geriatric Medicine, Univ. of Wales Coll. of Medicine, 1982–84; Dep. Chief MO, Welsh Office, 1984–87; Dir, Welsh Breast Cancer Screening Service, 1987–90. Mem., Audit Commn, 1998–99. Vice Pres., Marie Curie Cancer Care, 1998–; Chm., No Smoking Day, 1998–. *Publications:* papers on health promotion, health care of elderly, breast cancer screening, epidemiol. of old age in jls and text books; Calman-Hine report on cancer services. *Recreations:* travel, theatre, reading, canal cruising. *Address:* Commission for Health Improvement, Finsbury Tower, 103–105 Bunhill Row, EC1Y 8TG.

HINE, Air Chief Marshal Sir Patrick (Bardon), GCB 1989 (KCB 1983); GBE 1991; Air Officer Commanding-in-Chief, RAF Strike Command and Commander-in-Chief, United Kingdom Air Forces, 1988–91; Joint Commander, British Forces, Gulf War, 1990–91; Military Adviser to British Aerospace plc, 1992–99; *b* 14 July 1932; parents decd; *m* 1956, Jill Adèle (*née* Gardner); three *s. Educ:* Peter Symonds Sch., Winchester. Served with Nos 1, 93 and 111 Sqns, 1952–60; Mem., Black Arrows aerobatic team, 1957–59; commanded: No 92 Sqn, 1962–64; No 17 Sqn, 1970–71; RAF Wildenrath, 1974–75; Dir, Public Relations (RAF), 1975–77; RCDS 1978; SASO, HQ RAF, Germany, 1979; ACAS (Policy), 1979–83; C-in-C RAF Germany and Comdr, Second Allied Tactical Air Force, 1983–85; VCDS, 1985–87; Air Mem. for Supply and Orgn, 1987–88. Air ADC to the Queen, 1989–91. King of Arms, Order of the British Empire, 1997–. CIMgt; FRAeS. Winner, Carris Trophy, Hants, IoW and Channel Islands Golf Championship, and Brabazon Trophy, 1949; English Schoolboy Golf Internat., 1948–49; Inter-Services Golf, 1952–57. QCVSA 1960. *Recreations:* golf, ski-ing, caravanning, photography. *Clubs:* Royal Air Force; Colonels (Founder Mem.); Royal & Ancient, Brokenhurst Manor Golf, Seniors.

HINES, Barry Melvin, FRSL; writer; *b* 30 June 1939; *s* of Richard and Annie Hines; *m* (marr. diss.); one *s* one *d. Educ:* Ecclesfield Grammar Sch.; Loughborough Coll. of Educn (Teaching Cert.). FRSL 1977. Teacher of Physical Educn, London, 1960–62 and S Yorks, 1962–72; Yorkshire Arts Fellow in Creative Writing, Sheffield Univ., 1972–74; E Midlands Arts Fellow in Creative Writing, Matlock Coll. of Higher Educn, 1975–77; Sheffield City Polytechnic: Arts Council Fellow in Creative Writing, 1982–84; Hon. Fellow in Creative Writing, 1984; Hon. Fellow, 1985. *Television scripts:* Billy's Last Stand, 1971; Speech Day, 1973; Two Men from Derby, 1976; The Price of Coal (2 films), 1977; The Gamekeeper, 1979; A Question of Leadership, 1981; Threads, 1984; Shooting Stars, 1990; Born Kicking, 1992; *screenplays:* Kes, 1970; Looks and Smiles, 1981. *Publications:* (fiction): The Blinder, 1966; A Kestrel for a Knave, 1968; First Signs, 1972; The Gamekeeper, 1975; The Price of Coal, 1979; Looks and Smiles, 1981; Unfinished Business, 1983; The Heart of It, 1994; Elvis over England, 1998. *Address:* c/o The Agency, 24 Pottery Lane, Holland Park, W11 4LZ. *T:* (020) 7229 9216. *Club:* Hoyland Common Workingmen's (near Barnsley).

HINKLEY, Prof. David Victor, PhD; Professor of Statistics, University of California at Santa Barbara, since 1995; *b* 10 Sept. 1944; *s* of Eric Samson Hinkley and Edna Gertrude (*née* Alger); *m*; one *s* one *d. Educ:* Birmingham Univ. (BSc 1965); Imperial Coll., London (PhD 1969). MA Oxon 1990. Asst Lectr in Maths, Imperial Coll., London, 1967–69; Asst Prof. in Stats, Stanford Univ., 1969–71; Lectr in Maths, Imperial Coll., 1971–73; Associate Prof. and Prof. in Stats, Univ. of Minnesota, 1973–80; Prof. in Maths, Univ. of Texas, 1980–91; Prof. of Statistical Sci., and Fellow of St Anne's Coll., Oxford Univ., 1989–95. Editor: Annals of Statistics, 1980–82; Biometrika, 1991–92. *Publications:* Theoretical Statistics, 1973; Problems and Solutions in Theoretical Statistics, 1977; Statistical Theory and Modelling, 1990; Bootstrap Methods and Their Application, 1997; articles in statistical and scientific jls. *Recreations:* photography, tennis, botanical observation. *Address:* Department of Statistics and Applied Probability, University of California at Santa Barbara, CA 93106–3110, USA. *T:* (805) 8938331.

HINKLEY, Sarah Ann, (Sally), CBE 1995; Director, Performance Management Group, Cabinet Office, since 1999; *b* 28 March 1950; *d* of Eric David Booth and Mary Booth; *m* 1st, 1980, Nigel Dorling (marr. diss. 1988); one *s*; 2nd, 1998, Alan Hinkley; one step *d. Educ:* Kendal High Sch.; Callington Grammar Sch.; Girton Coll., Cambridge (BA 1972; MA). Joined Dept of the Environment, 1974: Private Sec. to Permanent Sec., 1980–81; Principal, 1981–86; Asst Sec., 1987; Hd, Central Policy Planning Unit, 1987–88; Dir of Finance and Resources, Historic Royal Palaces, 1989–92; Department of National Heritage, later of Culture, Media and Sport, 1992–99: Hd, Nat. Lottery Div. and Dir of Finance, 1992–94; Hd, Broadcasting Policy Div., 1994–95; Under Sec., 1995; Hd, Libraries, Galls and Museums Gp, 1995–98; Hd, Educn, Trng, Arts and Sports Gp, 1998–99. FRSA 1998. *Recreation:* family. *Address:* Cabinet Office, Admiralty Arch, The Mall, SW1A 2WH. *T:* (020) 7276 3000.

HINKS, Frank Peter; QC 2000; *b* 8 July 1950; *s* of Henry John Hinks and Patricia May Hinks (*née* Adams); *m* 1982, Susan Mary, *d* of Col J. A. Haire; three *s. Educ:* Bromley Grammar Sch.; St Catherine's Coll., Oxford (schol.; BA 1st Cl. Hons 1971; BCL 1st Cl. Hons 1972; MA). Called to the Bar, Lincoln's Inn, 1973; in practice at the Bar, 1974–. Churchwarden, St Peter and St Paul, Shoreham, 1995–. Liveryman, Innholders' Co. *Recreations:* writing and illustrating children's stories, collecting jugs, gardening. *Address:* The Old Vicarage, Shoreham, Sevenoaks, Kent TN14 7SB. *T:* (01959) 524480.

HINTON, Prof. Denys James, FRIBA; Chairman, Redditch New Town Development Corporation, 1978–85; *b* 12 April 1921; *s* of James and Nell Hinton; *m* 1971, Lynette Payne (*née* Pattinson); one *d. Educ:* Reading Sch.; Architectural Assoc. (MSc; AADip.). FRIBA. Asst, Wells Coates, 1950–52; Birmingham Sch. of Architecture: Lectr, 1952–57; Sen. Lectr, 1957–64; Dir, 1964–72; Prof. of Architecture, Univ. of Aston, 1966–81, now Emeritus. Sen. Partner, Hinton Brown Langstone, Architects, Warwick, 1960–86. Chairman: Architects Registration Council of UK, 1983–86; Fabric Adv. Cttee, St Philip's Cathedral, Birmingham, 1992–93; Pres., EC Architects' Directive Adv. Cttee, 1992–93; Vice-Pres. (formerly Vice-Chm.), Exec. Cttee, Internat. New Towns Assoc., 1980–85. *Publications:* Performance Characteristics of the Athenian Bouleterion, RIBA Athens Bursary, 1962; Great Interiors: High Victorian Period, 1967; contrib. RIBA and Architects Jl, papers on architectural education, Inst. Bulletin (worship and religious architecture), Univ. of Birmingham. *Recreations:* travel, moving house, water colours. *Address:* Hill Farm Barns, 33 Main Street, Greetham, near Oakham, Rutland LE15 7NJ. *T:* (01572) 813267.

HINTON, Prof. Geoffrey Everest, FRS 1998; FRSCan; PhD; Director, Gatsby Computational Neuroscience Unit, University College London, since 1998; *b* 6 Dec. 1947; *s* of Prof. Howard Everest Hinton, FRS and late Margaret Rose Hinton; *m* 1997, Jacqueline Ford; one *s* one *d. Educ:* King's Coll., Cambridge (BA Exptl Psychology 1970); Univ. of Edinburgh (PhD Artificial Intelligence 1978). Fellow: Sussex Univ., 1976–78; UCSD, 1978–80; Faculty Mem., Computer Sci. Dept, Carnegie-Mellon Univ., 1982–87; Fellow, Canadian Inst. for Advanced Res. and Prof. of Computer Science and Psychology, Univ. of Toronto, 1987–98. Pres., Cognitive Science Soc., 1992–93. Fellow, Amer. Assoc. for Artificial Intelligence, 1991; FRSCan 1996. Award for contribs to IT, IT Assoc. of Canada/NSERC, 1992. *Publications:* (ed jtly) Parallel Models of Human Associative Memory, 1989; Connectionist Symbol Processing, 1992; (ed jtly) Unsupervised Learning: foundations of neural computation, 1999; numerous papers and articles in learned jls. *Address:* Gatsby Computational Neuroscience Unit, University College London, 17 Queen Square, WC1N 3AR. *T:* (020) 7679 1178, *Fax:* (020) 7679 1173.

HINTON, Leslie Frank; Executive Chairman, News International plc, since 1995; a Director, Press Association, since 1996; *b* 19 Feb. 1944; *s* of Frank Arthur Hinton and Lilian Amy Hinton (*née* Bruce); *m* 1968, Mary Christine Weadick; four *s* one *d. Educ:* British Army schs in Germany, Libya, Egypt, Ethiopia and Singapore. Reporter, Adelaide News, SA, 1960–65; desk editor, British United Press, London, 1965–66; reporter, The Sun, 1966–69; writer editor, Adelaide News, 1969–70; reporter, The Sun, 1971–76; US corresp., News Internat., NYC, 1976–78; news editor, 1978–80, Managing Editor, 1980–82, The Star, NYC; Associate Editor, Boston Herald, 1982–85; Editor-in-Chief, Star Mag., 1985–87; Exec. Vice Pres., 1987–90, Pres., 1990–91, Murdoch Magazines, NYC; Pres. and Chief Exec. Officer, News America Publishing Inc., NYC, 1991–93; Chm. and Chief Exec. Officer, Fox Television Stations Inc. and Fox News Inc., LA, 1993–95. Dir, British Sky Broadcasting plc, 1999–. Chairman: Code of Practice Cttee, Press Complaints Commn, 1998–; Council, CBI, 1999–; Mem. Bd of Trustees, Amer. Sch. in London, 1999–. *Address:* News International plc, 1 Virginia Street, E1 9XY. *T:* (020) 7782 6000.

HINTON, Michael Herbert; JP; FCA; FICM; FRSA; FFA; ACIArb; *b* 10 Nov. 1934; *s* of late Walter Leonard Hinton and Freda Millicent Lillian Hinton; *m* 1st, 1955, Sarah Sunderland (marr. diss. 1982); one *s* two *d*; 2nd, 1984, Jane Margaret Manley, *d* of Arthur Crichton Howell. *Educ:* Ardingly Coll. Liveryman: Farmers' Co., 1964 (Master, 1981–82); Wheelwrights' Co.; Arbitrators' Co. (Master, 1998–99); Mem. Court of Common Council, 1970–71, Alderman, 1971–79, Ward of Billingsgate; Clerk to Wheelwrights' Co., 1965–71; Sheriff, City of London, 1977–78. JP City of London, 1971. *Recreations:* cricket, Association football, theatre, travel. *Address:* 37 Westgate Road, Beckenham, Kent BR3 5DT. *T:* (020) 8650 1996. *Clubs:* Farmers, MCC, City Livery (Pres., 1976–77).

HINTZ, B. Jürgen; Group Chief Executive, Novar plc (formerly Caradon plc), since 1998; *b* 3 May 1942; *s* of Karl-Heinz Hintz and Elsbeth Parr; *m* 2nd, 1996, Kirsty MacMaster; one *d* and one step-*d. Educ:* Univ. of N Carolina State (BSc). Physicist, 1964–75; Procter & Gamble Inc.: various positions, 1976–89; Dir, 1989–91; Chief Exec., CarnaudMetalBox, 1991–95. Non-executive Director: Apple Computers Inc., 1994–97; Inchcape plc, 1994–98. *Recreations:* ski-ing, tennis. *Address:* Novar plc, Caradon House, 24 Queens Road, Weybridge, Surrey KT13 9UX. *T:* (01932) 823518.

HIPKIN, John; Head of English, Meridian School, Royston, Herts, 1977–95; *b* 9 April 1935; *s* of Jack Hipkin and Elsie Hipkin; *m* 1963, Bronwyn Vaughan Dewey (marr. diss. 1985); four *s* one *d*; one *d. Educ:* Surbiton Grammar Sch. for Boys; LSE (BScEcon). Asst Teacher, 1957–65; Research Officer: King's Coll., Cambridge, 1965–68; Univ. of East Anglia, 1968–71; Sec., Schools Council Working Party on Whole Curriculum, 1973–74; Dir, Adv. Centre for Educn, 1974–77. Cambridge City Councillor (Lib Dem), 1992–. Chm. of Trustees, Winter Comfort for the Homeless, 2000–. *Publications:* (jtly) New Wine in Old Bottles, 1967; The Massacre of Peterloo (a play), 1968, 2nd edn 1974; (ed jtly) Education for the Seventies, 1970. *Recreations:* theatre, foreign travel, history, medieval music. *Address:* 15 Oxford Road, Cambridge CB4 3PH. *T:* (01223) 564126.

HIRD, Dame Thora, (Dame Thora Scott), DBE 1993 (OBE 1983); actress; *b* 28 May 1911; *d* of James Henry Hird and Mary Jane Mayor; *m* 1937, James Scott (*d* 1994); one *d. Educ:* The Misses Nelson's Prep. Sch., Morecambe, Lancs. Royalty Theatre Repertory Co., Morecambe; first appeared in West End of London, 1940–42: No Medals, Vaudeville; The Queen Came By, Duke of York's; Tobacco Road, Playhouse; The Trouble-Makers, Strand; The Same Sky, Duke of York's; The Love Match, Palace. Film contract, Ealing Studios, 1940; many *films include:* Blacksheep of Whitehall; They Came in Khaki; A Kind of Loving; Once a Jolly Swagman; Maytime in Mayfair; Wide-eyed and Legless; *TV series and serials:* Meet the Wife; The First Lady; In Loving Memory; Hallelujah!; Last of the Summer Wine; Flesh and Blood; Praise Be!; Thora on the Straight and Narrow; Goggle Eyes; many plays, incl. Cream Cracker under the Settee (BAFTA Award for Best TV Actress, 1988); Waiting for the Telegram (BAFTA Award for Best TV Actress, 1999); Lost for Words, 1999 (BAFTA Award for Best TV Actress, 2000). Pye Female Comedy Star Award, 1984. Hon. DLitt Lancaster, 1989; DUniv 1997. *Publications:* Scene and Hird (autobiog.), 1976; Praise Be Notebook, 1991; Praise Be Year Book, 1991; Praise Be Christmas Book, 1991; Praise Be Book of Prayers, 1992; Praise Be I Believe, 1993; Is it Thora?, 1996; Not in the Diary, 2000. *Recreations:* reading, gardening, travelling. *Address:* c/o Felix de Wolfe, Manfield House, 376–378 Strand, WC2R 0LR. *T:* (020) 7723 5561.

HIRSCH, Prof. Sir Peter (Bernhard), Kt 1975; MA, PhD; FRS 1963; Isaac Wolfson Professor of Metallurgy in the University of Oxford, 1966–92, Emeritus, 1992; Fellow, St Edmund Hall, Oxford, 1966–92, now Emeritus; *b* 16 Jan. 1925; *s* of Ismar Hirsch and

Regina Meyerson; *m* 1959, Mabel Anne Kellar (*née* Stephens), *widow* of James Noel Kellar; one step *s* one step *d*. *Educ:* Sloane Sch., Chelsea; St Catharine's Coll., Cambridge (Hon. Fellow, 1982). BA 1946; MA 1950; PhD 1951. Reader in Physics in Univ. of Cambridge, 1964–66; Fellow, Christ's Coll., Cambridge, 1960–66, Hon. Fellow, 1978. Has been engaged on researches with electron microscope on imperfections in crystalline structure of metals and on relation between structural defects and mechanical properties. Chairman: Metallurgy and Materials Cttee (and Mem., Eng. Bd), SRC, 1970–73; UKAEA, 1982–84 (pt-time Mem., 1982–94); Technical Adv. Gp on Structl Integrity, 1993–; Member: Elec. Supply Res. Council, 1969–82; Tech. Adv. Cttee, Advent, 1982–89; Tech. Adv. Bd, Monsanto Electronic Materials, 1985–88; Chm., Materials, Processes Adv. Bd, Rolls-Royce, 1996–2000. Chm., Isis Innovation Ltd, 1988–96; Director: Cogent Ltd, 1985–89; Rolls-Royce Associates, 1994–97; Oxford Med. Imaging Analysis, OMIA, 2000–01. FIC 1988. Hon. Fellow: RMS, 1977; Japan Soc. of Electron Microscopy, 1979; Japan Inst. of Metals, 1989. Associate Mem., Royal Acad. of Sci., Letters and Fine Arts, Belgium, 1995; Materials Res. Soc., India, 1990; For. Associate, US NAE, 2001. Hon. DSc: Newcastle, 1979; City, 1979; Northwestern, 1982; Hon. ScD East Anglia, 1983; Hon. DEng: Liverpool, 1991; Birmingham, 1993. Rosenhain Medal, Inst. of Metals, 1961; C. V. Boys Prize, Inst. of Physics and Physical Soc., 1962; Clamer Medal, Franklin Inst., 1970; Wihuri Internat. Prize, Helsinki, 1971; Royal Soc. Hughes Medal, 1973; Metals Soc. Platinum Medal, 1976; Royal Medal, Royal Soc., 1977; A. A. Griffith Medal, Inst. of Materials, 1979; Arthur Von Hippel Award, Materials Res. Soc., 1983; (jtly) Wolf Prize in Physics, Wolf Foundn, 1983–84; Dist. Scientist Award, Electron Microscopy Soc. of America, 1986; Holweck Prize, Inst. of Physics and French Physical Soc., 1988; Gold Medal, Japan Inst. of Metals, 1989; Acta Metallurgica Gold Medal, 1997. *Publications:* Electron Microscopy of Thin Crystals (with others), 1965; (ed) The Physics of Metals, vol. 2, Defects, 1975; (ed jtly) Progress in Materials Science, vol. 36, 1992; (ed) Topics in Electron Diffraction and Microscopy of Materials, 1999; numerous contribs to learned jls. *Recreation:* walking. *Address:* 104A Lonsdale Road, Oxford OX2 7ET.

HIRSCH, Prof. Steven Richard, FRCP; FRCPsych; Professor of Psychiatry, Imperial College School of Medicine (formerly Charing Cross and Westminster Medical School), since 1975; *b* 12 March 1937; *m* Theresa Hirsch; one *s* three *d*. *Educ:* Amherst Coll., Mass (BA Hons); Johns Hopkins Univ. (MD); London Univ. (MPhil). Res. worker, MRC Social Psychiatry, 1971–73; Hon. Sen. Registrar, Maudsley Hosp., 1971–73; Lectr in Psychiatry, Inst. of Psychiatry, Univ. of London, 1972–73; Sen. Lectr and Hon. Cons., Depts of Psychiatry, Westminster Hosp. and Queen Mary's Hosp., 1973–75. *Publications:* (ed with M. Shepherd) Themes and Variations in European Psychiatry: an anthology, 1974; (with J. Leff) Abnormalities in parents of schizophrenics: review of the literature and an investigation of communication defects and deviances, (monograph) 1975; (ed with R. Farmer) The Suicide Syndrome, 1980; (ed with P. B. Bradley) The Psychopharmacology and Treatment of Schizophrenia, 1986; Psychiatric Beds and Resources: factors influencing bed use and service planning (report of a working party, RCPsych), 1988; (ed with J. Harris) Consent and the Incompetent Patient: ethics, law and medicine, 1988; (ed with D. Weinberger) Schizophrenia, 1995, 2nd edn 2002. *Address:* Department of Psychiatry, Imperial College School of Medicine, Charing Cross Hospital, St Dunstan's Road, W6 8RP. *T:* (020) 8846 7390.

HIRST, Damien; artist; *b* Bristol, 7 June 1965; *s* of Mary Brennan; two *s* by Maia Norman. *Educ:* Goldsmiths' Coll., Univ. of London (BA Fine Art 1989). *Solo exhibitions include:* ICA, 1991; Emmanuel Perrotin, Paris, 1991; Cohen Gall., NY, 1992; Regen Projects, LA, 1993; Galerie Jablonka, Cologne, 1993; Milwaukee Art Mus., 1994; Dallas Mus., 1994; Kukje Gall., Seoul, 1995; White Cube Gall., 1995; Max Gandolph-Bibliothek, Salzburg, 1996; Gagosian Gall., NY, 1996; Bruno Bischofberger, Zurich, 1997; Astrup Fearnley, Oslo, 1997; Southampton City Art Gall., 1998; Tate Gall., 1999. Gp exhibitions in UK, Europe, USA and Australia. Co-founder and owner, Pharmacy, Notting Hill, 1998– (contemp. restaurant design award, Carlton London Restaurant Awards, 1999). Turner Prize, 1995. *Publications:* I Want to Spend the Rest of My Life Everywhere, With Everyone, One to One, Always, Forever, Now, 1997; Theories, Models, Methods, Approaches, Assumptions, Results and Findings, 2000; (illus.) Meaningless Static, by Paul Fryer, 2000. *Address:* (office) Science Ltd, 2 Bloomsbury Place, WC1A 2QA; c/o White Cube Gallery, 44 Duke Street, St James's, SW1Y 6DD.

HIRST, Rt Hon. Sir David (Cozens-Hardy), Kt 1982; PC 1992; a Lord Justice of Appeal, 1992–99; *b* 31 July 1925; *er s* of late Thomas William Hirst and Margaret Joy Hirst, Aylsham, Norfolk; *m* 1951, Pamela Elizabeth Molesworth Bevan, *d* of Col T. P. M. Bevan, MC; three *s* two *d*. *Educ:* Eton (Fellow, 1976–96); Trinity Coll., Cambridge. MA. Served 1943–47; RA and Intelligence Corps, Capt. 1946. Barrister, Inner Temple, 1951, Bencher, 1974, Reader, 1994, Treas., 1995; QC 1965; a Judge of the High Court, QBD, 1982–92. Vice-Chm. of the Bar, 1977–78, Chm., 1978–79. Member: Lord Chancellor's Law Reform Cttee; Council on Tribunals, 1966–80; Cttee to review Defamation Act, 1952, 1971–74; Chm., Spoliation Adv. Panel, 1999–; Hon. Life Mem., Amer. Bar Assoc. *Recreations:* theatre and opera, growing vegetables. *Address:* c/o Royal Courts of Justice, Strand, WC2A 2LL. *Clubs:* Boodle's, MCC.

See also J. W. Hirst.

HIRST, David Michael Geoffrey, FBA 1983; Professor of the History of Art, University of London at the Courtauld Institute, 1991–97, now Emeritus Professor of the History of Art; *b* 5 Sept. 1933; *s* of Walter Hirst; *m* 1st, 1960, Sara Vitali (marr. diss. 1970); one *s*; 2nd, 1972, Jane Martineau (marr. diss. 1984); 3rd, 1984, Diane Zervas. *Educ:* Stowe Sch.; New Coll., Oxford; Courtauld Inst. of Art (Hon. Fellow, 1998). Lectr, 1962–80, Reader, 1980–91, Courtauld Inst. Fellow at Villa I Tatti, 1969–70; Mem., Inst. for Advanced Study, Princeton, 1975. Mem., Pontifical Commn for Restoration of Sistine Ceiling, 1987–90. Arranged exhibn, Michelangelo Draftsman, Nat. Gall., Washington, 1988, Louvre, Paris, 1989; co-curated exhibn, The Young Michelangelo, Nat. Gall., 1994. *Publications:* Sebastiano del Piombo, 1981; Michelangelo and his Drawings, 1988 (Italian edn 1993); Michelangelo Draftsman, Milan, 1988 (French edn 1989); (jtly) The Young Michelangelo, 1994 (Italian edn 1997); many contribs to British and continental books and periodicals. *Address:* 3 Queensdale Place, W11 4SQ.

HIRST, Jonathan William; QC 1990; a Recorder, since 1997; *b* 2 July 1953; *s* of Rt Hon. Sir David (Cozens-Hardy) Hirst, *qv*; *m* 1974, Fiona Christine Mary Hirst (*née* Tyser); one *s* (and one *s* decd). *Educ:* Eton Coll.; Trinity Coll., Cambridge (MA). Called to the Bar, Inner Temple, 1975; Bencher, 1994. Mem., Gen. Council of the Bar, 1987– (Vice Chm., 1999, Chm., 2000; Chairman: Law Reform Cttee, 1992–94; Professional Standards Cttee, 1996–98). Governor: Taverham Hall Sch., Norfolk, 1991–95; London Goodenough Trust, 2001–. *Recreations:* shooting, gardening, other country pursuits. *Address:* Brick Court Chambers, 7–8 Essex Street, WC2R 3LD. *T:* (020) 7379 3550. *Clubs:* Boodle's; Norfolk (Norwich).

HIRST, Sir Michael (William), Kt 1992; LLB, CA; company director; business consultant; Founder, Michael Hirst Associates; Chairman, Scottish Conservative and Unionist Party, 1993–97; *b* 2 Jan. 1946; *s* of late John Melville Hirst and of Christina Binning Torrance or Hirst; *m* 1972, Naomi Ferguson Wilson; one *s* two *d*. *Educ:* Glasgow Acad., Glasgow; Univ. of Glasgow (LLB). CA 1970. Exchange Student, Univ. of Iceland, 1967; Partner, Peat, Marwick Mitchell & Co., 1978–83; Consultant, Peat Marwick UK, 1983–92. Pres., Glasgow Univ. Conservative Club, 1967; National Vice-Chm., Scottish Young Conservatives, 1971–73; Chm., Scottish Conservative Candidates Assoc., 1978–81; Vice-Chairman: Pty Organisation Cttee, 1985; Conservative Party in Scotland, 1987–89; Pres., Scottish Cons. & Unionist Assoc., 1989–92. Contested (C): Central Dunbartonshire, Feb. and Oct. 1974; E Dunbartonshire, 1979; Strathkelvin and Bearsden, 1987 and 1992. MP (C) Strathkelvin and Bearsden, 1983–87. PPS to Parly Under-Secs of State, DoE, 1985–87. Mem., Select Cttee on Scottish Affairs, 1983–87. Director: Children's Hospice Assoc., Scotland, 1993–; Princess Louise Scottish Hosp., 1980–; Member: Bd of Trustees, British Diabetic Assoc., 1988– (Hon. Sec., 1993–98; Vice Chm., 1998–); Court, Glasgow Caledonian Univ., 1993–98 (Chm., Audit Cttee, 1993–98). Chm., Laurel Park Sch. Educnl Trust, 1988–. FRSA 1993. *Recreations:* golf, walking, skiing. *Address:* Glentirran, Kippen, Stirlingshire FK8 3JA. *T:* (01786) 870283. *Clubs:* Carlton; The Western (Glasgow).

HIRST, Neil Alexander Carr; Deputy Director General, Energy, Department of Trade and Industry, since 1998; *b* 16 May 1946; *s* of Theodore James Hirst and Valerie Adamson Hirst; *m* 1984, Caroline Rokeby Collins; two *d*. *Educ:* Canford Sch.; Lincoln Coll., Oxford (BA 1st Cl. Hons PPE); Cornell Univ., USA (Telluride Schol., MBA). Jun. reporter, Eastbourne Gazette and Herald Chronicle, 1964–65; entered Civil Service, 1970: Asst Principal, Min. of Technol., 1970–73; Asst Private Sec. to Ministers for Industry and Energy and Sec. of State for Trade, 1973–75; Principal, Oil and Gas Div., then Atomic Energy Div., Dept. of Energy, 1975–80; on secondment to Private Finance Dept, Goldman Sachs, NY, 1981; returned to Dept of Energy for public flotation of Britoil, 1982; Asst Sec., Atomic Energy Div., 1983–85; Counsellor (Energy), Washington DC, 1985–88; Oil and Gas Div., Dept of Energy, 1988–92; Department of Trade and Industry: coal privatisation legislation, 1992–94; Labs Unit (privatisation of Nat. Engrg Lab. and Nat. Chemical Lab.), 1995; Under Sec. and Hd, Atomic Energy Div., 1995; Dir, Nuclear Industries, 1996–98. Mem., UKAEA, 1996–; Chm., Nuclear Safety Wkg Gp of the G8 Summit nations, 1998. Mem., Dorset Natural Hist. and Archaeol Soc. *Recreations:* gardening, music, theatre, walking. *Address:* 3 Stockwell Park Road, SW9 0AP. *T:* (020) 7735 9615; 59 Corfe Road, Stoborough, near Wareham, Dorset BH20 5AE. *Club:* Oxford and Cambridge.

HIRST, Prof. Paul Heywood; Professor of Education, University of Cambridge, 1971–88, now Emeritus, and Fellow of Wolfson College (formerly University College), Cambridge, since 1971; *b* 10 Nov. 1927; *s* of late Herbert and Winifred Hirst, Birkby, Huddersfield. *Educ:* Huddersfield Coll.; Trinity Coll., Cambridge. BA 1948, MA 1952, Certif. Educn 1952, Cantab; DipEd 1955, London; MA Oxon (by incorporation), Christ Church, Oxford, 1955. Asst Master, William Hulme's Grammar Sch., Manchester, 1948–50; Maths Master, Eastbourne Coll., 1950–55; Lectr and Tutor, Univ. of Oxford Dept of Educn, 1955–59; Lectr in Philosophy of Educn, Univ. of London Inst. of Educn, 1959–65; Prof. of Educn, King's Coll., Univ. of London, 1965–71. Visiting Professor: Univ. of British Columbia, 1964, 1967; Univ. of Malawi, 1969; Univ. of Puerto Rico, 1984; Univ. of Sydney, 1989; Univ. of Alberta, 1989; Inst. of Educn, Univ. of London, 1991–96. De Carle Lectr, Univ. of Otago, 1976; Fink Lectr, Univ. of Melbourne, 1976. Vice-Pres., Philosophy of Educn Soc. of GB; Member: UGC Educn Sub-Cttee, 1971–80; Educn Cttee, 1972–82, Academic Policy Cttee, 1981–87, Chm., Research Cttee, 1988–92, CNAA; Swann Cttee of Inquiry into Educn of Children from Ethnic Minorities, 1981–85. Chm., Univs Council for Educn of Teachers, 1985–88. Mem. Court, Univ. of Derby, 1996–. Hon. Mem., Royal Norwegian Soc. of Scis and Letters, 1996. Hon. DEd CNAA, 1992; Hon. DPhil Cheltenham and Gloucester Coll. of Higher Educn, 2000. *Publications:* (with R. S. Peters) The Logic of Education, 1970; (ed with R. F. Dearden and R. S. Peters) Education and the Development of Reason, 1971; Knowledge and the Curriculum, 1974; Moral Education in a Secular Society, 1974; (ed) Educational Theory and its Foundation Disciplines, 1984; (with V. J. Furlong) Initial Teacher Training and the Role of the School, 1988; (ed with P. A. White) Philosophy of Education: major themes in the analytic tradition, 1998; papers in: Philosophical Analysis and Education (ed R. D. Archambault), 1965; The Study of Education (ed J. W. Tibble), 1965; The Concept of Education (ed R. S. Peters), 1966; Religious Education in a Pluralistic Society (ed M. C. Felderhof), 1985; Education, Values and Mind (ed D. E. Cooper), 1986; Partnership in Initial Teacher Training (ed M. Booth *et al*), 1990; Beyond Liberal Education (ed R. Barrow and P. White), 1993; The Aims of Education (ed R. Marples), 1999; Education in Morality (ed J. M. Halstead and T. H. McLaughlin), 1999. *Recreation:* music, especially opera. *Address:* Flat 3, 6 Royal Crescent, Brighton BN2 1AL. *T:* (01273) 684118. *Club:* Athenæum.

HISCOX, Robert Ralph Scrymgeour; Chairman, Hiscox plc, since 1996; *b* 4 Jan. 1943; *s* of Ralph Hiscox, CBE and Louisa Jeanie Hiscox (*née* Boal); *m* 1st, 1966, Lucy Mills (marr. diss. 1978; she *d* 1996); two *s*; 2nd, 1985, Lady Julia Elizabeth Meade, 3rd *d* of Earl of Clanwilliam; three *s*. *Educ:* Rugby Sch.; Corpus Christi Coll., Cambridge (MA). ACII. Member of Lloyd's, 1967–98 (Dep. Chm., 1993–95; Dep. Chm., First Market Bd, 1993–95); Chairman: Lloyd's Underwriting Agents' Assoc., 1991; Lloyd's Corporate Capital Assoc., 1998–99; Lloyd's Market Assoc., 1999–2000. Director: Roberts & Hiscox, 1977–; Hiscox Hldgs Ltd, 1987–; R. K. Harrison Hldgs Ltd, 1990–99; Penrose Forbes Ltd, 1992–99; Hiscox Investment Mgt Ltd, 1995–; Hiscox Insce Co., 1996–; and other cos in Hiscox Gp. Mem., Mus. and Galls Commn, 1996–2000; Treas. and Trustee, Campaign for Museums, 1998–; Treasurer, Friends of the Tate Gallery, 1990–93. Vice Patron, Royal Soc. of British Sculptors, 1999–. Trustee: Wilts Bobby Van Trust, 1998–; 24 Hour Mus. Gov., St Francis Sch., Pewsey, 1995–97. *Recreations:* family life, country life, the arts. *Address:* Hiscox plc, 1 Great St Helen's, EC3A 6HX. *T:* (020) 7448 6011, *Fax:* (020) 7448 6598; *e-mail:* robert.hiscox@hiscox.com; Rainscombe Park, Oare, Marlborough, Wilts SN8 4HZ. *T:* (01672) 563491, *Fax:* (01672) 564120. *Club:* Boodle's.

HISLOP, George Steedman, CBE 1976; PhD; FREng, FIMechE; FRSE; Director, Aviall Airline Services (Caledonian), 1978–94; *b* 11 Feb. 1914; *s* of George Alexander Hislop and Marthesa Maria Hay; *m* 1942, Joan Daphne, *d* of William Beer and Gwendoline Fincken; two *s* one *d*. *Educ:* Clydebank High Sch.; Royal Technical Coll., Glasgow (ARTC); Cambridge Univ. (PhD). BScEng London. CEng, FIMechE 1949; FRAeS 1955; FREng (FEng 1976); FRSE 1976; FRSA 1959. A&AEE, RAF Boscombe Down, 1939–45; RAE, Farnborough, 1945–46; BEA, 1947–53; Chief Engr/Dir, Fairey Aviation Ltd, 1953–60; Westland Aircraft Ltd, 1960–79: Technical Dir (Develt), 1962–66; Dep. Man. Dir, 1966–68; Man. Dir, 1968–72; Vice-Chm., 1972–76. Chm., CEI, 1979–80 (Vice-Chm., 1978–79); Mem., Airworthiness Requirements Bd, CAA, 1976–83 (Chm., 1982–83). Vis. Prof., Univ. of Strathclyde, 1978–84. Mem. Council, RAeS, 1960–83 (Pres., 1973–74; Hon. FRAeS, 1983); Gov., Inveresk Res. Foundn, 1980–90. LRPS 1992. Hon. DSc Strathclyde, 1976. *Publications:* contrib. R & M series and RAeS Jl. *Recreations:* hill walking, photography, bird watching. *Address:* Hadley, St John's Hill, Old Coulsdon, Surrey CR5 1HD. *T:* (020) 8660 1008. *Clubs:* Royal Air Force, MCC.

HISLOP, Ian David; Editor, Private Eye, since 1986; writer and broadcaster; *b* 13 July 1960; *s* of late David Atholl Hislop and Helen Hislop; *m* 1988, Victoria Hamson; one *s* one *d*. *Educ:* Ardingly College; Magdalen College, Oxford (BA Hons Eng. Lang. and Lit.; Underhill Exhibn; Violet Vaughan Morgan Scholarship). Joined Private Eye, 1981, Dep. Editor, 1985–86. Columnist, The Listener, 1985–89; Television critic, The Spectator, 1994–96; Columnist, Sunday Telegraph, 1996–. *Radio:* Newsquiz, 1985–90; 4th Column, 1992–96; Lent Talk, 1994; (scriptwriter, with Nick Newman) Gush, 1994; The Hislop Vote, 2000; A Revolution in 5 Acts, 2001; *television:* scriptwriter: Spitting Image, 1984–89; (with Nick Newman) The Stone Age, 1989; Briefcase Encounter, 1990; The Case of the Missing, 1991; He Died a Death, 1991; Harry Enfield's Television Programme, 1990–92; Harry Enfield and Chums, 1994–98; Mangez Merveillac, 1994; Dead on Time, 1995; Gobble, 1996; Confessions of a Murderer, 1999; performer, Have I Got News For You, 1990–; documentary presenter: Canterbury Tales, 1996; School Rules, 1997; Pennies from Bevan, 1998; Great Railway Journeys East to West, 1999. *Publications:* various Private Eye collections, 1985–; contribs to newspapers and magazines on books, current affairs, arts and entertainment. *Address:* c/o Private Eye, 6 Carlisle Street, W1V 5RG. *T:* (020) 7437 4017.

HITCH, Brian, CMG 1985; CVO 1980; HM Diplomatic Service, retired; Director, Diploma in European Studies, and Fellow of Kellogg College (formerly Rewley House), University of Oxford, 1991–96, now Fellow Emeritus; *b* 2 June 1932; *m* 1954, Margaret Kathleen Wooller; two *d*. *Educ:* Wisbech Grammar Sch. (FRCO, LRAM); Magdalene Coll., Cambridge. Joined FO, 1955; 3rd/2nd Sec., Tokyo, 1955–61; FO, 1961–62; 2nd/1st Sec., Havana, 1962–64; 1st Sec., Athens, 1965–68; 1st Sec. and Head of Chancery, Tokyo, 1968–72; Asst Head, Southern European Dept, FCO, 1972–73; Dep. Head, later Head, Marine and Transport Dept, FCO, 1973–75; Counsellor, Bonn, 1975–77 and Algiers, 1977–80; Consul-Gen., Munich, 1980–84; Minister, Tokyo, 1984–87; High Comr to Malta, 1988–91. *Recreation:* music. *Address:* 19 Moreton Road, Oxford OX2 7AX. *T:* (01865) 556764.

HITCHCOCK, Dr Anthony John Michael; Head of Safety and Transportation Department, Transport and Road Research Laboratory, 1978–89; *b* 26 June 1929; *s* of Dr Ronald W. Hitchcock and Hilda (*née* Gould); *m* 1st, 1953, Audrey Ellen Ashworth (*d* 1990); one *s* two *d*; 2nd, 1992, Louise Nickel (*d* 1999). *Educ:* Bedales; Manchester Grammar Sch.; Trinity Coll., Cambridge; Univ. of Chicago. PhD, BA; MInstP; MCIT. Asst, Univ. of Chicago, 1951–52; AEA, 1953–67; Department of Transport: Head of Traffic Dept, 1967–71, Head of Transport Ops Dept, 1971–75, TRRL; Head, Res. Policy (Transport) Div., DoE/DoT, 1975–78. Vis. Researcher, Program for Advanced Technol. on the Highway, Univ. of Calif at Berkeley, 1990–94. Vis. Prof., Transport Studies, Cranfield Inst. of Technology, 1978–81. *Publications:* Nuclear Reactor Control, 1960; research reports and articles in learned jls. *Recreation:* bridge. *Address:* Seal Point, 2 Oakfield Place, Witney, Oxon OX28 4NH.

HITCHEN, Brian, CBE 1990; Chairman, Brian Hitchen Communications Ltd, since 1996; Chairman and Publisher, Kerry Life Ltd, since 1996; *b* 8 July 1936; *s* of Fred and Alice Hitchen, Lancs; *m* 1962, Ellen Josephine O'Hanlon, Kildare, Eire; one *s* one *d*. *Educ:* Hegginbottom Sch., Ashton-under-Lyne, Lancs, and elsewhere. Served Army, WO, Whitehall, 1954–56. Copy Boy, Daily Despatch, 1951; Gen. Reporter Bury Times 1952–54, Reporter, Manchester Evening News, 1957; Reporter, 1958–63, Foreign Correspondent, Paris Bureau, 1963–64, Daily Mirror; For. Corresp., Mirror US Bureaux, New York and Washington, 1964–72; Dep. News Editor, Daily Mirror, 1972; News Editor, Daily Express, 1973–76; Asst Editor, National Enquirer, USA, 1976, European Bureau Chief, 1977; Asst Editor, Now! magazine, 1978–80; London Editor, The Daily Star, 1981–86; Dep. Editor, Sunday Express, 1986–87; Ed., Daily Star, 1987–94; Ed., Sunday Express, Classic mag. and Sunday Express Magazine, 1994–95; Chm. and Publisher, Irish Country Life Ltd, 1996–2000. Director: Airspeed Internat. Corp., 1973–93; Express Newspapers, 1988–96; Independent Star, Eire, 1988–95. Member: Press Complaints Commn, 1991–95; Defence, Press and Broadcasting Adv. Cttee, 1993–96; NPA Code of Conduct Cttee, 1994–95. Press Officer, Lifeboat, Shoreham-by-Sea, W Sussex. Mem. Cttee, Friends of Airborne Forces Charity, 1996–. Saudi–British Jt Cultural Cttee, 2001–. *Publications:* Everything off the Mantlepiece, 1997; Eye of the Storm, 2000. *Recreations:* watercolours, fly-fishing, golf. *Address:* 32 Palmeira Square, Hove, East Sussex BN3 2JP. *Clubs:* Reform; Brighton and Hove Golf.

HITCHEN, John David; a Recorder of the Crown Court, since 1978; *b* 18 July 1935; *s* of late Harold Samuel and Frances Mary Hitchen; *m* 1966, Pamela Ann Cellan-Jones. *Educ:* Woodhouse Grove Sch., nr Bradford; Pembroke Coll., Oxford (BA(Hons)). Called to Bar, Lincoln's Inn, 1961. *Recreations:* music, reading. *Address:* 39 Rutland Drive, Harrogate, Yorks HG1 2NX. *T:* (01423) 566236.

HITCHENS, Christopher Eric; author and journalist; *b* 13 April 1949; *s* of late Comdr Eric Ernest Hitchens and Yvonne Jean Hitchens (*née* Hickman); *m* 1st, 1981, Eleni Meleagrou; one *s* one *d*; 2nd, 1991, Carol Blue; one *d*. *Educ:* Leys Sch., Cambridge; Balliol Coll., Oxford (BA PPE 1970). Social sci. corresp., THES, 1971–73; writer and Asst Editor, New Statesman, 1973–81; columnist and corresp. in Washington, 1982–; Columnist: The Nation (NY), 1982–; Vanity Fair (NY), 1982–; contributor to London Rev. of Books, 1989–. Mellon Prof. of English, Univ. of Pittsburgh, 1997. Lannan Literary Award for Non-Fiction, 1992. *Publications:* Karl Marx and the Paris Commune, 1971; James Callaghan, 1976; Hostage to History: Cyprus from the Ottomans to Kissinger, 1984; Imperial Spoils: the curious case of the Elgin Marbles, 1986; Prepared for the Worst: selected essays, 1989; Blood, Class and Nostalgia: Anglo-American ironies, 1990; For the Sake of Argument: selected essays, 1993; When the Borders Bleed: the struggle of the Kurds, 1994; The Missionary Position: Mother Teresa in theory and practice, 1995; No One Left to Lie To, 1999; Unacknowledged Legislation, 2001; The Trial of Henry Kissinger, 2001. *Recreations:* reading, travel, smoking, drinking, disputation. *Address:* 2022 Columbia Road NW, Washington, DC 20009, USA. *T:* (202) 3874842.

HITCHENS, Rear Adm. Gilbert Archibald Ford, CB 1988; Director General Ship Refitting, Ministry of Defence, 1985–87, retired; *b* 11 April 1932; *m* 1961, Patricia Hamilton; one *s* one *d*. BA Hons. Joined Royal Navy, 1950; Commander, 1968; Guided Weapons Staff Officer, Min. of Technology, 1968–70; Exec. Officer, RNEC, 1970–72; Senior Officer while building and Weapon Engineer Officer, HMS Sheffield, 1973–75; MoD (Navy), 1975–77; Naval Attaché, Tokyo and Seoul, 1977–79; Asst Dir, Manpower Requirements, MoD (Navy), 1979–80; Dir, Officers' Appts (Eng.), 1980–82; Captain, HMS Defiance, 1982–84; ADC to the Queen, 1984; CSO Engrg to C-in-C Fleet, 1984–85. Mem., Plymouth DHA, 1989–90. Admiralty Gov., Royal Naval Benevolent Trust, 1989–96. Chm. Govs, Devonport High Sch. for Boys, 1993–97. Liveryman, Ironmongers' Co., 1994. *Recreation:* any activity in the high hills.

See also T. M. Hitchens.

HITCHENS, Timothy Mark, LVO 1997; Assistant Private Secretary to the Queen, since 1998; *b* 7 May 1962; *s* of Rear Adm. Gilbert Archibald Ford Hitchens, *qv*; *m* 1985, Sara Kubra; one *s* one *d*. *Educ:* Dulwich Coll.; Christ's Coll., Cambridge (BA). Foreign and Commonwealth Office, 1983–; Tokyo, 1985–89; Private Sec. to Minister of State, FCO, 1991–94; Speechwriter to Foreign Sec., 1994–95; First Sec., Islamabad, 1995–97. *Recreations:* walking, gardening. *Address:* Buckingham Palace, SW1A 1AA.

HITCHIN, Prof. Nigel James, DPhil; FRS 1991; Savilian Professor of Geometry, University of Oxford, since 1997; Fellow of New College, Oxford, since 1997; *b* 2 Aug. 1946; *s* of Eric Wilfred Hitchin and Bessie (*née* Blood); *m* 1973, Nedda Vejarano Bernal; one *s* one *d*. *Educ:* Ecclesbourne Sch., Duffield; Jesus Coll., Oxford (BA 1968; Hon. Fellow, 1998); Wolfson Coll., Oxford (MA, DPhil 1972). Res. Asst, Inst. for Advanced Study, Princeton, 1971–73; Instructor, Courant Inst., New York Univ., 1973–74; SRC Res. Asst, 1974–77, SRC Advanced Res. Fellow, 1977–79, Oxford Univ.; Fellow and Tutor in Maths, St Catherine's Coll., Oxford, 1979–90; Prof. of Maths, Univ. of Warwick, 1990–94; Rouse Ball Prof. of Maths, and Fellow of Gonville and Caius Coll., Univ. of Cambridge, 1994–97. Vis. Prof., SUNY, Stony Brook, 1983. London Mathematical Society: Pres., 1994–96; Jun. Whitehead Prize, 1981; Sen. Berwick Prize, 1990; Sylvester Medal, Royal Soc., 2000. *Publications:* Monopoles, Minimal Surfaces and Algebraic Curves, 1987; (with M. F. Atiyah) The Geometry and Dynamics of Magnetic Monopoles, 1988; (with G. B. Segal and R. S. Ward) Integrable Systems: twistors, loop groups and Riemann surfaces, 1999; articles in learned jls. *Address:* 26 Lonsdale Road, Oxford OX2 7EW.

HITCHING, Alan Norman; His Honour Judge Hitching; a Circuit Judge, since 1987; Resident Judge, Blackfriars Crown Court, since 1998; *b* 5 Jan. 1941; *s* of late Norman Henry Samuel Hitching and Grace Ellen Hitching; *m* 1967, Hilda Muriel (*née* King) (*d* 2000); one *d* two *s*. *Educ:* Forest Sch., Snaresbrook; Christ Church, Oxford (BA 1962; Radcliffe Exhibnr and Dixon Scholar, 1962; BCL 1963; MA). Harmsworth Entrance Scholar, Middle Temple, 1960; Astbury Scholar and Safford Prize, Middle Temple, 1964; called to the Bar, Middle Temple, 1964; Standing Counsel, Inland Revenue, SE Circuit, 1972–87; a Recorder, 1985–87. Cropwood Fellow, Inst. of Criminology, Cambridge, 1990. Vice-Pres., John Grooms Assoc. for the Disabled, 1991– (Chm., 1981–89; Vice-Chm., 1978–81 and 1989–91). Licensed Reader, Dio. of Chelmsford, 1987–. *Address:* 9 Monkhams Drive, Woodford Green, Essex IG8 0LG. *T:* (020) 8504 4260; Blackfriars Crown Court, Pocock Street, SE1 0BJ. *T:* (020) 7922 5800.

HITCHINGS, Prof. Roger Alan, FRCS; FRCOphth; Ophthalmic Surgeon, since 1978, Consultant, since 1981, Director, Research and Development, since 2000, Moorfields Eye Hospital; Professor of Glaucoma and Allied Studies, Institute of Ophthalmology, University College London, since 1999; *b* 30 May 1942; *s* of Alan and Mary Hitchings; *m* 1966, Virmati Talwar; two *d*. *Educ:* Steyning Grammar Sch.; Royal Free Hosp. (MB BS). FRCS 1971; FRCOphth 1988. Resident Surgical Officer, Moorfields Eye Hosp., 1969–73; Res. Fellow, Wilts Eye Hosp., 1973–75; Sen. Lectr, Univ. of London, 1975–79; Consultant Ophthalmic Surgeon, KCH, 1979–81. Pres., Eur. Glaucoma Soc., 2000–. *Publications:* Atlas of Clinical Ophthalmology, 1984, 2nd edn 1994; The Refractory Glaucomas, 1995; Glaucoma: a practical guide, 2000; contrib. papers on glaucoma and allied subjects. *Recreations:* gardening, travel, food. *Address:* Moorfields Eye Hospital, City Road, EC1V 2PD.

HIVES, family name of **Baron Hives.**

HIVES, 3rd Baron *cr* 1950, of Duffield, co. Derby; **Matthew Peter Hives;** *b* 25 May 1971; *s* of Hon. Peter Anthony Hives (*d* 1974) and of Dinah (*née* Wilson-North); *S* uncle, 1997. *Heir: uncle* Hon. Michael Bruce Hives [*b* 12 March 1926; *m* 1951, Janet Rosemary (*née* Gee); two *s* one *d*].

HNATYSHYN, Rt Hon. Ramon John; PC (Can.) 1979; CC 1990; CMM 1990; CD 1990; QC (Can.) 1988; Governor General and Commander-in-Chief of Canada, 1990–95; Senior Partner, Gowling Lafleur Henderson LLP (formerly Gowling, Strathy & Henderson), since 1995; *b* 16 March 1934; *s* of John Hnatyshyn and Helen Constance Hnatyshyn (*née* Pitts); *m* 1960, Karen Gerda Nygaard Andreasen; two *s*. *Educ:* Victoria Public Sch.; Nutana Collegiate Inst., Univ. of Saskatchewan (BA 1954; LLB 1956). Royal Canadian Air Force: trng, 1951–56; 23 Wing Auxiliary, 1956–58. Called to the Bar, Saskatchewan, 1957, Ontario, 1986; QC Sask, 1973; practised to 1990; Private Sec. and Exec. Asst to Senate Leader of Govt, 1958–60; Lectr in Law, Univ. of Saskatchewan, 1966–74; MP (PC Party) Saskatoon-Biggar, 1974, Saskatoon West, 1979, 1980, 1984 elections; Dep. House Leader of Official Opposition, 1976; Minister of State for Science and Technology, 1979; Minister of Energy, Mines and Resources, 1979–80; Opposition Critic for Justice, 1980–84, and Solicitor Gen., 1984; Govt House Leader, 1984–86; Minister responsible for Regulatory Affairs, 1986; Minister of Justice and Attorney General of Canada, 1986–88. Pres., Queen's Privy Council for Canada, 1985–86. KStJ (Prior for Canada, 1990–95). *Address:* (office) Suite 2600, 160 Elgin Street, Ottawa, ON K1P 1C3, Canada.

HO, Eric Peter, CBE 1981; Chairman, Public Service Commission, Hong Kong, 1987–91, retired; *b* 30 Dec. 1927; *s* of Sai-Ki Ho and Doris (*née* Lo); *m* 1956, Grace Irene, *d* of Mr and Mrs A. V. Young; two *s* one *d*. *Educ:* Univ. of Hong Kong (BA 1950). Inspector of Taxes (under training), London, 1950–53; Hong Kong Civil Service, 1954–87: Sec. for Social Services, 1977–83; Sec. for Trade and Industry, 1983–87. RCDS, London, 1976. *Recreations:* swimming, lawn tennis. *Address:* 26 Greenways Drive, Sunningdale, Berks SL5 9QS.

HOAD, Air Vice-Marshal Norman Edward, CVO 1972; CBE 1969; AFC 1951 and Bar, 1956; artist; *b* 28 July 1923; *s* of Hubert Ronald Hoad and Florence Marie (*née* Johnson); two *s*. *Educ:* Brighton. Joined RAF, 1941, pilot trng, S Rhodesia; Lancaster pilot until shot down and taken prisoner in Germany, 1944; various flying and instructional duties, 1945–51; Sqdn Ldr 1951; OC No 192 Sqdn, 1953–55; psc 1956; Wing Comdr, HQ 2 ATAF, 1957–59; pfc 1960; OC No 216 Sqdn, 1960–62; jssc 1963; Gp Capt., MoD, 1963–65; idc 1966; Stn Comdr: RAF Lyneham, 1967, RAF Abingdon, 1968; Defence and Air Attaché, British Embassy, Paris, 1969–72; Dir, Defence Policy (A), 1972–74; Chief of Staff, 46 Gp, RAF Strike Comd, April-Oct. 1974; AOC No 46 Group, and Comdr, UK Jt Airborne Task Force, 1974–75; Senior RAF Mem., RCDS, 1976–78. Director, Air League, 1978–82. Founder Mem., Guild of Aviation Artists; Chm., Soc. of Equestrian Artists. MIMgt (MBIM 1970). *Address:* Little Meadow, Stowupland, Stowmarket, Suffolk IP14 5DF. *T:* (01449) 612006. *Club:* Royal Air Force.

HOAD, Pamela Joan; *see* Gordon, P. J.

HOAR, Rev. Ronald William Cecil; Chairman, Manchester and Stockport Methodist District, 1979–95; President of the Methodist Conference, 1991–92; *b* 31 Oct. 1931; *s* of Cecil Herbert William and Lilian Augusta Hoar; *m* 1956, Peggy Jean (*née* Stubbington); three *s* two *d*. *Educ:* Shedfield Church of England Primary Sch., Hants; Prices Sch., Fareham, Hants; Richmond Coll., Univ. of London (BD). Methodist Minister: Wells, Somerset, 1955–58; Bermondsey, London, 1958–62; Westminster and Chelsea, 1962–67; Bristol Mission, 1967–76; Great Yarmouth and Gorleston, 1976–79. *Publications:*

Methodism in Chelsea to 1963, 1963; A Good Ideal: a history of the Bristol Methodist Mission, 1973; Advertising the Gospel, 1991. *Recreations:* DIY, watching sport, oil painting, gardening. *Address:* 43 Green Lanes, Prestatyn, Denbighshire LL19 7BH. *T:* (01745) 886923.

HOARE, Sir Antony; *see* Hoare, Sir C. A. R.

HOARE, Rev. Brian Richard; Methodist Minister, since 1971; Methodist Evangelism Secretary, 1996–2000; President of the Methodist Conference, 1995–96; *b* 9 Dec. 1935; *s* of William Charles Hoare and Kathleen Nora Hoare (*née* Thwaites); *m* 1962, Joyce Eleanor Davidson; one *s* one *d. Educ:* Southwell Minster Grammar Sch., Notts; Westminster Coll., London (Teacher's Cert.); Richmond Coll., Univ. of London (BD 1971). Ops Clerk, RAF, 1954–56. Teacher, Col Frank Seely Secondary Sch., Calverton, Notts, 1959–62; Travelling Sec., subsequently Nat. Sec., Colls of Educn Christian Union, Inter-Varsity Fellowship, London, 1962–68. Chaplain Hunmanby Hall Sch., Filey, 1971–74; Minister, Hull Methodist Mission, 1974–77; New Testament Tutor, Cliff Coll., Sheffield, 1977–86; Superintendent Minister, Longton Central Hall, Stoke-on-Trent, 1986–88; Divl Sec. 1988–89, Dep. Gen. Sec. 1989–95, Home Mission Div. Member: World Methodist Council, Nairobi, 1986, Singapore, 1991, Rio de Janeiro, 1996; World Methodist Exec. Cttee, Bulgaria, 1992, Estonia, 1994. Has served on numerous Methodist cttees. *Publications:* (ed) Methods of Mission, 1979; Evangelism in New Testament Practice and Methodist Tradition, 1984; Hymns and Songs for Worship, 1985; Celebrate and Sing, 1991; 20 Things to do in a Decade of Evangelism, 1991; By the Way: six studies in incidental evangelism, 1995; New Creation: a full length musical presentation, 1995; Singing Faith, 1998; (ed) Leisure and Mission, 2000; hymns and songs (words and music) and tunes published in a variety of books. *Recreations:* music, literature, travel, walking. *Address:* 5 Flaxdale Close, Knaresborough, N Yorks HG5 0NZ.

HOARE, Sir (Charles) Antony (Richard), (Tony), Kt 2000; FRS 1982; Senior Researcher, Microsoft Research Ltd, Cambridge, since 1999; *b* 11 Jan. 1934; *s* of late Henry S. M. Hoare and Marjorie F. Hoare; *m* 1962, Jill Pym; one *s* one *d* (and one *s* decd). *Educ:* King's Sch., Canterbury; Merton Coll., Oxford (MA, Cert. Stats). Computer Div., Elliott Brothers, London, Ltd, 1959–68: successively Programmer, Chief Engr, Tech. Man., Chief Scientist; National Computer Centre, 1968; Prof. of Computer Science, QUB, 1968–77; Oxford University: Fellow, Wolfson Coll., 1977–99; Prof. of Computation, then James Martin Prof. of Computing, 1977–99; Dir, Univ. Computing Lab., 1982–87. Lee Kuan Yew Distinguished Visitor, Singapore, 1992. Dist. FBCS 1978; MAE 1989; For. Mem., Accademia Nazionale dei Lincei, 1988; Corresp. Mem., Bavarian Acad. of Scis, 1997. Hon. Fellow: Kellogg Coll., Oxford, 1999; Darwin Coll., Cambridge, 2001. Hon. DSc: Southern California, 1979; Warwick, 1985; Pennsylvania, 1986; Belfast, 1987; York, 1989; Essex 1991; Bath, 1993; Oxford Brookes, 2000. A. M. Turing Award, Assoc. Comp. Mach., 1980; Harry Goode Meml Award, Amer. Fedn of Inf. Processing Socs, 1981; Faraday Medal, IEE, 1985; Computer Pioneer Award, IEEE, 1991; Kyoto Prize, Inamori Foundn, 2000. *Publications:* Structured Programming (with O.-J. Dahl and E. W. Dijkstra), 1972; Communicating Sequential Processes, 1985; Essays in Computing Science, 1988; (with H. Jifeng) Unifying Theories of Programming, 1998; articles in Computer Jl, Commun. ACM, and Acta Informatica; *festschrift:* A Classical Mind, 1994. *Recreations:* walking, reading, listening to music. *Address:* (office) St George House, 1 Guildhall Street, Cambridge CB2 3NH.

HOARE, Christopher Henry St John, (Toby); Group Chief Executive, Bates UK Ltd, since 1999; *b* 2 Feb. 1960; *s* of J. Michael Hoare and Ann St J. Hoare; *m* 1986, Sarah Jane Dixon-Smith; two *s* one *d. Educ:* Harrow. Distillers Co. Ltd, 1979–80; Express Newspapers, 1980–84; Centaur Communications, 1984–85; Dorland Advertising, 1985–87; Young & Rubicam, 1987–99. Freeman, City of London, 1987; Liveryman, Co. of Distillers, 1982. *Recreations:* shooting, golf, opera. *Address:* 130 Kensington Park Road, W11 2EP. *T:* (020) 7221 5159; Little Codham Hall, Shalford, Essex CM7 5JD. *Clubs:* Garrick; Royal Newmarket & Worlington Golf.

HOARE, Henry Cadogan; Chairman, C. Hoare & Co., Bankers, since 1988; *b* 23 Nov. 1931; *s* of late Henry Peregrine Rennie Hoare and of Lady Beatrix Fanshawe, *d* of 6th Earl Cadogan, CBE; *m* 1st, 1959, Pamela Bunbury (marr. diss. 1970); two *s* one *d*; 2nd, 1977, Caromy Maxwell Macdonald. *Educ:* Eton; Trinity Coll., Cambridge (MA). Career in banking. *Address:* c/o C. Hoare & Co., 37 Fleet Street, EC4P 4DQ.

HOARE, John Michael; independent consultant, health services management, since 1990; *b* 23 Oct. 1932; *s* of Leslie Frank Hoare and Gladys Hoare; *m* 1963, Brita Hjalte; one *s* one *d. Educ:* Raynes Park; Christ's Coll., Cambridge (BA). Asst Sec., United Bristol Hosps, 1961; House Governor, St Stephen's Hosp., 1963; Asst Clerk, St Thomas' Hosp., 1965; Administrator, Northwick Park Hosp., 1967; Wessex Regional Health Authority: Administrator, 1974–84; Gen. Man., 1984–89; Quality Advr, 1989–90. Mem., Defence Medical Services Inquiry, 1971–73. *Recreations:* reading, walking, music, squash.

HOARE, Hon. Marcus Bertram, CMG 1965; Justice of Supreme Court of Queensland, 1966–80; *b* 3 March 1910; *s* of John George and Emma Hoare; *m* 1936, Eileen Parker; four *s. Educ:* Brisbane Grammar Sch. Solicitor, 1933; Barrister-at-Law, 1944; QC (Australia) 1960. *Address:* 13 Mortlake Road, Graceville, Brisbane, Qld 4075, Australia. *T:* (7) 33794181.

HOARE, Sir Peter Richard David, 8th Bt *cr* 1786; *b* 22 March 1932; *s* of Sir Peter William Hoare, 7th Bt, and Laura Ray (*d* 1992), *o d* of Sir John Esplen, 1st Bt, KBE; *S* father, 1973; *m* 1st, 1961, Jane (marr. diss. 1967), *o d* of late Daniel Orme; 2nd, 1978, Katrin Alexa, Lady Hodson (marr. diss. 1982), *o d* of late Erwin Bernstiel; 3rd, 1983, Angela Francesca Ayarza Valdovinos de la Claustra, *d* of late Fidel Fernando Ayarza. *Educ:* Eton. *Recreations:* travelling, shooting, skiing. *Heir: b* David John Hoare [*b* 8 Oct. 1935; *m* 1st, 1965, Mary Vanessa (marr. diss. 1978), *y d* of Peter Gordon Cardew; one *s*; 2nd, 1984, Virginia Victoria Graham Labes, *d* of late Michael Menzies]. *Address:* c/o Crèdit Andorrà, Avinguda Princep Benlloch 25, Andorra la Vella, Principality of Andorra. *Club:* Royal Automobile.

HOARE, Rt Rev. Rupert William Noel; Dean of Liverpool, since 2000; *b* 3 March 1940; *s* of Julian Hoare and Edith Hoare (*née* Temple); *m* 1965, Gesine (*née* Pflüger); three *s* one *d. Educ:* Rugby School; Trinity Coll., Oxford (BA 1961, MA 1967); Kirchliche Hochschule, Berlin; Westcott House and Fitzwilliam House, Cambridge (BA 1964); Birmingham Univ. (PhD 1973). Deacon 1964, priest 1965, Dio. Manchester; Curate of St Mary, Oldham, 1964–67; Lecturer, Queen's Theological Coll., Birmingham, 1968–72; Rector, Parish of the Resurrection, Manchester, 1972–78; Residentiary Canon, Birmingham Cathedral, 1978–81; Principal, Westcott House, Cambridge, 1981–93; Bishop Suffragan of Dudley, 1993–99. Canon Theologian of Coventry Cathedral, 1970–75. *Publications:* (trans. jtly) Bultmann's St John, 1971; (contrib.) Queen's Sermons, 1973, Queen's Essays, 1980; The Trial of Faith, 1988; articles in Theology. *Recreations:* hill walking, sailing, gardening, listening to music. *Address:* Liverpool Cathedral, L1 7AZ. *T:* (0151) 709 6271.

HOARE, Sir Timothy Edward Charles, 8th Bt *cr* 1784; OBE 1996; Director: Career Plan Ltd, since 1970; New Metals and Chemicals Ltd, since 1968; *b* 11 Nov. 1934; *s* of Sir Edward O'Bryen Hoare, 7th Bt and Nina Mary (*d* 1995), *d* of late Charles Nugent Hope-Wallace, MBE; *S* father, 1969; *m* 1969, Felicity Anne, *o d* of late Peter Boddington; one *s* twin *d. Educ:* Radley College; Worcester College, Oxford (MA Modern Hist.); Birkbeck Coll., London (MA Manpower Studies). FLS 1980; FZS 1982. Dir, World Vision of Britain, 1983–95. Mem., Church Assembly, 1960–70; General Synod of Church of England: Mem., 1970–2000; Mem., Standing Cttee, 1981–98; Chairman: Law of Marriage Gp, 1984–88 (report, An Honourable Estate); Clergy Conditions of Service Steering Gp, 1991–98. Member: Chadwick Commn on Church and State, 1964–70; ACCM, 1971–86; Crown Appointments Commn, 1987–92. Treas., dio. of London, 1994–. Deleg., WCC, Canberra, 1991. Trustee, Intercontinental Church Soc., 1975–98. Mem. Council, St John's Coll., Durham Univ., 1995–2000; Gov., Canford Sch., 1965–. *Publications:* (contrib.) Hope for the Church of England, 1986; (contrib.) New Dictionary of Christian Ethics and Pastoral Theology, 1995; (contrib.) Our National Life: a Christian perspective on the state of the nation, 1998. *Recreations:* the work of God in nature, and of man in art. *Heir: s* Charles James Hoare, *b* 15 March 1971. *Address:* 10 Belitha Villas, N1 1PD. *Clubs:* National (Chm.), MCC.

HOARE, Toby; *see* Hoare, C. H. St J.

HOBAN, Brian Michael Stanislaus; Head Master of Harrow, 1971–81; *b* 7 Oct. 1921; 2nd *s* of late Capt. R. A. Hoban; *m* 1947, Jasmine, 2nd *d* of J. C. Holmes, MC, Charterhouse, Godalming; one *s* one *d* (and one *d* decd). *Educ:* Charterhouse (Scholar); University Coll., Oxford (Sch.). 2nd Cl. Hon. Mods, 1947; 2nd Cl. Lit. Hum., 1949; BA 1949, MA 1957. Served War of 1939–45: Capt., Westminster Dragoons; NW Europe, 1944–45 (despatches); demobilised, Nov. 1945. Capt. Northants Yeomanry, TA, 1950–56. Asst Master: Uppingham Sch., 1949–52; Shrewsbury Sch., 1952–59; Headmaster, St Edmund's Sch., Canterbury, 1960–64; Head Master, Bradfield Coll., 1964–71. Pt-time Chm., CSSBs, 1984–91. Hon. Associate Mem., HMC, 1981– (Hon. Treasurer, 1975–80). Sometime CACTM and ACCM Lay Selector for dios of Canterbury and London. Sometime Mem., Central Adv. Bd, RAF Coll., Cranwell; Governor: Wellington Coll., 1981–92; St Edmund's Sch., Canterbury, 1975–96; St Margaret's Sch., Bushey, 1975–97. Pres., The Carthusian Soc., 1987–92. JP Berks, 1967–71. *Publication:* (with Donald Swann) Jesu Parvule, 1965. *Recreations:* music, cooking, watching amateur cricket, gardening. *Address:* Upcot, Wantage Road, Streatley, Berks RG8 9LD. *T:* (01491) 873419. *Clubs:* East India, Devonshire, Sports and Public Schools; Vincent's (Oxford).

HOBAN, Mark Gerard; MP (C) Fareham, since 2001; chartered accountant; *b* 31 March 1964; *s* of Tom Hoban and Maureen Hoban (*née* Orchard); *m* 1994, Fiona Jane Barrett. *Educ:* London Sch. of Econs (BSc Econs 1985). ACA 1988. With Coopers & Lybrand, then PricewaterhouseCoopers, 1985–2001, Sen. Manager, 1992–2001. Contested (C) South Shields, 1997. *Recreations:* cooking, entertaining, reading, travel. *Address:* House of Commons, SW1A 0AA.

HOBAN, Russell Conwell, FRSL 1988; writer; *b* 4 Feb. 1925; *s* of Abram Hoban and Jenny Dimmerman; *m* 1st, 1944, Lillian Aberman (marr. diss. 1975; she *d* 1998); one *s* three *d*; 2nd, 1975, Gundula Ahl; three *s. Educ:* Lansdale High Sch.; Philadelphia Museum Sch. of Industrial Art. Served US Army, 1943–45: 339th Inf., 85th Div., Italy (Bronze Star Medal, 1945). Various jobs, 1945–56; free-lance illustration, 1956–65; copywriter with Doyle, Dane, Bernbach, New York, 1965–67; resident in London, 1969–. Drama: (television) Come and Find Me, 1980; (stage) The Carrier Frequency, 1984; (radio) Perfect and Endless Circles, Radio 3, 1995; By a River in the Mind, Radio 4, 1999; opera: The Second Mrs Kong (music by Sir Harrison Birtwistle), Glyndebourne, 1994; stories for BBC Radio 4. *Publications: children's books:* What Does It Do and How Does It Work?, 1959; The Atomic Submarine, 1960; Bedtime for Frances, 1960, 2nd edn 1995; Herman the Loser, 1961; The Song in My Drum, 1962; London Men and English Men, 1963; Some Snow Said Hello, 1963; A Baby Sister for Frances, 1964, 2nd edn 1993; Nothing To Do, 1964; Bread and Jam for Frances, 1964, 2nd edn 1993; The Sorely Trying Day, 1964; Tom and the Two Handles, 1965; The Story of Hester Mouse, 1965; What Happened When Jack and Daisy Tried To Fool the Tooth Fairies, 1965; Goodnight, 1966; Henry and the Monstrous Din, 1966; Charlie the Tramp, 1966; The Little Brute Family, 1966; Save My Place, 1967; The Mouse and His Child, 1967 (filmed, 1977); The Stone Doll of Sister Brute, 1968; A Birthday for Frances, 1968, 2nd edn 1995; Ugly Bird, 1969; Best Friends for Frances, 1969, 2nd edn 1994; Harvey's Hideout, 1969; The Mole Family's Christmas, 1969; A Bargain for Frances, 1970, 2nd edn 1992; Emmet Otter's Jug-Band Christmas, 1971 (filmed for TV, 1977); The Sea-Thing Child, 1972, rev. edn 1999; Letitia Rabbit's String Song, 1973; How Tom Beat Captain Najork and His Hired Sportsmen, 1974 (Whitbread Literary Award); Ten What?, 1974; Dinner at Alberta's, 1975; Crocodile and Pierrot, 1975; A Near Thing for Captain Najork, 1975; The Twenty-Elephant Restaurant, 1977; Arthur's New Power, 1978; The Dancing Tigers, 1979; La Corona and Other Tin Tales, 1979; Ace Dragon Ltd, 1980; Flat Cat, 1980; The Serpent Tower, 1981; The Great Fruit Gum Robbery, 1981; They Came from Aargh!, 1981; The Flight of Bembel Rudzuk, 1982; The Battle of Zormla, 1982; Jim Frog, 1983; Big John Turkle, 1983; Charlie Meadows, 1984; Lavinia Bat, 1984; The Rain Door, 1986; The Marzipan Pig, 1986; Ponders, 1988; Monsters, 1989; Jim Hedgehog's Supernatural Christmas, 1989; Jim Hedgehog and the Lonesome Tower, 1990; M.O.L.E. (Much Overworked Little Earthmover), 1993; The Court of the Winged Serpent, 1994; Monster Film, 1995; Trouble on Thunder Mountain, 1998; Jim's Lion, 2001; *novels:* The Lion of Boaz-Jachin and Jachin-Boaz, 1973; Kleinzeit, 1974; Turtle Diary, 1975 (filmed, 1985); Riddley Walker, 1980 (John W. Campbell Meml Award, 1981, Best Internat. Fiction, Aust. Sci. Fiction Achievement Award, 1983; adapted for stage, 1986); Pilgermann, 1983; The Medusa Frequency, 1987; Fremder, 1996; The Trokeville Way, 1996; Mr Rinyo-Clacton's Offer, 1998; Angelica's Grotto, 1999; Amaryllis Night and Day, 2001; *verse:* The Pedalling Man and Other Poems, 1968, 2nd edn 1991; Egg Thoughts and Other Frances Songs, 1972, 2nd edn 1994; (contrib.) Six of the Best (ed A. Harvey), 1989; The Last of the Wallendas and Other Poems, 1997; *anthology:* The Moment Under the Moment, 1992; stories and essays in Fiction Magazine and Granta; *films:* (also narrated): Deadsy, 1989; Door, 1989. *Recreation:* rewriting yesterday's pages. *Address:* David Higham Associates Ltd, 5–8 Lower John Street, Golden Square, W1R 4HA. *T:* (020) 7437 7888, *Fax:* (020) 7437 1072.

HOBART (Australia), Archbishop of, (RC), since 1999; **Most Rev. Adrian Leo Doyle;** *b* 16 Nov. 1936; *s* of George Leo Doyle and Gertrude Mary (*née* O'Donnell). *Educ:* Urbaniana Univ., Rome (ThL, PhL); Gregorian Univ., Rome (DCL). Ordained priest, Rome, 1961; Parish Priest, Sandy Bay, Tasmania, 1974–90; VG, Archdio. of Hobart, 1997–99; apptd Coadjutor Archbishop of Hobart, 1997, ordained bishop, 1998. Judge: Regl Marriage Tribunal, Victoria and Tasmania, 1968–; Nat. Appeal Tribunal, Aust. and NZ, 1974–. *Recreations:* golf, walking, reading. *Address:* GPO Box 62, Hobart, Tas 7001, Australia. *T:* (3) 62251920. *Club:* Athenæum (Hobart).

HOBART, Sir John Vere, 4th Bt *cr* 1914, of Langdown, Co. Southampton; *b* 9 April 1945; *s* of Lt-Comdr Sir Robert Hampden Hobart, 3rd Bt, RN and Sylvia (*d* 1965), *d* of Harry Argo; *heir-pres.* to Earl of Buckinghamshire, *qv*; *S* father, 1988; *m* 1980, Kate, *o d* of late George Henry Iddles; two *s*. *Heir: s* George Hampden Hobart; *b* 10 June 1982. *Address:* 63 Queens Road, Cowes, Isle of Wight PO31 8BW.

HOBART-HAMPDEN, family name of **Earl of Buckinghamshire**.

HOBBS, Prof. (Frederick David) Richard, FRCGP; Professor and Head of Department of Primary Care and General Practice, since 1992, and Head of Division of Primary Care, Public and Occupational Health, since 1998, University of Birmingham; *b* 2 Nov. 1953; *s* of Frederick Derek Hobbs and Nancy Elizabeth (*née* Wilde); *m* 1977, Jane Marilyn Porter; one *s* one *d*. *Educ:* King Edward VI Camp Hill Sch., Birmingham; Bristol Univ. (MB, ChB 1977). MRCGP 1981, FRCGP 1990. House officer posts, Bath Royal United Hosp., 1977–78; Sen. house officer posts, Selly Oak Hosp., Birmingham, 1978–80; GP trainee, Univ. Health Centre, Birmingham, 1980–81; Principal in general practice, Bellevue Med. Centre, Birmingham, 1981– (part-time, 1992–); Birmingham University: part-time Sen. Lectr in General Practice, 1985–92; Asst Dean, Sch. of Medicine, 1993–96. *Publications:* (with M. Drury) Treatment and Prognosis in General Practice, 1990; (with B. Stillwell): Nursing in general practice, 1990; Practice Nurse Programme, 1990; (with M. Barrowcliffe) Managing Practice Information, 1992; (with L. Beeley) Treatment: a handbook of drug therapy, 1993; (with C. Bradley) Prescribing in Primary Care, 1998; over 300 research contribs to learned jls incl. Lancet, BMJ, Brit. Jl Gen. Pract., Family Practice, Brit. Jl Cardiol., Gut, Jl RSM. *Recreations:* gardening, travel, interests in music (passive), wine and good food. *Address:* Department of Primary Care and General Practice, Medical School, University of Birmingham, Edgbaston, Birmingham B15 2TT. *T:* (0121) 414 6764.

HOBBS, Herbert Harry, CB 1956; CVO 1972; Director, Ancient Monuments and Historic Buildings, 1970–72, retired; *b* 7 Nov. 1912; *s* of late Bertie Hobbs and Agnes Dora (*née* Clarke); *m* 1937, Joan Hazel Timmins (*d* 1979); two *s* one *d*. *Educ:* Bedford Sch.; Corpus Christi Coll., Oxford. Entered War Office, 1935; Comptroller of Lands and Claims, 1956–60; Asst Under-Sec. of State (Works), War Office, 1960–63; Under-Sec., MPBW, later DoE, 1963–72. Medal of Freedom with bronze palm (USA), 1946. *Recreation:* music. *Address:* Blenheim Lodge Residential Home, North Road, Minehead, Somerset TA24 5QB. *T:* (01643) 705350.

HOBBS, Jennifer Lynn, MBE 1992; Principal, St Mary's College, since 1999, and Director, International Office, since 1992, University of Durham; *b* 5 March 1944; *d* of Henry Edwin Hobbs and Jean Hobbs (*née* Kennedy). *Educ:* St Paul's Girls' Sch., London; Newnham Coll., Cambridge (BA (Hons) Geog 1966; MA 1970). VSO teacher, Malacca Girls' High Sch., Malaysia, 1966–68; Geography Editor, Overseas Educ. Dept, Macmillan Education, 1968–73; British Council, 1973–94: various posts in UK; Nepal, 1979–83; Yugoslavia/Croatia, 1988–92; on secondment, Univ. of Durham, 1992–94. *Recreations:* singing, playing piano and clarinet, classical music, various sports, walking, birdwatching, gardening. *Address:* St Mary's College, University of Durham, Elvet Hill Road, Durham DH1 3LR. *T:* (0191) 374 7119. *Club:* Royal Commonwealth Society.

HOBBS, John Charles; Chief Insurance Officer, Department of Health and Social Security, 1971–76; *b* 28 May 1917; British; *m* 1961, Doris Gronow. *Educ:* Portsmouth Southern Grammar Sch.; Portsmouth Coll. of Technology. 1st cl. hons BSc, 1936; 1st cl. hons BSc (Spec.) Maths, 1944. FIS 1950. Asst Principal, 1946; Principal, 1947; Asst Sec., 1957.

HOBBS, Prof. Kenneth Edward Frederick, ChM, FRCS; Professor of Surgery, Royal Free Hospital School of Medicine, University of London, and Consultant Surgeon, Royal Free Hampstead NHS Trust (formerly Royal Free Hospital), 1973–98, then Emeritus Professor; Chairman, Joint Board of Surgery, University College London Medical School and Royal Free Hospital School of Medicine, 1993–98; Dean, University of London Faculty of Medicine, 1994–98; *b* 28 Dec. 1936; *s* of late Thomas Edward Ernest Hobbs and Gladys May Hobbs (*née* Neave). *Educ:* West Suffolk County Grammar Sch., Bury St Edmunds; Guy's Hosp. Med. Sch., Univ. of London (MB BS 1960). ChM Bristol 1970; FRCS 1964. Lectr in Surgery, Univ. of Bristol, 1966–70; Surgical Res. Fellow, Harvard Univ., 1968–69; Sen. Lectr in Surgery, Univ. of Bristol, 1970–73; University of London: Vice-Dean, Faculty of Medicine, 1986–90; Mem. Senate, then Council, 1985–98; Chm., Acad. Adv. Bd in Medicine, 1986–90; Dep. Chm., Acad. Council Standing Sub-Cttee in Medicine, 1986–90. Mem., Systems Bd, MRC, 1982–86; Chm., Grants Cttee A, MRC, 1984–86; Member: Med. Sub-Cttee, UGC, 1986–89; Med. Cttee, UFC, 1991–92; GMC, 1996– (Dep. Chm., Professional Conduct Cttee, 1999–); Mason Med. Res. Foundn, 1988– (Chm., 1993–). Vis. Prof., Univs in China, Ethiopia, S Africa, Europe, USA, West Indies. Secretary: Patey Soc., 1979–82; 1942 Club, 1985–88; Trustee and Bd Mem., Stanley Thomas Johnson Foundn, Berne, 1976– (Chm., 1997–). FRSocMed 1973. *Publications:* chapters on aspects of liver surgery in textbooks; contribs to professional jls. *Recreations:* gourmet dining, the countryside. *Address:* The Rookery, New Buckenham, Norfolk NR16 2AE. *T:* (01953) 860558. *Club:* Royal Society of Medicine.

HOBBS, Maj.-Gen. Sir Michael (Frederick), KCVO 1998; CBE 1982 (OBE 1979; MBE 1975); Governor, Military Knights of Windsor, since 2000; Director, Outward Bound Trust, since 1995; *b* 28 Feb. 1937; *s* of late Brig. Godfrey Pennington Hobbs and Elizabeth Constance Mary Hobbs; *m* 1967, Tessa Mary Churchill; one *s* two *d*. *Educ:* Eton College. Served Grenadier Guards, 1956–80; Directing Staff, Staff Coll., 1974–77; MoD, 1980–82; Commander 39 Inf. Bde, 1982–84; Dir of PR (Army), 1984–85; Commander, 4th Armoured Div., 1985–87; retired. Dir, Duke of Edinburgh's Award, 1988–98. *Address:* Mary Tudor Tower, Windsor Castle, Windsor, Berks SL4 1NJ. *T:* (01753) 850802.

HOBBS, Peter Thomas Goddard; HM first lay Inspector of Constabulary, 1993–98; *b* 19 March 1938; *s* of late Reginald Stanley Hobbs, BEM, Gloucester and of Phyllis Gwendoline (*née* Goddard); *m* 1964, Victoria Christabel, *d* of late Rev. Alan Matheson, Clifton Campville, Staffs; one *d*. *Educ:* Crypt Sch., Glos; Exeter Coll., Oxford (Waugh Scholar; MA). Nat. Service, 2nd Lt, RASC, 1957–59; Capt., RCT, TA, 1959–68. With ICI Ltd, 1962–79 (Jt Personnel Manager, Mond Div.); Gp Personnel Dir, Wellcome Foundn and Wellcome PLC, 1979–92. Chemical Industries Association: Dep. Chm., Pharmaceuticals and Fine Chemical Jt Industrial Council, 1979–89; Chairman: Trng Cttee, 1985–89; Employment Affairs Bd, 1989–91; Mem. Council, 1989–92; Chm., Chem. Industry Educn Centre, Univ. of York, 1992–94. Dir, Employment Conditions Abroad Ltd, 1984–91 and 1993. Confederation of British Industry: Member: Task Force on Vocational Educn and Trng, 1989–90; Educn and Trng Cttee, 1990–94; Business in the Community: Member, Target Team: for Industrial/Educn Partnerships, 1988–90; for Priority Hiring, 1988–91; Founder Chm., Employers' Forum on Disability, 1986–93; Member: Nat. Adv. Council on Employment for People with Disabilities, 1991–93; Learning from Experience Trust, 1988– (Chm., 1992–93 and 1998–). Member: Council, Contemporary Applied Arts, 1990–92; Industry Adv. Gp, Nat. Curriculum Council, 1990–92; Personnel Standards Lead Body, 1992–94; Council, EDEXCEL (formerly BTEC), 1995–98. Non-exec. Dir, Forensic Sci. Service, 1996–. Director: and Dep. Chm., Roffey Park Inst., 1989–93; Centre for Enterprise, London Business Sch., 1989–92; Mem. Adv. Council, Mgt Centre Europe, Brussels, 1989–97. CIPD 1988 (Internat. Vice Pres., 1987–89, 1990–91); FInstD 1989 (Mem., Employment Cttee, 1989–93); FRSA 1992. Dr *hc* IMC, 2000. *Recreations:* history, topography, opera, turning the soil. *Address:* 105 Blenheim Crescent, W11 2EQ. *T:* (020) 7727 3054, *Fax:* (020) 7221 9542. *Club:* Oxford and Cambridge.

HOBBS, Richard; *see* Hobbs, F. D. R.

HOBBS, Prof. Roger Edwin, PhD, DSc; FIStructE, FICE; Professor of Engineering Structures, Imperial College of Science, Technology and Medicine, London, since 1990; *b* 24 Feb. 1943; *s* of Edwin Daniel Hobbs and Phyllis Eileen (*née* Chapman); *m* 1st, 1965, Barbara Ann Dalton (*d* 1987); one *s* two *d*; 2nd, 1989, Dorinda Elizabeth Mitchell. *Educ:* Imperial Coll., London (PhD 1966; DSc Eng 1996). FIStructE 1990; FICE 1995; FCGI 1996. Imperial College, London: Res. Asst, 1966–70; Lectr in Civil Engrg, 1970–83; Sen. Lectr, 1983–86; Reader in Structural Engrg, 1986–90; Hd, Dept of Civil Engrg, 1994–97. *Publications:* technical papers on steel structures, wire and high strength fibre ropes, offshore pipelines. *Recreations:* walking, France, preferably in combination. *Address:* Civil Engineering Department, Imperial College of Science, Technology and Medicine, University of London, SW7 2BU. *T:* (020) 7594 6043.

HOBDAY, Sir Gordon (Ivan), Kt 1979; Lord Lieutenant and Keeper of the Rolls for Nottinghamshire, 1983–91; Chancellor, Nottingham University, 1979–92 (President of the Council, 1973–82); *b* 1 Feb. 1916; *e s* of late Alexander Thomas Hobday and Frances Cassandra (*née* Meads); *m* 1940, Margaret Jean Joule (*d* 1995); one *d*. *Educ:* Long Eaton Grammar Sch.; UC Nottingham. BSc, PhD London; FRSC. Joined Boots Co., 1939; Dir of Research, 1952–68; Man. Dir, 1970–72; Chm., 1973–81; Chm., Central Independent Television, 1981–85; Dir, Lloyds Bank, 1981–86. A Dep. Chm., Price Commn, 1977–78. Pres., Portland Trng Coll., 1990–93. DL Notts, 1981. KStJ 1983. Hon. LLD Nottingham, 1977. *Recreations:* handicrafts, gardening. *Address:* Newstead Abbey Park, Nottingham NG15 8GD.

HOBDAY, Peter James; journalist and broadcaster; *b* 16 Feb. 1937; *s* of Arthur John Hobday and Dorothy Ann Hobday (*née* Lewis); *m* 1st, 1959, Tamara Batcharnikoff (*d* 1984); one *s* one *d*; 2nd, 1996, Victoria Fenwick. *Educ:* St Chad's Coll., Wolverhampton; Leicester Univ. Wolverhampton Express and Star, 1960; Business magazine, 1960–61; The Director, 1961–74; joined BBC, 1970: World Service, 1970–74; Financial World Tonight, 1974–80, Moneybox, 1977–80, Radio 4; Money Programme, 1979–80, Newsnight, 1980–82, BBC TV; Today programme, Radio 4, 1982–96; Masterworks, Radio 3, 1996–2000. Hon. Dr de Montfort, 1996. *Publications:* Man the Industrialist, 1970; Saudi Arabia Today, 1974; In the Valley of the Fireflies, 1995; Managing the Message, 2000. *Recreations:* growing olives in Italy, drinking Umbrian wine, reading, music. *Address:* 67 Highlever Road, W10 6PR. *Clubs:* Athenæum, Royal Automobile.

HOBDEN, Reginald Herbert, DFC 1944; HM Diplomatic Service, retired; *b* 9 Nov. 1919; *s* of William Richard and Ada Emily Hobden; *m* 1945, Gwendoline Ilma Vowles; two *s* one *d*. *Educ:* Sir William Borlase's Sch., Marlow. Apptd Colonial Office, Dec. 1936. Served War of 1939–45 (despatches, DFC): RAFVR, Sept. 1940–Jan. 1946 (Sqdn Ldr). Returned to Colonial Office, 1946; seconded to Dept of Technical Co-operation, 1961; First Sec., UK Commn, Malta, 1962–64; HM Diplomatic Service, Nov. 1964: CRO until April 1968; Head of British Interests Section, Canadian High Commn, Dar es Salaam, April 1968; British Acting High Comr, Dar es Salaam, July-Oct. 1968, and Counsellor, Dar es Salaam, Oct. 1968–69; Counsellor (Economic and Commercial), Islamabad, 1970–75; Inst. of Develt Studies, Sussex Univ., 1975; High Comr, Lesotho, 1976–78. Clerk in Clerk's Dept, House of Commons, 1978–84. *Recreations:* chess, bridge. *Address:* 14 Belmont Close, Uxbridge, Mddx UB8 1RF. *T:* (01895) 234754.

HOBHOUSE OF WOODBOROUGH, Baron *cr* 1998 (Life Peer), of Woodborough in the co. of Wiltshire; **John Stewart Hobhouse,** Kt 1982; PC 1993; a Lord of Appeal in Ordinary, since 1998; *b* 31 Jan. 1932. *Educ:* Christ Church, Oxford (BCL 1958; MA 1958). Called to the Bar, Inner Temple, 1955; QC 1973; a Judge of the High Court, Queen's Bench Div., 1982–93; a Lord Justice of Appeal, 1993–98. *Address:* House of Lords, SW1A 0PW.

HOBHOUSE, Sir Charles (John Spinney), 7th Bt *cr* 1812, of Broughton-Gifford, Bradford-on-Avon and of Monkton Farleigh, Wiltshire; *b* 27 Oct. 1962; *s* of Sir Charles Chisholm Hobhouse, 6th Bt, TD and of Elspeth Jean, *yr d* of late Thomas George Spinney; *S* father, 1991; *m* 1993, Katrina (marr. diss. 1997), *d* of Maj.-Gen. Sir Denzil Macarthur-Onslow, CBE, DSO and of Lady Macarthur-Onslow. *Recreations:* sport, travel. *Heir: uncle* John Spencer Hobhouse [*b* 15 Nov. 1910; *m* 1940, Mary, *yr d* of late Llewelyn Robert, MD]. *Address:* Monkton Farleigh Manor, Bradford-on-Avon, Wilts BA15 2QE.

HOBHOUSE, (Mary) Hermione, MBE 1981; FSA; writer and conservationist; General Editor, Survey of London, 1983–94; *d* of late Sir Arthur Lawrence Hobhouse and Konradin, *d* of Rt Hon. Frederick Huth Jackson; *m* 1958, Henry Trevenen Davidson Graham (marr. diss. 1988); one *s* one *d*. *Educ:* Ladies' Coll., Cheltenham; Lady Margaret Hall, Oxford (Hons Mod. Hist.). Researcher/Writer, Associated-Rediffusion TV and Granada TV, 1957–65; Tutor in Architectural History, Architectural Assoc. Sch., London, 1973–78; Sec., Victorian Soc., 1977–82. Member: Royal Commn for Exhibn of 1851, 1983–98; Council, Nat. Trust, 1983–; Council, Soc. of Antiquaries, 1984–87; London DAC, 1988–92; Council, Royal Albert Hall, 1988–. *Publications:* Thomas Cubitt: Master Builder, 1971 (Hitchcock Medal, 1972); Lost London, 1971; History of Regent Street, 1975; Oxford and Cambridge, 1980; Prince Albert: his life and work, 1983; (ed) Survey of London, vol. 42, Southern Kensington: Kensington Square to Earls Court, 1986, vol. 17, County Hall, 1991, vols 42 and 43, Poplar, Blackwall and the Isle of Dogs, 1994; London Survey'd: the work of the Survey of London 1894–1994, 1994; The Crystal Palace and the Great Exhbition, Art, Science and Productive Industry: the history of the Royal Commission for the Great Exhibition of 1851; contrib. Architectural Jl, Architectural Review. *Recreations:* gardening, looking at buildings of all periods. *Address:* Westcombe Stables, Evercreech, Shepton Mallet, Somerset BA4 6ES. *T:* (01749) 830465. *Club:* Reform.

HOBHOUSE, Penelope, (Mrs John Malins); gardener, garden writer and garden consultant, since 1976; *b* 20 Nov. 1929; *d* of late Captain J. J. L.-C. Chichester-Clark, DSO and Bar, MP and Marion Chichester-Clark (later Mrs C. E. Brackenbury); *m* 1st, 1952, Paul Hobhouse (marr. diss. 1982; he *d* 1994); two *s* one *d*; 2nd, 1983, Prof. John Malins (*d* 1992). *Educ:* Girton Coll., Cambridge (BA Hons Econs, 1951). National Trust tenant of Tintinhull House garden, 1980–93. VMH 1996. *Publications:* The Country Gardener, 1976, revd edn 1989; The Smaller Garden, 1981; Gertrude Jekyll on Gardening, 1983; Colour in your Garden, 1985; The National Trust: A Book of Gardening, 1986; Private Gardens of England, 1986; Garden Style, 1988; Painted Gardens,

1988; Borders, 1989; The Gardens of Europe, 1990; Flower Gardens, 1991; Plants in Garden History, 1992; Penelope Hobhouse on Gardening, 1994; Penelope Hobhouse's Garden Designs, 1997; Penelope Hobhouse's Natural Planting, 1997; A Gardener's Journal, 1997; Gardens of Italy, 1998. *Recreations:* reading Trollope and Henry James, Italy. *Address:* The Coach House, Bettiscombe, Bridport, Dorset DT6 5NT.

See also Sir R. Chichester-Clark, Baron Moyola.

HOBKIRK, Michael Dalgliesh; *b* 9 Dec. 1924; *s* of Roy and Phyllis Hobkirk; *m* 1952, Lucy Preble; two *d. Educ:* Marlborough Coll.; Wadham Coll., Oxford. BA (Social Studies), MA 1949. Served War of 1939–45: Army (RAC, RAEC, Captain), 1943–47. Civil Service: War Office, 1949–63; MoD, 1963–70; Directing Staff, Nat. Defence Coll., 1970–74; Brookings Instn, Washington, DC, USA, 1974–75; Lord Chancellor's Dept, 1975–80 (Principal Establishment and Finance Officer, 1977–80); Asst Under-Sec. of State, MoD, 1980–82. Sen. Fellow, Nat. Defense Univ., Washington, DC, USA, 1982–83. *Publication:* (contrib.) The Management of Defence (ed L. Martin), 1976; The Politics of Defence Budgeting, 1984; Land, Sea or Air?, 1992. *Address:* 48 Woodside Avenue, Beaconsfield, Bucks HP9 1JH. *Club:* Oxford and Cambridge.

HOBLEY, Brian, FSA; historical and archaeological researcher and writer; Director, Hobley Archaeological Consultancy Services Ltd, 1989–92; *b* 25 June 1930; *s* of William Hobley and Harriet (*née* Hobson); *m* (marr. diss. 1992); one *s* one *d*; partner, Dr Elizabeth Greene. *Educ:* Univ. of Leicester (BA Hons 1965); Univ. of Oxford (MSt 1994). FSA 1969; AMA 1970. Field Officer, Coventry Corp., 1965; Keeper, Dept Field Archaeology, Coventry Museum, 1970; Chief Urban Archaeologist, City of London, 1973–89. Lectr, Birmingham Univ. Extra-mural Dept, 1965–74. Chm. Standing Cttee, Arch. Unit Managers, 1986–89; Jt Sec., British Archaeologists and Developers Liaison Gp, 1986–89. MIMgt (MBIM 1978); MIFA 1982. *Publications:* (ed jtly) Waterfront Archaeology in Britain and Northern Europe, 1981; Roman Urban Defences in the West, 1983; Roman Urban Topography in Britain and the Western Empire, 1985; Roman and Saxon London: a reappraisal, 1986; British Archaeologists and Developers Code of Practice, 1986; The Rebirth of Towns in the West AD 700–1050, 1988; reports in learned jls incl. Proc. 7th, 8th, 9th and 12th Internat. Congresses of Roman Frontier Studies, Tel Aviv, Univ. Israel and Bucharest Univ., Rumania on excavations and reconstructions at The Lunt Roman fort, Baginton near Coventry. *Recreations:* classical music, chess. *Address:* 16 Basildon Court, 28 Devonshire Street, W1G 6PP.

HOBMAN, David Burton, CBE 1983; Director, Age Concern England (National Old People's Welfare Council), 1970–87; *b* 8 June 1927; *s* of J. B. and D. L. Hobman; *m* 1954, Erica Irwin; one *s* one *d. Educ:* University College Sch.; Blundell's. Community work, Forest of Dean, 1954–56; British Council for Aid to Refugees, 1957; Nat. Council of Social Service, 1958–67; Visiting Lectr in Social Admin, Nat. Inst. for Social Work, 1967; Dir, Social Work Adv. Service, 1968–70. Vis. Prof., Sch. of Social Work, McGill Univ., Montreal, 1977; Vis. Fellow, Univ. of Sussex, 1994–97. Member: BBC/ITA Appeals Adv. Council, 1965–69; Steering Cttee, Enquiry into Homelessness, Nat. Asstce Bd, 1967–68; Adv. Council, Nat. Corp. for Care of Old People, 1970–74; Metrication Bd, 1974–80; Lord Goodman's Cttee Reviewing Law of Charity, 1975–76; Chairman: Social Welfare Commn Conf. of Bishops, 1968–71; Family Housing Assoc., 1969–70; Oftel Adv. Cttee for Disabled and Elderly Persons, 1984–92; Home Concern Housing Assoc., 1985–87; Jt Chm., Age Concern Inst. of Gerontology, KCL, 1986–87; Consultant, UN Div. of Social Affairs, 1968–69; Observer, White House Congress on Ageing, 1971–; Pres., Internat. Fedn on Ageing, 1977–80, 1983–87 (Vice-Pres., 1974–77); Member: Personal Social Services Council, 1978–80; Exec. Cttee, Nat. Council of Voluntary Orgns, 1981–83; Anchor Housing, 1984–86; Exec. Sec., Charities Effectiveness Review Trust, 1987–92. Producer, Getting On (television programme), 1987–88. Special Advr, British delegn to World Assembly on Ageing, 1982. Mem. Adv. Bd, Saga Magazine, 1985–98; Dir, Cinetel Ltd. Governor: Newman Comp. Sch., Hove, 1971–76 (Chm.); Volunteer Centre, 1975–79; Conciliator, Sheltered Housing Adv. and Conciliation Service, 1990–94; Counsellor, Helen Hamlyn Foundn, 1991–98; Company Ombudsman, Peverel Gp, 1995–. President's Medal, British Geriatrics Soc., 1998. KSG. *Publications:* A Guide to Voluntary Service, 1964, 2nd edn 1967; Who Cares, 1971; The Social Challenge of Ageing, 1978; The Impact of Ageing, 1981; The Coming of Age, 1989; Planning Your Retirement, 1990; Intergenerational Solidarity—fact and fiction, 1993; The More We Are Together: a study of partnerships in later life, 1995; numerous papers, broadcasts. *Recreations:* reading, writing, grandchildren. *Address:* Robinswood, George's Lane, Storrington, Pulborough, W Sussex RH20 3JH. *T:* (01903) 742987.

HOBSBAWM, Prof. Eric John Ernest, CH 1998; FBA 1976; Emeritus Professor of Economic and Social History, University of London, since 1982; *b* 9 June 1917; *s* of Leopold Percy Hobsbawm and Nelly Grün; *m* 1962, Marlene Schwarz; one *s* one *d. Educ:* Vienna; Berlin; St Marylebone Grammar Sch.; Univ. of Cambridge (BA, PhD). Lectr, Birkbeck Coll., 1947; Fellow, King's Coll., Cambridge, 1949–55, Hon. Fellow, 1973; Reader, Birkbeck Coll., 1959, Prof., 1970–82. Hon. DPhil Univ. of Stockholm, 1970; Hon. DHL: Univ. of Chicago, 1976; New Sch. of Social Res., 1982; Bard Coll., 1986; Hon. LittD: UEA, 1982; York Univ., Canada, 1986; Columbia, 1997; Oxon, 2001; Hon. DLit London, 1993; DU Essex, 1996; *Dhc:* Univ. of Pisa, 1987; Univ. of Buenos Aires, 1998; Universidad de Artes e Ciencias Sociales, Santiago de Chile, 1998; Univ. of the Republic, Montevideo, 1999; Univ. of Turin, 2000. Foreign Hon. Mem., American Academy of Arts and Sciences, 1971; Hon. Mem., Hungarian Acad. of Sciences, 1979. Palmes Académiques, France, 1993; Comdr, Order of Southern Cross (Brazil), 1996. *Publications:* Labour's Turning Point, 1948; Primitive Rebels, 1959; (*pseud.* F. Newton) The Jazz Scene, 1959; The Age of Revolution, 1962; Labouring Men, 1964; (ed) Karl Marx, Precapitalist Formations, 1964; Industry and Empire, 1968; (with G. Rudé) Captain Swing, 1969; Bandits, 1969; Revolutionaries, 1973; The Age of Capital, 1975; (with T. Ranger) The Invention of Tradition, 1983; Worlds of Labour, 1984; The Age of Empire, 1987; Politics for a Rational Left, 1989; Nations and Nationalism since 1780, 1990; Echoes of the Marseillaise, 1990; Age of Extremes: the short Twentieth Century, 1994; On History, 1997; Uncommon People: resistance, rebellion and jazz, 1998; (with A. Polito) The New Century, 2000; contribs to jls. *Recreation:* travel. *Address:* Birkbeck College, Malet Street, WC1E 7HX. *T:* (020) 7580 6622.

See also J. N. Hobsbawm.

HOBSBAWM, Julia Nathalie; Chief Executive, Hobsbawm Macaulay Communications Ltd, since 2001 (Chair, 1993–2001); *b* 15 Aug. 1964; *d* of Prof. Eric John Ernest Hobsbawm, *qv* and Marlene (*née* Schwarz); partner, Alaric Bamping; one *s* one *d. Educ:* Camden Sch. for Girls; Poly. of Central London. Asst, Martin Dunitz Med. Publrs, 1982; Publicity Officer, Penguin Books, 1983; Head of Publicity, Virago Press, 1985–87; Researcher: Books by my Bedside, Thames TV, 1987–89; Wogan, BBC, 1989–90; Forward Planning Editor, John Gau Productions, 1990–91; Fundraising Consultant, 1000 Club and High Value Donors, Labour Party, 1991–92; founded Julia Hobsbawm Associates, 1992, then, with Sarah Macaulay, Hobsbawm Macaulay Communications, 1993. *Publication:* (with Robert Gray) The Cosmopolitan Guide to Working in PR and Advertising, 1996. *Recreation:* conversation. *Address:* Hobsbawm Macaulay Communications Ltd, Cavendish House, 51–55 Mortimer Street, W1W 8HP. *T:* (020) 7612 1555. *Clubs:* Groucho, Soho House.

HOBSLEY, Prof. Michael, TD 1969; PhD; FRCS; David Patey Professor of Surgery, University of London, 1986–94 (Professor of Surgery, 1984–94), now Emeritus Professor; Head, Department of Surgery, University College and Middlesex School of Medicine, University College London, 1984–93; *b* 18 Jan. 1929; *s* of Henry Hobsley and Sarah Lily Blanchfield; *m* 1953, Jane Fairlie Cambell; one *s* three *d. Educ:* La Martinière Coll., Calcutta; Sidney Sussex Coll., Cambridge (MA, MB, MChir); Middlesex Hosp. Med. Sch. PhD London, 1961; DSc London, 1989. FRCS 1958. Training posts in RAMC and at Middlesex, Whittington and Chace Farm Hosps, 1951–68; Comyns Berkeley Fellow, Gonville and Caius Coll., Cambridge and Mddx Hosp. Med. Sch., 1965–66; posts at Mddx Hosp. and Med. Sch., 1968–: Hon. Consultant Surgeon, 1969–; Reader in Surgical Science, 1970–75; Prof. of Surg. Science, 1975–83; Dir, Dept of Surgical Studies, 1983–88. Howard C. Naffziger Surg. Res. Fellow, Univ. of Calif, 1966; Windermere Foundn Travelling Prof. of Surgery, 1984; Glaxo Visitor, Univ. of Witwatersrand, 1985; Vis. Professor: Univ. of Calif, 1980; Univ. of Khartoum, 1976; McMaster Univ., 1982; Monash Univ., 1984; Univ. of Louisville, 1995. Non-exec. Mem., Enfield HA, 1990–93. Pres., British Soc. of Gastroenterology, 1992–93; Chm., Assoc. of Profs of Surgery, 1990–94. Royal College of Surgeons: Hunterian Prof., 1962–63; Penrose May Tutor, 1973–78; Sir Gordon Taylor Lectr, 1980; Examr, 1968–94. Examiner: Univ. of London, 1978–94; Univ. of Nigeria, 1977–94; Univ. of the WI, 1978–94; Univ. of Bristol, 1986–88; Univ. of Cambridge, 1986–94; St Mary's Hosp. Med. Sch., 1989–91; St George's Hosp. Med. Sch., 1990–93; Univ. of Birmingham, 1992–94; Univ. of Newcastle, 1992–94. Mem., Professional and Linguistics Assessment Bd and Chm., Multiple Choice Questions Panel, 1993–97; Trustee, and Chm. Academic Council, Inst. of Sports Medicine, 1995–. Hon. Fellow: Assoc. of Surgeons of India, 1983; Amer. Surgical Assoc., 1989. FRSocMed 1960. *Publications:* Pathways in Surgical Management, 1979, 2nd edn 1986; Disorders of the Digestive System, 1982; Colour Atlas of Parotidectomy, 1983; Physiology in Surgical Practice, 1992; articles in BMJ, Lancet, British Jl of Surgery, Gut, Klinische Wochenschrift. *Recreation:* cricket. *Address:* Fieldside, Barnet Lane, Totteridge, N20 8AS. *T:* (020) 8445 6507. *Clubs:* Athenæum, MCC.

HOBSON, Anthony Robert Alwyn, DLitt; FBA 1992; bibliographical historian; *b* 5 Sept. 1921; *s* of Geoffrey Dudley Hobson, MVO and Gertrude Adelaide, *d* of Rev. Thomas Vaughan, Rector of Rhuddlan, Flintshire; *m* 1959, Elena Pauline Tanya (*d* 1988), *d* of Igor Vinogradoff; one *s* two *d. Educ:* Eton Coll. (Oppidan Scholar); New Coll., Oxford (MA); DLitt Oxon, 1992. Served Scots Guards, 1941–46, Captain; Italy, 1943–46 (mentioned in despatches). Joined Sotheby & Co., 1947: Dir, 1949–71, Associate, 1971–77. Sandars Reader in Bibliography, Univ. of Cambridge, 1974–75; Franklin Jasper Walls Lectr, Pierpont Morgan Library, NY, 1979; Vis. Fellow, All Souls Coll., Oxford, 1982–83; Rosenbach Fellow, Univ. of Pennsylvania, 1990; Lyell Reader in Bibliography, Univ. of Oxford, 1990–91. President: Bibliographical Soc., 1977–79; Association internationale de Bibliophilie, 1985–99; Hon. Pres., Edinburgh Bibliographical Soc., 1971–; Trustee: Eton Coll. Collections Trust, 1977–97; Lambeth Palace Library, 1984–90. Hon. Fellow, Pierpont Morgan Library, 1983–; For. Associate, Ateneo Veneto, 1987–. Cavaliere Ufficiale, Al Merito della Repubblica Italiana, 1979. *Publications:* French and Italian Collectors and their Bindings, 1953; Great Libraries, 1970; Apollo and Pegasus, 1975; Humanists and Bookbinders, 1989 (Premio Felice Feliciano, Verona, 1991; Triennial Prize, Internat. League of Antiquarian Booksellers, 1991); (with Paul Culot) Italian and French Sixteenth-century Bookbindings, 1990; Renaissance Book Collecting: Jean Grolier and Diego Hurtado de Mendoza, their books and bindings, 1999; contrib. The Library, TLS, etc. *Recreations:* travel, opera, visiting libraries founded before 1800. *Address:* The Glebe House, Whitsbury, Fordingbridge, Hants SP6 3QB. *T:* (01725) 518221. *Clubs:* Brooks's, Beefsteak, Roxburghe; Grolier (New York); Société des Bibliophiles François (Paris).

HOBSON, David Constable, CBE 1991; Chartered Accountant; Partner, Coopers & Lybrand, 1953–84, Senior Partner, 1975–83; *b* 1 Nov. 1922; *s* of late Charles Kenneth and Eileen Isabel Hobson; *m* 1961, Elizabeth Anne Drury; one *s* one *d. Educ:* Marlborough Coll.; Christ's Coll., Cambridge (Scholar). MA. ACA 1950; FCA 1958. Served War, REME, 1942–47 (Captain). Joined Cooper Brothers & Co. (later Coopers & Lybrand), 1947; Mem., Exec. Cttee, Coopers & Lybrand (International), 1973–83. Chairman: Cambrian & General Securities, 1986–89; Fleming High Income Investment Trust, 1991–93 (Dir, 1989–93); Dir, The Laird Gp, 1985–98. Inspector (for Dept of Trade), London & County Securities Group Ltd, 1974; Advr, Prime Minister's Policy Unit, 1983–86. Member: Accounting Standards Cttee, 1970–82; City Capital Markets Cttee, 1980–84; Nat. Biological Standards Bd, 1983–88; Building Socs Commn, 1986–92; Board Mem. (repr. UK and Ireland), Internat. Accounting Standards Cttee, 1980–85. Hon. Treasurer, Lister Inst., 1986–98. Member of Council: Marlborough Coll., 1967–92 (Chm., 1987–92); Francis Holland Schools, 1975–95. *Recreations:* travel, gardening, reading, occasional golf. *Address:* Magnolia, Chiswick Mall, W4 2PR. *T:* (020) 8994 7511. *Club:* Reform.

HOBSON, John; Director, Construction Industry, Department of Trade and Industry, since 2001; *b* 30 March 1946; *s* of late John Leslie Hobson and of Beatrice Edith Hobson; *m* 1970, Jeanne Gerrish (marr. diss. 1996); one *s* one *d. Educ:* Northampton Grammar Sch.; Manchester Grammar Sch.; King's Coll., Cambridge (MA Mathematics). Joined Min. of Transport, 1967; Asst Private Sec. to Sec. of State for the Environment, 1970–72; Private Sec. to Head of CS, 1974–78; Assistant Secretary: Dept of Transport, 1979–80; DoE, 1980–86; Under-Sec., subseq. Dir, DoE, subseq. DETR, 1986–2001 (Dir of Construction, 1997–2001). *Address:* Department of Trade and Industry, Eland House, Bressenden Place, SW1E 5DU.

HOBSON, John Graham; QC 2000; a Recorder, since 2000; *b* 11 Feb. 1946; *s* of late John Herbert Hobson and Lilian May Hobson (*née* Mott); *m* 1976, Shirley June Palmer; one *s* one *d. Educ:* Monkton Combe Sch.; St John's Coll., Cambridge (LLM). Admitted Solicitor, 1968; Director: W Stepney Neighbourhood Law Centre, 1973–75; Southwark Law Project, 1975–80; called to the Bar, Inner Temple, 1980; Supplementary Panel of Counsel to Treasury, 1992–2000; Standing Counsel to Rent Assessment Panel, 1997–2000; Asst Recorder, 1999–2000. Special Advr, NI Affairs Cttee for Enquiry into Planning System in NI, H of C, 1995–96. *Recreations:* playing the 'cello, rowing, fishing, watching football. *Address:* 4–5 Gray's Inn Square, Gray's Inn, WC1R 5JP. *Clubs:* London Rowing; Christchurch Angling.

HOBSON, Prof. Marian Elizabeth, FBA 1999; Professor of French, Queen Mary and Westfield College, University of London, since 1992; *b* 10 Nov. 1941; *d* of Baron Hobson and Doris Mary Hobson; *m* 1968, Michel Jeanneret; one *s. Educ:* Newnham Coll., Cambridge. Asst Lectr in French, Univ. of Warwick, 1966–71; Maître-assistante, Univ. of Geneva, 1974–76; Fellow of Trinity Coll., Cambridge (first woman Fellow), 1977–92; Univ. Lectr, Univ. of Cambridge, 1985–92. Chevalier des palmes académiques (France),

1997. *Publications:* The Object of Art, 1982; Jacques Derrida: opening lines, 1998. *Address:* Department of French, Queen Mary and Westfield College, E1 4NS. *T:* (020) 7775 3372.

HOBSON, Peter; Chairman, Business Task Force, Objective One Partnership for Cornwall and Scilly, since 2000; *b* 2 Oct. 1944; *er s* of late William Hobson and Sheila (*née* Surtees); *m* 1976, Amanda Rosemary (marr. diss. 1997), *d* of Michael Thomas Emilius Clayton, CB, OBE. *Educ:* Rossall Sch.; Queen's Coll., Oxford (Fletcher Exhibnr; BA LitHum 1967; MA 1972). Wellington College: Classics Dept, 1968–86; Housemaster, 1971–86; Industrial Liaison Officer, 1978–86; Headmaster: Giggleswick Sch., 1986–93; Charterhouse, 1993–95. Chairman: ISIS N, 1991–93; ISIS London and SE, 1995. Schoolmaster Fellow, Queen's Coll., Oxford, 1982. *Recreations:* travel, life in Cornwall, reading biography, watching sport. *Address:* Chy-Pedyr, Commercial Road, St Keverne, Helston, Cornwall TR12 6LY.

HOCHHAUSER, Andrew Romain; QC 1997; FCIArb; *b* 16 March 1955; *s* of late Jerome Romain, MD, FRCSE and of Ruth Hochhauser. *Educ:* Highgate Sch.; Univ. of Bristol (LLB Hons); London Sch. of Econs (LLM Hons). FCIArb 1995. Called to the Bar, Middle Temple, 1977 (Harmsworth Scholar), Bencher, 2000. Part-time Mem., Law Faculty, LSE, 1979–86. *Recreations:* collecting paintings, swimming. *Address:* Essex Court Chambers, 24 Lincoln's Inn Fields, WC2A 3ED. *T:* (020) 7813 8000. *Club:* Reform.

HOCHHAUSER, Victor, CBE 1994; impresario; *b* 27 March 1923; *m* 1949, Lilian Hochhauser (*née* Shields); three *s* one *d*. *Educ:* City of London Coll. Impresario for: David Oistrakh; Sviatoslav Richter; Mstislav Rostropovich; Emil Gilels; Leonid Kogan; Margot Fonteyn; Natalia Makarova; Nureyev Festival; Bolshoi Ballet season at Covent Garden, 1963, 1969, 1999; Kirov Ballet, Royal Opera House, 1961, 1966, 2001; Kirov Ballet, 1993, 1995, 1997, 1998, 2000; Birmingham Royal Ballet, 1994–95; Royal Ballet season, London Coliseum, 1998; concerts, Royal Albert Hall, Barbican and Royal Festival Hall; Peking Opera and other Chinese companies, 1972–; presenter, Aida, Earls Court, 1988, Birmingham Arena, 1991. *Recreations:* reading, swimming, sleeping. *Address:* 4 Oak Hill Way, NW3 7LR. *T:* (020) 7794 0987.

HOCKADAY, Sir Arthur (Patrick), KCB 1978 (CB 1975); CMG 1969; Secretary and Director-General, Commonwealth War Graves Commission, 1982–89; *b* 17 March 1926; *s* of late William Ronald Hockaday and Marian Camilla Hockaday, *d* of Rev. A. C. Evans; *m* 1955, Peggy (*d* 1998), *d* of late H. W. Prince. *Educ:* Merchant Taylors' Sch.; St John's Coll., Oxford. BA (1st cl. Lit. Hum.) 1949, MA 1952. Apptd to Home Civil Service, 1949; Admty, 1949–62; Private Sec. to successive Ministers of Defence and Defence Secretaries, 1962–65; NATO Internat. Staff, 1965–69 (Asst Sec. Gen. for Defence Planning and Policy, 1967–69); Asst Under-Sec. of State, MoD, 1969–72; Under-Sec., Cabinet Office, 1972–73; Dep. Under-Sec. of State, MoD, 1973–76; 2nd Permanent Under-Sec. of State, MoD, 1976–82. Chm., British Group, Council on Christian Approaches to Defence and Disarmament, 1989–99. Chm., Gallipoli Meml Lecture Trust, 1990–93. *Publications:* (contrib.) Ethics and Nuclear Deterrence, 1982; The Strategic Defence Initiative, 1985; (contrib.) Ethics and European Security, 1986; (contrib.) Ethics and International Relations, 1986; (contrib.) Just Deterrence, 1990; (contrib.) The Crescent and the Cross, 1998; occasional articles and reviews. *Recreation:* fell-walking. *Address:* 11 Hitherwood Court, Hitherwood Drive, SE19 1UX. *T:* (020) 8670 7940. *Clubs:* Naval and Military, Civil Service.

HOCKÉ, Jean-Pierre; international consultant; United Nations High Commissioner for Refugees, 1986–89; *b* 31 March 1938; *s* of Charles and Marie Rose Hocké; *m* 1961, Michèle Marie Weber; two *s*. *Educ:* Univ. of Lausanne (grad. Econ. and Business Admin). With commercial firms in Switzerland and Nigeria, 1961–67; joined Internat. Cttee of Red Cross, 1968: Hd of Operations Dept, 1973; Mem., Directorate, 1981. Mem., Jean Monnet Foundn, Lausanne, 1984–; Vice-Chm., CASIN (internat. negotiations inst.), Geneva, 1986–; Chm., Bd, InterAssist, Bern, 1990–. Chm., Property Commn refugees and displaced, Bosnia, 1996–. Hon. Dr Lausanne, 1987. *Address:* 4 rue Amiral Duquesne, 1170 Aubonne, Switzerland. *T:* (21) 8088583; *e-mail:* hocke@sefanet.ch.

HOCKENHULL, Arthur James Weston, OBE 1966; HM Diplomatic Service, retired; *b* 8 Aug. 1915; *s* of late Frederick Weston Hockenhull and late Jessie Gibson Kaye Hockenhull (*née* Mitchell); *m* 1955, Rachel Ann Kimber; two *d*. *Educ:* Clifton Coll.; Exeter Coll., Oxford (MA). HM Overseas Civil Service; various appts in Far East, Cyprus and British Guiana, 1936–57. Interned by Japanese, in Singapore, 1942–45; First Sec., UK Commn, Singapore, 1958–63; Counsellor, British High Commn, Malaysia, 1964–68; HM Consul-Gen., Houston, 1969–74. *Recreations:* golf, gardening, swimming. *Club:* Oxford and Cambridge.

HOCKIN, Rt Rev. William Joseph; *see* Fredericton, Bishop of.

HOCKING, Philip Norman; *b* 27 Oct. 1925; *s* of late Fred Hocking, FIOB; *m* 1950, Joan Mable (marr. diss. 1970), *d* of Horace Ernest Jackson, CBE, Birmingham; three *d*. *Educ:* King Henry VIII Sch., Coventry; Birmingham Sch. of Architecture. Formerly Dir of building and develt cos. Mem. Coventry City Council, 1955–60. Prominent Mem. Young Con. Movement. MP (C) Coventry South, 1959–64; PPS to Minister of State, FO, 1963–64. Contested Coventry S, 1964 and 1966. Chm., Conservative Back Benchers' Housing and Local Govt Cttee, 1962–64. Life Mem., Shropshire Sheep Breeders' Soc.; show judge of sheep. *Recreations:* gardening, field sports, hunting with foot hound packs (Chm., Leadon Vale Basset Hounds, 1992–99), observing nature. *Address:* 2A Homepiece Cottages, Snowshill, Broadway, Worcs WR12 7JX.

HOCKLEY; *see* Farrar-Hockley.

HOCKLEY, Rev. Canon Raymond Alan; Canon Residentiary, Precentor, Succentor Canonicorum and Chamberlain of York Minster, 1976–95, Canon Emeritus, since 1995; *b* 18 Sept. 1929; 2nd *s* of late Henry Hockley and Doris (*née* Stonehouse); unmarried. *Educ:* Firth Park School, Sheffield; Royal Academy of Music, London; Westcott House, Cambridge. MA, LRAM. Macfarren Schol., Royal Acad. of Music, 1951–54; Charles Lucas Medal, William Corder Prize, Cuthbert Nunn Prize, etc; Theodore Holland Award, 1955. Clements Memorial Prize for Chamber Music by a British subject, 1954. Curate of St Augustine's, Sheffield, 1958–61; Priest-in-charge of Holy Trinity, Wicker, with St Michael and All Angels, Neepsend, 1961–63; Chaplain of Westcott House, Cambridge, 1963–68; Fellow, Chaplain and Dir of Studies in Music, Emmanuel Coll., Cambridge, 1968–76. Works performed include: Songs for Tenor, Soprano; String Quartet; Divertimento for piano duet; Cantata for Easter and the Ascension; Symphony; Suite for Orchestra; Mass for Choir and Organ; various anthems and motets; incidental music for plays. Other works include: two more Symphonies, A Woman's Last Word for three sopranos; Mysterium Dei, oratorio; ten Suites for piano; Canticles for Men's Voices. *Publications:* Six Songs of Faith; New Songs for the Church; Intercessions at Holy Communion; contribs to theological and musical jls. *Address:* St Clare, Sneaton Castle, Whitby, Yorkshire YO21 3QN. *T:* (01947) 821856.

HOCKMAN, Stephen Alexander; QC 1990; *b* 4 Jan. 1947; *s* of Nathaniel and Trude Hockman; *m* 1998, Elizabeth St Hill Davies. *Educ:* Eltham Coll.; Jesus Coll., Cambridge (MA). Called to the Bar, Middle Temple, 1970, Bencher, 1996. Leader, SE Circuit, 2000–. *Recreations:* philosophy, politics, the arts. *Address:* 6 Pump Court, Temple, EC4Y 7AR. *T:* (020) 7797 8400. *Club:* Royal Automobile.

HOCKNEY, David, CH 1997; RA 1991 (ARA 1985); artist; *b* Bradford, 9 July 1937; *s* of late Kenneth and Laura Hockney. *Educ:* Bradford Grammar Sch.; Bradford Sch. of Art; Royal Coll. of Art. Lecturer: Maidstone Coll. of Art, 1962; Univ. of Iowa, 1964; Univ. of Colorado, 1965; Univ. of California, Los Angeles, 1966, Berkeley, 1967. One-man shows: Kasmin Ltd, London, 1963, 1965, 1966, 1968, 1969, 1970, 1972; Alan Gallery, New York, 1964–67; Museum of Modern Art, NY, 1964–68; Stedlijk Museum, Amsterdam, 1966; Whitworth Gallery, Manchester, 1969; Louvre, Paris, 1974; Galerie Claude Bernard, Paris, 1975 and 1985; Nicholas Wilder, LA, 1976; Galerie Neundorf, Hamburg, 1977; Warehouse Gall., 1979; Knoedler Gall., 1979, 1981, 1982, 1983, 1984, 1986 and 1988; André Emmerich Gall., 1979, 1980, annually 1982–95; Tate, 1986, 1988; Hayward Gall., 1983 and 1985; L. A. Louver, LA, 1986, 1989 and 1995, etc; Annely Juda, 1997; touring show of drawings and prints: Munich, Madrid, Lisbon, Teheran, 1977; USA and Canada, 1978; Tate, 1980; Saltaire, Yorks, New York and LA, 1994; drawing retrospective, Hamburg, London, LA, 1996; Retrospective Exhibitions: Whitechapel Art Gall., 1970; LA County Museum of Art, Metropolitan Mus. of Art, Tate Gall., 1988–89; Manchester City Art Galls, 1996. Exhibitions of photographs: Hayward Gall., 1983; Nat. Mus. of Photography, Film and Television, 1991. 1st Prize, John Moores Exhibn, Liverpool, 1967. Designer: The Rake's Progress, Glyndebourne, 1975, La Scala, 1979; The Magic Flute, Glyndebourne, 1978; L'Enfant et les sortilèges and Nightingale, Double Bill, and Varii Capricci, Covent Garden, 1983; Tristan und Isolde, LA, 1987; Turandot, Chicago, San Francisco, Die Frau ohne Schatten, Covent Garden, 1992, LA, 1993; designing costumes and sets for Parade and Stravinsky triple bills, Metropolitan Opera House, NY, 1981. Films: A Bigger Splash, 1975; A Day on the Grand Canal with the Emperor of China or surface is illusion but so is depth, 1988. Hon. DLitt Oxford, 1995. Shakespeare Prize, Hamburg Foundn, 1983; First Prize, Internat. Center of Photography, NY, 1985; Silver Progress Medal, RPS, 1988; Praemium Imperiale, Japan Art Assoc., 1989; Fifth Annual Gov's Award for Visual Arts in California, 1994. *Publications:* (ed and illustrated) 14 Poems of C. P. Cavafy, 1967; (illustrated) Six Fairy Tales of the Brothers Grimm, 1969; 72 Drawings by David Hockney, 1971; David Hockney by David Hockney (autobiog.), 1976; The Blue Guitar, 1977; David Hockney: Travels with Pen, Pencil and Ink: selected prints and drawings 1962–77, 1978; Paper Pools, 1980; (with Stephen Spender) China Diary, 1982; Hockney Paints the Stage, 1983; David Hockney: Cameraworks, 1984 (Kodak Photography Book Award); David Hockney: A Retrospective, 1988; Hockney on Photography (conversations with Paul Joyce), 1988; Hockney's Alphabet, 1991 (ed Stephen Spender); That's the Way I See It (autobiog.), 1993; Hockney on Art: photography, painting and perspective, 1999; Secret Knowledge: rediscovering the lost techniques of the old masters, 2001. *Address:* c/o 7508 Santa Monica Boulevard, Los Angeles, CA 90046, USA.

HODDER, Prof. Bramwell William, PhD; Professor of Geography, School of Oriental and African Studies, University of London, 1970–83, now Emeritus; *b* 25 Nov. 1923; *s* of George Albert Hodder and Emily Griggs, Eastbourne; *m* 1971, Elizabeth Scruton (*see* E. Hodder); two step *d*; three *s* two *d* by previous marriages. *Educ:* Oldershaw, Wallasey; Oriel Coll., Oxford (MA, BLitt); PhD London. Served War, 1942–47, commissioned in Infantry (Cameronians), Lieut. Lecturer, Univ. of Malaya, Singapore, 1952–56; Lectr/Sen. Lectr, Univ. of Ibadan, Nigeria, 1956–63; Lectr, Univ of Glasgow, 1963–64; Lectr/Reader, Queen Mary Coll., Univ. of London, 1964–70. Chm., Commonwealth Geog. Bureau, 1968–72; Hon. Dir, 1981–82, Mem. Exec. Council, 1981–84, Internat. African Inst. Joint Hon. Pres., World Expeditionary Assoc., 1972–. *Publications:* Man in Malaya, 1959; Economic Development in the Tropics, 1968, 3rd edn 1980; (jtly) Markets in West Africa, 1969; (jtly) Africa in Transition, 1967; (jtly) Economic Geography, 1974; Africa Today, 1979; articles in various learned jls. *Recreations:* music, hill walking. *Address:* 8 Maitland House, Barton Road, Cambridge CB3 9JY. *T:* (01223) 301086.

See also I. R. Hodder.

HODDER, Elizabeth; Commissioner, Equal Opportunities Commission, since 1996 (Deputy Chairwoman, 1996–2000); Chairman, Lifespan Healthcare NHS Trust, since 2000 (non-executive Director, since 1993); *b* 5 Sept. 1942; *er d* of John Scruton and Beryl Haynes, High Wycombe; *m* 1st, 1962, Barry Quirke (marr. diss. 1970); two *d*; 2nd, 1971, Bramwell Hodder, *qv*; three step *s* two step *d*. *Educ:* High Wycombe High Sch.; Queen Mary Coll., Univ. of London. Member: Nat. Consumer Council, 1981–87; Building Societies Ombudsman Council, 1987–; Code of Banking Practice Review Cttee, 1992–; Comr and Chm., Consumers' Cttee, Meat and Livestock Commn, 1992–98. Founder and Hon. Pres., Nat. Stepfamily Assoc., 1985–; several positions in local and national organs. *Publications:* The Step-parents' Handbook, 1985; Stepfamilies Talking, 1989. *Recreations:* Italy, cooking, painting, hill-walking. *Address:* 8 Maitland House, Barton Road, Cambridge CB3 9JY. *T:* (01223) 301086.

See also R. V. Scruton.

HODDER, Prof. Ian Richard, PhD; FBA 1996; Professor of Archaeology, University of Cambridge, since 1996 (on leave, 1999–2001); Fellow of Darwin College, Cambridge, since 1990; *b* 23 Nov. 1948; *s* of Bramwell William Hodder *qv*, and Noreen Victoria Hodder; *m* 1st, 1975, Françoise Marguerite Hivernel; two *s*; 2nd, 1987, Christine Ann Hastorf; two *s*. *Educ:* Inst. of Archaeology, London (BA 1971); Peterhouse, Cambridge (PhD 1975). Lectr, Dept of Archaeology, University of Leeds, 1974–77; University of Cambridge: Univ. Asst, then Univ. Lectr, Dept of Archaeology, 1977–90; Reader in Prehistory, 1990–96; Dir, Cambridge Archaeol. Unit, 1990–. Adjunct Asst Prof. of Anthropology, SUNY, 1984–89; Visiting Professor: Dept of Anthropology, Univ. of Minnesota (and Adjunct Prof.), 1986–93; Van Giffen Inst. for Pre- and Proto-history, Amsterdam, 1980; Univ. of Paris I, Sorbonne, 1985; Fellow, Centre for Advanced Study in Behavioural Scis, Calif, 1987. *Publications:* Spatial Analysis in Archaeology (with C. Orton), 1976; Symbols in Action, 1982; The Present Past, 1982; Reading the Past, 1986; The Domestication of Europe, 1990; Theory and Practice in Archaeology, 1992; The Archaeological Process, 1998. *Recreations:* music (playing violin and piano), tennis, golf, sailing, travel. *Address:* Department of Archaeology, Downing Street, Cambridge CB2 3DZ.

HODDER-WILLIAMS, Paul, OBE 1945; TD; publisher; *b* 29 Jan. 1910; *s* of late Frank Garfield Hodder Williams, sometime Dean of Manchester, and late Sarah Myfanwy (*née* Nicholson); *m* 1936, Felicity (*d* 1986), 2nd *d* of late C. M. Blagden, DD, sometime Bishop of Peterborough; two *s* two *d*. *Educ:* Rugby; Gonville and Caius Coll., Cambridge (MA). Joined Hodder & Stoughton Ltd, 1931; Dir, 1936, Chm., 1961–75, Consultant, 1975–93. Served with HAC (Major, 1942), 99th (London Welsh) HAA Regt RA (Lt-Col Comdg, 1942–45). *Address:* Bradbury House, Windsor End, Beaconsfield, Bucks HP9 2JW. *T:* (01494) 672609.

HODDINOTT, Prof. Alun, CBE 1983; DMus; Hon. RAM; FRNCM; Professor of Music, University College, Cardiff, 1967–87, now Emeritus (Fellow, 1983); *b* 11 Aug. 1929; *s* of Thomas Ivor Hoddinott and Gertrude Jones; *m* 1953, Beti Rhiannon Huws; one *s*. *Educ:* University Coll. of S Wales and Mon. Lecturer: Cardiff Coll. of Music and Drama, 1951–59; University Coll. of S Wales and Mon, 1959–65; Reader, University of Wales, 1965–67. Member: BBC Music Central Adv. Cttee, 1971–78; Welsh Arts Council, 1968–74; Member Council: Welsh Nat. Opera, 1972–75; Composers' Guild of GB, 1972–; Nat. Youth Orchestra, 1972–. Chm., Welsh Music Archive, 1977–78, 1983–87. Artistic Dir, 1967–89, Pres., 1990–, Cardiff Music Festival. Governor: Welsh Nat. Theatre, 1968–74; St John's Coll., 1991–. FRNCM 1981; Fellow, Welsh Coll. of Music and Drama, 1991. Hon. DMus Sheffield, 1993. Walford Davies Prize, 1954; Arnold Bax Medal, 1957; John Edwards Meml Award, 1967; Hopkins Medal, St David's Soc., NY, 1980; Glyndwr Medal, 1997. *Publications: opera:* The Beach of Falesá, 1974; The Magician, 1975; What the Old Man does is always right, 1975; The Rajah's Diamond, 1979; The Trumpet Major, 1981; Tower, 1999; *choral:* Rebecca, 1961; oratorio, Job, 1962; Medieval Songs, 1962; Danegeld, 1964; Four Welsh Songs, 1964; Cantata: Dives and Lazarus, 1965; An Apple Tree and a Pig, 1968; Ballad, Black Bart, 1968; Out of the Deep, 1972; The Tree of Life, 1971; Four Welsh Songs, 1971; The Silver Swimmer, 1973; Sinfonia Fidei, 1977; Dulcia Iuventutis, 1978; Voyagers, 1978; Hymnus ante Somnum, 1979; Te Deum, 1982; Charge of the Light Brigade, 1983; In Parasceve Domini, 1983; King of Glory, 1984; Bells of Paradise, 1984; Jubilate, 1985; Lady and Unicorn, 1985; In Gravescentem Aetatem, 1985; Ballad of Green Broom, 1985; Christ is Risen, 1986; Sing a New Song, 1986; Flower Songs, 1986; In Praise of Music, 1986; The Legend of St Julian, 1987; Lines from Marlowe's Dr Faustus, 1988; Emynau Pantycelyn, 1990; Advent Carols, 1990; Vespers Canticle, 1992; Gloria, 1992; Three Motets, 1993; Missa Sancti David, 1994; Three Hymns for mixed choir and organ, 1994; Shakespeare Songs for unaccompanied voices, 1994; The Poetry of Earth, 1995; Missa Camargue, 1996; Magnificat and Nunc Dimittis, 1996; *vocal:* Roman Dream, 1968; Ancestor Worship, 1972; Ynys Mon, 1975; A Contemplation upon Flowers, 1976; Six Welsh Songs, 1982; The Silver Hound, 1986; Songs of Exile (tenor and orch.), 1989; The Silver Swimmer (soprano and ensemble), 1994; Five Poems of Becquer (baritone and piano), 1994; One Must Always Have Love: songs for high voice and piano, 1994; Tymhorau: four poems of Gwyn Thomas (baritone and piano), 1995; The Poetry of Earth (baritone and harp), 1997; Grongar Hill (baritone and ensemble), 1998; To the Poet (Pushkin songs, for baritone and piano), 1999; La Serenissima Cycle for baritone and piano, 2000; *orchestral:* Symphonies: no 1 1955, no 2 1962, no 3 1968, no 4 1969, no 5 1975, no 6 1984, no 7, for organ and orch., 1989, no 8, for brass and percussion, 1992, no 9, A Vision of Eternity, 1993, no 10 1999; Nocturne, 1952; Welsh Dances I, 1958, II 1969; Folk Song Suite, 1962; Variations, 1963; Night Music, 1966; Sinfonietta I, 1968, II, 1969, III, 1970, IV, 1971; Fioriture, 1968; Investiture Dances, 1969; Divertimento, 1969; the sun, the great luminary of the universe, 1970; the hawk is set free, 1972; Welsh Airs and Dances for Symphonic Band, 1975; Landscapes, 1975; French Suite, 1977; Passaggio, 1977; Nightpiece, 1977; Lanterne des Morts, 1981; Five Studies, 1983; Four Scenes, 1983; Quodlibet, 1984; Hommage à Chopin, 1985; Welsh Dances–3rd Suite, 1985; Scena, 1986; Fanfare with Variants; Concerto for Orchestra; Star Children, 1989; Celebration Dances, 1999; *concertos:* Clarinet I, 1951, II, 1987; Oboe, 1954; Harp, 1958; Viola, 1958; Piano I, 1950, II, 1960, III, 1966; Violin, 1961; Organ, 1967; Horn, 1969; Nocturnes and Cadenzas (cello), 1969; Ritornelli (trombone), 1974; The Heaventree of Stars, for violin and orchestra, 1980; Doubles (oboe); Scenes and Interludes (trumpet), 1985; Violin, Cello, Piano (Triple Concerto); Divisions (horn); Noctis Equi (cello and orch.), 1989; MISTRAL: concerto for violin and orch., 1995; Shining Pyramid (trumpet and orch.), 1995; Dragon Fire (timpani and percussion), 1998; concerto for percussion and brass, 2000; *chamber:* Septet, 1956; Sextet, 1960; Variations for Septet, 1962; Wind Quartet, 1963; String Quartet, 1965, no 2 1984, no 3 1988, no 4 1996, no 5 2001; Nocturnes and Cadenzas for Clarinet, Violin and Cello, 1968; Divertimento for 8 instruments, 1968; Piano Trio, 1970, no 2 1985, no 3 1996; Piano Quintet, 1972; Scena for String Quartet, 1979; Ritornelli for Brass Quintet, 1979; Ritornelli for four double basses, 1981; Masks for oboe, bassoon, piano, 1985; Divertimenti for flute, bassoon, double-bass and percussion, 1985; Sonata for Four Clarinets; chorales, variants and fanfares, 1992; Wind Quintet, 1993; six Bagatelles for string quartet, 1994; Bagatelles for wind quintet, 1999; Doubles, quintet for oboe, piano and string trio, 2000; *instrumental:* sonatas for: piano, 1959, 1962, 1965, 1966, 1968, 1972, 1984, 1986, 1989 (two), 1993, 1994, 2000; harp, 1964; clarinet and piano, 1967, 1996; violin and piano, 1969, 1970, 1971, 1976, 1992, 1997; cello and piano, 1970, 1977, 1996; horn and piano, 1971; organ, 1979; two pianos, 1986; flute and piano, 1991; oboe and harp, 1995; sonatinas for: clavichord, 1963; 2 pianos, 1978; guitar, 1978; Suite for Harp, 1967; Fantasy for Harp, 1970; Italian Suite for Recorder and Guitar, 1977; Nocturnes and Cadenzas for Solo Cello, 1983; Bagatelles for Oboe and Harp, 1983; Passacaglia and Fugue for Organ, 1986; Little Suite (trumpet and piano), 1988; Sonata Notturna for Harp, 1990; Tempi: sonata for harp, 1997; Island of Dragons Variants for cello, 1998; Lizard: variants for recorder. *Address:* Tan-y-Rhiw, 64 Gowerton Road, Three Crosses, Swansea SA4 3PX.

HODDINOTT, Rear-Adm. Anthony Paul, CB 1994; OBE 1979; Executive Director, International Bar Association, 1995–2000; Naval Attaché and Commander British Naval Staff, Washington, 1990–94; retired; *b* 28 Jan. 1942; *s* of Comdr Peter Hoddinott, RN and Marjorie Hoddinott (*née* Kent); *m* 1965, Ellen Ruby Burton (Rue); one *s* two *d*. *Educ:* St Michael's, Otford; Bloxham; BRNC Dartmouth. Served HM Ships Chawton, Trump, Dreadnought, Repulse, Porpoise; in Comd, HMS Andrew, 1973–75; Staff of Comdr Third Fleet, USN, 1975–76; in Comd, HMS Revenge, 1976–79; Comdr, Submarine Tactics and Weapons Gp, 1979–81; in Comd, HMS Glasgow, 1981–83 (South Atlantic, 1982); Asst Dir, Naval Warfare, 1983–85; NATO Defence Coll., Rome, 1985; Dep. UK Mil. Rep. to NATO, Brussels, 1986–88; COS (Submarines), 1988–90. Dir, Warship Preservation Trust, 1995–; Trustee, RN Submarine Mus., 1999– (Chm., Soc. of Friends, 1999–). *Recreations:* theatre, golf, swimming, family, travel. *Address:* 45 Oaklands Road, Petersfield, Hants GU32 2EY. *Club:* Naval.

HODDLE, Glenn; Manager, Tottenham Hotspur Football Club, since 2001; *b* 27 Oct. 1957; *s* of Derek Hoddle and Teressa (*née* Roberts); *m* 1979, Christine Anne Stirling (marr. diss. 1999); one *s* two *d*; *m* 2000, Vanessa Shean. *Educ:* Burnt Mill Sch., Harlow. Professional football player: Tottenham Hotspur, 1976–86 (won FA Cup, 1981, 1982, UEFA Cup, 1984); AS Monaco, 1986–91 (won French Championship, 1988); Player/Manager: Swindon Town, 1991–93; Chelsea, 1993–96; Coach, England Football Team, 1996–99; Manager, Southampton, 2000–01. 53 England caps, 1980–88; represented England in World Cup, Spain, 1982, Mexico, 1986. *Publications:* Spurred to Success (autobiog.), 1998; (with David Davies) Glenn Hoddle: the World Cup 1998 Story, 1998. *Address:* Tottenham Hotspur Football Club, 748 High Road, N17 0AP.

HODGE, Sir Andrew (Rowland), 3rd Bt *cr* 1921, of Chipstead, Kent; *b* 4 Dec. 1968; *o s* of Sir John Rowland Hodge, 2nd Bt, MBE and of his 4th wife, Vivien Jill, *d* of A. S. Knightley. *Educ:* Stella Maris Coll., Malta; Benjamin Britten High Sch., Suffolk. Estate agent, 1986–91 and 1993–94. *Recreations:* tennis, ski-ing.

HODGE, David Ralph; QC 1997; a Recorder, since 2000; *b* 13 July 1956; *er s* of Ralph Noel Hodge, CBE and Jean Margaret Hodge. *Educ:* St Margaret's, Liverpool; University Coll., Oxford (BA Jurisprudence 1977; BCL 1978). Called to the Bar, Inner Temple, 1979; admitted to Lincoln's Inn, 1980 (Bencher, 2000); an Asst Recorder, 1998–2000. Chm., Lincoln's Inn Bar Representation Cttee, 1997–98. *Publications:* contrib. chapter on Chancery Matters to Law and Practice of Compromise, 4th edn, 1996. *Recreations:* wine, Wodehouse, watercolours. *Address:* 9 Old Square, Lincoln's Inn, WC2A 3SR. *T:* (020) 7405 4682.

HODGE, Henry Egar Garfield, OBE 1993; **His Honour Judge Hodge;** a Circuit Judge, since 1999; Chief Immigration Adjudicator, since 2001; *b* 12 Jan. 1944; *s* of late Raymond Garfield Hodge and Ruth (*née* Egar); *m* 1st, 1971, Miranda Tufnell (marr. diss. 1975); 2nd, 1978, Margaret Eve Hodge, *qv*; two *d*, and one step *s* one step *d*. *Educ:* Chigwell Sch., Essex; Balliol Coll., Oxford (BA Law 1965). Admitted solicitor, 1970; Legal Sec., Justice, 1971; Solicitor and Dep. Dir, CPAG, 1972–77; Sen. Partner, Hodge Jones & Allen, Solicitors, 1977–99; Asst Recorder, 1993–97; a Recorder, 1997–99. Mem. (Lab), Islington Borough Council, 1974–78 (Vice-Chm., Housing Cttee, 1976–78). Member: Lord Chancellor's Legal Aid Adv. Cttee, 1977–83; Matrimonial Causes Rules Cttee, 1986–90. Law Society: Mem. Council, 1984–96 (Legal Aid Specialist); Chm., Courts and Legal Services Cttee, 1987–90; Chairman: Race Relns Cttee, 1992–94; Equal Opportunities Cttee, 1994–95. Dep. Chm., Legal Aid Bd, 1996–99; Member: Supplementary Benefits Commn, 1978–80; Social Security Adv. Cttee, 1980–92; Civil Justice Council, 1998–2000. Chairman: NCCL, 1974–75; Nat. CAB Trng Cttee, 1982–84; Camden CAB, 1983–88. Vice-Chm., Soc. of Labour Lawyers, 1992–99; Dep. Vice-Pres., Law Soc. of England and Wales, 1994–95. Contested (Lab) Croydon S, Feb. 1974. Gov., Coll. of Law, 1991–. Gov., Middx Univ., 1996–. *Publications:* Legal Rights, 1974; numerous articles on legal aid and legal rights. *Recreations:* Arsenal supporter, motor-cycling, golf, gardening. *Address:* Immigration Appellate Authority, Field House, Bream's Buildings, EC4A 1DZ.

HODGE, Sir James (William), KCVO 1996; CMG 1996; HM Diplomatic Service; Consul-General, Hong Kong and (non-resident) Macau, since 2000; *b* 24 Dec. 1943; *s* of late William Hodge and Catherine Hodge (*née* Carden); *m* 1970, Frances Margaret, *d* of late Michael Coyne and of Teresa Coyne (*née* Walsh); three *d*. *Educ:* Holy Cross Academy, Edinburgh; Univ. of Edinburgh (MA(Hons) English Lang. and Lit.). Commonwealth Office, 1966; Third Secretary, Tokyo, 1967; Second Secretary (Information), Tokyo, 1970; FCO, 1972; First Sec. (Development, later Chancery), Lagos, 1975; FCO, 1978; First Sec. (Economic), 1981, Counsellor (Commercial), 1982, Tokyo; Counsellor: Copenhagen, 1986; FCO, 1990; RCDS, 1994; Minister, British Embassy, Peking, 1995–96; Ambassador to Thailand and (non-resident) to Lao People's Democratic Republic, 1996–2000. Kt Grand Cross (1st cl.), Order of the White Elephant (Thailand), 1996. *Recreations:* books, music. *Address:* c/o Foreign and Commonwealth Office, SW1A 2AH. *Clubs:* MCC; Hong Kong, Hong Kong Country, Foreign Correspondents', China (Hong Kong); Macau Jockey.

HODGE, John Dennis; President, J. D. Hodge & Co., International Management and Aerospace Consultants, since 1987; *b* 10 Feb. 1929; *s* of John Charles Henry Hodge and Emily M. Corbett Hodge; *m* 1952, Audrey Cox; two *s* two *d*. *Educ:* Northampton Engineering Coll., University of London (now The City Univ.). Vickers-Armstrong Ltd, Weybridge, England (Aerodynamics Dept), 1950–52; Head, Air Loads Section, Avro Aircraft Ltd, Toronto, Canada, 1952–59; Tech. Asst to Chief, Ops Div., Space Task Group, NASA, Langley Field, Va, USA, 1959; Chief, Flight Control Br., Space Task Group, NASA, 1961; Asst Chief of Flight Control, 1962, Chief, Flight Control Div., Flight Ops Directorate, NASA, MSC, 1963–68; Manager, Advanced Missions Program, NASA, Manned Spacecraft Centre, 1968–70; Dir, Transport Systems Concepts, Transport Systems Center, 1970; Vice-Pres., R&D, The Ontario Transportation Develt Corp., 1974–76; Department of Transportation, Washington, 1976–82; Chief, R&D Plans and Programs Analysis Div., 1976–77; Actg Dir, Office of Policy, Plans and Admin, 1977–79; Associate Administrator, for Policy, Plans and Program Management, Res. and Special programs Admin, 1979–82; Dir, Space Station Task Force, NASA, Washington, 1982–84; Dep. Associate Administrator for Space Station, NASA, Washington, 1984–85, Actg Associate Administrator, 1985–86. FAIAA 1991. Hon. ScD, The City Univ., London, Eng., 1966; NASA Medal for Exceptional Service, 1967 and 1969; Dept of Transportation Meritorious Achievement Award, 1974; Special Achievement Award, 1979; Presidential Rank Award of Meritorious Executive, NASA, 1985. *Publications:* contribs to NASA publications and various aerospace jls. *Recreations:* reading, golf. *Address:* 1105 Challendon Road, Great Falls, VA 22066, USA.

HODGE, Sir Julian Stephen Alfred, Kt 1970; Merchant banker; Chairman: Avana Group Ltd, 1973–81; Carlyle Trust (Jersey) Ltd, since 1977; St Aubins Investment Co. Ltd, since 1986; Founder and Chairman, Bank of Wales, 1971–85; Chairman, Bank of Wales (Jersey) Ltd, 1974–87; Director, Bank of Wales (IoM) Ltd, 1974–85; *b* 15 Oct. 1904; *s* of late Alfred and Jane Hodge; *m* 1951, Moira (*née* Thomas); two *s* one *d*. *Educ:* Cardiff Technical Coll. Certified Accountant, 1930. Fellow, Inst. of Taxation, 1941–. Founded Hodge & Co., Accountants and Auditors; Man. Dir, 1963–75, Exec. Chm., 1975–78, Hodge Group Ltd; former Chairman: Julian S. Hodge & Co. Ltd; Gwent Enterprises Ltd; Hodge Finance Ltd; Hodge Life Assurance Co. Ltd; Carlyle Trust Ltd, 1962–85; Dir, Standard Chartered Bank, 1973–75. Founder and Chairman: The Jane Hodge Foundation, 1962; Sir Julian Hodge Charitable Trust, 1964; Chairman: Aberfan Disaster Fund Industrial Project Sub-Cttee; Member: Welsh Economic Council, 1965–68; Welsh Council, 1968–79; Council, Univ. of Wales Inst. of Science and Technology (Treasurer, 1968–76; Pres., 1981–85); Foundation Fund Cttee, Univ. of Surrey; Duke of Edinburgh Conf., 1974; Prince of Wales Cttee, 1979–85. Pres., S Glamorgan Dist, St John Ambulance Bde; Trustee, Welsh Sports Trust. Former Governor, All Hallows (Cranmore Hall) Sch. Trust Ltd. FTII 1941. FRSA. Hon. LLD Univ. of Wales, 1971. KStJ 1977 (CStJ 1972); KSG 1978. *Publication:* Paradox of Financial Preservation, 1959. *Recreations:* golf, walking, reading, gardening. *Address:* Clos des Seux, Mont du Coin, St Aubin, St Brelade, Jersey, JE3 8BE. *Clubs:* Victoria (St Helier, Jersey); La Moye Golf (Jersey).

HODGE, Margaret Eve, MBE 1978; MP (Lab) Barking, since June 1994; Minister of State, Department for Education and Skills, since 2001; *b* 8 Sept. 1944; *d* of late Hans and Lisbeth Oppenheimer; *m* 1st, 1968, Andrew Watson (marr. diss. 1978); one *s* one *d*; 2nd, 1978, Henry Egar Garfield Hodge, *qv*; two *d*. *Educ:* Bromley High Sch.; Oxford High Sch.; LSE (BSc Econ 1966). Teaching and internat. market research, 1966–73. London Borough of Islington: Councillor, 1973–94; Chair of Housing, 1975–79; Dep. Leader, 1981; Leader, 1982–92. Chair: Assoc. of London Authorities, 1984–92; London Res. Centre, 1985–92; Vice-Chair, AMA, 1991–92. Member: HO Adv. Cttee on Race Relations, 1988–92; Local Govt Commn, 1993–94; Board, Central and Inner London North TEC, 1990–92; Labour Party Local Govt Cttee, 1983–92. Parly Under-Sec. of State, DfEE, 1998–2001. Chair: Educn Select Cttee, H of C, 1997–98; London Gp of Labour MPs, 1996–98; former mem., govt and local govt bodies. Sen. Consultant, Price

Waterhouse, 1992–94. Director: London First, 1992; (non-exec.) UCH and Middlesex Hosp., 1992–94. Chair: Circle 33 Housing Trust, 1993–96; Fabian Soc., 1997–98. Gov., LSE, 1990–; Mem. Council, Univ. of London, 1994–98. Hon. Fellow, Polytechnic of North London. Hon. DCL City, 1993. *Publications:* Quality, Equality and Democracy, 1991; Beyond the Town Hall, 1994; Elected Mayors and Democracy, 1997; contribs to numerous jls and newspapers. *Recreations:* family, opera, piano, travel, cooking. *Address:* c/o House of Commons, SW1A 0AA.

HODGE, Michael, MBE 1975; HM Diplomatic Service, retired; *b* 12 June 1944; *s* of late Howard Jack Hodge and Iris Amy Hodge (*née* Treasure); *m* 1966, Wilhelmina Marjorie Glover; one *s* one *d. Educ:* Cotham Grammar Sch., Bristol. With Prison Commn, 1961–62; joined HM Diplomatic Service, 1962: FO, 1962–65; Third Sec., Belgrade, 1965–67; Commercial Officer, Paris, 1968–70; Third, later Second, Sec., Bahrain Residency, 1970–72; Second Secretary: (Information), Kaduna, 1972–73; (Commercial), Kampala, 1973–74; FCO, 1974–78; First Sec. (Econ.), Copenhagen, 1978–82; FCO, 1983–87; on loan to ICI Agrochemicals, 1987–89; First Sec. (Commercial), Paris, 1989–92; Head, Services Planning and Resources Dept, FCO, 1992–96; Consul Gen., Chicago, 1996–99. Kt, First Class, Order of Dannebrog (Denmark), 1978. *Recreations:* music, photography, steam railways. *Club:* National Liberal.

HODGE, Michael John Davy V.; *see* Vere-Hodge.

HODGE, Patricia; actress; *b* 29 Sept. 1946; *d* of Eric and Marion Hodge; *m* 1976, Peter Owen; two *s. Educ:* Wintringham Girls' Grammar Sch., Grimsby; St Helen's Sch., Northwood, Mddx; Maria Grey Coll., Twickenham; London Acad. of Music and Dramatic Art. Theatre début, No-one Was Saved, Traverse, Edinburgh, 1971; *West End theatre* includes: Popkiss, Globe, 1972; Two Gentlemen of Verona (musical), 1973; Pippin, Her Majesty's, 1973; Hair, Queen's, 1974; The Mitford Girls, Globe, 1981 (transf. from Chichester); Benefactors, Vaudeville, 1984; Noël and Gertie, Comedy, 1989–90; Shades, Albery, 1992; Separate Tables, Albery, 1993; The Prime of Miss Jean Brodie, Strand, 1994; A Little Night Music, RNT, 1995; Heartbreak House, Almeida, 1997; Money (Best Supporting Actress, Laurence Olivier Awards, 2000), Summerfolk, RNT, 1999; Noises Off, RNT, 2000; *other appearances* include: The Beggar's Opera, Nottingham Playhouse, 1975; Pal Joey, and Look Back In Anger, Oxford Playhouse, 1976; Then and Now, Hampstead, 1979; As You Like It, Chichester Fest., 1983; Lady in the Dark, Edinburgh Fest., 1988; *television plays and films* include: The Girls of Slender Means, 1975; The Naked Civil Servant, 1975; Hay Fever, 1984; The Death of the Heart, 1985; Hotel du Lac, 1986; Heat of the Day, 1988; The Shell Seekers, 1989; The Secret Life of Ian Fleming, 1989; The Moonstone, 1997; *television series and serials* include: Rumpole of the Bailey, 7 series, 1978–90; Edward and Mrs Simpson, 1978; Holding the Fort, 3 series, 1979–82; The Other 'Arf, 1979–80, 1981; Nanny, 1980; Jemima Shore Investigates, 1982; The Life and Loves of a She-Devil, 1986; Rich Tea and Sympathy, 1991; The Cloning of Joanna May, 1992; The Legacy of Reginald Perrin, 1996; *films* include: Betrayal, 1983; The Leading Man, 1996; Jilting Joe, 1997. Hon. DLitt Hull, 1996. *Address:* c/o Paul Lyon-Maris, ICM Ltd, Oxford House, 76 Oxford Street, W1N 0AX. *T:* (020) 7636 6565.

HODGE, Patrick Stewart; QC (Scot.) 1996; Commissioner (part time), Scottish Law Commission, since 1997; a Judge of the Courts of Appeal of Jersey and Guernsey, since 2000; *b* 19 May 1953; *s* of George Mackenzie Hodge and Helen Russell Hodge; *m* 1983, Penelope Jane Wigin; two *s* one *d. Educ:* Croftinloan Sch.; Trinity Coll., Glenalmond; Corpus Christi Coll., Cambridge (Scholar, BA); Edinburgh Univ. (LLB). Scottish Office, 1975–78; admitted Faculty of Advocates, 1983; Standing Junior Counsel: to Dept of Energy, 1989–91; to Inland Revenue in Scotland, 1991–96. Procurator to Gen. Assembly of Ch of Scotland, 2000–. Gov., Merchiston Castle Sch., Edinburgh, 1998–. *Publication:* Scotland and the Union, 1994. *Recreations:* opera, ski-ing. *Address:* 21 Lynedoch Place, Edinburgh EH3 7PY. *T:* (0131) 220 6914. *Club:* Bruntsfield Links Golfing Society.

HODGES, C(yril) Walter; free-lance writer, book illustrator, theatrical historian and designer; *b* 18 March 1909; *s* of Cyril James and Margaret Mary Hodges; *m* 1936, Greta (*née* Becker); two *s. Educ:* Dulwich Coll.; Goldsmiths' Coll. Sch. of Art. Commenced as stage designer, 1929, then illustrator for advertising, magazines (esp. Radio Times) and children's books; began writing, 1937; served with Army, 1940–46 (despatches); has designed stage productions (Mermaid Theatre, 1951, 1964), permanent Elizabethan stage, St George's Theatre, 1976; exhibns (Lloyds, UK Provident Instn; retrospective of theatre designs, Folger Shakespeare Library, Washington, 1988); mural decorations painted for Chartered Insce Inst., UK Provident Instn; Art Dir, Encyclopædia Britannica Films, 1959–61; reconstruction drawings for model of excavated Elizabethan Rose Theatre, Museum of London, 1989–91; consultant designer, Globe Theatre, Alexander Mills, N Carolina, USA, 1993–. Judith E. Wilson Lectr in Poetry and Drama, Cambridge, 1974; Co-ordinator, Symposium for the Reconstruction of Globe Playhouse, 1979, Adjunct Prof. of Theatre, 1980–83, Wayne State University, USA; Vis. Scholar, Univ. of Maryland, 1983. Hon. DLitt Sussex, 1979. Kate Greenaway Medal for illustration, 1965; Hons List, Hans Christian Andersen Internat. Award, 1966. *Publications:* Columbus Sails, 1939; The Flying House, 1947; Shakespeare and the Players, 1948; The Globe Restored, 1953 (rev. edn 1968); The Namesake, 1964; Shakespeare's Theatre, 1964; The Norman Conquest, 1966; Magna Carta, 1966; The Marsh King, 1967; The Spanish Armada, 1967; The Overland Launch, 1969; The English Civil War, 1972; Shakespeare's Second Globe, 1973; Playhouse Tales, 1974; The Emperor's Elephant, 1975; Plain Lane Christmas, 1978; The Battlement Garden, 1979; (ed) The Third Globe, 1981; Enter the Whole Army: the presentation of Shakespeare's plays in the theatres of his time, 1999; contributor: Shakespeare Survey; Theatre Notebook; (illus.) The New Cambridge Shakespeare, 1984–. *Recreations:* music (listening), letters (writing), museums (visiting). *Address:* 36 Southover High Street, Lewes, Sussex BN7 1HX. *T:* (01273) 476530.

HODGES, Elaine Mary, OBE 1975; HM Diplomatic Service; Counsellor, Foreign and Commonwealth Office, 1981–83; retired; *b* 12 Nov. 1928; *d* of late Lancelot James Hodges and Edith Mary (*née* Crossland). *Educ:* Nottingham High School for Girls; St Anne's Coll., Oxford (BA Hons, MA). Joined Foreign Office, 1952; served in: Germany, 1952–53; Switzerland, 1955–56; Warsaw, 1959; New Delhi, 1963–64; Paris, 1967–69; Brussels, 1974–79. *Recreations:* gardening, antiques, travel. *Address:* 46 Westbridge Road, SW11 3PW. *T:* (020) 7228 3771.

HODGES, Gerald; Director of Finance, City of Bradford Metropolitan Council, 1974–85; *b* 14 June 1925; *s* of Alfred John Hodges and Gertrude Alice Hodges; *m* 1950, Betty Maire (*née* Brading); one *s* (and one *s* decd). *Educ:* King's Sch., Peterborough. CPFA. Accountancy Asst, Bexley Borough Council, 1941–48, and Eton RDC, 1948–49; Sen. Accountancy Asst, Newcastle upon Tyne, 1949–53; Chief Accountant, Hemel Hempstead, 1953–56; Dep. Treas., Crawley UDC, 1956–70; Treas., Ilkley UDC, 1970–74. Pres., Soc. of Metropolitan Treasurers, 1984–85. Gen. Comr, Inland Revenue, 1985–. Hon. Treasurer: Yorkshire Arts, 1973–86; Univ. of Bradford, 1986–97; Chm., Bradford Flower Fund Homes; Trustee, Bradford Disaster Appeal, 1985. *Publications:* occasional articles in professional jls. *Recreations:* travelling, ornithology, reading. *Address:* 23 Victoria Avenue, Ilkley, West Yorks LS29 9BW. *T:* (01943) 607346.

HODGES, Lew; Director of Finance and Planning, Arts & Business, since 2001; *b* 29 Feb. 1956. *Educ:* University Coll. London (BA (Hons) Classics); MBA London Business Sch., 1990. Chartered Accountant 1981. Subsidy Officer, then Asst Dir of Finance, Arts Council, 1981–87; Head of Finance, CNAA, 1987–89; Finance Dir, Arts Council of GB, subseq. of England, 1989–96; Dir, Corporate Services, Sports Council, 1996–97; Hd of Finance, RNT, 1997–2000; Dir of Finance and Mgt Resources, London Arts, 2000–01. Mem., Inner London Probation Cttee, 1996–. *Address:* Arts & Business, Nutmeg House, 60 Gainsford Street, Butler's Wharf, SE1 2NY.

HODGES, Air Chief Marshal Sir Lewis (Macdonald), KCB 1968 (CB 1963); CBE 1958; DSO 1944 and Bar 1945; DFC 1942 and Bar 1943; DL; *b* 1 March 1918; *s* of late Arthur Macdonald Hodges and Gladys Mildred Hodges; *m* 1950, Elisabeth Mary, *e d* of late G. H. Blackett, MC; two *s. Educ:* St Paul's Sch.; RAF Coll., Cranwell. Bomber Command, 1938–44; SE Asia (India, Burma, Ceylon), 1944–45; Palestine, 1945–47; Air Ministry and Min. of Defence, 1948–52; Bomber Command, 1952–59; Asst Comdt, RAF Coll., Cranwell, 1959–61; AO i/c Admin., Middle East Comd, Aden, 1961–63; Imperial Def. Coll., 1963; SHAPE, 1964–65; Ministry of Defence, Asst Chief of Air Staff (Ops), 1965–68; AOC-in-C, RAF Air Support Comd, 1968–70; Air Mem. for Personnel, MoD, 1970–73; Dep. C-in-C, Allied Forces Central Europe, 1973–76, retired. Air ADC to the Queen, 1973–76. Dir, Pilkington Bros Ltd (Optical Div.), 1979–83; Governor, BUPA Med. Foundn Ltd, 1973–85; Chm. of Governors, Duke of Kent School, 1979–86; Chm., RAF Benevolent Fund Educn Cttee, 1979–86; Pres., RAF Escaping Soc., 1979–; Pres., Royal Air Forces Assoc., 1981–84. DL Kent, 1992. Grand Officier, Légion d'Honneur (France), 1988 (Commandeur, 1950); Croix de Guerre (France), 1944. *Recreations:* gardening, shooting, bee-keeping. *Address:* c/o Lloyds TSB, High Street, Tonbridge, Kent. *Clubs:* Royal Air Force (Vice Patron, 1993–), Special Forces.

HODGES, Mark Willie; Head of the Office of Arts and Libraries, 1982–84; *b* 23 Oct. 1923; *s* of William H. and Eva Hodges; *m* 1948, Glenna Marion (*née* Peacock); one *s* one *d. Educ:* Cowbridge Grammar Sch.; Jesus Coll., Oxford (MA 1948). Served War, RN, 1942–45. Lectr, Univ. of Sheffield, 1950–54; DSIR, 1954–56; Asst Scientific Attaché, Washington, 1956–61; Office of Minister for Science, 1961–64; Sec., Royal Commn on Med. Educn, 1965–68; Asst Sec., DES, 1968–79 (Arts and Libraries Br., 1977–79); Office of Arts and Libraries, 1979–84, Under Sec., 1982, Dep. Sec., 1983. Member: South Bank Theatre Bd, 1982–93 (Chm., 1984–93); Council, Royal Albert Hall, 1983–93; Council and Management Cttee, Eastern Arts Assoc., 1986–89. *Recreations:* woodwork, computer programming, listening to music. *Address:* The Corner Cottage, Church Way, Little Stukeley, Cambs PE28 4BQ. *T:* (01480) 459266.

HODGES, Nicholas Rudy; Chief Executive Officer, London International Group plc, 1993–99; *b* 26 Aug. 1939; *s* of Edward William Hodges and Gwendoline Winifred Hayward (*née* Golding); *m* 1st, 1959, Valerie Joyce Dyke (marr. diss. 1988; now Hedges); one *s* two *d*; 2nd, 1988, Christine Winifred Mary Dodd. *Educ:* Colchester Royal Grammar Sch. Salesman and Mktg, Nestlé Ltd, 1961–63; Kimberley Clark Ltd: Salesman, 1963–65; Product and Mktg Manager, 1965–67; Area Manager, 1967–69; Regl Manager, 1969–72; Regl Manager, Golden Wonder Ltd, 1972–74; Sales Dir, Johnson & Johnson Consumer, 1974–80; Man. Dir, Sangers, 1980–82; London International Group: Sales/Mktg Dir, 1982–88; World Wide Mkt Dir, Hosp. Products, 1988–90; European Man. Dir, 1990–93. Sen. non-exec. Dir and Dep. Chm., Taylor-Nelson Sofres, 1998–; Dep. Chm., SSL International PLC, 1999–. Liveryman: Glovers' Co., 1986–; Co. of World Traders, 1989– (Mem. Court, 1999–). MCIM (MInstM 1972); MInstD 1984. *Recreations:* good food and wine, golf, fishing, horse racing (owner). *Address:* Russett House, 8 Main Drive, Gerrards Cross SL9 7PS. *Clubs:* Royal Automobile, Dorchester; Royal Dornoch Golf, Burnham Beeches Golf, Kingswood Golf.

HODGES, Prof. Richard Andrew, OBE 1995; PhD; FSA 1984; Professor of Visual Arts, and Director, Institute of World Archaeology, School of World Arts and Museology, University of East Anglia, since 1995; *b* 29 Sept. 1952; *s* of Roy Clarence Hodges and Joan (*née* Hartnell); *m* 1976, Deborah Peters (marr. diss. 1998); one *s* one *d. Educ:* City of Bath Boys' Sch.; Univ. of Southampton (BA, PhD). Sheffield University: Lectr in Prehistory and Archaeology, 1976–86; Sen. Lectr, 1986–93; Prof., 1993–95. Leverhulme Res. Fellow, 1980, Dir, 1988–95 (on secondment), British Sch. at Rome; Dir, Prince of Wales's Inst. of Architecture, 1996–98. Special Advr to Minister of Culture, Albania, 1999; Advr to Packard Humanities Inst. proj., Albania, 2000–01. Visiting Professor: in Medieval Studies, SUNY-Birmingham, 1983; in Medieval Archaeology, Siena Univ., 1984–87; in Archaeology, Copenhagen Univ., 1987–88. Director: Roystone Grange landscape project, Derbyshire, 1978–88; San Vincenzo excavations, S Italy, 1980–98; co-director: Sheffield-Siena archaeological project, Montarrenti, Tuscany, 1982–87; Butrint excavations, Albania, 1994–. Scientific Dir, Butrint Foundn, 1995–. *Publications:* Walks in the Cotswolds, 1976; The Hamwih Pottery, 1981; (with G. Barker) Archaeology and Italian Society, 1981; Dark Age Economics, 1982, 2nd edn 1989; (with P. Davey) Ceramics and trade, 1983; (with D. Whitehouse) Mohammed, Charlemagne and the origins of Europe, 1983; (with John Mitchell) San Vincenzo al Volturno, 1985; Primitive and Peasant Markets, 1988; (with B. Hobley) Rebirth of the town in the West, 1988; The Anglo-Saxon Achievement, 1989; Wall to Wall History, 1991 (British Archaeological Book of the Year, 1992); (with K. Smith) Recent Developments in the Archaeology of the Peak District, 1991; (ed) San Vincenzo 1, 1993; (ed) San Vincenzo 2, 1995; (with J. Mitchell) La Basilica di Iosue a San Vincenzo al Volturno, 1995; Light in the Dark Ages, 1997; (with W. Bowden) The Sixth Century, 1998; Towns and Trade in the Age of Charlemagne, 2000; Visions of Rome: Thomas Ashby, archaeologist, 2000. *Recreations:* hill walking, music, watching cricket. *Address:* School of World Arts and Museology, University of East Anglia, Norwich NR4 7TJ.

HODGETTS, Robert Bartley; Clerk to Worshipful Company of Glaziers, 1979–85; *b* 10 Nov. 1918; *s* of late Captain Bartley Hodgetts, MN and Florence Hodgetts (*née* Stagg); *m* 1st, 1945, A. K. Jeffreys; one *d*; 2nd, 1949, Frances Grace, *d* of late A. J. Pepper, Worcester; two *d. Educ:* Merchant Taylors' Sch., Crosby; St John's Coll., Cambridge (Scholar, MA). Served RNVR (A), 1940–45. Asst Principal, Min. of Nat. Insce, 1947; Principal 1951; Asst Sec. 1964; Under-Sec., DHSS, 1973–78. *Recreations:* watching cricket and Rugby football. *Address:* 9 Purley Bury Close, Purley, Surrey CR8 1HW. *T:* (020) 8668 2827.

HODGKIN, Sir Howard, Kt 1992; CBE 1977; painter; *b* 6 Aug. 1932; *m* 1955, Julia Lane; two *s. Educ:* Camberwell Sch. of Art; Bath Academy of Art. Taught at Charterhouse Sch., 1954–56; taught at Bath Academy of Art, 1956–66; occasional tutor, Slade Sch. of Art and Chelsea Sch. of Art. Vis. Fellow in Creative Art, Brasenose Coll. Oxford, 1976–77. A Trustee: Tate Gall., 1970–76; National Gall., 1978–85. Mem., Exec. Cttee, Nat. Art Collections Fund, 1988–90. One-man exhibitions include: Arthur Tooth & Sons, London, 1962, 1964, 1967; Kasmin Gallery, 1969, 1971, 1976; Arnolfini Gall., Bristol, 1970, 1975; Dartington Hall, 1970; Galerie Müller, Cologne, 1971; Kornblee Gall., NY, 1973; Museum of Modern Art, Oxford, 1976, 1977; Serpentine Gall., London and provincial tour, Waddington Gall., 1976; André Emmerich Gall., Zürich and NY,

1977; Third Sydney Biennale, Art Gall. of NSW, 1979; Waddington Galls, 1972, 1980, 1988; Knoedler Gall. NY, 1981, 1982, 1984, 1988, 1990, 1993–94; Bernard Jacobson NY, 1980, 1981, LA, 1981, London, 1982; Tate Gall., 1982, 1985; Bath Fest., 1984; Phillips Collection, Washington DC, 1984; XLI Venice Biennale, 1984; Yale Centre for British Art, New Haven, 1985; Kestner-Gesellschaft, Hanover, 1985; Whitechapel Art Gall., 1985; Michael Werner Gall., Cologne, 1990; Nantes, Barcelona, Edinburgh and Dublin tour, 1990–91; Anthony D'Offay Gall., 1993, 1999–2000; Alan Cristea Gall., London, 1995; Metropolitan Mus. of Art, NY, 1995–96, and tour, incl. Hayward Gall., 1996–97 (retrospective); Gal. Lawrence Rubin, Zurich, 1996, 1997; Gagosian Gall., NY, 1998; Haas and Fuchs Gal., Berlin, 1998; Gall. Lawrence Rubin, Milan, 2001; Dulwich Picture Gall., 2001. Group Exhibitions include: The Human Clay, Hayward Gall., 1976; British Painting 1952–1977, RA, 1977; A New Spirit in Painting, RA, 1981; Hard Won Image, Tate Gall., 1984; An International Survey of Recent Paintings and Sculpture, Mus. of Mod. Art, 1984; NY, Carnegie International, Mus. of Art, Carnegie Inst., 1985–86; British Art in 20th Century, RA, 1987; Here and Now, Serpentine Gall., 1994; and in exhibns in: Australia, Austria, Belgium, Canada, Denmark, France, Germany, GB, Holland, India, Italy, Japan, Malta, Norway, Sweden, Switzerland, USA. Designs for: Pulcinella, Ballet Rambert, 1987; Piano, Royal Ballet, 1989; mural for British Council building, New Delhi, 1992. Works in public collections: Arts Council of GB; British Council, London; Contemp. Arts Soc.; Kettering Art Gall.; Peter Stuyvesant Foundn; São Paulo Museum; Oldham Art Gall.; Tate; V&A Museum; Swindon Central Lib.; Bristol City Art Gall.; Walker Art Center, Minneapolis; Nat. Gall. of S Aust., Adelaide; Fogg Art Museum, Cambridge, Mass; BM; Louisiana Museum, Denmark; Museum of Modern Art, Edinburgh; Southampton Art Gall.; Museum of Modern Art, and Metropolitan Mus. of Art, NY; Mus. of Art, Carnegie Inst.; Whitworth Art Gall., Manchester; City of Manchester Art Galls; Govt Picture Collection, London; Saatchi Collection, London; Nat. Gall. of Washington. Hon. Fellow, Brasenose Coll., Oxford, 1988. Hon. DLitt: London, 1985; Oxford, 2000. 2nd Prize, John Moore's Exhibn, 1976 and 1980; Turner Prize, 1985. *Address:* c/o Joanna Thornberry, Anthony d'Offay Gallery, 20 Dering Street, W1S 1AJ.

HODGKIN, Prof. Jonathan Alan, PhD; FRS 1990; Professor of Genetics, and Fellow of Keble College, Oxford University, since 2000; *b* 24 Aug. 1949; *s* of Sir Alan Hodgkin, OM, KBE, FRS and of Marion Hodgkin, *d* of late F. P. Rous. *Educ:* Bryanston Sch., Dorset; Merton Coll., Oxford (BA); Darwin Coll., Cambridge (PhD). SRC Res. Fellowship, 1974–76; Staff Scientist, MRC Lab. of Molecular Biology, 1977–2000. Vis. Prof., Univ. of Wisconsin, 1990. Mem., EMBO, 1989. *Publications:* contribs to scientific jls. *Recreations:* archaeology, cooking, cinema. *Address:* 82a Lonsdale Road, Oxford OX2 7ER. *T:* (01865) 552340.

HODGKIN, Mark William Backhouse; Chief Executive, WestLB Panmure (formerly Panmure Gordon) Ltd, since 1996; *b* 26 Jan. 1949; *s* of David Kenneth and Brigit Louise Hodgkin; *m* 1978, Madeleine Alison Newton; three *d. Educ:* Australian National Univ. (BEc). A. Fifer Ltd, 1972–74; Laurence Prust & Co., 1974–76; Man. Dir, Rivkin & Co. (Overseas), 1976–92; Vice Pres., Bankers Trust, 1992–93; Man. Dir, West Merchant Bank (WestLB Gp), 1993–98. *Recreations:* sailing, theatre, opera. *Address:* 3 Cannon Place, NW3 1EH.

HODGKINS, David John, CB 1993; Director, Resources and Planning, Health and Safety Executive, 1992–94; *b* 13 March 1934; *s* of late Rev. Harold Hodgkins and Elsie Hodgkins; *m* 1963, Sheila Lacey; two *s. Educ:* Buxton Coll.; Peterhouse, Cambridge. BA 1956, MA 1960. Entered Min. of Labour as Asst Principal, 1956; Principal: Min. of Lab., 1961–65; Treasury, 1965–68; Manpower and Productivity Services, Dept of Employment, 1968–70; Assistant Secretary: Prices and Incomes Div., Dept of Employment, 1970–72; Industrial Relns Div., 1973–76; Under Secretary, Overseas and Manpower Divisions, Dept of Employment, 1977–84; Safety Policy Div., HSE, 1984–92. Mem., Employment Appeal Tribunal, 1996–. *Publication:* Sir Edward Watkin: the second railway king, 2001. *Address:* Four Winds, Batchelors Way, Amersham, Bucks HP7 9AJ. *T:* (01494) 725207. *Club:* Royal Commonwealth Society.

HODGKINSON, Sir Derek; *see* Hodgkinson, Sir W. D.

HODGKINSON, Michael Stewart; Chief Executive, BAA plc, since 1999; *b* 7 April 1944; *s* of Stewart Gordon Hodgkinson and Ruth Phyllis Hodgkinson; *m* 1988, Elspeth Holman; one *s* two *d. Educ:* Nottingham Univ. (BA Hons Industrial Econs). ACMA 1969. Finance: Ford of Europe, 1965–69; British Leyland, 1969–75; Finance and Admin Dir, Leyland Cars Engrg, 1975–78; Man. Dir, Land Rover Ltd, 1978–83; Gp Dir, Watney Mann & Truman Brewers, 1983–85; Dep. Chief Exec., Express Dairies, 1985–89; Chief Exec., Grand Metropolitan Foods, Europe, 1989–92; Gp Airports Dir, BAA plc, 1992–99. *Recreations:* golf, theatre, travel. *Address:* BAA plc, 130 Wilton Road, SW1V 1LQ. *T:* (020) 7932 6769.

HODGKINSON, Neil Robert; Editor and Director, Yorkshire Evening Post, since 1999; *b* 28 May 1960; *s* of Robert Hodgkinson and Faith Hodgkinson; *m* 1st, 1984, Jacqueline Dawn Proctor; 2nd, 1993, Christine Elizabeth Talbot; 3rd, 2000, Emma Louise Schofield; one *s. Educ:* Baines Grammar Sch., Poulton-le-Fylde; Central Lancashire Poly. (Dip. Journalism). Trainee journalist to Dep. News Editor, W Lancs Evening Gazette, 1979–87; News Editor, then Dep. Editor, Lancs Evening Post, 1987–92; Dep. Ed., Yorkshire Evening Post, 1992–96; Editor, Lancs Evening Post, 1996–99. *Recreations:* football, cricket, tennis. *Address:* Yorkshire Evening Post, Wellington Street, Leeds, W Yorks LS1 1RF. *T:* (0113) 243 2701.

HODGKINSON, Air Chief Marshal Sir (William) Derek, KCB 1971 (CB 1969); CBE 1960; DFC 1941; AFC 1942; *b* 27 Dec. 1917; *s* of late Ernest Nicholls Hodgkinson; *m* 1939, Nancy Heather Goodwin; one *s* one *d. Educ:* Repton. Joined RAF 1936; served war of 1939–45, POW Germany, 1942–45; OC 210 and 240 (GR) Sqns; DS Aust. Jt Anti-Sub. Sch. and JSSC, 1946–58; Gp Captain, 1958; OC RAF St Mawgan, 1958–61; Staff of CDS, and ADC to the Queen, 1961–63; Air Cdre, 1963; IDC, 1964; Comdt RAF Staff Coll., Andover, 1965; Air Vice-Marshal, 1966; ACAS, Operational Requirements, 1966–68; SASO, RAF Training Command, 1969; Air Marshal, 1970; AOC-in-C, Near East Air Force, Commander British Forces Near East, and Administrator, Sovereign Base Areas, Cyprus, 1970–73; Air Secretary, 1973–76; Air Chief Marshal, 1974; retired 1976. Report on RAF Officer Career Structure, 1969. Pres., Regular Forces Employment Assoc., 1982–86 (Vice-Chm., 1977–80; Chm., 1980–82). *Recreations:* fishing, cricket. *Clubs:* Royal Air Force, MCC.

HODGSON, family name of **Baron Hodgson of Astley Abbotts**.

HODGSON OF ASTLEY ABBOTTS, Baron *cr* 2000 (Life Peer), of Nash in the co. of Shropshire; **Robin Granville Hodgson,** CBE 1992; Chairman, Granville Baird Ltd (formerly Granville plc), since 1995 (Director, since 1972; Group Chief Executive, 1979–95); Director, Johnson Bros & Co. Ltd, Walsall, since 1970; *b* 25 April 1942; *s* of late Henry Edward and of Natalie Beatrice Hodgson; *m* 1982, Fiona Ferelith, *o d* of K. S. Allom, Dorking, Surrey; three *s* one *d* (and one twin *s* decd). *Educ:* Shrewsbury Sch.; Oxford Univ. (BA Hons 1964); Wharton Sch. of Finance, Univ. of Pennsylvania (MBA 1969). Investment Banker, New York and Montreal, 1964–67; Industry in Birmingham, England, 1969–72; Director: Community Hospitals plc, 1982–85 and 1995–; Domnick Hunter Gp, 1992–; Staffordshire Building Soc., 1995–. Mem., W Midlands Industrial Develt Bd, 1989–97. Contested (C) Walsall North, Feb. and Oct. 1974; MP (C) Walsall North, Nov. 1976–1979. Chm., Birmingham Bow Gp, 1972–73; National Union of Conservative Associations: Mem. Exec. Cttee, 1988–98; Vice Pres., 1995–96; Chm., 1996–98; Chm., W Midlands Area, 1991–94. Dep. Chm., Cons. Party, 1998–2000; Chairman: Nat. Cons. Convention, 1998–2000; Trustees, Cons. Party Pension Fund. Member: Council for the Securities Industry, 1980–85; Securities and Investments Board, 1985–89; Dir, SFA, 1991–; Chm., Nat. Assoc. of Security Dealers and Investment Managers, 1979–85. Trustee: Shrewsbury Sch. Foundn; St Peter's Coll., Oxford; Associate, St George's House, Windsor. Liveryman, Goldsmiths' Co., 1983. *Publication:* Britain's Home Defence Gamble, 1978. *Recreations:* squash, fishing, theatre. *Address:* 15 Scarsdale Villas, W8 6PT. *T:* (020) 7937 2964; Nash Court, Ludlow, Salop SY8 3DG. *T:* (01584) 811677.

HODGSON, (Adam) Robin; DL; Chief Executive, Hampshire County Council, 1985–95; *b* 20 March 1937; *s* of Thomas Edward Highton Hodgson, CB; *m* 1962, Elizabeth Maureen Linda Bovenizer; one *s* two *d. Educ:* William Ellis Sch., London; Worcester Coll., Oxford (MA 1969); BSc Open Univ. 1997. Admitted Solicitor, 1964. Asst Solicitor, LCC and GLC, 1964–66; Sen. Asst Solicitor, Oxfordshire CC, 1966–71; Asst Clerk, Northamptonshire CC, 1972–74; Dep. County Sec., E Sussex CC, 1974–77; Dep. Chief Exec. and Clerk, Essex CC, 1977–85. Chm., Winchester Diocesan Bd of Finance, 1996–. Mem. Council, Univ. of Southampton, 1996–; Governor, Univ. of Portsmouth, 1996–. Mem. Gen. Chiropractic Council, 1996–. DL Hampshire, 1996. *Recreations:* music, drama, geology. *Address:* Tara, Dean Lane, Winchester, Hampshire SO22 5RA. *T:* (01962) 862115.

HODGSON, Ven. Derek; *see* Hodgson, Ven. J. D.

HODGSON, Hon. Sir Derek; *see* Hodgson, Hon. Sir W. D. T.

HODGSON, George Charles Day, CMG 1961; MBE 1950; lately an Administrative Officer, Nyasaland; retired from HMOCS, Nov. 1964; Secretary, Old Diocesans' Union, Diocesan College, Rondebosch, Cape, South Africa, 1964–86 (Patron, 2001); *b* 21 Sept. 1913; *s* of late P. J. Hodgson and of A. E. Joubert; *m* 1st, 1940, Edna Orde (*d* 1977), *d* of late G. H. Rushmere; one *s*; 2nd, 1978, Cecile Paston Dewar (*née* Foster). *Educ:* Diocesan Coll., Rondebosch, Capetown, S Africa; Rhodes Univ., Grahamstown, S Africa; Cambridge Univ. Joined Colonial Administrative Service as Cadet, 1939. Military Service, 1940–42; Lieut, 1st Bn King's African Rifles. Returned to duty as Distr. Officer, Nyasaland, 1943; seconded for special famine relief duties in Nyasaland, 1949–50; Provincial Commissioner, 1952; Adviser on Race Affairs to Govt of Federation of Rhodesia and Nyasaland, 1958–59; Nyasaland Govt Liaison Officer to Monckton Commn, 1960; Permanent Sec., Ministry of Natural Resources and Surveys, Nyasaland, 1961–62; Permanent Sec., Ministry of Transport and Communications, Nyasaland, 1963–64. *Recreations:* Rugby football, cricket, golf. *Address:* 308 Grosvenor Square, College Road, Rondebosch, 7700, South Africa. *Clubs:* Royal Cape Golf, Western Province Cricket (Cape Town).

HODGSON, Gordon Hewett; Master of the Supreme Court, Queen's Bench Division, 1983–2000; *b* 21 Jan. 1929; *s* of late John Lawrence Hodgson and Alice Joan Hodgson (*née* Wickham); *m* 1958, Pauline Audrey Gray; two *s. Educ:* Oundle School; University College London. LLB (Hons). National Service, RAEC, 1947–49; called to the Bar, Middle Temple, 1953; private practice, South Eastern Circuit, 1954–83; Asst Boundary Commissioner, 1976; Asst Recorder, 1979. Mem. Cttee, Bentham Club, 1987– (Chm., 1990–95). *Publication:* (ed jtly) Supreme Court Practice, 1991, 1995 and 1999. *Recreations:* gardening, enjoying Tuscany. *Address:* PO Box 28, Hemel Hempstead HP3 0XX. *T:* (01442) 833407. *Clubs:* East India; Bar Yacht.

HODGSON, Guy Andrew Keith; District Judge (Magistrates' Courts) (formerly Stipendiary Magistrate), Bradford, 1993–2000; *b* 19 March 1946; *s* of Herbert and Kathleen Hodgson; *m* 1968, Kay Bampton; three *s. Educ:* Pocklington Sch.; Nottingham Poly. (LLB London Ext.). Articled to M. M. Rossfield, Solicitor, York; Legal Asst, Thames Valley Police, 1970–71; Asst Prosecutor, Suffolk Police, 1971–72; Asst Solicitor, Gotelee & Goldsmith, Ipswich, 1972–74; Partner, Close Thornton, Darlington, 1974–93. *Recreations:* travel, reading, painting, hobby farming, vintage tractors, family interests, professional pipe smoker, canal narrow boats.

HODGSON, Howard Osmond Paul; author and scriptwriter; *b* 22 Feb. 1950; *s* of late Osmond Paul Charles Hodgson and of Sheila Mary (*née* Ward; now Mrs Baker); *m* 1st, 1972, Marianne Denise Yvonne (marr. diss. 1998), *d* of Samuel Katibien, Aix-en-Provence, France; two *s* one *d* (and one *s* decd); 2nd, 1999, Christine Mary, *d* of A. F. Pickles. *Educ:* Aiglon Coll., Villars, Switzerland. DipFD 1970; MBIFD; Affiliated MRSH, 1970. Asst Man., Hodgson & Sons Ltd, 1969–71; life assce exec., 1971–75; acquired: Hodgson & Sons Ltd, 1975 (floated USM, 1986); Ingalls from House of Fraser, 1987; launched Dignity in Destiny Ltd, 1989; merger with Pompes Funèbres Générales, France, Kenyon Securities and Hodgson Hldgs plc to form PFG Hodgson Kenyon Internat. plc, 1989; launched: Bereavement Support Service, 1990; PHKI Nat. Training Sch., 1990; retd, 1991, to pursue career in broadcasting and writing. Chief Executive: Halkin Hldgs, 1993; Hoskins Brewery plc, 1993; Ronson plc, 1995–97 (acquired Ronson plc and LGW plc, 1994, Home Shopping Marketing Ltd and associated cos, the business of DCK Marketing Ltd and Smiths Packaging Ltd, 1995; Group renamed Ronson plc, 1995; resigned, 1997); CEO, Colibri Internat., 1998–2001. Presenter, How Euro Are You, BBC2, 1991–92; panellist, Board Game, Radio 4, 1992–2001. Hon. Vice Pres., Royal Soc. of St George, 1989. USM Entrepreneur of the Year, 1987. *Publications:* How to Become Dead Rich, 1992; Six Feet Under, 2000 (film script, 2001); Exhumed Innocent?, 2002. *Recreations:* cricket, yachting, ski-ing, history. *Address:* Belvedere House, The Belvederes, Chaddesley Glen, Poole, Dorset BH13 7PB. *Club:* Royal Motor Yacht.

HODGSON, Prof. Humphrey Julian Francis, DM; FRCP; Dame Sheila Sherlock Professor of Medicine, Royal Free and University College Medical School of University College London, since 1999; *b* 5 April 1945; *s* of Harold Robinson Hodgson and Celia Frances Hodgson (*née* Hodgson); *m* 1971, Shirley Victoria Penrose; one *s* one *d. Educ:* Westminster Sch.; Christ Church, Oxford (BA, BSc); St Thomas's Hosp. Med. Sch. (BM BCh, DM). FRCP 1983. Trng posts at St Thomas' and Royal Free Hosps, 1970–76; Radcliffe Travelling Fellow, University Coll., Oxford, at Massachusetts Gen. Hosp., Boston, 1977; Consultant Physician, Hammersmith Hosp., 1977–99; Royal Postgraduate Medical School, London: Sen. Lectr in Medicine, 1978–89; Reader, 1989–91; Prof. of Gastroenterology, 1991–95; Vice Dean, 1986–97; Prof. of Medicine, RPMS, then ICSM, 1995–99; Jt Med. Dir, Hammersmith Hosps NHS Trust, 1994–97. Acad. Registrar, RCP, 1992–97. Chm., Scientific Co-ordinating Cttee, Arthritis Res. Campaign (formerly

Arthritis and Rheumatism Council for Res.), 1996–. *Publications:* Textbook of Gastroenterology, 1984; Gastroenterology: clinical science and practice, 1994. *Recreations:* walking, reading, academic travel. *Address:* Department of Medicine, Royal Free and University College Medical School, Rowland Hill Street, NW3 2PF. *T:* (020) 7433 2850; 40 Onslow Gardens, N10 3JU. *T:* (020) 8883 8297.

HODGSON, Ven. (John) Derek; Archdeacon of Durham, 1993–97, now Emeritus, and Canon Residentiary of Durham Cathedral, 1983–97, now Emeritus; *b* 15 Nov. 1931; *s* of Frederick and Hilda Hodgson; *m* 1956, Greta Wilson; two *s* one *d. Educ:* King James School, Bishop Auckland; St John's Coll., Durham (BA Hons History); Cranmer Hall, Durham (Dip. Theology). Short service commission, DLI, 1954–57. Deacon 1959, priest 1960; Curate: Stranton, Hartlepool, 1959–62; St Andrew's, Roker, 1962–64; Vicar: Stillington, 1964–66; Consett, 1966–75; Rector of Gateshead, 1975–83; RD of Gateshead, 1976–83; Hon. Canon of Durham, 1978–83; Archdeacon of Auckland, 1983–93. Chm. of Govs, Durham Sch., 1997–2001; Vice-Provost, Northern Div., Woodard Schs Corp., 1999–2001. *Recreations:* walking, music, theatre, sport. *Address:* 45 Woodside, Barnard Castle, Co. Durham DL12 8DZ. *T:* (01833) 690557.

HODGSON, Keith Stephen, OBE 1997; Director, Management Support Unit, Board of Inland Revenue, since 1998; *b* 29 Oct. 1946; *s* of Leonard Arthur and Florence Hodgson; *m* 1969, Jean Moran. *Educ:* Wolverhampton Municipal Grammar Sch. Min. of Transport, 1965–68; Board of Inland Revenue, 1968–; Private Sec. to Chm. of Bd, CS Pay Res. Unit, 1978–81; Dep. Controller of Stamps, 1982–90; Dir, Stamp Office, 1990–98. FRSA 1998. *Publications:* (contrib.) Managing Change in the New Public Sector, 1994; (contrib.) Creating a Good Impression: three hundred years of the Stamp Office and Stamp Duties, 1994. *Recreations:* Freemasonry, wine, Rugby, ski-ing. *Address:* East Horsley, Surrey; Chandolin, Val d'Anniviers, Valais, Switzerland.

HODGSON, Sir Maurice (Arthur Eric), Kt 1979; Chairman, British Home Stores plc, 1982–87, and Chief Executive, 1982–85; *b* 21 Oct. 1919; *s* of late Walter Hodgson and of Amy Hodgson (*née* Walker); *m* 1945, Norma Fawcett; one *s* one *d. Educ:* Bradford Grammar Sch.; Merton Coll., Oxford (Hon. Fellow, 1979). MA, BSc; FREng, FIChemE; CChem, FRSC. Joined ICI Ltd Fertilizer & Synthetic Products Gp, 1942; seconded to ICI (New York) Ltd, 1955–58; Head of ICI Ltd Technical Dept, 1958; Develt Dir, ICI Ltd Heavy Organic Chemicals Div., 1960, Dep. Chm., 1964; Gen. Man., Company Planning, ICI Ltd, 1966; Commercial Dir and Planning Dir, ICI Ltd, 1970; Dep. Chm., ICI Ltd, 1972–78, Chm., 1978–82; Director: Carrington Viyella Ltd, 1970–74; Imperial Chemicals Insce Ltd, 1970–78 (Chm. 1972); Dunlop Holdings plc, 1982–84 (Chm. 1984); Storehouse, 1985–89; Member: Internat. Adv. Bd, AMAX Inc., 1982–85; European Adv. Council, Air Products and Chemicals Inc., 1982–84; Council, Lloyd's of London, 1987–94. Chm., Civil Justice Review Adv. Cttee, 1985–88; Member: Court, British Shippers' Council, 1978–82; Council, CBI, 1978–82; Internat. Council, Salk Inst., 1978–97; Court, Univ. of Bradford, 1979–90. Vis. Fellow, Sch. of Business and Organizational Studies, Univ. of Lancaster, 1970–80. Governor, London Grad. Sch. of Business Studies, 1978–87. Hon. DUniv Heriot-Watt, 1979; Hon. DTech Bradford, 1979; Hon. DSc Loughborough, 1981; Hon. FUMIST, 1979. Messel Medal, Soc. of Chemical Industry, 1980; George E. Davis Medal, IChemE, 1982. *Recreations:* horse-racing, swimming, fishing.

HODGSON, Patricia Anne, (Mrs George Donaldson), CBE 1995; Chief Executive, Independent Television Commission, since 2000; *b* 19 Jan. 1947; *d* of Harold Hodgson and Pat Smith; *m* 1979, George Donaldson; one *s. Educ:* Brentwood High Sch.; Newnham Coll., Cambridge (MA; Associate Fellow, 1994–97); LRAM (Drama) 1968. Conservative Res. Dept, Desk Officer for public sector industries, 1968–70; freelance journalism and broadcasting in UK and USA during seventies; Chm., Bow Gp, 1975–76; Editor, Crossbow, 1976–80. BBC: joined as educn producer for Open Univ. (part of founding team pioneering distance learning techniques), 1970; most of prodn career in educn, specialising in history and philosophy, with spells in current affairs on Today and Tonight; Secretariat, 1982–83, Dep. Sec., 1983–85, The Sec., 1985–87; Hd of Policy & Planning, 1987–92; Dir of Policy & Planning, 1993–2000; Dir of Public Policy, 2000. Member: Competition (formerly Monopolies and Mergers) Commn, 1993–99; Statistics Commn, 2000–. Dir, BARB, 1987–98. Mem., (C) Haringey BC, 1974–77. Mem., London Arts Bd, 1991–96; Trustee, Prince's Youth Business Trust, 1992–95. Mem. Adv. Bd, Judge Inst., Cambridge, 1996–. *Television series* include: English Urban History, 1978; Conflict in Modern Europe, 1980; Rome in the Age of Augustus, 1981. *Publications:* (ed) Paying for Broadcasting, 1992; (ed) Public Purposes in Broadcasting, 1999; articles in various newspapers and jls. *Recreation:* quietness. *Address:* Independent Television Commission, 33 Foley Street, W1P 7LB. *T:* (020) 7306 7825. *Club:* Reform.

HODGSON, Robin; *see* Hodgson, A. R.

HODGSON, Col Terence Harold Henry, DSO 1945; MC 1944; TD 1953; DL; FSVA; Vice Lord-Lieutenant of Cumbria, 1983–91; *b* 10 Dec. 1916; *s* of late Michael C. L. Hodgson, Grange-over-Sands; *m* 1st, 1942, Joan Winsome Servant (marr. diss. 1969; she *d* 1974); 2nd, 1972, Doreen Jacqueline Pollit Brünzel (*d* 1985); two *s* three *d* (and one *s* decd); 3rd, 1985, Elizabeth Robinson. *Educ:* Kendal Grammar Sch. FSVA 1953; FRSH 1954. Served War with Border Regt, Ceylon, India and Burma; Comdr, 4th Bn Border Regt, TA, 1953–56; Dep. Comdr, 126 Inf. Bde, TA, 1956–59; Col TA, 1959; Hon. Colonel: King's Own Royal Border Regt, 1976–82; Cumbria Cadet Force, 1977–86. Dir, Cartmel Steeplechasers Ltd, 1959–98; Local Dir, Royal Insurance, 1960–. Chairman: Governors, Kirkbie Kendal Sch., 1970–86; Kendal Almshouse Charities, 1975–86; Cumbria Appeal Cttee, Army Benevolent Fund, 1987–93. Past Pres., Cumberland and Westmorland Rugby Union. DL Westmorland, 1958. FRICS 2001. *Recreations:* Rugby football, horse racing. *Address:* The Esplanade, Abbotsrood, Grange-over-Sands, Cumbria LA11 7HH. *T:* (015395) 32843. *Club:* Army and Navy.

HODGSON, Ven. Thomas Richard Burnham; Archdeacon of West Cumberland, 1979–91, now Archdeacon Emeritus; *b* 17 Aug. 1926; *s* of Richard Shillito Hodgson and Marion Thomasina Bertram Marshall; *m* 1952, Margaret Esther, *o d* of Evan and Caroline Margaret Makinson; one *s* one *d. Educ:* Heversham Grammar School; London Coll. of Divinity, Univ. of London. BD, ALCD. Deacon 1952, priest 1953, dio. Carlisle; Curate of Crosthwaite, Keswick, 1952–55; Curate of Stanwix, Carlisle, 1955–59; Vicar of St Nicholas', Whitehaven, 1959–65; Rector of Aikton, 1965–67; Vicar of Raughtonhead with Gaitsgill, 1967–73; Hon. Canon of Carlisle, 1973–91; Vicar of: Grange-over-Sands, 1973–79; Mosser, 1979–83. Mem., General Synod of C of E, 1983–90. Domestic Chaplain to Bishop of Carlisle, 1967–73, Hon. Chaplain 1973–79; Director of Ordination Candidates, 1970–74; RD of Windermere, 1976–79; Surrogate, 1962–91. *Publication:* Saying the Services, 1989. *Recreations:* listening to music, watching drama, geology, meteorological observing, watercolour painting. *Address:* 58 Greenacres, Wetheral, Carlisle CA4 8LD. *T:* (01228) 561159.

HODGSON, Hon. Sir (Walter) Derek (Thornley), Kt 1977; a Judge of the High Court of Justice, Queen's Bench Division, 1977–92; *b* 24 May 1917; *s* of late Walter Hodgson, Whitefield, Manchester; *m* 1951, Raymonde Valda (*née* de Villiers) (*d* 1965); no *c. Educ:* Malvern Coll.; Trinity Hall, Cambridge. Scholar, Trinity Hall; Harmsworth Scholar, Middle Temple; 1st Cl. Law Tripos, Part II, 1938; 1st Cl. LLB, 1939. Served throughout War 1939–46, Royal Artillery; Burma 1942–45; released with rank of Captain, 1946. Called to Bar, Middle Temple, 1946 (Master of the Bench, 1967); QC 1961. Member: Senate of Inns of Court, 1966–69; Gen. Council of the Bar, 1965–69. Judge of the Salford Hundred Court of Record, 1965–71; a Law Comr, 1971–77; a Recorder of the Crown Court, 1972–77. Member: Lord Chancellor's Cttees on: Legal Educn, 1968–71; Contempt of Court, 1971–74; Butler Cttee on Mentally Abnormal Offenders, 1973–75; Parole Board, 1981–83 (Vice-Chm., 1982–83). Chm., Howard League Wkg Pty on Forfeiture (report published as The Profits of Crime and their Recovery, 1984). *Recreation:* travel. *Address:* Carpmael Building, Middle Temple Lane, EC4Y 7AT. *T:* (020) 7583 1613. *Clubs:* Oxford and Cambridge, MCC; Tennis and Racquets (Manchester); Hawks (Cambridge).

HODGSON, William Donald John; General Manager, Independent Television News, 1960–82 (Director, 1972–86); *b* 25 March 1923; *s* of James Samuel Hodgson and Caroline Maud Albrecht; *m* 1946, Betty Joyce Brown; two *s* six *d. Educ:* Beckenham Grammar School. Served Beds and Herts Regt, 1940–42; pilot, RAF and Fleet Air Arm, 1942–46. Documentary and feature film editor (with Jean Renoir on The River, Calcutta), 1946–50; Organiser, Festival of Britain Youth Programme, 1950–51; Asst Sec., Central Bureau for Educational Visits and Exchanges, 1951–54; Asst Gen. Man., Press Assoc., 1954–60; Dir of Develt, ITN, 1982–86. Dir, UPITN Corp., 1967–73. Executive Producer: Battle for the Falklands, 1982; Theft of a Thoroughbred, 1983; Victory in Europe, 1985; writer and producer, Welcome to the Caley (Royal Caledonian Schs), 1987. *Recreations:* grandchildcare, private flying, cricket, swimming. *Address:* 38 Lakeside, Wickham Road, Beckenham, Kent BR3 6LX. *T:* (020) 8650 8959.

HODKINSON, Prof. Henry Malcolm, DM; FRCP; Barlow Professor of Geriatric Medicine, University College London, 1985–91, now Emeritus; *b* 28 April 1931; *s* of Charles and Olive Hodkinson; *m* 1st, (marr. diss.); four *d*; *m* 2nd, 1986, Judith Marie Bryant, *qv. Educ:* Manchester Grammar Sch.; Brasenose Coll., Oxford (DM 1975); Middlesex Hospital; Westminster Univ. (Dip. in Law, 2000). FRCP 1974. Consultant Physician in Geriatrics to: Enfield and Tottenham Gps of Hosps, 1962–70; Northwick Park Hosp., 1970–78 (also Mem., Scientific Staff of Clin. Res. Centre); Sen. Lectr in Geriatric Medicine, 1978–79, Prof. of Geriatric Medicine, 1979–84, RPMS. Vice Pres., Research into Ageing, 1996– (Governor, 1983–96). *Publications:* An Outline of Geriatrics, 1975, 2nd edn 1981 (trans. Spanish, Dutch, German, Italian and Japanese); Common Symptoms of Disease in the Elderly, 1976, 2nd edn 1980 (trans. Turkish); Biochemical Diagnosis of the Elderly, 1977; (ed) Clinical Biochemistry of the Elderly, 1984; (with J. M. Hodkinson) Sherratt? A Natural Family of Staffordshire Figures, 1991; approx. 100 papers in learned jls, 1961–. *Recreations:* English glass and ceramics. *Address:* 8 Chiswick Square, Burlington Lane, Chiswick, W4 2QG. *T:* (020) 8747 0239.

HODKINSON, James Clifford; Chief Executive, New Look Retailers Ltd, 1998–2000; *b* 21 April 1944; *s* of John and Lily Hodkinson; *m* 1969, Janet Lee; one *d. Educ:* Salesian Coll., Farnborough. Trainee Manager F W Woolworth Ltd, London, 1962–71; Manager, B & Q, Bournemouth, 1972–74; Sales Manager, B & Q (Retail) Ltd, 1974–76; Man. Dir, B & Q (Southern) Ltd, 1976–79; Dir, 1976–79, Ops Dir, 1979–84, Ops and Personnel Dir, 1984–86, B & Q (Retail) Ltd; Man. Dir, 1986–89, Chief Exec., 1989–92, B & Q plc; Internat. Develt Dir, Kingfisher plc, 1992–94; Chm. and Chief Exec., B & Q plc, 1994–98. *Recreations:* shooting, golf. *Clubs:* Annabelle's; Parkstone Golf.

HODKINSON, Judith Marie, (Mrs H. M. Hodkinson); *see* Bryant, J. M.

HODSON, Christopher Robert; His Honour Judge Hodson; a Circuit Judge, since 1993; *b* 3 Nov. 1946; *s* of James and Elizabeth Hodson; *m* 1970, Jean Patricia Anne Dayer; one *s* one *d. Educ:* King's Sch., Worcester. Called to the Bar, Lincoln's Inn, 1970; practised, Birmingham, 1971–93; a Recorder, 1988–93. *Address:* 6 Fountain Court, Steelhouse Lane, Birmingham B4 6DR. *T:* (0121) 233 3282.

HODSON, Clive, CBE 1992; FCCA; FCIT; Chairman, LRT Pension Fund Trustee Co. Ltd, since 1998; *b* 9 March 1942; *s* of late Stanley Louis Hodson and of Elsie May Hodson (*née* Stratford); *m* 1976, Fiona Mary Pybus; one *s* one *d. Educ:* Erith Grammar Sch. FCCA 1967; FCIT 1969; ATII 1968. LT, 1960–69; Asst Sec. and Accountant, London Country Bus Services Ltd, 1970–74; Mgt Accountant, LT, 1974–78; London Buses Ltd: Finance Dir, 1978–89; Man. Dir, 1989–95; Chm., 2000; Managing Director: LT Buses, 1994–2000; London Bus Services Ltd, 2000. Chairman: Victoria Coach Station Ltd, 1995–2000; London River Services Ltd, 1998–2000. Mem., LTB, 1995–2000. LT Project Dir, Bus Privatisation, 1993–95; Project Dir, Croydon Tramlink, 1995–2000; Freeman, City of London, 1995; Liveryman, Co. of Carmen, 1995. *Recreations:* travel, walking, reading. *Address:* 55 Broadway, Westminster, SW1H 0BD.

HODSON, Daniel Houghton, FCT; Chairman, Medialink International, since 1999; *b* 11 March 1944; *s* of late Henry Vincent Hodson and of Margaret Elizabeth (*née* Honey); *m* 1979, Diana Mary Ryde; two *d. Educ:* Eton; Merton Coll., Oxford (MA Hons PPE). FCT 1979. Chase Manhattan Bank, 1965–73; joined Edward Bates & Sons Ltd, 1973, Dir 1974–76; Unigate plc: Gp Treas., 1976–81; Gp Finance Dir, 1981–87; Pres., Unigate Inc., 1986–87; Chief Exec., 1987–88, Chm. 1988, Davidson Pearce Gp plc; Dep. Chief Exec., Nationwide Building Soc., 1989–92; Chief Exec., LIFFE, 1993–98. Director: The Post Office, 1984–95; Ransomes plc, 1993–98; Independent Insurance Gp plc, 1995–; London Clearing House, 1996–98; Rolfe and Nolan plc, 1999–; Reliance Environmental Services Ltd, 1999–; Berry Palmer and Lyle Hldgs Ltd, 2000–. Chm., European Cttee, Options and Futures Exchanges, 1996–98. Association of Corporate Treasurers: Chm., 1985–86; Pres., 1992–93. Gresham Prof. of Commerce, 1999–Sept. 2002. Chm., Design and Artists Copyright Soc., 1999–. Dep. Chm., Classical Opera Co., 1997–. Governor: Yehudi Menuhin Sch., 1984–; King Alfred's Coll., Winchester, 2000–; Peter Symonds' Coll., Winchester, 2000–. Founding Editor, Corporate Finance and Treasury Management, 1984–. *Recreations:* music, travel, ski-ing, gardening. *Address:* Treyford Manor, Midhurst, W Sussex GU29 0LD. *T:* (01730) 825436. *Club:* Brooks's.

HODSON, Denys Fraser, CBE 1981; arts consultant, since 1992; Director, Arts and Recreation, Thamesdown Borough Council, 1974–92; *b* 23 May 1928; *s* of late Rev. Harold Victor Hodson, MC and Marguerite Edmée Ritchie; *m* 1954, Julie Compton Goodwin; one *s* one *d. Educ:* Marlborough Coll.; Trinity Coll., Oxford (MA). After a career in commerce and industry, apptd first Controller of Arts and Recreation, Swindon Bor. Council, 1970. Chairman: Southern Arts Assoc., 1974–80 and 1985–87; Council, Regional Arts Assocs, 1975–80; Chief Leisure Officers' Assoc., 1974 and 1982–84; Chm., Public Arts Commns Agency, 1993–2000; Vice-Chm., Arts Council of GB, 1989–94 (Mem., 1987–94); a Director: Oxford Playhouse Co., 1974–86; Oxford Stage Co., 1988–89; Chairman: Brewery Arts, 1994–98; Arts Research Ltd, 1999–; Vice-Pres., Voluntary Arts Network, 1998– (Vice-Chm., 1992–94; Chm., 1994–98); a Governor: BFI, 1976–87; Wyvern Arts Trust, 1984–95. *Publications:* (contrib.) Arts Centres, 1981;

(contrib.) The Future of Leisure Services, 1988; conf. papers and articles. *Recreations:* bird-watching, fishing, the arts. *Address:* Manor Farm House, Fairford, Glos GL7 4AR. *T:* (01285) 712462.

HODSON, Prof. Frank, BSc London 1949; PhD Reading 1951; Professor of Geology in the University of Southampton, 1958–81, now Emeritus; *b* 23 Nov. 1921; *s* of late Matthew and Gertrude Hodson; *m* 1945, Ada Heyworth; three *d. Educ:* Burnley Grammar Sch.; Reading Univ.; London Univ. (external student). Demonstrator, Reading Univ., 1947–49; Lecturer, Reading Univ., 1949–58. Dean, Faculty of Science, 1972–74, and 1976–77, Public Orator, 1970–73, Univ. of Southampton. Murchison Fund, Geol. Soc., 1962; Founder Mem. and first Hon. Sec., Palaeontol. Assoc., 1957. Pres. Sect. C (geology), British Assoc. for Adv. of Science, 1975. Hon. Mem. Geol. Soc. de Belg. *Publications:* geological papers in publications of learned societies. *Recreation:* book collecting.

HODSON, John; Chairman, Singer & Friedlander Group, since 2000 (Director, since 1987; Chief Executive, 1993–99); *b* 19 May 1946; *s* of Arthur and Olga Hodson; *m* 1971, Christina McLeod; one *s* two *d. Educ:* Worcester Coll., Oxford (PPE). Joined Singer & Friedlander, 1969: Asst Dir, 1974–83; Dir, 1983–; Head of Investment Dept, 1985–90. Non-executive Director: Miller Fisher Gp plc; Intrinsic Value PLC; Prestbury Gp plc. *Recreations:* tennis, family. *Address:* (office) 21 New Street, Bishopsgate, EC2M 4HR. *T:* (020) 7523 5912.

HODSON, Sir Michael (Robin Adderley), 6th Bt *cr* 1789; Captain, Scots Guards, retired; *b* 5 March 1932; *s* of Major Sir Edmond Adair Hodson, 5th Bt, DSO, and Anne Elizabeth Adderley (*d* 1984), *yr d* of Lt-Col Hartopp Francis Charles Adderley Cradock, Hill House, Sherborne St John; *S* father, 1972; *m* 1st, 1963, Katrin Alexa (marr. diss. 1978), *d* of late Erwin Bernstiel, Dinas Powis, Glamorgan; three *d*; 2nd, 1978, Catherine, *d* of late John Henry Seymour, Wimpole St, W1. *Educ:* Eton. *Heir: b* Patrick Richard Hodson [*b* 27 Nov. 1934; *m* 1961, June, *o d* of H; M. Shepherd-Cross; three *s*]. *Address:* Nantyderry House, Nantyderry, Monmouthshire NP7 9DW.

HODSON, Thomas David Tattersall; His Honour Judge Hodson; a Circuit Judge, since 1987; a Senior Circuit Judge and Honorary Recorder of Newcastle upon Tyne, since 1997; *b* 24 Sept. 1942; *s* of late Thomas Norman Hodson and Elsie Nuttall Hodson; *m* 1969, Patricia Ann Vint; two *s* one *d. Educ:* Sedbergh Sch.; Manchester Univ. (LLB). Leader Writer, Yorkshire Post, 1964–65; called to the Bar, Inner Temple 1966, Bencher, 2001; in practice on Northern Circuit, 1967–87; Junior, 1969; a Recorder, 1983–87. Mem., Parole Bd, 1996–97; Chm., Northumbria Area Criminal Justice Strategy Cttee, 2001–. Pres., S Lancs Br., Magistrates' Assoc., 1994–96. Mem. Court, Univ. of Newcastle upon Tyne, 2000–. *Publication:* One Week in August: the Kaiser at Lowther Castle, August 1895, 1995. *Recreations:* music, genealogy, fell-walking. *Address:* The Law Courts, The Quayside, Newcastle upon Tyne NE1 3LA. *T:* (0191) 201 2000.

HOEKMAN, Johan Bernard; Knight, Order of Netherlands Lion; Officer, Order of Orange Nassau; Netherlands Ambassador to the Court of St James's, 1990–94, and concurrently to Iceland; *b* 11 Sept. 1931; *m* 1957, Jeanne van Gelder; three *s* one *d. Educ:* Univ. of Groningen (degree in Social Geography). Foreign Service, 1961; served Baghdad, Washington, Jeddah; Counsellor, Cairo, 1972–74; Deputy, later Head, Dept for Financial Economic Develt Co-operation, Min. of Foreign Affairs, 1974–80; Ambassador, Dakar, 1980–81, Paramaribo, 1981–84; Dir-Gen. for Internat. Co-operation, 1984–88; Ambassador, Paramaribo, 1988–90. Holds foreign decorations. *Address:* Staten Laan 102, 2582 GV The Hague, Netherlands.

HOERNER, John Lee; Chief Executive, Clothing, Tesco, since 2001; *b* 23 Sept. 1939; *s* of Robert Lee Hoerner and Lulu Alice (*née* Stone); *m* 1st 1959, Susan Kay Morgan (marr. diss. 1971); one *s* one *d*; 2nd, 1973, Anna Lea Thomas. *Educ:* Univ. of Nebraska (BS, BA). Hahnes Department Stores: senior buying and merchandising positions: Hovland Swanson, Lincoln, Neb, 1959–68; Woolf Bros, Kansas City, Mo, 1968–72; Hahnes, NJ, 1972–73; Pres. and Chief Exec. Officer, First 21st Century Corp., Hahnes, 1974–81; Chief Executive Officer: H. & S. Pogue Co., Cincinnati, Ohio, 1981–82; L. S. Ayres & Co., Indianapolis, Ind., 1982–87; Burton Group, subseq. Arcadia Group, 1987–2000: Chairman: Debenhams, 1987–92; Harvey Nichols, 1988–91; Gp Chief Exec., 1992–2000. Non-exec. Dir, BAA, 1998–. Mem., Council of Trustees, Dogs' Home, Battersea, 1991– (Vice-Chm., 1995–). *Recreations:* riding, flying. *Address:* Cornwell Glebe, Cornwell, Chipping Norton, Oxon OX7 6TX. *T:* (01608) 658549; *e-mail:* john.hoerner@zoom.co.uk. *Clubs:* Groucho; Air Squadron.

HOEY, Catharine Letitia; MP (Lab) Vauxhall, since June 1989; *b* 21 June 1946; *d* of Thomas Henry and Letitia Jane Hoey. *Educ:* Lylehill Primary Sch.; Belfast Royal Acad.; Ulster Coll. of Physical Educn (Dip. in PE); City of London Coll. (BSc Econs). Lectr, Southwark Coll., 1972–76; Sen. Lectr, Kingsway Coll., 1976–85; Educnl Advr, London Football Clubs, 1985–89. PPS to Minister of State (Minister for Welfare Reform), DSS, 1997–98; Parliamentary Under-Secretary of State: Home Office, 1998–99; DCMS (Minister for Sport), 1999–2001. *Recreations:* watching soccer, keeping fit. *Address:* House of Commons, SW1A 0AA. *T:* (020) 7219 3000. *Club:* Surrey CC (Mem. Cttee).

HOFF, Harry Summerfield; *see* Cooper, William.

HOFFBRAND, Prof. (Allan) Victor, DM, DSc; FRCP, FRCPath; Professor of Haematology and Honorary Consultant, Royal Free Hospital School of Medicine, 1974–96, now Emeritus Professor, Royal Free and University College Medical School; *b* 14 Oct. 1935; *s* of late Philip Hoffbrand and Minnie (*née* Freedman); *m* 1963, Irene Jill Mellows; two *s* one *d. Educ:* Bradford Grammar Sch.; Queen's Coll., Oxford (BA 1956; MA 1960; BM BCh 1959; DM 1972); Royal London Hospital; DSc London 1987. FRCP 1976; FRCPath 1980. Jun. hosp. posts, Royal London Hosp., 1960–62; Res. and Registrar posts, RPMS, 1962–66; Lectr, St Bartholomew's Hosp., 1966–67; MRC Fellow, New England Med. Centre, Boston, 1967–68; Sen. Lectr, RPMS, 1968–74. Visiting Professor: Sanaa, Yemen, 1986; Armed Forces Inst. Path., Rawalpindi, 1988; Royal Melbourne Hosp., 1991. Lectures: Los Braun Meml, Johannesburg, 1978; Sir Stanley Davidson, Edinburgh, 1983; G. Izak Meml, Jerusalem, 1984; K. J. R. Wightman, Toronto, 1988. Chairman: Standing Intercollegiate Cttee on Oncology, 1993–94; Jt Haematology Cttee, RCP, RCPath, 1994–97; Member: Systems Bd, MRC, 1986–89; Council, RCPath, 1987–90; Council, Royal Free Sch. of Med., 1991–94; Council, Eur. Haematology Assoc., 1994–99. Med. Advr, Leukaemia Res. Fund. Member: Amer. Soc. Haematology; Brit. Soc. Haematology; Internat. Soc. Haematology. FMedSci 2000; Hon. FRCPE 1986. Jt Editor, Revs in Clinical and Experimental Hematology, 2000–. Member, Editorial Board: Brit. Jl Haematology (Chm.); Clinical Haematology; Leukaemia Res.; Leukaemia and Lymphoma; Haematologica; Qly Jl Medicine; Jl Lab. and Clin. Medicine, Lancet Oncology. *Publications:* (ed with S. M. Lewis) Postgraduate Haematology, 1972, 4th edn 1998; (ed) Recent Advances in Haematology, 1977, 8th edn 1996; (with J. E. Pettit): Essential Haematology, 1980, 4th edn 2001; Blood Diseases Illustrated, 1987; Sandoz Atlas of Clinical Haematology, 1988, 2nd edn 1994, 3rd edn, as Color Atlas of Clinical Hematology, 2000; (with A. B. Mehta) Haematology at a Glance, 2000; papers on megaloblastic anaemia, iron chelation, leukaemia and related disorders. *Recreations:* music, antiques, chess, bridge. *Address:* Department of Haematology, Royal Free Hospital, NW3 2QG. *T:* (020) 7435 1547.

HOFFENBERG, Sir Raymond, (Bill), KBE 1984; President, Wolfson College, Oxford, 1985–93; Professor of Medical Ethics, University of Queensland, 1993–95; *b* 6 March 1923; *m* 1949; two *s. Educ:* Univ. of Cape Town (MB, ChB 1948; MD, PhD). FRCP 1971; FRCPE, FRCPI. Wartime Service with S African Armed Forces, N Africa and Italy. Sen. Lectr, Dept of Medicine, Univ. of Cape Town, 1955–67; banned by S African Govt, 1967; emigrated to UK, 1968. Sen. Scientist, MRC (UK), 1968–72; William Withering Prof. of Medicine, Univ. of Birmingham, 1972–85. Mem. MRC, 1978–82. Chm. Council, British Heart Foundn, 1987–93. Royal College of Physicians: Pres., 1983–89; Harveian Orator, 1991. *Publications:* Clinical Freedom, 1987 (Rock Carling Fellowship, Nuffield Provincial Hospitals Trust); papers on endocrinology and metabolism. *Address:* 304/57A Newstead Terrace, Newstead, Qld 4006, Australia.

HOFFMAN, Dustin Lee; actor; *b* 8 Aug. 1937; *s* of Harry Hoffman and Lillian Hoffman; *m* 1st, 1969, Anne Byrne (marr. diss. 1980); two *d*; 2nd, 1980, Lisa Gottsegen; two *s* two *d. Educ:* Santa Monica City Coll.; Pasadena Playhouse. Stage début in Sarah Lawrence Coll. prodn, Yes is For a Very Young Man; Broadway début, A Cook for Mr General, 1961; appeared in: Harry, and Noon and Night, Amer. Place Theatre, NY, 1964–65; Journey of the Fifth Horse, and Star Wagon, 1965; Fragments, Berkshire Theatre Festival, Stockbridge, Mass, 1966; Eh?, 1966–67; Jimmy Shine, Broadway, 1968–69; Death of a Salesman, Broadway, 1984; London début, Merchant of Venice, Phoenix, 1989. Dir, All Over Town, Broadway, 1974. Films: The Graduate, 1967; Midnight Cowboy, 1969; John and Mary, 1969; Little Big Man, 1971; Who Is Harry Kellerman and Why Is He Saying Those Terrible Things About Me?, 1971; Straw Dogs, 1972; Alfredo, Alfredo, 1972; Papillon, 1973; Lenny, 1974; All The President's Men, 1975; Marathon Man, 1976; Straight Time, 1978; Agatha, 1979; Kramer vs Kramer, 1979 (Academy Award); Tootsie, 1983; Death of a Salesman, 1985 (Emmy Award); Ishtar, 1987; Rain Man, 1989 (Academy Award; Golden Globe Award); Family Business, 1990; Billy Bathgate, 1991; Hook, 1992; Accidental Hero, 1993; Outbreak, 1995; American Buffalo, 1996; Sleepers, 1996; Mad City, 1997; Wag the Dog, 1997; Sphere, 1998. Record: Death of a Salesman. Obie Award as best off-Broadway actor, 1965–66, for Journey of the Fifth Horse; Drama Desk, Theatre World, and Vernon Rice Awards for Eh?, 1966; Oscar Award nominee for The Graduate, Midnight Cowboy, and Lenny. *Address:* Punch Productions, 1926 Broadway, Suite 305, New York, NY 10023, USA.

HOFFMAN, Gary Andrew; Managing Director, Customer Service and Delivery, Barclays Bank plc, since 1999; *b* 21 Oct. 1960; *m* (marr. diss.). *Educ:* Queens' Coll., Cambridge. With Barclays Bank plc, 1982–: Man. Dir, Telephone Banking, 1995–98; Chief Exec., UK Retail Banking, 1998. *Recreations:* running, watching Coventry City FC.

HOFFMAN, Rev. Canon Stanley Harold, MA; Chaplain in Ordinary to the Queen, 1976–87; Hon. Canon of Rochester Cathedral, 1965–80, now Emeritus; *b* 17 Aug. 1917; *s* of Charles and Ellen Hoffman, Denham, Bucks; *m* 1943, Mary Mifanwy Patricia (*d* 1991), *d* of late Canon Creed Meredith, Chaplain to the Queen, and Mrs R. Creed Meredith, Windsor; one *s* one *d. Educ:* The Royal Grammar Sch., High Wycombe, Bucks; St Edmund Hall, Oxford (BA 1939, MA 1943); Lincoln Theol Coll., 1940–41. Deacon, 1941; Priest, 1942; Curate: Windsor Parish Ch., 1941–44; All Saints, Weston, Bath, 1944–47; Chertsey (in charge of All SS), 1947–50; Vicar of Shottermill, Haslemere, Sy, 1951–64; Diocesan Director of Education, Rochester, 1965–80; Warden of Readers, 1974–80. Proctor in Convocation, Church Assembly, 1969–70; Exam. Chaplain to Bp of Rochester, 1973–80. Member: Kent Educn Cttee, 1965–80; Bromley Educn Cttee, 1967–80; Kent Council of Religious Educn, 1965–80; Archbps' Commn on Christian Initiation, 1970. Vice-Chm., Christ Church Coll., Canterbury, 1973–80. Hon. MA Kent, 1982. *Publications:* Morning Shows the Day: the making of a priest (autobiog.), 1995; part author: A Handbook of Thematic Material, 1968; Christians in Kent, 1972; Teaching the Parables, 1974; contrib. various pubns on Preaching and Religious Educn; numerous Dio. study papers. *Recreations:* music, walking. *Address:* Zansizzey, Trevone, Padstow, Cornwall PL28 8QJ. *T:* (01841) 520864.

HOFFMANN, family name of **Baron Hoffmann.**

HOFFMANN, Baron *cr* 1995 (Life Peer), of Chedworth in the County of Gloucestershire; **Leonard Hubert Hoffmann,** Kt 1985; PC 1992; a Lord of Appeal in Ordinary, since 1995; *b* 8 May 1934; *s* of B. W. and G. Hoffmann; *m* 1957, Gillian Lorna Sterner; two *d. Educ:* South African College Sch., Cape Town; Univ. of Cape Town (BA); The Queen's Coll., Oxford (Rhodes Scholar; MA, BCL, Vinerian Law Scholar; Hon. Fellow, 1992). Advocate of Supreme Court of S Africa, 1958–60. Called to the Bar, Gray's Inn, 1964, Bencher, 1984; QC 1977; a Judge, Courts of Appeal of Jersey and Guernsey, 1980–85; a Judge of the High Court of Justice, Chancery Div., 1985–92; a Lord Justice of Appeal, 1992–95. Non-permanent Judge, HK Court of Final Appeal, 1998–. Stowell Civil Law Fellow, University Coll., Oxford, 1961–73 (Hon. Fellow, 1995). Member: Royal Commn on Gambling, 1976–78; Council of Legal Educn, 1983–92 (Chm., 1989–92). Pres., British-German Jurists Assoc., 1991–. Dir, ENO, 1985–90, 1991–94. Chm., Arts Council Adv. Cttee on London Orchs, 1993. Hon. DCL: City, 1992; UWE, 1995. *Publication:* The South African Law of Evidence, 1963. *Address:* Surrey Lodge, 23 Keats Grove, NW3 2RS.

HOFFMANN, Prof. Roald; Frank H. T. Rhodes Professor of Humane Letters, Cornell University, since 1996; *b* 18 July 1937; *s* of Hillel Safran and Clara (*née* Rosen, who *m* 2nd, Paul Hoffmann); *m* 1960, Eva Börjesson; one *s* one *d. Educ:* Columbia Univ. (BA); Harvard Univ. (MA, PhD). Junior Fellow, Society of Fellows, Harvard Univ., 1962–65; Associate Professor, to Professor, 1965–74, John A. Newman Prof. of Physical Science, 1974–96, Cornell Univ. Member: Nat. Acad. of Sciences; Amer. Acad. of Arts and Sciences. Foreign Member: Royal Soc., 1984; Indian Nat. Acad. of Sciences; Royal Swedish Acad. of Sciences; USSR Acad. of Sciences; Finnish Acad. of Sciences. Hon. DTech Royal Inst. of Technology, Stockholm, 1977; Hon. DSc: Yale, 1980; Hartford, 1982; Columbia, 1982; City Univ. of NY, 1983; Puerto Rico, 1983; La Plata, 1984; Uruguay, 1984; State Univ. of NY at Binghamton, 1985; Colgate, 1985; Rennes, 1986; Ben Gurion, 1989; Lehigh Univ., 1989; Carleton Coll., 1989; Maryland, 1990; Athens 1991; Thessaloniki, 1991; Bar Ilan, 1991; St Petersburg, 1991; Barcelona, 1992; Ohio State, 1993. Nobel Prize for Chemistry, 1981. *Publications:* The Conservation of Orbital Symmetry, 1970; The Metamict State (poetry), 1987; Solids and Surfaces, 1988; Gaps and Verges (poetry), 1990; Chemistry Imagined, 1993; The Same and Not the Same, 1995; Old Wine, New Flasks, 1997; Memory Effects (poetry), 1999; (with Carl Djerassi) Oxygen (drama), 2000; many scientific articles. *Address:* Department of Chemistry, Cornell University, Ithaca, NY 14853, USA.

HOFMANN, Hansgeorg B.; Deputy Chairman, Kleinwort Benson Group plc, 1995–97 (Chairman, Group Executive Committee, 1997); Member, Board of Managing Directors,

Dresdner Bank AG, Frankfurt, 1995–97; *b* Munich, 2 June 1943; *m* 1971, Leonor Bahner; two *s*. Merrill Lynch, London and NY, 1979–87; Shearson Lehman Hutton Internat., London, 1987–89; Dresdner Bank AG, Frankfurt, 1989–97. Non-exec. Dir, SGL Carbon AG, 1996–.

HOFMEYR, Murray Bernard; Member, Executive Committee, Anglo American Corporation of South Africa Limited, 1972; Chairman, Johannesburg Consolidated Investment Co. Ltd, 1987; *b* 9 Dec. 1925; *s* of William and Margareta Hofmeyr; *m* 1953, Johanna Hendrika Hofmeyr (*née* Verdurmen); two *s* two *d*. *Educ:* BA (Rhodes), MA (Oxon). Joined Anglo American Corp., 1962; in Zambia, 1965–72; in England, 1972–80; Man. Dir, 1972–76, Chm. and Man. Dir, 1976–80, Charter Consolidated Ltd. *Recreations:* golf, tennis; Captain Oxford Univ. Cricket, 1951; played Rugby for England, 1950. *Address:* 20 Pinelands, 46 First Road, Hyde Park, Johannesburg 2196, South Africa.

HOFMEYR, Stephen Murray; QC 2000; *b* 10 Feb. 1956; *s* of late Jan Murray Hofmeyr and of Stella Mary Hofmeyr (*née* Mills); *m* 1980, Audrey Frances Cannan; two *s* one *d*. *Educ:* Diocesan Coll., Rondesbosch; Univ. of Cape Town (BCom, LLB); University Coll., Oxford (MA Juris.). Advocate, Supreme Court of S Africa; called to the Bar, Gray's Inn, 1982; Attorney and Conveyancer, Supreme Court of S Africa, 1984–85; in practice at the Bar, 1987–. *Recreations:* walking, ski-ing, tennis. *Address:* Acre Holt, One Tree Hill Road, Guildford GU4 8PJ. *T:* (01483) 834733; 7 King's Bench Walk, Temple, EC4Y 7DS. *Clubs:* Vincent's (Oxford); St George's Hill Lawn Tennis (Weybridge).

HOGAN, Prof. Brigid Linda Mary, PhD; FRS 2001; Professor of Cell Biology, Vanderbilt Univesity Medical School, since 1988; Investigator, Howard Hughes Medical Institute, since 1993; *b* 28 Aug. 1943; *d* of Edmond Hogan and Joyce Hogan (*née* Willcox). *Educ:* Wycombe High Sch. for Girls; Newnham Coll., Cambridge (MA, PhD 1968). Postdoctoral Fellowship, MIT, 1968–70; Lectr, Univ. of Sussex, 1970–74; ICRF, London, 1974–84; NIMR, London, 1985–88. Fellow, Amer. Acad. of Arts and Scis, 2001. *Address:* Department of Cell Biology, Vanderbilt University Medical School, 1161 21st Avenue S, Nashville, TN 37232-2175, USA.

HOGAN, Michael Henry; Member, Gaming Board for Great Britain, 1986–94 (Secretary, 1980–86); *b* 31 May 1927; *s* of James Joseph Hogan and Edith Mary Hogan; *m* 1st, 1953, Nina Spillane (*d* 1974); one *s* three *d*; 2nd, 1980, Mollie Burtwell. *Educ:* Ushaw Coll.; LSE. Certif. Social Sci., Certif. Mental Health. Asst Warden, St Vincent's Probation Hostel, 1949–50; London Probation Service, 1953–61; Home Office Inspectorate, 1961–80, Chief Probation Inspector, 1972–80. *Recreation:* golf. *Address:* Yew Tree Cottage, The Street, Capel, Surrey RH5 5LD. *T:* (01306) 711523.

HOGAN, Sir Patrick, KNZM 1999; CBE 1991; Proprietor, Cambridge Stud, since 1975; *b* 20 Oct. 1939; *s* of Thomas Hogan and Sarah Margaret Small; *m* 1961, Justine Alice Heath; two *d*. *Educ:* Goodwood Sch., Cambridge, NZ; St Peter's Convent Sch., Cambridge; Marist Brothers, Hamilton. Partner, with brother, Fencourt Thoroughbred Stud, 1965–75; estabd Cambridge Stud in partnership with wife, 1975. Pres., NZ Thoroughbred Breeders Assoc., 1993–96; Dir, NZ Thoroughbred Mktg Bd, 1997–99. Patron: Cambridge Chamber of Commerce, 1990–; Equine Res. Foundn, 1992; Epilepsy Foundn of NZ Inc., 1995. Formerly Pres., Cambridge Jockey Club Inc. *Recreations:* tennis, Rugby, racing, fishing. *Address:* Discombe Road, Cambridge, New Zealand. *Clubs:* Cambridge, Hautapu Rugby Football (Cambridge); Waikato Racing (Hamilton); Auckland Racing.

HOGARTH, (Arthur) Paul, OBE 1989; RA 1984 (ARA 1974); RE 1988; RDI 1979; painter, illustrator and draughtsman; *b* Kendal, Cumbria, 4 Oct. 1917; *s* of Arthur Hogarth and Janet Bownass; *m* 1963, one *s*. *Educ:* St Agnes Sch., Manchester; Coll. of Art, Manchester; St Martin's Sch. of Art, London. Travels in: Poland and Czechoslovakia, 1953; USSR and China, 1954; Rhodesia and S Africa, 1956; Ireland, with Brendan Behan, 1959; USA, 1961–79. Senior tutor of Drawing: Cambridge Sch. of Art, 1959–61; RCA, 1964–71; Associate Prof., Philadelphia Coll. of Art, 1968–69; Vis. Lectr, RCA, 1971–81. Hon. Pres., Assoc. of Illustrators, 1982. Exhibitions: one-man, Leicester Gall., London, 1955; Agnews, London, 1957; Amer. Embassy, London, 1964; retrospectives, Time-Life Bldg, London, 1968; World of Paul Hogarth, Arts Council, RCA Gall., 1970; Travels through the Seventies, Kyle Gall., London; The Other Hogarth, Northern Arts Council, 1985–86; Paul Hogarth at 80, RA, 1997; Cold War Reports: drawings 1947–67, Norfolk Inst. of Art & Design, Eastern Arts Council, 1989–90; Escape to the Sun: the travels of D. H. Lawrence, Univ. of Nottingham Arts Centre, 1996; exhibits regularly at Francis Kyle Gall., London. Sen. Fellow, RE, 1991. FRSA 1984. Dr RCA, 1971. Hon. DArts Manchester Metropolitan, 1999. *Publications:* Defiant People, 1953; Looking at China, 1956; People Like Us, 1958; (illus.) Brendan Behan's Island, 1962; Creative Pencil Drawing, 1964 (6th edn 1979); (illus.) Brendan Behan's New York, 1964; (with Robert Graves) Majorca Observed, 1965; (with M. Muggeridge) London à la Mode, 1966; Artist as Reporter, 1967, revised and enlarged edn, 1986; (with A. Jacob) Russian Journey, 1969; Drawing People, 1971; Artists on Horseback, 1972; Drawing Architecture, 1973; Paul Hogarth's American Album, 1974; Creative Ink Drawing, 1974 (5th edn 1979); Walking Tours of Old Philadelphia, 1976; Walking Tours of Old Boston, 1978; (with Stephen Spender) America Observed, 1979; Arthur Boyd Houghton, 1982; (with Graham Greene) Graham Greene Country, 1986; (with Laurence Durrell) The Mediterranean Shore, 1988; (with Peter Mayle) Illustrated Year in Provence, 1992; (with John Betjeman) In Praise of Churches, 1996; Drawing on Life (autobiog.), 1997. *Address:* c/o Royal Academy of Arts, Piccadilly, W1V 0DS. *Club:* Arts.

HOGARTH, James, CB 1973; Under-Secretary, Scottish Home and Health Department, 1963–74, retired; *b* 14 Aug. 1914; *s* of George Hogarth; *m* 1940, Katherine Mary Cameron; two *s* one *d*. *Educ:* George Watson's, Edinburgh; Edinburgh Univ.; Sorbonne, Paris. Joined Dept of Health for Scotland as Asst Principal, 1938; Principal, 1944; Asst Sec., 1948; Under-Sec., 1963. *Publications:* Payment of the General Practitioner, 1963; translations from French, German, Russian, etc. *Recreation:* travel. *Address:* 3 Oswald Road, Edinburgh EH9 2HE. *T:* (0131) 667 3878.

HOGARTH, Paul; *see* Hogarth, A. P.

HOGBEN, Ven. Peter Graham; Archdeacon of Dorking, 1982–90, now Archdeacon Emeritus; *b* 5 July 1925; *s* of Harold Henry and Winifred Minnie Hogben; *m* 1948, Audree Sayers; two *s*. *Educ:* Harvey Grammar School, Folkestone; Bishops' College, Cheshunt. Served Royal Engineers, 1943–47 (three years in Far East). Office Manager for two firms of Agricultural Auctioneers in Kent and Herts, 1948–59; theological college, 1960–61; ordained, 1961; Asst Curate of Hale, 1961–64; Vicar of Westborough, Guildford, 1964–71; Chaplain to WRAC, 1964–71; Vicar of Ewell, 1971–82; Editor, Guildford Diocesan Leaflet, 1978–82; Hon. Canon of Guildford, 1979–90, Canon Emeritus, 1990. RD of Epsom, 1980–82. *Recreations:* walking, gardening, water colour painting. *Address:* 3 School Road, Rowledge, Farnham, Surrey GU10 4EJ. *T:* (01252) 793533.

HOGBIN, Walter, CBE 1990; FREng, FICE; Consultant, Taylor Woodrow, 1997–99; Chairman, Taylor Woodrow International Ltd, 1983–96; *b* 21 Dec. 1937; *s* of Walter Clifford John Hogbin and Mary Hogbin; *m* 1968, Geraldine Anne-Marie Castley; two *s*. *Educ:* Kent Coll., Canterbury; Queens' Coll., Cambridge (MA). Joined Taylor Woodrow, 1961; Taylor Woodrow International Ltd: Divl Dir, 1975–77; Dir, 1977–79; Man. Dir, 1979–85; Dir, 1984–96, Jt Man. Dir, 1988–92, Taylor Woodrow plc; Chm., Taylor Woodrow Construction Supervisory Bd, 1991–93. Vice-Pres., Europ. Construction Industry Fedn, 1992–94; Member: Adv. Council, ECGD, 1983–88; Overseas Projects Bd, 1986–91; Export Gp for Construction Ind., 1980–97 (Chm., 1988–90); Europ. Internat. Contractors Fedn, 1988–97 (Pres., 1994–97). Col, Engr and Logistic (formerly Transport) Staff Corps, RE, 1986–2000. FREng (FEng 1994). FRSA. Telford Gold Medal, ICE, 1979. *Recreations:* golf, gardening. *Address:* Codrington Court, Codrington, S Glos BS37 6RY. *Club:* Athenæum.

HOGG, family name of **Hailsham Viscountcy** and of **Barons Hailsham of Saint Marylebone, Hogg of Cumbernauld** and **Baroness Hogg**.

HOGG, Baroness *cr* 1995 (Life Peer), of Kettlethorpe, in the county of Lincolnshire; **Sarah Elizabeth Mary Hogg;** Chairman: Frontier Economics, since 1999; Foreign and Colonial Smaller Companies Investment Trust, since 1997 (Director, since 1995); 3i Group, since 2002 (Director, since 1997; Deputy Chairman, 2000–02); a Governor, BBC, since 2000; *b* 14 May 1946; *d* of Baron Boyd-Carpenter, PC; *m* 1968, Rt Hon. Douglas Martin Hogg, *qv*; one *s* one *d*. *Educ:* St Mary's Convent, Ascot; Lady Margaret Hall, Oxford University (Hon. Fellow, 1994). 1st Cl. Hons PPE. Staff writer, Economist, 1967, Literary Editor, 1970, Economics Editor, 1977; Economics Editor, Sunday Times, 1981; Presenter, Channel 4 News, 1982–83; Econs Editor, and Dep. Exec. Editor, Finance and Industry, The Times, 1984–86; Asst Editor, and Business and City Editor, The Independent, 1986–89; Econs Editor, Daily Telegraph and Sunday Telegraph, 1989–90; Hd, Prime Minister's Policy Unit, 1990–95; Dir, 1995–97, Chm., 1997–99, London Economics. Director: London Broadcasting Co., 1982–90; Royal Nat. Theatre, 1988–91. Non-executive Director: Nat. Provident Instn, 1996–99; GKN, 1996–; The Energy Group, 1996–98; Scottish Eastern Investment Trust, 1998–99; P&O, 1999–; Martin Currie Portfolio Investment Trust, 1999–. Member: Internat. Adv. Bd, Nat. Westminster Bank, 1995–98; Adv. Bd, Bankinter, 1995–98. Member: House of Lords Select Cttee on Sci. and Technol., 1996–99; H of L Monetary Policy Cttee, 2000–. Member Council: REconS, 1996–; Hansard Soc., 1995–. Governor: Centre for Economic Policy Research, 1985–92; IDS, 1987. Fellow, Eton Coll., 1996–. Hon. MA Open Univ., 1987; Hon. DLitt Loughborough, 1992. Wincott Foundation Financial Journalist of the Year, 1985. *Publication:* (with Jonathan Hill) Too Close to Call, 1995. *Address:* House of Lords, SW1A 0PW.

See also Hon. Sir T. P. J Boyd-Carpenter.

HOGG OF CUMBERNAULD, Baron *cr* 1997 (Life Peer), of Cumbernauld in North Lanarkshire; **Norman Hogg;** Lord High Commissioner, General Assembly, Church of Scotland, 1998 and 1999; *b* 12 March 1938; *s* of late Norman Hogg, CBE, LLD, DL, JP, and Mary Wilson; *m* 1964, Elizabeth McCall Christie. *Educ:* Causewayend Sch., Aberdeen; Ruthrieston Secondary Sch., Aberdeen. Local Government Officer, Aberdeen Town Council, 1953–67, District Officer, National and Local Govt Officers Assoc., 1967–79. MP (Lab) Dunbartonshire East, 1979–83, Cumbernauld and Kilsyth, 1983–97. Mem., Select Cttee on Scottish Affairs, 1979–82; Scottish Labour Whip, 1982–83; Chm., Scottish Parly Lab Gp, 1981–82; Dep. Chief Opposition Whip, 1983–87; Scottish Affairs spokesman, 1987–88; Member: Chairman's Panel, 1988–97; Public Accounts Cttee, 1991–92. Mem., H of L Select Cttee on Delegated Powers and Deregulation, 1999–. Chm., British Israel Parly Gp, 1998–. Chm., Bus Appeals Body, 2000–. Hon. Pres., YMCA Scotland, 1998–; Hon. Vice Pres., CCJ, 1997–. Patron, Scottish Centre for Children with Motor Impairments, 1998–. Hon. LLD Aberdeen, 1999. *Recreation:* music. *Address:* House of Lords, SW1A 0PW.

HOGG, Sir Christopher (Anthony), Kt 1985; Chairman: Reuters Group (formerly Reuters Holdings) PLC, since 1985 (Director, since 1984); Allied Domecq, since 1996; *b* 2 Aug. 1936; *s* of Anthony Wentworth Hogg and late Monica Mary (*née* Gladwell); *m* 1st, 1961, Anne Patricia (*née* Cathie) (marr. diss. 1997); two *d*; 2nd, 1997, Miriam Stoppard, *qv*. *Educ:* Marlborough Coll.; Trinity Coll., Oxford (MA; Hon. Fellow 1982); Harvard Univ. (MBA). National Service, Parachute Regt, 1955–57. Harkness Fellow, 1960–62; IMEDE, Lausanne, 1962–63; Hill, Samuel Ltd, 1963–66; IRC, 1966–68; Courtaulds plc, 1968–96: Chief Exec., 1979–91; Chm., 1980–96; Chm., Courtaulds Textiles, 1990–95. Dir, SmithKline Beecham, subseq. Glaxo SmithKline, 1993–; Dep. Chm., Allied Domecq, 1995–96. Member: Indust. Develt Adv. Bd, 1976–81; Cttee of Award for Harkness Fellowships, 1980–86; Internat. Council, J. P. Morgan, 1988–; Court, Bank of England, 1992–96. Chm. Bd, RNT, 1995–. Trustee, Ford Foundn, 1987–99. For. Hon. Mem., Amer. Acad. of Arts and Scis, 1991. Hon. FCSD 1987; Hon. Fellow, London Business Sch., 1992; Hon. FCGI 1992. Hon. DSc: Cranfield Inst. of Technol., 1986; Aston, 1988. BIM Gold Medal, 1986; Centenary Medal, Soc. of Chemical Industry, 1989; Hambro Businessman of the Year, 1993. *Publication:* Masers and Lasers, 1963. *Recreations:* theatre, reading, walking, ski-ing. *Address:* Reuters Group PLC, 85 Fleet Street, EC4P 4AJ.

HOGG, David Alan, CB 1997; Solicitor and Legal Adviser, Department for Transport, Local Government and the Regions (formerly Department of the Environment, Transport and the Regions), since 1997; *b* 8 Oct. 1946; *s* of Donald Kenneth Hogg and Alwyn Lilian Hogg (*née* Chinchen); *m* 1st, 1969, Geraldine Patricia Smith (marr. diss. 1979); one *s* one *d*; 2nd, 1981, Pauline Pamela Papworth; two *s*. *Educ:* Brighton Coll.; Coll. of Law. Admitted solicitor, 1969; in private practice, 1969–78; Treasury Solicitor's Department: Sen. Legal Asst, 1978–85; Asst Treasury Solicitor, 1985–89; Dept of Energy, 1989–90; Treasury Solicitor's Department: Principal Asst Solicitor and Hd, Litigation Div., 1990–93; Dep. Treasury Solicitor, 1993–97. *Recreations:* inland waterways, theatre, reading, watching sport. *Address:* Department for Transport, Local Government and the Regions, Eland House, Bressenden Place, SW1E 5DU.

HOGG, Rt Hon. Douglas (Martin); PC 1992; QC 1990; MP (C) Sleaford and North Hykeham, since 1997 (Grantham, 1979–97); *b* 5 Feb. 1945; *er s* of Baron Hailsham of Saint Marylebone, *qv*; *m* 1968, Sarah Boyd-Carpenter (*see* Baroness Hogg); one *s* one *d*. *Educ:* Eton (Oppidan Schol.); Christ Church, Oxford (Schol.; Pres., Oxford Union). Called to the Bar, Lincoln's Inn, 1968 (Kennedy Law Schol.). Mem., Agric. Select Cttees, 1979–82; PPS to Chief Sec., HM Treasury, 1982–83; an Asst Govt Whip, 1983–84; Parly Under-Sec. of State, Home Office, 1986–89; Minister of State (Minister for Industry and Enterprise), DTI, 1989–90; Minister of State, FCO, 1990–95; Minister of Agriculture, Fisheries and Food, 1995–97. *Address:* House of Commons, SW1A 0AA.

HOGG, Gilbert Charles; solicitor and regulatory consultant, since 1995; *b* 11 Feb. 1933; *s* of Charles and Ivy Ellen Hogg; *m* 1st, Jeanne Whiteside; one *s* one *d*; 2nd, 1979, Angela Christina Wallace. *Educ:* Victoria University Coll., Wellington, NZ (LLB 1956). Called to the New Zealand Bar and admitted Solicitor, 1957; admitted Solicitor, GB, 1971.

Served RNZAC (TF), 1955–62 (Lieut). Partner, Phillips, Shayle-George and Co., Solicitors, Wellington, 1960–66; Sen. Crown Counsel, Hong Kong, 1966–70; Editor, Business Law Summary, 1970–73; Divl Legal Adviser, BSC, 1974–79; British Gas Corporation, subseq. British Gas: Dir of Legal Services, 1979–84; Sec., 1984–90; Dir, Regulatory Ops, 1990–95. Mem., Competition Commn (formerly Monopolies and Mergers Commn), 1998–. Mem., Professional Ethics Cttee, 1994–97, and Council, Energy Section, 1993–98, Internat. Bar Assoc. Chairman: Phoenix House, 1996–; Charterhouse-in-Southwark, 1999–; Trustee, IBA Educn Trust, 1995–98. *Publication:* A Smell of Fraud (novel), 1974. *Address:* 73 Ellerby Street, SW6 6EU. *T:* (020) 7736 8903.

HOGG, Vice-Adm. Sir Ian (Leslie Trower), KCB 1968 (CB 1964); DSC 1941, Bar to DSC 1944; *b* 30 May 1911; 3rd *s* of Col John M. T. Hogg, IA, and Elma (*née* Brand); *m* 1945, Mary G. J., *e d* of Col and Mrs Marsden; two *s*. *Educ:* Cheltenham Coll. Entered Royal Navy, 1929; specialised in Navigation, 1937; HMS Cardiff, 1939; HMS Penelope, 1940; HMAS Napier, 1941–43; HMS Mauritius, 1944–45; Master of the Fleet, 1946–47; British Admiralty Delegation, Washington, DC, 1948–49; HMS Sluys, in comd, 1950–51; Staff of C-in-C Med., 1952–53; Captain RN, Dec. 1953; Brit. Joint Staff, Washington, DC, 1955–57; idc 1958; Staff of Chief of Defence Staff, 1959–60; Cdre, Cyprus, 1961–62; Dir, Chief of Defence Staff's Commonwealth Exercise, 1962–63; Rear-Adm. 1963; Flag Officer, Medway, and Admiral Superintendent, HM Dockyard, Chatham, 1963–66; Vice-Adm. 1966; Defence Services Sec., 1966–67; Vice-Chief of the Defence Staff, 1967–70, retired. Comptroller, Royal Soc. of St George, 1971–74; Dir, Richard Unwin Internat. Ltd, 1975–86. *Address:* 21 Chapel Side, Titchfield, Hants PO14 4AP. *T:* (01329) 847515.

HOGG, Hon. Dame Mary (Claire), (Hon. Dame Mary Koops), DBE 1995; **Hon. Mrs Justice Hogg;** a Judge of the High Court of Justice, Family Division, since 1995; *b* 15 Jan. 1947; *d* of Rt Hon. Baron Hailsham of St Marylebone, *qv*; *m* 1987, Eric Koops (LVO 1997); one *s* one *d*. *Educ:* St Paul's Girls' Sch. Called to the Bar, Lincoln's Inn, 1968 (Bencher, 1995), NI, 1993; QC 1989; Asst Recorder, 1986–90; Recorder, 1990–95. Mem. Council, Children's Soc., 1990–95; Trustee, Harrison Homes, 1986–. Gov., Univ. of Westminster, 1992– (Poly. of Central London, 1983–92). Hon. LLD Westminster, 1995. FRSA 1991. Freeman, City of London, 1981. *Address:* Royal Courts of Justice, Strand, WC2A 2LL.

HOGG, Sir Michael Edward L.; *see* Lindsay-Hogg.

HOGG, Rear-Adm. Peter Beauchamp, CB 1980; Head of British Defence Liaison Staff and Defence Adviser, Canberra, 1977–80, retired; *b* 9 Nov. 1924; *s* of Beauchamp and Sybil Hogg; *m* 1951, Gabriel Argentine Alington; two *s* two *d*. *Educ:* Connaught House, Weymouth; Bradfield Coll., Berks; Royal Naval Engineering Coll., Keyham. Lieut, HMS Sirius, 1947–49; Advanced Engrg Course, RNC Greenwich, 1949–51; HMS Swiftsure and HMS Pincher, 1951–53; Lt Comdr, Loan Service with Royal Canadian Navy, 1953–56; Staff of RN Engrg Coll., Manadon, 1956–58; Comdr (Trng Comdr), HMS Sultan, 1959–62; Marine Engr Officer, HMS Hampshire, 1962–64; JSSC, Latimer, 1964; Ship Dept, Bath, 1965–67; Captain, Ship Dept, Bath, 1968–69; CO, HMS Tyne, 1970–71; RCDS, 1972; CO, HMS Caledonia, 1973–74; Dir of Naval Recruiting, 1974–76. Sec., Sixth Centenary Appeal, and Bursar i/c building works, Winchester Coll., 1980–88. Chairman: Hereford Cathedral Fabric Adv. Cttee, 1991–; Herefordshire Historic Churches Trust, 1996–. *Address:* c/o National Westminster Bank, 14 Old Town Street, Plymouth PL1 1DG.

HOGG, Sir Piers Michael James, 9th Bt cr 1846, of Upper Grosvenor Street, Middlesex; *b* 25 April 1957; *e s* of Sir Michael Hogg, 8th Bt and of Elizabeth Anne Thérèse, *e d* of Sir Terence Falkiner, 8th Bt; *S* father, 2001; *m* 1982, Vivien (marr. diss. 1996), *y d* of Dr Philip Holman; one *s* one *d*. *Educ:* St Paul's Sch. *Heir: s* James Edward Hogg, *b* 11 Sept. 1985.

HOGG, Prof. Richard Milne, FBA 1994; Smith Professor of English Language and Medieval Literature, University of Manchester, since 1980; *b* 20 May 1944; *s* of Charles Milne Hogg and Norenne Hogg (*née* Young); *m* 1969, Margaret Kathleen White; two *s*. *Educ:* Royal High Sch., Edinburgh; Univ. of Edinburgh (MA, Dip. Gen. Linguistics, PhD). Lecturer in English Language: Univ. van Amsterdam, 1969–73; Univ. of Lancaster, 1973–80. Leverhulme Major Res. Fellow, 2000–02. Gen. Editor, Cambridge History of the English Language, 1992–; Jt Editor, English Language and Linguistics, 1997–. *Publications:* English Quantifier Systems, 1977; Metrical Phonology, 1986; A Grammar of Old English, 1992; contribs to learned jls. *Recreation:* Altrincham Football Club. *Address:* Department of English and American Studies, University of Manchester, Oxford Road, Manchester M13 9PL. *T:* (0161) 275 3164.

HOGG, Rear-Adm. Robin Ivor Trower, CB 1988; FNI, FIMgt; Managing Director: Raidfleet Ltd, since 1988; Shinbond Ltd, since 1998; Robstar Productions Ltd, since 1998; *b* 25 Sept. 1932; *s* of Dudley and Nancy Hogg; *m* 1st, 1958, Susan Bridget Beryl Grantham; two *s* two *d*; 2nd, 1970, Angela Sarah Patricia Kirwan. *Educ:* The New Beacon, Sevenoaks; Bedford School. Directorate of Naval Plans, 1974–76; RCDS 1977; Captain RN Presentation Team, 1978–79; Captain First Frigate Sqdn, 1980–82; Director Naval Operational Requirements, 1982–84; Flag Officer, First Flotilla, 1984–86; COS to C-in-C Fleet, 1986–87, retd. CEO, Colebrand Ltd, 1988–97. *Recreation:* private life. *Address:* c/o Barclays Bank, Blenheim Gate, 22/24 Upper Marlborough Road, St Albans AL1 3AL. *T:* (01727) 863315.

HOGGARD, Robin Richard; HM Diplomatic Service; Counsellor (Management) and Consul General, Tokyo, since 1998; *b* 26 Nov. 1956; *s* of George Lawrence Hoggard and Frances Mary Christine Hoggard (*née* Stephenson); *m* 1988, Tonoko Komuro; one *s*. *Educ:* Cheadle Hulme Sch.; Univ. of Newcastle upon Tyne (BA Hons Politics 1979); SOAS, Univ. of London (MSc 1982). FCO, 1982; Tokyo, 1984–89; FCO, 1989–91; DTI, 1991–93; UK Deleg. to NATO, 1994–98. *Address:* c/o Foreign and Commonwealth Office, SW1A 2AH.

HOGGART, Richard (Herbert), LittD; Warden, Goldsmiths' College, University of London, 1976–84; *b* 24 Sept. 1918; 2nd *s* of Tom Longfellow Hoggart and Adeline Emma Hoggart; *m* 1942, Mary Holt France; two *s* one *d*. *Educ:* elementary and secondary schs, Leeds; Leeds Univ. (MA, LittD 1978). Served 1940–46, RA; demobilised as Staff Capt. Staff Tutor and Sen. Staff Tutor, University Coll. of Hull and University of Hull, 1946–59; Sen. Lectr in English, University of Leicester, 1959–62; Prof. of English, Birmingham Univ., 1962–73, and Dir, Centre for Contemporary Cultural Studies, 1964–73; an Asst Dir-Gen., Unesco, 1970–75. Vis. Fellow, Inst. of Development Studies, Univ. of Sussex, 1975. Visiting Prof., University of Rochester (NY), USA, 1956–57; Reith Lectr, 1971. Member: Albemarle Cttee on Youth Services, 1958–60; (Pilkington) Cttee on Broadcasting, 1960–62; Arts Council, 1976–81 (Chm., Drama Panel, 1977–80; Vice-Chm., 1980–82); Statesman and Nation Publishing Co. Ltd, 1977–81 (Chm., 1978–81); Chairman: Adv. Council for Adult and Continuing Educn, 1977–83; European Museum of the Year Award, 1977–95; Broadcasting Research Unit, 1981–91; Book Trust, 1995–97 (Vice-Chm., 1997–); Vice-Chm., Unesco Forum, 1997–. Patron, Nat. Book Cttee, 1998–. Governor, Royal Shakespeare Theatre, 1962–88. Pres., British Assoc. of Former UN Civil Servants, 1979–86. Hon. Professor: UEA, 1984; Univ. of Surrey, 1985; Hon. Fellow: Sheffield Polytechnic, 1983; Goldsmiths' Coll., 1987; DUniv: Open, 1973; Surrey, 1981; Leeds Metropolitan, 1995; Hon DèsL: Univ. of Bordeaux, 1975; Paris, 1987; Hon. LLD: CNAA, 1982; York (Toronto), 1988; Sheffield, 1999; Hon. LittD East Anglia, 1986; Hon. DLitt: Leicester, 1988; Hull, 1988; Keele, 1995; Leeds Metropolitan, 1995; Westminster, 1996; East London, 1998; Sheffield, 1999; Hon. DLit London, 2000. *Publications:* Auden, 1951; The Uses of Literacy, 1957; W. H. Auden, 1957; W. H. Auden—A Selection, 1961; chap. in Conviction, 1958; chapter in Pelican Guide to English Literature, 1961; Teaching Literature, 1963; chapter in Of Books and Humankind, 1964; The Critical Moment, 1964; How and Why Do We Learn, 1965; The World in 1984, 1965; Essays by Divers Hands XXXIII; Guide to the Social Sciences, 1966; Technology and Society, 1966; Essays on Reform, 1967; Your Sunday Paper (ed), 1967; Speaking to Each Other: vol. I, About Society; vol. II, About Literature, 1970; Only Connect (Reith Lectures), 1972; An Idea and Its Servants, 1978; (ed with Janet Morgan) The Future of Broadcasting, 1982; An English Temper, 1982; (ed) The Public Service Idea in British Broadcasting: main principles, 1986; Writers on Writing, 1986; (jtly) The British Council and The Arts, 1986; (with Douglas Johnson) An Idea of Europe, 1987; A Local Habitation (autobiog.), 1988; (ed) Liberty and Legislation, 1989; (ed) Quality in Television: programmes, programme makers, systems, 1989; A Sort of Clowning: life and times 1940–59 (autobiog.), 1990; An Imagined Life: life and times 1959–91 (autobiog.), 1992; Townscape with Figures, 1994; The Way We Live Now, 1995; First and Last Things, 1999; Richard Hoggart en France (essays), ed J.-C. Passeron, 1999; Between Two Worlds, 2001; numerous introductions, articles, pamphlets and reviews. *Recreation:* pottering about the house and garden. *Address:* 19 Mount Pleasant, Norwich NR2 2DH.
See also S. D. Hoggart.

HOGGART, Simon David; Parliamentary Reporter, The Guardian, since 1993; *b* 26 May 1946; *s* of Richard Hoggart, *qv*; *m* 1983, Alyson Clare Corner; one *s* one *d*. *Educ:* Hymer's College, Hull; Wyggeston Grammar Sch., Leicester; King's College, Cambridge. MA. Reporter, The Guardian, 1968–71, N Ireland corresp., 1971–73, political corresp., 1973–81; feature writer, The Observer, 1981–85; political columnist, Punch, 1979–85; US correspondent, 1985–89, columnist, 1989–92, Political Editor, 1992–93, The Observer. Chairman, The News Quiz, Radio 4, 1996–. *Publications:* (with Alistair Michie) The Pact, 1978; (with David Leigh) Michael Foot: a portrait, 1981; On the House, 1981; Back on the House, 1982; House of Ill Fame, 1985; (ed) House of Cards, 1988; America: a user's guide, 1990; House of Correction, 1994; (with Michael Hutchinson) Bizarre Beliefs, 1995; (with Steve Bell) Live Briefs, 1996. *Recreations:* reading, writing, occasional broadcasting. *Address:* Parliamentary Press Gallery, House of Commons, SW1A 0AA. *T:* (020) 7219 4700.

HOGGE, Maj.-Gen. (Arthur) Michael (Lancelot), CB 1979; DL; *b* 4 Aug. 1925; *s* of late Lt-Col A. H. F. Hogge, Punjab Regt, Indian Army, and Mrs K. M. Hogge; *m* 1952, Gunilla Jeane Earley; two *s*. *Educ:* Wellington Coll.; Brasenose Coll., Oxford. Commissioned, Oct. 1945; 6th Airborne Armoured Recce Regt and 3rd Hussars, Palestine, 1945–48; regimental appts, 3rd Hussars, BAOR, 1948–58; Queen's Own Hussars, BAOR, and Staff appts, 1958–65; comd Queen's Own Hussars, UK and Aden, 1965–67; Col GS, Staff Coll., 1969–71; Royal Coll. of Defence Studies, 1972; Dir of Operational Requirements, MoD, 1973–74, rank of Brig.; Dir Gen. Fighting Vehicles and Engineer Equipment, 1974–77; Dep. Master-General of the Ordnance, 1977–80; Gen. Man., Regular Forces Employment Assoc., 1981–87. Vice-Pres., Surrey Branch, SSAFA, 1996– (Chm., 1992–96). DL Surrey, 1993. *Recreations:* sailing, horticulture.

HOGGER, Henry George; HM Diplomatic Service; Ambassador to Syria, since 2000; *b* 9 Nov. 1948; *s* of late Rear-Adm. Henry Charles Hogger, CB, DSC and Ethel Mary Hogger; *m* 1972, Fiona Jane McNabb; two *s* two *d*. *Educ:* Winchester Coll.; Trinity Hall, Cambridge (MA Hons). Joined FCO 1969; MECAS, Lebanon, 1971–72; served Aden, Caracas, Kuwait; FCO, 1978–82; Head of Chancery, Abu Dhabi, 1982–86; FCO, 1986–89; Counsellor and Dep. Head of Mission, Amman, 1989–92; High Comr, Namibia, 1992–96; Head, Latin America, later Latin America and Caribbean Dept, FCO, 1996–2000. Mem., Inst. of Advanced Motorists. *Recreations:* golf, sailing, music, travel. *Address:* c/o Foreign and Commonwealth Office, SW1A 2AH.

HOGGETT, Anthony John Christopher, PhD; QC 1986; a Recorder, since 1988; *b* 20 Aug. 1940; *s* of late Christopher Hoggett and Annie Marie Hoggett; *m* 1968, Brenda Marjorie Hale (*see* Rt Hon. Dame Brenda Hale) (marr. diss. 1992); one *d*. *Educ:* Leeds Grammar Sch.; Hymers Coll., Hull; Clare Coll., Cambridge (MA, LLB); PhD Manchester. Asst Juridique, Inst. of Comparative Law, Paris, 1962–63; Lectr in Law, Univ. of Manchester, 1963–69; called to Bar, Gray's Inn, 1969, Head of Chambers, 1985–96; Asst Recorder, 1982. Res. Fellow, Univ. of Michigan, 1965–66. Mem., Civil Service Final Selection Bd for Planning Inspectors, 1987–91. Dir, Europ. Youth Parlt Internat., 1993–. Mem. Adv. Council, Rural Bldgs Preservation Trust, 1994– (Trustee, 2000–). Mem. Editl Bd, Envmtl Law Reports, 1992–. *Publications:* articles in Criminal Law Rev., Mod. Law Rev. and others. *Recreations:* swimming, music, walking. *Address:* Flat 29, Chepstow House, Chepstow Street, Manchester M1 5JF. *T:* (0161) 236 7973; 128 Offord Road, N1 1PF.

HOGWOOD, Christopher Jarvis Haley, CBE 1989; harpsichordist, conductor, musicologist, writer, editor and broadcaster; Founder and Director, Academy of Ancient Music, since 1973; *b* 10 Sept. 1941; *s* of Haley Evelyn Hogwood and Marion Constance Higgott. *Educ:* Pembroke Coll., Cambridge (MA; Hon. Fellow, 1992); Charles Univ., Prague. With Acad. of St Martin-in-the-Fields, 1965–76; Founder Mem., Early Music Consort of London, 1965–76; Artistic Director: King's Lynn Festival, 1976–80; Handel & Haydn Soc., Boston, USA, 1986–2001 (Conductor Laureate, 2001–); Summer Mozart Fest., Nat. Symphony Orch., USA, 1993–2001; Dir of Music, St Paul Chamber Orchestra, USA, 1987–92, Prin. Guest Conductor, 1992–98; Associate Dir, Beethoven Academie, Antwerp, 1998–; Principal Guest Conductor: Kammerorchester Basel, 2000–; Orquesta Ciudad de Granada, 2001–. Visiting Professor: RAM, 1992–; KCL, 1992–96; Hon. Prof. of Music, Keele Univ., 1986–90. Keyboard and orchestral recordings. Mem. Editl Bd, Early Music, 1993–97; Chm. Adv. Bd, C. P. E. Bach Complete Works, 1999–. Freeman, Co. of Musicians, 1989. FRSA 1982. Hon. RAM 1995; Hon. Fellow, Jesus Coll., Cambridge, 1989. Hon. DMus Keele, 1991. Walter Willson Cobbett Medal, Co. of Musicians, 1986; Distinguished Musician Award, ISM, 1997; Martinu Medal, Bohuslav Martinu Foundn, Prague, 1999. *Publications:* Music at Court (Folio Society), 1977; The Trio Sonata, 1979; Haydn's Visits to England (Folio Society), 1980; (ed with R. Luckett) Music in Eighteenth-Century England, 1983; Handel, 1984; (ed) Holmes' Life of Mozart (Folio Society), 1991. *Address:* 10 Brookside, Cambridge CB2 1JE. *T:* (01223) 363975.

HOLBOROW, Eric John, MD, FRCP, FRCPath; Emeritus Professor of Immunopathology and Honorary Consultant Immunologist, London Hospital Medical College, E1, retired 1983; *b* 30 March 1918; *s* of Albert Edward Ratcliffe Holborow and Marian Crutchley; *m* 1943, Cicely Mary Foister; two *s* one *d*. *Educ:* Epsom Coll.; Clare

Coll., Cambridge; St Bart's Hosp. MA, MD (Cantab). Served War of 1939–45, Major, RAMC. Consultant Bacteriologist, Canadian Hosp., Taplow, 1953; Mem. Scientific Staff, MRC Rheumatism Unit, Taplow, 1957; Director, 1975; Head, MRC Group, Bone and Joint Res. Unit, London Hosp. Med. Coll., 1976–83. Visiting Prof., Royal Free Hosp. Med. Sch., 1975. Bradshaw Lectr, RCP, 1982. Chm., Smith Kline Foundn, 1987–89 (Trustee, 1977–89). Editor, Jl Immunol. Methods, 1971–85. *Publications:* Autoimmunity and Disease (with L. E. Glynn), 1965; An ABC of Modern Immunology, 1968, 2nd edn 1973; (with W. G. Reeves) Immunology in Medicine, 1977, 2nd edn 1983; (with A. Maroudas) Studies in Joint Disease, vol. 1, 1981, vol. 2, 1983; Fingest: stony ground, 1999; books and papers on immunology. *Recreations:* glebe terriers, ecclesiastical records.

See also J. *Holborow.*

HOLBOROW, Jonathan; Editor, Mail on Sunday, 1992–98; Member, Editorial Integrity Board, Express Newspapers, since 2000; *b* 12 Oct. 1943; *s* of Prof. Eric John Holborow, *qv* and Cicely Mary (*née* Foister); *m* 1st, 1965, Susan Ridings (*d* 1993); one *s* one *d*; 2nd, 1994, Vivien Ferguson. *Educ:* Charterhouse. Reporter, Maidenhead Advertiser, 1961–65; Lincs Echo, 1965–66; Lincoln Chronicle, 1966–67; Daily Mail, Manchester, 1967–69; Scottish News Editor, Daily Mail, Glasgow, 1969–70; Daily Mail, Manchester: Northern Picture Editor, 1970–72; Northern News Editor, 1972–74; Daily Mail, London: Dep. News Editor, 1974–75; News Editor, 1975–80; Editor, Cambrian News, Aberystwyth, 1980–82; Asst Editor, then Associate Editor, Mail on Sunday, 1982–86; Dep. Editor, Today, 1986–87; Daily Mail: Asst Editor, then Associate Editor, 1987–88; Dep. Editor, 1988–92; Dir, Associated Newspapers Ltd, 1992–98. *Recreation:* golf. *Address:* Upper Ensign House, Selling Road, Old Wives Lees, Canterbury CT4 8BB.

HOLBOROW, Prof. Leslie Charles, MA; Vice-Chancellor, Victoria University of Wellington, 1985–98, now Emeritus Professor; *b* 28 Jan. 1941; *s* of George and Ivah Vivienne Holborow; *m* 1965, Patricia Lynette Walsh; one *s* two *d. Educ:* Henderson High Sch.; Auckland Grammar Sch.; Univ. of Auckland (MA 1st Cl. Hons Philosophy); Oxford Univ. (BPhil). Jun. Lectr, Auckland Univ., 1963; Commonwealth schol. at Merton Coll., Oxford, 1963–65; Lectr, then Sen. Lectr, Univ. of Dundee (until 1967 Queen's Coll., Univ. of St Andrews), 1965–74, Mem. Court, 1972–74; University of Queensland, Brisbane: Prof. of Philosophy, 1974–85; Pres., Academic Bd, 1980–81; Pro-Vice-Chancellor (Humanities), 1983–85. Pres., Qld Br., Aust. Inst. of Internat. Affairs, 1984–85; Nat. Pres., NZ Inst. of Internat. Affairs, 1987–90; Member: NZ Cttee for Pacific Economic Co-operation, 1986–97; Bd, Inst. of Policy Studies, 1986–98; Bd, NZ Inst. of Econ. Res., 1986–91; Bd, Victoria Univ. Foundn, 1990–98; NZ Cttee for Security Co-operation in Asia Pacific, 1994–. Chair: NZ Vice-Chancellors' Cttee, 1990, 1996; Cttee on Univ. Academic Progs, 1993–95; Member: Council, ACU, 1990–91, 1996; Educn Sub-Commn, UNESCO Commn for NZ, 1997–2000. Member: Musica Viva Nat. Bd, 1984–85; Bd of Management, Music Fedn of NZ, 1987–90. Trustee, NZ String Quartet, 1990–; Chm., NZ String Quartet Foundn, 1999–. Hon. LLD Victoria Univ. of Wellington, 1998. *Publications:* various articles in philosophical and legal jls. *Recreations:* tramping, sailing, listening to music. *Address:* 29 Upoko Road, Hataitai, Wellington, New Zealand. *Clubs:* Wellington, Victoria University Staff (Wellington).

HOLBOROW, Lady Mary (Christina); JP; Lord-Lieutenant of Cornwall, since 1994; *b* 19 Sept. 1936; *d* of 8th Earl of Courtown, OBE, TD, DL, and Christina Margaret Tremlett (*née* Cameron); *m* 1959, Geoffrey Jermyn Holborow, OBE; one *s* one *d. Educ:* Tudor Hall Sch., Banbury. Mem., Regional Board, TSB, 1981–87; Director: SW Water, 1989–95; Devon and Cornwall TEC, 1990–96; TSW Broadcasting, 1990–91. Vice-Chm., Cornwall and Isles of Scilly HA, 1990–2000; SW Regl Chm., FEFC, 1993–94; Chairman: Cornwall Macmillan Service, 1982–; Cornwall Rural Develt Cttee, 1987–99. Patron or Pres., numerous charitable orgns in Cornwall. JP Cornwall 1970. DStJ 1987 (Comr, St John Ambulance, 1982–87). *Address:* Ladock House, Ladock, Truro, Cornwall TR2 4PL. *T:* (01726) 882274.

HOLBROOK, David Kenneth, FEA; author; *b* 9 Jan. 1923; *o s* of late Kenneth Redvers and late Elsie Eleanor Holbrook; *m* 1949, Margot Davies-Jones; two *s* two *d. Educ:* City of Norwich Sch.; Downing Coll., Cambridge (Exhibr). Intell., mines and explosives officer, ER Yorks Yeo., Armd Corps, 1942–45. Asst Editor, Our Time, 1948; Asst Editor, Bureau of Current Affairs, 1949; Tutor organiser, WEA, 1952–53; Tutor, Bassingbourn Village Coll., Cambs, 1954–61; Fellow, King's Coll., Cambridge, 1961–65; Sen. Leverhulme Res. Fellow, 1965; College Lectr in English, Jesus Coll., Cambridge, 1968–70; Compton Poetry Lectr, Hull Univ., 1969 (resigned); Writer in Residence, Dartington Hall, 1970–73 (grant from Elmgrant Trust); Downing Coll., Cambridge: Asst Dir, English Studies, 1973–75; Fellow and Dir of English Studies, 1981–88, Emeritus Fellow, 1988–; Leverhulme Emeritus Res. Fellow, 1988–90. Hooker Distinguished Vis. Prof., McMaster Univ., Ontario, 1984. Founding FEA 2000. Arts Council Writers Grants, 1970, 1976, 1979. Mem. Editorial Bd, New Universities Qly, 1976–86. *Publications: poetry:* Imaginings, 1961; Against the Cruel Frost, 1963; Object Relations, 1967; Old World, New World, 1969; Moments in Italy, 1976; Chance of a Lifetime, 1978; Selected Poems, 1980; Bringing Everything Home, 1999; *fiction:* Lights in the Sky Country, 1963; Flesh Wounds, 1966; A Play of Passion, 1978; Nothing Larger than Life, 1987; Worlds Apart, 1988; A Little Athens, 1990; Jennifer, 1991; The Gold in Father's Heart, 1992; Even If They Fail, 1994; Getting it Wrong with Uncle Tom, 1998; *on education:* English for Maturity, 1961; English for the Rejected, 1964; The Secret Places, 1964; The Exploring Word, 1967; Children's Writing, 1967; English in Australia Now, 1972; Education, Nihilism and Survival, 1977; English for Meaning, 1980; Education and Philosophical Anthropology, 1987; Further Studies in Philosophical Anthropology, 1988; *literary criticism:* Llareggub Revisited, 1962; The Quest for Love, 1965; The Masks of Hate, 1972; Dylan Thomas: the code of night, 1972; Sylvia Plath: poetry and existence, 1976; Lost Bearings in English Poetry, 1977; The Novel and Authenticity, 1987; Images of Woman in Literature, 1989; The Skeleton in the Wardrobe: the fantasies of C. S. Lewis, 1991; Edith Wharton and the Unsatisfactory Man, 1991; Where D. H. Lawrence was Wrong about Woman, 1991; Charles Dickens and The Image of Woman, 1993; Tolstoy, Women and Death, 1997; Wuthering Heights: a drama of being, 1997; A Study of George MacDonald and the Image of Woman, 2000; Lewis Carroll: nonsense against sorrow, 2001; *music criticism:* Gustav Mahler and the Courage to Be, 1975; *general:* Children's Games, 1957; Human Hope and the Death Instinct, 1971; Sex and Dehumanization, 1972; The Pseudo-revolution, 1972; (ed) The Case Against Pornography, 1972; Evolution and the Humanities, 1987; (ed) What is it to be Human?: report on a philosophy conference, 1990; Creativity and Popular Culture, 1994; *anthologies:* edited: Iron, Honey, Gold, 1961; People and Diamonds, 1962; Thieves and Angels, 1963; Visions of Life, 1964; (with Elizabeth Poston) The Cambridge Hymnal, 1967; Plucking the Rushes, 1968; (with Christine Mackenzie) The Honey of Man, 1975; *opera libretti:* (with Wilfrid Mellers) The Borderline, 1958; (with John Joubert) The Quarry, 1967; *festschrift:* Powers of Being: David Holbrook and his work, ed E. Webb, 1996. *Recreations:* painting, cooking. *Address:* 1 Tennis Court Terrace, Cambridge CB2 1QX.

HOLBROOKE, Richard Charles; United States Representative to the United Nations, 1999–2001; *b* 2 April 1941; *s* of Dan Holbrooke and Trudi (*née* Moos); two *s*; *m* 1995, Kati Marton. *Educ:* Brown Univ. (BA). Foreign Service Officer in Vietnam and related posts, 1962–66; White House Vietnam staff, 1966–67; Special Asst to Under Secs of State Nicholas Katzenbach and Elliot Richardson, and Mem., US Delegn to Paris peace talks on Vietnam, 1967–69; Dir, Peace Corps, Morocco, 1970–72; Man. Dir, Foreign Policy mag., 1972–76; Consultant, President's Commn on Orgn of Govt for Conduct of Foreign Policy, 1974–75; Contrib. Ed., Newsweek, 1974–75; Co-ordinator, Nat. Security Affairs, Carter-Mondale Campaign, 1976; Asst Sec. of State for E Asian and Pacific Affairs, 1977–81; Vice-Pres., Public Strategies, 1981–85; Man. Dir, Lehman Bros, 1985–93; Ambassador to Germany, 1993–94; Asst Sec. of State for Eur. and Canadian Affairs, 1994–96; Vice-Chm., Credit Suisse First Boston Corp., 1996–99; Advr, Baltic Sea Council, 1996–97; Special Presidential Envoy for Cyprus, to Yugoslavia, 1997–98. Numerous hon. degrees, including: Maryland, and Heidelberg, 1994; Georgetown, 1996; Amer. Univ. of Paris, 1996; Central Euro-Atlantic Bucaresti, Romania, 1996; Tufts, 1997; Brown, 1997; Amer. Univ. in Athens, 1998; Lawrence, 1998; Dayton, 1998. Dist. Public Service Award, Dept of Defense, 1994 and 1996; Excellence in Diplomacy Award, Amer. Acad. of Diplomacy, 1996; Gold Medal for Dist. Service to Humanity, Nat. Inst. of Social Scis, 1996; Citation of Honor, USAF Assoc., 1996; Nahum Goldmann Award, World Jewish Congress, 1996; America's First Freedom Award, 1996; Sec. of State's Dist. Service Award, 1996; Manfred Woerner Award, FRG, 1997; Humanitarian of Year Award, American Jewish Congress, 1998; Nat. Diplomatic Award, Foreign Policy Assoc., 1998; Community Service Award, Mt Sinai Med. Center, 1999. *Publications:* (jtly) Counsel to the President, 1991; To End a War, 1998; contrib. various articles and essays. *Recreations:* tennis, ski-ing. *Address:* Council on Foreign Relations, 58 East 68th Street, New York, NY 10021, USA. *T:* (212) 4349644.

HOLCROFT, Sir Peter (George Culcheth), 3rd Bt *cr* 1921; JP; *b* 29 April 1931; *s* of Sir Reginald Culcheth Holcroft, 2nd Bt, TD, and Mary Frances (*d* 1963), *yr d* of late William Swire, CBE; *S* father, 1978; *m* 1956, Rosemary Rachel (marr. diss. 1987), *yr d* of late G. N. Deas; three *s* one *d. Educ:* Eton. High Sheriff of Shropshire, 1969; JP 1976. *Recreation:* the countryside. *Heir: s* Charles Antony Culcheth Holcroft [*b* 22 Oct. 1959; *m* 1986, Mrs Elizabeth Carter, *y d* of John Raper, Powys; one *s* one *d*]. *Address:* Berrington House, Berrington, Shrewsbury SY5 6HA.

HOLDEN, Amanda Juliet; musician, writer; *b* 19 Jan. 1948; *d* of Sir Brian Warren and Dame Josephine Barnes, DBE; *m* 1971, Anthony Holden, *qv* (marr. diss. 1988); three *s. Educ:* Benenden Sch.; Lady Margaret Hall, Oxford (MA); Guildhall Sch. of Music and Drama (LGSM); American Univ., Washington (Hall of Nations Schol.; MA); ARCM; LRAM. Music staff: St Michael's Comprehensive, Watford, 1970–72; Watford Sch. of Music, 1971–75; Guildhall Sch., 1973–85; Founder, Music Therapy Dept, Charing Cross Hosp., London, 1973–75. Mem., Opera Adv. Bd, Royal Opera House, 1998. Has translated more than 40 opera libretti, 1985–, including: Les Boréades (Rameau), Alcina, Ariodante (Handel), La Finta Giardiniera, Il re pastore, Idomeneo, Die Entführung, The Marriage of Figaro, La Clemenza di Tito, l'Elisir d'amore, Maria Stuarda, Beatrice and Benedict, Lohengrin, Rigoletto, Aida, Falstaff, Faust (Gounod), The Pearl Fishers, Werther, La Bohème, Tosca, Madam Butterfly, Il Trittico, Carmen, Don Giovanni; *cartoon film script:* Rhinegold, 1995; *play translation*, Kleist, Amphitryon; *adaptations for concert hall:* The Epic of Gilgamesh (Martinu); Der Freischütz, *libretti:* The Selfish Giant (after Wilde); The Silver Tassie (after O'Casey) (Outstanding Achievement in Opera (jtly), Laurence Olivier Awards, 2001). *Publications:* The Magic Flute (arr. for children), 1990; (contrib.) The Mozart Compendium, 1990; (trans.) Lohengrin, 1993; (ed) The Viking Opera Guide, 1993; (ed) The Penguin Opera Guide, 1995, 2nd edn 1997; (ed) The New Penguin Opera Guide, 2001. *Recreations:* piano duets, walking by the sea, motoring. *Address:* 107 Sotheby Road, N5 2UT. *T:* (020) 7226 4866.

HOLDEN, Anthony Ivan; writer; *b* 22 May 1947; *s* of late John Holden and Margaret Lois Holden (*née* Sharpe); *m* 1st, 1971, Amanda Juliet Warren (*see* A. J. Holden) (marr. diss. 1988); three *s*; 2nd, 1990, Cynthia Blake, *d* of Mrs George Blake, Brookline, Mass. *Educ:* Tre-Arddur House Sch., Anglesey; Oundle Sch.; Merton Coll., Oxford (MA Hons Eng. Lang. and Lit.; Editor, Isis). Trainee reporter, Thomson Regional Newspapers, Evening Echo, Hemel Hempstead, 1970–73; home and foreign corresp., Sunday Times, 1973–77; columnist (Atticus), Sunday Times, 1977–79; Washington corresp. and US Editor, Observer, 1979–81; Features Editor and Asst Editor, The Times, 1981–82; freelance journalist and author, 1982–85 and 1986–; Exec. Editor, Today, 1985–86. Fellow, Center for Scholars and Writers, NY Public Liby, 1999–2000. Broadcaster, radio and TV; TV documentaries include: The Man Who Would Be King, 1982; Charles at Forty, 1988; Anthony Holden on Poker, 1992; Who Killed Tchaikovsky, 1993. Young Journalist of 1972; commended for work in NI, News Reporter of the Year, British Press Awards, 1976; Columnist of the Year, British Press Awards, 1977. Opera translations: Don Giovanni, 1985; La Bohème, 1986; The Barber of Seville, 1987. *Publications:* (trans. and ed) Aeschylus' Agamemnon, 1969; (contrib.) The Greek Anthology, 1973; (trans. and ed) Greek Pastoral Poetry, 1974; The St Albans Poisoner, 1974, 2nd edn 1996; Charles, Prince of Wales, 1979; Their Royal Highnesses, 1981; Of Presidents, Prime Ministers and Princes, 1984; The Queen Mother, 1985, 3rd edn 1995; Don Giovanni, 1987; Olivier, 1988; Charles, 1988; Big Deal, 1990, 2nd edn 1995; (ed) The Last Paragraph, 1990; A Princely Marriage, 1991; The Oscars, 1993; The Tarnished Crown, 1993; (contrib.) Power and the Throne, 1994; Tchaikovsky, 1995; Diana: her life and legacy, 1997; Charles: a biography, 1998; William Shakespeare: his life and work, 1999; (ed jtly) The Mind Has Mountains, 1999; (ed jtly) There are Kermodians, 1999. *Recreations:* poker, Arsenal FC, Lancashire CC. *Address:* c/o Rogers Coleridge White, 20 Powis Mews, W11 1JN. *T:* (020) 7221 3717.

HOLDEN, His Honour Derek; a Circuit Judge, 1984–2000; a Chairman, Immigration Appeal Tribunal, since 2000; *b* 7 July 1935; *s* of Frederic Holden and Audrey Holden (*née* Hayes); *m* 1961, Dorien Elizabeth Holden (*née* Bell); two *s. Educ:* Cromwell House; Staines Grammar Sch. Served Army; Lieut East Surrey Regt, 1953–56. Qualified as Solicitor, 1966; Derek Holden & Co., Staines, Egham, Camberley, Feltham and Ashford, 1966–84; Consultant, Batt Holden & Co., 1966–84; Partner, Black Lake Securities, 1978–84; Principal, Dorien Property Co., 1974–84. A Recorder, 1980–84; President: Social Security Appeal Tribunals and Medical Appeal Tribunals, 1990–92; Vaccine Damage Tribunals, 1990–92; Disability Appeals Tribunal, 1992; Child Support Tribunal, 1993; Chm., Tribunals Cttee, Judicial Studies Bd, 1991–93; Mem., Criminal Injuries Compensation Appeal Panel, 2000–; Chm., Indep. Tribunal for Office of Supervision of Standards of Telephone Inf. Services, 2001–. Mem., Royal Yachting Assoc., 1975– (Dept of Trade Offshore Yachtmaster Instr with Ocean Cert.; Open Water Diving Cert., 2000); Principal, Chandor Sch. of Sailing, Lymington, 1978–85. *Recreations:* sailing, snow–boarding, photography, music. *Address:* c/o Reading County Court, Friar Street, Reading, Berks RG1 1HE. *Clubs:* Western (Glasgow); Leander, Remenham (Henley); Burway Rowing (Laleham); Eton Excelsior Rowing (Windsor); Staines Boat; Port Solent Yacht, Royal Solent Yacht (Yarmouth, IoW).

HOLDEN, Sir Edward, 6th Bt *cr* 1893; Consultant Anæsthetist, Darlington & Northallerton Group Hospitals, 1957–74; *b* 8 Oct. 1916; *s* of Sir Isaac Holden Holden, 5th

Bt, and Alice Edna Byrom (*d* 1971); *S* father, 1962; *m* 1942, Frances Joan, *e d* of John Spark, JP, Ludlow, Stockton-on-Tees; two adopted *s*. *Educ:* Leys Sch. and Christ's Coll., Cambridge (MA); St Thomas's Hosp. MRCS; LRCP 1942; DA Eng., 1946; FRCA (FFARCS, 1958). Formerly Vis. Anæsth., Cumb. Infirm., Carlisle; Cons. Anæsth. W Cumb. Hospital Group. Mem. Council, Harlow Car Gardens. *Recreations:* fishing and gardening. *Heir: b* Paul Holden [*b* 3 March 1923; *m* 1950, Vivien Mary Oldham; one *s* two *d*]. *Address:* 40 South End, Osmotherley, Northallerton, N Yorks DL6 3BL. *Club:* Farmers'.

HOLDEN, Sir John David, 4th Bt *cr* 1919; *b* 16 Dec. 1967; *s* of David George Holden (*d* 1971) (*e s* of 3rd Bt), and of Nancy, *d* of H. W. D. Marwood, Foulrice, Whenby, Brandsby, Yorks; *S* grandfather, 1976; *m* 1987, Suzanne Cummings; three *d*. *Heir: uncle* Brian Peter John Holden [*b* 12 April 1944; *m* 1984, Bernadette Anne Lopez, *d* of George Gerard O'Malley].

HOLDEN, John Stewart; Chief Executive, Companies House and Registrar of Companies for England and Wales, since 1996; *b* 23 July 1945; *s* of William Stewart Holden and Jenny Holden (*née* Brelsford); *m* 1st, 1970, Pamela (marr. diss. 1984); 2nd, 1984, Margaret Newport. *Educ:* Merchant Taylors'; Emmanuel Coll., Cambridge (BA Hons Natural Scis/Law 1967; MA). British Petroleum and subsidiaries, 1964–93: Manager, Gas (Western Hemisphere), 1981–84; Area Oil Co-ordinator and Dir, BP (Schweiz) AG, 1984–87; Dir, Alexander Duckham & Co., 1991–93; Manager, European Lubricants & Bitumen, 1991–93; Develt Dir, Electricity Pool, 1994–96. Registrar of Political Parties, 1998–2000. Mem., Bradford-on-Avon Rotary Club. *Publications:* The Watlington Branch, 1974; The Manchester and Milford Railway, 1979. *Recreations:* microlight flying, music, industrial history and archaeology. *Address:* Brunswick House, Bath Road, Bradford-on-Avon, Wilts BA15 1SL.

HOLDEN, Patrick Brian, MA, FCIS; Chairman: Ainsfield PLC, since 1991; Holden Homes (Southern) Ltd, since 1984; Director, Mortimer Growth II plc, since 1997; *b* 16 June 1937; *s* of Reginald John and Winifred Isabel Holden; *m* 1972, Jennifer Ruth (*née* Meddings), MB, BS. *Educ:* Allhallows Sch. (Major Schol.); St Catharine's Coll., Cambridge (BA Hons Law 1960, MA 1963). FCIS 1965. Served Royal Hampshire Regt, 1955–57 regular commn), seconded 1 Ghana Regt, RWAFF. Fine Fare Group: Sec., 1960–69; Legal and Property Dir, 1965–69; Pye of Cambridge Gp, 1969–74; Dir, Pye Telecom. Ltd, 1972–74; Dir and Sec., Oriel Foods Gp, 1975–81; Gp Sec., Fisons plc, 1981–83. Sec., New Town Assoc., 1974–75. *Publications:* A-Z of Dog Training and Behaviour, 1999; The Old School House: a Dickensian school, 2000; Agility: a step by step guide, 2001. *Recreations:* dogs, bridge, walking. *Address:* The Old School House, Lower Green, Tewin, Herts AL6 0LD. *T:* (01438) 717573. *Club:* Naval and Military.

HOLDEN-BROWN, Sir Derrick, Kt 1979; Chairman, Allied-Lyons PLC, 1982–91 (Chief Executive, 1982–88); Director, Allied Breweries, 1967–91 (Chairman, 1982–86); *b* 14 Feb. 1923; *s* of Harold Walter and Beatrice Florence (*née* Walker); *m* 1950, Patricia Mary Ross Mackenzie; one *s* one *d*. *Educ:* Westcliff. Mem., Inst of Chartered Accountants of Scotland. Served War, Royal Navy, 1941–46, Lt RNVR, Coastal Forces. Chartered Accountant, 1948; Hiram Walker & Sons, Distillers, 1949; Managing Director: Cairnes Ltd, Brewers, Eire, 1954; Grants of St James's Ltd, 1960; Dir, Ind Coope Ltd, 1962; Chm., Victoria Wine Co., 1964; Finance Dir, 1972, Vice-Chm., 1975–82, Allied Breweries; Director: Sun Alliance & London Insurance plc, 1977– (Vice Chm., 1983, Dep. Chm., 1985–92); Midland Bank, 1984–88. Chm., FDIC, 1984–85 (Dep. Chm. 1974–76). President: Food and Drink Fedn, 1985–86; Food Manufacturers' Fedn Inc., 1985. Chairman: Brewers' Soc., 1978–80 (Master, Brewers' Co., 1987–88); White Ensign Assoc., 1987–90; Portsmouth Naval Heritage Trust, 1989–. *Recreations:* sailing, offshore cruising. *Address:* Copse House, Milford-on-Sea, Lymington, Hants SO41 0PS. *T:* (01590) 642247. *Clubs:* Boodle's; Royal Yacht Squadron; Royal Lymington Yacht.

HOLDER, Sir (John) Henry, 4th Bt *cr* 1898, of Pitmaston, Moseley, Worcs; Production Director and Head Brewer, Elgood & Sons Ltd, North Brink Brewery, Wisbech, 1975–93, retired; *b* 12 March 1928; *s* of Sir John Eric Duncan Holder, 3rd Bt and Evelyn Josephine (*d* 1994), *er d* of late William Blain; *S* father, 1986; *m* 1st, 1960, Catharine Harrison (*d* 1994), *yr d* of late Leonard Baker; twin *s* one *d*; 2nd, 1996, Josephine Mary, *d* of late A. Elliott and *widow* of G. Rivett. *Educ:* Eton Coll.; Birmingham Univ. (Dip. Malting and Brewing); Dip. in Safety Management, British Safety Council. Diploma Mem., Inst. of Brewing. National Service, RAC; commnd 5th Royal Tank Regt, 1947. Shift Brewer, Mitchells & Butlers Ltd, 1951–53; Brewer, Reffels Bexley Brewery Ltd, 1953–56; Asst Manager, Unique Slide Rule Co., 1956–62; Brewer, Rhymney Brewery Co. Ltd, 1962–75. *Recreations:* sailing, computing. *Heir: er* twin *s* Nigel John Charles Holder, *b* 6 May 1962. *Address:* Westering, Holt Road, Cley next the Sea, Holt, Norfolk NR25 7UA. *Club:* Brancaster Staithe Sailing (King's Lynn).

HOLDERNESS, Baron *cr* 1979 (Life Peer), of Bishop Wilton in the County of Humberside; **Richard Frederick Wood;** PC 1959; DL; *b* 5 Oct. 1920; 3rd *s* of 1st Earl of Halifax, KG, PC, OM, GCSI, GCMG, GCIE, TD; *m* 1947, Diana, *d* of late Col E. O. Kellett, DSO, MP, and Hon. Mrs W. J. McGowan; one *s* one *d*. *Educ:* Eton; New College, Oxford. Hon. Attaché, British Embassy, Rome, 1940; served War of 1939–45 as Lieutenant, KRRC, 1941–43; retired, wounded, 1943; toured US Army hospitals, 1943–45; New College, Oxford, 1945–47. MP (C) Bridlington, Yorkshire, 1950–79; Parliamentary Private Secretary: to Minister of Pensions, 1951–53; to Minister of State, Board of Trade, 1953–54; to Minister of Agriculture and Fisheries, 1954–55; Joint Parliamentary Secretary: Ministry of Pensions and National Insurance, 1955–58; Ministry of Labour, 1958–59; Minister of Power, October 1959–63, of Pensions and National Insurance, Oct. 1963–64; Minister of Overseas Develt, ODM, June-Oct. 1970, FCO, 1970–74. Dir, Hargreaves Group Ltd, 1974–86; Regional Dir, Yorkshire and Humberside regional board, Lloyds Bank, 1981–90. Chairman: Disablement Services Authy, 1987–91; Adv. Gp on Rehabilitation, DoH, 1991–96. Pres., Queen Elizabeth's Foundn for the Disabled, 1983–96. DL E Riding Yorks, 1967. Hon. LLD: Sheffield Univ., 1962; Leeds, 1978; Hull, 1982. Hon. Colonel: Queen's Royal Rifles, 1962; 4th (Volunteer) Bn Royal Green Jackets, 1967–89. *Address:* Flat Top House, Bishop Wilton, York YO42 1RY. *T:* (01759) 368266.

See also Sir E. N. Brooksbank, Bt.

HOLDERNESS, Sir Martin (William), 4th Bt *cr* 1920, of Tadworth, Surrey; Director, AMR Financial Management Ltd, independent financial advisers and investment managers, since 1992; *b* 24 May 1957; *s* of Sir Richard William Holderness, 3rd Bt and of Pamela Mary Dawsett (*née* Chapman); *S* father, 1998; *m* 1984, Elizabeth Dorothy, BSc, DipHV, Dip Counselling, *d* of Dr William and Dr Maureen Thornton, Belfast; one *s* one *d*. *Educ:* Bradfield Coll., Berkshire; Portsmouth Poly. (BA Accountancy 1979). CA 1983; MSFA 1995. Articled KMG Thomson McLintock, 1978–83; financial adviser, 1984–. *Recreations:* theatre, films, football, family life. *Heir: s* Matthew William Thornton Holderness, *b* 23 May 1990. *Address:* Cuckman's Farm, Ragged Hall Lane, St Albans, Herts AL2 3NP. *Club:* Two Brydges.

HOLDGATE, Sir Martin (Wyatt), Kt 1994; CB 1979; PhD; FIBiol; President, Zoological Society of London, since 1994; *b* 14 Jan. 1931; *s* of late Francis Wyatt Holdgate, MA, JP, and Lois Marjorie (*née* Bebbington); *m* 1963, Elizabeth Mary (*née* Dickason), *widow* of Dr H. H. Weil; two *s*. *Educ:* Arnold Sch., Blackpool; Queens' Coll., Cambridge. BA Cantab 1952; MA 1956; PhD 1955; FIBiol 1967. Jt Leader and Senior Scientist, Gough Is Scientific Survey, 1955–56; Lecturer in Zoology: Manchester Univ., 1956–57; Durham Colleges, 1957–60; Leader, Royal Society Expedition to Southern Chile, 1958–59; Asst Director of Research, Scott Polar Research Institute, Cambridge, 1960–63; Senior Biologist, British Antarctic Survey, 1963–66; Dep. Dir (Research), The Nature Conservancy, 1966–70; Director: Central Unit on Environmental Pollution, DoE, 1970–74; Inst. of Terrestrial Ecology, NERC, 1974–76; Dep. Sec., 1976, Dir-Gen. of Res., 1976–79, Chief Scientist, 1979–85, Depts of the Environment and of Transport; Dep. Sec., Environment Protection and Chief Envmt Scientist, DoE, and Chief Scientific Advr, Dept of Transport, 1985–88; Dir Gen., IUCN, 1988–94. Hon. Professorial Fellow, UC Cardiff, 1976–83. Member: NERC, 1976–87; SERC (formerly SRC), 1976–86; ABRC, 1976–88; Bd, World Resources Inst., Washington, 1985–94; China Council for Internat. Co-operation on Envmt and Develt, Beijing, 1992–94; Chairman: Review of Scientific Civil Service, 1980; Renewable Energy Adv. Gp, 1992; Energy Adv. Panel, 1993–96; Internat. Inst. for Envmt and Develt, 1994–99; Co-Chm., Intergovtl Panel on Forests, UN Commn on Sustainable Develt, 1995–97; Mem., Royal Commn on Envmtl Pollution, 1994–2001; Trustee, Nat. Heritage Meml Fund and Heritage Lottery Fund, 1995–98. Chm., British Schools Exploring Society, 1967–78; Vice-Pres., Young Explorer's Trust, 1981–90 (Chm., 1972, 1979–81). President: Governing Council, UN Environment Prog., 1983–84; Global 500 Forum, 1992–97; Chm., Commonwealth Expert Gp on Climate Change, 1988–89. Chm., Governing Council, Athnold Sch., 1997–. Hon. Fellow, RHBNC, 1997. Hon. DSc: Durham, 1991; Sussex, 1993; Lancaster, 1995. Bruce Medal, RSE, 1964; UNEP Silver Medal, 1983; UNEP Global 500, 1988; Patron's Medal, RGS, 1992; Livingstone Medal, RSGS, 1993. Comdr, Order of the Golden Ark (Netherlands), 1991. *Publications:* A History of Appleby, 1956, 2nd edn 1970; Mountains in the Sea, The Story of the Gough Island Expedition, 1958; (ed jtly) Antarctic Biology, 1964; (ed) Antarctic Ecology, 1970; (with N. M. Wace) Man and Nature in the Tristan da Cunha Islands, 1976; A Perspective of Environmental Pollution, 1979; (ed jtly) The World Environment 1972–82, 1982; (ed jtly) The World Environment 1972–92, 1992; From Care to Action: making a sustainable world, 1996; The Green Web: a union for world conservation, 1999; numerous papers and articles on Antarctica, environment and conservation. *Address:* Fell Beck, Hartley, Kirkby Stephen, Cumbria CA17 4JH. *Club:* Athenæum.

HOLDING, John Francis; HM Diplomatic Service, retired; company director and business adviser, New Zealand, since 1996; *b* 12 August 1936; *s* of late Francis George Holding, CA, Inland Revenue, and Gwendoline Elizabeth Holding (*née* Jenkins); *m* 1st, 1970, Pamela Margaret Straker-Nesbit (marr. diss. 1984); two *d*; 2nd, 1993, Susan Ann Clark (marr. diss. 1999). *Educ:* Colwyn Bay Grammar Sch.; LSE (externally). Mil. service, 1955–57; Min. of Housing and Local Govt, 1957; CRO (later FCO), 1964; served Karachi, Islamabad and Kinshasa; First Sec., 1973; Canberra, 1973–78; The Gambia, 1978–80; Grenada and Barbados, 1984–87; Dep. High Comr, Dhaka, 1987–90; Consul-General, Auckland, and Dir, UK Trade Promotion in NZ, 1990–96. *Recreations:* tennis, walking, photography, pianoforte. *Address:* 36 Bell Road, Remuera, Auckland 1005, New Zealand; 16 Kingsmead Close, Teddington, Middlesex TW11 9EP.

HOLDING, Malcolm Alexander; HM Diplomatic Service, retired; Consul-General, Naples, 1986–90; *b* 11 May 1932; *s* of Adam Anderson Holding and Mary Lillian (*née* Golding); *m* 1955, Pamela Eve Hampshire; two *d*. *Educ:* King Henry VIII Sch., Coventry. Foreign Office, 1949–51; HM Forces, 1951–53; FO, 1953–55; Middle East Centre for Arab Studies, 1956–57; Third Secretary (Commercial), Tunis, 1957–60; Second Sec. (Commercial), Khartoum, 1960–64; Second, later First Sec. (Commercial), Cairo, 1964–68; Consul, Bari, 1969; FCO, 1970–73; First Sec., British Dep. High Commission, Madras, 1973–75; FCO, 1976–78; Canadian National Defence Coll., Kingston, Ontario, 1978–79; Counsellor (Commercial), Rome, 1979–81; Consul-Gen., Edmonton, 1981–85. Commendatore, Order of Merit of the Republic of Italy, 1980. *Recreations:* sailing, skiing. *Address:* Theatre Cottage, Powderham, Exeter EX6 8JJ.

HOLDRIDGE, Ven. Bernard Lee; Archdeacon of Doncaster, 1994–2001; *b* 24 July 1935; *s* of Geoffrey and Lucy Medlow Holdridge. *Educ:* Grammar Sch., Thorne; Lichfield Theol Coll. Ordained deacon, 1967, priest, 1968; Curate, Swinton, S Yorks, 1967–71; Vicar, St Jude, Hexthorpe, Doncaster, 1971–81; Rector, St Mary, Rawmarsh with Parkgate, 1981–88; RD of Rotherham, 1986–88; Vicar, Priory Church of St Mary and St Cuthbert, Worksop, with St Giles, Carburton and St Mary the Virgin, Clumber Park, dio. of Southwell, 1988–94. Dignitary in Convocation, 1999–. Chairman: DAC for Care of Churches and Churchyards, Southwell, 1990–94; ACS, 1998–. Guardian, Shrine of Our Lady of Walsingham, 1996–. *Recreations:* foreign travel, reading, theatre, a glass of wine with friends. *Address:* 354 Thorne Road, Wheatley Hills, Doncaster DN2 5AH. *T:* (01302) 341331.

HOLDSWORTH, Sir (George) Trevor, Kt 1982; CVO 1997; Chairman, Institute for Manufacturing, 1999–2000; *b* 29 May 1927; *s* of late William Albert Holdsworth and Winifred Holdsworth (*née* Bottomley); *m* 1st, 1951, Patricia June Ridler (*d* 1993); three *s*; 2nd, 1995, Jenny Watson. *Educ:* Hanson Grammar Sch., Bradford; Keighley Grammar Sch. FCA 1950. Rawlinson Greaves & Mitchell, Bradford, 1944–51; Bowater Paper Corp., 1952–63 (financial and admin. appts; Dir and Controller of UK paper-making subsids); joined Guest, Keen & Nettlefolds (later GKN plc), 1963; Dep. Chief Accountant, 1963–64; Gp Chief Accountant, 1965–67; General Man. Dir, GKN Screws & Fasteners Ltd, 1968–70; Dir, 1970–88; Gp Controller, 1970–72; Gp Exec. Vice Chm., Corporate Controls and Services, 1973–74; Dep. Chm., 1974–77; Man. Dir and Dep. Chm., 1977–80; Chm., 1980–88. Chairman: Allied Colloids Gp, 1983–96; British Satellite Broadcasting, 1987–90; National Power, 1990–95; Beauford, 1991–99; Lambert Howarth Gp, 1993–98; Director: Equity Capital for Industry, 1976–84; THORN EMI, 1977–87; Midland Bank plc, 1979–88; Prudential Corp., 1986–96 (Jt Dep. Chm., 1988–92); Owens-Corning Fiberglas Corp., 1994–98. Member: AMF Inc. Europ. Adv. Council, 1982–85; European Adv. Bd, Owens Corning Fiberglas Inc., 1990–93; Adv. Bd, LEK, 1992–99. Confederation of British Industry: Mem. Council, 1974–; Mem., Econ. and Financial Policy Cttee, 1978–80; Mem., Steering Gp on Unemployment, 1982; Mem., Special Programmes Unit, 1982; Chm., Tax Reform Working Party, 1984–86; Dep. Pres., 1987–88; Pres., 1988–90. Chairman: Review Body on Doctors' and Dentists' Remuneration, 1990–93; Adv. Council, Foundn for Manufacturing and Industry, 1993–99; Dep. Chm., Financial Reporting Council, 1990–93; Mem., Business in the Community, 1984–92; British Institute of Management: Mem. Council, 1974–84; Vice-Chm., 1978; Mem., Bd of Fellows, 1979; Chm., 1980–82; a Vice-Pres., 1982–; Gold Medal, 1987. Vice Pres., Engineering Employers' Fedn, 1980–88; Jt Dep. Chm., Adv. Bd, Inst. of Occupational Health, 1980; Duke of Edinburgh's Award: Mem., Internat. Panel, 1980 (Chm., 1987); Internat. Trustee, 1987–94; UK Trustee, 1988–96; Member: Exec. Cttee, SMMT, 1980–83; Engineering Industries Council, 1980–88 (Chm., 1985); Court of British Shippers' Council, 1981–89; British-North American Cttee, 1981–85; Council, RIIA, 1983–88; Internat. Council of INSEAD, 1985–92; Eur. Adv. Cttee, New York Stock Exchange, 1985–97. Chm., Wigmore Hall Trust, 1992–99; Member: Council, Royal Opera House Trust (Trustee, 1981–84); Council, Winston Churchill Meml Trust, 1985–96. Hon. Pres., Council of Mechanical and Metal Trade Assocs, 1987. Dir, UK–Japan 2000 Gp, 1987. Trustee: Anglo-German Foundn for the Study of Industrial Society, 1980–92; Brighton Fest. Trust, 1980–90 (Chm. 1982–87); Philharmonia Trust, 1982–93; Thrombosis Res. Trust, 1989–98. Governor, Ashridge Management Coll., 1978; Chancellor, Bradford Univ., 1992–97. Vice-Pres., Ironbridge Gorge Museum Develt Trust, 1981–. Internat. Counsellor, Conference Bd, 1984. CIEx 1987. FRSA 1988. Freeman, City of London, 1977; Liveryman, Worshipful Co. of Chartered Accountants in England and Wales, 1978. Hon. DTech Loughborough, 1981; Hon. DSc: Aston, 1982; Sussex, 1988; Hon. DEng: Bradford, 1983; Birmingham, 1992; Hon. DBA Internat. Management Centre, Buckingham, 1986. Chartered Accountants Founding Socs' Centenary Award, 1983; Hon. CGIA 1989. *Recreations:* music, theatre. *Club:* Athenæum.

HOLDSWORTH, Rev. Dr John Ivor; Principal and Warden, St Michael's Theological College, Llandaff, since 1997; *b* 10 Feb. 1949; *s* of Harold Holdsworth and Edith Mary Holdsworth; *m* 1971, Susan Annette Thomas; one *s* one *d. Educ:* Leeds Grammar Sch.; University Coll. of Wales, Aberystwyth (BA); University Coll., Cardiff (BD, MTh); St David's University Coll., Lampeter (PhD 1992). Ordained deacon 1973, priest 1974; Curate, St Paul's, Newport, 1973–77; Vicar: Abercrave and Callwen, 1977–86; Gorseinon, 1986–97. Presenter, HTV Wales Religious Affairs, 1988–. *Recreations:* walking, beekeeping, armchair supporter of Leeds United and Yorkshire County Cricket Club, broadcasting. *Address:* The Old Registry, 51 Cardiff Road, Llandaff, Cardiff CF5 2DQ. *T:* (029) 2056 3379.

HOLDSWORTH, Sir Trevor; *see* Holdsworth, Sir G. T.

HOLDSWORTH HUNT, Christopher; Founder Director and Managing Director, Peel, Hunt plc (formerly Peel, Hunt & Co. Ltd), since 1989; *b* 2 Aug. 1942; *s* of late Peter Holdsworth Hunt and Monica (*née* Neville); *m* 1st, 1969, Charlotte Folin (marr. diss. 1974); 2nd, 1976, Joanne Lesley Starr Minoprio (*née* Reynolds); two *s. Educ:* Summer Fields, St Leonards; Eton Coll.; Tours Univ. Commnd Coldstream Guards, 1961–64. Joined Murton & Adams, Stockjobbers, 1964; firm acquired by Pinchin Denny, 1969; Partner, Pinchin Denny, 1971; firm acquired by Morgan Grenfell, 1986; Dir, Morgan Grenfell Securities, 1987–88. *Recreations:* opera, ballet, theatre, golf, tennis, walking. *Address:* 105 Elgin Crescent, W11 2JF. *T:* (020) 7221 5755. *Clubs:* White's, City of London, Vanderbilt; Berkshire Golf; Swinley Forest Golf.

HOLE, Very Rev. Derek Norman; Provost of Leicester, 1992–99, now Emeritus; *b* 5 Dec. 1933; *s* of Frank Edwin Hole and Ella Evelyn Hole (*née* Thomas). *Educ:* Public Central Sch., Plymouth; Lincoln Theological College. Deacon, 1960; Priest, 1961; Asst Curate, St Mary Magdalen, Knighton, 1960–62; Domestic Chaplain to Archbishop of Cape Town, 1962–64; Asst Curate, St Nicholas, Kenilworth, 1964–67; Rector, St Mary the Virgin, Burton Latimer, 1967–73; Vicar, St James the Greater, Leicester, 1973–92; Chaplain to the Queen, 1985–92. Hon. Canon, Leicester Cathedral, 1983–92. Rural Dean, Christianity South, Leicester, 1983–92; Chm., House of Clergy, 1986–94; Vice-Pres., Diocesan Synod, 1986–94; Mem., Bishop's Council, 1986–99. Chaplain to: Lord Mayor of Leicester, 1976–77, 1994–95, 1996–97; High Sheriffs of Leics, 1980–85, 1987, 1999–2000 and 2001– April 2002; Leicester High Sch., 1984–92; Haymarket Theatre, Leicester, 1980–83, 1993–95; Leicester Br., RAFA, 1978–92; Master of Merchant Taylors' Co., 1995–96; Leicester Guild of Freemen, 1997–99; Royal Soc. of St George, 2000–. Commissary to Bishop of Wellington, NZ, 1998–. Priest Associate, Actors' Church Union, 1995–; Vice-Pres., English Clergy Assoc., 1993–. Chm. Leicester Diocesan Redundant Churches Uses Cttee, 1985–99. Mem., Leicester Charity Orgn Soc. 1983–; Trustee: Leicester Church Charities, 1983–; Leicester GS, 2000– (Gov., 1992–2000); Leics Historic Churches Preservation Trust, 1989–; Bernard Fawcett Meml Trust, 1993–; North Meml Homes, 1999–; Pres., Leicester Rotary Club, 1987–88; Vice-President: Leics County Scout Council, 1992–99; Leics Guild of the Disabled, 1994–99; Leicester Cathedral Old Choristers' Assoc., 1999–. Mem., Victorian Soc., 1986–; Hon. Life Mem., Leics Br., BRCS, 1995. Governor: Alderman Newton's Sch., Leicester, 1976–82; Alderman Newton Foundn, 1993–2000; Leicester High Sch., 1992–. Mem. (Ind.), Burton Latimer UDC, 1971–73. Sen. Fellow, De Montfort Univ., 1998–. Hon. DLitt De Montfort, 1999. *Recreations:* music, walking, reading biographies and Victorian history. *Address:* 25 Southernhay Close, Leicester LE1 3TW. *T:* and *Fax:* (0116) 270 9988; *e-mail:* dnhole@leicester.anglican.org. *Clubs:* Leicestershire (Leicester); Royal Western Yacht.

HOLES, Prof. Clive Douglas, PhD; Khalid Bin Abdullah Al-Saud Professor for the Study of the Contemporary Arab World, University of Oxford, since 1997; Fellow, Magdalen College, Oxford, since 1997; *b* 29 Sept. 1948; *s* of Douglas John Holes and Kathryn Mary (*née* Grafton); *m* 1980, Gillian Diane Pountain; two *s. Educ:* High Arcal Grammar Sch., Dudley, Worcs; Trinity Hall, Cambridge (BA Hons 1969; MA 1973); Univ. of Birmingham (MA 1972); Wolfson Coll., Cambridge (PhD 1981). UNA volunteer teacher, Bahrain, 1969–71; British Council Officer, Kuwait, Algeria, Iraq, Thailand and London, 1971–76 and 1979–83; Lectr in Arabic and Applied Linguistics, Univ. of Salford, 1983–85; Dir, Lang. Centre, Sultan Qaboos Univ., Oman, 1985–87; University of Cambridge: Lectr in Islamic Studies, 1987–96; Reader in Arabic, 1996; Fellow, Trinity Hall, 1989–96. Fellow: British Soc. for Middle Eastern Studies, 1989; Anglo-Oman Soc., 1990; Bahrain-British Soc., 1991. Mem., Philological Soc., 1984–. *Publications:* Colloquial Arabic of the Gulf and Saudi Arabia, 1984, 3rd edn 1992; Language Variation and Change in a Modernising Arab State, 1987; Gulf Arabic, 1990; Breakthrough Arabic, 1992; (ed) Perspectives on Arabic Linguistics, Vol. 5, 1993; Modern Arabic: structures, functions and varieties, 1995; Dialect, Culture and Society in Eastern Arabia, Vol. I, 2001; articles in professional jls concerned with Arabic language, culture, society and literature. *Recreations:* keeping fit, rowing, running, cricket, watching Wolverhampton Wanderers FC, visiting the Middle East. *Address:* Magdalen College, Oxford OX1 4AU. *T:* (01865) 278239.

HOLGATE, David John; QC 1997; *b* 3 Aug. 1956; *s* of John Charles Holgate and Catherine Philbin Holgate (*née* Rooney). *Educ:* Davenant Foundation Grammar Sch., Loughton; Exeter Coll., Oxford (BA Hons 1977). Called to the Bar, Middle Temple, 1978; admitted to Hong Kong Bar, 2001. Mem., Supplementary Panel, Jun. Counsel to the Crown (Common Law), 1986–97; Standing Jun. Counsel to the Inland Revenue in rating valuation matters, 1990–97. *Recreations:* music, particularly opera, travel, reading. *Address:* 4 Bream's Buildings, EC4A 1AQ. *T:* (020) 7353 5835, *Fax:* (020) 7430 1677; *e-mail:* clerks@4breams.co.uk. *Club:* Travellers.

HOLGATE, Dr Sidney, CBE 1981; Founder Master of Grey College, University of Durham, 1959–80; Member, Academic Advisory Committee, Open University, 1969–81 (Vice-Chairman, 1972–75; Chairman, 1975–77); *b* Hucknall, Notts, 9 Sept. 1918; *e s* of late Henry and Annie Elizabeth Holgate; *m* 1942, Isabel Armorey; no *c. Educ:* Henry Mellish Sch., Nottingham; Durham Univ. (Open Scholar, Hatfield Coll., Durham, 1937; Univ. Mathematical Scholarship, 1940; BA (1st Cl. Hons Mathematics) 1940; DThPT 1941; MA 1943; PhD 1945). Commnd RAFVR (Trng Br.), 1942–45. Asst Master, Nottingham High Sch., 1941–42; Lecturer in Mathematics, University of Durham, 1942–46; Sec. of the Durham Colls, 1946–59; Pro-Vice-Chancellor, Univ. of Durham, 1964–69. Member: Schools Council Gen. Studies Cttee, 1967–70; Chm., BBC Radio Durham Council, 1968–72; Vice-Chm., BBC Radio Newcastle Council, 1972–74. Hon. DUniv. Open, 1980. *Publications:* mathematical papers in Proc. Camb. Phil. Soc. and Proc. Royal Soc. *Recreations:* cricket and other sports, railways, bridge. *Address:* Rookstone, 46 North End, Durham DH1 4LW.

HOLGATE, Prof. Stephen Townley, MD, DSc; FRCP, FRCPE, FRCPath, FMedSci; CBiol, FIBiol; Medical Research Council Clinical Professor of Immunopharmacology, University of Southampton, and Hon. Consultant Physician, School of Medicine, Southampton General Hospital, since 1987; *b* 2 May 1947; *s* of William Townley Holgate and Margaret Helen (*née* Lancaster); *m* 1972, Elizabeth Karen Malkinson; three *s* one *d. Educ:* London Univ. (BSc 1968; MB BS 1971; MD 1979); DSc Soton 1991. FRCP 1984; FRCPE 1995; FRCPath 1999; CBiol, FIBiol 1999. House Physician and Surgeon, Charing Cross Hosp., 1971–72; Sen. Hse Physician, Nat. Hosp. for Nervous Diseases and Brompton Hosp., 1972–74; Registrar in Medicine, Salisbury and Southampton Gen. Hosps, 1974–76; Lectr in Medicine, 1976–80, Sen. Lectr, 1980–86, Reader and Prof. (personal Chair), 1986–87, Univ. of Southampton. MRC/Wellcome Trust Res. Fellow, Harvard Univ., 1978–80. Founder FMedSci, 1998. FRSA 1997. Hon. MB BS: Ferrara, Italy, 1997; Jallegonian, Poland, 1999. Rhône Poulenc Rorer World Health Award, 1995; (jtly) King Faisal Internat. Prize in Medicine, 1999. *Publications:* (ed jtly) Asthma and Rhinitis: implications for diagnosis and treatment, 1995; (ed jtly) Allergy, 1999; (ed jtly) Difficult Asthma, 1999; (jtly) Health Effects of Air Pollutants, 1999. *Recreations:* gardening, jogging, cricket. *Address:* Westmead, 29 Cupernham Lane, Romsey, Hants SO51 7JJ. *T:* (01794) 515676.

HOLLAMBY, David James; HM Diplomatic Service; Governor and Commander-in-Chief, St Helena and Dependencies, since 1999; *b* 19 May 1945; *s* of Reginald William Hollamby and Eva May Hollamby (*née* Ponman); *m* 1971, Maria Helena Guzmán; two step *s. Educ:* Albury Manor Sch., Surrey. Joined Foreign Office, 1964: Beirut, 1967–69; Latin American Floater, 1970–72; Third Sec. and Vice Consul, Asunción, 1972–75; Second Sec., FCO, 1975–78; Vice Consul (Commercial), NY, 1978–82; Consul (Commercial), Dallas, 1982–86; First Secretary: FCO, 1986–90; Rome, 1990–94; Asst Hd, Western Eur. Dept, FCO, 1994–96; Dep. Hd, W Indian and Atlantic Dept, FCO, 1996–98; Dep. Hd, Overseas Territories Dept, FCO, 1998–99. *Recreations:* travel, reading, music, golf, ski-ing. *Address:* c/o Foreign and Commonwealth Office, King Charles Street, SW1A 2AH.

HOLLAND, Hon. Sir Alan (Douglas), Kt 1995; Judge, High Court (formerly Supreme Court) of New Zealand, 1978–94, retired; *b* 20 June 1929; *s* of Clarence Cyril Holland and Marjorie Evelyn Holland; *m* 1961, Felicity Ann Ower; one *s. Educ:* Waitaki Boys' High Sch.; Canterbury Coll., Univ. of New Zealand (LLB). Part-time Lectr in Law and Commerce Faculties of Canterbury Univ., 1953–63; Partner, Wynn Williams & Co., Solicitors, Christchurch, 1956–78. Pres., Canterbury Dist Law Soc., 1973 (Mem. Council, 1963–73); Mem. Council and associated cttees, NZ Law Soc., 1970–74. *Recreations:* general. *Address:* 39 McDougall Avenue, Christchurch 8001, New Zealand. *T:* (3) 3557102. *Club:* Christchurch.

HOLLAND, Rt Rev. Alfred Charles; Bishop of Newcastle, NSW, 1978–92; *b* 23 Feb. 1927; *s* of Alfred Charles Holland and Maud Allison; *m* 1954, Joyce Marion Embling; three *s* one *d. Educ:* Raine's Sch., London; Univ. of Durham (BA 1950; DipTh 1952). RNVR, 1945–47; Univ. of Durham, 1948–52; Assistant Priest, West Hackney, London, 1952–54; Rector of Scarborough, WA, 1955–70; Asst Bishop, Dio. Perth, WA, 1970–77. Chaplain, St George's Coll., Jerusalem, 1993. Life Member: Stirling Rugby Football Club, 1969; Durham Univ. Society, 1984. *Publications:* Luke Through Lent, 1980; (ed) The Diocese Together, 1987. *Recreations:* reading, painting. *Address:* 21 Sullivan Crescent, Wanniassa, ACT 2903, Australia. *Club:* Australian (Sydney).

HOLLAND, Anthony; *see* Holland, J. A.

HOLLAND, Hon. Sir Christopher (John), Kt 1992; **Hon. Mr Justice Holland;** a Judge of the High Court of Justice, Queen's Bench Division, since 1992; a Judge of the Employment Appeal Tribunal, since 1994; *b* 1 June 1937; *er s* of late Frank and Winifred Mary Holland; *m* 1967, Jill Iona Holland; one *s* one *d. Educ:* Leeds Grammar Sch.; Emmanuel Coll., Cambridge (MA, LLB). National Service (acting L/Cpl), 3rd Royal Tank Regt, 1956–58. Called to the Bar, Inner Temple, 1963, Bencher, 1985; commenced practice on North Eastern Circuit (Presiding Judge, 1993–97); QC 1978; a Recorder, 1992. Mem., Criminal Injuries Compensation Bd, 1992. Vice Chm., Cttee of Inquiry into Outbreak of Legionnaires' Disease at Stafford, 1985. Chm., Lower Washburn Parish Council, 1975–91. *Address:* c/o Royal Courts of Justice, Strand, WC2A 2LL.

HOLLAND, Sir Clifton Vaughan, (Sir John), AC 1988; Kt 1973; BCE; CPEng, FTSE, Hon. FIEAust, FAIM, FAIB; Chairman, John Holland Holdings Limited, 1963–86; *b* Melbourne, 21 June 1914; *s* of Thomas and Mabel Ruth Elizabeth Holland; *m* 1942, Emily Joan Atkinson; three *s* one *d. Educ:* Flinders State Sch.; Frankston High Sch.; Queen's Coll., Univ. of Melbourne (BCE); Monash Univ. (Hon. DEng 1978). Junior Engineer, BP, 1936–39. Served War of 1939–45, RAE and 'Z' Special Force, Middle East, SW Pacific (Lt-Col). Construction Engr, BP Aust. 1946–49; Founder, John Holland (Constructions) Pty Ltd, 1949, Man. Dir 1949–73, Chm., 1949–86; Chm., Process Plant Constructions Pty Ltd, 1949–82; Director: T & G Life Soc., 1972–82; Aust. and NZ Banking Gp, 1976–81. Foundn Pres., Australian Fedn of Civil Contractors (Life Mem., 1971); Chm., Nat. Construction Industry Conf. Organising Cttee, 1982; Mem., Construction Industry Res. Bd, 1982. Chm., Econ. Consultative Adv. Gp to the Treasurer, 1975–81; Mem., Rhodes Scholar Selection Cttee, 1970–73; Mem. Bd, Royal Melbourne Hosp., 1963–79; Nat. Chm., Outward Bound, 1973–74, Chm. Victorian Div., 1964–77; Councillor, Inst. of Public Affairs, 1980; Mem., Churchill Fellowship Selection Cttee, 1968–82; Director: Winston Churchill Meml Trust, 1976–82 (Chm., Vic. Br., 1977–82); Child Accident Prevention Foundn of Australia, 1979–81; Chairman: La Trobe Centenary Commemoration Council, 1975–76; Matthew Flinders Bi-Centenary Council, 1973–75; History Adv. Council of Victoria, 1975–85; Loch Ard Centenary Commemoration Cttee, 1976–78; Citizens' Council, 150th Anniversary Celebrations, Victoria, 1979–82; Victorian Cttee for Anzac Awards, 1982–; Nat. Chm., Queen's Silver Jubilee Trust for Young Australians, 1981–87 (Vic. Chm., 1977–80; Life Mem., 1992); Mem., Centenary Test Co-ordinating Cttee, 1976–77. Dep. Chm., Melbourne Univ. Engineering Sch. Centenary Foundn and Appeal Cttee, 1982–90. Director: Corps of Commissionaires (Victoria) Ltd, 1978–89; Australian Bicentenary Celebrations, 1980–82 (Vic. Chm., 1980–82). Pres., Stroke Res. Foundn, 1983–90; Patron: Bone Marrow Foundn, 1992–; Voluntary Euthanasia Soc. of Victoria, 1996–;

Children First Foundn, 2000–. Construction projects include: Jindabyne pumping station; Westgate Bridge; Tasman Bridge restoration, New Parliament House. Foundation Fellow, Australian Acad. of Technological Scis. Hon. DEng Monash, 1976. Peter Nicoll Russell Meml Medal, 1974; Kernot Meml Medal, Univ. of Melbourne, 1976; Consulting Engineers Advancement Soc. Medal, 1983. *Recreations:* golf, music, gardening, cricket. *Address:* Hurst Lodge II, 33 George Road, Flinders, Vic 3929, Australia. *Clubs:* Australian, Naval and Military (Melbourne); Royal Melbourne Golf, Frankston Golf, Flinders Golf.

HOLLAND, David Cuthbert Lyall, CB 1975; Librarian of the House of Commons, 1967–76; *b* 23 March 1915; *yr s* of Michael Holland, MC, and Marion Holland (*née* Broadwood); *m* 1949, Rosemary Griffiths, *y d* of David Ll. Griffiths, OBE; two *s* one *d*. *Educ:* Eton; Trinity Coll., Cambridge (MA). War service, Army, 1939–46; PoW. Appointed House of Commons Library, 1946. Chm., Study of Parlt Gp, 1973–74. *Publications:* book reviews, etc. *Recreation:* book collecting. *Address:* The Barn, Milton Street, Polegate, East Sussex BN26 5RP. *T:* (01323) 870379. *Club:* Athenæum.

HOLLAND, Rt Rev. Edward; Area Bishop of Colchester, 1995–2001; *b* 28 June 1936; *s* of Reginald Dick Holland and Olive Holland (*née* Yeoman). *Educ:* New College School; Dauntsey's School; King's College London (AKC). National Service, Worcestershire Regt, 1955–57; worked for Importers, 1957–61; KCL, 1961–65. Deacon 1965, priest 1966, Rochester; Curate, Holy Trinity, Dartford, 1965–69; Curate, John Keble, Mill Hill, 1969–72; Precentor, Gibraltar Cathedral, and Missioner for Seamen, 1972–74; Chaplain at Naples, Italy, 1974–79; Vicar of S Mark's, Bromley, 1979–86; Suffragan Bishop of Gibraltar in Europe, 1986–95. Mem., Churches Conservation Trust, 1998–2001. *Recreations:* travel, being entertained and entertaining. *Address:* 37 Parfrey Street, Hammersmith, W6 9EW. *T:* (020) 8746 3638. *Club:* National Liberal.

HOLLAND, Edward Richard Charles, OBE 1983 (MBE 1969); HM Diplomatic Service, retired; *b* 26 March 1925; *s* of Cecil Francis Richard Holland and Joyce Mary (*née* Pyne); *m* 1952, Dorothy Olive Branthwaite (*d* 1997); two *s*. *Educ:* Launceston Coll. Served RAF, 1943–48. Joined FO, 1948; served in Batavia, Bangkok, Oslo, Prague and Helsinki, 1949–57; Consul, Saigon, 1957; FO, 1959; Cape Town, 1962; First Sec., Monrovia, 1964; Consul: Stuttgart, 1969; Düsseldorf, 1971; FCO, 1972; First Sec., Islamabad, 1977; Consul-Gen., Alexandria, 1981–82. *Recreations:* gardening, playing with computer, reading. *Address:* 25 Stafford Road, Seaford, E Sussex BN25 1UE. *T:* (01323) 897631. *Clubs:* Civil Service; Seaford Constitutional.

HOLLAND, Einion; *see* Holland, R. E.

HOLLAND, Frank Robert Dacre; Chairman, C. E. Heath PLC, 1973–84, Non-Executive Director, 1984–86; *b* 24 March 1924; *s* of Ernest Albert Holland and Kathleen Annie (*née* Page); *m* 1948, Margaret Lindsay Aird; one *d*. *Educ:* Whitgift Sch., Croydon. Joined C. E. Heath & Co. Ltd, 1941; entered Army, 1942; Sandhurst, 1943; commissioned 4th Queen's Own Hussars, 1944; served, Italy, 1944–45, Austria and Germany, 1945–47; returned to C. E. Heath & Co. Ltd, 1947; Joint Managing Director, North American Operation, 1965; Director, C. E. Heath & Co. Ltd, 1965, Dep. Chm., 1969. Director: British Aviation Insce Co., 1974–84; Trade Indemnity plc, 1974–86; Greyhound Corp., USA, 1974–87. Liveryman, Insurers' Co., 1980– (Master, 1985–86). *Recreations:* travel, gardening. *Address:* Moatside, 68 Ashley Road, Walton-on-Thames, Surrey KT12 1HR. *T:* (01932) 227591. *Clubs:* Oriental, Cavalry and Guards.

HOLLAND, Sir Geoffrey, KCB 1989 (CB 1984); Vice-Chancellor, Exeter University, since 1994; *b* 9 May 1938; *s* of late Frank Holland, CBE and of Elsie Freda Holland; *m* 1964, Carol Ann Challen. *Educ:* Merchant Taylors' Sch., Northwood; St John's Coll., Oxford (BA 1st cl. Hons; MA; Hon. Fellow, 1991). 2nd Lieut, RTR, 1956–58. Entered Min. of Labour, 1961, Asst Private Sec., 1964–65; Principal Private Sec. to Sec. of State for Employment, 1971–72; Manpower Services Commission: Asst Sec., Hd of Planning, 1973; Dir of Special Progs, 1977; Dep. Sec., 1981; Dir, 1981; Second Perm. Sec., 1986; Perm. Sec., Dept of Employment, subseq. Employment Dept Gp, 1988–93; Perm. Sec., DFE, 1993. Dir, Shell UK, 1994–98. Mem., Nat. Cttee of Inquiry into Higher Educn, 1996–97. Chm., Govt's Sustainable Develt Educn Panel, 1998–. Liveryman, Merchant Taylors' Co., 1967– (Master, 2000–01). CIMgt (CBIM 1987). Fellow, Eton Coll., 1994–; Hon. Fellow, Polytechnic of Wales, 1986. Hon. FIPD (Hon. FITD 1986; Pres., IPD, 1998–2000); Hon. FCGI 1994. Hon. LLD Sheffield, 1994. *Publications:* Young People and Work, 1977; many articles on manpower, educn, training, management etc in professional jls. *Recreations:* journeying, opera, exercising the dog. *Address:* Northcote House, The Queen's Drive, Exeter EX4 4QJ. *Club:* East India, Devonshire, Sports and Public Schools.

HOLLAND, Sir John; *see* Holland, Sir C. V.

HOLLAND, (John) Anthony; Chairman: Northern Ireland Parades Commission, since 2000; Standards Board for England, since 2001; Joint Insolvency Monitoring Unit, since 2001; *b* 9 Nov. 1938; *s* of John and Dorothy Rita Holland; *m* 1963, Kathleen Margaret Anderson; three *s*. *Educ:* Ratcliffe Coll., Leics; Nottingham Univ. (LLB 1959); Financial Planning Cert., Chartered Insce Inst., 1997; MPhil UWE 1998. Admitted Solicitor of Supreme Court, 1962; notary public. Joined Foot & Bowden, 1964, Partner, 1964–90, Sen. Partner, 1990–97; Principal Ombudsman, PIA, 1997–2000. Chairman: Young Solicitors Gp, Law Soc., 1972; Social Security Appeals Tribunal, 1974–97; South Western Regl Adv. Council, BBC, 1984–87; a Chm., SFA, 1993–; Member: Council, Law Soc., 1976–95 (Vice-Pres., 1989–90; Pres., 1990–91); Marre Cttee on future of the Legal Profession, 1986–88; Council, Justice, 1991– (Chm., Exec. Bd, 1996–99); Mem. Council, Howard League for Penal Reform, 1992–; Hon. Mem., SPTL, 1992. President: Plymouth Law Soc., 1986–87; Cornwall Law Soc., 1988–89. Member: Plymouth Diocesan Finances Cttee, 1986–94; Univ. of Nottingham Vice Chancellor's Adv. Bd, 1990–. Chm., Plymouth Chamber of Commerce and Industry, 1994–96. Governor: Plymouth Coll., 1976–93; Coll. of Law, 1991–97. Hon. Mem., Canadian Bar Assoc., 1990. *Publications:* (jtly) Principles of Registered Land Conveyancing, 1966; (jtly) Landlord and Tenant, 1968; (Jt Adv. Ed.) Mines and Quarries Section, Butterworth's Encyclopædia of Forms and Precedents, 1989–; (Gen. Ed.) Cordery on Solicitors, 9th edn, 1995. *Recreations:* opera, literature, journalism, broadcasting. *Address:* Parades Commission for Northern Ireland, 12th Floor, Windsor House, 6–12 Bedford Street, Belfast BT2 7EL; 262 Lauderdale Tower, Barbican, EC2Y 8BY. *T:* (020) 7638 5044. *Club:* Royal Western Yacht (Plymouth).

HOLLAND, John Lewis; Managing Director, Herts & Essex Newspapers, since 1990; *b* 23 May 1937; *s* of George James Holland and Esther Holland; *m* 1958, Maureen Ann Adams; one *s* one *d*. *Educ:* Nottingham Technical Grammar Sch. Trainee Reporter, Nottingham Evening News, subseq. Jun. Reporter, Mansfield Br. Office, 1953–55; Sports Reporter, Mansfield Reporter Co., 1955–56; Sports Reporter, subseq. Sports Editor, Aldershot News Group, 1956–59; News Editor, West Bridgford & Clifton Standard, Nottingham, 1959–61; Chief Sports Sub Editor, Bristol Evening Post, and Editor, Sports Green 'Un (sports edn), 1961–64; Editor, West Bridgford & Clifton Standard, Nottingham, and Partner, Botting & Turner Sports Agency, Nottingham, 1964–66; Birmingham Evening Mail: Dep. Sports Editor, 1966–71; Editor, Special Projects Unit (Colour Prodn Dept), 1971–75; Editor, 1975–79, and Gen. Man., 1979–81, Sandwell Evening Mail; Marketing/Promotions Gen. Man., Birmingham Post & Mail, 1981–82; Editor, The Birmingham Post, 1982–86. Director: Birmingham Post & Mail Circulation and Promotions, 1986–88; Birmingham Post & Mail Publications and Promotions, 1988–90; Birmingham Convention and Visitor Bureau, 1982–90. President: Chartered Inst. of Marketing, 1989–90; Chiltern Newspaper Proprietors Assoc., 1995–99 (Vice-Pres., 1994–95). Mem., Hertford Business Club, 1994–2000. *Recreations:* journalism, most sports (more recently playing golf), keeping horses, gardening, keep fit. *Address:* Carob Lodge, Marathounda, PO Box 60151, Paphos 8101, Cyprus. *Clubs:* Press (Birmingham); Heydon Grange Golf (Captain, 1998–99) (Royston); Tsada Golf, Secret Valley Golf (Cyprus).

HOLLAND, Sir Kenneth (Lawrence), Kt 1981; CBE 1971; QFSM 1974; Consultant, Fire Safety Engineering, since 1981; Director: Gent Ltd, 1981–93; Bas/Firelaw Ltd, since 1993; *b* 20 Sept. 1918; *s* of Percy Lawrence and Edith Holland; *m* 1941, Pauline Keith (*née* Mansfield); two *s* one *d*. *Educ:* Whitcliffe Mount Grammar Sch., Cleckheaton, Yorks. Entered Fire Service, Lancashire, 1937; Divisional Officer: Suffolk and Ipswich, 1948; Worcestershire, 1952; Dep. Chief Fire Officer, Lancashire, 1955; Chief Fire Officer: Bristol, 1960; West Riding of Yorkshire, 1967; HM Chief Inspector of Fire Services, 1972–80. Chm., Firelaw Ltd, 1988–93. President: Fire Brigade Soc., 1969; IFireE, 1969; Commonwealth Overseas Fire Services Assoc., 1983–90; Assoc. of Structural Fire Protection Contractors and Manufacturers, 1986–90; Nat. Assoc. for Safety in the Home, 1988–90; Trustee: Fire Services Res. Trng Trust, 1983–; Ivy Owen Award Trust, 1989–2000; Chairman: ISO Technical Cttee TC/21 Fire Equipment, 1983–94; Loss Prevention Certification Bd, 1984–92; Multi-technics Council, BSI, 1984–90; Visitor, Fire Res. Station, 1984–90. Chm., British Fire Services Assoc., 1964–65; Vice Pres., Fire Services Nat. Benevolent Fund, 1973–. Hon. Treasurer, Poole Arts Fedn, 1985–88. Pres., Past Rotarians Club, Bournemouth, 1995. Freeman, City of London, 1981. OStJ 1964. Defence Medal; Fire Brigade Long Service and Good Conduct Medal. *Recreations:* sports, gardening, the Arts. *Club:* Royal Over-Seas League.

HOLLAND, Kevin John William C.; *see* Crossley-Holland.

HOLLAND, Norman James Abbott, IEng, FIEIE; Group Standards Manager, Philips UK, 1983–90; President, British National Electrotechnical Committee, 1993–99; *b* 16 Dec. 1927; *s* of James George Holland and May Stuart Holland; *m* 1951, Barbara Florence Byatt; one *s* one *d*. *Educ:* Sir Walter St John's Grammar Sch.; Regent Street Polytechnic. UK Delegate: IEC Council, 1987–92 (Delegn Leader, 1993–99; Mem. Bd, 1998–99); CENELEC Gen. Assembly, 1987–92 (Delegn Leader, 1993–99); Chm., Electrotechnical Sector Bd, 1993–99, Mem., Standards Bd, 1993–99, BSI. Member: IEC Finance Cttee, 1985–91; Engrg Council, 1985–91; Bd, Electronic Engrg Assoc., 1985–92 (Chm., Standards Policy Gp); NACCB, 1987–92. *Recreation:* golf. *Address:* 12 Pine Road, Chandler's Ford, Hants SO53 1LP. *Club:* Hockley Golf.

HOLLAND, Sir Philip (Welsby), Kt 1983; retired; *b* 14 March 1917; *s* of late John Holland, Middlewich, Cheshire; *m* 1943, Josephine Alma Hudson (*d* 1999); one *s*. *Educ:* Sir John Deane's Grammar Sch., Northwich. Enlisted RAF 1936; commissioned 1943. Factory Manager, Jantzen Knitting Mills, 1946–47; Management Research, 1948–49; Manufacturers' Agent in Engineering and Refractories Products, 1949–60. Contested (C) Yardley Div. of Birmingham, Gen. Election, 1955; MP (C): Acton, 1959–64; Carlton, 1966–83; Gedling, 1983–87. PPS: to Minister of Pensions and Nat. Insurance, 1961–62; to Chief Sec. to Treasury and Paymaster-Gen., 1962–64; to Minister of Aviation Supply, 1970; to Minister for Aerospace, 1971; to Minister for Trade, 1972. Pres., Cons. Trade Union Nat. Adv. Cttee, 1972–74. Personnel Manager, The Ultra Electronics Group of Companies, 1964–66; Personnel Consultant to Standard Telephones and Cables Ltd, 1969–81. Chm., Cttee of Selection, H of C, 1979–84; Standing Cttee Chm., 1983–87. Councillor, Royal Borough of Kensington, 1955–59. Rector's Warden, St Margaret's Church, Westminister, 1990–95. *Publications:* The Quango Explosion (jtly), 1978; Quango, Quango, Quango, 1979; Costing the Quango, 1979; The Quango Death List, 1980; The Governance of Quangos, 1981; Quelling the Quango, 1982; (jtly) A–Z Guide to Parliament, 1988; Lobby Fodder?, 1988; St Margaret's Westminster, 1993; The Hunting of the Quango, 1994. *Recreations:* travel, writing. *Address:* 53 Pymers Mead, West Dulwich, SE21 8NH.

HOLLAND, Richard; District Judge (Magistrates' Courts) (formerly Stipendiary Magistrate), Leicestershire, since 1999; *b* 23 Jan. 1951; *s* of Clifford Holland and Mary Holland (*née* Gledhill, now Smithies). *Educ:* Colne Valley High Sch., W Yorks; Queen Mary Coll., Univ. of London (BA Hons 1971). Admitted Solicitor 1974. Articled Clerk, Magistrates' Courts Service, WR of Yorks, 1972–74; Sen. Court Clerk, 1974–75, Dep. Justices' Clerk, 1975–79, Oldham; Justices' Clerk, Rochdale, 1979–89; Justices' Clerk, and Clerk to the Magistrates' Courts Cttee, Wakefield Met. Dist, 1990–97; Justices' Clerk and Chief Exec., Leeds City, 1997–99. *Recreations:* birdwatching, canal boating, the sport of Kings, feigning indolence. *Address:* Leicester City Magistrates' Court, PO Box 1, Pocklingtons Walk, Leicester LE1 9BE. *T:* (0116) 255 3666.

HOLLAND, (Robert) Einion, FIA; Chairman: Pearl Assurance PLC, 1983–89; Pearl Group PLC, 1985–89 (Director, since 1985); *b* 23 April 1927; *s* of late Robert Ellis Holland and Bene Holland; *m* 1955, Eryl Haf Roberts (*d* 1988); one *s* two *d*. *Educ:* University Coll. of N Wales, Bangor (BSc). FIA 1957. Joined Pearl Assurance Co. Ltd, 1953: Dir, 1973; Chief Gen. Manager, 1977–83. Chm., Industrial Life Offices Assoc., 1976–78; Director: Aviation & General Insurance Co. Ltd, 1972–89 (Chm. 1976–78, 1984–85); British Rail Property Board, 1987–90; Community Reinsurance Corp. Ltd, 1973–89 (Chm., 1973–76); Crawley Warren Group, 1987–99; Pearl American Corp., 1972–84; Scottish Legal Life Assurance Soc. Ltd, 1995–97. Member: Welsh Develt Agency, 1976–86; CS Pay Research Unit Bd, 1980–81; Council, Univ. of Wales, 1990–95. *Recreations:* golf and Welsh literature. *Address:* 55 Corkscrew Hill, West Wickham, Kent BR4 9BA. *T:* (020) 8777 1861.

HOLLAND, Stuart (Kingsley); political economist; Chief Executive, Alter-Europe; Director, Associate Research in Economy and Society Ltd, since 1993; *b* 25 March 1940; *y s* of late Frederick Holland and May Holland, London; *m* 1976, Jenny Lennard; two *c*. *Educ:* state primary schs; Christ's Hosp.; Univ. of Missouri (Exchange Scholar); Balliol Coll., Oxford (Domus Scholar; 1st Cl. Hons Mod. History); St Antony's Coll., Oxford (Sen. Scholar; DPhil Econs). Econ. Asst, Cabinet Office, 1966–67; Personal Asst to Prime Minister, 1967–68; Res. Fellow, Centre for Contemp. European Studies, Univ. of Sussex, 1968–71, Assoc. Fellow and Lectr, 1971–79. Vis. Scholar, Brookings Instn, Washington, DC, 1970. Adviser to Commons Expenditure Cttee, 1971–72; Special Adviser to Minister of Overseas Develt, 1974–75. MP (Lab) Vauxhall, 1979–89; Opposition frontbench spokesman on overseas develt and co-operation, 1983–87, on treasury and economic affairs, 1987–89; Prof. of Econs, Eur. Univ. Inst., Florence, 1989–93. Res. Specialist, RIIA, 1972–74; Associate, Inst. of Develt Studies, 1974– (Gov., 1983–91). Consultant: Econ. and Social Affairs Cttee, Council of Europe, 1973; Open Univ., 1973. Rapporteur,

Trades Union Adv. Cttee, OECD, 1977. Chm., Public Enterprise Gp, 1973–75. European Community Commission: Mem., Expert Cttee on Inflation, 1975–76; Consultant to Directorate Gen. XVI, 1989; Dir, Proj. on Econ. and Social Cohesion, 1991–93; Adviser: to Merger Task Force, DG IV, 1991–93; to Region of Tuscany, 1992–96. Member: Council, Inst. for Workers' Control, 1974–; UN Univ. Working Party on Socio-Cultural Factors in Develt, Tokyo, 1977. Lubbock Lectr, Oxford Univ., 1975; Tom Mann Meml Lectr, Australia, 1977. Mem., Labour Party, 1962–; Mem. sub-cttees (inc. Finance and Econ. Policy, Indust. Policy, EEC, Economic Planning, Defence, Development Cooperation, Public Sector), Nat. Exec. Cttee, Labour Party, 1972–89; Executive Member: Labour Coordinating Cttee, 1978–81; European Nuclear Disarmament Campaign, 1980–83; Mem., Economic Cttee, Socialist International, 1984–. Hon. MRTPI 1980. Dr *hc* Roskilde Univ., Denmark, 1992. *Publications:* (jtly) Sovereignty and Multinational Corporations, 1971; (ed) The State as Entrepreneur, 1972; Strategy for Socialism, 1975; The Socialist Challenge, 1975; The Regional Problem, 1976; Capital versus the Regions, 1976; (ed) Beyond Capitalist Planning, 1978; Uncommon Market, 1980; (ed) Out of Crisis, 1983; (with Donald Anderson) Kissinger's Kingdom, 1984; (with James Firebrace) Never Kneel Down, 1984; The Market Economy, 1987; The Global Economy, 1987; The European Imperative: economic and social cohesion in the 1990s, 1993; Towards a New Bretton Woods: alternatives for the global economy, 1994; (with Ken Coates) Full Employment for Europe, 1995; contrib. symposia; articles in specialist jls and national and internat. press. *Recreation:* singing in the bath. *Address:* 12 St Gabriel's Manor, Cormont Road, SE5 9RH. *T:* (020) 7793 1442, *Fax:* (020) 7793 1492; *e-mail:* michelix@ats.it.

HOLLAND, Brother Tristam (Keith), SSF; Anglican Franciscan friar; *b* 20 March 1946; *s* of late George Holland and Eva Holland (*née* Pinion-Clark). *Educ:* Eastwood Hall Park Sch.; Trinity Coll., Cambridge (MA). Joined Society of St Francis, 1967; Guardian, Fiwila Friary and Leprosarium, Zambia, 1973–76; Provincial Sec., 1976–83, Gen. Sec., 1983–97, SSF. Member: Liturgical Commn of C of E, 1991–; Gen. Synod, C of E, 1994–. Editor, Franciscan Qly Magazine, 1994–. Mem., Labour Party. *Publications:* Celebrating Common Prayer, 1992; The Daily Office SSF, 1992; Exciting Holiness, 1997; The Word of the Lord, 4 vols, 1998; The Gospel of the Lord, 1999. *Recreations:* reading novels, music, travel. *Address:* Hilfield Friary, Dorchester, Dorset DT2 7BE. *T:* (01300) 341160, *Fax:* (01300) 341293; *e-mail:* tristam@ssf.orders.anglican.org.

HOLLAND, Prof. Walter Werner, CBE 1992; MD; FRCP, FRCPE, FRCGP, FRCPath, FFPHM; Professor of Public Health Medicine, 1991–94, now Emeritus, and Hon. Director, 1968–94, Social Medicine and Health Service Research Unit, United Medical and Dental Schools of Guy's and St Thomas' Hospitals (formerly St Thomas's Hospital Medical School); *b* 5 March 1929; *s* of Henry Holland and Hertha Zentner; *m* 1964, Fiona Margaret Auchinleck Love; three *s*. *Educ:* St Thomas's Hosp. Med. Sch., London (BSc Hons 1951; MB, BS Hons 1954; MD 1964). FFCM 1972; FRCP 1973; FRCGP 1982; FRCPE 1990; FRCPath 1992. House Officer, St Thomas' Hosp., 1954–56; MRC Clin. Res. Fellow, London Sch. of Hygiene, 1959–61; Lectr, Johns Hopkins Univ., Md, USA, 1961–62; St Thomas's Hospital Medical School, later United Medical and Dental Schools of Guy's and St Thomas' Hospitals: Sen. Lectr, Dept of Medicine, 1962–64; Reader and Chm., Dept of Clin. Epidemiol. and Social Medicine, 1965–68; Prof. of Clin. Epidemiol., 1968–91. Fogarty Scholar-in-Residence, NIH, Bethesda, Md, 1984–85; Sawyer Scholar-in-Residence, Case Western Reserve Med. Sch., Cleveland, Ohio, 1985. Vis. Prof., LSE, 1998–. Queen Elizabeth, Queen Mother Lectr, FPHM, 1995; Harben Lectr, 1995; Rock Carling Lectr, Nuffield Trust, 1997. President: Internat. Epidemiol Assoc., 1987–90; Faculty of Public Health (formerly Community) Medicine, RCP, 1989–92. Non-exec. Mem., Glos HA, 1992–96. FKC 1999. Life Mem., Soc. of Scholars, Johns Hopkins Univ., 1970; Hon. Mem., Amer. Epidemiol Soc., 1985. Hon. FFPHMI 1993; Hon. Fellow, UMDS, 1996. Dr *hc* Univ. of Bordeaux, 1981; Free Univ. of Berlin, 1990. *Publications:* Data Handling in Epidemiology, 1970; Air Pollution and Respiratory Disease, 1972; Epidemiology and Health, 1977; Health Care and Epidemiology, 1978; Measurement of Levels of Health, 1979; Evaluation of Health Care, 1983; Chronic Obstructive Bronchopathies, 1983; Oxford Textbook of Public Health, 1984, 2nd edn 1991; (with Susie Stewart) Screening in Health Care, 1990; pubns on health services res., epidemiol methods and on respiratory disease. *Recreations:* reading, walking. *Address:* 11 Ennerdale Road, Kew, Richmond, Surrey TW9 3PG. *Club:* Athenæum.

HOLLAND-HIBBERT, family name of **Viscount Knutsford**.

HOLLAND-MARTIN, Robert George, (Robin); Director, Henderson (formerly Henderson Administration Group) plc, 1983–98; *b* 6 July 1939; *y s* of late Cyril Holland-Martin and Rosa, *d* of Sir Gerald Chadwyck-Healey, 2nd Bt, CBE; *m* 1976, Dominique, 2nd *d* of Maurice Fromaget; two *d*. *Educ:* Eton. Cazenove & Co., 1960–74 (partner, 1968–74); Finance Director, Paterson Products Ltd, 1976–86; Consultant, Newmarket Venture Capital plc (formerly Newmarket Co.), 1982–94. Non-executive Director: Dorling Kindersley Hldgs plc, 1992–2000; Fine Art Soc. plc, 1995–; Grupo Picking Pack SA (Spain), 1998–. Hon. Dep. Treasurer, Cons. and Unionist Party, 1979–82. Mem., Trustee Bd (formerly Council), Metropolitan Hospital-Sunday Fund, 1964– (Chm., 1977–); Mem. Council, Homoeopathic Trust, 1970–90 (Vice Chm., 1975–90). Victoria & Albert Museum: Mem. Adv. Council, 1972–83; Mem. Cttee, Associates of V&A, 1976–85 (Chm., 1981–85); Dep. Chm., Trustees, 1983–85. Mem., Visiting Cttee for Royal Coll. of Art, 1982–93 (Chm., 1984–93). Trustee, Blackie Foundn Trust, 1971–96 (Chm., 1987–96; Pres., 1998–). *Address:* 18 Tite Street, SW3 4HZ. *T:* (020) 7352 7871. *Clubs:* White's, Royal Automobile.

HOLLANDER, Charles Simon; QC 1999; a Recorder, since 2000; *b* 1 Dec. 1955; *s* of Paul and Eileen Hollander; *m* 1986, Heather Pilley; two *s* two *d*. *Educ:* University College Sch.; King's Coll., Cambridge (BA 1977; MA 1981). Called to the Bar, Gray's Inn, 1978; in practice at the Bar, 1978–. *Publications:* jointly: Documentary Evidence, 1985, 6th edn 1997; Phipson on Evidence, 15th edn 2000; Conflicts of Interest and Chinese Walls, 2000. *Recreations:* tennis, food, wine. *Address:* Brick Court Chambers, 7/8 Essex Street, WC2R 3LD. *T:* (020) 7379 3550.

HOLLANDS, Maj.-Gen. Graham Spencer; Chief Executive, West Kent College, since 1994; *b* 14 Feb. 1942; *s* of Ernest Darrell Hollands and Gwendoline Isobel Hollands (*née* Matheson); *m* 1968, Lesley Clair Billam; one *s* one *d*. *Educ:* King Edward VI Sch., Bath; RMA Sandhurst; RMCS; Staff Coll., Camberley. Commissioned RA, 1963; served BAOR and UK; MoD, 1980–81; CO 25 Field Regt RA, 1981–84; CO 3rd Regt RHA, 1984–85; COS Artillery Div., HQ 1 (BR) Corps, 1985–86; Comdr, British Trng Teams, Nigeria, 1986–87; CRA 2nd Inf. Div., 1987–89; DCOS, HQ BAOR, 1989–92; Comdr Artillery, 1st British Corps, 1992–94. *Recreations:* golf, ski-ing, country pursuits. *Address:* National Westminster Bank, March Branch, March, Cambs PE15 8TN.

HOLLENDEN, 4th Baron *cr* 1912, of Leigh, Kent; **Ian Hampden Hope-Morley;** part-owner and Trustee, The Hampden Estate; *b* 23 Oct. 1946; *e s* of 3rd Baron Hollenden and of Sonja (*née* Sundt); *S* father, 1999; *m* 1st, 1972, Beatrice (*née* d'Anchald) (marr. diss. 1985); one *s* one *d*; 2nd, 1988, Caroline (*née* Ash); two *s*. *Educ:* Maidwell Hall; Eton Coll. Shipbroker: Asmarine SA, Paris, 1969–72; Eggar Forrester, London, 1972–77; Mktg Mgr, British Shipbuilders, 1977–79; Shipbroker, Galbraith Wrightson, 1979–86; Proprietor, The Hampden Wine Company, Thame, 1988–98. *Recreations:* shooting, ski-ing. *Heir: s* Hon. Edward Hope-Morley, *b* 9 April 1981. *Address:* The Estate Office, Great Hampden, Great Missenden, Bucks HP16 9RE. *Club:* Brooks's.

HOLLENWEGER, Prof. Walter Jacob; Professor of Mission, University of Birmingham, 1971–89; *b* 1 June 1927; *s* of Walter Otto and Anna Hollenweger-Spörri; *m* 1951, Erica Busslinger. *Educ:* Univs. of Zürich and Basel. Dr theol Zürich 1966 (and degrees leading up to it). Stock Exchange, Zürich, and several banking appts, until 1948. Pastor, 1949–57; ordained, Swiss Reformed Church, 1961. Study Dir, Ev. Acad., Zürich, 1964–65; Research Asst, Univ. of Zürich, 1961–64; Exec. Sec., World Council of Churches, Geneva, 1965–71; regular guest prof. in Switzerland, Germany and USA. Hon. Fellow, Selly Oak Colls, Birmingham, 1996. Prize for Theol., Sexau, Germany, 1995; Lifetime Achievement Award, Soc. for Pentecostal Studies, USA, 1999. *Publications:* Handbuch der Pfingstbewegung, 10 vols, 1965/66; (ed) The Church for Others, 1967 (also German, Spanish and Portuguese edns); (ed) Die Pfingstkirchen, 1971; Kirche, Benzin und Bohnensuppe, 1971; The Pentecostals, 1972, 1988 (also German and Spanish edns); Pentecost between Black and White, 1975 (also German and Dutch edns); Glaube, Geist und Geister, 1975; (ed) Studies in the Intercultural History of Christianity, 100 vols, 1975–; Evangelism Today, 1976 (also German edn); (with Th. Ahrens) Volkschristentum und Volksreligion in Pazifik, 1977; Interkulturelle Theologie, vol. I, 1979, vol. II, 1982, vol. III, 1988 (abridged French edn); Erfahrungen in Ephesus, 1979; Wie Grenzen zu Brücken werden, 1980; Besuch bei Lukas, 1981; Conflict in Corinth—Memoirs of an Old Man, 1982 (also German, Italian, Indonesian and French edns; musical and drama edn, 1999); Jüngermesse/Gomer: Das Gesicht des Unsichtbaren, 1983 (music edns 1994 and 1995); Zwingli zwischen Krieg und Frieden, 1983, 1988; Das Fest der Verlorenen, 1984; Der Handelsreisende Gottes, 1985 (music edn 1994); Das Wagnis des Glaubens, 1986 (music edn 1993); Weihnachtsoratorium, 1986; Mirjam, Mutter, and Michal: Die Frauen meines Mannes (zwei Monodramen), 1987 (music edn 1994); Bonhoeffer Requiem, 1990 (music edn 1992); Ostertanz der Frauen/Veni Creator Spiritus, 1990; Kommet her zu mir/Die zehn Aussätzigen, 1990; Fontana (musical), 1991; Jona (musical), 1992; Hiob im Kreuzfeuer der Religionen, 1993; Jürg Rathgeb (oratorio), 1993; Der Kommissar auf biblischer Spurensuche, 1993; Ruth, die Ausländerin, 1993; Kamele und Kapitalisten, 1994; Johannestexte, 1995; Scherben, 1996; Pentecostalism, 1997 (also German edn); Maria von Wedemeyer, 1997; Nympha und Onesimus, 1999; Neuer Himmel—neue Erde, 1999. *Address:* 3704 Krattigen, Switzerland. *T:* (33) 6544302.

HOLLEY, Rear Adm. Ronald Victor, CB 1987; FRAeS; Independent Inspector, Lord Chancellor's Panel, 1992–2001; *b* 13 July 1931; *s* of late Mr and Mrs V. E. Holley; *m* 1954, Sister Dorothy Brierley, QARNNS; two *s* twin *d*. *Educ:* Rondebosch, S Africa; Portsmouth GS; RNEC Manadon; RAFC Henlow (post graduate). MIMechE, MIEE; FRAeS 1988. Served HM Ships Implacable, Finisterre, Euryalus, Victorious, Eagle (899 Sqdn); NATO Defence Coll., Rome, 1968; Naval Plans, 1969–71; Aircraft Dept, 1971–73; Air Engr Officer, HMS Seahawk, 1973–75; Naval Asst to Controller of the Navy, 1975–77; RCDS, 1978; Seaman Officer Develt Study, 1979; Dir, Helicopter Projects, Procurement Exec., 1979–82; RNEC in command, 1982–84; Gen. Naval Mem., Directing Staff, RCDS, 1984–85; Dir Gen. Aircraft (Navy), 1985–87. Tech. Dir, Shell Aircraft, 1987–92. Sec., European Helicopter Operators Cttee, 1988–91. President: RN Volunteer Bands, 1983–87; RN Amateur Fencing Assoc., 1986–87 (Chm., 1983–86). Mem., Parly Gp for Engrg Develt, 1993–. Henson and Stringfellow Lectr, RAeS, 1987. *Publications:* contribs to Naval Jls, and Seaford House Papers, 1978. *Recreation:* the Philharmonic Orchestra.

HOLLEY, (William) Stephen, CBE 1979; General Manager, Washington Development Corporation, 1965–80; *b* 26 March 1920; *m* 1947, Dinah Mary Harper; three *s*. *Educ:* King William's Coll. Student Accountant, 1937–39. War service, RA (TA), 1939–45 (Major). Colonial Service, and Overseas Civil Service, 1945–64; Mem. Legislature and State Sec., Head of Civil Service, Sabah, Malaysia, 1964. Hon. ADK (Malaysia). DL Tyne and Wear, 1975–81. *Publications:* Washington—Quicker by Quango, 1983; Entente Cordiale, 1990; Godverse and Oddverse, 1998; contribs to Sarawak Museum Jl and press articles on New Town Development. *Recreations:* golf, writing, gardening, theatre. *Address:* Forge Cottage, The Green, Abthorpe, Northants NN12 8QP. *Club:* Royal Commonwealth Society.

HOLLICK, family name of **Baron Hollick**.

HOLLICK, Baron *cr* 1991 (Life Peer), of Notting Hill in the Royal Borough of Kensington and Chelsea; **Clive Richard Hollick;** Chief Executive, United News & Media plc, since 1996; *b* 20 May 1945; *s* of Leslie George Hollick and Olive Mary (*née* Scruton); *m* 1977, Susan Mary (*née* Woodford); three *d*. *Educ:* Taunton's Sch., Southampton; Univ. of Nottingham (BA Hons). Joined Hambros Bank Ltd, 1968, Dir, 1973–96; Chairman: Shepperton Studios Ltd, 1976–84; Garban Ltd (USA), 1983–97; Meridian Broadcasting Ltd, 1992–96; Chief Exec., Mills & Allen Internat., subseq. MAI PLC, 1974–96; Director: Logica plc, 1987–91; Avenir Havas Media SA, 1989–92; Satellite Information Systems Ltd, 1990–94; British Aerospace, 1992–97; Anglia Television, 1994–97; TRW Inc., 2000–. Special Advr to Pres. of BoT and Sec. of State for Trade and Industry, 1997–98. Member: Nat. Bus Co. Ltd, 1984–91; Adv. Cttee, Dept of Applied Econs, Univ. of Cambridge, 1989–97; Financial Law Panel, 1993–97; Commn on Public Policy and British Business, 1995–97. Chm., Galleon Trust, 1992–97. Founding Trustee, Inst. for Public Policy Res., 1988–. Gov., LSE, 1997–. Hon. LLD Nottingham, 1993. *Recreations:* reading, theatre, cinema, tennis, countryside. *Address:* House of Lords, SW1A 0PW.

HOLLIDAY, Sir Frederick (George Thomas), Kt 1990; CBE 1975; FRSE; Chairman, Northumbrian Water Group, since 1993 (Director, since 1991); *b* 22 Sept. 1935; *s* of late Alfred C. and Margaret Holliday; *m* 1957, Philippa Mary Davidson; one *s* one *d*. *Educ:* Bromsgrove County High Sch.; Sheffield Univ. BSc 1st cl. hons Zool. 1956; FIBiol 1970, FRSE 1971. Fisheries Research Trng Grant (Develt Commn) at Marine Lab., Aberdeen, 1956–58; Sci. Officer, Marine Lab., Aberdeen, 1958–61; Lectr in Zoology, Univ. of Aberdeen, 1961–66; Prof. of Biology, 1967–75, Dep. Principal, 1972, Acting Principal, 1973–75, Univ. of Stirling; Prof. of Zoology, Univ. of Aberdeen, 1975–79; Vice-Chancellor and Warden, Univ. of Durham, 1980–90. Member: Scottish Cttee, Nature Conservancy, 1969; Council, Scottish Field Studies Assoc., 1970–78 (Pres., 1981–); Council, Scottish Marine Biol Assoc., 1967–85 (Pres., 1979–85); Scottish Wildlife Trust (Vice-Pres.); Council, Freshwater Biol Assoc., 1969–72, and 1993–2000 (Pres., 1995–2001); NERC Oceanography and Fisheries Research Grants Cttee, 1971; Council, NERC, 1973–79; Nature Conservancy Council, 1975–80 (Dep. Chm., 1976–77, Chm., 1977–80); Scottish Economic Council, 1975–80; Council, Marine Biol Assoc. UK, 1975–78 (Vice-Pres., 1994–); Oil Develt Council for Scotland, 1976–78; Standing Commn on Energy and the Environment, 1978–82; Adv. Cttee, Leverhulme Trust Res. Awards, 1978–95 (Chm., 1989–95); PCFC, 1989–93; Awards Council, Royal Anniv. Trust, 1993–95; Council, Water Aid, 1994–98; Envmtl Cttee, CBI, 1994–; Chm., Independent Review of Disposal of Radioactive Waste at Sea, 1984; Ind. Chm., Jt Nature

Conservation Cttee, 1991. Dir, Shell UK, 1980–99; Mem., Shell UK Audit Cttee, 1993–94; Chairman: Investors' Cttee, Northern Venture Partnership Fund, 1990–2001; Northern Venture Capital Fund, 1996–; Go-Ahead Gp, 1998– (Dir, 1997–); Dep. Chm., Northern Regional Bd, Lloyd's Bank, 1989–91 (Mem., 1985–91; Chm., 1986–89); Director: Northern Investors Ltd, 1984–90; BRB, 1990–94 (Chm., BR (Eastern), 1986–90); Union Railways, 1993–97; Lyonnaise des Eaux SA, 1996–97; Lyonnaise Europe plc, 1996–2000; Suez Lyonnaise des Eaux, 1997–2001; Wisespeke Plc, 1997–98; Brewin Dolphin Gp, 1998–. Trustee, Nat. Heritage Meml Fund, 1980–91; Vice-Pres., Civic Trust for NE; Pres., British Trust for Ornithology, 1996–2001. Member: Bd of Governors, Rowett Res. Inst., 1976–84; Scottish Civic Trust, 1984–87. DUniv Stirling, 1984; Hon. DSc: Sheffield, 1987; Cranfield, 1991. DL Durham, 1985–90. *Publications:* (ed and contrib.) Wildlife of Scotland, 1979; numerous on fish biology and wildlife conservation in Adv. Mar. Biol., Fish Physiology, Oceanography and Marine Biology, etc. *Recreations:* ornithology, bee keeping, walking, gardening. *Address:* Northumbrian Water, Abbey Road, Pity Me, Durham DH1 5FJ. *T:* (0191) 301 6406. *Clubs:* Royal Commonwealth Society; Northern Counties (Newcastle upon Tyne).

HOLLIDAY, Leslie John, FCIOB, CIMgt; Chairman and Chief Executive, John Laing plc, 1982–85 (Director, 1978); Chairman, John Laing Construction Ltd, 1980–85 (Director, 1966); *b* 9 Jan. 1921; *s* of John and Elsie Holliday; *m* 1943, Kathleen Joan Marjorie Stacey; two *s*. *Educ:* St John's, Whitby. FCIOB 1969; CIMgt (CBIM 1982). Denaby & Cadby Colliery, 1937–40; served Merchant Navy, 1940–45; joined John Laing & Son Ltd, 1947, Dir 1977; Chairman: Laing Homes Ltd, 1978–81; Super Homes Ltd, 1979–81; Laing Management Contracting Ltd, 1980–81; John Laing Internat. Ltd, 1981–82; Director: Declan Kelly Holdings, 1985–89; RM Douglas Holdings, 1986–89; Admiral Homes Ltd, 1989–; Redrow Gp, 1989–92. Mem., EDC for Bldg, 1979–82. Freeman, City of London, 1984; Liveryman, Plaisterers' Co., 1984–. *Recreations:* yachting, golf. *Address:* 6 Priestland Gardens, Castle Village, Berkhamsted, Herts HP4 2GT. *Club:* Berkhamsted Golf.

HOLLIDAY, Dr Robin, FRS 1976; Chief Research Scientist, Commonwealth Scientific and Industrial Research Organisation (Australia), 1988–97; *b* 6 Nov. 1932; *s* of Clifford and Eunice Holliday; *m* 1st, 1957, Diana Collet (*née* Parsons) (marr. diss. 1983); one *s* three *d*; 2nd, 1986, Lily Irene (*née* Huschtscha); one *d*. *Educ:* Hitchin Grammar Sch.; Univ. of Cambridge (BA, PhD); Fulbright Scholar, 1962. Member, Scientific Staff: Dept of Genetics, John Innes Inst., Bayfordbury, Herts, 1958–65; Division of Microbiology, Nat. Inst. for Med. Research, 1965–70; Head, Div. of Genetics, Nat. Inst. for Med. Research, 1970–88. Mem., EMBO, 1982. For. Fellow, INSA, 1995. Lord Cohen Medal, 1987. *Publications:* The Science of Human Progress, 1981; Genes, Proteins and Cellular Aging, 1986; Understanding Ageing, 1995; Slaves and Saviours, 2000; over 250 scientific papers on genetic recombination, repair, gene expression and cellular ageing. *Recreations:* sculpture, writing. *Address:* 12 Roma Court, West Pennant Hills, NSW 2125, Australia. *T:* (2) 98733476, *Fax:* (2) 98712159; *e-mail:* randl.holliday@bigpond.com.

HOLLIGER, Heinz; oboist, composer and conductor; *b* Langenthal, Switzerland, 1939; *m* Ursula Holliger, harpist. *Educ:* Berne Conservatoire; Paris; Basle; studied with Cassagnaud, Lefêbure, Veress, Pierlot and Boulez. Played with Basle Orch., 1959–63; Prof. of oboe, Freiburg Music Acad., 1965–. Has appeared as soloist and conductor at all major European music festivals, and with Chamber Orch. of Europe, English Chamber Orch., etc; has directed all major Swiss orchs, Cleveland Orch., Philharmonia, Vienna Philharmonic, CBSO, etc. Has inspired compositions by Berio, Penderecki, Stockhausen, Henze, Martin and others. *Compositions include:* Der magische Tänzer, Trio, Dona nobis pacem, Pneuma, Psalm, Cardiophonie, Kreis, Siebengesang, H for wind quintet, string quartet Atembogen, Scardanelli-Cycle, Gesänge der Frühe, (S)irato for orch., Violin Concerto. Has won many international prizes, including: Geneva Competition first prize, 1959; Munich Competition first prize, 1961; Sonning Prize; Frankfurt Music Prize; Ernst von Siemens Prize. *Address:* Konzertgesellschaft, Hochstrasse 51/Postfach, 4002 Basel, Switzerland.

HOLLINGHURST, Edmund, FREng, FICE, FIStructE; FIHT; Director and Partner, since 1986, and Joint Managing Director, Gifford & Partners; *b* 27 June 1944; *s* of Rev. Dr George Frederick Hollinghurst and Rachel Hollinghurst (*née* Cooper); *m* 1986, Glenys Helen Davis; three *d*. *Educ:* Dragon Sch., Oxford; Kingswood Sch., Bath; Sidney Sussex Coll., Cambridge (MA). CEng 1971; FIHT 1985; FICE 1995; FIStructE 1995; FREng (FEng 1997). Trainee, Ove Arup & Partners, 1962–63; Engineer: Ninham Shand, Cape Town, SA, 1965–66; Ove Arup & Partners, London, Africa and Middle East, 1967–70; Kier Ltd, UK and overseas, 1970–73; Gifford & Partners, 1973–86, seconded as staff consultant, Asian Develt Bank, 1978. Mem., Royal Fine Art Commn, 1996–99. Major designs include: Bray Viaduct, Devon; Kwai Chung, Hong Kong; Dee Crossing, Wales; Second Severn Crossing; Camel Estuary Bridge, Cornwall; Kingston Bridge, Glasgow; River Tyne Millennium Bridge. Fédération Internationale de la Précontrainte Design Award, for Bray Viaduct, 1994. *Publications:* contrib. to ICE and IStructE texts. *Recreation:* sailing. *Address:* Carlton House, Ringwood Road, Woodlands, Southampton SO40 7HT. *T:* (023) 8081 3461.

HOLLINGS, Sir (Alfred) Kenneth, Kt 1971; MC 1944; Judge of the High Court of Justice, Family Division (formerly Probate, Divorce and Admiralty Division), 1971–93; *b* 12 June 1918; *s* of Alfred Holdsworth Hollings and Rachel Elizabeth Hollings; *m* 1949, Harriet Evelyn Isabella, *d* of W. J. C. Fishbourne, OBE, Brussels; one *s* one *d*. *Educ:* Leys Sch., Cambridge; Clare Coll., Cambridge. Law Qualifying and Law Tripos, Cambridge, 1936–39; MA. Served RA (Shropshire Yeomanry), 1939–46. Called to Bar, Middle Temple, 1947 (Harmsworth Schol.); Master of the Bench, 1971. Practised Northern Circuit; QC 1966; Recorder of Bolton, 1968; Judge of County Courts, Circuit 5 (E Lancs), 1968–71; Presiding Judge, Northern Circuit, 1975–78. *Recreations:* walking, swimming, music. *Clubs:* Garrick, Hurlingham; Tennis and Racquets (Manchester).

HOLLINGSWORTH, Michael Charles; Chief Executive, Venture Television Ltd, since 1989 (trading as Venture Artistes, Venture Broadcasting, and Venture Correspondents); Managing Director, Liberty Broadcasting, since 1996; *b* 22 Feb. 1946; *s* of Albert George Hollingsworth and Gwendoline Marjorie Hollingsworth; *m* 1st, 1968, Patricia Margaret Jefferson Winn (marr. diss. 1987); one *d*; 2nd, 1989, Anne Margaret Diamond (marr. diss. 1999); four *s* (and one *s* decd). *Educ:* Carlisle Grammar Sch. Programme Editor, Anglia Television, 1964–67; Producer, BBC Local Radio, 1967–74; Northern Editor, Today, Radio Four, 1974–75; Editor, News and Current Affairs: Southern Television Ltd, 1975–79; ATV Network/Central, 1979–82; Sen. Producer, Current Affairs, BBC TV, 1982–84; Dir of Programmes, TV-am Ltd, 1984–86; Man. Dir, Music Box Ltd, 1986–89. Agent and consultant to television and radio cos. *Recreation:* DIY (house renovation). *Address:* (office) Po Box 299, Oxford OX2 6LN. *T:* (07000) 402001, *Fax:* (07000) 402002.

HOLLINGTON, Robin Frank; QC 1999; *b* 30 June 1955; *s* of late Reginald Barrie Hollington and of Eleanor Gwendoline Hollington (*née* Paxton); *m* 1988, Jane Elizabeth Cadogan Gritten; one *s*. *Educ:* Haileybury; University Coll., Oxford (MA); Univ. of Pennsylvania (LLM). Called to the Bar, Lincoln's Inn, 1979. *Publication:* Minority Shareholders' Rights, 1990, 3rd edn 1999. *Recreations:* Real tennis, lawn tennis, golf. *Address:* New Square Chambers, 12 New Square, Lincoln's Inn, WC2A 3SW. *T:* (020) 7419 8000. *Clubs:* Royal Automobile, MCC; Walton Heath Golf.

HOLLINGWORTH, Clare, OBE 1984; Correspondent in Hong Kong for Sunday Telegraph, since 1981; Research Associate (formerly Visiting Scholar), Centre of Asian Studies, University of Hong Kong, since 1981; *b* 10 Oct. 1911; *d* of John Albert Hollingworth and Daisy Gertrude Hollingworth; *m* 1st, 1936, Vyvyan Derring Vandeleur Robinson (marr. diss. 1951); 2nd, 1952, Geoffrey Spencer Hoare (*d* 1966). *Educ:* Girls' Collegiate Sch., Leicester; Grammar Sch., Ashby de la Zouch, Leics; Sch. of Slavonic Studies, Univ. of London. On staff, League of Nations Union, 1935–38; worked in Poland for Lord Mayor's Fund for Refugees from Czechoslovakia, 1939; Correspondent in Poland for Daily Telegraph: first to report outbreak of war from Katawice; remained in Balkans as Germans took over; moved to Turkey and then Cairo, 1941–50, covering Desert Campaigns, troubles in Persia and Iraq, Civil War in Greece and events in Palestine; covered trouble spots from Paris for Manchester Guardian, 1950–63, incl. Algerian War, Egypt, Aden and Vietnam (Journalist of the Year Award and Hannan Swaffer Award, 1963); Guardian Defence Correspondent, 1963–67; Daily Telegraph: foreign trouble shooter, 1967–73, covering war in Vietnam; Correspondent in China, 1973–76; Defence Correspondent, 1976–81. Hon. DLitt Leicester, 1993. James Cameron Award for Journalism, 1994. *Publications:* Poland's Three Weeks War, 1940; There's a German Just Behind Me, 1945; The Arabs and the West, 1951; Mao and the Men Against Him, 1984; Front Line, 1990. *Recreations:* visiting second-hand furniture and bookshops, collecting modern pictures and Chinese porcelain, music. *Address:* 19 Dorset Square, NW1 6QB. *T:* (020) 7262 6923; 302 Ridley House, 2 Upper Albert Road, Hong Kong. *T:* 28681838. *Clubs:* Cercle de l'Union Interalliée (Paris); Foreign Correspondents (Hong Kong and Tokyo).

HOLLINGWORTH, John Harold; *b* 11 July 1930; *s* of Harold Hollingworth, Birmingham; *m* 1969, Susan Barbara (marr. diss. 1985), *d* of late J. H. Walters, Ramsey, IoM. *Educ:* Chigwell House Sch.; King Edward's Sch., Edgbaston. MP (C) All Saints Division of Birmingham, 1959–64; contested (C) Birmingham, All Saints, 1966 and 1970. Chairman: Birmingham Young Conservatives, 1958–62; Edgbaston Div. Conservative Assoc., 1967–72; Vice-Chm., Birmingham Conservative Assoc., 1958–61, 1972–78 (Vice-Pres. 1960–66). Dir and Gen. Manager, Cambridge Symphony Orch. Trust, 1979–82 (Gov., 1982–92); Dir, Thaxted Fest. Foundn, 1987–93. Chm., Elmdon Trust Ltd, 1984–91; dir of other cos; mem. of various charitable activities. Trustee, 1991–98, Hon. Chief Exec., 1992–93, Hon. Treas., 1993–98, British Performing Arts Medicine Trust. Member: Viola d'Amore Soc. of GB; ESU. *Publications:* contributions to political journals. *Recreations:* exercising Rough Collie dogs, planning third British Empire. *Address:* 10 Hamel Way, Widdington, Saffron Walden, CB11 3SJ. *T:* (01799) 542445. *Club:* Lansdowne.

HOLLINGWORTH, Rt Rev. Dr Peter John, AC 2001 (AO 1988); OBE 1976; Governor General of the Commonwealth of Australia, since 2001; *b* 10 April 1935; *m* 1960, Kathleen Ann Turner; three *d*. *Educ:* Murrumbeena and Lloyd Street State Schools; Scotch Coll., Melbourne; Trinity Coll., Univ. of Melbourne (BA 1958; MA 1980); Australian Coll. of Theol. (ThL 1959); Univ. of Melbourne (Dip. Social Studies, 1970). Commercial Cadet, Broken Hill Pty, 1952–53. Ordained, 1960; Priest in charge, St Mary's, N Melbourne, 1960–64; Brotherhood of St Laurence: Chaplain and Dir of Youth Work, 1964–70; Assoc. Dir, 1970–79; Exec. Dir, 1980–90; Canon, St Paul's Cathedral, Melbourne, 1980; Bishop in the Inner City, dio. of Melbourne, 1985–90; Archbishop of Brisbane and Metropolitan, Province of Queensland, 1990–2001. Chairman: Social Responsibilities Commn, Gen. Synod, Anglican Church of Aust., 1990–98; Nat. Council for the Centenary of Fedn, 2000. Mem., Australian Assoc. of Social Workers, 1970–78. FAIM 1997; Fellow, Trinity Coll., Melbourne, 1998. Hon. LLD: Monash, 1986; Melbourne, 1990; DUniv: Griffith, 1993; Qld Univ. of Technol., 1994; Univ. of Central Qld, 1995; DLitt Univ. of Southern Qld, 1999; DLitt Lambeth 2001. ChStJ 1998–2001; Nat. ChLJ 1998–2001; GCLJ 1998. Australian of the Year, 1991. *Publications:* Australians in Poverty, 1978; The Powerless Poor, 1972; The Poor: victims of affluence, 1975; Public Thoughts of an Archbishop, 1996. *Recreations:* writing, reading, swimming, music, the arts. *Address:* Government House, Canberra, ACT 2600, Australia.

HOLLINS, Rear-Adm. Hubert Walter Elphinstone, CB 1974; marine consultant; *b* 8 June 1923; *s* of Lt-Col W. T. Hollins; *m* 1963, Jillian Mary McAlpin; one *s* one *d*. *Educ:* Stubbington House; Britannia RNC Dartmouth. Cadet RN, 1937; Comdr 1957; Captain 1963; Rear-Adm. 1972; comd HM Ships Petard, Dundas, Caesar and Antrim; Flag Officer, Gibraltar, 1972–74; Admiral Commanding Reserves, 1974–77; Gen. Man., ME Navigation Aids Service, Bahrain, 1977–84. Younger Brother of Trinity House; Mem., Trinity House Lighthouse Bd, 1985–91. Commodore, Bahrain Yacht Club, 1981–83. Master Mariner. Trustee, Royal Merchant Navy Sch., Bearwood, 1985–92; President: Newbury RN Assoc., 1985–90; Newbury Sea Cadet Corps, 1985–91 (Patron, 1991). Vice Patron, Gallantry Medallists' League, 1995–. *Recreation:* fishing. *Address:* Waunllan, Llandyfriog, Newcastle Emlyn, Cardiganshire SA38 9HB. *T:* (01239) 710456.

HOLLINS, Peter Thomas; Chief Executive, British Energy, 1998–2001; *b* 22 Nov. 1947; *m* 1973, Linda Pitchford; two *d*. *Educ:* 2nd. Cl. Hons Chem. British Oxygen, 1970–73; ICI UK, 1973–89; ICI Holland, 1989–92; EVC Brussels, 1992–98. *Recreations:* fluent in Dutch, German, and French, classical music, travelling, Rugby, hill-walking. *Address:* Flat 61, Harlequin Court, 6 Thomas More Street, E1W 1AR.

HOLLIS, family name of **Baroness Hollis of Heigham.**

HOLLIS OF HEIGHAM, Baroness *cr* 1990 (Life Peer), of Heigham in the City of Norwich; **Patricia Lesley Hollis;** PC 1999; DL; DPhil; Parliamentary Under-Secretary of State, Department for Work and Pensions, since 2001; *b* 24 May 1941; *d* of (Harry) Lesley (George) Wells and Queenie Rosalyn Wells; *m* 1965, (James) Martin Hollis, FBA (*d* 1998); two *s*. *Educ:* Plympton Grammar Sch.; Cambridge Univ. (MA); Univ. of California; Columbia Univ., NY; Nuffield Coll., Oxford (DPhil). Harkness Fellow, 1962–64; Nuffield Scholar, 1964–67. University of East Anglia: Lectr, 1967, then Reader, and Sen. Fellow in Modern Hist.; Dean, School of English and American Studies, 1988–90. Councillor: Norwich City Council, 1968–91 (Leader, 1983–88); Norfolk CC, 1981–85. Member: Regional Econ. Planning Council, 1975–79; Govt Commn on Housing, 1975–77; RHA, 1979–83; BBC Regional Adv. Cttee, 1979–83. Vice-President: ADC, 1990–; AMA, 1990–97; Assoc. of Envmtl Health Officers, 1992–; NFHA, 1993–. Dir, Radio Broadland, 1983–97. Nat. Comr, English Heritage, 1988–91; Mem. Press Council, 1989–90. Contested (Lab) Gt Yarmouth, Feb. and Oct. 1974, 1979. An opposition whip, 1990–97; opposition frontbench spokesperson on social security, disability, local govt and housing, 1992–97; Parly Under-Sec. of State, DSS, 1997–2001. FRHistS. DL Norfolk, 1994. Hon. DLitt: Anglia Poly. Univ., 1995; London Guildhall, 2001; DUniv Open, 2000. *Publications:* The Pauper Press, 1970; Class and Conflict, 1815–50, 1973; Pressure from Without, 1974; Women in Public 1850–1900, 1979; (with

Dr B. H. Harrison) Robert Lowery, Radical and Chartist, 1979; Ladies Elect: women in English local government 1865–1914, 1987; Jennie Lee: a life, 1997. *Recreations:* boating, singing, domesticity. *Address:* House of Lords, SW1A 0PW. *T:* (020) 7219 3000.

HOLLIS, Sir Anthony Barnard, Kt 1982; a Judge of the High Court of Justice, Family Division, 1982–97; *b* 11 May 1927; *er s* of late Henry Lewis Hollis and of Gladys Florence Hollis (*née* Barnard); *m* 1956, Pauline Mary (*née* Skuce); one step *d. Educ:* Tonbridge Sch.; St Peter's Hall, Oxford (Hon. Fellow, St Peter's Coll., 1993). Called to the Bar, Gray's Inn, 1951 (Bencher, 1979); QC 1969; a Recorder of the Crown Court, 1976–82. Chm., Family Law Bar Assoc., 1974–76. *Recreation:* golf. *Address:* Hook Hill, Hook Hill Lane, Woking, Surrey GU22 0QB. *Clubs:* Garrick; Woking Golf; Royal St George's Golf (Sandwich).

HOLLIS, Rt Rev. Crispian; *see* Portsmouth, Bishop of, (RC).

HOLLIS, Daniel Ayrton; QC 1968; a Recorder of the Crown Court, 1972–96; *b* 30 April 1925; *m* 1st, 1950, Gillian Mary Turner (marr. diss., 1961); one *d* (one *s* decd); 2nd, 1963, Stella Hydleman; one *s. Educ:* Geelong Grammar Sch., Australia; Brasenose Coll., Oxford. Served N Atlantic and Mediterranean, 1943–46. Lieut-Commander, RNVR. Called to Bar, Middle Temple, 1949; Bencher, 1975; Treas., 1994; Head of Chambers, 1968–95. A Comr, CCC, 1971; a Dep. High Ct Judge, 1982–93. Mem., Criminal Injuries Compensation Bd, 1995–2000. Mem., Home Sec.'s Adv. Bd on Restricted Patients, 1986–92. *Address:* 22 St James's Square, SW1Y 4JH; 8 place Fontaine Vieille, La Garde Freinet 83680, France. *Club:* Travellers.

HOLLIS, Geoffrey Alan; Director, Drew Associates, since 1997; *b* 25 Nov. 1943; *s* of late William John Hollis and of Elsie Jean Hollis (*née* Baker); *m* 1967, Ann Josephine Prentice; two *s. Educ:* Hastings Grammar Sch.; Hertford Coll., Oxford (MA); Polytechnic of Central London (Dip. Management Studies). International Computers, 1966; International Publishing Corp., 1967; Gulf Oil, 1969; MAFF, 1974–96; seconded to FCO, First Sec., 1977–80, UK Perm. Rep., EC, Brussels; Under Sec. and Hd of Meat, later Livestock Gp, 1991–96. Non-executive Director: Lucas Ingredients (Dalgety plc), 1991–95; E and N Herts HA, 1998–2001; Mem., Welwyn Hatfield Primary Care Trust, 2001–. Admitted to Co. of Clockmakers, 1997. *Recreations:* chess, golf, horology. *Address:* 12 Lodge Drive, Hatfield, Herts AL9 5HN.

HOLLIS, Ven. Gerald; Archdeacon of Birmingham, 1974–84; *b* 16 May 1919; *s* of Canon Walter Hollis and Enid (*née* Inchbold); *m* 1946, Doreen Emmet Stancliffe; one *s* three *d. Educ:* St Edward's Sch., Oxford; Christ Church, Oxford (MA); Wells Theological College. RNVR, 1940–45. Curate: All Saints, Stepney, E1, 1947–50; i/c St Luke's, Rossington, 1950–55; Rector, Armthorpe, 1955–60; Vicar of Rotherham and Rural Dean, 1960–74. Hon. Canon, Birmingham Cathedral, 1984–. Mem. Gen. Synod, C of E, 1975–84. *Publication:* Rugger: do it this way, 1946. *Recreation:* gardening. *Address:* 68 Britford Lane, Salisbury, Wilts SP2 8AH. *T:* (01722) 338154. *Club:* Vincent's (Oxford).

HOLLIS, Keith Martin John; His Honour Judge Hollis; a Circuit Judge, since 2000; *b* 9 June 1951; *s* of Eric and Joan Hollis; *m* 1979, Mariana Roberts; one *s* one *d. Educ:* Whitgift Sch., Croydon. Admitted Solicitor, 1975; Partner, Davies Brown & Co., Solicitors, 1976–82; Sole Principal, then Sen. Partner, Hollis Wood & Co., Solicitors, 1982–92; Dist Judge, 1992–2000. Dir of Studies, Commonwealth Magistrates' and Judges' Assoc., 1999–. *Recreations:* music, walking, gardening. *Address:* c/o Dartford County Court, Home Gardens, Dartford, Kent DA1 1DX. *Club:* Royal Commonwealth Society.

HOLLIS, Posy; *see* Simmonds, P.

HOLLIS, Most Rev. Reginald; Rector, St Paul's Church, New Smyrna Beach, Florida, 1994–97; *b* 18 July 1932; *s* of Jesse Farndon Hollis and Edith Ellen Lee; *m* 1957, Marcia Henderson Crombie; two *s* one *d. Educ:* Selwyn Coll., Cambridge; McGill Univ., Montreal. Chaplain and Lectr, Montreal Dio. Theol Coll., 1956–60; Chaplain to Anglican Students, McGill Univ.; Asst Rector, St Matthias' Church, Westmount, PQ, 1960–63; Rector, St Barnabas' Church, Pierrefonds, PQ, 1963–70; Rector, Christ Church, Beaconsfield, PQ, 1971–74; Dir of Parish and Dio. Services, Dio. Montreal, 1974–75; Bishop of Montreal, 1975; Metropolitan of the Ecclesiastical Province of Canada and Archbishop of Montreal, 1989–90; Asst Bishop, dio. of Central Florida and Episcopal Dir, Anglican Fellowship of Prayer, 1990–94. Hon. DD 1975. *Publication:* Abiding in Christ, 1987. *Address:* 203–250 Douglas Street, Victoria, BC V8V 2P4, Canada.

HOLLIS, Rt Rev. (Roger Francis) Crispian; *see* Portsmouth, Bishop of, (RC).

HOLLMAN, Arthur, MD; FRCP; FLS; Consultant Cardiologist, University College Hospital, London, 1962–87, now Consulting Cardiologist; Consultant Cardiologist, Hospital for Sick Children, London, 1978–88, now Consulting Cardiologist; Hon. Senior Lecturer, University College London Medical School (formerly University College and Middlesex School of Medicine), since 1962; *b* 7 Dec. 1923; *s* of W. J. and I. R. Hollman; *m* 1949, Catharine Elizabeth Large; three *d* (and one *d* decd). *Educ:* Tiffin Boys' Sch., Kingston upon Thames; University Coll. London (Fellow, 1978); UCH Med. Sch. (MD). FRCP 1967. FLS 1983. Jun. hosp. appts, London, Banbury and Taplow, 1946–57; Bilton Pollard Fellow of UCH Med. Sch. at Children's Meml Hosp., Montreal, 1951–52; Clinical Asst, National Heart Hosp., 1954–56; Sen. Registrar and Asst Lectr, Royal Postgraduate Med. Sch., 1957–62; Hon. Consultant Cardiologist, Kingston Hosp., 1964–87. Advisor in Cardiology: to Mauritius Govt, 1966–86; to Republic of Seychelles, 1974–94. Councillor, RCP, 1976–79. Thomas Lewis Lectr, British Cardiac Soc., 1981. Member: Adv. Cttee, Chelsea Physic Garden, 1971–98; Council, British Heart Foundn, 1975–80; British Cardiac Soc. (Mem. Council, Asst Sec., and Sec., 1971–76; Archivist, 1993–); Assoc. of Physicians of GB and Ireland. Pres., Osler Club, 1983–84. Curator of herb garden, Barbers' Co., 1995–. President's Medal, RCP, 1998. *Publications:* Plants in Medicine, 1989, 3rd edn 1996; Plants in Cardiology, 1992; Sir Thomas Lewis: pioneer cardiologist and clinical scientist, 1997; (ed jtly) British Cardiology in the 20th Century, 2000; articles on the history of cardiology and medicinal plants. *Recreations:* gardening, especially medicinal plants; medical history. *Address:* Seabank, Chick Hill, Pett, Hastings, East Sussex TN35 4EQ. *T:* (01424) 813228. *Club:* Athenæum.

HOLLOM, Sir Jasper (Quintus), KBE 1975; Chairman: Eagle Star Holdings PLC, 1985–87; Eagle Star Insurance Co. Ltd, 1985–87; *b* 16 Dec. 1917; *s* of Arthur and Kate Louisa Hollom; *m* 1954, Patricia Elizabeth Mary Ellis. *Educ:* King's Sch., Bruton. Entered Bank of England, 1936; appointed Deputy Chief Cashier, 1956; Chief Cashier, 1962–66; Director, 1966–70, 1980–84; Deputy Governor, 1970–80. Director: BAT Industries plc, 1980–87; Portals Hldgs plc, 1980–88. Chairman: Panel on Take-overs and Mergers, 1980–87; Council for the Securities Industry, 1985–86; Commonwealth Develt Finance Co. Ltd, 1980–86; Pres., Council of Foreign Bondholders, 1983–89. *Address:* The Long Barn, Alexanders Lane, Privett, Alton, Hants GU34 3PW. *T:* (01730) 828417.

HOLLOWAY, Hon. Sir Barry (Blyth), KBE 1984 (CBE 1974); *b* 26 Sept. 1934; *s* of Archibald and Betty Holloway; *m* 1990, Fua Evelin; one *s* four *d*, and three *s* four *d* by previous marriage. *Educ:* Launceston Church Grammar Sch., Tasmania; Sch. of Pacific Administration, Sydney, 1957; Univ. of Papua New Guinea. Dip., Pacific Admin. District Officer in Papua New Guinea, 1953–64. Elected to first PNG Parliament, 1964; Foundn Mem., Pangu Pati, 1966; MP Eastern Highlands Province. Member of various parliamentary cttees, incl. Public Accounts; Speaker of Parliament, 1972–77; Finance Minister, 1977–80; Minister for Educn, 1982–85. Policy Co-ordinator, Planning, Prime Minister's Dept, 1995–96. Chairman of Constituent Assembly responsible for the formation of Constitution of the Independent State of Papua New Guinea, 1974–75. Consultant, World Bank, to establish Anti-Corruption Commn, PNG, 1997–98; Alternate Exec. Dir, Asian Develt Bank, Manila, Philippines, 1999–. Director of various companies. *Recreations:* reading, agriculture. *Address:* PO Box 6361, Boroko, Papua New Guinea. *T:* 3231611.

HOLLOWAY, Frank, FCA; Managing Director, Supplies and Transport, 1980–83 and Board Member, 1978–83, British Steel Corporation; *b* 20 Oct. 1924; *s* of Frank and Elizabeth Holloway; *m* 1949, Elizabeth Beattie; two *d. Educ:* Burnage High Sch., Manchester. Served War, Royal Navy, 1943–46. Various senior finance appts in The United Steel Companies Ltd and later in British Steel Corp., 1949–72. Managing Director: Supplies and Production Control, 1973–76, Finance and Supplies, 1976–80, British Steel Corp. *Recreations:* cricket, collecting books.

HOLLOWAY, Frederick Reginald Bryn; His Honour Judge Holloway; a Circuit Judge, since 1992; *b* 9 Jan. 1947; *s* of William Herbert Holloway and Audrey (*née* Hull-Brown); *m* 1974, Barbara Bradley; two *s. Educ:* Mill Mead, Shrewsbury; Wrekin Coll., Wellington, Salop; Coll. of Law. Entered chambers in Liverpool, 1972; Asst Recorder, 1984–89; Recorder, 1989–92. *Recreations:* gardening, Shrewsbury Town FC, cricket, tennis. *Address:* Queen Elizabeth II Law Courts, Derby Square, Liverpool L2 1XA.

HOLLOWAY, James Essex; Director, Scottish National Portrait Gallery, since 1997; *b* 24 Nov. 1948; *s* of Roland David Holloway and Nancy Briant Holloway (*née* Evans). *Educ:* Marlborough Coll.; Courtauld Inst. of Art, London Univ. (BA Hons). Res. Asst, Nat. Gall. of Scotland, 1972–80; Asst Keeper, Nat. Mus. of Wales, 1980–83; Dep. Keeper, Scottish Nat. Portrait Gall., 1983–97. *Publications:* The Discovery of Scotland, 1978; James Tassie, 1986; Jacob More, 1987; William Aikman, 1988; Patrons and Painters: art in Scotland 1650–1760, 1989; The Norie Family, 1994. *Recreations:* motorbikes, India. *Address:* Scottish National Portrait Gallery, 1 Queen Street, Edinburgh EH2 1JD. *T:* (0131) 624 6401. *Clubs:* New, Puffin's (Edinburgh).

HOLLOWAY, Reginald Eric, CMG 1984; HM Diplomatic Service, retired; *b* 22 June 1932; *s* of late Ernest and Beatrice Holloway; *m* 1958, Anne Penelope, *d* of late Walter Robert and Doris Lilian Pawley; one *d. Educ:* St Luke's, Brighton. Apprentice reporter, 1947–53; served RAF, 1953–55; journalist in Britain and E Africa, 1955–61; Press Officer, Tanganyika Govt, 1961–63; Dir, British Inf. Service, Guyana, 1964–67; Inf. Dept, FCO, 1967–69 (Anguilla, 1969); 2nd, later 1st Sec., Chancery in Malta, 1970–72; E African Dept, FCO, 1972–74; Consul and Head of Chancery, Kathmandu, 1974–77 (Chargé d'Affaires *ai*, 1975 and 1976); Asst Head, S Asian Dept, FCO, 1977–79; Counsellor, 1979; Inspector, 1979–81; Consul-Gen., Toronto, 1981–85; Sen. British Trade Comr, Hong Kong, 1985–89, and Consul-Gen. (non-resident), Macao, 1986–89; Consul-Gen., Los Angeles, 1989–92. Business consultant, 1992–97; tree farmer, 1998–2001. Chm., Canadian Urban Inst., 1993–98. *Recreations:* woodworking, old press cameras. *Address:* 152 Burch Drive, Rural Route 3, Minden, ON K0M 2K0, Canada.

HOLLOWAY, Rt Rev. Richard Frederick; Bishop of Edinburgh, 1986–2000 and Primus of the Episcopal Church in Scotland, 1992–2000; *b* 26 Nov. 1933; *s* of Arthur and Mary Holloway; *m* 1963, Jean Elizabeth Kennedy, New York; one *s* two *d. Educ:* Kelham Theol Coll.; Edinburgh Theol Coll.; Union Theol Seminary, New York (STM); BD (London). FRSE 1995. Curate, St Ninian's, Glasgow, 1959–63; Priest-in-charge, St Margaret and St Mungo's, Glasgow, 1963–68; Rector, Old St Paul's, Edinburgh, 1968–80; Rector, Church of the Advent, Boston, Mass, USA, 1980–84; Vicar, St Mary Magdalen's, Oxford, 1984–86. Gresham Prof. of Divinity, 1997–2001. Mem., Human Fertilisation and Embryo Authority, 1991–97; Chm., Edinburgh Voluntary Orgns Council, 1991–95. FRSA 1992; FRSE 1995. DUniv Strathclyde, 1994; Hon. DLitt Napier, 2000; Hon. DD: Aberdeen, 1995; Glasgow, 2001. *Publications:* Let God Arise, 1972; New Vision of Glory, 1974; A New Heaven, 1978; Beyond Belief, 1982; Signs of Glory, 1983; The Killing, 1984, 2nd edn as Behold Your King, 1995; (ed) The Anglican Tradition, 1984; Paradoxes of Christian Faith and Life, 1984; The Sidelong Glance, 1985; The Way of the Cross, 1986; Seven to Flee, Seven to Follow, 1987; Crossfire: faith and doubt in an age of certainty, 1988; Another Country, Another King, 1991; Who Needs Feminism?, 1991; Anger, Sex, Doubt and Death, 1992; The Stranger in the Wings, 1994; (jtly) Churches and How to Survive Them, 1994; Limping Towards the Sunrise, 1995; Dancing on the Edge, 1997; Godless Morality, 1999; Doubts and Loves: what is left of Christianity, 2001. *Recreations:* long-distance walking, reading, cinema, music. *Address:* 6 Blantyre Terrace, Edinburgh EH10 5AE.

HOLLOWAY, Dr Robin Greville; composer; Fellow of Gonville and Caius College, Cambridge, since 1969, and Reader in Music, University of Cambridge, since 1999; *b* 19 Oct. 1943; *s* of Robert Charles Holloway and Pamela Mary Jacob. *Educ:* St Paul's Cathedral Choir Sch.; King's Coll. Sch., Wimbledon; King's Coll., Cambridge (MA 1968; PhD 1972; MusD 1976); New Coll., Oxford. Lectr in Music, Cambridge Univ., 1975–99. *Compositions* include: Garden Music, 1962; First Concerto for Orchestra, 1966–69; Scenes from Schumann, 1969–70; Evening with Angels, 1972; Domination of Black, 1973–74; Sea Surface full of Clouds, 1974–75; Clarissa, 1976 (premièred ENO, 1990); Romanza, 1976; The Rivers of Hell, 1977; Second Concerto for Orchestra, 1978–79; Serenade in C, 1979; Aria, 1980; Peer Gynt, 1980–97; Brand, 1981; Women in War, 1982; Second Idyll, 1983; Seascape and Harvest, 1984; Viola Concerto, 1984; Serenade in E flat, 1984; Ballad for harp and orch., 1985; Inquietus, 1986; Double Concerto for clarinet and saxophone, 1988; The Spacious Firmament, 1989; Violin Concerto, 1990; Boys and Girls Come Out to Play, 1992; Gilded Goldbergs, 1992–98; Third Concerto for Orchestra, 1994; Canterbury Concerto for clarinet and orch., 1997; Scenes from Antwerp, 1998; Double Bass Concerto, 1998; Symphony, 1999. *Publications:* Wagner and Debussy, 1978; numerous articles and reviews. *Recreation:* playing on two pianos. *Address:* Gonville and Caius College, Cambridge CB2 1TA. *T:* (01223) 335424.

HOLLOWELL, Rt Rev. Barry Craig Bates; *see* Calgary, Bishop of.

HOLLOWS, Dame Sharon, DBE 2001; Head Teacher, Calverton School, since 1994; *b* 14 Dec. 1958; *d* of Jack and Margaret Hollows; one *s* one *d. Educ:* Haslingden Grammar Sch.; W London Inst. of Higher Educn; Greenwich Univ. (MA Ed). Teacher, London, 1978–94. Mem., Standards Task Force, 2000–. *Recreations:* running, eating, walking, gardening. *Address:* Calverton School, King George Avenue, Custom House, E16 3ET. *T:* (020) 7476 3076.

HOLM, Sir Carl Henry, (Sir Charles Holm), Kt 1987; OBE 1975; land developer, dairy farmer, cane farmer; *b* 1 Aug. 1915; *s* of Frederick Otto Holm and Johanna Jamieson (formerly Stickens); *m* 1st, 1938, Myrtle Phyllis Murtha (*d* 1987); one *s*; 2nd, 1988, Joyce Elaine Blackbeard (*née* Shell). *Educ:* Baralaba State Sch.; Ipswich Boys' Sch.; Pimpana State Sch.; Coomera State Sch. Sgt, Volunteer Defence Corp., 1942–45. Albert Shire Council: Councillor, 1967–82; Mem., Town Planning Cttee, 1975–82; Chm., Works Cttee, 1975–82; National Party of Australia: first Senior Vice-Pres., Qld, 1972–90; Federal Sen. Vice-Pres., 1975–; Past Chm., Tranport Cttee; Past Chm., Conservation Cttee. Queensland Dairymen's Organisation: Mem., 1946–96; Chm., SE District Council, 1961–96; Mem., State Council, 1972–96; Mem., State Milk Exec., 1967–; Chm., United Milk Producers Co-operative Assoc., 1972–96; Pres., Metrop. Milk Producers Co-operative Assoc., 1976–79, Dir, 1979–96. *Recreation:* riding horses. *Address:* 4919 The Parkway, Sanctuary Cove, Qld 4212, Australia. *T:* (7) 55779085. *Club:* National (Southport, Qld) (Foundn Mem. and Chm., 1973–91).

HOLM, Sir Ian, Kt 1998; CBE 1989; actor, since 1954; *b* 12 Sept. 1931; *s* of Dr James Harvey Cuthbert and Jean Wilson Cuthbert; *m* 1st, 1955, Lynn Mary Shaw (marr. diss. 1965); two *d*; and one *s* one *d*; 2nd, 1982, Sophie Baker (marr. diss. 1986); one *s*; 3rd, 1991, Penelope Wilton *qv*; one step *d*. *Educ:* Chigwell Grammar Sch., Essex. Trained RADA, 1950–53 (interrupted by Nat. Service); joined Shakespeare Memorial Theatre, 1954, left after 1955; Worthing Rep., 1956; tour, Olivier's Titus Andronicus, 1957; re-joined Stratford, 1958: roles include: Puck; Ariel; Gremio; Lorenzo; Prince Hal; Henry V; Duke of Gloucester; Richard III; The Fool in Lear; Lennie in The Homecoming (also on Broadway, 1966) (Evening Standard Actor of the Year, 1965); left RSC, 1967; Moonlight, Almeida, 1993 (Evening Standard Actor of the Year, Critics Circle Award); King Lear, RNT, 1997 (Olivier award for Best Actor, 1998); The Homecoming, Comedy, 2001. Major film appearances include: Young Winston, The Fixer, Oh! What a Lovely War, The Bofors Gun, Alien, All Quiet on the Western Front, Chariots of Fire (Best Supporting Actor: Cannes, 1981; BAFTA, 1982); Return of the Soldier; Greystoke; Brazil; Laughterhouse; Dance With a Stranger; Wetherby; Dreamchild; Another Woman; Hamlet; Kafka; Naked Lunch; Blue Ice; Mary Shelley's Frankenstein, 1994; The Madness of King George, Big Night, Night Falls on Manhattan, 1995; Lochness, 1996; A Life Less Ordinary, The Sweet Hereafter, The Fifth Element, 1997; Simon Magus, eXistenZ, The Match, Joe Gould's Secret, 1998; Esther Kahn, Beautiful Joe, 1999; Bless the Child, Fellowship of the Ring, 2001. TV series include: J. M. Barrie in trilogy The Lost Boys (RTS Best Actor Award, 1979); We, the Accused, 1980; The Bell, 1981; Game, Set and Match, 1988; other TV appearances include: Lech Walesa in Strike, 1981; Goebbels in Inside the Third Reich, 1982; Mr and Mrs Edgehill, 1985; The Browning Version, 1986; Uncle Vanya, 1990; The Last Romantics, 1991; The Borrowers, 1992; The Deep Blue Sea, 1994; Landscape, 1995; King Lear, 1997; Alice Through the Looking Glass, 1998. *Recreations:* tennis, walking, general outdoor activities. *Address:* c/o Julian Belfrage Associates, 46 Albermarle Street, W1X 4PP.

HOLMAN, Hon. Sir (Edward) James, Kt 1995; **Hon. Mr Justice Holman;** a Judge of the High Court of Justice, Family Division, since 1995; *b* 21 Aug. 1947; *o s* of late Dr Edward Theodore Holman and of Mary Megan Holman, MBE (*née* Morris), formerly of Ringwood, Hants, and Manaccan, Cornwall; *m* 1979, Fiona Elisabeth, *er d* of Dr Ronald Cathcart Roxburgh, FRCP; two *s* one *d*. *Educ:* Dauntsey's; Exeter College, Oxford (BA Jurisp., MA). Called to the Bar, Middle Temple, 1971, Bencher, 1995; QC 1991; Western Circuit; in practice, 1971–95; Standing Counsel to HM Treasury (Queen's Proctor), 1980–91; a Recorder, 1993–95; Family Div. Liaison Judge, Western Circuit, 1995–. A Legal Assessor, UK Central Council for Nursing, Midwifery and Health Visiting, 1983–95. Member: Family Proceedings Rules Cttee, 1991–95; Supreme Court Procedure Cttee, 1992–95; ex-officio Mem., Bar Council, 1992–95. Chm., Family Law Bar Assoc., 1992–95 (Sec., 1988–92). Mem., Council, RYA, 1980–83, 1984–87, 1988–91. *Recreations:* sailing, ski-ing, music. *Address:* Royal Courts of Justice, Strand, WC2A 2LL. *Clubs:* Royal Ocean Racing (Mem. Cttee, 1984–87); Royal Yacht Squadron.

HOLMAN, Richard Christopher; His Honour Judge Holman; a Circuit Judge, since 1994; Designated Civil Judge, since 1998; *b* 16 June 1946; *s* of Frank Harold Holman and Joan (*née* Attrill); *m* 1969, Susan Whittaker, MBE; two *s*. *Educ:* Watford Grammar Sch. for Boys; Eton Coll.; Gonville and Caius Coll., Cambridge (MA 1968). Admitted as solicitor, 1971; Partner, Foysters, later Davies Wallis Foyster, 1973–94, Man. Partner, 1988–89; Dep. Dist Registrar of High Court and Dep. Registrar of County Court, 1982–88; Asst Recorder, 1988–92; a Recorder, 1992–94. Member: NW Legal Aid Area Cttee, 1980–94; Civil Procedure Rule Cttee, 1997–. Mem. Council, Manchester Law Soc., 1983–90. Gov., Pownall Hall Sch., Wilmslow, 1990–98 (Chm., 1993–98). *Recreations:* golf, gardening, theatre, music. *Address:* Courts of Justice, Crown Square, Manchester M3 3FL. *T:* (0161) 954 1800. *Club:* Wilmslow Golf (Captain, 1999).

HOLMBERG, Eric Robert Reginald; Deputy Chief Scientist (Army), Ministry of Defence, 1972–77; *b* 24 Aug. 1917; *s* of Robert and May Holmberg; *m* 1940, Wanda Erna Reich; one *s* one *d*. *Educ:* Sandown (Isle of Wight) Grammar Sch.; St John's Coll., Cambridge (MA); Imperial Coll., London (PhD). Joined Mine Design Department, Admiralty, 1940; Admiralty Gunnery Establishment, 1945; Operational Research Department, Admiralty, 1950; appointed Chief Supt Army Operational Research Group, 1956; Dir, Army Operational Science and Res., subseq. Asst Chief Scientist (Army), MoD, 1961–72. *Publications:* The Trouble with Relativity, 1986; papers in Proc. Royal Astronomical Society. *Address:* 29 Westmoreland Road, Barnes, SW13 9RZ. *T:* (020) 8748 2568.

HOLME, family name of **Baron Holme of Cheltenham**.

HOLME OF CHELTENHAM, Baron *cr* 1990 (Life Peer), of Cheltenham in the County of Gloucestershire; **Richard Gordon Holme,** CBE 1983; PC 2000; Member, Advisory Board, NTL plc, since 2000; *b* 27 May 1936; *s* of J. R. Holme and E. M. Holme (*née* Eggleton); *m* 1958, Kathleen Mary Powell; two *s* two *d*. *Educ:* Royal Masonic Sch.; St John's Coll., Oxford; Harvard Business Sch. (PMD). Commnd 10th Gurkha Rifles, Malaya, 1954–56. Vice-Chm., Liberal Party Exec., 1966–67; Pres., Liberal Party, 1980–81; contested: East Grinstead (L) 1964 and by-election, 1965; Braintree (L) Oct. 1974; Cheltenham (L) 1983, (L/Alliance) 1987. Lib Dem spokesman on NI, H of L, 1992–99; Chm., Lib Dem Gen. Elect. Campaign, 1997. Dir, Campaign for Electoral Reform, 1976–85; Sec., Parly Democracy Trust, 1977–; Chm., Constitutional Reform Centre, 1985–94; Hon. Treasurer, Green Alliance, 1978–90. Chairman: DPR Publishing (formerly Dod's Publishing and Research), 1988–98; Black Box Publishing, 1988–95; Hollis Directories, 1989–98; Brasseys Ltd, 1996–98; Dep. Chm., ITC, 1999; Director: Political Quarterly, 1988–; RTZ-CRA, later Rio Tinto plc, 1995–98. Chm., Broadcasting Standards Commn, 1999–2000. Vis. Prof. in Business Administration, Middlesex Polytechnic, 1990–94. Associate Mem., Nuffield Coll., 1985–89; Exec. Mem., Campaign for Oxford, 1990–. Vice-Chm., Hansard Soc. for Parly Govt, 1991–. Chairman: English Coll. Foundn, Prague, 1991–; Adv. Bd, British American Proj., 1999–; Mem. Council, ODI, 1998–. Trustee, Citizenship Foundn, 1994–. Chancellor, Univ. of Greenwich, 1998–. *Publications:* No Dole for the Young, 1975; A Democracy Which Works, 1978; The People's Kingdom, 1987; (ed jtly) 1688–1988, Time for a New Constitution, 1988. *Address:* House of Lords, SW1A 0PW. *Club:* Brooks's, Reform.

HOLME, Maj.-Gen. Michael Walter, CBE 1966; MC 1945; *b* 9 May 1918; *s* of Thomas Walter Holme and Ruth Sangster Holme (*née* Rivington); *m* 1948, Sarah Christian Van Der Gucht; one *s* two *d*. *Educ:* Winchester College. Directing Staff, Staff Coll., Camberley, 1952–55; Comdr 1st Bn 3rd East Anglian Regt, 1960–62; Comdr Land Forces Persian Gulf, 1963–66; Chief of Staff, Western Comd, 1966–67; Divisional Brig., The Queen's Div., 1968–69; GOC Near East Land Forces, 1969–72, retired; Dep. Col, The Royal Anglian Regiment, 1970–77. *Recreations:* various. *Address:* Glen Cottage, 145 Park Road, Camberley, Surrey GU15 2LL. *Club:* Army and Navy.

HOLMER, Paul Cecil Henry, CMG 1973; HM Diplomatic Service, retired; Ambassador to Romania, 1979–83; *b* 19 Oct. 1923; *s* of late Bernard Cecil and Mimi Claudine Holmer; *m* 1946, Irene Nora, *e d* of late Orlando Lenox Beater, DFC; two *s* two *d*. *Educ:* King's Sch., Canterbury; Balliol Coll., Oxford. Served in RA, 1942–46. Entered Civil Service, 1947; Colonial Office, 1947–49; transferred to HM Foreign Service, 1949; FO, 1949–51; Singapore, 1951–55; FO, 1955–56; served on Civil Service Selection Bd, 1956; FO, 1956–58; Moscow, 1958–59; Berlin, 1960–64; FO, 1964–66; Counsellor, 1966; Dep. High Comr, Singapore, 1966–69; Head of Security Dept, FCO, 1969–72; Ambassador, Ivory Coast, Upper Volta and Niger, 1972–75; Minister and UK Dep. Perm. Rep. to NATO, 1976–79. Dir, African Develt Fund, 1973–75.

HOLMES, Prof. Andrew Bruce, FRS 2000; Director, Melville Laboratory for Polymer Synthesis, since 1994, and Professor of Organic and Polymer Chemistry, since 1998, Cambridge University; Fellow, Clare College, Cambridge, since 1973; *b* 5 Sept. 1943; *s* of late Bruce Morell Holmes and Frances Henty Graham Holmes; *m* 1971, Jennifer Lesley; three *s*. *Educ:* Scotch Coll., Melbourne; Univ. of Melbourne (BSc, MSc); University Coll. London (PhD 1971); ScD Cantab 1997. Royal Soc. European Postdoctoral Fellow, ETH Zürich, 1971–72; University of Cambridge: Demonstrator, 1972–77; Lectr, 1977–94; Reader in Organic and Polymer Chemistry, 1995–98; Dir, Cambridge Quantum Fund, 1995–; Mem., CUP Syndicate, 2000–. Principal Ed., Jl Materials Res., 1994–99; Chm., Editl Bd, Chemical Communications, 2000–; Member: Bd of Editors, Organic Syntheses, Inc., 1996–2001; Editl Bd, New Jl of Chemistry, 2000–; International Advisory Board: Macromolecular Chem. and Physics, 1999–; Jl Mater. Chem., 1996–. Vis. Fellow, La Trobe Univ., 1977; Visiting Professor: Univ. of Calif, Berkeley, 1984; Univ. of Calif, Irvine, 1991; Royal Soc. Leverhulme Sen. Res. Fellow, 1993–94. Alfred Bader Award, 1994, Materials Chem. Award, 1995, RSC. *Publications:* contribs to various learned chem., physics and materials sci. jls on subject of synthesis of polymeric materials and of natural products. *Recreations:* musical appreciation, walking, ski-ing. *Address:* Melville Laboratory for Polymer Synthesis, Pembroke Street, Cambridge CB2 3RA. *T:* (01223) 334370, *Fax:* (01223) 334866; Department of Chemistry, Lensfield Road, Cambridge CB2 1EW, *T:* (01223) 336404, *Fax:* (01223) 336362; *e-mail:* abh1@cus.cam.ac.uk.

HOLMES, Anthony, CBE 1982; Head of Passport Department, Home Office (formerly Chief Passport Officer, Foreign and Commonwealth Office), 1980–88, retired; *b* 4 Sept. 1931; *s* of Herbert and Jessie Holmes; *m* 1954, Sheila Frances Povall. *Educ:* Calday Grange Grammar School. Joined HM Customs and Excise, 1949; served HM Forces, 1950–52; Passport Office, 1955; Dep. Chief Passport Officer, 1977. *Recreations:* golf, sailing. *Address:* Hilbre, Mill Road, West Chiltington, Pulborough, West Sussex RH20 2PZ. *Clubs:* West Sussex Golf (Pulborough); El Paraiso Golf (Estepona, Spain).

HOLMES, Barry Trevor; HM Diplomatic Service, retired; business development and PR consultant, since 1993; *b* 23 Sept. 1933; *s* of Edwin Holmes and Marion (*née* Jones); *m* 1st, 1956, Dorothy Pitchforth (marr. diss. 1989); three *d*; 2nd, 1992, Sherie Shortridge. *Educ:* Bishopshalt Grammar School. Entered HM Foreign Service, 1950; Personnel Services Dept, 1950–53; Foreign Office, 1955–58; Quito, 1958–62; FO, 1962–65; Vancouver, 1965–68; First Secretary, FCO, 1968–72; Nairobi, 1972–75; FCO, 1975–80; Commercial Counsellor, Helsinki, 1980–85; Consul-Gen., Atlanta, 1985–92. Dir, British Amer. Business Gp, Atlanta, 1994–99. Pres., ESU Atlanta Br., 1996–97. Internat. Vice-Pres., Rotary Club of Atlanta, 2001–02. National Service: Captain, Royal Artillery, Egypt, 1953–55. *Recreations:* chess, light opera, walking. *Address:* 1707 West Wesley Road NW, Atlanta, GA 30327, USA.

HOLMES, Christopher John, CBE 1998; Director, Shelter, since 1995; *b* 13 July 1942; *s* of Gordon Holmes and Doris Holmes (*née* Waite); *m* 1969, Ann Warden (marr. diss. 1989); one *s* one *d*; partner, Hattie Llewelyn-Davies; one *s* one *d*. *Educ:* Clare Coll., Cambridge (MA Hons Econs 1964); Univ. of Bradford (Dip. in Industrial Admin 1966). Asst Gen. Sec., Student Christian Movement, 1964–65; John Laing Construction, 1966–68; NE Islington Community Project, then N Islington Housing Rights Project, 1969–74; Dep. Dir, Shelter, 1974–76; Director: Soc. for Co-operative Dwellings, 1976–79; E London Housing Assoc., 1979–82; CHAR, 1982–87; Consultant, Priority Estates Project, 1988–89; Dir of Housing, London Borough of Camden, 1990–95. Mem., Nat. Consumer Council, 1975–80. *Recreations:* my family, reading, walking, theatre, cricket. *Address:* 1 Carpenters Yard, Park Street, Tring, Herts HP23 6AR.

HOLMES, David, CB 1985; Director, Corporate Resources, British Airways plc, 1996–99; Chairman, British Airways Regional, 1998–99; *b* 6 March 1935; *s* of late George A. Holmes and Annie Holmes; *m* 1963, Ann Chillingworth; one *s* two *d*. *Educ:* Doncaster Grammar Sch.; Christ Church, Oxford (MA). Asst Principal, Min. of Transport and Civil Aviation, 1957; Private Sec. to Jt Parly Sec., 1961–63; HM Treasury, 1965–68; Principal Private Sec. to Minister of Transport, 1968–70; Asst Sec., 1970, Under Sec., 1976, Dep. Sec., 1982–91, Dept of Transport; Dir, Govt and Industry Affairs, British Airways, 1991–95. FRAeS. *Recreation:* music. *Address:* Dormer Lodge, 31 Little Park Gardens, Enfield, Middx EN2 6PQ. *Club:* Royal Automobile.

HOLMES, David Robert; Registrar, University of Oxford, and Professorial Fellow, St John's College, Oxford, since 1998; *b* 2 May 1948; *s* of Leslie Howard Holmes and Joyce Mary Holmes (*née* Stone); *m* 1st, 1974, Lesley Ann Crone (marr diss. 1989); one *s* one *d*; 2nd, 1989, Susan Bayley. *Educ:* Preston GS; Merton Coll., Oxford (MA; Hon. Fellow, 2000). University of Warwick: Admin. Asst, 1970–74; Asst Registrar, 1974–78; seconded as Asst Registrar, Univ. of Sheffield, 1975–76; Sen. Asst Registrar, 1978–82; University of Liverpool: Acad. Sec., 1982–86; Dep. Registrar and Acad. Sec., 1987–88; Registrar and Sec., Univ. of Birmingham, 1988–98. *Publications:* (contrib.) Beyond the Limelight, 1986; Perspectives, Policy and Practice in Higher Education, 1998. *Recreations:* reading the classics, squash, cricket, golf, tennis, music, gardening. *Address:* 20 Goodby Road, Moseley, Birmingham B13 8NJ. *T:* (0121) 249 9714; Flat 4, 3 Bradmore Road, Oxford OX2 6QW. *T:* (01865) 452024. *Club:* Athenæum.
See also Sir J. E. Holmes.

HOLMES, David Vivian; Member, Broadcasting Complaints Commission, 1987–92; *b* 12 Oct. 1926; *s* of Vivian and Kathleen St Clair Holmes; *m* 1st, 1957, Rhoda Ann, *d* of late Col N. J. Gai; two *d*; 2nd, 1979, Linda Ruth Alexander (*née* Kirk). *Educ:* Ipswich Sch.; Allhallows Sch. Served KRRC, 1944–47. Evening Standard, 1951–56; Reporter, BBC News, 1956–61; BBC political reporter, 1961–72; Asst Head, BBC Radio Talks and Documentary Programmes; launched Kaleidoscope arts programme, 1973; Political Editor, BBC, 1975–80; Chief Asst to Dir-Gen., BBC, 1980–83; Sec. of the BBC, 1983–85. Chm., Parly Lobby Journalists, 1976–77. Member: Council, Hansard Soc., 1981–83; MoD Censorship Study Gp, 1983; Exec. Cttee, Suffolk Historic Churches Trust, 1989–90. Founder and Organiser, Blyth Valley Chamber Music concerts, 1988–2000. *Recreations:* history of 17th century Dissent, gardening. *Address:* 5 Salters Lane, Walpole, Halesworth, Suffolk IP19 9BA. *T:* (01986) 784412. *Club:* Farmers.

HOLMES, Prof. (Edward) Richard, CBE (mil.) 1998 (OBE (mil.) 1988); TD 1979 (Bar 1985, 2nd Bar 1996); JP; PhD; Professor of Military and Security Studies, since 1995, and Co-Director, Security Studies Institute, since 1989, Cranfield University; *b* 29 March 1946; *s* of Edward William Holmes and Helen Holmes; *m* 1975, Katharine Elizabeth Saxton; two *d. Educ:* Forest Sch.; Emmanuel Coll., Cambridge (MA); Northern Illinois Univ.; Reading Univ. (PhD 1975). Royal Military Academy, Sandhurst: Lectr, Dept of War Studies, 1969–73; Sen. Lectr, 1973–84; Dep. Hd of Dept, 1984–86; Lt Col (non-Regular Perm. Staff), CO 2nd Bn, Wessex Regt (Vols), 1986–88. Writer and presenter, various TV documentaries, including: War Walks, 1996; War Walks 2, 1997; The Western Front, 1999; Battlefields, 2001. Territorial Army: enlisted Essex Yeo., 1964; commnd 1966; Brig., 1994–; Dir, Reserve Forces and Cadets, 1997–2000; Col, The Princess of Wales's Royal Regt, 1999–. JP Hants. Comdr 1st cl., Order of the Dannebrog (Denmark). *Publications:* (with P. Young) The English Civil War, 1974; The Little Field Marshal: Sir John French, 1984; Firing Line, 1985 (US edn as Acts of War, 1986), 4th edn 1994; (with J. Keegan) Soldiers, 1985; Riding the Retreat, 1995; War Walks, 1996; War Walks 2, 1997; The Western Front, 1999; Battlefields, 2001; (Gen. Ed.) The Oxford Companion to Military History, 2001. *Recreation:* riding. *Address:* Security Studies Institute, Royal Military College of Science, Shrivenham, Swindon, Wilts SN6 8LA. *T:* (01793) 785474. *Club:* Army and Navy.

HOLMES, Sir Frank (Wakefield), Kt 1975; JP; company director; consultant; Emeritus Professor, since 1985, Visiting Fellow, since 1986, and Chairman, 1989–91, Institute of Policy Studies, Victoria University of Wellington; *b* 8 Sept. 1924; *s* of James Francis Wakefield and Marie Esme Babette Holmes; *m* 1947, Nola Ruth Ross; two *s. Educ:* Waitaki Boys' Jun. High Sch. (Dux 1936); King's High Sch. (Dux 1941); Otago Univ.; Auckland University Coll. (Sen. Schol. 1948); Victoria University Coll. MA (1st Cl. Hons) 1949. Flying Officer, Royal NZ Air Force, 1942–45 (despatches). Economic Div., Prime Minister's and External Affairs Depts 1949–52; Lectr to Prof., Victoria Univ. of Wellington, 1952–67; Macarthy Prof. of Economics, 1959–67; Dean, Faculty of Commerce, 1961–63; Economics Manager, Tasman Pulp & Paper Co Ltd, 1967–70; Victoria Univ. of Wellington: Prof. of Money and Finance, 1970–77; Vis. Prof. and Convener, Master of Public Policy Programme, 1982–85. Adviser, Royal Commn on Monetary, Banking and Credit Systems, 1955; Consultant, Bank of New Zealand, 1956–58 and 1964–67; Chm., Monetary and Economic Council, 1961–64 and 1970–72; Jt Sec., Cttee on Universities, 1959; Mem., NZ Council Educnl Research, 1965–77 (Chm. 1970–74); Chairman: Adv. Council on Educnl Planning and Steering Cttee, Educnl Develt Conf., 1973–74; NZ Govt Task Force on Economic and Social Planning, 1976; NZ Planning Council, 1977–82; Asia 2000 Foundn, NZ, 1994–96 (Hon. Advr, 1996–); Cttee Advising on Professional Educn, 1995–98; Dep. Chm., Inst. of Policy Studies, 1984–89. President: NZ Assoc. of Economists, 1961–63; Economic Section, ANZAAS, 1967, Education Section, 1979; Central Council, Economic Soc. of Australia and NZ, 1967–68; NZ Inst. of Internat. Affairs, 1998–2000. Chairman: South Pacific Merchant Finance Ltd, 1985–89 (Dir, 1984–89); Hugo Consulting Group Ltd, 1989– (Exec. Dir., 1986–); State Insurance Ltd, 1990–94; Norwich Holdings Ltd, 1990–94; Norwich Union Life Insce (NZ) Ltd, 1993–94; Director: National Bank of NZ Ltd, 1982–95; Norwich Union Life Insce Soc. 1983–92 (Chm., 1990–92); Lloyds Bank NZA Ltd, Sydney, 1992–95. Mem., Internat. Organising Cttee, Pacific Trade and Develt Confs, 1982–. FRSA; FNZIM 1986; Fellow, NZ Inst. of Dirs, 1995 (Distinguished Fellow, 1999). Life Member: VUW Students' Assoc., 1967; Australia–NZ Business Council, 1998. JP 1960. Hon. LLD Otago, 1997. *Publications:* Money, Finance and the Economy, 1972; Government in the New Zealand Economy, 1977, 2nd edn 1980; Closer Economic Relations with Australia, 1986; Partners in the Pacific, 1988; (ed) Stepping Stones to Freer Trade, 1989; (jtly) Meeting the East Asia Challenge, 1989; Meeting the European Challenge, 1991; NAFTA, CER and a Pacific Basin Initiative, 1992; A New Approach to Central Banking, 1994; CER: Trends and Linkages, 1994; New Zealand and ASEAN, 1995; Trans-Tasman Co-operation, 1996; The Thoroughbred Among Banks in New Zealand, 1999; pamphlets and articles on econs, finance, educn and internat. affairs. *Recreations:* touring, walking, swimming, music. *Address:* 61 Cheviot Road, Lowry Bay, Lower Hutt, New Zealand. *T:* Wellington (4) 5684719. *Club:* Wellington (Wellington).

HOLMES, Prof. George Arthur, PhD; FBA 1985; Chichele Professor of Medieval History, University of Oxford, and Fellow of All Souls College, 1989–94; *b* 22 April 1927; *s* of late John Holmes and Margaret Holmes, Aberystwyth; *m* 1953, Evelyn Anne, *d* of late Dr John Klein and Audrey Klein; one *s* two *d* (and one *s* decd). *Educ:* Ardwyn County Sch., Aberystwyth; UC, Aberystwyth; St John's Coll., Cambridge (MA, PhD). Fellow, St John's Coll., Cambridge, 1951–54; Tutor, St Catherine's Society, Oxford, 1954–62; Fellow and Tutor, St Catherine's Coll., Oxford, 1962–89 (Vice-Master, 1969–71; Emeritus Fellow, 1990). Mem., Inst. for Advanced Study, Princeton, 1967–68. Vis. Prof., Harvard Univ. Centre for Italian Renaissance Studies, Florence, 1995–. Chm. Bd, Warburg Inst., London Univ., 1993–95. Chm., Victoria County Hist. Cttee, Inst. of Hist. Res., 1979–89. Jt Editor, English Historical Review, 1974–81; Delegate, Oxford Univ. Press, 1982–91. Serena Medal for Italian Studies, British Acad., 1993. *Publications:* The Estates of the Higher Nobility in Fourteenth-Century England, 1957; The Later Middle Ages, 1962; The Florentine Enlightenment 1400–1450, 1969; Europe: hierarchy and revolt 1320–1450, 1975; The Good Parliament, 1975; Dante, 1980; Florence, Rome and the Origins of the Renaissance, 1986; (ed) The Oxford Illustrated History of Medieval Europe, 1988; The First Age of the Western City 1300–1500, 1990; (ed) Art and Politics in Renaissance Italy, 1993; Renaissance, 1996; (ed) The Oxford Illustrated History of Italy, 1997; articles in learned jls. *Recreations:* walking in the country, looking at pictures. *Address:* Highmoor House, Bampton, Oxon OX18 2HY. *T:* (01993) 850408.

HOLMES, George Dennis, CB 1979; FRSE; Director-General and Deputy Chairman, Forestry Commission, 1977–86, retired; *b* 9 Nov. 1926; *s* of James Henry Holmes and Florence Holmes (*née* Jones); *m* 1953, Sheila Rosemary Woodger; three *d. Educ:* John Bright's Sch., Llandudno; Univ. of Wales (BSc (Hons)); FRSE 1982; FICFor. Post-grad Research, Univ. of Wales, 1947; appointed Forestry Commission, 1948; Asst Silviculturist, Research Div., 1948; Asst Conservator, N Wales, 1962; Dir of Research, 1968; Comr for Harvesting and Marketing, 1973. Mem., Scottish Legal Aid Bd, 1989–94. Hon. Prof., Univ. of Aberdeen, 1984. Chm., Capability Scotland (formerly Scottish Council for Spastics), 1986–97. Hon. DSc Wales, 1985. *Publications:* contribs to Forestry Commission pubns and to Brit. and Internat. forestry jls. *Recreations:* golf, fishing. *Address:* 7 Cammo Road, Barnton, Edinburgh EH4 8EF. *T:* (0131) 339 7474.

HOLMES, Sir John (Eaton), KBE 1999; CMG 1997; CVO 1998; HM Diplomatic Service; Ambassador to France, since 2001; *b* 29 April 1951; *s* of Lesley Howard Holmes and Joyce Mary (*née* Stone); *m* 1976, Margaret Penelope Morris; three *d. Educ:* Preston Grammar Sch.; Balliol Coll., Oxford (BA 1st Cl. Hons Lit. Hum., MA). Joined HM Diplomatic Service, 1973; FCO, 1973–76; 3rd Sec., then 2nd Sec., Moscow, 1976–78; Near East and N Africa Dept, FCO, 1978–82; Asst Private Sec. to Foreign Sec., 1982–84; 1st Sec. (Economic), Paris, 1984–87; Asst Hd of Soviet Dept, FCO, 1987–89; seconded to Thomas de la Rue & Co., 1989–91; Counsellor, Econ. and Commercial, New Delhi, 1991–95; Head of European Union Dept (External), FCO, 1995; on secondment as Private Sec. (Foreign Affairs), 1996–99 and Principal Private Sec., 1997–99, to the Prime Minister; Ambassador to Portugal, 1999–2001. *Recreations:* sport (tennis, squash, cricket, golf), music, reading. *Address:* c/o Foreign and Commonwealth Office, SW1A 2AH.
See also D. R. Holmes.

HOLMES, Dr John Ernest Raymond; Director, Quality and Performance, United Kingdom Atomic Energy Authority, 1989–90; *b* Birmingham, 13 Aug. 1925; *s* of late Dr John K. Holmes and of Ellen R. Holmes; *m* 1949, Patricia Clitheroe; one *s* one *d. Educ:* King Edward's School, Birmingham; University of Birmingham (BSc, PhD). Asst Lectr in Physics, Manchester Univ., 1949–52; Research Scientist, AERE Harwell, 1952–59; Atomic Energy Establishment, Winfrith: Research Scientist, 1959–66; Chief Physicist, 1966–73; Dep. Dir, 1973–86; Dir, 1986–89. *Publications:* technical papers on nuclear power. *Address:* Thatches, Church Street, Barton St David, Somerset TA11 6BU. *T:* (01458) 850659.

HOLMES, Prof. Kenneth Charles, PhD; FRS 1981; Director of the Department of Biophysics, Max-Planck-Institute for Medical Research, Heidelberg, since 1968; Professor of Biophysics, Heidelberg University, since 1972; *b* 19 Nov. 1934; *m* 1957, Mary Scruby; one *s* three *d. Educ:* St John's Coll., Cambridge (MA 1959); London Univ. (PhD 1959). Res. Associate, Childrens' Hosp., Boston, USA, 1960–61; Mem., Scientific Staff, MRC Lab. of Molecular Biology, Cambridge, 1962–68. Mem., European Molecular Biol. Organisation. Scientific mem., Max Planck Gesellschaft, 1972–; Corresp. Mem., Soc. Royale des Scis, Liège. *Publications:* (with D. Blow) The Use of X-ray Diffraction in the Study of Protein and Nucleic Acid Structure, 1965; papers on virus structure, molecular mechanism of muscular contraction and the structure of actin. *Recreations:* rowing, singing. *Address:* Biophysics Department, Max-Planck-Institute for Medical Research, Jahnstrasse 29, 69120 Heidelberg, Germany. *T:* (6221) 486270.

HOLMES, Maurice Colston, OBE 1985; Director, Safety, British Railways Board, 1989–92; *b* 15 Feb. 1935; *s* of Charles Edward Holmes and Ellen Catherine Mary Holmes (*née* Colston); *m* 1985, Margaret Joan Wiscombe. *Educ:* Presentation Coll., Reading. British Rail: Divl Man., Liverpool Street, 1976–79; Chief Operating Man., 1979–80, Dep. Gen. Man., 1980–82, Southern Region; Dir of Operations, BRB, 1982–88. Dir and Trustee, Railway Pension Trustee Co. Ltd, 1994–96. Pres., British Transport Pension Fedn, 1993–. Col, RE, Engrg and Logistic Staff Corps (TA), 1990–2001. *Recreations:* travel, transport, gardens. *Address:* 9 High Tree Drive, Earley, Reading, Berks RG6 1EU. *T:* (0118) 966 8887.

HOLMES, Michael Harry; Chief Executive, Chesterton International plc, 1997–2001; *b* 10 March 1945; *s* of Harry Albert Holmes and Doris Rachel (*née* Linihan); *m* 1968, Ellen van Caspel; three *s. Educ:* Alleyn's Sch., Dulwich; Gonville and Caius Coll., Cambridge (MA). Costain Civil Engineering Ltd, 1966–70; Ready Mixed Concrete Ltd, 1970–73; Pioneer Concrete Ltd, 1973–77; Rentokil Group plc, 1977–95: Regl Man. Dir, UK Property Services, 1988–91; Regl Man. Dir, N America, Caribbean and E Africa, 1992–95; self-employed, 1995–97. *Recreations:* fishing, sailing, old cars, motorcycles, theatre. *Address:* Beechcroft, Hophurst Hill, Crawley Down, W Sussex RH10 4LW. *T:* (01342) 716101. *Club:* Oriental.

HOLMES, Michael John; Member (UK Ind) South West Region, England, European Parliament, since 1999; *b* 6 June 1938; adopted *s* of Albert and Elsie Holmes; *m* 1974, Carolyn Allen Jee; two *s* one *d. Educ:* Sevenoaks Sch. SSC, Royal Warwicks Regt, 1958–60. Sales and Mkting Exec., Sunday Times, Evening Standard, and Observer, 1962–69; Owner Publisher, Independent Gp of Free Newspapers, 1970–87; voluntary and charity work, 1987–99. Leader, UK Independence Party, 1998–2000. *Recreations:* travel, reading, politics. *Address:* Venards House, North Gorley, Fordingbridge, Hants SP6 2PJ. *T:* (01425) 654117, *Fax:* (01425) 653534.

HOLMES, Prof. Patrick, PhD; Professor of Hydraulics, Imperial College of Science, Technology and Medicine, since 1983; Dean, City and Guilds College, 1988–91; *b* 23 Feb. 1939; *s* of Norman Holmes and Irene (*née* Shelbourne); *m* 1963, Olive (*née* Towning); one *s* one *d. Educ:* University Coll. of Swansea, Univ. of Wales (BSc 1960, PhD 1963). CEng, MICE. Res. Engr, Harbour and Deep Ocean Engrg, US Navy Civil Engrg Lab., Port Hueneme, Calif, 1963–65; Lectr, Dept of Civil Engrg, Univ. of Liverpool, 1966–72, Sen. Lectr, 1972–74, Prof. of Maritime Civil Engrg, 1974–83. Vis. Prof., Univ. of the WI, Trinidad, 2001. Chm., Environment Cttee, SERC, 1981–85. Pres., Conf. of European Schs of Advanced Engrg Educn and Res., 1993–95. Hon. Mem., C&G, 1992 (FCGI 1999). *Publications:* (ed) Handbook of Hydraulic Engineering (English edn), by Lencastre, 1987; articles on ocean and coastal engineering, wave motion, wave loading, coastal erosion and accretion, and harbour and breakwater design, in Proc. ICE and Proc. Amer. Soc. of Civil Engrs. *Recreations:* golf, yachting, walking, choral music. *Address:* Department of Civil Engineering, Imperial College of Science, Technology and Medicine, SW7 2AZ; West Winds, The Green, Steeple Morden, near Royston, Herts SG8 0ND. *T:* (01763) 852582.

HOLMES, Paul Robert; MP (Lib Dem) Chesterfield, since 2001; *b* 16 Jan. 1957; *s* of Frank and Dorothy Holmes; *m* 1978, Raelene Palmer. *Educ:* York Univ. (BA Hons Hist); Sheffield Univ. (PGCE). Teacher, Chesterfield Boys' High Sch., 1979–84; Hd of History, Buxton Coll., 1984–90; Hd of Sixth Form, Buxton Community Sch., 1990–2001. Mem., Chesterfield BC, 1987–95, 1999–2001. *Recreations:* reading, walking, history. *Address:* (office) 12a Old Hall Road, Brampton, Chesterfield S40 3RG. *T:* (01246) 234879.

HOLMES, Sir Peter (Fenwick), Kt 1988; MC 1952; Managing Director, 1982–93 and Chairman, Committee of Managing Directors, 1992–93, Royal Dutch/Shell Group; Director, Shell Transport and Trading Co., 1982–2001 (Chairman, 1985–93); *b* 27 Sept. 1932; *s* of Gerald Hugh Holmes and Caroline Elizabeth Holmes; *m* 1st, 1955, Judith Millicent (*née* Walker) (marr. diss. 1999); three *d*; 2nd, 1999, Mary Lois Holmes; one step *d. Educ:* Trinity Coll., Cambridge (MA). Various posts in Royal Dutch/Shell Group, 1956–93, including: Gen. Man., Shell Markets, ME, 1965–68; Chief Rep., Libya, 1970–72; Man. Dir, Shell-BP, Nigeria, 1977–81; Pres., Shell Internat. Trading, 1981–83. Pres., Hakluyt Foundn, 1997–. Trustee, WWF-UK, 1989–96. FRGS. Hon. DSc Cranfield, 1993. *Publications:* Mountains and a Monastery, 1958; Nigeria, Giant of Africa,

1985; Turkey, A Timeless Bridge, 1988. *Recreations:* mountaineering, ski-ing, travel to remote areas, fishing, photography, 19th century travel books. *Address:* c/o Shell Centre, SE1 7NA. *T:* (020) 7934 5611. *Clubs:* Athenæum, Alpine, Himalayan, Climbers, Kandahar.

HOLMES, Peter Rodney; HM Diplomatic Service, retired; *b* 29 July 1938; *m* Anne Cecilia Tarrant; one *s* three *d*. Diplomatic Service: served Strasbourg, Belgrade, Paris, Cento, Ankara; Stockholm, 1974; Consul, Douala, 1978; Dep. Head of Mission, Bahrain, 1983; Commercial Counsellor, Santiago, 1987; Ambassador to Honduras, 1995–98. *Address:* 2 Sandringham Close, Alton, Hampshire GU34 1QF.

HOLMES, Peter Sloan; Director, Sheridan Group, since 2000; Chief Executive, Sheridan Millennium Ltd; *b* 8 Dec. 1942; *s* of George H. G. and Anne S. Holmes; *m* 1966, Patricia McMahon; two *s*. *Educ:* Rossall Sch.; Magdalen Coll., Oxford (BA English Lang. and Lit.). Teacher, Eastbourne Coll., 1965–68; Head of English, Grosvenor High Sch., Belfast, 1968–71; Lectr, then Sen. Lectr, Stranmillis Coll. of Educn, Belfast, 1971–75; Department of Education for Northern Ireland: Inspector, 1975–83 (Sen. Inspector, 1980; Staff Inspector, 1982); Asst Sec., 1983–87; Under Sec., 1987; Dep. Sec., 1996–2000. Chm., Arts & Business NI, 2000–. *Recreations:* singing, cycling, gliding. *Address:* 63 Spa Road, Ballynahinch, Co. Down BT24 8PT. *T:* (028) 9756 2332. *Club:* Oxford and Cambridge.

HOLMES, Richard; *see* Holmes, E. R.

HOLMES, Richard Gordon Heath, OBE 1992; FBA 1997; FRSL; writer; *b* 5 Nov. 1945; *s* of Dennis Patrick Holmes and Pamela Mavis Holmes (*née* Gordon). *Educ:* Downside Sch.; Churchill Coll., Cambridge (BA). FRSL 1975. Reviewer and historical features writer for The Times, 1967–92. Mem. Cttee, Royal Literary Fund. Vis. Fellow, Trinity Coll., Cambridge, 2000; Prof. of Biographical Studies, UEA, 2001. Lectures: Ernest Jones Meml, British Inst. of Psycho-Analysis, 1990; John Keats Meml, RCS, 1995; Johan Huizinga Meml, Univ. of Leiden, 1997. *Publications:* Thomas Chatterton: the case re-opened, 1970; One for Sorrow (poems), 1970; Shelley: the pursuit, 1974 (Somerset Maugham Award, 1977); Gautier: my fantoms (trans.), 1976; Inside the Tower (radio drama documentary), 1977; (ed) Shelley on Love, 1980; Coleridge, 1982; (with Peter Jay) Nerval: the chimeras, 1985; Footsteps: adventures of a romantic biographer, 1985; (ed) Mary Wollstonecraft and William Godwin, 1987; (ed with Robert Hampson) Kipling: something of myself, 1987; De Feministe en de Filosoof, 1988; Coleridge: vol. 1, Early Visions (Whitbread Book of the Year Prize), 1989, vol. 2, Darker Reflections (Duff Cooper Memorial Prize), 1998; To the Tempest Given (radio drama documentary), 1992; Dr Johnson & Mr Savage, 1993 (James Tait Black Meml Prize, 1994); The Nightwalking (radio drama documentary), 1995 (Sony Award); (ed) Coleridge: selected poems, 1996; The Romantic Poets and their Circle, 1997; Clouded Hills (radio documentary), 1999; Runaway Lives (radio documentary), 2000; Sidetracks: explorations of a romantic biographer, 2000. *Recreations:* sailing, hill-walking, rooftop gardening, stargazing. *Address:* c/o HarperCollins, 77 Fulham Palace Road, W6 8JB.

HOLMES, Robin Edmond Kendall; Head of Judicial Appointments, Lord Chancellor's Department, 1992–98; *b* 14 July 1938; *s* of Roy Frederick George Holmes; *m* 1964, Karin Kutter; two *s*. *Educ:* Wolverhampton Grammar Sch.; Clare Coll., Cambridge (BA); Birmingham Univ. (LLM). Articles, Wolverhampton CBC, 1961–64; admitted solicitor, 1964; Min. of Housing and Local Govt, subseq. DoE, 1965–73 and 1976–82; Colonial Secretariat, Hong Kong, 1973–75; Lord Chancellor's Dept, 1982–98; Grade 3, 1983–98; Circuit Administrator, Midland and Oxford Circuit, 1986–92. *Recreation:* travelling.

HOLMES, Roger de Lacy; Chief Executive, St John Ambulance, since 2002; *b* 15 Jan. 1948; *s* of Stephen and Muriel Holmes; *m* 1970, Jennifer Anne Heal; one *s* one *d*. *Educ:* Huddersfield New Coll.; Balliol Coll., Oxford (BA). DTI, 1969–74; Dept of Prices and Consumer Protection, 1974–77; Dept of Industry, 1977–79; Asst to Chm., British Leyland, 1980–82; Company Sec., Mercury Communications, 1982–83; Jt Sec and Dir, Corporate Affairs, ICL, 1984; Exec. Dir, Dunlop Holdings, 1984–85; Euroroute, 1985–86; Chloride Group: Man. Dir, Power Electronics, 1986–88; Corporate Affairs Dir, 1989–92; Dep. Master and Comptroller, Royal Mint, 1993–2001. Non-exec. Dir, Cygnet Health Care, 1993–2000. *Recreation:* golf. *Address:* St John Ambulance National HQ, 27 St John's Lane, EC1M 4BU. *T:* (020) 7324 4025.

HOLMES, Timothy Charles; HM Diplomatic Service; Deputy Head of Mission, since 1997, and Consul-General, since 2000, The Hague; *b* 26 April 1951; *s* of late Ronald William Holmes and Barbara Jean (*née* Mickleburgh); *m* 1973, Anna-Carin Magnusson; one *s* one *d*. *Educ:* Bec Sch.; Selwyn Coll., Cambridge (MA); Univ. of Aix-Marseille. Joined FCO, 1974; Second, later First, Sec., Tokyo, 1976–80; seconded to Invest in Britain Bureau, Dept of Industry, 1981–83; FCO, 1983–86; First Sec., Islamabad, 1986–90; FCO, 1990–94; Dep. Head of Mission and Commercial and Econ. Counsellor, Seoul, 1994–97. *Publication:* The Wild Flowers of Islamabad, 1990. *Recreations:* botany, ornithology, reading. *Address:* c/o Foreign and Commonwealth Office, King Charles Street, SW1A 2AH.

HOLMES, Prof. William; Professor of Agriculture, Wye College, University of London, 1955–87, Professor Emeritus, since 1985, Fellow, 1993; *b* Kilbarchan, Renfrewshire, 16 Aug. 1922; *s* of William John Holmes, Bank Manager; *m* 1949, Jean Ishbel Campbell, BSc; two *d*. *Educ:* John Neilson Sch., Paisley; Glasgow Univ.; West of Scotland Agricultural Coll. BSc (Agric), NDD, 1942; NDA (Hons), 1943; PhD Glasgow, 1947; DSc London, 1966. FIBiol 1974. Asst Executive Officer, S Ayrshire AEC, 1943–44; Hannah Dairy Research Inst.: Asst in Animal Husbandry, 1944–47; Head of Department of Dairy and Grassland Husbandry, 1947–55. Member, Cttee on Milk Composition in the UK, 1958–60; Governor, Grassland Research Inst., 1960–75; Pres., British Grassland Soc., 1968–69 (1st recipient, British Grassland Soc. Award, 1979); Pres., British Soc. of Animal Production, 1969–70; Member technical cttees of ARC, JCO MAFF, MMB and MLC, 1960–90. Pres., Wye Gardeners' Soc., 1988–2000. Correspondent Étranger, Acad. d'Agric. de France, 1984. Ed., Jl Wye Coll. Agricola Club, 1987–97. *Publications:* (ed) Grass, its production and utilization, 1980, 2nd edn 1989; (ed) Grassland Beef Production, 1984; papers in technical agricultural journals. *Recreations:* woodland ecology, gardening, beekeeping, travel. *Address:* Amage, Wye, Kent TN25 5DF. *T:* (01233) 812372.

HOLMES, Prof. William Neil; Professor of Physiology, University of California, since 1964; *b* 2 June 1927; *s* of William Holmes and Minnie Holmes (*née* Lloyd); *m* 1955, Betty M. Brown, Boston, Mass; two *s* two *d*. *Educ:* Adams Grammar Sch., Newport, Salop; Liverpool Univ. (BSc, MSc, PhD, DSc); Harvard Univ., Cambridge, Mass. National Service, 2nd Bn RWF, 1946–48. Visiting Scholar in Biology, Harvard Univ., 1953–55; Post-grad. Research Schol., Liverpool Univ., 1955–56; ICI Fellow, Glasgow Univ., 1956–57; Asst Prof. of Zoology, 1957–63, Associate Prof. of Zoology, 1963–64, Univ. of British Columbia, Canada; John Simon Guggenheim Foundn Fellow, 1961–62; Visiting Professor of Zoology: Univ. of Hull, 1970; Univ. of Hong Kong, 1973, 1982–83 and 1987. Scientific Fellow, Zoological Soc. of London, 1967; External examiner: for undergraduate degrees, Univ. of Hong Kong, 1976–79, 1985–88; for higher degrees, Univs of Hong Kong and Hull, 1976–; Consultant to: Amer. Petroleum Inst., Washington, DC (environmental conservation), 1972–74; US Nat. Sci. Foundn (Regulatory Biology Prog.), 1980–83; US Bureau of Land Management (petroleum toxicity in seabirds), 1982–. Mem. Editorial Bd, American Journal of Physiology, 1967–70. Member: Endocrine Soc., US, 1957–; Soc. for Endocrinology, UK, 1955–; Amer. Physiological Soc., 1960–; Zoological Soc. of London, 1964–. *Publications:* numerous articles and reviews in Endocrinology, Jl of Endocrinology, Gen. and Comp. Endocrinology, Cell and Tissue Res., Archives of Environmental Contamination and Toxicology, Environmental Res., Jl of Experimental Biology. *Recreations:* travel, old maps and prints, carpentry and building. *Address:* 117 East Junipero Street, Santa Barbara, CA 93105, USA. *T:* (805) 6827256. *Club:* Tennis (Santa Barbara).

HOLMES à COURT, family name of **Baron Heytesbury**.

HOLMES à COURT, Janet Lee, AO 1985; Chairman, Heytesbury Pty Ltd, Australia, since 1990 (Chairman of all companies in the group, including Heytesbury Beef Pty, John Holland Group, Vasse Felix Winery); *b* 29 Nov. 1943; *m* 1966, (Michael) Robert (Hamilton) Holmes à Court (*d* 1990); three *s* one *d*. *Educ:* Perth Modern Sch.; Univ. of Western Australia (BSc Chemistry). Former Chemistry Teacher, Perth. Chairman: Australian Children's TV Foundn, 1983–; Black Swan Theatre Co., Perth, 1991–. Mem. Bd, Reserve Bank of Australia, 1992–97. Veuve Clicquot Business Woman of the Year, 1996. *Address:* Heytesbury Pty Ltd, PO Box 7225, Cloisters Square, Perth, WA 6850, Australia.

HOLMES SELLORS, Patrick John; *see* Sellors.

HOLMPATRICK, 4th Baron *cr* 1897; **Hans James David Hamilton;** *b* 15 March 1955; *s* of 3rd Baron Holmpatrick and Anne Loys Roche (*d* 1998), *o d* of Commander J. E. P. Brass, RN (retd); *S* father, 1991; *m* 1984, Mrs Gill du Feu, *e d* of K. J. Harding; one *s* and one step *s*. *Heir:* *b* Hon. Ion Henry James Hamilton, *b* 12 June 1956.

HOLROYD, Air Marshal Sir Frank (Martyn), KBE 1989; CB 1985; FREng; Chairman, Composite Technology Ltd, since 1992; *b* 30 Aug. 1935; *s* of George L. Holroyd and Winifred H. Holroyd (*née* Ford); *m* 1958, Veronica Christine, *d* of Arthur Booth; two *s* one *d*. *Educ:* Southend-on-Sea Grammar Sch.; Cranfield Inst. of Technology (MSc). FIEE; FRAeS; FREng (FEng 1992). Joined RAF, 1956; Fighter Comd units, 1957–60; Blind Landing Development RAE Bedford, 1960–63; Cranfield Inst. of Tech., 1963–65; HQ Fighter Comd, 1965–67; Far East, 1967–69; Wing Comdr, MoD, 1970–72; RAF Brize Norton, 1972–74; Gp Captain Commandant No 1 Radio School, 1974–76; SO Eng. HQ 38 Gp, 1976–77; Air Cdre Director Aircraft Engrg, MoD, 1977–80; RCDS 1981; Dir Weapons and Support Engrg, MoD, 1982, Air Vice-Marshal 1982; DG Strategic Electronics Systems, MoD (Procurement Exec.), 1982–86; AO Engrg, Strike Comd, 1986–88; Chief Engr, 1988–91, and Chief of Logistics Support, 1989–91, RAF. Chairman: AVR Communications Ltd, 1992–95; Elettronica (UK) Ltd, 1992–95; Dep. Chm., Military Aircraft Spares Ltd, 1999–; Director: Admiral plc, 1992–2000; Ultra Electronics Hldgs, 1995–; REW Communications Ltd, 1995–96; Airinmar Ltd, 1996–2000. Mem., Engrg Council, 1990–2000. Pres., RAeS, 1992–93. Member: Court, 1988–, and Council, 1990–97 (Vice Chm., 1997–), Inst. of Technology, now Univ., Cranfield; Adv. Council, RMCS, Shrivenham, 1988–91; BBC Engrg Adv. Bd, 1984–90. Trustee, Macrobert Award Trust, Royal Acad. of Engrg, 1993–98. CIMgt (Mem., Companions Bd, 1991–99). *Recreations:* travel, gardening, maintaining 14th century house, shooting (game birds). *Club:* Royal Air Force.

HOLROYD, John Hepworth, CB 1993; CVO 1999; Secretary for Appointments to the Prime Minister, and Ecclesiastical Secretary to the Lord Chancellor, 1993–99; *b* 10 April 1935; *s* of Harry Holroyd and Annie Dodgshun Holroyd; *m* 1963, Judith Mary Hudson; one *s* one *d*. *Educ:* Kingswood Sch., Bath; Worcester Coll., Oxford (Open Schol.; BA(Hist.); MA 1987). Joined MAFF, 1959; Asst. Sec., 1969–78; Under Secretary, 1978; Resident Chm., Civil Service Selection Bd, 1978–80; Dir of Establishments, MAFF, 1981–85; Cabinet Office: Under Sec., European Secretariat, 1985–89; First CS Comr and Dep. Sec., 1989–93. Gov., Kingswood Sch., 1985–. Lay Reader: St Albans Abbey; Gloucester Cathedral, 2001–. Trustee, St Albans Cathedral Trust, 1980–2001. DL Herts, 1999–2001. *Recreations:* music, carpentry, bee-keeping, travel. *Address:* The Miller's House, 2 Miller's Green, Gloucester GL1 2BN.

See also W. A. H. Holroyd.

HOLROYD, Margaret, (Mrs Michael Holroyd); *see* Drabble, M.

HOLROYD, Michael (de Courcy Fraser), CBE 1989; author; *b* London, 27 Aug. 1935; *s* of Basil Holroyd and Ulla (*née* Hall); *m* 1982, Margaret Drabble, *qv*. *Educ:* Eton Coll.; Maidenhead Public Library. Vis. Fellow, Pennsylvania State Univ., 1979. Chm., Soc. of Authors, 1973–74; Chm., Nat. Book League, 1976–78; Pres., English PEN, 1985–88. Chm., Strachey Trust, 1990–95. Member: BBC Archives Adv. Cttee, 1976–79; Arts Council of England (formerly of GB), 1992–95 (Vice-Chm., 1982–83, Chm., 1992–95, Literature Panel); Chm., Public Lending Right Adv. Cttee, 1997–2000. Vice-Pres., Royal Literary Fund, 1997–. Nat. Gov., Shaw Fest. Theatre, Ontario, 1993–. FRSL 1968 (Mem. Council, 1977–87; Chm. Council, 1998–2001); FRHistS; FRSA. Hon. DLitt: Ulster, 1992; Sheffield, 1993; Warwick, 1993; East Anglia, 1994; LSE, 1998. Heywood Hill Prize, 2001. *Publications:* Hugh Kingsmill: a critical biography, 1964; Lytton Strachey, 2 vols, 1967, 1968, rev. edn 1994; A Dog's Life: a novel, 1969; (ed) The Best of Hugh Kingsmill, 1970; (ed) Lytton Strachey By Himself, 1971; Unreceived Opinions, 1973; Augustus John, 2 vols, 1974, 1975, rev. edn 1996; (with M. Easton) The Art of Augustus John, 1974; (ed) The Genius of Shaw, 1979; (ed with Paul Levy) The Shorter Strachey, 1980; (ed with Robert Skidelsky) William Gerhardie's God's Fifth Column, 1981; (ed) Essays by Divers Hands, vol. XLII, 1982; Bernard Shaw: Vol. I, The Search for Love 1856–1898, 1988; Vol. II, The Pursuit of Power 1898–1918, 1989; Vol. III, The Lure of Fantasy 1918–1950, 1991; Vol. IV, The Last Laugh 1950–1991, 1992; Vol. V, The Shaw Companion, 1992; abridged edn, 1997; Basil Street Blues, 1999; Works on Paper, 2002; various radio and television scripts. *Recreations:* listening to stories, watching people dance, avoiding tame animals, being polite, music, siestas. *Address:* c/o A. P. Watt Ltd, 20 John Street, WC1N 2DL.

HOLROYD, William Arthur Hepworth, FHSM; Chief Executive, North Durham Health Authority, 1992–93; *b* 15 Sept. 1938; *s* of late Rev. Harry Holroyd and Annie Dodgshun Holroyd; *m* 1967, Hilary Gower; three *s*. *Educ:* Kingswood Sch., Bath; Trinity Hall, Cambridge (MA History); Manchester Univ. (DSA). Hospital Secretary: Crewe Memorial Hosp., 1963–65; Wycombe General Hosp., 1965–67; secondment to Dept of Health, 1967–69; Dep. Gp Sec., Blackpool and Fylde HMC, 1969–72; Regional Manpower Officer, Leeds RHB, 1972–74; District Administrator, York Health Dist, 1974–82; Regional Administrator, Yorkshire RHA, 1982–85; Dist Gen. Man., Durham HA, 1985–92. Non-exec. Dir, York Waterworks, plc, 1996–99. Member: National Staff Cttee for Admin. and Clerical Staff in NHS, 1973–82; General Nursing Council for England and Wales, 1978–83; English Nat. Board for Nursing, Midwifery and Health

Visiting, 1980–87; NHS Trng Authority, 1988–91. Director, Methodist Chapel Aid Assoc. Ltd, 1978– (Chm., 2000–). Mem. Bd of Visitors, HM Prison Full Sutton, 1995–. *Publication:* (ed) Hospital Traffic and Supply Problems, 1968. *Recreations:* walking, music, visiting the Shetland Isles.

See also J. H. Holroyd.

HOLROYDE, Geoffrey Vernon; Director, Coventry (formerly Coventry Lanchester) Polytechnic, 1975–87); *b* 18 Sept. 1928; *s* of late Harold Vincent Holroyde and Kathleen Olive (*née* Glover); *m* 1960, Elizabeth Mary, *d* of Rev. E. O. Connell; two *s* two *d*. *Educ:* Wrekin Coll.; Birmingham Univ. (BSc); Birmingham Conservatoire (BMus 1995); ARCO. Royal Navy, 1949–54 and 1956–61; School-master, Welbeck Coll., 1954–56; English Electric, becoming Principal of Staff Coll., Dunchurch, 1961–70; British Leyland, Head Office Training Staff, 1970–71; Head, Sidney Stringer Sch. and Community Coll., Coventry, 1971–75; Higher Educn Adviser to Training Commn, 1987–88; Dir, GEC Management Coll., Dunchurch, 1989–92. Chairman: Industrial Links Adv. Gp to Cttee of Dirs of Polytechnics, 1980–87; National Forum for the Performing Arts in Higher Educn, 1987–91; Develt Training Steering Gp, 1983–88; Mem., W Midlands RHA, 1985–89 (Chm., Non Clinical Res. Cttee; Vice-Chm., AIDS Task Force); Mem., RSA Educn Industry Forum, 1986–90. Dir of Music, St Mary's Church, Warwick, 1962–72; Dir, Coventry Cathedral Chapter House Choir, 1982–95; Asst Dir, Warwickshire County Youth Chorale, 1999–. Mem., Exec. Cttee, British Fedn of Young Choirs, 1993–95. Member: Council, Upper Avon Navigation Trust, 1994–2001; Steering Cttee, Assoc. of Inland Navigation Authorities, 1997–. Governor, 1978–91, Trustee, 1979–91, Chm., Governing Body, 1984–89, Brathay Hall Trust; Chm. Trustees, St Mary's Hall, Warwick, 1984–90; Governor: Mid Warwicks Coll. of Further Educn, 1976–87; Kings School, Worcester, 1983–88. Hon. Life Mem., RSCM, 1970. *Publications:* Managing People, 1968; Delegations, 1968; Communications, 1969; Organs of St Mary's Church, Warwick, 1969. *Recreations:* music (organ and choir), canals, sailing, outdoor pursuits. *Address:* 38 Coten End, Warwick CV34 4NP. *T:* (01926) 492329.

HOLROYDE, Timothy Victor; QC 1996; a Recorder, since 1997; *b* 18 Aug. 1955; *s* of Frank Holroyde and Doreen Holroyde; *m* 1980, Miranda Elisabeth Stone; two *d*. *Educ:* Bristol Grammar Sch.; Wadham Coll., Oxford (BA Hons Juris.). Called to the Bar, Middle Temple, 1977; in practice on Northern Circuit, 1978–. *Recreations:* squash, tennis. *Address:* Exchange Chambers, Pearl Assurance House, Derby Square, Liverpool L2 9XX. *T:* (0151) 236 7747.

HOLT, Alexis Fayrer B.; *see* Brett-Holt.

HOLT, Dr Andrew Anthony; Head, Information Services Division, Department of Health, since 1990; *b* 4 Jan. 1944; *s* of Josef Holzmann and Livia Holzmann; *m* 1969, Janet Margery; three *s*. *Educ:* Latymer Upper Sch.; University Coll. London (BSc Maths 1965; PhD 1969). ICI Paints Div., 1968–70; entered Civil Service, 1970: Principal, Treasury, 1974–78; Head, Operational Research: Inland Revenue, 1978–87; DHSS, 1987–90. Tutor, Open Univ., 1972–. *Publications:* contrib. to jls or society papers. *Address:* Department of Health, Skipton House, 80 London Road, Elephant and Castle, SE1 6LH.

HOLT, Constance, CBE 1975; Area Nursing Officer, Manchester Area Health Authority (Teaching), 1973–77; *b* 5 Jan. 1924; *d* of Ernest Biddulph and of Ada Biddulph (*née* Robley); *m* 1975, Robert Lord Holt, OBE, FRCS. *Educ:* Whalley Range High Sch. for Girls, Manchester; Manchester Royal Infirmary (SRN); Queen Charlotte's Hosp., London; St Mary's Hosp., Manchester (SCM); Royal Coll. of Nursing, London Univ. (Sister Tutor Dipl.); Univ. of Washington (Florence Nightingale Schol., Fulbright Award). Nursing Officer, Min. of Health, 1959–65; Chief Nursing Officer: United Oxford Hosps, 1965–69; United Manchester Hosps, 1969–73. Pres., Assoc. of Nurse Administrators (formerly Assoc. of Hosp. Matrons), 1972–. Reader licensed by Bishop of Sodor and Man. Hon. Lectr, Dept of Nursing, Univ. of Manchester, 1972. Hon. MA Manchester, 1980. *Publications:* articles in British and internat. nursing press. *Recreations:* reading, gardening, music. *Address:* Seabank, Marine Terrace, Port St Mary, Isle of Man IM9 5EQ.

HOLT, Prof. David, (Tim), CB 2000; PhD; FSS; Professor of Social Statistics, University of Southampton, since 2000; *b* 29 Oct. 1943; *s* of late Ernest Frederick Holt and Catherine Rose (*née* Finn); *m* 1966, Jill Blake; one *s* one *d*. *Educ:* Coopers' Company's Sch.; Exeter Univ. (BSc Maths 1966; PhD Mathematical Stats 1969). FSS 1973. Res. Fellow, Univ. of Exeter, 1969–70; Survey Statistician, Statistics Canada, 1970–73 (Consultant, 1974–75); University of Southampton: Lectr in Social Stats, 1973–80; Leverhulme Prof. of Social Stats, 1980–99; Dean, Social Sci. Faculty, 1981–83; Dep. Vice Chancellor, 1990–95; Dir, CSO, 1995–96; Hd, Govt Statistical Service, 1995–2000; Dir, ONS, and Registrar Gen. for England and Wales, 1996–2000. Consultant: NZ Dept of Stats, 1981; OPCS, 1983, 1987, 1991; ESRC, 1990; Australian Bureau of Stats, 1990; Scientific Advr to Chief Scientist, DHSS, 1983–88. Vis. Fellow, Nuffield Coll., Oxford, 1995–. Associate Editor: Jl Royal Statistical Soc. B, 1983–88; Survey Methodology, 1988–; Editor, Jl Royal Statistical Soc. A: Stats and Society, 1991–94. Vice-President: Internat. Assoc. of Survey Statisticians, 1989–91 (Scientific Sec., 1985–87); UN Statistical Commn, 1997–99; Mem., Internat. Statistical Inst., 1985 (Vice-Pres., 1999–2001); Fellow, Amer. Statistical Assoc., 1990; Founding Academician, Acad. of Social Scis, 1999. Trustee, Newitt Trust, 1990–. Hon. DSc (SocSci) Southampton, 1999. *Publications:* (jtly) Analysis of Complex Surveys, 1989; papers in academic jls. *Recreations:* orienteering, travelling. *Address:* Department of Social Statistics, University of Southampton, Southampton SO17 1BJ. *T:* (023) 8059 2527; *e-mail:* tholt@socsci.soton.ac.uk.

HOLT, Denise Mary; HM Diplomatic Service; Director, Personnel, Foreign and Commonwealth Office, since 1999; *b* 1 Oct. 1949; *d* of William Dennis and Mary Joanna Mills; *m* 1987, David Holt; one *s*. *Educ:* New Hall Sch., Chelmsford; Bristol Univ. (BA Hons French, Spanish, Politics). Res. Analyst, FCO, 1970–84; First Sec., Dublin, 1984–87; Head of Section, FCO, 1988–90; First Sec., Brasilia, 1991–93; Dep. Hd, Eastern Dept, FCO, 1993–94; Asst Dir, Personnel, 1996–98; Dep. Hd of Mission, Dublin, 1998–99. *Recreations:* reading, cooking, needlework. *Address:* c/o Foreign and Commonwealth Office, King Charles Street, SW1A 2AH. *T:* (020) 7008 0580. *Club:* Stephen's Green (Dublin).

HOLT, Sir James (Clarke), Kt 1990; FSA 1967; FBA 1978; Professor of Medieval History, Cambridge University, 1978–88; Master of Fitzwilliam College, Cambridge, 1981–88 (Hon. Fellow, 1988; Life Fellow, 2000); *b* 26 April 1922; *s* of late Herbert and Eunice Holt; *m* 1950, Alice Catherine Elizabeth Suley (*d* 1998); one *s*. *Educ:* Bradford Grammar Sch.; Queen's Coll., Oxford (Hastings Schol.; Hon. Fellow, 1996). MA 1947; 1st cl. Modern Hist.; DPhil 1952. Served with RA, 1942–45 (Captain). Harmsworth Sen. Schol., Merton Coll., Oxford, 1947; Univ. of Nottingham: Asst Lectr, 1949; Lectr, 1951; Sen. Lectr, 1961; Prof. of Medieval History, 1962; Reading University: Prof. of History, 1966–78; Dean, Faculty of Letters and Soc. Scis, 1972–76; Professorial Fellow, Emanuel Coll., Cambridge, 1978–81 (Hon. Fellow, 1985). Vis. Prof., Univ. of Calif, Santa Barbara, 1977; Vis. Hinkley Prof., Johns Hopkins Univ., 1983; Vis. JSPS Fellow, Japan, 1986. Raleigh Lectr, British Acad., 1975. Mem., Adv. Council on Public Records, 1974–81. Pres., Royal Historical Soc., 1980–84; Life Pres., Pipe Roll Soc., 1999; Vice-Pres., British Academy, 1987–89. Corres. Fellow, Medieval Acad. of America, 1983. Hon DLitt: Reading, 1984; Nottingham, 1996. Comdr, Order of Civil Merit (Spain), 1988. *Publications:* The Northerners: a study in the reign of King John, 1961, 2nd edn 1992; Praestita Roll 14–18 John, 1964; Magna Carta, 1965, 2nd edn 1992; The Making of Magna Carta, 1966; Magna Carta and the Idea of Liberty, 1972; The University of Reading: the first fifty years, 1977; Robin Hood, 1982, 2nd edn 1989; (ed with J. Gillingham) War and Government in the Middle Ages, 1984; Magna Carta and Medieval Government, 1985; (with R. Mortimer) Acta of Henry II and Richard I, 1986; (ed) Domesday Studies, 1987; Colonial England 1066–1215, 1997; papers in English Historical Review, Past and Present, Economic History Review, Trans Royal Hist. Soc. *Recreations:* mountaineering, cricket, fly-fishing, music. *Address:* 5 Holben Close, Barton, Cambridge CB3 7AQ. *T:* (01223) 264923. *Clubs:* Oxford and Cambridge, National Liberal, MCC; Wayfarers' (Liverpool).

HOLT, (James) Richard (Trist); President, Pensions Appeal Tribunals (England & Wales), 1993–98; *b* 17 Aug. 1924; *s* of George Richard Holt and Gladys Floyd Holt (*née* Bennetts); *m* 1st, 1952, Helen Worswick (marr. diss); one *s* one *d*; 2nd, 1977, Patricia Mary Hartley. *Educ:* Giggleswick Sch.; Queen's Coll., Oxford (MA 1950); London Univ. (ext. LLB 1952). Served Royal Signals, 1942–47, commnd 1945. Articled clerk, 1941; admitted solicitor, 1951; called to the Bar, Gray's Inn, 1973. Part-time Chairman: Med. Appeal Tribunals, 1979–96; Vaccine Damage Tribunals, 1982–96; Pensions Appeal Tribunals, 1985–98; Disability Appeal Tribunals, 1992–96; Immigration Appeals Adjudicator, 1982–90; Mem., Mental Health Act Commn, 1985–86. Contested (C), Rossendale, 1959. *Publication:* contrib. Law Soc. Gazette. *Recreations:* walking, reading history. *Address:* The Hey Farm, Newton-in-Bowland, near Clitheroe, Lancs BB7 3EE. *T:* (01200) 446213. *Club:* Army and Navy.

HOLT, John Frederick; His Honour Judge Holt; a Circuit Judge, since 1998; *b* 7 Oct. 1947; *s* of Edward Basil Holt and Monica Holt; *m* 1970, Stephanie Ann Watson; three *s*. *Educ:* Ampleforth; Bristol Univ. (LLB). Called to the Bar, Lincoln's Inn, 1970; barrister, E Anglian Chambers, 1970–98 (Head of Chambers, 1993–98); Asst Recorder, 1989–92; a Recorder, 1992–98. ECB cricket coach. *Recreations:* village cricket, classic motor cars. *Address:* c/o Group Manager, Chelmsford Group of Courts, 1st Floor, Steeple House, Church Lane, Chelmsford CM1 1NH. *Clubs:* Strangers (Norwich); MG Car; Twinstead Cricket.

HOLT, John Michael, MD, FRCP; Consultant Physician, John Radcliffe Hospital (formerly Radcliffe Infirmary), Oxford, 1974–2000, now Emeritus; Fellow, 1968–2000, now Emeritus, and Vice Principal, 1999–2000, Linacre College, Oxford; *b* 8 March 1935; *s* of late Frank Holt, BSc and of Constance Holt; *m* 1959, Sheila Margaret Morton; one *s* three *d*. *Educ:* St Peter's Sch., York; Univ. of St Andrews. MA Oxon; MD St Andrews; MSc Queen's Univ. Ont. Registrar and Lectr, Nuffield Dept of Medicine, Radcliffe Infirmary, Oxford, 1964–66, Cons. Physician 1968; Chm., Medical Staff, Oxford Hosps, 1982–84. University of Oxford: Med. Tutor, 1967–73; Dir of Clinical Studies, 1971–76; Mem., Gen. Bd of Faculties, 1987–91; Chm., Clinical Medicine Bd, 1992–94. Civilian Advr in Medicine, RAF, 1991–2000. Formerly Examiner in Medicine: Univ. of Oxford; Hong Kong; London; Glasgow; Dublin; RCP. Censor, RCP, 1995–97. Member: Assoc. of Physicians; Soc. of Apothecaries; Cttee on Safety of Medicines, 1979–86; Oxford RHA, 1984–88. Editor, Qly Jl of Medicine, 1975–92. *Publications:* papers on disorders of blood and various med. topics in BMJ, Lancet, etc. *Recreation:* sailing. *Address:* Old Whitehill, Tackley, Oxon OX5 3AB. *T:* (01869) 331241. *Clubs:* Oxford and Cambridge; Royal Cornwall Yacht (Falmouth).

HOLT, Prof. John Riley, FRS 1964; Professor of Experimental Physics, University of Liverpool, 1966–83, now Emeritus; *b* 15 Feb. 1918; *er s* of Frederick Holt and Annie (*née* Riley); *m* 1949, Joan Silvester Thomas (*d* 2001); two *s*. *Educ:* Runcorn Secondary Sch.; University of Liverpool; PhD 1941; British Atomic Energy Project, Liverpool and Cambridge, 1940–45; University of Liverpool: Lecturer, 1945–53, (Senior Lecturer, 1953–56) Reader, 1956–66. *Publications:* papers in scientific journals on nuclear physics and particle physics. *Recreation:* gardening. *Address:* Rydalmere, Stanley Avenue, Higher Bebington, Wirral CH63 5QE. *T:* (0151) 608 2041.

HOLT, Her Honour Mary; a Circuit Judge, 1977–95; *d* of Henry James Holt, solicitor, and of Sarah Holt (*née* Chapman); unmarried. *Educ:* Park Sch., Preston; Girton Coll., Cambridge (MA, LLB, 1st cl. Hons). Called to the Bar, Gray's Inn, 1949 (Atkin Scholar). Practised on Northern circuit. Former Vice-Chm., Preston North Conservative Assoc.; Member: Nat. Exec. Council, 1969–72; Woman's Nat. Advisory Cttee, 1969–70; representative, Central Council, 1969–71. MP (C) Preston N, 1970–Feb. 1974. Contested (C) Preston N, Feb. and Oct. 1974. Dep. Pres., Lancs Br., BRCS, 1976–95. Freedom of Cities of Dallas and Denton, Texas, 1987. Badge of Honour, BRCS, 1989. *Publication:* 2nd edn, Benas and Essenhigh's Precedents of Pleadings, 1956. *Recreation:* walking. *Club:* Royal Over Seas League.

HOLT, Sir Michael, Kt 1995; CBE 1981; FCA; Chairman, Eastern Area Conservative Provincial Council, 1992–96; *b* 23 Dec. 1927; *s* of Frank Holt, MM, FCA and Helen Gertrude Holt (*née* Wheeler); *m* 1955, Janet Michelle Simon; two *s* one *d*. *Educ:* Epsom Coll.; Downing Coll., Cambridge (MA, LLM). Called to the Bar, Inner Temple, 1953; qualified as Chartered Accountant, 1958; Sen. Partner, Arthur Goddard & Co., Chartered Accountants, 1966–83. Dir, Lay and Wheeler Gp Ltd, 1983, and other cos. External Mem., Lloyds, 1983–96. Member: NE Essex HA, 1982–89, 1990–93; Bd of Govs, St John's Hosp. for Diseases of the Skin, 1980–82. Conservative Party: Hon. Treas., Colchester Assoc., 1965–76; Chm., 1983–85, Vice Pres., 1985–95, N Colchester Assoc.; Vice Pres., N Essex Assoc., 1995–; Hon. Treas., 1975–80, Vice Chm., then Dep. Chm., 1986–92, Eastern Area Provincial Council; Pres., N Essex and S Suffolk Eur. Constituency Council, 1994–99; Vice Chm., 1985–86, Chm., 1986–90, Pres., 1991–94, NE Essex European Cons. Council; Mem. Exec. Cttee, Nat. Union of Cons. and Unionist Assocs, 1975–83, 1986–98. *Recreations:* politics, gardening, book collecting. *Address:* The Tower House, Bildeston, Suffolk IP7 7ER. *T:* (01449) 741313. *Clubs:* St Stephen's Constitutional; Colchester and District Conservative.

HOLT, Oliver Charles Thomas; Chief Sports Correspondent, The Times, since 2000; *b* 22 May 1966; *s* of Thomas and Eileen Holt; *m* 1995, Sarah Llewellyn-Jones; one *d*. *Educ:* Christ Church, Oxford (BA Hons Modern Hist.). Reporter, Daily Post & Echo, Liverpool, 1990–93; Motor Racing Corresp., 1993–97, Football Corresp., 1997–2000, The Times. *Publication:* The Bridge, 1998. *Recreations:* Marlon Brando, Bob Dylan, Stockport County. *Address:* c/o The Times, 1 Pennington Street, E1 9XN.

HOLT, Prof. Peter Malcolm, FBA 1975; FSA; Professor of History of the Near and Middle East, University of London, 1975–82, now Professor Emeritus; *b* 28 Nov. 1918; *s* of Rev. Peter and Elizabeth Holt; *m* 1953, Nancy Bury (*née* Mawle); one *s* one *d*. *Educ:* Lord Williams's Grammar Sch., Thame; University Coll., Oxford (Schol.) (MA, DLitt).

Sudan Civil Service: Min. of Education, 1941–53; Govt Archivist, 1954–55. School of Oriental and African Studies, London, 1955–82; Prof. of Arab History, 1964–75. FRHistS 1973; FSA 1980. Hon. Fellow, SOAS, 1985. Gold Medal of Science, Letters and Arts, Repub. of Sudan, 1980. *Publications:* The Mahdist State in the Sudan, 1958, 2nd edn 1970; A Modern History of the Sudan, 1961, 4th edn (with M. W. Daly) as A History of the Sudan from the Coming of Islam to the Present Day, 1988, 5th edn 2000; (co-ed with Bernard Lewis) Historians of the Middle East, 1962; Egypt and the Fertile Crescent, 1966; (ed) Political and Social Change in Modern Egypt, 1968; (co-ed with Ann K. S. Lambton and Bernard Lewis) The Cambridge History of Islam, 1970; Studies in the History of the Near East, 1973; (ed) The Eastern Mediterranean Lands in the period of the Crusades, 1977; The Memoirs of a Syrian Prince, 1983; The Age of the Crusades, 1986; trans. P. Thorau, The Lion of Egypt, 1992; Early Mamluk Diplomacy, 1995; The Sudan of the three Niles, 1999; trans. C. Cahen, The Formation of Turkey, 2001; articles in: Encyclopaedia of Islam, Bulletin of SOAS, Sudan Notes and Records, Der Islam, English Historical Rev., etc. *Address:* Dryden Spinney, Bletchington Road, Kirtlington, Kidlington, Oxon OX5 3HF. *T:* (01869) 350477. *Club:* Oxford and Cambridge.

HOLT, Richard; *see* Holt, J. R. T.

HOLT, Prof. Stephen Campbell, OBE 2000; PhD; Rector and Chief Executive, Roehampton Institute, London, 1988–99, now Emeritus Professor, University of Surrey Roehampton; *b* 27 Sept. 1935; *s* of late E. S. Holt and E. C. Holt; *m* 1st, 1959, Moira Jill Ditchburn (marr. diss.); two *s* one *d*; 2nd, 1989, Anne Ashcroft, two step *d*. *Educ:* Mill Hill Sch.; Emmanuel Coll., Cambridge (MA); PhD Manchester 1966. Nat. Service, RM, 1954–56, 2nd Lieut; worked in family hosiery business, The Holt Hosiery Co., 1959–61; research, Dept of Govt, Univ. of Manchester, 1961–63; Asst Lectr and Lectr, Dept of Political Theory and Instns, Univ. of Sheffield, 1963–69; Vis. Prof., Univ. of Colorado, 1969–70; University of Bradford: Prof. of Eur. Studies, 1970–80; Pro Vice-Chancellor, 1976–78; University of Kent at Canterbury: Prof. of Eur. Studies, 1980–88; Pro Vice-Chancellor, 1986–88. Vis. Prof., Coll. of Europe, Bruges, 1984–88. CEDR Registered Mediator, 2001. Chm., Horsham Dist Community Mediation Service. Hon. Fellow, St Mary's Coll., Twickenham, 2000. DUniv Surrey, 1999. *Publications:* The Common Market, 1967; Six European States, 1970; (with J. E. Farquharson) Europe from Below, 1975; articles in acad. jls. *Recreations:* reading, cosmology, theology. *Club:* Oxford and Cambridge.

HOLT, Stuart; Headmaster, Clitheroe Royal Grammar School, since 1991; *b* 12 Sept. 1943; *s* of Alan and Irene Holt; *m* 1968, Valerie Hollows; one *s* one *d*. *Educ:* Leeds Univ. (BSc 2nd Cl. Hons Zool., MPhil); Univ. of Lancaster (MA Educn). Biol. Master, Adwick Sch., Doncaster, 1968–71; Hd of Biol., King's Sch., Pontefract, 1971–73; Hd of Sci., Whitley High Sch., Wigan, 1973–78; Dep. Hd Curriculum, Wright Robinson High Sch., Manchester, 1978–84; Headmaster, Failsworth Sch., Oldham, 1984–91. Mem., Rotary Internat. *Recreations:* theatre, photography, Italy, fell-walking, cabinet making. *Address:* Clitheroe Royal Grammar School, York Street, Clitheroe, Lancs BB7 2DJ. *T:* (01200) 423118.

HOLT, Thelma Mary Bernadette, CBE 1994; Managing Director, Thelma Holt Ltd, since 1990; *b* 4 Jan. 1932; *d* of David Holt and Ellen Finagh (*née* Doyle); *m* 1st, 1956, Patrick Graucob (marr. diss. 1968); 2nd, 1969, David Pressman (marr. diss. 1970). *Educ:* St Ann's Sch., Lytham; RADA. Actress, 1953; Founder, Open Space Theatre (with Charles Marowitz), 1968; Dir, Round House Theatre, 1977; Exec. Producer, Theatre of Comedy, 1983; Head of Touring and Commercial Exploitation, Royal Nat. Theatre, 1985 (Laurence Olivier/Observer Award for Outstanding Achievement, 1987); Exec. Producer, Peter Hall Co., 1989; formed Thelma Holt Ltd, 1990, productions include: The Three Sisters, 1990; Tango at the End of Winter, 1991; Electra, Hamlet, Les Atrides, La Baruffe Chiozotte, Six Characters in Search of an Author, The Tempest, 1992; Much Ado About Nothing, 1993; Peer Gynt, The Clandestine Marriage, 1994; The Seagull, A Midsummer Night's Dream, Antony and Cleopatra, The Glass Menagerie, 1995; Observe the Sons of Ulster Marching Towards the Somme, A Doll's House, 1996; The Maids, Les Fausses Confidences, Oh Les Beaux Jours, Shintoku-Maru, 1997; The Relapse, 1998; Macbeth, King Lear, 1999; Miss Julie, 2000; Semi-Monde, 2001. Member: Arts Council, 1993–98 (Chm., Drama Adv. Panel, 1994–98); Council, RADA, 1985–. Director: Theatre Investment Fund Ltd, 1982–; Citizens Theatre, Glasgow, 1989– (Vice-Pres., 1997–). Cameron Mackintosh Vis. Prof. of Contemporary Theatre, Oxford Univ., 1998; Fellow, St Catherine's Coll., Oxford, 1998. Patron, OUDS, 2001. Governor, Middlesex Univ., 1996–. DUniv Middlesex, 1994; Hon. MA: Open, 1988; Oxford, 1998. *Recreation:* bargain hunting at antique fairs. *Address:* Waldorf Chambers, 11 Aldwych, WC2B 4DG. *T:* (020) 7379 0438, *Fax:* (020) 7836 9832; *e-mail:* thelma@dircon.co.uk.

HOLT, Tim; *see* Holt, David.

HOLTAM, Rev. Nicholas Roderick; Vicar of St Martin-in-the-Fields, since 1995; *b* 8 Aug. 1954; *s* of late Sydney Holtam and Kathleen (*née* Freeberne); *m* 1981, Helen Harris; three *s* one *d*. *Educ:* Latymer Grammar Sch., Edmonton; Collingwood Coll., Univ. of Durham (BA Geog.; MA Theol.); King's Coll. London (BD, AKC); Westcott House, Cambridge. Ordained deacon, 1979, priest, 1980; Asst Curate, St Dunstan and All Saints, Stepney, 1979–82; Tutor, Lincoln Theol Coll., 1983–87; Vicar, Christ Church and St John with St Luke, Isle of Dogs, 1988–95. FRSA 1999. *Recreations:* walking, cycling, reading, exploring London. *Address:* 6 St Martin's Place, WC2N 4JJ. *T:* (020) 7930 0089.

HOLTBY, Very Rev. Robert Tinsley, FSA; Dean of Chichester, 1977–89, Dean Emeritus, 1989; *b* 25 Feb. 1921; *o s* of William and Elsie Holtby, Thornton-le-Dale, Yorkshire; *m* 1947, Mary, *er d* of late Rt Rev. Eric Graham; one *s* two *d*. *Educ:* York Minster Choir Sch.; Scarborough Coll. and High School. St Edmund Hall, Oxford, 1939; MA (2nd Class Mod. Hist.), 1946; BD 1957. Choral Scholar, King's Coll., Cambridge, 1944; MA (2nd Class Theol.), 1952. Cuddesdon Theological Coll. and Westcott House, Cambridge, 1943–46. FSA 1990. Deacon, 1946; Priest, 1947. Curate of Pocklington, Yorks, 1946–48. Chaplain to the Forces, 1948–52: 14/20th King's Hussars, Catterick; Singapore; Priest-in-charge, Johore Bahru. Hon. CF, 1952–; Acting Chaplain, King's Coll., Cambridge, 1952; Chaplain and Asst Master, Malvern Coll., 1952–54; Chaplain and Assistant Master, St Edward's Sch., Oxford, 1954–59; Canon Residentiary of Carlisle and Diocesan Dir of Educn, 1959–67, Canon Emeritus, 1967–; Gen. Sec., Nat. Soc. for Promoting Religious Education, 1967–77; Sec., Schs Cttee, 1967–74, Gen. Sec., 1974–77, Church of England Bd of Educn. Vis. Fellow, W Sussex Inst. of Higher Educn, 1990–93. Select Preacher: Cambridge, 1984; Oxford, 1989. Chm., Cumberland Council of Social Service, 1962–67. Chaplain to High Sheriff of Cumberland, 1964, 1966. *Publications:* Daniel Waterland, A Study in 18th Century Orthodoxy, 1966; Carlisle Cathedral Library and Records, 1966; Eric Graham, 1888–1964, 1967; Carlisle Cathedral, 1969; Chichester Cathedral, 1980; Robert Wright Stopford, 1988; Bishop William Otter, 1989; Eric Milner-White, 1991; The Minster School, York, 1994. *Recreations:* music, walking, history. *Address:* 4 Hutton Hall, Huttons Ambo, York YO60 7HW. *T:* (01653) 696366.

HOLTHAM, Gerald Hubert; Chief Investment Officer, Morley Fund Management; *b* Aberdare, 28 June 1944; *s* of late Denis Arthur Holtham and Dilys Maud Holtham (*née* Bull); *m* 1st, 1969, Patricia Mary Blythin (marr. diss. 1976); one *d*; 2nd, 1979, Edith Hodgkinson; one *s* one *d*. *Educ:* King Edward's Sch., Birmingham; Jesus Coll., Oxford (BA 1st Cl. PPE); Nuffield Coll., Oxford (MPhil Econ). ODI, 1973–75; Economist, OECD, Paris, 1975–82; Head, Gen. Econ. Div., Dept of Econs, OECD, 1982–85; Vis. Fellow, Brookings Inst., Washington, 1985–87; Chief Internat. Economist, Shearson Lehman, 1988–91; Econs Fellow, Magdalen Coll., Oxford, 1991–92; Chief Economist, Lehman Brothers, Europe, 1992–94; Dir, IPPR, 1994–98; Dir, Global Startegy, Norwich Union Investment Mgt, 1998. Vis. Prof., Univ. of Strathclyde, 1990–; Affiliated Prof., London Business Sch., 1992–99. *Publications:* (with Roger Busby) Main Line Kill (novel), 1967; (with Arthur Hazlewood) Aid and Inequality in Kenya, 1975; (jtly) Empirical Macroeconomics for Interdependent Economies, 1988; (with Ralph Bryant and Peter Hooper) External Deficits and the Dollar, 1988; articles on economics in learned jls. *Recreations:* gardening, windsurfing, listening to jazz. *Address:* 13 Lansdowne Gardens, SW8 2EQ. *T:* (020) 7622 8673.

HOLTON, Michael; Assistant Secretary, Ministry of Defence, 1976–87, retired; *b* 30 Sept. 1927; 3rd *s* of late George Arnold Holton and Ethel (*née* Fountain); *m* 1st, 1951, Daphne Bache (marr. diss. 1987); one *s* two *d*; 2nd, 1987, Joan Catherine Thurman (*née* Hickman), (OBE 1994), Huddersfield. *Educ:* Finchley County Grammar Sch.; London Sch. of Economics. RAFVR, 1946–48; Min. of Food, 1948–54; Air Ministry, 1955–61; MoD, 1961–68; Sec., Countryside Commn for Scotland, 1968–70; Sec., Carnegie UK Trust, 1971–75. Sec., European Conservation Year Cttee for Scotland, 1970; Mem. Council, 1976–93, Hon. Sec., 1988–93, RSNC; Member: YHA, 1946–; Consultative Cttee, Family Fund, 1973–75; Bd, Cairngorm Chairlift Co., 1973–95; Museums Assoc., 1976–95; Inverliever Lodge Trust, 1979–90. Hon. Secretary: RAF Mountaineering Assoc., 1952–54; British Mountaineering Council, 1954–59 (Hon. Mem., 1997–); RAF Mountain Rescue Assoc., 1993–95 (Hon. Mem., 1996–). *Publication:* Training Handbook for RAF Mountain Rescue Teams, 1953. *Address:* 4 Ludlow Way, Hampstead Garden Suburb, N2 0LA. *T:* (020) 8444 8582. *Clubs:* Athenæum, Alpine; Himalayan.

HOLWELL, Peter, FCA; Consultant, Chatham Historic Dockyard Trust, 1999–2001; *b* 28 March 1936; *s* of Frank Holwell and Helen (*née* Howe); *m* 1959, Jean Patricia Ashman; one *s* one *d*. *Educ:* Palmers Endowed Sch., Grays, Essex; Hendon Grammar Sch.; London Sch. of Econs and Pol Science (BSc Econ). FCA 1972; MBCS 1974; FRSocMed 1991. Articled Clerk, 1958–61, Management Consultant, 1961–64, Arthur Andersen and Co.; University of London: Head of Computing, Sch. Exams Bd, 1964–67; Head of University Computing and O & M Unit, 1967–77; Sec. for Accounting and Admin. Computing, 1977–82; Clerk of the Court, 1982–85; Principal, 1985–97; Dir, School Exams Council, 1988–94; Mem., Univ. of London Exams and Assessments Council, 1991–96. Chm., UCCA Computing Gp, 1977–82. Chm., City and E London FHSA, 1994–96. Director: Zoo Operations Ltd, 1988–92; London E Anglian Gp Ltd, 1990–93; Non-exec. Mem., NE Thames RHA, 1990–94. Consultant, POW Sch. of Architecture and the Bldg Arts, 1998–99. FZS, 1988–2001 (Treas., 1991–92). Chm., St Mark's Res. Foundn and Educnl Trust, 1995–2000; Trustee, Samuel Courtauld (formerly Home House) Trust, 1985–97. Mem. Council, Sch. of Pharmacy, Univ. of London, 1996–; Vice-Chm., Wye Coll., 1996–2000. *Recreations:* walking, music, horology. *Address:* Hookers Green, Bishopsbourne, Canterbury, Kent CT4 5JB. *Clubs:* Athenæum, Royal Society of Medicine.

HOLZACH, Dr Robert; Hon. Chairman, Union Bank of Switzerland, 1988–96; *b* 28 Sept. 1922. *Educ:* Univ. of Zürich (Dr of Law). Union Bank of Switzerland: trainee, Geneva, London, 1951–52; Vice-Pres., 1956; Senior Vice-Pres., Head of Commercial Div., Head Office, 1962; Mem., Exec. Board, 1966; Exec. Vice-Pres., 1968; President, 1976; Chm. of Board, 1980–88. *Publication:* Herausforderungen, 1988. *Address:* c/o Union Bank of Switzerland, Bahnhofstrasse 45, 8001 Zurich, Switzerland. *T:* (1) 2341111.

HOM, Ken; BBC-TV presenter; author; *b* 3 May 1949; *s* of late Thomas Hom and of Ying Fong Hom. *Educ:* Univ. of Calif, Berkeley. Public television producer, 1974–75; cookery teacher, 1975–78; Cookery prof., Calif. Culinary Acad., San Francisco, 1978–82; Presenter, BBC-TV series: Ken Hom's Chinese Cookery, 1984; Hot Chefs, 1991; Ken Hom's Hot Wok, 1996; Ken Hom Travels with a Hot Wok, 1998; Foolproof Chinese Cookery, 2000. *Publications:* Ken Hom's Encyclopaedia of Chinese Cookery Techniques, 1984 (US edn as Chinese Technique, 1981); Ken Hom's Chinese Cookery, 1984, rev. edn 2001; Ken Hom's Vegetable and Pasta Book, 1987; Ken Hom's East Meets West Cuisine, 1987; Fragrant Harbour Taste, 1988; Asian Vegetarian Feast, 1988; Ken Hom's Quick and Easy Chinese Cookery, 1988; The Taste of China, 1989; The Cooking of China, 1992; Ken Hom's Chinese Kitchen, 1993; Ken Hom's Hot Wok, 1996; Ken Hom's Asian Ingredients and Posters, 1997; Ken Hom Travels with a Hot Wok, 1997; Easy Family Dishes: a memoir with recipes, 1998 (Andre Simon Award, 1999; US edn as Easy Family Recipes from a Chinese-American Childhood, 1998); Ken Hom Cooks Thai, 1999; Foolproof Chinese Cookery, 2000; Quick Wok, 2001. *Recreations:* Bordeaux vintage wine, bicycling, reading. *Address:* c/o William Levene Ltd, 167 Imperial Drive, Harrow, Middx HA2 7JP. *T:* (020) 8868 4355, *Fax:* (020) 8429 3668. *Club:* Monte's.

HOMA, Peter Michael, CBE 2000; Chief Executive, Commission for Health Improvement, since 1999; *b* 3 Jan. 1957; *s* of late Karol Anthony Homa and of Anne Kathleen Homa (*née* Dixon); *m* 1985, Carol Pamela Brunt; one *s* one *d*. *Educ:* Ernest Bevin Sch., London; Univ. of Sussex (BA Hons Econs 1979); Univ. of Hull (MBA 1993); Henley Management Coll. and Brunel Univ. (DBA 1998). MHSM 1985, FHSM 1999. Self-employed, 1979–81; nat. admin. trainee, SW Thames RHA, 1981–82; Operational Services Adminr, St George's Hosp., London, 1983–84; Dep. Unit Adminr, Bristol Children's and Maternity Hosps, 1984–86; Dep. Unit Gen. Manager, Acute Services, Bromsgrove and Redditch HA, 1986–89; Leicester Royal Infirmary: Associate Gen. Manager, 1989–90; Unit. Gen. Manager, 1990–93; Chief Exec., Leicester Royal Infirmary NHS Trust, 1993–98; Hd, Nat. Patients' Access Team, NHS Exec., 1998–99. Pres., IHSM, 1998–99 (Vice-Chm., 1996–97; Chm., 1997–98). Hon. Lectr, Health Services Management, Univ. of Leicester, 1997–; Vis. Prof., Dept of Health, LSE, 2000–. Pres., Leicester Royal Infirmary Drama, Operatic and Literary Soc., 1991–98. *Recreations:* running, cycling, climbing, reading, writing, picture framing. *Address:* (office) Finsbury Tower, 103–105 Bunhill Row, EC1Y 8TG. *T:* (020) 7448 9246, *Fax:* (020) 7448 9311; *e-mail:* peterhoma@chi.nhs.uk.

HOMAN, Maj.-Gen. John Vincent, CB 1980; CEng, FIMechE; Facilities Manager, Matra Marconi Space (formerly Marconi Space Systems), Portsmouth, 1982–92; *b* 30 June 1927; *s* of Charles Frederic William Burton Homan and Dorothy Maud Homan; *m* 1953, Ann Bartlett; one *s* two *d*. *Educ:* Haileybury; RMA Sandhurst; RMCS Shrivenham. BSc (Eng). Commnd, REME, 1948; Lt-Col 1967; Comdr REME 2nd Div., 1968–70; Col 1970; MoD 1970–72; CO 27 Comd Workshop REME, 1972–74; Brig. 1974; Dep. Dir, Electrical and Mechanical Engineering, 1st British Corps, 1974–76; Dir of Equipment Management, MoD, 1976–77; Dir Gen., Electrical and Mechanical Engrg, MoD,

1978–79; Maj.-Gen. 1978; Sen. Army Mem., RCDS, 1980–82. Col Comdt, REME, 1982–88. *Address:* Roedean, 25 The Avenue, Andover, Hants SP10 3EW. *T:* (01264) 351196. *Club:* Army and Navy.

HOMAN, Rear-Adm. Thomas Buckhurst, CB 1978; *b* 9 April 1921; *s* of late Arthur Buckhurst Homan and Gertrude Homan, West Malling, Kent; *m* 1945, Christine Oliver; one *d*. *Educ:* Maidstone Grammar Sch. RN Cadet, 1939; served War of 1939–45 at sea; Comdr 1958; Sec., British Defence Staff, Washington, 1961; Captain 1965; Defence Intell. Staff, 1965; Sec. to Comdr Far East Fleet, 1967; idc 1970; Dir Naval Officer Appts (S), 1971; Captain HMS Pembroke, 1973; Rear-Adm. 1974; Dir Gen., Naval Personal Services, 1974–78. Sub-Treasurer, Inner Temple, 1978–85. *Recreations:* reading, theatre, staying at home, cooking. *Address:* 602 Hood House, Dolphin Square, SW1V 3NJ. *T:* (020) 7798 8434. *Club:* Army and Navy.

HOME; *see* Douglas Home, and Douglas-Home, family name of Baroness Dacre and Earl of Home.

HOME, 15th Earl of *cr* 1605; **David Alexander Cospatrick Douglas-Home,** CVO 1997; CBE 1991; Baron Home 1473; Baron Dunglass 1605; Baron Douglas (UK) 1875; Chairman: Coutts & Co., since 1999; Coutts (Switzerland), since 2000 (Director, since 1999); *b* 20 Nov. 1943; *o s* of Baron Home of the Hirsel (Life Peer), KT, PC (who disclaimed his hereditary peerages for life, 1963) and Elizabeth Hester (*d* 1990), *d* of Very Rev. C. A. Alington, DD; *S* father, 1995; *m* 1972, Jane Margaret, *yr d* of late Col J. Williams-Wynne, CBE, DSO; one *s* two *d*. *Educ:* Eton College; Christ Church, Oxford (BA 1966). Director: Morgan Grenfell & Co. Ltd, 1974–99; Morgan Grenfell Egyptian Finance Co. Ltd, 1975–77; Morgan Grenfell (Scotland), then Deutsche Morgan Grenfell (Scotland) Ltd, 1978–99 (Chm., 1986–99); Morgan Grenfell (Asia) Ltd, 1978–82 (Dep. Chm., 1979–82); Arab Bank Investment Co., 1979–87; Agricultural Mortgage Corp., 1979–93; Arab-British Chamber of Commerce, 1975–84; Tandem Group (formerly EFG plc), 1981–96 (Chm., 1993–96); Credit for Exports, 1984–94; Deutsche Morgan Grenfell (Hong Kong), 1989–99; Deutsche Morgan Grenfell Asia Pacific Holdings Pte Ltd, 1989–99; Morgan Grenfell Thai Co., 1990–96; K & N Kenanaga Bhd, 1995–99; Kenanga DMG Futures Sdn Bhd, 1995–99; Deutsche Morgan Grenfell Group plc, 1996–99 (Chm., Jan.–March, 1999); Chairman: Morgan Grenfell Export Services, 1984–99; Morgan Grenfell Internat. Ltd, 1987–99; Cegelec Controls Ltd, 1991–94; K & N Kenanga Holdings Bhd, 1993–99; Grosvenor Estate Hldgs, 1993–99; MAN Ltd, 2000–; Trustee, Grosvenor Estate, 1993–. Chm., Committee for Middle East Trade, 1986–92 (Mem., 1973–75). Governor: Ditchley Foundn, 1977–; Commonwealth Inst., 1988–98. Trustee, RASE, 1999–. Elected Mem., H of L, 1999. *Recreations:* outdoor sports. *Heir:* Lord Dunglass, *qv*. *Address:* 99 Dovehouse Street, SW3 6JZ. *T:* (020) 7352 9060; The Hirsel, Coldstream, Berwickshire TD12 4LP. *T:* (01890) 882345. *Club:* Turf.

HOME, Anna Margaret, OBE 1993; Chief Executive, Children's Film and Television Foundation, since 1998; *b* 13 Jan. 1938; *d* of James Douglas Home and Janet Mary (*née* Wheeler). *Educ:* Convent of Our Lady, St Leonard's-on-Sea, Sussex; St Anne's Coll., Oxford (MA (Hons) Mod. Hist.). BBC Radio Studio Man., 1960–64; Res. Asst, Dir, Producer, Children's TV, 1966–70; Exec. Producer, BBC Children's Drama Unit, 1970–81: responsible for series such as Lizzie Dripping, Bagthorpe Saga, Moon Stallion; started Grange Hill, 1977; Controller of Programmes SE, later Dep. Dir of Programmes, TVS (one of the original franchise gp), 1981–86; Hd of Children's Programmes, BBC TV, 1986–98. Chm., 2nd World Summit on TV for Children, London, 1998. FRTS 1987. Pye Award for distinguished services to children's television, 1984; Eleanor Farjeon Award for services to children's literature, 1989; Judges Award, RTS, 1993; Lifetime Achievement Award, Women in Film and TV, 1996; BAFTA Special Award for Lifetime Achievement in Children's Programmes, 1997. *Publication:* Into the Box of Delights: a history of children's television, 1993. *Recreations:* theatre, literature, travel, gardening. *Address:* 3 Liberia Road, N5 1JP.

HOME, Prof. George, BL; FCIBS; Professor of International Banking, Heriot-Watt University, Edinburgh, 1978–85, Professor Emeritus, since 1985; *b* 13 April 1920; *s* of George Home and Leah Home; *m* 1946, Muriel Margaret Birleson; two *s* one *d*. *Educ:* Fort Augustus Village Sch.; Trinity Academy, Edinburgh; George Heriot's Sch., Edinburgh; Edinburgh Univ. (BL 1952). FCIBS; FIMgt. Joined Royal Bank of Scotland, 1936; served RAF, 1940–46; Dep. Man. Dir, Royal Bank of Scotland Ltd, 1973–80; Dep. Gp Man. Dir, Royal Bank of Scotland Gp Ltd, 1976–80; Director: Williams & Glyn's Bank Ltd, 1975–80; The Wagon Finance Corp. plc, 1980–85. Vice-Pres., Inst. of Bankers in Scotland, 1977–80. Chm., George Heriot's Trust, 1989–96. *Recreations:* fishing, gardening, reading, travel. *Address:* Bickley, 12 Barnton Park View, Edinburgh EH4 6HJ. *T:* (0131) 312 7648.

HOME, Sir William (Dundas), 14th Bt *cr* 1671 (NS), of Blackadder, Co. Berwick; consultant tree surgeon and horticulturalist; *b* 19 Feb. 1968; *s* of late John Home, *er s* of 13th Bt, and of Nancy Helen, *d* of H. G. Elliott, Perth, WA (she; *m* 1993, Rt Hon. Sir John Gorton, *qv*); *S* grandfather, 1992; *m* 1995, Dominique Meryl, *d* of Sydney Fischer, OBE; one *s* one *d*. *Educ:* Cranbrook Sch., Sydney, NSW. Member: Internat. Soc. of Arboriculture, 1991 (Founding Mem., Australian Chapter, 1997); Aust. Inst. of Horticulture, 1992; Nat. Arborists' Assoc. of Aust., 1999. *Recreations:* golf, scuba diving, fishing, tennis. *Heir:* *s* Thomas John Home, *b* 24 Nov. 1996. *Address:* 53 York Road, Queen's Park, NSW 2022, Australia. *Club:* Royal Sydney Golf (Sydney).

HOME ROBERTSON, John David; Member (Lab) East Lothian, Scottish Parliament, since 1999; Convener, Holyrood Progress Group, since 2000; *b* 5 Dec. 1948; *s* of late Lt-Col J. W. Home Robertson and Mrs H. M. Home Robertson; *m* 1977, Catherine Jean Brewster; two *s*. *Educ:* Ampleforth Coll.; West of Scotland Coll. of Agriculture. Farmer. Mem., Berwicks DC, 1975–78; Mem., Borders Health Bd, 1976–78. Chm., Eastern Borders CAB, 1977. MP (Lab) Berwick and E Lothian, Oct. 1978–83, E Lothian, 1983–2001. Opposition Scottish Whip, 1983–84; opposition spokesman on agric., 1984–87, 1988–90, on Scotland, 1987–88; PPS to Minister of Agriculture, Fisheries and Food, 1997–98; PPS to Minister for Cabinet Office, 1998–99; Member: Select Cttee on Scottish affairs, 1980–83; Select Cttee on Defence, 1990–97; British-Irish Parly Body, 1993–99. Chm., Scottish Gp of Lab MPs, 1983. Dep. Minister for Rural Affairs, Scottish Exec., 1999–2000. Founder, Paxton Trust, 1989. *Address:* Scottish Parliament, George IV Bridge, Edinburgh EH99 1SP. *T:* (0131) 348 5839. *Clubs:* East Lothian Labour, Prestonpans Labour.

HONDERICH, Prof. Edgar Dawn Ross, (Ted), PhD; Grote Professor of the Philosophy of Mind and Logic, University College London, 1988–98; *b* 30 Jan. 1933; *s* of John William Honderich and Rae Laura Armstrong, Baden, Canada; *m* 1st, 1964, Pauline Ann Marina Goodwin (marr. diss. 1972), *d* of Paul Fawcett Goodwin and Lena Payne, Kildare; one *s* one *d*; 2nd, 1989, Jane Elizabeth O'Grady, *d* of Major Robert O'Grady and Hon. Joan Ramsbotham, Bath. *Educ:* Kitchener Sch., Kitchener, Canada; Lawrence Park Sch., Toronto; University Coll., Univ. of Toronto (BA 1959); University Coll. London (PhD 1968). Literary Editor, Toronto Star, 1957–59; Lectr in Phil., Univ. of Sussex, 1962–64; Lectr in Phil., 1964–73, Reader in Phil., 1973–83, Prof. of Phil., 1983–88, and Head of Dept of Philosophy, 1988–93, UCL; Chm., Bd of Phil Studies, Univ. of London, 1986–89. Vis. Prof., Yale Univ., and CUNY, 1970. Editor: Internat. Library of Philosophy and Scientific Method, 1966–98; Penguin philosophy books, 1967–98; The Arguments of the Philosophers, 1968–98; The Problems of Philosophy: their past and present, 1984–98; radio, television, journalism. *Publications:* Punishment: the supposed justifications, 1969, 4th edn 1989; (ed) Essays on Freedom of Action, 1973; (ed) Social Ends and Political Means, 1976; Violence for Equality: inquiries in political philosophy (incorporating Three Essays on Political Violence, 1976), 1980, 2nd edn 1989; (ed with Myles Burnyeat) Philosophy As It Is, 1979; (ed) Philosophy Through Its Past, 1984; (ed) Morality and Objectivity, 1985; A Theory of Determinism: the mind, neuroscience, and life-hopes, 1988, 2nd edn, as The Consequences of Determinism, 1990; Mind and Brain, 1990; Conservatism, 1990; How Free Are You? The Determinism Problem, 1993 (trans. German, Japanese, Chinese, Swedish, Italian, Polish, Romanian); (ed) The Oxford Companion to Philosophy, 1995; Philosopher: a kind of life, 2000; phil articles in Amer. Phil Qly, Analysis, Inquiry, Jl of Theoretical Biol., Mind, Phil., Pol Studies, Proc. Aristotelian Soc., etc. *Recreations:* cycling, wine. *Address:* Fountain House, Gould's Ground, Frome BA11 3DW. *T:* (01373) 466854. *Club:* Garrick.

HONDROS, Ernest Demetrios, CMG 1996; DSc; FRS 1984; Director: Petten Establishment, Commission of European Communities' Joint Research Centre, 1985–95; Institute of Advanced Materials, Petten (Netherlands) and Ispra (Italy), 1988–95; Visiting Professor, Department of Materials, Imperial College of Science, Technology and Medicine, since 1988; *b* 18 Feb. 1930; *s* of Demetrios Hondros and Athanasia Paleologos; *m* 1968, Sissel Kristine Garder-Olsen; two *s*. *Educ:* Univ. of Melbourne (DSc MSc); Univ. of Paris (Dr d'Univ.). CEng, FIM. Research Officer, CSIRO Tribophysics Laboratory, Melbourne, 1955–59; Research Fellow, Univ. of Paris, Lab. de Chimie Minérale, 1959–62; National Physical Laboratory: Sen. Research Officer, Metallurgy Div., 1962–65; Principal Res. Fellow, 1965–68; Sen. Principal Res. Officer (Special Merit), 1974; Supt, Materials Applications Div., 1979–85. Membre d'Honneur, Société Française de Métallurgie, 1986; Mem., Academia Europaea, 1988. Hon. DSc London, 1997. Rosenhain Medallist, Metals Soc., 1976; Howe Medal, Amer. Soc. for Metals, 1978; A. A. Griffiths Medal and Prize, Inst. of Metals, 1987. *Publications:* numerous research papers and reviews in learned jls. *Recreations:* music, literature, walking. *Address:* 37 Ullswater Crescent, Kingston Vale, SW15 3RG. *T:* and *Fax:* (020) 8549 9526.

HONE, David; landscape and portrait painter; President, Royal Hibernian Academy of Arts, 1978–83; *b* 14 Dec. 1928; *s* of Joseph Hone and Vera Hone (*née* Brewster); *m* 1962, Rosemary D'Arcy; two *s* one *d*. *Educ:* Baymount School; St Columba's College; University College, Dublin. Studied art at National College of Art, Dublin, and later in Italy. Hon. RA, HRSA (ex-officio). *Recreations:* walking dogs, photography. *Address:* 25 Lower Baggot Street, Dublin 2, Ireland. *T:* (1) 6763746.

HONE, Michael Stuart, OBE 1993 (MBE 1978); JP; HM Diplomatic Service, retired; Ambassador and Consul-General, Iceland, 1993–96; *b* 19 May 1936; *s* of William John Hone and Marguerite (*née* Howe); *m* 1st, 1957; three *s*; 2nd, 1983, Dr Elizabeth Ann Balmer; one *s* one *d*. *Educ:* Westham Secondary Sch. Entered RN 1951; joined CRO, 1961; served Kingston, Nairobi, Lisbon, Bridgetown; FCO 1972; served Beirut, Baghdad, Canberra; Resident British Rep., St Vincent and Grenadines; Chief Secretary, St Helena, 1990. *Recreations:* family, walking, golf, water colour painting, stained glass. *Address:* Hillcroft, Station Approach, Crowhurst, Sussex TN33 9DB. *T:* (01424) 830444.

HONE, Richard Michael; QC 1997; a Recorder, since 1991; *b* 15 Feb. 1947; *s* of Maj. Gen. Sir Ralph Hone, KCMG, KBE, MC, TD, QC and Sybil Mary Hone (*née* Collins); *m* 1st, Sarah Nicholl-Carne (marr. diss. 1998); two *s*; 2nd, Diana Pavel; two *s*. *Educ:* St Paul's Sch. (Schol.); University Coll., Oxford (MA). Called to the Bar, Middle Temple, 1970 (Bencher, 1994; Cocks' Referee, 1988–94); Asst Recorder, 1987–91. Mem., Bar Professional Conduct Cttee, 1993–97; Chm., Jt Regulations Cttee, Inns of Court and Bar, 1995–2000; Legal Mem., Mental Health Review Tribunals, 2000–. KStJ 2000 (Asst Dir of Ceremonies, 1996). *Recreations:* wine, travel, fine art, photography. *Address:* Crown Office Chambers, Temple, EC4Y 7EP. *T:* (020) 7797 8100; 7 Caroline Place Mews, W2 4AQ. *Clubs:* Boodle's, Pratt's.

HONE, Robert Monro, MA; Headmaster, Exeter School, 1966–79; *b* 2 March 1923; *s* of late Rt Rev. Campbell R. Hone; *m* 1958, Helen Isobel, *d* of late Col H. M. Cadell of Grange, OBE; three *d*. *Educ:* Winchester Coll. (Scholar); New Coll., Oxford (Scholar). Rifle Brigade, 1942–45. Asst Master, Clifton Coll., 1948–65 (Housemaster, 1958–65). *Address:* 3 The Orchard, Throwleigh, Okehampton, Devon EX20 2HT.

HONEY, Elizabeth; *see* Filkin, E.

HONEY, Michael John; Chief Executive, London Ambulance Service, 1996–2000; *b* 28 Nov. 1941; *s* of Denis Honey and Mary Honey (*née* Henderson); four *d*; *m* 1996, Elizabeth Filkin, *qv*. *Educ:* Clifton College; Regent Street Polytechnic (DipArch); Columbia Univ. MArch (Urban Design); MSc (City Planning). City Planner, Boston Redevelopment Authority, 1968–70; Corporate Planning Manager, Bor. of Greenwich, 1970–74; Head, Exec. Office, Bor. of Croydon, 1974–80; Chief Executive: Bor. of Richmond upon Thames, 1980–88; LDDC, 1988–90; Gloucestershire CC, 1990–96. *Recreations:* flying, sailing.

HONEY, Air Vice-Marshal Robert John, CB 1991; CBE 1987; *b* 3 Dec. 1936; *s* of F. G. Honey; *m* 1956, Diana Chalmers; one *s* one *d*. *Educ:* Ashford Grammar Sch. Joined RAF as pilot, 1954; served: Germany, 1956–59; Singapore, 1961–64; Canada, 1968–69; India, 1982; UK intervening years; Dep. Commander RAF Germany, 1987–89; Air Sec., 1989–94. Dir, RAF Sports Bd, 1994–2001. Mountaineering expedns to Mulkila, India, 1979, Masherbrum, Pakistan, 1981. *Recreations:* climbing, mountaineering, ski-ing. *Club:* Royal Air Force.

HONEYCOMBE, Gordon; *see* Honeycombe, R. G.

HONEYCOMBE, Sir Robert (William Kerr), Kt 1990; FRS 1981; FREng; Goldsmiths' Professor of Metallurgy, University of Cambridge, 1966–84, now Emeritus; *b* 2 May 1921, *s* of William and Rachel Honeycombe (*née* Kerr); *m* 1947, June Collins; two *d*. *Educ:* Geelong Coll.; Univ. of Melbourne. Research Student, Department of Metallurgy, University of Melbourne, 1941–42; Research Officer, Commonwealth Scientific and Industrial Research Organization, Australia, 1942–47; ICI Research Fellow, Cavendish Laboratory, Cambridge, 1948–49; Royal Society Armourers and Brasiers' Research Fellow, Cavendish Laboratory, Cambridge, 1949–51; Senior Lecturer in Physical Metallurgy, University of Sheffield, 1951–55; Professor, 1955–66. Fellow of Trinity Hall, Cambridge, 1966–73, Hon. Fellow, 1975; Pres. 1973–80, Fellow, 1980–88, Emeritus Fellow, 1988, Clare Hall, Cambridge. Pres., Instn of Metallurgists, 1977; Pres., Metals Soc., 1980–81; Vice-Pres., Royal Institution, 1977–78; Treas., 1986–92, a Vice Pres., 1986–92, Royal Soc. Visiting Professor: University of Melbourne, 1962; Stanford

Univ., 1965; Monash Univ., 1974; Hatfield Meml Lectr, Sheffield Univ., 1979. FREng (FEng 1980). Hon. Member: Iron and Steel Inst. of Japan, 1979; Soc. Française de Métallurgie, 1981; Japan Inst. of Metals, 1983 (Gold Medallist, 1983); Indian Inst. of Metals, 1984. Mem. Ct of Assts, Goldsmiths' Co., 1977– (Prime Warden, 1986–87). Hon. DAppSc Melbourne, 1974; Hon. DMet Sheffield, 1983; Dr *hc* Montanistischen Wissenschaften Leoben, 1990. Rosenhain Medal of Inst. of Metals, 1959; Sir George Beilby Gold Medal, 1963; Ste-Claire-Deville Medal, 1971; Inst. of Metals Lectr and Mehl Medallist, AIME, 1976; Sorby Award, Internat. Metallographic Soc., 1986. *Publications:* The Plastic Deformation of Metals, 1968, 2nd edn 1984; Steels—Microstructure and Properties, 1981, 2nd edn (with H. K. D. H. Bhadeshia) 1995; papers in Proc. Royal Soc., Metal Science, etc. *Recreations:* gardening, photography, walking. *Address:* Barrabool, 46 Main Street, Hardwick, Cambridge CB3 7QS. *T:* (01954) 210501.

HONEYCOMBE, (Ronald) Gordon; author, playwright, television presenter, actor and narrator; *b* Karachi, British India, 27 Sept. 1936; *s* of Gordon Samuel Honeycombe and Dorothy Louise Reid Fraser. *Educ:* Edinburgh Acad.; University Coll., Oxford (MA English). National Service, RA, mainly in Hong Kong, 1955–57. Announcer: Radio Hong Kong, 1956–57; BBC Scottish Home Service, 1958; actor: with Tomorrow's Audience, 1961–62; with RSC, Stratford-on-Avon and London, 1962–63; Newscaster with ITN, 1965–77; Newscaster, TV-am, 1984–89. Acted in TV plays, series and shows including: That Was the Week that Was, 1964; The Brack Report, 1982; CQ, 1984; Numbats, 1994; appearances as TV presenter include: (also writer) A Family Tree and Brass Rubbing (documentaries), 1973; The Late Late Show (series), and Something Special (series), 1978; (also ed and jt writer) Family History (series), 1979; appearances as TV narrator include: Arthur C. Clarke's Mysterious World (series), 1980; A Shred of Evidence, 1984; stage appearances include: Play-back 625, Royal Court, 1970; Paradise Lost, York and Old Vic, 1975; Suspects, Swansea, 1989; Aladdin, Wimbledon, 1989–90, Bournemouth, 1990–91; Run For Your Wife!, tour, 1990; The Taming of the Shrew, 1998; film appearances include: The Medusa Touch; The Fourth Protocol; Let's Get Skase. Author of stage productions: The Miracles, Oxford, 1960 and (perf. by RSC), Southwark Cath., 1963 and Consett, 1970; The Princess and the Goblins (musical), Great Ayton, 1976; Paradise Lost, York, Old Vic and Edinburgh Fest., 1975–77; Waltz of my Heart, Bournemouth, 1980; Lancelot and Guinevere, Old Vic, 1980; author of TV plays: The Golden Vision, 1968; Time and Again, 1974 (Silver Medal, Film and TV Fest., NY, 1975); The Thirteenth Day of Christmas, 1986; radio dramatisations (all Radio 4): Paradise Lost, 1975; Lancelot and Guinevere, 1976; A King shall have a Kingdom, 1977; devised Royal Gala performances: God save the Queen!, Chichester, 1977; A King shall have a Kingdom, York, 1977. Directed and prod, The Redemption, Fest. of Perth, 1990. *Publications: non-fiction:* Nagasaki 1945, 1981; Royal Wedding, 1981; The Murders of the Black Museum, 1982; The Year of the Princess, 1982; Selfridges, 1984; TV-am's Official Celebration of the Royal Wedding, 1986; More Murders of the Black Museum, 1993; The Complete Murders of the Black Museum, 1995; *documentary novels:* Adam's Tale, 1974; Red Watch, 1976; Siren Song, 1992; *fiction:* The Redemption (play), 1964; Neither the Sea nor the Sand, 1969; Dragon under the Hill, 1972; The Edge of Heaven, 1981; contrib. national newspapers and magazines. *Recreations:* bridge, crosswords. *Address:* c/o Jules Bennett, PO Box 25, Moreton-in-Marsh, Glos GL56 9YJ. *T:* (07000) 458537.

HONEYMAN, Gitta; *see* Sereny, G.

HONEYSETT, Martin; cartoonist and illustrator, since 1969; *b* 20 May 1943; *s* of Donovan Honeysett and Kathleen Ethel Ivy Probert; *m* 1970, Maureen Elizabeth Lonergan (marr. diss. 1988); one *s* one *d* (and one *s* decd). *Educ:* Selhurst Grammar Sch.; Croydon Art Coll. (for one year). After leaving Art Coll., 1961, spent several years in NZ and Canada doing variety of jobs; returned to England, 1968; started drawing cartoons part-time, 1969; became full-time freelance, working for Punch, Private Eye and other magazines and newspapers, 1972; illustrator of series of books by the author/poet, Ivor Cutler. *Publications:* Private Eye Cartoonists No 4, 1974; Honeysett at Home, 1976; The Motor Show Book of Humour, 1978; The Not Another Book of Old Photographs Book, 1981; Microphobia, 1982; The Joy of Headaches, 1983; Fit for Nothing, 1984; Animal Nonsense Rhymes, 1984; The Best of Honeysett, 1985; (with Ivor Cutler): Gruts, 1961, repr. 1986; Life in a Scotch Sitting Room, vol. 2, 1984, 2nd edn 1998; Fremsley, 1987; Glasgow Dreamer, 1990, 2nd edn 1998. *Recreations:* walking, swimming. *Address:* 2 Burnham Cottages, Tram Road, Rye Harbour, East Sussex TN31 7TZ. *T:* (01797) 224355.

HONIGMANN, Prof. Ernst Anselm Joachim, DLitt; FBA 1989; Joseph Cowen Professor of English Literature, University of Newcastle upon Tyne, 1970–89, now Professor Emeritus; *b* Breslau, Germany, 29 Nov. 1927; *s* of Dr H. D. S. Honigmann and U. M. Honigmann (*née* Heilborn); *m* 1958, Dr Elsie M. Packman (*d* 1994); two *s* one *d*. *Educ:* Glasgow Univ. (MA 1948; DLitt 1966); Merton Coll., Oxford (BLitt 1950). Asst Lectr, 1951, Lectr, Sen. Lectr and Reader, 1954–67, Glasgow Univ.; Fellow, Shakespeare Inst., Birmingham Univ., 1951–54; Reader, Univ. of Newcastle upon Tyne, 1968–70. Jt Gen. Ed., The Revels Plays, 1976–2000. *Publications:* The Stability of Shakespeare's Text, 1965; Shakespeare: Seven Tragedies, the dramatist's manipulation of response, 1976; Shakespeare's Impact on his Contemporaries, 1982; Shakespeare: the lost years, 1985, 2nd edn 1998; John Weever: a biography, 1987; Myriad-minded Shakespeare, 1989, 2nd edn 1998; The Texts of Othello, 1996; *editor:* King John, 1954; Milton's Sonnets, 1966; The Masque of Flowers, 1967; Richard III, 1968; Twelfth Night, 1971; Paradise Lost, Book 10 (with C. A. Patrides), 1972; Shakespeare and his Contemporaries: essays in comparison, 1986; (with Susan Brock) Playhouse Wills 1558–1642, 1993; Othello, 1996. *Recreations:* grandchildren, gardening, travel. *Address:* 18 Wilson Gardens, Newcastle upon Tyne NE3 4JA.

HONORÉ, Prof. Antony Maurice; QC 1987; DCL Oxon; FBA 1972; Regius Professor of Civil Law, University of Oxford, 1971–88; Fellow, 1971–89, Acting Warden, 1987–89, All Souls College, Oxford; *b* 30 March 1921; *o s* of Frédéric Maurice Honoré and Marjorie Erskine (*née* Gilbert); *m* 1st, Martine Marie-Odette Genouville; one *s* one *d*; 2nd, Deborah Mary Cowen (*née* Duncan). *Educ:* Diocesan Coll., Rondebosch; Univ. of Cape Town; New Coll., Oxford (Rhodes Scholar, 1940); DCL Oxon 1969. Union Defence Forces, 1940–45; Lieut, Rand Light Infantry, 1942. BCL 1948. Vinerian Scholar, 1948. Advocate, South Africa, 1951; called to Bar, Lincoln's Inn, 1952, Hon. Bencher, 1971. Lectr, Nottingham Univ., 1948; Rhodes Reader in Roman-Dutch Law, 1957–70, Fellow of Queen's Coll., Oxford, 1949–64, of New Coll., 1964–70. Visiting Professor: McGill, 1961; Berkeley, 1968. Lectures: Hamlyn, Nottingham, 1982; J. H. Gray, Cambridge, 1985; Blackstone, Oxford, 1988; H. L. A. Hart, University Coll., Oxford, 1992; Maccabean, British Acad., 1998. Member: Internat. Acad. of Comparative Law, 1994; Accademia Costantiniana, 1994. Corresp. Member: Bavarian Acad. of Scis, 1992; Serbian Phil. Soc., 1988; Hon. Fellow, Harris Manchester Coll., Oxford. Hon. LLD: Edinburgh, 1977; South Africa, 1984; Stellenbosch, 1988; Cape Town, 1990. *Publications:* (with H. L. A. Hart) Causation in the Law, 1959, 2nd edn 1985 (trans. Japanese, 1991); Gaius, 1962; The South African Law of Trusts, 1965, 4th edn 1992; Tribonian, 1978; Sex Law, 1978; (with J. Menner) Concordance to the Digest Jurists, 1980; Emperors and Lawyers, 1981, 2nd edn 1994; The Quest for Security, 1982; Ulpian, 1982; Making Law Bind, 1987; About Law, 1996 (trans. Arabic and Ukranian, 1999); Law in the Crisis of Empire, 1998; Responsibility and Fault, 1999; *festschriften:* The Legal Mind (ed N. MacCormick and P. Birks), 1986; Relating to Responsibility (ed P. Carl and J. Gardner), 2001. *Address:* 94C Banbury Road, Oxford OX2 6JT. *T:* (01865) 559684.

HONOUR, (Patrick) Hugh, FRSL; writer; *b* 26 Sept. 1927; *s* of late Herbert Percy Honour and Dorothy Margaret Withers. *Educ:* King's Sch., Canterbury; St Catharine's Coll., Cambridge (BA). Asst to Dir, Leeds City Art Gall. and Temple Newsam House, 1953–54. Guest Curator for exhibn, The European Vision of America, National Gall. of Art, Washington, Cleveland Museum of Art, and, as L'Amérique vue par l'Europe, Grand Palais, Paris, 1976. FRSL 1972. Corresp. FBA 1986 (Serena Medal, 1995). *Publications:* Chinoiserie, 1961 (2nd edn 1973); Companion Guide to Venice, 1965 (rev. edn 1997); (with Sir Nikolaus Pevsner and John Fleming) The Penguin Dictionary of Architecture, 1966 (5th rev. edn as Penguin Dictionary of Architecture and Landscape Architecture, 1998); Neo-classicism, 1968 (4th edn 1977); The New Golden Land, 1976; (with John Fleming) The Penguin Dictionary of Decorative Arts, 1977 (rev. edn 1989); Romanticism, 1979; (with John Fleming) A World History of Art, 1982 (Mitchell Prize, 1982) (USA as The Visual Arts: a history, 5th edn 1999); The Image of the Black in Western Art IV, from the American Revolution to World War I, 1989 (Anisfield-Wolf Book Award in Race Relations, 1990); (with John Fleming) The Venetian Hours of Henry James, Whistler and Sargent, 1991; (ed) Edizione Nazionale delle Opere di Antonio Canova, vol. I, Scritti, 1994; Carnets Khmers, 1998. *Recreation:* gardening.

HONYWOOD, Sir Filmer (Courtenay William), 11th Bt *cr* 1660; FRICS; Regional Surveyor and Valuer, South Eastern Region, Central Electricity Generating Board, 1978–88; *b* 20 May 1930; *s* of Col Sir William Wynne Honywood, 10th Bt, MC, and Maud Naylor (*d* 1953), *d* of William Hodgson Wilson, Hexgreave Park, Southwell, Notts; *S* father, 1982; *m* 1956, Elizabeth Margaret Mary Cynthia (*d* 1996), *d* of Sir Alastair George Lionel Joseph Miller of Glenlee, 6th Bt; two *s* two *d*. *Educ:* Downside; RMA Sandhurst; Royal Agricultural College, Cirencester (MRAC Diploma). Served 3rd Carabiniers (Prince of Wales' Dragoon Guards). Farmed, 1954–64 (Suffolk Co. Dairy Herd Prodn Awards, 1955 and 1956); joined Agricl Land Service, MAFF, Maidstone, 1964; Asst Land Comr, 1966; Surveyor, Cockermouth, Cumbria, 1973–74; Senior Lands Officer, South Eastern Region, CEGB, 1974–78; pt time Sen. Valuer, Inland Revenue Valuation Service, Folkestone, 1989–90. Consultant on agricultural compensation/restoration, UK Nirex Ltd, 1988–90; Land Agency consultant, Nuclear Electric plc, 1993–94. Examiner in Agriculture: Incorporated Soc. of Estates & Wayleaves Officers, 1989–95; Soc. of Surveying Technicians, 1996–97. *Heir:* *s* Rupert Anthony Honywood, *b* 2 March 1957. *Address:* Greenway Forstal Farmhouse, Hollingbourne, Maidstone, Kent ME17 1QA. *T:* (01622) 880418.

HOOD, family name of **Viscounts Bridport** and **Hood**.

HOOD, 8th Viscount *cr* 1796, of Whitley, co. Warwick; **Henry Lyttelton Alexander Hood;** Bt 1778; Baron (Ire.) 1782, GB 1795; Partner, Hunters, Solicitors, since 1991; *b* 16 March 1958; *e s* of 7th Viscount Hood and of Diana Maud Hood, CVO (*née* Lyttelton); *S* father, 1999; *m* 1991, Flora, *yr d* of Comdr M. B. Casement, OBE, RN; three *s* one *d* (of whom one *s* one *d* are twins). *Educ:* Edinburgh Univ. (MA 1981). Qualified as solicitor, 1987. *Heir:* *s* Hon. Archibald Lyttelton Samuel Hood, *b* 16 May 1993. *Address:* 4 Alexander Street, W2 5NT.

HOOD, Prof. Christopher Cropper, DLitt; FBA 1996; Gladstone Professor of Government, Oxford University, since 2001; Fellow of All Souls College, Oxford, since 2001; *b* 5 March 1947; *s* of David White Hood and Margaret Cropper; *m* 1979, Gillian Thackwray White; two *d*. *Educ:* Univ. of York (BA 1968; DLitt 1987); Univ. of Glasgow (BLitt 1971). Lectr in Politics, Glasgow Univ., 1972–77 and 1979–86; Res. Fellow, Univ. of York, 1977–79; Prof. of Govt and Public Administration, Univ. of Sydney, 1986–89; Prof. of Public Admin and Public Policy, LSE, 1989–2000. Vis. Res. Fellow, Zentrum für Interdisziplinäre Forschung, Univ. of Bielefeld, 1982 and 1989; Sen. Teaching Fellow, Nat. Univ. of Singapore, 1984–85. *Publications:* Limits of Administration, 1976; (ed jtly) Big Government in Hard Times, 1981; (with A. Dunsire) Bureaumetrics, 1981; The Tools of Government, 1983; Administrative Analysis, 1986; (ed jtly) Delivering Public Services in Western Europe, 1988; (with A. Dunsire) Cutback Management in Public Bureaucracies, 1989; (with M. W. Jackson) Administrative Argument, 1991; Explaining Economic Policy Reversals, 1994; (ed jtly) Rewards at the Top, 1994; The Art of the State, 1998; (with C. Scott *et al*) Regulation inside Government, 1999; (jtly) Telecommunications Regulation, 1999. *Address:* All Souls College, Oxford OX1 4AL. *T:* (01865) 279379.

HOOD, Sir Harold (Joseph), 2nd Bt *cr* 1922, of Wimbledon, Co. Surrey; TD; Circulation Director: Universe, 1953–60; Catholic Herald, 1961–87; *b* 23 Jan. 1916; *e s* of Sir Joseph Hood, 1st Bt, and Marie Josephine (*d* 1956), *e d* of Archibald Robinson, JP, Dublin; *S* father, 1931; *m* 1946, Hon. Ferelith Rosemary Florence Kenworthy, *o d* of 10th Baron Strabolgi and Doris, *o c* of late Sir Frederick Whitley-Thomson, MP; two *s* two *d* (and one *s* decd). *Educ:* Downside Sch. Mem. Editorial Staff, The Universe, 1936–39; Asst Editor, The Catholic Directory, 1950, Managing Ed., 1959–60; Editor, The Catholic Who's Who, 1952 Edition. 2nd Lieutenant 58th Middx Battalion RE (AA) (TA) 1939; Lieut RA, 1941. GCSG (Holy See) 1986; (KSG 1964; KCSG 1978); Kt of Magistral Grace, SMO Malta, 1972. *Heir:* *s* John Joseph Harold Hood, *b* 27 Aug. 1952. *Address:* 31 Avenue Road, NW8 6BS. *T:* (020) 7722 9088. *Clubs:* Royal Automobile, MCC.

HOOD, James; MP (Lab) Clydesdale, since 1987; *b* 16 May 1948; *m* 1967, Marion McCleary; one *s* one *d*. *Educ:* Lesmahagow High Sch.; Motherwell Tech. Coll.; Nottingham Univ. WEA. Miner, Nottingham, 1968–87; NUM official, 1973–87 (Mem., NEC, 1990–92); Leader, Nottingham striking miners, 1984–85. Member: Ollerton Parish Council, 1973–87; Newark and Sherwood Dist Council, 1979–87. Mem., Select Cttee on European Legislation, 1987– (Chm., 1992–); founder Chm., All Party Gp on ME (Myalgic Encephalomyetis), 1987–92; Chm., Miners' Parly Gp, 1991–92; Convenor: Home Affairs Cttee, 1992–97; Scottish Lab. Gp of MPs, 1995–96; sponsor of three Private Members' Bills on under-age drinking, a Bill on ME, and a Bill on road transport safety. *Recreations:* reading, gardening. *Address:* House of Commons, SW1A 0AA. *T:* (020) 7219 4585; Ras-al-Ghar, 57 Biggar Road, Symington, Lanarkshire ML12 6FT. *Club:* Lesmahagow Miners Welfare Social (Hon. Mem.).

HOOD, Rear-Adm. John, CBE 1981; CEng, FIMechE; Director General Aircraft (Naval), 1978–81; *b* 23 March 1924; *s* of Charles Arthur Hood, architect, and Nellie Ormiston Brown Lamont; *m* 1948, Julia Mary Trevaskis (*d* 1993); three *s*. *Educ:* Plymouth Coll.; RN Engineering Coll., Keyham. Entered Royal Navy, 1945; RNEC, 1945–48; served in Illustrious, 1948; RN Air Stations, Abbotsinch, Anthorn, RAF West Raynham (NAFDU), 1948–51; HQ Min. of Supply, 1951–53; Air Engineer Officer, 1834 Sqdn, 1953–55, Aeroplane and Armament Experimental Estabt, 1955–57; Staff of Dir Aircraft Maintenance and Repair, 1957–59; AEO, HMS Albion, 1959–61; Sen. Air Engr, RNEC,

Manadon, 1961–62; Development Project Officer, Sea Vixen 2, Min. of Aviation, 1962–65; AEO, RNAS, Lossiemouth, 1965–67; Staff of Dir of Officer Appointments (E), 1967–69; Defence and Naval Attaché, Argentina and Uruguay, 1970–72; Sen. Officers War Course, 1973; Asst Dir, Naval Manpower Requirements (Ships), 1974–75; Head of Aircraft Dept (Naval), 1975–78. Comdr 1962, Captain 1969, Rear-Adm. 1979. *Recreations:* sailing, gardening. *Club:* RN Sailing Association.

HOOD, (Martin) Sinclair (Frankland), FSA; FBA 1983; archaeologist; *b* 31 Jan. 1917; *s* of late Lt-Comdr Martin Hood, RN, and late Mrs Martin Hood, New York; *m* 1957, Rachel Simmons; one *s* two *d*. *Educ:* Harrow; Magdalen Coll., Oxford. FSA 1953. British Sch. at Athens: student, 1947–48 and 1951–53; Asst Dir, 1949–51; Dir, 1954–62; Vice-Pres., 1996–. Student, British Inst. Archaeology, Ankara, 1948–49. Geddes-Harrower Vis. Prof. of Greek Art and Archaeology, Univ. of Aberdeen, 1968. Took part in excavations at: Dorchester, Oxon, 1937; Compton, Berks, 1946–47; Southwark, 1946; Smyrna, 1948–49; Atchana, 1949–50; Sakca-Gozu, 1950; Mycenae, 1950–52; Knossos, 1950–51, 1953–55, 1957–61, 1973 and 1987; Jericho, 1952; Chios, 1952–55. Hon. Dr, Univ. of Athens, 2000. *Publications:* The Home of the Heroes: The Aegean before the Greeks, 1967; The Minoans, 1971; The Arts in Prehistoric Greece, 1978; various excavation reports and articles. *Address:* The Old Vicarage, Great Milton, Oxford OX44 7PB. *T:* (01844) 279202. *Club:* Athenæum.

HOOD, Prof. Neil, CBE 2000; FRSE; Professor of Business Policy, University of Strathclyde, since 1979; *b* 10 Aug. 1943; *s* of Andrew Hood and Elizabeth Taylor Carruthers; *m* 1966, Anna Watson Clark; one *s* one *d*. *Educ:* Wishaw High Sch.; Univ. of Glasgow. MA, MLitt; FRSE 1987. Res. Fellow, Scottish Coll. of Textiles, 1966–68; Lectr, later Sen. Lectr, Paisley Coll. of Technol., 1968–78; Economic Advr, Scottish Economic Planning Dept, 1979; University of Strathclyde: Associate Dean, 1982–85, Dean, 1985–87, Strathclyde Business Sch.; Co-Dir, 1983–87, Dir, 1992–2001, Strathclyde Internat. Business Unit; Special Advr to Dep. Principal (Develt), then Principal (Develt), 1991–94. Dir, Locate In Scotland, 1987–89, and Dir, Employment and Special Initiatives, 1989–90, Scottish Develt Agency (on secondment). Vis. Prof. of Internat. Business, Univ. of Texas, Dallas, 1981; Vis. Prof., Stockholm Sch. of Economics, 1983–89. Trade Adviser, UNCTAD-GATT, 1980–85; Economic Consultant to Sec. of State for Scotland, 1980–87; Consultant to: Internat. Finance Corp., World Bank, 1982–84, 1991–; UN Centre on Transnational Corporations, 1982–84. Mem., Irvine Develt Corp., 1985–87. Non-executive Director: Euroscot Meat Exports Ltd, 1983–86; Scottish Develt Finance Ltd, 1984–90, 1993–96; Lanarkshire Industrial Field Executive Ltd, 1984–86; Prestwick Holdings PLC, 1986–87; Lamberton (Hldgs) Ltd, 1989–92; GA (Hldgs) Ltd, 1990–92; Shanks & McEwan Gp PLC, 1990–94; First Charlotte Assets Trust plc, 1990–92; Charlotte Marketing Services Ltd, 1991–94; Kwik-Fit plc, 1991–; I & S UK Smaller Cos Trust plc, 1992–98; Grampian Hldgs plc, 1993–; I & S Trustlink Ltd, 1994–97; Chm., John Dickie Gp Ltd, 1995–2000; Dep. Chm., British Polythene Industries plc, 1998–. Investment Advr, Castleforth Fund Managers Ltd, 1984–88; Corporate Advr, Scottish Power plc, 1990–; Chairman: Scottish Adv. Council, FI Gp, 1992–97 (non exec. Dir, 1997–); Scottish Equity Partners Ltd, 2000–; Dep. Chm., Scottish Enterprise, 2001–; Mem., Scottish Business Forum, 1998–2000. Member: various boards, CNAA, 1971–83; Industry and Employment Cttee, ESRC, 1985–87. Pres., European Internat. Business Assoc., 1986. Fellow, European Inst. of Advanced Studies in Management, Brussels, 1985–87. *Publications:* (with S. Young): Chrysler UK: Corporation in transition, 1977; Economics of Multinational Enterprise, 1979; European Development Strategies of US-owned Manufacturing Companies Located in Scotland, 1980; Multinationals in Retreat: the Scottish experience, 1982; Multinational Investment Strategies in the British Isles, 1983; (ed) Industrial Policy and the Scottish Economy, 1984; (with P. Draper, I. Smith and W. Stewart) Scottish Financial Sector, 1987; (ed with J. E. Vahlne) Strategies in Global Competition, 1987; (with S. Young and J. Hamill) Foreign Multinationals and the British Economy, Impact and Policy, 1988; (ed with S. Shaw) Marketing in Evolution, 1996; (ed with R. Kilis and J. E. Vahlne) Transition in the Baltic States, 1997; (ed with J. Birkinshaw) Multinational Corporate Evolution and Subsidiary Development, 1998; (ed with S. Young) The Globalisation of Multinational Enterprise and Economic Development, 1999; articles on internat. business, marketing, economic development and business policy, in various jls. *Recreations:* reading, writing, swimming, golf, gardening. *Address:* 95 Mote Hill, Hamilton ML3 6EA. *T:* (01698) 424870.

HOOD, Nicholas; *see* Hood, W. N.

HOOD, Peter Charles Freeman G.; *see* Gregory-Hood.

HOOD, Prof. Roger Grahame, CBE 1995; DCL; FBA 1992; Professor of Criminology, University of Oxford, since 1996; Director of the Centre for Criminological Research, and Fellow of All Souls College, Oxford, since 1973; *b* 12 June 1936; 2nd *s* of Ronald and Phyllis Hood; *m* 1963, Barbara Blaine Young (marr. diss. 1985); one *d*; *m* 1985, Nancy Stebbing (*née* Lynah). *Educ:* King Edward's Sch., Five Ways, Birmingham; LSE (BSc Sociology); Downing Coll., Cambridge (PhD); DCL Oxon 1999. Research Officer, LSE, 1961–63; Lectr in Social Admin, Univ. of Durham, 1963–67; Asst Dir of Research, Inst. of Criminology, Univ. of Cambridge, 1967–73; Fellow of Clare Hall, Cambridge, 1969–73; Reader in Criminology, Oxford Univ., 1973–96; Sub-Warden, All Souls Coll., Oxford, 1994–96. Vis. Prof., Univ. of Virginia Sch. of Law, 1980–90. Expert Consultant, UN, on death penalty, 1988, 1995–96 and 2000. Member: Parole Bd, 1972–73; SSRC Cttee on Social Sciences and the Law, 1975–79; Judicial Studies Bd, 1979–85; Parole System Review, 1987–88; Foreign Seretary's Death Penalty Panel, 1998–. Pres., British Soc. of Criminology, 1986–89. Hon. QC 2000. Sellin-Glueck Award, Amer. Soc. of Criminology, 1986. *Publications:* Sentencing in Magistrates' Courts, 1962; Borstal Re-assessed, 1965; (with Richard Sparks) Key Issues in Criminology, 1970; Sentencing the Motoring Offender, 1972; (ed) Crime, Criminology and Public Policy: Essays in Honour of Sir Leon Radzinowicz, 1974; (with Sir Leon Radzinowicz) Criminology and the Administration of Criminal Justice: a bibliography, 1976; (with Sir Leon Radzinowicz) A History of English Criminal Law, vol. 5, The Emergence of Penal Policy, 1986; The Death Penalty: a world-wide perspective, 1989, 2nd edn 1996; Race and Sentencing, 1992; (with Stephen Shute) The Parole System at Work, 2000. *Address:* 63 Iffley Road, Oxford OX4 1EF. *T:* (01865) 246084.

HOOD, Samuel Harold; Director, Defence Operational Analysis Establishment, Ministry of Defence, 1985–86; *b* 21 Aug. 1926; *s* of Samuel N. and Annie Hood; *m* 1959, Frances Eileen Todd; two *s* four *d*. *Educ:* Larne Grammar Sch., Co. Antrim; Queen's Univ., Belfast (BA Hons Maths). Joined Civil Service, staff of Scientific Advr, Air Min., 1948; Staff of Operational Res. Br., Bomber Comd, 1950; Scientific Officer, BCDU, RAF Wittering, 1954; Operational Res. Br., Bomber Comd, 1959; Staff of Chief Scientist (RAF), 1964; joined DOAE, 1965; Supt, Air Div., DOAE, 1969; Dir, Defence Sci. Divs 1 and 7, MoD, 1974; Head, Systems Assessment Dept, RAE, 1981. *Recreations:* walking, gardening, bird watching. *Address:* 26 Langford Drive, Mapua, Motueka 7150, Nelson, New Zealand.

HOOD, Sinclair; *see* Hood, M. S. F.

HOOD, (William) Nicholas, CBE 1991; Chairman, Wessex Water, 1989–99; *b* 3 Dec. 1935; *s* of Sir Tom Hood, KBE, CB, TD and of Joan, *d* of Richmond P. Hellyar; *m* 1st, 1963, Angela Robinson (marr. diss. 1990); one *s* one *d*; 2nd, 1994, Ann E. H. Reynolds. *Educ:* Clifton Coll. FIWEM 1992. CIMgt (CBIM 1990). Served DCLI, 1955–57. NEM General Insce Assoc. Ltd and Credit Insce Assoc. Ltd, 1958–64; G. B. Britton UK Ltd, eventually Sales and Marketing Dir, 1964–70; UBM Gp Plc, eventually Dir of Central Reg., 1970–84; Man. Dir, UBM Overseas Ltd, 1972–82; Dir, HAT Gp Ltd, 1984–86; Chm., Wessex Water Authy, 1987–89. Director: Bremhill Industries Plc, 1987–93; Winterthur Life UK (formerly Provident Life Assoc.) Ltd, 1988–; Western Adv. Bd, Nat. Westminster Bank, 1990–92; CU Environmental Trust Plc, 1992–98; APV plc, 1994–97; QHIT plc, 1998–; Brewin Dolphin plc, 2000–; Dep. Chm., Azurix, 1998–99; Chairman: MHIT plc, 1998–; Frogmat Ltd, 2001–. Dep. Chm., BITC, 1993–. Mem., DTI/DoE Adv. Cttee on Business and the Envmt, 1991–93. Chm., Water Aid Council, 1990–95; Chm., Water Services Assoc., 1995; Pres., IWSA, 1997–99 (Vice-Pres., 1993–97); Member: Water Trng Council, 1987–99; Foundn for Water Res., 1989–99; Sustainability South West, 2000–. Director: Harbourside Centre, 1996–99; Harbourside Foundn, 1998–; Clifton College Services Ltd, 2000. Chairman: Bristol 2000, 1995–98; @ Bristol, 1998–. Mem., Prince of Wales Council, 1993–. Chm. Trustees, Bristol Cancer Help Centre, 2000–; Trustee, West Country Rivers, 2000–. *Recreations:* fishing, painting. *Address:* @ Bristol, Anchor Road, Harbourside, Bristol BS1 5DB. *T:* (0117) 915 7225. *Clubs:* Army and Navy, Boodle's.

HOOK, David Morgan Alfred, FREng; Consultant, G. Maunsell & Partners, (Managing Director, 1984–88; Deputy Chairman, 1989–90); *b* 16 April 1931; *m* 1957, Winifred (*née* Brown); two *s* one *d*. *Educ:* Bancroft's School; Queens' College, Cambridge (MA). FICE, FIStructE; FREng (FEng 1985). Holland & Hannen and Cubitts, 1954–58; Nuclear Civil Constructors, 1958–62; G. Maunsell & Partners (Consulting Engineers), 1962–, Partner, 1968–. Liveryman, Engineers' Co., 1985. *Publications:* papers in Jl of IStructE. *Recreations:* golf, bridge. *Club:* Oxford and Cambridge.

HOOK, Neil Kenneth, MVO 1983; HM Diplomatic Service; Consul-General, Osaka, since 2001; *b* 24 April 1945; *s* of George Edward Hook and Winifred Lucy Hook (*née* Werrell); *m* 1973, Pauline Ann Hamilton; one *s* one *d*. *Educ:* Varndean Grammar Sch., Brighton; Sheffield Univ. (Dip. Management Studies). Joined Diplomatic Service, 1968; served FCO, Moscow, Tokyo; Dhaka, 1980–83; S Africa Dept, FCO, 1984; S Asia Dept, FCO, 1985–86; Tokyo, 1987–92; N America Dept, FCO, 1993–95; Ambassador to Turkmenistan, 1995–98; FCO, 1998–99; High Court, Swaziland, 1999–2001. *Recreations:* ballads, bridge, Hash House Harriers, photography. *Address:* c/o Foreign and Commonwealth Office, SW1A 2AH.

HOOKER, Michael Ayerst, PhD; Development Director, Newton Prep (school for intellectually gifted children), since 1998; *b* 22 Jan. 1923; *s* of late Albert Ayerst Hooker, late of Broomsleigh Park, Seal Chart, Kent, and Marjorie Mitchell Hooker (*née* Gunson). *Educ:* Marlborough; St Edmund Hall, Oxford (MA 1944); Univ. of the Witwatersrand (PhD 1952). Home Guard, Oxford Univ. Sen. Trng Corps and Army Cadet Force (TARO), 1940–48. British Council, 1945–47; Schoolmaster, England and S Africa, 1947–51; London Diocesan Bd of Educn, 1952–66; Visual Aids and Public Relations, 1953–59; Chmn, Fedn of Conservative Students, 1944; Party Candidate (C) Coventry East, 1955; various offices, Conservative Commonwealth Council, 1955–60. Wells Organisation, fund raising in UK and NZ, 1957–58; Man. Dir, Hooker Craigmyle & Co. Ltd (first institutional fund raising consultants in UK), 1959–72; Man. Dir, Michael Hooker and Associates Ltd, 1972–79; Develt Dir, The Look Wide Trust, 1979–80; Chief Exec. Gov., Truman and Knightley Educn Trust, 1981–87 (Gov., 1977–87); Exec. Dir, 1988–91, Sen. Educnl Advr, 1991–93, Jerwood Award; Dir, Donnington Grove Inter-Faith Prog., 1991–2001; Cultural Dir, Shi-tennoji International, 1992–98. From 1957, has helped to raise nearly £70 million for various good causes, incl. 13 historic cathedrals, univs, colleges, schools, medical causes, welfare charities, etc. Mem., Adv. Cttee on Charitable Fund Raising, Nat. Council of Social Service, 1971–73. Jt Founder and Chm., Friends of Friends, subseq. Routledge Soc., 1985–90; Chm., Dame Flora Robson Meml Cttee, 1994–96; Vice-Pres., Donnington Grove Soc., 1999–; Trustee: Ross McWhirter Foundn, 1976–98 (a Vice-Pres., 1999–); Dicey Trust, 1978–93; Jerwood Oakham Foundn, 1981–92; Police Convalescence and Rehabilitation Trust, 1985–92; Hon. Councillor, NSPCC, 1981–; Governor: Oakham Sch., 1971–83; Shi-tennoji Sch., 1986–2001; All Hallows House, 1991–98; Newton Prep. 1991–93. Patron: Elton John AIDS Foundn, 1993–98; Martlets Hospice, 1997–; Brighton & Hove Inter-Faith Contact Gp, 1999–. *Publications:* various pamphlets and broadcasts on charities, historic churches, educnl issues, law and taxation, Christian stewardship of money. *Address:* Flat 8, 85 Marine Parade, Brighton BN2 1AJ. *T:* (01273) 624265, *Fax:* (01273) 624304.

HOOKER, Prof. Morna Dorothy, DD; Lady Margaret's Professor of Divinity, University of Cambridge, 1976–98; Fellow of Robinson College, Cambridge, since 1976; *b* 19 May 1931; *d* of Percy Francis Hooker, FIA, and Lily (*née* Riley); *m* 1978, Rev. Dr W. David Stacey, MA (*d* 1993). *Educ:* Univ. of Bristol (research schol.); Univ. of Manchester (research studentship). MA (Bristol 1956, Oxford 1970 and Cambridge 1976); PhD (Manchester 1966); DD (Cambridge 1993). Research Fellow, Univ. of Durham, 1959–61; Lectr in New Testament Studies, King's Coll., London, 1961–70; Lectr in Theology, Oxford, and Fellow, Linacre Coll., 1970–76 (Hon. Fellow, 1980); Lectr in Theology, Keble Coll., 1972–76. Visiting Fellow, Clare Hall, Cambridge, 1974; Visiting Professor: McGill Univ., 1968; Duke Univ., 1987 and 1989. FKC 1979. Lectures: T. W. Manson meml, 1977; A. S. Peake meml, 1978; Henton Davies, 1979; Ethel M. Wood, 1984; James A. Gray, Duke Univ., 1984; W. A. Sanderson, Melbourne, 1986; Didsbury, Manchester, 1988; Brennan, Louisville, 1989; St Paul's, 1989; Perkins, Texas, 1990; Shaffer, Yale, 1995; John Albert Hall, Victoria, BC, 1996; Smyth, Columbia Decatur, 1996; Chuen King, Hong Kong, 2001. Pres., SNTS, 1988–89. Jt Editor, Jl of Theological Studies, 1985–. Hon. Fellow, Westminster Coll., Oxford, 1996. Hon. DLitt Bristol, 1994; Hon. DD Edinburgh, 1997. *Publications:* Jesus and the Servant, 1959; The Son of Man in Mark, 1967; (ed jtly) What about the New Testament?, 1975; Pauline Pieces, 1979; Studying the New Testament, 1979; (ed jtly) Paul and Paulinism, 1982; The Message of Mark, 1983; Continuity and Discontinuity, 1986; From Adam to Christ, 1990; A Commentary on the Gospel according to St Mark, 1991; Not Ashamed of the Gospel, 1994; The Signs of a Prophet, 1997; Beginnings, 1997; contribs to New Testament Studies, Jl of Theological Studies, Theology, Epworth Review, etc. *Recreations:* Molinology, walking, music. *Address:* Robinson College, Grange Road, Cambridge CB3 9AN.

HOOKER, Ronald George, CBE 1985; FREng; CIMgt; FRSA; Chairman: Management & Business Services Ltd, since 1972; EAC Ltd, since 1993; company directorships; *b* 6 Aug. 1921; *m* 1954, Eve Pigott; one *s* one *d*. *Educ:* Wimbledon Technical Coll.; London Univ. (external). Hon. FIEE (FIProdE 1980); FREng (FEng 1984). CIMgt (CBIM 1972). Apprentice, Philips Electrical Ltd, 1937–41, Develt Engr, 1945–48; FBI, 1948–50; Dir and Gen. Man., Brush Electrical Engineering Co. Ltd, 1950–60; Man. Dir, K & L Steelfounders & Engineers Ltd, 1960–65; Man. Dir, Associated Fire Alarms Ltd,

1965–68; Chm. and Man. Dir, Crane Fruehauf Trailers Ltd, 1968–71; Dir of Manufacture, Rolls Royce (1971) Ltd, 1971–73; Chm. and Man. Dir, John M. Henderson (Holdings) Ltd, 1973–75; Chm., Thomas Storey Ltd, 1984–96. Dir, Computing Devices Hldgs Ltd, 1986–. Pres., Engrg Employers' Fedn, 1986–88 (Mem. Management Bd, 1977–); Mem., Engrg Council, 1982–86. Past Pres., IProdE, 1974–75 (Hon. Life MIProdE 1980). Freeman, City of London. *Publications:* papers on management and prodn engrg to BIM, ICMA, IProdE and IMechE. *Recreations:* gardening, reading, music. *Address:* Loxborough House, Bledlow Ridge, near High Wycombe, Bucks HP14 4AA. *T:* (01494) 481486. *Clubs:* Athenæum, Lansdowne.

HOOKS, Air Vice-Marshal Robert Keith, CBE 1979; CEng, FRAeS; RAF retired; *b* 7 Aug. 1929; *s* of late Robert George Hooks and Phyllis Hooks; *m* 1954, Kathleen (*née* Cooper); one *s* one *d. Educ:* Acklam Hall Sch.; Constantine Coll., Middlesbrough. Bsc(Eng) London. Commissioned RAF, 1951; served at RAF stations West Malling, Fassberg, Sylt, 1952–55; RAF Technical Coll., Henlow, 1956; Fairey Aviation Co., 1957–58; Air Ministry, 1958–60; Skybolt Trials Unit, Eglin, Florida, 1961–63; Bomber Command Armament Sch., Wittering, 1963–65; OC Engrg Wing, RAF Coll., Cranwell, 1967–69; HQ Far East Air Force, 1969–71; Supt of Armament A&AEE, 1971–74; Director Ground Training, 1974–76; Director Air Armament, 1976–80; Vice-Pres. (Air), Ordnance Board, 1980; Dir Gen. Aircraft 2, MoD (Procurement Exec.), 1981–84; Divl Dir (European Business), Westland Helicopters, 1984–85; Projects Dir, Helicopter Div., Westland plc, 1985–87. Dep. Man. Dir, E H Industries Ltd, 1987–94. *Address:* 34 Thames Crescent, Maidenhead, Berks SL6 8EY. *Club:* Royal Air Force.

HOOKWAY, Sir Harry (Thurston), Kt 1978; Pro-Chancellor, Loughborough University of Technology, 1987–93; *b* 23 July 1921; *s* of William and Bertha Hookway; *m* 1956, Barbara Olive (*d* 1991), *o d* of late Oliver and Olive Butler; one *s* one *d. Educ:* Trinity Sch. of John Whitgift; London Univ. (BSc, PhD). Various posts in industry, 1941–49; DSIR, 1949–65; Asst Dir, National Chemical Laboratory, 1959; Dir, UK Scientific Mission (North America), Scientific Attaché, Washington, DC, and Scientific Adviser to UK High Comr, Ottawa, 1960–64; Head of Information Div., DSIR, 1964–65; CSO, DES, 1966–69; Asst Under-Sec. of State, DES, 1969–73; Dep. Chm. and Chief Exec., The British Library Bd, 1973–84; Chairman: Publishers Databases Ltd, 1984–87; LA Publishing Ltd, 1986–89. Chairman: UNESCO Internat. Adv. Cttee for Documentation, Libraries and Archives, 1975–79; British Council Libraries Adv. Cttee, 1982–86; President: Inst. of Information Scientists, 1973–76; Library Assoc., 1985. Mem., Royal Commn on Historical Monuments (England), 1981–89. Governor, British Inst. for Recorded Sound, 1981–86. Dir, Arundel Castle Trustees Ltd, 1976–. Hon. FLA, 1982; Hon. FIInfSc. Hon. LLD Sheffield, 1976; Hon. DLitt Loughborough, 1980. Gold Medal, Internat. Assoc. of Library Assocs, 1985. *Publications:* various contribs to jls of learned societies. *Recreations:* music, travel. *Address:* 3 St James Green, Thirsk, N Yorks YO7 1AF. *Club:* Athenæum.

HOOLAHAN, Anthony Terence; QC 1973; a Recorder of the Crown Court, 1976–97; a Social Security Commissioner, 1986–97; a Child Support Commissioner, 1993–98; *b* 26 July 1925; *s* of late Gerald and Val Hoolahan; *m* 1949, Dorothy Veronica Connochie; one *s* one *d* (and one *d* decd). *Educ:* Dorset House, Littlehampton, Sussex; Framlingham Coll., Suffolk; Lincoln Coll., Oxford (MA). Served War, RNVR, 1943–46. Oxford Univ., 1946–48. Called to Bar, Inner Temple, 1949, Bencher, 1980; called to the Bar of Northern Ireland, 1980, QC (Northern Ireland) 1980. Chairman: Richmond Soc., 1976–80; Trustees, Richmond Museum, 1988–95. Gov., St Elizabeth's Sch., Richmond, 1990–. *Publications:* Guide to Defamation Practice (with Colin Duncan, QC), 2nd edn, 1958; contrib. to Halsbury's Laws of England, Atkin's Court Forms. *Recreation:* swimming. *Address:* Fair Lawn, Ormond Avenue, Richmond, Surrey TW10 6TN.

HOOLE, John George Aldick; Director, Barbican Art Galleries, 1998–2001; *b* 3 Feb. 1951; *s* of John Aldick Hoole and Pamela Betty Coleman; *m* 1975, Lindsey G. Rushworth; one *s* one *d. Educ:* Univ. of East Anglia (BA Hons History of Art). Asst Keeper of Art, Southampton Art Gall., 1974–78; Asst Dir, Museum of Modern Art, Oxford, 1978–82; Curator, Barbican Art Gall., 1982–98. *Recreations:* parenthood, books. *Address:* 54 Western Road, Oxford OX1 4LG. *T:* (01865) 245268.

HOOLEY, Prof. Christopher, FRS 1983; Distinguished Research Professor, Department of Mathematics, University of Wales College of Cardiff, since 1995; *b* 7 Aug. 1928; *s* of Leonard Joseph Hooley, MA, BSc, and Barbara Hooley; *m* 1954, Birgitta Kniep; two *s. Educ:* Wilmslow Preparatory Sch.; Abbotsholme Sch.; Corpus Christi Coll., Cambridge (MA, PhD, ScD). Captain, RAEC, 1948–49 (SO III, British Troops in Egypt). Fellow, Corpus Christi Coll., Cambridge, 1955–58; Lectr in Mathematics, Univ. of Bristol, 1958–65; Prof. of Pure Mathematics, Univ. of Durham, 1965–67; University College, Cardiff, subseq. University of Wales, Cardiff: Prof. of Pure Maths, 1967–95; Hd of Dept of Pure Maths, 1967–88; Dean of Faculty of Science, 1973–76; Dep. Principal, 1979–81; Hd of Sch. of Maths, 1988–95; Dep. Principal, 1991–94. Visiting Member: Inst. for Advanced Study, Princeton, 1970–71, and Fall Terms, 1976, 1977, 1982, 1983; Institut des Hautes Etudes Scientifiques, Paris, 1984. Adams Prize, Cambridge, 1973; Sen. Berwick Prize, London Mathematical Soc., 1980. *Publications:* Applications of Sieve Methods to the Theory of Numbers, 1976; (ed with H. Halberstam) Recent Progress in Analytic Number Theory, 1981; memoirs in diverse mathematical jls. *Recreations:* classic cars; antiquities. *Address:* Rushmoor Grange, Backwell, Bristol BS48 3BN. *T:* (01275) 462363.

HOOLEY, Frank Oswald; retired; *b* 30 Nov. 1923; *m* 1945, Doris Irene Snook; two *d. Educ:* King Edward's High Sch., Birmingham; Birmingham Univ. Admin. Asst, Birmingham Univ., 1948–52; Sheffield Univ.: Asst Registrar, 1952–65; Sen. Asst Registrar, 1965–66; Registrar, Fourah Bay Coll., Sierra Leone, 1960–62 (secondment from Sheffield); Sen. Admin. Asst, Manchester Poly., 1970–71; Chief Admin. Offr, Sheffield City Coll. of Educn, 1971–74. Res. Asst to John Tomlinson, MEP, 1984–88. MP (Lab) Sheffield, Heeley, 1966–70 and Feb. 1974–1983. Chm., Parly Liaison Gp for Alternative Energy Strategies, 1978; formerly Member, Select Committees on Public Accounts, Estimates, Sci. and Technol., Overseas Aid, Foreign Affairs, and Procedure. Contested (Lab) Stratford-on-Avon, 1983. Vice-Chm., Sutton Coldfield Lab. Party, 1988–98; Chm., Brecon and Radnorshire Lab. Party, 2000–. Chairman: Co-ordinating Cttee, Internat. Anti-Apartheid Year, 1978; Central Reg., UNA, 1994–98; Mem., UK Commn, UNESCO, 1999–2000. Governor: Bishop Vesey Sch., 1989–98; Banners Gate Jun. Sch., 1993–98. Trustee, Sutton Coldfield Municipal Charities, 1986–98. *Address:* 50 Caenbrook Meadow, Presteigne, Powys LD8 2NE. *T:* (01544) 260790.

HOOLEY, John Rouse; DL; Chief Executive, West Sussex County Council, 1975–90; Clerk to the Lieutenancy of West Sussex, 1976–90; *b* 25 June 1927; *s* of Harry and Elsie Hooley; *m* 1953, Gloria Patricia Swanston; three *s* one *d. Educ:* William Hulme's Sch., Manchester; Lincoln Coll., Oxford; Manchester Univ. LLB London. Admitted Solicitor (Hons), 1952. Served Lancashire Fusiliers, 1946–48. Asst Solicitor, Chester, Carlisle and Shropshire, 1952–65; Asst Clerk, Cornwall, 1965–67; Dep. Clerk and Dep. Clerk of the Peace, W Sussex, 1967–74; County Sec., W Sussex, 1974–75. Member: Chichester HA, 1990–95 (Chm., 1993–95); W Sussex HA, 1995–96. Chm., Downland Housing Gp, 1998–. DL W Sussex, 1991. *Recreations:* gardening, music. *Address:* Bosvigo, Lavant Road, Chichester PO19 1RQ.

HOON, Rt Hon. Geoffrey (William); PC 1999; MP (Lab) Ashfield, since 1992; Secretary of State for Defence, since 1999; *b* 6 Dec. 1953; *s* of Ernest and June Hoon; *m* 1981, Elaine Ann Dumelow; one *s* two *d. Educ:* Nottingham High Sch.; Jesus College, Cambridge (MA). Called to the Bar, Gray's Inn, 1978. Labourer at furniture factory, 1972–73; Lectr in Law, Leeds Univ., 1976–82. Vis. Prof. of Law, Univ. of Louisville, 1979–80. In practice at Nottingham, 1982–84. An Opposition Whip, 1994–95; opposition spokesman on IT, 1995–97; Parly Sec., 1997–98, Minister of State, 1998–99, Lord Chancellor's Dept; Minister of State, FCO, 1999. European Parliament: Mem. (Lab) Derbyshire, 1984–94; Mem., Legal Affairs Cttee, 1984–94; President: Standing Delegn to China, 1987–89; Standing Delegn to US, 1989–92. Chm., Friends of Music, 1992–94; Vice-Chm. and Gov., Westminster Foundn, 1994–97. *Recreations:* football, squash, running, cinema, music. *Address:* House of Commons, SW1A 0AA; 8 Station Street, Kirkby-in-Ashfield, Notts NG17 7AR.

HOOPER, family name of **Baroness Hooper**.

HOOPER, Baroness *cr* 1985 (Life Peer), of Liverpool and of St James's in the City of Westminster; **Gloria Dorothy Hooper;** *b* 25 May 1939; *d* of late Frances and Frederick Hooper. *Educ:* University of Southampton (BA Hons Law); Universidad Central, Quito, Ecuador (Lic. de Derecho Internacional). Admitted to Law Society, Solicitor, 1973; Partner, Taylor Garrett, 1974–84. MEP (C) Liverpool, 1979–84; contested (C) Merseyside West, European Parly elecn, 1984. Baroness in Waiting, 1985–87; Parly Under Sec. of State, DES, 1987–88, Dept of Energy, 1988–89, DoH, 1989–92; Dep. Speaker, H of L, 1993–. Mem., Parly Delegns to Council of Europe and WEU, 1992–97. Pres., Canning House, 1997–. FRGS 1982; Fellow, Industry and Parlt Trust, 1983; FRSA 1986. *Publications:* Cases on Company Law, 1967; Law of International Trade, 1968. *Recreations:* theatre and walking. *Address:* House of Lords, Westminster, SW1A 0PW. *T:* (020) 7219 3000.

HOOPER, Hon. Sir Anthony, Kt 1995; **Hon. Mr Justice Hooper;** a Judge of the High Court of Justice, Queen's Bench Division, since 1995; *b* 16 Sept 1937; *s* of late Edwin Morris Hooper and of Greta Lillian Chissim; *m* 1st, Margrethe Frances (*née* Hansen) (marr. diss. 1986); one *s* one *d*; 2nd, Heather Christine (*née* Randall). *Educ:* Sherborne; Trinity Hall, Cambridge (Scholar; MA, LLB). 2nd Lieut, 7th RTR, 1956–57. Called to the Bar, Inner Temple, 1965, Bencher, 1993; admitted to Law Society of British Columbia, 1969; QC 1987; a Recorder, 1986–95; Presiding Judge, NE Circuit, 1997–2000. Asst Lectr and Lectr, Univ. of Newcastle upon Tyne, 1962–65; Asst and Associate Prof., Faculty of Law, Univ. of British Columbia, 1965–68; Prof. Associé, Univ. de Laval, 1969–70; Prof., Osgoode Hall Law Sch., York Univ., 1971–73. Visiting Professor: Univ. de Montréal, 1972, 1973; Osgoode Hall, 1984. Chm. Govs, Inns of Court Sch. of Law, 1996–99. *Publications:* (ed) Harris's Criminal Law, 21st edn 1968; articles in legal jls. *Address:* Royal Courts of Justice, Strand, WC2A 2LL.

See also R. Hooper.

HOOPER, Dr John David, CEng; CDir; Chief Executive, Royal Society for the Prevention of Accidents, since 1997; *b* 22 March 1947; *s* of Wilfred John Hooper and Vera Hooper; *m* 3rd, 1991, Veronica Jane Bligh; one *s* four *d* by previous marriages. *Educ:* Bath Univ. (BSc 1972); Salford Univ. (MSc 1982); Columbia Pacific Univ. (PhD 1985). CEng 1980. Apprentice engr, UKAEA, 1964–69; Project Engr, United Glass Ltd, 1969–74; Sen. Project Engr, Cadbury Schweppes Ltd, 1974–78; Dep. Gp Chief Engr, Gp Energy Manager and Sales Manager, Glaxo Pharmaceuticals PLC, 1978–85; Chief Exec., Chartered Inst. Building, 1985–87; Dir, Pan European Ops, Carlson Mktg Gp, Inc., 1987–90; Business Strategy Manager, Scottish Hydro Electric PLC, 1990–94; Chief Exec., British Sports Fedn, 1994–97. FIMgt (FInstM 1985); FInstD 1985. Mem., ACENVO, 1997. Patron, Lifeskills Learning for Living, 1997–. Advr, Business in the Arts, 1993–. FRSA 1999. *Publications:* Heat Energy Recovery in the Pharmaceutical Industry, 1982; Energy Management and Marketing in the Pharmaceutical Industry, 1985. *Recreations:* flying light aircraft, DIY. *Address:* Tedstone Heights, Tedstone Delamere, Bromyard, Herefordshire HR7 4PS.

HOOPER, Ven. Michael Wrenford; Archdeacon of Hereford, since 1997; *b* 2 May 1941; *m* 1968, Rosemary Anne Edwards; two *s* two *d. Educ:* Crypt Sch., Gloucester; St David's Coll., Lampeter; St Stephen's House, Oxford. Ordained deacon, 1965, priest, 1966; Asst Curate, St Mary Magdalene, Bridgnorth, Shropshire, dio. of Hereford, 1965–70; Vicar of Minsterley and Rector of Habberley, 1970–81; Rural Dean of Pontesbury, 1976–81; Rector and Rural Dean of Leominster, 1981–97; Prebendary of Hereford Cathedral, 1981–. *Recreations:* walking, cycling, dogs, reading, music. *Address:* Archdeacon's House, The Close, Hereford HR1 2NG. *T:* (01432) 272873.

HOOPER, Noel Barrie; Judge of the High Court, Hong Kong, 1981–93; *b* 9 Nov. 1931; twin *s* of late Alfred Edward Hooper and Constance Violet Hooper; *m* 1959, Pauline Mary (*née* Irwin); two *d. Educ:* Prince of Wales Sch., Kenya; St Peter's Hall, Oxford (BA 1954). Called to the Bar, Gray's Inn, 1956. Advocate of High Court, Uganda, 1956–61; Magistrate, Basutoland, 1961–64 and Hong Kong, 1964–68; Sen. Magistrate, Hong Kong, 1968–73; Principal Magistrate, 1973–76; Dist Judge, 1976–81; Comr of the Supreme Court of Brunei, 1983–86, 1986–89, 1990–93, 1994–. *Recreations:* tennis, cricket, golf, reading. *Clubs:* MCC; Corhampton Golf; Forty.

HOOPER, Richard; Chairman, Radio Authority, since 2000 (Member, 1990–94); Managing Partner, Hooper Communications, since 1988; *b* 19 Sept. 1939; *s* of late Edwin Morris Hooper and Greta Lillian (*née* Goode); *m* 1964, Meredith Jean Rooney; two *s* one *d. Educ:* Sherborne Sch.; Worcester Coll., Oxford (BA German and Russian, 1963; MA). National Service, 2nd Lieut 7th RTR, BAOR, 1958–59. Gen. trainee, BBC, 1963; Radio Producer, BBC Further Educn, 1964–66; Harkness Fellow, USA, 1967–68; Sen. Radio and TV Producer, BBC Open Univ. Prodns, 1969–72; Dir, National Develt Prog. in Computer Assisted Learning, 1973–77; Man. Dir, Mills & Allen Communications, 1978–79; Dir, Prestel, Post Office Telecommunications, 1980–81; Chief Exec., Value Added Systems and Services, BT, 1982–86; Man. Dir, Super Channel, 1986–88. Non-exec. Chm., IMS Gp plc, 1997–; non-executive Director: MAI, 1993–96; United News & Media, 1996–97; LLP Gp plc, 1997–98; Informed Sources Internat., 1997–99; Superscape plc, 2000–; Sen. non-exec. Dir, Informa Gp plc, 1999–. Special Staff Consultant to President Lyndon Johnson's Commn on Instructional Technology, 1968. Chm., The Pluralists, 1992–. MInstD 1993; FRSA 1994. *Publications:* (ed) Colour in Britain, 1965; (ed) The Curriculum, Context, Design and Development, 1971; Unnatural Monopolies, 1991; contrib. to books and jls. *Recreations:* the family, theatre, golf. *Clubs:* Garrick; Vincent's (Oxford).

See also Sir A. Hooper.

HOOPER, Toby Julien Anderson; QC 2000; a Recorder, since 2000; *b* 14 Dec. 1950; *o s* of Lt Col Denys Anderson Hooper and Paula Hooper (*née* Glascoe); *m* 1981, Anna, *d* of Dr Brian Locke, FRCR and Rachel Locke; one *s* two *d*. *Educ:* Downside Sch.; Durham Univ. (BA Hons 1972). Called to the Bar, Inner Temple, 1973, Bencher, 2000; in practice at the Bar, 1974–; Asst Recorder, 1998–2000. Bar Council: Additional Mem., Fees Collection Cttee, 1990–97, Remuneration Cttee, 1998– (Vice-Chm. (Civil), 2000–); Mem. (as SE Circuit Rep.), 2000–; Chm., Pupillage Bd, 2001–; Mem., Inner Temple Advocacy Trng Cttee, 1998–; Chm., Continuing Educn Cttee, Personal Injuries Bar Assoc., 1999–; Rep., SE Circuit, Inns' Advocacy Trng Cttee, 2000–. Hon. Sec., Incorp. Inns of Court Mission (Gainsford Youth Club, Covent Garden), 1979–90. Hon. Sec., Thomas More Soc., 1994–97; Mem. Council, St Gregory's Soc., 1997–; Trustee, St Gregory's Charitable Trust, 1998–. *Publications:* (ed) Inner Temple Advocacy Handbook, 1998, 4th edn 2001; (Gen. Ed.) Bar Council Taxation and Retirement Benefits Handbook, 3rd edn 2000; (contrib.) Butterworth's Professional Negligence Service, 2000–. *Recreations:* choral singing, walking. *Address:* 12 King's Bench Walk, Temple, EC4Y 7EL. *T:* (020) 7583 0811. *Club:* Bank of England Sports.

HOOSON, family name of **Baron Hooson**.

HOOSON, Baron *cr* 1979 (Life Peer), of Montgomery in the County of Powys and of Colomendy in the County of Clwyd; **Hugh Emlyn Hooson;** QC 1960; a Recorder of the Crown Court, 1972–93 (Recorder of Swansea, 1971); *b* 26 March 1925; *s* of late Hugh and Elsie Hooson, Colomendy, Denbigh; *m* 1950, Shirley Margaret Wynne, *d* of late Sir George Hamer, CBE; two *d*. *Educ:* Denbigh Gram. Sch.; University Coll. of Wales; Gray's Inn (Bencher, 1968; Vice-Treasurer, 1985; Treasurer, 1986). Called to Bar, 1949; Wales and Chester Circuit (Junior, 1954–55; Leader, 1971–74); Dep. Chm., Flint QS, 1960–71; Dep. Chm., Merioneth QS, 1960–67, Chm., 1967–71; Recorder of Merthyr Tydfil, 1971. MP (L) Montgomery, 1962–79. Leader, 1966–79, Pres., 1983–86, Welsh Liberal Party. Vice-Chm. Political Cttee, North Atlantic Assembly, 1975–79. Dir (non-exec.), Laura Ashley (Holdings), 1985–96 (Chm., 1995–96); Chm., Severn River Crossing, 1991–2000. President: Royal Nat. Eisteddfod of Wales, Newtown, 1965; Llangollen Internat. Eisteddfod, 1987–93; Wales International, 1995–98. Gov., Inst. of Grassland and Envmtl Res., 1989–92. Hon. Professorial Fellow, Univ. of Wales Aberystwyth (formerly UCW), 1971–. *Address:* Summerfield, Llanidloes, Powys SY18 6AQ. *T:* (01686) 412298; *T:* (office) (020) 7219 5226; (home) (020) 7405 4160.

HOOTON, Patrick Jonathan; His Honour Judge Hooton; a Circuit Judge, since 1994; *b* 30 June 1941; *s* of late John Charles Hooton, CMG, MBE, QC (Bermuda) and of Patricia Jessica Hooton (*née* Manning); *m* 1st, 1970, Anne Josephine Wells; one *s*; 2nd, 1980, Jocelyn Margaret East; one *s* one *d*. *Educ:* Downside Sch., Somerset; Trinity Coll., Cambridge. Commonwealth Develt Corp., 1964–68; Van Moppes & Co., 1969–71; called to the Bar, Gray's Inn, 1973; practised on Western Circuit, 1973–94. Mem., Club Taurino, 1994–. *Recreations:* field sports, sailing, ski-ing, Southampton FC and Hampshire CC. *Clubs:* Lawyers' Fishing; Hampshire CC.

HOPCROFT, George William; HM Diplomatic Service, retired; consultant on international relations; *b* 30 Sept. 1927; *s* of late Frederick Hopcroft and Dorothy Gertrude (*née* Bourne); *m* 1951, Audrey Joan Rodd; three *s* one *d*. *Educ:* Chiswick Grammar Sch.; London Univ. (BCom); Brasenose Coll., Oxford; INSEAD, Fontainebleau. Auditor with Wm R. Warner, 1946; entered Export Credits Guarantee Dept, 1946; Asst Trade Comr, Madras, 1953–57; Sen. Underwriter, ECGD, 1957–65; joined FO, 1965; First Sec. (Commercial), Amman, 1965–69; First Sec. (Econ.), Bonn, 1969–71; First Sec. (Comm.), Kuala Lumpur, 1971–75; FCO, 1975–78; Counsellor (Comm. and Econ.), Bangkok, 1978–81; FCO 1981. Founder Mem., Export and Overseas Trade Adv. Panel (EOTAP), 1982–; operational expert in for. affairs, attached to Govt of Belize, 1982–83. *Recreations:* leisure and circumnavigation, German and French literature, song, film, sport (Civil Service ½ mile champion, 1947), serendipity. *Clubs:* Civil Service; British (Bangkok).

HOPE, family name of **Barons Glendevon** and **Hope of Craighead, Marquess of Linlithgow** and **Baron Rankeillour**.

HOPE OF CRAIGHEAD, Baron *cr* 1995 (Life Peer), of Bamff in the District of Perth and Kinross; **James Arthur David Hope;** PC 1989; a Lord of Appeal in Ordinary, since 1996; *b* 27 June 1938; *s* of Arthur Henry Cecil Hope, OBE, WS, Edinburgh and Muriel Ann Neilson Hope (*née* Collie); *m* 1966, Katharine Mary Kerr, *d* of W. Mark Kerr, WS, Edinburgh; twin *s* one *d*. *Educ:* Edinburgh Acad.; Rugby Sch.; St John's Coll., Cambridge (Open Schol. 1956, BA 1962, MA 1978; Hon. Fellow, 1995); Edinburgh Univ. (LLB 1965). National Service, Seaforth Highlanders, 1957–59 (Lieutenant 1959). Admitted Faculty of Advocates, 1965; Standing Junior Counsel in Scotland to Board of Inland Revenue, 1974–78; Advocate-Depute, 1978–82; QC (Scotland) 1978; Dean, Faculty of Advocates, 1986–89; Lord Justice-Gen. of Scotland and Lord Pres. of Court of Session, 1989–96. Chm., Med. Appeal Tribunal, 1985–86; Legal Chm., Pensions Appeal Tribunal, 1985–86. Mem., Scottish Cttee on Law of Arbitration, 1986–89. Chm., Mem. Bd of Trustees, Nat. Liby of Scotland, 1989–96. Chm. Bd, Inst. of Advanced Legal Studies, 2000–. President: Stair Soc., 1993–; Internat. Criminal Law Assoc., 2000–2001. Chm., Sub-Cttee E (Law and Instns), H of L Select Cttee on EU, 1998–. Hon. Prof. of Law, Aberdeen, 1994–. Hon. Member: Canadian Bar Assoc., 1987; SPTL, 1991; Hon. Fellow, Amer. Coll. of Trial Lawyers, 2000. Hon. Bencher: Gray's Inn, 1989; Inn of Court of NI, 1995. Chancellor, Strathclyde Univ., 1998– (Fellow, 2000). Hon. LLD: Aberdeen, 1991; Strathclyde, 1993; Edinburgh, 1995. *Publications:* (ed jtly) Gloag & Henderson's Introduction to the Law of Scotland, 7th edn 1968, asst editor, 8th edn 1980 and 9th edn 1987, (contrib.) 11th edn 2001; (ed jtly) Armour on Valuation for Rating, 4th edn 1971, 5th edn 1985; (with A. G. M. Duncan) The Rent (Scotland) Act 1984, 1986; (contrib.) Stair Memorial Encyclopaedia of Scots Law. *Recreations:* walking, ornithology, music. *Address:* 34 India Street, Edinburgh EH3 6HB. *T:* (0131) 225 8245; House of Lords, SW1A 0PW. *T:* (020) 7219 3202. *Club:* New (Edinburgh).

HOPE, Alan; JP; Leader, West Midlands County Council Opposition Group (C), 1981–86; *b* 5 Jan. 1933; *s* of George Edward Thomas Hope and Vera Hope; *m* 1960, Marilyn Dawson; one *s* one *d*. *Educ:* George Dixon Grammar Sch., Birmingham. Councillor, Birmingham CC, 1964–73; West Midlands County Council: Councillor, 1973; Leader, 1980–81; Chairman: Trading Standards, 1977–79; Finance, 1979–80. JP Birmingham 1974. *Address:* Whitehaven, 7 Rosemary Drive, Little Aston Park, Sutton Coldfield, West Midlands B74 3AG. *T:* (0121) 353 3011. *Club:* Royal Commonwealth Society.

HOPE, Bob, (Leslie Townes Hope), Hon. KBE 1998 (Hon. CBE 1976); Congressional Gold Medal, US, 1963; film, stage, radio, TV actor; *b* England, 29 May 1903; family migrated to US, 1907; *m* 1934, Dolores Reade; two adopted *s* two adopted *d*. *Educ:* Fairmont Gram. Sch. and High Sch., Cleveland, O. Started career as dance instructor, clerk, amateur boxer; formed dancing act for Fatty Arbuckle review. After Mid-West tours formed own Company in Chicago; toured New York and joined RKO Vaudeville and Keith Circuit; first important stage parts include: Ballyhoo, 1932; Roberta, 1933; Ziegfield Follies, 1935; first radio part, 1934. Entered films, 1938. *Films include:* Big Broadcast of 1938; Some Like It Hot; The Cat and the Canary; Road to Singapore; The Ghost Breakers; Road to Zanzibar; Star Spangled Rhythm; Nothing but the Truth; Louisiana Purchase; My Favorite Blonde; Road to Morocco; Let's Face It; Road to Utopia; Monsieur Beaucaire; My Favorite Brunette; They Got Me Covered; The Princess and the Pirate; Road to Rio; Where There's Life; The Great Lover; My Favorite Spy; Road to Bali; Son of Paleface; Here Come the Girls; Casanova's Big Night; The Seven Little Foys; The Iron Petticoat; That Certain Feeling; Beau James; The Facts of Life; Bachelor in Paradise; The Road to Hong Kong; Call Me Bwana; A Global Affair; Boy, Did I Get a Wrong Number!; Eight on the Run; How to Commit Marriage; Cancel My Reservation. *TV series:* The Bob Hope Show, 1950–93; numerous guest appearances. Five Royal Command Performances. Awarded 44 honorary degrees; more than a thousand awards and citations for humanitarian and professional services. KCSG 1998. *Publications:* They've Got Me Covered, 1941; I Never Left Home, 1944; So This is Peace, 1946; This One's on Me, 1954; I Owe Russia $1200, 1963; Five Women I Love, 1966; The Last Christmas Show, 1974; Road to Hollywood, 1977; Confessions of a Hooker, 1985; Don't shoot, it's only me, 1990. *Address:* Hope Enterprises, Inc., 3808 Riverside Drive, Burbank, CA 91505, USA.

HOPE, Christopher, FRSL; writer; *b* 26 Feb. 1944; *s* of Dennis Tully and Kathleen Mary Hope (*née* McKenna); *m* 1967, Eleanor Klein; two *s*. *Educ:* Christian Brothers College, Pretoria; Univ. of Natal (BA Hons 1970); Univ. of Witwatersrand (MA 1973). FRSL 1990. Pringle Prize, English Acad. of Southern Africa, 1972; Cholmondeley Award, Soc. of Authors, 1974; Arts Council Bursary, 1982; Travelex, Travel Writers' Award, 1997. *Publications:* Cape Drives, 1974; A Separate Development, 1981 (David Higham Prize for Fiction); In the Country of the Black Pig, 1981; Private Parts and Other Tales, 1982 (rev. edn as Learning to Fly and Other Tales, 1990) (Internat. PEN Silver Pen Award); Kruger's Alp, 1984 (Whitbread Prize for Fiction); Englishmen, 1985; The Hottentot Room, 1986; Black Swan, 1987; White Boy Running, 1988 (CNA Award, S Africa); My Chocolate Redeemer, 1989; Moscow! Moscow!, 1990; Serenity House, 1992; The Love Songs of Nathan J. Swirsky, 1993; Darkest England, 1996; (ed jtly) New Writing, 1996; Me, the Moon and Elvis Presley, 1997; Signs of the Heart: love and death in Languedoc, 1999; Heaven Forbid, 2002; contribs to BBC, newspapers, jls. *Recreation:* getting lost. *Address:* c/o Rogers, Coleridge & White, 20 Powis Mews, W11 1JN.

HOPE, Sir Colin (Frederick Newton), Kt 1996; MA; FREng, FIMechE, FIMI; Executive Chairman, T & N plc, 1995–98; *b* 17 May 1932; *s* of Frederick and Mildred Hope; *m* 1959, Gillian Carden; two *s*. *Educ:* Stowe Sch.; St Catharine's College, Cambridge (MA). CEng, FREng (FEng 1995). Glacier Metal Co., 1963–70; Managing Dir, 1970–73, Exec. Chm., 1973–75, Covrad; Director: Engineering Group, Dunlop, 1975–79; Tyres UK Dunlop, 1979–82; Tyres Europe Dunlop Holdings, 1982–84; Chief Exec., Dunlop Engineering International, 1984–85; Gp Man. Dir, 1985–89, Chm. and Chief Exec., 1989–95, Turner & Newall, subseq. T & N plc. Chairman: Bryant Gp, 1992–2001; Ibstock Johnsen, 1993–97 (Dir, 1989–). Pres., SMMT, 1991–93. Trustee, Nat. Motor Mus., 1991–. Hon. DSc Cranfield, 1998. *Recreations:* theatre, music, vintage motor cars. *Address:* Hornby Cottage, High Street, Welford-on-Avon, Warwickshire CV37 8EF. *T:* (01665) 576142. *Club:* Royal Automobile.

HOPE, Most Rev. and Rt Hon. David Michael; *see* York, Archbishop of.

HOPE, Sir John (Carl Alexander), 18th Bt *cr* 1628 (NS), of Craighall; *b* 10 June 1939; *s* of Sir Archibald Philip Hope, 17th Bt, OBE, DFC, AE and of Ruth, *y d* of Carl Davis; *S* father, 1987; *m*1968, Merle Pringle, *d* of late Robert Douglas, Holbrook, Ipswich; one *s* one *d*. *Educ:* Eton. *Heir:* *s* Alexander Archibald Douglas Hope, *b* 16 March 1969. *Address:* 9 Westleigh Avenue, SW15 6RF.

HOPE, Marcus Laurence Hulbert, OBE 1998; HM Diplomatic Service; Consul-General, Montreal, 1998–Feb. 2002; *b* 2 Feb. 1942; *s* of late Laurence Frank Hope, OBE; *m* 1980, Uta Maria Luise Müller-Unverfehrt; one *s*. *Educ:* City of London Sch.; Sydney C of E Grammar Sch.; Univ. of Sydney (BA); Univ. of London (BA Hons). Joined HM Diplomatic Service, 1965; Third Sec., CRO, 1965; MECAS, 1966; Second Sec., Tripoli, 1968; FCO, 1970; First Sec., 1972; Head of Chancery, Dubai, 1974; First Sec. (Commercial), Bonn, 1976; FCO, 1980; NATO Defence Coll., Rome, 1984; Counsellor, Beirut, 1984–85; Counsellor and Head of Chancery, Berne, 1985–89; Dep. Head of Mission and Counsellor (Commercial and Aid), Jakarta, 1989–92; Hd, Western Europe Dept, FCO, 1992–95; Ambassador to Zaire, also (non-resident) to the Congo, 1996–98. *Recreation:* classical guitar. *Address:* c/o Foreign and Commonwealth Office, King Charles Street, SW1A 2AH.

HOPE, Philip Ian; MP (Lab and Co-op) Corby, since 1997; *b* 19 April 1955; *s* of A. G. Hope and Grace Hope; *m* 1980, Allison, *d* of John and Margaret Butt; one *s* one *d*. *Educ:* Wandsworth Comp. Sch.; St Luke's Coll., Exeter Univ. (BEd). Teacher, Kettering Sch. for Boys; Youth Policy Advr, NCVO; Hd, Young Volunteer Resources Unit, Nat. Youth Bureau; Mgt and Community Work Consultant, Framework, 1985–96; Dir, Framework in Print publishing co-operative. Member (Lab and Co-op): Kettering BC, 1983–87; Northants CC, 1993–97. Contested (Lab and Co-op) Kettering, 1992. PPS to Minister of State for Housing and Planning, 1999–2001, to Dep. Prime Minister, 2001–. Member: Public Accounts Select Cttee, 1997–98; NI Grand Cttee, 1997–; Cttee of Selection, 1999–; Chairman: All-Party Parly Gp for charities and voluntary orgns, 1997–; All-Party Lighting Gp, 2001–. Vice Chm., PLP Social Security Deptl Cttee, 1997–; Mem., Leadership Campaign Team with responsibility for educn, 1997–99. *Publications:* Making Best Use of Consultants, 1993; (jtly) Performance Appraisal, 1995; various curriculum and training packs for schs and youthworkers and information booklets for young people. *Recreations:* tennis, juggling, computing, gardening. *Address:* House of Commons, SW1A 0AA.

HOPE, Prof. Ronald Anthony, (Tony), PhD; FRCPsych; Professor of Medical Ethics, University of Oxford, since 2000; Fellow, St Cross College, Oxford, since 1990; *b* 16 March 1951; *s* of Ronald Sidney Hope and Marion Nutall Hope (*née* Whittaker); *m* 1981, Sally Louise Hirsh; two *d*. *Educ:* Dulwich Coll.; New Coll., Oxford (Bosanquet Open Schol. in Medicine; MA, PhD 1978; BM BCh 1980). FRCPsych 1997. W. H. Rhodes Travel Schol., 1969; doctoral res. in neurobiol. at NIMR, 1973–76; preclinical trng, Middx Hosp., 1976–77; clinical trng, Univ. of Oxford, 1977–80; House surgeon, Royal United Hosp., Bath, 1980–81; House physician, John Radcliffe Hosp., Oxford, 1981; SHO-Registrar rotation in Psychiatry, Oxford, 1981–85; Wellcome Trust Trng Fellow in Psychiatry, Oxford hosps, 1985–87; University of Oxford: Clin. Lectr in Psychiatry, 1987–90; Leader, Oxford Practice Skills Project, 1990–95; Lectr in Practice Skills, 1995–2000; Reader in Medicine, 1996–2000; Dir, Ethox (Oxford Centre for Ethics and Communication in Health Care Practice), 1999–; Hon. Consultant Psychiatrist, Warneford Hosp. Oxford, 1990–. Res. Prize and Medal, RCPsych, 1989. *Publications:* Oxford Handbook of Clinical Medicine, 1985 (trans. 9 langs), 4th edn 1998; Essential Practice in Patient-Centred Care, 1995; Manage Your Mind, 1995 (trans. 3 langs); contrib. numerous papers and chapters, mainly in fields of Alzheimer's Disease and med.

ethics. *Recreations:* family, literature, wine, walking. *Address:* Ethox Centre, Institute of Health Sciences, Old Road, Oxford OX3 7LF. *T:* (01865) 226936; St Cross College, Oxford OX1 3LZ.

HOPE, Tony; *see* Hope, R. A.

HOPE-DUNBAR, Sir David, 8th Bt *cr* 1664; *b* 13 July 1941; *o s* of Sir Basil Douglas Hope-Dunbar, 7th Bt, and of his 2nd wife, Edith Maude Maclaren (*d* 1989), *d* of late Malcolm Cross; *S* father, 1961; *m* 1971, Kathleen, *yr d* of late J. T. Kenrick; one *s* two *d*. *Educ:* Eton; Royal Agricultural College, Cirencester. ARICS 1966. Founder, Dunbar & Co., now Allied Dunbar PLC. *Recreations:* fishing, shooting. *Heir: s* Charles Hope-Dunbar, *b* 11 March 1975. *Address:* Banks Farm, Kirkcudbright DG6 4XF. *T:* (01557) 330424.

HOPE JOHNSTONE, family name of **Earl of Annandale and Hartfell**.

HOPE-MORLEY, family name of **Baron Hollenden**.

HOPE-WALLACE, (Dorothy) Jaqueline, CBE 1958; *b* 1909; 2nd *d* of Charles Nugent Hope-Wallace and Mabel Chaplin. *Educ:* Lady Margaret Hall, Oxford. Entered Ministry of Labour, 1932; transferred to National Assistance Board, 1934; Under-Sec., 1958–65; Under-Sec., Min. of Housing and Local Govt, 1965–69, retired. Commonwealth Fellow, 1952–53. Comr, Public Works Loan Bd, 1974–78; Member Board: Corby Develt Corp., 1969–80; Inst. for Recorded Sound, 1971–74, 1979–83 (Chm. 1975–76); Nat. Corp. for Care of Old People (now Centre for Policy on Ageing), 1973–81 (Chm., 1978–80); Mem., Nat. Sound Archive Adv. Cttee, 1983–84. Mem. Bd of Govs, UCH, 1970–74; Pres., Friends of UCH, 1999– (Chm., 1973–85). *Recreations:* arts, travel. *Address:* 17 Ashley Court, Morpeth Terrace, SW1P 1EN.

HOPETOUN, Earl of; Andrew Victor Arthur Charles Hope; *b* 22 May 1969; *s* and *heir* of Marquess of Linlithgow, *qv*; *m* 1993, Skye, *e d* of Major Bristow Bovill; twin *s* two *d*. *Educ:* Eton; Exeter Coll., Oxford. A Page of Honour to the Queen Mother, 1985–87. *Heir: s* Viscount Aithrie, *b* 25 July 2001. *Address:* c/o Hopetoun House, South Queensferry, West Lothian EH30 9SL.

HOPEWELL, John Prince; Consultant Surgeon, Royal Free Hospital, 1957–86 (Hon. Consulting Surgeon (Urology), since 1986); *b* 1 Dec. 1920; *s* of Samuel Prince and Wilhelmina Hopewell; *m* 1st, 1959, Dr Natalie Bogdan (*d* 1975); one *s* one *d*; 2nd, 1984, Dr Rosemary Radley-Smith. *Educ:* Bradfield Coll., Berks; King's Coll. Hosp., London. RAMC, 1945–48. Postgrad. education at King's Coll. Hosp. and Brighton, Sussex, and Hosp. for Sick Children, Gt Ormond Street. Formerly Cnslt Surgeon, Putney Hosp. and Frimley Hosp., Surrey. Mem., Hampstead DHA, 1982–85; Chm., Camden Div., BMA, 1985–93; Past Chairman: Med. Cttee, Royal Free Hosp.; N Camden Dist Med. Cttee; Chm., Hon. Med. Staff Cttee, Hosp. of St John and St Elizabeth, 1993–95. Founder Mem., British Transplantation Soc., 1972; Member: Internat. Soc. of Urology; British Assoc. Urol. Surgeons; Past President: Chelsea Clinical Soc.; Section of Urology, RSM, 1982–83; Fellowship of Postgrad. Medicine. Founder Mem., Assoc. of Univ. Hospitals. Hon. Mem., NY Section, AUA. Hunterian Prof., RCS, 1958. Mem. Court of Examiners, RCSE, 1969–75. Member: Friends of St Helena; Soc. of Ornamental Woodturners. *Publications:* Three Clinical Cases of Renal Transplantation, British Medical Jl, 1964, and contribs to various medical journals. *Address:* Old Vicarage, Langrish, Petersfield, Hants GU32 1QY. *T:* (01730) 261354.

HOPGOOD, Richard Simon; Director of Policy and Deputy Secretary-General, Archbishops' Council, since 1999; *b* 7 Oct. 1952; *s* of Ronald and Daphne Hopgood; *m* 1988, Elizabeth Wakefield; one *d*. *Educ:* Christ's Hosp.; Wadham Coll., Oxford (BA). On staff of Church Comrs, 1977–98 (Dep. Sec., Policy and Planning, 1994–98). *Recreations:* reading, photography, cycling. *Address:* Archbishops' Council, Church House, Great Smith Street, SW1P 3NZ. *T:* (020) 7898 1530.

HOPKIN, Sir Bryan; *see* Hopkin, Sir W. A. B.

HOPKIN, Prof. Deian Rhys, PhD; FRHistS; Vice-Chancellor and Chief Executive, South Bank University, since 2001; *b* 1 March 1944; *s* of late Islwyn Hopkin and Charlotte Hopkin (nee Rees); *m* 1st, 1966, Orian Jones (marr. diss. 1989); two *d*; 2nd, 1989, Lynne Hurley; two *s*. *Educ:* Llandovery Coll.; University Coll. of Wales, Aberystwyth (BA 1965; PhD 1981). FRHistS 1985. Lectr, 1967–84, Sen. Lectr, 1984–91, Hd of Dept, 1989–91, Dept of History, UCW Aberystwyth; Staff Tutor, Open Univ., 1974–76; Dean, Human Scis, 1992–96, Vice-Provost, 1996–2001, City of London Poly., then London Guildhall Univ. Chm., Cityside Regeneration Ltd, 1997–. Member: Council, Nat. Liby of Wales, 1975–88; Gen. Adv. Council, BBC, 1988–95; Exec., UK Arts and Humanities Service, 1996–. Mem., London Eur. Progs Cttee, 2000–. Mem., Hackney Community Coll. Corp., 2000–. Freeman: City of London, 2000; Co. of Inf. Technologists, 2000. FRSA 1997. Trustee, Bishopsgate Foundn, 1999–. *Publications:* (ed jtly) History and Computing, 1987; (ed jtly) Class, Community and the Labour Movement: Wales and Canada 1850–1930, 1989; (ed jtly) The Labour Party in Wales 1900–2000, 2000; contrib. articles to Internat. Rev. Social Hist., Llafur, etc. *Recreations:* music (especially jazz), writing, broadcasting. *Address:* South Bank University, 103 Borough Road, SE1 0AA. *T:* (020) 7815 6004.

HOPKIN, John Raymond; DL; **His Honour Judge Hopkin;** a Circuit Judge, since 1979; *b* 23 June 1935; *s* of George Raymond Buxton Hopkin and Muriel Hopkin; *m* 1965, Susan Mary Limb; one *s* one *d*. *Educ:* King's Sch., Worcester. Called to Bar, Middle Temple, 1958; in practice at the Bar, 1959–. A Recorder of the Crown Court, 1978–79. A Chm. of Disciplinary Tribunals, Council of Inns of Court, 1987–. Mem. Bd, Law Sch., Nottingham Trent Univ., 1998–; Chm. of Governors, Nottingham High Sch. for Girls, 1992–. DL Notts, 1996. *Recreations:* fell walking and climbing, gardening, golf, the theatre. *Address:* c/o The Crown Court, Canal Street, Nottingham NG1 7EJ. *Club:* Nottingham and Notts Services.

HOPKIN, Royston Oliver, CMG 1995; Chairman and Managing Director, Spice Island Beach Resort (formerly Spice Island Inn), since 1987; Owner, Blue Horizons Cottage Hotel, since 1978; *b* 10 Jan. 1945; *s* of late Curtis Hopkin and Audrey Hopkin; *m* 1st, 1975, Floreen Hope (decd); one *s* one *d*; 2nd, 1983, Betty Grell-Hull; one *d*. *Educ:* Grenada Boys' Secondary Sch. British Amer. Insce Co., 1963–65; joined family business, Ross Point Inn, 1965, Manager, 1969–78. Dir, George F. Huggins & Co. Ltd, 2001–. Member: Grenada Tourist Bd, 1965–83; Grenada Bd of Tourism, 1998–2001; Pres., Grenada Hotel Assoc., 1969–89; Caribbean Hotel Association: Dir, 1970–; Pres., 1994–96; Chm., 1996–98; Chm., Memship Policy Cttee, 2000–; Caribbean Tourism Organization: Dir, 1990–98; Exec. Cttee, 1994–98. Vice-Chm., Caribbean Alliance (formerly Action) for Sustainable Tourism, 1996–. Mem. Bd of Trustees, Queen Elizabeth Home, Grenada, 1996–. Numerous awards incl. Caribbean Hotelier of the Year, 1991. *Recreations:* reading, tennis. *Address:* Mace Point Villa, True Blue, Box 41, St George's, Grenada, West Indies. *T:* (home) 4444584; (business) 4444258; *e-mail:* hopkin@caribsurf.com.

HOPKIN, Sir (William Aylsham) Bryan, Kt 1971; CBE 1961; Hon. Professorial Fellow, University College, Swansea, since 1988; *b* 7 Dec. 1914; *s* of late William Hopkin and Lilian Hopkin (*née* Cottelle); *m* 1938, Renée Ricour; two *s*. *Educ:* Barry (Glam.) County Sch.; St John's Coll., Cambridge (Hon. Fellow, 1982); Manchester Univ. Ministry of Health, 1938–41; Prime Minister's Statistical Branch, 1941–45; Royal Commn on Population, 1945–48; Econ. Sect., Cabinet Office, 1948–50; Central Statistical Office, 1950–52; Dir, Nat. Inst. of Econ. and Soc. Research, 1952–57; Sec., Council on Prices, Productivity, and Incomes, 1957–58; Dep. Dir, Econ. Sect., HM Treasury, 1958–65; Econ. Planning Unit, Mauritius, 1965; Min. of Overseas Devlt, 1966–67; Dir-Gen. of Economic Planning, ODM, 1967–69; Dir-Gen., DEA, 1969; Dep. Chief Econ. Adviser, HM Treasury, 1970–72; Prof. of Econs, UC Cardiff, 1972–82 (on leave of absence, Head of Govt Economic Service and Chief Economic Advr, HM Treasury, 1974–77). Mem., Commonwealth Develt Corp., 1972–74. Chm., Manpower Services Cttee for Wales, 1978–79. *Address:* Bedford Charterhouse, Kimbolton Road, Bedford MK42 2PU. *T:* (01234) 267757.

HOPKINS, Alan Cripps Nind, MA Cantab, LLB Yale; Chairman, Wellman Engineering Corporation, 1972–83 (Director, 1968); *b* 27 Oct. 1926; *s* of late Rt Hon. Sir Richard V. N. Hopkins, GCB and Lady Hopkins; *m* 1st, 1954, Margaret Cameron (from whom divorced, 1962), *d* of E. C. Bolton, Waco, Texas, USA; one *s*; 2nd, 1962, Venetia, *d* of Sir Edward Wills, 4th Bt; twin *s*. *Educ:* Winchester Coll.; King's Coll., Cambridge; Yale University Law Sch., USA. BA Cantab 1947, MA 1950; LLB Yale 1952. Barrister, Inner Temple, 1948. MP (C and Nat L) Bristol North-East, 1959–66; PPS to Financial Sec. to Treasury, 1960–62. *Recreation:* travelling. *Address:* Chalet Topaze, 1972 Anzere, Valais, Switzerland. *T:* (27) 3981651. *Club:* Brooks's.

HOPKINS, Sir Anthony; *see* Hopkins, Sir P. A.

HOPKINS, Anthony Strother, CBE 1996; BSc(Econ); FCA; Chairman, Laganside Corporation, since 1997 (Deputy Chairman, 1995–96); *b* 17 July 1940; *s* of Strother Smith Hopkins, OBE, and Alice Roberta Hopkins; *m* 1965, Dorothy Moira (*née* McDonough); one *s* two *d*. *Educ:* Campbell Coll., Belfast; Queen's University of Belfast (BScEcon). Manager, Thomson McLintock & Co., Chartered Accountants, London, 1966–70; Principal, Dept of Commerce, N Ireland, 1970–74; Northern Ireland Development Agency, 1975–82, Chief Executive, 1979–82; Under Secretary, 1982–88, Second Perm. Sec., 1988–92, Dept of Economic Development for N Ireland; Dep. Chief Exec., 1982–88, Chief Exec., 1988–92, Industrial Develt Bd for NI; Sen. Partner, Deloitte & Tonche (formerly Touche Ross & Co.), NI, Chartered Accountants, 1992–2001. Chm., MMB for NI, 1995–; Dep. Chm., Probation Bd for NI, 1997–98. Member: NI Tourist Bd, 1992–98; Council, NI Chamber of Commerce and Industry, 1992–95; Bd of Advrs, Hambro NI Ventures, 1995–. Vis. Prof., Univ. of Ulster, 1992–. Mem. Adv. Bd, Ulster Business Sch., 1992–99. Member, Appeal Committee: Relate, 1994–97; Mencap (NI), 1997–; Hon. Treas., Prince's Trust NI Appeal, 1995–97. CIMgt (CBIM 1990; Chm. NI Regl Bd, 1992–97). *Recreations:* golf, tennis, sailing. *Club:* Royal Belfast Golf (Co. Down).

HOPKINS, Antony, CBE 1976; composer and conductor; *b* 21 March 1921; *s* of late Hugh and of Marjorie Reynolds; adopted *c* of Major and Mrs T. H. C. Hopkins since 1925; *m* 1947, Alison Purves (*d* 1991). *Educ:* Berkhamsted Sch.; Royal Coll. of Music. Won Chappell Gold Medal and Cobbett Prize at RCM, 1942; shortly became known as composer of incidental music for radio; numerous scores composed for BBC (2 for programmes winning Italia prize for best European programme of the year, 1952 and 1957). Composed music for many productions at Stratford and in West End. Dir, Intimate Opera Co., 1952–, and has written a number of chamber operas for this group; *ballets:* Etude and Café des Sports, for Sadler's Wells; *films (music) include:* Pickwick Papers, Decameron Nights, Cast a Dark Shadow, Billy Budd; John and the Magic Music Man (narr. and orch.; Grand Prix, Besançon Film Festival, 1976). Regular broadcaster with a series of programmes entitled Talking about Music. Hon. FRCM 1964; Hon. RAM 1979; Hon. Fellow, Robinson Coll., Cambridge, 1980. DUniv. Stirling, 1980. *Publications:* Talking about Symphonies, 1961; Talking about Concertos, 1964; Music All Around Me, 1968; Lucy and Peterkin, 1968; Talking about Sonatas, 1971; Downbeat Guide, 1977; Understanding Music, 1979; The Nine Symphonies of Beethoven, 1980; Songs for Swinging Golfers, 1981; Sounds of Music, 1982; Beating Time (autobiog.), 1982; Pathway to Music, 1983; Musicamusings, 1983; The Concertgoer's Companion: Vol. I, 1984, Vol. II, 1985, one vol. edn, 1993; The Seven Concertos of Beethoven, 1996. *Recreations:* motoring, golf. *Address:* Woodyard Cottage, Ashridge, Berkhamsted, Herts HP4 1PS. *T:* (01442) 842257.

HOPKINS, Prof. Antony Gerald, PhD; FBA 1996; Walter Prescott Webb Professor of History, University of Texas at Austin, since 2002; *b* 21 Feb. 1938; *s* of George Henry Hopkins and Queenie Ethel (*née* Knight); *m* 1964, Wendy Beech; two *s*. *Educ:* St Paul's Sch.; QMC, Univ. of London (BA); SOAS (PhD). Asst Lectr, Lectr, then Reader, 1964–77, Prof. of Economic History, 1977–88, Univ. of Birmingham; Prof. of Internat. History, Grad. Inst. of Internat. Studies, Univ. of Geneva, 1988–94; Smuts Prof. of Commonwealth History, Univ. of Cambridge, 1994–2001. DUniv Stirling, 1996. Forkosch Prize, Amer. Historical Assoc., 1995. *Publications:* An Economic History of West Africa, 1973, revd 1988; (with P. J. Cain) British Imperialism: innovation and expansion 1688–1914, 1993, 2nd edn as British Imperialism 1688–2000, 2001; (with P. J. Cain) British Imperialism: crisis and deconstruction 1914–90, 1993; (ed) Globalization in World History, 2002; articles in learned jls. *Recreation:* worrying. *Address:* Department of HIstory, University of Texas, Garrison 101, B7000, Austin, TX 78712–1163, USA.

HOPKINS, Prof. Colin Russell, PhD; Professor of Molecular Cell Biology, Imperial College of Science, Technology and Medicine, since 2000; *b* 4 June 1939; *s* of Bleddyn Hopkins and Vivienne Russell (*née* Jenkins); *m* 1964, Hilary Floyd; one *s* one *d*. *Educ:* UC, Swansea, Univ. of Wales (BSc; PhD 1964). University of Liverpool: Asst Lectr, Dept of Physiol., Med. Sch., 1964–66; Lectr, Dept of Histology, 1966–70; Sen. Lectr, Dept of Histology and Cell Biol. (Medical), 1971–75; Fulbright Fellow, Dept of Cell Biol., 1970, Fulbright Travelling Schol. and Vis. Associate Prof., 1971–72, Rockefeller Univ., NY; Prof. and Head, Dept of Medical Cell Biol., Univ. of Liverpool, 1975–86; Rank Prof. of Physiological Biochem., ICSTM, 1986–91; Dir, MRC Lab. for Molecular Cell Biol., UCL, 1991–2000. *Publications:* Cell Structure and Function, 1964; numerous scientific papers. *Recreations:* natural history, music. *Address:* Department of Biochemistry, Imperial College of Science, Technology and Medicine, Exhibition Road, SW7 2AZ. *T:* (020) 7589 5111; *e-mail:* colinhopkins@comp.com.

HOPKINS, David Rex Eugène; Director of Quality Assurance/Administration, Ministry of Defence, 1983–90; *b* 29 June 1930; *s* of late Frank Hopkins and Vera (*née* Wimhurst); *m* 1955, Brenda Joyce Phillips; two *s* one *d* (one *d* decd). *Educ:* Worthing High Sch.; Christ Church, Oxford (MA 1950; Dip. in Econs and Pol. Science, 1951). National Service Commn, RA, 1952; service in Korea. Asst Principal, WO, 1953; Principal, WO, 1957, MoD 1964; Asst Sec., 1967; Home Office, 1969–70; RCDS, 1971; Defence Equipment Secretariat, 1972; Dir, Headquarters Security, 1975; Financial Counsellor, UK

Delegn to NATO, 1981–83. *Recreations:* church work, archaeological digging, fell-walking, military history. *Address:* 16 Hitherwood Drive, SE19 1XB. *T:* (020) 8670 7504.

HOPKINS, Elizabeth Ann; Clerk, House of Lords, 1998–2000; *b* 25 Sept. 1941; *d* of Philip G. H. Hopkins and Edith A. I. (Nessie) Hopkins (*née* Holmes). *Educ:* Parkstone Grammar Sch.; King Edward VI High Sch., Birmingham; Lady Margaret Hall, Oxford (BA Hons); Univ. of Ibadan (MSc); Univ. of Sussex (DPhil). Asst Lectr, Univ. of Sussex, 1965–68; Res. Officer, Inst. of Develt Studies, Sussex, 1968–72; Economist, Govt of Zambia, 1972–76; DoE, 1977–86; Dept of Transport (Channel Tunnel; Internat. Aviation), 1986–90; Regl Dir (SW), Depts of the Envmt and of Transport, 1990–93; Dir of Finance, Dept of Transport, 1993–95; Financial Mgt Advr, Dept of Transport, S Africa, 1995–96; Clerk/Advr, H of C Select Cttee on Eur. Legislation, 1997–98. *Recreation:* travel. *Address:* 33 Barkston Gardens, SW5 0ER. *T:* (020) 7370 7981.

HOPKINS, John Humphrey David; Golf Correspondent, The Times, since 1993; *b* 26 March 1945; *s* of Leslie Charles Hopkins and late Mary Eileen Hopkins (*née* Ellis); *m* 1970, Suzanne Ernestine Kommenda (marr. diss. 1998); one *s* one *d*. *Educ:* Llandaff Cathedral Sch., Cardiff (Choral Schol.); Wrekin Coll., Telford, Salop. Sunday Times: Rugby Corresp., 1976–80; Golf Corresp., 1980–91; golf and Rugby writer, Financial Times, 1991–93. *Publications:* Life with the Lions, 1977; The British Lions, 1980; Nick Faldo in Perspective, 1985; Golf: the four Majors, 1988; Golfer's Companion, 1990; Golf in Wales: the Centenary 1895–1995, 1995. *Recreations:* squash, golf, Rugby, theatre, reading. *Address:* c/o The Times, 1 Pennington Street, E1 9XN. *T:* (020) 7782 5944. *Clubs:* Royal Automobile, MCC; Jesters; Royal Porthcawl.

HOPKINS, Julian; *see* Hopkins, R. J.

HOPKINS, Keith; *see* Hopkins, M. K.

HOPKINS, Kelvin Peter; MP (Lab) Luton North, since 1997; *b* 22 Aug. 1941; *s* of late Prof. Harold Horace Hopkins, FRS and of Joan Avery Frost; *m* 1965, Patricia Mabel Langley; one *s* one *d*. *Educ:* Nottingham Univ. (BA Hons Politics, Economics, Maths with Stats). Economic Dept, TUC, 1969–70 and 1973–77; Lectr, St Albans Coll. of Further Educn, 1971–73; Policy and Res. Officer, NALGO, then UNISON, 1977–94. Hon. Fellow, Univ. of Luton, 1993. *Publications:* NALGO papers. *Recreations:* music, photography, theatre, wine, sailing on the Norfolk Broads. *Address:* House of Commons, Westminster, SW1A 0AA. *T:* (020) 7219 6670; (home) (01582) 722913. *Clubs:* Luton Socialist, Lansdowne (Luton).

HOPKINS, Sir Michael (John), Kt 1995; CBE 1989; RA 1992; RIBA; RWA; Founding Partner, Michael Hopkins & Partners, 1976; *b* 7 May 1935; *s* of late Gerald and Barbara Hopkins; *m* 1962, Patricia Ann Wainwright (*see* P. A. Hopkins); one *s* two *d*. *Educ:* Sherborne Sch.; Architectural Assoc. (AA Dip. 1964). RIBA 1966; RWA 1989. Worked in offices of Sir Basil Spence, Leonard Manasseh and Tom Hancock; partnership with Norman Foster, 1969–75 and with Patricia Hopkins, 1976–; *projects include*: own house and studio, Hampstead, 1976 (RIBA Award, 1977; Civic Trust Award, 1979); brewery bldg for Greene King, 1979 (RIBA, and FT Awards, 1980); Patera Bldg System, 1984; Res. Centre for Schlumberger, Cambridge, 1984 (FT Award, 1985; RIBA, and Civic Trust Awards, 1988); infants sch., Hampshire, 1986 (RIBA, and Civic Trust Awards, 1988); Bicentenary Stand, Lord's Cricket Ground, 1987 (RIBA, Civic Trust Awards, 1988); R&D Centre, Solid State Logic, 1988 (RIBA Award, 1989; Civic Trust Award, 1990); London office and country workshop for David Mellor, 1989 and 1991 (FT, and RIBA Awards, 1989; Civic Trust Award, 1990; RIBA Award, 1993); redevelt of Bracken House, St Paul's, for Ohbayashi Corp., 1992 (RIBA Award, 1992; FT Award, 1993; Civic Trust Award, 1994); offices at New Square, Bedfont Lakes, 1992 (FT Award, 1993); Glyndebourne Opera House, 1994 (RIBA, and Royal Fine Art Commn Awards, 1994; Civic Trust and FT Awards, 1995); Inland Revenue Centre, Nottingham, 1995 (Civic Trust Award, 1997); Queen's Bldg, Emmanuel Coll., Cambridge, 1995 (RIBA, and Royal Fine Art Commn Awards, 1996); Jewish Care residential home for the elderly, 1996; Saga Gp HQ, 1999; new campus, Nottingham Univ., 1999; William Younger Centre, 1999; Wildscreen @ Bristol 2000, 1999; Portcullis House, Westminster, 2000; *current projects*: new Hall, Haberdashers' Co.; Norwich Millennium Project. Exhibited, Venice Biennale, 1991. Member: Royal Fine Art Commn, 1986–99; London Adv. Cttee, English Heritage, 1990–93; Architectural Adv. Gp, Arts Council, 1992–95. Pres., Architectural Assoc., 1997–99 (Vice Pres., 1987–93); Trustee: Thomas Cubitt Trust, 1987–; British Mus., 1993–. Hon. FAIA 1996; Hon.FRIAS 1996. Hon. Mem., Bund Architekten, 1996. Dr *hc* RCA 1994; Hon. DLitt Nottingham, 1995; Hon. DTech London Guildhall, 1996. *Recreations:* sailing, Catureglio. *Address:* 49A Downshire Hill, NW3 1NX. *T:* (020) 7435 1109; (office) 27 Broadley Terrace, NW1 6LG. *T:* (020) 7724 1751.

HOPKINS, Prof. (Morris) Keith, FBA 1984; Professor of Ancient History, University of Cambridge, 1985–2001; Fellow, since 1985, and Vice-Provost, since 2000, King's College, Cambridge; *b* 20 June 1934; *s* of late Albert Thomas Hopkins and Hélène Dorothy Pratt; *m* 1st, 1963, Juliet (marr. diss. 1989), *d* of Sir Henry Phelps Brown, MBE, FBA; two *s* one *d*; 2nd, 1991, Jennifer Simmons; two *d*. *Educ:* Brentwood School; King's College, Cambridge. BA 1958; MA 1961. Asst Lectr in Sociology, Leicester Univ., 1961–63; Research Fellow, King's College, Cambridge, 1963–67; Lectr and Senior Lectr in Sociology, LSE, 1963–67, 1970–72; Prof. of Sociology: Univ. of Hong Kong, 1967–69; Brunel Univ., 1972–85 (Dean, Faculty of Social Sciences, 1981–85). Mem., Inst. for Advanced Study, Princeton, 1969–70, 1974–75, 1983. *Publications:* Hong Kong: The Industrial Colony (ed), 1971; Conquerors and Slaves, 1978; Death and Renewal, 1983; A World Full of Gods, 1999. *Recreations:* drinking wine, gardening. *Address:* King's College, Cambridge CB2 1ST. *T:* (01223) 331100.

HOPKINS, Patricia Ann, (Lady Hopkins); Partner, Michael Hopkins & Partners, since 1976; *b* 7 April 1942; *d* of Denys Wainwright, MB, Dsc, FRCS and Dr Shelagh Wainwright, MB, ChB; *m* 1962, Michael John Hopkins (*see* Sir Michael Hopkins); one *s* two *d*. *Educ:* Wycombe Abbey Sch.; Architectural Assoc. (AA Dip. 1968). Own practice, 1968–76; in partnership with Michael Hopkins, 1976–. Buildings include: own house and studio, Hampstead, 1976 (RIBA Award, 1977; Civic Trust Award, 1979); Hopkins office, Marylebone, London, 1985; Fleet Velmead Infants Sch., Hants, 1986 (RIBA Award, Civic Trust Award, 1988); Masterplan, 1988, Raphael Cartoon Gall., 1993, V&A Mus.; Glyndebourne Opera House, 1994 (RIBA Award, Royal Fine Art Commn Award, 1994; Civic Trust Award, FT Award, 1995); Queen's Bldg, Emmanuel Coll., Cambridge, 1995 (RIBA Award, Royal Fine Art Commn Award, 1996); Jewish Care residential home for the elderly, 1996; projects include: Ickworth House; Preachers Court, Charterhouse; Wildscreen @ Bristol; Haberdashers' Hall; Manchester City Art Gall.; Royal Acad. Member: Nat. Lottery Bd, Arts Council of England, 1994–; Foundn Campaign Bd, AA, 1994–. Trustee, Nat. Gall., 1998–. Gov., Queen's Coll., Harley St, 1997–. Hon. FRIAS 1996; Hon. FAIA 1997. Hon. DTech London Guildhall, 1996. *Recreations:* family, friends, Black Heath, Catureglio. *Address:* 49A Downshire Hill, NW3 1NX. *T:* (020) 7435 1109; (office) 27 Broadley Terrace, NW1 6LG. *T:* (020) 7724 1751.

HOPKINS, Sir (Philip) Anthony, Kt 1993; CBE 1987; actor since 1961; *b* Port Talbot, S Wales, 31 Dec. 1937; *s* of late Richard and of Muriel Hopkins; *m* 1st, 1968, Petronella (marr. diss. 1972); one *d*; 2nd, 1973, Jennifer, *d* of Ronald Lynton. *Educ:* Cowbridge, S Wales; RADA; Cardiff Coll. of Drama. London debut as Metellus Cimber in Julius Caesar, Royal Court, 1964; National Theatre: Juno and the Paycock, A Flea in Her Ear, 1966; The Dance of Death, The Three Sisters, As You Like It (all male cast), 1967; The Architect and the Emperor of Assyria, A Woman Killed with Kindness, Coriolanus, 1971; Macbeth, 1972; Pravda, 1985 (Laurence Olivier/Observer Award for outstanding achievements, 1985; (jtly) Best Actor, British Theatre Assoc. and Drama Magazine Awards, 1985; Royal Variety Club Stage Actor Award, 1985); King Lear, 1986; Antony and Cleopatra, 1987. Other stage appearances include: The Taming of the Shrew, Chichester, 1972; Equus, USA, 1974–75, 1977 (Best Actor Award, NY Drama Desk, Amer. Authors and Celebrities Forum Award, Outer Critics Circle Award, 1975; LA Drama Critics' Award, 1977); The Tempest, LA, 1979; Old Times, New York, 1984; The Lonely Road, Old Vic, 1985; M. Butterfly, Shaftesbury, 1989; Director: Dylan Thomas: return journey, Lyric, Hammersmith, 1992; August, Theatr Clwyd, 1994. *Films:* The Lion in Winter, 1968; The Looking Glass War, 1969; Hamlet, 1969; When Eight Bells Toll, 1971; Young Winston, 1972; A Doll's House, 1973; The Girl from Petrovka, 1974; All Creatures Great and Small, 1974; Juggernaut, 1974; Audrey Rose, 1977; A Bridge Too Far, 1977; International Velvet, 1978; Magic, 1978; The Elephant Man, A Change of Seasons, 1980; The Bounty (Variety Club Film Actor Award), 1984; The Good Father, 1986; 84 Charing Cross Road (Best Actor Award, Moscow Film Fest.), 1986; The Dawning, 1988; A Chorus of Disapproval, 1989; Desperate Hours, 1991; The Silence of the Lambs, 1991; (Acad., BAFTA and NY Film Critics Circle, Awards for Best Actor, 1992); Freejack, Howard's End, Chaplin, 1992; Bram Stoker's Dracula, The Trial, The Innocent, The Remains of the Day, 1993 (BAFTA Best Actor Award); Shadowlands, 1994; The Road to Wellville, Legends of the Fall, 1995; Nixon, 1996; August (also dir), 1996; Surviving Picasso, 1996; Amistad, 1998; The Edge, 1998; The Mask of Zorro, 1998; Meet Joe Black, 1999; Instinct, 1999; Titus, 2000; Hannibal, 2001. *American television films:* QB VII, 1973; Dark Victory, 1975; Bruno Hauptmann in The Lindbergh Kidnapping Case (Emmy Award), 1976; The Voyage of the Mayflower, 1979; The Bunker (Emmy Award, 1981), The Acts of Peter and Paul, 1980; The Hunchback of Notre Dame, 1981; The Arch of Triumph, 1984; Hollywood Wives, 1984; Guilty Conscience, 1984; The Tenth Man, 1988; To Be the Best, 1991; *BBC television:* Pierre Bezukhov in serial, War and Peace (SFTA Best TV Actor award), 1972; Kean, 1978; Othello, 1981; Little Eyolf, 1982; Guy Burgess in Blunt (film), 1987; Donald Campbell in Across the Lake, 1988; Heartland, 1989; Gwyn Thomas: A Few Selected Exits, 1993; Indep. TV performances incl. A Married Man (series), 1983. Hon. Fellow, St David's Coll., Lampeter, 1992. Hon. DLitt Wales, 1988. Commandeur, Ordre des Arts et des Lettres (France), 1996. *Recreations:* reading, walking, piano.

HOPKINS, (Richard) Julian; Director, ORBIS USA, ORBIS International, New York, since 1994; *b* 12 Oct. 1940; *s* of late Richard Robert Hopkins, CBE and Grace Hilda (*née* Hatfield); *m* 1971, Maureen Mary (*née* Hoye); two *s* one *d*. *Educ:* Bedford School. Asst Manager, London Palladium, 1963; Central Services Manager, BBC, 1965; joined RSPCA as Accounts Manager, 1972, appointed Admin. and Finance Officer, 1976; Exec. Dir, 1978–82; Gen. Manager, Charity Christmas Card Council, 1982–83; Finance Dir, War on Want, 1984–88; Dir, CARE Britain, 1988–94. Dir, and Mem. Exec. Cttee, World Soc. for Protection of Animals, 1980–82; Mem., Farm Animal Welfare Council, 1980–83. FIMgt. *Recreation:* all theatre, but especially opera, concert-going. *Address:* ORBIS, 330 West 42nd Street, New York, NY 10036, USA. *T:* (212) 2442525.

HOPKINS, Russell, OBE 1989; FDSRCS; Consultant Oral and Maxillo-Facial Surgeon, Cardiff Royal Infirmary, 1968–95; Director of Medical Audit, South Glamorgan Health Authority, 1991–95; *b* 30 April 1932; *s* of Charles Albert Hopkins and Frances Doris Hopkins; *m* 1970, Jill Margaret Pexton; two *s* one *d*. *Educ:* Barnard Castle Sch.; King's Coll., Durham Univ. (BDS 1956); Royal Free Hosp., London Univ. LRCP, MRCS 1964; FDSRCS 1961. Gen. dental practice, 1956–58; SHO, Oral Surgery, Nottingham Gen. Hosp., 1958–59; Registrar, Oral Surgery, St Peter's Hosp., Chertsey, 1959–61; Sen. Registrar, Royal Victoria Infirmary, Newcastle upon Tyne, 1965–68; Consultant, 1970–95, Gen. Manager, 1985–91, Univ. Hosp. of Wales, Cardiff. Member: Central Cttee, Hosp. Med. Services, 1975–88; Jt Consultant Cttee, London, 1980–93 (Chm., Welsh Sub-Cttee, 1986–93); Chairman: Med. Bd, S Glamorgan, 1980–82; Welsh Council, BMA, 1991–94 (Chm., Welsh Consultant and Specialist Cttee, 1989–93); BMA Gen. Managers' Gp, 1988–90; Glan-Y-Môr NHS Trust, 1995–99; Brô Morgannwg NHS Trust, 1999–. Pres., BAOMS 1992–93; Mem., Eur. Assoc. of Max.-Fac. Surgery; Fellow, BMA, 1998. Ext. Examr, Univ. of Hong Kong, 1990–93. *Publications:* Pre-Prosthetic Oral Surgery, 1986; chapters in numerous medical works. *Recreations:* golf, sea fishing, walking, photography, reading. *Address:* 179 Cyncoed Road, Cardiff CF23 6AH. *T:* (home) (029) 2075 2319. *Club:* Cardiff and County (Cardiff).

HOPKINS, Sidney Arthur; Managing Director, Guardian Royal Exchange plc, 1990–94; *b* 15 April 1932; *m* 1955, Joan Marion Smith; one *d*. *Educ:* Battersea Grammar Sch. ACII. Joined Royal Exchange Assce, 1948, Man., Organisation and Methods, 1966; Guardian Royal Exchange Assurance Ltd: Chief Claims Man. (UK), 1974; Man., Home Motor, 1976; Asst Gen. Man. (Life), 1979; Guardian Royal Exchange Assurance plc: Asst Gen. Man. (Field Operations), 1983; Gen. Man. (UK), 1985; Guardian Royal Exchange (UK) Ltd: Man. Dir, 1987; Guardian Royal Exchange plc: Dir, 1986; Dep. Chief Exec., 1989. Dir, Residuary MMB, 1994–. Freeman, City of London; Liveryman, Company of Insurers. *Recreations:* sports, films. *Address:* Woodlands, 8 Littleworth Lane, Esher, Surrey KT10 9PF. *Club:* Royal Automobile.

HOPKINSON, family name of **Baron Colyton**.

HOPKINSON, Ven. Barnabas John; Archdeacon of Wilts, since 1998; *b* 11 May 1939; *s* of Prebendary Stephan Hopkinson and late Mrs Anne Hopkinson; *m* 1968, Esmé Faith (*née* Gibbons); three *d*. *Educ:* Emanuel School; Trinity Coll., Cambridge (MA); Lincoln Theological Coll. Curate: All Saints and Martyrs, Langley, Manchester, 1965–67; Great St Mary's, Cambridge, 1967–70; Chaplain, Charterhouse School, 1970–75; Team Vicar of Preshute, Wilts, 1975–81; RD of Marlborough, 1977–81; Rector of Wimborne Minster, Dorset, 1981–86; RD of Wimborne, 1985–86; Archdeacon of Sarum, 1986–98; Priest-in-charge, Stratford-sub-Castle, 1987–98. Canon of Salisbury Cathedral, 1983–. *Recreation:* gardening. *Address:* Sarum House, High Street, Urchfont, Devizes SN10 4QH. *T:* (01380) 840373, *Fax:* (01380) 848247; *e-mail:* adwilts@salisbury.anglican.org.

HOPKINSON, Prof. Brian Ridley, FRCS; Professor of Vascular Surgery, University of Nottingham, since 1996; Consultant Surgeon, Queen's Medical Centre, Nottingham; *b* 26 Feb. 1938; *s* of Edward Alban Ernest Hopkinson and May Olive Hopkinson (*née* Redding); *m* 1962, Margaret Ruth Bull; three *s* one *d*. *Educ:* Birmingham Univ. (MB ChB 1961; ChM 1972). FRCS 1964. Hse Surgeon, 1961–62, Resident Surgical Officer, 1964–65, Hallam Hosp., W Bromwich; Registrar, Cardiac Surgery, Queen Elizabeth Hosp., Birmingham, 1965–66; Buswell Res. Fellow, Buffalo, NY, 1966–67; Sen. Surgical

Registrar, Birmingham Gen. Hosp. and Wolverhampton Royal Infirmary, 1967–69; Lectr in Surgery, Univ. of Birmingham, 1969–73; Consultant Gen. Surgeon specialising in vascular surgery, Queen's Med. Centre, Nottingham, 1973–96. Hon. Prof., Chinese Med. Univ., Shenyang, China, 1999. Various BMA posts including: Sec. and Chm., Nottingham Div., 1975–83; Chm., Trent Regl Council, 1992–95; Chm., Regl Consultant and Specialist Cttee, 1987–92; Chm., Annual Reps' Meeting, 1998–2001. Licensed Lay Reader, C of E, St Jude's, Mapperley. *Publications:* Endovascular Surgery for Aortic Aneurysms, 1997; Operative Atlas of Endovascular Aneurysm Surgery, 1999; contrib. Lancet. *Recreations:* swimming, motor caravanning, coal fired steamboats. *Address:* Lincolnsfield, 18 Victoria Crescent, Private Road, Sherwood, Nottingham NG5 4DA. *T:* (0115) 960 4167.

HOPKINSON, Bryan; Director, Montenegro Project, Podgorica, International Crisis Group, since 2000; *b* 24 Nov. 1956; *s* of Brian Hopkinson and Florance Hopkinson (*née* Richardson), Huddersfield; *m* 1987, Stephanie Burd (*née* Perkins). *Educ:* King James's Grammar Sch., Huddersfield; King's Coll., Cambridge (BA, MA). Joined FCO, 1980; Kampala, 1981–84; songwriter and musician, 1985–87; rejoined FCO, 1987; Lisbon, 1989–93; FCO, 1993–95; Ambassador to Bosnia-Hercegovina, 1995–96; Hon. Dir, British Council, Sarajevo, 1995–96; Dir, Bosnia Proj., Sarajevo, Jan.–July 1999, Kosovo Proj., Pristina, July–Dec. 1999, Internat. Crisis Gp. *Publications:* numerous Balkans reports. *Recreations:* walking, music, board and computer games. *Address:* 9 St George's Court, Newark, Notts NG24 1NW. *T:* (01636) 672899.

HOPKINSON, Prof. David Albert, MD; Professor of Human Biochemical Genetics, University College London, 1993–2000; now Emeritus; Director, Medical Research Council Human Biochemical Genetics Unit, 1976–2000; *b* 26 June 1935; *s* of George Albert and Lily Hopkinson; *m* 1st, 1959, Josephine Manze; two *s* one *d*; 2nd, 1980, Yvonne Edwards. *Educ:* Chesterfield Grammar Sch.; St Catharine's Coll., Cambridge; Royal London Hosp. Med. Coll. (MA, MD). Royal London Hospital: House Surgeon and House Physician, 1959–60; Jun. Lectr, Biochem., 1960; Resident Pathologist, 1961; Scientific Staff, MRC Human Biochemical Genetics Unit, 1962–2000. Hon. Life Mem., Internat. Forensic Haemogenetics Soc., 1992. *Publication:* Handbook of Enzyme Electrophoresis in Human Genetics, 1976. *Recreations:* vegetable gardening, hill and mountain walking, furniture restoration, watching Rugby. *Address:* Swan Cottage, 42 Church Street, Great Missenden, Bucks HP16 0AZ.

HOPKINSON, David Hugh; editorial consultant, The Times, since 1995; *b* 9 June 1930; *er s* of late C. G. Hopkinson; *m* Patricia Ann Eaton; one *s* one *d*; and three *s* one *d* by previous marriage. *Educ:* Sowerby Bridge Grammar Sch. Entered journalism on Huddersfield Examiner, 1950; Yorkshire Observer, 1954; Yorkshire Evening News, 1954; Evening Chronicle, Manchester, 1956; Chief Sub-Editor, Sunday Graphic, London, 1957; Asst Editor, Evening Chronicle, Newcastle upon Tyne, 1959; Chief Asst Editor, Sunday Graphic, 1960; Dep. Editor, Sheffield Telegraph, 1961, Editor, 1962–64; Editor, The Birmingham Post, 1964–73; Dir, Birmingham Post & Mail Ltd, 1967–80; Editor, Birmingham Evening Mail, 1974–79; Editor-in-Chief, Evening Mail series, 1975–79, Birmingham Post and Evening Mail, 1979–80; The Times: Asst to Editor, 1981; Chief Night Ed., 1982–89; Dep. Man. Ed., 1990–95. Mem., Lord Justice Phillimore's Cttee inquiring into law of contempt. National Press Award, Journalist of the Year, 1963. *Address:* c/o The Times, 1 Pennington Street, E98 1TT.

HOPKINSON, David Hugh Laing, CBE 1986; RD 1965; DL; Deputy Chairman and Chief Executive, M&G Group PLC, 1979–87; Chairman, Harrisons and Crosfield, 1988–91 (Deputy Chairman, 1987–88, Director, 1986–91); Deputy Chairman, ECC Group (formerly English China Clays), 1986–91 (Director, since 1975); *b* 14 Aug. 1926; *s* of late Cecil Hopkinson and Leila Hopkinson; *m* 1951, Prudence Margaret Holmes, OBE, JP, DL; two *s* two *d*. *Educ:* Wellington Coll.; Merton Coll., Oxford (BA 1949). RNVR and RNR, 1944–65. A Clerk of the House of Commons, 1948–59; Robert Fleming, 1959–62; M&G Investment Management, 1963–87 (Chm., 1975–87); Director: Lloyds Bank Southern Regional Board, 1977–88; BR (Southern) Bd, 1978–87 (Chm., 1983–87); Wolverhampton and Dudley Breweries, 1987–96; Mem., Adv. Gp of Governor of Bank of England, 1984. Mem., Housing Corp., 1986–88. Director: English Chamber Orchestra and Music Soc., 1970–89; Charities Investment Managers, 1970–; Merchants Trust, 1976–99; RTZ Pension Trustees, 1993–99; SE Arts Board, 1994–97. Member: General Synod of C of E, 1970–90; Central Bd of Finance, 1970–90; a Church Comr, 1973–82, 1984–94; Mem., Chichester Dio. Bd of Finance, 1970– (Chm., 1977–88);Chm., Chichester Cathedral Finance Cttee, 2000–. Chm., Church Army Bd, 1987–89. Trustee: Nat. Assoc. of Almshouses; Chichester Cathedral Development Trust; Pallant House Gall., Chichester (Chm. of Trustees); Royal Pavilion, Brighton; RAM Foundn; Edward James Foundn (Chm.). Governor: Sherborne Sch., 1970–96 (Vice-Chm., Bd, 1987–96); Wellington Coll., 1978–96. DL 1986, High Sheriff, 1987–88, W Sussex. Hon. Fellow, St Anne's Coll., Oxford, 1984–. *Recreations:* travelling, walking, opera. *Address:* St John's Priory, Poling, Arundel, W Sussex BN18 9PS. *T:* (01903) 882393. *Club:* Brooks's.

HOPKINSON, George William; writer and speaker on international relations; *b* 13 Sept. 1943; *s* of William Hartley Hopkinson and Mary (*née* Ashmore); *m* 1973, Mary Agnes Coverdale (marr. diss. 1997); one *s*. *Educ:* Tupton Hall Grammar Sch.; Pembroke Coll., Cambridge (BA 1965; MA 1969). Inland Revenue, 1965–73; CSD, 1973–81; HM Treasury, 1981–86; Ministry of Defence, 1986–97: Hd, Defence Arms Control Unit, 1988–91; Vis. Fellow, Global Security Programme, Cambridge Univ., 1991–92 (on secondment); Hd, Defence Lands Service, 1992–93; Asst Under-Sec. of State (Policy) 1993–97; Royal Institute of International Affairs: Hd of Internat. Security Prog., 1997–99; Dep. Dir and Dir of Studies, 1999–2000. Associate Fellow: RUSI, 1997–; RIIA, 2000–; Sen. Vis. Fellow, WEU Inst., Paris, 2001. *Publications:* The Making of British Defence Policy, 2000; contribs to books on security policy, international affairs and arms control; occasional papers. *Recreations:* reading, walking. *Address:* Heaven's Door, Rimpton, Somerset BA22 8AN. *Clubs:* Oxford and Cambridge, National Liberal.

HOPKINSON, Giles, CB 1990; Under-Secretary, Departments of the Environment and Transport, 1976–90, retired; *b* 20 Nov. 1931; *s* of late Arthur John Hopkinson, CIE, ICS, and of Eleanor (*née* Richardson); *m* 1956, Eleanor Jean Riddell; three *d*. *Educ:* Marlborough Coll.; Leeds Univ. (BSc). E. & J. Richardson Ltd, 1956–57; Forestal Land, Timber and Rly Co. Ltd, 1957–58; DSIR: Scientific Officer, 1958–61; Sen. Scientific Officer, 1961–64; Private Sec. to Perm. Sec., 1963–64; Principal, MoT, 1964–71; Asst Sec., DoE, 1971; Under-Secretary: DoE, 1976; Dept of Transport (Ports and Freight Directorate), 1979; Dir, London Region, PSA, DoE, 1983–90. *Recreations:* music, painting, restoration of antique furniture, church bellringing. *Address:* 12 Barn Hill, Stamford, Lincs PE9 2AE. *Club:* Royal Commonwealth Society.

HOPKINSON, Maj.-Gen. John Charles Oswald Rooke, CB 1984; Director, British Field Sports Society, 1984–93; *b* 31 July 1931; *s* of Lt-Col John Oliver Hopkinson and Aileen Disney Hopkinson (*née* Rooke); *m* 1956, Sarah Elizabeth, *d* of Maj.-Gen. M. H. P. Sayers, OBE; three *s* one *d*. *Educ:* Stonyhurst Coll.; RMA, Sandhurst. sc 1963, jssc 1968, rcds 1979. Commanding Officer, 1st Bn Queen's Own Highlanders, 1972–74 (despatches); Dep. Comdr 2nd Armoured Division, and Comdr Osnabrück Garrison, 1977–78; Director Operational Requirements 3 (Army), 1980–82; Chief-of-Staff, HQ Allied Forces Northern Europe, 1982–84. Colonel, Queen's Own Highlanders, 1983–94. Chm., Wye Salmon Fishery Owners Assoc., 1993–; Vice-Chm., Atlantic Salmon Trust, 1995–. Dir, Green Bottom Property Co. Ltd, 1995–. Trustee, Wye Foundn, 1996–. *Recreations:* shooting, fishing, sailing. *Address:* Bigsweir, Gloucestershire. *Club:* Army and Navy.

HOPKINSON, John Edmund; Judge of the High Court, Hong Kong, 1985–89, retired; *b* 25 Oct. 1924; *s* of Captain E. H. Hopkinson, OBE, RN and Mrs E. H. Hopkinson; *m* 1961, Inge Gansel; one *s* one *d*. *Educ:* Marlborough Coll., Wilts; Pembroke Coll., Cambridge (MA). Called to the Bar, Lincoln's Inn, 1949. Served War, RN, 1943–46: Ordinary Seaman, Midshipman RNVR, 1943; Sub-Lt RNVR, 1944–46. Prudential Assurance Co., 1949–50; Legal Asst, Colonial Office, 1950–55; Hong Kong, 1962–89: Crown Counsel, 1962; Principal Crown Counsel, 1972; Dist Judge, 1974. *Recreations:* golf, tennis, ski-ing, music. *Address:* 41 Clavering Avenue, SW13 9DX. *Clubs:* Roehampton; Royal Cinque Ports Golf.

HOPKINSON, Simon Charles; restaurateur, chef, writer; *b* 5 June 1954; *s* of Bruce and late Dorothie Hopkinson. *Educ:* St John's Coll. Sch., Cambridge (chorister); Trent Coll., Derbyshire. Normandie Hotel, Birtle, 1972; Hat and Feather Restaurant, Knutsford, 1973; St Non's Hotel, St David's, 1973–74; Druidstone Hotel, Broadhaven, 1974–75; chef and proprietor: Shed Restaurant, Dinas, 1975–77; Hoppy's Restaurant, 1977–78; Egon Ronay Inspector, 1978–80; private chef, London, 1980–83; Hilaire Restaurant, Kensington, 1983–87; co-proprietor, Bibendum, 1987– (head chef, 1987–95). Cookery writer for The Independent and Food Illustrated. Awards: Glenfiddich, 1995, 1997; André Simon Meml, 1995. *Publications:* (with Lindsey Bareham) Roast Chicken and Other Stories, 1994; (contrib.) The Conran Cook Book, 1997; (with Lindsey Bareham) The Prawn Cocktail Years, 1997; Gammon & Spinach, 1998; Roast Chicken and Other Stories: Second Helpings, 2001. *Recreations:* poker, wine. *Address:* c/o David Higham Associates, 5–8 Lower John Street, Golden Square, W1R 4HA. *T:* (020) 7437 7888.

HOPKIRK, Joyce, (Mrs W. J. Lear); Director, Editors' Unlimited, since 1990; *b* 2 March; *d* of Walter Nicholson and Veronica (*née* Keelan); *m* 1st, 1962, Peter Hopkirk; one *d*; 2nd, 1974, William James Lear; one *s*. *Educ:* Middle Street Secondary Sch., Newcastle upon Tyne. Reporter, Gateshead Post, 1955; Founder Editor, Majorcan News, 1959; Reporter, Daily Sketch, 1960; Royal Reporter, Daily Express, 1961; Ed., Fashion Magazine, 1967; Women's Ed., Sun, 1967; Launch Ed., Cosmopolitan, 1971–72 (launched 1972); Asst Ed., Daily Mirror, 1973–78; Women's Ed., Sunday Times, 1982; Editl Dir, Elle, 1984; Asst Ed., Sunday Mirror, 1985; Ed.-in-Chief, She Magazine, 1986–89; Founder Ed., Chic Magazine 1994. Mem., Competition Commn, 1999–. Co-Chm., PPA Awards, 1998. Editor of the Year, 1972; Women's Magazines Editor of the Year, 1988. FRSA. *Publications:* Successful Slimming, 1976; Successful Slimming Cookbook, 1978; (jtly) Splash!, 1995; (jtly) Best of Enemies, 1996; (jtly) Double Trouble, 1997; Unfinished Business, 1998; Relative Strangers, 1999; The Affair, 2000. *Recreations:* conversation, sleeping, gardening, hockey, ski-ing, boating. *Address:* Gadespring, 109 Piccotts End, Hemel Hempstead, Herts HP1 3AT. *T:* (01442) 245608; Jury's Gap, Sussex. *Address:* Puerto Andraitx, Mallorca.

HOPKIRK, Peter; author and traveller; *b* 15 Dec. 1930; *s* of Rev. Frank Stuart Hopkirk and Mary Hopkirk; *m* 1970, Kathleen Partridge; one *s* one *d*. *Educ:* Dragon Sch., Oxford; Marlborough. Military service, 1949–51: Subaltern, 4th (Uganda) Bn, KAR; served ex-Italian Somaliland and Kenya. Reporter, Sunday Express, London, 1954–56 (Algerian War, 1956); Ed., Drum (W African news mag.), 1956–57; ITN reporter and newscaster, London, 1958–59; foreign corresp., Daily Express, 1959–62: NY Bureau, 1960–61 (imprisoned Havana, 1961, Bay of Pigs invasion); Beirut corresp., 1962 (expelled); various writing assignments abroad, 1962–64, incl. China, Africa (visiting Albert Schweitzer at Lambaréné leper hosp.), and resident corresp., Istanbul; joined IPC newspapers, London, 1964; assigned to open group's first Moscow bureau, but visa blocked by Soviets; staff reporter, The Times, London, 1966–85: Chief Reporter, later ME and FE specialist (hijacked by Arab terrorists, 1974). Sir Percy Sykes Meml Medal, RSAA, 1999. *Publications:* Foreign Devils on the Silk Road, 1980; Trespassers on the Roof of the World, 1982; Setting the East Ablaze, 1984; The Great Game, 1990; On Secret Service East of Constantinople, 1994; Quest for Kim, 1996; trans of books in 14 langs. *Recreations:* Asian travel, book-hunting. *Address:* c/o John Murray, 50 Albemarle Street, W1X 4BD.

HOPPEN, Prof. (Karl) Theodore, PhD; FBA 2001; Professor of History, University of Hull, since 1996; *b* 27 Nov. 1941; *s* of Paul Ernst Theodore Hoppen and Edith Margaretha Hoppen (*née* Van Brussel); *m* 1970, Alison Mary Buchan; one *s* two *d*. *Educ:* Glenstal Abbey Sch., Co. Limerick; University Coll., Dublin (BA 1961; MA 1964); Trinity Coll., Cambridge (PhD 1967). University of Hull: Asst Lectr, 1966–68; Lectr, 1968–74; Sen. Lectr, 1974–86; Reader, 1986–96. Benjamin Duke Fellow, Nat. Humanities Center, NC, 1985–86; Vis. Fellow, Sidney Sussex Coll., Cambridge, 1988; Res. Reader in Humanities, British Acad., 1994–96. *Publications:* The Common Scientist in the Seventeenth Century, 1970; (ed) Papers of the Dublin Philosophical Society 1683–1709, 1982; Elections, Politics and Society in Ireland 1832–1885, 1984; Ireland since 1800: conflict and conformity, 1989, 2nd edn 1999; (contrib.) New Oxford History of England, 1998; contrib. numerous articles to learned jls. *Recreation:* idleness. *Address:* Department of History, University of Hull, Hull HU6 7RX. *T:* (01482) 346311, (01482) 465490. *Club:* Oxford and Cambridge.

HOPPER, Prof. Andrew, PhD; FREng, FIEE; Managing Director, AT&T Laboratories Cambridge (formerly Olivetti-Oracle Research Laboratory, Cambridge), since 1986; Professor of Communications Engineering, University of Cambridge, since 1997; Fellow, Corpus Christi College, Cambridge, since 1981; *b* Warsaw, Poland, 9 May 1953; *s* of William John Hopper and Maria Barbara Wyrzykowska; *m* 1988, Dr Alison Gail Smith; one *s* one *d*. *Educ:* Quintin Kynaston Sch., London; University Coll. of Swansea (BSc); Trinity Hall, Cambridge (PhD 1978). FREng (FEng 1996); FIEE 1993. University of Cambridge: Res. Asst, 1977–79; Asst Lectr, 1979–83; Lectr, 1983–92; Reader in Computer Technol., 1992–98. Res. Dir, Acorn Computers Ltd, Cambridge, 1979–84; Director: Qudos Ltd, Cambridge, 1985–89; Virata Corp. (formerly Advanced Telecommunications Modules Ltd), 1993–; Acorn Computer Gp plc, Cambridge, 1996–98; Telemedia Systems Ltd, Cambridge, 1998– (Chm., 1995–98); Adaptive Broadband Ltd, 1998–; Chm., Cambridge Broadband Ltd, 2000–; Vice-Pres., Res., Ing. C. Olivetti & C., SpA, Italy, 1993–98. Clifford Paterson Lecture, Royal Soc., 1999. *Publication:* (jtly) Local Area Network Design, 1986. *Recreations:* ski-ing (Univ. of Cambridge Half Blue), flying, farming. *Address:* AT&T Laboratories Cambridge, 24A Trumpington Street, Cambridge CB2 1QA. *T:* (01223) 343000.

HOPPER, Andrew Christopher Graham; QC 2001; *b* 1 Oct. 1948; *s* of late Hugh Christopher Hopper and Doreen Adele Hopper (*née* Harper); *m* 1980, Rosamund Heather Towers. *Educ:* Monkton Combe Sch., Bath. Admitted solicitor, 1972; Higher Courts

(Civil) Qualification 1994; Partner, Adams & Black, Cardiff, 1972–88 (Sen. Partner, 1982–88); HM Dep. Coroner for S Glamorgan, 1977–83; estabd own practice, 1988; Consultant: Cartwrights Adams & Black, Cardiff, 1988–; Jay Benning & Peltz, 1997–2000; Geoffrey Williams and Christopher Green, Cardiff, 1998–; Radcliffes, 2001–. Mem., Disciplinary Prosecuting Panel, Law Soc., 1979–. *Publications:* (ed) Cordery on Solicitors, 9th edn, 1995, 10th edn, 1999; (contrib.) Legal Problems in Emergency Medicine, 1996; (ed) Guide to Professional Conduct of Solicitors, 8th edn, 1999. *Recreation:* mostly Burgundy. *Address:* PO Box 7, Pontyclun, Mid Glamorgan CF72 9XN. *Club:* East India.

HOPPER, William Joseph; Executive Chairman, WJ Hopper & Co. Ltd, investment bankers, and placing agents, since 1996; *b* 9 Aug. 1929; *s* of I. Vance Hopper and Jennie Josephine Hopper; one *d* by a former marriage. *Educ:* Langside Elementary Sch., Glasgow; Queen's Park Secondary Sch., Glasgow; Glasgow Univ. (MA 1st Cl. Hons (Mod. Langs) 1953). Financial Analyst, W. R. Grace & Co., NY, 1956–59; London Office Manager, H. Hentz & Co., Members, NY Stock Exchange, 1960–66; Gen. Manager, S. G. Warburg & Co. Ltd, 1966–69; Director: Hill Samuel & Co. Ltd, 1969–74; Morgan Grenfell & Co. Ltd, 1974–79 (Adviser, 1979–86) (bond issue for EIB selected as Deal of the Year by Institutional Investor, 1976); Wharf Resources Ltd, Calgary, 1984–87; Manchester Ship Canal Co., 1985–87; Chm., Robust Mouldings, 1986–90; Exec. Chm., Shire Trust, 1986–91; Advr, Yamaichi Internat. (Europe), 1986–88. MEP (C), Greater Manchester West, 1979–84. Co-founder (1969) and first Chm. (now Mem., Exec. Cttee), Inst. for Fiscal Studies, London; Treasurer, Action Resource Centre, 1985–94; Trustee: Nat. Hosp. for Nervous Diseases Develt Fund, 1986–90; Hampstead, Wells and Campden Trust, 1989–2000. Chm. Cttee of Management, Rosslyn Hill Unitarian Chapel, 1995–98. Mem., London Dist and SE Provincial Assembly of Unitarian and Free Christian Churches, 2000–. Governor, Colville Primary Sch., Notting Hill Gate, 1978–80. *Publication:* A Turntable for Capital, 1969. *Recreations:* listening to music, garden design. *Address:* 9a Flask Walk, Hampstead, NW3 1HJ. *T:* (020) 7435 6414, *Fax:* (020) 7431 5568; *e-mail:* wjhopper@compuserve.com. *Club:* Garrick.

HOPWOOD, Prof. Anthony George; Peter Moores Director, Saïd Business School, University of Oxford, since 1999; American Standard Companies Professor of Operations Management and Student of Christ Church, University of Oxford, since 1997; *b* 18 May 1944; *s* of late George and Violet Hopwood; *m* 1967, Caryl Davies; two *s*. *Educ:* Hanley High School; LSE (BSc Econ); Univ. of Chicago (MBA, PhD). Fulbright Fellow, Univ. of Chicago, 1965–70; Lectr in Management Accounting, Manchester Business Sch., 1970–73; Senior Staff, Admin. Staff Coll., Henley, 1973–76; Professorial Fellow, Oxford Centre for Management Studies, 1976–78; ICA Prof. of Accounting and Financial Reporting, London Business Sch., 1978–85; Arthur Young, subseq. Ernst and Young, Prof. of Internat. Accounting and Financial Management, LSE, 1985–95; Oxford University: Prof. of Management Studies, and Fellow, Templeton Coll., 1995–97; Dep. Dir, Sch. of Mgt Studies, later Saïd Business Sch., 1995–98; Visitor, Ashmolean Mus., 2000–. Vis. Prof. of Management, European Inst. for Advanced Studies in Management, Brussels, 1972– (Pres., 1995–); Associate Fellow, Industrial Relations Research Unit, Univ. of Warwick, 1978–80; Amer. Accounting Assoc. Dist. Internat. Vis. Lectr, 1981; Distinguished Vis. Prof. of Accounting, Pennsylvania State Univ., 1983–88. Mem., Management and Industrial Relations Cttee, SSRC, 1975–79; Chm., Management Awards Panel, SSRC, 1976–79; Pres., European Accounting Assoc., 1977–79 and 1987–88; Member: Council, Tavistock Inst. of Human Relations, 1981–91; Research Bd, ICA, 1982–98; Dir, Greater London Enterprise Bd, 1985–87. Accounting Advr, EC, 1989–90; Accounting Cons., OECD, 1990–91. Editor-in-Chief, Accounting, Organizations and Society, 1976–. Hon. DEcon: Turku Sch. of Econs, Finland, 1989; Gothenburg, 1992; Hon. DSc Lincolnshire and Humberside, 1999; Hon. Dr Mercaturae. Copenhagen Business Sch., 2000. *Publications:* An Accounting System and Managerial Behaviour, 1973; Accounting and Human Behaviour, 1973; (with M. Bromwich) Essays in British Accounting Research, 1981; (with M. Bromwich and J. Shaw) Auditing Research, 1982; (with M. Bromwich) Accounting Standard Setting, 1983; (with H. Schreuder) European Contributions to Accounting Research, 1984; (with C. Tomkins) Issues in Public Sector Accounting, 1984; (with M. Bromwich) Research and Current Issues in Management Accounting, 1986; Accounting from the Outside: the collected papers of Anthony G. Hopwood, 1988; International Pressures for Accounting Change, 1989; (with M. Page and S. Turley) Understanding Accounting in a Changing Environment, 1990; (with M. Bromwich) Accounting and the Law, 1992; (with P. Miller) Accounting as Social and Institutional Practice, 1994; articles in learned and professional jls. *Address:* Saïd Business School, University of Oxford, Radcliffe Infirmary, Woodstock Road, Oxford OX2 6HE. *T:* (01865) 228470.

HOPWOOD, Sir David (Alan), Kt 1994; FRS 1979; John Innes Professor of Genetics, University of East Anglia, Norwich, 1968–98, now Emeritus Professor of Genetics; Head of the Genetics Department, John Innes Centre, 1968–98, now Emeritus Fellow; *b* 19 Aug. 1933; *s* of Herbert Hopwood and Dora Hopwood (*née* Grant); *m* 1962, Joyce Lilian Bloom; two *s* one *d*. *Educ:* Purbrook Park County High Sch., Hants; Lymm Grammar Sch., Cheshire; St John's Coll., Cambridge (MA, PhD). DSc (Glasgow). Whytehead Major Scholar, St John's Coll., Cambridge, 1951–54; John Stothert Bye-Fellow, Magdalene Coll., Cambridge, 1956–58 (Hon. Fellow, 1991); Res. Fellow, St John's Coll., 1958–61; Univ. Demonstrator, Univ. of Cambridge, 1957–61; Lectr in Genetics, Univ. of Glasgow, 1961–68. Pres., Genetical Soc. of GB, 1985–87. Foreign Fellow, Indian Nat. Science Acad., 1987. Hon. Professor: Chinese Acad. of Med. Scis, 1987; Insts of Microbiology and Plant Physiology, Chinese Acad. of Scis, 1987; Huazhong Agricl Univ., Wuhan, China, 1989. Hon. FIBiol 2001. Hon. Fellow: UMIST, 1990; Magdalene Coll., Cambridge, 1992. Hon. Member: Spanish Microbiol. Soc., 1985; Hungarian Acad. of Scis, 1990; Soc. for Gen. Microbiol., 1990; Kitasato Inst., Tokyo, 1997. Hon. DSc: Eidgenössische Technische Hochschule, Zürich, 1989; UEA, 1998. Mendel Medal, Czech Acad. of Scis, 1995. *Publications:* numerous articles and chapters in scientific jls and books. *Recreations:* cooking, gardening. *Address:* John Innes Centre, Colney Lane, Norwich NR4 7UH. *T:* (01603) 450000, *Fax:* (01603) 450045.

HORAM, John Rhodes; MP (C) Orpington, since 1992; *b* 7 March 1939; *s* of Sydney Horam, Preston; *m* 1987, Judith Jackson. *Educ:* Silcoates Sch., Wakefield; Univ. of Cambridge. Marketing Executive, Rowntree & Co., 1960–62; leader and feature writer: Financial Times, 1962–65; The Economist, 1965–68; Man. Dir, Commodities Research Unit Ltd, 1968–70 and 1983–92; Dep. Chm., CRU Internat. Ltd, 1992–95, 1997–. MP Gateshead West, 1970–83 (Lab, 1970–81, SDP, 1981–83). Parly Under-Sec. of State, Dept of Transport, 1976–79; Labour spokesman on econ. affairs, 1979–81; Parly spokesman on econ. affairs, SDP, 1981–83; Parly Sec., OPSS, 1995; Parly Under-Sec. of State, DoH, 1995–97. Chm., Envmtl Audit Select Cttee, 1997–. Joined Conservative Party, Feb. 1987. *Address:* 6 Bovingdon Road, SW6 2AP.

HORBURY, Rev. Prof. William, PhD, DD; FBA 1997; Professor of Jewish and Early Christian Studies, University of Cambridge, since 1998; Fellow of Corpus Christi College, Cambridge, since 1978; *b* 6 June 1942; *m* 1966, Katharine Mary, *d* of late Rt Rev. D. R. Feaver; two *d*. *Educ:* Charterhouse; Oriel Coll., Oxford (MA 1967); Clare Coll., Cambridge (MA 1968; PhD 1971); Westcott House, Cambridge; DD Cantab 2000. Res. Fellow, Clare Coll., Cambridge, 1968–72; ordained deacon, 1969, priest, 1970; Vicar, Great Gransden, and Rector, Little Gransden, 1972–78; Cambridge University: Dean of Chapel, Corpus Christi Coll., 1978–85; Univ. Lectr in Divinity, 1984–96; Reader, 1996–98; Dir, Jewish Inscriptions Project, Divinity Faculty, 1989–95. NSM, St Botolph, Cambridge, 1990–. Pres., British Assoc. for Jewish Studies, 1996. *Publications:* (ed jtly) Suffering and Martyrdom in the New Testament, 1981; (ed jtly) Essays in Honour of Ernst Bammel, 1983; (ed) *Templum Amicitiae*: essays on the Second Temple, 1991; (jtly) Jewish Inscriptions of Graeco-Roman Egypt, 1992; (jtly) The Jewish-Christian Controversy, 1996; Jews and Christians in Contact and Controversy, 1998; Jewish Messianism and the Cult of Christ, 1998; (ed) Hebrew Study from Ezra to Ben-Yehuda, 1999; (ed jtly) The Cambridge History of Judaism, vol. iii, The Early Roman Period, 1999; Christianity in Ancient Jewish Tradition, 1999; articles in Vetus Testamentum, Jl of Theol Studies, New Testament Studies, Palestine Exploration Qly, Jewish Studies Qly, and other jls. *Recreations:* railways, cats. *Address:* Corpus Christi College, Cambridge CB2 1RH; 5 Grange Road, Cambridge CB3 9AS. *T:* (01223) 363529.

See also W. A. Feaver.

HORD, Brian Howard, CBE 1989; FRICS; company director; chartered surveyor; Director General, Bureau of European Building Consultants and Experts, 1991–95; *b* 20 June 1934; *s* of late Edwin Charles and Winifred Hannah Hord; *m* 1960, Christine Marian Lucas; two *s*. *Educ:* Reedham Sch.; Purley Grammar Sch. County Planning Dept, Mddx CC, 1950–51; Surveyor, private practice, 1951–57; National Service, RAF, 1957–59; Estates Surveyor, United Drapery Stores, 1959–66; Richard Costain Ltd, 1966–70; Director, Capcount UK Ltd, principal subsid. of Capital & Counties Property Co. Ltd, 1970–75; Partner, Howard Hord & Palmer, Chartered Surveyors, 1975–84. Chm., Bexley HA, 1986–92. Member: London Rent Assessment Panel, 1985–; London Regl Passengers' Cttee, 1997–2000. Contested (C) Darlington, Feb. and Oct. 1974. MEP (C) London West, 1979–84; Whip of European Democratic Gp, 1982–83; Mem., Agric. and Budgets Cttees, EP. *Publication:* (jtly) Rates-Realism or Rebellion. *Recreations:* photography, top-fruit growing, bee-keeping. *Address:* Whitesides, Pilgrims Way East, Otford, Sevenoaks, Kent TN14 5QN.

HORDEN, Prof. John Robert Backhouse, FSA, FSAScot, FRSL; Emeritus Professor of Bibliographical Studies, University of Stirling, since 1988; Editor, Dictionary of Scottish Biography; *o s* of late Henry Robert Horden and Ethel Edith Horden (*née* Backhouse), Warwicks; *m* 1948, Aileen Mary (*d* 1984), *o d* of late Lt Col and Mrs W. J. Douglas, Warwicks and S Wales; one *s*. *Educ:* Oxford, Cambridge, Heidelberg, Sorbonne, Lincoln's Inn. Revived and ed The Isis, 1945–46. Previously: Tutor and Lectr in English Literature, Christ Church, Oxford; Director, Inst. of Bibliography and Textual Criticism, Univ. of Leeds; Dir, Centre for Bibliographical Studies, Univ. of Stirling. Vis. professorial appts, Univs of Pennsylvania State, Saskatchewan, Erlangen-Nürnberg, Texas at Austin, Münster; Cecil Oldman Meml Lectr in Bibliography and Textual Criticism, 1971. Hon. Life Mem., Modern Humanities Res. Assoc., 1976. DHL (*hc*) Indiana State Univ., 1974. Marc Fitch Prize for Bibliography, 1979. Devised new academic discipline of Publishing Studies and designed first British degree course at Univ. of Leeds, 1972 (MA); initiated first British degree in Public Relations (MSc), Univ. of Stirling, 1987. *Publications:* Francis Quarles: a bibliography of his works to 1800, 1953; (ed) Francis Quarles' Hosanna and Threnodes, 1960, 3rd edn 1965; John Quarles (1625–1665): an analytical bibliography, 1960; Arthur Warwick's Spare Minutes (1634): an analytical bibliography, 1965; (ed) Annual Bibliography of English Language and Literature, 1967–75; (ed) English and Continental Emblem Books (22 vols), 1968–76; Art of the Drama, 1969; (ed) George Wither's A Collection of Emblemes, 1973; Everyday Life in Seventeenth-century England, 1974; (contrib.) New Cambridge Bibliography of English Literature, 1974; Techniques of Bibliography, 1977; (ed) Dictionary of Concealed Authorship, vol. 1, 1980 (1st vol. of rev. Halkett and Laing); (initiator and first editor) Index of English Literary Manuscripts (11 vols), 1980–97; John Freeth: political ballad writer and inn keeper, 1985, 2nd edn 1993; (ed) Bibliographia, 1992; (ed jtly) Francis Quarles' Emblemes and Hieroglyphikes, 1993; numerous contribs to learned jls. *Recreations:* golf (represented England, Warwicks, Oxford, and Cambridge), music, painting. *Address:* Department of English Studies, University of Stirling, Stirling FK9 4LA. *T:* (01786) 467495. *Clubs:* Athenæum; Vincent's (Oxford); Hawks' (Cambridge).

HORDEN, Richard, RIBA; Chairman, Horden Cherry Lee Architects Ltd, since 1999; Managing Director, Richard Horden Associates, since 1985; *b* 26 Dec. 1944; *s* of Peter Horden and Irene Horden (*née* Kelly); *m* 1972, Kathleen Gibson Valentine (*d* 1998); one *s* one *d*. *Educ:* Perrott Hill Sch.; Bryanston Sch.; Architectural Assoc. (AA Dip.). RIBA 1974. Work with Sir Norman Foster, 1974–84: Design Assistant for the Sainsbury Centre for Visual Arts, UEA; Stansted Airport; estabd Richard Horden Associates, 1985. RIBA Commendation for Courtyard House, Poole, 1974; FT Award and RIBA Nat. Award for Architecture for Queen's Stand, Epsom, 1993. *Publications:* Light Tech: towards a light architecture, 1995; Richard Horden: architecture and teaching, 1999. *Recreations:* yachting, ski-ing, running. *Address:* Horden Cherry Lee Architects Ltd, 34 Bruton Place, W1J 6NR. *T:* (020) 7495 4119. *Club:* Royal Motor Yacht (Poole).

HORDER, Dr John Plaistowe, CBE 1981 (OBE 1971); FRCP, FRCPE, FRCGP, FRCPsych; general practitioner of medicine, 1951–81, retired; President, National Centre for the Advancement of Interprofessional Education, since 1995 (Chairman, 1987–94); *b* 9 Dec. 1919; *s* of Gerald Morley Horder and Emma Ruth Horder; *m* 1940, Elizabeth June Wilson; two *s* two *d*. *Educ:* Lancing Coll.; University Coll., Oxford (BA 1945); London Hosp. (BM BCh 1948). FRCP 1972 (MRCP 1951); FRCGP 1970 (MRCGP 1957); FRCPsych 1980 (MRCPsych 1975); FRCPE 1982. Consultant, 1959, Travelling Fellow, 1964, WHO; Lectr, London School of Economics and Pol. Sci., 1964–69; Sir Harry Jeffcott Vis. Prof., Univ. of Nottingham, 1975; Visiting Professor: Royal Free Hosp. Med. Sch., 1982–91; Zagreb Univ., 1990–. Samuel Gee Lectr, RCP, 1991. Consultant Adviser, DHSS, 1978–84. Pres., Medical Art Soc., 1990–93. Pres., RCGP, 1979–82 (John Hunt Fellow, 1974–77; Wolfson Travelling Prof., 1978); Hon. FRSocMed 1983 (Vice-Pres., 1987–89; Pres., Sect. of Gen. Practice, 1970). Hon. Fellow: Green Coll., Oxford, 1988; QMW, 1997. Hon. MD Free Univ. Amsterdam, 1985. Hon. Mem., Coll. of Family Physicians of Canada, 1982. *Publications:* ed and co-author: The Future General Practitioner—learning and teaching, 1972; General Practice under the National Health Service 1948–1997, 1998. *Recreations:* painting, music. *Address:* 98 Regent's Park Road, NW1 8UG. *T:* (020) 7722 3804.

HORDERN, (Alfred) Christopher (Willoughby); QC 1979; **His Honour Judge Hordern;** a Circuit Judge, since 1983; *m*; one *s* two *d*. *Educ:* Oxford Univ. (MA). Called to the Bar, Middle Temple, 1961; a Recorder of the Crown Court, 1974–83. *Address:* c/o South Eastern Circuit Office, New Cavendish House, 18 Maltravers Street, WC2R 3EU.

HORDERN, Rt Hon. Sir Peter (Maudslay), Kt 1985; PC 1993; DL; Chairman, Fina (formerly Petrofina (UK)), 1987–98 (Director, 1973–98); *b* 18 April 1929; British; *s* of C.

H. Hordern, MBE; *m* 1964, Susan Chataway; two *s* one *d*. *Educ:* Geelong Grammar Sch., Australia; Christ Church, Oxford, 1949–52 (MA). Mem. of Stock Exchange, London, 1957–74. Chm., Foreign & Colonial Smaller Cos (formerly Foreign & Colonial Alliance Investment), 1986–97 (Dir, 1976–99); Dir, TR Technology, 1975–98. MP (C) Horsham, 1964–74 and 1983–97, Horsham and Crawley, 1974–83. Chm., Cons. Parly Finance Cttee, 1970–72; Member: Exec., 1922 Cttee, 1968–97 (Jt Sec., 1988–97); Public Accts Cttee, 1970–97; Public Accounts Commn, 1984–97 (Chm., 1988–97). Mem. Bd, British Liby, 1996–99. DL West Sussex, 1988. *Recreations:* golf, reading and travel.

HORE-RUTHVEN, family name of **Earl of Gowrie**.

HORLICK, Vice-Adm. Sir Edwin John, (Sir Ted), KBE 1981; FREng, FIMechE, MIMarE; part-time consultant; *b* 28 Sept. 1925; *m* Jean Margaret (*née* Covington) (*d* 1991); four *s*. *Educ:* Bedford Modern Sch. Joined RN, 1943; Sqdn Eng. Officer, 2nd Frigate Sqdn, 1960–63; Ship Dept, MoD, 1963–66; First Asst to Chief Engineer, HM Dockyard, Singapore, 1966–68; Asst Dir Submarines, 1969–72; SOWC 1973; Fleet Marine Engineering Officer, Staff of C-in-C Fleet, 1973–75; RCDS 1976; Dir Project Team Submarine/Polaris, 1977–79; Dir Gen. Ships, 1979–83; Chief Naval Engineer Officer, 1981–83. FREng (FEng 1983). *Recreations:* golf, Rugby administration, DIY. *Address:* Garden Apt, 74 Great Pulteney Street, Bath BA2 4DL. *Club:* Army and Navy.

HORLICK, Sir James Cunliffe William, 6th Bt *cr* 1914, of Cowley Manor, Gloucester; *b* 19 Nov. 1956; *o s* of Sir John James Macdonald Horlick, 5th Bt and of June, *d* of Douglas Cory-Wright, CBE; *S* father, 1995; *m* 1st, 1985, Fiona Rosalie (marr. diss. 1998), *e d* of Andrew McLaren; three *s*; 2nd, 1999, Mrs Gina Hudson. *Educ:* Eton. *Heir: s* Alexander Horlick, *b* 8 April 1987.

HORLICK, Sir Ted; *see* Horlick, Sir Edwin John.

HORLOCK, Henry Wimburn Sudell; Underwriting Member of Lloyd's, 1957; Director, Stepping Stone School, 1962–87; *b* 19 July 1915; *s* of Rev. Henry Darrell Sudell Horlock, DD, and Mary Haliburton Laurie; *m* 1960, Jeannetta Robin, *d* of F. W. Tanner, JP. *Educ:* Pembroke Coll., Oxford (MA). Army, 1939–42. Civil Service, 1942–60. Court of Common Council, City of London, 1969–2001 (Chm., West Ham Park Cttee, 1979–82; Chm., Police Cttee, 1987–90); Deputy, Ward of Farringdon Within, 1978–99; Sheriff, City of London, 1972–73; Chm., City of London Sheriffs' Soc., 1985–; Liveryman: Saddlers Co., 1937–, Master, 1976–77; Plaisterers' Co. (Hon.), 1975–; Fletchers' Co., 1977–; Gardeners' Co., 1980–; Member: Parish Clerks' Co., 1966–, Master, 1981–82; Guild of Freemen, 1972–, Master, 1986–87; Farringdon Ward Club, 1970–, Pres., 1978–79; United Wards Club, 1972–, Pres., 1980–81; City Livery Club, 1969–, Pres., 1981–82; City of London Br., Royal Society of St George, 1972–, Chm., 1989–90. Commander: Order of Merit, Federal Republic of Germany, 1972; National Order of the Aztec Eagle of Mexico, 1973; Order of Wissam Alouite, Morocco, 1987. *Recreations:* Freemasonry, gardening, travel. *Address:* Copse Hill House, Lower Slaughter, Glos GL54 2HZ. *T:* (01451) 820276; 97 Defoe House, Barbican, EC2Y 8DN. *T:* (020) 7588 1602. *Clubs:* Athenæum, Guildhall, City Livery.

HORLOCK, Sir John (Harold), Kt 1996; FRS 1976; FREng; Vice-Chancellor, 1981–90, and Fellow, since 1991, Open University; *b* 19 April 1928; *s* of Harold Edgar and Olive Margaret Horlock; *m* 1953, Sheila Joy Stutely; one *s* two *d*. *Educ:* Edmonton Latymer Sch.; (Scholar) St John's Coll., Cambridge (Hon. Fellow 1989). 1st Class Hons Mech. Sci. Tripos, Pt I, 1948, Rex Moir Prize; Pt II, 1949; MA 1952; PhD 1955; ScD 1975. Design and Development Engineer, Rolls Royce Ltd, Derby, 1949–51; Fellow, St John's Coll., Cambridge, 1954–57 and 1967–74; Univ. Demonstrator, 1952–56; University Lecturer, 1956–58, at Cambridge Univ. Engineering Lab.; Harrison Prof. of Mechanical Engineering, Liverpool Univ., 1958–66; Prof. of Engineering, and Dir of Whittle Lab., Cambridge Univ., 1967–74; Vice-Chancellor, Univ. of Salford, 1974–80. Visiting Asst Prof. in Mech. Engineering, Massachusetts Inst. of Technology, USA, 1956–57; Vis. Prof. of Aero-Space Engineering, Pennsylvania State Univ., USA, 1966. Chm., ARC, 1979–80 (Mem., 1960–63, 1969–72); Member: SRC, 1974–77; Cttee of Inquiry into Engineering Profession, 1977–80; Engineering Council, 1981–83; Chm., Adv. Cttee on Safety in Nuclear Installations, 1984–93. Director: BICERA Ltd, 1964–65; Cambridge Water Co., 1971–74; British Engine Insurance Ltd, 1979–84; Gaydon Technology Ltd, 1978–88; Open University Educational Enterprises Ltd, 1981–88; National Grid Co., 1989–94. A Vice-Pres., 1981–83, 1992–97, Treas., 1992–97, Royal Soc. Calvin Rice Lectr, ASME, 1994. FREng (FEng 1977); FIMechE; Fellow ASME; Foreign Associate, US Nat. Acad. of Engrg. Hon. Fellow, UMIST, 1991 (a Pro-Chancellor, 1995–). Hon. DSc: Heriot-Watt, 1980; Salford, 1981; CNAA, 1991; de Montfort, 1995; Cranfield, 1997; Hon. ScD East Asia, 1987; Hon. DEng Liverpool, 1987; DUniv Open, 1991. Clayton Prize, 1962, Thomas Hawksley Gold Medal, 1969, Arthur Charles Main Prize, 1997, IMechE; R. Tom Sawyer Award, ASME, 1997. *Publications:* The Fluid Mechanics and Thermodynamics of Axial Flow Compressors, 1958; The Fluid Mechanics and Thermodynamics of Axial Flow Turbines, 1966; Actuator Disc Theory, 1978; (ed) Thermodynamics and Gas Dynamics of Internal Combustion Engines, vol. I, 1982, vol. II, 1986; Cogeneration—Combined Heat and Power, 1987; Combined Power Plants, 1992; (ed) Energy for the Future, 1995; contribs to mech. and aero. engineering jls and to Proc. Royal Society. *Recreations:* music, watching sport. *Address:* 2 The Avenue, Ampthill, Bedford MK45 2NR. *T:* (01525) 841307. *Clubs:* Athenæum, MCC.

See also T. J. Horlock.

HORLOCK, Timothy John; QC 1997; a Recorder, since 2000; *b* 4 Jan. 1958; *s* of Sir John Horlock, *qv*; *m*; three *s*. *Educ:* Manchester Grammar Sch.; St John's Coll., Cambridge (MA). Called to the Bar, Middle Temple, 1981; Asst Recorder, 1997–2000. *Recreations:* football, tennis, cricket. *Address:* 9 St John Street, Manchester M3 4DN.

HORN, Bernard Philip; Director, 1995–2000, and Executive Director, Group Operations, 1996–2000, National Westminster Bank Plc; *b* 22 April 1946; *s* of late Robert Horn and Margaret Mary Horn; *m* 1988, Clare Margaret Gilbert; one *s* two *d*; and two *s* one *d* by previous marriage. *Educ:* Catholic Coll., Preston; John Dalton Faculty of Technol., Manchester (DMS); Harvard Business Sch. With National Westminster Bank, 1965–2000: Sen. Internat. Exec., Corp. Financial Services, 1986–88; Chief of Staff, 1989–90; Gen. Manager, Gp Strategy and Communications, 1990–91; Chief Exec., Internat. Businesses, 1991–96. Chm., Public Private Finance Ltd; non-executive Director: Netik plc; Cubic-C Ltd; Rock Project & Construction Management Ltd. FCIB 1991; FRSA 1991. *Recreations:* keeping fit, opera, theatre, my Morgan+8, piano (playing for own enjoyment), the trials, tribulations, delights and successes of my children. *Address:* Netik plc, Sir John Lyn House, High Timber Street, EC4V 3LS; *e-mail:* bphorn@globalnet.co.uk. *Clubs:* Royal Automobile, Harbour.

HORN, Prof. Gabriel, MA, MD, ScD; FRS 1986; Master of Sidney Sussex College, Cambridge, 1992–99, Emeritus Fellow, since 1999; Fellow of King's College, Cambridge, 1962–74, 1978–92 and since 1999; *b* 9 Dec. 1927; *s* of late Abraham and Anne Horn; *m* 1st, 1952, Ann Loveday Dean Soper (marr. diss. 1979); two *s* two *d*; 2nd, 1980, Priscilla Barrett. *Educ:* Handsworth Technical Sch. and Coll., Birmingham (Nat. Cert. in Mech. Engrg); Univ. of Birmingham (BSc Anatomy and Physiology; MD, ChB). MA, ScD Cantab. Served in RAF (Educn Br.), 1947–49. House appts, Birmingham Children's and Birmingham and Midland Eye Hosps, 1955–56; University of Cambridge: Univ. Demonstrator in Anat., 1956–62; Lectr in Anat., 1962–72; Reader in Neurobiology, 1972–74; Prof. and Head of Dept of Anat., Univ. of Bristol, 1974–77; Cambridge University: Prof. of Zoology, 1978–95, now Emeritus Prof.; Hd of Dept, 1979–94; Dep. Vice-Chancellor, 1994–98; Chairman: Core Cttee, Govt Policy Prog., 1998–; Review Cttee on Origin of BSE, 2001. Sen. Res. Fellow in Neurophysiol., Montreal Neurol Inst., McGill Univ., 1957–58; Leverhulme Res. Fellow, Laboratoire de Neurophysiologie Cellulaire, France, 1970–71. Vis. Prof. of Physiol Optics, Univ. of Calif, Berkeley, 1963; Vis. Res. Prof., Ohio State Univ., 1965; Vis. Prof. of Zool., Makerere University Coll., Uganda, 1966; Dist. Vis. Prof., Univ. of Alberta, Edmonton, Canada, 1988; Vis. Miller Prof., Univ. of Calif, Berkeley, USA, 1989. Charnock Bradley Lectr, Edinburgh Univ., 1988; Crisp Lectr, Univ. of Leeds, 1990. Dir, Cambridge Consultants Ltd, 1966–69; Sen. Consultant, PA Technology, 1976–86; Mem., Scientific Adv. Bd, Parke-Davis, 1988–99 (Chm., 1996). Member: Biol Sciences Cttee, SRC, 1973–75; Jt MRC and SRC Adv. Panel on Neurobiol., 1971–72; Res. Cttee, Mental Health Foundn, 1973–78; Council, Anatomical Soc., 1976–78; Adv. Gp, ARC Inst. of Animal Physiology, Babraham, 1981–87; AFRC, 1991–94; Chairman: Mgt Cttee, Wellcome Trust and CRC Inst. of Cancer and Develtl Biol., 1990–97; BBSRC Wkg Party on Biol. of Spongiform Encephalopathies, 1991–95; Animal Scis and Psychol. Res. Grants Cttee, BBSRC, 1994–96. Dir, Co. of Biologists, 1980–93. Foreign Fellow, Acad. of Scis, Republic of Georgia, 1997; Hon. Mem., Anatomical Soc. of GB and Ireland, 1997. Hon. DSc Birmingham, 1999. Kenneth Craik Award in Physiol Psychol., 1962; Royal Medal, Royal Soc., 2001. *Publications:* (ed with R. A. Hinde) Short-Term Changes in Neural Activity and Behaviour, 1970; Memory, Imprinting and the Brain, 1985; (ed with J. R. Krebs) Behavioural and Neural Aspects of Learning and Memory, 1991; contrib. scientific jls, mainly on topics in neurosciences. *Recreations:* walking, cycling, music, riding. *Address:* Sub-Department of Animal Behaviour, Department of Zoology, University of Cambridge, Madingley, Cambridge CB3 8AA.

HORN, Gyula, PhD; MP (MSzP) Republic of Hungary, since 1990; Prime Minister of Hungary, 1994–98; *b* 5 July 1932; *s* of Geza Horn and Anna Csornyei; *m* Anna Kiraly; one *s* one *d*. *Educ:* Rostow Inst. Econs, USSR; Polit. Acad., Budapest (PhD 1976). Official, Min. of Finance, Budapest, 1954–59; desk officer, Min. of Foreign Affairs, 1959–61; Embassy Secretary, Diplomatic Mission: Sofia, 1961–63; Belgrade, 1963–69; Staff Mem., then Hd, Internat. Dept, Hungarian Socialist Workers Party (MSZMP), Budapest, 1969–85; State Sec., Min. of Foreign Affairs, 1985–89; Minister of Foreign Affairs, 1989–90; Chm., Foreign Affairs Cttee, Hungarian Parlt, 1990–93. Founder and Pres., Hungarian Socialist Party (MSzP), 1989– (Chm., 1990–). Mem., Hungarian Soc. of Political Scis. Mem., European Hon. Senate, 1991–. Glass of Understanding, Kassel; Karl Prize for work towards European unification, Aachen, 1991. Golden Labour Award of Merit (Hungary); Grand Cross (FRG). *Publications:* Development of East-West Relations in the 70s, 1970; Yugoslavia: our neighbour, 1971; Social and Political Changes in Albania since World War II, 1973; Pikes (autobiog.), 1991; Cölöpök, 1991; Freiheit die ich meine, 1991; Those Were the 90s, 1999; books on E-W relations in the Seventies, European security and co-operation and develt of internat. contacts; contrib. numerous articles to professional jls. *Address:* National Assembly, 1055 Budapest, Kossuth Lajos tér 1, Hungary.

HORN, Dr Heinz; Chairman: Executive Board, Ruhrkohle AG, 1985–95; Supervisory Board, Rütgerswerke AG, 1989–95; *b* 17 Sept. 1930; *m*; two *s* two *d*. *Educ:* Univs of Frankfurt and Munster. Financial Dir, Eschweiler Bergwerks-Verein, 1965–68; Member, Executive Board: Krupp Industrie und Stahlbau, 1968–72; Eisen & Metall AG, 1972–74; Mem., Exec. Bd, later Chm., Eschweiler Bergwerks-Verein, 1974–83; Dep. Chm., Exec. Bd, Ruhrkohle AG, 1983–85. *Address:* c/o Ruhrkohle AG, Rellinghauser Strasse 1, 45128 Essen, Germany.

HORN, Dr Pamela Lucy Ray; author; freelance lecturer, since 1991; *b* 2 May 1936; *d* of Gilbert L. Jones and Marjorie H. Jones; *m* 1963, Clifford Alfred Horn. *Educ:* Girls' High Sch., Burton on Trent; Leicester Univ. (BSc Econ. 1964; PhD 1968). Sec., Derbys CC, 1954–58; Assistant Lecturer: Burton on Trent Tech. Coll., 1958–59; Derby & Dist Coll. of Technol., 1959–63; part-time Lectr in Econ. and Social Hist., Oxford Poly., 1967–91. *Publications:* Joseph Arch, 1971; (ed) Agricultural Trade Unionism in Oxfordshire, 1974; The Victorian Country Child, 1974, 3rd edn 1997; The Rise and Fall of the Victorian Servant, 1975, 2nd edn 1995; Labouring Life in the Victorian Countryside, 1976, 2nd edn 1995; Education in Rural England, 1978; (ed) Village Education in 19th Century Oxfordshire, 1979; The Rural World 1780–1850, 1980; The Changing Countryside, 1984; Rural Life in England in the First World War, 1984; Life and Labour in Rural England 1780–1850, 1987; Around Abingdon in Old Photographs, 1987; The Victorian and Edwardian Schoolchild, 1989; Victorian Countrywomen, 1991; Ladies of the Manor, 1991, 2nd edn 1997; High Society, 1992; Children's Work and Welfare 1780–1890, 1994; Women in the 1920's, 1995; The Victorian Town Child, 1997; Pleasures and Pastimes in Victorian Britain, 1999; Life Below Stairs in the Twentieth Century, 2001; contributor to several books. *Recreations:* walking, gardening, foreign travel. *Address:* 11 Harwell Road, Sutton Courtenay, Abingdon, Oxon OX14 4BN. *T:* (01235) 847424.

HORNBY, Sir Derek (Peter), Kt 1990; *b* 10 Jan. 1930; *s* of F. N. Hornby and V. M. Pardy; *m* 1st, 1953, Margaret Withers (marr. diss.); one *s* one *d*; 2nd, 1971, Sonia Beesley; one *s* one *d*. *Educ:* Canford School. With Mobil Oil, Mars Industries and Texas Instruments; Xerox Corp., 1973 (Dir, Internat. Ops); Exec. Dir, Rank Xerox, 1980–84; Chm., Rank-Xerox (UK), 1984–90. Mem. Bd, British Rail, 1985–90; Civil Service Comr, 1986–90; Chairman: BOTB, 1990–95 (Mem., 1987–95; Chm., N Amer. Gp, 1987); NACCB, 1980–84. Chairman: Video Arts, 1993–96; Partnership Sourcing Ltd, 1993–98; London & Continental Railways, 1994–98; IRG, 1997–2000; Director: Cogent Elliott, 1988–; London and Edinburgh Insurance Gp, 1989–96; Kode International, 1989–97; Dixons, 1990–97; Sedgwick Group, 1993–98; Pillar Properties plc, 1994–; Morgan Sindall Ltd, 1995– (Chm., 1995–2000). Mem. Bd, Savills, 1988–95. Pres., Shaw Trust, 1995–. Chm. Govs, Priors Court Sch. for Autism, 1999–. CIMgt (Chm., 1990–93). FRSA. Hon. DSc Aston, 1993. *Recreations:* Real tennis, theatre, cricket. *Address:* Badgers Farm, Idlicote, Shipston-on-Stour, Warwicks CV36 5DT. *Clubs:* Garrick, MCC; Leamington Real Tennis.

See also R. D. Harris.

HORNBY, Derrick Richard; *b* 11 Jan. 1926; *s* of late Richard W. Hornby and Dora M. Hornby; *m* 1948, June Steele; two *s* one *d*. *Educ:* University Coll., Southampton (DipEcon). Early career in accountancy; Marketing Dir, Tetley Tea Co. Ltd, 1964–69; Man. Dir, Eden Vale, 1969–74; Chm., Spillers Foods Ltd, 1974–77; Divisional Managing Director: Spillers Internat., 1977–80; Spillers Grocery Products Div., 1979–80; Chm., Carrington Viyella Ltd, 1979. Pres., Food Manufrs Fedn Incorp., 1977–79; Mem., Food and Drinks EDC. Member Council: CBI, to 1979; Food and Drinks Industry Council, to 1979. Chairman: Appeal Fund, Nat. Grocers Benefit Fund, 1973–74; London Animal

Trust, 1978–80. FIMgt, FIGD, ACommA. *Recreations:* golf, fly-fishing. *Address:* 4 Clipper Close, Warsash, Southampton SO31 9BJ.

HORNBY, Prof. James Angus; Professor of Law in the University of Bristol, 1961–85, now Emeritus; *b* 15 Aug. 1922; twin *s* of James Hornby and Evelyn Gladys (*née* Grant). *Educ:* Bolton County Grammar Sch.; Christ's Coll., Cambridge. BA 1944, LLB 1945, MA 1948 Cantab. Called to Bar, Lincoln's Inn, 1947. Lecturer, Manchester Univ., 1947–61. *Publications:* An Introduction to Company Law, 1957, 5th edn 1975; contribs to legal journals. *Recreations:* listening to music, reading, walking. *Address:* 7 Henbury Gardens, Henbury Road, Bristol BS10 7AJ. *Club:* Oxford and Cambridge.

HORNBY, Keith Anthony Delgado; His Honour Judge Hornby; a Circuit Judge, since 1995; *b* 18 Feb. 1947; *s* of late James Lawrence Hornby and of Naomi Ruth Hornby (*née* Delgado); *m* 1970, Judith Constance Fairbairn; two *s* one *d*. *Educ:* Oratory Sch.; Trinity Coll., Dublin (BA Hons Legal Sci.). Lectr in Commercial Law, PCL, 1969–70; called to the Bar, Gray's Inn, 1970; practised on SE Circuit, 1970–95; Asst Recorder, 1988–92; Recorder, 1992–95. *Recreations:* art, theatre, cricket, squash, golf. *Address:* Bow County Court, 96 Romford Road, Stratford, E15 4EG. *T:* (020) 8555 3421. *Club:* Hurlingham.

HORNBY, Richard Phipps, MA; Chairman, Halifax Building Society, 1983–90 (Director, 1976; Vice-Chairman, 1981–83); *b* 20 June 1922; *e s* of late Rt Rev. Hugh Leycester Hornby, MC; *m* 1951, Stella Hichens; two *s* one *d* (and one *s* decd). *Educ:* Winchester Coll.; Trinity Coll., Oxford (Scholar). Served in King's Royal Rifle Corps, 1941–45. 2nd Cl. Hons in Modern History, Oxford, 1948 (Soccer Blue). History Master, Eton Coll., 1948–50; with Unilever, 1951–52; with J. Walter Thompson Co., 1952–63, 1964–81 (Dir, 1974–81); Director: McCorquodale plc, 1982–86; Cadbury Schweppes plc, 1982–93. Contested (C) West Walthamstow: May 1955 (gen. election) and March 1956 (by-election); MP (C) Tonbridge, Kent, June 1956–Feb. 1974. PPS to Rt Hon. Duncan Sandys, MP, 1959–63; Parly Under-Sec. of State, CRO and CO, Oct. 1963–Oct. 1964. Member: BBC Gen. Adv. Council, 1969–74; Cttee of Inquiry into Intrusions into Privacy, 1970–72; British Council Exec. Cttee, 1971–74. *Recreations:* shooting, fishing, walking. *Address:* Ebble Thatch, Bowerchalke, near Salisbury, Wilts SP5 5BW.

HORNBY, Sir Simon (Michael), Kt 1988; Director, 1974–94, Chairman, 1982–94, W. H. Smith Group (formerly W. H. Smith & Son (Holdings) plc); Director: Pearson plc (formerly S. Pearson & Son Ltd), 1978–97; Lloyds TSB Group (formerly Lloyds Bank), 1988–99; Lloyds Abbey Life PLC, 1991–97 (Chairman, 1992–97); *b* 29 Dec. 1934; *s* of late Michael Hornby and Nicolette Joan, *d* of Hon. Cyril Ward, MVO; *m* 1968, Sheran Cazalet. *Educ:* Eton; New Coll., Oxford; Harvard Business Sch. 2nd Lieut, Grenadier Guards, 1953–55. Entered W. H. Smith & Son, 1958, Dir, 1965; Gp Chief Exec., W. H. Smith & Son (Holdings), 1978–82. Mem. Exec. Cttee, 1966–93, Property Cttee, 1979–86, Council 1976–2001, National Trust; Mem. Adv. Council, Victoria and Albert Museum, 1971–75; Council, RSA, 1985–90; Trustee, British Museum, 1975–85; Chairman: Design Council, 1986–92; Assoc. for Business Sponsorship of the Arts, 1988–97; Nat. Literary Trust, 1993–2001; President: Book Trust, 1990–96 (Dep. Chm., 1976–78, Chm., 1978–80, NBL); Newsvendors' Benevolent Instn, 1989–94; RHS, 1994–2001 (Mem. Council, 1992–2001); Chelsea Soc., 1994–2000. DUniv Stirling, 1992; Hon. DLitt Hull, 1994; Reading, 1996. *Recreations:* gardening, golf. *Address:* The Ham, Wantage, Oxon OX12 9JA. *T:* (01235) 770222.

HORNE, Sir (Alan) Gray (Antony), 3rd Bt *cr* 1929; *b* 11 July 1948; *s* of Antony Edgar Alan Horne (*d* 1954) (*o s* of 2nd Bt), and of Valentine Antonia, *d* of Valentine Dudensing; *S* grandfather, 1984; *m* 1980, Cecile Rose, *d* of Jacques Desplanche. *Heir:* none. *Address:* Château du Basty, Thenon, Dordogne, France.

HORNE, Alistair Allan, CBE 1992; LittD; author, journalist, lecturer; *b* 9 Nov. 1925; *s* of late Sir (James) Allan Horne and Lady (Auriol) Horne (*née* Hay), *widow* of Capt. Noel Barran; *m* 1st, 1953, Renira Margaret (marr. diss. 1982), *d* of Adm. Sir Geoffrey Hawkins, KBE, CB, MVO, DSC; three *d*; 2nd, 1987, Hon. Mrs Sheelin Eccles. *Educ:* Le Rosey, Switzerland; Millbrook, USA; Jesus Coll., Cambridge (MA); LittD Cantab 1993. Served War of 1939–45: RAF, 1943–44; Coldstream Gds, 1944–47; Captain, attached Intelligence Service (ME). Foreign Correspondent, Daily Telegraph, 1952–55. Founded Alistair Horne Res. Fellowship in Mod. History, St Antony's Coll., Oxford, 1969, Hon. Fellow, 1988. Fellow, Woodrow Wilson Center, Washington, DC, USA, 1980–81. Lectures: Lees Knowles, Cambridge, 1982; Goodman, Univ. of West Ontario, 1983. Member: Management Cttee, Royal Literary Fund, 1969–; Franco-British Council, 1979–; Cttee of Management, Soc. of Authors, 1979–82; Trustee, Imperial War Museum, 1975–82. FRSL. Chevalier, Légion d'Honneur (France), 1993. *Publications:* Back into Power, 1955; The Land is Bright, 1958; Canada and the Canadians, 1961; The Price of Glory: Verdun 1916, 1962 (Hawthornden Prize, 1963); The Fall of Paris: The Siege and The Commune 1870–71, 1965, rev. 2nd edn 1990; To Lose a Battle: France 1940, 1969, rev. 2nd edn 1990; Death of a Generation, 1970; The Terrible Year: The Paris Commune, 1971; Small Earthquake in Chile, 1972, rev. 2nd edn 1990; A Savage War of Peace: Algeria 1954–62, 1977 (Yorkshire Post Book of Year Prize, 1978; Wolfson Literary Award, 1978), 3rd edn 1996; Napoleon, Master of Europe 1805–1807, 1979; The French Army and Politics 1870–1970, 1984 (Enid Macleod Prize, 1985); Macmillan: the official biography, Vol. I, 1894–1956, 1988, Vol. 2, 1957–1986, 1989; A Bundle from Britain, 1993; (with David Montgomery) The Lonely Leader: Monty 1944–45, 1994; How Far from Austerlitz?: Napoleon 1805–1815, 1996; (ed) Telling Lives, 2000; *contribs to books:* Combat: World War I, ed Don Congdon, 1964; Impressions of America, ed R. A. Brown, 1966; Marshal V. I. Chuikov, The End of the Third Reich, 1967; Sports and Games in Canadian Life, ed N. and M. L. Howell, 1969; Decisive Battles of the Twentieth Century, ed N. Frankland and C. Dowling, 1976; The War Lords: Military Commanders of the Twentieth Century, ed Field Marshal Sir M. Carver, 1976; Regular Armies and Insurgency, ed R. Haycock, 1979; Macmillan: a life in pictures, 1983; contribs various periodicals. *Recreations:* thinking about ski-ing, painting, gardening, travel, communing with dogs. *Address:* The Old Vicarage, Turville, near Henley-on-Thames, Oxon RG9 6QU. *Clubs:* Garrick, Beefsteak.

HORNE, David Oliver, FCA; Chairman and Chief Executive, Lloyds Merchant Bank, 1987–92; *b* 7 March 1932; *s* of Herbert Oliver Horne, MBE and Edith Marion Horne (*née* Sellers); *m* 1959, Joyce Heather (*née* Kynoch); two *s* two *d*. *Educ:* Fettes College, Edinburgh. Director: S. G. Warburg & Co., 1966–70; Williams & Glyn's Bank, 1970–78; Lloyds Bank International, 1978–85; Managing Dir, Lloyds Merchant Bank, 1985–87. Dep. Chm., Serif, 1993–97; Director: Waterman Partnership Hldgs, 1992–; Black Arrow Gp, 1993–. *Recreation:* golf. *Address:* Four Winds, 5 The Gardens, Esher, Surrey KT10 8QF. *T:* (01372) 463510.

HORNE, Frederic Thomas; Chief Taxing Master of the Supreme Court, 1983–88 (Master, 1967–83); *b* 21 March 1917; *y s* of Lionel Edward Horne, JP, Moreton-in-Marsh, Glos; *m* 1944, Madeline Hatton; two *s* two *d*. *Educ:* Chipping Campden Grammar Sch. Admitted a Solicitor (Hons), 1938. Served with RAFVR in General Duties Branch (Pilot), 1939–56. Partner in Iliffe Sweet & Co., 1956–67. Mem., Lord Chancellor's Adv. Cttee on Legal Aid, 1983–91; Chm., Working Party on the Simplification of Taxation, 1980–83 (Horne Report, 1983). Pres., Assoc. of Law Costs Draftsmen, 1991–97. *Publications:* Cordery's Law Relating to Solicitors, 7th edn (jtly) 1981, 8th edn 1987; (contrib.) Atkins Encyclopaedia of Court Forms, 2nd edn, 1983; (ed jtly) The Supreme Court Practice, 1985 and 1988 edns; (contrib.) Private International Litigation, 1987. *Recreations:* cricket, music, archaeology. *Address:* Dunstall, Quickley Lane, Chorleywood, Herts WD3 5AF. *Club:* MCC.

HORNE, Sir Gray; *see* Horne, Sir A. G. A.

HORNE, Marilyn (Bernice); mezzo-soprano; *b* 16 Jan. 1934; *m* 1960, Henry Lewis (marr. diss.); one *d*; *m* Nicola Zaccaria. *Educ:* Univ. of Southern California. US opera début, 1954; sings at Covent Garden, La Scala, Metropolitan Opera and other major venues; rôles include Adalgisa, Amneris, Carmen, Eboli, Isabella, Mignon, Orlando, Rosina, Tancredi, concerts and recitals. *Address:* c/o Colombia Artists Management, Wilford Division, 165 West 57th Street, New York, NY 10019-2201, USA.

HORNE, Dr Nigel William, FREng, FIEE; Chairman, Alcatel UK Ltd, since 1992; *b* 13 Sept. 1940; *s* of late Eric Charles Henry and Edith Margaret Horne; *m* 1965, Jennifer Ann Holton; one *s* two *d*. *Educ:* John Lyon Sch., Harrow; Univ. of Bristol (BScEng 1962); Univ. of Cambridge (PhD 1968). FREng (FEng 1982); FIEE 1984. GEC Telecommunications, 1958–70; Management Systems Manager, 1970–72; Manufg Gen. Manager, 1972–75; Dir and Gen. Manager, Switching, 1976–82; Managing Dir, GEC Inf. Systems, 1982–83; Director: Technical and Corporate Develt, STC, 1983–90; Abingworth, 1985–90; LSI Logic, 1986–90; FI Gp, 1992–98; FI Gp Employees Trust, 1998–; Wireless Systems Internat. Ltd, 1995–; Foresight VCT Plc, 1997–; Onyvax Ltd, 1997–; Parc Technologies Ltd, 1999–; IT Partner, KPMG Peat Marwick, 1990–92. Vis. Prof., Univ. of Bristol, 1990–98. Member: Nat. Electronics Council, 1985–90; EC Esprit Adv. Bd, 1988–93; ACOST, Cabinet Office, 1991–93; EC Strategy Bd, DGIII, 1994–98; Ind. Review, Higher Educn Pay and Conditions, 1998; British N American Cttee, 1998–; Chairman: Computing and Control Div., IEE, 1988–89; DTI/SERC IT Adv. Bd, 1988–91. FRSA. Freeman, City of London; Liveryman, Inf. Technologists' Co.; Mem., Engineers' Co. Hon. DEng Bristol, 1992; Hon. DSc: Hull, 1992; City, 1995. Caballeros del Monasteria de Juste (Spain), 1992. *Publications:* papers in learned jls. *Recreations:* piano, walking, gardening. *Address:* Alcatel Ltd, 67–69 New Bond Street, W1Y 9DF. *Club:* Athenæum.

HORNE, Robert Drake; First Assistant Secretary, Department of Education (formerly Employment and Education), Training and Youth Affairs, Canberra, 1998–2001; *b* 23 April 1945; *s* of late Harold Metcalfe Horne and Dorothy Katharine Horne; *m* 1972, Jennifer Mary (*née* Gill); three *d*. *Educ:* Mill Hill Sch.; Oriel Coll., Oxford (MA Classics). Asst Master, Eton Coll., Windsor, 1967–68; DES, later DFE, then DFEE, 1968–97; seconded to Cabinet Office, 1979–80; Under Sec., 1988–97; Dir of Finance and Planning, Employment Service, 1995–97. *Recreations:* cycling, sun-soaking. *Address:* 53 Gulfview Road, Blackwood, SA 5051.

HORNER, Douglas George; Chairman, Mercantile Credit Company, 1980–84; Vice-Chairman, 1979–81, Director, 1975–84, Barclays Bank UK Limited; *b* Dec. 1917; *s* of Albert and Louise Horner; *m* 1941, Gwendoline Phyllis Wall; one *s*. *Educ:* Enfield Grammar Sch. Commissioned, Royal Norfolk Regt, 1940. Asst Manager/Manager at various bank branches, 1954–71; Local Dir, Lombard Street, 1971; Regional Gen. Manager, London, 1973; Gen. Man., 1975; Senior Gen. Man., 1977; Dir Barclays Bank plc, 1977–83. *Recreations:* golf, gardening.

HORNER, Frederick, DSc; CEng, FIEE; Director, Appleton Laboratory, Science Research Council, 1977–79; *b* 28 Aug. 1918; *s* of late Frederick and Mary Horner; *m* 1946, Elizabeth Bonsey; one *s* one *d*. *Educ:* Bolton Sch.; Univ. of Manchester (Ashbury Scholar, 1937; Fairbairn Engrg Prize, 1939; BSc 1st Cl. Hons 1939; MSc 1941; DSc 1968). CEng, FIEE 1959. On staff of DSIR, NPL, 1941–52; UK Scientific Mission, Washington DC, 1947; Radio Research Station, later Appleton Lab. of SRC, 1952–79, Dep. Dir, 1969–77; Admin. Staff Coll., Henley, 1959. Delegate: Internat. Union of Radio Science, 1950–90 (Chm., Commn VIII, 1966–69); Internat. Radio Consultative Cttee, 1953–90 (Internat. Chm., Study Group 2, 1980–90). Member: Inter-Union Commn on Frequency Allocations for Radio Astronomy and Space Science, 1965–92 (Sec., 1975–82); Electronics Divl Bd, IEE, 1970–76. Mem. Council: RHC, 1979–85 (Vice-Chm., 1982–85); RHBNC, 1985–89; Hon. Associate, Physics, RHC, 1975–85. Diplôme d'Honneur, Internat. Radio Cons. Cttee, 1989. *Publications:* more than 50 scientific papers. *Recreations:* genealogy, gardening. *Address:* Gordano Lodge, Clevedon Road, Weston-in-Gordano, Bristol BS20 8PZ.

HORNSBY, Timothy Richard, MA; a National Lottery Commissioner; *b* 22 Sept. 1940; *s* of late Harker William Hornsby and Agnes Nora French; *m* 1971, Dr Charmian Rosemary Newton; one *s* one *d*. *Educ:* Bradfield Coll.; Christ Church, Oxford Univ. (MA 1st C1. Hons Modern History). Harkness Fellow, USA, at Harvard, Columbia, Henry E. Huntington Research Inst., 1961–63; Asst Prof., Birmingham Southern Coll., Alabama, 1963–64; Research Lectr, Christ Church, Oxford, 1964–65; Asst Principal, Min. of Public Building and Works, 1965–67; Private Sec. to Controller General, 1968–69; HM Treasury, 1971–73; Prin., then Asst Sec., DoE, 1975; Dir, Ancient Monuments and Historic Buildings, 1983–88, and Dir of Rural Affairs, 1984–88, DoE; Dir Gen., Nature Conservancy Council, 1988–91; Dir, Construction Policy Directorate, DoE, 1991; Chief Executive: Royal Bor. of Kingston upon Thames, 1991–95; Nat. Lottery Charities Bd, 1995–2001. FRSA. *Recreations:* conservation, skiing, talking. *Address:* The Willows, Dulwich Common, SE21 7EW. *T:* (020) 8693 7379. *Club:* Athenæum.

HOROWITZ, Gillian Mary, (Mrs M. Horowitz); *see* Darley, G. M.

HOROWITZ, Michael; QC 1990; a Recorder, since 1991; *b* 18 Oct. 1943; *s* of late David Horowitz and Irene Horowitz; *m* 1986, Gillian Mary Darley, *qv*; one *d* (one *s* decd). *Educ:* St Marylebone Grammar School; Pembroke College, Cambridge (BA 1966; LLB 1967). Pres., Cambridge Union Soc., 1967; English-Speaking Union Debating Tour of USA, 1967. Called to the Bar, Lincoln's Inn, 1968, Bencher, 1997; Asst Recorder, 1987. Senate of Inns of Court and Bar, 1982–85; Mem., Professional Conduct Cttee, Bar Council, 1997–2000. Dir, Bar Mutual Indemnity Fund. *Publications:* (contrib.) Rayden on Divorce, 17th edn 1997; Essential Family Practice, 2000. *Recreations:* reading history, listening. *Address:* 1 Mitre Court Buildings, Temple, EC4Y 7BS. *T:* (020) 7797 7070.

HOROWITZ, Prof. Myer, OC 1990; EdD; Adjunct Professor of Education, University of Victoria, since 1998; Professor Emeritus of Education, since 1990, President Emeritus, since 1999, University of Alberta; *b* 27 Dec. 1932; *s* of Philip Horowitz and Fanny Cotler; *m* 1956, Barbara, *d* of Samuel Rosen and Grace Midvidy, Montreal; two *d*. *Educ:* High Sch., Montreal; Sch. for Teachers, Macdonald Coll.; Sir George Williams Univ. (BA); Univ. of Alberta (MEd); Stanford Univ. (EdD). Teacher, Schs in Montreal, Sch. Bd,

Greater Montreal, 1952–60. McGill University: Lectr in Educn, 1960–63; Asst Prof., 1963–65; Associate Prof., 1965–67; Asst to Dir, 1964–65; Prof. of Educn, 1967–69 and Asst Dean, 1965–69; University of Alberta: Prof. and Chm., Dept Elem. Educn, 1969–72; Dean, Faculty of Educn, 1972–75; Vice-Pres. (Academic), 1975–79; Pres., 1979–89. Hon. Dr: McGill, 1979; Concordia, 1982; Athabasca, 1989; British Columbia, 1990; Alberta, 1990; Victoria, 2000; Brock, 2000. *Address:* A269 MacLaurin Building, University of Victoria, PO Box 3010, Victoria, BC V8W 3N4, Canada.

HORRELL, John Ray, CBE 1979; TD; DL; farmer; *b* 8 March 1929; *er s* of late Harry Ray Horrell and of Phyllis Mary Horrell (*née* Whittome); *m* 1951, Mary Elizabeth Noëlle Dickinson; one *s* one *d.* Dir, Horrell's Farmers Ltd. Mem., Board, Peterborough New Town Develt Corp., 1970–88; formerly Mem. Oakes and Taylor Cttees of Enquiry. Member: Cambs (formerly Huntingdon and Peterborough) CC, 1963– (Chm., 1971–77; Chm., Educn Cttee; Leader, 1989–93); Peterborough City Council, 1996–; Chairman: Council of Local Educn Authorities, 1976–79; ACC, 1981–83 (Vice-Chm., 1979–81); E of England Agricl Soc., 1984–87. Mem. Council, CGLI, later C&G, 1975–96. Major, TA; a Vice-Chm., 1977–86, Chm., 1986–91, E Anglia TA&VRA. FRSA 1981. High Sheriff, Cambs, 1981–82; DL Cambs, 1973. *Address:* The Grove, Longthorpe, Peterborough PE3 6LZ. *T:* (01733) 262618.

HORRELL, Roger William, CMG 1988; OBE 1974; HM Diplomatic Service, retired; *b* 9 July 1935; *s* of William John Horrell and Dorice Enid (*née* Young); *m* 1970, Patricia Mildred Eileen Smith (*née* Binns) (marr. diss. 1975); one *s* one *d. Educ:* Shebbear College; Exeter College, Oxford. MA. Served in Devonshire Regt, 1953–55; HM Colonial Service, Kenya, 1959–64; joined Foreign Office, 1964; Economic Officer, Dubai, 1965–67; FCO, 1967–70; First Sec., Kampala, 1970–73; FCO, 1973–76; First Sec., Lusaka, 1976–80; Counsellor, FCO, 1980–93. *Recreations:* cricket, reading, walking, bridge. *Address:* 51 Oatlands Drive, Weybridge, Surrey KT13 9LU. *Club:* Reform.

HORRIDGE, Prof. (George) Adrian, FRS 1969; FAA 1971; Professor, Research School of Biological Sciences, Australian National University, 1969–92, Emeritus Professor, since 1993; *b* Sheffield, England, 12 Dec. 1927; *s* of George William Horridge and Olive Stray; *m* 1954, Audrey Anne Lightburne; one *s* four *d. Educ:* King Edward VII Sch., Sheffield. Fellow, St John's Coll., Cambridge, 1953–56; on staff, St Andrews Univ., 1956–69; Dir, Gatty Marine Laboratory, St Andrews, 1960–69. Vis. Fellow, Churchill Coll., Cambridge, 1993–94. *Publications:* Structure and Function of the Nervous Systems of Invertebrates (with T. H. Bullock), 1965; Interneurons, 1968; (ed) The Compound Eye and Vision of Insects, 1975; Monographs of the Maritime Museum at Greenwich nos 38, 39, 40, 54, 1979–82; The Prahu: traditional sailing boat of Indonesia, 1982 (Oxford in Asia); Sailing Craft of Indonesia, 1985 (Oxford in Asia); Outrigger Canoes of Bali & Madura, Indonesia, 1986; (contrib.) The Austronesians, 1995; contribs numerous scientific papers to jls, etc, on behaviour and nervous systems of lower animals, and vision of the honeybee. *Recreations:* optics, mathematics, marine biology; sailing, language, arts, boat construction in Indonesia. *Address:* PO Box 475, Canberra City, ACT 2601, Australia. *T:* (2) 62812762, *Fax:* (2) 61253808; *e-mail:* horridge@rsbs.anu.edu.au.

HORROCKS, Prof. Geoffrey Charles, PhD; Fellow, St John's College, Cambridge, since 1983; Professor of Comparative Philology, University of Cambridge, since 1997; *b* 3 Feb. 1951; *s* of Roland Horrocks and Marjorie Horrocks (*née* Atkinson); *m* 1973, Gillian Elizabeth Tasker; two *d. Educ:* Manchester Grammar Sch.; Downing Coll., Cambridge (BA 1972; PhD 1978). Employee Relns Manager, Mobil North Sea Ltd, 1972–73; Res. Fellow, Downing Coll., Cambridge, 1976–77; Lectr in Linguistics, SOAS, 1977–83; Lectr in Classics, Univ. of Cambridge, 1983–97. *Publications:* Space and Time in Homer, 1981; Generative Grammar, 1987; Greek: a history of the language and its speakers, 1997; contrib. numerous articles in jls of general, theoretical and historical linguistics, and Classics. *Recreations:* travel, guitar, football, gardening, gossip, talking to the members of my family (in no particular order). *Address:* St John's College, Cambridge CB2 1TP. *T:* (01223) 338600.

HORROCKS, Jane; actress; *b* 18 Jan. 1964; *d* of John and Barbara Horrocks; partner, Nick Vivian; one *s* one *d. Educ:* Fearns Co. Secondary Sch., Rossendale, Lancs; RADA (Dip.). *Films:* The Dressmaker, 1989; Life is Sweet, 1991 (Best Supporting Actress, LA Critics Award, 1992); Little Voice, 1998; Born Romantic, 2001; *plays:* The Rise and Fall of Little Voice, RNT and Aldwych, 1992–93; Cabaret, Donmar Warehouse, 1993–94; *television:* Suffer the Little Children, 1994 (Best Actress Award, RTS, 1995); Absolutely Fabulous, 1992–94, 2001; The Flint Street Nativity, 1999; Mirrorball, 2000. *Address:* c/o Peters Fraser & Dunlop, Drury House, 34–43 Russell Street, WC2B 5HA. *T:* (020) 7344 1010, *Fax:* (020) 7836 9544. *Club:* Groucho.

HORROCKS, Paul John; Editor, Manchester Evening News, since 1997; *b* 19 Dec. 1953; *s* of Joe and Eunice Horrocks; *m* 1976, Linda Jean Walton; two *s* one *d*, and one step *d. Educ:* Bolton Sch. Reporter, Daily Mail, 1974; Manchester Evening News: gen. reporter, 1975–80; crime corresp., 1980–87; news editor, 1987–91; Asst Editor, 1991–95; Dep. Editor, 1995–97. Dir, Soc. of Editors. Vice-Pres., Community Foundn for Greater Manchester, 2000–. Member: Organising Council, Commonwealth Games, Manchester 2002, 1998–; Manchester Enterprises Partners' Council. Patron, Francis House Children's Hospice. *Recreations:* sailing, golf, Rugby Union. *Address:* Manchester Evening News, 164 Deansgate, Manchester M60 2RD.

HORROCKS, Peter John Gibson. Head of Current Affairs, BBC, since 2000; *b* 8 Oct. 1959; *s* of James Nigel Gibson Horrocks and Ellen Elizabeth Gibson Horrocks; *m* 1987, Katharine Rosemary Rogers; two *s* one *d. Educ:* King's Coll. Sch., Wimbledon; Christ's Coll., Cambridge (BA). BBC: Dep. Ed., Panorama, 1988–90; Editor: Election '92; Public Eye, 1992–94; Here and Now, 1994; Newsnight, 1994–97; Election '97; Panorama, 1992–2000. *Address:* c/o BBC White City, Wood Lane, W12 7RJ.

HORROCKS, Raymond, CBE 1983; Chairman: Owenbell Ltd, 1987–2000; Chloride Group, 1988–99 (Director, 1986–99; Chief Executive, 1989–91); *b* 9 Jan. 1930; *s* of Elsie and Cecil Horrocks; *m* 1953, Pamela Florence Russell; three *d. Educ:* Bolton Municipal Secondary School. Textile Industry, 1944–48 and 1950–51; HM Forces, Army, Intelligence Corps, 1948–50; Sales Rep., Proctor & Gamble, 1951–52; Merchandiser, Marks & Spencer, 1953–58; Sub Gp Buying Controller, Littlewoods Mail Order Stores, 1958–63; various plant, departmental and divisional management positions, Ford Motor Co., 1963–72; Regional Dir, Europe and Middle East, Materials Handling Gp, Eaton Corp., 1972–77; Chm. and Man. Dir, Austin Morris Ltd, 1978–80; Man. Dir, BL Cars, 1980–81; Chm. and Chief Exec., BL Cars Gp, 1981–82; Exec. Dir and Bd Mem., BL, 1981–86; Gp Chief Exec., Cars, 1982–86; Chairman: Unipart Group Ltd, 1981–86; Austin Rover Gp Hldgs, 1981–86; Jaguar Cars Holdings Ltd, 1982–84; Kay Consultancy Group, 1989–91; Dir, Nuffield Services, 1982–86; non-executive Director: Jaguar plc, 1984–85; The Caravan Club, 1983–87; Electrocomponents, 1986–99; Lookers, 1986–99; WOL Hldgs Ltd, 1988–89; Burtree Caravans, 1988–96; Applied Hldgs (UK) Pty, 1988–96; Smith Millington Motor Co. Ltd (formerly SMAC Gp), 1988–96 (Chm., 1988–89); Applied Chemicals, 1988–96 (Dep. Chm., 1988–94); Jabiru UK, 1989–96. Member: Council, CBI, 1981–86; Europe Cttee, CBI, 1985–86. FIMI; CIMgt. *Recreations:* fly fishing, gardening, walking. *Address:* Far End, Riverview Road, Pangbourne, Reading, Berks RG8 7AU.

HORSBRUGH, Ian Robert; Principal, Guildhall School of Music & Drama, since 1988; *b* 16 Sept. 1941; *s* of Walter and Sheila Horsbrugh; *m* 1965, Caroline Everett; two *s* two *d. Educ:* St Paul's Sch.; Guildhall Sch. of Music and Drama (AGSM); Royal Coll. of Music (ARCM). FGSM 1988; FRCM 1988; FRSAMD 1993; FRNCM 1993. Head of Music: St Mary's Sch., Hendon, 1969–72; Villiers High Sch., Southall, 1972–79; Dep. Warden, ILEA Music Centre, 1979–84; Vice-Dir, Royal Coll. of Music, 1985–88. Mem., Music Panel and Chm., New Music Sub-Cttee, Arts Council, 1981–87; Member: Music Adv. Cttee, British Council, 1987–; Steering Cttee, Nat. Studio for Electronic Music, 1986–89; Bd, City Arts Trust, 1989–; Management Bd, London Internat. String Quartet Competition, 1989–; Council, NYO, 1989–; Arts and Entertainment Training Council, 1990–94; Dep. Chm., London Arts Bd, 1991–99; Vice-Pres., Nat. Assoc. of Youth Orchestras, 1989–; Pres., Assoc. of European Conservatoires, 1996–; Trustee, Parkhouse Award, 1990– (Chm., 1990–92). Treasurer, 1977–79, Chm., 1979–84, New Macnaghten Concerts. Hon. RAM 1993; FRSA. Hon. DMus: City, 1995; New England Conservatory, Boston, Mass. *Publication:* Leoš Janáček: the field that prospered, 1981. *Recreations:* watching Rugby football and cricket, reading, walking, cycling. *Address:* Guildhall School of Music & Drama, Barbican, Silk Street, EC2Y 8DT. *T:* (020) 7382 7141. *Club:* MCC.

HORSBRUGH-PORTER, Sir John (Simon), 4th Bt *cr* 1902; *b* 18 Dec. 1938; *s* of Col Sir Andrew Marshall Horsbrugh-Porter, 3rd Bt, DSO and Bar, and Annette Mary (*d* 1992), *d* of Brig.-Gen. R. C. Browne-Clayton, DSO; *S* father, 1986; *m* 1964, Lavinia Rose, *d* of Ralph Turton; one *s* two *d. Educ:* Winchester College; Trinity Coll., Cambridge (BA Hons History). Formerly, School Master. *Recreations:* literature, music. *Heir:* *s* Andrew Alexander Marshall Horsbrugh-Porter, *b* 19 Jan. 1971. *Address:* Bowers Croft, Coleshill, Amersham, Bucks HP7 0LS. *T:* (01494) 724596.

HORSBURGH, John Millar Stewart; QC (Scot.) 1980; Sheriff of Lothian and Borders at Edinburgh, since 1990; *b* 15 May 1938; *s* of late Alexander Horsburgh and Helen Margaret Watson Millar or Horsburgh; *m* 1966, Johann Catriona Gardner, MB, ChB, DObst RCOG; one *s* one *d. Educ:* Hutchesons' Boys' Grammar Sch., Glasgow; Univ. of Glasgow (MA Hons, LLB). Admitted to Scots Bar, 1965; Advocate-Depute, 1987–89. Part-time Mem., Lands Tribunal for Scotland, 1985–87. *Address:* 8 Laverockbank Road, Edinburgh EH5 3DG. *T:* (0131) 552 5328.

HORSEY, Gordon; JP; a District Judge, 1991–94; *b* 20 July 1926; *s* of late E. W. Horsey, MBE, and of H. V. Horsey; *m* 1951, Jean Mary (*née* Favill); one *d. Educ:* Magnus Grammar Sch., Newark, Notts; St Catharine's Coll., Cambridge. BA, LLB. Served RN, 1944–45, RE, 1945–48 (Captain). Admitted solicitor, 1953; private practice in Nottingham, 1953–71; Registrar: Coventry County Court, 1971; Leicester County Court, 1973; a Recorder, 1978–84. JP Leics, 1975. *Recreation:* fly-fishing. *Address:* The Old Woodyard, 55 Swithland Lane, Rothley, Leics LE7 7SG. *T:* (0116) 230 2545.

HORSFALL, Sir John (Musgrave), 3rd Bt *cr* 1909; MC 1946; TD 1949 and clasp 1951; JP; *b* 26 Aug. 1915; *s* of Sir (John) Donald Horsfall, 2nd Bt, and Henrietta (*d* 1936), *d* of William Musgrave; *S* father, 1975; *m* 1940, Cassandra Nora Bernardine, *d* of late G. E. Wright; two *s* one *d. Educ:* Uppingham. Major, Duke of Wellington's Regt. Dir, Skipton Building Society, 1960–85, retd. Mem. Skipton RDC, 1952–74; Pres. Skipton Divl Conservative Assoc., 1966–79. Pres., Worsted Spinners Fedn, 1961–64. JP North Yorks, 1959. *Heir:* *s* Edward John Wright Horsfall [*b* 17 Dec. 1940; *m* 1965, Rosemary, *d* of Frank N. King; three *s*]. *Address:* Greenfield House, Embsay, Skipton, North Yorkshire BD23 6SD. *T:* (01756) 794560.

HORSFIELD, Maj.-Gen. David Ralph, OBE 1962; FIEE; *b* 17 Dec. 1916; *s* of late Major Ralph B. and Morah Horsfield (*née* Baynes); *m* 1948, Sheelah Patricia Royal Eagan; two *s* two *d. Educ:* Oundle Sch.; RMA Woolwich; Clare Coll., Cambridge Univ. (MA). Commnd in Royal Signals, 1936; British troops, Egypt, 1939–41; comd Burma Corps Signals, 1942; Instr, Staff Coll., Quetta, 1944–45; comd 2 Indian Airborne Signals, 1946–47; Instr, RMA Sandhurst, 1950–53 (Company Comdr to HM King Hussein of Jordan); comd 2 Signal Regt, 1956–59; Principal Army Staff Officer, MoD, Malaya, 1959–61; Dir of Telecommunications (Army), 1966–68; ADC to the Queen, 1968–69; Deputy Communications and Electronics, Supreme HQ Allied Powers, Europe, 1968–69; Maj.-Gen. 1969; Chief Signal Officer, BAOR, 1969–72; Col Comdt, Royal Signals, 1972–78. Pres., Indian Signals Assoc. of GB, 1978–; Vice Pres., Nat. Ski Fedn, 1978–81. *Recreations:* ski-ing (British Ski Champion, 1949), the visual arts. *Address:* Preybrook Farm, Preywater Road, Wookey, Wells BA5 1LE. *T:* (01749) 673241. *Club:* Ski Club of Great Britain.

HORSFIELD, Peter Muir Francis; QC 1978; *b* 15 Feb. 1932; *s* of Henry Taylor Horsfield, AFC, and Florence Lily (*née* Muir); *m* 1962, Anne Charlotte, *d* of late Sir Piers Debenham, 2nd Bt, and Lady (Angela) Debenham; three *s. Educ:* Beaumont; Trinity Coll., Oxford (BA 1st Cl. Hons Mods and Greats). Served RNR, 1955–57; Lieut RNR, 1960. Called to the Bar, Middle Temple, 1958, Bencher, 1984; in practice at Chancery Bar, 1958–94. Pt-time Chm., VAT Tribunals and Special Comr of Income Tax, 1993–. *Recreation:* painting (one-man show, Cassian de Vere Cole Fine Arts, 1997). *Club:* Garrick.

HORSFORD, Maj.-Gen. Derek Gordon Thomond, CBE 1962 (MBE 1953); DSO 1944 and Bar 1945; *b* 7 Feb. 1917; *s* of late Captain H. T. Horsford, The Gloucestershire Regt, and Mrs V. E. Horsford; *m* 1st, 1948, Sheila Louise Russell Crawford (*d* 1995); one *s* (and one step *s* two step *d*); 2nd, 1996, Gillian Patricia Moorhouse, *d* of K. O'B. Horsford; two step *s. Educ:* Clifton Coll.; RMC, Sandhurst. Commissioned into 8th Gurkha Rifles, 1937; despatches 1943 and 1945; comd 4/1 Gurkha Rifles, Burma, 1944–45; transf. to RA, 1948; Instructor Staff Coll., 1950–52; transf. to King's Regt, 1950; GSO1, 2nd Infantry Div., 1955–56; comd 1st Bn, The King's Regt, 1957–59; AAG, AG2, War Office, 1959–60; Comdr 24th Infantry Brigade Group, Dec. 1960–Dec. 1962; Imperial Defence Coll., 1963; Brig., Gen. Staff, HQ, BAOR, 1964–66. Maj.-Gen. 1966; GOC 50 (Northumbrian) Div./Dist, 1966–67; GOC Yorks Dist, 1967–68; GOC 17 Div./Malaya District, 1969–70; Maj.-Gen., Brigade of Gurkhas, 1969–71; Dep. Comdr Land Forces, Hong Kong, 1970–71, retired. Col, The King's Regt, 1965–70; Col, The Gurkha Transport Regt, 1973–78. Sec., Council, League of Remembrance, 1973–85. *Recreations:* travel, reading.

HORSHAM, Area Bishop of, since 1993; **Rt Rev. Lindsay Goodall Urwin,** OGS; *b* 13 March 1956. *Educ:* Camberwell GS, Australia; Ripon Coll., Cuddesdon. Ordained deacon, 1980, priest, 1981; Curate, St Peter, Walworth, 1980–83; Vicar, St Faith, N Dulwich, 1983–88; Diocesan Missioner, Chichester, 1988–93. Nat. Chm., Church Union, 1995–98. Member: OGS, 1991– (UK Provincial, 1996–); Coll. of Evangelists, 1999–. *Publication:* (ed jtly) Youthful Spirit, 1999. *Address:* Bishop's House, 21 Guildford

Road, Horsham RH12 1LU. *T:* (01403) 211139, *Fax:* (01403) 217349; *e-mail:* bishhorsham@clara.net.

HORSHAM, Archdeacon of; *see* Filby, Ven. W. C. L.

HORSHAM, Jean, CBE 1979; Deputy Parliamentary Commissioner for Administration, 1981–82, retired; Chairman, Solicitors Complaints Bureau, 1986–89; *b* 25 June 1922; *d* of Albert John James Horsham and Janet Horsham (*née* Henderson). *Educ:* Keith Grammar Sch. Forestry Commn, 1939–64, seconded to Min. of Supply, 1940–45; Min. of Land and Natural Resources, 1964–66; Min. of Housing and Local Govt, 1966; Office of Parly Comr for Administration, 1967–82. Member: Subsidence Compensation Review Cttee, 1983–84; Law Soc. Professional Purposes Cttee, 1984–86; Council on Tribunals, 1986–92; Chorus Enquiry at Royal Opera House, 1988–89; Tribunals Cttee, Judicial Studies Bd, 1990–92. *Address:* 14 Cotelands, Croydon, Surrey CRO 5UD. *T:* (020) 8681 0806.

HORSLEY, Rev. Canon Alan Avery; Provost of St Andrew's Cathedral, Inverness, 1988–91; Canon Emeritus, Peterborough Cathedral, since 1986; *b* 13 May 1936; *s* of Reginald James and Edith Irene Horsley; *m* 1966, Mary Joy Marshall, MA; two *d. Educ:* St Chad's Coll., Durham (BA 1958); Birmingham Univ.; Pacific Western Univ., Calif (MA 1984; PhD 1985); Queen's Coll., Birmingham. Deacon 1960, priest 1961, Peterborough; Assistant Curate: Daventry, 1960–63; St Giles, Reading, 1963–64; St Paul's, Wokingham, 1964–66; Vicar of Yeadon, dio. Bradford, 1966–71; Rector of Heyford and Stowe Nine Churches, dio. Peterborough, 1971–78; RD of Daventry, 1976–78; Vicar of Oakham with Hambleton and Egleton (and Braunston and Brooke from 1980), 1978–86; Non-Residentiary Canon of Peterborough Cathedral, 1979–86; Chaplain: Catmose Vale Hosp., 1978–86; Rutland Memorial Hosp., 1978–86; Vicar of Lanteglos-by-Fowey, dio. Truro, 1986–88; Priest in Charge: St Mary in the Fields, Culloden, 1988–91; St Paul, Strath Nairn, 1988–91; Vicar, Mill End and Heronsgate with West Hyde, 1991–2001; acting RD, Rickmansworth, 1998–2000, RD, 2000–01. Permission to officiate, dio. TNO, 1998–. *Publications:* (with Mary J. Horsley) A Lent Course, 1967, 2nd edn 1982; Lent with St Luke, 1978, 3rd edn 1997; Action at Lanteglos and Polruan, 1987; The Parish Church at Mill End, Rickmansworth, Hertfordshire: Pt I, 1999, 2nd edn 2000; Pt II, 2000; contribs to Rutland Record Soc. Jl. *Recreations:* music, piano and organ, cultivation of flowers, historical research. *Address:* Boswartha, Porthleven, Helston, Cornwall TR13 9EU. *T:* (01326) 562404.

HORSLEY, Air Marshal Sir (Beresford) Peter (Torrington), KCB 1974; CBE 1964; LVO 1956; AFC 1945; idc; psc; pfc; *b* 26 March 1921; *s* of late Capt. Arthur Beresford Horsley, CBE; *m* 1st, 1943, Phyllis Conrad Phinney (marr. diss. 1976); one *s* one *d*; 2nd, 1976, Ann MacKinnon, *d* of Gareth and Frances Crwys-Williams; two step *s* two step *d. Educ:* Wellington Coll. Joined Royal Air Force, 1940; served in 2nd TAF and Fighter Command. Adjt Oxford Univ. Air Sqdn, 1948; Commands: No 9 and No 29 Sqdns, RAF Wattisham, RAF Akrotiri. Equerry to Princess Elizabeth and to the Duke of Edinburgh, 1949–52; Equerry to the Queen, 1952–53; Equerry to the Duke of Edinburgh, 1953–56. Dep. Comdt, Jt Warfare Establishment, RAF Old Sarum, 1966–68; Asst CAS (Operations), 1968–70; AOC No 1 (Bomber) Gp, 1971–73; Dep. C-in-C, Strike Comd, 1973–75. Retired RAF, 1975. Chairman: National Printing Ink Co., 1987–; Osprey Aviation Ltd, 1991–; Director: Horsley Hldgs, 1985–; RCR Internat., 1984–. Pres., Yorkshire Sports, 1986–. Croix de Guerre, 1944. Holds Orders of Christ (Portugal), North Star (Sweden), and Menelik (Ethiopia). *Publications:* (as Peter Beresford) Journal of a Stamp Collector, 1972; Sounds From Another Room (autobiog.), 1997. *Recreations:* ski-ing, philately. *Address:* c/o Barclays Bank, High Street, Newmarket CB8 8NH. *Club:* Hopetown Sailing.

HORSLEY, Colin, OBE 1963; FRCM 1973; Hon. RAM 1977; pianist; Professor, Royal College of Music, London, 1953–90; *b* Wanganui, New Zealand, 23 April 1920. *Educ:* Royal College of Music. Debut at invitation of Sir John Barbirolli at Hallé Concerts, Manchester, 1943. Soloist with all leading orchestras of Great Britain, the Royal Philharmonic Soc. (1953, 1959), Promenade Concerts, etc. Toured Belgium, Holland, Spain, France, Scandinavia, Malta, Ceylon, Malaya, Australia and New Zealand. Festival appearances include Aix-en-Provence, International Contemporary Music Festival, Palermo, British Music Festivals in Belgium, Holland and Finland. Vis. Prof., Royal Manchester Coll., later RNCM, 1964–80. Broadcasts frequently, and has made many records. *Recreation:* gardening. *Address:* Belmont, Dreemskerry, Maughold, Isle of Man IM7 1BF. *T:* (01624) 813095.

HORSLEY, (George) Nicholas (Seward); Chairman, 1970–86, Deputy Chairman, 1986–88, Northern Foods plc, retired; non-executive Chairman, Millway Foods Limited, 1988–89; *b* 21 April 1934; *s* of Alec Stewart Horsley and Ida Seward Horsley; *m* 1st, 1958, Valerie Anne Edwards (marr. diss. 1975); two *s* one *d*; 2nd, 1975, Sabita Sarkar (marr. diss. 1987); 3rd, 1988, Alwyne Marjorie Law. *Educ:* Keswick Grammar Sch.; Bootham Sch., York; Worcester Coll., Oxford (BA). Freelance journalist, 1957–58. Northern Dairies Ltd: Trainee Manager, 1958; Director, 1963; Vice-Chairman, 1968–70 (Northern Dairies Ltd changed its name to Northern Foods Ltd in 1972). Chm., News on Sunday Publishing, 1986–87. Pres., Dairy Trade Fedn, 1975–77 and 1980–85. Chm., BBC Consultative Group on Industrial and Business Affairs, 1980–83; Mem., BBC Gen. Adv. Council, 1980–83. *Recreations:* music, bridge, watching cricket, reading. *Address:* Barbados, West Indies.

HORSLEY, Sir Peter; *see* Horsley, Sir B. P. T.

HORSLEY, Stephen Daril; Consultant in Public Health, Morecambe Bay Health Authority, since 1994; *b* 23 June 1947; *s* of Donald Vincent Horsley and Marie Margaret Horsley; *m* 1974, Vivienne Marjorie Lee; one *s* two *d. Educ:* Guy's Hosp.; Manchester Business Sch. (MBSc 1985). FRCP 1988 (MRCP 1976); FFPHM. Gen. Hosp. Medicine, Truro, 1971–75; Community Medicine, Yorks RHA, 1975–79; District Community Physician, E Cumbria HA, 1979–82; District MO, S Cumbria HA, 1982–85; Specialist in Community Medicine, Oxford RHA, 1985–86; Regl MO, N Western RHA, 1986–94. Hon. Prof. of Public Health, Lancaster Univ., 1997. *Publications:* contribs to BMJ, Community Medicine. *Recreations:* wind surfing, walking. *Address:* Ulverston, Cumbria.

HORSMAN, Malcolm; *b* 28 June 1933. Director, Slater Walker Securities Ltd, 1967–70; Chairman: Ralli International Ltd, 1969–73; Alice Hoffman Homes Ltd, later Hoffman De Visme Foundn, 1992–98; Director: The Bowater Corporation Ltd, 1972–77; Tozer Kemsley & Millbourn (Holdings) Ltd, 1975–82. Member: Study Group on Local Authority Management Structures, 1971–72; South East Economic Planning Council, 1972–74; Royal Commission on the Press, 1974–77; Institute of Contemporary Arts Ltd, 1975–78; Council, Oxford Centre for Management Studies, 1973–84; Chm., British Centre, Internat. Theatre Inst., 1982–84 (Mem. Exec. Council, 1980–87). Visiting Fellow, Cranfield Univ. (formerly Cranfield Institute of Technology)/The School of Management, 1977–97. Vis. Lectr, Univ. of Transkei, 1977. Chm., Nat. Youth Theatre, 1982–90 (Dep. Chm. 1971–82); Director: Hackney New Variety Ltd (Hackney Empire Trust), 1995–97; Gate Theatre, 1997–; Member: Court, RCA, 1977–80; Editorial Bd, DRAMA, 1978–81; Royal Court Develt Cttee, 1995–98; Council, Birthright, 1974–85; Council, Anti-Slavery Internat., 1998–2000. Chm., Open School Trust, 1998–2000. *Clubs:* Reform; Harlequins Rugby Football.

HORSMAN, Michael John; Director, Office of Manpower Economics, since 1992; *b* 3 March 1949; *s* of Graham Joseph Vivian Horsman and Ruth (*née* Guest); *m* 1977, Dr Anne Margaret Marley; three *s. Educ:* Dollar Acad.; Glasgow Univ. (MA Hist. and Politics, 1st cl. Hons, 1971); Balliol Coll., Oxford (Snell Exhibnr, Brackenbury Scholar). Entered Civil Service, 1974; Private Sec. to Chm., MSC, 1978–79; Dept of Employment, 1979–84, on secondment to Unilever, 1981–82; Dir, PER, 1984–85; Hd, Finance Policy, and Resource Controller, MSC, 1985–87; Hd, Ops Br., Employment Service, 1987–89; Regl Dir, London and SE, Employment Service, 1989–92. *Recreations:* historical research, literature, cycling. *Address:* Office of Manpower Economics, Oxford House, 76 Oxford Street, W1N 9FD. *T:* (020) 7467 7200.

HORT, Sir Andrew (Edwin Fenton), 9th Bt *cr* 1767, of Castle Strange, Middlesex; *b* 15 Nov. 1954; *e s* of Sir James Fenton Hort, 8th Bt and of Joan, *d* of Edward Peat; *S* father, 1995; *m* 1986, Mary, *d* of Jack Whibley; one *s* one *d. Heir: s* James John Fenton Hort, *b* 26 Nov. 1989. *Address:* Westerlee, 77 Fortis Green, E Finchley, N2 9JD.

HORTON, Dr Eric William; retired; livestock farmer, 1983–93; Director of Regulatory Affairs, Glaxo Group Research Ltd, 1980–83, Member Board, 1982–83; Director, Willow & Wicket Computer Cricket Ltd, 1994–2000; *b* 20 June 1929; *e s* of late Harold and Agnes Horton; *m* 1956, Thalia Helen (*d* 1999), *er d* of late Sir George Lowe; two *s* one *d. Educ:* Sedbergh; Edinburgh Univ. BSc, MB, ChB, PhD, DSc, MD, FRCPE. Mem. Scientific Staff, MRC, Nat. Inst. for Med. Res., London, 1958–60; Dir of Therapeutic Res. and Head of Pharmacology, Miles Labs Ltd, Stoke Poges, 1960–63; Sen. Lectr in Physiology, St Bartholomew's Hosp., London, 1963–66; Wellcome Prof. of Pharmacology, Sch. of Pharmacy, Univ. of London, 1966–69; Prof. of Pharmacology, Univ. of Edinburgh, 1969–80. Hon. Sen. Res. Fellow, Med. Coll. of St Bartholomew's Hosp., London, 1980; Hon. Lectr in Pharmacol., Royal Free Hosp. Med. Sch., London, 1960–63. Member, Governing Body, Inveresk Res. Foundn (formerly International), 1971–80; Non-executive Director: Inveresk Res. Internat. Ltd, 1977–80; GLP Systems Ltd, 1978–80. Member: Adv. Cttee on Pesticides, MAFF, 1970–73; Biological Research and Cell Boards, MRC, 1973–75; Pharmacy Panel, SRC, 1980–81; Editorial Bd, British Jl of Pharmacology, 1960–66; Editorial Bd, Pharmacological Reviews, 1968–74. Hon. Treasurer, Brit. Pharmacological Soc., 1976–80. Hon. Sec., Edin. Univ. RFC, 1949–50. Baly Medal, RCP, 1973. *Publications:* Prostaglandins, 1972; papers in learned jls on peptides and prostaglandins. *Recreations:* listening to music, computer programming.

HORTON, Geoffrey Robert; Economic Consultant, Horton 4 Consulting, since 1998; *b* 23 July 1951; *s* of late Leonard Horton and Joan Horton; *m* 1991, Dianne Alexandra Craker; two *d. Educ:* Bristol Grammar Sch.; Exeter Coll., Oxford (MA); University Coll. London (MSc Econ). Economic asst, HM Treasury, 1974–76; Lectr in Econs, University Coll. of Swansea, 1976–78; Economic Advr, HM Treasury, 1978–85; Chief Economist, DRI (Europe) Ltd, 1985–88; Sen. Economic Advr, Dept of Energy, 1988–90; Sen. Consultant (part-time), Nat. Economic Research Associates, 1990–92; Dir (part-time), Regulation and Business Affairs, Office of Electricity Regulation, 1990–95; Dir Gen (part-time), Electricity Supply for NI, 1992–95; Dir of Consumer Affairs, OFT, 1995–98. *Publications:* articles and research papers on economics. *Recreations:* reading, cooking, sailing. *Address:* 43 Grove Park, Camberwell, SE5 8LG. *T:* (020) 7733 6587; *e-mail:* ghorton@easynet.co.uk.

HORTON, Matthew Bethell; QC 1989; *b* 23 Sept. 1946; *s* of Albert Leslie Horton, BSc, FRICS and Gladys Rose Ellen Harding; *m* 1972, Liliane Boleslawski (marr. diss. 1984); one *s* one *d. Educ:* Sevenoaks School; Trinity Hall, Cambridge (Open Exhibn, Hist.; Squire Law Scholar; 1st Cl. Hons Law 1967; MA 1967; LLM 1968); Astbury Scholar, Middle Temple, 1968. Called to the Bar, Middle Temple, 1969. Western Circuit; Mem., Parly Bar Mess. Member: Cttee, Jt Planning Law Conf.; European Environmental Law Cttee, Internat. Bar Assoc.; Admin. Law Cttee of Justice. *Recreations:* ski-ing, windsurfing, tennis. *Address:* 2 Mitre Court Buildings, Temple, EC4Y 7BX. *T:* (020) 7583 1380. *Club:* Tramp.

HORTON, Dr Richard Charles, FRCP; Editor, The Lancet, since 1995; *b* 29 Dec. 1961; *s* of Charles Kenneth Horton and Clarice Audrey Ward; *m* 1998, Ingrid Johanna Wolfe; one *d. Educ:* Bristol GS; Univ. of Birmingham (BSc, MB ChB). FRCP 1997. Sen. House Officer, Queen Elizabeth Hosp., Birmingham, 1987–88; Clin. Res. Fellow, Royal Free Hosp., London, 1988–90; Asst Editor, 1990–93, N American Editor, 1993–95, The Lancet. Med. Columnist, The Observer, 1996–98. Affiliate Lectr, Univ. of Cambridge, 1996–; Bradford Hill Meml Lectr, 1999; Curtis Meinert Hon. Lectr. Visiting Professor: Cleveland Clinic, USA, 1997; LSHTM, 2000–; Duke Univ., USA, 2000; Arthur Thomson Vis. Prof., Univ. of Birmingham, 2000; Arnold Johnson Vis. Prof., McMaster Univ., Canada, 2000. Writer and Presenter, The Citadel (TV), 1998. Member: Evaluation Gp, Acheson Ind. Inquiry into Inequalities in Health, 1998; UK Cttee, Publication Ethics, 1997–; Internat. Cttee, Med. Jl Editors, 1995–; Editl Policy Cttee, Council of Biol. Editors, 1997–99. Pres., World Assoc. of Med. Editors, 1995–96. Fellow, Amer. Acad. for Advancement of Sci., 1997; Founder FMedSci 1998. *Publications:* (with M. J. Kendall) Preventing Coronary Artery Disease, 1994, 2nd edn 1998; (with M. J. Kendall and N. M. Kaplan) Difficult Hypertension, 1995; res. pubns in cardiovascular pharmacol., gastroenterol. and journalology; reviews and essays in New York Review of Books, London Review of Books, TLS. *Recreation:* horizontal reflection. *Address:* The Lancet, 84 Theobalds Road, WC1X 8RR. *T:* (020) 7611 4046.

HORTON, Sir Robert (Baynes), Kt 1997; *b* 18 Aug. 1939; *s* of late William Harold Horton and of Dorothy Joan Horton (*née* Baynes); *m* 1962, Sally Doreen (*née* Wells); one *s* one *d. Educ:* King's School, Canterbury; University of St Andrews (BSc); Massachusetts Inst. of Technology (SM; Sloan Fellow, 1970–71). British Petroleum, 1957–92: General Manager, BP Tankers, 1975–76; Gen. Manager, Corporate Planning, 1976–79; Chief Exec. Officer, BP Chemicals, 1980–83; a Man. Dir, 1983–86 and 1988–92; Chm. and Chief Exec. Officer, 1990–92; Chm., Standard Oil, 1986–88; Vice-Chm., BRB, 1992–93; Chm., Railtrack, 1993–99. Director: ICL plc, 1982–84; Pilkington Brothers plc, 1985–86; National City Corp., 1986–88; Emerson Electric Company, 1987–; Partner Re, 1993–; Premier Farnell plc, 1995–; Estate Incomes Ltd, 1998–. Pres., Chemicals Industry Assoc., 1982–84; Vice-Chm., BIM, 1985–91 (CIMgt (CBIM 1982)); Member: SERC, 1985–86; UFC, 1989–92; Bd and Management Cttee, Amer. Petroleum Inst., 1986–88; US Business Roundtable, 1986–88; Nat. Petroleum Council, USA, 1986–88. Pres., BESO, 1993–97. Trustee: Cleveland Orchestra, 1986–93; MIT Corp., 1987–97; Case Western Reserve Univ., 1987–93; Chairman: Tate Foundation, 1988–92; Business in the Arts, 1988–96. Chancellor, Univ. of Kent at Canterbury, 1990–95. Gov., King's Sch., Canterbury, 1984–. FCIT 1994. Hon. FIChemE 1990; Hon. FCGI 1992. Hon. LLD: Dundee, 1988; Aberdeen, 1992; Hon. DCL Kent, 1990; Hon. DBA N London Poly., 1991; Hon. DSc Cranfield, 1992; DUniv Open, 1993; Hon. DCL Kingston, 1994.

Corporate Leadership Award, MIT, 1987; Civic Award, Cleveland, 1988; SCI Gold Medal, 1990. *Recreations:* music, country activities. *Address:* Stoke Abbas, South Stoke, Reading, Berks RG8 0JT. *Clubs:* Athenæum; Leander; Huntercombe Golf.

HORWICH, Prof. Alan, PhD; FRCR, FRCP; Professor of Radiotherapy, since 1986, and Director of Clinical Research, since 1994, Institute of Cancer Research and Royal Marsden Hospital; Warden, Royal College of Radiologists, since 1998; *b* 1 June 1948; *s* of William and Audrey Horwich; *m* 1981, Pauline Amanda Barnes; two *s* one *d*. *Educ:* William Hulme's Grammar Sch., Manchester; University College Hosp. Med. Sch. (MB BS 1971; PhD 1981). MRCP 1974, FRCP 1994; FRCR 1981. Postgrad. medicine, London, 1971– 74; Fellowship in Oncology, Harvard, 1975; res. on ribonucleic acid tumour viruses, ICRF, 1976–79; radiation oncology, Royal Marsden Hosp. and Inst. of Cancer Res., 1979–; Dean, Inst. of Cancer Res., 1992–97. Chm., MRC Testicular Tumour Working Party, 1988–94. Civilian Consultant to RN, 1989–. *Publications:* Testicular Cancer: investigation and management, 1991, 2nd edn 1996; Combined Radiotherapy and Chemotherapy in Clinical Oncology, 1992; Oncology: a multidisciplinary text book, 1995; numerous articles in med. jls on urological cancers and lymphomas. *Address:* Royal Marsden Hospital, Downs Road, Sutton, Surrey SM2 5PT. *T:* (020) 8642 6011.

See also P. G. Horwich.

HORWICH, Prof. Paul Gordon, PhD; Professor of Philosophy, University College London, since 1994; *b* 7 Feb. 1947; *s* of William Horwich and Audrey (*née* Rigby). *Educ:* Brasenose Coll., Oxford (BA Physics); Yale Univ. (MA Physics & Phil.); Cornell Univ. (MA, PhD Phil. 1975). Massachusetts Institute of Technology: Asst Prof. in Philosophy, 1973–80; Associate Prof., 1980–87; Prof. of Philosophy, 1987–95. *Publications:* Probability and Evidence, 1982; Asymmetries in Time, 1987; Truth, 1992, 2nd edn 1998; Meaning, 1998. *Recreations:* opera, ski-ing, summers in Tuscany. *Address:* Department of Philosophy, University College London, Gower Street, WC1E 6BT. *Club:* Blacks.

See also A. Horwich.

HORWOOD-SMART, Rosamund, (Mrs R. O. Bernays); QC 1996; a Recorder, since 1995; *b* 21 Sept. 1951; *d* of late John Horwood-Smart and of Sylvia Horwood-Smart; *m* 1st, 1983, Richard Blackford (marr. diss. 1994); one *s* one *d*; 2nd, 1996, Richard O. Bernays. *Educ:* Felixstowe Coll.; Cambridgeshire High Sch. for Girls; Inns of Court Sch. of Law. Called to the Bar, Inner Temple, 1974, Bencher, 1998. Trustee: Nat. Music Day, 1992–98; Prisoners of Conscience Fund, 1990–. Gov., Internat. Students House, 1980–(Chm. Govs, 2000). Hon. Editor, Wig & Pen, 1998–. *Recreations:* music, gardening. *Address:* 18 Red Lion Court, EC4A 3EB. *T:* (020) 7520 6000.

HOSE, John Horsley, CBE 1987; Forest Craftsman, Forestry Commission, 1975–88 (Forest Worker, 1949, Skilled Forest Worker, 1950); President, National Union of Agricultural and Allied Workers, 1978–82; *b* 21 March 1928; *s* of Harry and Margaret Eleanor Hose; *m* 1st, 1967, Margaret Winifred Gaskin (marr. diss. 1987); 2nd, 1987, Linda Sharon Morris. *Educ:* Sneinton Boulevard Council Sch.; Nottingham Bluecoat Sch. Architects' Junior Asst, 1943–46. National Service, with Royal Engineers, 1946–48. Chm., Nat. Trade Gp, Agricultural and Allied Workers/TGWU, 1982–86 (Mem., 1982–89); Mem., Gen. Exec. Council, TGWU, 1986–88. *Recreations:* reading, drinking real ale. *Address:* 140 Sneinton Dale, Nottingham NG2 4HJ. *T:* (0115) 958 0494.

HOSKER, Edmund Nigel Ronald; Director, Finance and Resource Management, Department of Trade and Industry, since 2000; *b* 25 April 1958; *s* of Ronald Reece Hosker and Hilda Gertrude Hosker (*née* Harrington); *m* 1983, Elizabeth Miranda Thornely; three *d*. *Educ:* Slough Grammar Sch.; St Catharine's Coll., Cambridge (BA Hons Eng. 1979). Joined Department of Trade and Industry, 1979: Private Sec. to Minister for Industry and subseq. to Sec. of State for Trade and Industry, 1983–84; Principal, 1984; on secondment to British Embassy, Washington, 1990–94; Asst Sec., 1994; transf. to Cabinet Office, 1995–97; Dir of Finance, DTI, 1997–2000. *Recreations:* reading, music. *Address:* Department of Trade and Industry, 1 Victoria Street, SW1H 0ET.

HOSKER, Sir Gerald (Albery), KCB 1995 (CB 1987); HM Procurator General, Treasury Solicitor and Queen's Proctor, 1992–95; *b* 28 July 1933; *s* of Leslie Reece Hosker and Constance Alice Rose Hosker (*née* Hubbard); *m* 1956, Rachel Victoria Beatrice Middleton; one *s* one *d*. *Educ:* Berkhamsted Sch., Berkhamsted, Herts. Admitted Solicitor, 1956; Corporate Secretary 1964; Associate of the Faculty of Secretaries and Administrators 1964. Articled to Derrick Bridges & Co., 1951–56; with Clifford-Turner & Co., 1957–59; entered Treasury Solicitor's Dept as Legal Asst, 1960; Sen. Legal Asst, 1966; Asst Solicitor, 1973; Under Sec. (Legal), 1982; Dep. Treasury Solicitor, 1984–87; Solicitor to the DTI, 1987–92. Conducted enquiry into: Customs and Excise aspects of Simon de Danser case, 1999; C. W. Cheney Pension Fund for DSS, 2001; Public Inquiry Comr, Falkland Is, 1999–2000. Mem. Bd, Inst. of Advanced Legal Studies, Univ. of London, 1992–95; Governor, Lyonsdown Sch., New Barnet, 1996–. Trustee, RAF Mus., 1998–. FRSA 1964. Hon. QC 1991. *Recreations:* the study of biblical prophecy, swimming. *Address:* Queen Anne's Chambers, 28 Broadway, SW1H 9JS. *Club:* Royal Over-Seas League.

HOSKING, Barbara Nancy, CBE 1999 (OBE 1985); Deputy Chairman, Westcountry Television, 1997–99 (non-executive Director, 1992–99); *b* 4 Nov. 1926; *d* of late William Henry Hosking and Ada Kathleen Hosking (*née* Murrish). *Educ:* West Cornwall School for Girls, Penzance; Hillcroft College, Surbiton; and by friends. Secretary to Town Clerk, Council of Isles of Scilly, and local corresp. for BBC and Western Morning News, 1945–47; Editl Asst, The Circle, Odeon and Gaumont cinemas, 1947–50; Asst to Inf. Officer, Labour Party, 1952–55; Asst to Gen. Manager, Uruwira Minerals Ltd, Tanzania, 1955–57; Res. Officer, Broadcasting Section, Labour Party, 1958–65; Science Press Officer, DES, 1965; Press Officer, Min. of Technology, 1967; Press and Publicity Officer, Metrication Board, 1970; Senior Inf. Officer, 10 Downing Street, 1970; Principal Inf. Officer, DoE, 1972; Private Sec. to Parly Secs, Cabinet Office, 1973; Chief Inf. Officer, DoE, 1974–77; Controller of Inf. Services, IBA, 1977–86; Political Consultant, Yorkshire TV, 1987–92. Mem. (Lab), Islington BC, 1962–64. Non-exec. Dir, Camden and Islington Community Health Services NHS Trust, 1992–93. Pres., Media Soc., 1987–88; Jt Vice-Chm., NCVO, 1987–92. Mem. Council, Family Policy Studies Centre, 1994–97. Trustee: Charities Aid Foundn, 1987–92; 300 Gp, 1988–91; Nat. Literacy Trust, 1993–99. Associate, Women's Advertising Club of London, 1994–. Patron, Clean-Break Theatre Co., 1992–. Hon. Vice Pres., London Cornish Assoc., 1992; Bard, Gorsedd Kernow. Radio broadcaster, incl. BBC Radio 4 Any Questions. FRTS 1988; FRSA (Mem. Council, 1992–96). DUniv Ulster, 1996. Special citation, Internat. Women's Forum, NY, 1983, Boston, 1996. *Publications:* contribs to Punch, New Scientist, Spectator. *Recreations:* opera, lieder, watching politics, watching sport. *Address:* 9 Highgate Spinney, Crescent Road, N8 8AR. *T:* (020) 8340 1853. *Club:* Reform.

HOSKING, Prof. Geoffrey Alan, FBA 1993; FRHistS; Professor of Russian History, since 1984, and Leverhulme Personal Research Professor, since 1999, University of London; *b* 28 April 1942; *s* of Stuart William Steggall Hosking and Jean Ross Hosking; *m* 1970, Anne Lloyd Hirst; two *d*. *Educ:* Maidstone Grammar Sch.; King's Coll., Cambridge (MA, PhD); St Antony's Coll., Oxford. FRHistS 1998. Asst Lectr in Government, 1966–68, Lectr in Government, 1968–71, Univ. of Essex; Vis. Lectr in Political Science, Univ. of Wisconsin, Madison, 1971–72; Lectr in History, Univ. of Essex, 1972–76; Sen. Research Fellow, Russian Inst., Columbia Univ., New York, 1976; Sen. Lectr and Reader in Russian History, Univ. of Essex, 1976–84; Dep. Dir, SSEES, London Univ., 1996–98. Vis. Prof., Slavisches Inst., Univ. of Cologne, 1980–81. BBC Reith Lectr, 1988 (The Rediscovery of Politics: authority, culture and community in the USSR). Member: Council, Writers and Scholars Educnl Trust, 1985–; Overseas Policy Cttee, British Acad., 1994–2000; Jury, Booker Prize for Russian Fiction, 1993. Member: Internat. Academic Council, Mus. of Contemporary History (formerly Mus. of the Revolution), Moscow, 1994–; Admin. Bd, Moscow Sch. of Pol Studies, 1992–; Exec. Cttee, Britain-Russia Centre, 1994–2000. Trustee, J. S. Mill Inst., 1992–96; Governor, Camden Sch. for Girls, 1989–94. Member: Editl Bd, Jl of Contemporary History, 1988–99; Editl Cttee, Nations and Nationalism, 1994–; Editl Bd, Nationalities Papers, 1997–. *Publications:* The Russian Constitutional Experiment: Government and Duma 1907–14, 1973; Beyond Socialist Realism: Soviet fiction since Ivan Denisovich, 1980; A History of the Soviet Union, 1985, 3rd edn 1992 (Los Angeles Times Hist. Book Prize, 1986); The Awakening of the Soviet Union, 1990, 2nd edn 1991; (with J. Aves and P. J. S. Duncan) The Road to Post-Communism: independent political movements in the Soviet Union 1985–91, 1992; Russia: people and Empire 1552–1917, 1997; (ed with George Schöpflin) Myths and Nationhood, 1997; (ed with Robert Service) Russian Nationalism Past and Present, 1998; (ed with Robert Service) Reinterpreting Russia, 1999; Russia and the Russians: a history, 2001. *Recreations:* music, chess, walking. *Address:* School of Slavonic and East European Studies, University College London, Senate House, Malet Street, WC1E 7HU. *T:* (020) 7862 8571.

HOSKING, John Everard, CBE 1990; JP; DL; Chairman, Agra Europe (London) Ltd, 1989–94 (Director and Chief Executive, 1974–89); Vice-President, Magistrates' Association, since 1990 (Chairman of Council, 1987–90); *b* 23 Oct. 1929; *s* of J. Everard Hosking, OBE and E. Margaret (*née* Shaxson); *m* 1953, Joan Cecily Whitaker, BSc; two *s*. *Educ:* Marlborough Coll.; Wye Coll., London Univ. (BScA 1953). NDA 1954. Farming and forestry in Kent, 1953–69; Man. Dir, Eastes and Loud Ltd, 1965–69; Director: Newgrain-Kent, 1969–74; Ashford Corn Exchange Co., 1965–69; Agroup Ltd, 1987–94; Bureau Européen de Recherches SA, 1987–90; European Intelligence Ltd, 1987–94. Tax Comr, 1980–. Chairman: Centre for European Agricultural Studies Assoc., 1977–83; Kent Br., Magistrates' Assoc., 1973–78; Kent Magistrates' Courts Cttee, 1984–88; Member: Kent Police Authority, 1970–74; Lord Chancellor's Adv. Cttee on the Appointment of Magistrates, 1977–89; Central Council, Magistrates' Courts Cttees, 1980–83; Bar Council Professional Conduct Cttee, 1983–86; Senate of Inns of Court and the Bar Disciplinary Tribunal, 1983–86; Council, Commonwealth Magistrates' and Judges' Assoc., 1989–92; Lord Chief Justice's Working Party on Mode of Trial, 1989; Lord Chancellor's Adv. Cttee on Legal Educn and Conduct, 1991–94. Vice-Pres., Kent Magistrates' Assoc., 1999– (Chm., 1973–78). Pres., Wye Coll. Agricola Club, 1995–. Governor: Ashford Sch., 1976– (Chm., 1994–); Wye Coll., Univ. of London, 1995–2000; Mem. Governing Council, Church Schs Co., 1999–. JP Kent, 1962 (Chm., Ashford Bench, 1975–85); DL Kent, 1992. British Univs Ploughing Champion, 1952. *Publications:* (ed) Rural Response to the Resource Crisis in Europe, 1981; The Agricultural Industry of West Germany, 1990. *Recreations:* the arts, the countryside. *Address:* Pett House, Charing, Kent. *Club:* Farmers'.

HOSKINS, Prof. Brian John, CBE 1998; PhD; FRS 1988; Professor of Meteorology, University of Reading, since 1981; *b* 17 May 1945; *s* of George Frederick Hoskins and Kathleen Matilda Louise Hoskins; *m* 1968, Jacqueline Holmes; two *d*. *Educ:* Bristol Grammar Sch.; Trinity Hall, Cambridge (BA 1966; MA, PhD 1970). FRMetS 1970 (Hon. FRMets 2001); Fellow, Amer. Meteorol Soc, 1985. Post-doctoral Fellow, Nat. Center for Atmospheric Res., Boulder, Colo, 1970–71; Vis. Scientist, GFD Program, Univ. of Princeton, 1972–73; Univ. of Reading: Post-doctoral Fellow, 1971–72, Gp Leader, 1973–, Atmospheric Modelling Gp; Reader in Atmospheric Modelling, 1976–81; Head, Dept of Meteorol., 1990–96. Special Advr to Sec. of State for Transport, 1990. Member: NERC, 1988–94; Meteorol Cttee, Meteorol Office, 1994– (Chm., SAC, 1995–); Jt Scientific Cttee, World Climate Res. Prog., 1995–; Royal Commn on Envmtl Pollution, 1998–; Council, Royal Soc., 2000–2001; Chair, Royal Soc. Global Envmtl Res. Cttee, 1999–. Pres., IAMAS, 1991–95. Mem., Academia Europaea, 1989; Corresp. Academician, Real Acad. de Ciencias y Artes de Barcelona, 1994. Starr Meml Lecture, MIT, 1989; Bernard Haurwitz Meml Lecture, Amer. Meteorol Soc., 1995. Royal Meteorological Society: Pres., 1998–2000; Symons Meml Lecture, 1982; L. F. Richardson Prize, 1972; Buchan Prize, 1976; Charles Chree Silver Medal, Inst. of Physics, 1987; Carl-Gustaf Rossby Res. Medal, Amer. Meteorol Soc., 1988; Vilhelm Bjerknes Prize, Eur. Geophys. Soc., 1997. *Publications:* (ed with R. P. Pearce) Large-scale Dynamical Processes in the Atmosphere, 1983; 100 papers in meteorol jls. *Recreations:* music, sport, gardening. *Address:* 32 Reading Road, Wokingham, Berks RG41 1EH. *T:* (0118) 979 1015.

HOSKINS, Robert William, (Bob); actor; *b* 26 Oct. 1942; *s* of Robert Hoskins and Elsie Lilian Hoskins; *m* 1st, 1970, Jane Livesey; one *s* one *d*; 2nd, 1982, Linda Banwell; one *s* one *d*. *Educ:* Stroud Green School. *Stage:* Intimate Theatre, Palmers Green, 1966; Victoria, Stoke on Trent, 1967; Century Travelling Theatre, 1969; Royal Court, 1972; Doolittle in Pygmalion, Albery, 1974; RSC season, Aldwych, 1976; The World Turned Upside Down, NT, 1978; Has Washington Legs?, NT, 1978; True West, NT, 1981; Guys and Dolls, NT, 1981; Old Wicked Songs, Gielgud, 1996; *television:* On the Move, 1976; Pennies from Heaven, 1978; Flickers, 1980; The Dunera Boys, 1985; The Changeling, 1993; World War II: When Lions Roared, 1993; David Copperfield, 1999; *films:* Zulu Dawn, 1980; The Long Good Friday, 1981; The Honorary Consul, 1982; Lassiter, 1984; Cotton Club, 1984; Sweet Liberty, 1986; Mona Lisa, 1986 (Best Actor award, Cannes Fest.; Golden Globe Award); A Prayer for the Dying, 1988; The Raggedy Rawney (writer, dir, actor), 1988; Who Framed Roger Rabbit, 1988; The Lonely Passion of Judith Hearne, 1989; Heart Condition, 1990; Mermaids, 1991; The Favour, the Watch and the Very Big Fish, 1992; Hook, 1992; The Inner Circle, 1992; Super Mario Brothers, 1993; Nixon, 1996; The Rainbow (dir, actor), 1996; Michael, 1996; Cousin Bette, 1996; TwentyFourSeven, 1997; The Secret Agent (producer, actor), 1998; Captain Jack, Parting Shots, Felicia's Journey, 1999; Enemy at the Gates, 2001. *Recreations:* photography, gardening, playgoing. *Address:* c/o ICM, Oxford House, 76 Oxford Street, W1N 0AX.

HOSKYNS, Sir Benedict (Leigh), 16th Bt, *cr* 1676; *b* 27 May 1928; *s* of Rev. Sir Edwyn Clement Hoskyns, 13th Bt, MC, DD and Mary Trym (*d* 1994), *d* of Edwin Budden, Macclesfield; *S* brother 1956; *m* 1953, Ann Wilkinson; two *s* two *d*. *Educ:* Haileybury; Corpus Christi Coll., Cambridge; London Hospital. BA Cantab 1949; MB, BChir Cantab 1952. House Officer at the London Hospital, 1953. RAMC, 1953–56. House Officer at Royal Surrey County Hospital and General Lying-In Hospital, York Road, SE1, 1957–58; DObstRCOG 1958; in general practice, 1958–93. *Heir: s* Edwyn Wren Hoskyns [*b* 4 Feb. 1956; *m* 1981, Jane, *d* of John Sellars; one *s* one *d*. *Educ:* Nottingham Univ. Medical School (BM, BS); MRCP, FRCPCH. Cons. Paediatrician, Leicester Gen.

Hosp, 1993–]. *Address:* Russell House, Wherry Corner, High Street, Manningtree, Essex CO11 1AP. *T:* (01206) 396432.

HOSKYNS, Sir John (Austin Hungerford Leigh), Kt 1982; Director-General, Institute of Directors, 1984–89; Chairman: The Burton Group plc, 1990–98; Arcadia Group plc, 1998; *b* 23 Aug. 1927; *s* of Lt-Colonel Chandos Benedict Arden Hoskyns and Joyce Austin Hoskyns; *m* 1956, Miranda Jane Marie Mott; two *s* one *d.* *Educ:* Winchester College. Served in The Rifle Brigade, 1945–57 (Captain); IBM United Kingdom Ltd, 1957–64; founded John Hoskyns & Co. Ltd, later part of Hoskyns Group plc (Chm. and Man. Dir), 1964–75; Director: ICL plc, 1982–84; AGB Research plc, later Pergamon AGB plc, 1983–89; Clerical Medical & General Life Assurance Soc., 1983–98; McKechnie plc, 1983–93; Ferranti Internat. plc, 1986–94; EMAP, 1993–98 (Chm., 1994–98). Hd of PM's Policy Unit, 1979–82. Hon. DSc Salford, 1985; DU Essex, 1987. *Publication:* Just In Time: inside the Thatcher revolution, 2000. *Recreations:* opera, shooting. *Address:* c/o Child & Co., 1 Fleet Street, EC4Y 1BD. *Clubs:* Travellers, Green Jackets.

HOSSAIN, Ajmalul; QC 1998; *b* 18 Oct. 1950; *s* of Asrarul Hossain, barrister and Senior Advocate, Supreme Court of Bangladesh, and late Rabia Hossain; *m* 1970, Nasreen Ahmed; two *s.* *Educ:* King's Coll., London (LLB Hons 1976; LLM 1977). FCIArb 1994. Called to the Bar, Lincoln's Inn, 1976 (Buchanan Prize); SE Circuit; in practice at the Bar, Bangladesh, 1977–, England, 1978–; Supreme Court of Bangladesh: enrolled in High Court Div., 1977, Appellate Div., 1986; Senior Advocate, 1998. Pt-time Chm., Southampton Reg., Employment (formerly Industrial) Tribunals, 1995–; Mem., City Disputes Panel, London, 1994–. Member: Supreme Court Bar Assoc., Bangladesh, 1986; Employment Law Bar Assoc., 1995. *Recreations:* travelling, bridge. *Address:* Bedford Row Chambers, 29 Bedford Row, WC1R 4HE. *T:* (020) 7404 1044, *Fax:* (020) 7831 0626; A. Hossain & Associates, 3B Outer Circular Road, Maghbazar, Dhaka 1217, Bangladesh. *T:* (2) 8311492, *Fax:* (2) 9344356.

HOTHAM, family name of **Baron Hotham.**

HOTHAM, 8th Baron *cr* 1797; **Henry Durand Hotham;** Bt 1621; DL; *b* 3 May 1940; *s* of 7th Baron Hotham, CBE, and Lady Letitia Sibell Winifred Cecil (*d* 1992), *er d* of 5th Marquess of Exeter, KG; *S* father, 1967; *m* 1972, Alexandra Stirling Home, *d* of late Maj. Andrew S. H. Drummond Moray; two *s* one *d.* *Educ:* Eton; Cirencester Agricultural Coll. Late Lieut, Grenadier Guards; ADC to Governor of Tasmania, 1963–66. DL Humberside, 1981. *Heir:* *s* Hon. William Beaumont Hotham, *b* 13 Oct. 1972. *Address:* South Dalton Hall, South Dalton, Beverley, Yorks HU17 7PW; Scorborough Hall, Driffield, Yorks YO25 9AZ.

HOTHFIELD, 6th Baron *cr* 1881; **Anthony Charles Sackville Tufton;** Bt 1851; *b* 21 Oct. 1939; *s* of 5th Baron Hothfield, TD and Evelyn Margarette (*d* 1989), *e d* of late Eustace Charles Mordaunt; *S* father, 1991; *m* 1975, Lucinda Marjorie, *d* of Captain Timothy John Gurney; one *s* one *d.* *Educ:* Eton; Magdalene Coll., Cambridge (MA). MICE. *Recreations:* Real tennis, lawn tennis, bridge, shooting. *Heir:* *s* Hon. William Sackville Tufton, *b* 14 Nov. 1977. *Address:* Drybeck Hall, Appleby, Cumbria CA16 6TF. *Clubs:* Hawks (Cambridge); Jesters; almost every Real tennis club.

HOTSPUR; *see* McGrath, J. A.

HOTTEN, Christopher Peter; QC 1994; a Recorder, since 1990; *b* 7 July 1949; *s* of Alan John Hotten and Ida Lydia Hotten; *m* 1973, Lone Elisabeth Nielsen; one *s* two *d.* *Educ:* Hornchurch Grammar Sch.; Leicester Univ. (LLB). Called to the Bar, Inner Temple, 1972. *Recreations:* golf, tennis, snooker. *Address:* 7 Bedford Row, WC1R 4BU. *Club:* Stetchford (Birmingham).

HOTTER, Hans; opera and concert singer, retired 1972, but still gives occasional concert performances; teaches masterclasses in USA, Japan, Great Britain, Austria, Germany and other countries; *b* Offenbach, Germany, 19 Jan. 1909; *m* 1936, Helga Fischer; one *s* one *d.* *Educ:* Munich. Concert career began in 1929 and opera career in 1930. Prof. at Vienna Musik-Hochschule, 1977–80. Mem. of Munich, Vienna and Hamburg State Operas; guest singer in opera and concerts in all major cities of Europe and USA; concert tours in Australia; for 10 years, connected with Columbia Gramophone Co., England; guest singer, Covent Garden Opera, London, 1947–72. Festivals: Salzburg, Edinburgh and Bayreuth. *Relevant publication:* Hans Hotter: man and artist, by Penelope Turing, 1984. *Address:* Bayerische Staatsoper, 80539 München, Germany.

HOTUNG, Sir Joseph (Edward), Kt 1993; Chairman, Ho Hung Hing Estates Ltd, since 1962; *b* 25 May 1930; *s* of Edward Sai-kim Hotung and Maud Alice (*née* Newman); *m* 1957, Mary Catherine McGinley (marr. diss. 1969); two *s* two *d.* *Educ:* St Francis Xavier Coll., Shanghai; St Louis Coll., Tientsin; Catholic Univ. of America (BA); Univ. of London (LLB). With Marine Midland Bank, 1957–60. Director: HSBC Hldgs plc, 1991–98; Hongkong & Shanghai Banking Corp. Ltd, 1991–96; Hongkong Electric Hldgs Ltd, 1984–97; China & Eastern Investment Co. Ltd, 1989–98; Mem., Adv. Council, Phillips Auctioneers, 2000–. Member: Judicial Services Commn, 1990–97; Inland Revenue Bd of Review, 1989–95. University of Hong Kong: Mem. Council, 1984–96; Mem., Finance Cttee, 1986–96; Chm. and Trustee, Staff Terminal Benefits Scheme, 1987–96; Mem. Council, Business Sch., 1990–96; Chm., Arts Develt Council, Hong Kong, 1994–96; Dir, E Asian Hist. of Sci. Foundn, 1991–; Member: UK Adv. Council, Asia House, London, 1993–2000; Governing Body, SOAS, 1997–; Council, St George's Hosp. Med. Sch., London Univ., 2001–; Vis. Cttee, Freer Gall. of Art, Washington, 1990–. Trustee: British Mus., 1994–; Asia Soc., NY, 1991–97; MMA, NY, 2000– (Mem., Vis. Cttee, 1986–; Chm's Council, 1998–; Life Fellow). Vice-Chm., Friends of the Culture and Civilisation of China, USA, 2000–. Hon. Fellow, Hong Kong Univ., 1995. Hon. DLitt Hong Kong, 1997. NACF Award, 1993; Montblanc de la Culture Award, Hong Kong, 1996. *Recreation:* Oriental art. *Address:* 1215 Prince's Building, 10 Chater Road, Central, Hong Kong. *T:* 25229929. *Clubs:* Reform, Beefsteak; Hong Kong (Hong Kong); Century Assoc. (New York).

HOUGH, George Hubert, CBE 1965; PhD; FRAeS; Chairman: Forthstar Ltd, since 1980; Abasec Ltd, since 1988; *b* 21 Oct. 1921; *m* Hazel Ayrton (*née* Russel); one *s* two *d.* *Educ:* Winsford Grammar Sch.; King's Coll., London. BSc (Hons Physics), PhD. Admiralty Signals Estabt, 1940–46. Standard Telecommunication Laboratories Ltd (ITT), 1946–51 (as external student at London Univ. prepared thesis on gaseous discharge tubes); de Havilland Propellers Ltd: early mem. Firestreak team in charge of develt of guidance systems and proximity fusing, 1951–59; Chief Engr (Guided Weapons), 1959; Chief Executive (Engrg), 1961; Dir, de Havilland Aircraft Co., 1962; Hawker Siddeley Dynamics Ltd: Technical Dir, 1963; Dep. Managing Dir, 1968; Man. Dir, 1977; Dep. Chief Exec., Dynamics Group British Aerospace, 1977. Chairman and Chief Executive: British Smelter Constructions Ltd, 1978–80; Magnetic Components Ltd, 1986–89; Fernau Hldgs Ltd, 1989–94; Fernau Avionics Ltd, 1989–94; Director: Sheepbridge Engrg Ltd, 1977–79; Scientific Finance Ltd, 1979–84; Programmed Neuro Cybernetics (UK) Ltd, 1979–85; Landis & Gyr Ltd, 1980–85; Leigh Instruments Ltd (Canada), 1987–88. *Publication:* (with Dr P. Morris) The Anatomy of Major Projects, 1987. *Recreation:* golf. *Address:* Trelyon, Rock, near Wadebridge, Cornwall PL27 6LB. *T:* (01208) 863454.

HOUGH, Prof. James Harley, PhD; CPhys, FInstP; FRAS; Head of Physical Sciences, since 1987, Professor of Astrophysics, since 1989, and Dean of Natural Sciences, since 1998, University of Hertfordshire (formerly Hatfield Polytechnic); *b* 2 July 1943; *s* of John Harley Hough and Sarah Ann (*née* Lomax); *m* 1966, Monica Jane Dent; one *s* one *d.* *Educ:* Prince Henry's GS, Otley, Yorks; Univ. of Leeds (BSc 1st Cl. Hons; PhD 1967). FRAS 1997; FInstP 1998. Res. Fellow, Univ. of Calgary, 1967–71; SERC Res. Fellow, Univ. of Durham, 1971–72; Hatfield Polytechnic: Lectr, 1972–83; Reader in Astronomy, 1983–89. Particle Physics and Astronomy Research Council: Mem. Council 1997–2000; Chm., Educn and Trng Panel, 1998–; Mem. or Chm., numerous SERC/PPARC Cttees and Bds, 1980–. *Publications:* PPARC reports on future of UK Ground-Based Astronomy; numerous scientific papers in learned jls, mostly on active galaxies, star formation, interstellar dust, astronomical polarimetry. *Recreations:* gardening, walking. *Address:* Faculty of Natural Sciences, University of Hertfordshire, Hatfield AL10 9AB. *T:* (01707) 284500.

HOUGH, John Patrick; Secretary, Institute of Chartered Accountants in England and Wales, 1972–82; *b* 6 July 1928; *s* of William Patrick Hough, MBE, Lt-Comdr RN and Eva Harriet Hough; *m* 1956, Dorothy Nadine Akerman; four *s* one *d.* *Educ:* Purbrook High School. FCA, MIMC, FBCS. Articled M. R. Cobbett & Co., Portsmouth, 1950–53; Derbyshire & Co., 1953–54; Turquand Youngs & Co., 1954–57; Computer Specialist, IBM United Kingdom Ltd, 1957–61; Consultant 1961–62, Partner 1962–69, Robson Morrow & Co.; Dep. Sec., Inst. of Chartered Accountants in England and Wales, 1969–71. *Recreations:* music, food. *Address:* 5 South Row, Blackheath, SE3 0RY; Coastguard Cottage, Newtown, Newport, Isle of Wight PO30 4PA. *Club:* London Rowing.

HOUGH, Julia Marie, (Judy); *see* Taylor, Judy.

HOUGH, Stephen; concert pianist; *b* 22 Nov. 1961; *s* of Colin Hough and Annetta (*née* Johnstone). *Educ:* Chetham's Sch. Music, Manchester; Royal Northern Coll. of Music (Fellow, 1993); Juilliard Sch. Numerous recitals and concerto appearances with LSO, LPO, RPO, Philharmonia, Chicago SO, Philadelphia Orchestra, Cleveland Orchestra, LA Philharmonic, San Francisco SO; Boston SO, Orchestre Nat. de France, Deutsches Symphonie Orchester; festival performances incl.: Ravinia, Mostly Mozart, Hollywood Bowl, Blossom, Proms, Le Grange de Meslay, La Roque d'Antheron, Edinburgh, Salzburg, Tanglewood. *Recordings:* Hummel Piano Concertos; 3 Liszt Recitals; 3 Piano Albums; Schumann Recital; Brahms Piano Concertos Nos 1 and 2; Complete Britten Piano Music; Schubert Sonatas; Mendelssohn Piano Concertos; (with Robert Mann) Complete Beethoven and Brahms Violin Sonatas; Scharwenka Piano Concerto No 4, and Sauer Piano Concerto No 1 (Gramophone Record of the Year, 1996); (with Steven Isserlis) Cello Sonatas of Grieg and Rubinstein; Piano Concertos of Lowell Liebermann; Brahms Sonata; (with Michael Collins and Steven Isserlis) Clarinet Trios; piano music of York Bowen, Franck and Mompou; music of Corigliano Tsoutakis, Copland and Weber. RNCM Dayas Gold Medal, 1981; Internat. Terence Judd Award, 1982; Naumburg Internat. Piano Competition, 1983. KHS 1998. *Publications:* vols of transcriptions incl. Rodgers and Hammerstein, 1999, Franck, Choral No 3, 2000. *Recreation:* reading. *Address:* Harrison Parrott Ltd, 12 Penzance Place, W11 4PA.

HOUGHAM, John William, CBE 1996; Commissioner and Deputy Chairman, Disability Rights Commission, since 2000; *b* 18 Jan. 1937; *s* of William George Hougham and Emily Jane (*née* Smith); *m* 1961, Peggy Edith Grove; one *s* one *d.* *Educ:* Sir Roger Manwood's Sch., Sandwich; Leeds Univ. (BA Hons). National Service: commnd 2nd Lieut RA, 1955–57. British Home Stores, 1960–63; Ford Motor Company Ltd, 1963–93: Director: Industrial Relns, Ford España SA, 1976–80; Industrial Relns, Mfg, Ford of Europe Inc., 1982–86; Personnel, and Exec. Bd Mem., 1986–93. Mem. Bd, Personnel Mgt Services Ltd, 1989–93. Chm., ACAS, 1993–2000; Member: Review Body on Doctors' and Dentists' Remuneration, 1992–93; Adv. Bd of CS Occupational Health Service, 1992–96; Employment Appeal Tribunal, 1992–93 and 2000–. Member: Engrg ITB, 1987–90; IPM Nat. Cttee for Equal Opportunities, 1987–92; CBI Employment Policy Cttee, 1987–93; Council, CRAC, 1988–2000; Bd, Trng and Employment Agency for NI, 1990–93; Council, Engrg Trng Auth., 1990–93; Chairman: Employment Occupational Standards Council, 1994–97; Employment NTO, 1997–2001; Adv. Cttee, ESRC Future of Work Prog., 1998–. Vis. Prof., Univ. (formerly Poly.) of E London, 1991–; Vis. Fellow, City Univ., 1991–. Pres., Manpower Soc., 1997–2001; Mem. Adv. Council, Involvement & Participation Assoc., 1997– (Vice-Pres., 1994–97); Chm. Disciplinary Cttee, British Health Trades Assoc., 2000–. Governor: St George's C of E Sch., Gravesend, 1990–; Gravesend GS for Boys, 1990–. Reader, dio. of Rochester, 1998–. CCIPD (CIPM 1986); CIMgt 1986; FRSA 1998. Freeman, City of London, 1995. Member, Editorial Advisory Board: Human Resource Mgt Jl, 1991–2000; People Mgt Mag., 1993–. Hon. LLD Leeds, 1997; Hon. DBA De Montfort, 1997. *Publication:* (contrib.) Legal Intervention in Industrial Relations (ed William McCarthy), 1992. *Recreations:* collecting books on Kent, watching cricket and Rugby football, family history, amateur dramatics. *Address:* 12 Old Road East, Gravesend, Kent DA12 1NQ. *T:* (01474) 352138, *Fax:* (01474) 355526. *Club:* Harlequin Football.

HOUGHTON, Brian Thomas, CB 1991; Director, International Division (formerly International Tax Policy Division), Inland Revenue, 1987–91; *b* 22 Aug. 1931; *s* of Bernard Charles Houghton and Sadie Houghton; *m* 1953, Joyce Beryl (*née* Williams); three *s* one *d.* *Educ:* City Boys' Sch., Leicester; Christ's Coll., Cambridge (Scholar; BA (Mod. Langs); MA 1957). Inland Revenue, 1957; Private Sec. to Chief Sec., HM Treasury, 1966–68; Assistant Secretary: Inland Revenue, 1968–75; HM Treasury, 1975–77; Under Sec., 1977, Principal Finance Officer and Dir of Manpower, Inland Revenue, 1977–83; Policy Div. Dir, Inland Revenue, 1983–87. Consultant, OECD, 1991–93. Vis. Professorial Fellow, QMW, 1992–97. *Recreation:* sailing. *Address:* 19 Rookes Lane, Lymington, Hants SO41 8FP. *T:* (01590) 670375.

HOUGHTON, Herbert; Director: Stenhouse Holdings Ltd, 1979–83; Reed Stenhouse Cos Ltd, 1977–86; Chancellor Insurance Co. Ltd, 1984; *b* 4 Oct. 1920; *s* of Herbert Edward and Emily Houghton; *m* 1st, 1939, Dorothy Ballantyne (*d* 1981); one *s* one *d*; *m* 2nd, 1991, Catharine W. Duffy. *Educ:* William Hulmes' Grammar School. Director, Cockshoots Ltd, 1955; Man. Dir, Stenhouse Northern Ltd, 1968; Chairman: Sir Wm Garthwaite (Holdings) Ltd, 1973; Sten-Re Ltd, 1973; Director and Chief Executive, A. R. Stenhouse & Partners Ltd, 1977; Dir, British Vita Co. Ltd, 1969–84. *Recreations:* overseas travel, golf, reading, gardening. *Address:* 2 Orchard Court, Grindleford, Sheffield S30 1JH. *T:* (01433) 631142; 554 Palm Way, Gulf Stream, FL 33483, USA.

HOUGHTON, Dr John; JP; Director, Teesside Polytechnic, 1971–79, retired (Principal, Constantine College of Technology, 1961–70); *b* 12 June 1922; *s* of George Stanley Houghton and Hilda (*née* Simpson); *m* 1951, Kathleen Lamb; one *s* one *d.* *Educ:* King Henry VIII Sch., Coventry; Hanley High Sch.; Coventry Techn. Coll.; King's Coll.,

Cambridge; Queen Mary Coll., London Univ. BSc (hons) Engrg 1949; PhD 1952. CEng, MIMechE, FRAeS. Aircraft Apprentice, Sir W. G. Armstrong-Whitworth Aircraft Ltd, 1938–43; design and stress engr, 1943–46; student at univ. (Clayton Fellow), 1946–51; Lectr, Queen Mary Coll., London Univ., 1950–52; Sen. Lectr and Head of Aero-Engrg, Coventry Techn. Coll., 1952–57; Head of Dept of Mech. Engrg, Brunel Coll. Advanced Technology, 1957–61. Freeman, City of Coventry, 1943. JP Middlesbrough, 1962. *Publications:* (with D. R. L. Smith) Mechanics of Fluids by Worked Examples, 1959; various research reports, reviews and articles in professional and learned jls. *Recreations:* keen sportsman (triple Blue), do-it-yourself activities, gardening, pottery, oil painting. *Club:* Middlesbrough Rotary.

HOUGHTON, Sir John (Theodore), Kt 1991; CBE 1983; FRS 1972; Chief Executive (formerly Director General) of the Meteorological Office, 1983–91; Chairman, Royal Commission on Environmental Pollution, 1992–98 (Member, 1991–98); *b* 30 Dec. 1931; *s* of Sidney M. Houghton, schoolmaster, and Miriam Houghton; *m* 1st, 1962, Margaret Edith Houghton (*née* Broughton) (*d* 1986), MB, BS, DPH; one *s* one *d*; 2nd, 1988, Sheila Houghton (*née* Thompson). *Educ:* Rhyl Grammar Sch.; Jesus Coll., Oxford (Scholar). BA hons Physics 1951, MA, DPhil 1955. Research Fellow, RAE Farnborough, 1954–57; Lectr in Atmospheric Physics, Oxford Univ., 1958–62; Reader, 1962–76; Professor, 1976–83; Fellow, Jesus Coll., Oxford, 1960–83, Hon. Fellow 1983; on secondment as Dir (Appleton), 1979–83, and Dep. Dir, 1981–83, Rutherford Appleton Laboratory, SERC, Hon. Scientist, 1992–. Member: Astronomy, Space and Radio Bd, SERC (formerly SRC), 1970–73 and 1976–81; Exec. Cttee, WMO, 1983–91 (Vice-Pres., 1987–91); Astronomy and Planetary Sci. Bd, SERC, 1987–93; Meteorological Cttee, 1975–80; Jt Organising Cttee, Global Atmospheric Res. Programme, 1976–79; Exec. Management Bd, British Nat. Space Centre, 1986–91; UK Govt Panel on Sustainable Develt, 1994–2000; Chairman: Jt Scientific Cttee, World Climate Research Programme, 1981–84; Earth Observation Adv. Cttee, ESA, 1982–93; Scientific Assessment, Intergovtl Panel for Climate Change, 1988–; Jt Scientific and Tech. Cttee, Global Climate Observing System, 1992–95. Pres., RMetS, 1976–78 (Hon. Mem.); MAE 1988; Fellow, Optical Soc. of America; Hon. Mem., Amer. Met. Soc. FInstP; Lectures: Cherwell-Simon Meml, 1983–84, Halley, 1992, Templeton, 1992, Oxford Univ.; Bakerian, Royal Soc., 1991. Hon. Fellow, Univ. of Wales, Lampeter, 1994. Hon. DSc: Wales, 1991; UEA, 1993; Leeds, 1995; Heriot-Watt, 1996; Greenwich, 1997; Glamorgan, 1998; Reading, 1999; Birmingham, 2000; DUniv Stirling, 1992. Buchan Prize, RMetS, 1966; Charles Chree medal and prize, Inst. of Physics, 1979; (with F. W. Taylor, C. D. Rodgers and G. D. Peskett) Rank Prize for opto-electronics, 1989; Symons Meml Medal, RMetS, 1991; Glazebrook Medal and Prize, Inst. of Phys, 1990; Global 500 Award, UN Envmt Programme, 1994; Gold Medal, RAS, 1995; Internat. Meteorological Orgn Prize, 1998. *Publications:* (with S. D. Smith) Infra-Red Physics, 1966; The Physics of Atmospheres, 1977, 2nd edn 1986; (with F. W. Taylor and C. D. Rodgers) Remote Sounding of Atmospheres, 1984; Does God play dice?, 1988; Global Warming: the complete briefing, 1994, 2nd edn 1997; The Search for God: can science help?, 1995; papers in learned jls on atmospheric radiation, spectroscopy, remote sounding from satellites and climate change. *Recreations:* walking, sailing. *Address:* IPCC Unit, Hadley Centre, Meteorological Office, London Road, Bracknell, Berks RG12 2SY.

HOUGHTON, Peter; Director, Eastern Region, NHS Executive, Department of Health, since 1999; *b* 7 Dec. 1957; *s* of late Peter Houghton and of Verde Cicely Houghton. *Educ:* Barnsley Grammar Sch.; Keble Coll., Oxford (BA Classics); Aberdeen Univ. (Cert. Health Econs 1988). NHS nat. admin trainee, 1981–83; Dep. Administrator, Royal Nat. Orthopaedic Hosp., London, 1983–85; Gen. Manager, Mental Health and Learning Disability Services, Cambridge, 1985–91; Chief Exec., Hinchingbrooke Healthcare NHS Trust, Huntingdon, 1991–93; Actg Dir of Planning, E Anglian RHA, 1993–94; Dir, Strategic Develt, Anglia and Oxford Reg., NHS Exec., 1994–99. Mem., Inst. Health Mgt, 1984. *Recreations:* classical music and opera, travel, gardening, cycling. *Address:* 1 All Saints Close, Gazeley, Newmarket, Suffolk CB8 8WS. *T:* (01638) 750808.

HOUGHTON, Maj.-Gen. Robert Dyer, CB 1963; OBE 1947; MC 1942; DL; *b* 7 March 1912; *s* of late J. M. Houghton, Dawlish, Devon; *m* 1940, Dorothy Uladh (*d* 1995), *y d* of late Maj.-Gen. R. W. S. Lyons, IMS; two *s* one *d*. *Educ:* Haileybury Coll. Royal Marines Officer, 1930–64; Col Comdt, Royal Marines, 1973–76. Gen. Sec., Royal UK Beneficent Assoc., 1968–78. DL East Sussex, 1977. *Recreations:* gardening, sailing, model engineering. *Address:* Vert House, Whitesmith, near Lewes, East Sussex BN8 6JQ. *Club:* Army and Navy.

HOULDEN, Rev. Prof. (James) Leslie; Professor of Theology, King's College, London, 1987–94, now Emeritus; *b* 1 March 1929; *s* of late James and Lily Alice Houlden. *Educ:* Altrincham Grammar Sch.; Queen's Coll., Oxford. Asst Curate, St Mary's, Hunslet, Leeds, 1955–58; Chaplain, Chichester Theological Coll., 1958–60; Chaplain Fellow, Trinity Coll., Oxford, 1960–70; Principal, Cuddesdon Theol Coll., later Ripon Coll., Cuddesdon, 1970–77; King's College, London: Lectr, 1977; Sen. Lectr in New Testament Studies, 1985; Dean, Faculty of Theology and Religious Studies, 1986–88; Head, Dept of Biblical Studies, 1988–89; Actg Dean, 1993–94; FKC 1994. Hon. Canon of Christ Church Oxford, 1976–77. Member: Liturgical Commn, 1969–76; Doctrine Commn of C of E, 1969–76; Gen. Synod of C of E, 1980–90. Editor, Theology, 1983–91. *Publications:* Paul's Letters from Prison, 1970; (ed) A Celebration of Faith, 1970; Ethics and the New Testament, 1973; The Johannine Epistles, 1974; The Pastoral Epistles, 1976; Patterns of Faith, 1977; Explorations in Theology 3, 1978; What Did the First Christians Believe?, 1982; Connections, 1986; Backward into Light, 1987; (ed) The World's Religions, 1988; History, Story and Belief, 1988; (ed) Dictionary of Biblical Interpretation, 1990; Truth Untold, 1991; (ed) Austin Farrer: the essential sermons, 1991; Bible and Belief, 1991; Jesus: a question of identity, 1992; (ed jtly) Austin Farrer, Words for Life, 1993; (ed) The Interpretation of the Bible in the Church, 1995; (ed) Companion Encyclopedia of Theology, 1995; The Public Face of the Gospel, 1997; *contributed to:* The Myth of God Incarnate, 1977; Incarnation and Myth, 1979; Alternative Approaches to New Testament Study, 1985; The Reality of God, 1986; A New Dictionary of Christian Ethics, 1986; The Trial of Faith, 1988; God's Truth, 1988; Embracing the Chaos, 1990; Tradition and Unity, 1991; Using the Bible Today, 1991; Fundamentalism and Tolerance, 1991; Anchor Bible Dictionary, 1992; The Resurrection of Jesus Christ, 1993; Crossing the Boundaries, 1994; Divine Revelation, 1997; New Soundings, 1997; Theological Liberalism, 2000; reviews and articles in learned jls. *Address:* 5 The Court, Temple Balsall, Knowle, Solihull B93 0AN. *Club:* Athenæum.

HOULDER, Bruce Fiddes; QC 1994; a Recorder, since 1991; *b* 27 Sept. 1947; *s* of late Charles Alexander Houlder and Jessie Houlder (*née* Fiddes); *m* 1974, Stella Catherine Mattinson; two *d*. *Educ:* Felsted Sch., Dunmow. Called to the Bar, Gray's Inn, 1969, Bencher, 2001. Mem., Bar Council, 1995–97, 1998– (Vice Chm., Professional Standards Cttee and Public Affairs Cttee, 1996–98; Chm., Public Affairs Cttee, 1999); Chm., Criminal Bar Assoc. of England and Wales, 2001–July 2002 (Vice Chm., 2000–01). Member: Internat. Bar Assoc.; Amer. Bar Assoc. Fellow, Soc. of Advanced Legal Studies. *Recreations:* painting, sailing, walking, theatre, music. *Address:* 6 King's Bench Walk, Temple, EC4Y 7DR. *T:* (020) 7583 0410.

HOULDER, John Maurice, CBE 1977 (MBE (mil.) 1941); Chairman, Houlder Offshore Engineering Ltd, since 1984; *b* 20 Feb. 1916; *m* 1981, Rody, *d* of late Major Luke White. Private Pilot's Licence, 1938–; instrument rating, 1949–; Lessee, Elstree Aerodrome, 1951–. Chm., Houlder Diving Research Facility Ltd, 1978–. Vis. Prof., Dept of Ship and Marine Technol., Univ. of Strathclyde, 1982–. Chm., London Ocean Shipowners Joint Dock Labour Piecework Cttee, 1950–60; first Chm., River Plate Europe Freight Conf., 1961–70; Chm., Bulk Cargo Cttee, Continental River Plate Conf., 1954–70. Member: Gen. Cttee, 1961–, Exec. Board, 1970–93, and Technical Cttee, 1970–95, Lloyds Register of Shipping; Light Aircraft Requirements Cttee, CAA, 1955–84; Adv. Cttee on R&D to Sec. of State for Energy, 1987–90. Member, Council: RSPB, 1974–79; RINA, 1981–87; Pres., Soc for Underwater Technology, 1978–80 (President's Award, 1987). Hon. DSc Strathclyde, 1986. Stanley Gray Award, Inst. of Marine Engrs, 1982. *Recreations:* ski-ing, flying, bird-watching, computer programming. *Address:* 59 Warwick Square, SW1V 2AL. *T:* (020) 7834 2856, *Fax:* (020) 7834 1647. *Clubs:* Air Squadron; Kandahar Ski, 1001.

HOULDSWORTH, Sir Richard (Thomas Reginald), 5th Bt *cr* 1887, of Reddish and Coodham; Farm Manager since 1988; *b* 2 Aug. 1947; *s* of Sir Reginald Douglas Henry Houldsworth, 4th Bt, OBE, TD and Margaret May (*d* 1995), *d* of late Cecil Emilius Laurie; *S* father, 1989; *m* 1st, 1970, Jane Elizabeth (marr. diss. 1982), *o d* of Alistair Orr; two *s*; 2nd, 1992, Ann Catherine Tremayne; one *s*. *Educ:* Bredon School, Tewkesbury, Glos; Blanerne School, Denholm, Roxburghshire. *Recreations:* shooting, fishing, tennis, squash, horse racing. *Heir: s* Simon Richard Henry Houldsworth, *b* 6 Oct. 1971. *Address:* Kirkbride, Glenburn, Crosshill, Ayrshire KA19 7QA. *T:* (01655) 740202.

HOULIHAN, Michael Patrick, FRGS; Chief Executive, (formerly Director), Museums and Galleries of Northern Ireland, since 1998; *b* 27 Sept. 1948; *s* of Michael Houlihan and Kathleen (*née* Small); *m* 1969, Jane Hibbert; one *s* one *d*. *Educ:* St Francis Xavier's Coll., Liverpool; Univ. of Bristol (BA Hons Hist.). FRGS 1994. Imperial War Museum: Research Asst, 1971–75, Dep. Keeper, 1975–76, Dept of Exhibits; Keeper, Dept of Permanent Exhibns, 1976–84; Dep. Dir, 1984–94, Dir, 1994–98, Horniman Mus. and Gardens. Member: British Commn for Military Hist., 1982–; NI Cttee, British Council, 1998–; Bd, NI Mus Council, 1998. Trustee, Nat. Self-Portrait Collection of Ireland, 1998–. Mem. Council, Goldsmiths Coll., Univ. of London, 1997–98. FRSA 1989. *Publications:* Trench Warfare 1914–18, 1974; (with B. Yale) No Man's Land, 1984. *Recreations:* military history, cycling, Romanesque architecture, battlefields. *Address:* Ulster Museum, Botanic Gardens, Belfast BT9 5AB.

HOULSBY, Prof. Guy Tinmouth, PhD; FREng; Professor of Civil Engineering, and Fellow of Brasenose College, Oxford, since 1991; *b* 28 March 1954; *s* of late Lt Col Thomas Tinmouth Houlsby, TD and of Vivienne May Houlsby (*née* Ford); *m* 1985, Jenny Lucy Damaris Nedderman; two *s*. *Educ:* Trinity College, Glenalmond; St John's College, Cambridge (MA, PhD). CEng 1983, FREng 1999; FICE 1997. Engineer, Binnie and Partners, 1975–76, Babtie Shaw and Morton, 1976–77; Research Student, Cambridge, 1977–80; Oxford University: Jun. Res. Fellow, Balliol Coll., 1980–83; Lectr in Engineering, 1983–91; Fellow, Keble College, 1983–91. *Publications:* contribs to learned jls on soil mechanics. *Recreations:* ornithology, woodwork, Northumbrian small pipes. *Address:* 25 Purcell Road, Marston, Oxford OX3 0HB. *T:* (01865) 722128.

HOULT, Helen Isabel; *see* Cleland, H. I.

HOUNSFIELD, Sir Godfrey (Newbold), Kt 1981; CBE 1976; FRS 1975; Consultant to Laboratories, Central Research Laboratories of EMI Group (formerly Thorn EMI Central Research Laboratories), Hayes, Middx, since 1986 (Head of Medical Systems section, 1972–76; Chief Staff Scientist, 1976–77, Senior Staff Scientist, 1977–85); Consultant (part-time), National Heart & Chest Hospitals, Chelsea, since 1986; *b* 28 Aug. 1919; *s* of Thomas Hounsfield, Newark, Notts. *Educ:* Magnus Grammar Sch., Newark; City and Guilds Coll., London (Radio Communications qualif.); Faraday House Electrical Engineering Coll. (Diploma); grad. for IEE. Volunteered for RAF, 1939; served 1939–46 (incl. period as Lectr at Cranwell Radar Sch.); awarded Certificate of Merit (for work done in RAF), 1945. Attended Faraday House, where he studied elec. and mech. engrg, 1947–51. Joined EMI Ltd, 1951, working initially on radar systems and, later, on computers; led design team for the first large, all transistor computer to be built in Great Britain, the EMIDEC 1100, 1958–59; invented the EMI-scanner computerised transverse axial tomography system for X-ray examination, 1969–72 (first used at Atkinson Morley's Hosp., Wimbledon, and now used at leading hosps throughout the world, known as CAT or CT scanning); the technique can be applied to cranial examinations and the whole of the body; the system has overcome obstacles to the diagnosis of disease in the brain which have continued since Roentgen's day (1895); it includes a patient-scanning unit; developer of a new X-ray technique (the EMI-scanner system) which won the 1972 MacRobert Award of £25,000 for the invention, and a Gold Medal for EMI Ltd; working on Nuclear Magnetic Resonance Imaging, 1976–; Magnetic Resonance Imaging Advr, Nat. Heart Hosp. and Brompton Hosp.; formerly Professorial Fellow in Imaging Sciences, Manchester Univ. Hon. FRCP 1976; Hon. FRCR 1976; Hon. FREng (Hon. FEng 1994). Dr Medicine (*hc*) Universität Basel, 1975; Hon. DSc: City, 1976; London, 1976; Hon. DTech Loughborough, 1976. Wilhelm-Exner Medal, Austrian Industrial Assoc., 1974; Ziedses des Plantes Medal, Physikalisch Medizinische Gesellschaft, Würzburg, 1974; Prince Philip Medal Award, CGLI, 1975; ANS Radiation Industry Award, Georgia Inst. of Technology, 1975; Lasker Award, Lasker Foundn, 1975; Duddell Bronze Medal, Inst. Physics, 1976; Golden Plate Award, Amer. Acad. of Achievement, 1976; Reginald Mitchell Gold Medal, Stoke-on-Trent Assoc. of Engrs, 1976; Churchill Gold Medal, 1976; Gairdner Foundn Award, 1976; (jtly) Nobel Prize for Physiology or Medicine, 1979; Ambrogino d'Oro Award, City of Milan, 1980; Deutsche Roentgen Plakette, Deutsche Roentgen Museum, 1980. *Publications:* contribs: New Scientist; Brit. Jl of Radiology; Amer. Jl of Röntgenology. *Recreation:* mountain walking. *Address:* Central Research Laboratories, Dawley Road, Hayes, Middx UB3 1HH. *T:* (020) 8848 6404; 15 Crane Park Road, Twickenham TW2 6DF. *T:* (020) 8894 1746.

HOURSTON, Sir Gordon (Minto), Kt 1997; FRPharmS; Chairman, United Biscuits plc, 1999–2000 (non-executive Director, 1995–99); *b* 24 July 1934; *s* of William A. M. Hourston and Vera W. (*née* Minto); *m* 1962, Sheila Morris; two *s*. *Educ:* Daniel Stewart's Coll., Edinburgh; Heriot-Watt Univ. FRPharmS 1982 (MRPharmS 1957). Joined Boots The Chemists, 1958: Dir, 1978; Dep. Man. Dir, 1984–88; Chm. and Man. Dir, 1988–95; Dir, Boots Co. plc, 1981–95. Chm., Roseleys plc, 1996–. Chm., Company Chemists' Assoc., 1988–95. Chm., Armed Forces Pay Rev. Body, 1993–99 (Mem., 1989–99); Mem., Sen. Salaries Rev. Body, 1993–99. Trustee, Pharmacy Practice Res. Trust, 1999–. *Recreations:* golf, walking, modern history, reading. *Address:* 7 Firs Road, Edwalton, Nottingham NG12 4BY.

HOUSDEN, Peter James; Director General for Schools, Department for Education and Skills, since 2001; *b* 7 Dec. 1950. Teacher, Madeley Court Sch., Telford, 1975–79; Professional Asst, Humberside LEA, 1979–82; Asst Dir of Educn, Notts LEA, 1982–86; Sen. Educn Officer, Lancs LEA, 1986–88; Dep. Chief Educn Officer, Notts LEA, 1988–91; Dir of Educn, 1991–94, Chief Exec., 1994–2001, Notts CC. Mem., Chartermark Panel, 1997–. Advr, LGA, 1997–2001. Chm., Nottingham Drug Action Team, 1994–2000; Mem., Adv. Council on Misuse of Drugs, 1998–. Associate Fellow, Warwick Univ. Business Sch., 1996–. *Address:* Department for Education and Skills, Sanctuary Buildings, Great Smith Street, SW1P 3BT. *T:* (020) 7925 6504.

HOUSE, Lt-Gen. Sir David (George), GCB 1977 (KCB 1975); KCVO 1985; CBE 1967; MC 1944; Gentleman Usher of the Black Rod, House of Lords, 1978–85; Serjeant-at-Arms, House of Lords, and Secretary to the Lord Great Chamberlain, 1978–85; *b* 8 Aug. 1922; *s* of A. G. House; *m* 1947, Sheila Betty Darwin; two *d. Educ:* Regents Park Sch., London. War service in Italy; and thereafter in variety of regimental (KRRC and 1st Bn The Royal Green Jackets) and staff appts. Comd 51 Gurkha Bde in Borneo, 1965–67; Chief BRIXMIS, 1967–69; Dep. Mil. Sec., 1969–71; Chief of Staff, HQ BAOR, 1971–73; Dir of Infantry, 1973–75; GOC Northern Ireland, 1975–77. Colonel Commandant: The Light Division, 1974–77; Small Arms School Corps, 1974–77. Dir, Yorks and Humberside, Lloyds Bank, 1985–91. *Address:* Dormer Lodge, Aldborough, near Boroughbridge, N Yorks YO5 9EP. *Club:* Army and Navy.

HOUSE, Ven. Francis Harry, OBE 1955; MA; Officer Royal (Hellenic) Order of Phoenix, 1947; Archdeacon of Macclesfield, 1967–78, now Archdeacon Emeritus; Rector of St James, Gawsworth, 1967–78; *b* 9 Aug. 1908; *s* of late Canon William Joseph House, DD; *m* 1938, Margaret Neave; two *d. Educ:* St George's Sch., Harpenden; Wadham Coll., Oxford; Cuddesdon Theological Coll. Sec. of Student Christian Movement of Gt Britain and Ireland, 1931–34; Deacon, 1936; Priest, 1937. Asst Missioner, Pembroke Coll. (Cambridge) Mission, Walworth, 1936–37; Travelling sec. of World's Student Christian Federation, Geneva, 1938–40; Curate of Leeds Parish Church, 1940–42; Overseas Asst, Religious Broadcasting Dept, BBC, London, 1942–44; representative of World Student Relief in Greece, 1944–46; Sec. Youth Dept World Council of Churches, Geneva, and World Conference of Christian Youth, Oslo, 1946–47; Head of Religious Broadcasting BBC, London, 1947–55; Associate Gen. Sec. of the World Council of Churches, Geneva, 1955–62; Vicar of St Giles, Pontefract, 1962–67. Select Preacher, Cambridge Univ., 1949. Member: Gen. Synod of Church of England, 1970–78; Gen. Synod's Commn on Broadcasting, 1971–73; Bd for Mission and Unity, 1971–80 (Vice-Chm., 1971–75). *Publications:* The Russian Phoenix, 1988; articles contributed to: The Student Movement, The Student World, East and West, the Ecumenical Review, Theology, Crucible, One in Christ, etc. *Address:* 11 Drummond Court, Far Headingley, Leeds LS16 5QE. *T:* (0113) 278 3646.

HOUSE, Prof. John Peter Humphry, PhD; Professor, Courtauld Institute of Art, University of London, since 1995 (Deputy Director, 1996–99); *b* 19 April 1945; *s* of Madeline Edith Church and Arthur Humphry House; *m* 1968, Jill Elaine Turner; two *s. Educ:* Westminster Sch.; New Coll., Oxford (BA); Courtauld Inst. of Art (MA, PhD). Lecturer: UEA, 1969–76; UCL, 1976–80; Lectr, 1980–87, Reader, 1987–95, Courtauld Inst., London Univ. Slade Prof. of Fine Art, Univ. of Oxford, 1986–87; British Acad. Res. Reader, 1988–90. Organiser: Impressionism Exhibn, RA, 1974; Landscapes of France exhibn, Hayward Gall., 1995; Co-organiser: Post Impressionism exhibn, RA, 1979–80; Renoir exhibn, Arts Council, 1985. *Publications:* Monet, 1977, 2nd edn 1981; Monet: nature into art, 1986; (jtly) Impressionist and Post-Impressionist Masterpieces from the Courtauld Collection, 1987; (jtly) Impressionism for England: Samuel Courtauld as Patron and Collector, 1994; Renoir: la promenade, 1997; author/co-author, exhibition catalogues; articles in Burlington Magazine, Art History, Art in America. *Recreation:* second hand bookshops. *Address:* Courtauld Institute of Art, University of London, Somerset House, Strand, WC2R 0RN. *T:* (020) 7848 2777; *e-mail:* john.house@courtauld.ac.uk.

See also E. H. O. Parry.

HOUSE, Roger Keith; a District Judge (Magistrates' Courts) (formerly Metropolitan Stipendiary Magistrate), since 1995; Chairman, Youth Court, since 1995; *b* 24 Jan. 1944; *s* of Donald Stuart House and Kathleen Mary House; *m* 1971, Elizabeth Anne Hall; two *s. Educ:* Wychwood Prep. Sch.; Sherborne. Admitted Solicitor, 1972; Asst Solicitor with various firms, 1972–76; sole practitioner, 1976–95. *Recreations:* singing, reading, walking the countryside, shooting, surfing. *Address:* c/o Camberwell Magistrates' Court, Camberwell Green, SE5 7UP. *T:* (020) 7805 9868.

HOUSLAY, Prof. Miles Douglas, PhD; FRSE; Gardiner Professor of Biochemistry, University of Glasgow, since 1984; *b* 25 June 1950; *s* of Edwin Douglas Houslay and Georgina Marie Houslay; *m* 1972, Rhian Mair Gee; two *s* one *d. Educ:* UC Cardiff (BSc Hons Biochem. 1971); King's Coll., Cambridge (PhD Biochem. 1974). FRSE 1986. ICI Res. Fellow, Dept Pharmacol., Univ. of Cambridge, 1974; Res. Fellow, Queens' Coll., Cambridge, 1975; Lectr in Biochem., 1976–82, Reader, 1982–84, UMIST. Ed.-in-Chief, Cellular Signalling, 1987–. Chairman: Cell Bd Grant Panel, MRC, 1990–93; Project Grant Panel, Wellcome Trust, 1996–2000, BHF, 1997–99; former Member: Grant Panels for MRC, AFRC and Brit. Diabetic Assoc.; RAE panels, HEFC, 1992, 1996. Selby Fellow, Aust. Acad. Scis, 1984. Minshull Meml Lectr, Univ. of Edinburgh, 1990. Trustee, BHF, 1997. Founder, FMedSci, 1998. Colworth Medal, Biochem. Soc., 1984; Most Cited Scientist in Scotland, Edinburgh Sci. Fest. Award, 1992. *Publications:* Dynamics of Biological Membranes, 1982; numerous contribs on cell signalling systems to learned jls. *Recreations:* walking (hill, coastal and desert), reading, driving, cooking, music, eating out. *Address:* Division of Biochemistry and Molecular Biology, Wolfson and Davidson Buildings, Institute of Biomedical and Life Sciences, University of Glasgow, Glasgow G12 8QQ. *T:* (0141) 330 5903.

HOUSSEMAYNE du BOULAY, (Edward Philip) George, CBE 1985; FRCR, FRCP; Professor of Neuroradiology, University of London at Institute of Neurology, 1975–84, now Emeritus; Hon. Research Fellow, Zoological Society of London (Head, X-Ray Department, Nuffield Laboratories, Institute of Zoology, 1965–86); Director, Radiological Research Trust, since 1985; *b* 28 Jan. 1922; *yr s* of Philip Houssemayne du Boulay and Mercy Tyrrell (*née* Friend); *m* 1944, Vivien M. Glasson (marr. diss.); four *s* (and two *s* decd); *m* 1968, Pamela Mary Verity; two *d. Educ:* Christ's Hospital; King's Coll., London; Charing Cross Hosp. (Entrance Schol. 1940; MB, BS, DMRD). Served RAF (Medical), 1946–48; Army Emergency Reserve, 1952–57. House appts, Charing Cross Hosp. and Derby City Hosp., 1945–46; Registrar (Radiology), Middlesex Hosp., 1948–49; Sen. Registrar (Radiology): St Bartholomew's Hosp., 1949–54; St George's Hosp., 1951–52; Consultant Radiologist: Nat. Hosp. for Nervous Diseases, Maida Vale, 1954–68; Bartholomew's Hosp., 1954–71; Nat. Hosp. for Nervous Diseases, Queen Square, 1968–75 (Head, Lysholm Radiol Dept, 1975–84). Editor, Neuroradiology, 1974–91. Pres., Brit. Inst. of Radiology, 1976–77, Appeal Co-ordinator 1976–84; Hon. Member: Société Française de Neuroradiologie; Amer. Soc. of Neuroradiology; Swedish Soc. of Neuroradiology; German Soc. Neuroradiology. Trustee, Nat. Hosp. Develt Foundn. Glyn Evans Meml Lectr, RCR, 1970; Ernestine Henry Lectr, RCP, 1976. Hon. FACR. Hon. DSc Leicester Polytechnic, 1992. Barclay Medal, BIR, 1968. *Publications:* Principles of X-Ray Diagnosis of the Skull, 1965, 2nd edn 1979; (jtly) 4th edn of A Text Book of X-Ray Diagnosis by British Authors: Neuroradiology Vol. 1, 5th edn 1984; (jtly) The Cranial Arteries of Mammals, 1973; (jtly) An Atlas of Normal Vertebral Angiograms, 1976; works in specialist jls. *Recreation:* gardening. *Address:* Old Manor House, Brington, Huntingdon, Cambs PE28 5AF. *T:* (01832) 710353.

HOUSSEMAYNE du BOULAY, Sir Roger (William), KCVO 1982 (CVO 1972); CMG 1975; HM Diplomatic Service, retired; Vice Marshal of the Diplomatic Corps, 1975–82; *b* 30 March 1922; *s* of Charles John Houssemayne du Boulay, Captain, RN, and Mary Alice Veronica, *née* Morgan; *m* 1957, Elizabeth, *d* of late Brig. Home, late RM, and Molly, Lady Pile; one *d*, and two step *s. Educ:* Winchester; Oxford. Served RAFVR, 1941–46 (Pilot). HM Colonial Service, Nigeria, 1949–58; HM Foreign, later Diplomatic, Service, 1959; FO, 1959; Washington, 1960–64; FCO 1964–67; Manila, 1967–71; Alternate Director, Asian Development Bank, Manila, 1967–69, and Director, 1969–71; Counsellor and Head of Chancery, Paris, 1971–73; Resident Comr, New Hebrides, 1973–75. Adviser: Solomon Is Govt, 1986; Swaziland Govt, 1992. *Address:* Anstey House, near Buntingford, Herts SG9 0BJ.

HOUSTON, Maj.-Gen. David, CBE 1975 (OBE 1972); JP; Lord-Lieutenant of Sutherland, since 1991; *b* 24 Feb. 1929; *s* of late David Houston and late Christina Charleson Houston (*née* Dunnett); *m* 1959, Jancis Veronica Burn; two *s. Educ:* Latymer Upper Sch. Commissioned, Royal Irish Fusiliers, 1949; served Korea, Kenya, BAOR, N Africa; Staff Coll., Camberley, 1961; commanded 1 Loyals and newly amalgamated 1st QLR, 1969–71; in comd 8th Inf. Bde, Londonderry, N Ireland, 1974–75; Mem. RCDS, 1976; Military Attaché and Commander, British Army Staff, Washington, 1977–79; HQ UKLF, 1979–80; Pres., Regular Commissions Bd, 1980–83; retd 1984. Hon. Col, Manchester and Salford Univs OTC (TA), 1985–90; Col, The Queen's Lancashire Regt, 1983–92. DL Sutherland, 1991; JP Sutherland, 1991. *Recreations:* fishing, golf. *Address:* c/o Bank of Scotland, Dornoch, Sutherland IV25 3ST.

HOUSTON, James Caldwell, CBE 1982; MD, FRCP; Physician to Guy's Hospital, 1953–82, now Emeritus Physician; Dean, United Medical and Dental Schools, Guys and St Thomas's Hospitals, 1982–84 (Hon. Fellow, 1993; Dean, Medical and Dental Schools, Guy's Hospital, 1965–82); *b* 18 Feb. 1917; *yr s* of late David Houston and Minnie Walker Houston; *m* 1946, Thelma Cromarty Cruickshank, MB, ChB, 2nd *d* of late John Cruickshank, CBE; four *s. Educ:* Mill Hill Sch.; Guy's Hosp. Medical Sch. MRCS, LRCP 1939; MB, BS (London) 1940; MRCP 1944; MD 1946; FRCP 1956. Late Major RAMC; Medical Registrar, Guy's Hospital, 1946. Asst Ed., 1954, Jt Ed., 1958–67, Guy's Hosp. Reports. Member: Bd of Governors, Guy's Hosp., 1965–74; SE Metropolitan Regional Hosp. Bd, 1966–71; Lambeth, Lewisham and Southwark AHA (Teaching), 1974–78; Court of Governors, London Sch. of Hygiene and Tropical Med., 1969–84; Senate, Univ. of London, 1970–84; Bd of Faculty of Clinical Medicine, Cambridge Univ., 1975–81; Cttee of Vice-Chancellors and Principals, 1977–80; Chm., Collegiate Council, Univ. of London, 1976–79; Special Trustee, Guy's Hosp., 1974–82; Trustee, Hayward Foundn, 1978–2001. Dir, Clerical, Medical & Gen. Life Assurance Soc., 1965–87; Vice-Pres., Medical Defence Union, 1970–92. *Publications:* Principles of Medicine and Medical Nursing (jtly), 1956, 5th edn 1978, A Short Text-book of Medicine (jtly), 1962, 8th edn 1984; articles in Quart. Jl Med., Brit. Med. Bull., Lancet, etc. *Recreations:* golf, gardening. *Address:* Discovery Cottage, 1 Mews Street, E1W 1UG. *T:* (020) 7481 8912.

HOUSTOUN-BOSWALL, Sir (Thomas) Alford, 8th Bt *cr* 1836; founder and Chairman, The Harrodian School, since 1993; international economics and business consultant; *b* 23 May 1947; *s* of Sir Thomas Houstoun-Boswall, 7th Bt, and of Margaret Jean, *d* of George Bullen-Smith; *S* father, 1982; *m* 1971, Eliana Michele (marr. diss. 1996), *d* of Dr John Pearse, New York; one *s* one *d. Educ:* Lindisfarne College. Partner, Rosedale-Engel, Houstoun-Boswall Partnership, Bermuda; Director, Stair & Co., New York (specialising in fine 18th century English furniture and works of art); Pres., Houstoun-Boswall Inc. (Fine Arts), New York. Lecturer, New York Univ. and Metropolitan Museum of Art, New York. *Heir: s* Alexander Alford Houstoun-Boswall, *b* 16 Sept. 1972. *Address:* The Harrodian School, Lonsdale Road, SW13 9QN; 18 rue Basse, 06410 Biot, France; 15 East 77 Street, New York, NY 10021, USA.

HOVELL-THURLOW-CUMMING-BRUCE, family name of **Baron Thurlow**.

HOVEN, Helmert Frans van den; Knight, Order of Netherlands Lion, 1978; Commander, Order of Orange Nassau, 1984; Hon. KBE 1980. Chairman, Unilever NV, 1975–84; Vice-Chairman, Unilever Ltd, 1975–84; *b* 25 April 1923; *m* 1st, 1950, Dorothy Ida Bevan (marr. diss. 1981); one *s*; 2nd, 1981, Cornelia Maria van As. *Educ:* Grammar and Trade schs in The Netherlands. Joined Unilever NV, Rotterdam, 1938; transf. to Unilever Ltd, London, 1948, then to Turkey, 1951, becoming Chm. of Unilever's business there, 1958; Chm., Unilever's Dutch margarine business, Van den Bergh en Jurgens BV, 1962; sen. marketing post, product gp, Margarine, Edible Fats and Oils, 1966; Mem. Bds of Unilever, and responsible for product gp, Sundry Foods and Drinks, 1970; Dir, Fidelity Investments, 1984–; non-executive Director: Hunter Douglas NV, 1984–; Colt Telecom Gp plc, 1995–; formerly: Mem. Supervisory Bd of Shell; Chm. Supervisory Bds of ABN/Amro Bank and various other cos; Mem., Eur. Adv. Bd, AT & T and Rockwell. Pres., ICC, Paris, 1984–86. Mem. Council, North Western (Kellogg) Business Sch., 1984–. *Recreations:* summer and winter sports in general. *Address:* Marevista 35, 2202 BX, Noordwijk, Netherlands.

HOVING, Thomas; President, Hoving Associates, Inc., since 1977; Editor-in-Chief, Connoisseur, 1982–91; *b* 15 Jan. 1931; *s* of late Walter Hoving and Mary Osgood (*née* Field); *m* 1953, Nancy Melissa Bell; one *d. Educ:* Princeton Univ. BA Highest Hons, 1953; Nat. Council of the Humanities Fellowship, 1955; Kienbusch and Haring Fellowship, 1957; MFA 1958; PhD 1959. Dept of Medieval Art and The Cloisters, Metropolitan Museum of Art: Curatorial Asst, 1959; Asst Curator, 1960; Associate Curator, 1963; Curator, 1965; Commissioner of Parks, New York City, 1966; Administrator of Recreation and Cultural Affairs, New York City, 1967; Dir, Metropolitan Museum of Art, 1967–77. Distinguished Citizen's Award, Citizen's Budget Cttee, 1967. Hon. Mem. AIA, 1967. Hon. LLD, Pratt Inst., 1967; Dr *hc*: Princeton; New York Univ. Middlebury and Woodrow Wilson Awards, Princeton. *Publications:* The Sources of the Ada Group Ivories (PhD thesis), 1959; Guide to The Cloisters, 1962; The Chase and The Capture, 1976; Two Worlds of Andrew Wyeth, 1977; Tutankhamun, the Untold Story, 1978; King of the Confessors, 1981; Masterpiece (novel), 1986; Discovery (novel), 1989; Making the Mummies Dance: inside the Metropolitan Museum of Art, 1993; (introd.) Andrew Wyeth: autobiography, 1995; False Impressions: the hunt for big time art fakes, 1996; Greatest Works of Art of Western Civilization, 1997; Art for Dummies, 1999; The Art of Dan Namingha, 2000; articles in Apollo magazine and Metropolitan Museum of Art Bulletin. *Recreations:* sailing, ski-ing, bicycling, flying. *Address:* (office) Hoving Associates, 150 East 73rd Street, New York, NY 10021, USA.

HOW, Timothy Francis; Chief Executive, Majestic Wine PLC, since 1989; *b* 29 Dec. 1950; *s* of Mervyn Henry How and Margaret Helen How; *m* 1975, Elizabeth Mary Howard; four *d*. *Educ:* Churchill Coll., Cambridge (MA); London Business Sch. (MSc Business Studies). Gen. Manager, Polaroid (UK) Ltd, 1979–83; Man. Dir, Bejam Gp PLC, 1983–89. *Recreation:* sailing. *Address:* 47 Battlefield Road, St Albans, Herts AL1 4DB. *T:* (01727) 857884. *Clubs:* Oxford and Cambridge Sailing, Brancaster Staithe Sailing.

HOWARD; *see* Fitzalan-Howard.

HOWARD, family name of **Earls of Carlisle, Effingham,** and **Suffolk,** and of **Barons Howard of Penrith** and **Strathcona**.

HOWARD DE WALDEN, Barony *cr* 1597; in abeyance since 1999. *Co-heiresses:* Hon. Mary Hazel Caridwen Czernin [*b* 12 Aug. 1935; *m* 1957, Count Joseph Czernin; one *s* five *d*]; Hon. Blanche Susan Fionodbhar Buchan [*b* 6 Oct. 1937; *m* 1961, Captain David William Sinclair Buchan of Auchmacoy; four *s* one *d*]; Hon. Jessica Jane Vronwy White [*b* 6 Aug. 1941; *m* 1966, Adrian Tancred White; four *s*]; Hon. Camilla Anne Bronwen Acloque [*b* 1 April 1947; *m* 1971, Guy Acloque; one *s* twin *d*].

HOWARD OF EFFINGHAM, Lord; Edward Mowbray Nicholas Howard; *b* 11 May 1971; *s* and *heir* of Earl of Effingham, *qv*, and *s* of Anne M. Howard (who *m* 1978, Prof. P. G. Stein, *qv*). *Educ:* Oundle; Bristol Univ. Currency Options trader with ANZ Investment Bank. *Address:* The Miller's Cottage, Eades Mill, Great Witchingham, Norfolk NR9 5PQ.

HOWARD OF PENRITH, 3rd Baron *cr* 1930, of Gowbarrow, co. Cumberland; **Philip Esme Howard;** Chairman, Esperia Capital Management Ltd, since 1999; *b* 1 May 1945; *e s* of 2nd Baron Howard of Penrith and of Anne (*née* Hotham, *widow* of Anthony Bazley); *S* father, 1999; *m* 1969, Sarah Sophia Walker; two *s* two *d*. *Educ:* Ampleforth Coll.; Christ Church, Oxford. Journalist, Scotsman, then Daily Mail, 1967–71; Dir, Deltec Trading Co. Ltd, 1972–77; Partner, Phillips and Drew, 1977–84; Man. Dir, Lehman Brothers, 1984–97. *Heir: s* Hon. Thomas Philip Howard, *b* 8 June 1974. *Address:* 45 Erpingham Road, SW15 1BQ. *T:* (020) 8789 7604. *Clubs:* Turf, Portland.

HOWARD, Alan (Mackenzie), CBE 1998; actor; Associate Artist, Royal Shakespeare Company, since 1967; *b* 5 Aug. 1937; *s* of late Arthur John Howard and of Jean Compton Mackenzie; *m* 1st, Stephanie Hinchcliffe Davies (marr. diss. 1976); 2nd, Sally Beauman; one *s*. *Educ:* Ardingly Coll. Belgrade Theatre, Coventry, 1958–60, parts incl. Frankie Bryant in Roots (also at Royal Court and Duke of York's); Wesker Trilogy, Royal Court, 1960; A Loss of Roses, Pembroke, Croydon, 1961; The Changeling, Royal Court, 1961; The Chances, and The Broken Heart, inaugural season, Chichester Festival, 1962; Virtue in Danger, Mermaid and Strand, 1963; Bassanio in The Merchant of Venice, Lysander in A Midsummer Night's Dream, in tour of S America and Europe, 1964; Simon in A Heritage and its History, Phoenix, 1965; Angelo in Measure for Measure, Bolingbroke in Richard II, Nottingham, 1965–66; Cyril Jackson in The Black and White Minstrels, Traverse, Edinburgh, 1972, Hampstead, 1973; A Ride Across Lake Constance, Hampstead and Mayfair, 1973; The Silver King, Chichester, 1990; Scenes from a Marriage, Chichester, transf. Wyndhams, 1990; Kings, 1991; Waiting for Godot, Old Vic, 1997; King Lear, Old Vic, 1997; The Play about the Baby, Almeida, 1998; Lulu, Almeida, 2001; *Royal Shakespeare Company:* joined company, 1966, playing Orsino in Twelfth Night, Lussurioso in The Revenger's Tragedy; 1967: Jaques in As You Like It (also LA, 1968), Young Fashion in The Relapse; 1968: Edgar in King Lear, Achilles in Troilus and Cressida, Benedick in Much Ado about Nothing; 1969: Benedick (also in LA and San Francisco), Achilles, Lussurioso, and Bartholomew Cokes in Bartholomew Fair; 1970: Mephistophilis in Dr Faustus, Hamlet, Theseus/Oberon in A Midsummer Night's Dream, Ceres in The Tempest; 1971: Theseus/Oberon (NY debut); 1971–72: Theseus/Oberon, Nikolai in Enemies, Dorimant in The Man of Mode, The Envoy in The Balcony; 1972–73: Theseus/Oberon, in tour of E and W Europe, USA, Japan, Australia; 1974: Carlos II in The Bewitched; 1975: Henry V, Prince Hal in Henry IV parts I and II; 1976: Prince Hal (SWET Award for Best Actor in revival), Henry V in tour of Europe and USA, Jack Rover in Wild Oats (also Piccadilly); 1977: Henry V, Henry VI parts I, II and III, Coriolanus (Plays and Players London Critics Award, SWET Award for Best Actor in revival, Evening Standard Best Actor Award, 1978); 1978: Antony in Antony and Cleopatra; 1979: Coriolanus in tour of Europe, The Children of the Sun; 1980: title rôles in Richard II and Richard III (Variety Club Best Actor Award); 1981–82: Neschastlivsev in The Forest; Good (Standard Best Actor Award, 1981); 1985: Nikolai in Breaking the Silence; *Royal National Theatre:* Prof. Higgins in Pygmalion, 1992; title rôle in Macbeth, 1993; Calogero in La Grande Magia, 1995; Player in Rosencrantz and Guildenstern are Dead, 1995; title rôle, Oedipus Plays, 1996; Khludov in Flight, 1998; Sloper in The Heiress, 2000. Best Actor (jt), 1981, Drama (British Theatre Assoc.) awards for Richard II, Good and The Forest. *Films include:* The Heroes of Telemark; Work is a Four Letter Word; The Return of the Musketeers; The Cook, The Thief, his Wife and her Lover. *Television appearances include:* The Way of the World; Comet Among the Stars; Coriolanus; The Holy Experiment; Poppyland; Sherlock Holmes, Evensong, The Double Helix, 1986; A Perfect Spy, 1987; The Dog it Was That Died, 1988. *Radio includes:* Soames in Forsyte Chronicles, 1990–91. *Address:* c/o Julian Belfrage Associates, 46 Albermarle Street, W1X 4PP. *T:* (020) 7491 4400.

HOWARD, Ann; freelance opera singer (mezzo-soprano), since 1971; *b* 22 July 1936; *d* of William Alfred and Gladys Winifred Swadling; *m* 1954, Keith Giles; one *d*. *Educ:* privately; with Topliss Green, Rodolfa Lhombino (London) and Dominic Modesti (Paris) via scholarship from Royal Opera House, Covent Garden. Principal Mezzo-Soprano, Sadler's Wells Opera, 1964–73. Main rôles: Carmen, Dalila (Samson et Dalila), Azucena (Il Trovatore), Amneris (Aida), Fricka (Das Rheingold and Die Walküre), La Grande Duchesse de Gerolstein, Brangäne (Tristan und Isolde), Kabanicha (Kátya Kabanová), Gingerbread Witch (Hansel and Gretel), Eboli (Don Carlos), Katisha (Mikado), La Belle Hélène, Babulenka (The Gambler), Fairy Queen (Iolanthe), Dulcinée (Don Quichotte), Hérodiade, Klytemnestra (Electra), Isabella (Italian Girl in Algiers), Old Lady (Candide), Prince Orlofsky (Die Fledermaus), Hostess and Marina (Boris Godunov), Step-Mother (Into the Woods), Auntie (Peter Grimes), Baba (Rake's Progress), Emma Jones (Street Scene); world premières: Madam Leda (The Mines of Sulphur), Sadler's Wells, 1965; Mrs Danvers (Rebecca), Opera North, 1983; Caliban (The Tempest), Santa Fé Festival Opera, USA, 1985; Mrs Worthing (The Plumber's Gift), ENO, 1989; 2nd Official (The Doctor of Myddfai), WNO, 1996; British premières: Cassandra (The Trojans, Pts 1 and 2), Scottish Opera, 1969; Mescalina (Le Grand Macabre), ENO, 1982; début Metropolitan Opera, NY, 1994 (Auntie); also performances in France, Italy, Belgium, Austria, Germany, USA (incl. series of Gilbert and Sullivan operas at Performing Arts Center, NY State Univ., 1993–98), Canada, Mexico, Chile, Portugal; many recordings and videos; teaches privately. *Recreations:* gardening, cooking. *Address:* c/o Stafford Law Associates, 6 Barham Close, Weybridge, Surrey KT13 9PR. *T:* (01932) 854489, *Fax:* (01932) 858521.

HOWARD, Anthony Michell, CBE 1997; journalist and broadcaster; Obituaries Editor, The Times, 1993–99; *b* 12 Feb. 1934; *s* of late Canon Guy Howard and Janet Rymer Howard; *m* 1965, Carol Anne Gaynor. *Educ:* Westminster Sch.; Christ Church, Oxford. Chm., Oxford Univ. Labour Club, 1954; Pres., Oxford Union, 1955. Called to Bar, Inner Temple, 1956. Nat. Service, 2nd Lieut, Royal Fusiliers, 1956–58; Political Corresp., Reynolds News, 1958–59; Editorial Staff, Manchester Guardian, 1959–61 (Harkness Fellowship in USA, 1960); Political Corresp., New Statesman, 1961–64; Whitehall Corresp., Sunday Times, 1965; Washington Corresp., Observer, 1966–69 and Political Columnist, 1971–72; Asst Editor, 1970–72, Editor, 1972–78, New Statesman; Editor, The Listener, 1979–81; Dep. Editor, The Observer, 1981–88; Presenter: Face the Press, Channel Four, 1982–85; The Editors, Sky News TV, 1989–90; Reporter, BBC TV News and Current Affairs (Panorama and Newsnight), 1989–92; Chief political book reviewer, Sunday Times, 1990–. Hon. LLD Nottingham, 2001. Gerald Barry Award, What the Papers Say, 1999. *Publications:* (contrib.) The Baldwin Age, 1960; (contrib.) Age of Austerity, 1963; (with Richard West) The Making of the Prime Minister, 1965; (ed) The Crossman Diaries: selections from the Diaries of a Cabinet Minister, 1979; Rab: the life of R. A. Butler, 1987; Crossman: the pursuit of power, 1990; (contrib.) Secrets of the Press, 1999. *Address:* 11 Campden House Court, 42 Gloucester Walk, W8 4HU. *T:* (020) 7937 7313; Dinham Lodge, Ludlow, Shropshire SY8 1EH. *T:* (01584) 878457. *Clubs:* Garrick, Beefsteak.

HOWARD, Charles Anthony Frederick; QC 1999; *b* 7 March 1951; *s* of late Hon. John Algernon Frederick Charles Howard and Naida Howard (later Mrs Geoffrey Royal); *m* 1st, 1978, Geraldine Dorman (marr. diss.); one *s* one *d*; 2nd, 1999, Rosie Boycott, *qv*; one step *d*. *Educ:* Sherborne Sch.; St John's Coll., Cambridge (Open Hist. Schol.; BA 1972; MA 1976; McMahon Student). Called to the Bar, Inner Temple, 1975. Mem., Family Law Bar Assoc. *Recreations:* cricket, tennis, gardening, walking, films. *Address:* 1 King's Bench Walk, Temple, EC4Y 7DB. *T:* (020) 7736 1500. *Club:* Groucho.
See also Earl of Effingham.

HOWARD, Rear-Adm. Christopher John, (Jack); human resources consultant, since 1997; Chief of Staff, C-in-C Naval Home Command, 1987–89, retired; *b* 13 Sept. 1932; *s* of late Claude Albert Howard and Hilda Mabel Howard (*née* Norton); *m* 1st, 1960, Jean Webster (marr. diss. 1987); two *d*; 2nd, 1987, Hilary Troy; one *s* one *d*. *Educ:* Newton Abbot Grammar School; King's College London; Imperial College, London. MSc, DIC. MIEE. Entered RN 1954; served in HM Ships Ocean, Pukaki, Roebuck, Urchin, Tenby; Officer i/c RN Polaris School, 1978–80; Dean, RN Engineering College, 1980–82; Dir, Naval Officer Appts (Instructor), 1982–84; Commodore, HMS Nelson, 1985–87. NDC Latimer, 1975; Chief Naval Instructor Officer, 1987. Consultant, PA Consulting Group, 1989–91; Dir of Ops, Devon and Cornwall TEC, 1992–97. *Recreations:* shooting, Rugby. *Club:* Army and Navy.

HOWARD, Sir David Howarth Seymour, 3rd Bt *cr* 1955, of Great Rissington, co. Gloucester; Managing Director, since 1971 and Chairman, since 1999, Charles Stanley & Co., Stockbrokers; Lord Mayor of London, 2000–01; *b* 29 Dec. 1945; *s* of Sir Edward Howard, 2nd Bt, GBE; *S* father, 2001; *m* 1968, Valerie Picton Crosse, *o d* of Derek W. Crosse; two *s* two *d*. *Educ:* Radley Coll., Worcester Coll., Oxford (MA Hons). Mem., Sutton LBC, 1974–78; Common Councilman, City of London, 1972–86, Alderman, 1986–, Sheriff, 1997–98; Master, Gardeners' Co., 1990–91. Chm., London Gardens Soc., 1996–. Mem. Council, City Univ., 1995–. FSI. *Recreation:* gardening. *Heir: s* Robert Picton Seymour Howard, *b* 28 Jan. 1971. *Address:* 8 Monkwell Square, EC2Y 5BN. *T:* (020) 7739 8200. *Clubs:* City Livery, United Wards, Lime Street Ward.

HOWARD, David John; Director, Excise and Central Policy, HM Customs and Excise, 1994–2000; *b* 1 June 1941; *s* of late Albert Henry Howard and Olive Mary Howard (*née* Chase); *m* 1969, Anne Westmore; two *s* two *d*. *Educ:* Whitgift Sch., Croydon. Exchequer and Audit Dept, 1960–69; HM Customs and Excise, 1969–72: Asst Principal, 1969; Principal, 1969–75; Private Sec. to Chief Sec. to HM Treasury, 1972–74; Customs & Excise, 1974–91: Asst Sec., 1976–84; Director: VAT Control, 1985–87; Personnel, 1987–90; Organisation, 1990–91; Dep. Dir of Savings, Principal Estabt and Finance Officer, Dept for Nat. Savings, 1991–94. Chm. Govs, Coulsdon High Sch., 1993–. *Recreations:* vintage films, walking.

HOWARD, Dr Deborah Janet, FSA, FSAScot; Reader in Architectural History, University of Cambridge, since 1996; Fellow of St John's College, Cambridge, since 1992; *b* 26 Feb. 1946; *d* of Thomas Were Howard, OBE and Isobel Howard (*née* Brewer); *m* 1975, Prof. Malcolm Sim Longair, *qv*; one *s* one *d*. *Educ:* Loughton High Sch. for Girls; Newnham Coll., Cambridge (BA 1st Cl. Hons Architecture and Fine Arts 1968; MA 1972); Courtauld Inst. of Art, Univ. of London (MA 1969; PhD 1973). FSA 1984; FSAScot 1991. Leverhulme Fellow in History of Art, Clare Hall, Cambridge, 1972–73; Lectr in History of Art, UCL, 1973–76; pt-time Lectr, 1982–90, Sen. Lectr, 1990–91, Reader, 1991, Dept of Architecture, Univ. of Edinburgh; pt-time Lectr, Courtauld Inst. of Art, Univ. of London, 1991–92; Librarian, Faculty of Architecture and History of Art, Univ. of Cambridge, 1992–96. Member: Royal Fine Art Commn for Scotland, 1987–95; Royal Commn on Ancient and Historical Monuments of Scotland, 1990–99; Chm., Soc. of Architectl Historians of GB, 1997–2000. Trustee, British Archtl Liby Trust, 2001–. Hon. FRIAS 1995. *Publications:* (jtly) The Art of Claude Lorrain, 1969; Jacopo Sansovino: architecture and patronage in Renaissance Venice, 1975, 2nd edn 1987; The Architectural History of Venice, 1980, 2nd edn 1987; (ed and jtly) The Architecture of the Scottish Renaissance, 1990; (ed) William Adam, 1990; (ed) Scottish Architects Abroad, 1991; Scottish Architecture from the Reformation to the Restoration 1560–1660, 1995; (ed) Architecture in Italy 1500–1600 by Wolfgang Lotz, 2nd edn, 1995; Venice & the East: the impact of the Islamic world on Venetian architecture, 2000; numerous articles and book reviews in learned jls. *Recreations:* mountain walking, music, photography, gardening. *Address:* Faculty of Architecture and History of Art, University of Cambridge, 1 Scroope Terrace, Cambridge CB2 1PX. *T:* (01223) 332977; St John's College, Cambridge CB2 1TP. *T:* (01223) 339360.

HOWARD, Rev. Canon Donald; Provost, St Andrew's Cathedral, Aberdeen, 1978–91, retired; *b* 21 Jan. 1927; *s* of William Howard and Alexandra Eadie (*née* Buchanan); unmarried. *Educ:* Hull Coll. of Technology; London Univ. (BD, AKC). AFRAeS, 1954–58. Design Engineer, Blackburn Aircraft, 1948–52; Hunting Percival Aircraft, 1952–54; English Electric Co., 1954–55. Assistant Minister, Emmanuel Church, Saltburn-by-the-Sea, Yorks, 1959–62; Rector and Mission Director, Dio. Kimberley and Kuruman, S Africa, 1962–65; Rector of St John the Evangelist, East London, S Africa, 1965–72; Rector of Holy Trinity Episcopal Church, Haddington, Scotland, 1972–78. Honorary Canon: Christ Church Cathedral, Hartford, Conn, USA, 1978–91; St Andrew's Cathedral, Aberdeen, 1991. *Address:* 42 Waterside, Bondgate, Ripon, North Yorkshire HG4 1RA. *T:* (01765) 692144.

HOWARD, Hon. Edmund Bernard Carlo, CMG 1969; LVO 1961; HM Diplomatic Service, retired; *b* 8 Sept. 1909; *s* of 1st Baron Howard of Penrith, PC, GCB, GCMG, CVO, and Lady Isabella Giustiniani-Bandini (*d* of Prince Giustiniani-Bandini, 8th Earl of Newburgh); *m* 1936, Cécile Geoffroy-Dechaume; three *s* one *d* (and one *d* decd). *Educ:* Downside Sch.; Newman Sch., Lakewood, NJ; New Coll., Oxford. Called to the Bar,

1932; Sec., Trustees and Managers, Stock Exchange, 1937. Served in HM Forces, KRRC, 1940–45. Joined HM Diplomatic Service, 1947; served in: Rome, 1947–51; Foreign Office, 1951–53; Madrid, 1953–57; Bogotá, 1957–59; Florence, 1960–61; Rome, 1961–65; Consul-Gen., Genoa, 1965–69. Comdr, Order of Merit, Italy, 1973. *Publications:* Genoa: history and art in an old seaport, 1971 (Duchi di Galliera prize, 1973); trans. The Aryan Myth, 1974; Italia: the art of living Italian style, 1996. *Recreations:* travel, gardening. *Address:* Jerome Cottage, Marlow Common, Bucks SL7 2QR. *T:* (01628) 482129.

HOWARD, Elizabeth Jane, CBE 2000; FRSL; novelist; *b* 26 March 1923; *d* of David Liddon and Katharine M. Howard; *m* 1st, 1942, Peter M. Scott (marr. diss. 1951; later Sir Peter Scott, CH, CBE, FRS (*d* 1989)); one *d*; 2nd, 1959, James Douglas-Henry; 3rd, 1965, Kingsley Amis (later Sir Kingsley Amis, CBE) (marr. diss. 1983; he *d* 1995). *Educ:* home. FRSL 1994. Trained at London Mask Theatre Sch. Played at Stratford-on-Avon, and in repertory theatre in Devon; BBC, Television, modelling, 1939–46; Sec. to Inland Waterways Assoc., 1947; subsequently writing, editing, reviewing, journalism and writing plays for television, incl. serials of After Julius in three plays and Something in Disguise in six plays. John Llewellyn Rhys Memorial Prize for The Beautiful Visit, 1950. Hon. Artistic Dir, Cheltenham Literary Festival, 1962; Artistic co-Dir, Salisbury Festival of Arts, 1973. Film script, The Attachment, 1986. *Publications:* The Beautiful Visit, 1950; The Long View, 1956; The Sea Change, 1959; After Julius, 1965; Something in Disguise, 1969 (TV series, 1982); Odd Girl Out, 1972; Mr Wrong, 1975; (ed) A Companion for Lovers, 1978; Getting It Right, 1982 (Yorkshire Post Prize) (film script, 1985); (jtly) Howard and Maschler on Food: cooking for occasions, 1987; The Light Years, 1990; Green Shades (anthology), 1991; Marking Time, 1991; Confusion, 1993; Casting Off, 1995; Anthology on Marriage, 1997; Falling, 1999. *Recreations:* music, gardening, enjoying all the arts, travelling, natural history. *Address:* c/o Jonathan Clowes, Iron Bridge House, Bridge Approach, NW1 8BD.

HOWARD, Prof. Ian George, RSA 1998; Professor of Fine Art, University of Dundee, since 1995 (Personal Chair); Principal, Edinburgh College of Art, since 2001; *b* 7 Nov. 1952; *s* of Harold Geoffrey Howard and Violet Howard (*née* Kelly); *m* 1977, Ruth D'Arcy; two *d*. *Educ:* Aberdeen Grammar Sch.; Univ. of Edinburgh; Edinburgh Coll. of Art. MA Hons Fine Art 1975; Post Grad. Dip. 1976. Lectr in Painting, Gray's Sch. of Art, Aberdeen, 1977–86; Head of Painting, Duncan of Jordanstone Coll. of Art, Dundee, 1986–95; Mem., Faculty of Fine Art, British Sch. at Rome, 1996–; Dean, Duncan of Jordanstone Coll. of Art and Design, 1999–2001. Dir, Dundee Contemporary Arts Ltd, 1997–. Numerous exhibns internationally; work in collections, including: Scottish Arts Council; Arts Council of England; Contemporary Art Soc.; Edinburgh City Art Centre; Hunterian Art Gall., Glasgow; Robert Fleming, London; Royal Scottish Acad. *Publications:* Heretical Diagrams, 1995; Emblemata, 1998. *Recreations:* travel, cooking, picking wild mushrooms. *Address:* Principal's Office, Edinburgh College of Art, Lauriston Place, Edinburgh EH3 9DF. *T:* (0131) 221 6001.

HOWARD, Rear-Adm. Jack; *see* Howard, Rear-Adm. C. J.

HOWARD, James Boag, CB 1972; Assistant Under-Secretary of State, Home Office, 1963–75; *b* 10 Jan. 1915; *yr s* of William and Jean Howard, Greenock; *m* 1943, Dorothy Jean Crawshaw (*d* 2000); two *d*. *Educ:* Greenock High Sch.; Glasgow Univ. (MA, BSc; 1st cl. Hons Mathematics and Natural Philosophy). Asst Principal, Home Office, 1937; Private Sec. to Permanent Sec., Ministry of Home Security, 1940–41; Principal, 1941; Asst Sec., 1948. *Address:* 12 Windhill, Bishop's Stortford, Herts CM23 2NG. *T:* (01279) 651728.

HOWARD, (James) Kenneth, RA 1991 (ARA 1983); painter; *b* 26 Dec. 1932; *s* of Frank and Elizabeth Howard; *m* 1st Ann Howard (*née* Popham), dress designer (marr. diss. 1974); 2nd, 1990, Christa Gaa (*née* Köhler), RWS (*d* 1992); 3rd, 2000, Dora Bertolutti. *Educ:* Kilburn Grammar School; Hornsey School of Art; Royal College of Art (ARCA). NEAC 1962 (Pres., 1998); ROI 1966; RWA 1981; RWS 1983. British Council scholarship to Florence, 1958–59; taught various London Art Schools, 1959–73; Official Artist for Imperial War Museum in N Ireland, 1973, 1978; painted for the British Army in N Ireland, Germany, Cyprus, Hong Kong, Brunei, Nepal, Belize, Norway, Lebanon, Canada, Oman, 1973–; one man exhibitions: Plymouth Art Centre, 1955; John Whibley Gallery, 1966, 1968; New Grafton Gallery, 1971–; Jersey, 1978, 1980, 1983; Hong Kong, 1979; Nicosia, 1982; Delhi, 1983; Lowndes Lodge Gall., 1987, 1989, 1990, 1991; Sinfield Gall., 1991, 1993, 1995; Bankside Gall., 1996; Everard Reid Gall., Johannesburg, 1998. Works purchased by Plymouth Art Gall., Imperial War Mus., Guildhall Art Gall., Ulster Mus., Nat. Army Mus., Hove Mus., Sheffield Art Gall., Southend Mus.; commissions for UN, BAOR, Drapers' Co., Stock Exchange, States of Jersey, Banque Paribas, Royal Hosp. Chelsea. Hon. ROI 1988; Hon. RBA 1989; RSBA 1991. First Prize: Hunting Group Award, 1982; Sparkasse Karlsruhe, 1985. Gen. Editor, Art Class series, 1988. *Publications:* contribs to: The War Artists, 1983; 60th Vol. of The Old Water-Colour Societies' Club, 1985; Painting Interiors, 1989; Art of Landscape and Seascape, 1989; Visions of Venice, 1990; Venice: the artist's vision, 1990; 20th Century Painters and Sculptors, 1991; Oils Masterclass, 1996; (jtly) Inspired by Light, 1998; Dictionary of Artists in Britain since 1945, 1998; *relevant publication:* The Paintings of Ken Howard, by Michael Spender, 1992. *Recreations:* cinema, opera. *Address:* 8 South Bolton Gardens, SW5 0DH. *T:* (020) 7373 2912; (studio) St Clements Studio, Mousehole, Cornwall TR19 6TR. *T:* (01736) 731596. *Clubs:* Arts, Chelsea Arts.

HOWARD, Hon. John Winston; MP (L) for Bennelong, NSW, since 1974; Prime Minister of Australia, since 1996; *b* 26 July 1939; *m* 1971, Alison Janette Parker; two *s* one *d*. *Educ:* Canterbury Boys' High Sch.; Sydney Univ. Solicitor of NSW Supreme Court. Minister for Business and Consumer Affairs, Australia, 1975; Minister assisting Prime Minister, May 1977; Minister for Special Trade Negotiations, July 1977; Federal Treasurer, 1977–83; Leader, Parly Liberal Party, and Leader of the Opposition, Australia, 1985–89, 1995–96 (Dep. Leader, 1983–85). Chm., Manpower and Labour Market Reform Gp, 1990–. *Recreations:* reading, tennis, cricket. *Address:* Parliament House, Canberra, ACT 2600, Australia; Kirribilli House, 109 Kirribilli Avenue, Kirribilli, NSW 2061, Australia. *Club:* Australian (Sydney).

HOWARD, Prof. Jonathan Charles, DPhil; FRS 1995; Professor of Genetics, Institute for Genetics, University of Cologne, since 1994; *b* 24 June 1943; *s* of John Eldred Howard and Marghanita (*née* Laski); *m* 1990, Maria Leptin; two *s*. *Educ:* Westminster Sch.; Magdalen Coll., Oxford (BA Zool. 1964; DPhil Medicine 1969). Mem., Scientific Staff, MRC, at Cellular Immunology Res. Unit, Sir William Dunn Sch. of Pathology, Univ. of Oxford, 1968–73; Weir Jun. Res. Fellow, University Coll., Oxford, 1970–73; Babraham Institute, Cambridge: Mem. Staff, Dept of Immunology, 1974–94; Head of Dept, 1985–94; Res. Fellow, Clare Hall, Cambridge, 1975–78; sabbaticals at: Depts of Pathology and Cell Biol., Stanford Univ., 1983, 1987; Div. of Biol., CIT, 1983; EMBL, 1992. Mem., EMBO, 1993. *Publications:* Darwin, 1982; papers in learned jls on immunology and evolution. *Recreation:* fishing. *Address:* Institut für Genetik, Universität zu Köln, Zülpicher Strasse 47, 50674 Köln, Germany. *T:* (221) 4704864; Heinestrasse 19, 50931 Köln, Germany. *T:* (221) 4200320.

HOWARD, Kenneth; *see* Howard, J. K.

HOWARD, Margaret; freelance broadcaster, since 1969; presenter, with Classic FM, 1992–99; *b* 29 March 1938; *d* of John Bernard Howard and Ellen Corwena Roberts. *Educ:* St Mary's Convent, Rhyl, N Wales; St Teresa's Convent, Sunbury; Guildhall Sch. of Music and Drama; Indiana Univ., Bloomington, USA. LGSM; LRAM 1960. BBC World Service Announcer, 1967–69; Reporter: The World This Weekend, BBC Radio 4, 1970–74; Edition, BBC TV, 1971; Tomorrow's World, BBC TV, 1972; Editor and Presenter: Pick of the Week, BBC Radio 4, 1974–91; Classic Reports, Classic FM, 1992–94; Howard's Week, Classic FM, 1994–97; Presenter: It's Your World, BBC World Service, 1981–86; Masterclass, Classic FM, 1994–99; Interviewer/Presenter, Strictly Instrumental, occasional series, 1980–85. Radio critic, The Tablet; columnist, The Universe; record columnist, Chic magazine. Female UK Radio Personality of the Year, Sony Awards, 1984; Sony Radio Awards Roll of Honour, 1988; Voice of the Listener Award for excellence, 1991; Radio Personality of the Year, TRIC Awards, 1996. *Publications:* Margaret Howard's Pick of the Week, 1984; Court Jesting, 1986. *Recreations:* riding, tasting wine, walking the Jack Russell. *Address:* 215 Cavendish Road, SW12 0BP. *T:* (020) 8673 7336.

HOWARD, Rt Hon. Michael; PC 1990; QC 1982; MP (C) Folkestone and Hythe, since 1983; *b* 7 July 1941; *s* of late Bernard Howard and of Hilda Howard; *m* 1975, Sandra Clare, *d* of Wing-Comdr Saville Paul; one *s* one *d* (and one step *s*). *Educ:* Llanelli Grammar School; Peterhouse, Cambridge. MA, LLB; President of the Union, 1962. Major Scholar, Inner Temple, 1962; called to the Bar, Inner Temple, 1964, Bencher, 1992. Junior Counsel to the Crown (Common Law), 1980–82; a Recorder, 1986. Contested (C) Liverpool, Edge Hill, 1966 and 1970; Chm., Bow Group, 1970–71. PPS to Solicitor-General, 1984–85; Parly Under-Sec. of State, DTI, 1985–87; Minister of State, DoE, 1987–90; Secretary of State for: Employment, 1990–92; the Environment, 1992–93; the Home Dept, 1993–97; Opposition frontbench spokesman on foreign affairs, 1997–99; Shadow Chancellor, 2001–. Jt Sec., Cons. Legal Cttee, 1983–84; Jt Vice-Chm., Cons. Employment Cttee, 1983–84; Vice-Chm., Soc. of Cons. Lawyers, 1985. *Recreations:* watching football (Swansea, Liverpool) and baseball (New York Mets). *Address:* House of Commons, SW1A 0AA. *T:* (020) 7219 5493. *Clubs:* Carlton, Pratt's, Coningsby (Chm., 1972–73).

HOWARD, Sir Michael (Eliot), Kt 1986; CBE 1977; MC 1943; DLitt; FBA 1970; FRHistS; Emeritus Professor of Modern History, University of Oxford, since 1989; *b* 29 Nov. 1922; *y s* of late Geoffrey Eliot Howard, Ashmore, near Salisbury, and of Edith Julia Emma, *o d* of Otto Edinger. *Educ:* Wellington; Christ Church, Oxford (BA 1946, MA 1948; Hon. Student, 1990). Served War, Coldstream Guards, 1942–45. Asst Lecturer in History, University of London, King's Coll., 1947; Lecturer, 1950; Lecturer, then Reader, in War Studies, 1953–63; Prof. of War Studies, 1963–68; University of Oxford: Fellow of All Souls Coll., 1968–80; Chichele Prof. of History of War, 1977–80; Regius Prof. of Modern History and Fellow of Oriel Coll., 1980–89 (Hon. Fellow, 1990); Robert A. Lovett Prof. of Military and Naval Hist., Yale Univ., 1989–93. Vis. Prof. of European History, Stanford Univ., 1967. Ford's Lectr in English History, Oxford, 1971; Radcliffe Lectr, Univ. of Warwick, 1975; Trevelyan Lectr, Cambridge, 1977; Leverhulme Lectr, 1996; Lee Kuan Yew Distinguished Visitor, Nat. Univ. of Singapore, 1996. FKC. Pres. and co-Founder, Internat. Institute for Strategic Studies; Vice-President: Council on Christian Approaches to Defence and Disarmament; Army Records Soc. For. Hon. Mem., Amer. Acad. of Arts and Scis, 1983. Hon. LittD Leeds, 1979; Hon. DLit London, 1988; Hon. DHumLit Lehigh Univ., Pa, USA, 1990. Chesney Meml Gold Medal, RUSI, 1973; NATO Atlantic Award, 1989. *Publications:* The Coldstream Guards, 1920–46 (with John Sparrow), 1951; Disengagement in Europe, 1958; Wellingtonian Studies, 1959; The Franco-Prussian War, 1961 (Duff Cooper Memorial Prize, 1962); The Theory and Practice of War, 1965; The Mediterranean Strategy in the Second World War, 1967; Studies in War and Peace, 1970; Grand Strategy, vol IV (in UK History of 2nd World War, Military series), 1971 (Wolfson Foundn History Award, 1972); The Continental Commitment, 1972; War in European History, 1976; (with P. Paret) Clausewitz On War, 1977; War and the Liberal Conscience, 1978; (ed) Restraints on War, 1979; The Causes of Wars, 1983; Clausewitz, 1983; Strategic Deception in World War II, 1990; The Lessons of History, 1991; (ed with W. R. Louis) The Oxford History of the Twentieth Century, 1998; The Invention of Peace, 2000. *Address:* The Old Farm, Eastbury, Hungerford, Berks RG17 7JN. *Clubs:* Athenæum, Garrick.

HOWARD, Michael Newman; QC 1986; a Recorder, since 1993; *b* 10 June 1947; *s* of late Henry Ian Howard and of Tilly Celia Howard. *Educ:* Clifton College; Magdalen College, Oxford (MA, BCL). Lecturer in Law, LSE, 1970–74; called to the Bar, Gray's Inn, 1971, Bencher, 1995; in practice at Bar, 1971–; Leader of Admiralty Bar, 1999–. Visiting Professor: Law, Univ. of Essex, 1987–92; Maritime Law, UCL, 1996–99. Mem. of Panel, Lloyd's Salvage Arbitrators, 1987–. *Publications:* Phipson on Evidence, ed jtly, 12th edn 1976 to 14th edn 1990, Gen. Ed., 15th edn 2000; *contributions to:* Frustration and Force Majeure, 1991, 2nd edn 1995; *Consensus ad Idem:* essays for Guenter Treitel, 1996; Halsbury's Laws of England, 4th edn (Damages); articles and reviews in legal periodicals. *Recreations:* books, music, sport. *Address:* 4 Essex Court, Temple, EC4Y 9AJ. *T:* (020) 7797 7970. *Clubs:* Royal Automobile, Oxford and Cambridge.

HOWARD, Michael Stockwin; organ recitalist and recording artist; *b* London, 14 Sept. 1922; *er s* of Frank Henry Howard (viola, Internat. String Quartet; Foundn principal, Beecham's Philharmonic) and Florence Mabel Howard. *Educ:* Ellesmere; Royal Acad. of Music; privately. Organist, Tewkesbury Abbey, 1943–44; Dir of Music, Ludgrove; Founder, Renaissance Society, and conductor, Renaissance Singers, 1944–64; Organist and Magister Choristarum, Ely Cath., 1953–58; Dir, Cantores in Ecclesia, 1964–86; Dir of Music, St Marylebone Parish Church, 1971–79; Organist to the Franciscans of Rye, 1979–83; Rector Chori, St Michael's Abbey, Farnborough, 1984–86. Performer at: Proms; Bath Fest.; Cheltenham Fest.; internat. fests incl. Czechoslovakia; broadcaster and writer. Hon. ARAM 1976. Prix Musicale de Radio Brno, 1967; Charpentier Grand Prix du Disque, 1975. Cavaillé-Coll organ recordings incl. principal works of César Franck. *Publications:* A Tribute to Cavaillé-Coll, 1985; Thine Adversaries Roar . . . (autobiographical observations), 2001. *Recreations:* steam railway traction, listening, reading. *Address:* 1 Somerset Villas, Corseley Road, Groombridge, Tunbridge Wells, Sussex TN3 9RR.

HOWARD, Air Vice-Marshal Peter, CB 1989; OBE 1957; FRCP, FRAeS; Commandant, RAF Institute of Aviation Medicine, 1975–88; The Senior Consultant, RAF, 1987–88; *b* 15 Dec. 1925; *s* of late Edward Charles Howard and Doris Mary Howard (*née* Cure); *m* 1950, Norma Lockhart Fletcher; one *s* one *d*. *Educ:* Farnborough Grammar Sch.; St Thomas's Hosp. Med. Sch. (MB BS 1949, PhD 1964); FRCP 1977; FFOM 1981; FRAeS 1973. House Physician, 1950, Registrar, 1951. St Thomas' Hosp.; RAF Medical Branch, 1951–88; RAF Consultant in Aviation Physiology, 1964; RAF

Consultant Adviser in Occupational Medicine, 1983–85; Dean of Air Force Medicine, 1985–87. QHP 1982–88. Chm., Defence Med. Services Postgraduate Council, 1986–87; Registrar, Faculty of Occupational Medicine, RCP, 1986–91. *Publications:* papers and chapters in books on aviation physiology, medicine, occupational medicine. *Recreations:* fly fishing, computing. *Address:* 135 Aldershot Road, Church Crookham, Hants GU13 0JU. *T:* (01252) 617309. *Club:* Royal Air Force.

HOWARD, Peter Milner; Editor, Jane's Defence Industry, since 2001; *b* 27 June 1937; *s* of Thomas Roland Howard and Margaret A. Howard (*née* Potter); *m* 1965, Janet Crownshaw; one *s* one *d*. *Educ:* St Thomas C of E Sch., Heaton Chapel; Dialstone Lane Mod. Sec., Stockport; Woodseats Co., Sheffield; Sheffield Coll. of Commerce and Tech. (NCTJ Prof. Cert. 1960). Copy boy, reporter, sports reporter and sub-editor, The Star, Sheffield, 1952–58; Nat. Service, Army, 1958–60; The Star, Sheffield: sports reporter and sub-editor, 1960–73; Sports Editor, 1973–75; Inf. Officer, MoD, 1975–83; Sen. Inf. Officer and Editor, Soldier Mag., 1983–85; Jane's Defence Weekly: Features Editor, 1985–87; Man. Editor, 1987–89; Editor, 1989–95; Man. Editor, Military and Tri-Service Gp, 1995–98, Editor, Jane's Navy Internat., 1998–2001, Jane's Inf. Gp. *Recreations:* military history, military music, golf, walking. *Address:* Mildmay Cottage, Hawkley Road, West Liss, Hants GU33 6JL. *T:* and *Fax:* (01730) 893307.

HOWARD, Philip Nicholas Charles, FRSL; leader writer, columnist, and word watching, The Times, since 1992; *b* 2 Nov. 1933; *s* of Peter Dunsmore Howard and Doris Emily Metaxa; *m* 1959, Myrtle, *d* of Sir Reginald Houldsworth, 4th Bt, OBE, TD; two *s* one *d*. *Educ:* Eton Coll. (King's Scholar); Trinity Coll., Oxford (Major Scholar; first cl. Lit. Hum; MA). Glasgow Herald, 1959–64; The Times, 1964–: reporter, writer, columnist; Literary Ed., 1978–92. Member: Classical Assoc.; Horatian Soc.; Soc. of Bookmen; Literary Soc.; Flaccidae. Founder Patron, Friends of Classics, 1991. FRSL 1987. Liveryman, Wheelwrights' Co. London Editor, Verbatim, 1977–. *Publications:* The Black Watch, 1968; The Royal Palaces, 1970; London's River, 1975; New Words for Old, 1977; The British Monarchy, 1977; Weasel Words, 1978; Words Fail Me, 1980; A Word in Your Ear, 1983; The State of the Language, English Observed, 1984; (jtly) The Times Bicentenary Stamp Book, 1985; We Thundered Out, 200 Years of The Times 1785–1985, 1985; Winged Words, 1988; Word-Watching, 1988; (jtly) London, The Evolution of a Great City, 1989; A Word in Time, 1990; (ed) The Times Bedside Book, 1991; Reading a Poem, 1992; (ed) The Times Bedside Book, 1992. *Recreations:* walking, reading, talking, music, the classics, beagles not beagling, Jack Russells, stand at Twickenham. *Address:* Flat 1, 47 Ladbroke Grove, W11 3AR. *T:* (020) 7727 1077. *Clubs:* Garrick; Ad Eundem (Oxford and Cambridge).

HOWARD, Robert, (Bob); Northern Regional Secretary, Trades Union Congress, 1980–2000; *b* 4 April 1939; *s* of Robert and Lily Howard; *m* 1984, Valerie Stewart; two *s* one *d*. *Educ:* Gregson Lane County Primary Sch.; Deepdale Secondary Modern Sch.; Queen Elizabeth's Grammar Sch., Blackburn, Lancs; Cliff Training Coll., Calver via Sheffield, Derbyshire. British Leyland, Lancs, 1961–68: Member, Clerical and Admin. Workers' Union Br. Exec.; Councillor, Walton le Dale UDC, 1962–65; GPO, Preston, Lancs, 1969–80: Telephone Area UPW Telecomms Representative Member: Jt Consultative Council, Jt Productivity Council, Council of PO Unions Area Cttee, Delegate to Preston Trades Council; Secretary, Lancashire Assoc. of Trades Councils, 1977–79; created 14 specialist cttees for LATC; appointment as N Reg. Sec., TUC, 1980, by Gen. Sec., TUC, first full-time secretary to a TUC region. Member: Industrial Tribunals, 1979–80; Northumbria Regional Cttee, Nat. Trust, 1989–; Council, Northern Exams Assoc., 1986–; Board: Durham Univ. Business Sch., 1987–; Tyneside TEC, 1989–99; Northern Develt Co., 1991–99; Nat. Resource for Innovative Trng Res. and Employment Ltd, later Northern Informatics, 1995–99. Northern Region Coordinator, Jobs March, 1983; Exec. Organiser, Great North Family Gala Day, 1986–90. JP Duchy of Lancaster, 1969–74. *Publications:* North-East Lancashire Structure Plan—The Trades Councils' View (with Peter Stock), 1979; Organisation and Functions of TUC Northern Regional Council, 1980. *Recreations:* fell walking, opera, ballet, classical music, camping, cricket, football, spectating outdoor sports, reading, chess. *Address:* 8 Caxton Way, North Lodge, Chester le Street, County Durham DH3 4BW. *Club:* Durham CC.

HOWARD, Stephen Lee; Group Chief Executive, Cookson Group plc, since 1997; *b* 25 March 1953; *s* of Richard and Marilyn Howard; *m* 1976, Holly Grothe; three *s*. *Educ:* Michigan State Univ. (BA 1975); Univ. of Michigan Law Sch. (JD *cum laude* 1978). In practice as lawyer, Providence, RI, 1978–85; Cookson America Inc.: General Counsel, 1985–86; Vice-Pres., Corporate Develt and General Counsel, 1986–91; Cookson Group plc: Chief Exec., Gp Develt, 1991–92; Dir and Chief Exec., Engineered Prods Div. and Gp Corporate Develt, 1992–94; Chief Exec., Ceramic and Engineered Prods Div. and Gp Corporate Develt, 1994–97; Gp Jt Man. Dir, 1995–97. Member: RI Bar Assoc., 1978–; American Bar Assoc. MInstD 1997. *Recreations:* tennis, basketball. *Address:* Cookson Group plc, The Adelphi, 1–11 John Adam Street, WC2N 6HJ. *T:* (020) 7766 4500. *Clubs:* Royal Automobile; Hope (Providence); Agawam Hunt (E Providence).

HOWARD, Victoria; *see* Barnsley, V.

HOWARD, William Brian; Deputy Chairman, Northern Foods plc, 1988–97 (Director, 1987–97); Deputy Chairman, 1984–87, Joint Managing Director, 1976–86, Marks & Spencer plc; *b* 16 July 1926; *s* of William James and Annie Howard; *m* 1952, Audrey Elizabeth (*née* Jenney); one *s* one *d*. *Educ:* Revoe Junior Sch., Blackpool; Blackpool Grammar Sch.; Manchester Univ. (BA (Hons) Mod. Hist., Economics and Politics); Harvard Graduate Business Sch., 1973. Royal Signals, 1944–47. Marks & Spencer Ltd, 1951–87; Dir, 1973–87. A Church Comr, 1977–93. *Address:* Crawley Farm, Ballinger, Great Missenden, Bucks HP16 9LQ. *Club:* MCC.

HOWARD-DOBSON, Gen. Sir Patrick John, GCB 1979 (KCB 1974; CB 1973); *b* 12 Aug. 1921; *s* of late Canon Howard Dobson, MA; *m* 1946, Barbara Mary Mills; two *s* one *d*. *Educ:* King's Coll. Choir Sch., Cambridge; Framlingham College. Joined 7th Queen's Own Hussars, Egypt, Dec. 1941; served in: Burma, 1942; Middle East, 1943; Italy, 1944–45; Germany, 1946; psc 1950; jssc 1958; comd The Queen's Own Hussars, 1963–65 and 20 Armoured Bde, 1965–67; idc 1968; Chief of Staff, Far East Comd, 1969–71; Comdt, Staff Coll., Camberley, 1972–74; Military Secretary, 1974–76; Quartermaster General, 1977–79; Vice-Chief of Defence Staff (Personnel and Logistics), 1979–81; ADC Gen. to the Queen, 1978–81. Col Comdt, ACC, 1976–82. Nat. Pres., Royal British Legion, 1981–87. Virtuti Militari (Poland), 1945; Silver Star (US), 1945. *Recreations:* sailing, golf. *Address:* 1 Drury Park, Snape, Saxmundham, Suffolk IP17 1TA. *Clubs:* Royal Cruising; Senior Golfers' Society.

HOWARD-DRAKE, Jack Thomas Arthur; Assistant Under-Secretary of State, Home Office, 1974–78; *b* 7 Jan. 1919; *o s* of Arthur Howard and Ruby (*née* Cherry); *m* 1947, Joan Mary, *o d* of Hubert and Winifred Crook; one *s* two *d*. *Educ:* Hele's Sch., Exeter. Asst Inspector, Ministry of Health Insurance Dept, 1937–39 and 1946–47. Served War, RA, 1939–46 (Major, despatches). Colonial Office: Asst Principal, 1947; Principal, 1949; Private Sec. to Sec. of State, 1956–62; Asst Sec., 1962; Asst Sec., Cabinet Office, 1963–65; Asst Sec., Home Office, 1965–72; Asst Under-Sec. of State, NI Office, 1972–74. Chairman: Oxfordshire Local History Assoc., 1984–91; Wychwoods Local History Soc., 1984–92. *Publications:* Oxford Church Courts: Depositions 1542–1550, 1991, 1570–1574, 1993, 1581–1586, 1994, 1589–1593, 1997, 1592–1596, 1998, 1603–1606, 1999. *Recreations:* gardening, local history, golf. *Address:* 26 Sinnels Field, Shipton-under-Wychwood, Chipping Norton, Oxon OX7 6EJ. *T:* (01993) 830792.

HOWARD-JOHNSTON, Angela Maureen; *see* Huth, A. M.

HOWARD-LAWSON, Sir John (Philip), 6th Bt *cr* 1841, of Brough Hall, Yorkshire; *b* 6 June 1934; *s* of Sir William Howard Lawson, 5th Bt and Joan Eleanor (*d* 1989), *d* of late Arthur Cowie Stamer, CBE; assumed by Royal Licence surname and arms of Howard, 1962, of Howard-Lawson, 1992; *S* father, 1990; *m* 1960, Jean Veronica (*née* Marsh) (*d* 2001); two *s* one *d*. *Educ:* Ampleforth. *Heir: s* Philip William Howard [*b* 28 June 1961; *m* 1st, 1988, Cara Margaret Browne (marr. diss. 1992); 2nd, 1993, Isabel Anne Oldridge de la Hey; one *d*]. *Address:* Hunter Hall, Great Salkeld, Penrith, Cumbria CA11 9NA. *T:* (01768) 897135.

HOWARTH OF BRECKLAND, Baroness *cr* 2001 (Life Peer), of Parson Cross in the County of South Yorkshire; **Valerie Georgina Howarth,** OBE 1999; Chief Executive, ChildLine, 1987–2001; *b* 5 Sept. 1940. *Educ:* Abbeydale Girls' Grammar Sch.; Univ. of Leicester. Caseworker, Family Welfare Assoc., 1963–68; London Borough of Lambeth: Sen. Child CareWorker and Trng Officer, 1968–70; Area Co-ordinator, 1970–72; Chief Co-ordinator of Social Work, 1972–76; Asst Dir of Personal Services, 1976–82; Dir of Social Services, London Borough of Brent, 1982–86. Board Member: Food Standards Agency, 2000–; Nat. Care Standards Commn, 2001–. Vice Chairman: John Grooms Assoc. for Disabled People; Faithfull Foundn; Chm., Stop It Now. Trustee, Michael Sieff Foundn. *Address:* House of Lords, SW1A 0PW.

HOWARTH, Rt Hon. Alan Thomas, CBE 1982; PC 2000; MP (Lab) Newport East, since 1997 (MP Stratford-on-Avon, 1983–97, C, 1983–95, Lab, 1995–97); *b* 11 June 1944; *e s* of late T. E. B. Howarth, MC, TD and Margaret Howarth; *m* 1967, Gillian Martha (marr. diss. 1996), *d* of Mr and Mrs Arthur Chance, Dublin; two *s* two *d*. *Educ:* Rugby Sch. (scholar); King's Coll., Cambridge (major scholar in History; BA 1965). Sen. Res. Asst to Field-Marshal Montgomery on A History of Warfare, 1965–67; Asst Master, Westminster Sch., 1968–74; Private Sec. to Chm. of Conservative Party, 1975–79; Dir, Cons. Res. Dept, 1979–81; Vice-Chm., Conservative Party, 1980–81. PPS to Dr Rhodes Boyson, MP, 1985–87; an Asst Govt Whip, 1987–88; Lord Comr of HM Treasury, 1988–89; Parliamentary Under-Secretary of State: DES, 1989–92 (Schools Minister, 1989–90; Minister for Higher Educn and Sci., 1990–92); DFEE, 1997–98 (Employment Minister and Minister for Disabled People); DCMS, 1998–2001. Secretary: Cons. Arts and Heritage Cttee, 1984–85; PLP Social Security Cttee, 1996–97; Member: Nat. Heritage Select Cttee, 1992–93; Social Security Select Cttee, 1996–97; Intelligence and Security Cttee, 2001–; Chm., All Party Parly Gp on Charities and Vol. Sector, 1992–97; Treasurer, All Party Arts and Heritage Gp, 1993–97. Chm., Friends, Huntington's Disease Assoc., 1988–97; Mem. Adv. Council, Nat. Listening Library, 1992–97; Vice-Pres., British Dyslexia Assoc., 1994–97. Mem. Court: Univ. of Warwick, 1987–97; Univ. of Birmingham, 1992–97. Mem. Bd., Inst. of Historical Res., 1992–97. Governor, Royal Shakespeare Theatre, 1984–97. *Publications:* (jtly) Monty at Close Quarters, 1985; jt author of various CPC pamphlets. *Recreations:* books, the arts, hill-walking. *Address:* House of Commons, SW1A 0AA.

HOWARTH, Elgar; freelance musician; *b* 4 Nov. 1935; *s* of Oliver and Emma Howarth; *m* 1958, Mary Bridget Neary; one *s* two *d*. *Educ:* Manchester Univ. (MusB); Royal Manchester Coll. of Music (ARMCM 1956; FRMCM 1970). Royal Opera House, Covent Garden (Orchestra), 1958–63; Royal Philharmonic Orchestra, 1963–69; Mem., London Sinfonietta, 1968–71; Mem., Philip Jones Brass Ensemble, 1965–76; freelance conductor, 1970–; Principal Guest Conductor, Opera North, 1985–88; Musical Advisor, Grimethorpe Colliery Brass Band, 1972–. Hon. RAM 1989; FRNCM 1994; FWCMD 1997; FRCM 1999. Hon. Fellow, UC Salford, 1992. DUniv: Birmingham, 1993; York, 1999; Hon. DMus Keele, 1995. Olivier Award for Outstanding Achievement in Opera (for Die Soldaten, and The Prince of Hamburg, ENO), 1997. *Publications:* various compositions mostly for brass instruments. *Address:* 27 Cromwell Avenue, N6 5HN.

HOWARTH, George Edward; MP (Lab) Knowsley North and Sefton East, since 1997 (Knowsley North, Nov. 1986–1997); *b* 29 June 1949; *m* 1977, Julie Rodgers; two *s* one *d*. *Educ:* Liverpool Polytechnic. Formerly: engineer; teacher; Chief Exec., Wales TUC's Co-operative Centre, 1984–86. Former Mem., Huyton UDC; Mem., Knowsley BC, 1975–86 (Dep. Leader, 1982). Parliamentary Under-Secretary of State: Home Office, 1997–99; NI Office, 1999–2001. *Address:* House of Commons, SW1A 0AA.

HOWARTH, (James) Gerald (Douglas); MP (C) Aldershot, since 1997; *b* 12 Sept. 1947; *s* of late James Howarth and of Mary Howarth, Hurley, Berks; *m* 1973, Elizabeth Jane, *d* of late Michael and of Muriel Squibb, Crowborough, Sussex; two *s* one *d*. *Educ:* Haileybury and ISC Jun. Sch.; Bloxham Sch.; Southampton Univ. (BA Hons). Commnd RAFVR, 1968. Gen. Sec., Soc. for Individual Freedom, 1969–71; entered internat. banking, 1971; Bank of America Internat., 1971–77; European Arab Bank, 1977–81 (Manager, 1979–81); Syndication Manager, Standard Chartered Bank, 1981–83; Dir, Richard Unwin Internat., 1983–87; Jt Man. Dir, Taskforce Communications, 1993–96. Dir, Freedom Under Law, 1973–77; estabd Dicey Trust, 1976. Mem., Hounslow BC, 1982–83. MP (C) Cannock and Burntwood, 1983–92. Parliamentary Private Secretary: to Parly Under-Sec. of State for Energy, 1987–90; to Minister for Housing and Planning, 1990–91; to Rt Hon. Margaret Thatcher, MP, 1991–92. Member: Select Cttee on Sound Broadcasting, 1987–92; Home Affairs Select Cttee, 1997–2001; Defence Select Cttee, 2001–. Vice-Chm., Parly Aerospace Gp, 1997–; Jt Sec., Cons. Parly Aviation Cttee, 1983–87; Vice-Chm., Cons. Parly Envmt, Transport and the Regions Cttee, 1997–99; Jt Vice-Chm., Cons. Parly Home Affairs Cttee, 2000–. Mem. Exec., 1922 Cttee, 1999–. Britannia Airways Parly Pilot of the Year, 1988. Contributor to No Turning Back Gp pubns. *Recreations:* flying (private pilot's licence, 1965), squash, walking up hills, normal family pursuits. *Address:* House of Commons, SW1A 0AA. *T:* (020) 7219 5650.

HOWARTH, Judith; soprano; *b* 11 Sept. 1962. *Educ:* Royal Scottish Acad. of Music and Drama. Rôles include: *Royal Opera:* 1985–86: Oscar, in Un Ballo in Maschera (also in Florida); Elvira, in L'Italiana in Algeri; Iris, in Semele; 1989–: Adele, in Die Fledermaus; Ännchen, in Der Freischutz; Gilda, in Rigoletto; Liu, in Turandot; Marguerite de Valois, in Les Huguenots; Marzelline, in Fidelio; Morgana, in Alcina; Musetta, in La Bohème; Norina, in Don Pasquale; *Opera North:* 1992–: Cressida, in Troilus and Cressida; Norina; Susanna, in Le Nozze di Figaro; other rôles and productions include: Violetta, in La Traviata, Glyndebourne Touring Opera; Anne Trulove, in The Rake's Progress, Brussels; Marie, in La Fille du Régiment, Geneva; Hasse's Solimano and Cavilli's La Didone, Berlin; Madame Mao, in Nixon in China, ENO. Many concerts and festival appearances, incl. Salzburg, Aix-en-Provence, Edinburgh. *Address:* c/o Askonas Holt, Lonsdale Chambers, 27 Chancery Lane, WC2A 1PF.

HOWARTH, Nigel John Graham; His Honour Judge Howarth; a Circuit Judge, since 1992; *b* 12 Dec. 1936; *s* of Vernon and Irene Howarth; *m* 1962, Janice Mary Hooper; two *s* one *d*. *Educ:* Manchester Grammar Sch,; Manchester Univ. (LLB, LLM). Called to the Bar, Gray's Inn, 1960; private practice at Chancery Bar, Manchester, 1961–92; Actg Deemster, IOM, 1985, 1989; a Recorder, 1989–92. Chm., Northern Chancery Bar Assoc., 1990–92. Pres., Manchester Incorp. Law Library Soc., 1985–87. Vice Pres., Disabled Living, 1993–. *Recreations:* music, theatre, fell walking, Assoc. football (Altrincham FC).

HOWARTH, Peter; Editor, Esquire, since 1996; *b* 12 Sept. 1964; partner, Tracey Brett; two *s*. *Educ:* Gonville and Caius Coll., Cambridge (BA English 1986). Projects Manager, Paul Smith Ltd, 1986–88; Head of Menswear, Nicole Farhi, 1988–91; Style Ed., 1991–93, Style Dir, 1993–95, GQ; Editor, Arena, 1995–96. *Publications:* (ed) Fatherhood, 1997; articles in Blitz, The Guardian, etc. *Address:* National Magazine Company Ltd, National Magazine House, 72 Broadwick Street, W1V 2BP. *T:* (020) 7439 5000.

HOWARTH, Peter James, CBE 1995; Managing Director, Royal Mail, 1992–96, and Board Member, 1991–96, Post Office; *b* 27 July 1935; *s* of late Sidney and Margaret Howarth; *m* 1964, Susan Mary Briggs; one *s* one *d*. *Educ:* St Joseph's Coll., Blackpool. Entered Post Office, 1953; held junior and middle management positions; Head Postmaster, Manchester, 1979–85; Chm., NW Postal Bd, 1985–86; Gen. Manager, West and London Letters Territories, 1986–88; Dir Ops, Royal Mail, 1988–91; Asst Man. Dir, Royal Mail, 1991; Man. Dir, Parcelforce, 1991–92. Mem., Billericay Mayflower Rotary Club. *Recreations:* golf, fishing, reading. *Address:* Timbers, 38 Stock Road, Billericay, Essex CM12 0BE. *Club:* Stock Brook Manor Golf (Billericay).

HOWARTH, Robert Lever; Leader, Labour Group, Bolton Metropolitan Borough, since 1975; Leader, Bolton Metropolitan Borough Council, since 1980; *b* 31 July 1927; *s* of James Howarth and Bessie (*née* Pearson); *m* 1952, Josephine Mary Doyle; one *s* one *d*. *Educ:* Bolton County Grammar Sch.; Bolton Technical Coll. Draughtsman with Hawker Siddeley Dynamics. MP (Lab) Bolton East, 1964–70. Lectr in Liberal Studies, Leigh Technical Coll., 1970–76; Senior Lectr in General Studies, Wigan Coll. of Technology, 1977–87. Dep. Chm., 1986–87, Chm., 1987–88, Manchester Airport. *Recreations:* gardening, reading, walking, films. *Address:* 93 Markland Hill, Bolton, Lancs BL1 5EQ. *T:* (01204) 844121.

HOWARTH, Stephen Frederick; HM Diplomatic Service; Minister, Paris, since 1998; *b* 25 Feb. 1947; *s* of Alan Howarth and Alice Howarth (*née* Wilkinson); *m* 1966, Jennifer Mary Chrissop; one *s* two *d*. *Educ:* Switzerland; Rossall Sch.; Norwich Sch. Joined HM Diplomatic Service, 1966; FCO, 1966–71; Vice Consul, Rabat, 1971–74; Second Sec., Washington, 1975–80; Second, later First, Sec., Near East and N Africa Dept, FCO, 1980–82; seconded to Ecole Nationale d'Admin, Paris, 1982–83; Asst Head, Trade Relations and Export Dept, FCO, 1983–84; Dep. Head of Mission, Dakar, 1984–88; Asst Head of Cultural Relations Dept, FCO, 1989–90; Counsellor and Dep. Head, Perm. Under Sec.'s Dept, FCO, 1990–92; Head of Consular Dept, later Div., 1993–98. *Publications:* contribs. to jl of Institut Internat. de l'Admin Public, ENA Mensuel, Paris. *Recreations:* books, walking, landscape, architecture, gardens. *Address:* c/o Foreign and Commonwealth Office, King Charles Street, SW1A 2AH.

HOWATCH, Susan; writer; *b* 14 July 1940; *d* of George Stanford Sturt and Ann Sturt (*née* Watney); *m* 1964, Joseph Howatch (separated 1975); one *d*. *Educ:* Sutton High Sch. GPDST; King's Coll. London (LLB 1961; FKC 1999). Established Starbridge Lectureship in Theology and Natural Science, Cambridge University, 1992. *Publications:* The Dark Shore, 1965; The Waiting Sands, 1966; Call in the Night, 1967; The Shrouded Walls, 1968; April's Grave, 1969; The Devil on Lammas Night, 1970; Penmarric, 1971; Cashelmara, 1974; The Rich are Different, 1977; Sins of the Fathers, 1980; The Wheel of Fortune, 1984; A Question of Integrity, 1997; The High Flyer, 1999; *Starbridge novels:* Glittering Images, 1987; Glamorous Powers, 1988; Ultimate Prizes, 1989; Scandalous Risks, 1991; Mystical Paths, 1992; Absolute Truths, 1994. *Recreation:* reading theology. *Address:* c/o Gillon Aitken Associates Ltd, 29 Fernshaw Road, SW10 0TG. *T:* (020) 7351 7561.

HOWDEN, Alan Percival; Advisor, Programme Acquisition, BBC TV, since 1999; *b* 28 Aug. 1936; *s* of C. P. Howden and Marian Grindell; *m* 1981, Judith South; one *d*. *Educ:* Sale Grammar Sch.; UMIST (BSc Tech Mech. Engrg). Joined BBC, 1964: Exec., 1966–67, Head, 1977–83, Purchased Programmes; Gen. Manager, later Head, Programme Acquisition, 1983–97; Controller, Prog. Acquisition, 1997–99. Mem. Bd, BBC Enterprises, 1989–94. British Film Institute: Gov., 1994–; Chm., Film Educn Rev. Cttee for DCMS, 1998–; British Federation of Film Societies: Vice-Chm., 1965–80; Chm., 1980–82; Vice Pres., 1982–. *Recreations:* theatre, early music, English countryside. *Address:* BBC Broadcast, Room C115, Centre House, Wood Lane, W12 7SB. *T:* (020) 8225 6726. *Club:* Soho House.

HOWDEN, Timothy Simon; Director: Finning International Inc., since 1998; SSL International plc, since 1999; Hyperion Insurance Group, since 2000; *b* 2 April 1937; *s* of Phillip Alexander and Rene Howden; *m* 1st, 1958, Penelope Mary Wilmott (marr. diss. 1984); two *s* one *d*; 2nd, 1999, Lois Robin Chesney. *Educ:* Tonbridge Sch. Served RA, 1955–57, 2nd Lieut. Floor Treatments Ltd, 1957–59; joined Reckitt & Colman, 1962; France, 1962–64; Germany, 1964–70; Dir, Reckitt & Colman Europe, 1970–73; Ranks Hovis McDougall, 1973–92: Dir, RHM Flour Mills, 1973–75; Man. Dir, RHM Foods, 1975–81; Chm. and Man. Dir, British Bakeries, 1981–85; Planning, then Dep. Man. Dir, 1985–89; Man. Dir, 1989–92; Gp Chief Exec. for Europe, The Albert Fisher Group, 1992–96; CEO, Albert Fisher Inc., N America, 1996–97. *Recreations:* ski-ing, scuba diving, tennis, sailing. *Address:* Flat 72, Berkeley House, Hay Hill, W1X 7LH. *T:* (01628) 484121. *Club:* Annabel's.

HOWDLE, Prof. Peter David, MD; FRCP; Professor of Clinical Education, University of Leeds, since 1996; Consultant Physician, St James's University Hospital, Leeds, since 1987; *b* 16 June 1948; *s* of George Henry Howdle and Mary Jane Howdle (*née* Baugh); *m* 1972, Susan Ruth Lowery. *Educ:* King's Sch., Pontefract; Univ. of Leeds Med. Sch. (BSc 1969; MB ChB 1972; MD 1985). FRCP 1992. Jun. med. appts, St James's Univ. Hosp., Leeds, 1972–82; Lectr in Medicine, 1982–87, Sen. Lectr, 1987–96, Univ. of Leeds. Hd, Acad. Unit of Gen. Surgery, Medicine and Anaesthesia, Univ. of Leeds Med. Sch., 1999–. Vis. Lectr (Fulbright Schol.), Harvard Univ., 1984–85. *Publications:* Comprehensive Clinical Hepatology, 2000; contrib. articles on gastroenterology. *Recreations:* classical music, modern literature, Methodist history and liturgy. *Address:* Department of Academic Medicine, Clinical Sciences Building, St James's University Hospital, Leeds LS9 7TF. *T:* (0113) 206 5256.

HOWE, family name of **Baron Howe of Aberavon** and **Baroness Howe of Idlicote**.

HOWE, 7th Earl *cr* 1821; **Frederick Richard Penn Curzon;** Baron Howe, 1788; Baron Curzon, 1794; Viscount Curzon, 1802; farmer; Chairman, London and Provincial Antique Dealers' Association, since 1999; *b* 29 Jan. 1951; *s* of Chambré George William Penn Curzon (*d* 1976) (*g s* of 3rd Earl) and Enid Jane Victoria Curzon (*née* Fergusson) (*d* 1997); *S* cousin, 1984; *m* 1983, Elizabeth Helen Stuart, DL; one *s* three *d*. *Educ:* Rugby School; Christ Church, Oxford (MA Hons Lit. Hum.; Chancellor's Prize for Latin Verse, 1973). AIB. Entered Barclays Bank Ltd, 1973; Manager, 1982; Sen. Manager, 1984–87. Director: Adam & Co., 1987–90; Provident Life Assoc. Ltd, 1988–91. A Lord in Waiting (Govt Whip), 1991–92; front bench spokesman, H of L, on employment and transport, 1991, on environment and defence, 1992; Parly Sec., MAFF, 1992–95; Parly Under-Sec. of State, MoD, 1995–97; opposition front bench spokesman on health, H of L, 1997–; elected Mem., H of L, 1999. Governor: King William IV Naval Foundation, 1984–; Milton's Cottage, 1985–; Trident Trust, 1985–; Member: Cttee of Mgt, RNLI, 1997– (Pres., Chilterns Br., 1985–); Council of Mgt, Restoration of Appearance and Function Trust, 2000–; President: S Bucks Assoc. for the Disabled, 1984–; Nat. Soc. for Epilepsy, 1986– (Vice-Pres., 1984–86); Penn Country Br., CPRE, 1986–92; Abbeyfield Beaconsfield Soc., 1991–. Patron, Demand, 2000–. *Recreation:* spending time with family. *Heir:* *s* Viscount Curzon, *qv*. *Address:* c/o House of Lords, SW1A 0PW.

HOWE OF ABERAVON, Baron *cr* 1992 (Life Peer), of Tandridge, in the County of Surrey; **Richard Edward Geoffrey Howe,** CH 1996; Kt 1970; PC 1972; QC 1965; *b* 20 Dec. 1926; *er s* of late B. E. Howe and Mrs E. F. Howe, JP (*née* Thomson), Port Talbot, Glamorgan; *m* 1953, Elspeth Rosamund Morton Shand (*see* Baroness Howe of Idlicote); one *s* two *d*. *Educ:* Winchester Coll. (Exhibitioner); Trinity Hall, Cambridge (Scholar, MA, LLB; Hon. Fellow, 1992); Pres., Trinity Hall Assoc., 1977–78. Lieut Royal Signals 1945–48. Chm. Cambridge Univ. Conservative Assoc., 1951; Chm. Bow Group, 1955; Managing Dir, Crossbow, 1957–60, Editor 1960–62. Called to the Bar, Middle Temple, 1952, Bencher, 1969, Reader, 1993; Mem. General Council of the Bar, 1957–61; Mem. Council of Justice, 1963–70. Dep. Chm., Glamorgan QS, 1966–70. Contested (C) Aberavon, 1955, 1959; MP (C): Bebington, 1964–66; Reigate, 1970–74; Surrey East, 1974–92. Sec. Conservative Parliamentary Health and Social Security Cttee, 1964–65; an Opposition Front Bench spokesman on labour and social services, 1965–66; Solicitor-General, 1970–72; Minister for Trade and Consumer Affairs, DTI, 1972–74; opposition front bench spokesman on social services, 1974–75, on Treasury and economic affairs, 1975–79; Chancellor of the Exchequer, 1979–83; Sec. of State for Foreign and Commonwealth Affairs, 1983–89; Lord Pres. of the Council, Leader of H of C, and Dep. Prime Minister, 1989–90. Chm., Interim Cttee, IMF, 1982–83. Chm., Framlington Russian Investment Fund, 1994–; Director: Sun Alliance & London Insce Co. Ltd, 1974–79; AGB Research Ltd, 1974–79; EMI Ltd, 1976–79; BICC plc, 1991–97; Glaxo Hldgs, 1991–95; Glaxo Wellcome plc, 1995–96. Special Advr, Internat. Affairs, Jones, Day, Reavis and Pogue, 1991–2000; Member: J. P. Morgan Internat. Adv. Council, 1992–2001; Adv. Council, Bertelsmann Foundn, 1992–97; Fuji Wolfensohn Internat. European Adv. Bd, 1996–98; Carlyle Gp Eur. Adv. Bd, 1997–; Carlyle Gp Internat. Adv. Council, 1997–; Fuji Bank Internat. Adv. Council, 1999–. Member: (Latey) Interdeptl Cttee on Age of Majority, 1965–67; (Street) Cttee on Racial Discrimination, 1967; (Cripps) Cons. Cttee on Discrimination against Women, 1968–69; Chm. Ely Hospital, Cardiff, Inquiry, 1969. Visitor, SOAS, Univ. of London, 1991–2001; Vis. Fellow, John F. Kennedy Sch. of Govt, Harvard Univ., 1991–92; Herman Phleger Vis. Prof., Stanford Law Sch., Calif, 1993. Member, International Advisory Council: Inst. of Internat. Studies, Stanford Univ., Calif, 1990–; Centre for Eur. Policy Studies, 1992–; Chm., Adv. Bd, English Centre for Legal Studies, Warsaw Univ., 1992–99; Vice-President: RUSI, 1991–; English Coll. Foundn in Prague, 1992–. President: Cons. Political Centre Nat. Adv. Cttee, 1977–79; Nat. Union of Cons. and Unionist Assocs, 1983–84; Jt Pres., Wealth of Nations Foundn, 1991–. Mem., Adv. Council, Presidium of Supreme Rada of Ukraine, 1991–97. Mem. Council of Management, Private Patients' Plan, 1969–70; Mem., Steering Cttee, Project Liberty, 1991–97; Patron, Enterprise Europe, 1990–. Pres., Assoc. for Consumer Res., 1992– (an Hon. Vice-Pres., 1974–92). Hon. Fellow: Amer. Bar Foundn, 2000; Chartered Inst. of Taxation, 2000. Hon. Freeman, Port Talbot, 1992. Hon. LLD Wales, 1988; Hon. DCL City, 1993. Joseph Bech Prize, FVS Stifting, Hamburg, 1993. Grand Cross, Order of Merit (Portugal), 1987; Grand Cross, Order of Merit (Germany), 1992. *Publications:* Conflict of Loyalty (memoirs), 1994; various political pamphlets for Bow Group and Conservative Political Centre. *Address:* House of Lords, SW1A 0PW. *Clubs:* Athenæum, Garrick.

HOWE OF IDLICOTE, Baroness *cr* 2001 (Life Peer), of Shipston-on-Stour in the County of Warwickshire; **Elspeth Rosamund Morton Howe,** CBE 1999; JP; Chairman: Broadcasting Standards Commission, 1997–99 (Chairman, Broadcasting Standards Council, 1993–97); BOC Foundation for the Environment and Community, since 1990; President, UNICEF UK, since 1993; *b* 8 Feb. 1932; *d* of late Philip Morton Shand and Sybil Mary (*née* Sissons); *m* 1953, Baron Howe of Aberavon, *qv*; one *s* two *d*. *Educ:* Bath High Sch.; Wycombe Abbey; London Sch. of Econs and Pol Science (BSc 1985). Vice-Chm., Conservative London Area Women's Adv. Cttee, 1966–67, also Pres. of the Cttee's Contact Gp, 1973–77; Mem., Conservative Women's Nat. Adv. Cttee, 1966–71. Member: Lord Chancellor's Adv. Cttee on appointment of Magistrates for Inner London Area, 1965–75; Lord Chancellor's Adv. Cttee on Legal Aid, 1971–75; Parole Board, 1972–75. Dep. Chm., Equal Opportunities Commn, 1975–79. Co-opted Mem., ILEA, 1967–70; Member: Briggs Cttee on Nursing Profession, 1970–72; Justice Cttee on English Judiciary, 1992. Chairman: Hansard Soc. Commn on Women at the Top, 1989–90; The Quality of Care, Local Govt Management Bd Inquiry and Report, 1991–92; Archbishop's Commn on Cathedrals, 1992–94. Director: Kingfisher (formerly Woolworth Holdings) PLC, 1986–2000; United Biscuits (Holdings) PLC, 1988–94; Legal & General Group, 1989–97; Chm., Opportunity 2000 Target Team, Business in the Community, 1990–99. President: Peckham Settlement, 1976–; Women's Gas Fedn, 1979–93; Fedn of Personnel Services, subseq. of Recruitment and Employment Services, 1980–94; Member Council: NACRO, 1974–93; PSI, 1983–92; St George's House, Windsor, 1987–92; Vice-Pres., Pre-Sch. Playgroups Assoc., 1979–83. Trustee, Westminster Foundn for Democracy, 1992–96. Has served as chm. or mem. of several sch. governing bodies in Tower Hamlets; Governor: Cumberlow Lodge Remand Home, 1967–70; Wycombe Abbey, 1968–90; Froebel Educn Inst., 1968–75; LSE, 1985–; Open Univ., 1996– (Vice Chm. Council, 2001–); Mem. Bd of Governors, James Allen's Girls' Sch., 1988–93. JP Inner London Juvenile Court Panel, 1964–92 (Chm. of Court, 1970–90). Hon. LLD: London, 1990; Aberdeen, 1993; Liverpool, 1994; DUniv: Open, 1993; South Bank, 1996; Hon. DLitt: Bradford, 1990; Sunderland, 1995. *Publication:* Under Five (a report on pre-school education), 1966. *Address:* PO Box 23825, SE15 5ZL.
See also B. M. H. Shand.

HOWE, Hon. Brian Leslie, AM 2001; Sanderson Fellow, United Faculty of Theology, Ormond College, University of Melbourne, since 1996; *b* 28 Jan. 1936; *s* of John P. Howe and Lillian M. Howe; *m* 1962, Renate Morris; one *s* two *d*. *Educ:* Melbourne High Sch.; Melbourne Univ. (BA, DipCrim); McCormick Theol Seminary, Chicago (MA). Ordained Minister of Methodist Church, 1963; parishes at Eltham, Morwell and Fitzroy, 1960–69; Dir, Centre for Urban Research and Action, Fitzroy, and Lectr in Sociology, Swinburne Inst. of Technology, 1970–77. Professorial Associate, Centre for Public Policy,

Univ. of Melbourne, 1996–99; Woodrow Wilson School of Public and International Affairs, Princeton University: Res. Fellow, Centre of Domestic and Comparative Policy Studies, 1997; Frederick H. Schultz Class of 1951 Prof., 1998. MP (ALP) Batman, Vic, 1977–96; Minister: for Defence Support, 1983–84; for Social Security, 1984–89; for Community Services and Health, 1990–91; for Health, Housing and Community Services, 1991–93; for Housing, Local Govt and Community (then Human) Services, 1993–94; for Housing and Regional Develt, 1994–96; Minister assisting the Prime Minister for Social Justice, 1988–93, for Commonwealth-State Relations, 1991–93; Dep. Prime Minister of Australia, 1991–95. *Recreations:* golf, reading, films, Australian Rules football. *Address:* 6 Brennand Street, North Fitzroy, Vic 3068, Australia.

HOWE, Prof. Christopher Barry, MBE 1997; PhD; FBA 2001; Professor of Economics with reference to Asia, University of London, since 1979; *b* 3 Nov. 1937; *s* of Charles Roderick Howe and Patricia (*née* Creeden); *m* 1967, Patricia Anne Giles; one *s* one *d*. *Educ:* William Ellis Sch., London; St Catharine's Coll., Cambridge (MA). PhD London. Economic Secretariat, FBI, 1961–63; Sch. of Oriental and African Studies, London Univ., 1963–: Head, Contemp. China Inst., 1972–78. Member: Hong Kong Univ. and Polytechnic Grants Cttee, 1974–93; UGC, 1979–84; ESRC Res. Develt Gp, 1987–88; Hong Kong Res. Grants Council, 1991–99. Chm., Japan and SE Asia Business Gp, 1983–87. *Publications:* Employment and Economic Growth in Urban China 1949–57, 1971; Industrial Relations and Rapid Industrialisation, 1972; Wage Patterns and Wage Policy in Modern China 1919–1972, 1973; China's Economy: a basic guide, 1978; (ed) Studying China, 1979; (ed) Shanghai: revolution and development, 1980; (ed) The Readjustment in the Chinese Economy, 1984; (ed) China and Japan: history, trends and prospects, 1990; The Origins of Japanese Trade Supremacy, 1996; (ed with C. H. Feinstein) Chinese Technology Transfer in the 1990s, 1997; (with R. A. Ash and Y. Y. Kueh) China's Economic Reform, 2001. *Recreations:* music, Burmese cats, walking. *Address:* 12 Highgate Avenue, N6 5RX. *T:* (020) 8340 8104.

HOWE, Prof. Daniel Walker; Rhodes Professor of American History, and Fellow of St Catherine's College, Oxford, since 1992; *b* 10 Jan. 1937; *s* of Maurice Langdon Howe and Lucie Walker Howe; *m* 1961, Sandra Shumway; two *s* one *d*. *Educ:* Harvard (BA); Magdalen Coll., Oxford (MA); Univ. of California at Berkeley (PhD). Lieut, US Army, 1959–60. Yale University: Instructor, 1966–68; Asst Prof., 1968–73; University of California at Los Angeles: Associate Prof., 1973–77; Prof., 1977–92; Chm., History Dept, 1983–87. Harmsworth Vis. Prof., Oxford, 1989–90. Fellow: Charles Warren Center, Harvard, 1970–71; Nat. Endowment for Humanities, 1975–76; Guggenheim Foundn, 1984–85; Res. Fellow, Huntington Library, 1991–92. *Publications:* The Unitarian Conscience, 1970, 2nd edn 1988; The Political Culture of the American Whigs, 1980; Making the American Self, 1997; articles in learned jls. *Recreation:* music. *Address:* St Catherine's College, Oxford OX1 3UJ. *T:* (01865) 271700; 3814 Cody Road, Sherman Oaks, CA 91403, USA.

HOWE, Prof. Denis; Professor of Aircraft Design, 1973–92, College of Aeronautics, Cranfield Institute of Technology, now Professor Emeritus, Cranfield University; *b* 3 Sept. 1927; *s* of Alfred and Alice Howe; *m* 1st, 1954, Audrey Marion Wilkinson; two *s* three *d*; 2nd, 1981, Catherine Bolton. *Educ:* Watford Grammar Sch.; MIT (SM); College of Aeronautics (PhD). CEng, FIMechE, FRAeS. Project Engineer, Fairey Aviation Co., 1945–54; College of Aeronautics, Cranfield Institute of Technology: Lectr, Sen. Lectr and Reader, 1954–73; Head of College, 1986–90; Dean of Engineering, 1988–91. *Publications:* Aircraft Conceptual Design Synthesis, 2000; contribs to learned jls. *Recreations:* gardening, church administration. *Address:* 57 Brecon Way, Bedford MK41 8DE. *T:* (01234) 56747.

HOWE, Derek Andrew, CBE 1991; public affairs and political consultant; company director; *b* 31 Aug. 1934; *o s* of late Harold and Elsie Howe; *m* 1st, 1958, Barbara (*née* Estill); two *d*; 2nd, 1975, Sheila (*née* Digger), MBE (*d* 1990); one *s*; 3rd, 1996, Penny (*née* James). *Educ:* City of Leeds Sch.; Cockburn High Sch., Leeds. Journalist, Yorkshire Evening News, 1951–61; Conservative Central Office, 1962–70; Parliamentary Liaison Officer, 1970–73; Special Adviser, 1973–75; Press Officer, Leader of HM Opposition, 1975–79; special adviser to: Paymaster Gen., 1979–81; Chancellor of Duchy of Lancaster, 1981; Political Secretary, 10 Downing Street, 1981–83 and Special Adviser to Leader of the House of Commons, 1982–83. Chm., Churchill Clinic, 1996–99 (Dep. Chm., 1995–96). Trustee, London Youth Trust, 1985– (Chm. Trustees, 1988–). Freeman of the City of London. *Recreations:* gardening, reading, philately, Freemasonry. *Address:* The Vines, Kimpton, near Andover, Hampshire SP11 8NU. *Club:* St Stephen's Constitutional.

HOWE, Eric James, CBE 1990; Data Protection Registrar, 1984–94; *b* 4 Oct. 1931; *s* of Albert Henry Howe and Florence Beatrice (*née* Hale); *m* 1967, Patricia Enid (*née* Schollick); two *d*. *Educ:* Stretford Grammar Sch.; Univ. of Liverpool (BA Econs 1954). FIDPM 1990; FBCS 1972. NCB, 1954–59; British Cotton Industry Res. Assoc., 1959–61; English Electric Computer Co., 1961–66; National Computing Centre, 1966–84: Dep. Dir, 1975–84; Mem. Bd of Dirs, 1976–84. Chairman: National Computer Users Forum, 1977–84; Focus Cttee for Private Sector Users, DoI, 1982–84; Member: User Panel, NEDO, 1983–84; Council, British Computer Soc., 1971–74 and 1980–83; NW Regional Council, CBI, 1977–83; Bd, N Wales Housing Assoc., 1997–. Rep. UK, Confedn of Eur. Computer Users Assocs, 1980–83. *Recreations:* gardening, golf.

HOWE, Prof. Geoffrey Leslie, TD 1962 (Bars 1969 and 1974); Professor of Oral Surgery and Oral Medicine, 1987–96, and Dean, 1988–96, Jordan University of Science and Technology; *b* 22 April 1924; *e s* of late Leo Leslie John Howe, Maidenhead, Berks; *m* 1948, Heather Patricia Joan Hambly (*d* 1997); (one *s* decd). *Educ:* Royal Dental and Middlesex Hospitals. LDS RCS 1946; LRCP, MRCS 1954; FDS RCS 1955; MDS Dunelm, 1961; FFD RCSI 1964; FICD 1981. Dental and Medical Sch. Prizeman; Begley Prize, RCS, 1951; Cartwright Prize, RCS, 1961. Dental Officer, Royal Army Dental Corps, 1946–49. House appointments, etc., Royal Dental and Middlesex Hospitals, 1949–55. Registrar in Oral Surgery, Eastman Dental Hosp. (Institute of Dental Surgery), 1955–56; Senior Registrar in Oral Surgery, Plastic and Oral Surgery Centre, Chepstow, Mon, 1956; Senior Registrar in Oral Surgery, Eastman Dental Hospital, 1956–59; Professor of Oral Surgery, University of Newcastle upon Tyne (formerly King's Coll., University of Durham), 1959–67; Prof. of Oral Surgery, Royal Dental Hosp., London Sch. of Dental Surgery, 1967–78 (Dean of School, 1974–78); Prof. of Oral Surgery and Oral Medicine, and Dean of Dental Studies, Univ. of Hong Kong, 1978–83; Dir, Prince Philip Dental Hosp., 1981–83. Cons. Oral Surgeon, United Newcastle upon Tyne Hosps, 1959–67; Chm., Central Cttee for Hosp. Dental Services, 1971–73; Vice-Pres., BDA, 1979– (Vice-Chm., 1971–73; Chm., 1973–78); Pres., Internat. Assoc. of Oral Surgeons, 1980–83. Hon. Col Comdt, RADC, 1975–89. OStJ. *Publications:* The Extraction of Teeth, 1961, 2nd edn 1970; Minor Oral Surgery, 1966, 3rd edn 1985; (with F. I. H. Whitehead) Local Anaesthesia in Dentistry, 1972, 3rd edn 1990; contribs to: Medical Treatment Yearbook, 1959; Modern Trends in Dental Surgery, 1962, and to numerous medical and dental journals. *Recreations:* sailing; Territorial Army Volunteer Reserve (lately Col, OC 217 (L) Gen. Hosp. RAMC (V), graded Cons. Dental Surgeon RADC, TAVR). *Address:* 70 Croham Manor Road, South Croydon, Surrey CR2 7BF. *Clubs:* Savage, Gents, Oral Surgery; Hong Kong; Hong Kong Yacht.

HOWE, Geoffrey Michael Thomas; Director: Fleming Overseas Investment Trust plc, since 1999; Gateway Electronic Components Ltd, since 2000; *b* 3 Sept. 1949; *s* of Michael Edward Howe and Susan Dorothy Howe (*née* Allan); *m* 1995, Karen Mary Webber (*née* Ford); two *d*. *Educ:* Manchester Grammar Sch.; St John's Coll., Cambridge (MA). Solicitor. Stephenson Harwood, 1971–75; joined Clifford Chance, 1975; Partner, Corporate Dept, 1980; Man. Partner, 1989–97; Gen. Counsel and Dir, Robert Fleming Hldgs Ltd, 1998–2000. *Recreations:* cricket, golf, opera, wine, antiques. *Address:* 11 Highbury Terrace, N5 1UP.

HOWE, Ven. George Alexander; Archdeacon of Westmorland and Furness, since 2000; *b* 22 Jan. 1952; *s* of Eugene Howe and Olivia Lydia Caroline Howe (*née* Denroche); *m* 1980, Jane Corbould; one *s* one *d*. *Educ:* Liverpool Inst. High Sch.; Univ. of Durham (BA 1973); Westcott House Cambridge. Ordained deacon, 1975, priest, 1976; Curate: St Cuthbert, Peterlee, 1975–79; St Mary, Norton, Stockton-on-Tees, 1979–81; Vicar, Utd Benefice of Hart with Elwick Hall, 1981–85; Rector, St Edmund, Sedgefield, 1985–91; Rural Dean of Sedgefield, 1988–91; Vicar, Holy Trinity, Kendal, 1991–2000; Rural Dean of Kendal, 1994–99. Hon. Canon, Carlisle Cathedral, 1994–. Bishop's Advr for Ecumenical Affairs, dio. of Carlisle, 2001–. *Recreations:* listening to The Archers, walking the dog, good food and wine, cartology. *Address:* The Vicarage, Windermere Road, Lindale, Grange-over-Sands, Cumbria LA11 6LB. *T:* (015395) 34717.

HOWE, Prof. G(eorge) Melvyn, PhD, DSc; FRSE, FRGS, FRSGS, FRMetS; Professor of Geography, University of Strathclyde, 1967–85, now Emeritus; *b* Abercynon, 7 April 1920; *s* of Reuben and Edith Howe, Abercynon; *m* 1947, Patricia Graham Fennell, Pontypridd; three *d*. *Educ:* Caerphilly Boys' Grammar Sch.; UCW Aberystwyth (BSc 1940; BSc 1st cl. hons Geog. and Anthrop., 1947; MSc 1949; PhD 1957); DSc Strathclyde 1974. Served with RAF, 1940–46: Meteorological Br., 1940–42; commnd Intell. (Air Photographic Interpretation) Br., 1942–46, in Middle East Comd. Lectr, later Sen. Lectr, in Geography, UCW Aberystwyth, 1948; Reader in Geog., Univ. of Wales, 1964. Vis. Prof. (Health and Welfare, Canada), 1977. Mem. Council, Inst. of British Geographers (Pres., 1985); Mem. Medical Geography Cttee, RGS, 1960–; British Rep. on Medical Geog. Commn of IGU, 1970–; Mem., British Nat. Cttee for Geography, Royal Soc., 1978–83. Gill Memorial Award, RGS, 1964. *Publications:* Wales from the Air, 1957, 2nd edn 1966; (with P. Thomas) Welsh Landforms and Scenery, 1963; National Atlas of Disease Mortality in the United Kingdom, 1963, 2nd edn 1970; The Soviet Union, 1968, 2nd edn 1983; The USSR, 1971; Man, Environment and Disease in Britain, 1972, 2nd edn 1976; (ed and contrib.) Atlas of Glasgow and the West of Scotland, 1972; (contrib.) Wales (ed E. G. Bowen), 1958; (contrib.) Modern Methods in the History of Medicine (ed E. Clarke), 1970; (ed with J. A. Loraine, and contrib.) Environmental Medicine, 1973, 2nd edn 1980; (contrib.) Environment and Man (ed J. Lenihan and W. W. Fletcher), 1976; (ed and contrib.) A World Geography of Human Diseases, 1977; (ed and contrib.) Global Geocancerology, 1986; People, Environment, Disease and Death in Britain, 1997; articles in geographical, meteorological, hydrological and medical jls. *Recreation:* travel. *Address:* Hendre, 50 Heol Croes Faen, Nottage, Porthcawl CF36 3SW. *T:* (01656) 772377. *Club:* Royal Air Force.

HOWE, Jack, RDI 1961; FRIBA 1953; Architect and Industrial Designer; *b* 24 Feb. 1911; *s* of Charles Henry and Florence Eleanor Howe; *m* 1960, Margaret Crosbie Corrie (*d* 1979); one *s* one *d* (by former marriage); *m* 1981, Jennifer Mary Dixon (*née* Hughes D'Aeth). *Educ:* Enfield Grammar Sch.; Polytechnic Sch. of Architecture. FSIAD 1955. Asst to E. Maxwell Fry, 1933–37; Chief Asst to Walter Gropius and Maxwell Fry, 1937–39; Drawing Office Manager to Holland, Hannan & Cubitts Ltd for Royal Ordnance Factories at Wrexham and Ranskill, 1939–43; Associate Partner, Arcon, 1944–48; private practice, 1949; Partnership with Andrew Bain, 1959–76. Architectural work includes: Highbury Quadrant Primary School, (LCC); Windmill House, Lambeth (LCC Housing Scheme); Television Research Lab. for AEI Ltd; Kodak Pavilion, Brussels Exhibn, 1958; Official Architects for British Trade Fair, Moscow, 1961; Industrial Designs include: Diesel Electric Locomotives and Express Pullman Trains; also Rly equipment. Industrial Design Consultant to various large firms and to BR Board. Mem. Design Index Cttee and Street Furniture Cttee, Design Council (formerly CoID), 1956–; Member: Cttee on Traffic Signs, Min. of Transport, 1962, 1963; Nat. Council for Diplomas in Art and Design. Pres., SIAD, 1963–64; Master of Faculty, RDI, 1975–77. Duke of Edinburgh's design prize, 1969. *Publications:* articles for various architectural and design jls. *Recreations:* music, theatre. *Address:* 4 Leopold Avenue, Wimbledon, SW19 7ET. *T:* (020) 8946 7116.

HOWE, John Francis, CB 1996; OBE 1974; Executive Director, Thales (formerly Thomson-CSF Racal) plc, and Director of Defence Strategy, Thales (formerly Thomson Racal) Defence Ltd, 2000–May 2002 (on secondment); *b* 29 Jan. 1944; *s* of late Frank and Marjorie Howe; *m* 1981, Angela Ephrosini (*née* Nicolaides); one *d* one step *d*. *Educ:* Shrewsbury Sch.; Balliol Coll., Oxford (Scholar; MA). Pirelli General Cable Works, 1964; joined MoD as Asst Principal, 1967; Principal, 1972; Civil Adviser to GOC NI, 1972–73; Private Sec. to Perm. Under-Sec. of State, 1975–78; Asst Sec., 1979; seconded to FCO as Defence Counsellor, UK Delegn to NATO, 1981–84; Head, Arms Control Unit, MoD, 1985–86; Private Sec. to Sec. of State for Defence, 1986–87; Asst Under-Sec. of State (Personnel and Logistics), 1988–91; Dep. Under-Sec. of State (Civilian Management), 1992–96; Dep. Chief of Defence Procurement (Support), 1996–2000. *Recreations:* travel, garden labour, paintings. *Club:* Athenæum.

HOWE, Air Vice-Marshal John Frederick George, CB 1985; CBE 1980; AFC 1961; Commandant-General, RAF Regiment and Director General of Security (RAF), 1983–85, retired; *b* 26 March 1930; *m* 1961, Annabelle Gowing; three *d*. *Educ:* St Andrew's Coll., Grahamstown, SA. SAAF, 1950–54 (served in Korea, 2nd Sqdn SAAF and 19 Inf. Regt, US Army, 1951); 222 Sqdn, Fighter Comd, 1956; 40 Commando RM, Suez Campaign, 1956; Fighter Command: Flt Comdr, 222 Sqdn, 1957; Flt Comdr, 43 Sqdn, 1957–59; Sqdn Comdr, 74 Sqdn, 1960–61; Air Staff, HQ Fighter Command, 1961–63; RAF Staff Coll., 1964; USAF Exchange Tour at Air Defence Comd HQ, Colorado Springs, 1965–67; 229 Operational Conversion Unit, RAF Chivenor, 1967–68; OC 228 OCU, Coningsby, 1968–69; Central Tactics and Trials Org., HQ Air Support Comd, 1969–70; MoD, 1970–72; Station Comdr, RAF Gutersloh, 1973–74; RCDS, 1975; Gp Capt. Ops, HQ No 11 Gp, 1975–77; Comdt, ROC, 1977–80; Comdr, Southern Maritime Air Region, 1980–83. Hon. Colonel: Field Sqns (Airfield Damage Repair) (Vol.) (South), 1988–93; 77 Engr Regt (Vol.), 1993. American DFC 1951; Air Medal 1951. *Recreations:* country pursuits, ski-ing, sailing. *Clubs:* Royal Air Force; Norfolk (Norwich).

HOWE, Josephine Mary O'C.; *see* O'Connor Howe.

HOWE, Martin, CB 1995; PhD; Director, Competition Policy Division, Office of Fair Trading, 1984–96; *b* 9 Dec. 1936; *s* of late Leslie Wistow Howe and Dorothy Vernon

Howe (*née* Taylor Farrell); *m* 1959, Anne Cicely Lawrenson; three *s*. *Educ:* Leeds Univ. (BCom (Accountancy), PhD). Asst Lectr, Lectr, Sen. Lectr, in Economics, Univ. of Sheffield, 1959–73; Senior Economic Adviser: Monopolies Commn, 1973–77; Office of Fair Trading, 1977–80; Asst Secretary, OFT and DTI, 1980–84. Special Prof., Univ. of Nottingham Business Sch., 1994–. *Publications:* Equity Issues and the London Capital Market (with A. J. Merrett and G. D. Newbould), 1967; articles on variety of topics in learned and professional jls. *Recreations:* theatre (including amateur dramatics), cricket, gardening. *Address:* 6 Mansdale Road, Redbourn, Herts AL3 7DN. *T:* (01582) 792074.

HOWE, Martin Russell Thomson; QC 1996; *b* 26 June 1955; *s* of late Colin Howe, FRCS and Dr Angela Howe, *d* of Baron Brock, surgeon; *m* 1989, Lynda Barnett; one *s* three *d*. *Educ:* Winchester Coll. (Schol.); Trinity Hall, Cambridge (BA, Pt I Engrg, Pt II Law; Baker Prize for Engrg, 1974; MA). Called to the Bar, Middle Temple, 1978 (Harmsworth Exhibnr); in practice, specialising in intellectual property and European law, 1980–. Councillor (C), London Borough of Hammersmith and Fulham, 1982–86 (Chm., Planning Cttee, 1985–86). Contested (C) Neath (S Wales), 1987. *Publications:* Europe and the Constitution after Maastricht, 1992; (ed) Russell-Clarke on Industrial Designs, 6th edn, 1998; contrib. Halsbury's Laws of England, 1986, 1995, 2000; Protecting the Foundations of Nationhood, 2001; numerous articles in legal jls and pamphlets on European constitutional issues and intellectual property law. *Address:* c/o National Westminster Bank plc, Law Courts Branch, 217 Strand, WC2R 1AL.

HOWE, His Honour Ronald William; Director of Appeals, General Dental Council, 1999–Dec. 2002; a Circuit Judge, 1991–97; *b* 19 June 1932; *s* of William Arthur and Lilian Mary Howe; *m* 1956, Jean Emily Goodman; three *s* one *d*. *Educ:* Morpeth Sch.; Coll. of Law, London. Admitted Solicitor, 1966; partner with Ronald Brooke & Co., Ilford, then Brooke, Garland & Howe, 1966–75; Registrar of County Court, subseq. Dist Judge, 1975–91. Mem., Judicial Studies Bd, 1990–91 (Mem., Civil and Family Cttee, 1988–91; former tutor); Advocacy Trng Advr, Law Soc., 1998–2000. *Recreations:* gardening, IT, badminton, golf (an increasing passion), cycling.

HOWE, Stephen Douglas; Editor, since 1991, Associate Publisher, since 2000, Farmers Weekly; *b* 28 Feb. 1948; *m* 1971, Susan Jane Apps; one *s* one *d*. *Educ:* Brymore Sch., Somerset; Seale-Hayne Coll. (DipAgr); NDA, Dip Farm Management. Lectr in Crop Husbandry and Farm Manager, Lackham Coll. of Agric., Wilts, 1969–72; Power Farming magazine: Management Specialist, 1972–82; Managing Editor, 1982–85; Agricultural Machinery Jl, 1985–87; Editor, Crops, 1987–91. Governor: Inst. of Grassland and Environmental Res., 1996–2000; Nat. Fedn of Young Farmers, 1999–2000. Pres., Eurofarm, 1999–. Fellow, Guild of Agricultural Journalists, 1991. Hon. DArts Plymouth, 2000. *Recreations:* gardening, sailing, farming, flying. *Address:* Springfield Cottage, Byers Lane, South Godstone, Surrey RH9 8JH. *T:* (01342) 893018. *Club:* Farmers'.

HOWELL, family name of **Baron Howell of Guildford**.

HOWELL OF GUILDFORD, Baron *cr* 1997 (Life Peer), of Penton Mewsey in the co. of Hampshire; **David Arthur Russell Howell;** PC 1979; journalist and economist; *b* 18 Jan. 1936; *s* of late Colonel A. H. E. Howell, DSO, TD, DL and Beryl Howell, 5 Headfort Place, SW1; *m* 1967, Davina Wallace; one *s* two *d*. *Educ:* Eton; King's Coll., Cambridge. BA 1st class hons Cantab, 1959. Lieut Coldstream Guards, 1954–56. Joined Economic Section of Treasury, 1959; resigned, 1960. Leader Writer and Special Correspondent, The Daily Telegraph, 1960; Chm. of Bow Gp, 1961–62; Editor of Crossbow, 1962–64; contested (C) Dudley, 1964. MP (C) Guildford, 1966–97. A Lord Comr of Treasury, 1970–71; Parly Sec., CSD, 1970–72; Parly Under-Sec.: Dept of Employment, 1971–72; NI Office, March–Nov. 1972; Minister of State: NI Office, 1972–74; Dept of Energy, 1974; Secretary of State: for Energy, 1979–81; for Transport, 1981–83. Chairman: Select Cttee on Foreign Affairs, 1987–97; H of L Sub-Cttee on EC Foreign and Security Policy, 1999–2000. H of L Opposition spokesman on foreign affairs, 2000–. Chairman: Cons. One Nation Gp, 1987–97; UK-Japan 21st Century (formerly 2000) Group, 1990–2001. Sen. Vis. Fellow, PSI, 1983–85; Vis. Fellow, Nuffield Coll., Oxford, 1993–2001. Dir of Conservative Political Centre, 1964–66. Director: Jardine Insurance Brokers, 1991–97; Monks Investment Trust, 1993–; John Laing Plc, Adv. Dir, Warburg Dillon Read (formerly SBC Warburg), 1997–2000; Advr, Japan Central Railway Co., 2001–. Mem., Internat. Adv. Council, Swiss Bank Corp., 1988–97. Governor, Sadler's Wells Trust, 1995–98; Trustee, Shakespeare Globe Theatre, 2000–. *Publications:* (co-author) Principles in Practice, 1960; The Conservative Opportunity, 1965; Freedom and Capital, 1981; Blind Victory: a study in income, wealth and power, 1986; The Edge of Now, 2000; various pamphlets and articles. *Recreations:* writing, history, gardening. *Address:* House of Lords, SW1A 0PW. *Club:* Beefsteak.

See also G. G. O. Osborne.

HOWELL, Air Vice-Marshal Evelyn Michael Thomas, CBE 1961; CEng, FRAeS; *b* 11 Sept. 1913; *s* of Sir Evelyn Berkeley Howell, KCIE, CSI; *m* 1st, 1937, Helen Joan, *o d* of late Brig. W. M. Hayes, CBE, FRICS (marr. diss. 1972); one *s* three *d*; 2nd, 1972, Rosemary, *e d* of I. A. Cram, CEng, MICE; one *s* one *d*. *Educ:* Downside Sch.; RAF Coll., Cranwell. Commissioned, 1934; Dir of Air Armament Research and Devt, Min. of Aviation, 1960–62; Comdt, RAF Techn. Coll., 1963–65; SASO, HQ Technical Training Command RAF, 1966–67; retired, 1967. Gen. Manager, Van Dusen Aircraft Supplies, Oxford, Minneapolis, St Louis, Helsingborg, 1967–79. Mem. Livery of Clothworkers' Co., 1938. *Recreations:* swimming, conservation, boating. *Address:* 6 Summerhill, Kendal, Cumbria LA9 4JU. *Club:* Royal Air Force.

HOWELL, Gareth, CBE 1993; PhD; CChem; Director, British Council, Malaysia, 1990–95; *b* 22 April 1935; *s* of Amwel John and Sarah Blodwen Howell; *m* 1957, Margaret Patricia Ashelford; one *s* two *d*. *Educ:* Ferndale Grammar Sch., Rhondda; University College London; Inst. of Education, Univ. of London. BSc, PhD; PGCE London. MRSC. Asst Master, Canford Sch., Wimborne, Dorset, 1957–61; Lectr, Norwich City Coll., 1961–65; British Council: Science Educn Officer, London, 1965–66; Science Educn Officer, Nigeria, 1966–70; Head, Science Educn Section, 1970–74; Director, Science and Technology Dept, 1974; Representative, Malawi, 1974–76; on secondment to Min. of Overseas Development as Educn Adviser, 1976–79; Counsellor and Dep. Educn Adviser, British Council Div., British High Commn, India, 1979–83; Controller: Sci., Technol. and Educn Div., 1983–87; Americas, Pacific and E Asia Div., 1987–90. *Recreations:* photography, philately, gardening, tennis, walking, travel. *Address:* 9 Alderway, West Cross, Swansea SA3 5PD.

HOWELL, Gwynne Richard, CBE 1998; Principal Bass, Royal Opera House, since 1971; *b* Gorseinon, S Wales, 13 June 1938; *s* of Gilbert and Ellaline Howell; *m* 1968, Mary Edwina Morris; two *s*. *Educ:* Pontardawe Grammar Sch.; Univ. of Wales, Swansea (BSc; Hon. Fellow 1986); Manchester Univ. (DipTP); MRTPI 1966. Studied singing with Redvers Llewellyn while at UCW; pt-time student, Manchester RCM, with Gwilym Jones, during DipTP trng at Manchester Univ.; studied with Otakar Kraus, 1968–72. Planning Asst, Kent CC, 1961–63; Sen. Planning Officer, Manchester Corp., 1965–68, meanwhile continuing to study music pt-time and giving public operatic performances which incl. the rôle of Pogner, in Die Meistersinger; as a result of this rôle, apptd Principal Bass at Sadler's Wells, 1968; also reached final of BBC Opera Singers competition for N of Eng., 1967. In first season at Sadler's Wells, sang 8 rôles, incl. Monterone and the Commendatore; appearances with Hallé Orch., 1968 and 1969; Arkel in Pelleas and Melisande, Glyndebourne and Covent Garden, 1969; Goffredo, in Il Pirato, 1969. *Royal Opera House, Covent Garden:* début as First Nazarene, Salome, 1969–70 season; the King, in Aida; Timur, in Turandot; Mephisto, in Damnation of Faust; Prince Gremin, in Eugene Onegin; High Priest, in Nabucco; Reinmar, in Tannhauser, 1973–74 (later rôle, Landgraf); Colline, in La Boheme; Pimen, in Boris Godunov; Ribbing, Un ballo in maschera; Padre Guardiano, in La forza del destino; Hobson, in Peter Grimes, 1975; Sparafucile, in Rigoletto, 1975–76 season; Ramfis in Aida, 1977; Tristan und Isolde, 1978, 1982; Luisa Miller, 1978; Samson et Delilah, 1981; Fiesco in Simon Boccanegra, 1981; Pogner in Die Meistersinger, 1982; Arkel in Pelléas et Mélisande, 1982; Dossifei in Khovanshchina, 1982; Semele, 1982; Die Zauberflöte, 1983; Raimondo, in Lucia di Lammermoor, 1985; Rocco in Fidelio, 1986; Marcel in Les Huguenots, 1991; Daland in Der Fliegende Holländer, 1992; Katya Kabanova, 1994; Stiffelio, 1995; Mathis der Maler, 1995; The Bartered Bride, 1998; Greek Passion, 2000; *English National Opera:* Don Carlos, Die Meistersinger, 1974–75; The Magic Flute, Don Carlos, 1975–76; Duke Bluebeard's Castle, 1978, 1991; The Barber of Seville, 1980; Tristan and Isolde, 1981; Hans Sachs in Die Meistersinger, 1984; Parsifal, 1986; Don Carlos, 1992; Banquo in Macbeth, 1993; Fidelio, 1996; Mary Stuart, 1998; Silver Tassie (world première), 2000; *Metropolitan Opera House, New York:* début as Lódovico in Otello, and Pogner in Die Meistersinger, 1985; *Bastille, Paris:* début in Parsifal, 1997; *sacred music:* Verdi and Mozart Requiems, Missa Solemnis, St Matthew and St John Passions; sings in Europe and USA; records for BBC and for major recording companies. *Recreations:* tennis, squash, golf, Rugby enthusiast, gardening. *Address:* 197 Fox Lane, N13 4BB. *T:* and *Fax:* (020) 8886 1981.

HOWELL, Prof. John Bernard Lloyd, CBE 1991; Chairman, Southampton and SW Hampshire District Health Authority, 1983–98; Foundation Professor of Medicine, University of Southampton, 1969–91, now Emeritus (Dean of the Faculty of Medicine, 1978–83); Hon. Consultant Physician, Southampton General Hospital, 1969–91, now Emeritus; *b* 1 Aug. 1926; *s* of late David John Howells and Hilda Mary Hill, Ynystawe, Swansea; *m* 1952, Heather Joan Rolfe; two *s* one *d*. *Educ:* Swansea Grammar Sch.; Middx Hosp. Med. Sch. (Meyerstein Scholar 1946). BSc, MB, BS, PhD; FRCP. House Officer posts, Middx and Brompton Hosps; MO RAMC, 1952–54; Lectr in Physiol Medicine, 1954–56, in Pharmacol Medicine, 1958–60, Middlesex Hosp. Med. Sch.; Manchester Royal Infirmary: Sen. Lectr in Medicine and Hon. Consultant Physician, 1960–66; Consultant Physician, 1966–69. Eli Lilly Travelling Fellow, Johns Hopkins Hospital, 1957–58; Goulstonian Lectr, RCP, 1966. Member: Physiol Soc., 1956–; Med. Res. Soc., 1956–; Assoc. of Physicians of GB and Ire., 1964–; GMC, 1978–83. President: British Thoracic Soc., 1988–89; BMA, 1989–90 (Chm., Bd of Sci. and Educn, 1991–98). Mem. Soc. of Scholars, Johns Hopkins Univ., 1998–. Hon. Life Mem., Canadian Thoracic Soc., 1978; Hon. FACP 1982. Hon. DSc Southampton, 1994. *Publications:* (ed jtly) Breathlessness, 1966; chapters in: Cecil and Loeb's Textbook of Medicine, 13th edn 1970, 14th edn 1974; Recent Advances in Chest Medicine, 1976; Thoracic Medicine, 1981; Oxford Textbook of Medicine, 1982; Respiratory Medicine, 1995; Asthma and Rhinitis, 1995; papers on respiratory physiology and medicine and health care. *Recreations:* France, DIY, wine. *Address:* The Coach House, Bassett Wood Drive, Southampton SO16 3PT. *T:* and *Fax:* (023) 8076 8878.

HOWELL, John Frederick; Senior Research Fellow, Overseas Development Institute (Director, 1987–97); *b* 16 July 1941; *s* of late Frederick Howell and Glenys Griffiths; *m* 1993, Paula Wade; two *s*, and one step *s*. *Educ:* Univ. of Wales (BA Hons 1963); Univ. of Manchester (MA Econ. Dist. 1965); Univ. of Reading, (external; PhD). Lectr, Univ. of Khartoum, 1966–73; correspondent, Africa Confidential, 1971–75; Sen. Lectr and Head of Pol. and Admin. Studies, Univ. of Zambia, 1973–77; Overseas Development Institute, 1977–; seconded as Advr, Min. of Agric. and Land Affairs, S Africa, 1997–2001. Vis Lectr, Mananga Agric. Management Centre, Swaziland, 1978–80; Vis. Prof. in Agricl Develt, Wye Coll., Univ. of London, 1988–96. Consultant on aid and agricl devel: World Bank; FAO; Commonwealth Secretariat; DFID in S Africa, India, Nepal, Nigeria, Brazil, Tanzania, Sudan; Adviser: All-Party Parly Gp on Overseas Develt, 1985–86; Princess Royal's Africa Review Gp, 1987–89. Mem. Council, VSO, 1991–97. Pres., UK Chapter, Soc. of Internat. Develt, 1991–93. *Publications:* Local Government and Politics in the Sudan, 1974; (ed) Borrowers and Lenders: rural financial markets and institutions in developing countries, 1980; Administering Agricultural Development for Small Farmers, 1981; (ed) Recurrent Costs and Agricultural Development, 1985; (ed) Agricultural Extension in Practice, 1988; (with Alex Duncan) Structural Adjustment and the African Farmer, 1992. *Address:* Overseas Development Institute, 111 Westminster Bridge Road, SE1 7JD.

HOWELL, Maj.-Gen. Lloyd, CBE 1972; Consultant, Technical Education Development, University College, Cardiff, 1980–86 (Fellow, 1981); *b* 28 Dec. 1923; *s* of Thomas Idris Howell and Anne Howell; *m* 1st, 1945, Hazel Barker (*d* 1974); five *s* three *d*; 2nd, 1975, Elizabeth June Buchanan Husband (*née* Atkinson); two step *s*. *Educ:* Barry Grammar Sch.; University Coll. of S Wales and Monmouthshire (BSc); Royal Military Coll. of Science. CEng, MRAeS. Commissioned RA, 1944; Field Regt, RA, E Africa, 1945–46; Staff, Divl HQ, Palestine, 1946–47; RAEC 1949; Instr, RMA Sandhurst, 1949–53; TSO II Trials Estabt, 1954–57; SO II (Educn), Divl HQ, BAOR, 1957–59; DS, Royal Mil. Coll. of Science, 1960–64; SEO, Army Apprentices Coll., 1964–67; Headmaster/Comdg, Duke of York's Royal Mil. Sch., 1967–72; Col (Ed), MoD (Army), 1972–74; Chief Educn Officer, HQ UKLF, 1974–76; Dir, Army Educn, 1976–80. Col Comdt, RAEC, 1982–86. Dir (non-exec.), Building Trades Exhibitions Ltd, 1980–93. Mem. Council, CGLI, 1977–90; Mem., Ct of Governors, Cardiff Univ. (formerly UWCC), 1980–. Hon. MA Open Univ., 1980. *Recreations:* gardening, golf, reading. *Address:* c/o HSBC, The Forum, Old Town, Swindon, Wilts SN3 1QT.

HOWELL, Michael Edward, CMG 1989; OBE 1980; HM Diplomatic Service; High Commissioner, Mauritius, 1989–93; *b* 2 May 1933; *s* of Edward and Fanny Howell; *m* 1958, Joan Little; one *s* one *d*. *Educ:* Newport High Sch. Served RAF, 1951–53. Colonial Office, 1953; CRO, 1958; Karachi, 1959; 2nd Secretary: Bombay, 1962; UK Delegn to Disarmament Cttee, Geneva, 1966; 1st Sec. (Parly Clerk), FCO, 1969; Consul (Comm.), New York, 1973; ndc 1975; FCO, 1976; Hd of Chancery, later Chargé d'Affaires, Kabul, 1978; Consul-General: Berlin, 1981; Frankfurt, 1983; High Comr to Papua New Guinea, 1986. *Recreation:* tennis. *Address:* c/o Foreign and Commonwealth Office, SW1A 2AH.

HOWELL, Patrick Leonard; QC 1990; *b* 4 Dec. 1942; *s* of Leonard Howell, MC, and Mary Isobel (*née* Adam); *m* 1966, Sandra Marie McColl; two *s* one *d*. *Educ:* Radley; Christ Church, Oxford (MA); London Sch. of Econs and Pol Science (LLM). Called to the Bar: Inner Temple, 1966; Lincoln's Inn, 1968. Teaching Fellow, Osgoode Hall Law Sch., Toronto, 1965–66. Social Security Comr and Child Support Comr, 1994–; a Judge, Employment Appeal Tribunal, 1999–. *Recreation:* building things. *Address:* Office of the Social Security Commissioners, 83 Farringdon Street, EC4A 4DH. *T:* (020) 7353 5145.

HOWELL, Paul Frederic; farmer; Special Operations Manager WRG plc, since 2000; *b* 17 Jan. 1951; *s* of Sir Ralph Howell, *qv*; *m* 1987, Johanna Youlten Turnbull; two *s*. *Educ:* Gresham's Sch., Holt, Norfolk; St Edmund Hall, Oxford (MA Agric. and Econ.). Conservative Research Dept, 1973–75. MEP (C) Norfolk, 1979–94; contested (C) Eur. Parly elecns, 1994. Mem., Agricl, Foreign Affairs and Fisheries Cttees, European Parlt, 1979–94; spokesman for EDG: on youth culture, educn, information and sport, 1984–86; on agriculture, 1989–92; on fisheries, 1989–94; Mem. and EDG spokesman, Regl Cttee, 1992–94; Member, European Parliament's delegation: to Central America, 1987–94; to Soviet Union, 1989–91; to CIS, 1991–94; to Russia, Ukraine, Georgia, Armenia and Azerbaijan, 1993–94; Vice-Chm., Europ. Parlt/Comecon Delegn, 1984; Pres., Council of Centre for Eur. Educn, 1985–87. Chm., Riceman Insurance Investments plc, 1995–99. Mem. Council, and Trustee, RSPB, 1992–95; Trustee, Nuffield Russia Trust, 1991–. *Recreations:* all sports. *Address:* The White House Farm, Bradenham Road, Scarning, East Dereham, Norfolk NR19 2LA.

HOWELL, Peter Adrian; Senior Lecturer, Department of Classics, Royal Holloway and Bedford New College, University of London, 1994–99 (Lecturer, 1985–94), now Hon. Research Fellow; *b* 29 July 1941; *s* of Lt-Col Harry Alfred Adrian Howell, MBE and Madge Maud Mary, *d* of Major-Gen. R. L. B. Thompson, CB, CMG, DSO. *Educ:* Downside School; Balliol College, Oxford (BA 1963; MA; MPhil 1966). Asst Lectr and Lectr, Dept of Latin, Bedford Coll., Univ. of London, 1964–85. Dep. Chm., Jt Cttee, Nat. Amenity Socs, 1991–93; Member: Cttee, Victorian Soc., 1968– (Chm., 1987–93); Westminster Cathedral Art Cttee, 1974–91, 1993–; Dept of Art and Architecture, Liturgy Commn, RC Bishops' Conf., 1977–84; Churches Cttee, English Heritage, 1984–88; RC Historic Churches Cttee for Wales and Herefordshire, 1995–; Westminster Diocesan Historic Churches Cttee, 1995–99. *Publications:* Victorian Churches, 1968; (with Elisabeth Beazley) Companion Guide to North Wales, 1975; (with Elisabeth Beazley) Companion Guide to South Wales, 1977; A Commentary on Book I of the Epigrams of Martial, 1980; (ed with Ian Sutton) The Faber Guide to Victorian Churches, 1989; (ed and trans.) Martial: the Epigrams Book V, 1995; articles in Architectural History, Country Life. *Recreations:* art, architecture, music. *Address:* 127 Banbury Road, Oxford OX2 6JX. *T:* (01865) 515050.

HOWELL, Sir Ralph (Frederic), Kt 1993; *b* 25 May 1923; *m* 1950, Margaret (*née* Bone); two *s* one *d*. *Educ:* Diss Grammar Sch., Norfolk. Navigator/Bomb-aimer, RAF, 1941–46; farmer, 1946–. Mem., European Parlt, 1974–79. MP (C) N Norfolk, 1970–97. Member: Treasury and Civil Service Select Cttee, 1981–87; Select Cttee on Employment, 1994–97. Vice-Chm., Cons. Parly Finance Cttee, 1979–84; Chairman: Cons. Parly Employment Cttee, 1984–87; Cons. Parly Agriculture Cttee, 1988; Mem. Exec., 1922 Cttee, 1984–90; Mem., Council of Europe and WEU, 1987–97. *Publications:* Why Work, 1976, 2nd edn 1981; Why Not Work, 1991; Putting Britain Back to Work, 1995. *Club:* Farmers'.
See also P. F. Howell.

HOWELL, Rupert Cortlandt Spencer, FIPA; Founder, 1987, and Chairman, since 1999, HHCL & Partners (formerly Howell Henry Chaldecott Lury Ltd); Joint Chief Executive, Chime Communications plc, since 1997; President, Institute of Practitioners in Advertising, since 1999; *b* 6 Feb. 1957; *s* of Lt Col F. R. Howell, MBE, RE retd, and S. D. L. Howell (*née* McCallum); *m* 1987, Claire Jane Ashworth; one *s* one *d*. *Educ:* Wellington Coll.; Univ. of Warwick (BSc Mgt Scis). FIPA 1995. Mkting trainee, Lucas Service Overseas, 1978; Account Exec., Mathers Advertising, 1979–81; Account Supervisor, Grey Advertising, 1981–83; Young & Rubicam: Account Dir, 1983–84; New Business Dir, 1985–86; Hd, Client Services, 1987; Man. Partner, 1987–97, Jt Chief Exec., 1997–98, Howell Henry Chaldecott Lury Ltd, subseq. HHCL & Partners. *Recreations:* golf, ski-ing (participating); cricket, Rugby Union, soccer (spectating); cinema. *Address:* HHCL & Partners, Kent House, 14–17 Market Place, Great Titchfield Street, W1N 7AJ. *T:* (020) 7436 3333. *Clubs:* MCC, Lord's Taverners, Thirty; Wentworth (Surrey).

HOWELL, Prof. Simon Laurence, PhD, DSc; Professor of Physiology, King's College London, since 1985; Head, Guy's, King's and St Thomas' School of Biomedical Sciences, King's College London, since 1998; *b* 29 June 1943; *s* of Laurence James Howell and Joan Kathleen Rosemary (*née* Wheelwright); *m* 1969, Linda Margaret Chapman; one *d*. *Educ:* St John's Sch., Leatherhead; Chelsea Coll., London (BSc Hons 1964); KCL (PhD 1967); DSc London 1983. Res. Fellow, Univ. of Sussex, 1968–78; Lectr, Charing Cross Hosp. Med. Sch., London, 1978–80; Reader, Queen Elizabeth Coll., London, 1980–85; Hd, Biomed. Scis Div., KCL, 1988–98. Minkowski Prize, Eur. Assoc. Study of Diabetes, 1983. *Publications:* (jtly) Biochemistry of the Polypeptide Hormones, 1985; (jtly) Diabetes and its Management, 5th edn 1996; The Biology of the Pancreatic B Cell, 1999. *Recreations:* gardening, opera. *Address:* Guy's, King's and St Thomas' School of Biomedical Sciences, King's College London, Guy's Campus, SE1 9UL.

HOWELLS, family name of **Baron Geraint** and **Baroness Howells of St Davids**.

HOWELLS OF ST DAVIDS, Baroness *cr* 1999 (Life Peer), of Charlton in the London Borough of Greenwich; **Rosalind Patricia-Anne Howells,** OBE 1994; Vice Chair, London Voluntary Services Council; *b* Grenada, WI, 10 Jan. 1931; *m* 1955, John Charles Howells; two *d*. *Educ:* St Joseph's Convent, Grenada; South West London Coll. (Cert. Welfare and Counselling); City Univ., Washington. Formerly Dep. High Comr for Grenada in London; Equal Opportunities Dir, Greenwich Council for Racial Equality, 1980–87; Chair, Lewisham Racial Equality Council, 1994–97; Mem., Commn on Future of Multi-Ethnic Britain. Governor, Avery Hill Coll., later Thames Poly., then Univ. of Greenwich, 1985–97. Trustee: West Indian Standing Conf.; City Parochial Foundn; Museum of Ethnic Arts; Women of the Year Cttee; Stephen Lawrence Charitable Trust. DUniv Greenwich, 1998. *Recreations:* travelling, adventurous food, all types of music. *Address:* c/o House of Lords, SW1A 0PW.

HOWELLS, Anne Elizabeth, FRMCM; opera, concert and recital singer; Professor, Royal Academy of Music, since 1997; *b* 12 Jan. 1941; *d* of Trevor William Howells and Mona Hewart; *m* 1st, 1966, Ryland Davies, *qv* (marr. diss. 1981); 2nd, 1981, Stafford Dean (marr. diss. 1996); one *s* one *d*; 3rd, 1999, Peter R. Fyson. *Educ:* Sale County Grammar Sch.; Royal Northern (subseq. Royal Manchester) Coll. of Music (ARMCM; Hon. Fellow); studied under Frederick Cox and Vera Rosza. Three seasons (Chorus), with Glyndebourne, 1964–66; at short notice given star rôle there in Cavalli's L'Ormindo, 1967; rôles there also include: Dorabella in Così fan Tutte; Cathleen in (world première of) Nicholas Maw's Rising of the Moon, 1970; the Composer in Ariadne; Diana in Calisto; under contract, 1969–71, subseq. Guest Artist, Royal Opera, Covent Garden; sings with Scottish Opera, ENO and major orchs in UK; recitals in Brussels and Vienna; operatic guest performances incl. La Scala (Milan), Chicago, Metropolitan (NY), San Francisco, Geneva, Brussels, Salzburg, Amsterdam, Hamburg (W German début), W Berlin, Paris. Rôles include: Lena in (world première of) Richard Rodney Bennett's Victory; Rosina in Barber of Seville; Cherubino in Marriage of Figaro; Zerlina in Don Giovanni; Giulietta in The Tales of Hoffmann; Orsini in Lucrezia Borgia; Ascanius in Benvenuto Cellini; Helen in King Priam; Judit in Bluebeard's Castle; Octavian in Der Rosenkavalier (video recording), 1985; Annius in La Clemenza di Tito (film of Salzburg prodn); Lady Hautdesert in (world première of) Gawain, 1994. *Recreations:* theatre, cinema, reading. *Address:* c/o IMG, Media House, 3 Burlington Lane, W4 2JH.

HOWELLS, Sir Eric (Waldo Benjamin), Kt 1993; CBE 1986; farmer and landowner, since 1966; *b* 9 Aug. 1933; *s* of Vincent Vaughan Howells and Amy (*née* Jones); *m* 1960, Margaret Maisie Edwards; one *s* twin *d*. Sec. and Gen. Manager of a limited co., 1959–66; Director: Carmarthen and Pumsaint Farmers Ltd, 1997–; Welsh Milk Ltd, 2000–. Chm., Whitland and Dist Abattoir Cttee, 2001–. Former Chm., Pembrokeshire NFU. Mem., Llanddewi Velfrey Parish, subseq. Community, Council (Chm., 1967, 1974, 1981, 1988, 1995, 2001); Chm., 1978–87, Pres., 1987–90, Pembrokeshire Cons. and Unionist Assoc.; Wales Area Conservative Party: Treas., 1984–88; Dep. Chm., 1988–90; Chm., 1990–95; Pres., 1996–99; Life Vice-Pres. Chm., Wales Area Cons. European Co-ordinating Cttee, 1992–95; Mem. of numerous other local and nat. Cons. and other bodies; regular broadcaster on radio and television in English and Welsh. Deacon and Treas., Bethel Congregational Chapel, Llanddewi Velfry, 1974–. *Recreations:* music, bee keeping, DIY, reading, writing. *Address:* Meadow View, Llanddewi Velfrey, Narberth, Pembrokeshire SA67 7EJ. *T:* (01994) 240205.

HOWELLS, Gwyn; Director General, Meat and Livestock Commission, since 1999; *b* 21 May 1949; *s* of late Emrys Howells and Edith Frances (*née* Taylor); *m* 1976, Margaret Anne Farrall (*d* 1995); one *s* one *d*. *Educ:* Lewis Sch. for Boys, Pengam; City of London Poly. (BSc Econs 1970). Sen. Brand Manager, Gallaher Ltd, 1971–82; Dir, Brand and Trade Mktg, Courage Ltd, 1982–89; Marketing Director: Reebok UK Ltd, 1989–92; Meat and Livestock Commn, 1992–99. *Recreations:* Rugby football, tennis, theatre. *Address:* Meat and Livestock Commission, PO Box 44, Winterhill House, Snowdon Drive, Milton Keynes MK6 1AX. *T:* (01908) 844220. *Clubs:* Hampstead Rugby Football, Rhymney Rugby Football.

HOWELLS, Kim Scott, PhD; MP (Lab) Pontypridd, since Feb. 1989; Parliamentary Under-Secretary of State, Department for Culture, Media and Sport, since 2001; *b* 27 Nov. 1946; *s* of Glanville James and Joan Glenys Howells; *m* 1983, Eirlys Howells (*née* Davies); two *s* one *d*. *Educ:* Mountain Ash Grammar Sch.; Hornsey College of Art; Cambridge College of Advanced Technology (BA (Jt Hons)); Warwick Univ. (PhD). Steel-worker, 1969–70; Coal-miner, 1970–71; Lectr, 1975–79; Research Officer: Swansea Univ., 1979–82; NUM, S Wales Area, 1982–89. Opposition Front bench spokesman on aid and develt, 1993–94, on foreign affairs, 1994, on home affairs, 1994–95, on trade and industry, 1995–97; Parliamentary Under-Secretary of State: DFEE, 1997–98; DTI, 1998–2001. Mem., British Mountaineering Council. *Recreations:* climbing, jazz, cinema, literature, art. *Address:* House of Commons, SW1A 0AA. *Clubs:* Llantwit Fadre Cricket, Pontypridd Rugby Football (Pontypridd); Hopkinstown Cricket (Pontypridd).

HOWES, Sir Christopher (Kingston), KCVO 1999 (CVO 1997); CB 1993; Second Commissioner and Chief Executive of the Crown Estate, 1989–2001; Member: HRH Prince of Wales's Council, since 1990; Council, Duchy of Lancaster, since 1993; *b* 30 Jan. 1942; *yr s* of late Leonard Howes, OBE and Marion Howes (*née* Bussey); *m* 1967, Clare Cunliffe; one *s* one *d* (and one *s* one *d* decd). *Educ:* Gresham's Sch.; Coll. of Estate Management, Univ. of London (BSc 1965); Univ. of Reading (MPhil 1976). ARICS 1967, FRICS 1977. Valuation and Planning Depts, GLC, 1965–67; Partner and Sen. Partner, Chartered Surveyors, Norwich, 1967–79; Department of the Environment: Dep. Dir, Land Economy, 1979–81; Chief Estates Officer, 1981–85; Dir, Land and Property Div., 1985–89. Sen. Vis. Fellow, Sch. of Envtl Scis, UEA, 1975; Vis. Lectr, Univs of Reading, 1976, Aberdeen 1980–; Vis. Prof., Bartlett Sch. of Architecture and Planning, UCL, 1984–. Mem., Sec. of State for the Envmt's Thames Adv. Cttee, 1995–98. Member: CNAA Surveying Bd, 1978–82; Planning and Develt Divl Council, RICS, 1983–92; Policy Review Cttee, RICS, 1984–90; RIBA Awards Gp, 1997–; Norfolk Archaeological Trust, 1979–; Council, British Property Fedn, 1992–. Jt Chm., World Land Policy Congress, London, 1986. Hon. Mem., Cambridge Univ. Land Soc., 1989–. Founder Mem., Norwich Third World Centre, 1970; dir of various housing assocs, 1970–80; non-exec. Dir, Norwich & Peterborough Building Soc., 1998–; Chm., Rivercastle Ltd; Member, Advisory Board: Barclays Private Banking; Aldeburgh Productions. Dir, Theatre Royal Trust, 1969–79; Steward and Hon Surveyor to Dean and Chapter, Norwich Cathedral, 1973–79; Trustee, British Architectural Library Trust, 1997–; Member: Court of Advisers, St Paul's Cathedral, 1980–99; Court, UEA, 1992–; Court of Advisers, HRH The Prince of Wales's Inst. of Architecture, 1992–99. Norwich CC, 1969–73; JP Norfolk 1973–80. Hon. FRIBA 1995. Hon. LittD E Anglia, 2000. Mem. of various editorial bds. *Publications:* (jtly) Acquiring Office Space, 1975; Value Maps: aspects of land and property values, 1979; Economic Regeneration (monograph), 1988; Urban Revitalization (monograph), 1988; papers on land and property policy in learned jls. *Recreations:* music, art, architecture, sailing. *Address:* (office) 8 Upper Grosvenor Street, W1K 2LY. *T:* (020) 7493 3666, *Fax:* (020) 7493 4666. *Clubs:* Athenæum, Garrick; Norfolk (Norwich); Aldeburgh Yacht; Aldeburgh Golf.

HOWES, Sally Ann; actress (stage, film and television); *b* 20 July; *d* of late Bobby Howes; *m* 1958, Richard Adler (marr. diss.); *m* 1969, Andrew Maree (marr. diss.). *Educ:* Glendower, London; Queenswood, Herts; privately. *Films include:* Thursday's Child, 1943; Halfway House, 1943; Dead of Night, 1945; Nicholas Nickleby, 1947; Anna Karenina, 1948; My Sister and I; Fools Rush In; History of Mr Polly, 1949; Stop Press Girl; Honeymoon Deferred; The Admirable Crichton, 1957; Chitty, Chitty Bang Bang, 1968. First appeared West End stage in (revue) Fancy Free, at Prince of Wales's, and at Royal Variety Performance, 1950. *Stage Shows include:* Caprice (musical debut); Paint Your Wagon; Babes in the Wood; Romance by Candlelight; Summer Song; Hatful of Rain; My Fair Lady; Kwamina, NY; What Makes Sammy Run?, NY; Brigadoon (revival), NY City Center, 1962; Sound of Music, Los Angeles and San Francisco, 1972; Lover, St Martin's; The King and I, Adelphi, 1973, Los Angeles and San Francisco, 1974; Hans Andersen, Palladium, 1977; Hamlet (tour), 1983; The Dead, NY, 2000. Has appeared on television: in England from 1949 (Short and Sweet Series, Sally Ann Howes Show, etc); in USA from 1958 (Dean Martin Show, Ed Sullivan Show, Mission Impossible, Marcus Welby MD); Play of the Week; Panel Shows: Hollywood Squares; Password; Bell Telephone Hour; US Steel Hour, etc. *Recreations:* reading, riding, theatre.

HOWICK OF GLENDALE, 2nd Baron *cr* 1960; **Charles Evelyn Baring;** a Director, Northern Rock plc (formerly Northern Rock Building Society), 1987–2001; a Managing Director, Baring Brothers & Co. Ltd, 1969–82; *b* 30 Dec. 1937; *s* of 1st Baron Howick of Glendale, KG, GCMG, KCVO, and of Lady Mary Cecil Grey, *er d* of 5th Earl Grey; *S* father, 1973; *m* 1964, Clare Nicolette, *y d* of Col Cyril Darby; one *s* three *d*. *Educ:* Eton; New Coll., Oxford. Director: The London Life Association Ltd, 1972–82; Swan Hunter Group Ltd, 1972–79. Member: Exec. Cttee, Nat. Art Collections Fund, 1973–86; Council, Friends of Tate Gall., 1973–78; Adv. Cttee, Westonbirt Arboretum, 1995–. Dir, Chelsea Physic Garden, 1994–. Mem. Council, Baring Foundn, 1982–99; Trustee: Northern Rock Foundn, 1997–; Royal Botanic Gdns, Edinburgh, 2001–. *Heir: s* Hon. David Evelyn Charles Baring, *b* 26 March 1975. *Address:* Howick, Alnwick, Northumberland NE66 3LB. *T:* (01665) 577624; 42 Bedford Gardens, W8 7EH. *T:* (020)

7221 0880.
See also Sir E. H. T. Wakefield.

HOWIE, family name of **Baron Howie of Troon.**

HOWIE OF TROON, Baron *cr* 1978 (Life Peer), of Troon in the District of Kyle and Carrick; **William Howie;** civil engineer, publisher, journalist; Director: (Internal Relations), Thomas Telford Ltd, 1987–96 (General Manager, 1976–87); PMS Publications Ltd, since 1996; SETO, since 1996; *b* Troon, Ayrshire, 2 March 1924; *er s* of late Peter and Annie Howie, Troon; *m* 1951, Mairi Margaret, *o d* of late Martha and John Sanderson, Troon; two *d* two *s*. *Educ:* Marr Coll., Troon; Royal Technical Coll., Glasgow (BSc, Diploma). MP (Lab) Luton, Nov. 1963–70; Asst Whip, 1964–66; Lord Comr of the Treasury, 1966–67; Comptroller, HM Household, 1967–68. A Vice-Chm., Parly Labour Party, 1968–70. MICE 1951, FICE 1984; Member: Council, Instn of Civil Engineers, 1964–67; Cttee of Inquiry into the Engineering Profession, 1977–80; President: Assoc. of Supervisory and Exec. Engrs, 1980–85; Assoc. for Educnl and Trng Technol., 1982–93; Indep. Publishers Guild, 1987–93; Vice-President: PPA, 1990–; Combustion Engrg Assoc., 1999–. Member: Governing Body, Imperial Coll. of Science and Technology, 1965–67; Pro-Chancellor, City Univ., 1984–91 (Mem. Council 1968–91). MSocIS (France), 1978. Hon. FIStructE 1995; Hon. FABE 2000. Hon. DSc City Univ., 1992; Hon. LLD Strathclyde, 1994. *Publications:* (jtly) Public Sector Purchasing, 1968; Trade Unions and the Professional Engineer, 1977; Trade Unions in Construction, 1981; (ed jtly) Thames Tunnel to Channel Tunnel, 1987. *Recreation:* opera. *Address:* 34 Temple Fortune Lane, NW11 7UL. *T:* (020) 8455 0492. *Clubs:* Luton Labour, Lighthouse, Architecture.

HOWIE, Prof. Archibald, CBE 1998; PhD; FRS 1978; Professor of Physics, Cavendish Laboratory, University of Cambridge, since 1986; Fellow of Churchill College, Cambridge, since 1960; *b* 8 March 1934; *s* of Robert Howie and Margaret Marshall McDonald; *m* 1964, Melva Jean Scott; one *d* (one *s* decd). *Educ:* Kirkcaldy High Sch.; Univ. of Edinburgh (BSc); California Inst. of Technology (MS); Univ. of Cambridge (PhD). English Speaking Union, King George VI Memorial Fellow (at Calif. Inst. of Technology), 1956–57; Cambridge University: Research Scholar, Trinity Coll., 1957–60; Research Fellow, Churchill Coll., 1960–61; Cavendish Laboratory: ICI Research Fellow, 1960–61; Demonstrator in Physics, 1961–65; Lecturer, 1965–79; Reader, 1979–86; Hd of Dept of Physics, 1989–97. Visiting Scientist, Nat. Research Council, Canada, 1966–67; Vis. Prof. of Physics, Univ. of Aarhus, Denmark, 1974. Dir, NPL Management Ltd, 1995–. Pres., Internat. Fedn of Socs for Electron Microscopy, 1999–. Hon. FRMS 1978 (Pres., 1984–86); Hon. FRSE 1995. Hon. Dr (Physics): Bologna, 1989; Thessaloniki, 1995. Distinguished Scientist Award, Electron Microscopy Soc. of America, 1991; Guthrie Medal, Inst. of Physics, 1992; Royal Medal, Royal Soc., 1999; (jtly with M. J. Whelan): C. V. Boys Prize, Inst. of Physics, 1965; Hughes Medal, Royal Soc., 1988. *Publications:* (co-author) Electron Microscopy of Thin Crystals, 1965, 2nd edn 1977; papers on electron microscopy and diffraction in scientific jls. *Recreations:* gardening, wine-making. *Address:* 194 Huntingdon Road, Cambridge CB3 0LB. *T:* (01223) 570977.

HOWIE, Prof. John Garvie Robertson, CBE 1996; MD, PhD; FRCGP, FRCPE, FMedSci; Professor of General Practice, University of Edinburgh, 1980–2000; *b* 23 Jan. 1937; *s* of Sir James Howie and of Isabella Winifred Mitchell, BEd; *m* 1962, Elizabeth Margaret Donald; two *s* one *d*. *Educ:* High School of Glasgow; Univ. of Glasgow (MD); PhD Aberdeen. House officer, 1961–62; Laboratory medicine, 1962–66; General practitioner, Glasgow, 1966–70; Lectr/Sen. Lectr in General Practice, Univ. of Aberdeen, 1970–80. Founder FMedSci 1998. *Publications:* Research in General Practice, 1979, 2nd edn 1989; A Day in the Life of Academic General Practice, 1999; articles on appendicitis, prescribing and general medical practice and education, in various jls. *Recreations:* golf, gardening, music. *Address:* 4 Ravelrig Park, Balerno, Midlothian EH14 7DL. *T:* (0131) 449 6305; *e-mail:* John.Howie@ed.ac.uk.

HOWIE, Prof. John Mackintosh, CBE 1993; Regius Professor of Mathematics, University of St Andrews, 1970–97; Dean, Faculty of Science, 1976–79; *b* 23 May 1936; *s* of Rev. David Y. Howie and Janet McD. Howie (*née* Mackintosh); *m* 1960, Dorothy Joyce Mitchell Miller; two *d*. *Educ:* Robert Gordon's Coll., Aberdeen; Univ. of Aberdeen; Balliol Coll., Oxford. MA, DPhil, DSc; FRSE 1971. Asst in Mathematics: Aberdeen Univ., 1958–59; Glasgow Univ., 1961–63; Lectr in Mathematics, Glasgow Univ., 1963–67; Visiting Asst Prof., Tulane Univ., 1964–65; Sen. Lectr in Mathematics, Stirling Univ., 1967–70; Visiting Professor: Monash Univ., 1979; N Illinois Univ., 1988; Univ. of Lisbon, 1996. Mem., Cttee to Review Examination Arrangements (Dunning Cttee), 1975–77; Chairman: Scottish Central Cttee on Mathematics, 1975–82; Cttee to Review Curriculum and Exams in Fifth and Sixth Years (Howie Cttee), Scottish Office Educn Dept, 1990–92. Vice-Pres., London Mathematical Soc., 1984–86. Chm., Bd of Governors, Dundee Coll. of Educn, 1983–87. DUniv Open, 2000. Keith Prize for 1979–81, RSE, 1982. *Publications:* An Introduction to Semigroup Theory, 1976; Automata and Languages, 1991; Fundamentals of Semigroup Theory, 1995; Real Analysis, 2001; articles in British and foreign mathematical jls. *Recreations:* music, gardening. *Address:* Longacre, 19 Strathkinness High Road, St Andrews, Fife KY16 9UA. *T:* (01334) 474103.

HOWIE, Prof. Robert Andrew, PhD, ScD; FGS; FKC; Lyell Professor of Geology, Royal Holloway and Bedford New College, University of London, 1985–87, now Emeritus Professor of Mineralogy; *b* 4 June 1923; *s* of Robert Howie; *m* 1st, 1952, Honor Eugenie (marr. diss. 1998), *d* of Robert Taylor; two *s*; 2nd, 1998, Irene, *d* of G. R. Ancliff. *Educ:* Bedford Sch.; Trinity Coll., Cambridge (MA, PhD, ScD). FGS 1950. Served War, RAF, 1941–46. Research, Dept of Mineralogy and Petrology, Univ. of Cambridge, 1950–53; Lectr in Geology, Manchester Univ., 1953–62; King's College, London: Reader in Geol., 1962–72; Prof. of Mineralogy, 1972–85; Fellow 1980; Dean, Faculty of Science, Univ. of London, 1979–83; Chairman: Academic Council, Univ. of London, 1983–86; Computer Policy Cttee, Univ. of London, 1987–93; Vice-Chm., Bd of Management, Univ. of London Computer Centre, 1989–93. Mem., Commonwealth Scholarships Commn, 1988–96. Geological Society: Mem. Council, 1968–71, 1972–76; Vice-Pres., 1973–75. Mineralogical Society: Mem. Council, 1958–61, 1963–; Gen. Sec., 1965; Ed., Mineralogical Abstracts, 1966– (designated Principal Ed., 1971–); Vice-Pres., 1975–77; Pres., 1978–80; Managing Trustee, 1978–87. Fellow, Mineral Soc. of America, 1962 (Dist. Public Service Award, 1999). Member: Gemmological Assoc and Gem Testing Lab. of GB, 1968– (Pres., 1996–2000; Hon. FGA 1996); Council, Internat. Mineral Assoc., 1974–82; Senate, Univ. of London, 1974–78, 1980–90; Court, Univ. of London, 1984–89. Hon. Mem., Mineralogical Soc. of India, 1973, of USSR, 1982, of France, 1986, of Bulgaria, 1991. Murchison Medal, Geol Soc., 1976. *Publications:* Rock-forming Minerals (with Prof. W. A. Deer and Prof. J. Zussman), 5 vols, 1962–63 (2nd edn in 10 vols, 1978–); An Introduction to the Rock-forming Minerals, 1966, 2nd edn 1992; scientific papers dealing with charnockites and with silicate mineralogy. *Recreations:* mineral collecting, writing abstracts. *Address:* Ashcroft, Glebe Close, Church Street, Bonsall, Matlock, Derbyshire DE4 2AE. *Club:* Geological.

HOWIE, Robert Bruce McNeill, QC (Scot.) 2000; *b* 24 Aug. 1960; *s* of Dr William Bruce McNeill Howie, OBE, and Dr Theresa Grant or Howie; *m* 1996 , Deidre Elizabeth Hughes Clark or Haigh; one *s*. *Educ:* Aberdeen Grammar Sch.; Aberdeen Univ. (LLB, DLP). Admitted Advocate, 1986. *Address:* 41a Fountainhall Road, Edinburgh EH9 2LN.

HOWITT, Anthony Wentworth; Senior Consultancy Partner, Peat, Marwick, Mitchell & Co., Management Consultants, 1957–84; *b* 7 Feb. 1920; *o s* of late Sir Harold Gibson Howitt, GBE, DSO, MC, and late Dorothy Radford; *m* 1951, June Mary Brent. *Educ:* Uppingham; Trinity Coll., Cambridge (MA). FCA, FCMA, JDipMA, CBIM, FIMC, FBCS. Commissioned RA; served in UK, ME and Italy, 1940–46 (Major). With Peat, Marwick, Mitchell & Co., Chartered Accountants, 1946–57. British Consultants Bureau: Vice-Chm., 1981–83; Mem. Council, 1968–75 and 1979–84; led mission to Far East, 1969. Member Council: Inst. of Management Consultants, 1964–77 (Pres., 1967–68); Inst. of Cost and Management Accountants, 1966–76 (Pres., 1972–73; Gold Medal, 1991); Management Consultants Assoc., 1966–84 (Chm., 1976); Mem., Devlin Commn of Inquiry into Industrial Representation, 1971–72. Member: Bd of Fellows of BIM, 1973–76; Adv. Panel to Overseas Projects Gp, 1973–76; Price Commn, 1973–77; Domestic Promotions Cttee, British Invisible Exports Council, 1984. Member Council: Anglo-Jordanian Soc., 1983–96; Anglo-Indonesian Soc., 1991–; Anglo-Arab Assoc., 1993–. Mem., Court of Assistants, Merchant Taylors' Co., 1971– (Master 1980–81). *Publications:* papers and addresses on professional and management subjects. *Recreations:* fox-hunting, tennis, golf. *Address:* 17 Basing Hill, Golders Green, NW11 8TE. *Clubs:* Army and Navy; MCC; Harlequins.

HOWITT, Fowler; *see* Howitt, W. F.

HOWITT, Richard Stuart; Member (Lab) Eastern Region, England, European Parliament, since 1999 (Essex South, 1994–99); *b* 5 April 1961. *Educ:* Lady Margaret Hall, Oxford (BA); Univ. of Hertfordshire (DMS). Community worker, 1982–94. Mem. (Lab), Harlow DC, 1984–94 (Leader, 1991–94). Contested (Lab) Billericay, 1987. Hon. Pres., SE Econ. Develt Strategy Assoc., 1994– (Chm., 1986–94); Hon. Vice-President: ADC, 1994–97; LGA, 1997–; Trustee, Centre for Local Econ. Strategies, 1994–. Mem., Labour Party Nat. Policy Forum and NEC Local Govt sub-cttee, 1994–. European Parliament: First Vice-Pres., Regl Affairs Cttee, 1997–99 (Mem., 1994–96); Pres., All-Party Disability Gp, 1999–; Rapporteur: Europe and UN Social Summit, 1995; European Funding for Local and Regl Authorities, 1995; European Refugee Policy, 1996; Guidelines for Effective European Projects, 1998; European Code of Conduct for Enterprises, 1999. *Address:* Labour European Office, Labour Hall, Collingwood Road, Witham, Essex CM8 2EE. *T:* (01376) 51700, *Fax:* (01376) 501900; *e-mail:* richard.howitt@geo2.poptel.org.uk.

HOWITT, W(illiam) Fowler, DA (Dundee); FRIBA; architect and hospital planning consultant, retired; *b* Perth, Scotland, May 1924; *s* of late Frederick Howitt, Head Postmaster, Forfar; *m* 1951, Ann Elizabeth, *o d* of late A. J. Hedges, Radipole, Dorset; three *s* one *d*. *Educ:* Perth Academy. Royal Marines, 1943–46. Sch. of Architecture, Dundee, 1948; RIBA Victory Scholar, 1949. Asst Louis de Soissons, London (housing and flats), 1949–52; Prin. Asst to Vincent Kelly, Dublin (hosps and offices), 1952–55; Architect to St Thomas' Hosp. (Hosp. rebuilding schemes, flats, offices), 1955–64; Partner, Cusdin Burden and Howitt, Architects, 1965–90. Projects include: design and supervision of Coll. of Medicine and King Khalid Hosp., King Saud Univ., Riyadh, Saudi Arabia; design of teaching hospitals: Abuja city and Niger State, Nigeria; children's hospitals, Anambra and Imo States, Nigeria; Addenbrooke's Hosp., Cambridge; Royal Victoria Hosp., Belfast, planning consultancy, 1980–: gen. hosps, Sharjah and Fujairah, UAE; King Fahad Medical City, Riyadh, Saudi Arabia; Polyclinico Teaching Hosp., Milan; private hosp., Milan; gen. hosps Como and Varese. *Recreations:* reading, golf. *Address:* 32 Gloucester Road, Teddington, Middx TW11 0NU. *T:* (020) 8977 5772; 143 Allée des Goelands, 62730 Marck, France. *T:* 321854252.

HOWKINS, John, MD; FRCS; Gynæcological Surgeon to St Bartholomew's Hospital, 1946–69 (Hon. Consultant Gynæcologist since 1969), to Hampstead General Hospital 1946–67 (Hon. Consultant Gynæcologist, since 1968), and to Royal Masonic Hospital, 1948–73; *b* 17 Dec. 1907; *m* 1940, Lena Brown; one *s* two *d*. *Educ:* Shrewsbury Sch.; London Univ. Arts Scholar, Middlesex Hospital, 1926; MRCS, LRCP 1932; MB, BS London, 1933; FRCS 1936; MS London, 1936; MD (Gold Medal) London, 1937; MRCOG 1937, FRCOG 1947. House Surgeon and Casualty Surgeon, Middlesex Hosp., 1932–34; RMO, Chelsea Hosp. for Women, 1936; Gynæcological Registrar, Middlesex Hosp., 1937–38; Resident Obstetric Surg., St Bartholomew's Hosp., 1938 and 1945; Temp. Wing-Comdr, RAFVR Med. Br., 1939–45. Hunterian Prof., RCS 1947. William Meredith Fletcher Shaw Lectr, RCOG, 1975. Sometime Examiner in Midwifery to Univs of Cambridge and London, RCOG, Conjoint Bd of England. Chm. Council, Ski Club of Great Britain, 1964–67 (Hon. Life Member, 1968, Trustee, 1969–); Mem., Gynaecological Travellers' Club. *Publications:* Shaw's Textbook of Gynæcology, 7th edn 1956 to 9th edn 1971; Shaw's Textbook of Operative Gynaecology, 2nd edn 1960 to 5th edn (jtly) 1983; (jtly) Bonney's Textbook of Gynæcological Surgery, 7th edn 1964, 8th edn 1974. *Recreations:* ski-ing, salmon fishing, sheep farming. *Address:* Caen Hen, Abercegir, Machynlleth, Powys, Wales SY20 8NR. *Clubs:* Ski Club of Great Britain; Wilks XV (Hon. Mem.).

HOWKINS, John Anthony; consultant and writer; *b* 3 Aug. 1945; *s* of Col Ashby Howkins and Lesley (*née* Stops); *m* 1st, 1971, Jill Liddington; 2nd, 1977, Annabel Whittet. *Educ:* Rugby Sch.; Keele Univ.; Architectural Association's Sch. of Architecture (Dip.). Marketing Manager, Lever Bros, 1968–70; founder, TV4 Gp, 1971; TV/Radio Editor, Books Editor, Time Out, 1971–74; Sec., Standing Conf. on Broadcasting, 1975–76; Editor, InterMedia, Journal of IIC, 1975–84. Gov., London Internat. Film Sch., 1976– (Chm., 1979–84); Member: Interim Action Cttee on the Film Industry, DTI, 1980–84; British Screen Adv. Council, DTI, 1985– (Dep. Chm., 1991–); Vice-Chm. (New Media), Assoc. of Independent Producers, 1984–85. Exec. Editor, National Electronics Review, 1981–99; TV Columnist, Illustrated London News, 1981–83; Exec. Dir, Internat. Inst. of Communications, 1984–89. Chm., Tornado Productions, 2000–; Director: Television Investments, 1993–; Equator Gp plc, 1999–; Project Dir, World Learning Network, 1996–. Specialist Advr, Select Cttee on European Communities, House of Lords, 1985–87; Adviser: Broadcasting Reform Commn, Poland, 1989–90; Polish-Radio-and-Television, 1991–94; Minister of Film, Poland, 1991–92; Chm., Adv. Bd, Createc, 1996–2000; Co-ordinator, Eur. Audiovisual Conf., 1997–98. Associate, Coopers Lybrand Deloitte, 1990–91. Special European Consultant, HBO Inc. (and other Time Warner Inc. cos), 1981–85 and 1989–95. UK Rep., Transatlantic Dialogue on Broadcasting and Information Soc., 1998–. *Publications:* Understanding Television, 1977; The China Media Industry, 1980; Mass Communications in China, 1982; New Technologies, New Policies, 1982; Satellites International, 1987; (with Michael Foster) Television in '1992': a guide to Europe's new TV, film and video business, 1989; Four Global Scenarios on Information/Communication Technology and Development, 1997; The Creative Economy, 2001. *Address:* E6 Albany, Piccadilly, W1J 0AR. *T:* (020) 7434 1400; *e-mail:* howkins@compuserve.com.

HOWLAND, Lord; Andrew Ian Henry Russell; Partner, Bloomsbury Stud, since 1985; Director: Tattersalls Ltd, since 1992; Newmarket Racecourses Trust, since 1996; *b* 30 March 1962; *s* and *heir* of Marquess of Tavistock, *qv*; *m* 2000, Louise, *d* of late Donald Crammond and of Dowager Lady Delves Broughton; one *d*. *Educ:* Heatherdown; Harrow; Harvard. *Recreations:* shooting, golf, racing. *Address:* 6 Fairlawns, Dullingham Road, Newmarket, Suffolk CB8 9JS; (office) Tattersalls Ltd, Terrace House, High Street, Newmarket, Suffolk CB8 9BT. *Clubs:* Jockey; AD (Cambridge, Mass).

HOWLAND JACKSON, Anthony Geoffrey Clive; Chairman, General Insurance Standards Council, since 1999; Director, Hiscox PLC, since 1997; *b* 25 May 1941; *s* of late Arthur Geoffrey Howland Jackson and of Pamela (*née* Wauton); *m* 1963, Susan Ellen Hickson; one *s* two *d*. *Educ:* Sherborne Sch. Chief Executive: H. Clarkson Insurance Hldgs, 1979–81; Clarkson Puckle, 1981–83; Dir, Gill & Duffus plc, 1983–87; Man. Dir, Bain Clarkson Ltd, 1987; Dep. Chm. and Chief Exec., 1987–93, Chm., 1993–94, Hogg Group plc; Chm., Bain Hogg plc, 1994–97. Dir, AON UK Hldgs, 1997–99. Lloyd's: Mem., 1976–; Mem., Regulatory Bd, 1993–; Chm., Lloyd's Insurance Brokers' Cttee, 1996, 1998, 1999. Mem., Worshipful Co. of Insurers, 1981–. *Recreations:* shooting, cricket, racing, golf. *Address:* General Insurance Standards Council, 110 Cannon Street, EC4N 6EU. *Club:* Turf.

HOWLETT, Anthony Douglas, RD 1971; Remembrancer of the City of London, 1981–86; *b* 30 Dec. 1924; *s* of late Ernest Robert Howlett and Catherine (*née* Broughton), Grantham, Lincs; *m* 1952, Alfreda Dorothy Pearce, *yr d* of Arthur W. Pearce, Hove, Sussex. *Educ:* King's Sch., Rochester; Wellingborough; King's Sch., Grantham; Trinity Coll., Cambridge. BA Hons 1948, LLB 1949, MA 1950. Served War, 1939–46, RNVR; RNVSR, 1951–60; RNR, 1960–75 (Lt Comdr 1968). Hon. Mem., HMS President. Called to the Bar, Gray's Inn, 1950; joined Legal Br., BoT, 1951; Sen. Legal Assistant, 1960; Asst Solicitor, 1972, i/c Export Credit Guarantees Br., 1972–75, i/c Merchant Shipping Br., 1975–81. UK delegate: London Diplomatic Conf. on Limitation of Liability for Maritime Claims, 1976; Geneva Diplomatic Conf. on Multi-Modal Transport, 1980, and other internat. maritime confs. Vice-Chm., Enfield HA, 1987–93; Chm., Enfield Dist Res. Ethics Cttee, 1990–93. Founder Mem., Sherlock Holmes Soc. of London, 1951 (Chm., 1960–63, 1986–89; Pres., 1992–); Trustee, Crowborough Conan Doyle Trust Ltd, 1997–2001; Member: City Pickwick Club, 1988–; James Hilton Soc., 2001–. Freedom of City of London, 1981; Liveryman, Scriveners' Co., 1981–. OStJ 1986. Order of King Abdul Aziz (II) (Saudi Arabia), 1981; Order of Oman (III), 1982; Comdr, Order of Orange-Nassau (Netherlands), 1982; Officier, Légion d'Honneur (France), 1984; Comdr, Order of the Lion of Malaŵi, 1985; Order of Qatar (III), 1985. *Publications:* articles on Conan Doyle and Holmesiana. *Recreations:* book browsing, Sherlock Holmes, opera, photography, sailing and maritime history, foreign travel. *Address:* Rivendell, 37 Links Side, Enfield, Middlesex EN2 7QZ. *T:* (020) 8363 5802. *Club:* Naval.

HOWLETT, Elizabeth, (Elizabeth Robson); Member (C) Merton and Wandsworth, London Assembly, Greater London Authority, since 2000; Professor of Singing, Royal College of Music, since 1989; *b* 17 Jan. 1938; *d* of Walter James Robson and Lizzie Mason Robson (*née* Houston); *m* 1962, Neil Baillie Howlett (marr. diss. 1987); two *d*. *Educ:* Royal Scottish Acad. of Music (Sir James Caird Jun. and Sen. Scholarships; DRSAMD). Leading Lyric Soprano, Sadler's Wells Opera Co., 1961–65; Leading Soprano, Royal Opera House, Covent Gdn, 1965–70; Soprano, Staatsoper, Hamburg, 1970–74; guest engagements in Europe, S Africa, Japan, Korea, Canada, USA, Scottish Opera, WNO, Opera North, ENO, 1974–. Nat. and Internat. Examr, 1997–; Adjudicator, Festivales Musicales, Buenos Aires, 1995–. Mem. (C) Wandsworth BC, 1986– (Chairman: Social Services Cttee, 1989–92; Educn Cttee, 1992–98; Chief Whip, 1999–2000); Mayor of Wandsworth, 1998. Mem., Inner London Probation Bd, 1995–2001. Non-exec. Dir and Chm., Nat. Hosp. for Neurol. and Neurosurgery, 1990–96. Founder and Trustee, Margaret Dick Award for young Scottish singers, 1982–; Trustee, Foundn for Young Musicians, 1996–. Hon. Vice Patron, Ystradgynlais Male Voice Choir, 1985–. JP Wimbledon, 1985. Freeman, City of London, 1999. Eschanson of Roi René Award, Aix-en-Provence, 1970. *Recreations:* walking, theatre, music. *Address:* Greater London Authority, Romney House, 43 Marsham Street, SW1P 3PY. *Club:* Wimbledon.

HOWLETT, Gen. Sir Geoffrey (Hugh Whitby), KBE 1984 (OBE 1972); MC 1952; Chairman: Leonard Cheshire Foundation, 1990–95; Services Sound & Vision Corporation, 1991–99 (Vice-Chairman, 1989–91); *b* 5 Feb. 1930; *s* of Brig. B. Howlett, DSO, and Mrs Joan Howlett (later Latham); *m* 1955, Elizabeth Anne Aspinal; one *s* two *d*. *Educ:* Wellington Coll.; RMA, Sandhurst. Commnd Queen's Own Royal W Kent Regt, 1950; served, 1951–69: Malaya, Berlin, Cyprus and Suez; 3 and 2 Para, 16 Parachute Bde and 15 Para (TA); RAF Staff Coll. and Jt Services Staff Coll.; Mil. Asst to CINCNORTH, Oslo, 1969–71; CO 2 Para, 1971–73; RCDS, 1973–75; Comd 16 Parachute Bde, 1975–77; Dir, Army Recruiting, 1977–79; GOC 1st Armoured Div., 1979–82; Comdt, RMA, Sandhurst, 1982–83; GOC SE District, 1983–85; C-in-C Allied Forces Northern Europe, 1986–89, retd. Colonel Commandant: ACC, 1981–89; Parachute Regt, 1983–90. Comr, Royal Hosp., Chelsea, 1989–95. President: CCF, 1989–2000; Army Benevolent Fund for Dorset, 1992–2000; Regular Forces Employment Assoc., 1993–97 (Vice-Chm., 1989–90; Chm., 1990–93); Army Cricket Assoc., 1984–85; Combined Services Cricket Assoc., 1985; Stragglers of Asia Cricket Club, 1989–94. Visitor, Milton Abbey Sch., 2001– (Chm. of Govs, 1994–2000). Liveryman, Cooks' Co., 1991–. Cross of Merit, 1st cl. (Lower Saxony), 1982. *Recreations:* cricket, shooting, racing. *Address:* c/o Lloyds TSB, Tonbridge, TN9 1DB. *Clubs:* Naval and Military, MCC.

HOWLETT, Air Vice-Marshal Neville Stanley, CB 1982; RAF retired, 1982; Member: Lord Chancellor's Panel of Independent Inquiry Inspectors, 1982–95; Pensions Appeal Tribunal, 1988–2000; *b* 17 April 1927; *s* of Stanley Herbert Howlett and Ethel Shirley Howlett (*née* Pritchard); *m* 1952, Sylvia, *d* of J. F. Foster; one *s* one *d*. *Educ:* Liverpool Inst. High Sch.; Peterhouse, Cambridge. RAF pilot training, 1945–47; 32 and 64 (Fighter) Squadrons, 1948–56; RAF Staff Coll. Course, 1957; Squadron Comdr, 229 (Fighter) OCU, 1958–59; OC Flying Wing, RAF Coltishall, 1961–63; Directing Staff, RAF Staff Coll., 1967–69; Station Comdr, RAF Leuchars, 1970–72; RCDS, 1972; Dir of Operations (Air Defence and Overseas), 1973–74; Air Attaché, Washington DC, 1975–77; Dir, Management Support of Intelligence, MoD, 1978–80; Dir Gen. of Personal Services (RAF), MoD, 1980–82. Vice-Pres., RAFA, 1984– (Chairman: Exec. Cttee, 1990–97; Central Council, 1999–). *Recreations:* golf, fishing. *Address:* Milverton, Bolney Trevor Drive, Lower Shiplake, Oxon RG9 3PG. *Clubs:* Royal Air Force; Phyllis Court (Henley); Huntercombe Golf.

HOWLETT, Ronald William, OBE 1986; Managing Director, Cwmbran Development Corporation, 1978–88, retired; *b* 18 Aug. 1928; *s* of Percy Edward Howlett and Lucy Caroline Howlett; *m* 1st, 1954, Margaret Megan Searl (marr. diss. 1990); two *s*; 2nd, 1996, Judith Lloyd Wade-Jones, *d* of Lt-Col N. L. Wade, OBE, TD. *Educ:* University Coll. London. BSc Eng (Hons); CEng; FICE. Crawley Develt Corp., 1953–56; Exec. Engr, Roads and Water Supply, Northern Nigeria, 1956–61; Bor. of Colchester, 1961–64; Cwmbran Develt Corp., 1964–65; Bor. of Slough, 1965–69; Dep. Chief Engr and Chief Admin. Officer, Cwmbran Develt Corp., 1969–78. *Recreations:* fishing, music. *Address:* Llangronwin, Llanbadoc, Usk, Monmouthshire NP5 1TL. *T:* (01291) 673493.

HOWSON, Peter John; painter, since 1981; *b* 27 March 1958; *s* of Tom and Janet Howson; *m* 1983, Frances Nevay (marr. diss.); *m* 1989, Terry Cullen; one *d*. *Educ:* Glasgow Sch. of Art (BA Hons 1981). Official British War Artist in Bosnia, 1993–95; The Times War Artist, Kosovo, 1999. DUniv Strathclyde. *Address:* c/o Flowers East, 199–205 Richmond Road, E8 3NJ.

HOYLAND, John, RA 1991 (ARA 1983); *b* 12 Oct. 1934; *s* of John Kenneth and Kathleen Hoyland; *m* 1957, Airi Karkkainen (marr. diss. 1968); one *s*. *Educ:* Sheffield Coll. of Art (NDD 1956); Royal Academy Schs (RA Cert. 1960). Taught at: Hornsey Coll. of Art, 1960–62; Chelsea Sch. of Art, 1962–69, Principal Lectr, 1965–69; St Martin's Sch. of Art, 1974–77; Slade Sch. of Art, 1974–77, 1980, 1983, resigned 1989; Charles A. Dana Prof. of Fine Arts, Colgate Univ., NY, 1972. Artist in residence: Studio Sch., NY, 1978; Melbourne Univ., 1979. Selector: Hayward Annual, 1979; RA Silver Jubilee exhibn, 1979; organized and curated Hans Hofman exhibn, Lateworks, Tate Gall., 1988. *One-man exhibitions* include: Marlborough New London Gall., 1964; Whitechapel Gall., 1967; Waddington Galls, 1967, annually 1969–71 and 1973–76, 1978, 1981, 1983, 1985, 1990; retrospectives: Serpentine Gall., 1979; RA, 1999 and in Canada, USA, Brazil, Italy, Portugal, W Germany and Australia. *Group exhibitions* include: Tate Gall., 1964; Hayward Gall., 1974; Walker Art Gall., Liverpool (in every John Moores exhibn, 1963–); British Art in the 20th Century, Royal Acad., 1987; Waddington Gall., 1987; Tate Gall. of Liverpool, 1993; Barbican Gall., 1993; also in Belgium, France, Japan and Norway. Work in public collections incl. RA, Tate Gall., V&A Mus. and other galls and instns in UK, Europe, USA and Australia. *TV appearances:* 6 Days in September, BBC TV, 1979; Signals, Channel 4, 1989. Designs for Zansa, Ballet Rambert, 1986. Gulbenkian Foundn purchase award, 1963; Peter Stuyvesant travel bursary, 1964; John Moores Liverpool exhibn prize, 1965, 1st prize, 1983; Open Paintings exhibn prize, Belfast, 1966; (jtly) 1st prize, Edinburgh Open 100 exhibn, 1969; 1st prize, Chichester Nat. Art exhibn, 1975; Arts Council purchase award, 1979; Athena Art Award, 1987. Order of the Southern Cross (Brazil), 1986. *Relevant publication:* John Hoyland, by Mel Gooding, 1990. *Address:* 41 Charterhouse Square, EC1M 6EA.

HOYLE, family name of **Baron Hoyle**.

HOYLE, Baron *cr* 1997 (Life Peer), of Warrington in the co. of Cheshire; **Eric Douglas Harvey Hoyle;** consultant; *b* 17 Feb. 1930; *s* of late William Hoyle and Leah Ellen Hoyle; *m* 1953, Pauline Spencer (*d* 1991); one *s*. *Educ:* Adlington C of E Sch.; Horwich and Bolton Techn. Colls. Engrg apprentice, British Rail, Horwich, 1946–51; Sales Engr, AEI, Manchester, 1951–53; Sales Engr and Marketing Executive, Charles Weston Ltd, Salford, 1951–74. Mem., Manchester Regional Hosp. Bd, 1968–74; Mem., NW Regional Health Authority, 1974–75. Contested (Lab): Clitheroe, 1964; Nelson and Colne, 1970 and Feb. 1974; MP (Lab): Nelson and Colne, Oct. 1974–1979; Warrington, July 1981–1983; Warrington N, 1983–97. Chm., PLP, 1992–97 (Mem., Trade and Industry Cttee, 1987–92); Mem., Select Cttee on Trade and Industry, 1984–92. Mem. Nat. Exec., Labour Party, 1978–82, 1983–85. A Lord in Waiting (Govt Whip), 1997–99. Pres., ASTMS, 1977–81, 1985–88 (Vice-Pres., 1981–85), MSF, 1988–91 (Jt Pres., 1988–90; Pres., 1990–91); Chm., ASTMS Parly Cttee, 1975–76. Pres., Adlington Cricket Club, 1974–; Chm., Warrington Rugby League Club, 1999–. JP 1958. *Recreations:* sport, cricket, theatre-going, reading. *Address:* House of Lords, SW1A 0PW.
See also Hon. L. H. Hoyle.

HOYLE, Prof. Eric; Professor of Education, 1971–96, now Professor Emeritus, and Senior Research Fellow, since 1996, Graduate School of Education, University of Bristol; *b* 22 May 1931; *s* of Percy and Bertha Hoyle; *m* 1954, Dorothy Mary Morley; one *s* two *d*. *Educ:* Preston Grammar Sch.; Univ. of London (BSc Sociology, MA). Taught, Harehills Secondary Sch., Leeds, 1953–58 (Head of English Dept, 1956–58); Head, English Dept, Batley High Sch., 1958–60; Lectr and Sen. Lectr in Educn, James Graham Coll., Leeds, 1961–64; Lectr and Sen. Lectr in Educn, Univ. of Manchester, 1965–71; Bristol University: Hd, Sch. of Educn, 1971–91; Dean, Faculty of Educn, 1974–77, 1983–86. Vis. Prof., Sch. of Management, Univ. of Lincs and Humberside, 1995–. Member: Avon Educn Cttee, 1977–80; Educnl Res. Bd, SSRC, 1973–78 (Vice-Chm., 1976–78); Bd of Management, NFER, 1976–94; Council, Exec. Council for Educn of Teachers, 1971 (Mem. Exec., 1978–81, 1987–90); Adviser to Public Schools Commn, 1968–70; consultant and advr on educnl mgt and professional develt of teachers to UNESCO, World Bank etc, SE Asia and Africa, 1972–. Editor, World Yearbook of Educn, 1980–86; founding Co-Editor, Research in Educn, 1969. *Publications:* The Role of the Teacher, 1969; (with J. Wilks) Gifted Children and their Education, 1974; The Politics of School Management, 1986; (with Peter John) Professional Knowledge and Professional Practice, 1995; contribs to professional jls. *Recreations:* music, reading, collecting first editions, walking, cooking. *Address:* 1 The Crescent, Henleaze, Bristol BS9 4RN. *T:* (0117) 962 0614; Graduate School of Education, University of Bristol, 35 Berkeley Square, Bristol BS8 1JA. *T:* (0117) 928 3000.

HOYLE, Hon. Lindsay (Harvey); MP (Lab) Chorley, since 1997; *b* 10 June 1957; *s* of Baron Hoyle, *qv*; *m* 1st, Lynda Anne Fowler (marr. diss. 1982); 2nd, Catherine Swindley; two *d*. *Educ:* Adlington County Sch.; Lord's Coll., Bolton. Owner of building co.; Man. Dir, textile printing co. Mem. (Lab) Chorley BC, 1980–98 (Dep. Leader, 1995–97; Chair, Economic Develt and Tourist Cttee); Mayor, 1997–98. Member: Trade and Industry Select Cttee, 1998–; H of C Catering Cttee, 1997–; All Pty Rugby League Gp, 1997– (Vice Chm., 1997–); All Pty Cricket Gp, 1997– (Treas., 1998–); Vice Chm., All Pty Tourism Gp, 1999–. Mem., Royal Lancs Agricl Show Soc. *Recreations:* Rugby League (former Chm., Chorley, now Lancashire, Lynx), cricket, football. *Address:* House of Commons, SW1A 0AA. *T:* (020) 7219 3000. *Clubs:* Adlington Cricket, Chorley Cricket.

HOYLE, Martin Trevor William Mordaunt; Radio Critic and Media Writer, Financial Times, since 1994; Classical Music and Opera Editor, Time Out, since 1988; *s* of Capt. T. W. Hoyle and Dora Marie (*née* Muller). *Educ:* Egypt and Canada; Clifton Coll.; Wadham Coll., Oxford (BA); Bristol Old Vic Sch.; Poly. of Central London Business Sch. Music Critic, Bristol Evening Post, 1963–67; freelance researcher, BBC TV 1965–; Sub-editor, John Calder Publishers, 1979–82; Theatre Critic, Financial Times, 1983–90; freelance writer on theatre, music, TV, film, books for Financial Times, Time Out, The Times, Mail on Sunday, Herald, The House, Independent on Sunday; reviews for Meridian (BBC World Service). *Publication:* The World of Opera: Mozart, 1996. *Recreation:* shouting at cyclists. *Address:* The Financial Times, 1 Southwark Bridge, SE1 9HL. *T:* (020) 7873 3000. *Club:* Chelsea Arts.

HOYLE, Susan; General Manager, The Place, since 1998; *b* 7 April 1953; *d* of Roland and Joan Hoyle. *Educ:* Univ. of Bristol (BA Drama and French). Education Officer, London Festival Ballet, 1980–83; Administrator, Extemporary Dance Th., 1983–86; Dance and Mime Officer, 1986–89, Dir of Dance, 1989–94, Arts Council of GB; Dep. Sec.-Gen., Arts Council of England, 1994–97; Head of Arts, British Council, France, 1997–98. Dir,

Shobana Jeyasingh Dance Co., 1998–. Mem., Franco-British Council, 2001. *Address:* (office) 17 Duke's Road, WC1H 9PY.

HOYT, Hon. William Lloyd; Chief Justice of New Brunswick, 1993–98; *b* 13 Sept. 1930; *m* 1954, Joan Millier; three *d. Educ:* Woodstock High Sch.; Acadia Univ. (BA, MA); Emmanuel Coll., Cambridge (BA Hons, MA; Hon. Fellow, 2001). Called to New Brunswick Bar, 1957; QC (NB) 1972; Associate, Limerick & Limerick, 1957–59; Partner, Limerick, Limerick & Hoyt and successor firm, Hoyt, Mockler, Allen & Dixon, 1959–81; Judge, 1981–84, Court of Appeal, 1984–98, New Brunswick. Mem., Bloody Sunday Tribunal of Inquiry (UK), 1998–. Member: Fredericton Barristers' Soc., 1957–81 (Pres., 1970–71); New Brunswick Barristers' Soc., 1957–81 and 1999– (Council, 1970–72, 1975–79); Cttee on Canadian Constitution, Canadian Bar Assoc., 1977–78; Director: Canadian Inst. for Admin of Justice, 1979–83; Canadian Judges' Conf., 1985–89; Chm., New Brunswick Judicial Council, 1993–98 (Vice-Chm., 1988–93). *Publications:* Married Women's Property, 1961; Professional Negligence, 1973.

HOYTE, Hugh Desmond, SC; President, Co-operative Republic of Guyana, 1985–92; Leader, People's National Congress; *b* 9 March 1929; *s* of George Alphonso Hoyte and Gladys Marietta Hoyte; *m* Joyce Hoyte. *Educ:* St Barnabas Anglican Sch.; Progressive High Sch.; Univ. of London (BA extl 1950, LLB 1959). Called to the Bar, Middle Temple, 1959. QC 1970, now SC. Civil servant and teacher; practised at Guyana Bar, 1960–; Chm., Legal Practitioners' Cttee, 1964; Mem., Nat. Elections Commn, 1966. Elected to Parliament, 1968; Minister: Home Affairs, 1969–70; Finance, 1970–72; Works and Communications, 1972–74; Economic Develt, 1974–80; Vice-Pres., Economic Planning and Finance, 1980–83, Production, 1983–84; First Vice-Pres. and Prime Minister, 1984. *Recreations:* reading, music, swimming, walking. *Address:* 14 North Road, Bourda, Georgetown, Guyana.

HUANG, Dr Christopher Li-Hur; Reader in Cellular Physiology, Cambridge University, since 1996; Fellow, New Hall, Cambridge, since 1979; *b* 28 Dec. 1951; *s* of Rayson Lisung Huang, *qv. Educ:* Methodist Boys' Sch., Kuala Lumpur; Nat. Jun. Coll., Singapore; Queen's Coll., Oxford (Florence Heale Scholar; Benefactors Prize; BA, BM, BCh, MA; DM 1985; DSc 1995); Gonville and Caius Coll., Cambridge (MA; PhD 1980; MD 1986; ScD 1995). House Physician, Nuffield Dept of Medicine, Oxford Univ., 1977–78; Cambridge University: MRC Schol., Physiological Lab., 1978–79; Asst Lectr, 1979–84; Lectr in Physiol., 1984–96; New Hall, Cambridge: Lectr in Physiol., 1979–; Dir of Studies in Med. Sci., 1981–. Hon. Res. Fellow, RCS, 1985–88; Hon. Sen. Res. Fellow, St George's Hosp. Med. Sch., London Univ., 1991–. Procultura Foundn Vis. Prof., Debrecen Univ., Hungary, 1996; Vis. Prof., Mount Sinai Med. Sch., NY, 2001. Consulting Ed., John Wiley, 1986–; Mem. Editl Bd, 1990–98, Distributing Ed., 1991–94, Jl Physiol.; Chairman, Editorial Board: Monographs of Physiol Soc., 1994–99; Biological Revs, 2000– . Council Mem., 1994–, Biol Sec., 2000–, Cambridge Philosophical Soc. Manager, Prince Philip Scholarship Fund, 1986–. Brian Johnson Prize in Pathology, Univ. of Oxford, 1976; Lepra Award, Brit. Leprosy Relief Assoc., 1977; Rolleston Meml Prize for Physiological Res., Oxford Univ., 1980; Gedge Prize in Physiol., Cambridge Univ., 1981. *Publications:* Companion to Neonatal Medicine, 1982; Companion to Obstetrics, 1982; Companion to Gynaecology, 1985; Research in Medicine: a guide to writing a thesis in the medical sciences, 1990, 2nd edn 1999; Intramembrane Charge Movements in Striated Muscle, 1993; (ed jtly) Applied Physiology for Surgery and Critical Care, 1995, original scientific papers and reviews on striated muscle activation, peripheral nerve growth and repair, physiol magnetic resonance imaging, and cellular triggering processes in osteoclasts. *Recreations:* music, playing the violin. *Address:* New Hall, Huntingdon Road, Cambridge CB3 0DF.

HUANG, Rayson Lisung, Hon. CBE 1976; DSc, DPhil; FRCPE; Vice-Chancellor, University of Hong Kong, 1972–86; *b* 1 Sept. 1920; *s* of Rufus Huang; *m* 1949, Grace Wei Li; two *s. Educ:* Munsang Coll., Hong Kong; Univ. of Hong Kong (BSc); Univ. of Oxford (DPhil, DSc); Univ. of Chicago. DSc (Malaya) 1956. FRCPE 1984. Demonstrator in Chemistry, Nat. Kwangsi Univ., Kweilin, China, 1943; Post-doctoral Fellow and Research Associate, Univ. of Chicago, 1947–50; Univ. of Malaya, Singapore: Lecturer in Chemistry, 1951–54; Reader, 1955–59; Univ. of Malaya, Kuala Lumpur: Prof. of Chemistry, 1959–69, and Dean of Science, 1962–65; Vice-Chancellor, Nanyang Univ., Singapore, 1969–72. Chm. Council, ACU, 1980–81; Pres., Assoc. of SE Asian Instns of Higher Learning, 1970–72, 1981–83. MLC Hong Kong, 1977–83. Mem. Drafting Cttee (Beijing) and Vice Chm. Consulting Cttee (Hong Kong), for the Basic Law for Special Administrative Region of Hong Kong, 1985–90. Mem. Adv. Bd, IBM China/Hong Kong Corp., 1989–93. Vice Chm. Council, Shantou Univ., China, 1987–94; Life Member: Court, Univ. of Hong Kong; Bd of Trustees, Croucher Foundn, Hong Kong; Life Trustee, Rayson Huang Foundn, Kuala Lumpur, 2001. JP. Hon. DSc Hong Kong, 1968; Hon. LLD East Asia, Macao, 1987. Order of the Rising Sun (Japan), 1986. *Publications:* Organic Chemistry of Free Radicals, 1974 (London); A Lifetime in Academia (autobiog.), 2000; about 50 research papers on chemistry of free radicals, molecular rearrangements, etc, mainly in Jl of Chem. Soc. (London). *Recreations:* music, violin playing. *Address:* Raycrest II, 10 The Stables, Selly Park, Birmingham B29 7JW. *Club:* Hong Kong.

See also C. L.-H. Huang.

HUBBARD, family name of **Baron Addington**.

HUBBARD, David; *see* Hubbard, R. D. C.

HUBBARD, Michael Joseph; QC 1985; a Recorder of the Crown Court, since 1984; *b* 16 June 1942; *m* 1967, Ruth Ann; five *s. Educ:* Lancing College. Admitted Solicitor, 1966; called to the Bar, Gray's Inn, 1972; Western Circuit; Prosecuting Counsel to Inland Revenue, 1983–85. *Recreation:* messing about in boats (yacht Wild Confusion). *Address:* (chambers) 1 Paper Buildings, Temple, EC4Y 7EP.

HUBBARD, (Richard) David (Cairns), OBE 1995; Chairman: London and Manchester Group, 1993–98 (Director, 1989–98); Exco plc, 1996–98 (Deputy Chairman, 1995); *b* 14 May 1936; *s* of late John Cairns Hubbard and Gertrude Emilie Hubbard; *m* 1964, Hannah Neale (*née* Dennison); three *d. Educ:* Tonbridge. FCA. Commissioned, Royal Artillery, 1955–57; Peat Marwick Mitchell & Co., 1957–65; Cape Asbestos Co., 1965–74; Bache & Co., 1974–76; Powell Duffryn, 1976–96 (Chm., 1986–96); Chm., Andrew Sykes Group, 1991–94; non-executive Director: Blue Circle Industries, 1986–96; City of London Investment Trust (formerly TR City of London Trust), 1989–; Slough Estates, 1994–; Medical Defence Union Ltd, 1998–2000; Mem., Southern Adv. Bd, Nat. Westminster Bank, 1988–91. Mem., Bd of Crown Agents for Oversea Govts and Admins, 1986–88. Mem. Council, Inst. of Dirs, 1991–97. Chm., CRC Council, 1996–98 (Council Mem., 1982–98). Liveryman, Skinners' Co.; Freeman, City of London. *Recreation:* golf. *Address:* Meadowcroft, Windlesham, Surrey GU20 6BJ. *T:* (01276) 472198. *Clubs:* Royal & Ancient Golf (St Andrews); Berkshire Golf (Pres., 1999–), Lucifer Golfing Society.

HUBBARD-MILES, Peter Charles, CBE 1981; self-employed small businessman, since 1948; *b* 9 May 1927; *s* of Charles Hubbard and Agnes (*née* Lewis); *m* 1948, Pamela Wilkins; two *s* three *d. Educ:* Lewis' Sch., Pengam. Served RAF, 1945–48. County Councillor, Mid Glamorgan CC (formerly Glamorgan CC), 1967 (Leader, Conservative Group, 1974–83); Leader, Cons. Gp, Ogwr Borough Council, 1974–83, first Cons. Mayor 1979–80. Chm., Wales Cons. Local Govt Adv. Council, 1979–83. Contested (C) Bridgend, 1987. MP (C) Bridgend, 1983–87. PPS to Sec. of State for Wales, 1985–87. Chm. Governors, Bridgend Tech. Coll., 1977–81. *Recreations:* theatre, showbusiness. *Address:* 1 Cleviston Gardens, Newton, Porthcawl CF36 5RW.

HUBEL, Prof. David Hunter, MD; John Franklin Enders University Professor, Harvard Medical School, since 1982; *b* Canada, 27 Feb. 1926; US citizen; *s* of Jesse H. Hubel and Elsie M. Hunter; *m* 1953, S. Ruth Izzard; three *s. Educ:* McGill Univ. (BSc Hons Maths and Physics, 1947); McGill Univ. Med. Sch. (MD 1951). Rotating Intern, Montreal Gen. Hosp., 1951–52; Asst Resident in Neurology, Montreal Neurol Inst., 1952–53, and Fellow in Electroencephalography, 1953–54; Asst Resident in Neurol., Johns Hopkins Hosp., 1954–55; Res. Fellow, Walter Reed Army Inst. of Res., 1955–58; Res. Fellow, Wilmer Inst., Johns Hopkins Univ. Med. Sch., 1958–59; Harvard Medical School: Associate in Neurophysiology and Neuropharmacology, 1959–60; Asst Prof. of Neurophys. and Neuropharm., 1960–62; Associate Prof. of Neurophys. and Neuropharm., 1962–65; Prof. of Neurophys., 1965–67; George Packer Berry Prof. of Physiol. and Chm., Dept of Physiol., 1967–68; George Packer Berry Prof. of Neurobiol., 1968–82. George Eastman Vis. Prof., Univ. of Oxford, and Fellow, Balliol Coll., 1990–91. Sen. Fellow, Harvard Soc. of Fellows, 1971–; Mem., Bd of Syndics, Harvard Univ. Press, 1979–83. Associate, Neurosciences Res. Program, 1974. Fellow, Amer. Acad. of Arts and Sciences, 1965; Member: Amer. Physiol Soc., 1959; National Acad. of Sciences, USA, 1971; Deutsche Akademie der Naturforscher Leopoldina, DDR, 1971; Soc. for Neuroscience, 1970; Assoc. for Res. in Vision and Ophthalmology, 1970; Amer. Philosophical Soc., 1982; Sigma Xi-Scientific Res. Soc., 1995; Foreign Mem., Royal Soc., 1982; Foreign MAE, 1995; Hon. Member: Physiol Soc., 1983; Amer. Neurol Assoc.; Spanish Soc. of Ophth., 1997. Lectures: George H. Bishop, Washington Univ., St Louis, 1964; Bowditch, Amer. Physiol Soc., 1966; Jessup, Columbia Univ., 1970; Ferrier, Royal Soc., 1972; James Arthur, Amer. Mus. of Nat. Hist., 1972; Harvey, Rockefeller Univ., 1976; Grass Foundn, Soc. for Neuroscience, 1976; Weizmann Meml, Weizmann Inst. of Science, Israel, 1979; Vanuxem, Princeton Univ., 1981; Hughlings Jackson, Montreal Neurol Inst., 1982; first David Marr, Cambridge Univ., 1982; first James S. McDonnell, Washington Univ. Sch. of Medicine, 1982; James A. F. Stevenson Meml, Univ. of W Ont, 1982; Keys Meml, Trinity Coll., Toronto, 1983; Nelson, Univ. of Calif. Davis, 1983; Deane, Wellesley Coll., 1983; first James M. Sprague, Univ. of Pa, 1984; Vancouver Inst., Univ. of BC, 1985. Hon. DSc: McGill, 1978; Manitoba, 1983; Oxford, 1994; Hon. DHL Johns Hopkins, 1990. Awards: Res. to Prevent Blindness Trustees, 1971; Lewis S. Rosenstiel for Basic Med. Res., Brandeis Univ., 1972; Friedenwald, Assoc. for Res. in Vision and Ophthalmol., 1975; New England Ophthalmol Soc. Annual, 1983; Paul Kayser Internat. Award of Merit for Retina Res., 1989. Prizes: Karl Spencer Lashley, Amer. Phil Soc., 1977; Louisa Gross Horwitz, Columbia Univ., 1978; Dickson in Medicine, Univ. of Pittsburgh, 1979; Ledlie, Harvard Univ., 1980; Nobel in Medicine or Physiol., 1981; Helen Keller, Hellen Keller Eye Res. Foundn, 1995. *Publications:* Eye, Brain and Vision, 1987; articles in scientific jls. *Recreations:* music, photography, astronomy, amateur radio, Japanese. *Address:* Harvard Medical School, 220 Longwood Avenue, Boston, MA 02115, USA. *T:* (617) 4321655.

HUBER, Prof. Robert; Director, Max-Planck-Institut für Biochemie, and Scientific Member, Max-Planck Society, since 1972; *b* 20 Feb. 1937; *s* of Sebastian and Helene Huber; *m* 1960, Christa Essig; two *s* two *d. Educ:* Grammar Sch. and Humanistisches Gymnasium, München; Technische Univ., München (Dr rer. nat. 1963). Lecturer, 1968, Associate Prof., 1976–, Technische Univ., München. Scientific Mem., Max-Planck Soc. Editor, Jl of Molecular Biology, 1976–. Member: EMBO (also Mem. Council); Deutsche Chem. Ges.; Ges. für Biologische Chem.; Bavarian Acad. of Scis, 1988; Deutsche Akademie der Naturforscher Leopoldina; Accademia Nazionale dei Lincei, Rome; Orden pour le mérite für Wissenschaft und Künste; Corresp. Mem., Croatian Acad. of Scis and Arts; Fellow, Amer. Acad. of Microbiology, 1996; Associate Fellow, Third World Acad. of Scis, 1995; Foreign Associate, Nat. Acad. of Scis, USA, 1995; Foreign Mem., Royal Soc., 1999. Hon. Member: Amer. Soc. of Biolog. Chemists; Swedish Soc. for Biophysics; Japanese Biochem. Soc. Dr *hc*: Catholic Univ. of Louvain, 1987; Univ. of Ljubljana, Jugoslavia, 1989; Univ. Tor Vergata, Rome, 1991; Univ. of Lisbon, 2000; Univ. of Barcelona, 2000. E. K. Frey Medal, Ges. für Chirurgie, 1972; Otto-Warburg Medal, Ges. für Biolog. Chem., 1977; Emil von Behring Medal, Univ. of Marburg, 1982; Keilin Medal, Biochem. Soc., 1987; Richard Kuhn Medal, Ges. Deutscher Chem., 1987; (jtly) Nobel Prize for Chemistry, 1988; E. K. Frey-E. Werle Gedächtnismedaille, 1989; Kone Award, Assoc. of Clin. Biochemists, 1990; Sir Hans Krebs Medal, FEBS, 1992; Linus Pauling Medal, 1993–94; Distinguished Service Award, Miami Winter Symposia, 1995; Max Tishler Prize, Harvard Univ., 1997; Max Bergmann Medal, 1997. Bayerischer Maximiliansorden für Wissenschaft und Kunst, 1993; Das Grosse Verdienstkreuz mit Stern und Schulterband (Germany), 1997. *Publications:* numerous papers in learned jls on crystallography, immunology and structure of proteins. *Recreations:* cycling, hiking, skiing. *Address:* Max-Planck Institut für Biochemie, Am Klopferspitz 18a, 82152 Martinsried, Germany. *T:* (089) 85782677/8.

HUCKER, Michael; His Honour Judge Hucker; a Circuit Judge, since 1994; *b* 25 Oct. 1937; *o s* of Ernest George Hucker, CBE and Mary Louise Hucker (*née* Jowett); *m* 1961, Hazel Zoë Drake, JP; one *s* one *d* (and one *s* decd). *Educ:* St Dunstan's Coll.; LSE. Regular Commission, RE, 1957; served BAOR, Cameroons, Malaysia, NI, MoD; attached Army Legal Services, 1974–76; retired 1976. Called to the Bar, Lincoln's Inn, 1974, Gibraltar, 1988; in practice, London and SE Circuit, 1977–94, Head of Chambers, 1978–91; Counsel for Army and Air Force Boards in CMAC and House of Lords, 1979–94; Recorder, 1992–94. Chm., Lord Chancellor's Adv. Cttee for SW London, 1996–2000. Freeman, City of London, 1978. *Address:* The Crown Court, 6–8 Penrhyn Road, Kingston-upon-Thames KT1 2BB. *T:* (020) 8240 2500.

HUCKER, Rev. Michael Frederick, MBE 1970; Principal Chaplain, Church of Scotland and Free Churches, Royal Air Force, 1987–90; Secretary, Forces Board, Methodist Church, 1990–96; *b* 1 May 1933; *s* of William John and Lucy Sophia Hucker; *m* 1961, Katherine Rosemary Parsons; one *s* one *d. Educ:* City of Bath Boys' Sch.; Bristol Univ. (MA); London Univ. (BD). Ordained Methodist minister, 1960; commnd as RAF chaplain, 1962. QHC 1987–90. Mem. Bd, Orbit Housing Assoc., 1996–. *Recreations:* gardening, music. *Address:* 1 Central Buildings, Westminster, SW1H 9NH.

HUCKFIELD, Leslie (John); owner of Leslie Huckfield Research (consultancy and advice in external funding), since 1997; *b* 7 April 1942; *s* of Ernest Leslie and Suvla Huckfield. *Educ:* Prince Henry's Grammar Sch., Evesham; Keble Coll., Oxford; Univ. of Birmingham. Lectr in Economics, City of Birmingham Coll. of Commerce, 1963–67. Advertising Manager, Tribune, 1983; Co-ordinator, CAPITAL (transport campaign against London Transport Bill), 1983–84. Prin. Officer, External Resources, St Helen's Coll., Merseyside, 1989–93; European Officer, Merseyside Colls, 1994–95; Eur. Funding Manager, Wirral Metropolitan Coll., 1995–97. Contested (Lab) Warwick and Leamington, 1966; MP (Lab) Nuneaton, March 1967–1983. PPS to Minister of Public Building and Works, 1969–70; Parly Under-Secretary of State, Dept of Industry, 1976–79. MEP (Lab) Merseyside E, 1984–89. Member: Nat. Exec. Cttee, Labour Party, 1978–82; W Midlands Reg. Exec. Cttee, Labour Party, 1978–82; Political Sec., Nat. Union Lab. and Socialist Clubs, 1979–81. Chairman: Lab. Party Transport Gp, 1974–76; Independent Adv. Commn on Transport, 1975–76; Pres., Worcs Fedn of Young Socialists, 1962–64; Member: Birmingham Regional Hosp. Bd, 1970–72; Political Cttee, Co-op. Retail Soc. (London Regional), 1981–93. *Publications:* various newspaper and periodical articles. *Recreation:* running marathons. *Address:* PO Box 1200, Coventry CV4 7YA. *T:* (024) 7669 2999, *Fax:* (024) 7669 0380; *e-mail:* research@huckfield.com.

HUCKLE, Alan Edden; HM Diplomatic Service; Head of Overseas Territories Department, Foreign and Commonwealth Office, and Commissioner (non-resident), British Antarctic Territory and British Indian Ocean Territory, since 2001; *b* 15 June 1948; *s* of late Albert Arthur Huckle and of Ethel Maud Pettifer Huckle (*née* Edden); *m* 1973, Helen Myra Gibson; one *s* one *d. Educ:* Rugby Sch.; Lower Sch. of John Lyon, Harrow; Univ. of Warwick (BA 1st Cl. Hons Hist. 1969; MA Renaissance Studies 1970). Leverhulme Trust Schol., 1971; British Sch. at Rome Schol., 1971; Personnel Mgt Div., CSD, 1971–74; Asst Private Sec. to Sec. of State for NI, Belfast, 1974–75; Machinery of Govt Div., CSD, 1975–78; Pol Affairs Div., NI Office, Belfast, 1978–80; FCO, 1980–83; Exec. Dir, British Inf. Services, NY, 1983–87; Hd of Chancery, Manila, 1987–90; Dep. Hd, Arms Control and Disarmament Dept, FCO, 1990–92; Counsellor and Dep. Hd of Delegn to CSCE, Vienna, 1992–96; Head: Dependent Territories Regl Secretariat, Bridgetown, 1996–98; OSCE/Council of Europe Dept, FCO, 1998–2001. *Recreations:* hill-walking, armchair mountaineering. *Address:* c/o Foreign and Commonwealth Office, King Charles Street, SW1A 2AH. *T:* (020) 7270 2741. *Club:* Royal Commonwealth Society.

HUCKSTEP, Prof. Ronald Lawrie, CMG 1971; MD; FRCS, FRCSE, FRACS, FTSE; Professor of Traumatic and Orthopaedic Surgery, University of New South Wales, 1972–92, now Emeritus Professor and Emeritus Orthopaedic Consultant, Prince of Wales/Prince Henry Hospital Group; Chairman of Departments of Orthopaedic Surgery and Director of Accident Services, Prince of Wales and Prince Henry Hospitals, Sydney, Australia, 1972–92; Consultant Orthopaedic Surgeon, Royal South Sydney and Sutherland Hospitals, 1972–92; *b* 22 July 1926; *er s* of late Herbert George Huckstep and Agnes Huckstep (*née* Lawrie-Smith); *m* 1960, Margaret Ann, *e d* of late Ronald Græme Macbeth, DM, FRCS; two *s* one *d. Educ:* Cathedral Sch., Shanghai, China; Queens' Coll., Cambridge; Middx Hosp. Med. Sch., London. MA, MB, BChir (Cantab) 1952; MD (Cantab) 1957; FRCSE 1957; FRCS 1958; FAOrthA 1972; FRACS 1973. Registrar and Chief Asst, Orthopaedic Dept, St Bartholomew's Hosp., and various surgical appts Middx and Royal Nat. Orthopaedic Hosps, London, 1952–60; Hunterian Prof., RCS, 1959–60; Makerere Univ. Coll., Kampala, Uganda: Lectr, 1960–62, Sen. Lectr, 1962–65 and Reader, 1965–67, in Orthopaedic Surgery, with responsibility for starting orthopaedic dept in Uganda; Prof. of Orthopaedic Surgery, Makerere Univ., Kampala, 1967–72. Became Hon. Cons. Orthopaedic Surgeon, Mulago and Mengo Hosps, and Round Table Polio Clinic, Kampala; Adviser on Orthopaedic Surgery, Ministry of Health, Uganda, 1960–72. Vis. Prof. of Surgery, Univ. of Sydney, 1995–. Corresp. Editor: Brit. and Amer. jls of Bone and Joint Surgery, 1965–72; Jl Western Pacific Orthopædic Assoc.; British Jl of Accident Surgery. Fellow, British Orthopaedic Assoc., 1967; Hon. Fellow: Western Pacific Orthopaedic Assoc., 1968; Assoc. of Surgeons of Uganda, 1993. Commonwealth Foundn Travelling Lectr, 1970, 1978–79 and 1982. FRSocMed; FTSE (FTS 1982). Patron Med. Soc., Univ. of NSW; Founder, World Orthopaedic Concern, 1973 (Hon. Mem. 1978); Vice-Pres., Australian Orthopaedic Assoc., 1982–83 (Betts Medal, 1983); Pres., Coast Med. Assoc., Sydney, 1985–86; Chairman, Fellow or Mem. various med. socs and of assocs, councils and cttees concerned with orthopaedic and traumatic surgery, accident services and rehabilitation of physically disabled. Inventions incl. Huckstep femoral fracture nail, hip, knee, shoulder and circlip. Irving Geist Award, 11th World Congress, Internat. Soc. for Rehabilitation of the Disabled, 1969; James Cook Medal, Royal Soc. of NSW, 1984; Sutherland Medal, Australian Acad. of Technological Scis, 1986; Paul Harris Fellow and Medal, Rotary Internat., 1987; Humanitarian Award, Orthopaedics Overseas, 1991. Hon. MD NSW, 1988. Hon. Mem., Mark Twain Soc., 1978. Rotary Vocational Service Award, 1994. *Publications:* Typhoid Fever and Other Salmonella Infections, 1962; A Simple Guide to Trauma, 1970, 5th edn 1995 (trans. Italian 1978, Japanese 1982); Poliomyelitis, A Guide for Developing Countries, Including Appliances and Rehabilitation, 1975 (ELBS and repr. edns 1979, 1983, French edn 1983); A Simple Guide to Orthopaedics, 1993; Colour Test in Orthopaedics and Trauma, 1994; various booklets, chapters in books, papers and films on injuries, orthopaedic diseases, typhoid fever, appliances and implants. *Recreations:* photography, designing orthopaedic appliances and implants for cripples in developing and developed countries, swimming, travel. *Address:* 108 Sugarloaf Crescent, Castlecrag, Sydney, NSW 2068, Australia. *T:* (612) 99581786, *Fax:* (612) 99672971. *Club:* Australian (Sydney).

HUDD, Roy; actor; *b* 16 May 1936; *s* of Harold Hudd and Evelyn Barham; *m* 1st, 1963, Ann Lambert (marr. diss. 1983); one *s*; 2nd, 1988, Deborah Flitcroft. *Educ:* Croydon Secondary Technical School. Entered show business, 1957, as half of double act Hudd & Kay; Butlin Redcoats; started as a solo comedian, 1959; first pantomine, Empire Theatre, Leeds, 1959; 4 years' concert party Out of the Blue, 1960–63; first radio broadcast Workers Playtime, 1960; *stage includes:* The Merchant of Venice, 1960; The Give Away, 1969; At the Palace, 1970; Young Vic Co. seasons, 1973, 1976, 1977; Oliver!, 1977; Underneath the Arches, 1982 (SWET Actor of the Year); Run For Your Wife, 1986, 1989; The Birth of Merlin, Theatre Clwyd, 1989; The Fantasticks, 1990; Midsummer Night's Dream, 1991; Friends Like This, 1998; A Funny Thing Happened on the Way to the Forum, 1999; Hard Times, Haymarket, 2000; Theft, 2001; *films include:* Blood Beast Terror, 1967; Up Pompeii; The Seven Magnificent Deadly Sins; Up the Chastity Belt; The Garnet Saga; An Acre of Seats in a Garden of Dreams, 1973; The Sweet Life, 1998; Kind of Hush, 1998; Purely Belter, 2000; *television series include:* Not So Much a Programme, More a Way of Life, 1964; Illustrated Weekly Hudd, 1966–68; Roy Hudd Show, 1971; Comedy Tonight, 1970–71; Up Sunday, 1973; Pebble Mill, 1974–75; Hold the Front Page, 1974–75; The 60 70 80 show, 1974–77; Movie Memories, 1981–85; Halls of Fame, 1985; The Puppet Man, 1985; Cinderella, 1986; Hometown, 1987, 1988–89; What's My Line?, 1990; Lipstick On Your Collar, 1993; Common as Muck, 1994–96; What's My Line, 1994–96; Karaoke, 1996; *radio series:* The News Huddlines, 1975–; *author of stage shows:* Victorian Christmas, 1978; Just a Verse and Chorus, 1979; Roy Hudd's Very Own Music Hall, 1980; Beautiful Dreamer, 1980; Underneath the Arches, 1982; While London Sleeps, 1983; They Called Me Al, 1987; numerous pantomimes, 1980–. Columnist, Yours magazine, 1991–. Chm., Entertainment Artistes Benevolent Fund, 1980–90. President: British Music Hall Soc., 1992–; TRIC, 2000–01. King Rat, Grand Order of Water Rats, 1989, 2000. Variety Club BBC Radio Personality, 1976, 1993; Gold Badge of Merit, BASCA, 1981; Sony Gold Award, 1990; British Comedy Lifetime Achievement, LWT, 1990; EMAP Columnist of the Year, 1995; Crystal Award for services to entertainment, Inst. of Entertainment & Arts Mgt, 1995. *Publications:* Music Hall, 1976; Roy Hudd's Book of Music Hall, Variety and Show Biz Anecdotes, 1993; Roy Hudd's Who's Who in Variety 1945–60, 1997. *Recreations:* collecting old songs, sleeping. *Address:* 652 Finchley Road, NW11 7NT. *T:* (020) 8458 7288. *Clubs:* Garrick, Green Room.

HUDGHTON, Ian Stewart; Member (SNP) Scotland North East, European Parliament, since 1998; *b* 19 Sept. 1951; *m* 1981, Lily M. Ingram; one *s* one *d* (and one *s* decd). *Educ:* Forfar Acad.; Kingsway Technical Coll., Dundee. Partner and Jt Proprietor, then Proprietor, F. Hudghton & Son, Painters and Decorators, 1971–95. Mem., Cttee of Regions, 1998. Member (SNP): Angus DC, 1986–96 (Housing Convener, 1988–96); Angus Council, 1995–99 (Leader, 1995–99); Tayside Regl Council, 1994–96 (Depute Leader, 1994–96). *Recreations:* family, theatre, music, hill walking. *Address:* (office) 70 Rosemount Place, Aberdeen AB25 2XJ. *T:* (01224) 623150.

HUDSON, Prof. Anne Mary, DPhil; FRHistS; FBA 1988; Professor of Medieval English, Oxford, since 1989; Fellow of Lady Margaret Hall, Oxford, since 1963; *b* 28 Aug. 1938; *d* of late R. L. and K. M. Hudson. *Educ:* Dartford Grammar Sch. for Girls; St Hugh's Coll., Oxford (BA English cl. I; MA; DPhil 1964). FRHistS 1976. Lectr in Medieval English, 1961–63, Tutor, 1963–91, LMH, Oxford; Oxford University: CUF Lectr, 1963–81; Special Lectr, 1981–83; British Acad. Reader in the Humanities, 1983–86; Lectr in Medieval English, 1986–89. Exec. Sec., 1969–82, Mem. Council, 1982–, EETS. Sir Israel Gollancz Prize, British Acad., 1985, 1991. *Publications:* (ed) Selections from English Wycliffite Writings, 1978; (ed) English Wycliffite Sermons, i, 1983, iii, 1990, iv and v (with P. Gradon), 1996; Lollards and their Books, 1985; (ed jtly) From Ockham to Wyclif, 1987; The Premature Reformation, 1988; (ed) Two Wycliffite Texts, 1993. *Address:* Lady Margaret Hall, Oxford OX2 6QA.

HUDSON, Prof. Anthony Hugh, PhD; Professor of Common Law, Liverpool University, 1977–92, now Emeritus (Dean of Faculty of Law, 1971–78 and 1984–91); *b* 21 Jan. 1928; *s* of late Dr Thomas A. G. Hudson and Bridget Hudson; *m* 1962, Joan O'Malley; one *s* three *d. Educ:* St Joseph's Coll., Blackpool; Pembroke Coll., Cambridge (LLB 1950, MA 1953); PhD Manchester 1966. Called to Bar, Lincoln's Inn, 1954. Lecturer in Law: Hull Univ., 1951–57; Birmingham Univ., 1957–62; Manchester Univ., 1962–64; Liverpool University: Sen. Lectr, 1964–71; Professor of Law, 1971–77. *Publications:* (jtly) Hood Phillips: A First Book of English Law, 7th edn 1977, 8th edn 1988; (jtly) Commercial Banking Law, 1978; (jtly) Stevens and Borrie Mercantile Law, 17th edn 1978; contribs on common and commercial law to various legal books and periodicals. *Recreations:* gardening, walking, history. *Address:* 18 Dowhills Road, Blundellsands, Liverpool L23 8SW. *T:* (0151) 924 5830.

HUDSON, Barrie; *see* Hudson, N. B.

HUDSON, (Eleanor) Erlund, RE 1946 (ARE 1938); RWS 1949 (ARWS 1939); ARCA 1937; artist; *b* 18 Feb. 1912; *d* of Helen Ingeborg Olsen, Brookline, Boston, USA, and Harold Hudson. *Educ:* Torquay; Dorking; Royal College of Art (Diploma 1937, Travelling Scholarship 1938). Former Mem. Chicago Print Soc. and Soc. of Artist Print-Makers. Studied and travelled in Italy, summer 1939. Interrupted by war. Exhibited in London, Provinces, Scandinavia, Canada, USA, etc; works purchased by War Artists Advisory Council, 1942–43. Formerly Artistic Dir and designer, Brooking Ballet Sch., W1. *Recreations:* music, country life. *Address:* 6 Hammersmith Terrace, W6 9TS. *T:* (020) 8748 3778; Meadow House, Old Bosham, W Sussex. *T:* (01243) 573558.

HUDSON, Erlund; *see* Hudson, E. E.

HUDSON, Prof. George, FRCP, FRCPath; Professor of Experimental Haematology, University of Sheffield, 1975–89, now Emeritus; *b* 10 Aug. 1924; *s* of George Hudson, blacksmith, and Edith Hannah (*née* Bennett); *m* 1955, Mary Patricia Hibbert (decd); one *d. Educ:* Edenfield C of E Sch.; Bury Grammar Sch.; Manchester Univ. (MSc, MB, ChB); MD, DSc Bristol. House Officer, Manchester Royal Inf., 1949–50; Demonstr in Anatomy, Univ. of Bristol, 1950–51; RAMC, 1951–53; University of Bristol: Lectr, later Reader, in Anatomy, 1953–68; Preclinical Dean, 1963–68; Vis. Prof., Univ. of Minnesota (Fulbright Award), 1959–60; Sheffield University: Admin. Dean, 1968–83; Hon. Clinical Lectr in Haematology, 1968–75; Head, Dept of Haematology, 1981–89; Postgrad. Dean, 1984–91. Hon. Cons. Haematologist, United Sheffield Hosps, 1969–89. Chm., Conf. of Deans of Provincial Med. Schs, 1980–82; Member: Sheffield RHB, 1970–74; Sheffield HA, 1974–84; DHSS Working Party on NHS Adv. and Representative Machinery, 1980–81; Council for Postgraduate Med. Educn for England and Wales, 1980–83. Hon. LLD Sheffield, 1993. *Publications:* papers in medical and scientific jls on haematological subjects. *Recreations:* lay reader since 1953, history of medicine, cavies, garden. *Address:* Box Cottage, Hill Bottom, Whitchurch Hill RG8 7PU. *T:* (0118) 984 2671.

HUDSON, Ian Francis, CB 1976; Deputy Secretary, Department of Employment, 1976–80; *b* 29 May 1925; *s* of Francis Reginald Hudson and Dorothy Mary Hudson (*née* Crabbe); *m* 1952, Gisela Elisabeth Grettka; one *s* one *d. Educ:* City of London Sch.; New Coll., Oxford. Royal Navy, 1943–47. Customs and Excise, 1947–53; Min. of Labour, 1953–56, 1959–61, 1963–64; Treasury, 1957–58; Dept of Labour, Australia, 1961–63; Asst Sec., 1963; DEA, 1964–68; Under-Sec., 1967; Dept of Employment, 1968–73; Dep. Sec. 1973; Sec., Pay Board, 1973–74; Sec., Royal Commn on Distribution of Income and Wealth, 1974–76.

See also J. A. Hudson.

HUDSON, James Ralph, CBE 1976; FRCS; Surgeon, Moorfields Eye Hospital, 1956–81, now Honorary Consulting Surgeon; Ophthalmic Surgeon, Guy's Hospital, 1963–76; Hon. Ophthalmic Surgeon: Hospital of St John and St Elizabeth, 1953–86; King Edward VII Hospital for Officers, 1970–86; Teacher of Ophthalmology, Guy's Hospital, 1964–76, Institute of Ophthalmology, University of London, 1961–81; Consultant Adviser in Ophthalmology, Department of Health and Social Security, 1969–82; *b* 15 Feb. 1916; *o s* of late William Shand Hudson and Ethel Summerskill; *m* 1946, Margaret May Oulpé; two *s* two *d. Educ:* The King's Sch., Canterbury; Middlesex Hosp. (Edmund Davis Exhibnr), Univ. of London. MRCS, LRCP 1939; MB, BS London 1940; DOMS (England) 1948; FRCS 1949; FRCOphth (FCOphth 1988; Hon. FCOphth 1990). Res. Med. Appts, Tindal House Emergency Hosp. (Middx Hosp. Sector), 1939–42. RAFVR Med. Service, 1942–46; Sqdn Ldr, 1944–46. Moorfields Eye Hosp., Clin. Asst, 1947, Ho. Surg., 1947–49, Sen. Resident Officer, 1949, Chief Clin. Asst, 1950–56; Middlesex Hosp., Clin. Asst Ophth. Outpatients, 1950–51; Ophth. Surg., W Middlesex Hosp., 1950–56, Mount Vernon Hosp., 1953–59. Civil Consultant in Ophthalmology to RAF, 1970–82. Examr in Ophthalmology (Dipl. Ophth. of Examg Bd of Eng., RCP and RCS, 1960–65; Mem. Court of Examrs, RCS, 1966–72). FRSocMed 1947 (Vice-Pres. Sect. of Ophthalmology, 1965); Member: Ophthal Soc. UK, 1948–88 (Hon. Sec. 1956–58, Vice-Pres., 1969–71, Pres., 1982–84); Faculty of Ophthalmologists, 1950–88 (Mem. Council,

1960–82; Hon. Sec. 1960–70; Vice-Pres., 1970–74; Pres., 1974–77; Rep. on Council of RCS, 1968–73; Hon. Mem., 1982–); Soc. Française d'Ophtal., 1950– (membre délégué étranger, 1970–92); Cttee d'Honneur Les Entretiens Annuels d'Ophtalmologie, 1970–; Internat. Council of Ophthalmology, 1978–86; UK Rep., Union Européenne des Médecins Spécialistes (Ophthalmology Section), 1973–91 (Pres., 1982–86); Hon. Fellow, Royal Aust. Coll. Ophthalmologists; Pilgrims of Gt Britain; Hon. Steward, Westminster Abbey, 1972–88. Liveryman, Soc. of Apothecaries, and Freeman of City of London. *Publications:* (with T. Keith Lyle) chapters in Matthews's Recent Advances in the Surgery of Trauma; contrib. to chapters in Rob and Rodney Smith's Operative Surgery, 1969; articles in: Brit. Jl of Ophthalmology; Trans Ophth. Soc. UK; Proc. Royal Soc. Med. *Recreations:* motoring, travel. *Address:* Flat 2, 17 Montagu Square, W1H 1RD. *T:* (020) 7487 2680.

HUDSON, John Arthur, CB 1970; Deputy Under-Secretary of State, Department of Education and Science, 1969–80; *b* 24 Aug. 1920; *s* of Francis Reginald Hudson and Dorothy Mary (*née* Crabbe); *m* 1960, Dwynwen Davies; one *s* one *d*. *Educ:* City of London Sch.; Jesus Coll., Oxford. Served Royal Corps of Signals, 1941–45 (despatches). Entered Ministry of Education, 1946. Mem., South Bank Theatre Bd, 1967–89. *Address:* The Rosary, Green Lane, Leominster, Herefordshire HR6 8QN. *T:* (01568) 614413.
See also I. F. Hudson.

HUDSON, Prof. John Pilkington, CBE 1975 (MBE (mil.) 1943); GM 1944 and Bar 1945; BSc, MSc, PhD; NDH; FIBiol; now Emeritus Professor; former Director, Long Ashton Research Station, and Professor of Horticultural Science, University of Bristol, 1967–75; *b* 24 July 1910; *o s* of W. A. Hudson and Bertha (*née* Pilkington); *m* 1936, Mary Gretta, *d* of late W. N. and Mary Heath, Westfields, Market Bosworth, Leics; two *s*. *Educ:* New Mills Grammar Sch.; Midland Agricultural Coll.; University Coll., Nottingham. Hort. Adviser, E Sussex CC, 1935–39. Served War, 1939–45, Royal Engineers Bomb Disposal (Major). Horticulturist, Dept of Agric., Wellington, NZ, 1945–48; Lecturer in Horticulture, University of Nottingham Sch. of Agric., 1948–50; Head of Dept of Horticulture, University of Nottingham, 1950–67 (as Prof. of Horticulture, 1958–67, Dean, Faculty of Agriculture and Horticulture, 1965–67); seconded part-time to Univ. of Khartoum, Sudan, to found Dept of Horticulture, 1961–63. Associate of Honour, Royal New Zealand Institute of Horticulture, 1948. Chm., Jt Advisory Cttee on Agricultural Education (HMSO report published, 1973); Mem., RHS Exam. Bd; PP and Hon. Mem., Hort. Educn Assoc. Hon. Fellow: RASE, 1977; Inst. of Hort., 1985. VMH, 1976. Editor, Experimental Agriculture, 1965–82; Past Mem. Editorial Bds, Jl Hort. Sci., SPAN. *Publications:* (ed) Control of the Plant Environment, 1957; numerous technical instructions on dealing with unexploded bomb fuses, where unambiguity was a matter of life and death; many contribs on effects of environment on plant growth and productivity to scientific jls. *Recreations:* choral singing, gardening, walking, talking with my friends. *Address:* The Spinney, Ladywell, Wrington, Bristol BS40 5LT.
See also R. A. Hudson.

HUDSON, Keith William, FRICS; Technical Secretary, Cost Commission, Comité Européen des Economistes de la Construction, 1989–94; *b* 2 June 1928; *s* of William Walter Hudson and Jessie Sarah Hudson; *m* 1952, Ailsa White; two *s* two *d*. *Educ:* Sir Charles Elliott Sch.; Coll. of Estate Management. FRICS 1945. Served Army, 1948–50 (Lieut). Private practice, 1945–48 and 1950–57, Min. of Works, Basic Grade, 1957–64; Min. of Health (later DHSS), 1964–86: Main Grade, 1964–66; Sen. Grade, 1966–74; Superintending, 1974–76; Dir B, 1976–79; Under Sec., 1979; Dir of Construction and Cost Intelligence, and Chief Surveyor, DHSS, 1979–86, retd. *Publications:* articles in Chartered Surveyor and in Building. *Recreations:* painting, walking. *Address:* Silver Birch, Mill Lane, Felbridge, East Grinstead, West Sussex RH19 2PE. *T:* (01342) 325817.

HUDSON, Kirsty; *see* McLeod, K.

HUDSON, Prof. Liam, MA, PhD; psychologist and writer; partner, Balas Copartnership, since 1987; *b* 20 July 1933; *er s* of Cyril and Kathleen Hudson; *m* 1st, 1955, Elizabeth Ward; 2nd, 1965, Bernadine Jacot de Boinod; three *s* one *d*. *Educ:* Whitgift Sch.; Exeter Coll., Oxford. Post-graduate and post-doctoral research, Psychological Laboratory, Cambridge, 1957–65, and Research Centre, King's Coll., Cambridge, 1965–68; Fellow, King's Coll., Cambridge, 1966–68; Bell Prof. of Educnl Scis, Univ. of Edinburgh, 1968–77 and Dir, Res. Unit on Intellectual Develt, 1964–77; Prof. of Psychology, Brunel Univ., 1977–87. Mem., Inst. for Advanced Study, Princeton, 1974–75; Vis. Prof., Tavistock and Portman Clinics, London, 1987–96. Tanner Lectures, Yale Univ., 1997. Maurice Hille Award, SIAD, 1983. *Publications:* Contrary Imaginations, 1966; Frames of Mind, 1968; (ed) The Ecology of Human Intelligence, 1970; The Cult of the Fact, 1972; Human Beings, 1975; The Nympholepts, 1978; Bodies of Knowledge, 1982; Night Life, 1985; The Way Men Think, 1991; Intimate Relations, 1995. *Recreations:* painting and photography, making things, otherwise largely domestic. *Address:* 34 North Park, Gerrards Cross, Bucks SL9 8JN.

HUDSON, Lucian; Director, Communications Directorate, Department for Environment, Food and Rural Affairs, since 2001; *b* 5 July 1960; *s* of John and Vanda Hudson; *m* 1982, Margaret Prythergch. *Educ:* Ecole Montalembert, Paris; Lycée Français de Londres; St Catherine's Coll., Oxford (BA (Hons) PPE); London Business Sch. Professional communicator with expertise in strategic communications and crisis mgt; launched and managed 10 new content-driven ventures in UK, Europe, N and S America, India, Far East; BBC: producer and sen. producer, Nine O'Clock News, 1988–93; night editor, Breakfast News, editor, TV news, 1993–94; strand editor, 70 live events and breaking news specials inc. first 6 hrs of death of Diana, Princess of Wales, BBC World, 1994–97; hd of programming, launched new cable channels, BBC Worldwide, 1997–99; Dir of e-Communications Gp, Cabinet Office, 2000–01; seconded to MAFF to run media ops during foot and mouth disease, 2001. Founding editorial dir, Justpeople.com, 1999–2000. Chm., Rory Peck Trust, 1998–2000. FRSA. *Recreations:* joining up government, building professional alliances, reading and travelling, watching Rugby, enjoying the sporting and business success of friends and family. *Address:* Department for Environment, Food and Rural Affairs, Nobel House, 17 Smith Square, SW1P 3JR. *Clubs:* London Capital, Institute of Directors.

HUDSON, (Norman) Barrie, CB 1996; Director, International Development Affairs (formerly Under Secretary, International Division), Overseas Development Administration, 1993–97, retired; *b* 21 June 1937; *s* of William and Mary Hudson; *m* 1963, Hazel (*née* Cotterill); two *s* one *d*. *Educ:* King Henry VIII Sch., Coventry; Univ. of Sheffield (BA Hons 1958); University Coll., London (MScEcon 1960). Economist, Tube Investments Ltd, 1960; Economist, Economist Intell. Unit, 1962; National Accounts Statistician (UK Technical Assistance to Govt of Jordan), 1963; Statistician, ODM, 1966; Econ. Adviser, ME Develt Div., Beirut, 1967; Overseas Development Administration: Econ. Adviser, 1972, Sen. Econ. Adviser, 1973; Head, SE Asia Develt Div., Bangkok, 1974; Asst Sec., 1977; Under Sec. (Principal Establishments Officer), 1981; Under Sec. for Africa, 1986. Trustee, SCF, 1998–. *Recreations:* theatre, reading, music, watching football and cricket. *Address:* The Galleons, Sallows Shaw, Sole Street, Cobham, Kent DA13 9BP. *T:* (01474) 814419.

HUDSON, Pamela May; *see* Hudson-Bendersky, P. M.

HUDSON, Peter Geoffrey; Member, Panel of Chairmen, Civil Service Selection Board, 1987–94; *b* 26 July 1926; *s* of late Thomas Albert Hudson and late Gertrude Hudson; *m* 1954, Valerie Mary, *yr d* of late Lewis Alfred Hart and late Eva Mary Hart; two *s* one *d*. *Educ:* King Edward VII Sch., Sheffield; Queen's Coll., Oxford (Hastings Scholar, MA). Gold Medallist, Royal Schs of Music, 1940. Sub-Lt RNVR, 1944–46 (Bletchley Park, 1944–45). Min. of Transport, 1949; Private Sec. to Minister of Transport and Civil Aviation, 1951–53; Principal, Min. of Transport and Civil Aviation, 1953–57; Admin. Staff Coll., Henley, 1957; British Civil Air Attaché, SE Asia and Far East, 1958–61; Asst Sec., Overseas Policy Div. and Estabt Div., Min. of Aviation and BoT, 1963–68; Counsellor (Civil Aviation), British Embassy, Washington, 1968–71; Under-Sec., DTI, 1971–84; Dir of Resources, British Tourist Authority and English Tourist Bd, 1984–86. Indep. Advr to Lady Marre Cttee on Future of Legal Profession, 1987–88. Vice Chm., Bromley CAB, 1989–95. Governor, Coll. of Air Trng, Hamble, 1974–75. *Recreation:* music. *Address:* Candle Hill, Raggleswood, Chislehurst, Kent BR7 5NH. *T:* (020) 8467 1761.

HUDSON, Peter John, CB 1978; Deputy Under-Secretary of State (Finance and Budget), Ministry of Defence, 1976–79; *b* 29 Sept. 1919; *o s* of late A. J. Hudson; *m* 1954, Joan Howard FitzGerald (*d* 1998); one *s* one *d*. *Educ:* Tollington Sch.; Birkbeck Coll., London. Exchequer and Audit Dept, 1938; RNVR, 1940–46 (Lieut); Asst Principal, Air Min., 1947; Private Sec. to Perm. Under Sec. of State for Air, 1948–51; Asst Sec., 1958; Head of Air Staff Secretariat, 1958–61; Imperial Defence Coll., 1962; Head of Programme and Budget Div., MoD, 1966–69; Under-Sec., Cabinet Office, 1969–72; Asst Under-Sec. of State, MoD, 1972–75; Dep. Under-Sec. of State (Air), MoD, 1975–76. *Address:* Folly Hill, Haslemere, Surrey GU27 2EY. *T:* (01428) 642078. *Club:* Royal Air Force.

HUDSON, Prof. Raymond, PhD, DSc; Professor of Geography, University of Durham, since 1990; *b* 7 March 1948; *s* of John and Jean Hudson; *m* 1975, Geraldine Holder; one *s* one *d*. *Educ:* Bristol Univ. (BA 1st Cl. Hons 1969; PhD 1974; DSc 1996). University of Durham: Lectr in Geog., 1972–83; Sen. Lectr, 1983–87; Reader, 1987–90; Head of Geog. Dept, 1992–97; Dir, Centre for European Studies, 1990–99; Chair, Internat. Centre for Regl Regeneration and Develt Studies, Univ. of Durham, 1999–. Chairman: Conf. of Heads of Geog. Depts in HE Instns in UK, 1995–99; Human Geog. Subject Area, ERSC, 1999–. Vice-Pres., RGS with IBG, 1999–2000. Editor, European Urban and Regional Studies, 1994–. Hon. DSc Roskilde, 1987. Edward Heath Award, RGS, 1989. *Publications:* (with D. Pocock) Images of the Urban Environment, 1978; (contrib. and ed, jtly) Regions in Crisis, 1980; (with D. W. Rhind) Land Use, 1980; (contrib. and ed, jtly) Regional Planning in Europe, 1982; (contrib. and ed, jtly) Redundant Spaces in Cities and Regions, 1983; (jtly) An Atlas of EEC Affairs, 1984; (contrib. and ed, jtly) Uneven Development in Southern Europe, 1985; (with A. Williams) The United Kingdom, 1986; Wrecking a Region, 1989; (with D. Sadler) The International Steel Industry, 1989; (with A. Williams) Divided Britain, 1989; (jtly) A Tale of Two Industries, 1991; (jtly) A Place called Teesside, 1994; (ed and contrib., jtly) Towards a New Map of Automobile Manufacturing in Europe?, 1995; (with M. Dunford) Successful European regions, 1996; (contrib. and ed jtly) Divided Europe, 1998; (jtly) Digging up Trouble: environment, protest and opencast coal mining, 2000; Production, Place and Environment: changing perspectives in economic geography, 2000; (jtly) Coalfields Regeneration: dealing with the consequences of industrial decline, 2000; Producing Places, 2001; numerous articles in scientific and scholarly jls. *Recreations:* reading, walking, keeping fit, travel. *Address:* 7 Oliver Place, Merryoaks, Durham DH1 3QS. *T:* (0191) 386 2963; (office) (0191) 374 2452.

HUDSON, Prof. Richard Anthony, FBA 1992; Professor of Linguistics, University College London, since 1989; *b* 18 Sept. 1939; *s* of Prof. John Pilkington Hudson, *qv*; *m* 1970, Gaynor Evans; two *d*. *Educ:* Loughborough Grammar Sch.; Corpus Christi Coll., Cambridge (BA); Sch. of Oriental and African Studies, London (PhD). University College London: Research Asst, Linguistics, 1964–70; Lectr 1970, Reader 1980, Dept of Phonetics and Linguistics. *Publications:* English Complex Sentences: an introduction to systemic grammar, 1971; Arguments for a Non-Transformational Grammar, 1976; Sociolinguistics, 1980; Word Grammar, 1984; An Invitation to Linguistics, 1984; English Word Grammar, 1990; Teaching Grammar: a guide for the national curriculum, 1992; Word Meaning, 1995; English Grammar, 1998; articles in jls. *Recreations:* running, walking, cycling, music. *Address:* Department of Phonetics and Linguistics, University College London, Gower Street, WC1E 6BT. *T:* (020) 7380 7172.

HUDSON, Richard Bayliss, RDI 1999; stage designer; *b* 9 June 1954; *s* of Peter Obank Hudson and Ella Joyce Bayliss. *Educ:* Peterhouse Sch., Rhodesia; Wimbledon Sch. of Art (BA Hons 1976). Designer of sets and costumes, 1986–, for major theatre companies in Britain, and for Royal Opera, ENO, Glyndebourne, Chicago Lyric Opera, La Fenice, Vienna State Opera, Bayerische Staatsoper; designs include: King Lear and Candide, Old Vic (Olivier award for season), 1988; A Night at the Chinese Opera, Kent Opera, 1990; The Queen of Spades, 1992, Eugene Onegin, 1994, Manon Lescaut, 1997, Le Nozze di Figaro and Don Giovanni, 2000, Glyndebourne; Die Meistersinger, Royal Opera, 1993; The Cherry Orchard, RSC, 1995; The Lion King, Broadway, 1997 (Tony Award, 1998), also London, Tokyo, Osaka, Toronto, Los Angeles, Hamburg; Samson et Dalila, Met. Opera, New York, 1998; Guillaume Tell and Ernani, Vienna State Opera, 1998; Peter Grimes, Amsterdam, 2000; Pique Dame, Chicago Lyric Opera, 2000; Tamerlano, Maggio Musicale Fiorentino, 2001; The Cunning Little Vixen, Opera North, 2001; Khovanshchina, Opéra de Paris, 2001. British Scenographic Comr, Orgn Internat. des Scénographes, Techniciens et Architectes de Théâtre, 1996–. FRSA 1999. *Address:* c/o Judy Daish Associates, 2 St Charles Place, W10 6EG.

HUDSON, Prof. Robert Francis, PhD; FRS 1982; Professor of Organic Chemistry, University of Kent at Canterbury, 1967–85 (part-time, 1981–85), now Emeritus; *b* 15 Dec. 1922; *s* of late John Frederick Hudson and Ethel Hudson; *m* 1945, Monica Ashton Stray (*d* 2000); one *s* twin *d*. *Educ:* Brigg Grammar Sch.; Imperial Coll. of Science and Technol., London (BSc, ARCS, PhD, DIC). Asst Lectr, Imperial Coll., London, 1945–47; Consultant, Wolsey Ltd, Leicester, 1945–50; Lectr, Queen Mary Coll., London, 1947–59; Res. Fellow, Purdue Univ., 1954; Gp Dir, Cyanamid European Res. Inst., Geneva, 1960–66. Vis. Professor: Rochester, USA, 1970; Bergen, 1971; CNRS, Thiais, Paris, 1973; Calgary, 1975; Mainz, 1979; Queen's, Kingston, Ont, 1983. Lectures: Frontiers, Case-Western Reserve Univ., USA, 1970; Nuffield, Canada, 1975; Quest, Queen's, Ont, 1983. Vice-Pres., Inst. of Science Technol., 1970–76; Member: Council, Chemical Soc., 1967–70 (Foundn Chm., Organic Reaction Mechanism Gp, 1973); Dalton Council, 1973–76; Perkin Council, 1980–83. *Publications:* (with P. Alexander) Wool—its physics and chemistry, 1954, 2nd edn 1960; Structure and Mechanism in Organophosphorus Chemistry, 1965; papers mainly in Jl of Chem. Soc., Helvetica

Chimica Acta and Angewandte Chemie. *Address:* 37 Puckle Lane, Canterbury, Kent CT1 3LA. *T:* (01227) 761340. *Club:* Athenæum.

HUDSON, Thomas Charles, CBE 1975; Chairman, ICL Ltd, 1972–80; Chartered Accountant (Canadian); *b* Sidcup, Kent, 23 Jan. 1915; British parents; *m* 1st, 1944, Lois Alma Hudson (marr. diss. 1973); two *s* one *d*; 2nd, 1986, Susan Gillian van Kan. *Educ:* Middleton High Sch., Nova Scotia. With Nightingale, Hayman & Co, Chartered Accountants, 1935–40. Served War, Royal Canadian Navy, Lieut, 1940–45. IBM Canada, as Sales Rep., 1946–51 (transf. to IBM, UK, as Sales Manager, 1951, and Managing Dir, 1954–65). Plessey Company: Financial Dir, 1967; Dir, 1969–76; Dir, ICL, 1968. Councillor for Enfield, GLC, 1970–73. *Recreations:* tennis, ski-ing, gardening. *Address:* Hele Farm, North Bovey, Devon TQ13 8RW. *T:* (01647) 440249. *Club:* Carlton.

HUDSON-BENDERSKY, Pamela May, CBE 1988; JP; Regional Nursing Director, North West Thames Regional Health Authority, 1985–88, retired; *b* 1 June 1931; *d* of late Leonard Joshua Hudson and of Mabel Ellen Hudson (now Baker); *m* 1987, David Bendersky, NY State and Kansas City. *Educ:* South West Essex High School. SRN. Nursing Officer, Charing Cross Hosp., 1966–67; Matron, Fulham Hosp., 1967–70; Principal Regl Nursing Officer, SE Thames RHB, 1970–73; Area Nursing Officer, Lambeth, Southwark and Lewisham AHA(T), 1973–82; Regional Nursing Officer, NW Thames RHA, 1982–85. Member, Alcohol Education and Research Council, 1982–87. JP: Inner London SE Div., 1983–88; N Glos (formerly Cheltenham) Petty Sessional Div., 1989–2001 (Chm., 1998–2001). *Publications:* contribs to nursing profession jls. *Recreations:* embroidery, theatre, gardening. *Address:* Uluru, 13 Northcot Lane, Draycott, near Moreton-in-Marsh, Glos GL56 9LR. *T:* (01386) 700142.

HUDSON DAVIES, (Gwilym) Ednyfed; *see* Davies.

HUDSON-WILKIN, Rev. Rose Josephine; Vicar, Holy Trinity, Dalston and All Saints, Haggerston, since 1998; Member, Broadcasting Standards Commission, since 1998; *b* 19 Jan. 1961; *m* 1983, Rev. Kenneth Wilkin; one *s* two *d*. *Educ:* Montego Bay High Sch.; Church Army Coll.; W Midlands Ministerial Trng Course; Birmingham Univ. (BPhil Ed 2000). Lay Trng Officer, Anglican Dio. Jamaica, 1982; ordained deacon, 1991, priest, 1994; Curate, St Matthew, Wolverhampton, 1991–94; Priest, Good Shepherd, W Bromwich, 1995–98; Officer for Black Anglican Concerns, Lichfield Dio., 1995–98. Mem., Gen. Synod of C of E, 1995–98; (Chm., Cttee for Minority Ethnic Anglican Concerns, 1999–). Mem., Theol Bd, WCC, 1996–98; Chm., Worldwide Cttee, SPCK, 1998–. *Recreations:* theatre, cooking, entertaining, tennis. *Address:* The Vicarage, Livermere Road, E8 4EZ.

HUEBNER, Michael Denis, CB 1994; Director General, Judicial Group, and Secretary of Commissions, Lord Chancellor's Department, 1998–2000; Deputy Clerk of the Crown in Chancery, 1993–2000; *b* 3 Sept. 1941; *s* of late Dr Denis William Huebner and Rene Huebner (*née* Jackson); *m* 1965, Wendy Ann, *d* of Brig. Peter Crosthwaite; one *s* one *d*. *Educ:* Rugby Sch.; St John's Coll., Oxford (BA Modern History). Called to the Bar, Gray's Inn, 1965, Bencher, 1994; Master of the House, 2001–. Lord Chancellor's Department, 1966–68; Law Officers' Dept, 1968–70; rejoined Lord Chancellor's Dept, 1970: Asst Solicitor, 1978; Under Sec., Circuit Administrator, NE Circuit, 1985–88; Prin. Estabt and Finance Officer, 1988–89; Dep. Sec., Judicial Appts, 1989; Sec. of Commns, 1989–91; Hd of Law and Policy Gps, 1991–93; Head, 1993–95, Chief Exec., 1995–98, Court Service. Trustee, St Luke's Community Trust, 2000–. *Publications:* brief guide to Ormesby Hall (Nat. Trust); contrib. (jtly) Courts, Halsbury's Laws of England, 4th edn 1975; legal articles in New Law Jl. *Recreations:* looking at pictures, architecture, theatre going. *Club:* Athenæum.

HUFFINLEY, Beryl; Chairman, Luban Action for Peace; formerly: President, National Assembly of Women; Vice President, British Peace Assembly; *b* 22 Aug. 1926; *d* of Wilfred and Ivey Sharpe; *m* 1948, Ronald Brown Huffinley. Secretary: Leeds Trades Council, 1966; Yorkshire and Humberside TUC Regional Council, 1974. Chairman: Leeds and York Dist Cttee, T&GWU, 1974; Regional Cttee, T&GWU No 9 Region, 1972. Member: Regional Econ. Planning Council (Yorkshire and Humberside), 1975–79; Leeds AHA, 1977; Press Council, 1978–84. Exec. Cttee, Labour Action for Peace. Trustee Yeadon Trade Council Club. *Address:* Cornerways, South View, Menston, Ilkley, West Yorks LS29 6JX. *T:* (01943) 875115. *Club:* Trades Council (Leeds).

HUFTON, Prof. Olwen, (Mrs B. T. Murphy), PhD; FBA 1993; Leverhulme Personal Research Professor, since 1997, and Senior Research Fellow, Merton College, since 1997, Oxford University; *d* of Joseph Hufton and Caroline Hufton; *m* 1965, Brian Taunton Murphy; two *d*. *Educ:* Hulme Grammar Sch., Oldham; Royal Holloway Coll., Univ. of London (BA 1959; Hon. Fellow, 2000); UCL (PhD 1962); DLitt Reading, 1999. Lectr, Univ. of Leicester, 1963–66; Reading University: Lectr, then Reader, 1966–75; Prof. of Modern Hist., 1975–88; Vis. Fellow, All Souls Coll., Oxford, 1986–87; Prof. of Modern Hist. and Women's Studies, Harvard Univ., 1987–91; Prof. of History, Eur. Univ. Inst., Florence, 1991–97. *Publications:* Bayeux in the Late Eighteenth Century, 1967; The Poor of Eighteenth Century France, 1974; Europe, Privilege and Protest, 1730–1789, 1980; Women and the Limits of Citizenship in the French Revolution, 1992; The Prospect before Her: a history of women in Western Europe, vol. 1, 1500–1800, 1995; articles in Past and Present, Eur. Studies Rev., and French Hist. Studies. *Address:* 40 Shinfield Road, Reading, Berks RG2 7BW. *T:* (0118) 987 1514.

HUGGINS, family name of **Viscount Malvern**.

HUGGINS, Sir Alan (Armstrong), Kt 1980; Justice of Appeal: British Antarctica, since 1988 (President, since 2000); Falkland Islands, since 1988 (President, since 1991); British Indian Ocean Territory (President), since 1991; *b* 15 May 1921; *yr s* of late William Armstrong Huggins and Dare (*née* Copping); *m* 1st, 1950, Catherine Davidson (marr. diss.), *d* of late David Dick; two *s* one *d*; 2nd, 1985, Elizabeth Low, *d* of late Christopher William Lumley Dodd, MRCS, LRCP. *Educ:* Radley Coll.; Sidney Sussex Coll., Cambridge (MA). TARO (Special List), 1940–48 (Actg Major); Admiralty, 1941–46. Called to Bar, Lincoln's Inn, 1947. Legal Associate Mem., TPI, 1949–70. Resident Magistrate, Uganda, 1951–53; Stipendiary Magistrate, Hong Kong, 1953–58; District Judge, Hong Kong, 1958–65. Chm., Justice (Hong Kong Br.), 1965–68; Judicial Comr, State of Brunei, 1966–2001 (Pres., 2001); Judge of Supreme Court, Hong Kong, 1965–76; Justice of Appeal, Hong Kong, 1976–80; Vice-Pres., Court of Appeal, Hong Kong, 1980–87; Justice of Appeal: Gibraltar, 1988–96; St Helena, 1988–97; Bermuda, 1989–2000; Mem., Ct of Final Appeal, HKSAR, China, 1997–. Hon. Lectr, Hong Kong Univ., 1979–87. Chm., Adv. Cttee on Legal Educn, 1972–87. Diocesan Reader, Dio. of Hong Kong and Macao, 1954–87; Reader, Dio. of Exeter, 1988–. Past Pres., YMCAs of Hong Kong. Hon. Life Governor, Brit. and For. Bible Soc; Hon. Life Mem., Amer. Bible Soc. Liveryman, Leathersellers' Company, 1942–91. *Recreations:* forestry, boating, archery, amateur theatre, tapestry. *Address:* Widdicombe Lodge, Widdicombe, Kingsbridge, Devon TQ7 2EF. *T:* (01548) 580727. *Club:* Royal Over-Seas League.

HUGGINS, Rt Rev. Philip James; *see* Grafton, NSW, Bishop of.

HUGH-JONES, Sir Wynn Normington, (Sir Hugh Jones), Kt 1984; LVO 1961; Joint Hon. Treasurer, Liberal Party, 1984–87; *b* 1 Nov. 1923; *s* of Huw Hugh-Jones and May Normington; *m* 1st, 1958, Ann (*née* Purkiss) (marr. diss. 1987); one *s* two *d*; 2nd, 1987, Oswynne (*née* Buchanan). *Educ:* Ludlow; Selwyn Coll., Cambridge (Scholar; MA) Served in RAF, 1943–46. Entered Foreign Service (now Diplomatic Service), 1947; Foreign Office, 1947–49; Jedda, 1949–52; Paris, 1952–56; FO, 1956–59; Chargé d'Affaires, Conakry, 1959–60; Head of Chancery, Rome, 1960–64; FO, 1964–66, Counsellor, 1964; Consul, Elizabethville (later Lubumbashi), 1966–68; Counsellor and Head of Chancery, Ottawa, 1968–70; FCO, 1971, attached Lord President's Office; Cabinet Office, 1972–73; Director-Gen., ESU, 1973–77; Sec.-Gen., Liberal Party, 1977–83. A Vice-Chm., European-Atlantic Gp, 1985–92; Vice-Pres., Lib. Internat. British Gp, 1995–98 (Patron, 1998–). Chm., Avebury in Danger, 1988–89. Gov., Queen Elizabeth Foundn for Disabled People, 1985–2001; Trustee, Wilts Community Foundn, 1991–93. FIMgt. *Recreations:* golf, gardening. *Address:* Fosse House, Avebury, Wilts SN8 1RF. *Clubs:* English-Speaking Union; N Wilts Golf.

HUGH SMITH, Sir Andrew (Colin), Kt 1992; Chairman, London Stock Exchange (formerly International Stock Exchange), 1988–94 (Member, 1970, Member of Council, 1981–91); Chairman, Barloworld (formerly Barlow International) Plc, since 2000; *b* 6 Sept. 1931; *s* of late Lt-Comdr Colin Hugh Smith and Hon. Mrs C. Hugh Smith; *m* 1964, Venetia, *d* of Lt-Col Peter Flower; two *s*. *Educ:* Ampleforth; Trinity Coll., Cambridge (BA). Called to Bar, Inner Temple, 1956; Hon. Bencher, 1995. Courtaulds Ltd, 1960–68; with Capel-Cure Carden (later Capel-Cure Myers), 1968–85; ANZ Merchant Bank, 1985–88. Chairman: Holland & Holland, 1987–95; Penna plc, then Penna Consulting Plc, 1995–2001; Eur. Adv. Bd, Accenture (formerly Andersen Consulting), 1995–; Director: Matheson Lloyds Investment Trust, 1994–97; Barloworld. (formerly J. Bibby & Sons, then Barlow Internat.), 1997–; Barlow Ltd, 1998–. Vice-Chm., GBDA, 1990–; Hon. Treas., Malcolm Sargent Cancer Fund for Children, 1992–. *Recreations:* gardening, shooting, fishing, reading. *Clubs:* Brooks's, Pratt's.

See also H. O. Hugh Smith.

HUGH SMITH, Col Henry Owen, LVO 1976; Defence Adviser to British High Commissioner, Nairobi, 1987–90; *b* 19 June 1937; *s* of Lt-Comdr Colin Hugh Smith and late Hon. Mrs C. Hugh Smith. *Educ:* Ampleforth; Magdalene Coll., Cambridge. BA Hons 1961. Commnd Royal Horse Guards, 1957; Blues and Royals, 1969; psc 1969; served Cyprus and Northern Ireland (wounded); Equerry in Waiting to The Duke of Edinburgh, 1974–76; CO The Blues and Royals, 1978–80; GSO1, MoD, 1980–87. Chm., BLESMA, 1996–. *Recreation:* sailing. *Clubs:* Boodle's, Pratt's; Royal Yacht Squadron, Royal Cruising.

See also Sir A. C. Hugh Smith.

HUGHES, family name of **Barons Hughes of Woodside** and **Islwyn**.

HUGHES OF WOODSIDE, Baron *cr* 1997 (Life Peer), of Woodside in the City of Aberdeen; **Robert Hughes;** *b* Pittenweem, Fife, 3 Jan. 1932; *m* 1957, Ina Margaret Miller; two *s* three *d*. *Educ:* Robert Gordon's Coll., Aberdeen; Benoni High Sch., Transvaal; Pietermaritzburg Tech. Coll., Natal. Emigrated S Africa, 1947, returned UK, 1954. Engrg apprentice, S African Rubber Co., Natal; Chief Draughtsman, C. F. Wilson & Co. (1932) Ltd, Aberdeen, until 1970. Mem., Aberdeen Town Council, 1962–70; Convener: Health and Welfare Cttee, 1963–68; Social Work Cttee, 1969–70. Mem., AEEU (formerly AEU), 1952–. Contested (Lab) North Angus and Mearns, 1959; MP (Lab) Aberdeen North, 1970–97. Member: Standing Cttee on Immigration Bill, 1971; Select Cttee, Scottish Affairs, 1971 and 1992–97; introd. Divorce (Scotland) Bill 1971 (failed owing to lack of time); Parly Under-Sec. of State, Scottish Office, 1974–75; sponsored (as Private Member's Bill) Rating (Disabled Persons) Act 1978; Principal Opposition Spokesman: on agriculture, 1983–84; on transport, 1985–88 (Jun. Opp. Spokesman, 1981–83); Mem., PLP Shadow Cabinet, 1985–88. Chm., Aberdeen City Labour Party, 1961–69. Vice-Chm., Tribune Gp, 1984–85. Founder Mem. and Aberdeen Chm., Campaign for Nuclear Disarmament; Vice-Chm., 1975–76, Chm., 1976–94, Anti-Apartheid Movement; Member: GMC, 1976–79; Movement for Colonial Freedom, 1955 (Chm. Southern Africa Cttee); Scottish Poverty Action Group; Aberdeen Trades Council and Exec. Cttee, 1957–69; Labour Party League of Youth, 1954–57; Chm., 1994–99, Hon. Pres., 1999–, Action for Southern Africa. *Recreation:* golf. *Address:* House of Lords, SW1A 0PW.

HUGHES, Alan; Managing Director, Whitechapel Bell Foundry Ltd (established 1570), since 1982; *b* 25 Aug. 1948; *s* of William A. Hughes and Florence I. Hughes; *m* 1985, Kathryn Smith; two *d*. *Educ:* Christ's Hosp. Church bell founder, 1966–. Freeman, City of London, 1984; Liveryman, Founders' Co., 2000. *Address:* Whitechapel Bell Foundry Ltd, 32 & 34 Whitechapel Road, E1 1DY.

HUGHES, Aneurin Rhys; Ambassador and Head of Delegation of European Commission to Australia and New Zealand, since 1995; *b* 11 Feb. 1937; *s* of William and Hilda Hughes; *m* 1964, Jill (*née* Salisbury); two *s*. *Educ:* University College of Wales, Aberystwyth (BA). President, National Union of Students, 1962–64. Research in S America, 1964–66; HM Diplomatic Service, 1967–73: served, Singapore and Rome; Commission of the European Communities, 1973–: Head of Division for Internal Coordination in Secretariat-General, 1973–77; Adviser to Dir. Gen. for Information, 1977–80; Chef de Cabinet to Mr Ivor Richard, Comr responsible for Employment, Social Affairs and Educn, 1981–85; Adviser to Dir Gen. for Information, and Chm., Selection Bd for Candidates from Spain and Portugal, 1985–87; Amb. and Head of Delegn in Norway, 1987–95. Organiser, Conf. on Culture, Economy and New Technologies, Florence, 1986–87. *Recreations:* squash, golf, music, hashing. *Address:* European Commission Delegation, 18 Arkana Street, Yarralumla, Canberra, ACT 2600, Australia.

HUGHES, Hon. Sir Anthony (Philip Gilson), Kt 1997; **Hon. Mr Justice Hughes;** a Judge of the High Court of Justice, Family Division, since 1997; *b* 11 Aug. 1948; *s* of late Patrick and Patricia Hughes; *m* 1972, Susan Elizabeth March; one *s* one *d*. *Educ:* Tettenhall Coll., Staffs; Van Mildert Coll., Durham (BA 1969). Sometime Lectr, Durham Univ. and QMC. Called to the Bar, Inner Temple, 1970, Bencher, 1997; a Recorder, 1988–97; QC 1990. Presiding Judge, Midland and Oxford Circuit, 2000–. *Recreations:* garden labouring and mechanics, campanology. *Address:* Royal Courts of Justice, Strand, WC2A 2LL. *Clubs:* Athenæum; Worcester Rowing.

HUGHES, Dr Antony Elwyn; consultant, since 1996; Director, Engineering and Science, and Deputy Chief Executive, Engineering and Physical Sciences Research Council, 1994–96; *b* 9 Sept. 1941; *s* of Ifor Elwyn Hughes and Anna Betty Hughes (*née* Ambler); *m* 1963, Margaret Mary Lewis; one *s* two *d* (and one *s* decd). *Educ:* Newport High Sch., Gwent; Jesus Coll., Oxford (MA; DPhil). CPhys; FInstP. Harkness Fellow, Cornell Univ., 1967–69. United Kingdom Atomic Energy Authority, Atomic Energy Research Establishment (Harwell): Scientific Officer, 1963–67; Sen. Scientific Officer, 1969–72; Principal Scientific Officer, 1972–75; Leader: Defects in Solids Gp, 1973; Solid

State Sciences Gp, 1978; Individual Merit Appointment, 1975–81; Sen. Personal Appointment, 1981–83; Head, Materials Physics Div., 1983–86; Dir, Underlying Res. and Non-Nuclear Energy Res., 1986–87; Authority Chief Scientist and Dir, Nuclear Res., 1987–88. Science and Engineering Research Council: Dir, Labs, 1988–91; Dir, Progs, and Dep. Chm., 1991–93; acting Chief Exec., 1993–94. Mem., NI Higher Educn Council, 1993–. Member Council: Royal Instn of GB, 1995–98; Careers Res. and Adv. Centre, 1994–. *Publications:* Real Solids and Radiation, 1975; (ed) Defects and their Structure in Non-Metallic Solids, 1976; review articles in Contemporary Physics, Advances in Physics, Jl of Materials Science, Jl of Nuclear Materials, Reports on Progress in Physics. *Recreations:* hill walking, watching Rugby and cricket, playing the trumpet, gardening. *Address:* Kingswood, King's Lane, Harwell, Didcot, Oxfordshire OX11 0EJ. *T:* (01235) 835301.

HUGHES, Beverley June; MP (Lab) Stretford and Urmston, since 1997; Parliamentary Under-Secretary of State, Home Office, since 2001; *b* 30 March 1950; *d* of Norman Hughes and Doris Hughes (*née* Gillard); *m* 1973, Thomas K. McDonald; one *s* two *d*. *Educ:* Manchester Univ. (BSc Hons, MSc); Liverpool Univ. (DSA, DASS). Merseyside Probation Service, 1973; Manchester University: Res. Fellow, 1976; Lectr, Sen. Lectr and Head of Dept of Social Policy and Social Work, 1981–97. Mem. (Lab), Trafford MBC, 1986–97 (Leader, 1995–97). Parly Under-Sec. of State, DETR, 1999–2001. *Publication:* Community Care and Older People, 1995. *Recreations:* jazz, walking, family. *Address:* House of Commons, SW1A 0AA. *T:* (020) 7219 3000.

HUGHES, Catherine Eva, CMG 1984; HM Diplomatic Service, retired; Principal, Somerville College, Oxford, 1989–96; *b* 24 Sept. 1933; *d* of Edmund Ernest Pestell and Isabella Cummine Sangster; *m* 1991, Dr (John) Trevor Hughes. *Educ:* Leeds Girls' High Sch.; St Hilda's Coll., Oxford (MA). FO, 1956; Third Sec., The Hague, 1958; Second Sec., Bangkok, 1961; FO, 1964; First Sec., UK Delegn to OECD, Paris, 1969; FCO, 1971; St Antony's Coll., Oxford, 1974; Counsellor, East Berlin, 1975–78; Cabinet Office, 1978–80; Diplomatic Service Inspector, 1980–82; Minister (Economic), Bonn, 1983–87; Asst Under-Sec. (Public Depts), FCO, 1987–89. *Address:* 2 Bishop Kirk Place, Oxford OX2 7HJ. *Club:* Reform.

See also J. E. Pestell.

HUGHES, Sir David (Collingwood), 14th Bt *cr* 1773; heraldic sculptor; Managing Director, Louis Lejeune Ltd, since 1978; *b* 29 Dec. 1936; *s* of Sir Richard Edgar Hughes, 13th Bt and Angela Lilian Adelaide Pell (*d* 1967); *S* father, 1970; *m* 1964, Rosemary Ann Pain, MA, LLM, *d* of late Rev. John Pain; three *s* (and one *s* decd). *Educ:* Oundle; Magdalene College, Cambridge (MA). National Service, RN, 1955–57. United Steel Cos Ltd, 1960–65; Unicam Instruments Ltd (subsequently Pye Unicam Ltd), export executive, 1965–70, E Europe manager, 1970–73. Builder, 1974–76. *Recreations:* shooting, fishing. *Heir: s* Thomas Collingwood Hughes, MSc, MBA, MRCP, FRCS [*b* 16 Feb. 1966; *m* 1996, Marina Louise Barbour, DPhil, MRCP, FRACP, *d* of Richard Barbour, Albany, WA]. *Address:* The Berristead, Wilburton, Ely, Cambs CB6 3RP. *T:* (01353) 740770. *Clubs:* Flyfishers'; Cambridge County (Cambridge).

HUGHES, (David Evan) Peter, MA; part-time teacher, Westminster School, since 1994; *b* 27 April 1932; *s* of late Evan Gwilliam Forrest-Hughes, OBE; *m* 1956, Iris (*née* Jenkins); one *s* one *d* (and one *d* decd). *Educ:* St Paul's Sch.; St John's Coll., Oxford (Gibbs Schol. in Chemistry; MA). National Service, 5 RHA, 1954. Assistant Master, Shrewsbury School, 1956; Head of Chemistry, 1958, Science, 1965; Nuffield Foundation, 1967–68; Second Master, Shrewsbury Sch., 1972; Headmaster, St Peter's Sch., York, 1980–84; Head of Science, Westminster Sch., 1984–89; Dir, Understanding Science Project, and Leverhulme Res. Fellow, Imperial Coll. and Westminster Sch., 1989–94. Chief Examr, Univ. of Cambridge Local Exam. Syndicate, 1968–. Chm., Friends' Cttee, Imperial Coll., 1992–94. *Publications:* Advanced Theoretical Chemistry (with M. J. Maloney), 1964; Chemical Energetics, 1967; (ed) Awareness of Science, 4 vols, 1993–94. *Recreations:* music, bridge, hill-walking. *Address:* Flat 1, 63 Millbank, SW1P 4RW.

HUGHES, David Glyn; National Agent, 1979–88, Senior National Officer, 1986–88, the Labour Party; *b* 1 March 1928; *s* of Richard and Miriam Hughes; *m* 1958, Mary Atkinson; one *d*. *Educ:* Darwin St Secondary Modern Sch. Apprentice, later fitter and turner, 1944–52; Labour Party Agent: Northwich, Bolton, Tonbridge, Portsmouth, 1952–69; Asst Regional Organiser, 1969–75, Regional Organiser, 1975–79, Northern Region. *Recreations:* gardening, walking. *Address:* Pembury, 7 Hayes Mead Road, Hayes, Bromley, Kent BR2 7HR. *T:* (020) 8462 1659. *Club:* Stella Maris Social (Life-Mem.) (Washington, Tyne and Wear).

HUGHES, David John, FRSL; writer; *b* 27 July 1930; *o s* of late Gwilym Fielden Hughes and of Edna Frances Hughes; *m* 1st, 1958, Mai Zetterling; 2nd, 1980, Elizabeth Westoll; one *s* one *d*. *Educ:* Eggar's Grammar Sch., Alton; King's College Sch., Wimbledon; Christ Church, Oxford (MA; Editor, Isis). FRSL 1986. Editorial Asst, London Magazine, 1953–55; Reader with Rupert Hart-Davis, 1956–60; Editor, Town magazine, 1960–61; script-writer and stills photographer of BBC documentaries and Scandinavian feature-films directed by Mai Zetterling, 1960–72; Editor, New Fiction Society, 1975–78, 1981–82. Asst Visiting Professor: Writers' Workshop, Univ. of Iowa, 1978–79, 1987; Univ. of Alabama, 1979; Vis. Assoc. Prof., Univ. of Houston, 1986. Film Critic, Sunday Times, 1982–83; Fiction Critic, 1982–99, Theatre Critic, 1996, Mail on Sunday. Mem. Council, RSL, 1989–96 (Life Vice Pres., 1998). Editor, Letters, jl of RSL, 1992–96. *Publications: fiction:* A Feeling in the Air, 1957; Sealed with a Loving Kiss, 1958; The Horsehair Sofa, 1961; The Major, 1964; The Man Who Invented Tomorrow, 1968; Memories of Dying, 1976; A Genoese Fancy, 1979; The Imperial German Dinner Service, 1983; The Pork Butcher, 1984 (Welsh Arts Council Fiction Prize, 1984; W. H. Smith Literary Award, 1985; filmed as Souvenir, 1989); But for Bunter, 1985; The Little Book, 1996; (ed) Winter's Tales: New Series I, 1985; (ed with Giles Gordon): Best Short Stories, annually 1986–95; The Best of Best Short Stories 1986–1995, 1995; *non-fiction:* J. B. Priestley, an informal study, 1958; The Road to Stockholm (travel), 1964; The Seven Ages of England (cultural history), 1967; The Rosewater Revolution, 1971; Evergreens, 1976; Himself & Other Animals: a portrait of Gerald Durrell, 1997; The Lent Jewels, 2002. *Address:* 163 Kennington Road, SE11 6SF. *Clubs:* Savile; Surrey CC.

HUGHES, His Honour David Morgan; a Circuit Judge, 1972–98; *b* 20 Jan. 1926; *s* of late Rev. John Edward Hughes and Mrs Margaret Ellen Hughes; *m* 1956, Elizabeth Jane Roberts; one *s* two *d*. *Educ:* Beaumaris Grammar Sch.; LSE (LLB). Army, 1944 48: Captain, Royal Welch Fusiliers; attached 2nd Bn The Welch Regt; Burma, 1945–47. London Univ., 1948–51; Rockefeller Foundn Fellowship in Internat. Air Law, McGill Univ., 1951–52; called to Bar, Middle Temple, 1953; practised Wales and Chester Circuit; Dep. Chm., Caernarvonshire QS, 1970–71; a Recorder, Jan.–Nov. 1972; Dep. Chm., Agricultural Lands Tribunal, 1972; Mem., Mental Health Review Tribunal, 1989–98. Pres., Council, HM Circuit Judges for England and Wales, 1995. *Recreations:* tennis, cricket, gardening. *Address:* Bryn, Kelsall, Cheshire CW6 0PA. *T:* (01829) 751349.

HUGHES, David Richard; Political Editor, Daily Mail, since 1994; *b* 3 April 1951; *s* of John Arfon Hughes and Lilian Elvira Hughes (*née* Jones); *m* 1973, Christine O'Brien; two *s*. *Educ:* Cowbridge Grammar Sch.; Univ. of Leicester (BA Hons Hist.). Reporter, Merthyr Express, 1973–76; Leader Writer, 1976–79, Political Corresp., 1979–84, Western Mail; Political Reporter, Daily Mail, 1984–86; Political Corresp., 1986–89, Chief Political Corresp., 1989–92, Sunday Times; Editor, Western Mail, 1992–94. *Recreations:* Rugby, music, family, surfing. *Address:* 7 Southfield Gardens, Strawberry Hill, Twickenham TW1 4SZ. *T:* (020) 8892 5726.

HUGHES, Dr David Treharne Dillon, FRCP; Consultant Physician, Royal London (formerly London) Hospital, 1970–96; Director, Respiratory Medicine, Royal Hospitals NHS Trust, 1994–96; Head, Department of Clinical Investigation, Wellcome Research Laboratories, 1978–93; *b* 31 Oct. 1931; *s* of Maj.-Gen. W. D. Hughes, CB, CBE; *m* 1959, Gloria Anna Bailey; one *s* two *d*. *Educ:* Cheltenham Coll.; Trinity Coll., Oxford (BSc, MA); London Hosp. Medical Coll. (BM BCh); RPMS. MRCP 1959, FRCP 1972. Jun. hosp. posts, London Hosp., 1957–59; Capt. RAMC, 1959–61 (jun. med. specialist, BMH Hong Kong); Res. Fellow, Univ. of Calif, 1963–64; jun. hosp. appts, London Hosp., 1964–70. Mem., GMC, 1993–96. Past President: Internat. Soc. Internal Medicine; Hunterian Soc. Chm., Bd of Govs, Moving Theatre Trust, 1994–. Master, Soc. of Apothecaries, 1992–93. *Publications:* Tropical Health Science, 1967; Human Biology and Hygiene, 1969; Lung Function for the Clinician, 1981; numerous scientific papers on respiratory function and chest disease. *Recreations:* cricket, rowing, horse racing. *Address:* 94 Overbury Avenue, Beckenham, Kent BR3 6PY. *T:* (020) 8650 3983; Littleport Farm, Sedgeford, Norfolk PE36 5LR. *T:* (01485) 570955. *Clubs:* Savage; Leander (Henley-on-Thames).

HUGHES, Hon. Sir Davis, Kt 1975; Agent-General for New South Wales, in London, 1973–78; *b* 24 Nov. 1910; *m* 1940, Joan Philip Johnson; one *s* two *d*. *Educ:* Launceston High Sch., Tasmania; Phillip Smith Teachers' Coll., Hobart, Tas. Teacher, Tasmania, incl. Friends' Sch., Hobart, 1930–35; Master, Caulfield Grammar Sch., Melbourne, 1935–40. Served War, Sqdn Ldr, RAAF, Australia and overseas, 1940–45. Dep. Headmaster, Armidale Sch., Armidale, NSW, 1946–49; Mayor of Armidale, 1953–56. MLA, NSW, 1950–53 and 1956–65; Minister for Public Works, NSW, 1965–73. Aust. Rep., 1978–83, Dir, 1980–83, Société Génerale Australia Ltd; Rep., Derek Crouch Aust. Ltd, 1978–84. Hon. DEd Newcastle, NSW, 1996. Freeman: City of Armidale, NSW, 1965; City of London, 1975. *Recreations:* tennis, golf, fishing, racing. *Address:* 53 The Manor, 6 Tarragal Glen Road, Erina, NSW 2250, Australia. *Club:* Australasian Pioneers (Sydney).

HUGHES, Dr (Edgar) John; HM Diplomatic Service; Ambassador to Venezuela, since 2000; *b* 27 July 1947; *s* of William Thomas Hughes and Martha Hughes (*née* Riggs); *m* 1982, Lynne Evans; two *s*. *Educ:* Lewis Sch., Pengam, Wales; LSE (BSc Econ 1969); Lehigh Univ., USA (MA 1970); Pembroke Coll., Cambridge (Univ. of Cambridge Sara Norton Res. Prize in Amer. Hist., 1972; PhD 1973). FCO, 1973–79; on secondment to Cabinet Office, 1979–81; First Sec., UK Delegn to CSCE, Madrid, 1981–82; FCO, 1982–83; First Sec. and Head of Chancery, Santiago, 1983–85, First Sec. (Inf.), Washington, 1985–89; Counsellor and Hd of Aviation and Maritime Dept, FCO 1990–93; Dep. Hd of Mission, Norway, 1993–97 ; Change Manager, FCO, 1997–99; on secondment to BAE Systems, 1999–2000. *Publications:* The Historian as Diplomat (with P. A. Reynolds), 1976; articles in internat. affairs jls. *Recreations:* running, ski-ing, tennis, watching Rugby, reading. *Address:* c/o Foreign and Commonwealth Office, SW1A 2AH. *Club:* Rhymney Rugby Football.

HUGHES, Edmwnd Goronwy M.; *see* Moelwyn-Hughes.

HUGHES, Prof. George Morgan; Professor of Zoology, Bristol University, 1965–85, now Emeritus; *b* 17 March 1925; *s* of James Williams Hughes and Edith May Hughes; *m* 1954, Jean Rosemary, *d* of Rowland Wynne Frazier and Jessie Frazier; two *s* one *d*. *Educ:* Liverpool Collegiate Sch.; King's Coll., Cambridge (Scholar; Frank Smart Prize, 1946; Martin Thackeray Studentship, 1946–48; MA, PhD, ScD). Cambridge Univ. Demonstrator, 1950–55, Lectr, 1955–65; successively Bye-Fellow, Research Fellow and Fellow of Magdalene Coll., Cambridge, 1949–65; University of Bristol: Head of Dept of Zoology, 1965–70; Head of Res. Unit for Comparative Animal Respiration, 1970–90. Research Fellow, California Inst. of Technology, 1958–59; Visiting Lectr in Physiology, State Univ. of New York, at Buffalo, 1964; Visiting Professor: Duke Univ., 1969; Japan Society for the Promotion of Science, Kochi, Kyoto, Kyushu and Hokkaido Univs, 1974; Univ. of Regensburg, 1977; Univs of Bhagalpur and Bretagne Occidentale, 1979; Kuwait, 1983; Nairobi, 1985. Invited Prof., Nat. Inst. of Physiolog. Sciences, Okazaki, 1980; Hon. Prof., Univ. of Wales Coll. of Cardiff, 1991–99. Mem., Internat. Cœlacanth Expdn, 1972. *Publications:* Comparative Physiology of Vertebrate Respiration, 1963; (jtly) Physiology of Mammals and other Vertebrates, 1965; (jtly) Air-breathing Fishes of India, 1992; (ed) several symposium vols; papers in Jl of Experimental Biology and other scientific jls, mainly on respiration of fishes. *Recreations:* travel, Welsh genealogy, photography; hockey for Cambridge Univ., 1945, and Wales, 1952–53. *Address:* 11 Lodge Drive, Long Ashton, Bristol BS41 9JF. *T:* (01275) 393402.

HUGHES, Very Rev. Geraint Morgan Hugh; Dean of Brecon, 1998–2000; *b* 21 Nov. 1934; *s* of late Ven. Hubert Hughes, Archdeacon of Gower, and late Blodwen Hughes; *m* 1959, Rosemary Criddle; one *s* one *d*. *Educ:* Brecon Grammar Sch.; Keble Coll., Oxford (BA 1958; MA 1963); St Michael's Coll., Llandaff. Nat. Service, RAF, 1953–55. Ordained deacon, 1959, priest, 1960; Curate: Gorseinon, 1959–63; Oystermouth, 1963–68; Rector: Llanbadarn Fawr Group, 1968–76; Llandrindod with Cefnllys, 1976–98; Canon of Brecon Cathedral, 1989–98; RD of Maelienydd, 1995–98. Chaplain, Mid and West Wales Fire Bde, 1996–. Paul Harris Fellow, Rotary Club, 1991. SBStJ 1995. *Recreations:* gardening, computing. *Address:* Hafod, Cefnllys Lane, Penybont, Llandrindod Wells, Powys LD1 5SW. *T:* (01597) 851830.

HUGHES, Rev. Dr Gerard Joseph, SJ; Master, Campion Hall, University of Oxford, since 1998; *b* 6 June 1934; *s* of Henry B. Hughes and Margaret (*née* Barry). *Educ:* Campion Hall, Oxford (MA Greats 1962); Heythrop Coll. (STL 1967); Univ. of Michigan (PhD 1970). Entered Society of Jesus, 1951; ordained priest, 1967; Heythrop College, University of London: Lectr in Philosophy, 1970–98; Head, Dept of Philosophy, 1974–96; Vice-Principal, 1984–98. *Publications:* Authority in Morals, 1978; (ed) The Philosophical Assessment of Theology, 1987; The Nature of God, 1995. *Recreations:* classical music, gardening. *Address:* Campion Hall, Oxford OX1 1QS. *T:* (01865) 286101.

HUGHES, Glyn Tegai, MA, PhD; Warden of Gregynog, University of Wales, 1964–89; *b* 18 Jan. 1923; *s* of Rev. John Hughes and Keturah Hughes; *m* 1957, Margaret Vera Herbert (*d* 1996), Brisbane, Qld; two *s*. *Educ:* Newtown and Towyn County Sch.; Liverpool Institute; Manchester Grammar Sch.; Corpus Christi Coll., Cambridge (Schol., MA, PhD). Served War, Royal Welch Fusiliers, 1942–46 (Major). Lector in English, Univ. of Basel, 1951–53; Lectr in Comparative Literary Studies, Univ. of Manchester, 1953–64, and Tutor to Faculty of Arts, 1961–64. Contested (L) Denbigh Div., elections 1950, 1955 and 1959. Mem., Welsh Arts Council, 1967–76; Nat. Governor for Wales, BBC, and Chm., Broadcasting Council for Wales, 1971–79; Member: Bd, Channel Four Television Co., 1980–87; Welsh Fourth TV Channel Authy., 1981–87. Chm., Welsh

Broadcasting Trust, 1988–96; Vice-Pres., N Wales Arts Assoc., 1977–94; Chm., Undeb Cymru Fydd, 1968–70. Hon. Fellow, Univ. of Wales Aberystwyth, 2000. Methodist local preacher, 1942–. *Publications:* Eichendorffs Taugenichts, 1961; Romantic German Literature, 1979; (ed) Life of Thomas Olivers, 1979; Williams Pantycelyn, 1983; (with David Esslemont) Gwasg Gregynog: a descriptive catalogue, 1990; articles in learned journals and Welsh language periodicals. *Recreation:* book-collecting. *Address:* Rhyd-y-gro, Tregynon, Newtown, Powys SY16 3PR. *T:* (01686) 650609.

HUGHES, Dr Graham Robert Vivian, FRCP; Consultant, and Head, Lupus Research Unit, St Thomas' Hospital, since 1985; *b* 26 Nov. 1940; *s* of G. Arthur Hughes and Elizabeth Emily Hughes; *m* 1966, Monica Ann Austin; one *s* one *d*. *Educ:* Cardiff High Sch. for Boys; London Hosp. Med. Coll. (MB BS 1967; MD 1973). Trng posts, London Hosp., 1967–69; Vis. Fellow, Columbia Univ., NY, 1969–70; Sen. Registrar, Hammersmith Hosp., 1970–73; Consultant, Univ. Hosp. of WI, Kingston, Jamaica, 1974; Consultant, and Reader in Medicine, Hammersmith Hosp., 1975–85. Ed., Lupus, 1991–; mem., editl bds of numerous jls. Consultant, RAF, 1985–. Life Pres., Lupus UK, 1985; Chm., Hughes Syndrome Foundn. Rheumatology World Prize, Internat. League against Rheumatism, 1993. *Publications:* Connective Tissue Diseases, 1977, 4th edn 1994; Modern Topics in Rheumatology, 1977; Clinics in Rheumatic Diseases: Systemic Lupus Erythematosus, 1982; Lupus: a guide for patients, 1985; Lecture Notes in Rheumatology, 1986; Problems in the Rheumatic Diseases: lessons from patients, 1988; Phospholipid Binding Antibodies, 1991; Autoimmune Connective Tissue Diseases, 1993; Antibodies to Endothelial Cells and Vascular Damage, 1993; Hughes Syndrome, 1998; Lupus: the facts, 2000; Hughes Syndrome: a patients guide, 2001; contrib. numerous papers on lupus and related diseases. *Recreations:* tennis, golf, sailing, piano (classical and jazz). *Address:* Lupus Research Unit, Rayne Institute, St Thomas' Hospital, SE1 7EH.

HUGHES, (Harold) Paul; Director of Finance, BBC, 1971–84; Director, Lazard Select Investment Trust Ltd, 1988–2001; *b* 16 Oct. 1926; *o s* of Edmund and Mabel Hughes; *m* 1955, Beryl Winifred Runacres; one *s* one *d*. *Educ:* Stand Grammar Sch., Whitefield, near Manchester. Certified Accountant. Westminster Bank Ltd, 1942–45; Royal Marines and Royal Navy, 1945–49; Arthur Guinness Son & Co. Ltd, 1950–58; British Broadcasting Corporation: Sen. Accountant, 1958–61; Asst Chief Accountant, Finance, 1961–69; Chief Accountant, Television, 1969–71; Pension Fund Consultant, 1984–89; Chm., BBC Enterprises Ltd, 1979–82; Chm., Visnews Ltd, 1984–85; Chief Exec., BBC Pension Trust Ltd, 1987–89. Chm, Pan European Property Unit Trust, 1987–96; Director: Kleinwort Benson Farmland Trust (Managers) Ltd, 1976–89; Keystone Investment Co. PLC, later Mercury Keystone Investment Trust PLC, 1988–96. *Recreations:* opera, gardening. *Address:* 26 Downside Road, Guildford, Surrey GU4 8PH. *T:* (01483) 569166.

HUGHES, (Harold) Victor, CBE 1989; FRAgS; Principal, Royal Agricultural College, Cirencester, 1978–90, Principal Emeritus 1990; *b* 2 Feb. 1926; *s* of Thomas Brindley Hughes and Hilda Hughes (*née* Williams). *Educ:* Tenby County Grammar Sch.; UCW, Aberystwyth (BSc). FRAgS 1980. Lectr, Glamorgan Training Centre, Pencoed, 1947–49; Crop Husbandry Adv. Officer, W Midland Province, Nat. Agricultural Adv. Service, 1950; Lectr in Agric., RAC, 1950–54; Vice Principal, Brooksby Agricultural Coll., Leics, 1954–60; Royal Agricultural College: Farms Dir and Principal Lectr in Farm Management, 1960–76; Vice Principal and Farms Dir, 1976–78. Hon. ARICS 1984. FIAgrM 1992. *Publications:* articles in learned jls and agric. press. *Recreation:* shooting. *Address:* No 17 Quakers Row, Coates, Cirencester, Glos GL7 6JX.

HUGHES, Henry Andrew Carne M.; *see* Meyric Hughes.

HUGHES, Howard; World Managing Partner, Price Waterhouse, 1992–98; *b* 4 March 1938; *s* of Charles William Hughes and Ethel May Hughes (*née* Howard); *m* 1st, 1964, Joy Margaret Pilmore-Bedford (*d* 1984); two *s* one *d*; 2nd, 1988, Christine Margaret Miles; one *s*. *Educ:* Rydal School. FCA. Articled Bryce Hanmer & Co., Liverpool, 1955; joined Price Waterhouse, London, 1960: Partner, 1970; Dir, London Office, 1982; Managing Partner, UK, 1985–91; Member: World Bd, 1988–98; World Mgt Cttee, 1990–98. Auditor, Duchy of Cornwall, 1983–98. Mem., Agricl Wages Bd, 1990–99. Chairman: Royal London Soc. for the Blind, 2000– (Mem. Council, 1985–); Exec. Cttee, British Heart Foundn, 2000– (Mem. Council, 1996–). Chm. Govs, Dorton House Sch., 1998–; Trustee and Chm. Finance Cttee, Utd Westminster Schs, 1999–. *Recreations:* golf, music. *Address:* Witham, Woodland Rise, Seal, Sevenoaks, Kent TN15 0HZ. *T:* (01732) 761161, *Fax:* (01732) 763553. *Clubs:* Carlton, MCC; Wildernesse Golf (Sevenoaks).

HUGHES, Iain Hamilton-Douglas; QC 1996; a Recorder, since 2000; *b* 7 Dec. 1950; *s* of late John Sidney Mather and of Jessica Hamilton-Douglas; *m* 1978, Claudia Madeleine, *yr d* of Baron Ackner, *qv*; one *s* one *d* (and one *s* decd). *Educ:* Moseley Hall Grammar Sch., Cheadle; Univ. of Bristol (LLB). Called to the Bar, Inner Temple, 1974; Bencher, 2001. Asst Recorder, 1997–2000. Chm., Professional Negligence Bar Assoc., 2000–01 (Vice-Chm., 1997–99). *Publication:* (ed) Jackson and Powell on Professional Negligence, 3rd edn 1992, 4th edn 1997, and annual supplements. *Recreations:* theatre, cinema, pottering in workshop. *Address:* 4 New Square, Lincoln's Inn, WC2A 3RJ. *T:* (020) 7822 2000.

HUGHES, Ian Noel; HM Diplomatic Service; Deputy Head of Mission and Consul General, Mexico, since 2000; *b* 5 Dec. 1951; *s* of Robert John Hughes and Sylvia Betty Hughes (*née* Lewis); *m* 1978, Tereasa June Tinguely; two *s* one *d*. *Educ:* Khormaksar, Aden; St John's, Singapore. FCO, 1971–74; Latin America Floater, 1974–76; Vice-Consul: Kabul, 1976–80; Warsaw, 1980–82; S Pacific Dept, FCO, 1982–85; Second Sec. and Vice-Consul, Tegucigalpa, 1985–88; First Sec. (Political), Berne, 1988–90; News Dept, FCO, 1991–93; First Sec. (Press/Information), New Delhi, 1993–97; Dep. Hd, Near East and N Africa Dept, FCO, 1997–2000. *Recreations:* reading, history, travel, playing golf badly. *Address:* c/o Foreign and Commonwealth Office, King Charles Street, SW1A 2AH. *Club:* Royal Over-Seas League.

HUGHES, Prof. Ieuan Arwel, FRCP, FRCPCH, FMedSci; Professor and Head of Department of Paediatrics, University of Cambridge, since 1989; Fellow of Clare Hall, Cambridge, since 1994; *b* 9 Nov. 1944; *s* of Arwel Hughes and Enid Phillips (*née* Thomas); *m* 1969, Margaret Maureen Davies; two *s* one *d*. *Educ:* Univ. of Wales Coll. of Medicine, Cardiff (MB, BCh, MD); MA Cantab, 1991. MRCP 1971, FRCP 1984; FRCPC 1974; FRCPCH 1997; MRSocMed. Medical Registrar, UCH, 1970–72; Senior Paediatric Resident, Dalhousie Univ., Canada, 1972–74; Endocrine Research Fellow, Manitoba Univ., Canada, 1974–76; MRC Fellow, Tenovus Inst., Cardiff, 1976–78; Consultant Paediatrician, Bristol, 1978–79; Senior Lectr in Child Health, 1979–85, Reader in Child Health, 1985–89, Univ. of Wales Coll. of Medicine, Cardiff. Mem., DoH Cttee on Toxicity of Chemicals in Food, Consumer Products and the Envmt (Phytoestrogen Working Gp). President: European Soc. for Paediatric Endocrinology, 1993– (Sec., 1987–92); Assoc. of Clinical Profs of Paediatrics, 1995–99; Mem. Council, Soc. for Endocrinology. Mem., Ralph Vaughan Williams Soc. Founder FMedSci 1998. *Publications:* Handbook of Endocrine Tests in Children, 1986; articles on paediatric endocrine disorders, steroid biochemistry and mechanism of steroid hormone action. *Recreations:* music (choral singing, bassoon, piano, concert-going), travel, hill walking, squash. *Address:* c/o Department of Paediatrics, Level 8, Addenbrooke's Hospital, Hills Road, Cambridge CB2 2QQ; 4 Latham Road, Cambridge CB2 2EQ.

HUGHES, Sir Jack (William), Kt 1980; chartered surveyor; Director, South Bank Estates and subsidiary companies, since 1960; Consultant, Jones, Lang, Wootton, 1976–99 (a Senior Partner, 1949–76); *b* 26 Sept. 1916; 2nd *s* of George William Hughes and Isabel Hughes, Maidstone, Kent; *m* 1st, 1939, Marie-Theresa (Slade School scholar) (*d* 1987), *d* of Graham Parmley and Jessie Thompson; 2nd, 1994, Helena, *d* of Franciszek and Katrzyna Kanik. *Educ:* Maidstone Grammar Sch.; Univ. of London. BSc (Est. Man.); BA Hons Open 1994. FRICS; FRIPHH. Served with Special Duties Br., RAF, 1940–46; demobilised Squadron Leader. Chairman: Bracknell Develt Corp., 1971–82; Property Adv. Gp, DoE, 1978–82; Director: URPT, 1961–86; MEPC, 1971–86; Housing Corporation (1974) Ltd, 1974–77; BR Property Bd, 1976–86; BR Investment Co., 1981–84; Property and Reversionary Investments, 1982–87; TR Property Investment Trust and subsid. cos, 1982–91; Brighton Marina Co. (Rep., Brighton Corp.), 1974–86; Undercliff Hldgs Ltd, 1986–93; Mem. Cttee, Mercantile Credit Gp Property Div.; Mem. Cttee of Management, Charities Property Unit Trust, 1967–74; Chm., South Hill Park Arts Centre Trust, 1972–79; Member: Adv. Gp to DoE on Commercial Property Develt, 1974–78; DoE Working Party on Housing Tenure, 1976–77. Founder Mem., Continuing Professional Develt Foundn (Mem. Adv. Bd, 1980–). A Vice-Pres., Pestalozzi Children's Village Trust, 1994–. Trustee, New Towns Pension Fund, 1975–82. Freeman, City of London, 1959–; Liveryman, Painter Stainers Guild, 1960–. FICPD 1998; FRSA. *Publications:* (jtly) Town and Country Planning Act 1949 (RICS); (Chm. of RICS Cttee) The Land Problem: a fresh approach; (co-ed) Glossary of Property Terms, 1990; techn. articles on property investment, develt and finance. *Recreations:* golf, travel, reading. *Address:* Challoners, The Green, Rottingdean, Brighton, Sussex BN2 7DD. *Club:* Royal Air Force.

HUGHES, James Ernest, PhD; FREng; Director, 1973–85 and Managing Director and Chief Executive, 1983–84, Johnson Matthey PLC; *b* 3 Nov. 1927; *s* of Herbert Thomas Hughes and Bessie Beatrice Hughes; *m* 1950, Hazel Aveline (*née* Louguet-Layton); three *d*. *Educ:* Spring Grove Sch.; Imperial Coll., London Univ, (BSc, ARSM (Bessemer Medalist); DIC); PhD London 1952. FIM, MIMM; FREng (FEng 1981). Associated Electrical Industries, 1952–63; Johnson Matthey PLC, 1963–85. Vis. Professor, Univ. of Sussex, 1974–80. President: Inst. of Metals, 1972–73; Metals Soc., 1981–82; Instn of Metallurgists, 1982–83. FRSA 1978. *Publications:* scientific papers in learned jls. *Recreations:* antiques, music, gardening. *Address:* Newlyn, Purse Caundle, Sherborne, Dorset DT9 5QY.

HUGHES, Janis; Member (Lab) Glasgow Rutherglen, Scottish Parliament, since 1999; *b* 1 May 1958; *d* of Thomas Nish and Janet (*née* Cumming); *m* (marr. diss.). *Educ:* Queen's Park Sch., Glasgow; Western Coll. of Nursing, Glasgow. Nursing: Royal Hosp. for Sick Children, Glasgow, 1980–82; Victoria Infirmary, Glasgow, 1982–86; Belvidere Hosp., Glasgow, 1986–88; Health Service Adminr, Renal Unit, Glasgow Royal Infirmary, 1988–99. Steward, 1980–83, Sec., Glasgow Royal Infirmary Br., 1993–99, NUPE, then UNISON. *Recreations:* reading, cooking. *Address:* 8 Upper Bourtree Court, Rutherglen G73 4HT. *T:* (0141) 634 7430.

HUGHES, John; *see* Hughes, E. J. and Hughes, R. J.

HUGHES, John; *b* 29 May 1925; *m*; two *s*. *Educ:* Durham. Served with Fleet Air Arm, 1943–45. Apprentice joiner; then miner and mechanic; worked for GEC, and Unipart (TGWU convener). Mem., Coventry City Council, 1974–82; Chm., Coventry NE Lab Party, 1978–81. MP (Lab) Coventry North East, 1987–92; contested (Ind. Lab) Coventry North East, 1992. *Address:* 15 Stafford Close, Bulkington, Bedworth, Nuneaton, Warwicks CV12 9QX.

HUGHES, Prof. John, PhD; FRS 1993; Director, Parke-Davis Neuroscience Research Centre (formerly Parke-Davis Research Unit), Cambridge University Forvie Site, Cambridge, since 1983; Senior Research Fellow, Wolfson College, University of Cambridge, since 1983; Vice President, Drug Discovery, Warner-Lambert, Europe, since 1988; *b* 6 Jan. 1942; *s* of Joseph and Edith Hughes; *m* 1967, Madelaine Carol Jennings (marr. diss. 1981); one *d*; three *s* one *d*; *m* 1997, Ann Rosemary Elizabeth, *d* of Joseph and Norma Mutty; one step *s* one step *d*. *Educ:* Mitcham County Grammar Sch. for Boys; Chelsea Coll., London (BSc); Inst. of Basic Med. Sciences, London (PhD). MA Cantab, 1988. Res. Fellow, Yale Univ. Med. Sch., 1967–69; University of Aberdeen: Lectr in Pharmacology, 1969–77; Dep.-Dir, Drug Res. Unit, 1973–77; Imperial College, London University: Reader in Pharmacol Biochemistry, 1977–79; Prof. of Pharmacol Biochemistry, 1979–82; Vis. Prof., 1983–. Hon. Professor: of Neuropharmacology, Univ. of Cambridge, 1989–; of Pharmacol., Aberdeen Univ., 1998–. Member: Substance Abuse Cttee, Mental Health Foundn, 1986–; Scientific Cttee, Assoc. of British Pharmaceutical Industry, 1990–95; Bd, Nat. Inst. for Biol Standards and Control, 1999–; Chm., Res. Cttee, Chronic Fatigue Syndrome (formerly Persistent Virus Disease) Res. Foundn, 1992– (Trustee of the Foundn, 1997–). Mem. Council, Internat. Sch. Neuroscience, 1988–. Editor: Brit. Jl Pharmacol., 1977–83; Brain Res., 1976–; Jt Chief Exec. Editor, Neuropeptides, 1980–. J. Y. Dent Meml Lectr, Soc. for Study of Drug Addiction, 1976; Oliver-Sharpey Lectr, RCP, 1980; Gaddum Lectr and Medal, British Pharmacol Soc., 1982. Mem., Royal Acad. of Medicine, Belgium, 1983. Dr *hc* Univ. of Liège, 1978. Sandoz Prize, British Pharmacol Soc., 1975; Pacesetter Award, US Nat. Inst. on Drug Abuse, 1977; Lasker Prize, Albert and Mary Lasker Foundn, NY, 1978; Scientific Medal, Soc. for Endocrinology, 1980; W. Feldberg Foundn Award, 1981; Lucien Dautrebande Prize, Fondation de Pathophysiologie, Belgium, 1983; Lilly Award, European Coll. of Neuropsychopharmacology, 1992. *Publications:* Centrally Acting Peptides, 1978; Opioids Past, Present and Future, 1984; (ed jtly) The Neuropeptide Cholecystokinin (CCK), 1989; articles in Nature, Science, Brit. Jl Pharmacol., and Brain Res. *Recreations:* family, friends, gardening. *Address:* Parke-Davis Neuroscience Research Centre, Cambridge University Forvie Site, Robinson Way, Cambridge CB2 2QB. *T:* (01223) 210929.

HUGHES, Very Rev. John Chester; Vicar of Bringhurst with Great Easton and Drayton, 1978–87; *b* 20 Feb. 1924; *m* 1950, Sybil Lewis McClelland; three *s* two *d* (and one *s* decd). *Educ:* Dulwich Coll.; St John's Coll., Durham (BA 1948; DipTh 1950; MA 1951). Curate of Westcliffe-on-Sea, Essex, 1950–53; Succentor of Chelmsford Cathedral, 1953–55; Vicar of St Barnabas, Leicester, 1955–61; Vicar of Croxton Kerrial with Branston-by-Belvoir, 1961–63; Provost of Leicester, 1963–78. ChStJ 1974. *Publication:* The Story of Launde Abbey, 1998. *Address:* 29 High Street, Hallaton, Market Harborough, Leics LE16 8UD. *T:* (01858) 555622.

HUGHES, John Dennis; Consultant, Trade Union Research Unit; Principal, Ruskin College, Oxford, 1979–89 (Tutor in Economics and Industrial Relations, 1957–70, and Vice Principal, 1970–79); *b* 28 Jan. 1927; *m* 1949, Violet (*née* Henderson); four *d*. *Educ:* Westminster City Sch.; Lincoln Coll., Oxford (MA). Lieut, RAEC, 1949–50. Extramural Tutor, Univs of Hull and Sheffield, 1950–57. Founded, Trade Union Res. Unit, 1970; Dep. Chm., Price Commn, 1977–79. Non-exec. Dir, BRB, 1997–99. Member: Industrial

Develt Adv. Bd, 1975–79; Nat. Consumer Council, 1982–94; Ind. Mem., Rail Passengers Council, 2001–. Governor, London Business Sch., 1979–92. Mem. Council, St George's House, 1978–83; Trustee Dir, NUMAST (formerly Merchant Navy and Airline Officers Assoc.), 1981–. *Publications:* Trade Union Structure and Government, 1968; (with R. Moore) A Special Case? Social Justice and the Miners, 1972; (with H. Pollins) Trade Unions in Great Britain, 1973; Industrial Restructuring: some manpower aspects, 1976; Britain in Crisis, 1981; The Social Charter and the European Single Market, 1991; contrib. Eur. Labour Forum jl. *Recreation:* cycling. *Address:* Rookery Cottage, Stoke Place, Old Headington, Oxford OX3 9BX. *T:* (01865) 763076.

HUGHES, John Richard Poulton; DL; County Clerk and Chief Executive, Staffordshire County Council, and Clerk to the Lieutenancy, 1978–83; *b* 21 Oct. 1920; *s* of Rev. John Evan Hughes and Mary Grace Hughes; *m* 1943, Mary Margaret, *e d* of Thomas Francis Thomas; one *s*. *Educ:* Bromsgrove Sch.; LLB Hons London; DPA; LMRTPI. Solicitor. Served War, RN and RNVR, 1940–46; discharged with rank of Lieut, RNVR. Articled in private practice, 1937–40; Asst Solicitor: West Bromwich County Borough Council, 1947–48; Surrey CC, 1948–50; Staffs County Council: Sen. Asst Solicitor, subseq. Chief Asst Solicitor, and Dep. Clerk, 1950–74; Dir of Admin, 1974–78; Sec., Staffs Probation and After Care Cttee, 1978–83. Sec., Staffs Historic Bldgs Trust, 1983–89; Trustee and Advr, Soc. for the Prevention of Solvent Abuse, 1984– (Vice-Pres., 1989). DL Staffs, 1979. *Recreations:* forestry, antiques restoration, sailing, fishing. *Address:* Plas Isa Cottage, Llanbedr Dyffryn Clwyd, near Ruthin, Clwyd LL15 1UP.

See also Sir T. P. Hughes.

HUGHES, Judith Caroline Anne; QC 1994; **Her Honour Judge Judith Hughes;** a Circuit Judge, since 2001; a Deputy High Court Judge, since 1997; *b* 13 Oct. 1950; 3rd *d* of Frank and Eva Hughes; *m* 1977, Mark G. Warwick (marr. diss. 1998); two *d*. *Educ:* Univ. of Leeds (LLB 1973). Called to the Bar, Inner Temple, 1974 (Bencher, 1994); Asst Recorder, 1991–95; a Recorder, 1995–2001. Vice Chm., Legal Services Cttee, Bar Council, 1999. Trustee: Gilbert Place Centre, 1995–98; Children's Soc., 1996–; Help African Schs to Educate, 2000 (Chm., 2001). *Publication:* (jtly) Butterworths Guide to Family Law, 1996. *Recreations:* theatre, reading, handicrafts, travel, gardening. *Address:* Snaresbrook Crown Court, 75 Hollybush Hill, E11 1QW.

HUGHES, Kevin Michael; MP (Lab) Doncaster North, since 1992; *b* 15 Dec. 1952; *s* of Leonard and Annie Hughes; *m* 1972, Lynda Saunders; one *s* one *d*. *Educ:* local state schs; Sheffield Univ. (3 yrs day release). Coal miner, 1970–90. Branch delegate, 1981–90, Mem., Yorks Area Exec. Cttee, 1983–86, NUM. Councillor, Doncaster MBC, 1986–92 (Chm., Social Services, 1987–92). An Asst Govt Whip, 1997–2001. *Recreations:* golf, walking, listening to opera. *Address:* House of Commons, SW1A 0AA. *Clubs:* Doncaster Trade Union and Labour; Skellow Grange Workingmen's.

HUGHES, Prof. Leslie Ernest, FRCS, FRACS; Professor of Surgery, University of Wales College of Medicine (formerly Welsh National School of Medicine), 1971–92; *b* 12 Aug. 1932; *s* of Charles Joseph and Vera Hughes; *m* 1955, Marian Castle; two *s* two *d*. *Educ:* Parramatta High Sch.; Sydney Univ. MB, BS (Sydney); DS (Queensland), 1975; FRCS, 1959; FRACS, 1959. Reader in Surgery, Univ. of Queensland, 1965–71. Hunterian Prof., RCS, 1986. Eleanor Roosevelt Internat. Cancer Fellow, 1970. President: Welsh Surgical Soc., 1991–93; Surgical Res. Soc., 1992–94; Hist. of Medicine Soc. of Wales, 2000. Audio-visual Aid Merit Award, Assoc. of Surgeons of GB and Ireland, 1983, 1986. Educn Editor and Chm., Editl Bd, European Jl of Surgical Oncology, 1992–97. *Publications:* (jtly) Benign Disorders of the Breast, 1988, 2nd edn 1999; numerous papers in medical jls, chiefly on immune aspects of cancer, and diseases of the colon. *Recreations:* music, travel. *Address:* Brook House, 14 Millwood, Lisvane, Cardiff CF14 0TL.

HUGHES, Lewis Harry, CB 1996; Deputy Auditor General for Wales, since 2000; *b* 6 March 1945; *s* of Reginald Harry Hughes, retired MoD official, and Gladys Lilian Hughes; *m* 1975, Irene June Nash, violinist and teacher; one *s*. *Educ:* Devonport High Sch. for Boys; City of London Coll. CIPFA. Exchequer and Audit Dept, 1963–83 (Associate Dir, 1982–83); National Audit Office, 1983–2000: Dir of Health Audit and of Defence Audit to 1990; Asst Auditor Gen., 1991–2000. *Recreations:* golf, music, family life. *Address:* 1 Wood End Road, Harpenden, Herts AL5 3EB. *T:* (01582) 764992. *Club:* Tavistock Golf.

HUGHES, Louis Ralph; President and Chief Operating Officer, Lockheed Martin Corporation, since 2000; *b* Cleveland, Ohio, 10 Feb. 1949. *Educ:* General Motors Inst., Flint (BMechEng); Harvard Univ. (MBA). General Motors Corp., 1973–2000: financial staff, 1973; Asst Treasurer, 1982; Vice-Pres., of Finance, Gen. Motors of Canada, 1985; Vice-Pres. of Finance, General Motors Europe, Zürich, 1987; Chm. and Man. Dir, Adam Opel AG, Rüsselsheim, 1989; Pres., General Motors Europe, 1992; Exec. Vice Pres., 1992–2000; Pres., Internat. Ops, 1994–98. *Recreations:* ski-ing, climbing, cuisine, antiques. *Address:* Lockheed Martin Corp., 6801 Rockledge Drive, Bethesda, MD 20817-1877, USA.

HUGHES, Merfyn; *see* Hughes, T. M.

HUGHES, Michael, CBE 1998; Chief Investment Officer, Baring Asset Management Ltd, since 2000 (Director, 1998–2000); *b* 26 Feb. 1951; *s* of late Leonard and Gwyneth Mair Hughes; *m* 1978, Jane Ann Gosham; two *d*. *Educ:* Univ. of Manchester (BA Econs); London School of Economics and Political Science (MSc Econs). Economist, BP Pension Fund, 1973–75; Partner and Chief Economist, de Zoete and Bevan, Stockbrokers, 1976–86; Dir, BZW Securities, 1986–89; Man. Dir, BZW Strategy, 1989–98; Chm., Barclays Capital Pension Fund, 1995–2000. Chm., Financial Panel, Foresight Prog., DTI, 1994–97; Mem., ESRC, 1995–98. Mem. Council, Univ. of Essex, 1997–. *Recreations:* horses, gardening. *Address:* c/o Baring Asset Management, 155 Bishopsgate, EC2M 3XY. *T:* (020) 7628 6000. *Club:* National Liberal.

HUGHES, Nigel Howard, FREng; Chairman, Airworthiness Requirements Board, Civil Aviation Authority, since 1998 (Member, since 1992); *b* 11 Aug. 1937; *s* of late William Howard Hughes and of Florence Hughes (*née* Crawshaw); *m* 1962, Margaret Ann Fairmaner; three *d*. *Educ:* St Paul's Sch.; Queen's Coll., Oxford (MA). CEng, FIMechE; FRAeS 1993; FREng (FEng 1995). Pilot Officer, RAF, 1956–58. RAE, Bedford, 1961–73; Head of Radio and Navigation Div., 1973–77, Head of Flight Systems Dept, 1977–80, RAE, Farnborough; MoD Central Staffs, 1980–82; Asst Chief Scientific Advr (Projects), MoD, 1982–84; Dep. Chief Scientific Advr, MoD, 1985–86; Dir, RSRE, 1986–89; Chief Exec., Defence Res. Agency, 1989–91; Dir of Technol., Smiths Industries Aerospace and Defence Systems Ltd, 1992–97. *Recreations:* Rolls-Royce enthusiast; model engineering, amateur radio, music. *Address:* Civil Aviation Authority, Aviation House, Gatwick Airport South, W Sussex RH6 0YR.

HUGHES, Owain Arwel; orchestral conductor, since 1970; Principal Conductor, Aalborg Symphony Orchestra, Denmark, since 1995; *b* 21 March 1942; *s* of Arwel Hughes and Enid Hughes (*née* Thomas); *m* 1966, Jean Lewis; one *s* one *d*. *Educ:* Howardian High Sch., Cardiff; University Coll., Cardiff (BA Hons); Royal Coll. of Music. Has conducted all major UK orchs and their choirs and also orchs throughout Europe; Associate Conductor: BBC Welsh Symphony Orch, 1980–86; Philharmonia Orch., London, 1985–90; Musical Dir, Huddersfield Choral Soc., 1980–86; Founder and Artistic Dir, Annual Welsh Proms, 1986–. Television: Blodeugerdd (series), BBC Wales, 1974–76; Development of English Choral Tradition, 1975; Music in Camera, 1976–86; Much Loved Music Show, 1977–83; Requiem series, 1987; Easter series, 1988. Has made numerous recordings and videos. Vice-Pres., NCH Action for Children, 1988–. Founding Fellow, George Thomas Soc., 1989. FWCMD 1995. Hon. Fellow: Univ. of Glamorgan (formerly Poly. of Wales), 1986; UC, Cardiff, 1991. Hon. DMus: CNAA, 1986; Wales, 1991. Gold Medal, Welsh Tourist Bd, 1988. *Recreations:* Rugby, cricket, golf. *Address:* (manager) Michael Emmerson, London Artists, 10 Guild Street, Stratford-upon-Avon, Warwicks CV37 6RE. *T:* (01789) 261561; *e-mail:* londartist@aol.com.

HUGHES, Paul; *see* Hughes, H. P.

HUGHES, Peter; *see* Hughes, D. E. P.

HUGHES, Peter Thomas; QC 1993; a Recorder, since 1992; a Deputy High Court Judge, since 2001; *b* 16 June 1949; *s* of late Peter Hughes, JP, and of Jane Blakemore Hughes (*née* Woodward); *m* 1974, Christine Stuart Taylor; one *s* one *d*. *Educ:* Bolton Sch.; Bristol Univ. (LLB Hons). Called to the Bar, Gray's Inn, 1971; Mem., Wales and Chester Circuit, 1971– (Junior, 1991; Treas., 1999–2000); Asst Recorder, 1988–92. Chairman: Medical Appeal Tribunals, 1988–93; Registered Homes Tribunals, 1993– (Lead Chm., 2000–); Mental Health Review Tribunals, 1999–. Mem., Gen. Council of the Bar, 1993–98. *Recreations:* fell-walking, books, taming an unruly garden. *Address:* Tanfield Chambers, Francis Taylor Building, Temple, EC4Y 7BY. *T:* (020) 7797 7250, *Fax:* 020 7797 7299; 22 Nicholas Street, Chester CH1 2NX. *T:* (01244) 323886. *Clubs:* Army and Navy, Royal Over-Seas League; Lancashire County Cricket.

HUGHES, Philip; *see* Hughes, R. P.

HUGHES, Philip Arthur Booley, CBE 1982; artist; Director, Thames and Hudson Ltd, since 1991; *s* of Leslie Booley Hughes and Elizabeth Alice Hughes (*née* Whyte); *m* 1964, Psiche Maria Anna Claudia Bertini; two *d*, and two step *d*. *Educ:* Bedford Sch.; Clare Coll., Cambridge (BA). Engineer, Shell Internat. Petroleum Co., 1957–61; Computer Consultant, SCICON Ltd (formerly CEIR), 1961–69; Co-Founder, Logica, 1969: Man. Dir, 1969–72; Chm., 1972–90; Dir, 1990–95. Vis. Prof., UCL, 1981–90. Member: SERC, 1981–85; Nat. Electronics Council, 1981–88. Governor, Technical Change Centre, 1980–88. Mem. Council, RCA, 1988–92. Trustee: Design Museum, 1990–96; Inst. for Public Policy Res., 1988–99; Nat. Gall., 1996– (Chm., Bd of Trustees, 1996–99). Exhibn of paintings with Beryl Bainbridge, Monks Gall., Sussex, 1972; exhibited: Contemp. British Painting, Madrid, 1983; Contemp. Painters, Ridgeway Exhibn Museum and Art Gall., Swindon, 1986; one-man exhibitions: Parkway Focus Gall., London, 1976; Angela Flowers Gall., London, 1977; Gal. Cance Manguin, Vaucluse, France, 1979, 1985, 2000; Francis Kyle Gall., London, 1979, 1982, 1984, 1987, 1989, 1992, 1994, 1997, 2000; Gal. La Tour des Cardinaux, Vaucluse, France, 1993; Mus. of Contemp. Art, Monterrey, Mexico, 1997; Mus. Rufino Tamayo, Mexico City, 1998; Tate St Ives, 2000; V&A Mus., 2001; retrospectives: Inverness Mus. and Art Gall., 1990; Ambassade d'Australie, Paris, 1995; Drill Hall Gall., Canberra, 1998; Volvo Gall., Sydney, George Adams Gall., Melbourne, 1999. CompOR 1985. Hon. Fellow, QMC, 1987. DUniv Stirling, 1985; Hon. DSc: Kent, 1988; London, 2000. *Publications:* Patterns in the Landscape, 1998; articles in nat. press and learned jls on management scis and computing.

HUGHES, Major Richard Charles, MBE 1951; TD 1945; Director, Federation of Commodity Associations, 1973–78; *b* 24 Dec. 1915; *s* of late Frank Pemberton Hughes and Minnie Hughes, Northwich. *Educ:* Wrekin Coll., Wellington, Telford. TA commn, 4/5th (E of C) Cheshire Regt, 1935; regular commn, 22nd (Cheshire) Regt, 1939. Served War of 1939–45: 2 i/c 5th, 2nd and 1st Bns 22nd (Cheshire) Regt. Palestine, 1945–47; S/Captain MS and DAAG Western Comd, 1948–51; Korea, 1954; GSO2 Sch. of Infantry, 1955–56; Sec. of Sch. of Inf. Beagles, 1955–56; retd pay, 1958. Sec. to Sugar Assoc. of London, British Sugar Refiners Assoc. and Refined Sugar Assoc., 1958–78; formed British Sugar Bureau and apptd Sec., 1964–66. Hon. Treas., W Kensington Environment Cttee, 1974–75; Mem. Barons Keep Management Cttee, 1975. Member: City Liaison Cttee, Bank of England and City EEC Cttee, 1975; City Adv. Panel to City Univ., and Adviser to City of London Polytechnic, 1975; City Communications Consultative Gp, 1976. *Recreations:* travel, sailing, antiques. *Address:* Stone Cottage, 3 Bell Meadow Court, Tarporley, Cheshire, CW6 0DT.

HUGHES, Richard John C.; *see* Carey-Hughes.

HUGHES, Robert Gurth; General Secretary, Federation of Ophthalmic and Dispensing Opticians, since 1997; *b* 14 July 1951; *s* of late Gurth Martin Hughes and Rosemary Dorothy Hughes (*née* Brown), JP; *m* 1986, Sandra Kathleen (*née* Vaughan); four *d*. *Educ:* Spring Grove Grammar Sch.; Harrow Coll. of Technology and Art. Trainee, then Film Producer, BAC Film Unit, 1968–73; News Picture Editor, BBC Television News, 1973–87. Greater London Council: Mem., 1980–86; Opposition Dep. Chief Whip, 1982–86; Opposition spokesman on arts and recreation, 1984–86. MP (C) Harrow West, 1987–97; contested (C) same seat, 1997. PPS to Rt Hon. Edward Heath, 1988–90, to Minister of State, DSS, 1990–92; an Asst Govt Whip, 1992–94; Parly Sec., OPSS, Cabinet Office, 1994–95. National Chm., Young Conservatives, 1979–80. A Governor, BFI, 1990–92. Hon. DSc Anglia Poly. Univ., 1998. *Recreations:* watching cricket, listening to music.

HUGHES, (Robert) John; journalist; Syndicated Columnist, The Christian Science Monitor, since 1985; Editor, since 1997, and Chief Operating Officer, since 1999, Deseret News, Salt Lake City; Director, International Media Studies Program, Brigham Young University, Utah, since 1991 (on leave of absence, since 1997); *b* Neath, S Wales, 28 April 1930; *s* of Evan John Hughes and Dellis May Hughes (*née* Williams); *m* 1st, 1955, Vera Elizabeth Pockman (marr diss. 1987); one *s* one *d*; 2nd, 1988, Peggy Janeane Chu; one *s*. *Educ:* Stationers' Company's Sch., London. Reporter, sub-editor, corresp. for miscellaneous London and S African newspapers and news agencies (Natal Mercury, Durban, Daily Mirror, Daily Express, Reuter, London News Agency), 1946–54; joined The Christian Science Monitor, Boston, USA, 1954: Africa Corresp., 1955–61; Asst Foreign Editor, 1962–64; Far East Corresp., 1964–70; Man. Editor, 1970; Editor, 1970–76; Editor and Manager, 1976–79; Pres. and Publisher, Hughes Newspapers Inc., USA, 1979–81, 1984–85; Associate Dir, US Information Agency, 1981–82; Dir, Voice of America, 1982; Asst Sec. of State for Public Affairs, USA, 1982–84; Pres., Concord Communications Inc., 1989–91; Asst Sec.-Gen., UN, 1995 (on leave of absence); special advr on communications to Sec.-Gen., UN, 1996–. Chairman: Presidential Commn on US Govt Internat. Broadcasting, 1991; Congressional Commn on Broadcasting to China, 1992. Nieman Fellow, Harvard Univ., 1961–62. Pres., Amer. Soc. of Newspaper Editors, 1978–79. Pulitzer Prize for Internat. Reporting, 1967; Overseas Press Club of America award for best daily newspaper or wire service reporting from abroad, 1970; Sigma Delta Chi's Yankee Quill Award, 1977. Hon. LLD Colby Coll., 1978; Hon. DH Southern Utah, 1995. *Publications:* The New Face of Africa, 1961; Indonesian Upheaval (UK as The End of Sukarno), 1967; articles in magazines and encyclopaedias. *Recreations:* reading, walking, raising Labrador retrievers. *Address:* Deseret News, PO Box 1257, Salt Lake City, UT 84110, USA. *Clubs:* Foreign Correspondents', Hong Kong Country (Hong Kong); Overseas Press (New York).

HUGHES, (Robert) Philip; His Honour Judge Philip Hughes; a Circuit Judge, since 1998; Designated Family Judge at Warrington; *b* 4 June 1947; *s* of late Peredur and Myra Hughes; *m* 1973, Kathleen, (Katie), Dolan; two *s*. *Educ:* Valley Sch., Anglesey; Wrekin Coll., Shropshire. Called to the Bar, Gray's Inn, 1971; in practice at the Bar, 1971–98; Asst Recorder, 1990–93; a Recorder, 1993–98; Wales and Chester Circuit. Asst Boundary Comr, 1996–98. *Recreations:* sailing, vegetable gardening, theatre. *Address:* The Law Courts, Legh Street, Warrington WA1 1UR. *T:* (01925) 256700. *Club:* Holyhead Sailing.

HUGHES, Robert Studley Forrest; Senior Writer (Art Critic), Time Magazine, New York, since 1970; *b* Sydney, Aust., 28 July 1938; *s* of Geoffrey E. F. Hughes and Margaret Sealey Vidal; *m* (marr. diss. 1981); one *s*; *m* 1981, Victoria Whistler (marr. diss. 2000). *Educ:* St Ignatius' Coll., Riverview, Sydney; Sydney Univ. (architecture course, unfinished). Contributed articles on art to The Nation and The Observer, Sydney, 1958–62; to Europe, 1964, living in Italy until 1966, when moved to London; freelancing for Sunday Times, BBC and other publications/instns, 1966–70. TV credits include: Landscape with Figures, ten-part series on Australian art for ABC, Australia; Caravaggio, Rubens and Bernini, for BBC, 1976–77; The Shock of the New, eight-part series for BBC, 1980; American Visions, BBC 2, 1996. Mem., Amer. Acad. of Arts and Scis, 1993. Hon. Dr Fine Arts, Sch. of Visual Arts, NY, 1982; Hon. DLitt Melbourne, 1997. Frank Jewett Mather Award, Coll. Art Assoc. of America, 1982, 1985; Golden Plate Award, Amer. Acad. of Achievement, 1988; El Brusi Prize, Barcelona Olympiad, 1992; Dimbleby Award for lifetime achievement in broadcasting, 1997. *Publications:* The Art of Australia, 1966; Heaven and Hell in Western Art, 1969; The Shock of the New (BBC publication), 1980, rev. edn 1991; The Fatal Shore, 1987; Frank Auerbach, 1990; Nothing If Not Critical, 1991; Barcelona, 1992; Culture of Complaint: the fraying of America, 1993; American Visions, 1997; A Jerk on One End, 1999. *Recreations:* gardening, shooting, river and sea fishing, cooking. *Address:* Time Magazine, 1271 Avenue of the Americas, New York, NY 10020, USA.

HUGHES, Robert Valentine, CBE 1999; FCIS; Chairman, Horserace Betting Levy Board, since 1998; *b* 13 Feb. 1943; *s* of Robert Canning Hughes and Betty Bertha Hughes; *m* 1968, Eryl Lumley. *Educ:* Univ. of Birmingham (DMS 1976; MSocSc 1979). FCIS 1982. Review Leader (Performance Rev.), W Midlands Co. Transport and Engrg Dept, 1977–81; Birmingham District Council: Principal Asst to Chief Exec., 1981–83; Develt and Promotion Officer, 1983–84; Town Clerk and Chief Exec., Great Grimsby BC, 1984–88; Chief Exec., Kirklees Metropolitan Council, 1988–98. Pres., SOLACE, 1997–98. FRSA 1990. *Recreations:* composing music (jazz), cooking, ski-ing, horse-racing. *Address:* Horserace Betting Levy Board, 52 Grosvenor Gardens, SW1W 0AU. *T:* (020) 7353 0043.

HUGHES, Ronald Frederick, CEng, FICE; quality management consultant, since 1992; Systems Consultant, London Underground Ltd, 1992; *b* 21 Oct. 1927; *s* of Harry Frederick and Kate Hughes; *m* 1957, Cecilia Patricia, *d* of Maurice Nunis, MCS, State Treasurer, Malaya, and Scholastica Nunis; two *s* one *d*. *Educ:* Birmingham Central Technical College; Bradford College of Technology. Articled pupil, Cyril Boucher and Partners, 1943; Royal Engineers Engineering Cadet, 1946; commissioned RE, 1950; service in Malaya, 1950–53. Res. Asst, BISRA, 1954; Civil Engineer, H. W. Evans & Co. Ltd, Malaya, 1955, Man. Dir, 1958; War Office, 1959; Head of War Office Works Group, Singapore, 1963; Works Adviser to C-in-C, FARELF, 1964; District Civil Engineer, Malaya, 1966; Property Services Agency: Regional Site Control Officer, Midland Region, 1969; Principal Engineer, Post Office Services, 1970; Area Works Officer, Birmingham, 1977; Asst Dir, 1979, Dir, 1983–87, Civil Engineering Services; Dir and Quality Systems Manager, Mott MacDonald Consultants, 1987–92. Dir, Construction Industry Computing Assoc., 1982–86; Member: Standing Cttee for Structural Safety, 1985–88; Maritime Bd, ICE, 1985–90; Nat. Jt Consultative Cttee for Building, 1986–88; Member Council: Construction Industry Res. and Inf. Assoc., 1984–88; BSI, 1985; Perm. Internat. Assoc. of Navigation Congresses, 1983–; Parly Maritime Gp, 1988–; Vice Pres., Concrete Soc., 1989–. *Recreations:* squash, photography, music. *Address:* 9A The Street, West Horsley, Surrey KT24 6AY. *T:* (01483) 282182. *Clubs:* Naval; Effingham (Surrey).

HUGHES, Prof. Sean Patrick Francis, MS; FRCS, FRCSEd, FRCSI, FRCSEd (Orth); Professor of Orthopaedic Surgery, since 1991 and Head, Surgery, Anaesthesia and Intensive Care, since 1997, Imperial College School of Medicine (formerly Royal Postgraduate Medical School), University of London; Clinical Director, Surgery and Anaesthesia, Hammersmith Hospitals NHS Trust, since 1998; Hon. Consultant Orthopaedic Surgeon, Hammersmith Hospitals, since 1991; Hon. Consultant, National Hospital for Nervous Diseases, Queen Square, since 1994; *b* 2 Dec. 1941; *s* of late Patrick Joseph Hughes and of Kathleen Ethel Hughes (*née* Bigg); *m* 1972, Felicity Mary (*née* Anderson); one *s* two *d*. *Educ:* Downside Sch.; St Mary's Hospital, Univ. of London (MB BS, MS). Senior Registrar in Orthopaedics, Middlesex and Royal National Orthopaedic Hosp., 1974–76; Research Fellow in Orthopaedics, Mayo Clinic, USA, 1975; Sen. Lectr, and Dir Orthopaedic Unit, RPMS, Hammersmith Hosp., 1977–79; George Harrison Law Prof. of Orthopaedic Surgery, Univ. of Edinburgh, 1979–91; Chief of Orthopaedic Service, Hammersmith Hosps NHS Trust, 1995–98. Hon. Civilian Consultant, RN. Vice President: RCSE, 1994–97 (Mem. Council, 1984–97); Assoc. Res. Circulation Bone, 1994–97; Mem. Council, British Orthopaedic Assoc., 1989–92. Fellow: Brit. Orthopaedic Assoc.; Royal Soc. Med.; Member: Orthopaedic Research Soc.; British Orth. Res. Soc. (Pres., 1995–97); Soc. Internat. de Chirurgie Orth. et de Traumatologie; World Orth. Concern; Internat. Soc. for Study of the Lumbar Spine. *Publications:* Astons Short Text Book of Orthopaedics, 2nd edn 1976 to 5th edn (jtly) 1997; Basis and Practice of Orthopaedics, 1981; Basis and Practice of Traumatology, 1983; Musculoskeletal Infections, 1986; (ed jtly) Orthopaedics: the principles and practice of musculoskeletal surgery, 1987; (ed jtly) Orthopaedic Radiology, 1987; papers on blood flow and mineral exchange, fracture healing, bone scanning, antibiotics and infection in bone, external fixation of fractures, surgery of the lumbar and cervical spine. *Recreations:* walking, ski-ing, music. *Address:* 24 Fairfax Road, W4 1EW. *T:* (020) 8995 2039. *Clubs:* Athenæum, Naval.

HUGHES, Shirley, (Mrs J. S. P. Vulliamy), OBE 1999; free-lance author/illustrator; *b* 16 July 1927; *d* of Thomas James Hughes and Kathleen Dowling; *m* 1952, John Sebastian Papendiek Vulliamy; two *s* one *d*. *Educ:* West Kirby High Sch. for Girls; Liverpool Art Sch.; Ruskin Sch. of Art, Oxford. Illustrator/author; overseas edns or distribn in France, Spain, W Germany, Denmark, Holland, Sweden, Aust., NZ, Japan, USA, China and Canada. Lectures to Teacher Trng Colls, Colls of Further Educn, confs on children's lit. and to children in schs and libraries; overseas lectures incl. tours to Aust. and USA. Mem., Cttee of Management, 1983–86, Chm., Children's Writers and Illustrators Gp, 1994–96, Soc. of Authors; Member: Public Lending Right Registrar's Adv. Cttee, 1984–88; Library and Information Services Council, 1989–92. FRSL 2000. Hon. FLA 1997. Children's Rights Other Award, 1976; Kate Greenaway Award, 1978; Silver Pencil Award, Holland, 1980; Eleanor Farjeon Award for services to children's lit., 1984. *Publications:* illustrated about 200 books for children of all ages; written and illustrated: Lucy and Tom's Day, 1960, 2nd edn 1979; The Trouble with Jack, 1970, 2nd edn 1981; Sally's Secret, 1973, 3rd edn 1976; Lucy and Tom go to School, 1973, 4th edn 1983; Helpers, 1975, 2nd edn 1978; Lucy and Tom at the Seaside, 1976, 3rd edn 1982; Dogger, 1977, 4th edn 1980; It's Too Frightening for Me, 1977, 4th edn 1982; Moving Molly, 1978, 3rd edn 1981; Up and Up, 1979, 3rd edn 1983; Here Comes Charlie Moon, 1980, 3rd edn 1984; Lucy and Tom's Christmas, 1981; Alfie Gets in First, 1981, 2nd edn 1982; Charlie Moon and the Big Bonanza Bust-up, 1982, 2nd edn 1983; Alfie's Feet, 1982, 2nd edn 1984; Alfie Gives a Hand, 1983; An Evening at Alfie's, 1984; Lucy and Tom's abc, 1984; A Nursery Collection, 6 vols, 1985–86; Chips and Jessie, 1985; Another Helping of Chips, 1986; Lucy and Tom's 123, 1987; Out and About, 1988; The Big Alfie and Annie Rose Story Book, 1988; Angel Mae, 1989; The Big Concrete Lorry, 1989; The Snowlady, 1990; Wheels, 1991; The Big Alfie Out-of-Doors Story Book, 1992; Bouncing, 1993; Giving, 1993; Stories by Firelight, 1993; Chatting, 1994; Hiding, 1994; Rhymes for Annie Rose, 1995; Enchantment in the Garden, 1996; Alfie and the Birthday Surprise, 1997; The Lion and the Unicorn, 1998; Abel's Moon, 1999; Alfie's Numbers, 1999; The Shirley Hughes Collection, 2000; (ed) Mother and Child Treasury, 1998. *Recreations:* looking at paintings, dressmaking, writing books for children.

HUGHES, Simon Henry Ward; MP (Lib Dem) Southwark North and Bermondsey, since 1997 (MP Southwark and Bermondsey, Feb. 1983–1997, L, 1983–88, Lib Dem, 1988–97); barrister; *b* 17 May 1951; *s* of late James Henry Annesley Hughes and of Sylvia (Paddy) Hughes (*née* Ward). *Educ:* Llandaff Cathedral Sch., Cardiff; Christ Coll., Brecon; Selwyn Coll., Cambridge (BA 1973, MA 1978); Inns of Court Sch. of Law; Coll. of Europe, Bruges (Cert. in Higher European Studies, 1975). Trainee, EEC, Brussels, 1975–76; Trainee and Mem. Secretariat, Directorate and Commn on Human Rights, Council of Europe, Strasbourg, 1976–77. Called to the Bar, Inner Temple, 1974; in practice, 1978–. Vice-Pres., Southwark Chamber of Commerce, 1987– (Pres., 1984–87). Spokesman: (L), on the environment, 1983–Jan. 1987 and June 1987–March 1988; (Alliance), on health, Jan.–June 1987; (Lib Dem), on education and science, 1988–90, on envmt, 1988–94, on natural resources, 1992–94, on community and urban affairs and young people, 1994–95, on social welfare, 1995–97, on health, 1995–99, on home affairs, 1999–. Mem., Accommodation and Works Select Cttee, 1992–97. Jun. Counsel, Lib. Party application to European Commn on Human Rights, 1978–79; Chm., Lib. Party Adv. Panel on Home Affairs, 1981–83; Vice-Chm., Bermondsey Lib. Assoc., 1981–83. Jt Pres., British Youth Council, 1983–84. President: Young Liberals, 1986–88 (Vice-Pres., 1983–86, Mem. 1973–78); Democrats Against Apartheid, 1988–; Vice-President: Union of Liberal Students, 1983–88 (Mem., 1970–73); Southwark Chamber of Commerce, 1987– (Pres., 1984–87); Student Democrats, 1988–; Vice-Chm., Parly Youth Affairs Lobby, 1984–. Member: the Christian Church; Gen. Synod of Church of England, 1984–85; Southwark Area Youth Cttee; Council of Management, Cambridge Univ. Mission, Bermondsey; Anti-Apartheid Movement. Trustee: Salmon Youth Centre, Bermondsey; Rose Theatre Trust; Gov., St James C of E Sch., Bermondsey. Hon. Fellow, South Bank Univ., 1992. Member to Watch Award, 1985. *Publications:* pamphlets on human rights in Western Europe, the prosecutorial process in England and Wales, Liberal values for defence and disarmament. *Recreations:* music (including raves), theatre, sport (Millwall and Hereford FC, Glamorgan CCC, Wales RFU), the open air. *Address:* House of Commons, SW1A 0AA. *T:* (020) 7219 6256; 6 Lynton Road, Bermondsey, SE1 5QR.

HUGHES, Stephen Edward; Director of Finance, London Borough of Brent, since 1999; *b* 18 Feb. 1954; *s* of Lawrence Edward Hughes and Dorothy Hughes (*née* Merricks); *m* 1991, Marian Nicholls; one step *s* one step *d*. *Educ:* Lincoln Grammar Sch.; Tettenhall Coll., Wolverhampton; Peterhouse, Cambridge (BA Hons Econs). CPFA 1997. Res. Officer, Internat. Wool Secretariat, 1976–79; Economist, Coventry CC, 1979–81; Principal Officer (Finance), AMA, 1981–84; Dep. Sec., ALA, 1984–90; seconded to Policy Unit, Islington LBC, 1990–92; Principal Asst Dir of Finance, 1992–97, Head of Finance and Property Services, 1997–98, Islington LBC; Divl Manager, Local Govt Taxation, DETR, 1998–99. Mem. (Lab), Didcot Town Council, 1987–95 (Chair, Finance Cttee, 1991–93; Dep. Leader, 1991–95). *Publications:* contribs to various local govt jls. *Recreations:* golf, chess, Go, surfing the net. *Address:* Brent Town Hall, Forty Lane, Wembly, Middx HA9 9EZ. *T:* (020) 8937 1424.

HUGHES, Stephen Skipsey; Member (Lab) North East Region, England, European Parliament, since 1999 (Durham, 1984–99); *b* 19 Aug. 1952; *m* 1988, Cynthia Beaver; one *s* one *d*, and one *s* twin *d* by previous marriage. *Educ:* St Bede's School, Lanchester; Newcastle Polytechnic (DMA). European Parliament: Dep. Ldr, Lab. Pty, 1991–93; Substitute Member: Legal Affairs Cttee, 1989–94; Citizens Rights Cttee, 1989–94; Mem., Environment Cttee, 1984–94; former Member: Rules Cttee; Security and Defence Cttee; Mem., Intergroup on Nuclear Disarmament, 1988– (Chm., 1988–90); Chm., 1994–99, Socialist Co-ordinator, 1999–, Social Affairs and Employment Cttee. Vice-President: Fedn of Industrial Develt Authorities, 1990–; Assoc. of District Councils, 1990–. *Address:* (office) County Hall, Durham DH1 5UR; (home) 19 Oakdene Avenue, Darlington, Co. Durham DL3 7HR.

HUGHES, Thomas Lowe; Trustee, since 1971, and President Emeritus, since 1991, Carnegie Endowment for International Peace, Washington (President, 1971–91); *b* 11 Dec. 1925; *s* of Evan Raymond Hughes and Alice (*née* Lowe); *m* 1st, 1955, Jean Hurlburt Reiman (*d* 1993); two *s*; 2nd, 1995, Jane Dudley Casey Kuczynski. *Educ:* Carleton Coll., Minn (BA); Balliol Coll., Oxford (Rhodes Schol., BPhil); Yale Law Sch. (LLB, JD). USAF, 1952–54 (Major). Member of Bar: Supreme Court of Minnesota; US District Court of DC; Supreme Court of US. Professional Staff Mem., US Senate Sub-cttee on Labour-Management Relations, 1951; part-time Prof. of Polit. Sci. and Internat. Relations, Univ. of Southern California, Los Angeles, 1953–54, and George Washington Univ., DC, 1957–58; Exec. Sec. to Governor of Connecticut, 1954–55; Legislative Counsel to Senator Hubert H. Humphrey, 1955–58; Admin. Asst to US Rep. Chester Bowles, 1959–60; Staff Dir of Platform Cttee, Democratic Nat. Convention, 1960; Special Asst to Under-Sec. of State, Dept of State, 1961; Dep. Dir of Intelligence and Research, Dept of State, 1961–63; Dir of Intell. and Res. (Asst Sec. of State), 1963–69; Minister and Dep. Chief of Mission, Amer. Embassy, London, 1969–70; Mem., Planning and Coordination Staff, Dept of State, 1970–71. Vis. Sen. Res. Fellow, German Histl Inst., Washington, 1997–. Chm., Nuclear Proliferation and Safeguards Adv. Panel, Office of Technology Assessment, US Congress; Chm., Bd of Editors, Foreign Policy Magazine; Sec., Bd of Dirs, German Marshall Fund of US; Dir, Arms Control Assoc. Chairman: Oxford-Cambridge Assoc. of Washington; US-UK Bicentennial Fellowships Cttee on the Arts. Member Bds of Visitors: Harvard Univ. (Center for Internat. Studies); Princeton Univ. (Woodrow Wilson Sch. of Public and Internat. Affairs); Georgetown Univ. (Sch. of Foreign Service); Bryn Mawr Coll. (Internat. Adv. Bd.); Univ. of Denver (Soc. Sci.

Foundn); Atlantic Council of US (Exec. Cttee). Member Bds of Advisers: Center for Internat. Journalism, Univ. of S Calif; Coll. of Public and Internat. Affairs, Amer. Univ., Washington, DC; Washington Strategy Seminar; Cosmos Club Jl (Chm.). Member Bds of Trustees: Civilian Military Inst.; Amer. Acad. of Political and Social Sci.; Amer. Cttee, IISS; Hubert H. Humphrey Inst. of Public Affairs; Amer. Inst. of Contemp. German Studies, Washington, DC; Arthur F. Burns Fellowship Program. Mem. Adv. Bd, Fundacion Luis Munoz Marin, Puerto Rico. Member: Internat. Inst. of Strategic Studies; Amer. Assoc. of Rhodes Scholars; Amer. Political Sci. Assoc.; Amer. Bar Assoc.; Amer. Assoc. of Internat. Law; Amer. For. Service Assoc.; Amer. Acad. of Diplomacy; Internat. Studies Assoc.; Washington Inst. of Foreign Affairs (Pres.); Trilateral Commn; Assoc. for Restoration of Old San Juan, Puerto Rico; Soc. Mayflower Descendants. Arthur S. Flemming Award, 1965. Hon. LLD: Washington Coll., 1973; Denison Univ., 1979; Florida Internat. Univ., 1986; Hon. HLD: Carleton Coll., 1974; Washington and Jefferson Coll., 1979. KStJ 1984. *Publications:* occasional contribs to professional jls, etc. *Recreations:* swimming, tennis, music, 18th century engravings. *Address:* 5636 Western Avenue, Chevy Chase, MD 20815, USA. *T:* (301) 6561420. *Clubs:* Yale, Century Association, Council on Foreign Relations (New York); Cosmos (Washington).

HUGHES, (Thomas) Merfyn; QC 1994; **His Honour Judge Merfyn Hughes;** a circuit Judge, since 2001; *b* 8 April 1949; *s* of John Medwyn Hughes and Blodwen Jane Hughes (*née* Roberts); *m* 1977, Patricia Joan, *d* of John Talbot, surgeon, Brentwood; two *s* one *d.* *Educ:* Rydal Sch., Colwyn Bay; Liverpool Univ. (LLB Hons 1970); Council of Legal Educn. Called to the Bar, Inner Temple, 1971; in practice at the Bar, Chester, 1971–94, Temple, 1994–2001; Asst Recorder, 1987–91; a Recorder, 1991–2001; Leading Counsel to Local Authorities, Waterhouse Tribunal on Child Abuse, 1996–98; Pres., Mental Health Review Tribunal, 1999–. Chm., Chester Bar Cttee, 1999–2001; Mem., Wales and Chester Circuit Mgt Bd, 1999–2001. Contested (Lab) Caernarfon, 1979. *Recreations:* sailing, Rugby. *Address:* The Law Courts, Chester Castle, Chester CH1 2AN. *Clubs:* Royal Anglesey Yacht; Bangor Rugby Union Football.

HUGHES, Sir Trevor Denby L.; *see* Lloyd-Hughes.

HUGHES, Sir Trevor (Poulton), KCB 1982 (CB 1974); FICE; Chairman: Building and Civil Engineering Holidays Scheme Management Ltd, 1987–99; Building and Civil Engineering Benefits Scheme Trustee Ltd, 1987–99; *b* 28 Sept. 1925; *y s* of late Rev. John Evan and Mary Grace Hughes; *m* 1st, 1950, Mary Ruth Walwyn (marr. diss.); two *s*; 2nd, 1978, Barbara June Davison. *Educ:* Ruthin Sch. RE, 1945–48, Captain 13 Fd Svy Co. Municipal engineering, 1948–61; Min. of Transport, 1961–62; Min. of Housing and Local Govt: Engineering Inspectorate, 1962–70; Dep. Chief Engineer, 1970–71; Dir, 1971–72 and Dir-Gen., 1972–74, Water Engineering, DoE; Dep. Sec., DoE, 1974–77; Dep. Sec., Dept of Transport, 1977–80; Perm. Sec., Welsh Office, 1980–85. Mem., British Waterways Bd, 1985–88. Vice-Chm., Public Works Congress Council, 1975–89, Chm., 1989–91. Chief British Deleg., Perm. Internat. Assoc. of Navigation Congresses, 1985–91; Mem., Water Panel, Monopolies and Mergers Commn, 1991–97. A Vice-Pres., ICE, 1984–86. Hon. Fellow, Univ. of Glamorgan (formerly Poly. of Wales), 1986. Hon. FCIWEM. *Recreations:* music, gardening, reading. *Address:* Clearwell, 13 Brambleton Avenue, Farnham, Surrey GU9 8RA. *T:* (01252) 714246.

See also J. R. P. Hughes.

HUGHES, Victor; *see* Hughes, H. V.

HUGHES, William, CB 1953; Chairman, Tooting Youth Project, 1981–87; *b* 21 Aug. 1910; *o s* of late William Hughes, Bishop's Stortford, Herts, and of Daisy Constance, *y d* of Charles Henry Davis; *m* 1941, Ilse Erna, *o d* of late E. F. Plohs; one *s* one *d.* *Educ:* Bishop's Stortford Coll.; Magdalen Coll., Oxford (demy). Board of Trade, 1933; Asst Sec., 1942; Under-Sec., 1948–63 (Sec., Monopolies and Restrictive Practices Commission, 1952–55); Second Sec., 1963–71. Consultant to British Overseas Trade Bd, 1972–73; Under-Sec., Prices Commn, 1973–75; Dep. Sec., DTI, 1970–71. *Recreation:* music. *Address:* 250 Trinity Road, SW18 3RQ. *T:* (020) 8870 3652; Page's, Widdington, Essex CB11 3SN. *Clubs:* Reform; Leander.

HUGHES, William Frederick; Director General, National Crime Squad, since 2001; *b* 11 Aug. 1950; *s* of Douglas William and Alice Maud Hughes; *m* 1974, Lesley Margaret Hicks; two *s.* *Educ:* Univ. of Aston in Birmingham (BSc Hons Mech. Engrg 1973). PC to Superintendent, Thames Valley Police, 1975–91; Asst Chief Constable, W Yorks Police, 1991–97; Dep. Chief Constable, Herts Constabulary, 1997–2001. *Recreations:* aviation, personal computers, music. *Address:* National Crime Squad, PO Box 2500, SW1V 2WF. *T:* (020) 7238 2525.

HUGHES, William Young, CBE 1987; Chief Executive, 1976–98, and Chairman, 1985–98, Grampian Holdings plc; Chairman, Aberforth Smaller Companies Trust plc, since 1990; *b* 12 April 1940; *s* of Hugh Prentice Hughes and Mary Henderson Hughes; *m* 1964, Anne Macdonald Richardson; two *s* one *d.* *Educ:* Firth Park Grammar Sch., Sheffield; Univ. of Glasgow (BSc Hons Pharmacy, 1963). MPS 1964. Research, MRC project, Dept of Pharmacy, Univ. of Strathclyde, 1963–64; Lectr, Dept of Pharmacy, Heriot-Watt Univ., 1964–66; Partner, R. Gordon Drummond (group of retail chemists), 1966–70; Man. Dir, MSJ Securities Ltd (subsid. of Guinness Gp), 1970–76; Grampian Holdings, Glasgow, 1977–98 (holding co. in transport, tourism and retail). Dir, Royal Scottish Nat. Hosp. and Community NHS Trust, subseq. Central Scotland Healthcare NHS Trust, 1992–97; Mem. Council, Strathcarron Hospice, 2000–. Chairman: CBI Scotland, 1987–89; Prince's Scottish Youth Business Trust, 2000–; Mem. Governing Council, Scottish Business in the Community, 1986–. Hon. Chm., European Summer Special Olympic Games (1990), Strathclyde, 1988–91. Pres., Work Wise, 1994–. Treas., Scottish Conservative Party, 1993–98 (Dep. Chm., 1989–92). *Recreation:* golf. *Address:* The Elms, 12 Camelon Road, Falkirk FK1 5RX. *Club:* Glenbervie Golf.

HUGHES-HALLETT, James Wyndham John, FCA; Chairman: Swire Pacific Ltd, since 1999; John Swire & Sons (HK) Ltd, since 1999; Cathay Pacific Ltd, since 1999; The China Navigation Co. Ltd, since 1993; *b* 10 Sept. 1949; *s* of Michael Wyndham Norton Hughes-Hallett and Penelope Ann Hughes-Hallett; *m* 1991, Lizabeth Louise Hall; two *d.* *Educ:* Eton Coll.; Merton Coll., Oxford (BA). FCA 1973. Articled Clerk, Dixon, Wilson, Tubbs and Gillett, 1970–73; freelance chartered accountant, 1974–76; various posts in Japan, Taiwan, Hong Kong and Australia, Swire Gp, 1976–2000. *Recreations:* reading, skiing, walking. *Address:* c/o John Swire and Sons (HK) Ltd, 35 Floor, 2 Pacific Place, 88 Queensway, Hong Kong. *T:* 28408306. *Club:* Hong Kong.

HUGHES JONES, Dr Nevin Campbell, FRS 1985; on scientific staff, Medical Research Council, 1954–88; Fellow of Hughes Hall, Cambridge, 1987–90, now Emeritus; *b* 10 Feb. 1923; *s* of William and Millicent Hughes Jones; *m* 1952, Elizabeth Helen Dufty; two *s* one *d.* *Educ:* Berkhampsted Sch., Herts; Oriel Coll., Univ. of Oxford; St Mary's Hosp. Med. School. MA, DM, PhD; FRCP. Medical posts held at St Mary's Hosp., Paddington, Radcliffe Infirmary, Oxford, and Postgrad. Med. Sch., Hammersmith, 1947–52; Member: MRC's Blood Transfusion Unit, Hammersmith, 1952–79 (Unit transferred to St Mary's Hosp. Med. Sch., Paddington, as MRC's Experimental Haematology Unit, 1960); MRC's Mechanisms in Immunopathology (formerly in Tumour Immunity) Unit, Cambridge, 1979–88. *Publication:* Lecture Notes on Haematology, 1970, 6th edn 1996. *Recreations:* making chairs, walking the Horseshoe Path on Snowdon. *Address:* 65 Orchard Road, Melbourn, Royston, Herts SG8 6BB. *T:* (01763) 260471.

HUGHES-MORGAN, His Honour Maj.-Gen. Sir David (John), 3rd Bt *cr* 1925; CB 1983; CBE 1973 (MBE 1959); a Circuit Judge, 1986–98; *b* 11 Oct. 1925; *s* of Sir John Hughes-Morgan, 2nd Bt and Lucie Margaret (*d* 1987), *d* of late Thomas Parry Jones-Parry; *S* father, 1969; *m* 1959, Isabel Jean (*d* 1994), *d* of J. M. Lindsay; three *s.* *Educ:* RNC, Dartmouth. Royal Navy, 1943–46. Admitted solicitor, 1950. Commissioned, Army Legal Services, 1955; Brig., Legal Staff, HQ UKLF, 1976–78; Dir, Army Legal Services, BAOR, 1978–80, MoD, 1980–84; a Recorder, 1983–86. *Heir: s* Ian Parry David Hughes-Morgan [*b* 22 Feb. 1960; *m* 1992, Julia, *er d* of R. J. S. Ward]. *Address:* Chorleywood Lodge, Rickmansworth Road, Chorleywood, Herts WD3 5BY.

HUGHES-YOUNG, family name of **Baron St Helens**.

HUGHESDON, Charles Frederick, AFC 1944; FRAeS; *b* 10 Dec. 1909; *m* 1st, 1937, Florence Elizabeth (actress, as Florence Desmond) (*d* 1993), *widow* of Captain Tom Campbell Black; one *s*; 2nd, 1993, Carol Elizabeth, *widow* of Baron Havers, PC; two step *s.* *Educ:* Raine's Foundation School. Entered insurance industry, 1927; learned to fly, 1932; Flying Instructor's Licence, 1934; commnd RAFO, 1934; Commercial Pilot's Licence, 1936. Joined Stewart, Smith & Co. Ltd, 1936; RAF Instructor at outbreak of war; seconded to General Aircraft as Chief Test Pilot, 1939–43; rejoined RAF, 1943–45 (AFC). Rejoined Stewart, Smith & Co. Ltd, 1946; retired as Chm. of Stewart Wrightson 1976. Dir, Aeronautical Trusts Ltd; Chm., The Charles Street Co. Hon. Treas., RAeS, 1969–85. Upper Freeman, City of London; Member: GAPAN; Gunmakers' Guild. Order of the Cedar, Lebanon, 1972. *Recreations:* shooting, horseracing, riding (dressage). *Address:* Leckhampstead House, Leckhampstead, near Newbury, Berks RG20 8QH; 5 Grosvenor Square, W1X 9LA. *T:* (020) 7493 1494. *Clubs:* Garrick, Royal Air Force, Royal Thames Yacht, Lloyd's Yacht.

See also Hon. N. A. Havers, Hon. P. N. Havers.

HUGHFF, Victor William, FIA, CIMgt; Chief General Manager, Norwich Union Life Insurance Society, 1984–89; *b* 30 May 1931; *s* of William Scott Hughff and Alice Doris (*née* Kerry); *m* 1955, Grace Margaret (*née* Lambert) one *s* one *d.* *Educ:* City of Norwich School. Served in RAF, 1951–53; commnd in Secretarial Br., National Service List. Joined Norwich Union Life Insce Soc., 1949; Assistant Actuary, 1966; General Manager and Actuary, 1975; Main Board Director, 1981–89. Director: Stalwart Assurance Group, 1989–93; Congregational & General Insurance, 1989–2001; United Reformed Church Ministers' Pension Trust Ltd, 1993–; Norwich Centre Projects Ltd, 1994–. Liveryman, Actuaries' Co., 1990–. Elder of United Reformed Church, 1972–. *Recreations:* tennis, badminton. *Address:* 18 Hilly Plantation, Thorpe St Andrew, Norwich NR7 0JN. *T:* (01603) 434517.

HUGILL, John; QC 1976; a Recorder of the Crown Court, 1972–96; *b* 11 Aug. 1930; *s* of late John A. and Alice Hugill; *m* 1956, Patricia Elizabeth Hugill (*née* Welton); two *d.* *Educ:* Sydney C of E Grammar Sch., NSW; Fettes Coll.; Trinity Hall, Cambridge (MA). 2nd Lieut RA, 1948–49. Called to the Bar, Middle Temple, 1954 (Bencher, 1984); Northern Circuit, 1954; Assistant Recorder, Bolton, 1971; a Dep. High Court Judge, 1993–95. Chairman: Darryn Clarke Inquiry, 1979; Stanley Royd Inquiry, 1985. Member: Criminal Injuries Compensation Bd, 1998–2000; Criminal Injuries Compensation Appeals Panel, 2000–March 2002. Member: Senate of the Inns of Court and the Bar, 1984–86; Gen. Council of the Bar, 1987–89. Hon. Legal Advr, Clay Pigeon Shooting Assoc., 1992–. *Recreation:* talking and reading about yachting. *Address:* Peel Court Chambers, 45 Hardman Street, Manchester M3 3HA.

HUGILL, Michael James; Assistant Master, Westminster School, 1972–86; *b* 13 July 1918; 2nd *s* of late Rear-Adm. R. C. Hugill, CB, MVO, OBE, and Winifred (*née* Backwell). *Educ:* Oundle; King's Coll., Cambridge (Exhibitioner; BA 1939; MA 1943). War Service in the RN; Mediterranean, Home and Pacific Fleets, 1939–46; rank on demobilisation, Lieut-Comdr. Mathematics Master, Stratford Grammar Sch., 1947–51; Senior Mathematics Master, Bedford Modern Sch., 1951–57; Headmaster, Preston Grammar Sch., 1957–61; Headmaster, Whitgift School, Croydon, 1961–70; Lectr, Inst. of Education, Keele Univ., 1971–72. *Publication:* Advanced Statistics, 1985. *Address:* 4 Glenmore, Kersfield Road, SW15 3HL. *Club:* Army and Navy.

HUHNE, Christopher; Member (Lib Dem) South East Region, England, European Parliament, since 1999; *b* 2 July 1954; *s* of Peter Ivor Paul Huhne and Ann Gladstone Murray; *m* 1984, Vicky Pryce (*née* Courmouzis); two *s* one *d*, and two step *d.* *Educ:* Université de Paris-Sorbonne (Certificat 1972); Magdalen Coll., Oxford (BA 1st Cl. Hons PPE 1975). Freelance journalist, India, 1975–76; Liverpool Daily Post and Echo, 1976–77; Brussels Corresp., Economist, 1977–80; Economics Leader Writer, 1980–84, Economics Editor, 1984–90, Guardian; Business Editor and Asst Editor, Independent on Sunday, 1990–91; Economic Columnist and Business and City Editor, Independent and Independent on Sunday, 1991–94; Founder and Man. Dir, sovereign ratings div., Ibca Ltd, 1994–97; Gp Man. Dir, Fitch Ibca Ltd, 1997–99; Vice-Chm., sovereign and internat. public finance, Fitch Ratings Ltd, 1999–. Mem. Council, REconS, 1993–98. Contested (SDP/Lib Dem Alliance): Reading E, 1983; Oxford W and Abingdon, 1987. Liberal Democrats: Chair, Press and Broadcasting Policy Panel, 1994–95; Econ. Advr, General Election, 1997; Mem., Econ. Policy Commn, 1998; Mem. Adv. Bd, Centre for Reform, 1998–; Jt Chair, Policy Panel on Global Stability, Security and Sustainability, 1999–2000; Chm., Expert Commn on Britain's adoption of Euro, 2000. European Parliament: spokesman, European Lib Dem and Reformist Gp, Econ. and Monetary Affairs Cttee, 1999–; Substitute Mem., Budget Cttee, 1999–. Pres., Oxfordshire Br., European Movt, 2000–; Mem. Council, Britain in Europe. Young Financial Journalist of the Year, 1981, Financial Journalist of the Year, 1990, Wincott Awards. Contributing Editor, The International Economy; columnist, Evening Standard, 1999–. *Publications:* (jtly) Debt and Danger: the world financial crisis, 1984, 2nd edn 1987; Real World Economics, 1990; (jtly) The Ecu Report, 1991; Both Sides of the Coin: the case for the Euro, 1999, 2nd edn 2001. *Recreations:* family, exercise, cinema. *Address:* European Parliament Office, 2 Queen Anne's Gate, SW1H 9AA. *T:* (020) 7227 4319, *Fax:* (020) 7233 3959; *e-mail:* chuhneoffice@cix.co.uk; European Parliament, Rue Wiertz, 1047 Brussels, Belgium. *T:* (2) 2845221, *Fax:* (2) 2849221. *Clubs:* National Liberal, Hurlingham.

HUISMANS, Sipko; Special Adviser to Chairman, Texmaco, Indonesia, since 1996; *b* 28 Dec. 1940; *s* of Jouko and Roelofina Huismans; *m* 1969, Janet; two *s* one *d.* *Educ:* primary sch., Holland; secondary sch., Standerton, S Africa; Stellenbosch Univ., S Africa (BA Com). Shift chemist, Usutu Pulp Co. Ltd, 1961–68; Gen. Man., Springwood Cellulose Co., 1968–74; Man. Dir, Courtaulds Central Trading, 1974–80; Dir, 1980–96, Man. Dir, 1982–84, Courtaulds Fibres; Dir, 1984–96, Man. Dir, 1990–91, Chief Exec., 1991–96,

Courtaulds PLC; Chairman: Internat. Paints Ltd, 1987–90; Courtaulds Chemical and Industrial Exec., 1988–96. Non-executive Director: Vickers, 1996–; Imperial Tobacco, 1996–. *Recreations:* motor racing, sailing, competition. *Clubs:* Royal Lymington Yacht, Royal Southampton Yacht.

HULDT, Prof. Bo Kristofer Andreas; Professor and Director, Department of Strategic Studies, Swedish National Defence College, since 1997; *b* 24 April 1941; *s* of Bo and Martha Huldt; *m* Ingrid Mariana Neering; two *d*. *Educ:* Lund Univ., Sweden (PhD Hist.); Augustana Coll., USA (BA); graduate work, Princeton. Asst and Associate Prof. of History, Lund and Växjö Univs, 1974–79; Res. Associate, Swedish Secretariat for Future Studies, 1975–78; Swedish Institute of International Affairs: Res. Associate, 1979; Asst Dir, 1983; Dep. Dir and Dir of Studies, 1985; Dir, 1988–97 (on leave of absence, 1992–95); Dir, IISS, 1992–93; Dir, Dept of Security Policy, Strategy and Mil. Hist., Royal Swedish Mil. Staff and War Coll., Stockholm, 1994–95. Special Consultant to Swedish Dept of Defence, 1981–82. Pres., Swedish Nat. Defence Assoc., 1997–2000. Member: Swedish Royal Acad. of War Science, 1984; Swedish Royal Naval Acad., 1991. Editor, Yearbooks of Swedish Inst. of Internat. Affairs, 1983–92. *Publications:* Sweden, the United Nations and Decolonization, 1974; (jtly) Sweden in World Society, 1978; World History 1945–65, Norwegian edn, 1982, Swedish and Finnish edns, 1983, Icelandic edn, 1985, French edn, 1995; contribs to learned jls on history, internat. politics and security. *Recreations:* shooting, literature. *Address:* Swedish National Defence College, Box 27805, 11593 Stockholm, Sweden.

HULL, Bishop Suffragan of, since 1998; **Rt Rev. Richard Michael Cokayne Frith;** *b* 8 April 1949; *s* of Roger Cokayne Frith and Joan Agnes Frith; *m* 1975, Jill Richardson; two *s* two *d*. *Educ:* Marlborough Coll., Wiltshire; Fitzwilliam Coll., Cambridge (BA 1972; MA 1976); St John's Coll., Nottingham. Ordained: deacon, 1974, priest 1975; Asst Curate, Mortlake with East Sheen, Southwark, 1974–78; Team Vicar, Thamesmead, Southwark, 1978–83; Team Rector, Keynsham, Bath and Wells, 1983–92; Archdeacon of Taunton, 1992–98. *Recreations:* cricket, squash, theatre. *Address:* Hullen House, Woodfield Lane, Hessle, East Yorks HU13 0ES. *Club:* MCC.

HULL, Prof. Sir David, Kt 1993; FRCP, FRCPCH; Foundation Professor of Child Health, University of Nottingham, 1972–96; *b* 4 Aug. 1932; *s* of late William and Nellie Hull; *m* 1960, Caroline Elena Lloyd; two *s* one *d*. *Educ:* Univ. of Liverpool (BSc Hons, MB ChB). DCH, DObstRCOG; FRCP 1974; FRCPCH 1996. Lectr in Paediatrics, Oxford, 1963–66; Consultant Paediatrician, Hosp. for Sick Children, London, 1966–72; Sen. Lectr, Inst. of Child Health, Univ. of London, 1966–72. President: Neonatal Soc., 1987–91; British Paediatric Assoc., 1991–94. *Publications:* (with D. I. Johnston) Essential Paediatrics, 1981, 4th edn 1999; (with A. D. Milner) Hospital Paediatrics, 1984, 3rd edn 1997; (with E. F. St J. Adamson) Nursing Sick Children, 1984; (with L. Polnay) Community Paediatrics, 1984, 2nd edn 1993. *Recreations:* gardening, walking, drawing. *Address:* Oak House, 3 Lanark Close, Wollaton Park, Nottingham NG8 1BQ.
See also Derek Hull.

HULL, Air Vice-Marshal David Hugill, FRCP; Dean of Air Force Medicine and Clinical Director, RAF, 1994–96, retired; *b* 21 Aug. 1931; *s* of late T. E. O. and M. E. Hull (*née* Dinsley); *m* 1957, Ann Thornton-Symington; two *d*. *Educ:* Rugby; Trinity Hall, Cambridge; St Thomas' Hosp. MA, MB BChir. Royal Waterloo and Kingston upon Thames Hosps, 1956–57; RAF 1957; Consultant in Medicine, PMRAF Hosp., Akrotiri, 1966–67; RAF Hosp., Cosford, 1967–74; Exchange Consultant, Aeromedical Consultation Service, USAF Sch. of Aerospace Medicine, 1974–77; PARAF Hosp., Wroughton, 1977–82; Consultant Advr in Medicine, RAF, 1983–93; Reader, Clinical Aviation Medicine, RAF IAM, 1981–93. QHS, 1991–96. Lady Cade Medal, RCS, 1973. Hon. Texas Citizen, 1977. OStJ 1997. *Publications:* chapters in books on aviation and aerospace medicine; papers in professional jls. *Recreations:* sailing, gardening, cross-country ski-ing. *Address:* 20 Chedworth Gate, Broome Manor, Swindon, Wilts SN3 1NE. *Club:* Royal Air Force.

HULL, Prof. Derek, FRS 1989; FREng, FIM, FPRI; Senior Fellow, University of Liverpool, since 1991; Goldsmiths' Professor of Metallurgy, University of Cambridge, 1984–91, now Professor Emeritus; Fellow, Magdalene College, Cambridge, 1984–91; *b* 8 Aug. 1931; *s* of late William and Nellie Hull (*née* Hayes); *m* 1953, Pauline Scott; one *s* four *d*. *Educ:* Baines Grammar School, Poulton-le-Fylde; Univ. of Wales (PhD, DSc). AERE, Harwell and Clarendon Lab., Oxford, 1956–60; University of Liverpool: Senior Lectr, 1960–64; Henry Bell Wortley Prof. of Materials Engineering, 1964–84; Dean of Engineering, 1971–74; Pro-Vice-Chancellor, 1983–84. Dist. Vis. Prof. and Senior Vis. NSF Fellow, Univ. of Delaware, 1968–69; Monash Vis. Prof., Univ. of Monash, 1981; Andrew Laing Lecture, NECInst, 1989. FREng (FEng 1986). Hon. Fellow, University Coll. Cardiff, 1985. Hon. DTech Tampere Univ. of Technology, Finland, 1987. Rosenhain Medal, 1973, A. A. Griffith Silver Medal, 1985, Inst. of Metals; Medal of Excellence in Composite Materials, Univ. of Delaware, 1990. *Publications:* Introduction to Dislocations, 1966, 4th edn 2001; An Introduction to Composite Materials, 1981, 2nd edn 1996; Fractography: observing, measuring and interpreting fracture surface topography, 1999; numerous contribs to Proc. Royal Soc., Acta Met., Phil. Mag., Jl Mat. Sci., MetalScience, Composites. *Recreations:* golf, music, fell-walking. *Address:* Department of Materials Science and Engineering, University of Liverpool, PO Box 147, Liverpool L69 3BX. *Club:* Heswall Golf.
See also Sir David Hull.

HULL, John Folliott Charles, CBE 1993; Chairman, 1997–98, Deputy Chairman, 1976–97 and 1998–99, Land Securities plc; *b* 21 Oct. 1925; *er s* of Sir Hubert Hull, CBE, and Judith, *e d* of P. F. S. Stokes; *m* 1951, Rosemarie Waring; one *s* three *d*. *Educ:* Downside; Aberdeen Univ.; Jesus Coll., Cambridge (Titular Schol.; 1st cl. hons Law; Keller Prize; MA). RA, 1944–48 (attached Royal Indian Artillery, 1945–48). Called to Bar, Inner Temple, 1952, *ad eund* Lincoln's Inn, 1954. J. Henry Schroder Wagg & Co. Ltd, 1957–72, 1974–85: a Man. Dir, 1961–72; Dep. Chm., 1974–77; Chm., 1977–83; Dir, 1984–85; Schroders plc: Dir, 1969–72, 1974–85; Dep. Chm., 1977–85. Director: Lucas Industries plc, 1975–90; Legal and General Assurance Soc., 1976–79; Legal & General Group plc, 1979–90; Goodwood Racecourse Ltd, 1987–93. Dir-Gen., City Panel on Take-overs and Mergers, 1972–74 (Dep. Chm., 1987–99); Chm., City Company Law Cttee, 1976–79. Lay Mem., Stock Exchange, 1983–84. Mem., Council, Manchester Business Sch., 1973–86. *Recreation:* reading 19th century novelists. *Address:* 33 Edwardes Square, W8 6HH. *T:* (020) 7603 0715. *Club:* MCC.
See also Duke of Somerset.

HULL, John Grove; QC 1983; **His Honour Judge Hull;** a Circuit Judge, since 1991; *b* 21 Aug. 1931; *s* of Tom Edward Orridge Hull and Marjory Ethel Hull; *m* 1961, Gillian Ann, *d* of Leslie Fawcett Stemp; two *d*. *Educ:* Rugby School; King's College, Cambridge. BA (1st cl. in Mech. Scis Tripos) 1953, MA 1957; LLB 1954. National Service, commissioned RE, 1954–56; called to the Bar, Middle Temple, 1958 (Cert. of Honour, Bar Final), Bencher, 1989; in practice, common law Bar, 1958–91; a Recorder, 1984–91. *Recreations:* gardening, English literature.

HULL, Robert; Director, Joint Services (formerly Common Services Organisation), European Economic and Social Committee and European Committee of the Regions, since 1998; *b* 23 Jan. 1947; *s* of John Whitfield Hull and Marguerite (*née* Stace); *m* 1972, Christine Elizabeth Biffin; one *s* two *d*. *Educ:* Dame Allan's Sch., Newcastle upon Tyne; Univ. of Leicester (BA Hist. 1968); Manchester Business Sch. (MBA 1973). UKAEA, 1968–69; PO Telecommunications, 1969–71; North of England Develt Council, 1973–74; EC Commission, 1974–79: Customs Service, 1974–76; Ext. Relns, SE Asia, 1976–79; Civil Servant, Scottish Office, 1979–82; European Commission, 1982–98: Ext. Relns, ME, 1982–86; Asst to Dir Gen., Financial Instns and Co. Law, 1986–90; Head, Policy Co-ordination Unit for Envmt, 1990–98. Contested (C) Durham, EP elecn, 1989. *Publications:* various articles on EU ext. relns, financial services, envmt and sustainable develt, lobbying the EU. *Recreations:* sailing, ski-ing, music, theatre. *Address:* European Economic and Social Committee, 2 rue Ravenstein, 1000 Brussels, Belgium. *T:* (2) 5469316. *Club:* International (Brussels).

HULL, Robert David, (Rob), PhD; Director for Qualifications and Young People (formerly Qualifications and Occupational Standards), Department for Education and Skills (formerly Department for Education and Employment), since 1998; *b* 17 Dec. 1950; *s* of David Archibald Hull and Rosalie Joy Hull (*née* Cave); *m* 1973, Sarah, (Sally), Ann, *d* of Frank Bernard Cockett, *qv*; one *s* one *d*. *Educ:* Royal Grammar Sch., Guildford; Jesus Coll., Cambridge (BA 1st cl. Hons Mathematics; MA; PhD Linguistics 1975). Civil Service Dept, 1974–81; Dept of Educn and Science, later Dept for Educn, 1982–94; Sec., HEFCE, 1994–98 (on secondment). Mem., NIHEC, 1994–98. Gov., Holloway Sch., 1999–. *Recreations:* chess, digital photography. *Address:* 27 Myddelton Square, EC1R 1YE. *Club:* Barbican Chess.

HULLAH, Rt Rev. Peter Fearnley; *see* Ramsbury, Area Bishop of.

HULME, Bishop Suffragan of, since 1999; **Rt Rev. Stephen Richard Lowe;** *b* 3 March 1944; *s* of Leonard Ernest Lowe and Marguerite Helen Lowe; *m* 1967; one *s* one *d*. *Educ:* Leeds Grammar School; Reading School; London Univ. (BSc Econs); Ripon Hall, Oxford. Curate, St Michael's Anglican Methodist Church, Gospel Lane, Birmingham, 1968–72; Minister-in-Charge, Woodgate Valley Conventional District, 1972–75; Team Rector of East Ham, 1975–88; Archdeacon of Sheffield, 1988–99. Hon. Canon, Chelmsford Cathedral, 1985–88; Chelmsford Diocesan Urban Officer, 1986–88. Travelling Fellowship, Winston Churchill Meml Trust, 1980. A Church Comr, 1992–99 (Member: Bd of Govs, 1994–99; Bishoprics Cttee, 1995–99). Member: Gen. Synod of C of E, 1991–99, 2000–; Churches Council for Britain and Ire., 1991–96; Exec., Central Bd of Finance, Gen. Synod, 1993–96; Archbishop's Commn on Orgn of C of E, 1994–95; Bishops' Adv. Gp on urban priority areas, 1993–97; Bishoprics and Cathedrals Cttee; Bishops' Urban Panel, 2001–; Trustee, Church Urban Fund, 1991–97 (Chm., Grants Cttee, 1993–96). Chm., Sheffield Somalian Refugees Trust, 1990–94. Mem., Duke of Edinburgh Commonwealth Study Conf., 1989. Paul Cadbury Travelling Fellowship on Urban Empowerment, 1996. *Publication:* Churches' Role in Care of the Elderly, 1974. *Recreations:* watching football, music, cinema, theatre and travel. *Address:* 14 Moorgate Avenue, Withington, Manchester M20 1HE. *T:* (0161) 445 5922, *Fax:* (0161) 448 9687; *e-mail:* 100737.634@compuserve.com.
See also P. M. Lowe.

HULME, Geoffrey Gordon, CB 1984; consultant, Office of Health Economics, Chartered Institute of Public Finance, since 1991; *b* 8 March 1931; *s* of Alfred and Jessie Hulme; *m* 1956, Shirley Leigh Cumberlidge; one *s* one *d*. *Educ:* King's Sch., Macclesfield; Corpus Christi Coll., Oxford (MA, 1st Cl Hons Mod. Langs). Nat. Service, Intelligence Corps, 1949–50; Oxford, 1950–53; Ministry of Health, subseq. Department of Health and Social Security, latterly Department of Health: Asst Principal, 1953–59; Principal, 1959–64; Principal Regional Officer, W Midlands, 1964–67; Asst Sec., 1967–74; Under-Sec., 1974–81; Principal Finance Officer, 1981–86; Dep. Sec., 1981–91; seconded to Public Finance Foundn as Dir, Public Expenditure Policy Unit, 1986–91. Vice-Chm., Disabled Living Foundn, 2000–. *Recreations:* most of the usual things and collecting edible fungi. *Address:* Stone Farm, Little Cornard, Sudbury, Suffolk CO10 0NW; 314 Metro Central Heights, 119 Newington Causeway, SE1 4DB. *T:* (020) 7407 5520. *Club:* Royal Automobile.

HULME, Margaret Jean; *see* Snowling, M. J.

HULME, Rev. Paul; Minister, New River Circuit, North London, since 1997; *b* 14 May 1942; *s* of Harry Hulme and Elizabeth Hulme; *m* 1976, Hilary Frances Martin; three *s*. *Educ:* Hatfield House, Yorks; Didsbury Theological Coll., Bristol (BA). Minister: Bungay, Suffolk, 1968–70; Brighton, 1970–75; Newquay, Cornwall, 1975–79; Taunton, 1979–86; Enfield, 1986–88; Supt Minister, Wesley's Chapel, London, 1988–96. Chaplain, Sussex Univ., 1970–75. Freeman, City of London, 1990. *Recreations:* walking, music. *Address:* Parkside, 41 Ashford Avenue, Crouch End, N8 8LN. *Club:* National Liberal.

HULSE, Christopher, CMG 1992; OBE 1982; HM Diplomatic Service; Ambassador to the Swiss Confederation, and concurrently (non-resident) to the Principality of Liechtenstein, 1997–2001; *b* 31 July 1942; *s* of Eric Cecil Hulse and late Joan Mary Hulse (*née* Tizard); *m* 1966, Dimitra, *d* of Brig. D. Carayannakos, Sparta, Greece; one *d*. *Educ:* Woking Grammar Sch.; Trinity Coll., Cambridge (BA 1964). Entered Foreign Office, 1964; UN Dept, FO, 1964–67; Third Sec., later Second Sec., Prague, 1967–70; Eastern European and Soviet Dept, FCO, 1970–72; First Sec., Bangkok, 1973; Western European Dept, FCO, 1973–77; UK Delegn to NATO, Brussels, 1977–80; UK Delegn to CSCE Conf., Madrid, 1980–81; Asst Hd, Defence Dept, FCO, 1981–82; Counsellor, NATO Defence Coll., Rome, 1983; Political Counsellor and Consul-Gen., Athens, 1983–88; Hd of Eastern European, subseq. Central European Dept, FCO, 1988–92; Permt Rep., UN, Vienna, 1992–97. *Recreations:* books, music, walking, gardening, carpentry. *Address:* c/o Foreign and Commonwealth Office, SW1A 2AH.

HULSE, Sir Edward (Jeremy Westrow), 10th Bt *cr* 1739, of Lincoln's Inn Fields; DL; *b* 22 Nov. 1932; *er s* of Sir Westrow Hulse, 9th Bt and his 1st wife Philippa Mabel Hulse (decd) (*née* Taylor, later Lamb); *S* father, 1996; *m* 1957, Verity Ann Pilkington; one *s* one *d*. *Educ:* Eton; Sandhurst. Late Captain, Scots Guards. High Sheriff, Hampshire, 1978; DL Hampshire, 1989. *Recreations:* tennis, shooting. *Heir: s* Edward Michael Westrow Hulse [*b* 10 Sept. 1959; *m* 1986, Doone Brotherton; three *s* three *d*]. *Address:* Breamore House, near Fordingbridge, Hampshire SP6 2DF. *T:* (01725) 512233. *Club:* White's.

HULSE, Dr Russell Alan; Principal Research Physicist, Plasma Physics Laboratory, Princeton University, since 1992; *b* 28 Nov. 1950; *s* of Alan Earle Hulse and Betty Joan Hulse (*née* Wedemeyer). *Educ:* The Cooper Union, NY (BS Physics 1970); Univ. of Massachusetts, Amherst (MS Physics 1972; PhD Physics 1975; DSc 1994). National Radio Astronomy Observatory, 1975–77; Plasma Physics Lab., Princeton Univ., 1977–, Dist. Res. Fellow, 1994. Fellow, Amer. Physical Soc., 1993. (Jtly) Nobel Prize in Physics, 1993. *Publications:* papers in professional jls and conf. procs in fields of pulsar astronomy, controlled fusion plasma physics and computer modeling. *Recreations:* cross-country ski-ing, canoeing, nature photography, bird watching, other outdoor activities, clay target shooting, music. *Address:* Princeton University, Plasma Physics Laboratory, James Forrestal Research Campus, PO Box 451, Princeton, NJ 08543, USA. *T:* (609) 2432621.

HUM, Christopher Owen, CMG 1996; HM Diplomatic Service; Ambassador to the People's Republic of China, from March 2002; *b* 27 Jan. 1946; *s* of late Norman Charles Hum and of Muriel Kathleen (*née* Hines); *m* 1970, Julia Mary, second *d* of Hon. Sir Hugh Park; one *s* one *d*. *Educ:* Berkhamsted Sch.; Pembroke Coll., Cambridge (Foundn Scholar; 1st Cl. Hons; MA); Univ. of Hong Kong. Joined FCO, 1967; served in: Hong Kong, 1968–70; Peking, 1971–73; Office of the UK Perm. Rep. to the EEC, Brussels, 1973–75; FCO, 1975–79; Peking, 1979–81; Paris, 1981–83; Asst Head, Hong Kong Dept, FCO, 1983–85; Counsellor, 1985; Dep. Head, Falkland Is Dept, FCO, 1985–86; Head, Hong Kong Dept, FCO, 1986–89; Counsellor (Political) and Hd of Chancery, UK Mission to UN, New York, 1989–92; Asst Under-Sec. of State (Northern Asia), 1992–94, (Northern Asia and Pacific), 1994–95; Ambassador to Poland, 1996–98; Dep. Under-Sec. of State and Chief Clerk, FCO, 1998–2001. Gov., SOAS, 1998–2001. *Recreations:* music (piano, viola), walking. *Address:* c/o Foreign and Commonwealth Office, King Charles Street, SW1A 2AH. *Club:* Art and Business (Poznan).

HUMBLE, James Kenneth, OBE 1996; fair trading consultant, since 1998; non-executive Director: National Consumer Council, since 1997; Wine Standards Board, since 1999; *b* 8 May 1936; *s* of Joseph Humble and Alice (*née* Rhodes); *m* 1962, Freda (*née* Holden); three *d*. Served RN, 1954–56. Weights and Measures, Oldham, 1952–62; Fed. Min. of Commerce and Industry, Nigeria, 1962–66; Chief Trading Standards Officer, Croydon, 1966–74; Asst Dir of Consumer Affairs, Office of Fair Trading, 1974–79; Dir of Metrication Bd, 1979–80; Dir, Nat. Metrological Co-ordinating Unit, 1980–87; Chief Exec., Local Auths Co-ordinating Body on Food and Trading Standards, 1982–98. Sec., Trade Descriptions Cttee, Inst. of Trading Standards, 1968–73; Examr, Dip. in Trading Standards, 1978–94; Vice Chm., Council of Europe Cttee of Experts on Consumer Protection, 1976–79. Member: Council for Vehicle Servicing and Repair, 1972–75; Methven Cttee, 1974–76; OECD Cttee, Air Package Tours, 1978–79; BSI Divl Council, 1976–79; Eden Cttee on Metrology, 1984; Food Codes Cttee, DoH, 1998–; Group Chairman: World Conf. on Safety, Sweden, 1989; Yugoslavian Conf. on Fair Trading, 1992; Member: European Consumer Product Safety Assoc., 1987–97; W European Legal Metrology Co-operation, 1989–98; European Forum Food Law Enforcement Practitioners, 1990–98; Consumer Congress, 1998–. Organiser, First European Metrology Symposium, 1988. Conf. papers to USA Western States Conf. on Weights and Measures, 1989. FITSA 1974– (Vice Pres., 1997–); FRSA 1996. Sport, Devonport Services, 1954–56; Captain, Oldham Rugby Union, 1957–59; Professional Rugby, Leigh RFC, 1959–65. *Publications:* (contrib.) Marketing and the Consumer Movement, 1978; European Inspection, Protection and Control, 1990; contrib. to various jls. *Recreations:* bridge, golf, opera. *Address:* 153 Upper Selsdon Road, Croydon, Surrey CR2 0DU. *T:* (020) 8657 6170.

HUMBLE, Jovanka, (Joan); JP; MP (Lab) Blackpool North and Fleetwood, since 1997; *b* 3 March 1951; *d* of Jovo and Darinka Piplica; *m* 1972, Paul Nugent Humble; two *d*. *Educ:* Lancaster Univ. (BA Hons). DHSS, 1972–73; Inland Revenue, 1973–77. Mem. (Lab), Lancs CC, 1985–97. *Recreations:* gardening, cooking, reading. *Address:* (constituency office) 216 Lord Street, Fleetwood FY7 6SW. *T:* (01253) 877346.

HUME, Sir Alan (Blyth), Kt 1973; CB 1963; *b* 5 Jan. 1913; *s* of late W. Alan Hume; *m* 1943, Marion Morton Garrett; one *s* one *d*. *Educ:* George Heriot's Sch.; Edinburgh Univ. Entered Scottish Office, 1936. Under-Sec., Scottish Home Department, 1957–59; Asst Under-Sec. of State, Scottish Office, 1959–62; Under-Sec., Min. of Public Bldg and Works, 1963–64; Secretary, Scottish Develt Dept, 1965–73. Chairman: Ancient Monuments Bd, Scotland, 1973–81; Edinburgh New Town Conservation Cttee, 1975–90. *Recreations:* golf, fishing. *Address:* 12 Oswald Road, Edinburgh EH9 2HJ. *T:* (0131) 667 2440. *Clubs:* English-Speaking Union; New (Edinburgh).

HUME, James Bell; Under-Secretary, Scottish Office, 1973–83; *b* 16 June 1923; *s* of late Francis John Hume and Jean McLellan Hume; *m* 1950, Elizabeth Margaret Nicolson. *Educ:* George Heriot's Sch., Edinburgh; Edinburgh Univ. (MA Hons History, 1st Cl.). RAF, 1942–45. Entered Scottish Office, 1947; Jt Sec., Royal Commn on Doctors' and Dentists' Remuneration, 1958–59; Nuffield Trav. Fellowship, 1963–64; Head of Edinburgh Centre, Civil Service Coll., 1969–73. *Publication:* Mandarin Grade 3, 1993. *Recreations:* dance music, walking, enjoying silence. *Address:* 2/9 Succoth Court, Succoth Park, Edinburgh EH12 6BZ. *T:* (0131) 346 4451. *Club:* New (Edinburgh).

HUME, John; MP (SDLP) Foyle, since 1983; Member (SDLP) Northern Ireland, European Parliament, since 1979; *b* 18 Jan. 1937; *s* of Samuel Hume; *m* 1960, Patricia Hone; two *s* three *d*. *Educ:* St Columb's Coll., Derry; St Patrick's Coll., Maynooth, NUI (MA). Res. Fellow in European Studies, TCD; Associate Fellow, Centre for Internat. Affairs, Harvard, 1976. Pres., Credit Union League of Ireland, 1964–68; MP for Foyle, NI Parlt, 1969–73; Member (SDLP): Londonderry: NI Assembly, 1973–75; NI Constitutional Convention, 1975–76; NI Assembly, 1982–86; Foyle, NI Assembly, 1998–2000; Minister of Commerce, NI, 1974. Leader, SDLP, 1979–2001. Mem. (SDLP) New Ireland Forum, 1983–84. Contested (SDLP) Londonderry, UK elections, Oct. 1974. Member: Cttee on Regl Policy and Regl Planning, European Parlt, 1979–; ACP-EEC Jt Cttee, 1979–; Bureau of European Socialist Gp, 1979–. Mem., Irish T&GWU (now Services, Industrial, Professional & Technical Union). Hon. DLitt: Massachusetts, 1985; Catholic Univ. of America, 1986; St Joseph's Univ., Philadelphia, 1986; Tusculum Coll., Tennessee, 1988. St Thomas More Award, Univ. of San Francisco, 1991; (jtly) Nobel Peace Prize, 1998; Freedom of Londonderry, 2000. *Address:* (office) 5 Bayview Terrace, Derry, N Ireland BT48 7EE. *T:* (028) 7126 5340, *Fax:* (028) 7136 3423.

HUME, Dr Robert, FRCPE, FRCPGlas, FRCPI, FRCPath, FRCSE; Consultant Physician, Southern General Hospital, Glasgow, 1965–93; *b* 6 Jan. 1928; *m* 1958, Kathleen Ann Ogilvie; two *s* one *d*. *Educ:* Univ. of Glasgow (MB, ChB, MD, DSc). FRCPGlas 1968; FRCPE 1969; FRCPath 1992; FRCSE 1992; FRCPI 1993. Nat. Service in India and Germany, 1946–48, commnd into Gordon Highlanders. Glasgow University: Hutcheson Res. Scholar, 1955–56; Hall Fellow, 1956–58; Hon. Clinical Sub-Dean, 1985–93. Dir, HCI Internat. Med. Centre, 1996–. Pres., RCPSGlas, 1990–92. Chm., Jt Cttee on Higher Med. Trng for UK Colls, 1990–93. Mem., Acad. of Medicine, Malaysia, 1991. Hon. FACP; Hon. FRACP; Hon. FCSSA; Hon. FRCP&S (Canada). *Publications:* on haematological and vascular diseases. *Recreations:* hill-walking, swimming, reading, art appreciation, gardening, talking. *Address:* 6 Rubislaw Drive, Bearsden, Glasgow G61 1PR. *T:* (0141) 942 5331. *Clubs:* Royal Commonwealth Society; Royal Scottish Automobile (Glasgow).

HUMFREY, Charles Thomas William, CMG 1999; HM Diplomatic Service; Ambassador to Republic of Korea, since 2000; *b* 1 Dec. 1947; *s* of Brian and Marjorie Humfrey; *m* 1971, Enid Thomas; two *s* one *d*. *Educ:* The Lodge Sch., Barbados (Barbados Scholar, 1966); St Edmund Hall, Oxford (BA; Webb Medley Jun. Prize, 1968). FCO 1969; Tokyo, 1971–76; SE Asian Dept, FCO, 1976–79; Private Sec. to Minister of State, 1979–81; UK Mission, NY, 1981–85; Southern African Dept, FCO, 1985–87; Counsellor, Ankara, 1988–90; Counsellor (Econ.), Tokyo, 1990–94; Head of African Dept (Southern), FCO, 1994–95; Minister, Tokyo, 1995–99. *Address:* c/o Foreign and Commonwealth Office, SW1A 2AH.

HUMM, Roger Frederick; non-executive Director, Alexanders Holdings plc, since 2000 (Vice-Chairman and Chief Executive, 1992–2000); Director, Imperial Hospitals Ltd, since 1991; *b* 7 March 1937; *s* of Leonard Edward Humm, MBE, and Gladys Humm; *m* 1966, Marion Frances (*née* Czechman) (marr. diss.). *Educ:* Hampton Sch., Hampton, Middx; Univ. of Sheffield (BA Hons Econ). Graduate trainee, Ford Motor Co. Ltd (UK), 1960, Sales Manager, 1973; Marketing Dir, 1977, Internat. Gp Dir, N Europe, 1978, Ford of Europe Inc.; Exec. Dir of Sales, 1980, Man. Dir, 1986–90, Ford Motor Co. Ltd; Director: Henry Ford & Son Ltd (Cork), 1978–90; Ford Motor Credit Co. Ltd, 1980–90. FRSA 1987; CIMgt; FInstD; FIMI. Liveryman, Worshipful Co. of Carmen, 1986; Freeman, City of London, 1986. *Recreations:* golf, scuba diving, writing. *Address:* The Clock House, Kelvedon, Essex CO5 9DG. *Clubs:* Royal Automobile, Lord's Taverners, Variety Club of Great Britain; Harlequins.

HUMMEL, Frederick Cornelius, MA, DPhil, BSc; Head of Forestry Division, Commission of the European Communities, 1973–80, retired; *b* 28 April 1915; *s* of Cornelius Hummel, OBE, and Caroline Hummel (*née* Riefler); *m* 1st, 1941, Agnes Kathleen Rushforth (marr. diss. 1961); one *s* (and one *s* decd); 2nd, 1961, Floriana Rosemary Hollyer; three *d*. *Educ:* St Stephan, Augsburg, Germany; Wadham Coll., Oxford. District Forest Officer, Uganda Forest Service, 1938–46; Forestry Commn, 1946–73; Mensuration Officer, 1946; Chief, Management Sect., 1956; released for service with FAO as Co-Dir, Mexican Nat. Forest Inventory, 1961–66; Controller, Management Services, Forestry Commn, 1966–68, Comr for Harvesting and Marketing, 1968–73. Hon. Member: Société Royale Forestière de Belgique; Asociación para el Progreso Forestal, Spain; Corresponding Member: Mexican Acad. of Forest Scis; Italian Acad. of Forest Scis; Soc. of Forestry, Finland. Dr *hc* Munich, 1978. Bernard Eduard Fernow Plaquette, (jtly) Amer. Forestry Assoc. and Deutscher Forstverein, 1986; Alexander von Humboldt Gold Medal, 1995. *Publications:* Forest Policy, 1984; Biomass Forestry in Europe, 1988; Forestry Policies in Europe: an analysis, 1989; Memories of Forestry and Travel, 2001. *Address:* Ridgemount, 8 The Ridgeway, Guildford, Surrey GU1 2DG. *T:* (01483) 572383. *Club:* Oxford and Cambridge.

HUMPHREY, Prof. Caroline, (Lady Rees), PhD; FBA 1998; Fellow, King's College, Cambridge, since 1978; Professor of Asian Anthropology, University of Cambridge, since 1998; *b* 1 Sept. 1943; *d* of Prof. C. H. Waddington, CBE, FRS and M. J. Waddington; *m* 1st, 1967, Nicholas Humphrey (marr. diss. 1977); 2nd, 1986, Sir Martin Rees, *qv*. *Educ:* St George's High Sch., Edinburgh; Girton Coll., Cambridge (BA 1965; PhD 1973); Leeds Univ. (MA Mongolian Studies 1971). University of Cambridge: Research Fellow, Girton Coll., 1971–74; Sen. Asst in Res., Scott Polar Res. Inst., 1973–78; Asst Lectr, 1978–83; Lectr, 1983–95; Reader, 1995–98. British Acad. Research Reader, 1990–92; Vis. Fellow, Inst. for Humanities, Univ. of Michigan, 1992. Staley Prize in Anthropology, Sch. of Amer. Res., USA, 1990. *Publications:* Karl Marx Collective: economy, society and religion in a Siberian collective farm, 1983, rev. edn 1998; (with J. Laidlaw) The Archetypal Actions of Ritual, 1994; Shamans and Elders: experience, knowledge and power among the Daur Mongols, 1996; (with D. Sneath) The End of Nomadism?: pastoralism and the state in Inner Asia, 1998. *Recreation:* classical music. *Address:* River Farm House, Latham Road, Cambridge CB2 2EJ. *Address:* (01223) 369043.

HUMPHREYS, Arthur Leslie Charles, CBE 1970; Director: Knowledge Engineering (UK) Ltd (formerly Computer Associated Systems Ltd), since 1982; Charles Babbage Institute, since 1978; *b* 8 Jan. 1917; *s* of late Percy Stewart Humphreys and late Louise (*née* Weston); *m* 1st, 1943, Marjorie Irene Murphy-Jones (decd); two *s* one *d*; 2nd, 1975, Audrey Norah Urquhart (*née* Dunningham) (decd); 3rd, 1994, Marion Terry Rushton (*née* Greest). *Educ:* Catford Grammar Sch.; Administrative Staff Coll., Henley. International Computers & Tabulators Ltd: Dir, 1963–83; Dep. Man. Dir, 1964; Man. Dir, 1967; ICL Ltd: Dir, 1968–82; Man. Dir, 1968–72; Dep. Chm., 1972–77; Dir, Data Recording Instrument Co. Ltd, 1957–84. *Recreations:* table tennis, bridge, music. *Address:* 24 Middle Street, Thriplow, Royston, Herts SG8 7RD. *T:* (01763) 208594.

HUMPHREYS, Prof. Colin John, FREng, FIM, FInstP; Goldsmiths' Professor of Materials Science, University of Cambridge, since 1992 (Professor of Materials Science, 1990–92); Professor of Experimental Physics, Royal Institution of Great Britain, since 1999; Director, Rolls-Royce University Technology Centre, since 1994; Fellow of Selwyn College, Cambridge, since 1990; *b* 24 May 1941; *s* of Arthur William Humphreys and Olive Annie (*née* Harton); *m* 1966, Sarah Jane Matthews; two *d*. *Educ:* Luton Grammar Sch.; Imperial Coll., London (BSc); Churchill Coll., Cambridge (PhD); Jesus Coll., Oxford (MA). Sen. Res. Officer 1971–80, Lectr 1980–85, in Metallurgy and Science of Materials, Univ. of Oxford; Sen. Res. Fellow, Jesus Coll., Oxford, 1974–85; Henry Bell Wortley Prof. of Materials Engrg and Hd of Dept of Materials Sci. and Engrg, Liverpool Univ., 1985–89; Hd, Dept of Materials Sci. and Metallurgy, Univ. of Cambridge, 1991–95. Visiting Professor: Univ. of Illinois, 1982–86; Arizona State Univ., 1979. Lectures: D. K. C. MacDonald Meml, Toronto, 1993; Hume-Rothery Meml, Oxford, 1997; Gladstone, London, 1999; Hatfield Meml, Sheffield, 2000; Royal Acad. of Engrg Sterling, Singapore and Malaysia, 2001. Chm., Commn on Electron Diffraction, and Mem. Commn on Internat. Tables, Internat. Union of Crystallography, 1984–87. Member: SERC, 1988–92 (Chm., Materials Sci. and Engrg Commn, 1988–92; Mem., Science Bd, 1990–92); Adv. Cttee, Davy-Faraday Labs, Royal Instn, 1989–92; Scientific Adv. Cttee on Advanced Materials for EC Internat. Scientific Co-opn Prog., 1990–; Metallurgy and Materials Panel, RAE 2001, HEFCE; DTI Nat. Adv. Cttee on Electronic Materials and Devices, 1999–. Member Council: RMS, 1988–89; Inst. of Metals, 1989–91; President: Physics sect., BAAS, 1998–99; Inst. of Materials, 2002–(Mem. Council, 1992–; Sen. Vice-Pres., 2000–01). Fellow in Public Understanding of Physics, Inst. of Phys, 1997–98; Selby Fellow, Aust. Acad. of Scis, 1997. Hon. Pres., Canadian Coll. for Chinese Studies, 1996–; Member Court: Univ. of Bradford, 1990–92; Univ. of Cranfield, 1992–. Freeman, City of London, 1994. FREng (FEng 1996); MAE 1991. Hon. DSc Leicester, 2001. RSA Medal, 1963; Reginald Mitchell Meml Lecture and Medal, 1989; Rosenhain Medal and Prize, Inst. of Metals, 1989; Templeton Award, 1994; Elegant Work Prize, Inst. of Materials, 1996; Kelvin Medal and Prize, Inst. of Physics, 1999; Gold Medal, Fedn of Eur. Materials Socs, 2001. Editor, Reports on Progress in Physics, 2001–. *Publications:* (ed) High Voltage Electron Microscopy, 1974; (ed) Electron Diffraction 1927–77, 1978; Creation and Evolution, 1985 (trans. Chinese 1988); patents and numerous sci. and tech. pubns mainly on electron microscopy, semiconductors, superconductors and nanometre scale electron beam lithography. *Recreations:* chronology of ancient historical events, contemplating gardening. *Address:* Department of Materials Science and Metallurgy, Pembroke Street, Cambridge CB2 3QZ. *T:* (01223) 334457.

HUMPHREYS, Emyr Owen, FRSL; author; *b* 15 April 1919; *s* of William and Sarah Rosina Humphreys, Prestatyn, Flints; *m* 1946, Elinor Myfanwy, *d* of Rev. Griffith Jones, Bontnewydd, Caerns; three *s* one *d*. *Educ:* University Coll., Aberystwyth; University Coll., Bangor (Hon. Fellow, Univ. of Wales, 1987). Gregynog Arts Fellow, 1974–75; Hon. Prof., English Dept, Univ. Coll. of N Wales, Bangor, 1988. FRSL 1993. Hon. DLitt Wales, 1990. *Publications:* The Little Kingdom, 1946; The Voice of a Stranger, 1949; A Change of Heart, 1951; Hear and Forgive, 1952 (Somerset Maugham Award, 1953); A Man's Estate, 1955; The Italian Wife, 1957; Y Tri Llais, 1958; A Toy Epic, 1958 (Hawthornden Prize, 1959); The Gift, 1963; Outside the House of Baal, 1965; Natives, 1968; Ancestor Worship, 1970; National Winner, 1971 (Welsh Arts Council Prize, 1972); Flesh and Blood, 1974; Landscapes, 1976; The Best of Friends, 1978; Penguin Modern Poets No 27, 1978 (Soc. of Authors Travelling Award, 1979); The Kingdom of Brân, 1979; The Anchor Tree, 1980; Pwyll a Riannon, 1980; Miscellany Two, 1981; The Taliesin Tradition, 1983 (Welsh Arts Council Non-Fiction Prize, 1984); Jones: a novel, 1984; Salt of the Earth, 1985; An Absolute Hero, 1986; Darn o Dir, 1986; Open Secrets, 1988; The Triple Net, 1988; The Crucible of Myth, 1990; Bonds of Attachment, 1991 (Book of the Year, Welsh Arts Council, 1992); Outside Time, 1991; Brodyr a Chwiorydd, 1994; Unconditional Surrender, 1996; The Gift of a Daughter, 1998; Collected Poems, 1999; Dal Pen Rheswm, 1999; Ghosts and Strangers, 2001. *Recreation:* walking. *Address:* Llinon, Penyberth, Llanfairpwll, Ynys Môn, Gwynedd LL61 5YT.

HUMPHREYS, Janet, (Mrs V. W. Humphreys); *see* Anderson, Janet.

HUMPHREYS, Kate; *see* Priestley, K.

HUMPHREYS, Dr Keith Wood, CBE 1992; Chairman, The Technology Partnership plc, since 1998; *b* 5 Jan. 1934; *s* of William and Alice Humphreys; *m* 1964, Tessa Karen Shepherd; three *d*. *Educ:* Manchester Grammar School; Trinity Hall, Cambridge (MA, PhD). FRSC; CIMgt. Managing Dir, Plastics Div., Ciba-Geigy (UK), 1972–78; Jt Managing Dir, Ciba-Geigy (UK), 1979–82; Managing Dir, 1982–84, Chm. and Man. Dir, 1984–95, May & Baker, later Rhône-Poulenc Ltd. Director: Hickson Internat. plc, 1995–2000; BIP Ltd, 1996–. Mem., BBSRC, 1994–98. *Recreations:* music, tennis, mountain walking.

HUMPHRIES, Barry; *see* Humphries, J. B.

HUMPHRIES, Christopher, CBE 1998; Director-General, City & Guilds of London Institute, since 2001; *b* 31 Aug. 1948; *s* of John Joseph Humphries and Neridah Merle Humphries; *m* 1996, Hazel Maxwell Cross; one *s* two *d*. *Educ:* Univ. of NSW (BA 1972). Media Resources Officer, ILEA, 1975–79; Producer, Promedia, 1979–82; IT Prog. Manager, 1982–84, Asst Dir, 1984–87, CET; Production Manager, ICL Interactive Learning Services, 1987–88; Educn Business Unit Manager, Acorn Computers Ltd, 1988–91; Chief Exec., Hertfordshire TEC, 1991–94; Dir, then Chief Exec., TEC Nat. Council, 1994–98; Dir-Gen., British Chambers of Commerce, 1998–2001. Chairman: Nat. Skills Task Force, 1998–2000; UK Skills, 2000–; Member: Nat. Learning and Skills Council, 2000–; Nat. Adult Learning Cttee, 2000–. *Address:* City & Guilds of London Institute, 1 Giltspur Street, EC1A 9DD.

HUMPHRIES, David Ernest; defence science consultant; Director, Materials Research Laboratory, Defence Science and Technology Organisation, Melbourne, Australia, 1992–94; *b* 3 Feb. 1937; *er s* of late Ernest Augustus Humphries and Kathleen Humphries; *m* 1959, Wendy Rosemary Cook; one *s* one *d*. *Educ:* Brighton Coll.; Corpus Christi Coll., Oxford (Scholar; MA). RAE Farnborough: Materials Dept, 1961; Avionics Dept, 1966; Head of Inertial Navigation Div., 1974; Head of Bombing and Navigation Div., 1975; Head of Systems Assessment Dept, 1978; Dir Gen. Future Projects, MoD PE, 1981–83; Chief Scientist (RAF) and Dir Gen. of Res. (C), MoD, 1983–84; Dir Gen. Res. Technol., MoD (PE), 1984–86; Asst Chief Scientific Advr (Projects and Research), MoD, 1986–90; Dir, Australian Aeronautical Res. Lab., 1990–92. *Recreations:* music, theatre. *Address:* Little Follies, Liphook Road, Headley, Bordon, Hants GU35 8LL.

HUMPHRIES, Gerard William; His Honour Judge Humphries; a Circuit Judge since 1980; *b* 13 Dec. 1928; *s* of late John Alfred Humphries and Marie Frances Humphries (*née* Whitwell), Barrow-in-Furness; *m* 1957, Margaret Valerie (*d* 1999), *o d* of late W. W. Gelderd and Margaret Gelderd (*née* Bell), Ulverston; four *s* one *d*. *Educ:* St Bede's Coll., Manchester; Manchester Univ. (LLB Hons). Served RAF, 1951–53, Flying Officer. Called to Bar, Middle Temple, 1952; admitted to Northern Circuit, 1954; Asst Recorder of Salford, 1969–71; a Recorder of the Crown Court, 1974–80. Chairman: Medical Appeals Tribunal, 1976–80; Vaccine Damage Tribunals, 1979–80. Charter Mem., Serra Club, N Cheshire, 1963– (Pres. 1968, 1973, 1995–96). Trustee: SBC Educnl Trust, 1979– (Chm., 1979–90); Serra Foundn, 1998–. Foundn Governor, St Bede's Coll., Manchester, 1978–. KCHS 1996 (KHS 1986). *Publication:* The Stations of the Cross: stations for vocation, 1995. *Recreations:* tennis, golf, music, caravanning, gardening, lecturing on New Testament trials and other subjects.

HUMPHRIES, John Anthony Charles, OBE 1980; Senior Partner, Travers Smith Braithwaite, 1980–95; *b* 15 June 1925; *s* of Charles Humphries; *m* 1951, Olga June, *d* of Dr Geoffrey Duckworth, MRCP; four *d*. *Educ:* Fettes; Peterhouse, Cambridge (1st Law). Served War, RNVR, 1943–46. Solicitor (Hons), 1951. Chairman: Water Space Amenity Commn, 1973–83; Southern Council for Sport and Recreation, 1987–92; Vice-Pres., Inland Waterways Assoc., 1973– (Chm., 1970–73); Mem. Inland Waterways Amenity Adv. Council, 1971–89; Adviser to HM Govt on amenity use of water space, 1972; Member: Nat. Water Council, 1973–83; Thames Water Authy, 1983–87. Mem., Sports Council, 1987–88. Chm., Evans of Leeds plc, 1982–97; Mem., London Bd, Halifax Building Soc., 1985–92; Dep. Chm., Environment Council, 1985–94. Chm., Lothbury Property Trust, 1996–99. Vice Chm., Council, Surrey Univ., 1995–99. Governor, Sports Aid Foundn, 1990–96. Trustee, Thames Salmon Trust, 1987–. *Recreations:* inland waters, gardening. *Address:* 21 Parkside, Wimbledon, SW19 5NA. *T:* (020) 8946 3764. *Clubs:* Naval, City.

HUMPHRIES, (John) Barry, AO 1982; music-hall artiste and author; *b* 17 Feb. 1934; *s* of J. A. E. Humphries and L. A. Brown; *m* 1959, Rosalind Tong; two *d*; *m* 1979, Diane Millstead; two *s*; *m* 1990, Lizzie, *d* of Sir Stephen (Harold) Spender, CBE, CLit. *Educ:* Melbourne Grammar Sch.; Univ. of Melbourne. Repertory seasons, Union Theatre, Melbourne, 1953–54; Phillip Street Revue Theatre, Sydney, 1956; Demon Barber, Lyric, Hammersmith, 1959; Oliver!, New, 1960, Piccadilly, 1968; Treasure Island, Mermaid, 1968; London Palladium, 1997. One-man shows (author and performer): A Nice Night's Entertainment, 1962; Excuse I, 1965; Just a Show, Australia, 1968, Fortune Theatre, 1969; A Load of Olde Stuffe, 1971; At Least You Can Say That You've Seen It, 1974; Housewife Superstar, 1976; Isn't It Pathetic at His Age, 1979; A Night with Dame Edna, 1979; An Evening's Intercourse with Barry Humphries, 1981–82; Tears Before Bedtime, 1986; Back with a Vengeance, 1987; Look At Me When I'm Talking To You!, 1994; Rampant in Whitehall, Les Patterson Has a Stand Up, 1996; New Edna, the Spectacle, 1998; Edna's Royal Tour, 1998, NY, 2000 (Special Tony Award); Remember You're Out, 1999; Nat. American Tour, 2001. TV series, The Dame Edna Experience, 1987. Numerous plays, films, broadcasts and recordings. Pres., Frans de Boever Soc. (Belgium). DUniv Griffith Univ., Qld, 1994. *Publications:* Bizarre, 1964; Innocent Austral Verse, 1968; (with Nicholas Garland) The Wonderful World of Barry McKenzie, 1970; (with Nicholas Garland) Bazza Holds His Own, 1972; Dame Edna's Coffee Table Book, 1976; Les Patterson's Australia, 1979; Treasury of Australian Kitsch, 1980; A Nice Night's Entertainment, 1981; Dame Edna's Bedside Companion, 1982; The Traveller's Tool, 1985; (with Nicholas Garland) The Complete Barry McKenzie, 1988; My Gorgeous Life: the autobiography of Dame Edna Everage, 1989; The Life and Death of Sandy Stone, 1991; More Please (autobiog.), 1992; Women in the Background (novel), 1995. *Recreations:* kissing, inventing Australia, trailing his coat. *Address:* c/o Duet Productions, 2nd Floor, 20 Young Street, Neutral Bay, NSW 2089, Australia. *Clubs:* Garrick, Beefsteak; Grolier (New York).

HUMPHRIES, John Charles Freeman; Founder, 1987, and Director, since 1993, British Bone Marrow Donor Appeal; Editor, Western Mail, 1988–92; *b* 2 Jan. 1937; *s* of Charles Montague Humphries and Lilian Clara Humphries; *m* 1959, Eliana Paola Julia Mifsud; two *s* one *d*. *Educ:* St Julian's High Sch., Newport, Gwent. Western Mail: News Editor, 1966–73; Dep. Editor, 1973–80; Thomson Regional Newspapers: European Bureau Chief, 1980–86; London/City Editor, 1986–87; Launch Editor, Wales on Sunday, 1989. Chief Exec., Cymru Annibynnol Ind. Wales Party, 2000–. *Recreations:* walking, opera, reading, Rugby, gardening. *Address:* Plas Cwm Coed, Usk Road, Tredunnock, Gwent NP5 1PE.

HUMPHRYS, John; Presenter: Today Programme, Radio 4, since 1987; On the Record, BBC TV, since 1993; On the Ropes, Radio 4, since 1994; *b* 17 Aug. 1943; *s* of George and Winifred Humphrys; *m* 1965, Edna Wilding (marr. diss. 1991); one *s* one *d*; partner, Valerie Sanderson; one *s*. *Educ:* Cardiff High School. BBC TV: Washington Correspondent, 1971–77; Southern Africa Correspondent, 1977–80; Diplomatic Correspondent, 1980–81; Presenter, 9 o'Clock News, 1981–86. Hon. Fellow, Cardiff Univ., 1998. Hon DLitt Abertay Dundee, 1996; Hon. MA Wales, 1998; Hon. LLD St Andrews, 1999. *Publications:* Devil's Advocate, 1999; The Great Food Gamble, 2001. *Recreations:* music, attempting to play the 'cello, would-be organic farmer. *Address:* c/o News Centre, BBC TV Centre, W12 7RJ.

HUNNISETT, Dr Roy Frank, FSA, FRHistS; on staff of Public Record Office, 1953–88; *b* 26 Feb. 1928; *s* of Frank Hunnisett and Alice (*née* Budden); *m* 1st, 1954, Edith Margaret Evans (marr. diss. 1989); 2nd, 1989, Janet Heather Stevenson. *Educ:* Bexhill Grammar Sch.; New Coll., Oxford (1st Cl. Hons Mod. Hist., 1952; Amy Mary Preston Read Scholar, 1952–53; MA, DPhil 1956). FRHistS 1961; FSA 1975. Lectr, New Coll., Oxford, 1957–63. Royal Historical Society: Alexander Prize, 1957; Mem. Council, 1974–77; Vice-Pres., 1979–82; Selden Society: Mem. Council, 1975–84, 1987–; Vice-Pres., 1984–87; Treasurer, Pipe Roll Soc., 1973–87. *Publications:* Calendar of Inquisitions Miscellaneous: (ed jtly) vol. IV, 1957 and vol. V, 1962; (ed) vol. VI, 1963 and vol. VII, 1968; The Medieval Coroners' Rolls, 1960; The Medieval Coroner, 1961; (ed) Bedfordshire Coroners' Rolls, 1961; (ed) Calendar of Nottinghamshire Coroners' Inquests 1485–1558, 1969; (contrib.) The Study of Medieval Records: essays in honour of Kathleen Major, 1971; Indexing for Editors, 1972; Editing Records for Publication, 1977; (ed jtly and contrib.) Medieval Legal Records edited in memory of C.A.F. Meekings, 1978; (ed) Wiltshire Coroners' Bills 1752–1796, 1981; (ed) Sussex Coroners' Inquests 1485–1558, 1985; (ed) Sussex Coroners' Inquests 1558–1603, 1996, and 1603–1688, 1998; articles and revs in historical and legal jls. *Recreations:* Sussex, music, cricket. *Address:* 23 Byron Gardens, Sutton, Surrey SM1 3QG. *T:* (020) 8661 2618.

HUNSDON OF HUNSDON, Baron; *see* Aldenham, Baron.

HUNSWORTH, John Alfred; Director, Banking Information Service, 1954–81; *b* 23 Dec. 1921; *s* of late Fred Sheard Hunsworth and Lillian Margaret (*née* Wetmon); *m* 1972, Phyllis Sparshatt (*d* 1994). *Educ:* Selhurst Grammar Sch.; LSE (BCom). Served War, 1941–46: commnd E Surrey Regt; served 2nd Punjab Regt, Indian Army, 1942–45. Dep. Editor, Bankers' Magazine, 1948–54. Freeman, City of London. *Publications:* contrib. prof. jls. *Recreations:* gardening, world travel, philately; formerly lawn tennis and Rugby football. *Address:* 29 West Hill, Sanderstead, Surrey CR2 0SB. *T:* (020) 8657 2585. *Clubs:* Reform, Royal Over-Seas League; Surrey County Cricket.

HUNT, family name of **Barons Hunt of Chesterton, Hunt of Kings Heath, Hunt of Tanworth** and **Hunt of Wirral**.

HUNT OF CHESTERTON, Baron *cr* 2000 (Life Peer), of Chesterton in the co. of Cambridgeshire; **Julian Charles Roland Hunt,** CB 1998; PhD; FRS 1989; Professor in Climate Modelling, University College London, since 1999; *b* 5 Sept. 1941; *s* of Roland Charles Colin Hunt, CMG; *m* 1965, Marylla Ellen Shephard; one *s* two *d*. *Educ:* Westminster Sch.; Trinity Coll., Cambridge (BA 1963; PhD 1967); Univ. of Warwick. Post-doctoral res., Cornell Univ., USA, 1967; Res. Officer, Central Electricity Res. Labs, 1968–70; University of Cambridge: Fellow, 1966–, Sen. Res. Fellow, 1998–99, Trinity Coll.; Lectr in Applied Maths and in Engrg, 1970–78; Reader in Fluid Mechanics, 1978–90; Prof., 1990–92, Hon. Prof., 1992–, in Fluid Mechanics; Chief Exec., Meteorol Office, 1992–97. Vis. Scientist, Cerfacs, Toulouse, 1997, 1998; Visiting Professor: Colorado State Univ., 1975; NC State Univ., and Envmtl Protection Agency, 1977; Univ. of Colorado, 1980; Nat. Center for Atmospheric Res., Boulder, Colo, 1983; Arizona State Univ., 1997–98; Stanford Univ., 1998; J. M. Burgers Prof., Tech. Univ., Delft, 1998–. Founder Dir, 1986–91, Dir, 1997–, Cambridge Envmtl Res. Consultants Ltd. Pres., IMA, 1993–95 (Hon. Sec., 1984–89; Vice-Pres., 1989–93); Mem. Man. Bd, European Res. Community for Flow Turbulence and Combustion, 1988–95; Mem. Exec. Council, WMO, 1992–97; Mem., NERC, 1994–96. Councillor, Cambridge CC, 1971–74 (Leader, Labour Gp, 1972). Hon. DSc: Salford, 1995; Bath, 1996; UEA, 1997; Grenoble, Uppsala, Warwick, 2000. L. F. Richardson Medal, Eur. Geophysical Soc., 2001. *Publications:* (contrib.) New Applications of Mathematics, ed C. Bondi, 1991; scientific pubns in Jl of Fluid Mechanics, Atmospheric Envmt, Qly Jl of Royal Meteorol Soc., Proc. Royal Soc. *Address:* Department of Space and Climate Physics, University College London, Gower Street, WC1E 6BT.

HUNT OF KINGS HEATH, Baron *cr* 1997 (Life Peer), of Birmingham in the co. of West Midlands; **Philip Alexander Hunt,** OBE 1993; Parliamentary Under-Secretary of State, Department of Health, since 1999; *b* 19 May 1949; *s* of Rev. Philip Lacey Winter Hunt and Muriel Hunt; *m* 1st, 1974 (marr. diss.); one *d*; 2nd, 1988, Selina Ruth Helen Stewart; three *s* one *d*. *Educ:* City of Oxford High Sch.; Oxford Sch.; Leeds Univ. (BA). MHSM. Oxford RHB, 1972–74; Nuffield Orthopaedic Centre, 1974–75; Mem., Oxfordshire AHA, 1975–77; Sec. Edgware/Hendon Community Health Council, 1975–78; Asst Sec., 1978–79, Asst Dir, 1979–84, NAHA; Dir, NAHA, then NAHAT, 1984–97; Chief Exec., NHS Confedn, 1997. Sen. Policy Advr, Sainsbury Centre for Mental Health, 1997; Sen. Policy Associate, King's Fund, 1998. Member: Oxford City Council, 1973–79; Birmingham City Council, 1980–82. A Lord in Waiting (Govt Whip),

1998–99. Co-Chm., All-Party Gp on Public Health and Primary Care, 1997–98. Member: Council, Internat. Hosp. Fedn, 1986–91; King's Fund Inst. Adv. Cttee, 1991–93; Council, Assoc. for Public Health, 1992 (Co-Chm., 1994). Pres., FPA, 1998. *Publications:* The Health Authority Member (discussion paper) (with W. E. Hall), 1978; articles in Health Service publications. *Recreations:* music, cycling, swimming, football. *Address:* House of Lords, SW1A 0PW.

HUNT OF TANWORTH, Baron *cr* 1980 (Life Peer), of Stratford-upon-Avon in the county of Warwickshire; **John Joseph Benedict Hunt,** GCB 1977 (KCB 1973; CB 1968); Secretary of the Cabinet, 1973–79; Chairman, Prudential Corporation, 1985–90; *b* 23 Oct. 1919; *er s* of Major Arthur L. Hunt and Daphne Hunt; *m* 1st, 1941, Hon. Magdalen Mary Lister Robinson (*d* 1971), *yr d* of 1st Baron Robinson; two *s* (and one *d* decd); 2nd, 1973, Madeleine Frances, *d* of Sir William Hume, CMG, FRCP, and *widow* of Sir John Charles, KCB, FRCP; one step *s* one step *d*. *Educ:* Downside; Magdalene College, Cambridge (Hon. Fellow, 1977). Served Royal Naval Volunteer Reserve, 1940–46, Lieut; Convoy escort, Western Approaches and in Far East. Home Civil Service, Admin. Class, 1946; Dominions Office, 1946; Priv. Sec. to Parly Under-Sec., 1947; 2nd Sec., Office of UK High Comr in Ceylon, 1948–50; Principal, 1949; Directing Staff, IDC, 1951–52; 1st Sec., Office of UK High Comr in Canada, 1953–56; Private Secretary to Sec. of Cabinet and Perm. Sec. to Treasury and Head of Civil Service, 1956–58; Asst Secretary: CRO, 1958; Cabinet Office, 1960; HM Treasury, 1962–67, Under-Sec., 1965; Dep. Sec., 1968 and First Civil Service Comr, Civil Service Dept, 1968–71; Third Sec., Treasury, 1971–72; Second Permanent Sec., Cabinet Office, 1972–73. Dir, 1980–92, Dep. Chm., 1982–85, Prudential Corp.; Dep. Chm., Prudential Assurance Co. Ltd, 1982–85; Chairman: Banque Nat. de Paris plc, 1980–97; BNP UK Hldgs, 1991–97; Dir, IBM (UK) Ltd, 1980–90; Adv. Dir, Unilever plc, 1980–90. Chairman: Sub-Cttee A, H of L European Communities Select Cttee, 1992–95; H of L Select Cttee on Relations between Central and Local Govt, 1995–96. Chm., Disasters Emergency Cttee, 1981–89. Chm., Inquiry into Cable Expansion and Broadcasting Policy, 1982. Chm., European Policy Forum, 1992–98. Chm., Ditchley Foundn, 1983–91. Dir, The Tablet Publishing Co. Ltd, 1984–99 (Chm., 1984–96). Pres., Local Govt Assoc., 1997–2001. Officier, Légion d'Honneur (France), 1987; Kt Comdr, Order of Pius IX (Holy See), 1997. *Recreation:* gardening. *Address:* 8 Wool Road, Wimbledon, SW20 0HW. *T:* (020) 8947 7640.

HUNT OF WIRRAL, Baron *cr* 1997 (Life Peer), of Wirral in the co. of Merseyside; **David James Fletcher Hunt,** MBE 1973; PC 1990; Senior Partner, Beachcroft Wansbroughs, solicitors; *b* 21 May 1942; *s* of late Alan Nathaniel Hunt, OBE and Jessie Edna Ellis Northrop Hunt; *m* 1973, Patricia, (Paddy), Margery (*née* Orchard); two *s* two *d*. *Educ:* Liverpool Coll.; Montpellier Univ.; Bristol Univ. (LLB); Guildford Coll. of Law. Solicitor of Supreme Court of Judicature, admitted 1968; Partner: Stanleys & Simpson North, 1977–88; Beachcroft Stanleys, 1988–99; Beachcroft Wansbroughs, 1999–; Partner, then Consultant, Stanley Wansbrough & Co., 1965–85; Director: BET Omnibus Services Ltd, 1980–81; Solicitors Indemnity Mutual Insce Assoc. Ltd, 2001–. Chm., Assoc. of Ind. Financial Advisers, 1999–. Contested (C) Bristol South, 1970, Kingswood, 1974; MP (C) Wirral, March 1976–1983, Wirral West, 1983–97; contested (C) Wirral West, 1997. PPS to Sec. of State for Trade, 1979–81, to Sec. of State for Defence, 1981; an Asst Govt Whip, 1981–83; a Lord Comr of HM Treasury, 1983–84; Parly Under-Sec. of State, Dept of Energy, 1984–87; Treasurer of HM Household and Dep. Chief Whip, 1987–89; Minister for Local Govt and Inner Cities, DoE, 1989–90; Secretary of State: for Wales, 1990–93; for Employment, 1993–94; Chancellor, Duchy of Lancaster and Minister for Public Service and Sci., 1994–95. Chm., Cons. Shipping and Shipbuilding Cttee, 1977–79; Vice-Chairman: Parly Youth Lobby, 1978–80; Parly War Crimes Gp, 2000–; Vice-Pres., Cons. Group for Europe, 1984–87 (Vice-Chm., 1978–81; Chm, 1981–82); Pres., All Party Parly Gp on Occupational Safety and Health, 1999–. Chm., Inter-Parly Council against Anti-Semitism, 1996–. Chm., Bristol Univ. Conservatives, 1964–65; winner of Observer Mace for British Universities Debating Competition, 1965–66; Nat. Vice-Chm., FUCUA, 1965–66; Chm., Bristol City CPC, 1965–68; Nat. Vice-Chm., YCNAC, 1967–69; Chm., Bristol Fedn of YCs, 1970–71; Chm., British Youth Council, 1971–74 (Pres., 1978–80); Vice-Pres., Nat. YCs, 1986–88 (Chm., 1972–73); Vice-Chairman: Nat. Union of Cons. and Unionist Assocs, 1974–76; Cons. Party, 1983–85. Pres., Tory Reform Gp, 1991–97. Vice-Pres., Nat. Playbus Assoc., 1981–. Member: South Western Economic Planning Council, 1972–76; CBI Council, 1999–. Mem. Adv. Cttee on Pop Festivals, 1972–75. Trustee, Holocaust Educnl Trust, 1998–; Dep. Chm., ESU, 2000– (Gov., 1999–). Mem., Rotary Club, London, 2000–. *Publications:* Europe Right Ahead, 1978; A Time for Youth, 1978; Towards 2000 and Beyond, 1990; Right Ahead: conservatism and the social market, 1994. *Recreations:* cricket, walking. *Address:* Beachcroft Wansbroughs, 100 Fetter Lane, EC4A 1ES. *T:* (020) 7894 6066, *Fax:* (020) 7894 6158. *Club:* Hurlingham.

HUNT, Alan Charles, CMG 1990; HM Diplomatic Service, retired; High Commissioner in Singapore, 1997–2001; *b* 5 March 1941; *s* of John Henry Hunt and Nelly Elizabeth Hunt (*née* Hunter); *m* 1978, Meredith Margaret Claydon; two *d*. *Educ:* Latymer Upper School, Hammersmith; Univ. of East Anglia. First Cl. Hons BA in European Studies. Clerical Officer, Min. of Power, 1958–59; FO, 1959–62; Vice-Consul, Tehran, 1962–64; Third Sec., Jedda, 1964–65; floating duties, Latin America, 1965–67; University, 1967–70; Second, later First Sec., FCO, 1970–73; First Sec., Panama, 1973–76; FCO 1976–77; First Sec. (Commercial), Madrid, 1977–81; FCO, 1981–83; Counsellor (Econ. and Commercial), Oslo, 1983–87; Head of British Interests Section, subseq. Chargé d'Affaires, Buenos Aires, 1987–90; Counsellor, FCO, 1990–91; Consul-Gen., Düsseldorf, and Dir-Gen. of Trade and Investment Promotion in Germany, 1991–95; Sen. Directing Staff (Civilian), RCDS, 1995–96; Dir of Trade and Investment Promotion, FCO, and Dep. Dir-Gen. for Export Promotion, DTI, 1996–97. *Recreations:* tennis, golf, skiing, travel, reading, music. *Club:* Royal Commonwealth Society.

HUNT, Anthony Blair, DLitt; FBA 1999; Fellow and Tutor in French, St Peter's College, and Lecturer in Mediaeval French Literature, Oxford University, since 1990; *b* 21 March 1944; *s* of Norman Blair Hunt and Dorothy Gaskell Hunt (*née* Mottershead). *Educ:* Birkenhead Sch.; Worcester Coll., Oxford (BLitt, MA 1971); St Andrews Univ. (DLitt 1991). University of St Andrews: Asst Lectr, 1968–72; Lectr, 1972–79; Reader, 1979–90; British Acad. Res. Reader, 1986–88. Vis. Prof. of Mediaeval Studies, Westfield Coll., London Univ., 1986–88. FSA 1986. Foreign Mem., Norwegian Acad. of Sci. and Letters, 1999. *Publications:* Rauf de Linham, Kalender, 1983; Chrétien de Troyes, Yvain, 1986; Les giupartiz des eschez, 1986; Plant Names of Medieval England, 1989; Popular Medicine in Thirteenth-Century England, 1990; Teaching and Learning Latin in Thirteenth-Century England, 1991; The Medieval Surgery, 1992; Anglo-Norman Medicine, vol. 1, 1994, vol. 2, 1997; Le Livre de Catun, 1994; Villon's Last Will, 1996; Sermons on Joshua, 1998; Three Receptaria from Medieval England, 2001; 1999; articles in learned jls, contribs to collective vols, etc. *Recreations:* fell-walking, playing the double bass, opera. *Address:* St Peter's College, Oxford OX1 2DL. *T:* (01865) 278852.

HUNT, Anthony James, CEng; FIStructE; Chairman: Anthony Hunt Associates, since 1988; YRM plc, 1993–94; *b* 1932; *s* of late James Edward Hunt and of Joan Margaret (*née* Cassidy); *m* 1st, 1957, Patricia Daniels (marr. diss. 1972; remarried 1975; marr. diss. 1982); one *s* one *d*; 3rd, 1985, Diana Joyce Collett. *Educ:* Salesian Coll., Farnborough; Westminster Tech. Coll. CEng 1961. FIStructE 1973. Articled via Founders' Co. to J. L. Wheeler Consulting Engr, 1948–51; F. J. Samuely and Partners, Consulting Engrs, 1951–59; Morton Lupton, Architects, 1960–62; founded Anthony Hunt Associates, Consulting Engrs, 1962; acquired by YRM plc, Bldg Design Consultants, 1988; became separate limited co., 1997. Major buildings: Sainsbury Centre for the Visual Arts, Norwich, 1978, 1993; Willis Faber Dumas HQ, Ipswich, 1975; Inmos Micro Electronics Factory, Gwent, 1982; Schlumberger Cambridge Research, 1985; Waterloo Internat. Terminal, 1993; Law Faculty, Cambridge, 1995; Nat. Botanic Gdn, Wales, 1998; New Mus. of Scotland, Edinburgh, 1998; Lloyd's Register of Shipping, London, 1998–99; Eden Project, Cornwall, 1998–99. Willis Vis. Prof. of Architecture, Sheffield Univ., 1994–. FRSA 1989. Hon. FRIBA 1989. Hon. DLitt Sheffield, 1999. Gold Medallist, IStructE, 1995. *Publications:* Tony Hunt's Structures Notebook, 1997; Tony Hunt's Sketchbook, 1999. *Recreations:* furniture restoration, music, sailing, ski-ing. *Address:* Anthony Hunt Associates, Gloucester House, 60 Dyer Street, Cirencester, Glos GL7 2PF. *Clubs:* Chelsea Arts, Oriental.

HUNT, Arthur James, OBE 1971; FRTPI, FRICS; Chief Reporter for Public Inquiries, Scottish Office, 1974–79; *b* 18 Nov. 1915; *s* of Edward Henry and Norah Hunt; *m* 1946, Fanny Betty Bacon; one *s* three *d*. *Educ:* Tauntons Sch., Southampton. Ordnance Survey, 1938–44; Planning Officer with West Sussex, Kent and Bucks County Councils, 1944–48; Asst County Planning Officer, East Sussex CC, 1948–52; Town Planning Officer, City of Durban, SA, 1953–61; Sen. and Principal Planning Inspector, Min. of Housing and Local Govt, 1961–68; Mem., Roskill Commn on the Third London Airport, 1968–70; Superintending Inspector, Dept of the Environment, 1971–74. *Recreations:* sailing, gardening, caravan touring. *Address:* Pentlands, 4 West Avenue, Middleton-on-Sea, West Sussex PO22 6EF.

HUNT, Barbara L.; *see* Leigh-Hunt.

HUNT, Bernard John, MBE 1977; Professional Golfer, Foxhills Golf and Country Club, since 1975; *b* 2 Feb. 1930; *s* of John and Lilian Hunt; *m* 1955, Margaret Ellen Clark; one *s* two *d*. *Educ:* Atherstone Grammar Sch. Mem., Ryder Cup team, 1953, 1957–69 (Captain, 1973, 1975); Winner: H. Vardon Trophy, 1958, 1960, 1965; over 30 major tournaments, incl. Dunlop Masters, 1963, 1965, and German, French, Brazilian and Belgian Opens. Captain, PGA, 1966, 1995, 1996. *Recreations:* golf, badminton. *Address:* Foxhills Golf and Country Club, Stonehill Road, Ottershaw, Surrey KT16 0EL.

HUNT, Christopher H.; *see* Holdsworth-Hunt.

HUNT, Christopher John, FSA; Director and University Librarian, John Rylands University Library of Manchester, since 1991; *b* 28 Jan. 1937; *s* of Richard John Hunt and Dorothy (*née* Pendleton); *m* 1963, Kathleen Mary Wyatt. *Educ:* Rutlish Sch., Merton; Univ. of Exeter (BA); King's Coll., Univ. of Durham (MLitt). FSA 1995. Asst Librarian, Univ. of Newcastle upon Tyne, 1960–67; Sub Librarian, Univ. of Manchester, 1967–74; University Librarian: James Cook Univ. of N Queensland, 1974–81; La Trobe Univ., 1981–85; Librarian, British Library of Political and Economic Science, LSE, 1985–91. Chairman: Internat. Cttee for Social Sci. Inf. and Documentation, 1989–; Library Panel, Wellcome Trust, 1993–99 (Mem., 1988–99). Curator of Libraries, Univ. of Oxford, 2000–. Academic Gov., LSE, 1989–91; Mem. Council, Univ. of Manchester, 2000–; Feoffee of Chetham's Hosp. and Library, Manchester, 1993–. *Publications:* The Leadminers of the Northern Pennines, 1970; The Book Trade in Northumberland and Durham to 1860, 1975; papers in professional and learned jls. *Recreations:* book collecting, scuba diving, wine. *Address:* John Rylands University Library, Oxford Road, Manchester M13 9PP. *T:* (0161) 275 3700; 18 Stanneylands Road, Wilmslow, Cheshire SK9 4ER.

HUNT, (David) Peter; His Honour Judge Peter Hunt; a Circuit Judge, since 1997; Designated Family Judge, Leeds Care Centre, since 2000; *b* 25 April 1951; *s* of late Rev. Charles Christopher Hunt and of Edna Hunt; *m* 1984, Cherryl Janet Nicholson; two *s*. *Educ:* Grangefield Grammar Sch., Stockton-on-Tees; Keble Coll., Oxford (MA). Called to the Bar, Gray's Inn, 1974; in practice at the Bar, 1974–97; Junior, North Eastern Circuit, 1981–82; a Recorder, 1993–97. Member: Gen. Council of the Bar, 1981–84; Family Proceedings Cttee, 2001–. Chm., Inquiry into multiple abuse of nursery sch. children, Newcastle, 1993–94. *Publication:* (with M. L. Rakusen) Distribution of Assets on Divorce, 1979, 3rd edn 1990. *Address:* Leeds Combined Court, The Courthouse, 1 Oxford Row, Leeds LS1 3BG. *T:* (0113) 238 0040.

HUNT, David Roderic Notley; QC 1987; a Recorder, since 1991; *b* 22 June 1947; *s* of Dr Geoffrey Notley Hunt and Deborah Katharine Rosamund Hunt; *m* 1974, Alison Connell Jelf; two *s*. *Educ:* Charterhouse School; Trinity College, Cambridge (MA Hons). Called to the Bar, Gray's Inn, 1969, Bencher, 1996. *Recreations:* sailing, ski-ing, golf. *Address:* Blackstone Chambers, Blackstone House, Temple, EC4Y 9BW. *T:* (020) 7583 1770.

HUNT, Derek Simpson; Chairman: MFI Furniture Group Plc, 1987–2000 (Chief Executive, 1987–94); MFI Furniture Centres Ltd, 1987–2000 (Managing Director, 1987–90); *b* 9 June 1939; *s* of late John William Hunt and of Elizabeth (*née* Simpson); *m* 1967, Sandra Phyllis Jones; two *s*. *Educ:* Queen Elizabeth Grammar Sch., Darlington, Co. Durham. Joined MFI as Retail Area Controller, 1972; Branch Ops Controller, 1973; Dir, MFI Furniture Centres, 1974; MFI Furniture Group: Dir, 1976; Man. Dir, 1981; Chm., 1984; during merger with Asda, also Chief Exec. and Dep. Chm., Asda-MFI, 1985–87; returned to MFI and effected management buy-out, 1987. Gov., Ashridge Management Coll., 1986–95. Vice Pres., NCH Action for Children (formerly Nat. Children's Home), 1989–. Founding Fellow, Nat. Children's Home George Thomas Soc., 1989. Hon. Fellow, Manchester Polytechnic, 1988. *Recreations:* sailing, Rugby Union, golf. *Address:* c/o Southon House, 333 The Hyde, Edgware Road, Colindale, NW9 6TD. *T:* (020) 8200 8000.

HUNT, Donald Frederick, OBE 1993; FRCO; Principal, Elgar School of Music, since 1997; Master of the Choristers and Organist, Worcester Cathedral, 1975–96; *b* 26 July 1930; *m* 1954, Josephine Benbow; two *s* two *d*. *Educ:* King's School, Gloucester. ARCM; ARCO 1951; FRCO(CHM) 1954. Asst Organist, Gloucester Cathedral, 1947–54; Director of Music: St John's Church, Torquay, 1954–57; Leeds Parish Church, 1957–75; Leeds City Organist, 1973–75. Chorus Dir, Leeds Festival, 1962–75; Conductor: Halifax Choral Soc., 1957–88; Leeds Philharmonic Soc., 1962–75; Worcester Festival Choral Soc., 1975–97; Worcester Three Choirs Festival, 1975–96; Elgar Chorale, 1980–; Elgar Camerata, 1999–; Guest Conductor, Cape Town Philharmonia, 1997–; Artistic Director: Bromsgrove Festival, 1981–91; N Staffs Triennial Fest., 1999. Hon DMus Leeds 1975. *Publications:* S. S. Wesley: cathedral musician, 1990; Festival Memories, 1996; Elgar and the Three Choirs Festival, 1999; *compositions:* Magnificat and Nunc Dimittis, 1972; Missa Brevis, 1973; Versicles and Responses, 1973; God be gracious, 1984; Missa Nova, 1985; Mass for Three Voices, 1986; A Song of Celebration, 1995; Hymnus Paschalis, 1999;

anthems and carols. *Recreations:* cricket, poetry, travel. *Address:* 13 Bilford Avenue, Worcester WR3 8PJ. *T:* (01905) 756329; *e-mail:* dhunt2126@aol.com.

HUNT, (Henry) Holman, CBE 1988; Deputy Chairman, 1985–91, Member, 1980–91, Monopolies and Mergers Commission; *b* 13 May 1924; *s* of Henry Hunt and Jessie Brenda Beale; *m* 1954, Sonja Blom; one *s* two *d*. *Educ:* Queens Park Sch., Glasgow; Glasgow Univ. (MA). FCMA, FIMC, FBCS, FInstAM. Caledonian Insce Co., 1940–43; RAF, 1943–46; Glasgow Univ., 1946–50; Cadbury Bros, 1950–51; PA Management Consultants: Consultant, 1952–57; Manager, Office Organisation, 1958–63; Dir, Computer Div., 1964–69; Bd Dir, 1970–83; Man. Dir, PA Computers and Telecommunications, 1976–83. Pres., Inst. of Management Consultants, 1974–75. FRSA 1988. *Recreations:* music, reading, walking, travel, photography. *Address:* 28 The Ridings, Epsom, Surrey KT18 5JJ. *T:* (01372) 720974. *Club:* Caledonian.

HUNT, James; *see* Hunt, P. J.

HUNT, Prof. John David, PhD; FRS 2001; Professor of Materials, University of Oxford, since 1996; Fellow and Tutor in Metallurgy, St Edmund Hall, Oxford, since 1968; *b* 12 Dec. 1936; *s* of Frederick John Hunt and Eleanor Hunt; *m* 1961, Ann Mercy Carroll; one *s* one *d* (and one *s* decd). *Educ:* Wellington Sch., Som; Christ's Coll., Cambridge (BA 1960; PhD 1963). Sen. Scientist, Bell Telephone Labs, Murray Hill, NJ, 1963–65; SSO, UKAEA, Harwell, 1965–66; Lectr, Dept of Metallurgy, 1966–90, Reader in Physical Metallurgy, 1990–96, Univ. of Oxford. Hon. Prof., Key Solidification Lab. of China, N Western Poly. Univ., Xian, China, 1996. Mathewson Gold Medal, 1967, Bruce Chalmers Award, 1996, Amer. Inst. Metallurgical Engrs; Rosenhain Medal and Prize, Inst. Metals, 1981; Armourers' and Brasiers' Award, Royal Soc., 2001. *Publications:* numerous contribs on solidification theory and experiment to learned jls. *Recreations:* keeping livestock, growing ferns, walking. *Address:* Church Farm House, Church Road, Northleigh, Witney, Oxon OX29 6TX.

HUNT, Sir John (Leonard), Kt 1989; *b* 27 Oct. 1929; *s* of late William John Hunt and Dora Maud Hunt, Keston, Kent; unmarried. *Educ:* Dulwich Coll. Councillor, Bromley Borough Council, 1953–65; Alderman, Bromley Borough Council, 1961–65; Mayor of Bromley, 1963–64. Contested (C) S Lewisham, 1959. MP (C): Bromley, 1964–74; Ravensbourne, 1974–97. Member: Select Cttee on Home Affairs (and Mem., Sub-Cttee on Race Relations and Immigration), 1979–87; Speaker's Panel of Chairmen, 1980–97. Chm., Indo-British Parly Gp, 1979–91; UK Rep. at Council of Europe and WEU, 1973–77 and 1988–97. Jt Pres., British-Caribbean Assoc., 1998– (Jt Chm., 1968–77 and 1984–97). Mem., BBC Gen. Adv. Council, 1975–87. Pres., Inst. of Administrative Accountants, subseq. of Financial Accountants, 1970–88. Mem. of London Stock Exchange, 1958–70. Freeman, City of London, 1986; Freeman, Haberdashers' Co., 1986. *Recreations:* foreign travel, good food. *Address:* 164 Sutherland Avenue, W9 1HR.

HUNT, John Maitland, MA, BLitt; Headmaster of Roedean, 1971–84; *b* 4 March 1932; *s* of Richard Herbert Alexander Hunt and Eileen Mary Isabelle Hunt (*née* Witt); *m* 1969, Sarah, *d* of Lt-Gen. Sir Derek Lang, KGB, DSO, MC; two *s*. *Educ:* Radley College; Wadham College, Oxford. BA 1956; BLitt 1959; MA 1960. Assistant Master, Stowe School, 1958–70 (Sixth Form tutor in Geography). Chm., Bd of Managers, Common Entrance Exam. for Girls' Schs, 1974–81. *Publications:* various articles on fine arts and architecture. *Recreations:* estate management, fine arts, writing, travel. *Address:* Logie, Dunfermline, Fife KY12 8QN. *Club:* Royal Commonwealth Society.

HUNT, John Michael Graham, OBE 2000; Chief Executive and Secretary, British Dental Association, since 1993; *b* 5 Feb. 1942; *s* of Robert Graham Hunt and Patricia Mary Hunt; *m* 1966, Jill Mason Williams; one *s* two *d*. *Educ:* Guy's Hosp. Dental Sch., Univ. of London (BDS 1965). LDS RCS 1965. Resident House Officer, Guy's Hosp., 1965; Fulbright Travelling Schol., Clinical Dental Fellow, Eastman Dental Centre, NY, 1966–67; London Hospital Dental Institute: Registrar, Conservative Dentistry, 1967–70; Lectr in Oral Surgery, 1968–70; General Dental Practice, Torquay, 1970–80; Clinical Dental Surgeon, Prince Philip Dental Hosp., Univ. of Hong Kong, 1980–84; Dental Officer, 1984–89, Sen. Dental Officer, 1989–93, DoH. Hon. Lectr, London Hosp. Med. Coll., 1989–93; Speaker, FDI, World Dental Fedn, 1999–. FRSA. *Recreations:* walking, ski-ing, tennis, sailing. *Address:* British Dental Association, 64 Wimpole Street, W1M 8AL. *T:* (020) 7935 0875. *Club:* Royal Society of Medicine.

HUNT, Judith Anne, OBE 1999; Special Advisor, Local Government Association, since 1999; Special Advisor, since 1999 and Senior Consultant, since 2000, Improvement and Development Agency; *b* 13 Sept. 1945; *d* of Philip E. Riley and late Amy Riley; *m* 1st, 1967, Alan J. Hunt (marr. diss. 1979); two *d*; 2nd, 1988, Daniel W. Silverstone. *Educ:* Cheadle Hulme Sch.; Leeds Univ. (BA Hons). Lectr, Stockport Coll. and Salford Coll. of Technology, and teacher, Salford, 1967–74; Nat. Organiser, 1974–80 and Asst Gen. Sec., 1980–82, AUEW (TASS); Equal Opportunities Advr and Dep. Head, Personnel Services, GLC, 1982–84; Dir of Personnel (Staffing), GLC, 1984–86; Acting Dir of Personnel, ILEA, 1986–87; Chief Executive: London Borough of Ealing, 1987–93; Local Govt Mgt Bd, 1993–99. CS Comr, 1995–98; Mem. Adv. Council, CS Coll., 1995–99. Chm., Camden and Islington HA, 2000–. Parent Governor, ILEA; Member: Governing Body, Ruskin Coll.; Exec. Council, Solace; Women's Nat. Commn, 1976–82; ESRC Res. Priorities Bd, 1995–; Council, Inst. of Employment Studies; W London TEC; W London Leadership, 1989–93; London First, 1992–95. Trustee, Common Purpose, 1994–. FRSA. *Publications:* Organising Women Workers, 1985; (ed) Jackie West: work, women and the labour market; contribs to jls. *Recreations:* books, gardening, opera, theatre. *Address:* 10 St Ann's Gardens, NW5 4ER. *Club:* Reform.

HUNT, Brig. Kenneth, OBE 1955; MC 1943; Vice-President, International Institute for Strategic Studies, 1988–2000 (Deputy Director, 1967–77); *b* 26 May 1914; *s* of late John Hunt and Elizabeth Hunt; *m* 1939, Mary Mabel Crickett (*d* 1995); two *s* (and one *d* decd). *Educ:* Chatham House Sch., Ramsgate; sc Camberley; idc. Commissioned into Royal Artillery, 1940; served, Africa, Italy, Austria, with HAC, 1 RHA and 2 RHA, 1942–46 (despatches thrice); Bt Lt-Col 1955; CO 40 Fd Regt RA, 1958–60; CRA 51 Highland Div., 1961–63; IDC 1963; Dep. Standing Gp Rep. to N Atlantic Council, 1964–66; resigned commission, 1967. Dir, British Atlantic Cttee, 1978–81. Specialist Adviser to House of Commons Defence Cttee, 1971–84. Visiting Professor: Fletcher Sch. of Law, Cambridge, Mass, 1975; Univ. of S California, 1978–79; Univ. of Surrey, 1978–87. Mem. Council, RUSI, 1977; Fellow, Inst. of Security, Tokyo, 1979–. Freeman, City of London, 1977; Mem., HAC. Hon. Dr (PolSci), Korea Univ., 1977. Order of Rising Sun (Japan), 1984. *Publications:* NATO without France, 1967; The Requirements of Military Technology, 1967; Defence with Fewer Men, 1973; (ed) The Military Balance, 1967–77; (jtly) The Third World War, 1978; (jtly) Asian Security, annually, 1979–89; Europe in the Western Alliance, 1988; contribs to learned jls, and chapters in books, in UK, USA, E Asia. *Recreations:* fly-fishing, listening to music. *Address:* 6 Canal Walk, Hungerford, Berkshire RG17 0EQ. *T:* (01488) 683996. *Clubs:* Army and Navy; International House of Japan (Tokyo).

HUNT, Maj.-Gen. Malcolm Peter John, OBE 1984; Royal Marines retired, 1992; General Secretary, Association of British Dispensing Opticians, 1995–99; *b* 19 Nov. 1938; *s* of Peter Gordon Hunt and Rachel Margaret Hunt (*née* Owston); *m* 1962, Margaret Peat (*d* 1996); two *s*. *Educ:* St John's Sch., Leatherhead; Staff Coll., Camberley. Joined Royal Marines, 1957; service in Malta, Aden and NI; OC RM Detachment, HMS Nubian, 1966–68; Instructor, Army Staff Coll., 1979–81; CO, 40 Commando RM, 1981–83 (Falklands, NI); Internat. Mil. Staff, HQ NATO, 1984–87; Dir, NATO Defence Commitments Staff, MoD, 1987–90; Comdr, British Forces Falkland Islands, 1990–91. Exec. Dir, Nat. Back Pain Assoc., 1993–94. Member: Metropolitan Police Cttee, 1995–2000; Gen. Optical Council, 1999–. Gov., St John's Sch., Leatherhead, 1993– (Vice-Chm., 1997–). FRSA 1993. Freeman, City of London, 1999; Liveryman, Co. of Spectacle Makers, 2000. *Recreations:* golf, politics, reading, theatre. *Address:* 20 Kent Road, East Molesey, Surrey KT8 9JZ.

HUNT, Margaret Corinna; *see* Phillips, M. C.

HUNT, Martin Robert, RDI 1981; Partner, Queensberry Hunt (formerly Queensberry Hunt Levien), design consultancy, since 1966; *b* 4 Sept. 1942; *s* of Frederick and Frances Hunt; *m* 1st, 1963, Pauline Hunt; one *s* one *d*; 2nd, 1980, Glenys Barton; one *s*. *Educ:* Monmouth. DesRCA, FCSD. Graduated RCA 1966 (Hon. Fellow 1987); formed Queensberry Hunt Partnership, 1966. Part time Tutor, 1968, Head of Glass Sch., 1974–86, Vis. Prof., 1997–2000, Royal Coll. of Art; Vis. Prof., De Montfort Univ., 1997–. Master, Faculty of RDI, 2001–. *Recreation:* sailing. *Address:* Queensberry Hunt, 63 Penfold Street, NW8 8PQ. *T:* (020) 7535 7120.

HUNT, Maurice William; Deputy Director-General, 1989–97, and Secretary, 1986–97, Confederation of British Industry; *b* 30 Aug. 1936; *s* of Maurice Hunt and Helen Hunt (*née* Andrews); *m* 1960, Jean Mary Ellis; one *s* one *d*. *Educ:* Selhurst Grammar School, Croydon; LSE (BSc Econ). ACIB. Nat. Service, RAF, 1955–57. ANZ Bank, 1953–66; Joint Iron Council, 1966–67; Board of Trade, 1967; Asst Sec., DTI, 1974; RCDS 1982; Dir, Membership, CBI, 1984; Exec. Dir (Ops), CBI, 1987. *Recreations:* walking, gardening, sailing. *Address:* Hurstbury, Blackhill, Lindfield, W Sussex RH16 2HE. *T:* (01444) 487598.

HUNT, Adm. Sir Nicholas (John Streynsham), GCB 1987 (KCB 1985); LVO 1961; DL; Chairman, Chatham Historic Dockyard Trust, since 1998; *b* 7 Nov. 1930; *s* of Brig. and Mrs J. M. Hunt; *m* 1966, Meriel Eve Givan; two *s* one *d*. *Educ:* BRNC, Dartmouth. CO HMS Burnaston, HMS Palliser, HMS Troubridge, HMS Intrepid, and BRNC, Dartmouth; Asst Private Sec. to Princess Marina, Duchess of Kent; Executive Officer, HMS Ark Royal, 1969–71; RCDS 1974; Dir of Naval Plans, 1976–78; Flag Officer, Second Flotilla, 1980–81; Dir-Gen., Naval Manpower and Training, 1981–83; Flag Officer, Scotland and NI, and Port Admiral Rosyth, 1983–85; C-in-C, Fleet, and Allied C-in-C, Channel and Eastern Atlantic, 1985–87, retd. Rear-Adm. of the UK, 1994–97, Vice Adm. of the UK and Lt of the Admiralty, 1997–2001. Dep. Man. Dir (Orgn and Develt), Eurotunnel, 1987–89; Dir-Gen., Chamber of Shipping, 1991–97. Chairman: SW Surrey DHA, 1990–95; Nuffield Hosps, 1996–2001. Comr, CWGC, 1988–92; Vice-Pres., ESU of Malta, 1988. Freeman, City of London, 1988. DL Surrey, 1996. *Recreation:* family. *Clubs:* Boodle's, Royal Navy of 1765 and 1785; Woodroffe's.

HUNT, Prof. Norman Charles, CBE 1975; Professor of Business Studies, 1967–84, Vice-Principal, 1980–84, University of Edinburgh, now Emeritus Professor; *b* 6 April 1918; *s* of Charles Hunt and Charlotte (*née* Jackson), Swindon, Wilts; *m* 1942, Lorna Mary, 2nd *d* of Mary and William Arthur Mann, Swindon, Wilts; two *s*. *Educ:* Commonweal Sch.; Swindon Coll.; University of London (Sir Edward Stern Schol., BCom 1st cl. hons); PhD (Edinburgh). On Staff (Research Dept and Personal Staff of Chief Mechanical Engineer), GWR Co., 1934–45; Lectr in Organisation of Industry and Commerce, University of Edinburgh, 1946–53; Dir of Studies in Commerce, 1948–53; Prof. of Organisation of Industry and Commerce, 1953–66; Dean of Faculty of Social Sciences, 1962–64. Member: Departmental Cttee on Fire Service, 1967–70; Rubber Industry NEDC, 1968–71; UGC, 1969–78 (Vice-Chm., 1974–76); ODM Working Party on Management Educn and Training in Developing Countries, 1968–69; Bd of Governors (and Chm., Management Develt Cttee), Council for Technical Educn and Training in Overseas Countries, 1971–75; Police Adv. Bd for Scotland, 1971–75; Council for Tertiary Educn in Scotland, 1979–84; CNAA, 1979–84. Consultant: UNIDO, 1973–; Hong Kong Baptist Coll., 1984–87; Hong Kong Management Assoc., 1986–98. Chairman: R. and R. Clark Ltd, 1967–70; William Thyne Ltd, 1967–70; Director: William Thyne (Holdings) Ltd, 1963–70; William Thyne (Plastics) Ltd, 1967–70; INMAP Ltd, 1984–86; UnivEd Technologies Ltd, 1984–98 (Chm. 1984–86); Edinburgh Res. and Innovation Ltd, 1998–2000. Hon. DLitt Loughborough, 1975. *Publications:* Methods of Wage Payment in British Industry, 1951; (with W. D. Reekie) Management in the Social and Safety Services, 1974; articles in economic and management jls on industrial organisation, industrial relations, and management problems. *Recreations:* photography, motoring, foreign travel. *Address:* 65 Ravelston Dykes Road, Edinburgh EH4 3NU.

HUNT, Hon. Sir (Patrick) James, Kt 2000; **Hon. Mr Justice Hunt;** a Judge of the High Court, Queen's Bench Division, since 2000; *b* 26 Jan. 1943; *s* of Thomas Ronald Clifford Hunt and Doreen Gwyneth Katarina Hunt; *m* 1969, Susan Jennifer Goodhead, JP; one *s* three *d*. *Educ:* Ashby de la Zouch Boys' Grammar Sch.; Keble Coll., Oxford (MA Mod. History). Called to the Bar, Gray's Inn, 1968, Bencher, 1994; in practice on Midland and Oxford Circuit, from London chambers; Leader, Midland and Oxford Circuit, 1996–99 (Dep. Leader, 1992–96); a Recorder, 1982–2000; QC 1987; a Dep. High Court Judge, 1994–2000. Mem., Gen. Council of the Bar, 1989–91, 1996–99. Legal Assessor to Disciplinary Cttee, RCVS, 1990–2000; Chm., Code of Protection Appeal Bd, Assoc. of British Pharmaceutical Industry, 1999–2000. *Recreations:* singing, gardening, stonework. *Address:* Royal Courts of Justice, Strand, WC2A 2LL. *Clubs:* Royal Automobile; Northants County; Nottingham United Services.

HUNT, Peter; *see* Hunt, D. P.

HUNT, Peter Lawrence, CMG 2001; HM Diplomatic Service; *b* 10 June 1945; *s* of late Lawrence Hunt and Catherine Hunt (*née* Bree); *m* 1972, Anne Langhorne Carson; two *s* two *d*. *Educ:* St Anselm's Coll.; Birkbeck Coll., Univ. of London (BA Hons). Joined HM Diplomatic Service, 1962: African floater duties, 1967–69; Managua, 1970–73; FCO, 1973–78; Second Sec., (Commercial), Caracas, 1978–82; First Secretary: FCO, 1982–87; Dep. Head of Mission and Consul, Montevideo, 1987–90; Dep. Head, S Atlantic and Antarctic Dept and Dep. Comr, British Antarctic Territory, 1990–93; Minister-Counsellor, Dep. Head of Mission, and Consul-Gen., Santiago, 1993–96; Consul-Gen., Istanbul, 1997–2001. *Recreations:* chess, golf, tennis, hill-walking. *Address:* c/o Foreign and Commonwealth Office, King Charles Street, SW1A 2AH.

HUNT, Philip Bodley; Director, Welsh Office Industry Department, 1975–76; *b* 28 July 1916; *s* of Bernard and Janet Hunt; *m* 1940, Eleanor Margaret Parnell (*d* 1989); three *s* one *d*. *Educ:* Sedbergh Sch.; Christ Church, Oxford (Boulter Exhibnr; 1st cl. PPE; MA). Joined

Board of Trade, 1946; Trade Commissioner, Montreal, 1952; Principal Trade Commissioner, Vancouver, 1955; Commercial Counsellor, Canberra, 1957; returned Board of Trade, 1962; Dept of Economic Affairs, 1964–65; Director, London & SE Region, BoT, 1968; Dir, DTI Office for Wales, 1972–75. Chm., S Wales Marriage Guidance Council, 1974–83; Mem. Nat. Exec., Nat. Marriage Guidance Council, 1977–83; Dept Mem. of Panel, County Structure Plans of S and W Glamorgan, 1978, of Gwent and Mid Glamorgan, 1979; Vice-Pres., Develt Corporation for Wales, 1980–83. Chm., John Macmurray Fellowship, 1993–. Silver Jubilee Medal, 1977. *Publication:* John Macmurray and the BBC: 1930–1941, 1995. *Recreation:* life and works of John Macmurray. *Address:* 8 Prospect Place, Camden Road, Bath BA1 5JD. *T:* (01225) 466982.

HUNT, Sir Rex (Masterman), Kt 1982; CMG 1980; HM Diplomatic Service, retired; Civil Commissioner, Falkland Islands, 1982–Sept. 1985, and High Commissioner, British Antarctic Territory, 1980–85 (Governor and Commander-in-Chief, Falkland Islands, 1980–82; Governor, Oct. 1985); *b* 29 June 1926; *s* of H. W. Hunt and Ivy Masterman; *m* 1951, Mavis Amanda Buckland; one *s* one *d*. *Educ:* Coatham Sch.; St Peter's Coll., Oxford (BA). Served with RAF, 1944–48; Flt Lt RAFO. Entered HM Overseas Civil Service, 1951; District Comr, Uganda, 1962; CRO, 1963–64; 1st Sec., Kuching, 1964–65; Jesselton, 1965–67; Brunei, 1967; 1st Sec. (Econ.), Ankara, 1968–70; 1st Sec. and Head of Chancery, Jakarta, 1970–72; Asst, ME Dept, FCO, 1972–74; Counsellor, Saigon, 1974–75, Kuala Lumpur, 1976–77; Dep. High Comr, Kuala Lumpur, 1977–79. Hon. Air Cdre, City of Lincoln Sqn, RAuxAF, 1987–97. Hon. Freeman, City of London, 1981. *Publication:* My Falkland Days, 1992. *Recreations:* golf, gardening. *Address:* Old Woodside, Broomfield Park, Sunningdale, Berks SL5 0JS. *Club:* Wentworth.

HUNT, Richard Bruce; Chairman, R. B. Hunt and Partners Ltd, 1966–95; Deputy Chairman, Howe Robinson and Co. Ltd, 1990–97; *b* 15 Dec. 1927; *s* of Percy Thompson Hunt and Thelma Constance Hunt; *m* 1972, Ulrike Dorothea Schmidt; two *d*. *Educ:* Christ's Hospital. FICS. Served Royal Signals, 1946–48; joined Merchant Bankers Ralli Brothers, 1949–66; formed own company, R. B. Hunt and Partners, 1966. Chm., Baltic Exchange Ltd, 1985–87 (Dir, 1977–80, re-elected, 1981–87). Liveryman, Shipwrights' Co. *Recreations:* golf, ski-ing. *Address:* Howe Robinson and Co. Ltd, 77 Mansell Street, E1 8AF. *T:* (020) 7488 3444. *Clubs:* Hurlingham, Royal Wimbledon Golf; Royal Lymington Yacht.

HUNT, (Richard) Tim(othy), PhD; FRS 1991; Principal (formerly Senior) Scientist, Imperial Cancer Research Fund, since 1990; Fellow of Clare College, Cambridge, since 1968; *b* 19 Feb. 1943; *s* of Richard William Hunt and Katherine Eva Rowland; *m* 1st, 1971, Missy Cusick (marr. diss. 1974); 2nd, 1995, Prof. Mary Katharine Levinge Collins; two *d*. *Educ:* Dragon Sch.; Magdalen Coll. Sch., Oxford; Clare Coll., Cambridge (BA Nat. Sci. 1964; PhD 1968). Univ. Lectr in Biochem., Cambridge, 1981–90 (Junior Proctor, 1982–83). Mem., EMBO; MAE 1998. Founder FMedSci 1998. Foreign Hon. Mem., Amer. Acad. of Arts and Scis, 1997; Foreign Associate, US Nat. Acad. of Scis, 1999. (Jtly) Nobel Prize for Physiology or Medicine, 2001. *Publications:* Molecular Biology of the Cell Problems (with John Wilson), 1989, 2nd edn 1994; The Cell Cycle: an introduction (with Andrew Murray), 1993; articles in cell and molecular biology jls. *Recreations:* cooking, eating, walking. *Address:* Imperial Cancer Research Fund, Clare Hall Laboratories, South Mimms, Herts EN6 3LD. *T:* (020) 7269 3981, *Fax:* (020) 7269 3804; *e-mail:* tim.hunt@icrf.icnet.uk.

HUNT, Robert Alan, OBE 1984; QPM 1992; Assistant Commissioner, Territorial Operations Department, Metropolitan Police, 1990–95; *b* 6 July 1935; *s* of Peter and Minnie Hunt; *m* 1956, Jean White; one *s* three *d*. *Educ:* Dulwich Coll.; London Univ. (LLB external 1970). Served in RA. Joined Metropolitan Police, 1955: Chief Superintendent, 1973; Comdr, 1976; Dep. Asst Comr, 1981. *Recreations:* music—traditional and light classical, reading, the family. *Address:* 7 Ashley Drive, Banstead, Surrey SM7 2AG. *T:* (01737) 356467.

HUNT, Sir Robert (Frederick), Kt 1979; CBE 1974; DL; Chairman, Dowty Group PLC, 1975–86; Deputy Chairman, Rover Group (formerly BL plc), 1982–90 (Director, 1980–90); Director, Charter Consolidated, 1983–90; *b* 11 May 1918; *s* of late Arthur Hunt, Cheltenham and Kathleen Alice Cotton; *m* 1st, 1947, Joy Patricia Molly (*d* 1984), *d* of late Charles Leslie Harding, Cheltenham; four *d*; 2nd, 1987, Joyce Elizabeth Baigent, *d* of Otto Leiske. *Educ:* Pates Grammar Sch., Cheltenham; N Glos Techn. Coll. Apprenticed Dowty Equipment Ltd, 1935; Chief Instructor to Co.'s Sch. of Hydraulics, 1940; RAF Trng Comd, 1940; Export Man., Dowty Equipment Ltd, 1946; Vice-Pres. and Gen. Man., 1949, Pres., 1954, Dowty Equipment of Canada Ltd; Dir, Dowty Gp Ltd, 1956, Dep. Chm., 1959–75, Chief Exec., 1975–83. Dir, Eagle Star Hldgs plc, 1980–87. Chm., Bd of Trustees, Improvement District of Ajax, Ont., 1954; Dir, Ajax and Pickering Gen. Hosp., 1954; Chm., Cheltenham Hosp. Gp Man. Cttee, 1959; Chm., Glos AHA, 1974–81; Pres., 1967–68, Treas., 1973, Vice-Pres., 1976, Pres., 1977–78, SBAC. FREng (FEng 1982); FCASI 1976; FRAeS 1968, Hon. FRAeS 1981. Hon. DSc Bath, 1979. DL Glos, 1977; Hon. Freeman of Cheltenham, 1980. *Recreations:* family interests, golf, gardening. *Address:* Maple House, Withington, Glos GL54 4DA. *T:* (01242) 890344. *Club:* New (Cheltenham).

HUNT, Terence, CBE 1996; Chief Executive (formerly National Director), NHS Supplies, 1991–2000; *b* 8 Aug. 1943; *s* of Thomas John Hunt and Marie Louise Hunt (*née* Potter); *m* 1967, Wendy Graeme George; one *s* one *d*. *Educ:* Huish's Grammar Sch., Taunton. Associate Mem. Inst. of Health Service Management. Tone Vale Group HMC, 1963–65; NE Somerset HMC, 1965–67; Winchester Gp HMC, 1967–69; Lincoln No 1 HMC, 1969–70; Hosp. Sec., Wycombe General Hosp., 1970–73; Dep. Gp Sec., Hillingdon Hosp., 1973–74; Area General Administrator, Kensington and Chelsea and Westminster AHA(T), 1974–77; District Administrator: NW Dist of KCW AHA(T), 1977–82; Paddington and N Kensington, 1982–84; Regl Gen. Manager, NE Thames RHA, 1984–91. Member: Steering Gp on Undergrad. Med. and Dental Educn and Res., 1987–91; NHS Central R&D Cttee, 1991–94; Hosp. Cttee, EEC, 1991–93; Med. Cttee, UFC, 1989–91. Member: Twyford & Dist Round Table, 1975–84 (Chm., 1980–81; Pres., 1988–89); Cttee, Reading Town Regatta, 1984–95 (Treas., 1984–86; Chm., 1989–93). Member: Council of Govs, London Hosp. Med. Coll., 1985–91; Council, UCL, 1985–91. CIMgt. Freeman, 1991, Liveryman, 1998, Barbers' Co. *Recreations:* sculling, cycling, all things practical with metal and wood. *Address:* 36 Old Bath Road, Charvil, Reading, Berks RG10 9QR. *T:* (0118) 934 1062. *Club:* Royal Society of Medicine.

HUNT, Tim; *see* Hunt, R. T.

HUNT, William George, TD 1988 (and Clasp 1994); Windsor Herald of Arms, since 1999; *b* 8 Dec. 1946; *s* of Frank Williams Hunt, TD, and Mary Elizabeth Leyland Hunt (*née* Orton), JP; *m* 1998, Michaela Wedel; one *s*. *Educ:* Liverpool Coll.; Univ. of Southampton (BA); Univ. of Constance; Univ. of Lausanne; Univ. of Caen (Dip.). FCA 1979. Mentor, Salem Sch., 1967–69; Audit Manager, Arthur Young McClelland Moores, 1970–83; Financial Controller and Partnership Sec., Frere Cholmeley, 1983–92; Finance Dir, Hopkins & Wood, 1993–95; Portcullis Pursuivant of Arms, 1992–99. Clerk, HM Commn of Lieutenancy for City of London, 1990–. Dir, Heraldry Soc., 1998–. Treas., HAC Biographical Dictionary (1537–1914) Trust, 1993–. Freeman, City of London; Founder Mem., Treas., 1976–78, Chm., 1978–79, Soc. of Young Freemen of City of London; Maj. and Mem., Ct of Assts, 1988–2000, HAC; Mem., Ct of Assts, 1996–, Master, 2000–01, Co. of Makers of Playing Cards. SBStJ 1999. *Publications:* Guide to the Honourable Artillery Company, 1987; (ed jtly) Dictionary of British Arms, Vol. 1, 1992. *Recreation:* orders and decorations. *Address:* College of Arms, Queen Victoria Street, EC4V 4BT. *T:* (020) 7329 8755. *Club:* City Livery (Clerk, 1996–98, Dep. Clerk, 1998–).

HUNT-DAVIS, Brig. Miles Garth, CVO 1998; CBE 1990 (MBE 1977); Private Secretary, since 1993, and Treasurer, since 2000, to HRH The Duke of Edinburgh (Assistant Private Secretary, 1991–92); *b* Johannesburg, SA, 7 Nov. 1938; *s* of late Lt-Col Eric Hunt-Davis, OBE, ED and Mary Eleanor Turnbull (*née* Boyce); *m* 1965, Anita (Gay) Ridsdale, *d* of Francis James Ridsdale; two *s* one *d*. *Educ:* St Andrew's Coll., Grahamstown, SA. Commnd 6th QEO Gurkha Rifles, 1962; active service in Borneo and Malaya, 1964–66; student, Canadian Land Forces Comd and Staff Coll., 1969–70; Bde Maj., 48 Gurkha Inf. Bde, 1974–76; Comdt, 7th Duke of Edinburgh's Own Gurkha Rifles, 1976–79; School of Infantry: Chief Instructor, Tactics Wing, 1979–80; GSO 1 Tactics, 1980–82; Instr, Staff Coll., Camberley, 1982–83; Commander: British Gurkhas, Nepal, 1985–87; Bde of Gurkhas, 1987–90; retd, 1991. Col, 7th Duke of Edinburgh's Own Gurkha Rifles, 1991–94. Chm., Gurkha Bde Assoc., 1991–. Trustee, Gurkha Welfare Trust (UK), 1987–. *Publication:* (with Col E. D. Powell-Jones) Abridged History of the 6th Queen Elizabeth's Own Gurkha Rifles, 1974. *Recreations:* golf, walking, elephant polo. *Address:* Nottingham Cottage, Kensington Palace, W8 4PY. *T:* (home) (020) 7937 6258, (office) (020) 7930 4832. *Clubs:* Army and Navy, Beefsteak; Hong Kong Golf.

HUNTER, Hon. Lord; John Oswald Mair Hunter, VRD; a Senator of the College of Justice in Scotland, 1961–86; *b* 21 Feb. 1913; *s* of John Mair Hunter, QC (Scot.) and Jessie Donald Frew; *m* 1st, 1939, Doris Mary Simpson (*d* 1988); one *s* one *d*; 2nd, 1989, Mrs Angela Marion McLean. *Educ:* Edinburgh Acad.; Rugby; New Coll., Oxford (BA 1934, MA 1961); Edinburgh Univ. (LLB 1936, LLD 1975). Entered RNVR, 1933; served War 1939–45 (despatches); Lt-Comdr RNVR; retired list 1949. Called to Bar, Inner Temple, 1937; admitted to Faculty of Advocates, 1937; QC (Scot.) 1951. Advocate Depute (Home), 1954–57; Sheriff of Ayr and Bute, 1957–61. Chairman: Deptl Cttee on Scottish Salmon and Trout Fisheries, 1962–65; Lands Valuation Appeal Court, 1966–71; Scottish Law Commn, 1971–81; Scottish Council on Crime, 1972–75; Dep. Chm., Boundary Commn for Scotland, 1971–76. Pres., Scottish Univs Law Inst., 1972–77; Member: Scottish Records Adv. Council, 1966–81; Statute Law Cttee, 1971–81; Chm., later Hon. Pres., Cttee, RNLI (Dunbar), 1969–80 and 1981–2001; Hon. Pres., Scottish Assoc. for Study of Delinquency, 1971–88.

HUNTER, Air Vice-Marshal Alexander Freeland Cairns, CBE 1982 (OBE 1981); AFC 1978; DL; Chairman: Home Group, since 1998; Paramount Homes Ltd, since 1998; Deputy Chairman: Annington Holdings plc, since 1996; Urban Housing Trust Ltd, since 2001; *b* 8 March 1939; *s* of late H. A. C. and L. E. M. Hunter; *m* 1964, Wilma Elizabeth Bruce Wilson. *Educ:* Aberdeen Grammar Sch.; Aberdeen Univ. (MA 1960, LLB 1962). Commissioned RAFVR 1959; RAF 1962; flying training 1962; Pilot, 81 (PR) Sqn, FEAF, 1964–67; Central Flying Sch., 1967–68; Instructor, Northumbrian Univ. Air Sqn, 1968–69; Asst Air Attaché, Moscow, 1971–73; RAF Staff Coll., 1974; Flight Comdr, 230 Sqn, 1975–77; OC 18 Sqn, RAF Germany, 1978–80; Air Warfare Course, 1981; MoD (Air), 1981; OC RAF Odiham, 1981–83; Gp Captain Plans, HQ Strike Comd, 1983–85; RCDS 1986; Dir of Public Relations (RAF), 1987–88; Comdt, RAF Staff Coll., 1989–90; Comdr British Forces Cyprus and Adminr of Sovereign Base Areas, 1990–93. Chm., Home Housing Assoc., 1995–98; Member, Board: North Housing Assoc. Ltd, 1993–95 (Vice Chm. (NE), 1994); Warden Housing Assoc., 1996–98. Chairman: Home in Scotland Ltd, 1998–2000; Kenton Bar Bunker Co. Ltd, 1999–; Director: Clyde Helicopters Ltd, 1993–95; Newcastle Bldg Soc., 1993–; Newcastle Bank (Gibraltar), 1995–99; Great NE Air Ambulance Trading Co. Ltd, 2000–. Vice Chm. (Air): N of England, RFCA (formerly TAVRA), 1996–; Council of RFCAs (formerly TAVRAs), 1999–. Hon. Col, Tyne-Tees Regt, 1999–. DL Northumberland, 1994. OStJ 1994 (Chm. Council, Northumbria, 1998–2000). *Recreations:* shooting, fishing, hill-walking, military history. *Address:* c/o Clydesdale Bank, Business Banking Centre, Wakefield Road, Carlisle CA3 0HE. *Clubs:* Royal Air Force; Northern Counties (Newcastle upon Tyne); Tanglin (Singapore).

HUNTER, Sir Alistair (John), KCMG 1994 (CMG 1985); DL; HM Diplomatic Service, retired; Chairman, British Music Rights, since 1998; *b* 9 Aug. 1936; *s* of Kenneth Clarke Hunter and Joan Tunks; *m* 1st, 1963; one *s* two *d*; 2nd, 1978, Helge Milton (*née* Kahle). *Educ:* Felsted; Magdalen Coll., Oxford. Royal Air Force, 1955–57; CRO, 1961–65; Private Sec. to Permanent Under-Sec., 1961–63; 2nd Sec., Kuala Lumpur, 1963–65; 1st Sec. (Commercial), Peking, 1965–68; seconded to Cabinet Office, 1969–70; FCO, 1970–73; 1st Sec., Rome, 1973–75; FCO, 1975–80; Hd of Chancery, Bonn, 1980–85; seconded to DTI as Under Sec., Overseas Trade, 1985–88; Consul-Gen., Düsseldorf, and Dir-Gen. of British Trade and Investment Promotion in FRG, 1988–91; Consul-Gen., NY, and Dir-Gen. of Trade and Investment, USA, 1991–96. Exec. Chm., British-Amer. Chamber of Commerce, London, 1996–98. Chairman: E Kent Forum, 1998–; Manston Airport Consultative Cttee, 1999–; Dir, PRS, 1996–; Dep. Chm., Locate in Kent, 1996–. Chm., Theatre Royal Margate Trust, 2000–. Trustee, Horniman Mus. and Gdns, 1996–99. DL Kent, 2001. *Address:* Bay View House, 2A Bay View Road, Broadstairs CT10 2EA.

HUNTER, Andrew Robert Frederick; MP (C) Basingstoke, since 1983; company director and consultant; *b* 8 Jan. 1943; *s* of late Sqdn Leader Roger Edward Hunter, DFC and Winifred Mary Hunter (*née* Nelson); *m* 1972, Janet, *d* of late Samuel Bourne of Gloucester; one *s* one *d*. *Educ:* St George's Sch., Harpenden; Durham Univ.; Jesus Coll., Cambridge; Westcott House, Cambridge. In industry, 1969; Asst Master, St Martin's Sch., Northwood, 1970–71; Asst Master, Harrow Sch., 1971–83. Contested (C) Southampton, Itchen, 1979. PPS to Minister of State, DoE, 1985–86. Mem., NI Select Cttee, 1994–2001, Dep. Chm., Cons. NI Cttee, 1997– (Chm., 1992–97). Sponsored Private Members' Bills: Control of Smoke Pollution Act, 1989; Timeshare Act, 1992; Noise and Statutory Nuisance Act, 1993; Dogs (Fouling of Land) Act, 1996; Road Traffic (Vehicle Testing) Act, 1999. Member: NFU; Countryside Alliance. Vice-Pres., Nat. Prayer Book Soc., 1987–. Mem., Court, Univ. of Southampton, 1983–. Hon. Mem., Soc. of the Sealed Knot, 1990–. *Recreations:* horse riding, watching cricket and Rugby football. *Address:* House of Commons, SW1A 0AA. *T:* (020) 7219 5216. *Clubs:* Pratt's, St Stephen's Constitutional, Carlton.

HUNTER, Angela Jane; Director of Communications, BP, since 2002; *b* 29 July 1955; *d* of Arthur John, (Mac), Hunter and Joy Lorraine Hunter; *m* 1980, Nick Cornwall; one *s* one *d*. *Educ:* St Leonard's Sch., St Andrews, Fife; Brighton Poly. (BA 1987). Teacher of

English as a foreign language, 1976–78; Legal Asst, 1978–80; Res. Asst to Tony Blair, MP, 1986–90, Head of Office, 1990–97; Special Asst to Prime Minsiter, 1997–2001; Dir of Govt Relations, Prime Minister's Office, 2001. *Recreations:* diving, ski-ing. *Address:* BP plc, Britannia House, 1 Finsbury Cricus, EC2M 7BA.

HUNTER, Rt Rev. Anthony George Weaver; *b* 3 June 1916; *s* of Herbert George Hunter and Ethel Frances Weaver; *m* 1st, 1948, Joan Isobel Marshall (*d* 1981); 2nd, 1982, Emlyn Marianne Garton (*née* Dent) (*d* 2001). *Educ:* Wanstead; Leeds Univ. (BA); Coll. of the Resurrection, Mirfield. Deacon, 1941; Priest, 1942; Curate of St George's, Jesmond, 1941–43; Orlando Mission Dist, 1943–47; Johannesburg Coloured Mission, 1947–48; Curate of St George's, Jesmond, 1948–49; Vicar of Ashington, 1949–60; Proctor in Convocation, 1959–60; Vicar of Huddersfield, 1960–68; Rural Dean of Huddersfield, 1960–68; Hon. Canon of Wakefield, 1962–68; Proctor in Convocation, 1962–68; Bishop of Swaziland, 1968–75; Rector of Hexham, Dio. Newcastle, 1975–79; Asst Bishop, Dio. Newcastle, 1976–80; Supernumerary Bishop, 1980–81; Acting Archdeacon of Lindisfarne, 1981; retd Oct. 1981. OStJ. *Recreations:* walking, gardening, travel. *Address:* The West Wing, Sandwood House, Spaldington, East Yorks DN14 7NG. *T:* (01420) 422424.

HUNTER, Anthony John; Director of Social Services, Housing and Public Protection, East Riding of Yorkshire Council, since 1995; *b* 9 March 1954; *s* of Robert and Elizabeth Hunter; *m* 1986, Tatyana Fomina; one *s* one *d*. *Educ:* Doncaster Grammar Sch.; Queen's Coll., Oxford (MA PPE 1976); Nottingham Univ. (MA Applied Social Studies, CQSW, 1980); Sheffield Poly. (DMS 1984). Social Worker and Social Services Manager: Doncaster MBC, 1976–84; Barnsley MBC, 1985–86; Res. and Develt Manager, Barnardo's, 1986–89; Health and Social Care Consultant, Price Waterhouse, 1989–95. *Publications:* articles on social care, local govt develt and change mgt issues in social work and local govt jls. *Recreations:* football, rock'n'roll singing, playing computer games with my children. *Address:* East Riding of Yorkshire Council, County Hall, Beverley HU17 9BA. *T:* (01482) 885562.

HUNTER, Anthony Rex; *see* Hunter, Tony.

HUNTER, Archibald Sinclair; DL; CA; Senior Partner, Scotland, KPMG, 1992–99, now Consultant; President, Institute of Chartered Accountants of Scotland, 1997–98; *b* 20 Aug. 1943; *s* of late John Lockhart Hunter and Elizabeth Hastings (*née* Sinclair); *m* 1969, Patricia Ann Robertson; two *s* one *d*. *Educ:* Queen's Park Sch., Glasgow. CA 1966. With Mackie & Clark, Glasgow, 1966; joined Thomson McLintock, 1966: Partner, 1974–87; Glasgow Office Managing Partner, 1983–87; Glasgow Office Managing Partner, KPMG Peat Marwick, 1987–92. Director: Macfarlane Gp, 1998–; Clydeport plc, 1999–. Dir, Beatson Inst., 1999–. Mem. Court, Univ. of Strathclyde, 1999–. DL Renfrewshire, 1995. *Recreations:* golf, swimming, hill-walking. *Address:* KPMG, 24 Blythswood Square, Glasgow G2 4QS. *T:* (0141) 226 5511. *Clubs:* Royal Scottish Automobile, Williamwood Golf (formerly Capt.) (Glasgow); Western Gailes Golf (Ayrshire).

HUNTER, Rt Rev. Barry Russell, AM 1992; Bishop of Riverina, 1971–92; permission to officiate, diocese of Newcastle, NSW, since 1996; *b* Brisbane, Queensland, 15 Aug. 1927; *s* of late John Hunter; *m* 1961, Dorothy Nancy, *d* of B. P. Sanders, Brisbane; three *d*. *Educ:* Toowoomba Grammar Sch.; St Francis' Theological Coll., Brisbane; Univ. of Queensland (BA, ThL). Assistant Curate, St Matthew's, Sherwood, 1953–56; Member, Bush Brotherhood of St Paul, Cunnamulla, Queensland, 1956–61; Rector, St Cecilia's, Chinchilla, 1961–66; Rector, St Gabriel's, Biloela, 1966–71; Archdeacon of the East, Diocese of Rockhampton, 1969–71; Locum Tenens in parish of Cudal, NSW, 1992–96. DLitt (*hc*) Charles Sturt Univ., 1994. *Recreation:* music. *Address:* 27 Telopea Drive, Taree, NSW 2430, Australia.

HUNTER, David Peter; Director, Agricultural Strategy, EU and International Policy Directorate, Department for Environment, Food and Rural Affairs, since 2001; *b* 31 Dec. 1948; *o s* of Mr and Mrs D. Hunter, Southampton; *m* 1973, Judith, *d* of Mr and Mrs G. A. Baker, Worcester; two *s* two *d*. *Educ:* Regent's Park Sch.; Shirley Sch.; King Edward VI Sch., Southampton; Magdalen Coll., Oxford (MA). MAFF, 1972; Cabinet Office, 1982; rejoined MAFF, 1983; Head: Beef Div., 1984; Trade Policy and Tropical Products Div., 1987; Agencies and Citizen's Charter Div., 1993; EU and Livestock Gp, 1996; Agricl Gp, MAFF, subseq. DEFRA, 1998–2001. *Recreations:* theatre, vegetables, Soton FC. *Address:* Department for Environment, Food and Rural Affairs, Whitehall Place, SW1A 2HH. *T:* (020) 7270 8679. *Club:* Lion & Unicorn Players (Petersfield).

HUNTER, Evan; writer; *b* New York, 15 Oct. 1926; *s* of Charles F. Lombino and Marie Lombino; *m* 1st, 1949, Anita Melnick (marr. diss.); three *s*; 2nd, 1973, Mary Vann Finley (marr. diss.); one step *d*; 3rd, 1997, Dragica Dimitrijevic. *Educ:* Cooper Union; Hunter Coll. (BA 1950). Served USNR. Literary Father of the Year, 1961; Phi Beta Kappa. Grand Master Award, Mystery Writers of America, 1986; Cartier Diamond Dagger Award, CWA, 1998. *Publications include: as Evan Hunter:* The Blackboard Jungle, 1954; Second Ending, 1956; Strangers When We Meet, 1958; A Matter of Conviction, 1959; The Remarkable Harry, 1960; The Wonderful Button, 1961; Mothers and Daughters, 1961; Happy New Year, Herbie, 1963; Buddwing, 1964; The Paper Dragon, 1966; A Horse's Head, 1967; Last Summer, 1968; Sons, 1969; Nobody Knew They Were There, 1971; Every Little Crook and Nanny, 1972; The Easter Man, 1972; Seven, 1972; Come Winter, 1973; Streets of Gold, 1974; The Chisholms, 1976; Me and Mr Stenner, 1977; Walk Proud, 1978; Love, Dad, 1981; Far From the Sea, 1983; Lizzie, 1984; Criminal Conversation, 1994; Privileged Conversation, 1996; Candyland, 2001; *as Ed McBain:* Cop Hater, 1956; The Mugger, 1956; The Pusher, 1956; The Con Man, 1957; Killer's Choice, 1958; Killer's Payoff, 1958; Lady Killer, 1958; Killer's Wedge, 1959; 'Til Death, 1959; King's Ransom, 1959; Give the Boys a Great Big Hand, 1960; The Heckler, 1960; See Them Die, 1960; Lady, Lady, I Did It, 1961; The Empty Hours, 1962; Like Love, 1962; Ten Plus One, 1963; Ax, 1964; The Sentries, 1965; He Who Hesitates, 1965; Doll, 1965; Eighty Million Eyes, 1966; Fuzz, 1968; Shotgun, 1969; Jigsaw, 1970; Hail, Hail, the Gang's All Here!, 1971; Sadie When She Died, 1972; Let's Hear It for the Deaf Man, 1972; Death of a Nurse, 1972; Hail to the Chief, 1973; Bread, 1974; Where There's Smoke, 1975; Blood Relatives, 1975; So Long as You Both Shall Live, 1976; Guns, 1976; Long Time No See, 1977; Goldilocks, 1978; Calypso, 1979; Ghosts, 1980; Even the Wicked, 1980; Rumpelstiltskin, 1981; Heat, 1981; Beauty and the Beast, 1982; Ice, 1983; Jack and the Beanstalk, 1984; Lightning, 1984; Snow White and Rose Red, 1985; Eight Black Horses, 1985; Cinderella, 1986; Another Part of the City, 1986; Poison, 1987; Tricks, 1987; Puss in Boots, 1987; McBain's Ladies, 1988; The House that Jack Built, 1988; Lullaby, 1989; McBain's Ladies, Too, 1989; Downtown, 1989; Vespers, 1990; Mary, Mary, 1992; Mischief, 1993; There was a Little Girl, 1994; Romance, 1995; Gladly the Cross-Eyed Bear, 1996; Nocturne, 1997; The Last Best Hope, 1998; The Big Bad City, 1999; The Last Dance, 2000; Candyland, 2001; *screenplays:* Strangers When We Meet, 1959; The Birds, 1962; Fuzz, 1972; Walk Proud, 1979; Dream West (TV mini-series), 1986; *plays:* The Easter Man, 1964; The Conjuror, 1969. *Recreation:* travelling. *Address:* Curtis Brown, 28/29 Haymarket, SW1Y 4SP.

HUNTER, Rear-Adm. Ian Alexander, CB 1993; Chief of Naval Staff, New Zealand, 1991–94; *b* 23 Oct. 1939; *s* of late A. A. Hunter and O. R. Hunter; *m* 1965, Hilary R. Sturrock; two *s*. *Educ:* Christchurch Boys' High Sch.; BRNC Dartmouth. Joined RNZN 1957; served HMNZS Otago, HMS Tabard, USS Arneb, HMNZS Rotoiti (Antarctic), N Ireland Anti-Submarine Sch., HM Ships Torquay and Eastbourne, HMNZ Ships Taranaki, Blackpool, Canterbury, Waikato (Command), Southland (Command); posts with Chief of Naval Staff; RCDS 1985; ACDS (Develt Plans), 1987–88; Commodore Auckland, 1988–91 (concerned with Govt financial reforms for RNZN, restructuring Dockyard, orgn of Whitbread Round the World Yacht Race). Pres., Sea Cadet Assoc. of NZ, 1998–. Trustee, Wellington Civic Trust, 1994– (Dep. Chm., 1995; Chm., 1996–); Chm. of Friends, Wellington Maritime Mus., 1995–. *Address:* 108B Messines Road, Karori, Wellington, New Zealand.

HUNTER, Sir Ian (Bruce Hope), Kt 1983; MBE 1945; Impresario; President, Askonas Holt Ltd, since 1998; Chairman, Tempo Video Ltd, since 1984; *b* 2 April 1919; *s* of late W. O. Hunter; *m* 1st, 1949, Susan (*d* 1977), *d* of late Brig. A. G. Russell; four *d*; 2nd, 1984, Lady Showering, *widow* of Sir Keith Showering. *Educ:* Fettes Coll., Edinburgh; abroad as pupil of Dr Fritz Busch and at Glyndebourne. Served War of 1939–45, Lt-Col. Asst to Artistic Dir, Edinburgh Festival, 1946–48; Artistic Administrator, Edinburgh Festival, 1949–50; Artistic Dir, Edinburgh Festival, 1951–55; Chm. and Chief Exec., 1953–88, Pres. and Dir, 1988–98, Harold Holt Ltd. Director, Bath Festivals, 1948, 1955, 1958–68; Adviser, Adelaide Festivals, 1960–64; Dir-Gen., Commonwealth Arts Festival, 1965; Artistic Director: Festivals of the City of London, 1962–80; Brighton Festivals, 1967–83; (with Yehudi Menuhin) Windsor Festivals, 1969–72; Hong Kong Arts Festivals, 1973–75; Malvern Festival, 1977–82; American Festival, 1985; Festival of German Arts, London, 1987. Dir, British Nat. Day Entertainment, Expo' 67. Dir, Live Music Now, 1983–. Member: Opera/Ballet Enquiry for Arts Council, 1967–69; Arts Administration Course Enquiry for Arts Council, 1970–71; Arts Council Trng Cttee, 1974–76; Centenary Appeal Cttee, RCM, 1982–; Adv. Cttee, Britain Salutes New York, 1983; Chairman: Entertainments Cttee, Queen's Silver Jubilee Appeal; Musicians' Benevolent Fund, 1987–95. Royal Concert Cttee, 1988–93. Pres., British Arts Festivals Assoc., 1978–81; Dep. Chm., Stravinsky Festival Trust; Trustee, Chichester Festival Theatre Trust, until 1988; Founder and Trustee, Young Concert Artists Trust, 1984–; Chm. of Governors, London Festival Ballet (later English National Ballet), 1984–89; Vice-Chm., Japan Fest. UK 1991, 1989–92; Mem. Cttee, Spanish Arts Festival, London, 1994; Vice-Pres., Yehudi Menuhin Sch. R. B. Bennett Commonwealth Prize for 1966. FRCM 1991 (Hon. RCM 1984); Hon. Mem., GSMD, 1975. FRSA (Mem. Council, 1968–73, 1976–83; Chm. Council, 1981–83; a Vice-Pres., 1981–). Mem. Ct of Assistants, Musicians' Co., 1981–84. Hon. DMus Bath, 1996. *Recreations:* gardening, painting. *Address:* c/o Askonas Holt, Lonsdale Chambers, 27 Chancery Lane, WC2A 1PF. *T:* (020) 7400 1700. *Club:* Garrick.

HUNTER, Ian Gerald Adamson; QC 1980; SC (NSW) 1994; a Recorder, since 1986; *b* 3 Oct. 1944; *s* of late Gerald Oliver Hunter and Jessie Hunter; *m* 1975, Maggie (*née* Reed) (marr. diss. 1999); two *s*. *Educ:* Reading Sch.; Pembroke Coll., Cambridge (Open Scholar, Squire Univ. Law Scholar, Trevelyan Scholar, BA (double first in Law), MA, LLB); Harvard Law Sch. (Kennedy Memorial Scholar, LLM). Called to the Bar, Inner Temple, 1967 (Duke of Edinburgh Entrance Scholar, Major Scholar), Bencher, 1986; Mem. Bar, NSW, 1993; Avocat à la cour de Paris, 1995. CEDR Accredited Mediator, 1998–. Chm., Consolidated Regulations and Transfer Cttee, Senate of Inns of Court, 1986–87 (Mem., 1982–85); Member: International Relations Cttee, Bar Council, 1982–90; Exec. Cttee, Bar Council, 1985–86. Mem. and Rapporteur, Internat. Law Assoc. Anti-Trust Cttee, 1968–72; Pres., Union Internat. des Avocats, 1989 (UK Vice-Pres., 1982–86; first Vice Pres., 1986–; Dir of Studies, 1990–91); Vice Pres., Franco-British Lawyers Soc., 1996–99; Pres., Anglo-Australasian Lawyers Soc., 1998–; Treas., Bar Pro Bono Unit, 1997–99; Hon. Mem., Canadian Bar Assoc., 1990. *Publications:* articles on public international law. *Recreations:* bebop, other good music, French cooking. *Address:* Essex Court Chambers, 24 Lincoln's Inn Fields, WC2A 3ED. *T:* (020) 7813 8000.

HUNTER, Brig. Ian Murray, CVO 1954; AM 1994; MBE 1943; ED 1996; psc 1943; fsc (US) 1955; FAIM; FAICD; FIM; Chairman, since 1970, and Managing Director, since 1981, Allied Rubber Products (Qld) Pty Ltd; *b* Sydney, Aust., 10 July 1917; *s* of late Dr James Hunter, Stranraer, Scotland; *m* 1947, Rosemary Jane Batchelor; two *s* two *d*. *Educ:* Cranbrook Sch., Sydney; RMC, Duntroon. Lieut Aust. Staff Corps, and AIF, 1939; 2/1 MG Bn, 1939–40; T/Capt. 1940; Staff Capt., 25 Inf. Bde, 1940–41; Middle East Staff Coll., Haifa, 1941; DA QMG (1), HQ 6 Div., 1941–42; T/Major 1942; AQMG, NT Force (MBE), 1942–43; Staff Sch. (Aust.), 1943; Gen. Staff 3 Corps and Advanced HQ Allied Land Forces, 1943–44; Lieut-Col 1945; Instructor, Staff Sch., 1945; AQMG, and Col BCOF, 1946–47; AQMG, AHQ and JCOSA, 1947; AA&QMG, HQ, 3 Div., 1948–50; Royal Visit, 1949; Exec. Commonwealth Jubilee Celebrations, 1950–51; CO 2 Recruit Trg Bn, 1952; CO 4 RAR, 1953; Executive and Commonwealth Marshal, Royal Visit, 1952, and 1954; Command and Gen. Staff Coll., Fort Leavenworth, USA, 1954–55; Military Mission, Washington, 1955–56; Officer i/c Admin, N Comd, 1956–59; Comd 11 Inf. Bde, 1959–60; Command 2nd RQR, 1960–62; Chief of Staff 1st Div., 1963; Commandant, Australian Staff Coll., 1963–65; Comdr, Papua New Guinea Comd, 1966–69; DQMG, Army HQ, 1969. Indep. Mem., Presbyterian Church Property Commn, 1974–84. Chm., Australian Red Cross Soc. (Qld), 1990–94. FAIM 1964; FAICD 1990; FIM 1993; Fellow, Australian Plastic and Rubber Inst., 1994. *Recreations:* golf, squash, swimming, riding. *Address:* Box 3053, Stafford Delivery Centre, Qld 4053, Australia; Garthland, 5 Sword Street, Ascot, Brisbane, Queensland 4007, Australia; Finchley, Hargreaves Street, Blackheath, NSW 2785, Australia. *Clubs:* Australian (Sydney); Queensland (Brisbane); Royal Sydney Golf.

HUNTER, James, CBE 2001; PhD; Chairman, Highlands and Islands Enterprise, since 1998; *b* 22 May 1948; *s* of Donald and Jean Hunter; *m* 1972, Evelyn Ronaldson; one *s* one *d*. *Educ:* Oban High Sch.; Aberdeen Univ. (MA Hons 1971); Edinburgh Univ. (PhD 1974). Res. Fellow, Aberdeen Univ., 1974–76; journalist: Press and Jl, 1976–81; Sunday Standard, 1981–82; freelance journalist and broadcaster, 1982–85; Founding Dir, Scottish Crofters' Union, 1985–90; freelance writer, historian and broadcaster, 1990–. Chm., Skye and Localsh Enterprise, 1995–98; Member: Bd, Highlands and Is Enterprise, 1991–95; North Areas Bd, Scottish Natural Heritage, 1992–98; Scottish Tourist Bd, 1995–98; Council, NT for Scotland, 1995–98; Convention of the Highlands and Is, 1996–. Mem., BBC's Broadcasting Council for Scotland, 1999–. *Publications:* The Making of the Crofting Community, 1976; For the People's Cause, 1986; Skye: the island, 1986; The Claim of Crofting, 1991; Scottish Highlanders: a people and their place, 1992; A Dance Called America: the Scottish Highlands, the United States and Canada, 1994; On the Other Side of Sorrow: nature and people in the Scottish Highlands, 1995; Glencoe and the Indians, 1996 (US edn as Scottish Highlanders, Indian Peoples); Last of the Free: a millennial history of the Highlands and Islands of Scotland, 1999; Culloden and the Last Clansman, 2001. *Recreations:* hillwalking, swimming. *Address:* Rowanbrae, Kiltarlity, Beauly, Inverness-shire IV4 7HT. *T:* (01463) 741644.

HUNTER, Surg. Rear-Adm. (D) John, CB 1973; OBE 1963; Director of Naval Dental Services, Ministry of Defence, 1971–74; *b* 21 Aug. 1915; *s* of Hugh Hunter and Evelyn Marian Hunter (*née* Jessop), Hale, Cheshire; *m* 1947, Anne Madelaine Hardwicke, Friarmayne, Dorset; three *s* two *d*. *Educ:* Bowdon Coll., Cheshire; Manchester Univ. LDS 1939. Surg. Lieut (D) RNVR 1940; HMS Kenya and 10th Cruiser Sqdn, 1941–42; HMS Howe, British Pacific Fleet, 1944–47; transf. to RN; HMS Forth on Staff of Rear-Adm. Destroyers, Mediterranean (Surg. Lt-Comdr), 1948–50; Dartmouth, Royal Marines; Surg. Comdr, Staff of Flag Officer Flotillas Mediterranean, 1956; service ashore in Admty, 1960–63; Surg. Captain (D), Staff of C-in-C Mediterranean, 1965–66; Staff of C-in-C Plymouth Comd, 1967–68; Fleet Dental Surgeon on Staff of C-in-C Western Fleet, 1969–70. QHDS 1971–74. Mem., South Hams DC, 1979–83. Chm., River Yealm Harbour Authority, 1982–85. *Recreations:* ocean racing, cruising, shooting. *Address:* Horsewells, Newton Ferrers, Plymouth PL8 1AT. *T:* (01752) 872254. *Clubs:* Royal Ocean Racing; Royal Western Yacht.

HUNTER, His Honour John; a Circuit Judge, 1980–93; *b* 12 April 1921; *s* of Charles and Mary Hunter; *m* 1956, Margaret Cynthia Webb; one *s* two *d*. *Educ:* Fitzwilliam House, Cambridge (MA). Called to the Bar, Lincoln's Inn, 1952. Served War, Army, 1939–46. Industry, 1952–62; practised at the Bar, 1962–80. *Recreations:* sailing, gardening. *Address:* 230 Compass House, Smugglers Way, SW18 1DQ. *Club:* London Rowing.

HUNTER, Prof. John Angus Alexander, OBE 1997; MD; Grant Professor of Dermatology, University of Edinburgh, 1981–99, now Emeritus; *b* 16 June 1939; *s* of Dr John Craig Alexander Hunter and Alison Hay Shand Alexander; *m* 1968, Ruth Mary Farrow; one *s* two *d*. *Educ:* Loretto Sch., Musselburgh; Pembroke Coll., Cambridge (BA 1960); Univ. of Edinburgh (MB ChB 1963; MD 1977 (Gold Medal)). FRCPE 1978. Gen. med. posts, Edinburgh, 1963–66; Research Fellow in Dermatology: Inst. of Dermatology, London, 1967; Univ. of Minnesota, 1968–69; Lectr, Dept of Dermatology, Univ. of Edinburgh, 1970–74; Consultant Dermatologist, Lothian Health Bd, 1974–80. Hon. Member: British Assoc. of Dermatologists, 1999; Dermatological Socs of N America, Greece, Germany, Poland, Austria and USA. *Publications:* (jtly) Common Diseases of the Skin, 1983; (jtly) Clinical Dermatology, 1989, 2nd edn 1994; (jtly) Skin Signs in Clinical Medicine, 1997; (ed jtly) Davidson's Principles and Practice of Medicine, 18th edn, 1999; numerous articles in dermatol jls. *Recreations:* golf, gardening, music. *Address:* Leewood, Rosslyn Castle, Roslin, Midlothian EH25 9PZ. *T:* (0131) 440 2181; *e-mail:* jaa.hunter@virgin.net. *Clubs:* Hawks (Cambridge); Hon. Company of Edinburgh Golfers.

HUNTER, John Garvin; Permanent Secretary, Department for Social Development, Northern Ireland Civil Service, since 1999; *b* 9 Aug. 1947; *s* of Garvin and Martha Hunter; *m* 1976, Rosemary Alison Haire; one *s* two *d*. *Educ:* Merchant Taylors' Sch., Liverpool; Queen's Univ., Belfast (BA); Cornell Univ., NY (MBA). Asst Principal, NICS, 1970; Department of Health and Social Services: Dep. Principal, 1973; Harkness Fellow, 1977–79; Principal Officer, 1979; Asst Sec., 1982; Dir Gen., Internat. Fund for Ireland, 1986; Under Sec., 1988; Chief Exec., Mgt Exec., Health and Personal Social Services, NI, 1990–96; Dir of Personnel, NICS, 1997–99. *Publications:* contribs to conf. papers on the conflict in NI and on health service planning. *Recreations:* Corrymeela Community, church, swimming, Belfast Philharmonic Choir. *Address:* Department for Social Development, Churchill House, Victoria Square, Belfast BT1 4SD.

HUNTER, John Murray, CB 1980; MC 1943; *b* 10 Nov. 1920; *s* of Rev. Dr John Hunter and Frances Hunter (*née* Martin); *m* 1948, Margaret (*d* 1997), *d* of late Stanley Cursiter, CBE, RSW, RSA, and Phyllis Eda (*née* Hourston); two *s* three *d*. *Educ:* Fettes Coll.; Clare Coll., Cambridge. Served Army, 1941–45: Captain, The Rifle Bde. Served in Diplomatic Service at Canberra, Bogotá, Baghdad, Prague, Buenos Aires and in FCO (Head of Consular Dept, 1966, and of Latin America Dept, 1971–73); idc 1961, sowc 1965, jssc (Senior Directing Staff), 1967–69. Sec., 1973–75, Comr for Admin and Finance, 1976–81, Forestry Commn. Vice-Chm., 1981–83, Chm., 1983–86, Edinburgh West End Community Council. Scottish Tourist Guide, 1983–97. *Recreations:* music, reading; formerly Rugby football (Cambridge 1946, Scotland 1947), curling. *Address:* 14–37 Maxwell Street, Edinburgh EH10 5HU.

HUNTER, John Oswald Mair; *see* Hunter, Hon. Lord.

HUNTER, Prof. John Rotheram, PhD; FSA, FSAScot; Professor of Ancient History and Archaeology, University of Birmingham, since 1996; *b* 4 Jan. 1949; *s* of William Rotherham Hunter and Stella Maud Hunter (*née* Atthill); *m* 1971, Margaret Suddes; three *s* one *d*. *Educ:* Merchant Taylors' Sch., Crosby; Univ. of Durham (BA 1970; DipArch 1971; PhD 1977); Univ. of Lund. FSAScot 1980; MIFA 1985; FSA 1986. Lectr, 1974–83, Sen. Lectr, 1983–95, Reader, 1995–96, in Archaeology, Univ. of Bradford. Cathedral Archaeologist, Bradford Cathedral, 1990–99. *Publications:* Rescue Excavations on the Brough of Birsay, Orkney, 1986; (with I. B. M. Ralston) Archaeological Resource Management in the UK, 1993; (with C. Roberts and A. Martin) Studies in Crime: an introduction to forensic archaeology, 1996; Fair Isle: the archaeology of an island community, 1996; (with I. B. M. Ralston) The Archaeology of Britain: an introduction, 1998. *Recreations:* rowing, watching football, walking the dog. *Address:* Department of Ancient History and Archaeology, University of Birmingham, Birmingham B15 2TT. *T:* (0121) 414 5498.

HUNTER, Keith Robert, OBE 1981; British Council Director, Italy, 1990–96; *b* 29 May 1936; *s* of Robert Ernest Williamson and Winifred Mary Hunter; *m* 1st, 1959, Ann Patricia Fuller (marr. diss. 1989); one *s* two *d*; 2nd, 1991, Victoria Solomonidis. *Educ:* Hymers Coll., Hull; Magdalen Coll., Oxford (MA). Joined British Council, 1962; Lectr, Royal Sch. of Admin, Phnom Penh, 1960–64; Schs Recruitment Dept, 1964–66; SOAS, 1966–67; Asst Rep., Hong Kong, 1967–69; Dir, Penang, 1970–72; Dep. Rep., Kuala Lumpur, 1972–74; London Univ. Inst. of Educn, 1974–75; Rep., Algeria, 1975–78; First Sec. (Cultural), subseq. Cultural Counsellor (British Council Rep.), China, 1979–82; Sec. of Bd, and Hd of Dir-Gen.'s Dept, 1982–85; Controller, Arts Div., 1985–90. Trustee, British Sch. at Rome, 1997–2001. Chm., Parkhouse Award, Parkhouse Award Trust, 1999–. *Recreation:* music. *Address:* 15 Queensdale Road, W11 4SB.

HUNTER, Sir Laurence (Colvin), Kt 1995; CBE 1987; FRSE 1986; Professor of Applied Economics, University of Glasgow, since 1970; *b* 8 Aug. 1934; *s* of Laurence O. and Jessie P. Hunter; *m* 1958, Evelyn Margaret (*née* Green); three *s* one *d*. *Educ:* Hillhead High Sch., Glasgow; Univ. of Glasgow (MA); University Coll., Oxford (DPhil). Asst, Manchester Univ., 1958–59; National Service, 1959–61; Post-Doctoral Fellow, Univ. of Chicago, 1961–62; University of Glasgow: Lectr, 1962; Sen. Lectr, 1967; Titular Prof., 1969; Vice-Principal, 1982–86; Dir of External Relations, 1987–90; Dir, Business Sch., 1996–99. Member: Ct of Inquiry into miners' strike, 1972; Council, Advisory, Conciliation and Arbitration Service, 1974–86; Royal Commn on Legal Services in Scotland, 1976–80; Council, ESRC, 1989–92; Chairman: Post Office Arbitration Tribunal, 1974–92; Police Negotiating Bd, 1987–99 (Dep. Chm., 1980–86). Pres., Scottish Econ. Soc., 1993–96; Treas., RSE, 1999–. DUniv Paisley, 1999. *Publications:* (with G. L. Reid) Urban Worker Mobility, 1968; (with D. J. Robertson) Economics of Wages and Labour, 1969, 2nd edn (with C. Mulvey), 1981; (with G. L. Reid and D. Boddy) Labour Problems of Technological Change, 1970; (with A. W. J. Thomson) The Nationalised Transport Industries, 1973; (with R. B. McKersie) Pay, Productivity and Collective Bargaining, 1973; (with L. Baddon *et al.*) People's Capitalism, 1989; other pubns in economics and industrial relations. *Recreations:* golf, painting. *Address:* 23 Boclair Road, Bearsden, Glasgow G61 2AF. *T:* (0141) 563 7135.

HUNTER, Prof. Michael Cyril William, FSA, FRHistS; Professor of History, Birkbeck College, University of London, since 1992; *b* 22 April 1949; *s* of Francis Hunter and Olive Hunter (*née* Williams). *Educ:* Christ's Hospital; Jesus Coll., Cambridge (BA 1971, MA 1975); Worcester Coll., Oxford (DPhil 1975). Research Fellow: Worcester Coll., Oxford, 1972–75; Univ. of Reading, 1975–76; Birkbeck College, University of London: Lectr in History, 1976–84; Reader in History, 1984–92. Longstanding activist on issues concerning historic preservation. *Publications:* John Aubrey and the Realm of Learning, 1975; Science and Society in Restoration England, 1981; The Victorian Villas of Hackney, 1981; (with Annabel Gregory) An Astrological Diary of the Seventeenth Century, 1988; Establishing the New Science, 1989; (jtly) Avebury Reconsidered, 1991; The Royal Society and its Fellows 1660–1700, 1982, rev. edn 1994; Robert Boyle by Himself and his Friends, 1994; Science and the Shape of Orthodoxy, 1995; (ed) Preserving the Past, 1996; (ed) Archives of the Scientific Revolution, 1998; (ed with Edward B. Davis) The Works of Robert Boyle, vols 1–7, 1999, vols 8–14, 2000; Robert Boyle: scrupulosity and science, 2000; (ed jtly) The Correspondence of Robert Boyle, 6 vols, 2001; The Occult Laboratory, 2001. *Recreations:* book-collecting, motorcycling, historic buildings. *Address:* Exmouth House, Exmouth Place, Hastings, East Sussex TN34 3JA. *T:* (01424) 430727; Department of History, Birkbeck College, Malet Street, WC1E 7HX. *T:* (020) 7631 6299.

HUNTER, Muir Vane Skerrett; QC 1965; Lt-Col (Hon.); MA Oxon; MRI; Barrister-at-Law; *b* 19 Aug. 1913; *s* of late H. S. Hunter, Home Civil Service, and Bluebell M. Hunter, novelist; *m* 1st, 1939, Dorothea Eason, JP (*d* 1986), *e d* of late P. E. Verstone; one *d*; 2nd, 1986, Gillian Victoria Joyce Petrie, *d* of late Dr Alexander Petrie, CBE, MD, FRCS, FRCP. *Educ:* Westminster Sch.; Christ Church, Oxford (Scholar). Called to the Bar, Gray's Inn, 1938 (*ad eundem* Inner Temple, 1965); Holker Senior Scholar; Bencher, Gray's Inn, 1976. Served 1940–46: Royal Armoured Corps; GS Intelligence, GHQ (India); GSO 1 attd War and Legislative Depts, Mil. Judge of Anti-Corruption Tribunals, Govt of India; returned to the Bar, 1946; standing counsel (bankruptcy) to Bd of Trade, 1949–65; Dep. Chm., Advisory Cttee on Service Candidates, HO, 1960–95; Member: EEC Bankruptcy Adv. Cttee, Dept of Trade, 1973–76; Insolvency Law Review Cttee, Dept of Trade, 1977–82; Advr, Law Reform Commn, Kenya Govt, 1991–96; Consultant on law reform, Govt of The Gambia/USAID, 1992. Vis. Prof. of Insolvency Law, Bournemouth Univ., 1997–. Founder-Chairman, N Kensington Neighbourhood Law Centre, 1969–71; Mem., Exec. Cttee, British-Polish Legal Assoc., 1991–97; Hon. Mem. of Council, Justice. Amnesty/ICJ International Observer: Burundi, 1962; Rhodesia, 1969; Turkey, 1972. Gov., Royal Shakespeare Theatre, 1978, now Hon. Life Gov.; Mem. Council, Royal Shakespeare Theatre Trust, 1978–97; Pres., East Street Poets, Blandford, 1995–97; Sec., Kickstart Poets of Salisbury, 2000–01. Chairman: Gdansk Hospice Fund, 1989–92; Polish Hospices Fund, 1992–. Hon. Legal Advr, Nairobi Hospice, Kenya, 1989–92. Hon. Life Mem., Commercial Law League of America, 1985. Mem. Editl Board, Insolvency Law & Practice, 1985–95; Editl Consultant, Sweet & Maxwell Ltd, 1999–. (Jtly) Aid and Co-operation Medals, Polish Govt, 1996. Hon. LLD. *Publications:* Senior Editor, Williams on Bankruptcy, 1958–78, Williams and Muir Hunter on Bankruptcy, 1979–84, Muir Hunter on Personal Insolvency, 1987–; Emergent Africa and the Rule of Law, 1963; Jt Editor: Halsbury's Laws, 4th edn, Vol 3; Atkins' Forms, Vol 7; Editor, Kerr, The Law and Practice as to Receivers and Administrators, 17th edn, 1988; Part Editor, Butterworth's Civil Court Precedents (formerly County Court Precedents and Pleadings), 1984–; (contrib.) Tears in the Fence (poetry), 1994; The Grain of My Life (poetry), 1997; contrib. Jl of Business Law. *Recreations:* writing poetry, theatre, travel, music. *Address:* (chambers) 3–4 South Square, Gray's Inn, WC1R 5HP. *T:* (020) 7696 9900, *Fax:* (020) 7696 9911; Hunterston, Donhead St Andrew, Shaftesbury, Dorset SP7 9EB, *T:* (01747) 828779, *Fax:* (01747) 828045; *e-mail:* mvshunterqc.@aol.com. *Clubs:* Hurlingham; Oxford Union.

HUNTER, Paul Anthony, FRCS, FRCOphth; Consultant Ophthalmic Surgeon, King's College Hospital, since 1982; President, Royal College of Ophthalmologists, since 2000; *b* 22 Nov. 1944; *s* of Gordon Nicholson Hunter and Kathleen Margaret (*née* Tyldesley); *m* 1971, Elizabeth Alex Pearse; one *s* one *d*. *Educ:* Leys Sch., Cambridge; Queens' Coll., Cambridge (BA Hons 1966; MB BChir 1969); Middlesex Hosp. Med. Sch. DO RCP&RCS 1974. FRCS 1977; FRCOphth 1993. Resident Surgical Officer, Moorfields Eye Hosp., 1976–79; Sen. Registrar, Middx Hosp., 1980–81; Hon. Lectr, King's Coll. Med. Sch., London Univ., 1982–. *Publications:* (ed jtly) Atlas of Clinical Ophthalmology, 1988, 2nd edn 1994; contribs on cornea and external eye disease to professional jls. *Recreations:* travel, ski-ing, gardening. *Address:* 148 Harley Street, W1G 7LG. *T:* (020) 7935 1207.

HUNTER, Philip Brown, TD; Chairman, John Holt & Co. (Liverpool) Ltd, 1967–71; *b* 30 May 1909; *s* of Charles Edward Hunter and Marion (*née* Harper); *m* 1937, Joyce Mary (*née* Holt); two *s* two *d*. *Educ:* Birkenhead Sch.; London University. Practised as Solicitor, 1933–80. Chm., Guardian Royal Exchange Assurance (Sierra Leone) Ltd, 1972–79; Director: Cammell Laird & Co. Ltd, 1949–70 (Chm. 1966–70); John Holt & Co. (Liverpool) Ltd, 1951–71 (Exec. Dir, 1960); Guardian Royal Exchange, 1969–79; Guardian Assurance Co. Ltd, 1967–69; Royal Exchange (Nigeria) Ltd, 1972–79; Lion of Africa Insurance Co. Ltd, 1972–79; Enterprise Insurance Co. Ltd, Ghana, 1972–79. *Address:* Bryn Hyfryd, Lixwm, Holywell, Flintshire CH8 8LT. *T:* (01352) 780054.

HUNTER, Dr Philip John, CBE 1999; Director of Education (formerly Chief Education Officer), Staffordshire, 1985–2000; *b* 23 Nov. 1939; *m* Ruth Bailey; two *s* one *d*. *Educ:* Univ. of Durham (BSc 1962); Univ. of Newcastle upon Tyne (PhD 1965). Lectr, Univ. of Khartoum, 1965–67; Senior Scientific Officer: ARC, Cambridge, 1967–69; DES, 1969–71; Course Dir, CS Staff Coll., 1971–73; posts at DES, including science, schools, finance and Private Office, 1973–79; Dep. Chief Educn Officer, ILEA, 1979–85. Dir, Staffs TEC, 1990–; Member of Council: Keele Univ., 1987–99; BTEC, 1990–95; Member: Nat. Council for Educnl Technol., 1986–91; Nat. Curriculum Wkg Gp on Design and Technol., 1988–89; Design Council Educn Cttee, 1990–94; Qualifications and Curriculum Authy, 1997–. Chm., West Midlands Chief Educn Officers, 1995–97; Pres., Soc. of Educn Officers, 1998–99 (Vice-Pres., 1997). Vis. Prof. of Educn, Keele Univ., 1998–. Hon. DTech Staffs, 1999. *Publications:* (jtly) Terrestrial Slugs, 1970; (jtly) Pulmonates, 1978; (ed) Developing Education: fifteen years on, 1999; papers on ecology of invertebrates; contrib. educnl jls on educn policy matters. *Recreation:* gardening. *Address:* Upmeads, Newport Road, Stafford ST16 1DD.

HUNTER, Prof. Richard Lawrence, PhD; Regius Professor of Greek, Cambridge University, since 2001; Fellow, Trinity College, Cambridge, since 2001; *b* 30 Oct. 1953; *s* of John Lawrence Hunter and Ruth Munro Hunter; *m* 1978, Iris Temperli; one *s* one *d*.

Educ: Cranbrook Sch., Sydney; Univ. of Sydney (BA Hons 1974); Pembroke Coll., Cambridge (PhD 1979). University of Cambridge: Fellow, 1977–2001, Dir of Studies in Classics, 1979–99, Asst Tutor, 1985–87, Tutor for Admissions, 1987–93, Pembroke Coll.; Univ. Lectr in Classics, 1987–97; Reader in Greek and Latin Lit., 1997–2001. Visiting Professor: Princeton Univ., 1991–92; Univ. of Virginia, 1979, 1984. Ed., Jl of Hellenic Studies, 1995–2000. Corresp. Fellow, Acad. of Athens, 2001. *Publications:* Eubulus: the fragments, 1983; A Study of Daphnis and Chloe, 1983; The New Comedy of Greece and Rome, 1985; Apollonius of Rhodes, Argonautica III, 1989; The Argonautica of Apollonius, Literary Studies, 1993; trans., Jason and the Golden Fleece (The Argonautica), 1993; Theocritus and the Archaeology of Greek Poetry, 1996; (ed) Studies in Heliodorus, 1998; Theocritus: a selection, 1999; (with M. Fantuzzi) La poesia alessandrina, 2001; articles and reviews in learned jls. *Recreations:* travel, my children's pets. *Address:* Faculty of Classics, Sidgwick Avenue, Cambridge CB3 9DA. *T:* (01223) 335151, 335152.

HUNTER, Dr Tony, (Anthony Rex Hunter), FRS 1987; Professor, Molecular Biology and Virology Laboratory, Salk Institute, San Diego, California, since 1982; concurrently Adjunct Professor of Biology, University of California, San Diego; *b* 23 Aug. 1943; *s* of Ranulph Rex Hunter and Nellie Ruby Elsie Hunter (*née* Hitchcock); *m* 1969, Philippa Charlotte Marrack (marr. diss. 1974); *m* 1992, Jennifer Ann Maureen Price; two *s*. *Educ:* Felsted Sch., Essex; Gonville and Caius Coll., Cambridge (BA, MA, PhD). Research Fellow, Christ's Coll., Cambridge, 1968–71 and 1973–74; Salk Inst., San Diego: Res. Associate, 1971–73; Asst Prof., 1975–78; Associate Prof., 1978–82. American Cancer Soc. Res. Prof., 1992–. Assoc. Mem., EMBO, 1992. FRSA 1989; Fellow, Amer. Acad. of Arts and Scis, 1992; For. Associate, US Nat. Acad. of Scis, 1998. Katharine Berkan Judd Award, Meml Sloan-Kettering Cancer Center, 1992; Gairdner Foundn Internat. Award, 1994; Hopkins Meml Medal, Biochemical Soc., 1994; Mott Prize, Gen. Motors Cancer Res. Foundn, 1994; Feodor Lynen Medal, Univ. of Miami, 1999. *Publications:* numerous, in leading scientific jls. *Recreations:* white water rafting, exploring the Baja peninsula. *Address:* Molecular Biology and Virology Laboratory, The Salk Institute, 10010 North Torrey Pines Road, La Jolla, CA 92037, USA. *T:* (858) 4534100, ext. 1385, *Fax:* (858) 4574765; *e-mail:* hunter@salk.edu.

HUNTER, William Hill, CBE 1971; JP; DL; CA; Consultant, McLay, McAlister & McGibbon, Chartered Accountants, since 1991 (Partner, 1946–91); *b* 5 Nov. 1916; *s* of Robert Dalglish Hunter and Mrs Margaret Walker Hill or Hunter; *m* 1947, Kathleen, *d* of William Alfred Cole; one *s* (and one *s* decd). *Educ:* Cumnock Academy. Chartered Accountant, 1940. Served War: enlisted as private, RASC, 1940; commissioned RA, 1941; Staff Capt., Middle East, 1944–46. Director: Abbey National Building Soc. Scottish Adv. Bd, 1966–86; City of Glasgow Friendly Soc., 1966–88 (Pres., 1980–88); J. & G. Grant Glenfarclas Distillery, 1966–92. President: W Renfrewshire Conservative and Unionist Assoc., 1972–99; Scottish Young Unionist Assoc., 1958–60; Scottish Unionist Assoc., 1964–65. Contested (U) South Ayrshire, 1959 and 1964. Chairman: Salvation Army Adv. Bd in W Scotland, 1982–93 (Vice-Chm., 1972–82; Hon. Life Mem., 2001); Salvation Army Housing Assoc. (Scotland) Ltd, 1986–91. Hon. Financial Advr and Mem. Exec. Council, Erskine Hosp., 1972; Hon. Treasurer, Quarrier's Homes, 1979–94 (Acting Chm., 1989–92). Deacon Convener, Trades House of Glasgow, 1986–87. Hon. Vice-Pres., Royal Scottish Agricl Benevolent Inst., 1993–; Hon. Pres., Friends of Glasgow Botanic Gardens, 1994–. Session Clerk, Kilmacolm Old Kirk, 1967–72. JP 1970, DL 1987, Renfrewshire. *Recreations:* gardening, golf, swimming. *Address:* Armitage, Kilmacolm, Renfrewshire PA13 4PH. *T:* (01505) 872444. *Clubs:* Western, Royal Scottish Automobile (Glasgow).

HUNTER, William John, MB, BS; FRCP, FFOM; Director, Public Health, European Commission, 1999–2000; *b* 5 April 1937; *m*; two *s* one *d*. *Educ:* Westminster Medical Sch. (MB, BS). LRCP; FRCP 1995; MRCS; FFOM 1978. Commission of the European Communities: Principal Administrator, 1974–82; Hd of Div., Industrial Medicine and Hygiene, 1982–88; Dir, Public Health and Safety at Work, 1988–99. Hon. DG, EC. FRCPE. Hon. FFPHM 1997. OStJ 1993. *Publications:* many on public health and safety at work. *Recreations:* swimming, diving, music.

HUNTER, Winston Ronald O'Sullivan; QC 2000; a Recorder, since 2000; *b* 7 Sept. 1960; *m* 1988, Louise Mary Blackwell; three *s*. *Educ:* Leeds Univ. (LLB 1st Cl. Hons). Called to the Bar, Lincoln's Inn, 1985. *Recreations:* cricket, shooting, antiques. *Address:* 12 Byrom Street, Manchester M3 4PF. *T:* (0161) 829 2100.

HUNTER-BLAIR, Sir Edward (Thomas), 8th Bt *cr* 1786, of Dunskey; landowner and forester since 1964; *b* 15 Dec. 1920; *s* of Sir James Hunter Blair, 7th Bt and Jean Galloway (*d* 1953), *d* of T. W. McIntyre, Sorn Castle, Ayrshire; *S* father, 1985; *m* 1956, Norma (*d* 1972), *d* of late W. S. Harris; one adopted *s* one adopted *d*. *Educ:* Balliol Coll., Oxford (BA); Univ. of Paris (Diploma, French Lang. and Lit.). Temp. Civil Servant, 1941–43; journalist (Asst Foreign Editor), 1944–49; in business in Yorkshire, manager and director of own company, 1950–63. Mem. Council, Wyndham Trust, 1992–. Mem., Kirkcudbright CC, 1970–71. Mem. Cttee, Scottish Assoc. for Public Transport, 1993–. Former Pres., Dumfries and Galloway Mountaineering Club. 1939–45 Star, Gen. Service Medal, 1946. *Publications:* Scotland Sings, and A Story of Me, 1981; A Future Time (With an Earlier Life), 1984; A Mission in Life, 1987; Nearing the Year 2000, 1990; Our Troubled Future, 1993; articles on learned and other subjects. *Recreations:* gardening, hill-walking. *Heir: b* James Hunter Blair, *b* 18 March 1926. *Address:* Parton House, Castle Douglas, Scotland DG7 3NB. *T:* (01644) 470234. *Clubs:* Royal Over-Seas League; Western Meeting (Ayr).

HUNTER JOHNSTON, David Alan; *b* 16 Jan. 1915; *s* of James Ernest Johnston and Florence Edith Johnston (*née* Hunter); *m* 1949, Philippa Frances Ray; three *s* one *d*. *Educ:* Christ's Hospital; King's Coll., London. FKC 1970. Royal Ordnance Factories, Woolwich, 1936–39; S Metropolitan Gas Co., 1939–44; Min. of Economic Warfare (Economic and Industrial Planning Staff), 1944–45; Control Office for Germany and Austria, 1945–47; Sec. to Scientific Cttee for Germany, 1946; FO (German Section), Asst Head, German Gen. Economic Dept, 1947–49; HM Treasury, Supply, Estabt and Home Finance Divs, 1949–53. Central Bd of Finance of Church of England: Sec. (and Fin. Sec. to Church Assembly), 1953–59, and Investment Manager, 1959–65; concurrently, Dir, Local Authorities Mutual Investment Trust, 1961–65, and Investment Man. to Charities Official Investment Fund, 1963–65; a Man. Dir, J. Henry Schroder Wagg & Co. Ltd, 1965–74; Chairman: Schroder Executor & Trustee Co. Ltd, 1966–74; Reserve Pension Bd, 1974–75; Assoc. of Investment Trust Cos, 1975–77; Director: Trans-Oceanic Trust, subseq. Schroder Global Trust plc, 1965–88; Clerical, Medical & General Life Assurance Soc., 1970–74; Lindustries Ltd, 1970–79 and of other investment trust cos for many years. Mem., Monopolies Commn, 1969–73. A Reader, 1959–85, licensed in dio. St Albans, dio. Bath and Wells. *Publications:* Stewardship and the Gospel, 1995; Church Synod State and Crown, 1997; The Sheep Look Up... Theodicyana the Gospel. *Address:* Eastfield, North Perrott, Crewkerne, Somerset TA18 7SW. *T:* (01460) 75156. *Clubs:* Farmers', City of London.

HUNTER SMART, Norman; *see* Hunter Smart, W. N.

HUNTER SMART, (William) Norman, CA; Chairman, C. J. Sims Ltd, 1990–99; *b* 25 May 1921; *s* of William Hunter Smart, CA, and Margaret Thorburn Inglis; *m* 1st, 1948, Bridget Beryl Andreae (*d* 1974); three *s* (and one *s* decd); 2nd, 1977, Sheila Smith Stewart (*née* Speirs) (*d* 2000). *Educ:* George Watson's Coll., Edinburgh. Served War, 1939–45; 1st Lothians & Border Horse; Warwickshire Yeomanry; mentioned in despatches. Hays Allan, Chartered Accountants, 1950–86 (Senior Partner, 1983–86). Chm., Charterhouse Develt Capital Fund Ltd, 1987–96. Chm., Assoc. of Scottish Chartered Accountants in London, 1972–73; Institute of Chartered Accountants of Scotland: Council Mem., 1970–75; Vice-Pres., 1976–78; Pres., 1978–79. Member: Gaming Bd for GB, 1985–90; Scottish Legal Aid Bd, 1986–89. *Address:* Greenhouse Cottage, Lilliesleaf, Melrose, Roxburghshire TD6 9EP. *Club:* Caledonian.

HUNTING, Richard Hugh; Chairman, Hunting plc, since 1991 (Deputy Chairman, 1989–91); *b* 30 July 1946; *s* of late Charles Patrick Maule Hunting, CBE, TD and Diana, *d* of Brig. A. B. P. Pereira, DSO; *m* 1970, Penelope, *d* of Col L. L. Fleming, MBE, MC; one *s* two *d*. *Educ:* Rugby Sch.; Sheffield Univ. (BEng); Manchester Business Sch. (MBA). Joined Hunting Gp, 1972; worked at Hunting Surveys and Consultants, Field Aviation, E. A. Gibson Shipbrokers, Hunting Oilfield Services, Hunting Engineering; Director: Hunting Associated Industries, 1986–89 (Chm., 1989); Hunting Petroleum Services, 1989; Hunting plc, 1989–. Dir, Yule Catto & Co. plc, 2000–. Mem. Council, CBI, 1992–97. Trustee, Geffrye Mus., 1995– (Chm., 2000–); Chm., Battle of Britain Meml Trust, 2000– (Trustee, 1998–). Mem. Court, Ironmongers' Co., 1986– (Master, 1996). *Recreations:* arts, ski-ing, family history. *Address:* (office) 3 Cockspur Street, SW1Y 5BQ. *T:* (020) 7321 0123. *Club:* Travellers.

HUNTINGDON, 16th Earl of, *cr* 1529; **William Edward Robin Hood Hastings Bass,** LVO 1999; racehorse trainer, since 1976; *b* 30 Jan. 1948; *s* of Capt. Peter Robin Hood Hastings Bass (who assumed additional surname of Bass by deed poll, 1954) (*d* 1964); *g s* of 13th Earl and of Priscilla Victoria, *d* of Capt. Sir Malcolm Bullock, 1st Bt, MBE; *S* kinsman, 1990; *m* 1989, Sue Warner. *Educ:* Winchester; Trinity Coll., Cambridge. Trainer, West Ilsley Stables, Berks, 1989–. *Heir: b* Hon. Simon Aubrey Robin Hood Hastings Bass, *b* 2 May 1950. *Address:* Hodcott House, West Ilsley, near Newbury, Berks RG20 7AE.

HUNTINGDON, Bishop Suffragan of, since 1997; **Rt Rev. John Robert Flack;** *b* 30 May 1942; *s* of Edwin John Flack and Joan Annie Flack; *m* 1968, Julia Clare Slaughter; one *s* one *d*. *Educ:* Hertford Grammar Sch.; Univ. of Leeds (BA 1964); Coll. of the Resurrection, Mirfield. Ordained, deacon, 1966, priest, 1967; Assistant Curate: St Bartholomew, Armley, Leeds, 1966–69; St Mary the Virgin, Northampton, 1969–72; Vicar: Chapelthorpe (Wakefield dio.), 1972–81; Ripponden with Rishworth and Barkisland with West Scammonden, 1981–85; Brighouse, 1985–92 (Team Rector, 1988–92); Rural Dean of Brighouse and Elland, 1986–92; Archdeacon of Pontefract, 1992–97. Hon. Canon of Wakefield Cathedral, 1989–97. *Recreations:* cricket, Mozart. *Address:* 14 Lynn Road, Ely, Cambs CB6 1DA. *T:* (01353) 662137, *Fax:* (01353) 669357.

HUNTINGDON, Archdeacon of; *see* Beer, Ven. J. S.

HUNTINGFIELD, 7th Baron *cr* 1796 (Ire.); **Joshua Charles Vanneck;** Bt 1751; accountant, NFU Mutual, Cambridge, since 1993; *b* 10 Aug. 1954; *o s* of 6th Baron Huntingfield and of Janetta Lois, *er d* of Captain R. H. Errington, RN; *S* father, 1994; *m* 1982, Arabella Mary, *d* of A. H. J. Fraser, MC; four *s* one *d* (incl. twin *s*). *Educ:* West Downs, Winchester; Eton; Magdalene Coll., Cambridge (MA). ACA. With Gerald Eve & Co., London, 1976, Chestertons, London, 1977–82; Highland Wineries, Inverness, 1982–87; accountant, Deloitte Haskin & Sells, later Coopers & Lybrand, Cambridge, 1987–91. *Recreations:* family, history. *Heir: s* Hon. Gerard Charles Alastair Vanneck, *b* 12 March 1985. *Address:* 69 Barrons Way, Comberton, Cambridge CB3 7EQ. *Club:* Pratt's.

HUNTINGTON-WHITELEY, Sir Hugo (Baldwin), 3rd Bt *cr* 1918; DL; *b* 31 March 1924; *e* surv. *s* of Captain Sir Maurice Huntington-Whiteley, 2nd Bt, RN, and Lady (Pamela) Margaret Huntington-Whiteley (*d* 1976), 3rd *d* of 1st Earl Baldwin of Bewdley, KG, PC; *S* father, 1975; *m* 1959, Jean Marie Ramsay, JP 1973, DStJ; two *d*. *Educ:* Eton. Royal Navy, 1942–47. Chartered Accountant; Partner, Price Waterhouse, 1963–83. Mem. Ct of Assts, Goldsmiths' Co., 1982– (Prime Warden, 1989–90). Worcs: High Sheriff 1971; DL 1972. *Recreations:* music, travel. *Heir: b* (John) Miles Huntington-Whiteley, VRD, Lieut-Comdr RNR [*b* 18 July 1929; *m* 1960, Countess Victoria Adelheid Clementine Louise, *d* of late Count Friedrich Wolfgang zu Castell-Rudenhausen; one *s* two *d*]. *Address:* Ripple Hall, Tewkesbury, Glos GL20 6EY. *T:* (01684) 592431; 12 Stafford Terrace, W8 7BH. *T:* (020) 7937 2918. *Club:* Brooks's.

HUNTLEY, Andrew John Mack, FRICS; Chairman, Insignia Richard Ellis (formerly Richard Ellis, Chartered Surveyors), since 1993; *b* 24 Jan. 1939; *s* of William Mack Huntley and Murial Huntley (*née* Akehurst); *m* 1963, Juliet Vivien Collum; three *d*. *Educ:* Monkton Coombe Sch., Bath. FRICS 1963. Davis & Son, Bristol, 1956–58; D. Ward & Son, Plymouth, 1958–61; Davige & Partners, London, 1961–65; with Richard Ellis, subseq. Insignia Richard Ellis, 1965–. *Recreations:* shooting, tennis. *Address:* Ashurst, Fernhurst, Haslemere, Surrey GU27 3JB. *Club:* Boodle's.

HUNTLEY, Gillian Lesley; *see* Slater, G. L.

HUNTLY, 13th Marquess of, *cr* 1599 (Scot.); **Granville Charles Gomer Gordon;** Earl of Huntly, 1450; Earl of Aboyne, Baron Gordon of Strathavon and Glenlivet, 1660; Baron Meldrum (UK), 1815; Premier Marquess of Scotland; Chief of House of Gordon; *b* 4 Feb. 1944; *s* of 12th Marquess of Huntly and Hon. Mary Pamela Berry (*d* 1998), *d* of 1st Viscount Kemsley; *S* father, 1987; *m* 1st, 1972, Jane Elizabeth Angela (marr. diss. 1990), *d* of late Col Alistair Gibb and Lady McCorquodale of Newton; one *s* two *d*; 2nd, 1991, Mrs Catheryn Millbourn; one *d*. *Educ:* Gordonstoun. Chairman: Freecall Ltd, then Powernet Telecom plc, 1996–2000; Cock o' the North Liqueur Co. Ltd, 1998–; Dir, Hintlesham Hldgs Ltd, 1987–. Pres., Inst. of Commercial Mgt, 1986–. *Heir: s* Earl of Aboyne, *qv*. *Address:* Aboyne Castle, Aberdeenshire AB34 5JP. *T:* (01339) 887061.

See also Baron Cranworth.

HUNTSMAN, Peter William, FRICS; FAAV; Principal, College of Estate Management, University of Reading, 1981–92, Hon. Fellow, 1993; *b* 11 Aug. 1935; *s* of late William and Lydia Irene Huntsman (*née* Clegg); *m* 1st, 1961, Janet Mary Bell (marr. diss.); one *s* one *d*; 2nd, 1984, Cicely Eleanor (*née* Tamblin). *Educ:* Hymers Coll., Hull; Coll. of Estate Management, Univ. of London (BSc Estate Man.). Agricultural Land Service, Dorset and Northumberland, 1961–69; Kellogg Foundn Fellowship, Cornell Univ., USA, 1969–70; Principal Surveyor, London, ADAS, 1971–76; Divl Surveyor, Surrey, Middx and Sussex, 1976–81. Liveryman, Chartered Surveyors' Co., 1985; Freeman, City of London, 1985. Hon. FSVA 1993. *Publications:* (contrib.) Walmsley's Rural Estate Management, 6th edn 1978; contribs to professional jls. *Recreations:* sport, Dorset countryside, reading. *Address:* Radnor Cottage, Cauldon Avenue, Swanage, Dorset BH19 1PQ. *T:* (01929) 425857. *Club:* Farmers.

HUPPERT, Prof. Herbert Eric, ScD; FRS 1987; Professor of Theoretical Geophysics and Foundation Director, Institute of Theoretical Geophysics, Cambridge University, since 1989; Fellow of King's College, Cambridge, since 1970; *b* 26 Nov. 1943; *er c* of Leo Huppert and Alice Huppert (*née* Neuman); *m* 1966, Felicia Adina Huppert (*née* Ferster), PhD; two *s*. *Educ:* Sydney Boys' High Sch.; Sydney Univ. (BSc 1963); ANU (MSc 1964); Univ. of California at San Diego (MS 1966, PhD 1968); Univ. of Cambridge (MA 1971, ScD 1985). ICI Research Fellow, 1968–70; University of Cambridge: Asst Dir of Research, 1970–81; Lectr in Applied Maths, 1981–88; BP Venture Unit Sen. Res. Fellow, 1983–89; Reader in Geophysical Dynamics, 1988–89. Visiting research scientist: ANU; Univ. of California, San Diego; Canterbury Univ.; Caltech; MIT; Univ. of NSW; Woods Hole Oceanographic Inst.; Vis. Prof., Univ. of NSW, 1991–96. Mem., NERC, 1993–98. Lectures: Evnin, Princeton, 1995; Midwest Mechanics, 1996–97; Henry Charnock Dist., Southampton Oceanography Centre, 1999; Smiths Industries, Oxford Univ., 1999. Associate Editor, Jl Fluid Mechanics, 1971–90; Editor, Jl of Soviet Jewry, 1985–; Member, Editorial Board: Philosophical Trans of Royal Soc. (series A), 1994–99; Reports on Progress in Physics, 1997–2000. *Publications:* approximately 180 papers on applied mathematics, crystal growth, fluid mechanics, geology, geophysics, oceanography and meteorology. *Recreations:* my children, squash, tennis, mountaineering, cycling. *Address:* Institute of Theoretical Geophysics, Department of Applied Mathematics and Theoretical Physics, 20 Silver Street, Cambridge CB3 9EW; 46 De Freville Avenue, Cambridge CB4 1HT. *T:* (01223) 356071; (office) (01223) 337853, (01223) 333463, *Fax:* (01223) 337918; *e-mail:* hehl@esc.cam.ac.uk.

HURD, family name of **Baron Hurd of Westwell.**

HURD OF WESTWELL, Baron *cr* 1997 (Life Peer), of Westwell in the co. of Oxfordshire; **Douglas Richard Hurd,** CH 1996; CBE 1974; PC 1982; Deputy Chairman, Coutts & Co., since 1998; *b* 8 March 1930; *e s* of Baron Hurd (*d* 1966) and Stephanie Corner (*d* 1985); *m* 1st, 1960, Tatiana Elizabeth Michelle (marr. diss. 1982), *d* of A. C. Benedict Eyre, Westburton House, Bury, Sussex; three *s*; 2nd, 1982, Judy, *d* of Sidney and Pamela Smart; one *s* one *d*. *Educ:* Eton (King's Scholar and Newcastle Scholar; Fellow, 1981–96); Trinity Coll., Cambridge (Major Scholar). Pres., Cambridge Union, 1952. HM Diplomatic Service, 1952–66; served in: Peking, 1954–56; UK Mission to UN, 1956–60; Private Sec. to Perm. Under-Sec. of State, FO, 1960–63; Rome, 1963–66. Joined Conservative Research Dept, 1966; Head of Foreign Affairs Section, 1968; Private Sec. to Leader of the Opposition, 1968–70; Political Sec. to Prime Minister, 1970–74. MP (C): Mid-Oxon, Feb. 1974–1983; Witney, 1983–97. Opposition Spokesman on European Affairs, 1976–79; Minister of State, FCO, 1979–83; Minister of State, Home Office, 1983–84; Sec. of State for NI, 1984–85, for Home Dept, 1985–89; Sec. of State for Foreign and Commonwealth Affairs, 1989–95. Dir, NatWest Gp, 1995–99; Dep. Chm., NatWest Markets, 1995–98; Chm., British Invisibles, 1997–2000. Mem., Royal Commn on H of L reform, 1999. Chairman: Prison Reform Trust, 1997–; CEDR, 2001–; Canterbury Review Gp, 2000–01. Vis. Fellow, Nuffield Coll., Oxford, 1978–86. Chm. Booker Prize Judges, 1998. High Steward, Westminster Abbey, 2000–. *Publications:* The Arrow War, 1967; An End to Promises, 1979; The Search for Peace (televised), 1997; Ten Minutes to Turn the Devil (short stories), 1999; *novels:* Truth Game, 1972; Vote to Kill, 1975; The Shape of Ice, 1998; Image in the Water, 2001; with Andrew Osmond: Send Him Victorious, 1968; The Smile on the Face of the Tiger, 1969, repr. 1982; Scotch on the Rocks, 1971; War Without Frontiers, 1982; (with Stephen Lamport) Palace of Enchantments, 1985. *Recreation:* writing. *Address:* c/o House of Lords, SW1A 0PW. *Clubs:* Beefsteak, Pratt's, Travellers.

HURFORD, Peter (John), OBE 1984; organist; *b* 22 Nov. 1930; *e c* of H. J. Hurford, Minehead and Gladys Winifred Hurford (*née* James); *m* 1955, Patricia Mary Matthews, *e d* of late Prof. Sir Bryan Matthews, CBE, FRS; two *s* one *d*. *Educ:* Blundells Sch.; Royal Coll. of Music; Jesus Coll., Cambridge (MA, MusB). FRCO. Commnd, Royal Signals, 1954–56. Director of Music, Bablake Sch., Coventry and Conductor, Leamington Spa Bach Choir, 1956–57; Master of the Music, Cathedral and Abbey Church of St Alban, 1958–78; Conductor, St Albans Bach Choir, 1958–78; Founder, Internat. Organ Festival Soc., St Albans, 1963. Artist-in-Residence: Univ. of Cincinnati, 1967–68; Sydney Opera Ho., 1980, 1981, 1982; Acting Organist, St John's Coll., Cambridge, 1979–80; recital and lecture tours throughout Europe, USA, Canada, Japan, Philippines, Taiwan, Australia and NZ, 1960–; perf. the organ works of J. S. Bach, in 34 progs for BBC, 1980–82, and at 50th Edinburgh Fest., 1997. Vis. Prof. of Organ, Univ. of Western Ontario, 1976–77; Prof., RAM, 1982–88; Betts Fellow, Oxford Univ., 1992–93; Hon. Fellow in Organ Studies, Bristol Univ., 1997–98. Mem. Council, 1963–, Pres., 1980–82, RCO; Pres., IAO, 1995–97; Mem., Hon. Council of Management, Royal Philharmonic Soc., 1983–87. Has made numerous LP records and CDs, incl. complete organ works of J. S. Bach (Gramophone Award, 1979; Silver Disc, 1983), F. Couperin, G. F. Handel, P. Hindemith. Hon. FRSCM 1977; Hon. Mem., RAM, 1981; Hon. FRCM 1987. Hon. Dr, Baldwin-Wallace Coll., Ohio, 1981; Hon. DMus Bristol, 1992. *Publications:* Making Music on the Organ, 1988; Suite: Laudate Dominum; sundry other works for organ; Masses for Series III and Rite II of Amer. Episcopal Church; sundry church anthems. *Recreations:* walking, wine, silence. *Address:* Broom House, St Bernard's Road, St Albans, Herts AL3 5RA.

HURLEY, Dame Rosalinde, (Dame Rosalinde Gortvai), DBE 1988; LLB, MD; FRCPath; Professor of Microbiology, University of London, at Institute of Obstetrics and Gynaecology (Royal Postgraduate Medical School), 1975–95, now Professor Emeritus, Imperial College School of Medicine; Consultant Microbiologist, Queen Charlotte's Maternity Hospital, 1963–95, now Hon. Consultant; *b* 30 Dec. 1929; *o d* of late William Hurley and Rose Clancey; *m* 1964, Peter Gortvai, FRCS. *Educ:* Academy of the Assumption, Wellesley Hills, Mass, USA; Queen's Coll., Harley St, London; Univ. of London; Inns of Court. Called to the Bar, Inner Temple, 1958. House Surg., Wembley Hosp., 1955; Ho. Phys., W London Hosp., 1956; Sen. Ho. Officer, 1956–57, Registrar, 1957–58, Lectr and Asst Clin. Pathologist, 1958–62, Charing Cross Hosp. and Med. Sch. Chm., Medicines Commn, 1982–93; Mem., PHLS Bd, 1982–90 (Chm., Ethics Cttee, 1983–); Chm., Nuffield Council on Bioethics Working Gp on Human Tissues (report published, 1995). EP Rep., Management Bd, European Medicines Evaluation Agency. Examiner, RCPath, and univs at home and abroad; Mem. Council, 1977–, Asst Registrar, 1978–, and Vice-Pres., 1984–87, RCPath; Royal Society of Medicine: Pres., Section of Pathology, and Vice-Pres., 1979–; Mem. Council, 1980–; Hon. Sec., 1984–90; Chm., 1980–82, formerly Vice-Chm., Cttee on Dental and Surgical Materials; Pres., Assoc. of Clinical Pathologists, 1984– (Pres.-elect, 1983–84); Chm., Assoc. of Profs of Medical Microbiol., 1987–94; Chm. Board, Therapeutic Res. and Educn Orgn, 1994–. Mem. Governing Body, Postgrad. Med. Fed., 1985–90. FRCOG 1993. Hon. FFPM 1990; Hon. FRSM 1995; CBiol, Hon. FIBiol 1998. DUniv Surrey, 1984. C. ver Heyden de Lancey Prize, RSM, 1991; Medal, RCPath, 1999. *Publications:* (jtly) Candida albicans, 1964; (jtly) Symposium on Candida Infections, 1966; (jtly) Neonatal and Perinatal Infections, 1979; chapters in med. books; papers in med. and sci. jls. *Recreations:* gardening, reading. *Address:* 2 Temple Gardens, Temple, EC4Y 9AY. *T:* (020) 7353 0577.

HURN, Sir (Francis) Roger, Kt 1996; Chairman, Prudential plc, since 2000; Deputy Chairman, GlaxoSmithKline, since 2000 (Deputy Chairman, Glaxo Wellcome, 1997–2000); *b* 9 June 1938; *s* of Francis James Hurn and Joyce Elsa Hurn (*née* Bennett); *m* 1980, Rosalind Jackson; one *d*. *Educ:* Marlborough Coll. Engrg apprentice, Rolls Royce Motors, 1956; joined Smiths Industries, 1958. National Service, 1959–61. Smiths Industries: Export Dir, Motor Accessory Div., 1969; Man. Dir, Internat. Operations, 1974; Exec. Dir, 1976; Man. Dir, 1978; Chief Exec., 1981–96; Chm., 1991–98; Chm., GEC, subseq. Marconi, 1998–2001. Non-executive Director: Ocean Transport & Trading, 1982–88; Pilkington, 1984–94; S. G. Warburg Gp, 1987–95; ICI, 1993–2001. Chm. Govs, Henley Mgt Coll., 1996– (Gov., 1986–). Liveryman, Coachmakers and Coach Harness Makers' Co., 1979–. *Recreations:* outdoor pursuits, travel. *Address:* Prudential plc, Governor's House, Laurence Pountney Hill, EC4R 0HH.

HURRELL, Sir Anthony (Gerald), KCVO 1986; CMG 1984; HM Diplomatic Service, retired; *b* 18 Feb. 1927; *s* of late William Hurrell and Florence Hurrell; *m* 1951, Jean Wyatt; two *d*. *Educ:* Norwich Sch.; St Catharine's Coll., Cambridge. RAEC, 1948–50; Min. of Labour, 1950–53; Min. of Educn, 1953–64; joined Min. of Overseas Develt, 1964; Fellow, Center for International Affairs, Harvard, 1969–70; Head of SE Asia Develt Div., Bangkok, 1972–74; Under Secretary: Internat. Div. ODM, 1974–75; Central Policy Rev. Staff, Cabinet Office, 1976; Duchy of Lancaster, 1977; Asia and Oceans Div., ODA, 1978–83; Ambassador to Nepal, 1983–86. Pres., St Catharine's Soc., 1993–94. *Recreations:* bird-ringing, bird-watching, digging ponds, music. *Address:* Lapwings, Dunwich, Saxmundham, Suffolk IP17 3DR.

HURRELL, Air Vice-Marshal Frederick Charles, CB 1986; OBE 1968; Director General, Royal Air Force Medical Services and Deputy Surgeon General (Operations), 1986–87; retired 1988; *b* 24 April 1928; *s* of Alexander John Hurrell and Maria Del Carmen Hurrell (*née* De Biedma); *m* 1950, Jay Jarvis; five *d*. *Educ:* Royal Masonic School, Bushey; St Mary's Hosp., Paddington (MB BS 1952). MRCS, LRCP 1952; DAvMed 1970; MFOM 1981, FFOM 1987. Joined RAF 1953; served UK, Australia and Singapore; Dep. Dir, Aviation Medicine, RAF, 1974–77; British Defence Staff, Washington DC, 1977–80; CO Princess Alexandra Hosp., RAF Wroughton, 1980–82; Dir, Health and Research, RAF, 1982–84; PMO Strike Command, 1984–86. Dir of Appeals, RAF Benevolent Fund, 1988–95. Vice Pres., Royal Internat. Air Tattoo, 1997–. QHP 1984–88. FRAeS 1987. CStJ 1986. Chadwick Gold Medal, 1970. *Recreations:* painting, photography. *Address:* Hale House, 4 Upper Hale Road, Farnham, Surrey GU9 0NJ. *T:* (01252) 714190. *Club:* Royal Air Force.

HURST, Alan Arthur; MP (Lab) Braintree, since 1997; *b* 2 Sept. 1945; *s* of George Arthur Hurst and Eva Grace Hurst; *m* 1976, Hilary Caroline Burch; two *s* one *d*. *Educ:* Westcliff High Sch.; Univ. of Liverpool (BA Hons). Admitted Solicitor, 1975; Partner, Law, Hurst & Taylor, 1980–. Member (Lab): Southend BC, 1980–96; Essex CC, 1993–. Pres., Southend-on Sea Law Soc., 1992–93. *Recreations:* bird watching, local history, canvassing. *Address:* 28 Whitefriars Crescent, Westcliff-on-Sea, Essex SS0 8EU. *T:* (01702) 337864; Labour Hall, Collingwood Road, Witham, Essex CM8 2EE.

HURST, Sir Geoffrey Charles, Kt 1998; MBE 1977; Director, Aon Warranty Group (formerly London General Insurance), since 1995; professional football player, 1957–76; *b* 8 Dec. 1941; *s* of Charles and Evelyn Hurst; *m* 1964, Judith Helen Harries; three *d*. Professional Football Player: West Ham United, 1957–72; Stoke City, 1972–75; West Bromwich Albion, 1975–76; Player-Manager, Telford United, 1976–79; Manager, Chelsea, 1979–81; English Football International, 1966–72. Joined London General Insurance, 1981. *Publications:* The World Game, 1970; (with Michael Hart) 1966 and All That, 2001. *Recreations:* sport in general, family. *Address:* Dragonwyck, Old Avenue, St George's Hill, Weybridge, Surrey KT13 0PY.

HURST, George; conductor; *b* 20 May 1926; Rumanian father and Russian mother. *Educ:* various preparatory and public schs in the UK and Canada; Royal Conservatory, Toronto, Canada. First prize for Composition, Canadian Assoc. of Publishers, Authors and Composers, 1945. Asst Conductor, Opera Dept, Royal Conservatory of Music, Toronto, 1946; Lectr in Harmony, Counterpoint, Composition etc, Peabody Conservatory of Music, Baltimore, Md, 1947; Conductor of York, Pa, Symph. Orch., 1950–55, and concurrently of Peabody Conservatory Orch., 1952–55; Asst Conductor, LPO, 1955–57, with which toured USSR 1956; Associate Conductor, BBC Northern Symphony Orchestra, 1957; Principal Conductor, BBC Northern Symphony Orchestra (previously BBC Northern Orchestra), 1958–68; Artistic Adviser, 1968–73, Staff Conductor, 1968–88, Vice-Pres., 1979, Western Orchestral Soc. (Bournemouth SO and Bournemouth Sinfonietta); Prin. Conductor, Nat. SO of Ireland, 1990–91. Consultant, Nat. Centre of Orchestral Studies, 1980–87; RAM conducting studies consultant, 1983–; Principal Guest Conductor, BBC Scottish Symphony Orchestra, 1986–89. Since 1956 frequent guest conductor in Europe, Israel, Canada. *Publications:* piano and vocal music (Canada). *Recreations:* yachting, horse-riding.

HURST, Henry Ronald Grimshaw; Overseas Labour Adviser, Foreign and Commonwealth Office, 1976–81, retired; *b* 24 April 1919; *s* of Frederick George Hurst and Elizabeth Ellen (*née* Grimshaw); *m* 1st, 1942, Norah Joyce (*d* 1984), *d* of John Stanley Rothwell; one *s* one *d*; 2nd, 1986, Joy Oldroyde (*d* 1991). *Educ:* Darwen and Blackpool Grammar Schs; St Catharine's Coll., Cambridge (MA). Served War, Army, 1940–46. Colonial Service, 1946–70: Permanent Sec., Min. of Labour, Tanzania, 1962–64; Labour Adviser, Tanzania, 1965–68, and Malaŵi, 1969–70; Dep. Overseas Labour Adviser, FCO, 1970–76. *Recreations:* cricket, gardening, golf. *Address:* Flat 1, Meriden, Weston Road, Bath, Avon BA1 2XZ. *T:* (01225) 334429. *Clubs:* Civil Service; Lansdown Golf.

HURST, John Gilbert, FBA 1987; FSA 1958; Assistant Chief Inspector of Ancient Monuments, English Heritage (formerly Department of the Environment), 1980–87; *b* 15 Aug. 1927; *s* of late Charles Chamberlain and Rona Hurst; *m* 1955, Dorothy Gillian Duckett (*d* 1971); two *d*. *Educ:* Harrow; Trinity Coll., Cambridge (BA Hons Archaeol. 1951; MA 1954). Joined Ancient Monuments Inspectorate, Min. of Works, 1952; Asst Inspector, 1954, Inspector, 1964 (Medieval rescue excavations); Principal Inspector (rescue excavations), 1973–80; directed excavations: Northolt Manor, 1950–70; Norwich, 1951–55; Dir, Wharram Res. Project, 1953–90. Sec., (Deserted) Medieval Village Res. Gp, 1952–86; British Association for Advancement of Science (Sect. H Anthrop.): Sec., 1954–57; Recorder, 1958–62; Pres., 1974; Society for Medieval Archaeology: Treasurer, 1957–76; Pres., 1980–83; Hon. Vice-Pres., 1983–; Vice-Pres., Soc. of Antiquaries of London, 1969–73; President: Soc. for Post-Medieval Archaeology, 1970–72 (Hon. Life Mem., 1993); Medieval Pottery Res. Gp, 1977–80; Southwark and Lambeth Arch. Soc., 1982–84; Hon. Vice-Pres., Medieval Settlement Res. Gp, 1986–. Hon. MRIA 1991. DUniv York 1995. Hon. Mem., Asoc. Española de Arqueología Medieval, Madrid, 1993. Gen. Editor, Wharram Research Project Monographs, 1979–. Legal and General Silver Trowel Award, Archaeologist of the Year, 1990. *Publications include:* Deserted Villages of Oxfordshire, 1965 and Deserted Villages of Northamptonshire, 1966 (both with K. J. A. Allison and M. W. Beresford); (with M. W. Beresford) Deserted Medieval Villages: studies, 1971, 2nd edn 1989; (ed) B. Rackham, Medieval English Pottery, 2nd edn 1972;

(ed with H. Hodges and V. Evison) Medieval Pottery from Excavations, 1974; (with D. S. Neal and H. J. E. Van Beuningen) Pottery Produced and Traded in North West Europe 1350–1650, 1986; (with M. W. Beresford) Wharram Percy: deserted medieval village, 1990; numerous contribs to learned jls. *Recreations:* listening to music, gardening. *Address:* The Old Dairy, 14 Main Street, Great Casterton, Stamford, Lincs PE9 4AP. *T:* (01780) 757072.

HURST, Peter Thomas; Senior Costs Judge of the Supreme Court Costs Office (formerly Chief Master of the Supreme Court Taxing Office), since 1992 (Master, 1981–92); a Recorder, since 2000; *b* Troutbeck, Westmorland, 27 Oct. 1942; *s* of Thomas Lyon Hurst and Nora Mary Hurst; *m* 1968, Diane Irvine; one *s* two *d.* *Educ:* Stonyhurst College. LLB, MPhil London. Admitted as Solicitor of the Supreme Court, 1967; Partner: Hurst and Walker, Solicitors, Liverpool, 1967–77; Gair Roberts Hurst and Walker, Solicitors, Liverpool, 1977–81. *Publications:* (ed jtly) Butterworth's Costs Service, vol. 1, vol. 2, 1986–; (contrib.) Cordery on Solicitors, 8th edn 1988; (ed jtly) Legal Aid, 1994, Solicitors, 1995, Halsbury's Laws of England, 4th edn; Sweet & Maxwell's Civil Costs, 1995, 2nd edn 2000; (ed jtly) Legal Aid Practice 1996–97, 1996; (ed jtly) The New Civil Costs Regime, 1999; (ed jtly) Civil Procedure, 2000. *Recreation:* music. *Address:* Royal Courts of Justice, Strand, WC2A 2LL. *T:* (020) 7936 6000.

HURT, John; actor, stage, films and television; Director, United British Artists, since 1982; *b* 22 Jan. 1940; *s* of Rev. Arnould Herbert Hurt and Phyllis Massey; *m* 1984, Donna Peacock (marr. diss. 1990); *m* 1990, Jo Dalton (marr. diss. 1995); two *s.* *Educ:* The Lincoln Sch., Lincoln; RADA. Started as a painter. *Stage:* début, Arts Theatre, London, 1962; Chips With Everything, Vaudeville, 1962; The Dwarfs, Arts, 1963; Hamp (title role), Edin. Fest., 1964; Inadmissible Evidence, Wyndhams, 1965; Little Malcolm and his Struggle Against the Eunuchs, Garrick, 1966; Belcher's Luck, Aldwych (RSC), 1966; Man and Superman, Gaiety, Dublin, 1969; The Caretaker, Mermaid, 1972; The Only Street, Dublin Fest. and Islington, 1973; Travesties, Aldwych (RSC), 1974; The Arrest, Bristol Old Vic, 1974; The Shadow of a Gunman, Nottingham Playhouse, 1978; The Seagull, Lyric, Hammersmith, 1985; A Month in the Country, Albery, 1994; Krapp's Last Tape, New Ambassadors, 2000. *Films include:* With The Wild and the Willing, 1962; A Man for All Seasons, 1966; Sinful Davey, 1967; Before Winter Comes, 1969; In Search of Gregory, 1970; Mr Forbush and the Penguins, (Evans in) 10 Rillington Place, 1971; The Ghoul, Little Malcolm, 1974; East of Elephant Rock, 1977; The Disappearance, The Shout, Spectre, Alien, Midnight Express (BAFTA award, 1978), 1978; Heaven's Gate, 1979; The Elephant Man, 1980 (BAFTA award, 1981); History of the World Part 1, 1981; Partners, 1982; Champions, Nineteen Eighty-Four, The Osterman Weekend, The Hit, 1984; Jake Speed, Rocinate, 1986; Aria, 1987; White Mischief, 1988; Scandal, 1989; Frankenstein Unbound, The Field, 1990; King Ralph, Lapse of Memory, 1991; Dark at Noon, 1992; Second Best, 1994; Even Cowgirls Get the Blues, Rob Roy, 1995; Dead Man, Wild Bill, 1996; Contact, 1997; Love and Death on Long Island, 1998; All the Little Animals, You're Dead, 1999; Night Train, 2000; Lost Souls, Captain Corelli's Mandolin, 2001. *Television:* The Waste Places, 1968; The Naked Civil Servant, 1975 (Emmy Award, 1976); Caligula, in I Claudius (series), 1976; Treats, 1977; Crime and Punishment (series), 1979; Deadline, 1988; Poison Candy, 1988; Who Bombed Birmingham, 1990; Red Fox, 1991; Six Characters in Search of an Author, 1992. *Address:* c/o Julian Belfrage Associates, 46 Albemarle Street, W1X 4PP. *T:* (020) 7491 4400.

HURWITZ, His Honour Vivian Ronald; a Circuit Judge, 1974–91; *b* 7 Sept. 1926; *s* of Alter Max and Dora Rebecca Hurwitz; *m* 1963, Dr Ruth Cohen, Middlesbrough; one *s* two *d.* *Educ:* Roundhay Sch., Leeds; Hertford Coll., Oxford (MA). Served RNVR: Univ. Naval Short Course, Oct. 1944–March 1945, followed by service until March 1947. Called to Bar, Lincoln's Inn, 1952, practised NE Circuit. A Recorder of Crown Court, 1972–74. *Recreations:* bowls, bridge, music (listening), art (looking at), sport—various (watching).

HUSBAND, Prof. Thomas Mutrie, PhD; FREng, FIEE, FIMechE; Chairman: UKERNA, 1997–2000; East and North Herts NHS Trust, 2000–01; Vice-Chancellor, University of Salford, 1990–97; *b* 7 July 1936; *s* of Thomas Mutrie Husband and Janet Clark; *m* 1962, Pat Caldwell (*d* 2001); two *s.* *Educ:* Shawlands Acad., Glasgow; Univ. of Strathclyde (BSc(Eng), MA, PhD). Weir Ltd, Glasgow: Apprentice Fitter, 1953–58; Engr/Jun. Manager, 1958–62; sandwich degree student (mech. engrg), 1958–61; various engrg and management positions with ASEA Ltd in Denmark, UK and S Africa, 1962–65; postgrad. student, Strathclyde Univ., 1965–66; Teaching Fellow, Univ. of Chicago, 1966–67; Lectr, Univ. of Strathclyde, 1967–70; Sen. Lectr, Univ. of Glasgow, 1970–73; Prof. of Manufacturing Organisation, Loughborough Univ., 1973–81; Prof. of Engrg Manufacture, 1981–90, Dir of Centre for Robotics, 1982–90, Hd of Dept of Mech. Engrg, 1983–90, Imperial Coll., London Univ. Member: Standing Cttee for Educn, Training and Competence to Practise, Royal Acad. of Engrg (formerly Fellowship of Engrg), 1989–93; Engrg Technol. Adv. Cttee, DTI, 1990–93; Council, Engrg Council, 1992–95; Manufacturing Div. Bd, IEE, 1992–95. Non-executive Director: Royal Exchange Theatre, Manchester, 1993–97; Univs and Colls Employers Assoc., 1994–97. FREng (FEng 1988). Hon. DSc: Manchester, 1997; Salford, 1998. *Publications:* Work Analysis and Pay Structure, 1976; Maintenance and Terotechnology, 1977; Education and Training in Robotics, 1986; articles in Terotechnica, Industrial Relations Jl, Microelectronics and Reliability, etc. *Recreations:* watching Arsenal FC, music, theatre. *Address:* 113 Wilbury Road, Letchworth, Herts SG6 4JQ.

HUSBANDS, Sir Clifford (Straughn), GCMG 1996; KA 1995; CHB 1989; GCM 1986; Governor-General of Barbados, since 1996; *b* 5 Aug. 1926; *s* of Adam Straughn Husbands and Ada Augusta (*née* Griffith); *m* 1959, Ruby C. D. Parris; one *s* two *d.* *Educ:* Parry Sch., Barbados; Harrison Coll., Barbados; Middle Temple, Inns of Court, London. Called to the Bar, Middle Temple, 1952; in private practice, Barbados, 1952–54; Actg Dep. Registrar, Barbados, 1954; Legal Asst to Attorney Gen., Grenada, 1954–56; Magistrate: Grenada, 1956–57; Antigua, 1957–58; Crown Attorney, Magistrate and Registrar, Montserrat, 1958–60; Actg Crown Attorney, 1959, Actg Attorney Gen., 1960, St Kitts–Nevis–Anguilla; Asst to Attorney Gen., Barbados, 1960–67 (Legal Draughtsman, 1960–63); DPP, Barbados, 1967–76; QC Barbados 1968; Judge, Supreme Court, Barbados, 1976–91; Justice of Appeal, 1991–96. *Recreations:* music, swimming, photography, cricket. *Address:* Government House, St Michael, Barbados. *T:* 4292962/4292646. *Clubs:* Rally, Spartan (Barbados).

HUSH, Prof. Noel Sydney, AO 1993; DSc; FRS 1988; FAA; Foundation Professor and Head of Department of Theoretical Chemistry, University of Sydney, 1971–92, now Professor Emeritus; *b* 15 Dec. 1924; *s* of Sidney Edgar Hush and Adrienne (*née* Cooper); *m* 1949, Thea L. Warman (decd), London; one *s* one *d.* *Educ:* Univ. of Sydney (BSc 1946; MSc 1948); Univ. of Manchester (DSc 1959). FAA 1977. Res. Fellow in Chemistry, Univ. of Sydney, 1946–49; Lectr in Phys. Chem., Univ. of Manchester, 1950–54; Lectr, subseq. Reader in Chem., Univ. of Bristol, 1955–71. Visiting Professor: ANU, 1960; Florida State Univ., 1965; Case Western Reserve Univ., 1968; Cambridge Univ., 1981; Stanford Univ., 1987; Vis. Fellow, Cavendish Lab., 1971; Vis. Sen. Scientist, Brookhaven Nat. Lab., USA, 1959–. Mem., Aust. Res. Grants Cttee, 1984–90 (Chm., Chem. Cttee, 1987–90). Dir, Molecular Electronics Res. Ltd, 1997–. Foreign Mem., Amer. Acad. of Arts and Scis, 1999. Centenary Medal, RSC, 1990; Flinders Medal, 1994, Inaugural Award, David Craig Medal, 2000, Australian Acad. of Science. Adv. Editor, Chemical Physics, 1973–. *Publications:* (ed) Reactions of Molecules at Electrodes, 1971; papers in Jl of Chemical Physics, Chemical Physics, Jl of Amer. Chemical Soc. *Recreations:* literature, music, travel. *Address:* 170 Windsor Street, Paddington, Sydney, NSW 2021, Australia. *T:* (2) 93281685; Department of Theoretical Chemistry, University of Sydney, Sydney, NSW 2006. *T:* (2) 96923330. *Clubs:* Athenæum; Union (Sydney).

HUSKISSON, Edward Cameron, MD; FRCP; Consultant Rheumatologist, King Edward VII Hospital for Officers, since 1982; *b* 7 April 1939; *s* of Edward William Huskisson, Northwood, Middx and late Elinor Margot Huskisson (*née* Gibson); *m* 1990, Janice Elizabeth Louden; three *s* one *d.* *Educ:* Eastbourne Coll.; King's Coll., London (BSc); Westminster Hosp. Med. Sch. (MB BS 1964); MD London 1974. MRCS 1964; LRCP 1964, MRCP 1967, FRCP 1980. Consultant Physician and Head of Rheumatology, St Bartholomew's Hosp., 1976–93. *Publications:* (jtly) Joint Disease: all the arthropathies, 1973, 4th edn 1988; Repetitive Strain Injury, 1992. *Address:* 14A Milford House, 7 Queen Anne Street, W1G 9HN. *T:* (020) 7636 4278, *Fax:* (020) 7323 6829.

HUSKISSON, Robert Andrews, CBE 1979; Chairman, Lloyd's Register of Shipping, 1973–83 (Deputy Chairman, 1972–73); *b* 2 April 1923; *y s* of Edward Huskisson and Mary Huskisson (*née* Downing); *m* 1969, Alice Marian Swaffin. *Educ:* Merchant Taylors' Sch.; St Edmund Hall, Oxford. Served Royal Corps of Signals, 1941–47 (Major). Joined Shaw Savill & Albion Co. Ltd 1947; Dir 1966–72; Dep. Chief Exec., 1971–72; Director: Overseas Containers Ltd, 1967–72; Container Fleets Ltd, 1967–72; Cairn Line of Steamships Ltd, 1969–72. Director: SMIT Internat. Gp (UK) Ltd, 1982–87; Harland and Wolff plc, 1983–87; Lloyd's of London Press, 1983–89. President: British Shipping Fedn, 1971–72 (Chm. 1968–71); International Shipping Fedn, 1969–73; Chairman: Hotels and Catering EDC, 1975–79; Marine Technology Management Cttee, SRC, 1977–81. Dir, Chatham Historical Dockyard Trust, 1984–91; Chm., Essex Nuffield Hosp. Local Adv. Cttee, 1987–91. *Recreations:* golf, music. *Address:* Lanterns, Luppitt Close, Hutton Mount, Brentwood, Essex CM13 2JU. *Clubs:* Vincent's (Oxford); Thorndon Park Golf.

HUSSAIN, Karamat, SQA 1983; retired; Councillor (Lab) Mapesbury Ward, London Borough of Brent, 1971–86; Chairman, National Standing Conference of Afro-Caribbean and Asian Councillors, 1980–86 (Founder Member); *b* Rawalpindi, 1926; *m* Shamim. *Educ:* Aligarh Muslim Univ., India (BA Hons Humanities, MPhil). Political Educn Officer, Brent E, 1967–70. Brent Council: Chm., Planning Cttee, 1978–86; Vice Chm., Develt Cttee, 1978–86; Mem., Housing and Finance Cttees, 1978–86; Mayor of Brent, 1981–82 (Dep. Mayor, 1980–81); formerly Mem. and Vice-Chm., Brent Community Relations Council. Former Member: Regl Adv. Council on Higher Technical Educn, London and Home Counties; ASTMS. Gov., Willesden Coll. of Technology, 1971–86. *Recreation:* research in political philosophy. *Address:* Bungalow 14, Tregwilym Road, Rogerstone, Newport, Gwent NP1 9DW. *T:* (01633) 892187.

HUSSAIN, Mukhtar; QC 1992; a Recorder of the Crown Court, since 1989; *b* 22 March 1950; *s* of late Karam Dad and Rehmi Bi; *m* 1972, Shamim Akhtar Ali; three *d.* *Educ:* William Temple Secondary School. Came to UK, 1964. Called to the Bar, Middle Temple, 1971, Bencher, 2000; Asst Recorder, 1986–89; Head of Chambers, 1992–. Chm., Police Discipline Appeals Tribunal, 1997–; Member: Mental Health Review Tribunal, 2000–; CICB, 2000–; Bar Council, 2001. Presenter, Granada TV, 1982–87. *Recreations:* cricket, squash, bridge, golf, reading. *Address:* Lincoln House, 1 Brazennose Street, Manchester M2 5EL.

HUSSEY, family name of **Baron Hussey of North Bradley**.

HUSSEY OF NORTH BRADLEY, Baron *cr* 1996 (Life Peer), of North Bradley in the county of Wiltshire; **Marmaduke James Hussey;** Chairman, Board of Governors, BBC, 1986–96; Chairman, Royal Marsden Hospital, 1985–98; *b* 29 Aug. 1923; *s* of late E. R. J. Hussey, CMG and Mrs Christine Hussey; *m* 1959, Lady Susan Katharine Waldegrave (*see* Lady Susan Hussey); one *s* one *d.* *Educ:* Rugby Sch.; Trinity Coll., Oxford (Scholar, MA; Hon. Fellow 1989). Served War of 1939–45, Grenadier Guards, Italy. Joined Associated Newspapers, 1949, Dir 1964; Man. Dir, Harmsworth Publications, 1967–70; Thomson Organisation Exec. Bd, 1971–82; Chief Exec., Times Newspapers Ltd, 1971–82; Jt Chm., Great Western Radio, 1985–86; Dir, William Collins plc, 1985–89. Chairman: Ruffer Investment Management Ltd, 1995–; Cadweb, 1996–; Director: Colonial Mutual Gp, 1985–97; Dialog Corp., 1996–2000. Mem. Bd, British Council, 1983–96. Mem., Select Cttee on EC, H of L, 1997–. Member: Govt Working Party on Artificial Limb and Appliance Centres in England, 1984–86; Management Cttee and Educn Cttee, King Edward's Hosp. Fund for London, 1987–99; Chm., King's Fund London Commn, 1991–92, 1995. President: Royal Bath and West of England Soc., 1990–91; Somerset, RBL, 1999– (Patron, 1999–). Trustee: Rhodes Trust, 1972–91; Royal Acad. Trust, 1988–96. *Publication:* Chance Governs All (autobiog.), 2001. *Address:* Waldegrave House, Chewton Mendip, near Bath, Somerset BA3 4PD; Flat 15, 47 Courtfield Road, SW7 4DB. *T:* (020) 7370 1414. *Club:* Brooks's.

See also Sir Francis Brooke, Bt.

HUSSEY, Derek Robert; Member (UU) Tyrone West, Northern Ireland Assembly, since 1998; *b* 12 Sept. 1948; *s* of Sidney Robert Hussey and Rachael Hussey (*née* Maguire); *m* 1st, (marr. diss.); one *s*; 2nd, Karen (*née* Vaughan); one *d.* *Educ:* Model Sch., Omagh; Omagh Acad.; Stranmillis Coll., Belfast (Cert Ed). Head of Business Studies, Castlederg High Sch., 1972–98, retired. Mem. (Ind. U 1989–97, UU 1997–), Strabane DC. Mem., N Ireland Forum, 1996–98. Dep. Whip, UUP, NI Assembly, 1998–99. *Recreations:* country and western music, soccer, Rugby, ski-ing, Ulster-Scots history and culture. *Address:* 48 Main Street, Castlederg, Co. Tyrone, N Ireland BT81 7AT. *T:* (028) 8167 9299, *Fax:* (028) 8167 9288; *e-mail:* derek.hussey.co@niassembly.gov.uk.

HUSSEY, Prof. Joan Mervyn, MA, BLitt, PhD; FSA; FRHistS; Professor of History in the University of London, at Royal Holloway College, 1950–74, now Emeritus. *Educ:* privately; Trowbridge High Sch.; Lycée Victor Duruy, Versailles; St Hugh's Coll., Oxford. Research Student, Westfield Coll., London, 1932–34; Internat. Travelling Fellow (FUW), 1934–35; Pfeiffer Research Fellow, Girton, 1934–37; Gamble Prize, 1935. Asst Lectr in Hist., Univ. of Manchester, 1937–43; Lectr in Hist., 1943–47, Reader in Hist., 1947–50, at Bedford Coll., Univ. of London. Visiting Prof. at Amer. Univ. of Beirut, 1966. Leverhulme Foundn Emeritus Res. Fellow, 1974. Pres., Brit. Nat. Cttee for Byzantine Studies, 1961–71; Hon. Vice-Pres., Internat. Cttee for Byzantine Studies, 1976. Governor, Girton Coll., Cambridge, 1935–37; Mem. Council, St Hugh's Coll., Oxford, 1940–46; Mem. Council, Royal Holloway Coll., 1966–86. Hon. Fellow, St Hugh's Coll., Oxford, 1968; Hon. Res. Associate, RHBNC, 1986. Hon. Fellow, Instituto Siciliano di Studi Bizantini, 1975. *Publications:* Church and Learning in the Byzantine Empire 867–1185, 1937 (repr. 1961); The Byzantine World, 1957, 3rd edn 1966; Cambridge Medieval History IV, Pts I and II: ed and contributor, 1966–67; The Finlay Papers, 1973;

The Orthodox Church in the Byzantine Empire, 1986, rev. edn 1990; (ed) Journals and Correspondence of George Finlay, 2 vols, 1995; reviews and articles in Byzantinische Zeitschrift, Byzantinoslavica, Trans Roy. Hist. Soc., Jl of Theological Studies, Jahrbuch der Österreichischen Byzantinistik, Enc. Britannica, Chambers's Enc., New Catholic Enc., New DNB, etc. *Address:* 16 Clarence Drive, Englefield Green, Egham, Surrey TW20 0NL.

HUSSEY, Lady Susan Katharine, DCVO 1984 (CVO 1971); Lady-in-Waiting to the Queen, since 1960; *b* 1 May 1939; 5th *d* of 12th Earl Waldegrave, KG, GCVO; *m* 1959, Marmaduke Hussey (*see* Baron Hussey of North Bradley); one *s* one *d*. *Address:* Flat 15, 45/47 Courtfield Road, SW7 4DB. *T:* (020) 7370 1414.
See also Sir Francis Brooke, Bt.

HUSTLER, Dr Margaret Joan; Headmistress, Harrogate Ladies' College, since 1996; *b* 1 Nov. 1949; *d* of Harry Hustler and Dorothy (*née* Kaye); *m* 1976, David Thomas Wraight; three *s* five *d*. *Educ:* Marist Convent, London; Westfield Coll., London Univ. (BSc Hons); Royal Holloway Coll., London Univ. (PhD Biochem). Teacher, Lady Eleanor Holles Sch., Hampton, 1977–85; Dep. Headmistress, Atherley Sch., Southampton, 1985–89; Headmistress, St Michael's Sch., Limpsfield, 1989–96. *Recreations:* walking, sewing, knitting, reading. *Address:* Harrogate Ladies' College, Clarence Drive, Harrogate, N Yorks HG1 2QG. *T:* (01423) 504543.

HUSTON, Felicity Victoria; Commissioner, House of Lords Appointments Commission, since 2000; Partner, Huston & Co., Tax Consultants, since 1994; *b* 28 May 1963; *d* of Jim McCormick and Joy McCormick (*née* Day); *m* 1992, Adrian Robert Arthur Huston, JP; two *s*. *Educ:* Strathearn Sch., Belfast; Campbell Coll., Belfast; Nottingham Univ. (BA Hons 1985). HM Inspector of Taxes, 1988–94. Mem., Industrial Tribunals Panel, 1999–2000. Member: Consumer Panel, PIA, 1996–98; PO Users' Council, NI, 1996–2000; Gen. Consumer Council, 1996–2000 (Dep. Chm., 1999–2000); Chm., NI Consumer Cttee for Electricity, 2000–. Mem. Bd, NI Charities Adv. Cttee, 1998–2000; Hon. Treas., Clifton House (Belfast Charitable Soc.), 1995–. Chm., Point Fields Th. Co., 1996. *Recreations:* cookery, family, pets. *Address:* c/o Huston & Co., 473 Upper Newtownards Road, Belfast BT4 3LJ. *T:* (028) 9080 6080; *e-mail:* felicity@huston.co.uk. *Club:* Ulster Reform (Belfast).

HUTCHINGS, Gregory Frederick; Chief Executive, Tomkins PLC, 1984–94 and 2000 (Director, 1993–2000; Chairman, 1995–2000). *Educ:* Uppingham Sch.; University of Aston (BSc, MBA). Bd Mem., RNT, 1996–; Gov., Mus. of London, 1999–. Hon. DBA Sunderland.

HUTCHINS, Patricia; freelance writer and illustrator of children's books, since 1964; *b* 18 June 1942; *d* of Edward and Lily Victoria Goundry; *m* 1966, Laurence Edward Hutchins; two *s*. *Educ:* Darlington Art Sch.; Leeds Coll. of Art (NDD). Asst Art Dir, J. Walter Thompson Advertising Agency, 1962–64. Kate Greenaway Medal, 1974. *Publications:* Rosie's Walk, 1968; Tom and Sam, 1968; The Surprise Party, 1968; Clocks and More Clocks, 1970; Changes, Changes, 1971; Titch, 1971; Goodnight Owl, 1972; The Wind Blew, 1974; The Silver Christmas Tree, 1974; The House That Sailed Away, 1975; Don't Forget the Bacon, 1976; Happy Birthday Sam, 1979; Follow That Bus!, 1978; One-Eyed Jake, 1978; The Best Train Set Ever, 1978; The Mona Lisa Mystery, 1981; One Hunter, 1982; King Henry's Palace, 1983; You'll soon Grow into them, Titch, 1983; The Curse of the Egyptian Mummy, 1983; The Very Worst Monster, 1985; The Tale of Thomas Mead, 1986; The Doorbell Rang, 1986; Where's the Baby?, 1987; Which Witch is Which?, 1989; Rats!, 1989; What Game Shall We Play?, 1990; Tidy Titch, 1991; Silly Billy, 1992; My Best Friend, 1992; Little Pink Pig, 1993; Three Star Billy, 1994; Titch and Daisy, 1996; Shrinking Mouse, 1997; It's My Birthday, 1999. *Recreations:* music, reading, gardening, cooking. *Address:* Random House, 20 Vauxhall Bridge Road, SW1V 2SA. *Club:* Chelsea Arts.

HUTCHINSON; *see* Hely-Hutchinson.

HUTCHINSON, family name of **Baron Hutchinson of Lullington**.

HUTCHINSON OF LULLINGTON, Baron *cr* 1978 (Life Peer), of Lullington in the County of E Sussex; **Jeremy Nicolas Hutchinson;** QC 1961; *b* 28 March 1915; *o s* of late St John Hutchinson, KC; *m* 1st, 1940, Dame Peggy Ashcroft (marr. diss. 1966; she *d* 1991); one *s* one *d*; 2nd, 1966, June Osborn. *Educ:* Stowe Sch.; Magdalen Coll., Oxford. Called to Bar, Middle Temple, 1939, Bencher 1963. RNVR, 1939–46. Practised on Western Circuit, N London Sessions and Central Criminal Court. Recorder of Bath, 1962–72; a Recorder of the Crown Court, 1972–76. Member: Cttee on Immigration Appeals, 1966–68; Cttee on Identification Procedures, 1974–76. Prof. of Law, RA, 1987–. Mem., Arts Council of GB, 1974–79 (Vice-Chm., 1977–79); Trustee: Tate Gallery, 1977–84 (Chm., 1980–84); Chantrey Bequest, 1977–99. *Address:* House of Lords, Westminster, SW1A 0PW. *Club:* MCC.

HUTCHINSON, His Honour Arthur Edward; QC 1979; a Circuit Judge, 1984–2000; *b* 31 Aug. 1934; *s* of late George Edward Hutchinson and Kathleen Hutchinson; *m* 1967, Wendy Pauline Cordingley, one *s* two *d*. *Educ:* Silcoates Sch.; Emmanuel Coll., Cambridge (MA). Commissioned, West Yorkshire Regt, 1953; served in Kenya with 5th Fusiliers, 1953–54. Called to Bar, Middle Temple, 1958; joined NE Circuit, 1959; a Recorder, 1974–84. *Recreations:* cricket, gardening, music.

HUTCHINSON, Elisabeth Helen; Economic and Domestic Secretariat, since 1998, Legislative Programme Manager, since 2000, Cabinet Office; *b* 24 June 1964; *d* of Andrew and Monica Hutchinson; partner, Michael Wicksteed. *Educ:* Univ. of York (BA Hons). Lord Chancellor's Dept, 1987-98; Private Sec. to Lord Chancellor, 1997–98; Dep. Sec., Sierra Leone Arms Investigation, June–July 1998. *Address:* Cabinet Office, 70 Whitehall, SW1A 2AS.

HUTCHINSON, (George) Malcolm, CB 1989; CEng, FIEE; Chairman, Atomic Weapon Establishment Management Ltd, since 1990; *b* 24 Aug. 1935; *s* of Cecil George Hutchinson and Annie Hutchinson; *m* 1958, Irene Mary Mook; four *d*. *Educ:* Pocklington Sch.; Queens' Coll., Cambridge (MA). Develt Engr, Metropolitan Vickers, 1957; short service commn, 1958, regular commn, 1961, REME; RMCS, 1967; sc Camberley, 1968; CO 12 Armd Workshop, REME, 1968–70; Staff appts, 1970–74; British Liaison Officer, USA Army Materiel Comd, 1974–76; Comdr REME 1 British Corps troops, 1977–79; REME staff, 1979–82; Project Man., Software Systems, 1982–85; Dep. to DGEME, 1985–86; Dir Procurement Strategy MoD(PE), 1986–88; Vice Master-Gen. of the Ordnance, 1988–90. Mem., Defence Prospect Team, 1990. Procurement and logistic consultant, 1991–92. Managing Director: DLR, 1992–97; Docklands Rly Mgt Ltd, 1997–99. Mem., Engrg Council, 1993–99. Pres., IEEIE, 1990–94. Col Comdt, REME, 1991–96. *Recreations:* Rugby, cricket, sailing. *Address:* Rectory Cottage, Little Ann, Andover, Hants SP11 7NR.

HUTCHINSON, Prof. George William, MA, PhD, Cantab; Professor of Physics, Southampton University, 1960–85, now Emeritus; *b* Feb. 1921; *s* of George Hutchinson, farmer, and Louisa Ethel (*née* Saul), Farnsfield, Notts; *m* 1943, Christine Anne (marr. diss. 1970), *d* of Matthew Rymer and Mary (*née* Proctor), York; two *s*. *Educ:* Abergele Grammar Sch.; Cambridge. MA 1946, PhD 1952, Cantab. State Schol. and Schol. of St John's Coll., Cambridge, 1939–42. Research worker and factory manager in cotton textile industry, 1942–47; Cavendish Lab., Cambridge, 1947–52; Clerk-Maxwell Schol. of Cambridge Univ., 1949–52; Nuffield Fellow, 1952–53, and Lecturer, 1953–55, in Natural Philosophy, University of Glasgow; Research Assoc. of Stanford Univ., Calif, 1954. Lecturer, 1955, Sen. Lectr, 1957, in Physics, University of Birmingham. Member: Nat. Exec. Cttee, AUT, 1978–84; Nat. Council, CND, 1981–84; Internat. Sec., Scientists Against Nuclear Arms, 1985–90; Exec. Cttee, British Peace Assembly, 1988–92 (Acting Chm., 1990–92; Chm., 1992); Exec. Cttee, World Disarmament Campaign UK, 1988– (Jt Chm., 1999–). Exec. Cttee, Labour Action for Peace, 1990– (Membership Sec., 1992–97). Duddell Medal, Physical Soc., 1959. FRAS; FRSA. *Publications:* papers on nuclear and elementary particle physics, nuclear instrumentation and cosmic rays, and disarmament and peace. *Recreations:* music, travel. *Address:* Physical Laboratory, University of Southampton, Southampton SO9 5NH. *T:* (023) 8059 5000.

HUTCHINSON, (John) Maxwell, PPRIBA; architect, writer, broadcaster; *b* 3 Dec. 1948; *s* of late Frank Maxwell Hutchinson and Elizabeth Ross Muir (*née* Wright); marr. diss. *Educ:* Wellingborough Prep. Sch.; Oundle; Scott Sutherland Sch. of Arch., Aberdeen; Architectural Assoc. Sch. of Arch. (AA Dip. 1972); RIBA 1972. Founder, Hutchinson and Partners, Chartered Architects, 1972, Chm., 1987–93; Dir, The Hutchinson Studio Architects, 1993–. Chairman: Permarock Products Ltd, Loughborough, 1985–95. Royal Institute of British Architects: Mem. Council, 1978–93, Sen. Vice Pres., 1988–89, Pres., 1989–91; Chairman: East Midlands Arts Bd Ltd, 1991–95; Industrial Bldg Bureau, 1987–89; Vice-Chm., Construction Industry Council, 1990–92. Vis. Prof., Architecture, QUB, 1989–93; Special Prof. of Architecture, Nottingham Univ., 1993–96; Vis. Prof., Westminster Univ., 1998–. Chm., British Architectural Library Trust, 1991–99; Mem. Council, RSCM, 1997–2000. Associate Mem., PRS, 1988. Hon. Fellow: Greenwich Univ., 1990; Royal Soc. of Ulster Architects, 1991. *Compositions:* The Kibbo Kift, Edinburgh Fest., 1976; The Ascent of Wilberforce III, Lyric Hammersmith, 1982; Requiem in a Village Church (choral), 1986; St John's Cantata, 1987. *Publication:* The Prince of Wales: right or wrong?, 1989. *Recreations:* playing the guitar loudly, cooking. *Address:* 1 Back Hill, Clerkenwell, EC1R 5EN. *Club:* Athenæum.

HUTCHINSON, Malcolm; *see* Hutchinson, G. M.

HUTCHINSON, Prof. Marcus Henry Ritchie, PhD; FInstP; Professor of Laser Physics, Imperial College of Science, Technology and Medicine, since 1989; Director, Central Laser Facility, Rutherford Appleton Laboratory, since 1997; *b* 2 Dec. 1945; *s* of Marcus Henry McCracken Hutchinson and Maud Hutchinson; *m* 1973, Gillian Ruth Harris; one *s* two *d*. *Educ:* Coleraine Academical Instn; Queen's Univ. of Belfast (BSc 1st cl. Hons Physics 1968; PhD Physics 1971). FInstP 1998. Imperial College, London: Lectr in Physics, 1973–83; Sen. Lectr, 1983–86; Reader in Optics, 1986–89; Dir, Blackett Lab. Laser Consortium, 1986–97; Associate Dir, Centre for Photomolecular Scis, 1992–. Vis. Res. Prof., Univ. of Illinois at Chicago, 1986. Mem., SERC Physics Cttee, 1990–92. *Publications:* contrib. numerous scientific papers and articles in physics. *Recreations:* walking, gardening. *Address:* 16 Chiltern Hills Road, Beaconsfield, Bucks HP9 1PL.

HUTCHINSON, Maxwell; *see* Hutchinson, J. M.

HUTCHINSON, Patricia Margaret, CMG 1981; CBE 1982; HM Diplomatic Service, retired; *b* 18 June 1926; *d* of late Francis Hutchinson and Margaret Peat. *Educ:* abroad; St Paul's Girls' Sch.; Somerville Coll., Oxford (PPE, MA, Hon Fellow, 1980). ECE, Geneva, 1947; Bd of Trade, 1947–48; HM Diplomatic Service, 1948: 3rd Sec., Bucharest, 1950–52; Foreign Office, 1952–55; 2nd (later 1st) Sec., Berne, 1955–58; 1st Sec. (Commercial), Washington, 1958–61; FO, 1961–64; 1st Sec., Lima, 1964–67 (acted as Chargé d'Affaires); Dep. UK Permanent Rep. to Council of Europe, 1967–69; Counsellor: Stockholm, 1969–72; UK Delegn to OECD, 1973–75; Consul-Gen., Geneva, 1975–80; Ambassador to Uruguay, 1980–83; Consul-Gen., Barcelona, 1983–86. Pres., Somerville ASM, 1988–91. *Recreations:* music, reading. *Address:* 118A Ashley Gardens, SW1P 1HL. *Club:* Oxford and Cambridge.

HUTCHINSON, Prof. Philip, FREng; CPhys; Head of School of Mechanical Engineering, since 1987, Deputy Vice Chancellor, since 1996, and Principal, Royal Military College of Science, since 1996, Cranfield University (formerly Institute of Technology) (Pro Vice-Chancellor, 1996–99); *b* 26 July 1938; *s* of George and Edna Hutchinson; *m* 1960, Joyce Harrison; one *s* one *d*. *Educ:* King James 1st Grammar Sch., Bishop Auckland, Co. Durham; King's Coll., Univ. of Durham (BSc); Univ. of Newcastle upon Tyne (PhD). MInstP. SO and SSO, Theoretical Phys. Div., AERE, Harwell, 1962–69; Vis. Fellow, Chem. Engrg Dept, Univ. of Houston, Texas, 1969–70; AERE, Harwell: SSO and PSO, Theoretical Phys Div., 1970–75; Hd of Thermodynamics and Fluid Mechanics Gp, Engrg Scis Div., 1975–80; Hd of Engrg Phys Br., Engrg Scis Div., 1980–85; Hd of Engrg Scis Div., 1985–87; Hd, Harwell Combustion Centre, 1980–87. Visiting Professor: Imperial Coll., London, 1980–85; Univ. of Leeds, 1985–. Chairman: Exec. Cttee on Fundamental Res. in Combustion, 1977–81, Exec. Cttee on Energy Efficiency and Emissions Reduction in Combustion, 1997–98, Internat. Energy Agency; Combustion Phys Gp of InstP, 1985–89; MRI 1989; Mem., Combustion Inst., 1977–; Past Mem., Watt Cttee on Energy, representing InstP and Combustion Inst. respectively; Founding Bd Mem., Europ. Research Community on Flow Turbulence and Combustion, 1988 (Chm., 1994–2000; Treas., 2000–). 27th Leonardo da Vinci Lectr for IMechE, 1983. FREng (FEng 1997). Hon. DTech Lund, 1999. *Publications:* papers in learned jls on statistical mechanics, fluid mechanics, combustion and laser light scattering. *Recreations:* squash, music, reading, Go, gadgets. *Address:* School of Engineering, Cranfield University, Cranfield, Beds MK43 0AL. *Club:* Reform.

HUTCHINSON, His Honour Richard Hampson; a Circuit Judge, 1974–2000; *b* 31 Aug. 1927; *s* of late John Riley Hutchinson and May Hutchinson; *m* 1954, Nancy Mary (*née* Jones); two *s* three *d*. *Educ:* St Bede's Grammar Sch., Bradford; UC Hull. LLB London. National Service, RAF, 1949–51. Called to Bar, Gray's Inn, 1949; practised on NE Circuit, 1951–74. Recorder: Rotherham, 1971–72; Crown Court, 1972–74; Hon. Recorder of Lincoln, 1991–2000; Resident Judge, Lincoln Crown Court. Mem., County Court Rules Cttee, 1990–94; Technical Rep., Central Council of Probation Cttees, 1989–2000. *Recreations:* reading, conversation, history. *Address:* c/o Lincoln Combined Court Centre, 360 High Street, Lincoln LN5 7RL.

HUTCHINSON, Hon. Sir Ross, Kt 1977; DFC 1944; Speaker, Legislative Assembly, Western Australia, 1974–77, retired; MLA (L) Cottesloe, 1950–77; *b* 10 Sept. 1914; *s* of Albert H. Hutchinson and Agnes L. M. Hutchinson; *m* 1939, Amy Goodall Strang; one *s* one *d*. *Educ:* Wesley Coll. RAAF, 1942–45. School teacher, 1935–49. Chief Sec., Minister for Health and Fisheries, 1959–65; Minister for Works and Water Supplies, 1965–71.

Australian Rules Football, former Captain Coach; East Fremantle, West Perth and South Fremantle; Captain Coach, WA, 1939. *Recreations:* tennis, reading. *Address:* 42 Griver Street, Cottesloe, WA 6011, Australia. *T:* (8) 93842680. *Club:* Royal King's Park Tennis (Perth, WA).

HUTCHISON, family name of **Baroness Kennedy of the Shaws**.

HUTCHISON, Rt Rev. Andrew; *see* Montreal, Bishop of.

HUTCHISON, Geordie Oliphant; Managing Director, Calders & Grandidge, timber importers and manufacturers, 1974–96; *b* 11 June 1934; *s* of late Col Ronald Gordon Oliphant Hutchison and of Ruth Gordon Hutchison-Bradburne; *m* 1964, Virginia Barbezat; two *s* one *d*. *Educ:* Eton Coll. Served RN, 1952–54: commnd as aircraft pilot, 1953. Calders Ltd, 1954–59; Calders & Grandidge Ltd, 1959–96: Dir, 1969. Comr, Forestry Commn, 1981–89. High Sheriff, Lincs, 1998. *Recreations:* golf, shooting. *Address:* Swallowfield House, Welby, Grantham, Lincs NG32 3LR. *T:* (01400) 230510. *Club:* Royal and Ancient Golf (St Andrews).

HUTCHISON, Lt-Comdr Sir (George) Ian Clark, Kt 1954; Royal Navy, retired; Member of the Queen's Body Guard for Scotland, Royal Company of Archers; *b* 4 Jan. 1903; *e s* of late Sir George Clark Hutchison, KC, MP, Eriska, Argyllshire; *m* 1926, Sheena (*d* 1966), *o d* of late A. B. Campbell, WS; one *d*. *Educ:* Edinburgh Academy; RN Colleges, Osborne and Dartmouth. Joined Navy as Cadet, 1916; Lieut, 1926; Lieut-Comdr 1934; specialised in torpedoes, 1929; emergency list, 1931; Mem., Edinburgh Town Council, 1935–41; Chm., Public Assistance Cttee, 1937–39; contested Maryhill Div. of Glasgow, 1935; rejoined Navy Sept. 1939; served in Naval Ordnance Inspection Dept, 1939–43; MP (U) for West Div. of Edinburgh, 1941–59. Mem. National Executive Council of British Legion (Scotland), 1943–51; Governor of Donaldson's Sch. for the Deaf, Edinburgh, 1937–75; Mem. Cttee on Electoral Registration, 1945–46; Mem. Scottish Leases Cttee, 1951–52. DL County of City of Edinburgh, 1958–84. *Recreations:* golf, fishing, walking, philately. *Address:* 16 Wester Coates Gardens, Edinburgh EH12 5LT. *T:* (0131) 337 4888. *Club:* New (Edinburgh).
See also J. V. Paterson.

HUTCHISON, Lt-Comdr Sir Ian Clark; *see* Hutchison, Sir G. I. C.

HUTCHISON, Rt Hon. Sir Michael, Kt 1983; PC 1995; a Lord Justice of Appeal, 1995–99; *b* 13 Oct. 1933; *s* of Ernest and Frances Hutchison; *m* 1957, Mary Spettigue; two *s* three *d*. *Educ:* Lancing; Clare College, Cambridge (MA). Called to Bar, Gray's Inn, 1958, Bencher, 1983; a Recorder, 1975–83; QC 1976; a Judge of the High Court, QBD, 1983–95; Judge, Employment Appeal Tribunal, 1984–87; Presiding Judge, Western Circuit, 1989–92. Surveillance Comr, 1998–. Member: Judicial Studies Bd, 1985–87; Parole Bd, 1987–89.

HUTCHISON, Sir Peter Craft, 2nd Bt *cr* 1956; CBE 1992; FRSE; Chairman: Hutchison & Craft Ltd, Insurance Brokers, Glasgow, 1979–96; Forestry Commission, since 1994; *b* 5 June 1935; *s* of Sir James Riley Holt Hutchison, 1st Bt, DSO, TD, and Winefryde Eleanor Mary (*d* 1988), *d* of late Rev. R. H. Craft; *S* father, 1979; *m* 1966, Virginia, *er d* of late John Millar Colville, Gribloch, Kippen, Stirlingshire; one *s*. *Educ:* Eton; Magdalene Coll., Cambridge. Mem., Scottish Tourist Bd, 1981–87; Mem., 1987–98, Vice-Chm., 1989–98, British Waterways Bd; Chm., Loch Lomond and Trossachs Wkg Party, 1991–92. Chm. of Trustees, Royal Botanic Gdn, Edinburgh, 1985–94; Mem. Bd, Scottish Natural Heritage, 1994. Hon. Pres., Royal Caledonian Horticultural Soc., 1994–. Deacon, Incorporation of Hammermen, 1984–85. FRSE 1997. *Heir: s* James Colville Hutchison [*b* 7 Oct. 1967; *m* 1996, Jane, *d* of Peter Laidlaw]. *Address:* Broich, Kippen, Stirlingshire FK8 3EN.

HUTCHISON, Sir Robert, 3rd Bt *cr* 1939, of Thurle, Streatley, co. Berks; independent financial adviser, since 1978; *b* 25 May 1954; *er s* of Sir Peter Hutchison, 2nd Bt and of Mary-Grace (*née* Seymour); *S* father, 1998; *m* 1987, Anne Margaret, *e d* of Sir (Godfrey) Michael (David) Thomas, Bt, *qv*; two *s*. *Educ:* Orwell Park Sch., Ipswich; Marlborough Coll. With J. & A. Scrimgeour Ltd, 1973–78. *Recreations:* golf, tennis, watching Association Football, family life. *Heir: s* Hugo Thomas Alexander Hutchison, *b* 16 April 1988. *Address:* Hawthorn Cottage, Lower Road, Grundisburgh, Woodbridge, Suffolk IP13 6UQ. *Clubs:* Ipswich & Suffolk (Ipswich), Woodbridge Golf.

HUTCHISON, Robert Edward; Keeper, Scottish National Portrait Gallery, 1953–82, retired; *b* 4 Aug. 1922; *y s* of late Sir William Hutchison; *m* 1946, Heather, *d* of late Major A. G. Bird; one *s* one *d*. *Educ:* Gresham's Sch., Holt. Served War, 1940–46, Infantry and RA; Asst Keeper, Scottish National Portrait Gallery, 1949. Hon. MA Edinburgh, 1972. *Publication:* (with Stuart Maxwell) Scottish Costume 1550–1850, 1958. *Address:* Ivory Court, Langriggs, Haddington, East Lothian EH41 4BY. *T:* (01620) 823213.

HUTCHISON, Prof. Terence Wilmot, FBA 1992; Professor of Economics, University of Birmingham, 1956–78, now Emeritus Professor; Dean of the Faculty of Commerce and Social Science, 1959–61; *b* 13 Aug. 1912; *m* 1st, 1935, Loretta Hack (*d* 1981); one *s* two *d*; 2nd, 1983, Christine Donaldson. *Educ:* Tonbridge Sch.; Peterhouse, Cambridge. Lector, Univ. of Bonn, 1935–38; Prof., Teachers' Training Coll., Bagdad, 1938–41. Served Indian Army, in intelligence, in Middle East and India, 1941–46; attached to Govt of India, 1945–46. Lecturer, University Coll., Hull, 1946–47; Lecturer, 1947–51 and Reader, 1951–56, London Sch. of Economics. Visiting Professor: Columbia Univ., 1954–55; Univ. of Saarbrücken, 1962, 1980; Yale Univ., 1963–64; Dalhousie Univ., 1970; Keio Univ., Tokyo, 1973; Univ. of WA, 1975; Univ. of California, Davis, 1978; Visiting Fellow: Univ. of Virginia, 1960; Aust. Nat. Univ., Canberra, 1967. Mem. Council, Royal Economic Soc., 1967–72. *Publications:* The Significance and Basic Postulates of Economic Theory, 1938 (2nd edn 1960); A Review of Economic Doctrines 1870–1929, 1953; Positive Economics and Policy Objectives, 1964; Economics and Economic Policy 1946–66, 1968; Knowledge and Ignorance in Economics, 1977; Keynes *v* the Keynesians, 1977; Revolutions and Progress in Economic Knowledge, 1978; The Politics and Philosophy of Economics, 1981; Before Adam Smith, 1988; Changing Aims in Economics, 1992; The Uses and Abuses of Economics, 1994; The Methodology of Economics and the Formalist Revolution, 2000; articles, reviews in jls. *Address:* 75 Oakfield Road, Selly Park, Birmingham B29 7HL. *T:* (0121) 472 2020.
See also Ven. W. C. L. Filby.

HUTH, Angela Maureen, (Mrs J. D. Howard-Johnston); writer; *b* 29 Aug. 1938; *d* of late Harold Edward Strachan Huth and Bridget Huth (*née* Nickols); *m* 1961, Quentin Hugh Crewe, (marr. diss. 1970; he *d* 1998); one *d* (one *s* decd); *m* 1978, James Douglas Howard-Johnston; one *d* (one *s* decd). *Educ:* Lawnside, Gt Malvern, Worcs; Beaux Arts, Paris; Annigoni Sch. of Painting, Florence; Byam Shaw Art Sch., London. Harpers Bazaar, 1957–58; Art dept, J. Walter-Thompson, 1958–59; Queen mag., 1959–61; reporter, Man Alive, BBC, 1965–67; BBC TV presenter, How It Is, 1969–70; Kaleidoscope, Radio 4, 1970; freelance, 1968–. Radio and TV: plays: The Drip (radio); I didn't take my mother (radio); Special Co-respondent; The Emperor's New Hat; The Summer House; Virginia Fly is Drowning; Sun Child; documentaries: The English Woman's Wardrobe, 1987; Land Girls, 1995; stage plays: The Understanding, 1982; The Trouble with Old Lovers, 1995. FRSL 1975. *Publications:* Nowhere Girl, 1970; Virginia Fly is Drowning, 1972; Sun Child, 1975; South of the Lights, 1977; Monday Lunch in Fairyland and Other Stories, 1978; The Understanding (play), 1982; Wanting, 1984; The English Woman's Wardrobe (non-fiction), 1986; Eugenie in Cloud Cuckoo Land (for children), 1986; Such Visitors and Other Stories, 1989; Invitation to the Married Life, 1991; Land Girls, 1994; The Trouble with Old Lovers (play), 1995; Another Kind of Cinderella, 1996; Wives of the Fishermen, 1998; Easy Silence, 1999. *Recreations:* collecting antique paste jewellery, re-visiting favourite places in Britain. *Address:* Pullens End, Pullens Lane, Headington, Oxford OX3 0BZ. *T:* (01865) 769498.

HUTSON, John Whiteford, OBE 1966; HM Diplomatic Service, retired; Consul-General, Casablanca, 1984–87; *b* 21 Oct. 1927; *s* of John Hutson and Jean Greenlees Laird; *m* 1954, Doris Kemp; one *s* two *d*. *Educ:* Hamilton Academy; Glasgow Univ. (MA (Hons)). MIL 1987. HM Forces, 1949–51; Foreign Office, 1951; Third Secretary, Prague, 1953; FO, 1955; Second Sec., Berlin, 1956; Saigon, 1959; First Sec., 1961; Consul (Commercial) San Francisco, 1963–67; First Sec. and Head of Chancery, Sofia, 1967–69; FCO, 1969; Counsellor, 1970; Baghdad, 1971–72; Inspector, FCO, 1972–74; Head, Communications Operations Dept, FCO, 1974–76; Counsellor (Commercial), Moscow, 1976–79; Consul-Gen., Frankfurt, 1979–83. *Recreation:* British diplomatic oral history project.

HUTT, Ven. David Handley; Sub-Dean and Archdeacon, since 1999, Canon and Steward, since 1995, Westminster Abbey; *b* 24 Aug. 1938; *s* of late Frank and of Evelyn Hutt. *Educ:* Brentwood; RMA Sandhurst; King's College London (Hanson Prize for Christian Ethics; Barry Prize for Theology; AKC). Regular Army, 1957–64. KCL, 1964–68. Deacon 1969, priest 1970; Curate: Bedford Park, W4, 1969–70; St Matthew, Westminster, 1970–73; Priest Vicar and Succentor, Southwark Cathedral, 1973–78; Sen. Chaplain, King's Coll., Taunton, 1978–82; Vicar: St Alban and St Patrick, Birmingham, 1982–86; All Saints, Margaret St, 1986–95. Pres., Sion Coll., 1996–97. Nat. Co-ordinator, Affirming Catholicism, 1990–98. *Publications:* miscellaneous theol articles and reviews. *Recreations:* gardening, cooking, music, theatre. *Address:* 5 Little Cloister, SW1P 3PL. *T:* (020) 7654 4815, *Fax:* (020) 7654 4825; *e-mail:* david.hutt@westminster-abbey.org.

HUTT, Jane Elizabeth; Member (Lab) Vale of Glamorgan, and Minister (formerly Secretary) for Health and Social Services, National Assembly for Wales, since 1999; *b* 15 Dec. 1949; *d* of late Prof. Michael Stewart Rees Hutt and of Elizabeth Mai Hutt; *m* 1984, Michael John Hillary Trickey; two *d*. *Educ:* Highlands Sch., Eldoret, Kenya; Rosemead Sch., Littlehampton; Univ. of Kent (BA Hons 1970); London Sch. of Econs (CQSW 1972); Bristol Univ. (MSc Mgt Develt and Social Responsibility 1995). Community worker: IMPACT (Town Planners & Architects), Wales, 1972–74; Polypill (Community Projects Foundn), Wales, 1975–77; Co-ordinator, Welsh Women's Aid, 1978–88; Director: Tenant Participation Adv. Service, (Wales), 1988–92; Chwarae Teg (Wales), 1992–99. Hon. Fellow, UWIC, 1996. *Publications:* Opening the Town Hall: an introduction to local government, 1989; Making Opportunities: a guide for women and employers, 1992. *Recreations:* music, reading. *Address:* National Assembly for Wales, Cardiff Bay, Cardiff CF99 1NA. *T:* (029) 2082 5111.

HUTTER, Prof. Otto Fred, PhD; Regius Professor of Physiology, University of Glasgow, 1971–90, now Emeritus; *b* 29 Feb. 1924; *s* of Isak and Elisabeth Hutter; *m* 1948, Yvonne T. Brown; two *s* two *d*. *Educ:* Chajes Real Gymnasium, Vienna; Bishops Stortford Coll., Herts; University Coll., London (BSc, PhD). Univ. of London Postgrad. Student in Physiology, 1948; Sharpey Scholar, UCL, 1949–52; Rockefeller Travelling Fellow and Fellow in Residence, Johns Hopkins Hosp., Baltimore, 1953–55; Lectr, Dept of Physiology, UCL, 1953–61; Hon. Lectr, 1961–70. Visiting Prof., Tel-Aviv Univ., 1968, 1970; Scientific Staff, Nat. Inst. for Medical Research, Mill Hill, London, 1961–70. Hon. Mem., Physiological Soc., 1992. Hon. DSc Glasgow Caledonian, 1994. *Publications:* papers on neuromuscular and synaptic transmission, cardiac and skeletal muscle, in physiological jls. *Address:* Institute of Physiology, University of Glasgow, Glasgow G12 8QQ. *T:* (0141) 330 4496.

HUTTON, family name of **Baron Hutton**.

HUTTON, Baron *cr* 1997 (Life Peer), of Bresagh in the county of Down; **James Brian Edward Hutton,** Kt 1988; PC 1988; a Lord of Appeal in Ordinary, since 1997; *b* 29 June 1931; *s* of late James and Mabel Hutton, Belfast; *m* 1975, Mary Gillian Murland (*d* 2000); two *d*; *m* 2001, Lindy, *widow* of Christopher H. Nickols. *Educ:* Shrewsbury Sch.; Balliol Coll., Oxford (1st Cl. final sch. of Jurisprudence; Hon. Fellow, 1988); Queen's Univ. of Belfast. Called to the Northern Ireland Bar, 1954; QC (NI) 1970; Bencher, Inn of Court of Northern Ireland, 1974; called to English Bar, 1972. Junior Counsel to Attorney-General for NI, 1969; Legal Adviser to Min. of Home Affairs, NI, 1973; Sen. Crown Counsel in NI, 1973–79; Judge of the High Court of Justice (NI), 1979–88; Lord Chief Justice of NI, 1988–97. Hon. Bencher: Inner Temple, 1988; King's Inns, Dublin, 1988. Mem., Jt Law Enforcement Commn, 1974; Dep. Chm., Boundary Commn for NI, 1985–88. Visitor, Univ. of Ulster, 1999–. Hon. LLD QUB, 1992. *Address:* House of Lords, SW1A 0PW.

HUTTON, Alasdair Henry, OBE 1990 (MBE 1986); TD 1977; Director: Impact Weather Services, since 1999; European Editions, since 1999; writer and narrator of public events, UK and overseas; *b* 19 May 1940; *s* of Alexander Hutton and Margaret Elizabeth (*née* Henderson); *m* 1975, Deirdre Mary Cassels (*see* D. M. Hutton); two *s*. *Educ:* Dollar Academy; Brisbane State High Sch., Australia. Radio Station 4BH, Brisbane, 1956; John Clemenger Advertising, Melbourne, 1957–59; Journalist: The Age, Melb., 1959–61; Press and Journal, Aberdeen, Scotland, 1962–64; Broadcaster, BBC: Scotland, N Ireland, London, Shetland, 1964–79. MEP (C) S Scotland, 1979–89; European Democratic Gp spokesman on regional policy, 1983–87, on budgetary control, 1987–89; contested (C) S Scotland, EP elecn, 1989 and 1994. Contested (C) Roxburgh and Berwickshire, Scottish Parly elecn, 1999. Man. Consultant, Coutts Career Consultants, Scotland, 1994–97; European Adviser: IOM Parlt, 1997–; Scottish Police Coll., 1997–. Board Member: Scottish Agricl Coll., 1990–95; UK 2000 Scotland, 1991–96. Chm., Crime Concern, Scotland, 1990–95. Member: Internat. Relns Cttee, Law Soc. of Scotland, 1991–99; Church and Nation Cttee, Church of Scotland, 1992–96; Social Security Adv. Cttee, 1996–99. Presenter, The Business Programme, BBC Radio Scotland, 1989–90; Narrator, Edinburgh Mil. Tattoo, 1992–. Mem., Queen's Body Guard for Scotland, Royal Co. of Archers. Member: Border Union Agricl Soc.; Royal Highland and Agricl Soc. of Scotland. Life Member: John Buchan Soc.; Edinburgh Sir Walter Scott Club. Trustee, Community Service Volunteers, 1985–. Founding Fellow and Trustee, Inst. of Contemp. Scotland, 2001–. Elder, Kelso N, Church of Scotland. *Publication:* 15 Para 1947-1993, 1993. *Address:* Rosebank, Shedden Park Road, Kelso, Roxburghshire TD5 7PX. *T:* and *Fax:* (01573) 224369; *e-mail:* AlasdairHutton@compuserve.com. *Club:* New (Edinburgh).

HUTTON, Anthony Charles, CB 1995; Director, Public Management Service, OECD, Paris, since 2000; *b* 4 April 1941; *s* of Charles James Hutton and Athene Mary (*née* Hastie); *m* 1963, Sara Flemming; two *s* one *d*. *Educ:* Brentwood School; Trinity College, Oxford (MA). HM Inspector of Taxes, 1962; joined Board of Trade, 1964; Private Sec. to 2nd Perm. Sec., 1967–68; Principal Private Sec. to Sec. of State for Trade, 1974–77; Asst Sec., DoT, 1977, DTI, 1983; Under Sec., 1984–91; Dep. Sec., 1991–96; Principal Estabt and Finance Officer, 1991–97; Dir Gen., Resources and Services, 1996–97; Dir Gen., Trade Policy, DTI, 1997–2000. *Recreations:* music, reading, 20th century history. *Address:* (office) OECD, 2 rue André Pascal, 75775 Paris Cedex 16, France. *T:* (1) 45249060; *e-mail:* tony.hutton@oecd.org. *Club:* Athenæum.

HUTTON, Brian Gerald; Secretary, 1976–88, Deputy Librarian, 1983–88, National Library of Scotland (Assistant Keeper, 1974–76); *b* Barrow-in-Furness, 1 Nov. 1933; *s* of James and Nora Hutton; *m* 1958, Serena Quartermaine May; one *s* one *d*. *Educ:* Barrow Grammar Sch.; Nottingham Univ. (BA Hons Hist. 1955); University Coll. London (Dip. Archive Admin. and Churchill Jenkinson prizeman, 1959); Oxford Brookes Univ. (LLB 1st Cl. 1996). National Service as Russian Linguist, RN, 1955–57. Asst Archivist, Herts County Record Office, 1959–60; Asst Keeper and Dep. Dir, Public Record Office, N Ireland, also Administrator, Ulster Hist. Foundn and Lectr in Archive Admin., Queen's Univ., Belfast, 1960–74. County Sec., Bucks CPRE, 1990–93. Chm., Friends of Oxfordshire Museums, 1991–96; Mem. Exec. Cttee, Bucks Record Soc., 1999–. Lectr in local history studies and on legal topics. Commissioned, Kentucky Colonel, 1982. *Publications:* contribs to library and archive jls. *Recreations:* walking in Chilterns, visiting art galleries, listening to music. *Address:* Elma Cottage, The Green, Kingston Blount, Oxon OX39 4SE. *T:* (01844) 354173; La Casa Bianca, Groppoli, Tuscany, Italy. *Club:* New (Edinburgh).

HUTTON, Deirdre Mary, CBE 1998; Chairman, National Consumer Council, since 2001 (Vice-Chairman, 1997–2000); *b* 15 March 1949; *d* of Kenneth Alexander Home Cassels and Barbara Kathleen Cassels; *m* 1975, Alasdair Henry Hutton, *qv*; two *s*. *Educ:* Sherborne Sch. for Girls; Hartwell House Coll. Researcher, Glasgow Chamber of Commerce, 1975–80; freelance researcher, 1980–86; Scottish Consumer Council: Mem. Council, 1987–89; Vice Chm., 1990–91; Chm., 1991–99. Vice Chm., Borders Local Health Council, 1991–94; Chairman: Enterprise Music Scotland Ltd, 1992–95 (also Founder); Rural Forum (Scotland) Ltd, 1992–99; Council, PIA Ombudsman, 1997–2000 (Dep. Chm., 1995–97); DTI Foresight Panel on Food Chain and Crops for Industry, 1999–2000; Vice-Chm., Scottish Envmt Protection Agency, 1999–; Member: Music Cttee, Scottish Arts Council, 1985–91; Scottish Consultative Council on the Curriculum, 1987–91; Parole Bd for Scotland, 1993–97; Minister's Energy Adv. Panel, DTI, 1997–99; Sec. of State for Scotland's Constitutional Steering Gp on Scottish Parliament, 1998; Sec. of State's Competitiveness Council, DTI, 1999–2000; Sustainable Develt Commn, 2000–. Non-executive Director: Edinburgh Festival Theatres Ltd, 1997–99; Borders Health Bd, 1997–; FSA, 1998–. DUniv Stirling, 2000. *Recreations:* reading, eating, talking, music. *Address:* Rosebank, Shedden Park Road, Kelso, Roxburghshire TD5 7PX. *T:* (01573) 224368.

HUTTON, Gabriel Bruce; His Honour Judge Hutton; a Circuit Judge, since 1978; *b* 27 Aug. 1932; *y s* of late Robert Crompton Hutton, and Elfreda Bruce; *m* 1st, 1963, Frances Henrietta Cooke (*d* 1963); 2nd, 1965, Deborah Leigh Windus; one *s* two *d*. *Educ:* Marlborough; Trinity Coll., Cambridge (BA). Called to Bar, Inner Temple, 1956; Dep. Chm., Glos QS, 1971. A Recorder of the Crown Court, 1972–77. Liaison Judge for Glos, 1987–, and Resident Judge for Gloucester Crown Court, 1990–. Chm., Glos and Wilts Area Criminal Justice Liaison Cttee, 1992–. Chm., Glos Br., CPRE, 1993–. *Recreations:* hunting (Chm., Berkeley Hunt), shooting, fishing. *Address:* Chestal, Dursley, Glos. *T:* (01453) 543285.

HUTTON, (Hubert) Robin, OBE 1993; Director-General, British Merchant Banking and Securities Houses Association, 1988–92; *b* 22 April 1933; *e s* of late Kenneth Douglas and of Dorothy Hutton; *m* 1st, 1956, Valerie Riseborough (marr. diss. 1967); one *s* one *d*; 2nd, 1969, Deborah Berkeley; two step *d*. *Educ:* Merchant Taylors' Sch.; Peterhouse, Cambridge (Scholar). MA Cantab 1960. Royal Tank Regt, 1952–53 (commnd). Economic Adviser to Finance Corp. for Industry Ltd, 1956–62; economic journalist and consultant; Dir, Hambros Bank Ltd, 1966–70; Special Adviser: to HM Govt, 1970–72; to Min. of Posts and Telecommunications, 1972–73. Chm., Cttee of Inquiry into Public Trustee Office, 1971; Dir of Banking, Insurance and Financial Instns in EEC, Brussels, 1973–78; Exec. Dir, S. G. Warburg & Co. Ltd, 1978–82; Chm., Soc. des Banques S. G. Warburg et Leu SA, Luxembourg, 1979–82; Director-General: Accepting Houses Cttee, 1982–87; Issuing Houses Assoc., 1983–88. Director: Ariel Exchange Ltd, 1982–86; Associated Book Publishers PLC, 1982–87; Northern Rock plc (formerly Northern Rock Building Soc.), 1986–2001; Rock Asset Management Ltd, Rock Asset Management (Unit Trust) Ltd, 1988–93; Singer & Friedlander Hldgs Ltd, 1993–; Chairman: LondonClear Ltd, 1987–89; Homes Intown plc, 1989–94. Dir, IMRO, 1986–2000; Lay Mem., Disciplinary Cttee, ICAEW, 1988–98; Member: Exec. Cttee, BBA, 1982–92 (Chm., Securities Cttee, 1987–91); Council of Foreign Bondholders, 1983–89; Adv. Cttee, European Business Inst., 1983–94; Chm., Nat. Adv. Cttee on Telecommunications for England, 1985–93. FRSA 1990. *Recreations:* cricket, ski-ing, gardening, travel. *Address:* Church Farm, Athelington, Suffolk IP21 5EJ. *T:* (01728) 628361. *Club:* MCC.

HUTTON, Janet; nursing/management adviser, self-employed consultant, 1988–99; *b* 15 Feb. 1938; *d* of Ronald James and Marion Hutton. *Educ:* Gen. Infirmary at Leeds Sch. of Nursing. SRN 1959. Ward Sister, Leeds Gen. Infirmary, 1962–64, 1966–68; Nursing Sister, Australia, 1964–66; Commng Nurse, Lister Hosp., Stevenage, 1968–71; Planning and Develts Nurse, N London, 1971–73; Divl Nursing Officer, Colchester, 1973–79; Dist Nursing officer, E Dorset, 1979–83; Regl Nursing Officer, 1983–88, Quality Assurance Manager, 1986–88, Yorks RHA. Trustee, Sue Ryder Care, 1998–. *Recreations:* music, needlework, tennis (spectator and participant). *Address:* Fringill, Daleside Park, Darley, Harrogate HG3 2PX. *Club:* Soroptimist International of Great Britain and Ireland (Harrogate).

HUTTON, Rt Hon. (John) Matthew Patrick; PC 2001; MP (Lab) Barrow and Furness, since 1992; Minister of State, Department of Health, since 1999; *b* 6 May 1955; *m*; three *s* one *d* (and one *s* decd). *Educ:* Magdalen Coll., Oxford (BA, BCL). Research Associate, Templeton Coll., Oxford, 1980–81; Sen. Lectr, Newcastle Poly., 1981–92. Parly Under-Sec. of State, DoH, 1998–99. Contested (Lab): Penrith and Borders, 1987; Cumbria and Lancs N (European Parlt), 1989. *Publications:* articles on labour law in Industrial Law Jl. *Recreations:* football, cricket, cinema, music. *Address:* House of Commons, SW1A 0AA; (office) 22 Hartington Street, Barrow-in-Furness, Cumbria LA14 5SL. *T:* (01229) 431204. *Clubs:* Cemetery Cottages Working Men's, Barrow Labour (Barrow-in-Furness).

HUTTON, Prof. John Philip, MA; Professor of Economics and Econometrics, since 1982, and Head of Department of Economics and Related Studies, since 2001, University of York; *b* 26 May 1940; *s* of Philip Ernest Michelson Hutton and Hester Mary Black Hutton; *m* 1964, Sandra Smith Reid; one *s* one *d*. *Educ:* Daniel Stewart's Coll., Edinburgh; Edinburgh Univ. (MA 1st Cl.). York University: Junior Research Fellow, 1962; Lecturer, 1963; Sen. Lectr, 1973; Reader, 1976. Economic Adviser, HM Treasury, 1970, 1971; Advr to Malaysian Treasury, 1977, Mem., Technical Assistance Mission, Kenya, 1990, IMF; Consultant to: NEDO, 1963; Home Office, 1966; Royal Commission on Local Govt in England and Wales, 1967; NIESR, 1980. Chairman, HM Treasury Academic Panel, 1980, 1981; Mem. Council, Royal Economic Soc., 1981–86. Jt Managing Editor, Economic Journal, 1980–86; Jt Editor, Bulletin of Economic Research, 1986–91; Associate Editor, Applied Economics, 1986–. *Publications:* contribs to learned jls, incl. Economic Jl, Rev. of Economic Studies, Oxford Economic Papers. *Recreation:* family. *Address:* 1 The Old Orchard, Fulford, York Y01 4LT. *T:* (01904) 638363.

HUTTON, Kenneth; Chairman, Peterborough Development Agency, 1987–92; *b* 11 May 1931; *s* of Wilks and Gertrude Hutton; *m* 1981, Georgia (*née* Hutchinson); one *s*, and two step *s* one step *d*. *Educ:* Bradford Belle Vue Grammar School; Liverpool University (Thomas Bartlett Scholar; BEng). FICE; FIHT. Graduate Asst, Halifax CBC, 1952–54; Royal Engineers, 1954–56; Sen Engineer, Halifax CBC, 1956–59; Sen. Asst Engineer, Huddersfield CBC, 1959–63; Asst Chief Engineer, Skelmersdale Develt Corp., 1963–66; Dep. Chief Engineer, Telford Develt Corp., 1966–68; Chief Engineer, 1968–84, Gen. Manager, 1984–88, Peterborough Develt Corp. Gov., Peterborough Enterprise Programme, 1988–92. *Recreations:* swimming, bridge, woodworking. *Address:* 4 Sunningdale, Orton Waterville, Peterborough PE2 5UB.

HUTTON, Prof. Peter, PhD; FRCP, FRCA; Professor of Anaesthesia, and Head, Department of Anaesthesia and Intensive Care, University of Birmingham, since 1986; Hon. Consultant Anaesthetist, University Hospital Birmingham NHS Trust, since 1986; President, Royal College of Anaesthetists, since 2000; *b* 9 Nov. 1947; *s* of Peter Hutton and Lily Hutton (*née* Draper); *m* 1973, Barbara Meriel Johnson; two *s* two *d*. *Educ:* Morecambe GS; Birmingham Univ. (BSc 1st Cl. Hons Mech. Engrg 1969, PhD 1973; MB ChB 1978). FRCA 1982; FRCP 2001. SERC Res. Fellow, Birmingham Univ., 1969–72; jun. doctor trng posts in anaesthesia and medicine, Birmingham and Bristol, 1978–82; Clinical Lectr in Anaesthesia, Univ. of Bristol and Hon. Sen. Registrar, Avon AHA, 1982–86. Mem., Jt Cttee for Higher Trng in Anaesthesia, 1988–92. Pres., Anaesthetic and Recovery Nurses Assoc., 1989–90; Council Member: Assoc. Anaesthetists of GB and Ireland, 1989–92; RCAnaes, 1993– (Sen. Vice Pres., 1999–2000); Vice-Chm., Acad. of Med. Royal Colls, 2001–. Founder FMedSci 1998. *Publications:* (with G. M. Cooper) Guidelines in Clinical Anaesthesia, 1985; (ed. with C. Prys-Roberts) Monitoring in Anaesthesia and Intensive Care, 1994; (ed jtly) Fundamental Principles and Practice of Anaesthesia, 2001; contrib. numerous scientific and rev. papers. *Recreations:* family, woodwork, fell-walking. *Address:* University Department of Anaesthesia, North 5, Queen Elizabeth Hospital, University Hospital Birmingham NHS Trust, Edgbaston, Birmingham B15 2TH. *T:* (0121) 627 2060, *Fax:* (0121) 627 2062.

HUTTON, Robin; *see* Hutton, H. R.

HUTTON, William Nicholas; Chief Executive, Industrial Society, since 2000; *b* 21 May 1950; *s* of William Thomas Hutton and Dorothy Anne (*née* Haynes); *m* 1978, Jane Anne Elizabeth Atkinson; one *s* two *d*. *Educ:* Chislehurst and Sidcup GS; Bristol Univ. (BSocSc); INSEAD (MBA). With Phillips & Drew, Stockbrokers, 1971–77; Sen. Producer, Current Affairs, BBC Radio 4, 1978–81; Dir and Producer, Money Programme, BBC 2, 1981–83; econs corresp., Newsnight, BBC 2, 1983–88; Ed., European Business Channel, 1988–90; The Guardian: Econs Ed., 1990–95; Asst Ed., 1995–96; The Observer: Ed., 1996–98; Ed.-in-Chief, 1998–99; Contributing Ed. and columnist, 2000–. Vis. Fellow, Nuffield Coll., Oxford, 1995; Vis. Prof., Manchester Business Sch., 1996–99. Chm., Employment Policy Inst., 1995–. Hon. DLitt: Kingston, 1995; De Montfort, 1996; Strathclyde, London Guildhall, UCE, 1997. Political Journalist of Year, What The Papers Say, 1993. *Publications:* The Revolution That Never Was: an assessment of Keynesian economics, 1986; The State We're In, 1995; The State To Come, 1997; The Stakeholding Society, 1998; (with Anthony Giddens) On the Edge: living with global capitalism, 2000. *Recreations:* family, reading, squash, tennis, cinema, writing. *Address:* Industrial Society, Robert Hyde House, 48 Bryanston Square, W1H 7LN. *T:* (020) 7479 2158.

HUXLEY, Sir Andrew Fielding, OM 1983; Kt 1974; FRS 1955; MA, Hon. ScD Cantab; Master, 1984–90, Fellow, 1941–60 and since 1990, Trinity College, Cambridge (Hon. Fellow, 1967–90); *b* 22 Nov. 1917; *s* of late Leonard Huxley and Rosalind Bruce; *m* 1947, Jocelyn Richenda Gammell Pease; one *s* five *d*. *Educ:* University College Sch.; Westminster Sch. (Hon. Fellow, 1991); Trinity Coll., Cambridge (MA). Operational research for Anti-Aircraft Command, 1940–42, for Admiralty, 1942–45. Demonstrator, 1946–50, Asst Dir of Research, 1951–59, and Reader in Experimental Biophysics, 1959–60, in Dept of Physiology, Cambridge Univ.; Dir of Studies, Trinity Coll., Cambridge, 1952–60; Jodrell Prof., 1960–69 (now Emeritus), Royal Soc. Research Prof., 1969–83, UCL (Hon. Fellow, 1980). Lectures: Herter, Johns Hopkins Univ., 1959; Jesup, Columbia Univ., 1964; Alexander Forbes, Grass Foundation, 1966; Croonian, Royal Society, 1967; Review Lectr on Muscular Contraction, Physiological Soc., 1973; Hans Hecht, Univ. of Chicago, 1975; Sherrington, Liverpool, 1977; Florey, ANU, 1982; John C. Krantz Jr, Maryland Univ. Sch. of Medicine, 1982; Darwin, Darwin Coll., Cambridge, 1982; Romanes, Oxford, 1983; Fenn, IUPS XXIX Internat. Congress, Sydney, 1983; Blackett, Delhi, 1984; Green Coll., Oxford, 1986; Tarner, Trinity Coll., Cambridge, 1988; Maulana Abul Kalam Azad Meml, Delhi, 1991; C. G. Bernhard, Stockholm, 1993; Davson Meml, Amer. Physiol. Soc., 1998. Fullerian Prof. of Physiology and Comparative Anatomy, Royal Institution, 1967–73; Cecil H. and Ida Green Vis. Prof., Univ. of British Columbia, 1980. President: BAAS, 1976–77; Royal Soc., 1980–85 (Mem. Council, 1960–62, 1977–79, 1980–85); Internat. Union of Physiological Scis, 1986–93; Vice-Pres., Muscular Dystrophy Gp of GB, 1980–. Member: ARC, 1977–81; Nature Conservancy Council, 1985–87. Trustee: BM (Nat. Hist.), 1981–91; Science Museum, 1984–88. Hon. Member: Physiolog. Soc., 1979; Amer. Soc. of Zoologists, 1985; Japan Acad., 1988; Hon. MRIA, 1986; Foreign Associate: Nat. Acad. of Scis, USA, 1979; Amer. Philosophical Soc., 1975; Foreign Hon. Member: Amer. Acad. of Arts and Sciences, 1961; Royal Acad. of Medicine, Belgium, 1978; Foreign Fellow, Indian Nat. Science Acad., 1985; Hon. MRI, 1981; Associate Mem., Royal Acad. of Scis, Letters and Fine Arts, Belgium, 1978; Mem., Leopoldina Academy, 1964; Foreign Member: Danish Acad. of Sciences, 1964; Dutch Soc. of Sciences, 1984. Hon. Fellow: Imperial Coll., London, 1980; Darwin Coll., Cambridge, 1981; QMW, London, 1987; RHBNC, London, 1994. Hon. FIBiol 1981; Hon. FRSC (Canada) 1982; Hon. FRSE 1983; Hon. FREng (Hon. FEng 1986); Hon. FMedSci 1999. Hon. MD: University of the Saar, 1964; Ulm, 1993; Charles Univ., Prague, 1998; Hon. DSc: Sheffield, 1964; Leicester, 1967; London, 1973; St Andrews, 1974; Aston, 1977; Western Australia, 1982; Oxford, 1983; Pennsylvania, 1984; Harvard, 1984; Keele, 1985; East Anglia, 1985; Humboldt, E Berlin, 1985; Maryland, 1987; Brunel, 1988; Hyderabad, 1991; Glasgow, 1993; Witwatersrand, 1998; Hon. LLD: Birmingham, 1979; Dundee, 1984; DUniv York, 1981; Hon. DHL New York, 1982; Hon. Dr: Marseille Fac. of Medicine, 1979; Toyama Med. and Pharm. Univ., Japan, 1995. Nobel Prize for Physiology or Medicine (jtly), 1963; Copley Medal, Royal Soc., 1973; Swammerdam Medal, Soc. for Natural Sci., Medicine and Surgery, Amsterdam, 1997.

Grand Cordon, Order of Sacred Treasure (Japan), 1995. *Publications:* Reflections on Muscle (Sherrington Lectures XIV), 1980; (contrib.) The Pursuit of Nature, 1977; papers in the Journal of Physiology, etc. *Recreations:* walking, shooting, designing scientific instruments. *Address:* Manor Field, 1 Vicarage Drive, Grantchester, Cambridge CB3 9NG. *T:* and *Fax:* (01223) 840207; Trinity College, Cambridge. *T:* (01223) 338586.

HUXLEY, Air Vice-Marshal Brian, CB 1986; CBE 1981; Deputy Controller, National Air Traffic Services, 1985–86; retired 1987; *b* 14 Sept. 1931; *s* of Ernest and Winifred Huxley; *m* 1955, Frances (*née* Franklin); two *s*. *Educ:* St Paul's Sch.; RAF College, Cranwell. Commissioned 1952; No 28 Sqdn, Hong Kong, 1953–55; qual. Flying Instructor, 1956; Cranwell, Central Flying Sch. and No 213 Sqdn, 1956–65; MoD, 1966–68; Chief Flying Instr, Cranwell, 1969–71; Commanding RAF Valley, 1971–73; RAF Staff Coll., 1973–74; RCDS 1975; Defence Intelligence Staff, 1976–77; AOC Mil. Air Traffic Ops, 1978–80; Dir of Control (Airspace Policy), and Chm., Nat. Air Traffic Management Adv. Cttee, 1981–84. Mem., CAA Ops Adv. Cttee, 1987–99. Chm., Review of Helicopter Offshore Safety and Survival, 1993–94. *Publications:* contribs to Children's Encyclopaedia Britannica, 1970–72, and to Railway Modeller, 1974–. *Recreations:* Flying Officer RAFVR(T), model-making. *Club:* Royal Air Force.

HUXLEY, Prof. George Leonard, FSA; MRIA; Hon. Professor, Trinity College Dublin, since 1989 (Research Associate, 1983–89); Professor Emeritus, Queen's University, Belfast, since 1988; *b* Leicester, 23 Sept. 1932; *s* of late Sir Leonard Huxley, KBE and Ella M. C., *d* of F. G. and E. Copeland; *m* 1957, Davina Best; three *d*. *Educ:* Blundell's Sch.; Magdalen Coll., Oxford. 2nd Mods, 1st Greats, Derby Scholar 1955. Commnd in RE, 1951, Actg Op. Supt, Longmoor Mil. Rly. Fellow of All Souls Coll., Oxford, 1955–61; Asst Dir, British School at Athens, 1956–58; Prof. of Greek, QUB, 1962–83; Dir, Gennadius Library, Amer. Sch. of Classical Studies, Athens, 1986–89. Harvard University: Vis. Lectr, 1958 and 1961; Loeb Lectr, 1986; Leverhulme Fellow, European Sci. Foundn, 1980–81; Vis. Lectr, St Patrick's Coll., Maynooth, 1984–85 and 1993; Vis. Prof., UCSD, 1990. Mem. of Exec., NI Civil Rights Assoc., 1971–72. Member: Irish Nat. Cttee, Greek and Latin Studies, 1972–86, 1991–99 (Chm., 1976–79); Irish Adv. Cttee, Liverpool Univ. Inst. of Irish Studies, 1996–; Exec., Nat. Library of Ireland Soc., 1997–2000; Member, Managing Committee: British Sch. at Athens, 1967–79; Amer. Sch. of Classical Studies, Athens, 1991–; Irish Mem., Standing Cttee on Humanities, European Science Foundn, Strasbourg, 1978–86. Royal Irish Academy: Sec., Polite Literature and Antiquities Cttee, 1979–86; Sen. Vice-Pres., 1984–85 and 1999–2000; Vice-Pres., 1997–98; Hon. Librarian, 1990–94; Special Envoy, 1994–97; Hon. Pres., Classical Assoc. of Ireland, 1999; Mem., Bureau, Fédn Internat. d'Etudes Classiques, 1981–89 (Senior Vice-Pres. 1984–89); Mem., Internat. Commn, Thesaurus Linguae Latinae, Munich, 1999–2001; MAE 1990. Patron, Irish Inst. of Hellenic Studies, Athens, 1998–. Hon. LittD TCD, 1984; Hon. DLit QUB, 1996. Cromer Greek Prize, British Acad., 1963. *Publications:* Achaeans and Hittites, 1960; Early Sparta, 1962; The Early Ionians, 1966; Greek Epic Poetry from Eumelos to Panyassis, 1969; (ed with J. N. Coldstream) Kythera, 1972; Pindar's Vision of the Past, 1975; On Aristotle and Greek Society, 1979; Homer and the Travellers, 1988; articles on Hellenic and Byzantine subjects. *Recreation:* siderodromophilia. *Address:* School of Classics, Trinity College, Dublin 2, Ireland; Forge Cottage, Church Enstone, Oxfordshire OX7 4NN. *Club:* Athenæum.

HUXLEY, Hugh Esmor, MBE 1948; MA, PhD, ScD; FRS 1960; Professor of Biology, 1987–97, now Emeritus, and Director, 1988–94, Rosenstiel Basic Medical Sciences Research Center, Brandeis University, Boston, Mass; *b* 25 Feb. 1924; *s* of late Thomas Hugh Huxley and Olwen Roberts, Birkenhead, Cheshire; *m* 1966, Frances Fripp, *d* of G. Maxon, Milwaukee; one *d*, and two step *s* one step *d*. *Educ:* Park High Sch., Birkenhead; Christ's Coll., Cambridge (Exhibitioner and Scholar; Hon. Fellow 1981). Natural Science Tripos, Cambridge, 1941–43 and 1947–48 (Pt II Physics); BA 1948, MA 1950, PhD 1952, ScD 1964. Served War of 1939–45, Radar Officer, RAF Bomber Command and Telecommunications Research Establishment, Malvern, 1943–47; Mem. Empire Air Armaments Sch. Mission to Australia and NZ, 1946. Research Student, MRC Unit for Molecular Biology, Cavendish Lab., Cambridge, 1948–52; Commonwealth Fund Fellow, Biology Dept, MIT, 1952–54; Research Fellow, Christ's Coll., Cambridge, 1953–56; Mem. of External Staff of MRC, and Hon. Res. Associate, Biophysics Dept, UCL, 1956–61; Fellow, King's Coll., Cambridge, 1961–67; Scientific Staff, MRC Lab. of Molecular Biol., Cambridge, 1961–87, Dep. Dir, 1977–87; Fellow, Churchill Coll., Cambridge, 1967–87. Ziskind Vis. Prof., Brandeis Univ., 1971; Lectures: Harvey Soc., New York, 1964–65; Hooke, Univ. of Texas, 1968; Dunham, Harvard Med. Sch., 1969; Croonian, Royal Soc., 1970; Mayer, MIT, 1971; Penn, Pennsylvania Univ., 1971; Carter-Wallace, Princeton Univ., 1973; Adam Muller, State Univ. of NY, 1973; Pauling, Stanford, 1980; Jesse Beams, Virginia, 1980; Ida Beam, Iowa, 1981; Staples, Univ. of Maine, 1994; Davson, Amer. Physiol. Soc., 1994. Member: Council, Royal Soc., 1973–75, 1984–85; President's Adv. Bd, Rosentiel Basic Med. Scis Center, Brandeis Univ., 1971–77; Scientific Adv. Council, European Molecular Biol. Lab., 1976–81. Mem., German Acad. of Sci., Leopoldina, 1964; Hon. Member: Amer. Soc. of Biol Chem., 1976; Amer. Assoc. of Anatomy, 1981; Amer. Physiol. Soc., 1981; Amer. Soc. of Zoologists, 1986; Foreign Hon. Member: Amer. Acad. of Arts and Scis, 1965; Danish Acad. of Scis, 1971; Foreign Associate, US Nat. Acad. of Scis, 1978. Hon. ScD: Harvard, 1969; Leicester, 1989; Hon. DSc: Chicago, 1974; Pennsylvania, 1976. Feldberg Foundation Award for Experimental Medical Research, 1963; William Bate Hardy Prize (Camb. Phil. Soc.) 1965; Louisa Gross Horwitz Prize, 1971; Internat. Feltrinelli Prize, 1974; Gairdner Foundn Award, 1975; Baly Medal, RCP, 1975; Royal Medal, 1977, Copley Medal, 1997, Royal Soc.; E. B. Wilson Award, Amer. Soc. Cell Biology, 1983; Albert Einstein Award, World Cultural Council, 1987; Franklin Medal, Franklin Inst., Philadelphia, 1990; Distinguished Scientist Award, Electron Microscope Soc. of America, 1991. *Publications:* contrib. to learned jls. *Recreations:* ski-ing, sailing. *Address:* Rosenstiel Basic Medical Sciences Research Center, Brandeis University, Waltham, MA 02254, USA. *T:* (617) 7362490.

HUXLEY, Rev. Keith; Rector of Gateshead, Diocese of Durham, 1983–97; Chaplain to the Queen, 1981–98; *b* 17 Sept. 1933; *s* of George and Eluned Huxley. *Educ:* Birkenhead Sch.; Christ's Coll., Cambridge (MA); Cuddesdon Theol Coll. Curate: St Mary's, Bowdon, 1959–61; Christ Church, Crewe, 1961–62; Chester Diocesan Youth Chaplain, 1962–68; Leader, Runcorn Ecumenical Team Ministry, 1968–75; Vicar, St Andrew's, Runcorn, 1968–73; Rector, East Runcorn Team Ministry, 1973–77; Home Secretary, Bd for Mission and Unity, C of E, 1977–83; RD of Gateshead, 1988–93. Secretary: NE Ecumenical Gp, 1983–94; Durham Ecumenical Relations Gp, 1985–97. Mem., Rotary Club, Gateshead, 1983–. *Recreation:* ornithology. *Address:* 2 Chaucer Close, Gateshead, Tyne and Wear NE8 3NG. *T:* (0191) 477 3094.

HUXLEY, Paul, RA 1991 (ARA 1987); artist; Professor of Painting, Royal College of Art, 1986–98, now Emeritus; Treasurer, Royal Academy, since 2000; *b* 12 May 1938; *m* 1st, 1957, Margaret Doria Perryman (marr. diss. 1972); two *s*; 2nd, 1990, Susan Jennifer Metcalfe. *Educ:* Harrow Coll. of Art; Royal Acad. Schs (Cert.). Harkness Fellow, 1965–67; Vis. Prof., Cooper Union, New York, 1974; Vis. Tutor, RCA, 1974–85. Member: Serpentine Gallery Cttee, 1971–74; Art Panel and Exhibns Sub-Cttee, Arts Council of GB, 1972–76; Trustee, Tate Gall., 1975–82. Mem. Council, British Sch. at Rome, 2000–. Commnd by London Transport to design 22 ceramic murals for King's Cross Underground Stn, 1984; commnd by Rambert Dance Co. to design sets and costumes for Cat's Eye, 1992. *One-man exhibitions:* Rowan Gall., London, 1963, 1965, 1968, 1969, 1971, 1974, 1978, 1980; Juda Rowan Gall., London, 1982; Kornblee Gall., New York, 1967, 1970; Galeria da Emenda, Lisbon, 1974; Forum Kunst, Rottweil, W Germany, 1975; Mayor Rowan Gall., 1989; Galerie zur alten deutschen Schule, Switzerland, 1992; Gillian Jason Gall., 1993; Gardner Art Centre, Sussex Univ., 1994; Jason & Rhodes Gall., London, 1998; *group exhibitions:* Whitechapel Art Gall., London, and Albright-Knox Gall., Buffalo, NY, 1964; Paris Biennale, and Marlborough-Gerson Gall., New York, 1965; Galerie Milano, Milan, 1966; Carnegie Inst., Pittsburgh, 1967; UCLA, Calif (also USA tour), and touring show of Mus. of Modern Art, New York, 1968; Mus. am Ostwall, Dortmund (also Eur. tour), and Tate Gall., 1969; Walker Art Gall., Liverpool, 1973; Hayward Gall., 1974; São Paulo Bienal, and Forum Gall., Leverkusen, 1975; Palazzo Reale, Milan, 1976; Royal Acad., 1977; Nat. Theatre, 1979; Arts Council tour, Sheffield, Newcastle upon Tyne and Bristol, 1980; Museo Municipal, Madrid, and Eastern Arts 4th Nat. Exhibn and British tour, 1983; Juda Rowan Gall., 1985; Kunstlerhaus, Vienna, 1986; Mappin Art Gall., Sheffield, 1988; British Council tour, Eastern Europe, 1990–93; South Bank Centre, and Arts Council tour, 1992–93; Barbican Gall., London, 1993; British Council tour, Africa, 1994–96; Gallery 7, HK, 1996; Gulbenkian Foundn Center for Modern Art, Lisbon, 1997; Pallant House Gall., Chichester, 1998; Kettle's Yard, Cambridge, 1999; Rhodes+Mann, London, 2000; *works in public collections:* Tate Gall., V&A Mus., Arts Council of GB, British Council, Royal Acad., RCA, Contemp. Arts Soc., Camden Council, Govt Art Collection, Nuffield Foundn, London; Whitworth Art Gall., Manchester; Graves Art Gall., Sheffield; Walker Art Gall., Liverpool; City Art Gall., Leeds; Creasey Collection of Modern Art, Salisbury; Leics Educn Authority; Fitzwilliam Mus., Cambridge; Ulster Mus., Belfast; Art Gall. of NSW, and Mus. of Contemp. Art, Sydney; Art Gall. of SA, Adelaide; Albright-Knox Gall., Buffalo, Neuberger Mus., Purchase, and MOMA, NY; Centro Cultural Arte Contemporaneo, Mexico City; Art Gall. of Ontario, Toronto; Moroccan Govt Collection, Asilah; Szépmüvészeti Mus., Budapest; Technisches Mus., Vienna. *Publication:* (ed) Exhibition Road: painters at the Royal College of Art, 1988. *Address:* 2 Dalling Road, W6 0JB.

HUXLEY, Dr Peter Arthur, PhD; CBiol; FIBiol; agroforestry education consultant, since 1992; *b* 26 Sept. 1926; *s* of Ernest Henry Huxley and Florence Agnes (*née* King); *m* 1st, 1954, Betty Grace Anne Foot (marr. diss. 1980); three *s* one *d*; 2nd, 1980, Jennifer Margaret Bell (*née* Pollard); one *s* one *d*. *Educ:* Alleyn's Sch.; Edinburgh Univ.; Reading Univ. (BSc, PhD). FIBiol 1970. RNVR, 1944–46. Asst Lectr to Sen. Lectr, Makerere University Coll., Uganda, 1954–64; Dir of Res., Coffee Res. Foundn, Kenya, 1965–69; Prof. of Horticulture, Univ. of Reading, 1969–74; Prof. of Crop Science, Univ. of Dar es Salaam/FAO, 1974–76; Agric. Res. Adviser/FAO, Agric. Res. Centre, Tripoli, 1977–78; International Council for Research in Agroforestry, Nairobi, 1979–92: Dir, Res. Develt Div., 1987–90; Principal Res. Advr, 1991–92. Mem., Tropical Agricl Assoc., UK; Associate Mem., Oxford Forestry Inst. *Publications:* (ed jtly) Soils Research in Agroforestry, 1980; (ed jtly) Plant Research and Agroforestry, 1983; (ed) Manual of Research Methodology for the Exploration and Assessment of Multipurpose Trees, 1983; (ed jtly) Multipurpose trees: selection and testing for agroforestry, 1989; (ed jtly) Tree-crop Interactions: a physiological approach, 1996; (ed jtly) Agroforestry for Sustainable Development in Sri Lanka, 1996; (ed jtly) Glossary for Agroforestry, 1997; (compiled and ed jtly) Tropical Agroforestry, 1999; approx. 135 pubns in agric., horticult., agroforestry, meteorol and agricl botany jls. *Recreations:* cooking, music and music-making (double bass), canal narrowboating. *Address:* Flat 4, 9 Linton Road, Oxford OX2 6UH.

HUXTABLE, Gen. Sir Charles Richard, KCB 1984 (CB 1982); CBE 1976 (OBE 1972; MBE 1961); DL; Commander-in-Chief, United Kingdom Land Forces, 1988–90; Aide-de-Camp General to the Queen, 1988–90; *b* 22 July 1931; *m* 1959, Mary, *d* of late Brig. J. H. C. Lawlor; three *d*. *Educ:* Wellington Coll.; RMA Sandhurst; Staff College, Camberley; psc, jssc. Commissioned, Duke of Wellington's Regt, 1952; Captain, 1958, Major, 1965; GS02 (Ops), BAOR, 1964–65; GS01 Staff College, 1968–70; CO 1 DWR, 1970–72; Col, 1973; MoD, 1974; Brig., Comd Dhofar Bde, 1976–78; Maj.-Gen., 1980; Dir, Army Staff Duties, 1982–83; Comdr, Training and Arms Dirs (formerly Training Estabts), 1983–86; QMG, 1986–88. Colonel: DWR, 1982–90; Col, Royal Irish Regt, 1992–96; Colonel Commandant: The King's Div., 1983–88; UDR, 1991–92. Pres., Ex-Services Mental Welfare Soc., 1990–. DL N Yorks, 1994. *Address:* c/o Lloyds TSB, 23 High Street, Teddington, Middlesex TW11 8EX.

HUYDECOPER, Jonkheer (Jan Louis) Reinier, Hon. GCVO 1982 (Hon. KCVO 1972); Commander, Order of Orange Nassau, 1986 (Officer, 1966); Chevalier, Order of Netherlands Lion, 1980; Ambassador of the Netherlands to the Court of St James's, and concurrently to Iceland, 1982–86; *b* 23 Feb. 1922; *s* of Jonkheer Louis Huydecoper and Jonkvrouwe Laurence B. W. Ram; *m* 1944, Baroness Constance C. van Wassenaer; one *s* two *d*. *Educ:* Univ. of Utrecht (LLM). Banking, 1942–44; Legal Dept, Min. of Finance, The Hague, 1945–46; entered Min. of For. Affairs, 1946; UN, NY, 1946; Ottawa, 1947–48; Mil. Mission, Berlin, 1949–50; Bonn, 1950–52; London, 1952–56; Djakarta, 1956–59; Washington, 1959–62; Rome, 1962–66; Min. of For. Affairs, 1966–70; London, 1970–73; Ambassador, Hd of Delegn to Conf. on Security and Co-operation in Europe, Helsinki and Geneva, 1973–74; Ambassador: Moscow, 1974–77; Lisbon, 1978–80; Inspector of For. Service, Min. of For. Affairs, 1981–82. Holds various foreign orders. *Address:* Wassenaarseweg 132, 2596 EA, The Hague, Netherlands.

HYAM, Michael Joshua; His Honour Judge Hyam; Recorder of London, since 1998; a Senior Circuit Judge, since 1998; *b* 18 April 1938; *s* of Isaac J. Hyam and Rachel Hyam; *m* 1968, Diana Mortimer; three *s*. *Educ:* Westminster Sch.; St Catharine's Coll., Cambridge (MA). Called to Bar, Gray's Inn, 1962, Bencher, 1999; a Recorder, 1983–84; practised on SE Circuit, 1962–84; a Circuit Judge, 1984–98; Resident Judge, and Designated Family Judge, Norwich, 1991–98. Member: Council of Legal Education, 1980–86; Ethical Cttee, Cromwell Hosp., 1983–92; Chm., Area Criminal Justice Liaison Cttee, 1992–98. Gov., Dulwich Coll. Prep. Sch., 1986–92. HM Lieut, City of London, 1999–; Liveryman, Curriers' Co., 1998–; Hon. Liveryman, Fruiterers' Co., 1999. *Publication:* Learning the Skills of Advocacy, 1990, 4th edn 1999. *Recreations:* book collecting, cricket, gardening, yeast cookery. *Address:* Central Criminal Court, EC4M 7EH. *T:* (020) 7248 3277, *Fax:* (020) 7489 8451. *Clubs:* Garrick, MCC.

HYAMS, Daisy Deborah, (Mrs C. Guderley), OBE 1974; *b* 25 Nov. 1912; *d* of Hyman Hyams and Annie Burnett; *m* 1936, Sidney Hart; no *c*; *m* 1975, C. Guderley. *Educ:* Coborn Grammar Sch. for Girls, Bow. FGI. Joined Tesco, 1931; Man. Dir, Tesco (Wholesale) Ltd, 1965–82; Dir, Tesco Stores PLC, 1969–82. *Recreations:* travel, reading. *Address:* 10 Noblefield Heights, Great North Road, Highgate, N2 0NX. *T:* (020) 8348 1591.

HYDE, Lord; George Edward Laurence Villiers; with Knight Frank; *b* 12 Feb. 1976; *s* and *heir* of 7th Earl of Clarendon, *qv*. *Educ:* Royal Agricl Coll. (BSc Hons). MRICS. Page of Honour to the Queen. *Address:* c/o Holywell House, Swanmore, Hants SO32 2QE.

HYDE, Helen Yvonne, MA; Headmistress, Watford Grammar School, since 1987; *b* 11 May 1947; *d* of Henry and Tilly Seligman; *m* 1968, Dr John Hyde; two *d*. *Educ:* Parktown Girls' High Sch., Johannesburg; Witwatersrand Univ. (BA 1967; BA Hons 1969); King's Coll., London (MA 1974). Teacher of French, 1970, Head of Modern Languages, 1978, Acland Burghley; Dep. Headmistress, Highgate Wood, 1983. Treas., Assoc. of Heads of Foundn and Aided Schs, 1995–. *Recreations:* tapestry, exercise, theology. *Address:* Watford Grammar School, Lady's Close, Watford, Herts WD1 8AE.

HYDE, Margaret Sheila; Director, Esmée Fairbairn Foundation, since 1994; *b* 11 Sept. 1945; *er d* of late Gerry Tomlins and Sheila (*née* Thorpe); *m* 1966, Derek Hyde (marr. diss. 1976). *Educ:* Watford Grammar Sch. for Girls; London Sch. of Econs and Political Science (DSA 1969; BSc Hons Social Admin 1971; Mostyn Lloyd Meml Prize, 1969; Janet Beveridge Award, 1971). Blackfriars Settlement, 1965–67; Home Office, 1972–77: served in Probation, Prison and Gen. Depts, 1972–76; Private Sec. to Perm. Under Sec. of State, 1976–77; Head of Information, NCVO, 1977–85; Chief Exec., Action Resource Centre, 1985–91 (Trustee, 1992–94); Dep. Sec. Gen., Arts Council of GB, 1991–92; Prog. Consultant, Internat. Save the Children Alliance and Save the Children UK, 1992–94. Mem., Exec. Cttee, 300 Gp, 1984–87 (Treas., 1985–87). Mem., Exec. Cttee, Assoc. of Charitable Foundns, 1995–99 (Vice Chm., 1997–99); Trustee: Peter Bedford Trust, 1983–92 (Chm., 1985–87); Charities Effectiveness Review Trust, 1986–91. Mem. Ct of Govs, LSE, 1987–. FRSA 1991 (Mem. Council, 1994–99). *Recreation:* hill walking. *Address:* 178 Dalling Road, W6 0EU. *Club:* Reform.

HYDE-CHAMBERS, Fredrick Rignold; Director, Industry and Parliament Trust, since 1987; Secretary-General, International Association of Business and Parliament, since 1997; *b* 12 May 1949; *s* of late Derek Christie Hyde-Chambers and Margaret M. Rignold; *m* 1976, Audrey Christine Martin (*née* Smith); two *s*. *Educ:* Buckingham Coll., Harrow; Arts Educnl Sch. Child actor, TV and stage, 1958–64; The Tibet Relief Fund, UK, 1965–68; Gen. Sec., Buddhist Soc., 1968–72; Private Sec. to MPs, 1974–80; Industry and Parliament Trust, 1980–. Co-Founder and Hon. Advr, All-Party Parly Tibet Gp. Member: Bd, Inst. of Citizenship; Adv. Bd, State Legis. Leaders' Foundn, USA; Board, Arts Inform; Council, Buddhist Soc.; Tibet Soc.; Trustee, Ap Tibet. Script writer and consultant, BBC TV and Channel 4 documentaries. First Novel Award, Authors' Club, 1988; Airey Neave Trust Human Rights Scholarship, 1989. *Publications:* The Mouse King, 1976; (with Audrey Hyde-Chambers) Tibetan Folktales, 1979, repr. 1996 (Japan, 1997); Tibet and China, 1988; Lama, 1988 (also USA, Germany, Sweden, Argentina and France). *Recreations:* Tortoises, my two children. *Address:* Industry and Parliament Trust, 1 Buckingham Place, SW1E 6HR. *T:* (020) 7976 5311; 12 Gloucester Court, Swan Street, SE1 1DQ. *T:* (020) 7407 5244.

HYDE-PARKER, Sir Richard William; *see* Parker.

HYLAND, (James) Graham (Keith); QC 1998; a Recorder, since 1996; *b* 11 Jan. 1955; *s* of Reginald Keith Hyland and Evelyn (*née* Graham); *m* 1st, 1979, Angela Lancaster (marr. diss. 1993); one *s*; 2nd, 1995, Jane Alison Davies; one *d*. *Educ:* Heath Grammar Sch., Halifax; Newcastle upon Tyne Poly. (BA Law 1977). Called to the Bar, Inner Temple, 1978. *Recreations:* walking, music, reading, wine, cricket and Association Football (watching). *Address:* Broadway House, 9 Bank Street, Bradford BD1 1TW. *T:* (01274) 722560; 2 Paper Buildings, Temple, EC4Y 7ET. *Clubs:* Bradford; Octave (Elland); South Caernarvonshire Yacht.

HYLTON, 5th Baron *cr* 1866; **Raymond Hervey Jolliffe,** MA; ARICS; *b* 13 June 1932; *er s* of 4th Baron Hylton and Perdita Rose Mary (*d* 1996), *d* of late Raymond Asquith and *sister* of 2nd Earl of Oxford and Asquith, *qv*; *S* father, 1967; *m* 1966, Joanna Ida Elizabeth, *d* of late Andrew de Bertodano; four *s* one *d*. *Educ:* Eton (King's Scholar); Trinity Coll., Oxford (MA). Lieut R of O, Coldstream Guards. Asst Private Sec. to Governor-General of Canada, 1960–62; Trustee, Shelter Housing Aid Centre 1970–76; Chairman: Catholic Housing Aid Soc., 1972–73; Nat. Fedn of Housing Assocs, 1973–76; Housing Assoc. Charitable Trust; Help the Aged Housing Trust, 1976–82; Hugh of Witham Foundn, 1978–; Vice-Pres., Age Concern (Nat. Old People's Welfare Council), 1971–77; President: SW Reg. Nat. Soc. for Mentally Handicapped Children, 1976–79; NI Assoc. for Care and Resettlement of Offenders, 1989. An indep. mem. of H of L; Member, All Party Parliamentary Group: on Penal Affairs; on Human Rights; British-Russian; British-Armenian; British-Albanian; British-Palestine; elected Mem., H of L, 1999. Chm., Partners in Hope (formerly St Francis and St Sergius Trust Fund), 1993–2001. Founder and Mem., Mendip and Wansdyke Local Enterprise Gp, 1979–85. Hon. Treas., Study on Human Rights and Responsibilities in Britain and N Ireland, 1985–88. Mem., Nat. Steering Gp, Charter '87, 1987–99; Signatory of Charter '88 and of Charter '99. Trustee: Christian Internat. Peace Service, 1977–82; Acorn Christian Healing Trust, 1983–98; Action around Bethlehem among Children with Disabilities, 1993–2000; Chm., Moldovan Initiatives Cttee of Mgt, 1993–; Member: Council for Advancement of Arab-British Understanding; RIIA. Governor, Christian Coll. for Adult Educn, 1972–. Mem., Frome RDC, 1968–72. DL Somerset, 1975–90. Hon DSc (SocSc) Southampton, 1994. *Heir:* *s* Hon. William Henry Martin Jolliffe, *b* April 1967. *Address:* Kingmans Farm, Hemington, Bath, Somerset BA3 5UR.

HYLTON-FOSTER, family name of **Baroness Hylton-Foster**.

HYLTON-FOSTER, Baroness *cr* 1965, of the City of Westminster (Life Peer); **Audrey Pellew Hylton-Foster,** DBE 1990; British Red Cross Society: Director, Chelsea Division, 1950–60; President and Chairman, London Branch, 1960–83, Patron, since 1984; Hon. Consultant, National Headquarters, 1984–86; Convenor, Cross Bench Peers, 1974–95; *b* 19 May 1908; *d* of 1st Viscount Ruffside, PC, DL (*d* 1958), and Viscountess Ruffside (*d* 1969); *m* 1931, Rt Hon. Sir Harry Hylton-Foster, QC (*d* 1965); no *c*. *Educ:* St George's, Ascot; Ivy House, Wimbledon. Pres., Research into Blindness Fund, 1965–76. *Recreations:* gardening, fishing. *Address:* The Coach House, Tanhurst, Leith Hill, Holmbury St Mary, Dorking, Surrey RH5 6LU. *T:* (01306) 711975.

HYMAN, Howard Jonathan; Chairman, Hyman Associates, since 1997; *b* 23 Oct. 1949; *s* of late Joe Hyman and Corrine Irene (*née* Abrahams); *m* 1972, Anne Moira Sowden; two *s* one *d*. *Educ:* Bedales Sch., Hants; Manchester Univ. (MA Hons Econs 1972). ACA 1975, FCA 1982. Price Waterhouse: articled clerk, 1972–75; Partner, 1984; seconded to HM Treasury as specialist privatisation adviser, 1984–87; Founder and Partner i/c of Privatisation Services Dept, 1987–90; Head of Corporate Finance, Europe, 1990; Member: E European Jt Venture Bd, 1990–94; European Mgt Bd, 1991–94; China Bd, 1993–94; World Gen. Council, 1992–94; World Head, Corporate Finance, 1994; Dep. Chm., Charterhouse Bank Ltd, 1994–96; Man. Dir, Charterhouse plc, 1994–96. Freeman, City of London, 1997. *Publications:* Privatisation: the facts, 1988; The Implications of Privatisation for Nationalised Industries, 1988; chapters in: Privatisation and Competition, 1988; Privatisation in the UK, 1988; articles in Electrical Rev., Equities Internat., Public Finance and Accountancy, Business and Govt, Administrator. *Recreations:* Chinese culture and language, walking, golf, watching cricket, reading, gardening, classical music. *Address:* 1 Cato Street, W1H 5HG. *T:* (020) 7258 0404. *Clubs:* Reform, MCC; Cirencester Golf, Coombe Hill Golf.

HYMAN, Robin Philip; publisher; Chairman, Calmann & King Ltd, since 1991; *b* 9 Sept. 1931; *s* of late Leonard Hyman and Helen Hyman (*née* Mautner); *m* 1966, Inge Neufeld; two *s* one *d*. *Educ:* Henley Grammar Sch.; Christ's Coll., Finchley; Univ. of Birmingham (BA (Hons) 1955). National Service, RAF, 1949–51. Editor, Mermaid, 1953–54; Bookselling and Publishing: joined Evans Brothers Ltd, Publishers, 1955: Dir, 1964; Dep. Man. Dir, 1967; Man. Dir, 1972–77; Chm., Bell & Hyman Ltd, 1977–86, which merged with Allen & Unwin Ltd, 1986, to form Unwin Hyman Ltd, Man. Dir, 1986–88, Chm. and Chief Exec., 1989–90. Mem. Editorial Bd, World Year Book of Education, 1969–73. Publishers' Association: Mem. Council, 1975–92; Treasurer, 1982–84; Vice-Pres., 1988–89, 1991–92; Pres., 1989–91; Member: Exec. Cttee, Educnl Publishers' Council, 1971–76 (Treas., 1972–75); Publishers' Adv. Cttee, British Council, 1989–92; BBC Gen. Adv. Council, 1992–97. Dir, Spiro Inst., 1991–98. Trustee, ADAPT, 1997–. Mem., First British Publishers' Delegn to China, 1978. FRSA. *Publications:* A Dictionary of Famous Quotations, 1962; (with John Trevaskis) Boys' and Girls' First Dictionary, 1967; Bell & Hyman First Colour Dictionary, 1985; Universal Primary Dictionary (for Africa), 1976; (with Inge Hyman) 11 children's books, incl. Barnabas Ball at the Circus, 1967; Runaway James and the Night Owl, 1968; The Hippo who Wanted to Fly, 1973; The Magical Fish, 1974; Peter's Magic Hide-and-Seek, 1982. *Recreations:* theatre, reading, travel. *Address:* 101 Hampstead Way, NW11 7LR. *T:* (020) 8455 7055. *Clubs:* Garrick, MCC, Samuel Pepys.

HYND, Ronald; choreographer; Ballet Director, National Theater, Munich, 1970–73 and 1984–86; *b* 22 April 1931; *s* of William John and Alice Louisa Hens; *m* 1957, Annette Page, *qv*; one *d*. *Educ:* erratically throughout England due to multiple wartime evacuation. Joined Rambert School, 1946; Ballet Rambert, 1949; Royal Ballet (then Sadlers Well's Ballet), 1952, rising from Corps de Ballet to Principal Dancer, 1959; danced Siegfried (Swan Lake), Florimund (Sleeping Beauty), Albrecht (Giselle), Poet (Sylphides), Tsarevitch (Firebird), Prince of Pagodas, Moondog (Lady and Fool), Tybalt (Romeo), etc; produced first choreography for Royal Ballet Choreographic Group followed by works for London Festival Ballet, Royal Ballet, Dutch National Ballet, Munich Ballet, Houston Ballet, Australian Ballet, Tokyo Ballet, Nat. Ballet of Canada, Grands Ballets Canadiens, Santiago Ballet, Cincinnati Ballet, Pact Ballet, Malmö Ballet, Ljubljania Ballet, Northern Ballet, Ballet of La Scala, Milan, Bonn Ballet, Vienna State Ballet, Amer. Ballet Theatre, Deutsche Oper Berlin, Royal Danish Ballet. *Ballets include:* Le Baiser de la Fée, 1968, new production 1974; Pasiphaë, 1969; Dvorak Variations, 1970; Wendekreise, 1972; In a Summer Garden, 1972; Das Telefon, 1972; Mozartiana, 1973; Charlotte Brontë, 1974; Mozart Adagio, 1974; Galileo (film), 1974; Orient/Occident, 1975; La Valse, 1975; Valses Nobles et Sentimentales, 1975; The Merry Widow, 1975, nine subseq. prodns incl. Amer. Ballet Th. at Met. Opera, NY, 1997 and Royal Danish Ballet, 1998; L'Eventail, 1976; The Nutcracker (new version for Festival Ballet), 1976, new prodns for Ballet de Nice, 1997, La Scala, 2000; ice ballets for John Curry, 1977; Rosalinda, 1978, eleven subseq. prodns incl. Berlin, 1998; La Chatte, 1978; Papillon, 1979; The Seasons, 1980; Alceste, 1981; Scherzo Capriccioso, 1982; Le Diable a Quatre, 1984; Fanfare fur Tänzer, 1985; Coppelia (new prodn for Festival Ballet), 1985, new prodns for Santiago and Berlin, 2000; Ludwig-Fragmente Eines Rätsels, 1986; The Hunchback of Notre Dame, 1988; Ballade, 1988; Liaisons Amoureuses, 1989; Sleeping Beauty (new prodn for English Nat. Ballet), 1993; A Pacific Northwest Ballet, 2001; *musical:* Sound of Music, 1981; *TV productions:* The Nutcracker, The Sanguine Fan (Fest. Ballet); The Merry Widow (Nat. Ballet of Canada). *Recreations:* the gramophone, garden. *E-mail:* ronaldhynd@talk21.com.

HYND, Mrs Ronald; *see* Page, Annette.

HYNES, Ann Patricia, (Mrs T. P. Hynes); *see* Dowling, A. P.

HYNES, Prof. Richard Olding, FRS 1989; Professor of Biology, since 1983, and Director of Center for Cancer Research, since 1991, Massachusetts Institute of Technology; Investigator, Howard Hughes Medical Institute, since 1988; *b* 29 Nov. 1944; *s* of Hugh Bernard Noel Hynes and late Mary Elizabeth Hynes; *m* 1966, Fleur Marshall; two *s*. *Educ:* Trinity Coll., Cambridge (BA 1966; MA 1970); MIT (PhD Biology 1971). Res. Fellow, Imperial Cancer Res. Fund, 1971–74; Massachusetts Institute of Technology: Asst Prof., 1975–78, Associate Prof., 1978–83, Dept of Biology and Center for Cancer Res.; Associate Hd, 1985–89, Head, 1989–91, of Biology Dept. Hon. Res. Fellow, Dept of Zoology, UCL, 1982–83. Guggenheim Fellow, 1982. Mem., Inst. of Medicine, US NAS, 1995; Mem., US NAS, 1996. FAAAS, 1987; Fellow, Amer. Acad. of Arts and Scis, 1994. Gairdner Internat. Award, Gairdner Foundn, Toronto, 1997. *Publications:* (ed) Surfaces of Normal and Malignant Cells, 1979; (ed) Tumor Cell Surfaces and Malignancy, 1980; Fibronectins, 1990; over 200 articles in professional jls. *Recreations:* reading, music, gardening, ski-ing. *Address:* E17-227, Massachusetts Institute of Technology, Cambridge, MA 02139, USA. *T:* (617) 2536422, *Fax:* (617) 2538357.

HYNES, Prof. Samuel, DFC 1945; PhD; Woodrow Wilson Emeritus Professor of Literature, Princeton University, since 1990; *b* 29 Aug. 1924; *s* of Samuel Hynes and Margaret Turner Hynes; *m* 1944, Elizabeth Igleheart; two *d*. *Educ:* Univ. of Minnesota (AB 1947); Columbia Univ. (PhD 1956). Pilot, US Marine Corps: 2nd Lieut, 1943–46; Capt., then Major., 1952–53. Instructor to Prof. of English, Swarthmore Coll., 1949–52 and 1954–68; Professor: Northwestern Univ., 1968–76; Princeton Univ., 1976–90. Woodrow Wilson Prof. of Literature, 1977–90. FRSL 1978. Air Medal, 1945. *Publications:* (ed) Further Speculations by T. E. Hulme, 1955; The Pattern of Hardy's Poetry, 1961; The Edwardian Turn of Mind, 1962; William Golding, 1964; (ed) The Author's Craft and Other Critical Writings of Arnold Bennett, 1968; (ed) Romance and Realism, 1970; Edwardian Occasions, 1972; The Auden Generation, 1976; (ed) Complete Poetical Works of Thomas Hardy, Vol. I 1982, Vol. II 1984, Vol. III 1985, Vols. IV and V 1995; (ed) Thomas Hardy, 1984; Flights of Passage: reflections of a World War II aviator, 1988; A War Imagined, 1990; (ed) Joseph Conrad: complete short fiction, 4 vols, 1992–93; The Soldiers' Tale: bearing witness to modern war, 1997. *Address:* 130 Moore Street, Princeton, NJ 08540, USA. *T:* (609) 9211930.

HYSLOP; *see* Maxwell-Hyslop.

HYSLOP, Fiona Jane; Member (SNP) Lothians, Scottish Parliament, since 1999; *b* 1 Aug. 1964; *d* of Thomas Hyslop and Margaret Birrell; *m* 1994; one *s* one *d*. *Educ:* Ayr Acad.; Glasgow Univ. (MA Hons 1985); Scottish Coll. of Textiles (Post Grad. Dip. 1986). Mkting Manager, Standard Life, 1986–99. Mem., SNP, 1986– (Mem., Nat. Exec., 1990–). Contested (SNP): Edinburgh Leith, 1992; Edinburgh Central, 1997. *Address:* Scottish Parliament, Edinburgh EH99 1SP. *T:* (0131) 348 5920.

HYTNER, Benet Alan; QC 1970; a Recorder of the Crown Court, 1972–97; Judge of Appeal, Isle of Man, 1980–97; *b* 29 Dec. 1927; *s* of late Maurice and Sarah Hytner, Manchester; *m* 1954, Joyce Myers (marr. diss. 1980); three *s* one *d*. *Educ:* Manchester Grammar Sch.; Trinity Hall, Cambridge (Exhibr). MA. National Service, RASC, 1949–51 (commnd). Called to Bar, Middle Temple, 1952, Bencher, 1977, Reader, 1995; Leader, Northern Circuit, 1984–88. Member: Gen. Council of Bar, 1969–73, 1986–88; Senate of Inns of Court and Bar, 1977–81, 1984–86. *Recreations:* fell walking, music, theatre, reading. *Address:* 22 Old Buildings, Lincoln's Inn, WC2A 3UJ.

See also N. R. Hytner.

HYTNER, Nicholas Robert; theatre and film director; *b* 7 May 1956; *s* of Benet Hytner, *qv* and Joyce Hytner. *Educ:* Manchester Grammar School; Trinity Hall, Cambridge (MA). Associate Director: Royal Exchange Theatre, Manchester, 1985–89; RNT, 1989–97; director of many theatre and opera productions including: *theatre:* As You Like It, 1985, Edward II, 1986, The Country Wife, 1986, Don Carlos, 1987, Royal Exchange; Measure for Measure, 1987, The Tempest, 1988, RSC; Ghetto, National Theatre, 1989; Miss Saigon, Drury Lane, 1989, Broadway, 1991; Volpone, Almeida, 1990; King Lear, RSC, 1990; The Wind in the Willows, NT, 1990; The Madness of George III, NT, 1991; The Recruiting Officer, NT, 1992; Carousel, NT, 1992, Shaftesbury, 1993, NY, 1994; The Importance of Being Earnest, Aldwych, 1993; The Cripple of Inishmaan, NT, 1997; Twelfth Night, NY, 1998; Lady in the Van, Queen's 1999; Cressida, Albery, 2000; Orpheus Descending, Donmar Warehouse, 2000; The Winter's Tale, Mother Clapp's Molly House, RNT, 2001; *opera:* English National Opera: Rienzi, 1983; Xerxes, 1985 (Laurence Olivier and Evening Standard Awards); The Magic Flute, 1988; The Force of Destiny, 1992; King Priam, Kent Opera, 1983; Giulio Cesare, Paris Opera, Houston Grand Opera, 1987; Le Nozze di Figaro, Geneva Opera, 1989; La Clemenza di Tito, Glyndebourne, 1991; Don Giovanni, Bavarian State Opera, 1994; The Cunning Little Vixen, Paris, 1995; *films:* The Madness of King George, 1994 (Evening Standard and BAFTA Awards for Best British Film); The Crucible, 1997; The Object of My Affection, 1998. Awards for Best Director: Evening Standard, 1989; Critics Circle, 1989; Olivier, 1993; Tony, 1994. *Address:* c/o Peters, Fraser and Dunlop, Drury House, 34-43 Russell Street, WC2B 5HA.

I

IACOBESCU, George; Chief Executive Officer, Canary Wharf Group plc, since 1997; *b* 9 Nov. 1945; *m* 1976, Gabriela ; one *d. Educ:* Lyceum D. Cantemiu (BSc 1963); Univ. of Civil & Industrial Engrg, Bucharest (Masters degree in professional engrg 1968). Project Dir, Olympia Center and Neiman Marcus Bldgs, Chicago, 1981-84; Vice-Pres., Develt and Construction, World Financial Center, 1984-87; Vice-Pres., Construction, 1987-92; Dir, CWL, 1993-95; Dep. CEO, Canary Wharf Gp plc, 1995-97. MInstD. *Recreations:* jazz, opera, antiques, football, tennis. *Address:* Canary Wharf Group plc, 1 Canada Square, E14 5AB. *T:* (020) 7418 2209.

IBBOTSON, Peter Stamford; broadcasting and media consultant; *b* 13 Dec. 1943; *s* of Arthur Ibbotson and Ivy Elizabeth (*née* Acton); *m* 1975, Susan Mary Crewdson; two *s* one *d. Educ:* Manchester Grammar Sch.; St Catherine's Coll., Oxford (BA Modern History). BBC: Editor, Newsweek, 1978–82; Editor, Panorama, 1983–85; Asst Head, Television Current Affairs, 1985–86; Chief Asst to Dir of Programmes, Television, 1986–87; Dep. Dir of Progs, TV, 1987–88; Dir of Corporate Affairs, Carlton Television Ltd, 1991–94. Director: UK Radio Develts Ltd, 1990–94; Film and Television Completions PLC, 1990–98. Corporate Consultant, Channel 4, 1988–91 and 1994–. Dir, BARB, 1987–88. Gov., ESU, 2000–. *Publication:* (jtly) The Third Age of Broadcasting, 1978. *Recreations:* silviculture, reading, photography. *Address:* Newnham Farm, Wallingford, Oxon OX10 8BW. *T:* (01491) 833111. *Clubs:* Beefsteak, Royal Automobile.

IBBOTSON, Roger; His Honour Judge Ibbotson; a Circuit Judge, since 2001; *b* 2 Jan. 1943; *s* of Harry and Lily Ibbotson; *m* 1967, Susan Elizabeth Dalton; three *d. Educ:* Cockburn High Sch., Leeds Univ. of Manchester (LLB); Articled clerk, Burton and Burton, Leeds, 1963-66; Asst Solicitor, 1966-70, Partner, 1970-2001, Booth & Co, later Addleshaw Booth & Co.; Asst Recorder, 1994-98; Recorder, 1998-2001. Pres., Leeds Law Soc., 1996-97; Council Mem., Law Soc., 1997-2001. *Recreations:* walking, reading, occasional golf. *Address:* Leeds Combined Court Centre, 1 Oxford Row, Leeds, LS1 3BG. *T:* (0113) 283 0040. *Club:* Leeds.

IBBOTT, Alec, CBE 1988; HM Diplomatic Service, retired; *b* 14 Oct. 1930; *s* of Francis Joseph Ibbott and Madge Winifred Ibbott (*née* Graham); *m* 1964, Margaret Elizabeth Brown; one *s* one *d.* Joined Foreign (subseq. Diplomatic) Service, 1949; served in HM Forces, 1949–51; FCO, 1951–54; ME Centre for Arab Studies, 1955–56; Second Secretary and Vice Consul, Rabat, 1956–60; Second Secretary, FO, 1960–61; Second Sec. (Information), Tripoli, 1961; Second Sec., Benghazi, 1961–65; First Sec. (Information), Khartoum, 1965–67; First Sec., FO (later FCO), 1967–71; Asst Political Agent, Dubai, 1971; First Secretary, Head of Chancery and Consul: Dubai, 1971–72; Abu Dhabi, 1972–73; First Secretary and Head of Chancery: Nicosia, 1973–74; FCO, 1975–77; Carácas, 1977–79; Counsellor, Khartoum, 1979–82; seconded to IMS Ltd, 1982–85; Ambassador to Liberia, 1985–87; High Comr to the Republic of The Gambia, 1988–90. Chief Exec., Southern Africa Assoc., 1992–95; Gen. Manager, UK Southern Africa Business Assoc., 1994–95. Mem. Council, Anglo-Arab Assoc., 1992–. Trustee, Charlton Community Develt Trust, 1995–. *Address:* 15a Sanderstead Hill, South Croydon, Surrey CR2 0HD.

IBBS, Sir (John) Robin, KBE 1988; Kt 1982; Chairman: Lloyds TSB Group PLC, 1995–97; Lloyds Bank, 1993–97 (Director, 1985–97; Deputy Chairman, 1988–93); *b* 21 April 1926; *o s* of late Prof. T. L. Ibbs, MC, DSc, FInstP and of Marjorie Ibbs (*née* Bell); *m* 1952, Iris Barbara, *d* of late S. Hall; one *d. Educ:* West House Sch.; Gresham's Sch.; Upper Canada Coll., Toronto; Univ. of Toronto; Trinity Coll., Cambridge (MA Mech. Scis). Instr Lieut, RN, 1947–49. Called to the Bar, Lincoln's Inn, 1952 (Hon. Bencher 1999). C. A. Parsons & Co. Ltd, 1949–51; joined ICI, 1952; Dir, 1976–80 and 1982–88; on secondment as Head, Central Policy Review Staff, Cabinet Office, 1980–82; Advr to Prime Minister on Efficiency and Effectiveness in Govt, 1983–88; Chm., Lloyds Merchant Bank Hldgs, 1989–92; Dep. Chm., Lloyds Bank Canada, 1989–90. Dir, IMI, 1972–76. Chm., Adv. Council, PA Search and Selection, 1997–98. Member: Governing Body and Council, British Nat. Cttee of ICC, 1976–80; Industrial Develt Adv. Bd, DoI, 1978–80; Council, CBI, 1982–87 (Mem. Companies Cttee, 1978–80); Council, CIA, 1976–79, 1982–87 (Vice Pres., 1983–87; Hon. Mem., 1987); Chemicals EDC, NEDO, 1982–88; Council, RIIA, Chatham House, 1983–89; Top Salaries Review Body, 1983–89; Adv. Cttee on Business Appts, 1991–98; second Mem., Sierra Leone Arms Investigation, 1998; Leader, Review of H of C Services, 1990. Pres., Bankers Club, 1994–95. Vice Pres., CIB, 1993–97 (FCIB 1993). Trustee and Dep. Chm., Isaac Newton Trust, 1988–99. Mem. Court, Cranfield Inst. of Technology, 1983–88; Chm. of Council, UCL, 1989–95; Mem. Council, Foundn for Sci. and Technol., 1997–. CIMgt (CBIM 1985). Hon. Fellow UCL, 1993. Hon. DSc Bradford, 1986; Hon LLD Bath, 1993. BIM Special Award, 1989. *Address:* c/o Lloyds TSB Group, 71 Lombard Street, EC3P 3BS. *Clubs:* Oxford and Cambridge (Trustee, 1989–), Naval and Military.

IDALIE, Zoë, (Mme Heinric Idalie); *see* Oldenbourg-Idalie, Z.

IDDESLEIGH, 4th Earl of, *cr* 1885; **Stafford Henry Northcote;** Bt 1641; Viscount St Cyres, 1885; Vice Lord-Lieutenant of Devon, since 1999; Director, Devon & Exeter Steeplechases Ltd, since 1975 (Vice Chairman, 1990–98); *b* 14 July 1932; *er s* of 3rd Earl of Iddesleigh and Elizabeth (*d* 1991), *er d* of late F. S. A. Lowndes and late Marie Belloc; *S* father, 1970; *m* 1955, Maria Luisa Alvarez-Builla y Urquijo (Condesa del Real Agrado in Spain), OBE, DL, *d* of late Don Gonzalo Alvarez-Builla y Alvera and Viscountess Exmouth, *widow* of 9th Viscount Exmouth; one *s* one *d. Educ:* Downside. 2nd Lieut, Irish Guards, 1951–52. Director: Television South West, 1982–92; Gemini Radio Ltd, 1993–98; Orchard Media Ltd, 1996–98; UDT, 1983–87; TSB Gp, 1986–87; TSB Commercial Hldgs, 1987; Mem., SW Region, TSB GP Bd (Chm., 1983–87). DL Devon, 1979. Kt SMO Malta. *Heir: s* Viscount St Cyres, *qv. Address:* Shillands House, Upton Pyne Hill, Exeter, Devon EX5 5EB. *T:* (01392) 258916. *Club:* Army and Navy.

IDDON, Dr Brian, CChem, FRSC; MP (Lab) Bolton South East, since 1997; *b* 5 July 1940; *s* of John Iddon and Violet (*née* Stazicker); *m* 1st, 1965, Merrilyn Ann Muncaster (marr. diss. 1989); two *d*; 2nd, 1995, Eileen Harrison; two step *s. Educ:* Univ. of Hull (BSc Chem. 1961; PhD Organic Chem. 1964; DSc 1981). FRSC (FCS 1959); CChem 1980. Temp. Lectr in Organic Chem., 1964–65, Sen. Demonstrator, 1965–66, Univ. of Durham; University of Salford: Lectr in Organic Chem., 1966–78; Sen. Lectr, 1978–86; Reader, 1986–97. Has lectured worldwide, incl. lect. The Magic of Chemistry presented to schs and univs in UK and Europe, 1968–98. Has made TV and radio broadcasts. Mem. (Lab) Bolton MDC, 1977–98 (Vice-Chm., 1980–82, Chm., 1986–96, Housing Cttee). *Publications:* (jtly) Radiation Sterilization of Pharmaceutical and Biomedical Products, 1974; The Magic of Chemistry, 1985; contrib. chapters in books; numerous papers and reviews and articles in learned jls incl. Jl Chem. Soc., Perkin Trans, Tetrahedron, Chem. Comm., Sch. Sci. Rev., Heterocycles. *Recreations:* gardening, philately, cricket (spectator). *Address:* House of Commons, SW1A 0AA. *T:* (020) 7219 4064, *Fax:* (020) 7219 2653. *Clubs:* Derby Ward Labour (Life Mem.); Bradford Ward Labour.

IDIENS, Dale; Acting Director, National Museums of Scotland; *b* 13 May 1942; *d* of Richard Idiens and Ruth Christine Idiens (*née* Hattersley). *Educ:* High Wycombe High Sch.; Univ. of Leicester. BA (Hons); DipEd. Department of Art and Archaeology, Royal Scottish Museum, later National Museums of Scotland: Asst Keeper in charge of Ethnography, 1964; Dep. Keeper, 1979; Keeper, Dept of Hist. and Applied Art, 1983; Depute Dir (Collections), 1992; Depute Dir, 2000. *Publications:* Traditional African Sculpture, 1969; Ancient American Art, 1971; (ed with K. G. Ponting) African Textiles, 1980; The Hausa of Northern Nigeria, 1981; Pacific Art, 1982; (contrib.) Indians and Europe, an Interdisciplinary Collection of Essays, 1987; Cook Islands Art, 1990; (contrib.) No Ordinary Journey: John Rae, Arctic explorer 1813–1893, 1993; articles and papers in Jl of the Polynesian Soc., African Arts, Textile History; reviews and lectures. *Recreations:* travel, film, wine. *Address:* Sylvan House, 13 Sylvan Place, Edinburgh EH9 1LH. *T:* (0131) 667 2399. *Club:* Naval and Military.

IDLE, Eric; actor and writer; *b* 29 March 1943; *m* 1st, Lynn Ashley (marr. diss.); one *s*; 2nd, Tania Kosevich; one *d. Educ:* Royal Sch., Wolverhampton; Pembroke Coll., Cambridge (BA 1965; Pres., Cambridge Footlights, 1964–65). Pres., Prominent Features. *Stage* includes: I'm Just Wild About Harry, Edinburgh Fest., 1963; Monty Python Live at Drury Lane, 1974; Monty Python Live at the Hollywood Bowl, 1980; The Mikado, ENO, 1987, Houston Opera House, 1989; *television* includes: joint writer: The Frost Report, 1967; Marty Feldman, 1968–69; joint writer and actor: Monty Python's Flying Circus, 4 series, 1969–74; Rutland Weekend Television, 1978; actor: Do Not Adjust Your Set, 1968–69; Around the World in 80 Days, 1989; Nearly Departed, 1989; *films* include: joint writer and actor: And Now for Something Completely Different, 1970; Monty Python and the Holy Grail, 1974; Life of Brian, 1978; The Meaning of Life, 1982; Splitting Heirs, 1993; actor: The Adventures of Baron Munchausen, 1988; Nuns on the Run, 1990; Casper, 1995; Wind in the Willows, 1996. *Publications: novels:* Hello Sailor, 1975; The Road to Mars, 1999. *Address:* Prominent Features, 68a Delancey Street, NW1 7RY; c/o ICM Ltd, Oxford House, 76 Oxford Street, W1N 0AX.

IDLE, Prof. Jeffrey Robert, PhD; CChem, FRSC, EurChem; CBiol, FIBiol, EurProBiol; Professor in Medicine and Molecular Biology, Norwegian University of Science and Technology, 1996–2001 (on leave of absence); Consultant in Medical Genetics, Regional Hospital, Trondheim, 1996–99; *b* 17 Sept. 1950; *s* of Robert William Idle and Margaret Joyce Idle (*née* Golightly); *m* Samar El-Sallab (marr. diss.); one *d. Educ:* Hatfield Polytechnic (BSc 1972, BSc Hons 1973); St Mary's Hosp. Med. Sch. (PhD 1976). CChem 1987; FRSC 1987; CBiol 1999; FIBiol 1999; EurChem 2000; EurProBiol 2000. St Mary's Hospital Medical School, London: Lectr in Biochem., 1976; Lectr in Biochemical Pharmacol., 1976–83; Wellcome Trust Sen. Lectr, 1983–88; Reader in Pharmacogenetics, 1985–88; University of Newcastle upon Tyne: Prof. of Pharmacogenetics, 1988–95; Hd, Sch. of Clinical Med. Scis, 1992–95; Hd, Dept of Pharmacol. Scis, 1992–95. Hon. Prof. of Clinical Pharmacology, Med. Sch., Univ. of Extremadura, Badajoz, Spain. Dir, Nivy Blacksmith Music sro, 1999–. Founding Editor and Editor-in-Chief, Pharmacogenetics, 1991–98. Chief Executive: Genotype Ltd, 1993–95; VitOmega Internat., 1995–98. *Publications:* articles in internat. scientific and med. jls. *Recreations:* language and culture of the Middle East, music. *Address:* Zlata ul. 34, 36005 Karlovy Vary, Czech Republic.

IDRIS, Kamil E., PhD; Director General, World Intellectual Property Organization, since 1997 (Deputy Director General, 1994–97); *b* 26 Aug. 1945; *s* of Eltayeb and Amuna Haj Hussein; *m* 1986, Azza Mohyeldin Ahmed; one *s* three *d. Educ:* Univ. of Cairo (BA Philosophy, Pol Sci. and Econ. Theories); Univ. of Geneva (PhD Internat. Law); Univ. of Ohio (Master Internat. Law and Internat. Affairs); Inst. of Public Admin, Khartoum (DPA); Univ. of Khartoum (LLB). Part-time Journalist, El-Ayam and El-Sahafa (newspapers), Sudan, 1971–79; Lecturer: in Philosophy and Jurisp., Univ. of Cairo, 1976–77; in Jurisp., Ohio Univ., 1978; Asst Dir, Res. Dept, subseq. Dep. Dir, Legal Dept, Min. of Foreign Affairs, Sudan, 1978; Vice-Consul in Switzerland, and Legal Advr, Sudan Perm. Mission to UN Office, Geneva, 1979–82; Sen. Prog. Officer, Develt Co-operation and External Relns Bureau for Africa, 1982–85, Dir, Develt Co-operation and External Relns Bureau for Arab and Central and European Countries, 1984–94, WIPO. Prof. of Public Internat. Law, Univ. of Khartoum; Sec. Gen., Internat. Union for the Protection of New Varieties of Plants. Advocate and Comr of Oaths, Republic of Sudan. Member: UN Internat. Law Commn, 1991–96; Sudan Bar Assoc.; African Jurists Assoc. Comdr, Ordre Nat. du Lion (Senegal), 1998. *Publications:* articles on law, econs, jurisp. and aesthetics in jls. *Address:* (office) 34 Chemin des Colombettes, 1211 Geneva, Switzerland. *T:* (22) 3389111.

IEVERS, Frank George Eyre, CMG 1964; Postmaster-General, East Africa, 1962–65, retired; *b* 8 May 1910; *s* of Eyre Francis and Catherine Ievers; *m* 1936, Phyllis Robinson; two *s*. *Educ:* Dover Coll. Asst Traffic Supt, Post Office, 1933; Traffic Supt, East Africa, 1946; Telecommunications Controller, 1951; Regional Dir, 1959. *Recreations:* golf, photography. *Address:* 20 Heron Close, Worcester WR2 4BW. *T:* (01905) 427121. *Clubs:* Nairobi (Kenya); Sudan (Khartoum).

IFE, Prof. Barry William, CBE 2000; PhD; Cervantes Professor of Spanish, since 1988, Vice-Principal, since 1997, King's College London; *b* 19 June 1947; *s* of Bernard Edward Ife and Joan Mary (*née* Thacker); *m* 1st, 1968, Anne Elizabeth Vernon (marr. diss. 1985); 2nd, 1986, Christine Mary Whiffen (marr. diss. 1998); two *s*. *Educ:* King's Coll., London (BA Hons 1968; FKC 1992); Birkbeck Coll., London (PhD 1984). ALCM 1965. Asst Lectr in Spanish, 1969–71, Lectr, 1971–72, Univ. of Nottingham; Lectr in Spanish, Birkbeck Coll., London, 1972-88; Hd, Sch. of Humanities, KCL, 1989–96. Leverhulme Res. Fellow, 1983–85. Gov., RAM, 1998–. Hon. FRAM 2001. *Publications:* Dos Versiones de Piramo y Tisbe, 1974; Francisco de Quevedo: La Vida del Buscón, 1977; Anthology of Early Keyboard Methods, 1981; Domenico Scarlatti, 1985; Reading and Fiction in Golden-Age Spain, 1985; Early Spanish Keyboard Music, 1986; Antonio Soler: Twelve Sonatas, 1989; Christopher Columbus: Journal of the First Voyage, 1990; Lectura y Ficción, 1992; Letters from America, 1992; Miguel de Cervantes: Exemplary Novels, 1993; Corpus of Contemporary Spanish, 1995; Don Quixote's Diet, 2000; contrib. articles and reviews to Bull. Hispanic Studies, MLR, Jl Inst. Romance Studies, TLS and others. *Recreations:* music, literature, sorting things out. *Address:* King's College London, Strand, WC2R 2LS; Queen's Head House, 70 Seckford Street, Woodbridge, Suffolk IP12 4LZ. *T:* (01394) 382958; *e-mail:* barry.ife@kcl.ac.uk.

IGGO, Prof. Ainsley, PhD, DSc; FRCPE; FRS 1978; FRSE; Professor of Veterinary Physiology, University of Edinburgh, 1962–90, now Emeritus; *b* 2 Aug. 1924; *s* of late Lancelot George Iggo and late Catherine Josefine Fraser; *m* 1952, Betty Joan McCurdy, PhD, *d* of late Donald A. McCurdy, OBE; three *s*. *Educ:* Gladstone Sch., NZ; Southland Technical High Sch., NZ; Lincoln Coll., NZ (Sen. Scholar; MAgrSc 1947); Univ. of Otago (BSc 1949). PhD Aberdeen, 1954; DSc Edinburgh, 1962. FRSE 1962; FRCPE 1985. Asst Lectr in Physiology, Otago Univ. Med. Sch., 1948–50; NZ McMillan Brown Trav. Fellow, Rowett Inst., 1950–51; Lectr in Physiol., Univ. of Edinburgh Med. Sch., 1952–60; Nuffield Royal Soc. Commonwealth Fellow, ANU, 1959; Royal Soc. Locke Res. Fellow, 1960–62; Dean, Faculty of Veterinary Med., Univ. of Edinburgh, 1974–77 and 1985–90. Vis. Professor: Univ. of Ibadan, Nigeria, 1968; (also Leverhulme Res. Fellow) Univ. of Kyoto, 1970; Univ. of Heidelberg, 1972. Chm., IUPS Somatosensory Commn, 1974–. Mem. Council: RCVS, 1975–78 and 1985–90; Royal Soc., 1982–83; Pres., Internat. Assoc. for Study of Pain, 1980–83. Governor, E of Scotland Coll. of Agriculture, 1968–77. Hon. DSc Pennsylvania; Hon. DVM&S Edinburgh, 1993. *Publications:* (ed) Sensory Physiology: Vol. II, Somatosensory System, 1973; articles on neurophysiol topics in Jl Physiol., etc. *Recreations:* bee-keeping, gardening. *Address:* 5 Relugas Road, Edinburgh EH9 2NE. *T:* (0131) 667 4879.

IGNARRO, Prof. Louis J.; PhD; Professor, Department of Molecular and Medical Pharmacology, University of California, Los Angeles, since 1985; *b* 31 May 1941; *m* 1st (marr. diss.); one *d*; 2nd, 1997, Sharon Elizabeth Williams. *Educ:* Long Beach High Sch.; Columbia Univ. (BA 1962); Univ. of Minnesota (PhD 1966). Post-doctoral Fellow, NIH, 1966-68; Hd, Biochem. and Anti-inflammatory Prog., Geigy Pharmaceuticals, 1968-73; Asst Prof., 1973-79, Prof., 1979-85, Dept of Pharmacol., Sch. of Medicine, Tulane Univ. Mem., US Nat. Acad. of Scis. Nobel Prize for Medicine (jtly), 1998. *Publications:* articles in scientific jls. *Address:* Department of Molecular and Medical Pharmacology, University of California, 10833 Le Conte Avenue, Los Angeles, CA 90095, USA.

IGNATIEFF, Michael, PhD; writer; *b* 12 May 1947; *s* of George Ignatieff and Alison (*née* Grant); *m* 1st, 1977, Susan Barrowclough (marr. diss. 1998); one *s* one *d*; 2nd, 1999, Suzanna Zsohar. *Educ:* Upper Canada Coll., Toronto; Univ. of Toronto (BA 1969); Cambridge Univ. (MA 1978); Harvard Univ. (PhD 1975). Asst Prof. of History, Univ. of BC, 1976–78; Sen. Res. Fellow, King's Coll., Cambridge, 1978–84; Vis. Fellow, Ecole des Hautes Etudes, Paris, 1985; Alistair Horne Fellow, St Antony's Coll., Oxford, 1993–95; Visiting Professor: Univ. of Calif, Berkeley, 1997; LSE, 1998–2000; Carr Prof. of Human Rights Policy, Kennedy Sch. of Govt, Harvard Univ., 2000–. Presenter: Voices, Channel 4, 1986; Thinking Aloud, BBC TV Series, 1987–88; The Late Show, BBC TV, 1989–95; Blood and Belonging, BBC, 1993; Trial of Freedom, C4, 1999; The Future of War, BBC, 2000. Editorial Columnist, The Observer, 1990–93. Hon. DPhil Stirling, 1996. *Publications:* A Just Measure of Pain, 1978; The Needs of Strangers, 1984; The Russian Album, 1987 (Canadian Governor General's Award, 1988; Heinemann Prize, RSL, 1988); Asya, 1991; Scar Tissue, 1993; Blood and Belonging, 1993; The Warrior's Honour: ethnic war and the modern conscience, 1998; Isaiah Berlin: a life, 1998; Virtual War: Kosovo and beyond, 2000; The Rights Revolution, 2000; Human Rights as Politics and Idolatry, 2001. *Recreations:* tennis, talking, wine, theatre, music. *Address:* c/o A. P. Watt Ltd, 20 John Street, WC1N 2DR.

IKERRIN, Viscount; Arion Thomas Piers Hamilton Butler; *b* 1 Sept. 1975; *s* and *heir* of 10th Earl of Carrick, *qv*.

ILCHESTER, 9th Earl of, *cr* 1756; **Maurice Vivian de Touffreville Fox-Strangways;** Baron Ilchester of Ilchester, Somerset, and Baron Strangways of Woodsford Strangways, Dorset, 1741; Baron Ilchester and Stavordale of Redlynch, Somerset, 1747; Group Captain, Royal Air Force, retired; Vice-Chairman, County Border News Ltd and Bromley News Ltd, since 1995 (Managing Director, 1984–95); *b* 1 April 1920; *s* of 8th Earl of Ilchester and Laure Georgine Emilie (*d* 1970), *d* of late Evanghelos Georgios Mazaraki, sometime Treasurer of Suez Canal Company; *S* father, 1970; *m* 1941, Diana Mary Elizabeth, *e d* of late George Frederick Simpson, Cassington, Oxfordshire. *Educ:* Kingsbridge Sch. CEng; MRAeS; FINucE (Pres., 1982–84); FIMgt. Served RAF, 1936–76 (Gp Captain). Vice Chm., Biggin Hill Airport Consultative Cttee, 1976–95. Dir, 1982–90, Vice Chm., 1985–86, Nottingham Building Soc. Mem., H of L Select Cttee on Science and Technology, 1984–89. President: Soc. of Engineers, 1974 (Hon. FSE 1989); Biggin Hill Br., 1973–, SE Area, 1978–, RAFA; Darent River Preservation Soc., 1993–; Grant Maintained Schools Foundn, 1991–99; Cannock Sch., 1992–95 (Chm. Govs, 1978–92); Kent and Downs Reg. Newspaper Soc., 1994–95; Westerham Br., RBL, 1996–. President: 285 Sqn, ATC, 1973–; 2427 Sqn, ATC, 1977–. Liveryman, GAPAN. Hon. FCP 1994. *Recreations:* outdoor activities, enjoyment of the arts. *Heir: b* Hon. Raymond George Fox-Strangways [*b* 11 Nov. 1921; *m* 1941, Margaret Vera, *d* of late James Force, North Surrey, BC; two *s*]. *Address:* Farley Mill, Westerham, Kent TN16 1UB. *T:* (01959) 562314. *Club:* Royal Air Force.

ILERSIC, Prof. Alfred Roman; Emeritus Professor of Social Studies, Bedford College, University of London, since 1984 (Professor, 1965–84); *b* 14 Jan. 1920; *s* of late Roman Ilersic and Mary (*née* Moss); *m* 1st, 1944, Patricia Florence Bertram Liddle (marr. diss. 1976); one *s* one *d*; 2nd, 1976, June Elaine Browning. *Educ:* Polytechnic Sec. Sch., London; London Sch. of Economics, Lectr in Econs, University Coll. of S West, Exeter, 1947–53; Lectr in Social Statistics, Bedford Coll., 1953; Reader in Economic and Social Statistics, Bedford Coll., London, 1963. Vis. Prof., Univ. of Bath, 1983–87. Mem., Cost of Living Adv. Cttee, 1970–88. Chm., Inst. of Statisticians, 1968–70. Mem., Wilts CC, 1989–93. Hon. Mem., Rating and Valuation Assoc., 1968. *Publications:* Statistics, 1953; Government Finance and Fiscal Policy in Post-War Britain, 1956; (with P. F. B. Liddle) Parliament of Commerce 1860–1960, 1960; Taxation of Capital Gains, 1962; Rate Equalisation in London, 1968; Local Government Finance in Northern Ireland, 1969. *Recreations:* listening to music, walking.

ILIFFE, family name of **Baron Iliffe**.

ILIFFE, 3rd Baron *cr* 1933, of Yattendon; **Robert Peter Richard Iliffe;** Chairman, Yattendon Investment Trust PLC, since 1984; *b* Oxford, 22 Nov. 1944; *s* of late Hon. W. H. R. Iliffe and Mrs Iliffe; *S* uncle, 1996; *m* 1966, Rosemary Anne Skipwith; three *s* one *d* (of whom one *s* one *d* are twins). *Educ:* Eton; Christ Church, Oxford. Subsidiary cos of Yattendon Investment Trust: Marina Developments Ltd; Cambridge Newspapers Ltd; Herts & Essex Newspapers Ltd; Burton Daily Mail Ltd; Staffordshire Newsletter. Chm., Yattendon Estates Ltd, 1987–; former Chairman: Birmingham Post and Mail Ltd; Coventry Newspapers Ltd; Dir, Scottish Provincial Press Ltd, 1990–. Member of Council, RASE, 1972– (Chm., 1994–98). High Sheriff of Warwicks, 1983–84. *Recreations:* yachting, shooting, fishing, old cars. *Heir: s* Hon. Edward Richard Iliffe, *b* 13 Sept. 1968. *Address:* Barn Close, Yattendon, Thatcham, Berks RG18 0UX.

ILIFFE, Prof. John, FBA 1989; Professor of African History, University of Cambridge, since 1990; Fellow of St John's College, Cambridge, since 1971; *b* 1 May 1939; 2nd *s* of late Arthur Ross Iliffe and Violet Evelyn Iliffe. *Educ:* Framlingham Coll.; Peterhouse, Cambridge (BA 1961; MA; PhD 1965; LittD 1990). Lectr, then Reader, in History, Univ. of Dar-es-Salaam, 1965–71; University of Cambridge: Asst Dir of Res. in Hist., 1971–80; Reader in African Hist., 1980–90. *Publications:* Tanganyika under German Rule, 1969; A Modern History of Tanganyika, 1979; The Emergence of African Capitalism, 1983; The African Poor: a history, 1987; Famine in Zimbabwe, 1989; Africans: the history of a continent, 1995; East African Doctors: a history of the modern profession, 1998. *Recreation:* cricket. *Address:* St John's College, Cambridge CB2 1TP. *T:* (01223) 338714. *Club:* MCC.

ILLINGWORTH, David Gordon, CVO 1987 (LVO 1980); MD, FRCPE; retired; Surgeon Apothecary to HM Household at Holyrood Palace, Edinburgh, 1970–86; *b* 22 Dec. 1921; *yr s* of Sir Gordon Illingworth; *m* 1946, Lesley Beagrie, Peterhead; two *s* one *d*. *Educ:* George Watson's Coll.; Edinburgh University. MB, ChB Edinburgh, 1943; MRCPE 1949; MD (with commendation) 1963; FRCPE 1965; FRCGP 1970. Nuffield Foundn Travelling Fellow, 1966. RN Medical Service, 1944–46 (2nd Escort Gp); medical appts, Edinburgh Northern Hosps Group, 1946–82. Dep. CMO, Scottish Life Assurance Co., 1973–92. Hon. Sen. Lectr in Rehabilitation Studies, Dept of Orthopaedic Surgery, Edinburgh Univ., 1977–82; Lectr in Gen. Practice Teaching Unit, Edinburgh Univ., 1965–82. Member: Cancer Planning Group, Scottish Health Service Planning Council, 1976–81; Tenovus, Edinburgh, 1978–92; ASH, Royal Colleges Jt Cttee, 1978–82; Specialty Sub-Cttee on Gen. Practice, 1980–82; Nat. Med. Cons. Cttee, 1980–82. AFOM, RCP, 1980. Mem., Harveian Soc. Life Governor, Imperial Cancer Res. Fund, 1978. *Publications:* Practice (jtly), 1978; (contrib.) By Royal Command, ed H. Buckton, 1997; contribs to BMJ, Jl of Clinical Pathology, Gut, Lancet, Medicine. *Recreations:* golf, gardening. *Address:* 19 Napier Road, Edinburgh EH10 5AZ. *T:* (0131) 229 8102. *Clubs:* University (Edinburgh); Bruntsfield Links Golfing Soc.

ILLINGWORTH, David Jeremy, FCA; Partner, KPMG (formerly KMG Thomson McLintock), since 1975; Vice-President, 2001–June 2002, Deputy President, from June 2002, Institute of Chartered Accountants in England and Wales; *b* Stockport, Cheshire, 28 April 1947; *s* of late Prof. Charles Raymond Illingworth and Joan Ellen Mary Illingworth; *m* 1968, Annie Vincenza Bailey; two *d*. *Educ:* Stockport Sch.; Emmanuel Coll., Cambridge (BA 1968). ACA 1971, FCA 1972. Trainee, KMG Thomson McLintock, 1968–71. Member: Cttee, Manchester Soc. of Chartered Accountants, 1983– (Pres., 1992–93); Council, ICAEW, 1997–. NW Regl Council Mem., CBI, 1993–. Mem. Cttee, Duke of Westminster Awards for Business and Industry in the NW, 1995–. Gov., Hulme Grammar Schs, Oldham, 1992–. *Recreations:* travel, golf, music, theatre, opera, walking. *Address:* Alphin, 7 Park Lane, Greenfield, Oldham OL3 7DX. *T:* (01457) 875971. *Clubs:* St James' (Manchester); Saddleworth Golf (Oldham).

ILLINGWORTH, Raymond, CBE 1973; cricketer; Manager, Yorkshire County Cricket Club, 1979–84; Chairman of Selectors, Test and County Cricket Board, 1994–96; and Manager, England Cricket Team, 1995–96; *b* 8 June 1932; *s* of late Frederick Spencer Illingworth and Ida Illingworth; *m* 1958, Shirley Milnes; two *d*. *Educ:* Wesley Street Sch., Farsley, Pudsey. Yorkshire County cricketer; capped, 1955. Captain: MCC, 1969; Leics CCC, 1969–78; Yorks CCC, 1982–83. Toured: West Indies, 1959–60; Australia twice (once as Captain), 1962–63 and 1970–71. Played in 66 Test Matches (36 as Captain). Hon. MA Hull, 1983; Hon. Dr Leeds Metropolitan, 1997. *Publications:* Spinners Wicket, 1969; The Young Cricketer, 1972; Spin Bowling, 1979; Captaincy, 1980; Yorkshire and Back, 1980; (with Kenneth Gregory) The Ashes, 1982; The Tempestuous Years 1977–83, 1987; One Man Committee, 1996. *Recreations:* golf, bridge. *Address:* The Mistle, 4 Calverley Lane, Farsley, Pudsey, West Yorkshire LS28 5LB.

ILLMAN, John, CMG 1999; HM Diplomatic Service, retired; Ambassador to Peru, 1995–99; *b* 26 Oct. 1940; *s* of Reginald Thomas Illman and Hilda Kathleen Illman (*née* Targett); *m* 1962, Elizabeth Hunter Frame; one *s* two *d*. *Educ:* Reading Sch.; St Andrews Univ. Joined Foreign Office, 1961: Leopoldville, later Kinshasa, 1963–66; Dublin, 1967–71; Paris, 1971–73; First Sec., FCO, 1973–75; Buenos Aires, 1975–79; Lagos, 1979–82; Commonwealth Co-ordination Dept, FCO, 1982–86; Dep. Head of Mission and Consul-Gen., Algiers, 1986–90; Consul-Gen., Marseilles and for Principality of Monaco, 1990–94. *Recreations:* squash, tennis, Rugby, cricket, amateur dramatics. *Clubs:* Royal Commonwealth Society, Candlewick Ward.

ILLSLEY, Anthony Kim; non-executive Director: EasyJet, since 2000; Capital Radio, since 2000; *b* 8 July 1956. *Educ:* Loughborough Grammar Sch.; Bath Univ. (BSc Business Admin). Mktg and Sales Trainee, subseq. Gp Brand Manager, Colgate Palmolive, 1979–84; joined Pepsico, 1984: European Mktg Manager, subseq. Ops Dir, Pepsicola International; resp. for business in France, Belgium and Scandinavia, Pepsi-Cola; European Regl Dir, 7-Up Div., Pepsico; President: Pepsicola Japan; Asia Pacific Div., Hong Kong; Walkers Snack Foods UK Ltd, 1995–98; CEO, Telewest Communications, 1998–2000. *Recreation:* motorsport.

ILLSLEY, Eric Evlyn; MP (Lab) Barnsley Central, since 1987; *b* 9 April 1955; *s* of John and Maude Illsley; *m* 1978, Dawn Webb; two *d*. *Educ:* Barnsley Holgate Grammar Sch.;

Leeds Univ. (LLB Hons 1977). NUM, Yorkshire Area: Compensation Officer, 1978–81; Asst Head of General Dept, 1981–84; Head of Gen. Dept and Chief Admin. Officer, 1984–87. An Opposition Whip, 1991–94; Opposition spokesperson: on health, 1994–95; on local govt, April–Oct. 1995; on NI, 1995–97. Member, Select Committee: on televising proceedings of H of C, 1988–91; on Energy, 1987–91; on Procedure, 1991–; on Foreign Affairs, 1997–; Jt Chm., All Party Parly Glass Gp, 1989–; Vice Chm., All Party Parly Gp on Occupnl Pensions, 1997– (Treas., 1993–97); Vice-Pres., Parly and Scientific Cttee, 1998– (Jt Hon. Sec., 1994–95; Jt Dep. Chm., 1995–98). Sec., Barnsley Constit. Lab. Pty, 1980–83 (Treas., 1979–80); Sec. and Election Agent, Yorks S Eur. Constit. Lab. Pty, 1983–87; Treas., Yorks Gp of Lab. MPs, 1988–. Member Executive Committee: CPA, 1997–; IPU, 1997–. *Recreation:* gymnasium. *Address:* House of Commons, Westminster, SW1A 0AA. *T:* (office) (01226) 730692.

ILLSLEY, Prof. Raymond, CBE 1979; PhD; Professorial Fellow in Social Policy, University of Bath, since 1984; *b* 6 July 1919; *s* of James and Harriet Illsley; *m* 1948, Jean Mary Harrison; two *s* one *d. Educ:* St Edmund Hall, Oxford (BA 1948). PhD Aberdeen 1956. Served War, 1939–45: active service in GB and ME, 1939–42; PoW, Italy and Germany, 1942–45. Econ. Asst, Commonwealth Econ. Cttee, London, 1948; Social Res. Officer, New Town Develt Corp., Crawley, Sussex, 1948–50; Sociologist, MRC, working with Dept of Midwifery, Univ. of Aberdeen, as Mem., Social Med. Res. Unit and later Mem., Obstetric Med. Res. Unit, 1951–64; Prof. of Sociology, Univ. of Aberdeen, 1964–75, Prof. of Medical Sociology, 1975–84. Dir, MRC Medical Sociology Unit, 1965–83. Vis. Prof., Cornell Univ., NY, 1963–64; Vis. Scientist, Harvard Univ., 1968; Sen. Foreign Scientist, National Sci. Foundn, Boston Univ., 1971–72; Vis. Prof., Dept of Sociology, Boston Univ., 1971–72, Adjunct Prof., 1972–76. Chairman: Scottish TUC Inquiry on Upper Clyde Shipbuilders Ltd, 1971; Social Sciences Adv. Panel, Action for the Crippled Child, 1971–76; Health Services Res. Cttee, Chief Scientist's Org., SHHD, 1976–84. Member: Sec. of State's Scottish Council on Crime, 1972–76; Exec. Cttee, Nat. Fund for Res. into Crippling Diseases, 1972–76; Chief Scientist's Cttee, SHHD, 1973–85; EEC Cttee on Med. Res., 1974–77; SSRC, 1976–78 (Chairman: Sociol. and Soc. Admin Cttee, 1976–79; Social Affairs Cttee, 1982–85); Chief Scientist's Adv. Cttee, DHSS, 1980–81; European Adv. Cttee for Med. Res., WHO, 1981–85. Rock Carling Fellow, Nuffield Prov. Hosps Trust, 1980. Hon. DSc Univ. of Hull, 1984; DUniv Stirling, 1987; Hon. dr med. Copenhagen, 1992. *Publications:* Mental Subnormality in the Community: a clinical and epidemiological study (with H. Birch, S. Richardson, D. Baird et al), 1970; Professional or Public Health, 1980; (with R. G. Mitchell) Low Birth Weight, 1984; articles in learned jls on reproduction, migration, social mobility, mental subnormality. *Recreation:* rough husbandry. *Address:* Tisbut House, Box Hill, Wilts SN13 8HG. *T:* (01225) 742313.

ILLSTON, Prof. John Michael, CEng, FICE; Director of the Hatfield Polytechnic, 1982–87, Professor and Professor Emeritus, 1987, Fellow, 1991; *b* 17 June 1928; *s* of Alfred Charles Illston and Ethel Marian Illston; *m* 1951, Olga Elizabeth Poulter; one *s* two *d. Educ:* Wallington County Grammar Sch.; King's Coll., Univ. of London (BScEng, PhD, DScEng; FKC 1985). CEng, FICE 1975. Water engr, then schoolmaster, 1949–59; Lectr, Sen. Lectr and Reader in Civil Engrg, King's Coll., London, 1959–77; Dir of Studies in Civil Engrg, Dean of Engrg, and Dep. Dir, Hatfield Polytechnic, 1977–82. Member: Commonwealth Scholarships Commn, 1983–92; Engrg Bd, SERC, 1983–86; Engrg Council, 1981–90; Council, BTEC, 1986–89; Chm., CNAA Cttee for Engrg, 1987–91; Visitor, Building Res. Stn, 1989–95. Chairman: Govs, Bishop Wordsworth Sch., 1994–98; Salisbury Br., CRUSE Bereavement Care, 1998–2001. *Publications:* (with J. M. Dinwoodie and A. A. Smith) Concrete, Timber and Metals, 1979; (ed) Construction Materials, 2nd edn 1994; contrib. Cement and Concrete Res. and Magazine of Concrete Res. *Address:* 10 Merrifield Road, Ford, Salisbury, Wilts SP4 6DF.

IMBERT, family name of **Baron Imbert**.

IMBERT, Baron *cr* 1999 (Life Peer), of New Romney, in the county of Kent; **Peter Michael Imbert,** Kt 1988; QPM 1980; Lord-Lieutenant of Greater London, since 1998; Commissioner, Metropolitan Police, 1987–93 (Deputy Commissioner, 1985–87); *b* 27 April 1933; *s* of late William Henry Imbert and of Frances May (*née* Hodge); *m* 1956, Iris Rosina (*née* Dove); one *s* two *d. Educ:* Harvey Grammar Sch., Folkestone, Kent; Holborn College of Law, Languages and Commerce. Joined Metropolitan Police, 1953; Asst Chief Constable, Surrey Constabulary, 1976, Dep. Chief Constable, 1977; Chief Constable, Thames Valley Police, 1979–85. Metropolitan Police Anti-Terrorist Squad, 1973–75; Police negotiator at Balcome Street siege, Dec. 1975; visited Holland following Moluccan sieges, and Vienna following siege of OPEC building by terrorists, Dec. 1975. Lectures in UK and Europe to police and military on terrorism and siege situations; lecture tours to Australia, 1977, 1980 and 1986, to advise on terrorism and sieges, and to Canada, 1981 re practical effects on police forces of recommendations of Royal Commn on Criminal Procedure; Vis. Internat. Fellow, Australian Police Staff College, 1994 and 1997. Leader, Internat. Criminal Justice Delegn to Russia, 1993. Sec., Nat. Crime Cttee-ACPO Council, 1980–83 (Chm., 1983–85). Non-executive Director: Securicor Gp, 1993–2001; Camelot Gp, 1994–; non-exec. Chm., Retainagroup, 1995–; Chm., Capital Eye Security, 1997–. Member: Gen. Advisory Council, BBC, 1980–87; Criminal Justice Consultative Cttee, 1992–93; Mental Health Foundn, Cttee of Inquiry into Care in the Community for the Severely Mentally Ill, 1994; Academic Consultative Cttee, King George VI and Queen Elizabeth Foundn of St Catharine's, Cumberland Lodge, Windsor, 1983–2001; Ministerial Adv. Gp, Royal Parks, 1993–2001; Public Policy Cttee, RAC, 1993–. Trustee, Queen Elizabeth Foundn of St Catharine's, 1988–2001. Chm., Surrey CCC Youth Trust, 1993–96; Pres., Richmond Horse Show, 1993–99. Gov., Harvey Grammar Sch., 1994–. CIMgt (CBIM 1982). DL Greater London, 1994. Hon. DLitt Reading, 1987; Hon. DBA IMCB, 1989. *Publications:* occasional articles and book reviews. *Recreations:* bad bridge, coarse golf, talking about my grandchildren. *Address:* c/o The Lieutenancy Office, City Hall, PO Box 240, Victoria Street, SW1A 1AA.

IMBERT-TERRY, Sir Michael Edward Stanley, 5th Bt *cr* 1917, of Strete Ralegh, Whimple, Co. Devon; *b* 18 April 1950; *s* of Major Sir Edward Henry Bouhier Imbert-Terry, 3rd Bt, MC, and of Jean (who *m* 1983, Baron Sackville, *qv*), *d* of late Arthur Stanley Garton; *S* brother, 1985; *m* 1975, Frances Dorothy, *d* of late Peter Scott, Ealing; two *s* two *d. Educ:* Cranleigh. *Heir: s* Brychan Edward Imbert-Terry, *b* 1975.

IMBODEN, Dr Christoph Niklaus; consultant ecologist; *b* 28 April 1946; *s* of Max Imboden and Elisabeth Imboden-Stahel; *m* 1970, Eve Elisabeth Staub; one *s* one *d. Educ:* Univ. of Basel (PhD). New Zealand Wildlife Service: Sen. Scientist, 1977; Asst Dir (Research), 1978; Dir-Gen., ICBP, later BirdLife Internat., 1980–96. Premio Gaia, Sicily, 1993; RSPB Conservation Medal, 1993. Officer, Order of the Golden Ark (Netherlands), 1996. *Publications:* papers on ornithology, ecology, conservation. *Recreations:* classical music, birdwatching, hill-walking, travelling. *Address:* 8 Church Lane, Girton, Cambridge CB3 0JP.

IMISON, Dame Tamsyn, DBE 1998; education strategist; Headteacher, Hampstead School, 1984–2000; *b* 1 May 1937; *m* 1958, Michael Imison; two *d* (one *s* decd). *Educ:* Hitchin Girls' GS; Milham Ford Sch., Oxford; Somerville Coll., Oxford (Hon. Fellow, 1999); Queen Mary Coll., London (BSc Hons Zoology 1964); Ruskin Sch. of Drawing and Fine Art, Oxford; Inst. of Education, London Univ. (PGCE 1972; Hon. Fellow, 2001); Open Univ. (Cert. of Prof. Develt in Educn 1994; MA Educn 1996). Freelance scientific, exhibn and illustration work for Oxford Mus., British Mus. (Natural History), and Publisher's Editor, Elsevier, 1960–70; Teacher: Brentford Sch. for Girls, 1972–76; Pimlico Sch., 1976–79; Abbey Wood Sch., 1979–84. Member: Secondary Exam. Council, 1986–88 (Chair, A Level and GCSE Biology and Music Cttees); Secondary Heads Council, 1993–98; SHA Exec., 1994–98; various DES Steering Gps; Adv. Gp on Raising Achievement of Ethnic-minority Children; ASE, 1972–; BEMAS, 1984–; Dir, CRAC Council, 1996–; Mem., Nat. Adv. Cttee on Creativity and Cultural Educn, 1997–99; Founder, Nat. Schs Playwright Commning Gp, 1995–; Heads' Appraiser, GDST, 1998–; Dir, Lifelong Learning Foundn, 1999–; Trustee: Menerva (formerly 300 Gp) Educnl Trust, 1990–99; Soc. for Furtherance of Critical Philosophy (also Chair); I Can (Special Needs charity), 1997–; Little Angel Theatre, 2001–. Mem. Council, UCS, 1995–. Patron, Students Exploring Marriage, 2001. Scientific Fellow, Zoological Soc. of London, 1966; FRSA 1995. *Publications:* (contrib.) Education 14–19: critical perspectives, 1997; (contrib.) New Teachers in an Urban Comprehensive School, 1997; Managing ICT in the Secondary School, 2001; scientific illustrations in textbooks. *Recreations:* fun, theatre, painting, gardening, walking, swimming, sailing. *Address:* 28 Almeida Street, N1 1TD. *T:* (020) 7689 0493; Hilltop, Rissemere, Reydon, Southwold, Suffolk IP18 6SP. *T:* (01502) 723624; *e-mail:* tamsyn@sthwold.demon.co.uk.

IMRAN KHAN, (Imran Ahmad Khan Niazi); *see* Khan.

IMRAY, Sir Colin (Henry), KBE 1992; CMG 1983; HM Diplomatic Service, retired; Director, Overseas Relations, St John Ambulance, 1997–98; *b* 21 Sept. 1933; *s* of late Henry Gibbon Imray and Frances Olive Imray; *m* 1957, Shirley Margaret Matthews; one *s* three *d. Educ:* Highgate Sch.; Hotchkiss Sch., Conn; Balliol Coll., Oxford (2nd cl. Hons PPE, MA). Served in Seaforth Highlanders and RWAFF, Sierra Leone, 1952–54. CRO, 1957; Canberra, 1958–61; CRO, 1961–63; Nairobi, 1963–66; FCO, 1966–70; British Trade Comr, Montreal, 1970–73; Counsellor, Head of Chancery and Consul-Gen., Islamabad, 1973–77; RCDS, 1977; Commercial Counsellor, Tel Aviv, 1977–80; Rayner Project Officer, 1980; Dep. High Comr, Bombay, 1980–84; Asst Under-Sec. of State (Dep. Chief Clerk and Chief Inspector), FCO, 1984–85; High Commissioner: Tanzania, 1986–89; Bangladesh, 1989–93; Sec. Gen., Order of St John, 1993–97. Chm., Royal Over-Seas League, 2000–. KStJ 1993. *Address:* Holbrook House, Reading Road, Wallingford OX10 9DT. *Clubs:* Travellers, Royal Over-Seas League.

INCH, Thomas David, OBE 2000; CChem, FRSC; Secretary-General, Royal Society of Chemistry, 1993–2000; *b* 25 Sept. 1938; *s* of Thomas Alexander Inch and Sarah Lang Graves Inch; *m* 1964, Jacqueline Vivienne Pudner; one *d. Educ:* St Austell Grammar Sch.; Univ. of Birmingham (BSc 1st Cl. Hons Chem. 1960; PhD 1963; DSc 1971). Salters Fellow, Univ. of Birmingham, 1963–64; Vis. Fellow, NIH, USA, 1964–65; Chemical Defence Estabt, MoD, 1965–87 (RCDS 1985); Gen. Manager, Research Business Development, BP Research, 1987–90; Vice-Pres., R&D, BP America, 1990–93. Director: BP Ventures, 1987–89; Edison Polymer Innovation Corp., 1990–92; Ohio Science and Technology Commn, 1992. Chm., Nat. Adv. Cttee, Chemical Weapons Convention, 1997–. *Publications:* papers and reviews on chemistry and related topics. *Recreation:* golf. *Address:* 16 Ashlands, Ford, Salisbury SP4 6DY. *Club:* High Post Golf.

INCHBALD, Michael John Chantrey, FCSD; architectural and interior designer; design consultant, since 1983; *b* 8 March 1920; *s* of late Geoffrey H. E. Inchbald and Rosemary, *d* of Arthur Ilbert and *niece* of Sir Courtenay Ilbert, GCB, KCSI, CIE; *m* 1955, Jacqueline Bromley (marr. diss. 1964; *see* J. A. Duncan); one *s* one *d*; *m* 1964, Eunice Haymes (marr. diss. 1970). *Educ:* Sherborne; Architect. Assoc. Sch. of Architecture. FCSD (MSIA 1947). Director, Michael Inchbald Ltd, 1953–83. Work exhibited: Triennale, Milan; V & A Mus.; Design Centres London, New York, Helsinki. Design projects for: Bank of America; Crown Estate Comrs; Cunard; Dunhill worldwide; Ferragamo; Imperial Group; Justerini & Brooks; Law Soc.; John Lewis; Manufacturers Hanover Bank; Manufacturers Hanover Trust Bank; John Player; Plessey Co.; Pratt Burnard Engineering; Savoy Group—Berkeley, Claridges and Savoy hotels, and the restaurant complex Stones Chop House; Scottish Highland Industries; Trust House Forte—Post House, London Airport and several restaurants; Wolsey; ships, QE2, Carmania, Franconia and Windsor Castle; royal and private yachts and houses. Consultant to furniture and carpet manufacturers. Consulted *re* changes at Buckingham Palace; other projects, for the Duc de la Rochefoucauld, 13th Duke of St Albans, 8th Marquess of Ailesbury, 6th Marquess of Bristol, 17th Earl of Perth, 9th Earl of Dartmouth, 2nd Earl St Aldwyn, 3rd Baron Gisborough, 6th Baron Kilmarnock, 7th Baron Latymer, and 4th Baron St Levan. Inchbald schs founded under his auspices, 1960. Winner of four out of four nat. design competitions entered, including: Shapes of Things to Come, 1946; Nat. Chair Design Competition, 1955. Freeman, Clockmakers' Co., 1985. *Publications:* contrib. Arch. Rev., Arch. Digest, Connaissance des Arts, Connoisseur, Country Life, Harpers/Queen, House & Garden, Internat. Lighting Rev., Tatler, and Vogue. *Recreations:* arts, travel, antiques. *Address:* Stanley House, 10 Milner Street, SW3 2PU. *T:* (020) 7584 8832.

INCHCAPE, 4th Earl of, *cr* 1929; **Kenneth Peter Lyle Mackay,** AIB; Viscount Glenapp 1929; Viscount Inchcape 1924; Baron Inchcape 1911; Director: Inchcape Family Investments Ltd, since 1985; Assam Investments Ltd, since 1985; Assam Company Ltd, since 1995; Gray Dawes Travel Ltd; *b* 23 Jan. 1943; *er s* of 3rd Earl of Inchcape, and of his 1st wife, Mrs Aline Thorn Hannay, *d* of Sir Richard Pease, 2nd Bt; *S* father, 1994; *m* 1966, Georgina, *d* of late S. C. Nisbet and Mrs G. R. Sutton; one *s* two *d. Educ:* Eton. Late Lieut 9/12th Royal Lancers. Master, Grocers' Co., 1993–94; Prime Warden, Shipwrights' Co., 1998–99. *Recreations:* shooting, fishing, golf, farming. *Heir: s* Viscount Glenapp, *qv*. *Address:* Manor Farm, Clyffe Pypard, Swindon, Wilts SN4 7PY; 63E Pont Street, SW1X 0BD. *Clubs:* White's, Oriental, Pratt's; New (Edinburgh); Royal Sydney (Sydney, NSW).

INCHIQUIN, 18th Baron of, *cr* 1543; **Conor Myles John O'Brien;** (The O'Brien); Bt 1686; Prince of Thomond; Chief of the Name; *b* 17 July 1943; *s* of Hon. Fionn Myles Maryons O'Brien (*d* 1977) (*y s* of 15th Baron) and of Josephine Reine, *d* of late Joseph Eugene Bembaron; *S* uncle, 1982; *m* 1988, Helen, *d* of Gerald Fitzgerald O'Farrell; two *d. Educ:* Eton. Served as Captain, 14th/20th King's Hussars. *Heir: cousin* Murrough Richard O'Brien [*b* 25 May 1910; *m* 1st, 1942, Irene Clarice (marr. diss. 1951), *o d* of H. W. Richards; 2nd, 1952, Joan, *d* of Charles Pierre Jenkinson and *widow* of Captain Woolf Barnato; one *s* one *d*]. *Address:* Thomond House, Dromoland, Newmarket on Fergus, Co. Clare, Ireland.

INCHYRA, 2nd Baron *cr* 1962, of St Madoes, Co. Perth; **Robert Charles Reneke Hoyer Millar;** Chairman, National Association of Clubs for Young People (formerly NABC—Clubs for Young People), since 1994; *b* 4 April 1935; *er s* of 1st Baron Inchyra, GCMG, CVO and Elizabeth de Marees van Swinderen; *S* father, 1989; *m* 1961, Fiona Mary, *d* of Major E. C. R. Sheffield; one *s* two *d. Educ:* Eton; New Coll., Oxford. J. Henry

Schroder Wagg & Co., 1958–64; Barclays Bank, 1964–88: Local Dir, Newcastle upon Tyne, 1967–75; Reg. Gen. Man., 1976–81; Dep. Chm., Barclays Bank Trust Co., 1982–85; Gen. Man. and Dir, UK Financial Services, 1985–88; Sec. (later Dir) Gen., BBA, 1988–94. Chm., Johnson Fry European Utilities Trust plc, 1994–; Dir, Witan Investment Co., 1979–. *Heir: s* Hon. Christian James Charles Hoyer Millar [*b* 12 Aug. 1962; *m* 1992, Caroline, *d* of Robin Swan; one *s* one *d*]. *Address:* Rookley Manor, Kings Somborne, Stockbridge, Hants SO20 6QX. *T:* (01794) 388319. *Clubs:* White's, Pratt's.

IND, Jack Kenneth; Teacher, Eastbourne College, 2001–Aug. 2002; Headmaster of Dover College, 1981–91; *b* 20 Jan. 1935; *s* of late Rev. William Price Ind and Mrs Doris Maud Ind (*née* Cavell); *m* 1964, Elizabeth Olive Toombs; two *s* two *d*. *Educ:* Marlborough Coll.; St John's Coll., Oxford (BA Hons Mods, 2nd Cl. Class. Lit. and Lit. Hum.). Assistant Master: Wellingborough Sch., 1960–63; Tonbridge Sch., 1963–81 (Housemaster, 1970–81) and 1991–92; Eastbourne Coll., 1992–93; Teacher, Gymnásium, Nové Zámky, Slovakia, 1994; Assistant Teacher: Talbot Heath Sch., Bournemouth, 1996–97; Eastbourne Coll., 1997–98; Teacher, Prior Park Coll., Bath, 1999–2001. Trustee, HMC projects in Central and Eastern Europe. *Recreations:* tennis, Rugby football, music, reading. *Address:* Salvete, 39 Sandridge Road, Melksham, Wilts SN12 7BQ. *T:* (01225) 709925.

IND, Rt Rev. William; *see* Truro, Bishop of.

INDIAN OCEAN, Archibishop of the, since 1995; **Most Rev. Remi Joseph Rabenirina;** Bishop of Antananarivo, since 1984; *b* 6 March 1938; *s* of Joseph Razafindrabe and Josephine Ramanantenasoa; *m* 1971, Elizabeth Razaizanany; two *s* four *d*. *Educ:* Protestant Church schs; St Paul's Theol Coll., Ambatoharanana, Madagascar; Univ. of Madagascar; St Chad's Theol Coll., Lichfield; Ecumenical Inst. of Bossey, Switzerland. School teacher, 1958–61; Parish Priest: St James', Toamasina, 1967–68; St Matthew's, Antsiranana, 1968–73; St John's, Ambohimangakely (Antananarivo), 1973–84; Diocesan Chancellor, Antananarivo, 1982–84. Chevalier de l'Ordre National (Malagasy). *Publications:* (in Malagasy) An Open Door: a short history of the beginning of the Anglican Church in Northern Madagascar, 1969; (trans.) J. C. Fenton, Preaching the Cross, 1990; Some of the Saints (biogs of Saints remembered in the Anglican Church Calendar, Madagascar), 1998. *Recreations:* reading, writing. *Address:* Evêché Anglican Ambohimanoro, 101 Antananarivo, Madagascar. *T:* (20) 2220827.

INGAMELLS, John Anderson Stuart; art historian; *b* 12 Nov. 1934; *s* of late George Harry Ingamells and Gladys Lucy (*née* Rollett); *m* 1964, Hazel Wilson; two *d*. *Educ:* Hastings Grammar School; Eastbourne Grammar School; Fitzwilliam House, Cambridge. National Service, Army (Cyprus), 1956–58; Art Asst, York Art Gallery, 1959–63; Asst Keeper, Dept of Art, National Museum of Wales, 1963–67; Curator, York Art Gallery, 1967–77; Asst to the Director, 1977–78, Director, 1978–92, Wallace Collection. Mem. Exec. Cttee, NACF, 1992–97. *Publications:* The Davies Collection of French Art, 1967; The English Episcopal Portrait, 1981; (ed) Dictionary of British and Irish Travellers in Italy 1701–1800, 1997; (ed jtly) The Letters of Sir Joshua Reynolds, 2001; numerous catalogues, including: Philip Mercier (with Robert Raines), 1969; Portraits at Bishopthorpe Palace, 1972; Paintings by Allan Ramsay (ed), 1999; museum catalogues at York, Cardiff and the Wallace Collection; articles in Apollo, Connoisseur, Burlington Magazine, Walpole Soc., etc. *Address:* 39 Benson Road, SE23 3RL.

INGE, family name of **Baron Inge**.

INGE, Baron *cr* 1997 (Life Peer), of Richmond in the co. of North Yorkshire; **Field Marshal Peter Anthony Inge,** KG 2001; GCB 1992 (KCB 1988); DL; Chief of the Defence Staff, 1994–97; Constable, HM Tower of London, 1996–2001; *b* 5 Aug. 1935; *s* of Raymond Albert Inge and late Grace Maud Caroline Inge (*née* Du Rose); *m* 1960, Letitia Marion Beryl, *yr d* of late Trevor and Sylvia Thornton-Berry; two *d*. *Educ:* Summer Fields; Wrekin College; RMA Sandhurst. Commissioned Green Howards, 1956; served Hong Kong, Malaya, Germany, Libya and UK; ADC to GOC 4 Div., 1960–61; Adjutant, 1 Green Howards, 1963–64; student, Staff Coll., 1966; MoD, 1967–69; Coy Comdr, 1 Green Howards, 1969–70; student, JSSC, 1971; BM 11 Armd Bde, 1972; Instructor, Staff Coll., 1973–74; CO 1 Green Howards, 1974–76; Comdt, Junior Div., Staff Coll., 1977–79; Comdr Task Force C/4 Armd Bde, 1980–81; Chief of Staff, HQ 1 (BR) Corps, 1982–83; GOC NE District and Comdr 2nd Inf. Div., 1984–86; Dir Gen. Logistic Policy (Army), MoD, 1986–87; Comdr 1st (Br.) Corps, 1987–89; Comdr Northern Army Gp, and C-in-C, BAOR, 1989–92; CGS 1992–94. ADC Gen. to the Queen, 1991–94. Colonel, The Green Howards, 1982–94. Col Comdt: RMP, 1987–92; APTC, 1988–97. Non-exec. Dir, Racal Electronics plc, 1997–2000. Comr, Royal Hosp. Chelsea, 1998–; Trustee, Historic Royal Palaces, 1999–. Pres., Army Benevolent Fund, 1998–; Mem. Council, St George's House, Windsor Castle, 1998–. Hon. DCL Newcastle, 1995. DL N Yorks, 1994. *Recreations:* cricket, walking, music and reading, especially military history. *Address:* c/o House of Lords, SW1A 0PW. *Clubs:* Boodle's, Beefsteak, Army and Navy, MCC.

INGE, George Patrick Francis, FRICS; Chairman, FPD Savills (formerly Savills Land & Property) Ltd, 1992–2000; *b* 31 Aug. 1941; *s* of late John William Wolstenholme Inge and Alison Lilias Inge; *m* 1977, Joyce (*née* Leinster); one *s* one *d*. *Educ:* Old Malthouse Prep. Sch., Dorset; Sherborne Sch. Joined Alfred Savill & Sons, 1960; Partner, 1968; Man. Partner, Savills, 1985; Chief Exec., 1987–91, and Chm., 1987–95, Savills Plc. Non-exec. Chm., Severn Trent Property Ltd, 1995–; non-exec. Dir, Westbury plc, 1995–. Governor: Old Malthouse Sch., Dorset, 1977–98 (Chm., 1986–98); Cothill House Sch., 1989–; Nottingham Trent Univ., 1994–96; Downe House Sch., 1996– (Chm., 1999–). *Recreations:* shooting, fishing, golf. *Address:* The Old Vicarage, Little Milton, Oxford OX44 7QB. *T:* (01844) 279538. *Clubs:* Buck's, Flyfishers', Farmers'.

INGE-INNES-LILLINGSTON, George David, CVO 1993; CBE 1986; DL; MA; a Crown Estates Commissioner, 1974–93; *b* 13 Nov. 1923; *s* of late Comdr H. W. Innes-Lillingston, RN, and Mrs Innes-Lillingston, formerly of Lochalsh House, Balmacara, Kyle, Ross-shire; *m* 1st, 1946, Alison Mary (*d* 1947), *er d* of late Canon F. W. Green, MA, BD, Norwich; one *d*; 2nd, 1955, Elizabeth Violet Grizel Thomson-Inge, *yr d* of late Lt-Gen. Sir William Thomson, KCMG, CB, MC; two *s* one *d*. *Educ:* Stowe, Buckingham; Merton Coll., Oxford (MA Hons Agric.). Served War as Lieut RNVR, 1942–45, Lt-Comdr RNR, 1966. Member: Agricultural Land Tribunal, 1962–72; Minister's Agricultural Panel for W Midlands, 1972–76; Council for Charitable Support, 1985–90; Chairman: N Birmingham and District Hosps, 1968–74; Agric. and Hort. Cttee, BSI, 1980–86; President: Staffs Agricultural Soc., 1970–71; CLA, 1979–81 (Pres., Staffs Br., 1983–94). Dir, Lands Improvement Gp Ltd, and associated cos, 1983–91; Chm., Croxden Horticultural Products Ltd, 1986–91. Chm., Midland Reg., STA, 1983–94. Trustee, Lichfield Cathedral, 1980–99. FRAgS 1986. JP 1967–74, DL 1969, Staffs; High Sheriff, Staffs, 1966. Bledisloe Gold Medal for Landowners, RASE, 1991. *Recreation:* growing trees. *Address:* The Old Kennels, Thorpe Constantine, Tamworth, Staffs B79 0LH. *T:* (01827) 830224. *Clubs:* Boodle's, Farmers', Royal Thames Yacht; Royal Highland Yacht (Oban).

INGESTRE, Viscount; James Richard Charles John Chetwynd-Talbot; *b* 11 Jan. 1978; *s* and *heir* of 22nd Earl of Shrewsbury and Waterford, *qv*. *Educ:* Shrewsbury Sch.; Royal Agricl Coll.

INGHAM, Sir Bernard, Kt 1990; Chairman, Bernard Ingham Communications, since 1990; *b* 21 June 1932; *s* of Garnet and Alice Ingham; *m* 1956, Nancy Hilda Hoyle; one *s*. *Educ:* Hebden Bridge Grammar Sch., Yorks. Reporter: Hebden Bridge Times, 1948–52; Yorkshire Post and Yorkshire Evening Post, Halifax, 1952–59; Yorkshire Post, Leeds, 1959–61; Northern Industrial Correspondent, Yorkshire Post, 1961; Reporter, The Guardian, 1962–65; Labour Staff, The Guardian, London, 1965–67; Press and Public Relns Adviser, NBPI, 1967–68; Chief Inf. Officer, DEP, 1968–73; Dir of Information: Dept of Employment, 1973; Dept of Energy, 1974–77; Under Sec., Energy Conservation Div., Dept of Energy, 1978–79; Chief Press Sec. to Prime Minister, 1979–90; Head, Govt Inf. Service, 1989–90. Columnist: The Express (formerly Daily Express), 1991–98; PR Week, 1994–. Dir, Burley Ingham Consultancy, 1999–; non-executive Director: McDonald's Restaurants Ltd, 1991–; Hill and Knowlton (UK) Ltd, public relations counsel, 1991–. Vis. Fellow, Univ. of Newcastle, 1989–; Visiting Professor: Middlesex Univ. Business Sch., 1998–; Univ. of Huddersfield, 2001–. Pres., British Franchise Assoc., 1993–. Sec., Supporters of Nuclear Energy, 1998–. Mem. Council Univ. of Huddersfield, 1994–2000. Hon. DLitt Buckingham, 1997; DUniv Middlesex, 1999. *Publications:* Kill The Messenger, 1991; Yorkshire Millennium, 1999. *Recreations:* walking, gardening, reading. *Address:* 9 Monahan Avenue, Purley, Surrey CR8 3BB. *T:* (020) 8660 8970, *Fax:* (020) 8668 4357. *Club:* Reform.

INGHAM, Christopher John; HM Diplomatic Service; Ambassador to Republic of Uzbekistan and (non-resident) to Republic of Tajikistan, since 1999; *b* 4 June 1944; *s* of Dr Roland Ingham and Dorothy Ingham; *m* 1968, Jacqueline Anne Clarke; one *s* two *d*. *Educ:* St John's Coll., Cambridge (MA). Mgt trainee, Cadbury Bros Ltd, 1966–68; joined HM Diplomatic Service, 1968: Moscow, 1972–74; Calcutta, 1974; Kuwait, 1974–76; FCO, 1976–80; Dep. Perm. Rep. to IAEA/UNIDO, Vienna, 1980–85; FCO, 1985–87; Hd, Commercial Section, Mexico City, 1987–89; FCO, 1989–91; Counsellor and Dep. Hd of Mission, Bucharest, 1991–95; Counsellor, EU and Economic, Madrid, 1995–99. *Recreations:* hill-walking, choral singing. *Address:* c/o Foreign and Commonwealth Office, King Charles Street, SW1A 2AH.

INGHAM, Prof. Kenneth, OBE 1961; MC 1946; Professor of History, 1967–84, Part-time Professor of History, 1984–86, now Emeritus Professor, and Head of History Department, 1970–84, University of Bristol; *b* 9 Aug. 1921; *s* of Gladson and Frances Lily Ingham; *m* 1949, Elizabeth Mary Southall; one *s* one *d*. *Educ:* Bingley Grammar Sch.; Keble Coll., Oxford (Exhibitioner). Served with West Yorks Regt, 1941–46 (despatches, 1945). Frere Exhibitioner in Indian Studies, University of Oxford, 1947; DPhil 1950. Lecturer in Modern History, Makerere Coll., Uganda, 1950–56, Prof., 1956–62; Dir of Studies, RMA, Sandhurst, 1962–67. MLC, Uganda, 1954–61. *Publications:* Reformers in India, 1956; The Making of Modern Uganda, 1958; A History of East Africa, 1962; The Kingdom of Toro in Uganda, 1975; Jan Christian Smuts: the conscience of a South African, 1986; Politics in Modern Africa, 1990; Obote: a political biography, 1994; contrib. to Encyclopædia Britannica, Britannica Book of the Year. *Address:* The Woodlands, 94 West Town Lane, Bristol BS4 5DZ.

INGHAM, Rt Rev. Michael; *see* New Westminster, Bishop of.

INGHAM, Stuart Edward; Chief Executive, United Leeds Teaching Hospitals NHS Trust, 1991–98; *b* 9 Oct. 1942; *s* of Edward Ingham and Dorothy Mary (*née* Pollard); *m* 1969, Jane Stella Wilkinson; one *s* one *d*. *Educ:* Canon Slade Grammar Sch., Bolton. AHSM 1970. Bolton and District HMC: Trainee in Hosp. Admin, 1965–66; HCO, 1966–67; Dep. Gen. Supt, Ancoats Hosp., 1967–69; Sen. Admin Asst, Royal Bucks and Associated HMC, 1969–70; Hospital Secretary: Harefield Hosp., 1970–73; St James's Univ. Hosp., Leeds, 1973–74; Leeds Area Health Authority (Eastern): General Administrator, 1974–77; Dist Administrator, 1977–82; York Health Authority: Dist Administrator, 1982–84; Dist Gen. Manager, 1985–88; Dist Gen. Manager, Leeds Western HA, 1988–90. *Recreation:* equestrian sports. *Address:* The Turnings, Woodacre Crescent, Bardsey, Leeds LS17 9DQ. *T:* (01937) 572673.

INGILBY, Sir Thomas (Colvin William), 6th Bt *cr* 1866; FAAV; managing own estate; *b* 17 July 1955; *s* of Sir Joslan William Vivian Ingilby, 5th Bt, DL, JP, and of Diana, *d* of late Sir George Colvin, CB, CMG, DSO; *S* father, 1974; *m* 1984, Emma Clare Roebuck, *d* of Major R. R. Thompson, Whinfield, Strensall, York; four *s* one *d*. *Educ:* Aysgarth Sch., Bedale; Eton Coll.; Royal Agricultural Coll., Cirencester. MRAC; MRICS; MBII. Joined Army, May 1974, but discharged on death of father; Assistant: Stephenson & Son, York, 1978–80; Strutt & Parker, Harrogate, 1981–83. Chairman: Harrogate Mgt Centre Ltd, 1991–99; Action Harrogate Ltd, 1992–98. Chm., Mktg Ops and Vice-Chm., Private Sector Members Cttees, Yorks Tourist Bd, 1999–. Founder and Nat. Co-ordinator, Stately Homes Hotline, 1988–2001; Pres., Council for Prevention of Art Theft, 1991–; Chm., Yorkshire's Great Houses, Castles and Gardens, 1995–; Jt Chm., Great Inns of Britain, 1996–. Mem., Ripon Area Deanery Synod, 2000–; Chm., Dio. of Ripon and Leeds Church Tourism Initiative, 2001–. President: Nidderdale Amateur Cricket League, 1979–; Harrogate Gilbert and Sullivan Soc., 1988–. Mem., British Deer Farmers Assoc. Pres., Millennium Appeal, Queen Margaret's Sch., Escrick. Internat. Hon. Citizen, New Orleans, 1979. *Recreations:* cricket, tennis, reading, writing, lecturing. *Heir:* *s* James William Francis Ingilby, *b* 15 June 1985. *Address:* Ripley Castle, Ripley, near Harrogate, North Yorkshire HG3 3AY. *T:* (01423) 770152; *e-mail:* sirthomas@ripleycastle. co.uk.

INGLE, Alan Richmond, CMG 2000; HM Diplomatic Service; Counsellor, Foreign and Commonwealth Office, since 2000; *b* 16 Oct. 1939; *s* of late Henry Ingle and of Helen Ingle (*née* Keating); *m* 1963, Gillian Hall; one *s* one *d*. *Educ:* Stand Grammar Sch. and Prince Rupert Sch., Wilhelmshaven. Entered BoT, 1957; Accra (Trade Commn Service), 1961–65; FO, 1965–66; Kingston, 1966–70; Third Sec., Christchurch, 1970–74; Second Secretary: FCO, 1974–77; (Commercial), Singapore, 1977–81; First Sec., FCO, 1981–83; Consul and Dir, British Inf. Services, NY, 1983–88; First Sec., FCO 1988–93; Counsellor (Mgt), Lagos and Abuja, 1993–96; Hd of Delegn, Jt Mgt Office, Brussels, 1996–2000. *Address:* Martins Cottage, Furley, Axminster, Devon EX13 7TR. *T:* (01404) 881735. *Club:* Royal Over-Seas League.

INGLEBY, 2nd Viscount *cr* 1955, of Snilesworth; **Martin Raymond Peake;** landowner; Director, Hargreaves Group Ltd, 1960–80; *b* 31 May 1926; *s* of 1st Viscount Ingleby, and Joan, Viscountess Ingleby (*d* 1979); *S* father, 1966; *m* 1952, Susan (*d* 1996), *d* of late Henderson Russell Landale; four *d* (one *s* decd). *Educ:* Eton; Trinity Coll., Oxford (MA). Called to the Bar, Inner Temple, 1956. Sec., Hargreaves Group Ltd, 1958–61. Administrative Staff Coll., 1961. CC Yorks (North Riding), 1964–67. Mem., N Yorks Moors Nat. Park Planning Cttee, 1968–78. *Heir:* none. *Address:* Snilesworth, Northallerton, North Yorks DL6 3QD.

INGLEDOW, Anthony Brian, OBE 1969; HM Diplomatic Service, retired; Counsellor, Foreign and Commonwealth Office, 1983–93; *b* 25 July 1928; *s* of Cedric Francis Ingledow and Doris Evelyn Ingledow (*née* Worrall); *m* 1956, Margaret Monica, *d* of Sir Reginald Watson-Jones, FRCS; one *s* one *d*. *Educ:* St Bees School; London Univ. Served HM Forces, 1947–49. Joined Colonial Administrative Service, Nigeria, 1950; District Officer: Auchi, 1954; Oyo, 1956; Secretariat, Ibadan, 1958, retired 1960; joined HM Diplomatic Service, 1961; 2nd Secretary, Khartoum, 1962; FO, 1964; 1st Secretary, Aden, 1966; Lagos, 1967; FCO, 1970; Dakar, 1972; FCO, 1975. *Recreations:* reading, travel. *Address:* c/o Lloyds TSB, 8–10 Waterloo Place, SW1Y 4BE. *Club:* Athenæum.

INGLEFIELD-WATSON, Lt-Col Sir John (Forbes), 5th Bt *cr* 1895, of Earnock, Co. Lanarks; *b* 16 May 1926; *s* of Sir Derrick William Inglefield Watson, Bt, TD (who changed family surname to Inglefield-Watson by Deed Poll, 1945) and Margrett Georgina (*née* Robertson-Aikman, later Savill) (*d* 1995); *S* father, 1987. *Educ:* Eton College. MIMgt. Enlisted RE, 1944; short course, Trinity Coll., Cambridge, 1944–45; commnd RE, 1946; served in Iraq, Egypt, Kenya, Libya, Cyprus, Germany, N Ireland; psc 1958; Major 1959; Lt-Col 1969; retired 1981. Association Football Referee: Class I, 1954; Chm. Army FA Referees Cttee, 1974–78; FA Staff Referee Instructor, 1978–. Mem. Council, Kent County FA, 1975–81; Hon. Vice-Pres., Army FA, 1982–92. *Recreations:* Association football refereeing; philately. *Heir: cousin* Simon Conran Hamilton Watson [*b* 11 Aug. 1939; *m* 1971, Madeleine Stiles (*d* 1998), *e d* of late Wagner Mahlon Dickerson]. *Address:* The Ross, Hamilton, Lanarkshire ML3 7UF. *T:* (01698) 283734.

INGLESE, Anthony Michael Christopher; Deputy Treasury Solicitor, since 1997; *b* 19 Dec. 1951; *s* of Angelo Inglese and Dora Inglese (*née* Di Paola); *m* 1974, Jane Elizabeth Kerry Bailes; one *s* one *d*. *Educ:* Salvatorian Coll., Harrow Weald; Fitzwilliam Coll., Cambridge (MA, LLB). Called to the Bar, Gray's Inn, 1976; Legal Advr's Br., Home Office, 1975–86; Legal Secretariat to Law Officers, 1986–88; Legal Advr's Br., Home Office, 1988–91; Legal Dir, OFT, 1991–95; Legal Advr, MoD (Treasury Solicitor's Dept), 1995–97. *Address:* Treasury Solicitor's Department, Queen Anne's Chambers, 28 Broadway, SW1H 9JS. *Club:* Institute of Contemporary Arts.

INGLEWOOD, 2nd Baron *cr* 1964; **(William) Richard Fletcher-Vane;** DL; Member (C) North West Region, England, European Parliament, since 1999; *b* 31 July 1951; *e s* of 1st Baron Inglewood, TD and Mary (*d* 1982), *e d* of Major Sir Richard George Proby, 1st Bt, MC; *S* father, 1989; *m* 1986, Cressida, *y d* of late Desmond Pemberton-Pigott, CMG; one *s* two *d*. *Educ:* Eton; Trinity Coll., Cambridge (MA); Cumbria Coll. of Agriculture and Forestry. ARICS. Called to the Bar, Lincoln's Inn, 1975. Member: Lake Dist Special Planning Bd, 1984–90 (Chm., Develt Control Cttee, 1984–89); NW Water Authority, 1987–89. Contested (C) Houghton and Washington, 1983; Durham, European Parlt, 1984; MEP (C) Cumbria and Lancashire N, 1989–94; contested (C) Cumbria and Lancashire N, Eur. Parly elecns, 1994. Cons. spokesman on legal affairs, EP, 1989–94; Dep. Whip, EDG, 1992–94, Chief Whip, 1994. A Lord in Waiting (Govt Whip), 1994–95; Captain of HM Yeomen of the Guard (Dep. Govt Chief Whip), 1995; Parly Under-Sec. of State, DNH, 1995–97; elected Mem., H of L, 1999. DL Cumbria, 1993. *Heir: s* Hon. Henry William Frederick Fletcher-Vane, *b* 24 Dec. 1990. *Address:* Hutton-in-the-Forest, Penrith, Cumbria CA11 9TH. *T:* (01768) 484500, *Fax:* (01768) 484571. *Clubs:* Pratt's, Travellers.

INGLIS, Sir Brian Scott, AC 1988; Kt 1977; FTSE; Chairman: Optus Communications, 1992–96; Scalzo Automotive Research Ltd, 1986–95; *b* Adelaide, 3 Jan. 1924; *s* of late E. S. Inglis, Albany, WA; *m* 1953, Leila, *d* of E. V. Butler; three *d*. *Educ:* Geelong Church of England Grammar School; Trinity Coll., Univ. of Melbourne (BSc; Mem. Council, 1985). Served War of 1939–45; Flying Officer, RAAF, 453 Sqdn, 1942–45. Director and Gen. Manufacturing Manager, 1963–70, first Australian Man. Dir, Ford Motor Co. of Australia Ltd, 1970–81, Vice-Pres., 1981–83, Chm. 1981–85; Chm., Ford Asia-Pacific Inc., 1983–84. Chairman: Newcrest Mining (formerly Newmont Holdings), 1985–94; Aerospace Technologies of Aust. Pty Ltd, 1987–94; Amcor, 1989–94 (Dep. Chm., 1988–89; Dir, 1984–94); non-exec. Dir, Australian Paper, 1994–98. Chm., Defence Industry Cttee, 1984–87 (Mem., 1982–87). Chm., Centre for Molecular Biology and Medicine, Monash Univ. Hon. LLD Monash. James N. Kirby Medal, IProdE, 1979; Kernot Medal, Faculty of Engrg, Univ. of Melbourne, 1979. *Address:* 10 Bowley Avenue, Balwyn, Victoria 3103, Australia. *Clubs:* Australian (Melbourne); Barwon Heads Golf.

INGLIS, George Bruton; Senior Partner, Slaughter and May, 1986–92; *b* 19 April 1933; *s* of late Cecil George Inglis and Ethel Mabel Inglis; *m* 1968, Patricia Mary Forbes; three *s*. *Educ:* Winchester College; Pembroke College, Oxford (MA). Solicitor. Partner, Slaughter and May, 1966–92. *Recreation:* gardening.

INGLIS, Heather Hughson; *see* Swindells, H. H.

INGLIS, Ian Grahame, CB 1983; Chairman, State Grants Commission, Tasmania, since 1990; *b* 2 April 1929; *s* of late William and Ellen Jean Inglis; *m* 1952, Elaine Arlene Connors; three *s* one *d*. *Educ:* Hutchins Sch., Hobart; Univ. of Tasmania (BComm). Agricl Economist, Tasmanian Dept. of Agric., 1951–58; Economist, State Treasury, 1958–69; Chairman: Rivers and Water Supply Commn, and Metropolitan Water Bd, 1969–77; NW Regl Water Authority, 1977; State Under Treasurer, Tas, 1977–89. Dir, TGIO Ltd (formerly Tasmanian Govt Insce Bd), 1989–96. Chm., Retirement Benefits Fund Investment Trust, 1989–95. Member: Ambulance Commn of Tasmania, 1959–65; Tasmanian Grain Elevators Bd, 1962–65; Clarence Municipal Commn, 1965–69; Motor Accidents Insurance Bd, 1991–95. Dir, Comalco Aluminium (Bell Bay) Ltd, 1980–95. *Recreations:* yacht-racing, gardening, bridge. *Address:* 5 Sayer Crescent, Sandy Bay, Hobart, Tas 7005, Australia. *T:* (3) 62231928. *Clubs:* Tasmanian, Royal Yacht of Tasmania (Hobart).

INGLIS, Prof. Kenneth Stanley, DPhil; Professor of History, Australian National University, 1977–94, retired; *b* 7 Oct. 1929; *s* of S. W. Inglis; *m* 1st, 1952, Judy Betheras (*d* 1962); one *s* two *d*; 2nd, 1965, Amirah Gust. *Educ:* Univ. of Melbourne (MA); Univ. of Oxford (DPhil). Sen. Lectr in History, Univ. of Adelaide, 1956–60; Reader in History, 1960–62; Associate Prof. of History, Australian National Univ., 1962–65; Prof., 1965–66; Prof. of History, Univ. of Papua New Guinea, 1966–72, Vice-Chancellor, 1972–75; Professorial Fellow in Hist., ANU, 1975–77. Vis. Prof. of Australian Studies, Harvard, 1982; Vis. Prof., Univ. of Hawaii, 1985; Vis. Fellow, St John's Coll., Cambridge, 1990–91. Hon. DLitt Melbourne, 1996. Jt Gen. Editor, Australians: a historical library, 1987–88. *Publications:* Hospital and Community, 1958; The Stuart Case, 1961; Churches and the Working Classes in Victorian England, 1963; The Australian Colonists, 1974; This is the ABC: the Australian Broadcasting Commission, 1932–1983, 1983; The Rehearsal: Australians at War in the Sudan 1885, 1985; (ed and introduced) Nation: the life of an independent journal 1958–1972, 1989; Sacred Places: war memorials in the Australian landscape, 1998; Anzac Remembered: selected writings, 1998; Observing Australia, 1959–1999, 1999. *Address:* PO Box 5, O'Connor, Canberra, ACT 2602, Australia.

INGLIS, Richard Anthony Girvan; His Honour Judge Inglis; a Circuit Judge, since 1996; *b* 28 Dec. 1947; *s* of Angus Inglis and Kathleen Flora Inglis; *m* 1976, Heather Hughson Swindells, *qv*; one *s*. *Educ:* Marlborough Coll.; Selwyn Coll., Cambridge (BA 1969). Called to the Bar, Middle Temple, 1971; Jun., Midland and Oxford Circuit, 1984; Recorder, 1993–96. *Recreations:* garden, music, church bell ringing. *Address:* Lincoln Combined Court Centre, 360 High Street, Lincoln LN5 7RL. *Club:* Lansdowne.

INGLIS of Glencorse, Sir Roderick (John), 10th Bt *cr* 1703 (then Mackenzie of Gairloch); MB, ChB; *b* 25 Jan. 1936; *s* of Sir Maxwell Ian Hector Inglis of Glencorse, 9th Bt and Dorothy Evelyn (*d* 1970), MD, JP, *d* of Dr John Stewart, Tasmania; *S* father, 1974; *m* 1960, Rachel (marr. diss. 1975), *d* of Lt-Col N. M. Morris, Dowdstown, Ardee, Co. Louth; twin *s* one *d* (and *e s* decd); *m* 1975 (marr. diss. 1977); one *d*. *Educ:* Winchester; Edinburgh Univ. (MB, ChB 1960). *Heir: s* Ian Richard Inglis, *b* 9 Aug. 1965. *Address:* 18 Cordwalles Road, Pietermaritzburg, Natal 3201, S Africa.

INGLIS-JONES, Nigel John; QC 1982; Barrister-at-Law; *b* 7 May 1935; 2nd *s* of Major John Alfred Inglis-Jones and Hermione Inglis-Jones; *m* 1st, 1965, Lenette Bromley-Davenport (*d* 1986); two *s* two *d*; 2nd, 1987, Ursula Culverwell; one *s*. *Educ:* Eton; Trinity Coll., Oxford (BA). Nat. Service with Grenadier Guards (ensign). Called to the Bar, Inner Temple, 1959, Bencher, 1981. A Recorder, 1976–93. Dep. Social Security Comr, 1993–; Gen. Comr of Income Tax, 1992–. *Publication:* The Law of Occupational Pension Schemes, 1989. *Recreations:* gardening, fishing, collecting English drinking glass. *Address:* 21 Elms Crescent, SW4 8QE. *T:* (020) 7622 3043. *Club:* MCC.

INGMAN, David Charles, CBE 1993; Chairman, British Waterways Board, 1987–93; *b* 22 March 1928; *s* of Charles and Muriel Ingman; *m* 1951, Joan Elizabeth Walker; two *d*. *Educ:* Grangefield Grammar Sch., Stockton-on-Tees; Durham Univ. (BSc, MSc). Imperial Chemical Industries, 1949–85: Dir, then Dep. Chm., Plastics Div., 1975–81; Gp Dir, Plastics and Petrochemicals Div., 1981–85; Chm. and Chief Exec., Bestobell, 1985–86. Dir, Engineering Services Ltd, 1975–78; Alternative Dir, AECI Ltd, SA, 1978–82; Non-exec. Dir, Negretti-Zambra, 1979–81. Mem., Nationalised Industries Chairmen's Gp, 1987–93. *Recreations:* golf, walking, travel.

INGOLD, Cecil Terence, CMG 1970; DSc 1940; Professor of Botany in University of London, Birkbeck College, 1944–72; Vice-Master, Birkbeck College, 1965–70, Fellow, 1973; *b* 3 July 1905; *s* of late E. G. Ingold; *m* 1933, Leonora Mary Kemp; one *s* three *d*. *Educ:* Bangor (Co. Down) Grammar Sch.; Queen's Univ., Belfast. (BSc 1925). Asst in Botany, QUB, 1929; Lectr in Botany, University of Reading, 1930–37; Lecturer-in-charge of Dept of Botany, University Coll., Leicester, 1937–44; Dean of Faculty of Science, London Univ., 1956–60. Dep. Vice-Chancellor, London Univ., 1966–68, Chm. Academic Council, 1969–72. Chm., University Entrance and School Examinations Council, 1958–64; Vice-Chm., Inter-Univ. Council for Higher Educn Overseas, 1969 74. Chm., Council Freshwater Biolog. Assoc., 1965–74; Pres., Internat Mycological Congress, 1971. Hooker Lectr, Linnean Soc., 1974. Hon. FLS 2000. Hon. DLitt Ibadan, 1969; Hon. DSc Exeter, 1972; Hon. DCL Kent, 1978. Linnean Medal (Botany), 1983; de Bary Medal (Mycology), Internat. Mycological Assoc., 1996; Millennium Gold Medal, 15th Internat. Botanical Congress, 1999. *Publications:* Spore Discharge in Land Plants, 1939; Dispersal in Fungi, 1953; The Biology of Fungi, 1961; Spore Liberation, 1965; Fungal Spores: their liberation and dispersal, 1971. *Address:* 1 The Rowans, West End, Cholsey, Oxon OX10 9LN.

See also T. Ingold.

INGOLD, Dr Keith Usherwood, OC 1994; FRS 1979; FRSC 1969; Distinguished Research Scientist, Steacie Institute for Molecular Sciences, since 1991; *b* Leeds, 31 May 1929; *s* of Christopher Kelk Ingold and Edith Hilda (*née* Usherwood); *m* 1956, Carmen Cairine Hodgkin; one *s* one *d* (and one *s* decd). *Educ:* University Coll. London (BSc Hons Chem., 1949; Fellow, 1987); Univ. of Oxford (DPhil 1951). Emigrated to Canada, 1951; Post-doctorate Fellow (under Dr F. P. Lossing), Div. of Pure Chem., Nat. Res. Council of Canada, 1951–53; Def. Res. Bd Post-doctorate Fellow (under Prof. W. A. Bryce), Chem. Dept, Univ. of BC, 1953–55; National Research Council of Canada: joined Div. of Appl. Chem., 1955; Head, Hydrocarbon Chem. Section of Div. of Chem., 1965; Associate Dir, Div. of Chemistry, 1977–90. Adjunct Professor: Brunel Univ., 1983–94; Univ. of Guelph, 1985–87; Carleton Univ., 1991–; Van Arkel Vis. Prof., Leiden Univ., Holland, 1992; Vis. Lectr, Japan Soc. for Promotion of Science, 1982. Hon. Treas., RSC, 1979–81; Canadian Society for Chemistry: Vice-Pres., 1985–87, Pres., 1987–88. Hon. Mem., Argentinian Soc. for Res. in Organic Chem., 1997. Lectures: Frontiers in Chem., Case Western Res. Univ., and Frank Burnett Dains Meml, Univ. of Kansas, 1969; J. A. McRae Meml, Queen's Univ., Ont, 1980; Canadian Industries Ltd, Acadia Univ., NS, Imperial Oil, Univ. of Western Ont, and Douglas Hill Meml, Duke Univ., NC, 1987; Rayson Huang, Univ. of Hong Kong, 1988; 3M University, Univ. of Western Ont, Peter de la Mare Meml, Univ. of Auckland, and Gilman, Iowa State Univ., 1993; Marjorie Young Bell, Mount Allison Univ., NB, and Bergman, Yale Univ., 1994; Weissberger-Williams, Kodak Res. Center, Rochester, NY, and Stanley J. Cristol, Univ. of Colorado, 1995; (first) Cheves Walling, Gordon Res. Conf., 1997; Max T. Rogers, Michigan State Univ., 2000. Hon. FRSE 2001. Hon. DSc: Univ. of Guelph, 1985; St Andrews, 1989; Carleton, 1992; McMaster, 1995; Hon. LLD: Mount Allison, New Brunswick, 1987; Dalhousie, 1996; Dr *hc* Ancona, 1999. Award in Petroleum Chem., ACS, 1968; Award in Kinetics and Mechanism, Chem. Soc., 1978; Medal of Chem. Inst. of Canada, 1981, Syntex Award for Physical Organic Chemistry, CIC, 1983; Centennial Medal, RSC, 1982; Henry Marshall Tory Medal, RSC, 1985; Pauling Award, ACS, 1988; Humboldt Res. Award, Alexander von Humboldt Foundn, W Germany, 1989; Alfred Bader Award in Organic Chem., Canadian Soc. for Chem., 1989; Sir Christopher Ingold Lectureship Award, RSC, 1989; VERIS Award, Vitamin E Res. Inf. Services, 1989; Lansdowne Visitor Award, Univ. of Victoria, Canada, 1990; Mangini Prize in Chem., Univ. of Bologna, 1990; Davy Medal, Royal Soc., 1990; Izaak Walton Killam Meml Prize, Canada Council, 1992; Arthur C. Cope Scholar Award, 1992, James Flack Norris Award in Physical Organic Chemistry, 1993, Amer. Chem. Soc. Silver Jubilee Medal, 1977; Angelo Mangini Medal, Italian Chem. Soc., 1997; Canada Gold Medal for Sci. and Engrg, Natural Scis and Engrg Res. Council of Canada, 1998; Royal Medal, Royal Soc., 2000. *Publications:* over 450 scientific papers in field of physical organic chemistry, partic. free-radical chemistry. *Recreation:* ski-ing. *Address:* 72 Ryeburn Drive, Ottawa ON K1V 1H5, Canada. *T:* (613) 8221123; (office) (613) 9900938.

INGOLD, Prof. Timothy, PhD; FBA 1997; FRSE; Professor of Anthropology, University of Aberdeen, since 1999; *b* 1 Nov. 1948; *s* of Cecil Terence Ingold, *qv*; *m* 1972, Anna Kaarina Väli-Kivistö; three *s* one *d*. *Educ:* Churchill Coll., Cambridge (BA 1st cl. Hons 1970; PhD Social Anthropol. 1976). Department of Social Anthropology, University of Manchester: Lectr, 1974–85; Sen. Lectr, 1985–90; Prof., 1990–99 (Max Gluckman Prof. of Social Anthropology, 1995–99); Hd of Dept, 1993–97. British Academy Res. Readership, 1997–99; Adjunct Prof., Univ. of Tromsø, Norway, 1997–2000. Corresp. Mem., Finnish Literary Soc., 1993. FRSE 2000. Rivers Meml Medal, RAI, 1989; Jean-Marie Delwart Foundn Award, Royal Belgian Acad. of Scis,

1994. *Publications:* The Skolt Lapps today, 1976; Hunters, pastoralists and ranchers, 1980; Evolution and social life, 1986; The appropriation of nature, 1986; (ed) What is an animal?, 1988; (ed jtly) Hunters and gatherers, 2 vols, 1988; (ed jtly) Tools, language and cognition in human evolution, 1993; (ed) Companion encyclopedia of anthropology, 1994; (ed) Key debates in anthropology, 1996; The Perception of the Environment, 2000; articles in academic books and learned jls. *Recreation:* music ('cello and piano). *Address:* Department of Sociology, University of Aberdeen AB24 3QY. *T:* (01224) 274350.

INGRAHAM, Rt Hon. Hubert Alexander; PC 1993; Prime Minister, Commonwealth of the Bahamas, since 1992; Member, National Assembly, since 1977 (PLP, 1977–86, Ind, 1987–90, FNM, since 1990); *b* 4 Aug. 1947; *m* Delores Velma Miller; five *c. Educ:* Cooper's Town Public Sch.; Southern Senior Sch.; Govt High Sch. Evening Inst., Nassau. Called to Bahamas Bar, 1972; Sen. Partner, Christie, Ingraham & Co. Formerly: Mem., Air Transport Licensing Authy; Chm., Real Property Tax Tribunal. Chm., Bahamas Mortgage Corp., 1982. Mem., Progressive Liberal Party, 1975–86; Minister of Housing, Nat. Insurance and Social Services, 1982–84; Leader, Free National Movement, 1990; Leader of Opposition, 1990–92. *Address:* Office of the Prime Minister, PO Box CB–10980, Nassau, Bahamas.

INGRAM, Adam; Member (SNP) South of Scotland, Scottish Parliament, since 1999; *b* 1 May 1951; *m* Gerry; three *s* one *d. Educ:* Kilmarnock Acad.; Paisley Coll. (BA Hons Business Economics, 1980). Family Bakery Business, 1971–76; Researcher and Lectr, Paisley Coll.; Sen. Economic Asst, Manpower Services Commn; Hd of Res., Development Options Ltd; Economic Develt consultant, 1990–99. Joined SNP, 1983 (Mem., Nat. Exec. Cttee, 1994–99). *Address:* Scottish Parliament, Edinburgh EH99 1SP.

INGRAM, Rt Hon. Adam (Paterson); PC 1999; JP; MP (Lab) East Kilbride, since 1987; Minister of State, Ministry of Defence, since 2001; *b* 1 Feb 1947; *s* of Bert Ingram and Lousia Paterson; *m* 1970, Maureen Georgina McMahon. *Educ:* Cranhill Secondary School. Commercial apprentice, 1965, computer programmer, 1966–69, J. & P. Coats, Glasgow; programmer/analyst, Associated British Foods, 1969–70; programmer/systems analyst, SSEB, 1970–77; Trade Union Official, NALGO, 1977–87. Sec., Jt Trades Union Side, Gas Staffs and Senior Officers, Scottish Gas, 1978–82; Chair, East Kilbride Constituency Labour Party, 1981–85; Councillor, E Kilbride DC, 1980–87, Leader, 1984–87. An Opposition Whip, Feb.–Nov. 1988 (responsible for Scottish business and Treasury matters); PPS to Leader of the Opposition, 1988–92; Minister of State, NI Office, 1997–2001. Front bench spokesman on social security, 1993–95, on sci. and technol., 1995–97; Mem., Select Cttee on Trade and Industry, 1992–93; Vice-Chm., British–Japanese All-Party Parly Gp, 1992–97; Sec., British–Singapore All-Party Parly Gp, 1992–97. JP East Kilbride, 1980. *Recreations:* fishing, cooking, reading. *Address:* House of Commons, SW1A 0AA. *T:* (020) 7219 4093.

INGRAM, Christopher John; Chairman, Tempus Group plc (formerly CIA Media Communications Group plc), since 1976; *b* 9 June 1943; *s* of Thomas Frank Ingram and Gladys Agnes Ingram; *m* 1964, Janet Elizabeth Rye; one *s* one *d. Educ:* Woking Grammar Sch. KMP, 1970–72; Man. Dir, TMD Advertising, 1972–76; founded Chris Ingram Associates, later CIA Gp plc, 1976. *Recreations:* theatre, football, art, eating out, travel. *Address:* Tempus Group plc, 1 Pemberton Row, EC4A 3BG.

INGRAM, Prof. David Stanley, OBE 1999; Master, St Catharine's College, Cambridge, since 2000; *b* 10 Oct. 1941; *s* of Stanley Arthur Ingram, tool maker and Vera May Ingram (*née* Mansfield); *m* 1965, Alison Winifred Graham; two *s. Educ:* Yardley Grammar School, Birmingham; Univ. of Hull (BSc, PhD); MA, ScD Cantab. CBiol, FIBiol 1986; FLS 1991; FRSE 1993; FIHort 1997; FRCPE 1998. Research Fellow, Univ. of Glasgow Dept of Botany, 1966–68; ARC Unit of Develt Botany, Cambridge, 1969–74; University of Cambridge: Research Fellow, Botany Sch., 1968–69; Univ. Lectr, 1974–88; Reader in Plant Pathology, 1988–90; Mem. Gen. Board, 1984–88; Fellow, Downing Coll., Cambridge, 1974–90 (Dean, 1976–82; Tutor for Graduate Students, 1982–88; Dir of Studies in Biology, 1976–89; Hon. Fellow, 2000); Regius Keeper, Royal Botanic Garden, Edinburgh, 1990–98 (Hon. Fellow, 1998); Advr to Univ. of Edinburgh on public understanding of science, 1998–; Chm., Cttee for Interdisciplinary Envmtl Studies, Cambridge Univ., 2001–. Visiting Professor: Univ. of Glasgow, 1991–; of Envmtl Sci and Horticulture, Napier Univ., 1998–; Hon. Prof., Univ. of Edinburgh, 1992– (Mem. Adv. Cttee, Div. of Biol Scis, 1991–98); Prof. of Horticulture, RHS, 1995–2000. Chairman: Scientific Council, Sainsbury Lab. for Plant Pathology, 1990–92; Science and Plants for Schools Trust, 1991–98; Science and Plants for Schs, Scotland, 1998–2000; Scientific and Horticultural Advice Cttee, RHS, 1995–2000 (Mem., Scientific Cttee, 1992–95); Adv. Cttee, Darwin Initiative for Survival of the Species, 1999–; Member: Adv. Cttee, St Andrews Botanic Garden, 1990–95; Exec. Cttee, Scotland's Nat. Gardens Scheme, 1990–96; Adv. Cttee on SSSI in Scotland, 1992–98; Council, Linnean Soc., 1992–95 (Vice Pres., 1993–94); Council, Internat. Assoc. of Botanic Gardens; main Bd and Scientific Adv. Cttee, Scottish Natural Heritage, 1999–2000; Jt Nature Conservation Cttee, 1999–2000. Trustee: Grimesthorpe and Drummond Castle Trust, 1990–98; John Fife Meml Trust, 1990–98; Younger Botanic Garden Trust, 1990–2000; Royal Botanic Garden (Sibbald) Trust, 1990–98; Botanic Gardens Conservation International, 1991–98; Scottish Sci. Trust, 1998–99 (Mem. Scientific Adv. Cttee, 1999–); Dynamic Earth Proj., 1998–2000; World Conservation Monitoring Centre 2000, 2001–. President: 7th Internat. Congress of Plant Pathology, 1994–98; British Soc. for Plant Pathology, 1998; Hon. Vice-Pres., Royal Caledonian Horticultural Soc., 1990. Hon. Fellow, Myerscough Coll., 2001. Hon. FRSGS 1998. Member: Editl Cttee, Flora of China, 1992–98; Editorial Board: Biol Revs, 1984–98, 2001–; Annals of Botany, 1992–; Advances in Plant Path, 1992–95. DUniv Open, 2000. *Publications:* (with D. N. Butcher) Plant Tissue Culture, 1974; (with J. P. Helgeson) Tissue Culture Methods for Plant Pathologists, 1980; (with A. Friday) Cambridge Encyclopedia of Life Sciences, 1985; (with P. H. Williams) Advances in Plant Pathology, vol. 1, 1982—vol. 9, 1993; (with A. Hudson) Shape and Form in Plants and Fungi, 1994; (with N. F. Robertson) Plant Disease, 1999; many papers dealing with research in plant pathology, plant tissue culture and botany, in learned jls. *Recreations:* listening to classical music and jazz, theatre, ceramics, gardening, travel, reading, strolling around capital cities. *Address:* St Catharine's College, Cambridge CB2 1RL. *Club:* Caledonian.

INGRAM, Edward John W.; *see* Winnington-Ingram.

INGRAM, Sir James (Herbert Charles), 4th Bt *cr* 1893; *b* 6 May 1966; *s* of (Herbert) Robin Ingram (*d* 1979) and of Shiela, *d* of late Charles Peczenik; *S* grandfather, 1980; *m* 1998, Aracea Elizabeth, *d* of Graham Pearce. *Educ:* Eton; Cardiff Univ. *Recreations:* golf, shooting. *Heir: half b* Nicholas David Ingram, *b* 12 June 1975. *Address:* 8 Lochaline Street, W6 9SH.

INGRAM, Sir John (Henderson), Kt 1994; CBE 1984; FIMechE, FIPENZ; company director; *b* 3 Sept. 1924; *s* of John Garden Ingram and Irene Caro Ingram (*née* Simpson); *m* 1952, Rosemary Clara Cuningham; three *d. Educ:* Nelson Coll., NZ; Canterbury Univ., Christchurch, NZ (BE; Dist. Alumnus, 1999). FIPENZ (FNZIE 1969; Dist. FIPENZ 1997); FAusIMM 1975; FIMechE 1991. Served RNZAF, NZ and Pacific, 1943–45. Man. Dir, NZ Steel Ltd, 1969–86; Dir, Nat Bank of NZ, 1983–95; Chm., Auckland Uniservices Ltd, 1988–99. Chm., Youth Skills NZ, 1989–97; Mem., Auckland HA, 1990–91. President: Inst. of Professional Engrs, NZ, 1976–77; Auckland Manufacturers' Assoc., 1989–91. Mem., Waitangi Tribunal, 1993–98. Mem. Council, 1979–96, Pro Chancellor, 1982–83 and 1995–96, Fellow, 1997, Univ. of Auckland. Commemoration Medal, NZ, 1990. *Publications:* contrib. papers in Inst. of Professional Engrs, NZ Jl, Conf. papers IISI, Inst. of Engrs, Australia, Aust. Inst. of Metals. *Recreations:* garden, ski-ing. *Address:* 6 Glenbrook Street, Remuera, Auckland 5, New Zealand. *T:* (9) 5200167. *Club:* Northern (Auckland).

INGRAM, Paul; Head of Agricultural Services, Barclays Bank plc, 1988–94; *b* 20 Sept. 1934; *s* of John Granville Ingram and Sybil Ingram (*née* Johnson); *m* 1957, Jennifer (*née* Morgan) (*d* 1988); one *s* one *d. Educ:* Manchester Central High School; University of Nottingham (BSc 1956). Dept of Conservation and Extension, Fedn of Rhodesia and Nyasaland, 1956–63; Nat. Agricl Adv. Service, later ADAS, MAFF, 1965–; County Livestock Officer, Lancs, 1969–70; Policy Planning Unit, MAFF, 1970–72; Farm Management Adviser, Devon, 1972–76; Regional Farm Management Adviser, Wales, 1976–77; Dep. Sen. Livestock Advr, 1977–79, Sen. Agricl Officer, 1979–85, Chief Agricl Officer, 1985–87, Dir of Farm and Countryside Service, 1987–88, ADAS. *Address:* 36 Ceylon Road, W14 0PY.

INGRAM, Robert Alexander; Chief Operating Officer, and President, Pharmaceutical Operations, GlaxoSmithKline, since 2000; *b* 6 Dec. 1942; *s* of Myra L. Ingram; *m* 1962, Carolyn Jean Hutson; three *s. Educ:* Eastern Illinois Univ. (BSc Business Admin); Lumpkin Coll. of Business. Sales rep., 1965; Merrell Dow Pharmaceuticals: various sales mgt, then govt and public affairs posts; Vice Pres., Public Affairs, until 1985; Vice Pres., Govt Affairs, Merck & Co. Inc., 1985–88; Pres., Merck Frosst Canada Inc., 1988–90; joined Glaxo Inc., 1990: Exec. Vice Pres., Admin and Regulatory Affairs, 1990–93; Exec. Vice Pres., then Pres. and Chief Operating Officer, 1993–94; Pres. and CEO, 1994–99; Chm., Glaxo Wellcome Inc., and Chief Exec., Glaxo Wellcome plc, 1997–2000; Chm., Glaxo Inc., 1999–2000. Director: Wachovia Corp., 1997–; TheraCom, 1998–; Northern Telecom Ltd (NORTEL), 1999–. Hon. LLD: Eastern Illinois, 1988; Univ. of Scis, Philadelphia, 1999. *Recreations:* Formula One motor racing, Porsche restoration. *Address:* GlaxoSmithKline, Five Moore Drive, PO Box 13398, Research Triangle Park, NC 27709–3398, USA. *Club:* Royal Automobile.

INGRAM, Stanley Edward; solicitor; *b* 5 Dec. 1922; *o s* of late Ernest Alfred Stanley Ingram and Ethel Ann Ingram; *m* 1948, Vera (*née* Brown); one *s* one *d. Educ:* Charlton Central School. Articled clerk with Wright & Bull, Solicitors; admitted Solicitor, 1950. Served RAF, 1942–46. Legal Asst, Min. of Nat. Insurance, 1953; Sen. Legal Asst, Min. of Pensions and Nat. Insurance, 1958; Asst Solicitor, 1971, Under Sec. (Legal), 1978–83, DHSS. Member Council: Civil Service Legal Soc. and of Legal Section of First Division Assoc., 1971–82; Mem., Salaried Solicitors' Cttee of Law Society, 1978–81. Secretary: Romsey Gp, CS Retirement Fellowship, 1989–97; Test Valley Croquet Club, 1995– (Treas., 1994–95); Winchester Croquet Club, 1998–; Romsey Abbey Probus Club, 2000– (Vice-Pres., 1996; Pres., 1997). *Recreations:* gardening, playing croquet. *Address:* 2 Little Woodley Farm, Winchester Hill, Romsey, Hants SO51 7NU. *Club:* Law Society.

INGRAM, Tamara; Chairman and Chief Executive, McCann-Erickson London, since 2002; *b* 1 Oct. 1960; *d* of John Ingram and Sonia (*née* Bolson); *m* 1989, Andrew Millington; one *s* one *d. Educ:* Queen's Coll., Harley St; Univ. of E Anglia (BA Hons Eng.). Joined Saatchi & Saatchi, 1985: Account Exec., 1985–87; Supervisor, 1987–88; Dir, 1988–89; Bd Account Dir, 1989–90; Gp Account Dir, 1990–93; Exec. Bd Dir, 1993–95; Saatchi & Saatchi Advertising Ltd: Jt CEO, 1995–99; Chief Exec., 1999–2001; Chm., 2001. Member Council: IPA, 1995–; Mktg Soc., 1995–. *Recreations:* the arts, my family. *Address:* McCann-Erickson House, 7–11 Herbrand Street, WC1N 1EX.

INGRAM, Prof. Vernon Martin, FRS 1970; John and Dorothy Wilson Professor of Biology, Massachusetts Institute of Technology, since 1988; *b* Breslau, 19 May 1924; *s* of Kurt and Johanna Immerwahr; *m* 1st, 1950, Margaret Young; one *s* one *d*; 2nd, 1984, Elizabeth Hendee. *Educ:* Birkbeck Coll., Univ. of London. PhD Organic Chemistry, 1949; DSc Biochemistry, 1961. Analytical and Res. Chemist, Thos Morson & Son, Mddx, 1941–45; Lecture Demonstrator in Chem., Birkbeck Coll., 1945–47; Asst Lectr in Chem., Birkbeck Coll., 1947–50; Rockefeller Foundn Fellow, Rockefeller Inst., NY, 1950–51; Coxe Fellow, Yale, 1951–52; Mem. Sci. Staff, MRC Unit for Molecular Biology, Cavendish Lab., Cambridge, 1952–58; Assoc. Prof. 1958–61, Prof. of Biochemistry, 1961–, MIT; Lectr (part-time) in Medicine, Columbia, 1961–73; Guggenheim Fellow, UCL, 1967–68. Jesup Lectr, Columbia, 1962; Harvey Soc. Lectr, 1965. Mem., Amer. Acad. of Arts and Sciences, 1964. Fellow, Amer. Assoc. for Advancement of Science, 1987. William Allen Award, Amer. Soc. for Human Genetics, 1967. *Publications:* Haemoglobin and Its Abnormalities, 1961; The Hemoglobins in Genetics and Evolution, 1963; The Biosynthesis of Macromolecules, 1965, new edn, 1971; articles on human genetics, nucleic acids, differentiation and molecular biology of aging and developmental neurobiology, Alzheimer's Disease, in Nature, Jl Mol. Biol., Jl Cell Biol., Develt Biol., Jl Biol Chem., Brain Research, etc. *Recreations:* music; photographer of abstract images. *Address:* Massachusetts Institute of Technology, Massachusetts Avenue, Cambridge, Mass 02139, USA. *T:* (617) 2533706.

INGRAMS, family name of **Baroness Darcy de Knayth**.

INGRAMS, Leonard Victor, OBE 1980; Partner, L.V. Ingrams & Co. Ltd, since 1998; *b* 1 Sept. 1941; *s* of late Leonard St Clair Ingrams and Victoria Susan Beatrice (*née* Reid); *m* 1964, Rosalind Ann Moore; one *s* three *d. Educ:* Stonyhurst Coll.; Corpus Christi Coll., Oxford (1st Cl. Classics (Mods) 1961; 1st Cl. Lit.Hum. 1963; MA; Derby Schol. 1963; Sen. Schol. 1964; BLitt). Asst Lectr, QMC, 1965–67; joined Baring Bros, 1967, Man. Dir, 1975–81; Sen. Advr, Saudi Arabian Monetary Agency, 1974–79, Chief Advr to Gov., 1981–84; Dir, Robert Fleming Hldgs, 1985–96; Sen. Vice-Pres., Arab Banking Corp, 1996–98. Director: Deutschland Investment Corp., 1996–99 (Chm., 1990–96); Czech and Slovak Investment Corp., 1996– (Chm., 1992–96). Chm., Garsington Opera Ltd, 1990–; Mem., Mozart 2006 Cttee, Salzburg, 2000–. FRSA 1997. Pro Europa Foundn of Culture Prize, 2000. *Publications:* (ed) International Bond Portfolio Management, 1988; contribs to various vols of Oxyrhynchus Papyri. *Recreations:* gardening, music. *Address:* (office) Suite 3, 32 Davies Street, W1K 4ND; Garsington Manor, Garsington, Oxford OX44 9DH. *T:* (01865) 361234. *Club:* Beefsteak.

See also R. R. Ingrams.

INGRAMS, Richard Reid; journalist; Editor, Private Eye, 1963–86, Chairman, since 1974; Editor, The Oldie, since 1992; *b* 19 Aug. 1937; *s* of late Leonard St Clair Ingrams and Victoria (*née* Reid); *m* 1962, Mary Morgan (marr. diss. 1993); one *s* one *d* (and one *s* decd). *Educ:* Shrewsbury; University Coll., Oxford. Joined Private Eye, 1962; columnist, Observer, 1988–90, 1992–. *Publications:* (with Christopher Booker and William Rushton) Private Eye on London, 1962; Private Eye's Romantic England, 1963; (with John Wells)

Mrs Wilson's Diary, 1965; Mrs Wilson's 2nd Diary, 1966; The Tale of Driver Grope, 1968; (with Barry Fantoni) The Bible for Motorists, 1970; (ed) The Life and Times of Private Eye, 1971; (as Philip Reid, with Andrew Osmond) Harris in Wonderland, 1973; (ed) Cobbett's Country Book, 1974; (ed) Beachcomber: the works of J. B. Morton, 1974; The Best of Private Eye, 1974; God's Apology, 1977; Goldenballs, 1979; (with Fay Godwin) Romney Marsh and the Royal Military Canal, 1980; (with John Wells) Dear Bill: the collected letters of Denis Thatcher, 1980; (with John Wells) The Other Half: further letters of Denis Thatcher, 1981; (with John Wells) One for the Road, 1982; (with John Piper) Piper's Places, 1983; (ed) The Penguin Book of Private Eye Cartoons, 1983; (with John Wells) My Round!, 1983; (ed) Dr Johnson by Mrs Thrale, 1984; (with John Wells) Down the Hatch, 1985; (with John Wells) Just the One, 1986; John Stewart Collis: a memoir, 1986; (with John Wells) The Best of Dear Bill, 1986; (with John Wells) Mud in Your Eye, 1987; The Ridgeway, 1988; You Might As Well Be Dead, 1988; England (anthology), 1989; (with John Wells) Number 10, 1989; On and On . . ., 1990; (ed) The Oldie Annual, 1993; (ed) The Oldie Annual 2, 1994; Malcolm Muggeridge: the authorized biography, 1995; (ed) I Once Met, 1996; (ed) The Oldie Annual 3, 1997; (ed) Jesus: authors take sides (anthology), 1999; (ed) The Oldie Annual 4, 1999. *Recreation:* piano. *Address:* c/o The Oldie, 45 Poland Street, W1V 4AU.

See also L. V. Ingrams.

INGRESS BELL, Philip; *see* Bell.

INGROW, Baron *cr* 1982 (Life Peer), of Keighley in the County of West Yorkshire; **John Aked Taylor,** Kt 1972; OBE 1960; TD 1951; DL; JP; Life President, Timothy Taylor & Co. Ltd, since 1995 (Chairman and Managing Director, 1954–95); Lord-Lieutenant and Custos Rotulorum of West Yorkshire, 1985–92 (Vice Lord-Lieutenant, 1976–85); *b* 15 Aug. 1917; *s* of Percy Taylor, Knowle Spring House, Keighley, and Gladys Broster (who *m* 2nd, 1953, Sir (John) Donald Horsfall, 2nd Bt); *m* 1949, Barbara Mary (*d* 1998), *d* of Percy Wright Stirk, Keighley; two *d. Educ:* Shrewsbury Sch. Served War of 1939–45: Duke of Wellington's Regt and Royal Signals, Major; Norway, Middle East, Sicily, NW Europe and Far East. Mem., Keighley Town Council, 1946–67 (Mayor, 1956–57; Chm., Educn Cttee, 1949–61; Chm., Finance Cttee, 1961–67); Mem. Council, Magistrates' Assoc., 1957–86 (Vice-Chm., Exec. Cttee, 1975–76; Chm., Licensing Cttee, 1969–76; Hon. Treasurer, 1976–86; Vice-Pres., 1986–; Past Pres. and Chm., WR Br.; Life Vice-Pres., W Yorks Br.); Chm., Keighley Conservative Assoc., 1952–56 and 1957–67 (Pres., 1971–76, Jt Hon. Treas., 1947–52, and Chm., Young Conservatives, 1946–47); Chm., Yorkshire West Conservative European Constituency Council, 1978–84 (Pres., 1984–85); Chm., Yorkshire Area, Nat. Union of Conservative and Unionist Assocs, 1966–71 (Vice-Chm., 1965–66); Chm., Exec. Cttee of Nat. Union of Conservative and Unionist Assocs, 1971–76 (Mem. 1964–83); Pres., Nat. Union of Conservative and Unionist Assocs 1982–83 (Hon. Vice-Pres., 1976–). Gen. Comr of Income Tax, 1965–92. Vice-Pres., Yorks and Humberside TAVRA, 1985–88, and 1991–92 (Pres., 1988–91). Mem. Court, Univ. of Leeds, 1986–92. Pres., Council of Order of St John, S and W Yorks, 1985–92; KStJ 1986. JP Borough of Keighley 1949; DL West (formerly WR) Yorks, 1971. DUniv Bradford, 1990. *Address:* Fieldhead, Keighley, West Yorkshire BD20 6LP. *T:* (01535) 603895.

INKIN, Sir Geoffrey (David), Kt 1993; OBE 1974 (MBE 1971); Chairman, Cardiff Bay Development Corporation, 1987–2000; *b* 2 Oct. 1934; *e s* of late Noel D. Inkin and Evelyn Margaret Inkin; *m* 1st 1961, Susan Elizabeth Sheldon (marr. diss. 1998); three *s*; 2nd, 1998, Mrs Susan Inglefield. *Educ:* Dean Close Sch.; RMA, Sandhurst; Staff Coll., Camberley; Royal Agricl Coll., Cirencester. Commnd The Royal Welch Fusiliers, 1955; served Malaya, 1955–57 and Cyprus, 1958–59 (despatches); commanded 1st Bn The Royal Welch Fusiliers, 1972–74. Member: Gwent CC, 1977–83; Gwent Police Authority, 1979–83; Mem. Bd, 1980–83, Chm., 1983–87, Cwmbran Develt Corp.; Chm., Land Authy for Wales, 1986–98; Mem. Bd, Welsh Devlt Agency, 1984–87. Gov., Haberdashers' Monmouth Schs, 1977–90; Mem. Bd, WNO, 1987–91, 1993–95; Member Council: UWIST, 1987–88; Cardiff Univ., 1988–. Patron, Butler Trust. Parly Cand. (C) Ebbw Vale, 1977–79. Mem., RICS, 1994. Gwent: DL, 1983–91; High Sheriff, 1987–88. Hon. Dr Univ. of Glamorgan, 1996. *Address:* Castle Upon Alun, St Brides Major, Bridgend CF32 0TN. *T:* (01656) 880298. *Clubs:* Brooks's; Cardiff and County (Cardiff).

INMAN, Derek Arthur; His Honour Judge Inman; a Circuit Judge, since 1993; *b* 1 Aug. 1937; *s* of Arthur and Marjorie Inman; *m* 1st, 1963, Sarah Juliet Cahn (marr. diss. 1982); one *s* two *d*; 2nd, 1983, Elizabeth (*née* Dickinson), *widow* of Lt-Col C. Thomson. *Educ:* Roundhay Sch., Leeds; RNC, Dartmouth. RN; served in HM Ships Sheffield, Belfast and Bulwark; Staff of C-in-C Home Fleet; Sec. to Comdr Naval Forces Gulf and HMS Hermione; retired as Lieut Comdr, 1974. Called to the Bar, Middle Temple, 1968; in Chambers at 2 Harcourt Bldgs, 1974–93. *Recreations:* watching cricket and Rugby, compulsory gardening. *Address:* c/o Lloyd's Bank, High Street, Godalming, Surrey GU7 1AT.

INMAN, Edward Oliver, OBE 1998; FRAeS; Director (formerly Keeper) of Duxford Airfield, Imperial War Museum, since 1978; *b* 12 Aug. 1948; *s* of John Inman and Peggy Inman (*née* Beard); *m* 1st, 1971 (marr. diss. 1982); one *s* one *d*; 2nd, 1984, Sherida Lesley (*née* Sturton); one *d*, and two step *d. Educ:* King's College Sch., Wimbledon; Gonville and Caius Coll., Cambridge (MA); School of Slavonic and East European Studies, London (MA). FRAeS 1999. Joined Imperial War Museum as Res. Asst, 1972; Asst Keeper 1974; Keeper of Exhibits (Duxford) 1976. Gov., 2nd Air Div. Meml Liby, Norwich, 1990–. Mem. Bd, Cultural Heritage NTO (formerly Mus. Trng Inst.), 1998–. *Recreations:* squash, travel, time with the family. *Address:* c/o Imperial War Museum, Duxford, Cambridge CB2 4QR. *T:* (01223) 835000.

INMAN, Herbert, CBE 1977; Regional Administrator, Yorkshire Regional Health Authority, 1973–77; Hon. Adviser to the Sue Ryder Foundation, since 1977, and Member of Council, 1986–89; Member, Executive Committee, Sue Ryder Homes, 1983–88 (Chairman, 1983–87); *b* 8 Jan. 1917; *s* of Matthew Herbert Inman and Rose Mary Earle; *m* 1939, Beatrice, *d* of Thomas Edward Lee and Florence Lee; twin *s. Educ:* Wheelwright Grammar Sch., Dewsbury; Univ. of Leeds. FHSM (Nat. Pres. 1968–69); DPA. Various hosp. appts, Dewsbury, Wakefield and Aylesbury, 1933–48; Dep. Gp Sec., Leeds (A) Gp HMC and Dep. Chief Admin. Officer, 1948–62; Gp Sec. and Chief Admin. Officer, Leeds (A) Gp HMC, 1962–70; Gp Sec. and Chief Admin. Officer, Leeds (St James's) Univ. HMC, 1970–73. *Publications:* occasional articles in Hospital and Health Services jls. *Recreations:* Rugby and cricket (spectator), travel, gardening, swimming. *Address:* 7 Potterton Close, Barwick in Elmet, Leeds LS15 4DY. *T:* (0113) 281 2538.

INMAN, Melbourne Donald; QC 1998; a Recorder, since 1999; *b* 1 April 1957; *s* of Melbourne and Norah Inman. *Educ:* Bishop Vesey's Grammar Sch.; Regent's Park Coll., Oxford (MA). Called to the Bar, Inner Temple, 1979; Asst Recorder, 1996–99. *Recreations:* ski-ing, listening to the piano. *Address:* 1 Fountain Court, Steelhouse Lane, Birmingham B4 6DR. *T:* (0121) 236 5721.

INMAN, Roger, OBE (mil.) 1945 (MBE (mil.) 1944); TD 1945; Vice Lord-Lieutenant of South Yorkshire, 1981–90; Joint Managing Director, since 1951, and Chairman, since 1997, Harrison Fisher Group; *b* 18 April 1915; *y s* of S. M. Inman, Sheffield; *m* 1939, Christine Lucas, *e d* of Lt-Col J. Rodgers, Sheffield; two *s. Educ:* King Edward VII Sch., Sheffield. Commissioned into 71st (WR) Field Bde, RA TA, 1935; served War, with RA and General Staff, Western Desert, Middle East, Italy, 1939–46; released, 1946, with rank of Lt-Col; reformed and commanded 271 (WR) Fd Regt, RA TA, 1947–51; Brevet Col 1953; Hon. Col, Sheffield Artillery Volunteers, 1964–70; Member, W Riding T&AFA, 1947–; Vice-Chm., Yorkshire and Humberside TA&VRA, 1973–80. JP 1954 (Chm. Sheffield City Bench, 1974–80), DL 1967, West Riding. General Commissioner of Income Tax, 1969–90; Chm. of Comrs, Don Div. of Sheffield, 1975–90. Chm., Guardians of Standard of Wrought Plate within the Town of Sheffield, 1988–98. *Recreation:* golf. *Address:* Flat 1, Mayfield View, 15 Whitworth Road, Sheffield S10 3HD. *Club:* Hallamshire Golf (Sheffield).

INNES, Alistair Campbell M.; *see* Mitchell-Innes.

INNES of Coxton, Sir David (Charles Kenneth Gordon), 12th Bt *cr* 1686 (NS); consultant in electronics for petro-chemical and power generation fields; *b* 17 April 1940; *s* of Sir Charles Innes of Coxton, 11th Bt and Margaret Colquhoun Lockhart (*d* 1992), *d* of F. C. L. Robertson; *S* father, 1990; *m* 1969, Majorie Alison, *d* of E. W. Parker; one *s* one *d. Educ:* Haileybury Coll.; City & Guilds Coll. of Imperial Coll., London Univ. BSc(Eng); ACGI. Technical Dir, Peak Technologies, 1974–78; Man. Dir, Peak Combustion Controls, 1978–81. *Recreations:* electronics, aeronautics, astronomy. *Heir: s* Alastair Charles Deverell Innes, *b* 17 Sept. 1970. *Address:* 28 Wadham Close, Shepperton, Middlesex TW17 9HT. *T:* (01932) 228273.

INNES of Edingight, Sir Malcolm (Rognvald), KCVO 1990 (CVO 1981); Orkney Herald of Arms Extraordinary, since 2001; *b* 25 May 1938; 3rd *s* of late Sir Thomas Innes of Learney, GCVO, LLD, and Lady Lucy Buchan, 3rd *d* of 18th Earl of Caithness; *m* 1963, Joan, *o d* of Thomas D. Hay, CA, Edinburgh; three *s. Educ:* Edinburgh Acad.; Univ. of Edinburgh (MA, LLB). WS 1964. Falkland Pursuivant Extraordinary, 1957; Carrick Pursuivant, 1958; Lyon Clerk and Keeper of the Records, 1966; Marchmont Herald, 1971; Lord Lyon King of Arms, 1981–2001; Sec., Order of the Thistle, 1981–2001. Mem., Queen's Body Guard for Scotland (Royal Company of Archers), 1971. Pres., Heraldry Soc. of Scotland. Trustee, Sir William Fraser's Foundn. KStJ. Grand Officer of Merit, SMO Malta. *Recreation:* visiting places of historic interest. *Clubs:* New, Puffins (Edinburgh).

INNES, Sir Peter (Alexander Berowald), 17th Bt *cr* 1628, of Balvenie; FICE; Director, Scott Wilson Kirkpatrick & Co. Ltd (formerly Scott Wilson Kirkpatrick and Partners), Consulting Engineers, 1995–2000 (Partner, 1987–95); *b* 6 Jan. 1937; *s* of Lt-Col Sir (Ronald Gordon) Berowald Innes, 16th Bt, OBE and Elizabeth Haughton (*d* 1958), *e d* of late Alfred Fayle; *S* father, 1988; *m* 1959, Julia Mary, *d* of A. S. Levesley; two *s* one *d. Educ:* Prince of Wales School, Nairobi, Kenya; Bristol Univ. (BSc). Scott Wilson Kirkpatrick & Co. Ltd (formerly Scott Wilson Kirkpatrick and Partners), 1964–2000; Associate, 1982–87. Responsible for several airport projects in UK, Africa and Middle East, including major military airbases. Lt-Col Engr and Logistic (formerly Transport) Staff Corps, RE (TA). *Heir: s* Alexander Guy Berowald Innes, *b* 4 May 1960. *Address:* The Wheel House, Nations Hill, Kings Worthy, Winchester SO23 7QY. *T:* (01962) 881024. *Club:* S Winchester Golf.

INNES, Peter Maxwell; HM Diplomatic Service; Consul-General, Melbourne, since 1998; *b* 9 Aug. 1941; *s* of James Innes and Agnes Margaret Innes (*née* Dea); *m* 1965, Robina Baillie Walker; one *s* one *d. Educ:* Morrison's Acad., Crieff. Min. of Aviation, 1960–72; Department of Trade and Industry, 1972–77; Asst Airport Manager, Aberdeen Airport, 1972–73; on secondment to British Embassy, Washington, 1973–76; joined FCO, 1977; Seoul, 1979–83; FCO, 1983–85; First Sec. (Agric.), Dublin, 1985–89; FCO, 1989–92 (EC Monitoring Mission in Bosnia, 1991); Dir, British Information Services, NY, 1992–97; FCO, 1997–98. *Recreations:* reading, walking, travel, watching sport of all kinds. *Address:* c/o Foreign and Commonwealth Office, King Charles Street, SW1A 2AH. *Clubs:* Athenæum, Melbourne, Royal Automobile of Victoria, Savage (Melbourne).

INNES, Sheila Miriam; consultant (education and media); *b* 25 Jan. 1931; *d* of late Dr James Innes, MB, ChB, MA and of Nora Innes. *Educ:* Talbot Heath School, Bournemouth; Lady Margaret Hall, Oxford (Exhibnr; BA Hons Mod. Langs; MA). BBC Radio Producer, World Service, 1955–61; BBC TV producer: family programmes, 1961–65; further education, 1965–73; exec. producer, further education, 1973–77; Head, BBC Continuing Educn, TV, 1977–84; Controller, BBC Educnl Broadcasting, 1984–87; Dir, BBC Enterprises Ltd, 1986–87; Chief Exec., 1987–89, Dep. Chm., 1989–92, Open Coll. Non-exec. Dir, Brighton Health Care NHS Trust, 1993–96. Chairman: Cross-Sector Cttee for Development and Review, BTEC, 1986–87; Cross-Sector Cttee for Product Develt, BTEC, 1989–92; British Gas Training Awards, 1988–92. Member: Gen. Board, Alcoholics Anonymous, 1980–; Board of Governors, Centre for Information on Language Teaching and Research, 1981–84; Council, Open Univ., 1984–87; Council for Educational Technology, 1984–87; EBU Educational Working Party, 1984–87; Educn Cttee, 1990–95, Women's Adv. Gp, 1992–95, RSA; Standing Conf. on Schools' Science and Technol., 1990–93 (Mem. Council, 1993–98); Age Concern Training Validation (later Quality) Cttee, 1992–94; IMgt Management Develt Proj., 1992–95. Vice-Pres., Educn Sect., BAAS, 1990–. Mem., Clothing and Allied Products ITB Management 2000 Cttee of Enquiry, 1989. Patron, One World Broadcasting Trust, 1988–98. Gov., Talbot Heath Sch., Bournemouth, 1989–95. Mem., RTS, 1984; FRSA 1986; FITD 1987; CIMgt 1987. Hon. DLitt South Bank, 1992. *Publications:* BBC publications; articles for language jls and EBU Review. *Recreations:* music (classical and jazz), country pursuits, swimming, sketching, photography, travel, languages. *Address:* Wychwood, Barcombe, East Sussex BN8 5TP. *T:* (01273) 400268. *Clubs:* Reform; Oxford Society.

INNES, Lt-Col William Alexander Disney; DL; Vice Lord-Lieutenant of Banffshire, 1971–86; *b* 19 April 1910; 2nd *s* of late Captain James William Guy Innes, CBE, DL, JP, RN, of Maryculter, Kincardineshire; *m* 1939, Mary Alison (*d* 1997), *d* of late Francis Burnett-Stuart, Howe Green, Hertford; two *s*; *m* 2001, Patricia Joan (*née*) Callender), *widow* of George Gordon. *Educ:* Marlborough Coll., RMC, Sandhurst. Gordon Highlanders: 2nd Lieut, 1930; Captain 1938; Temp. Major 1941; Major, 1946; Temp. Lt-Col, 1951; retd, 1952. Served War of 1939–45: Far East (PoW Malaya and Siam, 1942–45). Chm., Banffshire T&AFA, 1959. DL 1959–87, JP 1964–86, Banffshire. *Recreation:* gardening. *Address:* Heath Cottage, Aberlour, Banffshire AB38 9QD. *T:* (01340) 871266.

INNES, William James Alexander; Assistant Under Secretary of State, 1985–94, Head of Fire and Emergency Planning Department, 1992–94, Home Office, retired; *b* 11 Oct. 1934; *s* of late William Johnstone Innes and Helen Margaret Meldrum Porter; *m* 1st, 1959, Carol Isabel Bruce (marr. diss. 1983); one *s* one *d*; 2nd, 1992, Mrs Ann Harrold. *Educ:* Robert Gordon's Coll., Aberdeen; Aberdeen Univ. (MA). Served Royal Air Force, 1956,

Officer Commanding 45 Sqdn, 1967–70. Principal, Home Office, 1972; Private Sec. to Home Sec., 1974–76; Asst Sec., 1977; Asst Under Sec. of State, seconded to NI Office, 1985–88; Dir of Operational Policy, Prison Dept, Home Office, 1988–90; Dir of Custody, Prison Service HQ, Home Office, 1990–92. *Recreations:* opera, theatre, golf. *Address:* Nightingales, Nightingale Lane, Maidenhead, Berks SL6 7QL. *Clubs:* Royal Air Force; Burnham Beeches Golf.

INNES-KER, family name of **Duke of Roxburghe**.

INSALL, Donald William, CBE 1995 (OBE 1981); FSA, RWA, FRIBA, FRTPI; architect and planning consultant; Director, Donald Insall Associates Ltd (formerly Donald W. Insall & Associates), since 1958 (Founder, 1958; Principal, 1958–81; Chairman, 1981–98); *b* 7 Feb. 1926; *o s* of late William R. Insall and Phyllis Insall, Henleaze, Bristol; *m* 1964, Amy Elizabeth, MA, *er d* of Malcolm H. Moss, Nanpantan, Leics; two *s* one *d*. *Educ:* Bristol Univ.; RA; Sch. of Planning, London (Dip. (Hons)); SPAB Lethaby Schol. 1951. FRIBA 1968, FRTPI 1973. Coldstream Guards, 1944–47. Architectural and Town-Planning Consultancy has included town-centre studies, civic and univ., church, domestic and other buildings, notably in conservation of historic towns and buildings (incl. restoration of ceiling, House of Lords, and Windsor Castle after fire, 1992); Medal (Min. of Housing and Local Govt), Good Design in Housing, 1962. Visiting Lecturer: RCA, 1964–69; Internat. Centre for Conservation, Rome, 1969–; Coll. d'Europe, Bruges, 1976–81; Catholic Univ. of Leuven, 1982–; Adjunct Prof., Univ. of Syracuse, 1971–81. Mem., Council of Europe Working Party, 1969–70; Nat. Pilot Study, Chester: A Study in Conservation, 1968; Consultant, Chester Conservation Programme, 1970–87 (EAHY Exemplar; European Prize for Preservation of Historic Monuments, 1981; Europa Nostra Medals of Honour, 1983 and 1989). Member: Historic Buildings Council for England, 1971–84; Grants Panel, EAHY, 1974; Council, RSA, 1976–80 (FRSA, 1948); Council, SPAB, 1979–; Ancient Monuments Bd for England, 1980–84; UK Council, ICOMOS, 1998–; Royal Parks Adv. Bd, 2000–; Comr, Historic Bldgs and Monuments Commn, 1984–89; Member: Standing Adv. Cttee, Getty Grant Program, 1988–92; EC Expert Cttee on Architectural Heritage, 1990, 1993–; DNH Inquiry into Fire Protection at Royal Palaces, 1993; Vice-Chm., Conf. on Trng in Architectural Conservation, 1990– (Hon. Sec., 1959–89); Vice-Pres., Bldg Crafts and Conservation Trust, 1994–. Member: Archtl Adv. Cttee, Westminster Abbey, 1993–98; Fabric Adv. Cttee, Southwark Cathedral, 1992–, Canterbury Cathedral, 1997–. RIBA: Banister Fletcher Medallist, 1949; Neale Bursar, 1955; Examnr, 1957; Competition Assessor, 1971. Conferences: White House (Natural Beauty), 1965; Historic Architectural Interiors, USA, 1988, 1993; Singapore, 1994. Lecture Tours: USA, 1964, 1972 (US Internat. Reg. Conf. on Conservation); Mexico, 1972; Yugoslavia, 1973; Canada, 1974, 1999; Argentina, 1976; India, 1979; Portugal, 1982. Hon. Freeman, City of Chester, 2000. European Architectural Heritage Year Medal (for Restoration of Chevening), 1973; Harley J. McKee Award, Assoc. for Preservation Technol. Internat, 1999; People in Conservation Award, RICS, 1999; Europa Nostra Medal of Honour, 2000; Plowden Medal, Royal Warrant Holders' Assoc., 2001. Silver Jubilee Medal, 1977. *Publications:* (jtly) Railway Station Architecture, 1966; (jtly) Conservation Areas 1967; The Care of Old Buildings Today, 1973; Historic Buildings: action to maintain the expertise for their care and repair, 1974; Conservation in Action, 1982; Conservation in Chester, 1988; contrib. to Encyclopædia Britannica, professional, environmental and internat. jls. *Recreations:* visiting, sketching, photographing and enjoying places; appreciating craftsmanship; Post-Vintage Thoroughbred Cars (Mem., Rolls Royce Enthusiasts' Club). *Address:* 73 Kew Green, Richmond, Surrey TW9 3AH; (office) 19 West Eaton Place, Eaton Square, SW1X 8LT. *T:* (020) 7245 9888. *Club:* Athenæum.

INSCH, Elspeth Virginia, OBE 1998; Headmistress, King Edward VI Handsworth School, Birmingham, since 1989; *b* 21 Aug. 1949; *d* of John Douglas Insch and Isabella Elizabeth Campbell (*née* Brodie). *Educ:* Newarke Girls' Sch., Leicester; Birkbeck Coll., Univ. of London (BSc); Univ. of Edinburgh (MPhil, DipEd, PGCE). Demonstrator, Univ. of Edinburgh, 1970–73; Teacher: Abington High Sch., Leics, 1974–77; Nottingham High Sch. for Girls (GPDST), 1977–84; Dep. Head, Kesteven and Sleaford High Sch. for Girls, 1984–89. Consultant, Springbank Sand and Gravel Co. Ltd, 1970–79. Pres., Assoc. of Maintained Girls' Schools, 1999–2000; Mem. Cttee, Nat. Grammar Schools Assoc., 1990–. FRGS, 1968 (Mem., Educn Cttee, 1994–). Fellow, Winston Churchill Meml Trust, 1980; Trustee, Grantham Yorke Trust, 1990–. *Address:* King Edward VI Handsworth School, Rose Hill Road, Birmingham B21 9AR.

INSKIP, family name of **Viscount Caldecote**.

INSOLE, Douglas John, CBE 1979; Marketing Director, Trollope & Colls Ltd, 1975–91; *b* 18 April 1926; *s* of John Herbert Insole and Margaret Rose Insole; *m* 1948, Barbara Hazel Ridgway (*d* 1982); two *d* (and one *d* decd). *Educ:* Sir George Monoux Grammar Sch.; St Catharine's Coll., Cambridge (MA). Cricket: Cambridge Univ., 1947–49 (Captain, 1949); Essex CCC, 1947–63 (Captain, 1950–60); played 9 times for England; Vice-Captain, MCC tour of S Africa, 1956–57. Chairman: Test Selectors, 1965–68; TCCB, later ECB, 1975–78 (Chm., Cricket Cttee, 1968–87; Chm., Internat. Cttee, 1988–2000); Mem., MCC Cttee, 1955–94; Manager, England cricket team, Australian tours, 1978–79 and 1982–83. Soccer: Cambridge Univ., 1946–48; Pegasus, and Corinthian Casuals; Amateur Cup Final medal, 1956. Member: Sports Council, 1971–74; FA Council, 1979– (Life Vice-Pres., 1999). Pres., Essex CCC, 1994–. JP Chingford, 1962–74. *Publication:* Cricket from the Middle, 1960. *Recreations:* cricket, soccer. *Address:* 8 Hadleigh Court, Crescent Road, Chingford, E4 6AX. *T:* (020) 8529 6546. *Club:* MCC (Trustee, 1988–94; Hon. Life Vice Pres., 1995).

INSTANCE, Caroline Mary; Chief Executive, Occupational Pensions Regulatory Authority, since 1996; *b* 4 May 1957; *d* of William Henry and Hilary Willatt; *m* 1st (marr. diss. 1995); one *s* one *d*; 2nd, 1998, John Instance; two step *d*. *Educ:* Henley Grammar Sch.; Sheffield Univ. (BSc Hons Psychol. 1978). MIPD. With Rank Orgn, 1978–82; United Friendly, 1982–96 (Human Resources Dir, 1993–96). *Recreations:* family life, enjoying countryside, theatre, cinema, good food and wine, teasing lawyers and actuaries. *Address:* Occupational Pensions Regulatory Authority, Invicta House, Trafalgar Place, Brighton BN1 4DW. *T:* (01273) 627618; *e-mail:* caroline.instance@opra.gov.uk. *Club:* Opra Sports and Social.

INVERFORTH, 4th Baron *cr* 1919, of Southgate; **Andrew Peter Weir;** *b* 16 Nov. 1966; *s* of 3rd Baron Inverforth and of Jill Elizabeth, *o d* of late John W. Thornycroft, CBE; S father, 1982; *m* 1992, Rachel Sian Shapland Davies; one *d*. *Educ:* Marlborough College; Trinity Coll., Cambridge; London Hosp. Med. Coll. MB BS 1994. *Heir: uncle* Hon. John Vincent Weir, *b* 8 Feb. 1935.

INVERNESS (St Andrew's Cathedral), Provost of; *see* Grant, Very Rev. M. E.

INVERURIE, Lord; James William Falconer Keith; Master of Kintore; *b* 15 April 1976; *s* and *heir* of Earl of Kintore, *qv*. *Address:* The Stables, Keith Hall, Inverurie, Aberdeenshire AB51 0LD.

INWOOD, Ven. Richard Neil; Archdeacon of Halifax, since 1995; *b* 4 March 1946; *s* of Cyril and Sylvia Inwood; *m* 1969, Elizabeth Joan Abram; three *d*. *Educ:* University Coll., Oxford (MA, BSc Chem.); Univ. of Nottingham (BA Theol.). Teacher, Uganda, 1969; Works R & D chemist, Dyestuffs Div., ICI, 1970–71; ministerial trng, St John's Coll., Nottingham, 1971–74; ordained deacon, 1974, priest, 1975; Curate: Christ Church, Fulwood, Sheffield, 1974–78; All Souls, Langham Place, W1, 1978–81; Vicar, St Luke's, Bath, 1981–89; Hon. Chaplain, Dorothy House Foundn, Bath, 1984–89; Rector, Yeovil with Kingston Pitney, 1989–95; Prebendary of Wells, 1990–95. *Publications:* Biblical Perspectives on Counselling, 1980; (jtly) The Church, 1987. *Recreations:* fell walking, gardening, music, family. *Address:* 2 Vicarage Gardens, Rastrick, Brighouse, West Yorks HD6 3HD. *T:* (01484) 714553, *Fax:* (01484) 711897.

ION, Dr Susan Elizabeth, FREng, FIM, FINucE; Director of Technology and Operations, British Nuclear Fuels Ltd, since 1996; *b* 3 Feb. 1955; *d* of Lawrence James Burrows and Doris Burrows (*née* Cherry); *m* 1980, John Albert Ion. *Educ:* Penwortham Girls' Grammar Sch., Preston, Lancs; Imperial Coll., London (BSc 1st Cl. Hons, DIC; PhD Materials Sci./Metallurgy 1979). FREng (FEng 1996). British Nuclear Fuels Ltd: Hd, R & D, Fuel Div., 1990–92; Dir, Technol. Devlt, 1992–96; Mem., Company Executive, 1996–. Mem., PPARC, 1994–2000. Hinton Medal for Outstanding Contribn to Nuclear Engrg, INucE, 1993. *Recreations:* ski-ing, fell walking, playing the violin. *Address:* British Nuclear Fuels Ltd, Risley, Warrington, Cheshire WA3 6AS.

IPSWICH, Viscount; Henry Oliver Charles FitzRoy; *b* 6 April 1978; *s* and *heir* of Earl of Euston, *qv*.

IPSWICH, Bishop of; *see* St Edmundsbury and Ipswich.

IPSWICH, Archdeacon of; *see* Gibson, Ven. T. A.

IRBY, family name of **Baron Boston**.

IRBY, Charles Leonard Anthony, FCA; Director, since 1999, and Chairman, since 2000, Aberdeen Asset Management plc; Senior UK Adviser, ING Barings, since 1999; *b* 5 June 1945; *s* of Hon. Anthony P. Irby and Mary Irby (*née* Apponyi); *m* 1971, Sarah Jane Sutherland; one *s* one *d*. *Educ:* Eton Coll. FCA 1979. Binder Hamlyn & Co., Chartered Accountants, 1965–69; Joseph Sebag & Co., Stockbrokers, 1971–74; Baring Brothers & Co. Ltd, 1974–95 (Dir, 1985–95); Baring Brothers Asia Ltd, 1976–79; Dir, Baring Brothers Internat. Ltd, 1995–99 (Dep. Chm., 1997–99); Man. Dir, ING Barings, 1995–99. Director: E. C. Harris, 2001–; QBE Insurance GP Ltd, 2001–. Mem., Panel on Takeovers and Mergers, 1998–99. Chm., Corporate Finance Cttee, London Investment Bankers' Assoc., 1998–99. Mem. Council, King Edward VII's Hosp. Sister Agnes, 2000–. *Recreations:* travel, photography. *Address:* 125 Blenheim Crescent, W11 2EQ. *T:* (020) 7221 2979. *Club:* City of London.

IREDALE, Peter, PhD; FInstP, FIEE; Chairman: Oxfordshire Health Authority, 1996–2001; Four Counties Public Health Resources Unit, 1997–2000; *b* Brownhills, Staffs, 15 March 1932; *s* of late Henry Iredale and Annie (*née* Kirby); *m* 1957, Judith Margaret (*née* Marshall); one *s* three *d*. *Educ:* King Edward VIth Grammar Sch., Lichfield; Univ. of Bristol (BSc, PhD). AERE Harwell (subseq. Harwell Laboratory), 1955–92: research: on Nuclear Instrumentation, 1955–69; on Non Destructive Testing, 1969–70; Computer Storage, 1970–73; Commercial Officer, 1973–75; Gp Leader, Nuclear Instrumentation, 1975–77; Dep. Hd, Marketing and Sales Dept, 1977–79; Hd of Marine Technology Support Unit, 1979–81; Chm., UK Wave-Energy Steering Cttee, 1979–84; Dir, Engrg, 1981–84; Dir, Engrg and Non Nuclear Energy, 1984–86; Dep. Dir, 1986–87, Dir, 1987–90, Harwell Lab.; Dir, Culham/Harwell Sites, UKAEA, 1990–92. Chairman: Oxfordshire DHA, 1992–96; Devlt Bd, Oxford Inst. of Health Scis, 1993–2001. Supernumerary Fellow, 1991–99, Mem. of Common Room, Wolfson Coll., Oxford. Hon. DSc Oxford Brookes, 1993. *Publications:* papers on high energy physics, nuclear instrumentation. *Recreations:* family, music, working with wood, gardening. *Address:* 25 Kirk Close, Oxford, OX2 8JL.

IREDALE, Prof. Roger Oliver, PhD; Professor of International Education, 1993–96, now Professor Emeritus, and Director (formerly Dean), Faculty of Education, 1994–96, University of Manchester; Senior Consultant, Iredale Development International, since 1996; *b* 13 Aug. 1934; *s* of Fred Iredale and Elsie Florence (*née* Hills); *m* 1968, Mavis Potter; one *s* one *d*. *Educ:* Harrow County Grammar Sch.; Univ. of Reading (BA 1956, MA 1959, PhD 1971; Hurry Medal for Poetry; Early English Text Soc's Prize; Seymour-Sharman Prize for Literature; Graham Robertson Travel Award); Peterhouse Coll., Univ. of Cambridge (Cert. Ed. 1957). Teacher, Hele's Sch., Exeter, 1959–61; Lectr and Senior Lectr, Bishop Otter Coll., Chichester, 1962–70; British Council Officer and Maître de Conférences, Univ. of Algiers, 1970–72; Lectr, Chichester Coll. of Further Educn, 1972–73; British Council Officer, Madras, 1973–75; Dir of Studies, Educl Admin., Univ. of Leeds, 1975–79; Educn Adviser, 1979–83, Chief Educn Advr, 1983–93, ODA. Member: Commonwealth Scholarship Commn, 1984–93; Unesco-Unicef Jt Cttee, 1991–96; Comr, Sino-British Friendship Scholarship Scheme Commn, 1986–96. Governor: Sch. of Oriental and African Studies, 1983–95; Queen Elizabeth House, Oxford, 1986–87; Commonwealth of Learning, 1988–93. Trustee, 1993–98, non-exec. Dir, 1998–, CfBT Educn Services. Trustee, War on Want, 1998–2000. Hon. FCP 1995. Poetry Society's Greenwood Prize, 1974. *Publications:* Turning Bronzes (poems), 1974; Out Towards the Dark (poems), 1978; articles in Comparative Education and other jls; poems for BBC Radio 3 and in anthologies and jls. *Recreations:* poetry writing, restoring the discarded. *Address:* Northsyde House, 17 High Street, West Coker, Yeovil BA22 9AP. *T:* (01935) 864422.

IRELAND, Norman Charles; Chairman, BTR, 1993–96 (Director, 1969–96); *b* 28 May 1927; *s* of Charles and Winifred Ireland; *m* 1953, Gillian Margaret (*née* Harrison) (*d* 2001); one *s* one *d*. *Educ:* England, USA, India. CA (Scot.); Chartered Management Accountant. With Richard Brown & Co., Edinburgh, 1944–50; Brown Fleming & Murray, London, 1950–54; Avon Rubber Co., Melksham, 1955–64; Chief Accountant, United Glass, 1964–66; Finance Dir, BTR, 1967–87; Chm., Bowater plc, 1987–93. Chairman: The Housing Finance Corp., 1988–93; Intermediate Capital Gp, 1989–93; Dir, Meggitt, 1987–93. *Recreations:* gardening, ballet, opera, music.

IRELAND, Patrick Gault de C.; *see* de Courcy-Ireland.

IRELAND, Ronald David; QC (Scotland) 1964; Sheriff Principal of Grampian, Highland and Islands, 1988–93; *b* 13 March 1925; *o s* of William Alexander Ireland and Agnes Victoria Brown. *Educ:* George Watson's Coll., Edinburgh; Balliol Coll., Oxford (Scholar); Edinburgh Univ. Served Royal Signals, 1943–46. BA Oxford, 1950, MA 1958; LLB Edinburgh, 1952. Passed Advocate, 1952; Clerk of the Faculty of Advocates, 1957–58; Aberdeen University: Prof. of Scots Law, 1958–71; Dean of Faculty of Law, 1964–67; Hon. Prof., Faculty of Law, 1988–; Sheriff of Lothian and Borders (formerly Lothians and Peebles) at Edinburgh, 1972–88. Governor, Aberdeen Coll. of Education, 1959–64 (Vice-Chm., 1962–64). Comr, under NI (Emergency Provisions) Act, 1974–75. Member: Bd of Management, Aberdeen Gen. Hosps, 1961–71 (Chm., 1964–71); Departmental Cttee on Children and Young Persons, 1961–64; Cttee on the Working of the Abortion Act, 1971–74; Hon. Sheriff for Aberdeenshire, 1963–88. Member: North Eastern Regional Hosp. Bd, 1964–71 (Vice-Chm. 1966–71); After Care Council, 1962–65; Nat. Staff Advisory Cttee for the Scottish Hosp. Service, 1964–65; Chm., Scottish Hosps Administrative Staffs Cttee, 1965–72. Dir, Scottish Courts Admin, 1975–78. Hon. LLD Aberdeen, 1994. *Address:* 6A Greenhill Gardens, Edinburgh EH10 4BW. *Clubs:* New (Edinburgh); Royal Northern and University (Aberdeen); Highland (Inverness).

IRETON, Barrie Rowland, CB 2000; Director-General, Programmes, Department for International Development (formerly Overseas Development Administration, Foreign and Commonwealth Office), since 1996; *b* 15 Jan. 1944; *s* of Philip Thomas Ireton, CBE, and Marjorie Rosalind Ireton; *m* 1965, June Collins; one *s* one *d* (and one *s* decd). *Educ:* Alleyn's Grammar Sch., Stevenage; Trinity Coll., Cambridge (MA); London School of Economics (MSc 1970). Economic Statistician, Govt of Zambia, 1965–68; Economist, Industrial Develt Corp., Zambia, 1968–69; Development Sec., The Gambia, 1970–73; Overseas Development Administration; Economic Advr, 1973–76; Sen. Economic Advr, 1976–84; Asst Sec., 1984–88; Under Sec., 1988–96; Principal Finance Officer, 1988–93; Hd, Africa Div., 1993–96. *Recreations:* tennis, gardening, walking. *Address:* Department for International Development, 1 Palace Street, SW1E 5HE.

IRONS, Jeremy; actor; *b* 19 Sept. 1948; *s* of late Paul Dugan Irons and of Barbara Anne Brereton (*née* Sharpe); *m* 1st (marr. diss.); 2nd, 1978, Sinead Cusack; two *s*. *Educ:* Sherborne; Bristol Old Vic Theatre Sch. *Theatre* appearances include: Bristol Old Vic Theatre Co., 1968–71; Godspell, Round House, transf. Wyndham's, 1971; The Taming of the Shrew, New Shakespeare Co., Round House, 1975; Wild Oats, RSC, 1976–77; The Rear Column, Globe, 1978; The Real Thing, Broadway, 1984 (Tony Award for Best Actor); The Rover, Mermaid, 1986; A Winter's Tale, RSC, 1986; Richard II, RSC, 1986; *television* appearances include: The Pallisers; Love for Lydia; Brideshead Revisited, 1981; The Captain's Doll, 1983; Longitude, 2000; *films* include: The French Lieutenant's Woman, 1981; Moonlighting, 1982; Betrayal, 1982; Swann in Love, 1983; The Wild Duck, 1983; The Mission, 1986; A Chorus of Disapproval, 1988; Dead Ringers, 1988; Danny Champion of the World, 1988; Reversal of Fortune, 1990; Australia, 1991; Kafka, 1992; Waterland, 1992; Damage, 1993; M. Butterfly, 1994; The House of the Spirits, 1994; Die Hard: with a vengeance, 1995; Stealing Beauty, 1996; Lolita, 1997; The Man in the Iron Mask, 1998; Chinese Box, 1998; Dungeons and Dragons, 2001. Member: Gaia Foundn; European Film Acad.; Patron: Prison Phoenix Trust; Archway Foundn. *Address:* c/o Hutton Management, 4 Old Manor Close, Askett, Bucks HP27 9NA.

IRONS, Norman MacFarlane, CBE 1995; JP; DL; CEng; Lord Provost and Lord Lieutenant of Edinburgh, 1992–96; Partner, IFP Consulting Engineers, since 1983; *b* 4 Jan. 1941; *s* of Dugald Paterson Irons and Anne Galbraith Irons (*née* Rankin); *m* 1966, Anne Wyness Buckley; one *s* one *d*. *Educ:* George Heriot's Sch.; Borough Road Coll.; Napier Tech. Coll. CEng; MCIBSE 1968; MIMechE 1973. Building Services Engr, 1962–. Mem. (SNP) City of Edinburgh Council, 1976–96. JP 1983, DL 1988, Edinburgh. Pres., Lismore RFC, 1989–94. Hon. Consul for Denmark, 1999. Paul Harris Fellow, Rotary Internat., 1996. Hon. FRCSE 1994. Hon. DLitt Napier, 1993; DUniv Heriot-Watt, 1997. Royal Order of Merit (Norway), 1994. *Recreations:* enjoying life with wife, Rugby. *Address:* 11 Laughtonhall Drive, Edinburgh EH12 5TS. *T:* (0131) 337 6154. *Club:* New (Edinburgh).

IRONSIDE, family name of **Baron Ironside**.

IRONSIDE, 2nd Baron *cr* 1941, of Archangel and of Ironside; **Edmund Oslac Ironside;** Defence Consultant, Rolls-Royce Industrial Power Group, 1989–95; *b* 21 Sept. 1924; *o s* of 1st Baron Ironside, Field Marshal, GCB, CMG, DSO, and Mariot Ysabel Cheyne (*d* 1984); *S* father, 1959; *m* 1950, Audrey Marigold, *y d* of late Lt-Col Hon. Thomas Morgan-Grenville, DSO, OBE, MC; one *s* one *d*. *Educ:* Tonbridge Sch. Joined Royal Navy, 1943; retd as Lt, 1952. English Electric Gp, 1952–63; Cryosystems Ltd, 1963–68; International Research and Development Co., 1968–84; Market Co-ordinator (Defence), NEI plc, 1984–89. Vice-Pres., Parly and Scientific Cttee, 1984–87 (Dep. Chm., 1974–77); Chm., All Party Defence Study Gp, 1995–99 (Hon. Sec., 1992–95). Mem., Organising Cttee, British Library, 1971–72. President: Electric Vehicle Assoc., 1976–83; European Electric Road Vehicle Assoc., 1980–82; Vice-Pres., Inst. of Patentees and Inventors, 1977–91; Chm., Adv. Cttee, Science Reference Lib., 1976–84. Governor, Tonbridge Sch. and others; Member: Court, 1971–96, Council, 1987–89, City Univ.; Court, 1982–, Council, 1982–87, Essex Univ. Master, Skinners' Co., 1981–82. Hon. FCGI (CGIA 1986). *Publication:* (ed) High Road to Command: the diaries of Major-General Sir Edmund Ironside, 1920–22, 1972. *Heir:* *s* Hon. Charles Edmund Grenville Ironside [*b* 1 July 1956; *m* 1st, 1985, Hon. Elizabeth Law (marr. diss. 2001), *e d* of Lord Coleraine, *qv*; one *s* two *d*; 2nd, 2001, Katherine Rowley]. *Address:* Priory House, Old House Lane, Boxted, Colchester, Essex CO4 5RB. *Club:* Royal Ocean Racing.

IRVINE, family name of **Baron Irvine of Lairg**.

IRVINE OF LAIRG, Baron *cr* 1987 (Life Peer), of Lairg in the District of Sutherland; **Alexander Andrew Mackay Irvine;** PC 1997; Lord High Chancellor of Great Britain, since 1997; *b* 23 June 1940; *s* of Alexander Irvine and Margaret Christina Irvine; *m* 1974, Alison Mary, *y d* of Dr James Shaw McNair, MD, and Agnes McNair, MA; two *s*. *Educ:* Inverness Acad.; Hutchesons' Boys' Grammar Sch., Glasgow; Glasgow Univ. (MA, LLB); Christ's Coll., Cambridge (Scholar; BA 1st Cl. Hons with distinction; LLB 1st Cl. Hons; George Long Prize in Jurisprudence; Hon. Fellow, 1996). Called to the Bar, Inner Temple, 1967, Bencher, 1985; QC 1978; a Recorder, 1985–88; Dep. High Court Judge, 1987–97. Univ. Lectr, LSE, 1965–69. Contested (Lab) Hendon North, 1970. Opposition spokesman on legal and home affairs, 1987–92; Shadow Lord Chancellor, H of L, 1992–97. Joint President: Industry and Parlt Trust, 1997–; British-Amer. Parly Gp, 1997–; IPU, 1997–; CPA, 1997–; Pres., Magistrates' Assoc. Church Comr. Trustee, John Smith Meml Trust, 1992–97; Foundn Trustee, Whitechapel Art Gall., 1990–; Trustee, Hunterian Collection, 1997–. Mem. Cttee, Friends of the Slade, 1990–. Hon. Bencher, Inn of Court of NI, 1998. Fellow, US Coll. of Trial Lawyers, 1998; Hon. Fellow, Soc. for Advanced Legal Studies, 1997. Hon. Mem., Polish Bar, 2000. Hon. LLD Glasgow, 1997–; Dr *hc* Siena, 2000. *Recreations:* cinema, theatre, collecting paintings, travel. *Address:* Lord Chancellor's Office, House of Lords SW1A 0PW. *Club:* Garrick.

IRVINE, Alan Montgomery, RDI 1964; DesRCA, ARIBA; architect in private practice; *b* 14 Sept. 1926; *s* of Douglas Irvine and Ellen Marler; *m* 1st, 1955; one *s*; 2nd, 1966, Katherine Mary Buzas; two *s*. *Educ:* Regent Street Polytechnic, Secondary Sch. and Sch. of Architecture; Royal College of Art. RAF (Aircrew), 1944–47. Worked in Milan with BBPR Gp, 1954–55. In private practice since 1956, specialising in design of interiors, museums and exhibitions; partnership Buzas and Irvine, 1965–85. Accredited correspondent to NASA, Apollo 13 Mission, 1970. Work has included interior design for Schroder Wagg & Co., Lazards, Bovis, S Australian Govt, Nat. Enterprise Bd; Mem. of design team for QE2, 1966. Various exhibns for V&A Museum, Tate Gallery, Royal Academy, Imperial War Museum, RIBA, British Council, British Museum, Wellcome Inst., Olivetti, Fiat etc including: Treasures of Cambridge, 1959; Book of Kells, 1961; Internat. Exhibn of Modern Jewellery, 1961; Architecture of Power, 1963; Mellon Collection, 1969; Art and the E India Trade, 1970; Age of Charles I, 1972; Internat. Ceramics, 1972; Pompeii AD79, 1976; Gold of El Dorado, 1978; Medals: Mirror of History, 1979; Horses of San Marco (London, NY, Milan, Berlin), 1979–82; Great Japan Exhibition, 1981; Art and Industry, 1982; Cimabue Crucifix (London, Madrid, Munich), 1982–83; Treasures of Ancient Nigeria, 1983; The Genius of Venice, 1983; Leonardo da Vinci: studies for the Last Supper (Milan, Sydney, Toronto, Barcelona, Tokyo), 1984; Art of the Architect, 1984; Re dei Confessori (Milan, Venice), 1985; C. S. Jagger: War and Peace Sculpture, 1985; Queen Elizabeth II: portraits of 60 years, 1986; Eye for Industry, 1986; Glass of the Caesars (London, Cologne, Rome), 1988; Michelangelo Drawings, Louvre, 1989; Conservation Today, 1989; Paul de Lamerie, 1990; Lion of Venice (London, Amsterdam), 1991; David Smith Medals, 1991; Leonardo and Venezia, Venice, 1992. Museum work includes: Old Master Drawings Gallery, Windsor Castle, 1965; New Galleries for Royal Scottish Museum, 1968; Crown Jewels display, Tower of London, 1968; Heinz Gallery for Architectural Drawings, RIBA, London, 1972; Museum and Art Gallery for Harrow School, 1975; Heralds' Museum, London, 1980; Housesteads Roman Fort Mus., 1982; Al Shaheed Museum, Baghdad, 1983; Cabinet War Rooms, London, 1984; West Wing Galls, Nat. Maritime Mus., Greenwich, 1986; Beatrix Potter Museum, Cumbria, 1988; George III Gall., Science Mus., 1993; English Sculpture Gall., V&A Mus., 1999; Fleming Foundn Gall., London, 2001; Monumental Tower, Bologna Airport, 2001; Treasuries at: Winchester Cathedral, 1968; Christ Church, Oxford, 1975; Winchester Coll., 1982; Lichfield Cath., 1993. Retrospective personal exhibitions: RIBA Heinz Gall., 1989; Portraits from Detroit: US cars 1940s–60s, photographs by Alan Irvine, RCA, 1996. Consultant designer to Olivetti, Italy, 1979–89; Consultant architect to British Museum, 1981–84. Mem., Crafts Council, 1984–86. Liveryman, Worshipful Co. of Goldsmiths. Hon. Fellow, RCA. *Recreations:* travel, photography. *Address:* 2 Aubrey Place, St John's Wood, NW8 9BH. *T:* (020) 7328 2229. *Club:* London Collie.

IRVINE, Rev. Christopher Paul; Principal, College of the Resurrection, Mirfield, since 1998; *b* 17 Dec. 1951; *s* of Joseph Ernest Irvine and Phyllis Irvine; *m* 1978, Rosemary Hardwicke; two *d*. *Educ:* Univ. of Nottingham (BTh); Univ. of Lancaster (MA); Kelham Theol Coll. Ordained deacon and priest, 1976; Asst Curate, St Mary, Stoke Newington, 1977–80; Anglican Chaplain, Sheffield Univ., 1980–85; Chaplain, St Edmund Hall, Oxford, 1985–90; Tutor, 1985–90, Vice-Principal, 1991–94, St Stephen's House, Oxford; Vicar, Cowley St John, Oxford, 1994–98. *Publications:* Worship, Church and Society, 1993; (ed) Celebrating the Easter Mystery, 1996; (ed) They shaped our Worship, 1998. *Recreations:* reading modern novels, poetry, gardening, film. *Address:* College of the Resurrection, Mirfield, W Yorks WF14 0BW. *T:* (01924) 481908.

IRVINE, Sir Donald (Hamilton), Kt 1994; CBE 1987 (OBE 1979); MD; FRCGP; Principal in General Practice, Ashington, 1960–95; Regional Adviser in General Practice, University of Newcastle, 1973–95; President, General Medical Council, 1995–2002; *b* 2 June 1935; *s* of late Dr Andrew Bell Hamilton Irvine and Dorothy Mary Irvine; *m* 1960; two *s* one *d*; *m* 1986, Sally Fountain. *Educ:* King Edward Sixth Grammar Sch., Morpeth; Medical Sch., King's Coll., Univ. of Durham (MB BS); DObstRCOG 1960; MD Newcastle 1964; FRCGP 1972 (MRCGP 1965). House Phys. to Dr C. N. Armstrong and Dr Henry Miller, 1958–59. Chm. Council, RCGP, 1982–85 (Vice-Chm., 1981–82); Hon. Sec. of the College, 1972–78; Jt Hon. Sec., Jt Cttee on Postgraduate Trng for General Practice, 1976–82; Fellow, BMA, 1976; Mem., Gen. Medical Council, 1979 (Chm., Cttee on Standards and Medical Ethics, 1985–95); Governor, MSD Foundn, 1982–89 (Chm., Bd of Governors, 1983–89). Vice-Pres., Medical Defence Union, 1974–78. Vis. Professor in Family Practice, Univ. of Iowa, USA, 1973; (first) Vis. Prof. to Royal Australian Coll. of General Practitioners, 1977; Vis. Cons. on Postgrad. Educn for Family Medicine to Virginia Commonwealth Univ., 1971, Univ. of Wisconsin-Madison, 1973, Medical Univ. of S Carolina, 1974. Mem., Audit Commn, 1990–96. Founder FMedSci 1998. *Publications:* The Future General Practitioner: learning and teaching, (jtly), 1972 (RCGP); Managing for Quality in General Practice, 1990; (ed jtly) Making Sense of Audit, 1991, 2nd edn 1997; (with Sally Irvine) The Practice of Quality, 1996; chapters to several books on gen. practice; papers on clinical and educnl studies in medicine, in BMJ, Lancet, Jl of RCGP. *Recreations:* bird watching, gardening, walking, watching television. *Address:* Mole End, Fairmoor, Morpeth NE61 3JL; Flat 1, Rossetti House, 106–110 Hallam Street, W1N 6JE.

IRVINE, His Honour James Eccles Malise; a Circuit Judge, 1972–96 (Leicester County and Crown Courts, 1972–82; Oxford and Northampton Combined Courts Centres, 1982–96); *b* 10 July 1925; *y s* of late Brig.-Gen. A. E. Irvine, CB, CMG, DSO, Wotton-under-Edge; *m* 1954, Anne, *e d* of late Col G. Egerton-Warburton, DSO, TD, JP, DL, Grafton Hall, Malpas; one *s* one *d*. *Educ:* Stowe Sch. (Scholar); Merton Coll., Oxford (Postmaster; MA Oxon 1953). Served Grenadier Guards, 1943–46 (France and Germany Star); Hon. Captain Grenadier Guards, 1946. Called to Bar, Inner Temple, 1949 (Poland Prizeman in Criminal Law, 1949); practised Oxford Circuit, 1949–71; Prosecuting Counsel for Inland Revenue on Oxford Circuit, 1965–71; Dep. Chm., Glos QS, 1967–71. Lay Judge of Court of Arches of Canterbury and Chancery Court of York, 1981–2000. Pres. Oxon Br., Grenadier Guards Assoc., 1990–. Pres., Heyford and Dist. Br., RBL, 1999–. *Publication:* Parties and Pleasures: the Diaries of Helen Graham 1823–26, 1957. *Address:* 2 Harcourt Buildings, Temple, EC4Y 9DB.

IRVINE, Very Rev. John Dudley; Dean of Coventry Cathedral, since 2001; *b* 2 Jan. 1949; 3rd *s* of Rt Hon. Sir Arthur Irvine, QC, MP and Eleanor Irvine; *m* 1972, Andrea Mary Carr; three *s* one *d*. *Educ:* Sussex Univ. (BA (Hons) Law, 1970); Wycliffe Hall, Oxford (BA (Hons) Theol., 1980; MA 1985). Called to the Bar, Middle Temple, 1973; in practice, Inner Temple, 1973-78. Ordained deacon, 1981, priest, 1982; Curate, Holy Trinity, Brompton with St Paul's, Onslow Sq., 1981-85; Priest i/c, 1985-95, Vicar, 1995-2001, St Barnabas, Kensington. *Recreations:* travel, film, theatre, walking. *Address:* The Deanery, 11 Priory Row, Coventry CV1 5ES. *T:* (024) 7626 7045, *Fax:* (024) 7663 1448; *e-mail:* dean@coventrycathedral.org.

See also M. F. Irvine.

IRVINE, John Ferguson, CB 1983; charities financial consultant; Chief Executive, Industrial Therapy Organisation (Ulster), 1984–94; *b* 13 Nov. 1920; *s* of Joseph Ferguson Irvine and Helen Gardner; *m* 1st, 1945, Doris Partridge (*d* 1973); one *s* one *d*; 2nd, 1980, Christine Margot Tudor; two *s* and two step *s*. *Educ:* Ardrossan Acad.; Glasgow Univ. (MA). RAF, 1941–46; Scottish Home Dept, 1946–48; NI Civil Service, 1948–66; Chief Exec., Ulster Transport Authority, 1966–68; Chief Exec., NI Transport Holding Co., 1968; NI Civil Service, 1969–83; Dep. Sec., DoE, NI, 1971–76; Permanent Secretary: attached NI Office, 1977–80; Dept of Manpower Services, 1980–81; DoE for NI, 1981–83. Chm. Management Cttee, 1974–75, and Vice-Chm. General Council, 1975, Action Cancer; Chm., Down Care and Aftercare Cttee, 1992–; Member: NI Marriage Guidance Council (Chm., 1976–78); Council, PHAB (NI), 1984–86; Council, PHAB (UK), 1984–86; Trustee, Heart Fund, Royal Victoria Hosp., Belfast, 1986–88. Mem.,

Downpatrick Inter-Church Caring Project, 1996–. *Recreations:* swimming, yoga, Majorca, football. *Address:* 7 Bullseye Park, Downpatrick, Co. Down BT30 6RX.

IRVINE, John Jeremy; Middle East Correspondent, ITN, since 2000; *b* 2 June 1963; *s* of Dr Kenneth Irvine and Jacqueline Irvine; *m* 1992, Libby McCann; one *s* one *d*. *Educ:* Brackenber House Prep. Sch., Belfast; Campbell Coll., Belfast. Reporter: Tyrone Constitution, Omagh, 1983-87; Ulster TV, Belfast, 1987-94; Ireland Corresp., ITN, 1987-2000. *Recreation:* golf. *Address:* c/o ITN, 200 Gray's Inn Road, WC1X 8XZ; 39 Deramore Drive, Belfast BT9 5JS. *Club:* Malone Golf (Belfast).

IRVINE, Prof. (John) Maxwell, DL; PhD; CPhys, FInstP; FRAS; FRSE; Professor of Physics, University of Manchester, since 2001; *b* 28 Feb. 1939; *s* of John MacDonald Irvine and Joan Paterson (*née* Adamson); *m* 1962, Grace Ritchie; one *s*. *Educ:* George Heriot's Sch., Edinburgh; Edinburgh Univ. (BSc Math. Phys. 1961); Univ. of Michigan (MSc 1962); Univ. of Manchester (PhD 1964). FInstP 1971; CPhys 1985; FRAS 1986; FRSE 1993. English-Speaking Union Fellow, Univ. of Michigan, 1961–62; Asst Lectr, Univ. of Manchester, 1964–66; Res. Associate, Cornell Univ., 1966–68; University of Manchester: Lectr, 1968–73; Sen. Lectr, 1973–76; Reader, 1976–83; Prof. of Theoretical Physics, 1983–91; Dean of Science, 1989–91; Principal and Vice-Chancellor, Aberdeen Univ., 1991–96; Vice-Chancellor and Principal, Univ. of Birmingham, 1996–2001. Chairman: CVCP Information Systems Sector Gp, 1996–98; Cttee of Scottish Univ. Principals, 1994–96; W Midlands Regl Innovation Strategy Gp, 1996–2001; Jt Information Systems Cttee, 1998–. Director: Grampian Enterprise Ltd, 1992–96; Rowett Res. Inst., 1992–96. Member: Nuclear Physics Bd, SERC, 1983–88 (Chm., Nuclear Structure Cttee, 1984–88); Bd, Scottish Council for Develt and Industry, 1992–96; Scottish Econ. Council, 1993–96; Scottish Cttee, British Council, 1994–96; BT Scottish Forum, 1994–96; Bd, HEQC, 1994–97; Univ. and Colls Employers Assoc., 1995–2001; UCAS, 1995–2001; Bd, PHLS, 1997–. Member Council: ACU 1994– (Chm., 1995; Treas., 1998–); CVCP, 1996–2001; NERC, 1998–2001. Vice-Pres., 1982–87, Mem. Council, 1981–87, 1988–94, Inst. of Physics. Gov., ESU, 1999–. FRSA 1993; CIMgt 1996. DL West Midlands, 1999. Hon. FRCSEd 1995. Hon. DSc Coll. of William and Mary in Va, 1995; Hon. DEd Robert Gordon Univ., 1995; DUniv Edin., 1995; Hon. LLD Aberdeen, 1997. *Publications:* The Basis of Modern Physics, 1967 (trans. Dutch and French, 1969); Nuclear Structure Theory, 1972; Heavy Nuclei, Superheavy Nuclei and Neutron Stars, 1975; Neutron Stars, 1978; research articles on nuclear physics, astrophysics and condensed matter physics. *Recreations:* hill walking, tennis, bridge. *Address:* Shuster Laboratory, University of Manchester, Manchester M13 9PL.

IRVINE, Very Rev. (John) Murray; Provost and Rector of Southwell Minster, 1978–91, Emeritus, since 1991; Priest-in-Charge of Edingley and Halam, 1978–91; Priest-in-Charge of Rolleston with Fiskerton and Morton and Upton, 1990–91; *b* 19 Aug. 1924; *s* of Andrew Leicester Irvine and Eleanor Mildred (*née* Lloyd); *m* 1st, 1961, Pamela Shirley Brain (*d* 1992); one *s* three *d*; 2nd, 2000, Miriam Ruth van Laun (*née* Davis). *Educ:* Charterhouse; Magdalene Coll., Cambridge; Ely Theological Coll. BA 1946, MA 1949. Deacon, 1948; Priest, 1949; Curate of All Saints, Poplar, 1948–53; Chaplain of Sidney Sussex Coll., Cambridge, 1953–60; Selection Sec. of CACTM, 1960–65; Canon Residentiary, Prebendary of Hunderton, Chancellor and Librarian of Hereford Cathedral, and Dir of Ordination Training, Diocese of Hereford, 1965–78; Warden of Readers, 1976–78. *Address:* 9 Salston Barton, Strawberry Lane, Ottery St Mary, Devon EX11 1RG. *T:* (01404) 815901.

IRVINE, Michael Fraser; barrister; *b* 21 Oct. 1939; *s* of Rt Hon. Sir Arthur Irvine, PC, QC, MP, and Eleanor Irvine. *Educ:* Rugby; Oriel College, Oxford (BA). Called to the Bar, Inner Temple, 1964. Contested (C): Bishop Auckland, 1979; Ipswich, 1992; MP (C) Ipswich, 1987–92. PPS to Attorney-Gen., 1990–92. *Recreation:* hill walking in Scotland. *Address:* 3 Hare Court, Temple, EC4Y 7BJ. *T:* (020) 7415 7800.

IRVINE, Very Rev. Murray; *see* Irvine, Very Rev. J. M.

IRVINE, Norman Forrest; QC 1973; a Recorder of the Crown Court, 1974–86; *b* 29 Sept. 1922; *s* of William Allan Irvine and Dorcas Forrest; *m* 1964, Mary Lilian Patricia Edmunds (*née* Constable); one *s*. *Educ:* High Sch. of Glasgow; Glasgow Univ. BL 1941. Solicitor (Scotland), 1943. Served War, 1942–45: Lieut Royal Signals, Staff Captain. HM Claims Commn, 1945–46; London Claims Supt, Provincial Insurance Co. Ltd, 1950–52. Called to Bar, Gray's Inn, 1955. *Recreations:* reading, piano, writing. *Address:* 11 Upland Park Road, Oxford OX2 7RU.

IRVINE, Prof. Robin Francis, FRS 1993; Royal Society Research Professor, Department of Pharmacology, University of Cambridge, since 1996; *b* 10 Feb. 1950; *s* of Charles Donald Irvine and June (*née* Ievers); *m* 1973, Sandra Jane Elder; two *s*. *Educ:* Stroud Sch., Romsey; Sherborne Sch., Dorset; St Catherine's Coll., Oxford (MA Biochem. 1972); Corpus Christi Coll., Cambridge (PhD Botany 1976). SRC Res. Student, ARC Unit of Developmental Botany, Cambridge, 1972–75; Beit Meml Fellow, ARC Inst. of Animal Physiol., Babraham, 1975–78; Mem. of Scientific Staff, 1978–95, UG5, 1993–95, AFRC Inst. of Animal Physiol. and Genetics Res., subseq. AFRC Babraham Inst., Cambridge. Mem., Wellcome Trust Cell and Molecular Panel, 1989–92. Council, Royal Soc., 1999–2001. Morton Lectr, Biochem. Soc., 1994. FIBiol 1998; Founder FMedSci 1998. Member Editorial Board, Biochemical Jl, 1988–96; Cell, 1994–; Current Biology, 1994–; Molecular Pharmacology, 2000–. *Publications:* (ed) Methods in Inositide Research, 1990; contribs to Nature, Biochem. Jl and other scientific jls. *Recreations:* playing the lute and guitar, music (especially pre-1650), ornithology, reading. *Address:* Department of Pharmacology, Tennis Court Road, Cambridge CB2 1QJ. *T:* (01223) 339683.

IRVINE, Sarah Frances; *see* Beamish, S. F.

IRVING, Clifford; *see* Irving, E. C.

IRVING, Edward, ScD; FRS 1979; FRSC 1973; Research Scientist, Pacific Geoscience Centre, Sidney, BC, 1981–92, Emeritus since 1992; *b* 27 May 1927; *s* of George Edward and Nellie Irving; *m* 1957, Sheila Ann Irwin; two *s* two *d*. *Educ:* Colne Grammar Sch.; Cambridge Univ., 1948–54 (BA, MA, MSc, ScD). Served Army, 1945–48. Research Fellow, Fellow and Sen. Fellow, ANU, 1954–64; Dominion Observatory, Canada, 1964–66; Prof. of Geophysics, Univ. of Leeds, 1966–67; Res. Scientist, Dominion Observatory, later Earth Physics Br., Dept of Energy, Mines and Resources, Ottawa, 1967–81; Adjunct Professor: Carleton Univ., Ottawa, 1975–81; Univ. of Victoria, 1985–94. FRAS 1958; Fellow: Amer. Geophysical Union, 1976 (Walter H. Bucher Medal, 1979); Geological Soc. of America, 1979 (Arthur L. Day Medal, 1997); For. Associate, NAS, US, 1998. Hon. FGS 1989. Hon. DSc: Carleton, 1979; Memorial Univ. of Newfoundland, 1986; Victoria, 1999. Gondwanaland Medal, Mining, Geological and Metallurgical Soc. of India, 1962; Logan Medal, Geol Assoc. of Canada, 1975; J. T. Wilson Medal, Canadian Geophys. Union, 1984; Alfred Wegener Medal, European Geoscience Union, 1995. *Publications:* Paleomagnetism, 1964; numerous contribs to learned jls. *Recreations:* gardening, carpentry, choral singing. *Address:* Pacific Geoscience Centre, 9860 West Saanich Road, Box 6000, Sidney, BC V8L 4B2 Canada. *T:* (250) 3636508; 9363 Carnoustie Crescent, Sidney, BC V8L 5G7. *T:* (250) 6569645; *e-mail:* tirving@pgc-gsc.nrcan.gc.ca.

IRVING, (Edward) Clifford, CBE 1981; Member, Legislative Council, Isle of Man, 1987–95; *b* 24 May 1914; *s* of late William Radcliffe Irving and Mabel Henrietta (*née* Cottier); *m* 1941, Nora, *d* of Harold Page, Luton; one *s* one *d*. *Educ:* Isle of Man; Canada. Member: House of Keys, 1955–61, 1966–81, 1984–87 (Acting Speaker, 1971–81); Executive Council, IOM Govt, 1968–81 (Chm., 1977–81). Member, IOM Government Boards: Airports, 1955–58; Assessment, 1955–56; Social Security, 1956; Local Govt, 1956–62; Tourist, 1956–62; Finance, 1966–71; Member: Industrial Adv. Council, 1961–62, 1971–81, 1987–94; CS Commn, 1976–81. Chairman: IOM Tourist Bd, 1971–81; IOM Sports Council, 1971–81; IOM Harbours Bd, 1985–87. Chairman: Bank of Wales (IOM), 1985–87; Etam (IOM), 1985–; Refuge (IOM) Ltd, 1988–92; Director: Bank of Scotland (IOM) Ltd, 1987–95 (Chm., 1987–89); Bank of Scotland Nominees (IOM) Ltd, 1987–95 (Chm., 1987–89). President: Wanderers Male Voice Choir; Manx Nat. Powerboat Club; Manx Parascending Club; IOM Angling Assoc.; Douglas Br., RNLI; Douglas and Dist Angling Club; Douglas Bay Yacht Club; Past Rotarians' Club of IOM, 1996–97; Past Patron: Manx Variety Club; IOM TT Races. *Recreations:* powerboating, angling. *Address:* Highfield, Belmont Road, Douglas, Isle of Man IM1 4NR. *T:* (01624) 673652. *Clubs:* Douglas and District Angling; Douglas Bay Yacht.

IRVING, John Winslow; novelist; *b* Exeter, New Hampshire, 2 March 1942; *s* of Colin Franklin Newell Irving and Frances Winslow Irving; *m* 1st, 1964, Shyla Leary (marr. diss. 1981); two *s*; 2nd, 1987, Janet Turnbull; one *s*. *Educ:* Phillips Exeter Acad., USA; Univ. of New Hampshire (BA 1965); Univ. of Iowa (MFA 1967). Professor of English: Windham Coll., 1967–72; Univ. of Iowa, 1972–75; Mount Holyoke Coll., 1975–78; Brandeis Univ., 1978–79. Wrestling Coach: Northfield Mt Hermon Sch., 1981–83; Fessenden Sch., 1983–86; Vermont Acad., 1987–89. Rockefeller Foundn Award, 1972; Nat. Endowment for the Arts Award, 1974; Guggenheim Foundn Fellowship, 1978. *Publications:* Setting Free the Bears, 1968; The Water-Method Man, 1972; The 158-Pound Marriage, 1974; The World According to Garp, 1978 (Nat. Book Award, USA, 1979); The Hotel New Hampshire, 1981; The Cider House Rules, 1985 (screenplay, 1999; Best Screenplay Award, Nat. Bd of Review, 1999; Academy Award for best adapted screenplay, 2000); A Prayer for Owen Meany, 1989; A Son of the Circus, 1994; Trying to Save Piggy Snead, 1996; A Widow for One Year, 1998; My Movie Business: a memoir, 1999; The Fourth Hand, 2001. *Address:* c/o The Turnbull Agency, POB 757, Dorset, VT 05251, USA. *Club:* New York Athletic.

IRVING, Sir Miles (Horsfall), Kt 1995; MD; FRCS, FRCSE; Professor of Surgery, University of Manchester, 1974–99, now Emeritus; Chairman, Newcastle upon Tyne NHS Hospitals Trust, since 1998; *b* 29 June 1935; *s* of Frederick William Irving and Mabel Irving; *m* 1965, Patricia Margaret Blaiklock; two *s* two *d*. *Educ:* King George V Sch., Southport; Liverpool Univ. (MB, ChB 1959; MD 1962; ChM 1968); Sydney Univ., Australia; MSc Manchester Univ., 1977. FRCS 1964; FRCSE 1964. Robert Gee Fellow, Liverpool Univ., 1962; Phyllis Anderson Fellow, Sydney Univ., 1967; St Bartholomew's Hospital, London: Chief Asst in Surgery, 1969–71; Reader in Surgery, Asst Dir of Professorial Surgical Unit, and Hon. Consultant Surgeon, 1972–74. Hon. Consultant Surgeon: Hope Hosp., Salford, 1974–99; Manchester Royal Infirmary, 1993–95; to the Army, 1989–July 2002. Hunterian Prof., 1967, Hunterian Orator, 1993, RCS; Sir Gordon Bell Meml Orator, NZ, 1982. Regl Dir of R&D, N Western RHA, 1992–94; Chm., Standing Gp on Health Technol., DoH, 1993–99; Nat. Dir, NHS Health Technol. Prog., 1994–99; Member: Expert Adv. Gp on AIDS, DoH, 1991–96; MRC Health Services and Public Health Res. Bd, 1993–96. Member: Council, RCS, 1984–95; GMC, 1989–92; President: Ileostomy Assoc. of GB and Ireland, 1982–92; Assoc. of Surgeons of GB and Ireland, 1995–96; Internat. Surgical Gp, 1995–96; Section of Coloproctology, RSM, 1997–98; Assoc. of Coloproctology of GB and Ireland, 1998–99; Manchester Med. Soc., 1999–2000. Founder FMedSci 1998. Hon. Fellow: Amer. Assoc. for Surgery of Trauma, 1985; Amer. Surgical Assoc., 2000; Hon. FFAEM 1995; Hon. FRCSCan; FRCSGlas *ad eund*; Hon. FACS 2000. Hon. Member: Assoc. Française de Chirurgie, 1996; Romanian Soc. of Surgeons. Hon. DSc Salford, 1996; DSc (*hc*) Sibiu Univ., Romania, 1997. Moynihan Medal, Assoc. of Surgeons of GB and Ire., 1968; Pybus Medal, N of England Surgical Soc., 1986; John Loewenthal Medal, Sydney Univ., 1993; Canet Medal, Inst. of Mech. Incorp. Engrs, 1995; Bryan Brooke Medal, Ileostomy Assoc. of GB and Ire., 1996; Presidents Medal, British Soc. of Gastroenterology, 1999. Hon. Col 201 (Northern) Fd Hosp. Vol., 1999–. *Publications:* Gastroenterological Surgery, 1983; Intestinal Fistulas, 1985; ABC of Colorectal Diseases, 1993; Introduction to Minimal Access Surgery, 1995. *Recreations:* thinking about and occasionally actually climbing mountains, reading The Spectator, opera. *Address:* Juniper, The Old Stables, Aydon Road, Corbridge, Northumberland NE45 5EH. *T:* (01434) 634243.

IRWIN, Lord; James Charles Wood; *b* 24 Aug. 1977; *s* and *heir* of 3rd Earl of Halifax, *qv*. Royal Marines. *Address:* Garrowby, York YO41 1QD.

IRWIN, Lt Gen. Alistair Stuart Hastings, CBE 1994 (OBE 1987); General Officer Commanding Northern Ireland, since 2000; *b* 27 Aug. 1948; *s* of late Brig. Angus Digby Hastings Irwin, CBE, DSO, MC and of Elizabeth Bryson Irwin (*née* Cumming); *m* 1972, Nicola Valentine Blomfield Williams; one *s* two *d*. *Educ:* Wellington Coll.; St Andrews Univ. (MA); Staff Coll., Quetta, Pakistan (BSc Hons Univ. of Baluchistan, 1980). Commnd The Black Watch (RHR), 1970; Staff Coll., Quetta, Pakistan, 1980; CO 1st Bn, The Black Watch, 1985–88; Instructor, Staff Coll., Camberley, 1988–92; Comd, 39 Inf. Bde, 1992–94; Dir Land Warfare, MoD, 1994–95; Prog. Dir, PE, MoD, 1996; Comdt, RMCS, 1996–99; Military Sec., 1999–2000. Col Comdt, Scottish Div., 2000–; Hon. Col Tayforth Univs OTC, 1998–. Mem., Royal Co. of Archers (Queen's Bodyguard for Scotland), 1989–. Pres., Army Angling Fedn, 1997–. *Recreations:* shooting, fishing, walking, photography, bad golf. *Address:* c/o Adam & Co. plc, 22 Charlotte Square, Edinburgh EH2 4DF. *Clubs:* Boodle's; Highland Brigade.

IRWIN, Maj.-Gen. Brian St George, CB 1975; Director General, Ordnance Survey, 1969–77, retired; *b* 16 Sept. 1917; *s* of late Lt-Col Alfred Percy Bulteel Irwin, DSO, and late Eileen Irwin (*née* Holberton); *m* 1939, Audrey Lilla (*d* 1994), *d* of late Lt-Col H. B. Steen, IMS; two *s*. *Educ:* Rugby Sch.; RMA Woolwich; Trinity Hall, Cambridge (MA). Commnd in RE, 1937; war service in Western Desert, 1941–43 (despatches); Sicily and Italy, 1943–44 (despatches); Greece, 1944–45; subseq. in Cyprus, 1956–59 (despatches) and 1961–63; Dir of Military Survey, MoD, 1965–69. Col Comdt, RE, 1977–82. FRICS (Council 1969–70, 1972–76); FRGS (Council 1966–70; Vice-Pres., 1974–77). *Recreations:* sailing, golf, gardening, genealogy. *Address:* 16 Northerwood House, Swan Green, Lyndhurst, Hants SO43 7DT. *T:* (023) 8028 3499. *Club:* Army and Navy.

IRWIN, David; Chief Executive, Small Business Service, since 2000; *b* 5 Sept. 1955; *s* of Hew Irwin and Ann (*née* Tattersfield); *m* 1983, Jane Christine Kinghorn; one *s* one *d*. *Educ:* Worksop Coll.; Durham Univ. (BSc (Hons) Engrg Sci and Mgt 1977); Cambridge Univ.

(Adv. Course Prodn Methods and Mgt 1978); Newcastle Univ. (MBA 1986). Develt Engr, Hydraulic Hose Div., Dunlop, 1978–80; Co-founder and Dir, Project North East, 1980–2000. FIMgt 1984; FCMC 1993; Fellow Inst. Business Counsellors, 1989; FRSA 1993. *Publications:* Financial Control, 1991; Planning to Succeed in Business, 1995; Financial Control for Non Financial Managers, 1995; Make Your Business Grow, 1998; On Target, 1999. *Recreations:* squash, photography. *Address:* c/o Small Business Service, 1 Victoria Street, SW1H 0ET. *T:* (020) 7215 5558. *Club:* Northern Rugby Football (Newcastle upon Tyne).

IRWIN, Flavia; *see* de Grey, F.

IRWIN, Helen Elizabeth; Principal Clerk, Table Office, House of Commons, since 2001; *b* 21 April 1948; *d* of Walter William Taylor and late Kathleen Taylor (*née* Moffoot); *m* 1972, Robert Graham Irwin; one *d*. *Educ:* Whalley Range Grammar Sch., Manchester; King's Coll., London (BA Hons Hist. 1969); SSEES, Univ. of London (MA Soviet Studies 1970). Asst Clerk, H of C, 1970–72; Admin Asst, Univ. of St Andrews, 1972–75; a Clerk, House of Commons, 1977–: Cttee of Public Accounts, 1977–81; served in Table Office, 1981–85; Social Services Cttee, 1985–89; Health Cttee, 1989–91; Foreign Affairs Cttee, 1991–94; Principal Clerk, Committee Office, 1994–99; Clerk of Bills, 1999–2001. Mem. Council, Hansard Soc., 1990–99. *Publications:* occasional contribs to books on parliamentary practice and procedure. *Recreations:* family, friends, travel. *Address:* Table Office, House of Commons, SW1A 0AA. *T:* (020) 7219 3312.

IRWIN, Ian Sutherland, CBE 1982; Executive Chairman (formerly also Chief Executive), Scottish Transport Group, since 1987; *b* Glasgow, 20 Feb. 1933; *s* of Andrew Campbell Irwin and Elizabeth Ritchie Arnott; *m* 1959, Margaret Miller Maureen Irvine; two *s*. *Educ:* Whitehill Sen. Secondary Sch., Glasgow; Glasgow Univ. BL; CA, IPFA, FCIT, CIMgt, FInstD. Commercial Man., Scottish Omnibuses Ltd, 1960–64; Gp Accountant, Scottish Bus Gp, 1964–69; Gp Sec., 1969–75, Dep. Chm. and Man. Dir, 1975–87, Scottish Transport Gp; Chairman: Scottish Bus Gp Ltd, 1975–; Caledonian MacBrayne Ltd, 1975–90; STG Properties Ltd (formerly Scottish Transport Investments Ltd), 1975–; STG Pension Funds, 1975–; Dir, Scottish Mortgage & Trust plc, 1986–99. Pres., Bus and Coach Council, 1979–80; Hon. Vice-Pres., Internat. Union of Public Transport; Member Council: CIT, 1978–87 (Vice Pres., 1984–87); CBI, 1987–93. Hon. Col, 154 Regt RCT (V), 1986–93. *Publications:* various papers. *Recreations:* golf, foreign travel, reading. *Address:* 10 Moray Place, Edinburgh EH3 6DT. *T:* (0131) 225 6454. *Clubs:* MCC; Bruntsfield Links Golfing Soc.

IRWIN, Dr Michael Henry Knox; Chairman, Voluntary Euthanasia Society, 1996–99 (Vice-Chairman, 1995); *b* 5 June 1931; *s* of late William Knox Irwin, FRCS and of Edith Isabel Mary Irwin; *m* 1958, Elizabeth Naumann (marr. diss. 1982); three *d*; partner, Angela Farmer. *Educ:* St Bartholomew's Hosp. Med. Coll., London (MB, BS 1955); Columbia Univ., New York (MPH 1960). House Phys. and House Surg., Prince of Wales' Hosp., London, 1955–56; MO, UN, 1957–61; Dep. Resident Rep., UN Technical Assistance Bd, Pakistan, 1961–63; MO, 1963–66, SMO, 1966–69, and Med. Dir, 1969–73, United Nations; Dir, Div. of Personnel, UNDP, 1973–76; UNICEF Rep., Bangladesh, 1977–80; Sen. Advr (Childhood Disabilities), UNICEF, 1980–82; Sen. Consultant, UN Internat. Year of Disabled Persons, 1981; Med. Dir, UN, UNICEF and UNDP, 1982–89; Director, Health Services Dept, IBRD, 1989–90; Westside Action, 1991–93. Founder, Doctors for Assisted Dying, 1998. Pres., Assistance for Blind Children Internat., 1978–84. Consultant, Amer. Assoc. of Blood Banks, 1984–90; Advr, ActionAid, 1990–91; Vice Pres., UNA, 1999– (Vice-Chm., 1995–96; Chm., 1996–98); Chm., UK Cttee, UNHCR, 1997–May 2002; Vice Pres., Nat. Peace Council, 1996–2000. Vice-Pres., 2000–02, Pres., Sept. 2002–, World Fedn of Right-to-Die Socs. Contested (Living Will Campaign) Kensington and Chelsea, Nov. 1999. Mem. Editl Adv. Panel, Medicine and War, 1985–95. Officer Cross, Internat. Fedn of Blood Donor Organizations, 1984. *Publications:* Check-ups: safeguarding your health, 1961; Overweight: a problem for millions, 1964; Travelling without Tears, 1964; Viruses, Colds and Flu, 1966; Blood: new uses for saving lives, 1967; The Truth About Cancer, 1969; What Do We Know about Allergies?, 1972; A Child's Horizon, 1982; Aspirin: current knowledge about an old medication, 1983; Can We Survive Nuclear War?, 1984; Nuclear Energy: good or bad?, 1985; Peace Museums, 1991; Double Effect, 1997; *novel:* Talpa, 1990. *Recreations:* politics, windmills, writing. *Address:* 9 Waverleigh Road, Cranleigh, Surrey GU6 8BZ.

IRWIN, Rear-Adm. Richard Oran, CB 1995; Member, Criminal Injuries Compensation Appeals Panel, since 2000; *b* 3 Sept. 1942; *s* of Lt Col Richard Arthur Irwin, TD and Catherine Millicent (*née* Palmer); *m* 1965, Coreen Jill Blackham, *d* of Rear-Adm. J. L. Blackham, *qv*; one *s* one *d*. *Educ:* Sherborne; Dartmouth; RN Engrg Coll., Manadon (BSc Engrg). FIEE 1986. Served in 7th, 3rd and 10th Submarine Sqdns, 1968–78; on Naval Staff, 1978–81; on staff of Flag Officer, Submarines, 1981–83; on staff, Strategic Systems Exec., 1983–86; RCDS, 1987; Dir, Nuclear Systems, 1988–91; Captain, HMS Raleigh, 1991–92; Chief, Strategic Systems Exec., MoD, 1992–95; RN retd, 1996. Mem., DFEE Panel of Ind. Assessors, 1996–. Chm., W Sussex HA, 1996–2000. Non-exec. Dir, Halmatic Ltd, 1996–98. Chm., Queen Alexandra Hosp. Home, 1998–. Member: RNSA; Assoc. of Retired Naval Officers; Chm., Friends of Royal Naval Mus. and HMS Victory, 1999–. Gov., Kingsham Primary Sch., 1996–; Pres., Old Shirburnian Soc., 1999–2000. Officer, Legion of Merit (US), 1996. *Recreations:* sailing, squash, tennis, ski-ing, bridge. *Address:* Linden Lodge, Salthill Road, Chichester PO19 3PY. *Clubs:* Lansdowne; Chichester Lawn Tennis and Squash; Emsworth Bridge.

IRWIN, Stephen John; QC 1997; a Recorder, since 2000; *b* 5 Feb. 1953; *s* of late John McCaughey Irwin and of Norma Gordon Irwin; *m* 1978, Deborah Rose Ann Spring; one *s* two *d*. *Educ:* Methodist Coll., Belfast; Jesus Coll., Cambridge (BA Hons 1975). Called to the Bar: Gray's Inn, 1976; Northern Ireland, 1997. *Publications:* Medical Negligence: a practitioner's guide, 1995; legal articles in learned jls. *Recreations:* walking, Irish history, music, verse. *Address:* Doughty Street Chambers, 10 Doughty Street, WC1N 2PL. *T:* (020) 7404 1313.

ISAAC, Anthony John Gower, CB 1985; fiscal consultant; a Deputy Chairman, Board of Inland Revenue, 1982–91 (a Commissioner of Inland Revenue, 1973–77 and 1979–91); *b* 21 Dec. 1931; *s* of Ronald and Kathleen Mary Gower Isaac; *m* 1963, Olga Elizabeth Sibley; one *s* two *d* (and two *d* decd). *Educ:* Malvern Coll.; King's Coll., Cambridge (BA). HM Treasury, 1953–70: Private Sec. to Chief Sec. to Treasury, 1964–66; Inland Revenue, 1971; on secondment to HM Treasury, 1976–78. Mem., Tax Law Rev. Cttee, 1994–. *Publications:* A Local Income Tax, 1992; A Comment on the Viability of the Allowance for Corporate Equity, 1997. *Recreations:* gardening, fishing.

ISAAC, James Keith, CBE 1985; FCIT, FILT; Hon. President, International Union of Public Transport, since 1997 (Vice-President, 1989–93; President, 1993–97); Director, London Transport Buses Ltd, 1994–99; *b* 28 Jan. 1932; *s* of late Arthur Burton Isaac and Doreen (*née* Davies); *m* 1957, Elizabeth Mary Roskell; two *d*. *Educ:* Leeds Grammar Sch. Mem., Inst. of Traffic Admin; FCIT 1978. Asst to Traffic Manager, Aldershot and Dist Traction Co. Ltd, 1958–59; Asst Traffic Man., Jamaica Omnibus Services Ltd, Kingston, Jamaica, 1959–64; Dep. Traffic Man., Midland Red (Birmingham and Midland Motor Omnibus Co. Ltd), Birmingham, 1965–67; Traffic Manager: North Western Road Car Co. Ltd, Stockport, Cheshire, 1967–69; Midland Red, Birmingham, 1969–73; Dir of Ops, 1973–77, Dir Gen., 1977–86, W Midlands Passenger Transp. Exec., Birmingham; Man. Dir, 1986–90, Chief Exec., 1986–92, Chm., 1986–94, West Midlands Travel Ltd. Chm., Bus and Coach Services Ltd, 1986–90. Chm., Internat. Commn on Transport Economics, 1981–88; President: Omnibus Soc., 1982; Bus and Coach Council, 1985–86; Mem. Council, CIT, 1982–85. *Recreations:* golf, walking, reading, travel, grandchildren. *Address:* 24B Middlefield Lane, Hagley, Stourbridge, West Midlands DY9 0PX. *T:* (01562) 884757. *Clubs:* Army and Navy; Rotary of Hagley (Worcs); Churchill and Blakedown Golf (near Kidderminster).

ISAAC, Maurice Laurence Reginald, MA; Headmaster, Latymer Upper School, Hammersmith, W6, 1971–88; *b* 26 April 1928; *s* of late Frank and Lilian Isaac; *m* 1954, Anne Fielden; three *d*. *Educ:* Selhurst Grammar Sch., Croydon; Magdalene Coll., Cambridge. BA Hist. Tripos, 1950; MA 1955, Cambridge; Certif. in Educn, 1952. Asst Master: Liverpool Collegiate Sch., 1952–56; Bristol Grammar Sch., 1956–62; Head of History, Colchester Royal Grammar Sch., 1962–65; Headmaster, Yeovil Sch., 1966–71. Mem. Council, Francis Holland Schools Trust, 1982–95. *Publications:* A History of Europe, 1870–1950, 1960; contributor to The Teaching of History, 1965. *Address:* Glebe House, Crowcombe, near Taunton, Somerset TA4 4AA. *T:* (01984) 618230. *Club:* East India.

ISAAC, Prof. Peter Charles Gerald; Professor of Civil and Public Health Engineering, 1964–81, now Emeritus, and Head of Department of Civil Engineering, 1970–81, University of Newcastle upon Tyne; Partner, Watson Hawksley (consulting engineers), 1973–83; *b* 21 Jan. 1921; *s* of late Herbert George Isaac and Julienne Geneviève (*née* Hattenberger); *m* 1950, Marjorie Eleanor White; one *s* one *d*. *Educ:* Felsted Sch.; London and Harvard Universities. BSc(Eng), SM; DLitt Newcastle, 1997. Asst Engineer, GWR, 1940–45; Lecturer in Civil Engineering, 1946; Senior Lecturer in Public Health Engineering, 1953, Reader, 1960, Univ. of Durham; Dean of Faculty of Applied Science, Univ. of Newcastle upon Tyne, 1969–73; Sandars Reader in Bibliography, Univ. of Cambridge, 1983–84. Member: Industrial Health Adv. Cttee, Min. of Lab. and Nat. Service, 1959–66; Working Party on Sewage Disposal, 1969–70; WHO Expert Adv. Panel on Environmental Health, 1976–87; specialist advr, House of Lords Select Cttee on Sci. and Technol. II (Hazardous Waste), 1980–81 and House of Lords Select Cttee on Sci. and Technol. I (Water), 1982; DoE Long-Term Water-Research Requirements Cttee. Bibliographical Society: Mem. Council, 1970–74, 1979–83; Vice-Pres., 1984–94; Pres., 1994–96; Hon. Editor of Monographs, 1982–89. Chairman: History of the Book Trade in the North, 1965–; British Book Trade Index; Printing Historical Soc., 1989–91; Pres., Assoc. of Indep. Libraries, 1997–2000. Member of Council: ICE, 1968–71, 1972–75, 1977–80; IPHE, 1973–87 (Pres., 1977–78); Pres., British Occupational Hygiene Soc., 1962–63 (Hon. Mem., 1993); Mem. Bd, CEI, 1978–79. Trustee, Asian Inst. Technology, Bangkok, 1968–82 (Vice-Chm., 1979–82). Hon. Mem., Lit. and Philos. Soc., Newcastle upon Tyne. Director: Thorne's Students' Bookshop Ltd, 1969–74; Environmental Resources Ltd, 1972–74. Freeman, Co. of Stationers and Newspaper Makers, 1984, Liveryman, 1986, Renter Warden, 1998–99. FSA 1987; FICE 1956 (AMICE 1946); Hon. FIPHE 1986. Clemens Herschel Prize in Applied Hydraulics, 1952; Telford Premium, 1957; Thomas Bedford Award, 1978; Gold Medal, IPHE, 1987. *Publications:* Electric Resistance Strain Gauges (with W. B. Dobie), 1948; Public Health Engineering, 1953; Trade Wastes, 1957; Waste Treatment, 1960; River Management, 1967; William Davison of Alnwick: pharmacist and printer, 1968; Farm Wastes, 1970; Civil Engineering–The University Contribution, 1970; Management in Civil Engineering, 1971; Davison's Halfpenny Chapbooks, 1971; (ed) The Burman Alnwick Collection, 1973; William Davison's New Specimen, 1990; Six Centuries of the Provincial Book Trade in Britain, 1990; William Bulmer: the fine printer in context, 1993; (ed with B. McKay) Images and Texts, 1997; (ed with B. McKay) The Reach of Print, 1998; (ed with B. McKay) The Human Face of the Book Trade, 1999; (ed) Newspapers in the Northeast, 1999; (ed with B. McKay) The Mighty Engine, 2000; (ed with B. McKay) The Moving Market, 2001; contribs to various learned and technical jls. *Recreations:* bibliography, printing, book-trade history. *Address:* 10 Woodcroft Road, Wylam, Northumberland NE41 8DJ. *T:* (01661) 853174; *e-mail:* peterisaac@britishlibrary.net. *Clubs:* Royal Commonwealth Society, Penn.

ISAAC, Rear-Adm. Robert Arthur, CB 1989; Director General Marine Engineering, Ministry of Defence (Procurement Executive), 1986–89; consultant (business with Japan), 1989–97; *b* 21 Feb. 1933; *s* of Frank and Florence Isaac; *m* 1960, Joy Little; one *s* one *d*. *Educ:* Oakham Sch.; Royal Naval Engrg Coll. (Dartmouth Special Entry). CEng, FIMechE, FIMarE. Entered RN, 1951; HMS Albion, 1957–59; HM Submarines Scotsman, Aurochs, nuclear trng, and HM Submarine Warspite, 1959–69; Dir Gen. Ships, MoD, 1970–74; HMS Blake, 1974–76; 2nd Sea Lord's Dept, MoD, 1976–78; Captain 1977; Naval Attaché, Tokyo and Seoul, 1979–81; Project Dir, Surface Ships, MoD (PE), 1981–84; HMS Thunderer, RNEC in comd, 1984–86; Rear-Adm. 1986. *Recreations:* sport, gardening. *Clubs:* Naval, Army and Navy.

ISAACS, family name of **Marquess of Reading**.

ISAACS, Dame Albertha Madeline, DBE 1974; former Senator, now worker for the community, in the Bahamas; *b* Nassau, Bahamas, 18 April 1900; *d* of late Robert Hanna and Lilla (*née* Minns); *m*; three *s* one *d*. *Educ:* Cosmopolitan High Sch. and Victoria High Sch., Nassau. Member: Progressive Liberal Party, Senator, 1968–72; also of PLP's Nat. Gen. Council, and of Council of Women. Mem. of a Good Samaritan Group. *Address:* PO Box SS 5031, Nassau, N.P., Bahamas.

ISAACS, Dr Anthony John; Consultant in Clinical Audit, Education and Training, Barnet Health Authority, since 1995; Consultant Endocrinologist, Chelsea & Westminster Hospital, since 1993; *b* 22 Oct. 1942; *s* of Benjamin H. Isaacs, BSc and Lily Isaacs (*née* Rogol); *m* 1st, 1971, Jill Kathleen Elek; three *s*; 2nd, 1986, Dr Edie Friedman; one *d*. *Educ:* Wanstead County High Sch.; Hertford Coll., Oxford (Open Exhibnr; Domus Scholar; BA Animal Physiology, 1st Cl. Hons 1965; MA 1968; BM, BCh 1968); Westminster Med. Sch. (Barron Schol.); MSc (Public Health Medicine), London, 1992. MRCP 1971, FRCP 1997. House posts, Westminster, Whittington and Hammersmith Hosps, 1968–70; Med. Registrar, Westminster Hosp., 1971–73; Research Fellow (Endocrinology), Royal Free Hosp., 1973–75; Sen. Med. Registrar, Westminster Hosp., 1975–84; SMO, Medicines Div., 1984–85, PMO, and Med. Assessor, Cttee on Safety of Medicines, 1985–86, SPMO/Under Sec., and Hd, Med. Manpower and Educn Div., 1986–91, DHSS, subseq. DoH; Regl Consultant (Service Policy and Clinical Audit), NE Thames, later N Thames RHA, 1993–95; Consultant Endocrinologist, Charing Cross Hosp., 1993–95. Hon. Consultant Phys. (Endocrinology), UC and Middx Hosps, 1986–96. Vice-Chm., Jt Planning Adv. Cttee, 1986–91; Member: Steering Gp for Implementation of Achieving a Balance (and Co-Chm., Technical sub-gp), 1986–91; 2nd Adv. Cttee on Med. Manpower Planning, 1986–89; Steering Gp on Undergrad. Med. and Dental Educn and Res., 1987–91 (Chm., Implementation Task Gp, 1989–90 and Working Gp, 1990–91); Ministerial Gp on Junior Doctors' Hours, 1990–91. Chairman: Barnet Health Promoting Schs, later Barnet Healthy Schs Scheme, Steering Gp, 1995–; Barnet Cardiovascular Strategy Steering Gp (formerly Barnet Coronary Heart Disease, Stroke and Smoking Focus Gp), 1995–; Barnet Adv. Gp on Palliative Care Services, 1996–. Hon. Vis. Fellow, LSHTM, 1992–93. Chm., New End Sch. PTA, 1983–85; Parent Governor, 1987–92, Partnership (formerly First) Gov., 1992–, Hendon Sch. Mem., Soc. for Endocrinology, 1998–. DFPHM 1999. *Publications:* Anorexia Nervosa (with P. Dally and J. Gomez), 1979; papers in med. jls on rheumatol and endocrinol topics. *Recreations:* music, cinema, table tennis, chess, travel. *Address:* Barnet Health Authority, Hyde House, The Hyde, NW9 6QQ.

ISAACS, Sir Jeremy (Israel), Kt 1996; General Director, Royal Opera House, Covent Garden, 1988–97 (Member, Board of Directors, 1985–97); Chief Executive, Jeremy Isaacs Productions, since 1998; *b* 28 Sept. 1932; *s* of Isidore Isaacs and Sara Jacobs; *m* 1st, 1958, Tamara (*née* Weinreich) (*d* 1986), Cape Town; one *s* one *d*; 2nd, 1988, Gillian Mary Widdicombe. *Educ:* Glasgow Acad.; Merton Coll., Oxford (MA). Pres. of the Union, Hilary, 1955. Television Producer, Granada TV (What the Papers Say, All Our Yesterdays), 1958; Associated-Rediffusion (This Week), 1963; BBC TV (Panorama), 1965; Controller of Features, Associated Rediffusion, 1967; with Thames Television, 1968–78: Controller of Features, 1968–74; Producer, The World at War, 1974; Director of Programmes, 1974–78; Chief Exec., Channel Four TV Co., 1981–87; TV programmes: A Sense of Freedom, STV; Ireland, a Television History, BBC; Cold War, CNN; Millennium, CNN, 1999; interviewer, Face to Face, BBC. Chm., Artsworld Channels Ltd, 2000–. Dir, Glasgow 1999, 1996–99. Chm., Salzburg Festival Trust, 1997–; Trustee, IPPR, 1989–99. Member: Somerset House Trust, 1997–; Council, UEA, 1997–2000. Dir, Open College, 1987–92. Governor, BFI, 1979–84 (Chm., BFI Production Bd, 1979–81). Pres., RTS, 1997–2000. Organised A Statue for Oscar Wilde, Adelaide Street, 1998. James MacTaggart Meml Lectr, Edinburgh TV Fest., 1979. FRSA 1983; Fellow: BAFTA, 1985; BFI, 1986; FRSAMD 1989; FGSM 1989. Hon. DLitt: Strathclyde, 1984; CNAA, 1987; Bristol, 1988; Hon. LLD Manchester, 1999. Desmond Davis Award for outstanding creative contrib. to television, 1972; George Polk Meml Award, 1973; Cyril Bennett Award for outstanding contrib. to television programming, RTS, 1982; Lord Willis Award for Distinguished Service to Television, 1985; Directorate Award, Internat. Council of Nat. Acad. of TV Arts and Scis, NY, 1987; Lifetime Achievement Award, Banff, 1988. Commandeur de l'Ordre des Arts et des Lettres (France), 1988; Mem., Ordre pour le Mérite (France), 1993. *Publications:* Storm over Four: a personal account, 1989; (jtly) Cold War, 1998; Never Mind the Moon: my time at the Royal Opera House, 1999. *Recreations:* reading, walking. *Club:* Garrick.

ISAACS, Stuart Lindsay; QC 1991; a Recorder, since 1997; *b* 8 April 1952; *s* of late Stanley Leslie Isaacs and of Marquette Isaacs; *m* 2000, Melodie, *e d* of Mannie and Judy Schuster; one *s*. *Educ:* Haberdashers' Aske's Sch., Elstree; Downing Coll., Cambridge (Law, Double 1st cl. Hons); Univ. Libre de Bruxelles (License spécial en droit européen, grande distinction). Called to the Bar, Lincoln's Inn, 1975, Bencher, 1999; admitted NY Bar, 1985. An Asst Recorder, 1992–97. Member: Internat. Panel of Arbitrators, Singapore Internat. Arbitration Centre, 1998–; Restricted Patients Panel, Mental Health Review Tribunal, 2000–. Mem. Law Adv. Cttee, British Council, 1996–99. Consultant Editor: Butterworth's EC Case Citator, 1991–; Banking Law Reports, 1996–98. *Publications:* EC Banking Law, 1985, 2nd edn 1994; Banking and the Competition Law of the EEC, 1978. *Recreations:* travel, languages. *Address:* 3–4 South Square, Gray's Inn, WC1R 5HP. *T:* (020) 7696 9900, *Fax:* (020) 7696 9911.

ISAACSON, Laurence Ivor, CBE 1998; Joint Founder and Deputy Chairman, Groupe Chez Gérard PLC, since 1986; *b* 1 July 1943; *s* of Henry Isaacson and Dorothy (*née* Levitt). *Educ:* London Sch. of Econs (BSc Econ). FHCIMA 1996. Mgt trainee, Unilever, London and Rotterdam, 1964–67; Doyle Dane Bernbach Advertising, 1967–70; Foote Cone & Belding Advertising, 1970–72; Jt Founder and Man. Dir, Creative Business Ltd, 1972–83; Dir, Kennedy Brookes Plc, 1983–86. Chm., MAP Travel-Canada, 2001–. Mem. Adv. Bd, UK in NY, 2001. Chairman: Contemp. Dance Trust, 1988–94; BOC Covent Gdn Fest. of Opera and Music Theatre, 1993–; London Restaurant Week, 1999; Dir and Mem. Council, Arts & Business (formerly ABSA), 1987–; Dir, RSC Foundn, 1998–2000; non-exec. Dir, Ambassador Theatre Gp, 2000–; Gov., RSC, 2000–. Dir, London Tourist Bd, 1994–; Mem., London First Visitors Council, 1994–98. Dir, Crusaid, 1994–. FRSA 1997. *Address:* 5 Chalcot Crescent, NW1 8YE. *T:* (020) 7586 3793; 30 Crosby Street, Soho, New York, NY 10013, USA; *e-mail:* laurencei@aol.com. *Clubs:* Garrick, Groucho, Home House (Founding Partner and Dir, 1999–).

ISAACSON, Prof. Peter Gersohn, DM, DSc; FRCPath; Professor of Morbid Anatomy, University College London, since 1982; *b* 24 Nov. 1936; *s* of Robert and Freda Isaacson; *m* 1959, Maria de Lourdes Abranches Pinto; one *s* three *d*. *Educ:* Prince Edward Sch., Salisbury, Rhodesia; Univ. of Cape Town (MB ChB); DM Southampton, 1980; DSc London, 1992. FRCPath 1972. Sen. Lectr, then Reader, Southampton Univ. Med. Sch., 1974–82. Founder FMedSci 1998. Hon. MD Free Univ. of Berlin, 1998. San-Salvatore Prize, Lugano, 1999. *Publications:* Biopsy Pathology of the Lymphoreticular System, 1983; Oxford Textbook of Pathology, 1993; Extranodal Lymphoma, 1994; numerous contribs to med. jls. *Address:* Department of Histopathology, Rockefeller Building, University Street, WC1E 6JJ. *T:* (020) 7209 6045.

ISAAMAN, Gerald Michael, OBE 1994; journalist and consultant; Editorial Consultant, Home Counties Newspapers plc, 1994–99; Editor, 1968–94, and General Manager, 1990–94, Hampstead and Highgate Express; *b* 22 Dec. 1933; *s* of Asher Isaaman and Lily Finklestein; *m* 1962, Delphine Walker, *e d* of Cecile and Arnold Walker; one *s*. *Educ:* Dame Alice Owen's Grammar School. Reporter, North London Observer Series, 1950, Hampstead and Highgate Express, 1955. Director: Pipistrel Retail Solutions, 1994–; Pipistrel Education Systems, 1994–; non-exec. Dir, Whittington Hosp. NHS Trust, 1994–98. Founder Trustee, Arkwright Arts Trust, 1971; Chairman: Camden Arts Trust Management Board, 1970–82; Exhibns Cttee, Camden Arts Centre, 1971–82; Russell Housing Soc., 1976–82; Trustees, King's Cross Disaster Fund, 1987–89; Dep. Chm., Assoc. of British Editors, 1996– (Mem. Council, 1985–93); Member: Press Complaints Commn, 1993–95; Bd, Camden Trng Centre, 1997–; Camden Festival Trust, 1982–; Cheltenham Literary Fest. Cttee, 1998–; Patron and Trustee, Hamden Trust, 1995–; Patron, Ledbury Poetry Fest., 1997–. FRSA 1992. Special presentation, for distinguished services to journalism, British Press Awards, 1994. *Recreations:* cooking breakfast, listening to jazz, work. *Address:* 10 Salmon Mews, West End Lane, NW6 1RH. *T:* and *Fax:* (020) 7431 5525; *e-mail:* gerald@isaaman.com. *Club:* Garrick.

ISEPP, Martin Johannes Sebastian; Head of Music Studies, National Opera Studio, 1979–95; Chief Guest Coach, Glyndebourne Festival Opera, since 1994; *b* Vienna, 30 Sept. 1930; *s* of Sebastian and Helene Isepp; *m* 1966, Rose Henrietta Harris; two *s*. *Educ:* St Paul's Sch.; Lincoln Coll., Oxford; Royal Coll. of Music, London (ARCM 1952). Studied piano with Prof. Leonie Gombrich, 1939–52. English Opera Gp, 1954–57; Glyndebourne Fest. Opera, 1957– (Head of Music Staff, 1973–93); Head of Opera Trng Dept, Juilliard Sch. of Music, New York, 1973–78; Hd, Acad of Singing, Banff Sch. of Fine Arts, Alberta, Canada, 1982–93. As accompanist, began career accompanying mother, Helene Isepp (the singer and voice teacher); has accompanied many of the world's leading singers and instrumentalists, notably Elisabeth Schwarzkopf, Elisabeth Söderström, Janet Baker and John Shirley-Quirk; harpsichordist with Handel Opera Soc. of New York in most of their Handel Festivals, 1966–; master classes in opera and song at Amer. univs, incl. Southern Calif, Ann Arbor, Maryland, Minnesota and Colorado, 1975–; lieder courses, Britten-Pears Sch. for Advanced Musical Studies, Aldeburgh, 1988–; coached Peking Opera and Peking Conservatory in Mozart operas, 1983; opera prodns, Centre de la Voix, Fondation Royaumont, France, 1992–; annual opera course (Music Dir), Walton Foundn, Ischia, Italy, 1992–95; classes in opera and song, Pacific Music Fest., Sapporo, Japan, 1995–. As conductor: Le Nozze di Figaro, Glyndebourne Touring Op., 1984; Don Giovanni, Glyndebourne Touring Op., 1986; Abduction from the Seraglio, Washington Op., 1986–87; Asst Conductor, Met. Op., NY, 1994–. Hon. DMus Wake Forest, NC, 2001. Carroll Donner Stuchell Medal for Accompanists, Harriet Cohen Internat. Musical Foundn, 1965. *Recreations:* photography, walking. *Address:* 37A Steele's Road, NW3 4RG. *T:* (020) 7722 3085.

ISHAM, Sir Ian (Vere Gyles), 13th Bt *cr* 1627; *b* 17 July 1923; *s* of Lt-Col Vere Arthur Richard Isham, MC (*d* 1968) and Edith Irene (*d* 1973), *d* of Harry Brown; *S* cousin, Sir Gyles Isham, 12th Bt, 1976. Served War of 1939–45, Captain RAC. *Heir:* *b* Norman Murray Crawford Isham, OBE [*b* 28 Jan. 1930; *m* 1956, Joan, *d* of late Leonard James Genet; two *s* one *d*]. *Address:* 40 Turnpike Link, Croydon, Surrey CR0 5NX.

ISHERWOOD, John David Gould, CMG 2001; consultant solicitor, since 1991; *b* 8 Feb. 1936; *s* of Frank Hilton Isherwood and Beatrice Marion Isherwood (*née* Gould); *m* 1967, Anne Isobel Inglis; one *s* one *d*. *Educ:* Cheltenham Coll.; Merton Coll., Oxford (MA 1963; MSt 1997); Stanford Univ., California. Lieut, RA, 1954–56. Admitted Solicitor, 1964; VSO, 1964–68; Solicitor, 1969, Sen. Partner, 1985-91, Barker, Son & Isherwood, Andover. Mem., Law Soc. Trustee: Oxfam 1968-98 (Chm., Exec. Cttee, 1979-85); Wateraid, 1981- (Chm., 1995-2001); NCVO, 1996-. Chm., Hampshire Archives Trust, 2001-. *Recreations:* local history, theatre, travel. *Address:* Chalcot, Penton Mewsey, Andover, Hants SP11 0RQ.

ISHIGURO, Kazuo, OBE 1995; FRSL; author; *b* 8 Nov. 1954; *s* of Shizuo and Shizuko Ishiguro; *m* 1986, Lorna Anne MacDougall; one *d*. *Educ.* Univ. of Kent (BA English/Philosophy); Univ. of East Anglia (MA Creative Writing). Began publishing short stories, articles, in magazines, 1980; writer of TV plays, 1984–. Mem. Jury, Cannes Film Festival, 1994. FRSL 1989. Hon. DLitt: Kent, 1990; UEA, 1995. Premio Scanno for Literature, Italy, 1995; Premio Mantova, Italy, 1998. Chevalier de l'Ordre des Arts et des Lettres (France), 1998. *Publications:* A Pale View of Hills, 1982 (Winifred Holtby Prize, RSL); An Artist of the Floating World, 1986 (Whitbread Book of the Year, Whitbread Fiction Prize); The Remains of the Day, 1989 (Booker Prize; filmed 1993); The Unconsoled, 1995 (Cheltenham Prize, 1995); When We Were Orphans, 2000. *Recreations:* music; playing piano and guitar. *Address:* c/o Faber & Faber, 3 Queen Square, WC1N 3AU.

ISHIHARA, Takashi, First Class, Order of the Rising Sun (Japan), 1991; Hon. KBE 1990; Counsellor, Nissan Motor Co., Ltd, since 1992 (Chairman, 1985–92); *b* 3 March 1912; *s* of Ichiji and Shigeyo Ishihara; *m* 1943, Shizuko Nakajo; one *s*. *Educ:* Law Dept, Tohoku Univ. (grad 1937). Joined Nissan Motor Co., Ltd, 1937; promoted to Gen. Man. of Planning and Accounting Depts respectively; Dir of Finance and Accounting, 1954; Man. Dir, 1963; Exec. Man. Dir, 1969; Exec. Vice Pres., 1973; Pres., 1977; Pres., Nissan Motor Corp. in USA, 1960–65; Chm., Nissan Motor Manufacturing Corp., USA, 1980–82. Exec. Dir, Keidanren (Fedn of Econ. Orgns), 1977–85; Chm., Keizai Doyukai (Japan Assoc. of Corporate Execs), 1985–91; Dir, Nikkeiren (Japan Fedn of Employers Assocs), 1978–85; President: Japan Automobile Manufacturers Assoc., Inc., 1980–86; Japan Motor Industrial Fedn, Inc., 1980–86. Hon. DCL Durham, 1987. Blue Ribbon Medal (Japan), 1974; First Order of Sacred Treasure (Japan), 1983; Grand Cross (Spain), 1985. *Recreations:* reading, golf, ocean cruising. *Address:* Nissan Motor Co., 17–1 Ginza 6–chome, Chuo-ku, Tokyo 104, Japan; 20–3, 2–chome, Shiroganedai, Minato-ku, Tokyo 108, Japan.

ISLE OF MAN, Archdeacon of; *see* Partington, Ven. B. H.

ISLE OF WIGHT, Archdeacon of; *see* Banting, Ven. K. M. L. H.

ISLES, Maj.-Gen. Donald Edward, CB 1978; OBE 1968; DL; *b* 19 July 1924; *s* of Harold and Kathleen Isles; *m* 1948, Sheila Mary Stephens (formerly Thorpe); three *s* one *d*. *Educ:* Roundhay; Leeds Univ.; RMCS. jssc 1961. Italian campaign, Palestine, Egypt, Sudan, Syria, with 1st Bn, Duke of Wellington's Regt, 1944–47; Asst Mil. Attaché, Paris, 1963–65; CO, 1DWR, BAOR and UN Forces in Cyprus, 1965–67; AMS, MoD, 1968; Col GS, MoD, 1968–71; Dir of Munitions, Brit. Defence Staff Washington, 1972–75; Dir-Gen. Weapons (Army), 1975–78, retired. Dep. Man. Dir, British Manufacture & Res. Co., 1979–89. Col, The Duke of Wellington's Regt, 1975–82; Col Comdt, The King's Div., 1975–79; Vice-Chm., Yorks and Humberside TA&VRA, 1984–87. Hon. Colonel: 3rd Bn, Yorkshire Volunteers, 1977–83; Leeds Univ. OTC, 1985–90. Mem., Court, Leeds Univ., 1987–95. Pres., Lincs and S Humberside RBL, 1990–96; Patron, Lincs RBL, 1996. DL Lincs, 1990. *Recreations:* shooting, tennis. *Club:* Army and Navy.

ISLWYN, Baron *cr* 1997 (Life Peer), of Casnewydd in the co. of Gwent; **Royston John Hughes;** DL; *b* 9 June 1925; *s* of John Hughes, Coal Miner; *m* 1957, Florence Marion Appleyard; three *d*. *Educ:* Ruskin Coll., Oxford. Mem. Coventry City Council, 1962–66; various offices in Transport and General Workers' Union, 1959–66. MP (Lab): Newport, Gwent, 1966–83; Newport E, 1983–97. PPS to Minister of Transport, 1974–75; Mem., Speaker's panel, 1982–84, 1991–97; opposition frontbench spokesman on Welsh affairs, 1984–88. Joint Chairman: All Party Roads Gp, 1983–97; All Party Motors Gp, 1986–97; Chairman: PLP Sports Gp, 1974–83; PLP Steel Group, 1978–87, 1994–97; Parly Gp, TGWU, 1979–82. Chm., Welsh Grand Cttee, 1982–84, 1991–97. Exec. Mem., IPU, 1987–97 (Treas., 1990–92). Deleg., Council of Europe and WEU, 1991–97. Jt Chm., Rugby Union Gp, 1993–97; Pres., Newport Athletic Club, 1997–; Vice President: Crawshays RFC; Glamorgan CCC. DL Gwent, 1992. *Recreations:* gardening, watching Rugby and cricket. *Address:* Chapel Field, Chapel Lane, Abergavenny, Gwent NP7 7BT. *T:* (01873) 856502. *Clubs:* Royal Automobile (Mem., Public Policy Cttee, 1983–97); Pontllanfraith Workingmen's Social.

ISMAY, Walter Nicholas; Managing Director, Worcester Parsons Ltd, 1975–82, retired; *b* 20 June 1921; *s* of late John Ismay, Maryport, Cumberland. *Educ:* Taunton's Sch., Southampton; King's Coll., University of London (BSc). Royal Aircraft Establishment, 1939–40; Ministry of Supply, 1940–43; Served Army (Capt., General List), 1943–46; Imperial Chemical Industries, Metals Division, 1948–58 (Technical Dir, 1957–58); Dir, Yorkshire Imperial Metals, 1958–67; Dep. Chm. Yorkshire Imperial Plastics, 1966–67; Dep. Chm. and Man. Dir, Milton Keynes Develt Corp., 1967–71; McKechnie Britain

Ltd, 1972–75. FIMechE. *Recreation:* sailing. *Address:* 39 Courtenay Place, Lymington, Hampshire SO41 3NQ. *T:* (01590) 673032. *Club:* Royal Lymington Yacht.

ISOLANI, Casimiro Peter Hugh Tomasi, CBE 1975 (OBE 1960; MBE (mil.) 1945); LVO 1961; HM Diplomatic Service, retired; *b* 2 Sept. 1917; *s* of late Umberto Tomasi Isolani, Bologna, and late Georgiana Eleanor Lyle-Smyth, Great Barrow, Ches; *m* 1943, Karin Gunni Signe Zetterström (*d* 1996), *d* of Henry Zetterström, Gothenburg; one *s*. *Educ:* Aldenham Sch.; Clare Coll., Cambridge; Major open schol., 1936, 1st cl. Mod. and Med. Lang. Tripos 1; Senior Foundn schol., 1937; BA 1939. Commnd RA 1940, Intell. Corps 1941; attached 1st Canadian Div., 1943 (Sicily, Italy landings); Psychol Warfare Br., 1944; GS1 (Civil Liaison, Liaison Italian Resistance), 1945; Hon. Partisan, Veneto Corpo Volontari della Liberta; FO 1946; Vice-Consul, Bologna, 1946; Attaché, later 1st Sec. (Information), British Embassy, Rome, 1947–61; resigned Foreign Service; Dep. Dir, Inst. for Strategic Studies, 1961–63; rejoined Foreign Service; Regional Information Officer, Paris, 1963–72; Counsellor (Information), British Embassy (and UK delegn NATO and UK Representation, EEC), Brussels, 1972–77. United Nations University: Rep. (Europe), 1978–85; Sen. Consultant, 1985–87. *Address:* 44 Pont Street, SW1X 0AD. *T:* (020) 7584 1543. *Clubs:* Royal Anglo-Belgian, Special Forces.

ISRAEL, Prof. Jonathan Irvine, DPhil; FBA 1992; Professor of Dutch History and Institutions, University College London, since 1985; *b* 22 Jan. 1946; *s* of David and Miriam Israel; *m* 1985, Jenny Tatjana Winckel; one *s* one *d*. *Educ:* Kilburn Grammar Sch.; Queens' Coll., Cambridge; St Antony's Coll., Oxford (DPhil 1972). Lectr, Hull Univ., 1972–74; Lectr, 1974–81, Reader, 1981–84, UCL. *Publications:* Race, Class and Politics in Colonial Mexico, 1975; The Dutch Republic and the Hispanic World, 1982; European Jewry in the Age of Mercantilism 1550–1750, 1985; Dutch Primacy in World Trade 1585–1740, 1989; Empires and Entrepots: the Dutch, the Spanish monarchy and the Jews 1585–1713, 1990; (ed) The Anglo-Dutch Movement: essays on the Glorious Revolution and its world impact, 1991; The Dutch Republic, 1995; Conflicts of Empires: Spain, the Low Countries and the struggle for world supremacy 1585–1713, 1997. *Address:* Department of History, University College London, Gower Street, WC1E 6BT. *T:* (020) 7387 7050.

ISRAEL, Rev. Dr Martin Spencer, FRCPath; Priest-in-Charge, Holy Trinity with All Saints Church, South Kensington, 1983–97; *b* 30 April 1927; *s* of Elie Benjamin Israel, ophthalmic surgeon, and Minnie Israel. *Educ:* Parktown Boys' High Sch., Johannesburg; Univ. of the Witwatersrand (MB ChB). MRCP 1952, FRCPath 1972. Ho. Phys., Hammersmith Hosp., 1952; Registrar in Pathology, Royal Hosp., Wolverhampton, 1953–55; service in RAMC, 1955–57; Lectr and Sen. Lectr in Pathology, 1958–82, Hon. Sen. Lectr 1982–, RCS. Ordained priest in C of E, 1975. President: Guild of Health, 1983–90; Churches' Fellowship for Psychical and Spiritual Studies, 1983–98. *Publications: medical:* General Pathology (with J. B. Walter), 1963, 6th edn 1987; *spiritual matters:* Summons to Life, 1974; Precarious Living, 1976; Smouldering Fire, 1978; The Pain that Heals, 1981; Living Alone, 1982; The Spirit of Counsel, 1983; Healing as Sacrament, 1984; The Discipline of Love, 1985; Coming in Glory, 1986; Gethsemane, 1987; The Pearl of Great Price, 1988; The Dark Face of Reality, 1989; The Quest for Wholeness, 1989; Creation, 1989; Night Thoughts, 1990; A Light on the Path, 1990; Life Eternal, 1993; Dark Victory, 1994; Angels—Messengers of Grace, 1995; Exorcism: the removal of evil influences, 1997; Doubt: the way of growth, 1997; Happiness That Lasts, 1999; (with Neil Broadbent) Learning to Love, 2001. *Recreations:* music, conversation. *Address:* 21 Soudan Road, SW11 4HH. *T:* (020) 7622 5756.

ISRAEL, Prof. Werner, OC 1994; FRS 1986; Adjunct Professor of Physics, University of Victoria, since 1997; *b* 4 Oct. 1931; *s* of Arthur Israel and Marie Kappauf; *m* 1958, Inge Margulies; one *s* one *d*. *Educ:* Cape Town High Sch.; Univ. of Cape Town (BSc 1951, MSc 1954); Dublin Inst. for Advanced Studies; Trinity Coll., Dublin (PhD 1960). Lectr in Applied Maths, Univ. of Cape Town, 1954–56; University of Alberta: Asst Prof., 1958; Associate Prof., 1964; Prof. of Maths, 1968–71; Prof. of Physics, 1972–96; Univ. Prof., 1985–96. Sherman Fairchild Dist. Schol., CIT, 1974–75; Vis. Prof., Dublin Inst. for Advanced Studies, 1966–68; Sen. Visitor, Dept of Applied Maths and Theoretical Physics, Univ. of Cambridge, 1975–76; Maître de Recherche Associé, Inst. Henri Poincaré, Paris, 1976–77; Visiting Professor: Berne, 1980; Kyoto, 1986, 1988; Vis. Fellow, Gonville and Caius Coll., Cambridge, 1985. Fellow, Canadian Inst. for Advanced Research, 1986–. Pres., Internat. Soc. of Gen. Relativity and Gravitation, 1998–2001. Hon. DSc: Queen's, Kingston, Ont, 1987; Victoria, BC, 1999; Dr *hc* Tours, 1994. *Publications:* (ed) Relativity, Astrophysics and Cosmology, 1973; (ed with S. W. Hawking) General Relativity: an Einstein centenary survey, 1979; (ed with S. W. Hawking) 300 Years of Gravitation, 1987; numerous papers on black hole physics, general relativity, relativistic statistical mechanics. *Recreation:* music. *Address:* Department of Physics and Astronomy, University of Victoria, Victoria, BC V8W 3P6, Canada. *T:* (250) 7217708.

ISRAELACHVILI, Prof. Jacob Nissim, FRS 1988; FAA; Professor of Chemical Engineering and Materials Science, Department of Chemical Engineering and Materials Department, University of California, Santa Barbara, since 1986; *b* 19 Aug. 1944; *s* of Haim and Hela Israelachvili; *m* 1971, Karina (*née* Haglund); two *d*. *Educ:* Univ. of Cambridge (MA; PhD 1972). FAA 1982. Post-doctoral res. into surface forces, Cavendish Lab., Cambridge, 1971–72; EMBO Res. Fellow, Biophysics Inst., Univ. of Stockholm, 1972–74; Res. Fellow, subseq. Professorial Fellow, Res. Sch. of Physical Scis, Inst. of Advanced Studies, ANU, Canberra, 1974–86. Council Mem., 1983–87, Vice-Pres., 1986–87, Internat. Assoc. of Colloid and Interface Scientists. Foreign Associate, US NAE, 1996. Pawsey Medal, 1977, Matthew Flinders Lectr medallist, 1986, Aust. Acad. of Sci.; (jtly) David Syme Res. Prize, 1983. *Publications:* Intermolecular and Surface Forces: with applications to colloidal and biological systems, 1985, 2nd edn 1991; about 200 pubns in learned jls, incl. Nature, Science, Procs Royal Soc. *Recreation:* history of science. *Address:* 2233 Foothill Lane, Santa Barbara, CA 93105, USA. *T:* (residence) (805) 9639545, (office) (805) 8938407.

ISSERLIS, Steven John, CBE 1998; 'cellist; *b* 19 Dec. 1958; *s* of George and late Cynthia Isserlis; lives with Pauline Mara; one *s*. *Educ:* City of London School; International 'Cello Centre; Oberlin College. London recital début, Wigmore Hall, 1977; London concerto début, with English Chamber Orchestra, 1980; concerts in Europe, N America, Australia, 1978–; tours in USSR, 1984–; débuts, 1990–, in New York, Chicago, LA, Paris, Berlin, etc; numerous recordings. Awards for recordings include: Gramophone Award (Contemporary Music), for John Tavener's The Protecting Veil, 1992; Deutsche Schallplattenpreis, for Schumann Cello Concerto, 1998; Classic CD Award, for Haydn Concertos, 1999. Piatigorsky Artist Award, USA, 1993; Instrumentalist Award, Royal Philharmonic Soc., 1993; Schumann Prize, City of Zwickau, 2000. *Publication:* Why Beethoven Threw the Stew (for children), 2001. *Recreations:* talking on the telephone, eating too much, regretting it, watching videos, reading, panicking about upcoming concerts, sleeping, jet-lag, telling people how tired I am, wondering if I should have any more worthwhile recreations. *Address:* c/o Harrison & Parrott, 12 Penzance Place, W11 4PA. *T:* (020) 7229 9166.

ISSING, Dr Otmar; Member, Executive Board, European Central Bank, since 1998; *b* 27 March 1936. *Educ:* Univ. of Würzburg (BA Econs; PhD 1961). Res. Asst, Inst. of Econs and Social Scis, 1960–66, Lectr, 1965–67, Univ. of Würzburg; Temp. Prof., Univ. of Marburg, 1965–66; Professor: Faculty of Econs and Social Scis, and Dir, Inst. for Internat. Econ. Relns, Univ. of Erlangen-Nuremberg, 1967–73 (Temp. Prof., 1966–67); of Econs, Monetary Econs and Internat. Econ. Relns, Univ. of Würzburg, 1973–90 (Hon. Prof., 1991–); Mem. Directorate, Deutsche Bundesbank, 1990–98. Co-founder and Jt Ed., WiSt (scientific jl), 1972–90. Hon. doctorates from: Bayreuth, 1996; Constance, 1998; Frankfurt am Main, 1999. *Publications* include: Leitwährung und internationale Währungsordnung, 1965; Indexklauseln und Inflation, Vorträge und Aufsätze, 1973; Einführung in die Geldtheorie, 1974, 11th edn 1998 (trans. Chinese and Bulgarian); Investitionslenkung in der Marktwirtschaft?, 1975; (jtly) Kleineres Eigentum: Grundlage unserer Staats- und Wirtschaftsordnung, 1976; Einführung in die Geldpolitik, 1981, 6th edn 1996; Internationale Währungsordnung, 1991; Von der D-Mark zum Euro, 1998; contrib. learned jls. *Address:* European Central Bank, Kaiserstrasse 29, 60311 Frankfurt, Germany. *T:* (69) 13440.

ISTEAD, Maj.-Gen. Peter Walter Ernest, CB 1989; OBE 1978; GM 1966; DL; Chief Executive, Institute of Brewing, 1990–96; *b* 7 Aug. 1935; *s* of Walter and Marie Istead; *m* 1961, Jennifer Mary Swinson; one *s* one *d*. *Educ:* Whitgift Trinity Sch., Croydon. Enlisted as boy soldier into Scots Guards, 1952; commnd Queen's Royal Regt, 1954; seconded to KAR, 1954–56; transf. RAOC, 1957; HQ 16 Parachute Bde, 1958–62; sc 1968; Directing Staff, Staff Coll., Camberley, 1971–73; DCS, 4 Armd Div., 1978–81; RCDS, 1982; Dir, Admin. Planning (Army), 1983–86; Comdr Supply, BAOR, 1986–87; Dir Gen., Logistic Policy (Army), 1987–90. Hon. Col Comdt, RAOC, 1989–92. Freeman, City of London, 1986; Liveryman, Co. of Gold and Silver Wyre Drawers, 1990. DL Greater London, 1997. *Recreation:* angling. *Address:* Wandsworth, London.

IUUL, Michael Christian Stig; Managing Director and Chief Executive Officer, Carlsberg Asia Ltd, Singapore, since 2001; *b* Copenhagen, 26 Jan. 1943; *s* of Stig A. Iuul and Grethe (*née* Gerlach); *m* Annie Ingeborg Scavenius; two *s*. *Educ:* Herlufsholm Sch.; Univ. of Copenhagen (MA Econs); Univ. of Paris; Univ. of Rome. International Bank for Reconstruction and Development: Planning Consultant, 1970–74; Industrial Economist, then Chief Economist, projects in Ghana, 1971, and Malaysia, 1972–74; joined Carlsberg A'S, Copenhagen, 1974: Manager, Sinebrychoff AB, Helsinki, 1975–76; Man. Dir, Carlsberg Brewery Ltd, Northampton, 1977–85; Gp Man. Dir and CEO (Internat. Ops), 1985–2001. Chm., Carlsberg-Tetley Ltd; Director: Th. Wessel & Vett Ltd. Ridder af Dannebrog (Denmark). *Recreations:* tennis, ski-ing, yachting. *Address:* Grosvenor Road, SW1; Carlsberg Asia Ltd, 501 Orchard Road, Wheelock Place 08–02A/03, Singapore 238880. *Club:* Royal Thames Yacht.

IVAMY, Prof. Edward Richard Hardy; Professor of Law, University of London, 1960–86, now Emeritus; *b* 1 Dec. 1920; *o s* of late Edward Wadham Ivamy and late Florence Ivamy; *m* 1965, Christine Ann Frances, *o d* of William and late Frances Culver; one *s*. *Educ:* Malvern Coll.; University Coll., London. Served War of 1939–45, RA: 67 Field Regt, N Africa, Italy and Middle East; 2nd Lieut 1942; Temp. Capt. 1945; Staff Capt., GHQ, Cairo, 1946. LLB (1st cl. hons) 1947; PhD 1953; LLD 1967. Barrister, Middle Temple, 1949. University Coll., London: Asst Lectr in Laws, 1947–50; Lectr, 1950–56; Reader in Law, 1956–60; Dean of Faculty of Laws, 1964 and 1965; Fellow, 1969. Hon. Sec., Soc. of Public Teachers of Law, 1960–63; Hon. Sec., Bentham Club, 1953–58; Governor, Malvern Coll., 1982–. *Publications:* Show Business and the Law, 1955; (ed) Payne and Ivamy's Carriage of Goods by Sea, 7th edn 1963–13th edn, 1989; Hire-Purchase Legislation in England and Wales, 1965; Casebook on Carriage of Goods by Sea, 1965, 6th edn 1985; Casebook on Sale of Goods, 1966, 5th edn 1987; (ed) Chalmers's Marine Insurance Act 1906, 6th edn 1966–10th edn 1993; General Principles of Insurance Law, 1966, 6th edn 1993; (ed) Topham and Ivamy's Company Law, 13th edn 1967–16th edn 1978; Casebook on Commercial Law, 1967, 3rd edn 1979; Fire and Motor Insurance, 1968, 5th edn 1997; Casebook on Insurance Law, 1969, 4th edn 1984; Marine Insurance, 1969, 4th edn 1985; Casebook on Shipping Law, 1970, 4th edn 1987; Casebook on Partnership, 1970, 2nd edn 1982; Casebook on Agency, 1971, 3rd edn 1987; Personal Accident, Life and Other Insurances, 1973, 2nd edn 1980; (ed) Underhill's Partnership, 10th edn 1975 to 12th edn 1985; (ed) Halsbury's Laws of England, 4th edn 1978, vol. 25 (Insurance), 1977 and 1994, vol. 43 (Shipping and Navigation), 1983 and 1997; Dictionary of Insurance Law, 1981; Dictionary of Company Law, 1983, 2nd edn 1985; Insurance Law Handbook, 1983; Dictionary of Shipping Law, 1984; Encyclopaedia of Shipping Law Sources (UK), 1985; Encyclopedia of Oil and Natural Gas Law, 1986; Encyclopedia of Carriage Law Sources, 1987; Merchant Shipping (Liner Conferences) Act 1982, 1987; Merchant Shipping Act 1970, 1987; Merchant Shipping Act 1979, 1987; (ed) Mozley and Whiteley's Law Dictionary, 10th edn 1988 and 11th edn 1993; contrib. to Encyclopædia Britannica, Chambers's Encyclopædia, Current Legal Problems, Jl of Business Law; Annual Survey of Commonwealth Law, 1967–77. *Recreations:* railways, cricket, tennis. *Address:* 7 Egliston Mews, SW15 1AP. *T:* (020) 8785 6718.

IVANYI, Prof. Juraj, MD; PhD; Head (formerly Director), Tuberculosis and Related Infections Unit, MRC Clinical Sciences Centre, 1984–97; Professor of Mycobacteriological Immunology, Royal Postgraduate Medical School, University of London, 1990–97; *b* 20 June 1934; *s* of Dr Arnold Ivanyi and Maria (*née* Keszner); *m* 1960, Dr Ludmila Svobodova. *Educ:* Charles Univ., Prague (MD); Acad. of Scis, Prague (PhD 1963). Czechoslovak Acad. of Scis, Prague, 1961–68; Wellcome Res. Labs, Beckenham, 1969–84; MRC, Hammersmith Hosp., 1984–97. Vis. Prof., Dept of Oral Med. and Pathology, Guy's, King's and St Thomas' Med. and Dental Sch., KCL at Guy's Hosp., 1998–. Hon. Mem., Slovak Soc. for Immunology, 1995. *Publications:* numerous in field of immunology. *Recreations:* theatre, ski-ing. *Address:* 3 Grotes Place, Blackheath, SE3 0QH. *T:* (020) 8318 1088.

IVEAGH, 4th Earl of, *cr* 1919; **Arthur Edward Rory Guinness;** Bt 1885; Baron Iveagh 1891; Viscount Iveagh 1905; Viscount Elveden 1919; *b* 10 Aug. 1969; *s* of 3rd Earl of Iveagh and of Miranda Daphne Jane, *d* of Maj. Michael Smiley; *S* father, 1992; *m* 2001, Clare Hazell. *Heir: b* Hon. Rory Michael Benjamin Guinness, *b* 12 Dec. 1974.

IVENS, Michael William, CBE 1983; Consultant, Aims of Industry, 1994–2001 (Director, 1971–94); Director, Foundation for Business Responsibilities, 1967–92; *b* 15 March 1924; *s* of Harry Guest Ivens and Nina Ailion; *m* 1st, 1950, Rosalie Turnbull (marr. diss. 1971); two *s* one *d* (and one *s* decd); 2nd, 1971, Katherine Laurence; two *s*. Jt Editor, Twentieth Century, 1967; Hon. Vice-Pres., Junior Hosp. Doctors Assoc., 1969; Director: Standard Telephone, 1970; Working Together Campaign, 1972–73. Jt Founder and Vice-Pres., Freedom Assoc.; Jt Founder and Trustee, Foundn for the Study of Terrorism, 1986; Member: Adv. Bd, US Industrial Council Educn Foundn, 1980–; Council and Hon. Treas., Poetry Soc., 1989–91; Adv. Cttee, Airey Neave Foundn, 1990–. *Publications:* Practice of Industrial Communication, 1963; Case Studies in Management, 1964; Case Studies in Human Relations, 1966; Case for Capitalism, 1967; Industry and Values, 1970; Which Way?, 1970; Prophets of Freedom and Enterprise, 1975; (ed jtly) Bachman's Book of Freedom Quotes, 1978; *poetry:* Another Sky, 1963; Last Waltz, 1964; Private and Public, 1968; Born Early, 1975; No Woman is an Island, 1983; New Divine Comedy, 1990; columns and articles under pseudonym Yorick. *Recreation:* campaigning. *Address:* 2 Mulgrave Road, NW10 1BT.

IVERSEN, Prof. Leslie Lars, PhD; FRS 1980; Professor of Pharmacology and Director, Wolfson Centre for Age-Related Diseases, King's College London, since 1999; Visiting Professor of Pharmacology: University of Oxford, since 1996; Imperial College School of Medicine, since 1997; *b* 31 Oct. 1937; *s* of Svend Iversen and Anna Caia Iversen; *m* 1961, Susan Diana (*née* Kibble) (*see* S. D. Iversen); one *s* one *d* (and one *d* decd). *Educ:* Trinity Coll., Cambridge (BA Biochem, PhD Pharmacol). Harkness Fellow, United States: with Dr J. Axelrod, Nat. Inst. of Mental Health, and Dr E. Kravitz, Dept of Neurobiology, Harvard Med. Sch., 1964–66; Fellow, Trinity Coll., Cambridge, 1964–84; Locke Research Fellow of Royal Society, Dept of Pharmacology, Univ. of Cambridge, 1967–71; Dir, MRC Neurochemical Pharmacology Unit, Cambridge, 1971–82; Dir, Merck, Sharp & Dohme Neurosci. Res. Centre, Harlow, 1982–95; Sen. Vis. Scientist, Dept of Pharmacology, Univ. of Oxford, 1995–96. Foreign Associate, Nat. Acad. of Scis (USA), 1986. *Publications:* The Uptake and Storage of Noradrenaline in Sympathetic Nerves, 1967; (with S. D. Iversen) Behavioural Pharmacology, 1975, 2nd edn 1981; The Science of Marijuana, 2000. *Recreations:* reading, gardening. *Address:* Department of Pharmacology, University of Oxford, Mansfield Road, Oxford OX1 3QT.

IVERSEN, Prof. Susan Diana, PhD, ScD; Professor of Psychology, since 1993, and a Pro-Vice-Chancellor, since 1998, Oxford University; Fellow of Magdalen College, Oxford, since 1993; *b* 28 Feb. 1940; *d* of Jack Bertram Kibble and Edith Margaret Kibble; *m* 1961, Leslie Lars Iversen, *qv*; one *s* one *d* (and one *d* decd). *Educ:* Girton Coll., Cambridge (BA Zoology, PhD Exp. Psych, ScD). NATO Science Fellow, Nat. Inst. Mental Health and Dept of Pharmacology, Harvard Med. Sch., 1964–66; Fellow: Girton Coll., Cambridge, 1964–75; Jesus Coll., Cambridge, 1981–93; Dept of Exp. Psychology, Cambridge, 1966–83; Merck Sharp & Dohme, Neuroscience Research Centre, Harlow, 1983–93; Prof. and Head of Dept of Experimental Psychol., Oxford Univ., 1993–2000. Member: Council, SERC, 1991–94; BBSRC, 1994–97. *Publications:* (with L. L. Iversen) Behavioural Pharmacology, 1975, 2nd edn 1981; (ed with L. L. Iversen and S. H. Snyder) Handbook of Psychopharmacology, 20 vols. *Recreations:* history, wildlife, modern art, theatre. *Address:* University Offices, Wellington Square, Oxford OX1 2JD.

IVES, Charles John Grayston, (Bill); Informator Choristarum, Organist, and Tutor in Music, Magdalen College, Oxford, since 1991; Fellow of Magdalen College, since 1991; *b* 15 Feb. 1948; *s* of Harold James Ives and Catherine Lilla Ives; *m* 1st, 1972, Bethan Eleri Jones (marr. diss. 1986); one *s* one *d*; 2nd, 1988, Janette Ann (*née* Buqué). *Educ:* King's Sch., Ely; Selwyn Coll., Cambridge. Asst Dir of Music, Reed's Sch., Cobham, 1971–76; Lectr in Music, Coll. of Further Educn, Chichester, 1976–78; tenor, The King's Singers, 1978–85; freelance composer, 1985–91. Examr, Associated Bd of Royal Schs of Music, 1988–. *Publications:* (as Grayston Ives) musical compositions of sacred choral music, including Canterbury Te Deum (commnd for Enthronement of Archbishop George Carey, Canterbury Cathedral, 1991). *Recreations:* books, wine, travel. *Address:* Magdalen College, Oxford OX1 4AU. *T:* (01865) 276007.

IVES, Prof. Kenneth James, CBE 1996; FREng; FICE; Chadwick Professor of Civil Engineering, University College London, 1984–92, retired; *b* 29 Nov. 1926; *s* of Walter Ives and Grace Ives (*née* Curson); *m* 1952, Brenda Grace Tilley; one *s* one *d*. *Educ:* William Ellis Grammar School, London; University College London (BSc Eng, PhD, DSc Eng; Fellow, 1996). FREng (FEng 1986); FICE 1983. Junior Engineer, Metropolitan Water Board, London, 1948–55; Lectr, Reader, Prof., University Coll. London, 1955–92. Research Fellow, Harvard Univ., 1958–59; Visiting Professor: Univ. of North Carolina, 1964; Delft Technical Univ., 1977; Consultant Expert Adviser, WHO, 1966–92. Mem., Badenoch Cttee on Cryptosporidium in Water Supplies, 1989–95. Gans Medal, Soc. for Water Treatment, 1966; Gold Medal, Filtration Soc. Internat, 1983; Jenkins Medal, IAWPRC, 1990; Freese Award, ASCE, 1994. *Publications:* Scientific Basis of Filtration, 1975; Scientific Basis of Flocculation, 1978; Scientific Basis of Flotation, 1984; contribs to sci. and eng. jls on water purification. *Recreation:* ballroom dancing. *Address:* Department of Civil and Environmental Engineering, University College London, Gower Street, WC1E 6BT. *T:* (020) 7387 7050.

IVISON, David Malcolm; Director, British Metallurgical Plant Constructors' Association, since 1994; *b* 22 March 1936; *s* of John and Ruth Ellen Ivison; *m* 1961, Lieselotte Verse; one *s* one *d*. *Educ:* King Edward VI School, Lichfield; RMA Sandhurst; Staff College, Camberley. Army, Gurkha Transport Regt, 1955–83 (Lt-Col). Tate & Lyle, 1984–85; Chief Exec., Inst. of Road Transport Engrs, 1985–89. *Recreations:* learning languages, tennis, reading. *Address:* 1 Dundaff Close, Camberley, Surrey GU15 1AF. *T:* (01276) 27778.

IVORY, Brian Gammell, CBE 1999; CA; Chairman, Highland Distillers (formerly The Highland Distilleries Co.) plc, 1997–1999; *b* 10 April 1949; *s* of late Eric James Ivory and Alice Margaret Joan, *d* of Sir Sydney James Gammell; *m* 1981, Oona Mairi Macphie Bell-MacDonald (*see* O. M. M. Ivory); one *s* one *d*. *Educ:* Eton College; Magdalene College, Cambridge (MA). The Highland Distilleries Co.: Dir, 1978–; Man. Dir, 1988–94; Gp Chief Exec., 1994–97; Director: Rémy Cointreau SA, 1991–; Bank of Scotland, 1998–2001; Scottish American Investment Co. plc, 2000–; Retec Europe, 2001–. Vice-Chm., Scottish Arts Council, 1988–92; Mem., Arts Council of GB, 1988–92. Chm. Trustees, Nat. Galls of Scotland, 2000–. Founder and Chm., The Piping Centre, 1996–. Mem., Royal Co. of Archers (Queen's Bodyguard for Scotland), 1996–. FRSA 1993; FRSE 2001. Freeman, City of London, 1996. *Recreations:* the arts, farming, hill walking. *Address:* 12 Ann Street, Edinburgh EH4 1PJ. *Club:* New (Edinburgh).

IVORY, James Francis; film director; Partner in Merchant Ivory Productions, since 1961; *b* 7 June 1928; *s* of Edward Patrick Ivory and Hallie Millicent De Loney. *Educ:* Univ. of Oregon (BA Fine Arts); Univ. of Southern California (MFA Cinema). Guggenheim Fellow, 1974. Collaborator with Ruth Prawer Jhabvala and Ismail Merchant on the following films: The Householder, 1963; Shakespeare Wallah, 1965; The Guru, 1969; Bombay Talkie, 1970; Autobiography of a Princess, 1975; Roseland, 1977; Hullabaloo over Georgie and Bonnie's Pictures, 1978; The Europeans, 1979; Jane Austen in Manhattan, 1980; Quartet, 1981; Heat and Dust, 1983; The Bostonians, 1984; A Room With a View, 1986; Mr and Mrs Bridge, 1990; Howards End, 1992; The Remains of the Day, 1993; Jefferson in Paris, 1995; Surviving Picasso, 1996; A Soldier's Daughter Never Cries, 1998; The Golden Bowl, 2000; collaborator with Ismail Merchant (producer) on: (with Nirad Chaudhuri) Adventures of a Brown Man in Search of Civilization, 1971; (with George W. S. Trow and Michael O'Donoghue) Savages, 1972; (with Walter Marks) The Wild Party, 1975; (with Kit Hesketh-Harvey) Maurice, 1987; (with Tama Janowitz) Slaves of New York, 1989; (other films: (with Terence McNally) The Five Forty Eight, 1979; documentaries: Venice, Theme and Variations, 1957; The Sword and the Flute, 1959; The Delhi Way, 1964. D. W. Griffith Award, Directors Guild of America, 1995. Commandeur, Ordre des Arts et des Lettres (France), 1996. *Publication:* Autobiography of a Princess (Also Being the Adventures of an American Film Director in the Land of the Maharajas), 1975. *Recreation:* looking at pictures. *Address:* PO Box 93, Claverack, NY 12513, USA. *T:* (office) (212) 5828049.

IVORY, Oona Mairi Macphie; DL; Director, Royal Scottish Academy of Music and Drama, since 1989; *b* 21 July 1954; *d* of late Archibald Ian Bell-Macdonald and Mary Rae (*née* Macphie); *m* 1981, Brian Gammell Ivory, *qv*; one *s* one *d*. *Educ:* Royal Scottish Acad. of Music and Drama; King's Coll., Cambridge (MA); Royal Acad. of Music. ARCM. Dir, 1988–97, Chm., 1995–97, Scottish Ballet. Founder and Dir, Piping Centre, 1996– (Dep. Chm., 1999–). FRSA. DL Edinburgh, 1998. *Recreations:* the arts, sailing, hill-walking. *Address:* 12 Ann Street, Edinburgh EH4 1PJ.

IVORY, Thomas Peter Gerard; QC 1998; *b* 29 Sept. 1956; *s* of late Patrick Ivory and of Rosaleen Ivory; *m* 1985, Deborah Mary Stinson. *Educ:* St Patrick's Coll., Knock, Belfast; St Catharine's Coll., Cambridge (BA 1977; MA). Called to the Bar, Lincoln's Inn, 1978. Fellow, St Catharine's Coll., Cambridge, 1983–90. *Recreation:* golf. *Address:* 1 Essex Court, Temple, EC4Y 9AR. *T:* (020) 7583 2000.

J

JABALÉ, Rt Rev. (John) Mark, OSB; Bishop Coadjutor of Menevia, (RC), since 2000; *b* 16 Oct. 1933; *s* of John and Arlette Jabalé. *Educ:* Belmont Abbey Sch.: Fribourg Univ. (LèsL); St Mary's Coll., London (DipEd). Belmont Abbey School: Games Master and House Master, 1963–69; Headmaster, 1969–83; built Monastery of the Incarnation, in Tambogrande, Perú; Prior, 1986–93, Abbot, 1993–2000, Belmont Abbey. Steward and Mem., Cttee of Management, Henley Royal Regatta. *Recreations:* computers, rowing. *Address:* Belmont Abbey, Hereford HR2 9RZ. *T:* (01432) 277386. *Club:* Leander (Henley-on-Thames).

JACK, Hon. Sir Alieu (Sulayman), Grand Commander, 1972, and Chancellor, 1972–83, National Order of The Gambia; Kt 1970; Speaker, House of Representatives of the Republic of The Gambia, 1962–72, and 1977–83, retired; *b* 14 July 1922; *m* 1946, Yai Marie Cham; four *s* four *d* (and one *d* decd). *Educ:* St Augustine's School. Entered Gambia Civil Service, 1939; resigned and took up local appt with NAAFI, 1940–44; Civil Service, 1945–48; entered commerce, 1948; Man. Dir, Gambia National Trading Co. Ltd, 1948–72. Mem., Bathurst City Council, 1949–62. Minister for Works and Communications, The Gambia, 1972–77. Represented The Gambia Parlt at various internat. gatherings. Comdr, National Order of Senegal, 1967; Comdr, Order of Merit of Mauritania, 1967; Commander, Order of Fed. Republic of Nigeria, 1970; Kt Grand Band, Liberia, 1977. *Recreation:* golf. *Address:* PO Box 376, Banjul, The Gambia. *T:* (home) 92204, (office) 28431. *Club:* Bathurst (Banjul).

JACK, Sir David, Kt 1993; CBE 1982; PhD; FRS 1992; FRSE; pharmacologist; *b* 22 Feb. 1924; *s* of Andrew Jack and Mary McDougal Jack (*née* Maiden); *m* 1952, Lydia Downie Brown; two *d. Educ:* Markinch and Buckhaven Schools, Fife; Univ. of Glasgow (BSc); Univ. of London (PhD); Royal Technical Coll., Glasgow. FRSC, FIBiol, FRPharmS; FRSE 1978. Lectr in Pharmacology, Glasgow Univ. and RTC Glasgow, 1948–51; Scientist, Glaxo Labs, 1951–53; Head of Product Develt, Smith Kline and French, 1953–61; Res. Dir, Allen & Hanburys, 1961–73; Man. Dir, Allen & Hanburys Res., 1973–78; R&D Dir, Glaxo Holdings, 1978–87; associated with new medicines for asthma (Queen's Awards for salbutamol, 1973, inhaled beclomethasone dipropionate, 1975), hypertension, peptic ulcer (Queen's Award for ranitidine, 1985), nausea and migraine (Queen's Award for sumatriptan, 1996). Hon. Mem., British Pharm. Soc., 1990. Hon. DL Dundee, 1991. Hon. DSc: Strathclyde, 1982; Bath, 1987; CNAA, 1987; Liverpool, 1998; London, 1999. Harrison Medal, Royal Pharm. Soc., 1969; Medicinal Chem. Medal, RSC, 1980; Award for Drug Discovery, Soc. for Drug Research, 1985; Lilly Prize Medal, British Pharm. Soc., 1989; Mullard Medal, Royal Soc., 1991; Galen Medal, Soc. of Apothecaries, 1995; Host-Madsen Medal, Internat. Pharmaceutical Fedn, 1995. *Publications:* papers in Br. Jl Pharmacology. *Recreations:* asthma therapy, gardening, golf. *Address:* 6 The Slype, Gustard Wood, Wheathampstead, Herts AL4 8RY. *T:* (01582) 832241.

JACK, Sir David (Emmanuel), GCMG 1991; MBE 1975; Governor General, St Vincent and The Grenadines, 1989–96; *b* 16 July 1918; *s* of John Fitzroy Jack and Margaret Lewis Jack; *m* 1946, Esther Veronica McKay; two *s* two *d* (and one *s* decd). *Educ:* Stubbs Govt School; La Salle Extension Univ., Chicago (Dip. Higher Accountancy). Teacher's Cert., St Vincent Educn Dept. School Teacher, 1934–43; Engine Operator, Shell Oil Refinery, 1943–45; Commercial Accounting, 1945–69; Gen. Manager, A'Root Ind., 1969–79; in business and politics, 1979–84; elected to Parliament, 1984; Minister, 1984–89. Methodist local preacher, 1940–96. *Recreations:* carpentry, music. *Address:* PO Box 381, New Montrose, St Vincent and The Grenadines. *T:* 4561270.

JACK, David M.; *see* Morton Jack.

JACK, Ian Grant; Editor, Granta, since 1995; *b* 7 Feb. 1945; *s* of Henry Jack and Isabella Jack (*née* Gillespie); *m* 1st, 1979, Aparna Bagchi (marr. diss. 1992); 2nd, 1998, Rosalind Sharpe; one *s* one *d. Educ:* Dunfermline High School, Fife. Trainee journalist, Glasgow Herald, 1965; reporter, Cambuslang Advertiser and East Kilbride News, 1966; journalist, Scottish Daily Express, 1966–70; Sunday Times, 1970–86; Observer and Vanity Fair (NY), 1986–88; Dep. Editor, 1989–91, Exec. Editor, 1991–92, Editor, 1992–95, Independent on Sunday. Journalist of the Year, Granada TV What The Papers Say award, 1985; Colour Magazine Writer of the Year, 1985, Reporter of the Year, 1988, British Press Awards; Nat. Newspaper Editor of the Year, Newspaper Focus Awards, 1992. *Publications:* Before the Oil Ran Out, 1987; The Crash That Stopped Britain, 2001. *Address:* Granta Publications, 2–3 Hanover Yard, Noel Road, N1 8BE. *Club:* India International Centre (New Delhi).

JACK, Prof. Ian Robert James, FBA 1986; Professor of English Literature, University of Cambridge, 1976–89, Emeritus 1989; Fellow of Pembroke College, Cambridge, 1961–89, Emeritus 1989; *b* 5 Dec. 1923; *s* of John McGregor Bruce Jack, WS, and Helena Colburn Buchanan; *m* 1st, 1948, Jane Henderson MacDonald (marr. diss.); two *s* one *d*; 2nd, 1972, Margaret Elizabeth Crone; one *s. Educ:* George Watson's Coll. (John Welsh Classical Schol., 1942); Univ. of Edinburgh (James Boswell Fellow, 1946; MA 1947); Merton Coll., Oxford (DPhil 1950; Hon. Fellow, 1998); LittD Cantab 1973. Brasenose College, Oxford: Lectr in Eng. Lit., 1950–55; Sen. Res. Fellow, 1955–61; Cambridge University: Lectr in English, 1961–73; Reader in English Poetry, 1973–76; Librarian, Pembroke Coll., 1965–75. Vis. Professor: Alexandria, 1960; Chicago (Carpenter Prof.), 1968–69; California at Berkeley, 1968–69; British Columbia, 1975; Virginia, 1980–81; Tsuda Coll., Tokyo, 1981; New York Univ. (Berg Prof.), 1989; de Carle Lectr, Univ. of Otago, NZ, 1964; Warton Lectr in English Poetry, British Acad., 1967; Guest Speaker, Nichol Smith Seminar, ANU, 1976; Guest Speaker, 50th anniversary meeting of English Literary Soc. of Japan, 1978; Leverhulme Emeritus Fellow, 1990, 1991; numerous lecture-tours for British Council and other bodies. President: Charles Lamb Soc., 1970–80; Browning Soc., 1980–83; Johnson Soc., Lichfield, 1986–87; Vice-Pres., Brontë Soc., 1973–. General Editor: Brontë novels (Clarendon edn), 7 vols, 1969–92; The Poetical Works of Browning, 1983–95. *Publications:* Augustan Satire, 1952; English Literature 1815–1832 (Vol. X, Oxf. Hist. of Eng. Lit.), 1963; Keats and the Mirror of Art, 1967; Browning's Major Poetry, 1973; The Poet and his Audience, 1984; *edited:* Sterne: A Sentimental Journey, etc, 1968; Browning: Poetical Works 1833–1864, 1970; (with Hilda Marsden) Emily Brontë: Wuthering Heights, 1976; The Poetical Works of Browning: co-edited: (with M. Smith) Vol. 1 (Pauline, Paracelsus), 1983; (with M. Smith) Vol. 2 (Sordello), 1984; (with R. Fowler) Vol. 3 (Bells and Pomegranates i–vi), 1988; (with R. Fowler and M. Smith) Vol. 4 (Bells and Pomegranates, vii–viii, Christmas-Eve and Easter-Day), 1991; (with R. Inglesfield) Vol. 5 (Men and Women), 1995; contrib. TLS, RES, etc. *Recreations:* collecting books, travelling hopefully, thinking about words. *Address:* Highfield House, High Street, Fen Ditton, Cambridgeshire CB5 8ST. *T:* (01223) 292697; Pembroke College, Cambridge CB2 1RF. *Club:* MCC.

JACK, Prof. (James) Julian (Bennett), PhD; FRS 1997; Professor of Physiology, since 1996, and Fellow of University College, since 1966, University of Oxford; *b* Invercargill, NZ, 25 March 1936. *Educ:* Univ. of Otago (MMedSc, PhD); Magdalen Coll., Oxford (BM 1963; MA). Rhodes Scholarship, 1960–63; House Officer, Radcliffe Infirmary, Oxford, 1963–64; Foulerton Gift Res. Fellow, Royal Soc., 1964–68; University of Oxford: Weir Jun. Res. Fellow in Natural Sci., UC, 1966; Lectr in Physiology, 1970–94; Reader in Cellular Neurosci., 1994–96. Mem. Council, Action Res., 1988–91; Gov., Wellcome Trust, 1987– (Dep. Chm. of Govs, 1994–99). Founder FMedSci 1998; FRCP 1999. Hon. FRSNZ 1999. *Address:* University Laboratory of Physiology, Parks Road, Oxford OX1 3PT. *T:* (01865) 272537; 16 Merton Street, Oxford OX1 4JE. *T:* (01865) 790637.

JACK, Rt Hon. (John) Michael; PC 1997; MP (C) Fylde, since 1987; *b* 17 Sept. 1946; *m* 1976, Alison Jane Musgrave; two *s. Educ:* Bradford Grammar Sch.; Bradford Tech. Coll.; Leicester Univ. BA(Econs); MPhil. Shipping, subseq. Advertising, Depts, Procter & Gamble, 1970–75; PA to Sir Derek Rayner, Marks & Spencer, 1975–80; Sales Dir, L. O. Jeffs Ltd, 1980–87. Mem., Mersey RHA, 1984–87. Contested (C) Newcastle upon Tyne Central, Feb. 1974. PPS to Minister of State, DOE, 1988–89, to Minister of Agric., Fisheries and Food, 1989–90; Parly Under Sec. of State, DSS, 1990–92; Minister of State: Home Office, 1992–93; MAFF, 1993–95; Financial Sec. to HM Treasury, 1995–96; Opposition front bench spokesman on health, 1997, on agric., fisheries and food, 1998. Member: Agriculture Select Cttee, 1999–; Tax Law Rewrite Steering Cttee, 1999–; Exec., 1922 Cttee, 1999–. Sec., Cons. Back-bench Transport Cttee, 1987–88; Chm., Cons. Back-bench sub-cttee on Horticulture and Markets, 1987–88; Sec., Cons. NW Members Gp, 1988–90. Nat. Chm., Young Conservatives, 1976–77. Trustee: MedAlert, 1990–; Lytham Community Sports Assoc., 1997. Vice-Pres., Think Green, 1989–90. President: Clifton Hosp. League of Friends, 1991–; Lytham St Annes ATC 2486 Sqdn, 1991–; Lytham Road Runners Club, 1999–. *Recreations:* dinghy sailing, vegetable growing, motor sport, boule. *Address:* House of Commons, SW1A 0AA.

JACK, Julian; *see* Jack, (James) J. B.

JACK, Prof. Kenneth Henderson, OBE 1997; PhD, ScD; FRS 1980; CChem, FRSC; Professor of Applied Crystal Chemistry, University of Newcastle upon Tyne, 1964–84, now Emeritus Professor, and Director of Wolfson Research Group for High-Strength Materials, 1970–84; Leverhulme Emeritus Fellow, 1985–87; *b* 12 Oct. 1918; *e s* of late John Henderson Jack, DSC, and Emily (*née* Cozens), North Shields, Northumberland; *m* 1942, Alfreda Hughes (*d* 1974); two *s. Educ:* Tynemouth Municipal High Sch.; King's Coll., Univ. of Durham, Newcastle upon Tyne (BSc 1939, DThPT 1940, MSc 1944); Fitzwilliam Coll., Univ. of Cambridge (PhD 1950, ScD 1978). Experimental Officer, Min. of Supply, 1940–41; Lectr in Chemistry, King's Coll., Univ. of Durham, 1941–45, 1949–52, 1953–57; Sen. Scientific Officer, Brit. Iron and Steel Res. Assoc., 1945–49; research at Crystallographic Lab., Cavendish Laboratory, Cambridge, 1947–49; Research Engr, Westinghouse Elec. Corp., Pittsburgh, Pa, 1952–53; Research Dir, Thermal Syndicate Ltd, Wallsend, 1957–64. Consultant, Cookson Group, 1986–94. Hon. Prof. of Materials Engrg, Univ. of Wales Swansea, 1996–. Lectures: J.W. Mellor Meml, Brit. Ceramic Soc., 1973; Harold Moore Meml, Metals Soc., 1984; W. Hume-Rothery Meml, Oxford Metallurgical Soc., 1986; Sosman Meml, Amer. Ceramic Soc., 1989. Fellow, Amer. Ceramic Soc., 1984; Membre d'Honneur, Société Française de Métallurgie, 1984; Mem., Internat. Acad. of Ceramics, 1990; Hon. Member: Materials Res. Soc. of India, 1991; Ceramic Soc. of Japan, 1991. Saville-Shaw Medal, Soc. of Chem. Industry, 1944; Sir George Beilby Meml Award, Inst. of Metals, RIC and Soc. of Chem. Industry, 1951; Kroll Medal and Prize, Metals Soc., 1979; (with Dr R.J. Lumby) Prince of Wales Award for Industrial Innovation and Production, 1984; Armourers & Brasiers' Co. Award, Royal Soc., 1988; World Materials Congress Award, ASM Internat., 1988; A. A. Griffith Silver Medal and Prize, Inst. of Metals, 1989; Centennial Award, Ceramic Soc. of Japan, 1991. *Publications:* papers in scientific jls and conf. proc. *Address:* 147 Broadway, Cullercoats, Tyne and Wear NE30 3TA. *T:* (0191) 257 3664.

JACK, Dr Malcolm Roy; Clerk of the Journals, House of Commons, since 2001; *b* 17 Dec. 1946; *s* of late Iain Ross Jack and Alicia Maria Eça da Silva, Hong Kong. *Educ:* school in Hong Kong; Univ. of Liverpool (Hong Kong Govt Scholar; BA Hons 1st Class); LSE, Univ. of London (PhD). A Clerk, House of Commons, 1967–; Private Sec. to Chm. of Ways and Means, 1977–80; Clerk to Agriculture Select Cttee, 1980–88; Clerk of Supply, 1989–91; Clerk of Standing Cttees, 1991–95; Sec. to H of C Commn, 1995–2001. Presidential Advr, OSCE Parly Assembly, 1992–96. Chm., Beckford Soc., 1996–; Sec., Johnson Club, 1998–; Mem., Highgate Literary and Scientific Instn. *Publications:* The Social and Political Thought of Bernard Mandeville, 1987; Corruption and Progress: the eighteenth-century debate, 1989; (ed with Anita Desai) The Turkish Embassy Letters of Lady Mary Wortley Montagu, 1993; (ed) Vathek and Other Stories: a William Beckford Reader, 1993; (ed) The Episodes of Vathek of William Beckford, 1994; William Beckford: an English Fidalgo, 1996; Sintra: a glorious Eden, 2002; articles and essays in books, learned and literary jls; reviews in TLS, APN Lisbon. *Recreations:* the Enlightenment (except in England), Dr Samuel Johnson, Luso-Brasilian life, letters and drama, Tang and Ming horses, the civic virtue of bees, fine arts, travel. *Address:* Journals Office, House of Commons, SW1A 0AA. *Club:* East India.

JACK, Rt Hon. Michael; *see* Jack, Rt Hon. J. M.

JACK, Hon. Sir Raymond (Evan), Kt 2001; **Hon. Mr Justice Jack;** a Judge of the High Court, Queen's Bench Division, since 2001; *b* 13 Nov. 1942; *s* of Evan and Charlotte Jack; *m* 1976, Elizabeth Alison, *d* of Rev. Canon James Seymour Denis Mansel, KCVO; one *s* two *d. Educ:* Rugby; Trinity Coll., Cambridge (MA). Called to Bar, Inner Temple, 1966, Bencher, 2000; QC 1982; a Recorder, 1989–91; a Circuit Judge, 1991–2001; Judge of the Bristol Mercantile Court, 1994–2001. *Publication:* Documentary Credits, 1991, 3rd edn 2000. *Recreations:* words and wood. *Address:* Royal Courts of Justice, Strand, WC2A 2LL.

JACK, Prof. Robert Barr, CBE 1988; Partner, McGrigor Donald, Solicitors, Glasgow, Edinburgh and London, 1957–93 (Joint Senior Partner, 1986–90; Senior Partner, 1990–93); *b* 18 March 1928; *s* of Robert Hendry Jack and Christina Alexandra Jack; *m* 1958, Anna Thorburn Thomson; two *s. Educ:* Kilsyth Acad.; High Sch., Glasgow; Glasgow Univ. MA 1948, LLB 1951. Admitted a solicitor in Scotland, 1951; Prof. of Mercantile Law, Glasgow Univ., 1978–93. Member: Company Law Cttee of Law Society of Scotland, 1971–95 (Convener, 1978–85); Scottish Law Commn, 1974–77. Scottish observer on Dept of Trade's Insolvency Law Review Cttee, 1977–82; Mem., DoT Adv. Panel on Company Law, 1980–83; Chm., Review Cttee on Banking Services Law, 1987–89. Lay Member: Council for the Securities Industry, 1983–85; Stock Exchange Council, 1984–86; Independent Mem. Bd, Securities Assoc., later SFA, 1987–94; Mem. Bd, SIB, 1994–97; UK Mem., Panel of Arbitrators, ICSID, 1989–95; Member: Takeover Panel, 1992–2001; Financial Law Panel, 1993–; MSI 1993. Chairman: Brownlee plc, Timber Merchants, Glasgow, 1984–86 (Dir, 1974–86); Joseph Dunn (Bottlers) Ltd, Soft Drink Manufacturers, Glasgow, 1983–2001; Scottish Mutual Assce 1992–98 (Dir, 1987–98); Dep. Chm., Scottish Metropolitan Property, 1991–98 (Dir, 1980–98); Director: Clyde Football Club Ltd, 1980–96; Bank of Scotland, 1985–96; Gartmore Scotland Investment Trust, 1991–2001; Glasgow Develt Agency, 1992–97. Pres., Scottish Nat. Council of YMCAs, 1983–98 (Chm., 1966–73). Mem., SHEFC, 1992–96. Chm., The Turnberry Trust, 1983–; Governor, Hutchesons' Educational Trust, Glasgow, 1978–87 (Chm. 1980–87); Mem. Bd of Govs, Beatson Inst. for Cancer Res., Glasgow, 1989–; Chm., Audit Commn, Glasgow Univ., 1996–. Mem., W of Scotland Adv. Bd, Salvation Army, 1995–. Trustee, Football Trust, 1998–2000. DUniv Glasgow, 2001. *Publications:* lectures on various aspects of company, insolvency and banking law and financial services regulation law. *Recreations:* golf, hopeful support of one of Scotland's less fashionable football teams; a dedicated lover of Isle of Arran. *Address:* 50 Lanton Road, Newlands, Glasgow G43 2SR. *T:* (0141) 637 7302, *Fax:* (0141) 637 8115; *e-mail:* robertjack@talk21.com. *Clubs:* Caledonian; Western (Glasgow); Pollok Golf; Shiskine Golf and Tennis (Isle of Arran) (Captain 1973–75).

JACK, Stuart Duncan Macdonald, CVO 1994; HM Diplomatic Service; Minister, Tokyo, since 1999; *b* 8 June 1949; *s* of William Harris Jack and Edith Florence Jack (*née* Coker); *m* 1977, Mariko Nobechi; one *s* two *d. Educ:* Westcliff High Sch. for Boys; Merton Coll., Oxford (BA 1971). VSO, Laos, 1971; joined HM Diplomatic Service, 1972: Eastern European and Soviet Dept, FO, 1972–73; Tokyo, 1974–79; Far Eastern Dept, FCO, 1979–81; Moscow, 1981–84; on secondment with Bank of England, 1984–85; Tokyo, 1985–89; Overseas Inspector, 1989–92; Consul Gen., St Petersburg, 1992–95; Hd of Research and Analysis, FCO, 1996–99. *Recreations:* reading, photography, music. *Address:* c/o Foreign and Commonwealth Office, King Charles Street, SW1A 2AH.

JACK, Dr William Hugh, CB 1988; management consultant, 1994–2000; Comptroller and Auditor General, Northern Ireland Audit Office, 1989–94; *b* 18 Feb. 1929; *s* of John Charles Jack and Martha Ann Jack; *m* 1953, Beatrice Jane Thompson; three *s* one *d. Educ:* Ballymena Acad.; Univ. of Edinburgh (BSc(For); PhD); Queen's Univ., Belfast (BSc (Econ)). MICFor 1959. Min. of Agriculture for NI, 1948–49; Colonial Forest Service, Gold Coast/Ghana, 1949–59 (Conservator of Forests, 1957); Dept of Agriculture for NI, 1959–89 (Permanent Sec., 1983). CIMgt. *Publications:* various articles in forestry research and economic jls. *Recreations:* walking, reading. *Address:* 22 Viewfort Park, Belfast BT17 9JY.

JACKAMAN, Michael Clifford John; Chairman of Grand Appeal, Royal Hospital for Sick Children, Bristol, 1995–2001; Chairman, Allied Domecq (formerly Allied-Lyons) plc, 1991–96 (Vice-Chairman, 1988–91); *b* 7 Nov. 1935; *s* of Air Cdre Clifford Thomas Jackaman, OBE and Lily Margaret Jackaman; *m* 1960, Valerie Jane Pankhurst; one *s* one *d. Educ:* Felsted Sch., Essex; Jesus Coll., Cambridge (MA Hons). Lieut RA, 1955–56. Dep. Man. Dir, Harveys of Bristol, 1976–78; Marketing Dir, Allied Breweries, 1978–83; Dir, Allied Domecq (formerly Allied Lyons) plc, 1978–; Chairman: Hiram Walker Allied Vintners, 1983–91; John Harvey & Sons Ltd, 1983–93; Mem., Council of Admin, Château Latour, 1983–93; Director: Fintex of London Ltd, 1986–92; Rank Orgn, 1992–97; Kleinwort Benson Gp, 1994–98. Governor, Bristol Polytechnic, 1988–91. Dir, Th. Royal, Bath, 1999–. Vice Pres., Internat. Wine and Spirits Comp. Liveryman, Distillers' Co.; Grand Master, Keepers of the Quaich (Scotland); Commanderie des Bontemps du Médoc et des Graves (France); Confraria do Vinho do Porto (Portugal). Hon. DBA UWE, 1993. *Recreations:* stoneware pottery, painting, etching, theatre, tennis. *Club:* Army and Navy.

JACKLIN, Anthony, CBE 1990 (OBE 1970); professional golfer, 1962–85 and 1988–99; Director of Golf, San Roque Club, 1988–90; *b* 7 July 1944; *s* of Arthur David Jacklin; *m* 1st, 1966, Vivien (*d* 1988); two *s* one *d*; 2nd, 1988, Astrid May Waagen; one *s*, one step *s* one step *d*. Successes include: British Assistant Pro Championship, 1965; Pringle Tournament, 1967; Dunlop Masters, 1967; Greater Jacksonville Open, USA, 1968; British Open Championship, 1969; US Open Championship, 1970; Benson & Hedges, 1971; British Professional Golfers Assoc., 1972, 1982; Gtr Jacksonville Open, 1972; Bogota Open, 1973 and 1974; Italian Open, 1973; Dunlop Masters, 1973; Scandinavian Open, 1975; Kerrygold International, 1976; English National PGA Championship, 1977; German Open, 1979; Jersey Open, 1981; PGA Champion, 1982; Ryder Cup player, 1967–80, Team Captain, Europe, 1983–89. Life Mem., PGA (Hon. Life Mem., European Tournament Players Div.). *Publications:* Golf with Tony Jacklin, 1969; The Price of Success, 1979; (with Peter Dobereiner) Jacklin's Golfing Secrets, 1983; Tony Jacklin: the first forty years, 1985; (with Bill Robertson) Your Game and Mine, 1990. *Recreation:* shooting. *Address:* 1175 51st West, Bradenton, FL 34209, USA. *Clubs:* Potters Bar Golf; Hon. Mem. of others.

JACKLIN, William, (Bill), RA 1991 (ARA 1989); *b* 1 Jan. 1943; *s* of Harold and Alice Jacklin; *m* 1st, 1979, Lesley Sarina Berman (marr. diss. 1993); 2nd, 1993, Janet Ann Russo. *Educ:* Walthamstow Sch. of Art; Royal College of Art (NDD, MARCA). Part-time Lectr at various art colleges, 1967–75; Arts Council Bursary, 1975; lives and works in New York, 1985–; Artist in Residence, British Council, Hong Kong, 1993–94. One man exhibns, London galleries, 1970–, USA, 1985–, Hong Kong, 1995; retrospective exhibn, Mus. of Modern Art, Oxford, 1992; frequent shows in internat. exhibns; works in major collections including Arts Council, British Mus., Metropolitan Mus. NY, Mus. of Modern Art NY, Tate Gall., V&A. *Publications:* catalogues to one man exhibns, London and New York; *relevant publication:* Bill Jacklin (monograph), by John Russell-Taylor, 1997. *Recreation:* planting trees. *Address:* c/o Marlborough Fine Art, 6 Albemarle Street, W1X 4BY. *T:* (020) 7629 5161. *Club:* Chelsea Arts.

JACKLING, Sir Roger Tustin, KCB 2001 (CB 1995); CBE 1982; Second Permanent Under-Secretary of State, Ministry of Defence, since 1996; *b* 23 Nov. 1943; *s* of Sir Roger Jackling, GCMG and late Joan (*née* Tustin) (Lady Jackling); *m* 1976, Jane Allen Pritchard; two *s. Educ:* Wellington Coll.; New York Univ. (BA); Jesus Coll., Oxford. Asst Principal, MoD, 1969, Principal, 1972; London Executive Prog., London Business Sch., 1974; Sec. of State's Office, MoD, 1976–79; Asst Sec. and Hd of DS11, 1979–82; Prime Minister's Office, 1983; Head of DS7/Resources and Programmes (Army), MoD, 1983–85; Fellow, Center for Internat. Affairs, Harvard Univ., 1985–86; Principal, CS Coll., 1986–89; Asst Under-Sec. of State (Progs), MoD, 1989–91; Dep. Under-Sec. of State (Resources, Progs and Finance), MoD, 1991–96. Member Council: RIPA, 1987–92; RUSI, 1993–96. *Recreations:* books, theatre, playing golf, watching cricket. *Address:* c/o Ministry of Defence, Whitehall, SW1. *Clubs:* Garrick; Highgate Golf, Faversham Golf.

JACKSON, Alan Robert, AO 1991; Chairman: Australian Trade Commission, since 1996; Austrim Nylex (formerly Austrim) Ltd, since 1990 (Chief Executive, 1990–2001); *b* 30 March 1936; *m* 1962, Esme Adelia Giles; four *d.* FCA, FASA, FAIM, FCPA. Accountant to Man. Dir, Mather & Platt, 1952–77; Man. Dir, 1977–90, Chm., 1990–97, BTR Nylex Ltd; Man. Dir and Chief Exec. Officer, BTR plc, 1991–95. Director: Australia Reserve Bank, 1990–2001; Seven Network Ltd, 1995–; Titan Petrochemicals and Polymers Berhad (Malaysia), 1997–. Dir, St Frances Xavier Cabrini Hosp., 1995–. *Recreations:* tennis, golf. *Address:* Austrade, AIDC Tower, 201 Kent Street, Sydney, NSW 2000, Australia; Level 4 East Tower, 608 St Kilda Road, Melbourne, Vic 3004, Australia.

JACKSON, Albert Leslie Samuel; JP; Chairman, Birmingham Technology Ltd (Aston Science Park), since 1984; *b* 20 Jan. 1918; *s* of Bert Jackson and Olive Powell; *m* Gladys Burley; one *s* one *d. Educ:* Handsworth New Road Council Sch. War service, Radio Mechanic, RAF. Mem., Birmingham CC, 1952–86; Lord Mayor, 1975–76, Dep. Lord Mayor, 1978–79, Birmingham. Dir and Cttee Chm., NEC, 1984–87; Dir, National Exhibition Centre (Developments) PLC, 1997–. JP 1968. Hon. DSc Aston, 1999. *Recreations:* chess, sailing. *Address:* Dickies Meadow, Dock Lane, Bredon, near Tewkesbury GL20 7LG. *T:* (01684) 772541.

JACKSON, Anthony Geoffrey Clive H.; *see* Howland Jackson.

JACKSON, Mrs (Audrey) Muriel W.; *see* Ward-Jackson.

JACKSON, Sir Barry (Trevor), Kt 2001; MS, FRCS; Serjeant Surgeon to The Queen, 1991–2001; Consultant Surgeon: St Thomas' Hospital, 1973–2001; Queen Victoria Hospital, East Grinstead, 1977–98; King Edward VII Hospital for Officers, since 1983; President-elect, Royal Society of Medicine, 2001–July 2002, President, from July 2002; *b* 7 July 1936; *er s* of Arthur Stanley Jackson and Violet May (*née* Fry); *m* 1962, Sheila May Wood; two *s* one *d. Educ:* Sir George Monoux Grammar Sch.; King's College London; Westminster Med. Sch. (Entrance Scholar). MB, BS 1963; MRCS, LRCP 1963; MS 1972; FRCS 1967; FRCP 1999. Down Bros Ltd, 1952–54; RAF 1954–56; junior surgical appts, Gordon Hosp., St James' Hosp., Balham, St Peter's Hosp., Chertsey, St Helier Hosp., Carshalton, St Thomas' Hosp. Surgeon to the Royal Household, 1983–91; Hon. Consultant in Surgery to the Army, 1990–. Royal College of Surgeons: Arris & Gale Lectr, 1973; Vicary Lectr, 1994; Bradshaw Lectr, 1998; Examr Primary FRCS, 1977–83; Mem. Court of Examrs, 1983–89; Mem. Council, 1991–2001; Pres., 1998–2001; Asst Editor 1984–91, Editor, 1992–97, Annals RCS; Pres., Assoc. of Surgeons of GB and Ireland, 1994–95 (Mem. Council, 1982–85; Hon. Sec., 1986–91; Vice Pres., 1993–94); Mem. Council, RSocMed, 1987–92 (Pres., Sect. of Coloproctology, 1991–92); Mem., GMC, 1999–. External examr in surgery: Khartoum, 1981, 1997; Ibadan, 1982; Colombo, 1984, 1988; Abu Dhabi, 1989. Mem., W Lambeth HA, 1982–83; Special Trustee: St Thomas' Hosp., 1982–84, 1994–99; Guy's Hosp., 1996–99; Trustee, Smith & Nephew Foundn, 1995–; Chm., SE Thames Regional Med. Adv. Cttee, 1983–87. Mem. Council of Govs, UMDS of Guy's and St Thomas' Hosps, 1989–94. Liveryman, Barbers' Co. (Mem., Ct of Assts, 1995–). Hon. FRCSI, 1999; Hon. FRCSEd, 1999; Hon. FDSRCS, 1999; Hon. FACS, 2000; Hon. FRACS, 2000. Hon. DSc Hull, 2001. *Publications:* contribs to surgical jls and textbooks (surgery of gastro-intestinal tract). *Recreations:* book collecting, reading, medical history, music, especially opera. *Address:* The Consulting Rooms, York House, 199 Westminster Bridge Road, SE1 7UT. *T:* (020) 7928 5485. *Club:* Athenæum.

JACKSON, Betty, MBE 1987; RDI 1988; Designer Director, Betty Jackson Ltd, since 1981; *b* 24 June 1949; *d* of Arthur and Phyllis Gertrude Jackson; *m* 1985, David Cohen; one *s* one *d. Educ:* Bacup and Rawtenstall Grammar Sch.; Birmingham Coll. of Art (DipAD fashion and textiles). Freelance fashion illustrator, 1971–73; design asst, 1973–75; chief designer, Quorum, 1975–81. Part-time Tutor, 1982–90, Vis. Prof., 1998–, RCA. Fellow, Birmingham Polytechnic, 1989; Univ. of Central Lancs, 1992. Hon. Fellow, RCA, 1989. Awards include: British Designer of the Year, Harvey Nichols and British Fashion Council, 1985; Viyella, 1987; Fil d'Or, Internat. Linen, 1989; Contemporary Designer of the Year, British Fashion Awards, 1999. *Address:* Betty Jackson Ltd, 1 Netherwood Place, Netherwood Road, W14 0BW. *T:* (020) 7602 6023; Betty Jackson Retail, 311 Brompton Road, SW3 2DY. *T:* (020) 7589 7884. *Club:* Groucho.

JACKSON, Very Rev. Brandon Donald; Dean of Lincoln, 1989–97, now Emeritus; *b* 11 Aug. 1934; *s* of Herbert and Millicent Jackson; *m* 1958, Mary Lindsay, 2nd *d* of John and Helen Philip; two *s* one *d. Educ:* Stockport School; Liverpool Univ.; St Catherine's Coll. and Wycliffe Hall, Oxford (LLB, DipTh). Curate: Christ Church, New Malden, Surrey, 1958–61; St George, Leeds, 1961–65; Vicar, St Peter, Shipley, Yorks, 1965–77; Provost of Bradford Cathedral, 1977–89. Religious Adviser to Yorkshire Television, 1969–79; Church Commissioner, 1971–73; Mem., Marriage Commn, 1975–78; Examining Chaplain to Bishop of Bradford, 1974–80. Chm., Wensleydale CPRE. Member Council: Wycliffe Hall, Oxford, 1971–85; St John's Coll., Nottingham, 1987–89; Governor: Harrogate College, 1974–86; Bradford Grammar Sch., 1977–89; Bishop Grosseteste Coll., Lincoln, 1989–97; Lincoln Christ's Hosp. Sch., 1989–97. Hon. DLitt Bradford, 1990. *Recreations:* sport (mainly watching), jogging, fell-walking, fishing, enjoying grandchildren, routine house maintenance and repair, reading, thinking, speaking. *Address:* Little Spigot, West Witton, Leyburn, N Yorks DL8 4LP. *T:* (01969) 624589; *e-mail:* brandon.littlespigot@debrett.net.

JACKSON, Caroline Frances; Member (C) South West Region, England, European Parliament, since 1999 (Wiltshire, 1984–94; Wiltshire North and Bath, 1994–99); *b* 5 Nov. 1946; *d* of G. H. Harvey; *m* 1975, Robert Victor Jackson, *qv*; one *s* decd. *Educ:* School of St Clare, Penzance; St Hugh's and Nuffield Colleges, Oxford. MA, DPhil. Elizabeth Wordsworth Research Fellow, St Hugh's College, Oxford, 1972. Oxford City Councillor, 1970–73; contested (C) Birmingham, Erdington, 1974. European Parliament: Secretariat of Cons. Group, 1974–84; Chm., Envmt, Consumer Protection and Public Health Cttee, 1999–. Dir, Peugeot Talbot (UK) Ltd, 1987–99. Mem., Nat. Consumer Council, 1982–84. *Publications:* A Students Guide to Europe, 1988; Europe's Environment, 1989; The End of the Throwaway Society, 1998; Playing by the Green Rules, 2000. *Recreations:* walking, painting, tennis, golf. *Address:* Euro-office, 14 Bath Road, Swindon, Wilts SN1 4BA. *T:* (01793) 422663, *Fax:* (01793) 422664.

JACKSON, Christopher Murray; Chairman: Natural Resources International Ltd, since 1997; Wellmeade Ltd, since 1999; *b* 24 May 1935; *s* of Rev. Howard Murray Jackson and Doris Bessie Jackson (*née* Grainger); *m* 1971, Carlie Elizabeth Keeling; one *s* one *d*. *Educ:* Kingswood Sch., Bath; Magdalen Coll., Oxford (Open Exhibnr, BA Hons (Physics) 1959, MA 1964); Goethe Univ., Frankfurt; London Sch. of Economics. National Service, commnd RAF, Pilot, 1954–56. Unilever, 1959–69, Sen. Man., 1967; Save and Prosper Gp, 1969–71; D. MacPherson Gp, 1971–74; Dir, Corporate Development Spillers Ltd, 1974–80; Chairman: CJA Consultants Ltd, 1995–2001; European Broadcasting Network plc, 1997–99. Contested (C): East Ham South, 1970; Northampton North, Feb. 1974. MEP (C) Kent E, 1979–94; contested (C) Kent E, EP elecns, 1994; Hon. MEP, 1994–; European Parliament: spokesman, on develt and co-op., 1981–87, on foreign affairs, 1991–92, on econ. affairs, 1992–94; Cons. spokesman on agric., 1987–89; Chm., Intergroup on Frontier Controls, 1987–94; Co-Pres., Working Gp on Population and Develt, 1990–94; Mem., Bureau of EDG, 1984–91; Dep. Ldr, Cons. Members, 1989–91; Rapporteur-General, ACP-EEC Jt Assembly, 1985–86. Chm., Countryside (formerly Nat. Agricl Countryside) Forum, 1995–98. Mem., Cons. Nat. Union Exec. Cttee, 1995–98. Dir, Politics International Ltd, 1995–98. Vice President: Assoc. of Dist Councils, 1980–95; Assoc. of Local Councils, 1984–95; Assoc. of Port Health Authorities, 1989–99. Treas., St Martin-in-the-Fields, 1975–77. Pres., Kent Hotels and Restaurants Assoc., 1988–94. Chm. Bd of Govs, Bethany Sch, Goudhurst, 1999–. *Publications:* Towards 2000—people centred development, 1986 (major report); (ed) Your European Watchdogs, 1990; Shaking the Foundations: Britain and the New Europe, 1991; The Maastricht Summit, 1992; Whose Job is it Anyway?—decentralisation (or subsidiarity) and the EC, 1992; Working for the European Community, 1990, 2nd edn 1992; EDG Briefs on cars, Third World, and world hunger; pamphlets on Britain and Europe. *Recreations:* music, gardening, ski-ing, sailing. *Address:* (office) 8 Wellmeade Drive, Sevenoaks, Kent TN13 1QA. *T:* (01732) 741117, *Fax:* (01732) 743061; *e-mail:* cj@cjac.co.uk.

JACKSON, Daphne Diana; Assistant Personnel Officer, City Engineer's Department, City of Birmingham, 1986–93; *b* 8 Oct. 1933; *d* of Major Thomas Casey, MC, South Lancs Regt, and Agnes Nora Casey (*née* Gradden); *m* 1953, John Hudleston Jackson. *Educ:* Folkestone County Grammar School for Girls; South West London College. ACIS. Westminster Bank, 1951–53; Kent Educn Cttee, 1953–57; Pfizer Ltd, Sandwich, 1957–67; Southern Transformer Products, 1967–68; Borough of Hounslow, 1968–86, Personnel and Central Services Officer, Borough Engr and Surveyor's Dept, 1978–86. Mem., NACRO Employment Adv. Cttee, 1984–86; Chm., Gen. Adv. Council to IBA, 1985–89 (Mem., 1980). Mem., Soroptimists International (Pres., Stratford-upon-Avon, 1995–96). Mem., Cleeve Prior PCC, 1991–; Gov., Cleeve Prior C of E Controlled First Sch., 1989–; Chm. Mgt Cttee, Cleeve Prior Meml Village Hall, 1994–97. Freeman, City of London, 1980; Liveryman, Chartered Secretaries and Administrators Co., 1980. *Recreations:* bereavement counselling, learning about antiques, reading. *Address:* 3 Manor Court, Cleeve Prior, Evesham, Worcs WR11 5LQ. *T:* (01789) 772817.

JACKSON, Prof. David Cooper; Chairman, Immigration Appeal Tribunal, since 1996 (Vice-President, 1984–96); Professor of Law (part time), 1984–98, now Emeritus, and Director, Institute of Maritime Law, 1987–90, University of Southampton; *b* 3 Dec. 1931; *s* of late Rev. James Jackson and Mary Emma Jackson; *m* Roma Lilian (*née* Pendergast). *Educ:* Ashville Coll., Harrogate; Brasenose Coll., Oxford. MA, BCL; Senior Hulme Scholar, 1954; LLD Southampton, 1997. Called to the Bar, Inner Temple, 1957, and Victoria, Australia, 1967. Bigelow Fellow, Univ. of Chicago, 1955; Fellow, Assoc. of Bar of City of New York, 1956; National Service, 1957–59; Senior Lectr, Univ. of Singapore, 1963–64; Sir John Latham Prof. of Law, Monash Univ., 1965–70 (Carnegie Travelling Fellow, 1969); Prof. of Law, Southampton Univ., 1970–83 (Dean of Law, 1972–75, 1978–81; Dep. Vice-Chancellor, 1982–83); Consultant, UNCTAD, 1980, 1983. Visiting Professor: Queen Mary Coll., London, 1969; Arizona State Univ., 1976; Melbourne Univ., 1976. JP Hants 1980–84. Editor, World Shipping Laws, 1979– (and contrib.). *Publications:* Principles of Property Law, 1967; The Conflicts Process, 1975; Enforcement of Maritime Claims, 1985, 3rd edn 2000; Civil Jurisdiction and Judgments: maritime claims, 1987; Immigration Law and Practice, 1996, 2nd edn 1999; articles in legal jls, Australia, UK, USA. *Recreations:* walking, travel, theatre.

JACKSON, Dirik George Allan; His Honour Judge Dirik Jackson; a Circuit Judge, since 2000; *b* 10 June 1946; *s* of Allan Jackson and Catharina Maria Anna Jackson (*née* de Boer); *m* 1984, Nicola Bryant; two *s* one *d*. *Educ:* Tonbridge Sch.; Trinity Coll., Cambridge (BA, LLB). Called to the Bar, Lincoln's Inn, 1969; in practice, 1970–2000; Asst Recorder, 1987–92; Recorder, 1992–2000. *Recreations:* music, exploring the Internet, squash, roller-blading, windsurfing in warm waters. *Address:* Woolwich Crown Court, 2 Belmarsh Road, SE28 0EY.

JACKSON, Donald, MVO 1985; artist calligrapher; Scribe to Crown Office, since 1964; *b* 14 Jan. 1938; *s* of Wilfred Jackson and Helena Ruth Jackson (*née* Tolley); *m* 1962, Mabel Elizabeth Morgan; one *s* one *d*. *Educ:* Bolton Sch. of Art; City & Guilds, London; Central Sch. of Art; Goldsmiths' Coll. FSSI 1960 (Chm., 1973). Preparer of Letters Patent and Royal Charters under Great Seal, incl. 1974 redesignated Royal Cities, towns and boroughs in England and Wales; Dir, Calligraphy Centre, 1984; Artistic Dir, The St John's Bible (handwritten and illuminated Bible in seven vols to mark Millennium, for St John's Univ. and Benedictine Abbey, Minn), 1997–. Vis. Prof. of Art, California State Univ., 1976–77; lectr in USA and Australia. 30-year personal retrospective exhibn, Painting with Words, in USA, Puerto Rico, Hong Kong, Europe, 1988–91; work in public and private collections. Founding Trustee, Irene Wellington Educnl Trust, 1987. Presenter, and producer with Jeremy Bennet, Alphabet (film series), 1979. Liveryman, Scriveners' Co., 1973 (Master, 1997–98). *Publications:* The Story of Writing, 1980, 3rd edn 1994; (jtly) The Calligraphers' Handbook, 1985; (jtly) More than Fine Writing, 1986. *Recreations:* people watching, travel, graphic arts, architecture, country sports. *Address:* The Hendre Hall, The Hendre, Monmouth NP25 5HB. *T:* (01600) 716565.

JACKSON, Sir Edward; *see* Jackson, Sir J. E.

JACKSON, Francis Alan, OBE 1978; Organist and Master of the Music, York Minster, 1946–82, Organist Emeritus, since 1988; *b* 2 Oct. 1917; *s* of W. A. Jackson; *m* 1950, Priscilla, *d* of Tyndale Procter; two *s* one *d*. *Educ:* York Minster Choir Sch.; Sir Edward Bairstow. Chorister, York Minster, 1929–33; ARCO, 1936; BMus Dunelm 1937; FRCO (Limpus Prize), 1937; DMus Dunelm 1957. Organist Malton Parish Church, 1933–40. Served War of 1939–45, with 9th Lancers in Egypt, N Africa and Italy, 1940–46. Asst Organist, York Minster, 1946; Conductor York Musical Soc., 1947–82; Conductor York Symphony Orchestra, 1947–80. Pres. Incorp. Assoc. of Organists, 1960–62; Pres., RCO, 1972–74. Hon. FRSCM 1963; Hon. Fellow, Westminster Choir Coll., Princeton, NJ, 1970; Hon. FRNCM, 1982. DUniv York, 1983. Order of St William of York, 1983. *Publications:* organ music, including 4 sonatas, symphony, organ concerto, church music, songs, monodramas. *Recreation:* gardening. *Address:* Nether Garth, East Acklam, Malton, N Yorks YO17 9RG. *T:* (01653) 658395.

JACKSON, Prof. Frank Cameron; Professor of Philosophy, 1986–90 and since 1992, Deputy Vice-Chancellor (Research), since 2001, Australian National University; *b* 31 Aug. 1943; *s* of Allan Cameron Jackson and Ann Elizabeth Jackson; *m* 1966, Morag Elizabeth Fraser; two *d*. *Educ:* Melbourne Univ. (BA, BSc, 1966); LaTrobe Univ. (PhD 1975). Temp. Lectr, Adelaide Univ., 1967; Lectr, Sen. Lectr, then Reader, LaTrobe Univ., 1968–77; Prof., Monash Univ., 1978–86 and 1991; Dir, Inst. of Advanced Studies, ANU, 1998–2001. Corresp. FBA 2000. *Publications:* Perception, 1977; Conditionals, 1987; (with D. Braddon-Mitchell) Philosophy of Mind and Cognition, 1996; From Metaphysics to Ethics, 1998; Mind, Method, and Conditionals, 1998. *Recreations:* reading, tennis. *Address:* Philosophy Program, Research School of Social Sciences, Australian National University, ACT 0200, Australia. *Club:* Reid Tennis (Canberra).

JACKSON, Glenda May, CBE 1978; MP (Lab) Hampstead and Highgate, since 1992; *b* Birkenhead, 9 May 1936; *d* of Harry and Joan Jackson; *m* 1958, Roy Hodges (marr. diss. 1976); one *s*. *Educ:* West Kirby Co. Grammar Sch. for Girls; RADA. Actress, 1957–92; with various repertory cos, 1957–63, stage manager, Crewe Rep.; joined Royal Shakespeare Co., 1963. Dir, United British Artists, 1983. Parly Under-Sec. of State, DETR, 1997–99. Pres., Play Matters (formerly Toy Libraries Assoc.), 1976–. *Plays:* All Kinds of Men, Arts, 1957; The Idiot, Lyric, 1962; Alfie, Mermaid and Duchess, 1963; Royal Shakespeare Co.: Theatre of Cruelty Season, LAMDA, 1964; The Jew of Malta, 1964; Marat/Sade, 1965, NY and Paris, 1965; Love's Labour's Lost, Squire Puntila and his Servant Matti, The Investigation, Hamlet, 1965; US, Aldwych, 1966; Three Sisters, Royal Ct, 1967; Fanghorn, Fortune, 1967; Collaborators, Duchess, 1973; The Maids, Greenwich, 1974; Hedda Gabler, Australia, USA, London, 1975; The White Devil, Old Vic, 1976; Stevie, Vaudeville, 1977; Antony and Cleopatra, Stratford, 1978; Rose, Duke of York's, 1980; Summit Conference, Lyric, 1982; Great and Small, Vaudeville, 1983; Strange Interlude, Duke of York's, 1984; Phedra, Old Vic, 1984, Aldwych, 1985; Across from the Garden of Allah, Comedy, 1986; The House of Bernarda Alba, Globe, 1986; Macbeth, NY, 1988; Scenes from an Execution, Almeida, 1990; Mother Courage, Mermaid, 1990; *films:* This Sporting Life, 1963; Marat/Sade, 1967; Negatives, 1968; Women in Love (Oscar Award, 1971), 1970; The Music Lovers, 1971; Sunday, Bloody Sunday, 1971; The Boyfriend, 1972; Mary, Queen of Scots, 1972; Triple Echo, 1972; Il Sorviso de Grande Tentatore (The Tempter), 1973; Bequest to the Nation, 1973; A Touch of Class (Oscar Award, 1974), 1973; The Maids, 1974; The Romantic Englishwoman, 1974; Hedda Gabler, 1975; The Incredible Sarah, 1976; House Calls, 1978; Stevie, 1978; The Class of Miss MacMichael, 1978; Lost and Found, 1979; Hopscotch, 1980; Return of the Soldier, 1982; Health, 1982; Giro City, 1982; Sacharov, 1983; Turtle Diary, 1985; Business as Usual, 1987; Beyond Therapy, 1987; Salome's Last Dance, 1988; The Rainbow, 1989; The Secret Life of Sir Arnold Bax, 1992; *TV:* Elizabeth in Elizabeth R, 1971; The Patricia Neal Story (Amer.). Best film actress awards: Variety Club of GB, 1971, 1975, 1978; NY Film Critics, 1971; Nat. Soc. of Film Critics, US, 1971. *Recreations:* cooking, gardening, reading Jane Austen. *Address:* c/o House of Commons, SW1A 0AA.

JACKSON, Gordon; *see* Jackson, W. G.

JACKSON, Helen Margaret; MP (Lab) Sheffield, Hillsborough, since 1992; *b* 19 May 1939; *d* of Stanley Price and Katherine (*née* Thornton); *m* 1960, Keith Jackson (marr. diss. 1998); two *s* one *d*. *Educ:* St Hilda's Coll., Oxford (BA Hons Mod. Hist., MA); C. F. Mott Coll. of Educn, Prescot (Cert Ed 1972). Asst Librarian, 1961; mother, housewife and voluntary worker, 1961–72; teacher, 1972–80; City Cllr, Sheffield, 1980–91 (Chm., Public Works and Econ. Develt Cttees). Founder Mem. and Chair, Centre for Local Economic Strategies, 1986–91. PPS to Sec. of State for NI, 1997–2001. Member: Envmt Select Cttee, 1992–97; Modernisation of H of C Select Cttee, 1997–2001; Transport, Local Govt and the Regions Select Cttee, 2001–; Chair: All-Party Parly Water Gp, 1993–97; Parly Envmt Gp, 1997–; All-Party Parly Gp on S Africa, 1997–; Co-Chair, PLP Women's Gp, 1992–97; Sec., PLP Gp on Envmtl Protection, 1995–97; Vice-Chair, PLP, 2001– (Mem., Parly Cttee, Labour Party); Mem., NEC, Labour Pty, 1999–. UK Parly Rep., Assoc. of Eur. Parliamentarians for Africa, 1997–. *Recreations:* walking, music. *Address:* House of Commons, SW1A 0AA.

See also Christopher Price.

JACKSON, Ian (Macgilchrist), BA Cantab, MB, BChir, FRCS, FRCOG; Obstetric and Gynæcological Surgeon, Middlesex Hospital, 1948–79, retired; Gynæcological Surgeon: Chelsea Hospital for Women, 1948–79; King Edward VII Hospital for Officers, 1961–84; Royal Masonic Hospital, 1963–79; Consulting Gynæcologist, King Edward VII Hospital, Midhurst, 1959; Consultant Obstetrician and Gynæcologist, RAF, 1964–83; *b* Shanghai, 11 Nov. 1914; *s* of Dr Ernest David Jackson; *m* 1943 (marr. diss. 1967); two *s* one *d*; *m* 1970, Deirdre Ruth Heitz. *Educ:* Marlborough Coll.; Trinity Hall, Cambridge (scholar; double 1st cl. hons, Nat. Sci. tripos pts I, II). London Hospital: open scholarship, 1936; house appointments, 1939; First Asst, Surgical and Obstetric and Gynæcol Depts, 1940–43. Served as Surgical Specialist, RAMC, 1943–47 (Major); Parachute Surgical Team, 224 Para. Field Amb.; Mobile Surgical Unit, 3 Commando Brigade. Royal College of Obstetricians and Gynæcologists: Council, 1951–61, 1962–70; Hon. Sec., 1954–61; Chm., Examination Cttee, 1962–65, Hon. Treas., 1966–70; Hon. Librarian, RSM, 1969–75. Examiner for Univs of Cambridge, Oxford, and London, Conjoint Bd and RCOG. Mem., Court of Assts, Worshipful Soc. of Apothecaries, 1966, Senior Warden 1977, Master 1978, Hon. Treas., 1985–89; President: Chelsea Clinical Soc., 1979; Sydenham Medical Club, 1987–90. Order of the Star of Africa (Liberia), 1969; Grand Officer of Order of Istiqlal, Jordan, 1970. *Publications:* British Obstetric and Gynæcological Practice (jtly), 1963; Obstetrics by Ten Teachers (jtly), 1966, 2nd edn 1972; Gynæcology by Ten Teachers (jtly), 1971; numerous contribs to medical literature. *Recreations:* fishing, golf, photography. *Address:* 23 Springfield Road, NW8 0QJ. *T:* (020) 7624 3580.

JACKSON, Jane Therese, (Tessa); Director, Scottish Arts Council, since 1999; *b* 5 Nov. 1955; *d* of John Nevill Jackson and Viva Christian Therese Jackson (*née* Blomfield). *Educ:* Univ. of East Anglia (BA Hons Fine Art); Univ. of Manchester (Dip. Museum Studies); Univ. of Bristol (MA Film and TV Prodn), 1998. Art Editor, OUP, 1979–80; Exhibns

Organiser, SPAB, 1981–82; Curator, Eyemouth Museum, 1982; Curator, Collins Gallery, Univ. of Strathclyde, 1982–88; Visual Arts Officer, Glasgow 1990—European City of Culture, 1988–91; Dir, Arnolfini, Bristol, 1991–99. *Publications:* (with John R. Hume) George Washington Wilson and Victorian Glasgow, 1983; (jtly) Signs of the Times: art and industry in Scotland 1750–1985, 1985; (ed jtly) A Platform for Partnership (Glasgow City Council), 1991. *Recreations:* travel, walking, architecture. *Address:* Scottish Arts Council, 12 Manor Place, Edinburgh EH3 7DD. *T:* (0131) 226 6051.

JACKSON, John Bernard Haysom; Chairman: Celltech Group, since 1982; Wyndeham Press Group plc, since 1990; Xenova Group plc, since 1990; Hilton Group, since 1994 (Vice Chairman, 1991–94; Director, since 1980); Oxford Technology Venture Capital Trust plc, since 1997; *b* 26 May 1929; *m* 1st, 1955, Ann Nichols (marr. diss. 1984); one *s* two *d*; 2nd, 1984, Rowena Thomas. *Educ:* King's School, Canterbury; Queens' Coll., Cambridge (BA, LLB). Called to the Bar, Inner Temple. Philips Electronics, 1952–80 (Dir, 1966–94); Non-solicitor Chm., Mishcon de Reya, 1992–; Dep. Chm., BHP Ltd and Billiton plc, which merged 2001 to form BHP Billiton plc (Dir, 1997–); Director: WPP Group plc, 1993–; Brown & Jackson plc, 1994–. Chm., Countryside Alliance, 1999–; Trustee, One World Action, 1998–. Chm. and co-owner, History Today magazine, 1981–. *Publications:* A Bucket of Nuts and a Herring Net, 1979, 2nd edn as A Little Piece of England: a small holding from scratch, 2000; (contrib.) Even Paranoids have Enemies, 1998. *Recreations:* growing rare plants, breeding butterflies, fishing, painting, writing.

JACKSON, Sir (John) Edward, KCMG 1984 (CMG 1977); HM Diplomatic Service, retired; *b* 24 June 1925; *s* of late Edward and Margaret Jackson; *m* 1952, Eve Stainton Harris, *d* of late George James Harris, MC and Mrs Friede Rowntree Harris, York; two *s* one *d*. *Educ:* Ardingly; Corpus Christi Coll., Cambridge. RNVR (Sub-Lt), 1943–46; joined Foreign (now Diplomatic) Service, 1947; FO, 1947–49; 3rd Sec., Paris, 1949–52; 2nd Sec., FO, 1952–56; 1st Sec., Bonn, 1956–59; Guatemala City, 1959–62; FO, 1963–68; Counsellor, 1968; NATO Defence Coll., Rome, 1969; Counsellor (Political Adviser), British Mil. Govt, Berlin, 1969–73; Head of Defence Dept, FCO, 1973–75; Ambassador to Cuba, 1975–79; Head of UK Delegn to Negotiations on Mutual Reduction of Forces and Armaments and Associated Measures in Central Europe, with personal rank of Ambassador, 1980–82; Ambassador to Belgium, 1982–85. Chm., Brecon Beacons Natural Waters Ltd, later Spadel Ltd, 1985–96 (Vice-Chm., Consultancy Bd, 1997–2000); Director: Herbert Mueller Ltd and associated cos, 1987–90. Dir, Armistice Festival, 1986–89. Chm., Anglo-Belgian Soc., 1987–2001; Dep. Chm., Belgo-Luxembourg Chamber of Commerce, 1987–. Trustee, Imperial War Museum, 1986–95. Vice-Pres., Internat. Yehudi Menuhin Foundn (formerly Internat. Menuhin Assoc.), 1991–99. *Recreations:* the arts. *Address:* 17 Paultons Square, SW3 5AP. *Clubs:* Royal Anglo-Belgian (Dir, 1993–), Hurlingham.

JACKSON, John Henry; Clerk to the Governors, Dulwich College and Alleyn's School, since 1998; Company Secretary, BG plc (formerly British Gas), 1990–97; *b* 7 Aug. 1948; *s* of late John and of May Jackson; *m* 1975, Patricia Mary Robinson; one *s* one *d*. *Educ:* Trinity School, Croydon; St Catherine's College, Oxford (MA). FCIS. Joined SE Gas Board, 1970; Asst Sec., 1977, Sen. Asst Sec., 1983, British Gas Corp., later British Gas plc. Mem. UK and Internat. Councils, ICSA, 1996– (a Chief Examr, 1997–2000). Non-exec. Dir, Queen Victoria Hosp. NHS Trust, E Grinstead, 1996–98. *Address:* Governors' Office, 87 College Road, SE21 7HH. *T:* (020) 8299 6400.

JACKSON, (John) Patrick; Homesearch consultant, since 2000; *b* 18 Sept. 1940; *s* of Godfrey Jackson and Mary Jackson (*née* Worthington); *m* 1st, 1963, Marieliese de Vos van Steenwyk (marr. diss.); three *d* (and one *d* decd); 2nd, 1978, Hélène Mellotte; two *d*. *Educ:* Worksop Coll.; Midhurst Grammar Sch.; New Coll., Oxford (MA); Moscow Univ. (postgrad. studies); London Univ. Inst. of Educn (postgrad. Cert Ed). British Council, 1963–96: English Language Teaching Inst., London, 1964–66; Asst Dir, Bahrain, 1966–69; Asst Cultural Attaché, Moscow, 1969–71; Dep. Dir, Higher Educn Dept, 1971–73; Regl Dir, Calcutta, 1973–75; Dir, N Europe Dept, 1975–79; Rep., Senegal, 1979–83; Regl Dir, São Paulo, 1983–88; Dep. Controller, Home Div., 1988–91; Dir, Exchanges and Training Div., 1991–93; Dir, Portugal, 1993–96; early retirement, 1996; kidney transplant, 1997; Baggage Agent, Gatwick Handling Ltd, 1997–2000. *Recreations:* birdwatching, proofreading, languages, bridge. *Address:* Two Houses, Hollow Lane, Dormansland, Surrey RH19 3PS.

JACKSON, Judith Mary; QC 1994; *b* 18 Sept. 1950; *d* of Thomas Worthington Jackson and Betty Jackson (*née* Kinsey); one *d*. *Educ:* Queen Mary College, London. LLB, LLM. Called to the Bar, Inner Temple, 1975; Bencher, Lincoln's Inn, 2001. Dir, Bar Mutual Insce Fund Ltd, 1999–. Chm., Young Barristers' Cttee, 1984–85. *Recreations:* music, cycling, dog-walking. *Address:* 9 Old Square, Lincoln's Inn, WC2A 3SR. *T:* (020) 7405 4682.

JACKSON, (Kevin) Paul; Managing Director, Granada Media Australia, and Chief Executive, Red Heart Productions, since 2000; *b* 2 Oct. 1947; *s* of late T. Leslie Jackson and of Jo (*née* Spooney); *m* 1981, Judith Elizabeth Cain; two *d*. *Educ:* Gunnersbury Grammar Sch.; Univ. of Exeter (BA 1970); Stanford Univ. (Exec. Program 1993). Stage manager: Marlowe Theatre, Canterbury, 1970; Thorndike Theatre, Leatherhead, 1971. BBC Television: Production Assistant, 1971–79; Producer, 1979–82: programmes include: The Two Ronnies, Three of a Kind (BAFTA Award 1982), Carrot's Lib, The Young Ones (BAFTA Award 1984), Happy Families; freelance producer and director, 1982–84: programmes include: Cannon & Ball, Girls On Top; Producer and Chm., Paul Jackson Prodns Ltd, 1984–86: programmes include: Red Dwarf, Don't Miss Wax, Saturday Live; Man. Dir, Noel Gay TV, 1987–91: progs include The Appointments of Dennis Jennings (Oscar for Best Live Action Short, 1989); Dir of Progs, 1991, Man. Dir, 1993–94, Carlton TV; Man. Dir, Carlton UK Productions, 1994–96; Head, then Controller, BBC Entertainment, 1997–2000. Chairman: RTS, 1994–96; Comic Relief, 1987–98; Charity Projects, 1992–98; Trustee: Pilotlight, 1996– (Chm., 1996–2000); Pilotlight Australia, 2000–. Academic Visitor, Exeter Univ., 1996. FInstD 1992; FRTS 1993. Hon. Fellow, Exeter Univ., 1999. *Recreations:* my family, theatre, Rugby, travel, food and wine. *Address:* c/o Capel and Land Ltd, 29 Wardour Street, W1D 6PS. *Club:* Groucho.

JACKSON, Very Rev. Lawrence, AKC; Provost of Blackburn, 1973–92, Provost Emeritus 1992; *b* Hessle, Yorks, 22 March 1926; *s* of Walter and Edith Jackson; *m* 1955, Faith Anne, *d* of Philip and Marjorie Seymour; four *d*. *Educ:* Alderman Newton's Sch.; Leicester Coll. of Technology; King's Coll., Univ. of London (AKC 1950); St Boniface Coll., Warminster. Asst Curate, St Margaret, Leicester, and Asst Chaplain, Leicester Royal Infirmary, 1951–54; Vicar of: Wymeswold, Leicester, 1954–59; St James the Greater, Leicester, 1959–65; Coventry (Holy Trinity), 1965–73. Canon of Coventry Cath., 1967–73; Rural Dean of Coventry N, 1969–73. Senior Chaplain: Leicester and Rutland ACF, 1955–65; Warwickshire ACF, 1965–73; Chaplain, Coventry Guild of Freemen, 1968–73; Dio. Chaplain, CEMS, 1969–71. Mem., Gen. Synod of C of E, 1975–92; a Church Comr, 1981–92. Dir, The Samaritans of Leicester, 1960–65; Pres., Coventry Round Table, 1968; Governor, Queen Elizabeth Grammar Sch., Blackburn, 1973–92. Pres., Midlands Club Cricket Conf., 1995. Freeman, City of London, 1982; Liveryman, Fruiterers' Co., 1982. *Publication:* Services for Special Occasions, 1982. *Recreations:* music, archæology, architecture, countryside, after dinner speaking. *Address:* Northcot, Brook Lane, Newbold-on-Stour, Stratford-upon-Avon, Warwicks CV37 8UA. *T:* (01789) 450721. *Clubs:* Forty, Lighthouse; Lord's Taverners'.

JACKSON, Michael; Chairman, Results Plus Ltd, since 1998; *b* 12 March 1948; *s* of Stanley Jackson and Maisie Joan Jackson. *Educ:* Salford Univ. (BSc Electronics). Hawker Siddeley, 1970–73; Vice Pres., Citibank NA, 1973–86; Sen. Vice Pres., Bank of America, 1986–90; Chief Exec., Birmingham Midshires Bldg Soc., 1990–98. Non-exec. Dir, Gallifords plc, 1997–. Hon. DBA Wolverhampton, 1997. *Recreations:* genealogy, music, sport. *Address:* Results Plus Ltd, Ivy Cottage, Strawmoor Lane, Oaken, Wolverhampton WV8 2HY.

JACKSON, Gen. Sir Michael David, (Sir Mike), KCB 1998 (CB 1996); CBE 1992 (MBE 1979); DSO 1999; Commander-in-Chief, Land Command, since 2000; Aide-de-Camp General to the Queen, since 2001; *b* 21 March 1944; *s* of George Jackson and Ivy (*née* Bower); *m* 1985, Sarah Coombe; two *s* one *d*. *Educ:* Stamford Sch.; RMA Sandhurst; Birmingham Univ. (BSocSc 1967). Commnd Intelligence Corps, 1963; transf. to Parachute Regt, 1970; Staff Coll., 1976; Bde Major, Berlin, 1977–78; ndc 1981; Directing Staff, Staff Coll., 1981–83; Comd 1st Bn Parachute Regt, 1984–86; Sen. DS, Jt Service Defence Coll., 1986–88; Services Fellow, Wolfson Coll., Cambridge, 1989; Comdr, 39 Inf. Bde, 1990–92; Dir Gen. Personal Services (Army), MoD, 1992–94; GOC 3 (UK) Div., 1994–95; Comdr, Implementation Force Multinat. Div. SW, Bosnia Herzegovina, 1995–96; Dir Gen., Develt and Doctrine, MoD, 1996–97; Comdr, ACE Rapid Reaction Corps, 1997–2000; Comdr, Kosovo Force, March–Oct. 1999. Col Comdt, Parachute Regt, 1998–; Hon. Col, Rifle Vols, TA, 1999–. Freeman, City of London, 1988. *Recreations:* travel, music, ski-ing, tennis. *Address:* RHQ The Parachute Regiment, Browning Barracks, Aldershot, Hants GU11 2BU. *Club:* St Moritz Tobogganing.

JACKSON, Michael Richard; President and Chief Executive, USA Entertainment, since 2001; *b* 11 Feb. 1958; *s* of Ernest Jackson and Margaret (*née* Kearsley). *Educ:* King's Sch., Macclesfield; Poly. of Central London (BA (Hons) Media Studies). Organiser, Channel Four Gp, 1979; Producer, The Sixties, 1982; Independent Producer, Beat Productions Ltd, 1983–87, produced Whose Town is it Anyway?, Open the Box, The Media Show; joined BBC Television; Editor: The Late Show (BFI Television Award), 1988–90; Late Show Productions, 1990–91, progs incl. The Nelson Mandela Tribute, Tales from Prague (Grierson Documentary Award), Moving Pictures, The American Late Show (PBS), Naked Hollywood (BAFTA Award, Best Factual Series); Head of Music and Arts, BBC Television, 1991–93; progs produced, 1991–, incl. Sounds of the Sixties, The Lime Grove Story, TV Hell; Controller, BBC 2, 1993–96; Controller, BBC 1 and BBC Dir of Television, 1996–97; Dir of Progs, 1997–98, Chief Exec., 1997–2001, C4; Chm., Film Four Ltd, 1997–2001. Non-exec. Dir, EMI Gp, 1999–; Chm., Photographers' Gall., 2001–. FRTS 1997. Hon. DLitt Westminster, 1995. *Recreations:* reading, films, collecting photography, walking. *Address:* USA Networks, 42nd Floor, 152 West 57th Street, New York, NY 10019, USA.

JACKSON, Air Vice-Marshal Michael Richard, CB 1998; Executive Director, Oracle Corporation, since 1998; Director General, Ministry of Defence, 1996–98; *b* 28 Dec. 1941; *s* of Felix Ralph Jackson and Margaret Jackson (*née* Marshall); *m* 1967, Kay Johnson; two *s*. *Educ:* Cardinal Vaughan Sch.; RAF Coll., Cranwell. Joined RAF, 1965: sqdn flying duties, 1965–69; navigation instructor, 1969–70; Exchange Officer, USA, 1971–74; RAF Staff Coll., 1974; Sqdn Comdr, 1975–77; Mem., Directing Staff, Army Staff Coll., Camberley, 1977–80; Ops Wing Comdr, 1981–84; Defence and Air Attaché, Warsaw, 1985–87; Unit Comdr, 1987–89; Defence Fellow, Rand Corp. and Cambridge Univ., 1989–90; Dir, MoD Central Staffs, 1991–95. *Recreations:* music, walking, gardening. *Address:* c/o RAF Record Office, MoD Innsworth, Gloucester GL3 1EZ. *Club:* Royal Air Force.

JACKSON, (Michael) Rodney; a Recorder, 1985–2001; Consultant, Andrew M. Jackson & Co., Solicitors, 1994–2001 (Partner, 1964–94; Senior Partner, 1992–94); *b* 16 April 1935; *s* of John William Jackson and Nora Jackson (*née* Phipps); *m* 1968, Anne Margaret, *d* of Prof. E. W. Hawkins, *qv*; two *s*. *Educ:* Queen Elizabeth Grammar Sch., Wakefield; Queens' Coll., Cambridge (MA, LLM). Admitted Solicitor of the Supreme Court, 1962; Notary Public, 1967; Solicitor Advocate, 1996. *Recreations:* fell walking, railway photography. *Address:* 11 The Paddock, Swanland, North Ferriby, E Yorks HU14 3QW. *T:* (01482) 633278.

JACKSON, Sir Michael (Roland), 5th Bt *cr* 1902; MA; CEng, MIEE; FIQA; *b* 20 April 1919; *s* of Sir W. D. Russell Jackson, 4th Bt, and Kathleen (*d* 1975), *d* of Summers Hunter, CBE, Tynemouth; *S* father 1956; *m* 1st, 1942, Hilda Margaret (marr. diss. 1969), *d* of late Cecil George Herbert Richardson, CBE, Newark; one *s* one *d*; 2nd, 1969, Hazel Mary, *d* of late Ernest Harold Edwards. *Educ:* Stowe; Clare Coll., Cambridge. Served War of 1939–45; Flight-Lt, Royal Air Force Volunteer Reserve. *Heir: s* Thomas St Felix Jackson [*b* 27 Sept. 1946; *m* 1980, Victoria, *d* of George Scatliff, Wineham, Sussex; two *d*].

JACKSON, Michael Walter; Under Secretary and Head of Marine Directorate, Department of Transport, 1993–94, retired; *b* 5 April 1934; *s* of late William Henry Jackson and Nellie Jackson; *m* 1963, Mary Bruce Hope Sinclair; one *s* one *d*. *Educ:* Queen Elizabeth Grammar Sch., Wakefield; Queen's Coll., Oxford (MA Lit. Hum.). UKAEA, 1959–68; joined MoT, 1968; Assistant Secretary: MoT, 1973–76; PSA, 1976–80; Dept of Transport, 1980–93. *Recreations:* hill-walking, opera. *Address:* Tranby Croft, Greystoke Gill, Penrith, Cumbria CA11 0UQ. *T:* (01768) 483848.

JACKSON, Mrs Muriel W.; *see* Ward-Jackson.

JACKSON, Sir Neil Keith, 9th Bt *cr* 1815, of Arlsey, Bedfordshire; *b* 12 May 1952; *s* of Sir Keith Arnold Jackson, 8th Bt and of Pauline Mona (*née* Climo); *S* father, 2000; *m* 1973, Sandra Whitehead; two *s*. *Heir: s* Stephen Keith Jackson, *b* 27 Sept. 1973.

JACKSON, Sir Nicholas (Fane St George), 3rd Bt *cr* 1913; organist, harpsichordist and composer; Director, Concertante of London, since 1987; *b* 4 Sept. 1934; *s* of Sir Hugh Jackson, 2nd Bt, and Violet Marguerite Loftus (*d* 2001), *y d* of Loftus St George; *S* father, 1979; *m* 1972, Nadia Françoise Genevieve (*née* Michard); one *s*. *Educ:* Radley Coll.; Wadham Coll., Oxford; Royal Acad. of Music. LRAM; ARCM. Organist: St Anne's, Soho, 1963–68; St James's, Piccadilly, 1971–74; St Lawrence, Jewry, 1974–77; Organist and Master of the Choristers, St David's Cathedral, 1977–84. Musical Dir, St David's Cathedral Bach Fest., 1979; Dir, Bach Festival, Santes Creus, Spain, 1987–89. Organ recitals and broadcasts: Berlin, 1967; Paris, 1972, 1975; USA (tour), 1975, 1978, 1980 and 1989; Minorca, 1977; Spain, 1979; Madrid Bach Festival, 1980; RFH, 1984; concert tours of Spain and Germany, annually 1980–. Début as harpsichordist, Wigmore Hall, 1963; directed Soho Concertante, Queen Elizabeth Hall, 1964–72. Mem. Music Cttee, Welsh Arts Council, 1981–84. Examiner, Trinity Coll. of Music, 1985–99. Recordings: Mass for a Saint's Day, 1971; organ and harpsichord music, incl. works by Arnell, Bach, Couperin, Langlais, Mozart, Vierne and Walther; Spanish organ music; own organ music, recorded at Chartres Cath., 2000. Hon. Patron, Hertford Coll. Music Soc., 1996–. Master, Drapers' Co., 1994–95; Liveryman, Musicians' Co., 1985. Hon. Fellow, Hertford Coll., Oxford, 1995. *Publications: compositions:* Mass for a Saint's Day, 1966; 20th Century Merbecke, 1967; 4 Images (for organ), 1971; Solemn Mass, 1977; Divertissement (organ), 1983; Organ Mass, 1984; 2 Organ Sonatas, 1985; Suite, for brass quintet and organ, 1986; The Reluctant Highwayman (opera), 1992 (world première, 1995); (completed) Bach's Fugue, BWV 906, 1996. *Recreations:* sketching, writing. *Heir:* *s* Thomas Graham St George Jackson, *b* 5 Oct. 1980.

JACKSON, Oliver James V.; *see* Vaughan-Jackson.

JACKSON, Patrick; *see* Jackson, J. P.

JACKSON, Patrick; *see* Jackson, W. P.

JACKSON, Paul; *see* Jackson, K. P.

JACKSON, Peter Arthur Brian; QC 2000; a Recorder, since 2000; *b* 9 Dec. 1955; *s* of late Guy Jackson and of Amanda Jackson (now Park); *m* 1983, Deborah Sanderson; two *d*. *Educ:* Marlborough Coll.; Brasenose Coll., Oxford (BA Hons). Called to the Bar, Inner Temple, 1978; barrister specialising in family law, 1978–. Gov., Camden Sch. for Girls, 2000–. *Recreations:* music, narrow boating, copying old masters. *Address:* 4 Paper Buildings, Temple, EC4Y 7EX. *T:* (020) 7583 0816. *Clubs:* Irish, Portmarnock Golf (Dublin).

JACKSON, Peter John; Chief Executive, Associated British Foods plc, since 1999; *b* 16 Jan. 1947; *s* of Jack and Joan Jackson; *m* 1974, Anne Campbell; two *s* one *d*. *Educ:* Leeds Univ. (BA Econs). Industrial Relations Officer, BSC, 1968–71; Res. Officer, Commn on Industrial Relns, 1971–73; Personnel Manager, Guthrie Industries Europe, 1973–76; Perkins Engines: Indust. Relns Manager, 1976–80; Personnel Dir, 1980–83; Man. Dir, Rolls Royce Diesels, 1983–84; Dir and Gen. Manager, Gp Parts and Distribn, 1985–87; joined Associated British Foods, 1987; British Sugar plc: Exec. Dir, 1987–88; Dep. Man. Dir, 1988–89; Chief Exec., 1989–99. *Recreations:* garden, golf, Sheffield United. *Address:* Associated British Foods plc, Weston Centre, Bowater House, 68 Knightsbridge, SW1X 7LQ. *T:* (020) 7589 6363. *Club:* Farmers'.

JACKSON, Peter John Edward; His Honour Judge Jackson; a Circuit Judge, since 1992; *b* 14 May 1944; *s* of late David Charles Jackson and of Sarah Ann (*née* Manester); *m* 1967, Ursula, *y d* of late Paul and Henny Schubert, Hamburg, W Germany; two *d*. *Educ:* Brockley County Grammar Sch.; Sprachen und Dolmetscher Inst., Hamburg; London Univ. (LLB Hons 1967); Tübingen Univ., Germany (Dr jur. 1987). Called to the Bar, Middle Temple, 1968 (Blackstone Scholar; Churchill Prize; Bencher, 1999); called to the Bar of NI, 1982. Dep. Circuit Judge, 1979–81; Asst Recorder, 1982–83; a Recorder, 1983–92; Attorney Gen.'s List of Prosecuting Counsel, 1985–92; Partner, Campbell and Jackson Internat. Arbitral and Legal Consultants, Brussels, Stuttgart, Paris, 1985–90; Overseas Mem., Law Offices of Dr Brauner and Colleagues, Stuttgart, 1982–92. Mem., Arbitration Panel, ICC, 1990–92; Co-opted Mem., Internat. Practice Cttee, Bar Council, 1991–92; Trainer, Middle Temple Advocacy, 1998–. Approved Supervisor, Judicial and Legal Trainees in England, German Ministries of Justice and German Attorneys' Assoc., 1987–. Speaker/Chm., legal seminars in England and overseas, 1987–; speaker, German Judges Acad., Berlin and Trier, 1994–. Chm., St Leonard's Soc., Ilford, 1993–2001. Gov., Newbold Coll., Bracknell, 1991–95. ACIArb 1983. *Recreations:* gardens, German Law, the German language, travel. *Address:* 3 Pump Court, Temple, EC4Y 7AJ. *T:* (020) 7353 0711; 70372 Stuttgart (Bad Cannstatt), Seelbergstrasse 8, Germany. *T:* (0711) 954646-0, *Fax:* (0711) 954646-46.

JACKSON, Peter (Michael); Senior Lecturer, in Industrial Studies, Institute of Extra-mural Studies, National University of Lesotho, 1980; *b* 14 Oct. 1928; *s* of Leonard Patterson Jackson; *m* 1961, Christine Thomas. *Educ:* Durham Univ.; University Coll., Leicester. Lecturer, Dept of Sociology, University of Hull, 1964–66; Fellow, Univ. of Hull, 1970–72; Tutor, Open Univ., 1972–74; Senior Planning Officer, S Yorks CC, 1974–77. MP (Lab) High Peak, 1966–70; contested (Lab) Birmingham North, European Parly elecns, 1979. Member: Peak Park Jt Planning Bd, 1973–77, 1979–82; Derby CC, 1973–77. *Recreations:* numismatics, book collecting, ski-ing. *Address:* 82 Vandon Court, Petty France, SW1H 9HG. *Club:* Maseru (Lesotho).

JACKSON, Richard Michael, CVO 1983; HM Diplomatic Service, retired; Ambassador to Costa Rica, 1995–97; *b* 12 July 1940; *s* of Richard William Jackson and Charlotte (*née* Wrightson); *m* 1961, Mary Elizabeth Kitchin; one *s* one *d*. *Educ:* Queen Elizabeth Grammar Sch., Darlington; Paisley Grammar Sch.; Glasgow Univ. (MA Hons 1961). Joined Home Civil Service, 1961; Scottish Office, 1961–70; seconded to MAFF, 1971–72; seconded to FCO and served in The Hague, 1973–74; trans. to HM Diplomatic Service, 1974; European Integration Dept (External), FCO, 1975–76; Panama City, 1976–79; Arms Control and Disarmament Dept, FCO, 1979–81; Buenos Aires, 1981–82; Falkland Islands Dept, FCO, 1982; Stockholm, 1982–87; Dep. Head of Mission, Seoul, 1987–91; Ambassador to Bolivia, 1991–95. *Recreations:* conservation, birdwatching, real ale. *Address:* Casilla 6320, Santa Cruz, Bolivia.

JACKSON, Robert Victor; MP (C) Wantage, since 1983; *b* 24 Sept. 1946; *m* 1975, Caroline Frances Harvey (*see* C. F. Jackson); one *s* decd. *Educ:* Falcon Coll., S Rhodesia; St Edmund Hall, Oxford (H. W. C. Davis Prize, 1966; 1st Cl. Hons Mod. Hist. 1968); President Oxford Union, 1967. Prize Fellowship, All Souls Coll., 1968 (Fellow, 1968–86). Councillor, Oxford CC, 1969–71; Political Adviser to Sec. of State for Employment, 1973–74; Member, Cabinet of Sir Christopher Soames, EEC Commn, Brussels, 1974–76; Chef de Cabinet, President of EEC Economic and Social Cttee, Brussels, 1976–78; Mem. (C) Upper Thames, European Parlt, 1979–84; Special Adviser to Governor of Rhodesia (Lord Soames), 1979–80; European Parlt's Rapporteur-Gen. on 1983 European Community Budget. Parly Under Sec. of State, DES, 1987–90, Dept of Employment, 1990–92, Office of Public Service and Sci., 1992–93. Mem., Select Cttee on Sci. and Technol., 1999–. Mem., UK Delegn, Council of Europe and WEU, 2000–. Contested (C) Manchester Central Div., Oct. 1974. Co-Chm., CAABU, 2001–. Editor: The Round Table: Commonwealth Jl of Internat. Relations, 1970–74; International Affairs (Chatham House), 1979–80. *Publications:* South Asian Crisis: India, Pakistan, Bangladesh 1972, 1975; The Powers of the European Parliament, 1977; The European Parliament: Penguin Guide to Direct Elections, 1979; Reforming the European Budget, 1981; Tradition and Reality: Conservative philosophy and European integration 1982; From Boom to Bust?—British farming and CAP reform, 1983; Political Ideas in Western Europe Today, 1984. *Recreations:* reading, music, walking. *Address:* House of Commons, SW1A 0AA.

JACKSON, Rodney; *see* Jackson, M. R.

JACKSON, Prof. Roy, DSc; FRS 2000; Class of 1950 Professor of Engineering and Applied Science, Princeton University, 1983–98, now Professor Emeritus; *b* 6 Oct. 1931; *s* of Harold and Ellen Jackson; *m* 1957, Susan Margaret Birch (*d* 1991); one *s* one *d*. *Educ:* Trinity Coll., Cambridge (BA 1954, MA 1959); Univ. of Edinburgh (DSc 1968). ICI Ltd, 1955–61; Reader in Chemical Engrg, Univ. of Edinburgh, 1961–68; A. J. Hartsock Prof. of Chemical Engrg, Rice Univ., 1968–77; Prof. of Chemical Engrg, Univ. of Houston, 1977–82; Sherman Fairchild Dist. Schol., CIT, 1982–83. Alpha Chi Sigma Award, 1980, Thomas Baron Award, 1993, AIChE. *Publications:* Transport in Porous Catalysts, 1977; The Dynamics of Fluidized Particles, 2000. *Recreations:* sailing, water colour painting. *Address:* 311 Johnson Street, New Bern, NC 28560, USA. *T:* (252) 5142493.

JACKSON, Roy Arthur; Assistant General Secretary, Trades Union Congress, 1984–92; *b* 18 June 1928; *s* of Charles Frederick Jackson and Harriet Betsy (*née* Ridewood); *m* 1956, Lilian May Ley; three *d*. *Educ:* North Paddington Central Sch.; Ruskin Coll., Oxford (DipEcon Pol Sci (Distinction)); Worcester Coll., Oxford (BA Hons, PPE). Post Office Savings Bank, 1942; RN, Ord. Signalman, 1946–48. Trades Union Congress: joined Educn Dept, 1956; Dir of Studies, 1964; Head of Educn, 1974–84. Member: Albemarle Cttee of Youth Service, 1958–60; Open Univ. Cttee on Continuing Educn, 1975–76; Adv. Cttee for Continuing and Adult Educn, 1977–83; Schools Council Convocation, 1978–82; Further Educn Unit, DES, 1980–; Employment Appeal Tribunal, 1992–99; TUC Comr, MSC, 1987–88. Non-exec. Dir, Remploy Ltd, 1992–99. *Recreations:* walking, reading, gardening. *Address:* 27 The Ryde, Hatfield, Herts AL9 5DQ. *T:* (01707) 890566.

JACKSON, Hon. Sir Rupert (Matthew), Kt 1999; **Hon. Mr Justice Jackson;** a Judge of the High Court of Justice, Queen's Bench Division, since 1999; *b* 7 March 1948; *s* of late George Henry Jackson and Nancy Barbara Jackson (*née* May); *m* 1975, Claire Corinne Potter; three *d*. *Educ:* Christ's Hospital; Jesus College, Cambridge (MA, LLB). Pres., Cambridge Union, 1971. Called to the Bar, Middle Temple, 1972, Bencher, 1995; QC 1987; a Recorder, 1990–98; a Dep. High Court Judge, 1993–98. Chm., Professional Negligence Bar Assoc., 1993–95. *Publication:* Jackson and Powell on Professional Negligence, 1982, 4th edn 1997. *Address:* Royal Courts of Justice, Strand, WC2A 2LL. *Club:* Reform.

JACKSON, Prof. Stephen Philip, PhD; Frederick James Quick Professor of Biology, Department of Zoology, Cambridge University, since 1995; Senior Scientist, Wellcome/CRC Institute, Cambridge University, since 1996; *b* 17 July 1962; *s* of Philip George Jackson and Marian Margaret (*née* Smith); *m* 1991, Teresa Margaret Clarke; two *s*. *Educ:* Univ. of Leeds (BSc 1st Cl. Hons Biochem. 1983); Univ. of Edinburgh (PhD Molecular Biol. 1987). Postgraduate research: Imperial Coll., London, 1983–85; Univ. of Edinburgh, 1985–87; Postdoctoral Fellow, Univ. of Calif, Berkeley, 1987–91; Research Gp Leader, Wellcome/CRC Inst., Univ. of Cambridge, 1991–95. Founder, and CSO, KuDOS Pharmaceuticals Ltd, 1997–. Tenovus Medal Lecture, Tenovus-Scotland, 1997. Eppendorf European Investigator Award, 1995; Colworth Medal, Biochemical Soc., 1997. *Publications:* numerous research papers and review articles in leading scientific jls, particularly in areas of transcription and DNA repair. *Recreations:* walking and camping, travel, gardening, Nottingham Forest Football Club supporter, contemporary music. *Address:* Wellcome/CRC Institute, University of Cambridge, Tennis Court Road, Cambridge CB2 1QR. *T:* (office) (01223) 334102.

JACKSON, Dr Sylvia; Member (Lab) Stirling, Scottish Parliament, since 1999; *b* 3 Dec. 1946; *d* of Herbert Edward Woodforth and Lucy Franklin; *m* 1970, Michael Peart Jackson; one *s* one *d*. *Educ:* Brigg Girls' High Sch.; Univ. of Hull (BSc Hons Chemistry; PGCE; BPhil Educn); Univ. of Stirling (PhD Educn). Teacher of chemistry and physics, schools in Hull, Alva, Stirling, Cumbernauld and Kirkintilloch; Asst Sci. Advr, Edinburgh CC and Lothian Regl Council; Res. Fellow, Univ. of Stirling; Lectr, Moray House Inst. of Educn, Univ. of Edinburgh. *Publications:* Introducing Science (series of 12 pupil books and 6 teacher guides); contribs to jls, mainly dealing with professional develt of teachers. *Recreations:* running, keeping fit, reading. *Address:* Scottish Parliament, Edinburgh EH99 1SP.

JACKSON, Tessa; *see* Jackson, J. T.

JACKSON, Sir Thomas; *see* Jackson, Sir W. T.

JACKSON, Thomas; General Secretary, Union of Communication Workers (formerly Post Office Workers), 1967–82; bookseller; *b* 9 April 1925; *s* of George Frederick Jackson and Ethel Hargreaves; *m* 1st, 1947, Norma Burrow (marr. diss. 1982); one *d*; 2nd, 1982, Kathleen Maria Tognarelli; one *d*. *Educ:* Jack Lane Elementary Sch. Boy Messenger, GPO, 1939; Royal Navy, 1943; Postman, 1946; Executive Mem., Union of Post Office Workers, 1955; Asst Sec., Union of Post Office Workers, 1964. HM Government Dir, British Petroleum, 1975–83. Member: Gen. Council of TUC, 1967–82 (Chm., 1978–79; Chm., Internat. Cttee, 1978–82); Press Council, 1973–76; Annan Cttee on the Future of Broadcasting, 1974–77; CRE, 1977–78; Broadcasting Complaints Commn, 1982–87; Yorks Water Authority, 1983–89. Non-exec. Dir, Yorks Water plc, 1989–94. Member: Court and Council, Sussex Univ., 1974–78; Council, Bradford Univ., 1987–90. Chm., Ilkley Literature Fest., 1984–87. A Governor: BBC, 1968–73; NIESR, 1974–85. Hon. LLD Leeds, 1995. *Recreations:* cooking, photography. *Address:* 22 Parish Ghyll Road, Ilkley, West Yorks LS29 9NE.

JACKSON, (Walter) Patrick, CB 1987; Under-Secretary, Department of Transport, 1981–89, retired; *b* 10 Feb. 1929; *m* 1952, Kathleen Roper; one *s* one *d*. *Educ:* University Coll., Oxford. John Lewis Partnership, 1952–66; Principal, Min. of Transport and DoE, 1966–72; Asst Sec., DoE, 1972–78; Under Sec. and Regional Dir (E Midlands), DoE and Dept of Transport, 1978–81. *Publications:* The Last of the Whigs, 1994; Education Act Forster, 1997. *Recreations:* concert- and theatre-going, historical research.

JACKSON, (William) Gordon; QC (Scot) 1990; Member (Lab) Glasgow Govan, Scottish Parliament, since 1999; *b* 5 Aug. 1948; *s* of Alexander Jackson and Margaret Shillinglaw or Jackson; *m* 1972, Anne Stevely; one *s* two *d*. *Educ:* Ardrossan Academy; St Andrews Univ. (LLB). Advocate, 1979; called to the Bar, Lincoln's Inn, 1989; Advocate Depute, Scotland, 1987–90. *Address:* Scottish Parliament, Edinburgh EH99 1SP.

JACKSON, William Theodore, CBE 1967 (MBE 1946); ARIBA; MRTPI; Director of Post Office Services, Ministry of Public Building and Works, 1969–71, retired; *b* 18 July 1906; *y s* of Rev. Oliver Miles Jackson and Emily Jackson; *m* 1932, Marjorie Campbell; one *s* two *d*. *Educ:* Cheltenham Grammar Sch.; Regent St Poly. ARIBA 1931; MRTPI 1942. Dublin Chief Asst, 1932–36; Chief Architect, Iraq Govt, i/c of design and construction of Mausoleum for King Feisal, and other projects, 1936–39; Dir, Special Repair Service, Min. of Works, 1940–45; Min. of Public Building and Works, 1946–71: Dir, Mobile Labour Force, 1946–50; Dir of Maintenance, 1950–56; seconded to World Bank as Advr to Development Plan organisation, 1957–59; Regional Dir, Home Counties, 1959–61; Dir, Headquarters Services, 1962–69. *Recreations:* gardening, painting. *Address:* 26 Roding Close, Elmbridge Road, Cranleigh, Surrey GU6 8TE. *T:* (01483) 276273.

JACKSON, Sir (William) Thomas, 8th Bt *cr* 1869; farmer, declined 1990; *b* 12 Oct. 1927; *s* of Sir William Jackson, 7th Bt, and Lady Ankaret Jackson (*d* 1945), 2nd *d* of 10th Earl of Carlisle; *S* father, 1985; *m* 1951, Gilian Malise, *d* of John William Stobart, MBE; three *s*. *Educ:* Mill Hill School; Royal Agricultural Coll., Cirencester. Qualified Associate Chartered Land Agents Soc., later ARICS; resigned, 1969. Nat. Service, 1947–49, 2/Lt Border Regt; Gen. Reserve as Lieut. Land Agent in various firms and on private estates till 1969, when he left the profession and started farming. Chairman: Cumberland Branch, CLA, 1984–86; Whitehaven Branch, NFU, 1983–85. *Recreation:* painting. *Heir: e s* (William) Roland Cedric Jackson, PhD [*b* 9 Jan. 1954; *m* 1977, Nicola Mary, *yr d* of Prof. Peter Reginald Davis, PhD, FRCS; three *s*]. *Address:* Fell End, Mungrisdale, Penrith, Cumbria CA11 0XR.

JACKSON, Yvonne Brenda, OBE 1985; DL; Chairman, West Yorkshire Metropolitan County Council, 1980–81; *b* 23 July 1920; *d* of Charles and Margaret Wilson; *m* 1946, Edward Grosvenor Jackson; twin *s* one *d*. *Educ:* Edgbaston C of E Coll., Birmingham; Manchester Teachers' Trng Coll. (Dip. Domestic Science and qualified teacher). School Meals Organizer, West Bromwich, Staffs, 1942–45. Mem., W Riding CC, 1967–73 (local govt reorganisation); Mem. W Yorks CC, 1973–86; Chm., Fire and Public Protection Cttee, 1977–80; Deputy Leader and Shadow Chairman: Fire Cttee, 1981–86; Trading Standards Cttee, 1981–86; Police Cttee, 1982–86. Chm., Yorks Electricity Consultative Council, 1982–90; Mem., Yorks RHA, 1982–87. Mem. Exec. Cttee, Nat. Union of Cons. Assocs, 1981–88 (Dep. Chm., Yorks Area Finance and Gen. Purposes Cttee, 1982–88; Divl Pres., Elmet, 1985–93). Mem. Council and Court, Leeds Univ. DL W Yorks, 1983, High Sheriff, 1986–87. *Recreations:* badminton, fishing; formerly County hockey and tennis player; former motor rally driver (competed in nat. and internat. events inc. Monte Carlo, Alpine and Tulip rallies). *Address:* East Garth, School Lane, Collingham, W Yorks LS22 5BQ. *T:* (01937) 573452.

JACKSON-LIPKIN, Miles Henry, (Li Pak-Kim); QC (Hong Kong) 1974; SC 1997; JP; a Judge of the High Court of Hong Kong, 1981–87; *b* Liverpool, 24 May 1924; *s* of late I. J. Jackson-Lipkin, MD and F.A. Patley; *m* Lucille Yun-Shim Fung, DCLJ, barrister; one *s*. *Educ:* Harrow; Trinity Coll., Oxford. FCIArb 1986; Mem., HKIArb; Chartered Arbitrator, Canada, Hong Kong and UK. Called to the Bar, Middle Temple, 1951; admitted Hong Kong Bar, 1963, NSW Bar, 1980. Comr, Supreme Court of Negara Brunei Darussalam, 1984–87. Panel Member: Inland Revenue Bd of Review, Hong Kong, 1975; London Court of Internat. Arbitration, 1994–; WIPO, 1995–; British Columbia Arbitration Mediation Inst., 1995–; Hong Kong Internat. Arbitration Centre Mediation Gp, 1996–. Chm. Exec. Cttee, and Man. Dir, Hong Kong Children and Youth Services, 1978–. Member: Medico-Legal Soc., 1952; Justice, 1956; Council of Honour, Monarchist League, 1969; Council, Constitutional Monarchy Assoc., 1995; Founder Member: Hong Kong Br., Justice, 1963; Hong Kong Medico-Legal Soc., 1974 (Mem. Cttee, 1976–). Vice-Chm., Hong Kong Island Br., Internat. Wine and Food Soc. Hon. Mem., Chinese Soc. for Wind Engrg. Liveryman: Meadmakers' Co. (Edinburgh), 1984; Arbitrators' Co., 1986; Freeman, City of London, 1986. JP Hong Kong, 1977. GLJ 1998 ((Grand Priory of Lochore); KCLJ 1983; KLJ 1977; CLJ 1973). *Publications:* The Beaufort Legitimation, 1957; Scales of Justice, 1958; Israel Naval Forces, 1959. *Recreations:* gardening, heraldry, classical music, philately, walking. *Address:* 11C Ewan Court, 56 Kennedy Road, Hong Kong; 62 Eaton Terrace, SW1W 8TZ; 309 The Capilano, 2024 Fullerton Avenue, West Vancouver, BC V7P 3G4, Canada. *Clubs:* Naval and Military, MCC; Hong Kong, Hong Kong Cricket, Hong Kong Golf, Hong Kong Jockey, American, Arts, Classic Car, (Hon.) Shanghai Fraternity Assoc. (Hong Kong).

JACKSON-STOPS, Timothy William Ashworth, FRICS; Chairman, 1978–98, Consultant, since 1998, Jackson-Stops & Staff; *b* 1942; *s* of late Anthony and Jean Jackson-Stops; *m* 1987, Jenny MacArthur; two *s*. *Educ:* Eton; Agricultural Coll., Cirencester. Jackson-Stops & Staff, 1967–: Dir, 1974. *Recreations:* ski-ing, sailing, shooting. *Address:* Wood Burcote Court, Towcester, Northants NN12 7JP. *T:* (01327) 350443.

JACOB, David Oliver Ll.; *see* Lloyd Jacob.

JACOB, Prof. François; Croix de la Libération; Grand-Croix de la Légion d'Honneur; biologist; Head of Cellular Genetics Unit, Pasteur Institute, 1960–91; Professor of Cellular Genetics, at the College of France, 1964–91; *b* Nancy (Meurthe & Moselle), 17 June 1920; *m* 1st, 1947, Lysiane Bloch (*d* 1984); three *s* one *d*; 2nd, 1999, Geneviève Barrier. *Educ:* Lycée Carnot, France. DenM 1947; DèsS 1954. Pasteur Institute: Asst, 1950–56; Head of Laboratory, 1956–60; Prof., 1960–; Pres., 1982–88. Member: Acad. of Scis, Paris, 1977; Acad. Française, Paris, 1996. Charles Léopold Mayer Prize, Acad. des Sciences, Paris, 1962; Nobel Prize for Medicine, 1965. Foreign Member: Royal Danish Acad. of Letters and Sciences, 1962; Amer. Acad. of Arts and Sciences, 1964; Nat. Acad. of Scis, USA, 1969; Royal Soc., 1973; Acad. Royale de Médecine, Belgique, 1973; Acad. of Sci., Hungary, 1986; Royal Acad. of Sci., Madrid, 1987. Holds hon. doctorates from several univs, incl. Chicago, 1965. *Publications:* La Logique du Vivant, 1970 (The Logic of Life, 1974); Le Jeu des Possibles, 1981 (The Possible and the Actual, 1982); La Statue Intérieure, 1987 (The Statue Within, 1988); La Souris, la Mouche et l'Homme, 1997 (Of Flies, Mice and Men, 1998); various scientific. *Recreation:* painting. *Address:* 25 rue du Dr Roux, 75724 Paris, Cedex 15, France.

JACOB, Frederick Henry; CBiol; retired; Director, Ministry of Agriculture, Fisheries and Food's Pest Infestation Control Laboratory, 1968–77; *b* 12 March 1915; *s* of Henry Theodore and Elizabeth Jacob; *m* 1941, Winifred Edith Sloman (decd); one *s* one *d*. *Educ:* Friars Sch., Bangor; UC North Wales. BSc, MSc; CBiol, FIBiol. Asst Entomologist: King's Coll., Newcastle upon Tyne, 1942–44; Sch. of Agriculture, Cambridge, 1944–45; Adviser in Agric. Zoology, UC North Wales, 1945–46; Adv. Entomologist, Min. of Agriculture and Fisheries, Nat. Agric. Adv. Service, N Wales, 1946–50; Head of Entomology Dept, MAFF, Plant Pathology Lab., 1950–68. Pres., Assoc. of Applied Biologists, 1976–77. *Publications:* papers mainly on systematics of Aphididae in learned jls. *Recreations:* hill walking, fishing, gardening. *Address:* Hillside, Almondbury Common, Huddersfield HD4 6SN. *Clubs:* Climbers; Wayfarers (Liverpool).

JACOB, Hon. Sir Robert Raphael Hayim, (Sir Robin), Kt 1993; **Hon. Mr Justice Jacob;** a Judge of the High Court of Justice, Chancery Division, since 1993; *b* 26 April 1941; *s* of Sir Isaac Hai, (Sir Jack) Jacob, QC; *m* 1967, Wendy Jones; three *s*. *Educ:* King Alfred Sch., Hampstead; Mountgrace Secondary Comprehensive Sch., Potters Bar; St Paul's Sch.; Trinity Coll., Cambridge (BA, MA); LSE (LLB). Called to the Bar, Gray's Inn, 1965 (Atkin Scholar; Bencher, 1989); teacher of law, 1965–66; pupillage with Nigel (now Lord) Bridge, 1966–67, with A. M. Walton, 1967; entered chambers of Thomas Blanco White, 1967; Junior Counsel to Treasury in Patent Matters, 1976–81; QC 1981. Dep. Chm., Copyright Tribunal, 1989–93; apptd to hear appeals to Sec. of State under the Trade Marks Acts, 1988–93. Governor: LSE, 1994–; Expert Witness Inst., 1996–. Hon. Vis. Prof. of Law, Univ. of Birmingham, 1999–. Hon. Fellow, St Peter's Coll., Oxford, 1998. Jt Editor, Encyclopedia of UK and European Patent Law, 1977–. *Publications:* Kerly's Law of Trade Marks (ed jtly), 1972, 1983 and 1986 edns; Patents, Trade Marks, Copyright and Designs (ed jtly), 1970, 1978, 1986; Editor, Court Forms Sections on Copyright (1978), Designs and Trade Marks (1975–86); section on Trade Marks (ed jtly), 4th edn, Halsbury's Laws of England, 1985, 1995; Guidebook of Intellectual Property, 1993. *Recreations:* Arsenal FC, photography, country garden. *Address:* Royal Courts of Justice, Strand, WC2A 2LL.

JACOB, Ven. William Mungo, PhD; Archdeacon of Charing Cross, since 1996; *b* 15 Nov. 1944; *s* of John William Carey Jacob and Mary Marsters Dewar. *Educ:* King Edward VII School, King's Lynn; Hull Univ. (LLB); Linacre Coll., Oxford (MA); Exeter Univ. (PhD). Deacon 1970, priest 1971; Curate of Wymondham, Norfolk, 1970–73; Asst Chaplain, Exeter Univ., 1973–75; Lecturer, Salisbury and Wells Theological Coll., 1975–80, Vice-Principal, 1977–80; Sec. to Cttee for Theological Education, ACCM, 1980–86; Warden, Lincoln Theol Coll., 1986–96; Canon of Lincoln Cathedral, 1986–96. Ed., Theology, 1998–. *Publications:* (ed with P. Baelz) Ministers of the Kingdom, 1985; (contrib.) Religious Dissent in East Anglia, 1991; (contrib.) The Weight of Glory, 1991; (ed with N. Yates) Crown and Mitre, 1993; Lay People and Religion in the Early Eighteenth Century, 1996; The Making of the Anglican Church Worldwide, 1997; (contrib.) Studies in Church History, vols 16, 28, 30. *Address:* 15A Gower Street, WC1E 6HW. *T:* (020) 7323 1992.

JACOBI, Sir Derek (George), Kt 1994; CBE 1985; actor; *b* 22 Oct. 1938; *s* of Alfred George Jacobi and Daisy Gertrude Masters. *Educ:* Leyton County High Sch.; St John's Coll., Cambridge (MA Hons; Hon. Fellow, 1987). Artistic Associate, Old Vic Co. (formerly Prospect Theatre Co.), 1976–81; associate actor, RSC; Artistic Dir, Chichester Fest. Th., 1995–96. Vice-Pres., Nat. Youth Theatre, 1982–. *Stage:* Birmingham Repertory Theatre, 1960–63 (first appearance in One Way Pendulum, 1961); National Theatre, 1963–71; Prospect Theatre Co., 1972, 1974, 1976, 1977, 1978; Hamlet (for reformation of Old Vic Co., and at Elsinore), 1979; Benedick in Much Ado About Nothing (Tony Award, 1985), title rôle in Peer Gynt, Prospero in The Tempest, 1982, title rôle in Cyrano de Bergerac, 1983 (SWET Award; Plays and Players Award), RSC; Breaking the Code, Haymarket, 1986, Washington and NY 1987; Dir, Hamlet, Phoenix, 1988; title rôle in Kean, Old Vic, 1990; title rôle in Becket, Haymarket, 1991; Byron, in Mad, Bad and Dangerous to Know, Ambassadors, 1992; Macbeth, RSC, 1993; title rôle in Hadrian VII, Playing the Wife, Chichester, 1995; Uncle Vanya, Chichester, 1996, NY, 2000; God Only Knows, Vaudeville, 2001; *appearances include: TV:* She Stoops to Conquer, Man of Straw, The Pallisers, I Claudius, Philby, Burgess and Maclean, Richard II, Hamlet, Inside the Third Reich, Mr Pye, Cadfael; *films:* 1971–: Odessa File; Day of the Jackal; The Medusa Touch; Othello; Three Sisters; Interlude; The Human Factor; Charlotte; The Man Who Went Up in Smoke; Enigma; Little Dorrit (Best Actor Award, Evening Standard); Henry V; The Fool; Dead Again; Hamlet; Love is the Devil (Best Actor Award, Evening Standard); Gladiator. *Awards:* BAFTA Best Actor, 1976–77; Variety Club TV Personality, 1976; Standard Best Actor, 1983. *Address:* c/o ICM Ltd, Oxford House, 76 Oxford Street, W1N 0AX.

JACOBI, Sir James (Edward), Kt 1989; OBE 1978; Medical Practitioner (private practice), since 1960; *b* 26 Aug. 1925; *s* of Edward William Jacobi and Doris Stella Jacobi; *m* 1946, Joy; one *s* two *d*; *m* 1974, Nora Maria; two *s*. *Educ:* Maryborough State High School; Univ. of Queensland (MB, BS, PhC). Clerk, Public Service, 1941; RAAF, 1943–46; served navigator-wireless operator, Beaufighter Sqdn, SW Pacific. Apprentice pharmaceutical chemist, 1946–50; pharm. chem., 1950–54, and Univ. student, 1954–60; Resident MO, Brisbane, 1961; MO, Dept of Health, Papua New Guinea, 1962–63; GP Port Moresby, 1963–. *Recreation:* Past President, PNG Rugby Football League. *Address:* Jacobi Medical Centre, Box 1551, Boroko, Papua New Guinea. *T:* 3255355. *Clubs:* United Services (Brisbane); City Tattersalls, NSW Leagues (Sydney); Brisbane Polo; Papua (Port Moresby).

JACOBS, family name of **Baron Jacobs**.

JACOBS, Baron *cr* 1997 (Life Peer), of Belgravia in the City of Westminster; **David Anthony Jacobs,** Kt 1988; FCA; *b* Nov. 1931; *s* of Ridley and Ella Jacobs; *m* 1954, Evelyn Felicity Patchett; one *s* one *d*. *Educ:* Clifton Coll.; London Univ. (BCom). Chairman: Nig Securities Gp, 1957–72; Tricoville Gp, 1961–90, 1992–94; British Sch. of Motoring, 1973–90. Contested (L) Watford, Feb. and Oct. 1974. Jt Treas., Liberal Party, 1984–87; Vice-Pres., Soc. & Lib. Dem., 1988; Chm., Federal Exec., Soc. & Lib. Dem., 1988. *Recreations:* golf, reading, theatre, opera, travel. *Address:* 9 Nottingham Terrace, NW1 4QB. *T:* (020) 7486 6323. *Clubs:* Coombe Hill Golf (Surrey); Palm Beach Country (USA).

JACOBS, David Lewis, CBE 1996; radio and television broadcaster; *b* 19 May 1926; *s* of David Jacobs and Jeanette Victoria Jacobs; *m* 1st, 1949, Patricia Bradlaw (marr. diss. 1972); three *d* (one *s* decd); 2nd, 1975, Caroline Munro (*d* 1975); 3rd, 1979, Mrs Lindsay Stuart-Hutcheson. *Educ:* Belmont Coll.; Strand Sch. RN, 1944–47. First broadcast, Navy Mixture, 1944; Announcer, Forces Broadcasting Service, 1944–45; Chief Announcer, Radio SEAC, Ceylon, 1945–47; Asst Stn Dir, Radio SEAC, 1947; News Reader, BBC Gen. Overseas Service, 1947, subseq. freelance. Major radio credits include: Book of Verse, Housewives' Choice, Journey into Space, Dateline London, Grande Gingold, Curioser and Curioser, Puffney Post Office, Follow that Man, Man about Town, Jazz Club, Midday Spin, Music Through Midnight, Scarlet Pimpernel, Radio 2 DJ Show, Pick of the Pops, Saturday Show Band Show, Melodies for You (12 years), Saturday Star Sounds, Any Questions (Chm. for 17 years), Any Answers; Internat. Fest. of Light Music. TV credits incl.: Focus on Hocus, Vera Lynn Show, Make up your Mind, Tell the Truth, Juke Box Jury, Top of the Pops, Hot Line, Miss World, Top Town, David Jacobs' Words and Music, Sunday Night with David Jacobs, Little Women, There Goes that Song Again, Make a Note, Where are they Now, What's My Line, Who What or Where, Frank Sinatra Show, Mario Lanza Show, Walt Disney Christmas Show, Wednesday Show, Wednesday Magazine, Eurovision Song Contest, TV Ice Time, Twist, A Song for Europe, Ivor Novello Awards, Aladdin, Airs and Graces, Tell Me Another, Those Wonderful TV Times, Blankety Blank, Come Dancing, Questions (TVS), Primetime, Countdown, Holiday Destinations (Sky). Numerous film performances incl. Golden Disc, You Must Be Joking, It's Trad Dad, Stardust; former commentator, British Movietone News. 6 Royal Command Performances; 6 yrs Britain's Top Disc Jockey on both BBC and Radio Luxembourg; Variety Club of Gt Brit., BBC TV Personality of Year, 1960, and BBC Radio Personality of the Year, 1975; Sony Gold Award for Outstanding Contribution to Radio over the Years, 1984; RSPCA Richard Martin Award, 1978. Chairman: Kingston FM, 1994–95; Thames FM, 1995–. Director: Duke of York's Theatre, 1979–85; Man in the Moon (UK) Ltd, 1986–; Video Travel Guides, 1990–91; Tom Smith Crackers, 1997–98; private banking section, Guinness Mahon, 1997–98. Director: Kingston Theatre Trust, 1991– (Chm., 1990–); College of Driver Educn, 1991–96. Vice-President: Stars Organisation for Spastics (Past Chm.); Soc. of Stars, 1996–; Mem. Council, RSPCA, 1969–77, Vice-Chm. 1975–76; Vice-Pres., The St John Ambulance London (Prince of Wales's), 1985–97. Past Pres., Nat. Children's Orch.; Vice-Pres., Wimbledon Girls Choir. Chm., Think British Council, 1985–89 (Dep. Chm., 1983–85); Vice-Pres., Invest in Britain Campaign, 1992– (Chm., 1989–92). President: Kingston upon Thames Royal

British Legion, 1984–; SW London Area, SSAFA 1995; Jt Pres., SW London Community Foundn, 1994–; Vice-President: Royal Star and Garter Home, Richmond, 1988–; Friends of Chelsea and Westminster Hosp., 1993–; Patron: Age Resource, 1990–; Kingston Wel-Care Assoc., 1995; Pres., Kingston Alcohol Adv. Service, 1993–; Vice Pres., Kingston Arts Council; Trustee, Dine-a-Mite, 1994–. Life Gov., ICRF, 1995. DL Greater London, 1983, Kingston upon Thames, 1984–2001 (representative); High Steward, 2001. DUniv Kingston, 1994. *Publications:* (autobiog.) Jacobs' Ladder, 1963; Caroline, 1978; (with Michael Bowen) Any Questions?, 1981. *Recreations:* talking and listening, hotels. *Address:* 203 Pavilion Road, SW1X 0BJ. *Clubs:* Garrick, St James'.

JACOBS, Edward John; Social Security and Child Support Commissioner, since 1998; *b* 20 Nov. 1952; *m* Jill, *d* of W. J. Langford. *Educ:* Paston Sch.; Univ. of Southampton. Called to the Bar, Inner Temple, 1976. *Publications:* Effective Exclusion Clauses, 1990; (with M. Jones) Company Meetings: law and procedure, 1991; (with G. Douglas) Child Support: the legislation, 1993, 4th edn 1999; contrib. articles to legal jls. *Recreation:* ancient and medieval murder. *Address:* Office of the Social Security and Child Support Commissioners, Harp House, 83–86 Farringdon Street, EC4A 4DH. *T:* (020) 7353 5145.

JACOBS, Francis Geoffrey; an Advocate General, Court of Justice of the European Communities, since 1988; *b* 8 June 1939; *s* of late Cecil Sigismund Jacobs and Louise Jacobs (*née* Fischhof); *m* 1st, 1964, Ruth (*née* Freeman); one *s*; 2nd, 1975, Susan Felicity Gordon (*née* Cox); one *s* three *d*. *Educ:* City of London Sch.; Christ Church, Oxford; Nuffield Coll., Oxford. MA, DPhil. Called to the Bar, Middle Temple, 1964, Bencher, 1990; in part-time practice, 1974–88; QC 1984; Lectr in Jurisprudence, Univ. of Glasgow, 1963–65; Lectr in Law, LSE, 1965–69; Secretariat, European Commn of Human Rights, and Legal Directorate, Council of Europe, Strasbourg, 1969–72; Legal Sec., Court of Justice of European Communities, Luxembourg, 1972–74; Prof. of European Law, Univ. of London, 1974–88; King's College, London: Dir, Centre of European Law, 1981–88; Vis. Prof., 1989–; Fellow, 1990. Hon. Sec. UK Assoc. for European Law, 1974–81 (a Vice-Pres., 1988–); UK Deleg., Conf. of Supreme Administrative Courts, EEC, 1984–88; Mem., Admin. Tribunal, Internat. Inst. for Unification of Private Law, Rome; Chm., Adv. Bd (European Law sect.), British Inst. of Internat. and Comparative Law, 1999–. Cooley Lectr, 1983, Bishop Lectr, 1989, Univ. of Mich. Governor: British Inst. of Human Rights, 1985–; Inns of Court Sch. of Law, 1996–. Hon. LLD Birmingham, 1996; Hon. DCL City, 1997. Hon. Texan, 2000. Commandeur de l'Ordre de Mérite, Luxembourg, 1983. Founding Editor, Yearbook of European Law, 1981–88; Mem. Editorial Board: Yearbook of European Law; Cahiers de Droit Européen; Common Market Law Review; European Law Review; European Business Orgn Law Review; Jl of Internat. Econ. Law; Jl of Envmtl Law; King's Coll. Law Jl; Revue des Affaires européennes/Law and Eur. Affairs; Rivista di Diritto Europeo. Gen. Ed., Oxford EC Law Library (formerly Oxford European Community Law series), 1986–. *Publications:* Criminal Responsibility, 1971; The European Convention on Human Rights, 1975, 2nd edn (with Robin C. A. White), 1996; (jtly) References to the European Court, 1975; (ed) European Law and the Individual, 1976; (jtly) The Court of Justice of the European Communities, 1977; (jtly) The European Union Treaty, 1986; (joint editor): The European Community and GATT, 1986; The Effect of Treaties in Domestic Law, 1987; Liber Amicorum Pierre Pescatore, 1987; European Community Law in English Courts, 1998; (contrib.) de Smith, Woolf and Jowell, Judicial Review of Administrative Action, 1995. *Recreations:* family life, books, music, nature, travel. *Address:* Court of Justice of the European Communities, Kirchberg, Luxembourg; Wayside, 15 St Alban's Gardens, Teddington, Mddx TW11 8AE. *T:* (020) 8943 0503.

JACOBS, Rabbi Irving, PhD; Principal, Jews' College, London, 1990–93; *b* 2 Aug. 1938; *s* of Solomon Jacobs and Bertha (*née* Bluestone); *m* 1963, Ann Klein; one *s* three *d*. *Educ:* Jews' Coll., London; Univ. of London (BA, PhD); Rabbinical Dip. Jews' College, London: Res. Fellow, 1966–69; Lectr, 1969–75; Sen. Lectr, 1975–84; Dean, 1984–90. *Publications:* The Midrashic Process, 1995; articles on Midrash Apocryphal lit. and Jewish liturgy in scholarly jls. *Address:* 28 Elmstead Avenue, Wembley, Middx HA9 8NX. *T:* (020) 8248 5777.

JACOBS, Jeffrey; Executive Director, Policy and Partnerships, Greater London Authority, since 2001; *b* 20 July 1949; *s* of late Sydney and Jane Jacobs; *m* 1974, Mary Jane Whitelegg; one *s* one *d*. *Educ:* Enfield Grammar Sch. Joined Ministry of Housing and Local Government, later Department of the Environment, 1965: Asst Private Sec. to Sec. of State for Envmt, 1979–82; Head: Housing Policies Studies Div., 1987–90; Envmt Agency Project Team, 1990–92; Manchester Olympic Unit, 1992–94; Regeneration Div., 1994–97; Principal Private Sec. to Dep. Prime Minister, 1997–98; Dir, Planning Directorate, DETR, 1998–2001. Fellow, Hubert H. Humphrey Inst., Minneapolis, 1986–87. *Recreations:* sport, walking. *Address:* Greater London Authority, Romney House, 43 Marsham Street, SW1P 3PY.

JACOBS, Prof. John Arthur; Hon. Professor, Institute of Earth Studies, University of Wales (formerly University College of Wales), Aberystwyth, since 1989; Professor of Geophysics, 1974–83, and Fellow, Darwin College, since 1976 (Vice Master, 1978–82), University of Cambridge; *b* 13 April 1916; *m* 1st, 1941, Daisy Sarah Ann Montgomerie (*d* 1974); two *d*; 2nd, 1974, Margaret Jones (marr. diss. 1981); 3rd, 1982, Ann Grace Wintle. *Educ:* Univ. of London. BA 1937, MA 1939, PhD 1949, DSc 1961. Instr Lieut RN, 1941–46; Lectr, Royal Holloway Coll., Univ. of London, 1946–51; Assoc. Prof., Univ. of Toronto, 1951–57; Prof., Univ. of British Columbia, 1957–67; Dir, Inst. of Earth Sciences, Univ. of British Columbia, 1961–67; Killam Meml Prof. of Science, Univ. of Alberta, 1967–74; Dir, Inst. of Earth and Planetary Physics, Univ. of Alberta, 1970–74. Res. Fellow, RHBNC, 1987–89. Sec., Royal Astronomical Soc., 1977–82; Harold Jeffreys Lectr, RAS, 1983. FRSC 1958; DSc *hc* Univ. of BC, 1987. Centennial Medal of Canada, 1967; Medal of Canadian Assoc. of Physicists, 1975; J. Tuzo Wilson Medal, Canadian Geophys. Union, 1982; John Adam Fleming Medal, Amer. Geophys. Union, 1994; Price Medal, RAS, 1994. *Publications:* (with R. D. Russell and J. T. Wilson) Physics and Geology, 1959, 2nd edn 1974; The Earth's Core and Geomagnetism, 1963; Geomagnetic Micropulsations, 1970; A Textbook on Geonomy, 1974; The Earth's Core, 1975, 2nd edn 1987; Reversals of the Earth's Magnetic Field, 1984, 2nd edn 1994; Deep Interior of the Earth, 1992. *Recreations:* walking, music. *Address:* Institute of Earth Studies, University of Wales, Aberystwyth, Dyfed SY23 3DB. *T:* (01970) 622646.

JACOBS, John Robert Maurice, OBE 1997; golf entrepreneur; *b* 14 March 1925; *s* of Robert and Gertrude Vivian Jacobs; *m* 1949, Rita Wragg; one *s* one *d*. *Educ:* Maltby Grammar School. Asst Professional Golfer, Hallamshire Golf Club, 1947–49; Golf Professional: Gezira Sporting Club, Cairo, 1949–52; Sandy Lodge Golf Club, 1952–64; Man. Dir, Athlon Golf, 1967–75; Professional Golfers' Association: Tournament Dir-Gen., 1971–76, Advr to Tournament Div., 1977; European Ryder Cup Captain, 1979–81 (player, 1955); Golf Instructor: Golf Digest Magazine Schs, 1971–76; Golf Magazine Schs, US, 1977. Adviser to: Walker Cup Team; Spanish and French nat. teams; Past Adviser to: Curtis Cup Team; English Golf Union team; Scottish Union team; German, Swedish and Italian teams. Golf Commentator, ITV, 1967–87. Currently associated with John Jacobs' Practical Golf Schools, based in USA. Golf adviser to Golf World Magazine, 1962–86. Pres., PGA of Europe, 1999–2000. *Publications:* Golf, 1961; Play Better Golf, 1969; Practical Golf, 1973; John Jacobs Analyses the Superstars, 1974; Golf Doctor, 1979; The Golf Swing Simplified, 1993; Golf in a Nutshell, 1995; 50 Greatest Golf Lessons of the Century, 1999. *Recreations:* shooting, fishing. *Address:* Stable Cottage, Chapel Lane, Lyndhurst, Hants SO43 7FG. *T:* (023) 8028 2743. *Clubs:* Sandy Lodge Golf, New Forest Golf, Brokenhurst Manor Golf, Bramshaw Golf, Burley Golf; Lake Nona Golf and Country (Florida), Hamptworth Golf and Country.

JACOBS, Hon. Sir Kenneth (Sydney), KBE 1976; Justice of High Court of Australia, 1974–79; *b* 5 Oct. 1917; *s* of Albert Sydney Jacobs and Sarah Grace Jacobs (*née* Aggs); *m* 1952, Eleanor Mary Neal; one *d*. *Educ:* Knox Grammar Sch., NSW; Univ. of Sydney (BA, LLB). Admitted to NSW Bar, 1947; QC 1958; Supreme Court of NSW: Judge, 1960; Judge of Appeal, 1966; Pres., Court of Appeal, 1972. *Publication:* Law of Trusts, 1958. *Recreations:* printing and bookbinding; gardening. *Address:* Crooks Lane Corner, Axford, Marlborough, Wilts SN8 2HA.

JACOBS, Rabbi Dr Louis, CBE 1990; Rabbi, New London Synagogue, since 1964; Visiting Professor, University of Lancaster, since 1987; *b* 17 July 1920; *s* of Harry and Lena Jacobs; *m* 1944, Sophie Lisagorska; two *s* one *d*. *Educ:* Manchester Central High Sch.; Manchester Talmudical Coll.; BA Hons, PhD, London. Rabbinical Ordination; Rabbi, Central Synagogue, Manchester, 1948–54; New West End Synagogue, 1954–60; Tutor, Jews' Coll., London, 1959–62; Dir, Society Study of Jewish Theology, 1962–64. Vis. Prof., Harvard Divinity Sch., 1985–86. Hon. Fellow: UCL, 1988; Leo Baeck Coll., 1988. Hon. DHL: Spertus Coll., Chicago, 1987; Hebrew Union Coll., Cincinnati, 1989; Jewish Theol. Seminary, NY, 1989; Hon. DLitt Lancaster, 1991. Hon. Citizen: Texas, 1961; New Orleans, 1963. *Publications:* Jewish Prayer, 1955; We Have Reason to Believe, 1957; Guide to Rosh Hashanah, 1959; Guide to Yom Kippur, 1959; Jewish Values, 1960; (trans.) The Palm Tree of Deborah, 1960; Studies in Talmudic Logic, 1961; (trans.) Tract on Ecstasy, 1963; Principles of Jewish Faith, 1964; Seeker of Unity, 1966; Faith, 1968; Jewish Law, 1968; Jewish Ethics, Philosophy and Mysticism, 1969; Jewish Thought Today, 1970; What Does Judaism Say About . . .?, 1973; A Jewish Theology, 1973; Theology in the Responsa, 1975; Hasidic Thought, 1976; Hasidic Prayer, 1977; Jewish Mystical Testimonies, 1977; TEKYU: the unsolved problem in the Babylonian Talmud, 1981; The Talmudic Argument, 1985; A Tree of Life, 1985; Holy Living, 1990; Helping with Inquiries (autobiog.), 1989; God, Torah, Israel, 1990; Structure and Form of the Babylonian Talmud, 1991; Religion and the Individual, 1991; The Jewish Religion: a companion, 1995; Concise Companion to the Jewish Religion, 1999; Beyond Reasonable Doubt, 1999; Ask the Rabbi, 1999; contribs to learned jls, collections and festschriften. *Recreations:* reading thrillers, watching television, hill walking. *Address:* 27 Clifton Hill, St John's Wood, NW8 0QE. *T:* (020) 7624 1299.

JACOBS, Prof. Patricia Ann, OBE 1999; FRS 1993; Director, Wessex Regional Genetics Laboratory, since 1988; *b* 8 Oct. 1934; *d* of Cyril Jacobs and Sadie Jacobs (*née* Jones); *m* 1972, Newton Ennis Morton; three step *s* two step *d*. *Educ:* St Andrews Univ. (BSc 1st Cl. Hons 1956; D'Arcy Thomson Medal 1956; DSc 1966; Sykes Medal 1966). FRSE 1977; FRCPath 1987; FRCPE 1998. Res. Asst, Mount Holyoke Coll., USA, 1956–57; Scientist, MRC, 1957–72; Prof., Dept of Anatomy and Reproductive Biology, Univ. of Hawaii Sch. of Medicine, 1972–85; Prof. and Chief of Div. of Human Genetics, Dept of Pediatrics, Cornell Univ. Med. Coll., 1985–87. Hon. Prof. of Human Genetics, Univ. of Southampton Med. Sch., 1993. Mem., MRC, 1996–98. Founder FMedSci 1998. Allan Award, Amer. Soc. of Human Genetics, 1981; Regents Medal, Univ. of Hawaii, 1983. *Publications:* numerous articles in learned jls. *Recreations:* walking, botany, gardening. *Address:* Wessex Regional Genetics Laboratory, Salisbury District Hospital, Salisbury SP2 8BJ. *T:* (01722) 336262.

See also Peter A. Jacobs.

JACOBS, Peter Alan; non-executive Chairman: Healthcall Ltd, since 1998; L. A. Fitness (formerly L. A. Leisure), since 1999; *b* 22 Feb. 1943; *s* of Cyril and Sadie Jacobs; *m* 1966, Eileen Dorothy Naftalin; twin *s* one *d*. *Educ:* Glasgow Univ. (BSc Hons MechEng); Aston Univ. (Dip. Management Studies). Tube Investments: grad. trainee, 1965–67; Production Controller, Toy Div., 1968–70; Pedigree Petfoods: Production Shift Manager, 1970–72; Purchasing Dept, 1972–81; Production Manager, 1981–83; Sales Dir, Mars Confectionery, 1983–86; Berisford International: Man. Dir, British Sugar, 1986–89; Chief Exec., Berisford and Chm., British Sugar, 1989–91; Chief Exec., BUPA, 1991–98; non-exec. Chm., Hillsdown Holdings plc, 1999. Non-executive Director: Allied Domecq, 1998–; Bank Leumi (UK), 1999–; Virtual Communities Inc., 1999–2000. *Recreations:* tennis, theatre, music. *Address:* 2 Norfolk Road, NW8 6AX. *Club:* Royal Automobile.

See also Patricia A. Jacobs.

JACOBS, Peter John; His Honour Judge Jacobs; a Circuit Judge, since 1997; *b* 16 April 1943; *s* of Herbert Walter Jacobs and Emma Doris Jacobs; *m* 1975, Dr Ruth Edwards; two *s*. *Educ:* King Edward VII Sch., King's Lynn; University Coll., Cardiff (BA Hons 1964). Schoolmaster: Barry Boys' Grammar Sch., 1965–68; Cathays High Sch., 1968–72; called to the Bar, Gray's Inn, 1973; practice, 1973–97; Standing Counsel to Inland Revenue, 1995–97. Mem. (L), Barry Borough Council, 1966–69. *Recreations:* watching Norwich City Football Club, fine art, Norfolk railways and churches, gardening. *Address:* Cardiff Crown Court, Cathays Park, Cardiff CF1 3PG. *Clubs:* Norwich City Football; Cardiff Lawn Tennis.

JACOBS, Richard David; QC 1998; *b* 21 Dec. 1956; *s* of late Elliott Jacobs, chartered accountant, and of Ruth Jacobs (*née* Ellenbogen); *m* 1990, Pamela Fine; one *s* two *d*. *Educ:* Highgate Sch.; Pembroke Coll., Cambridge. Called to the Bar, Middle Temple, 1979. *Recreations:* tennis, Arsenal FC, theatre, piano. *Address:* Essex Court Chambers, 24 Lincoln's Inn Fields, WC2A 3ED. *T:* (020) 7813 8000. *Clubs:* MCC, Royal Automobile.

JACOBSON, Prof. Dan; novelist, critic; Professor Emeritus, University College London, since 1994; *b* 7 March 1929; *s* of Michael Hyman Jacobson and Liebe Jacobson (*née* Melamed); *m* 1954, Margaret Dunipace Pye; two *s* one *d*. *Educ:* Kimberley Boys' High Sch., SA; Univ. of Witwatersrand, Johannesburg (BA 1949). Fellow in Creative Writing, Stanford Univ., Calif, 1956–57; University College London: Reader in English, 1979–86; Prof. of English, 1986–94. Vis. Prof., Syracuse Univ., NY, 1965–66; Visiting Fellow: State Univ. of NY, 1972; Humanities Research Centre, ANU, 1981. Lectures: Ernest Jones Meml, British Inst. of Psycho-Analysis, 1988; Ethel M. Wood, Univ. of London, 1990; Bernard Krikler Meml, Wiener Liby, 1995; Lord Northcliffe, UCL, 2001. FRSL 1974–99. Hon. DLitt Witwatersrand, 1997. Llewellyn Rhys Award, Book Trust, 1958; W. Somerset Maugham Award, Soc. of Authors, 1962. Mary Elinore Smith Poetry Prize, Amer. Scholar, 1992. *Publications: fiction:* The Trap, 1955; A Dance in the Sun, 1956; The Price of Diamonds, 1957; The Evidence of Love, 1960; The Beginners, 1966; The Rape of Tamar, 1970; Inklings: selected stories, 1973; The Wonder-Worker, 1973; The Confessions of Josef Baisz, 1977 (H. H. Wingate Award, Jewish Chronicle, 1979); Her Story, 1987; Hidden in the Heart, 1991; The God-Fearer, 1992; *criticism:* The Story of the Stories, 1982; Adult Pleasures, 1988; *autobiography:* Time and Time Again, 1985 (J. R.

Ackerley Prize, PEN, 1986); *travel:* The Electronic Elephant, 1994; *memoir:* Heshel's Kingdom, 1998; *translation:* H. van Woerden, A Mouthful of Glass, 2000. *Recreations:* tennis, walking, reading, talking. *Address:* c/o A. M. Heath & Co., 79 St Martin's Lane, WC2N 4AA. *T:* (020) 7229 0113. *Clubs:* Athenæum; Templars Tennis.

JACOBSON, Howard Eric; novelist; critic; *b* 25 Aug. 1942; *s* of Max Jacobson and Anita (*née* Black); *m* 1st, 1964, Barbara Starr (marr. diss.); one *s*; 2nd, 1978, Rosalin Sadler. *Educ:* Stand Grammar Sch., Whitefield; Downing Coll., Cambridge (BA, MA). Lectr in English Lit., Univ. of Sydney, Australia, 1965–67; Tutor in English, Selwyn Coll., Cambridge, 1968–72; Sen. Lectr, Wolverhampton Poly., 1974–80. Writer and presenter, TV documentaries: Into the Land of Oz, 1991; Yo, Mrs Askew, 1991; Roots Schmoots, 1993; Sorry, Judas, 1993; Seriously Funny, 1997; Howard Jacobson Takes on the Turner, 2000; contrib. to Late Show, 1989–, Late Rev., 1995–. TV critic, The Correspondent, 1989–90; columnist, The Independent, 1998–. Mem. Editl Bd, Modern Painters, 1990–. *Publications:* (with W. Sanders) Shakespeare's Magnanimity, 1978; In the Land of Oz, 1987; Roots Schmoots, 1993; Seeing with the Ear (Peter Fuller Meml Lecture), 1993; Seriously Funny, 1997; *novels:* Coming from Behind, 1983; Peeping Tom, 1984; Redback, 1986; The Very Model of a Man, 1992; No More Mister Nice Guy, 1998; The Mighty Walzer, 1999; Who's Sorry Now, 2002. *Address:* c/o Peters Fraser & Dunlop, Drury House, 34–43 Russell Street, WC2B 5HA. *T:* (020) 7344 1000. *Clubs:* Chelsea Arts, Groucho.

JACOBUS, Prof. Mary Longstaff, DPhil; Professor of English (Grace 2), and Fellow of Churchill College, University of Cambridge, since 2000; *b* 4 May 1944; *d* of Marcus Jacobus and Diana (*née* Longstaff); *m* 1981, A. Reeve Parker; one *s* one *d*. *Educ:* Oxford High Sch. for Girls, GPDST; Lady Margaret Hall, Oxford (BA 1st Cl. Hons English 1965, MA; DPhil 1970; Hon. Fellow, 2000). Oxford University: Randall McIver Jun. Res. Fellow, 1968–70, Fellow and Tutor in English, 1971–80, Lady Margaret Hall; Lectr, English Faculty, 1972–80; Lectr, Manchester Univ., 1970–71; Cornell University: Associate Prof. of English, 1980–82; Prof. of English, 1982–89; John Wendell Anderson Prof. of English and Women's Studies, 1989–2000. Hon. Res. Fellow, LMH, Oxford, 1980–2000. Guggenheim Fellow, 1988–89. *Publications:* Tradition and Experiment in Wordsworth's Lyrical Ballads (1798), 1976; (ed) Women Writing and Women Writing About Women, 1979; Reading Woman: essays in feminist criticism, 1986; (ed jtly) Body/Politics: women and the discourse of science, 1989; Romanticism, Writing and Sexual Difference: essays on The Prelude, 1989; First Things: the maternal imaginary in literature, art and psychoanalysis, 1996; Psychoanalysis and the Scene of Reading, 1999. *Address:* Churchill College, Cambridge CB3 0DS. *T:* (01223) 336000.

JACOMB, Sir Martin (Wakefield), Kt 1985; Chairman: Delta plc, since 1993; Share plc, since 2001; *b* 11 Nov. 1929; *s* of Hilary W. Jacomb and Félise Jacomb; *m* 1960, Evelyn Heathcoat Amory; two *s* one *d*. *Educ:* Eton Coll.; Worcester Coll., Oxford (MA Law 1953; Hon. Fellow, 1994). 2nd Lieut, RA, 1948–49. *T:* and *Fax:* Called to the Bar, Inner Temple, 1955; practised at the Bar, 1955–68. Kleinwort Benson Ltd, 1968–85; Dep. Chm., Barclays Bank PLC, 1985–93; Chairman: Barclays de Zoete Wedd, 1986–91; Postel Investment Management, 1991–95; Prudential Corp., 1995–2000 (Dir, 1994–2000); Director: The Telegraph plc (formerly Daily Telegraph), 1986–95; Rio Tinto plc (formerly RTZ Corp.), 1988–; Marks and Spencer, 1991–2000; Canary Wharf Group PLC, 1999–. A Dir, Bank of England, 1986–95. Chm., British Council, 1992–98. External Mem., Finance Cttee, OUP, 1971–95. Trustee, Nat. Heritage Meml Fund, 1982–97. Chancellor, Univ. of Buckingham, 1998–. Hon. Bencher, Inner Temple, 1987. Hon. Dr: Humberside, 1993; Buckingham, 1997; Hon. DCL Oxford, 1997. *Recreations:* theatre, family bridge, the outdoors.

JACQUES, Dr David Lawson; Programme Director, Conservation (Landscapes and Gardens), Architectural Association, since 2000; *b* 29 Sept. 1948; *s* of Greville Lawson Jacques and Anne Grace Jacques; *m* 1973, Rosalind Catherine Denny; two *d*. *Educ:* Univ. of Leeds (MSc Transportation Engrg 1972); Poly of N London (DipTP 1977); Courtauld Inst., Univ. of London (PhD 1999). MIHT 1977; MRTPI 1981. Land Use Consultants, 1973–76; Jacques Miller Partnership, 1977–78; Associate, Travers Morgan Planning, 1978–87; Inspector of Historic Parks and Gardens, English Heritage, 1987–93; Consultant on historic landscapes, parks and gardens, 1993– (eg. Privy Garden, Hampton Court); Lectr (pt-time) Landscapes and Gardens, Dept of Archaeol., Univ. of York, 1994–98. Vis. Prof., De Montfort Univ., 1999–. Mem. Council, 1975–2001, Chm., 1998–2000, Garden Hist. Soc.; Mem., English Heritage Gdns Adv. Cttee, 1984–87; International Council on Monuments and Sites: Co-ordinator, Landscapes Wkg Gp, 1991–95; Corresp. Mem., Internat. Cttee for Gdns and Sites, 1991–; Chm., UK Historic Gdns and Landscapes Cttee, 1993–98. Trustee and Chm., Gdns Cttee, Castle Bromwich Hall Gdns Trust, 1985–87; Chm., Bishop's Park Co-ordinating Gp, 1985–87; Trustee, Landscape Design Trust, 1994–; Chm., Staffs Gdns and Parks Trust, 1994–97. Chm., Hammersmith and Fulham Liberal Democrats, 1987–93. *Publications:* Georgian Gardens: the reign of nature, 1983, repr. 1990; (with A. J. Van der Horst) The Gardens of William and Mary, 1988; Strategic Guidance for Heritage Land in London, 1988; Essential to the pracktick part of phisick: the London apothecaries 1540–1617, 1994; The Millenial Landscape, 2001; contrib. chapters in books and articles to jls incl. Jl Gdn Hist. Soc., Landscape Design, Country Life, Jl Envmtl Mgt, Landscape Res., Jl RTPI, Monuments Historiques, English Heritage Conservation Bull., Die Gartenkunst, Arte dei Giardini, Internat. Jl Heritage Studies, Jl Architectural Conservation, Schriftenreihe des Deutschen Rates fur Landespflege, Tuinjournaal and Architectural Hist. *Recreations:* narrow boats, croquet, visiting historic gardens. *Address:* Sugnall Hall, Sugnall, Stafford ST21 6NF. *T:* (01785) 851711. *Club:* Farmers'.

JACQUES, Peter Roy Albert, CBE 1990; Secretary, TUC Social Insurance and Industrial Welfare Department, since 1971; *b* 12 Aug. 1939; *s* of George Henry Jacques and Ivy Mary Jacques (*née* Farr); *m* 1965, Jacqueline Anne Sears; one *s* one *d*. *Educ:* Archbishop Temple's Secondary Sch.; Newcastle upon Tyne Polytechnic (BSc Sociology); Univ. of Leicester. Building labourer, 1955–58; market porter, 1958–62; Asst, TUC Social Insce and Industrial Welfare Dept, 1968–71. Member: Industrial Injuries Adv. Council, 1972; Nat. Insce Adv. Cttee, 1972–78; Health and Safety Commn, 1974–95; Royal Commn on the Nat. Health Service, 1976–79; EEC Cttee on Health-Safety, 1976; NHS London Adv. Cttee, 1979; Social Security Adv. Cttee, 1980–95; Health Educn Council, 1984–87; Civil Justice Review Adv. Cttee, 1985–; Royal Commn on Envmtl Pollution, 1989–95; Employment Appeal Tribunal, 1996–. Jt Sec., BMA/TUC Cttee, 1972; Secretary: TUC Social Health and Envmt Protection Cttee (formerly Social Insurance and Industrial Welfare Cttee), 1972–93; TUC Health Services Cttee, 1979–; TUC Special Advr, 1992–95. Vice-Chm., Redbridge and Waltham Forest HA, 1996–99. Mem. Exec. Cttee, Royal Assoc. for Disability and Rehabilitation, 1975–. *Publications:* responsible for TUC pubns Health-Safety Handbook; Occupational Pension Schemes. *Recreations:* reading, yoga, walking, camping, vegetable growing. *Address:* 7 Starling Close, Buckhurst Hill, Essex IG9 5TN. *T:* (020) 8505 5327.

JAEGER, Prof. Leslie Gordon, FRSE 1966; Research Professor of Civil Engineering and Applied Mathematics, Technical University of Nova Scotia, 1988–92, Emeritus 1992; *b* 28 Jan. 1926; *s* of Henry Jaeger; *m* 1st, 1948, Annie Sylvia Dyson; two *d*; 2nd, 1981, Kathleen Grant. *Educ:* King George V Sch., Southport; Gonville and Caius Coll., Cambridge. PhD, DSc (Eng) London. Royal Corps of Naval Constructors, 1945–48; Industry, 1948–52; University College, Khartoum, 1952–56; Univ. Lectr, Cambridge, 1956–62; Fellow and Dir of Studies, Magdalene Coll., Cambridge, 1959–62; Prof. of Applied Mechanics, McGill Univ., Montreal, 1962–65; Regius Prof. of Engineering, Edinburgh Univ., 1965–66; Prof. of Civil Engineering, McGill Univ., 1966–70; Dean, Faculty of Engineering, Univ. of New Brunswick, 1970–75; Academic Vice-Pres., Acadia Univ., NS, 1975–80; Vice-Pres. (Res.), Technical Univ. of NS, 1980–88. Pres., Canadian Soc. for Civil Engrg, 1992–93. Hon. Prof. of Civil Engrg, Tong Ji Univ., Shanghai, 1987; Hon. Rector, Usman Inst. of Technol., Karachi, 1993. DEng *hc*: Carleton Univ., Ottawa, 1991; Meml Univ., Newfoundland, 1994; Technical Univ. of NS, 1995. Telford Premium, ICE, 1959; A. B. Sanderson Award, 1983, P. L. Prattey Award, 1994, Canadian Soc. for Civil Engrg; Gzowski Medal, 1985, Julian C. Smith Medal, 1996, Engrg Inst. of Canada. *Publications:* The Analysis of Grid Frameworks and Related Structures (with A. W. Hendry), 1958; Elementary Theory of Elastic Plates, 1964; Cartesian Tensors in Engineering Science, 1965; (with B. Bakht) Bridge Analysis Simplified, 1985; (with B. Bakht) Bridge Analysis by Microcomputer, 1989; various papers on grillage analysis in British, European and American Journals. *Recreations:* golf, curling, contract bridge. *Address:* PO Box 1000, Halifax, NS B3J 2X4, Canada. *T:* (902) 4779571. *Club:* Saraguay (Halifax, Canada).

JAFFERJEE, Aftab Asger; Senior Treasury Counsel, Central Criminal Court, since 2001; *b* 25 June 1956; *s* of Asger Jafferjee and Tara Kajiji. *Educ:* St Paul's Sch., Darjeeling; Rugby Sch.; Durham Univ. (BA Hons). Called to the Bar, Inner Temple, 1980; Jun. Treasury Counsel, 1997–2001. Member: Professional Conduct Cttee of Bar (of England and Wales), 1994–96; Cttee, Criminal Bar Assoc., 1995–97. *Recreations:* cuisine, travel, theatre (Founder, Castle Th. Co., Durham, 1977). *Address:* 2 Harcourt Buildings, Temple, EC4Y 9DB. *T:* (020) 7353 2112.

JAFFRAY, Alistair Robert Morton, CB 1978; Deputy Under-Secretary of State, Ministry of Defence, 1975–84; *b* 28 Oct. 1925; *s* of late Alexander George and Janet Jaffray; *m* 1st, 1953, Margaret Betty Newman (decd); two *s* one *d*; 2nd, 1980, Edna Mary, *e d* of late S. J. Tasker, Brasted Chart. *Educ:* Clifton Coll.; Corpus Christi Coll., Cambridge. BA First Cl. Hons., Mod. Langs. Served War, RNVR, 1943–46. Apptd Home Civil Service (Admty), 1948; Private Sec. to First Lord of Admty, 1960–62; Private Sec. to successive Secretaries of State for Defence, 1969–70; Asst Under-Sec. of State, MoD, 1971, Dep. Sec. 1975; Sec. to Admty Bd, 1981–84. Governor, Clifton Coll., 1980–; Chm. Management Cttee, Royal Hospital Sch., Holbrook, 1985–91. *Address:* Okeford, 10 Lynch Road, Farnham, Surrey GU9 8BZ.

JAFFRAY, Sir William Otho, 5th Bt *cr* 1892; *b* 1 Nov. 1951; *s* of Sir William Edmund Jaffray, 4th Bt, TD, JP, DL; *S* father, 1953; *m* 1981, Cynthia Ross Corrington, Montreal, Canada (marr. diss. 1997); three *s* one *d*. *Educ:* Eton. Mem., United Names Cttee against Soc. of Lloyd's, 1996–2000. *Heir: s* Nicholas Gordon Alexander Jaffray, *b* 18 Oct. 1982.

JAFFRÉ, Philippe Serge Yves; Chevalier de la Légion d'Honneur; Ordres du Mérite et du Mérite Agricole; Chariman, Europatweb, since 2000; *b* 2 March 1945; *s* of Yves-Frédéric Jaffré and Janine Jaffré (*née* Alliot); *m* 1974, Elisabeth Coulon; one *s* two *d*. *Educ:* Faculté of Law, Paris; Inst. d'études politiques, Paris (diploma); Ecole Nat. d'Administration (Bachelor of Law). Inspecteur des Finances, 1974; Dept of the Treasury, 1977–88; Gen. Sec., Comité Interministeriel pour l'Aménagement des Structures Industrielles, 1978; Tech. Advr to Minister of Economy, 1979; Dep. Dir, Dept of Govt Holdings, 1984; Head of Dept for Monetary and Financial affairs, 1986–88; Dir, Banque Stern, 1988; Chief Exec. Officer, Crédit Agricole, 1988–93; Chm. and Chief Exec. Officer, Elf Aquitaine, 1993–99. *Publication:* La Monnaie et la politique Monétaire, 1990. *Recreation:* golf. *Address:* 9 rue de Valois, 75001 Paris, France.

JAFFREY, Saeed, OBE 1995; actor and writer; *b* 8 Jan. 1929; *s* of late Dr Hamid Hussain Joffrey and Hadia Begum Joffrey; *m* 1st, 1958, Madhur Bahadur (marr. diss. 1966); three *d*; 2nd, 1980, Jennifer Irene Sorrell. *Educ:* Allahabad Univ. (MA Medieval Hist. 1950); Catholic Univ., Washington DC (MFA Drama 1958). First Indian actor to tour USA in Shakespeare, 1958, and to appear on Broadway, in A Passage to India, 1962; *films* include: The Wilby Conspiracy, 1974; The Man Who Would Be King, 1975; The Chess Players, 1977 (Best Actor Awards, Filmfare, and Filmworld, 1978); Touch Wood, 1981; Masoom, 1982; Gandhi, 1982; My Beautiful Laundrette, 1985 (BAFTA award, 1986); A Passage to India, 1985; Ram Teri Ganga Maili, 1985; Henna, 1989; Masala (Canadian Acad. Award), 1992; *television* includes: Gangsters, 1975–77; Jewel in the Crown, Staying On, 1980–82; Far Pavilions, 1985; Partition, Tandoori Nights, 1985–87; Love Match, 1986; Killing on the Exchange, 1986; Rumpole, 1990; Little Napoleons, 1994–95; Common as Muck, 1996–97; Ravi Desai in Coronation Street, 1998–99; *theatre* includes: Captain Brassbound's Conversion, 1972; Midsummer Night's Dream, 1989; White Chameleon, 1991; My Fair Lady, 1997; The King & I, 2001;*radio* includes: wrote and presented first programme on India in America, Reflections of India, 1961–63; numerous plays incl. Art of Love (Kama Sutra), The Pump, Shakuntala, Savitri, A Suitable Boy, and The Silver Castle. *Publication:* Saeed: an actor's journey, 1998. *Recreations:* snooker, cartooning and caricatures, watching cricket and tennis. *Address:* c/o Magnolia Management, 136 Hicks Avenue, Greenford, Middx UB6 8HB. *T:* (020) 8578 2899.

JAGAN, Janet, OE 1993; President, Republic of Guyana, 1997–99; *b* Chicago, 20 Oct. 1920; *d* of Charles and Kathryn Roberts; *m* 1943, Dr Cheddi Jagan (*d* 1997), former President of Guyana; one *s* one *d*. *Educ:* Univ. of Detroit; Wayne Univ.; Michigan State Coll. Founder Mem., 1946, Political Affairs Cttee, which became People's Progressive Party, Guyana, in 1950: Exec. Mem., 1950–; Gen. Sec., 1950–70; Editor, Thunder (party jl), 1950–57; Internat. Affairs Sec., 1970–80. First woman elected to Georgetown CC, 1950; MP Guyana, 1953, 1957–61, 1963–64, 1976–97; Dep. Speaker, House of Assembly, 1953; imprisoned for six months, Sept. 1954–Feb. 1955; Minister of Labour, Health and Housing, 1957–61, of Home Affairs, 1963–64; Prime Minister of Guyana, May–Dec. 1997. Mem., Elections Commn, 1967–68. Pres., Union of Guyanese Journalists, 1970–90. Editor, Mirror newspaper, 1973–97. Gandhi Gold Medal for Democracy, Peace and Women's Rights, UNESCO, 1997. Order of the Liberator (Venezuela), 1998. *Publications:* History of the PPP, 1960; Army Intervention in 1973 Elections, 1973; *for children:* When Grandpa Cheddi was a Boy, 1993; Patricia the Baby Manatee and other stories, 1995; Children's Stories of Guyana's Freedom Struggles, 1995; Anastasia the Anteater and other stories, 1997. *Recreation:* swimming. *Address:* 65 Plantation Bel Air, Georgetown, Guyana; HQ of People's Progressive Party, 41 Robb Street, Georgetown, Guyana. *T:* 72095.

JAGGER, Ven. Ian; Archdeacon of Auckland, Diocese of Durham, since 2001; *b* 17 April 1955; *m* 1993, Ruth Green; one *s*. *Educ:* Huddersfield New Coll.; King's Coll., Cambridge (BA 1977, MA 1981); St John's Coll., Durham (BA 1980, MA 1987).

Ordained deacon, 1982, priest, 1983; Curate, St Mary, Twickenham, 1982–85; Team Vicar, Willen, Milton Keynes, 1985–94; Team Rector, Fareham, 1994–98; RD Fareham, 1996–98; Canon Residentiary, Portsmouth Cathedral, 1998–2001. *Address:* 2 Etherley Lane, Bishop Auckland, Co. Durham DL14 7QR. *T:* (01388) 451635.

JAGLAND, Thorbjørn; MP (Lab) Norway, since 1993; Ministry of Foreign Affairs, since 2000; *b* 5 Nov. 1950; *m* 1975, Hanne Grotjord; two *s*. *Educ:* Univ. of Oslo. Leader, Labour Youth League, 1977–81; Labour Party of Norway: Res. and Analysis Sec., 1981–86; Party Sec., 1986–92; Leader, 1992–. Prime Minister of Norway, 1996–97. *Publications:* My European Dream, 1990; New Solidarity, 1993; Letters, 1995. *Recreations:* ski-ing, outdoor activities, literature. *Address:* Ministry of Foreign Affairs, POB 8114 Dep, 0032 Oslo, Norway. *T:* 22243600.

JAGO, David Edgar John; Communar of Chichester Cathedral, 1987–92; *b* 2 Dec. 1937; *s* of late Edgar George Jago and of Violet Jago; *m* 1st, 1963, Judith Lissenden, DPhil (*d* 1995); one *s* one *d*; 2nd, 1997, Gertraud Marianne, (Gerty), Apfelbeck. *Educ:* King Edward's Sch., Bath; Pembroke Coll., Oxford (MA). National Service, RA, 1956–58. Asst Principal, Admiralty, 1961; Private Sec. to Permanent Under Sec. of State (RN), 1964–65; Principal 1965; Directing Staff, IDC, 1968–70; Private Sec. to Parly Under Sec. of State for Defence (RN), 1971–73; Ministry of Defence: Asst Sec., 1973; Asst Under Sec. of State: Aircraft, 1979–82; Naval Staff, 1982–84; Under Sec., Cabinet Office, 1984–86. Gov., Bedgebury Sch., 1996–2000. *Recreations:* theatre, opera, military history, supporting Arsenal FC. *Club:* Oxford and Cambridge.

JAHN, Dr Wolfgang; Managing Director, Commerzbank AG, Düsseldorf, 1969–84; *b* 27 Sept. 1918; *s* of Dr Georg Jahn and Ella (*née* Schick); *m* 1949, Gabriele (*née* Beck); two *s* one *d*. *Educ:* Zürich Univ.; Berlin Univ.; Heidelberg Univ. (DrEcon). Industrial Credit Bank, Düsseldorf, 1949–54; IBRD, Washington, 1954–57; Commerzbank AG, Düsseldorf, 1957–84. *Address:* c/o Commerzbank AG, PO Box 101137, 40002 Düsseldorf, Germany.

JAHODA, Prof. Gustav, FBA 1988; FRSE; Professor of Psychology, University of Strathclyde, 1964–85, now Emeritus Professor; *b* 11 Oct. 1920; *s* of late Olga and Leopold Jahoda; *m* 1950, Jean Catherine (*née* Buchanan) (*d* 1991); three *s* one *d*. *Educ:* Vienna, Paris, Univ. of London. MScEcon, PhD. FRSE 1993. Tutor, Oxford Extra-Mural Delegacy, 1946–68; Lectr, Univ. of Manchester, 1948–51; Univ. of Ghana, 1952–56; Sen. Lectr, Univ. of Glasgow, 1956–63. Visiting Professor, Universities of: Ghana, 1968; Tilburg, 1984; Kansai, Osaka, 1985; Ecole des Hautes Etudes, Paris, 1986; Saarbrücken, 1987; New York, 1987; Geneva, 1990. Fellow, Netherlands Inst. of Advanced Studies, 1980–81; Hon. Fellow, Internat. Assoc. for Cross-Cultural Psychology (Pres., 1972–74); Membre d'Honneur, Assoc. pour la Recherche Inter-culturelle, 1986. *Publications:* White Man, 1961, 2nd edn 1983; The Psychology of Superstition, 1969, 8th edn 1979; Psychology and Anthropology, 1982 (French edn 1989; Japanese edn 1992); (with I. M. Lewis) Acquiring Culture, 1988; Crossroads between Culture and Mind, 1992; Images of Savages, 1999; contribs to learned jls. *Recreations:* fishing, gardening. *Address:* c/o Department of Psychology, University of Strathclyde, Glasgow G1 1RD. *Club:* University of Strathclyde Staff.

JAINE, Tom William Mahony; Proprietor, Prospect Books, since 1993; freelance writer; *b* 4 June 1943; *s* of William Edwin Jaine and Aileen (*née* Mahony); *m* 1st, 1965, Susanna F. Fisher; 2nd, 1973, Patience Mary Welsh (decd); two *d*; 3rd, 1983, Sally Caroline Agnew; two *d*. *Educ:* Kingswood Sch., Bath; Balliol Coll., Oxford (BA Hons). Asst Registrar, Royal Commn on Historical Manuscripts, 1967–73; Partner, Carved Angel Restaurant, Dartmouth, 1974–84; publisher, The Three Course Newsletter (and predecessors), 1980–89; Editor, Good Food Guide, 1989–93. Wine and Food Writer of the Year, Glenfiddich Awards, 2000. *Publications:* Cooking in the Country, 1986; Cosmic Cuisine, 1988; Making Bread at Home, 1995; Building a Wood-Fired Oven, 1996; contribs Sunday Telegraph, etc. *Recreations:* baking, buildings. *Address:* Allaleigh House, Blackawton, Totnes, Devon TQ9 7DL.

JAKEMAN, Prof. Eric, FRS 1990; Professor of Applied Statistical Optics, University of Nottingham, since 1996; *b* 3 June 1939; *s* of Frederick Leonard Jakeman and Hilda Mary Hays; *m* 1968, Glenys Joan Cooper; two *d*. *Educ:* Brunts Grammar Sch., Mansfield; Univ. of Birmingham (BSc, PhD). FInstP 1979. Asst Res. Physicist, UCLA, 1963–64. DRA (formerly RRE, subseq. RSRE), 1964–95 (DCSO, 1985–95). Hon. Sec., Inst. of Physics, 1994– (Vice-Pres. for Publications, 1989–93); Mem. Exec. Cttee, European Physical Soc., 1990–94. Fellow, Optical Soc. of America, 1988. Maxwell Medal and Prize, Inst. of Physics, 1977; (jtly) MacRobert Award, 1977; (jtly) Instrument Makers' Co. Award. *Publications:* numerous contribs to learned jls. *Recreations:* gardening, music, beekeeping. *Address:* Saxeten, Guarlford Road, Malvern, Worcs WR14 3QT; University of Nottingham, University Park, Nottingham NG7 2RD.

JALLOH, Sulaiman T.; *see* Tejan-Jalloh.

JAMES; *see* Streatfeild-James.

JAMES, family name of **Baron Northbourne**.

JAMES OF HOLLAND PARK, Baroness *cr* 1991 (Life Peer), of Southwold in the County of Suffolk; **Phyllis Dorothy White, (P. D. James),** OBE 1983; JP; FRSL; author; *b* 3 Aug. 1920; *d* of Sidney Victor James and Dorothy Amelia James (*née* Hone); *m* 1941, Connor Bantry White (*d* 1964); two *d*. *Educ:* Cambridge Girls' High Sch. Administrator, National Health Service, 1949–68; Civil Service: apptd Principal, Home Office, 1968; Police Dept, 1968–72; Criminal Policy Dept, 1972–79. Associate Fellow, Downing Coll., Cambridge, 1986. A Gov., BBC, 1988–93; Member: BBC Gen. Adv. Council, 1987–88; Arts Council, 1988–92 (Chm., Literature Adv. Panel, 1988–92); Bd, British Council, 1988–93 (Mem., Literature Cttee, 1988–93). Chm., Booker Prize Panel of Judges, 1987. Pres., Soc. of Authors, 1997– (Chm., 1984–86); Mem., Detection Club. JP: Willesden, 1979–82; Inner London, 1984. FRSL 1987; FRSA. Hon. Fellow, St Hilda's Coll., Oxford, 1996. Hon. DLitt: Buckingham, 1992; Hertfordshire, 1994; Glasgow, 1995; Durham, 1998; Portsmouth, 1999; Hon. DLit London, 1993; DU Essex, 1996. Awarded many major prizes for crime writing in GB, America, Italy and Scandinavia; Grand Master award, Mystery Writers of America, 1999. *Publications:* Cover Her Face, 1962 (televised 1985); A Mind to Murder, 1963 (televised 1995); Unnatural Causes, 1967 (televised 1993); Shroud for a Nightingale, 1971 (televised 1984); (with T. A. Critchley) The Maul and the Pear Tree, 1971; An Unsuitable Job for a Woman, 1972 (filmed 1982; televised 1998); The Black Tower, 1975 (televised 1986); Death of an Expert Witness, 1977 (televised 1983); Innocent Blood, 1980; The Skull beneath the Skin, 1982; A Taste for Death, 1986 (televised 1988); Devices and Desires, 1989 (televised 1991); The Children of Men, 1992; Original Sin, 1994 (televised 1997); A Certain Justice, 1997 (televised 1998); A Time to be in Earnest: a fragment of autobiography, 1999; Death in Holy Orders, 2001; (ed with Harriet Harvey Wood) Sightlines, 2001. *Recreations:* exploring churches, walking by the sea. *Address:* c/o Greene & Heaton Ltd, 37 Goldhawk Road, W12 8QQ.

JAMES, Anne Eleanor S.; *see* Scott-James.

JAMES, Anthony Trafford, CBE 1979; PhD; FRS 1983; Member of Executive Committee of Unilever Research Colworth Laboratory, also Head of Division of Biosciences, 1972–85; *b* Cardiff, Wales, 6 March 1922; *s* of J. M. and I. James; *m* 1st, 1945, O. I. A. Clayton (*d* 1980); two *s* one *d*; 2nd, 1983, L. J. Beare; one *s*. *Educ:* University College Sch.; Northern Polytechnic; University Coll. London (BSc, PhD), Fellow 1975; Harvard Business Sch. (AMP). MRC Junior Fellowship at Bedford Coll., Univ. of London (with Prof. E. E. Turner, subject: Antimalarials), 1945–47; Jun. Mem. staff, Lister Inst. for Preventive Med., London (with Dr R. L. M. Synge, Nobel Laureate, subject: Structure of Gramicidin S), 1947–50; Mem. scientific staff, Nat. Inst. for Med. Res., London (special appt awarded, 1961), 1950–62 (with Dr A. J. P. Martin, FRS, Nobel Laureate, 1950–56); Unilever Research Lab., Sharnbrook: Div. Manager and Head of Biosynthesis Unit, 1962–67; Head of Div. of Plant Products and Biochemistry, 1967–69; Gp Manager, Biosciences Gp, 1969–72. Industrial Prof. of Chemistry, Loughborough Univ. of Technology, 1966–71. Non-exec. Dir, Wellcome Foundn, 1985–92. Member: SRC, 1973–77; Food Sci. and Technol. Bd, MAFF, 1975–80; Manpower Cttee, SERC, 1981–84; ABRC, 1983–; Council, Royal Soc., 1988–90; Chairman: Food Composition, Quality and Safety Cttee, MAFF, 1975–80; Biotechnol. Management Cttee, SERC, 1981–85. Hon. Dr Dijon, 1981; Hon. DSc Cranfield Inst. of Technology, 1985. Has had various awards incl. some from abroad. *Publications:* New Biochemical Separations (ed A. T. James and L. J. Morris), 1964; Lipid Biochemistry—an introduction (M. I. Gurr and A. T. James), 1972. *Recreations:* glass engraving, antique collecting, gardening. *Address:* 9 High Street, Harrold, Beds MK43 7DQ.

JAMES, (Arthur) Walter; Principal, St Catharine's, Windsor, 1974–82; *b* 30 June 1912; *s* of late W. J. James, OBE; *m* 1st, 1939, Elisabeth (marr. diss. 1956), *e d* of Richard Rylands Howroyd; one *d*; 2nd, 1957, Ann Jocelyn, *y d* of late C. A. Leavy Burton; one *d* and one adopted *s* two adopted *d*. *Educ:* Uckfield Grammar Sch.; Keble Coll., Oxford (Scholar); 1st Cl. Mod. Hist.; Liddon Student; Arnold Essay Prizeman. Senior Demy of Magdalen Coll., 1935; Scholar in Mediæval Studies, British School at Rome, 1935; Editorial staff, Manchester Guardian, 1937–46. NFS 1939–45. Contested (L) Bury, Lancs, 1945. Dep. Editor, The Times Educational Supplement, 1947–51, Editor, 1952–69; Special Advisor on Educn, Times Newspapers, 1969–71; also Editor, Technology, 1957–60. Reader in Journalism, Univ. of Canterbury, NZ, 1971–74. Member: BBC Gen. Advisory Council, 1956–64; Council of Industrial Design, 1961–66; Council, Royal Society of Arts, 1964; Cttee, British-American Associates, 1964; Governor, Central School of Art and Design, 1966. Woodard Lecturer, 1965. *Publications:* (Ed.) Temples and Faiths 1958; The Christian in Politics, 1962; The Teacher and his World, 1962; A Middle-class Parent's Guide to Education, 1964; (contrib.) Looking Forward to the Seventies, 1967. *Recreation:* gardening. *Address:* 1 Cumberland Mews, The Great Park, Windsor, Berks SL4 2JD. *T:* (01784) 431377. *Club:* National Liberal.

JAMES, Aubrey Graham Wallen; Deputy Chief Land Registrar, 1975–81; *b* 5 Jan. 1918; *s* of Reginald Aubrey James and Amelia Martha James; *m* 1952, Audrey Elizabeth, *er d* of Dr and Mrs A. W. F. Edmonds; two *s*. *Educ:* Nantgyle Grammar Sch.; London Univ. (LLB 1939). Solicitor, 1940. Served Second World War, 1940–46, Major, Cheshire Regt. Legal Asst, HM Land Registry, 1948; Asst Land Registrar, 1954; Land Registrar, 1963; Dist Land Registrar, Nottingham, 1963. Chm., E Midlands Region, CS Sports Council, 1970–75. *Recreations:* having had a life-long interest in several sporting activities, has developed, in latter years, a latent interest in art, and is Chairman of a thriving local art group. *Address:* 11 Playle Chase, Great Totham, Maldon CM9 8UT.

JAMES, Basil; Special Commissioner, 1963–82, Presiding Special Commissioner, 1982–83; *b* 25 May 1918; *s* of late John Elwyn James, MA (Oxon.), Cardiff, and Mary Janet (*née* Lewis), Gwaelodygarth, Glam; *m* 1943, Moira Houlding Rayner, MA (Cantab.), *d* of late Capt. Benjamin Harold Rayner, North Staffs Regt, and Elizabeth (*née* Houlding), Preston, Lancs; one *s* twin *d*. *Educ:* Llandovery Coll.; Canton High Sch., Cardiff; Christ's Coll., Cambridge (Exhibnr). Tancred Law Student, Lincoln's Inn, 1936; Squire Law Scholar, Cambridge, 1936. BA 1939; MA 1942. Called to Bar, Lincoln's Inn, 1940. Continuous sea service as RNVR officer in small ships on anti-submarine and convoy duties in Atlantic, Arctic and Mediterranean, 1940–45. King George V Coronation Scholar, Lincoln's Inn, 1946. Practised at Chancery Bar, 1946–63. Admitted to Federal Supreme Court of Nigeria, 1962. *Publications:* contrib. to Atkin's Court Forms and Halsbury's Laws of England. *Recreations:* music, gardening.

See also J. E. R. James.

JAMES, Cecil; *see* James, T. C. G.

JAMES, Charles Edwin Frederic; His Honour Judge Charles James; a Circuit Judge, since 1993; *b* 17 April 1943; *s* of Frederic Crockett Gwilym James and Marjorie Peggy James (*née* Peace); *m* 1968, Diana Mary Francis (*née* Thornton); two *s*. *Educ:* Trent College, Long Eaton, Derbyshire; Selwyn College, Cambridge. MA 1968. Called to the Bar, Inner Temple, 1965; practised on Northern Circuit, 1965–93; Jun. of Northern Circuit, 1966. A Recorder, 1982–93. *Recreation:* family pursuits. *Address:* Liverpool Combined Court Centre, Derby Square, Liverpool L2 1XA. *Clubs:* Cambridge University Cricket; Royal Liverpool Golf, Royal Mersey Yacht.

JAMES, Christopher John; Deputy Chairman, R. Griggs Group Ltd, 1994–2000 (Director, 1993–2000); *b* 20 March 1932; *s* of John Thomas Walters James, MC and Cicely Hilda James; *m* 1958, Elizabeth Marion Cicely Thomson; one *s* one *d*. *Educ:* Clifton Coll., Bristol; Magdalene Coll., Cambridge (MA). Served RA, 2nd Lieut, 1951–52; TA, 1952–60. Admitted Solicitor, 1958; Partner, Johnson & Co., Birmingham, 1960–87 (Sen. Partner, 1985–87); Dep. Sen. Partner, Martineau Johnson, 1987–89, Sen. Partner, 1989–94. Director: Birmingham Building Soc., then Birmingham Midshires Building Soc., 1980–96 (Dep. Chm., 1988–90; Chm., 1990–96); Police Mutual Assurance Soc., 1996–2001. Gen. Comr for Income Tax, 1974–82. Pres., Birmingham Law Soc., 1983–84. Chm., Kalamazoo Trust, 1997–2001. Mem. Council, Edgbaston High Sch. for Girls, 1980–90 (Chm., 1987–90); Gov., Clifton Coll., 1980–99. *Recreations:* photography, railways, golf.

JAMES, His Honour Christopher Philip; a Circuit Judge, 1980–97; *b* 27 May 1934; *yr s* of late Herbert Edgar James, CBE, and Elizabeth Margaret James (*née* Davies). *Educ:* Felsted School; Magdalene Coll., Cambridge (MA). Commnd RASC, 1953. Called to the Bar, Gray's Inn, 1959; a Recorder of the Crown Court, 1979; Judge of Woolwich County Court, 1982–92, of Lambeth County Court, 1992–97. *Address:* Flat 8, 93 Elm Park Gardens, SW10 9QW. *Club:* Oxford and Cambridge.

JAMES, Clive Vivian Leopold, AM 1992; writer and broadcaster; non-executive Chairman, Welcome Stranger.com, since 2000; *b* 7 Oct. 1939; *s* of Albert Arthur James and Minora May (*née* Darke). *Educ:* Sydney Technical High Sch.; Sydney Univ. (BA Hons); Pembroke Coll., Cambridge (MA). President of Footlights when at Cambridge. Dir, Watchmaker Prodns, 1994–99. Record albums as lyricist for Pete Atkin: Beware of the Beautiful Stranger; Driving through Mythical America; A King at Nightfall; The Road of Silk; Secret Drinker; Live Libel; The Master of the Revels; Touch has a Memory, 1991. Song-book with Pete Atkin: A First Folio. *Television series:* Cinema, Up Sunday, So It Goes, A Question of Sex, Saturday Night People, Clive James on Television, The Late Clive James, The Late Show with Clive James, Saturday Night Clive, The Talk Show with Clive James, Clive James—Fame in the Twentieth Century, Review of the Year, Sunday Night Clive, The Clive James Show, Clive James on Television (1997); *television documentaries:* Shakespeare in Perspective: Hamlet, 1980; The Clive James Paris Fashion Show, Clive James and the Calendar Girls, 1981; The Return of the Flash of lightning, 1982; Clive James Live in Las Vegas,1982; Clive James meets Roman Polanski, 1984; The Clive James Great American Beauty Pageant, 1984; Clive James in Dallas, 1985; Clive James Meets Katherine Hepburn, 1986; Clive James on Safari, 1986; Clive James and the Heroes of San Francisco, 1987; Clive James in Japan, 1987; Clive James meets Jane Fonda, Clive James on the 80s, 1989; Clive James meets Damon Hill, The Clive James Formula One Show, 1997; Clive James meets Mel Gibson, 1998; Clive James meets the Supermodels, 1998; Postcard series, 1989–: Rio, Chicago, Paris, Miami, Rome, Shanghai, Sydney, London, Cairo, New York, Bombay, Berlin, Buenos Aires, Nashville, Hong Kong, Mexico City, Las Vegas, Havana. Hon. DLitt Sydney, 1999. *Publications: non-fiction:* The Metropolitan Critic, 1974, 2nd edn 1994; The Fate of Felicity Fark in the Land of the Media, 1975; Peregrine Prykke's Pilgrimage through the London Literary World, 1976; Britannia Bright's Bewilderment in the Wilderness of Westminster, 1976; Visions Before Midnight, 1977; At the Pillars of Hercules, 1979; First Reactions, 1980; The Crystal Bucket, 1981; Charles Charming's Challenges on the Pathway to the Throne, 1981; From the Land of Shadows, 1982; Glued to the Box, 1982; Flying Visits, 1984; Snakecharmers in Texas, 1988; On Television, 1991; The Dreaming Swimmer, 1992; Fame, 1993; The Speaker in Ground Zero, 1999; Reliable Essays, 2001; Even As We Speak, 2001; Always Unreliable, 2001; *fiction:* Brilliant Creatures, 1983; The Remake, 1987; Brrm! Brrm!, 1991; The Silver Castle, 1996; *verse:* Fan-Mail, 1977; Poem of the Year, 1983; Other Passports: poems 1958–85, 1986; *autobiography:* Unreliable Memoirs, 1980; Falling Towards England: Unreliable Memoirs II, 1985; May Week Was in June: Unreliable Memoirs III, 1990.

JAMES, Rt Rev. Colin Clement Walter; Bishop of Winchester, 1985–95; *b* 20 Sept. 1926; *yr s* of late Canon Charles Clement Hancock James and Gwenyth Mary James; *m* 1962, Margaret Joan, (Sally), Henshaw; one *s* two *d*. *Educ:* Aldenham School; King's College, Cambridge (MA, Hons History); Cuddesdon Theological College. Assistant Curate, Stepney Parish Church, 1952–55; Chaplain, Stowe School, 1955–59; BBC Religious Broadcasting Dept, 1959–67; Religious Broadcasting Organizer, BBC South and West, 1960–67; Vicar of St Peter with St Swithin, Bournemouth, 1967–73; Bishop Suffragan of Basingstoke, 1973–77; Canon Residentiary of Winchester Cathedral, 1973–77; Bishop of Wakefield, 1977–85. Member of General Synod, 1970–95; Chairman: Church Information Cttee, 1976–79; C of E's Liturgical Commn, 1986–93. Chm., BBC and IBA Central Religious Adv. Cttee, 1979–84. President: Woodard Corp., 1978–93; RADIUS, 1980–93. Chm., USPG, 1985–88. Hon. DLitt Southampton, 1996. *Recreations:* theatre, travelling. *Address:* 5 Hermitage Road, Lansdown, Bath BA1 5SN. *T:* (01225) 312720.

JAMES, Colin John Irwin, FIPD; Chief Executive, Roads Service, Northern Ireland, since 1999; *b* 17 Sept. 1942; *s* of William and Evelyn James; *m* 1968, Monica Jean Patston; one *s* one *d*. *Educ:* Royal Belfast Academical Instn; Queen's Univ., Belfast (BSc Hons 1965); University Coll. London (MPhil 1967). FIPD 1988; MCIH 1992; MIHT 1999. GLC, 1967–71; DoE (NI), 1971–73; NI Housing Exec., 1973–94; joined Defence Housing Exec., 1994, Chief Exec., 1995–99. *Recreations:* cycling, photography. *Address:* (office) Roads Service, Clarence Court, 10–18 Adelaide Street, Belfast BT2 8GB.

JAMES, Sir Cynlais Morgan, (Sir Kenneth), KCMG 1985 (CMG 1976); HM Diplomatic Service, retired; Director General, Canning House, 1987–92; *b* 29 April 1926; *s* of Thomas James and Lydia Ann James (*née* Morgan); *m* 1953, Mary Teresa, *d* of R. D. Girouard and Lady Blanche Girouard; two *d*. *Educ:* Trinity Coll., Cambridge (MA). Service in RAF, 1944–47. Cambridge 1948–51. Entered Senior Branch of Foreign Service, 1951; Foreign Office, 1951–53; Third Sec., Tokyo, 1953–56; Second Sec., Rio de Janeiro, 1956–59; First Sec. and Cultural Attaché, Moscow, 1959–62; FO, 1962–65; Paris, 1965–69; promoted Counsellor, 1968; Counsellor and Consul-General, Saigon, 1969–71; Head of W European Dept, FCO, 1971–75; NATO Defence Coll., Rome, 1975–76; Minister, Paris, 1976–81; Ambassador to Poland, 1981–83; Asst Under Sec. of State, FCO, 1983; Ambassador to Mexico, 1983–86. Director: Thomas Cook, 1986–91; Latin American Investment Trust, 1990–96; Foreign and Colonial Emerging Markets, 1993–96; Polish Investment Trust, 1996–; Consultant, Darwin Instruments, 1986–; Advr, Amerada Hess Ltd, 1997–. Chairman: British-Mexican Soc., 1987–90; British Inst. in Paris, 1988–; Bd, Inst. of Latin American Studies, 1992–98; Mem., Franco-British Council, 1986–99. Hon. Dr Mexican Acad. of Internat. Law, 1984. Order of the Aztec, 1st cl. (Mexico), 1985; Order of Andres Bello, 1st cl. (Venezuela), 1990; Order of Merit (Chile), 1991; Chevalier, Legion of Honour (France), 1995. *Recreation:* tennis. *Address:* 63 Eccleston Square, SW1V 1PH. *Clubs:* Brooks's, Beefsteak, Pratt's, MCC; Travellers (Paris).

JAMES, Rt Rev. David Charles; *see* Pontefract, Bishop Suffragan of.

JAMES, Prof. David Edward; Professor (formerly Director) of Adult Education, since 1969, and Dean of Associated Institutions, since 1996, University of Surrey; *b* 31 July 1937; *s* of Charles Edward James and Dorothy Hilda (*née* Reeves); *m* 1963, Penelope Jane Murray; two *s* one *d*. *Educ:* Universities of Reading, Oxford, Durham, London (Bsc Hons Gen., BSc Hons Special, MEd, DipEd, DipFE); FRSH; FITD 1992. Lectr in Biology, City of Bath Tech. Coll. 1961–63; Lectr in Sci. and Educn, St Mary's Coll. of Educn, Newcastle upon Tyne, 1963–64; University of Surrey: Lectr in Educnl Psych., 1964–69; Hd, Dept of Educnl Studies, 1982–93. FRSA. *Publications:* A Student's Guide to Efficient Study, 1966, Amer. edn 1967; Introduction to Psychology, 1968, Italian edn 1972. *Recreation:* farming. *Address:* University of Surrey, Guildford, Surrey GU2 5XH.

JAMES, Dr (David) Geraint, FRCP; Consultant Ophthalmic Physician, St Thomas' Hospital, London, since 1973; Teacher, University of London, since 1979; *b* 2 Jan. 1922; *s* of David James and Sarah (*née* Davies); *m* 1951, Sheila Sherlock, *qv*; two *d*. *Educ:* Jesus Coll., Cambridge (MA 1945); Mddx Hosp. Med. Sch., London (MD 1953); Columbia Univ., NYC. FRCP 1964. Consultant Physician, Royal Northern Hosp., 1959–86 (Dean, 1968–86). Adjunct Prof. of Medicine, Univ. of Miami, Fla, 1973–, and Prof. of Epidemiology, 1981–; Adjunct Prof., Royal Free Hosp. Med. Sch., 1987–; Consulting Phys. to RN, 1972–86; Hon. Consultant Phys., US Veterans' Admin, 1978–; Hon. Consulting Phys., Sydney Hosp., Australia, 1969–79. President: Internat. Cttee on Sarcoidosis, 1987– (World Exec. Sec., 1980–86); Italian Congress on Sarcoidosis, 1983; World Assoc. of Sarcoidosis, 1987–; Vice-Pres., Fellowship of Postgrad. Medicine; Past President: Med. Soc. of London; Harveian Soc.; Osler Club (Hon. Fellow); Vice-Pres., London Glamorgan Soc., 1989–; Mem. Council, Cymmrodorion Soc. Lectures: Tudor Edwards, RCP and RCS, 1983; George Wise Meml, New York City, 1983. Foreign Corresponding Mem., French Nat. Acad. of Medicine, 1987; Hon. Corresp. Mem., Thoracic Socs of Italy, France, Dominican Republic and Portugal; Hon. FACP 1990; Hon. FRCOphth, 1994. Editor, Internat. Rev. of Sarcoidosis, 1984–. Freeman, City of London, 1961. Hon. LLD Wales, 1982. Chesterfield Medal, Inst. of Dermatology, London, 1957; Gold Medal, Barraquer Inst. of Ophthalmology, 1958; Carlo Forlanini Gold Medal, Italian Thoracic Soc., 1983. Gold Medal, Milan, 1987. Kt of Order of Christopher Columbus (Dominican Republic), 1987. *Publications:* Diagnosis and Treatment of Infections, 1957; Sarcoidosis, 1970; Circulation of the Blood, 1978; Atlas of Respiratory Diseases, 1981, 2nd edn 1992; Sarcoidosis and other Granulomatous Disorders, 1985; Textbook on Sarcoidosis and other Granulomatous Disorders, 1994; The Granulomatous Disorders, 1999. *Recreations:* history of medicine, international Welshness, Rugby football. *Address:* 149 Harley Street, W1N 1HG. *T:* (020) 7935 4444. *Club:* Athenæum.

JAMES, Dr David Gwynfor; Head of Meteorological Research Flight, Royal Aircraft Establishment, Farnborough, 1971–82; *b* 16 April 1925; *s* of William James and Margaret May Jones; *m* 1953, Margaret Vida Gower; two *d*. *Educ:* Univ. of Wales, Cardiff (BSc, PhD). Joined Meteorological Office, 1950; Met. Res. Flight, Farnborough, 1951; Forecasting Res., Dunstable, 1953; Christmas Island, Pacific, 1958; Satellite Lab., US Weather Bureau, 1961; Cloud Physics Res., Bracknell, 1966; Met. Res. Flight, RAE, 1971. Fellow, UC Cardiff, 1987. *Publications:* papers in Qly Jl Royal Met. Soc., Jl Atmospheric Sciences, Met. Res. Papers, and Nature. *Recreations:* golf, choral singing. *Address:* Tŷ'r Onnen, 56 Port Lion, Llangwm, Haverfordwest, Dyfed SA62 4JT.

JAMES, Derek Claude, OBE 1989; Director of Social Services, Leeds, 1978–89; *b* 9 March 1929; *s* of Cecil Claude James and Violet (*née* Rudge); *m* 1954, Evelyn (*née* Thomas); one *s* one *d*. *Educ:* King Edward's Grammar Sch., Camp Hill, Birmingham; Open Univ. (BA). Dip. in Municipal Admin. Local Government: Birmingham, 1946–60; Coventry, 1960–63; Bradford, 1963–69; Leeds, 1969–89. Mem., Yorks and Humberside RHA, 1976–82; Chm., Leeds Area Review Cttee (Child Abuse), 1978–89; Mem., Nat. Adv. Council on Employment of Disabled People, 1984–89; Pres., Nat. Assoc. of Nursery and Family Care, 1988–92; Chairman: Nightstop Homeless Persons Project, 1989–92; Nightstop Trust, Leeds, 1993–2000; Council, Disabled Living Centre, Leeds, 1997–; Vice-Chm., Nat. Family Service Units, 1992–96 (Mem. Nat. Cttee, 1992–96); Expert Panel Mem., Registered Homes Tribunal, 1990–96; Adviser: AMA Social Services Cttee, 1983–89; Physical Disablement Res. Liaison Gp, 1986–89. Sanctuary Housing Association: Chm., North and West Yorks Area Cttee, 1992–; Mem., North Divl Cttee, 1992–97; Mem., Central Council, 1993–97, 2001–; Chm., Care Cttee, 1998–. Non-exec. Dir, Neuroscis and Maxillo-Facial Surgery Subsid. Governing Body, United Leeds Teaching Hosps Trust, 1997–98. *Recreations:* watching sport, garden pottering, acceding to my grandchildren's wishes. *Address:* Hill House, Woodhall Hills, Calverley, Pudsey, West Yorks LS28 5QY. *T:* (0113) 2578044.

JAMES, Hon. Edison Chenfil; MP (UWP) Marigot, Dominica; Leader of the Opposition, since 2000; *b* 18 Oct. 1943; *s* of David and Patricia James; *m* 1970, Wilma; one *s* two *d*. *Educ:* North East London Poly. (BSc Hons); Univ. of Reading (MSc); Imperial Coll., London (Dip. Pest Management). Teacher, St Mary's Acad., 1973; Agronomist, Min. of Agriculture, Dominica, 1974–76; Farm Improvement Officer, Caribbean Develt Bank and Agric. and Indust. Develt Bank, 1976–80; Project Co-ordinator, Coconut Rehabilitation; Gen. Manager, Dominica Banana Marketing Corp., 1980–87; Man. Dir, Agric. Managing Corp., 1987–95. Prime Minister, Dominica, 1995–2000. *Recreations:* cricket, football, table tennis, politics, international affairs. *Address:* Parliament of Dominica, Roseau, Dominica, West Indies. *T:* 4482401. *Club:* Rotary Club of Dominica.

JAMES, Edward Foster, CMG 1968; OBE 1946; HM Diplomatic Service, retired; *b* 18 Jan. 1917; *s* of late Arthur Foster James; *m* 1985, Janet Mary Walls; one *s* two *d* by a previous marriage. Served HM Forces, 1939–46, India, Burma, Malaya, Indonesia; Lieut-Colonel (GSO1) (OBE, despatches twice). Joined HM Diplomatic Service, 1947; Rangoon, 1948; Hong Kong, 1951; Foreign Office, 1953; Rome, 1955; Foreign Office, 1958; Berlin, 1960; FO (later FCO), 1961–74. Exec. Dir, Inst. of Directors, 1975–76; Dep. Dir-Gen., CBI, 1976–83. Chm., Coastal Pollution Control plc, 1984–85; Dir, Tace plc, 1984–91. *Address:* 95 Gloucester Terrace, W2 3HB. *T:* (020) 7262 0139. *Club:* Boodle's.

JAMES, (Edwin) Kenneth (George); Chairman, Photon plc, 1986–89, retired; Chief Scientific Officer, Civil Service Department, 1970–76; *b* 27 Dec. 1916; *s* of late Edwin and Jessie Marion James; *m* 1941, Dorothy Margaret Pratt (*d* 1998); one *d*. *Educ:* Latymer Upper Sch.; Northern Polytechnic. BSc London; FRSC; FOR. Joined War Office, 1938; Chem. Defence Exper. Stn, 1942; Aust. Field Exper. Stn, 1944–46; Operational Research Gp, US Army, Md, 1950–54; Dir, Biol and Chem. Defence, WO, 1961; Army (later Defence) Op. Res. Estab., Byfleet, 1965; HM Treasury (later Civil Service Dept), 1968. Chm., PAG Ltd, 1984–87 (Dir, 1977–84). Silver Medal, Op. Res. Soc., 1979. *Recreation:* writing. *Address:* 5 Watersmeet Road, East Harnham, Salisbury, Wilts SP2 8JH. *T:* (01722) 334099. *Club:* Athenæum.

JAMES, Eleanor Mary; Lecturer in Mathematics, University College of Wales, Aberystwyth, 1957–92; *b* 31 Aug. 1935; *d* of Morris and Violet Mary Jones; *m* 1958, David Bryan James. *Educ:* Ardwyn Grammar Sch., Aberystwyth; University College of Wales, Aberystwyth (BSc 1955; PhD 1972). Member: Welsh Consumer Council, 1981–90; CECG, 1982–84; Consumer Develt Sub-Cttee, Nat. Consumer Council, 1983–85; Layfield Cttee of Enquiry, Local Govt Finance, 1974–76; Audit Commn for Local Authorities and NHS, 1988–91; Dyfed-Powys Police Authy, 1994–99. Member: N Wales Area Cttee, NACAB (formerly CAB), 1987–90, 1991–99 (Chm., Aberystwyth, 1988–93, 1998–2000); POUNC, 1991–97 (Chm., Council for Wales, 1991–97); Radioactive Waste Management Adv. Cttee, 1991–94; Wkg Pty, Churches' Enquiry into Unemployment and Future of Work, 1995–97; Chm., Wales Rural Forum, 1994–97; Campaign for the Protection of Rural Wales: Chm., Ceredigion Br., 1992–2000; Mem., Exec. Cttee, 1996–; Treas., 2001–. National Federation of Women's Institutes: Mem., Envmt and Public Affairs Sub-Cttee, 1981–84; Vice Chm., Fedn of Wales Sub-Cttee, 1991–94; Chm., Dyfed Ceredigion Fedn of WIs, 1993–96 (Treas., 1989–92). University College of Wales: Mem. Council, 1982–86; Mem., Court of Governors, 1982–; Treas., Old Students' Assoc., 1975–. *Publication:* (with T. V. Davies) Nonlinear Differential Equations, 1966. *Recreations:* walking, swimming, the WI. *Address:* Dolhuan, Llandre, Bowstreet, Ceredigion SY24 5AB. *T:* (01970) 828362.

JAMES, Rev. Canon Eric Arthur; an Extra Chaplain to HM the Queen, since 1995 (Chaplain, 1984–95); Hon. Director, Christian Action, 1990–96 (Director, 1979–90); *b* 14 April 1925; *s* of John Morgan James and Alice Amelia James. *Educ:* Dagenham County

High School; King's Coll. London (MA, BD; FKC 1986). Asst Curate, St Stephen with St John, Westminster, 1951–55; Chaplain Trinity Coll., Cambridge, 1955–59; Select Preacher to Univ. of Cambridge, 1959–60; Vicar of St George, Camberwell and Warden of Trinity College Mission, 1959–64; Director of Parish and People, 1964–69; Proctor in Convocation, 1964–72; Canon Precentor of Southwark Cathedral, 1964–73; Canon Residentiary and Missioner, Diocese of St Albans, 1973–83; Hon. Canon, 1983–90; Canon Emeritus, 1990. Preacher to Gray's Inn, 1978–97; Select Preacher to Univ. of Oxford, 1991–92. Commissary to Bishop of Kimberley, 1965–67, to Archbishop of Melanesia, 1969–93. Examining Chaplain to Bishop of St Albans, 1973–83, to Bishop of Truro, 1983–93. Hon. Bencher Gray's Inn, 1997. FRSA 1992. DD Lambeth, 1993. *Publications:* The Double Cure, 1957, 2nd edn 1980; Odd Man Out, 1962; (ed) Spirituality for Today, 1968; (ed) Stewards of the Mysteries of God, 1979; A Life of Bishop John A. T. Robinson: Scholar, Pastor, Prophet, 1987; (ed) God's Truth, 1988; Judge Not: a selection of sermons preached in Gray's Inn Chapel, 1989; Collected Thoughts: fifty scripts for BBC's Thought for The Day, 1990; (ed) A Last Eccentric: a symposium concerning the Rev. Canon F. A. Simpson: historian, preacher and eccentric, 1991; Word Over All: forty sermons 1985–1991, 1992; The Voice Said, Cry: forty sermons 1990–1993, 1994; A Time to Speak: forty sermons 1993–95, 1997; In Season, Out of Season: sermons 1996–97, 1999. *Address:* 11 Denny Crescent, SE11 4UY. *T:* (020) 7582 3068. *Clubs:* Reform, Royal Commonwealth Society.

JAMES, Evan Maitland; *b* 14 Jan. 1911; *er s* of late A. G. James, CBE, and late Helen James (*née* Maitland); *m* 1st, 1939, Joan Goodnow (*d* 1989), *d* of late Hon. J. V. A. MacMurray, State Dept, Washington, DC; one *s* two *d*; 2nd, 1992, Miriam Beatriz Porter, *d* of late George and Elizabeth Wansbrough. *Educ:* Durnford; Eton (Oppidan Scholar); Trinity Coll., Oxford (MA). Served War of 1939–45: War Reserve Police (Metropolitan), 1939; BBC Overseas (Propaganda Research) Dept, 1940–41; Ordinary Seaman/Lieut, RNVR, 1941–46. Clerk of the Merchant Taylors' Company, 1947–62; Steward of Christ Church, Oxford, 1962–78. *Address:* Upwood Park, Besselsleigh, Abingdon, Oxon OX13 5QE. *T:* (01865) 390535. *Club:* Travellers.

JAMES, Geraint; *see* James, D. G.

JAMES, Geraldine; actress; *b* 6 July 1950; *d* of Gerald Trevor Thomas and Annabella Doogan Thomas; adopted stage name, Geraldine James, 1972; *m* 1986, Joseph Sebastian Blatchley; one *d*. *Educ:* Downe House, Newbury; Drama Centre London Ltd. *Stage:* repertory, Chester, 1972–74, Exeter, 1974–75, Coventry, 1975; Passion of Dracula, Queen's, 1978; The White Devil, Oxford, 1981; Turning Over, Bush, 1984; When I was a Girl I used to Scream and Shout, Whitehall, 1987; Cymbeline, National, 1988; Merchant of Venice, Phoenix, 1989, NY (Drama Desk Best Actress Award), 1990; Death and the Maiden, Duke of York's, 1992; Lysistrata, Old Vic and Wyndham's, 1993; Hedda Gabler, Royal Exchange, Manchester, 1993; Give Me Your Answer Do!, Hampstead, 1998; Faith Healer, Almeida, 2001; *TV series:* The History Man, 1980; Jewel in the Crown, 1984; Blott on the Landscape, 1985; Echoes, 1988; Stanley and the Women, 1991; Band of Gold, 1994, 1995; Kavanagh QC, 1994, 1995, 1997, 1998; Over Here, 1995; Drover's Gold, 1996; Gold, 1997; Seesaw, 1998; The Sins, 2000; *TV films:* Dummy (Best Actress, BPG), 1977; Ex, Losing Track, 1991; A Doll's House, 1992; The Healer, 1994; Doggin' Around, 1994; My Life as a Fairy Tale, 2001; *films:* Sweet William, 1978; Night Cruiser, 1978; Gandhi, 1981; The Storm, 1985; Wolves of Willoughby Chase, 1988; The Tall Guy, 1989; She's Been Away, 1989 (Best actress, Venice Film Festival, 1989); If Looks Could Kill, 1990; The Bridge, 1990; Prince of Shadows, 1991; No Worries Australia, 1993; Words on the Window Pane, 1994; Moll Flanders, 1995; The Man Who Knew Too Little, 1998; All Forgotten, The Testimony of Taliesin Jones, The Luzhin Defence, 2000. *Recreation:* music. *Address:* c/o Julian Belfrage Associates, 46 Albemarle Street, W1X 4PP; c/o Robert Duva Associates, 200 W 57th Street, Suite 1407, New York, NY 10019, USA.

JAMES, Rt Rev. Graham Richard; *see* Norwich, Bishop of.

JAMES, Howell Malcolm Plowden, CBE 1997; Director, Brown, Lloyd, James Ltd, since 1997; *b* 13 March 1954; *s* of late T. J. and Virginia James. *Educ:* Mill Hill Sch., London. Head of Promotions, Capital Radio, 1978–82; Organiser, Help a London Child Charity, 1979–82; Head of Press and Publicity, TV-am, 1982–85; Special Adviser: Cabinet Office, 1985; Dept of Employment, 1985–87; DTI, 1987; Dir of Corporate Affairs, BBC, 1987–92; Dir of Corporate and Govt Affairs, Cable and Wireless, 1992–94; Pol Sec. to Prime Minister, 1994–97. Dir, Broadcast Audience Res. Bd, 1987–92. Dir, English Nat. Ballet Sch., 1990–96; Gov., George Eliot Sch., 1989–92; Mem., Ct of Govs, Mill Hill Sch., 1996–. Trustee, Queen Elizabeth's Foundn for Disabled People Develt Trust, 1992–96. *Recreations:* theatre, movies, food. *Address:* 25 Lower Belgrave Street, SW1W 0NR. *T:* (020) 7591 9610. *Club:* Garrick.

JAMES, Prof. Ioan Mackenzie, FRS 1968; MA, DPhil; Savilian Professor of Geometry, Oxford University, 1970–95, Professor Emeritus, since 1995; Fellow of New College, Oxford, 1970–95, Emeritus Fellow, 1995, Leverhulme Emeritus Fellow, 1996–98, Hon. Fellow, 1999; Editor, Topology, since 1962; *b* 23 May 1928; *o s* of Reginald Douglas and Jessie Agnes James; *m* 1961, Rosemary Gordon Stewart, *qv*; no *c*. *Educ:* St Paul's Sch. (Foundn Schol.); Queen's Coll., Oxford (Open Schol.). Commonwealth Fund Fellow, Princeton, Berkeley and Inst. for Advanced Study, 1954–55; Tapp Res. Fellow, Gonville and Caius Coll., Cambridge, 1956; Reader in Pure Mathematics, Oxford, 1957–69, and Senior Research Fellow, St John's Coll., 1959–69, Hon. Fellow, 1988. Hon. Prof., Univ. of Wales, 1989; Vis. Prof., Univ. of Paris, 1995–97. London Mathematical Society: Treasurer, 1969–79; Pres., 1985–87; Whitehead Prize and Lectr, 1978. Mem. Council, Royal Soc., 1982–83. Gov., St Paul's Schs, 1970–99. Hon. DSc Aberdeen, 1993. *Publications:* The Mathematical Works of J. H. C. Whitehead, 1963; The Topology of Stiefel Manifolds, 1976; Topological Topics, 1983; General Topology and Homotopy Theory, 1984; Aspects of Topology, 1984; Topological and Uniform Spaces, 1987; Fibrewise Topology, 1988; Introduction to Uniform Spaces, 1990; Handbook of Algebraic Topology, 1995; Fibrewise Homotopy Theory, 1998; Topologies and Uniformities, 1999; History of Topology, 1999; papers in mathematical and historical jls. *Address:* Mathematical Institute, 24–29 St Giles, Oxford OX1 3LB. *T:* (01865) 273541.

JAMES, Sir Jeffrey (Russell), KBE 2001; CMG 1994; HM Diplomatic Service, retired; *b* 13 Aug. 1944; *s* of Lewis Charles James and Ruth James; *m* 1965, Mary Longden; two *d*. *Educ:* Whitgift Sch.; Keele Univ. (BA Hons Internat. Relations). FCO 1967; served Tehran and Kabul; Dep. Political Advr, BMG Berlin, 1978; FCO 1982; Counsellor on loan to Cabinet Office, 1984; Counsellor and Head of Chancery, Pretoria/Cape Town, 1986; Counsellor (Economic and Commercial), New Delhi, 1988; Head, Edinburgh European Council Unit, FCO, 1992; Chargé d'Affaires, Tehran, 1993; High Comr, Nairobi, 1997–2001. *Recreations:* bird watching, golf, tennis, hill walking. *Address:* 7 Rockfield Close, Oxted, Surrey RH8 0DN. *Clubs:* Royal Commonwealth Society; Tandridge Golf.

JAMES, John A.; *see* Angell-James.

JAMES, John Christopher Urmston; Secretary, Lawn Tennis Association, since 1981 (Assistant Secretary, 1973–81); *b* 22 June 1937; *s* of John Urmston James and Ellen Irene James; *m* 1st, 1959, Gillian Mary Davies (marr. diss. 1982); two *s*; 2nd, 1982, Patricia Mary, *d* of late Arthur Leslie Walter White. *Educ:* St Michael's, Llanelli; Hereford Cathedral Sch. Harrods, 1954; Jaeger, 1961; Pringle, 1972. MInstD. *Recreations:* tennis, Rugby football, walking, architecture, the countryside, gardening, theatre. *Address:* c/o Lawn Tennis Association, The Queen's Club, West Kensington, W14 9EG. *T:* (020) 7381 7000. *Clubs:* Queen's, Questors, London Welsh, International of GB; West Hants (Bournemouth).

JAMES, John Douglas, OBE 1996; conservationist; Chief Executive, Woodland Trust, 1992–97; *b* 28 July 1949; *s* of late William Antony James, ERD, MA and of Agnes Winifred James (*née* Mitchell); *m* 1971, Margaret Patricia Manton. *Educ:* Spalding Grammar School; Dip. in Co. Direction, Inst. of Dirs, 1994; MBA Nottingham Univ. 1999. Articled pupil, William H. Brown & Son, 1967–68; Marketing Dept, Geest Industries, 1969–71; Marketing Dept, John Player & Sons, 1971–77; Nat. Develt Officer, 1977, (first) Director, 1980, Exec. Dir, 1985, Woodland Trust. Forestry Comr, 1998–. Co-owner, Focus Gall., Nottingham, 1995–. Nottingham Roosevelt Scholar, 1975 (Trustee, Nottingham Roosevelt Scholarship, 1997–); Churchill Fellow, 1980. Founder Mem., S Lincs Nature Reserves Ltd, 1968; Mem., Inst. of Charity Fundraising Managers. MInstD. FRSA 1995. *Publications:* articles in countryside and gardening jls. *Recreation:* woodland walks. *Address:* c/o Focus Gallery, 108 Derby Road, Nottingham NG1 5FB.

JAMES, John Henry; Chief Executive, Kensington & Chelsea and Westminster Health Authority (formerly Commissioning Agency), since 1992; *b* 19 July 1944; step *s* of George Arthur James and *s* of Doris May James; *m* 3rd, 1987, Anita Mary Stockton, *d* of Brian Scarth, QPM and Irene Scarth. *Educ:* Ludlow Grammar Sch.; Keble Coll., Oxford (BA Mod. Hist. 1965; postgrad. dip. in Econ. and Pol. Sci. 1966). AHSM 1991 (LHSM 1989). Entered Home Civil Service 1966; Asst Principal, Min. of Pensions and Nat. Insurance; Private Sec. to First Perm. Sec., 1969–71, Principal, 1971–74, DHSS; seconded to HM Treasury, 1974–76; Principal, 1976–78, Asst Sec., 1978–86, Under Sec., 1986–91, DHSS, later Dept of Health; Dir of Health Authority Finance, NHS Management Bd, 1986–89; General Manager: Harrow DHA, 1990–92; Parkside DHA, 1991–93. Co-ordinator, London Cardiac Specialty Rev., 1993. Non-Exec. Dir, Laing Homes Ltd, 1987–89. Member: Adv. Council, King's Fund Inst., 1990–93; NHS Res. Task Force, 1994; NHS Central R&D Council, 1994–99; MRC Health Services and Public Health Res. Bd, 1995–99; NHS Adv. Cttee on Resource Allocation, 1997–99; Accessible Transport Commn for London, 1998–; Nat. Strategic Gp tackling Racial Harassment in NHS, 1999–. FRSA 1994. *Publications:* Transforming the NHS, 1994; contributed: Oxford Textbook of Public Health, 1985, 2nd edn 1991; Health Care UK, 1993; Rationing of Health and Social Care, 1993; Information Management in Health Services, 1994; articles in jls. *Recreations:* chess, cricket, travel, food and wine, collecting edible fungi. *Address:* 1 Moreton Villas, Knoll Road, SW18 2DF.

JAMES, Sir John (Nigel Courtenay), KCVO 1997; CBE 1990; FRICS; Secretary and Keeper of the Records, Duchy of Cornwall, 1993–97; Trustee of the Grosvenor Estate, 1971–2000; a Crown Estate Commissioner, 1984–99; *b* 31 March 1935; *s* of Frank Courtenay James and Beryl May Wilford Burden; *m* 1961, Elizabeth Jane St Clair-Ford; one *s* one *d*. *Educ:* Sherborne Sch., Dorset. Chief Agent and Estate Surveyor, Grosvenor Estate, 1968–71. Director: Sun Alliance & London Insurance Gp, 1972–93 (a Vice-Chm., 1988–93); Woolwich Equitable Building Soc., 1982–89; Williams & Glyn's Bank plc, 1983–85; Royal Bank of Scotland, 1985–93. Member: Commn for the New Towns, 1978–86; Cttee of Management, RNLI, 1980– (Dep. Chm., 1999–); Council, Architectural Heritage Fund, 1983–2001 (Chm., 1999–2001); Prince of Wales' Council, 1984–97. Pres., RICS, 1980–81. Trustee, Henry Smith's Charity, 1991–. Gov., Sherborne Sch., 1990–. *Recreation:* sailing. *Club:* Brooks's.

JAMES, Jonathan Elwyn Rayner; QC 1988; a Recorder, since 1998; *b* 26 July 1950; *s* of Basil James, *qv*; *m* 1981, Anne Henshaw (*née* McRae); one *s*. *Educ:* King's College Sch., Wimbledon; Christ's Coll., Cambridge (MA, LLM); Brussels Univ. (Lic. Spécial en Droit Européen 1973). Called to Bar, Lincoln's Inn (Hardwicke Schol.), 1971, Bencher, 1994. Asst Recorder, 1994–98. Mem. Editl Bd, Entertainment Law Rev., 1990–. *Publications:* (co-ed) EEC Anti-Trust Law, 1975; (co-ed) Copinger and Skone James on Copyright, 12th edn 1980–14th edn 1998; (jt consulting editor) Encyclopaedia of Forms and Precedents, Vol. 15 (Entertainment), 1989. *Recreations:* DIY, opera, 007, squash, France. *Address:* 5 New Square, Lincoln's Inn, WC2A 3RJ. *T:* (020) 7404 0404.

JAMES, Sir Kenneth; *see* James, Sir C. M.

JAMES, Kenneth; *see* James, E. K. G.

JAMES, Lawrence Edwin; author, since 1985; *b* 26 May 1943; *s* of Arthur and Laura James; *m* 1967, Mary Charlotte Williams; two *s*. *Educ:* Weston-super-Mare GS; York Univ. (BA 1966); Merton Coll., Oxford (MLitt 1979). Schoolmaster: Merchant Taylors' Sch., Northwood, 1969–76; Sedbergh Sch., Cumbria, 1976–85. *Publications:* Crimea: the war with Russia in contemporary photographs, 1981; The Savage Wars: the British conquest of Africa 1870–1920, 1985; Mutiny, 1987; Imperial Rearguard: wars of empire 1919–1985, 1988; The Golden Warrior: the life and legend of Lawrence of Arabia, 1990, 2nd edn 1996; The Iron Duke: a military biography of the Duke of Wellington, 1992; Imperial Warrior: the life and times of Field-Marshal Viscount Allenby, 1993; The Rise and Fall of the British Empire, 1994, 2nd edn 1997; Raj: the making and unmaking of British India, 1997; Warrior Race: the British experience of war, 2001. *Recreations:* bird watching, maintenance of Newfoundland dog. *Address:* c/o Little, Brown, Brettenham House, Lancaster Gate, WC2E 7EN. *Club:* New (Edinburgh).

JAMES, Linda Elizabeth Blake; *see* Sullivan, L. E.

JAMES, Lionel Frederic Edward, CBE 1977 (MBE (mil.) 1944); Comptroller, Forces Help Society and Lord Roberts Workshops, 1970–82; *b* 22 Feb. 1912; *s* of late Frederic James, Westmount, Exeter; *m* 1st, 1933, Harriet French-Harley (decd); one *s* one *d*; 2nd, 1992, Aurea Maidment. *Educ:* Royal Grammar Sch., Worcester. Investment Co., 1933–39. Served War with Royal Engineers, 1939–46: BEF; Planning Staff, Sicilian Invasion; N Africa, Sicily, Greece and Italy (Major). Dep. Dir, Overseas Service, Forces Help Soc., 1946, Dir, 1948; Asst Sec. of Society, 1953, Company Sec., 1963. *Recreation:* vetting and restoration of art and antiques.

JAMES, Michael; *see* James, R. M. and Jayston, M.

JAMES, Michael Francis; a District Judge (Magistrates' Courts) (formerly Stipendiary Magistrate), West Midlands, since 1991; *b* 30 Oct. 1933; *s* of Francis and Eveline James; *m* 1958, Lois Joy Elcock. *Educ:* King Charles I Grammar Sch., Kidderminster. Admitted solicitor, 1956. National Service: commnd RAF, 1957; qualified as air navigator, 1958. Partner, Ivens Morton & Greville-Smith (later Morton Fisher), 1959–86; Sen. Partner, 1986–91. Vis. Fellow, UWE, 1996–99. *Recreations:* books, wine, walking, music. *Address:* Victoria Law Courts, Corporation Street, Birmingham B4 6QJ. *T:* (0121) 212 6600.

JAMES, Michael Leonard, (Michael Hartland); writer and broadcaster, since 1983; Chairman, Wade Hartland Films Ltd, 1991–2000; *b* 7 Feb. 1941; *s* of late Leonard and of Marjorie James, Portreath, Cornwall; *m* 1975, Jill Elizabeth (marr. diss. 1992), *d* of late George Tarján, OBE and Etelka Tarján, formerly of Budapest; two *d*. *Educ:* Latymer Upper Sch.; Christ's Coll., Cambridge. Entered British govt service, 1963; Private Sec. to Rt Hon. Jennie Lee, MP, Minister for the Arts, 1966–68; Principal, DES, 1968–71; Planning Unit of Rt Hon. Margaret Thatcher, MP, Sec. of State for Educn and Science, 1971–73; Asst Sec., 1973; DCSO 1974; Advr to OECD, Paris, and UK Governor, IIMT, Milan, 1973–75; specialist duties, 1975–78; Director, IAEA, Vienna, 1978–83; Advr on Internat. Relations, CEC, Brussels, 1983–85. Member: CSSB, 1983–93; Immigration Appeal Tribunal, 1987–; Professional Conduct Cttee, GMC, 2000–. Governor: East Devon Coll. of Further Educn, Tiverton, 1985–92; Colyton Grammar Sch., 1985–90; Chm. of Governors, Sidmouth Community Coll., 1998– (Gov.,1988–). Feature writer and book reviewer for The Times (thriller critic, 1989–90; travel correspondent, 1993–), Daily Telegraph (thriller critic, 1993–), Sunday Times and Guardian, 1986–. Television and radio include: Sonja's Report (ITV), 1990; Masterspy, interviews with Oleg Gordievsky (BBC Radio 4), 1991. FRSA 1982. Hon. Fellow, Univ. of Exeter, 1985. *Publications: as M. L. James:* (jtly) Internationalization to Prevent the Spread of Nuclear Weapons, 1980; articles on internat. relations and nuclear energy; *as Michael Hartland:* Down Among the Dead Men, 1983; Seven Steps to Treason, 1985 (SW Arts Lit. Award; dramatized for BBC Radio 4, 1990); The Third Betrayal, 1986; Frontier of Fear, 1989; The Year of the Scorpion, 1991; *as Ruth Carrington:* Dead Fish, 1998. *Address:* Cotte Barton, Branscombe, Devon EX12 3BH. *Clubs:* Athenæum, PEN, Detection; Honiton Working Men's (Devon).

JAMES, Prof. Michael Norman George, DPhil, FRS 1989; FRS(Can) 1985; Professor of Biochemistry, University of Alberta, since 1978, University Professor of Biochemistry, since 1993; *b* 16 May 1940; *s* of Claud Stewart Murray James and Mimosa Ruth Harriet James; *m* 1961, Patricia McCarthy; one *s* one *d*; *m* 1977, Anita Sielecki. *Educ:* Univ. of Manitoba (BSc, MSc); Linacre Coll., Oxford (DPhil). Asst Prof., Associate Prof., Univ. of Alberta, 1968–78. Mem., MRC of Canada Group in Protein Structure and Function, 1974. *Publications:* contribs to learned jls. *Address:* Department of Biochemistry, University of Alberta, Edmonton, AB T6G 2H7, Canada. *T:* (403) 4924550.

JAMES, Dame Naomi (Christine), DBE 1979; author and yachtswoman; *b* 2 March 1949; *d* of Charles Robert Power and Joan Power; *m* 1st, 1976, Robert Alan James (*d* 1983); one *d*; 2nd, 1990, Eric G. Haythorne (marr. diss.), *o s* of G. V. Haythorne, Ottawa, Canada. *Educ:* Rotorua Girls' High Sch., NZ; UC, Cork (BA Philosophy and Eng. Lit. 1997; MA Philosophy 1999). Hair stylist, 1966–71; language teacher, 1972–74; yacht charter crew, 1975–77. Sailed single handed round the world via the three great Capes, incl. first woman solo round Cape Horn, on 53 ft yacht, Express Crusader, Sept. 1977–June 1978; sailed in 1980 Observer Transatlantic Race, winning Ladies Prize and achieving women's record for single-handed Atlantic crossing, on 53 ft yacht Kriter Lady; won 1982 Round Britain Race with Rob James, on multihull Colt Cars GB. Formerly: Trustee, Nat. Maritime Museum; Council Mem., Winston Churchill Meml Trust. Royal Yacht Sqdn Chichester Trophy, 1978; NZ Yachtsman of the Year, 1978. *Publications:* Woman Alone, 1978; At One with the Sea, 1979; At Sea on Land, 1981; Courage at Sea, 1987. *Recreations:* riding, literature, philosophy. *Address:* Shore Cottage, Currabinny, Carrigaline, Co. Cork, Ireland. *Clubs:* Royal Dart Yacht (Dartmouth); Royal Lymington Yacht (Lymington); Royal Western Yacht (Plymouth).

JAMES, Prof. Oliver Francis Wintour, FRCP; Professor of Geriatric Medicine, since 1985, and Head, School of Clinical Medical Sciences, since 1994, University of Newcastle upon Tyne; Consultant Physician, Freeman Hospital, Newcastle, since 1977; *b* 23 Sept. 1943; *s* of Baron James of Rusholme and of Cordelia Mary (*née* Wintour); *m* 1965, Rosanna Foster; one *s* one *d*. *Educ:* Winchester; Balliol Coll., Oxford (MA 1964; BM BCh 1967); Middlesex Hosp. Med. Sch. Registrar and Fellow, Royal Free Hosp., 1971–74; University of Newcastle upon Tyne: First Asst in Medicine, 1974–75; Reader in Medicine (Geriatrics), 1975–85. Vis. Prof., Univs of Hong Kong, Indianapolis and St Louis. Chairman: Liver Section, EC Concerted Action on Cellular Aging, 1982–86; Jt Cttee for Higher Med. Trng, SAC in Geriatrics, 1992–95. Pres., Brit. Assoc. for Study of Liver, 1992–94. Royal College of Physicians: Censor, 1994–96; Sen. Vice Pres., 1997–. Founder FMedSci 1998. *Publications:* numerous papers and chapters on aspects of liver disease, geriatric medicine and training of physicians. *Recreations:* vegetable growing, wine, golf. *Address:* Sleightholmedale, Kirbymoorside, York YO6 6JG.

JAMES, P. D.; *see* Baroness James of Holland Park.

JAMES, Patrick Leonard, FRCS, FDS RCS; Hon. Consulting Oral and Maxillo-facial Surgeon: Royal London (formerly London) Hospital, Whitechapel (Senior Consultant Surgeon, 1963–91); North East Thames Regional Hospital Board Hospitals (Consultant Surgeon, 1963–91); Recognized Teacher in Oral Surgery, London University, since 1965; *b* 7 Jan. 1926; *s* of late John Vincent James and Priscilla Elsie James; *m* 1951, Jean Margaret, *er d* of Leslie and Ruth Hatcher; one *s* two *d*. *Educ:* King's Coll., London; London Hosp. FDSRCS 1958; FRCS 1985 (MRCS 1956); LRCP 1956. Served RAF, Flt Lieut, ME Comd, 1949–51. Sen. Registrar, Queen Victoria Hosp., E Grinstead, 1959–63; Hon. Consulting Oral and Maxillo-facial Surgeon: to London Hosp., Honey Lane Hosp., Waltham Abbey, Herts and Essex Hosp., Bishop's Stortford (Consultant Surgeon, 1963); to King George Hosp. (Consultant Surgeon, 1967); St Margaret's Hosp., Epping (Consultant Surgeon, 1966); Black Notley Hosp. (Consultant Surgeon, 1969); Hon. Civil Consultant (Oral and Maxillo-facial Surgery), RAF, 1989 (Civil Consultant in Oral Surgery, 1979–89). Exchange Fellow, Henry Ford Hosp., Detroit, Mich., 1962; Hunterian Prof., RCS, 1970–71. Member: Academic Bd, London Hosp. Med. Coll., 1968–71; Adv. Cttee in Plastic Surgery, NE Met. Reg. Hosp. Bd, 1969–77; NE Thames Reg. Manpower Cttee, 1975–78. Fellow: BAOS, 1963– (Mem. Council, 1971–74); Internat. Assoc. of Oral Surgs (BAOS Rep. on Council, 1974–78); Chm., Sci. Session, 6th Internat. Congress of Oral Surgs, Sydney, 1977; Associate Mem., Brit. Assoc. of Plastic Surgs, 1958–77. FRSocMed; Mem., Acad. of Expert Witnesses. Member: Council, Chelsea Clin. Soc; Bd of Governors, Eastman Hosp., 1983–84. Liveryman, Soc. of Apothecaries, 1969; Freeman, City of London, 1978. *Publications:* (chapter in Oral Surgery) Malignancies in Odontogenic Cysts, 1967; (chapter in Oral Surgery) Correction of Apertognathia with Osteotomies and Bone Graft, 1970; (chapter in Oral Surgery, vol. 7) Surgical Treatment of Mandibular Joint Disorders, 1978; numerous articles on surgical treatment of mandibular joint disorders, surgery of salivary glands and maxillo facial surgery in med. and surg. jls. *Recreations:* shooting, fishing, sailing (Cdre, United Hosps Sailing Club, 1968–75), ski-ing. *Address:* Meesden Hall, Meesden, Buntingford, Herts SG9 0AZ; 152 Harley Street, W1N 1HH. *T:* (020) 7935 4444. *Club:* Boodle's.

JAMES, Peter John; Principal, London Academy of Music and Dramatic Art, since 1994; *b* 27 July 1940; *s* of Arthur Leonard James and Gladys (*née* King); *m* 1st, 1964, Anthea Olive (marr. diss. 1972); one *d*; one *s* by Bernadette McKenna; 2nd, 1999, Alexandra Paisley. *Educ:* Birmingham Univ. (BA Hons English, Philosophy); Bristol Univ. (Postgrad. Cert. Drama). Founder Dir, Liverpool Everyman Theatre, 1964–71; Associate Dir, NT at Young Vic, 1971–73; Director: Crucible Theatre, Sheffield, 1974–81; Lyric Theatre, Hammersmith, 1981–94 (numerous first productions; Lyric Theatre Awards, 1986, 1992). Dir of plays, UK and overseas, incl. Russia. Former cttee memberships incl. Arts Council, European Theatre Convention, Internat. Theatre Inst. (Award for Excellence, 1990). *Recreations:* cooking, watching boxing and football matches. *Address:* LAMDA, Tower House, 226 Cromwell Road, SW5 0SR. *T:* (020) 7373 3465.

JAMES, Philip; *see* James, W. P. T.

JAMES, Richard Austin, CB 1980; MC 1945; Receiver for Metropolitan Police District, 1977–80; *b* 26 May 1920; *s* of late Thomas Morris James, Headmaster of Sutton Valence Sch., and Hilda Joan James; *m* 1948, Joan Boorer; two *s* one *d*. *Educ:* Clifton Coll.; Emmanuel Coll., Cambridge. British American Tobacco Co., 1938; Royal Engrs, 1939–41; Queen's Own Royal W Kent Regt, 1941–46; Home Office, 1948; Private Sec. to Chancellor of Duchy of Lancaster, 1960; Asst Sec., 1961; Dep. Receiver for Metropolitan Police District, 1970–73; Asst Under-Sec. of State, Police Dept, Home Office, 1974–76; Dep. Under-Sec. of State, 1980. Vice-Pres., Distressed Gentlefolk's Aid Assoc., 1992–96 (Gen. Sec., 1981–82; Mem., Council of Mgt, 1982–88); Mem., Cttee of Management, Sussex Housing Assoc. for the Aged, 1985–88. Pres., Brunswick Boys Club Trust, Fulham, 1990–95. Freeman, City of London, 1980. *Recreation:* cricket. *Address:* 5 Gadge Close, Thame, Oxfordshire OX9 2BD. *T:* (01844) 261776. *Clubs:* Athenæum, MCC.

JAMES, (Robert) Michael; UK Trade Adviser, International Tropical Timber Organisation, 1998–2000; *b* 2 Oct. 1934; *s* of late Rev. B. V. James and Mrs D. M. James; *m* 1959, Sarah Helen (*née* Bell); two *s* one *d*. *Educ:* St John's, Leatherhead; Trinity Coll., Cambridge (BA Hons History). Schoolmaster: Harrow Sch., 1958–60; Cranleigh Sch., 1960–62; joined CRO, 1962; 3rd Sec., Wellington, NZ, 1963–65; 1st Sec., Colombo, Sri Lanka, 1966–69; FCO, 1969–71; Dep. High Comr and Head of Chancery, Georgetown, Guyana, 1971–73; Econ. Sec., Ankara, Turkey, 1974–76; FCO, 1976–80; Commercial Counsellor and Deputy High Commissioner: Accra, 1980–83; Singapore, 1984–87; Dep. High Comr, Bridgetown, Barbados, 1987–90. Exec., Timber Trade Fedn, 1990–98; Dir, Forests Forever Campaign, 1990–98. *Recreations:* sport (cricket Blue, 1956–58), drawing, travel. *Address:* 17 North Grove, Highgate, N6 4SH. *T:* (020) 8245 3763. *Clubs:* MCC; Hawks (Cambridge); Hunstanton Golf, Highgate Golf.

JAMES, Rosemary Gordon; *see* Stewart, R. G.

JAMES, Roy Lewis, CBE 1998; External Professor, University of Glamorgan, since 1997; Visiting Research Fellow, University of Wales Institute, Cardiff, since 2000; *b* 9 Feb. 1937; *s* of David John and Eleanor James; *m* 1962, Mary Williams; one *d*. *Educ:* Llandysul Grammar School; University College of Wales, Aberystwyth (BSc Hons, DipEd). Asst Master, Strode's Grammar Sch., Egham, 1959–60; Head of Maths Dept, Lampeter Comp. Sch., 1960–62; Head of Maths Dept, Cyfarthfa Castle Sch., Merthyr Tydfil, 1962–70; HM Inspector of Schools, 1970–84, seconded as Sec., Schs Council Cttee for Wales, 1975–77; Staff Inspector, 1984–90; Chief Inspector of Schs (Wales), Welsh Office, 1990–92; HM Chief Inspector of Schs in Wales, 1992–97. Chairman: Techniquest (Wales) Educn Adv. Gp, 1997–; Awards Panel Wales (Teaching Awards), 2000–. Trustee, Teaching Awards Trust, 2000–. Admitted to Gorsedd of Bards, Nat. Eisteddfod of Wales, 1997. *Recreations:* travel, walking, reading, snooker. *Address:* Llys-Coed, 36 North Rise, Llanishen, Cardiff CF14 0RN.

JAMES, Prof. Dame Sheila (Patricia Violet); *see* Sherlock, Prof. Dame S. P. V.

JAMES, Sir Stanislaus (Anthony), GCSL 1992; GCMG 1992 (CMG 1990); OBE 1985; Governor General of Saint Lucia, West Indies, 1988–96; *b* 13 Nov. 1919; *s* of Raymond and Theresa James; *m* 1952, Lucille MacDonald; two *s* two *d*. *Educ:* St Mary's Coll., St Lucia; Govt Training Coll., Trinidad; Univ. of Wales, Swansea; Carleton Univ., Ottawa. Educn Dept, St Lucia, 1944–46; Head, Public Relations and Social Welfare Dept, Probation Officer, 1948–50; Chief Clerk, Govt Office, 1954–56; PR and Social Welfare Officer, 1956–65; Perm. Sec., Min. of Trade, Industry, Agric. and Tourism, Min. of Housing, Community, Social Affairs and Labour, Min. of Educn and Health, 1965–74; National Co-ordinator: for Non-Govt Orgns, 1974–88; for Emergency Services, 1979–88. *Recreation:* horticulture. *Address:* Sunny Acres, Choc, Castries, St Lucia, West Indies. *T:* 4519562.

JAMES, Stanley Francis; Head of Statistics Division 1, Department of Trade and Industry, 1981–84; *b* 12 Feb. 1927; *s* of H. F. James; unmarried. *Educ:* Sutton County Sch.; Trinity Coll., Cambridge. Maths Tripos Pt II; Dip. Math. Statistics. Research Lectr, Econs Dept, Nottingham Univ., 1951; Statistician, Bd of Inland Revenue, 1956; Chief Statistician: Bd of Inland Revenue, 1966; Central Statistical Office, 1968; Asst Dir, Central Statistical Office, 1970–72; Dir, Stats Div., Bd of Inland Revenue, 1972–77; Head, Econs and Stats Div. 6, Depts of Industry and Trade, 1977–81. Hon. Treasurer, Royal Statistical Soc., 1978–83. *Recreations:* travel, theatre, gardening. *Address:* 23 Hayward Road, Oxford OX2 8LN. *Club:* Royal Automobile.

JAMES, Stephen Lawrence; Consultant, Simmons & Simmons, Solicitors, since 1992 (Partner, 1961; Senior Partner, 1980–92); *b* 19 Oct. 1930; *s* of Walter Amyas James and Cecile Juliet (*née* Hillman); *m* 1st, 1955, Patricia Eleanor Favell James (marr. diss. 1986); two *s* two *d*; 2nd, 1998, Monique Whittome (*née* Borda). *Educ:* Clifton Coll.; St Catharine's Coll., Cambridge (BA History and Law). Mem., Gray's Inn, 1953, Bar finals, 1956; admitted Solicitor: England and Wales, 1959; Hong Kong, 1980. Director: Horace Clarkson PLC (formerly H. Clarkson (Holdings) PLC), 1975–; Shipping Industrial Holdings Ltd, 1972–82; Tradinvest Bank & Trust Co. of Nassau Ltd, 1975–85; Nodiv Ltd, 1975–78; Silver Line Ltd, 1978–82; Thompson Moore Associates Ltd, 1984–88; Greycoat PLC, 1994–99; Kiln Capital PLC, 1994–99. Mem., Law Soc., 1961–. *Recreations:* yachting, gardening. *Address:* (office) Simmons & Simmons, 21 Wilson Street, EC2M 2TX; 39 Markham Square, SW3 4XA; Widden, Shirley Holms, Lymington, Hampshire SO41 8NL. *Clubs:* Royal Thames Yacht; Royal Yacht Squadron (Cowes); Royal Lymington Yacht.

JAMES, Steven Wynne Lloyd; Circuit Administrator, North-Eastern Circuit, Lord Chancellor's Department, 1988–94; *b* 9 June 1934; *s* of late Trevor Lloyd James and Olwen James; *m* 1962, Carolyn Ann Rowlands (*d* 1995), *d* of late James Morgan Rowlands and of Mercia Rowlands; three *s*. *Educ:* Queen Elizabeth Grammar Sch., Carmarthen; LSE. LLB 1956. Admitted solicitor, 1959. Asst Solicitor in private practice, 1959–61; Legal Asst, HM Land Registry, 1961; Asst Solicitor, Glamorgan CC, 1962–70; Asst Clerk of the Peace, 1970–71; Lord Chancellor's Dept, 1971–94: Wales and Chester Circuit: Courts Administrator, (Chester/Mold), 1971–76; Asst Sec., 1976; Dep. Circuit Administrator, 1976–82; Under Sec., 1982; Circuit Adminstrator, 1982–88. *Address:* Westlake, 2 Heol-y-Bryn, The Knap, Barry, Vale of Glamorgan CF62 6SY. *T:* (01446) 420677. *Club:* Civil Service.

JAMES, (Thomas) Cecil (Garside), CMG 1966; Assistant Under-Secretary of State, Ministry of Defence, 1968–77; *b* 8 Jan. 1918; *s* of Joshua James, MBE, Ashton-under-Lyne; *m* 1941, Elsie Williams, Ashton-under-Lyne; one *s* two *d*. *Educ:* Manchester Grammar Sch.; St John's Coll., Cambridge. Prin. Priv. Sec. to Sec. of State for Air, 1951–55; Asst Sec., Air Min., 1955; Civil Sec., FEAF, 1963–66; Chief of Public Relations, MoD, 1966–68. RAF historian. Order of Merit (Poland), 1998. *Publications:* The Battle of Britain, The Official Narrative; The Growth of Fighter Command 1936–40. *Address:* 3 Dove Park, Uxbridge Road, Hatch End, Middx HA5 4EB. *T:* (020) 8428 6898. *Club:* Royal Over-Seas League.

JAMES, Thomas Garnet Henry, CBE 1984; FBA 1976; Keeper of Egyptian Antiquities, British Museum, 1974–88; *b* 8 May 1923; *s* of late Thomas Garnet James and Edith (*née* Griffiths); *m* 1956, Diana Margaret, *y d* of H. L. Vavasseur-Durell; one *s*. *Educ:* Neath Grammar Sch.; Exeter Coll., Oxford (Hon. Fellow, 1998). 2nd Cl. Lit. Hum. 1947; 1st Cl. Oriental Studies 1950, MA 1948. Served War of 1939–45, RA; NW Europe; 2nd Lieut 1943; Captain 1945. Asst Keeper, Dept of Egyptian and Assyrian Antiquities, 1951; Dep. Keeper (Egyptian Antiquities), 1974. Laycock Student of Egyptology, Worcester Coll., Oxford, 1954–60; Wilbour Fellow, Brooklyn Museum, 1964; Visiting Professor: Collège de France, 1983; Memphis State Univ., 1990. Vice-Pres., Egypt Exploration Soc., 1990– (Chm., 1983–89); Mem., German Archæological Inst., 1974. Foreign Corresp., l'Institut de France, 2000. Editor: Jl of Egyptian Archæology, 1960–70; Egyptological pubns of Egypt Exploration Soc., 1960–89. *Publications:* The Mastaba of Khentika called Ikhekhi, 1953; Hieroglyphic Texts in the British Museum I, 1961; The Hekanakhte Papers and other Early Middle Kingdom Documents, 1962; (with R. A. Caminos) Gebel es-Silsilah I, 1963; Egyptian Sculptures, 1966; Myths and Legends of Ancient Egypt, 1969; Hieroglyphic Texts in the British Museum, 9, 1970; Archæology of Ancient Egypt, 1972; Corpus of Hieroglyphic Inscriptions in the Brooklyn Museum, I, 1974; (ed) An Introduction to Ancient Egypt, 1979; (ed) Excavating in Egypt, 1982; (with W. V. Davies) Egyptian Sculpture, 1983; Pharaoh's People, 1984; Egyptian Painting, 1985; Ancient Egypt: the land and its legacy, 1988; Howard Carter, the Path to Tutankhamun, 1992; Egypt: the living past, 1992; A Short History of Ancient Egypt, 1996; Egypt Revealed, 1997; Tutankhamun: the eternal splendours of the boy Pharaoh, 2000; contributed to: W. B. Emery: Great Tombs of the First Dynasty II, 1954; T. J. Dunbabin: Perachora II, 1962; Cambridge Ancient History, 3rd edn, Vol. II, i, 1973, Vol III, ii, 1991; Encyclop. Britannica, 15th edn, 1974; (ed English trans.) H. Kees: Ancient Egypt, 1961; articles in Jl Egyptian Arch., etc; reviews in learned jls. *Recreations:* music, cooking. *Address:* 113 Willifield Way, NW11 6YE. *T:* (020) 8455 9221. *Club:* Oxford and Cambridge.

JAMES, Prof. Vivian Hector Thomas; Professor and Head of Department of Chemical Pathology, St Mary's Hospital Medical School, London University, 1973–90, now Professor Emeritus; Hon. Chemical Pathologist, Paddington and North Kensington Health Authority, since 1973; *b* 29 Dec. 1924; *s* of William and Alice James; *m* 1958, Betty Irene Pike. *Educ:* Latymer Sch.; London Univ. BSc, PhD, DSc; FRCPath 1977. Flying duties, RAF, 1942–46. Scientific Staff, Nat. Inst. for Med. Res., 1952–56; St Mary's Hospital Medical School, London: Lectr, Dept of Chemical Pathol., 1956; Reader, 1962; Prof. of Chem. Endocrinol., 1967; Chm., Div. of Pathology, St Mary's Hosp., 1981–85. Emeritus Fellow, Leverhulme Trust, 1991. Mem., Herts AHA, 1974–77. Secretary: Clin. Endocrinol. Cttee, MRC, 1967–72; Cttee for Human Pituitary Collection, MRC, 1972–76 (Chm., 1976–82); Endocrine Sect., RSocMed, 1972–76 (Pres., 1976–78); Gen. Sec., Soc. for Endocrinology, 1979–85 (Treas., 1986–91); Sec.-Gen., European Fedn of Endocrine Socs, 1986–; Chm., UKSport Expert Cttee, 1999–. Clinical Endocrinology Medal Lectr, Clin. Endocrinol. Trust, 1990; Jubilee Medal, Soc. for Endocrinology, 1992. Hon. MRCP 1989. Freeman, Haverfordwest, 1946. Fiorino d'oro, City of Florence, 1977. Editor, Clinical Endocrinology, 1972–74. Editor-in-Chief, 1993–2000, Founder Editor, 2000–, Endocrine-Related Cancer; Editl Advr, European Jl of Endocrinology, 1994–. *Publications:* (ed jtly) Current Topics in Experimental Endocrinology, 1971, 5th edn 1983; (ed) The Adrenal Gland, 1979, 2nd edn 1992; (ed jtly) Hormones in Blood, 1961, 3rd edn 1983; contribs to various endocrine and other jls. *Club:* Royal Society of Medicine.

JAMES, Walter; *see* James, A. W.

JAMES, Prof. Walter, CBE 1977; Dean and Director of Studies, Faculty of Educational Studies, 1969–77, Professor of Educational Studies, 1969–84, Open University; *b* 8 Dec. 1924; *s* of late George Herbert James and Mary Kathleen (*née* Crutch); *m* 1948, Joyce Dorothy Woollaston; two *s*. *Educ:* Royal Grammar Sch., Worcester; St Luke's Coll., Exeter; Univ. of Nottingham. BA 1955. School teacher, 1948–52; Univ. of Nottingham: Resident Tutor, Dept of Extra-Mural Studies, 1958–65; Lectr in Adult Educn, Dept of Adult Educn, 1965–69. Consultant on Adult Educn and Community Develt to Govt of Seychelles and ODA of FCO, 1973; Adviser: to Office of Educn, WCC, 1974–76; on Social Planning, to State of Bahrain, 1975; Council of Europe: UK Rep., Working Party on Develt of Adult Education, 1973–81; UK Rep. and Project Adviser, Adult Educn for Community Develt, 1982–87, Adult Educn for Social Change, 1988–93; Chairman: Nat. Council for Voluntary Youth Services, 1970–76; Review of Training of part-time Youth and Community Workers, 1975–77; Religious Adv. Bd, Scout Assoc., 1977–82; Inservice Training and Educn Panel for Youth and Community Service, 1978–82; Council for Educn and Trng in Youth and Community Work, 1982–85; Nat. Adv. Council for the Youth Service, 1985–88; Council for Local Non-Stipendiary Ministerial Training, dio. of Southwark, 1992–95; Eastbourne, Seaford and Wealden CHC, 1998–; Member: DES Cttee on Youth and Community Work in 70s, 1967–69; ILO Working Party on Use of Radio and TV for Workers' Educn, 1968; Gen. Synod, C of E, 1970–75; Exec. Cttee, Nat. Council of Social Service, 1970–75; Univs' Council for Educn of Teachers, 1970–84; Univs Council for Adult Educn, 1971–76; BBC Further Educn Adv. Council, 1971–75; Exec. Cttee and Council, Nat. Inst. of Adult Educn, 1971–77; Library Adv. Council for England, 1974–76; Adv. Council, HM Queen's Silver Jubilee Appeal, 1976–78; Bd of Educn, Gen. Synod of C of E, 1991–2001; Bd of Govs, S Eastern Museums Service, 1997–; SE Arts Bd, 1998; Trustee: Young Volunteer Force Foundn, 1972–77; Trident Educnl Trust, 1972–86; Community Projects Foundn, 1977–90; Community Develt Foundn, 1990–96; President: Inst. of Playleadership, 1972–74; Fair Play for Children, 1979–82; London and SE Regl Youth Work Unit, 1992–94. Councillor (Lib Dem), Eastbourne BC, 1994–98. *Publications:* (with F. J. Bayliss) The Standard of Living, 1964; (ed) Virginia Woolf, Selections from her essays, 1966; (contrib.) Encyclopaedia of Education, 1968; (contrib.) Teaching Techniques in Adult Education, 1971; (contrib.) Mass Media and Adult Education, 1971; (with H. Janne and P. Dominice) The Development of Adult Education, 1980; (with others) The 14 Pilot Experiments, Vols 1–3, 1984; Some Conclusions from the Co-operation of 14 Development Projects, 1985; Handbook on Co-operative Monitoring, 1986; The Uses of Media for Community Development, 1988; (contrib.) Tomorrow is Another Country: education in a postmodern world, 1996; (contrib.) Called to New Life, 1999. *Recreation:* living. *Address:* 25 Kepplestone, Staveley Road, Eastbourne BN20 7JZ. *T:* (01323) 417029.

JAMES, Prof. Wendy Rosalind, (Mrs D. H. Johnson), DPhil; FBA 1999; Professor of Social Anthropology, University of Oxford, since 1996; Fellow, St Cross College, Oxford, since 1972; *b* 4 Feb. 1940; *d* of William Stanley James and Isabel James (*née* Lunt); *m* 1977, Douglas Hamilton Johnson; one *s* one *d*. *Educ:* Kelsick Grammar Sch., Ambleside; St Hugh's Coll., Oxford (BA 1962; BLitt 1964; DPhil 1970). Lectr in Social Anthropol., Univ. of Khartoum, 1964–69; Leverhulme Res. Fellow, St Hugh's Coll., Oxford, 1969–71; Lectr in Social Anthropol., Univ. of Oxford, 1972–96. Vis. Lectr, Univ. of Bergen, 1971–72. *Publications:* 'Kwanim Pa: the making of the Uduk people, 1979; (ed with D. L. Donham) The Southern Marches of Imperial Ethiopia, 1986; The Listening Ebony: moral knowledge, religion and power among the Uduk of Sudan, 1988; (ed with D. H. Johnson) Vernacular Christianity, 1988; (ed) The Pursuit of Certainty: religious and cultural formulations, 1995; (ed jtly) Juan Maria Schuver's Travels in North East Africa 1880–1883, 1996; (ed with N. J. Allen) Marcel Mauss: a centenary tribute, 1998; (ed jtly) Anthropologists in a Wider World: essays on field research, 2000. *Recreations:* travel, vegetarian cookery, gardening. *Address:* Institute of Social and Cultural Anthropology, 51 Banbury Road, Oxford OX2 6PE. *T:* (01865) 274677, 559041.

JAMES, Prof. (William) Philip (Trehearne), CBE 1993; MD, DSc; FRCP, FRCPEd, FMedSci; FRSE; FIBiol; Director, Public Health Policy Group, since 1999; Research Professor, Aberdeen University, since 1983; *b* 27 June 1938; *s* of Jenkin William James and Lilian Mary James; *m* 1961, Jean Hamilton (*née* Moorhouse); one *s* one *d*. *Educ:* Ackworth Sch., Pontefract, Yorks; University Coll. London (BSc Hons 1959; DSc 1983); University Coll. Hosp. (MB, BS 1962; MD 1968). FRCP 1978; FRCPEd 1983; FRSE 1986; FIBiol 1988. Sen. House Physician, Whittington Hosp., London, 1963–65; Clin. Res. Scientist, MRC Tropical Metabolism Res. Unit, Kingston, Jamaica, 1965–68; Harvard Res. Fellow, Mass Gen. Hosp., 1968–69; Wellcome Trust Res. Fellow, MRC Gastroenterology Unit, London, 1969–70; Sen. Lectr, Dept of Human Nutrition, London Sch. of Hygiene and Trop. Medicine, and Hon. Consultant Physician, UCH, 1970–74; Asst Dir, MRC Dunn Nutrition Unit, and Hon. Consultant Physician, Addenbrooke's Hosp., Cambridge, 1974–82; Dir, Rowett Res. Inst., Aberdeen, 1982–99. Hon. Consultant on nutrition to Army, 1989–; Advr, Eur. Dirs of Agricl Res. on Diet and Health, 1995–. Chairman: FAO Consultation on internat. food needs, 1987; Nat. Food Alliance, 1988–90 (Pres., 1990–); Coronary Prevention Gp, 1988–95 (Pres., 1999–2000); WHO Consultation on world food and health policies, 1989; DoH Panel on Novel Foods, 1992–98; DoH Task Force on Obesity, 1994; RCPE Wkg Pty on Mgt of Obesity in NHS, 1994–97; Internat. Obesity Task Force, 1995–; Eur. Panel, Eur. Heart Foundn's Analysis of Cardiovascular Risk, 1994; Planning Gp, Eur. Young Nutrition Leadership Courses, 1994–; UN Commn on Food and Health, later Nutrition Needs in new Millennium, 1997–99; Assoc. of Profs of Human Nutrition, 1994–97; Member: MAFF Adv. Cttee on Novel Foods and Processes, 1986–; EC Scientific Cttee for Food, 1992–95; DoH (formerly MAFF) Nutrition Task Force, 1992–95; DoH Cttee on Med. Aspects of Food Policy, 1990–99; Internat. Panel on Diet and Cancer, World Cancer Res. Fund, 1994–97; BSE Cttee, 2001–; Ind. Mem., Scientific Steering Cttee, DGXXIV, Brussels, 1997–2000. Author, proposals on Food Standards Agency for Prime Minister, 1997 and EU, 1999. Founder FMedSci 1998. Hon. MFPHM 1994. FRSA 1988. Hon. MA Cantab, 1977. *Publications:* The Analysis of Dietary Fibre in Food, 1981; The Body Weight Regulatory System: normal and disturbed mechanisms, 1981; Assessing Human Energy Requirements, 1990; (ed) Human Nutrition and Diatetics, 1992, 2nd edn 1999; documents on European national nutrition policy and energy needs for Scottish Office, DoH, FAO, NACNE and WHO; scientific pubns on energy metabolism, salt handling, and heart disease in Lancet, Nature, Clin. Science. *Recreations:* talking, writing reports; eating, preferably in France. *Address:* 1 Gatti's Wharf, 5 New Wharf Road, N1 9RS; (office) 231 North Gower Street, NW1 2NS. *T:* (020) 7691 1900; *e-mail:* jeanhjames@aol.com(Philip James). *Club:* Athenæum.

JAMES, William Seymour; Chief Registrar in Bankruptcy, Royal Courts of Justice, since 2001 (Registrar in Bankruptcy, 1991–2001); *b* 11 Dec. 1945; *s* of late Arthur Dyfrig James and of Ann Pamela Mary James (*née* Pincham); *m* 1st, 1973, Pamela Margaret Lord (marr. diss. 1986); one *d*; 2nd, 1989, Susan Amy Barr (*née* Jones); two step *s*. *Educ:* St Edward's Sch., Oxford; College of Law, Guildford. Articled to L. W. S. Parry-Williams, Solicitor, Middlewich, 1966–71; Solicitor in private practice, 1971–91; Under-Sheriff, City of Gloucester, 1988–89. Asst Editor, Muir Hunter on Personal Insolvency, 1996–; Adv. Editor, Butterworths Encyclopaedia of Forms and Precedents, 1999–. *Recreations:* tennis, ski-ing, sailing. *Address:* Royal Courts of Justice, Strand, WC2A 2LL. *T:* (020) 7936 7319.

JAMES-MOORE, Jonathan Guy; Managing Director, Commedia Ltd, since 1999; *b* 22 March 1946; *s* of Wilfred Seward and Alana James-Moore; *m* 1975, Jenny Baynes; one *d*. *Educ:* Bromsgrove Sch.; Emmanuel Coll., Cambridge (MA). Founder Dir, Oxford & Cambridge Shakespeare Co., 1968–71; Gen. Manager, Sir Nicholas Sekers Theatre at Rosehill, 1971–72; Administrator: Mermaid Theatre, 1972–74; St George's Theatre, 1975–76; BBC Radio Light Entertainment, 1978–99: Hd of Light Entertainment, BBC Radio, later of Light Entertainment Radio, BBC Prodn, 1991–99. *Recreations:* collecting wine labels, escaping to Umbria. *Address:* 32A Primrose Gardens, NW3 4TN. *T:* (020) 7722 8951.

JAMESON, Antony; *see* Jameson, G. A.

JAMESON, Derek; news, TV and radio commentator; Co-Presenter, Jamesons, Radio 2, 1992–97; *b* 29 Nov. 1929; *e s* of Mrs Elsie Jameson; *m* 1st, 1948, Jacqueline Sinclair (marr. diss. 1966); one *s* one *d*; 2nd, 1971, Pauline Tomlin (marr. diss. 1978); two *s*; 3rd, 1988, Ellen Petrie. *Educ:* elementary schools, Hackney. Office boy rising to Chief Sub-editor, Reuters, 1944–60; Editor, London American, 1960–61; features staff, Daily Express, 1961–63; Picture Editor, Sunday Mirror, 1963–65; Asst Editor, Sunday Mirror, 1965–72; Northern Editor, Sunday and Daily Mirror, 1972–76; Managing Editor, Daily Mirror, 1976–77; Editor, Daily Express, 1977–79; Editor-in-Chief, The Daily Star, 1978–80; Editor, News of the World, 1981–84. Presenter: Radio 2 Jameson Show, 1986–91; Jameson Tonight, Sky TV, 1989–90. *Publications:* Touched by Angels (autobiog.), 1988; Last of the Hot Metal Men (autobiog.), 1990. *Recreations:* opera, music, reading. *Address:* Western Esplanade, Hove, Sussex BN41 1WE. *Fax:* (01273) 439626; *e-mail:* jameson@pavilion.co.uk.

JAMESON, Prof. (Guy) Antony, PhD; FRS 1995; Thomas V. Jones Professor of Engineering, Stanford University, since 1997; *b* 20 Nov. 1934; *s* of Brig. Guy Oscar Jameson and late Olive Maud Helen Jameson (*née* Turney); *m* 1st, 1964, Catharina Selander (marr. diss.); one *s* one *d*; 2nd, 1985, Charlotte Ansted. *Educ:* Trinity Hall, Cambridge (MA; PhD 1963). Nat. Service, 2nd Lieut, RE, 1953–55. Research Fellow, Trinity Hall, Cambridge, 1960–63; Economist, TUC, 1964–65; Chief Mathematician, Hawker Siddeley Dynamics, Coventry, 1965–66; Aerodynamics Engineer, Grumman Aerospace, Bethpage, NY, 1966–72; Courant Institute of Mathematical Sciences, New York University: Research Scientist, 1972–74; Prof. of Computer Sci., 1974–80; Prof. of Aerospace Engrg, 1980–82, James S. McDonnell Dist. Univ. Prof. of Aerospace Engrg, 1982–96, Princeton Univ. *Publications:* numerous articles in jls and conference proceedings. *Recreations:* squash, tennis, ski-ing. *Address:* Department of Aeronautics and Astronautics, Stanford University, Durand Building, Room D279, Stanford, CA 94305, USA.

JAMESON, John, CBE 1998; QFSM 1995; CIMgt; Firemaster, Strathclyde Fire Brigade, 1991–2000; *b* 12 April 1946; *s* of John Jameson and Catherine Clark Jameson; *m* 1970, Helen Mulvey; one *s* one *d.* *Educ:* St Aloysius and St Patrick's High Sch., Coatbridge. AIFireE 1995. Lanarkshire Fire Brigade, 1965–70; Glasgow Fire Service, 1970–75; Strathclyde Fire Brigade, 1975–: Asst Firemaster, 1987–88; Dep. Firemaster, 1988–91. CIMgt (FBIM 1991). Fire Brigade Long Service and Good Conduct Medal, 1985; Strathclyde Regl Medal for Bravery, 1987. Churchill Fellowship, 1983. *Recreations:* historic buildings, cooking. *Address:* Iona, 56 Dunellan Road, Douglas Mains Estate, Milngavie, Glasgow G62 7RE.

JAMIESON, Brian George, PhD; research management consultant, since 1997; *b* 7 Feb. 1943; *s* of George and Amy Jamieson; *m* 1966, Helen Carol Scott. *Educ:* Boroughmuir Sch.; Edinburgh Univ. (BSc, PhD). Research Assistant: Brigham Young Univ., Utah, 1967–68; Edinburgh Univ., 1968–70; Natural Environment Res. Council, 1970–73 and 1975–77; Principal, ARC, 1973–75; Cabinet Office, 1977–78; Agricultural and Food Research Council: Asst Sec., 1978–87; Dir, Central Office, 1987–91; Acting Sec., Oct.–Dec. 1990; Dir of Admin, 1991–94; Dep. Chief Exec., BBSRC, 1994–97. Mem., Univ. of Bristol Agriculture Cttee, 1997–. Mem., Remuneration Cttee, Royal Soc., 1995–2000. Mem. Bd of Mgt, Sarsen Housing Assoc., 1997–. Mem. Court, Univ. of Salford, 1996–98. *Publications:* papers on igneous petrology and research management. *Recreations:* running, keeping fit, ski-ing, travelling, family history. *Address:* 8 Orwell Close, Caversham, Reading, Berks RG4 7PU. *T:* (0118) 954 6652; *e-mail:* brianjamieson@compuserve.com. *Club:* Phyllis Court (Henley-on-Thames).

JAMIESON, Cathy; Member (Lab and Co-op) Carrick, Cumnock and Doon Valley, Scottish Parliament, since 1999; *b* 3 Nov. 1956; *d* of Robert and Mary Jamieson; *m* 1976, Ian Sharpe; one *s.* *Educ:* James Hamilton Acad., Kilmarnock; Glasgow Art Sch. (BA Hons Fine Art); Goldsmiths' Coll. (Higher Dip. Art); Glasgow Univ. (CQSW); Glasgow Poly. (Cert. Management). Social Worker, Strathclyde Regl Council, 1980–92; Principal Officer, Who Cares? Scotland, 1992–99. Mem., Scottish Exec. Cttee, 1996–, NEC 1998–99, Lab Party. *Address:* Scottish Parliament, Edinburgh EH99 1SP.

JAMIESON, David Charles; MP (Lab) Plymouth Devonport, since 1992; Parliamentary Under-Secretary of State, Department for Transport, Local Government and the Regions, since 2001; *b* 18 May 1947; *s* of Frank and Eileen Jamieson; *m* 1971, Patricia Hofton; two *s* one *d.* *Educ:* Tudor Grange Sch., Solihull; St Peter's, Birmingham; Open Univ. (BA). Teacher, Riland Bedford Sch., 1970–76; Head, Maths Dept, Crown Hills Sch., Leicester, 1976–81; Vice-Principal, John Kitto Community Coll., Plymouth, 1981–92. An Asst Govt Whip, 1997–98; a Lord Comr of HM Treasury (Govt Whip), 1998–2001. Mem., Select Cttee on Educn, 1992–97. Sponsored Private Mem's Bill for Activity Centres (Young Persons' Safety) Act, 1995. *Recreations:* music, tennis, gardening. *Address:* House of Commons, SW1A 0AA. *T:* (020) 7219 6252.

JAMIESON, Air Marshal Sir (David) Ewan, KBE 1986 (OBE 1967); CB 1981; Chief of Defence Staff, New Zealand, 1983–86, retired; *b* Christchurch, 19 April 1930; *s* of Judge R. D. Jamieson, CMG; *m* 1957, Margaret Elaine, *d* of L. J. Bridge; three *s* one *d.* *Educ:* Christchurch and New Plymouth Boys' High Sch. Joined RNZAF, 1949; OC Flying, Ohakea, 1964; CO Malaysia, 1965–66; Jt Services Staff Coll., 1969; CO Auckland, 1971–72; AOC Ops Group, 1974–76; RCDS 1977; Chief of Air Staff, RNZAF, 1979–83. *Address:* 14 Hinerau Grove, Taupo, New Zealand.

JAMIESON, Air Marshal Sir Ewan; *see* Jamieson, Air Marshal Sir D. E.

JAMIESON, Rt Rev. Hamish Thomas Umphelby; Bishop of Bunbury, 1984–2000; *b* 15 Feb. 1932; *s* of Robert Marshall Jamieson and Constance Marzetti Jamieson (*née* Umphelby); *m* 1962, Ellice Anne McPherson; one *s* two *d.* *Educ:* Sydney C of E Grammar Sch.; St Michael's House, Crafers (ThL); Univ. of New England (BA). Deacon 1955; Priest 1956. Mem. Bush Brotherhood of Good Shepherd, 1955–62. Parish of Gilgandra, 1957; Priest-in-Charge, Katherine, NT, 1957–62; Rector, Darwin, 1962–67; Canon of All Souls Cathedral, Thursday Island, 1963–67; Royal Australian Navy Chaplain, 1967–74; HMAS Sydney, 1967–68; HMAS Albatross, 1969–71; Small Ships Chaplain, 1972; HMAS Cerberus, 1972–74; Bishop of Carpentaria, 1974–84. Liaison Bp to the West and Chm. Australian Council, Missions to Seamen, 1992–2000. Chm. Nat. Exec., Anglican Renewal Ministries of Australia, 1984–2000; Exec. Mem., Internat. Charismatic Consultation on World Evangelisation, 1994–; Mem. Internat. Bd, Sharing of Ministries Abroad, 1998–. *Recreations:* reading, music, gardening. *Address:* 17 Bonnydoon Court, Cooloongup, WA 6168, Australia.

JAMIESON, Rear-Adm. Ian Wyndham, CB 1970; DSC 1945; Emeritus Fellow, Jesus College, Oxford, 1986 (Home Bursar and Fellow, 1972–86); *b* 13 March 1920; *s* of late S. W. Jamieson, CBE; *m* 1949, Patricia Wheeler, Knowle, Warwickshire; two *s* one *d.* *Educ:* RNC, Dartmouth. Served War of 1939–45: Anti Submarine Warfare Specialist, 1943. Comdr, 1953; Staff of RN Tactical Sch., 1953–56; HMS Maidstone, 1956–58; Dir, Jt Tactical Sch., Malta, 1958; Capt. 1959; Asst Dir, Naval Intelligence, 1959–61; Comd HMS Nubian and 6th Frigate Sqdn, 1961–64; Dir, Seaman Officers Appts, 1964–66; Comd Britannia RN Coll., Dartmouth, 1966–68; Rear-Adm. 1968; Flag Officer, Gibraltar, and Admiral Superintendent, HM Dockyard, Gibraltar; also NATO Comdr, Gibraltar (Mediterranean Area), 1968–69; C of S to C-in-C Western Fleet, 1969–71; retired. Mem., Southern Arts Council, 1985–91. Hon. MA Oxon, 1973. *Recreations:* hockey (Scotland and Combined Services), cricket, golf, tennis. *Address:* 7 Leicester Close, Henley-on-Thames, Oxon RG9 2LD. *Clubs:* Army and Navy, MCC.

JAMIESON, Kenneth Douglas, CMG 1968; HM Diplomatic Service, retired; *b* 9 Jan. 1921; *s* of late Rt Hon. Lord Jamieson, PC, KC, Senator of College of Justice in Scotland and Violet Rhodes; *m* 1946, Pamela Hall; two *s* one *d.* *Educ:* Rugby; Balliol Coll., Oxford. War Service: 5th Regt RHA, 1941–45; HQ, RA 7th Armoured Div., 1945–46. Joined Foreign Service, 1946; served in: Washington, 1948; FO, 1952; Lima, 1954; Brussels, 1959; FO, 1961; Caracas, 1963; Dir of Commercial Training, DSAO, 1968; Head of Export Promotion Dept, FCO, 1968–70; Minister and UK Dep. Permanent Representative, UN, NY, 1970–74; Ambassador to Peru, 1974–77; Sen. Directing Staff, RCDS, 1977–80. *Address:* Mill Hill House, Bucks Green, Rudgwick, W Sussex RH12 3HZ.

JAMIESON, Margaret; Member (Lab) Kilmarnock and Loudoun, Scottish Parliament, since 1999; *b* 6 April 1953; *d* of late George and Margaret Wallace; *m* 1974, Russell Jamieson; one *d.* *Educ:* Grange Acad.; Ayr Coll. Official for UNISON (formerly NUPE), 1979–99. Mem. Bd, E Ayrshire Employment Initiative, 1998–. Mem., Audit, and Health and Community Care Cttees, Scottish Parlt, 1999–. *Address:* Scottish Parliament, Edinburgh EH99 1SP; Kilmarnock and Loudoun Parliamentary Advice Centre, 32 Grange Street, Kilmarnock KA1 2DD. *T:* (01563) 520267.

JAMIESON, Rt Rev. Penelope Ann Bansall; *see* Dunedin, Bishop of.

JAMIESON, William Bryce; Executive Editor, The Scotsman, since 2000; Director, The Policy Institute, since 2000; *b* 9 June 1945; *s* of John Bryce Jamieson and Anne Jamieson (*née* Leckie); *m* 1971, Elaine Margaret Muller; one *s.* *Educ:* Sedbergh Sch., Yorks; Manchester Univ. (BA Econs). Sub Editor, Gwent Gazette, 1969–70; Chief Sub-Editor, Celtic Press, 1970–71; News Editor, Merthyr Express, 1971; Sub-Editor, Western Mail, 1971–73; Thomson Regional Newspapers: City Reporter, 1973–75; Economics Correspondent, 1975–76; City Reporter, Daily Express, 1976–78; City Editor, Thomson Regl Newspapers, 1978–86; Dep. City Editor, Today, 1986; Dep. City Editor, 1986–95, Econs Editor, 1995–2000, Sunday Telegraph. Regl Financial Journalist Wincott Award, 1979. *Publications:* Goldstrike: Oppenheimer empire in crisis, 1989; Britain Beyond Europe, 1994; UBS Guide to Emerging Markets, 1997; EU Enlargement: a coming home or poisoned chalice?, 1998; Britain: free to choose, 1998; Illustrated Guide to the British Economy, 1998. *Recreations:* reading, opera, gardening. *Address:* The Scotsman, 108 Holyrood Road, Edinburgh EH8 8AS. *T:* (0131) 620 8361. *Club:* Beaujolais.

JAMISON, James Kenneth, OBE 1978; Director, Arts Council of Northern Ireland, 1969–91; *b* 9 May 1931; *s* of William Jamison and Alicia Rea Jamison; *m* 1964, Joan Young Boyd; one *s* one *d.* *Educ:* Belfast College of Art (DA). Secondary school teacher, 1953–61; Art Critic, Belfast Telegraph, 1956–61; Art Organiser, Arts Council of Northern Ireland, 1962–64, Dep. Director, 1964–69. Hon. DLitt Ulster, 1989. *Publications:* miscellaneous on the arts in the North of Ireland. *Recreations:* the arts, travel. *Address:* 64 Rugby Road, Belfast BT7 1PT. *T:* (028) 9032 3063.

JAMMEH, Alhaji Yahya Abdulaziz Jemus Junkung; President, Republic of the Gambia, since 1996; *b* 25 May 1965; *m* 1998, Zineb Yahya Souma. *Educ:* Gambia High Sch. Joined Gambia Nat. Gendarmerie, 1984; commnd 1989; served: Special Intervention Unit, 1984–86; Mobile Gendarmerie Special Guards Unit, 1986–87; Gendarmerie Trng Sch., 1987–89; 2nd Lieut, 1989; OC, Mobile Gendarmerie, Jan.–June 1991; OC, Mil. Police Unit, June–Aug. 1991; Gambia Nat. Army, 1991–93; Lieut, 1992; Mil. Police Officers' Basic Course, Alabama, 1993–94; Capt., 1994; Chm., Armed Forces Provisional Ruling Council and Hd of State, 1994–96; Col, 1996; retd from Army, 1996. Chm., CILLS (Inter-states cttee for control of drought in Sahel), 1997–2000; Vice-Chm., Orgn of Islamic Conf., 2000–. Hon. DCL St Mary's, Halifax, Canada, 1999. Has received numerous awards and decorations from USA, Libya, China, Liberia and Senegal. *Recreations:* tennis, soccer, hunting, reading, correspondence, driving, riding motorcycles, music, movies, world events, animal rearing. *Address:* Office of the President, State House, Banjul, The Gambia.

JANES, (John) Douglas (Webster), CB 1975; Secretary, The Bach Choir, 1981–89; Deputy Secretary, Northern Ireland Office, 1974–79; *b* 17 Aug. 1918; *s* of late John Arnold Janes and Maud Mackinnon (*née* Webster); *m* 1st, 1943, Margaret Isabel Smith (*d* 1978); one *s* two *d*; 2nd, 1986, Mrs Joan Walker (*née* Bentley). *Educ:* Southgate County Sch., Mddx; Imperial Coll. of Science and Technology. 1st cl. BSc (Eng) London, ACGI, DIC. Entered Post Office Engineering Dept, Research Branch, 1939. Served Royal Signals, RAOC, REME, 1939–45: War Office, 1941–45; Major. Min. of Town and Country Planning, 1947; Min. of Housing and Local Govt, 1951; seconded to Min. of Power, 1956–58; HM Treasury, 1960–63; Min. of Land and Natural Resources, 1964–66; Prin. Finance Officer and Accountant Gen., Min. of Housing and Local Govt, 1968–70; Prin. Finance Officer (Local Govt and Develt), DoE, 1970–73, Dep. Sec., 1973; Chief Executive, Maplin Develt Authority, 1973–74. Chm., Home Grown Timber Adv. Cttee, 1981–93 (Mem., 1979–93); various management and organisation reviews, 1979–81. *Recreations:* singing, do-it-yourself.

JANES, Maj.-Gen. Mervyn, CB 1973; MBE 1944; *b* 1 Oct. 1920; *o s* of W. G. Janes; *m* 1946, Elizabeth Kathleen McIntyre; two *d.* *Educ:* Sir Walter St John's Sch., London. Commnd 1942; served with Essex Yeo. (104 Regt RHA), 1942–46, Middle East and Italy; psc 1951; served with 3 RHA, 1952–53; 2 Div., BMRA, 1954–55; Chief Instructor, New Coll., RMAS, 1956–57; Batt. Comd, 3 RHA, 1958–60; Asst Army Instructor (GSO1), Imperial Defence Coll., 1961–62; comd 1st Regt RHA, 1963–65; Comdr, RA, in BAOR, 1965–67; DMS2 (MoD(A)), 1967–70; GOC 5th Division, 1970–71; Dir, Royal Artillery, 1971–73. Col Comdt, RA, 1973–81. *Recreations:* music, ornithology. *Address:* Lucy's Cottage, North Street, Theale, Reading, Berks RG7 5EX. *Club:* Army and Navy.

JANKOVIĆ, Dr Vladeta; Ambassador of Federal Republic of Yugoslavia to the Court of St James's, since 2001; *b* 1 Sept. 1940; *s* of Dr Dragoslav and Bosiljka Janković; *m* 1970, Slavka Srdić; one *s* one *d.* *Educ:* Univ. of Belgrade (BA 1964; MA 1967; PhD Lit. 1975). University of Belgrade, Faculty of Philology: Asst Lectr, 1970–78; Lectr, 1978–83; Prof. of Classical Lit. and Comparative Hist. of Eur. Drama, 1983–2000; Hd, Dept of Comparative Lit. and Theory of Lit., 1992-2000. Lectr, Univ. of Ann Arbor, and Univ. of Columbia (Fulbright Schol.), 1987–88. Co-founder (with Vojislan Kostunica), Democratic Party of Serbia, 1992 (Vice-Pres., 1992–). MP Serbia, 1992–93; Mem., Fed. Parlt of Yugoslavia, 1996–2000; Chm., Foreign Affairs Cttee, Upper Chamber of Parlt, 2000–01. *Publications:* Menander's Characters and the European Drama, 1978; Terence, Comedies, 1978; The Laughing Animal: on classical comedy, 1987; Comedies of Hroswitha, 1988; Who's Who in Classical Antiquity, 1991, 2nd edn 1996; Myths and Legends, 1995, 4th edn 2000. Recreation: tennis. *Address:* Yugoslav Embassy, 5–7 Lexham Gardens, W8 5JJ; 25 Hyde Park Gate, SW7 5DS. *T:* (020) 7581 2140.

JANMAN, Timothy Simon; Director, Boyden International Recruiting, since 1997; *b* 9 Sept. 1956; *s* of Jack and Irene Janman; *m* 1990, Shirley Buckingham (marr. diss. 2000). *Educ:* Sir William Borlase Grammar Sch., Marlow, Bucks; Nottingham Univ. (BSc Hons Chemistry). Ford Motor Co., 1979–83; IBM UK Ltd, 1983–87; Manpower PLC: Nat. Account, subseq. Public Sector Business, Manager, 1993–95; Sen. Nat. Account Manager, 1995–97. Nat. Sen. Vice-Chm., FCS, 1980–81; Vice-President: Selsdon Gp, 1988– (Chm., 1983–87); Jordan is Palestine Cttee, 1988–. Mem., Southampton City Council, May–July 1987. MP (C) Thurrock, 1987–92; contested (C) Thurrock, 1992. Mem., Select Cttee on Employment, 1989–92. Vice-Chm., Cons. Backbench Employment Cttee, 1988–92 (Sec., 1987–88); Sec., Cons. Backbench Home Affairs Cttee, 1989–92. *Publications:* contribs to booklets and pamphlets. *Recreations:* restaurants, theatre. *Address:* 40 Weltje Road, Hammersmith, W6 9LT.

JANNER, family name of **Baron Janner of Braunstone**.

JANNER OF BRAUNSTONE, Baron *cr* 1997 (Life Peer), of Leicester in the co. of Leicestershire; **Greville Ewan Janner,** MA Cantab; QC 1971; barrister, author, lecturer, journalist and broadcaster; *b* 11 July 1928; *s* of Baron Janner and Lady Janner; *m* 1955, Myra Louise Sheink (*d* 1996), Melbourne; one *s* two *d.* *Educ:* Bishop's Coll. Sch., Canada;

St Paul's Sch. (Foundn Schol.); Trinity Hall, Cambridge (Exhbnr); Harvard Post Graduate Law School (Fulbright and Smith-Mundt Schol.); Harmsworth Scholar, Middle Temple, 1955. Nat. Service: Sgt RA, BAOR, War Crimes Investigator. Pres., Cambridge Union, 1952; Chm., Cambridge Univ. Labour Club, 1952; Internat. Sec., Nat. Assoc. of Labour Students, 1952; Pres., Trinity Hall Athletic Club, 1952. Contested (Lab) Wimbledon, 1955. MP (Lab) Leicester NW, 1970–74, Leicester W, 1974–97. Mem., Select Cttee on Employment, 1982–96 (Chm., 1992–96); Co-Chm., All Party Employment Gp, 1996–97; Chairman: All-Party Industrial Safety Gp, 1975–97; All-Party Magic Group, 1991–97; Founder, 1973, and former Chm., All-Party Cttee for Homeless and Rootless People; Founder, 1990, and Vice-Chm., 1990–92, All Party Race and Community Gp; Vice-Chairman: All-Party Parly Cttee for Jews in the Former Soviet Union (formerly Cttee for Release of Soviet Jewry), 1971–97; (Jt), British-Israel Parly Gp, 1983–; British-India Parly Gp, 1991–97 (Jt Vice-Chm., 1987–91); British-Spanish Parly Gp, 1987–97 (Sec., 1986); All-Party British-Romanian Gp, 1990–92; All-Party Parly Cttee for E Europ. Jewry, 1990–97; Sec., All-Party War Crimes Gp, 1987–97, 2000–; Founder and Pres. of World Exec., Inter-Party Council Against Anti-Semitism, 1990–97. President: National Council for Soviet Jewry, 1979–85; Bd of Deputies of British Jews, 1979–85; Commonwealth Jewish Council, 1983–; Vice-President: Assoc. for Jewish Youth, 1970–; Assoc. of Jewish Ex-Servicemen; IVS, 1983–; World Jewish Congress: European Vice-Pres., 1984–86; Mem. World Exec., 1986–; Vice-Pres., 1990–. Partner, JSB Associates, 1984–88; Chm., JSB Gp Ltd, 1988–97; non-exec. Dir, Ladbroke Plc, 1986–95. Member: Nat. Union of Journalists; Soc. of Labour Lawyers; Magic Circle; Internat. Brotherhood of Magicians; Pres., REACH, 1982–; Pres., Jewish Museum, 1985–2001; Mem. Bd of Dirs, Jt Israel Appeal, 1985–; Vice-Pres., Guideposts Trust, 1983–; Founder and Pres., Maimonides Foundn, 1992–; Chairman: Holocaust Educnl Trust, 1987–; Lord Forte Charitable Foundn, 1995–. Formerly Dir, Jewish Chronicle Newspaper Ltd; Trustee, Jewish Chronicle Trust. Hon. Mem., Leics NUM, 1986–. FIPD (FIPM 1976). Hon. PhD Haifa Univ., 1984; Hon. LLD De Montfort, 1998. *Publications:* 65 books, mainly on employment and industrial relations law, presentational skills, and on public speaking, including: Employment Letters; Complete Speechmaker; Complete Letterwriter; Janner on Presentation; Communication; Chairing; Meetings; One Hand Alone Cannot Clap. *Recreations:* magic, languages—speaks nine, learning Arabic. *Address:* House of Lords, SW1A 0PW. *Fax:* (020) 7222 2864; *e-mail:* lordj@netcomuk.co.uk.

JANSEN, Elly, (Mrs Elly Whitehouse-Jansen), OBE 1980; Founder and International Director, The Richmond Fellowship for community mental health, 1959–99; *b* 5 Oct. 1929; *d* of Jacobus Gerrit Jansen and Petronella Suzanna Vellekoop; *m* 1969, Alan Brian Stewart Whitehouse (known as George); three *d. Educ:* Paedologisch Inst. of Free Univ., Amsterdam; Boerhave Kliniek (SRN); London Univ. Founded: Richmond Fellowship of America, 1968, of Australia, 1973, of New Zealand, 1978, of Austria, 1979, of Canada, 1981, of Hong Kong, of India, of Israel, 1984, and of the Caribbean, 1987; Richmond Fellowship Internat., 1981; Richmond Fellowship branches in France, Malta, Peru, Bolivia, Uruguay, Costa Rica, Mexico, Ghana, Nigeria, Zimbabwe, Pakistan, Philippines, Nepal and Bangladesh, 1981–93; Fellowship Charitable Foundn (later Community Housing and Therapy), 1983. Organised internat. confs on therapeutic communities, 1973, 1975, 1976, 1979, 1984, and 1988; acted as consultant to many govts on issues of community care. Fellowship, German Marshall Meml Fund, 1977–78. *Publications:* (ed) The Therapeutic Community Outside the Hospital, 1980; (contrib.) Mental Health and the Community, 1983; (contrib.) Towards a Whole Society: collected papers on aspects of mental health, 1985; (contrib.) R. D. Laing: creative destroyer, 1997; contribs to Amer. Jl of Psychiatry, L'Inf. Psychiatrique, and other jls. *Recreations:* literature, music, interior design. *Address:* Clyde House, 109 Strawberry Vale, Twickenham, TW1 4SJ. *T:* (020) 8744 0374, *Fax:* (020) 8891 0500.

JANSEN, Sir Ross (Malcolm), KBE 1989 (CBE 1986); Chairman, Local Government Commission, New Zealand, 1998–2001; Mayor of Hamilton City, New Zealand, 1977–89; *b* 6 Sept. 1932; *m* 1957, Rhyl Robinson; three *s* three *d. Educ:* Horowhenua Coll., Levin (Dux *proxime accessit* 1950); Victoria Univ., Wellington (LLB 1957); Univ. of Waikato (DPhil 1994). NZ Univ. Law Moot Prize, 1956. Practised law in partnership. Hamilton, 1958–77. Hamilton City Council: Mem., 1965–74, 1977–89; Chairman: Planning Cttee, 1965–68; Works Cttee, 1968–74; Dep. Mayor, 1971–74. Chairman: Waikato United Council, 1986–89; Hamilton Industrial Develt Prog., 1966–68; NZ Bldg Industry Commn, 1986–89; Lottery Community Facilities Cttee, 1989–91; Waikato Regl Council, 1989–91; Midland Regl HA, 1992–98. President: Municipal Assoc. of NZ, 1984–89; NZ Local Govt Assoc., 1988–89. Mem. Council, Univ. of Waikato, 1977–. Winston Churchill Trust Fellowship in Town Planning, 1968. FRSA; ACIArb. Hon. Dr Waikato Univ., 1984. Hon. Chieftain of Western Samoa (for services to the Samoan Community). Commemoration Medal, NZ, 1990. *Recreations:* reading (poetry and history), tennis, gardening. *Address:* 363D Hibiscus Coast Highway, Orewa, New Zealand.

JANSONS, Mariss; conductor; Music Director, Pittsburgh Symphony Orchestra, since 1997; *b* Riga, Latvia, 14 Jan. 1943; *s* of Arvid Jansons. *Educ:* Leningrad Conservatory; studied in Vienna with Prof. Hans Swarowsky and in Salzburg with Herbert von Karajan. Leningrad Philharmonic (later renamed St Petersburg Philharmonic): Associate Conductor, 1973–85; Associate Principal Conductor, 1985–; Music Dir, Oslo Philharmonic Orch., 1979–2000; Principal Guest Conductor, LPO, 1992–. Has conducted leading orchestras of Europe and America incl. Boston and Chicago Symphony Orchestras, Berlin and Vienna Philharmonic, Royal Concertgebouw, etc. Has toured extensively in Europe, America and Japan. Prof. of Conducting, St Petersburg Conservatoire, 1992–. Numerous recordings. Eddison Award for recording of Shostakovich's 7th Symphony, Holland, 1989; Dutch Luister Award for recording of Berlioz Symphonie fantastique with Royal Concertgebouw Orch., 1982; Norwegian Culture Prize of Anders Jahre, 1991; Artist of the Year, EMI Classics, 1996. Comdr with Star, Royal Norwegian Order of Merit, 1995. *Address:* c/o IMG Artists Europe, 616 Chiswick High Road, W4 5RX.

JANUARY, Peter, PhD; HM Diplomatic Service; Foreign and Commonwealth Office, since 2001; *b* 13 Jan. 1952; *s* of Eric Frank January and Hetty Amelia January (*née* Green); *m* 2000, Catherine Helen Courtier Jones, MBE. *Educ:* Sexey's Sch., Bruton; Univ. of Reading (BA 1st Cl. Hons History and Italian); University Coll. London (PhD Italian History 1983). Asst Master, Chatham Grammar Sch. for Girls, 1975–80; joined FCO, 1983; First Sec. (Commercial), Hungary, 1985–88; FCO, 1988–91; Dep. Head of Mission, Mozambique, 1991–93; FCO, 1993–99; Ambassador to Albania, 1999–2001. *Recreations:* spending time with my wife, watching and reading about cricket, Shakespeare, Jacobean tragedy, European history, travel in Italy, poetry, British coins, Falkland Island stamps, canine company, daydreaming. *Address:* c/o Foreign and Commonwealth Office, King Charles Street, SW1A 2AH. *Club:* Somerset CC.

JANVRIN, Rt Hon. Sir Robin (Berry), KCVO 1998 (CVO 1994; LVO 1983); CB 1997; PC 1998; Private Secretary to the Queen and Keeper of the Queen's Archives, since 1999; *b* 20 Sept. 1946; *s* of Vice Adm. Sir Richard Janvrin, KCB, DSC; *m* 1977, Isabelle de Boissonneaux de Chevigny; two *s* two *d. Educ:* Marlborough Coll.; Brasenose Coll., Oxford (BA 1970; Hon. Fellow, 1999). Royal Navy, 1964–75; joined Diplomatic Service, 1975; First Secretary: UK Delegn to NATO, 1976–78; New Delhi, 1981–84; Counsellor, 1985; Press Sec. to the Queen, 1987–90; Asst Private Sec. to the Queen, 1990–95; Dep. Private Sec. to the Queen, 1996–99. *Recreations:* family, painting. *Address:* c/o Buckingham Palace, SW1A 1AA.

JANZON, Mrs Bengt; *see* Dobbs, Mattiwilda.

JAPAN, Emperor of; *see* Akihito.

JAQUES, Prof. Elliott; Research Professor in Management Sciences, George Washington University, since 1989; *b* 18 Jan. 1917; one *d. Educ:* Univ. of Toronto (BA, MA); Johns Hopkins Med. Sch. (MD); Harvard Univ. (PhD). Qual. Psycho-analyst (Brit. Psycho-An. Soc.) 1951. Rantoul Fellow in Psychology, Harvard, 1940–41; Major, Royal Can. Army Med. Corps, 1941–45; Founder Mem., Tavistock Inst. of Human Relations, 1946–51; private practice as psycho-analyst and industrial consultant, 1952–65; Brunel University: Head of Sch. of Social Sciences, 1965–70; Prof. of Sociology, 1970–82; Dir, Inst. of Orgn and Social Studies, 1970–85, now Prof. Emeritus of Social Sciences. Hon. Prof., Dept of Economics, Buenos Aires Univ. Adviser to BoT on organisation for overseas marketing, 1965–69; Mem. Management Study Steering Cttee on NHS Reorganisation, 1972; consultant on leadership develt, US Army, 1979–90; mgt consultancy res., 1990–. Harry Levinson Award, Amer. Psychol Assoc., 2000. *Publications:* The Changing Culture of a Factory, 1951; Measurement of Responsibility, 1956; Equitable Payment, 1961; (with Wilfred Brown) Product Analysis Pricing, 1964; Time-Span Handbook, 1964; (with Wilfred Brown) Glacier Project Papers, 1965; Progression Handbook, 1968; Work, Creativity and Social Justice, 1970; A General Theory of Bureaucracy, 1976; Health Services, 1978; Levels of Abstraction and Logic in Human Action, 1978; The Form of Time, 1982; Free Enterprise, Fair Employment, 1982; Requisite Organisation, 1989, 2nd edn 1996; Executive Leadership, 1991; Human Capability, 1994; The Life and Behavior of Living Organisms, 2001; The Great Social Power of the CEO, 2001; articles in Human Relations, New Society, Internat. Jl of Psycho-Analysis, etc. *Recreations:* art, music, skiing. *Address:* 6 Raven Lane, Gloucester, MA 01930, USA.

JARDINE of Applegirth, Sir Alexander Maule, (Sir Alec), 12th Bt *cr* 1672 (NS); 23rd Chief of the Clan Jardine; *b* 24 Aug. 1947; *s* of Col Sir William Edward Jardine of Applegirth, 11th Bt, OBE, TD, JP, DL, and of Ann Graham, *yr d* of late Lt-Col Claud Archibald Scott Maitland, DSO; *S* father, 1986; *m* 1982, Mary Beatrice, *d* of late Hon. John Michael Inigo Cross and of Mrs Anne Parker-Jervis, *d* of late Maj. Thomas Prain Douglas Murray, MBE, TD, JP, DL; three *s* two *d. Educ:* Gordonstoun; Scottish Agricl Coll., Aberdeen (DipFBOM 1988). Member of Queen's Body Guard for Scotland, Royal Co. of Archers. *Heir: s* William Murray Jardine, yr of Applegirth, *b* 4 July 1984. *Address:* Ash House, Thwaites, Millom, Cumbria LA18 5HY.

JARDINE, Sir Andrew (Colin Douglas), 5th Bt *cr* 1916; *b* 30 Nov. 1955; *s* of Brigadier Sir Ian Liddell Jardine, 4th Bt, OBE, MC, and of Priscilla Daphne, *d* of Douglas Middleton Parnham Scott-Phillips; *S* father, 1982; *m* 1997, Dr Claire Vyvien Griffith, *d* of Dr William and Dr Vyvien Griffith; two *d. Educ:* Charterhouse; Royal Agricultural Coll., Cirencester; Reading Univ. (BSc Hons 1996). MRICS (ARICS 1998). Commissioned Royal Green Jackets, 1975–78. With C. T. Bowring & Co. Ltd, 1979–81; with Henderson Administration Gp, 1981–92; Dir, Gartmore Investment Trust Management Ltd, 1992–93; with Strutt & Parker, 1996–99; Bathurst Estate, 2000–. MSI 1993. Mem., Queen's Body Guard for Scotland, Royal Company of Archers, 1990–. *Heir: b* Michael Ian Christopher Jardine [*b* 4 Oct. 1958; *m* 1982, Maria Milky Pineda; two *s*]. *Address:* Crabtree Barn, Duntisbourne Leer, Cirencester, Glos GL7 7AS. *T:* (01285) 821895. *Club:* Boodle's.

See also Sir J. R. G. Baird, Bt.

JARDINE, Sir (Andrew) Rupert (John) Buchanan-, 4th Bt *cr* 1885; MC 1944; DL; landowner and farmer; *b* 2 Feb. 1923; *s* of Sir John William Buchanan-Jardine, 3rd Bt and Jean Barbara (*d* 1989), *d* of late Lord Ernest Hamilton; *S* father, 1969; *m* 1950, Jane Fiona (marr. diss. 1975), 2nd *d* of Sir Charles Edmonstone, 6th Bt; one *s* one *d. Educ:* Harrow; Royal Agricultural College. Joined Royal Horse Guards, 1941; served in France, Holland and Germany; Major 1948; retired, 1949. Joint-Master, Dumfriesshire Foxhounds, 1950. JP Dumfriesshire, 1957; DL Dumfriesshire, 1978. Bronze Lion of the Netherlands, 1945. *Recreations:* country pursuits. *Heir: s* John Christopher Rupert Buchanan-Jardine [*b* 20 March 1952; *m* 1975, Pandora Lavinia, *d* of Peter Murray Lee; one *s* five *d*]. *Address:* Dixons, Lockerbie, Dumfriesshire DG11 2PR. *T:* (01576) 202508. *Club:* MCC.

JARDINE, James Christopher Macnaughton; Sheriff of Glasgow and Strathkelvin, 1979–95; *b* 18 Jan. 1930; *s* of James Jardine; *m* 1955, Vena Gordon Kight; one *d. Educ:* Glasgow Academy; Gresham House, Ayrshire; Glasgow Univ. (BL). National Service (Lieut RASC), 1950–52. Admitted as Solicitor, in Scotland, 1953. Practice as principal (from 1955) of Nelson & Mackay, and as partner of McClure, Naismith, Brodie & Co., Solicitors, Glasgow, 1956–69; Sheriff of Stirling, Dunbarton and Clackmannan, later N Strathclyde, at Dumbarton, 1969–79. A Vice-Pres., Sheriffs' Assoc., 1976–79. Sec., Glasgow Univ. Graduates Assoc., 1956–66; Mem., Business Cttee of Glasgow Univ. Gen. Council, 1964–67. Member: Consultative Cttee on Social Work in the Criminal Justice System (formerly Probation) for Strathclyde Region, 1980–94; Professional Advisory Cttee, Scottish Council on Alcoholism, 1982–85. *Recreation:* enjoyment of music and theatre.

JARDINE, Prof. Lisa Anne, PhD; Professor of Renaissance Studies, Queen Mary and Westfield College, University of London, since 1989; *b* 12 April 1944; *d* of Jacob Bronowski and Rita (*née* Coblenz); *m* 1st, 1969, Nicholas Jardine, *qv* (marr. diss. 1979); one *s* one *d*; 2nd, 1982, John Robert Hare; one *s. Educ:* Cheltenham Ladies' Coll.; Newnham Coll., Cambridge (BA Maths and English 1966; MA 1968; PhD 1973; Associate 1992); Univ. of Essex (MA 1967). Res. Fellow, Warburg Inst., Univ. of London, 1971–74; Lectr in Renaissance Literature, Univ. of Essex, 1974; Res. Fellow, Cornell Univ., 1974–75; University of Cambridge: Res. Fellow, Girton Coll., 1974–75; Fellow: King's Coll., 1975–76 (Hon. Fellow, 1995); Jesus Coll., 1976–89; Lectr in English, 1976–89; Reader in Renaissance English, 1989. Davis Center Fellow, Princeton Univ., 1987–88. Presenter, Night Waves, BBC Radio 3, 1992–96. Chair of Govs, Westminster City Sch., 1999–. Chair of Judges, Orange Prize for Fiction, 1997. FRHistS 1992; FRSA 1992. *Publications:* Francis Bacon: discovery and the art of discourse, 1974; Still Harping on Daughters: women and drama in the age of Shakespeare, 1983; (jtly) From Humanism to the Humanities: education and the liberal arts in fifteenth- and sixteenth-century Europe, 1986; (jtly) What's Left?: women in culture and the labour movement, 1989; Erasmus, Man of Letters, 1993; Reading Shakespeare Historically, 1996; Wordly Goods: a new history of the Renaissance, 1996; Erasmus, the Education of a Christian Prince, 1997; (jtly) Hostage to Fortune: the troubled life of Francis Bacon, 1998; Ingenious Pursuits: building the scientific revolution, 1999; Francis Bacon, A New Organon and Other Writings, 1999; (jtly) Global Interests: Renaissance art between East and West,

2000; contribs to newspapers, numerous articles in learned jls. *Recreations:* conversation, cookery, contemporary art. *Address:* 51 Bedford Court Mansions, Bedford Avenue, WC1B 3AA.

JARDINE, Prof. Nicholas, PhD; Professor of History and Philosophy of the Sciences, University of Cambridge, since 1992; Fellow, Darwin College, Cambridge, since 1975; *b* 4 Sept. 1943; *s* of Michael James Jardine and Jean Caroline (*née* Crook); *m* 1992, Marina Frasca-Spada; two *s* two *d* from previous marriages. *Educ:* Monkton Combe; King's Coll., Cambridge (BA 1965; PhD 1969). Jun. Res. Fellow, 1967–71, Sen. Res. Fellow, 1971–75, King's Coll., Cambridge; Royal Soc. Res. Fellow, 1968–73; University of Cambridge: Lectr, 1975–86; Reader, 1986–92. Mem., Internat. Acad. of Hist. of Sci., 1991–. Editor: Studies in Hist. and Philosophy of Sci., 1982–; Studies in Hist. and Philosophy of Biol and Biomedic. Scis, 1998–. *Publications:* (with R. Sibson) Mathematical Taxonomy, 1971; The Birth of History and Philosophy of Science, 1984, rev. edn 1988; The Fortunes of Inquiry, 1986; (ed jtly) Romanticism and the Sciences, 1990; The Scenes of Inquiry, 1991, 2nd edn 2000; (ed jtly) Cultures of Natural History, 1996; (ed jtly) Books and Sciences in History, 2000. *Recreation:* plant hunting. *Address:* 83 Alpha Road, Cambridge CB4 3DQ. *T:* (01223) 313734.

JARDINE, Ronald Charles C.; *see* Cunningham-Jardine.

JARDINE, Sir Rupert Buchanan-; *see* Jardine, Sir A. R. J. B.

JARMAN, Sir Brian, Kt 1998; OBE 1988; PhD; FRCP, FRCGP, FFPHM; Professor of Primary Health Care, Imperial College School of Medicine (formerly St Mary's Hospital Medical School), 1984–98, now Emeritus; *b* 9 July 1933; *m* 1963, Marina Juez Uriel; three *s*. *Educ:* Barking Abbey Sch.; St Catharine's Coll., Cambridge (Open Exhibn; BA Nat. Sci. 1954; MA 1957); Imperial Coll., London (DIC 1957, PhD 1960, Geophysics); St Mary's Hosp. Med. Sch., London Univ. (MB BS 1st Cl. Hons 1969). MRCP 1972, FRCP 1988; MRCGP 1978, FRCGP 1984; MFPHM 1994, FFPHM 1999. National Service, 2nd Lt, 19 Field Regt, RA, 1954–55, Army Opnl Res. Gp, 1955–56. Geophysicist: Royal Dutch Shell Oil Co., 1960–63; Geophysical Services Inc., 1963–64; House appts: St Mary's Hosp., London, 1969; St Bernard's Hosp., Gibraltar, 1970; Beth Israel Hosp., Harvard Med. Sch., 1970; Clin. Fellow, Harvard Univ., 1970; GP, London, 1971–; St Mary's Hospital Medical School, later Imperial College School of Medicine: pt-time Sen. Lectr, Dept of Gen. Practice, 1973–83; Hd of Community Health Scis Div., 1995–97; Hd, Div. of Primary Care and Population Health Scis, 1997–98. Med. Advr and Cons., Barnet FHSA, 1991–95. Member: Sci. Consultative Gp, BBC, 1983–89; Health Services Res. Cttee, MRC, 1987–89; Requirements Bd, Advanced Informatics in Medicine, EC, 1989–90; Kensington, Chelsea & Westminster FHSA, 1990–96; Standing Med. Adv. Cttee, 1998–. Mem. Council, RCP, 1995–98. Med. Mem., Bristol Royal Infirmary Inquiry, 1999–2001. Trustee, Wytham Hall Unit for the Homeless, 1979–; Chm., Trustees, Anna Freud Centre, 1995–. Founder FMedSci 1998. *Publications:* (ed and contrib.) Primary Care, 1988; contribs to books, papers, reviews, articles in med. jls, conf. proceedings. *Recreations:* music, reading, family, travel, squash, friends. *Address:* 62 Aberdare Gardens, NW6 3QD. *T:* (020) 7624 5502.

JARMAN, John Milwyn; QC 2001; *b* 30 April 1957; *s* of Thomas Jarman and Mary Elizabeth Jarman; *m* 1983, Caroline Anne Joyce Newman; two *s* one *d*. *Educ:* UCW, Aberystwyth (LLB 1st Cl. Hons); Sidney Sussex Coll., Cambridge (LLM). Called to the Bar, Gray's Inn, 1980; in practice, Cardiff, 1981–, specialising in chancery, planning and local government, and personal injuries law. *Recreations:* ski-ing, snooker, Welsh sport and affairs. *Address:* (chambers) 9 Park Place, Cardiff CF10 3DP. *T:* (029) 2038 2731.

JARMAN, Nicholas Francis Barnaby; QC 1985; barrister; a Recorder of the Crown Court, since 1982; *b* 19 June 1938; *s* of late A. S. Jarman and of Helene Jarman; *m* 1st, 1973, Jennifer Michelle Lawrence-Smith (marr. diss. 1978); one *d*; 2nd, 1989, Julia Elizabeth MacDougall (*née* Owen-John). *Educ:* Harrow; Christ Church, Oxford (MA Jurisprudence). Commnd RA, 1956–58 (JUO Mons, 1957). Called to the Bar, Inner Temple, 1965 (Duke of Edinburgh Scholar). Bar Chm., Bucks, Berks and Oxon Jt Liaison Cttee, 1986–96. *Recreations:* France, fly-fishing. *Address:* Mas Terrier Gibertes, Route d'Uzès, 30700 Flaux, France. *T:* (4) 66030308; 21A Parsons Green Lane, SW6 4HH; 4 King's Bench Walk, Temple, EC4Y 7DL. *T:* (020) 7353 3581.

JARMAN, Pauline; Member (Plaid Cymru) South Wales Central, National Assembly for Wales, since 1999; *b* 15 Dec. 1945; *m* Colin Jarman; two *s*. *Educ:* Mountain Ash Grammar Sch. Export Officer, AB Metals, 1962–65; Export/Import Officer, Fram Filters, 1965–68; self-employed retailer, 1976–88. Member: Cynon Valley BC, 1976–96 (Leader, Plaid Cymru Gp; Mayor, 1987–88); Mid-Glamorgan CC, 1981–96 (Leader, Plaid Cymru Gp; Leader of Council); Rhondda Cynon Taff CBC, 1995–. *Address:* National Assembly for Wales, Cardiff Bay, Cardiff CF99 1NA.

JARMAN, Richard Neville; arts consultant, since 2000; *b* 24 April 1949; *s* of late Dr Gwyn Jarman and of Pauline (*née* Lane). *Educ:* King's Sch., Canterbury; Trinity Coll., Oxford (MA English). Sadler's Wells Opera and ENO, 1971–76; Touring Officer, Dance, Arts Council, 1976–77; Edinburgh International Festival: Artistic Asst, 1978–82; Fest. Adminr, 1982–84; Gen. Adminr, London Fest. and English Nat. Ballet, 1984–90; Gen. Dir, Scottish Opera, 1991–97; Interim Gen. Manager, Arts Theatre, Cambridge, 1997–98; Artistic Dir, Royal Opera House, 1998–2000. Chm., Dance Umbrella, 1997–; Director: Cambridge Arts Th. Trust, 2000–; Canterbury Fest., 2001–. Gov., Central Sch. of Speech and Drama, 2000–. Trustee: British Performing Arts Medicine Trust, 1999–; Castle Trust, 2001–. FRSA. *Publications:* History of Sadler's Wells Opera, 1974; History of London Coliseum Theatre, 1979. *Recreations:* listening to music, going to the theatre, gardening, food and drink, travel, reading. *Address:* Barham Court, Rectory Lane, Barham, Canterbury, Kent CT4 6PD. *T:* (01227) 832873.

JARMAN, Roger Whitney; Under Secretary, Local Government Finance, Housing and Social Services Group, Welsh Office, 1994–95; *b* 16 Feb. 1935; *s* of Reginald Cecil Jarman and Marjorie Dix Jarman; *m* 1959, Patricia Dorothy Odwell; one *s*. *Educ:* Cathays High Sch., Cardiff; Univ. of Birmingham (BSocSc Hons; Cert. in Educn). Recruitment and Selection Officer, Vauxhall Motors Ltd, 1960–64; Asst Sec., Univ. of Bristol Appts Bd, 1964–68; Asst Dir of Recruitment, CSD, 1968–72; Welsh Office: Principal, European Div., 1972–74; Asst Sec., Devolution Div., 1974–78; Asst Sec., Perm. Sec.'s Div., 1978–80; Under Secretary: Land Use Planning Gp, 1980–83; Transport, Highways and Planning Gp, 1983–88; Transport, Planning, Water and Environment Gp, 1988; Housing, Health and Social Services Policy Gp, 1988–94. Standing Orders Comr, Nat. Assembly for Wales, 1998. Mem. Panel of Chairmen, RAS, 1995–; Lay Chm., NHS Complaints Procedure, 1996–; Bd Mem., Glamorgan and Gwent Housing Assoc., 1999–. Mem., Nat. Trust Cttee for Wales, 2000–. *Recreations:* walking, reading, wine and food. *Club:* Civil Service.

JAROSZEK, Jeremy; Director of Resources, London Borough of Barnet, since 1999; *b* 5 Dec. 1951; *s* of Walenty Jaroszek and Sylvia Jaroszek (*née* Stanley); *m* 1989, Rosemary Moon; one *s* one *d*. *Educ:* Vyners Sch.; Selwyn Coll., Cambridge (MA); Imperial Coll., London (MSc 1974). CPFA 1982. Greater London Council, 1974–85; Camden LBC, 1985–86; Dep. Dir of Finance, London Borough of Hillingdon, 1986–89; Dir of Finance, London Borough of Barnet, 1990–99. Treas., Middlesex Probation Service, 1990–2001. *Recreations:* ski-ing, stargazing, family pursuits. *Address:* (office) Town Hall, The Burroughs, Hendon, NW4 4BL. *T:* (020) 8359 2123.

JARRATT, Sir Alexander Anthony, (Sir Alex), Kt 1979; CB 1968; DL; Chancellor, University of Birmingham, since 1983; Chairman, Centre for Dispute Resolution, 1990–2000, President, since 2000; *b* 19 Jan. 1924; *o s* of Alexander and Mary Jarratt; *m* 1946, Mary Philomena Keogh; one *s* two *d*. *Educ:* Royal Liberty Gram. Sch., Essex; University of Birmingham. War Service, Fleet Air Arm, 1942–46. University of Birmingham, BCom, 1946–49. Asst Principal, Min. of Power, 1949, Principal, 1953, and seconded to Treas., 1954–55; Min. of Power: Prin. Priv. Sec. to Minister, 1955–59; Asst Sec., Oil Div., 1959–63; Under-Sec., Gas Div., 1963–64; seconded to Cabinet Office, 1964–65; Secretary to the National Board for Prices and Incomes, 1965–68; Dep. Sec., 1967; Dep. Under Sec. of State, Dept of Employment and Productivity, 1968–70; Dep. Sec., Min. of Agriculture, 1970. Man. Dir, IPC, 1970–73; Chm. and Chief Executive, IPC and IPC Newspapers, 1974; Chairman: Reed Internat., 1974–85 (Dir, 1970–85); Smiths Industries, 1985–91 (Dir, 1984–96); a Dep. Chm., Midland Bank, 1980–91; Jt Dep. Chm., Prudential Corp. plc, 1987–91, 1992–94 (Dir, 1985–94); Director: ICI, 1975–91; Thyssen-Bornemisza Group, 1972–89; Mem., Ford European Adv. Council, 1983–88. Confederation of British Industry: Mem., Council, 1972–92; Mem., President's Cttee, 1983–86; Chairman: Economic Policy Cttee, 1972–74; Employment Policy Cttee, 1983–86; Mem., NEDC, 1976–80. President: Advertising Assoc., 1979–83; PPA 1983–85. Chairman: Industrial Soc., 1975–79; Henley: The Management Coll., 1977–89; Gov., Ashridge Management Coll., 1975–91. Vice-Pres., Inst. of Marketing. Pres., Age Concern, Essex, 2000–. FRSA. DL Essex, 1995. Hon. CGIA 1990. Hon. DSc Cranfield, 1973; DUniv: Brunel, 1979; Essex, 1997; Hon. LLD Birmingham, 1982. *Recreations:* walking, the countryside, reading, music. *Address:* Barn Mead, Fryerning, Essex CM4 0NP.

JARRATT, Prof. Peter, CEng; FBCS; FSS; FIMA; Professor of Computing, University of Birmingham, 1975–2000, now Emeritus; *b* 2 Jan. 1935; *s* of Edward Jarratt and Edna Mary Jarratt; *m* 1972, Jeanette Debeir; one *s* two *d*. *Educ:* Univ. of Manchester (BSc, PhD). Programmer, Nuclear Power Plant Co. Ltd, 1957; Chief Programmer, Nuclear Power Gp, 1960; Lectr in Mathematics, Bradford Inst. of Technology, 1962; Asst Dir, Computing Lab., Univ. of Bradford, 1966; Dir, Computing Lab., Univ. of Salford, 1972; University of Birmingham: Dir, Computer Centre, 1975–91; Dep. Dean, Faculty of Science and Engrg, 1984; first Dean of Faculty of Science, 1985–88; Develt Advr to Vice-Chancellor, 1988–93. Director: Birmingham Res. and Develt Ltd, 1986–88; BISS Ltd, 1993–96; Carma Ltd, 1993–; Wang-Inet Ltd, 1996–97; Wang Global Ltd, 1997–99. Chm., Birmingham Inst. for Conductive Educn, 1987–90. Mem., Birmingham Lunar Soc., 1991–93. Gov., Royal Nat. Coll. for the Blind, 1986–95; Patron, Henshaw's Soc. for the Blind, 1993–. *Publications:* numerous res. papers on mathematics, computer sci. and risk mgt. *Recreations:* classical music, mountain walking, gardening, chess. *Address:* c/o The University of Birmingham, Edgbaston, Birmingham B15 2TT. *Club:* Athenæum.

JARRE, Maurice Alexis; French composer; *b* 13 Sept. 1924; *s* of André Jarre and Gabrielle Jarre (*née* Boullu); *m* 1984, Khong Fui Fong; one *s* one *d* by previous marriages. *Educ:* Lycée Ampère, Lyons; Univ. of Lyons; Univ. of Paris, Sorbonne; Conservatoire Nat. Supérieur de Musique. Musician, Radiodiffusion Française, 1946–50; Dir of Music, Théâtre Nat. Populaire, 1950–63. Work includes symphonic music, music for theatre and ballet; film scores include: Hôtel des Invalides, 1952; Sur le pont d'Avignon, 1956; Sundays and Cybele, 1962; The Longest Day, 1962; Lawrence of Arabia, 1962 (Acad. Award for best original score); Dr Zhivago, 1965 (Acad. Award for best original score); Gambit, 1966; The Fixer, 1968; Ryan's Daughter, 1970; El Condor, 1970; The Life and Times of Judge Roy Bean, 1972; The Man Who Would Be King, 1975; Jesus of Nazareth, 1977; Shogun, 1980; Firefox, 1982; The Year of Living Dangerously, 1983; A Passage To India, 1985 (Acad. Award for best original score); Mad Max 3, 1985; Witness, 1985; The Mosquito Coast, 1986; Tai-Pan, 1987; Fatal Attraction, 1987; Gorillas in the Mist, 1989; Dead Poets Society, 1989; Ghost, 1990; A Walk in the Clouds, 1995; La Jour et la Nuit, 1997; Sunshine, 1999; I Dreamed of Africa, 2000. Hon. Citizen: Lyon; Lille; Officier, Légion d'honneur (France); Commandeur des Arts et des Lettres (France); Comdr, Ordre Nat. du Mérite (France). *Address:* c/o Sacem, 225 avenue Charles de Gaulle, 92521 Neuilly-sur-Seine, France.

JARRETT, Rt Rev. Martyn William; *see* Beverley, Bishop Suffragan of.

JARRETT, Prof. William Fleming Hoggan, FRS 1980; FRSE 1965; Professor of Veterinary Pathology, 1968–91, Senior Research Fellow, since 1991, University of Glasgow; *b* 2 Jan. 1928; *s* of James and Jessie Jarrett; *m* 1952, Anna Fraser Sharp; two *d*. *Educ:* Lenzie Academy; Glasgow Veterinary Coll.; Univ. of Glasgow; PhD, FRCVS, FRCPath. Gold Medal, 1949; John Henry Steele Meml Medal, 1961; Steele Bodger Meml Schol. 1955. ARC Research Student, 1949–52; Lectr, Dept of Veterinary Pathology, Univ. of Glasgow Vet. Sch., 1952–53; Head of Hospital Path. Dept of Vet. Hosp., Univ. of Glasgow, 1953–61; Reader in Pathology, Univ. of Glasgow, 1962–65; seconded to Univ. of E Africa, 1963–64; Titular Prof. of Experimental Vet. Medicine, Univ. of Glasgow, 1965. Lectures: Leeuwenhoek, Royal Soc., 1986; McFadyean Meml, RVC, 1986. Fogarty Scholar, NIH, 1985. Hon. FRCPSGlas 1988. Dr *hc* Liège Univ., 1986; DUniv Stirling, 1988; Hon. DSc: East Anglia, 1989; Edinburgh, 1989; Hon. DVSc RVC, London, 1991. Centennial Award, Univ. of Pennsylvania, 1984; Makdougall Brisbane Prize, RSE, 1984; J.T. Edwards Meml Medal, RCVS, 1984; Feldberg Prize, 1987; Tenovus–Scotland Margaret McLellan Award, 1989; Saltire Award, 1989; WSAVA Waltham Internat. Award, 1991. *Publications:* various, on tumour viruses, Leukaemia and immunology. *Recreations:* sailing, ski-ing, mountaineering, music. *Address:* Auchineden House, Blanefield G63 9AX. *T:* and *Fax:* (01360) 770112. *Clubs:* Clyde Cruising; Glencoe Ski.

JARRING, Gunnar, PhD; Grand Cross, Order of the North Star, Sweden; Swedish Ambassador and Special Representative of the Secretary-General of the United Nations on the Middle East question, 1967–91; *b* S Sweden, 12 Oct. 1907; *s* of Gottfrid Jönsson and Betty Svensson; *m* 1932, Agnes, *d* of Prof. Carl Charlier, Lund; one *d*. *Educ:* Lund; Univ. of Lund (PhD). Family surname changed to Jarring, 1931. Associate Prof. of Turkish Langs, Lund Univ., 1933–40; Attaché, Ankara, 1940–41; Chief, Section B, Teheran, 1941; Chargé d'Affaires *ad interim:* Teheran and Baghdad, 1945; Addis Ababa, 1946–48; Minister: to India, 1948–51, concurrently to Ceylon, 1950–51; to Persia, Iraq and Pakistan, 1951–52; Dir, Polit. Div., Min. of Foreign Affairs, 1953–56; Permanent Rep. to UN, 1956–58; Rep. on Security Council, 1957–58; Ambassador to USA, 1958–64, to USSR, 1964–73, and to Mongolia, 1965–73. *Publications:* Studien zu einer osttürkischen Lautlehre, 1933; The Contest of the Fruits - An Eastern Turki Allegory, 1936; The Uzbek Dialect of Quilich, Russian Turkestan, 1937; Uzbek Texts from Afghan Turkestan, 1938;

The Distribution of Turk Tribes in Afghanistan, 1939; Materials to the Knowledge of Eastern Turki (vols 1–4), 1947–51; An Eastern Turki-English Dialect Dictionary, 1964; Literary Texts from Kashghar, 1980; Return to Kashghar, 1986; Prints from Kashghar, 1991; Central Asian Turkic Place-names, 1997. *Address:* Pontus Ols väg 7, 26040 Viken, Sweden.

JARROLD, Kenneth Wesley, CBE 1997; Chief Executive, County Durham Health Authority, since 1997; *b* 19 May 1948; *s* of William Stanley Jarrold and Martha Hamilton Jarrold (*née* Cowan); *m* 1973, Patricia Hadaway; two *s*. *Educ:* St Lawrence Coll., Ramsgate; Sidney Sussex Coll., Cambridge (Whittaker Schol.; BA Hons Hist. 1st cl.; Pres., Cambridge Union Soc.) Dip. IHSM (Hons Standard). E Anglian RHB, 1969–70; Briggs Cttee on Nursing, 1970–71; Dep. Supt, Royal Hosp., Sheffield, 1971–74; Hosp. Sec., Derbyshire Royal Infirmary, 1974–75; Sector Administrator, Nottingham Gen. and Univ. Hosps, 1975–79; Asst Dist Administrator (Planning), S Tees HA, 1979–82; Dist Administrator, 1982–84, Dist Gen. Manager, 1984–89, Gloucester HA; Regl Gen. Manager, Wessex RHA, 1990–94; Dir of Human Resources, NHS Exec., 1994–97. Mem., NHS Training Authy and Chm., Training Cttee, 1984–87; Chairman: Management Educn System by Open Learning Project Group, 1986–89, and 1991–93; Durham and Teesside Workforce Develt Confedn, 2001–. Pres., IHSM, 1985–86 (Mem., Nat. Council, 1977–89. Hon. Vis. Prof., Univs of York and Salford, 1998–. DUniv Open, 1999. *Publications:* Challenges for Health Services in the 1990s, 1990; (contrib.) Health Care Systems in Canada and the UK, 1994; Minding Our Own Business: healing division in the NHS, 1995; Servants and Leaders, 1998; articles in professional jls. *Address:* 20 Dunottar Avenue, Eaglescliffe, Stockton-on-Tees TS16 0AB.

JARROLD, Nicholas Robert; HM Diplomatic Service; Ambassador to Croatia, since 2000; *b* 2 March 1946; *s* of late A. R. Jarrold and D. V. Roberts; *m* 1972, Anne Catherine Whitworth; two *s*. *Educ:* Shrewsbury Sch.; Western Reserve Acad., Ohio (ESU Scholar); St Edmund Hall, Oxford (Exhibnr, MA). Entered Diplomatic Service, 1968: FCO, 1968–69; The Hague, 1969–72; Dakar, 1972–75; FCO, 1975–79; Nairobi, 1979–83; FCO, 1983–89; Counsellor and Dep. Head of Mission, Havana, 1989–91; Vis. Fellow, St Antony's Coll., Oxford, 1991–92; Counsellor (Economic and Commercial), Brussels and Luxembourg, 1992–96; Ambassador to Latvia, 1996–99. *Recreations:* reading history, cricket, the theatre. *Address:* c/o Foreign and Commonwealth Office, King Charles Street, SW1A 2AH. *Club:* Athenæum.

JARROW, Bishop Suffragan of, since 2002; **Rt Rev. John Lawrence Pritchard;** *b* 22 April 1948; *s* of late Rev. Canon Neil Lawrence Pritchard and Winifred Mary Coverdale (*née* Savill); *m* 1972, Susan Wendy Claridge; two *d*. *Educ:* St Peter's Coll., Oxford (MA (Law) 1973); St John's Coll., Durham (MLitt (Theol.) 1993). Ordained deacon, 1972, priest, 1973; Asst Curate, St Martin's-in-the Bull Ring, Birmingham, 1972–76; Diocesan Youth Chaplain and Asst Dir of Educn, dio. of Bath and Wells, 1976–80; Vicar, St George's, Wilton, Taunton, 1980–88; Dir of Pastoral Studies, 1989–93, Warden, 1993–96, Cranmer Hall, St John's Coll., Durham; Archdeacon of Canterbury, 1996–2001. Mem., Gen. Synod of C of E, 1999–2001. Bishops' Inspector, 1999–. *Publications:* Practical Theology in Action, 1996; The Intercessions Handbook, 1997; Beginning Again, 2000; Living the Gospel Stories Today, 2001. *Recreations:* photography, walking, travel, music, cricket, reading. *Address:* (until June 2002) c/o Diocesan Office, Auckland Castle, Market Place, Bishop Auckland, Co. Durham DL14 7QJ; (from June 2002) Bishop's House, Ivy Lane, Low Fell, Gateshead NE9 6QD.

JÄRVI, Neeme; Music Director, Detroit Symphony Orchestra, since 1990; Chief Conductor, Gothenburg Symphony Orchestra, Sweden, since 1982; *b* Tallinn, Estonia, 7 June 1937; *s* of August and Elss Järvi; *m* 1961, Liilia Järvi; two *s* one *d*. *Educ:* Estonia-Tallinn Conservatory of Music; Leningrad State Conservatory. Chief Conductor: Estonian Radio Symphony Orch., 1963–77 (Conductor, 1960–63); Estonia opera house, Tallinn, 1963–77; toured USA with Leningrad Phil. Orch., 1973 and 1977; Chief Conductor, Estonian State Symph. Orch., 1976–80; since emigration to USA in 1980 has appeared as Guest Conductor with New York Phil. Orch., Philadelphia Orch., Boston Symph., Chicago Symph., Los Angeles Phil., Met. Opera (New York) and in San Francisco, Cincinnati, Indianapolis, Minneapolis and Detroit; has also given concerts in Vienna, London, Canada, Sweden, Finland, Norway, Denmark, Holland, Switzerland and W Germany; Principal Guest Conductor, CBSO, 1981–84; Musical Dir and Principal Conductor, Scottish Nat. Orch., 1984–88, Conductor Laureate, 1989. 1st Prize, Internat. Conductors Competition, Accademia Santa Cecilia, Rome, 1971. Over 310 CDs including: works by Bartok, Dvorak, Medtner, Barber, Prokofiev (symphonic cycle), Shostakovich; complete works of Sibelius and all symphonies of Nielsen and Mahler (Toblach Prize for best recording, 1993, for No 3); Saul and David, opera by Nielsen; Don Giovanni; Schmidt symphonies. *Recreation:* traveller. *Address:* c/o Columbia Artists Management Inc., 165 West 57th Street, New York, NY 10019, USA.

JARVIE, Elizabeth (Marie-Lesley); QC (Scot.) 1995; Sheriff of Lothian and Borders at Edinburgh, since 1997; *b* 22 Jan. 1952; *d* of Dr James Leslie Rennie and Marie-Thérèse (*née* Loyseau de Mauléon); *m* 1976, John Jarvie; one *s* four *d*. *Educ:* Larbert High Sch., Stirlingshire; Univ. of Edinburgh (MA Hons, LLB). Apprentice, Biggert Baillie & Gifford WS, 1978–79; admitted to Scots Bar, 1981; Advocate-Depute, 1991–94. Part-time Chm., Social Security Appeal Tribunal, 1986–89. *Recreations:* ski-ing, music, lunching, news. *Address:* Rowallan, Barnton Avenue, Edinburgh EH4 6JJ. *T:* (0131) 336 2117.

JARVIS, Frederick Frank, (Fred); General Secretary, National Union of Teachers, 1975–89; Member of General Council, 1974–89, President, 1987, Trades Union Congress (Chairman, 1986–87); *b* 8 Sept. 1924; *s* of Alfred and Emily Ann Jarvis; *m* 1954, Elizabeth Anne Colegrove, Stanton Harcourt, Oxfordshire; one *s* one *d*. *Educ:* Plaistow Secondary Sch., West Ham; Oldershaw Grammar Sch., Wallasey; Liverpool Univ.; St Catherine's Society, Oxford. Dip. in Social Science with dist. (Liverpool Univ.); BA (Hons) in Politics, Philosophy and Economics (Oxon), MA (Oxon). Contested (Lab) Wallasey, Gen. Elec., 1951; Chm., Nat. Assoc. of Labour Student Organisations, 1951; Pres., Nat. Union of Students, 1952–54 (Dep. Pres., 1951–52); Asst Sec., Nat. Union of Teachers, 1955–59; Head of Publicity and Public Relations, 1959–70; Dep. Gen. Sec., NUT, 1970–74 (apptd Gen. Sec. Designate, March 1974). Pres., Eur. Trade Union Cttee for Educn, 1983–84, 1985–86 (Vice-Pres., 1981–83); Chairman, TUC Cttees: Local Govt, 1983–88; Educn Training, 1985–88; Chm., TUC Nuclear Energy Review Body, 1986–88. Member: Central Arbitration Cttee, 1985–94; Franco-British Council, 1986–98. Mem. Council, Nat. Youth Theatre; Trustee, Trident Trust; Mem. Bd, Univ. of First Age, Birmingham. Photographic exhibitions: Days of Rallies and Roses, London, Manchester, Norwich and Grantham, 1997; Politicians, Poppies and other Flowers, London, 1998; Monet's Garden—the lesser known Provence, London, Birmingham, 2000, Poole, Edinburgh, Alton, Provence, Oxford, 2001; Homage to the Hammers, London, 2001. FRSA. Hon. FEIS 1980; Hon. FCP 1982. *Publications:* The Educational Implications of UK Membership of the EEC, 1972; Education and Mr Major, 1993; Ed, various jls incl.: 'Youth Review', NUT Guide to Careers; NUT Univ. and Coll. Entrance Guide. *Recreations:* swimming, cycling, gardening, cinema, theatre, photography. *Address:* 92 Hadley Road, New Barnet, Herts EN5 5QR. *Club:* Ronnie Scott's.

JARVIS, James Roger; His Honour Judge Jarvis; a Circuit Judge, since 2000; *b* 7 Sept. 1944; *s* of Flt Lieut Douglas Bernard Jarvis, DFC, RAF (retd), and Elsie Vanessa Jarvis; *m* 1972, Kerstin Marianne Hall; one *s* two *d*. *Educ:* Latymer Upper Sch.; Brockenhurst County Grammar Sch.; Peter Symonds. Articled Clerk, Bernard Chill & Axtell; admitted Solicitor, 1969; joined Andrews McQueen, later McQueen Yeoman, 1972; Asst Solicitor, 1972–73; Partner, 1973–2000. *Recreations:* jogging, walking, reading. *Address:* c/o Combined Courts, Portsmouth PO1 2EB.

JARVIS, John Francis, CVO 2001; CBE 1993; Chairman and Chief Executive, Jarvis Hotels, since 1990; *b* 15 Feb. 1943; *s* of Thomas Jarvis and Mary Jarvis; *m* 1984, Sally Ann Garrod; one *s* two *d*. *Educ:* Scarborough Grammar Sch.; S Devon Hotel Coll. FHCIMA 1975. With Rank Orgn, 1965–75; Ladbroke Gp plc, 1975–90: Chairman: Ladbroke Hotels, Holidays and Entertainment, 1975–87; Texas Homecare, 1985–87; Hilton Internat., 1987–90; Prince's Trust-Action, 1993–98; Prince's Trust Trading, 1998–2000. Director: Shepperton Hldgs Ltd, 1995–2001; Apollo Leisure Gp, 1998–99; Non-exec. Chm., On Board Services Ltd, later Europ. Rail Catering (Hldgs) Ltd, 1995–97. Member: English Tourist Bd, 1983–96; BTA, 1995–2000; Chm., British Hospitality Assoc. Council, 2000–. Mem., Exec. Bd, Variety Club of GB, 1986–98. *Recreation:* tennis. *Address:* Jarvis Hotels, Castle House, Desborough Road, High Wycombe, Bucks HP11 2PR. *T:* (01494) 473800.

JARVIS, John Manners; QC 1989; a Recorder, since 1992; a Deputy High Court Judge, since 1998; *b* 20 Nov. 1947; *s* of late Donald Edward Manners Jarvis and Theodora Brixie Jarvis; *m* 1972, Janet Rona Kitson; two *s*. *Educ:* King's Coll. Sch., Wimbledon; Emmanuel Coll., Cambridge (MA (Law)). Called to Bar, Lincoln's Inn, 1970 (Bencher); practising barrister specialising in Commercial Law, particularly banking; Jt Hd of Chambers, 1999–. An Asst Recorder, 1987–92. Chm., Commercial Bar Assoc., 1995–97 (Treas., 1993–95); Mem., Bar Council, 1995–97. Gov., King's Coll. Sch., Wimbledon, 1987–. Overseas Editor, Jl of Banking and Finance—Law and Practice, 1990–. *Publications:* (jtly) Lender Liability, 1993; (contrib.) Banks, Liability and Risk, 2nd edn 1995. *Recreations:* tennis, horse-riding, sailing, ski-ing, cycling, music. *Address:* Eyeworth Lodge, Fritham, Lyndhurst, Hampshire SO43 7HJ. *T:* (023) 8081 3321, *Fax:* (023) 8081 4431; 3 Verulam Buildings, Gray's Inn, WC1R 5NT. *T:* (020) 7831 8441, *Fax:* (020) 7831 8479. *Club:* Hurlingham.

JARVIS, Martin, OBE 2000; actor; *b* 4 Aug. 1941; *s* of Denys Jarvis and Margot Jarvis; *m*; two *s*; *m* 1974, Rosalind Ayres. *Educ:* Whitgift School; RADA (Hons Dip., 1962, Silver Medal, 1962, Vanbrugh Award, 1962; RADA Associate, 1980). Nat. Youth Theatre, 1960–62; played Henry V, Sadler's Wells, 1962; Manchester Library Theatre, 1962–63; *stage:* Cockade, Arts, 1963; Poor Bitos, Duke of York's, 1963; Man and Superman, Vaudeville, 1966; The Bandwagon, Mermaid, 1970; The Rivals, USA, 1973; Hamlet (title rôle), Fest. of British Th., 1973; The Circle, Haymarket, 1976; She Stoops to Conquer, Canada, and Hong Kong Arts Festival, 1977; Caught in the Act, Garrick, 1981; Importance of Being Earnest, NT, 1982; Victoria Station, NT, 1983; The Trojan War Will Not Take Place, NT, 1983; Woman in Mind, Vaudeville, 1986; The Perfect Party, Greenwich, 1987; Henceforward, Vaudeville, 1989; Exchange, Vaudeville, 1990, Los Angeles, 1992; You Say Potato, Los Angeles, 1990; Twelfth Night, Playhouse, 1991; Leo in Love, Southampton, 1992; Just Between Ourselves, Greenwich, 1992; Make and Break, 1993, Man of the Moment, 1994, Los Angeles; On Approval, Playhouse, 1994; Table Manners, LA, 1995; The Doctor's Dilemma, Almeida, 1998; Skylight, LA, 1999; Passion Play, Donmar, 2000; By Jeeves, USA, 2001; recitals of Paradise Lost, Old Vic, Chichester and QEH, 1975–77; The Queen's Birthday Concert, Royal Festival Hall, 1996; narrator, Peter and the Wolf, Barbican, 1997; *films:* The Last Escape, Ike, The Bunker, Taste the Blood of Dracula, Buster; The Fool of the World and the Flying Ship, 1991 (Emmy Award); Emily's Ghost, 1992; Calliope; Absence of War, 1995; Titanic, 1997; The X-Ray Kid, Sex 'n' Death, 1999; Mrs Caldicot's Cabbage War, By Jeeves, 2001; *television series:* The Forsyte Saga, 1967; Nicholas Nickleby, 1968; Little Women, 1969; The Moonstone, 1971; The Pallisers, 1974; David Copperfield, 1975; Killers, 1976; Rings on Their Fingers, 1978–80; Breakaway, 1980; The Black Tower, 1985; Chelworth, 1988; Countdown, 1990; Murder Most Horrid, 1991; The Good Guys, 1992; Woof!, 1992; Library of Romance, 1992; Girl from Ipanema (British Comedy Award); Scarlet and Black, 1993; Brillat Saverin, 1994; Lovejoy, 1994; Murder She Wrote, 1995; Supply and Demand, 1998; Space Island One, 1998; Lorna Doone, 2000; Micawber, 2001; *radio:* numerous performances, incl. one-man series, Jarvis's Frayn; as Charles Dickens in series, The Best of Times; Gush, 1994; (and prod.) Speak After the Beep, 2 series, 1997; productions of plays; script writing and adaptations; commentaries for TV and film documentaries and for arts programmes; has adapted and read over 90 of Richmal Crompton's Just William stories for radio, TV and cassette; recorded one-man performance of David Copperfield for cassette, 1991; one-man perf., Oscar Wilde, 1996; co-produced cassette 2nd World War Poetry, 1993; produced and directed cassettes, Tales from Shakespeare; writer/presenter, Concorde Playhouse, 1994–97. Dir, Children's Film Unit, 1993–2000. Vice-Pres., Salamander Oasis Trust, 1990–. Sony Silver Award, 1991; NY Internat. Award, for contribn to broadcasting, 1994; British Talkies award, 1995, 1997, 1998; US Audie Award, 1999. *Publications:* Bright Boy, 1977; William Stories: a personal selection, 1992; Meet Just William, 1999; Acting Strangely (autobiog.), 1999; short stories for radio; contribs to many anthologies; articles in The Listener, Punch, Tatler, Daily Telegraph and London Evening Standard. *Recreations:* Beethoven, Mozart, growing lemons. *Address:* c/o London Management, 2–4 Noel Street, W1V 3RB.

JARVIS, Patrick William, CB 1985; CEng, FIEE, FIMarE; FRINA; RCNC; Deputy Controller (Warships), Ministry of Defence (Procurement Executive), and Head of Royal Corps of Naval Constructors, 1983–86; *b* 27 Aug. 1926; *s* of Frederick Arthur and Marjorie Winifred Jarvis; *m* 1951, Amy (*née* Ryley); two *s*. *Educ:* Royal Naval Coll., Greenwich; Royal Naval Engrg Coll., Keyham, Devonport. BScEng. Trade apprentice, HM Dockyard, Chatham, 1942–46; Design Engineer, Admiralty, Bath, 1946–62; Warship Electrical Supt, Belfast, 1962–63; Suptg Engr, MoD(N), Bath, 1963–72; Ship Department, MoD (PE), Bath: Asst Dir and Dep. Dir, 1972–78; Under Sec., 1978; Dir of Naval Ship Production, 1979–81; Dir of Ship Design and Engrg, and Dep. Head of Royal Corps of Naval Constructors, 1981–83; Dep. Sec., 1983. *Address:* Ranworth, Bathampton Lane, Bath BA2 6ST.

JASON, David, OBE 1993; actor; *b* 2 Feb. 1940; *s* of Arthur and Olwyn White; adopted stage name, David Jason, 1965; one *d* by Gill Hinchcliffe. Stage career began with a season in repertory, Bromley Rep.; *theatre includes:* Under Milk Wood, Mayfair, 1971; The Rivals, Sadler's Wells, 1972; No Sex Please … We're British!, Strand, 1972; Darling Mr London, tour, 1975; Charley's Aunt, tour, 1975; The Norman Conquests, Oxford Playhouse, 1976; The Relapse, Cambridge Theatre Co., 1978; Cinderella, 1979; The Unvarnished Truth, Mid/Far East tour, 1983; Look No Hans!, tour and West End, 1985; *films:* Under Milk Wood, 1970; Royal Flash, 1974; The Odd Job, 1978; Only Fools and

Horses; Wind in the Willows, 1983; *television includes:* Do Not Adjust Your Set, 1967; The Top Secret Life of Edgar Briggs, 1973–74; Mr Stabbs, 1974; Ronnie Barker Shows, 1975; Open All Hours, 1975; Porridge, 1975; Lucky Feller, 1975; A Sharp Intake of Breath, 1978; Del Trotter in Only Fools and Horses, 1981–91 (Best Light Entertainment Perf., BAFTA, 1990); Porterhouse Blue, 1986; Jackanory, 1988; A Bit of A Do, 1988–89; Single Voices: The Chemist, 1989; Amongst Barbarians, 1989; Pa Larkin in The Darling Buds of May, 1990–93; A Touch of Frost, 1992–; The Bullion Boys, 1993; All the King's Men, 1999; *voice work:* Dangermouse, Count Duckula, The Wind in the Willows. Awards include Best Actor Award, BAFTA, 1988; Special Recognition Award for Lifetime Achievement in Television, Nat. Television Awards, 1996; Best Comedy Perf. Award, BAFTA, 1997. *Recreations:* diving, flying, motorcycles. *Address:* c/o Richard Stone Partnership, 2 Henrietta Street, WC2E 8PS.

JASPAN, Andrew; Editor, Sunday Herald, since 1999; *b* 20 April 1952; *s* of Mervyn and Helen Jaspan; *m* 1991, Karen Jane Grant; two *s*. *Educ:* Beverley GS; Manchester Univ. (BA Hons Politics). Co-Founder, New Manchester Review, 1976–79; Daily Telegraph features, 1979; Fellowship, Journalists in Europe, Paris, 1980–81; freelance journalist, Daily Mirror and Daily Telegraph, 1982; News Sub-Ed., The Times, 1983–85; Asst News Ed., Sunday Times, 1985–88; Editor: Sunday Times Scotland, 1988–89; Scotland on Sunday, 1989–94; The Scotsman, 1994–95; The Observer, 1995–96; Publr and Man. Dir, The Big Issue, 1996–98. *Publications:* Exams and Assessment, 1975; Preparing for Higher Education, 1975. *Recreations:* tennis, travelling. *Address:* (office) c/o The Sunday Herald, 195 Albion Street, Glasgow G1 1QP. *Club:* Glasgow Art.

JASPER, Robin Leslie Darlow, CMG 1963; HM Diplomatic Service, retired; *b* 22 Feb. 1914; *s* of T. D. Jasper, Beckenham; *m* 1st, 1940, Jean Cochrane (marr. diss.; she *d* 2001); one *d*; 2nd, 1966, Diana Speed (*née* West); two step *d*. *Educ:* Dulwich; Clare Coll., Cambridge. Apprentice, LNER Hotels Dept, 1936–39; Bursar, Dominion Students Hall Trust (London House), 1939–40; RAFVR (Wing Comdr), 1940–45; Principal, India Office (later Commonwealth Relations Office), 1945; concerned with resettlement of the Sec. of State's Services in India, 1947–48; British Dep. High Commissioner, Lahore, Pakistan, 1949–52; Adviser to London Conferences on Central African Federation, and visited Central Africa in this connection, 1952–53; Counsellor, HM Embassy, Lisbon, 1953–55; visited Portuguese Africa, 1954; Commonwealth Relations Office, 1955–60 (Head of Information Policy Dept, 1958–60); attached to the United Kingdom delegation to the United Nations, 1955 and 1956; British Dep. High Commissioner, Ibadan, Nigeria, 1960–64; Counsellor, Commonwealth Office, 1965–67; Consul-Gen., Naples, 1967–71, retired 1972. Lived in Almuñécar, Granada, Spain, 1971–79. *Recreations:* tennis, Rugby fives, wind music, 17th Century Church Sculpture, claret, madrigals, mainstream jazz, psychotherapy. *Address:* Ashburnham Lodge, 62 London Road, St Leonard's-on-Sea, East Sussex TN37 6AS. *T:* (01424) 438575. *Clubs:* MCC, Jesters.

JAUNCEY, family name of **Baron Jauncey of Tullichettle**.

JAUNCEY OF TULLICHETTLE, Baron *cr* 1988 (Life Peer), of Comrie in the District of Perth and Kinross; **Charles Eliot Jauncey;** PC 1988; a Lord of Appeal in Ordinary, 1988–96; *b* 8 May 1925; *s* of late Captain John Henry Jauncey, DSO, RN, Tullichettle, Comrie, and Muriel Charlie, *d* of late Adm. Sir Charles Dundas of Dundas, KCMG; *m* 1st, 1948, Jean (marr. diss. 1969), *d* of Adm. Sir Angus Cunninghame Graham of Gartmore, KBE, CB; two *s* one *d*; 2nd, 1973, Elizabeth (marr. diss. 1977), *widow* of Major John Ballingal, MC; 3rd, 1977, Camilla, *d* of late Lt-Col Charles Cathcart of Pitcairlie, DSO; one *d*. *Educ:* Radley; Christ Church, Oxford (Hon. Student, 1990); Glasgow Univ. BA 1947, Oxford; LLB 1949, Glasgow. Served in War, 1943–46, Sub-Lt RNVR. Advocate, Scottish Bar, 1949; Standing Junior Counsel to Admiralty, 1954; QC (Scotland) 1963; Kintyre Pursuivant of Arms, 1955–71; Sheriff Principal of Fife and Kinross, 1971–74; Judge of the Courts of Appeal of Jersey and Guernsey, 1972–79; a Senator of College of Justice, Scotland, 1979–88. Hon. Sheriff-Substitute of Perthshire, 1962. Mem. of Royal Co. of Archers (Queen's Body Guard for Scotland), 1951. Mem., Historic Buildings Council for Scotland, 1971–92. *Recreations:* shooting, fishing, bicycling, genealogy. *Address:* Tullichettle, Comrie, Perthshire PH6 2HU. *T:* (01764) 670349; House of Lords, SW1A 0PW. *Club:* Royal (Perth).

JAVACHEFF, Christo; *see* Christo and Jeanne-Claude.

JAVACHEFF, Jeanne-Claude; *see* Christo and Jeanne-Claude.

JAWARA, Alhaji Sir Dawda Kairaba, Kt 1966; Hon. GCMG 1974; Grand Master, Order of the Republic of The Gambia, 1972; President of the Republic of The Gambia, 1970–94; Vice-President of the Senegambian Confederation, 1982; *b* Barajally, MacCarthy Island Div., 16 May 1924. *Educ:* Muslim Primary Sch. and Methodist Boys' Grammar Sch., Bathurst; Achimota Coll.; Glasgow Univ. FRCVS 1988 (MRCVS 1953); Dipl. in Trop. Vet. Med., Edinburgh, 1957. Veterinary Officer for The Gambia Govt, 1954–57, Principal Vet. Officer, 1957–60. Leader of People's Progressive Party (formerly Protectorate People's Party), The Gambia, 1960; MP 1960; Minister of Education, 1960–61; Premier, 1962–63; Prime Minister, 1963–70. Chairman: Permanent Inter State Cttee for Drought in the Sahel, 1977–79; Organisation pour la Mise en Valeur du Fleuve Gambie Conf., Heads of State and Govt, 1987–88; Authy of Heads of State and Govt, Economic Community of W African States, 1988–89. Patron, Commonwealth Vet. Assoc., 1967–. Hon. LLD Ife, 1978; Hon. DSc Colorado State Univ., USA, 1986. Peutinger Gold Medal, Peutinger-Collegium, Munich, 1979; Agricola Medal, FAO, Rome, 1980. Grand Cross: Order of Cedar of Lebanon, 1966; Nat. Order of Republic of Senegal, 1967; Order of Propitious Clouds of China (Taiwan), 1968; Nat. Order of Republic of Guinea, 1973; Grand Cordon of Most Venerable Order of Knighthood, Pioneers of Republic of Liberia, 1968; Grand Comdr, Nat. Order of Federal Republic of Nigeria, 1970; Comdr of Golden Ark (Netherlands), 1979; Grand Gwanghwa Medal of Order of Diplomatic Service (Republic of Korea), 1984; Nishan-i-Pakistan (Pakistan), 1984; Grand Officer of Nat. Merit, Islamic Republic of Mauritania, 1992; Grant Comdr, Nat. Order of Republic of Portugal, 1993. *Recreations:* golf, gardening, sailing. *Address:* 15 Birchen Lane, Haywards Heath, West Sussex RH16 1RY.

JAY, family name of **Baroness Jay of Paddington**.

JAY OF PADDINGTON, Baroness *cr* 1992 (Life Peer), of Paddington in the City of Westminster; **Margaret Ann Jay;** PC 1998; Leader of the House of Lords, 1998–2001; Minister for Women, 1998–2001; *b* 18 Nov. 1939; *er d* of Baron Callaghan of Cardiff, *qv*; *m* 1961, Hon. Peter Jay, *qv* (marr. diss. 1986); one *s* two *d*; *m* 1994, Prof. M. W. Adler, *qv*. Principal Opposition Spokesman on Health, H of L, 1995–97; Minister of State, DoH, 1997–98. Dir, Nat. Aids Trust, 1988–92. Non-executive Director: Carlton Television, 1996–97; Scottish Power, 1996–97. Mem., Kensington, Chelsea & Westminster HA, 1992–97; Chm., Nat. Assoc. of Leagues of Hosp. Friends, 1994. *Address:* c/o House of Lords, SW1A 0PW.

JAY, Sir Antony (Rupert), Kt 1988; CVO 1993; freelance writer and producer, since 1964; Chairman, Video Arts Ltd, 1972–89; *b* 20 April 1930; *s* of Ernest Jay and Catherine Hay; *m* 1957, Rosemary Jill Watkins; two *s* two *d*. *Educ:* St Paul's Sch. (scholar); Magdalene Coll., Cambridge (major scholar; BA (1st cl. Hons) Classics and Comparative Philology, 1952; MA 1955). 2nd Lieut Royal Signals, 1952–54. BBC, 1955–64: Editor, Tonight, 1962–63; Head of Talks Features, TV, 1963–64; (with Jonathan Lynn) writer of BBC TV series, Yes, Minister and Yes, Prime Minister, 1980–88. Mem., Cttee on Future of Broadcasting, 1974–77. FRSA 1992; CIMgt 1992. Hon. MA Sheffield, 1987; Hon. DBA IMCB, 1988. *Publications:* Management and Machiavelli, 1967, 2nd edn 1987; (with David Frost) To England with Love, 1967; Effective Presentation, 1970; Corporation Man, 1972; The Householder's Guide to Community Defence against Bureaucratic Aggression, 1972; (with Jonathan Lynn): Yes, Minister, Vol. 1 1981, Vol. 2 1982, Vol. 3 1983; The Complete Yes, Minister, 1984; Yes, Prime Minister, Vol. 1 1986, Vol. 2 1987; The Complete Yes, Prime Minister, 1989; Elizabeth R, 1992; (ed) Oxford Dictionary of Political Quotations, 1996, 2nd edn 2001; How to Beat Sir Humphrey, 1997. *Address:* c/o The Production Tree, 71 Masbro Road, W14 0LS. *T:* (020) 7610 5599.

JAY, Prof. Barrie Samuel, MD, FRCS; FRCOphth; Professor of Clinical Ophthalmology, University of London, 1985–92, now Emeritus; Consulting Surgeon, Moorfields Eye Hospital, since 1992 (Consultant Surgeon, 1969–92); Hon. Secretary: Academy of Medical Royal Colleges, 1994–99; Specialist Training Authority, Medical Royal Colleges, 1996–99; *b* 7 May 1929; *er s* of late Dr M. B. Jay and Julia Sterling; *m* 1954, Marcelle Ruby Byre; two *s*. *Educ:* Perse Sch., Cambridge; Gonville and Caius Coll., Cambridge (MA, MD); University Coll. Hosp., London. FRCS 1962; FCOphth 1988 (Hon. FRCOphth 1994). House Surgeon and Sen. Resident Officer, Moorfields Eye Hosp., 1959–62; Sen. Registrar, Ophthalmic Dept, London Hosp., 1962–65; Institute of Ophthalmology, University of London: Shepherd Res. Scholar, 1963–64; Mem., Cttee of Management, 1972–77, 1979–91; Clinical Sub-Dean, 1973–77; Dean, 1980–85; Ophthalmic Surgeon, The London Hosp., 1965–79. Consultant Advr in Ophthalmol., DHSS, 1982–88. Examiner: Dip. in Ophthal., 1970–75; British Orthoptic Council, 1970–78; Ophthalmic Nursing Bd, 1971–87; Mem. Ct of Examrs, RCS, 1975–80. Brit. Rep., Monospecialist Section of Ophthal., Eur. Union of Med. Specialists, 1973–85. Mem. Council: Section of Ophthal., RSM, 1965–77 (Editorial Rep., 1966–77); Faculty of Ophthalmologists, 1970–88 (Asst Hon. Sec., 1976–78; Hon. Sec., 1978–86; Pres., 1986–88); RCS (co-opted Mem. for Ophthalmology), 1983–88; Coll. of Ophthalmologists, 1988–92 (Vice-Pres., 1988–92); Nat. Ophthalmic Treatment Bd Assoc., 1971–75; Internat. Pediatric Ophthal. Soc., 1975–92; Ophthal. Soc. UK, 1985–88; Member: Ophthal. Nursing Bd, 1974–88; Orthoptists Bd, Council for Professions Supplementary to Medicine, 1977–92 (Vice Chm., 1982–88); Specialist Adv. Cttee in Ophthalmology, 1979–88 (Chm., 1982–88); Standing Med. Adv. Cttee, DHSS, 1980–84; Transplant Adv. Panel, DHSS, 1983–88. Trustee: Fight for Sight, 1973–94; Wolfson Foundn, 1986–92; Wolfson Family Charitable Trust, 1992–. Fellow, Eugenics Soc.; FRPSL (Hon. Sec., 1992–98; Vice-Pres., 1996–98; Pres., 1998–2000); Hon. FRCPCH 1996; Hon. Member: British Paediatric Assoc., 1995; Canadian Ophthalmol Soc. Mem., Ct of Assts, Soc. of Apothecaries (Master, 1995–96; Hon. Treas., 1999–); Liveryman: Co. of Barbers; Co. of Spectacle Makers. Mem., Bd of Governors, Moorfields Eye Hosp., 1971–90. Mem. Editorial Board: Ophthalmic Literature, 1962–91 (Asst Editor, 1977–78; Editor, 1978–85); British Jl of Ophthalmology, 1965–90; Jl of Medical Genetics, 1971–76; Metabolic Ophthalmology, 1975–78; Survey of Ophthalmology, 1976–; Ophthalmic Paediatrics and Genetics, 1981–94; Editor, Postal History, 1994–. *Publications:* contrib. on ophthalmology and genetics to med. jls. *Recreations:* postal history, gardening. *Address:* 10 Beltane Drive, SW19 5JR. *T:* (020) 8947 1771.
See also R. M. Jay.

JAY, John Philip Bromberg; Director, New Star Asset Management, since 2001; *b* 1 April 1957; *s* of Alec Jay and June (*née* Bromberg); *m* 1st, 1987, Susy Streeter (marr. diss. 1992); 2nd, 1992, Judi Bevan (*née* Leader); one *d*. *Educ:* University Coll. Sch.; Magdalen Coll., Oxford (BA Hons Mod. Hist.). Journalist, Western Mail, 1979–81; financial journalist: Thomson Regl Newspapers, 1981–84; Sunday Telegraph, 1984–86; City Editor, Sunday Times, 1986–89; City and Business Editor, Sunday Telegraph, 1989–95; Man. Ed., Business News, Sunday Times, 1995–2001. *Publication:* (with Judi Bevan) The New Tycoons, 1989. *Recreations:* ski-ing, cinema, theatre, walking. *Address:* 202 Rotherhithe Street, SE16 7RB. *T:* (020) 7252 1194.

JAY, Hon. Martin, CBE 2000; DL; Chief Executive, Vosper Thornycroft Holdings plc, since 1989; *b* 18 July 1939; *s* of Baron Jay, PC and of Margaret Christian Jay; *m* 1969, Sandra Mary Ruth Williams; one *s* two *d*. *Educ:* Winchester Coll.; New Coll., Oxford (MA). With BP, 1962–69; GEC plc, 1969–85 (Man. Dir, GEC Inf. Services, and Mem., Mgt Bd, 1980–85); Man. Dir, Lewmar plc, 1985–87; Man. Dir, Electronics Components Div., GEC plc, 1987–89. Mem., Nat. Defence Industries Council, 1997–; Pres., British Marine Equipt Council, 1997–. Chm., Rose Rd Children's Appeal. DL Hants, 2001. *Recreations:* sailing, gardening, tennis. *Address:* Bishops Court, Bishops Sutton, Alresford, Hants SO24 0AN. *T:* (01962) 732193.
See also Hon. P. Jay.

JAY, Sir Michael (Hastings), KCMG 1997 (CMG 1992); HM Diplomatic Service; Permanent Under-Secretary of State, Foreign and Commonwealth Office, and Head of the Diplomatic Service, from Feb. 2002; *b* 19 June 1946; *s* of late Alan David Hastings Jay, DSO, DSC, RN and of Vera Frances Effa Vickery, MBE; *m* 1975, Sylvia Mylroie (*see* S. Jay). *Educ:* Winchester Coll.; Magdalen Coll., Oxford (MA); School of Oriental and African Studies, London Univ. (MSc 1969). ODM, 1969–73; UK Delegn, IMF-IBRD, Washington, 1973–75; ODM, 1976–78; First Sec., New Delhi, 1978–81; FCO, 1981–85; Counsellor: Cabinet Office, 1985–87; (Financial and Commercial), Paris, 1987–90; Asst Under-Sec. of State for EC Affairs, FCO, 1990–93; Dep. Under-Sec. of State (Dir for EC and Economic Affairs), FCO, 1994–96; Ambassador to France, 1996–2001. Sen. Associate Mem., St Antony's Coll., Oxford, 1996. *Address:* c/o Foreign and Commonwealth Office, SW1A 2AH. *T:* (020) 7270 3000.

JAY, Hon. Peter; writer and broadcaster; *b* 7 Feb. 1937; *s* of Baron Jay, PC and of Margaret (Peggy) Christian Jay; *m* 1st, 1961, Margaret Ann (*see* Baroness Jay of Paddington) (marr. diss. 1986), *d* of Baron Callaghan of Cardiff, *qv*; one *s* two *d*; one *s*; 2nd, 1986, Emma, *d* of P. K. Thornton, *qv*; three *s*. *Educ:* Winchester Coll.; Christ Church, Oxford (MA 1st cl. hons PPE, 1960). President of the Union, 1960. Nuffield Coll., 1960. Midshipman and Sub-Lt RNVR, 1956–57. Asst Principal 1961–64, Private Sec. to Jt Perm. Sec. 1964, Principal 1964–67, HM Treasury; Economics Editor, The Times, 1967–77, and Associate Editor, Times Business News, 1969–77; Presenter, Weekend World (ITV Sunday morning series), 1972–77; The Jay Interview (ITV series), 1975–76; Ambassador to US, 1977–79; Dir Economist Intelligence Unit, 1979–83. Consultant, Economist Gp, 1979–81; Chm. and Chief Exec., TV-am Ltd, 1980–83 and TV-am News, 1982–83, Pres., TV-am, 1983–; Presenter, A Week in Politics, Channel 4, 1983–86; COS to Robert Maxwell (Chm., Mirror Gp Newspapers Ltd), 1986–89; Supervising Editor, Banking World, 1986–89 (Editor, 1984–86); Economics and Business

Editor, 1990–2001, Economics Editor, 2001, BBC. Presenter, The Road to Riches, BBC TV series, 2000. Chairman: NACRO Working Party on Children and Young Persons in Custody, 1976–77; NCVO, 1981–86 (Vice-Pres., 1986–92); Trustee, Charities Aid Foundn, 1981–86; Chm., Charities Effectiveness Review Trust, 1986–87. Vis. Scholar, Brookings Instn, Washington, 1979–80; Wincott Meml Lectr, 1975; Copland Meml Lectr, Australia, 1980; Shell Lectr, Glasgow, 1985. Hon. Prof., Univ. of Wales, Aberystwyth, 2001–. Governor, Ditchley Foundn, 1982–; Mem. Council, St George's House, Windsor, 1982–. Dir, New Nat. Theater, Washington, DC, 1979–81. Political Broadcaster of Year, 1973; Harold Wincott Financial and Economic Journalist of Year, 1973; RTS Male Personality of Year (Pye Award), 1974; SFTA Shell Internat. TV Award, 1974; RTS Home News Award, 1992. FRGS 1977. Hon. DH Ohio State Univ., 1978; Hon. DLitt Wake Forest Univ., 1979; Berkeley Citation, Univ. of Calif, 1979. *Publications:* The Budget, 1972; (contrib.) America and the World 1979, 1980; The Crisis for Western Political Economy and other Essays, 1984; (with Michael Stewart) Apocalypse 2000, 1987; Road to Riches, or The Wealth of Man, 2000; contrib. Foreign Affairs jl. *Recreation:* sailing. *Address:* Hensington Farmhouse, Woodstock, Oxon OX20 1LH. *T:* (01993) 811222, *Fax:* (01993) 812861; *e-mail:* peter@jay.prestel.co.uk. *Clubs:* Garrick; Royal Naval Sailing Association, Royal Cork Yacht.

See also Hon. M. Jay.

JAY, Robert Maurice; QC 1998; a Recorder, since 2000; *b* 20 Sept. 1959; *s* of Prof. Barrie Samuel Jay, *qv* and Marcelle Ruby Jay; *m* 1997, Deborah Jacinta Trenner; one *d*. *Educ:* King's Coll. Sch. (Open Schol.); New Coll., Oxford (Open Schol.; BA 1st cl. Hons Jurisp. 1980). Called to the Bar, Middle Temple, 1981; in practice at the Bar, 1981–. Jun. Counsel to the Crown (Common Law), 1989–98. *Recreations:* golf, opera, chess, bridge, politics. *Address:* 39 Essex Street, WC2R 3AT. *T:* (020) 7832 1111. *Clubs:* Royal Automobile; Coombe Hill Golf.

JAY, Sylvia, (Lady Jay); Director General, Food and Drink Federation, since 2001; *b* 1 Nov. 1946; *d* of William Edwin Mylroie and Edie Mylroie (*née* Chew); *m* 1975, Michael Hastings Jay (*see* Sir M. H. Jay). *Educ:* Nottingham Univ. (BA (Hons) Soc. Sci.); London Sch. of Econs. Home Civil Service: Admin. grade, ODA, 1971–87; secondments to French Ministère de la Coopération, 1988–89, to French Trésor, Paris, 1990, to EBRD, London, 1990–93; Clerk to European Union Sub-cttee A, H of L, 1994–96; accomp. husband, Ambassador to France, Paris, 1996–2000. Mem. Bd, Saint-Gobain, 2001–. Lay Mem., Professional Conduct and Complaints Cttee, General Council of the Bar, 2001–. *Recreations:* cooking, reading, sewing, walking, opera. *Address:* Food and Drink Federation, 6 Catherine Street, WC2B 5JJ. *T:* (020) 7836 2460.

JAYAWARDENA, Dr Lal; Chairman, World Bank-sponsored Global Development Network of Development Research Institutions, Washington; Senior Fellow, Social Scientists Association, Colombo; *b* 27 May 1934; *s* of Neville Ubesinghe Jayawardena and late Gertrude Mildred Jayawardena; *m* 1958, Kumari de Zoysa; one *s*. *Educ:* Royal Coll., Colombo; King's Coll., Cambridge (BA 1956; MA, PhD 1963; Hon. Fellow, 1989). Econs Affairs Officer, UN, 1963–66; Econ. Advr and Dir, Perspective Planning Div., Min. of Planning and Econ. Affairs, Colombo, 1963–71; Additional Sec., 1971–75, Sec. to Treasury, and Sec., 1975–78, Min. of Finance and Planning; Ambassador to Belgium, The Netherlands, Luxembourg and EC, 1978–82; Dir-Gen., Econ. Affairs, Min. of Foreign Affairs, 1982–85; Asst Sec.-Gen., UN, and Dir, World Inst. for Develt Econs Res., Helsinki, 1985–93; Econ. Advr to Pres. of Sri Lanka, 1994–99; Dep. Chm., Nat. Develt Council, 1996–99; High Comr for Sri Lanka in UK and concurrently to Republic of Ireland, 1999–2000. Rapporteur, Vice-Chm., then Chm., 1972–74, Second Vice-Chm., then First Vice-Chm., 1997–99, Deputies of Gp of Twenty-Four (G-24); Dep., Cttee of Twenty on Reform of Internat. Monetary System, 1972–74; Mem., Gp of Eminent Persons advising Brandt Commn on Internat. Develt Issues, 1978–80. *Publications:* (contrib.) The International Monetary and Financial System, ed G. K. Helleiner, 1996; contrib. and contrib. jtly numerous monographs in World Inst. for Develt Econs Res. Study Gp series; contrib. numerous articles on develt econs. *Recreations:* reading, music. *Address:* No 69 Gregory's Road, Colombo 7, Sri Lanka. *T:* (1) 692656, *Fax:* (1) 697792.

JAYSON, Prof. Malcolm Irving Vivian, MD; FRCP; Professor of Rheumatology and Director, University Centre for the Study of Chronic Rheumatism, University of Manchester, 1977–96, now Emeritus Professor; *b* 9 Dec. 1937; *s* of Joseph and Sybil Jayson; *m* 1962, Judith Tauber; two *s*. *Educ:* Middlesex Hosp. Med. Sch., Univ. of London (MB, BS 1961); MD Bristol, 1969; MSc Manchester, 1977. FRCP 1976. House Physician, 1961, House Surgeon, 1962, Middlesex Hosp.; House Physician: Central Middlesex Hosp., 1962; Brompton Hosp., 1963; Sen. House Officer, Middlesex Hosp, 1963; Registrar: Westminster Hosp., 1964; Royal Free Hosp., 1965; Lectr, Univ. of Bristol, Royal Nat. Hosp. for Rheumatic Diseases, Bath, and Bristol Royal Infirmary, 1967; Sen. Lectr, Univ. of Bristol, and Consultant, Royal Nat. Hosp. for Rheumatic Diseases, Bath, and Bristol Royal Infirmary, 1979. Visiting Professor: Univ. of Iowa, 1984; Univ. of Queensland, 1985; Univ. of Cairo, 1992. Gen. Sec., Internat. Back Pain Soc., 1986–; President: Soc. of Chiropodists, 1984; Arachnoiditis Self-Help Gp, 1989–; Pres., Internat. Soc. for Study of the Lumbar Spine, 1995–96. *Publications:* (with A. StJ. Dixon) Rheumatism and Arthritis, 1974, 8th edn 1991; The Lumbar Spine and Back Pain, 1976, 4th edn 1992; Back Pain: the facts, 1981, 3rd edn 1992; (with C. Black) Systemic Sclerosis: Scleroderma, 1988; contribs to Lancet, BMJ and other med. jls. *Recreations:* antiques (especially sundials), trout fishing. *Address:* The Gate House, 8 Lancaster Road, Didsbury, Manchester M20 2TY. *T:* (0161) 445 1729. *Club:* Royal Society of Medicine.

JAYSTON, Michael, (Michael James); actor; *b* 29 Oct. 1935; *s* of Aubrey Vincent James and Edna Myfanwy Llewelyn; *m* 1st, 1965, Lynn Farleigh (marr. diss. 1970); 2nd, 1970, Heather Mary Sneddon (marr. diss. 1977); 3rd, 1978, Elizabeth Ann Smithson; three *s* one *d*. *Educ:* Becket Grammar School, Nottingham; Guildhall Sch. of Music and Drama (FGSM). *Stage:* Salisbury Playhouse, 1962–63 (parts incl. Henry II, in Becket); Bristol Old Vic, 1963–65; RSC, 1965–69 (incl. Ghosts, All's Well That Ends Well, Hamlet, The Homecoming (NY), The Relapse); Equus, NT, 1973, Albery, 1977; Private Lives, Duchess, 1980; The Sound of Music, Apollo, 1981; The Way of the World, Chichester, 1984, Haymarket, 1985; Woman in Mind, Vaudeville, 1987; Dancing at Lughnasa, Garrick, 1992; The Wind in the Willows, NT, 1994; Easy Virtue, Chichester, 1999; *films include:* Midsummer Night's Dream, 1968; Cromwell, 1969; Nicholas and Alexandra, 1970; *television includes:* Beethoven, 1969; Mad Jack, 1970; Wilfred Owen, 1971; The Power Game, 1978; Tinker, Tailor, Soldier, Spy, 1979; Dr Who, 1986; A Bit of a Do, 1988, 1989; Haggard, 1990; Darling Buds of May, 1992; Outside Edge, 1995, 1996; Only Fools and Horses, 1996. Life Mem., Battersea Dogs Home. *Recreations:* cricket, darts, chess. *Address:* c/o Michael Whitehall, 125 Gloucester Road, SW7 4TE. *Clubs:* MCC, Lord's Taverners', Cricketers'; Sussex CC, Gedling Colliery CC (Vice-Pres.); Rottingdean CC (Pres.).

JEAFFRESON, David Gregory, CBE 1981; Deputy Chairman, Big Island Holdings (formerly Big Island Contracting) (HK) Ltd, since 1992; *b* 23 Nov. 1931; *s* of Bryan Leslie Jeaffreson, MD, FRCS, MRCOG and Margaret Jeaffreson; *m* 1959, Elisabeth Marie Jausions; two *s* two *d* (and one *d* decd). *Educ:* Bootham Sch., York; Clare Coll., Cambridge (MA). 2nd Lieut, RA, 1950. Dist Officer, Tanganyika, 1955–58; Asst Man., Henricot Steel Foundry, 1959–60; Admin. Officer, Hong Kong Govt, 1961; Dep. Financial Sec., 1972–76; Sec. for Economic Services, 1976–82; Sec. for Security, 1982–88; Comr, Independent Commn Against Corruption, 1988–92. *Recreations:* history, music, sailing, walking. *Address:* A2 Cherry Court, 12 Consort Rise, Hong Kong. *T:* 28188025. *Club:* Royal Hong Kong Yacht.

JEANES, Leslie Edwin Elloway, CBE 1982; Chief of Public Relations, Ministry of Defence, 1978–81, retired; *b* 17 Dec. 1920; *er s* of late Edwin Eli Jubilee Jeanes and of Mary Eunice Jeanes; *m* 1942, Valerie Ruth, *d* of Ernest and Ethel Vidler; one *d*. *Educ:* Westcliff High Sch. Entered Civil Service, 1939; Inf. Officer, DSIR, 1948–65; Chief Press Officer, Min. of Technol., 1965–68; Dep. Head of Inf., MoT, 1968–70; Head of News, DoE, 1970–73; Chief Inf. Officer, MAFF, 1973–78. *Recreations:* gardening, motoring, DIY. *Address:* 14 Whistley Close, Bracknell, Berks RG12 9LQ. *T:* (01344) 429429.

See also R. E. Jeanes.

JEANES, Ronald Eric; Deputy Director, Building Research Establishment, 1981–86; *b* 23 Sept. 1926; *s* of Edwin and Eunice Jeanes; *m* 1951, Helen Field (*née* Entwistle); one *s* one *d*. *Educ:* University Coll., Exeter (BSc 1951). Served HM Forces, 1945–48. Royal Naval Scientific Service, 1951–62; BRE, 1962–86. *Publications:* DoE and BRE reports. *Recreation:* amateur theatre. *Address:* 1 Wrensfield, Hemel Hempstead, Herts HP1 1RN. *T:* (01442) 258713.

See also L. E. E. Jeanes.

JEANNERET, Marian Elizabeth; *see* Hobson, M. E.

JEANNIOT, Pierre Jean, OC 1988; Director General and Chief Executive Officer, International Air Transport Association, since 1993; *b* Montpellier, France, 9 April 1933; *s* of Gaston and Renée Jeanniot; *m* 1979, Marcia David; two *s* one *d*. *Educ:* Sir George Williams Univ. (BSc); McGill Univ. (Management Prog.). Sperry Gyroscope, 1952–55; Air Canada, 1955–68; Vice-Pres., Computers and Communications, Québec Univ., 1969; Air Canada: Vice-Pres., Computer and Systems Services, 1970–76; subseq. Exec., sales, marketing, planning subsid. cos; Exec. Vice-Pres. and Chief Operating Officer, 1980; Pres. and CEO, 1984–90; Pres. and CEO, JINMAG Inc., 1990–92; Director, Bank of Nova Scotia. Pres., Canadian OR Soc., 1966; Chm., Air Transport Assoc. of Canada, 1984; Mem., Exec. Cttee and Chm., Strategic Planning Sub-Cttee, IATA, 1988–90. Chm., Council for Canadian Unity, 1991–94. University of Québec: Chm. Bd, 1972–78; Pres., Foundn, 1978–92; Chancellor, 1995–; Hon. Dr, 1988; Hon. LLD Concordia Univ., 1997. Chm. and participant, numerous charitable bodies. Chevalier, Légion d'Honneur (France), 1991; Independence Medal (First Order) (Kingdom of Jordan), 1995. *Address:* IATA, PO Box 416, 1215 Geneva 15 Airport, Switzerland. *T:* (22) 7992526.

JEANS, Christopher James Marwood; QC 1997; *b* 24 Jan. 1956; *s* of late David Marwood Jeans and of Rosalie Jean Jeans; *m* 1998, Judith Mary Laws; one *d*. *Educ:* Minchenden Sch.; King's Coll. London (LLB 1977); St John's Coll., Oxford (BCL 1979). Called to the Bar, Gray's Inn, 1980; Lectr, City of London Poly., 1981–83; in practice at the Bar, 1983–. Part-time Chm., Employment Tribunals, 1998–. Fellow, Inst. of Continuing Professional Develt, 1998. *Recreations:* football (Spurs), cricket, walking, swimming, cinema, theatre, arctic and world travel. *Address:* 11 King's Bench Walk, Temple, EC4Y 7EQ.

JEAPES, Maj.-Gen. Anthony Showan, CB 1987; OBE 1977; MC 1960; retired; Member, Lord Chancellor's Panel of Independent Inspectors, since 1991; *b* 6 March 1935; *s* of Stanley Arthur Jeapes; *m* 1959, Jennifer Clare White; one *s* one *d*. *Educ:* Raynes Park Grammar Sch.; RMA Sandhurst. Commissioned Dorset, later Devonshire and Dorset, Regt, 1955; joined 22 SAS Regt, 1958; attached US Special Forces, 1961; Staff College, 1966; Brigade Major, 39 Inf. Bde, NI, 1967; Sqn Comdr, 22 SAS Regt, 1968; Nat. Defence Coll., 1971; Directing Staff, Staff Coll., Camberley, 1972; CO 22 SAS Regt, 1974; Mem., British Mil. Adv. Team, Bangladesh, 1977; Dep. Comdr, Sch. of Infantry, 1979; Comdr, 5 Airborne Brigade, 1982; Comdr, Land Forces NI, 1985–87; GOC, SW Dist, 1987–90. Vice-Chairman: Romanian Orphanage Trust, 1991–99; European Children's Trust, 1995–99. *Publications:* SAS Operation Oman, 1980; SAS Secret War, 1996. *Recreations:* offshore sailing, deer management, country pursuits. *Address:* c/o National Westminster Bank, Warminster, Wilts BA12 9AW. *Club:* Army and Navy.

JEAVONS, (Robert) Clyde (Scott); Curator, National Film and Television Archive, British Film Institute, 1990–97; *b* 30 June 1939; *s* of Frank Rechab Scott-Jeavons and Olive Edith (*née* Robins); *m* 1st, 1963, Hilary Coopey (marr. diss.); one *d*; 2nd, 1977, Orly Yadin. *Educ:* Royal Russell Sch.; University Coll. London (BA Hons Scandinavian Studies). Asst Stage Manager, Det Norske Riksteatret, Norway, 1963; financial journalist, Investors' Rev., 1964; Chief Sub, Features Ed. and book reviewer and film critic, SHE mag., 1964–69; Dep. Curator and Hd, Film and TV Acquisitions, Nat. Film Archive, BFI, 1969–85; freelance author and film programmer, 1986–90. Member: Satyajit Ray Foundn; BAFTA; Critics' Circle; FRSA 1992. Hon. FBKS 1994. *Publications:* (with Michael Parkinson) A Pictorial History of Westerns, 1974; A Pictorial History of War Films, 1975; (with Jeremy Pascall) A Pictorial History of Sex in the Movies, 1976; British Film-Makers of the Eighties, 1990; contrib. Sight & Sound, Monthly Film Bull., Guardian, etc. *Recreations:* cricket, travel, dining, music, film, popular literature, reading the New Yorker. *Address:* Garden Flat, 110A Highbury New Park, N5 2DR. *T:* (020) 7226 6778. *Clubs:* Union; Brondesbury Cricket, Barnes Cricket (Hon. Mem.).

JEBB, family name of **Baron Gladwyn**.

JEBB, Dom (Anthony) Philip, MA; Prior, Downside Abbey, since 1991; Parish Priest, Radstock, since 1998; *b* 14 Aug. 1932; 2nd *s* of late Reginald Jebb and Eleanor, *d* of Hilaire Belloc. *Educ:* Downside; Christ's Coll., Cambridge, 1957–60 (MA Classics). Professed at Downside, 1951; priest, 1956; Curate, Midsomer Norton, 1960–62; teaching at Downside, 1960–97; House master, 1962–75; Dep. Head Master, 1975–80; Headmaster, 1980–91; Dir. of Sch. Appeal, 1996–98. Archivist and Annalist, English Benedictine Congregation, 1972–; Mem., EBC Theological Commn, 1969–82 (Chm., 1979–82); Delegate to General Chapter, EBC, 1981–2001; Mem., Central Cttee, 1987–88, Chm., SW Div., 1988, HMC; Member: Council, Somerset Records Soc., 1975–97; Cttee, Area 7, SHA, 1984–91; Court, Bath Univ., 1983–85. Trustee, Somerset Archaeol and Natural Hist. Soc., 1989–97 (Pres., 1993–94). Vice-Pres., SW Amateur Fencing Assoc., 1970–. Chaplain of Magistral Obedience, British Assoc., Sovereign Mil. Order of Malta, 1978–; Asst Chaplain, Shepton Mallet Prison, 1995–. Gov., St Antony's-Leweston Sch., 1980–97. *Publications:* Missale de Lesnes, 1964; Religious Education, 1968; Widowed, 1973, 2nd edn 1976; contrib. Consider Your Call, 1978, 2nd edn 1979; A Touch of God, 1982; (ed) By Death Parted, 1986; In a Quiet Garden, 1999; contribs to Downside Review, The Way, The Sword. *Recreations:* fencing, archaeology, astronomy, canoeing. *Address:* Downside Abbey, Stratton-on-the-Fosse, Radstock BA3 4RH. *T:* (01761) 235148.

JEDDERE-FISHER, Arthur; Solicitor, Customs and Excise, 1982–85; *b* 15 July 1924; *s* of late Major Harry and Sarah Jeddere-Fisher; *m* 1947, Marcia Vincent, *d* of Kenneth Clarence Smith; three *s* one *d*. *Educ:* Harrow Sch.; Christ Church, Oxford (MA). Served War of 1939–45, Air Engineer, Royal Navy, 1942–46 (despatches). Called to Bar, Inner Temple, 1949; Magistrate, Senior Magistrate and Chairman Land Tribunal, Fiji, 1953–69; joined Solicitor's Office, HM Customs and Excise, 1970, Principal Asst Solicitor, 1977–82. *Recreations:* the collection and use of historic machinery, cricket, bird photography. *Address:* Apsley Cottage, Kingston Blount, Chinnor OX39 4SJ. *T:* (01844) 351300. *Clubs:* MCC, Vintage Sports Car.

JEEPS, Richard Eric Gautrey, CBE 1977; Chairman, Sports Council, 1978–85; *b* 25 Nov. 1931; *s* of Francis Herbert and Mildred Mary Jeeps; *m* 1954, Jean Margaret Levitt (marr. diss.); three *d*. *Educ:* Bedford Modern Sch. Rugby career: Cambridge City, 1948–49; Northampton, 1949–62 and 1964; Eastern Counties, 1950–62; England, 1956–62 (24 caps); Barbarians, 1958–62; British Lions: SA, 1955; NZ, 1959; SA 1962; 13 Tests. Rugby Football Union: Mem. Cttee, 1962–78; Pres., 1976–77. Formerly: Mem., English Tourist Bd; Trustee, Sports Aid Trust. *Recreations:* Rugby Union football, sport. *Address:* Alcheringa, 1 Burwell Road, Exning, Suffolk CB8 7EX.

JEEVES, Prof. Malcolm Alexander, CBE 1992; FMedSci, FBPsS; PPRSE; Professor of Psychology, University of St Andrews, 1969–93, Hon. Research Professor, since 1993; *b* 16 Nov. 1926; *s* of Alderman Alexander Frederic Thomas Jeeves and Helena May Jeeves (*née* Hammond); *m* 1955, Ruth Elisabeth Hartridge; two *d*. *Educ:* Stamford Sch.; St John's Coll., Cambridge (MA, PhD). Commissioned Royal Lincs Regt, served 1st Bn Sherwood Foresters, BAOR, 1945–48. Cambridge University: Exhibnr, St John's Coll., 1948, Res. Exhibnr, 1952; Burney Student, 1952; Gregg Bury Prizeman, 1954; Kenneth Craik Res. Award, St John's Coll., 1955. Rotary Foundn Fellow, Harvard, 1953; Lectr, Leeds Univ., 1956; Prof. of Psychology, Adelaide Univ., 1959–69, and Dean, Faculty of Arts, 1962–64; Vice-Principal, St Andrews Univ., 1981–85; Dir, MRC Cognitive Neuroscience Res. Gp, St Andrews, 1984–89. Lectures: Abbie Meml, Adelaide Univ., 1981; Cairns Meml, Aust., 1986; New Coll., Univ. of NSW, 1987. Member: SSRC Psych. Cttee, 1972–76; Biol. Cttee, 1980–84, Science Bd, 1985–89, Council, 1985–89, SERC; MRC Neuroscience and Mental Health Bd, 1985–89; Council, 1984–88, Exec., 1985–87, Vice-Pres., 1990–93, Pres., 1996–99, RSE; ABRC Manpower Sub-Cttee, 1991–93; Pres., Section J, BAAS, 1988. Founder FMedSci 1998. Hon. Sheriff, Fife, 1986–. Hon. DSc: Edinburgh, 1993; St Andrews, 2000; DUniv. Stirling, 1999. Editor-in-Chief, Neuropsychologia, 1990–93. *Publications:* (with Z. P. Dienes) Thinking in Structures, 1965 (trans. French, German, Spanish, Italian, Japanese); (with Z. P. Dienes) The Effects of Structural Relations upon Transfer, 1968; The Scientific Enterprise and Christian Faith, 1969; Experimental Psychology: an introduction for Biologists, 1974; Psychology and Christianity: the view both ways, 1976 (trans. Chinese); (with G. B. Greer) Analysis of Structural Learning, 1983; (with R. J. Berry and D. Atkinson) Free to be Different, 1984; Behavioural Sciences: a Christian perspective, 1984; (with D. G. Myers) Psychology—through the eyes of faith, 1987; Mind Fields, 1994; Human Nature at the Millennium, 1997; (with R. J. Berry) Science, Life and Christian Belief, 1998; papers in sci. jls, mainly on neuropsychology and cognition. *Recreations:* music, fly fishing, walking. *Address:* Psychology Laboratory, The University, St Andrews KY16 9JU. *T:* (01334) 462057. *Club:* New (Edinburgh).

See also E. R. Dobbs.

JEEWOOLALL, Sir Ramesh, Kt 1979; Speaker, Mauritius Parliament, 1979–82 and since 1996; *b* 20 Dec. 1940; *s* of Shivprasad Jeewoolall; *m* 1971, Usweenee (*née* Reetoo); two *s*. *Educ:* in Mauritius; Inns of Court Sch. of Law. Called to the Bar, Middle Temple, 1968; practising at the Bar, 1969–71; Magistrate, 1971–72; practising at the Bar and Chm., Mauritius Tea Develt Authority, 1972–76. Mem., Mauritius Parlt, 1976–82 and 1987–91; Minister of Housing, Lands, Town and Country Planning and the Envmt, 1987–90; Dep. Speaker, 1977–79. Pres., CPA, 1996–97 (Vice-Pres., 1995–96). *Recreations:* reading, conversation, chess. *Address:* 92 Belle Rose Avenue, Quatre Bornes, Mauritius. *T:* 4645371.

JEFFARES, Prof. Alexander Norman, (Derry), Hon. AM 1988; MA, PhD, DPhil; Docteur de l'Université (*hc*) Lille, 1977; Hon. DLitt Ulster, 1990; FRSA 1963; FRSL 1965; FRSE 1981; Professor of English Studies, Stirling University, 1974–86, Hon. Professor, since 1986; Managing Director, Academic Advisory Services Ltd, since 1975; Director, Colin Smythe Ltd, since 1978; *b* 11 Aug. 1920; *s* of late C. Norman Jeffares, Dublin; *m* 1947, Jeanne Agnès, *d* of late E. Calembert, Brussels; one *d*. *Educ:* The High Sch., Dublin; Trinity Coll., Dublin (Hon. Fellow, 1978); Oriel Coll., Oxford. Lectr in Classics, Univ. of Dublin, 1943–44; Lector in English, Univ. of Groningen, 1946–48; Lectr in English, Univ. of Edinburgh, 1949–51; Jury Prof. of English Language and Literature, Univ. of Adelaide, 1951–56; Prof. of English Lit., Leeds Univ., 1957–74. Sec., Australian Humanities Res. Council, 1954–57; Corresp. Mem. for Great Britain and Ireland, 1958–70; Hon. Fellow, Aust. Acad. of the Humanities, 1970–. Mem. Council, RSE, 1985– (a Vice-Pres., 1988–89); Scottish Arts Council: Mem., 1979–84; Vice-Chm., 1980–84; Chm., Literature Cttee, 1979–83; Chm., Touring Cttee, 1983–84; Chm., Housing the Arts, 1980–84; Mem., Arts Council of GB, 1980–84. Chm., Book Trust Scotland (formerly NBL (Scotland)), 1984–89; Mem. Exec. Cttee, NBL, 1984–86; Mem. Bd, Book Trust, 1987–88. Pres., Internat. PEN Scottish Centre, 1986–89; Mem., Exec. Cttee, Scots Australian Council, 1992–. Vice-Pres., Film and Television Council of S Aust., 1951–56; Chairman: Assoc. for Commonwealth Literature and Language Studies, 1966–68, Hon. Fellow, 1971; Internat. Assoc. for Study of Anglo-Irish Literature, 1968–70, Co-Chm., 1971–73, Hon. Life Pres., 1973–; Dir, Yeats Internat. Summer Sch., Sligo, 1969–71. Hon. Res. Fellow, Royal Holloway, Univ. of London, 1996. Editor, A Review of English Literature, 1960–67; General Editor: Writers and Critics, 1960–73; New Oxford English Series, 1963–; Macmillan History of Literature, 1983–; (with Michael Alexander) Macmillan Anthologies of English Literature, 1989; York Classics, 1988–; York Insights, 1989–; Joint Editor, Biography and Criticism, 1963–73; Literary Editor, Fountainwell Drama Texts, 1968–75; Co-Editor, York Notes, 1980–; Editor: Ariel, A Review of Internat. English Literature, 1970–72; York Handbooks, 1984–. *Publications:* Trinity College, Dublin: drawings and descriptions, 1944; W. B. Yeats: man and poet, 1949, rev. edn 1996; Seven Centuries of Poetry, 1955, rev. edn 1960; (with M. Bryn Davies) The Scientific Background, 1958; The Poetry of W. B. Yeats, 1961; (ed with G. F. Cross) In Excited Reverie: centenary tribute to W. B. Yeats, 1965; Fair Liberty was All His Cry: a tercentenary tribute to Jonathan Swift 1667–1743, 1967; A Commentary on the Collected Poems of W. B. Yeats, 1968; (ed) Restoration Comedy, 4 vols, 1974; (with A. S. Knowland) A Commentary on the Collected Plays of W. B. Yeats, 1975; (ed) Yeats: the critical heritage, 1977; A History of Anglo-Irish Literature, 1982; A New Commentary on the Poems of W. B. Yeats, 1984; Brought up in Dublin (poems), 1987; Brought up to Leave (poems), 1987; (ed with Antony Kamm) An Irish Childhood, 1987; (ed with Antony Kamm) A Jewish Childhood, 1988; W. B. Yeats: a new biography, 1988, rev. edn 2001; (ed) Yeats's Poems, 1989, rev. edn 1996; (ed) W. B. Yeats: the love poems, 1990; (ed) W. B. Yeats: A Vision and related writings, 1990; (ed) W. B. Yeats: poems of place, 1991; (ed with Anna White) Always Your Friend: the Gonne-Yeats letters 1893–1938, 1992; (ed) Jonathan Swift: the selected poems, 1992; (with Brendan Kennelly) (ed) Joycechoyce, 1992; (ed jtly) Ireland's Women: writings past and present, 1994; (ed with Anna White) Maud Gonne, a servant of the Queen, 1994; Images of Imagination: Irish essays, 1996; (ed with Martin Gray) The Collins Dictionary of Quotations, 1995; (ed) Victorian Love Poems, 1996; A Pocket History of Irish Literature, 1997; (ed) Irish Love Poems, 1997; The Irish Literary Movement: character sketches, 1998; (ed) The Secret Rose: love poems by W. B. Yeats, 1998; (ed) Ireland's Love Poems: wonder and a wild desire, 2000; (ed) Oliver St John Gogarty: poems and plays, 2001; also: edns of works by Congreve, Farquhar, Goldsmith, Sheridan, Cowper, Maria Edgeworth, Disraeli, Whitman and Yeats; edns of criticisms of Swift, Scott and Yeats; various monographs on Swift, Goldsmith, George Moore, Yeats, Oliver St John Gogarty; contribs to learned jls. *Recreations:* drawing, motoring. *Address:* Craighead Cottage, Fife Ness, Crail, Fife KY10 3XN. *Clubs:* Athenæum, Royal Commonwealth Society.

JEFFCOTT, Prof. Leo Broof, PhD, DVSc; FRCVS; Professor of Veterinary Clinical Studies, and Dean of Veterinary School, University of Cambridge, since 1991; Professorial Fellow, Pembroke College, Cambridge, since 1993; *b* 19 June 1942; *s* of late Edward Ian Broof Jeffcott and of Pamela Mary (*née* Hull); *m* 1969, Tisza Jacqueline (*née* Hubbard); two *d*. *Educ:* Univ. of London (BVetMed 1967, PhD 1972); Univ. of Melbourne (DVSc 1989); MA Cantab 1994. FRCVS 1978. Animal Health Trust, Newmarket: Asst Pathologist, 1967–71; Clinician, 1972–77; Head, Clinical Dept, 1977–81; Professor: of Clinical Radiology, Swedish Univ. of Agricl Scis, Uppsala, 1981–82; of Veterinary Clinical Sciences, Univ. of Melbourne, 1982–91. Chm., Internat. Cttee for 5th Internat. Conf. on Equine Exercise Physiology, 1994–98; Mem. Bureau, FEI, 1998– (Chm., Vet. Cttee, 1998–). Lectures: Sir Frederick Hobday Meml, BEVA, 1977; Peter Hernqvist, Swedish Univ. of Agricl Scis, Skara, 1991; Share-Jones, RCVS, 1993. FEI Official Veterinarian: Seoul Olympics, 1988; World Equestrian Games, Stockholm, 1990, The Hague, 1994, Rome, 1998; Jerez, 2002; Barcelona Olympics, 1992; Atlanta Olympics, 1996; Sydney Olympics, 2000. Hon. FRVC 1997. VetMedDr *hc* Swedish Univ. of Agricl Scis, 2000. Norman Hall Medal for Research, RCVS, 1978; Internat. Prize of Tierklinik Hochmoor, Germany, 1981; Equine Veterinary Jl Open Award, BEVA, 1982; John Hickman Orthopaedic Prize, BEVA, 1991; Internat. Hall of Fame Award for Equine Res., Univ. of Kentucky, 1991; UK Equestrian Award for Scientific Achievement, 1994; Sefton Award for Services to Equestrian Safety, 1997. *Publications:* (with R. K. Archer) Comparative Clinical Haematology, 1977; (ed jtly) Equine Exercise Physiology 3, 1991; (with G. Dalin) Osteochondrosis in the 90s, 1993; (with A. F. Clarke) On to Atlanta '96, 1994; (with A. F. Clarke) Progress towards Atlanta '96: thermoregulatory responses during competitive exercise with performance horse, Vol. I 1995, Vol. II 1996; Equine Exercise Physiology 5, 1999; (ed jtly) Osteochondrosis and Musculoskeletal Development in the Foal Under the Influence of Exercise, 1999; (ed with P. D. Rossdale) A Tribute to Colonel John Hickman, 2001. *Recreations:* swimming, photography, equestrian sports. *Address:* Department of Clinical Veterinary Medicine, University of Cambridge, Madingley Road, Cambridge CB3 0ES. *T:* (01223) 337764.

JEFFERIES, David George, CBE 1990; FREng; Chairman: National Grid Group plc, 1990–99; Viridian Group (formerly Northern Ireland Electricity) plc, 1994–98; *b* 26 Dec. 1933; *s* of Rose and George Jefferies; *m* 1959, Jeanette Ann Hanson. *Educ:* SE Coll. of Technology. FREng (FEng 1989); FIEE, CIMgt, FInstE. Southern Electricity Board: Area Manager, Portsmouth, 1967–72; Staff Coll., Henley, 1970; Chief Engr, 1972–74; Dir, NW Region, CEGB, 1974–77; Dir Personnel, CEGB, 1977–81; Chm., London Electricity Bd, 1981–86; Dep. Chm., Electricity Council, 1986–89. Non-exec. Dir, Strategic Rail Authy, 1999–; Chairman: 24/Seven Utilities Service Co., 1999–; Smartlogik, 2000–; Costain, 2001–. Chm., Electricity Pension Scheme, 1986–97. Chm., Power Sector Working Gp, 1993–; Co-Chm., Indo-British Partnership, 1999–. President: Energy Industries Club, 1991–93; Inst. of Energy, 1994–96; Electricity Assoc., 1996–97; IEE, 1997–98; Electrical and Electronic Industries Benevolent Assoc., 1998–99. Liveryman, Wax Chandlers' Co., 1984–. Hon. DTech Brunel, 1992; Hon. LLD Manchester, 1993. *Recreations:* golf, gardening, music. *Address:* Espada, 30 Abbots Drive, Virginia Water, Surrey GU25 4SE. *Clubs:* Athenæum, Royal Automobile; Wentworth.

JEFFERIES, Roger David; Independent Housing Ombudsman, 1997–2001; *b* 13 Oct. 1939; *s* of George Edward Jefferies and Freda Rose Jefferies (*née* Marshall); *m* 1st, 1962, Jennifer Anne Southgate (marr. diss.); one *s* two *d*; 2nd, 1974, Margaret Sealy (marr. diss.); 3rd, 1984, Pamela Mary Elsey (*née* Holden); one *s*. *Educ:* Whitgift School; Balliol College, Oxford. BA, BCL; solicitor. Member: Law Society, 1965–; British and Irish Ombudsman Assoc., 1997–. Asst Solicitor, Coventry Corporation, 1965–68; Asst Town Clerk, Southend-on-Sea County Borough Council, 1968–70; Director of Operations, London Borough of Hammersmith, 1970–75; Chief Exec., London Borough of Hounslow, 1975–90; Under Secretary, DoE, 1983–85 (on secondment); Chief Exec., London Bor. of Croydon, 1990–93; Housing Assoc. Tenants' Ombudsman, 1993–97. Chm., Discipline Cttees, Lambeth, Southwark and Lewisham HA, 1998–. Non-exec. Dir, Nat. Clinical Assessment Authy, 2001–. Member: Regl Planning Bd, Arts Council of GB, 1986–88; Adv. Bd, Lewisham Theatre, 1994–99; Council, RIPA, 1982–88; Bd, Public Finance Foundn, 1987–93; Pres., SOLACE, 1990–91. Clerk: Mortlake Crematorium Bd, 1973–90; W London Waste Authy, 1986–90. Director: Extemporary Dance Co., 1989–91; Croydon Business Venture, 1991–93; Solotec, 1992–93. Hon. Sec., Commn for Local Democracy, 1993–96. Trustee, S African Advanced Educn Project, 1989–96. *Publication:* Tackling the Town Hall, 1982. *Recreations:* the novel, theatre, travel, an allotment, genealogy. *Address:* (office) Norman House, 105–109 Strand, WC2R 0AA. *T:* (020) 7836 3630.

JEFFERIES, Sheelagh, CBE 1987; Deputy Director General, 1983–87, Acting Director General, Jan.–June 1987, Central Office of Information; *b* 25 Aug. 1926; *d* of late Norman and Vera Jefferies. *Educ:* Harrogate Grammar Sch.; Girton Coll., Cambridge (MA); Smith Coll., Northampton, Mass, USA (MA). FIPR; FCAM. Archivist, RIIA, 1947–50, 1951–52; COI, 1953–60; Office of Chancellor of Duchy of Lancaster, 1960–61; Press Officer, Prime Minister's Office, 1961–67; Principal Inf. Officer, Privy Council Office, 1967–69; Chief Press Officer, Min. of Housing and Local Govt, 1969–71; Head of Parly Liaison Unit and later Head of News, DoE, 1971–74; Chief Inf. Officer, Dept of Prices and Consumer Protection, 1974–77; Central Office of Information: Dir, Overseas Press and Radio, 1977–78; Controller (Home), 1978–83. Press Consultant, WRVS, 1988–92. *Recreations:* reading, conversation. *Address:* 17 Beaumont Avenue, Richmond, Surrey TW9 2HE. *T:* (020) 8940 9229.

JEFFERIES, Stephen; Artistic Director, Hong Kong Ballet, since 1996; Senior Principal Dancer, Royal Ballet, 1979–95, Character Principal, 1994–95 (Principal Dancer, 1973–76 and 1977–79); *b* 24 June 1951; *s* of George and Barbara Jefferies; *m* 1972, Rashna Homji; one *s* one *d*. *Educ:* Turves Green Sch., Birmingham; Royal Ballet Sch. ARAD (Advanced Hons). Joined Sadler's Wells Royal Ballet, 1969; created 10 leading roles whilst with Sadler's Wells; joined National Ballet of Canada as Principal Dancer, 1976; created role of Morris, in Washington Square, 1977; returned to Royal Ballet at Covent Garden, 1977; *major roles include:* Prince in Sleeping Beauty, Swan Lake and Giselle, Prince Rudolf in

Mayerling, Petruchio in Taming of the Shrew, Romeo and Mercutio in Romeo and Juliet, Lescaut in Manon; lead, in Song and Dance, 1982; *roles created:* Yukinojo (mime role), in world première of Minoru Miki's opera An Actor's Revenge, 1979; male lead in Bolero, Japan, 1980 (choreographed by Yashiro Okamoto); Antonio in The Duenna, S Africa (chor. by Ashley Killar), 1980; lead, in Dances of Albion (chor. by Glen Tetley), 1980; Esenin in Kenneth Macmillan's ballet, Isadora, Covent Garden, 1981; lead, in L'Invitation au Voyage, Covent Garden, 1982; Consort Lessons, and Sons of Horos, 1986, Still Life at the Penguin Café, and The Trial of Prometheus, 1988 (chor. by David Bintley); title role in Cyrano (chor. by David Bintley), 1991. Choreographed ballets: Bits and Pieces, in Canada, 1977; Mes Souvenirs, in London, 1978; Magic Toyshop, 1987; Swan Lake, 1996, Giselle, 1997, Nutcracker, 1997, for Hong Kong Ballet. Rehearsal Dir, Rambert Dance Co., Jan.–July 1995 (on leave of absence). *Film:* Anna, 1988. *Recreations:* golf, football, sleeping, gardening, swimming and various other sports. *Address:* c/o Hong Kong Ballet Co., 60 Blue Pool Road, Happy Valley, Hong Kong.

JEFFERS, John Norman Richard, CStat; CBiol, FIBiol; FICFor; consultant; Visiting Professor: Mechanical, Materials and Manufacturing, University of Newcastle, since 1994; Mathematical Institute, University of Kent, since 1993; School of Mathematics, Statistics and Computing, University of Greenwich, since 1994; *b* 10 Sept. 1926; *s* of late Lt-Col John Harold Jeffers, OBE, and Emily Matilda Alice (*née* Robinson); *m* 1951, Edna May (*née* Parratt); one *d. Educ:* Portsmouth Grammar Sch.; Forestry Commission Forester Trng Sch., 1944–46. Forester in Forestry Commn Research Br., 1946–55; joined Min. of Agriculture, 1955, as Asst Statistician, after succeeding in limited competition to Statistician Class; rejoined Forestry Commn as Head of Statistics Section of Forestry Commn Research Br., 1956; Dir, Nature Conservancy's Merlewood Research Station, 1968; Dep. Dir, Inst. of Terrestrial Ecology, NERC, 1973, Dir, 1976–86. Editor, Internat. Jl of Sustainable Develt and World Ecology, 1994–. Hon. DSc Lancaster, 1988. *Publications:* Experimental Design and Analysis in Forest Research, 1959; Mathematical Models in Ecology, 1972; Introduction to Systems Analysis: with ecological applications, 1978; Modelling, 1982; Practitioner's Manual on the Modelling of Dynamic Change in Ecosystems, 1988; Microcomputers in Environmental Biology, 1990; numerous papers in stat., forestry and ecolog. jls. *Recreations:* military history and wargaming, amateur dramatics. *Address:* Glenside, Oxenholme, Kendal, Cumbria LA9 7RF. *T:* (01539) 734375. *Club:* Athenæum.

JEFFERSON, Bryan; *see* Jefferson, J. B.

JEFFERSON, Sir George Rowland, Kt 1981; CBE 1969; BSc Hons (London); FREng, Hon. FIMechE, FIEE, FRAeS; FRSA; CIMgt; FCGI; Chairman, 1981–87 and Chief Executive, 1981–86, British Telecommunications plc; *b* 26 March 1921; *s* of Harold Jefferson and Eva Elizabeth Ellen; *m* 1943, Irene Watson-Browne (*d* 1998); three *s. Educ:* Grammar Sch., Dartford, Kent. Engrg Apprentice, Royal Ordnance Factory, Woolwich, 1937–42; commnd RAOC, 1942; transf. REME, 1942; served 1942–45, Anti-Aircraft Comd on heavy anti-aircraft power control systems and later Armament Design Dept, Fort Halstead, on anti-aircraft gun mounting development; subseq. Mem. Min. of Supply staff, Fort Halstead, until 1952; joined Guided Weapons Div., English Electric Co. Ltd, 1952; Chief Research Engr, 1953; Dep. Chief Engr, 1958; Dir, English Electric Aviation Ltd, 1961 (on formation of co.); British Aircraft Corporation: Dir and Chief Exec., BAC (Guided Weapons) Ltd, 1963 (on formation of Corp.), Dep. Man. Dir, 1964, Mem. Board, 1965–77, Man. Dir, 1966–68, Chm. and Man. Dir, 1968–77; a Dir, British Aerospace, and Chm. and Chief Exec., Dynamics Gp, British Aerospace, 1977–80 (Mem., Organizing Cttee, 1976–77); Chm., Stevenage/Bristol and Hatfield/Lostock Divs, Dynamics Gp, 1978–80; Chm., BAC (Anti-Tank), 1968–78; Dep. Chm., Post Office, 1980; Chm., 1981–87, Chief Exec., 1981–86, British Telecommunications plc. Chairman: Matthew Hall, 1987–88; City Centre Communications, 1988–90; Videotron Corp., 1990–97. Director: British Aerospace (Australia) Ltd, 1968–80; British Scandinavian Aviation AB, 1968–80; Hawker Siddeley Dynamics, 1977–80; Engineering Sciences Data Unit Ltd, 1975–80; Babcock International, 1980–87; Lloyds Bank, 1986–89; AMEC, 1988–91. Member: NEB, 1979–80; NEDC, 1981–84; NICG, 1980–84; Member Council: SBAC, 1965–80; Electronic Engineering Assoc., 1968–72; RAeS, 1977–79 (Vice-Pres., 1979). Freeman of the City of London. Hon. DSc Bristol, 1984; DUniv Essex, 1985. *Address:* 449 Kingsway, Landsdale, Perth, WA 6065, Australia.

JEFFERSON, Joan Ena; *see* Appleyard, J. E.

JEFFERSON, (John) Bryan, CB 1989; CBE 1983; PPRIBA; Architectural Advisor to Department for Culture, Media and Sport (formerly National Heritage), 1993–2001; Visiting Professor, School of Architecture, Sheffield University, since 1992; *b* 26 April 1928; *s* of John Jefferson and Marjorie Jefferson (*née* Oxley); *m* 1st, 1954, Alison Gray (marr. diss. 1965); three *s*; 2nd, 1999, Jean Marsden. *Educ:* Lady Manners Sch., Bakewell; Sheffield Univ. DipArch 1954. ARIBA 1954. Morrison and Partners, Derby, 1955–57; established practice in Sheffield and London with Gerald F. Sheard, 1957; Sen. Partner, Jefferson Sheard and Partners, 1957–84; Dir-Gen. of Design, PSA, DoE, 1984–89; Chm., PSA Projects, DoE, 1989–92; Mem., Standing Cttee on Structl Safety, 1991–99. President: Sheffield Soc. of Architects, 1973–74; Concrete Soc., 1977–78; RIBA, 1979–81; Chm., RIBA Yorks Region, 1974–75. Trustee, Civic Trust, 1998–. Hon. FRAIC 1980; Hon. Mem., RICS 1987. Hon. DEng Bradford, 1986; Hon. LittD Sheffield, 1992. *Publications:* broadcasts; articles in lay and professional jls. *Recreations:* music, sailing offshore. *Address:* 6 St Andrews Mansions, Dorset Street, W1U 4EQ. *Clubs:* Royal Automobile; Royal Western Yacht.

JEFFERSON, Sir Mervyn Stewart D.; *see* Dunnington-Jefferson.

JEFFERSON, William Hayton, OBE 1985; Director, Portugal, British Council, and Cultural Counsellor, Lisbon, 1996–98; *b* 29 July 1940; *s* of late Stanley Jefferson and Josephine (*née* Hayton); *m* 1st, 1963, Marie-Jeanne Mazenq (marr. diss. 1986); three *s*; 2nd, 1986, Fadia Georges Tarraf; one *s. Educ:* Nelson-Thomlinson Grammar Sch., Wigton, Cumbria; Wadham Coll., Oxford (MA 1966). Russian teacher, 1963–66; with British Council, 1967–98: Tripoli, 1967–70; Kuwait, 1970–72; Algeria, 1972–75; Director: Qatar, 1975–79; Overseas Co-operation, London, 1979–82; United Arab Emirates, 1982–85; Algeria, 1985–90; Dir, Czechoslovakia, and Cultural Counsellor, Prague, 1990–96. Mem. (Ind), Allerdale Borough Council, Cumbria, 1999–; Chm., N Allerdale Regeneration Gp, 2001–. Gold Medal: Czech Scientific Univ., 1995; Palacky Univ., Olomouc, 1996; Silver Medal: Charles Univ., Prague, 1996; Masaryk Univ., Brno, 1996. *Recreations:* Cumbrian local history and dialect, wine, bowls. *Address:* 3 Marine Terrace, Silloth, Cumbria CA7 4BZ. *T:* (01697) 332526. *Club:* Silloth-on-Solway Bowls.

JEFFERSON SMITH, Peter, CB 1992; Trustee, South East London Community Foundation, since 1995; (Chair of Trustees, 1995–2000); *b* 14 July 1939; *m* 1964, Anna Willett; two *d. Educ:* Trinity College, Cambridge. HM Customs and Excise, 1960; Commissioner, 1980; Dep. Chm., 1988–94. *Address:* 22 Iveley Road, SW4 0EW. *T:* (020) 7622 8285.

JEFFERY, David John, CBE 2000; Chief Executive, British Marine Equipment Council, 2000–01; *b* 18 Feb. 1936; *s* of late Stanley John Friend Jeffery and Sylvia May (*née* Mashford); *m* 1959, Margaret (*née* Yates); one *s* two *d. Educ:* Sutton High Sch., Plymouth; Croydon Coll. of Technology. Nat. Service, RAOC, 1954–56; Admiralty Dir of Stores Dept, 1956–66; RN Staff Coll., 1967; MoD, 1968–70; on secondment, 1970–76: Treasury Centre for Admin. Studies, 1970–72; Management Science Training Adviser, Malaysian Govt, Kuala Lumpur, 1972–74; Civil Service Dept, 1974–76; MoD, 1976–83; RCDS, 1983; Dir, Armaments and Management Services, RN Supply and Transport Service 1984–86; Chief Exec. and Bd Mem., PLA, 1986–99. Chm., Estuary Services Ltd, 1988–. Director: UK Major Ports Ltd, 1993–99; British Ports Industry Trng Ltd, 1993–99 (Chm., 1998–99); Trustee Dir, Pilots' Nat. Pension Fund, 1987–95; Vice-Pres. of Conf., Internat. Assoc. of Ports and Harbors, 1995–97; Chairman: European Sea Ports Orgn, 1997–99; DTI Ports Sector Gp, 1998–; Mem., European Maritime Industries High Level Panel, 1994–95, Marine Foresight Panel, 1997–. Mem., Co. of Watermen and Lightermen of River Thames, 1987. Freeman, City of London, 1987. *Recreations:* theatre, music, travel, children's work with the local church. *Address:* The Old Coach House, Nunney, Frome BA11 4LZ.

JEFFERY, Maj.-Gen. Philip Michael, AC 1996 (AO (mil.) 1989); CVO 2000; MC 1971; Governor of Western Australia, 1993–2000; *b* 12 Dec. 1937; *s* of Philip Frederick Jeffery and Edna Mary Jeffery (*née* Johnson); *m* 1966, Marlena Joy Kerr; three *s* one *d. Educ:* Kent Street High Sch.; Royal Mil. Coll., Duntroon. Served Infantry, 1958–93: jun. regtl appts, 17 Nat. Service Trng Co. and SAS Regt, 1959–62; Operational Service, Malaya, Borneo and Vietnam, 1962–72; psc 1972; Commanding Officer: 2nd Bn Pacific Islands Regt, PNG, 1974–75; SAS Regt, Perth, 1976–77; jssc 1978; Dir, Special Forces, 1979–81; Comd, 1 Bde, Sydney, 1983–84; rcds 1985; comd, 1 Div., Brisbane, 1986–88; DCGS, Canberra, 1990–91; ACGS Materiel, 1991–93. Mem., United Services Inst., Canberra, 1978–. Hon. Dr Technology Curtin, 2000. Citizen of WA, 2000. KStJ 1994. *Recreations:* golf, fishing, music. *Address:* 18 Hampton Circuit, Yarralumla, Canberra, ACT 2600, Australia. *Clubs:* Commonwealth (Canberra); Royal Canberra Golf.

JEFFERY, Very Rev. Robert Martin Colquhoun; Canon and Sub-Dean of Christ Church, Oxford, since 1996; *b* 30 April 1935; *s* of Norman Clare Jeffery and Gwenyth Isabel Jeffery; *m* 1968, Ruth Margaret Tinling (*d* 1995); three *s* one *d. Educ:* St Paul's School; King's Coll., London (BD, AKC). Assistant Curate: St Aidan, Grangetown, 1959–61; St Mary, Barnes, 1961–63; Asst Sec., Missionary and Ecumenical Council of Church Assembly, 1964–68; Sec., Dept of Mission and Unity, BCC, 1968–71; Vicar, St Andrew, Headington, Oxford, 1971–78; RD of Cowley, 1973–78; Lichfield Diocesan Missioner, 1978–79; Archdeacon of Salop, 1980–87; Dean of Worcester, 1987–96, now Dean Emeritus. Mem., Gen. Synod of C of E, 1982–87 and 1988–96 (Member: Standing Cttee, 1990–96; Business Cttee, 1990–96); Mem., Crown Appointments Commn, 1996. FRSA 1992. Hon. DD Birmingham, 1999. *Publications:* (with D. M. Paton) Christian Unity and the Anglican Communion, 1965, 3rd edn 1968; (with T. S. Garret) Unity in Nigeria, 1964; (ed) Lambeth Conference 1968 Preparatory Information; Areas of Ecumenical Experiment, 1968; Ecumenical Experiments: A Handbook, 1971; Case Studies in Unity, 1972; (ed) By What Authority?, 1987; Anima Christi, 1994. *Recreations:* local history, cooking. *Address:* Christ Church, Oxford OX1 1DP.

JEFFERYS, Dr David Barrington, FFPM, FRCP, FRCPE; Chief Executive and Director, Medical Devices Agency, since 2000; *b* 1 Aug. 1952; *s* of Godfrey B. Jefferys and Joyce E. Jefferys; *m* 1985, Ann-Marie Smith; one *s* one *d. Educ:* St Dunstan's Coll.; Guy's Hosp. Med. Sch., Univ. of London (BSc Hons; MB BS 1976; MD 1983). FFPM 1990; FRCPE 1990; FRCP 1992. Medical posts at Guy's and St Thomas' Hosps, 1976–83; locum consultant physician, Tunbridge Wells, 1983–84; SMO, DoH, 1984–86; PMO and Principal Assessor to Cttee on Safety of Medicines, 1986; Medicines Control Agency: Business Manager, Eur. and New Drug Licensing, 1986–94; Dir, Licensing Div., 1994–2000. Vis. Prof. in Medicine, Univ. of Newcastle upon Tyne, 1994. UK Deleg to Cttee on Proprietary Medicinal Products, 1995–2000. Chm., Mutual Recognition Facilitation Gp, EU, 1997–98. Mem., British Inst. of Regulatory Affairs, 2000–. *Publications:* chapters in books and articles on medicines regulation, regulatory policy and quality assurance. *Recreations:* sport, theatre, music, art, Church affairs. *Address:* Medical Devices Agency, Hannibal House, Elephant and Castle, SE1 6TQ. *Club:* Surrey County Cricket.

JEFFORD, Barbara Mary, OBE 1965; actress; *b* Plymstock, Devon, 26 July 1930; *d* of late Percival Francis Jefford and Elizabeth Mary Ellen (*née* Laity); *m* 1953, Terence Longdon (marr. diss. 1961); *m* 1967, John Arnold Turner. *Educ:* Weirfield Sch., Taunton, Som. Studied for stage, Bristol and Royal Academy of Dramatic Art (Bancroft Gold Medal). *Royal Shakespeare Co.:* Stratford-on-Avon, 1950–54: Isabella in Measure for Measure; Anne Bullen in Henry VIII; Hero in Much Ado About Nothing; Lady Percy in Henry IV parts I and II; Desdemona in Othello; Rosalind in As You Like It; Helena in A Midsummer Night's Dream; Katharina in The Taming of the Shrew; Volumnia in Coriolanus, 1989 and 1990; Tatyana in Barbarians, 1990; Countess in All's Well That Ends Well, Mistress Quickly in The Merry Wives of Windsor, 1992; Katia in Misha's Party, 1993; Countess Terzky in Wallenstein, 1993–94; *Old Vic Company:* (1956–62) Imogen in Cymbeline; Beatrice in Much Ado About Nothing; Portia in The Merchant of Venice; Julia in Two Gentlemen of Verona; Tamora in Titus Andronicus; Lady Anne in Richard III; Queen Margaret in Henry VI parts I, II and III; Isabella in Measure for Measure; Regan in King Lear; Viola in Twelfth Night; Ophelia in Hamlet; Rosalind in As You Like It; St Joan; Lady Macbeth; Gwendoline in The Importance of Being Earnest; Beatrice Cenci; Lavinia in Mourning Becomes Electra; *for Prospect, at Old Vic:* (1977–79) Gertrude in Hamlet; Cleopatra in All for Love; Cleopatra in Antony and Cleopatra; Nurse in Romeo and Juliet; Anna in The Government Inspector; RSC Nat. Tour, 1980, Mistress Quickly in Henry IV pts 1 and 2; *National Theatre:* Gertrude in Hamlet, Zabina in Tamburlaine the Great, 1976; Mother in Six Characters in Search of an Author, Arina Bazarov in Fathers and Sons, Salathiel in Ting Tang Mine (Clarence Derwent Award, 1988), 1987. *Other London stage appearances include:* Andromache in Tiger at the Gates, Apollo, 1955, NY, 1956; Lina in Misalliance, Royal Court and Criterion, 1963; step-daughter in Six Characters in Search of an Author, Mayfair, 1963; Nan in Ride a Cock Horse, Piccadilly, 1965; Patsy Newquist in Little Murders, Aldwych, 1967; Mother Vauzou in Mistress of Novices, Piccadilly, 1973; Filumena, Lyric, 1979; Duchess of York in Richard II, and Queen Margaret in Richard III, Phoenix, 1988–89; Oenone in Phèdre, Albina in Britannicus, Albery, 1998, NY, 1999; Duchess of York in Richard II, and Volumnia in Coriolanus, Almeida at Gainsborough Studios, NY and Tokyo, 2000; *other stage appearances include:* Hedda Gabler, Medea, Phaedra, Oxford Playhouse, 1966; Lady Sneerwell in The School for Scandal, toured UK, 1995; Our Betters, Chichester, 1997; has toured extensively in UK, Europe, USA, Near East, Far East, Africa, Australia, Russia, Poland and Yugoslavia. *Films:* Ulysses, 1967; A Midsummer Night's Dream, 1967; The Shoes of the Fisherman, 1968; To Love a Vampire, 1970; Hitler: the last ten days, 1973; And the Ship Sails On, 1983; Why the Whales Came, 1988; Reunion, 1988; Where Angels Fear to Tread, 1991; The Ninth Gate, 1999. Has appeared in numerous television and radio plays. Pragnell Shakespeare Award, 1994. Silver Jubilee Medal, 1977. *Recreations:*

music, swimming, gardening. *Address:* c/o Peters, Fraser and Dunlop Ltd, Drury House, 34–43 Russell Street, WC2B 5HA.

JEFFREY, Joan; *see* MacNaughton, J.

JEFFREY, Dr Robin Campbell, FREng, FIChemE, FIMechE; Chairman and Chief Executive, British Energy, since 2001; *b* 19 Feb. 1939; *s* of Robert Stewart Martin Jeffrey and Catherine Campbell McSporran; *m* 1962, Barbara Helen Robinson; two *s* one *d*. *Educ:* Kelvinside Acad.; Royal Technical Coll. (Glasgow Univ.) (BSc); Pembroke Coll., Cambridge (PhD). With Babcock & Wilcox, 1956–79, Engrg Res. Manager, 1964–79; South of Scotland Electricity Board, later Scottish Power: Technical Services Manager, 1979–80; Torness Project Manager, 1980–88; Chief Engr, 1988–89; Man. Dir, Engrg Resources Business, 1989–92; Chief Exec., 1992–98, Chm., 1995–98, Scottish Nuclear Ltd; Dep. Chm., 1996–2001, Exec. Dir, N America, 1998–2001, British Energy. Board Member: London Transport, 1996–; London Underground Ltd, 1996–. Vis. Prof., Univ. of Strathclyde, 1994–. FREng (FEng 1992). *Publications:* (jtly) Open Cycle MHD Power Generation, 1969; pubns on energy related issues. *Recreations:* squash, tennis, ski-ing, playing musical instruments. *Address:* British Energy plc, 3 Redwood Crescent, Peel Park, E Kilbride G74 5PR. *Clubs:* Cambridge University Royal Tennis; Glasgow Academical Squash.

JEFFREY, William Alexander, CB 2001; Deputy Secretary, Northern Ireland Office, since 1998; *b* 28 Feb. 1948; *s* of Alexander and Joyce Jeffrey; *m* 1979, Joan MacNaughton, *qv*. *Educ:* Alan Glen's, Glasgow; Univ. of Glasgow (BSc Hons). Home Office, 1971–94: Private Sec. to Permanent Under Sec. of State, 1975–76; Principal, 1976–84; Assistant Secretary: Criminal Policy Dept, 1984–88; HM Prison Service, 1988–91; Asst Under Sec. of State, Immigration and Nationality Dept, 1991–94; Under Sec., Economic and Domestic Affairs Secretariat, Cabinet Office, 1994–98. *Recreations:* reading, hill-walking, watching football. *Address:* c/o Northern Ireland Office, 11 Millbank, SW1P 4QE.

JEFFREYS, family name of **Baron Jeffreys**.

JEFFREYS, 3rd Baron *cr* 1952, of Burkham; **Christopher Henry Mark Jeffreys;** stockbroker, since 2000; Director: Raphael Asset Management; Raphael Tutton & Saunders Ltd; *b* 22 May 1957; *s* of 2nd Baron Jeffreys and of Sarah Annabelle Mary, *d* of late Major Henry Garnett; *S* father, 1986; *m* 1985, Anne Elisabeth Johnson; one *s* one *d*. *Educ:* Eton. With: GNI Ltd, 1985–90; Raphael Zorn Hemsley, 1992–2000. *Recreations:* country sports. *Heir: s* Hon. Arthur Mark Henry Jeffreys, *b* 18 Feb. 1989. *Address:* The Corner House, Sewstern, Grantham, Lincs NG33 5RF. *T:* (01476) 861454.

JEFFREYS, Alan Howard; QC 1996; a Recorder, since 1993; *b* 27 Sept. 1947; *s* of late Hugh and Rachel Jeffreys; *m* 1975, Jane Olivia Sadler; one *s* one *d*. *Educ:* Ellesmere Coll.; King's College, London (LLB Hons). Called to the Bar, Gray's Inn, 1970; South Eastern Circuit; Asst Recorder, 1989. Mem., Criminal Injuries Compensation Appeals Authy (formerly Criminal Injuries Compensation Bd), 1999–. *Recreations:* fishing, golf, chess, music. *Address:* Farrar's Building, Temple, EC4Y 7BD. *T:* (020) 7583 9241. *Club:* Hurlingham.

JEFFREYS, Sir Alec John, Kt 1994; FRS 1986; Wolfson Research Professor of the Royal Society, University of Leicester, since 1991 (Professor of Genetics, since 1987); *b* 9 Jan. 1950; *s* of Sidney Victor Jeffreys and Joan (*née* Knight); *m* 1971, Susan Miles; two *d*. *Educ:* Luton Grammar School; Luton VIth Form College; Merton College, Oxford (Postmaster; Christopher Welch Schol.; BA, MA, DPhil 1975; Hon. Fellow, 1990). EMBO Research Fellow, Univ. of Amsterdam, 1975–77; Leicester University: Lectr, Dept of Genetics, 1977–84; Reader, 1984–87; Lister Inst. Res. Fellow, 1982–91. Member: EMBO, 1983; Human Genome Orgn, 1989. Editor, Jl of Molecular Evolution, 1985. Founder FMedSci 1998. Fellow, Forensic Sci. Soc. of India, 1989; Hon. Mem., Amer. Acad. of Forensic Scis, 1998. Hon. Fellow, Univ. of Luton, 1995. Colworth Medal for Biochemistry, Biochem. Soc., 1985; Davy Medal, Royal Soc., 1987; Linnean Soc. Bicentenary Medal, 1987; Analytika Prize, German Soc. for Clin. Chem., 1988; Press, Radio and TV Award, Midlander of the Year, 1989; Linnean Medal, 1994; Sir Frederick Gowland Hopkins Meml Medal, Biochem. Soc., 1996; Albert Einstein World of Science Award, World Cultural Council, 1996; Baly Medal, RCP, 1997; SCI Medal, 1997. UK Patents on genetic fingerprints. *Publications:* research articles on molecular genetics and evolution in Nature, Cell, etc. *Recreations:* walking, swimming, postal history, reading unimproving novels.

JEFFREYS, David Alfred; QC 1981; a Recorder of the Crown Court, 1979–99; *b* 1 July 1934; *s* of late Coleman and Ruby Jeffreys; *m* 1964, Mary Ann Elizabeth Long; one *s* one *d*. *Educ:* Harrow; Trinity Coll., Cambridge (BA Hons). Served, Royal Signals, 1952–54; City, 1958. Called to the Bar, Gray's Inn, 1958, Bencher, 1989; Junior Prosecuting Counsel to the Crown, Central Criminal Court, 1975; Sen. Prosecuting Counsel to the Crown, CCC, 1979–81; Jt Head, Hollis Whiteman Chambers, 1995–99, retd. Mem., Bar Council, 1977–80. *Address:* c/o Queen Elizabeth Building, Temple, EC4Y 9BS.

JEFFREYS, Prof. Elizabeth Mary; Bywater and Sotheby Professor of Byzantine and Modern Greek Language and Literature, and Fellow of Exeter College, Oxford, since 1996; *b* 22 July 1941; *d* of Lawrence R. Brown and Veronica Thompson; *m* 1965, Michael J. Jeffreys; one *d*. *Educ:* Blackheath High Sch. for Girls (GPDST); Girton Coll., Cambridge (MA (Class. Tripos)); St Anne's Coll., Oxford (BLitt; Hon. Fellow, 1997). Classics Mistress, Mary Datchelor Girls' Sch., 1965–69; Sen. Res. Fellow, Warburg Inst., London Univ., 1969–72; Vis. Fellow, Dumbarton Oaks Centre for Byzantine Studies, 1972–74, 1984; Res. Fellow, Ioannina Univ., Greece, 1974–76; part-time Lectr, univs in Sydney, Australia, 1976–86; Vis. Fellow, Humanities Centre, Canberra, 1978; Res. Fellow, Melbourne Univ., 1987–89; Res. Fellow, 1990–92, Australian Sen. Res. Fellow, 1993–95, Sydney Univ. Fellow, Australian Acad. of Humanities, 1993. *Publications:* Byzantine Papers, 1981; Popular Literature in Late Byzantium, 1983; The Chronicle of John Malalas: a translation, 1986; Studies in John Malalas, 1990; The War of Troy, 1996; Digenis Akritis, 1998; Through the Looking Glass, 2000. *Recreation:* walking. *Address:* Exeter College, Oxford OX1 3DP.

JEFFREYS, Mrs Judith Diana; Assistant Director (Keeper), the Tate Gallery, 1975–83; *b* 22 Sept. 1927; *d* of Prof. Philip Cloake, FRCP and Letitia Blanche (*née* MacDonald); *m* 1968, William John Jeffreys. *Educ:* Bedales; Courtauld Inst. of Art, Univ. of London (BA Hons History of Art). Tate Gallery: Asst Keeper, 1951–64; Publications Manager, 1960–65; Dep. Keeper, 1964–75. *Recreations:* reading, music, landscape gardening, water-colour painting. *Address:* Oak Ridge House, Sutton Mandeville, Salisbury, Wilts SP3 5LT.

JEFFRIES, Hon. Sir John (Francis), Kt 1993; Chairman, New Zealand Press Council, 1997–June 2002; *b* 28 March 1929; *s* of Frank Leon Jeffries and Mary Jeffries; *m* 1951, Joan Patricia Christensen; one *s* one *d*. *Educ:* St Patrick's Coll., Wellington; Victoria Univ. of Wellington (BA, LLB). Clerical, 1946–50; school teaching, 1950–55; Law, 1956–76; Judge of the High Court of New Zealand, 1976–92; NZ Police Complaints Authority, 1992–97. Chm., Air New Zealand, 1975. Wellington City Council, 1962–74; Dep. Mayor, Wellington, 1971–74. Chm., Nat. Housing Commn, 1973–75. Vice-Pres., NZ Law Soc., 1973–76; Member: Trust for Intellectually Handicapped, 1980–88; NZ Inst. of Mental Retardation, 1984–88. Mem., Internat. Court of Arbitration for Sport, 1999–; Comr of Security Warrants, 1999–Sept. 2002. Hon. Life Mem., Amer. Bar Assoc., 1974. *Recreations:* reading, music, sports generally, playing golf. *Address:* 44 Clutha Avenue, Khandallah, Wellington, New Zealand. *T:* (4) 4795732. *Clubs:* Wellington; Wellington Golf.

JEFFRIES, Lionel Charles; actor since 1949, screen writer since 1959, and film director since 1970; *b* 10 June 1926; *s* of Bernard Jeffries and Elsie Jackson; *m* 1951, Eileen Mary Walsh; one *s* two *d*. *Educ:* Queen Elizabeth's Grammar Sch., Wimborne, Dorset; Royal Academy of Dramatic Art (Dip., Kendal Award, 1947). War of 1939–45: commissioned, Oxf. and Bucks LI, 1945; served in Burma (Burma Star, 1945); Captain, Royal West African Frontier Force. Stage: (West End) *plays:* Carrington VC; The Enchanted; Blood Wedding; Brouhaha; Hello Dolly, Prince of Wales, 1984; See How They Run, Two Into One, Rookery Nook, Shaftesbury, 1985–86; Pygmalion, Broadway, 1987; The Wild Duck, Phoenix, 1990; *films* include: Bhowani Junction, Lust for Life, The Baby and The Battleship, 1956; Colditz Story, Doctor at Large, 1957; Law and Disorder, 1958; The Nun's Story, 1959; Idle on Parade; Two Way Stretch, The Trials of Oscar Wilde, 1960; Fanny, 1961; The Notorious Landlady (Hollywood), The Wrong Arm of the Law, 1962; The First Men in the Moon, 1964; The Truth about Spring, 1965; Arrivederci Baby, The Spy with a Cold Nose, 1966; Camelot (Hollywood), 1967; Chitty, Chitty, Bang Bang, 1968; Baxter, 1973 (also dir; Golden Bear Award for Best Film, Europe); The Prisoner of Zenda, 1979; Eyewitness, 1981; Ménage à Trois; Chorus of Disapproval, 1989; Danny Champion of the World; Ending Up; First and Last. Wrote and directed: The Railway Children, 1970 (St Christopher Gold Medal, Hollywood, for Best Film); The Amazing Mr Blunden, 1972 (Gold Medal for Best Screen Play, Internat. Sci. Fiction and Fantasy Film Fest., Paris, 1974); Wombling Free, 1977; co-wrote and directed: The Water Babies, 1979; *television:* Cream in my Coffee, 1980; Shillingbury Tales, 1981; Father Charlie; Tom, Dick, and Harriet, 1983; Rich Tea and Sympathy, 1991; Look at it This Way, 1993. *Recreations:* swimming, painting. *Address:* c/o Liz Hobbs, MBE Management Ltd, PO Box 124, Newark, Notts NG24 2RS.

JEFFRIES, Michael Makepeace Eugene, RIBA; Chairman, W. S. Atkins PLC, since 2001 (Chief Executive, 1995–2001); *b* 17 Sept. 1944; *s* of William Eugene Jeffries and Margaret Jeffries (*née* Makepeace); *m* 1966, Pamela Mary Booth; two *s* two *d*. *Educ:* Poly. of North London (DipArch Hons). RIBA 1973. Architectural Assistant: John Laing & Sons Ltd, 1963–67; Surrey CC, 1967–68; Gillespie & Steele, Trinidad, 1968–69; Deeks Bousell Partnership, London, 1969–73; Senior Architect: Bradshaw Gass & Hope, Lancs, 1973–75; W. S. Atkins Ltd, 1975–78; Man. Dir, ASFA Ltd, 1978; Dir, W. S. Atkins Gp Consultants Ltd, 1979–92; Mkting and Business Develt Dir, W. S. Atkins Ltd, 1992–95. Non-exec. Dir, De La Rue, 2000–. *Publications:* various technical papers in jls. *Recreations:* sailing, golf, water colour painting, antiquarian horology. *Address:* Sunset, 38 Dorset Lake Avenue, Lilliput, Poole, Dorset BH14 8JP. *T:* (01202) 706986. *Clubs:* Royal Automobile; Lake Yard Yacht (Poole).

JEFFS, Julian; QC 1975; arbitrator, author and editor; *b* 5 April 1931; *s* of Alfred Wright Jeffs, Wolverhampton, and Janet Honor Irene (*née* Davies); *m* 1966, Deborah, *d* of Peter James Stuart Bevan; three *s*. *Educ:* Mostyn House Sch.; Wrekin Coll.; Downing Coll., Cambridge (MA; Associate Fellow, 1986). MCIArb 1999. Royal Navy (nat. service), 1949–50. Sherry Shipper's Asst, Spain, 1956. Barrister, Gray's Inn, 1958 (Bencher 1981), Inner Temple, 1971; Midland and Oxford Circuit; Hong Kong Bar; retired from practice, 1991; a Recorder, 1975–96; a Dep. High Court Judge, Chancery Div., 1981–96. Chm., Patent Bar Assoc., 1980–89; Member: Senate of Inns of Court and Bar, 1984–85; Bar Council, 1988–89. Gen. Comr of Income Tax, 1983–91. Editor, Wine and Food, 1965–67; Mem., Cttee of Management, International Wine & Food Soc., 1965–67, 1971–82; Chm., 1970–72, Vice-Pres., 1975–91, Pres., 1992–96, Circle of Wine Writers. Dep. Gauger, City of London, 1979. Freeman, City of London. Lauréat de l'Office International de la Vigne et du Vin, 1962; Glenfiddich wine writer awards, 1974 and 1978. Mem., Gran Orden de Caballeros del Vino. General Editor, Faber's Wine Series. *Publications:* Sherry, 1961, 4th edn 1992; (an editor) Clerk and Lindsell on Torts, 13th edn 1969 to 16th edn 1989; The Wines of Europe, 1971; Little Dictionary of Drink, 1973; (jtly) Encyclopedia of United Kingdom and European Patent Law, 1977; The Wines of Spain, 1999. *Recreations:* freemasonry, wine, walking, old cars, musical boxes, follies, Iberian things. *Address:* Church Farm House, East Ilsley, Newbury, Berks. *T:* (01635) 281216, *Fax:* (01635) 281756. *Clubs:* Beefsteak, Garrick, Reform, Saintsbury.

JEFFS, Kenneth Peter, CMG 1983; FRAeS; consultant; *b* 30 Jan. 1931; *s* of Albert Jeffs and Theresa Eleanor Jeffs; *m* Iris Woolsey; one *s* two *d*. *Educ:* Richmond and East Sheen County Sch. jssc. National Service, RAF, 1949–51. Entered CS as Clerical Officer, Bd of Control, 1947; Air Min., 1952; Principal, 1964; JSSC, 1966–67; Private Secretary: to Under-Sec. of State (RN), MoD, 1969–71; to Minister of Defence, 1971–72; Asst Sec., Dir Defence Sales, MoD, 1972–75; Counsellor, Defence Supply, Washington, DC, 1976–79; Dir Gen. (Marketing), MoD, 1979–83; Exec. Vice-Pres., (Mil. Affairs), 1984–87, Dir, 1985–87, British Aerospace Inc.; Pres., MLRS Internat. Corp., 1987–92; Dir, Studley Associates, 1994–99. FRAeS 1985. *Recreations:* granddaughters, golf, horse racing. *Address:* Old Studley, Howell Hill Grove, Ewell, near Epsom, Surrey KT17 3ET. *Clubs:* Royal Automobile; Bude and North Cornwall Golf.

JEGER, Baroness *cr* 1979 (Life Peer), of St Pancras in Greater London; **Lena May Jeger;** *b* 19 Nov. 1915; *e d* of Charles and Alice Chivers, Yorkley, Glos; *m* 1948, Dr Santo Wayburn Jeger (*d* 1953); no *c*. *Educ:* Southgate County Sch., Middx; Birkbeck Coll., London University (BA; Hon. Fellow, 1994). Civil Service: Customs and Excise, Ministry of Information, Foreign Office, 1936–49; British Embassy Moscow, 1947; Manchester Guardian, later The Guardian, London Staff, 1951–54, 1961–79. Mem. St Pancras Borough Council, 1945–59; Mem. LCC for Holborn and St Pancras South, 1952–55. Mem., Nat. Exec. Cttee, Labour Party, 1968–80 (Vice-Chm., 1978–79; Chm., 1980). MP (Lab) Holborn and St Pancras South, Nov. 1953–1959 and 1964–74, Camden, Holborn and St Pancras South, 1974–79. Mem., Chairmen's Panel, House of Commons, 1971–79. Chm., Govt Working Party on Sewage Disposal, 1969–70. Member, Consultative Assembly: Council of Europe, 1969–71; WEU, 1969–71; UK delegate, Status of Women Commn, UN, 1967. *Address:* 9 Cumberland Terrace, Regent's Park, NW1 4HS.

JEHANGIR, Sir Cowasji, 4th Bt *cr* 1908, of Bombay; *b* 23 Nov. 1953; *er s* of Sir Hirji Jehangir, 3rd Bt and of Jinoo, *d* of K. H. Cama; *S* father, 2000; *m* 1988, Jasmine, *d* of Beji Billimoria; one *s* one *d*. *Educ:* Cathedral and John Connon Sch., Bombay; Elphinstone Coll., Bombay (BA Econ). National Radio and Electronics Co. Ltd, Bombay, 1976–80. Chm., Jehangir Hosp., Pune, 1989–. Hon. Dir, Centre for Photography as an Art Form, Bombay, 1986–. Mem. Senate, Univ. of Pune, 1992–95. Trustee, Sir Cowasji Jehangir Sch., Bombay. *Recreations:* wildlife, photography, jazz, squash. *Heir: s* Cowasji Jehangir, *b* 28 March 1990. *Address:* Readymoney House, 49 Nepean Sea Road, Mumbai 400 036,

India; 24 Kensington Court Gardens, Kensington Court Place, W8 5QF. *Clubs:* Willingdon Sports, Bombay Gymkhana (Bombay); Royal Western India Turf (Bombay and Pune); Poona (Pune).

JEJEEBHOY, Sir Jamsetjee, 7th Bt *cr* 1857; *b* 19 April 1913; *s* of Rustamjee J. C. Jamsetjee (*d* 1947), and Soonabai Rustomjee Byramjee Jeejeebhoy (*d* 1968); *S* cousin, Sir Jamsetjee Jejeebhoy, 6th Bt, 1968, and assumed name of Jamsetjee Jejeebhoy in lieu of Maneckjee Rustamjee Jamsetjee; *m* 1943, Shirin J. H. Cama; one *s* one *d*. *Educ:* St Xavier's Coll., Bombay (BA). Chairman: Sir Jamsetjee Jejeebhoy Charity Funds; Sir J. J. Parsee Benevolent Instn; Wadiaji's Atash-behram; M. F. Cama Athornan Instn; Iran League; Rustomjee Jamsetjee Jejeebhoy Gujarat Schools' Fund; Bombay Panjrapole; Zoroastrian Bldg Fund; Parsee Dhanda Rojgar Fund; K. R. Cama Oriental Instn; Framjee Cowasjee Inst.; Destitute Eranee's Charity Fund and Dharamshala; H. D. Saher Agiary and Charity Trust; Trustee: Byramjee Jeejeebhoy Parsee Charitable Instn; A. H. Wadia Charity Trust; Parsi Surat Charity Fund; Cowasji Behramji Divecha Charity Trust; Mem., Exec. Cttee, B. D. Petit Parsee Gen. Hosp.; Director: Enjay Estates Pvte Ltd, 1972–; Beaulieu Investments Pvte Ltd, 1975–; Palmera Investment Pvte Ltd, 1984–; Dawn Threads Pvte Ltd, 1984–. Hon. Freeman and Liveryman, Clockmakers' Co., 1995. *Heir: s* Rustom Jejeebhoy [*b* 16 Nov. 1957; *m* 1984, Delara, *d* of Jal N. Bhaisa; one *s*]. *Address:* (residence) Beaulieu, 95 Worli Sea Face, Mumbai 400025, India. *T:* 4930955; (office) Maneckjee Wadia Building, Mahatma Gandhi Road, Fort, Mumbai 400001. *T:* 2673843. *Clubs:* Willingdon Sports, Royal Western India Turf, Ripon, Western India Automobile Association (Mumbai).

JELLICOE, family name of **Earl Jellicoe**.

JELLICOE, 2nd Earl *cr* 1925; **George Patrick John Rushworth Jellicoe,** KBE 1986; DSO 1942; MC 1944; PC 1963; FRS 1990; Viscount Brocas of Southampton, 1925; Viscount Jellicoe of Scapa, 1918; Baron Jellicoe of Southampton (Life Peer), 1999; President, Crete Veterans Association, since 1990; *b* 4 April 1918; *o s* of Admiral of the Fleet 1st Earl Jellicoe and late Florence Gwendoline, *d* of Sir Charles Cayzer, 1st Bt; godson of King George V; *S* father, 1935; *m* 1st, 1944, Patricia Christine (marr. diss., 1966), *o d* of Jeremiah O'Kane, Vancouver, Canada; two *s* two *d*; 2nd, 1966, Philippa, *o d* of late Philip Dunne; one *s* two *d*. *Educ:* Winchester; Trinity Coll., Cambridge (Exhibnr). Hon. Page to King George VI; served War of 1939–45, Coldstream Guards, 1 SAS Regt, SBS Regt (despatches (three times), DSO, MC, Légion d'Honneur, Croix de Guerre, Greek War Cross). Entered HM Foreign Service, 1947; served as 1st Sec. in Washington, Brussels, Baghdad (Deputy Sec. General Baghdad Pact). Lord-in-Waiting, Jan.-June 1961; Jt Parly. Sec., Min. of Housing and Local Govt, 1961–62; Minister of State, Home Office, 1962–63; First Lord of the Admiralty, 1963–64; Minister of Defence for the Royal Navy, April-Oct. 1964; Deputy Leader of the Opposition, House of Lords, 1967–70; Lord Privy Seal and Minister in Charge, Civil Service Dept, 1970–73; Leader of the House of Lords, 1970–73. Chairman: Brit. Adv. Cttee on Oil Pollution of the Sea, 1968–70; 3rd Int. Conf. on Oil Pollution of the Sea, 1968. Chm., MRC, 1982–90. Chairman: Tate & Lyle, 1978–83 (Dir, 1974–93); Davy Corp., 1985–90; Booker Tate, 1988–91; Director: Sotheby's, 1973–85; Smiths Industries, 1973–86; Morgan Crucible, 1973–87; S. G. Warburg, 1973–88; Chm., European Capital Ltd, 1991–95. Chm., BOTB, 1983–86; President: London Chamber of Commerce and Industry, 1979–82; E European Trade Council, 1990–95 (Chm., 1986–90); Chm., 1978–86, Patron, 1986–, Anglo-Hellenic League; Chm., Greece Fund, 1988–94. A Governor, Centre for Environmental Studies, 1967–70; President: National Federation of Housing Societies, 1965–70; Parly and Scientific Cttee, 1980–83; Review of Prevention of Terrorism Act, 1983. President: BHF, 1990–95; RGS, 1993–97; SAS Regtl Assoc., 1996–2000. Chm. of Council, KCL, 1977–84; Chancellor, Southampton Univ., 1984–95. FKC 1979. Hon. LLD: Southampton, 1985; London; Long Island Univ., 1987. Grand Comdr, Order of Honour (Greece), 1992. *Recreations:* ski-ing, travel. *Heir: s* Viscount Brocas, *qv*. *Address:* Tidcombe Manor, Tidcombe, near Marlborough, Wilts SN8 3SL. *T:* (01264) 731225, *Fax:* (01264) 731418; Flat 5, 97 Onslow Square, SW7 3LT. *T:* (020) 7584 1551. *Clubs:* Brooks's, Special Forces.

See also Adm. Sir Charles Madden, Bt.

JELLICOE, Ann; *see* Jellicoe, P. A.

JELLICOE, (Patricia) Ann, (Mrs Roger Mayne), OBE 1984; playwright and director; *b* 15 July 1927; *d* of John Andrea Jellicoe and Frances Jackson Henderson; *m* 1st, 1950, C. E. Knight-Clarke (marr. diss. 1961); 2nd, 1962, Roger Mayne; one *s* one *d*. *Educ:* Polam Hall, Darlington; Queen Margaret's, York; Central Sch. of Speech and Drama (Elsie Fogarty Prize, 1947). Actress, stage manager and dir, London and provinces, 1947–51; privately commnd to study relationship between theatre architecture and theatre practice, 1949; founded and ran Cockpit Theatre Club to experiment with open stage, 1952–54; taught acting and directed plays, Central Sch., 1954–56; Literary Manager, Royal Court Theatre, 1973–75; Founder, 1979, Director, 1979–85 and Pres., 1986, Colway Theatre Trust to produce community plays; Life Pres., Dorchester Community Plays Assoc., 1999. *Plays:* The Sport of My Mad Mother (also dir. with George Devine), Royal Court, 1958; The Knack, Arts (Cambridge), 1961 (also dir. with Keith Johnstone), Royal Court, 1962, New York, 1964, Paris, 1967 (filmed, 1965; Palme d'Or, Cannes, 1965); Shelley or The Idealist (also dir.), Royal Court, 1965; The Rising Generation, Royal Court, 1967; The Giveaway, Garrick, 1969; Flora and the Bandits (also dir.), Dartington Coll. of Arts, 1976; The Bargain (also dir.), SW Music Theatre, 1979; *community plays:* (also directed): The Reckoning, Lyme Regis, 1978; The Tide, Seaton, 1980; (with Fay Weldon and John Fowles) The Western Women, Lyme Regis, 1984; Mark og Mønt (Money and Land), Holbæk, Denmark, 1988; Under the God, Dorchester, 1989; Changing Places, Woking, 1992; *plays for children:* (also directed): You'll Never Guess!, Arts, 1973; Clever Elsie, Smiling John, Silent Peter, Royal Court, 1974; A Good Thing or a Bad Thing, Royal Court, 1974; *translations:* Rosmersholm, Royal Court, 1960; The Lady from the Sea, Queen's, 1961; (with Ariadne Nicolaeff) The Seagull, Queen's, 1963; Der Freischütz, Sadlers Wells, 1964; *directed:* For Children, 1959; Skyvers, 1963; A Worthy Guest, 1974; (community plays): The Poor Man's Friend, Bridport, 1981; The Garden, Sherborne, 1982; Entertaining Strangers, Dorchester, 1985. *Publications:* Some Unconscious Influences in the Theatre, 1967; (with Roger Mayne) Shell Guide to Devon, 1975; Community Plays: how to put them on, 1987; *plays:* The Sport of My Mad Mother, 1958 (USA 1964); The Knack, 1962 (USA 1964; trans. various langs); Shelley or The Idealist, 1966; The Rising Generation, 1969; The Giveaway, 1970; 3 Jelliplays, 1975. *Recreations:* gardening, enjoying grandchildren. *Address:* Colway Manor, Lyme Regis, Dorset DT7 3HD.

JENCKS, Charles Alexander, PhD; landscape architect, designer and writer; *b* 21 June 1939; *s* of Gardner Platt Jencks and Ruth Pearl Jencks; *m* 1st, 1960, Pamela Balding (marr. diss. 1973); two *s*; 2nd, 1978, Margaret Keswick (*d* 1995); one *s* one *d*. *Educ:* Harvard University (BA Eng. Lit. 1961; BA, MA Arch. 1965); London University (PhD Arch. Hist., 1970). Architectural Association, 1968; writer on Post-Modern architecture, 1975–, Late-Modern architecture, 1978–; designer of furniture, gardens, and Alessi Tea and Coffee Set, 1983; numerous Univ. lectures, incl. Peking, Warsaw, Tokyo, USA, Paris; house designs incl. The Garagia Rotunda, 1976–77, The Elemental House, 1983, The Thematic House, 1984. Fulbright Schol., Univ. of London, 1965–67; Melbourne Oration, Australia, 1974; Bossom Lectr, RSA, 1980; Mem., Cttee for selection of architects, Venice Biennale, 1980; Curator, Post-Modern London, exhibn, 1991. Editor at Academy Editions, 1979–. Member: Architectural Assoc.; RSA. Gold Medal for Architecture, Nara, Japan, 1992; Gardener of the Year, Country Life, 1998. *TV films:* (wrote) Le Corbusier, BBC, 1974; (wrote and presented) Kings of Infinite Space (Frank Lloyd Wright and Michael Graves), 1983. *Publications:* Meaning in Architecture, 1969; Architecture 2000, 1971; Adhocism, 1972; Modern Movements in Architecture, 1973, 2nd edn 1985; Le Corbusier and the Tragic View of Architecture, 1974, 2nd edn 1987; The Language of Post-Modern Architecture, 1977, 6th edn 1991; Late-Modern Architecture, 1980; Post-Modern Classicism, 1980; Free-Style Classicism, 1982; Architecture Today (Current Architecture), 1982, 2nd edn 1988; Abstract Representation, 1983; Kings of Infinite Space, 1983; Towards a Symbolic Architecture, 1985; What is Post-Modernism? 1986, 3rd edn 1989; Post-Modernism—the new classicism in art and architecture, 1987; The Architecture of Democracy, 1987; The Prince, The Architects and New Wave Monarchy, 1988; The New Moderns, 1990; (ed) The Post Modern Reader, 1992; Heteropolis, Los Angeles, the Riots and the Strange Beauty of Heteroarchitecture, 1993; The Architecture of the Jumping Universe, 1995, 2nd edn 1997; Frank O. Gehry: cultural conservation and individual imagination, 1995; (ed jtly) Theories and Manifestos of Contemporary Architecture, 1997; Ecstatic Architecture, 1999; Le Corbusier and the Continual Revolution in Architecture, 2000; articles in Encounter, Connoisseur, l'Oeil, TLS. *Recreations:* travel, collecting Chinese (bullet-hole) rocks. *Address:* 19 Lansdowne Walk, W11 3AH; 519 Latimer Road, Santa Monica, CA 90402, USA.

JENKIN, family name of **Baron Jenkin of Roding**.

JENKIN OF RODING, Baron *cr* 1987 (Life Peer), of Wanstead and Woodford in Greater London; **Charles Patrick Fleeming Jenkin;** PC 1973; MA; Chairman, Foundation for Science and Technology, since 1997 (Vice-President, 1996–97); *b* 7 Sept. 1926; *s* of late Mr and Mrs C. O. F. Jenkin; *m* 1952, Alison Monica Graham; two *s* two *d*. *Educ:* Dragon Sch., Oxford; Clifton Coll.; Jesus Coll., Cambridge. MA (Cantab.) 1951. Served with QO Cameron Highlanders, 1945–48; 1st Class Hons in Law, Cambridge, 1951; Harmsworth Scholar, Middle Temple, 1951; called to the Bar, 1952. Distillers Co. Ltd, 1957–70. Member: Hornsey Borough Council, 1960–63; London Coun. of Social Service, 1963–67. MP (C) Wanstead and Woodford, 1964–87. An Opposition front bench spokesman on Treasury, Trade and Economics, 1965–70; Jt Vice-Chm., Cons. Parly Trade and Power Cttee, 1966–67; Chm., All Party Parly Group on Chemical Industry, 1968–70; Financial Sec. to the Treasury, 1970–72; Chief Sec. to Treasury, 1972–74; Minister for Energy, 1974; Opposition front bench spokesman: on Energy, 1974–76; on Soc. Services, 1976–79; Secretary of State: for Social Services, 1979–81; for Industry, 1981–83; for the Environment, 1983–85. Mem., Select Cttee on Sci. and Technol., H of L, 1996–2001 (Chm., Sub-Cttee II on Sci. and Soc., 1999–2000). Mem., Exec. Cttee, Assoc. of Cons. Peers, 1996–2000. President: National CPC Cttee, 1983–86; Greater London Area, Nat. Union of Cons. Assocs, 1989– (Vice-Pres., 1987–89). Chm., Friends' Provident Life Office, 1988–98 (Dep. Chm., Friends' Provident Life Office (Dir, 1986–88) and UK Provident Institution (Dir, 1987–88), 1987–88, when merged). Chm., Forest Healthcare NHS Trust, 1991–97. Director: Tilbury Contracting Gp Ltd, 1974–79; Royal Worcester Ltd, 1975–79; Continental and Industrial Trust Ltd, 1975–79; Chairman: Crystalate Hldgs PLC, 1988–90 (Dir, 1987–90); Lamco Paper Sales Ltd, 1987–93; Consultant, Thames Estuary Airport Co. Ltd, 1994–; Mem. Internat. Adv. Bd, Marsh and McLennan, 1993–98. UK Co-Chm., UK-Japan 2000 Gp, 1986–90 (Bd Mem., 1990–99); Vice-Pres., 1991 Japan Festival Cttee, 1987–91. Adviser: Andersen Consulting, Management Consultants, 1985–96; Sumitomo Trust and Banking Co. Ltd, 1989–; Member: UK Adv. Bd, Nat. Economic Res. Associates Inc., 1985–98; Supervisory Bd, Achmea Hldg NV, Netherlands, 1992–98. Member, Council: UK CEED, 1987–; Guide Dogs for the Blind Assoc., 1987–97; ICRF, 1991–97 (Dep. Chm., 1994–97); Chm., Visual Handicap Gp, 1990–98; Pres., Friends of Wanstead Hosp., 1987–91. Pres., British Urban Regeneration Assoc., 1990–96; Sen. Vice Pres., World Congress on Urban Growth and Develt, 1992–95; Vice President: Nat. Housing Fedn, 1992–2000; LGA, 1997–; Jt Pres., Assoc. of London Govt, 1995–. Chm. Trustees, Westfield Coll. Trust, 1988–2000 (Gov., Westfield Coll., 1964–70; Fellow, QMW, 1991); Gov., Clifton Coll., 1969– (Mem. Council, 1972–79; Pres. of School, 1994–99; Pres., Old Cliftonian Soc., 1987–89); Mem. Internat. Adv. Bd, Nijenrode Univ., Netherlands, 1994–98. Trustee, Monteverdi Choir, 1992–2001. Patron: St Clare West Essex Hospice Trust, 1991–; Stort Trust, 1991–. Freeman: City of London, 1985; London Bor. of Redbridge, 1988. FRSA 1985. Hon. FRSE 2001. Hon. LLD South Bank, 1997; Hon. DSc Ulster, 2001. *Recreations:* music, gardening, sailing, bricklaying. *Address:* House of Lords, SW1A 0PW. *T:* (020) 7219 6966, *Fax:* (020) 7219 0759; *e-mail:* jenkinp@parliament.uk. *Club:* West Essex Conservative (Wanstead).

See also Hon. B. C. Jenkin, Rear-Adm. D. C. Jenkin.

JENKIN, Hon. Bernard Christison; MP (C) Essex North, since 1997 (Colchester North, 1992–97); *b* 9 April 1959; *s* of Lord Jenkin of Roding, *qv*; *m* 1988, Anne Caroline, *d* of late Hon. Charles Strutt; two *s*. *Educ:* Highgate Sch.; William Ellis Sch.; Corpus Christi Coll., Cambridge (BA Hons Eng. Lit., MA). Ford Motor Co., 1983–86; 3i, 1986–88; Hill Samuel Bank, 1988–89; Legal & General Ventures, 1989–92. Contested (C) Glasgow Central, 1987. PPS to Sec. of State for Scotland, 1995–97; Opposition spokesman on constitutional affairs, 1997–98, on transport, 1998–99; Opposition front bench spokesman on transport, and for London, 1999–2001; Shadow Defence Sec., 2001–. Mem., Select Cttee on Social Security, 1992–97; Sec., Cons. Backbench Small Business Cttee, 1992–97; Jt Sec., Cons. Backbench Foreign Affairs Cttee, 1994–95. Pres., Cambridge Union Soc., 1982. *Recreations:* family, music (esp. opera), fishing, shooting, sailing, ski-ing, DIY, arguing the Conservative cause. *Address:* House of Commons, SW1A 0AA. *T:* (020) 7219 3000. *Club:* Colchester Conservative.

See also Baron Rayleigh.

JENKIN, Conrad; *see* Jenkin, D. C.

JENKIN, Rear Adm. (David) Conrad, CB 1983; Commandant, Joint Service Defence College (formerly National Defence College), 1981–84, retired; *b* 25 Oct. 1928; *s* of Mr and Mrs C. O. F. Jenkin; *m* 1958, Jennifer Margaret Nowell; three *s* one *d*. *Educ:* Dragon Sch., Oxford; RNC, Dartmouth. Entered RN at age of 13½, 1942; qual. in Gunnery, 1953; commanded: HMS Palliser, 1961–63; HMS Cambrian, 1964–66; HMS Galatea, 1974–75; HMS Hermes (aircraft carrier), 1978–79; Flag Officer, First Flotilla, 1980–81. Pres., Hong Kong Flotilla Assoc, 1999–. *Recreations:* sailing, ski-ing, do-it-yourself. *Address:* Knapsyard House, West Meon, Hants GU32 1LF. *T:* (01730) 829227.

See also Baron Jenkin of Roding.

JENKIN, Ian (Evers) Tregarthen, OBE 1984; Principal, Camberwell School of Art and Crafts, 1975–85; *b* 18 June 1920; *s* of Henry Archibald Tregarthen Jenkin, OBE and Dagmar Leggott. *Educ:* Stowe; Camberwell Sch. of Art and Crafts; Trinity Coll., Cambridge (MA Econ.); Slade Sch., University Coll. London. Served with Royal Artillery, 1939–46. Sec. and Tutor, Slade School, 1949–75; Curator, RA Schools, 1985–86; Co-founder, 1986, Dir, 1986–89, Pres., 1989–91, Vice-Pres., 1991–, Open Coll. of the Arts. Chm., Craft Initiative Wkg Pty, Gulbenkian Foundn, 1985–89; Member: Art Panel, Arts Council (Vice-Chm.), 1979–82; Crafts Council, 1981–84 (Chm., Educn Cttee); Art and Design Working Gp, Nat. Adv. Body for Public Sector Higher Educn, 1982–85; Council, British Sch. at Rome, 1981–90 (Mem. Mgt Cttee, 1990–95; Chm., Painting Faculty, 1981–86; Chm., 1986–90, Mem., 1994–98, Fine Art Faculty); Cttee for Paintings in Hosps, 1982–97; Exec. Cttee, C & G Art Sch., 1985–. Advisor, Member, Trustee, examiner, numerous educnl, art and conservation bodies; Trustee, Sir Stanley Spencer Meml Trust, 1982–; Chairman: E. Vincent Harris Fund for Mural Decoration, 1993–2001; Edwin Austin Abbey Meml Trust Fund for Mural Painting in GB, 1993–2001; Edwin Austin Abbey Meml Scholarships Council, 1994–98 (Mem., 1985–94 and 1998–2001). Pres., Dulwich Br., NADFAS, 1984–95; Vice-Pres., Nine Elms Gp of Artists, 1990–; Dir, Guild of St George, 1986–2000 (Companion, 1984). Hon. Fellow, W Surrey Coll. of Art and Design, 1994; Hon. Mem., C&G, 1995. FRSA. Hon. Dr Arts CNAA 1987. *Publications:* Disaster Planning and Preparedness: a survey of practices and procedures (British Liby R&D report), 1986; An Outline Disaster Control Plan (British Liby Inf. Guide), 1987; contribs to DNB. *Recreations:* gardening, painting. *Address:* Barn Cottage, Grove Farm, Fifield, Maidenhead, Berks SL6 2PF. *Club:* Athenæum.

JENKIN, Simon William Geoffrey; education consultant; Chief Education Officer, Devon County Council, 1989–98; *b* 25 July 1943; *s* of Dudley Cyril Robert Jenkin and Muriel Grace (*née* Mather); *m* 1973, Elizabeth Tapsell; two *d*. *Educ:* Univ. of London (BSc Econs); Jesus Coll., Oxford (DipEd). Lectr, 1967–72, Sen. Lectr, 1972–75, Bournemouth Coll. of Technology; Educn Officer, Essex CC, 1975–80; Area Educn Officer, NE Essex, 1980–83; Principal Educn Officer, Derbys CC, 1983–87; Dep. Chief Educn Officer, Devon CC, 1988–89. Mem., SW Regl Cttee, FEFCE, 1993–98. Dir, Cornwall and Devon Careers Co. Ltd, 1995–98. Advr, LGA, 1991–98. Gov., United World Coll. of the Atlantic, 1991–98. FRSA 1992. *Recreation:* my wife. *Address:* 34 Wonford Road, St Leonard's, Exeter, Devon EX2 4LD. *T:* (01392) 499798.

JENKINS, family name of **Barons Jenkins of Hillhead** and **Jenkins of Putney**.

JENKINS OF HILLHEAD, Baron *cr* 1987 (Life Peer), of Pontypool in the County of Gwent; **Roy Harris Jenkins,** OM 1993; PC 1964; FBA; Chancellor, University of Oxford, since 1987; President, Royal Society of Literature, since 1988; Co-President, Royal Institute of International Affairs, since 1993; Leader, Social and Liberal Democratic Peers, 1988–98; First Leader, Social Democratic Party, 1982–83 (Member of Joint Leadership, 1981–82); *b* 11 Nov. 1920; *o s* of late Arthur Jenkins, MP, and of Hattie Jenkins; *m* 1945, Jennifer Morris (*see* Dame Jennifer Jenkins); two *s* one *d*. *Educ:* Abersychan Grammar Sch.; University Coll., Cardiff (Hon. Fellow 1982); Balliol Coll., Oxford (Hon. Fellow 1969). Sec. and Librarian, Oxford Union Society; Chairman, Oxford Univ. Democratic Socialist Club; First Class in Hon. Sch. of Philosophy, Politics and Economics, 1941; DCL Oxford, 1987. Served War of 1939–45, in RA, 1942–46; Captain, 1944–46. Contested (Lab) Solihull Div. of Warwicks, at Gen. Election, 1945. Mem. of Staff of Industrial and Commercial Finance Corp. Ltd, 1946–48. Mem. Exec. Cttee of Fabian Soc., 1949–61; Chm., Fabian Soc., 1957–58; Mem. Cttee of Management, Soc. of Authors, 1956–60; Governor, British Film Institute, 1955–58; Adviser to John Lewis Partnership, 1954–62, Dir of Financial Operations, 1962–64. Dir, Morgan Grenfell Hldgs Ltd, 1981–82. MP (Lab): Central Southwark, 1948–50; Stechford, Birmingham, 1950–76; PPS to Sec. of State for Commonwealth Relations, 1949–50; Minister of Aviation, 1964–65; Home Sec., 1965–67, 1974–76; Chancellor of the Exchequer, 1967–70; Dep. Leader, Labour Party, 1970–72. Pres., European Commn, 1977–81. Contested: Warrington by-election as first Social Democratic candidate, July 1981; Glasgow Hillhead (SDP/Alliance), 1982. MP (SDP) Glasgow Hillhead, March 1982–1987. UK Deleg. to Council of Europe, 1955–57. Chm., Indep. Commn on the Voting System, 1997–98. Vice-Pres., Inst. of Fiscal Studies, 1970–. Formerly: Dep. Chm. Federal Union; Pres., Britain in Europe, Referendum Campaign, 1975; Chm., Labour European Cttee. A President of United Kingdom Council of the European Movement. Pres., UWIST, 1975–81. Trustee, Pilgrim Trust, 1973–98. Lectures: G. M. Young, Oxford, 1963; Henry L. Stimson, Yale, 1971; Jean Monnet, Florence, 1977; Dimbleby, 1979; Churchill, Luxembourg, 1980; Rede, Cambridge, 1988; George Ball, Princeton, 1989; Goodman, 1989; Leverhulme, Liverpool, 1990; Stephenson, Glasgow, 1992; Paul-Henri Spaak, Harvard, 1994; Romanes, Oxford, 1996; Nobel, Oslo, 1997; Eleanor Rathbone, Durham, 1998; Jean Monnet, Hull, 2000. Liveryman, Goldsmiths' Co.; Freeman, City of London, 1965. Freeman, City of Brussels, 1980. Hon. Foreign Mem., Amer. Acad. Arts and Scis, 1973. Hon. FBA 1993; Hon. Fellow: Berkeley Coll., Yale, 1972; St Antony's Coll., Oxford, 1987. Hon. LLD: Leeds, 1971; Harvard, 1972; Pennsylvania, 1973; Dundee, 1973; Loughborough, 1975; Bath, 1978; Michigan, 1978; Wales, 1979; Bristol, 1980; Hon. DLitt: Glasgow, 1972; City, 1976; Warwick, 1978; Reading, 1979; London, 2000; Hon. DCL: Oxford, 1973; Kent, 1992; Hon. DSc Aston, 1977; DUniv: Keele, 1977; Essex, 1978; Open, 1979; Hon. DPhil Katholieke Univ., Leuven, 1979; Hon. doctorates: Urbino, 1979; TCD, 1979; Georgetown, 1988; W Virginia, 1992; Glamorgan, 1994; Bologna, 1994; Sofia, 1998. Charlemagne Prize, 1972; Robert Schuman Prize, 1972; Prix Bentinck, 1978. Order of European Merit (Luxemburg), 1976; Grand Cross: Legion of Honour of Senegal, 1979; Legion of Honour of Mali, 1979; Order of Charles III (Spain), 1980; Order of Merit (Italy), 1990; Order of Infante D. Henrique (Portugal), 1993; Comdr, Legion of Honour (France), 1999. *Publications:* (ed) Purpose and Policy (a vol. of the Prime Minister's Speeches), 1947; Mr Attlee: An Interim Biography, 1948; (contrib.) New Fabian Essays, 1952; Pursuit of Progress, 1953; Mr Balfour's Poodle, 1954; Sir Charles Dilke: A Victorian Tragedy, 1958; The Labour Case (Penguin Special), 1959; Asquith, 1964; (contrib.) Hugh Gaitskell: a memoir, 1964; Essays and Speeches, 1967; Afternoon on the Potomac?, 1972; What Matters Now, 1972; Nine Men of Power, 1975; Partnership of Principle, 1985; Truman, 1986; Baldwin, 1987; Gallery of Twentieth Century Portraits, 1988; European Diary 1977–81, 1989; A Life at the Centre (autobiog.), 1991; Portraits and Miniatures, 1993; Gladstone (Whitbread Biography Award), 1995; The Chancellors, 1998; Churchill, 2001. *Address:* 2 Kensington Park Gardens, W11 3HB; St Amand's House, East Hendred, Oxon OX12 8LA. *Clubs:* Athenæum, Brooks's, Pratt's, Reform, Beefsteak, Oxford and Cambridge.

JENKINS OF HILLHEAD, Lady; *see* Jenkins, Dame M. J.

JENKINS OF PUTNEY, Baron *cr* 1981 (Life Peer), of Wandsworth in Greater London; **Hugh Gater Jenkins;** *b* 27 July 1908; *s* of Joseph Walter Jenkins and Florence Emily (*née* Gater), Enfield, Middlesex; *m* 1st, 1936, Marie (*née* Crosbie) (*d* 1989), *d* of Sqdn Ldr Ernest Crosbie and Ethel (*née* Hawkins); 2nd, 1991, Helena Maria (*d* 1994), *d* of Nicolas and Katerina Pavlidis, Athens. *Educ:* Enfield Grammar Sch. Personal exploration of employment and unemployment, and political and economic research, 1925–30; Prudential Assce Co., 1930–40. ROC, 1938; RAF: Fighter Comd, 1941; became GCI Controller (Flt Lt); seconded to Govt of Burma, 1945, as Dir Engl. Programmes, Rangoon Radio. Nat. Union of Bank Employees: Greater London Organiser, 1947; Res. and Publicity Officer; Ed., The Bank Officer, 1948; British Actors' Equity Assoc.: Asst Sec., 1950; Asst Gen. Sec., 1957–64. LCC: Mem. for Stoke Newington and Hackney N, 1958–65 (Public Control and Town Planning Cttees). Fabian Soc. lectr and Dir of Summer Schools in early post-war years; Chairman: H Bomb Campaign Cttee, 1954; Campaign for Nuclear Disarmament, 1979–81 (Vice-Pres., 1981–); CND, Aldermaston Marcher, 1957–63; Chm. Victory for Socialism, 1956–60; Mem. Exec. Cttee Greater London Labour Party. Contested (Lab): Enfield W, 1950; Mitcham, 1955; MP (Lab) Wandsworth, Putney, 1964–79; Minister for the Arts, 1974–76. Former Mem., Public Accounts Cttee. Member: Arts Council, 1968–71; Drama Panel, 1972–74; Nat. Theatre Bd, 1976–80; Dep. Chm., Theatres Trust, 1977–79, Dir, 1979–86, Consultant, 1986–, Life Pres., 1995. Theatres' Advisory Council: Jt Sec., 1963; Chm., 1964–74, 1976–86; Vice-Pres., 1986–95; Pres., 1996–. Occasional broadcasts and lectures on communications, theatrical and disarmament subjects. *Radio plays:* series, Scenes from an Autobiography: Solo Boy, 1983; When You and I Were Seventeen, 1985; A Day in September, 1986; In Time of War, 1986; Lost Tune from Rangoon, 1987; View to a Death, 1989. *Publications:* Essays in Local Government Enterprise (with others), 1964; The Culture Gap, 1979; Rank and File, 1980; various pamphlets; contrib. to Tribune, New Statesman, Guardian, etc. *Recreations:* reading, writing, talking, viewing, listening, avoiding retirement. *Address:* House of Lords, SW1A 0PW. *T:* (020) 7219 6706, (office) (020) 7836 8591.

JENKINS, Alan Roberts; editorial consultant; *b* 8 June 1926; *s* of Leslie Roberts Jenkins and Marjorie Kate Cawston; *m* 1st, 1949, Kathleen Mary Baker (*d* 1969); four *s*; 2nd, 1971, Helen Mary Speed; one *s*. *Educ:* Aylesbury Grammar Sch. Commnd Royal Berks Regt, 1945; Captain, W African Liaison Service, GHQ India; Staff Captain Public Relations, Royal W African Frontier Force, Lagos; DADPR W Africa Comd (Major). Reporter, Reading Mercury and Berkshire Chronicle, 1948; Sub-editor, Daily Herald; Daily Mail: Sub-editor; Night Editor, 1962–69; Northern Editor, 1969–71; Asst Editor, Evening Standard, 1971; Dep. Editor, Sunday People, 1971–72; Asst Editor, Sunday Mirror, 1972–77; Editor, Glasgow Herald, 1978–80; Editorial exec., The Times, 1981–89; Gp Consultant, The New Straits Times, Malaysia, 1989–92. *Address:* Old Rose Cottage, Kirkton of Balmerino, Fife DD6 8SA.

JENKINS, Alun; *see* Jenkins, T. A.

JENKINS, Archibald Ian; Member (Lib Dem) Tweeddale, Ettrick and Lauderdale, Scottish Parliament, since 1999; *b* 18 March 1941; *s* of Archibald Jenkins and Margaret (*née* Duncan); *m* 1967, Margery MacKay. *Educ:* Rothesay Acad., Isle of Bute; Glasgow Univ. (MA 1963; DipEd 1964). Teacher of English, Clydebank High Sch., 1964–70; Principal Teacher of English, Peebles High Sch., 1970–99. *Recreations:* golf, jazz, watching Rugby, reading. *Address:* 1 South Park Drive, Peebles EH45 9DR. *T:* (01721) 720528.

JENKINS, Prof. Aubrey Dennis; Professor of Polymer Science, University of Sussex, 1971–92, now Emeritus; *b* 6 Sept. 1927; *s* of Arthur William Jenkins and Mabel Emily (*née* Street); *m* 1st, 1950, Audrey Doreen Middleton (marr. diss. 1987); two *s* one *d*; 2nd, 1987, Jitka Horská, *er d* of late Josef Horský and of Anna Horská, Hradec Králové, Czechoslovakia. *Educ:* Dartford Grammar Sch.; Sir John Cass Technical Inst.; King's Coll., Univ. of London. BSc 1948, PhD 1951; DSc 1961. FRIC 1957. Research Chemist, Courtaulds Ltd, Fundamental Research Laboratory, Maidenhead, 1950–60; Head of Chemistry Research, Gillette Industries Ltd, Reading, 1960–64 (Harris Research Labs, Washington, DC, 1963–64); University of Sussex, 1964–92: Sen. Lectr in Chemistry, 1964–68; Reader, 1968–71; Dean, Sch. of Molecular Scis, 1973–78. Visiting Professor: Inst. of Macromolecular Chemistry, Prague, 1978 and 1986; Univ. of Massachusetts, Amherst, 1979. Member: Internat. Union of Pure and Applied Chemistry, Commn on Macromolecular Nomenclature, 1974–85 (Chm., 1977–85; Sec., Macromolecular Div., 1985–93); British Assoc. for Central and Eastern Europe (formerly GB/E Europe Centre), 1975–; British, Czech and Slovak Assoc., 1990–. Mem., Brighton HA, 1983–90. Examining chaplain to Bishop of Chichester, 1980–90. Hon. Fellow, Soc. of Organic Chemistry of Argentina, 1993. Heyrovský Gold Medal for Chemistry, Czechoslovak Acad. of Scis, 1990. *Publications:* Kinetics of Vinyl Polymerization by Radical Mechanisms (with C. H. Bamford, W. G. Barb and P. F. Onyon), 1958; Polymer Science, 1972; (with A. Ledwith) Reactivity, Mechanism and Structure in Polymer Chemistry, 1974; (with J. F. Kennedy) Macromolecular Chemistry, Vol. I 1980, Vol. II 1982, Vol. III 1984; Progress in Polymer Science (12 vols), 1967–85; (with J. N. Murrell) Properties of Liquids and Solutions, 1994; papers in learned jls. *Recreations:* music, travel, photography. *Address:* Vixens', 22A North Court, Hassocks, West Sussex BN6 8JS. *T:* (01273) 845410; *e-mail:* adjjj@jjadj.u-net.com.

JENKINS, Brian David; MP (Lab) Tamworth, since 1997 (SE Staffordshire, April 1996–1997); *b* 19 Sept. 1942; *s* of Hiram Jenkins and Gladys (*née* Morgan); *m* 1963, Joan Dix; one *s* one *d*. *Educ:* Aston Coll.; Coventry Coll.; Coleg Harlech; London Sch. of Econs (BSc Econ); Wolverhampton Poly. (PGCE). With CEGB, 1963–68; Jaguar Cars, 1968–73; Percy Lane, 1973–75; Lecturer: Isle of Man Coll., 1981–83; Tamworth Coll., 1983–96. Mem., GMB. Tamworth Borough Council: Mem. (Lab), 1985–96; Dep. Mayor, 1992–93; Mayor, 1993–94; Leader, 1995–96. Contested (Lab) SE Staffs, 1992. Mem., Tamworth Br., RBL. *Recreations:* music, reading, watching sport. *Address:* House of Commons, SW1A 0AA.

JENKINS, Sir Brian (Garton), GBE 1991; FCA; Chairman, Charities Aid Foundation, since 1998; a Deputy Chairman, Barclays Bank plc, since 2000; Lord Mayor of London, 1991–92; *b* 3 Dec. 1935; *s* of late Owen Garton Jenkins and Doris Enid (*née* Webber); *m* 1967, (Elizabeth) Ann Prentice; one *s* one *d*. *Educ:* Tonbridge; Trinity Coll., Oxford (State Scholar; MA; Hon. Fellow, 1992). FCA 1974. Served RA, Gibraltar, 1955–57 (2nd Lieut). With Cooper Brothers & Co., later Coopers & Lybrand, 1960–95; Chm., Woolwich Bldg Soc., later Woolwich plc, 1995–2000. Pres., ICAEW, 1985–86. Pres., London Chamber of Commerce, 1996–98; Mem., Financial Law Panel, 1993–. Vice-Pres., Foundn for Sci. and Technol., 2000–. Alderman, City of London (Ward of Cordwainer), 1980– (Sheriff, 1987–88); Liveryman: Chartered Accountants' Co., 1980– (Master, 1990–91); Merchant Taylors' Co., 1984– (Master, 1999–2000); Information Technologists' Co., 1985– (Master, 1994–95). Dep. Pres., 1996–97, Pres., 1997–98, BCS. Trustee: Community Service Volunteers, 1987–; Crimestoppers, 1996–; Nuffield Trust for the Forces of the Crown, 1997–. Hon. Bencher, Inner Temple, 1992. Hon. Mem., Baltic Exchange, 1993. Hon. DSc City Univ., 1991; Hon. DLitt London Guildhall Univ., 1991; Companion, De Montfort Univ., 1993; Hon. Fellow, Goldsmiths Coll., London, 1998. FBCS. CIMgt; FRSA. Centenary Award, Chartered Accountants Founding Socs, 1993. Grand Conseiller Tutélaire des Neuf Nations de Bruxelles, 1992. *Publication:* An Audit Approach to Computers, 1978, 4th edn 1992. *Recreations:* garden construction, old books, large jigsaw puzzles, ephemera. *Address:* Barclays Bank plc, 54 Lombard Street, EC3P 3AH. *Clubs:* Brooks's, City of London, City Livery.

JENKINS, Lt-Col Charles Peter de Brisay, MBE 1960; MC 1945; Clerk, Worshipful Company of Goldsmiths, 1975–88, retired; *b* 19 Aug. 1923; *s* of late Brig. A. de B. Jenkins and of Mrs Elizabeth Susan Jenkins; *m* 1949, Joan Mary, *e d* of late Col and Mrs C. N. Littleboy, Thirsk; one *s*. *Educ:* Cheltenham Coll.; Selwyn Coll., Cambridge. Commnd RE, 1944; served in Italy, 1944–45; subseq. Hong Kong, Kenya and Germany; jssc 1960; Instructor, Staff Coll., Camberley, 1961–63; Comdr, RE 1st Div., 1965–67; retd 1967. Asst Clerk, Goldsmiths' Co., 1968. Mem., Hallmarking Council, 1977–88; Vice-Chm., Goldsmiths' Coll. (Univ. of London) Council, 1983–91. Trustee Nat. Centre for Orchestral Studies, 1980–89. *Publication:* Unravelling the Mystery - the Story of the Goldsmith's Company in the Twentieth Century, 2000. *Recreations:* swimming, gardening, Wagner. *Address:* Oak Hill, South Brent, Devon TQ10 9JL.

JENKINS, Christopher; *see* Jenkins, J. C.

JENKINS, Christopher Dennis Alexander M.; *see* Martin-Jenkins.

JENKINS, Rev. Dr Daniel Thomas; Free Church Minister and theologian; *b* 9 June 1914; *s* of Evan and Eleanor Jenkins; *m* 1942, Agatha Helen Mary Cree; two *s* three *d*. *Educ:* Merthyr Tydfil Schs; Edinburgh Univ. (MA, BD); Yorkshire United Coll.; Mansfield Coll., Oxford (BA). Minister, Vineyard Congregational Ch, Richmond, Surrey, 1940–42; SCM, Univ. of Birmingham, 1942–45; Asst Editor, Christian Newsletter, London, 1945–48; Commonwealth Fund Fellow, NY, 1948–49; Minister: Oxted Congregational Ch, 1950–56; Kings Weigh House Congregational Ch, London, 1956–62; Chaplain and Reader, Univ. of Sussex, 1963–73; Minister, Regent Sq. URC, London, 1972–81; Weyerhaeuser Prof., Princeton Theol Seminary, USA, 1981–84. Associate Prof. of Theol., Univ. of Chicago, 1950–62; Vis. Prof., KCL, 1973–75. Hon. DD: Knox Coll., Toronto, 1957; Edinburgh, 1964. *Publications:* The Nature of Catholicity, 1942; Prayer and the Service of God, 1945; The Gift of Ministry, 1947; The Doctors' Profession, 1948; Tradition and the Spirit, 1950; Europe and America, 1951; Congregationalism, 1954; The Strangeness of the Church, 1955; The Protestant Ministry, 1958; Equality and Excellence, 1961; Beyond Religion, 1962; The Christian Belief in God, 1964; The Educated Society, 1966; The British: their identity and their religion, 1975; Christian Maturity and Christian Success, 1982. *Address:* 301 Willoughby House, Barbican, EC2Y 8BL.

See also K. M. Jenkins, S. D. Jenkins, B. J. Mack.

JENKINS, David, CBE 1977; MA; Librarian, National Library of Wales, 1969–79; *b* 29 May 1912; *s* of late Evan Jenkins and Mary (*née* James), Blaenclydach, Rhondda; *m* 1948, Menna Rhys, *o d* of late Rev. Owen Evans Williams, Penrhyn-coch, Aberystwyth; one *s* one *d*. *Educ:* Ardwyn Grammar Sch., Aberystwyth; UCW, Aberystwyth (BA Hons Welsh Lit. 1936, MA 1948; W. P. Thomas (Rhondda) Schol. 1936; Sir John Williams Research Student, 1937–38; Hon. Fellow). Served War of 1939–45, Army; Major, 1943; NW Europe. National Library of Wales: Asst, Dept MSS, 1939–48; Asst Keeper, Dept of Printed Books, 1949, Keeper, 1957, Sen. Keeper, 1962. Professorial Fellow, UCW Aberystwyth, 1971–79. Gen. Comr of Income Tax, 1968–87; Chairman: Mid-Wales HMC, 1969–70; Welsh Books Council, 1974–80 (Vice-Chm. 1971–74); Library Adv. Council (Wales), 1979–82; Member: Court of Governors, Univ. of Wales; Ct and Council, UC Aberystwyth and Lampeter; Adv. Council, British Library, 1975–82; BBC Archives Adv. Cttee, 1976–79; Hon. Soc. of Cymmrodorion; Pantyfedwen Trust, 1969–95; Coll. of Librarianship Wales; Governor: Ardwyn Grammar Sch., 1963–72; Penweddig Compreh. Sch., 1973–77. Editor: NLW Jl, 1968–79; Jl Welsh Bibliog. Soc., 1964–79; Ceredigion, Trans Cards Antiq. Soc., 1973–84. JP Aberystwyth 1959–82: Chm. Llanbadarn Bench 1965–69; Vice-Chm., Aberystwyth Bench, 1980; Member: Dyfed Magistrates' Courts Cttee, 1975–79; Dyfed-Powys Police Authority, 1977–81. Hon. DLitt Wales, 1979. Sir Ellis Griffith Meml Prize, Univ. of Wales, 1975. *Publications:* Cofiant Thomas Gwynn Jones, 1973, 2nd edn 1994 (Welsh Arts Council Prize, 1974); (ed) Erthyglau ac Ysgrifau Kate Roberts, 1978; Bardd a Bro: T. Gwynn Jones, Cyngor y Celfyddydau, 1984; Bro Dafydd ap Gwilym, 1992; O Blas Gogerddan i Horeb, 1993; (with G. Morgan) History of National Library of Wales to 1952, 2000; articles in NLW Jl, Bull. Bd of Celtic Studies and many other jls; contrib. Dictionary of Welsh Biography, Cydymaith i lenyddiaeth Cymru, DNB. *Recreation:* walking. *Address:* Maesaleg, Penrhyn-coch, Aberystwyth, Dyfed SY23 3EH. *T:* (01970) 828766.

JENKINS, Rt Rev. David Edward; Bishop of Durham, 1984–94; an Assistant Bishop, diocese of Ripon and Leeds, since 1994; *b* 26 Jan. 1925; *er s* of Lionel C. Jenkins and Dora (*née* Page); *m* 1949, Stella Mary Peet; two *s* two *d*. *Educ:* St Dunstan's Coll., Catford; Queen's Coll., Oxford (MA; Hon. Fellow, 1991). EC, RA, 1945–47 (Captain). Priest, 1954. Succentor, Birmingham Cath. and Lectr, Queen's Coll., 1953–54; Fellow, Chaplain and Praelector in Theology, Queen's Coll., Oxford, 1954–69; Dir, Humanum Studies, World Council of Churches, Geneva, 1969–73 (Consultant, 1973–75); Dir, William Temple Foundn, Manchester, 1973–78 (Jt Dir, 1979–84); Prof. of Theology, Univ. of Leeds, 1979–84, Emeritus Prof., 1985; Hon. Prof. of Divinity, Univ. of Durham, 1994–. Exam. Chaplain to Bps of Lichfield, 1956–69, Newcastle, 1957–69, Bristol, 1958–84, Wakefield, 1978–84, and Bradford, 1979–84; Canon Theologian, Leicester, 1966–82, Canon Emeritus, 1982–. Lectures: Bampton, 1966; Hale, Seabury-Western, USA, 1970; Moorehouse, Melbourne, 1972; Cadbury, Birmingham Univ., 1974; Lindsay Meml, Keele Univ., 1976; Heslington, York Univ., 1980; Drummond, Stirling Univ., 1981; Hibbert, Hibbert Trust, 1985; Hensley Henson, Oxford, 1987; Gore, Westminster Abbey, 1990; Samuel Ferguson, Manchester Univ., 1997. Chm., SCM Press, 1987–92; Trustee, SCM Press Trust, 1992–97. Hon. Fellow: St Chad's Coll., Durham, 1986; Univ. of Sunderland (formerly Sunderland Poly.), 1986. Hon. DD: Durham, 1987; Trinity Coll., Toronto, 1989; Aberdeen, 1990; Birmingham, 1996; Leeds, 1996; Hon. DLitt Teesside, 1994; Hon. DCL Northumbria, 1994. DUniv Open 1996. Jt Editor, Theology, 1976–82. *Publications:* Guide to the Debate about God, 1966; The Glory of Man, 1967; Living with Questions, 1969; What is Man?, 1970; The Contradiction of Christianity, 1976; God, Miracle and the Church of England, 1987; God, Politics and the Future, 1988; God, Jesus and Life in the Spirit, 1988; Still Living with Questions, 1990; (with Rebecca Jenkins) Free to Believe, 1991; Market Whys and Human Wherefores, 2000; contrib. Man, Fallen and Free, 1969, etc. *Recreations:* music, reading, walking, birdwatching. *Address:* Ashbourne, Cotherstone, Barnard Castle, Co. Durham DL12 9PR.

JENKINS, David Edward Stewart; Senior Partner, Lateral Research Consultants, since 1994; *b* 9 May 1949; *s* of late William Stephen Jenkins and of Jean Nicol Downie; *m* 1972, Maggie Steele, *d* of Dr C. H. and Mrs J. D. Lack; two *s* one *d*. *Educ:* Univ. of London Goldsmiths' College (BA(Soc) 1977); LSE. Warden, Ellison Hse Adult Probation Hostel, SE17, 1973–74; Lecturer: (part-time) in Sociology, Brunel Univ., 1980–81; (part-time) in Social Administration, LSE and Goldsmiths' Coll., 1980–81; in Criminology, Univ. of Edinburgh, 1981; Dir, Howard League, 1982–86; Res. Fellow, PSI, 1986–87; Res. Consultant to HM Chief Inspector of Prisons, 1987–95. Morris Ginsburg Fellow in Sociology, LSE, 1986–87. *Recreations:* music, swimming, cycling. *T:* (office) (01225) 445125.

JENKINS, David Hugh; Chief Executive, Dorset County Council, since 1999; *b* 28 April 1952; *s* of David Lyndhurst Jenkins and Charlotte Elizabeth Jenkins; *m* 1980, Ethna Geraldine Trafford; one *d*. *Educ:* Barry Boys' Comprehensive Sch.; Jesus Coll., Oxford (MA). Asst Master, Fairfield GS, Bristol, 1973–74; admitted solicitor, 1977; Articled Clerk then Asst Solicitor, Oxon CC, 1975–79; Solicitor, Commn for Local Admin in Wales, 1979–84; Asst Co. Sec., Hants CC, 1984–89; Dorset County Council: Dep. Co. Solicitor, 1989–91; Asst Chief Exec., 1991–93; Co. Solicitor, 1993–96; Dir, Corporate Services, 1996–99. Clerk to: Dorset Fire Authy, 1999–; Dorset Lieutenancy, 1999–; Sec., Dorset Probation Cttee, 1999–. Board Member: Dorset TEC, 1999–2001; Dorset Business Link, 1999–2001; Bournemouth SO, 2000–. *Recreations:* music, theatre. *Address:* County Hall, Dorchester, Dorset DT1 1XJ. *T:* (01305) 224195.

JENKINS, David John, MBE 1993; General Secretary, Wales Trades Union Congress, since 1983; *b* 21 Sept. 1948; *s* of William and Dorothy Jenkins; *m* 1976, Felicity Anne (*née* Wood); two *s* one *d*. *Educ:* Canton High Sch., Cardiff; Liverpool Univ. (BA Hons); Garnett Coll., London (CertEd). Industrial Sales Organiser, ITT (Distributors), 1970–74; steel worker, GKN, 1974; Lectr, Peterborough Tech. Coll., 1975–78; Research and Admin. Officer, Wales TUC, 1978–83. Pt-time Mem., Competition (formerly Monopolies and Mergers) Commission, 1993–; Mem., Employment Appeal Tribunal, 1994–. *Recreation:* finding time to spend with family. *Address:* 1 Cathedral Road, Cardiff CF1 9SD. *T:* (029) 2037 2345.

JENKINS, Maj.-Gen. David John Malcolm, CB 2000; CBE 1994; Under-Treasurer, Honourable Society of Gray's Inn, since 2000; *b* 2 Jan. 1945; *m* 1969, Ann Patricia Sharp; one *s* two *d*. *Educ:* Sherborne Sch.; Reading Univ. (BA Hons); Magdalene Coll., Cambridge (MPhil). Commissioned The Queen's Own Hussars, 1964; regimental service, 1964–75; RMCS and Staff Coll., 1976–77; Allied Staff, Berlin, 1983–85; CO, The Queen's Own Hussars, 1985–87; COS, 3 Armd Div., 1988–90; Comdr Armd 1 (Br) Corps, 1990–91; Dir, Military Ops, 1991–93; Commandant, RMCS, 1994–96; DG Land Systems, MoD, 1996–2000; Master Gen. of the Ordnance, 1998–2000. *Recreations:* ski-ing, country sports, music, military history. *Address:* Treasury Office, 8 South Square, Gray's Inn, WC1R 5ET. *Clubs:* Cavalry and Guards, Beefsteak.

JENKINS, Ven. David Thomas Ivor; Archdeacon of Westmorland and Furness, 1995–99, now Emeritus; *b* 3 June 1929; *s* of Edward Evan and Edith Olwen Jenkins; *m* 1st, 1953, Rosemary German (*d* 1990); one *d*; 2nd, 1992, Kathleen Theresa Sidey. *Educ:* King's Coll. London (BD, AKC); Birmingham Univ. (MA (Theol.)). Ordained deacon, 1953, priest, 1954; Asst Curate, St Mark's Bilton, Rugby, 1953–56; Vicar, St Margaret's, Wolston, Coventry, 1956–61; Asst Dir, Religious Educn, dio. of Carlisle, 1961–63; Vicar: St Barnabas, Carlisle, 1963–72; St Cuthbert's, Carlisle, 1972–91; Canon Residentiary, Carlisle Cathedral, 1991–95, Canon Emeritus, 2000. Sec., Carlisle Diocesan Synod and Bishop's Council, 1972–95; Diocesan Synod Sec., 1984–95; Sec., Synod of Convocation of York, 1985–. *Recreations:* golf, reading, good food and wine with friends, foreign travel. *Address:* Irvings House, Sleagill, Penrith, Cumbria CA10 3HD. *T:* (01931) 714400.

JENKINS, Prof. Edgar William, CChem, FRSC, Professor of Science Education Policy, University of Leeds, 1993–2000, now Emeritus; *b* 7 Jan. 1939; *s* of Lewis Morgan Jenkins and Eira Gwyn (*née* Thomas); *m* 1961, Isobel Harrison; two *d*. *Educ:* Univ. of Leeds (BSc, MEd). CChem, FRSC 1974. Teacher: Keighley Grammar Sch., 1961–62; Leeds Grammar Sch., 1962–67; University of Leeds: Lectr and Sen. Lectr, 1967–76; Reader in Science Education, 1980–92; Head, Sch. of Education, 1980–84, 1991–95; Dir, Centre for Studies in Science Educn, 1997–. Chm., Bd, Grad. Teacher Trng Registry, 1995–. JP W Yorks, 1977. Editor: Studies in Science Education, 1986–98; Internat. Jl of Technology and Design Education, 1994–2000. *Publications:* A Safety Handbook for Science Teachers, 1973, 4th edn 1991; From Armstrong to Nuffield, 1979; Inarticulate Science?, 1983; Technological Revolution?, 1985; A Magnificent Pile, 1985; Policy, Practice and Professional Judgement, 1993; Investigations by Order, 1996; Junior School Science Education since 1900, 1998; Learning from Others, 2000; Policy, Professionalism and Change, 2001; books for schools. *Recreations:* choral music, walking, lay administration of justice. *Address:* School of Education, The University, Leeds LS2 9JT. *T:* (0113) 233 4561.

JENKINS, Edward Nicholas; QC 2000; a Recorder, since 2000; *b* 27 May 1954; *m* 1979; one *s* one *d*. *Educ:* Trinity Hall, Cambridge (BA Hons). Called to the Bar, Middle Temple, 1977; Asst Recorder, 1999–2000. *Address:* 5 Paper Buildings, Temple, EC4Y 7HB. *T:* (020) 7583 6117.

JENKINS, Sir Elgar (Spencer), Kt 1996; OBE 1988; Chairman, Bath Mental Health Care NHS Trust, 1993–97; *b* 16 June 1935; *s* of late Spencer and Mabel Jenkins. *Educ:* Monmouth Sch.; St Edmund Hall, Oxford (Pres., Oxford Univ., Cons. Assoc., 1955); St Luke's Coll., Exeter; Open Univ. (BA, Teaching Cert). Commission, RAF, 1956–59. Asst Master, Bath and Bristol, 1962–73; Dep. Headmaster, Cardinal Newman Sch., then St Gregory's Catholic Comp. Sch., Bath, 1973–88. Chm., Bath and Dist HA, 1989–93. Member: Local Govt Mgt Bd, 1990–96; Nat. Adv. Cttee on Libraries, 1995–. Bath City Council: Mem. (C), 1966–72, 1973–96; Mayor, Leader of Council, Chm. of Cttees; Association of District Councils: Mem., 1985–96; Leader, Cons. Gp, 1991–96; Dep. Chm., 1991–93; Vice-Chm., 1993–96. Mem., Nat. Exec., Cons. Party, 1994–96. Contested (C) Ebbw Vale, 1970. Mem. Council, 1968–96, Mem. Court, 1968–, Bath Univ.; Chm. of Trustees, Bath Postal Mus., 1986–. Mem., Bath Archaeol Trust, 1994–. FRSA. *Recreations:* history, reading. *Address:* 22 Frankley Buildings, Bath BA1 6EG. *T:* (01225) 314834.

JENKINS, Elizabeth, OBE 1981; *b* 31 Oct. 1905. *Educ:* St Christopher's School, Letchworth; Newnham College, Cambridge. *Publications:* The Winters, 1931; Lady Caroline Lamb, a Biography, 1932; Harriet (awarded the Femina Vie Heureuse Prize), 1934; The Phoenix' Nest, 1936; Jane Austen, a Biography, 1938; Robert and Helen, 1944; Young Enthusiasts, 1946; Henry Fielding (The English Novelists Series), 1947; Six Criminal Women, 1949; The Tortoise and the Hare, 1954; Ten Fascinating Women, 1955; Elizabeth the Great (biography), 1958; Elizabeth and Leicester, 1961; Brightness, 1963; Honey, 1968; Dr Gully, 1972; The Mystery of King Arthur, 1975; The Princes in the Tower, 1978; The Shadow and the Light, 1983; A Silent Joy, 1992. *Address:* 121 Greenhill, Hampstead, NW3 5TY. *T:* (020) 7435 4642.

JENKINS, Emyr; *see* Jenkins, J. E.

JENKINS, Ffion Llywelyn; *see* Hague, F. L.

JENKINS, Very Rev. Frank Graham; Dean of Monmouth and Vicar of St Woolos, 1976–90; *b* 24 Feb. 1923; *s* of Edward and Miriam M. Jenkins; *m* 1950, Ena Doraine Parry; two *s* one *d*. *Educ:* Cyfarthfa Sec. Sch., Merthyr Tydfil; Port Talbot Sec. Sch.; St David's Coll., Lampeter (BA Hist); Jesus Coll., Oxford (BA Theol., MA); St Michael's Coll., Llandaff. HM Forces, 1942–46. Deacon 1950, priest 1951, Llandaff; Asst Curate,

Llangeinor, 1950–53; Minor Canon, Llandaff Cathedral, 1953–60; CF (TA), 1956–61; Vicar of Abertillery, 1960–64; Vicar of Risca, 1964–75; Canon of Monmouth, 1967–76; Vicar of Caerleon, 1975–76. *Address:* Rivendell, 209 Christchurch Road, Newport, Gwent NP9 7QL. *T:* (01633) 255278.

JENKINS, Prof. George Charles, MB, BS, PhD; FRCPE, FRCPath; Consultant Haematologist, The Royal London (formerly London) Hospital, 1965–92, now Hon. Consulting; Hon. Consultant, St Peter's Hospitals, 1972–86; Professor of Haematology in the University of London, 1974–92, now Emeritus; Consultant to the Royal Navy; *b* 2 Aug. 1927; *s* of late John R. Jenkins and Mabel Rebecca (*née* Smith); *m* 1956, Elizabeth, *d* of late Cecil J. Welch, London; one *s* two *d*. *Educ:* Wyggeston, Leicester; St Bartholomew's Hosp. Med. Coll. MB, BS, PhD; MRCS 1951; LRCP 1951; FRCPath 1975 (MRCPath 1964); FRCPE; FRSocMed. House Phys. and Ho. Surg., St Bart's Hosp., 1951–52. Sqdn Ldr, RAF Med. Br., 1952–54. Registrar in Pathology, St Bart's Hosp., 1954–57; MRC Research Fellow, Royal Postgraduate Med. Sch., 1957–60; Sen. Registrar, Haematology, London Hosp., 1960–63; Cons. Haematologist, N Middlesex Hosp., 1963–65. Examiner: Univ. of London, 1971–95; Univ. of Cambridge, 1984–95; Sen. Examiner, RCPath, 1971–92, Mem. Council, 1979–84, Vice-Pres., 1981–84. Member, subcttee on biologicals, 1976–86, cttee on dental and surgical materials, 1988–92, Cttee on Safety of Medicines. Pres., British Acad. of Forensic Scis, 1990–91 (Mem., 1977–; Chm. Exec. Council, 1985–89); Member: British Soc. for Haematology, 1962– (formerly Hon. Sec.; Pres., 1988–89); Internat. Soc. of Haematology, 1975–95; Assoc. of Clinical Pathologists, 1958–92. Gov. and Mem. Council, Home Farm Trust, 1993–. *Publications:* (jtly) Advanced Haematology, 1974; (jtly) Infection and Haematology, 1994; papers and contribs to med. and sci. books and jls. *Recreations:* theatre, music, talking to people.

JENKINS, Prof. Geraint Huw, PhD, DLitt; Director, University of Wales Centre for Advanced Welsh and Celtic Studies, since 1993; *b* 24 Jan. 1946; *s* of David Hugh Jenkins and Lilian Jenkins (*née* Phillips); *m* 1972, Ann Ffrancon; three *d*. *Educ:* Ardwyn Grammar Sch., Aberystwyth; UCW, Swansea (BA 1st Cl. Hons 1967); UCW, Aberystwyth (PhD 1974); Univ. of Wales (DLitt 1994). University of Wales, Aberystwyth: Lectr in Welsh Hist., 1968–81; Sen. Lectr, 1981–88; Reader, 1988–90; Prof. of Welsh Hist., 1990–93; Head of Welsh History, 1991–93. Member: Univ. of Wales Bd of Celtic Studies, 1985– (Chm., 1993–); Council and Court, Univ. of Wales, Aberystwyth, 1991–; Cardiganshire Antiquarian Soc. (Chm., 1998–). Editor: Ceredigion, 1985–95; Cof Cenedl, 1986–. *Publications:* Cewri'r Bêl-droed yng Nghymru, 1977; Literature, Religion and Society in Wales 1660–1730, 1978; Thomas Jones yr Almanaciwr, 1980; Hanes Cymru yn Cyfnod Modern Cynnar, 1983, rev. edn 1988 (Welsh Arts Council Prize, 1989); The Foundations of Modern Wales, 1987, rev. edn 1993; (ed jtly) Politics and Society in Wales 1840–1922, 1988; Llunio Cymru Fodern, 1989; The Making of Modern Wales, 1989; Cymru Ddoe a Heddiw, 1990; Wales Yesterday and Today, 1990; Cadw Tŷ mewn Cwmwl Tystion, 1990 (Welsh Arts Council Prize, 1991); Protestant Dissenters in Wales 1639–1689, 1992; The Illustrated History of the University of Wales, 1993; (ed jtly) Merêd: Casgliad o'i Ysgrifau, 1995; (ed) Y Gymraeg yn ei Disgleirdeb, 1997; (ed) The Welsh Language before the Industrial Revolution, 1997; (ed jtly) Cardiganshire in Modern Times, 1998; (ed) Iaith Carreg fy Aelwyd, 1998; (ed) Language and Community in the Nineteenth Century, 1998; (ed) Gwnewch Bopeth yn Gymraeg, 1999; Doc Tom: Thomas Richards, 1999; (ed) Welsh and its Social Domains 1801–1911, 2000; (ed jtly) Eu Hiaith a Gadwant?, 2000; (ed jtly) Let's Do Our Best for the Ancient Tongue, 2000. *Recreations:* music, sport, gardening. *Address:* University of Wales Centre for Advanced Welsh and Celtic Studies, National Library of Wales, Aberystwyth SY23 3HH. *T:* (01970) 626717.

JENKINS, Gilbert Kenneth; Keeper, Department of Coins and Medals, British Museum, 1965–78; *b* 2 July 1918; *s* of late Kenneth Gordon Jenkins and of Julia Louisa Jenkins (*née* Colbourne); *m* 1939, Cynthia Mary, *d* of late Dr Hugh Scott, FRS; one *s* two *d*. *Educ:* All Saints Sch., Bloxham; Corpus Christi Coll., Oxford. Open Classical Scholar (Corpus Christi Coll.), 1936; First Class Honour Mods, 1938. War Service in Royal Artillery, 1940–46 (SE Asia, 1944–46). BA, 1946. Asst Keeper, British Museum, 1947; Dep. Keeper, 1956. An Editor of Numismatic Chronicle, 1964. Mem., German Archaeological Inst., 1967; Corresp. Mem., Amer. Numismatic Soc., 1958; Hon. Mem., Swiss Numismatic Soc., 1979; Hon. FRNS, 1980. Akbar Medal, Numismatic Soc. of India, 1966; Royal Numismatic Soc. Medal, 1975; Archer Huntington Medal, Amer. Numismatic Soc., 1976. *Publications:* Carthaginian Gold and Electrum Coins (with R. B. Lewis), 1963; Coins of Greek Sicily, 1966; Sylloge Nummorum Graecorum (Danish Nat. Museum), part 42, N Africa (ed), 1969, part 43, Spain-Gaul (ed), 1979; The Coinage of Gela, 1970; Ancient Greek Coins, 1972; (with U. Westermark) The Coinage of Kamarina, 1980; (jtly) A catalogue of the Calouste Gulbenkian Collection of Greek Coins, part II, 1989; articles in numismatic periodicals. *Recreations:* music, cycling. *Address:* Cecil Court, 2–4 Priory Road, Kew, Richmond, Surrey TW9 3DG.

JENKINS, Hon. Dr Henry Alfred, AM 1991; retired; *b* 24 Sept. 1925; *s* of Henry Alfred Jenkins and Eileen Clare Jenkins (*née* McCormack); *m* 1951, Hazel Eileen Winter; three *s* one *d*. *Educ:* Ormond, Eltham and Heidelberg State Schools; Ivanhoe Grammar Sch.; Univ. of Melbourne (MSc, MB BS); Deakin Univ. (BA). Tutor, Univ. of Melbourne, 1946–52; RMO Alfred Hosp., 1953; Medical Practitioner, 1953–61; MLA (Lab) Reservoir Parliament of Victoria, 1961–69; MP (Lab) Scullin, Federal Parliament of Australia, 1969–85; Chm. of Committees and Dep. Speaker, House of Representatives, 1975–76, Speaker, 1983–85; Aust. Ambassador to Spain, 1986–88. *Recreations:* reading, hobby farming, community service. *Address:* 61 Mill Park Drive, Mill Park, Vic 3082, Australia. *Club:* Royal Automobile of Victoria.

JENKINS, Hugh Royston, CBE 1996; FRICS, FPMI; Chairman and Chief Executive, Prudential Portfolio Managers, and Director, Prudential Corporation, 1989–95; Chairman: Falcon Property Trust, since 1995; Development Securities plc, since 1999; *b* 9 Nov. 1933; *m* 1988, Mrs Beryl Kirk. *Educ:* Llanelli Grammar Sch.; National Service, Royal Artillery, 1954–56. Valuer, London County Council, 1956–62; Assistant Controller, 1962–68, Managing Director, 1968–72, Coal Industry (Nominees) Ltd; Dir Gen. of Investments, NCB, 1972–85. Vice Chm., National Assoc. of Pension Funds, 1979–80; Chief Exec. Officer, Heron Financial Corp., 1985–86; Gp Investment Dir, Allied Dunbar Assce, 1986–89; Dep. Chm. and Chief Exec., Allied Dunbar Unit Trusts, 1986–89; Chm., Dunbar Bank, 1988–89; Chm. and Chief Exec., Allied Dunbar Asset Management, 1987–89. Dep. Chm., 1996–97, Chm., 1997–98, Thorn plc; Director: Unilever Pensions Ltd, 1985–89; IBM Pensions Trust PLC, 1985–89; Heron International, 1985–89; EMI, 1995–2001; Rank Gp plc, 1995–2001; Johnson Matthey, 1996–. Chm., Property Adv. Gp, DoE, 1990–96; Member: The City Capital Markets Cttee, 1982; Private Finance Panel, 1994–95; Lay Mem. of the Stock Exchange, 1984–85. *Recreation:* golf. *Address:* c/o S. G. Hambros Trust Company Ltd, 41 Tower Hill, EC3N 4HA. *Club:* Garrick.

JENKINS, Surg. Rear Adm. Ian Lawrence, CVO 2000; QHS 1994; Medical Director General (Naval), Ministry of Defence, since 1999; *b* 12 Sept. 1944; *s* of Gordon Eaton Jenkins, MBE and Edith Jenkins (*née* Rouse); *m* 1968, Elizabeth Philippa Anne Lane; one *s* one *d*. *Educ:* Howardian Grammar Sch.; Welsh Nat. Sch. of Medicine (MB BCh 1968). *Club:* FRCS 1973. Joined RN, 1975; HMS Ark Royal, 1975; RN Hosp. Haslar, 1976, 1979; Newcastle Gen. Hosp., 1977–79; OC 1 RN Surg. Support Team (3rd Cdo Bde), 1976–79; RN Hosp. Gibraltar, 1979–82; Consultant Urological Surg., 1982–90, MO i/c, 1990–96, RN Hosp. Haslar; Prof. of Naval Surgery, RN and RCS, 1988–90; Defence Postgrad. Med. Dean and Comdt, Royal Defence Med. Coll., 1996–99. CStJ 2000. *Publications:* contribs to med. jls on urological subjects. *Recreations:* swimming, game fishing, music, painting in watercolour, travel. *Address:* Victory Building, HM Naval Base, Portsmouth PO1 3LS. *T:* (023) 9272 7800. *Club:* Naval.

JENKINS, Dr Ivor, CBE 1970; FREng; freelance Consultant, since 1979; Group Director of Research, Delta Metal Co. Ltd, 1973–78; Managing Director, 1973–77, Deputy Chairman, 1977–78, Delta Materials Research Ltd; *b* 25 July 1913; *m* 1941, Caroline Wijnanda James; two *s*. *Educ:* Gowerton Grammar Sch.; Univ. of Wales, Swansea (BSc, MSc, DSc; Hon. Fellow, UC Swansea, 1986). Bursar, GEC Research Labs, Wembley, 1934; Mem. Scientific Staff, GEC, 1935; Dep. Chief Metallurgist, Whitehead Iron & Steel Co., Newport, Mon, 1944; Head of Metallurgy Dept, 1946, Chief Metallurgist, 1952, GEC, Wembley; Dir of Research, Manganese Bronze Holdings Ltd, and Dir, Manganese Bronze Ltd, 1961–69; Dir of Research, Delta Metal Co., and Dir, Delta Metal (BW) Ltd, 1969–73. Vis. Prof., Univ. of Surrey, 1978–. FIM 1948 (Pres. 1965–66); Fellow, Amer. Soc. of Metals, 1974; Pres., Inst. of Metals, 1968–69; Mem., Iron and Steel Inst., 1937– (Williams Prize, 1946); FREng (FEng 1979). Platinum medallist, Metals Soc., 1978. *Publications:* Controlled Atmospheres for the Heat Treatment of Metals, 1946; (ed jtly) Selected Case Studies in Powder Metallurgy, 1991; (ed jtly) Powder Metallurgy: an overview, 1991; contribs to learned jls at home and abroad on metallurgical and related subjects. *Recreations:* music, gardening, swimming. *Address:* 31 Trotyn Croft, Aldwick Felds, Aldwick, Bognor Regis, Sussex PO21 3TX. *T:* (01243) 828749.

JENKINS, Sir (James) Christopher, KCB 1999 (CB 1987); First Parliamentary Counsel, 1994–99; *b* 20 May 1939; *s* of Percival Si Phillips Jenkins and Dela (*née* Griffiths); *m* 1962, Margaret Elaine Edwards, *yr d* of Rt Hon. L. John Edwards and Dorothy (*née* Watson); two *s* one *d*. *Educ:* Lewes County Grammar Sch.; Magdalen Coll., Oxford. Solicitor, 1965. Joined Office of Parly Counsel, 1967; at Law Commn, 1970–72 and 1983–86; Parly Counsel, 1978–91; Second Parly Counsel, 1991–94. Hon. QC 1994. *Address:* c/o Parliamentary Counsel Office, 36 Whitehall, SW1A 2AY.

JENKINS, Dame Jennifer; *see* Jenkins, Dame M. J.

JENKINS, John, LVO 1989; HM Diplomatic Service; Ambassador to Burma (Union of Myanmar), since 1999; *b* 26 Jan. 1955; *s* of John Malsbury Jenkins and Mabel Lilleen Norah Jenkins (*née* Gardiner); *m* 1982, Nancy Caroline Pomfret. *Educ:* St Philip's Grammar Sch., Birmingham; Becket Sch., Nottingham; Jesus Coll., Cambridge (BA 1977; PhD 1980). Joined FCO, 1980; Second, later First, Sec., Abu Dhabi, 1983–86; First Sec., FCO, 1986–89; Head of Chancery, Kuala Lumpur, 1989–92; First Sec., FCO, 1992–95; Counsellor and Dep. Head of Mission, Kuwait, 1995–98. *Recreations:* Nottingham Forest FC, walking, cycling, travel, opera, theatre, reading. *Address:* c/o Foreign and Commonwealth Office, King Charles Street, SW1A 2AH. *T:* (020) 7270 1500.

JENKINS, John David; QC 1990; a Recorder, since 1990; *b* 7 Dec. 1947; *s* of late Vivian Evan Jenkins, MBE and of Megan Myfanwy Evans; *m* 1972, Susan Elizabeth Wilkinson; two *s*. *Educ:* Ashville Coll., Harrogate; King's Coll. London (LLB Hons). Called to the Bar, Gray's Inn, 1970; in practice at the Bar, Wales and Chester Circuit, 1970–. *Recreations:* football, cricket, psephology. *Address:* (office) 30 Park Place, Cardiff CF1 3BA. *T:* (029) 2039 8421. *Club:* Pentyrch Cricket.

JENKINS, (John) Emyr; Chief Executive, Arts Council of Wales, 1994–98; *b* 3 May 1938; *s* of Llewellyn Jenkins and Mary Olwen Jenkins; *m* 1964, Myra Bonner Samuel; two *d*. *Educ:* Machynlleth County Sch.; UCW, Aberystwyth (BSc Physics). BBC Studio Manager, 1961–63; BBC Announcer and Newsreader, 1963–71; Anchorman, Heddiw (Daily TV Mag.), 1968–69; BBC Wales Programme Organiser, 1971–77; First Dir, Royal Nat. Eisteddfod of Wales, 1978–93; Dir, Welsh Arts Council, 1993–94. Mem., IBA Welsh Adv. Cttee, 1986–90. Foundn Chm., Mudiad Ysgolion Meithrin (Assoc. of Welsh Playgroups), 1971–73; Member: Welsh Lang. Educn Develt Cttee, 1987–88; Council, UCW Aberystwyth, 1982–86; Steering Cttee/Council, Voluntary Arts Network, 1988–94; Voluntary Arts Wales Cttee, 1999–2001; Mgt Cttee, Univ. of Wales Press, 1999–. Chm., Welsh Music Inf. Centre, 2000–. Gov., WCMD, 1998– (Dep. Chm., 2000–). FRSA 1992. Hon. FWCMD 1997. Hon. MA Wales, 1993. Hon. Mem., Gorsedd of Bards, 1982. Elder, Crwys Presbyterian Church of Wales, 1983. *Recreations:* music, theatre, walking, sport.

See also F. L. Hague.

JENKINS, John George, CBE 1971; farmer; *b* 26 Aug. 1919; *s* of George John Jenkins, OBE, FRCS and Alice Maud Jenkins, MBE; *m* 1948, Chloe Evelyn (*née* Kenward); one *s* three *d*. *Educ:* Winchester; Edinburgh University. Farmed in Scotland, 1939–62; farmed in England (Cambs and Lincs), 1957–. Pres., NFU of Scotland, 1960–61; Chm., Agricultural Marketing Development Exec. Cttee, 1967–73. Chm., United Oilseeds Ltd, 1984–87; Director: Childerley Estates Ltd, 1957–; Agricultural Mortgage Corporation Ltd, 1968–90. Compère, Anglia Television programme Farming Diary, 1963–80. *Publications:* contrib. Proc. Royal Soc., RSA Jl, etc. *Recreations:* bridge, music. *Address:* Childerley Hall, Dry Drayton, Cambridge CB3 8BB. *T:* (01954) 210271. *Club:* Farmers'.

JENKINS, John Owen, MBE 1978; FCSP; Chartered Physiotherapist; Senior Lecturer, St Mary's Hospital School of Physiotherapy, W2, 1975–88 (Lecturer, 1959); *b* 4 Nov. 1922; *s* of late J. O. Jenkins, JP, and M. E. Jenkins, Great House, Dilwyn, Hereford; *m* 1953, Catherine MacFarlane Baird, MCSP; three *d*. *Educ:* Worcester College for the Blind; NIB School of Physiotherapy, London. TMMG, TET, FCSP 1990. Chartered Society of Physiotherapy: Mem. Council, 1952–81; Chm., Finance and Gen. Purposes Cttee, 1955–79; Member: Education Cttee, 1953–71; Executive Cttee, 1955–79; Trustee, Members' Benevolent Fund, 1956–96. CSP Examiner, 1954–88; Pres., Orgn of Chartered Physiotherapists in Private Practice, 1980–86. Physiotherapy Representative: Min. of Health Working Party on Statutory Registration, 1954; Council for Professions Supplementary to Medicine, 1961–76; Chm., Physiotherapists' Board, 1962–76. Director, LAMPS, 1969–96, Chm., 1980–87, Pres., 1988–96; Trustee, Moira Pakenham-Walsh Foundn, 1978–96. Churchwarden, St James the Great, N20, 1974–81. *Publications:* contribs to Physiotherapy and Rehabilitation. *Recreation:* freemasonry (Pres., Southgate Masonic Centre, 1997). *Address:* The New House, 34A Ravensdale Avenue, N12 9HT. *T:* (020) 8445 6072.

JENKINS, John Robin, OBE 1999; writer; *b* Cambuslang, Lanarks, 11 Sept. 1912; *s* of late James Jenkins and Annie Robin; *m* 1937, Mary McIntyre Wyllie; one *s* two *d*. *Educ:* Hamilton Academy; Glasgow Univ. (MA Hons). *Publications:* (as Robin Jenkins) Happy for the Child, 1953; The Thistle and the Grail, 1954; The Cone-Gatherers, 1955; Guests of War, 1956; The Missionaries, 1957; The Changeling, 1958; Some Kind of Grace, 1960; Dust on the Paw, 1961; The Tiger of Gold, 1962; A Love of Innocence, 1963; The Sardana Dancers, 1964; A Very Scotch Affair, 1968; The Holy Tree, 1969; The Expatriates, 1971; A Toast to the Lord, 1972; A Far Cry from Bowmore, 1973; A Figure of Fun, 1974; A Would-be Saint, 1978; Fergus Lamont, 1979; The Awakening of George Darroch, 1985; Just Duffy, 1988; Poverty Castle, 1991; Willie Hogg, 1993; Leila, 1996; Lunderston Tales, 1996; Matthew and Sheila, 1998; Poor Angus, 2000; Childish Things, 2001. *Recreations:* travel, golf. *Address:* Fairhaven, Toward, by Dunoon, Argyll PA23 7UE. *T:* (01369) 870288.

JENKINS, Katharine Mary; Chairman, Kate Jenkins Associates; *b* 14 Feb. 1945; *d* of Daniel Thomas Jenkins, *qv* and Nell Jenkins; *m* 1967, Euan Sutherland, *qv* (marr. diss. 1995); one *s* one *d. Educ:* South Hampstead High Sch.; St Anne's Coll., Oxford (BA Hons); London School of Economics (MScEcon). Called to Bar, Inner Temple, 1971. Asst Principal, 1968, Principal, 1973, Dept of Employment; Central Policy Review Staff, 1976; Asst Sec., Dept of Employment, 1979; Dep. Head of Efficiency Unit, 1984; Hd, Prime Minister's Efficiency Unit, and Under Sec., Cabinet Office, 1986–89; Dir, Personnel, Royal Mail, 1989–91. Member: NHS Policy Bd, 1992–95; Audit Commn, 1993–99; Hansard Soc. Commn on Scrutiny Rôle of Parliament, 1999–2001. Dir, London and Manchester Gp, 1989–97. Special Trustee, St Thomas' Hosp., 1992–95. Mem., Barbican Centre Cttee, 2000–; Governor, 1990–, Mem. Council, 2000–, LSE; Governor, Alleyn's Sch., Dulwich, 1990–98. *Publications:* reports: Making Things Happen: the implementation of government scrutinies, 1985; Improving Management in Government: the next steps, 1988; Keeping Control: the management of public sector reform programmes, 1995. *Address:* 108 Andrewes House, Barbican, EC2Y 8AY.
See also S. D. Jenkins.

JENKINS, Dame (Mary) Jennifer, (Lady Jenkins of Hillhead), DBE 1985; Member of Council, National Trust, 1985–90 (Chairman, 1986–90); *b* 18 Jan. 1921; *d* of late Sir Parker Morris; *m* 1945, Baron Jenkins of Hillhead, *qv*; two *s* one *d. Educ:* St Mary's Sch., Calne; Girton Coll., Cambridge. Chm., Cambridge Univ. Labour Club. With Hoover Ltd, 1942–43; Min. of Labour, 1943–46; Political and Economic Planning (PEP), 1946–48; part-time extra-mural lectr, 1949–61; part-time teacher, Kingsway Day Coll., 1961–67. Chairman: Consumers' Assoc., 1965–76; Historic Buildings Council for England, 1975–84; Member: Exec. Bd, British Standards Instn, 1970–73; Design Council, 1971–74; Cttee of Management, Courtauld Inst., 1981–84; Ancient Monuments Bd, 1982–84; Historic Buildings and Monuments Commn, 1984–85 (Chm., Historic Buildings Adv. Cttee, 1984–85); Pres., Ancient Monuments Soc., 1985– (Sec., 1972–75). Chairman: N Kensington Amenity Trust, 1974–77; Royal Parks Review Gp, 1991–96; Architectural Heritage Fund, 1994–97; Adv. Panel, Heritage Lottery Fund, 1995–99. Trustee, Wallace Collection, 1977–83. Director: J. Sainsbury Ltd, 1981–86; Abbey National plc (formerly Abbey National Building Soc.), 1984–91. Liveryman, Goldsmiths' Co., 1980. Freeman, City of London, 1982. JP London Juvenile Courts, 1964–74. Hon. FRICS 1981; Hon. FRIBA 1982; Hon. MRTPI 1988; Hon. FLI 1995. Hon. LLD: London, 1988; Bristol, 1990; DUniv: York, 1990; Strathclyde, 1993; Hon. DCL Newcastle, 1992; Hon. DArch Oxford Brookes, 1993; Hon. DLitt Greenwich, 1998. *Publication:* (with Patrick James) From Acorn to Oak Tree, 1994. *Address:* St Amand's House, East Hendred, Oxon OX12 8LA.

JENKINS, Sir Michael (Nicholas Howard), Kt 1997; OBE 1991; Chairman: London Clearing House Ltd, since 1996 (Director, since 1991); E-Crossnet Ltd, since 1999; *b* 13 Oct. 1932; *s* of C. N. and M. E. S. Jenkins; *m* 1957, Jacqueline Frances Jones; three *s. Educ:* Tonbridge School; Merton College, Oxford (MA Jurisp.). Shell-Mex & BP, 1956–61; IBM UK, 1961–67; Partner, Robson, Morrow, Management Consultants, 1967–71; Technical Dir, Stock Exchange, 1971–77; Man. Dir, European Options Exchange, Amsterdam, 1977–79; Chief Executive, LIFFE, 1981–92; Chairman: London Commodity Exchange, 1992–96; Futures and Options Assoc., 1993–99. Director: Tradepoint Financial Networks plc, 1995–99; British Invisibles, 1998–2001; EasyScreen plc, 1999–. Trustee, British Brain and Spine Foundn, 1993–. Gov., Sevenoaks Sch., 1993–. *Recreations:* games, classical music and jazz, furniture making. *Address:* London Clearing House Ltd, Aldgate House, 33 Aldgate High Street, EC3N 1EA. *T:* (020) 7426 7000. *Club:* Wildernesse (Sevenoaks).

JENKINS, Sir Michael (Romilly Heald), KCMG 1990 (CMG 1984); Vice-Chairman, Dresdner Kleinwort Wasserstein (formerly Kleinwort Benson Group PLC, then Dresdner Kleinwort Benson), since 1996; *b* 9 Jan. 1936; *s* of Prof. Romilly Jenkins and Celine Juliette Haeglar; *m* 1968, Maxine Louise Hodson; one *s* one *d. Educ:* privately; King's Coll., Cambridge (Exhibr, BA). Entered Foreign (subseq. Diplomatic) Service, 1959; served in Paris, Moscow and Bonn; Deputy Chef de Cabinet, 1973–75, Chef de Cabinet, 1975–76, to Rt Hon. George Thomson, EEC; Principal Advr to Mr Roy Jenkins, Pres. EEC, Jan–Aug. 1977; Head of European Integration Dept (External), FCO, 1977–79; Hd of Central Adv. Gp, EEC, 1979–81; Dep. Sec. Gen., Commn of the Eur. Communities, 1981–83; Asst Under Sec. of State (Europe), FCO, 1983–85; Minister, Washington, 1985–87; Ambassador to the Netherlands, 1988–93; Exec. Dir, Kleinwort Benson Gp, 1993–96. Director: Aegon NV, 1995–; EO plc, 2000–; Advr, Sage International Ltd, 1998–. Member: European Exec. Cttee, Trilateral Commn, 1994–99; President's Adv. Council, Atlantic Council, 1994–. Chairman: Action Centre for Europe, 1995–; Dataroom, 2000–. *Publications:* Arakcheev, Grand Vizier of the Russian Empire, 1969; A House in Flanders, 1992; contrib. History Today. *Address:* c/o Dresdner Kleinwort Wasserstein, 20 Fenchurch Street, EC3P 3DB. *Clubs:* Brooks's, MCC (Treas., 1999–2000; Chm., Cttee, 2000–01; Trustee 2001–).

JENKINS, Neil Martin James; opera singer; tenor; music editor; *b* 9 April 1945; *s* of Harry James Jenkins and Mary Morrison Jenkins (*née* Terry); *m* 1st, 1969, Sandra Wilkes; one *s*; 2nd, 1982, Penny (*née* Underwood); one *s* and two step *s* one step *d. Educ:* Westminster Abbey Choir School; Dean Close School (music Scholar); King's College Cambridge (Choral Scholar; MA). Recital début, Kirkman Concert Series, Purcell Room, 1967; operatic début, Menotti's The Consul, Israel Festival, 1968; major rôles with English Music Theatre, Glyndebourne Fest. Opera, Kent Opera, New Sussex Opera, Scottish Opera, WNO; ENO; numerous recordings, film sound tracks and videos. Prof. of Singing, RCM, 1975–76; teacher, summer schools, incl. Canford and Wellington, 1989–. Pres., Grange Choral Soc., Hants; Vice-President: Hunts Philharmonic; Brighton Competitive Music Festival. Geoffrey Tankard Lieder Prize, 1967; NFMS Award, 1972. *Publications: choral music* (edited and arranged): The Carol Singer's Handbook, 1993; O Praise God, 1994; O Holy Night, 1994; Sing Solo Sacred, 1997; Bach, St Matthew Passion, 1997; Bach, St John Passion, 1998; Bach, Christmas Oratorio, 1999; Bach, Magnificat, 2000. *Recreations:* visiting ancient monuments, 18th Century music research. *Address:* c/o Music International, 13 Ardilaun Road, N5 2QR. *T:* (020) 7359 5813.

JENKINS, Peter Redmond; HM Diplomatic Service; Permanent Representative to the United Nations and other International Organizations, Vienna (with personal rank of Ambassador), since 2001; *b* 2 March 1950; *s* of Denys Arthur Reali Jenkins and Monique Marie-Louise Jenkins; *m* 1990, Angelina Chee-Hung Yang; one *s* one *d. Educ:* Downside Sch.; Corpus Christi Coll., Cambridge (BA Hons, MA); Harvard Univ. (Harkness Fellow). Joined HM Diplomatic Service, 1973: FCO, 1973–75; UK Mission to Internat. Orgns, Vienna, 1975–78; FCO, 1978–82; Private Sec. to HM Ambassador, Washington, 1982–84; FCO, 1984–87; Paris, 1987–91; Minister-Counsellor and Consul Gen., Brasilia, 1992–95; Dep. Perm. Rep., 1996–2001, and Minister, 1998–2001, UK Mission to UN, Geneva. *Address:* c/o Foreign and Commonwealth Office, King Charles Street, SW1A 2AH. *Club:* Brooks's.

JENKINS, Peter White; management consultant; *b* 12 Oct. 1937; *s* of John White Jenkins, OBE, and Dorothy Jenkins; *m* 1961, Joyce Christine Muter; one *s* one *d. Educ:* Queen Mary's Grammar Sch., Walsall; King Edward VI Grammar Sch., Nuneaton. CIPFA. Local govt service in Finance Depts at Coventry, Preston, Chester, Wolverhampton; Dep. Treasurer, Birkenhead, 1969–73; County Treasurer, Merseyside CC, 1973–84; Dir. of Finance, Welsh Water Authority, 1984–87. Hon. Treas., Brecon Cathedral, 1994–98. *Recreations:* walking, gardening, local history, reading. *Address:* 9 Camden Crescent, Brecon, Powys LD3 7BY.

JENKINS, Richard Peter Vellacott; His Honour Judge Richard Jenkins; a Circuit Judge, since 1989; *b* 10 May 1943; *s* of late Gwynne Jenkins and of Irene Lilian Jenkins; *m* 1975, Agnes Anna Margaret Mullan; one *s* one *d. Educ:* Edge Grove School, Aldenham; Radley College; Trinity Hall, Cambridge (MA). Called to the Bar, Inner Temple, 1966; Midland Circuit, 1968–72; Midland and Oxford Circuit, 1972–89 (Remembrancer and Asst Treasurer, 1984–89); a Recorder, 1988–89; Magistrates' Liaison Judge for Lincs and S Humberside, 1995–; Designated Family Judge, Lincoln, 1998–. Mem., Humberside Probation Cttee Policy Sub-Cttee, 1996–2000. Chairman: Lincolnshire Family Mediation Service, 1997–; Lincs Area Criminal Justice Strategy Cttee, 2000–. Mem., Sleaford Music Club. Liveryman, Co. of Barbers, 1967–. *Address:* Hall Barn, Far End, Boothby Graffoe, Lincoln LN5 0LG. *Club:* MCC.

JENKINS, Richard Thomas, OBE 1986; HM Diplomatic Service, retired; Ambassador to Georgia, 1998–2001; *b* 19 Aug. 1943; *s* of Vincent Arthur Wood Jenkins and Edna Jenkins (*née* Frith); *m* 1976, Maurizia Marantonio; two *s. Educ:* Plaistow Co. GS; Nottingham Univ. (BA Hons 1964); Warsaw Univ.; Glasgow Univ. Entered HM Diplomatic Service, 1967; FCO, 1967–70; Warsaw, 1970; FCO, 1970–76; Second, subseq. First Sec., E Berlin, 1976–79; Res. Dept, FCO, 1979–83; First Sec. (Commercial), Warsaw, 1983–85; Head, Central European Sect., 1985–89, Dep. Head, Jt Assistance Unit (Know How Fund), 1989–94, FCO Res. Dept; Dep. Head of Mission and Consul-Gen., Kiev, 1994–98. Mem., Fabian Soc. Freeman, City of London, 1998. Hon. Fellow, Univ. of E London, 1995.

JENKINS, Robin; *see* Jenkins, J. R.

JENKINS, Simon David; columnist, The Times, since 1992 (Editor, 1990–92); *b* 10 June 1943; *s* of Dr Daniel Thomas Jenkins, *qv* and Nell Jenkins; *m* 1978, Gayle Hunnicutt; one *s* and one step *s. Educ:* Mill Hill Sch.; St John's Coll., Oxford (BA Hons). Country Life magazine, 1965; Research Asst, Univ. of London Inst. of Educn, 1966; News Editor, Times Educational Supplement, 1966–68; Evening Standard, 1968–74; Insight Editor, Sunday Times, 1974–75; Dep. Editor, Evening Standard, 1976, Editor, 1976–78; Political Editor, The Economist, 1979–86; The Sunday Times: columnist, 1986–90; editor, Books Section, 1988–89. Member: British Railways Bd, 1979–90 (Chm., BR Environment Panel, 1984–90); LRT Bd, 1984–86; South Bank Bd, 1985–90; Calcutt Cttee on Privacy, 1989–90; Grade Cttee on Fear of Crime, 1989; Runciman Cttee on Misuse of Drugs Act 1971, 1998–2000. Chm., Commn for Local Democracy, 1994–95. Director: Municipal Journal Ltd, 1980–90; Faber & Faber, 1980–90. Mem. Council, Bow Group, and Editor of Crossbow, 1968–70; Member: Cttee Save Britain's Heritage, 1976–85; Historic Buildings and Monuments Commn, 1985–90 (Dep. Chm., 1988–90); Millennium Commn, 1994–2000; Mem. Council: Inst. of Contemporary Arts, 1976–85; Old Vic Co., 1979–81; Chm., Buildings Books Trust, 1994–; Dep. Chm., Thirties Soc., 1979–85; Founder and Dir, Railway Heritage Trust, 1985–90; Trustee, World Monuments Fund, 1995–98. Gov., Mus. of London, 1985–87. Hon. RIBA, 1997. Hon. Dr UCE, 1998; Hon. DLitt: London, 2000; City, 2001. What The Papers Say Journalist of the Year, 1988; Columnist of the Year, British Press Awards, 1993; Edgar Wallace Trophy for Outstanding Reporting, London Press Club, 1997; David Watt Meml Prize, Rio Tinto, 1998. *Publications:* A City at Risk, 1971; Landlords to London, 1974; (ed) Insight on Portugal, 1975; Newspapers: the power and the money, 1979; The Companion Guide to Outer London, 1981; (with Max Hastings) The Battle for the Falklands, 1983; Images of Hampstead, 1983; (with Anne Sloman) With Respect Ambassador, 1985; The Market for Glory, 1986; The Times Guide to English Style and Usage, 1992; The Selling of Mary Davies, 1993; Against the Grain, 1994; Accountable to None: the Tory nationalization of Britain, 1995; England's Thousand Best Churches, 1999. *Recreation:* old buildings. *Address:* c/o The Times, Pennington Street, E1 9XN. *Club:* Garrick.
See also K. M. Jenkins.

JENKINS, Stanley Kenneth; HM Diplomatic Service, retired; *b* 25 Nov. 1920; *s* of Benjamin and Ethel Jane Jenkins; *m* 1957, Barbara Mary Marshall Webb; four *d. Educ:* Brecon; Cardiff Tech. Coll. President, Nat. Union of Students, 1949–51. LIOB 1950. Served War, Royal Artillery and Royal Engineers, 1942–46, retiring as Major. Joined Foreign (later Diplomatic) Service, 1951; Singapore, 1953; Kuala Lumpur, 1955; FO, 1957; Singapore, 1959; Rangoon, 1961; FO, 1964; Nicosia, 1967; FO, 1970–78, Counsellor. *Publication:* So Much to Do, So Little Time (autobiog.), 2000. *Recreations:* gardening, tennis. *Address:* Willow Cottage, 1 Beehive Lane, Ferring, Worthing, W Sussex BN12 5NL. *T:* (01903) 247356. *Club:* Royal Commonwealth Society.

JENKINS, (Thomas) Alun; QC 1996; a Recorder, since 2000; *b* 19 Aug. 1948; *s* of Seward Thomas Jenkins and Iris, *d* of Alderman W. G. H. Bull, miner and sometime Chm. of Monmouthshire CC; *m* 1971, Glenys Maureen Constant; one *s* two *d. Educ:* Ebbw Vale Tech. Sch.; Bristol Univ. (LLB Hons 1971). Called to the Bar, Lincoln's Inn, 1972; in private practice, Bristol, 1972–, specialising in serious crime, esp. large scale drug importations, fraud, organised crime, and conspiracies; Head of Chambers, Queen Square, Bristol, 1995–. Asst Recorder, 1992–2000. *Recreations:* horse riding, horse racing, Rugby, motor cars, point to point, reading. *Address:* Queen Square Chambers, 56 Queen Square, Bristol BS1 4PR. *T:* (0117) 921 1966.

JENKINS, Thomas Harris, (Tom), CBE 1981; General Secretary, Transport Salaried Staffs' Association, 1977–82; *b* 29 Aug. 1920; *s* of David Samuel Jenkins and Miriam Hughes (*née* Harris); *m* 1946, Joyce Smith; two *d. Educ:* Port Talbot Central Boys' Sch.; Port Talbot County Sch.; Shrewsbury Technical Coll. (evenings); Pitmans Coll., London (evenings). MCIT 1980. Served War, RAMC, 1941–46 (Certif. for Good Service, Army, Western Comd, 1946). Railway clerk, 1937–41; railway/docks clerk, 1946–49. Full-time service with Railway Clerks' Assoc., subseq. re-named Transport Salaried Staffs' Assoc., 1949–82: Southern Reg. Divl Sec., 1959; Western Reg. Divl Sec., 1963; LMR Divl Sec., 1966; Sen. Asst Sec., 1968; Asst Gen. Sec., 1970, also Dep. to Gen. Sec., 1973. Member:

Cttee of Transport Workers in European Community, 1976–82; Transport Industry, Nationalised Industries, and Hotel and Catering Industry Cttees of TUC, 1977–82; Management and Industl Relns Cttee, SSRC, 1979–81; Air Transport and Travel Industry Trng Bd, 1976–82; Hotel and Catering Industry Trng Bd, 1978–82; Employment Appeal Tribunal, 1982–91; British Railways Midland and NW Reg. Bd, 1982–86; Police Complaints Bd, 1983–85; Central Arbitration Cttee, 1983–90; ACAS Arbitration Bd, 1983–90. Mem. Labour Party, 1946–; Mem., Lab. Party Transport Sub-Cttee, 1970–82. *Recreations:* watching cricket, athletics and Rugby football. *Address:* 23 The Chase, Edgware, Mddx HA8 5DW. *T:* (020) 8952 5314. *Clubs:* MCC, Middlesex County Cricket.

JENKINSON, Dr David Stewart, FRS 1991; Lawes Trust Fellow, Rothamsted Experimental Station, since 1988; Visiting Professor, University of Reading, since 1992; *b* 25 Feb. 1928; *s* of Hugh McLoughlin Jenkinson and Isabel Frances (*née* Glass); *m* 1958, Moira O'Brien; three *s* one *d. Educ:* Armagh Royal Sch.; Trinity Coll., Dublin (BA 1950; BSc 1950; PhD 1954). MRSC 1955. Asst Lectr, Univ. of Reading, 1955–57; on scientific staff, Rothamsted Exptl Station, 1957–88. Hannaford Res. Fellow, Univ. of Adelaide, 1976–77; Vis. Scientist, CSIRO, 1977. Lectures: Hannaford, Univ. of Adelaide, 1977; Distinguished Scholars, QUB, 1989; Univ. of Kent, 1992; Massey Ferguson Nat. Agricl Award, 1993. Hon. Mem., Soil Science Soc. of Amer., 1995. *Publications:* Nitrogen Efficiency in Agricultural Soils, 1988; numerous papers in jls of soil science, soil biochemistry and agronomy. *Recreations:* Irish history and literature, low input gardening. *Address:* 15 Topstreet Way, Harpenden, Herts AL5 5TU. *T:* (01582) 715744.

JENKINSON, Jeffrey Charles, MVO 1977; Chief Executive, Harwich Haven Authority, 1992–97; *b* 22 Aug. 1939; *s* of late John Jenkinson and Olive May Jenkinson; *m* 1962, Janet Ann (*née* Jarrett); one *s* two *d. Educ:* Royal Liberty Sch., Romford; City of London Coll. MCIT, MIMgt. National Service, RN, 1957–59. Port of London Authority: Port operations and gen. management, 1959–71; British Transport Staff Coll., 1972; PLA Sec., 1972–81; Dir of Admin, 1982–86; Bd Mem., 1982–92; Chief Exec., Property, 1987–92; Dir, Placon Ltd and other PLA gp subsid. cos, 1978–92. Dir, E London Small Business Centre Ltd, 1977–92; Mem. Bd, Globe Centre Ltd, 1992–96. Chm., Essex Area Envmt Gp, Envmt Agency, 1996–. Member: Bd, and Council, London Chamber of Commerce and Industry, 1989–92; Council, British Ports Assoc., 1993–96; Chm., Thames Riparian Housing Assoc., 1986–92; Member: Newham CHC, 1974–80; Committee of Management: Seamen's Gp of Hosps, 1972–74; Seamen's Hosp. Soc., 1974– (Hon. Treas., 1998–). Vice-Pres., Maritime Volunteer Service, 1997–. Freeman, City of London, 1975; Mem. Ct, Co. of Watermen and Lightermen of River Thames, 1990– (Master, 1998). *Recreations:* sailing, walking, music. *Address:* 18 Woodview Close, Colchester, Essex CO4 4UW. *T:* (01206) 845233.

JENKINSON, Sir John (Banks), 14th Bt *cr* 1661; *b* 16 Feb. 1945; *o s* of Sir Anthony Banks Jenkinson, 13th Bt and Frances (*d* 1996), *d* of Harry Stremmel; *S* father, 1989; *m* 1979, Josephine Mary Marshall-Andrew; one *s* one *d. Educ:* Eton; Univ. of Miami. *Heir: s* George Samuel Anthony Banks Jenkinson, *b* 8 Nov. 1980. *Address:* Hawkesbury Home Farm, Hawkesbury, Badminton, S Glos GL9 1AY.

JENKINSON, Kenneth Leslie; Headmaster, Colchester Royal Grammar School, since 2000 (Deputy Headmaster, 1994–2000); *b* 4 Oct. 1955; *s* of Reginald and Margaret Jenkinson; *m* 1979, Jacqueline Anne Loose; two *d. Educ:* Danum Grammar Sch., Doncaster; Univ. of Leeds (BA, PGCE); Univ. of Sheffield (MA); NPQH. Teacher, Modern Languages, Hayfield Sch., Doncaster, 1979–88; Head, Modern Languages, Blundell's Sch., Tiverton, 1988–94. *Recreations:* family, humour, sport. *Address:* Colchester Royal Grammar School, Lexden Road, Colchester, Essex CO3 3ND. *T:* (01206) 577971.

JENKINSON, Nigel Harrison; Deputy Director, Monetary Analysis and Statistics, Bank of England, since 1999; *b* 18 June 1955; *s* of Alan and Jean Jenkinson; *m* 1977, Jeanne Mellalieu; two *s. Educ:* Birmingham Univ. (BSocSc 1st cl. Hons Mathematics, Econs and Statistics); London Sch. of Economics (MSc Econometrics and Mathematical Econs (Dist)). Bank of England: Economist, 1977–90; Mem., Economic Unit, Secretariat of Cttee of Govs, European Union Central Banks, 1990–93 (on secondment); Dep. Head, Reserves Mgt, 1993–94; Head, Structural Economic Analysis Div., 1994–98; Mem., REconS. *Recreations:* football, cricket, reading. *Address:* Bank of England, Threadneedle Street, EC2R 8AH. *T:* (020) 7601 3000. *Club:* Colchester United Supporters Association.

JENKINSON, Philip; Chief Executive, and Clerk to the Lieutenancy, Devon County Council, since 1995; *b* 2 June 1948; *s* of Harold Jenkinson and Edith Florence Jenkinson (*née* Phillipson); *m* 1970, Sandra Elizabeth Cornish; four *s. Educ:* Manchester Grammar Sch.; Univ. of Exeter (LLB 1st Cl. Hons); Liverpool Poly. Trainee solicitor, Gillingham BC, Kent, 1970–72; admitted solicitor, 1972; Asst Solicitor, Bath CC, 1972–74; Solicitor, Devon CC, 1974–95. Dir, Prosper (formerly Devon and Cornwall TEC), 1995–. FRSA. *Recreations:* soccer referee, music. *Address:* County Hall, Exeter, Devon EX2 4QD. *T:* (01392) 383201.

JENKS, Sir (Maurice Arthur) Brian, 3rd Bt *cr* 1932, of Cheape in the City of London; chartered accountant in sole practice; *b* 28 Oct. 1933; *er s* of Sir Richard Atherley Jenks, 2nd Bt and of Marjorie Suzanne Arlette Jenks, *d* of Sir Arthur du Cros, 1st Bt; *S* father, 1993; *m* 1962, Susan Lois Allen; one *d* and one adopted *s. Educ:* Charterhouse. FCA. Qualified chartered accountant, 1956; Partner, Mann Judd & Co., subseq. Touche Ross & Co., 1960–93. Mem. Ct of Assts, Haberdashers' Co., 1961– (Master 1988–89 and 1992–93). *Publication:* Small Businesses: how to survive and succeed, 1989. *Recreations:* wine, racing, gardening. *Heir: b* Richard John Peter Jenks [*b* 28 June 1936; *m* 1963, Juniper Li-Yung, *e d* of Tan Sri Y. C. Foo; one *s* two *d*]. *Address:* Warren House, Savernake, Marlborough, Wilts SN8 3BQ. *T:* (01672) 870442.

JENKYNS, Henry Leigh; Under-Secretary, Department of the Environment, 1969–75; *b* 20 Jan. 1917; *y s* of H. H. Jenkyns, Indian Civil Service; *m* 1947, Rosalind Mary Home; two *s* one *d. Educ:* Eton, Balliol Coll., Oxford. War Service in Royal Signals; Lt-Col, East Africa Command, 1944. Treasury, 1945–66; Private Sec. to Chancellor, 1951–53. Treasury Representative in Australia and New Zealand, 1953–56; UK Delegation to OECD, Paris, 1961–63; Asst Under-Sec. of State, DEA, 1966–69; Chm., SE Economic Planning Bd, 1968–71. Mem., Southwark Diocesan Adv. Cttee for Care of Churches, 1977–78. Mem., Exmoor Study Team, 1977. *Recreations:* music, garden, sailing, mending things. *Address:* 3 Tower Lane, Aldeburgh, Suffolk IP15 5LN. *T:* (01728) 452357.

See also Very Rev. K. B. Jones.

JENNER, Ann Maureen; Guest Ballet Teacher: Victorian College of the Arts, Melbourne; Australian Ballet; Queensland Ballet; Australian Ballet School, and many other schools in Sydney and Melbourne; also guest choreographer; *b* 8 March 1944; *d* of Kenneth George Jenner and Margaret Rosetta (*née* Wilson); *m* 1980, Dale Robert Baker; one *s. Educ:* Royal Ballet Junior and Senior Schools. Royal Ballet Co., 1961–78: Soloist 1964; Principal Dancer 1970. Australian Ballet, 1978–80. Associate Dir, 1987, Dir, 1988–94, Nat. Theater Ballet Sch., Melbourne. Roles include: Lise, Fille Mal Gardée, 1966; Swanhilda, Coppelia, 1968; Cinderella, 1969; Princess Aurora, Sleeping Beauty, 1972; Giselle, 1973; Gypsy, Deux Pigeons, 1974; White Girl, Deux Pigeons, 1976; Juliet, Romeo and Juliet, 1977; Countess Larisch, Mayerling, 1978; Flavia, Spartacus, 1979; Kitri, Don Quixote, 1979; Anna, Anna Karenina, 1980; Poll, Pineapple Poll, 1980; one-act roles include: Symphonic Variations, 1967; Firebird, 1972; Triad, 1973; Les Sylphides; Serenade; Les Patineurs; Elite Syncopations, Concert, Flower Festival Pas de Deux, etc. Guest Teacher, San Francisco Ballet Co. and San Francisco Ballet Sch., 1985; Asst Dir, Dance World 301, Melbourne, 1996–97.

JENNER, Prof. Peter George, PhD, DSc; FRPharmS; Professor of Pharmacology, since 1989, and Head of Division of Pharmacology and Therapeutics, Guy's, King's and St Thomas' School of Biomedical Sciences, since 1998, King's College London; *b* 6 July 1946; *s* of late George Edwin Jenner and Edith (*née* Hallett); *m* 1973, Katherine Mary Philomena Snell; one *s. Educ:* Chelsea Coll., London Univ. (BPharm Hons 1967; PhD 1970; DSc 1987). FRPharmS 1994. Post-grad. Fellow, Dept of Pharmacy, Chelsea Coll., London, 1970–72; Lectr in Biochem., 1972–78, Sen. Lectr, 1978–85, Dept of Neurol., Inst. of Psychiatry, Univ. of London, 1972–78; Reader in Neurochem. Pharmacol., Inst. of Psychiatry and KCH Med. Sch., 1985–89; Hon. Sen. Lectr, Inst. of Neurol., 1988–; Head, Dept of Pharmacology, KCL, 1989–98. Dir, Exptl Res. Labs, Parkinson's Disease Soc., 1988–; Co-Dir, Neurodegenerative Diseases Res. Centre, 1993–. Adjunct Prof. of Neurology, Univ. of Miami, USA, 1997–. Parkinson's Disease Society: Mem. Council, 1993– (Hon. Sec. to Council, 1996–); Mem., Med. Adv. Panel, 1993–. Mem., Molecular and Cellular Pharmacol. Gp Cttee, Biochem. Soc., 1993. Mem., Bd of Mgt, Inst. of Epileptology, KCL, 1994–. *Publications:* (with B. Testa) Drug Metabolism: chemical and biochemical aspects, 1976; (ed with B. Testa) Concepts in Drug Metabolism, Part A 1980, Part B 1981; (ed jtly) Approaches to the Use of Bromocriptine in Parkinson's Disease, 1985; (ed jtly) Neurological Disorders, 1987; (ed) Neurotoxins and their Pharmacological Implications, 1987; (ed jtly) Disorders of Movement, 1989; contrib. Lancet, Jl Neurochem., Annals Neurol., Biochem. Pharmacol., Brain Res., Psychopharmacol., Neuroscience. *Recreations:* gardening, driving. *Address:* Neurodegenerative Diseases Research Centre, Division of Pharmacology and Therapeutics, Hodgkin Building, Guy's, King's and St Thomas' School of Biomedical Sciences, King's College London, Guy's Campus, London Bridge, SE1 1UL. *T:* (020) 7848 6011. *Club:* Athenæum.

JENNER, Air Marshal Sir Timothy (Ivo), KCB 2000 (CB 1996); FRAeS; Commander, NATO Combined Air Operations Centre 9, 2000; *b* 31 Dec. 1945; *s* of Harold Ivo Jenner and Josephine Dorothy Jenner; *m* 1968, Susan Lesley Stokes; two *d. Educ:* Maidstone Grammar Sch.; RAF Coll., Cranwell. FRAeS 1997. Wessex Sqdn Pilot and Instructor, UK, ME and Germany, 1968–75; Puma Pilot and Instructor, 1976–78; MoD Desk Officer, Helicopter, 1979–80; Army Staff Coll., Camberley, 1981; OC 33 Sqdn, 1982–84; Military Assistant to: ACDS (Commitments), 1985; DCDS (Programmes & Personnel), 1986; OC, RAF Shawbury, 1987–88; RCDS 1989; Dep. Dir, Air Force Plans, 1990–91; Dir, Defence Progs, 1992–93; AO Plans, HQ Strike Command, 1993; Asst Chief of Defence Staff (Costs Review), 1993–95; ACAS, 1995–98; COS and Dep. C-in-C, Strike Comd, 1998–2000. Pres., RAF Gliding and Soaring Assoc. *Recreations:* gliding, old cars, photography, mountain walking. *Address:* c/o Lloyds TSB, PO Box 1190, 7 Pall Mall, SW1Y 5NA. *Club:* Royal Air Force.

JENNETT, Frederick Stuart, CBE 1985; consultant architect and town planner in own firm, since 1990; *b* 22 April 1924; *s* of Horace Frederick Jennett and Jenny Sophia Jennett; *m* 1948, Nada Eusebia Phillips; two *d. Educ:* Whitchurch Grammar School; Welsh School of Architecture, UWIST (Dip. in Architecture (dist.)). FRIBA, MRTPI, FRSA. T. Alwyn Lloyd & Gordon, Architects, Cardiff, 1949; Cwmbran Develt Corp., 1951; Louis de Soissons Peacock Hodges & Robinson, Welwyn Garden City, 1955; S. Colwyn Foukes & Partners, Colwyn Bay, 1956; Associate, 1962, Partner, 1964, Sir Percy Thomas & Son, Bristol; Chm. and Sen. Partner, Percy Thomas Partnership, 1971–89; Consultant to Studio BAAD, architects, Hebden Bridge, 1990–93; garden design with Nada Jennett, Weston Park, Shropshire, 1990–. Experience ranges over new town neighbourhood planning, public housing and private houses; ecclesiastical, university and hospital projects in the UK and overseas, and refurbishment of historic/listed buildings. *Publications:* papers on hospital planning. *Recreations:* water colour painting, calligraphy, hill walking, running. *Address:* Portland Lodge, Lower Almondsbury, Bristol BS32 4EJ. *T:* (01454) 615175. *Club:* Royal Over-Seas League.

JENNETT, Prof. (William) Bryan, CBE 1992; FRCS; Professor of Neurosurgery, University of Glasgow, 1968–91, now Emeritus (Dean of the Faculty of Medicine, 1981–86); *b* 1 March 1926; *s* of Robert William Jennett and Jessie Pate Loudon; *m* 1950, Sheila Mary Pope; three *s* one *d. Educ:* Univ. of Liverpool (MB ChB 1949, MD 1960). House Physician to Lord Cohen of Birkenhead, 1949; Ho. Surg. to Sir Hugh Cairns, 1950; Surgical Specialist, RAMC, 1951–53; Registrar in Neurosurgery, Oxford and Cardiff, 1954–56; Lectr in Neurosurgery, Univ. of Manchester, 1957–62; Rockefeller Travelling Fellow, Univ. of California, LA, 1958–59; Cons. Neurosurgeon, Glasgow, 1963–68. Member: MRC, 1979–83; GMC, 1984–91; Chief Scientists' Cttee, 1983–; Inst. of Med. Ethics, 1986–. Mem. Ct, Univ. of Glasgow, 1988–91. Rock Carling Fellow, London, 1983. Hon. DSc St Andrews, 1993. *Publications:* Epilepsy after Blunt Head Injury, 1962, 2nd edn 1975; Introduction to Neurosurgery, 1964, 5th edn 1994; (with G. Teasdale) Management of Head Injuries, 1981; High Technology Medicine: benefits and burdens, 1984, 2nd edn 1986; The Vegetative State: medical facts, ethical and legal dilemmas, 2002; many papers in Lancet, BMJ and elsewhere. *Recreations:* cruising under sail, writing. *Address:* 83 Hughenden Lane, Glasgow G12 9XN. *T:* (0141) 334 5148. *Club:* Royal Society of Medicine.

JENNINGS, Anthony Francis; QC 2001; *b* 11 May 1960; *s* of Robert Jennings and Margaret (Irene) Jennings (*née* Conlon); *m* 1993, Louise McKeon; one *s* one *d. Educ:* St Patrick's Coll., Belfast; Univ. of Warwick (LLB Hons); Inns of Court Sch. of Law. Called to the Bar, Gray's Inn, 1983. *Publications:* (contributing ed.) Archbold, Criminal Pleading: evidence and practice, annually 1995–; (ed) Justice Under Fire: the abuse of Civil Liberties in Northern Ireland, 1988; (contrib.) Human Rights Practice, 2001; (contrib.) Criminal Justice, Police Powers and Human Rights, 2001; contrib. to jls on crime and human rights. *Recreations:* Italy, Irish literature, Liverpool FC. *Address:* Matrix Chambers, Griffin Building, Gray's Inn, WC1R 5LN. *T:* (020) 7404 3447. *Club:* Liverpool Supporters.

JENNINGS, Audrey Mary; Metropolitan Stipendiary Magistrate, 1972–99; *b* 22 June 1928; *d* of Hugh and Olive Jennings, Ashbrook Range, Sunderland; *m* 1961, Roger Harry Kilbourne Frisby, *qv* (marr. diss. 1980); two *s* one *d. Educ:* Durham High Sch.; Durham Univ. (BA); Oxford Univ. (DPA). Children's Officer, City and County of Cambridge, 1952–56. Called to Bar, Middle Temple, 1956 (Harmsworth Schol.); practised at Criminal Bar, London, 1956–61 and 1967–72. Occasional opera critic, Musical Opinion. *Recreations:* theatre, music, gardening, writing short stories.

JENNINGS, Colin Brian; HM Diplomatic Service; Chief Executive, Wilton Park Executive Agency, Foreign and Commonwealth Office, since 1996; *b* 27 Nov. 1952; *s* of Brian Jennings and Jean (*née* Thomas); *m* 1978, Jane Barfield. *Educ:* Hereford Cathedral

Sch.; Univ. of Leicester (BA 1975; MA 1976). Joined MoD, 1976; Procurement Executive, 1976–78; Defence Secretariat, 1979, Principal, 1982–83; Second Sec., UK Delegn to NATO, 1980–81 (on secondment); joined HM Diplomatic Service, 1983; Policy Planning Staff, FCO, 1983–86; First Sec. (Economic), Lagos, 1986–89; Asst, Central and Southern Africa Dept, FCO, 1990–92; Dep. High Comr, Nicosia, 1992–96. *Recreations:* tennis, watching Rugby, walking fox terriers. *Address:* Wilton Park, Wiston House, Steyning, West Sussex BN44 3DZ.

JENNINGS, Rt Rev. David Willfred Michael; *see* Warrington, Bishop Suffragan of.

JENNINGS, Elizabeth (Joan), CBE 1992; author; *b* 18 July 1926; *d* of Dr H. C. Jennings, Oxon. *Educ:* Oxford High Sch.; St Anne's Coll., Oxford. Asst at Oxford City Library, 1950–58; Reader for Chatto & Windus Ltd, 1958–60. *Publications: poetry:* Poems (Arts Council Prize), 1953; A Way of Looking, 1955 (Somerset Maugham Award, 1956); A Sense of the World, 1958; (ed) The Batsford Book of Children's Verse, 1958; Song for a Birth or a Death, 1961; a translation of Michelangelo's sonnets, 1961; Recoveries, 1964; The Mind Has Mountains, 1966 (Richard Hillary Prize, 1966); The Secret Brother (for children), 1966; Collected Poems, 1967; The Animals' Arrival, 1969 (Arts Council Bursary, 1969); (ed) A Choice of Christina Rossetti's Verse, 1970; Lucidities, 1970; Relationships, 1972; Growing Points, 1975; Consequently I Rejoice, 1977; After the Ark (for children), 1978; Selected Poems, 1980; Moments of Grace, 1980; (ed) The Batsford Book of Religious Verse, 1981; Celebrations and Elegies, 1982; In Praise of Our Lady (anthology), 1982; Extending the Territory, 1985; (contrib.) A Quintet (for children), 1985; Collected Poems, 1953–86, 1986 (W. H. Smith Award, 1987); Tributes, 1989; Times and Seasons, 1992; Familiar Spirits, 1994; A Spell of Words, 1997; Praises, 1998; Timely Issues, 2001; *prose:* Let's Have Some Poetry, 1960; Every Changing Shape, 1961; Robert Frost, 1964; Christianity and Poetry, 1965; Seven Men of Vision, 1976; also poems and articles in: New Statesman, New Yorker, Botteghe Oscure, Observer, Spectator, Listener, Vogue, The Independent, etc. *Recreations:* travel, looking at pictures, the theatre, the cinema, music, collecting, conversation. *Address:* c/o David Higham Associates Ltd, 5–8 Lower John Street, W1R 4HA. *Club:* Society of Authors.

JENNINGS, James, OBE 1998; JP; Convener, Strathclyde Regional Council, 1986–90; *b* 18 Feb. 1925; *s* of late Mark Jennings and Janet McGrath; *m* 1st, 1943, Margaret Cook Barclay (decd); three *s* two *d*; 2nd, 1974, Margaret Mary Hughes, JP; two *d*. *Educ:* St Palladius School, Dalry; St Michael's College, Irvine. In steel industry, 1946–79. Member: Ayr County Council, 1958 (Chairman: Police and Law Cttee, 1964–70; Ayrshire Jt Police Cttee, 1970–75; N Ayrshire Crime Prevention Panel, 1970–82); Strathclyde Regional Council, 1974–96 (Chm., Police and Fire Cttee, 1978–82, 1990–96; Vice-Convener, 1982–86); N Ayrshire Unitary Council, 1995– (Chm., Social Work Cttee, 1995–). Convention of Scottish Local Authorities: Rep. for Strathclyde, 1974–96; Chm., Protective Services Cttee, 1977–82; Mem., Exec. Policy Cttee, 1982–96. Chm., Official Side, Police Negotiating Bd, 1986–88, 1992–94 (Vice-Chm., 1984–86). Chm., Garnock Valley Develt Exec., 1988–. Contested (Lab) Perth and East Perthshire, 1966. Hon. Sheriff, Kilmarnock, 1991–. Hon. Vice-President: Royal British Legion Scotland (Dalry and District Branch); Scottish Junior FA, 1994. JP Cunninghame, 1969 (Chm., Cunninghame Justices Cttee, 1974–). Freeman, N Ayrshire, 1997. *Recreation:* local community involvement. *Address:* 4 Place View, Kilbirnie, Ayrshire KA25 6BG. *T:* (01505) 683339. *Club:* Garnock Labour (Chairman).

JENNINGS, Sir John (Southwood), Kt 1997; CBE 1985; PhD; FRSE; Director, Shell Transport and Trading Company plc, since 1987 (Chairman, 1993–97); Vice Chairman, Committee of Managing Directors, Royal Dutch/Shell Group of Companies, 1993–97; Managing Director, Royal Dutch/Shell Group of Companies, 1987–97; *b* 30 March 1937; *s* of George Southwood Jennings and Irene Beatrice Jennings; *m* 1961, Gloria Ann Griffiths (marr. diss. 1996); one *s* one *d*. *Educ:* Oldbury Grammar Sch.; Univ. of Birmingham (BSc Hons Geology, 1958); Univ. of Edinburgh (PhD Geology, 1961); London Business Sch. (Sloan Fellow, 1970–71). Various posts, Royal Dutch/Shell Group, 1962–, including: Gen. Man. and Chief Rep., Shell cos in Turkey, 1976–78; Man. Dir, Shell UK Exploration and Prodn, 1979–84; Exploration and Prodn Co-ordinator, Shell Internationale Petroleum Mij., The Hague, 1985–90. Non-executive Director: Robert Fleming Holdings, 1997–; Det Norske Veritas, 1997–2001; MITIE Gp, 1997–2000; Mem., Internat. Adv. Bds, Toyota, Bechtel Corp. Vice Chm., Governing Body, London Business Sch., 1993–97 (Mem., 1992–); Vice Pres., Liverpool Sch. of Tropical Medicine, 1991–97; Member Council: RIIA, 1994–97; Exeter Univ. FRSE 1992. Hon. FGS 1992. Hon. DSc: Edinburgh, 1991; Birmingham, 1997. Commandeur de l'Ordre National du Mérite (Gabon), 1989. *Recreations:* fly fishing, shooting, travel. *Address:* c/o Shell Centre, SE1 7NA. *T:* (020) 7934 5553. *Clubs:* Brooks's, Flyfishers'.

JENNINGS, Very Rev. Kenneth Neal; Dean of Gloucester, 1983–96, now Emeritus; *b* 8 Nov. 1930; *s* of Reginald Tinsley and Edith Dora Jennings; *m* 1972, Wendy Margaret Stallworthy; one *s* one *d*. *Educ:* Hertford Grammar School; Corpus Christi College, Cambridge (MA); Cuddesdon College, Oxford. Asst Curate, Holy Trinity, Ramsgate, 1956–59; Lecturer 1959–61, Vice-Principal 1961–66, Bishop's College, Calcutta; Vice-Principal, Cuddesdon Theological Coll., 1967–73; Vicar of Hitchin, 1973–76; Team Rector of Hitchin, 1977–82. *Recreations:* music, fell-walking. *Address:* The School House, Keasden, Clapham, Lancaster LA2 8EY. *T:* (01524) 251455.

JENNINGS, Rev. Peter; educational and interfaith consultant; Associate Minister, Cambridge Methodist Circuit, since 1998; *b* 9 Oct. 1937; *s* of Robert William Jennings and Margaret Irene Jennings; *m* 1963, Cynthia Margaret Leicester; two *s*. *Educ:* Manchester Grammar Sch.; Keble Coll., Oxford (MA); Hartley Victoria Methodist Theological Coll.; Manchester Univ. (MA). Ordained 1965. Minister: Swansea Methodist Circuit, 1963–67; London Mission (East) Circuit, 1967–78, and Tutor Warden, Social Studies Centre, 1967–74; Gen. Sec., Council of Christians and Jews, 1974–81; Associate Minister, Wesley's Chapel, 1978–81; Asst Minister, Walthamstow and Chingford Methodist Circuit, 1981–82; Superintendent Minister: Whitechapel Mission, 1982–91; Barking and Ilford Methodist Circuit, 1991–93; Dir, N E London Religious Educn Centre, 1993–98. Pastoral Tutor, Centre for Jewish-Christian Relns, Wesley House, Cambridge Univ., 1999–. *Publications:* papers and articles on aspects of Christian-Jewish relations. *Recreations:* photography, being educated by Tim and Nick. *Address:* 68 Melbourn Road, Royston, Herts SG8 7DG. *T:* and *Fax:* (01763) 230210.

JENNINGS, Sir Peter (Nevile Wake), Kt 2000; CVO 1999; Serjeant at Arms, House of Commons, 1995–99; *b* 19 Aug. 1934; *s* of late Comdr A. E. de B. Jennings, RN and Mrs V. Jennings, MBE; *m* 1958, Shirley Anne, *d* of late Captain B. J. Fisher, DSO, RN and Mrs C. C. Fisher; one *s* two *d*. *Educ:* Marlborough College; psc (m)†, osc (US). Commissioned 2/Lt, RM, 1952; retired as Major, 1976. Appointed to staff of House of Commons, 1976; Dep. Serjeant at Arms, H of C, 1982–95. Chm., Central London Br., SSAFA Forces Help, 2001–. Pres., Friends of St Mary's Church, Kintbury, 1995–96 (Chm., 1990–95). *Address:* c/o House of Commons, SW1A 0AA.

JENNINGS, Sir Robert (Yewdall), Kt 1982; QC 1969; MA, LLB Cantab; a Judge, 1982–95, and President, 1991–94, the International Court of Justice; *b* 19 Oct. 1913; *o s* of Arthur Jennings; *m* 1955, Christine, *yr d* of Bernard Bennett; one *s* two *d*. *Educ:* Belle Vue Secondary Sch., Bradford; Downing Coll., Cambridge (scholar; 1st cl. pts I & II Law Tripos; LLB; Hon. Fellow, 1982). Served War, Intelligence Corps, 1940–46; Hon. Major, Officers' AER. Called to the Bar, Lincoln's Inn, 1943 (Hon. Bencher, 1970). Whewell Scholar in Internat. Law, Cambridge, 1936; Joseph Hodges Choate Fellow, Harvard Univ., 1936–37; Asst Lectr in Law, LSE, 1938–39; Jesus College, Cambridge: Fellow, 1939, Hon. Fellow, 1982; Sen. Tutor, 1949–55; sometime Pres.; Whewell Prof. of Internat. Law, Cambridge Univ., 1955–81; Reader in Internat. Law, Council of Legal Educn, 1959–70. Pres., Eritrea/Yemen Arbitration, 1996–99; Appointing Authy, Iran–US Claims Tribunal, The Hague, 1999–. Member: Permanent Court of Arbitration, 1982–; Inst. of Internat. Law, 1967– (Vice-Pres., 1979; Pres., 1981–83; Hon. Mem., 1985–); Hon. Mem., Indian Soc. of Internat. Law; Hon. Life Mem., Amer. Soc. of Internat. Law (Manley O. Hudson Medal, 1993). Hon. LLD: Hull, 1987; Cantab, 1993; Leicester, 1995; Hon. Dr jur: Saarland, W Germany, 1988; La Sapienza, Rome, 1990; Hon. DCL Oxon, 1996. Joint Editor: International and Comparative Law Quarterly, 1956–61; British Year Book of International Law, 1960–82. *Publications:* The Acquisition of Territory, 1963; General Course on International Law, 1967; Collected Writings of Sir Robert Jennings, 2 vols, 1998; articles in legal periodicals. *Address:* Jesus College, Cambridge CB5 8BL. *T:* (01223) 39339. *Clubs:* Oxford and Cambridge; Haagsche (The Hague).

JENSEN, Most Rev. Peter; *see* Sydney, Archbishop of.

JEPHCOTT, Sir (John) Anthony, 2nd Bt *cr* 1962; *b* 21 May 1924; *s* of Sir Harry Jephcott, 1st Bt, and Doris (*d* 1985), *d* of Henry Gregory; *S* father, 1978; *m* 1st, 1949, Sylvia Mary, *d* of Thorsten Frederick Relling, Wellington, NZ; two *d*; 2nd, 1978, Josephine Agnes Sheridan. *Educ:* Aldenham; St John's Coll., Oxford; London School of Economics (BCom). Served with REME and RAEC, 1944–47. Director, Longworth Scientific Instrument Co. Ltd, 1946; Managing Director and Chairman, 1952–73; Managing Director and Chairman, Pen Medic Ltd (NZ), 1973–78. Hon. FFARACS 1990. *Publications:* A History of Longworth Scientific Instrument Co. Ltd, 1988; correspondence in Anaesthesia (UK), and Anaesthesia and Intensive Care (Australia). *Recreations:* gardening, photography. *Heir: b* Neil Welbourn Jephcott [*b* 3 June 1929; *m* 1st, 1951, Mary Denise (*d* 1977), *d* of Arthur Muddiman; two *s* one *d*; 2nd, 1978, Mary Florence Daly]. *Address:* 26 Sage Road, Kohimarama, Auckland 5, New Zealand.

JEREMIAH, Melvyn Gwynne, CB 1994; Chairman, Wages and Salary Commission, Republic of Namibia, 1995–97; *b* 10 March 1939; *s* of Bryn Jeremiah and Evelyn (*née* Rogers); *m* 1960, Lilian Clare (*née* Bailey) (marr. diss. 1966). *Educ:* Abertillery County Sch. Apptd to Home Office, 1958; HM Customs and Excise, 1963–75; Cabinet Office, 1975–76; Treasury, 1976–79; Principal Finance Officer (Under Sec.), Welsh Office, 1979–87; Under Sec., DHSS, later DoH, 1987–95; Chief Exec., Disablement Services Authy, 1987–91, on secondment from DoH. Special Advr to Govt of Repub. of Namibia, 1995–97. Sec., Assoc. of First Div. Civil Servants, 1967–70. *Recreation:* genealogy. *Club:* Reform.

JEROME, Hon. James Alexander; PC (Can.) 1981; Associate Chief Justice, Federal Court of Canada, 1980–98; lawyer, since 1958; *b* Kingston, Ont, 4 March 1933; *s* of Joseph Leonard Jerome and Phyllis Devlin; *m* 1958, Barry Karen Hodgins; two *s* two *d* (and one *s* decd). *Educ:* Our Lady of Perpetual Help Sch., Toronto; St Michael's Coll. High Sch., Toronto; Univ. of Toronto (BA 1954); Osgoode Hall. Alderman, Sudbury, Ont, 1966–67. MP, Sudbury, 1968–80; Parly Sec. to President of Privy Council, 1970–74; Speaker of the House of Commons, 1974–80. QC (Can.) 1976. Pres., Commonwealth Parly Assoc., 1976. *Recreations:* golf, piano.

JERRAM, (Jeremy) James, CBE 1995; Chairman, Railways Pension Scheme; *b* 7 Aug. 1939; *s* of Lionel Jerram and Kathleen (*née* Cochrane); *m* 1965, Ruth Middleton; four *d*. *Educ:* Selwyn Coll., Cambridge (MA). FCA 1966. Arthur Andersen & Co., 1963–71; Standard Telephones & Cables, 1971–87; finance dir, computer software cos, 1987–90; Bd Mem. for Finance, then Vice-Chm., BRB, 1991–2000. *Address:* Railways Pension Trustee Co., 55 Old Broad Street, EC2M 1RX. *T:* (020) 7256 8003.

JERSEY, 10th Earl of *cr* 1697; **George Francis William Child Villiers;** Viscount Grandison of Limerick (Ire.), 1620; Viscount Villiers of Dartford and Baron Villiers of Hoo, 1691; actor; *b* 5 Feb. 1976; *s* of George Henry Child Villiers, Viscount Villiers (*d* 1998), and of his 2nd wife, Sacha Jane Hooper Valpy (now Mrs Raymond Hubbard); *S* grandfather, 1998. *Educ:* Canford Sch.; Birmingham Sch. of Speech and Drama. *Heir: half-b* Hon. Jamie Charles Child Villiers, *b* 31 May 1994. *Recreations:* Rugby, squash, tennis, cricket, sailing. *Address:* 5 Mimosa Road, SW6. *Club:* Royal Automobile.

JERSEY, Dean of; *see* Seaford, Very Rev. J. N.

JERVIS, family name of **Viscount St Vincent**.

JERVIS, Roger P.; *see* Parker-Jervis.

JERVIS, Simon Swynfen, FSA; Director of Historic Buildings (formerly Historic Buildings Secretary), National Trust, since 1995; *b* 9 Jan. 1943; *s* of late John Swynfen Jervis and Diana (*née* Marriott); *m* 1969, Fionnuala MacMahon; one *s* one *d*. *Educ:* Downside Sch.; Corpus Christi Coll., Cambridge (schol.) Student Asst, Asst Keeper of Art, Leicester Mus. and Art Gall., 1964–66; Department of Furniture, Victoria and Albert Museum: Asst Keeper, 1966–75; Dep. Keeper, 1975–89; Actg Keeper, 1989; Curator, 1989–90; Dir, Fitzwilliam Mus., Cambridge, 1990–95. Guest Schol., J. Paul Getty Mus., 1988–89; Chm., Nat. Trust Arts Panel, 1987–95. Dir, Burlington Magazine, 1993– (Trustee, 1996–). Editor, Furniture History, 1987–92 (Chm., 1998–). Trustee: Royal Collection Trust, 1993–2001; Leche Trust, 1995–; Sir John Soane's Mus., 1999–. FSA 1983 (Pres., 1995–2001). *Publications:* Victorian Furniture, 1968; Printed Furniture Designs Before 1650, 1974; High Victorian Design, 1983; Penguin Dictionary of Design and Designers, 1984; many articles in learned jls. *Address:* c/o National Trust, 36 Queen Anne's Gate, SW1H 9AS. *T:* (020) 7222 9251. *Club:* Brooks's.

JESSEL, Sir Charles (John), 3rd Bt *cr* 1883; farmer; nutrition consultant, since 1987; *b* 29 Dec. 1924; *s* of Sir George Jessel, 2nd Bt, MC, and Muriel (*d* 1948), *d* of Col J. W. Chaplin, VC; *S* father, 1977; *m* 1st, 1956, Shirley Cornelia (*d* 1977), *o d* of John Waters, Northampton; two *s* one *d*; 2nd, 1979, Gwendolyn Mary (marr. diss. 1983), *d* of late Laurance Devereux, OBE, and *widow* of Charles Langer, MA. *Educ:* Eton; Balliol College, Oxford; Northants Inst. of Agric., Moulton, 1952 (Dip with distinction). Served War of 1939–45, Lieut 15/19th Hussars (despatches). Chm., Ashford Br., NFU, 1963–64; Mem., Exec. Cttee, Kent Br., NFU, 1960–73; Pres., Kent Br., Men of the Trees, 1979–85, and 1995–. Life Vice Pres., British Soc. of Dowsers, 1994 (Pres., 1987–93). Gov., Inst of Optimum Nutrition, 1994–98 (Chm., 1997–98). Member: British Inst. for Allergy and Envmtl Therapy, 1990–; (and co-founding Dir), British Assoc. of Nutritional Therapists,

1997–. Life Mem., Internat. Dendrology Soc. Hon. Fellow, Psionic Med. Soc., 1977 (Pres., 1995–). Dip., Inst. of Optimum Nutrition, 1987. JP Kent 1960–78. *Publication:* (ed) An Anthology of Inner Silence, 1990. *Recreations:* gardening, planting trees. *Heir: s* George Elphinstone Jessel [*b* 15 Dec. 1957; *m* 1st, 1988, Rose (marr. diss. 1993), *yr d* of James Coutts-Smith; 2nd, 1998, Victoria, *y d* of Captain A. J. B. Naish, CBE, RN]. *Address:* South Hill Farm, Hastingleigh, near Ashford, Kent TN25 5HL. *T:* (01233) 750325. *Club:* Cavalry and Guards.

JESSEL, Oliver Richard; Chairman of numerous companies in the Jessel Group, 1954–89; *b* 24 Aug. 1929; *s* of late Comdr R. F. Jessel, DSO, OBE, DSC, RN; *m* 1950, Gloria Rosalie Teresa (*née* Holden); one *s* five *d*. *Educ:* Rugby. Founded group of companies, 1954; opened office in City of London, 1960; Chm., London, Australian and General Exploration Co. Ltd., 1960–75; formed: New Issue Unit Trust and other trusts, 1962–68; Castle Communications, 1983; Standard Financial Holdings, 1987; responsible for numerous mergers, incl. Johnson & Firth Brown Ltd, and Maple Macowards Ltd; Chm., Charles Clifford Industries Ltd, 1978–81; reorganised Belvoir Petroleum Corp., 1987–89; Chm., Thomas Seager PLC, 1993–. *Address:* Tilts House, Boughton Monchelsea, Maidstone, Kent ME17 4JE.

JESSEL, Toby Francis Henry; *b* 11 July 1934; *y s* of late Comdr R. F. Jessel, DSO, OBE, DSC, RN; *m* 1st, 1967 (marr. diss. 1973); one *d* decd; 2nd, 1980, Eira Gwen, *y d* of late Horace and Marigwen Heath. *Educ:* Royal Naval Coll., Dartmouth; Balliol Coll., Oxford (MA). Sub-Lt, RNVR, 1954. (Co-opted) LCC Housing Cttee, 1961–65; Councillor, London Borough of Southwark, 1964–66; Mem. for Richmond-upon-Thames, GLC, 1967–73 (Chm., S Area Bd, Planning and Transportation Cttee, 1968–70). Contested (C): Peckham, 1964; Hull North, 1966. MP (C) Twickenham, 1970–97; contested (C) same seat, 1997. Mem., Nat. Heritage Select Cttee, 1992–97. Chairman: Cons. Parly Arts and Heritage Cttee, 1983–97 (Vice-Chm., 1979); Anglo-Belgian Parly Gp, 1983–97; Indo-British Parly Gp, 1991–97 (Hon. Sec., 1972–87; Vice-Chm., 1987); Treas., Anglo-Chilean Parly Gp, 1991–93. Parliamentary delegate: to India and Pakistan, 1971; to India, 1982, 1992, 1994; to Belgium, 1994; Member: Council of Europe, 1976–92; WEU, 1976–92. Hon. Sec., Assoc. of Adopted Cons. Candidates, 1961–66. Hon. Sec., Katyn Meml Fund, 1972–75. Mem. Metropolitan Water Bd, 1967–70; Mem., London Airport Consultative Cttee, 1967–70. Mem. Council, Fluoridation Soc., 1976–83. Dir, Warship Preservation Trust, 1994–. Member: Exec. Cttee and Organizing Cttee, European Music Year, 1985; Council, Assoc. of British Orchestras, 1991–. Liveryman, Worshipful Co. of Musicians. Chevalier, Ordre de la Couronne (Belgium), 1980; Order of Polonia Restituta (Polish Govt in Exile); Commander's Cross with Star, Order of Merit (Liechtenstein), 1979. *Recreations:* music (has performed Mozart, Beethoven and Schumann piano concertos; raised £30,000 for NSPCC, Nov. perf., 1993, and £40,000 Dec. perf., 1995), gardening, croquet (Longworth Cup, Hurlingham, 1961), ski-ing. *Address:* Old Court House, Hampton Court, East Molesey, Surrey KT8 9BW. *Clubs:* Garrick, Hurlingham.

See also O. R. Jessel, J. H. Walford.

JESSELL, Prof. Thomas Michael, PhD; FRS 1996; Professor, Department of Biochemistry and Molecular Biophysics, Columbia University, New York, since 1989; Investigator, Howard Hughes Medical Institute, since 1985; *b* 2 Aug. 1951; *s* of Andre Hubert Jessell and Bettina Maria Anna Jessell (*née* Arndt); *m* 1973, Jennet Ann Priestland (marr. diss. 1981); partner, Jane Dodd; three *d*. *Educ:* Chelsea Coll., Univ. of London (BPharm); Trinity Coll., Cambridge Univ. (PhD 1977). Harkness Fellow, Harvard Univ., 1978–80; Res. Fellow, Trinity Coll., Cambridge, 1979; Royal Soc. Locke Res. Fellow, St George's Hosp., London, 1980–81; Asst Prof., Dept of Neurobiol., Harvard Med. Sch., 1981–85; Associate Prof., Dept of Biochem. and Molecular Biophysics, Columbia Univ., 1985–89. Fellow, Amer. Acad. of Arts and Scis, 1992. Hon. DPhil Umeå, Sweden, 1998. *Publications:* edited with E. Kandel and J. Schwartz: Principles of Neural Science, 3rd edn 1991; Essentials of Neural Science, 1995; contrib. to scientific jls. *Recreation:* British art. *Address:* Columbia University, College of Physicians and Surgeons, 701 West 168th Street, New York, NY 10032, USA. *T:* (212) 3051531.

JESSOP, Alexander Smethurst; Sheriff of Grampian, Highland and Islands at Aberdeen, since 1990; *b* 17 May 1943; *s* of Thomas Alexander Jessop and Ethel Marion Jessop; *m* 1967, Joyce Isobel Duncan; two *s* one *d*. *Educ:* Montrose Acad.; Fettes Coll.; Aberdeen Univ. (MA, LLB). Solicitor in private practice, Montrose, 1966–76; Depute Procurator Fiscal, Perth, 1976–78; Asst Solicitor, Crown Office, 1978–80; Sen. Asst Procurator Fiscal, Glasgow, 1980–84; Regional Procurator Fiscal: Aberdeen, 1984–87; Glasgow, 1987–90. Mem., Scottish Legal Aid Bd, 1996–. External Examr, Aberdeen Univ, 1998–. *Recreation:* sport. *Address:* 1 Hillhead of Hedderwick, Hillside, Montrose DD10 9JS; Sheriff Court, Castle Street, Aberdeen AB10 1WP. *Club:* Royal Montrose Golf (Captain).

JEVONS, Prof. Frederic Raphael, AO 1986; Hon. Professorial Associate, Department of History and Philosophy of Science, University of Melbourne, Australia, since 1996; *b* 19 Sept. 1929; *s* of Fritz and Hedwig Bettelheim; *m* 1956, Grete Bradel; two *s*. *Educ:* Langley Sch., Norwich; King's Coll., Cambridge (Major Schol.). 1st Cl. Hons Nat. Scis Pt II (Biochem.) Cantab 1950; PhD Cantab 1953; DSc Manchester 1966. Postdoctoral Fellow, Univ. of Washington, Seattle, 1953–54; Fellow, King's Coll., Cambridge, 1953–59; Univ. Demonstrator in Biochem., Cambridge, 1956–59; Lectr in Biol Chem., Manchester Univ., 1959–66; Prof. of Liberal Studies in Science, Manchester Univ., 1966–75; Vice-Chancellor, Deakin Univ., Australia, 1976–85, subseq. Emeritus Prof.; consultant on distance educn in southern Africa, 1986–87; Prof. of Science and Technology Policy, Murdoch Univ., Australia, 1988–92. Simon Sen. Res. Fellow, Univ. of Manchester, 1992; Hon. Professorial Fellow, Dept of Mgt, Monash Univ., 1994–96. Chairman: Gen. Studies Cttee, Schools Council, 1974–75; Grad. Careers Council of Aust., 1976–80; Policy Cttee, Victorian Technical and Further Educn Off-Campus Network, 1985–88; Member: Jt Matriculation Bd, Manchester, 1969–75; Jt Cttee, SRC and SSRC, 1974–75; Educn Res. and Develt Cttee, Aust., 1980–81; Council, Sci. Mus. of Vic., 1980–83; Council, Mus. of Vic., 1983–87; Aust. Vice-Chancellors' Exec. Cttee, 1981–82; Standing Cttee on External Studies, Commonwealth Tertiary Educn Commn, Canberra, 1985–87; Aust. Sci. and Technol. Council, 1986–89. Interviewer for Civil Service Commn on Final Selection Bds, 1970–75; Adviser to Leverhulme project on educnl objectives in applied science, Strathclyde Univ., 1972–75; British Council tours in India, E Africa, Nigeria, 1972–75. Mem., Editorial Advisory Boards: R and D Management, 1972–76; Studies in Science Educn, 1974–84; Scientometrics, 1978–; Australasian Studies in History and Philosophy of Science, 1980–86. Life Gov., Geelong Hosp., 1986. DUniv Open, 1985; Hon. DLitt Deakin, 1986; Hon. DSc Manchester, 1986. Inaugural winner, UNESCO prize for science and technology policy, 1992. *Publications:* The Biochemical Approach to Life, 1964, 2nd edn 1968 (trans. Italian, Spanish, Japanese, German); The Teaching of Science: education, science and society, 1969; (ed jtly) University Perspectives, 1970; (jtly) Wealth from Knowledge: studies of innovation in industry, 1972; (ed jtly) What Kinds of Graduates do we Need?, 1972; Science Observed: science as a social and intellectual activity, 1973; Knowledge and Power, 1976; numerous papers on biochem., history of science, science educn and science policy. *Recreations:* music, theatre, reading. *Address:* Department of History and Philosophy of Science, University of Melbourne, Parkville, Vic 3052, Australia. *T:* (3) 93446556, *Fax:* (3) 93447959.

JEWELL, David John, MA, MSc; Master of Haileybury and Imperial Service College, 1987–96; *b* 24 March 1934; *s* of late Wing Comdr John Jewell, OBE, FRAeS, and Rachel Jewell, Porthleven, Cornwall; *m* 1958, Katharine Frida Heller; one *s* three *d*. *Educ:* Blundell's Sch., Tiverton; St John's Coll., Oxford. Honours Sch. of Natural Science (Chemistry), BA 1957, MA 1961; BSc Physical Sciences, 1959, MSc 1981. National Service with RAF, 1952–54. Head of Science Dept, Eastbourne Coll., 1958–62; Winchester Coll., 1962–67; Dep. Head, Lawrence Weston Comprehensive Sch., Bristol, 1967–70; Head Master, Bristol Cathedral Sch., 1970–78; Headmaster, Repton Sch., 1979–87. Vis. Prof., Rollins Coll., Florida, 1987. Chairman: HMC, 1990 (Chairman: Direct Grant Sub-Cttee, 1977–78; Professional Develt Cttee, 1987–89); Choir Schools' Assoc., 1976–77. Vice-Chm. of Govs, Truro Sch., 1994– (Gov., 1990–); Chm. of Govs, Blundell's Sch., 1996–2000 (Gov., 1994–). Mem. Council, Engrg and Marine Trng Authy, 1996–99. FRSA 1981. *Publications:* papers and articles in various scientific and educnl jls. *Recreations:* music, cricket, theology, Cornwall. *Address:* Coombe Orchard, Compton Martin, NE Somerset BS40 6JA. *T:* (01761) 221264. *Clubs:* East India, Devonshire, Sports and Public Schools, MCC, Lord's Taverners; Bristol Savages.

JEWELL, Prof. Derek Parry, DPhil; FRCP, FMedSci; Professor of Gastroenterology, University of Oxford, since 1999; Fellow, Green College, Oxford, since 1995; Consultant Physician, John Radcliffe Hospital, Oxford, since 1980; *b* 14 June 1941; *s* of Ralph Parry Jewell and Eileen Rose Jewell; *m* 1974, Barbara Margaret Lockwood; one *s* one *d*. *Educ:* Bristol Grammar Sch.; Pembroke Coll., Oxford (MA, DPhil 1972). FRCP 1979. Associate Prof. in Medicine, Stanford Univ., USA, 1973–74; Sen. Lectr in Medicine, Royal Free Sch. of Medicine, 1974–80; Sen. Lectr, 1980–97, Reader, 1997–99, Univ. of Oxford. FMedSci 1999. *Publications:* (with H. C. Thomas) Clinical Gastrointestinal Immunology, 1979; Challenges in Inflammatory Bowel Disease, 2001; (contrib.) Topics in Gastroenterol; numerous original papers. *Recreations:* music, reading, gardening. Address: Radcliffe Infirmary, Oxford OX2 6HE.

JEWERS, William George, CBE 1982 (OBE 1976); Managing Director, Finance, and Member, British Gas plc (formerly British Gas Corporation), 1976–87; *b* 18 Oct. 1921; *s* of late William Jewers and Hilda Jewers (*née* Ellison); *m* 1955, Helena Florence Rimmer; one *s* one *d*. *Educ:* Liverpool Inst. High Sch. for Boys. Liverpool Gas Co., 1938–41. Served War: RAFVR Observer (Flying Officer), 1941–46: Indian Ocean, 265 Sqdn (Catalinas), 1943–44; Burma 194 Sqdn (Dakotas), 1945. Liverpool Gas Co./NW Gas Bd, Sen. Accountancy Asst, 1946–52; W Midlands Gas Bd: Cost Acct, Birmingham and Dist Div., 1953–62; Cost Acct, Area HQ, 1962–65; Asst Chief Acct, 1965–66; Chief Acct, 1967; Dir of Finance, 1968; Gas Council, Dir of Finance, 1969–73; British Gas Corp., Dir of Finance, 1973–76. FCMA, FCCA, JDipMA, CompIGasE. *Publications:* papers and articles to gas industry jls. *Recreations:* music, reading. *Address:* 17 South Park View, Gerrards Cross, Bucks SL9 8HN. *T:* (01753) 886169.

JEWKES, Sir Gordon (Wesley), KCMG 1990 (CMG 1980); HM Diplomatic Service, retired; Director, Slough Estates plc, since 1992; *b* 18 Nov. 1931; *er s* of late Jesse Jewkes; *m* 1954, Joyce Lyons; two *s*. *Educ:* Barrow Grammar Sch.; Magnus Grammar Sch., Newark-on-Trent, and elsewhere. Colonial Office, 1948; commnd HM Forces, Army, 1950–52; Gen. Register Office, 1950–63; CS Pay Res. Unit, 1963–65; Gen. Register Office, 1965–68; transf. to HM Diplomatic Service, 1968; CO, later FCO, 1968–69; Consul (Commercial), Chicago, 1969–72; Dep. High Comr, Port of Spain, 1972–75; Head of Finance Dept, FCO, and Finance Officer of Diplomatic Service, 1975–79; Consul-General: Cleveland, 1979–82; Chicago, 1982–85; Gov., Falkland Is and High Comr, British Antarctic Territory, 1985–88; Dir-Gen. of Trade and Investment, USA, and Consul-Gen., NY, 1989–91. Dir, Hogg Group, 1992–94; Exec. Dir, Walpole Cttee, 1992–96. Member: Council, Univ. of Buckingham, 1996–2001; Marshall Aid Commemoration Commn, 1996–99; London Metropolitan Adv. Bd, Salvation Army, 1996–. *Recreations:* music, travel, walking. *Address:* 19 Furzefield Road, Beaconsfield, Bucks HP9 1PG. *T:* (01494) 681830.

JEWSON, Richard Wilson; DL; Chairman: Inter X (formerly Ideal Hardware) plc, since 1994; Anglian Housing Group Ltd, since 1996; Octagon Healthcare (Holdings) Ltd, since 1998; *b* 5 Aug. 1944; *s* of Charles Boardman and Joyce Marjorie Jewson; *m* 1965, Sarah Rosemary Spencer; one *s* three *d*. *Educ:* Rugby; Pembroke Coll., Cambridge (MA). Joined Jewson & Sons, 1965, Man. Dir, 1974–86; Meyer International: Dir, 1983–93; Group Man. Dir, 1986–91; Dep. Chm., 1990–91; Chm., 1991–93. Non-executive Director: Eastern Counties Newspapers Group Ltd, 1982– (Chm., 1996–); Pro Share (UK), 1991–95; Anglian Water, 1991– (Dep. Chm., 1994–); Delian Lloyds Investment Trust, 1993–95; Savills plc, 1994– (Chm., 1995–); Queens Moat Houses, 1994–(Chm., 2001–); Grafton Gp plc, 1994–; Miller Insurance Group Ltd, 1995–96; Angerstein Underwriting Trust, 1995–96. Mem., CBI London Region Cttee, 1986–93. CIMgt. DL Norfolk, 2000. *Recreations:* golf, Real tennis, gardening, opera, visual arts. *Address:* Dades Farm, Barnham Broom, Norfolk NR9 4BT. *T:* (01603) 759237, *Fax:* (01603) 757909. *Clubs:* Boodle's; Norfolk (Norwich); Royal West Norfolk Golf.

JHABVALA, Mrs Ruth Prawer, CBE 1998; author; *b* in Germany, of Polish parents, 7 May 1927; *d* of Marcus Prawer and Eleonora Prawer (*née* Cohn); came to England as refugee, 1939; *m* 1951, C. S. H. Jhabvala; three *d*. *Educ:* Hendon County Sch.; Queen Mary Coll., London Univ. Started writing after graduation and marriage, alternating between novels and short stories; occasional original film-scripts (with James Ivory and Ismail Merchant), including: Shakespeare-wallah, 1965; The Guru, 1969; Bombay Talkie, 1971; Autobiography of a Princess, 1975; Roseland, 1977; Hullabaloo over Georgie and Bonnie's Pictures, 1978; The Europeans (based on Henry James' novel), 1979; Jane Austen in Manhattan, 1980; Quartet (based on Jean Rhys' novel), 1981; Heat and Dust (based on own novel), 1983; The Bostonians (based on Henry James' novel), 1984; A Room with a View (based on E. M. Forster's novel), 1986 (Academy Award, 1987); Mr and Mrs Bridge (based on Evan Connell's novels), 1991; Howards End (based on E. M. Forster's novel), 1992 (Academy Award, 1993); Remains of the Day (based on Kazuo Ishiguro's novel), 1993; Jefferson in Paris, 1995; Surviving Picasso, 1996; A Soldier's Daughter Never Cries, 1998; The Golden Bowl (based on Henry James' novel), 2000; film script (with John Schlesinger), Madame Sousatzka, 1988. *Publications: novels:* To Whom She Will, 1955; The Nature of Passion, 1956; Esmond in India, 1958; The Householder, 1960; Get Ready for Battle, 1962; A Backward Place, 1965; A New Dominion, 1973; Heat and Dust, 1975 (Booker Prize, 1975); In Search of Love and Beauty, 1983; Three Continents, 1987; Poet and Dancer, 1993; Shards of Memory, 1995; *short story collections:* Like Birds, like Fishes, 1964; A Stronger Climate, 1968; An Experience of India, 1971; How I became a Holy Mother and other Stories, 1976; Out of India: selected stories, 1986; East into Upper East, 1998. *Recreation:* writing film-scripts. *Address:* 400 East 52nd Street, New York, NY 10022, USA.

See also Prof. S. S. Prawer.

JI Chaozhu; Under-Secretary General of the United Nations, 1991–96; *b* Shanxi Province, 30 July 1929; *s* of Dr Chi Kung-Chuan, Commissioner of Education, and Chang Tao-Jan; *m* 1957, Wang Xiangtong; two *s*. *Educ:* Primary and secondary schools in Manhattan; Harvard Univ. (reading Chemistry); Tsinghua Univ. (graduated 1952). English stenographer at Panmunjom, Korea, for Chinese People's Volunteers, 1952–54; English interpreter for Chinese leaders, incl. Chairman Mao, Premier Chou En-Lai, 1954–73; Dep. Dir, Translation Dept, Foreign Ministry, 1970–73; Counsellor, Liaison Office, Washington DC, 1973–75; Dep. Dir, Dept of Internat. Organisations and Confs, Foreign Min., 1975–79; Dep. Dir, Dept of American and Oceanic Affairs, Foreign Min., 1979–82; Minister-Counsellor, US Embassy, 1982–85; Ambassador to Fiji, Kiribati and Vanuatu, 1985–87; Ambassador to UK, 1987–91. *Recreations:* swimming, music. *Address:* 112–01 Queens Boulevard, Apt 18D, Forest Hills, NY 11375, USA.

JIANG, Enzhu; Minister, Liaison Office of the Central People's Government in Hong Kong Special Administrative Region, since 2000; *b* 14 Dec. 1938; *s* of Jiang Guohua and Yu Wen Guizhen; *m* 1967, Zhu Manli; one *s*. *Educ:* Beijing Foreign Languages Inst. Teacher, Beijing Foreign Languages Inst., 1964; London Embassy, People's Republic of China, 1964–77; Ministry of Foreign Affairs: Dep. Dir, 1978, Dir, 1983, Dep. Dir-Gen. and Dir-Gen., 1984–90, Dept of W European Affairs; Asst Minister, 1990–91; Vice Foreign Minister, 1991–95; Chinese Ambassador to UK, 1995–97; Dir, Xinhua News Agency (Hong Kong Br.), 1997–2000. Chief Negotiator for People's Republic of China in Sino-British talks over future of Hong Kong, 1993; a Dep. Hd, Prelim. Wkg Cttee of Preparatory Cttee, HKSAR, 1993–95. Res. Fellow, Center for Internat. Affairs, Harvard Univ., and Sen. Vis. Scholar, Brookings Inst., USA, 1981–82. *Address:* Liaison Office of the Central People's Government, 387 Queen's Road East, Wanchai, Hong Kong.

JIANG ZEMIN; President, People's Republic of China, since 1993; Chairman, Central Military Commission, since 1990; *b* Yangzhou City, Aug. 1926. *Educ:* Jiaotong Univ., Shanghai. Participated in student movement led by underground Party orgns, 1943; joined Communist Party of China, 1946. Associate engr, section chief and power workshop dir, factory Party sec., then First Dep. Dir, Shanghai Yimin No 1 Foodstuffs Factory; First Dep. Dir, Shanghai Soap Factory; Section Chief of electrical machinery, Shanghai No 2 Designing Sub-bureau, First Min. of Machine-building Industry; trainee, Stalin Automobile Plant, Moscow, 1955; Dep. Chief, Power Div., Dep. Chief Power Engr, and Dir, Power Plant, Changchun No 1 Auto Works, 1956–62; Dep. Dir, Shanghai Electric Equipt Res. Inst., 1962; Dir and actg Party sec., Wuhan Thermo-Tech. Machinery Res. Inst.; Dep. Dir, and Dir, Foreign Affairs Bureau, First Min. of Machine-building Industry; Vice-Chm. and Sec.-Gen., State Commns on Admin of Imports and Exports and on Admin of Foreign Investment, 1980–82; Vice Minister and Dep. Sec., Party Gp, later Minister and Sec., Party Gp, Min. of Electronics Industry, 1982–85. Mayor of Shanghai and Dep. Sec., later Sec., Shanghai Municipal Party Cttee, 1985. Communist Party of China Central Committee: Mem., 1982; Mem., Political Bureau, 1987 (Mem., Standing Cttee, 1989, Gen. Sec.); Chm., Military Cttee, 1989. *Address:* Office of the President, Beijing, People's Republic of China.

JILANI, Asaf; journalist and broadcaster; a pioneer of Urdu journalism in the UK. Senior Producer, South Asia Region (formerly Eastern) Service, BBC World Service, 1983–94; *b* 24 Sept. 1934; *s* of Abdul Wahid Sindhi and Noor Fatima Jilani; *m* 1961, Mohsina Jilani; two *s* one *d*. *Educ:* Jamia Millia, Delhi; Sindh Madrasa, Karachi; Karachi Univ. (BA, Economics and Persian). Sub-Editor, Daily Imroze, Karachi (Progressive Papers Ltd), 1952; Political Corresp., Daily Imroze, 1954; Special Corresp., Daily Jang, Karachi (posted in India), 1959–65; first Urdu journalist to be posted as a foreign correspondent; held prisoner in Delhi during India/Pakistan War, 1965; London Editor: Daily Jang (Karachi, Rawalpindi, Quetta); Daily News, Karachi, and Akhbar-Jehan, Karachi, 1965–73; Editor, Daily Jang, London (first Urdu Daily in UK), 1973–82. Iqbal Medal (Pakistan), for journalistic contribution to exposition of Islamic poetic philosopher Dr Mohammed Iqbal, during his centenary celebrations, 1979. *Publications:* Wast Asia, Nai Azadi Nay Challenge (Central Asian Journey, in Urdu; based on 21 prog. series for BBC World Service), 1994; Gaon Gaon Badalti Dunia (Changing Villages, in Urdu; based on 26 prog. series for BBC Urdu Service), 1998. *Recreations:* walking, swimming, painting. *Address:* 17 Leys Gardens, Cockfosters, Herts EN4 9NA.

JILLINGS, Godfrey Frank; Deputy Chairman: DBS Management plc, since 1996 (Director, since 1994); Gladedale Holdings plc, since 2000; *b* 24 May 1940; *s* of late Gerald Frank Jillings and Dorothy Marjorie Jillings; *m* 1967, Moira Elizabeth McCoy (*d* 1986); one *s*. *Educ:* Tiffin's Sch., Kingston; Inst. of Personnel Management. DMS; ACIB. S. G. Warburg & Co. Ltd, 1956–58; National Westminster Bank Ltd, 1958–90: Head of Industrial Section, 1983; Sen. Project Manager, 1985–86; Director: County Unit Trust Managers Ltd, 1986–87; Natwest Stockbrokers Ltd, 1986–89; Chief Exec., Natwest Personal Financial Management Ltd, 1987–89; Senior Exec., Group Chief Exec's Office, 1989–90; Chief Exec., FIMBRA, 1990–94; Dir, Financial Services Initiative, later Dir, London Office, WDA, 1994–97. A Dep. Chief Exec., PIA, 1992–94. Chm., John Gater Holdings Ltd, 1994–95; Director: Baronsmead VCT plc, 1995–; DBS Financial Management plc, 1997–; Baronsmead VCT 2 plc, 1998–. *Recreations:* travel, chess. *Address:* 47 Hurlingham Square, Peterborough Road, SW6 3DZ. *T:* (020) 7736 9083, *Fax:* (020) 7736 9098. *Club:* Royal Automobile.

JINKINSON, Alan Raymond; General Secretary, UNISON, 1993–96; *b* 27 Feb. 1935; *s* of Raymond and Maggie Jinkinson; *m* 1968, Madeleine Gillian Douglas (*d* 1995). *Educ:* King Edward VII Sch., Sheffield; Keble Coll., Oxford (BA Hons). National and Local Government Officers' Association: Education Dept, 1960; District Officer, 1967; District Orgn Officer, 1973; National Officer (Local Govt), 1976; Asst Gen. Sec., 1981; Dep. Gen. Sec., 1983; Gen. Sec., 1990. *Recreations:* cinema, jogging, walking. *Address:* 24 Holmdene Avenue, SE24 9LF. *T:* (020) 7274 5017.

JIRIČNA, Eva Magdalena, CBE 1994; RA 1997; RDI 1991; architect; Principal of own practice, since 1984; *b* 3 March 1939; *d* of Josef Jiričny and Eva Jiričná; *m* 1963, Martin Holub (marr. diss. 1973). *Educ:* Coll. of Architecture and Town Planners, Univ. of Prague (Engr Architect 1962); Acad. of Fine Arts, Prague (Acad. Architect 1967). Professional practice and management examination, RIBA, 1973. Main projects include: Joan & David Inc. Shops, UK, USA, Paris, Far East; Prague HQ, Andersen Consulting; Faith Zone, Millennium Dome; Kimberlin Library Extension, De Montfort Univ.; Orangery, Prague Castle; Hotel Rybna, Prague; Boodle & Dunthorne, Jewellers, Sloane St, Chester and Manchester; AMEC plc. Hon. FRCA 1989. *Address:* 3rd Floor, 38 Warren Street, W1T 6AE. *T:* (020) 7554 2400, *Fax:* (020) 7388 8022;; *e-mail:* mail@ejal.com.

JOACHIM, Rev. Dr Margaret Jane; Client Delivery Manager, EDS (Electronic Data Systems) Ltd, since 2000; Minister in Secular Employment, Diocese of London, since 1997; *b* 25 June 1949; *d* of late Reginald Carpenter and Joyce Margaret Carpenter; *m* 1970, Paul Joseph Joachim; one *d*. *Educ:* Brighton and Hove High School; St Hugh's College, Oxford (MA Geology); Univ. of Birmingham (PhD Geology); Southern Dioceses Ministerial Trng Scheme. FRES 1983; FGS 1991. Grammar school teacher, 1971–76; post-doctoral research Fellow, Univ. of Birmingham, 1976–79; computer consultant, 1979–84; Futures Database Manager, Rudolf Wolff & Co., 1984–87; EDS (Electronic Data Systems) Ltd: Manager, UK Insurance Services, 1988–91; Leadership and Professional Develt Instr, 1991–93; Sen. Relationship Manager (Insce), 1994–96; Manager, EMEA Year 2000 Services, 1997–2000; Asst Dir, Taskforce 2000, 1997 (on secondment). Training Officer, Liberal Parly Assoc., 1979–84; Mem., Exec. Cttee, Women's Liberal Fedn, 1984–85; Chair, Fawcett Soc., 1984–87 (Vice-Chair, 1993–95; Mem. Exec. Cttee, 1990–95); Trustee, Fawcett Trust, 1995–; Chair, internat. working gp to set up EEC Women's Lobby, 1988–90; Chair, 1989–90, Vice-Chair, 1990–92, WLD (formerly SLD Women's Orgn). Co-ordinator, Women into Public Life Campaign, 1987–88; Vice-Chair, 1989, Mem. Exec. Cttee, 1989–91, 300 Gp. Contested: (L) West Gloucestershire, 1979; (L/Alliance) Finchley, 1983; (L/Alliance) Epsom and Ewell, 1987. Ordained deacon, 1994, priest, 1995; Asst Curate (non-stipendiary), St Barnabas, Ealing, 1994–97, St Peter's, Mount Park, Ealing, 1998–. Moderator, CHRISM (Christians in Secular Ministry), 1999–. Mem., Exec. Cttee, Nat. Traction Engine Club, 1976–79; Founder, Steam Apprentice Club, 1978; Founder, Oxford Univ. Gilbert and Sullivan Soc., 1968. *Publications:* papers in: Studies in the Late-Glacial of North-West Europe, 1980; Holocene Palaeoecology and Palaeohydrology, 1986. *Recreations:* walking, reading, going to traction engine rallies, making jam, running 1954 MG TF. *Address:* 8 Newburgh Road, W3 6DQ. *T:* (020) 8723 4514; *e-mail:* margaret.joachim@dlondon.org.uk. *Club:* Reform.

JOB, Rev. (Evan) Roger (Gould); Canon Residentiary, Precentor and Sacrist, 1979–94, Vice Dean, 1991–94, Winchester Cathedral; *b* 15 May 1936; 2nd *s* of late Thomas Brian and Elsie Maud Job, Ipswich; *m* 1964, Rose Constance Mary, *o d* of late Stanley E. and Audrey H. Gordon, Hooton, Wirral; two *s*. *Educ:* Cathedral Choir School and King's Sch., Canterbury; Magdalen Coll., Oxford; Cuddesdon Theol Coll. BA 1960, MA 1964; ARCM 1955. Deacon 1962, priest 1963. Asst Curate, Liverpool Parish Church, 1962–65; Vicar of St John, New Springs, Wigan, 1965–70; Precentor of Manchester Cath., 1970–74; Precentor and Sacrist of Westminster Abbey, 1974–79; Chaplain of The Dorchester, 1976–79. Select Preacher, Univ. of Oxford, 1974, 1991. *Recreations:* gardening, piano. *Address:* Kitwood Farm-house, Ropley, Alresford, Hants SO24 0DB.

JOB, Sir Peter James Denton, Kt 2001; Chief Executive, Reuters Group PLC, 1991–2001; *b* 13 July 1941; *s* of late Frederick Job and of Marion Job (*née* Pickard); *m* 1966, Christine Cobley, *d* of Frederick Cobley; one *s* one *d*. *Educ:* Clifton College; Exeter College, Oxford (BA). Trainee Reuter journalist, 1963; reporter then manager in Paris, New Delhi, Kuala Lumpur, Jakarta and Buenos Aires, 1963–78; Man. Dir, Reuters Asia, based in Hong Kong, 1978–90; Dir, Reuters Gp, 1989–2001; Chm., Visnews Ltd, 1991–92. Non-executive Director: Grand Metropolitan, 1994–97; Glaxo Wellcome, 1997–99; Diageo, 1997–99; Schroders, 1999–; GlaxoSmithKline, 2000–; Inctanet, 2000–; TIBCO Software Inc., 2000–. Chm., Internat. Adv. Council, NASDAQ, 1999; Member: DTI Multimedia Adv. Gp, 1994–97; DTI Japan Trade Gp, 1994–98; HM Treasury Adv. Panel, 1995; High Level Adv. Gp on Information Society, EU, 1996; FCO Business Panel, 1998; INSEAD UK Nat. Council, 1993–; London/NY Alliance Bd, 2001–. Hon. Fellow, Green Coll., Oxford, 1995. Hon. DLitt Kent, 1998. *Recreations:* boating, golf, tennis, music, gardening, theatre, country sports. *Address:* 701 Rowan House, 9 Greycoat Street, SW1P 2QD. *Clubs:* Oriental; Hong Kong (Hong Kong); Tadmarton Golf.

JOBBINS, Robert, OBE 2001; media consultant, since 2001; Director of News, BBC World Service, 1996–2001; *b* 2 Nov. 1941; *s* of Henry Robert Jobbins and Miriam Jeffrey Jobbins; *m* 1st, 1962, Jenifer Ann Rowbotham (marr. diss. 1991); two *s*; 2nd, 1992, Jacqueline Duff. *Educ:* Rickmansworth Grammar Sch. BBC Foreign Correspondent: Cairo, 1977–83; Singapore, 1983–86; Head of BBC Arabic Service, 1986–89; Editor, BBC World Service News and Current Affairs, 1989–96. Ind. Mem., Essex Police Authy, 2001–. Chm., Rory Peck Trust, 2001–. *Recreations:* walking, medieval art, opera. *Address:* Blue House Cottage, Maldon Road, Bradwell on Sea, Essex CM0 7MR. *T:* (01621) 776507.

JOBERT, Michel; Commandeur de la Légion d'Honneur; Croix de Guerre (1939–45); politician, writer and lawyer; Founder and Leader, Mouvement des Démocrates, since 1974; *b* Meknès, Morocco, 11 Sept. 1921; *s* of Jules Jobert and Yvonne Babule; *m* Muriel Frances Green; one *s*. *Educ:* Lycées of Rabat and Meknès; Dip. de l'Ecole libre des sciences politiques; Ecole nationale d'Administration. Cour des comptes: Auditor, 1949; Conseiller Référendaire, 1953. Member of Ministerial Cabinets: Finance, Labour and Social Security, President of the Council, 1952–56; Director of the Cabinet of the High Commr of the Republic in French West Africa, 1956–58; Dir of Cabinet of Minister of State, 1959–61; Jt Dir, 1963–66, then Director, 1966–68, of the Prime Minister's Cabinet (Georges Pompidou); Pres., Council of Admin of Nat. Office of Forests, 1966–73; Administrator of Havas, 1968–73; Secretary-Gen., Presidency of the Republic, 1969–73; Minister for Foreign Affairs, 1973–74; Minister of State and Minister for Overseas Trade, 1981–83. Conseiller-maître, Cour des comptes, 1971– (Hon. Conseiller-maître, 1986). Arbitrator, Nat. Cttee, Internat. Chamber of Commerce, 1991. Former Board Member: SOFIRAD, Radio Monte-Carlo; French Radio and TV Organisation. Editor, La Lettre de Michel Jobert, 1974–84; Editorialiste, Paris ce Soir, Jan.–Feb. 1985. Prix de la Langue de France, 1989. *Publications:* Mémoires d'avenir, 1974; L'autre regard, 1976; Lettre ouverte aux femmes politiques, 1976; Parler aux Français, 1977; La vie d'Hella Schuster (novel), 1977; Maroc: extrême Maghreb du soleil couchant, 1978; La rivière aux grenades, 1982; Chroniques du Midi Libre, 1982; Vive l'Europe Libre, 1984; Par Trente-six chemins, 1984; Maghreb, à l'ombre de ses mains, 1985; Les Américains, 1987; Journal immédiat … et pour une petite éternité, 1987; Vandales!, 1990; Journal du Golfe, 1991; Ni dieu ni diable, 1993; Chroniques de l'Espérance 1988–1992, 1993; L'aveuglement du monde occidental, Chroniques de politique internationale 1993–1996, 1997; Les illusions immobiles, Chroniques de politique internationale 1996–1998, 1999. *Address:* (home) 21 quai Alphonse-Le Gallo, 92100 Boulogne-sur-Seine, France; (office) 108 quai Louis Blériot, 75016 Paris, France.

JOBLING, Captain James Hobson, RN; Metropolitan Stipendiary Magistrate, 1973–87; *b* 29 Sept. 1921; *s* of late Captain and Mrs J. S. Jobling, North Shields, Northumberland; *m* 1946, Cynthia, *o d* of late F. E. V. Lean, Beacon Park, Plymouth; one *s* one *d*. *Educ:* Tynemouth High Sch.; London Univ. (LLB Hons, 1971). Entered Royal Navy, 1940; HMS Furious, 1941; HMS Victorious, 1941–45; awarded Gedge Medal and Prize, 1946; called to Bar, Inner Temple, 1955; Comdr, 1960; JSSC course, 1961–62; Dir, Nat. Liaison, SACLANT HQ, USA, 1962–65; Chief Naval Judge Advocate, in rank of Captain, 1969–72; retd, 1973. Planning Inspector, DoE, 1973; a Dep. Circuit Judge, 1976–82. *Recreations:* gardening, walking. *Address:* Pinewell Lodge, Wood Road, Hindhead, Surrey GU26 6PT. *T:* (01428) 604426.

JOBS, Steven Paul; Joint Founder, 1975, Consultant, since 1995, and interim President, since 1997, Apple Computer Inc.; Chairman and Chief Executive Officer, Pixar Animation Studios, since 1986; *b* 1955; adopted *s* of Paul and Clara Jobs; one *d*; *m* 1991, Laurene Powell; one *s* one *d*. *Educ:* Homestead High Sch.; Reed Coll. Electronics engr; Video Game Designer, Atari Inc., 1974; Apple Computer Inc.: Jt Designer, Apple I computer, 1976; Chm., 1975–77, 1981–84; Dir, 1995–; Pres., NeXT Inc., 1985–96 (CEO). *Address:* c/o Apple Computer Inc., 1 Infinite Loop, Cupertino, CA 95014-2084, USA.

JOBSON, Roy; Director of Education, Edinburgh, since 1998; *b* 2 June 1947; *s* of James Jobson and Miriam H. Jobson; *m* 1971, Maureen Scott; one *s* two *d. Educ:* Bedlington Grammar Sch.; Univ. of Durham; Newcastle and Sunderland Polytechnics. Teacher: King's Sch., Tynemouth, 1970–73; Norham High Sch., 1973–74; Asst Sec., E Midland Regional Examining Bd, 1974–80; Asst Dir of Educn, Gateshead Metropolitan Borough Council, 1980–84; Dep. Chief Educn Officer, 1984–88, Chief Educn Officer, 1988–98, Manchester City Council. Adviser: AMA, 1993–97; LGA, 1997–98. Member: Jt Council for GCSE, 1989–93; NEAB, 1992–93; Soc. of Educn Officers, 1988–; Chm., ACEO, 1997–98. FRSA 1994. *Recreations:* children, family, church, music, dogs. *Address:* 4 Buckstone View, Edinburgh EH10 6PE. *T:* (0131) 469 3322.

JOCELYN, family name of **Earl of Roden.**

JOCELYN, Viscount; Shane Robert Henning Jocelyn; *b* 9 Dec. 1989; *s* and *heir* of Earl of Roden, *qv.*

JOFFE, family name of **Baron Joffe.**

JOFFE, Baron *cr* 2000 (Life Peer), of Liddington in the County of Wiltshire; **Joel Goodman Joffe,** CBE 1999; Chairman, Oxfam, since 1995; *b* 12 May 1932; *s* of Abraham Joffe and Dena Joffe (*née* Idelson); *m* 1962, Vanetta Pretorius; three *d. Educ:* Marist Brothers' Coll., Johannesburg; Univ. of Witwatersrand (BCom, LLB). Admitted Solicitor, Johannesburg, 1956; called to the Bar, S Africa, 1962; Human Rights lawyer, 1958–65; Dir and Sec., Abbey Life Assurance Co., 1965–70; Dir, Jt Man. Dir and Dep. Chm., Allied Dunbar Life Assurance Co., 1971–91. Chairman: Swindon Private Hosp., 1982–87; Swindon HA, 1988–93; Swindon and Marlborough NHS Trust, 1993–95. Mem., Royal Commn on Long Term Care for the Elderly, 1997–98. Special Advr to S African Minister of Transport, 1997–98. Trustee, 1980–, Hon. Sec., 1982–85, Exec. Cttee Chm., 1985–93, Oxfam; numerous other charitable organisations. DUniv Open, 1995. *Publication:* The Rivonia Trial, 1995. *Recreations:* tennis, ski-ing.

JOGEE, Dr Moussa, MBE 1996; Joint Deputy Chairman, Commission for Racial Equality, since 1999 (Commissioner, since 1994); *b* 11 Nov. 1930; *s* of Ebrahim Moosa and Aysha Ebrahim; *m* 1948, Fatma Seedat; three *s* two *d* (and one *d* decd). *Educ:* India; South Africa; Newbattle Abbey Coll., Edinburgh. Activist in South Africa against apartheid; Founder and Editor, Lalkar jl, South Africa; exiled to Britain, 1965; caterer and restaurateur, 1973–. Exec. Editor, Inter-Arts jl, 1986–91. FRSA 1996. JP, 1985. Hon. DLitt Edinburgh, 1996. Hind Ratan, India, 1989. *Recreations:* cricket, cooking, poetry (Urdu). *Address:* 13 Hopeward Court, The Stables, Dalgety Bay KY11 9TF. *T:* (01383) 821056; Commission for Racial Equality, 45 Hanover Street, Edinburgh EH2 2PJ. *T:* (0131) 226 5186.

JOHANNESBURG, Bishop of, since 2000; **Rt Rev. Brian Charles Germond;** *b* 21 Jan. 1947; *s* of Charles Alfred Germond and Dorothy Eileen Germond (*née* Impey); *m* 1971, Susan Patricia Strong; one *s* two *d. Educ:* King Edward VII Sch.; Univ. of SA (BA); St Paul's Theol Coll. (DipTh); Univ. of London (BD); McCormack Seminary (DMin). Ordained deacon, 1976, priest, 1977; Curate, St Martin-in-the-Veld, Johannesburg, 1976–80; Rector: St Barnabas Lichtenburg, St Andrews, Lichtenburg, and St John's, Zeerust, 1980–85; St Martin-in-the-Veld, 1987–2000; Archdeacon of Rosebank, 1989–2000. *Recreations:* birdwatching, woodworking. *Address:* PO Box 1131, Johannesburg 2000, RSA. *T:* (011) 3368724.

JÓHANNSSON, Kjartan, PhD; Secretary General, European Free Trade Association, since 1994; *b* 19 Dec. 1939; *s* of Johan and Astrid Dahl Thorsteinsson; *m* 1964, Irma Karlsdottir; one *d. Educ:* Reykjavik Coll.; Tech. Univ. of Stockholm; Univ. of Stockholm; Illinois Inst. of Tech., Chicago. Consulting Engr, Reykjavik, 1966–78; University of Iceland: Teacher, Faculty of Engrg and Sci., 1966–78; Prof., Faculty for Econs and Business Admin, 1980–89. Mem., Municipal Council, Hafnarfjördur, 1974–78; Mem. (SDP), Althing (Parlt of Iceland), 1978–89; Speaker, Lower Hse, 1988–89; Minister of Fisheries, 1978–80, also of Commerce, 1979–80; Ambassador and Perm. Rep. to UN and other internat. orgns, Geneva, 1989–94. Social Democratic Party: Mem., Party Council and Exec. Council, 1972–89; Vice-Chm., 1974–80; Chm., 1980–84. *Address:* c/o European Free Trade Association, 9 rue de Varembé, 1211 Geneva 20, Switzerland. *T:* (22) 7491335.

JOHANSEN-BERG, Rev. John; Founder Member, since 1984, Leader, since 1986, and International Director, since 2001, Community for Reconciliation; Moderator, Free Church Federal Council, 1987–88; *b* 4 Nov. 1935; *s* of John Alfred and Caroline Johansen-Berg, Middlesbrough; *m* 1971, Joan, *d* of James and Sally Ann Parnham, Leeds; two *s* one *d. Educ:* Acklam Hall Grammar Sch., Middlesbrough; Leeds Univ. (BA Hons Eng. Lit., BD); Fitzwilliam Coll., Cambridge Univ. (BA Theol Tripos, MA); Westminster Theol Coll. (Dip. Theol.). Tutor, Westminster Coll., Cambridge, 1961; ordained, 1962; pastoral charges: St Ninian's Presbyterian Church, Luton, 1962–70 (Sec., Luton Council of Churches); Founder Minister, St Katherine of Genoa Church, Dunstable (dedicated 1968); The Rock Church Centre, Liverpool (Presbyterian, then United Reformed), 1970–77, work begun in old public house, converted into Queens Road Youth Club, new Church Centre dedicated 1972, a building designed for youth, community and church use; Minister: St Andrew's URC, Ealing, 1977–86; Rubery URC, 1992–2001. Convener, Church and Community Cttee of Presbyterian C of E, 1970–72; Chm. Church and Society Dept, URC, 1972–79; Moderator of the Gen. Assembly of the URC, 1980–81. British Council of Churches: Mem., Assembly, 1987–90; formerly Member: Div. of Internat. Affairs; Div. of Community Affairs; Chm. Gp on Violence, Non-violence and Social Change (for Britain Today and Tomorrow Programme, 1977); Convenor, Commission on Non-Violent Action (report published 1973); Mem., Forum of Churches Together in England, 1990–97. Chm., Christian Fellowship Trust, 1981–87; Trustee, Nat. Assoc. of Christian Communities and Networks, 1989–2001; Mem., Exec., CCJ, 1989–97; Mem. Council, Centre for Study of Judaism and Jewish Christian Relns, 1989–96; Trustee, Fellowship of Reconciliation, 2000–. Founder Mem. and Sponsor, Christian Concern for Southern Africa, 1972–94; Founder Sponsor, Clergy Against Nuclear Arms, 1982– (Chm., 1986–90); Founder: Romania Concern, 1990; United Africa Aid, 1996; Ecumenical Order of Ministry, 1990; Jt Leader, Ecumenical Festivals of Faith in: Putney and Roehampton, 1978; Stroud, 1980; Banstead, 1983; North Mymms, 1985; Guildford, 1986; Jesmond, 1987; Worth Abbey, 1988; Palmers Green, 1990; Poole, and Ballyholme, 1991; Finchley, 1992; South Wallasey, 1994. Jt Editor, Jl of Presbyterian Historical Soc. of England, 1964–70. *Publications:* Arian or Arminian? Presbyterian Continuity in the Eighteenth Century, 1969; Prayers of the Way, 1987 (rev. edn 1992); Prayers of Pilgrimage, 1988; Prayers of Prophecy, 1990; Prayers for Pilgrims, 1993; A Celtic Collection, 1996; Pilgrims on the Edge, 1997. *Recreations:* mountain walking, badminton, drama. *Address:* 12 Rannoch Avenue, Worcester WR5 3UN. *T:* (01905) 351115.

JOHANSON, Rev. Dr Brian; Minister of Christ Church, United Reformed Church, Tonbridge, 1987–94; *b* 8 March 1929; *s* of Bernard Johanson and Petra Johanson; *m* 1st, 1955, Marion Shirley Giles (*d* 1994); one *s* two *d*; 2nd, 1995, Maureen Linnea Henderson. *Educ:* Univ. of South Africa (BA, DD); Univ. of London (BD). Parish Minister, S Africa, 1956–63; Sen. Lectr in Theology, 1964–69, Prof. of Theol., 1970–76, Univ. of SA; Minister of the City Temple, London, 1976–85; Dir of Ministerial Training, Presbyterian Church of Southern Africa, Johannesburg, 1985–86. Vis. Res. Fellow: Princeton Theol Seminary, 1970; Univ. of Aberdeen, 1976. *Publications:* univ. pubns in S Africa; booklets; essays in collections; articles in theol jls.

JOHANSON, Capt. Philip; Chief Secretary, Church Army, since 1990; *b* 10 April 1947; *s* of late Stanley Theodore Johanson and Betty Johanson. *Educ:* Alderman Cogan Sch., Hull; Wilson Carlile Coll. of Evangelism, London. Missioner, dio. of Coventry, 1972–75; Head of Missions, 1975–83, Dir of Evangelism, 1983–90, Church Army. Chm., African Pastors Trust, 1981–; Member: C of E Partnership for World Mission Cttee, 1990–; Portman House Trust, 1990–; Council, Evangelical Alliance, 1991–; C of E Board of Mission, 1997–. *Recreations:* theatre, music, travel, reading. *Address:* 28 Blackheath Grove, Blackheath, SE3 0DH. *T:* (020) 8297 2141. *Club:* Royal Commonwealth Society.

JOHN, Sir David (Glyndwr), KCMG 1999; Chairman, BOC Group, 1996–2002 (non-executive Director, 1993–2002); *b* 20 July 1938; *o s* of William Glyndwr John and Marjorie John (*née* Gaze); *m* 1964, Gillian Edwards; one *s* one *d. Educ:* Llandovery Coll., Dyfed; Christ's Coll., Cambridge (MA); Columbia Univ., NY (MBA); Harvard Univ. (SMP). 2nd Lieut, RA, 1957–59. United Steel Co., 1962–64; Rio Tinto Zinc Corp., 1966–73 (RTZ Consultants, Hardman & Holden); Redland plc, 1973–81 (Land Reclamation Co., Redland Indust. Services, Redland Purle); Inchcape, 1981–95; Main Bd Dir, 1988–95; Develt Dir, later Chief Exec., Gray Mackenzie & Co., Middle East, 1981–87; Chairman: Inchcape Bhd, Singapore, 1990–95 (Chief Exec., 1987–90); Inchcape Middle East, 1991–94; Inchcape Toyota, 1994–95; Premier Oil plc, 1998–. Non-executive Director: British Biotech plc, 1996–99; The St Paul Cos Inc., Minn, USA, 1996–; Balfour Beatty plc, 2000–. Dir, WDA, 2001–; Vice Chm., British Trade Internat., 1999–. Vice Pres. and Mem. Bd, POW Business Leaders Forum, 1996–99; Mem. President's Cttee, and Chm. Internat. Cttee, CBI, 1996–; Dir and Trustee, Council for Industry and Higher Educn, 1996–; Mem., Wilson Cttee on Export Promotion, 1998–99. Gov., SOAS, 1993–; Mem. Bd of Overseers, Columbia Business Sch., NY, 1996–; Trustee, Asia House, 2000–. CIMgt; FRSA. Freeman, City of London, 1997; Liveryman, Scientific Instrument Makers' Co., 1997–. *Recreations:* sailing, gardening, reading. *Address:* c/o HSBC Republic Bank (UK) Ltd, 31 Hill Street, W1J 5LS. *Clubs:* Oxford and Cambridge, Oriental.

JOHN, Dr David Thomas, (Dai), PhD; Vice Chancellor, University of Luton, since 1998; *b* 31 Oct. 1943; *s* of Trevor John and Violet Gwyneth; *m* 1966, Jennifer Christine Morris; one *s* two *d. Educ:* Univ. of London (BSc, PhD). *Educ:* Kingston Polytechnic, 1966–86: successively Asst Lectr, Lectr, Sen. Lectr, and Principal Lectr; Hd of Applied Sci. and Associate Dean of Sci.; Vice Principal, NE Surrey Coll. of Technology, 1987–89; Dep. Dir, Luton Coll. of Higher Educn, 1989–98. *Publications:* several books and chapters on geology and geomorphology; various sci. papers on Tertiary and Quaternary history of SE England and on soils. *Recreations:* music, reading, travel, squash, Rugby. *Address:* University of Luton, Park Square, Luton LU1 3JU; 1 Sturges Close, Walton Park, Milton Keynes MK7 7HJ. *T:* (01908) 675806.

JOHN, Sir Elton (Hercules), Kt 1998; CBE 1996; musician, composer; *b* 25 March 1947; *s* of Stanley Dwight and Sheila (now Farebrother); *né* Reginald Kenneth Dwight; changed name to Elton Hercules John; *m* 1984, Renate Blauel (marr. diss. 1988). *Educ:* Pinner County Grammar Sch.; Royal Acad. of Music, London. Played piano in Northwood Hills Hotel, 1964; joined local group, Bluesology, 1965; signed to Dick James Music as writer and singer, 1967; visited America for concert and was overnight success, 1970; formed Elton John Band, 1970; regularly tours America, Europe, Australia and Japan; first internat. pop singer to perform in Russia, 1979. Founder, Rocket Pictures, 1996. Vice-Pres. and Mem. Council, National Youth Theatre of GB, 1975–; Life Pres., Watford Football Club, 1990 (Dir, 1974; Chm., 1976–90 and 1997–); toured China with Watford Football Club, 1983. Founder and Pres., Elton John AIDS Foundn, 1993. Trustee, Wallace Collection, 1999–. *Hit Records include: albums:* Empty Sky, 1969; Elton John, Tumbleweed Connection, 1970; Friends, 11.17.70, Madman Across the Water, 1971; Honky Chateau, 1972; Don't Shoot Me, Goodbye Yellow Brick Road, 1973; Caribou, Greatest Hits, 1974; Captain Fantastic, Rock of the Westies, 1975; Here and There, Blue Moves, 1976; Greatest Hits vol. II, 1977; A Single Man, 1978; Victim of Love, 1979; 21 at 33, Lady Samantha, 1980; The Fox, 1981; Jump Up, 1982; Too Low for Zero, 1983; Breaking Hearts, 1984; Ice on Fire, 1985; Leather Jackets, 1986; Live in Australia, 1987; Reg Strikes Back, 1988; Sleeping with the Past, 1989; The Very Best of Elton John, 1990; Two Rooms, 1991; The One, 1992; Duets, 1993; The Lion King, 1994 (expanded into musical, 1997, Tony Award, 1998); Made in England, 1995; Love Songs, 1995; The Big Picture, 1997; Songs From the West Coast, 2001; *singles:* Your Song, 1971; Rocket Man, Crocodile Rock, 1972; Daniel, Goodbye Yellow Brick Road, 1973; Candle in the Wind, Don't Let the Sun Go Down On Me, The Bitch is Back, Lucy in the Sky with Diamonds, 1974; Philadelphia Freedom, Someone Saved My Life Tonight, 1975; Don't Go Breaking My Heart, Sorry Seems to be the Hardest Word, 1976; Ego, Part Time Love, Song for Guy, 1978; Little Jeannie, 1980; Nobody Wins, 1981; Blue Eyes, Empty Garden, Princess, 1982; I Guess that's Why They Call It the Blues, 1983; Sad Songs (Say So Much), Passengers, Who Wears These Shoes, 1984; Breaking Hearts, Act of War, Nikita, Wrap Her Up, 1985; Cry to Heaven, Heartache all over the World, Slow Rivers, 1986; Your Song (live), Candle in the Wind, (live) 1987, 1997; I Don't Wanna Go On With You Like That, 1988; Healing Hands, 1989; Sacrifice, 1990. *Films:* Goodbye to Norma Jean, 1973; To Russia with Elton, 1980; played Pinball Wizard, in Tommy, 1973. Hon. RAM 1997. Recipient of gold discs for all albums; Ivor Novello Awards, 1973, 1976, 1978, 1985 (twice), 1990, 1998 (twice). Brit Awards, 1991, 1995 and 1998; US Grammy Awards, 1991, 1998, 2000, 2001; Acad. Award for Best Original Song, 1995. Freedom of Nice, 1997; Freedom, Borough of Watford, 1998. *Recreations:* include playing tennis. *Address:* Twenty-First Artists, 1 Blythe Road, W14 0HG. *T:* (020) 7348 4800.

JOHN, Geoffrey Richards, CBE 1991; Chairman, Food From Britain, 1993–99; *b* 25 March 1934; *s* of Reginald and Mabel John; *m* 1961, Christine Merritt; two *d. Educ:* Bromsgrove School, Worcs; University College Cardiff (BA 1st cl. Hons Econs). Flying Officer, RAF, 1955–57; Cadbury Schweppes, 1957–74; Man. Dir, Spillers Foods, 1974–80; Chief Exec., Foods Div., Dalgety-Spillers, 1980–82; Chm. and Chief Exec., Allied Bakeries, 1982–87; Chm., Dairy Crest, 1988–94; Director: Associated British Foods, 1982–87; Frizzell Gp, 1991–92; Morland plc, 1993–99; NFU Services Ltd, 1999–. Mem., ARC, 1980–82; Chm., Meat and Livestock Commn, 1987–93. Dir, Hereford Hosps NHS Trust, 1994–99. Bromsgrove School: Pres., 1994–; Gov., 1965–94 (Chm.,

1982–91); Governor: Inst. of Grassland and Envmtl Res., 1996–98; Hereford Cathedral Sch., 1997–; Aston Univ., 1999–. *Recreations:* Rugby Football, music. *Address:* 15 Cantilupe Street, Hereford HR1 2NU. *Clubs:* Royal Air Force, Harlequin FC.

JOHN, Maldwyn Noel, FREng, FIEEE; Consultant, Kennedy & Donkin, 1994–97 (Chairman, 1987–94); *b* 25 Dec. 1929; *s* of Thomas Daniel John and Beatrice May John; *m* 1953, Margaret Cannell; two *s*. *Educ:* University College Cardiff. BSc 1st Cl. Hons, Elec. Eng. Metropolitan Vickers Elec. Co. Ltd, Manchester, 1950–59; Atomic Energy Authy, Winfrith, 1959–63; AEI/GEC, Manchester, as Chief Engineer, Systems Dept, Chief Engineer, Transformer Div., and Manager, AC Transmission Div., 1963–69; Chief Elec. Engineer, 1969–72, Partner, 1972–86, Kennedy & Donkin. President: IEE, 1983–84; Convention of Nat. Socs of Engineering of Western Europe, 1983–84; Dir Bd, Nat. Inspection Council for Electrical Installation Contractors, 1988–91; Mem., Overseas Projects Bd, 1987–91. FIEE 1969 (Hon. FIEE 1998); FREng (FEng 1979). Freeman, City of London, 1987. *Publications:* (jtly) Practical Diakoptics for Electrical Networks, 1969; (jtly) Power Circuit Breaker Theory and Design, 1975, 2nd edn 1982; papers in IEE Procs. *Recreation:* golf. *Address:* 65 Orchard Drive, Horsell, Woking, Surrey GU21 4BS. *T:* (01483) 825755.

JOHN, Stewart Morris, OBE 1992; FREng, FRAeS; Director, Aviation Exposure Management, since 1995; *b* 28 Nov. 1938; *s* of Ivor Morgan John and Lilian John; *m* 1961, Susan Anne Cody; one *s* one *d*. *Educ:* Porth Co. Grammar Sch.; N Staffs Tech. Coll.; Southall Tech. Coll. CEng 1977; FREng (FEng 1990); FRAeS 1977. BOAC: apprentice, 1955–60; on secondment to: Kuwait Airways, 1960–63; Malaysia-Singapore Airlines, as Chief Engr, Borneo, 1963–67; Develt Engr, 1967–70; Workshop Superintendent/Manager, 1970–73; Manager Maintenance, American Aircraft Fleet, 1973–77; Cathay Pacific Airways: Dep. Dir, Engrg, Hong Kong, 1977–80; Engrg Dir (Main Bd Mem.), 1980–94; Dep. Chm., Hong Kong Aircraft Engrg Co., 1982–94; Director: Taikoo Aircraft Engrg Co., Xiamen, China, 1992–; Rolls-Royce Commercial Aero Engines Ltd, 1994–98; British Aerospace Aviation Services, 1994–98; British Midland Aviation Services, 1995–2000; Hong Kong Aero Engine Services Ltd, 1996–98. President: Internat. Fedn of Airworthiness, 1993–96; RAeS, 1997–98. Trustee, Brooklands Mus., 1994–. FHKIE 1986. FRSA 1994; FInstD 1995. Mem., GAPAN, 1996–. *Recreations:* golf, classic cars, Rugby. *Address:* The Hollies, Pyle Hill, Mayford, Woking, Surrey GU22 0SR. *T:* (01483) 747465. *Clubs:* Burhill Golf; Hong Kong, Aviation, Shek O Golf (Hong Kong).

JOHN CHARLES, Rt Rev. Brother; *see* Vockler, Rt Rev. J. C.

JOHN PAUL II, His Holiness Pope, (Karol Jozef Wojtyla); *b* Wadowice, Poland, 18 May 1920; *s* of Karol Wojtyla. *Educ:* Jagiellonian Univ., Cracow; Pontificio Ateneo 'Angelicum' (Dr in Theology). Ordained Priest, 1946; Prof. of Moral Theology, Univs of Lublin and Cracow, 1954–58; titular Bishop of Ombi, and Auxiliary Bishop of Cracow, 1958; Vicar Capitular, 1962; Archbishop and Metropolitan of Cracow, 1964–78. Cardinal, 1967; elected Pope, 16 Oct. 1978. Formerly Member, Congregations Pro Institutione Catholica, Pro Sacramentis et Cultu Divino, and Pro Clero. *Publications:* The Goldsmith Shop (play), 1960; Love and Responsibility, 1962; Person and Act, 1969; The Foundations of Renewal, 1972; Sign of Contradiction, 1976; The Future of the Church, 1979; Easter Vigil and other poems, 1979; Collected Poems (trans. Jerzy Peterkiewicz), 1982; Crossing the Threshold of Hope (essays), 1994; The Place Within (trans. Jerzy Peterkiewicz), 1995; Gift and Mystery (autobiog.), 1996; Agenda for the Third Millennium, 1999. *Address:* Apostolic Palace, 00120 Vatican City.

JOHNS, Prof. David John, CBE 1998; FREng; Chairman, Prescription Pricing Authority, since 1998; *b* 29 April 1931. *Educ:* Univ. of Bristol (BSc Eng, MSc Eng, Aeronautical Engineering); Loughborough Univ. of Technology (PhD, DSc). FREng (FEng 1990); FRAeS, FAeSI, FHKIE. Bristol Aeroplane Co., 1950–57 (section leader); Project Officer, Sir W. G. Armstrong Whitworth Co., 1957–58; Lectr, Cranfield Inst. of Technology, 1958–63; Loughborough University of Technology: Reader, 1964–68; Prof. in Transport Technology, 1968–83; Senior Pro-Vice-Chancellor, 1982–83; (Foundation) Dir, City Polytechnic of Hong Kong, 1983–89; Vice-Chancellor and Principal, Univ. of Bradford, 1989–98. Dir, British Bd of Agrément, 1998–. Hon. Chm., Professional Develt Gp, RAeS, 1998–. Unofficial JP Hong Kong, 1987–89. *Publications:* Thermal Stress Analyses, 1965; contribs to learned jls. *Recreations:* bridge, theatre, music. *Fax:* (01423) 502561. *Clubs:* Athenæum; Hong Kong; Hong Kong Jockey.

JOHNS, Glynis; actress; *b* Pretoria, South Africa; *d* of late Mervyn Johns and Alice Maude (*née* Steel-Payne); *m* 1st, Anthony Forwood (marr. diss.); one *s*; 2nd, David Foster, DSO, DSC and Bar (marr. diss.); 3rd, Cecil Peter Lamont Henderson; 4th, Elliott Arnold. *Educ:* Clifton and Hampstead High Schs. First stage appearance in Buckie's Bears as a child ballerina, Garrick Theatre, London, 1935. Parts include: Sonia in Judgement Day, Embassy and Strand, 1937; Miranda in Quiet Wedding, Wyndham's, 1938 and in Quiet Weekend, Wyndham's, 1941; Peter in Peter Pan, Cambridge Theatre, 1943; Fools Rush In, Fortune; The Way Things Go, Phœnix, 1950; Gertie (title role), NY, 1952; Major Barbara (title role), NY, 1957; The Patient in Too True to Be Good, NY, 1962; The King's Mare, Garrick, 1966; Come as You Are, New, 1970; A Little Night Music, New York, 1973 (Tony award for best musical actress); Ring Round the Moon, Los Angeles, 1975; 13 Rue de l'Amour, Phœnix, 1976; Cause Célèbre, Her Majesty's, 1977 (Best Actress Award, Variety Club); Hayfever, UK; The Boy Friend, Toronto; The Circle, NY, 1989–90. Entered films as a child. *Films include:* South Riding, 49th Parallel, Frieda, An Ideal Husband, Miranda (the Mermaid), State Secret, No Highway, The Magic Box, Appointment with Venus, Encore, The Card, Sword and the Rose, Personal Affair, Rob Roy, The Weak and the Wicked, The Beachcomber, The Seekers, Poppa's Delicate Condition, Cabinet of Dr Caligari, Mad About Men, Josephine and Men, The Court Jester, Loser Takes All, The Chapman Report, Dear Bridget, Mary Poppins, Zelly and Me, Nuki, While You Were Sleeping. Also broadcasts; television programmes include: Star Quality; The Parkinson Show (singing Send in the Clowns); Mrs Amworth (USA); All You Need is Love; Across a Crowded Room; Little Gloria, Happy at Last; Sprague; Love Boat; Murder She Wrote; The Cavanaughs; starring role, Coming of Age (series). *Address:* c/o A. Morgan Maree, Jr, and Associates, Inc., 4727 Wilshire Boulevard, Suite 600, Los Angeles, CA 90010, USA.

JOHNS, Jasper; painter; *b* 15 May 1930; *s* of Jasper Johns and Jean Riley. *Educ:* Univ. of South Carolina. Works in collections of Tate Gall., NY Mus. of Modern Art, Buffalo, Cologne, Washington, Amsterdam, Stockholm, Dallas, Chicago, Baltimore, Basle, Cleveland, Minneapolis; one-man exhibitions principally in Leo Castelli Gallery, NY; others in UK, USA, Canada, France, Germany, Italy, Japan, Switzerland; retrospective exhibn, NY Mus. of Modern Art, 1996. Hon. RA; Mem., Amer. Acad. of Arts and Letters (Gold Medal, 1986); Pittsburgh Internat. Prize, 1958; Wolf Foundn Prize, 1986; Venice Biennale, 1988; Nat. Medal of Arts, 1990; Praemium Imperiale Award, Japan, 1993. Officier, Ordre des Arts et des Lettres (France), 1990. *Address:* c/o Leo Castelli Gallery, 59 East 79th Street, New York, NY 10021, USA.

JOHNS, Michael Alan, CB 2000; Chief Executive, Valuation Office Agency and a Commissioner of Inland Revenue, since 1997; *b* 20 July 1946; *s* of John and Kathleen Johns. *Educ:* Judd School, Tonbridge; Queens' College, Cambridge (MA Hist.). Inland Revenue, 1967–79; Central Policy Review Staff, 1979–80; Inland Revenue, 1980–84; seconded to Orion Royal Bank, 1985; Inland Revenue, 1986–; Under Sec., 1987; Dir, Oil and Financial Div., 1988–91; Dir, Central Div., 1991–93; Dir, Business Ops Div., 1993–97. Treasurer, Working Men's College, 1986–90. *Recreations:* ski-ing, teaching adults, moral philosophy. *Address:* Valuation Office Agency, New Court, Carey Street, WC2A 2JE.

JOHNS, Rev. Patricia Holly, MA; Non-stipendiary Curate, Marlborough Team Ministry, 1994–99; Priest in charge, Mildenhall, Marlborough, 1996–99; *b* 13 Nov. 1933; *d* of William and Violet Harris; *m* 1958, Michael Charles Bedford Johns (*d* 1965), MA; one *s* one *d*. *Educ:* Blackheath High Sch.; Girton Coll., Cambridge (BA 1956, MA 1959, CertEd with distinction 1957). Asst Maths Mistress; Cheltenham Ladies' Coll., 1957–58; Macclesfield Girls' High Sch., 1958–60; Asst Maths Mistress, then Head of Maths and Dir of Studies, St Albans High Sch., 1966–75; Sen. Mistress, and Housemistress of Hopeman House, Gordonstoun, 1975–80; Headmistress, St Mary's Sch., Wantage, 1980–94. Ordained deacon, 1990, priest, 1994. *Recreations:* choral singing, walking, travel. *Address:* Flat 1, Priory Lodge, 93 Brown Street, Salisbury, Wilts SP1 2BX. *T:* (01722) 328007.

JOHNS, Paul; management consultant, since 1994; Chief Executive, Fairtrade Foundation, 1992–94; *b* 13 March 1934; *s* of Alfred Thomas Johns and Margherita Johns; *m* 1st, 1956, Ruth Thomas (marr. diss. 1973); two *s* one *d*; 2nd, 1984, Margaret Perry. *Educ:* Kingswood School, Bath; Oriel College, Oxford (MA Hons Modern Hist.). Personnel Management, Dunlop Rubber Co., 1958–63 and Northern Foods Ltd, 1963–68; Senior Partner, Urwick Orr & Partners, 1968–83; Dir, Profile Consulting, 1983–89; Man. Dir, Traidcraft, 1988–91. Chairperson, 1985–87, Vice-Chairperson, 1987–88, CND. Consultant: to FA Premier League, 1994–; to humanitarian aid projects in Bosnia, 1994–. Lay preacher, Methodist Church; contrib. to Thought for the Day, BBC Radio 4. *Recreations:* photography, listening to music, watching football (keen supporter of Nottingham Forest). *Address:* 33 Burleigh Road, West Bridgford, Nottingham NG2 6FP.

JOHNS, Air Chief Marshal Sir Richard (Edward), GCB 1997 (KCB 1994; CB 1991); CBE 1985 (OBE 1978); LVO 1972; FRAeS; Constable and Governor of Windsor Castle, since 2000; *b* Horsham, 28 July 1939; *s* of late Lt-Col Herbert Edward Johns, RM and of Marjory Harley Johns (*née* Everett); *m* 1965, Elizabeth Naomi Anne Manning; one *s* two *d*. *Educ:* Portsmouth Grammar Sch.; RAF College, Cranwell. FRAeS 1997. Commissioned 1959; Night Fighter and Fighter/Reconnaissance Sqns, UK, Cyprus, Aden, 1960–67; Flying Instructional duties, 1968–71; Flying Instructor to Prince of Wales, 1970–71; OC 3 (Fighter) Sqn (Harrier), 1975–77; Dir, Air Staff Briefing, 1979–81; Station Comdr and Harrier Force Comdr, RAF Gütersloh, 1982–84; ADC to the Queen, 1983–84; RCDS 1985; SASO, HQ RAF Germany, 1985–88; SASO, HQ Strike Comd, 1989–91; AOC No 1 Gp, 1991–93; COS and Dep. C-in-C, Strike Comd and UK Air Forces, 1993–94; AOC-in-C Strike Comd, 1994; C-in-C, Allied Forces NW Europe, 1994–97; Chief of Air Staff, 1997–2000; Air ADC to the Queen, 1997–2000. Hon. Col, 73 Engr Regt (V), 1994–; Hon. Air Cdre, RAF Regt, 2000–. Freeman, City of London, 1999; Liveryman, GAPAN, 1999–. *Recreations:* military history, Rugby, cricket, equitation. *Address:* Windsor Castle, Windsor, Berks SL4 1NJ. *T:* (01753) 868286. *Club:* Royal Air Force.

JOHNSON, Alan Arthur; MP (Lab) Kingston-upon-Hull West and Hessle, since 1997; Minister of State, Department of Trade and Industry, since 2001; *b* 17 May 1950; *s* of late Lillian May and Stephen Arthur Johnson; *m* 1st, 1968, Judith Elizabeth Cox (marr. diss.); one *s* one d (and one *d* decd); 2nd, 1991, Laura Jane Patient; one *s*. *Educ:* Sloane Grammar School, Chelsea. Postman, 1968; UCW Branch Official, 1976; UCW Exec. Council, 1981; UCW National Officer, 1987–93; Gen. Sec., UCW, 1993–95; Jt Gen. Sec., CWU, 1995–97. PPS to Financial Sec. to the Treasury, 1997–99, to Paymaster General, 1999; Parly Under-Sec. of State, DTI, 1999–2001. Mem., Trade and Industry Select Cttee, 1997. Mem. Gen. Council, TUC, 1994–95; Exec. Mem., Postal, Telegraph and Telephone Internat., 1994–97; Mem., Labour Party NEC, 1995–97; Dir, Unity Trust Bank plc. Duke of Edinburgh Commonwealth Study Conf., 1992. Gov., Ruskin Coll., 1992–97. *Recreations:* music, tennis, reading, football, cookery, radio. *Address:* House of Commons, SW1A 0AA.

JOHNSON, Air Vice-Marshal Alan Taylor, FRAeS; Director of Occupational Health, Metropolitan Police, 1991–95; *b* 3 March 1931; *s* of Percy and Janet Johnson; *m* 1954, Margaret Ellen Mee; two *s* three *d* (and one *s* decd). *Educ:* Mexborough Grammar Sch.; Univ. of Sheffield (MB, ChB); DAvMed; FFOM, MFCM. Commnd RAF, 1957; MO, RAF Gaydon, 1957–59; Princess Mary's RAF Hosp., Akrotiri, Cyprus, 1959–61; No 1 Parachute Trng Sch., RAF Abingdon, 1961–65; RAF Changi, Singapore, 1965–67; RAF Inst. of Aviation Medicine, 1967–71; RAF Bruggen, Germany, 1971–74; Med. SO (Air) HQ RAF Support Comd, 1974–77; RAF Brize Norton, 1977–78; Chief of Aerospace Medicine HQ SAC Offutt AFB, USA, 1978–81; Dep. Dir of Health and Res. (Aviation Medicine), 1981–84; OC Princess Alexandra Hosp., RAF Wroughton, 1984–86; Asst Surg.-Gen. (Environmental Medicine and Res.), MoD, 1986; PMO, HQ RAF, Germany, 1986–88; PMO, HQ Strike Comd, RAF High Wycombe, 1988–91; retired. QHS 1986–91. OStJ 1976. *Recreations:* sport parachuting, music, cricket. *Address:* Hoo Cottage, School Lane, Buckden, St Neots, Cambs PE19 5TT. *Club:* Royal Air Force.

JOHNSON, (Alexander) Boris (de Pfeffel); MP (C) Henley, since 2001; Editor, The Spectator, since 1999; *b* 19 June 1964; *s* of Stanley Patrick Johnson, *qv* and Charlotte Johnson (*née* Fawcett); *m* 1993, Marina Wheeler; two *s* two *d*. *Educ:* Eton (King's Schol.); Balliol Coll., Oxford (Brackenbury Schol.; Pres., Oxford Union). LEK Partnership, one week, 1987; The Times, 1987–88; Daily Telegraph, 1988–99: EC Correspondent, 1989–94; Asst Ed. and Chief Pol Columnist, 1994–99. Commentator of the Year, What the Papers Say awards, 1997. *Publication:* Friends, Voters, Countrymen, 2001. *Recreation:* painting. *Address:* The Spectator, 56 Doughty Street, WC1N 2LL; House of Commons, SW1A 0AA. *Club:* Beefsteak.

JOHNSON, Prof. Anne Mandall, MD; FFPHM; Professor of Epidemiology, Royal Free and University College Medical School, University College London (formerly University College London Medical School), since 1996; *b* 30 Jan. 1954; *d* of Gordon Trevor Johnson and Helen Margaret Johnson; *m* 1996, John Martin Watson; one *s* one *d*. *Educ:* Newnham Coll., Cambridge (BA 1974; MA 1979; Associate, 1996–); Univ. of Newcastle upon Tyne (MB BS 1978; MD with commendation 1992); LSHTM (MSc 1984); MRCGP 1982; FFPHM 1993. House Officer, Newcastle upon Tyne, 1978–79; Sen. House Officer, vocational trng in Gen. Practice, Northumbria, 1979–83; Registrar in Community Medicine, NE Thames RHA, 1983–84; Lectr, Middlesex Hosp. Med. Sch., 1985–88; University College London Medical School: Sen. Lectr in Epidemiology and Hon. Consultant in Public Health Medicine, 1988–94; Reader in Epidemiology, 1994–96. Hon. Sen. Lectr, 1990–99, Vis. Prof., 1999–, LSHTM; Hon. Consultant in Public Health

Medicine, Camden and Islington NHS Trust, 1995–. Dir, MRC UK Co-ordinating Centre for Epidemiol Study of HIV and AIDS, 1989–99. Chm., Prison Health Res. Ethics Cttee, 1999– (Mem., 1996–); Member: Council, Inst. of Drug Dependency, London, 1990–98; MRC Adv. Bd, 1998–. Vis. Scholar, Univ. of Sydney, 1998. Editor, AIDS, 1994–2000. Hon. MRCP 1998. *Publications:* (jtly) Sexual Attitudes and Lifestyles, 1994; Sexual Behaviour in Britain, 1994; articles on HIV/AIDS and sexually transmitted diseases. *Recreation:* singing. *Address:* Centre for Infectious Disease Epidemiology, Royal Free and University College Medical School, Mortimer Market Centre, Mortimer Market, off Capper Street, WC1E 6AU. *T:* (020) 7380 9878.

JOHNSON, Anne Montgomery; Market Research, Harris Research Centre, 1983–92; *b* 12 June 1922; *y c* of late Frederick Harold Johnson and late Gertrude Le Quesne (*née* Martin). *Educ:* St John's, Bexhill-on-Sea; Queen Elizabeth Hosp. (SRN); Brompton Hosp. (BTA Hons); Simpson Memorial Maternity Pavilion, Edinburgh (SCM). Asst Matron, Harefield Hosp., 1956–59; Dep. Matron, St Mary's Hosp., Paddington, 1959–62; Matron, Guy's Hosp., 1962–68; Mem. Directing and Tutorial Staff, King Edward's Hosp. Fund for London, 1968–71; Regional Dir, Help the Aged, 1971–73; Matron, The Royal Star and Garter Home for Disabled Sailors, Soldiers and Airmen, 1975–82. Member: King's Fund Working Party, 'The Shape of Hospital Management 1980', 1966–67 (report publd 1967); Jt Cttee of Gen. Synod Working Party 'The Hospital Chaplain' (report publd 1974); Hosp. Chaplaincies Council, 1963–81; Nursing Cttee, Assoc. of Indep. Hosps, 1978–83. Gov., Orleans Park Sch., Twickenham, 1988–97. *Recreations:* straight theatre, travel. *Address:* Flat 5, 6 Cardigan Road, Richmond-on-Thames, Surrey TW10 6BJ.

JOHNSON, WO1 Barry, GC 1990; RAOC; Warrant Officer 1 (Staff Sergeant Major), 1986, retired 1992; *b* 25 Jan. 1952; *s* of Charles William Johnson and Joyce Johnson; *m* 1971, Linda Maria Lane; one *s* one *d*. Mem., Inst. of Explosives Engineers. Army Apprentices College, Chepstow, 1967; Royal Army Ordnance Corps, 1970; served in UK, BAOR, NI, Canada and Belize. *Club:* Victoria Cross and George Cross Association.

JOHNSON, Prof. Barry Edward, PhD; FRS 1978; Professor of Pure Mathematics, University of Newcastle upon Tyne, since 1969; *b* 1 Aug. 1937; *s* of Edward Johnson and Evelyn May (*née* Bailey); *m* 1st (marr. diss. 1979); two *s* one *d*; 2nd, 1990, Margaret Jones (*née* Brown). *Educ:* Epsom County Grammar Sch.; Hobart State High Sch.; Univ. of Tasmania (BSc 1956); Cambridge Univ. (PhD 1961). Instr, Univ. of Calif, Berkeley, 1961–62; Vis. Lectr, Yale Univ., 1962–63; Lectr, Exeter Univ., 1963–65; University of Newcastle upon Tyne: Lectr, 1965–68; Reader, 1968–69; Head of Dept of Pure Maths, 1976–83; Head of Sch. of Maths, 1983–86; Dean, Faculty of Sci., 1986–89. Vis. Prof., Yale Univ., 1970–71. Auditor, HEQC, 1993–. Mem., London Math. Soc. (Mem. Council, 1975–78; Pres., 1980–82). *Publications:* Cohomology of Banach Algebras, 1972; papers in Jl of London Math. Soc. and Amer. Jl of Maths. *Recreations:* reading, travel. *Address:* 63 Montagu Court, Gosforth, Newcastle upon Tyne NE3 4JL. *T:* (0191) 213 1013.

JOHNSON, Boris; *see* Johnson, A. B. de P.

JOHNSON, Brian; *see* Johnson, R. B.

JOHNSON, Prof. Brian Frederick Gilbert, PhD; FRS 1991; Professor of Inorganic Chemistry, University of Cambridge, since 1995; Master of Fitzwilliam College, Cambridge, since 1999; *b* 11 Sept. 1938; *s* of Frank and Mona Johnson; *m* 1962, Christine Draper; two *d*. *Educ:* Northampton Grammar Sch.; Univ. of Nottingham (BSc, PhD). Lecturer: Univ. of Manchester, 1965–67; UCL, 1967–70; Cambridge University: Lectr, 1970–78; Reader, 1978–90; Fitzwilliam College: Fellow, 1970–90, and 1995–99; Pres., 1988–89; Vice Master, 1989–90; Crum Brown Prof. of Inorganic Chem., Univ. of Edinburgh, 1991–95. Mem., EPSRC, 1994–99 (Chm., Public Understanding of Sci., Engrg and Technol. Steering Gp, 1998–). *Publication:* Transition Metal Clusters, 1982. *Recreations:* chemistry, walking, cycling, travel. *Address:* Department of Chemistry, Lensfield Road, Cambridge CB2 1EW; Master's Lodge, Fitzwilliam College, Cambridge CB3 0DG.

JOHNSON, Bruce Joseph F.; *see* Forsyth-Johnson.

JOHNSON, Charles Ernest; JP; Councillor (Lab), Salford, since 1986; *b* 2 Jan. 1918; adopted *s* of Henry and Mary Johnson; *m* 1942, Betty, *d* of William Nelson Hesford, farmer; one *s*. *Educ:* elementary school. Commenced work as apprentice coppersmith, 1932; called up to Royal Navy, 1940, demobilised, 1946. Councillor and Alderman, Eccles Town Council, 1952–73; Mayor, 1964–65; Chm. of various cttees, incl. Housing, for 14 years, and of Local Employment Cttee, for ten years; Councillor, Greater Manchester County Council, 1974–86 (Chairman, 1982–83). Mem., Police Authy, Gtr Manchester, 1986–88. Mem., Assoc. of Municipal Councils, 1958–. JP Eccles, 1965. 1939–45 Medal, Atlantic Medal, Africa Star, Victory Medal; Imperial Service Medal, 1978. *Recreations:* gardening, watching football, swimming. *Address:* 17 Dartford Avenue, Winton, Eccles, Manchester M30 8NF. *T:* (0161) 789 4229.

JOHNSON, Christopher Edmund; Director General, Defence Accounts, Ministry of Defence, 1984–89; *b* 17 Jan. 1934; *s* of late Christopher and Phyllis Johnson; *m* 1956, Janet Yvonne Wakefield; eight *s* three *d*. *Educ:* Salesian Coll., Chertsey; Collyer's Sch., Horsham. Sub Lt, RNVR, 1952–54. Exec. Officer, 1954–58, Higher Exec. Officer, 1959–65, War Office; Principal, MoD, 1965–71; UK Jt Comd Sec., ANZUK Force, Singapore, 1971–74; Ministry of Defence: Asst Sec., 1974–84; Asst Under Sec. of State, 1984. *Recreations:* gardening, reading. *Address:* Rohannon Farm, Weston, Bath, Avon BA1 4EY. *T:* (01225) 314247.

JOHNSON, Daniel, PhD; Counsel, McCarthy Tétrault, Barristers and Solicitors, since 1998; Chairman, Geneka Biotechnology Inc., since 1999; *b* Montreal, 24 Dec. 1944; *s* of Daniel Johnson (Premier of Quebec, 1966–68) and Reine (*née* Gagne); *m* 1993, Suzanne Marcil; one *s* one *d* from former marriage. *Educ:* Stanislas Coll., Montreal; Saint-Laurent Coll. (BA Univ. of Montreal); Univ. of Montreal (LLL); University Coll. London (LLM, PhD); Harvard Business Sch. (MBA). A lawyer. Corp. Sec., 1973–81, Vice-Pres., 1978–81, Power Corp. of Canada. Director: Great-West Life Assce Co., 1999–; Bombardier Inc., 1999–; Investors Gp, 1999–; Ecopia BioSciences Inc., 2000–. Mem. (L) Vaudreuil, Quebec Nat. Assembly, 1981–98; Minister of Industry and Commerce, 1985–88; Dep. House Leader, 1985–94; Pres., Treasury Bd and Minister responsible for Admin, 1988–89; Minister reponsible for Admin and CS and Chm., Treasury Bd, 1989–94; Prime Minister and Pres. Exec. Council, Jan.–Sept. 1994; Leader of Official Opposition, 1994–98. Leader, Quebec Liberal Party, 1993–98. *Address:* (office) Le Windsor, 1170 Peel Street, Montreal, QC H3B 4S8, Canada.

JOHNSON, Daniel Benedict; columnist and Associate Editor (Culture), The Daily Telegraph, since 1998; *b* 26 Aug. 1957; *s* of Paul Johnson, *qv* and Marigold Johnson, MBE (*née* Hunt); *m* 1988, Sarah Thompson, *d* of J. W. M. Thompson, *qv*; two *s* two *d*. *Educ:* Langley Grammar Sch.; Magdalen Coll., Oxford (BA 1st Cl. Hons Hist.). Res. Student, Peterhouse, Cambridge, 1978–81; Shakespeare Scholar, Berlin, 1979–80; taught German hist., QMC, 1982–84; Dir of Pubns, Centre for Policy Studies, 1983–84; Daily Telegraph: Leader Writer, 1986–87; Bonn Corresp., 1987–89; Eastern Europe Corresp., 1989; The Times: Leader Writer, 1990–91; Literary Editor, 1991–95; an Asst Editor, 1995–98. *Publications:* co-edited: German Neo-Liberals and the Social Market Economy, 1989; Thomas Mann: Death in Venice and other stories, 1991; Collected Stories, 2001; contrib. to New Yorker, NY Times, Wall St Jl, Washington Post, Civilisation, Commentary, Nat. Interest, Spectator, TLS, Lit. Review, Prospect, and other jls. *Recreation:* chess. *Address:* The Daily Telegraph, 1 Canada Square, E14 5DT; 46 Aldbourne Road, W12 0LN. *T:* (020) 8743 4995.

See also L. O. Johnson.

JOHNSON, Darren Paul; Member (Green), London Assembly, Greater London Authority, since 2000; Environment Advisor to Mayor of London, since 2000; *b* 20 May 1966; *s* of Alan Johnson and Joyce Johnson (*née* Abram, now Reynolds). *Educ:* Goldsmiths' Coll., Univ. of London (BA 1st Cl. Hons Politics and Econs 1997). Finance and admin posts, 1987–93. Mem., Green Party, 1987–; Elections Co-ordinator, Nat. Exec., 1993–95. *Recreations:* walking, cycling. *Address:* Greater London Authority, Romney House, 43 Marsham Street, SW1P 3PY. *T:* (020) 7983 4406.

JOHNSON, David Bryan; Chief Executive, Leeds Teaching Hospitals NHS Trust, since 1998; *b* 27 Feb. 1957; *s* of Audrey and Bernard Johnson; *m* 1980, Gillian Pobgee; one *s*. *Educ:* Sheffield Univ. (BA Hons Politics 1978). Nat. Management Trainee, NHS, 1980–83; Asst, then Dep. Administrator, Manchester Royal Infirmary, 1983–85; Unit Gen. Manager, Pontefract HA Acute and Maternity Services, 1985–90; Dir of Ops, 1990–92, Acting Chief Exec., Feb.–May 1992, St James's Univ. Hosp.; Chief Exec., St James's and Seacroft Univ. Hosps NHS Trust, 1992–98. *Recreations:* golf, swimming, football, cycling, travel. *Address:* Woodthorpe, 40 Thorp Arch Park, Thorp Arch, Wetherby, W Yorks LS23 7AN.

JOHNSON, David Burnham; QC 1978; a Recorder, 1984–98; *b* 6 Aug. 1930; *s* of late Thomas Burnham Johnson and of Elsie May Johnson; *m* 1968, Julia Clare Addison Hopkinson, *o d* of late Col H. S. P. Hopkinson, OBE; one *s* three *d*. *Educ:* Truro Sch.; Univ. of Wales. Solicitor and Notary Public, Oct. 1952. Commissioned, National Service, with Royal Artillery, 1952–54. Private practice as solicitor, Cardiff and Plymouth, 1954–67; called to Bar, Inner Temple, 1967, Bencher, 1985. *Recreations:* sailing, walking, shooting, reading, music. *Address:* 25 Murray Road, Wimbledon, SW19 4PD. *T:* (020) 8947 9188; (chambers) 20 Essex Street, WC2R 3AL. *T:* (020) 7583 9294. *Clubs:* Lansdowne; Royal Western Yacht (Plymouth).

JOHNSON, David Robert W.; *see* Wilson-Johnson.

JOHNSON, Donald Edwin, RIBA, FRTPI; Under Secretary, 1978–80, and Deputy Chief Planner, 1975–80, Department of the Environment; *b* 4 July 1920; *s* of Henry William Johnson and Ann Catherine (*née* Lake); *m* 1947, Thérèse Andrée Simone Marquant; two *s* one *d*. *Educ:* Haberdashers' Aske's, Hatcham; School of Architecture, Regent Polytechnic; APRR School of Planning. Served War, Royal Artillery and Royal Engineers, 1940–45. Planning Officer, Min. of Town and Country Planning, 1947; Sen. Planning Officer, 1950, Principal Planner, 1965, Asst Chief Planner, 1972. *Publications: fiction:* Project 38, 1963; Crooked Cross, 1964; Flashing Mountain, 1965; Devil of Bruges, 1966. *Address:* Flat D, 1 Morpeth Terrace, SW1P 1EW. *T:* (020) 7834 7300.

JOHNSON, Prof. Douglas William John; Professor of French History, University College London, 1968–90, now Emeritus; Visiting Professor, French Department, King's College, London, since 1993; *b* Edinburgh, 1 Feb. 1925; *o s* of John Thornburn Johnson and Christine Douglas Mair; *m* 1950, Madeleine Rébillard; one *d*. *Educ:* Royal Grammar Sch., Lancaster; Worcester Coll., Oxford (BA, BLitt); Ecole Normale Supérieure, Paris. Birmingham Univ.: Lectr in Modern History, 1949; Prof. of Modern History and Chm. of Sch. of History, 1963–68; Head of Dept of History, 1979–83, Dean, Faculty of Arts, 1979–82, UCL. Vis. Prof., Univs of Aix-en-Provence, Nancy, Paris, British Columbia, Toronto, Caen, Lyons, Montreal, Texas; Lectures: Zaharoff, Oxford Univ., 1989; Simon Cohen Meml, Kent Univ., 1990; Creighton, London Univ., 1991; Stenton, Reading Univ., 1995; Centenary, Univ. of Aston, 1996. Chm. Bd of Examrs in History, Univ. of London, 1973–75; Member: CNAA, 1974–79; Franco-British Council, 1976–; Scientific Council, Fondation Charles de Gaulle, 1993–. FRHistS. Hon. DSc Aston, 1996. Ordre Nat. du Mérite (France), 1980; Commandeur des Palmes Académiques (France), 1987; Officier de la Légion d'Honneur (France), 1997 (Chevalier, 1990). *Publications:* Guizot: Aspects of French History 1787–1874, 1963; France and the Dreyfus Affair, 1966; France, 1969; Concise History of France, 1970; The French Revolution, 1970; (ed) French Society and the Revolution, 1976; (ed jtly) Britain and France: Ten Centuries, 1980; (with Richard Hoggart) An Idea of Europe, 1987; (with Madeleine Johnson) The Age of Illusion, 1987; (with Geoffrey Best) The Permanent Revolution, 1988; Michelet and the French Revolution, 1990; How European are the French?, 1996; (ed. with Anne Corbett) A Day in June: Britain and de Gaulle 1940, 2001; (General Editor) The Making of the Modern World; (General Editor) The Fontana History of Modern France. *Recreations:* music, French politics. *Address:* 29 Rudall Crescent, NW3 1RR; 12 rue Delambre, Paris 75014, France. *Club:* Travellers.

JOHNSON, Emma Louise, MBE 1996; solo clarinettist; *b* 20 May 1966; *d* of Roger and Mary Johnson; *m* 1997, Chris West; (one *s* decd). *Educ:* Newstead Wood Sch.; Sevenoaks Sch.; Pembroke Coll., Cambridge (MA English Lit. and Music 1992). Concerts and tours in Europe, USA, Far East, Australia and Africa; guest appearances with major orchestras world-wide; compositions commnd from several leading British composers. Dir, chamber music gp; Prof. of Clarinet, RCM, 1997–. Numerous recordings, including the concertos of Mozart, Crusell, Weber, Finzi, Arnold and Berkeley; four recital discs. Winner, BBC Young Musicians, 1984; Bronze Medal, Eurovision Young Musicians Competition, 1984; Winner, Young Concert Artists Auditions, NY, 1991. *Publication:* "Encore!": compositions and transcriptions for clarinet and piano, 1994. *Recreations:* theatre, literature, art, gardening, bird watching, travel. *Address:* Christa Phelps Artist Management, 6 Malvern Road, E8 3LT. *T:* (020) 7254 1006.

JOHNSON, Prof. Francis Rea; Professor of Anatomy, London Hospital Medical College, 1968–86, now Emeritus; Pre-clinical Sub-Dean, 1979–86; *b* 8 July 1921; *s* of Marcus Jervis Johnson and Elizabeth Johnson; *m* 1951, Ena Patricia Laverty; one *s* one *d*. *Educ:* Omagh Academy, N Ire.; Queen's Univ., Belfast. MB, BCh, BAO 1945, MD 1949. House appts, Belfast City Hosp., 1946; Demonstrator in Anatomy and Physiology, QUB, 1947–50; Lectr in Anatomy, Sheffield Univ., 1950–57; Reader in Anatomy, London Hosp. Med. Coll., 1957–64; Prof. of Histology, London Hosp. Med. Coll., 1964–68. *Publications:* papers on histochemistry and ultrastructure of tissues and organs in various jls. *Recreations:* motoring, camping, gardening. *Address:* 11 Beacon Rise, Sevenoaks, Kent TN13 2NJ. *T:* (01732) 453343.

JOHNSON, Frank Robert; Parliamentary Sketch Writer, The Daily Telegraph, since 2000; *b* 20 Jan. 1943; *s* of late Ernest Johnson, pastry cook and confectioner, and Doreen (*née* Skinner); *m* 1998, Virginia, *widow* of Hon. Simon Fraser, Master of Lovat; two step *s* two step *d. Educ:* Chartesey Secondary Sch., Shoreditch; Shoreditch Secondary Sch. Messenger Boy, Sunday Express, 1959–60; Reporter on local and regional newspapers, 1960–69; Political Staff, Sun, 1969–72; Parly Sketch Writer and Leader Writer, Daily Telegraph, 1972–79; Columnist, Now! Magazine, 1979–81; The Times: Parly Sketch Writer, 1981–83; Paris Diarist, 1984; Bonn Corresp., 1985–86; Parly Sketch Writer, 1986–87; Associate Editor, 1987–88; The Sunday Telegraph: Associate Editor, 1988–93; Dep. Editor (Comment), 1993–94; Dep. Editor, 1994–95; Editor, The Spectator, 1995–99. Parly Sketch Writer of the Year Award, Granada, What The Papers Say, 1977; Columnist of the Year, British Press Awards, 1981. *Publications:* Out of Order, 1982; Frank Johnson's Election Year, 1983. *Recreations:* opera, ballet. *Address:* c/o The Daily Telegraph, 1 Canada Square, Canary Wharf, E14 5DT. *Clubs:* Garrick, Beefsteak.

See also Lord Lovat.

JOHNSON, Air Vice-Marshal Frank Sidney Roland, CB 1973; OBE 1963; CIMgt; *b* 4 Aug. 1917; *s* of Major Harry Johnson, IA, and Georgina Marklew; *m* 1943, Evelyn Hunt; two *s. Educ:* Trinity County Secondary Sch., Wood Green. Enlisted, 1935; served in UK and India; commnd, 1943; Germany (Berlin Airlift), 1948; Western Union Defence Organisation, 1955–57; Directing Staff, RAF Staff Coll., 1958–60; comd 113 MU, RAF Nicosia, 1960–63; Chief Instructor Equipment and Secretarial Wing, RAF Coll. Cranwell, 1963–64; Dep. Dir MoD, 1965–66; idc 1967; Chief Supply Officer, Fighter and Strike Comds, 1968–70; Dir-Gen. of Supply, RAF, 1971–73; Supply Manager, BAC, Saudi Arabia, 1974–76; Base Manager, BAC RSAF, Khamis Mushayt, Saudi Arabia, 1976–77, Dhahran, 1978–82. *Recreations:* golf, squash, hockey, cricket. *Club:* Royal Air Force.

JOHNSON, Frederick Alistair, PhD; FInstP; consultant, BAE Systems and other companies, since 2000; *b* Christchurch, NZ, 9 April 1928; *s* of Archibald Frederick Johnson and Minnie, *d* of William Frederick Pellew; *m* 1952, Isobel Beth, *d* of Horace George Wilson; two *d. Educ:* Christchurch Boys' High Sch.; Univ. of Canterbury, New Zealand (MSc, PhD). Rutherford Meml Fellow, 1952; Lectr, Univ. of Otago, 1952; post graduate research, Bristol Univ., 1953–55. Royal Radar Establishment, 1956–75: Individual Merit Promotion, 1964; Head of Physics Dept, 1968–73; Dep. Director, 1973–75; Dep. Dir, Royal Armament Research & Development Estabt, 1975–77; Dir of Scientific and Technical Intell., MoD, 1977–79; Chief Scientist (Royal Navy) and Dir Gen. Research A, MoD, 1980–84; Dir, Marconi Maritime Applied Res. Lab., and Chief Scientist, Marconi Underwater Systems Ltd, 1985–87; Technical Dir, GEC Research, later GEC-Marconi Res. Centre, 1987–95; Dir, Special Projects, GEC-Marconi, subseq. BAE Systems Res. Centre, 1995–2000. Visiting Professor, Massachusetts Inst. of Technology, 1967–68; Hon. Prof. of Physics, Birmingham Univ., 1969–75. *Publications:* numerous papers on spectroscopy, optics, lattice dynamics and ocean thermal energy conversion in Proc. Physical Soc. and Proc. Royal Soc. *Recreation:* sailing. *Address:* Otia Tuta, Grassy Lane, Sevenoaks, Kent TN13 1PL. *Club:* Athenæum.

JOHNSON, Gen. Sir Garry (Dene), KCB 1990; OBE 1977 (MBE 1971); MC 1965; Chairman: International Defence Advisory Board to the Baltic States, 1995–2000; International Security Advisory Board, since 1998; *b* 20 Sept. 1937; *m* 1962, Caroline Sarah Frearson; two *s. Educ:* Christ's Hospital. psc, ndc, rcds. Commissioned 10th Princess Mary's Own Gurkha Rifles, 1956; Malaya and Borneo campaigns, 1956–67; Royal Green Jackets, 1970; command, 1st Bn RGJ, 1976–79; Comdr, 11 Armoured Brigade, 1981–82; Dep. Chief of Staff, HQ BAOR, 1983; ACDS (NATO/UK), 1985–87; Comdr, British Forces Hong Kong, and Maj.-Gen., Bde of Gurkhas, 1987–89; MEC, Hong Kong Govt, 1987–89; Comdr Trng and Arms Dirs, 1989–91; Inspector Gen. Doctrine and Trng, 1991–92; C-in-C, AFNORTH, 1992–94. Colonel, 10th PMO Gurkha Rifles, 1985–94; Col Comdt, Light Div., 1990–94. Chm., TEC Nat. Council, 1995–99; Vice-Pres., Nat. Fedn of Enterprise Agencies, 1996–99. Chairman: Ogilby Trust, 1991–; Need in Nepal, 1997–; Trustee, Gurkha Welfare Trust, 1985– (Chm., 1987–89). Member: NACETT, 1995–99; Adv. Council, Prince's Youth Business Trust, 1995–99; NCIHE, 1996–99. FRGS 1993; FRAS 1994; FRSA 1994; FRUSI 1999. Hon. DSc Soton 1999. Order of Terra Mariana (Estonia), 1997; Order of Grand Duke Gediminas (Lithuania), 1999. *Publications:* Brightly Shone the Dawn, 1979; Inland from Gold Beach, 1999. *Address:* c/o Holt's Branch, Royal Bank of Scotland, Lawrie House, Victoria Road, Farnborough GU14 7NR. *Club:* Army and Navy.

JOHNSON, Prof. Garth Roston, PhD; FREng, FIMechE; Professor of Rehabilitation Engineering, University of Newcastle upon Tyne, since 1995; *b* 23 Jan. 1945; *s* of Daniel Cowan Johnson and Vera Olive Johnson; *m* 1978, Katherine Zaida Cooke; one *s. Educ:* Univ. of Leeds (BSc Hons; PhD 1974). CEng 1991, FIMechE 1991; FREng 2000. Res. engr, Adcock & Shipley, machine tool manufrs, Leicester, 1961–71; Res. Fellow, Rheumatology Res. Unit, Dept of Medicine, Univ. of Leeds, 1971–75; Tech. Dir, Orthotics and Disability Res. Centre, Derbys Royal Infirmary, 1975–81; University of Newcastle upon Tyne: William Leech Reader in Biomed. Engrg, Dept of Mechanical, Materials and Manufg Engrg, 1981–95; Tech. Dir, Centre for Rehabilitation and Engrg Studies, 1991–. *Publications:* (ed with M. P. Barnes) Upper Motor Neurone Syndrome and Spasticity, 2001; contrib. to learned jls incl. Proc. IMechE, Jl Biomechanics, Clin. Biomechanics. *Recreation:* music. *Address:* Centre for Rehabilitation and Engineering Studies, University of Newcastle upon Tyne, Stephenson Building, Newcastle upon Tyne NE1 7RU. *T:* (0191) 222 6196.

JOHNSON, Dr Gordon; President, Wolfson College, University of Cambridge, since 1994; Provost, Gates Cambridge Trust, since 2000; *b* 13 Sept. 1943; *s* of Robert Johnson and Bessie (*née* Hewson); *m* 1973, Faith Sargent Lewis, New Haven, Conn; three *s. Educ:* Richmond Sch., Yorks; Trinity Coll., Cambridge (BA 1964; MA, PhD 1968). Fellow, Trinity Coll., Cambridge, 1966–74; Selwyn College, Cambridge: Fellow, 1974–94; Tutor, 1975–92; Hon. Fellow, 1994; University of Cambridge: Lectr in History of S Asia, 1974–; Dir, Centre of S Asian Studies, 1983–2001; Chairman, Faculty of: Oriental Studies, 1984–87; Architecture and History of Art, 1985–; Educn, 1994–; Member: Library Syndicate, 1978–; Press Syndicate, 1981– (Chm., 1993–); Syndicate on Govt of Univ., 1988–89; Statutes and Ordinances Revision Syndicate, 1990–; Gen. Bd of Faculties, 1979–82 and 1985–90; Council, Senate, 1985–92 and 1999–. Trustee: Cambridge Commonwealth Trust, 1983–; Cambridge Overseas Trust, 1989–; Malaysian Commonwealth Studies Centre, 1999–. Gov., Comberton Village Coll., 1991–2001 (Chm., 1992–2001). Editor, Modern Asian Studies, 1971–; Gen. Editor, The New Cambridge History of India, 1979–. *Publications:* Provincial Politics and Indian Nationalism, 1973; University Politics: F. M. Cornford's Cambridge and his advice to the young academic politician, 1994; Cultural Atlas of India, 1995; Printing and Publishing for the University: three hundred years of the press syndicate, 1999. *Recreations:* reading, taking exercise. *Address:* Wolfson College, Cambridge CB3 9BB. *T:* (01223) 335900.

JOHNSON, Gordon Arthur; DL; Chief Executive, Lancashire County Council, 1998–2000; *b* 30 Aug. 1938; *y s* of Annie Elizabeth Johnson and William Johnson; *m* 1963, Jennifer Roxane Bradley; two *d. Educ:* Bournemouth Sch.; University College London (BA Hons Hist.). Solicitor. Kent CC, 1962–64; Staffs CC, 1964–73; Dep. Dir of Admin, W Yorks MCC, 1973–76; Dep. Clerk, 1977–90, Chief. Exec. Clerk, 1991–98, Lancs CC. Lancs County Electoral Returning Officer, 1991–2000; Clerk: Lancs Lieutenancy, 1991–2000; Lancs Police Authy, 1995–2000; Lancs Combined Fire Authy, 1998–2000; Secretary: Lancs Adv. Cttee, 1991–2000; Lord Chancellor's Adv. Cttee on Gen. Cmrs of Income Tax, 1991–2000; Lancs Probation Cttee; Lancs Cttee, Prince's Trust-Action; Co. Sec., Lancs County Enterprises Ltd, 1991–2000; Mem., MSC Area Manpower Bd, 1986–88; Chm., Soc. of County Secretaries, 1987–88 (Hon. Treasurer, 1977–86); Dir, LAWTEC, 1991–98. Adviser: LGA Policy and Strategy Cttee, 1997–2000; Assoc. of Police Authorities, 1997–2000. Mem. Court, Univ. of Lancaster, 1991–2000. DL Lancs, 2000. *Recreations:* motor cycling, travel, reading. *Address:* Beech House, 72 Higher Bank Road, Fulwood, Preston, Lancs PR2 8PH.

JOHNSON, Graham Rhodes, OBE 1994; concert accompanist; Professor of Accompaniment, Guildhall School of Music, since 1986; *b* 10 July 1950; *s* of late John Edward Donald Johnson and of Violet May Johnson (*née* Johnson). *Educ:* Hamilton High Sch., Bulawayo, Rhodesia; Royal Acad. of Music, London. FRAM 1984; FGSM 1988. Concert début, Wigmore Hall, 1972; has since accompanied Elisabeth Schwarzkopf, Jessye Norman, Victoria de los Angeles (USA Tour 1977), Dame Janet Baker, Sir Peter Pears, Felicity Lott, Margaret Price (USA Tour 1985), Peter Schreier, John Shirley Quirk, Mady Mesplé, Thomas Hampson, Robert Holl, Tom Krause, Sergei Leiferkus, Brigitte Fassbaender, Matthias Goerne, Christine Schäfer. Work with contemporaries led to formation of The Songmakers' Almanac (Artistic Director); has devised and accompanied over 150 London recitals for this group since Oct. 1976. Tours of US with Sarah Walker, Richard Jackson, and of Australia and NZ with The Songmakers' Almanac, 1981. Writer and presenter of major BBC Radio 3 series on Poulenc songs, and BBC TV programmes on Schubert songs (1978) and the songs of Liszt (1986). Lectr at song courses in Savonlinna (Finland), US and at Pears-Britten Sch., Snape; Artistic advr and accompanist, Alte Oper Festival, Frankfurt, 1981–82; Song Adviser, Wigmore Hall, 1992–; Chm. Jury, Wigmore Hall Internat. Singing Competition, 1997 and 1999. Festival appearances in Aldeburgh, Edinburgh, Munich, Hohenems, Salzburg, Bath, Hong Kong, Bermuda. Many recordings incl. those with Songmakers' Almanac, Martyn Hill, Elly Ameling, Arleen Auger, Janet Baker, Philip Langridge, Marjana Lipovsek, Ann Murray, Sarah Walker, Anthony Rolfe Johnson, and of Schubert Lieder, with various artists, 1988–. Hon. Mem., Royal Swedish Acad. of Music, 2000. Gramophone Award, 1989, 1996 and 1997; Royal Philharmonic Prize for Instrumentalist, 1998. *Publications:* (contrib.) The Britten Companion, ed Christopher Palmer, 1984; (contrib.) Gerald Moore, The Unashamed Accompanist, rev. edn 1984; (contrib.) The Spanish Song Companion, 1992; The Songmakers' Almanac: reflections and commentaries, 1996; A French Song Companion, 2000, reviews in TLS, articles for music jls. *Recreation:* eating in good restaurants with friends and fine wine. *Address:* 83 Fordwych Road, NW2 3TL. *T:* (020) 8452 5193.

JOHNSON, Heather Jean; *see* Mellows, H. J.

JOHNSON, Hugh Eric Allan; author, broadcaster and editor; *b* 10 March 1939; *s* of late Guy Francis Johnson, CBE and Grace Kittel; *m* 1965, Judith Eve Grinling; one *s* two *d. Educ:* Rugby Sch.; King's Coll., Cambridge (MA). Staff writer, Condé Nast publications, 1960–63; Editor, Wine & Food, and Sec., Wine and Food Soc., 1963–65; Wine Corresp., 1962–67, and Travel Editor, 1967, Sunday Times; Editor, Queen, 1968–70. President: The Sunday Times Wine Club, 1973–; Circle of Wine Writers, 1997–. Chairman: Saling Hall Press, 1975–; Conservation Cttee, Internat. Dendrology Soc., 1979–86; Winestar Productions Ltd, 1984–; The Hugh Johnson Collection Ltd, 1985–; Vice-Pres., Essex Gardens Trust, 1997–; Director: Société Civile de Château Latour, 1986–; Coldstream Winemakers Ltd, 1991–94. Editorial Director: Jl of RHS, 1975–89, Editl Cons., 1989–; The Plantsman, 1979–94. Wine Editor, Cuisine, New York, 1983–84; Wine Consultant: to Jardine Matheson Ltd, Hong Kong and Tokyo, 1985–; to British Airways, 1987–; to the Royal Tokaji Wine Co, 1990–; Hon. Trustee, Amer. Center for Wine, Food and the Arts, Calif, 2000. Gardening Correspondent, New York Times, 1986–87; series Editor, Touring in Wine Country, 1995–. Video, How to Handle a Wine, 1984 (Glenfiddich Trophy, 1984; reissued as Understanding Wine, 1989); TV series: Wine—a user's guide (KQED, San Francisco), 1986; Vintage—a history of wine (Channel 4 and WGBH, Boston), 1989; TV documentary, Return Voyage (Star TV, Hong Kong), 1992. Hon. Chm., Wine Japan (Tokyo exhibn), 1989–94. Docteur ès Vins, Acad. du Vin de Bordeaux, 1987. DUniv Essex, 1998. Carl-Friedrich von Rumor Gold Ring, German Gastronomic Acad., 1998; Veitch Meml Medal, RHS, 2000. *Publications:* Wine, 1966, rev. edn 1974; (ed) Frank Schoonmaker's Encyclopedia of Wine, English edn, 1967; The World Atlas of Wine, 1971, 5th edn (with Jancis Robinson) 2001; The International Book of Trees, 1973, rev. edn 1994; (with Bob Thompson) The California Wine Book, 1976; Hugh Johnson's Pocket Wine Book, annually 1977–; The Principles of Gardening, 1979, rev. edn as Hugh Johnson's Gardening Companion, 1996; Understanding Wine, 1980; (with Paul Miles) The Pocket Encyclopedia of Garden Plants, 1981; Hugh Johnson's Wine Companion, 1983, 4th edn 1997; How to Enjoy Your Wine, 1985, 2nd edn 1998; The Hugh Johnson Cellar Book, 1986; The Atlas of German Wines, 1986, rev. edn (with Stuart Pigott) 1995; Hugh Johnson's Wine Cellar, (US) 1986; (with Jan Read) The Wine and Food of Spain, 1987; (with Hubrecht Duijker) The Wine Atlas of France, 1987, rev. edn 1997; The Story of Wine, 1989 (ten awards, incl. Glenfiddich Wine Award, 1990, Grand Prix de la Communication de la Vigne et du Vin, 1992); Hugh Johnson's Pop-up Wine Book, 1989; (with James Halliday) The Art and Science of Wine, 1992; Hugh Johnson on Gardening: the best of Tradescant's Diary, 1993; Tuscany and its Wines, 2000; articles on gastronomy, travel and gardening. *Recreations:* trees, travelling, staying at home. *Address:* Saling Hall, Great Saling, Essex CM7 5DT; 73 St James's Street, SW1A 1PH; Domaine des Boutons, 03190 Hérisson, Allier, France. *Clubs:* Garrick, Saintsbury; Essex.

JOHNSON, Rt Rev. James Nathaniel; Bishop of St Helena, 1985–91; Hon. Assistant Bishop, Chelmsford Diocese, since 1997 (Assistant Bishop, 1992–97); *b* 28 April 1932; *s* of William and Lydia Florence Johnson; *m* 1953, Evelyn Joyce Clifford; one *s* one *d. Educ:* Primary and Secondary Selective School, St Helena; Church Army College; Wells Theol Coll. Deacon 1964, priest 1965; Curate of St Peter's, Lawrence Weston, dio. Bristol, 1964–66; Priest-in-charge of St Paul's Cathedral, St Helena, 1966–69, Vicar 1969–71; Domestic Chaplain to Bishop of St Helena, 1967–71; USPG Area Sec. for Diocese of Exeter and Truro, 1972–74; Rector of Combe Martin dio. Exeter, 1974–80; Hon. Canon of St Helena, 1975–; Vicar of St Augustine, Thorpe Bay, dio. Chelmsford, 1980–85; Rector of Byfield with Boddington and Aston-le-Walls, and Hon. Asst Bishop, Peterborough dio., 1991–92; Vicar of Hockley, Essex, 1992–97. Non-residentiary Canon, Chelmsford Cathedral, 1995–97, Canon Emeritus, 1997. *Recreations:* music, gardening, walking. *Address:* St Helena, 249 Woodgrange Drive, Southend-on-Sea, Essex SS1 2SQ. *T:* (01702) 613429.

JOHNSON, His Honour John Robin; a Circuit Judge, 1973–93; *b* 27 Nov. 1927; *s* of Sir Philip Bulmer Johnson, Hexham, Northumberland; *m* 1958, Meriel Jean, *d* of H. B. Speke, Aydon, Corbridge; one *s* one *d. Educ:* Winchester; Trinity Coll., Cambridge. Called to Bar, Middle Temple, 1950. Dep. Chm., Northumberland QS, 1966–71; a

Recorder of the Crown Court, 1972–73. *Address:* Kirk Fenwick, Cambo, Morpeth NE61 4BN.

JOHNSON, Sir John (Rodney), KCMG 1988 (CMG 1981); HM Diplomatic Service, retired; Chairman, Countryside Commission, 1991–95; Visiting Fellow, Kellogg College, Oxford, since 2000; *b* 6 Sept. 1930; *s* of Edwin Done Johnson, OBE and Florence Mary (*née* Clough); *m* 1956, Jean Mary Lewis; three *s* one *d. Educ:* Manchester Grammar Sch.; Oxford Univ. (MA). HM Colonial Service, Kenya, 1955–64; Dist Comr, Thika, 1962–64; Administrator, Cttee of Vice-Chancellors and Principals of UK Univs, 1965; First Sec., FCO, 1966–69; Head of Chancery, British Embassy, Algiers, 1969–72; Dep. High Comr, British High Commn, Barbados, 1972–74; Counsellor, British High Commn, Lagos, 1975–78; Head of W African Dept, FCO, and Ambassador (non-resident) to Chad, 1978–80; High Comr in Zambia, 1980–84; Asst Under Sec. of State (Africa), FCO, 1984–86; High Comr in Kenya, 1986–90; Dir, Foreign Service Prog., and specially elected Fellow, Keble Coll., Oxford Univ., 1990–95. Mem., Jt Nature Conservation Cttee, 1991–95. Chairman: Kenya Soc., 1992–98; Chilterns Conservation Bd, 2001–; President: Friends of Lake Dist, 1995–; Long Distance Walkers Assoc., 1995–; Vice-President: Royal African Soc., 1995–; YHA, 1995–; Chiltern Soc., 1995–; Vice-Chm., Chilterns Conf., 1996–2001. FRGS 1990. *Recreations:* walking, reaching remote places. *Address:* The Gables, High Street, Amersham, Bucks HP7 0DP. *Clubs:* Travellers, Alpine; Climbers; Mombasa.

JOHNSON, Kenneth James, OBE 1966; colonial administrator and industrialist; *b* 8 Feb. 1926; *s* of Albert Percy Johnson and Winifred Florence (*née* Coole); *m* 1951, Margaret Teresa Bontoft Jenkins; three *s* two *d. Educ:* Rishworth School, near Halifax; Wadham Coll., Oxford; LSE; SOAS. Indian Army (14 Punjab Regt), 1945–47. Colonial Admin. Service, Nigeria, 1949–61, senior appts in Min. of Finance and Min. of Commerce and Industry; Head of Economic Dept, later Dir of Industrial Affairs, CBI, 1961–70; Courtaulds Ltd, 1970–73: Chm. and Man. Dir, various subsidiary cos; Dep. Chm., Pay Board, 1973–74; Dunlop Group, 1974–85: Personnel Dir, 1974–79; Overseas Dir, Dunlop Holdings plc, 1979–84; Chm., Dunlop International AG, 1984–85; Chm., Crown Agents Pensions Trust, 1984–96. Member: Bd of Crown Agents for Oversea Govts and Administrations, 1980–88; Crown Agents Hldg and Realisation Bd, 1980–88. Chm., Farlington Sch. Trust, 1990–2000. FRSA 1972; FIPM 1976. *Recreation:* book-collecting. *Address:* Snappers Field, Shipley, Horsham, West Sussex RH13 7BQ. *Club:* Oriental.

JOHNSON, Prof. Kenneth Langstreth, PhD; FRS 1982; FREng; Professor of Engineering, Cambridge University, 1977–92, now Emeritus; Fellow of Jesus College, Cambridge, since 1957; *b* 19 March 1925; *s* of Frank Herbert Johnson and Ellen Howorth Langstreth; *m* 1954, Dorothy Rosemary Watkins; one *s* two *d. Educ:* Barrow Grammar Sch.; Manchester Univ. (MScTech, MA, PhD). FIMechE; FREng (FEng 1987). Engr, Messrs Rotol Ltd, Gloucester, 1944–49; Asst Lectr, Coll. of Technology, Manchester, 1949–54; Lectr, then Reader in Engrg, Cambridge Univ., 1954–77. Hon. FUMIST, 1993. Tribology Trust Gold Medal, IMechE, 1985; Mayo Hersey Award, ASME, 1991; William Prager Medal, Amer. Soc. Engrg Sci., 1999. *Publications:* Contact Mechanics, 1985; contrib. scientific and engrg jls, and Proc. IMechE. *Recreations:* mountain walking, swimming. *Address:* 1 New Square, Cambridge CB1 1EY. *T:* (01223) 355287.

JOHNSON, Prof. Louise Napier, FRS 1990; David Phillips Professor of Molecular Biophysics, and Professorial Fellow, Corpus Christi College, Oxford, since 1990; *b* 26 Sept. 1940; *m*; one *s* one *d. Educ:* Wimbledon High Sch. for Girls; University College London (BSc 1962; Fellow, 1993); Royal Institution, London (PhD 1965). Research Asst., Yale Univ., 1966; University of Oxford: Demonstrator, Zoology Dept, 1967–73; Lectr in Molecular Biophysics, 1973–90; Reader, 1990; Additional Fellow, Somerville College, 1973–90, Hon. Fellow, 1991. Member: Council, Royal Soc., 1998–2001; CCLRC, 1998–2001; Scientific Adv. Council, EMBL, 1994– (Chm., 1998–2001). Mem., EMBO, 1991. Trustee, Cambridge Crystallographic Data Base, 1996–. Gov., Westminster Sch., 1993–2001. Associate Fellow, Third World Acad. of Scis, 2000; MAE, 2001. Hon. DSc St Andrews, 1992. Kaj Linderström-Lang Prize, 1989; Charmian Medal, Royal Soc. Chem., 1997; Datta Medal, FEBS, 1998. *Publications:* Protein Crystallography (jtly with T. L. Blundell), 1976; papers on lysozyme, glycogen phosphorylase, kinases and cell cycle proteins, protein crystallography, enzyme mechanism and allosteric mechanisms. *Recreations:* family, horses. *Address:* Laboratory of Molecular Biophysics, Rex Richards Building, University of Oxford, South Parks Road, Oxford OX1 3QU.

JOHNSON, Luke Oliver; Chairman, Belgo Group plc, since 1997; *b* 2 Feb. 1962; *s* of Paul Johnson, *qv. Educ:* Langley Grammar Sch.; Magdalen Coll., Oxford. Stockbroking Analyst, Grieveson Grant, then Kleinwort Benson, 1983–88; Director: AoD, 1989–92; ICD, 1989–92; Crabtree Gp, 1992–94; PizzaExpress, 1992–95 and 1998–99 (Chm., 1996–98); My Kinda Town, 1994–96; American Port Services, 1995–98; Abacus Recruitment, 1995–99; Whittards of Chelsea, 1998–2001; NewMedia SPARK, 1999–; Nightfreight, 1999–2001; Acquisitor, 1999–; Manager, Intrinsic Value, 1999–. Gov., London Inst., 2000–. Columnist, Sunday Telegraph, 1997–. *Publications:* How to Get a Highly Paid Job in the City, 1987; Betting to Win, 1990, 2nd edn 1997. *Recreations:* writing, squash, tennis. *Address:* 52 Brook's Mews, W1Y 1LE. *T:* (020) 7499 5311. *Clubs:* Royal Automobile, Groucho, Cobden.
See also D. B. Johnson.

JOHNSON, Martin; Sports Feature Writer, Daily Telegraph, since 1995; *b* 23 June 1949; *s* of late Basil Johnson and of Bridget Johnson; *m* 1985, Teresa Mary Wright; one *s* one *d. Educ:* St Julian's High Sch., Newport, Mon.; Monmouth Sch. Ronald French Advertising Agency, Liverpool, 1970; South Wales Argus, Newport, 1970–73; Leicester Mercury, 1973–86; Cricket Corresp., The Independent, 1986–95. *Publications:* (ed) The Independent World Cup Cricket, 1987; (jtly) Gower: the autobiography, 1992; Rugby and All That: an irreverent history, 2000. *Recreation:* golf. *Address:* 3 Oadby Hill Drive, Oadby, Leicester LE2 5GF. *Club:* Cosby Golf.

JOHNSON, Prof. Martin Hume, PhD; Professor of Reproductive Sciences, University of Cambridge, since 1992; Fellow, Christ's College, Cambridge, since 1969; *b* 19 Dec. 1944; *s* of Reginald Hugh Ben and Joyce Florence Johnson. *Educ:* Cheltenham Grammar Sch.; Christ's Coll., Cambridge (MA, PhD). Jun. Res. Fellow, Christ's Coll., Cambridge, 1969; MRC Jun. Res. Fellow, 1970; Harkness Fellow, 1971; University of Cambridge: Lectr in Anatomy, 1974–84; Reader in Exptl Embryology, 1984–92; Head of Dept of Anatomy, 1995–99. Hon. Sen. Lectr in Obstetrics and Gynaecology, UMDS, 1991–95; Distinguished Vis. Fellow, La Trobe Univ., 1993; Vis. Prof., Sydney Univ., 1999–2001. Chm., Brit. Soc. for Developmental Biol., 1984–89; Mem., HFEA, 1994–99. Albert Brachet Prize, Belgian Royal Acad. Scis, Letters and Fine Arts, 1989. *Publications:* (with B. J. Everitt) Essential Reproduction, 1980, 5th edn 2000; contrib. to numerous scientific pubns. *Recreations:* opera, music. *Address:* Department of Anatomy, Downing Street, Cambridge CB2 3DY. *T:* (01223) 333772.

JOHNSON, Melanie Jane; JP; MP (Lab) Welwyn Hatfield, since 1997; Parliamentary Under-Secretary of State, Department of Trade and Industry, since 2001; *b* 5 Feb. 1955; *d* of David Guyatt Johnson and Mary Angela Johnson; one *s* twin *d* by William Jordan. *Educ:* University Coll. London (BA Jt Hons Phil. and Ancient Greek); King's Coll., Cambridge (postgrad. res.). Mem. Relns Officer, 1981–88, Retail Admin Manager, 1988–90, Cambridge Co-op. Soc.; Asst Gen. Manager (Quality Assurance), Cambs FHSA, 1990–92; Schools Inspector, 1993–97. Mem. (Lab) Cambs CC, 1981–97. PPS to Financial Sec., HM Treasury, 1999; Economic Sec., HM Treasury, 1999–2001. Member: Public Admin. Select Cttee, 1997–98; Home Affairs Select Cttee, 1998–99; Chm., All Party Parenting Gp, 1998–. Contested (Lab) Cambs, EP elecn, 1994. JP Cambridge, 1994. *Recreations:* family, films, gardening. *Address:* House of Commons, SW1A 0AA. *T:* (01707) 262920.

JOHNSON, Merwyn; *see* Johnson, W. M.

JOHNSON, Michael York-; *see* York, M.

JOHNSON, Dame Monica; *see* Golding, Dame (Cecilie) Monica.

JOHNSON, Neil Anthony, OBE 1989; TD 1985, bar 1992; Chairman, Motability Finance Ltd, since 2001; *b* 13 April 1949; *s* of Anthony and Dilys Johnson, Glamorgan; *m* 1st, 1971 (marr. diss. 1996); three *d*; 2nd, 1996, Elizabeth Jane Hunter Johnston (*née* Robinson); one *d*, and three step *d. Educ:* Canton High Sch., Cardiff; RMA Sandhurst. Graduate Trainee, Lex Gp, 1971–73; British Leyland Internat., 1973–75; Leyland Cars: Gen. Manager, Tech. Services and Marketing, 1975–77; Staff Dir, Marketing and Planning, 1977–79; Service Dir, 1979–80; Dir, Continental Europe Ops, BL, 1980–82; Dir, Sales and Marketing, Jaguar Cars, 1982–86; MoD, 1986–89; Main Bd Dir, Rover Gp, British Aerospace, resp. for European Ops, 1989–92; Dir-Gen., EEF, 1992–93; Gen. Sec., 1994–99, Chief Exec., 1996–99, RAC; Chief Exec., British and Amer. Chamber of Commerce, 2000–01. Chairman: Hornby plc, 2000– (Dep. Chm., 1998–2000); Cybit plc, 2001–; Director: Charter plc, 1994–; RAC Ltd, 1994–99; RAC Motor Sports Assoc., 1994–98; Tenon plc, 2000–. Chm., Speedway Control Bd, 1994–96. Territorial Army: Pembroke Yeomanry, 1971; 4th Bn RGJ, 1973; CO, 1986–89; ADC to the Queen, 1990; Hon. Col, 157 Transport Regt, RLC, 1993–2001; Hon. Col, F Co., London Regt, RGJ, 2000–. Member: Prime Minister's Panel of Advrs on Citizen's Charter, Cabinet Office, 1995–; UK Round Table on Sustainable Develt, 1997–98; Cleaner Vehicles Task Force, 1997–99. Mem., Nat. Employers' Liaison Cttee for the Reserve Forces, 1992–98. Trustee, Jaguar Daimler Heritage Trust, 1994–99. FIMI; CIMgt 1995; FRSA. Freeman, City of London, 1985; Asst, Court of Co. of Coachmakers and Coach Harness Makers, 1994. Rep. DL, City of Westminster, 1993. Ordre de l'Encouragement Publique (France), 1987. *Recreations:* town and country pursuits, fast British cars, slow Italian lunches. *Address:* 9 Catherine Wheel Yard, SW1A 1DR. *Clubs:* Royal Automobile, Army and Navy, Royal Green Jackets, Beefsteak; Cardiff & County (Cardiff); Woodroffe's.

JOHNSON, Nevil; Nuffield Reader in the Comparative Study of Institutions, University of Oxford, and Professorial Fellow, Nuffield College, 1969–96, now Emeritus Fellow; *b* 6 Feb. 1929; *s* of G. E. Johnson and Doris Johnson, MBE, Darlington; *m* 1957, Ulla van Aubel; two *s. Educ:* Queen Elizabeth Grammar Sch., Darlington; University Coll., Oxford (BA PPE 1952, MA 1962). Army service, 1947–49. Admin. Cl. of Home Civil Service: Min. of Supply, 1952–57; Min. of Housing and Local Govt, 1957–62; Lectr in Politics, Univ. of Nottingham, 1962–66; Sen. Lectr in Politics, Univ. of Warwick, 1966–69. Chm. Board, Faculty of Social Studies, Oxford, 1976–78. Visiting Professor: Ruhr Univ. of Bochum, 1968–69; Univ. of Munich, 1980. Mem., ESRC (formerly SSRC), 1981–87 (Chm., Govt and Law Cttee, 1982–86). Civil Service Comr (pt-time), 1982–85. Mem. Exec. Council, RIPA, 1965–87; Chm., Study of Parlt Gp, 1984–87. Hon. Editor, Public Administration, 1967–81. *Publications:* Parliament and Administration: The Estimates Committee 1945–65, 1967; Government in the Federal Republic of Germany, 1973; In Search of the Constitution, 1977 (trans. German, 1977); (with A. Cochrane) Economic Policy-Making by Local Authorities in Britain and Western Germany, 1981; State and Government in the Federal Republic of Germany, 1983; The Limits of Political Science, 1989 (trans. Spanish, 1991); articles in Public Admin, Political Studies, Parly Affairs, Ztschr. für Politik, Die Verwaltung, and Der Staat. *Recreations:* walking, swimming, gardening. *Address:* 2 Race Farm Cottages, Kingston Bagpuize, Oxon OX13 5AU. *T:* (01865) 820777.

JOHNSON, Prof. Newell Walter, MDSc, PhD; FDSRCS, FRACDS, FRCPath, FMedSci; Nuffield Research Professor of Dental Science, Royal College of Surgeons of England, since 1984; Professor of Oral Pathology, University of London, at Guy's, King's and St Thomas' Dental Institute of King's College London (formerly King's College School of Medicine and Dentistry), since 1994; specialist in oral medicine, oral pathology and periodontics; *b* 5 Aug. 1938; *s* of Otto Johnson and Lorna (*née* Guy); *m* 1965, Pauline Margaret Trafford (marr. diss. 1984); two *d. Educ:* University High Sch., Melbourne; Univ. of Melbourne (BDSc Hons 1960; MDSc 1963); Univ. of Bristol (PhD 1967). FDSRCS 1964; FRACDS 1966; FRCPath 1982; FFOP (RCPA) 1996. Res. Fellow in Pathology, Univ. of Melbourne, 1961–63; Lectr in Dental Surgery, UCL, 1963–64; Scientific Officer, MRC Dental Res. Unit, Bristol, 1964–67; London Hospital Medical College: Reader in Experimental Oral Path., 1968–76; Prof. of Oral Path., 1976–83; Hon. Dir, MRC Dental Res. Unit, 1983–93; Governor, 1983 (Chm., Academic Div. of Dentistry, 1983); Chm., London Hosp. Div. of Dentistry, 1981–83; Dir of Res. and Univ. Postgrad. Educn, Dental Inst., KCL, 1994–95. Hon. Consultant Dental Surgeon: Royal London (formerly London) Hosp., 1968–; King's Healthcare NHS Trust, 1993–. Consultant, Fédération Dentaire Internationale, 1984– (Comr, 1996–). Consultant in Oral Health, WHO, 1984–; Dir, WHO Collaborating Centre for Oral Cancer and Precancer, 1995–. Pres., British Soc. of Periodontology, 1992–93. Chm., UK Cttee, Royal Australasian Coll. of Dental Surgeons, 1981–83; FRSocMed (Mem. Council, Section of Odontology, 1972–91 (Pres., 1988–89)); Founder FMedSci 1998. Member, Editorial Board: Jl of Oral Pathology, 1982–93; Jl of Periodontal Research, 1986–96 (Associate Ed., 1993–); Jl of Clin. Periodontology, 1990–; Oral Oncology, 1992–; Editor in Chief, Oral Diseases, 1994–. *Publications:* (jtly) The Oral Mucosa in Health and Disease, 1975; (jtly) The Human Oral Mucosa: structure, metabolism and function, 1976; (jtly) Dental Caries: aetiology, pathology and prevention, 1979; (ed jtly) Oral Diseases in the Tropics, 1992; (ed) Detection of High Risk Groups for Oral Diseases, 3 vols, 1991; Oral Cancer, 2000; articles in scientific jls. *Recreations:* music, theatre, visual arts, yoga, the environment, the Third World. *Club:* Blizard.

JOHNSON, Nichola; Director of Museology, since 1993, Director, Sainsbury Centre for Visual Arts, since 1996, University of East Anglia; *b* 21 May 1945; *d* of John Nicholas Healey and Jessica (*née* Horrocks); *m* 1965, M. D. Johnson (marr. diss. 1971); one *s* one *d. Educ:* Ipswich High Sch.; Univ. of Sheffield (BA); Univ. of Essex (MA). Lectr, Dept of Art History, Univ. of Essex, 1980–83; Hd, Dept of Later London History, Mus. of London, 1983–93. *Publications:* contribs to professional jls and edited volumes. *Recreations:* music-making, driving in the USA, long-distance walking. *Address:* Sainsbury Centre for Visual Arts, University of East Anglia, Norwich NR4 7TJ. *T:* (01603) 593193.

JOHNSON, Sir Patrick Eliot, 8th Bt *cr* 1818, of Bath; *b* 11 June 1955; *s* of Sir Robin Eliot Johnson, 7th Bt and of Barbara Alfreda, *d* of late Alfred T. Brown; *S* father, 1989; *m* 1980, Rose (marr. diss. 1989), *d* of Olav Alfhein; twin *s*. *Heir: s* Richard Eliot Johnson, *b* 8 Jan. 1983.

JOHNSON, Paul (Bede); author; *b* 2 Nov. 1928; *s* of William Aloysius and Anne Johnson; *m* 1957, Marigold Hunt, MBE; three *s* one *d*. *Educ:* Stonyhurst; Magdalen Coll., Oxford. Asst Exec. Editor, Réalités, 1952–55; Editorial Staff, New Statesman, 1955, Dir, Statesman and Nation Publishing Co., 1965, Editor of the New Statesman, 1965–70. Member: Royal Commn on the Press, 1974–77; Cable Authority, 1984–90. *Publications:* The Suez War, 1957; Journey into Chaos, 1958; Left of Centre, 1960; Merrie England, 1964; Statesmen and Nations, 1971; The Offshore Islanders, 1972; (with G. Gale) The Highland Jaunt, 1973; Elizabeth I, 1974; A Place in History, 1974; Pope John XXIII, 1975 (Yorkshire Post Book of the Year Award, 1975); A History of Christianity, 1976; Enemies of Society, 1977; The National Trust Book of British Castles, 1978; The Recovery of Freedom, 1980; British Cathedrals, 1980; Ireland: Land of Troubles, 1980; Pope John Paul II and the Catholic Restoration, 1982; A History of the Modern World from 1917 to the 1980s, 1983, rev. edn 1991; The Pick of Paul Johnson, 1985; Oxford Book of Political Anecdotes, 1986; A History of the Jews, 1987; Intellectuals, 1988; The Birth of the Modern: world society 1815–30, 1991; Wake Up Britain! A Latterday Pamphlet, 1994; The Quest for God: a personal pilgrimage, 1996; To Hell With Picasso!: essays from the Spectator, 1996; A History of the American People, 1997; The Renaissance, 2000. *Recreations:* hill-walking, painting. *Address:* 29 Newton Road, W2 5JR. *T:* (020) 7229 3859; The Coach House, Over Stowey, near Bridgwater, Somerset TA5 1HA. *T:* (01278) 732393.

See also D. B. Johnson, L. O. Johnson.

JOHNSON, Paul Gavin; Chief Economist, and Director, Analytical Services, Department for Education and Skills (formerly Department for Education and Employment), since 2000; *b* 5 Jan. 1967; *s* of Robert and Joy Johnson; partner, Lorraine Dearden; two *s*. *Educ:* Keble Coll., Oxford (BA 1st. Cl. Hons PPE); Birkbeck Coll., London (MSc Econs). Inst. for Fiscal Studies, 1988–98 (Dep. Dir, 1996–98); Hd, Econs of Financial Regulation, FSA, 1999–2000. *Publications:* (jtly) Inequality in the UK, 1996; (jtly) Pension Systems and Retirement Incomes Across OECD Countries, 2001; contrib. numerous articles to econs jls and in press. *Address:* Department for Education and Skills, Sanctuary Buildings, Great Smith Street, SW1P 3BT.

JOHNSON, Sir Peter (Colpoys Paley), 7th Bt *cr* 1755, of New York in North America; author; publishing consultant; *b* 26 March 1930; *s* of Sir John Paley Johnson, 6th Bt, MBE, and of Carol, *d* of late Edmund Haas; *S* father, 1975; *m* 1st, 1956, Clare (marr. diss. 1973), *d* of late Dr Nigel Bruce; one *s* two *d*; 2nd, 1973, Caroline Elisabeth, *d* of late Sir John Hodsoll, CB; one *s*. *Educ:* Wellington Coll.; Royal Military Coll. of Science. Served RA, 1949; retired 1961, Captain. Dir, Sea Sure Ltd, 1965–73; Dir and Editor, Nautical Publishing Co. Ltd, 1970–81; Publishing Dir, Nautical Books, London, 1981–86. British Delegate, Internat. Offshore (Yachting) Council, 1970–79 (Chm. Internat. Technical Cttee, 1973–76); Ocean Racing Correspondent, Yachting World, London, 1971–81. Hon. Col, King's Royal Regt of NY (Canada), 1988–. *Publications:* Ocean Racing and Offshore Yachts, 1970, 2nd edn 1972; Boating Britain, 1973; Guinness Book of Yachting Facts and Feats, 1975; Guinness Guide to Sailing, 1981; This is Fast Cruising, 1985; The Encyclopedia of Yachting, 1989; Whitbread Round the World 1973–93, 1993; Yacht Clubs of the World, 1995; Yacht Rating, 1997. *Recreation:* sailing. *Heir: s* Colpoys Guy Johnson [*b* 13 Nov. 1965; *m* 1990, Marie-Louise, *d* of John Holroyd; three *s*]. *Address:* Dene End, Buckland Dene, Lymington, Hampshire SO41 9DT. *T:* (01590) 675921, *Fax:* (01590) 672885. *Clubs:* Royal Ocean Racing; Royal Yacht Squadron.

JOHNSON, Peter Michael; Chief Executive, George Wimpey PLC, since 2000; *b* 3 July 1947; *s* of late James and Nancy Johnson; *m* 1972, Janet Esther Ashman; two *s* one *d*. *Educ:* Bromley Grammar Sch.; St Edmund Hall, Oxford (MA PPE, BPhil Econs). With Unilever PLC, 1970–73; Redland PLC, 1973–96: Gp Treas., 1978–81; Dir of Planning, 1981–84; Man. Dir, Redland Bricks Ltd, 1984–88; Dir, Redland PLC, 1988–9; Chief Exec., Rugby Gp PLC, 1996–2000. Dir, David S. Smith (Hldgs), 1999–. President: Fédération Européene des Fabricants de Tuiles et de Briques, 1994–96; Nat. Council of Building Material Producers, 1997–2000. *Recreations:* music, tennis, cricket. *Address:* The Lydd, Sharpthorne, East Grinstead, Sussex RH19 4NS.

JOHNSON, Peter Michael; Headmaster, Millfield School, since 1998; *b* 21 Dec. 1947; *s* of Joseph William (Johnnie) Johnson and Dorothy Johnson; *m* 1969, Christine Anne Rayment; two *s*. *Educ:* Bec Grammar Sch.; Mansfield Coll., Oxford (Army Scholarship; MA Geog.; PGCE; Rugby Blue, 1968, 1969, 1970, Judo Blue, 1968, 1969). Commnd Parachute Bde, 1971; served 7 Parachute Regt, RHA, 1971–76 (emergency tours in NI, 1972 and 1974 (GSM)); retd in rank of Captain. Radley College: Asst Master, 1976–91; Housemaster, 1983–91; Headmaster, Wrekin Coll., 1991–98. Oxford Univ. Rep. on RFU Council, 1987–98; Trustee, Nat. Centre for Schs and Youth Rugby, 1992–. Capt., Northampton FC, 1978–79. *Recreations:* gardening, music, oenology, golf. *Address:* Millfield, Street, Somerset BA16 0YD. *T:* (01458) 442291. *Clubs:* East India; Vincent's (Oxford); Free Foresters.

JOHNSON, Peter William; Chief Executive, Inchcape plc, since 1999; *b* 2 Nov. 1947; *s* of Alfred and Emily Johnson; *m* 1973, Ann Gillian Highlby; one *s* one *d*. *Educ:* Hull Univ. (BSc Hons Econs). Mgt trainee, 1969, sen. mgt posts, 1970–79, British Leyland; Sales Dir, Austin-Morris, 1980–84; Export Dir, Austin-Rover, 1984–86; Sales Dir, Rover Gp, 1986–88; Chief Executive: Applied Chemicals, 1988–90; Marshall Gp, 1990–94; Inchcape Motors International, 1994–99. Vice Pres., Motor Agents Assoc., 1992–95. FIMI 1984 (Chm., 1991–95); MInstD 1990. *Recreations:* squash, golf, swimming, reading, travel. *Address:* Inchcape plc, 33 Cavendish Square, W1M 9HF. *T:* (020) 7546 8418. *Clubs:* Buckingham Golf, Brampton Park Golf; Hunts County Squash.

JOHNSON, Philip Cortelyou; architect, with own firm, 1953–67, with Johnson/Burgee Architects, since 1967; *b* Cleveland, Ohio, 8 July 1906; *s* of Homer H. Johnson and Louise Pope Johnson. *Educ:* Harvard (AB 1927, *cum laude*). Dir, Dept of Architecture, The Museum of Modern Art, New York, 1932–54, Trustee, 1958–; Graduate Sch. of Design, Harvard, 1940–43 (BArch). Has taught and lectured at: Yale Univ.; Cornell Univ.; Pratt Inst. (Dr Fine Arts, 1962). Mem. AIA (New York Chapter); Architectural League, NY. Hon. Dr Fine Arts Yale, 1978. Gold Medal, AIA, 1978; Pritzker Architecture Prize, 1979. *Publications:* Machine Art, 1934; Mies van der Rohe, 1st edn 1947, 2nd edn 1953; (with Henry-Russell Hitchcock) The International Style, Architecture since 1922, 1932, new edn 1966; (with others) Modern Architects, 1932; Architecture 1949–65, 1966; Philip Johnson Writings, 1979; contributor to Architectural Review. *Address:* Ponus Ridge Road, New Canaan, CT 06840, USA. *T:* (203) 9660565. *Clubs:* Athenæum; Century.

JOHNSON, Richard; National Hunt jockey; *b* 21 July 1977. Equal 10th in list of winning jockeys while still an apprentice, 1995–96; 2nd, 1998–99 and 1999–2000 seasons; winner, Cheltenham Gold Cup on Looks Like Trouble, 2000. *Address:* The Orchards, Toddington, Cheltenham, Glos GL54 5BY.

JOHNSON, Richard John M.; *see* McGregor-Johnson.

JOHNSON, Richard Keith; actor and producer; *b* 30 July 1927; *s* of Keith Holcombe and Frances Louisa Olive Johnson; *m* 1st, 1957, Sheila Sweet (marr. diss); one *s* one *d*; 2nd, 1965, Kim Novak (marr. diss.); 3rd, 1982, Marie-Louise Norlund (marr. diss.); one *s* one *d*. *Educ:* Parkfield School; Felsted School; RADA. RN, 1945–48. 1st stage appearance, Opera House, Manchester, 1944; repertory, Haymarket, 1944–45; *stage:* contract, Royal Shakespeare Theatre, 1957–62; Antony in Antony and Cleopatra, RSC, 1972–73, and 1992–93; NT, 1976–78; The War That Still Goes On, Young Vic, 1991; King, in All's Well that Ends Well, RSC, 1992–93; An Inspector Calls, Aldwych, 1994; The Rivals, Albery, 1994–95; Freddie in Gangster No 1, Almeida, 1995; Tyrone in Long Day's Journey into Night, Young Vic, 1996; Serebyakov in Uncle Vanya, Albery, 1996; Tusker in Staying On, nat. tour, 1997; Atticus in To Kill a Mockingbird, nat. tour, 1997; Sir Leonard Darwin in Plenty, Albery, 1999; Dr Dorn in The Seagull, RSC, 2000; Heinrich Mann in Tales from Hollywood, Donmar, 2001; *films:* MGM contract, 1959–65; acted in: The Haunting; Moll Flanders; Operation Crossbow; Khartoum; The Pumpkin Eater; Danger Route; Deadlier than the Male; Oedipus the King; Hennessy (also wrote original story); Aces High; The Four Feathers; Happy Days, 2000; Tomb Raider, 2001; produced: Turtle Diary; Castaway (Exec. Producer); The Lonely Passion of Judith Hearne; *television:* Rembrandt (title rôle); Hamlet (king); Antony and Cleopatra (Antony); The Member for Chelsea (title rôle); The Camomile Lawn (Oliver); Anglo-Saxon Attitudes (Gerald); Breaking the Code (Knox). Jt Founder, United British Artists, 1982. Member, Council: BAFTA, 1977–79; RADA, 2000–. *Recreations:* reading, gardening, travelling. *Address:* c/o Conway, Van Gelder Ltd, 18–21 Jermyn Street, SW1Y 6HP.

JOHNSON, (Robert) Brian, CBE 1990; QPM 1981; DL; Chief Constable, Lancashire Constabulary, 1983–95; *b* 28 July 1932; *s* of Robert and Hilda Johnson; *m* 1954, Jean Thew; two *d*. *Educ:* Stephenson Memorial Boys' Sch.; College of Commerce, Newcastle. Newcastle City Police: Police Cadet, 1948; Police Constable, 1952; Detective Constable, 1955; Detective Sergeant, 1962; Detective Inspector, 1966; Detective Chief Inspector, 1969; Detective Supt, Northumbria Police, 1971; Chief Supt, Northumbria Police, Home Office, 1976; Asst Chief Constable, Northumbria, 1977; Dep. Chief Constable, Lancashire, 1981. President: NW Area, National Assoc. of Retired Police Officers (also Pres., Blackpool Br.), 1983–95; ACPO, 1991–92; Lancs Assoc. of Boys Clubs, 1983–95; Lancs Outward Bound Assoc., 1983–95; Vice-Pres., Lancs Council for Voluntary Youth Services, 1985–; Patron: NW Counties Schools ABA, 1983–95; Blackburn Area, Road Safety Assoc., 1983–. DL Lancs, 1989. *Recreations:* reading, golf.

JOHNSON, Hon. Sir Robert (Lionel), Kt 1989; **Hon. Mr Justice Johnson;** a Justice of the High Court, Family Division, since 1989; *b* 9 Feb. 1933; *er s* of late Edward Harold Johnson, MSc, FRIC, and of Ellen Lydiate Johnson, Cranleigh; *m* 1957, Linda Mary, *er d* of late Charles William Bennie and Ena Ethel Bennie, Egglescliffe; one *s* two *d*. *Educ:* Watford Grammar Sch. (1940–51); London Sch. of Econs and Polit. Science. 5th Royal Inniskilling Dragoon Guards, 1955–57, Captain; ADC to GOC-in-C Northern Comd, 1956–57; Inns of Court Regt, 1957–64. Called to the Bar, Gray's Inn, 1957, Bencher, 1986; QC 1978; a Recorder, 1977–89. Jun. Counsel to Treasury in Probate Matters, 1975–78; Legal Assessor, GNC, 1977–82. Chairman: Bar Fees and Legal Aid Cttee, 1984–86 (Vice-Chm., 1982–84); Family Law Bar Assoc., 1984–86; Family Law Cttee, Justice, 1990–93; Mem., Bar Council, 1981–88; Vice Chm., 1987, Chm., 1988, Gen. Council of Bar. Member: Supreme Court Procedure Cttee, 1982–87; Law Soc. Legal Aid Cttee, 1981–87; No 1 Legal Aid Area Cttee, 1980–87; Co-Chm., Civil and Family Cttee, Judicial Studies Bd, 1989–94. Pres., English Chapter, Internat. Acad. of Matrimonial Lawyers, 1986–89. Sec., Internat. Cystic Fibrosis Assoc., 1984–90; Trustee: Cystic Fibrosis Res. Trust, 1964–; Robert Luff Charitable Foundn, 1977–. *Publications:* (with James Comyn) Wills & Intestacies, 1970; Contract, 1975; (with Malcolm Stitcher) Atkin's Trade, Labour and Employment, 1975. *Recreations:* charitable work, gardening. *Address:* Royal Courts of Justice, Strand, WC2A 2LL.

JOHNSON, Prof. Roger Paul, FREng; Professor of Civil Engineering, University of Warwick, 1971–98, now Emeritus; *b* 12 May 1931; *s* of Norman Eric Ernest Johnson and Eleanor Florence (*née* Paul); *m* 1958, Diana June (*née* Perkins); three *s*. *Educ:* Cranleigh Sch., Surrey; Jesus Coll., Cambridge (BA 1953; MA 1957). FIStructE 1972; FICE 1979; FREng (FEng 1986). Holloway Bros (London), Civil Engineering Contractor, 1953–55; Ove Arup and Partners, Consulting Engineers, 1956–59; Lectr in Engineering, Cambridge Univ., 1959–71. Visiting Professor: Univ. of Sydney, 1982–83; Univ. of Adelaide, 1995, 1999. *Publications:* Structural Concrete, 1967; Composite Structures of Steel and Concrete, vol. 1, 1975, 2nd edn 1994, vol. 2 (with R. J. Buckby), 1979, 2nd edn 1986; (with D. Anderson) Designers' Handbook to Eurocode 4, 1993; contribs to learned jls. *Recreations:* music, travel, mountain walking. *Address:* School of Engineering, University of Warwick, Coventry CV4 7AL. *T:* (024) 7652 3129.

JOHNSON, Stanley, CBE 1970; FCA; FCIT; Managing Director, British Transport Docks Board, 1967–75; *b* 10 Nov. 1912; *s* of late Robert and Janet Mary Johnson; *m* 1st, 1940, Sheila McLean Bald (*d* 1994); two *s* two *d*; 2nd, 1998, Ellen Elaine Sholten; three step *s* one step *d*. *Educ:* King George V Sch., Southport. Served as Lieut (S) RINVR, 1942–45. Joined Singapore Harbour Board, 1939; Asst Gen. Man. 1952; Chm. and Gen. Man. 1958–59; Chief Docks Man., Hull Docks, 1962; Asst Gen. Man. 1963, Mem. and Dep. Man. Dir 1966, British Transport Docks Board. Chm. Major Ports Cttee, Dock and Harbour Authorities Assoc., 1971–72. Mem., Exec. Council, British Ports Assoc., 1973–75; Vice-Pres., Internat. Assoc. of Ports and Harbours, 1975–77. Vice-Pres., CIT, 1973–75. *Recreations:* walking, reading, travel. *Address:* 70 Royal Oak Court, Apt 201, Vero Beach, FL 32962, USA.

JOHNSON, Stanley Patrick; author and environmentalist; *b* 18 Aug. 1940; *s* of Wilfred Johnson and Irène (*née* Williams); *m* 1st, 1963, Charlotte Offlow Fawcett (marr. diss.); three *s* one *d*; 2nd, 1981, Mrs Jennifer Kidd; one *s* one *d*. *Educ:* Sherborne Sch.; Exeter Coll., Oxford (Trevelyan Schol., Sen. Classics Schol.); Harkness Fellow, USA, 1963–64. MA Oxon 1963; Dip. Agric. Econs Oxon 1965. World Bank, Washington, 1966–68; Project Dir, UNA-USA Nat. Policy Panel on World Population, 1968–69; Mem. Conservative Research Dept, 1969–70; Staff of Internat. Planned Parenthood Fedn, London, 1971–73; Consultant to UN Fund for Population Activities, 1971–73; Mem. Countryside Commn, 1971–73; Head of Prevention of Pollution and Nuisances Div., EEC, 1973–77; Adviser to Head of Environment and Consumer Protection Service, EEC, 1977–79; Member (C) Wight and Hants E, Eur. Parlt, 1979–84; Advr to Dir Gen. for Envmt, Civil Protection and Nuclear Safety, EEC, 1984–90; Dir for Energy Policy, EEC, 1990; Special Advr, Coopers & Lybrand, Deloitte, 1991; Dir, Envmtl Resources Mgt, 1992–94. Newdigate Prize for Poetry, 1962; Richard Martin Award, RSPCA, 1982; Greenpeace Award, 1984. *Publications:* Life Without Birth, 1970; The Green Revolution, 1972; The Politics of the Environment, 1973; (ed) The Population Problem, 1973; The Pollution Control Policy of the EEC, 1979, 3rd edn 1989; Antarctica—the last great wilderness, 1985; (jtly) The Environmental Policy of the EEC, 1989, 2nd edn 1995; The Earth Summit: the United Nations Conference on Environment and Development, 1993; World Population—turning the tide, 1994; The Politics of Population, 1995; *novels:* Gold Drain, 1967; Panther Jones for President, 1968; God Bless America, 1974; The Doomsday Deposit, 1980; The Marburg Virus, 1982; Tunnel, 1984; The Commissioner, 1987; Dragon River, 1989; Icecap, 1999. *Recreations:* writing, travel. *Address:* Nethercote, Winsford, Minehead, Somerset TA24 7HZ; 60 Regent's Park Road, NW1 7SX. *T:* (020) 7722 4258, *Fax:* (020) 7483 1390.

See also A. B. de P. Johnson.

JOHNSON, Terry; playwright and director; *b* 20 Dec. 1955; *s* of Harry Douglas Johnson and Winifred Mary Johnson (*née* Wood); one *d* by Marion Bailey. *Educ:* Birmingham Univ. (BA 2nd cl. Drama and Th. Arts). Actor, 1971–75; *playwright:* Amabel, Bush Th., 1972; Insignificance, Royal Court (Most Promising Playwright, Evening Standard Award), 1982 (screenplay, 1985); Unsuitable for Adults, Bush, Cries from the Mammal House, Royal Ct, 1984; (jtly) Tuesday's Child, Stratford Th. Royal, 1986; Imagine Drowning, Hampstead (John Whiting Award), 1991; Hysteria, Royal Ct, 1993 (Meyer-Whitworth Award, 1993; Best Comedy, Olivier Award, and Best Play, Writers' Guild, 1994); (also dir.) Dead Funny, Savoy, 1994 (Best Play, Writers' Guild, 1994; Best New Play, Critics' Circle, and Playwright of the Year, Lloyds Pvte Banking, 1995); adaptation (also dir.), The London Cuckolds, 1997, (also dir.) Cleo, Camping, Emmanuelle and Dick, 1998 (Best Comedy, Olivier Award, 1999), RNT; adaptation (also dir.), The Graduate, Gielgud, 2000; plays also performed in USA, Europe, Australia, Canada and NZ; other *plays directed* include: The Memory of Water, Vaudeville, 1996; The Libertine, Chicago, 1996; Elton John's Glasses, Queen's, 1997; Sparkleshark, RNT, 1999; Entertaining Mr Sloane, Arts, 2001; *television:* (dir.) Way Upstream, 1988; wrote and directed: Blood and Water, 1995; Cor Blimey!, 2000; Not Only But Always, 2001; screenplay, The Bite, 1994. *Publications:* Insignificance, 1982; Cries from the Mammal House, 1984; Unsuitable for Adults, 1985; Tuesday's Child, 1987; Imagine Drowning, 1991; Hysteria, 1993; Dead Funny, 1994; Johnson: Plays One, 1993; The London Cuckolds, 1997; Johnson: Plays Two, 1998; Cleo, Camping, Emmanuelle and Dick, 1998; The Graduate, 2000.

JOHNSON, Sir Vassel (Godfrey), Kt 1994; CBE 1979 (OBE 1970); JP; Director: British American Bank, since 1983; Monetary Authority, Cayman Islands, 1997–2000; *b* 18 Jan. 1922; *s* of late Charles McKintha Johnson and of Theresa Virginia Johnson (*née* McDoom); *m* 1952, Rita Joanna Hinds; two *s* four *d* (and one *s* decd). *Educ:* Govt Secondary Sch., Grand Cayman; Bennett Coll., England; Wolsey Hall; Sussex Univ. Entered Cayman Is CS, 1942; transferred to Cayman Co. of Jamaica Home Guard, 1942–45; Clerical Officer, Dept of Treasury, Customs and PO, 1945–55; Asst to Dep. Treas., 1955–59; Clerk of Courts, 1959–60; Public Recorder, 1962–76; Treas. and Collector of Taxes, 1965–82; Hd of Exchange Control, 1966–80; Inspector of Banks and Trust Cos, 1966–73; Chm., Cayman Is Currency Bd, 1971–82; Mem., Exec. Council, resp. for Finance and Develt, 1972–82; Actg Gov., Cayman Is, 1977; Chm., Govt Vehicles Funding Scheme, 1977–82; retd from CS, 1983. Chm., Public Service Commn, 1983–84; MLA, George Town, 1984–88; Mem., Exec. Council, resp. for Develt and Nat. Resources, 1984–88. Cayman Airways Ltd: Founding Dir, 1968; Chm., 1971–77 and 1984–85; Chm., Cayman Is Corp. (Airport), 1969–77; Trustee, Swiss Bank & Trust Corp., 1983–97; Man. Dir, Montpelier Properties (Cayman) Ltd, 1983–97. JP Cayman Is, 1977. Chm., Bd of Govs, Cayman Prep. Sch., 1982–84 and 1993–95. Silver Jubilee Medal, 1977. *Publications:* Cayman Islands Economic and Financial Review 1904–1981, 1982; As I See It: how Cayman became a leading financial centre (autobiog.), 2001. *Recreations:* bridge, church work (Senior Elder, United Church). *Address:* PO Box 78G, Grand Cayman, Cayman Islands. *T:* 9499217, *Fax:* 9459326.

JOHNSON, Walter Hamlet; *b* Hertford, 21 Nov. 1917; *s* of John Johnson; *m* 1945. *Educ:* Devon House Sch., Margate. Councillor, Brentford and Chiswick for 6 years. Nat. Treasurer, 1965–77, Pres., 1977–81, Transport Salaried Staffs' Assoc. Joined Labour Party, 1945. Contested (Lab) Bristol West, 1955 and South Bedfordshire, 1959, in General Elections; also Acton (Lab), 1968, in by-election. MP (Lab) Derby South, 1970–83; an Assistant Govt Whip, 1974–75. Is particularly interested in welfare services, transport, labour relations and aviation matters; Chm., PLP Aviation Cttee, 1979–83. Principal Executive Assistant, London Transport, 1980–83 (formerly a Sen. Exec., Staff Trng). Governor, Ruskin Coll., Oxford, 1966–85. *Recreation:* sport. *Address:* 9 Milton Court, Haywards Heath RH16 1EY. *T:* (01444) 412629.

JOHNSON, Wendy Rosalind; *see* James, W. R.

JOHNSON, Prof. William, DSc, MA; FRS 1982; FREng, FIMechE; Professor of Mechanics, Engineering Department, Cambridge University, 1975–82, now Professor Emeritus; Professorial Fellow, Fitzwilliam College, Cambridge, 1975–82; *b* 20 April 1922; *er s* of James Johnson and Elizabeth Johnson (*née* Riley); *m* 1946, Heather Marie (*née* Thornber); three *s* two *d. Educ:* Central Grammar Sch., Manchester; Manchester Coll. of Science and Technology (BScTech; DSc 1960); BSc Maths, London (ext.); UCL (Hist. and Phil. of Sci. course, 1950; Fellow, 1982); MA Cantab. CEng, FREng (FEng 1983). Commnd REME, UK, Italy and Austria, 1943–47. Asst Principal, Administrative Grade, Home Civil Service, 1948–50; Lecturer, Northampton Polytechnic, London, 1950–51; Lectr in Engineering, Sheffield Univ., 1952–56; Senior Lectr in Mechanical Engineering, Manchester Univ., 1956–60; Prof. of Mechanical Engrg, 1960–75, Dir of Medical Engrg, 1973–75, UMIST. Visiting Professor: McMaster Univ., Canada, 1969; Springer Prof., Univ. of Calif, Berkeley, 1980; Singapore, 1982; Allied Irish Banks Prof., Univ. of Belfast, 1983; UMIST, 1983–94; Industrial Engrg Dept, Purdue Univ., Indiana, 1984 and 1985; Taiwan, 1985; United Technologies Dist. Prof. of Engrg, Purdue Univ., 1988 and 1989. Hon. Sec., Yorks Br. of IMechE, 1953–56, and Chm., NW Br., 1974–75; Vis. for DoI to Prodn Engrg Res. Assoc. and Machine Tool Res. Assoc., 1973–75; President: Manchester and Salford Med. Engrg Club, 1971–72; Manchester Assoc. of Engrs, 1972–73; Manchester Technol. Assoc., 1983–84. Founder, and Editor-in-Chief: Internat. Jl Mech. Sciences, 1960–87; Internat. Jl Impact Engineering, 1983–87; Chm., Internat. Jl Mech. Engrg Educn, 1960–84. For. Fellow, Nat. Acad. of Athens, 1982; For. Mem., Russian Acad. of Scis, Ural Br., 1993; Hon. Mem., Indian Nat. Acad. Engrg, 1999. Hon. DTech Bradford, 1976; Hon. DEng: Sheffield, 1986; UMIST, 1995. Premium Award, Jl RAeS, 1956; T. Constantine Medal, Manchester Assoc. of Engrs, 1962; Bernard Hall Prize (jt), IMechE, 1965–66 and 1966–67; James Clayton Fund Prize (jt), IMechE, 1972 and 1978; Safety in Mech. Engrg Prize, (jt) 1980, 1991; Silver Medal, Inst. of Sheet Metal Engrg, 1987; James Clayton Prize, IMechE, 1987; Gold Medal, Jl of Advanced Materials Processing Technology, 1995. *Publications:* Plasticity for Mechanical Engineers (with P. B. Mellor), 1962; Mechanics of Metal Extrusion (with H. Kudo), 1962; Plane Strain Slip Line Fields (with R. Sowerby and J. B. Haddow), 1970; Impact Strength of Materials, 1972; Engineering Plasticity (with P. B. Mellor), 1973; Lectures in Engineering Plasticity (with A. G. Mamalis), 1978; Crashworthiness of Vehicles (with A. G. Mamalis), 1978; Plane-Strain Slip-Line Fields for Metal-Deformation Processes (with R. Sowerby and R. Venter), 1982; papers in mechanics of metal forming, impact engineering, mechanics of sports and games, solids, medical and bioengineering, and history of engineering mechanics. *Recreations:* gardening, music. *Address:* Department of Mechanical Engineering, University of Manchester Institute of Science and Technology, PO Box 88, Manchester M60 1QD.

JOHNSON, (Willis) Merwyn; Agent General for Saskatchewan in the United Kingdom, 1977–83; *b* 9 May 1923; *s* of Robert Arthur Johnson and Gudborg Kolbinson; *m* 1946, Laura Elaine Aseltine; two *s* two *d. Educ:* McKenzie High Sch., Kindersley; Univ. of Saskatchewan. BSA, BA. MP for Kindersley, Parliament of Canada, 1953–57 and 1957–58. *Recreations:* fishing, golf. *Address:* 4044 Hollydene Place, Victoria, BC V8N 3Z7, Canada. *T:* (250) 4774110.

JOHNSON-FERGUSON, Sir Ian (Edward), 4th Bt *cr* 1906, of Springkell, Dumfries, of Kenyon, Newchurch-in-Culceth, Lancaster, and of Wiston, Lanark; *b* 1 Feb. 1932; *s* of Sir Neil Edward Johnson-Ferguson, 3rd Bt, TD and Sheila Marion (*d* 1985), *er d* of Col H. S. Jervis, MC; *S* father, 1992; *m* 1964, Rosemary Teresa, *yr d* of C. J. Whitehead; three *s. Educ:* Ampleforth Coll.; Trinity Coll., Cambridge (BA 1953); Imperial Coll., London (DIC Geophysics 1954). Royal Dutch Shell, 1954–62; IBM UK Ltd, 1963–90. *Heir: s* Major Mark Edward Johnson-Ferguson, RE [*b* 14 Aug. 1965; *m* 1995, Dr Julia Catherine, *d* of T. D. Getley; two *d*]. *Address:* Copthall Place, Upper Clatford, Andover, Hants SP11 7LR.

JOHNSON-GILBERT, Ronald Stuart, OBE 1976; Secretary, Royal College of Surgeons of England, 1962–88; *b* 14 July 1925; *s* of late Sir Ian A. Johnson-Gilbert, CBE and late Rosalind Bell-Hughes; *m* 1951, Ann Weir Drummond; three *d. Educ:* Edinburgh Acad.; Rugby; Brasenose Coll., Oxford (Classical Exhbnr and Open Schol., 1943; MA). Intelligence Corps, 1943–46. Trainee, John Lewis Partnership, 1950–51; Admin. Staff, RCS, 1951–88; Secretary: Faculties of Dental Surgery and of Anaesthetists, 1958; Jt Conf. of Surgical Colls, 1963–88; Internat. Fedn of Surgical Colls, 1967–74; Hon. Sec., Med. Commn on Accident Prevention, 1984–88. Mem. Ct of Patrons, RCS, 1990–; Hunterian Trustee, RCS, 1989–2000. Hon. FFARCS 1983; Hon. FRCS 1987; Hon. FDSRCS 1987; Hon. FRCSI 1989. John Tomes Medal, BDA, 1980; McNeill Love Medal, RCS, 1981; Royal Australasian Coll. of Surgeons Medal, 1982. *Recreations:* music, painting, literature, golf. *Address:* Home Farm, Castle Rising, near King's Lynn, Norfolk PE31 6AE.

JOHNSON-LAIRD, Prof. Philip Nicholas, FRS 1991; FBA 1986; Stuart Professor of Psychology, Princeton University, since 1994 (Professor pf Psychology, since 1989); *b* 12 Oct. 1936; *s* of Eric Johnson-Laird and Dorothy (*née* Blackett); *m* 1959, Maureen Mary Sullivan; one *s* one *d. Educ:* Culford Sch.; University Coll. London (Rosa Morison Medal, 1964; James Sully Schol., 1964–66; BA (Hons) 1964; PhD 1967; Fellow, 1994). MBPsS 1962. 10 years of misc. jobs, as surveyor, musician, hosp. porter (alternative to Nat. Service), librarian, before going to university. Asst Lectr, then Lectr, in Psychol., UCL, 1966–73; Reader, 1973, Prof., 1978, in Exptl Psychol., Univ. of Sussex; Asst Dir, MRC Applied Psychology Unit, Cambridge, 1983–89; Fellow, Darwin Coll., Cambridge, 1984–89. Vis. Mem., Princeton Inst. for Advanced Study, 1971–72; Vis. Fellow, Stanford Univ., 1980; Visiting Professor: Stanford Univ., 1985; Princeton Univ., 1986. Member: Psychol. Cttee, SSRC, 1975–79; Linguistics Panel, SSRC, 1980–82; Adv. Council, Internat. Assoc. for Study of Attention and Performance, 1984. Member: Linguistics Assoc., 1967; Exptl Psychol. Soc., 1968; Cognitive Sci. Soc., 1980; Assoc. for Computational Linguistics, 1981. Hon. DPhil: Göteborg, 1983; Padua, 1997; Madrid, 2000; Dublin, 2000. Spearman Medal, 1974, President's Award, 1985, BPsS. *Publications:* (ed jtly) Thinking and Reasoning, 1968; (with P. C. Wason) Psychology and Reasoning, 1972; (with G. A. Miller) Language and Perception, 1976; (ed jtly) Thinking, 1977; Mental Models, 1983; The Computer and the Mind, 1988; (with Ruth Byrne) Deduction, 1991; Human and Machine Thinking, 1993; contribs to psychol, linguistic and cognitive sci. jls, reviews in lit. jls. *Recreations:* talking, arguing, laughing, playing modern jazz. *Address:* Department of Psychology, Princeton University, Princeton, NJ 08540, USA. *T:* (609) 2584432.

JOHNSON SMITH, Rt Hon. Sir Geoffrey, Kt 1982; PC 1996; DL; *b* 16 April 1924; *s* of late J. Johnson Smith; *m* Jeanne Pomeroy, MD; two *s* one *d. Educ:* Charterhouse; Lincoln Coll., Oxford. Served War of 1939–45: Royal Artillery, 1942–47; Capt. RA, 1946. BA Hons, Politics, Philosophy and Economics, Oxford, 1949. Mem., Oxford Union Soc. Debating Team, USA, 1949. Information Officer, British Information Services, San Francisco, 1950–52; Mem. Production Staff, Current Affairs Unit, BBC TV, 1953–54; London County Councillor, 1955–58; Interviewer, Reporter, BBC TV, 1955–59. MP (C): Holborn and St Pancras South, 1959–64; East Grinstead, Feb. 1965–1983; Wealden, 1983–2001. PPS, Board of Trade and Min. of Pensions, 1960–63; Opposition Whip, 1965; Parly Under-Sec. of State for Defence for the Army, MoD, 1971–72; Parly Sec., CSD, 1972–74. Chm., Cons. Back-bench Defence Cttee, 1988–93 (Vice-Chm., 1980–88); Chm., Select Cttee on Members' Interests, 1980–95; Vice-Chm., 1922 Cttee, 1988–2001 (Mem. Exec., 1979–2001). A Vice-Chm., Conservative Party, 1965–71. Member: IBA Gen. Adv. Council, 1975–80; N Atlantic Assembly, 1980–2001 (Chm., Military Cttee, 1985–89; Leader, UK Delegn to Assembly, 1987–97; Treas., 1996–2001). Governor, BFI, 1980–88. Freeman, City of London, 1980. DL East Sussex, 1986. *Address:* Parkhurst, High Hurstwood, Uckfield, E Sussex TN22 4AG. *Club:* Travellers.

JOHNSTON; *see* Lawson Johnston.

JOHNSTON; *see* Russell-Johnston.

JOHNSTON, family name of **Baron Johnston of Rockport**.

JOHNSTON, Hon. Lord; Alan Charles Macpherson Johnston; a Senator of the College of Justice in Scotland, since 1994; *b* 13 Jan. 1942; *s* of Hon. Lord Dunpark, TD; *m* 1966, Anthea Jean Blackburn; three *s. Educ:* Edinburgh Academy; Loretto School; Jesus Coll., Cambridge (BA Hons); Edinburgh Univ. (LLB). Called to the Bar, 1967; QC (Scot.) 1980. Standing Junior, Scottish Home and Health Dept, 1974–79; Advocate Depute, 1979–82; Treasurer, 1977–89, Dean, 1989–94, Faculty of Advocates. Chairman: Industrial Tribunal, 1982–85; Med. Appeal Tribunal, 1985–89. *Publication:* (asst editor) Gloag and Henderson, Introduction to Scots Law, 7th edn 1968. *Recreations:* shooting, fishing, golf, walking. *Address:* 3 Circus Gardens, Edinburgh EH3 6TN. *Clubs:* University Pitt (Cambridge); New (Edinburgh).

JOHNSTON OF ROCKPORT, Baron *cr* 1987 (Life Peer), of Caversham in the Royal County of Berkshire; **Charles Collier Johnston,** Kt 1973; TD; *b* 4 March 1915; *e s* of late Captain Charles Moore Johnston and Muriel Florence Mellon; *m;* two *s; m* 1981, Mrs Yvonne Shearman. *Educ:* Tonbridge Sch., Kent. Commissioned TA, 1938; served War of 1939–45 (TD); Major RA, retd 1946. Managing Dir, 1948–76, Chm., 1951–77, of Standex International Ltd (formerly Roehlen-Martin Ltd), Engravers and Engineers, Ashton Road, Bredbury, Cheshire; Chairman: Thames & Kennet Marina Ltd, 1982–94; James Burn International, 1986–; Standex Holdings Ltd, 1986– (Dir 1983). Jt Hon. Treas.,

Conservative Party, 1984–87. Chm., Macclesfield Constituency Conservative Assoc., 1961–65; Hon. Treas., NW Conservatives and Mem. Conservative Bd of Finance, 1965–71; Chm., NW Area Conservatives, 1971–76; Pres., Nat. Union of Conservative and Unionist Assocs, 1986–87 (Mem. Exec. Cttee, 1965–, Chm. 1976–81). Nat. Chm., Cons. Friends of Israel, 1983–86. Mem., Boyd Commn, as official observers of elecns held in Zimbabwe/Rhodesia, April 1980. *Recreations:* spectator sports, travelling, gardening. *Address:* House of Lords, SW1A 0PW.

JOHNSTON, Alexander Graham; Sheriff of Strathkelvin at Glasgow, since 1985; *b* 16 July 1944; *s* of Hon. Lord Kincraig, *qv*; *m* 1st, 1972, Susan (marr. diss. 1982); two *s*; 2nd, 1982, Angela; two step *d*. *Educ:* Edinburgh Acad.; Strathallan Sch.; Univ. of Edinburgh (LLB); University Coll., Oxford (BA). Admitted as Solicitor and Writer to the Signet, 1971; Partner, Hagart and Burn-Murdoch, Solicitors, Edinburgh, 1972–82. Sheriff of Grampian, Highland and Isles, 1982–85. Editor, Scottish Civil Law Reports, 1987–92. Hon. Fellow, Inst. of Professional Investigators, 1980. *Recreations:* photography, computing and IT, bridge, puzzles. *Address:* 3 North Dean Park Avenue, Bothwell, Lanarkshire G71 8HH. *T:* (01698) 852177; *e-mail:* grahamjohnston1@netscapeonline.co.uk. *Clubs:* Oxford and Cambridge Golfing Society; Vincent's (Oxford).

JOHNSTON, Most Rev. Allen Howard, CMG 1978; LTh; *b* Auckland, NZ, 1912; *s* of Joseph Howard Johnston; *m* 1937, Joyce Rhoda, *d* of John A. Grantley, Auckland; four *d*. *Educ:* Seddon Memorial Technical College; St John's College, Auckland; Auckland Univ. College. Deacon, 1935; Priest, 1936. Assistant Curate of St Mark's, Remuera, 1935–37; Vicar of Dargaville, 1937–42; Vicar of Northern Wairoa, 1942–44; Vicar of Otahuhu, 1944–49; Vicar of Whangarei, 1949–53; Archdeacon of Waimate, 1949–53; Bishop of Dunedin, 1953–69; Bishop of Waikato, 1969–80; Primate and Archbishop of New Zealand, 1972–80. Fellow, St John's Coll., Auckland, 1970. Hon. LLD Otago, 1969. ChStJ 1974. *Address:* 207 Riddell Road, Auckland, New Zealand.

JOHNSTON, Angela Maureen Howard-; *see* Huth, A. M.

JOHNSTON, Callum William; Secretary and Chief Executive, Central Arbitration Committee, since 1999; *b* 15 Sept. 1946; *s* of James Johnston, OBE, and Mary Johnston (*née* Upchurch); *m* 1974, Sarah Motta; one *s* one *d*. *Educ:* Westcliff High Sch.; King Edward VII Sch., Lytham; Durham Univ. (BA Econs and Law 1968); Indiana Univ. (MBA 1970). Financial journalist and broadcaster, 1970–73; DTI, 1973–79 (Private Sec., 1975–79); Cabinet Office, 1979–86; Department of Trade and Industry: British Steel privatisation, 1986–89; UK and EU Co. Law Policy, 1989–90; on secondment to Leyland DAF plc, 1990–92; UK and EU Technol. and IT Security Policy, 1992–95; Pay Dir, 1995–98; Dir, Small Business Policy, 1998–99. *Recreations:* music, walking, cycling, collecting and using cameras, changing jobs. *Address:* Central Arbitration Committee, Discovery House, 28–42 Banner Street, EC1Y 8QE.

JOHNSTON, Catherine Elizabeth, CB 2000; Parliamentary Counsel, since 1994; *b* 4 Jan. 1953; *d* of Sir Alexander Johnston, GCB, KBE and Betty Joan Johnston (*née* Harris), CBE; *m* 1989, Brendan Patrick Keith; one *s* one *d*. *Educ:* St Paul's Girls' Sch.; St Hugh's Coll., Oxford (Scholar 1970; BA 1974). Admitted as solicitor, 1978; joined Parliamentary Counsel Office, 1980; with Law Commn, 1983–85 and 1990–92; on secondment to Office of Parly Counsel, Canberra, 1987–88. *Address:* Office of the Parliamentary Counsel, 36 Whitehall, SW1A 2AY.

JOHNSTON, Prof. David, MD, ChM; FRCS, FRCSE, FRCSGlas; Professor of Surgery and Head of Department, University of Leeds at Leeds General Infirmary, 1977–98; *b* Glasgow, 4 Sept. 1936; *s* of Robert E. and Jean Johnston; *m* (marr. diss); three *s* one *d*; *m* 1987, Dr Maureen Teresa Reynolds; two *s*. *Educ:* Hamilton Acad.; Glasgow Univ. (MB, ChB Hons; MD Hons, ChM). FRCSE 1963; FRCSGlas 1964; FRCS 1979. House Surgeon, Western Infirmary, Glasgow, 1961–62; Res. Asst and Registrar, Univ. Dept of Surg., Leeds Gen. Infirm., 1962–64; Lectr in Surg., Univ. of Sheffield, 1965–68; Sen. Lectr and Consultant, Univ. Dept of Surg., Leeds Gen. Infirm., 1968–75; Prof. of Surg. and Head of Dept, Univ. of Bristol (Bristol Royal Infirm.), 1975–77. *Publications:* papers on physiology and surgery of the stomach, colon and rectum, and on obesity. *Recreations:* reading, running, tennis, fishing. *Address:* 23 Shire Oak Road, Headingley, Leeds LS6 2DD. *T:* (0113) 275 4689.

JOHNSTON, David Alan H.; *see* Hunter Johnston.

JOHNSTON, David Carr; Chief Education Officer, Manchester City Council, since 1998; *b* 18 March 1944; *s* of William and Sarah Johnston; *m* 1969, Jennifer Anne Hopkinson; two *d*. *Educ:* Didsbury Coll. of Educn (Teacher's Cert. 1965); Sheffield Univ. (DipASE 1971); Sheffield Poly. (Dip Educn Mgt 1975); Leicester Univ. (MEd 1982). Asst Teacher, Trafford, Lancs, 1965–67, Sheffield primary schs, 1967–69; Dep. Hd, Park Hill Jun. Sch., Sheffield, 1969–72; Headteacher: Shirebrook Middle Sch., Sheffield, 1972–74; Ballifield Nursery, First and Middle Sch., Sheffield, 1974–79; School Advr, Derbys CC, 1979–84; Sen. Sch. Inspector, 1984–88, Dep. Chief Educn Officer, 1988–92, Manchester City Council; Dir of Educn and Leisure, Salford City Council, 1992–98. *Publications:* Managing Primary Schools, 1985; Managing Primary Schools in the 1990s, 1990. *Recreations:* music appreciation, fell walking, supporting Manchester City FC. *Address:* Education Department, Crown Square, Manchester M60 3BB. *T:* (0161) 234 7001.

JOHNSTON, Dr David Eric Lothian; advocate, since 1992; *b* 10 March 1961; *e s* of Thomas Lothian Johnston, *qv*, and Joan (*née* Fahmy). *Educ:* Daniel Stewart's and Melville Coll., Edinburgh; St John's Coll., Cambridge (BA 1982; MA 1986; PhD 1986). Research Fellow, 1985–89, Fellow, 1993–99, Christ's Coll., Cambridge; Regius Prof. of Civil Law, Univ. of Cambridge, 1993–99. Visiting Fellow: Univ. of Freiburg, 1985–86; Univ. of Michigan Law Sch., 1987; Univ. of Calif, Berkeley, Law Sch., 1996, 1998; Visiting Professor: Paris I, 1999; Paris V, 2000, 2001; Univ. of Osaka, 2000; Hon. Prof., Edinburgh Univ. Law Sch., 2000–. *Publications:* On a Singular Book of Cervidius Scaevola, 1987; The Roman Law of Trusts, 1988; Roman Law in Context, 1999; Prescription and Limitation, 1999; articles in learned jls mainly on Roman law and legal history. *Recreations:* music, travel, wine and food. *Address:* Advocates' Library, Parliament House, Edinburgh EH1 1RF. *T:* (0131) 226 5071.

JOHNSTON, David Lawrence, OBE 1997; CEng, FIEE; FIMgt; RCNC; Chairman, National Quality Assurance Ltd, since 1993 (Director, since 1989); *b* 12 April 1936; *s* of late Herbert David Johnston and Hilda Eleanor Johnston (*née* Wood); *m* 1959, Beatrice Ann Witten; three *d*. *Educ:* Lancastrian Sch., Chichester; King's Coll., Durham (BSc). FIEE 1980. Short Service Commn (Lieut), RN, 1959–62. Joined Ministry of Defence, 1962; Overseeing, Wallsend, 1962–63; Design, Bath, 1963–66; Production and Project Management, Devonport Dockyard, 1966–73; Dockyard Policy, Bath, 1973–76; Design, Bath, 1976–79; Production and Planning, Portsmouth Dockyard, 1979–81; Planning and Production, Devonport Dockyard, 1981–84; Asst Under-Sec. of State, and Man. Dir, HM Dockyard, Devonport, 1984–87; Chm. and Man. Dir, Devonport Dockyard Ltd, Management Buy-out Co., 1985–87; Dep. Chm., Devonport Management Ltd, 1987–88; management consultant, 1988–89; Dir Gen., Nat. Inspection Council for Electrical Installation Contracting, 1989–2001. Dep. Chm., NQA, USA Inc., 1998– (Dir, 1993–). Director: Nat. Supervisory Council, Intruder Alarms Ltd, 1989–90; Nat. Approval Council, Security Systems Ltd, 1990–96. Chm., BASEEFA Adv. Council, HSE, 1990–; Member: Electrical Equipment Certification Management Bd, HSE, 1990–; HSE Open Government Complaints Panel, 1995–; IEE Wiring Regulations Policy Cttee, 2001–. FIMgt (FBIM 1980). *Recreations:* gardening, walking, converting houses. *Address:* Chinley House, 1 Eaton Park Road, Cobham, Surrey KT11 2JG. *T:* (01932) 588269, *Fax:* (01932) 864472; National Quality Assurance Ltd, Warwick House, Houghton Hall Park, Houghton Regis, Dunstable, Beds LU5 5ZX. *T:* (01582) 539000.

JOHNSTON, Prof. David Lloyd; President and Vice-Chancellor, University of Waterloo, since 1999; *b* 28 June 1941; *s* of Lloyd Johnston and Dorothy Stonehouse Johnston; *m* 1963, Sharon Downey; five *d*. *Educ:* Harvard Univ., Cambridge, Mass; Cambridge Univ.; Queen's Univ. at Kingston, Ont. Asst Prof., Faculty of Law, Queen's Univ., Kingston, 1966–68; Faculty of Law, Univ. of Toronto: Asst Prof., 1968–69; Associate Prof., 1969–72; Prof., 1972–74; Dean and Prof., Faculty of Law, Univ. of Western Ont, 1974–79; Prof. of Law, 1979–99, Principal and Vice-Chancellor, 1979–94, McGill Univ. Chairman: Nat. Round Table on Envmt and the Economy, 1988–92; Information Highway Adv. Council, 1994–97; Canadian Inst. for Advanced Res., 1994–99; NeuroScience Network, 1994–98. LLD *hc* Law Soc. of Upper Canada, 1980. *Publications:* Computers and the Law (ed), 1968; Canadian Securities Regulation, 1977; (jtly) Business Associations, 1979, 2nd edn 1989; (with R. Forbes) Canadian Companies and the Stock Exchange, 1980; (jtly) Canadian Securities Regulation, Supplement, 1982; (jtly) Partnerships and Canadian Business Corporations, 1989; (jtly) If Quebec Goes, 1995; (jtly) Getting Canada Online: understanding the information highway, 1995; (jtly) Cyberlaw and Communication Law, 1997; articles and reports. *Recreations:* jogging, ski-ing, tennis. *Address:* University of Waterloo, Waterloo, ON N2L 3G1, Canada. *T:* (519) 8884400. *Clubs:* University (Toronto); University (Waterloo); Westmount Golf.

JOHNSTON, Hon. Donald (James); PC 1980; QC (Can.) 1985; Secretary-General, Organisation for Economic Co-operation and Development, since 1996; *b* 26 June 1936; *s* of Wilbur Austin Johnston and Florence Jean Moffat Tucker; *m* 1965, Heather Bell Maclaren; four *d*. *Educ:* McGill Univ. (BA, BCL; Gold Medallist 1958); Univ. of Grenoble (schol.). Joined Strikeman & Elliott, 1961; founder of law firm, Johnston, Heenan and Blaikie; Counsel, Heenan Blaikie, 1988–96; Lectr, Fiscal Law, McGill Univ., 1964–77; MP (L) St Henri-Westmount, 1978–88; Pres., Treasury Bd of Canada, 1980–82; Minister of State for Econ. and Regl Develt and for Sci. and Techn., 1982; Minister of Justice and Attorney-Gen., 1984. Pres., Liberal Party, 1990–94. Hon. DCL. *Publications:* How to Survive Canada's Tax Chaos, 1974; Up the Hill, 1986; (ed) With a Bang, Not a Whimper: Pierre Trudeau speaks out, 1988. *Recreations:* writing, tennis, piano. *Clubs:* Mount-Royal (Montreal); Montreal Indoor Tennis; Cercle du Bois de Boulogne (Paris).

JOHNSTON, Very Rev. Frederick Mervyn Kieran; Dean of Cork, 1967–71, retired; *b* 22 Oct. 1911; *s* of Robert Mills Johnston and Florence Harriet O'Hanlon; *m* 1938, Catherine Alice Ruth FitzSimons; two *s*. *Educ:* Grammar Sch., Galway; Bishop Foy Sch., Waterford; Trinity Coll., Dublin. BA 1933. Deacon, 1934; Priest, 1936; Curate, Castlecomer, 1934–36; Curate, St Luke, Cork, 1936–38; Incumbent of Kilmeen, 1938–40; Drimoleague, 1940–45; Blackrock, Cork, 1945–58; Bandon, 1958–67; Rector of St Fin Barre's Cathedral and Dean of Cork, 1967; Examng Chaplain to Bishop of Cork, 1960–78. *Address:* 24 Lapps Court, Hartlands Avenue, Cork, Republic of Ireland.

JOHNSTON, Frederick Patrick Mair, CBE 1993; Chairman, Johnston Press plc (formerly F. Johnston & Co. Ltd), 1973–April 2001 (Director, since 1959); *b* Edinburgh, 15 Sept. 1935; *e s* of late Frederick M. Johnston and Mrs M. K. Johnston, Falkirk; *m* 1961, Elizabeth Ann Jones; two *s*. *Educ:* Morrison's Acad., Crieff; Lancing Coll., Sussex; New Coll., Oxford (MA, Mod. Hist.). Commissioned in Royal Scots Fusiliers, 1955; served in E Africa with 4th (Uganda) Bn, KAR, 1955–56. Joined Editorial Dept of Liverpool Daily Post & Echo, 1959; joined The Times Publishing Co. Ltd, as Asst Sec., 1960–62; F. Johnston & Co. Ltd, subseq. Johnston Press plc: Asst Manager, 1962; Company Sec., 1969–73; Managing Dir, 1973–80; Chief Exec., 1980–91; Exec. Chm., 1991–97. Chm., Dunn & Wilson Ltd, 1976–97; Director: Scottish Mortgage and Trust plc, 1991–; Lloyds TSB Bank Scotland plc, 1996–; The Press Association Ltd, 1997–. Dir, FIEJ, 1990–96. President: Young Newspapermen's Assoc., 1968–69; Forth Valley Chamber of Commerce, 1972–73; Scottish Newspaper Proprietors' Assoc., 1976–78; Newspaper Soc., 1989–90; Chm., Newspapers Press Fund Appeal, 1995; Chm., Central Scotland Manpower Cttee, 1976–83; Mem., Press Council, 1974–88; Treasurer: Soc. of Master Printers of Scotland, 1981–86; CPU, 1987–91. Chm., Edinburgh Internat. Book Fest. (formerly Edinburgh Book Fest.), 1996–. FRSA 1992. *Recreations:* reading, travelling. *Address:* Johnston Press plc, 53 Manor Place, Edinburgh EH3 7EG. *Clubs:* Caledonian; New (Edinburgh).

JOHNSTON, Gordon MacKenzie, OBE 1996; HM Diplomatic Service, retired; *b* 24 June 1941; *s* of William Johnston and Betty Isabel Lamond (*née* MacKenzie); *m* 1963, Barbara Glenis Christie; one *s* one *d*. *Educ:* Robert Gordon's Coll., Aberdeen; Dingwall Acad. Joined HM Foreign, later Diplomatic, Service, 1959; FO, 1959–63; Berne, 1963–65; Pro-Consul, Tamsui, 1966–67; FCO, 1967–71; Entry Clearance Officer, Islamabad, 1971; FCO, 1972–74; Commercial Attaché, Paris, 1974–77; Second Sec., Georgetown, 1978–81; Press Officer, FCO, 1981–84; First Secretary: Commercial, Belgrade, 1984–88; Economic, Dublin, 1989–90; FCO, 1990–92; Ambassador, Slovenia, 1992–97; Counsellor (Commercial and Econ.), Stockholm, 1997–98. *Recreations:* golf, tennis, reading.

JOHNSTON, Lt Col Grenville Shaw, OBE 1986; TD (2 clasps) 1975; CA; Senior Partner, W. D. Johnston & Carmichael, since 1975; Vice Lord-Lieutenant, Moray, since 1996; *b* 28 Jan. 1945; *s* of Lt Col William Dewar Johnston, OBE, TD, CA and Margaret Raynor Adaline Johnston (*née* Shaw); *m* 1972, Marylyn Jean Picken; two *d*. *Educ:* Seafield Primary Sch., Elgin; Blairmore Prep. Sch., Huntly; Fettes Coll., Edinburgh. CA 1968. Apprentice with Scott-Moncrieff Thomson & Sheils, Edinburgh, 1963–68; Asst, Thomson McLintock & Co., Glasgow, 1968–70; with W. D. Johnston & Carmichael, 1970–. Mem. Council, ICA Scotland, 1993– (Jun. Vice Pres., 1998; Sen. Vice Pres., 1999–2000; Pres., 2000–01). Chm., Grampian & Shetland Cttee, Royal Jubilee and Prince's Trusts, 1980–91; Mem., Grampian Cttee, Prince's Scottish Youth Business Trust, 1989–97. Sec., Moray Local Health Council, 1975–91; Board Member: Moray Enterprise Trust, 1985–93; Moray Badenoch & Strathspey Local Enterprise Co. Ltd, 1990–93; Highlands and Is Airports Ltd, 2001–. Trustee, Nat. Museums of Scotland, 1998–. Vice-Chm., Gordonstoun Sch., 1985–99. Mem., Highland Area, TAVRA Assoc., 1980–99; Chm., Northern Area, 1999–2001, Highland Area, 2001–, RFCA. Lt Col, TA, 1982; Hon. Col, 3rd Highlanders, 1997–99. DL Moray, 1979. KCSG 1982. *Recreations:* fishing, ski-ing, shooting, hockey, occasional running, increasingly golf, tenor in Culbin Singers, Forres. *Address:* Spynie Kirk House, Spynie, Elgin, Moray IV30 3XJ. *T:* (01343) 542578. *Clubs:* Caledonian, Special Forces; New (Edinburgh).

JOHNSTON, Henry Butler M.; *see* McKenzie Johnston.

JOHNSTON, Hugh Philip, CB 1977; FREng; Deputy Secretary, Property Services Agency, Department of the Environment, 1974–87; *b* 17 May 1927; *s* of late Philip Rose-Johnston and Dora Ellen Johnston; *m* 1949, Barbara Frances Theodoridi; one *s* three *d*. *Educ:* Wimbledon Coll.; Faraday House. DFH (Hons). Air Ministry Works Dept: Asst Engr, 1951; Engr, 1956; Ministry of Public Buildings and Works: Prin. Engr, 1964; Asst Dir, 1969; Dir (Under-Sec.), Dept of Environment and Property Services Agency, Engrg Services Directorate, 1970. Pres., CIBSE, 1987–88. FREng (FEng 1989). *Recreations:* motoring, music. *Address:* 9 Devas Road, Wimbledon, SW20 8PD. *T:* (020) 8946 2021.

JOHNSTON, Ian; *see* Johnston, W. I. R.

JOHNSTON, Ian Alistair, CB 1995; PhD; Vice Chancellor and Principal, Glasgow Caledonian University, since 1998; *b* 2 May 1944; *s* of late Donald Dalrymple Johnston and Muriel Joyce Johnston (*née* Hill); *m* 1973, Mary Bridget Lube; one *s* one *d*. *Educ:* Royal Grammar Sch., High Wycombe; Birmingham Univ. (BSc, PhD). Joined Dept of Employment as Assistant Principal, 1969; Private Sec. to Permanent Secretary, Sir Denis Barnes, 1972–73; Principal, 1973; First Sec. (Labour Attaché), British Embassy, Brussels, 1976–77; Asst Sec. (Director, ACAS), 1978; Under-Sec. (Dir of Planning and Resources, MSC), 1984; Chief Exec., Vocational Educn Trng Gp, MSC, 1985; Dep. Dir Gen., MSC, subseq. Training Commn, then Training Agency, then Training Enterprise and Education Directorate of Department of Employment, 1987–92; Dir of Resources and Strategy (Dep. Sec.), Dept of Employment, 1992; Dir Gen., TEED, Dept of Employment, 1992–95; Dep. Principal, Sheffield Hallam Univ., 1995–98. Dir, CAPITB plc, 1999–. Hon. Treas. and Council Mem., Industrial Soc., 1992–. Mem., European Commn Expert Study Gp on Educn and Trng, 1995–99. Member, Council: BTEC/Univ. of London Exam. Bd, 1995–98; Council for Industry and Higher Educn, 2000–; Dir, Qualification for Industry, 1996–99. Gov. and Dep. Chm., Sheffield Hallam Univ. (formerly Sheffield Poly.), 1988–95; Bd Mem., then Dep. Chm., Univ. for Industry, 1998–; Trustee, Carnegie Trust for Univs of Scotland, 1998–. CIMgt 1993; FCIPD (FIPD 1993); FRSA 1995. *Publications:* contribs to learned jls on atomic structure of metals, 1966–69, and subseq. on public admin and educn and trng strategy. *Recreations:* birding, gardening, tennis. *Address:* Glasgow Caledonian University, Cowcaddens Road, Glasgow G4 0BA.

JOHNSTON, Prof. Ian Alistair, PhD; CBiol, FIBiol; FRSE; Director, Gatty Marine Laboratory, since 1985, Chandos Professor and Founding Head, Division of Environmental and Evolutionary Biology, School of Environmental and Evolutionary Biology, since 1997, University of St Andrews; *b* 13 April 1949. *Educ:* Univ. of Hull (BSc 1st cl. Hons Biological Chem. and Zoology 1970; PhD 1973). CBiol, FIBiol 1997. NERC Res. Fellow, Univ. of Bristol, 1973; University of St Andrews: Lectr, 1976–84, Reader, 1984, in Physiology; Prof., 1985–95; Founding Chm., Dept of Biology and Preclin. Medicine, 1987–91; Head, Sch. of Biological and Med. Scis, 1991–92; Mem. Court, 1997–July 2002. Vis. Prof., Univ. of Nairobi, 1993. Mem. Council, NERC, 1995–2000. FRSE 1987. Scientific Medal, Zool Soc., 1984. *Publications:* (contrib.) Essentials of Physiology, 3rd edn 1991 (trans. Spanish 1987, trans. Italian 1989, trans. French 1990); (ed jtly) Phenotypic and Evolutionary Adaptation of Animals to Temperature, 1996; (jtly) Environmental Physiology of Animals, 2000. *Address:* Division of Environmental and Evolutionary Biology, University of St Andrews, Gatty Marine Laboratory, St Andrews KY16 8LB. *T:* (01334) 463440.

JOHNSTON, James Campbell, CBE 1972; Chairman: Capel Court Corporation Ltd, 1969–84; Australian Foundation Investment Co., 1967–84; Director, National Mutual T&G Life Association of Australasia Ltd (formerly of T&G Mutual Life Society), 1976–84; *b* 7 July 1912; *s* of late Edwin and Estelle Johnston; *m* 1938, Agnes Emily, *yr d* of late Richard Thomas; two *s* one *d*. *Educ:* Prince Alfred Coll., Adelaide; Scotch Coll., Melbourne; University of Melbourne. Admitted to Inst. Chartered Accountants, Australia, 1933; joined J. B. Were & Son, Stock and Share Brokers, 1935, Sen. Partner, 1967–78; Stock Exchange of Melbourne: Mem., 1947; Chm., 1972–77; Hon. Fellow, Australian Stock Exchange, 1991. Comr, State Electricity Commn of Victoria, 1978–83. Chartered Accountant of the Year, 1984. *Address:* 2/714 Orrong Road, Toorak, Vic 3142, Australia. *Clubs:* Melbourne, Royal Melbourne Golf (Melbourne).

JOHNSTON, Maj.-Gen. James Frederick Junor, CB 1993; CBE 1984; Chairman, Westminster Gardens Ltd, since 1991; *b* 5 Aug. 1939; *s* of late William Johnston and Margaret Macrae Ward Johnston (*née* Junor). *Educ:* George Watson's College; Welbeck College; RMA Sandhurst. BSc, CEng, Eur Ing, FIMechE, psc, rcds. Commissioned REME, 1959; Comd 7 Field Workshop, 1974–76; Directing Staff, Staff Coll., 1976–79; Comd Maint., 3 Armd Div., 1979–81; Dep. Chief of Staff, 4 Armd Div., 1981–84; Asst Chief of Staff, HQ BAOR, 1986–89; Dir Manning (Army), 1989; Dir Gen., Army Manning and Recruiting, MoD, 1990–93, retd. Col Comdt, REME, 1994–2000. Chairman: Crown Housing Trust, 1993–94; Broomleigh Housing Assoc., 1996–97; Brooke Hospital for Animals, 1998–2000. Trustee of several charities. FInstD; FIMgt. *Recreations:* travel, photography, postal history, genealogy, animal welfare. *Address:* c/o Royal Bank of Scotland, Lawrie House, Victoria Road, Farnborough, Hants GU14 7NR. *Clubs:* Army and Navy, Cavalry and Guards; Fadeaways.

JOHNSTON, Jennifer, (Mrs David Gilliland), FRSL; author; *b* 12 Jan. 1930; *d* of late (William) Denis Johnston, OBE; *m* 1st, 1951, Ian Smyth; two *s* two *d*; 2nd, 1976, David Gilliland, *qv*. *Educ:* Park House Sch., Dublin; Trinity Coll., Dublin. FRSL 1979. Mem., Aosdána. Plays: Indian Summer, performed Belfast, 1983; The Porch, prod Dublin, 1986. Hon. DLitt: Ulster, 1984: TCD, 1992; QUB, 1993. *Publications:* The Captains and the Kings, 1972; The Gates, 1973; How Many Miles to Babylon?, 1974; Shadows on Our Skin, 1978 (dramatised for TV, 1979); The Old Jest, 1979 (filmed as The Dawning, 1988); (play) The Nightingale and not the Lark, 1980; The Christmas Tree, 1981; The Railway Station Man, 1984; Fool's Sanctuary, 1987; The Invisible Worm, 1991; The Illusionist, 1995; (contrib.) Finbar's Hotel, 1997; Two Moons, 1998; The Gingerbread Woman, 2000. *Recreations:* theatre, cinema, gardening, travelling. *Address:* Brook Hall, Culmore Road, Derry, N Ireland BT48 8JE. *T:* (01504) 351297.

JOHNSTON, Sir John (Baines), GCMG 1978 (KCMG 1966; CMG 1962); KCVO 1972; HM Diplomatic Service, retired; *b* 13 May 1918; *e s* of late Rev. A. S. Johnston, Banbury, Oxon; *m* 1969, Elizabeth Mary, *d* of late J. F. Crace; one *s*. *Educ:* Banbury Grammar Sch.; Queen's Coll., Oxford (Eglesfield Scholar). Served War, 1940–46: Adjt 1st Bn Gordon Highlanders, 1944; DAQMG HQ 30 Corps District, 1945. Asst Principal, Colonial Office, 1947; Principal, 1948; Asst Sec., West African Council, Accra, 1950–51; UK Liaison Officer with Commission for Technical Co-operation in Africa South of the Sahara, 1952; Principal Private Sec. to Sec. of State for the Colonies, 1953; Asst Sec., 1956; Head of Far Eastern Dept, Colonial Office, 1956; transferred to Commonwealth Relations Office, 1957; Dep. High Commissioner in S Africa, 1959–61; British High Commissioner: in Sierra Leone, 1961–63; in the Federation of Rhodesia and Nyasaland, 1963, Rhodesia, 1964–65; Asst, later Dep. Under-Secretary of State, FCO, 1968–71; British High Commissioner: in Malaysia, 1971–74; in Canada, 1974–78. A Governor, BBC, 1978–85. Chm., ARELS Exams Trust, 1982–94. Mem., Disasters Emergency Cttee, 1985–92. *Address:* 5 Victoria Road, Oxford OX2 7QF. *T:* (01865) 556927.

JOHNSTON, Lt-Col Sir John (Frederick Dame), GCVO 1987 (KCVO 1981; CVO 1977; MVO 1971); MC 1945; Comptroller, Lord Chamberlain's Office, 1981–87 (Assistant Comptroller, 1964–81); *b* 24 Aug. 1922; *m* 1949, Hon. Elizabeth Hardinge (*d* 1995), JP Windsor 1971, *d* of late 2nd Baron Hardinge of Penshurst, PC, GCB, GCVO, MC, and late Lady Hardinge of Penshurst; one *s* one *d*. *Educ:* Ampleforth. Served in Grenadier Guards, 1941–64. Extra Equerry to the Queen, 1965–. President: King George V Fund for Actors and Actresses; Hearing Dogs for Deaf People. *Publication:* The Lord Chamberlain's Blue Pencil, 1990. *Address:* Studio Cottage, The Great Park, Windsor, Berks SL4 2HP. *T:* (01784) 431627; Stone Hill, Newport, Pembrokeshire SA42 0QD. *T:* (01239) 820978. *Club:* Swinley Forest Golf.

JOHNSTON, Margaret; *see* Parker, Margaret Annette McCrie J.

JOHNSTON, Lt-Gen. Sir Maurice (Robert), KCB 1982; OBE 1971; Lord-Lieutenant of Wiltshire, since 1996; Deputy Chief of Defence Staff, 1982–83, retired 1984; *b* 27 Oct. 1929; *s* of late Brig. Allen Leigh Johnston, OBE, and Gertrude Geraldine Johnston (*née* Templer); *m* 1960, Belinda Mary Sladen; one *s* one *d*. *Educ:* Wellington College; RMA Sandhurst. rcds, psc. Commissioned RA, 1949; transf. The Queen's Bays, 1954; served in Germany, Egypt, Jordan, Libya, N Ireland, Borneo. Instr, Army Staff Coll., 1965–67; MA to CGS, 1968–71; CO 1st The Queen's Dragoon Guards, 1971–73; Comdr 20th Armoured Brigade, 1973–75; BGS, HQ UKLF, 1977–78; Senior Directing Staff, RCDS, 1979; Asst Chief of Gen. Staff, 1980; Dep. Chief of Defence Staff (Op. Reqs), 1981–82. Col, 1st The Queen's Dragoon Guards, 1986–91. Chairman: Secondary Resources plc, 1988–91; Detention Corp., 1988–94; Managing Director: Freshglen Ltd, Wraxall Gp, 1984–85; Unit Security Ltd, 1985–88; Director: Partek Cargotec Ltd, 1984–; Shorrock Guards Ltd, 1988–91. Governor: Dauntsey's Sch., Wilts, 1987–, St Mary's Sch., Calne, 1988–94. DL Wilts, 1990, High Sheriff, 1993–94. *Recreations:* fishing, shooting, gardening, music, glass engraving. *Address:* Ivy House, Worton, Devizes, Wilts SN10 5RU. *Club:* Army and Navy.

JOHNSTON, Very Rev. Michael Alexander Ninian C.; *see* Campbell-Johnston.

JOHNSTON, (Paul) Nicholas, FIMI; *b* 5 Jan. 1948; *s* of Joseph Leo Johnston and Winifred Vera Neale or Johnston; *m* 1st, 1972, Catherine MacPhee (marr. diss. 1993); one *s* two *d*; 2nd, 1993, Anna Jiménez-Olive; two *s*. *Educ:* North Kesteven Grammar Sch.; RMA Sandhurst. Dir, Eastern Hldgs Ltd, 1972–. Mem. (C) Scotland Mid and Fife, Scottish Parlt, 1999–2001. *Recreations:* cookery, history, gardening.

JOHNSTON, Peter William; Chief Executive, International Federation of Accountants, since 1999; *b* 8 Feb. 1943; *s* of late William Johnston and of Louisa Alice Johnston (*née* Pritchard); *m* 1967, Patricia Sandra Macdonald; one *s* one *d*. *Educ:* Univ. of Glasgow (MA, LLB). Partner, MacArthur & Co., Solicitors, Inverness, 1971–76; Procurator Fiscal Depute, Dumfries, 1976–78; Procurator Fiscal, Banff, 1978–86; Senior Procurator Fiscal Depute, Crown Office, Edinburgh, 1986–87; Asst Solicitor, Crown Office, 1987–89; Chief Exec. and Sec., ICAS, 1989–99. FRSA. *Recreations:* music, foreign languages, sailing. *Address:* Apt 40G Madison Belvedere, 10E 29th Street, New York, NY 10016, USA; International Federation of Accountants, 535 Fifth Avenue, New York, NY 10017, USA. *Club:* New (Edinburgh).

JOHNSTON, Rita Margaret; Premier, Province of British Columbia, 1991; *b* 22 April 1935; *d* of John and Annie Leichert; *m* 1951, George Johnston; one *s* two *d*. Businesswoman and Mem., Chamber of Commerce. Alderman, Surrey, BC, 1970–83; MLA for Surrey, 1983–91; Parly Sec. to Minister of Energy, Mines and Petroleum Resources, then to Minister of Municipal Affairs, 1983–86; Minister: Municipal Affairs and Transit, 1986–89, also Recreation and Culture, 1988–89; Transportation and Highways, 1989–90; Dep. Premier, 1990–91. *Address:* 480 Rockland Drive, Vernon, BC V1B 2X5, Canada.

JOHNSTON, Robert Alan, AC 1986; Governor, Reserve Bank of Australia, 1982–89; *b* 19 July 1924; *m* 1948, Verna, *d* of H. I. Mullin; two *s* two *d*. *Educ:* Essendon High School; University of Melbourne. BCom. Commonwealth Bank of Australia, 1940–60; RAAF, 1943–46; Reserve Bank of Australia, 1960–89: Dep. Manager and Manager, Investment Dept, 1964–70; Chief Manager, Internat. Dept, 1970–76; Adviser, 1973–82; Chief Representative, London, 1976–77; Exec. Dir, World Bank Group, Washington, 1977–79; Secretary, Reserve Bank of Aust., 1980–82. Director: Australian Mutual Prov. Soc., 1989–97; John Fairfax Gp Pty, 1989–90; Westpac Banking Corp., 1992–96. Pres., Cttee for Econ. Develt of Australia, 1990–94. Hon. DCom Melbourne, 1992.

JOHNSTON, Robert Gordon Scott, CB 1993; Executive Director, United Kingdom Major Ports Group, 1993–99; *b* 27 Aug. 1933; *s* of late Robert William Fairfield Johnston, CMG, CBE, MC, TD; *m* 1960, Jill Maureen Campbell; one *s* one *d*. *Educ:* Clifton; Clare Coll., Cambridge (1st Cl. Hons Classical Tripos, MA). MCIT 1994. 2/Lieut Scots Guards (National Service), 1955–57. Entered Air Min. as Asst Principal, 1957; Private Sec. to Parly Under Sec. of State for Air, 1959–62; transf. to MPBW, Def. Works Secretariat, 1963; Sec., Bldg Regulation Adv. Cttee, 1964; Principal Private Sec. to successive Ministers of Public Bldg and Works, 1965–68; seconded to Shell Internat. Chemical Co., Finance Div., 1968–70; Asst Dir of Home Estate Management, Property Services Agency, 1970–73; seconded to Cabinet Office, 1973–75; Asst Sec., Railways Directorate, Dept of Transport, 1975–79; Under Sec., DoE, 1979–93; seconded to Price Commn, 1979; Dir of Civil Accommodation, 1979–88, Dir, Defence Services, 1988–90, PSA; Man. Dir, PSA Internat., 1990–93. Rep. of Sec. of State for Envmt on Commonwealth War Graves Commn, 1988–93. Lay Chm., NHS Complaints Panel, 2000–. *Address:* 5 Methley Street, SE11 4AL.

JOHNSTON, Robert Smith; *see* Kincraig, Hon. Lord.

JOHNSTON, Prof. Ronald John, PhD; FBA 1999; Professor of Geography, Bristol University, since 1995; *b* 30 March 1941; *s* of Henry Louis Johnston and Phyllis Joyce (*née* Liddiard); *m* 1963, Rita Brennan; one *s* one *d*. *Educ:* Commonweal County Secondary Grammar Sch., Swindon; Univ. of Manchester (BA 1962; MA 1964); Monash Univ. (PhD 1967). Department of Geography, Monash University: Teaching Fellow, 1964; Sen. Teaching Fellow, 1965; Lectr, 1966; University of Canterbury, New Zealand: Lectr, 1967–68; Sen. Lectr, 1969–72; Reader, 1973–74; University of Sheffield: Prof. of Geography, 1974–92; Pro-Vice-Chancellor for Acad. Affairs, 1989–92; Vice-Chancellor, Essex Univ., 1992–95. AcSS 1999. DU Essex, 1996; Hon. LLD Monash, 1999. Murchison Award, 1985, Victoria Medal, 1990, RGS; Honors Award for Distinction in Res., Assoc. Amer. Geographers, 1991; Prix Vautrin Lud, Fest. Internat. de Geographie, 1999. *Publications:* (with P. J. Rimmer) Retailing in Melbourne, 1970; Urban Residential Patterns: an introductory review, 1971; Spatial Structures: an introduction to the study of spatial systems in human geography, 1973; The New Zealanders: how they live and work, 1976; The World Trade System: some enquiries into its spatial structure, 1976; (with B.

E. Coates and P. L. Knox) Geography and Inequality, 1977; Multivariate Statistical Analysis in Geography: a primer on the general linear model, 1978; Political, Electoral and Spatial Systems, 1979; (with P. J. Taylor) Geography of Elections, 1979; Geography and Geographers: Anglo-American human geography since 1945, 1979, 5th edn 1997; City and Society: an outline for urban geography, 1980; The Geography of Federal Spending in the United States of America, 1980; The American Urban System: a geographical perspective, 1982; Geography and the State, 1982; Philosophy and Human Geography: an introduction to contemporary approaches, 1983, 2nd edn 1986; Residential Segregation, the State and Constitutional Conflict in American Urban Areas, 1984; The Geography of English Politics: the 1983 General Election, 1985; On Human Geography, 1986; Bell-Ringing: the English art of change-ringing, 1986; Money and Votes: constituency campaign spending and election results, 1987; (jtly) The United States: a contemporary human geography, 1988; (with C. J. Pattie and J. G. Allsopp) A Nation Dividing?: the electoral map of Great Britain 1979–1987, 1988; Environmental Problems: nature, economy and state, 1989, 2nd edn 1996; (jtly) An Atlas of Bells, 1990; A Question of Place: exploring the practice of human geography, 1991; (ed) The Dictionary of Human Geography, 1989, 4th edn 2000; contrib. chapters in ed vols and numerous papers in learned jls. *Recreation:* bell-ringing. *Address:* School of Geographical Sciences, University of Bristol, Bristol BS8 1SS. *T:* (0117) 928 9116, *Fax:* (0117) 928 7878; *e-mail:* r.johnston@bristol.ac.uk.

JOHNSTON, Sir Thomas Alexander, 14th Bt *cr* 1626, of Caskieben; *b* 1 Feb. 1956; *s* of Sir Thomas Alexander Johnston, 13th Bt, and of Helen Torry, *d* of Benjamin Franklin Du Bois; *S* father, 1984. *Heir: cousin* William Norville Johnston [*b* 11 July 1922; *m* 1952, Kathrine Pauline, *d* of Herbert Sigfred Solberg; three *s* one *d*].

JOHNSTON, Thomas Lothian; DL; Principal and Vice-Chancellor of Heriot-Watt University, 1981–88; President, Royal Society of Edinburgh, 1993–96; *b* 9 March 1927; *s* of late T. B. Johnston and Janet Johnston; *m* 1956, Joan, *d* of late E. C. Fahmy, surgeon; two *s* three *d*. *Educ:* Hawick High Sch.; Univs of Edinburgh and Stockholm. MA 1951, PhD 1955, Edinburgh. FRSE 1979; FRSA 1981; CIMgt (CBIM 1983); FIPD (FIPM 1986); FEIS 1989. Served RNVR, 1944–47 (Sub-Lt). Asst Lectr in Polit. Economy, Univ. of Edinburgh, 1953–55, Lectr 1955–65; Res. Fellow, Queen's Univ., Canada, 1965; Prof. and Hd of Dept of Econs, Heriot-Watt Univ., 1966–76. Visiting Professor: Univ. of Illinois, 1962–63; Internat. Inst. for Labour Studies, Geneva, 1973; Western Australia Inst. of Technol., 1979. Sec., Scottish Econ. Soc., 1958–65 (Pres., 1978–81); Member: Scottish Milk Marketing Bd, 1967–72; Nat. Industrial Relations Court, 1971–74; Scottish Cttee on Licensing Laws, 1971–73; Scottish Telecommunications Bd, 1977–84; Scottish Economic Council, 1977–91; Council for Tertiary Educn in Scotland, 1979–83; Chm., Manpower Services Cttee for Scotland, 1977–80; Economic Consultant to Sec. of State for Scotland, 1977–81. Trustee, Nat. Galls of Scotland, 1989–95. Director: First Charlotte Assets Trust, 1981–92; Universities Superannuation Scheme, 1985–88; Scottish Life Assurance, 1989–97; Hodgson Martin Ltd, 1989–97. A Dir, Edinburgh Sci. Festival, 1989–91. Chairman: Scottish Cttee, Industry Year 1986; Scottish Cttee, Industry Matters, 1987–89; Scottish Cttee, RSA, 1991–95; Univ. Authorities Pay Panel, 1985–88. Chairman: Enquiry into staff representation, London Clearing Banks, 1978–79; Water Workers' Enquiry, 1983; Mem., Review Cttee for NZ Univs, 1987; Arbitrator; Overseas Corresp., Nat. Acad. of Arbitrators, USA. For. Mem., Swedish Royal Acad. of Engrg Scis, 1985. DL Edinburgh, 1987. Dr *hc* Edinburgh, 1986; Hon. DEd CNAA, 1989; Hon. LLD Glasgow, 1989; DUniv Heriot-Watt, 1989; Hon. DLitt Napier, 1997. Comdr, Royal Swedish Order of the Polar Star, 1985. *Publications:* Collective Bargaining in Sweden, 1962; (ed and trans.) Economic Expansion and Structural Change, 1963; (jtly) The Structure and Growth of the Scottish Economy, 1971; Introduction to Industrial Relations, 1981; numerous translations from Swedish; articles in learned jls. *Recreations:* gardening, walking. *Address:* 14 Mansionhouse Road, Edinburgh EH9 1TZ. *T:* (0131) 667 1439.

See also D. E. L. Johnston.

JOHNSTON, Very Rev. William Bryce; Minister of Colinton Parish Church, Edinburgh, 1964–91; an Extra Chaplain to the Queen in Scotland, since 1991 (Chaplain-in-Ordinary, 1981–91); *b* 16 Sept. 1921; *s* of William Bryce Johnston and Isabel Winifred Highley; *m* 1947, Ruth Margaret, *d* of Rev. James Arthur Cowley; one *s* two *d*. *Educ:* George Watson's Coll., Edinburgh; Edinburgh Univ. (MA Hons Classics 1942); New Coll., Edinburgh (BD (Dist.) 1945). Ordained as Chaplain to HM Forces, 1945; served in Germany and as Staff Chaplain, PoW Directorate, War Office, 1945–48; Minister: St Andrew's, Bo'ness, 1949; St George's, Greenock, 1955. Moderator of General Assembly of Church of Scotland, 1980–81. Convener: Board of St Colm's Coll., 1966–70; General Assembly: Cttee on Adult Educn, 1970; Church and Nation Cttee, 1972; Inter-Church Relations Cttee, 1978; Cttee on Role of Men and Women, 1976; Chm., Judicial Commn, 1988–93. Mem., British Council of Churches, 1970–90 (Chm., Exec. Cttee, 1981–84); Delegate to 5th Assembly of World Council of Churches, 1975; Cunningham Lectr, New Coll., 1968–71; Vis. Lectr in Social Ethics, Heriot-Watt Univ., 1966–88. Mem., Broadcasting Council for Scotland, 1983–87. President, Edinburgh Rotary Club, 1975–76. Trustee, Scottish Nat. War Memorial, 1981–94. Hon. DD Aberdeen, 1980; Hon. DLitt Heriot-Watt, 1989. *Publications:* (jtly) Devolution and the British Churches, 1978; (ed) Davies, Ethics and Defence, 1986; *translations:* K. Barth, Church Dogmatics, vol. 2, 1955; Calvin, Commentaries on Hebrews, 1 Peter, 1960; various Bible study pamphlets and theological articles for SCM, Scottish Jl of Theology. *Recreations:* organ music, bowls. *Address:* 15 Elliot Road, Edinburgh EH14 1DU. *T:* (0131) 441 3387. *Club:* New (Edinburgh).

JOHNSTON, Ven. William Francis, CB 1983; Rector, Winslow with Great Horwood and Addington, diocese of Oxford, 1991–95; *b* 29 June 1930; *m* 1963, Jennifer Morton; two *s* one *d*. *Educ:* Wesley Coll., Dublin; Trinity Coll., Dublin (BA 1955; MA 1969). Ordained 1955; Curate of Orangefield, Co. Down, 1955–59; commissioned into Royal Army Chaplains Dept, 1959; served, UK, Germany, Aden, Cyprus; ACG South East District, 1977–80; Chaplain-Gen. to the Forces, 1980–86; QHC 1980–86; Priest-in-charge, Winslow with Addington, 1987–91. *Recreations:* golf, fishing, gardening. *Address:* Lower Axehill, Chard Road, Axminster, Devon EX13 5ED. *T:* (01297) 33259.

JOHNSTON, (William) Ian (Ridley), CBE 2001; QPM 1995; Chief Constable, British Transport Police, since 2001; *b* 6 Sept. 1945; *s* of late William and of Alice Johnston; *m* 1968, Carol Ann Smith; two *s*. *Educ:* Enfield Grammar Sch.; LSE (BSc 1st Cl. Hons). Joined Metropolitan Police 1965; ranks of PC to Chief Supt, 1965–88; Staff Officer to Sir Peter Imbert, 1988–89; Senior Command Course, 1989; Asst Chief Constable, Kent, 1989–92; Dep. Asst Comr, 1992–94, Asst Comr, 1994–2001, Met Police. *Recreations:* jogging, tennis, football, squash. *Address:* British Transport Police HQ, 15 Tavistock Place, WC1H 9SJ. *Club:* Orpington Rovers Football.

JOHNSTON, William James; Secretary, Association of Local Authorities of Northern Ireland, 1979–82; Chairman, National House Building Council, Northern Ireland, 1989–95; *b* 3 April 1919; *s* of late Thomas Hamilton Johnston and of Mary Kathleen Johnston; *m* 1943, Joan Elizabeth Nancye (*née* Young); two *d*. *Educ:* Portora Royal Sch., Enniskillen. FCA(Ire.). Professional accountancy, 1937–44; Antrim CC, 1944–68, Dep. Sec., 1951–68; Dep. Town Clerk, Belfast, 1968–73, Town Clerk, 1973–79. Dir, NI Adv. Bd, Abbey Nat. Bldg Soc., 1982–89. Member: NI Adv. Council, BBC, 1965–69; Council, ICAI, 1967–71; NI Tourist Bd, 1980–85; Local Govt Staff Commn, 1974–85; Public Service Trng Council (formerly Public Service Trng Cttee), 1974–83 (Chm., 1974–83); Arts Council of NI, 1974–81. Chm., Extra Care for Elderly People (NI) Ltd, 1999–. NI Rep., Duke of Edinburgh's Commonwealth Study Conf., Canada, 1962. *Recreations:* golf, live theatre. *Address:* 19A Windsor Avenue, Belfast BT9 6EE. *T:* (028) 9066 9373; 4 Riverside Close, Cushendall, Ballymena BT44 0NR. *T:* (028) 2177 2013. *Club:* Ulster Reform (Belfast).

JOHNSTON, Sir William Robert Patrick K.; *see* Knox-Johnston.

JOHNSTONE; *see* Hope Johnstone, family name of Earl of Annandale and Hartfell.

JOHNSTONE, VANDEN-BEMPDE-, family name of **Baron Derwent**.

JOHNSTONE, Lord; David Patrick Wentworth Hope Johnstone; Master of Annandale and Hartfell; *b* 13 Oct. 1971; *s* and *heir* of Earl of Annandale and Hartfell, *qv*; *m* 2001, Penny, *d* of late John Macmillan. *Educ:* Stowe; St Andrews Univ. (BSc 1994).

JOHNSTONE, Alexander; Member (C) North East Scotland, Scottish Parliament, since 1999; *b* 31 July 1961; *m* 1981, Linda; one *s* one *d*. *Educ:* Mackie Acad., Stonehaven. Farmer, 1981–. *Address:* Tannachie, Stonehaven, Kincardine AB39 3UY.

JOHNSTONE, David; Director of Social Services, Devon County Council, since 1999; *b* 9 May 1951; *s* of David Armour Johnstone and Veronica Johnstone; *m* 1974, Andra Newton; one *s* two *d*. *Educ:* Middlesex Poly. (BA Hons Social Sci.); Newcastle upon Tyne Univ. (MBA). Joined Social Services Dept, Newcastle upon Tyne, 1974, Asst Dir, 1990–95; Dir of Social Services, Stockton on Tees, 1995–99. *Recreations:* sailing, athletics, walking, soccer, music, literature. *Address:* Devon County Council, County Hall, Topsham Road, Exeter EX4 6BL. *Clubs:* Tynemouth Sailing; Wallsend Harriers and Athletics.

JOHNSTONE, Prof. Eve Cordelia, MD; FRCPsych, FRCPGlas, FRCPE; Professor of Psychiatry, and Head, Department of Psychiatry, University of Edinburgh, since 1989; *b* 1 Sept. 1944; *d* of late William Gillespie Johnstone and Dorothy Mary Johnstone. *Educ:* Park Sch., Glasgow; Univ. of Glasgow (MB ChB 1967; DPM 1970; MD 1976). MRCP 1971; MRCPsych 1972, FRCPsych 1984; FRCPE 1992. House officer posts, 1967–68, trng posts in Psychiatry, 1968–72, Glasgow Hosp.; Lectr in Psychological Medicine, Glasgow Univ., 1972–74; Mem., Scientific Staff, MRC, Clin. Res. Centre and Northwick Park Hosp., Harrow, 1974–89 (Hon. Consultant, 1979–). Mem., MRC, 1996– (Chm., Neurosis and Mental Health Bd, 1999–2000). Founder FMedSci 1998. *Publications:* Searching for the Causes of Schizophrenia, 1994; (ed) Biological Psychiatry, 1996; (ed jtly) Schizophrenia: concepts and management, 1999; (ed jtly) Companion to Psychiatric Studies, 6th edn, 1998; numerous contribs to learned jls mainly relating to schizophrenia and other serious psychiatric disorders. *Recreations:* card-playing, gardening, listening to opera, foreign travel. *Address:* Department of Psychiatry, University of Edinburgh, Kennedy Tower, Royal Edinburgh Hospital, Edinburgh EH10 5HF. *T:* (0131) 537 6267.

JOHNSTONE, Sir (George) Richard (Douglas), 11th Bt *cr* 1700, of Westerhall, Dumfriesshire; Managing Director, Moat House Consultants Ltd; *b* 21 Aug. 1948; *er s* of Sir Frederic Allan George Johnstone, 10th Bt and of Doris Johnstone (*née* Shortridge); *S* father, 1994; *m* 1976, Gwyneth Susan Bailey; one *s* one *d*. *Educ:* Leeds Grammar Sch.; Magdalen Coll., Oxford (MA; Dip. Physical Anthropology). Production Control Manager, Wolsey Ltd, 1973; Section Head, ITT Consumer Products (UK) Ltd, 1979; Dir, Central Govt Gp, P-E International plc, 1988; Man. Dir, DBI Associates Ltd, 1990. *Recreations:* biking, travel, computing. *Heir: s* Frederic Robert Arthur Johnstone, *b* 18 Nov. 1981.

JOHNSTONE, Iain Gilmour; author and broadcaster; *b* 8 April 1943; *s* of Jack and Gilly Johnstone; *m* 1980, Mo Watson; one *s* two *d*. *Educ:* Campbell College, Belfast; Bristol Univ. (LLB Hons). Newscaster, ITN, 1966–68; Producer, BBC TV, 1968–74; Prof. of Broadcasting, Boston Univ., 1975; Man. Dir, Kensington Television, 1977; BBC presenter, Film 1983, 1984; film critic, The Sunday Times, 1983–93. Screenplays: Fierce Creatures (with John Cleese), 1996; Minx, 2001; The Evening News , 2001; (jtly) Oz and the Pom, 2001. *Publications:* The Arnhem Report, 1977; The Man With No Name, 1980; Cannes: The Novel, 1990; Wimbledon 2000, 1992; The James Bond Companion, 1999; (with Frédéric Lepage) Taming the Night, 2001. *Recreations:* lawn tennis, reading, London parks. *Address:* c/o Ed Victor Ltd, 6 Bayley Street, WC1B 3HB. *Clubs:* Garrick, Groucho, Queen's.

JOHNSTONE, Isobel Theodora, PhD; Curator, Arts Council Collection, since 1979; *b* 1944. *Educ:* James Gillespie's High School; Edinburgh Univ.; Edinburgh Coll. of Art (MA Hons Fine Art); Glasgow Univ. (PhD). Lectr in History of Art, Glasgow School of Art, 1969–73; Scottish Arts Council, 1975–79. Painter. *Publications:* (as Isobel Spencer): Walter Crane, 1975; articles on late 19th century and 20th century British art. *Address:* Hayward Gallery, Belvedere Road, SE1 8ZZ.

JOHNSTONE, Sir (John) Raymond, Kt 1993; CBE 1988; Chairman, Historic Buildings Council for Scotland, since 1995; Chairman, Atrium (formerly Lomond) Underwriting plc, since 1994; *b* 27 Oct. 1929; *s* of Henry James Johnstone of Alva, Captain RN and Margaret Alison McIntyre; *m* 1979, Susan Sara Gore, DL; five step *s* two step *d*. *Educ:* Eton Coll.; Trinity Coll., Cambridge (BA Maths). CA. Apprenticed Chiene & Tait, Chartered Accts, Edinburgh, 1951–54; Robert Fleming & Co. Ltd, London, 1955–59; Partner in charge of investment management, Brown Fleming & Murray CA (becoming Whinney Murray CA, 1965), Glasgow, 1959–68; Murray Johnstone Ltd, Glasgow, formed to take over investment management dept of Whinney Murray: Man. Dir, 1968–89; Chm., 1984–94; Pres., 1994–. Chm., Forestry Commn, 1989–94. Chm., Summit Gp, 1989–98; Director: Shipping Industrial Holdings, 1964–75; Scottish Amicable Life Assce Soc., 1971–97 (Chm., 1983–85); Dominion Insurance Co. Ltd, 1973–95 (Chm., 1978–95); Scottish Financial Enterprise, 1986–91 (Chm., 1989–91); Kiln plc, 1995–. Hon. Pres., Scottish Opera, 1986–98 (Dir, 1978–86; Chm., 1983–85); Patron, Nat. Galls of Scotland, 1996–(Chm., 1996–99). Member: Scottish Adv. Cttee, Nature Conservancy Council, 1987–89; Scottish Econ. Council, 1987–95. Chairman: Nuclear Trust, 1996–; Nuclear Generation Decommissioning Fund Ltd, 1996–. *Recreations:* fishing, music, farming. *Address:* Wards, Gartocharn, Dunbartonshire G83 8SB. *T:* (01389) 830321.

JOHNSTONE, Peter; HM Diplomatic Service; Governor of Anguilla, since 2000; *b* 30 July 1944; *m* 1969, Diane Claxton; one *s* one *d*. Joined FO, 1962; served: Berne, 1965–66; Benin City, 1966–68; Budapest, 1968–69; Maseru, 1969–72; FCO, 1973–77; Dacca,

1977–79; First Sec., Dublin, 1979–82; FCO, 1983–86; First Sec. (Commercial), Harare, 1986–89; Consul Gen., Edmonton, 1989–91; FCO, 1991–95; Counsellor (Commercial Develt), Jakarta, 1995–98; FCO, 1999. *Address:* c/o Foreign and Commonwealth Office, SW1A 2AH.

JOHNSTONE, Sir Raymond; *see* Johnstone, Sir J. R.

JOHNSTONE, Sir Richard; *see* Johnstone, Sir G. R. D.

JOHNSTONE, William, CBE 1981; *b* 26 Dec. 1915; *s* of late David Grierson Johnstone and Jessie Lang Johnstone (*née* Malcolm); *m* 1942, Mary Rosamund Rowden; one *s* two *d. Educ:* Dalry High Sch.; Glasgow Univ. (BSc (Agric)). NDA, NDD. Technical Officer, Overseas Dept of Deutches Kalisyndikat, Berlin, 1938–39; joined ICI, 1940; seconded to County War Agricl Exec. Cttees in SE England on food prodn campaigns, 1940–45; Reg. Sales Management, ICI, 1950–61; Commercial Dir, Plant Protection Ltd, 1961–63, Man. Dir, 1963–73; Dir, ICI Billingham/Agricl Div., 1961–73; Dep. Chm., ICI Plant Protection Div., 1974–77. Chm. Subsid. Cos: Solplant (Italy), 1967–73; Sopra (France), 1971–75; Zeltia Agraria (Spain), 1976–77; Vis. Dir, ICI (United States) Inc., 1974–77; retd from ICI, 1977. Chairman: Meat and Livestock Commn, 1977–80; British Agricl Export Council, 1977–84; Member: European Trade Cttee, BOTB, 1982–85; Sino-British Trade Council, 1983–85. *Address:* Oxenbourne Farm, East Meon, Petersfield, Hants GU32 1QL. *T:* (01730) 823216. *Club:* Farmers'.

JOHNSTONE, Rev. Prof. William, DLitt; Professor of Hebrew and Semitic Languages, University of Aberdeen, 1980–2001; *b* 6 May 1936; *s* of Rev. T. K. Johnstone and Evelyn Hope Johnstone (*née* Murray); *m* 1964, Elizabeth Mary Ward; one *s* one *d. Educ:* Hamilton Academy; Glasgow Univ. (MA 1st Cl. Hons Semitic Langs, BD Distinction in New Testament and Old Testament; DLitt 1998); Univ. of Marburg. University of Aberdeen: Lectr 1962, Sen. Lectr 1972, in Hebrew and Semitic Languages; Dean, Faculty of Divinity, 1984–87; Hd of Dept, Divinity with Religious Studies, 1998–2000. Member, Mission archéologique française: Ras Shamra, 1963, 1964, 1966; Enkomi, 1963, 1965, 1971; Member, Marsala Punic Ship Excavation, 1973–79. Pres., SOTS, 1990. *Publications:* Exodus, 1990; 1 and 2 Chronicles, 1997; Exodus and Chronicles, 1998; *translations:* Fohrer: Hebrew and Aramaic Dictionary of the Old Testament, 1973; (also ed and contrib.) William Robertson Smith: essays in reassessment, 1995; *contributions to:* Ugaritica VI, 1969, VII, 1978, Alasia I, 1972; Dictionary of Biblical Interpretation, 1990; Cambridge Companion to Biblical Interpretation, 1998; Festschriften for: W. McKane, 1986; R. Davidson, 1992; G. W. Anderson, 1993; C. H. W. Brekelmans, 1997; articles in Aberdeen Univ. Review, Atti del I Congresso Internazionale di Studi Fenici e Punici, Bibliotheca Ephemeridum Theologicarum Lovaniensium, Expository Times, Kadmos, Notizie degli Scavi, Palestine Exploration Qly, Trans. Glasgow Univ. Oriental Soc., Scottish Jl of Theology, Studia Theologica, Theology, Vetus Testamentum, Zeitschrift für die alttestamentliche Wissenschaft. *Recreation:* alternative work. *Address:* 37 Rubislaw Den South, Aberdeen AB15 4BD. *T:* (01224) 316022; Makkevet Bor, New Galloway, Castle Douglas DG7 3RN.

JOHNSTONE, William Neill, RDI 1989; Founder Chairman, Neill Johnstone Ltd, since 1986; Chairman, Fabric Design Consultants International; *b* 16 May 1938; *s* of Harry McCall Johnstone and Ethel Mary Neill; *m* 1st, (marr. diss.); two *d*; 2nd, 1991, Mara Lukic; one *s* one *d. Educ:* Forfar Acad.; Edinburgh Acad.; Univ. of Edinburgh; Scottish Coll. of Textiles; RCA. Designer, then Design Dir, R. G. Neill & Son, 1961–70; Man. Dir and Design Dir, Neill of Langholm, 1970–85; Design Dir, Illingworth Morris Gp and Co-ordinator of design training programme, 1982–85; Internat. Wool Secretariat Design Consultant, 1978–90. Chm., Confedn of British Wool Textiles Ltd Steering Cttee, 1982–85; Industrialist on Selection Panel, Designer Graduate Attachment Scheme, 1982–85. *Recreations:* climbing, hill walking, collecting Inuit carvings. *Address:* Neill Johnstone Ltd, William Street, Langholm DG13 0BN. *T:* (01387) 381122.

JOICEY, family name of **Baron Joicey**.

JOICEY, 5th Baron *cr* 1906, of Chester-le-Street, Co. Durham; **James Michael Joicey;** Bt 1893; *b* 28 June 1953; *s* of 4th Baron and of Elisabeth Marion Joicey (*née* Leslie Melville); *S* father, 1993; *m* 1984, Agnes Harriet Frances Mary, *yr d* of Rev. and Mrs W. M. D. Thompson; two *s* two *d. Educ:* Eton Coll.; Christ Church, Oxford. *Heir: s* Hon. William James Joicey, *b* 21 May 1990. *Address:* Etal Manor, Berwick-upon-Tweed TD15 2PU.

JOLL, James Anthony Boyd, FSA; Chairman, Sir Winston Churchill Archive Trust, since 2000; *b* 6 Dec. 1936; *s* of Cecil Joll, FRCS and Antonia (*née* Ramsden); *m* 1st, 1963, Thalia Gough (marr. diss. 1973); one *s* two *d*; 2nd, 1977, Lucilla Kingsbury; two *s. Educ:* Eton; Magdalen Coll., Oxford (MA). 2nd Lieut, 4th Queen's Own Hussars, 1955–57. Editorial staff, Financial Times, 1961–68, Jt Ed., Lex column, 1965–68; N. M. Rothschild & Sons, 1968–80, Dir, 1970–80; Exec. Dir, 1980–96, Finance Dir, 1985–96, Pearson plc. Chm., AIB Asset Mgt Hldgs, 1997–; Deputy Chairman: Jarvis Hotels, 1990–; Equitas Hldgs, 1996–; Dir, The Economist Newspaper, 1995–99. Chm., Museums and Galls Commn, 1996–2000; Mem., Urgent Issues Task Force, Accounting Standards Bd, 1991–95. Trustee, Wallace Collection, 1990–2000. Mem. Council, RCM, 2000–. *Recreation:* the gothic revival. *Address:* 26 Kensington Park Gardens, W11 2QS. *Club:* Boodle's.

JOLLIFFE, family name of **Baron Hylton**.

JOLLIFFE, Sir Anthony (Stuart), GBE 1982; *b* Weymouth, Dorset, 12 Aug. 1938; *s* of Robert and Vi Dorothea Jolliffe. *Educ:* Portchester Sch., Bournemouth. Qualified chartered accountant, 1964; articled to Morison Rutherford & Co.; commenced practice on own account in name of Kingston Jolliffe & Co., 1965, later, Jolliffe Cork & Co., Sen. Partner, 1976. Chairman: China Mgt for Industry Ltd; Fawley Capital; Jolliffe Internat.; Director: General Mediterranean Holdings; Next Generation Clubs Mgt Ltd; MV Sports; Richard Pearson Ltd. Chm., adv. cttees, ABN Ambro Capital Investment; adv. and jt venture projects, China, ME, Argentina. Chm., Stoke Mandeville NHS Trust, 1994–95. Alderman, Ward of Candlewick, 1975–84; Sheriff, City of London, 1980–81; Lord Mayor of London, 1982–83. Pres., London Chamber of Commerce, 1985–88. Formerly Treasurer: Relate; Britain in Europe. Pres., Soc. of Dorset Men, 1984–. KStJ 1983. *Recreations:* yachting, classic cars. *Clubs:* Garrick, City Livery (Pres., 1979–80), Saints and Sinners, Royal Automobile.

JOLLIFFE, Christopher, CBE 1971; Chairman, Abbeyfield Richmond Society, 1980–87; Director, Science Division, Science Research Council, 1969–72 (Director for University Science and Technology, 1965–69); *b* 14 March 1912; *s* of William Edwin Jolliffe and Annie Etheldreda Thompson; *m* 1936, Miriam Mabel Ash. *Educ:* Gresham's Sch., Holt; University Coll., London. Asst Master, Stowe Sch., 1935–37; Dept of Scientific and Industrial Research, 1937–65. Vice-Chm., Council for Science and Society, 1978–82; Dir, Leverhulme Trust Fund, 1976–77. *Address:* 8 Broomfield Road, Kew, Richmond, Surrey TW9 3HR. *T:* (020) 8940 4265.

JOLLIFFE, Maj.-Gen. David Shrimpton, QHP 1999; FRCP; Director General, Army Medical Services, since 2000; *b* 20 March 1946; *s* of John Hedworth Jolliffe and Gwendoline Frances Angela Jolliffe (*née* Shrimpton); *m* 1969, Hilary Dickinson; two *d. Educ:* Ratcliffe Coll., Leicester; King's Coll. Hosp., London (MB). FRCP 1987. Regl MO, 23 Para Field Amb., 1971–73, 2 Para, 1973–74; Cons. Dermatologist, Queen Elizabeth Mil. Hosp., 1980–82; Consultant Advr in Dermatology to the Army, 1982–86; Commanding Officer: British Mil. Hosp., Hong Kong, 1986–89; Cambridge Mil. Hosp., Aldershot, 1993–94; COS, Army Medical Directorate, 1996–99; Comdr, Med. HQ, Land Command, 1999–2000. *Publications:* contrib. papers on general and tropical dermatology to professional jls. *Recreations:* carpentry, computer technology. *Address:* Army Medical Directorate, Keogh Barracks, Ash Vale, Aldershot GU12 5RR. *T:* (01252) 340331; *e-mail:* red@pennswood.demon.co.uk.

JOLLIFFE, William Orlando, CPFA, FCA; County Treasurer of Lancashire, 1973–85; *b* 16 Oct. 1925; *s* of late William Dibble Jolliffe and Laura Beatrice Jolliffe; *m* 1st (marr. diss.); one *s* one *d*; 2nd, 1975, Audrey (*née* Dale); one step *d. Educ:* Bude County Grammar Sch. Chartered Accountant (first place in final exam. of (former) Soc. of Incorporated Accountants, 1956). Joined Barclays Bank Ltd, 1941. Served War of 1939–45 (HM Forces, 1944–48). Subseq. held various appts in Treasurers' depts of Devon CC, Winchester City Council, Doncaster CB Council, Bury CB Council (Dep. Borough Treas.), and Blackpool CB Council (Dep. 1959, Borough Treas., 1962). Mem. Council, Chartered Inst. of Public Finance and Accountancy, 1969–85 (Pres., 1979–80); Financial Adviser, ACC, 1976–85; Mem. Council (Pres. 1974–75), Assoc. of Public Service Finance Officers, 1963–76; Chm., Officers' Side, JNC for Chief Officers of Local Authorities in England and Wales, 1971–76; Mem. Exec. Cttee (Pres. 1970–71), NW Soc. of Chartered Accountants, 1966–76; Chm., NW and N Wales Region of CIPFA, 1974–76; Mem., Soc. of County Treasurers (Mem. Exec. Cttee, 1977–85); Hon. Treas., Lancashire Playing Fields Assoc., 1974–85. Financial Adviser to Assoc. of Municipal Corporations, 1969–74; Mem. (Govt) Working Party on Collab. between Local Authorities and the National Health Service, 1971–74. *Publications:* articles for Public Finance and Accountancy and other local govt jls. *Address:* 12 The Leylands, Lytham St Annes, Lancs FY8 5QS. *T:* (01253) 739358. *Club:* St Annes Old Links Golf.

JOLLY, Sir (Arthur) Richard, KCMG 2001; PhD; development economist; Professorial Fellow Emeritus, Institute of Development Studies, University of Sussex; Special Adviser to the Administrator, United Nations Development Programme, New York, 1996–2000; *b* 30 June 1934; *s* of late Arthur Jolly and Flora Doris Jolly (*née* Leaver); *m* 1963, Alison Bishop, PhD; two *s* two *d. Educ:* Brighton Coll.; Magdalene Coll., Cambridge (BA 1956, MA 1959); Yale Univ. (MA 1960, PhD 1966). Community Develt Officer, Baringo Dist, Kenya, 1957–59; Associate Chubb Fellow, Yale Univ., 1961–62; Res. Fellow, E Africa Inst. of Social Res., Makerere Coll., Uganda, 1963–64; Res. Officer, Dept of Applied Econs, Cambridge Univ., 1964–68 (seconded as Advr on Manpower to Govt of Zambia, 1964–66); Fellow, 1968–71, Professorial Fellow, 1971–81, Dir, 1972–81, Inst. of Develt Studies, Univ. of Sussex; Dep. Exec. Dir, Programmes, 1982–95, Actg Exec. Dir, 1995, UNICEF, New York. Advr on Manpower Aid, ODM, 1968; Sen. Economist, Min. of Develt and Finance, Zambia, 1970; Advr to Parly Select Cttee on Overseas Aid and Develt, 1974–75; ILO Advr on Planning, Madagascar, 1975; Member: Triennial Rev. Gp, Commonwealth Fund for Tech. Co-operation, 1975–76; UK Council on Internat. Develt, 1974–78; UN Cttee for Develt Planning, 1978–81; Special Consultant on N-S Issues to Sec.-Gen., OECD, 1978; sometime member and chief of ILO and UN missions, and consultant to various governments and international organisations. Sec., British Alpine Hannibal Expedn, 1959. Member: Founding Cttee, European Assoc. of Develt Insts, 1972–75; Governing Council, 1976–85, and N-S Round Table, SID, 1976– (Vice-Pres., 1982–85; Chm., N-S Round Table, 1988–). Mem., Editorial Bd, World Development, 1973–. Master, Curriers' Co., 1977–78. Hon. LittD E Anglia, 1988; Hon. DLitt Sussex, 1992. *Publications:* (jtly) Cuba: the economic and social revolution, 1964; Planning Education for African Development, 1969; (ed) Education in Africa: research and action, 1969; (ed jtly) Third World Employment, 1973; (jtly) Redistribution with Growth, 1974 (trans. French 1977); (ed) Disarmament and World Development, 1978, 3rd edn 1986; (ed jtly) Recent Issues in World Development, 1981; (ed jtly) Rich Country Interests in Third World Development, 1982; (ed jtly) The Impact of World Recession on Children, 1984; (ed jtly) Adjustment with a Human Face, 1987 (trans. French 1987, Spanish 1987); (ed jtly) The UN and the Bretton Woods Institutions, 1995; (ed jtly) Human Development Report, annually 1996–2000 (trans. French, Spanish); (ed jtly) Development with a Human Face, 1998; articles in professional and develt jls. *Recreations:* billiards, croquet, nearly missing trains and planes. *Address:* Institute of Development Studies, University of Sussex, Brighton, Sussex BN1 9RE. *T:* (01273) 606261; *e-mail:* r.jolly@ids.ac.uk.

JOLLY, James Falcon; Editor, Gramophone, since 1989; *b* 12 Feb. 1961; *s* of Gordon and Enid Jolly. *Educ:* Pinewood Sch., Bourton; Bradfield Coll.; Univ. of Bristol (BA Hons); Univ. of Reading (MA). Asst Editor, Gramophone, 1985–88; Producer, BBC Radio 3, 1988–89. *Publications:* contrib. British Music Yearbook, 1986–88, Good CD Guide, Gramophone, Independent, Le Monde de la Musique, New Grove Dictionary of Opera. *Recreations:* food, wine, travel, cinema, gardening. *Address:* The Old White Horse, Sparrows Herne, Bushey, Herts WD2 3EU. *T:* (020) 8950 4552; (office) 135 Greenford Road, Sudbury Hill, Harrow, Middx HA1 3YD.

JOLLY, Michael Gordon, CBE 2001; Chairman, The Tussaud's Group, since 1994 (Chief Executive Officer, 1994–2000); *b* 21 Sept. 1952; *s* of Ron and Joy Jolly; *m* 1975, Julia Catherine Gordon Sharp; one *s* one *d. Educ:* Henley-on-Thames Grammar Sch. Marketing and other positions, Cadbury-Schweppes plc, 1972–83; Tussaud's Group: Head, Marketing, 1983–87; Bd Dir, 1987–91; Chief Operating Officer, 1991–94. *Recreations:* golf, the Arts, bonsai.

JOLLY, Sir Richard; *see* Jolly, Sir A. R.

JOLLY, Air Cdre Robert Malcolm, CBE 1969; retired; *b* 4 Aug. 1920; *s* of Robert Imrie Jolly and Ethel Thompson Jolly; *m* 1946, Josette Jacqueline (*née* Baindeky); no *c. Educ:* Skerry's Coll., Newcastle upon Tyne. Commnd in RAF, 1943; served in: Malta, 1941–45; Bilbeis, Egypt, 1945; Shaibah, Iraq, 1945–46; Malta, 1946–49; Air Cdre 1971; Dir of Personal Services, MoD, 1970–72; Dir of Automatic Data Processing (RAF), 1973–75, retd. Man. Dir, Leonard Griffiths & Associates, 1975–77; Vice-Pres., MWS Consultants Inc., 1978–80; Gen. Man., Diebold Europe SA and Dir, Diebold Research Program Europe, 1983–84. Hon. Archivist, St Paul's Anglican Pro-Cathedral, Malta GC, 1992–. *Address:* Villa Grey Golf, 26 Triq Galata, High Ridge, St Andrews STJ 03, Malta GC. *T:* 370282. *Club:* Royal Air Force.

JOLOWICZ, Prof. John Anthony; QC 1990; Professor of Comparative Law, University of Cambridge, 1976–93; Fellow, Trinity College, Cambridge, since 1952; *b* 11 April 1926; *e s* of late Prof. Herbert Felix Jolowicz and Ruby Victoria Wagner; *m* 1957, Poppy Stanley; one *s* two *d. Educ:* Oundle Sch.; Trinity Coll., Cambridge (Scholar; MA; 1st Cl. Hons Law Tripos 1950). Served HM Forces (commnd RASC), 1944–48. Called to the Bar, Inner Temple and Gray's Inn, 1952; Bencher, Gray's Inn, 1978. Univ. of Cambridge: Asst Lectr in Law, 1955, Lectr, 1959; Reader in Common and Comparative Law, 1972. Professeur associé, Université de Paris 2, 1976; Lionel Cohen Lectr, Hebrew Univ. of Jerusalem, 1983. Pres., SPTL, 1986–87. Vice-Pres., Internat. Acad. of Comparative Law, 1994– (Pres., Common Law Gp, 1990–98). Corresp. Mem., Institut de France, Acad. des Sciences morales et politiques, 1989; MAE 1988. Hon. Dr Universidad Nacional Autónoma de México, 1985; Hon. LLD Buckingham, 2000. Editor, Jl of Soc. of Public Teachers of Law, 1962–80. *Publications:* (ed) H. F. Jolowicz's Lectures on Jurisprudence, 1963; Winfield and Jolowicz on Tort, 1971, 15th edn (ed W. V. H. Rogers) 1998; (with M. Cappelletti) Public Interest Parties and the Active Role of the Judge, 1975; (jtly) Droit Anglais, 1986, 2nd edn 1992; (jtly) Recourse against Judgments in the European Union, 1999; On Civil Procedure, 2000; contrib. to Internat. Encyc. of Comparative Law and to legal jls. *Address:* Trinity College, Cambridge CB2 1TQ. *T:* (01223) 338400; West Green House, Barrington, Cambridge CB2 5SA. *T:* (01223) 870495. *Clubs:* Royal Automobile; Leander (Henley-on-Thames).

JONAS, Christopher William, CBE 1994; FRICS; property strategy adviser to large corporations; President, Royal Institution of Chartered Surveyors, 1992–93; *b* 19 Aug. 1941; *s* of late Philip Griffith Jonas, MC and Kathleen Marjory Jonas (*née* Ellis); *m* 1968, Penny Barker (marr. diss. 1997); three *s* one *d*. *Educ:* Charterhouse; Coll. of Estate Management; London Business Sch. (Sloan Fellow). TA Inns of Court Regt, 1959–66. Jones Lang Wootton, 1959–67; Drivers Jonas: Partner, 1967–82; Managing Partner, 1982–87; Sen. Partner, 1987–95. Property Adviser, Staffs County Council, 1982–. Chairman: Economics Research Associates, USA, 1987–93; Education Capital Finance Ltd, 2000–; Director: SFA, 1988–91; BITC, 1991–; Railtrack Gp plc, 1994–; Tate Gall. Projects Ltd, 1997–2000 (Chm., 1998–2000); Services Bd, Bank of Scotland, 2000–(England Bd, 1998–2000); Sunrise Assisted Living, 1998–; Canary Wharf Group plc, 1999–; ENO, 1999–; Board Member: PLA, 1985–99; British Rail Property Bd, 1991–94; BR, 1993–94. Mem., FEFC, 1992–98. Chm., Ethics Standards Bd, Accountancy Foundn, 2001–. Member: Urban Land Inst., USA; Amer. Soc. of Real Estate Counselors. Trustee, Property Centre, City Univ. Member: Governing Body, Charterhouse, 1995–; Governing Council, UCL, 1997–. Liveryman: Clothworkers' Co. (Warden, 1994–96; Asst, 1996); Chartered Surveyors' Co. FInstD; FRSA. Hon. DSc De Montfort, 1997. *Recreations:* music (esp. Wagner), ski-ing, tennis. *Address:* 12 Barton Street, SW1P 3NE. *T:* (020) 7222 5141; *e-mail:* cwjonas@msn.com. *Club:* Toronto (Toronto).

See also R. W. Jonas.

JONAS, Sir Peter, Kt 2000; CBE 1993; General Director (Staatsintendant), Bavarian State Opera, since 1993; *b* 14 Oct. 1946; *s* of late Walter Adolf Jonas and Hilda May Jonas; *m* 1989, Lucy (separated 1998), *d* of Christopher and Cecilia Hull. *Educ:* Worth School; Univ. of Sussex (BA Hons); Royal Northern Coll. of Music (LRAM; FRNCM 2000); Royal Coll. of Music (CAMS; Fellow, 1989); Eastman Sch. of Music, Univ. of Rochester, USA. Asst to Music Dir, 1974–76, Artistic Administrator, 1976–85, Chicago Symphony Orch.; Dir of Artistic Admin, Orchestral Assoc. of Chicago (Chicago Symph. Orch., Chicago Civic Orch., Chicago Symph. Chorus, Allied Arts Assoc., Orchestra Hall), 1977–85; Man. Dir, subseq. Gen. Dir, ENO, 1985–93. Member: Adv. Bd, Hypo-Vereinsbank, 1994–; Bd of Governors, Bayerische Rundfunk, 1999–; Chm., German Speaking Opera Intendants Conf., 2000–. Member: Bd of Management, Nat. Opera Studio, 1985–93; Council, RCM, 1988–95; Council, London Lighthouse, 1990–94. FRSA 1989. Hon. DrMus Sussex, 1994. *Publications:* (with Mark Elder and David Pountney) Power House, 1992; (jtly) Eliten und Demokratie, 1999. *Recreations:* cinema, old master paintings, 20th century architecture, cricket. *Address:* Bayerische Staatsoper, Nationaltheater, Max-Joseph-Platz 2, 80539 München, Germany; Frundsbergstrasse 13, 80634 München, Germany. *Club:* Athenæum.

JONAS, Richard Wheen, FRICS; Senior Partner, Cluttons, since 1992; *b* 10 April 1943; *s* of late Philip Griffith Jonas, MC and of Kathleen Marjory (*née* Ellis); *m* 1973, Bettina Banton; two *d*. *Educ:* Charterhouse; Royal Agricl Coll. Strutt & Parker, 1965–70; Carter Jonas, 1970–73; Cluttons, 1973–: Partner, 1978–. Mem. Council, Roedean Sch., 2000–. Liveryman, Clothworkers' Co., 1965– (Warden, 1996). Gold Medal, RASE, 1967. *Recreations:* shooting, golf, ornithology. *Address:* Cluttons, 45 Berkeley Square, W1X 5DB. *T:* (020) 7408 1010. *Club:* City of London.

See also C. W. Jonas.

JONES; *see* Allen-Jones.

JONES; *see* Armstrong-Jones, family name of Earl of Snowdon.

JONES; *see* Clement-Jones, family name of Baron Clement-Jones.

JONES; *see* Duncan-Jones.

JONES; *see* Garel-Jones.

JONES; *see* Griffith-Jones.

JONES; *see* Gwynne Jones, family name of Baron Chalfont.

JONES; *see* Lloyd Jones and Lloyd-Jones.

JONES, family name of **Baron Jones**.

JONES, Baron *cr* 2001 (Life Peer), of Deeside in the County of Clwyd; **Stephen Barry Jones;** PC 1999; *b* 1937; *s* of late Stephen and Grace Jones, Mancot, Flintshire; *m* Janet Jones (*née* Davies); one *s*. MP (Lab): Flint East, 1970–83; Alyn and Deeside, 1983–2001. PPS to Rt Hon. Denis Healey, 1972–74; Parly Under-Sec. of State for Wales, 1974–79; Opposition spokesman on employment, 1980–83; Chief Opposition spokesman on Wales, 1983–87, 1988–92. Mem., Labour Shadow Cabinet, 1983–87 and 1988–92. Member: Speaker's Panel of Chairmen, 1993–2001; Prime Minister's Intelligence and Security Cttee, 1994–2001; Dep. Speaker, Westminster Hall, 2001; Chm., Speaker's Adv. Cttee on political parties, 1999; Mem., Speaker's Cttee on Electoral Commn, 2001. Mem., WEU and Council of Europe, 1971–74. Member: Govs, Nat. Mus., Wales, 1992–; Court, Univ. of Wales, 1992–; Nat. Liby of Wales, 1992–. *Address:* House of Lords, SW1A 0PW.

JONES, Adam M.; *see* Mars-Jones.

JONES, Adrianne Shirley, (Ann), MBE 1969; Women's Team Captain, Lawn Tennis Association, 1990–97; BBC tennis commentator, since 1970; *b* 17 Oct. 1938; *d* of Adrian Arthur Haydon and Doris (*née* Jordan); *m* 1962, Philip Frank Jones (*d* 1993); two *s* one *d*. *Educ:* King's Norton Grammar Sch., Birmingham. Finalist, World Table Tennis Championships: Ladies Doubles, 1954; Singles, Ladies Doubles, Mixed Doubles, 1957; Tennis Championships: Winner, French Open, 1961, 1966; Winner, Italian Open, 1966; Finalist, US, 1961, 1967; Wimbledon: Finalist, Ladies Singles, 1967; Winner, 1969; semi-finalist nine times. Chm., Women's Internat. Professional Tennis Council, 1977–84; Dir, European Ops, Women's Tennis Assoc., 1976–84. *Publications:* Tackle Table Tennis My Way, 1957; Tennis: a game to love, 1970. *Recreations:* all sports, reading, music. *Address:* (home) 85 Westfield Road, Edgbaston, Birmingham B15 3JF. *T:* (0121) 680 5586; (office) Lawn Tennis Association, Queen's Club, West Kensington, W14 9EG. *T:* (020) 7381 7072. *Clubs:* All England Lawn Tennis, Queen's; Edgbaston Priory.

JONES, Alan Wingate, FREng, FIEE; Chief Executive, BICC plc, 1995–99; *b* 15 Oct. 1939; *s* of Gilbert Victor Jones and Isobel Nairn Jones; *m* 1974, Judi Ann Curtis; one *s* one *d*. *Educ:* Sutton Valence Sch.; King's Coll., Cambridge (MA MechScis). GEC, 1961–73; Plessey Co. Plc, 1973–89: Man. Dir, Plessey Marine, 1975–79; Divl Man. Dir, Plessey Displays and Sensors, 1979–85; Internat. Dir, 1985–87; Man. Dir, Plessey Electronic Systems, 1987–89; Dir, Plessey Plc, 1985–89; Chief Exec., Westland Gp, 1989–95; Dir, GKN, 1994–95. Dir, Witan Investment Trust, 1996–; Chm., British Internat., 2000–. Mem., Financial Reporting Council, 1998–. FREng (FEng 1989); FRAeS 1993. *Recreations:* opera, shooting, sailing. *Address:* The Grange, North Cadbury, near Yeovil, Somerset BA22 7BY. *Club:* Royal Automobile.

JONES, Prof. Albert Stanley, PhD; DSc; Professor of Chemistry, University of Birmingham, 1969–87, now Emeritus; *b* 30 April 1925; *s* of Albert Ernest Jones and Florence Jones (*née* Rathbone); *m* 1st, 1950, Joan Christine Gregg (*d* 1992); one *s* one *d*; 2nd, 1996, Rev. Gillian Linda Gibson, BEd. *Educ:* Waverley Grammar Sch.; Univ. of Birmingham (BSc (1st Cl. Hons) 1944, PhD 1947, DSc 1957). Beit Memorial Fellow for Medical Research, 1949–52; University of Birmingham: Lectr in Chemistry, 1952–61; Sen. Lectr, 1961–63; Reader in Organic Chemistry, 1963–69. Chemical Society London: Birmingham Representative, 1959–62; Mem. Council, 1966–69; Chm., Nucleotide Group, 1967–72. *Publications:* 183 papers, incl. three review articles, in scientific jls, on various aspects of organic chemistry and biological chemistry, particularly concerning nucleic acid derivatives. *Recreations:* church activities, walking, music, reading. *Address:* Waverley, 76 Manor House Lane, Yardley, Birmingham B26 1PR. *T:* (0121) 743 2030.

JONES, Allen, RA 1986 (ARA 1981); artist; *b* 1 Sept. 1937; *s* of William Jones and Madeline Jones (*née* Aveson); *m* 1st, 1964, Janet Bowen (marr. diss. 1978); two *d*; 2nd, 1994, Deirdre Morrow. *Educ:* Ealing Grammar Sch. for Boys; Hornsey Sch. of Art (NDD; ATD); Royal Coll. of Art. Teacher of Lithography, Croydon Coll. of Art, 1961–63; Teacher of Painting, Chelsea Sch. of Art, 1966–68; Tamarind Fellow in Lithography, Los Angeles, 1968; Guest Professor: Hochschule für Bildenden Kunst, Hamburg, 1968–70; Univs of S Florida, 1970, Calif at Irvine, 1973, Los Angeles, 1977; Hochschule für Kunst Berlin, 1983; has travelled extensively. Sec., Young Contemporaries exhibn, London, 1961. One-man exhibitions include: Arthur Tooth and Sons, London, 1963, 1964, 1967, 1970; Richard Feigen Gall., NY, Chicago and LA, 1964, 1965, 1970; Marlborough Fine Art, London, 1972; Arts Council sponsored exhibn tour, UK, 1974; Waddington Galls, London, 1976, 1980, 1982, 1983, 1985, 1993; James Corcoran Gall., LA, 1977, 1987; UCLA Art Galls, LA, 1977; Graphic Retrospective 1958–78, ICA, 1978, tour incl. Waddington Galls, Toronto; Gall. Cavallino, Venice, 1981; Thorden and Wetterling, Gothenburg, 1983; Gall. Kammer, Hamburg, 1983, 1984; Gall. Wentzel, Cologne (sculpture), 1984; Gall. Patrice Trigano, Paris, 1985, 1986, 1989, 1998; Gall. Kaj Forsblom, Helsinki, 1985, 1999; Gall. Hete Hunermann, Dusseldorf, 1987, 1994; Charles Cowles Gall., NY, 1988; Heland Wetterling Gall., Stockholm, 1989; Gall. Wentzel, Cologne, 1992; Gall. Punto, Valencia, 1992; Gall. Levy, Hamburg and Madrid, 1993, 1995, 1997, 1999; Kunsthalle, Darmstadt, 1996; Galeria Civica, Modena, 1996; Thomas Gibson Fine Art, London, 1997; Trussardi, Milan, 1998; Ars Nova Mus. of Contemp. Art, Turku, 1999; Summerstage (sculpture), Vienna, 1999; Gall. d'Arte Maggiore, Bologna, 1999; Print Retrospective, Barbican Centre and tour to Norway, Czechoslovakia, Cyprus, S America, 1995–98; first Retrospective of Painting, 1959–79, Walker Art Gall., Liverpool, and tour of England and Germany, 1979; first internat. exhibn, Paris Biennale, 1961 (Prix des Jeunes Artists); first professional exhibn (with Howard Hodgkin), Two Painters, ICA, 1962; first UK mus. exhibn, Decade of Painting and Sculpture, Tate Gall., 1964; museum and group exhibns in UK and abroad include: New Generation, Whitechapel, 1964; London, The New Scene, Minneapolis, 1965; British Drawing/New Generation, NY, 1967; Documenta IV, Kassel, 1968; Pop Art Redefined, Hayward Gall., 1969; British Painting and Sculpture, Washington, 1970; Metamorphosis of Object, Brussels, and tour, 1971; Seibu, Tokyo, 1974; Hyperealist/Realistes, Paris, 1974; Arte Inglese Oggi, Milan, 1976; El color en la pintura Britanica, British Council S American tour, 1977; British Painting 1952–77, Royal Academy, 1977; Arts Council sponsored exhibn tour, UK, 1978, Wales, 1992; British Watercolours, British Council tour, China, 1982; The Folding Image, Washington and Yale, 1984; Pop Art 1955–1970, NY, then Aust. tour, 1985; 40 Years of Modern Art, Tate Gall., 1986; British Art in the Twentieth Century, Royal Academy, then Stuttgart, 1987; Pop Art, Tokyo, 1987; Picturing People, British Council tour, Hong Kong, Singapore, Kuala Lumpur, 1990; New Acquisitions, Kunstmus., Dusseldorf, 1990; Seoul Internat. Art Fest., 1991; British Art since 1930, Waddington Gall., 1991; BM, 1991, 1997; Pop Art, Royal Academy, 1991, then Cologne, Madrid and Montreal, 1992; From Bacon to Now, Florence; Nat. Portrait Gall., 1994; Centre Georges Pompidou, Paris, 1995; Treasure Island, Gulbenkian Foundn, Lisbon, 1997; The Pop '60s, Centro Cultural de Belém, Lisbon, 1997; Pop Impressions Europe/USA, MoMA NY, 1999; Pop Art: US/UK Connections 1956–1966, Menil Foundn, Houston, 2001; Les années pop, Centre Georges Pompidou, Paris, 2001; exhibited annually at Royal Acad., 1981–; murals and sculptures for public places include: Fogal, Basel and Zurich; Liverpool Garden Fest., 1984; Perseverance Works, Hackney, 1986; Citicorp/Canadian Nat. Bank, London Bridge City, 1987; Milton Keynes, 1990; BAA, Heathrow, 1990; Ivy Restaurant, London, 1990; Chelsea/Westminster Hosp., 1993; LDDC, 1994; Mezzo Restaurant, London, 1995; Swire Properties, Hong Kong, 1997; Sculpture at Goodwood, 1998; Chatsworth House, 2000; GlaxoSmithKline, London, 2001; television and stage sets include: O Calcutta!, for Kenneth Tynan, London and Europe, 1970; Manner Wir Kommen, WDR, Cologne, 1970; Understanding Opera, LWT, 1988; Cinema/Eric Satie, for Ballet Rambert, 1989; Signed in Red, for Royal Ballet, 1996. Television films have been made on his work. Trustee, British Mus., 1990–99. *Publications:* Allen Jones Figures, 1969; Allen Jones Projects, 1971; Waitress, 1972; Sheer Magic, 1979, UK 1980; Allen Jones, 1993; Allen Jones Prints, 1995; Allen Jones, 1997; articles in various jls. *Recreation:* gardening. *Address:* 41 Charterhouse Square, EC1M 6EA. *Fax:* (020) 7600 1204.

JONES, Alun; *see* Jones, R. A.

JONES, Dr Alun Denry Wynn, OBE 2001; CPhys, FInstP; Chief Executive, Institute of Physics, since 1990; *b* 13 Nov. 1939; *s* of Thomas D. and Ray Jones; *m* 1964, Ann Edwards; two *d*. *Educ:* Amman Valley Grammar Sch.; Christ Church, Oxford (MA, DPhil). CPhys, FInstP 1973. Sen. Student, Commission for Exhibn of 1851, 1964–66; Sen. Research Fellow, UKAEA, 1966–67; Lockheed Missiles and Space Co., California, 1967–70; Tutor, Open Univ., 1971–82; joined Macmillan and Co., Publishers, 1971; Dep. Editor, Nature, 1972–73; British Steel Corp., 1974–77; British Steel Overseas Services, 1977–81; Asst Dir, Technical Change Centre, 1982–85; Dep. Dir, 1986–87, Dir, 1987–90, Wolfson Foundn. Sec. of working party on social concern and biological advances, 1972–74, Mem., Section X Cttee, 1981–92, BAAS. British Library: Adv. Council, 1983–85; Document Supply Centre Adv. Cttee, 1986–89; Mem. Council, Nat. Library of Wales, 1987–94 (Gov., 1986–94). Dir, Sci. Council (formerly Council for Sci. and Technol. Insts), 1990–; Mem. Council, Assoc. of Schs' Sci., Engrg & Technol. (formerly Standing Conf. on Schs' Sci. & Technol.), 1992–2000 (Dep. Chm., 1996–2000). Governor: UCW, Aberystwyth, 1990–92; City Univ., 1991–. Fellow, Univ. of Wales, Aberystwyth, 2000. *Publication:* (with W. F. Bodmer) Our Future Inheritance: choice or chance, 1974. *Recreations:* gardening, theatre, cricket. *Address:* Institute of Physics, 76 Portland Place, W1N 3DH. *T:* (020) 7470 4800; 4 Wheatsheaf Close, Woking, Surrey GU21 4BP. *Club:* Athenæum.

JONES, Rt Rev. Alwyn Rice; Archbishop of Wales, 1991–99. Bishop of St Asaph, 1982–99; *b* 25 March 1934; *s* of John Griffith and Annie Jones, Capel Curig, Caernarvonshire; *m* 1968, Meriel Anne Thomas; one *d. Educ:* Llanrwst Grammar School, Denbighshire; St David's Coll., Lampeter (BA Hons Welsh 1955); Fitzwilliam House, Cambridge (BA 1957 Theology Tripos, MA 1961); St Michael's Coll., Llandaff. Deacon 1958, priest 1959, Bangor Cathedral; Asst Curate, Llanfairisgaer, 1958–62; Secretary for SCM in N Wales Colleges and SCM in schools, 1962–65; Director of Education, Diocese of Bangor, 1965–75; Chaplain, St Winifred's School, Llanfairfechan, 1965–67; Diocesan Warden of Ordinands, 1970–75; Vicar of Porthmadog, dio. Bangor, 1975–79; Exam. Chaplain to Archbishop of Wales, 1970–79; Hon. Canon, Bangor Cathedrals, 1974–78, Preb. of Llanfair, 1978–79; Dean of Brecon Cathedral, 1979–82. Mem., IBA Panel of Religious Advisers and Welsh Cttee, IBA, 1972–76; Asst Tutor in Religious Education, UCNW, Bangor, 1973–76. Pres., CCBI, 1997–2000. Fellow, Trinity Coll., Carmarthen, 1993. *Recreations:* music, walking. *Address:* 7 Llwyn Onn, Bishop's Walk, St Asaph, Denbighshire LL17 0SQ.

JONES, Angela; *see* Jones, S. A. M.

JONES, Ann; *see* Jones, Adrianne S.

JONES, Ann; Member (Lab) Vale of Clwyd, National Assembly for Wales, since 1999; *b* 4 Nov. 1953; *d* of Charles and Helen Sadler; *m* 1973, Adrian Jones; two *c. Educ:* Rhyl Grammar, then High, Sch. Fire Service Emergency Call Operator, 1976–99. Nat. Official, Fire Brigade's Union, 1982–99. Member (Lab): Rhyl Town Council, 1991–99 (Mayor of Rhyl, 1996–97); Denbighshire CC, 1995–99 (Lab spokesman on educn, 1995–98). Mem., N Wales Fire Authy, 1995–99. Welsh Assembly: Chm., Lab Mems, 1999–2000; Member: Econ. Develt Cttee, 1999–; N Wales Regl Cttee, 1999–; Health and Social Services Cttee. *Address:* 47 Kinmel Street, Rhyl LL18 1AG. *T:* (01745) 332813.

JONES, Anna Louise; *see* Bradley, A. L.

JONES, Prof. Anne; Founder and Managing Director, Lifelong Learning Systems Ltd, since 2000; Professor of Lifelong Learning, Brunel University, 1995–2001, now Emeritus; *b* 8 April 1935; *d* of Sydney Joseph and Hilda Pickard; *m* 1958, C. Gareth Jones (marr. diss. 1989); one *s* two *d. Educ:* Harrow Weald County Sch.; Westfield Coll., London (BA; Fellow, QMW, 1992); DipSoc, PGCE London. Assistant Mistress: Malvern Girls' Coll., 1957–58; Godolphin and Latymer Sch., 1958–62; Dulwich Coll., 1964; Sch. Counsellor, Mayfield Comprehensive Sch., 1965–71; Dep. Hd, Thomas Calton Sch., 1971–74; Head: Vauxhall Manor Sch., 1974–81; Cranford Community Sch., 1981–87; Under Sec. (Dir of Educn), Dept of Employment, 1987–91; management consultant, 1991–93; Brunel University: Prof. of Continuing Educn, 1991–97; Dir of Contg Educn, 1991–93; Hd of Dept of Contg Educn, 1993–97; Dir, Centre for Lifelong Learning, 1995–2001. Vis. Prof. of Educn, Sheffield Univ., 1989–. OFSTED Registered Inspector, 1993–. Chm., Parents in a Learning Soc., RSA, 1992–95. Director: CRAC, 1983–94; Grubb Inst. of Behavioural Studies, 1987–94. Occasional Mem., Selection Panel, Cabinet Office, 1993–. Advr, European Trng Foundn, 1995–. Chm., Menerva Educnl Trust, 1995–99. Member Council: QMW, 1991–; W London Inst. of Higher Educn, 1991–95; NICEC, 1991–95. FRSA 1984 (Mem. Council, 1986–94); FIMgt 1992; FICPD 1998. Hon. FCP 1990. *Publications:* School Counselling in Practice, 1970; Counselling Adolescents in School, 1977, 2nd edn as Counselling Adolescents, School and After, 1984; Leadership for Tomorrow's Schools, 1987; (with Jan Marsh and A. G. Watts): Male and Female, 1974, 2nd edn 1982; Living Choices, 1976; Time to Spare, 1980; contribs to various books. *Recreations:* walking, boating, gardening, theatre, opera. *Address:* (office) 23 Queen Street, Henley-on-Thames, Oxfordshire RG9 1AR. *T:* (01491) 578672, *Fax:* (01491) 571853; *e-mail:* annej@lls.co.uk.

JONES, Prof. Anthony Edward, FRCA; Co-Chief Executive, and President of the School of Art, Art Institute of Chicago, 1986–92 and since 1996; *b* 3 Aug. 1944; *s* of late Edward and Violet Jones; *m* 1st, 1972, Gwen Brandt (marr. diss. 1978); one *s*; 2nd, 1989, Patricia Jon Carroll. *Educ:* Goldsmiths' Coll., Univ. of London; Newport Coll. of Art, Newport (DipAD, BA); Tulane Univ., New Orleans (MFA). Artist-in-Residence, Loyola Univ., 1967–68; Teaching Fellow, Gloucester Coll. of Art, Cheltenham, 1968–69; Sen. Lectr and Dep. Head of Sculpture, Glasgow Sch. of Art, 1969–72; Chm., Dept of Art and Art Hist., Texas Christian Univ., 1972–80; Dir, Glasgow Sch. of Art, 1980–86; Rector, Royal Coll. of Art, 1992–96. Fulbright Scholar, USA, 1966–68. FRCA 1993; FRSA 1994; Hon. AIA 1991. Newbery Medal, Glasgow Univ., 1986. *Publications:* Chapel Architecture in the Merthyr Valley, 1964; Welsh Chapels (Capeli Cymru), 1984, 1996; Charles Rennie Mackintosh, 1990. *Recreation:* travel, reluctantly! *Address:* School of the Art Institute of Chicago, 37 South Wabash Avenue, Chicago, IL 60603, USA. *Clubs:* Chelsea Arts; University (Chicago).

JONES, Anthony Graham Hume; His Honour Judge Graham Hume Jones; a Circuit Judge, since 1993; Deputy Senior Judge, Sovereign Base Areas, Cyprus, since 1999; *b* 16 Aug. 1942; *s* of Rt Hon. Sir Edward Jones, PC and Margaret Anne Crosland (*née* Smellie); *m* 1966, Evelyn Ann Brice Smyth (*d* 1998), *o d* of Brice Smyth, Belfast; two *s* one *d. Educ:* Trinity Coll., Glenalmond; Trinity Coll., Dublin (BA 1966). Mardon, Son & Hall Ltd, 1966–71; called to the Bar, Gray's Inn, 1971; called to the Bar, NI, 1981; a Recorder, 1990–93. Vice-Pres., Avon Br., SSAFA, 1993–. Master, Antient Soc. of St Stephen's Ringers, 1999–2000. *Recreations:* sailing, golf. *Address:* Yeowood, Wrington, Bristol BS40 5NS; Craig-y-Mor, Trearddur Bay, Holyhead, Anglesey LL65 2UP. *Clubs:* Royal Ocean Racing; Trearddur Bay Sailing (Cdre, 1994–96); Royal County Down Golf, Burnham and Berrow Golf, Holyhead Golf.

JONES, Anthony W.; *see* Whitworth-Jones.

JONES, Rt Rev. Arthur Lucas Vivian; *see* Gippsland, Bishop of.

JONES, Prof. Arthur Stanley, CBE 1997; CBiol, FIBiol; consultant to agricultural and food industries, since 1997; Principal, Royal Agricultural College, Cirencester, 1990–97; *b* 17 May 1932; *s* of John Jones and Anne Jones (*née* Hamilton); *m* 1962, Mary Margaret Smith; three *s* one *d. Educ:* Gosforth Grammar Sch.; Durham Univ. (BSc); Aberdeen Univ. (PhD). Commnd Army, 2nd Lieut, 1955–57; Pilot Officer, RAFVR, 1958–62. Rowett Research Institute: Res. Scientist, 1959; Hd, Applied Nutrition Dept, 1966; Chm., Applied Scis Div., 1975; Dep. Dir, 1983; Governor, 1986–90; Strathcona-Fordyce Prof. of Agriculture, Univ. of Aberdeen, 1986–90; Head, Sch. of Agriculture, Aberdeen, and Principal, N of Scotland Coll. of Agriculture, 1986–90; Gov., Aberdeen Centre for Land Use, 1987–90. Mem., House of Lords Rural Econ. Gp, 1992–94. Chairman: Scottish Beef Develts Ltd, 1988–91; RAC Enterprises Ltd, 1992–97; Member: Council, RASE, 1991–97; Bd, Arable Res. Centres, 1992–96. Gov., Henley Coll. of Management, 1996– (Chm. Acad. Adv. Council, 1996–). Dir, Clan Grant Centre Trust Ltd, 1998–; Mem. Council and Hon. Treas., Clan Grant Soc., 1998–. Trustee: Trehane Trust, 1993–; Geoffrey Cragghill Meml Scholarship Trust, 1993–99; Ceres Foundn, 1996–. Hon. Prof., Univ. of Prague, 1994–. FRSA; FIMgt; FIAgrM; ARAgS. *Publications:* Nutrition of Animals of Agricultural Importance (vol. 17, Internat. Encyc. of Food and Nutrition) (ed D. P. Cuthbertson), 1967; 115 articles in learned jls. *Recreations:* yachting, flying, gardening. *Address:* Begsdell, Caskieben, Kinellar, Aberdeenshire AB21 0TB. *Clubs:* Farmers', Royal Air Force.

JONES, Rt. Hon. Aubrey; PC 1955; Director: Thomas Tilling Ltd, 1970–82; Cornhill Insurance Company Ltd, 1971–82 (Chairman, 1971–74); *b* 20 Nov. 1911; *s* of Evan and Margaret Aubrey Jones, Merthyr Tydfil; *m* 1948, Joan, *d* of G. Godfrey-Isaacs, Ridgehanger, Hillcrest Road, Hanger Hill, W5; two *s. Educ:* Cyfarthfa Castle Secondary Sch., Merthyr Tydfil; London School of Economics. BSc (Econ.) 1st Cl. Hons, Gladstone Memorial Prizewinner, Gerstenberg Post-grad. Schol., LSE. On foreign and editorial staffs of The Times, 1937–39 and 1947–48. Joined British Iron and Steel Federation, 1949; General Dir, June-Dec. 1955. Served War of 1939–45, Army Intelligence Staff, War Office and Mediterranean Theatre, 1940–46. Contested (C) SE Essex in General Election, 1945 and Heywood and Radcliffe (by-election), 1946; MP (U) Birmingham, Hall Green, 1950–65; Parliamentary Private Sec. to Minister of State for Economic Affairs, 1952, and to Min. of Materials, 1953; Minister of Fuel and Power, Dec. 1955–Jan. 1957; Minister of Supply, 1957–Oct. 1959. Joined Liberal Party, 1981. Mem., Plowden Cttee of Inquiry into Aircraft Industry, 1965–66. Chairman: Staveley Industries Ltd, 1964–65 (Dir 1962–65); Laporte Industries (Holdings) Ltd, 1970–72; Director: Guest, Keen & Nettlefolds Steel Company Limited, 1960–65; Courtaulds Ltd, 1960–63; Black & Decker, 1977–81. Chm., Nat. Bd for Prices and Incomes, 1965–70; Vice-Pres., Consumers' Assoc., 1967–72; leading consultant to: Nigerian Public Service Commn, 1973–74; Iranian Govt, 1974–78; Plessey Ltd, 1978–80; Mem. Panel of Conciliators, Internat. Centre for Settlement of Investment Disputes, 1974–81. Pres., Oxford Energy Policy Club, 1976–88. Regent Lectr, Univ. of California at Berkeley, 1968. Vis. Fellow: New Coll., Oxford, 1978; Sci. Policy Res. Unit, Univ. of Sussex, 1986–, Hon. Fellow, 1993; Sen. Res. Associate, St Antony's Coll., Oxford, 1979–82; Guest Scholar, Brookings Instn, Washington, DC, 1982. Fellow Commoner, Churchill Coll., Cambridge, 1972 and 1982–86. Hon. Fellow, LSE, 1959, Mem., Court of Governors, 1964–87. Hon. DSc Bath, 1968. Winston Churchill Meml Trust Award, 1985. *Publications:* The Pendulum of Politics, 1946; Industrial Order, 1950; The New Inflation: the politics of prices and incomes, 1973; (ed) Economics and Equality, 1976; (contrib.) My LSE, 1977; (contrib.) The End of the Keynesian Era, 1977; Oil: the missed opportunity, 1981; Britain's Economy: the roots of stagnation, 1985. *Address:* Arnen, 120 Limmer Lane, Felpham, Bognor Regis, West Sussex PO22 7LP. *T:* (01243) 582722.

JONES, Beti, CBE 1980; *b* 23 Jan. 1919; *d* of Isaac Jones and Elizabeth (*née* Rowlands). *Educ:* Rhondda County Sch. for Girls; Univ. of Wales. BA (Hons) History, Teaching Diploma. Grammar Sch. teaching, 1941–43; S Wales Organiser, Nat. Assoc. of Girls' Clubs, 1943–47; Youth Officer, Educn Branch, Control Commission, Germany, 1947–49; Children's Officer, Glamorgan CC, 1949–68; Chief Adviser on Social Work, Scottish Office, 1968–80. Fellow, University Coll., Cardiff, 1982 (Hon. Fellow, Dept of Social Administration, 1970). *Address:* 5 Belgrave Crescent, Edinburgh EH4 3AQ. *T:* (0131) 332 2696. *Clubs:* Royal Over-Seas League (London and Edinburgh).

JONES, Brinley; *see* Jones, Robert B.

JONES, Bryn Terfel, (Bryn Terfel); opera singer; bass baritone; *b* 9 Nov. 1965; *s* of Hefin and Nesta Jones; *m* Lesley Halliday; three *s. Educ:* Guildhall Sch. of Music and Drama (AGSM). Opera performances in major venues: WNO, 1990–; ENO, 1991–; Salzburg, 1992–; Covent Garden, 1992–; Vienna State Opera, 1993–; NY Metropolitan, 1994–; Sydney Opera House, 1999–; rôles include: Guglielmo, Jochanaan in Salome, Balstrode, Leporello, Figaro, Falstaff, and Scarpia. Hon. Fellow, Univ. of Wales Aberystwyth, 1995; Hon. FWCMD, 1995. Hon. DMus Univ. of Glamorgan, 1997. *Recreations:* golf, supporting Manchester United, collecting fob watches. *Address:* c/o Harlequin Agency, 203 Fidlas Road, Cardiff CF14 5NA. *T:* (029) 2075 0821.

JONES, Carwyn Howell; Member (Lab) Bridgend, since 1999, and Minister for Rural Affairs, since 2000, National Assembly for Wales; *b* 21 March 1967; *s* of Caron Wyn Jones and (Katherine) Janice Jones; *m* 1994, Lisa Josephine Murray. *Educ:* Aberystwyth Univ. (LLB). Called to the Bar, Gray's Inn, 1989. Tutor, Centre for Professional Legal Studies, Cardiff, 1997–99. Sec. for Agric. and Rural Develt, Nat. Assembly for Wales, 2000. *Recreations:* sport, reading, travel. *Address:* National Assembly for Wales, Cardiff Bay, Cardiff CF99 1NA. *T:* (029) 2089 8769. *Clubs:* Brynaman Rugby, Musselburgh Rugby.

JONES, Ceri Jayne, (Mrs T. C. Cuthbert); Editor, Investors Chronicle, since 1994; Editor-in-Chief, Personal Finance Division, Financial Times Business, since 1997; *b* 3 July 1958; *d* of David and Julie Jones; *m* 1984, Thomas Charles Cuthbert; three *s* one *d. Educ:* Keele Univ.; Liverpool Univ. (BA Hons 1982). Ed., Pensions & Employees Benefits, 1986; Ed., Pensions Management, 1986–87, Financial Advr, 1987–94, Financial Times magazines. *Publications:* articles in newspapers. *Recreations:* children, natural history, travel, aerobics. *Address:* Financial Times Business, Maple House, 149 Tottenham Court Road, W1P 9LL.

JONES, Charles Beynon Lloyd, CMG 1978; Chairman of Directors, David Jones Ltd, 1963–80; Consul General of Finland in Sydney, 1971–88; *b* 4 Dec. 1932; *s* of late Sir Charles Lloyd Jones and Lady (Hannah Beynon) Lloyd Jones, OBE. *Educ:* Cranbrook Sch., Sydney; Univ. of Sydney (not completed). Joined David Jones Ltd, 1951; Alternate Director, 1956; Director, 1957; Joint Managing Director, 1961. President: Retail Traders Assoc., NSW, 1976–78; Bd of Trustees, Art Gall. of NSW, 1980–83 (Trustee, 1972; Vice-Pres., 1976–80). Governor, London House for Overseas Graduates, 1983–92. Officer, Order of Merit, Republic of Italy (Cavaliere Ufficiale); Comdr, Order of the Lion, Finland. *Address:* Summerlees Farm, Yarramalong, NSW 2259, Australia.

JONES, Gen. Sir (Charles) Edward (Webb), KCB 1989; CVO 2001; CBE 1985; Gentleman Usher of the Black Rod and Serjeant-at-Arms, House of Lords, and Secretary to the Lord Great Chamberlain, 1995–2001; *b* 25 Sept. 1936; *s* of Gen. Sir Charles Phibbs Jones, GCB, CBE, MC and of Ouida Margaret Wallace; *m* 1965, Suzanne Vere Pige Leschallas; two *s* one *d. Educ:* Portora Royal School, Enniskillen. Commissioned Oxford and Bucks LI, 1956; 1st Bn Royal Green Jackets, 1958; served BAOR, 1968–70; served NI, 1971–72 (despatches 1972); Directing Staff, Staff Coll., 1972; CO 1st Bn RGJ, 1974–76; Comdr 6th Armd Brigade, 1981–83; Comdr, British Mil. Adv. and Training

Team, Zimbabwe, 1983–85; Dir Gen., TA and Organisation, 1985–87; Comdr, 3rd Armoured Div., 1987–88; QMG, MoD, 1988–91; UK Mil. Rep. to NATO, 1992–95. Colonel Commandant: RAEC, 1986–92; RGJ, 1988–95; Dep. Col Comdt, AGC, 1992–93. Comr, Royal Hosp. Chelsea, 1995–; Governor: Wellington Coll., 1997–; Eagle House Sch., 1999–. *Recreations:* golf, fishing. *Address:* Rose Lodge, Winchfield, Hook, Hants RG27 8BT. *T:* (01252) 842389. *Club:* Army and Navy.

JONES, Charles Ian McMillan; education consultant, since 1995; *b* 11 Oct. 1934; *s* of Wilfred Charles Jones and Bessie Jones (*née* McMillan); *m* 1962, Jennifer Marie Potter; two *s. Educ:* Bishop's Stortford Coll.; St John's Coll., Cambridge (CertEd 1959; MA 1962). FIMgt, FRSA. 2nd Lieut RA, 1953–55. Head of Geog. Dept, Bishop's Stortford Coll., 1960–70, Asst to Headmaster, 1967–70; Vice-Principal, King William's Coll., IoM, 1971–75; Head Master, Bedford School, 1975–86; Dir of Studies, BRNC, Dartmouth, 1986–88; Centre for British Teachers, subseq. CfBT Education Services: Project Dir, Brunei Darussalam, 1988–91, Malaysia, 1990–91; Regl Dir, Educn Services, SE Asia, 1991–94; Grants Adminstr, UK, 1995–97. OFSTED Trained Inspector, 1996–; ISI Trained Reporting Inspector; Assessor for Nat. Professional Qualification for Head Teachers, 1998–. Man., England Schoolboy Hockey XI, 1967–74; Man., England Hockey XI, 1968–69; Pres., English Schoolboys Hockey Assoc., 1980–88; Mem. IoM Sports Council, 1972–75. *Publications:* articles in Guardian. *Recreations:* hockey (Captain Cambridge Univ. Hockey XI, 1959; England Hockey XI, 1959–64, 17 caps; Gt Britain Hockey XI, 1959–64, 28 caps), cricket (Captain IoM Cricket XI, 1973–75), golf. *Address:* Churchgate Middle Barn, Briston Road, Wood Dalling, Norfolk NR11 6SN. *Clubs:* MCC; Hawks (Cambridge); Royal Norwich Golf; Pantai Mentiri Golf (Brunei).

JONES, Rt Rev. Christopher; *see* Elphin, Bishop of (RC).

JONES, Sir Christopher L.; *see* Lawrence-Jones.

JONES, Clement; *see* Jones, John C.

JONES, Clive Lawson, CBE 1997; Secretary General, European Energy Charter Conference, 1991–95; *b* 16 March 1937; *s* of Celyn John Lawson Jones and Gladys Irene Jones; *m* 1961, Susan Brenda (*née* McLeod); one *s* one *d. Educ:* Cranleigh School; University of Wales. BSc (Chemistry). With British Petroleum, 1957–61; Texaco Trinidad, 1961–68; Principal, Min. of Power, 1968–69; Min. of Technology, 1969–70; DTI, 1970–73; Asst Sec., Oil Emergency Group, 1973–74; Department Energy: Asst Sec., 1974–77; Under Sec., Gas Div., 1981–82; Counsellor (Energy), Washington, 1977–81; Dir for Energy Policy, EC, 1982–86; Dep. Dir Gen. for Energy, EC, 1987–94. Chm., European Consultative Cttees on Electricity and Gas Markets, 1990–91; Mem., Adv. Bd, Houston Energy Inst., 1996–. *Recreations:* ephemera, vintage paperbacks.

JONES, Clive William; Chief Executive, Carlton Television, since 1996; *b* 10 Jan. 1949; *s* of Kenneth David Llewellyn Jones and Joan Muriel Jones (*née* Withers); *m* 1st, 1971, Frances Mawer (marr. diss. 1988); two *s* one *d*; 2nd, 1988, Fern Britton (marr. diss. 2000); two *s* one *d. Educ:* Newbridge Grammar Sch.; LSE (BSc Econ.). Journalist, until 1978; with Yorks TV, 1978–82; Man. Editor, Editor, then Editor-in-Chief, TV-am Ltd, 1982–84; TVS: Controller, News, Current Affairs and Sport, 1984–87; Dep. Dir of Programmes, 1987–91; Dep. Man. Dir, 1991–92; Founding Man. Dir, London News Network, 1992–94; Man. Dir, Central Independent Television PLC, April–Dec. 1994; Man. Dir, Carlton UK Broadcasting Ltd, 1995. Chairman: London News Network, 1994–; Carlton Sales (formerly Carlton UK Sales), 1995–; Carlton 021, 1995–; Westcountry Television, 1998–; Moving Picture Co., 1999–; Superhire, 1999–; Set Pieces, 1999–; HTV, 2000–; Nyre, 2000. Dir, BARB, 1995–. Governor, Nat. Film and Television Sch., 1998–. FRTS 2000; FRSA 2000. *Recreations:* Rugby, golf, films. *Address:* 101 St Martin's Lane, WC2N 4AZ. *T:* (020) 7240 4000, *Fax:* (020) 7240 4174. *Clubs:* Reform; Birmingham Press; Winchester Rugby Football.

JONES, Courtney John Lyndhurst, OBE 1989 (MBE 1980); President, National Ice Skating Association, 1987–95; *b* 30 April 1933; *s* of Reginald Jones and Inez Jones (*née* Wilsher). *Educ:* Ringwood Grammar Sch.; Bournemouth Coll. of Art (NDD). NSA Gold Medals for Ice Dance and for Pair Skating, 1957; British Ice Dance Champion, with June Markham, 1956–57, with Doreen Denny, 1958–60; European Ice Dance Champion, with June Markham, 1957–58, with Doreen Denny, 1959–61; World Ice Dance Champion, with June Markham, 1957–58, with Doreen Denny, 1959–60. Free-lance fashion designer, 1977–. Mem., Internat. Skating Union Ice Dance Tech. Cttee, 1996–. Mem., US Figure Skating Hall of Fame, 1987; George Hasler Medal, Internat. Skating Union, 1991. *Recreations:* reading, music, the arts. *Address:* 1 Wesley Square, Lancaster Road, W11 1TP. *T:* (020) 7221 1705.

JONES, Daniel Gruffydd; Registrar and Secretary, University of Wales, Aberystwyth, 1990–99; *b* 7 Dec. 1933; *o s* of late Ifor Ceredig Jones and Gwendolen Eluned Jones; *m* 1969, Maureen Anne Woodhall; three *d. Educ:* Ardwyn Grammar Sch., Aberystwyth; University Coll. of N Wales, Bangor (BA). RAEC, 1957–59 (BAOR). Asst Principal, Min. of Housing and Local Govt, 1960; Private Sec. to Parly Sec., 1962–63; Principal, 1963; Private Sec. to Sec. of Cabinet, 1967–69; Asst Sec., 1969; Sec., Water Resources Bd, 1969–73; DoE, 1973; Sec., Prime Minister's Cttee on Local Govt Rules of Conduct, 1973–74; Under Sec., 1975; Prin. Finance Officer, Welsh Office, 1975–79; Director: Local Govt Directorate, DoE, 1980–82; Central Directorate of Envmtl Protection, DoE, 1982–86; Regl Dir, SE Reg., DoE and Dept of Transport, 1986–90. Mem., Royal Commn on the Ancient and Historical Monuments of Wales, 1991–2001. Chm., Hafod Adv. Cttee, Forest Enterprise, 1992–97. FRSA 1985. High Sheriff of Dyfed, 2000–2001. *Address:* Nantmelyn, Llangawsai, Aberystwyth SY23 1HD. *T:* (01970) 623351.

JONES, Prof. David, OBE 1986; FRCN; Professor, School of Nursing and Midwifery, University of Sheffield, 1995–2000, now Emeritus (Foundation Dean, 1995–98); *b* 27 July 1940; *s* of John Evan Jones and Edith Catherine (*née* Edwards); *m* 1962, Janet Mary Ambler; two *s* two *d. Educ:* Boys' Grammar Sch., Bala, N Wales; Univ. of Wales (BEd). SRN; RMN; RNT; FRCN 1998. Divl Nursing Officer, Gwynedd, 1974–78; Chief Admin. Nursing Officer, Gwynedd HA, 1979–87; first Chm., Welsh Nat. Bd for Nursing, Midwifery and Health Visiting, 1979–86; Chief Exec., English Nat. Bd for Nursing, Midwifery and Health Visiting, 1987–89; Principal, Sheffield and N Trent Coll. of Nursing and Midwifery, 1990–95. Non-exec. Dir, Conwy and Denbighshire NHS Trust, 1999–. *Recreations:* public affairs, countryside, family. *Address:* School of Nursing and Midwifery, 301 Glossop Road, Sheffield S10 2HL. *T:* (0114) 222 9865; The Cottage, Carrog, Corwen, Denbighshire LL21 9AP. *T:* (01490) 430255.

JONES, Sir David A.; *see* Akers-Jones.

JONES, David Alan; HM Diplomatic Service; High Commissioner, Sierra Leone, since 2000; *b* 26 Oct. 1953; *m* 1st, 1975, Jennifer Anne Wright (marr. diss. 1992); 2nd, 1994, Daphne Patricia Foley. Joined LCD, 1970; FCO, 1971–; served Tehran, 1975–78, Islamabad, 1978–81; MoD, 1981–83 (on loan); First Sec. (Commercial), Cairo, 1986–89; Dep. Head of Mission and Consul, Luanda, 1993–96; Dep. High Comr, Dar es Salaam, 1996–2000. *Address:* c/o Foreign and Commonwealth Office, SW1A 2AH.

JONES, David Charles, CBE 1999; FCCA, FCIS; Deputy Chairman, 2001–May 2002, Chairman, from May 2002, Next Plc; *b* 2 Feb. 1943; *s* of Frederick Charles Thomas Jones and Annie Marcella Jones; *m* 1968, Jeanette Ann Crofts; two *s* one *d. Educ:* King's Sch., Worcester. FCIS 1974; FCCA 1975. Joined Kays Mail Order Co. (part of Great Universal Stores), 1960, Finance Dir, 1971–77; Man. Dir, BMOC, 1977–80; Chief Exec., Grattan Plc, 1980–86; Next Plc: Dep. Chief Exec., 1986–88; Chief Exec., 1988–2001. *Recreations:* golf, snooker. *Address:* Hepworth House, Claypit Lane, Leeds LS2 8DE. *T:* (0113) 244 0265.

JONES, David Evan Alun, CBE 1985; DL; Commissioner for Local Administration in Wales, 1980–85; *b* 9 Aug. 1925; *s* of David Jacob Jones, OBE, Master Mariner, and Margaret Jane Jones; *m* 1952, Joan Margaret Erica (*née* Davies); two *s. Educ:* Aberaeron County Sch.; University Coll. of Wales, Aberystwyth (LLB; Sir Samuel Evans Prize, 1949). Solicitor. Served War, RAF, 1943–47 (Flt Lieut). Articled service, Exeter, 1949–52; asst solicitor posts with Ilford Bor., Southampton County Bor., Berks County and Surrey County Councils, 1952–61; Dep. Clerk, Denbighshire CC, subseq. Clerk of CC and Clerk of the Peace, 1961–74; Chief Exec., Gwynedd CC, 1974–80. Chm., All Wales Adv. Panel on Develt of Services for Mentally Handicapped People, 1985–90; Member: Broadcasting Council for Wales, 1980–85; Local Govt Boundary Commn for Wales, 1985–89; Prince of Wales's Cttee, 1985–92 (Chm., Gwynedd County Gp, 1990–92); Gwynedd HA, 1986–88. Pres., Gwynedd Voluntary Services, 1994–96; Chm., N Wales Masonic Benevolent Assoc., 1996–99. Dir, Nat. Welsh-Amer. Foundn, 1992–. Treasurer, Univ. of Wales, Bangor (formerly UCNW), 1988–2000. Asst Provincial Grand Master, N Wales, 1987–94. DL Gwynedd, 1988. *Recreations:* gardening, travel, a little golf. *Address:* Min-y-Don, West End, Beaumaris, Gwynedd LL58 8BG. *T:* (01248) 810225. *Club:* Baron Hill Golf (Beaumaris).

JONES, David George; Director General (formerly Assistant Under Secretary of State), Financial Management, Ministry of Defence, 1996–2001; *b* 31 May 1941; *s* of Frederick George Jones and Dorothy Jones (*née* Steele); *m* 1962, Leonie Usherwood Smith; three *s. Educ:* High Storrs Grammar Sch., Sheffield. Joined War Office as Exec. Officer, 1960; Asst Private Sec. to Army Minister, 1970–71; Principal, MoD Central Financial Planning Div., 1973–77; Private Sec. to Minister of State for Defence, 1977–80; Regl Marketing Dir, Defence Sales Organisation, 1980–84; Asst Sec., Air Systems Controllerate, 1984–85; Dep. Dir Gen., Al Yamamah Project Office, 1985–88; Dir Gen. Aircraft 2, Air Systems Controllerate, MoD (PE), 1988–89; Civil Sec., British Forces Germany, 1989–92; Dir Gen. Supplies and Transport (Naval), 1993–95, Dir Gen. Naval Bases and Supply, 1995–96, MoD. FILT (FILog 1994). *Recreations:* gardening, travel.

JONES, David Hugh; Associate Director, Royal Shakespeare Company, since 1966; *b* 19 Feb. 1934; *s* of John David Jones and Gwendolen Agnes Langworthy (*née* Ricketts); *m* 1964, Sheila Allen (marr. diss.); two *s. Educ:* Taunton Sch.; Christ's Coll., Cambridge (MA 1st Cl. Hons English). 2nd Lieut RA, 1954–56. Production team of Monitor, BBC TV's 1st arts magazine, 1958–62, Editor, 1962–64; joined RSC, 1964; Aldwych Co. Dir, 1968–72; Artistic Dir, RSC (Aldwych), 1975–77; Producer, Play of the Month, BBC TV, 1977–78; Artistic Dir, Brooklyn Acad. of Music Theatre Co., 1979–81; Adjunct Prof. of Drama, Yale Univ., 1981. Productions for RSC incl. plays by Arden, Brecht, Gorky, Granville Barker, Günter Grass, Graham Greene, Mercer, O'Casey, Shakespeare, and Chekhov; dir. prodns for Chichester and Stratford, Ontario, Festival Theatres; other productions include: Old Times, Theatre Royal, Haymarket, and Los Angeles (LA Dramalogue Award for direction), 1985; No Man's Land, NY, 1994; The Hothouse, Chichester Fest., 1995; Taking Sides, NY, 1996. Dir, films for BBC TV, including: biography of poet, John Clare, 1969; adaptations of Hardy and Chekhov short stories, 1972 and 1973; Pinter's screenplay, Langrishe, Go Down, 1978; Merry Wives of Windsor, Pericles, 1982–83; The Devil's Disciple, 1987; Look Back in Anger, 1989 (ACE Award); directed for American TV: The Christmas Wife, 1988; Sensibility and Sense, 1990; The End of a Sentence, 1991; Fire in the Dark, 1991; And Then There Was One, 1994; Is There Life Out There?, 1994; Sophie and the Moonhanger, 1995; The Irvine Fertility Scandal, 1996; Time to Say Goodbye?, 1997; An Unexpected Life, 1998; A Christmas Carol, 1999; Custody of the Heart, 2000. Feature films directed: Pinter's Betrayal, 1982; 84 Charing Cross Road (royal film performance), 1987 (Christopher and Scriptor Awards, 1988); Jacknife, 1989; Kafka's The Trial, 1993; The Confession, 1998. Obie Awards, NY, for direction of RSC Summerfolk, 1975, for innovative programming at BAM Theatre Co., 1980. *Publication:* (with Richard Nelson) Making Plays, 1995. *Recreations:* restaurants, reading modern poetry, exploring mountains and islands. *Address:* 250 West 27th Street (# 6B), New York, NY 10001–5908, USA.

JONES, Rt Rev. David Huw; Bishop of St Davids, 1996–2001; *b* 1 July 1934; *s* of Joseph Elfed and Ethel Jones; *m* 1959, Gwyneth Jones; two *d. Educ:* Pontardawe Grammar Sch.; University Coll. of North Wales, Bangor (BA); University Coll., Oxford (MA). Curate: Aberdare, 1959–61; Neath, 1961–65; Vicar: Crynant, 1965–69; Michaelstone-super-Avon, 1969–73; Sub-Warden, St Michael's Coll., Llandaff, 1973–78; Lectr in Sch. of Theology, Univ. of Wales, Cardiff, 1973–78 (Asst Dean, 1977–78); Vicar of Prestatyn, 1978–82; Dean of Brecon, Vicar of Brecon, Battle and Llanddew, 1982–93; Asst Bishop, dio. of St Asaph, 1993–96. *Publications:* (ed jtly and contrib.) This Land and People, 1979; Guide to Brecon Cathedral, 1988. *Recreations:* walking, bird watching, church crawling, supporting Neath RFC. *Address:* c/o St Davids Diocesan Office, Abergwili, Carmarthen SA31 2JG.

JONES, (David) Huw; Chief Executive, S4C (Welsh Fourth Channel), since 1994; *b* 5 May 1948; *s* of Idris Jones and Olwen Mair Lloyd Jones; *m* 1972, Sian Marylka Miarczynska; one *s* one *d. Educ:* Cardiff High Sch. for Boys; Jesus Coll., Oxford (BA, MA). Singer and TV presenter, 1968–76; Dir, Sain (Recordiau) Cyf, 1969–81; Man. Dir, Teledu'r Tir Glas, 1982–93; Director: Sgrin Cyf, 1996–; S4C Masnacho 1 Cyf, 1999; S4C 2 1999–; SDN Ltd, 1999–; Nat. Assembly of Wales Broadcasting Co., 2000–. Chairman: Barcud Cyf, 1981–93; TAC, 1984–86; Arianrhod Cyf, 1988–93; Celtic Film and TV Fest. Ltd, 2001–; Dir, Internat. Film Fest. Wales, 2000–. Mem., FEFC for Wales, 1992–95. FRTS 1999. Hon. Fellow, Univ. of Wales, Aberystwyth, 1997. *Recreations:* reading, cycling, walking. *Address:* S4C, Parc Ty Glas, Llanishen, Cardiff CF14 5DU. *T:* (029) 2074 7444.

JONES, Rev. David Ian Stewart; Headmaster, Bryanston School, 1974–82; *b* 3 April 1934; *s* of Rev. John Milton Granville Jones and Evelyn Moyes Stewart Jones (formerly Chedburn); *m* 1967, Susan Rosemary Hardy Smith; twin *s* and *d. Educ:* St John's Sch., Leatherhead; Selwyn Coll., Cambridge (MA). Commnd Royal Signals, 1952–54. Curate at Oldham Parish Church, 1959–62; Vicar of All Saints, Elton, Bury, 1963–66; Asst Conduct and Chaplain of Eton Coll., 1966–70; Conduct and Sen. Chaplain of Eton Coll., 1970–74; Rector-designate of Bristol City, 1982–85; Dir, Lambeth Endowed Charities, 1985–97. Chm., Inner Cities Young People's Proj., 1988–98. *Recreations:* reading, music.

Address: 4 Kensington Park, Milford-on-Sea, Lymington, Hants SO41 0WD. *T:* (01590) 641107. *Club:* East India, Devonshire, Sports and Public Schools.

JONES, David le Brun, CB 1975; *b* 18 Nov. 1923; *s* of Thomas John Jones and Blanche le Brun. *Educ:* City of London Sch.; Trinity Coll., Oxford. Asst Principal, Min. of Power, 1947; Principal, MOP, 1952; Asst Sec., Office of the Minister for Science, 1962; Asst Sec., MOP, 1963; Under-Sec., MOP, later Min. of Technology and DTI, 1968–73; Dep. Sec., DTI, later DoI, 1973–76; Cabinet Office, 1976–77; Dept of Energy, 1978–82; Dir, Long Term Office, Internat. Energy Agency, 1982–88. Trustee, Nat. Energy Foundn, 1989–99. *Recreations:* walking, reading, chess. *Address:* 47 Grove End Road, NW8 9NB. *Club:* Oxford and Cambridge.

JONES, David Lewis, FSA; Librarian, House of Lords, since 1991; *b* 4 Jan. 1945; *s* of late Gwilym Morgan Jones and of Joyce Jones (*née* Davies). *Educ:* Aberaeron County Sch.; Jesus Coll., Oxford (MA); Coll. of Librarianship, Wales. FSA 1998. Asst Librarian, Inst. of Histl Res., 1970–72; University of Wales, Aberystwyth: Asst Librarian, 1972–75; Law Librarian, 1975–77; Dep. Librarian, H of L, 1977–91. Hon. Sec., Honourable Soc. of Cymmrodorion, 1994–96. Trustee, Cross Inn, Llanon, Sch. and School-House, 1975–. Gorsedd y Beirdd (Aelod er Anrhydedd), 1996. Freeman, City of London, 1993; Liveryman, Stationers' and Newspapermakers' Co., 1994. *Publications:* Books in English on the Soviet Union 1917–73, 1975; Paraguay: a bibliography, 1979; Debates and proceedings of the British Parliaments: a guide to printed sources, 1986; (ed jtly) Peers, politics and power: the House of Lords 1603–1911, 1986; A parliamentary history of the Glorious Revolution, 1988. *Address:* 10 Heathfield Court, Heathfield Terrace, W4 4LP. *T:* (020) 8995 6029.

JONES, David Lloyd; QC 1999; a Recorder, since 1994; *b* 13 Jan. 1952; *s* of William Elwyn Jones and Annie Blodwen Jones (*née* Lloyd-Jones); *m* 1983, Annmarie Harris; one *s* one *d*. *Educ:* Pontypridd Boys' Grammar Sch.; Downing Coll., Cambridge (MA, LLB, Whewell Scholar). Called to the Bar, Middle Temple, 1975; Fellow, Downing Coll., Cambridge, 1975–91; Asst Recorder, 1989–94; Junior Crown Counsel (Common Law), 1997–99. Asst Comr, Parly Boundary Commn for Wales, 1996–; Mem., Lord Chancellor's Adv. Cttee on Hague Judgments Negotiations, 1997–. Mem., Council of Legal Educn, 1991–96; Governor, Inns of Court Sch. of Law, 1996–. Vis. Prof., City Univ., 1999–. *Publications:* articles in legal jls. *Recreation:* music. *Address:* Brick Court Chambers, 7–8 Essex Street,WC2R 3LD. *T:* (020) 7379 3550.

JONES, David M.; *see* Mansel-Jones.

JONES, David Martin, FIBiol; Director, North Carolina Zoological Park, since 1994; *b* 14 Aug. 1944; *s* of John Trevor Jones and Mair Carno Jones; *m* 1969, Janet Marian Woosley; three *s*. *Educ:* St Paul's Cathedral Choir Sch.; St John's Sch., Leatherhead; Royal Veterinary Coll., London (BSc, BVetMed). MRCVS. Veterinary Officer, Whipsnade, 1969; Sen. Veterinary Officer, 1975, Asst Dir of Zoos, 1981, Dir of Zoos, 1984, Gen. Dir, 1991, Dir, Conservation and Consultancy Div., 1992, Zoological Soc. of London. Trustee, WWF UK, 1986–92, 1993–96 (Chm., Conservation Review Gp, subseq. Conservation Cttee, 1990–94); Member Council: WWF UK, 1994–; WWF US, 1996–; Chm., Fauna and Flora Internat., 1987–94. Chairman: Brooke Hosp. for Animals, 1990–98, 2000– (Vice-Chm., 1973–90); N Carolina Rural Heritage Forum, 1995–; Yadkin Pee-Dee Lakes Project, 1998–; Uwharrie Heritage LLC, 1999–2001. *Publications:* over 100 papers on wildlife medicine, management and conservation, in veterinary, medical and zoological jls. *Recreations:* field conservation, travel, antiquarian books, driving, gardening. *Address:* North Carolina Zoological Park, 4401 Zoo Parkway, Asheboro, NC 27203, USA.

JONES, Dr (David) Timothy; Chairman, InnovOx, since 2001; Deputy Chairman, Education and Training Wales, since 2001; *b* 21 Aug. 1944; *s* of David Percy Jones and Elvair (*née* Evans); *m* 1968, Jean Margaret Whitehead; four *d*. *Educ:* Leeds Univ. (PhD Physical Chem.); INSEAD, Fontainebleau (MBA with Dist.). MRSC 1967. Gen. Manager, Deutsche BP, 1985–88; Dir, BP France, 1988–89; Chief Exec., BP Oil Supply and Trading, 1990; Dir, BP Oil Europe, 1990–93; Dep. Chm., 1993–2000, Chief Exec., 1996–2000, Lloyd's Register. Chm., Marine Panel, Foresight Initiative, DTI, 1999–. *Recreations:* watching Rugby, walking, golf.

JONES, Deborah Mary; Editor, The Ark (Catholic Study Circle for Animal Welfare), since 1999; Deputy Editor, Priests & People, 1991–96 and since 1999; *b* 5 April 1948; *d* of Thomas Jones and Glenys Jones. *Educ:* W Kirby Grammar Sch. for Girls; University Coll. of S Wales, Cardiff (BA Gen. Hons); Leeds Univ. (PGCE); Regina Mundi Pontifical Inst., Rome. Teacher of English and Classical Studies, Clacton Co. High Sch., 1972–78; Dir, Adult Educn, dio. E Anglia, 1980–96 (pt-time, 1992–96); Lectr in Religious Studies, Suffolk Coll., 1987–92; Editor, Catholic Herald, 1996–98. *Publications:* Focus on Faith, 1987, 2nd edn 1996; This is My Body, 1989; contrib. articles to The Tablet, Priests & People, Ecotheology. *Recreations:* Baroque opera, golf, water-colouring. *Address:* 12 Swan Court, Witney, Oxon OX28 6EA.

JONES, Della Louise Gething; mezzo-soprano; *d* of Eileen Gething Jones and late Cyril Vincent Jones; *m* 1988, Paul Vigars; one *s*. *Educ:* Neath Girls' Grammar School; Royal College of Music. GRSM; LRAM (singing), ARCM (piano); Kathleen Ferrier Scholarship. Mem., ENO, 1977–82, leading roles; 1982–: guest artist, ENO; sings with major British opera companies; overseas concert and operatic appearances in all major European countries, also Russia, Japan and USA; radio and TV; prolific recordings with all major recording cos. Hon. FWCMD 1995. Hon. Fellow, Univ. of Wales Swansea, 1999. *Recreations:* writing cadenzas, art galleries, animal welfare, soap operas. *Address:* c/o Music International, 13 Ardilaun Road, Highbury, N5 2QR. *T:* (020) 7359 5183.

JONES, Sir Derek A.; *see* Alun-Jones.

JONES, Derek John Claremont, CMG 1979; Senior Fellow, Trade Policy Research Centre, 1986–90; retired; *b* 2 July 1927; *er s* of Albert Claremont Jones and Ethel Lilian Jones (*née* Hazell); *m* 1st, 1951, Jean Cynthia Withams; one *s* two *d*; 2nd, 1970, Kay Cecile Thewlis; one *s*. *Educ:* Colston Sch., Bristol; Bristol Univ.; London Sch. of Economics and Political Science. Economic Asst, Economic Section, Cabinet Office, 1950–53; Second Sec., UK Delegn to OEEC/NATO, Paris, 1953–55; Asst Principal, Colonial Office, 1955–57; Principal, Colonial Office, 1957–66; First Secretary, Commonwealth Office, 1966–67; Counsellor (Hong Kong Affairs), UK Mission, Geneva, 1967–71; Government of Hong Kong: Dep. Economic Sec., 1971–73; Sec. for Economic Services, 1973–76; Sec. for the Environment, 1976–81; Sec. for Transport, 1981–82; Minister for Hong Kong Relns with EC and Member States, 1982–86. *Recreations:* reading, travel, conversation. *Address:* Cliff House, Trevaunance Cove, St Agnes, Cornwall TR5 0RZ. *T:* (01872) 552334. *Clubs:* Hong Kong, Hong Kong Jockey.

JONES, Derek R.; *see* Rudd-Jones.

JONES, Derek William; Director, Economic Affairs, National Assembly for Wales, since 1999; *b* 8 Dec. 1952; *s* of William Jones and Patricia Mary Jones (*née* Gill); *m* 1976, Fiona Christine Anne Laidlaw; two *s*. *Educ:* UC Cardiff, Univ. of Wales (BA Hons). Worked on regional policy, company law and privatisation, DTI, 1977–82; HM Treasury: Public Expenditure Control, 1982–84; Head, Financial Instns and Markets Br., 1984–87; Head, Japan Desk and Overseas Trade Policy Div., DTI, 1987–89; Welsh Office: Asst Sec., 1989; Head, Industrial Policy Div., 1989–92; Head, Finance Progs Div., 1992–94; Under Sec., 1994; Dir, Industry and Trng Dept, 1994–99. *Recreations:* family life, reading, blues guitar. *Address:* c/o National Assembly for Wales, Cathays Park, Cardiff CF10 3NQ. *T:* (029) 2082 3325.

JONES, Rt Rev. Derwyn Dixon, DD; Bishop of Huron, 1984–90; *b* 5 Aug. 1925; *s* of Rev. Walter Jones, DD, and Mary Rosalie Jones (*née* Dixon); *m* 1960, Arline Carole Dilamarter; one *s* one *d*. *Educ:* Univ. of Western Ontario (BA); Huron College (LTh, DD). Deacon 1946, priest 1947; Curate: Holy Trinity, Winnipeg, 1946–48; All Saints', Windsor, 1948–49; Rector, St Andrew's, Kitchener, 1949–52; Asst Rector, St Paul's Cathedral, London, Ont, 1952–55; Rector: Canon Davis Memorial Church, Sarnia, 1955–58; St Barnabas, Windsor, 1958–66; St Peter's, Brockville, 1966–69; St James, Westminster, London, Ont, 1969–82; Archdeacon of Middlesex, 1978–82; Suffragan Bishop of Huron, 1982; Coadjutor Bishop, 1983. *Recreation:* music. *Address:* 3–515 Proudfoot Lane, London, ON N6H 5N9, Canada. *T:* (519) 6575068. *Club:* London (London, Ont).

JONES, Digby Marritt; Director General, Confederation of British Industry, since 2000; *b* 28 Oct. 1955; *s* of Derek Alwyn Jones and Bernice Joyce Jones; *m* 1990, Patricia Mary Moody. *Educ:* Bromsgrove Sch.; UCL (LLB Hons). Admitted Solicitor, 1980. Joined Edge & Ellison, Solicitors, 1978; articled clerk, 1978–80; Asst Solicitor, 1980–81; Associate, 1981–84; Partner, 1984–98; Head of Corporate, 1987; Dep. Sen. Partner, 1990–95; Sen. Partner, 1995–98; Vice-Chm., Corporate Finance, KPMG Business Advisors, 1998–99. *Recreations:* involvement in Birmingham Hospice and CBSO, Rugby, ski-ing, military history, keeping fit by cycling (cycled from John O'Groats to Lands End in June 1998). *Address:* CBI, Centre Point, 103 New Oxford Street, WC1A 1DU. *T:* (020) 7395 8001.

JONES, Rev. Prof. Douglas Rawlinson; Lightfoot Professor of Divinity, University of Durham, 1964–85, now Emeritus; Residentiary Canon of Durham Cathedral, 1964–85, now Emeritus; *b* 11 Nov. 1919; *s* of Percival and Charlotte Elizabeth Jones; *m* 1946, Hazel Mary Passmore; three *s* two *d*. *Educ:* Queen Elizabeth's Hosp., Bristol; St Edmund Hall, Oxford; Wycliffe Hall, Oxford. Squire Scholar, 1938; BA 1941; MA 1945; deacon, 1942; priest, 1943. Curate of St Michael and All Angels, Windmill Hill, Bristol, 1942–45; Lectr, Wycliffe Hall, Oxford, 1945–50; Chaplain, Wadham Coll., Oxford, 1945–50; Lectr in Divinity, 1948–50; University of Durham: Lectr, 1951; Sen. Lectr, 1963. Mem., Gen. Synod of C of E, 1970–80 and 1982–85. Chairman of the Liturgical Commn, 1981–86. DD Lambeth, 1985. *Publications:* Haggai, Zechariah and Malachi, 1962; Isaiah, 56–66 and Joel, 1964; Instrument of Peace, 1965; Jeremiah, 1992; contrib. to: Peake's Commentary on the Bible, 1962; Hastings' Dictionary of the Bible, 1963; The Cambridge History of the Bible, 1963; Thomas Cranmer, 1990; Sacrifice and Redemption, 1991; articles in Jl of Theolog. Studies, Zeitschrift für die Alttestamentliche Wissenschaft, Vetus Testamentum, Theology, Scottish Jl of Theology. *Recreation:* carpentry. *Address:* Whitefriars, Kings Road, Longniddry, E Lothian EH32 0NN. *T:* (01875) 52149.

JONES, Prof. Douglas Samuel, MBE 1945; FRS 1968; Ivory Professor of Mathematics, University of Dundee, 1965–92, now Emeritus Professor; *b* 10 Jan. 1922; *s* of late J. D. Jones and B. Jones (*née* Streather); *m* 1950, Ivy Styles; one *s* one *d*. *Educ:* Wolverhampton Grammar Sch.; Corpus Christi Coll., Oxford (MA 1947; Hon. Fellow, 1980); DSc Manchester 1957. FIMA 1964, CMath 1992; FRSE 1967; CEng, FIEE 1989. Flt-Lt, RAFVR, 1941–45. Commonwealth Fund Fellow, MIT, 1947–48; Asst Lectr in Maths, University of Manchester, 1948–51; Lectr 1951–54, Research Prof. 1955, New York Univ.; Sen. Lectr in Maths, Univ. of Manchester, 1955–57; Prof. of Maths, Univ. of Keele, 1957–64. Vis. Prof., Courant Inst., 1962–63. Member: UGC, 1976–86 (Mem., 1971–86, Chm., 1976–86, Mathematical Scis Sub-Cttee); Computer Bd, 1977–82; Open Univ. Vis. Cttee, 1982–87. Member Council: Royal Soc., 1973–74; IMA, 1982–85, 1986–97 (Pres., 1988–89). Hon. DSc Strathclyde, 1975. Keith Prize, RSE, 1974; van der Pol Gold Medal, Internat. Union of Radio Sci., 1981; Naylor Prize, London Mathematical Soc., 1987. Trustee, Quarterly Jl of Mechanics and Applied Maths, 1980–92; Associate Editor: Jl IMA, 1964–; RSE, 1969–82; SIAM Jl on Applied Maths, 1975–92; Applicable Analysis, 1976–92; Mathematical Methods in the Applied Sciences, 1977–; Royal Soc., 1978–83; Methods and Applications of Analysis, 1992–; Jl of Engrg Maths, 1992–; Communications in Applied Analysis, 1997–. *Publications:* Electrical and Mechanical Oscillations, 1961; Theory of Electromagnetism, 1964; Generalised Functions, 1966; Introductory Analysis, vol. 1, 1969, vol 2, 1970; Methods in Electromagnetic Wave Propagation, 1979, 2nd edn 1994; Elementary Information Theory, 1979; The Theory of Generalised Functions, 1982; Differential Equations and Mathematical Biology, 1983; Acoustic and Electromagnetic Waves, 1986; Assembly Programming and the 8086 Microprocessor, 1988; 80×86 Assembly Programming, 1991; Introduction to Asymptotics, 1997; articles in mathematical and physical jls. *Recreations:* golf, walking, photography. *Address:* Department of Mathematics, The University, Dundee DD1 4HN. *T:* (01382) 344486; 1 The Nurseries, St Madoes, Glencarse, Perth PH2 7NX. *Club:* Oxford and Cambridge.

JONES, Sir Edward; *see* Jones, Sir C. E. W.

JONES, Edward Bartley; QC 1997; a Recorder, since 2000; *b* Oswestry, 24 Dec. 1952; *o s* of Meurig Bartley Jones and late Ruby Jones (*née* Morris). *Educ:* Cardiff High Sch.; Balliol Coll., Oxford (BA Hons Modern Hist. 1973). Called to the Bar, Lincoln's Inn, 1975; in practice as a Chancery/Commercial Barrister in Liverpool, 1976– (Hd, Commercial Dept, Exchange Chambers, Liverpool and Manchester, 1994–); Asst Recorder, 1996–2000. Part-time Lectr in Law, Liverpool Univ., 1977–81. Member: Northern Chancery Bar Assoc.; Northern Circuit Commercial Bar Assoc.; Chancery Bar Assoc. *Recreations:* ski-ing, opera, travel, golf, shooting. *Address:* Exchange Chambers, Pearl Assurance House, Derby Square, Liverpool L2 9XX. *T:* (0151) 236 7747; 4 Ralli Courts, Manchester M3 5FT. *T:* (0161) 833 2722; Laurel Grove, Carden, Malpas, Cheshire SY14 7HP. *T:* (01829) 250257. *Clubs:* Oxford and Cambridge; Portal (Tarporley).

JONES, Edward David Brynmor, RIBA; architect in private practice, since 1973; Principal, Jeremy Dixon. Edward Jones, since 1989; *b* 20 Oct. 1939; *s* of David Jones and Margot Derricourt; *m* 1st; one *s* two *d*; 2nd, Margot Griffin; one *s* two *d*. *Educ:* Haileybury and ISC; AA Sch. of Architecture (AADip Hons 1963); RIBA 1968; RAIC and Ont. Assoc. of Architects, Canada, 1983–89. Tutor, AA, PCL and UC Dublin, 1968–72; Sen. Tutor, Sch. of Environmental Design, RCA, 1973–83; Vis. Prof., 1973–82, Adjunct Prof., 1983–89, Univ. of Toronto; Visiting Professor: Cornell, Harvard, Princeton, Yale, Pennsylvania, Rice, Syracuse and Kent State (Florence) Univs, 1973–; Portsmouth Univ., 1994–98. RIBA External Examiner: AA 1985; Portsmouth Univ., Kingston Univ.,

Heriot-Watt Univ., 1990–93; Univ. of Wales, 1995–97; Univ. of Technol., Kingston, Jamaica, 1997–2000. Mem. AA Council, 1993–99 (Vice Pres., 1995); Hon. Librarian, AA, 1994–95. Competitions, first prize: Northampton County Offices, 1973; Mississauga City Hall, Canada, 1982–87; Bus Stn, Venice, 1990; other projects include: Royal Opera House, Covent Garden, 1983–99; buildings for: Henry Moore Foundn at Leeds, 1989–93 and Perry Green, 1989–; Darwin Coll., Cambridge, 1989, 1994; Robert Gordon Univ., Aberdeen, 1991; superstores for J. Sainsbury at Plymouth and Bath; Portsmouth Univ. (Dept of Sci.), 1992–96; housing in New Delhi, 1994; Nat. Portrait Gall., 1994–2000; Said Business Sch., Oxford Univ., 1996–; Somerset House, south terrace and central courtyard, 1998–2000; master plan for Nat. Gall., 1998–; rep. Britain at Biennale: Venice, 1980; Paris, 1981; Santiago, 1982. FRSA. Hon. Dr: Wales, 2001; Portsmouth, 2001. Governor-General's Award for Architecture (Canada), 1988. *Publications:* A Guide to the Architecture of London (with C. Woodward), 1983, 3rd edn 2000; contribs to arch. jls. *Recreations:* swimming, drawing and cooking mostly in Italy. *Address:* 41 Gloucester Crescent, NW1 7DL. *T:* (020) 7267 7015. *Club:* Royal Automobile.

JONES, Air Marshal Sir Edward G.; *see* Gordon Jones.

JONES, Edward W.; *see* Wilson Jones.

JONES, Eleri Wynne; Member, Independent Television Commission, with special responsibility for Wales, 1990–98; *b* 9 Aug. 1933; *d* of Ellis Edgar and Elen Mary Griffith; *m* 1960, Bedwyr Lewis Jones (*d* 1992); two *s* one *d*. *Educ:* Howell's Sch., Denbigh (Foundn Schol.); University Coll. of Wales, Aberystwyth; University Coll., Cardiff. BA (Wales); DipIPM. Journalist, Canada, 1956–57; Careers Officer, Gwynedd, 1957–64; Tutor, Marr. Guidance Council, 1978–87; Lectr, Gwynedd Technical Coll., 1980–84; Member: Welsh Fourth Channel Authy, 1984–91; Bd of Channel Four, 1987–90. Dir, Cais Ltd, 1993–. Member: Staff Commn for Local Govt Reorgn (Wales), 1994–97; HEFCW, 2000–. Mem., Council, Univ. of Wales, Aberystwyth, 1995–98, Univ. of Wales, Bangor, 1998–. Formerly trainer and practitioner in psychotherapy and counselling. *Recreations:* walking, travel, television, films. *Address:* 3 Y Berllan, Lôn Las, Menai Bridge, Anglesey LL59 5BT. *T:* (01248) 717811.

JONES, Elin; Member (Plaid Cymru) Ceredigion, National Assembly for Wales, since 1999; Chairman, Plaid Cymru, since 2000; *b* 1 Sept. 1966; *d* of John and Avril Jones. *Educ:* Llanwnnen Primary Sch.; Lampeter Comprehensive; UC Cardiff (BScEcon); Univ. of Wales, Aberystwyth (MSc). Research Officer, Dept of Agric. Econs, UCW, Aberystwyth, 1988–91; Econ. Develt Officer, Develt Bd for Rural Wales, 1991–98; Regl Develt Manager, WDA, 1998–99. Mayor of Aberystwyth, 1997–98. *Recreations:* music, Welsh culture. *Address:* (constituency office) 8 Heol y Dŵr, Aberaeron, Ceredigion SA46 0DG. *T:* (01545) 571688.

JONES, Elizabeth Sian; QC 2000; *b* 24 March 1960; *d* of John Oswald Jones and Margrette Rachel Jones; *m* 1997, John Clark; one *s* one *d*. *Educ:* Howell's Sch., Llandaf; Ryde Sch., IoW; King's Coll., Cambridge. Called to the Bar, Middle Temple, 1984; in practice at the Bar, 1984–. *Recreations:* singing, opera, yoga, family. *Address:* Serle Court, 6 New Square, Lincoln's Inn, WC2A 3QS. *T:* (020) 7242 6105.

JONES, Prof. Emrys, MSc, PhD (Wales); FRGS; Professor of Geography, University of London, at London School of Economics, 1961–84, now Emeritus; *b* Aberdare, 17 Aug. 1920; *s* of Samuel Garfield and Anne Jones; *m* 1948, Iona Vivien, *d* of R. H. Hughes; one *d* (and one *d* decd). *Educ:* Grammar Sch. for Boys, Aberdare; University Coll. of Wales, Aberystwyth. BSc (1st Class Hons in Geography and Anthropology), 1941; MSc, 1945; PhD, 1947; Fellow of the University of Wales, 1946–47; Asst Lectr at University Coll., London, 1947–50; Fellow, Rockefeller Foundation, 1948–49; Lectr at Queen's Univ., Belfast, 1950–58, Sen. Lectr, 1958; Reader, LSE, 1959–61. O'Donnel Lectr, Univ. of Wales, 1977. Chairman: Regional Studies Assoc., 1967–69; Council, Hon. Soc. of Cymmrodorion, 1984–89 (Mem., 1977–; Pres., 1989–); Mem. Council, RGS, 1973–77 (Vice-Pres., 1978–81). Mem. Council, University Coll. of Wales, Aberystwyth, 1978–85. Consultant on urbanisation and planning. Hon. Fellow, UCW, 1991. Hon. DSc Belfast, 1978; DUniv Open, 1990. Victoria Medal, RGS, 1977. *Publications:* Hon. Editor, Belfast in its Regional Setting, 1952; (jointly) Welsh Rural Communities, 1960; A Social Geography of Belfast, 1961; Human Geography, 1964; Towns and Cities, 1966; Atlas of London, 1968; (ed jtly) Man and his Habitat, 1971; (contrib.) The Future of Planning, 1973; (with E. van Zandt) The City, 1974; Readings in Social Geography, 1975; (with J. Eyles) Introduction to Social Geography, 1977; (Chief Editor) The World and its Peoples, 1979; Metropolis: the world's great cities, 1990; The Welsh in London 1500–2000, 2001; articles in geographical, sociological and planning jls. *Recreations:* books, music. *Address:* 51 Lower King's Road, Berkhamsted, Herts HP4 2AA. *T:* (01442) 875422. *Club:* Athenæum.

JONES, Prof. Emrys Lloyd, FBA 1982; Goldsmiths' Professor of English Literature, Oxford University, and Fellow, New College, Oxford, 1984–98; *b* 30 March 1931; *s* of Peter Jones and Elizabeth Jane (*née* Evans); *m* 1965, Barbara Maud Everett; one *d*. *Educ:* Neath Grammar Sch.; Magdalen Coll., Oxford (BA, MA). Tutor in English, Magdalen Coll., 1955–77; Reader in Eng. Lit., Oxford Univ., 1977–84; Fellow, Magdalen Coll., Oxford, 1955–84. Hon. DPhil Lund, 1994. *Publications:* (ed) Poems of Henry Howard, Earl of Surrey, 1964; Pope and Dulness, 1972; Scenic Form in Shakespeare, 1971; The Origins of Shakespeare, 1977; (ed) Antony and Cleopatra, 1977; (ed) The New Oxford Book of Sixteenth Century Verse, 1991; contribs to jls and books. *Recreations:* looking at buildings; opera. *Address:* New College, Oxford OX1 3BN. *T:* (01865) 279555.

JONES, Eric S.; *see* Somerset Jones.

JONES, Ernest Edward; Member, Doncaster Metropolitan Borough Council, 1980–2000; *b* 15 Oct. 1931; *s* of William Edward Jones and Eileen Gasser; *m* 1955, Mary Armstrong; one *s* one *d*. *Educ:* Bentley Catholic Primary Sch., Doncaster; Sheffield De La Salle Coll.; Hopwood Hall Coll. of Educn, Middleton, Lancs; Manch. Univ. Sch. of Educn; Management Studies Unit, Sheffield Polytech. Min. of Educn Teaching Certif. (CertEd); Univ. Dipl. in Science Studies (DipSc); Dipl. in Educn Management (DEM). School Master, 1953–92. Doncaster County Borough: Councillor, 1962–74 (Chm. Health Cttee, 1971–74; Chm. Social Services Cttee, 1972–73; served on 15 other cttees at various times). South Yorkshire CC: Mem. 1973–77; Dep. Chm., 1973–75; Chm., 1975–76; Chm., Rec., Culture and Health Cttee, 1973–75; Doncaster Metropolitan Borough Council: Chairman: Libraries, Museums and Arts Cttee, 1982–91; Further Educn Cttee, 1983–85; Social Service Cttee, 1998–2000; Mem., Educn Services Cttee, 1980–2000 (Vice-Chm., 1982–95). Chairman: Trent Regional Assoc. of Community Health Councils, 1988–90; Doncaster CHC, 1981–90; Co. and Council of Management, Northern Coll., 1986–88, 1991– (Vice-Chm., 1982–86, 1990–91); Doncaster College (formerly Inst. of Further and Higher Educn), 1985–93; Mem., Doncaster Coll. Corp., 1993–. Member: Nat. Health Exec. Council, 1964–74; Doncaster and Dist Water Bd, 1972–74; AMC (Social Services), 1972–74; Peak Park Planning Bd, 1973–77; Yorks and Humberside Museum and Art Gall. Service, 1973–77, 1984–; Yorks and Humberside Jt Libraries Cttee, 1973–75, 1983–; Yorks and Humberside Assoc. of Further and High Educn, 1982–; Yorks and Humberside Assoc. of Educn Authorities, 1982– (Chm., 1988–89); Council, Museums Assoc., 1986; S Yorks Jt Archaeol Cttee, 1987–91 (Chm., 1987–88); S Yorks Jt Archives Cttee, 1987–91 (Chm., 1987–88); NEAB, 1992–; S Yorks Fire and Civil Defence Authy, 1997–; Cttee, Yorks Tourist Bd, 1999–; Exec. Mem., Nat. Field Studies Council, 1988–. Exec. Mem., Yorks Arts Assoc., 1983–85; Former Member: Yorks Regional Land Drainage Cttee; Univ. of Hull Educn Delegacy; AMA; Yorks and Humberside Museums and Art Galleries Fedn; Yorks and Humberside Regional Sports Council; Yorks, Humberside and Cleveland Tourist Bd; Exec. Mem., Youth Assoc. of South Yorks. Member: Hull Univ. Ct, 1983–85; Sheffield Univ. Ct and Council, 1983–; Bradford Univ. Ct and Council, 1986–93; Governor: Sheffield Poly., 1982–90; Sheffield Hallam Univ., 1995–99. FRSH; FRSA 1980. *Recreations:* music and fine arts, general interest in sport, fell-walking, keen caravanner. *Address:* 11 Norborough Road, Doncaster, South Yorks DN2 4AR. *T:* (01302) 366122.

JONES, Eurfron Gwynne; Director of Education, BBC, 1992–94; *b* 24 Sept. 1934; *d* of William Gwynne Jones and Annie (*née* Harries); *m* 1968, Michael Coyle; one *s*. *Educ:* Aberdare Girls' Grammar Sch.; University Coll., Cardiff, Univ. of Wales (BSc (Zoology); PhD). Teaching Asst, Mount Holyoke Coll., Mass, 1955–56; joined BBC as gen. trainee, 1959; Producer, BBC Sch. Radio, Sch. Television and Continuing Educn, TV, 1959–75; freelance broadcaster, writer and cons., Media Cons. Internat. Children's Centre, Educn Commn of the States, 1975–83; Asst Hd, Sch. Radio, 1983–84; Hd of Sch. Television, 1984–87; Controller, Educnl Broadcasting, BBC, 1987–92. Member: Wyatt Commn on Violence, 1986; OU Council, 1987–94; Open Coll. Council, 1987–89; Council, Royal Instn, 1989–92, and 1994–97; COPUS, 1992–94; Educn Adv. Cttee, Nat. Museums and Galls of Wales, 1995–99; Res. Panel, Inst. of Welsh Affairs, 1996–; Chm., Digital Coll. for Wales, 1997–. Vis. Prof., Inst. of Educn, Univ. of London, 1994–97. FRTS 1994 (Mem., 1984–94; Vice Pres., 1996–). Fellow, Univ. of Wales Cardiff, 1996. Hon. LLD Exeter, 1990; DUniv Open, 1996. *Publications:* Children Growing Up, 1973; The First Five Years, 1975; How Did I Grow?, 1977; Television Magic, 1978; Lifetime I, Lifetime II, 1982; numerous articles on children and educn. *Recreations:* photography, swimming.

JONES, Ewan Perrins W.; *see* Wallis-Jones.

JONES, Sir Ewart (Ray Herbert), Kt 1963; DSc Victoria, PhD Wales, MA Oxon; FRS 1950, FRSC; Waynflete Professor of Chemistry, University of Oxford, 1955–78, now Emeritus; Fellow of Magdalen College, 1955–78, Hon. Fellow, 1978; *b* Wrexham, Denbighshire, 16 March 1911; *m* 1937, Frances Mary Copp (*d* 1999); one *s* two *d*. *Educ:* Grove Park Sch., Wrexham; University Coll. of North Wales, Bangor; Univ. of Manchester. Fellow of Univ. of Wales, 1935–37; Lecturer, Imperial Coll. of Science and Technology, 1938; Reader in Organic Chemistry, Univ. of London, and Asst Prof., 1945; Sir Samuel Hall Prof. of Chemistry, The University, Manchester, 1947–55. Arthur D. Little Visiting Prof. of Chemistry, MIT, 1952; Karl Folkers Lectr at Univs of Illinois and Wisconsin, 1957; Andrews Lectr, Univ. of NSW, 1960. Mem. Council for Scientific and Industrial Research, and Chm., Research Grants Cttee, 1961–65; Mem. SRC and Chm., Univ. Science and Technology Bd, 1965–69; Mem., Science Bd, 1969–72. Chemical Society: Tilden Lectr, 1949; Pedler Lectr, 1959; Robert Robinson Lectr, 1978; Dalton Lectr, 1985; Award for Service to the Society, 1973; Award in Natural Product Chem., 1974; Meldola Medal, Royal Institute of Chemistry, 1940, Davy Medal, Royal Society, 1966. Fritzsche Award, American Chemical Soc., 1962. President: Chemical Soc., 1964–66; RIC, 1970–72 (Chm., Chem. Soc./RIC Unification Cttee, 1975–80); Royal Soc. of Chemistry, 1980–82 (Millennium Fellow, 2000). Fellow, Imperial Coll., 1967; Foreign Mem. Amer. Acad. of Arts and Sciences, 1967. Chm., Anchor and Guardian Housing Assocs, 1979–84. Hon. DSc: Birmingham, 1965; Nottingham, 1966; New South Wales, 1967; Sussex, 1969; Salford, 1971; Wales, 1971; East Anglia, 1978; Ulster, 1978; Hon. LLD Manchester, 1972. *Publications:* scientific papers in Jl of the Chem. Soc. *Address:* 6 Sandy Lane, Yarnton, Kidlington, Oxon OX5 1PB. *T:* (01865) 372581.

JONES, Fielding; *see* Jones, N. F.

JONES, Fiona Elizabeth Ann; *b* 27 Feb. 1957; *m*; two *s*. *Educ:* Mary Help of Christians Convent, Liverpool. Journalist. MP (Lab) Newark, 1997–2001; contested (Lab) same seat, 2001.

JONES, Francis John; Chairman, Telford Development Corporation, 1987–91; Chairman, Shropshire Health Authority, 1979–90; *b* 28 June 1928; *s* of John Francis and Mary Emma Jones; *m* 1st, 1953, Angela Mary Kelly (marr. diss.); one *s* one *d*; 2nd, 1970, Jean Elsie Sansome; two step *s* two step *d*. *Educ:* Manchester Grammar Sch.; Manchester Univ. Various marketing and sales positions; West African Colonies, 1950–52; Proctor & Gamble, 1952–54; Beecham Group, 1954–57; Crosse & Blackwell/Nestlé, 1957–64; W. Symington, 1964–69; Chm., Telford Foods, 1970–84, retired. *Recreations:* reading, music, opera. *Address:* 2 Swan Hill Gardens, Shrewsbury SY1 1NT. *T:* (01743) 362159.

JONES, Fred, CB 1978; CBE 1966; Deputy Secretary, HM Treasury, 1975–80, retired; *b* 5 May 1920; *s* of late Fred Jones and of Harriet (*née* Nuttall); *m* 1954, Joy (*née* Field); two *s*. *Educ:* Preston Grammar Sch.; St Catherine's Coll., Oxford. Economist, Trades Union Congress, 1951–59; Tutor in Economics and Industrial Relations, Ruskin Coll., Oxford, 1960–62; Economist, National Economic Development Office, 1962–64; Dept of Economic Affairs: Senior Economic Adviser, 1964–66; Asst Sec., 1966–68; Asst Under-Sec. of State, 1968–69; HM Treasury, Asst Under-Sec. of State, 1969–75. *Recreations:* walking, gardening, reading. *Address:* 16 Higher Greenfield, Ingol, Preston, Lancs PR2 3ZX.

JONES, Gareth; *see* Jones, J. G.

JONES, Gareth, OBE 1991; Member (Plaid Cymru) Conwy, National Assembly for Wales, since 1999; *b* 14 May 1939. *Educ:* UC, Swansea (BA Hons Geography). Former Headmaster; educnl consultant. Mem., Conwy County Borough Council, 1998–. *Address:* National Assembly for Wales, Cardiff Bay, Cardiff CF99 1NA; Dolarfon, 21 Roumania Drive, Craig y Don, Llandudno LL30 1UY.

JONES, Prof. Gareth (Hywel); QC 1986; FBA 1982; Fellow of Trinity College, Cambridge, since 1961; Downing Professor of the Laws of England, Cambridge University, 1975–98; *b* 10 Nov. 1930; *o c* of late B. T. Jones, FRICS, and late Mabel Jones, Tylorstown, Glam; *m* 1959, Vivienne Joy, *o d* of late C. E. Puckridge, FIA, Debden Green, Loughton; two *s* one *d*. *Educ:* Porth County Sch.; University Coll. London (PhD; Hon. Fellow 1988); St Catharine's Coll., Cambridge (Scholar); Harvard Univ. (LLM). LLB London 1951; MA, LLB 1953, LLD 1972, Cantab. Choate Fellow, Harvard, 1953; Yorke Prize, 1960. Called to Bar, Lincoln's Inn, 1955 (Scholar); Hon. Bencher 1975. Lecturer: Oriel and Exeter Colls, Oxford, 1956–58; KCL, 1958–61; Trinity College, Cambridge: Lectr, 1961–75; Tutor, 1967; Sen. Tutor, 1972; Vice-Master, 1986–92 and 1996–99; Univ. Lectr, Cambridge, 1961–75; Chm., Faculty of Law, 1978–81; Chm., Fitzwilliam Mus. Syndicate, 1987–. Visiting Professor: Harvard, 1966 and 1975; Chicago, 1976–95;

California at Berkeley, 1967 and 1971; Indiana, 1971, 1975; Michigan, 1983, 1997, 1999, 2001; Georgia, 1983; Texas, 1993. Lectures: Harris, Indiana, 1981; Wright, Toronto, 1984; Lionel Cohen, Hebrew Univ., 1985; Butterworth, QMC, 1987; Nambyar, India, 1991; Richard O'Sullivan, Thomas More Soc., 1991; Hochelaga, Hong Kong. Mem., American Law Inst.; For. Mem., Royal Netherlands Acad. of Arts and Scis, 1991. *Publications:* (with Lord Goff of Chieveley) The Law of Restitution, 1966, 5th edn 1998; The History of the Law of Charity 1532–1827, 1969; The Sovereignty of the Law, 1973; (with Lord Goodhart) Specific Performance, 1986, 2nd edn 1996; various articles. *Address:* Trinity College, Cambridge CB2 1TQ. *T:* (01223) 338473; 9B Cranmer Road, Cambridge CB3 9BL. *T:* (01223) 363932. *Address:* Clay Street, Thornham Magna, Eye, Suffolk IP23 8HE. *Club:* Beefsteak.

JONES, Dr Gareth L.; Director of Human Resources and Internal Communications, BBC, since 1999; *b* 21 Aug. 1951; *s* of Les and Gwen Jones; *m* 1990, Shirley Rose Neal; one *s* two *d*. BSc Econ, MA, PhD. Lecturer in Economic and Social Studies: UEA, 1974–85; London Business Sch., 1985–93; Sen. Vice Pres., Polygram Internat., 1993–96; BT Prof. of Orgnl Develt, Henley Mgt Coll., 1996–99. *Publications:* (with R. E. Goffee) The Character of a Corporation, 1998; contrib. articles to Eur. Jl Mgt, Human Relns, Harvard Business Rev. *Recreations:* soccer, squash, pub-visiting. *Address:* c/o BBC, Broadcasting House, W1A 1AA.

JONES, Gareth S.; *see* Stedman Jones.

JONES, Geoffrey; *see* Jones, John G.

JONES, Prof. Geoffrey M.; *see* Melvill Jones.

JONES, Geoffrey Rippon R.; *see* Rees-Jones.

JONES, George Briscoe, CBE 1988; Director: Job Ownership Ltd, 1983–95; Partnership in Business Ltd, 1988–95; *b* 1 June 1929; *s* of late Arthur Briscoe Jones and Mary Alexandra Jones (*née* Taylor); *m* 1955, Audrey Patricia Kendrick (*d* 1999); two *d*. *Educ:* Wallasey and Caldy Grammar Schools. Army, 1947–49; Unilever, 1949–84 (on secondment to CDA, 1982–84); Dir, BOCM Silcocks, 1974–82; Chm., Unitrition, 1977–82; Director: Co-op. Develt Agency, 1982–90; Chrisamer Ltd, 1989–93. Mem., Plunkett Foundn, 1985–. Governor: QMW, 1993–95; Fort Hill Sch., 1993–95. *Recreations:* painting, sculpture, chess, bridge. *Address:* 32 Cleveland Drive, Little Sutton, South Wirral, Cheshire CH66 4XY.

JONES, George Quentin; Political Editor, Daily Telegraph, since 1988; *b* 28 Feb. 1945; *s* of John Clement Jones, *qv*; *m* 1st, 1972, Diana Chittenden (marr. diss. 1989); one *s* one *d*; 2nd, 1990, Teresa Grace Rolleston. *Educ:* Highfields Sch., Wolverhampton. Trainee journalist, Eastern Daily Press, 1963–67; journalist, S Wales Argus and Western Mail, 1967–69; Reuters, London, 1969; Parly Staff, The Times, 1969–73; Parly and Political Corresp., Scotsman, 1973–82; Political Correspondent: Sunday Telegraph, 1982–85; Sunday Times, 1985–86; Daily Telegraph, 1986–88. Regular broadcaster, BBC News and current affairs programmes, London Radio, Sky News. Chairman: Parly Lobby Journalists, 1987–88; Parly Press Gallery, 1996–97. Judge, Spectator Parliamentarian of the Year Awards, 1993–. *Recreations:* walking, cycling, travelling, time with family. *Address:* 92 Kyrle Road, SW11 6BA. *T:* (020) 7223 6646. *Club:* Athenæum.

JONES, Prof. George William, OBE 1999; Professor of Government, University of London, since 1976; *b* 4 Feb. 1938; *er s* of George William and Grace Annie Jones; *m* 1963, Diana Mary Bedwell; one *s* one *d*. *Educ:* Wolverhampton Grammar Sch.; Jesus Coll., Oxford; Nuffield Coll., Oxford. Oxf. BA 1960, MA 1965, DPhil 1965. Univ. of Leeds: Asst Lectr in Govt, 1963; Lectr in Govt, 1965; London School of Economics and Political Science: Lectr in Political Science, 1966; Sen. Lectr in Polit. Sci., 1971; Reader in Polit. Sci., 1974; Chm., Graduate Sch., 1990–93; Vice-Chm., Appts Cttee, 1996–99. Sec., 1965–68, Mem. Exec. Cttee, 1969–75, Polit. Studies Assoc. of the UK; Mem., Exec. Council, Hansard Soc., 1968–70; Member, Editorial Committee: Local Government Studies, 1970–98; The London Journal, 1973–80; Governance, 1987–92; Korean Jl of Public Policy, 1988–; Studies in Law and Politics, 1989–; Nonprofit Management and Leadership, 1989–; Hong Kong Jl of Public Admin, 1992–. Member: Layfield Cttee of Inquiry into Local Govt Finance, 1974–76; Exams Cttee, and Admin. Staff Qualifications Council, Local Govt Trng Bd, 1977–80; Political Science and Internat. Relns Cttee, SSRC, 1977–81; Jt Working Party on Internal Management of Local Authorities, 1992–93; Chm., Central-Local Govt Relations Panel, SSRC, 1978–81; Special Adviser, Select Cttee on Welsh Affairs, 1985–87. Member: Governing Council, Wolverhampton Polytechnic, 1978–83 (Hon. Fellow, 1986); Council, RIPA, 1984–90; Nat. Consumer Council, 1991–99 (Chm., Public Services Cttee, 1992–98); Beacon Councils Adv. Panel, 1999–; Vice-Pres., Assoc. of Councillors, 1980–. FRHistS 1980. Hon. Fellow, Inst. of Local Govt Studies, Birmingham Univ., 1979. *Publications:* Borough Politics, 1969; (with B. Donoughue) Herbert Morrison: portrait of a politician, 1973, repr. 2001; (ed with A. Norton) Political Leadership in Local Authorities, 1978; (ed) New Approaches to the Study of Central-Local Government Relationships, 1980; (with J. Stewart) The Case for Local Government, 1983, 2nd edn 1985; (ed jtly) Between Centre and Locality, 1985; (ed) West European Prime Ministers, 1991; (with Tony Travers *et al*) The Government of London, 1991; Local Government and the Social Market, 1991; (with Tony Travers *et al*) The Impact of Population Size on Local Authority Costs and Effectiveness, 1993; Local Government: the management agenda, 1993; (with Tony Travers) Attitudes to Local Government in Westminster and Whitehall, 1994; (with Tony Travers *et al*) The Role of the Local Authority Chief Executive in Local Governance, 1997; The New Local Government Agenda, 1997; (jtly) At the Centre of Whitehall, 1998; (jtly) Regulation Inside Government, 1999; contribs to Political Studies, Public Admin., Political Qly, Parliamentary Affairs, Government and Opposition, Jl of Admin Overseas; Local Govt Chronicle; Internat. Jl Public Sector Mgt; Public Money and Mgt. *Recreations:* cinema, politics. *Address:* Department of Government, London School of Economics, Houghton Street, WC2A 2AE. *T:* (020) 7955 7179; *e-mail:* g.w.jones@lse.ac.uk. *Club:* Beefsteak.

JONES, Geraint Anthony; QC 2001; *b* 5 April 1953; *s* of John and Lydia Jones; *m* 1976, Pauline Julia Gibson. *Educ:* Christ Coll., Brecon; Jesus Coll., Cambridge (MA). Called to the Bar, Middle Temple, 1976; in practice as barrister, specialising in chancery, commercial and professional negligence law, Cardiff, 1976–. *Recreations:* hill walking, sailing. *Address:* The Garth, Rosewood Close, Lisvane, Cardiff CF14 0EU.

JONES, Geraint Stanley, CBE 1993; international broadcasting consultant and producer, since 1994; Chief Executive, S4C, 1989–94; *b* 26 April 1936; *s* of Olwen and David Stanley Jones; *m* 1961, Rhiannon Williams; two *d*. *Educ:* Pontypridd Grammar Sch.; University Coll. of N Wales (BA Hons; DipEd; Hon. Fellow 1988). BBC-Wales: Studio Manager, 1960–62; Production Asst, Current Affairs (TV), 1962–65; TV Producer: Current Affairs, 1965–69; Features and Documentaries, 1969–73; Asst Head of Programmes, Wales, 1973–74; Head of Programmes, Wales, 1974–81; Controller, BBC Wales, 1981–85; Dir of Public Affairs, BBC, 1986–87; Man. Dir, Regl Broadcasting, BBC, 1987–89. Director: WNO, 1985–94; Welsh Film Council, 1992–97; Screen Wales, 1992–96; Wales Millennium Centre, 1999–; Chm., Sgrîn, Media Agency for Wales, 1999–. Mem., Arts Council of Wales, 1994–2000. Chm., EBU Television Commn, 1990–96. Chm., Ryan Davies Trust, 1977–; Member: UK Freedom from Hunger Campaign Cttee, 1978–97; BT Wales Adv. Forum, 1994–2001; British Council Film and TV Cttee, 1995–; UNA (Welsh Centre) Trust. Vice Pres., WCMD, 2000– (Chm., Bd of Govs, 1990–2000); Mem., Court and Council, Univ. of Wales, Aberystwyth, 1990–96. Chm., Welsh Nat. Lang. Centre, 1994–97. Vis. Prof., Internat. Acad. of Broadcasting, Montreux, 1994–. FRSA 1989; FRTS 1992. FWCMD 2000. Hon. LLD Wales, 1998; Hon. DLitt Glamorgan, 1999. *Recreations:* music, painting, horse riding. *Address:* 12 Lady Mary Road, Roath Park, Cardiff CF23 5NS. *Clubs:* Royal Over-Seas League; Cardiff and County (Cardiff).

JONES, Dr Gerald, FRCP; Senior Principal Medical Officer, Department of Health (formerly of Health and Social Security), 1984–95; *b* 25 Jan. 1939; *s* of John Jones and Gladys Jones (*née* Roberts); *m* 1st, 1964, Anne Heatley (*née* Morris) (marr. diss. 1987); one *s* two *d*; 2nd, 1990, Jutta Friese. *Educ:* Swansea Grammar School; Merton College, Oxford; London Hosp. Med. Coll. (BA, BM, BCh, PhD, MSc). Appointments in hosp. medicine, 1965–69; research with MRC, 1969–73; pharmaceutical industry, 1974–75; medical staff, DHSS, later DoH, 1975–95. *Publications:* papers on cardiopulmonary physiology, respiratory medicine, cellular immunology and drug regulation. *Recreations:* music, gardening, mathematics. *Address:* 58 Palace Road, N8 8QP.

JONES, Gerald Kenneth; Chief Executive, Wandsworth Borough Council, since 1987; *b* 16 June 1943; *s* of Sir Kenneth Jones, CBE, QC and of Menna (*née* Jones); *m* 1976, Janet Norma Dymock; three *s* one *d*. *Educ:* Royal Grammar Sch., Guildford; St John's Coll., Cambridge (MA 1965); Brunel Univ. (MTech 1972). Operational Res. Scientist, NCB, 1966–69; Mgt Consultant, RTZ Corp., 1969–72; Corporate Planner, Haringey Council, 1972–74; Wandsworth Council: Asst Dir, Admin, 1974–83; Dep. Chief Exec., 1983–87. *Publications:* contrib. technical and professional jls. *Recreations:* collecting antiquarian books, triathlon. *Address:* The Town Hall, Wandsworth High Street, SW18 2PU.

JONES, Glyn Parry, FCA; Chief Executive, Gartmore Investment Management plc, since 2000; *b* 17 March 1952; *m* 1976, Catherine Anne King; two *s* one *d*. *Educ:* Birkenhead Sch.; Gonville and Caius Coll., Cambridge (MA Econs and Social and Pol Scis). FCA 1976. Deloitte Haskins and Sells: Auditor, London, 1973–76; Consultant, Financial Mgt Consultancy, London, 1977–80; Man. Dir, Kenyan Consultancy, Nairobi, 1980–83; Partner, Midlands Consulting Practice, Birmingham, 1983–85; Partner in Charge, Financial Services Consulting, London, 1986–89; European Sector Leader, Financial Services, London, Coopers & Lybrand Mgt Consultants, 1989–91; Standard Chartered Bank: Divl Dir, Standard Chartered Equitor, Hong Kong, 1991–92; Gen. Manager, Internat. Private Banking, Hong Kong, 1993–97; Commercial Dir, NatWest Wealth Mgt, London, March–Oct. 1997; Chief Exec., Coutts Gp, 1997–2000. *Recreations:* tennis, squash, theatre. *Address:* Gartmore House, 8 Fenchurch Place, EC3M 4PH.

JONES, Rev. Canon Glyndwr; Secretary General, Mission to Seafarers (formerly Missions to Seamen), 1990–2000; a Chaplain to the Queen, since 1990; *b* 25 Nov. 1935; *s* of late Bertie Samuel Jones and of Elizabeth Ellen Jones; *m* 1st, 1961, Cynthia Elaine Jenkins (*d* 1964); 2nd, 1966, (Marion) Anita Morris; one *s* one *d*. *Educ:* Dynefor Sch., Swansea; St Michael's Theol Coll., Llandaff, Univ. of Wales (DipTh). Nat. Service, 1954–56: RAPC, attached 19 Field Regt RA; served Korea, Hong Kong; demobbed Sgt AER. Deacon 1962, priest 1963; Curate: Clydach, 1962–64; Llangyfelach with Morriston, 1964–67; Sketty, 1967–70; Rector, Bryngwyn with Newchurch and Llanbedr, Painscastle with Llandewi Fach, 1970–72; The Missions to Seamen: Port Chaplain, Swansea and Port Talbot, 1972–76; Sen. Chaplain, Port of London, 1976–81; Auxiliary Ministries Sec., Central Office, 1981–85; Asst Gen. Sec., 1985–90. Hon. Chaplain, Royal Alfred Seafarers Soc., 1987–93; Chaplain to Lay Sheriff of London, 1993–94, 1999–2000; Hon. Canon, St Michael's Cathedral, Kobe, Japan, 1988–. Commissary to Bp of Cyprus in the Gulf, 1996–2000; Hon. Mem., Co. of Master Mariners, 1990–2000; Freeman, City of London, 1990; Chaplain: Co. of Information Technologists, 1989–2000; Co. of Inn-holders, 1990–; Co. of Farriers, 1990– (Liveryman, 1999–); Co. of Carmen, 1990– (Liveryman, 1995–). *Recreations:* sport, music, reading, theatre, travel. *Address:* 5 The Close, Grays, Essex RM16 2XU. *Club:* Little Ship (Hon. Chaplain, 1996–).

JONES, Glynn, CBE 1992; Circuit Administrator, Western Circuit, Lord Chancellor's Department, 1987–93; *b* 5 March 1933; *s* of late Bertie Jones and Alice Maud Jones (*née* Griffiths); *m* 1957, Crystal Laura, *d* of late Edward William Kendall and Ivy Irene Kendall; one *s* one *d*. *Educ:* state schs in Monmouthshire; BA Open. Local Govt service, 1950–71; Lord Chancellor's Department: Crown Court, Newport, 1972, Winchester, 1973; Courts Administrator: Nottingham Group of Courts, 1976; South Wales Group of Courts, 1980. *Recreations:* Rugby Union football, golf. *Address:* 17 Rockfield Glade, Penhow, Newport, S Wales NP26 3JF. *T:* (01633) 400835. *Clubs:* Civil Service; St Pierre Golf and Country, Newport Golf.

JONES, Gordon Frederick; architect; *b* 25 Aug. 1929; *s* of Harold Frederick and Rose Isabel Jones; *m* 1954, Patricia Mary (*née* Rowley); one *s* one *d*. *Educ:* Saltley Grammar Sch.; The School of Architecture, Birmingham (DipArch 1950), and subseq. by BBC; Sch. of Planning, UCL (Cert. Landscape Design, 1963). RIBA 1950. FRSA. Architect: in local government, 1952; War Office, 1959; Asst City Architect, Sheffield, 1966; private practice, London, 1968; Property Services Agency, DoE: Architect, 1970; Head of Student Training Office, 1976; Head of Architectural Services, 1979–85; Res. Dir, 1985–90, Editor, 1990–93, Product Design Review. Dir, Building Centre, 1984–87. Chm. of Standards, BDB/–, BSI, 1984–87. *Recreations:* watching cats, listening to music, re-building houses. *Address:* Hilltop, Monkleigh, Devon EX39 5JT.

JONES, Graham Edward, MA; Headmaster, Repton School, since 1987; *b* 22 Sept. 1944; *s* of late Edward Thomas Jones and of Dora Rachel Jones; *m* 1976, Vanessa Mary Heloise (*née* Smith). *Educ:* Birkenhead Sch.; Fitzwilliam Coll., Cambridge (schol.; 1st cl. Hons Econs Tripos 1966). Asst Master, Hd of Economics and Politics, Housemaster, Charterhouse, 1967–87; secondment to British Petroleum, 1981. Awarder in Economics, Oxford and Cambridge Schs Examination Bd, 1979–91; Reviser in Economics, JMB, 1981–91; Chm. Examrs, Oxford and Cambridge and RSA Examinations, 1996–. FRSA 1988. *Publications:* various articles on economics and teaching economics. *Recreations:* painting, walking, music, cooking, the classics. *Address:* The Hall, Repton, Derby DE65 6FH. *T:* (01283) 559220.

JONES, Graham Julian; His Honour Judge Graham Jones; a Circuit Judge, since 1985; a Judge of Technology and Construction Court (formerly a Circuit Official Referee), since 1993; Resident and Designated Judge, Cardiff County Court, since 1994; a Designated Civil Judge, Cardiff, since 1998; *b* 17 July 1936; *s* of late David John Jones, CBE, and of Edna Lillie Jones; *m* 1961, Dorothy, *o d* of late James Smith and Doris Irene Tickle, Abergavenny; two *s* one *d*. *Educ:* Porth County Grammar Sch. (state scholarship); St John's Coll., Cambridge. MA, LLM (Cantab). Admitted Solicitor, 1961; Partner,

Morgan Bruce and Nicholas, 1961 (represented Parents and Residents Assoc., Aberfan Disaster, 1966). Dep. Circuit Judge, 1975–78; a Recorder, 1978–85. Pres., Pontypridd Rhondda and Dist Law Soc., 1973–75; Member Council: Cardiff Law Soc., 1975–78, 1984–85; Associated Law Socs of Wales, 1974–85 (Pres., 1982–84); Member: Lord Chancellor's Legal Aid Adv. Cttee, 1980–85; Adv. Bd, Centre for Professional Legal Studies, Cardiff Law Sch., 1995–. Mem. Court, UWCC, 1995–. *Recreations:* golf, boats. *Address:* c/o Civil Justice Centre, 2 Park Street, Cardiff. *Clubs:* Cardiff and County (Cardiff), Radyr Golf, Royal Porthcawl Golf.

JONES, (Graham) Wyn, QPM 1987; Assistant Commissioner of Police of the Metropolis, 1989–93; *b* Ystradgynlais, Brecon, 12 Oct. 1943; *s* of Thomas James and Mary Elizabeth (*née* Almrott); *m* 1970, Joan Goodbrook. *Educ:* Thornbury Grammar Sch.; Univ. of Exeter (LLB). Joined Glos Police, 1963; Chief Inspector, Glos, 1971; Supt, 1976; Chief Supt, Oxford, 1979; Asst Chief Constable (Ops), Thames Valley Police, 1982; Dep. Asst Comr (CID), New Scotland Yard, 1984; Dep. Asst Comr, 2 Area (East), Metropolitan Police, 1985. Comd Police Ops, Greenham Common, 1983–84, Wapping, 1985–86. Vis. Lectr on policing and public disorder to Police Foundn, USA, and to Germany. *Publications:* articles and contribs to jls on public disorder, forensic investigation, police and media. *Recreations:* ballet, opera, tennis, golf, horse riding.

JONES, Griffith R.; *see* Rhys Jones.

JONES, Gwilym Haydn; *b* 19 Jan. 1947; *s* of Evan Haydn Jones and Mary Elizabeth Gwenhwyfar Jones (*née* Moseley); *m* 1974, Linda Margaret (*née* John); one *s* one *d.* Dir, Bowring Wales Ltd, 1980–93. Councillor, Cardiff CC, 1969–72 and 1973–83. MP (C) Cardiff North, 1983–97; contested (C) same seat, 1997. PPS to Minister of State, Dept of Transport, 1991–92; Parly Under-Sec. of State, Welsh Office, 1992–97. Secretary: Welsh Cons. Members Gp, 1984–93; All Party Gp for Fund for Replacement of Animals in Medical Experiments, 1987–92. Founder Chm., Friendship Force in Wales, 1978–81; Vice Pres., Kidney Res. Unit for Wales Foundn, 1986–93. Rowed for Wales in Speaker's Regatta, 1986. Liveryman, Welsh Livery Guild, 1993–. *Recreations:* golf, model railways, watching Wales win at Rugby. *Clubs:* County Conservative, Cardiff and County, Rhiwbina Rugby, United Services Mess (Cardiff); Tongwynlais Football; Whitchurch Bowls, Whitchurch Golf.

JONES, Gwyn; *see* Jones, Miah G.

JONES, Gwyn Idris M.; *see* Meirion-Jones.

JONES, Gwyn Owain, CBE 1978; MA, DSc Oxon; PhD Sheffield; Director, National Museum of Wales, 1968–77; *b* 29 March 1917; *s* of Dr Abel John Jones, OBE, HMI, and Rhoda May Jones, Cardiff and Porthcawl; *m* 1st, 1944, Sheila Heywood (marr. diss.); two *d*; 2nd, 1973, Elizabeth Blandino. *Educ:* Monmouth Sch.; Port Talbot Secondary Sch.; Jesus Coll., Oxford (Meyricke Schol.). Glass Delegacy Research Fellow of University of Sheffield, later mem. of academic staff, 1939–41; Mem. UK Government's Atomic Energy project, 1942–46; Nuffield Foundation Research Fellow at Clarendon Laboratory, Oxford, 1946–49; Reader in Experimental Physics in University of London, at Queen Mary Coll., 1949–53; Prof. of Physics in Univ. of London, and Head of Dept of Physics at Queen Mary Coll., 1953–68; Hon. Fellow of Queen Mary and Westfield (formerly Queen Mary) Coll. Visiting Prof. Univ. of Sussex, 1964. Member. Court and Council, UWIST, 1968–74; Court, University Coll., Swansea, 1981–84; Hon. Professorial Fellow, University Coll., Cardiff, 1969–79. Yr Academi Gymreig (English Language Section) 1971 (Chm., 1978–81); Gorsedd y Beirdd (Aelod er Anrhydedd) 1974. Governor, Commonwealth Institute, 1974–77. FMA 1976. *Publications:* Glass, 1956; (in collab.) Atoms and the Universe, 1956; papers on solid-state, glass, low-temperature physics; *novels:* The Catalyst, 1960; Personal File, 1962; Now, 1965; A Close Family, 1998; *story sequence:* The Conjuring Show, 1981. *Address:* 12 Squitchey Lane, Summertown, Oxford OX2 7LB. *T:* (01865) 510363.

JONES, Dame Gwyneth, DBE 1986 (CBE 1976); a Principal Dramatic Soprano: Royal Opera House, Covent Garden, since 1963; Vienna State Opera, since 1966 (Hon. Member, 1989); Deutsche Oper Berlin, since 1966; Bavarian State Opera, since 1967; *b* 7 Nov. 1936; *d* of late Edward George Jones and late Violet (*née* Webster); *m* Till Haberfeld; one *d. Educ:* Twmpath Sec. Mod. Sch., Pontypool, Mon; Royal College of Music, London; Accademia Chigiana, Siena; Zürich Internat. Opera Studio; Maria Carpi Prof., Geneva. Oratorio and recitals as well as opera. Guest Artiste: La Scala, Milan; Berlin State Opera; Munich State Opera; Bayreuth Festival; Salzburg Festival; Verona; Tokyo; Zürich; Metropolitan Opera, New York; Paris; Geneva; Dallas; San Francisco; Los Angeles; Teatro Colon, Buenos Aires; Edinburgh Festival; Welsh National Opera; Rome; Hamburg; Cologne; Maggio Musicale, Florence; Chicago. Numerous recordings, radio and TV appearances. Pres., Richard Wagner Soc., 1990–. FRCM. Kammersängerin, Austria and Bavaria. Hon. DMus: Wales; Glamorgan. Shakespeare Prize, FVS Hamburg, 1987. Bundesverdienstkreuz (FRG), 1988; Comdr, Ordre des Arts et des Lettres (France), 1992. *Address:* PO Box, 8037 Zürich, Switzerland.

JONES, Gwynoro Glyndwr; Partner, Education Policy Publicity Consulting (education, policy and marketing consultancy), since 1993 (Managing Director, EPPC-Severn Crossing Ltd, since 1999); Lay Inspector of Schools, since 1993; *b* 21 Nov. 1942; *s* of J. E. and late A. L. Jones, Minyrafon, Foelgastell, Cefneithin, Carms; *m* 1967, A. Laura Miles (marr. diss. 1991); two *s* one *d. Educ:* Gwendraeth Grammar Sch.; Cardiff Univ. BSc Econ (Hons) Politics and Economics. Market Research Officer with Ina Needle Bearings Ltd, Llanelli, 1966–67; Economist Section, Wales Gas Bd, 1967–69; Public Relations Officer, Labour Party in Wales, March 1969–June 1970; West Glamorgan County Council: Dir of Res., 1974–77; Assistant Education Officer: Develt Forward Planning, 1977–88; Capital and Property, 1988–93. Dir, West Wales Business Services Ltd, 1998–; Advr, Investors in People, 1998–; External Assessor, Performance Mgt of Headteachers, 2000–. Vice-Pres., Dist Council Assoc., 1974; Mem., Council of European Municipalities, 1975–77; first Chm., Welsh Council of European Movt, 1995–97. Broadcaster and television interviewer, S4C. MP (Lab) Carmarthen, 1970–Sept. 1974; Member: House of Commons Expenditure Cttee, 1972–74; Council of Europe and WEU, 1974; PPS to Home Sec., 1974. Pres., Nat. Eisteddfod of Wales, 1974. Co-ordinator, Wales in Europe campaign, 1975; Sponsor, Wales Lab and TU Cttee for Europe, 1975; joined SDP, May 1981; contested: (SDP) Gower, Sept. 1982; (SDP/Alliance) Carmarthen, 1987; (Lib Dem) Hereford, 1992. Chairman: SDP Council for Wales, 1982–85, 1987–88; Alliance Cttee for Wales, 1983–88; Interim Chm., Welsh Soc & Lib Dem Exec., 1988; Member: Council for Social Democracy, 1982–88; SDP Nat. Cttee, 1982–85; SDP Orgn Cttee, 1987–88; Lib Dem Federal Exec., 1988–90; Vice Chm., Lib Dem Policy Cttee, 1988–89. *Publications:* booklets: The Record Put Straight, 1973; SDP and the Alliance in Wales 1981–1986, 1986; SLD Golden Opportunities, 1988; A Movement in Crisis, 1989. *Recreations:* sport (played Rugby for both 1st and 2nd class teams). *Address:* Flat 2, 8 Richmond Villas, Swansea SA1 6DQ. *T:* (01792) 458828; *e-mail:* gwynoro@baynet.co.uk.

JONES, Sir Harry (George), Kt 2000; CBE 1995; Member (Lab) and Leader, Newport County Borough Council, since 1995; *b* 29 April 1927; *s* of Edward and Alice Jones; *m* 1956, Hazel Kembrey; three *s. Educ:* St Woolos Sch.; Newport Tech. Coll. Officer, Merchant Navy, 1948. Apprentice engr, 1943; worked in aluminium ind., 1970s. Member (Lab), Newport DC, 1973–96 (Leader of Council, 1987–96; Mayor, 1990–91). Leader, Welsh LGA, 1986–; Vice-Chm., LGA, 1995–; Chm., Local Govt Mgt Bd, 1994. Mem., Welsh NEC, and Nat. Policy Cttee, Labour Party. Hon. Mem. Council, NSPCC, 1993–; Patron, Prince's Trust, 1995–. Hon. Mem., RSA. Hon. Fellow, UCW, Newport, 1999. *Recreations:* swimming, art, gardening. *Address:* 8 Beaufort Place, Newport, S Wales NP19 7NB. *T:* (01633) 769538; (office) (01633) 232121.

JONES, Rt Rev. Haydn Harold; Bishop of Venezuela, 1976–86; actor in films, television soap operas and commercials, since 1986; *b* 22 Aug. 1920; *s* of Charles Samuel and Blodwen Jones (*née* Williams), Penarth, Glam. *Educ:* Ordination training, Brotherhood of Saint Paul, Barton, Yorks. RAF, 1941–44. Deacon 1947, priest 1948, Diocese of Bradford. Curate of St Barnabas, Heaton, Bradford, 1947–49; Tor Mohun, Torquay, 1949–51; Chaplain RN, 1951–53; Licence to Officiate, Diocese of London, 1954–62, Diocese of Coventry, 1962–63; Curate of St Peter's, Coventry, 1963–64; Rector of Clutton, Diocese of Bath and Wells, 1964–76, with Cameley, 1975–76; Surrogate, 1972–76; Dean of St Mary's Cathedral, Caracas, 1976–85. *Recreations:* formerly tennis (rep. RN 1952), bridge, films, theatre. *Address:* College of St Barnabas, Blackberry Lane, Lingfield, Surrey RH7 6NJ. *T:* (01342) 871673.

JONES, Helen Mary; MP (Lab) Warrington North, since 1997; *b* 24 Dec. 1954; *d* of late Robert Edward Jones and of Mary Scanlan; *m* 1988, Michael Vobe; one *s. Educ:* Ursuline Convent, Chester; UCL; Chester Coll.; Univ. of Liverpool; Manchester Metropolitan Univ. BA, PGCE, MEd, CPE, LSF. Teacher of English; Develt Officer, Mind; Justice and Peace Officer, Liverpool; Solicitor. Contested (Lab): Shropshire N, 1983; Lancashire Central, EP elecn, 1984; Ellesmere Port and Neston, 1987. *Address:* House of Commons, SW1A 0AA.

JONES, Helen Mary; Member (Plaid Cymru) Llanelli, National Assembly for Wales, since 1999; *b* 29 June 1960; *d* of John Mertyn Jones and late Daphne Stuart; one *d. Educ:* Colchester County High Sch. for Girls, Essex; Llanfair Caereinion High Sch.; UCW Aberystwyth (BA Hist.). Special Educn Teacher, Gwent, 1982–87; Orgnr for Wales, ActionAid, 1987–91; various positions in youth, community and social work, 1991–96; Sen. Develt Manager (Dep. Dir), EOC, Wales, 1996–99. Former Mem., Nat. Assembly Adv. Gp. Contested (Plaid Cymru): Islwyn, 1992; Montgomery, 1997. *Address:* National Assembly for Wales, Cardiff Bay, Cardiff CF99 1NA.

JONES, Henry Arthur, CBE 1974; MA; Professor Emeritus, University of Leicester, since 1981 (Vaughan Professor of Education, 1967–81; Head of the Department of Adult Education, 1967–78; Pro-Vice-Chancellor, 1978–81); *b* 7 March 1917; *er s* of Henry Lloyd Jones; *m* 1st, 1942, Molly (*d* 1971), 4th *d* of Richard Shenton; two *s*; 2nd, 1972, Nancy Winifred (*née* Cox), *widow* of Lt R. B. B. Jack, RN. *Educ:* Chorlton Grammar Sch.; Manchester Univ. George Gissing Prizeman, Manchester Univ., 1936; Graduate Research Fellow, Manchester Univ., 1937, MA 1938. Served War of 1939–45 with Lancs Fusiliers and DLI, 1940–42. Sen. English Master, Chorlton Grammar Sch., 1942–47; Resident Staff Tutor, Manchester Univ., 1947–49; Asst Dir of Extra-Mural Studies, Liverpool Univ., 1949–52, Dep. Dir 1953–57; Principal, The City Literary Institute, 1957–67. Chairman: Assoc. for Adult Education, 1964–67; Adult Educn Cttee, IBA, 1973–77; Vice-Pres., Nat. Inst. of Adult Education (Exec. Chm., 1976–84); Hon. Life Mem., Educnl Centres Assoc.; Vice-Pres., Pre-retirement Assoc.; Member: Library Adv. Council, DES, 1965–68; Sec. of State's Cttee on Adult Educn, DES, 1968–72; Adv. Council for Adult and Continuing Educn, DES, 1977–83. Chm., Leics Consultative Cttee for Voluntary Orgns, 1974–77. Editor: Vaughan Papers in Educn, 1967–82; Studies in Adult Education, 1974–82. *Publications:* Adult Literacy: a study of the impact, 1978; The Concept of Success in Adult Literacy, 1978; Adult Literacy: the UK experience, 1978; Education and Disadvantage, 1978; Stage by Stage, 1993; Great Bowden: a village and its people, 1999. *Address:* Stokes House, Great Bowden, Market Harborough, Leics LE16 7HF. *T:* (01858) 462846.

JONES, (Henry) John (Franklin); writer; *b* 6 May 1924; *s* of late Lt-Col James Walker Jones, DSO, IMS, and Doris Marjorie (*née* Franklin); *m* 1949, Jean Verity Robinson; one *s* one *d. Educ:* Blundell's Sch.; Colombo Public Library; Merton Coll., Oxford. Served War, Royal Navy: Ordinary Seaman, 1943; Intell. Staff, Eastern Fleet, 1944. Merton Coll., Oxford: Harmsworth Sen. Scholar, 1948; Fellow and Tutor in Jurisprudence, 1949; Univ. Sen. Lectr, 1956; Fellow and Tutor in Eng. Lit., 1962; Prof. of Poetry, Univ. of Oxford, 1979–84. Dill Meml Lectr, QUB, 1983. Football Correspondent, The Observer, 1956–59. TV appearances include The Modern World, 1988. *Publications:* The Egotistical Sublime, 1954, 5th edn 1978; (contrib.) The British Imagination, 1961; On Aristotle and Greek Tragedy, 1962, 5th edn 1980; (contrib.) Dickens and the Twentieth Century, 1962; (ed) H. W. Garrod, The Study of Good Letters, 1963; John Keats's Dream of Truth, 1969, 2nd edn 1980; (contrib.) The Morality of Art, 1969; The Same God, 1971; Dostoevsky, 1983, 2nd edn 1985; Shakespeare at Work, 1995, 2nd edn 1999. *Address:* Garden Flat, 41 Buckland Crescent, NW3 5DJ. *T:* (020) 7586 1808; Yellands, Brisworthy, Shaugh Prior, Plympton, Devon PL7 5EL. *T:* (01752) 839310.

JONES, Sir Hugh; *see* Hugh-Jones, Sir W. N.

JONES, Hugh Duncan Hitchings; His Honour Judge Hugh Jones; a Circuit Judge, since 1991; *b* 25 May 1937; *s* of Norman Everard Jones and Ann Jones (*née* Hitchings); *m* 1966, Helen Margaret Payne; three *d. Educ:* Mountain Ash Grammar School (State Scholarship); University College London (LLB). Admitted Solicitor, 1961; Registrar, Cardiff County Court and Dist Registrar of the High Court, Cardiff Dist Registry, 1978; a Recorder, 1988–91. Mem., County Court Rules Cttee, 1994–97. *Recreations:* cricket, gardening, golf, holidays in France. *Address:* c/o Pontypridd County Court, Courthouse Street, Pontypridd, Mid Glam CF37 1JR. *Club:* Mountain Ash Golf.

JONES, Hugh (Hugo) Jarrett H.; *see* Herbert-Jones.

JONES, Ven. Hughie; *see* Jones, Ven. T. H.

JONES, Huw; *see* Jones, D. H.

JONES, Hywel Ceri, CMG 1999; Chairman of Executive Board, The European Policy Centre, Brussels, since 1999; *b* 22 April 1937; *m* 1967, Morwenna Armstrong; one *s* one *d. Educ:* UCW, Aberystwyth (BA French and Classics, DipEd; Hon. Fellow, 1990). Admin. appts, Sussex Univ., 1962–73; joined EC, 1973; Head, Dept for Educn and Youth Policies, 1973–79; Dir for Educn, Vocational Trng and Youth Policy, 1979–88; Dir, Task Force for Human Resources, Educn, Trng and Youth, 1989–93; Acting Dir-Gen., 1993–95, Dep. Dir-Gen., 1995–98, Employment, Social Policy and Indust. Relns. Vis. Fellow in Educn and Contemp. European Studies, Sussex Univ., 1973–80. DUniv: Sussex, 1991; Leuven, 1992; Open, 2000; Hon. LLD NCEA, Ireland, 1992. Gold Medal, Republic of Italy, 1987. *Recreations:* Rugby, cricket, snooker, theatre, travel. *Address:* 64

Vicarage Court, Vicarage Gate, W8 4HG; The European Policy Centre, Boulevard Charlemagne 42, 1000 Brussels, Belgium. *Club:* Reform.

JONES, Hywel Francis; Commissioner for Local Administration in Wales, 1985–91; *b* 28 Dec. 1928; *s* of late Brynmor and Beatrice Jones, Morriston, Swansea; *m* 1959, Marian Rosser Craven; one *d. Educ:* Bishop Gore Grammar School, Swansea; St John's College, Cambridge (BA 1949, MA 1953). IPFA 1953. Borough Treasurer's Dept, Swansea, 1949–56; Nat. Service, RAPC, 1953–55; Dep. County Treasurer, Breconshire, 1956–59; Asst County Treasurer, Carmarthenshire, 1959–66; Borough Treasurer, Port Talbot, 1966–75; Sec., Commn for Local Administration in Wales, 1975–85. Mem., Public Works Loan Board, 1971–75; Financial Adviser, AMC, 1972–74. Mem., Lord Chancellor's Adv. Cttee for West Glamorgan, 1990–97. Treasurer, Royal National Eisteddfod of Wales, 1975–95; Mem., Gorsedd of Bards, 1977 (Treasurer, 1992–). *Recreations:* music, reading, gardening. *Address:* Godre'r Rhiw, 1 Lon Heulog, Baglan, Port Talbot, West Glam SA12 8SY. *T:* (01639) 813822.

JONES, Rt Rev. Hywel James; Bishop of British Columbia, 1980–84; *b* 4 March 1918; *s* of Ifor James and Ann Jones; *m* 1946, Dorothy Margaret Wilcox; one *s* one *d. Educ:* Emmanuel Coll., Univ. of Saskatchewan (LTh). Deacon, then priest, 1942; Curate, Tofield, 1942; travelling priest, 1942–44; Incumbent of Parksville–Qualicum Beach, 1944–47; Colwood–Langford, 1947–56; Rector, St Mary the Virgin, Oak Bay, 1956–80. Hon. Canon of BC, 1959–68; Archdeacon of Quatsino, 1968–71, of Victoria, 1971–77; Archdeacon Emeritus, 1977–80. DD (*hc*) Emmanuel Coll., Univ. of Saskatchewan, 1980. *Recreations:* reading, music, gardening. *Address:* 2028 Frederick Norris Road, Victoria, BC V8P 2B2, Canada. *T:* (250) 5927658. *Club:* Union (Victoria, BC).

JONES, Ian Michael; Director, Regional Group, British Trade International, since 2000; *b* 5 Sept. 1949; *s* of Derek and Jean Jones; *m* 1976, Vivien Hepworth; two *s. Educ:* St Bartholomew's Grammar Sch., Newbury; Fitzwilliam Coll., Cambridge (BA Econs and Politics 1972). Home Office, 1972–83; DTI, 1983–85, Grade 5, 1985; Dept of Employment, 1985–89; Sec., BOTB, 1989–90; Department of Trade and Industry, 1989–2000: Regl Dir, SE Reg., 1990–94; Leader, London City Action Team, 1992–94; Grade 3, 1994; Head, Textiles and Retail Div., 1994–96; Head, Posts, Retail and Textiles Directorate, 1996; Chief Exec., Employment Tribunals Service, 1997–2000. FRSA. *Recreation:* cricket. *Address:* British Trade International, Kingsgate House, 66–74 Victoria Street, SW1E 6SW. *T:* (020) 7215 4933.

JONES, Rt Rev. Idris; *see* Glasgow and Galloway, Bishop of.

JONES, Ieuan Wyn; Member (Plaid Cymru) Ynys Môn, National Assembly for Wales, since 1999; President, Plaid Cymru, since 2000; *b* 22 May 1949; *s* of late John Jones and of Mair Elizabeth Jones; *m* 1974, Eirian Llwyd; two *s* one *d. Educ:* Pontardawe Grammar School; Ysgol-y-Berwyn, Y Bala, Gwynedd; Liverpool Polytechnic. LLB Hons. Qualified Solicitor, 1973; Partner in practice, 1974–87. Plaid Cymru National Vice-Chm., 1975–79, National Chm., 1980–82, 1990–92. MP (Plaid Cymru) Ynys Môn, 1987–2001. Mem. Select Committee: on Welsh Affairs, 1990–92, 1997–2001; on Agriculture, 1992–97. Contested (Plaid Cymru) Ynys Môn (Anglesey), 1983. *Publications:* Europe: the challenge for Wales, 1996; Thomas Gee (biog.), 1998. *Recreations:* sport, local history. *Address:* Ty Elwyn Roberts, 45 Bridge Street, Llangefni, Ynys Môn, Gwynedd LL77 7RZ. *T:* (01248) 723599.

JONES, Ilston Percival Ll.; *see* Llewellyn-Jones.

JONES, Jack L.; *see* Jones, James Larkin.

JONES, Jacqui; *see* Lait, J.

JONES, Prof. James Eirug Thomas, FRCPath; Courtauld Professor of Animal Health, Royal Veterinary College, University of London, 1984–93, now Emeritus Professor; *b* 14 June 1927; *s* of David John and Mary Elizabeth Jones; *m* 1953, Marion Roberts; one *s* one *d. Educ:* Ystalyfera County Sch.; Royal Vet. Coll. MRCVS 1950, FRCVS 1994; PhD 1973. Gen. vet. practice, 1950–53; vet. officer, Birmingham Corp., 1953–54; Lectr in Path., RVC, 1954–58; Res. Officer, Animal Health Trust, 1958–63; Fulbright Scholar, Univ. of Pennsylvania, 1963–64; vis. worker, 1964, Sen. Lectr, 1967, Reader in Animal Health, 1975–84, RVC. J. T. Edwards Meml Medal, RCVS, 1985; Bledisloe Vet. Award, RASE, 1994. *Publications:* numerous papers in sci. jls on infectious diseases of farm animals. *Recreations:* travel, Celtic history. *Address:* 283 Bury Street West, N9 9JN. *T:* (020) 8360 2146.

JONES, James Larkin, (Jack), CH 1978; MBE 1950; FCIT 1970; General Secretary, Transport and General Workers' Union, 1969–78; Member, TUC General Council, 1968–78; Chairman, TUC International, Transport and Nationalised Industries Committees, 1972–78; Deputy Chairman, National Ports Council, 1967–79; *b* 29 March 1913; *m* 1938, Evelyn Mary Taylor; two *s. Educ:* elementary sch., Liverpool. Worked in engineering and docks industries, 1927–39. Liverpool City Councillor, 1936–39; served in Spanish Civil War; wounded Ebro battle, Aug. 1938; Coventry District Sec., Transport and General Workers' Union, also District Sec., Confedn of Shipbuilding and Engineering Unions, 1939–55; Midlands Regional Sec., Transport and General Workers' Union, 1955–63, Executive Officer, 1963–69. Mem., Midland Regional Bd for Industry, 1942–46, 1954–63; Chm., Midlands TUC Advisory Cttee, 1948–63. Coventry City Magistrate, 1950–63; Executive Chm., Birmingham Productivity Cttee, 1957–63; Member: Labour Party Nat. Exec. Cttee, 1964–67; Nat. Cttee for Commonwealth Immigrants, 1965–69; NEDC, 1969–78; Council, Advisory, Conciliation and Arbitration Service, 1974–78; British Overseas Trade Board, 1974–79; Cttee of Inquiry into Industrial Democracy, 1976–77 (Chm., Labour Party Wkg Party on Industrial Democracy, 1967); Bd, Crown Agents, 1978–80; Royal Commn on Criminal Procedure, 1978–80; Jt Chm. (with Lord Aldington), Special Cttee on the Ports, 1972. Pres., EFTA Trade Union Council, 1972–73; Founder Mem., European TUC, 1973. Vice-President: ITF, 1974–79; Anti-Apartheid Movement, 1976–; Age Concern, England, 1978–; European Fed of Retired and Elderly Persons, 1991–; Pres., Retired Members Assocs, 1979–; Chm., Nat Pensioners' Convention, 1992–. Chm., Trustees, Nat. Museum of Labour History, 1988–. Vis. Fellow, Nuffield Coll., Oxford, 1970–78; Associate Fellow, LSE, 1978–82. Dimbleby Lecture, BBC, 1977. Hon. Fellow: Liverpool Poly. (later Liverpool John Moores Univ.), 1988; Central Lancs Univ., 1993. Hon. DLitt: Warwick, 1978; Coventry, 1996; DUniv Open, 2000. Freeman, City of London, 1979. Award of Merit, City of Coventry, 1978. *Publications:* (contrib.) The Incompatibles, 1967; (contrib.) Industry's Democratic Revolution, 1974; (with Max Morris) A–Z of Trade Unionism and Industrial Relations, 1982; Union Man (autobiog.), 1986. *Recreation:* walking. *Address:* 74 Ruskin Park House, Champion Hill, SE5 8TH. *T:* (020) 7274 7067.

JONES, (James) Roger; Head of Antiques Department, Colefax and Fowler, since 1994; *b* 30 May 1952; *s* of late Albert James Jones and Hilda Vera Jones (*née* Evans). *Educ:* Shrewsbury; St Catharine's Coll., Cambridge (Sen. Schol.; MA). Called to the Bar, Middle Temple, 1974 (Lloyd Jacob Meml Exhibnr; Astbury Schol.); practised Oxford and Midland Circuit, 1975–83. Joined Office of Parly Counsel, 1983; with Law Commn, 1988–91; Dep. Parly Counsel, 1991–94. *Recreation:* walking the dog. *Address:* Sibyl Colefax and John Fowler, 39 Brook Street, W1K 4JE.

JONES, Rt Rev. James Stuart; *see* Liverpool, Bishop of.

JONES, Hon. Jeffrey Richard, CBE 1978; MA; Chief Justice and President of the Court of Appeal, 1980–85, Kiribati; Member, Appeal Court, Solomon Islands, 1982 and Vanuatu, 1983; *b* 18 Nov. 1921; *s* of Rev. Thomas Jones and Winifred (*née* Williams); *m* 1955, Anna Rosaleen Carberry (*d* 2001); one *s* one *d. Educ:* Grove Park Sch., Wrexham; Denstone Coll., Staffs; Keble Coll., Oxford, 1940, 1946–49 (MA PPE); Council of Legal Educn, 1950–52. Served RAFVR, Flt Lieut (Pilot), 1940–46. Schoolmaster, Mountgrace Comprehensive, Potters Bar, 1953–55. Called to the Bar, Middle Temple, 1954; private practice, Zaria, Nigeria, 1955–57; Magistrate, 1957, High Court Judge, 1965, Sen. Puisne Judge, 1970, Northern Nigeria; Chief Justice, Kano State, N Nigeria, 1975, Chief Judge (change of title, decree 41 of 1976), 1976–80. President, Rotary Club, Kano, 1977. Editor, Northern Nigeria Law Reports, 1966–74. *Publications:* Some Cases on Criminal Procedure and Evidence in Northern Nigeria 1968, 1968; Some Cases on Criminal Procedure and Evidence in Northern Nigeria 1969, 1969, 2nd edn combining 1968–69, 1970; Criminal Procedure in the Northern States of Nigeria (annotated), 1975, repr. 1978, 2nd edn 1979. *Recreations:* painting, gardening, bridge, golf. *Address:* Bradley Cottage, Bradley Lane, Holt, near Trowbridge, Wilts BA14 6QE. *T:* (01225) 782004.

JONES, Jennifer, (Mrs Norton Simon); film actress (US); *b* Tulsa, Okla, 2 March 1919; *née* Phylis Isley; *d* of Philip R. Isley and Flora Mae (*née* Suber); *m* 1st, 1939, Robert Walker (marr. diss. 1945); two *s*; 2nd, 1949, David O. Selznick (*d* 1965); (one *d* decd); 3rd, 1971, Norton Simon (*d* 1993). *Educ:* schools in Okla and Tex; Northwestern Univ., Evanston, Illinois; American Academy of Dramatic Arts, New York City. Films include: Dick Tracy's G-Men, 1939; The New Frontier, 1939; The Song of Bernadette, 1943; Since You Went Away, 1944; Love Letters, 1945; The American Creed, 1946; Cluny Brown, 1946; Duel in the Sun, 1946; Portrait of Jenny, 1948; Madame Bovary, 1949; We Were Strangers, 1949; The Wild Heart, 1950; Ruby Gentry, 1952; Carrie, 1952; Indiscretion of an American Wife, 1953; Beat the Devil, 1954; Good Morning, Miss Dove, 1955; Love is a Many-Splendoured Thing, 1955; The Man in the Gray Flannel Suit, 1956; The Barretts of Wimpole Street, 1957; A Farewell to Arms, 1957; Tender is the Night, 1962; The Idol, 1966; Angel, Down We Go, 1969; The Towering Inferno, 1974. Awards include: American Academy of Motion Pictures, Arts and Sciences Award, 1943 (for Song of Bernadette); 4 other Academy nominations, etc. Pres., Norton Simon Mus., Pasadena, 1989–. Medal for Korean War Work.

JONES, Jennifer, (Jenny); Member (Green), London Assembly, Greater London Authority, since 2000; *b* 23 Dec. 1949; *d* of Percy and Christine Jones; *m* (marr. diss.); two *d. Educ:* Inst. of Archaeol., Univ. of London (BSc Envmtl Archaeol.). Archaeologist, 1990–99; Financial Controller, Metro Inspection Services, 1999–2000. *Recreations:* running, cinema, family and friends. *Address:* Greater London Authority, Romney House, 43 Marsham Street, SW1P 3PY. *T:* (020) 7983 4000.

JONES, Jennifer Grace; *b* 8 Feb. 1948; *d* of Ernest Bew and Ivy Blake; *m* 1974, John Alun Charles Jones; one *s. Educ:* Bradford Univ. (BA Hons, CQSW 1972); Birmingham Univ. (MSocSc 1987); Wolverhampton Univ. (ITD). Legal Sec., ICI, 1968–69; Social Worker, Oxford CC, 1972–74; Housing Advr, Oxford Housing Aid Centre and Birmingham Housing Dept, 1974–77; Trng Officer, Birmingham Housing Co-op, 1980–85; Researcher, Wolverhampton Council, 1985–87; Business Advr, Black Country CDA, 1987–97. Trng Manager and Co. Dir, 1995–97. Mem. (Lab) Wolverhampton BC, 1991–97. MP (Lab) Wolverhampton SW, 1997–2001. *Recreations:* swimming, gardening, keeping cats, writing. *Address:* 56 Goldthorn Road, Wolverhampton WV2 4PN.

JONES, John; *see* Jones, H. J. F.

JONES, (John) Clement, CBE 1972; FRSA 1970; writer, broadcaster, technical adviser to developing countries; *b* 22 June 1915; *o s* of Clement Daniel Jones; *m* 1939, Marjorie (*d* 1991), *d* of George Gibson, Llandrindod Wells; three *s. Educ:* Ardwyn, Aberystwyth; BA (Hons) Open Univ., 1983. Various journalistic positions; News Editor, Express and Star, Wolverhampton, 1955; Editor, 1960–71; Editorial Director, 1971–74; Exec. Dir, Beacon Broadcasting, Wolverhampton, 1974–83. Pres., Guild of British Newspaper Editors, 1966–67, Hon. Life Vice-Pres., 1972 (Hon. Fellow, 1997). Member: Press Council, 1965–74; Adv. Bd, Thomson Foundn, 1965–87; BBC W Midlands Adv. Council, 1971–75; (part-time) Monopolies and Mergers Commn (Newspaper Panel), 1973–86; W Midlands Arts Assoc., 1973–78; Exec. Cttee, Soc. Internat. Devel, 1974–78; Vice Chm., Lichfield Dio. Media Council, 1976–82; Mem. Council, and Chm. Press Freedom Cttee, Commonwealth Press Union, 1975–80; Chm., Media Panel, Commn for Racial Equality, 1981–84; Vice-Chm., British Human Rights Trust, 1975–78; Governor, British Inst. Human Rights, 1971–82. Mem. Senate, Open Univ., 1983–86. Founder Mem., Circle of Wine Writers, 1966. Pres., Staffordshire Soc., 1971–74. Founder and Pres., Frinton and Walton Heritage Trust, 1984–. *Publications:* UNESCO World Survey of Media Councils and Codes of Ethics, 1976; Racism and Fascism, 1981; Race and the Media: thirty years on, 1982; A History of the First Fifty Years of the Guild of Editors, 1995; pamphlets on local history, NE Anglia. *Recreations:* travel, gardening. *Address:* Sandy Cross, Ridgeway Road, Dorking, Surrey RH4 3AY. *T:* (01306) 877691; *e-mail:* clemjon@lineone.net. *Club:* Athenæum.

See also G. Q. Jones.

JONES, John Elfed, CBE 1987; DL; CEng, FIEE; Chairman, International Greetings plc, since 1996; *b* 19 March 1933; *s* of Urien Maelgwyn Jones and Mary Jones; *m* 1957, Mary Sheila (*née* Rosser); two *d. Educ:* Blaenau Ffestiniog Grammar Sch.; Denbighshire Technical Coll., Wrexham; Heriot Watts Coll., Edinburgh. Student apprentice, 1949–53, graduate trainee, 1953–55, CEGB; National Service, RAF, 1955–57 (FO); Rock Climbing Instr, Outward Bound Sch., Aberdyfi, 1957; Technical Engr with CEGB, 1957–59; Dep. Project Manager, Rheidol Hydro-Electric Project, 1959–61; Sen. Elec. Engr, Trawsfynydd Nuclear Power Station, 1961–63; Deputy Manager: Mid Wales Gp of Power Stations, 1963–67; Connah's Quay Power Station, 1967–69; Anglesey Aluminium Metal Ltd: Engrg Manager, 1969–73; Production Manager, 1973–76; Admin Director, 1976–77; Dep. Man. Dir, 1977–79; Industrial Dir, Welsh Office (Under Sec. rank), 1979–82. Chairman: Welsh Water Authy, later Welsh Water plc, 1982–93; British Water International Ltd, 1983–88. Dep. Chm., HTV Gp, 1991–96; Director: HTV Cymru/Wales Ltd, 1990–96 (Chm., 1992–96); W Midlands and Wales Regl Adv. Bd, National Westminster Bank, 1990–91; BMSS plc, 1993–96; Cwmni Rheilffordd Beddgelert Cyf., 1994–98; Cwmni Rheilffordd Caernarfon Cyf., 1994–. Chm. Adv. Gp, Nat. Assembly of Wales, 1997–99. Treasurer, Urdd Gobaith Cymru, 1964–67; Chm., Welsh Language Bd, 1988–93; Mem., Royal National Eisteddfod of Wales, 1981–90; Member: BBC Broadcasting Council for Wales, 1979–83; Council, Food from Britain, 1985–87; Prince of Wales Cttee, 1986–90. Pres., Univ. of Wales, Lampeter, 1992–98; Member: Court and Council: UCNW, Bangor, 1978–; Nat. Lib. of Wales, 1983–88; Coleg Harlech, 1983–88;

Court, Univ. Coll., Aberystwyth, 1984–. Mem., Civic Trust for Wales, 1982–88; Pres., CPRW, 1995–2001. FRSA 1984; CIMgt (CBIM 1990). DL Mid Glam, 1989. Hon. Fellow: Univ. of Wales, Aberystwyth, 1990; NE Wales Inst., 1996. Hon. Dr Glamorgan, 1997; Hon. LLD Wales, 2000. Hon. Col, Commonwealth of Kentucky, 1976. *Recreations:* fishing for salmon and trout, reading, attending Eisteddfodau. *Address:* Ty Mawr, Coity, Bridgend, Mid Glamorgan CF35 6BN.

JONES, John Ernest P.; *see* Powell-Jones.

JONES, John Francis A.; *see* Avery Jones.

JONES, Prof. (John) Gareth, MD; FRCP; FRCA; Professor of Anaesthesia, Cambridge University, 1990–99; *b* 20 Aug. 1936; *s* of late Dr John and Catherine Jones; *m* 1964, Susan Price; three *d*. *Educ:* Canton High Sch., Cardiff; Welsh Nat. Sch. of Medicine, Univ. of Wales (MB BCh 1960); MD Birmingham, 1967. MRCP 1963, FRCP 1983; FRCA (FFARCS 1970). Res. Fellow, Dept of Medicine, 1964–68, Lectr, Anaesthesia, 1968–70, Univ. of Birmingham; North Sen. Fellow, Cardiovascular Res. Inst., Univ. of California, San Francisco, 1970–74; Scientific Staff, MRC, Northwick Park, 1974–86; Prof. of Anaesthesia, Univ. of Leeds, 1986–91. Vis. Scientist, Chest Service, Univ. of California, San Francisco, 1977–78; Consultant, Baragwanath Hosp., Soweto, 1986. Royal College of Anaesthetists: Mem. Council, 1996–99; Ed., Newsletter, 1997–99. Ed., Cardiff Med. Grads Jl, 1999–. Hon. FANZCA 1992. *Publications:* Effects of Anaesthesia and Surgery on Pulmonary Mechanisms, 1984; (jtly) Aspects of Recovery from Anaesthesia, 1987; Depth of Anaesthesia, 1989, 2nd edn 1993; (jtly) The Upper Airway, 1995; res. papers on peri-operative Hypoxaemia, and the effect of gen. anaesthetics on cognitive function and the electroencephalogram. *Recreations:* model engineering, low flying. *Address:* 11 St George's Court, Cavendish Avenue, Cambridge CB1 4UP; Cambridge University Department of Anaesthesia, Addenbrooke's Hospital, Hills Road, Cambridge CB2 2QQ.

JONES, His Honour (John) Geoffrey; a Circuit Judge, 1975–96, a Deputy Circuit Judge, 1996–2001; *b* 14 Sept. 1928; *s* of Wyndham and Lilias Jones; *m* 1954, Sheila (*née* Gregory); three *s*. *Educ:* Brighton and Hove Grammar Sch.; St Michael's Sch., Llanelli; St David's Coll., Lampeter; University Coll., London. LLB London 1955; LLM London 1985. Army service, 1946–48, commnd into RASC, 1947. Electrical wholesale business, 1948–52. Called to Bar, Gray's Inn, 1956; practised Leicester, 1958–70 and London, 1970–75. Pres., Mental Health Review Tribunals, 1985–2000; Chm., Mental Health Rev. Tribunal for Wales, 1996–99. Hon. Sen. Academic Fellow, Leicester Polytechnic, 1989. Hon. LLD De Montfort, 1996. *Recreation:* golf. *Address:* c/o The County Court, Wellington Street, Leicester LE1 6HN.

JONES, Sir John Henry H.; *see* Harvey-Jones.

JONES, John Hubert E.; *see* Emlyn Jones.

JONES, John Knighton C.; *see* Chadwick-Jones.

JONES, John Lloyd, OBE 1995; farmer; Chairman, Countryside Council for Wales, since 2000; *b* 10 Nov. 1949; *s* of Arthur Egryn Jones and Elizabeth Jones (*née* Owen); *m* 1972, Anne Tudor Lewis; three *d*. *Educ:* Tywyn Primary Sch.; Llandovery Coll. Chairman: NFU Wales, 1993–98; NFU Parly Land Use and Envmt Cttee, England and Wales, 1998–2000. Chm., Welsh Adv. Cttee, Forestry Commn, 1994–2000. *Recreations:* woodland creation, gardening. *Address:* Hendy, Tywyn, Gwynedd LL36 9RU. *T:* (01654) 710457.

JONES, Air Vice-Marshal John Maurice, CB 1986; *b* 27 Jan. 1931; *s* of E. Morris Jones and Gladys Jones (*née* Foulkes); *m* 1962, Joan (*née* McCallum); one *s* one *d*. *Educ:* Liverpool Institute High Sch.; Univ. of Liverpool (BDS). LDSRCS, FDSRCS 1987. Hospital appt, Liverpool Dental Hosp., 1954; RAF Dental Branch: appts UK and abroad, incl. Christmas Island, Malta, Cyprus and Fontainebleau, 1955–73; Dep. Dir of RAF Dental Services, 1973; OC RAF Inst. of Dental Health and Training, 1976; Principal Dental Officer: HQ RAF Germany, 1979; HQ RAF Support Command, 1982; Dir, RAF Dental Services, 1982–88, and Dir, Defence Dental Services, MoD, 1985–88; QHDS, 1983–87. Sec., Ski Club of GB, 1988–91. Pres., RAF Squash Rackets Assoc., 1986–88. OBStJ 1978. *Recreations:* golf, fishing, ski-ing. *Address:* Wyckenhurst, St Michael's Close, Halton Village, Wendover, Bucks HP22 5NW. *T:* (01296) 624184. *Club:* Royal Air Force, Kandahar.

JONES, Sir John Prichard; *see* Prichard-Jones.

JONES, Prof. (John) Stephen, PhD; Professor of Genetics, University College London, since 1992; *b* 24 March 1944; *s* of Thomas Gwilym Jones and Lydia Anne Jones; partner, Norma Percy. *Educ:* Wirral Grammar Sch.; Univ. of Edinburgh (BSc, PhD). Postdoctoral Fellow, Univ. of Chicago, 1969–71; Lectr in Genetics, Royal Free Hosp. Med. Sch., 1971–78; Lectr then Reader in Genetics, UCL, 1978–92; Head of Dept of Genetics and Biometry, 1989–94. Reith Lectr, 1991. Faraday Medal, Royal Soc., 1996. *Publications:* (ed) Cambridge Encyclopedia of Human Evolution, 1992; The Language of the Genes, 1993 (Science Book Prize, 1994); In the Blood, 1996; Almost Like a Whale: the Origin of Species updated, 1999; Y: a book about men, 2002; scientific papers in learned jls. *Recreation:* not administrating. *Address:* Galton Laboratory, University College London, Gower Street, WC1E 6BT. *T:* (020) 7679 2000.

JONES, Dr Jonathan Dallas George; Senior Scientist, since 1988, and Hon. Professor, since 1998, Sainsbury Laboratory, John Innes Centre; *b* 14 July 1954; *s* of George Ronald Jones and Isabel Dallas Orr (*née* Pinkney); one *d*; *m* 1991, Dr Caroline Dean; one *s* one *d*. *Educ:* Univ. of Cambridge (BSc Nat. Scis 1976; PhD 1980). Post-doctoral Fellow, Harvard, 1981–82; Res. Scientist, Advanced Genetic Scis Inc., Oakland, Calif, 1983–88. *Publications:* contribs to Cell, Science, Plant Cell, Plant Jl, Genetics, Plant Physiol., etc. *Recreations:* sailing, wind-surfing, children. *Address:* Sainsbury Laboratory, John Innes Centre, Colney Lane, Norwich NR4 7UH. *T:* (01603) 450327.

JONES, Jonathan Owen; MP (Lab and Co-op) Cardiff Central, since 1992; *b* 19 April 1954; *s* of Gwynfor Owen Jones and Dorothy Mary (*née* Davies); *m* 1989, Allison Clement; two *s* one *d*. *Educ:* Univ. of East Anglia (BSc Hons Ecology); Cardiff Univ. (PGCE). Science and biology teacher, 1977–92. An Opposition Whip, 1993–97; a Lord Comr of HM Treasury (Govt Whip), 1997–98; Parly Under-Sec. of State, Welsh Office, 1998–99. *Recreations:* cooking, walking, watching Rugby, my family, caravanning. *Address:* House of Commons, SW1A 0AA. *T:* (office) (029) 2048 5471. *Club:* Roath Labour.

JONES, Julia P.; *see* Peyton-Jones.

JONES, Karen Ida Boalth S.; *see* Spärck Jones.

JONES, Prof. Kathleen; Professor of Social Policy, University of York, 1981–89 (Professor of Social Administration, 1965–81), now Emeritus Professor; *b* 7 April 1922; *d* of William Robert Savage and Kate Lilian Barnard; *m* 1944, Rev. David Gwyn Jones (*d* 1976); one *s*. *Educ:* North London Collegiate Sch.; Westfield Coll., Univ. of London (BA, PhD). Research Asst in Social Administration, Univ. of Manchester, 1951–53, Asst Lectr 1953–55; Sen. History Teacher, Victoria Instn, Kuala Lumpur, 1956–58, also Asst Lectr in History, Univ. of Malaya (part-time); Lectr in Social Administration, Univ. of Manchester, 1958–62, Sen. Lectr 1962–65. Chm., Social Scis Cttee, UK Commn for UNESCO, 1966–69. Mem., Gen. Synod of C of E, 1975–80; Member: Archbishops' Commn on Church and State, 1966–71; Lord Gardiner's Cttee on NI, 1974–75; Archbishops' Commn on Marriage, 1976–78; Mental Health Act Commn, 1983–86 (NE Chm., 1983–85). Chm., Assoc. of Psychiatric Social Workers, 1968–70; Chm., Social Admin Assoc., 1980–83. Hon. FRCPsych, 1976. *Publications:* Lunacy, Law and Conscience, 1955; Mental Health and Social Policy, 1960; Mental Hospitals at Work, 1962; The Compassionate Society, 1965; The Teaching of Social Studies in British Universities, 1965; A History of the Mental Health Services, 1972; Opening the Door: a study of new policies for the mentally handicapped, 1975; Issues in Social Policy, 1978; (ed) Living the Faith: a call to the Church, 1980; Ideas on Institutions, 1984; Eileen Younghusband: a biography, 1985; Experience in Mental Health, 1988; The Making of Social Policy, 1991; Asylums and After, 1993; Poems of St John of the Cross, 1993; (ed) Butler's Lives of the Saints: June, 1997; December, 1999; Women Saints, 1999; Saints of the Anglican Calendar, 2000; A Basic Dictionary of Saints, 2001; (series editor) International Library of Social Policy, 1968–85; (ed) Year Book of Social Policy in Britain, 1971–76. *Address:* 44 West Moor Lane, Heslington, York YO10 5ER. *T:* (01904) 411579.

JONES, Very Rev. Keith Brynmor; Dean of Exeter, since 1996; *b* 27 June 1944; *s* of John Brynmor Jones and Mary Emily Jones; *m* 1973, Viola Mary, *d* of H. L. Jenkyns, *qv*; three *d*. *Educ:* Selwyn Coll., Cambridge (BA 1965; MA 1969); Cuddesdon Coll., Oxford. Ordained deacon, 1969, priest, 1970; Asst Curate, Limpfield with Titsey, Surrey, 1969–72; Dean's Vicar, Cathedral and Abbey Church of St Alban, 1972–76; Priest-in-charge, 1976–79, Team Vicar, 1979–82, St Michael's, Boreham Wood; Vicar of St Mary-le-Tower, Ipswich, 1982–95. Rural Dean of Ipswich, 1992–95; Hon. Canon, St Edmundsbury Cathedral, 1993–95. *Recreations:* music, gardening, theatre, walking. *Address:* The Deanery, Exeter, Devon EX1 1HT. *T:* (01392) 252891, 272697.

JONES, Keith H.; *see* Hamylton Jones.

JONES, Dr Keith Howard, CB 1997; FRCP, FRCPE; Chief Executive, Medicines Control Agency, Department of Health, since 1989; *b* 14 Oct. 1937; *s* of Arthur Leslie Jones and Miriam Emily Jones; *m* 1962, Dr Lilian, (Lynne), Pearse; three *s*. *Educ:* Welsh Nat. Sch. of Medicine, Cardiff (MB, BCh 1960; MD 1966). FFPM 1989; FRCPE 1990; FRCP 1993. Posts in clinical and academic medicine, Cardiff, Edinburgh and Cambridge, 1960–67; Chief Toxicologist, Fisons Agrochemicals, 1967–70; Head, Safety Assessment, Beecham Res. Labs, 1970–79; Exec. Dir, Medical Affairs, Merck & Co., USA, 1979–89. Adjunct Prof. of Medicine, Thomas Jefferson Med. Sch., Philadelphia, 1985–89; Vis. Prof. of Pharmacology, Sch. of Pharmacy, Univ. of London, 1995–. UK Representative: EC Cttee for Pharmaceutical Medical Products, 1989–95; EC Pharmaceutical Cttee, 1989–; Chairman: EC Scientific Cttee for Medicinal Products and Med. Devices, 1997–2000; Mgt Bd, Eur. Medicines Evaluation Agency, 2001– (Mem., 1995–2000); Expert Mem., EC Scientific Steering Cttee on Consumer Health and Food Safety, 1997–. Fellow, NY Acad. of Sci., 1983. *Publications:* contribs to learned jls on issues of metabolic medicine, toxicology, drug develt and regulatory matters. *Recreations:* sailing, tennis. *Address:* Shelford, Headley Road, Leatherhead, Surrey KT22 8PT. *T:* (01372) 376747.

JONES, Keith O.; *see* Orrell-Jones.

JONES, Sir Keith (Stephen), Kt 1980; FRCSE; FRACS; *b* 7 July 1911; *s* of Stephen William and Muriel Elsy Jones; *m* 1936, Kathleen Mary Abbott; three *s*. *Educ:* Newington Coll.; Univ. of Sydney (MB, BS). General practitioner, Army MO, Surgeon; President, Aust. Medical Assoc., 1973–76; Chief MO, NSW State Emergency Service, 1966–74; Mem., NSW Medical Bd, 1971–81. Mem., Newington Coll. Council, 1951–72; Mem., Nat. Specialist Recognition Appeals Cttee, 1970–83 (Chm., 1980–83; Chm., Nat. Spec. Qualifications Cttee, 1980–83). Chairman: Australasian Medical Publishing Co., 1976–82; Manly Art Gall., 1982–85; President: Medical Benefits Fund of Aust., 1983–85; Blue Cross Assoc. of Aust., 1983–85. Acting Editor, Medical Jl of Aust., 1981. Fellow, Australian Coll. of Emergency Medicine, 1984; Hon. FRACGP 1975. Gold Medal, AMA, 1976. *Recreation:* swimming. *Address:* 123 Bayview Garden Village, Cabbage Tree Road, Bayview, NSW 2104, Australia. *T:* (2) 99972876.

JONES, Sir Kenneth (George Illtyd), Kt 1974; a Judge of the High Court, Queen's Bench Division, 1974–89; *b* 26 May 1921; *s* of late Richard Arthur Jones and Olive Jane Jones, Radyr, Cardiff; *m* 1st, 1947, Dulcie (*d* 1977); one *s* two *d*; 2nd, 1978, June Patricia (prev. marr. diss.), *o d* of late Leslie Arthur and Winifred Doxey, Harrogate. *Educ:* Brigg Gram. Sch.; University Coll., Oxford (1939–41, 1945–46), MA; Treas., Oxford Union Society, 1941; served in Shropshire Yeo. (76th Medium Regt RA), 1942–45; Staff Captain, HQ 13th Corps, 1945 (despatches). Called to Bar, Gray's Inn, 1946; joined Oxford Circuit, 1947; QC 1962; Mem. Gen. Council of the Bar, 1961–65, 1968–69; Bencher, 1969, Treas., 1987, Gray's Inn. Recorder of: Shrewsbury, 1964–66; Wolverhampton, 1966–71; the Crown Court, 1972; Dep. Chm., Herefordshire QS, 1961–71; a Circuit Judge, 1972–73. Dep. Chm., Boundary Commn for Wales, 1984–88. *Recreations:* theatre, opera, travel, sculpture, woodcarving, fishing. *Address:* 7 Radnor Close, Henley-on-Thames, Oxon RG9 2DA.

JONES, Kevan David; MP (Lab) Durham North, since 2001; *b* 25 April 1964. *Educ:* Univ. of Southern Maine, USA; Newcastle upon Tyne Poly. (BA). Political Officer, 1989–2001, Regl Organiser, 1992–99, Sen. Organiser, 1999–2001, GMB. Mem. (Lab) Newcastle upon Tyne CC, 1990–2001 (Chief Whip, Chair of Public Health, and Cabinet Mem. for Develt and Transport). Mem., H of C Defence Cttee, 2001–. Chair, 1998–2000, Vice-Chair, 2000–, Northern Regl Lab. Party. *Address:* c/o House of Commons, SW1A 0AA; (office) 9 Plawsworth Road, Sacriston, Co. Durham DH7 6HJ. *T:* (0191) 371 8834. *Club:* Sacriston Workmen's.

JONES, Lewis C.; *see* Carter-Jones.

JONES, Lindsay Harwood O.; *see* Owen-Jones.

JONES, Sir Lyndon (Hugh), Kt 1999; Principal and Chief Executive, Harris City Technology College, 1990–99; *b* 2 Feb. 1943; *s* of late David Hugh Jones and Victoria Maud (*née* Elias); *m* 1st, 1965, Gillian Fortnum (marr. diss. 1981); two *s* one *d*; 2nd, 1990, Sandra Lees; two step *d*. *Educ:* Cardiff High Sch. for Boys; UC Cardiff (BA); Univ. of Reading (Postgrad. DipEd); Birmingham Univ. (MEd). Hd of Music Dept, Pool Hayes Comprehensive Sch., 1965–70; Sen. Lectr in Music and Educn, Bingley Teacher Trng Coll., 1970–76; Hd, Arts Faculty, Doncaster Inst. Higher Educn, 1976–78; Dir of Arts, Richmond Tertiary Coll., 1978–82; Dep. Principal, Westminster Further Educn Coll.,

1982–85; Principal, S London Further Educn Coll., 1985–90. Chief Examr, GCE Music, London Univ., 1978–83. Tutor Mentor, Nat. Professional Qualifications for Headship, 1998; Trainer, Leadership Prog. for Serving Head Teachers, 1999. Volunteer interviewer, Pecan jobs project. Mem., NAHT, 1990. FIMgt 1976. Composer, The Prince and the Pauper, 1992. *Recreations:* playing the piano, composing, Rugby, mountaineering, opera, amateur chef and wine taster.

JONES, Dr Lynne Mary; MP (Lab) Birmingham, Selly Oak, since 1992; *b* 26 April 1951; two *s*. *Educ:* Birmingham Univ. (BSc, PhD Biochem.); Birmingham Polytechnic (Dip. Housing Studies). Joined Labour Party, 1974; ASTMS, then MSF, 1972. Birmingham City Councillor, 1980–94 (Chair, Housing Cttee, 1984–87). Former Exec. Mem., Labour Housing Gp. Mem., Select Cttee on Science and Technology, 1992–2001. *Address:* House of Commons, SW1A 0AA. *T:* (020) 7219 6971.

JONES, Dr Margaret Anne, OBE, 2001; Chief Executive, Brook Advisory Centres, 1988–2001; *b* 30 Oct. 1940; *d* of Cecil Newton Collard and Rita Ross Collard (*née* White); *m* 1974, Hugh Vaughan Price Jones. *Educ:* Methodist Ladies' Coll., Burwood, Australia; Univ. of New South Wales (BSc, MSc); University College London (PhD). Postdoctoral Res. Fellow, Univ. of Cambridge, 1970–71; Res. Fellow, Univ. of Bath, 1971–74; Resources Officer, Health Education Council, 1974–88. Lay Mem., Chiltern and S Bucks Primary Care Gp, 1999–. Mem., Indep. Adv. Gp, Teenage Pregnancy Unit, DoH, 2000–. Hon. DSc Southampton, 2000. *Recreations:* music, cooking.

JONES, Mark Ellis Powell; Director, Victoria & Albert Museum, since 2001; *b* 5 Feb. 1951; *s* of John Ernest Powell-Jones, *qv* and Ann Paludan; *m* 1983, Ann Camilla, *d* of Stephen Edelston Toulmin, *qv*; two *s* two *d*. *Educ:* Eton College; Worcester College, Oxford (MA); Courtauld Inst. of Art. Asst Keeper, 1974–90, Keeper, 1990–92, Dept of Coins and Medals, BM; Dir, Nat. Mus of Scotland, 1992–2001. Co-Founder, 1994–96, and Mem. Bd, 1996–, Scottish Cultural Resources Access Network. Director: Scottish Museums Council, 1992–; Edinburgh and Lothians Tourist Bd, 1998–2000. Member: Royal Mint Adv. Cttee, 1994–; Arts and Humanities Data Service Steering Cttee, 1997–99; Focus Gp, Nat. Cultural Strategy, 1999–2000. President: Fédn Internat. de la Médaille, 1994–; British Art Medal Soc., 1998– (Sec., 1982–94); Corresp. Mem., Amer. Numismatic Soc., 1990. Hon. Prof., Univ. of Edinburgh, 1997. Editor, The Medal, 1983–. FSA 1992; FRSE 1999. *Publications:* The Art of the Medal, 1977; Impressionist Painting, 1979; Catalogue of French Medals in the British Museum, I, 1982, II, 1988; Contemporary British Medals, 1986; (ed) Fake?: the art of deception, 1990; (ed) Why Fakes Matter, 1992; (ed) Designs on Posterity, 1994. *Address:* Victoria & Albert Museum, Cromwell Road, SW7 2RL.

JONES, Prof. Martin Kenneth, DPhil; FSA; George Pitt-Rivers Professor of Archaeological Science, University of Cambridge, since 1990; *b* 29 June 1951; *s* of John Francis Jones and Margaret Olive (*née* Baldwin); *m* 1985, Lucy Walker; one *s* one *d*. *Educ:* Eltham Coll., Univ. of Cambridge (MA); Univ. of Oxford (DPhil 1985). FSA 1991. Oxford Archaeological Unit, 1973–79; Res. Asst, Oxford Univ., 1979–81; Lectr, 1981–89, Sen. Lectr, 1989–90, Durham Univ. DUniv Stirling, 1999. *Publications:* The Environment of Man: the Iron Age to the Anglo-Saxon period, 1981; Integrating the Subsistence Economy, 1983; England before Domesday, 1986; Archaeology and the Flora of the British Isles, 1988; Molecular Information and Prehistory, 1999; The Molecule Hunt: archaeology and the search for ancient DNA, 2001. *Recreation:* dancing. *Address:* Department of Archaeology, Downing Street, Cambridge CB2 3DZ. *T:* (01223) 333520.

JONES, Martyn David; MP (Lab) Clwyd South, since 1997 (Clwyd South West, 1987–97); *b* 1 March 1947; *m* 1974, Rhona Bellis (marr. diss. 1991); one *s* one *d*. *Educ:* Liverpool and Trent Polytechnics. MIBiol. Microbiologist, Wrexham Lager Beer Co., 1968–87. Mem., Clwyd CC, 1981–89. An Opposition Whip, 1988–92; Opposition spokesman on food, agric. and rural affairs, 1994–95; Mem., Chairman's Panel, 1992–94. Mem., Select Cttee on Agriculture, 1987–94 and 1996–97; Chm., Select Cttee on Welsh Affairs, 1997–; Chm., Parly Labour Party Agriculture Cttee, 1987–94. *Address:* House of Commons, SW1A 0AA; Foundry Buildings, Gutter Hill, Johnstown, Wrexham, Clwyd LL14 1LU.

JONES, Maude Elizabeth, CBE 1973; Deputy Director-General, British Red Cross Society, 1970–77; *b* 14 Jan. 1921; 2nd *d* of late E. W. Jones, Dolben, Ruthin, North Wales. *Educ:* Brynhyfryd Sch. for Girls, Ruthin. Joined Foreign Relations Dept, Jt War Organisation BRCS and OStJ, 1940; Dep. Dir, Jun. Red Cross, BRCS, 1949; Dir, Jun. Red Cross, 1960; Dep. Dir-Gen. for Branch Affairs, BRCS, 1966. Member: Jt Cttee (and Finance and Gen. Purposes Sub-Cttee) OStJ and BRCS, 1966–77; Council of Nat. Council of Social Service; Council of FANY, 1966–77. Governor, St David's Sch., Ashford, Mddx. SSStJ 1959. *Recreations:* music, gardening, reading. *Address:* Dolben, Ruthin, Denbighshire, North Wales LL15 1RB. *T:* (01824) 702443. *Club:* New Cavendish.

JONES, Mervyn; author; *b* 27 Feb. 1922; *s* of Ernest Jones and Katharine (*née* Jokl); *m* 1948, Jeanne Urquhart; one *s* two *d*. *Educ:* Abbotsholme School; New York University. Assistant Editor: Tribune, 1955–59; New Statesman, 1966–68; Drama Critic, Tribune, 1959–67. *Publications:* No Time to be Young, 1952; The New Town, 1953; The Last Barricade, 1953; Helen Blake, 1955; On the Last Day, 1958; Potbank, 1961; Big Two, 1962; A Set of Wives, 1965; Two Ears of Corn, 1965; John and Mary, 1966; A Survivor, 1968; Joseph, 1970; Mr Armitage Isn't Back Yet, 1971; Life on the Dole, 1972; Holding On, 1973; The Revolving Door, 1973; Strangers, 1974; Lord Richard's Passion, 1974; The Pursuit of Happiness, 1975; Scenes from Bourgeois Life, 1976; Nobody's Fault, 1977; Today The Struggle, 1978; The Beautiful Words, 1979; A Short Time to Live, 1980; Two Women and their Man, 1982; Joanna's Luck, 1985; Coming Home, 1986; Chances, 1987; That Year in Paris, 1988; A Radical Life, 1991; Michael Foot, 1994; The Amazing Victorian, 1999. *Address:* Flat 1, 20 Brunswick Terrace, Hove, East Sussex BN3 1HJ. *T:* (01273) 328948.

JONES, Mervyn C.; *see* Colenso-Jones, G. M. B.

JONES, Mervyn Thomas; HM Diplomatic Service; Governor, Turks and Caicos Islands, since 2000; *b* 23 Nov. 1942; *s* of William Clifford Jones and Winifred Mary Jones (*née* Jenkins); *m* 1965, Julia Mary Newcombe; two *s*. *Educ:* Bishop Gore Grammar Sch., Swansea; University Coll., Swansea (BA Hons Eng.). Entered HM Diplomatic Service, 1964: FCO, 1964–66; Calcutta, 1966; Bonn, 1966–70; Warsaw, 1970–73; FCO, 1973–77; Oslo, 1977–80; First Sec. (Mgt), then Hd of Chancery, Bangkok, 1981–85; jsdc, 1985; on secondment to Commonwealth Secretariat as Asst Dir, Internat. Affairs Div., 1985–90; Dep. Consul Gen. and Consul (Commercial), LA, 1990–94; Asst Hd, Migration and Visa Dept, FCO, 1994–96; Counsellor (Commercial and Econ.), Brussels, and co-accredited to Luxembourg, 1996–99; Consul-Gen. and Dep. Head of Mission, Brussels, 1999–2000. *Recreations:* reading, cinema, music, walking, Rugby (Welsh). *Address:* c/o Foreign and Commonwealth Office, King Charles Street, SW1A 2AH.

JONES, Miah Gwynfor, (Gwyn Jones), PhD; Executive Chairman, Agenda Multimedia Ltd, since 2000; *b* 2 Dec. 1948; *s* of Robert Jones and Jane Irene Jones (*née* Evans); *m* 1976, Maria Linda Johnson; two *d*. *Educ:* Ysgol Eifionydd, Porthmadog; Univ. of Manchester (BSc 1st Cl. Hons); Univ. of Essex (PhD). FBCS 1987. British Steel Corp., 1974–77; ICL, 1977–81; Chm., Business Micro Systems, 1981–85; Chm. and Chief Exec., Corporate Technology Gp plc, 1985–87; Chm., L. G. Software, 1985–87; Director: ACT Computers PLC, 1989–95; Corporate Technologies, 1989–; Welsh Water Enterprises Ltd, 1990–93; Tesco plc, 1992–98; Invesco English and Internat. Trust plc, 1993–; HBO (formerly HBOL) (UK) Ltd, 1996–97; Real Radio Ltd, 2000–; Dep. Chm., Agenda Television Ltd, 1997–2000. Chm., Welsh Develt Agency, 1988–93; BBC Nat. Gov. for Wales, 1992–96; Dir, S4C Authy, 1992–96. Member: Council, Univ. of Wales, 1989–95; Court, UC of Swansea, 1989–95; Prince of Wales Cttee, 1989–92; Prince's Youth Business Trust, 1989–92. *Recreations:* boats, mountain walking. *Address:* Agenda Multimedia, Agenda Centre, Llanelli, S Wales SA15 3YE.

JONES, Michael Abbott; communications consultant; Director, Rapid Insure plc, since 2000; *b* 3 May 1944; *s* of Ronald and Irene Jones; *m* 1973, Wendy (*née* Saward); twin *d*. *Educ:* Felsted; Magdalen Coll., Oxford (BA, DipEd). Joined Life Offices' Assoc., 1968, Jt Sec. 1982; transf. to Assoc. of British Insurers on its formation, as Manager, Legislation, 1985, Chief Exec., 1987–93; Hd of Corporate Affairs, Sun Alliance, 1993–96; Hd of Gp Corporate Affairs, Royal & Sun Alliance Insurance Gp plc, 1996–98. *Recreations:* reading, photography, sailing, theatre. *Address:* 10 Parkhill Road, E4 7ED.

JONES, Michael Frederick; Associate Editor (Politics), The Sunday Times, since 1995; *b* 3 July 1937; *s* of late Glyn Frederick Jones and of Elizabeth (*née* Coopey); *m* 1959, Sheila Joan Dawes; three *s*. *Educ:* Crypt Grammar Sch., Gloucester. Reporter: Maidenhead Advertiser, 1956–59; Northern Echo, Darlington, 1959–61; Manchester Evening News, 1961–64; Labour reporter, Financial Times, 1964–65; Industrial reporter, Daily Telegraph, 1965–67; News Editor, later Asst Editor, Times Business News, 1967–70; Managing Editor, The Asian, Hong Kong, 1971; Sunday Times: Associate News Editor, 1972–75; political correspondent, 1975–84; Political Editor, 1984–95; Associate Editor, 1990–. Chm., Parly Press Gallery, 1989–91. Vis. Fellow, Goldsmiths Coll., London, 2000. *Publication:* (with Betty Boothroyd) Betty Boothroyd The Autobiography, 2001. *Recreations:* travel, reading history. *Address:* The Sunday Times, 1 Pennington Street, E1 9XW. *T:* (020) 7782 5834. *Club:* Buck's.

JONES, Rt Rev. Michael Hugh Harold B.; *see* Bedford-Jones.

JONES, Dr Nevin Campbell H.; *see* Hughes Jones.

JONES, Nigel David; MP (Lib Dem) Cheltenham, since 1992; *b* 30 March 1948; *m* 1981, Katy Grinnell; one *s* twin *d*. *Educ:* Prince Henry's Grammar Sch., Evesham. With Westminster Bank, 1965–67; computer programmer, ICL Computers, 1967–70; systems analyst, Vehicle and Gen. Insce, 1970–71; systems programmer, Atkins Computing, 1971; systems designer and consultant, ICL Computers, 1971–92. Contested (L) Cheltenham, 1979. Lib Dem spokesman on England, local govt and housing, 1992–93, science and technology, 1993–99, consumer affairs, 1995–97, culture, media and sport, 1997–99, internat. develt, 1999–. *Address:* House of Commons, SW1A 0AA.

JONES, Nigel John I.; *see* Inglis-Jones.

JONES, Rt Rev. Noël Debroy; *see* Sodor and Man, Bishop of.

JONES, Norman Arthur W.; *see* Ward-Jones.

JONES, Dr (Norman) Fielding, FRCP; Consultant Physician, St Thomas' Hospital, London, 1967–93, now Emeritus; *b* 3 May 1931; *s* of William John and Winifred Jones; *m* 1958, Ann Pye Chavasse; three *s*. *Educ:* Christ Coll., Brecon; King's Coll., Cambridge (MA 1957; MD 1966); St Thomas' Hosp., London. FRCP 1970. Rockefeller Fellow, Univ. of N Carolina, 1963–64. Physician, King Edward VII's Hosp. for Officers, 1977–95; Consulting Physician, Metropolitan Police, 1980–92; Hon. Consulting Physician: to the Army, 1980–93; to Royal Hosp., Chelsea, 1987–93; CMO, Equitable Life Assurance Soc., 1985–97. Vice Chm., West Lambeth HA, 1989–90. Royal College of Physicians: Sen. Censor and Vice Pres., 1989–90; Treasurer, 1991–96; Chm., Cttee on Renal Disease, 1980–92; Chm., Cttee on Legal Aspects of Medicine, 1990–93. Special Trustee, St Thomas' Hosp., 1990–94; Treas., Royal Medical Benevolent Fund, 1996–. Member: Med. Res. Soc., 1962–; Assoc. of Physicians of GB and Ire., 1968–. FRSA 1991. *Publications:* (ed) Recent Advances in Renal Disease, 1975; (ed with Sir Douglas Black) Renal Disease, 1979; (ed with D. K. Peters) Recent Advances in Renal Medicine, 1982. *Recreations:* iconology, music. *Address:* The Old Coach House, Forest Park Road, Brockenhurst, Hants SO42 7SW.

JONES, Norman Henry; QC 1985; **His Honour Judge Norman Jones;** a Circuit Judge, since 1992 (a Senior Circuit Judge, since 2000); *b* 12 Dec. 1941; *s* of late Henry Robert Jones and of Charlotte Isabel Scott Jones; *m* 1970, Trudy Helen Chamberlain; two *s* one *d*. *Educ:* Bideford Grammar School; North Devon Tech. Coll.; Univ. of Leeds (LLB, LLM). Called to the Bar, Middle Temple, 1968. A Recorder, 1987–92. Resident Judge at Bradford, 2000; Recorder of Leeds and Resident Judge at Leeds, 2001. *Recreation:* boating. *Address:* The Crown Court, Oxford Road, Leeds LS1 3BG.

JONES, Sir (Owen) Trevor, Kt 1981; formerly Councillor, Liverpool Metropolitan District Council; *b* 1927; *s* of Owen and Ada Jones, Dyserth. Mem., Liverpool City Council, 1968, Liverpool Metropolitan District Council, 1973–91 (Leader, 1981–83). Pres., Liberal Party, 1972–73; contested (L): Liverpool, Toxteth, Feb. 1974 and Gillingham, Oct. 1974. *Address:* 221 Queen's Drive, Liverpool L15 6YE.

JONES, Dame Pauline N.; *see* Neville-Jones.

JONES, Penry; Chief Assistant (Television) (formerly Deputy Head of Programme Services), IBA (formerly ITA), 1971–82, retired; *b* 18 Aug. 1922; *s* of Joseph William and Edith Jones; *m* Beryl Joan Priestley; two *d*. *Educ:* Rock Ferry High Sch.; Liverpool Univ. Gen. Sec., YMCA, Altrincham, 1940; Sec., SCM, Southern Univs, 1945; Industrial Sec., Iona Community, 1948; Religious Programmes Producer, ABC Television, 1958; Religious Programmes Officer of ITA, 1964; Head of Religious Broadcasting, BBC, 1967. Chm., Iona Heritage Trust, 1997–. *Recreations:* hill-walking, swimming, watching Rugby football. *Address:* Erraid House, Isle of Iona, Argyll PA76 6SJ. *T:* (01681) 700448.

JONES, Brig. Percival de Courcy, OBE 1953; Chief Secretary, The Royal Life Saving Society, 1965–75; *b* 9 Oct. 1913; *s* of P. de C. Jones, Barnsley; *m* 1st, 1947, Anne Hollins (marr. diss., 1951); one *s*; 2nd, 1962, Elaine Garnett. *Educ:* Oundle; RMC, Sandhurst. Commissioned KSLI 1933; Staff Coll., 1942; comd 1st Northamptons, Burma, 1945; Staff Coll. Instructor, 1949–50; AA & QMG, 11th Armoured Div., 1951–53; comd 1st KSLI, 1953–55; AQMG, War Office, 1955–58; NATO Defence Coll., 1958–59; Bde Comdr, 1959–62; retd 1962. Mem., Aylesbury Vale DC, 1976–79. Commonwealth Chief Sec.,

RLSS, 1965–75. Silver Medallion, Fedn Internat. de Sauvetage, 1976. *Recreation:* gardening. *Address:* 6 Port Hill Gardens, Shrewsbury, Shropshire SY3 8SH.

JONES, Peter B.; *see* Bennett-Jones.

JONES, Peter Benjamin Gurner, CB 1991; Under Secretary; Director of Personnel, Board of Inland Revenue, 1984–92; *b* 25 Dec. 1932; *s* of Gurner Prince Jones and Irene Louise Jones (*née* Myall); *m* 1962, Diana Margaret Henly; one *s* one *d. Educ:* Bancroft's Sch.; St Catherine's Society, Oxford (BA (Hons) English Language and Literature). Inspector of Taxes, 1957; Inspector (Higher Grade), 1963; Sen. Inspector, 1969; Principal Inspector, 1975; Sen. Principal Inspector, 1980; Dir of Data Processing, Bd of Inland Revenue, 1981–84. Hon. Nat. Chm., CS Retirement Fellowship, 1994–2000. *Clubs:* Hampshire Rugby Union, Swanage and Wareham RFC.

JONES, Prof. Peter Brian, PhD; Professor of Psychiatry and Head, Department of Psychiatry, University of Cambridge, since 2000; *b* 24 Jan. 1960; *s* of Owen Trevor Jones and Amy M. Anita Jones; *m* 1986, Caroline Lea-Cox; two *s. Educ:* Northampton Grammar Sch.; King's Coll., London (BSc Neuroanatomy); Westminster Med. Sch. (MB BS); London Sch. of Hygiene and Tropical Medicine (MSc Dist.); Inst. of Psychiatry (PhD 1997). MRCP 1987; MRCPsych 1990. House physician, Westminster Hosp., 1984; house surgeon, E Surrey Hosp., 1985; Casualty Officer, Westminster Hosp., 1985; SHO, Whittington Hosp., 1986–87; Med. Registrar, KCH, 1987; Registrar, Bethlem Royal and Maudsley Hosps, 1987–90; Sen. Registrar in Psychiatry, KCH, 1991; MRC Trng Fellow, 1991–93; Sen. Lectr, Inst. of Psychiatry, 1993–95 (Hon. Lectr, 1991–93); Hon. Consultant Psychiatrist, Bethlem Royal and Maudsley Hosps, 1993–95; University of Nottingham: Sen. Lectr in Psychiatric Epidemiol., 1995–96; Prof. of Psychiatry and Community Mental Health, 1997–2000; Head, Div. of Psychiatry, 1997–2000. SMO (part-time), R&D Div., DoH, 1994–96. Hon. Consultant Psychiatrist: and Dir, R&D, Nottingham Healthcare Trust, 1995–2000; Addenbrooke's NHS Trust, 2000–. *Publications:* contribs to learned jls on causation, clinical features, epidemiology and treatment of adult mental illness, and the psychoses, in particular. *Recreations:* playing the flute, climbing fells, going fishing, doing nothing. *Address:* Department of Psychiatry, University of Cambridge, Box 189, Addenbrooke's Hospital, Cambridge CB2 2QQ. *T:* (01223) 336960.

JONES, Peter Derek; Deputy Chairman, Civil Service Appeal Board, since 1992; Secretary: Council of Civil Service Unions, 1980–92; Civil Service National Whitley Council (Trade Union Side), 1963–92; *b* 21 May 1932; *s* of Richard Morgan Jones and Phyllis Irene (*née* Lloyd); *m* 1962, Noreen Elizabeth (*née* Kemp) (*d* 2001). *Educ:* Wembley County Grammar School. National Service and TA, Green Jackets/Parachute Regt, 1950–56; Civil Service, Nat. Assistance Bd, 1952–59; Asst Sec., Civil Service Nat. Whitley Council, 1959–63. Chm., Civil Service Housing Assoc. Ltd, 1988–97 (Dir, 1963–81; Vice Chm., 1981–88, 1997–99); Dir, Civil Service Building Soc., 1963–87. Vice-Pres., RIPA, 1991–92 (Chm., 1987–90; Vice-Chm., 1986–87; Mem. Exec. Council, 1981–85); Member: Adv. Council, Civil Service Coll., 1982–92; Tourism and Leisure Industries EDC, 1987–92; Adv. Council, CS Occupational Health Service, 1988–92; Employment (formerly Industrial) Tribunals, 1992–; Security Vetting Appeals Panel, 1997–; Chm., CIPFA Disciplinary Investigations Cttee, 2001–. Trustee: Inst. of Contemporary Brit. History, 1985–; CS Benevolent Fund, 1992–99. Editor: Whitley Bulletin, 1963–83; CCSU Bulletin, 1984–92. *Publications:* articles in RIPA and personnel management jls. *Recreations:* relaxing, reading, golf. *Address:* Chaseview, Rowlands Hill, Wimborne, Dorset BH21 2QQ. *T:* (01202) 888824, *Fax:* (01202) 888831. *Clubs:* Wig and Pen, Belfry; Mansion House (Poole).

JONES, Peter Eldon, FRIBA, FRTPI; architect in private practice, since 1996; *b* 11 Oct. 1927; *s* of Wilfrid Eldon Jones and Jessie Meikle (*née* Buchanan); *m* 1st, 1954, Gisela Marie von Arnswaldt; two *s* one *d*; 2nd, 1985, Claudia Milner-Brown (*née* Laurence). *Educ:* Surbiton County Grammar Sch.; Kingston Polytechnic; University College London. DipTP. Private practice, 1950–54; joined LCC Architects Dept, 1954; Dep. Schools Architect, LCC, 1960–65; Town Development Architect/Planner, 1965–71; Technical Policy Architect, GLC, 1971–74; Education Architect, ILEA, 1974–82; Acting Director of Architecture, 1980–82, Dir of Architecture and Superintending Architect of Metrop. Bldgs, 1982–86, GLC. Consultant, DES, subseq. DFE, 1988–92. Dir, Assoc. of Small Historic Towns and Villages of the UK, 1993–95. Director: Interior Transformation Ltd, 1985–87; Watkins Gray Peter Jones, 1986–91. Part-time Lectr in Architectl Design, Kingston Poly., 1986–90. Mem., EC Adv. Cttee on Educn and Training in Architecture, 1987–92. Pres., Soc. of Chief Architects of Local Authorities, 1984–85; Mem. Council, Chm. Membership Cttee, and Vice-Pres., RIBA, 1985–87. *Publications:* articles and papers on town development, educn building, housing design and planning. *Recreations:* building, travel, golf. *Address:* Dene Cottage, The Green, Pirbright, Surrey GU24 0JE. *Club:* Woking Golf.

JONES, Peter Ferry, MA, MChir, FRCS, FRCSE; Surgeon to the Queen in Scotland, 1977–85; Honorary Consulting Surgeon, Aberdeen Royal Infirmary and Royal Aberdeen Children's Hospital, Aberdeen (Consultant Surgeon, 1958–85); Clinical Professor of Surgery, University of Aberdeen, 1983–85, now Emeritus; *b* 29 Feb. 1920; *s* of Ernest and Winifred Jones; *m* 1950, Margaret Thomson; two *s* two *d. Educ:* Emmanuel Coll., Cambridge (MA); St Bartholomew's Hosp. Med. Sch., London (MB, MChir). FRCS 1948; FRCSE 1964. Served War, RAMC, 1944–46, Captain. House Surgeon, St Bartholomew's Hosp., 1943; Surg. Registrar, N Middlesex Hosp., 1948–51; Surg. Tutor, St Bartholomew's Hosp., 1951–53; Sen. Surg. Registrar, Central Middlesex Hosp. and the Middlesex Hosp., London, 1953–57; Reader in Surg. Paediatrics, Univ. of Aberdeen, 1965–83. *Publications:* Abdominal Access and Exposure (with H. A. F. Dudley), 1965; Emergency Abdominal Surgery in Infancy, Childhood and Adult Life, 1974, 2nd edn 1987, 3rd edn (jtly) 1998; (jtly) Integrated Clinical Science: Gastroenterology, 1984; A Colour Atlas of Colo-Rectal Surgery, 1985; papers on paediatric and gen. surgery in Brit. Jl of Surg., BMJ, Lancet, etc. *Recreations:* gardening, surgical history. *Address:* 7 Park Road, Cults, Aberdeen AB15 9HR. *T:* (01224) 867702.

JONES, Peter George Edward Fitzgerald, CB 1985; Director, Atomic Weapons Research Establishment, 1982–87, retired; Consultant to the Ministry of Defence, since 1987; *b* 7 June 1925; *s* of John Christopher Jones and Isobel (*née* Howell); *m* 1st; two *s*; 2nd, Jacqueline Angela (*née* Gilbert); two *s* one *d. Educ:* various schs; Dulwich Coll.; London Univ. (BSc (Special) Physics 1st Cl. Hons 1951). FInstP. Served RAF, flying duties, 1943–47. GEC Res. Labs, 1951–54; AWRE and Pacific Test Site, 1955–63; Asst Dir of Res., London Communications Security, 1963; Atomic Weapons Research Establishment: Supt, Electronics Res., 1964; Head, Electronics Div., 1966; Head, Special Projs, 1971; Chief, Warhead Develt, 1974; Principal Dep. Dir, 1980. *Recreation:* motoring. *Address:* Yew Tree Cottage, Upper Llanover, Abergavenny, Gwent NP7 9ER. *T:* (01873) 880779.

JONES, Peter Henry Francis; His Honour Judge Peter Jones; a Circuit Judge, since 2001; *b* 25 Feb. 1952; *s* of Eric Roberts Jones, MBE and late Betty Irene Jones (*née* Longhurst); *m* 1978, Anne Elizabeth (*née* Jones); two *d. Educ:* Bishop Gore Grammar Sch., Swansea; Newport High Sch., Gwent; Balliol Coll., Oxford (MA (Hons) Lit.Hum.). Admitted Solicitor of Supreme Court, 1977. Partner: Darlington and Parkinson, Solicitors, London, 1978–87; J. Howell and Co., Solicitors, Sheffield, 1987–95; Asst Recorder, 1993–97; a Stipendiary Magistrate, then Dist Judge (Magistrates' Courts), S Yorks, 1995–2001; a Recorder, 1997–2001. Member: Lord Chancellor's Legal Aid Adv. Cttee, 1983–92; Legal Aid Bd, 1992–95; Sentencing Adv. Panel, 1999–. *Recreations:* golf, tennis, books, watching Rugby Union. *Address:* c/o Sheffield Combined Court Centre, 50 West Bar, Sheffield S3 8PH. *Clubs:* Dethreau Boat; Scorpions Cricket; Druidstone (Dyfed).

JONES, Prof. Peter (Howard), FRSE, FSAScot; Director and Trustee, Foundation for Advanced Studies in the Humanities, since 1997; Professor of Philosophy, 1984–98, now Emeritus, and Director, Institute for Advanced Studies in the Humanities, 1986–2000, University of Edinburgh; *b* 18 Dec. 1935; *s* of Thomas Leslie Jones and Hilda Croesora (*née* Parkinson); *m* 1960, (Elizabeth) Jean, *yr d* of R. J. Roberton, JP; two *d. Educ:* Highgate Sch.; Queens' Coll., Cambridge. With British Council, 1960–61; Asst Lectr in Philosophy, Univ. of Nottingham, 1963–64; Lectr, then Reader in Philosophy, Univ. of Edinburgh, 1964–84. Visiting Professor of Philosophy: Univ. of Rochester, NY, 1969–70; Dartmouth Coll., NH, 1973, 1983; Carleton Coll., Minn, 1974; Oklahoma Univ., 1978; Baylor Univ., 1978; Univ. of Malta, 1993; Belarusian State Univ., 1997; Visiting Fellow: Humanities Res. Centre, ANU, 1984; Calgary Inst. for Humanities, 1992. Lothian Lectr, Edinburgh, 1993; Gifford Lectr, Univ. of Aberdeen, 1994–95; Loemker Lectr, Emory Univ., 1995–96. Mem., Spoliation Adv. Panel, 2000–. Trustee: Nat. Museums of Scotland, 1987–99 (Chm., Mus. of Scotland Client Cttee, 1991–99); Univ. of Edinburgh Develt Trust, 1990–98; Policy Inst., 1999–; Scots at War, 1999–; Morrison's Acad., 1984–98; Fettes Coll., 1995–. Member: UNESCO forum on tolerance, Tblisi, 1995–; UNESCO dialogue on Europe and Islam, 1997–. Member: Court, Univ. of Edinburgh, 1987–90; Council, RSE, 1992–95. Founder Mem., Hume Soc., 1974. FRSE 1989; FSAScot 1993. *Publications:* Philosophy and the Novel, 1975; Hume's Sentiments, 1982; A Hotbed of Genius, 1986, 2nd edn 1996; (ed) Philosophy and Science in the Scottish Enlightenment, 1988; (ed) The Science of Man in the Scottish Enlightenment, 1989; (ed) Adam Smith Reviewed, 1992; articles on philosophy, literature and culture. *Recreations:* opera, architecture, the arts, travel. *Address:* Foundation for Advanced Studies in the Humanities, 6 Greenhill Terrace, Edinburgh EH10 4BS. *T:* (0131) 447 6344, *Fax:* (0131) 446 9049. *Club:* New (Edinburgh).

JONES, Peter Ivan; Chairman, Horserace Totalisator Board, since 1997 (Director, 1995–97); *b* 14 Dec. 1942; *s* of Glyndwr and Edith Evelyn Jones; *m* 1st, 1964, Judith Watson (marr. diss. 1969); one *s* one *d*; 2nd, 1970, Elizabeth Gent; one *s* one *d. Educ:* Gravesend Grammar Sch.; London School of Economics (BSc Econs 1964). MIPA 1967. Chief Executive: Boase Massimi Pollitt, 1988–89; Omnicom UK plc, 1989–93 (Dir, Omnicom Inc., 1989–97); Pres., Diversified Agency Services, 1993–97. Dir, British Horseracing Bd, 1993–97; Mem., Horserace Betting Levy Bd, 1993–95. Chm., Dorset Police Authy, 1997–. Pres., Racehorse Owners Assoc., 1990–93. *Publications:* Trainers Record, annually 1973 to 1987 (Editor, 1982–87); (ed) Ed Byrne's Racing Year, annually 1980 to 1983. *Recreations:* horse racing, computer programming, watching sport. *Address:* Melplash Farmhouse, Melplash, Bridport, Dorset DT6 3UH. *T:* (01308) 488383. *Club:* Bridport and West Bay Golf.

JONES, Maj.-Gen. (Peter) John R.; *see* Russell-Jones.

JONES, Peter Llewellyn G.; *see* Gwynn-Jones.

JONES, Peter Trevor S.; *see* Simpson-Jones.

JONES, Philip Graham, CEng, FIChemE, FIExpE; Deputy Director of Technology and Health Sciences Division, Health and Safety Executive, 1986–95; *b* 3 June 1937; *s* of Sydney and Olive Jones; *m* 1961, Janet Ann Collins; one *s* three *d. Educ:* Univ. of Aston in Birmingham (BSc). Eur Ing 1989. Professional positions in UK explosives industry, 1961–68 and 1972–76; service with Australian Public Service, 1969–71, with UK Civil Service, 1976–95; HM Chief Inspector of Explosives, 1981–86. Mem., Accreditation Bd, 1987–90, Professional Develt Cttee, 1988–91, IChemE. Chairman: Nat. Certification Scheme for Inservice Inspection Bodies, 1995–98; Engrg Inspection Technical Cttee, UK Accreditation Service, 1996–. Safety Advr, Severn Valley Rly, 1995–. *Publications:* articles in The Chemical Engineer, Explosives Engineer, and railway jls. *Recreations:* walking, reading, curling.

JONES, Philip James, DPhil; FBA 1984; FRHistS; Fellow and Tutor, Modern History, 1963–89, Librarian, 1965–89, Brasenose College, Oxford, now Emeritus Fellow; *b* 19 Nov. 1921; *s* of John David Jones and Caroline Susan Jones (*née* Davies); *m* 1954, Carla Susini; one *s* one *d. Educ:* St Dunstan's College; Wadham College, Oxford (1st class Hons Mod. Hist. 1945, MA, DPhil). Senior Demy, Magdalen College, Oxford, 1945–49; Amy Mary Preston Road Scholar, 1946; Bryce Research Student, 1947; Asst in History, Glasgow Univ., 1949–50; Leeds University: Lectr in Med. Hist., 1950–61; Reader in Med. Hist., 1961–63; Eileen Power Meml Student, 1956–57. Corresp. Mem., Deputazione Toscana di Storia Patria, 1975–. Serena Medal for Italian Studies, British Acad., 1988. *Publications:* The Malatesta of Rimini, 1974; Economia e Societa nell'Italia medievale, 1980; contribs to: Cambridge Economic History, Vol. 1, 2nd edn, 1966; Storia d'Italia, vol. 2, 1974; Storia d'Italia, Annali, Vol. 1, 1978; The Italian City-State: from commune to signoria, 1997; articles and reviews in hist. jls. *Address:* 167 Woodstock Road, Oxford OX2 7NA. *T:* (01865) 557953.

JONES, Piers Nicholas L.; *see* Legh-Jones.

JONES, Raymond Edgar; HM Diplomatic Service, retired; *b* 6 June 1919; *s* of Edgar George Jones, Portsmouth; *m* 1942, Joan Mildred Clark; one *s* two *d. Educ:* Portsmouth Northern Grammar Sch. Entered Admiralty service as Clerical Officer, 1936; joined RAF, 1941; commissioned, 1943; returned to Admty as Exec. Officer, 1946; transf. to Foreign Service, 1948; Singapore, 1949; Second Sec., Rome, 1950; Bahrain, 1952; Rio de Janeiro, 1955; Consul, Philadelphia, 1958; FO, 1961; First Sec., Copenhagen, 1963; Consul, Milan, 1965; Toronto (Dir of British Week), 1966; Dep. High Comr, Adelaide, 1967–71; FCO, 1971–76; Consul-Gen., Genoa, 1976–79. *Recreations:* music, gardening. *Address:* Oaklands, 3 Old Hall Drive, Dersingham, Norfolk PE31 6JT.

JONES, Raymond Francis, OBE 1986; HM Diplomatic Service, retired; Chairman, Holywell Hook Heath Ltd, since 2001 (Director, since 1996); *b* 15 Nov. 1935; *s* of late Hugh and Jessie Jones; *m* 1957, Maurag Annat (*d* 1994); two *d. Educ:* Liverpool Collegiate Sch. Nat. Service, RAF, 1954–56. Joined Foreign Office, 1953; served Amman, Tokyo, Cairo, Accra, 1956–70; Second Sec., FCO, 1970–73; Consul, Seattle, 1973–78; First Sec., 1978; on loan to DoI, 1978–82; New Delhi, 1982–86; Dep. Consul-Gen., Chicago, 1986–91; High Comr, Honiara, Solomon Is, 1991–95. *Recreations:* music, sport, reading. *Address:* Flat 5, Holywell, Hook Heath Road, Woking GU22 0LA.

JONES, Rhona Mary; Chief Nursing Officer, St Bartholomew's Hospital, 1969–74, retired; *b* 7 July 1921; *d* of late Thomas Henry Jones and late Margaret Evelyn King; single. *Educ:* Liverpool; Alder Hey Children's Hosp.; St Mary's Hosp., Paddington. RSCN 1943; SRN 1945; SCM 1948. Post-Registration Training, and Staff Nurse, Queen Charlotte's Hosp., 1946–48; Ward Sister, 1948–50, Departmental Sister, 1950–52, St Mary's Hosp., Paddington; General Duty Nurse, Canada, 1952–53; Asst Matron, Gen. Infirmary, Leeds, 1953–57; Dep. Matron, Royal Free Hosp., London, 1957–59; Matron, Bristol Royal Hosp., 1959–67; Matron and Superintendent of Nursing, St Bartholomew's Hosp., 1968–69. Chm., Bristol Branch, Royal Coll. of Nursing, 1962–65; Member: Standing Nursing Adv. Cttee, Central Health Services Council, 1963–74; Exec. Cttee, Assoc. Nurse Administrators (formerly Assoc. Hosp. Matrons for England and Wales), 1963–74; Area Nurse Trng Cttee, SW Region, 1965–67; NE Metropolitan Area Nurse Training Cttee, 1969–74; E London Group Hosp. Management Cttee, 1969–74. Vice-Pres., Bristol Royal Hosp. Nurses League. *Recreations:* reading, travel, listening to music. *Address:* 26 Seaton Drive, Bedford MK40 3BG. *T:* (01234) 365868.

JONES, Air Vice-Marshal Rhys Tudor Brackley, CB 1990; FRCS; Senior Consultant, Royal Air Force Medical Branch, 1988–90; *b* 16 Nov. 1925; *s* of Sir Edgar Rees Jones, KBE and Lilian May Jones; *m* 1953, Irene Lilian, *d* of late Peter Valentine Spain Gammon; two *s*. *Educ:* King's Coll. Sch., Wimbledon; St Mary's Hosp., London (qualified 1950). House Surgeon to Mr Dickson-Wright and J. C. Goligher; joined RAF, 1952; Specialist in Surgery; Consultant, 1964; Hosp. service, Aden, Singapore, Germany, as gen. surgeon, special interest oncology; Hon. Consultant, Westminster Hosp., 1982; Cade Prof., RCS, 1981; Consultant Adviser in Surgery, 1982; Dean of Air Force Medicine, 1987. QHS, 1987–90. CStJ 1986. Lady Cade Medal, RCS, 1988. *Publications:* contribs to learned jls. *Address:* Westfield, Common Lane, Bale, near Fakenham, Norfolk NR21 0QD. *Club:* Royal Air Force.

JONES, Rev. Richard Granville; Chairman of East Anglia District, Methodist Church, 1983–93; President of the Methodist Conference, 1988–89; *b* 26 July 1926; *s* of Henry William and Ida Grace Jones; *m* 1955, Kathleen Stone; three *d*. *Educ:* Truro School, Cornwall; St John's Coll., Cambridge (MA); Manchester Univ. (BD). Instructor Officer, RN, 1947–49. Methodist Minister in Plymouth East, 1949–50; Area Sec., SCM, 1953–55; Minister: Sheffield North Circuit, 1955–59; Sheffield Carver Street, 1959–64; Birkenhead, 1964–69; Tutor, Hartley Victoria Coll., Manchester, 1969–78, Principal 1978–82; Minister, Fakenham and Wells Circuit, 1982–83. Editor, Epworth Review, 1991–. Hon. DD Hull, 1988. *Publications:* (ed) Worship for Today, 1968; (with A. Wesson) Towards a Radical Church, 1972; How goes Christian Marriage?, 1978; Groundwork of Worship and Preaching, 1980; Groundwork of Christian Ethics, 1984; What to Do?: Christians and ethics, 1999. *Recreations:* walking, reading, writing. *Address:* 35 Davies Road, West Bridgford, Nottingham NG2 5JE. *T:* (0115) 981 8597.

JONES, Richard Henry; QC 1996; a Recorder, since 2000; *b* 6 April 1950; *s* of Henry Ingham Jones and Betty Marian Jones; *m* 1989, Sarah Jane Wildsmith; one *s* one *d*. *Educ:* Moseley Grammar Sch., Birmingham; St Peter's Coll., Oxford (MA Jurisp.). Called to the Bar, Inner Temple, 1972; in practice, 1973–80; Legal Adviser: Crown Life Insurance Gp, 1980–82; Financial Times Gp, 1982–86; in practice, 1986–. *Recreations:* cricket and Rugby (spectating), sailing, ski-ing. *Address:* 3 Hare Court, Temple, EC4Y 7BJ. *T:* (020) 7415 7800. *Clubs:* Royal Automobile, MCC; Harlequins.

JONES, Richard M.; *see* Mansell-Jones.

JONES, (Robert) Alun; QC 1989; a Recorder, since 1992; *b* 19 March 1949; *s* of late Owen Glyn Jones and Violet Marion Jones (*née* Luxton); *m* 1974, Elizabeth Clayton; one *s* three *d*. *Educ:* Oldershaw Grammar Sch., Wallasey, Cheshire; Bristol Univ. (BSc 1970). Called to the Bar, Gray's Inn, 1972. Asst Recorder, 1988. Member: Senate of Inns of Court and the Bar, 1979–82; Gen. Council of the Bar, 1986–89; Sec., Criminal Bar Assoc., 1982–86. *Publication:* Jones on Extradition, 1995. *Recreations:* bridge, cricket, growing vegetables. *Address:* 3 Raymond Buildings, Gray's Inn, WC1R 5BH. *T:* (020) 7831 3833.

JONES, Robert Brannock; Chairman: Redrow plc, since 2000 (Director, since 1997); Framlington NetNet.Inc Investment Trust plc, since 2000; *b* 26 Sept. 1950; *s* of Ray Elwin Jones and Iris Pamela Jones; *m* 1989, Jennifer Anne, *d* of late Lewis Emmanuel Sandercock and of Iris Delphia Sandercock, Braunton, Devon. *Educ:* Merchant Taylors' Sch.; Univ. of St Andrews (MA Hons Modern History). Marketing Develt Exec., Tay Textiles Ltd, Dundee, 1974–76; Head of Res., NHBC, 1976–78; Housing Policy Adviser, Conservative Central Office, 1978–79; Parly Adviser, Fedn of Civil Engrg Contractors, 1979–83. Member: St Andrews Burgh Council, 1972–75; Fife CC, 1973–75; Chiltern DC, 1979–83; Dir, Freeport Leisure plc, 1998–. Vice-Pres., Assoc. of Dist Councils, 1983–94. MP (C) Hertfordshire West, 1983–97; contested (C) Hemel Hempstead, 1997. Parly Under-Sec. of State, DoE, 1994–95; Minister of State (Minister for Construction, Planning and Energy Efficiency), DoE, 1995–97. Chairman: Environment Select Cttee, 1992–94 (Mem., 1983–94); Cons. Party Orgn Cttee, 1986–94. Freeport Leisure plc, 1998–. Vice-Pres., Wildlife Hosp. Trust, 1985–. Freeman, City of London; Liveryman, Merchant Taylors' Co. *Publications:* New Approaches to Housing, 1976; Watchdog: guide to the role of the district auditor, 1978; Ratepayers' Defence Manual, 1980; Town and Country Chaos: critique of the planning system, 1982. *Recreations:* music, gardening, food and wine. *Address:* Palmer's Barn, Station Road, Long Marston, Tring, Herts HP23 4QS.

JONES, Dr (Robert) Brinley, CBE 2000; FSA; President, National Library of Wales, since 1996 (Member, Court and Council, 1974–82); Chairman, Cathedrals and Churches Commission of the Church in Wales, since 1994; *b* 27 Feb. 1929; *yr s* of John Elias Jones and Mary Ann Jones (*née* Williams); *m* 1971, Stephanie Avril Hall; one *s*. *Educ:* Tonypandy Grammar Sch.; University Coll. Cardiff (BA Wales 1st cl. Hons 1950; DipEd 1951; Fellow 1984); Jesus Coll., Oxford (DPhil 1960); Internat. Inst. for Advanced Studies, Clayton, Mo (MA 1984). FSA 1971. Commissioned RAF, 1955; Educn Officer, RAF Kidlington and Bicester, 1955–58. Asst Master, Penarth Grammar Sch., 1958–60; Lectr, UC Swansea, 1960–66; Asst Registrar, Univ. of Wales, 1966–69; Dir, Univ. of Wales Press, 1969–76; Warden, Llandovery Coll., 1976–88. Member: Literature Cttee, Welsh Arts Council, 1968–74, 1981–1987; Bd, British Council, 1987–96 (Chm., Welsh Cttee, 1987–96); Broadcasting Standards Council, 1988–91. Chairman: European Assoc. of Teachers, 1965; Dinefwr Tourism Gp, 1988–96; Carmarthenshire Tourist Forum, 1998–. Member: Court, Univ. of Wales, 1997–; Council, St David's UC (later Univ. of Wales), Lampeter, 1977–95 (Hon. Fellow 1987); Court, UC Swansea (later Univ. of Wales, Swansea), 1983–; Council, Univ. of Wales, Aberystwyth, 1997–; Court, Univ. of Wales, Cardiff, 1997–; Council, Trinity Coll., Carmarthen, 1984– (Vice-Chm., 1998–); Governing Body, Church in Wales, 1981– (Chairman: Provincial Validating Bd for Ministerial Educn, 1990–; Church in Wales Publications, 1998–); Managing Trustee, St Michael's Theol Coll., 1982–94. Hon. Mem., Druidic Order, Gorsedd of Bards, 1979–; Mem., Welsh Acad., 1981–; Vice-Pres., Llangollen Internat. Musical Eisteddfod, 1989–. Fellow, Royal Commonwealth Soc., 1988–91. Editor, The European Teacher, 1964–69. Hon. DD Faraston Theol Seminary, Longview, WA, 1993; Hon. DLitt Greenwich, 1997. *Publications:* The Old British Tongue, 1970; (ed and contrib.) Anatomy of Wales, 1972; (ed with M. Stephens) Writers of Wales, 1970– (100 titles published by 2000); (ed with R. Bromwich) Astudiaethau ar yr Hengerdd: studies in old Welsh poetry, 1978; Introducing Wales, 1978, 3rd edn 1988; Prifysgol Rhydychen a'i Chysylltiadau Cymreig, 1983; Certain Scholars of Wales, 1986; (ed with D. Ellis Evans) Cofio'r Dafydd, 1987; (contrib.) C. N. D. Cole, The New Wales, 1990; (introd.) Songs of Praises: the English hymns and elegies of William Williams Pantycelyn 1717–1791, 1991, 2nd edn 1995; Prize Days: a headmaster remembers his school 1976–1987, 1993; William Salesbury, 1994; A Lanterne to their Feete: remembering Rhys Prichard 1579–1644, 1994; Floreat Landubriense, 1998; The Particularity of Wales, 2001; articles and reviews in learned jls. *Recreations:* music, farming, walking. *Address:* Drovers Farm, Porthyrhyd, Llanwrda, Dyfed SA19 8DF. *T:* (01558) 650649.

JONES, Sir Robert (Edward), Kt 1989; author; sporting and political commentator; Founder Chairman, Robt Jones Investments Ltd, 1982–92; *b* 24 Nov. 1939; *s* of Edward Llewyllan and Joyce Lillian Jones; *m* (marr. diss.); two *s* five *d*. *Educ:* Victoria Univ. of Wellington. Leader, New Zealand Party, Gen. Elect., 1984. Chm., NZ Winter Olympics Cttee, 1988. New Zealand Commemoration Medal, 1990. *Publications:* New Zealand Boxing Yearbooks, 1972 and 1973; Jones on Property, 1977, 6th edn 1979; NZ The Way I Want It, 1978; Travelling, 1980; Letters, 1981; The Permit (a philosophic novel), 1984; Wimp Walloping, 1989; Prancing Pavonine Charlatans, 1990; 80's Letters, 1990; Punchlines, 1991; A Year of It, 1992; Treading Water, 1993; Prosperity Denied—How the Reserve Bank Harms New Zealand, 1996; Memories of Muldoon, 1997; Full Circle (novel), 2000. *Recreations:* reading, writing, gardening, trout-fishing, tennis, travel, golf, wind-surfing. *Address:* Melling, Lower Hutt, New Zealand; Darling Point, Sydney, Australia.

JONES, Robert Hefin, CVO 1969; PhD; Under Secretary, Welsh Office, 1980–92; *b* 30 June 1932; *s* of late Owen Henry and Elizabeth Jones, Blaenau Ffestiniog. *Educ:* Ysgol Sir Ffestiniog; University Coll. of Wales, Aberystwyth (BSc); University of London (PhD). Asst Master, Whitgift Sch., 1957–63; HM Inspector of Schools (Wales), 1963; seconded to Welsh Office as Sec., Prince of Wales Investiture Cttee, and Personal Asst to the Earl Marshal, 1967; Welsh Office: Principal, 1969; Asst Sec. 1972; Hd, Educn Dept, 1980–92. Member: HEFCW, 1992–95; Council on Tribunals, 1993–99. Dir, WNO, 1992–94; Mem., Welsh Cttee, Live Music Now, 1992–. *Recreations:* music, reading, cooking. *Address:* 34 The Grange, Llandaff, Cardiff CF5 2LH. *T:* (029) 2056 4573.

JONES, Prof. Robert Maynard, FBA 1993; Fellow, Yr Academi Gymreig, 1995; Professor of Welsh Language and Literature, University of Wales, 1980–89, now Professor Emeritus; *b* 20 May 1929; *s* of Sydney Valentine Jones and Mary Edith Jones; *m* 1952, Anne Elizabeth James; one *s* one *d*. *Educ:* Univ. of Wales (BA 1949; MA 1951; PhD 1965; DLitt 1979); Univ. of Ireland; Laval Univ., Québec. Teaching in Llanidloes and Llangefni, 1952–56; Lectr, Trinity Coll., Carmarthen, 1956–58; University of Wales, Aberystwyth: Lectr in Educn, 1958–66; Lectr, Sen. Lectr, Reader, Prof. and Head of Dept of Welsh Language and Literature, 1966–89. Chm., Yr Academi Gymreig (Welsh Acad. of Letters), 1975–79; Vice-President, UCCF, 1990–95. *Publications include:* Y Gân Gyntaf, 1957; Crwydro Môn, 1957; Nid yw Dŵr yn Plygu, 1958; I'r Arch, 1959; Y Tair Rhamant, 1960; Bod yn Wraig, 1960; Rhwng Taf a Thaf, 1960; Graddio Geirfa, 1962; Émile, 1963; Cyflwyno'r Gymraeg, 1964; Cymraeg i Oedolion, I & II, 1965–66; Y Dyn na Ddaeth Adref, 1966; Yr Ŵyl Ifori, 1967; Ci wrth y Drws, 1968; Highlights in Welsh Literature, 1969; Daw'r Pasg i Bawb, 1969; System in Child Language, 1970; Pedwar Emynydd, 1970; Sioc o'r Gofod, 1971; Allor Wydn, 1971; Traed Prydferth, 1973; Tafod y Llenor, 1974; (with M. E. Roberts) Cyfeiriadur i'r Athro Iaith I–III, 1974–79; Llenyddiaeth Gymraeg 1936–1972, 1975; Gwlad Llun, 1976; Llên Cymru a Chrefydd, 1977; Pwy laddodd Miss Wales, 1977; Seiliau Beirniadaeth, 4 vols, 1984–88; Hunllef Arthur, 1986; (with Gwyn Davies) The Christian Heritage of Welsh Education, 1986; (with Gwyn Thomas) The Dragon's Pen, 1986; Llenyddiaeth Gymraeg 1902–1936, 1987; Selected Poems (trans. Joseph P. Clancy), 1987; Blodeugerdd Barddas o'r 19 Ganrif, 1988; (with Rhiannon Ifans) Gloywi Iaith I–III, 1988; Casgliad o Gerddi, 1989; Crio Chwerthin, 1990; Dawn Gweddwon, 1991; Language Regained, 1993; Cyfriniaeth Gymraeg, 1994; Canu Arnaf, Vol. I, 1994, Vol. II, 1995; Crist a Chenedlaetholdeb, 1994; Epistol Serch a Selsig, 1997; Tair Rhamant Arthuraidd, 1998; Ysbryd y Cwlwm, 1998; Ynghylch Tawelwch, 1998; O'r Bedd i'r Crud, 2000; Mawl a'i Gyfeillion, 2000. *Recreation:* walking. *Address:* Tandderwen, Ffordd Llanbadarn, Aberystwyth SY23 1HB. *T:* (01970) 623603.

JONES, Robin Francis McN.; *see* McNab Jones.

JONES, Roger; *see* Jones, James R.

JONES, Roger Charles M.; *see* Moylan-Jones.

JONES, Roger Kenneth; management consultant, since 1998; Secretary, Co-operative Wholesale Society, 1996–98; *b* 10 Sept. 1947; *s* of George Ephraim Jones and Winifred Annie Jones; *m* 1972, Caroline Ruth Proctor; three *d*. *Educ:* Abbeydale Grammar Sch., Sheffield; Manchester Univ. (BA Hons Econs 1969). Called to the Bar, Gray's Inn, 1977; Asst Sec., Manchester Ship Canal Co., 1977–83; Dep. Sec., CWS Ltd, 1983–96; Secretary: Unity Trust Bank, PLC, 1984–92; Co-operative Bank PLC, 1992–96. Mem., UK Co-operative Council, 1991–98. Hon. Pres., Co-operative Law Assoc., 1999–.

JONES, Roger Spencer, OBE 1996; National Governor for Wales, BBC, since 1997; Chairman, Welsh Development Agency, since 2002; *b* 2 July 1943; *s* of Richard David Jones and Gwladys Jones; *m* 1970, Ann Evans; one *s* one *d*. *Educ:* Bala Boys' Grammar Sch.; Univ. of Wales (BPharm); Univ. of Bradford (MSc). MRPharmS 1968. Area Manager, then Marketing Planning Manager, Wellcome Foundn Ltd, 1968–82; Man. Dir, Nigeria, Smith Kline & French Ltd, 1982–83; with Penn Pharmaceuticals Ltd, 1983–2000 (Chm., 1986–2000). Chairman: Gwent TEC, 1993–98; TEC SE Wales, 1998–2000; Council of Welsh TECs, 1995–2001. Non-exec. Dir, Powys Healthcare NHS Trust, 1993–2000. Chm., Wales Inst. of Dirs, 1995–. Chm., Children in Need, 1999–. Pres., YMCA Wales, 2000–. DUniv Glamorgan, 1997; Hon. DSc Wales, 2000. *Recreations:* salmon and trout fishing, shooting, nature conservation. *Address:* Battle House, Battle, Brecon LD3 9RW. *T:* (01874) 611777. *Club:* Athenæum.

JONES, Prof. Ronald Mervyn, MD; FRCA; Director of Continuing Education and Professional Development, and Editor of Bulletin, Royal College of Anaesthetists, since 1999; *b* 24 April 1947; *s* of Comdr Glyn Owen Jones, RN and Doris Woodley Jones; *m* 1st, 1970, Angela Christine Parsonage (marr. diss.); one *s* one *d*; 2nd, 1989, Caroline Ann Marshall; two *d*. *Educ:* Devonport High Sch., Plymouth; Univ. of Liverpool (MB ChB 1971; MD 1990). FRCA 1978. Karolinska Inst., Stockholm, 1978; Univ. of Michigan, 1979–80; Consultant, Nottingham Hosps, 1981–82; Sen. Lectr and Hon. Consultant, Guy's Hosp. and Med. Sch., 1982–90; Foundn Prof. of Anaesthetics and Hd of Dept, ICSM at St Mary's, London, 1990–99. Mem. Council, Royal Coll. of Anaesthetists, 1997–. Academician, European Acad. Anaesthesiologists, 1984; Hon. Life Mem., Australian Soc. Anaesthetists, 1988. *Publications:* (ed jtly) Medicine for Anaesthetists, 3rd edn 1989; (ed jtly) Clinical Anaesthesia, 1996. *Recreations:* art history, sailing. *Address:* Royal College of Anaesthetists, 48–49 Russell Square, WC1B 4JY. *Club:* Old Sarum Flying.

JONES, Prof. Ronald Samuel, OBE 1998; JP; DVSc; FRCVS; FIBiol; Professor of Veterinary Anaesthesia, since 1991, and Head of Department of Anaesthesia, since 1995, University of Liverpool; *b* 29 Oct. 1937; *s* of Samuel and Gladys Jane Jones; *m* 1962, Pamela Evans; two *d. Educ:* High Sch. for Boys, Oswestry; Univ. of Liverpool (BVSc 1960; MVSc; DVA); DrMedVet Berne, 1980; DVSc Pretoria, 1991. FRCVS 1981; FIBiol 1987. University of Glasgow: house surgeon, 1960–61; Asst, 1961–62; University of Liverpool: Lectr, 1962–77; Sen. Lectr, 1977–86; Reader, 1986–90; Dean, Faculty of Vet. Sci., 1989–93. Visiting Professor: Univ. of Zurich, 1975; Cornell Univ., 1980, 1993; Univ. of Pretoria, 1994. Member: Home Office Adv. Council on the Misuse of Drugs, 1994–; Medicines Commn, 1997–. Royal College of Veterinary Surgeons: Mem. Council, 1986–98; Treas., 1993–95; Jun. Vice-Pres., 1995–96; Pres., 1996–97; Sen. Vice-Pres., 1997–98. Mem., EC Adv. Cttee of Vet. Trng, 1990–93. FRSA 1996. JP Liverpool City, 1981. John Henry Steele Medal, RCVS, 1989; Coll. Medal, Royal Coll. Anaesthetists, 1996. *Publications:* (jtly) Principles of Veterinary Therapeutics, 1994; contrib. chapters to books and vet. and med. jls. *Recreations:* horse-racing, fly-fishing, vegetable gardening. *Address:* 7 Birch Road, Prenton, Merseyside CH43 5UF. *T:* (0151) 653 9008. *Clubs:* Farmers', Royal Society of Medicine.

JONES, Group Captain Royden Anthony; RAF retired; Regional Chairman of Industrial Tribunals, London (Central) Region, 1975–86; *b* 11 June 1925; *s* of Daniel Richard Glyndwr Jones and Hilda Margaret Jones (*née* Carruthers); *m* 1st, 1948, Krystyna Emilia Kumor (decd); one *s*; 2nd, 1955, Peggy Elizabeth Martin; one *s. Educ:* Torquay Grammar Sch. Trooper, Household Cavalry, 1943; RMC, Sandhurst, 1944; Captain, Arab Legion armoured car squadron, 1945–48. Qualified as solicitor, 1949; joined RAF Legal Services as prosecuting officer, 1950; RAF Staff Coll., 1961; served as Dep. Dir of Legal Services (RAF), in Cyprus and Germany, retiring as Gp Captain, 1975. *Publication:* Manual of Law for Kenya Armed Forces, 1971. *Recreations:* country pursuits, reading, house maintenance, photography. *Address:* Hill Top House, Staunton Harold, Ashby-de-la-Zouch, Leics LE65 1RW. *T:* (01332) 862583. *Club:* Royal Air Force.

JONES, Samuel, CBE 1996; DL; Chairman, Westcountry Ambulance Service NHS Trust, since 1996; Town Clerk, Corporation of London, 1991–96; *b* 27 Dec. 1939; *s* of late Samuel Jones and Sarah Johnston Jones (*née* McCulloch); *m* 1964, Jean Ann Broadhurst; two *d. Educ:* Morpeth Grammar Sch.; Manchester Univ. (LLB); Kent Univ. (MA). Admitted Solicitor, 1964. Asst Solicitor, Macclesfield Bor. Council, 1964–67; Asst Town Clerk, Bedford Bor. Council, 1967–71; Head of Legal Div., Coventry CBC, 1971–73; Head of Admin and Legal Dept, Sheffield Dist Council, 1973–76; Chief Exec. and County Clerk, Leics CC, and Clerk of Lieutenancy, 1976–91. Mem., Council on Tribunals, 1996–. Chairman: Heathrow Airport Consultative Cttee, 1997–; N Devon Marketing Bureau, 1996–98. DL Leics, 1992. *Recreations:* dog and coastal walking. *Address:* Middleborough House, Croyde, Devon EX33 1PA. *T:* (01271) 890210.

JONES, Sarah Louise R.; *see* Rowland-Jones.

JONES, Schuyler, CBE 1998; DPhil; Director (formerly Curator and Head of Department of Ethnology and Prehistory), Pitt Rivers Museum, 1985–97, and Fellow of Linacre College, 1970–97, now Emeritus Professor, Oxford University; *b* 7 Feb. 1930; *s* of Schuyler Jones, Jr and Ignace Mead Jones; *m* 1st, 1955, Lis Margit Søndergaard Rasmussen; one *s* one *d*; 2nd, 1998, Lorraine Christine Da'Luz Vieira. *Educ:* Edinburgh Univ. (MA Hons Anthropology); Oxford Univ. (DPhil Anthropology). Anthropological expeditions to: Atlas Mountains, Southern Algeria, French West Africa, Nigeria, 1951; French Equatorial Africa, Belgian Congo, 1952; East and Southern Africa, 1953; Morocco High Atlas, Algeria, Sahara, Niger River, 1954; Turkey, Iran, Afghanistan, Pakistan, India, Nepal, 1958–59; ten expeditions to Nuristan in the Hindu Kush, 1960–70; to Chinese Turkestan, 1985; Tibet and Gobi Desert, 1986; Southern China, Xinjiang, and Pakistan, 1988; Western Greenland, 1991; Greenland and E Africa, 1993. Asst Curator, Pitt Rivers Mus., 1970–71; Asst Curator and Univ. Lectr in Ethnology, 1971–85. Mem. Council, Royal Anthropological Inst., 1986–89. Trustee, Horniman Mus., 1989–94. *Publications:* Sous le Soleil Africain, 1955 (Under the African Sun, 1956); Annotated Bibliography of Nuristan (Kafiristan) and The Kalash Kafirs of Chitral, pt 1 1966, pt 2 1969; The Political Organization of the Kam Kafirs, 1967; Men of Influence in Nuristan, 1974; (jtly) Nuristan, 1979; Afghanistan, 1992; Tibetan Nomads: environment, pastoral economy and material culture, 1996; numerous articles. *Recreation:* travel in remote places. *Address:* c/o Pitt Rivers Museum, University of Oxford, South Parks Road, Oxford OX1 3PP.

JONES, Sir Simon (Warley Frederick) Benton, 4th Bt *cr* 1919; JP; *b* 11 Sept. 1941; *o s* of Sir Peter Fawcett Benton Jones, 3rd Bt, OBE, and Nancy Benton Jones (*d* 1974); *S* father, 1972; *m* 1966, Margaret Fiona (OBE 1995, DL), *d* of David Rutherford Dickson; three *s* two *d. Educ:* Eton; Trinity College, Cambridge (MA). JP Lincolnshire, 1971 (Chm., Lincs Magistrates' Courts Cttee, 1996–2000); High Sheriff, Lincs, 1977. *Heir: s* James Peter Martin Benton Jones [*b* 1 Jan. 1973; *m* 1997, Lucy Briggs (marr. diss. 2000)]. *Address:* Irnham Hall, Grantham, Lincs NG33 4JD. *T:* (01476) 550212; 19 Sopley, Christchurch, Dorset BH23 7AX.

JONES, Stephen; *see* Jones, John S.

JONES, Stephen Morris; Chief Executive, Wigan Metropolitan Borough Council, since 1990; *b* 12 March 1948; *s* of Owain Morris Jones and late Sylvia Blanche Jones (*née* Moss); *m* 1970, Rosemary Diana Pilgrim; one *s* two *d. Educ:* Univ. of Manchester (BA Hons Town Planning, 1970). MRTPI 1972. Asst Chief Exec., Bolton MBC, 1978–85; Chief Exec., Blackburn BC, 1985–90. Mem., Soc. of Local Govt Chief Execs, 1985–. *Recreations:* family, walking, sport, reading. *Address:* Wigan Metropolitan Borough Council, Town Hall, PO Box 36, Library Street, Wigan WN1 1YN. *T:* (01942) 827001.

JONES, Stephen O.; *see* Oliver-Jones.

JONES, Stephen Roger Curtis; Chairman of Governors, Centre for Information on Language Teaching and Research, since 1996; *b* 31 March 1944; *s* of Roger Henry Curtis Jones and Kate Alice Jones (*née* Pearson); *m* 1973, Janet Corkett; two *d. Educ:* Brentwood Sch., Essex; Univ. of Southampton (BA Hons French 1967; MA French 1968); Cambridge/RSA Cert. TEFLA, 1996. MoD, 1968–71; UK Delegn to NATO, 1971–73; DES, 1973–81 (Private Sec. to Sec. of State, Rt Hon. Shirley Williams, 1976–78); Asst Dir, City of London Poly., 1982–85; Department of Education and Science: Staff Inspector, HM Inspectorate, 1986–88; Head, Internat. Relations Div., 1988–92; Head of Internat. Relns, Youth and Gen. Br., DFE, 1992–94. FRSA 2000. *Recreations:* walking, choral singing. *Address:* Marne, Southdown Road, Woldingham, Surrey CR3 7DP. *T:* (01883) 653145; 14 Ave Albert Ier, 34480 Pouzolles, France. *T:* and *Fax:* 467247611; *e-mail:* stephen.jones@wanadoo.fr.

JONES, Stewart Elgan; QC 1994; a Recorder, since 1990; *b* 20 Jan. 1945; *s* of late Gwilym John Jones and of Elizabeth (*née* Davies); *m* 1979, Jennifer Anne (*née* Syddall); two *d*, and one step *s* one step *d. Educ:* Cheltenham Coll.; Queen's Coll., Oxford (MA Mod. Langs). Called to the Bar, Gray's Inn, 1972; Mem., Western Circuit. *Recreations:* home, hearth, the great outdoors. *Address:* 3 Paper Buildings, Temple, EC4Y 7EU. *T:* (020) 7583 8055. *Club:* Athenæum.

JONES, Rev. Stewart William; Archbishop of Canterbury's Diocesan Chaplain and Tait Missioner, since 1997; Priest-in-charge, All Saints', Canterbury, since 2001; *b* 17 March 1957; *s* of William Jones and Nettie Jean Jones; *m* 1st, 1982, Susan Kathleen Griffith (*d* 1990); one *d*; 2nd, 1992, Julie Marie Perkin; one *s* one *d. Educ:* Heriot-Watt Univ. (BA Hons Business Orgn); Bristol Univ. (Dip. Social Admin); Trinity Coll., Bristol (BA Hons Theol.). Grad. mgt trainee, National Westminster Bank, 1979–80; worker, Bristol Cyrenians, 1980–81; Supervisor, Bristol Churches Community Prog., 1983–85; ordained deacon 1988, priest 1989; Curate, St Mary's, Stoke Bishop, Bristol, 1988–92; Priest-in-charge, St Luke's, Brislington, Bristol, 1992–97. *Publications:* The Teaching of Jesus, 1994; The Touch of Jesus, 1995. *Recreations:* swimming, cooking, sport on TV, films, reading. *Address:* All Saints' Vicarage, Military Road, Canterbury, Kent CT1 1PA.

JONES, Dr (Sybil) Angela (Margaret), (Mrs Michael Pearson), FFPHM; Consultant in Public Health Medicine, North (formerly North West) Thames Regional Health Authority, 1985–96; *b* 23 Aug. 1940; *d* of Cyril and Ida Jones; *m* 1964, Dr Michael Pearson; three *s* one *d. Educ:* Cranford House Sch.; King's College London (AKC); King's Coll. Hosp. (MB BS). Dist MO, Victoria Health Authy, 1982–85. Member: Tech. Sub-Gp of Achieving a Balance, 1988–92; Standing Cttee on Postgrad. Med. Educn, 1989–96 (Chm., working gp on Health of the Nation); Jt Planning Adv. Cttee, 1988–92; Chm., Regl Med. Manpower and Personnel Gp, 1988–92. *Publications:* articles on med. manpower and public health issues in learned jls. *Recreations:* opera, dining with friends. *Address:* Flat 8, 7 Weymouth Mews, W1N 3FS. *T:* (020) 7436 0999.

JONES, Terence Leavesley; Under-Secretary, Department of the Environment, 1974–84; *b* 24 May 1926; *s* of late Reginald Arthur Jones and Grace Jones; *m* 1966, Barbara Hall; one *s. Educ:* Nottingham High Sch.; Jesus Coll., Cambridge (MA). RNVR, 1944–46 (Sub-Lt). Asst Inspector of Ancient Monuments, Min. of Works, 1949; Principal, 1957; Sec., Historic Buildings Council for England, 1961–67; Asst Sec., 1967; on loan to Housing Corp., 1979–81. *Recreations:* music, archæology. *Address:* Meadow View, Woodlands Road, Mildenhall, Marlborough, Wilts SN8 2LP. *T:* (01672) 512481.

JONES, Prof. Terence Valentine, FREng; Donald Schultz Professor of Turbomachinery, since 1988, and Director, Technology Centre in Aerodynamics and Heat Transfer, since 1993, Oxford University; Professorial Fellow, St Catherine's College, Oxford, since 1988; *b* 14 Feb. 1939; *s* of Albert Duncalf Jones and Frances Jones; *m* 1962, Lesley Lillian (*née* Hughes); one *s* one *d. Educ:* William Hulme's Grammar School, Manchester; Lincoln College, Oxford (MA, DPhil 1966). Lecturer: Keble College, Oxford, 1971–77; Lincoln College, Oxford, 1976–80; Jesus College, Oxford, 1977–86; Rolls Royce Tutorial Fellow, St Anne's College, Oxford, 1979–88. Senior Academic Visitor, NASA Lewis Research Center, Ohio, 1986. FREng 2000. Royal Soc. Esso Energy Award, 1996. *Publications:* articles on turbomachinery, heat transfer and fluid dynamics in NATO, ASME and ARC jls and conf. procs. *Recreations:* hiking, paragliding. *Address:* Department of Engineering Science, Parks Road, Oxford OX1 3PJ. *T:* (01865) 288734.

JONES, Terry, (Terence Graham Parry Jones); writer, film director and occasional performer; *b* 1 Feb. 1942; *s* of Alick George Parry Jones and Dilys Louisa Newnes; *m* Alison Telfer; one *s* one *d. Educ:* Esher C of E Primary Sch.; Royal Grammar Sch., Guildford; St Edmund Hall, Oxford. *Television:* wrote for various TV shows, 1966–68; wrote and performed in series: Do Not Adjust Your Set, 1968–69; The Complete and Utter History of Britain, 1969; Monty Python's Flying Circus, 1969–75; wrote (with Michael Palin): Secrets (play), BBC TV, 1974; Ripping Yarns, 1976–79; presented: Paperbacks, BBC TV; Victorian Values, BBC Radio; wrote and directed The Rupert Bear Story (documentary), 1981; wrote, directed and presented, So This Is Progress, BBC TV, 1991; co-wrote and presented, Crusades, BBC TV, 1995; Ancient Inventions, 1999; Gladiators, the Brutal Truth, 2000. *Films:* And Now For Something Completely Different, 1971; directed (with Terry Gilliam), co-wrote and performed, Monty Python and the Holy Grail, 1975; directed, co-wrote and performed: Monty Python's Life of Brian, 1978; Monty Python's Meaning of Life, 1983 (Grand Prix Spécial du Jury, Cannes); directed Personal Services, 1986; wrote, directed and performed: Erik the Viking, 1989; The Wind in the Willows, 1996; Asterix and Obelix (English version), 2000. *Publications:* Chaucer's Knight, 1980, 3rd edn 1984; Fairy Tales, 1981, 4th edn 1987; The Saga of Erik the Viking, 1983, 3rd edn 1986; Nicobobinus, 1985, 2nd edn 1987; Goblins of the Labyrinth, 1986; The Curse of the Vampire's Socks, 1988; Attacks of Opinion, 1988; Fantastic Stories, 1992; (with Brian Froud) Lady Cottington's Pressed Fairy Book, 1994; (with Alan Ereira) Crusades, 1994; The Knight and the Squire, 1997; (with Brian Froud) Lady Cottington's Pressed Fairy Journal, 1998; The Lady and the Squire, 2000; Who Murdered Chaucer?, 2000; (with Michael Palin): Dr Fegg's Encyclopeadia (sic) of all World Knowledge, etc; Ripping Yarns, etc; contrib. to the various Monty Python books. *Recreation:* sleeping. *Address:* c/o Python (Monty) Pictures, 34 Thistlewaite Road, E5 0QQ.

JONES, Thomas E.; *see* Elder-Jones.

JONES, Thomas Glanville; barrister; a Recorder of the Crown Court, 1972–99; *b* 10 May 1931; *s* of late Evan James and Margaret Olive Jones; Welsh; *m* 1964, Valma Shirley Jones; three *s. Educ:* St Clement Dane's Grammar Sch.; University Coll., London (LLB). Called to Bar, 1956. Hd of Angel Chambers, 1972–. Chm., Jt Professional Cttees of Swansea Local Bar and Swansea Law Soc. and W Wales Law Soc., 1976–; Founder Mem. and Exec. Cttee Mem., Wales Medico-Legal Soc., 1990; Founder Mem. and Trustee, Swansea Legal Charitable Foundn, 1994. Exec. Mem., Swansea Festival of Music and the Arts, 1967; Pres., Guild for Promotion of Welsh Music, 1996– (Chm., 1970); Mem., Grand Theatre Trust, 1988–. *Recreations:* Welsh culture, Rugby, reading, music, poetry, gardening. *Address:* Angel Chambers, 94 Walter Road, Swansea SA1 5QA. *T:* (01792) 464623; Gelligron, 12 Eastcliff, Southgate, Swansea SA3 2AS. *T:* (01441) 283118. *Club:* Ffynone (Swansea).

JONES, Ven. (Thomas) Hughie; Archdeacon of Loughborough, 1986–92, now Emeritus; *b* 15 Aug. 1927; *s* of Edward Teifi Jones and Ellen Jones; *m* 1949, Beryl Joan Henderson; two *d. Educ:* William Hulme's Grammar School, Manchester; Univ. of Wales (BA, LLM); Univ. of London (BD); Univ. of Leicester (MA). Warden and Lectr, Bible Trng Inst., Glasgow, 1949–54; Minister, John Street Baptist Church, Glasgow, 1951–54; RE specialist, Leicester and Leics schs, 1955–63; Sen. Lectr in RE, Leicester Coll. of Educn, 1964–70; deacon 1966, priest 1967; Vice-Principal, Bosworth Coll., 1970–75; Principal, Hind Leys College, Leics, 1975–81; Rector, The Langtons and Stonton Wyville, 1981–86. Hon. Canon of Leicester Cathedral, 1983–86. Bishop's Officer, Clergy

Widows and Retired Clergy, Ecclesiastical Law Soc., 1996– (Vice-Chm., 1990; Hon. Exec. Officer, 1993–96); Member: Selden Soc., 1991; Canon Law Soc. of GB and Ireland, 1993. *Publications:* (contrib. OT articles) New Bible Dictionary, 1962, 2nd edn 1980; Old Testament, religious education and canon law articles in relevant jls. *Recreations:* entomology, genealogy, Welsh interests, canon law. *Address:* Four Trees, 68 Main Street, Thorpe Satchville, Melton Mowbray, Leics LE14 2DQ. *Clubs:* Carlton, Millbank; Leicestershire (Leicester).

JONES, Sir Tim; *see* Jones, Sir E. R. H.

JONES, Timothy; *see* Jones, D. T.

JONES, Timothy Aidan; HM Diplomatic Service; Ambassador to Armenia, since 1999; *b* 5 Sept. 1962; *s* of Dr Derek Hugh Powell Jones and Thelma Anne (*née* Gray); *m* 2001, Dr Christin Marshall. *Educ:* Bexhill Co. Grammar Sch.; Christ's Coll., Cambridge (BA Hons 1984). Joined HM Diplomatic Service, 1984: Vienna (CSCE), 1987–88; The Hague, 1988–92; FCO, 1992–94; EU Admin, Mostar, 1994–95; Dep. Head of Mission, Tehran, 1996–99. *Recreations:* swimming, cycling, idle curiosity. *Address:* c/o Foreign and Commonwealth Office, King Charles Street, SW1A 2AH.

JONES, Tom; *see* Woodward, T. J.

JONES, Sir Trevor; *see* Jones, Sir O. T.

JONES, Trevor; Chief Executive, NHS Scotland and Head of Health Department, Scottish Executive, since 2000; *b* 23 Dec. 1950; *s* of John Jones and Florence Mary Jones (*née* Rogerson); *m* 1974, Hazel Oliver. Local Govt Finance, 1969–78; Sen. Asst Regl Treas., Northern RHA, 1978; Dep. Treas., S Manchester HA, 1983; Waltham Forest Health Authority: Dir of Finance, 1986; Dist Gen. Manager, 1989–92; Chief Exec., Forest Healthcare NHS Trust, 1992–95; Gen. Manager, then Chief Exec., Lothian Health Bd, 1995–2000. Chm., Gen. Managers' Gp, Scottish Health Bd, 1998–2000. CPFA, FCCA, ACIS; MIMgt. *Recreations:* golf, squash, photography. *Address:* St Andrews House, Regent Road, Edinburgh EH1 3DG. *Clubs:* Durham CC; Sunderland AF.

JONES, Trevor David K.; *see* Kent-Jones.

JONES, Trevor Mervyn, PhD; FRSC, FPS; Director-General, Association of the British Pharmaceutical Industry, since 1994; *b* 19 Aug. 1942; *s* of Samuel James Jones and Hilda May Jones (*née* Walley); *m* 1966, Verity Ann Bates; one *s* one *d.* *Educ:* Wolverhampton Grammar Sch.; King's Coll. London (BPharm Hons 1964; PhD 1967; FKC 1994). CChem 1975; FRSC 1978; FPS 1987; MCPP 1982. Lectr, Univ. of Nottingham, 1967–72; Hd of Pharmaceutical Develt, Boots Co. Ltd, 1972–76; Develt Dir, Wellcome Foundation Ltd, 1976–87; R&D Dir and Mem. Bd, Wellcome plc, 1987–94. Director: Wellcome Biotechnology Ltd, 1983–93; Wellgen Inc. USA, 1990–93; Merlin Partners, 1996– (Chm., Scientific Adv. Bd, 1996–). Visiting Professor: KCL, 1984–; Univ. of Strathclyde, 1988–93; Adjunct Prof., Univ. of N Carolina, 1985–90. Non-executive Chairman: Health Reform Investment Trust plc, 1996–98; ReNeuron, 2000–; Chm., Kinetique Biomedical Seed Fund, 2001–. Member: Expert Cttees, British Pharmacopoeia, 1976–89; Pharmacy Res. Bd, CNAA, 1978–83; UK Govt Medicines Commn, 1982–94; Adv. Bd on Human Genome, Cabinet Office, 1991–96; Expert Wkg Party on Use of Tissues, Nuffield Council for Bioethics, 1992–97; Exec. Cttee, Internat. Fedn of Pharmaceutical Manufrs, 1994–; Bd of Mgt, European Fedn of Pharmaceutical Industry Assoc., 1994–; Nat. Biological Standards Bd Review, 1995–97; Pres., Internat. Commn on Technology, 1979–83, Mem., Pharmaceut. Scis Bd, 1980–84, 1996–, Fédn Internat. Pharmaceutique. Trustee: Epilepsy Res. Foundn, 1996–; Northwick Park Inst. of Med. Res., 1998–. Liveryman, Co. of Apothecaries, 1989–. Hon. FFPM 1995; Hon. Fellow, London Sch. of Pharmacy, 1998. Hon. PhD Athens, 1993; Hon. DSc: Strathclyde, 1994; Nottingham, 1998; Bath, 2000. Harrison Meml Medal, 1987, Charter Gold Medal, 1996, RPSGB; Gold Medal, Comenius Univ., 1992. *Publications:* Drug Delivery to the Respiratory Tract, 1987; Advances in Pharmaceutical Sciences, 1993. *Recreations:* golf, gardening, Wales RU. *Address:* Association of the British Pharmaceutical Industry, 12 Whitehall, SW1A 2DY. *T:* (020) 7747 1424. *Clubs:* Athenæum; Surrey CC.

JONES, Ven. Trevor Pryce; Archdeacon of Hertford, since 1997; *b* 24 April 1948; *s* of John Pryce Jones and Annie (*née* Jepson); *m* 1976, Susan Diane Pengelley; one *s* one *d.* *Educ:* Dial Stone Sch., Stockport; St Luke's Coll., Exeter; Univ. of Southampton (BEd, BTh); Salisbury and Wells Theol Coll. Asst Teacher and Lay Chaplain, Shaftesbury Grammar Sch., 1969–73; ordained deacon, 1976, priest, 1977; Asst Curate, Gloucester St George, Lower Tuffley, 1976–79; Warden, Bishop Mascall Centre, Ludlow, and Mem., Hereford Diocesan Educn Team, 1979–84; Diocesan Communications Officer, Hereford, 1981–86; Team Rector, Hereford S Wye Team Ministry, 1984–97. Prebendary, Hereford Cathedral, 1993–97; Hon. Canon, Cathedral and Abbey Church of St Alban, 1997. OCF, 1985–97. Chm., St Alban's and Oxford Ministry Course, 1998–. *Recreations:* country walks, vintage buses and trains. *Address:* St Mary's House, Church Lane, Stapleford, Hertford SG14 3NB. *T:* (01992) 581629, *Fax:* (01992) 558745; *e-mail:* archdhert@stalbansdioc.org.uk. *Club:* Royal Commonwealth Society.

JONES, Prof. Tudor Bowden, DSc; FInstP; CEng, FIEE; Professor of Ionospheric Physics, 1980–98, Head of Department of Physics and Astronomy, 1993–98, University of Leicester, now Professor Emeritus; *b* 8 Nov. 1934; *s* of Idris Jones and Tydvil Ann Jones (*née* Bowden); *m* 1960, Patricia Brown; two *s.* *Educ:* County Grammar Sch., Ystradgynlais; University Coll. of Wales, Swansea (BSc Hons, PhD, DSc). FInstP 1975; CEng 1987; FIEE 1987. Res. Asst, UCW, Aberystwyth, 1959; University of Leicester: Lectr in Physics, 1960–69; Sen. Lectr, 1969–75; Reader, 1975–80. PPARC Nat. Co-ordinator for Solar Terrestrial Physics, 1998–2001. Guest Res. Scientist at various Govt estabts in UK and overseas, 1970–; Sen. Resident Associate, Nat. Oceanic and Atmospheric Admin Lab., Boulder, Colo, 1971–72. Leverhulme Emeritus Fellowship, 2001–02. Appleton Lectr, IEE, 1997. Appleton Prize, Internat. Union of Radio Sci. and Royal Soc., 1993; Charles Chree Prize and Medal, Inst. of Physics, 1995. *Publications:* (ed) Oblique Incidence Radio Wave Propagation, 1966; numerous papers in scientific jls on ionospheric physics and radio wave propagation. *Recreation:* classical music. *Address:* Department of Physics and Astronomy, University of Leicester, University Road, Leicester LE1 7RH. *T:* (0116) 252 3561.

JONES, Prof. Vaughan Frederick Randal, FRS 1990; Professor of Mathematics, University of California, Berkeley, since 1985; *b* Gisborne, NZ, 31 Dec. 1952; *s* of J. H. Jones and J. A. Goodfellow (*née* Collins); *m* 1979, Martha Weare Jones (*née* Myers); one *s* two *d.* *Educ:* St Peter's Sch., Cambridge, NZ; Auckland Grammar Sch.; Univ. of Auckland (schol.; Gillies schol.; Phillips Industries Bursary; BSc, MSc 1st Cl. Hons); Ecole de Physique, Geneva (Swiss Govt schol.; F. W. W. Rhodes Meml schol.); Ecole de Mathématiques, Geneva (DèsSc Mathematics); Vacheron Constantin Prize, Univ. de Genève. Asst, Univ. de Genève, 1975–80; E. R. Hedrick Asst Prof., UCLA, 1980–81; University of Pennsylvania: Vis. Lectr, 1981–82; Asst Prof., 1981–84; Associate Prof., 1984–85. Alfred P. Sloan Res. Fellowship, 1983; Guggenheim Fellowship, 1986. Hon. Vice Pres., Internat. Guild of Knot-tyers, 1991. Fields Medal, 1990. *Publication:* Coxeter graphs and Towers of algebras, 1989. *Recreations:* music, tennis, squash, ski-ing. *Address:* Mathematics Department, University College Berkeley, Berkeley, CA 94720, USA. *T:* (415) 6424196.

JONES, Vera June, (Mrs Ernest Brynmor Jones); *see* Di Palma, V. J.

JONES, Walter; *see* Jones, William W. A.

JONES, Most Rev. Walter Heath, Archbishop and Metropolitan of Rupert's Land, 1987–94; *b* 25 Dec. 1928; *s* of Harry Heath Jones and Anne Grace Evelyn Jones (*née* Stoddart); *m* 1951, L. Marilyn Jones (*née* Lunney); one *s* three *d.* *Educ:* Univ. of Manitoba (BA); St John's College (LTh); Nashotah House (STM). Received into Episcopal Church of USA, 1958; Rector, St Mary's Church, Mitchell, S Dak, 1958–62; Vice-Pres. of Chapter, 1962–67; Dean of Calvary Cathedral, Sioux Falls, S Dak, 1968–70; Bishop of South Dakota, Sioux Falls, 1970–83; Bishop of Rupert's Land, 1983. Chancellor, St John's Coll., 1983–94 (Hon. Fellow, 1993). Hon. DD: St John's Coll., 1970; Nashotah House; Trinity Coll., 1990. Hon. Citizen of St Boniface, 1966; Bush Fellow, 1978. *Address:* 3782 Olympic Court, Rapid City, SD 57702, USA. *T:* (605) 3990921.

JONES, Wilfred, CMG 1982; HM Diplomatic Service, retired; *b* 29 Nov. 1926; *m* 1952, Millicent Beresford; two *s.* Joined Foreign Office, 1949; served in Tamsui, Jedda, Brussels, Athens and FCO, 1950–66; First Sec. (Admin), Canberra, 1966–68; FCO, 1968–71; Copenhagen, 1971–74, Blantyre, 1974–75; Lilongwe, 1975–77; FCO, 1977–81; High Comr to Botswana, 1981–86. *Recreations:* sailing, golf, tennis. *Address:* Conifers, 16 The Hummicks, Dock Lane, Beaulieu, Hants SO4 7YJ.

JONES, William George Tilston; independent telecommunications consultant, since 1990; *b* 7 Jan. 1942; *s* of late Thomas Tilston Jones and Amy Ethel Jones; *m* 1965, Fiona Mary; one *d.* *Educ:* Portsmouth Grammar School; Portsmouth Polytechnic (BSc; Hon. Fellow 1989). CEng, FIEE. Post Office Engineering Dept, 1960; Head, Electronic Switching Gp, 1969; Head, System X Develt Div., 1978; Dir, System Evolution and Standards, 1983; Chief Exec., Technology, BT, 1984; seconded as Exec. in Residence, Internat. Management Inst., Geneva, 1987; Sen. Strategy Adviser, BT, 1988. Member: IEE Electronics Divl Bd, 1984–89; Parly IT Cttee, 1985–87; Chairman: IT Adv. Bd, Polytechnic of Central London, 1984–87; Adv. Gp, Centre of Communication and Information Studies, 1988–89; SE Centre, IEE, 1989–90; Dir, Technology Studies, British Telecom, 1988–90. Governor, Polytechnic of Central London, 1985–89. *Publications:* contribs on telecommunications to learned jls. *Recreations:* theatre, tennis, camping, making furniture.

JONES, William Pearce A.; *see* Andreae-Jones.

JONES, (William) Walter (Alexander); Headmaster, Royal Grammar School, Worcester, since 1993; *b* 11 Sept. 1949; *s* of Rev. Eric Jones and Elizabeth Jones; *m* 1974, Frances Linda Grant; one *s* two *d.* *Educ:* Campbell Coll., Belfast; Queens' Coll., Cambridge (MA; PGCE); Inst. of Education, Univ. of London (MA). Asst Teacher, St Edward's C of E Comprehensive, Romford, 1973–75; Head of Economics, King's Coll. Sch., Wimbledon, 1976–87; Second Master, King's Sch., Bruton, 1987–93. *Publications:* contrib. to British Economic Survey. *Recreations:* Rugby, walking. *Address:* 13 St George's Square, Worcester WR1 1HX.

JONES, Wyn; *see* Jones, Graham W.

JONES, Sir Wynn Normington H.; *see* Hugh-Jones.

JONES PARRY, Dr Emyr, CMG 1992; HM Diplomatic Service; UK Permanent Representative, UK Delegation to NATO, since 2001; *b* 21 Sept. 1947; *s* of Hugh Jones Parry and Eirwen Jones Parry (*née* Davies); *m* 1971, Lynn Noble; two *s.* *Educ:* Gwendraeth Grammar Sch.; University Coll. Cardiff (BSc, Dip Crystallography); St Catharine's Coll., Cambridge (PhD). FO, 1973–74; First Sec., Ottawa, 1974–79; FO, 1979–82; First Sec., UK Rep. to EC, Brussels, 1982–86; Dep. Head, Office of Pres. of European Parlt, 1987–89; Head, EC Dept (External), FCO, 1989–93; Minister, British Embassy, Madrid, 1993–96; Dep. Pol Dir, FCO, 1996–97; Dir, EU, FCO, 1997–98; Political Dir, FCO, 1998–2001. *Publications:* various scientific articles. *Recreations:* gardening, theatre, reading, sport. *Address:* c/o Foreign and Commonwealth Office, King Charles Street, SW1A 2AH. *Club:* Glamorgan County Cricket.

JONES-PARRY, Tristram, MA; Head Master, Westminster School, since 1998; *b* 23 July 1947; *s* of Sir Ernest Jones-Parry and late Mary (*née* Powell). *Educ:* Westminster Sch.; Christ Church, Oxford (MA). Operational Researcher, NCB, 1968–70; Maths Teacher, Dulwich Coll., 1970–73; Head of Maths, Housemaster and Under Master, Westminster Sch., 1973–94; Headmaster, Emanuel Sch., 1994–98. *Recreations:* reading, walking, cycling, travelling. *Address:* Westminster School, 17 Dean's Yard, SW1P 3PB. *Clubs:* Athenæum, East India.

JONES-WILLIAMS, Dafydd Wyn, OBE 1970; MC 1942; TD 1954; DL; Commissioner for Local Administration for Wales (Local Ombudsman), 1974–79; *b* 13 July 1916; *s* of late J. Jones-Williams, Dolgellau; *m* 1945, Rosemary Sally, *e d* of late A. E. Councell, Blaenau Hall, Rhydymain; two *d.* *Educ:* Dolgellau Grammar Sch.; UCW Aberystwyth (LLB). Served 1939–45 with HAC and X Royal Hussars (Western Desert). Formerly comdg 446 (Royal Welch) AB, LAA Regt, RA (TA). Solicitor, 1939. Clerk of County Council, Clerk of Peace, and Clerk to Lieutenancy, Merioneth, 1954–70; Circuit Administrator, Wales and Chester Circuit, 1970–74. Member: Hughes-Parry Cttee on Legal Status of Welsh Language, 1963–65; Lord Chancellor's Adv. Cttee on Trng of Magistrates, 1974–81; Council on Tribunals, 1980–86; BBC Gen. Adv. Council, 1979–85. Formerly: Mem., Nature Conservancy (Chm., Cttee for Wales); Mem., Nat. Broadcasting Council for Wales; Chm., Merioneth and Montgomeryshire T&AFA. DL Merioneth, 1958. *Recreations:* golf, snooker, reading. *Address:* Bennar, Felin Isaf, Dolgellau, Gwynedd LL40 1ES. *T:* (01341) 422303. *Club:* Royal St Davids Golf.

JONKMAN, (Pieter Jan) Hans, Hon. GCVO 1982; Commander, Order of Orange Nassau; Cross of Honour, Order of House of Orange Nassau; Secretary-General of the Permanent Court of Arbitration, The Hague, 1990–99; *b* 2 June 1925; *s* of Jan A. Jonkman and Johanna L. M. de Bruïne; *m* 1959, Maria Elisabeth te Winkel; one *s* two *d.* *Educ:* Univ. of Leyden (law degree). Entered Min. of Foreign Affairs, 1955; served Paris, Pretoria, Leopoldville, Buenos Aires; Min. of Foreign Affairs, 1962–66; Brussels, Beirut, Jakarta; Min. of Foreign Affairs, 1975–80; Grand-Officer for Special Services of HM Queen of the Netherlands, 1980–82; Grand-Master, House of The Queen, 1982–87; Ambassador of the Netherlands to UK and concurrently to Iceland, 1987–90. Holds various foreign decorations. *Club:* Societeit de Witte (The Hague).

JOPLING, family name of **Baron Jopling**.

JOPLING, Baron *cr* 1997 (Life Peer), of Ainderby Quernhow in the co. of N Yorkshire; **Thomas Michael Jopling;** PC 1979; DL; farmer; *b* 10 Dec. 1930; *s* of Mark Bellerby Jopling, Masham, Yorks; *m* 1958, Gail, *d* of Ernest Dickinson, Harrogate; two *s*. *Educ:* Cheltenham Coll.; King's Coll., Newcastle upon Tyne (BSc Agric.). Mem., Thirsk Rural District Council, 1958–64; Mem. National Council, National Farmers' Union, 1962–64. Contested (C) Wakefield, 1959. MP (C): Westmorland, 1964–83; Westmorland and Lonsdale, 1983–97. PPS to Minister of Agriculture, 1970–71; an Asst Govt Whip, 1971–73; a Lord Comr, HM Treasury, 1973–74; an Opposition Whip, March-June 1974; an Opposition spokesman on agriculture, 1974–75, 1976–79; Shadow Minister of Agriculture, 1975–76; Parly Sec. to HM Treasury, and Chief Whip, 1979–83; Minister of Agriculture, Fisheries and Food, 1983–87. Mem., Select Cttee on Foreign Affairs, 1987–97; Chm., Select Cttee on Sittings of the House, 1991–92; Mem., H of L Select Cttee on European Legislation, 2000– (Mem. Sub-Cttee (D) Agric., 1998–2000, (C) Defence and Foreign Policy, 2000–; Chm., 2001–); Jt Sec., Cons. Parly Agric. Cttee, 1966–70. Hon. Sec., British Amer. Parly Gp, 1987– (Vice Chm., 1983–86). Mem., UK Delegn to NATO Assembly, 1987–97. Mem., UK Exec., Commonwealth Parly Assoc., 1974–79, 1987–97 (Vice Chm., 1977–79). Pres. Councils, EEC Agric. and Fishery Ministers, July–Dec. 1986; Leader, 1990–97, Mem., 2000–, UK Delegn to OSCE Parly Assembly. Mem. Cttee, Assoc. of Cons. Peers, 1997–2000. Pres., Auto Cycle Union, 1990–. DL Cumbria, 1991–97, N Yorks, 1998. Hon. DCL Newcastle, 1992. *Address:* Ainderby Hall, Thirsk, North Yorks YO7 4HZ. *T:* (01845) 567224. *Club:* Buck's.
See also J. Jopling.

JOPLING, Jay; Founder, White Cube, art gallery, 1993, and White Cube^2, 2000; *s* of Lord Jopling, *qv*; *m* 1997, Sam Taylor-Wood; one *d*. *Educ:* Eton; Univ. of Edinburgh (MA Art Hist. 1984). *Address:* White Cube^2, 48 Hoxton Square, N1 6PB. *T:* (020) 7930 5373.

JORDAN, family name of **Baron Jordan**.

JORDAN, Baron *cr* 2000 (Life Peer), of Bournville in the co. of West Midlands; **William Brian Jordan,** CBE 1992; General Secretary, International Confederation of Free Trade Unions, since 1995; *b* 28 Jan. 1936; *s* of Walter and Alice Jordan; *m* 1958, Jean Ann Livesey; three *d*. *Educ:* Secondary Modern Sch., Birmingham. Convener of Shop Stewards, Guest Keen & Nettlefolds, 1966; full-time AUEW Divl Organiser, 1976; Pres., AEU, then AEEU, 1986–95. Mem., TUC General Council, 1986–95 (Chm., Cttee on European Strategy, 1988–95). A Gov., BBC, 1988–98. Member: NEDC, 1986–92; Engrg Industry Training Bd, 1986–91; Council, Industrial Soc., 1987–; RIIA, 1987–; ACAS, 1987–95; Nat. Trng Task Force, 1989–92; Engrg Trng Authy, 1991–; NACETT, 1993–95; English Partnerships, 1993–. President: European Metal-Workers Fedn, 1986–95; Exec., Internat. Metalworkers Fedn, 1986–95. Governor: London School of Economics, 1987–; Manchester Business School, 1987–92; Ashridge Management Coll., 1992–; Mem. Ct of Govs, Henley Coll., 1991–. Hon. CGIA 1989. DUniv Central England, 1993; Hon. DSc Cranfield, 1995. *Recreations:* reading, keen supporter of Birmingham City FC. *Address:* ICFTU, Boulevard du Roi Albert II, 5, Bte 1, 1210 Brussels, Belgium.

JORDAN, Prof. Carole, PhD; FRS 1990; FInstP; Professor of Physics, University of Oxford, since 1996; Wolfson Tutorial Fellow in Natural Science, Somerville College, Oxford, since 1976; *b* 19 July 1941; *d* of Reginald Sidney Jordan and Ethel May Jordan (*née* Waller). *Educ:* Harrow County Grammar School for Girls; University College London (BSc 1962; PhD 1965; Fellow 1991). FInstP 1973. Post-Doctoral Research Associate, Jt Inst. for Lab. Astrophysics, Boulder, Colorado, 1966; Asst Lectr, Dept of Astronomy, UCL, attached to Culham Lab., UKAEA, 1966–69; Astrophysics Research Unit, SRC, 1969–76; Oxford University: Lectr in Physics, 1976–94; Reader, Dept of Physics (Theoretical Physics), 1994–96. Member: SERC, 1985–90 (Chm., Solar System Cttee, 1983–86; Mem., Astronomy, Space and Radio Bd, 1979–86; Mem., Astronomy and Planetary Sci. Bd, 1986–90); PPARC, 1994–97. Pres., Royal Astronomical Soc., 1994–96 (Sec., 1981–90; Vice-Pres., 1990–91, 1996–97). DUniv Surrey, 1991. *Publications:* scientific papers on astrophysical plasma spectroscopy and structure and energy balance in cool star coronae, in learned jls. *Address:* Department of Physics (Theoretical Physics), 1 Keble Road, Oxford OX1 3NP. *T:* (01865) 273980.

JORDAN, Edmund Patrick; Chief Executive Officer, Jordan Grand Prix, since 1991; *b* 30 March 1948; *s* of Patrick Jordan and Eileen Jordan; *m* 1979, Marie McCarthy; two *s* two *d*. *Educ:* Synge Street Sch., Dublin; Coll. of Commerce, Dublin. Winner, Irish Kart Championship, 1971; single seater racing in FF1600, 1974; winner, Irish Formula Atlantic Championship, 1978; teamed up with Stefan Johannson, Marlboro Team Ireland, for British Formula 3 Championship, 1978; Formula 2, 1979; test drove McLaren F1 car, 1979; retired from single seater racing, 1980; Founder: Eddie Jordan Racing, 1979; Jordan Grand Prix, 1991. Irish Sporting Ambassador, 1999. *Recreations:* golf, music, ski-ing. *Address:* Jordan Grand Prix, Silverstone, Northants NN12 8TJ. *T:* (01327) 850800. *Clubs:* Sunningdale Golf; Oxfordshire Golf; Sotogrande Golf.

JORDAN, Francis Leo, (Frank), CBE 1989; QPM 1982; Chief Constable of Kent, 1982–89, retired; *b* 15 June 1930; *s* of Leo Thomas and Mary Jordan; *m* 1951, Ruth Ashmore; one *s* two *d*. *Educ:* St Joseph's Coll., Trent Vale, Stoke-on-Trent. CBIM. Staffordshire Police to rank of Chief Supt, 1950; seconded to Cyprus Police during EOKA emergency, 1956–58; Sen. Course in Criminology, Cambridge Univ., 1972; Sen. Comd Course, Police Staff Coll., 1973; Staff Officer to Home Office Police Inspectorate, 1975; Asst Chief Constable, West Midlands Police, 1976; Dep. Chief Constable of Kent, 1979. Mem., Parole Bd, 1990–93. Mem., Kent County Cttee, SSAFA, 1985–89. FRSA 1990. OStJ 1988. *Recreations:* walking, old buildings, churches, etc, travel. *Club:* Royal Over-Seas League.

JORDAN, Gerard Michael, CEng; Site Director, AEA Technology Dounreay (formerly Director, Dounreay Nuclear Power Establishment, United Kingdom Atomic Energy Authority), 1987–92; *b* 25 Sept. 1929; *s* of Arthur Thomas and Ruby Eveline Jordan; *m* 1955, Vera Peers; one *s* one *d*. *Educ:* Grange Sch., Birkenhead; Univ. of Liverpool. BEng; CEng, MIMechE, 1974. Marine Engrg Officer, 1950–55; Gp Engr, Messrs Thomas Hedley Ltd, 1956–59; United Kingdom Atomic Energy Authority: Principal Professional and Technical Officer, 1959–73; Band Grade Officer, 1973–80; Asst Dir (Safety and Reliability Div.), 1980; Asst Dir (Engrg and Safety Dounreay), 1980–84; Dep. Dir (Engrg Northern Div.), 1984–85; Dir of Engrg (Northern Div.), 1985–87. *Publications:* Handbook on Criticality Data, 1974, 2nd edn 1979; various papers in Trans IMechE, Trans IChemE, Trans INucE. *Recreations:* hobby electronics, DIY, fishing.

JORDAN, Graham Harold Ben; Deputy Under-Secretary of State (Science and Technology), Ministry of Defence, since 1997; *b* 1 April 1945; *s* of Harold Jordan and Violet Emily Jordan (*née* Wakefield); *m* 1977, Jean Anne Swale. *Educ:* Chislehurst and Sidcup Grammar Sch.; Downing Coll., Cambridge (Schol.; BA 1966 Nat. Scis and Chem. Eng; MA 1970); Brunel Univ. (MTech 1974 Op. Res.). DOAE, 1967–77; Dept of Chief Scientist, RAF, 1977–78; Supt, Land Air Studies Div., DOAE, 1978–82; Supt Royal Aircraft Establishment: Supt, Air to Air Weapons Div., 1982–85; Head, Defensive Weapons Dept, 1985–87; Head, Civil Service Personnel Policy Div., HM Treasury, 1987–90; Scientific Advr (Command Inf. Systems), MoD, 1990–91; Asst Chief Scientific Advr (Capabilities), MoD, 1991–95; Dep. Chief Scientist (Scrutiny and Analysis), MoD, 1995; Dir of Central IT Unit, Cabinet Office (OPS), 1995–97. *Publication:* (with Lee and Cawsey) Learning from Experience (report), 1988. *Recreations:* riding, small scale farming, home maintenance, music. *Address:* Main Building, Whitehall, SW1A 2HB.

JORDAN, Marc Lowis Aron; Managing Director, Acoustiguide Ltd, since 1999; *b* 12 July 1955; *s* of late Philip Jordan, MICE and Dr Louise Jordan (*née* Jackson); *m* 2000, Olivia, *d* of late Terence Kilmartin, CBE and Joanna Kilmartin; one *s*. *Educ:* William Ellis Sch.; Univ. of Exeter (BA Hons English Lit.); Courtauld Inst. of Art (MA Hist. of Art); London Business Sch. (MBA). Res. Assistant, Nat. Portrait Gallery, 1979–80; Cataloguer, Dept of Watercolours and Drawings, Phillips Auctioneers, 1981–82; Grove Dictionary of Art: Area Editor, 1985–88; Dep. Editor, 1988–92; Commissioning Editor, Phaidon Press, 1992–95; Publisher, Harvey Miller Publishers, 1998–99. Trustee, Hackney Historic Buildings Trust, 2000–; Mem., London Regl Cttee, Heritage Lottery Fund, 2001–. *Publications:* contribs to Apollo, Burlington Magazine, The Times, NY Times, TLS. *Recreation:* gardening. *Address:* c/o Acoustiguide Ltd, 52 Doughty Street, WC1N 2LS. *Club:* Groucho.

JORDAN, Michael Anthony; Chairman and Senior Partner, Cork Gully, Chartered Accountants, 1983–93; Partner, Coopers & Lybrand, Chartered Accountants, 1980–93; *b* 20 Aug. 1931; *s* of Charles Thomas Jordan and Florence Emily (*née* Golder); *m* 1st, 1956, Brenda Gee (marr. diss. 1989); one *s* one *d*; 2nd, 1990, Dorothea Rosine Estelle Coureau (*d* 2000). *Educ:* Haileybury. FCA 1956. Joined R. H. March Son & Co., 1958, Partner, 1959–68; Partner: Saker & Langdon Davis, 1963–93; W. H. Cork Gully & Co., 1968–80. Jt Inspector for High Court of IoM into the affairs of the Savings & Investment Bank Ltd, 1983. Gov., Royal Shakespeare Co., 1979–. *Publication:* (jtly) Insolvency, 1986. *Recreations:* opera, DIY, gardening. *Address:* Ballinger Farm, Ballinger, near Great Missenden, Bucks. *T:* (01494) 863298.

JORDANOVA, Prof. Ludmilla Jane, PhD; FRHistS; Professor of Visual Arts, University of East Anglia, since 1996; *b* 10 Oct. 1949; *d* of Ivan Nicholai Jordanov and Phyllis Elizabeth Jordanova (*née* Brown); *m* 1970, Simon Thomas Emmerson (marr. diss. 1974); two *d* by Karl Michael Figlio. *Educ:* Oxford High Sch. for Girls; New Hall, Cambridge (BA 1971; MA, PhD 1977); Univ. of Essex (MA 1987). FRHistS 1989. Res. Fellow, New Hall, Cambridge, 1975–78; Res. Officer, Wellcome Unit for History of Medicine, Univ. of Oxford, 1978–79; Lectr, 1980–88, Sen. Lectr, 1988–91, Prof., 1991–93, Dept of Hist., Univ. of Essex; Prof., Dept of Hist., Univ. of York, 1993–96. Pres., British Soc. for Hist. of Sci., 1998–2000; Mem. Council, RHistS, 1993–97. FRSocMed 1999. Trustee, Nat. Portrait Gall., 2001–. *Publications:* Lamarck, 1984; Sexual Visions: images of gender in science and medicine between the Eighteenth and Twentieth Centuries, 1989; Nature Displayed: gender, science and medicine 1760-1820, 1999; Defining Features: scientific and medical portraits 1660-2000, 2000; History in Practice, 2000; several edited vols, book reviews, contribs to learned jls. *Recreations:* friendship, travel, listening to music, art, museums, galleries. *Address:* School of World Art Studies and Museology, University of East Anglia, Norwich NR4 7TJ. *T:* (01603) 593768; 8 Ferrymans Court, Yarmouth Road, Norwich NR7 0EF.

JOSCELYNE, Richard Patrick; British Council Director, Japan, 1991–94; *b* 19 June 1934; *s* of Dr Patrick C. Joscelyne and Rosalind Whitcombe; *m* 1st, 1961, Vera Lucia Mello (marr. diss. 1988); one *s* one *d*; 2nd, 1988, Irangani Dias. *Educ:* Bryanston; Queens' Coll., Cambridge. Teaching posts in France, Brazil and Britain, 1958–62. British Council: Montevideo, 1962; Moscow, 1967; Madrid, 1969; Director, North and Latin America Dept, 1973; Representative, Sri Lanka, 1977; Controller, Overseas Div. B (America, Pacific and Asia Div.), 1980; Controller, Finance Div., 1982; Representative, Spain, 1987. *Address:* The Lake House, 8 Lagoon Court, Samford, Qld 4520, Australia. *T:* (7) 32891710.

JOSEPH, (Hon. Sir) James Samuel, (3rd Bt *cr* 1943, of Portsoken, City of London); *b* 27 Jan. 1955; *o s* of Baron Joseph, CH (Life Peer) and of Hellen Louise (*née* Guggenheimer); *S* to baronetcy of father, 1994, but does not use the title.

JOSEPH, Leslie; QC 1978; *b* 13 Aug. 1925; *s* of Benjamin Francis Joseph and Sarah Edelman; *m* 1964, Ursula Mary Hamilton (*d* 1988); one *s* two *d*. *Educ:* Haberdashers' Aske's, Hampstead; University Coll. London (LLB Hons). Served Army, 1943–47: Infantry, 1943–45 (Sgt); AEC, 1945–47. Called to the Bar, Middle Temple, 1953, Bencher, 1986; Master of the Revels, 1989–2000. Chairman: Common Professional Examn Bd, 1996–98 (Vice Chm., 1995–96); Bar Vocational Stage Sub-Cttee, 1996; Bar Vocational Course Validation Panel, 1997. Gov., Inns of Court Sch. of Law, 1996–97. *Recreations:* wine, water, cooking for friends. *Address:* 34 Upper Park Road, NW3 2UT. *T:* (020) 7722 3390.

JOSEPH, Thomas John Cedric; His Honour Judge Joseph; a Circuit Judge, since 1994; Resident Judge, Croydon Crown Court, since 1998; *b* 25 Aug. 1938; *s* of Thomas Rees Joseph and Katherine Ann Joseph; *m* 1960 Mary Weston; three *d*. *Educ:* Cardigan GS; LSE (LLB). Called to the Bar, Gray's Inn, 1960; Crown Counsel, Nyasaland, 1962–64; practised at the Bar, 1964–94; Asst Recorder, 1987–92; Recorder, 1992–94. *Recreations:* music, golf, travel, collecting old wine glasses and using them. *Address:* Croydon Crown Court, Altyre Road, Croydon CR9 5AB. *T:* (020) 8410 4700. *Club:* Royal Wimbledon Golf.

JOSEPH, Wendy Rose; QC 1998; a Recorder, since 1999; *b* 11 March 1952; *d* of late Norman Joseph and of Carole Joseph (*née* Marks). *Educ:* Cathays High Sch., Cardiff; Westridge Sch. for Girls, Pasadena, Calif; New Hall, Cambridge (MA). Called to the Bar, Gray's Inn, 1975; Asst Recorder, 1995–99. *Recreation:* Mozart and the stars. *Address:* 6 King's Bench Walk, Temple, EC4Y 7DR. *T:* (020) 7583 0410.

JOSEPHSON, Prof. Brian David, FRS 1970; Professor of Physics, Cambridge University, since 1974; Fellow of Trinity College, Cambridge, since 1962; *b* 4 Jan. 1940; *s* of Abraham Josephson and Mimi Josephson; *m* 1976, Carol Anne Olivier; one *d*. *Educ:* Cardiff High School; Cambridge Univ. BA 1960, MA, PhD 1964, Cantab. FInstP. Asst Dir of Res. in Physics, 1967–72, Reader in Physics, 1972–74, Univ. of Cambridge. Res. Asst Prof., Illinois Univ., 1965–66; Vis., Fellow, Cornell Univ., 1971; Vis. Faculty Mem., Maharishi European Res. Univ., 1975; Visiting Professor: Wayne State Univ., 1983; Indian Inst. of Sci., Bangalore, 1984. Hon. MIEEE, 1982; For. Hon. Mem., Amer. Acad. of Arts and Scis, 1974. Hon. DSc: Wales, 1974; Exeter, 1984; Hon. PhD Bar-Ilan, 1999. Awards: New Scientist, 1969; Research Corp., 1969; Fritz London, 1970; Nobel Prize for Physics, 1973; Casys, 2000. Medals: Guthrie, 1972; van der Pol, 1972; Elliott Cresson, 1972; Hughes, 1972; Holweck, 1973; Faraday, 1982; Sir George Thomson, 1984. *Publications:* Consciousness and the Physical World, 1980 (ed jtly); The Paranormal and the Platonic Worlds (in Japanese), 1997; research papers on physics and theory of intelligence, paranormal phenomena, Platonism, the convergence of science and religion.

Recreations: mountain walking, ice skating. *Address:* Cavendish Laboratory, Madingley Road, Cambridge CB3 0HE. *T:* (01223) 337260, *Fax:* (01223) 337356; *e-mail:* bdj10@cam.ac.uk.

JOSHI, Prof. Heather Evelyn, FBA 2000; AcSS; Professor of Economic and Developmental Demography in Education, Institute of Education, London University, since 1998; *b* 21 April 1946; *d* of Guy Malcolm Spooner, MBE and Molly Florence Spooner, MBE; *m* 1st, 1969, Vijay Ramchandra Joshi (marr. diss. 1977); 2nd, 1982, Gregory Hans David Martin; one *s* one *d. Educ:* St Hilda's Coll., Oxford (BA 1967, MA); St Antony's Coll., Oxford (MLitt 1970). Jun. Res. Fellow, Oxford Inst. of Econs and Statistics, 1969–73; Econ. Advr, Govt Econ. Service, 1973–79; Res. Fellow, 1979–83, Sen. Res. Fellow, 1983–88, LSHTM; Sen. Res. Fellow, Birkbeck Coll., 1988–90; Sen. Lectr, LSHTM, 1990–93; Sen. Res. Fellow, subseq. Prof., City Univ., 1993–98. Principal Investigator, ESRC Millennium Cohort Study, 2000–. Pres., British Soc. for Population Studies, 1999–2001. *Publications:* (with V. R. Joshi) Surplus Labour and the City, 1976; (ed) The Changing Population of Britain, 1989; (with P. Paci) Unequal Pay for Women and Men, 1998; articles in economics, demography and social policy jls. *Recreations:* family life, listening to classical music. *Address:* Centre for Longitudinal Studies, Institute of Education, 20 Bedford Way, WC1H 0AL. *T:* (020) 7612 6874.

JOSIPOVICI, Prof. Gabriel David, FRSL; FBA 2001; Professor of English, School of European Studies, University of Sussex, since 1984; *b* 8 Oct. 1940; *s* of Jean Josipovici and Sacha (*née* Rabinovitch) (*d* 1996). *Educ:* Victoria Coll., Cairo; Cheltenham Coll.; St Edmund Hall, Oxford (BA 1st Cl. Hons 1961). FRSL 1998. School of European Studies, University of Sussex: Asst Lectr in English, 1963–65; Lectr, 1965–74; Reader (part-time), 1974–84. Weidenfeld Vis. Prof. in Eur. Comparative Lit., Univ. of Oxford, 1996–97. *Plays:* Dreams of Mrs Fraser, 1972; Evidence of Intimacy, 1973; Playback, 1973; A Life, 1974; Vergil Dying, 1976; A Moment, 1977; AG, 1977; Kin, 1982; Mr Vee, 1987; A Little Personal Pocket Requiem, 1989. *Publications: fiction:* The Inventory, 1968; Words, 1971; Mobius the Stripper, 1974; The Present, 1975; Migrations, 1977; The Air We Breathe, 1981; Conversations in Another Room, 1984; Contre-Jour, 1987; The Big Glass, 1989; In the Fertile Land, 1991; Steps, 1992; In a Hotel Garden, 1993; Moo Pak, 1994; Now, 1998; *non-fiction:* The World and the Book, 1971, 3rd edn 1994; The Lessons of Modernism, 1977, 2nd edn 1986; Writing and the Body, 1982; The Mirror of Criticism, 1983; The Book of God, 1987, 2nd edn 1989; Text and Voice, 1992; Touch: an essay, 1996; On Trust, 1999; A Life, 2001. *Recreations:* walking, swimming. *Address:* 60 Prince Edward's Road, Lewes, Sussex BN7 1BH.

JOSLIN, Peter David, QPM 1983; DL; Consultant: British Institute of Innkeeping; Mobilefone Group; Chief Constable of Warwickshire, 1983–98; *b* 26 Oct. 1933; *s* of Frederick William Joslin and Emma Joslin; *m* 1960, Kathleen Josephine Monaghan; two *s* one *d. Educ:* King Edward VI Royal Grammer School, Chelmsford; Essex University. BA Hons. Joined Essex Police, 1954–74 (Police Constable to Superintendent); Chief Superintendent, Divl Comdr, Leicestershire Constabulary, 1974–76; Asst Chief Constable (Operations), Leics Constab., 1976–77; Dep. Chief Constable, Warwicks Constabulary, 1977–83. Chm., Traffic Cttee, ACPO, 1989–92. Pres., Warwickshire Assoc. for the Blind, 1993–. Vice Chm., Prince Michael Road Safety Award Cttee, 1998–. CIMgt. DL Warwickshire, 1999. *Recreations:* sport (now mainly as a spectator), house renovation, good wines, after dinner speaking. *Address:* Nash House, 41 High Street, Kenilworth, Warks CV8 1LY. *T:* (01926) 511517.

JOSPIN, Lionel Robert; Prime Minister of France, since 1997; *b* 12 July 1937; *s* of Robert Jospin and Mireille Jospin (*née* Dandieu); *m*; one *s* one *d*; *m* 1994, Prof. Sylviane Agacinski; one step *s. Educ:* Institut d'Etudes Politiques, Paris; Ecole Nationale d'Administration. French Foreign Office, 1965–70; Prof. of Economics, Technical Univ. Inst., Paris-Sceaux, 1970–81; MP 1981–88; MEP 1984–88; French Socialist Party: Nat. Sec., various divs, 1973–81; First Sec., 1981–88 and 1995–; Minister of State, Nat. Educn and Sports, 1988–92; Minister plenipotentiary, Foreign Office, 1992. Member: Conseil général, Haute-Garonne, 1988–; Conseil régional, Midi-Pyrénées, 1992–. Grand-Croix, Ordre National du Mérite (France), 1997. *Publications:* L'invention du Possible, 1991; Propositions pour la France 1995–2000, 1995. *Recreations:* basketball, tennis. *Address:* Hôtel de Matignon, 57 rue de Varenne, 75700 Paris, France. *T:* 42757501.

JOSS, William Hay; a Recorder of the Crown Court, 1982–96; *b* 20 May 1927; *s* of William Taylor Barron Joss and Elizabeth Lindsay Lillie Joss; *m* 1961, Rosemary Sarah Joss; two *s. Educ:* Worksop Coll., Notts; Exeter Coll., Oxon (BA Jurisprudence). Served Army, commissioned into 14th/20th King's Hussars, 1945–48. Industry, production management, 1950–62; called to the Bar, Gray's Inn, 1957; practising barrister, 1962–96. *Recreations:* golf, music, literature. *Address:* 49 Village Road, Clifton Village, Nottingham NG11 8NP. *T:* (0115) 921 1894. *Club:* Nottingham and Notts United Services.

JOST, H. Peter, CBE 1969; DSc; CEng; FIMechE; FIM; Hon. FIEE; CIMgt; Chairman, K. S. Paul Products Ltd, 1973–2000 (Managing Director, 1955–89); Director of overseas companies; Hon. Industrial Professor, Liverpool John Moores University (formerly Liverpool Polytechnic), since 1983; Hon. Professor of Mechanical Engineering, University of Wales, since 1986; *b* 25 Jan. 1921; *o s* of late Leo and Margot Jost; *m* 1948, Margaret Josephine, *o d* of late Michael and Sara Kadesh, Norfolk Is, S Pacific; two *d. Educ:* City of Liverpool Techn. Coll.; Manchester Coll. of Technology. Apprentice, Associated Metal Works, Glasgow and D. Napier & Son Ltd, Liverpool; Methods Engr, K & L Steelfounders and Engrs Ltd, 1943; Chief Planning Engr, Datim Machine Tool Co. Ltd, 1946; Gen. Man. 1949, Dir 1952, Trier Bros Ltd; Lubrication Consultant: Richard Thomas & Baldwins Ltd, 1960–65; August Thyssen Hütte AG 1963–66; Chairman: Bright Brazing Ltd, 1969–76; Peppermill Brass Foundry Ltd, 1970–76; Centralube Ltd, 1974–77 (Man. Dir, 1955–77); Associated Technology Gp Ltd, 1976–; Engineering & General Equipment Ltd, 1977–; Director: Williams Hudson Ltd, 1967–75; Stothert & Pitt, 1971–85; Fuchs Lubritech International, 2000–. Chairman: Lubrication Educn and Res. Working Gp, DES, 1964–65; Cttee on Tribology, DTI, 1966–74; Industrial Technologies Management Bd, DTI, 1972–74; Dep. Chm., Cttee for Industrial Technologies, DTI, 1972–74; Member: Adv. Council on Technology, 1968–70; Cttee on Terotechnology, 1971–72; Consultative Gp on Sci. and Technol., FCO, 1994–. Hon. Associate, Manchester Coll. of Science and Technology, 1962; University of Salford: Privy Council's Nominee to Ct, 1970–83; Mem. Council, 1974–84; Mem. Court, Middlesex Univ., 1996–. Mem. Council: IProdE, 1973–91 (Vice-Pres., 1975–77, Pres., 1977–78; Chm., Technical Policy Bd and Mem., Exec. Policy Cttee, 1974; Hon. Fellow, 1980); IMechE, 1974–92 (Member: Technical Bd, 1975; Finance Bd, 1979– (Chm., 1988–91); Disciplinary Bd, 1979–; Vice-Pres., 1987–92); Council of Engineering Institutions: Mem. Bd, 1977–83; Mem. Exec., 1979–83 (Mem. External Affairs Cttee, 1974–80; Chm. Home Affairs Cttee, 1980–83); Mem., Parly and Scientific Cttee, 1973– (Hon. Sec., 1990–93; Vice-Pres., 1993–95 and 1998–2001; Vice Chm., 1995–98; Mem., Gen. Purposes Cttee, 1991–; Mem. Council (formerly Steering Cttee), 1983–). President: Internat. Tribology Council, 1973–; Manchester Technology Assoc., 1984–85; Chm., Manchester Technology Assoc. in London, 1976–90. Trustee, Michael John Trust, 1986–. CIMgt (CBIM 1984); Fellow, 1970, Life Fellow, 1986, ASME; FSME, USA, 1988 (Hon. Mem., 1977); Hon. MIPlantE, 1969; Hon. Member: Société Française de Tribologie, 1972; Gesellschaft für Tribologie, 1972; Chinese Mech. Engrg Soc., 1986; Russian (formerly USSR) Acad. of Engrg, 1991; Nat. Tribology Council of Bulgaria, 1991; Japanese Soc. of Tribologists, 1992; Slovak Tribology Soc., 1993; Ukrainian Acad. of Transport, 1994; Polish Tribolog. Soc., 1995; Belarus Acad. of Engrg and Technol., 1996; Hon. Life Mem., Soc. of Tribologists and Lubrication Engrs, USA, 1997 (Internat. Award, 1997). Rutherford Lectr, Manchester Technology Assoc., 1979; James Clayton Lectr, IMechE, 1981. Freeman, City of London, 1984; Liveryman, Engineers' Co., 1984. Hon. DSc: Salford, 1970; Slovak Technical Univ., 1987; Bath, 1990; Technical Univ. of Budapest, 1993; Belarus Acad. of Scis, 2000; Hon. DTech CNAA, 1987; Hon. DEng Leeds, 1989; San Fernando Valley Engineers Council (USA) Internat. Achievement Award, 1978; State of California State Legislature Commendation, 1978; Georg Vagelpohl Insignia, Germany, 1979. Sir John Larking Medal 1944, Derby Medal 1955, Liverpool Engrg Soc.; Hutchinson Meml Medal 1952, Silver Medal for Best Paper 1952–53, 1st Nuffield Award 1981, IProdE; Merit Medal, Hungarian Scientific Soc. of Mech. Engrs, 1983; Gold Medal, Slovak Tech. Univ., 1984; Colclough Medal and Prize, Inst. of Materials, 1992; Louwe Alberts Award, S African Inst. of Tribology, 1992. Gold Insignia, Order of Merit of Poland, 1986; Officer Cross, Order of Merit (Germany), 1992; Officier, Palmes Académiques (France), 1995; Decoration of Honour for Science and Art, 1st cl. (Austria), 2001. *Publications:* Lubrication (Tribology) Report of DES Cttee, 1966 (Jost Report); The Introduction of a New Technology, Report of DTI Cttee, 1973; Technology *vs* Unemployment, 1986; various papers in Proc. IMechE, Proc.IProdE, technical jls, etc. *Recreations:* music, opera, gardening. *Address:* Hill House, Wills Grove, Mill Hill, NW7 1QL. *T:* (020) 8959 3355. *Club:* Athenæum.

JOULWAN, Gen. George Alfred; Adjunct Professor, National Defense University, 2000–01; Olin Professor of National Security Studies, United States Military Academy, West Point, 1998–2000; Supreme Allied Commander, Europe, 1993–97; Commander-in-Chief, United States European Command, 1993–97; *b* 16 Nov. 1939; *m* Karen E. Jones; three *d. Educ:* US Mil. Acad., West Point (BS 1961); Loyola Univ. (Master of Pol Sci. 1968); US Army War Coll., Washington. Joined US Army, 1961; served Europe, US and Vietnam, 1962–73; Special Assistant: to the Pres., 1973–74; to Supreme Allied Comdr, SHAPE, 1974–75; Bn Comdr, Europe, 1975–77; US Army War College: student, 1977–78; Dir, Pol and Econ. Studies, 1978–79; Bde Comdr, Europe, 1979–81; COS, 3 Inf. Div., Europe, 1981–82; Exec. Officer to Chm., Jt Chiefs of Staff, Washington, 1982–86; US Army Europe and Seventh Army: DCS for Ops, 1986–88; Commanding General: 3rd Armoured Div., 1988–89; V Corps, 1989–90; C-in-C, US Southern Comd, Quarry Heights, Panama, 1990–93. Defense Distinguished Service Medal, with two Oak Leaf Clusters (USA); Distinguished Service Medal (USA); Silver Star (with Oak Leaf Cluster) (USA). Foreign orders include: Grand Cross, Order of Merit, Hessian Order of Merit (Germany); Legion of Honour, Legion of Merit (France); Cross of Gallantry with three Gold Stars (Vietnam). *Address:* 2107 Arlington Ridge Road, Arlington, VA 22202, USA.

JOURDAN, Dr Martin Henry, FRCS; Consultant Surgeon, Guy's Hospital, since 1977, and St Thomas' Hospital, since 1982; Reader in Surgery, University of London, since 1982; *b* 7 Oct. 1941; *s* of Henry George Jourdan and Jocelyn Louise (*née* Courteney); *m* 1966, May McElwain; two *s* two *d. Educ:* Bishopshalt Sch., Hillingdon; Guy's Hosp. Med. Sch. (MB BS; PhD 1970; MS 1980). LRCP 1966; FRCS 1974. Lectr in Physiol., Guy's Hosp., 1967–70; MRC Travelling Fellow, Univ. of Calif, Berkeley, 1971–72; Registrar, then Sen. Registrar in Surgery, Guildford, Norwich and Guy's Hosp., 1974–77. Chm., Examrs in Surgery, Univ. of London, 1989–91; Mem., Court of Examrs, RCS, 1987–2000. Master, Soc. Apothecaries, 2001–Aug. 2002. *Publications:* (contrib.) The New Aird's Companion in Surgical Studies, 2000; papers on surgical nutrition and bowel disease. *Recreations:* tennis, theatre, gardening, opera. *Address:* 55 Shirlock Road, Hampstead, NW3 2HR. *T:* (020) 7267 1582. *Club:* Athenæum.

JOWELL, Prof. Jeffrey Lionel; Professor of Public Law, since 1975, and Dean and Head of the Laws Faculty, since 1998, University College London; UK Member, Venice Commission (European Commission on Democracy through Law), since 2000 (Member, Governing Board, since 2001); *b* 4 Nov. 1938; *s* of Jack and Emily Jowell, Cape Town; *m* 1963, Frances Barbara, *d* of Helen Suzman, *qv*; one *s* one *d. Educ:* Cape Town Univ. (BA, LLB 1961); Hertford Coll., Oxford (BA 1963, MA 1969), Pres., Oxford Union Soc., 1963; Harvard Univ. Law Sch. (LLM 1966, SJD 1971). Called to Bar, Middle Temple, 1965 (Hon. Bencher, 1999). Research Asst, Harvard Law Sch., 1966–68; Fellow, Jt Center for Urban Studies of Harvard Univ. and MIT, 1967–68; Associate Prof. of Law and Admin. Studies, Osgoode Hall Law Sch., York Univ., Toronto, 1968–72; Leverhulme Fellow in Urban Legal Studies, 1972–74, and Lectr in Law, 1974–75, LSE; University College London: Dean, Faculty of Laws, 1979–89; Head of Dept, 1982–89; Vice Provost, 1992–99; Hon. Fellow, 1997. Chairman, Social Sciences and The Law Cttee, 1981–84, and Vice-Chm., Govt and Law Cttee, 1982–84, Social Science Res. Council; Asst Boundary Comr, 1976–85; Chm., Cttee of Heads of University Law Schools, 1984–86; Member: Cttee of Management, Inst. of Advanced Legal Studies, 1978–89; Standing Cttee, Oxford Centre for Socio-Legal Studies, 1980–84; Gp for Study of Comparative European Admin., 1978–86; Nuffield Cttee on Town and Country Planning, 1983–86; Council, Justice, 1997–; Lord Chancellor's Review of Crown Office List, 1999–2000. UK deleg., Cttee of Experts, CSCE, Oslo, 1991. Convenor of numerous internat. workshops and confs on constitutional law and human rights. Non-exec. Director: UCL Press, 1993–95; Camden and Islington Community Health Services NHS Trust, 1994–97. Trustee: John Foster Meml Trust, 1986–; Internat. Centre for Public Law, 1992–98; Bd, Inst. of Commonwealth Studies, 1994–99; Prince of Wales's Foundn (formerly Inst. of Architecture), 1997–99; Inst. of Philanthropy, 2000–. Lionel Cohen Lecture, Jerusalem, 1988; Vis. Prof., Univ. of Paris II, 1991; Hon. Prof., Univ. of Cape Town, 1999–. Hon. QC 1993. Hon. DJur Athens, 1987; Hon. LLD: Ritsumeikan, 1988; Cape Town, 2000. Member Editorial Bds: Public Law, 1977–93; Policy and Politics, 1976–83; Urban Law and Policy, 1978–83; Jl of Environmental Law, 1988–92; Public Law Review, 1995–; Judicial Review, 1996–; Jt Editor, Current Legal Problems, 1984–89. *Publications:* Law and Bureaucracy, 1975; (ed jtly) Welfare Law and Policy, 1979; (ed jtly) Lord Denning: the Judge and the Law, 1984; (ed jtly) The Changing Constitution, 1985, 4th edn 2000; (ed jtly) New Directions in Judicial Review, 1988; (with S. A. de Smith and H. Woolf) Judicial Review of Administrative Action, 1995; Principles of Judicial Review, 1999; articles and reviews on public law and planning law. *Recreations:* tennis, London, Exmoor. *Address:* University College London, Gower Street, WC1E 6BT. *T:* (020) 7679 1405.

JOWELL, Roger Mark, CBE 2001; AcSS; Director, European Social Survey, National Centre for Social Research, since 2001; Co-director, ESRC Centre for Research into Elections and Social Trends, since 1994; Fellow, Centre for Management and Policy Studies, Cabinet Office, since 2001; *b* 26 March 1942; *s* of Jack and Emily Jowell, Cape Town, SA; *m* 1st, 1970, Tessa Jane Helen Douglas Palmer (*see* Rt Hon. Tessa Jowell) (marr. diss. 1978); 2nd, 1979, Nighat Gilani (marr. diss. 1995); two *s*; 3rd, 1996, Sharon

Witherspoon. *Educ:* Cape Town Univ. (BA 1963). Researcher, Res. Services Ltd, 1964–68; Founder and Co-Dir, 1969–84, sole Dir, 1984–2001, Social and Community Planning Res., later Nat. Centre for Social Res. Mem., Commn on Taxation and Citizenship, 1999–2001. Visiting Professor: City Univ., 1980–88 and 2001–; LSE, 1993–. Founder Dir, British Social Attitudes Survey series, 1983–2001; Co-dir, British Election Studies, 1983–2000. Member, Editorial Boards: Jl Royal Statistical Soc., 1990–92; Electoral Studies, 1997–; Internat. Jl Mkt Res., 2001–. Formulated Internat. Code of Ethics for Statisticians, 1980–85. Founder Chm., Internat. Social Survey Prog., 1984–90; Chm., Assoc. Res. Centres in Social Scis, 1999–2001; Board Mem., Inf. Centre on Asylum and Refugees, 2001–; Trustee, IPPR, 2001–. Alderman, Camden BC, 1970–77; Mem., Internat. Statistical Inst., 1985; FSS 1978. AcSS 1999. Hon. LLD Oxford Brookes, 1999. *Publications:* (jtly) Britain into Europe, 1976; (jtly) Survey Research Practice, 1978; (jtly) How Britain Votes, 1985; (jtly) Understanding Political Change, 1991; (jtly) Labour's Last Chance?, 1994; (jtly) The Quality of Life in London, 1995; (jtly) The Rise of New Labour, 2001; (ed and contrib.) British Social Attitudes, annually 1984–2000; contribs to Jl Royal Stat. Soc., Public Opinion Qly, Amer. Behavioral Scientist, Parly Affairs, Eur. Sociol Rev., Jl Official Stats. *Recreations:* tennis, cricket. *Address:* National Centre for Social Research, 35 Northampton Square, EC1V 0AX. *T:* (020) 7549 9504.

JOWELL, Rt Hon. Tessa Jane Helen Douglas; PC 1998; MP (Lab) Dulwich and West Norwood, since 1997 (Dulwich, 1992–97); Secretary of State for Culture, Media and Sport, since 2001; *b* 17 Sept. 1947; *d* of Kenneth and Rosemary Palmer; *m* 1st, 1970, Roger Mark Jowell, *qv* (marr. diss. 1977); 2nd, 1979, David Mills; one *s* one *d*. *Educ:* St Margaret's Sch., Aberdeen; Aberdeen Univ. (MA); Edinburgh Univ. (DSA). Child Care Officer, Lambeth, 1969–71; psychiatric social worker training, Goldsmiths' Coll., London Univ., 1971–72; Psychiatric Social Worker, Maudsley Hosp., 1972–74; Asst Dir, Mind, 1974–86; Dir, Community Care Special Action Project, Birmingham, and Sen. Vis. Fellow, PSI, 1986–90; Dir, Community Care Prog., Joseph Rowntree Foundn, and Sen. Vis. Fellow, King's Fund Inst., 1990–92. Councillor, Camden, 1971–86. Chair, Social Services Cttee, AMA, 1984–86; Mem., Mental Health Act Commn, 1985–90. An Opposition Whip, 1994–95; frontbench Opposition spokesperson on health, and on women, 1995–97; Minister of State (Minister for Public Health), DoH, 1997–99; Minister for Women, H of C, 1998–2001; Minister of State, DfEE, 1999–2001. Vis. Fellow, Nuffield Coll., Oxford, 1995. *Publications:* articles and contribs in social work and social policy jls. *Recreations:* gardening, reading, music, Italy. *Address:* House of Commons, Westminster, SW1A 0AA.

JOWETT, Very Rev. Alfred, CBE 1972; Dean of Manchester, 1964–83; *b* 29 May 1914; *s* of Alfred Edmund Jowett; *m* 1939, Margaret, *d* of St Clair Benford; one *s* three *d*. *Educ:* High Storrs Grammar Sch., Sheffield; St Catharine's Coll., Cambridge; Lincoln Theological Coll. BA 1935; Certif. Educn 1936; MA 1959. Deacon 1944; Priest 1945. Curate of St John the Evangelist, Goole, 1944–47; Sec., Sheffield Anglican and Free Church Council and Marriage Guidance Council, 1947–51; Vicar of St George with St Stephen, Sheffield, 1951–60; Part-time Lecturer, Sheffield Univ. Dept of Education, 1950–60; Vicar of Doncaster, 1960–64; Hon. Canon of Sheffield Cathedral, 1960–64. Select Preacher, Oxford Univ., 1964 and 1979. Mem., Community Relations Commn, 1968–77 (Dep. Chm., 1972–77). A Church Comr, 1978–80. Hon. Fellow, Manchester Polytechnic, 1972. OStJ 1979. Hon. LittD Sheffield, 1982. Hon. Freeman, City of Manchester, 1984. *Publication:* (part-author) The English Church: a New Look, 1966. *Recreations:* theatre, music, extra-mural lecturing. *Address:* 37 Stone Delf, Sheffield S10 3QX. *T:* (0114) 230 5455.

JOWITT, Sir Edwin (Frank), Kt 1988; a Justice of the High Court, Queen's Bench Division, 1988–2000; *b* 1 Oct. 1929; *s* of Frank and Winifred Jowitt; *m* 1959, Anne Barbara Dyson; three *s* two *d*. *Educ:* Swanwick Hall Grammar Sch.; London Sch. of Economics. LLB London 1950. Called to Bar, Middle Temple, 1951, Bencher 1977; Member Midland and Oxford Circuit, 1952–80. Dep. Chm. Quarter Sessions: Rutland, 1967–71; Derbyshire, 1970–71; QC 1969; a Recorder of the Crown Court, 1972–80; a Circuit Judge, 1980–88; a Sen. Circuit Judge, 1987–88; Hon. Recorder, Birmingham, 1987–88; Presiding Judge, Midland and Oxford Circuit, 1996–99. *Recreations:* fell walking, cycling. *Address:* Church House, Desborough, Northants NN14 2NP.

JOWITT, Juliet Diana Margaret, (Mrs Thomas Jowitt); Director, Northern Ballet Theatre, since 2000; Member, Independent Broadcasting Authority, 1981–86; Director, Yorkshire Television, 1987–94; *b* 24 Aug. 1940; *yr d* of late Lt-Col Robert Henry Langton Brackenbury, OBE and Eleanor Trewlove (*née* Springman); *m* 1963, Frederick Thomas Benson Jowitt; one *s* one *d*. *Educ:* Hatherop Castle; Switzerland and Spain. Associate Shopping Editor, House and Garden and Vogue, 1966–69; Proprietor, Wood House Design (Interior Design) (formerly Colour Go Round), 1971–. Dir, YTV Holdings PLC, 1988–92. Member: Domestic Coal Consumers' Council, 1985–95; Potato Marketing Bd, 1986–90. Fellow, IDDA, 1995 (Mem., 1985; Mem. Council, 1989). JP North Yorkshire, 1973–89. *Address:* Thorpe Lodge, Littlethorpe, Ripon, N Yorkshire HG4 3LU.

JOXE, Pierre Daniel, Hon. KBE; Member, Constitutional Court, Paris, since 2001; *b* 28 Nov. 1934; *s* of Louis Joxe and Françoise-Hélène Joxe (*née* Halévy); *m* 3rd, 1981, Valérie Cayeux; two *s*, and two *d* from a previous marr. *Educ:* Lycée Henri-IV; Faculté de droit de Paris; Ecole Nat. d'Administration. Started career in Audit Office, 1962; elected Deputy for Saône-et-Loire, 1973, 1978, 1981, 1986, 1988; Mem., European Parlt, 1977–79; Minister of Industry, 1981; Minister of the Interior, 1984–86, 1988–91; Minister of Defence, 1991–93; Auditor General, Audit Office, Paris, 1993–2001. Mem. Exec., Socialist Party, 1971–. *Publications:* Parti socialiste, 1973; A propos de la France, 1997; L'Edit de Nantes: une histoire pour aujourd' hui, 1998. *Address:* (office) 2 rue de Montpensier, 75001 Paris, France.

JOY, David, CBE 1983; HM Diplomatic Service, retired; *b* 9 Dec. 1932; *s* of late Harold Oliver Joy and Doris Kate Buxton; *m* 1957, Montserrat Morancho Saumench, *o d* of Angel Morancho Garreta and Josefa Saumench Castells, Zaragoza, Spain; one *s* one *d*. *Educ:* Hulme Grammar Sch., Oldham, Lancs; St Catharine's Coll., Cambridge (MA). HMOCS, Northern Rhodesia, 1956–64; Zambia, 1964–70: Cabinet Office, 1964; Under Sec. (Cabinet), 1968; Under Sec., Min. of Commerce and Industry, 1970; Ashridge Management Coll., 1970; joined HM Diplomatic Service, 1971; FCO, 1971–73; First Sec. (Inf.), Caracas, 1973–75; Head of Chancery, Caracas, 1975–77; Asst Head, Mexican and Caribbean Dept, FCO, 1977–78; Counsellor and Head of Chancery, Warsaw, 1978–82; Counsellor and Head of British Interests Section, Buenos Aires, 1982–84; Head of Mexico and Central America Dept, FCO, 1984–87; Ambassador to Honduras and El Salvador, 1987–89; Consul Gen. Barcelona, 1989–92. *Recreations:* golf, tennis, personal computers, music, reading; *e-mail:* dmmjoy@excite.com. *Clubs:* Oxford and Cambridge; Cercle del Liceu (Barcelona); Rotary, La Peñaza Golf (Zaragoza); Key Biscayne Yacht (Florida).

JOY, Peter, OBE 1969; HM Diplomatic Service, retired; *b* 16 Jan. 1926; *s* of late Neville Holt Joy and Marguerite Mary Duff Beith; *m* 1953, Rosemary Joan Hebden; two *s* two *d*. *Educ:* Downhouse Sch., Pembridge; New Coll., Oxford. Served with RAF, 1944–47. Entered Foreign (subseq. Diplomatic) Service, 1952; 1st Sec., Ankara, 1959; 1st Sec., New Delhi, 1962; FO, 1965; 1st Sec., Beirut, 1968; FCO, 1973; Counsellor, Kuala Lumpur, 1979–80; Counsellor, FCO, 1980–86. *Recreations:* shooting, fishing. *Address:* The Old Rectory, Stoke Bliss, near Tenbury, Worcs WR15 8QJ. *T:* (01885) 410342; Carrick House, Eday, Orkney KW17 2AB.

JOY, Thomas Alfred, LVO 1979; President, Hatchards Ltd, 1985 (Managing Director, 1965–85); *b* 30 Dec. 1904; *s* of Alfred Joy and Annie Carpenter; *m* 1932, Edith Ellis. *Educ:* privately; Bedford House Sch., Oxford. Jun. Assistant, Bodleian Library, Oxford, 1919; indentured apprentice, 1919–25, buyer and cataloguer, 1925–35, J. Thornton & Son, University Booksellers, Oxford; Manager, Circulating Library, 1935–45, and Manager, Book Dept, 1942–45, Harrods; Army & Navy Stores: Manager, Book Dept, and founder of Library, 1945–56; Merchandise Manager, 1956; Dep. Managing Dir, 1956–65. Began Hatchards Authors of the Year parties, 1966. Employers' rep., Bookselling and Stationery Trade Wages Council, 1946–79, leader of employers' side, 1957; Member: Nat. Chamber of Trade, 1946–51; Wholesale Trades Adv. Cttee, 1946–51; 1948 Book Trade Cttee; Arts Council working party on obscene pubns, 1968–69, and sub-cttee on Public Lending Rights, 1970. President: Booksellers Assoc. of GB and Ire, 1957–58 (Hon. Life Pres., 1989); Book Trade Benevolent Soc., 1974–86 (Patron, 1986). Inaugurated Nat. Book Sale (first Chm. of Cttee, 1954–65). Hon. Life Mem., Soc. of Bookmen. FRSA 1967. Jubilee Medal, 1977. *Publications:* The Right Way to Run a Library Business, 1949; Bookselling, 1953; The Truth about Bookselling, 1964; Mostly Joy (autobiog.), 1971; The Bookselling Business, 1974; contribs to Bookseller and other trade jls. *Recreations:* reading, gardening. *Address:* 13 Cole Park Gardens, Twickenham, Middlesex TW1 1JB. *T:* (020) 8892 5660.

JOYCE, Prof. Bruce Arthur, DSc; FRS 2000; CPhys, FInstP; Professor of Semiconductor Materials, Department of Physics, Imperial College, London, 1988–2000, now Emeritus Professor of Physics and Senior Research Investigator; *b* 17 Oct. 1934; *s* of Frederick Charles James Joyce and Dorothy Joyce (*née* Crouch); *m* 1956, Beryl Ann Mead; three *s* one *d*. *Educ:* Birmingham Univ. (BSc 1956; DSc 1973). CPhys, FInstP 1973. Nat. Service Commn, RAF, 1956–58. Sen. Scientist, Allen Clark Res. Centre, Plessey Co., 1958–69; Sen. Principal Scientist, Philips Res. Labs, Redhill, 1969–88; Dir, Univ. of London IRC for Semiconductor Materials, ICSTM, 1988–99. *Publications:* contrib. numerous papers to learned jls. *Recreations:* hill-walking, athletics (track and road running), Rugby football, cricket, crosswords, gardening. *Address:* 15 Tennyson Rise, East Grinstead, W Sussex RH19 1SQ. *T:* (01342) 323059.

JOYCE, Eric Stuart; MP (Lab) Falkirk West, since Dec. 2000; *b* 13 Oct. 1960; *s* of Leslie Joyce and Sheila Joyce (*née* Christie); *m* 1st, 1978, Christina Louise Guest (marr. diss. 1982); 2nd, 1991, Rosemary Jones. *Educ:* Univ. of Stirling (BA Hons 1986); W London Inst. (PGCE 1987); Univ. of Bath (MA 1994); Univ. of Keele (MBA 1995). Served Army, 1978–99: Black Watch, 1978–81; RMA Sandhurst, 1987; commnd RAEC, 1987; served AGC; Maj. 1992. Public Affairs Officer, CRE, 1999–2000. *Publications:* Arms and the Man: renewing the armed services, 1997; (ed) Now's the Hour!: new thinking for Holyrood, 1999. *Recreations:* climbing, judo, most sports. *Address:* House of Commons, SW1A 0AA; (constituency office) 2 Lint Riggs, Falkirk FK1 1DG. *T:* (01324) 638919; *e-mail:* epicjoycemp@parliament.uk. *Club:* Camelon Labour (Falkirk).

JOYCE, Peter Robert, CB 2000; FCCA; Inspector General and Agency Chief Executive, The Insolvency Service 1989–2001; *b* 14 Jan. 1942; *s* of George Henry Joyce and Edith Doris Joyce; *m* 1st, 1965 (marr. diss. 1988); one *s* one *d*; 2nd, 1988, Marian Neal. *Educ:* Westwood's Grammar Sch., Northleach, Glos. FCCA 1970. Insolvency Service, Board of Trade, subseq. Department of Trade and Industry, 1960–2001: Examr, 1960–69; Sen. Examr, 1969–76; Asst Official Receiver and Chief Examr, 1976–82; Official Receiver and Principal Examr, 1982–85; Dep. Inspector General, 1985–89. Chairman: Internat. Assoc. of Insolvency Regulators, 1995–2001; World Bank Wkg Gp on Insolvency Regulatory Frameworks, 1999–2001. Mem. Council, Central Govt NTO, 1999–2001. Hon. FCIM 2000. *Recreations:* watching cricket, theatre and concerts, dining out, DIY. *Club:* Gloucestershire County Cricket.

JOYCE, Sir Robert John H.; *see* Hayman-Joyce.

JOYCE, William R., Jr; lawyer, since 1951; Director and Secretary-Treasurer, Battle of Britain Museum Foundation (USA), since 1976; President, Canterbury Institute Trust (USA), since 1989; Director and President, Hanaya Financial Corporation, Tokyo and Washington, since 1996; *b* 18 May 1921; *s* of William R. Joyce and Winifred Lowery; *m* 1956, Mary-Hoyt Sherman; one *s* two *d*. *Educ:* Loyola Univ. (BA); New York and Harvard Law Schs. JD. Lawyer, in private practice, New York City and Washington, DC; member of firm, Vance Joyce & Carbaugh, 1977–; Consul General *ad hon.*, Republic of Bolivia (Washington, DC), 1963–. Pres., Consular Corps of Washington, DC, 1982–. Member: Bd of Trustees, Holy Land Foundn, Jerusalem, 1999–; Bd of Dirs, Council on Egyptian-American Relns, 2000–. FRGS. Academician, Catholic Acad. of Scis, USA, 1999. Kt 1973, Kt Comdr (pro Merito Melitensi), Order of Malta, 1977; Kt, Equestrian Order of Holy Sepulchre, Jerusalem, 1976, KCHS 1999; Kt Comdr of Grace, Order of Constantine and S George (Borbon-Two Sicilies), Naples, 1977; Order of Condor of the Andes, Bolivia, 1978; Order of Simon Bolivar the Liberator, Bolivia, 1988. *Recreations:* sailing, golf. *Address:* (residence) 3700 Blackthorn Court, Chevy Chase, MD 20815–4942, USA. *T:* (301) 6573292. *Clubs:* The Brook, India House, Union, New York Yacht (New York City); Metropolitan, Chevy Chase (Washington); Cooperstown Country (New York); Royal Malta Yacht (Malta).

JOYNSON-HICKS, family name of **Viscount Brentford**.

JOYNT, Rt Rev. Michael Charles S.; *see* Scott-Joynt.

JUCKES, Robert William Somerville; QC 1999; a Recorder, since 1995; *b* 1 Aug. 1950; *s* of Dr William Renwick Juckes and Enid Osyth Juckes (*née* Hankinson); *m* 1974, Frances Anne MacDowel; three *s*. *Educ:* Marlborough Coll.; Exeter Univ. (BA Hons Sociol. and Law 1972). Called to the Bar, Inner Temple, 1974; in practice, Birmingham, 1975; Asst Recorder, 1992–95. *Recreations:* golf, tennis, cricket, novels of Patrick O'Brian, culturing three sons. *Address:* 3 Fountain Court, Steelhouse Lane, Birmingham B4 6DR. *Clubs:* Blackwell Golf (Bromsgrove); Priory Tennis (Edgbaston).

JUDA, Annely, CBE 1998; Director, Annely Juda Fine Art, since 1967; *b* 23 Sept. 1914; *m* 1939, Paul Juda (marr. diss. 1955); one *s* two *d*. *Educ:* von Meysenburg Sch., Kassel; Reimann Art Sch., London. Founded: Molton Gall., 1960; Hamilton Gall., 1963, Annely Juda Fine Art, 1967. *Publications:* specialised catalogues. *Recreation:* ski-ing. *Address:* 74 Windermere Avenue, N3 3RA. *T:* (020) 8346 0743. *Club:* Theatre.

JUDD, family name of **Baron Judd**.

JUDD, Baron *cr* 1991 (Life Peer), of Portsea in the County of Hampshire; **Frank Ashcroft Judd;** consultant on international affairs, Third World issues, conflict resolution and arms control; Senior Fellow, Saferworld, since 1994; Director, Oxfam, 1985–91; *b* 28 March

1935; *s* of late Charles Judd, CBE and Helen Judd, JP; *m* 1961, Christine Elizabeth Willington; two *d.* *Educ:* City of London Sch.; London Sch. of Economics. Sec.-Gen., IVS, 1960–66. Contested (Lab): Sutton and Cheam, 1959; Portsmouth West, 1964; MP (Lab) Portsmouth W, 1966–74, Portsmouth N, 1974–79; PPS: to Minister of Housing, 1967–70; to the Leader of the Opposition, 1970–72; Mem., Opposition's Front Bench Defence Team, 1972–74; Parliamentary Under-Secretary of State: for Defence (Navy), MoD, 1974–76; ODM 1976; Minister of State: for Overseas Develt, 1976–77; FCO, 1977–79; Mem., British Parly Delegn to Council of Europe and WEU, 1970–73, 1997–; Opposition front bench spokesperson, H of L, on for. affairs, 1991–92, on defence, 1995–97; principal spokesperson, on educn, 1992–94, on overseas develt co-operation, 1994–97. Indep. Advr to UK Delegn to UN Special Session on Disarmament, 1982. Associate Dir, Internat. Defence Aid Fund for Southern Africa, 1979–80; Dir, VSO, 1980–85. Chairman: Centre for World Development Educn, 1980–85; Internat. Council of Voluntary Agencies, 1985–90; World Econ. Forum Conf., Geneva, on the future of S Africa, 1990 and 1991; Member: Steering Cttee, World Bank—NGO Cttee, 1989–91; Internat. Commn on Global Governance, 1992–2001; WHO Task Force on Health and Develt, 1994–98; Internat. Working Gp on Human Duties and Responsibilities in the New Millennium, 1997–99. Pres., European–Atlantic Gp, 1999–2001. Past Chm., Fabian Soc. Chm., Oxford Diocesan Bd for Social Responsibility, 1992–95. Dir, Portsmouth Harbour Renaissance Bd, 1998–; Mem., NW Regl Cttee, Nat. Trust, 1996–; Vice-Pres., Council for Nat. Parks, 1998–; Nat. Pres., YMCA England, 1996–; Pres., Friends of RN Mus., 2001–. Trustee: Internat. Alert, 1994–2000 (Chm., 1997–2000); Selly Oak Colls, Birmingham, 1994–97 (Chm. Council, 1994–97); Member Council: ODI; Univ. of Lancaster, 1996–; Governor: LSE, 1982–; Westminster Coll., Oxford, 1991–98. Member: MSF; GMB. Freeman, City of Portsmouth, 1995. Hon. Fellow, Univ. of Portsmouth (formerly Portsmouth Poly.), 1978–; Sen. Fellow, De Montfort Univ., 1999–. Hon. DLitt: Bradford Univ., 1987; Portsmouth, 1997; Hon. LLD Greenwich, 1999. FRSA 1988. *Publications:* (jtly) Radical Future, 1967; Fabian International Essays, 1970; Purpose in Socialism, 1973; (jtly) Our Global Neighbourhood, 1995; various papers and articles on current affairs. *Recreations:* walking, family holidays. *Address:* House of Lords, SW1A 0PW. *Club:* Royal Commonwealth Society.

JUDD, Clifford Harold Alfred, CB 1987; Under Secretary, HM Treasury, 1981–87; *b* 27 June 1927; *s* of Alfred Ernest and Florence Louisa Judd; *m* 1951, Elizabeth Margaret Holmes; two *d.* *Educ:* Christ's Hospital; Keble Coll., Oxford. National Service, RA, 1946–48 (to 2/Lt). HM Treasury: Executive Officer, 1948, through ranks to Principal, 1964, Sen. Prin., 1969, Asst Sec., 1973. *Recreations:* cricket, golf, do-it-yourself. *Address:* 4 Colets Orchard, Otford, Kent TN14 5RA. *T:* (01959) 522398. *Clubs:* Forty; Sevenoaks Vine; Knole Park Golf.

JUDD, Eric Campbell, CBE 1974; LVO 1956; Chairman, West Africa Committee, 1976–85 (Vice-Chairman, 1963–76); *b* St Thomas, Ont, 10 Aug. 1918; *s* of Frederick William Judd, PhmB (Canada), and Marjorie Katherine (*née* Bell); *m* 1947, Janet Creswell (*née* Fish); two *s* one *d.* *Educ:* Wellington, Canada; St Thomas Collegiate; Toronto Univ. Trainee Manager, Cities Service Oil Co., Canada, 1937–40. RCAF and RAF, 1940–45: Canada, N Atlantic Ferry Comd, Europe, Malta, Middle East, Far East, W Indies; retd Sqdn Ldr RCAF Reserve, 1945. Joined Unilever Ltd, 1946; United Africa Co. Ltd, Nigeria, 1946–60, Chm., 1957–60; Dir, UAC Ltd London, 1960, Man. Dir, 1968; Dep. Chm. and Jt Man. Dir, UAC International, 1969–77. Mem. House of Assembly, Western Nigeria, 1955–56; Chm., BNEC Africa, 1969–72; Chm., Adv. Gp Africa BOTB, 1972–74. Mem. Council, 1975–88, a Vice-Pres., 1983–88, Royal African Soc. *Recreations:* golf, tennis, theatre, music, reading. *Address:* 2 Gerard Court, Hitherfield Lane, Lydekker Park, Harpenden, Herts AL5 4JA. *T:* (01582) 712617. *Club:* MCC.

JUDD, Judith Margaret; Associate Editor, Times Educational Supplement, since 2001; *b* 18 April 1949; *d* of John Berry and Joan Berry (*née* Edge); *m* 1973, Very Rev. Peter Somerset Margesson Judd, *qv*; one *s* one *d.* *Educ:* Bolton Sch.; St Anne's Coll., Oxford (BA Modern History). Reporter, 1972–74, Educn Reporter, 1974–75, Birmingham Post and Birmingham Mail; joined THES, 1975, News Editor, 1977–79; Reporter, 1979–82, Educn Correspondent, 1982–90, Observer; Education Correspondent: Independent on Sunday, 1990–93; Independent, 1991–93; Educn Ed., The Independent and The Independent on Sunday, 1993–2001. *Recreations:* gardening, reading, walking. *Address:* The Dean's House, 3 Harlings Grove, Chelmsford CM1 1YQ; Times Educational Supplement, Admiral House, 66–68 East Smithfield, E1W 1BX.

JUDD, Nadine; *see* Nerina, Nadia.

JUDD, Very Rev. Peter Somerset Margesson; Dean (formerly Provost) of Chelmsford Cathedral, since 1997; *b* 20 Feb. 1949; *s* of William Frank Judd and Norah Margesson Judd (*née* Margesson); *m* 1973, Judith Margaret Berry (*see* J. M. Judd); one *s* one *d.* *Educ:* Charterhouse Sch.; Trinity Hall, Cambridge (MA Architecture); Cuddesdon Coll., Oxford (Cert. Theol.). Ordained deacon, 1974, priest, 1975; Asst Curate, St Philip with St Stephen, Salford, 1974–76; Chaplain, 1976–81, Fellow, 1980–81, Clare Coll., Cambridge; Team Vicar of Hitcham and Dropmore, Burnham Team Ministry, dio. of Oxford, 1981–88; Vicar, St Mary the Virgin, Iffley, 1988–97; Rural Dean of Cowley, 1995–97. *Recreations:* architecture, art, listening to music, literature, drawing, cooking, fell walking. *Address:* The Dean's House, 3 Harlings Grove, Chelmsford CM1 1YQ. *T:* (01245) 354318.

JUDGE, Harry George, MA Oxon, PhD London; Fellow of Brasenose College, Oxford, since 1973; Senior Research Associate, University of Oxford Department of Educational Studies, since 1988 (Director, 1973–88); *b* 1 Aug. 1928; *s* of George Arthur and Winifred Mary Judge; *m* 1956, Elizabeth Mary Patrick; one *s* two *d.* *Educ:* Cardiff High Sch.; Brasenose Coll., Oxford. Asst Master, Emanuel Sch. and Wallington County Grammar Sch., 1954–59; Dir of Studies, Cumberland Lodge, Windsor, 1959–62; Head Master, Banbury Grammar Sch., 1962–67; Principal, Banbury Sch., 1967–73. Visiting Professor: MIT, 1977 and 1980–82; Carnegie–Mellon Univ., 1984–86; Univ. of Virginia, 1987; Michigan State Univ., 1988–93; Pennsylvania State Univ., 1995–96; Visiting Scholar: Harvard Univ., 1985–87; Carnegie Foundn, 1998–2000; Sachs Lectr, Teachers' Coll., Columbia Univ., 1993; Read Distinguished Chair Lectr, Kent State Univ., 1996. Member: Public Schools Commission, 1966–70; James Cttee of Inquiry into Teacher Training, 1971–72; Educn Sub-Cttee, UGC, 1976–80; Oxon Educn Cttee, 1982–87. Chairman: School Broadcasting Council, 1977–81; RCN Commn on Education, 1984–85. Gen. Editor, Oxford Illus. Encyclopedia, 1985–. *Publications:* Louis XIV, 1965; School Is Not Yet Dead, 1974; Graduate Schools of Education in the US, 1982; A Generation of Schooling: English secondary schools since 1944, 1984; The University and the Teachers: France, the United States, England, 1994; contribs on educational and historical subjects to collective works and learned jls. *Recreation:* canals. *Address:* Brasenose College, Oxford OX1 4AJ.

JUDGE, Ian; theatre director; *b* 21 July 1946; *s* of Jack and Marjorie Judge. *Educ:* King George V Grammar Sch., Southport; GSMD. Joined RSC as an asst dir, 1975; productions include: The Wizard of Oz, 1987; The Comedy of Errors, 1990; Love's Labour's Lost, 1993; Twelfth Night, 1994; A Christmas Carol, 1994; The Relapse, 1995; Troilus and Cressida, 1996; The Merry Wives of Windsor, 1996; *opera:* English National Opera: Faust, 1985; Cavalleria Rusticana and Pagliacci, 1987; Don Quichotte, 1994; La Belle Vivette, 1995; Mephistopheles, 1999; Opera North: Macbeth, 1987; Tosca, 1988; Boris Godunov, 1989; Attila, 1990; Show Boat, 1990 (also at London Palladium); Scottish Opera: Falstaff, 1991; Norma, 1993; Royal Opera House: The Flying Dutchman, 1992; Simon Boccanegra, 1997; Così Fan Tutte, Garsington, 1997; Eugene Onegin, Grange Park Opera, 2000; Los Angeles: Tosca, 1989; Madama Butterfly, 1991; Melbourne and Sydney: Faust, 1990; Tales of Hoffman, 1992; Macbeth, Cologne, 1992; La Bohème, Kirov, 2001; Falstaff, Paris, 2001; *theatre:* Chichester: Oh! Kay, 1984; A Little Night Music, 1990 (also Piccadilly Theatre); Henry VIII, 1991; Love for Love, 1996; West Side Story (Australian tour), 1994–96; Macbeth, Sydney Th. Co., 1999; The Mikado, Savoy Theatre, 2000. *Address:* c/o Simpson Fox Associates, 52 Shaftesbury Avenue, W1V 7DE. *T:* (020) 7434 9167.

JUDGE, Rt Hon. Sir Igor, Kt 1988; PC 1996; **Rt Hon. Lord Justice Judge;** a Lord Justice of Appeal, since 1996; Senior Presiding Judge for England and Wales, since 1998; *b* 19 May 1941; *s* of Raymond and Rosa Judge; *m* 1965, Judith Mary Robinson; one *s* two *d.* *Educ:* Oratory Sch., Woodcote; Magdalene Coll., Cambridge (Exhbnr, MA). Harmsworth Exhbnr and Astbury Scholar, Middle Temple. Called to the Bar, Middle Temple, 1963, Bencher, 1987; a Recorder, 1976–88; Prosecuting Counsel to Inland Revenue, 1977–79; QC 1979; a Judge of the High Court, QBD, 1988–96; Leader, 1988, Presiding Judge, 1993–96, Midland and Oxford Circuit. Member: Senate, Inns of Court and the Bar, 1980–83, 1984–86; Bar Council, 1987–88; Judicial Studies Bd, 1984–88, 1991–94 and 1996–98 (Chm. Criminal Cttee, 1991–93 and 1996–98). *Recreations:* history, music, cricket. *Address:* Royal Courts of Justice, Strand, WC2A 2LL.

JUDGE, Sir Paul (Rupert), Kt 1996; Chairman, Isoworth Ltd, since 1989; *b* 25 April 1949; *s* of late Rupert Cyril Judge and of Betty Rosa Muriel Judge (*née* Daniels), Forest Hill; *m*; two *s.* *Educ:* St Dunstan's Coll.; Trinity Coll., Cambridge (MA, Open Scholar); Wharton Business Sch., Univ. of Pennsylvania (MBA, Thouron Schol.). Cadbury Schweppes, 1973–86 (Group Planning Dir, 1984–86); Premier Brands: Man. Dir, 1986–87; Chm., 1987–89; Chm., Food from Britain, 1989–92; Director: Grosvenor Development Capital plc, 1989–93; Boddington Group plc, 1983–93; WPP plc, 1991–97; Schroder Income Growth Fund plc, 1995–. Dir Gen., Cons. Party, 1992–95; Ministerial Advr, Cabinet Office, 1995–96. Chm., Adv. Bd, Cambridge Univ. Inst. of Management Studies, 1991–; Trustee: Cambridge Foundn, 1991–2000 (Emeritus, 2000–); British Food Heritage Trust, 1997–; Businessdynamics (formerly Understanding Industry) Trust, 1998– (Chm. Trustees, 1999–); Amer. Mgt Assoc., 2000–; Mem. Council, Assoc. of MBAs, 1992– (Chm., 1997–); Chm., Wharton European Bd, 2000–. Vice Pres., Mkting Council, 2001–. Mem., Shakespeare's Globe Develt Council, 1999– (Dep. Chm., 2000–). Governor: Bromsgrove Sch., 1991–96; St Dunstan's Coll., 1997– (Dep. Chm., 1999–). FInstD; Fellow, Marketing Soc.; FRSA. Freeman, City of London; Liveryman, Marketors' Co., 1993. Hon. LLD Cantab, 1995. *Recreations:* family, travel. *Address:* 88 The Panoramic, 152 Grosvenor Road, SW1V 3JL. *Clubs:* Athenæum, Carlton; Mombasa (Kenya).

JUGNAUTH, Rt Hon. Sir Aneerood, KCMG 1988; PC 1987; QC (Mauritius) 1980; Prime Minister of Mauritius, 1982–95 and since 2000; *b* 29 March 1930; *m* Sarojini Devi Ballah; one *s* one *d.* *Educ:* Church of England School, Palma, Mauritius; Regent Coll., Quatre Bornes. Called to the Bar, Lincoln's Inn, 1954. Teacher, New Eton Coll., 1948; worked in Civil Service, 1949. MLA Rivière du Rempart, 1963–67, Piton-Rivière du Rempart, 1976, 1982, 1983, 1987 and 1991–; Town Councillor, Vacoas-Phoenix, 1964; Minister of State for Develt, 1965–67; Minister of Labour, 1967; Leader of the Opposition, 1976–82; Minister of Finance, 1983–84 and 1990–91; Dist Magistrate, 1967–69; Crown Counsel, 1969; Sen. Crown Counsel, 1971. Attended London Constitutional Conf., 1965. Leader, Mouvement Socialist Militant, 1983–. Dr *hc* Aix-en-Provence, 1985; Hon. DCL Mauritius, 1985. Order of Rising Sun (1st cl.) (Japan), 1988; Grand Officier, Ordre de la Légion d'Honneur (France), 1990. *Address:* Government House, Port Louis, Mauritius; La Caverne No 1, Vacoas, Mauritius.

JUKES, Rt Rev. John, OFMConv; STL; VG; Parish Priest, Huntly, RC Diocese of Aberdeen, since 2000; Retired Auxiliary Bishop of Southwark; Titular Bishop of Strathearn, since 1980; *b* 7 Aug. 1923; *s* of Francis Bernard Jukes and Florence Jukes (*née* Stampton). *Educ:* Blackheath; Rome. Professed in Order of Friars Minor Conventual, 1948; priest, 1952; Lectr in Canon Law, Franciscan Internat. Study Centre, Univ. of Kent at Canterbury, Rector, 1999–; Minister Provincial, English Province, 1979. Formerly: Episcopal Vicar for Religious, Southwark; Area Bishop with special responsibility for Deaneries of Canterbury, Chatham, Dover, Gravesend, Maidstone, Ramsgate and Tunbridge Wells; an Auxiliary Bp in Southwark, 1980–2000. Mem., RC Bishops' Conf. of England and Wales (Chm., World of Work Cttee, 1983–; Mem., Internat. Bio-Ethics Cttee, 1996–); Vice Pres., Christian Council on Defence and Disarmament. Chm. Governors, St Mary's UC, Surrey Univ., 1991–99. DUniv Surrey. *Publications:* contribs to Misc. Francescana, Studia Canonica, New Life, Clergy Rev., etc. *Recreation:* mountain walking and climbing. *Address:* St Margaret, 30 Chapel Street, Huntly AB54 8BS.

JULIAN, Prof. Desmond Gareth, CBE 1993; MD, FRCP; Consultant Medical Director, British Heart Foundation, 1987–93; *b* 24 April 1926; *s* of Frederick Bennett Julian and Jane Frances Julian (*née* Galbraith); *m* 1st, 1956, Mary Ruth Jessup (decd); one *s* one *d*; 2nd, 1988, Claire Marley. *Educ:* Leighton Park Sch.; St John's Coll., Cambridge; Middlesex Hosp. MB BChir (Cantab) 1948; MA 1953; MD 1954; FRCPE 1967; FRCP 1970; FRACP 1970; FACC 1985. Surgeon Lieut, RNVR, 1949–51. Med. Registrar, Nat. Heart Hosp., 1955–56; Res. Fellow, Peter Bent Brigham Hosp., Boston, 1957–58; Sen. Reg., Royal Inf., Edinburgh, 1958–61; Cons. Cardiologist, Sydney Hosp., 1961–64, Royal Inf., Edinburgh, 1964–74; Prof. of Cardiology, Univ. of Newcastle upon Tyne, 1975–86. Mem., MRC Systems Bd, 1980–84. Pres., British Cardiac Soc., 1985–87; Second Vice-Pres., RCP, 1990–91. Hon. MD: Gothenburg, 1987; Edinburgh, 1997. Gold Medal, European Soc. of Cardiology, 1998. Editor, European Heart Jl, 1980–88. *Publications:* Cardiology, 1972, 7th edn 1998; (ed) Angina Pectoris, 1975, 2nd edn 1984; Acute Myocardial Infarction, 1967; (ed) Diseases of the Heart, 1989, 2nd edn 1995; Coronary Heart Disease: the facts, 1991; contribs to med. jls, particularly on coronary disease. *Recreations:* walking, writing. *Address:* Flat 1, 7 Netherhall Gardens, NW3 5RN. *T:* (020) 7435 8254. *Club:* Garrick.

JULIEN, Michael Frederick, FCA; FCT; Chairman, First Choice Holidays PLC (formerly Owners Abroad Group plc), 1993–97; *b* 22 March 1938; *s* of late Robert Auguste François and Olive Rita (*née* Evans); *m* 1963, Ellen Martinsen; one *s* two *d.* *Educ:* St Edward's Sch., Oxford. Price Waterhouse & Co., 1958–67; other commercial appts, 1967–76; Gp Finance Dir, BICC, 1976–83; Exec. Dir, Finance and Planning, Midland Bank, 1983–86; Man. Dir, Finance and Administration, Guinness PLC, 1987–88; Gp Chief Exec., Storehouse PLC, 1988–92. Director (non-executive): Littlewoods Orgn plc,

1981–86; Guinness PLC, 1988–97; Medeva PLC, 1993–98; Oxford English Online Ltd, 1999–. *Recreations:* family, travel. *Address:* *e-mail:* mfjulien@julienco.com.

JULIUS, Dr Anthony Robert; Consultant, Mishcon de Reya, since 1998; *b* 16 July 1956; *s* of Morris and Myrna Julius; *m* 1st, 1979, Judith Bernie (marr. diss. 1998); two *s* two *d*; 2nd, 1999, Dina Rabinovitch. *Educ:* City of London Sch.; Jesus Coll., Cambridge (MA); University Coll. London (PhD 1992). Admitted Solicitor, 1981; Mishcon de Reya: Partner, 1984–98; Head of Litigation, 1988–98. Institute of Jewish Policy Research: Dir, 1996–2000; Mem. Council, 2000–; Chair, Law Cttee, 1998–2000; Mem., Appeals Cttee, Dermatrust, 1999–; foreword, report on holocaust denial and UK law, 2000. Chair, Diana, Princess of Wales Meml Fund, 1997–99; Mem., Fest. Council, The Word. Chm. Mgt Bd, Centre for Cultural Analysis, Theory and History, Univ. of Leeds, 2001–. *Publications:* T. S. Eliot, anti-Semitism, and literary form, 1995; (contrib.) Law and Literature, 1999; Idolizing Pictures, 2001. *Recreations:* cinema, cooking. *Address:* (office) 21 Southampton Row, WC1B 5HS. *T:* (020) 7440 7025. *Club:* Soho House.

JULIUS, DeAnne, PhD; Member, Court, Bank of England, since 2001; *b* 14 April 1949; *d* of Marvin G. Julius and Maxine M. Julius; *m* 1976, Ian Harvey; one *s* one *d*. *Educ:* Iowa State Univ. (BSc Econs 1970); Univ. of Calif at Davis (MA 1974; PhD Econs 1975). Economic Analyst, US CS, 1970–71; Lectr, Univ. of Calif at Santa Barbara, 1975; project economist, then econ. advr, World Bank, 1975–82; Man. Dir, Logan Associates Inc., 1983–86; Prog. Dir for Econs, RIIA, 1986–89; Chief Economist: Shell Internat., 1989–93; British Airways, 1993–97; Chm., British Airways Pension Investment Mgt Ltd, 1995–97. Mem., Monetary Policy Cttee, Bank of England, 1997–2001. Vis. Prof., Univ. of Durham, 1998–. Member: Cttee on Women in Econs, Royal Econ. Soc., 1998–; Nat. Learning and Skills Council, 2000–; Vice Chm., Inst. Develt Studies, 2000–; Chairman: Banking Code Review Gp, 2000–; Council, RIIA, 2000–. *Publications:* (jtly) Appropriate Sanitation Alternatives: a technical and economic appraisal, 1982; (jtly) The Monetary Implications of the 1992 Process, 1990; Global Companies and Public Policy: the growing challenge of foreign direct investment, 1990; (with A. Mashayekhi) Economics of Natural Gas: pricing, planning and policy, 1990. *Recreations:* ski-ing, sailing, tending bonsai. *Address:* Bank of England, Threadneedle Street, EC2R 8AH.

JUNCKER, Dr Jean-Claude; Prime Minister, Minister of State and Minister of Finance, Luxembourg, since 1995; *b* Redange-Attert, 9 Dec. 1954; *m* 1979, Christiane Frising. *Educ:* Secondary Sch., Clairefontaine, Belgium; Univ. of Strasbourg (Dr Public Law 1979). Parly Sec., Christian Social Party, 1979–82; State Sec. for Labour and Social Affairs, 1982–84; Minister of: Labour and Minister i/c Budget, 1984–89; Labour and of Finance, 1989–95; Labour and Employment, 1995–99. Pres., Christian Social Party, 1990–95. *Address:* Hôtel de Bourgogne, 4 rue de la Congrégation, 2910 Luxembourg. *T:* 4782101, *Fax:* 461720.

JUNGELS, Dr Pierre Jean Marie Henri, Hon. CBE 1989; Chief Executive, Enterprise Oil plc, 1997–2001; *b* 18 Feb. 1944; *s* of Henri and Jeanne Jungels; *m* 1988, Caroline Benc; one step *s* one step *d*; one *s* one *d* from former marriage. *Educ:* Univ. of Liège (Ing. Civ. 1967); California Inst. of Technology (PhD 1973). Petroleum Engr, Shell, 1973–74; Dist Manager, 1975–77, General Manager and Chief Exec., 1977–80, Petrangol (Angola); Man. Dir and Chief Exec., Petrofina UK, 1980–89; Exec. Dir, Downstream, Petrofina Gp, 1989–92; Exec. Dir, Exploration and Production, Petrofina Group, 1992–95; Man. Dir, Exploration and Production, British Gas, 1996. Past Pres., Inst. of Petroleum. *Recreation:* shooting. *Address:* Enborne Chase, Enborne, Newbury, Berks RG20 0HD.

JUNGIUS, Vice-Adm. Sir James (George), KBE 1977; Supreme Allied Commander Atlantic's Representative in Europe, 1978–80, retired; Vice Lord-Lieutenant of Cornwall, 1994–98; *b* 15 Nov. 1923; *s* of Major E. J. T. Jungius, MC; *m* 1949, Rosemary Frances Turquand Matthey; three *s*. *Educ:* RNC, Dartmouth. Served War of 1939–45 in Atlantic and Mediterranean; Commando Ops in Adriatic (despatches). Specialised in Navigation in 1946, followed by series of appts as Navigating Officer at sea and instructing ashore. Comdr, Dec. 1955; CO, HMS Wizard, 1956–57; Admlty, 1958–59; Exec. Officer, HMS Centaur, 1960–61; Captain, 1963; Naval Staff, 1964–65; CO, HMS Lynx, 1966–67; Asst Naval Attaché, Washington, DC, 1968–70; CO, HMS Albion, 1971–72; Rear-Adm., 1972; Asst Chief of Naval Staff (Operational Requirements), 1972–74; Vice-Adm., 1974; Dep. Supreme Allied Comdr Atlantic, 1975–77. County Pres., Cornwall, RBL, 1995–. Vice-Chm., SW War Pensions Cttee, 1996–. Fellow, Woodard Corp., 1988–95. Gov., Grenville Coll., 1981–96. CIMgt. DL Cornwall, 1982. CStJ 1995 (Chm., St John Council for Cornwall, 1987–95). *Address:* c/o National Westminster Bank, Wadebridge, Cornwall PL27 7DL. *Clubs:* Royal Navy Club of 1765 and 1785; Pilgrims; Royal Cornwall Yacht.

JUNOR, Penelope Jane, (Penny); journalist, writer and broadcaster; *b* 6 Oct. 1949; *d* of Sir John Junor and Pamela Mary (*née* Welsh); *m* 1970, James Stewart Leith; three *s* one *d*. *Educ:* Benenden Sch.; Univ. of St Andrews. Feature writer, 19 mag., 1970–71; reporter, Londoner's Diary, Evening Standard, 1971–74; freelance, 1974–; columnist, Private Eye, 1977–82; television: reporter, Collecting Now, 1981; Presenter: 4 What It's Worth, 1982–89; The Afternoon Show, 1984–85; The Travel Show, 1988–97. Gen. Ed., John Lewis Partnership, 1993–99. *Publications:* Newspaper, 1979; Diana, Princess of Wales, 1982; Babyware, 1982; Margaret Thatcher: wife, mother, politician, 1983; Burton, the Man Behind the Myth, 1985; Charles, 1987; (ed) What Every Woman Needs to Know, 1988; Queen Elizabeth II: a pictorial celebration of her reign, 1991; Charles and Diana: portrait of a marriage, 1991; The Major Enigma, 1993; Charles: victim or villain?, 1998. *Recreation:* tennis. *Address:* c/o Jane Turnbull, 13 Wendell Road, W12 9RS. *T:* (020) 8743 9580, *Fax:* (020) 8749 6079; Knight Ayton Management, 114 St Martin's Lane, WC2N 4AZ. *T:* (020)7836 5333, *Fax:* (020) 7836 8333. *Club:* Groucho.

JUPE, George Percival; Under Secretary, Ministry of Agriculture, Fisheries and Food, 1979–90; *b* 6 April 1930; *s* of Frederick Stuart Jupe and Elizabeth (*née* Clayton); unmarried. *Educ:* Sandown Grammar Sch., IoW; Hertford Coll., Oxford. Ministry of Agriculture, Fisheries and Food: Asst Principal, 1955; Principal, 1960; Asst Sec., 1970–79: Eggs and Poultry, and Potatoes Divs, 1970–74; Internat. Fisheries Div., 1975–78; Emergencies, Food Quality and Pest Controls Gp, 1979–85; Dir, ADAS Admin, 1985–88; Horticulture, Seeds, Plant Health and Flood Defence Gp, 1988–90. *Recreations:* hill walking, gardening, music. *Address:* Briar Cottages, Brook, Isle of Wight PO30 4EU.

JUPP, Sir Kenneth Graham, Kt 1975; MC 1943; a Judge of the High Court, Queen's Bench Division, 1975–90; *b* 2 June 1917; *s* of Albert Leonard and Marguerite Isabel Jupp; *m* 1947, Kathleen Elizabeth (*née* Richards); two *s* two *d*. *Educ:* Perse Sch., Cambridge; University Coll., Oxford (Sen. Class. Schol., 1936; 1st Cl. Hon. Mods (Classics) 1938; College Prize for Greek, 1939; MA Oxon (War Degree), 1945, avoided Finals by joining Army, 1939); Lincoln's Inn (Cholmeley Schol., 1939; Cassel Schol., 1946). Regimental Service in France, Belgium, N Africa and Italy, 1939–43; War Office Selection Board, 1943–46. Called to Bar, Lincoln's Inn, 1945, Bencher, 1973; QC 1966; Dep. Chm., Cambridge and Isle of Ely QS, 1965–71; a Recorder of the Crown Court, 1972–75; Presiding Judge, NE Circuit, 1977–81. Chm., Independent Schs Tribunal, 1964–67; conducted MAFF inquiry into Wool Marketing Scheme, 1965; Chm., Public Inquiry into Fire at Fairfield Home, Nottingham, 1975. *Publications:* Stealing Our Land, 1997; (trans. and ed) Anne-Robert Turgot, The Formation and Distribution of Wealth: reflections on capitalism, 1999; various pamphlets on theol and econ. subjects. *Recreations:* playing and singing, language. *Address:* Farrar's Building, Temple, EC4Y 7BD. *Club:* Garrick.

JUPPÉ, Alain Marie; Prime Minister of France, 1995–97; Mayor of Bordeaux, since 1995; Deputy for Bordeaux, since 1997; *b* 15 Aug. 1945; *s* of Robert Juppé and Marie Darroze; *m* 1st, 1965, Christine Leblond (marr. diss.); one *s* one *d*; 2nd, 1993, Isabelle Bodin; one *d*. *Educ:* Lycées Victor-Duruy, Mont-de-Marsan and Louis-le-Grand, Paris; Ecole Normale Superieure (Dr in Classical Langs); Inst. of Political Studies; Nat. Sch. of Admin. Finance Inspector, 1972; Asst to Prime Minister Jacques Chirac, 1976; Advr to Minister for Co-operation, 1976–78; MEP, 1984–86; Minister of Foreign Affairs, France, 1993–95. Rassemblement pour la République: Nat. Deleg., 1976–78; Nat. Sec., 1984–86; Dep. Minister of Finance, Govt Spokesman, 1986–88; Gen. Sec., 1988–95; Pres., 1995–97; Deputy for Paris, 1988–93. Adviser to Mayor of Paris, 1978; Dir of Finance and Economic Affairs, City of Paris, 1980–81; Mem., Paris City Council, 1983–95; Dep. Mayor of Paris, i/c Finance, 1983–95. *Publications:* La Tentation de Venise, 1993; Entre Nous, 1996; Montesquieu le Moderne, 1999. *Address:* Hôtel de Ville, place Pey-Berland, 33077 Bordeaux cedex, France.

JURINAC, (Srebrenka) Sena; opera singer; Member of Vienna State Opera, 1944–82, now Honorary; retired from stage, 1982; *b* Travnik, Yugoslavia, 24 Oct. 1921; *d* of Ludwig Jurinac, MD, and Christine Cerv. *Educ:* High Sch.; Musical Academy. Made first appearance on stage as Mimi with Zagreb Opera, 1942. Frequent appearances at Glyndebourne Festivals, 1949–56, as well as at the Salzburg Festivals. Guest appearances at La Scala, Covent Garden, San Francisco, Teatro Colón. Principal parts include: Donna Anna and Donna Elvira in Don Giovanni; Elisabeth in Tannhauser; Tosca; Jenufa; Marie in Wozzeck; Marschallin in Der Rosenkavalier; Composer in Ariadne auf Naxos; Elisabeth in Don Carlos; Desdemona in Othello. *Film:* Der Rosenkavalier, 1962. Singing teacher; frequent appearances as mem. of jury in singing competitions. Kammersängerin award, 1951; Ehrenkreuz für Wissenschaft und Kunst, 1961; Grosses Ehrenzeichen für Verdienste um die Republik Oesterreich, 1967. *Address:* Lerchenweg 10, 86356 Neusäss-Hainhofen, Germany.

JURY, Archibald George, CBE 1961; FRIBA; FRIAS; City Architect, Glasgow, 1951–72, retired; *b* 23 June 1907; *s* of late George John Jury and Mabel Sophie Jury (*née* Fisher); *m* 1931, Amy Beatrice Maw (MBE 1983); one *d*. *Educ:* Mount Radford, Exeter; SW School of Art. Architect to Council, Taunton, 1938–40, and 1945. Served War, 1940–45, with Corps of Royal Engineers (rank of Major). Chief Housing Architect, Liverpool, 1946–49; Dir of Housing, Glasgow, 1949–51; Dir of Planning, Glasgow, 1951–66. Organised the building of 100,000 houses, 100,000 school places and numerous civic buildings; responsible for the Glasgow Devpt Plan, 1960–80, and implementation of urban renewal programme and official architecture. Several Saltire Soc. awards for best-designed flats in Scotland. Chairman: Technical Panel, Scottish Local Authorities Special Housing Group, 1965–72; Technical Panel, Clyde Valley Planning Adv. Cttee, 1960–70; Pres., Glasgow Inst. of Architects, 1970–72. *Publications:* contrib. professional and technical journals.

K

KABERRY, Hon. Sir Christopher Donald, (Hon. Sir Kit), 2nd Bt *cr* 1960, of Adel cum Eccup, City of Leeds; Head of Finance, Union Railways, since 1990; *b* 14 March 1943; *s* of Lord Kaberry of Adel (Life Peer) and Lily Margaret (*d* 1992), *d* of Edmund Scott; *S* to baronetcy of father, 1991; *m* 1967, Gaenor Elizabeth Vowe, *d* of C. V. Peake; two *s* one *d*. *Educ:* Repton Sch. FCA 1967. Various overseas positions, Costain Group PLC, 1969–80; Financial Manager, United Buildings Factories, Bahrain, 1980–82; Resources Manager, Balfour Beatty Group, Indonesia and Bahamas, 1983–90. *Recreations:* walking, gardening, Land Rover driving. *Heir: s* James Christopher Kaberry [*b* 1 April 1970; *m* 1989, Juliet Clare Hill (marr. diss. 1995); two *s* one *d*]. *Address:* Rock View, Chiddingstone Hoath, Kent TN8 7BT.

KADIRGAMAR, Hon. Lakshman; President's Counsel; MP Sri Lanka; Minister of Foreign Affairs, Sri Lanka, since 1994. *Educ:* Univ. of Ceylon (LLB Hons); Balliol Coll., Oxford (BLitt). Called to the Bar, Inner Temple, 1958 (Hon. Bencher); Advocate, Supreme Court of Ceylon; Attorney, Sri Lanka; in legal practice, 1960–73; ILO, Geneva, 1973–75; WIPO, Geneva, 1976–88 (Dir, 1983); legal practice, Sri Lanka, 1988–94. *Recreation:* watching sports. *Address:* 3/3 Havelock Road, Colombo 5, Sri Lanka. *T:* (1) 580415. *Club:* National Liberal.

KADRI, Sibghatullah; QC 1989; barrister-at-law; President, Standing Conference of Pakistani Organisations in UK, 1978–90 (Secretary General, 1975–78); Member, Race Relations Committee, Senate, since 1983; *b* 23 April 1937; *s* of Haji Maulana Firasat Ullah Kadri and Begum Tanwir Fatima Kadri; *m* 1963, Carita Elisabeth Idman; one *s* one *d*. *Educ:* S. M. Coll., Karachi; Karachi Univ. Called to the Bar, Inner Temple, 1969, Bencher, 1997. Sec. Gen., Karachi Univ. Students Union, 1957–58; jailed without trial, for opposing military regime of Ayub Khan, 1958–59; triple winner, All Pakistan Students Debates, 1960; Gen. Sec., Pakistan Students' Fedn in Britain, 1961–62, Vice Pres., 1962–63; Pres., Inner Temple Students Assoc., 1969–70. Producer and broadcaster, BBC Ext. Urdu Service, 1965–68, and Presenter, BBC Home Service Asian Prog., 1968–70. In practice at the Bar, 1969– (Head of Chambers, 6 King's Bench Walk). Chm., Soc. of Afro-Asian and Caribbean Lawyers, UK, 1979–83. Vis. Lectr in Urdu, Holborn Coll., London, 1967–70. Org. Pakistani Def. Cttees during wave of 'Paki-bashing', 1970; active in immigrant and race-relations activities, 1970–; led Asian delegn to Prime Minister, June 1976; attended UN Conf., Migrant Workers in Europe, Geneva, 1975; led Pakistan delegn to 3rd Internat. Conf., Migrant Workers in Europe, Turin, 1977. Gen. Sec., Pakistan Action Cttee, 1973; Convenor, Asian Action Cttee, 1976. Vice Chm., All Party Jt Cttee Against Racism, 1978–80. Publisher, Scopo News, London, until 1984. FRSA 1991. *Publications:* articles in ethnic minority press on immigration and race relations. *Recreations:* family and reading. *Address:* 6 King's Bench Walk, Temple, EC4Y 7DR. *T:* (020) 7353 4931/2.

KAFITY, Rt Rev. Samir; Presidential Consultant, Palestinian Presidency Office, since 1998; Anglican Bishop in Jerusalem, 1984–98; *b* 21 Sept. 1933; *s* of Hanna and Nazha Kafity; *m* 1963, Najat Abed; two *d*. *Educ:* American Univ., Beirut (BA); Near East Sch. of Theol. (DipTh). Ordained deacon, 1957, priest, 1958; Parish priest: to the Arab congregation at St George's Cathedral, Jerusalem, 1957–59; St Andrew's Ramallah, 1959–64; St Peter's, Beir Zeit, then All Saints, Beirut, 1964–77; Lectr, Beir Zeit Univ.; Archdeacon of Jerusalem, 1977–82; Coadjutor Bp in Jerusalem, 1982; Pres. Bishop, Episcopal Church in Jerusalem and the ME, 1986–96, Former Pres. Bishop, 1997–. Member: Standing Cttee, ACC, 1965; Bd of Managers and Exec. Cttee, Near East Sch. of Theol., 1965; Council of Evangelical Community in Syria and Lebanon, 1965–77. Hon. Life Pres., ME Council of Churches (Sec., 1974–94, Pres., 1985). Hon. Canon, Cathedral Church of St John the Divine, NY, 1988. Member: Royal Hashemite Commn on Jerusalem; Moslem-Christian Council, Palestine. President: Supreme Council, Jerusalem YMCA (Chm., Jerusalem); Jerusalem Crippled Chidlren's Instn. Hon. STD Dickenson Coll., Pa, 1985; Hon. DD: Virginia Theol Seminary, 1986; Kent at Canterbury, 1998. KHS; KCLJ 1998; ChStJ. First recipient, Palestinian Jerusalem Medal, 1997. *Publications:* articles in Anglican and ecumenical jls. *Recreation:* travel. *Address:* 11964 Callado Road, San Diego, CA 92128, USA.

KAHAN, George; Director of Conciliation and Arbitration, Advisory, Conciliation and Arbitration Service, 1988–91; *b* 11 June 1931; *er s* of late Joseph Kahan and of Xenia (*née* Kirschner); *m* 1959, Avril Pamela Cooper; one *s*. *Educ:* St Paul's Sch. Nat. Service, RAF, 1950–51. Park Royal Woodworkers Ltd, 1951–74 (Dir, 1960–74); Principal: Dept. of Employment, 1975–76; Health and Safety Executive, Health and Safety Commn, 1976–80; Asst Sec., Dept of Employment, 1980–88. *Recreations:* lazing in the sun, reading, listening to music. *Address:* Half Timbers, The Thatchway, Rustington, Sussex BN16 2BN. *T:* (01903) 784070.

KAHN, Paula; Chair, Equality Works, since 2000; non-executive Director: English Language Services International Ltd, since 1998; New Ways to Work, since 1998; *b* 15 Nov. 1940; *d* of Cyril Maurice Kahn and Stella Roscoe. *Educ:* Chiswick County High Sch.; Bristol Univ. (BA Hons). Teacher, administrator, 1962–66; Longman Group, 1966–94: editor, publisher, Publishing Director, Divl Man. Dir, 1966–79; Managing Director: ELT Div., Dictionaries Div. and Trade and Ref. Div., 1980–85; Internat. Sector, 1986–88; Chief Exec. (Publishing), 1988–89; Chief Exec. and Chm., 1990–94; Project Dir, World Learning Network, 1995–96; Man. Dir, Phaidon Press, 1996–97. Non-executive Director: Inst. of Internat. Visual Arts, 1994–; Focus Central London, TEC, 1998–2001; ITDG Publishing, 1999–; Stonewall, 2000–. Member: English Teaching Adv. Cttee, British Council, 1990–98; Educn and Training Sector Gp, DTI, 1993–98. Mem., Islington CHC, 1998–. Vice-Pres., Publishers Assoc., 1994–95. Mem., Governing Body, SOAS, 1993–95; Governor: Elizabeth Garrett Anderson Sch., Islington, 1997–2000; Cripplegate Foundn, 2000–. FRSA 1993; CIMgt 1992. *Recreations:* cinema, theatre, France, books. *Address:* 4 Mica House, Barnsbury Square, N1 1RN.

KAHN-ACKERMANN, Georg; Secretary General, Council of Europe, 1974–79; *b* 4 Jan. 1918; *m* 1945, Rosmarie Müller-Diefenbach; one *s* three *d*. *Educ:* in Germany and Switzerland. Served in Armed Forces, 1939–45. Press Reporter and Editor from 1946; Commentator with Radio Bavaria and wrote for newspaper, Abendzeitung, 1950. Author of several books, a publisher's reader, and mem. Exec. Cttee of Bavarian Assoc. of Journalists. Dir, VG WORT, Munich, 1972–74; Vice-Chm., Bd of Deutschlandfunk (Cologne). Mem., Social Democratic Party (SDP), from 1946, and of the German Federal Parliament, 1953–57, 1962–69 and 1970–74. Previous appts include: Vice-Pres., Western European Union Assembly, 1967–70; Chm., Political Commn of Western European Union, 1971–74; Vice-Pres., Consultative Assembly of Council of Europe until elected Secretary General in 1974. Mem. Council, Deutsche Welthunger hilfe; Pres., VG WORT. *Recreation:* ski-ing. *Address:* Sterzenweg 3, 82541 Ammerland, Bayern, Germany.

KAHURANANGA, Rt Rev. Musa; *b* 1921; *s* of Samweli and Mariamu Kahurananga; *m* 1941, Raheli Lutozi; three *s* four *d* (and one *s* decd). *Educ:* Teachers' Training College, Katoke Bukoba. Teacher; Deacon 1952, Priest 1953; Asst Bishop in Diocese of Central Tanganyika, 1962; Archbishop of Tanzania, 1979–83; Bishop of Western Tanganyika, 1966–83. *Recreation:* farming. *Address:* PO Box 13, Kasulu, Tanzania.

KAIN, Prof. Roger James Peter, PhD, DLit; FSA; FBA 1990; Montefiore Professor of Geography, since 1991, and Head, School of Geography and Archaeology, since 1999, Exeter University; *b* 12 Nov. 1944; *s* of Peter Albert Kain and Ivy Kain; *m* 1970, Annmaree Wallington; two *s*. *Educ:* Harrow Weald County Grammar Sch.; University College London (BA; PhD 1973; DLit 1998). FSA 1992. Tutor, Bedford Coll., London, 1971–72; Exeter University: Lectr, 1972–88; Montefiore Reader in Geography, 1988–91. Vice-Pres., 1997–99, and Chm. Grants Cttee, 1999–2002, British Acad. Gill Meml Medal, RGS, 1990; Kenneth Nebenzahl Prize, Newberry Liby, Chicago, 1991. *Publications:* Planning for Conservation: an international perspective, 1984; The Tithe Surveys of England and Wales, 1985; An Atlas and Index of the Tithe Files of Mid-Nineteenth-Century England and Wales, 1986; (jtly) Cadastral Mapping in the Service of the State: a history of property mapping, 1992; (jtly) The Tithe Maps of England and Wales: a cartographic analysis and county-by-county catalogue, 1995 (McColvin Medal, LA, 1996); (jtly) English Cartography, 1997; (jtly) English Maps: a history, 1999; (ed) Historical Atlas of South-West England, 1999; (jtly) Tithe Surveys for Historians, 2000; Historic Parishes of England and Wales, 2001. *Recreations:* mountain walking, gardening, fishing. *Address:* School of Geography and Archaeology, Exeter University, Exeter EX4 4RJ. *T:* (01392) 263333.

KAISER, Michael Martin; President, John F. Kennedy Center for Performing Arts, Washington, since 2001; *b* 27 Oct. 1953; *s* of Harold and Marion Kaiser. *Educ:* Brandeis Univ. (BS); Sloan Sch., MIT (MSM). Pres., Kaiser Associates, 1981–85; Exec. Dir, Kansas City Ballet, 1985–87; Associate Dir, Pierpoint Morgan Library, 1987–91; Exec. Dir, Alvin Ailey American Dance Theatre, 1991–93; Pres., Kaiser-Engler Gp, 1994–95; Executive Director: American Ballet Theatre, 1995–98; Royal Opera House, 1998–2000. *Address:* c/o John F. Kennedy Center for Performing Arts, 2700 F Street NW, Washington, DC 20566–0001, USA.

KAISER, Philip M.; political and economic consultant; *b* 12 July 1913; *s* of Morris Kaiser and Temma Kaiser (*née* Sloven); *m* 1939, Hannah Greeley; three *s*. *Educ:* University of Wisconsin; Balliol Coll., Oxford (Rhodes Scholar). Economist, Bd of Governors, Fed. Reserve System, 1939–42; Chief, Project Ops Staff, also Chief, Planning Staff, Bd Economic Warfare and Foreign Econ. Admin., 1942–46; Expert on Internat. Organization Affairs, US State Dept., 1946; Exec. Asst to Asst Sec. of Labor in charge of internat. labor affairs, US Dept of Labor, 1947–49; Asst Sec. of Labor for Internat. Labor Affairs, 1949–53; mem., US Govt Bd of Foreign Service, Dept of State, 1948–53; US Govt mem., Governing Body of ILO, 1948–53; Chief, US delegn to ILO Confs, 1949–53; Special Asst to Governor of New York, 1954–58; Prof. of Internat. Relations and Dir, Program for Overseas Labor and Industrial Relations, Sch. of Internat. Service, American Univ., 1958–61; US Ambassador, Republic of Senegal and Islamic Republic of Mauritania, 1961–64; Minister, Amer. Embassy, London, 1964–69. Chm., Encyclopaedia Britannica International Ltd, 1969–75; Dir, Guinness Mahon Holdings Ltd, 1975–77. US Ambassador to Hungary, 1977–80, to Austria, 1980–81. Member: US Govt Interdepartmental Cttee on Marshall Plan, 1947–48; Interdepartmental Cttee on Greek-Turkish aid and Point 4 Technical Assistance progs, 1947–49. Sen. Consultant, SRI International, 1981–97. Professorial Lectr, Johns Hopkins Sch. of Adv. Internat. Studies, 1983–84; Woodrow Wilson Vis. Fellow, Hartford Univ. of W Hartford, Connecticut, 1983. Board Member: Soros Hungarian Foundn; Amer. Ditchley Foundn; Council of Amer. Ambassadors; Amer. Acad. of Diplomacy; Inst. for Diplomatic Studies; Partners for Democratic Change; Member: Council on Foreign Relations; Washington Inst. of Foreign Affairs; IISS. *Publication:* Journeying Far and Wide: a political and diplomatic memoir, 1993. *Recreations:* tennis, swimming, music. *Address:* 2101 Connecticut Avenue NW, Washington, DC 20008, USA.

KAJUMBA, Ven. Daniel Steven Kimbugwe; Archdeacon of Reigate, since 2001; *b* 20 Nov. 1952; *s* of Prince Adonia Kajumba, Buganda royal family, and Lady Esther Kajumba; family exiled to UK, 1971; *m* 1974, Tina Carole; one *s* one *d*. *Educ:* school in Uganda; Southwark Ordination Course; HND; BA (Open); DipTh; Dip. Inst Municipal Bldg Mgt. Employment before ordination included: Auxiliary Nurse, Bournemouth; Youth Officer, West Cliff Baptist Ch; Dep. Warden, Christian Alliance Centre; Prop., Poole Parkside and Edward Russell Old People's Homes. Ordained deacon, 1985, priest, 1986; Curate,

Goldington, Dio. St Albans, 1985–87; employment in Uganda, 1987–98, included: Man. Dir, Transocean; Gen. Mgr, Rio Hldgs Internat.; Kingdom of Buganda: Sec. Gen.; Minister for Public Relns, Functions and Protocol, and Foreign Affairs; Team Vicar, Horley St Francis, Dio. Southwark, 1999–2001. *Address:* (home) 84 Higher Drive, Purley, Surrey CR8 2HJ. *T:* (01293) 411333; (office) St Matthew's House, 100 George Street, Croydon CR0 1PE. *T:* (020) 8681 5496, *Fax:* (020) 8686 2074; *e-mail:* daniel.kajumba@dswark.org.uk.

KAKKAR, Prof. Vijay Vir, FRCS, FRCSE; Professor of Surgical Science, Guy's, King's and St Thomas' School of Medicine of King's College London (formerly King's College School of Medicine and Dentistry), since 1975, and National Heart and Lung Institute, since 1990, University of London; Director, Thrombosis Research Institute, since 1990; *b* 22 March 1937; *s* of Dr H. B. and Mrs L. W. Kakkar; *m* 1962, Dr Savitri Karnani; two *s*. *Educ:* Vikram Univ., Ujjain, India (MB, BS 1960). FRCS 1964; FRCSE 1964. Junior staff appts, 1960–64; Lectr, Nuffield Dept of Surgery, Univ. of Oxford, 1964–65; Dept of Surgery, King's College Hospital, London: Pfizer Res. Fellow and Hon. Sen. Registrar, 1965–68; Sen. Registrar, 1968–69; Lectr and Hon. Sen. Registrar, 1969–71; Sen. Lectr and Hon. Consultant Surgeon, 1972–76; Dir, Thrombosis Res. Unit, 1975–; Hon. Consultant Surgeon: King's Coll. Hosp. Gp, 1972–; Mayday Hosp., Croydon, 1984–; Hon. Cons. Vascular Surgeon, Royal Brompton Nat. Heart and Lung Hosps, 1990–. Vis. Prof., Harvard Univ. Med. Sch., Boston, 1972. Pres., British Soc. for Haemostasis and Thrombosis, 1984– (Founder Mem., 1980, Sec., 1982–83); Member: Eur. Thrombosis Res. Orgn; Concerted Action Cttee on Thrombosis, EEC; Internat. Soc. on Thrombosis and Haemostasis (Chm., Cttee on Venous Thromboembolism); Internat. Surg. Soc.; Assoc. of Surgeons of GB and NI; Vascular Surg. Soc. of GB; Pan-Pacific Surg. Assoc.; Internat. Soc. for Haematology; Internat. Soc. for Angiology; Surg. Res. Soc. of GB; Hon. Mem., Assoc. of Surgeons of India; Hon. Fellow: Acad. of Medicine of Singapore; Hellenic Surgical Soc. Hunterian Prof., RCS, 1969; Lectures: Gunnar Bauer Meml, Copenhagen, 1971; James Finlayson Meml, RCPGlas, 1975; Cross Meml, RCS, 1977; Wright-Schulte, Internat. Soc. on Thrombosis and Haemostasis, 1977; Freyer Meml, RCSI, 1981; Dos Santos, 1994. David Patey Prize, Surg. Soc. of GB and Ireland, 1971. Member Editorial Board: Haemostasis, 1982–; Clinical Findings, 1982–; Internat. Angiology, 1982–; Thrombosis Research, 1990–. *Publications:* (jtly) Vascular Disease, 1969; (jtly) Thromboembolism: diagnosis and treatment, 1972; (jtly) Heparin: chemistry and clinical usage, 1976; (jtly) Chromogenic Peptide Substrates: chemistry and clinical usage, 1979; Atheroma and Thrombosis, 1983; 500 pubns in jls on thromboembolism and vascular disease. *Recreations:* golf, skiing, cricket. *Address:* Thrombosis Research Institute, Emmanuel Kaye Building, Manresa Road, Chelsea, SW3 6LR. *T:* (020) 7351 8301. *Club:* Athenæum.

KALETSKY, Anatole; Associate Editor, since 1992, and columnist, The Times (Economics Editor, 1990–96); *b* Moscow, 1 June 1952; *s* of Jacob and Esther Kaletsky; *m* 1985, Fiona Murphy; two *s* one *d*. *Educ:* Melbourne High Sch., Australia; Westminster City Sch.; King's Coll., Cambridge (BA Maths); Harvard Univ. (MA Econs). Financial Writer, The Economist, 1976–79; Financial Times: Leader Writer, 1979–81; Washington Corresp., 1981–83; Internat. Econs Corresp., 1984–86; NY Bureau Chief, 1986–90; Moscow Assignment, 1990. Hon. Sen. Scholar, King's Coll., Cambridge, 1973–74; Kennedy Scholar, Harvard Univ., 1974–76. Mem., Adv. Bd, UK Know-How Fund for E Europe and former Soviet Union, 1991–; Dir, Kaletsky Economic Consulting, 1997–. Mem. Council, REconS, 1999–. Trustee, New Europe Res. Trust, 1999–. Specialist Writer of Year, British Press Awards, 1980, 1992; Commentator of the Year, What the Papers Say, 1996; Financial Journalist of the Year, Wincott Foundn Award, 1997. *Publications:* The Costs of Default, 1985; In the Shadow of Debt, 1992. *Recreations:* playing the violin, cinema, family life. *Address:* The Times, 1 Pennington Street, E1 9XN. *T:* (020) 7782 5000; Kaletsky Economic Consulting, 39 De Vere Gardens, W8 5AW. *T:* (020) 7589 6222.

KALLIPETIS, Michel Louis; QC 1989; a Recorder, since 1989; *b* 29 Aug. 1941; *s* of late Takis George Kallipetis and of Sheila Gallaly; *m* 1984, Dr Esther Inge Seidel. *Educ:* Cardinal Vaughan Sch.; University Coll., London. Exchequer and Audit Dept, 1960–63. Called to the Bar, Gray's Inn, 1968, Bencher, 1997. *Recreations:* opera, cooking, travel. *Address:* 3 King's Bench Walk North, Temple, EC4Y 7HR. *T:* (020) 7797 8600. *Clubs:* Reform, Royal Automobile.

KALMS, Sir (Harold) Stanley, Kt 1996; Chairman, 1972–Sept. 2002, President, from Sept. 2002, Dixons Group plc; *b* 21 Nov. 1931; *s* of Charles and Cissie Kalms; *m* 1954, Pamela Jimack (MBE 1995); three *s*. *Educ:* Christ's College, Finchley. Whole career with Dixons Group: started in 1948 in one store owned by father; went public, 1962; Man. Dir, 1962–72; Dir, British Gas, 1987–97. Chm., King's Healthcare NHS Trust, 1993–96. Director: Centre for Policy Studies, 1991– (Treas., 1993–98); Business for Sterling, 1998–. Vis. Prof., Business Sch., Univ. (formerly Poly.) of N London, 1991–. Mem., Funding Agency for Schs, 1994–97. Governor: Dixons Bradford City Technol. Coll., 1988–; NIESR, 1995–. Trustee: Industry in Educn, 1993–; Economic Educn Trust, 1993–. Hon. FCGI 1991; Hon. Fellow, London Business Sch., 1995. Hon. DLitt CNAA, 1991; DUniv N London, 1994; Hon. DEcon Richmond, 1996. *Recreations:* communal activities, opera, ballet. *Address:* Dixons Group plc, 29 Farm Street, W1X 7RD. *T:* (020) 7499 3494.

KALMUS, Prof. George Ernest, CBE 2000; FRS 1988; Associate Director, 1986–94, Director, 1994–97, Particle Physics, Rutherford Appleton Laboratory; Visiting Professor, Physics and Astronomy Department, since 1984, Fellow, since 1998, University College London; *b* 21 April 1935; *s* of late Hans Kalmus and Anna Kalmus; *m* 1957, Ann Christine Harland; three *d*. *Educ:* St Albans County Grammar Sch.; University Coll. London (BSc Hons, PhD). Res. Asst, Bubble Chamber Gp, UCL, 1959–62; Research Associate, Powell-Birge Bubble Chamber Gp, Lawrence Radiation Lab., Univ. of California, Berkeley, 1962–63 and 1964–67; Lectr, Physics Dept, UCL, 1963–64; Sen. Physicist, Lawrence Rad. Lab., 1967–71; Gp Leader, Bubble Chamber and Delphi Gps, Rutherford Appleton Lab., 1971–86. Mem., various Programme Cttees at CERN, 1974–; Mem., CERN Scientific Policy Cttee, 1990–96 (Chm., 1999–). *Publications:* numerous articles on experimental particle physics in Phys. Rev., Phys. Rev. Letters, Nuclear Phys., etc. *Recreations:* ski-ing, cycling, reading. *Address:* 16 South Avenue, Abingdon, Oxon OX14 1QH. *T:* (01235) 523340.

See also P. I. P. Kalmus.

KALMUS, Prof. Peter Ignaz Paul, OBE 2001; PhD; CPhys, FInstP; Professor of Physics, 1978–98, and Head of Physics Department, 1992–97, Queen Mary and Westfield (formerly Queen Mary) College, University of London, now Emeritus Professor; *b* 25 Jan. 1933; *s* of late Hans and Anna Kalmus; *m* 1957, Felicity (Trixie) Barker; one *s* one *d*. *Educ:* University Coll. London (BSc, PhD). CPhys, FInstP 1967. Res. Associate, University Coll. London, 1957–60; Lectr (part-time), Northern Poly. and Chelsea Poly., 1955–60; Physicist, Argonne Nat. Lab., USA, 1960–64; Queen Mary College, University of London: Lectr, 1964–66; Reader, 1966–78. Visiting Scientist: CERN, Geneva, 1961–62, 1970–71, 1981–82; Univ. of Chicago, 1965. Scientific Advr, UK Delegn to CERN, 1978–81; Member: SERC Nuclear Physics Bd, 1979–82, 1989–93; SERC Astronomy and Planetary Sci. Bd, 1990–93; PPARC Educn & Trng Cttee, 1994–98; PPARC Public Understanding of Sci. Panel, 1994–98. Member Council: Inst. of Physics, 1993–2000 (Vice-Pres., 1996–2000; Chm., High Energy Physics Gp, 1989–93); Royal Instn, 1989– (MRI 1989; Vice-Pres., 1997–99; Chm., Davy Faraday Lab. Res. Cttee, 1998–99); Member: Amer. Phys. Soc., 1963 (Fellow, 1995); European Phys. Soc., 1970 (Mem., High Energy Particle Physics Bd, 1994–98); BAAS, 1986 (Pres., Physics Sect., 1990–91); Commn on Particles and Fields, IUPAP, 1994– (Hon. Sec., 1996–99; Chm., 1999–). Rutherford Medal and Prize, Inst. Physics, 1988. *Publications:* numerous papers in scientific jls. *Recreations:* photography, swimming, listening to jazz. *Address:* Department of Physics, Queen Mary and Westfield College, Mile End Road, E1 4NS. *T:* (020) 7882 5042; *e-mail:* p.i.p.kalmus@qmw.ac.uk.

See also G. E. Kalmus.

KALO, Sir Kwamala, Kt 1983; MBE 1975; Director of Administrative College, Port Moresby, 1987–89; *b* 28 Feb. 1929; *s* of Kalo Navu and Navuga Kila; *m* 1951, Gimaralai Samuel; two *s* two *d*. *Educ:* up to secondary level in Papua New Guinea. Govt Primary School teacher, 1949; served in Dept of Education as classroom teacher, Headmaster, Inspector, Supt of Schools, Asst Sec. of Technical Educn, until 1979; represented Papua New Guinea in Trusteeship Council Meeting of UN, 1963; seconded to Public Services Commn as a Comr, 1979; High Comr for Papua New Guinea in New Zealand, 1983–86. Hon. Award, PNG Trng and Develt Soc., 1991. *Publication:* Sam Ila' Apa Gena Mari (Hymns by Sam Ila' Apa), 1989. *Address:* PO Box 8529, Boroko NCD, Port Moresby, Papua New Guinea.

KAMBA, Prof. Walter Joseph; Founding Dean, and UNESCO Professor of Human Rights, Democracy and Law, Faculty of Law, University of Namibia; *b* 6 Sept. 1931; *s* of Joseph Mafara and Hilda Kamba; *m* 1960, Angeline Saziso Dube; three *s*. *Educ:* University of Cape Town (BA, LLB); Yale Law School (LLM). Attorney of the High Court of Rhodesia (now Zimbabwe), 1963–66; Research Fellow, Institute of Advanced Legal Studies, London Univ., 1967–68; Lecturer, then Sen. Lectr, in Comparative Law and Jurisprudence, 1969–80, Dean of the Faculty of Law, 1977–80, Univ. of Dundee; Prof. of Law, 1980–91, Vice-Prin., 1980–81, Vice-Chancellor, 1981–91, Univ. of Zimbabwe; Inaug. Dist. Knight Prof. of Law and Educn, Univ. of Manitoba, 1992; Inaug. UNESCO Africa Prof., Utrecht Univ., 1992–96. Chm., Kingstons (booksellers and distributors) (Zimbabwe), 1984–. Chm., Bd of Governors, Zimbabwe Broadcasting Corp., 1987 (Vice-Chm., 1980–87); Member: Public Service Professional Qualifications Panel, Harare, 1981–83; Council, ACU, 1981–83 (Member: Working Party on future policy, 1981; Budget Review Cttee, 1982–83); Commonwealth Standing Cttee on student mobility, 1981–88; Exec. Bd, Assoc. of African Univs, 1984 (Chm., Finance and Admin. Cttee, 1985); Nat. Commn, Law and Popn Studies Project, Zimbabwe, 1986–; Chairman: Assoc. of Eastern and Southern African Univs, 1984–87; Bd, UNITWIN, 1992–; Vice-President: Internat. Assoc. of Univs, 1985–90; ACP-EEC Foundn for Cultural Co-op., Brussels, 1986 88; Mem., Zimbabwe Nat. Commn for UNESCO, 1987–. Mem., Univ. of Swaziland Commn on Planning, 1986. Legal Adviser, ZANU (Patriotic Front), until 1980; Chm., Electoral Supervisory Commn, 1984–94; Mem., S African Ind. Electoral Commn, 1994; Co-Chm., Malaŵi Nat. Constitutional Conf., 1995; Mem. Adv. Bd, Global Governance Review, 1994–. Trustee: Zimbabwe Mass Media Trust, 1981–; Conservation Trust of Zimbabwe, 1981–87; Legal Resources Foundn, Zimbabwe, 1984–90; African-American Inst., NY, 1985–; Zimbabwe Cambridge Trust, 1987–; Centre for Higher Educn Transformation, S Africa, 1995–; Internat. Trustee, Press Trust of Malaŵi, 1996–; Member: Bd of Trustees, Michael Gelfand Med. Res. Foundn, Zimbabwe, 1986–; Internat. Bd, United World Colls, 1985–87; Mem. Council: Univ. for Peace, Costa Rica, 1981–86; Univ. of Zambia, 1981–86; United Nations Univ., Tokyo, 1983–89 (Chm., Council, 1985–86; Mem., Cttee on Institutional and Programmatic Develt); Univ. of Lesotho, 1987–; Mem., Internat. Adv. Cttee, Synergos Inst., NY, 1987–; Patron, Commonwealth Legal Educn Assoc., 1986–; Governor, Ranche House Coll., Harare, 1980–; Member Board of Governors: Zimbabwe Inst. of Development Studies, 1981– (Chm. Bd, 1986–); Internat. Develt Res. Centre, Canada, 1986–; Commonwealth of Learning, 1988– (Vice-Chm., 1989–); Member: Nat. St John's Ambulance Council for Republic of Zimbabwe, 1982–87; Indep. Internat. Commn on Health Res. for Develt, 1987–; Bd, Internat. Cttee for Study of Educnl Exchange, 1988–; Exec. Cttee, Internat. Develt Res. Centre, Canada, 1989–. Hon. LLD: Dundee, 1982; Natal, 1995; Zimbabwe, 1998; Hon. DHL Rhode Is, 1991; Hon. DLett Charles Sturt, 1995. 50th anniv. Distinguished Service Award, Lesotho, 1995. Officier dans l'Ordre des Palmes Académiques (France). *Publications:* articles in Internat. and Comparative Law Quarterly, Juridical Review. *Recreation:* tennis. *Address:* Faculty of Law, University of Namibia, Private Bag 13301, 340 Mandume Ndemufayo Avenue, Pioneerspark, Windhoek, Namibia. *T:* (61) 30636220, *Fax:* (61) 20637030.

KAMIL, Geoffrey Harvey; His Honour Judge Kamil; a Circuit Judge, since 1993; *b* 17 Aug. 1942; *s* of Peter and Sadie Kamil; *m* 1968, Andrea Pauline Kamil (*née* Ellis); two *d*. *Educ:* Leeds Grammar Sch.; Leeds University (LLB). Admitted as Solicitor of the Supreme Court, 1968; Partner with J. Levi & Co., solicitors, Leeds, 1968–87; Asst Stipendiary Magistrate, 1985–87; Stipendiary Magistrate, W Midlands, 1987–90, W Yorks, 1990–93; Asst Crown Court Recorder, 1986–91; Recorder, 1991–93; Ethnic Minority Liaison Judge, Leeds and Bradford, 1998–; Liaison Judge, Wakefield and Pontefract, 1998–; Chm., Immigration Appeals Tribunal, 1998–. Member: Magisterial Cttee, Judicial Studies Bd, 1991–93; Centre for Criminal Justice Studies, Leeds Univ., 1992–; W Yorks Race Issues Adv. Gp, 1998–; Equal Treatment Adv. Cttee, Judicial Studies Bd, 2000–. Leeds Law Society: Mem. Cttee, 1983–87; Chm., Courts Cttee, 1983–87; Mem., Duty Solicitor Cttee, 1986–87; Mem., Leeds Bar/Law Soc. Liaison Cttee, 1983–87. Sec., Kirkstall Lodge Hostal for Ex-Offenders, 1976–87. *Recreations:* golf, swimming, pumping iron, the Lake District, classic cars, TV soap addict. *Address:* Bradford Court Centre, The Law Courts, Exchange Square, Drake Street, Bradford BD1 1JA. *Clubs:* Bradford (Bradford); Moor Allerton Golf (Leeds).

KAN, Prof. Yuet Wai, FRCP 1983; FRS 1981; Louis K. Diamond Professor of Hematology, since 1984, Investigator, Howard Hughes Medical Institute Laboratory, since 1976, and Head, Division of Molecular Medicine and Diagnostics, Department of Laboratory Medicine, since 1989, University of California, San Francisco; *b* 11 June 1936; *s* of Kan Tong Po and Kan Li Lai Wan; *m* 1964, Alvera L. Limauro; two *d*. *Educ:* Univ. of Hong Kong (MB, BS, DSc). Research Associate, Children's Hosp. Medical Center, Dept of Pediatrics, Harvard Medical Sch., Boston, Mass; Asst Prof. of Pediatrics, Harvard Medical Sch., 1970–72; Associate Prof. of Medicine, Depts of Medicine and Laboratory Medicine, Univ. of California, San Francisco, 1972–77; Chief, Hematology Service, San Francisco General Hospital, 1972–79; Prof. of Lab. Medicine and Medicine, Univ. of California, 1977–. Dir, Molecular Biology Inst., Univ. of Hong Kong, 1990–94 (Hon. Dir, 1988–90). Trustee, Croucher Foundn, 1992– (Chm., 1997–). Member: Nat. Acad. of Scis, USA, 1986; Academia Sinica, Taiwan, 1988; Foreign Mem., Chinese Acad. of Scis, 1996. Hon. MD Univ. of Cagliari, Sardinia, 1981; Hon. DSc: Chinese Univ. of Hong Kong, 1981; Univ. of Hong Kong, 1987; Open Univ. of Hong Kong. *Publications:*

contribs to: Nature, Genetics, Proc. of Nat. Academy of Sciences, Jl of Clinical Investigation, Blood, British Jl of Haematology, and others. *Recreations:* tennis, skiing. *Address:* U426, University of California San Francisco, San Francisco, CA 94143–0793, USA. *T:* (415) 4765841, *Fax:* (415) 4762956.

See also Sir Kan Yuet-Keung.

KAN Yuet-Keung, Sir, GBE 1979 (CBE 1967; OBE 1959); Kt 1972; JP; Chairman, Hong Kong Trade Development Council, 1979–83; Chairman, Bank of East Asia Ltd, 1963–83; *b* 26 July 1913; *s* of late Kan Tong Po, JP; *m* 1940, Ida; two *s* one *d*. *Educ:* Hong Kong Univ.; London Univ. BA Hong Kong 1934. Solicitor and Notary Public. Sen. Unofficial MLC 1968–72, Sen. Unofficial MEC 1974–80, Hong Kong. Pro-Chancellor, Chinese Univ. of Hong Kong, 1983–96 (Chm., Council, 1973–83). Hon. Fellow, LSE, 1980. Hon. LLD: Chinese Univ. of Hong Kong, 1968; Univ. of Hong Kong, 1973. Order of Sacred Treasure, 3rd Class, Japan; Officier de l'Ordre National du Mérite (France), 1978; Officer's Cross, Order of Merit 1st class (Germany), 1983; Grand Decoration of Honour in Gold with Star (Austria), 1983; Order of Sacred Treasure, 2nd class (Japan), 1983; Knight Grand Cross, Royal Order of Northern Pole Star (Sweden), 1983. *Recreations:* tennis, swimming, golf.

See also Yuet Wai Kan.

KANE, Professor George, FBA 1968; Professor of English Language and Medieval Literature, 1965–76 and Head of English Department, 1968–76, King's College, London, Professor Emeritus, University of London, since 1976; *b* 4 July 1916; *o s* of George Michael and Clara Kane; *m* 1946, Katherine Bridget, *o d* of Lt-Col R. V. Montgomery, MC; one *d* (one *s* decd). *Educ:* St Peter's Coll.; British Columbia University; Toronto Univ.; University Coll., London. BA (University of BC), 1936; Research Fellow, University of Toronto, 1936–37; MA (Toronto), 1937; Research Fellow, Northwestern Univ., 1937–38; IODE Schol., for BC, 1938–39. Served War of 1939–45: Artists' Rifles, 1939–40; Rifle Bde, 1940–46 (despatches). PhD (London), 1946; Asst Lecturer in English, University Coll., London, 1946, Lecturer, 1948, Reader in English, 1953, Fellow, 1971; Prof. of English Language and Literature and Head of English Dept, Royal Holloway College, London Univ., 1955–65; William Rand Kenan Jr Prof. of English in Univ. of N Carolina at Chapel Hill, 1976–87, Chm. of Div. of Humanities, 1980–83, Prof. Emeritus, 1987–. Fellow, KCL, 1976. Vis. Prof., Medieval Acad. of America, 1970, 1982, Corresp. Fellow, 1975, Fellow, 1978; Fellow: Amer. Acad. of Arts and Scis, 1977–91 (resigned); Nat. Humanities Center, 1987–88; Sen. Fellow, Southeastern Inst. of Medieval and Renaissance Studies, 1978. Member: Council, Early English Text Soc., 1969–88; Governing Body, SOAS, 1970–76; Council, British Acad., 1974–76; Governing Body, Univ. of N Carolina Press, 1979–84. Sir Israel Gollancz Memorial Prize, British Acad., 1963, 1999; Haskins Medallist, Med. Acad. of Amer., 1978. Lectures: Chambers Meml, UCL, 1965; Accademia Nazionale dei Lincei, Rome, 1976; John Coffin Meml, Univ. of London, 1979; M. W. Bloomfield Meml, Harvard, 1989; Tucker-Cruse Meml, Bristol Univ., 1991; Public Orator, Univ. of London, 1962–66; Annual Chaucer Lectr, New Chaucer Soc., 1980. Gen. editor of London Edn of Piers Plowman. *Publications:* Middle English Literature, 1951; (ed) Piers Plowman, the A Version, 1960, the B Version, 1975, the C Version, 1997; Piers Plowman: The Evidence for Authorship, 1965; Geoffrey Chaucer, 1984; Chaucer and Langland, 1989; (ed) Chaucer, The Legend of Good Women, 1995; articles and reviews. *Recreation:* fishing. *Clubs:* Athenæum, Flyfishers'.

KANT, Krishan; Vice-President of India, since 1997; *b* Amritsar, 28 Feb. 1927; *s* of Lala Achint Ram, sometime MP; *m* Suman Kant. *Educ:* Banaras Hindu Univ. (MSc Technol). Scientist, Council of Scientific and Industrial Res., New Delhi. Member: Rajya Sabha, 1966–77; Lok Sabha, 1977–80. Congress Party, subseq. Janata Party: former Sec. of Parly Party and of Exec. Cttee; Mem., Nat. Exec., 1977–88. Founder Gen. Sec., People's Union of Civil Liberties and Democratic Rights, 1976; former Mem. Exec. Council, Inst. of Defence Studies and Analysis. *Publications:* contrib. to newspapers and periodicals on national and international politics, culture and science policy. *Address:* Office of the Vice-President, 6 Maulana Azad Road, New Delhi 110011, India.

KAO, Charles Kuen, CBE 1993; PhD; FRS 1997; FREng, FIEE, FIEEE; Chairman and Chief Executive Officer, Transtech Services Ltd, since 1996; Vice Chancellor, Chinese University of Hong Kong, 1987–96, Hon. Professor, since 1996; *b* Shanghai, 4 Nov. 1933; holds dual US/UK nationality; *s* of Chun-Hsian Kao and late Tisung-Fong Ming; *m* 1959, May-Wan Wong; one *s* two *d*. *Educ:* Woolwich Poly. (BSc London); UCL (PhD 1965). FIEEE 1978; FIEE 1979; FREng (FEng 1989). Engr, Standard Telephone & Cables Ltd, 1957–60; Res. Scientist, then Res. Manager, Standard Telecom Labs Ltd, ITT Central Europ. Lab., 1960–70; Hd, Electronics Dept, Chinese Univ. of Hong Kong, 1970–74; Chief Scientist, 1974–81, Vice-Pres. and Dir of Engrg, 1982–83, Electro-Optical Products Div., ITT, Va; Exec. Scientist and Corporate Dir of Res., ITT Advanced Tech. Centre, Conn, 1983–87. Fellow: Royal Swedish Acad. of Engrg Sci., 1989; US Nat. Acad. of Engrg, 1990; Europ. Acad. Scis and Art; Academia Sinica, Taiwan, 1994; Chinese Acad. of Sci., 1996. Hon. DSc: Chinese Univ. of Hong Kong, 1985; Sussex, 1990; Durham, 1994; Hull, 1998; Yale, 1999; Dr *hc* Soka, 1991; Hon. DEng Glasgow, 1992; Padova, 1996. Numerous awards and prizes including: Alexander Graham Bell Medal, IEEE, 1985; Marconi Internat. Fellowship, 1985; Faraday Medal, IEE, 1989; Japan Prize, 1996; Prince Philip Medal, Royal Acad. of Engrg, 1996; Charles Stark Draper Prize, Nat. Acad. of Engrg, USA, 1999. *Publications:* Optical Fiber Technology II, 1981; Optical Fiber Systems: technology, design and applications, 1982; Optical Fiber, 1988; A Choice Fulfilled: the business of high technology, 1991. *Recreations:* tennis, hiking, pottery-making. *Address:* c/o Department of Information Engineering, Ho Sin Hang Engineering Building, Chinese University of Hong Kong, Shatin, New Territories, Hong Kong. *T:* 26037643, *Fax:* 26037663; *e-mail:* ckao@ie.cuhk.edu.hk.

KAPI, Hon. Sir Mari, Kt 1988; CBE 1983; Deputy Chief Justice of Papua New Guinea, since 1982; a Justice of the Court of Appeal: Solomon Islands, since 1982; Fiji, since 1992; *b* 12 Dec. 1950; *s* of Kapi 'Ila and Mea Numa; *m* 1973, Tegana Kapi; two *s* three *d*. *Educ:* Univ. of Papua New Guinea (LLB); SOAS, Univ. of London (LLM). Admitted to practice in PNG and Australia, 1974. Dep. Public Solicitor, 1976; Associate Public Solicitor, 1977; Public Solicitor, 1978; a Judge of Nat. and Supreme Courts of PNG, 1979. Cross of Solomon Islands, 1994. *Recreations:* tennis, touch Rugby. *Address:* PO Box 7018, Boroko, Papua New Guinea. *T:* 3259273.

KAPLAN, Neil Trevor, CBE 2001; QC (Hong Kong) 1982; arbitrator, mediator; *b* 1 Sept. 1942; *s* of Leslie Henry Kaplan and Sybil Sylvia Kaplan (*née* Gasson); *m* 1st, 1971, Barbara Jane Spector (marr. diss. 1997); one *s* one *d*; 2nd, 1998, Paula White. *Educ:* St Paul's Sch.; King's College London (LLB). FCIArb. Called to the Bar, Inner Temple, 1965, Bencher 1991; practised London, 1965–80; Dep. Principal Crown Counsel, Hong Kong, 1980, Principal Crown Counsel, 1982; private practice, Hong Kong Bar, 1984–90; Solicitor-barrister, Victoria, NSW, 1983; NY Bar, 1986; High Court Judge, Hong Kong, 1990–94; Judge in charge of Construction and Arbitration List, 1990–94. Vis. Prof., City Univ. of Hong Kong, 1995–97. Pres., CIArb, 1999–2000 (Chm., Hong Kong Branch, 1984–87 and 1989–90); Chairman: Hong Kong Internat. Arbitration Centre, 1991–; Disputes Rev. Bd, new Hong Kong airport, 1995–99; Post-Release Supervision Bd, 1996–; WTO Rev. Body, Hong Kong, 2000–; Dep. Chm., Justice, Hong Kong, 1988–90; Mem., Judicial Studies Bd, 1994–. Mem. Council, ICCA, 1995–. Liveryman, Arbitrators' Co., 1982–. JP Hong Kong, 1984. *Publications:* (jtly) Hong Kong Arbitration—Cases and Materials, 1991; (jtly) Arbitration in Hong Kong and China, 1994; articles on arbitration. *Recreations:* tennis, travel, food and wine, films, theatre, walking. *Address:* 10th Floor, Bank of East Asia Building, 10 Des Voeux Road, Central, Hong Kong. *T:* 28696301, *Fax:* 28696372; Essex Court Chambers, 24 Lincoln's Inn Fields, WC2A 3ED, *T:* (020) 7813 8000. *Clubs:* Athenæum, Royal Automobile, Old Pauline; Hong Kong, Hong Kong Cricket.

KAPLICKY, Jan; Founder and Partner, Future Systems, since 1979; *b* Prague, 18 April 1937; *s* of Josef Kaplicky and Jirina Kaplicka (*née* Florova); *m* 1991, Amanda Levete; one *s*. *Educ:* Coll. of Applied Arts and Architecture, Prague (DipArch 1962). Architect: private practice, Prague, 1964–68; Denys Lasdun & Partners, 1969–71; Piano & Rogers, 1971–73; Spencer & Webster, 1974–75 (Associate); Foster & Partners, 1977–83. *Projects* include: Space Station Wardroom Table (NASA Cert. of Recognition, 1989); MOMI Tent, 1991 (British Construction Industry Award, 1992); Stonehenge Visitor Centre (AJ/Bovis Royal Acad. Award), 1993; Hauer-King House, London, 1994 (Aluminium Imagination Award, Civic Trust, 1996); West India Quay Bridge, Canary Wharf, 1995 (Millennium Product Award, Civic Trust, and RIBA Award, 1998); Wild at Heart flower shop (RIBA Award), 1998; Comme des Garçons, NY and Tokyo, 1999; NatWest Media Centre, Lord's Cricket Ground (Millennium Product Award, and Aluminium Imagination Award, Civic Trust; Stirling Prize, RIBA), 1999; Marni shops, London, Milan, Tokyo, Paris. *Exhibitions* include: RIBA, 1982, 1991; Arch. Assoc., London, 1987; Storefront, NY, 1992; New Urban Environments, Tokyo, 1998; ICA, 1998; Nat. Gall., Prague, 1999; The Cube, Manchester, 1999; FS Originals, Faggionato Fine Arts, 2001. Broadcasts on TV and radio. *Publications:* For Inspiration Only, 1996; More for Inspiration Only, 1999; *relevant publicaions*: Future Systems, 1987; Future Systems: the story of tomorrow, 1993; Future Systems, ed M. Field, 1999; Unique Building, 2001; exhibn catalogues; articles in jls throughout the world. *Recreation:* history of modern architecture. *Address:* Future Systems, 20 Victoria Gardens, W11 3PE. *T:* (020) 7243 7670. *Club:* Architecture.

KAPOOR, Anish; artist and sculptor; *b* Bombay, 12 March 1954; *s* of Rear Adm. D. C. Kapoor and Mrs H. Kapoor. *Educ:* Hornsey Coll. Art; Chelsea Sch. Art. Lectr, Wolverhampton Polytechnic, 1979–83. Artist in Residence, Walker Art Gall., Liverpool, 1982–83. Mem., Arts Council of England, 1998–. One-man exhibitions include: Lisson Gall., London, 1982, 1984, 1985, 1988, 1989–90, 1993, 1998, 2000; Walker Art Gall., Liverpool, 1982, 1983; Barbara Gladstone Gall., NY, 1984, 1986, 1989, 1990, 1998; Tate Gall., London, 1990–91; San Diego Mus. Contemporary Art, 1992; Tel Aviv Mus. of Art, 1993; Nat. Gall. of Canada, Ottawa, 1993; retrospective exhibn, Hayward Gall., 1998; and others in Europe, USA, Australia and Japan; contrib. numerous group exhibns in Britain, Europe, USA, Canada, Australia and Japan, incl. Tate Gall., London, 1983, 1991; Art Inst., Chicago, 1990; Expo '92, Seville, 1992. Turner Prize, 1991. *Address:* c/o Lisson Gallery, 67 Lisson Street, NW1 5DA.

KARACHI, Archibishop of, (RC), since 1994; **Most Rev. Simeon Anthony Pereira;** *b* 19 Oct. 1927. Ordained priest, 1951; consecrated Bishop, 1971; Bishop of Islamabad-Rawalpindi, 1973–93; Co-adjutor Bishop of Karachi, 1993–94. *Address:* Archbishop's House, St Patrick's Cathedral, Shahrah-e-Iraq, Karachi 74400, Pakistan.

KARASIN, Grigory Borisovich; Ambassador of the Russian Federation to the Court of St James's, since 2000; *b* 23 Aug. 1949; *m* 1971, Olga V. Karasina; two *d*. *Educ:* Coll. of Oriental Langs, Moscow State Univ. Joined USSR Diplomatic Service, 1972: served: Senegal, 1972–76; Australia, 1979–85; UK, 1988–92; Dir, Dept of Africa, 1992–93, Dept of Inf. and Press, 1993–96, Min. of Foreign Affairs; Dep. Minister of Foreign Affairs, Russian Fedn, 1996–2000. *Address:* Embassy of the Russian Federation, 13 Kensington Palace Gardens, W8 4QX. *T:* (020) 7229 3620. *Club:* Athenæum.

KARK, (Arthur) Leslie, MA (Oxon); FRSA; author, barrister; President, Lucie Clayton Colleges, 1951–95; Founder, Lucie Clayton Secretarial College, 1965; Chairman, Chartmill Roche Ltd; *b* 12 July 1910; *s* of Victor and Helena Kark, Johannesburg; *m* 1st, 1935, Joan Tetley (marr. diss., 1956); two *d*; 2nd, 1956, Evelyn Gordine, (Lucie Clayton) (*d* 1997); one *s* one *d*. *Educ:* Clayesmore; St John's Coll., Oxford. Called to Bar, Inner Temple, 1932; Features Editor of World's Press News, 1933; Editor of Photography, 1934; Public Relations Officer to Advertising Association, 1935; Features Editor News Review, 1936–39; London Theatre Critic, New York Herald Tribune; News Editor, Ministry of Information, 1940. Served War of 1939–45, RAF, 1940–46; Air-gunner; Wing Commander in Command of Public Relations (Overseas) Unit; author, Air Ministry's official book on Air War, Far East. Associate Editor, Courier Magazine, 1947–51; Dir of Public Relations for Australian Trade Comr, 1959–63. Short stories and novels translated into French, Swedish, German, Polish, etc. *Publications:* The Fire Was Bright, 1944; Red Rain, 1946; An Owl in the Sun, 1948; Wings of the Phœnix, 1949; On the Haycock, 1957. *Recreations:* fly-fishing, golf. *Address:* 9 Clareville Grove, SW7 5AU. *T:* (020) 7370 6349; Roche House, Sheep Street, Burford, Oxon OX18 4LS. *T:* (01993) 823007. *Club:* Oxford and Cambridge.

KARK, Austen Steven, CBE 1987; Managing Director, External Broadcasting (now World Service), BBC, 1985–86; *b* 20 Oct. 1926; *s* of late Major Norman Kark and Ethel Kark, formerly of Eaton Place, London, and Johannesburg; *m* 1st, 1949, Margaret Solomon (marr. diss. 1954); two *d*; 2nd, 1954, Nina Mary Bawden, *qv*; one *d* one step *s* (and one step *s* decd). *Educ:* Upper Canada Coll., Toronto; Nautical Coll., Pangbourne; RNC; Magdalen Coll., Oxford (MA). Served RN and RIN, 1943–46. Directed first prodn in UK of Sartre's The Flies, Oxford, 1948; trained in journalism, Belfast Telegraph, L'Illustré, Zofingen, Switzerland; Courier, Bandwagon, London Mystery Magazine; free-lance journalist and broadcaster, London and New York, 1952–54; joined BBC, 1954; scriptwriter; Producer, External Services; Head of S European Service, 1964; Head of E European (and Russian) Service, 1972; Editor, World Service, 1973; Controller, English Services, and Editor, World Service, 1974; advised Lord Soames on election broadcasting, Rhodesia, and chaired enquiry into future of radio and television in Zimbabwe, 1980; Dep. Man. Dir, External Broadcasting, BBC, 1981–85. Broadcasting consultant, 1987–; Chm., CPC Guidebooks, 1988–. Mem. UK Delegn, CSCE London Information Forum, 1989. Trustee, Commonwealth Journalists Assoc. Trust., 1992–. Member: RIIA; Soc. of Authors. *Publications:* Attic in Greece, 1994; The Forwarding Agent, 1999. *Recreations:* Real tennis, mosaics, The Ægean, grandchildren. *Address:* 22 Noel Road, N1 8HA; 19 Kapodistriou, Nauplion 21100, Greece. *Clubs:* Oriental, MCC, Queen's, Royal Tennis Court, Bushmen (ex-Chairman).

KARK, Leslie; *see* Kark, A. L.

KARK, Nina Mary, (Mrs A. S. Kark); *see* Bawden, N. M.

KARLE, Jerome, PhD; Chief Scientist, Laboratory for the Structure of Matter, since 1968; *b* NY, 18 June 1918; *s* of Louis Karfunkle and Sadie Helen Kun; *m* 1942, Isabella, *d* of Zygmunt and Elizabeth Lugoski; three *d*. *Educ:* Abraham Lincoln High Sch.; City Coll. of NY (BS 1937); Harvard Univ. (AM 1938); Univ. of Michigan (MS 1942; PhD 1943). Research Associate, Manhattan Project, Chicago, 1943–44; US Navy Project, Michigan, 1944–46; Head, Electron Diffraction Section, Naval Res. Lab., 1946–58, Head of Diffraction Branch, 1958–68. Prof. (part-time), Univ. of Maryland, 1951–70. Pres., Amer. Crystallographic Assoc., 1972; Chm., US Nat. Cttee for Crystallography, NAS and Nat. Res. Council, 1973–75; Pres., Internat. Union of Crystallography, 1981–84. Fellow, Amer. Phys. Soc.; Mem., NAS. Nobel Prize for Chemistry, 1985 (jtly). *Publications:* articles in learned jls on study of atoms, molecules, crystals and solid surfaces by diffraction methods. *Recreations:* stereo-photography, swimming, ice skating. *Address:* Laboratory for the Structure of Matter, Code 6030, Naval Research Laboratory, Washington, DC 20375–5341, USA. *T:* (202) 7672665.

KARMEL, Emeritus Prof. Peter Henry, AC 1976; CBE 1967; Chairman, National Institute of the Arts, Australian National University, since 1992; *b* 9 May 1922; *s* of Simeon Karmel; *m* 1946, Lena Garrett; one *s* five *d*. *Educ:* Caulfield Grammar Sch.; Univ. of Melbourne (BA); Trinity Coll., Cambridge (PhD). Research Officer, Commonwealth Bureau of Census and Statistics, 1943–45; Lectr in Econs, Univ. of Melbourne, 1946; Rouse Ball Res. Student, Trinity Coll., Cambridge, 1947–48; Sen. Lectr in Econs, Univ. of Melbourne, 1949; Prof. of Econs, 1950–62, Emeritus, 1965, Univ. of Adelaide; Principal-designate, Univ. of Adelaide at Bedford Park (subseq. Flinders Univ. of SA), 1961–66; Vice-Chancellor, Flinders Univ. of SA, 1966–71; Chancellor, Univ. of Papua and New Guinea, 1969–70 (Chm., Interim Council, 1965–69); Chairman: Univs Commn, 1971–77; Commonwealth Tertiary Educn Commn, 1977–82; Vice-Chancellor, ANU, 1982–87. Chairman: Aust. Inst. of Health, 1987–92; Nat. Council on AIDS, 1988–92. Mem. Council, Univ. of Adelaide, 1955–69; Vis. Prof. of Econs, Queen's Univ., Belfast, 1957–58; Mem. Commonwealth Cttee: on Future of Tertiary Educn, 1961–65; of Economic Enquiry, 1963–65; Mem., Australian Council for Educn Research, 1968– (Pres., 1979–99); Chairman: Cttee of Enquiry into Educn in SA, 1969–70; Interim Cttee for Aust. Schools Commn, 1972–73; Cttee of Enquiry on Med. Schs, 1972–73; Cttee of Enquiry on Open Univ., 1973–74; Australia Council, 1974–77; Cttee on Post-Secondary Educn in Tasmania, 1975–76; Quality of Educn Review Cttee, 1984–85; Member: Commonwealth Govt Cttee to Review Efficiency and Effectiveness in Higher Educn, 1985–86; Adv. Cttee of Cities Commn, 1972–74; CSIRO Adv. Council, 1979–82; Australian Stats Adv. Council, 1988–97. Leader, OECD Review of US Educn Policy, 1978–79 and NZ Educn Policy, 1982. Pres., Acad. of Social Sciences in Australia, 1987–90 (FASSA 1952); Chm., Canberra Inst. of the Arts, 1988–91. Mem. Council, Chinese Univ. of Hong Kong, 1990–94. FACE 1969. Hon. LLD: Univ. of Papua and New Guinea, 1970; Univ. of Melbourne, 1975; Univ. of Queensland, 1985; ANU, 1996; Hon. LittD Flinders Univ. of SA, 1971; Hon. DLit Murdoch Univ., 1975; Hon. DLitt Macquarie, 1992; DU Newcastle, NSW, 1978. Mackie Medal, 1975; Aust. Coll. of Educn Medal, 1981. *Publications:* Applied Statistics for Economists, 1957, 1962 (1970 edn with M. Polasek, 4th edn 1977), Portuguese edn, 1972; (with M. Brunt) Structure of the Australian Economy, 1962, repr. 1963, 1966; (with G. C. Harcourt and R. H. Wallace) Economic Activity, 1967 (Italian edn 1969); articles in Economic Record, Population Studies, Jl Royal Statistical Assoc., Australian Jl of Education, and other learned jls. *Address:* 4/127 Hopetoun Circuit, Canberra, ACT 2600, Australia.

KARMILOFF-SMITH, Prof. Annette Dionne, FBA 1993; Head, Neurocognitive Development Unit, Institute of Child Health, since 1998; Visiting Professor of Psychology, University College London, since 1982; *b* 18 July 1938; *d* of late Jack Smith and Doris Ellen Ruth Smith (*née* Findlay); *m* 1966, Igor Alexander Karmiloff (marr. diss. 1991); two *d*. *Educ:* Edmonton County GS; Inst Français de Londres; Holborn Coll. of Law and Langs (Dip. Internat. Conf. Interpreting); Geneva Univ. (Dr of exptl and genetic psychol.). Internat. Conf. Interpreter, UN, 1966–70; Res. Consultant, UNWRA-UNESCO Inst. of Educn, Beirut, 1970–72; Res. Collaborator, Internat. Centre for Genetic Epistemiol., Geneva, 1972–76; Vis. Res. Associate, Max Planck Inst. for Psycholinguistics, Nijmegen, 1978–83; Sen. Res. Scientist (with Special Appt status), MRC Cognitive Development Unit, 1982–98. Vis. Prof., Univs of Sussex, Brussels, Munich, Chicago, Tel-Aviv and Barcelona, 1979–88. Sloan Fellow: Yale Univ., 1978; Univ. of Berkeley, 1981. MAE 1991; FMedSci 1999. FRSA 1997. BPsS Book Award, 1995. *Publications:* A Functional Approach to Child Language, 1979, 2nd edn 1981; (jtly) Child Language Research in ESF Countries, 1981; Beyond Modularity: a developmental perspective on cognitive science, 1992; Baby It's You, 1994; (jtly) Rethinking Innateness: connectionism in a developmental framework, 1996; (jtly) Everything Your Baby Would Ask, 1999; (jtly) Pathways to Language from Foetus to Adolescent, 2001; many chapters, and articles in learned jls. *Recreations:* writing/reading poetry, working out, going on multiple diets, writing a satire (Powerful Minds in Flabby Bodies). *Address:* River Quin Barn, Gravelly Lane, Braughing, Ware, Herts SG11 2RD. *T:* (01920) 821414; (work) (020) 7905 2754.

KARPINSKI, Marek Romuald K.; *see* Korab-Karpinski.

KARRAN, Graham, QFSM 1985; Managing Director, Graham Karran & Associates Ltd, since 1991; *b* 28 Nov. 1939; *s* of Joseph Karran and Muriel Benson; *m* 1960, Thelma Gott; one *s* one *d*. *Educ:* Bootle Grammar Sch.; Liverpool College of Building. Estate Management, 1958–60; Southport Fire Bde, 1960–63; Lancashire County Fire Bde, 1963–74; Greater Manchester Fire Service, 1974–78; Cheshire County Fire Service, 1978–80; Derbyshire Fire Service, 1980–83; Chief Fire Officer, W Yorks Fire Service, 1983–90. *Publications:* articles in English and Amer. Fire jls. *Recreations:* music, beachcombing. *T:* (business) (01484) 607212, *Fax:* (01484) 608736.

KARSH, Yousuf, CC 1990 (OC 1968); portrait photographer since 1932; *b* Mardin, Armenia-in-Turkey, 23 Dec. 1908; parents Armenian; Canadian Citizen; *m* 1939, Solange Gauthier (*d* 1961); *m* 1962, Estrellita Maria Nachbar. *Educ:* Sherbrooke, PQ Canada; studied photography in Boston, Mass., USA. Portrayed Winston Churchill in Canada's Houses of Parliament, 1941; King George VI, 1943; HM Queen (then Princess) Elizabeth and the Duke of Edinburgh, 1951; HH Pope Pius XII, 1951; also portrayed, among many others: Shaw, Wells, Einstein, Sibelius, Somerset Maugham, Picasso, Eden, Eisenhower, Tito, Eleanor Roosevelt, Thomas Mann, Bertrand Russell, Attlee, Nehru, Ingrid Bergmann, Lord Mountbatten of Burma, Augustus John, Pope John Paul II; 20 portraits used on postage stamps of 15 countries. One man exhibitions: Men Who Make our World, Pav. of Canada, Expo. 67; Montreal Mus. of Fine Arts, 1968; Boston Mus. of Fine Arts, 1968; Corning Mus., 1968; Detroit Inst. of Arts, 1969; Corcoran Gall. of Art, Washington, 1969; Macdonald House, London, 1969; Seattle Art Museum; Japan (country-wide), and Honolulu, 1970, in Europe and USA annually, 1971–; exhibn acquired in toto by: Museum of Modern Art, Tokyo; Nat. Gall. of Australia; Province of Alberta, Canada, 1975–76; numerous exhibns throughout US, 1971–75, 1976–77; Ulrich Museum, Wichita, Kansas, 1978; Museum of Science and Industry, Chicago, 1978; Evansville Museum, Ind., 1979; Palm Springs Desert Museum, 1980; inaugural exhibn, Museum of Photography, Film and TV, Bradford, 1983; NY, 1983; Nat. Portrait Gall., 1983, 1991; Edinburgh, 1984; Internat. Center of Photography, NY, 1983; Helsinki, 1984; Minneapolis Museum, 1985; Syracuse Museum, 1985; Sarasota (Florida) Museum, 1986; 80th birthday gala exhibn, Barbican, London, and in France, Germany, Spain, Switzerland, 1988; Muscarelle Mus. of Art, William and Mary Coll., Williamsburg, Virginia, 1987; Castle Buda Palace, Budapest, 1989; Nat. Gall. of Canada, 1989; Gulbenkian Foundn, Lisbon, 1989; Copenhagen, Brussels, Zurich, 1989; Vancouver Art Mus., 1990; Vero Beach, Fla, 1991; Montreal Mus. of Fine Arts, 1992; Internat. Centre of Photography, NY, 1992; Corcoran Gall., Washington, 1993; Minton Mus., Charlotte, NC, 1993; Tribute Exhibn, Bradford, 1993; Canadian Embassy, Washington, 1994; Mus. of Fine Arts, Boston, 1996; Detroit Art Inst., 1996–97; Canadian Embassy, London, 1998; Charlottetown Fest., PEI, 1998; Nat. Portrait Gall. of Australia, 1999; Boston-Nagoya Mus. of Fine Arts, Japan, 2000; German Historical Mus., Berlin, 2000 (catalogue pub. as Heroes of Light and Shadow, 2001); Canadian Cultural Center, Rio de Janeiro, 2000. Visiting Professor: Ohio Univ., 1967–69; Emerson Coll., Boston, 1972–73, 1973–74; Photographic Advisor, Internat. Exhibn, Expo '70, Osaka, Japan; Judge, UN 40th anniversary internat. poster contest, 1985. Trustee, Photographic Arts and Scis Foundn, 1970. FRPS; Fellow Rochester Sci. Mus. RCA 1975. Gift of portfolio of artists' photographs to Bretholtz Center for patients and families, Brigham and Women's Hosp., Boston. Eponymous annual lect. inaugurated at Mus. of Fine Arts, Boston, 1998; estab. annual Karsh Prize for Photography, Sch. of Mus. of Fine Arts, Boston. Holds 27 hon. degrees. Canada Council Medal, 1965; Centennial Medal, 1967; Master of Photographic Arts, Prof. Photogrs of Canada, 1970; First Gold Medal, Nat. Assoc. Photog. Art, 1974; Life Achievement Award, Encyclopaedia Britannica, 1980; Silver Shingle Award, Law Sch., Boston Univ., 1983; Lotos Medal of Merit, Lotos Club of NY, 1989; first Creative Edge Award, NY Univ., 1989; Gold Medal, Americas Soc., 1989; Master Photographer, Internat. Center of Photography, 1990; Jerusalem Prize in the Arts, Bezalel Acad., Israel, 1997; Fox-Talbot Award, British Inst. of Prof. Photography, 1998. *Publications:* Faces of Destiny, 1947; (co-author) This is the Mass, 1958; Portraits of Greatness, 1959; (co-author) This is Rome, 1960; (co-author) This is the Holy Land, 1961; (autobiog.) In Search of Greatness, 1962; (co-author) These are the Sacraments, 1963; (co-author) The Warren Court; Karsh Portfolio, 1967; Faces of our Time, 1971; Karsh Portraits, 1976; Karsh Canadians, 1979; Karsh: a fifty year retrospective, 1983, rev. edn, a sixty year retrospective, 1996; American Legends, 1992. *Recreations:* tennis, bird-watching, archæology, music. *Address:* 2 Commonwealth Avenue, Boston, MA 02116, USA. *T:* (J. Fielder) (831) 3734569. *Clubs:* Garrick; Rideau (Ottawa); Century, Dutch Treat (NY).

KARSTEN, Ian George Francis; QC 1990; **His Honour Judge Ian Karsten;** a Circuit Judge, since 1999; *b* 27 July 1944; *s* of late Dr Frederick Karsten and of Edith Karsten; *m* 1984, Moira Elizabeth Ann O'Hara; one *s* two *d*. *Educ:* William Ellis School, Highgate; Magdalen College, Oxford (MA, BCL); Diplômé, Hague Acad. of Internat. Law. Called to the Bar, Gray's Inn, 1967; Midland and Oxford Circuit; commenced practice 1970; Lectr in Law, Southampton Univ., 1966–70, LSE, 1970–88; a Recorder, 1994–99. UK Deleg. to Hague Conf. on Private Internat. Law (Convention on the Law Applicable to Agency) (Rapporteur), 1973–77; Leader, UK Delegn to Unidroit Conf. on Agency in Internat. Sale of Goods, Bucharest, 1979, Geneva, 1983. *Publications:* Conflict of Laws, Halsbury's Laws of England, 4th edn (jtly), 1974; Report on the Convention on the Law Applicable to Agency (Hague Conf.), 1979; articles and notes in legal jls. *Recreations:* opera, travel, chess. *Address:* Crown Court at Middlesex Guildhall, Little George Street, SW1P 3BB. *T:* (020) 7799 2131.

KASER, Prof. Michael Charles, DLitt; General Editor, International Economic Association, since 1986; Hon. Professor and Senior Research Fellow, Institute for German Studies, University of Birmingham, since 1994; Reader in Economics, University of Oxford, and Professorial Fellow of St Antony's College, 1972–93 (Sub-Warden, 1986–87), now Reader Emeritus and Emeritus Fellow; *b* 2 May 1926; *er s* of Charles Joseph Kaser and Mabel Blunden; *m* 1954, Elisabeth Anne Mary, *er d* of Cyril Gascoigne Piggford; four *s* one *d*. *Educ:* King's Coll., Cambridge (Exhibr); DLitt Oxon 1993. Foreign Service, London and Moscow, 1947–51; UN Secretariat, Econ. Commn for Europe, Geneva, 1951–63; Faculty Fellow, St Antony's Coll., Oxford, 1963–72; Dir, 1988–93, Sen. Res. Assoc., 1997–, Inst. of Slavonic Studies (formerly Inst. of Russian, Soviet and E European Studies), Univ. of Oxford; Associate Fellow, Templeton Coll., Oxford, 1983–. Hon. Fellow, Divinity Faculty, Univ. of Edinburgh, 1993–96. Visiting Professor of Economics: Inst. Universitaire des Hautes Etudes Internats, Geneva, 1959–63; Univ. of Michigan, 1966; Vis. Faculty (formerly Fellow), Henley Management Coll., 1987–; Vis. Lectr, Cambridge Univ., 1967–68, 1977–78 and 1978–79; Vis. Lectr, INSEAD, Fontainebleau, 1959–82, 1988–92. Specialist Advr, Foreign Affairs Cttee, H of C, 1985–87. Oxford Univ. Latin Preacher, 1982. Convenor/Chm., Nat. Assoc. for Soviet and East European Studies, 1965–73, Chm., Jt Cttee with BUAS, 1980–84; Vice-Chm., Internat. Activities Cttee (Vice-Chm., Area Studies Panel, SSRC) ESRC, 1980–84; Chm., Co-ordinating Council, Area Studies Assocs, 1986–88 (Mem., 1980–93 and 1995; Sec., 1980–84, Vice-Chm., 1984–86); Governor, Plater Coll., Oxford, 1968–95, Emeritus Governor, 1995–; Chairman: Acad. Council, Wilton Park (FCO), 1986–92 (Mem., 1985–); Acad. Cttee, St Catharine's, Cumberland Lodge, 1991– (Mem., 1973–); Sir Heinz Koeppler Trust, 1992– (Mem., 1987–). President: British Assoc. for Slavonic and East European Studies, 1988–91 (Vice-Pres., 1991–93); British Assoc. of Former UN Civil Servants, 1994–; Chairman: Standing Cttee on E European Affairs, European Econ. Assoc., 1990–93; Keston Inst., 1994–. Member: Council, Royal Econ. Soc., 1976–86, 1987–90; Council, RIIA, 1979–85, 1986–92; Internat. Soc. Sci. Council, UNESCO, 1980–91; Council, SSEES, 1981–87; Sec., British Acad. Cttee for SE European Studies, 1988–93 (Mem., 1970–75, 1983–93). Steering Cttee, Königswinter Anglo-German Confs, 1969–90 (Chm., Oxford Organizing Cttee, 1975–78). Pres., Albania Soc. of Britain, 1992–95; Trustee, King George VI and Queen Elizabeth Foundn, 1987–. Missions for various internat. agencies, 1955–, incl. EC to Moscow, 1991, UNICEF to Albania, 1991, Turkmenistan and Uzbekistan, 1992, and IMF to Kyrgyzstan, 1998. Editorial Boards: Member: Central Asian Survey; Slavonic and East European Rev.; former Member: Econ. Jl; Jl of Industrial Econs; Soviet Studies; Oxford Rev. of Educn; CUP E European Monograph Series; World Develt; European Econ. Rev.; Energy Econs. Hon. DSocSc Birmingham, 1994. KSG 1990. Knight's Cross, Order of Merit (Poland), 1999; Order of Naim Frashëri (Albania), 1999. *Publications:* Comecon: Integration Problems of the Planned Economies, 1965, 2nd edn 1967; (ed) Economic Development for Eastern Europe, 1968; (with J. Zieliński) Planning in East Europe, 1970; Soviet Economics, 1970; (ed, with R. Portes) Planning and Market Relations, 1971; (ed, with H. Höhmann and K. Thalheim) The New Economic Systems of Eastern Europe, 1975; (ed, with A. Brown) The Soviet Union since the Fall of Khrushchev, 1975, 2nd edn 1978; Health Care in the Soviet Union and Eastern Europe, 1976; (ed with A. Brown) Soviet Policy for the 1980s, 1982; (ed jtly) The Cambridge Encyclopaedia of Russia and the Soviet Union, 1982, revd edn as The Cambridge Encyclopaedia of Russia and the Former Soviet Union, 1994; Gen. Ed., The Economic History of Eastern Europe 1919–1975, vols I and II (1919–49), vol. III (1949–75), 1985–86; (ed with E. A. G. Robinson) Early Steps in Comparing East-West Economies, 1992; (ed with D. Phillips)

Education and Economic Change in Eastern Europe and the Former Soviet Union, 1992; (with S. Mehrotra) The Central Asian Economies after Independence, 1992; Privatization in the CIS, 1995; The Economies of Kazakstan and Uzbekistan, 1997; papers in economic jls and symposia. *Address:* 31 Capel Close, Oxford OX2 7LA. *T:* (01865) 515581. *Club:* Reform.

KASMIN, John; art dealer, since 1960; *b* 24 Sept. 1934; *s* of Vera D'Olzewski and David Kosminsky (known as Kaye); *m* 1959, Jane Nicholson (marr. diss.); two *s*. *Educ:* Magdalen College School, Oxford. Adventurous and varied jobs in New Zealand, 1952–56; art gallery assistant, London, 1956–60; Founder Director: Kasmin Ltd, 1961– (in partnership with late Marquess of Dufferin and Ava); Knoedler Kasmin Ltd, 1977–92. *Recreations:* reading, walking in landscapes, museums, cities. *Address:* c/o Kasmin Ltd, 34 Warwick Avenue, W9 2PT.

KASPAROV, Garry Kimovich; chess player; *b* Baku, Azerbaijan, 13 April 1963; *né* Harry Weinstein; *s* of Kim Moiseyevich Weinstein and Klara Kasparova; *m* 1st, 1989, Maria Arapova (marr. diss. 1994); one *d*; 2nd, 1996, Yulia Vovk; one *s*. Youngest world chess champion, 1985; retained title, 1986, 1987, 1990, 1993, 1995; lost title, 2000. Resigned from FIDE and formed Professional Chess Assoc. (with Nigel Short); won first title, 1993; rejoined FIDE, 1994; won PCA World Championship, NY, 1995. Played supercomputer Deep Blue, Philadelphia, 1996 and NY, 1997, series drawn; played first Advanced chess against Topolov, Spain, 1998; played The World, 1999. Founded Kasparov Chess Acad., 1997. *Publications:* New World Chess Champion, 1985; The Test of Time, 1986; London-Leningrad Championship Games, 1987; (with Donald Trelford) Child of Change, 1987; Unlimited Challenge, 1990; (with Daniel King) Kasparov Against the World, 2000. *Address:* c/o SMSI, 249 Peruvian Avenue, F-2, Palm Beach, FL 33480, USA.

KATCHALSKI-KATZIR, Prof. Ephraim; *see* Katzir.

KATENGA-KAUNDA, Reid Willie; Malaŵi Independence Medal, 1964; Malaŵi Republic Medal, 1966; Political Adviser to State President, Malaŵi, since 1994; *b* 20 Aug. 1929; *s* of Gibson Amon Katenga Kaunda and Maggie Talengeske Nyabanda; *m* 1951, Elsie Nyabanda; one *s* three *d* (and one *s* one *d* decd). *Educ:* Ndola Govt Sch., Zambia; Inst. of Public Administration, Malaŵi; Trinity Coll., Oxford Univ.; Administrative Staff Coll., Henley; LSE. Sec., Nkhota Kota Rice Co-op. Soc. Ltd, 1952–62; Dist. Comr, Karonga, Malaŵi, 1964–65; Sen. Asst Sec., Min. of External Affairs, Zomba, Malaŵi, 1966; MP and Parly Sec., Office of the President and Cabinet, Malaŵi, 1966–68; Dep. Regional Chm., MCP, Northern Region, 1967–68; Under Sec., Office of the President and Cabinet, 1968–69; High Comr in London, 1969–70; Perm. Sec., Min. of Trade, Industry and Tourism, 1971–72; High Comr in London, 1972–73, and concurrently to the Holy See, Portugal, Belgium, Holland and France; business exec., 1975–94. Dep. Sec. Gen., 1992–99, Sec. Gen., 1999–, United Democratic Front, Malaŵi. Chm., Interparty Technical Cttee on Peace and Unity, 1999–. Dep. Chm., Ncheu and Mchinji Inquiry Commn, 1967. *Recreations:* reading, walking, cinema, Association football. *Address:* c/o PO Box 511, Blantyre, Malaŵi.

KATIN, Peter Roy; concert pianist; Professor, London College of Music and Media, Thames Valley University, since 2001; *b* 14 Nov. 1930; *m* 1954, Eva Zweig; two *s*. *Educ:* Henry Thornton Sch.; Westminster Abbey; Royal Academy of Music. First London appearance at Wigmore Hall, 1948. A leading Chopin interpreter. Performances abroad include most European countries, West and East, S and E Africa, Japan, Canada, USA, Hong Kong, India, New Zealand, Singapore, Malaysia. Many recordings, incl. complete sonatas of Mozart, complete nocturnes and impromptus of Chopin, complete preludes of Rachmaninov, complete lyric pieces of Grieg, fortepiano works of Clementi, Chopin and Schubert, and major works by Brahms, Mendelssohn, Scarlatti, Schubert, Schumann and Tchaikovsky. Professor: Royal Acad. of Music, 1956–59; RCM, 1992–2001. Vis. Prof. in piano, Univ. of Western Ontario, 1978–84. Founder: Katin Centre for Advanced Piano Studies, 1991; Katin Trio, 1997. Mem. Incorporated Soc. of Musicians (ISM). FRAM, ARCM. Hon. DMus De Montfort, 1994. Chopin Arts Award, NY, 1977. *Recreations:* reading, writing, theatre, tape recording, photography. *Address:* c/o Transart (UK) Ltd, 8 Bristol Gardens, W9 2JG. *T:* (020) 7286 7526, *Fax:* (020) 7266 2687; *e-mail:* transart@transartuk.com; Transart, 7 rue Hoche, 92300 Levallois Perret, France. *T:* (1) 47598709, *Fax:* (1) 47598700; *e-mail:* valmalete@dial.oleane.com.

KATKHUDA, Samih; His Honour Judge Katkhuda; a Circuit Judge, since 1995; *b* 15 Dec. 1941; *s* of Dr S. M. Katkhuda and U. Katkhuda (*née* Ciĉić); *m* 1968, Suzanne Gundred de Warrenne Crews; two *s*. *Educ:* King's Sch., Bruton, Som; Inns of Court Sch. of Law. Court Admin, CCC, Old Bailey, 1964–73; called to the Bar, Gray's Inn, 1974; in practice as barrister, 1974–96; a Recorder, 1994–96. *Publication:* Forms of Indictment, 1990. *Recreations:* music, travel, reading. *Address:* Snaresbrook Crown Court, 75 Hollybush Hill, Snaresbrook, E11 1QW. *Club:* Savage.

KATKOWSKI, Christopher Andrew Mark; QC 1999; *b* 16 Jan. 1957; *s* of Edward and Maria Katkowski; *m* 1976, Anna Thérèse Louise Gunstone. *Educ:* Fitzwilliam Coll., Cambridge (BA Law 1978; LLB 1979). Lectr in Law, City of London Poly., 1979–83; called to the Bar, Gray's Inn, 1982; in practice at the Bar, 1984–; Jun. Counsel to the Crown (Common Law), 1992–99. Mem., Attorney-Gen.'s Supplementary Panel, 1988–92. *Recreation:* switching-off. *Address:* 4 Breams Buildings, EC4Y 1AQ. *T:* (020) 7353 5835.

KATRITZKY, Prof. Alan Roy, DPhil, PhD, ScD; FRS 1980; FRSC; Kenan Professor of Chemistry, since 1980, and Director, Center for Heterocyclic Compounds, since 1986, University of Florida; *b* 18 Aug. 1928; *s* of Frederick Charles Katritzky and Emily Catherine (*née* Lane); *m* 1952, Agnes Juliane Dietlinde Kilian; one *s* three *d*. *Educ:* Oxford Univ. (BA, BSc, MA, DPhil); Cambridge Univ. (PhD, ScD). FRIC 1963. Lectr, Cambridge Univ., 1958–63; Fellow of Churchill Coll., Cambridge, 1960–63; Prof. of Chemistry, Univ. of E Anglia, 1963–80, Dean, Sch. of Chem. Sciences, UEA, 1963–70 and 1976–80. Foreign Member: Polish Acad. of Sci., 1991; Real Acad. Catalonia, Barcelona, 1995; Slovenian Acad., 2001. Foreign Fellow, RACI, 1983; FAAAS, 2000; Hon. Fellow: Italian Chem. Soc., 1978; Polish Chem. Soc., 1985; Internat. Soc. of Heterocyclic Chem., 1995. Hon. Prof., Beijing Inst. of Tech., China, 1995. Dr *hc:* Univ. Nacional, Madrid, 1986; Univ. Poznan, Poland, 1990; Medical Acad., Gdansk, 1994; Univ. of E Anglia, 1995; Univ. of Toulouse, 1996; Univ. of St Petersburg, 1997; Technical Univ., Bucharest, 1998; Rostov Univ., 2000; Univ. Ghent, 2001. Tilden Medal, Chem. Soc., 1975–76. Heterocyclic Award, RSC, 1983; Medals of Tartu State Univ., Estonia, USSR, 1986, 1992; Golden Tiger award, Exxon Corp., 1989; Inernat. Soc. of Heterocyclic Chemistry Award, 1993; Medal of Univ. of Thessaloniki, 1993; Florida Award, American Chem. Soc., 1995; Heyrowski Medal, Czech Acad., 1997; Kametani Prize, Japan, 1999. Cavaliere ufficiale, Order Al Merito Della Repubblica Italiana, 1975. *Publications:* (ed) Advances in Heterocyclic Chemistry, Vols 1–81, 1963–; (ed) Physical Methods in Heterocyclic Chemistry, Vols 1–6, 1963–72; Principles of Heterocyclic Chemistry, 1968 (trans. into French, German, Italian, Japanese, Russian, Polish and Spanish); Chemistry of Heterocyclic N-Oxides (monograph), 1970; Heteroaromatic Tautomerism (monograph), 1975; Handbook of Heterocyclic Chemistry, 1985, 2nd edn 2000; Heterocycles in Life and Society, 1998; Chm. Editorial Bd, Comprehensive Heterocyclic Chemistry (8 vols), 1985, 2nd edn (10 vols) 1996; Chm. Editorial Bd, Comprehensive Organic Functional Group Transformations (7 vols), 1995; scientific papers in Heterocylic Chem. *Recreations:* walking, travel, windsurfing. *Address:* Department of Chemistry, University of Florida, Gainesville, FL 32611, USA. *T:* (352) 3920554, *Fax:* (352) 3929199. *Club:* Oxford and Cambridge.

KATSAV, Moshe; President of Israel, since 2000; Member of Knesset, since 1977; *b* Iran, 1945; emigrated to Israel, 1951; *m* Gila; five *c*. *Educ:* Hebrew Univ. of Jerusalem. Newspaper reporter, Yediot Aharonot, 1966-68; Mem., Interior and Educn Cttees, Knesset, 1977-81; Dep. Minister of Housing and Construction, 1981-84; Minister: of Labour and Social Affairs, 1984-88; of Transportation, and Mem., Ministerial Cttee on Defence, 1988-92; Chm., Parly Cttee of Chinese-Israeli Friendship League, 1992-96; Dep. Prime Minister, Minister of Tourism, and Minister for Israeli-Arab Affairs, 1996-99; Chm., Ministerial Cttee for Nat. Events and Mem., Ministerial Cttee on Defence, 1996–99; Mem., Foreign Affairs and Defence Cttee, 1999-2000. Mem., Commn on adoptive children, 1978; Chm., Commn to determine higher educn tuition, 1982. Chairman, Likud Party: at Hebrew Univ., Jerusalem, 1969; in Knesset, 1992-96. Pres., B'nai B'rith Youth, 1968. Mayor, Kiryat Malachi, 1969 and 1974-81. Mem., Bd of Trustees, Ben-Gurion Univ., 1978. Hon. Dr Nebraska, 1998. *Publications:* contrib. articles in newspapers, Maariv and Yediot Aharonot. *Address:* The President's Residence, Jerusalem, Israel.

KATZ, Sir Bernard, Kt 1969; FRS 1952; Professor and Head of Biophysics Department, University College, London, 1952–78, now Emeritus, Hon. Research Fellow, 1978; *b* Leipzig, 26 March 1911; *s* of M. N. Katz; *m* 1945, Marguerite (*d* 1999), *d* of W. Penly, Sydney, Australia; two *s*. *Educ:* University of Leipzig (MD 1934). Biophysical research, University Coll., London, 1935–39; PhD London, and Beit Memorial Research Fellow, 1938; Carnegie Research Fellow, Sydney Hospital, Sydney, 1939–42; DSc London, 1943. Served War of 1939–45 in Pacific with RAAF, 1942–45; Flt-Lt, 1943. Asst Dir of Research, Biophysics Research Unit, University Coll., London, and Henry Head Research Fellow (Royal Society), 1946–50; Reader in Physiology, 1950–51. Lectures: Herter, Johns Hopkins Univ., 1958; Dunham, Harvard Coll., 1961; Croonian, Royal Society, 1961; Sherrington, Liverpool Univ., 1967; Fenn, IUPS, Glasgow, 1993. A Vice-Pres., Royal Society, 1965, Biological Secretary and Vice-President, 1968–76. Mem., Agric. Research Coun., 1967–77. For. Member: Royal Danish Academy Science and Letters, 1968; Accad. Naz. Lincei, 1968; Amer. Acad. of Arts and Sciences, 1969; For. Assoc., Nat. Acad. of Scis, USA, 1976; Hon. Member: Japanese Pharmacol. Soc., 1977; American Physiolog. Soc., 1985; Assoc. Mem., European Molecular Biol. Orgn, 1978; Corresp. Mem., Australian Acad. of Science, 1987. Fellow of University Coll., London. FRCP, 1968. Hon. FIBiol, 1978. Hon. DSc: Southampton, 1971; Melbourne, 1971; Cambridge, 1980; Hon. PhD Weizmann Inst., Israel, 1979; Hon. MD Leipzig, 1990. Feldberg Foundation Award, 1965; Baly Medal, RCP, 1967; Copley Medal, Royal Society, 1967; Nobel Prize (jtly) for Physiology and Medicine, 1970; Cothenius Medal, Deutsche Akademie der Wissenschaften, Leopoldina, 1989. Foreign Mem., Orden Pour le Mérite für Wissenschaften und Künste, 1982. *Publications:* Electric Excitation of Nerve, 1939; Nerve, Muscle and Synapse, 1966; The Release of Neural Transmitter Substances, 1969; papers on nerve and muscle physiology in Jl of Physiol., Proc. Royal Society, etc. *Recreation:* chess. *Address:* University College, WC1E 6BT.

KATZ, Philip Alec Jackson; QC 2000; a Recorder, since 2000; *b* 8 May 1953; *s* of Stanley Zeb Jackson (*née* Katz) and Anita Jackson; adopted patronymic Katz, 1976. *Educ:* Roundhay Grammar Sch., Leeds; University Coll., Oxford (MA). Called to the Bar, Middle Temple, 1976. *Address:* 9–12 Bell Yard, WC2A 2JR. *T:* (020) 7400 1800.

KATZIR, Prof. Ephraim (Katchalski), PhD; Institute Professor, Weizmann Institute of Science, since 1978; President, State of Israel, 1973–78; *b* Kiev, Ukraine, 16 May 1916; *s* of Yehuda and Tsila Katchalski; *m* 1938, Nina Gotlieb (decd); one *s* (two *d* decd). *Educ:* Rehavia High Sch., Jerusalem; Hebrew Univ., Jerusalem (chemistry, botany, zool., bacteriol.; MSc *summa cum laude* 1937; PhD 1941). Settled in Israel with parents, 1922; involved in Labour youth movement; Inf. Comdr, Jewish Self-Defence Forces (Hagana). Asst, Dept of Theoretical and Macromolecular Chem., Hebrew Univ., 1941–45; Res. Fellow, Polytechnic Inst., and Columbia Univ., NY, 1946–48; Actg Head, Dept of Biophys., Weizmann Inst. of Science, Rehovot, Israel, 1949–51, Head 1951–73 (mem. founding faculty of Inst.); Chief Scientist, Israel Def. Min., 1966–68; Head, Dept of Biotechnology, Tel Aviv Univ., 1980–88. Vis. Prof. of Biophys., Hebrew Univ., 1953–61; Guest Scientist, Harvard Univ., 1957–59; Vis. Prof., Rockefeller Univ., NY, and Univ. of Mich, Ann Arbor, 1961–65; Sen. Foreign Scientist Fellowship, UCLA, 1964; Battelle Seattle Res. Center, Washington, 1971; Regents Prof., Univ. of Calif., San Diego, 1979; First Herman F. Mark Chair in Polymer Sci., Poly. Inst., NY, 1979. President: World ORT Union, 1986–90; Cobiotech, 1989–95. Member: Biochem. Soc. of Israel; Israel Acad. of Sciences and Humanities; Israel Chem. Soc.; Council, Internat. Union of Biochem.; AAAS; Assoc. of Harvard Chemists; Leopoldina Acad. of Science, Germany; World Acad. of Art and Science; New York Acad. of Science (Life Mem.). Centennial Foreign Fellow, Amer. Chem. Soc.; For. Associate, Nat. Acad. of Sciences of USA. For. Member: The Royal Soc.; Amer. Philosoph. Soc.; Acad. des Scis, France, 1989. Hon. Fellow, Scientific Acad. of Argentina, 1986; Hon. Member: Amer. Acad. of Arts and Sciences; Amer. Soc. of Biol Chemists; Harvey Soc.; Romanian Acad. of Scis, 1991; Hon. MRI 1989. Hon. PhD: Hebrew Univ., 1973; Poly. Inst. of NY, 1975; Brandeis Univ., Univ. of Mich, and Hebrew Union Coll., 1975; Weizmann Inst. of Science, 1976; Northwestern Univ., Evanston, 1978; Harvard, 1978; McGill, 1980; ETH Zurich, 1980; Thomas Jefferson, 1981; Oxford, 1981; Miami, 1983; Technion, Israel Inst. of Technology, 1983; Univ. of Buenos Aires, 1986. Tchernikhovski Prize, 1948; Weizmann Prize, 1950; Israel Prize in Nat. Sciences, 1959; Rothschild Prize in Nat. Sciences, 1961; Linderstrøm Lang Gold Medal, 1969; Hans Krebs Medal, 1972; Alpha Omega Achievement Medal, 1979; Underwood Prescott Award, MIT, 1982; first Japan Prize, Science and Technol. Foundn of Japan, 1985; Internat. Enzyme Engineering Award, 1987. Hon. Founding Editor, Biopolymers, 1986– (Mem., Editorial Bd, 1963–86). Comdr, Legion of Honour (France), 1990. *Address:* Weizmann Institute of Science, Rehovot 76100, Israel.

KAUFFMANN, Prof. C. Michael, MA, PhD; FBA 1987; FMA; FSA; Professor of History of Art and Director, Courtauld Institute of Art, University of London, 1985–95, now Professor Emeritus; *b* 5 Feb. 1931; *s* of late Arthur and late Tamara Kauffmann; *m* 1954, Dorothea (*née* Hill); two *s*. *Educ:* St Paul's Sch.; Merton Coll., Oxford (Postmaster); Warburg Inst., London Univ. (Jun. Research Fellow). Asst Curator, Photographic Collection, Warburg Inst., 1957–58; Keeper, Manchester City Art Gall., 1958–60; Victoria and Albert Museum: Asst Keeper, 1960–75, Keeper, 1975–85, Dept of Prints & Drawings and Paintings; Asst to the Director, 1963–66; Visiting Associate Prof., Univ. of Chicago, 1969. Mem. Exec. Cttee, NACF, 1987–; Trustee, Nat. Museums and Galls on

Merseyside, 1986–99. *Publications:* The Baths of Pozzuoli: medieval illuminations of Peter of Eboli's poem, 1959; An Altar-piece of the Apocalypse, 1968; Victoria & Albert Museum: catalogue of foreign paintings, 1973; British Romanesque Manuscripts 1066–1190, 1975; Catalogue of Paintings in the Wellington Museum, 1982; John Varley, 1984; Studies in Medieval Art, 1992.

KAUFMAN, Rt Hon. Gerald (Bernard); PC 1978; MP (Lab) Manchester, Gorton, since 1983 (Manchester, Ardwick, 1970–83); *b* 21 June 1930; *s* of Louis and Jane Kaufman. *Educ:* Leeds Grammar Sch.; The Queen's Coll., Oxford. Asst Gen.-Sec., Fabian Soc., 1954–55; Political Staff, Daily Mirror, 1955–64; Political Correspondent, New Statesman, 1964–65; Parly Press Liaison Officer, Labour Party, 1965–70. Parly Under-Sec. of State, DoE, 1974–75, Dept of Industry, 1975; Minister of State, Dept of Industry, 1975–79; Shadow Envmt Sec., 1980–83; Shadow Home Sec., 1983–87; Shadow Foreign Sec., 1987–92. Chm., Select Cttee on Nat. Heritage, 1992–97, on Culture, Media and Sport, 1997–. Mem., Parly Cttee of PLP, 1980–92. Mem., Labour Party NEC, 1991–92. Mem., Royal Commn on H of L reform, 1999. Chm., Booker Prize Judges, 1999. HPk (Pakistan), 1999. *Publications:* (jtly) How to Live Under Labour, 1964; (ed) The Left, 1966; To Build the Promised Land, 1973; How to be a Minister, 1980, 2nd edn 1997; (ed) Renewal: Labour's Britain in the 1980s, 1983; My Life in the Silver Screen, 1985; Inside the Promised Land, 1986; Meet Me in St Louis, 1994. *Recreations:* travel, going to the pictures. *Address:* 87 Charlbert Court, Eamont Street, NW8 7DA. *T:* (office) (020) 7219 3000.

KAUFMAN, Prof. Matthew Howard, PhD, DSc; FRCPE; Professor of Anatomy, University of Edinburgh, since 1985 (Head of Department of Anatomy, 1985–95); *b* 29 Sept. 1942; *s* of Benjamin and Dora Kaufman; *m* 1973, Claire Lesley Kaufman (*née* Farrow); two *s*. *Educ:* Westminster City Sch.; Univ. of Edinburgh (MB ChB 1967; DSc 1984); Univ. of Cambridge (PhD 1973; MA 1975; ScD 1993). FRCPE 1996. Pre- and post-registration clinical posts, 1967–69; Research Associate, Inst. of Animal Genetics, Edinburgh, 1970; MRC Jun. Research Fellow, Physiol Lab., Cambridge, 1970–73; Royal Soc./Israel Acad. of Scis Research Fellow, and MRC Travelling Fellow, Weizmann Inst. of Science, 1973–75; University of Cambridge: Univ. Demonstrator, 1975–77; Lectr in Anatomy, 1977–85; Fellow and College Lectr in Anatomy, King's Coll., 1980–85. *Publications:* Early Mammalian Development: parthenogenetic studies, 1983; The Atlas of Mouse Development, 1992; (with J. B. L. Bard) The Anatomical Basis of Mouse Development, 1999; Surgeons at War, 2000; research papers in the fields of experimental and descriptive embryology, cytogenetics, developmental biology and teratology, medical history. *Recreations:* history of medicine, particularly of anatomy; the artefacts of phrenology, military surgery. *Address:* Section of Anatomy, Department of Biomedical Sciences, University Medical School, Teviot Place, Edinburgh EH8 9AG. *T:* (0131) 650 3113; *e-mail:* m.kaufman@ed.ac.uk.

KAUFMANN, Julia Ruth, OBE 1997; Commissioner, Postcomm, since 2000; freelance consultant for voluntary sector, since 2000; *b* 29 March 1941; *d* of Prof. Felix Kaufmann and Ruth Arnold; marr. diss.; two *s* one *d*. *Educ:* St George's Hosp., London (SRN); Sidney Webb Coll. (BEd London); Brunel Univ. (Dip. Social Policy and Admin). Advisory teacher, ILEA, 1974–76; Dir, Centre for Social Educn, 1976-78; Press Officer, 1978-79, Dir, 1979-87, Gingerbread; Dir, BBC Children in Need Appeal, 1987-2000. *Address:* 2 Carberry Road, SE19 3RU. *T:* (020) 8653 3877.

KAUL, Mahendra Nath, OBE 1975; Chairman, India's Restaurants Ltd, since 1997; *b* 28 July 1922; *s* of Dina Nath Kaul and Gauri Kaul; *m* 1955, Rajni Kapur, MA, MLS; one *d*. *Educ:* Univ. of the Punjab, India (BA). Joined Radio Kashmir of All India Radio, as news reader, actor and producer of dramas, 1949; appeared in two feature films and assisted in producing several documentaries, 1950–52; news reader and actor in three languages, also drama producer, All India Radio, New Delhi, 1952–55; joined Indian service of Voice of America, Washington DC, 1955, later becoming Editor of the service; joined external service of BBC, as newscaster, producer and dir of radio plays; producer/presenter, BBC TV prog. for Asian Viewers in UK, 1966–82. OBE awarded for services to race relations in Gt Britain. Received The Green Pennant from HRH The Duke of Edinburgh, awarded by Commonwealth Expedition (COMEX 10), 1980. *Recreations:* golf, cooking, boating, classical and light classical music, reading political works. *Address:* 109 Clive Court, Maida Vale, W9 1SF. *T:* (020) 7286 8131.

KAUNDA, Kenneth David; President of Zambia, Oct. 1964–1991 (Prime Minister, N Rhodesia, Jan.-Oct. 1964); Chancellor of the University of Zambia, 1966–91; *b* 28 April 1924; *s* of late David Julizgia and Hellen Kaunda, Missionaries; *m* 1946, Betty Banda; five *s* two *d* one adopted *s* (and two *s* decd). *Educ:* Lubwa Training Sch.; Munali Secondary Sch. Teacher, Lubwa Training Sch., 1943–44, Headmaster, 1944–47; Boarding Master, Mufulira Upper Sch., 1948–49. African National Congress: District Sec., 1950–52; Provincial Organising Sec., 1952–53; Sec.-Gen., 1953–58; Nat. Pres., Zambia African Nat. Congress, 1958–59; founded United Nat. Independence Party, 1958, Nat. Pres., 1960–91, re-elected, 1995–2000; Chm., Pan-African Freedom Movement for East, Central and South Africa, 1962; Minister of Local Government and Social Welfare, N Rhodesia, 1962–63. Chairman: Organization of African Unity, 1970, 1987; Non-aligned Countries, 1970. Hon. Doctor of Laws: Fordham Univ., USA, 1963; Dublin Univ., 1964; University of Sussex, 1965; Windsor Univ., Canada, 1966; University of Chile, 1966; Univ. of Zambia, 1974; Univ. of Humboldt, 1980; DUniv York, 1966. *Publications:* Black Government, 1961; Zambia Shall Be Free, 1962; Humanist in Africa, 1966; Humanism in Zambia and its implementation, 1967; Letter to My Children; Kaunda on Violence, 1980. *Recreations:* golf, music, table tennis, football, draughts, gardening and reading. *Address:* c/o UNIP, POB 30302, 10101 Lusaka, Zambia.

KAUNDA, Reid Willie K.; *see* Katenga-Kaunda.

KAUNTZE, Ralph, MBE 1944; MD; FRCP; Physician to Guy's Hospital, 1948–71, Consultant Physician Emeritus since 1971; *b* 5 June 1911; *s* of Charles Kauntze and Edith, *d* of Ralph Bagley; *m* 1st, 1935, Katharine Margaret (*d* 1993), *yr d* of late Ramsay Moodie; two *s* one *d*; 2nd, 1994, Enid M., *widow* of Lt-Col F. J. P. Dewhurst, RTR. *Educ:* Canford Sch.; Emmanuel Coll., Cambridge; St George's Hosp., London. William Brown Sen. Schol., St George's Hosp. 1932; MRCS, LRCP 1935; MA, MB, BCh Cantab 1937; MRCP 1939; MD Cantab 1946; FRCP 1950. Served, 1939–45, RAMC, chiefly Mediterranean area, Lt-Col O i/c Med. Div. Asst Dir of Dept of Med., Guy's Hosp., 1947–48, Physician to Cardiac Dept, 1956–71; Cons. Phys. to High Wycombe War Memorial Hosp., 1948–50; Dir Asthma Clinic, 1948–52, and of Dept of Student Health, 1950–63, Guy's Hosp.; Physician to Royal Masonic Hospital, 1963–76. Former Senior Cons. Phys. to: Commercial Union Assurance Co. Ltd; British & European Assurance Co.; European Assurance Co. Ltd. Hon. Vis. Phys., Johns Hopkins Hosp., Baltimore, 1958. Examiner in Medicine: RCP; London Univ. Mem. Brit. Cardiac Soc.; Mem. Assoc. of Physicians. *Publications:* contrib. med. jls. *Recreations:* farming, walking. *Address:* Arran House, rue de la Forge, St Martin, Jersey JE3 6BD. *T:* (01543) 854162.

KAUSIMAE, Sir David, KBE 1995 (OBE 1974); Founder and Deputy Chairman, Pacific Asia Evangelical Association, since 1976; *b* Solomon Is, 12 Oct. 1931; *s* of Joe Poraiwai and Patricia Hagar Keraapu; *m* 1951, Bethezel Kalifera; three *s* three *d*. No formal educn. MLC, Solomon Is, 1965–67; Member: Exec. Council, 1966; Forestry Rev. Cttee, 1968–69; Select Cttee on Tourist Bill, 1969–70; Governing Council, 1970–74; Chm., Natural Resources, Commerce and Industry, 1970–74; MLA, 1974–77; Minister of Foreign Trade, Commerce and Industry, 1974–75; Mem., Constitutional Cttee, 1975–76; Dep. Speaker, Nat. Parlt, 1976–77; Chairman: Special Cttee on Provincial Govt, 1977–79; Electoral Rev. Cttee, 1995; Mem., Police Force Rev. Cttee, 1989–90. Founder Mem., People's Alliance Party, 1976 (Pres., 1976). Chairman: Ports Authy, 1981–84 and 1989–91; Tourist Authy, 1991. Pres., S Pacific Ports Assoc., 1982–83. Chairman: 'Are'Are Maasina Develt Co. Ltd, 1970–80; Solomon Wholesale Union Ltd, 1972–73; Maasina Enterprises Ltd, 1973–74; Solomon Is Investment Ltd, 1973–75; Property Develt Co. Ltd, 1985–94; Sasape Mariner Ltd, 1985–86; Solomon Taiyo Ltd, 1986–87; Burns Philip Toyota (SI) Ltd, 1993–; Director: Concrete Industry Ltd, 1980–82; Central Bank of Solomon Is, 1990–92; Island Hotels Ltd, 1994–; King Solomon Hotel Ltd, 1994–; Gizo Hotel Ltd, 1994–. Chm., Praise the Lord Corp. Ltd, 1995–. Mem. Exec. Council, South Seas Evangelical Ch, 1972–73. Life Mem., CPA, 1966. *Address:* PO Box 335, Honiara, Solomon Islands; Maasina Hill, via Kiu Postal Agency, West 'Are'Are, Malaita Province, Solomon Islands. *T:* 22959. *Clubs:* Honiara Golf; Lions (Guadalcanal).

KAVANAGH, Prof. Dennis Anthony; Professor of Politics, University of Liverpool, since 1996; *b* 27 March 1941; *s* of Patrick Kavanagh and Agnes Kavanagh; *m* 1966, Monica Anne Taylor; one *s* three *d*. *Educ:* St Anselm's Coll., Birkenhead; Univ. of Manchester (BA, MA Econ). Asst Lectr, Univ. of Hull, 1965–67; Lectr, then Sen. Lectr, Univ. of Manchester, 1967–81; Prof. of Politics, Univ. of Nottingham, 1982–95. Ford Foundn Fellow, Univ. of Stanford, Calif, 1969–70; Visiting Professor: European Univ. Inst., Florence, 1977; Univ. of Calif, San Diego, La Jolla, 1979; Hoover Instn, Stanford Univ., 1985. Member Council, ESRC, 1991–94; Aurora, 1999–. Mem. Editl Bd, political jls. *Publications:* Constituency Electioneering in Britain, 1970; Political Culture, 1972; (with R. Rose) New Trends in British Politics: contemporary issues for research and discussions, 1977; The Politics of the Labour Party, 1982; Political Science and Political Behaviour, 1983; (ed) Comparative Politics and Government: essays in honour of S. E. Finer, 1984; British Politics, continuities and change, 1985, 4th edn 2000; Thatcherism and British Politics: the end of consensus?, 1987, 2nd edn 1990; Consensus Politics from Attlee to Thatcher, 1989, 2nd edn 1994; The Thatcher Effect, 1989; Personalities and Politics, 1990; Electoral Politics, 1992; (ed with A. Seldon) The Major Effect, 1995; Election Campaigning: the new marketing of politics, 1995; The Reordering of British Politics, 1997; (ed) Oxford Dictionary of Political Leadership, 1998; (with A. Seldon) The Powers Behind the Prime Minister, 1999; with David Butler: The British General Election of October 1974, 1975; The British General Election of 1979, 1980; The British General Election of 1983, 1984; The British General Election of 1987, 1988; The British General Election of 1992, 1992; The British General Election of 1997, 1997. *Recreations:* running, tennis, obituaries. *Address:* Department of Politics, Roxby Buildings, Liverpool L69 3BX. *T:* (0151) 794 2890; Lynton, Belgrave Road, Bowdon, Altrincham, Cheshire WA14 2NZ.

KAVANAGH, P. J., (Patrick Joseph Gregory Kavanagh), FRSL; writer; columnist: Times Literary Supplement, since 1997; The Spectator, 1983–97; *b* 6 Jan. 1931; *s* of H. E. (Ted) Kavanagh and Agnes O'Keefe; *m* 1st, 1956, Sally Philipps (*d* 1958); 2nd, 1965, Catherine Ward; two *s*. *Educ:* Douai Sch.; Lycee Jaccard, Lausanne; Merton Coll., Oxford (MA). British Council, 1957–59. Actor, 1959–70. Mem., Kingman Cttee of Inquiry into English Lang., 1986–88. *Publications: poems:* One and One, 1960; On the Way to the Depot, 1967; About Time, 1970; Edward Thomas in Heaven, 1974; Life before Death, 1979; Selected Poems, 1982; Presences (new and selected poems), 1987; An Enchantment, 1991; Collected Poems, 1992 (Cholmondely Prize, 1992); *novels:* A Song and Dance, 1968 (Guardian Fiction Prize, 1968); A Happy Man, 1972; People and Weather, 1979; Only by Mistake, 1986; *essays:* People and Places, 1988; *autobiography:* The Perfect Stranger, 1966 (Richard Hillary Prize, 1966); *travel autobiography:* Finding Connections, 1990; *for children:* Scarf Jack, 1978; Rebel for Good, 1980; *edited:* Collected Poems of Ivor Gurney, 1982; (with James Michie) Oxford Book of Short Poems, 1985; The Bodley Head G. K. Chesterton, 1985; Selected Poems of Ivor Gurney, 1990; A Book of Consolations, 1992; Voices in Ireland: a traveller's literary companion, 1994. *Recreation:* walking. *Address:* c/o Peters, Fraser, Dunlop, Drury House, 34–43 Russell Street, WC2B 5HA.

KAVANAGH, Patrick Bernard, CBE 1977; QPM 1974; Deputy Commissioner, Metropolitan Police, 1977–83; *b* 18 March 1923; *s* of late Michael Kavanagh and late Violet Kavanagh (*née* Duncan); *m* Beryl (*d* 1984), *er d* of late Lt-Comdr Richard Owen Williams, RNR and Annie (*née* McShiells); one *s* two *d*. *Educ:* St Aloysius Coll., Glasgow. Rifle Bde, 1941–43; Para. Regt, 1943–46 (Lieut). Manchester City Police (Constable to Supt), 1946–64; Asst Chief Constable, Cardiff City Police, 1964–69; Asst and Dep. Chief Constable, S Wales Constabulary, 1969–73; Asst Comr (Traffic), Metropolitan Police, 1974–77. Attended Administrative Staff Coll., Henley-on-Thames, 1961. Mem., Gaming Bd for GB, 1983–91. *Recreations:* walking, bird watching, music, crosswords. *Address:* c/o Metropolitan Police, 2 Bessborough Street, SW1V 2JF. *Club:* Royal Automobile.

KAWHARU, Prof. Sir (Ian) Hugh, Kt 1989; FRSNZ 1995; Professor, Maori Studies, and Head of Department of Anthropology, 1985–93, Professor Emeritus, and Director, James Henare Maori Research Centre, 1993–95, University of Auckland; *b* 18 Feb. 1927; *s* of Wiremu and Janet Paora Kawharu; *m* 1st, 1957, Nina; three *d*; 2nd, 1970, Freda; two *d*. *Educ:* Univ. of New Zealand (BSc); Univ. of Cambridge (MA); Univ. of Oxford (DPhil); Hon. Fellow, Exeter Coll., Oxford, 1993. Dept of Maori Affairs, housing welfare and trust admin, variously, 1953–65; Lectr, Dept of Anthropology, Univ. of Auckland, 1965–70; Prof. (personal chair), Social Anthropology and Maori Studies, Massey Univ., 1970–84. Consultant: FAO, 1961–63; NZ Govt, 1968–; Unesco, 1974–76; NZ Council for Educnl Res., 1976–89; NZ Maori Council, 1981–. Chm., Ngati Whatua Tribal Trusts, 1978–; Member: NZ Nat. Commn for Unesco, 1969–73; Royal Commn on the Courts, 1976–78; Waitangi Tribunal, 1986–94; Bd of Maori Affairs, 1987–90; Trust Bd, Auckland War Meml Mus., 1997–. Pres., Polynesian Soc., 1993–. Patron, Pitt-Rivers Mus. Soc., Oxford, 1991–. *Publications:* Orakei, a Ngati Whatua Community, 1975; Maori Land Tenure, 1977; (ed. and co-author): Administration in New Zealand's Multiracial Society, 1967; Conflict and Compromise, 1975; Trends in Ethnic Group Relations in Asia and Oceania, 1979; Waitangi: Maori and Pakeha Perspectives of the Treaty of Waitangi, 1989; contrib. to 10 vols of Waitangi Tribunal reports. *Recreation:* music. *Address:* University of Auckland, Private Bag 92019, Auckland, New Zealand. *T:* (9) 3737999.

KAY, Sir Andrew Watt, Kt 1973; retired; Regius Professor of Surgery, University of Glasgow, 1964–81; part-time Chief Scientist, Scottish Home and Health Department, 1973–81; *b* 14 Aug. 1916; of Scottish parentage; *m* 1st, 1943, Janetta M. Roxburgh (*d* 1990); two *s* two *d*; 2nd, 1992, Phyllis Gillies. *Educ:* Ayr Academy; Glasgow Univ. MB, ChB (Hons) with Brunton Memorial Prize, 1939; FRCSEd 1942; FRFPSG 1956 (Pres. 1972–); FRCS 1960; FRCSGlas 1967; FRSE 1971; MD (Hons) with Bellahouston Gold

Medal, 1944; Major Royal Army Medical Corps i/c Surgical Div., Millbank Military Hospital, 1946–48; ChM (Hons) 1949; Consultant Surgeon in charge of Wards, Western Infirmary, Glasgow, 1956–58; Asst to Regius Prof. of Surgery, Glasgow Univ., 1942–56; Prof. of Surgery, University of Sheffield, 1958–64. Sims Travelling Prof., Australasia, 1969; McLaughlin Foundn Edward Gallie Vis. Prof., Canada, 1970. Rock Carling Fellowship, 1977. Pres., Surgical Research Soc., 1969–71. Member: Royal Commission on Medical Education, 1965–68; MRC, 1967–71; Chm., Scottish Hosps Endowment Research Trust, 1983–89; Hon. Mem., The N Pacific Surgical Assoc. FRACS 1970; FRCSCan 1972; FCS(SoAf) 1972; Hon. Fellow: Norwegian Surgical Assoc., Belgian Surgical Soc.; Amer. Surg. Assoc., 1972; Hon. FACS, 1973; Hon. FRCSI, 1979. Hon. DSc: Leicester, 1973; Sheffield, 1975; Manchester, 1981; Nebraska, 1981; Hon. MD Edinburgh, 1981. Cecil Joll Prize, RCS, 1969; Gordon-Taylor Lectureship and Medal, 1970. *Publications:* (with R. A. Jamieson, FRCS) Textbook of Surgical Physiology, 1959 (2nd edn 1964); Research in Medicine: problems and prospects, 1977; several papers in medical and surgical jls on gastroenterological subjects. *Recreation:* gardening. *Address:* 5 Loch Road, Milngavie, Glasgow G62 8BB.

KAY, Prof. Anthony Barrington, (Barry), PhD, DSc; FRCPE, FRCP, FRCPath, FMedSci; Professor of Clinical Immunology and Director, Department of Allergy and Clinical Immunology and Hon. Consultant Physician, Royal Brompton Hospital and National Heart and Lung Institute, London, since 1980; *b* 23 June 1939; *s* of Anthony Chambers and Eva Gertrude (*née* Pearcey; she *m* 2nd H. Kay; now Mrs E. G. Reuben); *m* 1966, Rosemary Margaret Johnstone; three *d. Educ:* King's Sch., Peterborough; Edinburgh Univ. (MB, ChB 1963; DSc 1976); Jesus Coll., Cambridge (MA 1966; PhD 1970); Harvard Med. Sch. FRCPE 1975; FRCP 1980; FRCPath 1989. T. K. Stubbins Res. Fellow, RCP, 1969; Res. Fellow, Harvard Med. Sch., 1970–71; Lectr in Respiratory Diseases, Univ. of Edinburgh, 1972–74; Dep. Dir and Consultant, Immunology Div., Blood Transfusion Service, Royal Infirmary, Edinburgh, 1974–76; Sen. Lectr, then Reader, in Exptl Pathology, Dept of Pathology, Univ. of Edinburgh, 1977–79. President: European Acad. of Allergology and Clinical Immunology, 1989–92; Brit. Soc. of Allergy and Clinical Immunology, 1993–. Jt Editor, Clinical and Exptl Allergy, 1984–. FRSE 1993; FMedSci 1999. Hon. Fellow, Amer. Coll. of Allergy, 1986; Hon. Member: Amer. Assoc. of Physicians, 1988; Hungarian Soc. of Allergology and Clinical Immunology, 1990; Swiss Soc. of Allergology and Clinical Immunology, 1991; Belgian Soc. for Allergol. and Clin. Immunol., 1999. Hon. Dr Medicine and Surgery, Ferrara, 2000. Scientific Achievement Award, Internat. Assoc. of Allergology and Clinical Immunology, 1991. *Publications:* edited: Asthma: clinical pharmacology and therapeutic progress, 1986; Allergy and Inflammation, 1987; Allergic Basis of Asthma, 1988; Allergy and Asthma: new trends and approaches to therapy, 1989; Eosinophils, Allergy and Asthma, 1990; Eosinophils in Allergy and Inflammation, 1993; Allergy and Allergic Diseases, 1997; numerous scientific articles on allergy and asthma. *Recreations:* Baroque and modern bassoon, tennis, country walks. *Address:* Stamford Brook House, 12 Stamford Brook Avenue, W6 0YD. *T:* (020) 8741 5899. *Clubs:* Chelsea Arts, Hurlingham.

KAY, Bernard Hubert Gerard; HM Diplomatic Service, retired; *b* 7 July 1925; *s* of William and Alice Kay; *m* 1957, Teresa Jean Dyer; three *d. Educ:* St Bede's, Bradford; Wadham Coll., Oxford (MA, MLitt). Royal Navy, 1943–46. Foreign Office, 1955; served: Hong Kong, 1958–62; Singapore, 1964; Manila, 1965; New Delhi, 1967; Vientiane, 1968; Dacca, 1972; Ulan Bator, 1973; FCO, 1973–80. *Recreations:* Asia, books, mountains, the sea. *Address:* 6 Savona Close, Wimbledon, SW19 4HT.

KAY, Brian Christopher; broadcaster and musician; *b* 12 May 1944; *s* of Noel Bancroft Kay and Gwendoline Mary (*née* Sutton); *m* 1st, 1970, Sally Lyne; one *s* one *d;* 2nd, 1983, Gillian Fisher. *Educ:* Rydal Sch.; King's Coll., Cambridge (MA 1966); New Coll., Oxford (DipEd 1967). Bass Singer: Westminster Abbey Choir, 1968–71; King's Singers, 1968–82; Chorus Master, Huddersfield Choral Soc., 1983–93; Conductor: Cecilian Singers of Leicester, 1984–92; Cheltenham Bach Choir, 1989–97; Leith Hill Musical Fest., 1996–; Musical Dir, Bradford Fest. Choral Soc., 1998–. Presenter: Music in Mind, Radio 4, 1989–98; Brian Kay's Sunday Morning, Radio 3, 1992–; Comparing Notes, Radio 4, 1996–98. Friday Night is Music Night, Radio 2, 1998–. President: Nottingham Choral Trust; Harrogate Choral Soc.; Market Harborough Singers; Derbys Singers; Bristol Bach Choir. Vice-Pres., Assoc. of British Choral Dirs; Stars Orgn for Spastics. *Recreations:* gardening, reading. *Address:* c/o BBC Radio 3, Broadcasting House, W1A 1AA.

KAY, Prof. Harry, CBE 1981; PhD; Vice-Chancellor, University of Exeter, 1973–84 (Hon. Professor, 1984); *b* 22 March 1919; *s* of late Williamson T. Kay; *m* 1941, Gwendolen Diana, *d* of Charles Edward Maude; one *s* one *d. Educ:* Rotherham Grammar Sch.; Trinity Hall, Cambridge (1938–39, 1946–51). Served War of 1939–45 with Royal Artillery. Research with Nuffield Unit into Problems of Ageing, Cambridge, 1948–51; Psychologist of Naval Arctic Expedition, 1949. Lecturer in Experimental Psychology, Univ. of Oxford, 1951–59; Prof. of Psychology, Univ. of Sheffield, 1960–73. Visiting Scientist, National Institutes of Health, Washington, DC, 1957–58. Pro-Vice-Chancellor, University of Sheffield, 1967–71. Pres., British Psychological Soc., 1971–72. Hon. Director: MRC Unit, Dept of Psychology, Sheffield; Nat. Centre of Programmed Instruction for Industry, Sheffield. Member: SSRC, 1970–73; MRC, 1975–77 (Chm., Environmental Medicine Res. Policy Cttee, 1975–77); CNAA, 1974–79; Open Univ. Acad. Adv. Cttee; BBC Continuing Educn Adv. Cttee; Southern Univs Jt Bd (Chm., 1978–80); UCCA (Chm., 1978–84); NATO Human Factors Panel, 1972–75; GMC, 1984–89. Chairman: Central Council for Educn and Trng in Social Work, 1980–84; Bd of Management, Northcott Theatre, 1973–84. Hon. DSc: Sheffield, 1981; Exeter, 1985. Vernon Prize, 1962. *Publication:* (with B. Dodd and M. Sime) Teaching Machines and Programmed Instruction, 1968. *Recreations:* listening, Sir Walter Raleigh. *Address:* Coastguard House, 18 Coastguard Road, Budleigh Salterton EX9 6NU.

KAY, Prof. Humphrey Edward Melville, MD, FRCP, FRCPath; Haematologist, Royal Marsden Hospital, 1956–84; Professor of Haematology, University of London, 1982–84 (Professor Emeritus, since 1984); *b* 10 Oct. 1923; *s* of late Rev. Arnold Innes and Winifred Julia Kay; *m* 1st, 1950, April Grace Lavinia Powlett (*d* 1990); one *s* two *d;* 2nd, 1996, Sallie Diana (*née* Charlton), *widow* of Roy Perry, RI. *Educ:* Bryanston Sch.; St Thomas's Hospital. MB, BS 1945. RAFVR, 1947–49; junior appts at St Thomas's Hosp., 1950–56. Sec., MRC Cttee on Leukaemia, 1968–84; Dean, Inst. of Cancer Research, 1970–72. Editor, Jl Clinical Pathology, 1972–80. Member: Council, Wiltshire Wildlife Trust (formerly Wiltshire Trust for Nature Conservation), 1983–96; Nat. Badger Adv. Panel, 1988–98. Christopher Cadbury Medal, Wildlife Trusts, 1996. *Publications:* papers and chapters on blood diseases, etc; occasional poetry. *Recreation:* natural history including gardening. *Address:* New Mill Cottage, Pewsey, Wilts SN9 5LD.

KAY, Jervis; *see* Kay, R. J.

KAY, Prof. John Anderson, FBA 1997; economist; *b* 3 Aug. 1948; *s* of late James Scobie Kay and of Allison (*née* Anderson); *m* 1986, Deborah Freeman (marr. diss. 1995). *Educ:* Royal High Sch., Edinburgh; Univ. of Edinburgh (MA); Nuffield Coll., Oxford. Fellow of St John's Coll., 1970–, and Lectr in Econs, 1971–79, Univ. of Oxford; Res. Dir, 1979–81, Dir, 1981–86, Inst. for Fiscal Studies; London Business School: Prof., 1986–96; Dir, Centre for Business Strategy, 1986–91; Prof. of Mgt and Dir, Said Business Sch., Univ. of Oxford, 1997–99. Chm., Undervalued Assets Trust plc, 1994–; Director: London Econs Ltd, 1986–2000 (Chm., 1986–96); Halifax plc (formerly Halifax Building Soc.), 1991–2000; Foreign & Colonial Special Utilities Investment Trust Plc, 1993–; Value and Income Trust plc, 1994–. Mem., Council and Exec. Cttee, NIESR, 1989–97. Vice-Pres., Econs & Business Educn Assoc., 1996–. *Publications:* (with L. Hannah) Concentration in Modern Industry, 1977; (with M. A. King) The British Tax System, 1978, 6th edn 1997; (jtly) The Reform of Social Security, 1984; (jtly) The Economic Analysis of Accounting Profitability, 1987; Foundations of Corporate Success, 1993; Why Firms Succeed, 1995; The Business of Economics, 1996; contrib. articles in learned jls and columns in Financial Times. *Recreation:* walking, especially in France. *Address:* johnkay.com Ltd, PO Box 4036, W1A 6NZ. *T:* (020) 7224 8797, *Fax:* (020) 7402 1368.

KAY, Rt Hon. Sir John (William), Kt 1992; PC 2000; **Rt Hon. Lord Justice Kay;** a Lord Justice of Appeal, since 2000; *b* 13 Sept. 1943; *y s* of late C. Herbert Kay and Ida Kay; *m* 1966, Jeffa Connell; one *s* two *d. Educ:* Denstone; Christ's Coll., Cambridge (MA). Called to Bar, Gray's Inn, 1968, Bencher, 1992. Tutor in Law, Liverpool Univ., 1968–69; in practice on Northern Circuit, 1968–92; a Recorder, 1982–92; QC 1984; a Judge of the High Court of Justice, QBD, 1992–2000. Presiding Judge, Northern Circuit, 1994–97. Member: Gen. Council of Bar, 1988–92; Crown Ct Rules Cttee, 1995–; Judicial Studies Bd, 1998–2001 (Chm., Criminal Cttee). Chm., Criminal Justice Consultation Council, 2001–. *Recreations:* Rugby, genealogy, horse racing. *Address:* c/o Royal Courts of Justice, Strand, WC2A 2LL. *Club:* Waterloo Rugby Football (Pres., 1995–97).

KAY, Jolyon Christopher; HM Diplomatic Service, retired; Chairman, Southern Croquet Federation, since 1999; *b* 19 Sept. 1930; *s* of Colin Mardall Kay and Gertrude Fanny Kay; *m* 1956, Shirley Mary Clarke; two *s* two *d. Educ:* Charterhouse; St John's Coll., Cambridge (BA). MEng 1993. Chemical Engr, Albright and Wilson, 1954; UKAEA, Harwell, 1958; Battelle Inst., Geneva, 1961; Foreign Office, London, 1964; MECAS, 1965; British Interests Section, Swiss Embassy, Algiers, 1967; Head of Chancery and Information Adviser, Political Residency, Bahrain, 1968; FCO, 1970; Economic Counsellor, Jedda, 1974–77; Consul-Gen., Casablanca, 1977–80; Science, later Commercial, Counsellor, Paris, 1980–84; Counsellor and Consul-Gen., Dubai, 1985–90. Edtl Dir, London Insurance Insider, 1996–98. Convenor, Transport Gp, Oxfordshire CPRE, 1995–97. *Recreations:* acting, ski-ing, croquet. *Address:* Ickleton House, London Road, Blewbury, Oxfordshire OX11 9NZ. *T:* (01235) 850010.

KAY, Hon. Sir Maurice (Ralph), Kt 1995; **Hon. Mr Justice Maurice Kay;** a Judge of the High Court of Justice, Queen's Bench Division, since 1995; *b* 6 Dec. 1942; *s* of Ralph and Hylda Kay; *m* 1968, Margaret Angela Alcock; four *s. Educ:* William Hulme's Grammar Sch., Manchester; Sheffield Univ. (LLB, PhD). Called to the Bar, Gray's Inn, 1975; Bencher, 1995. Lecturer in Law: Hull Univ., 1967–72; Manchester Univ., 1972–73; Prof. of Law, Keele Univ., 1973–82. Practising barrister, 1975–95; an Asst Recorder, 1987–88; a Recorder, 1988–95; QC 1988. *Publications:* (author, contributor) numerous legal books and jls. *Recreations:* music, theatre, sport. *Address:* Royal Courts of Justice, Strand, WC2A 2LL. *Club:* Reform.

KAY, Neil Vincent; Director of Social Services, Sheffield, 1979–90 (Deputy Director, 1971–79); *b* 24 May 1936; *s* of Charles Vincent Kay and Emma Kay; *m* 1961, Maureen (*née* Flemons); one *s* two *d. Educ:* Woodhouse Grammar Sch.; Downing Coll., Cambridge (MA); Birmingham Univ. (Prof. Social Work Qual.). Social Worker (Child Care), Oxford CC, and Sheffield CC, 1960–66; Lectr and Tutor in Social Work, Extramural Dept, Sheffield Univ., 1966–71. *Address:* 22 Westwood Road, Sheffield S11 7EY. *T:* (0114) 230 1934.

KAY, Maj.-Gen. Patrick Richard, CB 1972; MBE 1945; RM retired; *b* 1 Aug. 1921; *y s* of late Dr and Mrs A. R. Kay, Blakeney, Norfolk; *m* 1944, Muriel Austen Smith; three *s* one *d. Educ:* Eastbourne Coll. Commissioned in Royal Marines, 1940; HMS Renown, 1941–43; 4 Commando Bde, 1944–45; Combined Ops HQ, 1945–48; Staff of Commandant-Gen., Royal Marines, 1948–50 and 1952–54; Staff Coll., Camberley, 1951; 40 Commando, RM, 1954–57; Joint Services Amphibious Warfare Centre, 1957–59; Plans Div., Naval Staff, 1959–62; CO, 43 Commando, RM, 1963–65; CO, Amphibious Training Unit, RM, 1965–66; Asst Dir (Jt Warfare) Naval Staff, 1966–67; Asst Chief of Staff to Comdt-Gen. RM, 1968; IDC, 1969; C of S to Comdt-Gen., RM, 1970–74, retired 1974. Dir of Naval Security, 1974–81. Sec., Defence, Press and Broadcasting Cttee, 1984–86. *Recreations:* gardening, golf. *Address:* c/o Barclays Bank, Fleet, Hants GU13 8BS.

KAY, (Robert) Jervis; QC 1996; *b* 25 Feb. 1949; *s* of late Philip Jervis Kay, VRD and Pamela Kay; *m* 1st, 1975, Rosemary Pollard (marr. diss. 1986); 2nd, 1988, Henrietta Kathleen Ward; one *s* three *d. Educ:* Wellington Coll.; Nottingham Univ. (LLB Hons). Called to the Bar, Lincoln's Inn, 1972; in practice at the Bar, 1973–. *Publications:* (Ed.) Atkins Court Forms, Vol. 3 Admiralty, 1979, 1990, 1994, 2000. *Recreation:* sailing. *Address:* 4 Field Court, Gray's Inn, WC1R 5EF. *Clubs:* Turf, MCC, Royal Ocean Racing; Royal London Yacht (Cowes).

KAY, Steven Walton; QC 1997; a Recorder, since 2000; *b* 4 Aug. 1954; *s* of late John Walton Kay and Eunice May Kay; *m* 1st (marr. diss.); one *s;* 2nd, 2000, Valerie (*née* Logan); one *d. Educ:* Epsom Coll.; Leeds Univ. (LLB). Called to the Bar, Inner Temple, 1977. Defence Counsel, first trial, Internat. Criminal Tribunal for former Yugoslavia, 1996. Sec., Criminal Bar Assoc., 1993–96; Mem., Internat. Bar Assoc; Treas., European Criminal Bar Assoc. *Recreations:* golf, walking. *Address:* 3 Gray's Inn Square, WC1R 5AH. *T:* (020) 7520 5600; Fairmile Lea, Portsmouth Road, Cobham, Surrey KT11 1BG. *T:* (01932) 589660.

KAY, William John; Personal Finance Editor, The Independent; *b* 12 Sept. 1946; *s* of William Jarvie Kay and Agnes Sutherland Walker; *m* 1968 (marr. diss. 1986); two *s;* partner, 1987, Lynne Bateson. *Educ:* Westminster City Sch.; The Queen's Coll., Oxford (MA). London Evening News, 1968; London Evening Standard, 1972; Daily Telegraph, 1977; Features Editor, Financial Weekly, 1979; Dep. Business Editor, Now!, 1979; Sen. Writer, Sunday Times Business News, 1981; City Editor, The Times, 1984; freelance, 1986; Financial Editor, Independent on Sunday, 1995; City Editor, Mail on Sunday, 1995–99. *Publications:* A–Z Guide to Money, 1983; Tycoons, 1985; Big Bang, 1986; (ed) The Stock Exchange: a market place for tomorrow, 1986; Battle for the High Street, 1987; (ed) Modern Merchant Banking, 1988; The Bosses, 1994; Lord of the Dance: the story of Gerry Robinson, 1999. *Recreations:* golf, cricket, travel, cheese, ice cream, Chelsea FC. *Address:* Independent House, 19 Marsh Wall, E14 9RS. *T:* (020) 7005 2000. *Club:* MCC.

KAY-SHUTTLEWORTH, family name of **Baron Shuttleworth**.

KAYE, Rev. Dr Bruce Norman; General Secretary, The Anglican Church of Australia General Synod, since 1994; *b* 30 June 1939; *s* of John Harold Kaye and Elsie Evelyn Kaye; *m* 1st, 1965, Rosemary Jeanette Hutchison (*d* 1979); one *s* one *d;* 2nd, 1983, Margaret

Louise Mathieson. *Educ:* Sydney Boys' High Sch.; Moore Theol Coll. (ThL 1963); Univ. of London (BD 1964); Univ. of Sydney (BA 1966); Univ. of Basel (Dr Theol 1976). Professional Officer, Sydney Water Bd, NSW, 1955–60. Deacon 1964, priest 1965; Curate, St Jude's, Dural, NSW, 1964–66; St John's College, University of Durham: Asst Tutor, 1968; Tutor, 1969; Tutor-Librarian, 1970–75; Sen. Tutor, 1975–82; Vice-Principal, 1979–82; Lectr, Faculty of Divinity, Univ. of Durham, 1970–82; Master, New Coll., Univ. of NSW, 1983–94; Founding Dir, New Coll. Inst. for Values Research, 1987–92. Vis. Fellow, Deutsche Akademische Austauschdienst, Freiberg, 1974; Vis. Fellow, Sch. of Sci. and Technol. Studies, Univ. of NSW, 1984–94; Fellow Commoner, Churchill Coll., and Vis. Schol., Faculty of Divinity, Univ. of Cambridge, 1991–92. *Publications:* Using the Bible in Ethics, 1976; The Supernatural in the New Testament, 1977; (ed) Obeying Christ in a Changing World, 1977; (ed) Law, Morality and the Bible, 1978; The Argument of Romans with Special Reference to Chapter 6, 1979; (ed) Immigration: what kind of Australia do we want?, 1989; A Church Without Walls: being Anglican in Australia, 1995; (ed) Authority and the Shaping of Tradition, 1997; Godly Citizens, 1999; Web of Meaning, 2000; contrib. numerous articles to theological and other learned jls. *Recreations:* theatre, golf, walking, reading. *Address:* The Anglican Church of Australia, General Synod Office, PO Box Q190, Queen Victoria Building, Sydney, NSW 1230, Australia. *Club:* Australian (Sydney).

KAYE, Dr Elaine Hilda; Headmistress, Oxford High School, GPDST, 1972–81; *b* 21 Jan. 1930; *d* of late Rev. Harold Sutcliffe Kaye and Kathleen Mary (*née* White). *Educ:* Bradford Girls' Grammar Sch.; Milton Mount Coll.; St Anne's Coll., Oxford; Sheffield Univ. (PhD 1995). Assistant Mistress: Leyton County High Sch., 1952–54; Queen's Coll., Harley Street, 1954–59; South Hampstead High Sch., GPDST, 1959–65; Part-time Tutor, Westminster Tutors, 1965–67; Dep. Warden, Missenden Abbey Adult Coll., 1967–72. Project Dir, Oxford Project for Peace Studies, 1989–92 (Vice-Chair and Editor, 1984–89); (non-stipendiary) Lectr in Theology (Church History), Mansfield Coll., Oxford, 1996–99 (College Historian, 1990–95). Pres., URC History Soc., 1997–. *Publications:* History of the King's Weigh House Church, 1968; History of Queen's College, Harley St, 1972; Short History of Missenden Abbey, 1973, 2nd edn 1992; (contrib.) Biographical Dictionary of Modern Peace Leaders, 1985; (ed) Peace Studies: the hard questions, 1987; C. J. Cadoux: theologian, scholar and pacifist, 1988; (with Ross Mackenzie) W. E. Orchard: a study in Christian exploration, 1990; Mansfield College, Oxford: its origin, history and significance, 1996; (contrib.) Oxford Dictionary of the Christian Church, 3rd edn 1997; For the Work of Ministry: Northern College and its predecessors, 1999; (contrib) Christian Thinking and Social Order, 1999. *Recreations:* music, walking, conversation. *Address:* 31 Rowland Close, Wolvercote, Oxford OX2 8PW.

KAYE, Geoffrey John; President, Allied Automotive Inc., since 1992; *b* 14 Aug. 1935; *s* of Michael and Golda Kaye; two *d.* *Educ:* Christ's College, Finchley. Started with Pricerite Ltd when business was a small private company controlling six shops, 1951; apptd Manager (aged 18) of one of Pricerite Ltd stores, 1953; Supervisor, Pricerite Ltd, 1955; Controller of all stores in Pricerite Ltd Gp, 1958; Director, 1963; Chairman and Man. Dir, 1966–73. *Recreations:* tennis, golf. *Address:* Independencia 34, Ajijic, Jalisco, Mexico.

KAYE, Sir John Phillip Lister L.; *see* Lister-Kaye.

KAYE, Lindsey Joy, (Mrs D. N. Kaye); *see* Kushner, L. J.

KAYE, Mary Margaret, (Mrs G. J. Hamilton), FRSL; authoress and illustrator; *d* of late Sir Cecil Kaye, CSI, CIE, CBE, and Lady Kaye; *m* Maj.-Gen. G. J. Hamilton, CB, CBE, DSO (*d* 1985); two *d.* *Publications: historical novels:* Shadow of the Moon, 1957, rev. edn 1979; Trade Wind, 1963, revd edn 1981; The Far Pavilions, 1978 (televised 1984); *detective novels:* Six Bars at Seven, 1940; Death Walks in Kashmir, 1953 (republished as Death in Kashmir, 1984); Death Walks in Berlin, 1955; Death Walks in Cyprus, 1956 (republished as Death in Cyprus, 1984); Later Than You Think, 1958 (republished as Death in Kenya, 1983); House of Shade, 1959 (republished as Death in Zanzibar, 1983); Night on the Island, 1960 (republished as Death in the Andamans, 1985); Death in Berlin, 1985; *for children:* The Potter Pinner Books (series), 1937–41; The Ordinary Princess, 1980, US 1984 (shown on BBC TV Jackanory, 1983, 1984); Thistledown, 1981; *autobiography:* Vol. I, The Sun in the Morning, 1990; Golden Afternoon: being the second part of Share of Summer, her autobiography, 1997; Vol. 3, Enchanted Evening, 1997; *edited:* The Golden Calm, 1980; Moon of Other Days, a personal choice of Kipling's verse, 1988; *illustrated:* The Story of St Francis; Children of Galilee; Adventures in a Caravan. *Recreation:* painting. *Club:* Army and Navy.

KAYE, Michael, OBE 1991; General Administrator, Young Concert Artists Trust, 1983–92; Festival Director, City of London Festival, 1984–94; *b* 27 Feb. 1925; *s* of Harry Kaye and Annie Steinberg; *m* 1st, 1950, Muriel Greenberg (marr. diss. 1959); one *d*; 2nd, 1962, Fay Bercovitch. *Educ:* Malmesbury Road, Bow; Cave Road, Plaistow; Water Lane, Stratford; West Ham Secondary Sch., E15. Served in Army, REME and Intelligence Corps, 1943–47. Journalism and Public Relations, 1947–53; Marketing and Public Relations in tobacco industry, 1953–61; PR Manager, later PR Director, Carreras-Rothmans, 1961–76; Director, Peter Stuyvesant Foundation, 1963–76; General Administrator, Rupert Foundn, 1972–76; Man. Dir, London Symphony Orchestra, 1976–80; Arts Dir, GLC, and Gen. Administrator, S Bank Concert Halls, 1980–83. Chm., Educn Cttee, British Assoc. of Concert Agents, 1989–92; Member: Exec. Cttee, Carl Flesch Internat. Violin Competition, 1984–95; Council, Centre for Study of Judaism and Jewish/Christian Relations, 1989–94. Trustee: Whitechapel Art Gallery, 1964–75; Youth & Music, 1970–78; A. M. Purnell Charitable Trust, 1994– (Trustee, 1994–, Chm., 1997–, Bath Mozartfest). Vice-Pres., Piano Trio Soc., 2000–. *Recreations:* photography, music (clarinet). *Address:* 3 Coppice Way, E18 2DU. *T:* (020) 8989 1281.

KAYE, Maj. Sir Paul (Henry Gordon), 5th Bt *cr* 1923, of Huddersfield, Co. York; Australian Army; *b* 19 Feb. 1958; *s* of Sir David Alexander Gordon Kaye, 4th Bt and of Adelle Francis Kaye (*née* Thomas); *S* father, 1994; *m* 1984, Sally Ann Louise Grützner. *Educ:* Downlands Coll., Toowoomba; Univ. of S Queensland (Dip. Applied Science (Rural Technol.) 1978). Lieut, Australian Regular Army, 1982; Captain, 1986; Major, 1991. Australian Service Medal, 1995; Multi-National Force and Observers Medal, 1995; Defence Force Service Medal, 1998. *Recreations:* horse riding, Rugby Union. *Heir:* *b* John Egidio Gordon Kaye, *b* 9 Sept. 1967. *Club:* Returned Services League (Canungra).

KAYE, Roger Godfrey, TD 1980 and Bar 1985; QC 1989, a Recorder, since 1994; *b* 21 Sept. 1946; *s* of late Anthony Harmsworth Kaye and Heidi Alice (*née* Jordy); *m* 1974, Melloney Rose, *d* of late Rev. H. M. Westall. *Educ:* King's Sch., Canterbury; Birmingham Univ. (LLB 1968). MCIArb 2000. Lectr in Law, Kingston Poly., 1968–73. Called to the Bar, Lincoln's Inn, 1970, Bencher, 1997; Jun. Treasury Counsel in Insolvency Matters, 1978–89; Dep. High Court Registrar in Bankruptcy, 1985–; Dep. High Court Judge, QBD and Chancery Div., 1990–. Deputy Chancellor: dio. of Southwark, 1995–99; dio. of St Albans, 1995–; Chancellor, dio. of Hereford, 2000– (Dep. Chancellor, 1997–2000). Chairman: Fees Collection Cttee, Bar Council, 1991–93 (Dep. Chm., 1990–91); Bristol & Cardiff Chancery Bar Assoc., 1990–95. Member: Professional Conduct Cttee, Bar Council, 1995–97; Panel of Chairmen, City Disputes Panel, 1997–. Varied TA service in Europe, 1967–97; Hon. Colonel: Intelligence and Security Gp (Volunteers), 1998–99; 3rd (Volunteer) Mil. Intelligence Bn, 1999–. FRSA 1995. *Recreation:* going home. *Address:* 24 Old Buildings, Lincoln's Inn, WC2A 3UP. *T:* (020) 7404 0946. *Clubs:* Army and Navy, Royal Automobile, Special Forces.

KAYE, Rosalind Anne, (Mrs J. A. Kaye); *see* Plowright, R. A.

KAYSEN, Prof. Carl; David W. Skinner Professor of Political Economy, Massachusetts Institute of Technology, 1977–90, now Emeritus (Director, Program in Science, Technology, and Society, 1981–87); *b* 5 March 1920; *s* of Samuel and Elizabeth Kaysen; *m* 1st, 1940, Annette Neutra (*d* 1990); two *d*; 2nd, 1994, Ruth Butler. *Educ:* Philadelphia Public Schs; Overbrook High Sch., Philadelphia; Pennsylvania, Columbia and Harvard Univs. AB Pa 1940; MA 1947, PhD 1954, Harvard. Nat. Bureau of Economic Research, 1940–42; Office of Strategic Services, Washington, 1942–43; Intelligence Officer, US Army Air Force, 1943–45; State Dept, Washington, 1945. Dep. Special Asst to President, 1961–63. Harvard University, 1947–66: Teaching Fellow in Econs, 1947; Asst Prof. of Economics, 1950–55; Assoc. Prof. of Economics 1955–57; Prof. of Economics, 1957–66; Assoc. Dean, Graduate Sch. of Public Administration, 1960–66; Lucius N. Littauer Prof. of Political Economy, 1964–66; Jr Fellow, Soc. of Fellows, 1947–50, Actg Sen. Fellow, 1957–58, 1964–65; Syndic, Harvard Univ. Press, 1964–66; Dir, Inst. for Advanced Study, Princeton, NJ, 1966–76, Dir Emeritus, 1976; Vice Chm., and Dir of Research, Sloan Commn on Govt and Higher Educn, 1977–79. Sen. Fulbright Res. Schol., LSE, 1955–56. Trustee: Pennsylvania Univ., 1967–; Russell Sage Foundn, 1979–89. *Publications:* United States *v* United Shoe Machinery Corporation, an Economic Analysis of an Anti-Trust Case, 1956; The American Business Creed (with others), 1956; Anti-Trust Policy (with D. F. Turner), 1959; The Demand for Electricity in the United States (with F. M. Fisher), 1962; The Higher Learning, The Universities, and The Public, 1969; (contrib.) Nuclear Energy Issues and Choices, 1979; A Program for Renewed Partnership (Sloan Commn on Govt and Higher Educn Report), 1980; (ed jtly and contrib.) Emerging Norms of Justified Intervention, 1995; (ed) The American Corporation Today, 1996; numerous articles on economic theory, applied economics, higher education, military strategy and arms control. *Address:* E38–614, Massachusetts Institute of Technology, Cambridge, MA 02139, USA.

KAZAN, Elia; author; independent producer and director of plays and films; *b* Constantinople, 7 Sept. 1909; *s* of George Kazan and Athena Sismanoglou; *m* 1st, 1932, Molly Thacher (*d* 1963); two *s* two *d*; 2nd, 1967, Barbara Loden (*d* 1980); one *s*; 3rd, 1982, Frances Rudge. *Educ:* Williams Coll. (AB); 2 years postgraduate work in Drama at Yale. Actor, Group Theatre, 1932–39; first London appearance as Eddie Fuseli in Golden Boy, St James, 1938. Directed *plays:* Skin of Our Teeth, 1942; All My Sons, A Streetcar Named Desire, 1947; Death of a Salesman, 1949; Camino Real, Tea and Sympathy, 1953; Cat on a Hot Tin Roof, 1955; Dark at Top of the Stairs, JB, 1958; Sweet Bird of Youth, 1959; After the Fall, 1964; But For Whom Charlie, 1964; The Changeling, 1964; Four times won best stage Director of Year, 1942, 1947, 1948, 1949. Directed *films:* Streetcar named Desire, 1951; Viva Zapata, 1952; Pinky, 1949; Gentleman's Agreement, 1948 (won Oscar, best Dir); Boomerang, 1947; A Tree Grows in Brooklyn, 1945; On the Waterfront, 1954 (won Oscar, best Dir); East of Eden, 1954; Baby Doll, 1956; A Face in the Crowd, 1957; Wild River, 1960; Splendour in the Grass, 1962; America, America, 1964; The Arrangement, 1969; The Visitors, 1972; The Last Tycoon, 1977. Three times won Best Picture of Year from New York Film Critics, 1948, 1952, 1955. Academy Award for Lifetime Achievement, 1999. *Publications:* America, America (novel), 1963; The Arrangement (novel), 1967; The Assassins, 1972; The Understudy, 1974; Acts of Love, 1978; The Anatolian, 1982; Elia Kazan, A Life (autobiog.), 1988; Beyond the Aegean, 1994; magazine articles in New York Times, Theatre Arts, etc. *Recreation:* tennis.

KEABLE-ELLIOTT, Dr (Robert) Anthony, OBE 1988; FRCGP; general practitioner, 1948–87; *b* 14 Nov. 1924; *s* of Robert Keable and Jolie Buck; *m* 1953, Gilian Mary Hutchison; four *s.* *Educ:* Sherborne Sch., Dorset; Guy's Hosp., London, 1943–48 (MB BS London). Founder Mem., Chiltern Medical Soc., 1956, Vice-Pres. 1958, Pres. 1964; Member, Faculty Board of Thames Valley, Faculty of Royal Coll. of General Practitioners, 1960; Upjohn Travelling Fellowship, 1962; Member: Bucks Local Med. Cttee, 1958–75 (Chm., 1964–68; Hon. Life Mem., 1975–); GMC, 1989–94. British Medical Association: Mem., 1948–; Mem. Council, 1974–94; Treasurer, 1981–87; Chm., Journal Cttee, 1987–93; Chm., Gen. Med. Services Cttee, 1966–72. Mem., Finance Corp. of General Practice, 1974–79. Mem., Soc. of Apothecaries, 1985–; Freeman, City of London, 1986. Asst Editor, Guy's Hospital Gazette, 1947–48. BMA Gold Medal, 1994. *Recreations:* sailing, golf, gardening. *Address:* Peels, Ibstone, near High Wycombe, Bucks HP14 3XX. *T:* (01491) 638385.

KEAL, Dr Edwin Ernest Frederick, FRCP; Honorary Consulting Physician, St Mary's and Brompton Hospitals, London; *b* 21 Aug. 1921; *s* of Frederick Archibald Keal and Mabel Orange Keal; *m* 1945, Constance Mary Gilliams; one *s.* *Educ:* Kingston High Sch., Hull; London Hospital Med. Coll. MB BS London 1952, DCH 1954, MD London 1971; FRCP 1973 (MRCP 1957). Service in RNVR (Exec. Lieut), 1939–46. Junior hosp. posts, London Hosp., 1952–59; Sen. Medical Registrar, Brompton Hosp., 1959–63; Consultant Physician: St Charles Hosp., London, 1963–77; Kensington Chest Clinic, 1963–86; Brompton Hosp., 1966–86; St Mary's Hosp., London, 1977–86; Cardiothoracic Institute: Sen. Lectr, 1972–77; Hon. Sen. Lectr, 1978–86; Dean, 1979–84. Hon. Consultant in Chest Diseases to the Army, 1979–86. Member: Bd of Governors, National Heart and Chest Hosps, 1975–85; Cttee of Management, Cardiothoracic Inst., 1978–84. *Publications:* chapters in various books, and articles, mainly related to diseases of the chest. *Recreations:* gardening, travel. *Address:* 55 Church Street, Orford, Woodbridge, Suffolk IP12 2NT. *T:* (01394) 450515.

KEALEY, Gavin Sean James; QC 1994; a Recorder, since 2000; *b* 2 Sept. 1953; *m* 1981, Karen Elizabeth Nowak; three *d.* *Educ:* Charterhouse; University Coll., Oxford (BA Jurisp.). Lectr in Law, King's Coll. London, 1976–77; called to the Bar, Inner Temple, 1977; Commercial Barrister, 1978. *Address:* 7 King's Bench Walk, Temple, EC4Y 7DS. *T:* (020) 7583 0404.

KEALEY, Dr (George) Terence (Evelyn); Vice-Chancellor, University of Buckingham, since 2001; *b* 16 Feb. 1952; *s* of Paul and Evelyn Kealey; *m* 1989, Sally Gritten; one *s* one *d.* *Educ:* Charterhouse Sch.; St Bartholomew's Hosp. Med. Sch. (MB BS 1975; BSc Biochem. 1976); Balliol Coll., Oxford (DPhil 1982); MA Cantab 1995. House physician, St Bartholomew's Hosp., 1976–77; MRC Trng Fellow, Nuffield Dept of Clinical Biochem., Oxford, 1977–82; Jun. Dean, Balliol Coll., Oxford, 1978–82; Sen. Registrar in Clinical Biochem. and Metabolic Medicine, Royal Victoria Infirmary, Newcastle upon Tyne, 1982–86; Wellcome Sen. Res. Fellow in Clinical Sci., Nuffield Dept of Clinical Biochem., Univ. of Oxford, 1986–88; Lectr, Dept of Clinical Biochem., Univ. of Cambridge, 1988–2001; Hon. Consultant Chemical Pathologist, Cambridge HA, 1988-2001. Mem., Skin Club. Hon. Fellow, Argentinian Soc. Dermatol., 1996. *Publications:* The Economic Laws of Scientific Research, 1996; contrib. papers in the molecular cell biol. of human skin develt. *Recreation:* playing with our *d* Helena and our *s* Teddy. *Address:* University of Buckingham, Hunter Street, Buckingham MK18 1EG. *T:* (01280) 820207.

KEALY, Robin Andrew, CMG 1991; HM Diplomatic Service; Ambassador to Tunisia, since 2002; *b* 7 Oct. 1944; *s* of Lt-Col H. L. B. Kealy, Royal Signals and Mrs B. E. Kealy; *m* 1987, Annabel Jane Hood; two *s*. *Educ:* Harrow Sch.; Oriel Coll., Oxford (Open Scholar; BA Lit. Hum. (1st Cl. Hons Mods); MA). Joined HM Diplomatic Service, 1967; FO, 1967; MECAS, 1968; Tripoli, 1970; Kuwait, 1972; ME Dept, FCO, 1975; Port of Spain, 1978; Commercial Sec., Prague, 1982; Asst, Aid Policy Dept, FCO, 1985; Counsellor and Consul Gen., Baghdad, 1987–90; Dir of Trade Promotion and Investment, Paris, 1990–95; Head, Aviation and Maritime Dept, FCO, 1995–97; Consul-Gen., Jerusalem, 1997–2001. *Recreations:* music, theatre, ski-ing, cooking, gardening. *Address:* c/o Foreign and Commonwealth Office, King Charles Street, SW1A 2AH. *Club:* Travellers.

KEANE, Desmond; QC 1981; QC (Hong Kong) 1982; QC (NSW) 1986; QC (NI) 1993; *b* 21 Aug. 1941; *er s* of late Henry Keane, MB, BCh, and of Patricia Keane; *m* 2001, Rachel Cheung Man Ching, barrister. *Educ:* Downside Sch.; Wadham Coll., Oxford (Schol.; MA Mod. Hist.). Called to the Bar, Middle Temple, 1964; a Recorder, 1979–91. *Recreations:* cricket umpiring, bridge. *Address:* Clock Chambers, 78 Darlington Street, Wolverhampton WV1 4LY. *T:* (01902) 313444, *Fax:* (01902) 421110.

KEANE, Fergal Patrick, OBE 1997; BBC Special Correspondent, since 1997; *b* 6 Jan. 1961; *s* of Eamon Patrick Keane and Maura Theresa (*née* Hassett); *m* 1986, Anne Frances Flaherty; one *s*. *Educ:* Terenure Coll., Dublin; Presentation Coll., Cork. Reporter: Limerick Leader, 1979–82; Irish Press, 1982–84; RTE, 1984–88; joined BBC, 1988: Ireland Corresp., 1988–90; Southern Africa Corresp., 1990–94; Asia Corresp., 1994–97. Radio Journalist of Year, Sony, 1994; Journalist of Year, RTS, 1994. BAFTA award, TV documentary, 1997. *Publications:* The Bondage of Fear, 1994; Season of Blood, 1995; Letter to Daniel, 1996; Letters Home, 1999; A Stranger's Eye, 2000. *Recreations:* fishing, sailing, reading. *Address:* c/o BBC Television, Wood Lane, W12 7RJ. *T:* (020) 8743 8000. *Clubs:* Foreign Correspondents' (Hong Kong); Royal Cork Yacht (Cork).

KEANE, Francis Joseph; Sheriff of Tayside, Central and Fife at Kirkcaldy, since 1998; *b* 5 Jan. 1936; *s* of Thomas and Helen Keane; *m* 1960, Lucia Corio Morrison; two *s* one *d*. *Educ:* Blairs Coll., Aberdeen; Gregorian Univ., Rome (PhL); Univ. of Edinburgh (LLB). Solicitor; Partner, McCluskey, Keane & Co., 1959; Depute Procurator Fiscal, Perth, 1961, Edinburgh, 1963; Senior Depute PF, Edinburgh, 1971; Senior Legal Asst, Crown Office, Edinburgh, 1972; PF, Airdrie, 1976; Regional PF, S Strathclyde, Dumfries and Galloway, 1980; Sheriff: of Glasgow and Strathkelvin, 1984–93; of Lothian and Borders at Edinburgh, 1993–98. Pres., PF Soc., 1982–84. *Recreations:* music, painting, tennis. *Address:* Sheriff Court House, Whytescauseway, Kirkcaldy KY1 1XQ.

KEANE, John B.; writer; *b* 21 July 1928; *s* of William B. Keane and Hannah (*née* Purtill); *m* Mary O'Connor; three *s* one *d*. *Educ:* Listowel Nat. Sch.; St Michael's Coll., Listowel, Co. Kerry. Chemist's asst, 1946–51; various jobs in UK, 1951–55; pub owner, Listowel, 1955–. Pres., Irish PEN, 1973–74. Life Mem., RDS, 1991. Hon. DLitt TCD, 1984; Hon. DFA Marymount Manhatten Coll. Independent Irish Life Award, 1986; Sunday Tribune Award, 1986; Fresh Amer. Lit. Award, 1988; Person of Year Award, 1991. *Publications:* include: Sive, 1959; The Street and Other Poems, 1961; Year of the Hiker, 1962; The Field, 1965 (filmed 1990); Big Maggie, 1967; The Crazy Wall, 1971; Letters Series of Books, 1967–91; *novels:* The Bodhran Makers, 1986; The Contractors; The High Meadow; Durango. *Recreations:* Gaelic football, Rugby, reading, walking. *Address:* 37 William Street, Listowel, Co. Kerry, Ireland. *Club:* Listowel GAA.

KEANE, Major Sir Richard (Michael), 6th Bt *cr* 1801; farmer; *b* 29 Jan. 1909; *s* of Sir John Keane, 5th Bart, DSO, and Lady Eleanor Hicks-Beach (*d* 1960), *e d* of 1st Earl St Aldwyn; *S* father, 1956; *m* 1939, Olivia Dorothy Hawkshaw; two *s* one *d*. *Educ:* Sherborne Sch.; Christ Church, Oxford. Diplomatic Correspondent to Reuters 1935–37; Diplomatic Corresp. and Asst to Editor, Sunday Times, 1937–39. Served with County of London Yeomanry and 10th Royal Hussars, 1939–44; Liaison Officer (Major) with HQ Vojvodina, Yugoslav Partisans, 1944; attached British Military Mission, Belgrade, 1944–45. Publicity Consultant to Imperial Chemical Industries Ltd, 1950–62. *Publications:* Germany: What Next?, (Penguin Special), 1939; Modern Marvels of Science (editor), 1961. *Recreation:* fishing. *Heir:* *s* John Charles Keane [*b* 16 Sept. 1941; *m* 1977, Corinne, *d* of Jean Everard de Harzir; two *s* one *d*]. *Address:* Cappoquin House, Cappoquin, County Waterford, Ireland. *T:* (58) 54004. *Club:* Kildare Street and University (Dublin).

KEANE, Hon. Ronan; Hon. Mr Justice Keane; Chief Justice of Ireland, since 2000; *b* 20 July 1932; *s* of John Patrick Keane and Katherine Gertrude Keane (*née* Boylan); *m* 1962, Ann Therese O'Donnell; one *s* two *d*. *Educ:* Blackrock Coll., Co. Dublin; University Coll., Dublin (BA 1953). Called to the Irish Bar, King's Inns, Dublin, 1954 (Bencher, 1979); in practice at the Bar, 1954–79; Jun. Counsel, 1954–70; Sen. Counsel, 1970–79; Judge: High Court of Ireland, 1979–96; Supreme Court of Ireland, 1996–2000. Chm., Irish Bar Council, 1974–75; Pres., Law Reform Commn, 1987–92. *Publications:* The Law of Local Government in the Republic of Ireland, 1982; Company Law in the Republic of Ireland, 1985, 2nd edn 1991; Equity and the Law of Trusts in the Republic of Ireland, 1988. *Recreations:* music, theatre, reading. *Address:* 39 Richmond Park, Monkstown, Co. Dublin, Ireland. *T:* (1) 2843618.

KEAR, Graham Francis; Under-Secretary, Department of Energy, 1974–80; *b* 9 Oct. 1928; *s* of Richard Walter Kear and Eva Davies; *m* 1978, Joyce Eileen Parks. *Educ:* Newport (St Julian's) High Sch., Mon; Balliol Coll., Oxford (BA). Min. of Supply, 1951–52 and 1954–57; UK Delegn to ECSC, 1953–54; Min. of Aviation, 1957–59 and 1960–63; NATO Maintenance Supply Agency, Paris, 1959–60; MoD, 1963–65; Cabinet Office, 1968–71; Min. of Aviation Supply/DTI, 1971–72; Fellow, Harvard Univ. Center for Internat. Affairs, 1972–73. Asst Sec., 1984–92, volunteer mem., 1992–, Abbeyfield Richmond Soc. *Recreation:* music. *Address:* 28 Eastbourne Road, Brentford, Mddx TW8 9PE. *T:* (020) 8560 4746.

KEAR, Dr Janet, (Mrs J. V. N. Turner), OBE 1993; ornithologist; Director of Centres, Wildfowl and Wetlands Trust, 1991–93, retired; *b* 13 Jan. 1933; *d* of Harold Kear and Constance May Kear (*née* Betteridge); *m* 1st, 1963, Geoffrey Vernon Matthews, *qv* (marr. diss. 1977); 2nd, 1993, John V. N. Turner. *Educ:* Walthamstow Hall, Sevenoaks; Caspar Jun. Coll., Caspar, Wyoming; King's Coll., London (BSc 1956); Girton Coll., Cambridge (PhD 1959). Wildfowl and Wetlands Trust: Research Scientist, 1959–74; PSO 1974; Avicultural Co-ordinator, 1974–77; Curator, Martin Mere Centre, 1977–90; Asst Dir, 1978–90; Mem., Mgt Cttee, 1988–93. Fellow, Zool Dept, Liverpool Univ., 1978–92. Wildlife Inspector, Scientific Authy for Animals, DoE, 1977–81. Council Mem., NCC, later NCCE, 1990–97 (Mem., Animal Cttee, 1981–). Mem. Council, 1965–76, Sec., 1966–73, Assoc. for Study of Animal Behaviour; Zoological Society of London International Zoo Yearbook: Mem., Editl Bd, 1974–79 and 1989–; Chm., 1980–88; Mem. 1974, Chm. 1975–83, Breeding and Conservation Sub-cttee, Zoo Fedn; Member: Avicl Soc. Council, 1975–77; British Trust for Ornithology Council, 1983–86; Res. Adv. Cttee, 1977–83, Council 1994–99, RSPB; International Union for Conservation of Nature: Chm., Endangered Waterfowl Gp, 1976–87; Mem., Captive Breeding Specialist Gp, 1979–92; Jersey Wildlife Preservation Trust: Mem., Scientific Adv. Cttee, 1979–; Dir, Summer Sch., 1993; Council Mem., 1994–; British Ornithologists' Union: Mem. Council, 1980–88; Vice-Pres., 1989–91; Pres., 1991–95; Medal, 1998; Mem., Internat. Ornithol Cttee, 1982– (Vice-Pres., XXII Internat. Ornith. Congress, Durban, 1998); Pres., Devon Bird Watching and Preservation Soc., 1995. Trustee, Nat. Mus and Galls on Merseyside, 1997–. Editor: Ibis, BOU Jl, 1980–88; Wildfowl, Jl of Wildfowl and Wetlands Trust, 1989–96. Hon. Fellow, Manchester Metropolitan Univ. (formerly Manchester Poly.), 1983; Hon. Prof., Liverpool John Moores Univ. (formerly Liverpool Poly.), 1990–. Hon. DSc Liverpool Poly., 1990. *Publications:* (ed with N. Duplaix-Hall) Flamingos, 1975; (with A. J. Berger) The Hawaiian Goose, 1980; Eric Hosking's Wildfowl, 1985; The Mute Swan, 1989; Man and Wildfowl (Natural World's Book of the Year), 1990; Swans, 1990; Ducks of the World, 1991. *Recreations:* reading, gardening, walking. *Address:* Jewells Lodge, Umberleigh, Devon EX37 9EY. *T:* (01769) 580057. *Club:* Naval and Military.

KEARLEY, family name of **Viscount Devonport**.

KEARNEY, Brian; Sheriff of Glasgow and Strathkelvin, since 1977; *b* 25 Aug. 1935; *s* of late James Samuel and Agnes Olive Kearney; *m* 1965, Elizabeth Mary Chambers; three *s* one *d*. *Educ:* Largs Higher Grade; Greenock Academy; Glasgow Univ. (MA, LLB). Qualified solicitor, 1960; Partner, Biggart, Lumsden & Co., Solicitors, Glasgow, 1965–74. Sheriff of N Strathclyde at Dumbarton (floating sheriff), 1974–77. Sometime tutor in Jurisprudence, and external examnr in legal subjects, Glasgow Univ.; Hon. Lectr, Social Work Dept, Dundee Univ., 1995–. Chm., Inquiry into Child Care Policies in Fife, 1989–92 (report published, 1992). Mem., Judicial Studies Cttee (Scotland), 1997–. Pres., Glasgow Juridical Soc., 1964–65; Chm., Glasgow Marriage Guidance Council, 1977–90; Hon. President: Glasgow Marriage Counselling Service, 1990–; Family Law Assoc., Scotland, 1999–. *Publications:* An Introduction to Ordinary Civil Procedure in the Sheriff Court, 1982; Children's Hearings and the Sheriff Court, 1987, 2nd edn 2000; (ed jtly) Butterworths' Scottish Family Law Service, 1995; articles in legal jls. *Recreations:* cutting sandwiches for family picnics, listening to music, reading, writing and resting. *Address:* Sheriff's Chambers, Sheriff Court House, 1 Carlton Place, Glasgow G5 9DA. *T:* (0141) 429 8888, *Fax:* (0141) 418 5185. *Club:* Glasgow Art.

KEARNEY, Hon. Sir William (John Francis), Kt 1982; CBE 1976; Judge of the Supreme Court of the Northern Territory, 1982–99; *b* 8 Jan. 1935; *s* of William John Kilbeg Kearney and Gertrude Ivylene Kearney; *m* 1959, Jessie Alice Elizabeth Yung; three *d*. *Educ:* Univ. of Sydney (BA, LLB); University Coll. London (LLM). Legal Service of Papua New Guinea, 1963–75; Sec. for Law, 1972–75; dormant Commn as Administrator, 1972–73, and as High Comr, 1973–75; Judge, Supreme Ct of PNG, 1976–82; Dep. Chief Justice, 1980–82. Aboriginal Land Comr, 1982–86. *Recreations:* travelling, literature. *Address:* 24 Sir George Back Street, Opua 0290, New Zealand.

KEARNS, David Todd; Deputy Secretary of Education, US Department of Education, 1991; *b* 11 Aug. 1930; *m* 1954, Shirley Cox; two *s* four *d*. *Educ:* Univ. of Rochester (BA). Served US Navy; IBM, 1954–71; Xerox Corp.: Corporate Vice Pres., 1971; Group Vice Pres. and Board of Dirs, 1976; Pres. and Chief Operating Officer, 1977; Chief Exec., 1982–91; Chm., 1985–91. Mem. Boards of Directors: Chase Manhattan Corp.; Time Inc.; Dayton Hudson Corp; Ryder System. Member: Council on Foreign Relations; Business Roundtable; Business Council; President's Commn on Executive Exchange. Trustee: Cttee for Economic Develt; Nat. Urban League. Member: Bd of Dirs, Junior Achievement; Bd of Visitors, Fuqua Sch. of Business Administration, Duke Univ.; Mem. Exec. Adv. Commn, William E. Simon Sch. of Business, and Trustee, Univ. of Rochester.

KEARNS, Dr William Edward, FFPHM; consultancy in health policy and public health, since 1993; *b* 10 July 1934; *s* of William Edward Kearns and Kathleen Wolfenden; *m* 1954, Beryl Cross; four *s* one *d* (and one *s* decd). *Educ:* Liverpool Coll.; Univ. of Liverpool (MB ChB); Univ. of London (MSc; DipTh 1995). MRCS, LRCP. Hosp. posts in cardiorespiratory physiology, gen. medicine and pathology, United Liverpool Hosps, 1958–70; NW Metropolitan Regional Hospital Board: Asst SMO, 1970–73; Regional Sci. Officer, 1973–74; Dist Community Physician, Kensington and Chelsea and Westminster AHA (Teaching), 1974–82; Hon. Sen. Lectr in Community Medicine, St Mary's Hosp. Med. Sch., 1975–86; Dist MO, Paddington and N Kensington HA, 1982–86; Regional MO and Dir of Health Care Policy, 1986–90, Dir of Public Health, 1990–92, CMO, 1990–93, NE Thames RHA. Reader, Neasden Parish Church (S Catherine); Sec. for Readers, dio. of London, 1996–; Oblate Novice, Monastery of Our Lady and St Benedict, Elmore Abbey, 1996–98; Oblate, Monastery of St Mary at the Cross, Edgware Abbey, 1998–. FRSA 1997. *Publications:* The Health Report, North East Thames Health Region, 1990, 1991; contribs to med. jls. *Recreations:* gardening for wild life conservation, grandparenting. *Address:* Five Midholm, Barn Hill, Wembley Park, Middx HA9 9LJ. *T:* (020) 8908 1511, *Fax:* (020) 8904 3884; *e-mail:* williamkearns@compuserve.com. *Club:* Royal Society of Medicine.

KEATES, Jonathan Basil; writer; Assistant English Master, City of London School, since 1974; *b* 7 Nov. 1946; *s* of Richard Herbert Basil Keates and Evangeline Sonia Wilcox. *Educ:* Bryanston Sch., Dorset (Schol.); Magdalen Coll., Oxford (MA); Exeter Univ. (PGCE). FRSL 1993. *Publications:* The Companion Guide to the Shakespeare Country, 1979; Allegro Postillions (James Tait Black Prize; Hawthornden Prize), 1984; Handel: the man and his music, 1985; The Strangers' Gallery, 1987; Italian Journeys, 1991; Stendhal, 1994 (Enid McLeod Prize, 1995); Henry Purcell, 1995; Soon To Be a Major Motion Picture, 1997; Smile Please, 2000. *Recreations:* Venice, libraries, music, friendship. *Address:* 23 Hightrees House, Nightingale Lane, SW12 8AQ. *T:* (020) 8675 6783.

KEATING, Frank; Sports Columnist, The Guardian, since 1976; *b* 4 Oct. 1937; *s* of Bryan Keating and Monica Marsh; *m* 1987, Jane Sinclair; one *s* one *d*. *Educ:* Belmont Abbey; Douai. Local newspapers, Stroud, Hereford, Guildford, Bristol, Southern Rhodesia, Gloucester and Slough, 1956–63; Editor, Outside Broadcasts, Rediffusion Television, 1963–67; Editor, Features, and Head of Special Projs, Thames Television, 1968–72; columnist: The Guardian, 1972–; Punch, 1979–90; The Spectator, 1990–96; The Oldie, 1997–. Astroturf Sportswriter of the Year, 1978; 'What the Papers Say' Sportswriter of the Year, 1979; Sports Council Magazine Writer of the Year, 1987; Specialist Writer of Year, Magazine Publishers Awards, 1988; Sports Journalist of the Year, British Press Awards, 1988. *Television series:* Maestro, BBC, 1981–85. *Publications:* Caught by Keating, 1979; Bowled Over, 1980; Another Bloody Day in Paradise, 1981; Up and Under, 1983; Long Days, Late Nights, 1984; High, Wide and Handsome, 1986; Gents and Players, 1986; Passing Shots, 1988; Sportswriter's Eye, 1989; Half-Time Whistle (autobiog.), 1992; The Great No Tens, 1994; (with Graham Gooch) Gooch: My Autobiography, 1995; Band of Brothers, 1996; Frank Keating's Sporting Century, 1998; contrib. New Statesman, BBC.

Recreation: roses. *Address:* Church House, Marden, near Hereford HR1 3EN. *T:* (01432) 880213. *Club:* Chelsea Arts.

KEATING, Henry Reymond Fitzwalter; author; *b* 31 Oct. 1926; *s* of John Hervey Keating and Muriel Marguerita Keating (*née* Clews); *m* 1953, Sheila Mary Mitchell; three *s* one *d*. *Educ:* Merchant Taylors' Sch.; Trinity Coll., Dublin. Journalism, 1952–60; Crime Reviewer for The Times, 1967–83. Chairman: Crime Writers' Assoc., 1970–71; Society of Authors, 1983–84; Pres., Detection Club, 1985. FRSL 1990. *Publications:* Death and the Visiting Firemen, 1959; Zen there was Murder, 1960; A Rush on the Ultimate, 1961; The Dog it was that Died, 1962; Death of a Fat God, 1963; The Perfect Murder, 1964 (filmed 1988); Is Skin-Deep, Is Fatal, 1965; Inspector Ghote's Good Crusade, 1966; Inspector Ghote Caught in Meshes, 1967; Inspector Ghote Hunts the Peacock, 1968; Inspector Ghote Plays a Joker, 1969; Inspector Ghote Breaks an Egg, 1970; Inspector Ghote goes by Train, 1971; The Strong Man, 1971; (ed) Blood on My Mind, 1972; Inspector Ghote Trusts the Heart, 1972; The Underside, 1974; Bats Fly Up for Inspector Ghote, 1974; A Remarkable Case of Burglary, 1975; Filmi, Filmi, Inspector Ghote, 1976; Murder Must Appetize, 1976; (ed) Agatha Christie: First Lady of Crime, 1977; A Long Walk to Wimbledon, 1978; Inspector Ghote Draws a Line, 1979; Sherlock Holmes: the man and his world, 1979; The Murder of the Maharajah, 1980; Go West, Inspector Ghote, 1981; (ed) Whodunit, 1982; The Lucky Alphonse, 1982; The Sheriff of Bombay, 1984; Mrs Craggs, Crimes Cleaned Up, 1985; Under a Monsoon Cloud, 1986; Writing Crime Fiction, 1986; The Body in the Billiard Room, 1987; Crime and Mystery: the 100 best books, 1987; Dead on Time, 1988; Inspector Ghote, His Life and Crimes, 1989; (ed) Bedside Companion to Crime, 1989; The Iciest Sin, 1990; (ed) Crime Wave 1, 1991; Cheating Death, 1992; (ed) The Man Who, 1992; The Rich Detective, 1993; Doing Wrong, 1994; The Good Detective, 1995; The Bad Detective, 1996; Asking Questions, 1996; The Soft Detective, 1997; In Kensington Gardens Once, 1997; Bribery, Corruption Also, 1999; Jack, the Lady Killer (verse), 1999; The Hard Detective, 2000; Breaking and Entering, 2000; A Detective in Love, 2001. *Recreation:* popping round to the post. *Address:* 35 Northumberland Place, W2 5AS. *T:* (020) 7229 1100.

KEATING, Kay Rosamond Blundell; a District Judge (Magistrates' Courts) (formerly Metropolitan Stipendiary Magistrate), since 1987; *b* 3 Oct. 1943; *d* of Geoffrey Blundell Jones and Avis Blundell Jones; *m* 1st, 1965, Edmund Deighton (decd); one *d* decd; 2nd, 1978, Donald Norman Keating, QC (*d* 1995); one *s*. *Educ:* St Hugh's College, Oxford (BA Jurisp. 1965; MA 1968). Called to the Bar, Gray's Inn, 1966. *Recreations:* travel, walking, tennis, riding, opera. *Address:* Horseferry Road Magistrates' Court, 70 Horseferry Road, SW1P 2AX.

KEATING, Dr Michael Stockton, AC 1996 (AO 1990); Fellow, Economics Department, Research School of Social Sciences, Australian National University, since 1997; *b* 25 Jan. 1940; *s* of Russell James Keating and Alice (*née* Skinner); *m* 1962, Rosemary Gardner; four *s*. *Educ:* Geelong Coll.; Univ. of Melbourne (BCom Hons); ANU (PhD). Hd, Growth Studies and Resource Allocation Div., OECD, 1976–78; First Asst Sec., Econ. Div., Dept of Prime Minister and Cabinet, Australia, 1979–82; Dep. Sec., Dept of Finance, 1982–83; Secretary: Dept of Employment and Industrial Relns, 1983–86; Dept of Finance, 1986–91; Dept of the PM and Cabinet, 1991–96. Adjunct Prof., Griffith Univ., 1997–. Board Mem., Australia Post, 1996–. Mem. Council, ANU, 1996–. DUniv Griffith. *Publications:* The Australian Workforce 1910–1911 to 1960–61, 1973; (jtly) The Making of Australian Economic Policy: 1983–88, 1989; (jtly) The Future of Governance, 2000; (jtly) Institutions on the Edge, 2000. *Recreations:* tennis, sailboarding, bushwalking, reading, golf. *Address:* 6 Ridley Street, Turner, ACT 2612, Australia. *T:* (2) 62496917.

KEATING, Hon. Paul John; Visiting Professor in Public Policy, University of New South Wales, since 1996; Prime Minister of Australia, 1991–96; *b* 18 Jan. 1944; *s* of Matthew and Minnie Keating; *m* 1975, Annita Johanna Maria Van Iersel; one *s* three *d*. *Educ:* De La Salle College, Bankstown, NSW. Research Officer, Federated Municipal and Shire Council Employees Union of Australia, 1967. MP (ALP) Blaxland, NSW, 1969–96; Minister for Northern Australia, Oct.-Nov. 1975; Shadow Minister for Agriculture, Jan.-March 1976, for Minerals and Energy, 1976–80, for Resources and Energy, 1980–83; Shadow Treasurer, Jan.-March 1983; Federal Treas. of Australia, 1983–91; Dep. Prime Minister, 1990–91. Member: Cabinet Expenditure Review Cttee (Dep. Chm.), 1987–91; Parly Structural Adjustment Cttee, 1987; Parly Social and Family Policy Cttee, 1983. Chm., Australian Loan Council, 1983–91. *Address:* GPO Box 2598, Sydney, NSW 2001, Australia.

KEATING, Roland Francis Kester, (Roly); Controller of Arts Commissioning and Digital Channels, BBC Television, since 2000; *b* 5 Aug. 1961; *s* of Donald Norman Keating and Betty Katharine Keating (*née* Wells); *m* 1989, Caroline Marguerite Cumine Russell; one *s* two *d*. *Educ:* Westminster Sch.; Balliol Coll., Oxford (BA Hons). Joined BBC as gen trainee, 1983: attachments to Radio Ulster, Kaleidoscope, Everyman, Newsnight progs; producer and dir, Music and Arts Dept, 1985-89; Editor: The Late Show, 1990-92; Bookmark, 1992-97; Executive Producer: (also devised and launched) One Foot in the Past, 1992; A History of British Art, 1996; The House Detectives, 1997; How Buildings Learn, 1997; Hd of Develt, Music and Arts, with special resp. for New Services, 1995; on secondment (part-time) to BBC Broadcast to develop new channel propositions for BBC Worldwide/Flextech jt venture, UKTV, 1996; Hd of Programming, UKTV, 1997-99; Controller, Digital Channels, BBC TV, 1999-2000. *Recreations:* children, reading, walking, being by the seaside. *Address:* BBC Television Centre, Wood Lane, W12 7RJ. *Club:* Soho House.

KEATINGE, Prof. William Richard, PhD; Professor of Physiology, Queen Mary and Westfield College, 1990–96, now Emeritus (Dean of Basic Medical Sciences, 1991–94); *b* 18 May 1931; *s* of Sir Edgar Keatinge, CBE; *m* 1955, M. E. Annette Hegarty (*d* 2000); one *s* two *d*. *Educ:* Upper Canada Coll.; Rugby Sch.; Cambridge Univ. (MA); St Thomas's Hospital (MB BChir). FRCP 1991. House Phys., St Thomas's Hospital, 1955–56; Surg.-Lt RN (Nat. Service), 1956–58; Jun. Research Fellow and Dir of Studies in Medicine, Pembroke Coll., Cambridge, 1958–60; Fellow, Cardiovascular Research Inst., San Francisco, 1960–61; MRC appt Radcliffe Infirmary, Oxford, 1961–68; Fellow of Pembroke Coll., Oxford, 1965–68; Reader in Physiology, 1968–71, Prof. of Physiol., 1971–90, London Hosp. Med. Coll. *Publications:* Survival in Cold Water, 1969; Local Mechanisms Controlling Blood Vessels, 1980; chapters in textbooks of physiology and medicine; papers in physiological and medical jls on temperature regulation and on control of blood vessels. *Recreations:* dinghy sailing, archaeology. *Address:* Queen Mary and Westfield College, Mile End Road, E1 4NS.

KEATLEY, Robert Leland; Editor, South China Morning Post, since 1999; *b* 14 Feb. 1935; *s* of Robert L. Keatley and Eva S. Keatley; *m* 1st, 1970, Anne Green (marr. diss.); one *s*; 2nd, 1982, Catharine Williams; two *d*. *Educ:* Univ. of Washington (BA); Stanford Univ. (MA). Diplomatic Corresp., Wall St Jl, Washington, 1969–77; Foreign Ed., Wall St Jl, NY, 1978; Editor: Asian Wall St Jl, Hong Kong, 1979–84; Wall St Jl Europe, Brussels, 1984–92; columnist and feature editor, Wall St Jl, Washington, 1992–98; Sen. Associate Editor, S China Morning Post, 1998–99. *Publication:* China: behind the mask, 1974. *Recreations:* hiking, jogging. *Address:* South China Morning Post, 16th Floor, Somerset House, 979 King's Road, Quarry Bay, Hong Kong. *Clubs:* Hong Kong, China, Ladies Recreation (Hong Kong).

KEAY, John Stanley Melville; author and history writer, since 1971; *b* 18 Sept. 1941; *s* of Capt. Stanley Walter Keay and Florence Jessie Keay (*née* Keeping); *m* 1972, Julia Margaret Atkins; two *s* two *d*. *Educ:* Ampleforth Coll.; Magdalen Coll., Oxford (BA Hons Modern Hist.). Various jobs in advertising, printing, journalism (freelance, mostly as special corresp. on India for The Economist), 1963-71; writer and presenter of radio documentaries, mainly on Asia, 1981-95. *Publications:* Into India, 1973, 3rd edn 1999; When Men and Mountains Meet, 1977, The Gilgit Game, 1979, combined as The Explorers of the Western Himalayas, 1996; India Discovered, 1981, 3rd edn 2001; Eccentric Travellers, 1983, 2nd edn 2001; Highland Drove, 1984; Explorers Extraordinary, 1985, 2nd edn 2001; (Gen. Ed.) The Royal Geographical Society History of World Exploration, 1991; The Honourable Company: a history of the East India Company, 1991; (ed with Julia Keay) Collins Encyclopaedia of Scotland, 1994, 2nd edn 2000; Indonesia: from Sabang to Merauke, 1995; Last Post: the end of Empire in the Far East, 1997, 2nd edn 2000; India: a history, 2000; The Great Arc, 2000. *Recreations:* weeding, walking, the warmer parts of Asia. *Address:* Succoth, Dalmally, Argyll PA33 1BB. *T:* (01838) 200250.

KEDDIE, Dr Alistair William Carnegie; Director, Environment, Innovation Services, Department of Trade and Industry, since 1999; *b* 1 Jan. 1943; *s* of Stuart Keddie and Ethel Carnegie Keddie; *m* 1966, Marjorie Scott Masterton; one *s* one *d*. *Educ:* Univ. of Glasgow (BSc Hons; PhD 1970). Res. Asst, then Asst Lectr, Dept of Astronomy, Univ. of Glasgow, 1967-70; res. mgt posts, 1970-77; Hd, Air Pollution Div., Warren Spring Lab., Stevenage, 1977-84; Department of Trade and Industry, 1984-: Hd, Innovation Unit, 1991-99. *Recreations:* walking, bird watching, music. *Address:* 24 Cromwell Road, Stevenage, Herts SG2 9HT; (01438) 360192.

KEE, Robert, CBE 1998; author and broadcaster; *b* 5 Oct. 1919; *s* of late Robert and Dorothy Kee; *m* 1st, 1948, Janetta (marr. diss. 1950), *d* of Rev. G. H. Woolley, VC; one *d*; 2nd, 1960, Cynthia (marr. diss. 1989), *d* of Edward Judah; one *s* one *d* (and one *s* decd); 3rd, 1990, Catherine Mary, *yr d* of Humphrey and Violet Margaret Trevelyan. *Educ:* Stowe Sch.; Magdalen Coll., Oxford (Exhibr, MA). RAF, 1940–46. Atlantic Award for Literature, 1946. Picture Post, 1948–51; Picture Editor, WHO, 1953; Special Corresp., Observer, 1956–57; Literary Editor, Spectator, 1957; Special Corresp., Sunday Times, 1957–58; BBC TV (Panorama, etc), 1958–62; Television Reporters International, 1963–64; ITV (Rediffusion, Thames, London Week-End, ITN, Yorkshire), 1964–78, Presenter, First Report, ITN's first lunch-time news prog., 1972–74; BBC, 1978–82; Presenter: Ireland: a television history (13 part television series), 1980; Panorama, BBC1, 1982; TV-am, 1983; Channel 4's Seven Days, 1984–88; miscellaneous BBC radio broadcasts, 1946–. Alistair Horne Research Fellow, St Antony's Coll., Oxford, 1972–73. BAFTA Richard Dimbleby Award, 1976. *Publications:* A Crowd Is Not Company, 1947, repr. 2000; The Impossible Shore, 1949; A Sign of the Times, 1955; Broadstrop In Season, 1959; Refugee World, 1961; The Green Flag, 1972, repr. 2000; Ireland: a history, 1980, revd edn 1995; The World We Left Behind, 1984; The World We Fought For, 1985; Trial and Error, 1986; Munich: the eleventh hour, 1988; The Picture Post Album, 1989; The Laurel and the Ivy: Parnell and Irish nationalism, 1993; many translations from German. *Recreations:* swimming, listening to music. *Address:* c/o Rogers, Coleridge and White, 20 Powis Mews, W11 1JN. *Club:* Reform.
See also William Kee.

KEE, His Honour William; a Circuit Judge, 1972–90; *b* 15 Oct. 1921; *yr s* of Robert and Dorothy Kee; *m* 1953, Helga Wessel Eckhoff; one *s* three *d*. *Educ:* Rottingdean Sch.; Stowe Sch. Served War, Army, 1941–46: attached 9th Gurkha Rifles, Dehra Dun, 1943; Staff Captain, Area HQ, 1945–46. Called to Bar, Inner Temple, 1948. Principal Judge for County Courts in Kent, 1985–90. Jt Chm., Independent Schools' Tribunal, 1971–72. *Publications:* (jt) Divorce Case Book, 1950; contributor to: titles in Atkin's Encyclopaedia of Court Forms; Halsbury's Laws of England. *Recreations:* listening to music, walking.
See also Robert Kee.

KEEBLE, Sir (Herbert Ben) Curtis, GCMG 1982 (KCMG 1978; CMG 1970); HM Diplomatic Service, retired; Ambassador at Moscow, 1978–82; *b* 18 Sept. 1922; *s* of Herbert Keeble and Gertrude Keeble, BEM; *m* 1947, Margaret Fraser; two *d* (and one *d* decd). *Educ:* Clacton County High Sch.; London University. Served HM Forces, 1942–47. Entered HM Foreign (subsequently Diplomatic) Service, 1947; served in Jakarta, 1947–49; Foreign Office, 1949–51; Berlin, 1951–54; Washington, 1954–58; Foreign Office, 1958–63; Counsellor and Head of European Economic Organisations Dept, 1963–65; Counsellor (Commercial), Berne, 1965–68; Minister, Canberra, 1968–71; Asst Under-Sec. of State, FCO, 1971–73; HM Ambassador, German Democratic Republic, 1974–76; Dep. Under Sec. of State (Chief Clerk), FCO, 1976–78. Special Adviser, H of C Foreign Affairs Cttee, 1985–86. A Governor, BBC, 1985–90. Chairman: Britain-Russia Centre (formerly GB-USSR Assoc.), 1985–95 (Vice Pres., 1995–); Foundn for Accountancy and Financial Management, 1993–2000; Thames Ditton Hosp. Foundn, 1996–2000; Member Council: RIIA, 1985–90; SSEES, 1985–90. *Publications:* (ed) The Soviet State, 1985; Britain and The Soviet Union, 1917–1989, 1990; (contrib.) Harold Macmillan: aspects of a political life, 1999; Britain, Russia and the Soviet Union, 2000. *Recreations:* sailing, painting. *Address:* Dormers, St Leonards Road, Thames Ditton, Surrey KT7 0RR. *T:* (020) 8398 7778. *Club:* Travellers.
See also S. C. Keeble.

KEEBLE, Major Robert, DSO 1940; MC 1945; TD 1946; Director: Associated Portland Cement Manufacturers Ltd, 1970–74; Aberthaw & Bristol Channel Portland Cement Co. Ltd, 1970–74; engaged in cement manufacture; *b* 20 Feb. 1911; *s* of late Edwin Percy and Alice Elizabeth Keeble; unmarried. *Educ:* King Henry VIII's Sch., Coventry. Commanded Royal Engineer Field Company; Territorial Army Commission, passed Staff Coll., Camberley, 1939; served in War of 1939–45 (despatches twice, twice wounded, DSO, MC, 1939–45 Star, African Star, France-Germany Star and Defence Medal, TD). Mem., Inst. Quarrying. Governor, Hull Univ. Hon. Brother, Hull Trinity House. Freeman of City of London and Liveryman of Company of Fanmakers. *Recreation:* fishing. *Address:* 15 Fernhill Close, Kenilworth CV8 1AN. *T:* (01926) 855668. *Club:* Army and Navy.

KEEBLE, Sally Curtis, (Mrs Andrew Porter); MP (Lab) Northampton North, since 1997; Parliamentary Under-Secretary of State, Department for Transport, Local Government and the Regions, since 2001; *b* 13 Oct. 1951; *d* of Sir Curtis Keeble, *qv* and Margaret Keeble; *m* 1990, Andrew Porter; one *s* one *d*. *Educ:* St Hugh's Coll., Oxford (BA Hons); Univ. of S Africa (BA Hons). Journalist, Daily News, Durban, SA, 1974–79; Reporter, Birmingham Post, 1979–83; Press Officer, Labour Party, 1983–84; Asst Dir, Ext. Relns, ILEA, 1984–86; Hd of Communications, GMB, 1986–90; Public Affairs Consultant, 1994–97. Mem. (Lab) Southwark BC, 1986–94 (Leader, 1990–93). Hon. Fellow, S Bank Univ. *Publications:* Collectors' Corner, 1984; Conceiving Your Baby: how medicine can help, 1995. *Recreations:* walking, antiques, reading. *Address:* House of Commons, SW1A 0AA; 8 Oakpark Close, Northampton NN3 5JG. *T:* (01604) 646310.

KEEFFE, Barrie Colin; dramatist; *b* 31 Oct. 1945; *s* of late Edward Thomas Keeffe and Constance Beatrice Keeffe (*née* Marsh); *m* 1st, 1969, Dee Sarah Truman (marr. diss. 1979); 2nd, 1981, Verity Eileen Proud (*née* Bargate) (*d* 1981); Guardian of her two *s*; 3rd, 1983, Julia Lindsay (marr. diss. 1993). *Educ:* East Ham Grammar School. Formerly actor with Nat. Youth Theatre; began writing career as journalist; Thames Television Award writer-in-residence, Shaw Theatre, 1977; Resident playwright, Royal Shakespeare Co., 1978; Associate Writer, Theatre Royal, Stratford East, 1986–91. Member: Board of Directors: Soho Theatre Co., 1978–; Theatre Royal, Stratford E, 1988–91; Patron, Greenwich Community Theatre, 1998. UN Ambassador, 1995. French Critics Prix Revelation, 1978; Giles Cooper Best Radio Plays, 1980; Mystery Writers of America Edgar Allan Poe Award, 1982. *Theatre plays:* Only a Game, 1973; A Sight of Glory, 1975; Scribes, 1975; Here Comes the Sun, 1976; Gimme Shelter, 1977; A Mad World My Masters, 1977, 1984; Barbarians, 1977; Frozen Assets, 1978; Sus, 1979; Bastard Angel, 1980; She's So Modern, 1980; Black Lear, 1980; Chorus Girls, 1981; Better Times, 1985; King of England, 1988; My Girl, 1989; Not Fade Away, 1990; Wild Justice, 1990; I Only Want to Be With You, 1995; The Long Good Friday, 1997; Shadows on the Sun, 2001; *television plays:* Substitute, 1972; Not Quite Cricket, 1977; Gotcha, 1977; Nipper, 1977; Champions, 1978; Hanging Around, 1978; Waterloo Sunset, 1979; King, 1984; *television series:* No Excuses, 1983; *film:* The Long Good Friday, 1981; also radio plays. *Publications: novels:* Gadabout, 1969; No Excuses, 1983; *plays:* Gimme Shelter, 1977; A Mad World My Masters, 1977; Barbarians, 1977; Here Comes the Sun, 1978; Frozen Assets, 1978; Sus, 1979; Bastard Angel, 1980; The Long Good Friday, 1984, new edn 1998; Better Times, 1985; King of England, 1988; My Girl, 1989; Wild Justice, Not Fade Away, Gimme Shelter, 1990; Barrie Keeffe Plays 1, 2001. *Recreation:* origami. *Address:* 110 Annandale Road, SE10 0JZ.

KEEGAN, (Elizabeth) Mary, FCA; Chairman, Accounting Standards Board, since 2001; *b* 21 Jan. 1953; *d* of Michael Keegan and Elizabeth Keegan (*née* Sarginson). *Educ:* Brentwood County High Sch. for Girls; Somerville Coll., Oxford (Caroline Haslett Meml Scholar, Coombs Exhibitioner; rowing blue; BA Natural Sci. 1974; MA 1977). ACA 1977, FCA 1983. Price Waterhouse, subseq. PricewaterhouseCoopers: articled London, 1974; Paris, 1979; Chicago, 1982; Partner, 1985–2001; Nat. Technical Partner, 1991–96; Dir Prrofessional Standards Europe, 1994–98; Hd Global Corporate Reporting Gp, 1998–2001. Member: Urgent Issues Task Force, Accounting Standards Bd, 1993–99; Standing Interpretations Cttee, Internat. Accounting Standards Cttee, 1997–; Internat. Forum on Accountancy Develt, 1999–2001; Chm., Financial Reporting Cttee., 1994–97, Mem. Council, 1994–97, ICAEW; Vice-Pres. and Mem. Council, Chm. Auditing Working Party, FEE, 1997–2001. FRSA. *Publications:* (jtly) The ValueReporting Revolution: moving beyond the earnings game, 2001; frequent contrib. to professional jls. *Recreations:* classical music, sailing. *Address:* Accounting Standards Board, Holborn Hall, 100 Gray's Inn Road, WC1X 8AL. *T:* (020) 7611 9702.

KEEGAN, Dame Geraldine (Mary Marcella), DBE 2000 (OBE 1995); Headmistress, St Mary's College, Londonderry, since 1987; Pro-Chancellor, University of Ulster, since 1997; *b* 17 Jan. 1941; *d* of Daniel Anthony McManus Keegan and Geraldine Catherine Veronica (*née* Halpin). *Educ:* St Mary's UC, Belfast (Cert Ed 1963); Univ. of Ulster (DipEd 1972); Univ. of Manchester (MEd 1975). Secondary sch. teacher of music, history and English, 1963–75; Sen. Lectr in Educnl Psychology, St Mary's UC, Belfast, 1975–85; Dep. Dir, NI Centre for Educn Mgt, 1985–87. FRSA 1995. *Recreations:* classical music, travel, fishing. *Address:* Balliniska House, Springtown, Londonderry BT48 0LX.

KEEGAN, Sir John (Desmond Patrick), Kt 2000; OBE 1991; FRSL; FRHistS; military historian; Defence Editor, The Daily Telegraph, since 1986; *b* 15 May 1934; *e s* of Francis Joseph Keegan and Eileen Mary Keegan (*née* Bridgman); *m* 1960, Susanne Ingeborg Everett; two *s* two *d*. *Educ:* King's Coll., Taunton; Wimbledon Coll.; Balliol Coll., Oxford (BA 1957; MA 1962; Hon. Fellow, 1999). Political Analyst, US Embassy, London, 1958–60; Sen. Lectr in Mil. Hist., RMA Sandhurst, 1960–86; corresp. from numerous countries, incl. Gulf, 1991. Delmas Vis. Dist. Prof. of Hist., Vassar Coll., 1997–98; Vis. Fellow, Princeton, 1984; Lectures: Lees Knowles, Cambridge, 1986; Eisenhower Meml, Kansas State, 1986; Brown Meml, Brown Univ., 1989; Whidden Meml, McMaster, 1990; Frum Meml, Toronto, 1994; Reith, BBC, 1998. Visitor, Hugh Sexey's Hosp., 1986–; Dir, E Somerset NHS Trust, 1991–97. Trustee: Nat. Heritage Meml Fund, 1994–2000; Heritage Lottery Fund, 1994–2000; Comr, Commonwealth War Graves Commn, 2001–. Contributing Editor: The New Republic, 1980–90; US News and World Report, 1986–. Hon. LLD New Brunswick, 1997; Hon. DLit QUB, 2000. Samuel Eliot Morison Prize, US Soc. for Mil. Hist., 1996. *Publications:* The Face of Battle, 1976; World Armies, 1978; Six Armies in Normandy, 1982; The Mask of Command, 1987; The Price of Admiralty, 1988, reissued as Battle at Sea, 1993; The Second World War, 1989; (ed) The Times Atlas of the Second World War, 1989; (ed) Churchill's Generals, 1991; A History of Warfare, 1993 (Duff Cooper Prize, 1994); Warpaths: travels of a military historian in North America, 1995; The Battle for History, 1996; The First World War, 1998 (Westminster Medal, 1999); War and Our World: the Reith Lectures, 1998; (ed) The Penguin Book of War: great military writings, 1999; contribs to DNB, Encyclopaedia Britannica. *Address:* The Manor House, Kilmington, near Warminster, Wilts BA12 6RD. *T:* (01985) 844856. *Clubs:* Garrick, Beefsteak, Pratt's; Brook (NY).

KEEGAN, (Joseph) Kevin, OBE 1982; professional footballer, 1966–84; Manager, Manchester City Football Club, since 2001; Coach, England Football Team, 1999–2000; *b* 14 Feb. 1951; *s* of late Joseph Keegan; *m* 1974, Jean Woodhouse; two *d*. Professional footballer with: Scunthorpe Utd, 1966–71; Liverpool, 1971–77; Hamburg, 1977–80; Southampton, 1980–82; Newcastle Utd, 1982–84. Internat. appearances for England, 1973–82, Captain, 1976–82. Manager, Newcastle Utd FC, 1992–97; Chief Operating Officer, Fulham FC, 1997–99. Football expert, Thames TV. Winners' medals: League Championships, 1973, 1976; UEFA Cup, 1973, 1976; FA Cup, 1974; European Cup, 1977. European Footballer of the Year, 1978, 1979. *Publications:* Kevin Keegan, 1978; Against the World: playing for England, 1979; Kevin Keegan: my autobiography, 1997. *Address:* c/o Manchester City Football Club, 195 Hut Road, Manchester, M14 7WN.

KEEGAN, Mary; *see* Keegan, E. M.

KEEGAN, William James Gregory; Economics Editor, since 1977, and Associate Editor, since 1983, The Observer; *b* 3 July 1938; *s* of William Patrick Keegan and Sheila Julia Keegan (*née* Buckley); *m* 1st, 1967, Tessa (*née* Young, *widow* of John Ashton) (marr. diss. 1982); two *s* two *d*; 2nd, 1992, Hilary, *d* of Maurice Stonefrost, *qv*; one *s* two *d*. *Educ:* Wimbledon Coll.; Trinity Coll., Cambridge (MA). National Service (Army), 1957–59 (commissioned). Journalist, Financial Times, Daily Mail and News Chronicle, 1963–67; Economics Correspondent, Financial Times, 1967–76; Economic Intell. Dept, Bank of England, 1976–77; Asst Editor and Business Editor, The Observer, 1981–83. Member: BBC Adv. Cttee on Business and Indust. Affairs, 1981–88; Council, Employment Inst., 1987–92; Adv. Bd, Dept of Applied Economics, Cambridge, 1988–92; Cttee for Soc. Scis., CNAA, 1991–92. Gov., NIESR, 1998–. Vis. Prof. of Journalism, 1989–, Hon. Res. Fellow, 1990–, Sheffield Univ. Hon. LittD Sheffield, 1995; Hon. DLitt City, 1998. *Publications:* Consulting Father Wintergreen, 1974; A Real Killing, 1976; (jtly) Who Runs the Economy?, 1978; Mrs Thatcher's Economic Experiment, 1984; Britain Without Oil, 1985; Mr Lawson's Gamble, 1989; The Spectre of Capitalism, 1992; 2066 and All That, 2000; contribs to The Tablet. *Address:* 76 Lofting Road, Islington, N1 1JB. *T:* (020) 7607 3590; The Observer, 119 Farringdon Road, EC1R 3ER. *T:* (020) 7278 2332. *Clubs:* Garrick, MCC.

KEEHAN, Michael Joseph; QC 2001; a Recorder, since 2000; *b* 31 March 1960; *s* of Michael and Alice Keehan; *m* 1988, Sarah Elizabeth Monk; two *d*. *Educ:* Birmingham Univ. (LLB). Called to the Bar, Middle Temple, 1982. *Recreations:* family life, gardening, walking. *Address:* St Ives Chambers, Whittall Street, Birmingham B4 6DH.

KEELING, Maj.-Gen. Andrew Myles, CB 1994; CBE 1992 (OBE 1988); freelance consultant, since 1996; *b* 4 July 1943; *s* of Richard George Maynard Keeling, OBE and Audrey Stuart Baxter (*née* Frederick); *m* 1965, Ann Margaret Grey Dudley (*d* 2001); one *s* two *d*. *Educ:* Rugby School. Commissioned 2nd Lieut RM, 1961; served 41, 42 and 45 Commandos, and training jobs at BRNC and RMA, 1963–75; student, Canadian Forces Command and Staff Coll., 1975–76; HQ 3 Cdo Bde RM, 1976–78; 41 Cdo, 1978–80; Bde Major, HQ 3 Cdo Bde, 1980–81; Directing Staff, NDC and JSDC, 1982–83; Jt Force HQ, 1984–85; CO 45 Cdo, 1985–87; MoD, 1987–89; Comd, 3 Cdo Bde, 1990–92; COS to Comdt-Gen. RM, 1992–93; Maj.-Gen., RM, 1992–94; retired RM, 1995. Rep. Col Comdt, RM, 1998–. Specialist Advr, Defence Select Cttee, H of C, 1997–98. Dir of Humanitarian Affairs, AMAR Internat. Charitable Foundn, 1995–96. President: City of Winchester Br., RMA, 1996–; SBS Assoc., 2001–; Naval Vice-Pres., CCF Assoc., 1995–; Mem. Council, St Dunstan's, 1995–. Sec., Salisbury Dio. Sudan Link, 2001–. Freeman, City of London, 1993. *Recreations:* sailing, walking. *Clubs:* Special Forces, MCC; Royal Marines Sailing (Hon. Life Vice-Commodore).

KEEMER, Peter John Charles; Assistant Auditor General, National Audit Office, 1989–93; *b* 27 Jan. 1932; *s* of late Frederick and Queenie Keemer; *m* 1954, Yvonne Griffin; one *s* one *d* (and one *s* decd). *Educ:* Price's Sch., Fareham; Univ. of Bath (MPhil). Exchequer and Audit Department: Asst Auditor and Auditor, 1950–62; Private Sec. to Comptroller and Auditor Gen., 1962–65; seconded to Parly Comr for Administration as Chief Exec. Officer, 1966–70; Chief Auditor, 1970; Dep. Dir, 1973; Dir, 1978–89 (seconded to European Court of Auditors as Director, 1978–86). External Auditor, European Univ. Inst., Florence, 1994–97. Mem., Conciliation Cttee, EC, 2001–. Mem., CIPFA, 1982. Chm., 1995–2001, Trustee, 1995–, Dir, 1997–, Breakthrough Breast Cancer; Mem. Council, Inst. of Cancer Res., 1994–2000 (Hon. Treas., 1996–2000). *Address:* How Green Cottage, How Lane, Chipstead, Surrey CR5 3LL. *T:* (01737) 553711; *e-mail:* keemer@globalnet.co.uk. *Club:* Royal Anglo-Belgian.

KEEN, Alan; *see* Keen, D. A.

KEEN, Ann Lloyd; MP (Lab) Brentford and Isleworth, since 1997; *b* 26 Nov. 1948; *d* of late John Fox and of Ruby Fox; one *s*; *m* 1980, (David) Alan Keen, *qv*; one step *s* one step *d*. *Educ:* Elfed Secondary Modern Sch., Clwyd; Univ. of Surrey (PGCE). Formerly: Hd, Faculty of Advanced Nursing, Queen Charlotte's Coll., Hammersmith; Gen. Sec., Community and District Nursing Assoc. Contested (Lab) Brentford and Isleworth, 1987, 1992. Hon. Prof. of Nursing, Thames Valley Univ. *Address:* House of Commons, SW1A 0AA.

KEEN, (David) Alan; MP (Lab and Co-op) Feltham and Heston, since 1992; *b* 25 Nov. 1937; one *s* one *d*; *m* 1980, Ann Lloyd (*see* Ann Keen); one step *s*. *Educ:* Sir William Turner's Sch., Redcar. Various posts as systems analyst, accountant and manager, 1963–92. Mem. (Lab) Hounslow BC, 1986–90. Mem., Select Cttee on Culture, Media and Sport. *Address:* House of Commons, SW1A 0AA.

KEEN, Kenneth Roger; QC 1991; **His Honour Judge Keen;** a Circuit Judge, since 2001; *b* 13 May 1946; *s* of Kenneth Henry Keen and Joan Megan Keen (*née* Weetman); *m* Mary Lorraine Raeburn; one *s* one *d* by previous marriage. *Educ:* Doncaster Grammar School. Qualified Solicitor, 1968; called to the Bar, Gray's Inn, 1976; practice on NE circuit; a Recorder, 1989. *Recreations:* tennis, travel, walking. *Address:* Sheffield Crown Court, 50 West Bar, Sheffield S3 8PH.

KEEN, Laurence John, OBE 2000; FSA, FRHistS; President, British Archaeological Association, since 1989; Consultant, John Stark & Crickmay Partnership, architects, since 1999; County Archaeological Officer, Dorset County Council, 1975–99; *b* 11 July 1943; *er s* of late John William Frederick Keen and Dorothy Ethel Keen (*née* French). *Educ:* Kilburn GS; St John's Coll., York (Cert Ed (Music) 1966); Inst. of Archaeology, Univ. of London (Postgrad. Dip. in European Archaeol. 1969; Gordon Childe Meml Prize); UCL (MPhil 1978). FRHistS 1974; FSA 1979; MIFA 1985; FSAScot 1995. Répetiteur, Lycée Mohammed V, Marrakech, 1962–63; Asst Master, Cundall Manor Sch., York, 1966–67; Dir, Southampton Archaeol Res. Cttee, 1972–75. Archaeol Cons., MPBW, then DoE, then English Heritage, 1964–. Director of excavations: Wardour Castle, Wilts; Blackfriars, Gloucester; Kingswood Abbey, Glos; Tattershall Coll., Lincs; Mountgrace Priory, Yorks; Beeston Castle, Cheshire; Prudhoe Castle, Northumberland; Sherborne Abbey, Dorset. Vis. Lectr in Archaeology, Univ. of Southampton, 1973–75. Winston Churchill Fellow, 1970; Hon. Research Fellow: Centre for South-Western Hist. Studies, Univ. of Exeter, 1995–98; UC of Ripon and York St John, 1995–. Member: Council, Soc. for Medieval Archaeology, 1973–76; DAC for Faculties, 1977–97, Diocesan Redundant Churches Cttee, 1985–97, Salisbury; Paintings Cttee, Council for the Care of Churches, 1979–96; Chm., Dorset Local Hist. Gp, 1985–99; Member, Council: Gloucester Cath. Fabric Cttee, 1991–; St George's Chapel (Windsor) Adv. Cttee, 1998– (Chm., 1999–); British Archaeol Assoc., 1973–76, 1978–81, 1984–87 (Vice-Pres., 1988; Reginald Taylor Essay Prize, 1969); Royal Archaeol Inst., 1982–85. Foreign Corresp. Associate Mem., Société Nat. des Antiquaires de France, 1990. Freeman, City of London, 1991; Freeman and Liveryman, Co. of Painter-Stainers, 1991. *Publications:* (jtly) William Barnes: the Dorset engravings, 1986 ((jtly) Mansel-Pleydell Essay Prize, Dorset Nat. Hist. & Archaeol. Soc., 1985), 2nd edn 1989; William Barnes: the Somerset engravings, 1989; (ed jtly) Historic Landscape of the Weld Estate, 1987; Dorset Domesday: an introduction, 1991; (ed jtly) Medieval Art and Architecture at Salisbury Cathedral, 1996; (ed) Almost the Richest City: Bristol in the Middle Ages, 1997; (jtly) Dorset from the Air, 1998; (ed) Studies in the Early History of Shaftesbury Abbey, 1999; (ed jtly) Windsor Castle: medieval archaeology, art and architecture of the Thames Valley, 2001; articles and reviews in nat. and county jls. *Recreations:* making music, entertaining, perfecting bread and butter pudding. *Address:* John Stark & Crickmay Partnership, 13–14 Princes Street, Dorchester, Dorset DT1 1TW. *T:* (01305) 262636; 7 Church Street, Dorchester, Dorset DT1 1JN. *T:* (01305) 265460. *Club:* Royal Over-Seas League.

KEEN, Lady Mary; *see* Keen, Lady P. M. R.

KEEN, Maurice Hugh, FSA; FBA 1990; Fellow of Balliol College, Oxford, 1961–2000, now Emeritus; *b* 30 Oct. 1933; *e s* of Harold Hugh Keen and Catherine Eleanor Lyle Keen (*née* Cummins); *m* 1968, Mary Agnes Keegan; three *d.* *Educ:* Winchester College; Balliol College, Oxford (BA 1st Cl. Mod. Hist. 1957). FSA 1987. Nat. Service 1952–54, commissioned Royal Ulster Rifles. Junior Res. Fellow, The Queen's Coll., Oxford, 1957–61; Tutor in Medieval History, Balliol Coll., Oxford, 1961–2000. External examr, Nat. Univ. of Ireland, 1971–78. Fellow, Winchester Coll., 1989–. Alexander Prize, RHistS, 1962. *Publications:* The Outlaws of Medieval Legend, 1961; The Laws of War in the Later Middle Ages, 1965; A History of Medieval Europe, 1968; England in the Later Middle Ages, 1973; Chivalry, 1984 (Wolfson Lit. Award for History, 1985); English Society in the later Middle Ages, 1990. *Recreations:* fishing, shooting. *Address:* 4 Walton Street, Oxford OX1 2HG. *Club:* Oxford and Cambridge.
See also G. L. Norman.

KEEN, Prof. Peter Marley, PhD; Professor of Pre-Clinical Veterinary Studies, Department of Pharmacology, University of Bristol, 1988–95, now Professor Emeritus; *b* 14 May 1930; *s* of Ernest Keen and Kathleen (*née* Marley); *m* 1956, Pauline Helen Franklin; four *d.* *Educ:* Wellington Sch., Somerset; Univ. of Bristol (BVSc); PhD London Univ. 1964. MRCVS 1955. Nat. Service, RAF, 1948–50. Veterinary practice, 1955–59; Lectr in Vet. Pharmacol., RVC, London, 1959–64; University of Bristol: Lectr, then Reader, in Vet. Pharmacol., 1964–88; Head of Vet. Sch., 1988–93; Dean of Medicine, 1993–95. *Publications:* articles in learned jls. *Recreations:* oil painting, pub walks, local architecture. *Address:* Old Orchard, Winscombe Hill, Winscombe BS25 1DF. *T:* (01934) 842026.

KEEN, Lady (Priscilla) Mary (Rose); garden designer, writer and lecturer; *b* 12 Feb. 1940; *d* of 6th Earl Howe and of Priscilla (*née* Weigall, who *m* 2nd, Harold Coriat); *m* 1962, Charles Keen; one *s* three *d.* *Educ:* Lawnside, Malvern; Lady Margaret Hall, Oxford. Gardening Columnist: Evening Standard, 1980–88; Perspectives, 1988–98; Independent on Sunday, 1988–98; freelance journalist: Gardening; Sunday Telegraph; designed Glyndebourne Opera House new gardens, 1992–93, and many large private commissions. National Trust: Member: Gardens Panel, 1982–; Thames and Chilterns Regl Cttee, 1982–92; Severn Regl Cttee, 1996–. Inspirational Garden Journalist of the Year, Garden Writer's Guild Awards, 1999. *Publications:* The Garden Border Book, 1987; The Glory of the English Garden, 1989; Colour Your Garden, 1991; Decorate Your Garden, 1993; Creating a Garden, 1996. *Recreation:* gardening. *Address:* The Old Rectory, Duntisbourne Rous, Cirencester, Glos GL7 7AP.

KEEN, Richard Sanderson; QC (Scot.) 1993; *b* 29 March 1954; *s* of Derek Michael Keen and Jean Sanderson Keen; *m* 1978, Jane Carolyn Anderson; one *s* one *d.* *Educ:* King's Sch., Rochester; Dollar Acad.; Edinburgh Univ. (LLB Hons 1976; Beckman Schol.). Admitted Faculty of Advocates, 1980; Standing Jun. Counsel in Scotland to DTI, 1986–93. Chm. Appeals Cttee, ICAS, 1996–. *Recreations:* golf, ski-ing, shooting, opera. *Address:* The Castle, Elie, Fife KY9 1DN. *T:* (01333) 330010; 39 Ann Street, Edinburgh EH4 1PL. *T:* (0131) 343 1935; Advocate's Library, Parliament House, Edinburgh EH1 1RF. *T:* (0131) 226 5071. *Clubs:* New (Edinburgh); Bruntsfield Links Golfing Society (Edinburgh).

KEENE, Rt Hon. Sir David (Wolfe), Kt 1994; PC 2000; **Rt Hon. Lord Justice Keene;** a Lord Justice of Appeal, since 2000; *b* 15 April 1941; *s* of Edward Henry Wolfe Keene and Lilian Marjorie Keene; *m* 1965, Gillian Margaret Lawrance; one *s* one *d.* *Educ:* Hampton Grammar Sch.; Balliol Coll., Oxford (Winter Williams Prizewinner, 1962; BA 1st Cl. Hons Law, 1962; BCL 1963). Called to the Bar, Inner Temple, 1964, Bencher, 1987; Eldon Law Scholar, 1965; QC 1980; a Recorder, 1989–94; a Deputy High Court Judge, 1993–94; a Judge of High Court of Justice, QBD, 1994–2000; a Judge, Employment Appeal Tribunal, 1995–2000. Chm. of Panel, Cumbria Structure Plan Examination in Public, 1980; conducted County Hall, London, Inquiry, 1987; Chairman: Planning and Envmtl Law Reform Working Gp, 1997–; Adv. Cttee on Equal Treatment, Judicial Studies Bd, 1998–. Chm., Planning Bar Assoc., 1994 (Vice-Chm., 1990–94). Visitor, Brunel Univ., 1995–2000. Hon. Fellow, Soc. of Advanced Legal Studies, 1998. Hon. LLD Brunel. *Recreations:* walking, opera, jazz, gardening. *Address:* Royal Courts of Justice, Strand, WC2A 2LL. *Club:* Athenæum.

KEENE, Prof. Derek John, DPhil; Leverhulme Professor of Comparative Metropolitan History, Institute of Historical Research, since 2001; *b* 27 Dec. 1942; *s* of Charles Henry Keene and Edith Anne Keene (*née* Swanston); *m* 1969, Suzanne Victoria Forbes (*see* S. V. Keene); one *s* one *d.* *Educ:* Ealing Grammar Sch.; Oriel Coll., Oxford (MA, DPhil). FRHistS. Researcher, 1968–74, Asst Dir, 1974–78, Winchester Research Unit; Dir, Social and Economic Study of Medieval London, 1987–99, Dir, Centre for Metropolitan History, 1987–2002, Inst. of Historical Research. Member: RCHM, 1987–99; Commn internat. pour l'histoire de villes, 1990–; Fabric Adv. Cttee, St Paul's Cathedral, 1991–; London Adv. Cttee, 1998–, Urban Panel, 2000–, English Heritage. *Publications:* Winchester in the Early Middle Ages (jtly), 1976; Survey of Medieval Winchester, 1985; Cheapside Before the Great Fire, 1985; (with V. Harding) A survey of documentary sources for property holding in London before the Great Fire, 1985; (with V. Harding) Historical Gazetteer of London before the Great Fire, 1987; (ed with P. J. Corfield) Work in Towns 850–1850, 1990; (jtly) A Medieval Capital and its Grain Supply: agrarian production and distribution in the London region *c* 1300, 1993; contribs to learned jls and to collections of essays. *Recreations:* metropolises, walking uphill, making and repairing things. *Address:* 162 Erlanger Road, SE14 5TJ. *T:* (020) 7639 5371.

KEENE, John Robert R.; *see* Ruck-Keene.

KEENE, Dr Suzanne Victoria, FIIC; Course Director, Museum Studies, University College London, since 2001; *b* 21 July 1944; *d* of Lt-Comdr Lachlan Andrew Forbes, RN and Adelaide Talbot Suzanne Forbes; *m* 1969, Derek John Keene, *qv*; one *s* one *d.* *Educ:* various schools; University Coll. London (Dip. Archaeol Conservation; Gordon Childe Prize, Inst. of Archaeol., 1969; PhD 1993). FIIC 1985. Archaeol Asst, British Sch. at Rome, 1964–66; Winchester Research Unit: Archaeol Conservator, 1969–75; Ed., Medieval Finds pubn, 1975–77; Museum of London: Hd of Section, Archaeol Conservation, 1979–86; Hd of Conservation, 1986–92; Hd of Collections Mgt, Science Mus., 1992–2000. Mem., Exec. Cttee, 1970–74, Gen. Sec., 1972–76, UK Inst. for Conservation; Mem., Panel on Archaeol Collections, Area Mus. for S Eastern England, 1976–90. Mem., UK Nat. Cttee, ICOM, 1993–99. Member: Working Parties, English Heritage and Mus and Galls Commn, 1988–90 and 1992; Working Gp on Mus and Nat. Grid for Learning, DCMS, 1998–; Bd, London Museums Agency, 2001–. Trustee, Tank Mus., 1998–. *Publications:* Managing Conservation in Museums, 1996; Digital Collections: museums in the information age, 1998; contrib. numerous articles on museum digitisation and conservation. *Recreations:* beautiful country-side, reading novels, films, the internet. *Address:* Institute of Archaeology, 31–34 Gordon Square, WC1H 0PY.

KEENLYSIDE, Simon John; baritone; *b* London, 3 Aug. 1959; *s* of Raymond Keenlyside and Ann Leonie Hirsch. *Educ:* St John's Coll., Cambridge (BA Zoology 1983); Royal Northern Coll. of Music. With Scottish Opera, 1989–94 (rôles incl. Marcello, Danilo, Guglielmo, Figaro in Barber of Seville, Billy Budd, Papageno and Belcore); *débuts:* Royal Opera, Covent Garden, 1989 (Silvio in Pagliacci); ENO, 1990 (Guglielmo in Così fan tutte); WNO, 1991 (Falke); San Francisco, 1993 (Olivier in Capriccio); Geneva, 1993 (Papageno in Die Zauberflote); Paris Opéra (Papageno), Australian Opera (Figaro) and La Scala, Milan, 1995; Glyndebourne, 1996 (Guglielmo); Metropolitan Opera, NY (Belcore in L'elisir d'amore); other rôles incl. Count Almaviva, Don Giovanni, Orfeo, Hamlet, Pelléas, Dandini in La Cenerentola, Wolfram in Tannhäuser, Yeletski in Queen of Spades, Oreste in Iphigénie en Tauride, Ubalde in Armide, Ford in Falstaff. Frequent concerts and recitals; recordings incl. operas, recitals of Schubert, Strauss and Mahler, and Schumann lieder. *Recreations:* a passion for all things zoological, diving, walking, painting, fly fishing. *Address:* c/o Askonas Holt, Lonsdale Chambers, 27 Chancery Lane, WC2A 1PF. *T:* (020) 7400 1700.

KEEP, Charles Reuben; Chairman and Managing Director, Resource Management Associates Ltd, since 1992; Chairman and Chief Executive, Bellair Holdings Ltd (formerly Bellair Cosmetics plc), since 1984; *b* 1932; *m*; one *d.* *Educ:* HCS, Hampstead. Joined Lloyds & Scottish Finance Ltd, 1956, Director, 1969; Man. Dir, International Factors Ltd, 1970; Group Man. Dir, Tozer Kemsley & Millbourn (Holdings) Ltd, 1973–77; Chm., Tozer Kemsley & Millbourn Trading Ltd, 1978–80; Director: Tozer Standard & Chartered Ltd, 1973–77; Barclays Tozer Ltd, 1974–77; Manufacturers Hanover Credit Corp., 1977–80; Chm., Export Leasing Ltd, Bermuda 1974–77; Pres., France Motors sa Paris, 1974–81. *Address:* The Oaks, 20 Forest Lane, Chigwell, Essex IG7 5AE. *T:* (020) 8504 3897. *Club:* Chigwell Golf.

KEETCH, Paul Stuart; MP (Lib Dem) Hereford, since 1997; *b* 21 May 1961; *s* of late John Norton Keetch and Agnes, (Peggy), Keetch; *m* 1991, Claire Elizabeth Baker; one *s.* *Educ:* Boys' High Sch., Hereford; Hereford Sixth Form Coll. With Midland Bank, then various water hygiene cos, 1979–95; Dir, MarketNet, 1996–. OSCE monitor to Albanian elections, 1996. Political and media advr to Lithuanian and Bosnian political parties, 1995–96. Joined Liberal Party, 1975; Mem. (Lib Dem) Hereford CC, 1983–86. Lib Dem spokesman on: health, 1997; employment and training, 1997–99; defence, 2001–. Member: Educn and Employment Select Cttee, 1997–99; Armed Forces Bill Select Cttee, 2001; Envmtl Audit Cttee, 1999–2001. All Party Groups: Founder, Cider Gp, 1997–; Sec., Albanian Gp, 1997–; Mem., Defence Studies Gp, 1997–; Sec., Electoral Reform Gp, 1997–; Vice-Chm., Childcare Gp, 1998–. Dir, and Mem. Council, Electoral Reform Soc., 1997–. Mem., CPA, 1997–. Hon. Pres., Staffordshire Univ. Lib Dem Gp, 1996. Patron, St Michael's Hospice, Hereford, 1997; Pres., Hereford Hosp. Radio, 1998–; Vice-President: Nat. Childminding Assoc., 1998–; Westfields FC, Hereford, 1997–; Pres., Barrs Court Sch., Hereford. Member: IISS; RUSI, 1999–. *Recreations:* swimming, entertaining, building model warships. *Address:* House of Commons, SW1A 0AA. *T:* (020) 7219 5163, *Fax:* (020) 7219 1184; *e-mail:* paulkeetch@cix.co.uk. *Clubs:* National Liberal; Hereford and County Liberal, Herefordshire Farmers; Herefordshire County Cricket (Life Mem.).

KEIGHLEY, Prof. Michael Robert Burch, FRCS, FRCSE; Barling Professor of Surgery, University of Birmingham, since 1988; *b* 12 Oct. 1943; *s* of late Dr Robert Arthur Spink Keighley and of Dr Jacqueline Vivian Keighley; *m* Dr Dorothy Margaret; one *s* one *d.* *Educ:* Monkton Combe Sch.; St Bartholomew's Hosp., Univ. of London (MB BS 1967; MS 1976). FRCS 1970; FRCSE 1970. Prof. of Surgery, General and Dental Hosps, Univ. of Birmingham, 1984–88. Boerhaave Prof. of Surgery, Univ. of Leiden, 1985; Eyber's Vis. Prof., Univ. of OFS, 1987; Vis. Prof., Harvard Univ., 1990; Penman Vis. Prof., Univ. of Cape Town, 1992; Vis. Prof., St Mark's Hosp., London, 1995; Rupert Turnbull Prof., Washington Univ., 1996. Mem., Christian Med. Fellowship, 1967–. Hon. Fellow, Brazilian Coll. of Surgeons, 1991. Jacksonian Prize, RCS, 1979; Hunterian Prof., RCS, 1979. *Publications:* Antimicrobial Prophylaxis in Surgery, 1979; Inflammatory Bowel Diseases, 1981, 3rd edn 1995; Gastrointestinal Haemorrhage, 1983; Textbook of Gastroenterology, 1985, 2nd edn 1994; Surgery of the Anus, Rectum and Colon, 1994, 2nd edn 1999; Atlas of Colorectal Surgery, 1996. *Recreations:* painting, music, sailing, climbing. *Address:* University of Birmingham, Department of Surgery, Queen Elizabeth Hospital, Edgbaston, Birmingham B15 2TH. *T:* (0121) 627 2274, *Fax:* (0121) 472 1230; Whalebone Cottage, Vicarage Hill, Tanworth in Arden, Warwicks B94 5AN, *T:* (01564) 742903, *Fax:* (01564) 742705. *Clubs:* Athenæum, Royal Society of Medicine.

KEIGHLEY, Thomas Christopher, TSSF; independent health care consultant, since 2001; *b* 4 May 1951; *s* of late John Charles Keighley and of Frances Louise Keighley (*née* Leary); *m* 1st, 1974, Anne Gibson (marr. diss. 1978); 2nd, 1979, Elizabeth Redfern (marr. diss. 1989); 3rd, 1990, Amanda Gunner; one step *s* one step *d.* *Educ:* St Michael's Coll., Kirkby Lonsdale; Preston Sch. of Nursing (SRN 1974; RMN 1976); Charles Frear Sch. of Nursing (NDN Cert. 1976); Huddersfield Polytechnic (RCNT 1979); Dip. Nursing, London Univ., 1981; BA Hons Open Univ. 1985. Aux. Nurse, Deepdale Hosp., Preston, 1970; Staff Nurse, Preston Royal Infirmary, 1974; Community Charge Nurse, NW Leics, 1976; Clinical Teacher: Maidstone, 1977; Cambridge HA, 1979; RCN Adviser, Research, 1982; Dist Dir of Nursing, 1986, of Nursing and Quality, 1988, Waltham Forest; Regl Dir of Nursing, Yorkshire Health, 1990–95; Dir, Inst. of Nursing, Univ. of Leeds, 1993–96; Dir of Internat. Devely, Sch. of Healthcare Studies, Univ. of Leeds, 1997–2001. Associate Researcher, Lincoln Theol Inst., Sheffield Univ., 1998–. Mem., EU Adv. Cttee on Training for Nursing, 1990–2000. Winifred Raphael Meml Lecture, RCN Res. Soc., 1988. TSSF, 2001–. Editor, Nursing Management, 1997–. *Publications:* articles on nursing and health care. *Recreations:* opera, art, walking, rug making. *Address:* The Old Chapel, Middlesmoor, Pateley Bridge, Harrogate, N Yorks HG3 5ST.

KEIGHTLEY, Maj.-Gen. Richard Charles, CB 1987; Chairman, Dorset (formerly West Dorset) Health Authority, 1988–95 and since 1998; *b* 2 July 1933; *s* of General Sir Charles Keightley, GCB, GBE, DSO, and late Lady (Joan) Keightley (*née* Smyth-Osbourne); *m* 1958, Caroline Rosemary Butler, *er d* of Sir Thomas Butler, 12th Bt, CVO, DSO, OBE; three *d.* *Educ:* Marlborough Coll.; RMA, Sandhurst. Commissioned into 5th Royal Inniskilling Dragoon Guards, 1953; served Canal Zone, BAOR, N Africa, Singapore, Cyprus; sc Camberley, 1963; comd 5th Royal Inniskilling Dragoon Guards, 1972–75; Task Force Comdr, 3 Armd Div., 1978–79; RCDS 1980; Brigadier General Staff HQ UKLF, 1981; GOC Western Dist, 1982–83; Comdt, RMA Sandhurst, 1983–87. Col, 5th Royal Inniskilling Dragoon Guards, 1986–91. Defence Consultant, Portescap (UK), 1987–92. Chm., Dorset Healthcare NHS Trust, 1996–98. Pres., Dorset Br., Royal British Legion, 1990–. Chm., Combined Services Polo Assoc., 1982–86. *Recreations:* field sports, cricket, farming. *Address:* White Kennels, Tarrant Gunville, Blandford, Dorset DT11 8JQ.

KEIR, James Dewar; QC 1980; Director, Open University Educational Enterprises Ltd, 1983–88; Chairman, City and East London Family Practitioner Committee, 1985–89; part-time Member, Monopolies and Mergers Commission, 1987–92; *b* 30 Nov. 1921; *s* of David Robert Keir and Elizabeth Lunan (*née* Ross); *m* 1948, Jean Mary, *e d* of Rev. and Mrs E. P. Orr; two *s* two *d.* *Educ:* Edinburgh Acad.; Christ Church, Oxford (MA 1948). Served War, 1941–46: ME, Italy; Captain, The Black Watch (RHR). Called to the Bar, Inner Temple, 1949; Yarborough-Anderson Scholar, Inner Temple, 1950. Legal Adviser,

United Africa Co. Ltd, 1954–66, Sec., 1966; Dep. Head of Legal Services, Unilever Ltd, 1973; Jt Sec., Unilever PLC and Unilever NV, 1976–84; Dir, UAC Internat. Ltd, 1973–77. Chm., 1969–72, Pres., 1980–82, Bar Assoc. for Commerce, Finance and Industry; Member: Bar Council, 1971–73; Senate of Inns of Ct and Bar, 1973–78. Chairman: Pharmacists Rev. Panel, 1986–97; Professional Cttee, Royal Coll. of Speech and Language Therapists, 1993–2001. *Recreations:* ski-ing, Rugby, opera, reading. *Address:* 15 Clays Close, East Grinstead, West Sussex RH19 4DJ. *T:* (01342) 323189. *Club:* Caledonian.

KEITH, family name of **Barons Keith of Castleacre** and **Keith of Kinkel** and of **Earl of Kintore**.

KEITH OF CASTLEACRE, Baron *cr* 1980 (Life Peer), of Swaffham in the County of Norfolk; **Kenneth Alexander Keith,** Kt 1969; merchant banker and industrialist; *b* 30 Aug. 1916; *er s* of late Edward Charles Keith, Swanton Morley House, Norfolk; *m* 1st, 1946, Lady Ariel Olivia Winifred Baird (marr. diss., 1958), 2nd *d* of 1st Viscount Stonehaven, PC, GCMG, DSO, and Countess of Kintore; one *s* one *d*; 2nd, 1962, Mrs Nancy Hayward (marr. diss. 1972; she *d* 1990), Manhasset, New York; 3rd, 1973, Mrs Marie Hanbury (*d* 2001), Burley-on-the-Hill, Rutland. *Educ:* Rugby Sch. Trained as a Chartered Accountant. 2nd Lt Welsh Guards, 1939; Lt-Col 1945; served in North Africa, Italy, France and Germany (despatches, Croix de Guerre with Silver Star). Asst to Dir Gen. Political Intelligence Dept, Foreign Office, 1945–46. Partner, 1946, Dir, 1948, Man. Dir, 1951, Philip Hill & Partners Ltd; Chairman: Philip Hill Investment Trust Ltd, 1967–87; Hill Samuel Group Ltd, 1970–80; Chm. and Chief Exec., Rolls Royce Ltd, 1972–80; Vice-Chm., BEA, 1964–71; Director: Beecham Gp Ltd, 1949–87 (Vice-Chm., 1970–87, Chm., 1986–87); Eagle Star Insurance Co., 1955–75; Nat. Provincial Bank, 1967–69; Times Newspapers Ltd, 1967–81; British Airways, 1971–72; Standard Telephones and Cables, subseq. STC, 1977–89 (Chm., 1985–89); Bank of Nova Scotia Ltd, 1978–87. Member: NEDC, 1964–71; CBI/NEDC Liaison Cttee, 1974–78; Pres., BSI, 1989–94; Vice-Pres., EEF. Chairman: Economic Planning Council for East Anglia, 1965–70; Governor, Nat. Inst. of Economic and Social Research. Council Mem. and Dir, Manchester Business Sch. President: Royal Norfolk Agricl Assoc., 1989; RoSPA, 1989–93. FIMgt; FRSA. Hon. Companion, RAeS. *Recreations:* farming, shooting, golf. *Address:* 9 Eaton Square, SW1 9DB. *T:* (020) 7730 4000; The Wicken House, Castle Acre, King's Lynn, Norfolk PE32 2BP. *T:* (01760) 755225. *Club:* White's.

KEITH OF KINKEL, Baron *cr* 1977 (Life Peer), of Strathtummel; **Henry Shanks Keith,** GBE 1997; PC 1976; a Lord of Appeal in Ordinary, 1977–96; *b* 7 Feb. 1922; *s* of late Baron Keith of Avonholm, PC (Life Peer); *m* 1955, Alison Hope Alan Brown, JP, MA; four *s* (including twin *s*) one *d*. *Educ:* Edinburgh Academy; Magdalen Coll., Oxford (MA; Hon. Fellow 1977); Edinburgh Univ. (LLB). War of 1939–45 (despatches); commnd Scots Guards, Nov. 1941; served N Africa and Italy, 1943–45; released, 1945 (Capt.). Advocate, Scottish Bar, 1950; Barrister, Gray's Inn, 1951, Bencher 1976; QC (Scotland), 1962. Standing Counsel to Dept of Health for Scotland, 1957–62; Sheriff Principal of Roxburgh, Berwick and Selkirk, 1970–71; Senator of Coll. of Justice in Scotland, 1971–77. Chairman: Scottish Valuation Adv. Coun., 1972–76 (Mem., 1957–70); Cttee on Powers of Revenue Depts, 1980–83; Dep. Chm., Parly Boundary Commn for Scotland, 1976; Member: Law Reform Cttee for Scotland, 1964–70; Cttee on Law of Defamation, 1971–74; Mem. Panel of Arbiters: European Fisheries Convention, 1964–71; Convention for Settlement of Investment Disputes, 1968–71. *Address:* House of Lords, SW1A 0PW. *Club:* Flyfishers'.

KEITH, Hon. Sir (Brian) Richard, Kt 2001; **Hon. Mr Justice Keith;** a Judge of the High Court, Queen's Bench Division, since 2001; *b* 14 April 1944; *s* of Alan Keith, OBE, broadcaster, and Pearl Keith (*née* Rebuck); *m* 1978, Gilly, *d* of late Air Cdre Ivan de la Plain, CBE; one *s* one *d*. *Educ:* University College School, Hampstead; Lincoln College, Oxford (MA). John F. Kennedy Fellow, Harvard Law School, 1966–67; called to the Bar, Inner Temple, 1968, Bencher, 1996; in practice, 1969–91; Assistant Recorder, 1988; QC 1989; a Recorder, 1993–2001. A Judge of the Supreme Court of Hong Kong, 1991–97; a Judge of the Court of First Instance, High Court of Hong Kong, 1997–99; Presiding Judge, Admin. Law List, High Court of Hong Kong, 1997–99; a Judge of the Court of Appeal, Hong Kong, 1999–2001. Hon. Lectr, Univ. of Hong Kong, 1994–2001. Mem., Judicial Studies Bd, Hong Kong, 1994–2001. *Recreations:* travel, tennis, cinema. *Address:* Royal Courts of Justice, Strand, WC2A 2LL. *Club:* Hong Kong.

KEITH, Rt Hon. Sir Kenneth (James), KBE 1988; PC 1998; **Rt Hon. Justice Keith;** a Judge of the Court of Appeal: New Zealand, since 1996; Western Samoa, since 1982; Cook Islands, since 1982; Niue, since 1995; *b* 19 Nov. 1937; *s* of Patrick James Keith and Amy Irene Keith (*née* Witheridge); *m* 1961, Jocelyn Margaret Buckett; two *s* two *d*. *Educ:* Auckland Grammar Sch.; Auckland Univ.; Victoria Univ. of Wellington (LLM); Harvard Law Sch. Barrister and Solicitor, High Court of New Zealand; QC (NZ) 1994. NZ Dept of External Affairs, 1960–62; Victoria Univ. of Wellington, 1962–64, 1966–91, Prof. of Law, 1974–91, now Emeritus; UN Secretariat, NY, 1968–70; NZ Inst. of Internat. Affairs, 1972–74; Pres., NZ Law Commn, 1991–96. Permanent Ct of Arbitration, 1985–. Mem., Internat. Fact Finding Commn (Geneva Conventions), 1991–. Associate Mem., Inst de Droit Internat., 1997–. *Publications:* (ed) Human Rights in New Zealand, 1968; The Extent of the Advisory Jurisdiction of the International Court, 1971; contrib. to Amer. Jl of Internat. Law, Internat. and Comparative Law Qly, NZ Univs Law Rev., etc. *Recreations:* walking, reading, music. *Address:* PO Box 1606, Wellington, New Zealand. *T:* (4) 9143540.

KEITH, Penelope Anne Constance, (Mrs Rodney Timson), OBE 1989; actress; *b* 2 April; *d* of Frederick A. W. Hatfield and Constance Mary Keith; *m* 1978, Rodney Timson. *Educ:* Annecy Convent, Seaford, Sussex; Webber Douglas Sch., London. First prof. appearance, Civic Theatre, Chesterfield, 1959; repertory, Lincoln, Salisbury and Manchester, 1960–63; RSC, Stratford, 1963, and Aldwych, 1965; rep., Cheltenham, 1967; Maggie Howard in Suddenly at Home, Fortune Theatre, 1971; Sarah in The Norman Conquests, Greenwich, then Globe Theatre, 1974; Lady Driver in Donkey's Years, 1976; Orinthia in The Apple Cart, Chichester, then Phoenix Theatre, 1977; Epifania in The Millionairess, Haymarket, 1978; Sarah in Moving, Queen's Theatre, 1981; Maggie in Hobson's Choice, Haymarket, 1982; Lady Cicely Waynflete in Captain Brassbound's Conversion, Haymarket, 1982; Judith Bliss in Hay Fever, Queen's, 1983; The Dragon's Tail, Apollo, 1985; Miranda, Chichester, 1987; The Deep Blue Sea, Haymarket, 1988; Dear Charles, Yvonne Arnaud, Guildford, 1990; The Merry Wives of Windsor, Chichester, 1990; Lady Bracknell in The Importance of Being Earnest, UK tour, 1991; On Approval, UK tour, 1992; Glyn and It, Richmond, 1994; Monsieur Amilcar, Chichester, 1995; Mrs Warren's Profession, Richmond, 1997; Good Grief, nat. tour, 1998; Star Quality, Apollo, 2001; directed: Relatively Speaking, nat. tour, 1992; How the Other Half Loves, nat. tour, 1994; *film:* The Priest of Love, 1980. Television plays and series include: The Good Life, 1974–77; The Norman Conquests, 1977; To the Manor Born, 1979, 1980 and 1981; Sweet Sixteen, 1983; Moving, 1985; Executive Stress, 1986–88; No Job for a Lady, 1990–92; presenter: What's My Line?, 1988; Growing Places, 1989. Mem., HFEA, 1990–96. Pres., Actors Benevolent Fund, 1990–. Governor: Queen Elizabeth's Foundn for the Disabled, 1989–; Guildford Sch. of Acting, 1991–. Trustee, Yvonne Arnaud Theatre, 1992–. High Sheriff, Surrey, 2002. Awards: BAFTA, 1976 and 1977; SWET, 1976; Variety Club of GB, 1976 and 1979. *Recreations:* gardening, theatre-going. *Address:* c/o London Management, 2–4 Noel Street, W1V 3RB. *T:* (020) 7287 9000.

KEITH, Shona; *see* McIsaac, S.

KELBURN, Viscount of; courtesy title of heir of Earl of Glasgow, not used by current heir.

KELL, Prof. Douglas Bruce, DPhil; FIBiol; Professor of Microbiology, since 1992, and Director of Research, since 1997, Institute of Biological Sciences, University of Wales, Aberystwyth; *b* 7 April 1953; *s* of William Howard Kell and Nancy Kell (*née* Finniston); *m* 1989, Dr Antje Wagner; one *s* two *d*. *Educ:* Bradfield Coll., Berks (Top Schol.); St John's Coll., Oxford (BA Hons Biochem. Upper 2nd Cl. with Dist. in Chem. Pharmacol.; MA, DPhil 1978). FIBiol 1999. UCW, Aberystwyth, then University of Wales, Aberystwyth: SRC Postdoctoral Res. Fellow, 1978–80; SERC Advanced Fellow, 1981–83; New Blood Lectr, 1983–88; Reader, 1988–92. Fleming Lectr, Soc. for Gen. Microbiol., 1986. Founding Director: Aber Instruments, 1988– (Queen's Award for Export Achievement 1998); Aber Genomic Computing, 2000–. Mem. Council, BBSRC, 2000–. *Publications:* numerous scientific pubns. *Recreation:* gazing at landscapes, real and imagined. *Address:* c/o Institute of Biological Sciences, Cledwyn Building, University of Wales, Aberystwyth SY23 3DD. *T:* (01970) 622334; *e-mail:* dbk@aber.ac.uk.

KELLAND, John William, LVO 1977; QPM 1975; Overseas Police Adviser and Inspector General of Dependent Territories' Police, Foreign and Commonwealth Office, 1985–91; *b* 18 Aug. 1929; *s* of William John Kelland and Violet Ethel (*née* Olsen); *m* 1st, 1960, Brenda Nancy (*née* Foulsham) (decd); 2nd, 1986, Frances Elizabeth (*née* Byrne); one step *d*. *Educ:* Sutton High Sch.; Plymouth Polytechnic. FIMgt. RAF, 1947–49. Constable, later Insp., Plymouth City Police, 1950–67; Insp., later Supt, Devon & Cornwall Constabulary, 1968–72; Asst Chief Constable, Cumbria Constabulary, 1972–74; Dir, Sen. Comd Courses, Nat. Police Coll., Bramshill, 1974–75 and 1978–80; Comr, Royal Fiji Police, 1975–78; 1981–85: Management Consultant and Chm., CSSBs; Sen. Consultant, RIPA; Sen. Lectr, Cornwall Coll.; Facilitator, Interpersonal Skills, Cornwall CC Seminars. Mem., Cornwall & Isles of Scilly FHSA, 1992–93. Mem., Royal St George Soc. (Plymouth and W Devon). Chm., Old Suttonian Assoc. *Publications:* various articles in learned jls. *Recreations:* Rugby football, choral singing, wildlife. *Club:* Civil Service.

KELLAS, Arthur Roy Handasyde, CMG 1964; HM Diplomatic Service, retired; High Commissioner in Tanzania, 1972–74; *b* 6 May 1915; *s* of Henry Kellas and Mary Kellas (*née* Brown); *m* 1952, Katharine Bridget, *d* of Sir John Le Rougetel, KCMG, MC; two *s* one *d*. *Educ:* Aberdeen Grammar Sch.; Aberdeen Univ.; Oxford Univ.; Ecole des Sciences Politiques. Passed into Diplomatic Service, Sept. 1939. Commissioned into Border Regt, Nov. 1939. War of 1939–45: Active Service with 1st Bn Parachute Regt and Special Ops, Af. and Gr, 1941–44 (despatches twice). Third Sec. at HM Embassy, Tehran, 1944–47; First Sec. at HM Legation, Helsingfors, 1948–50; First Sec. (press) at HM Embassy, Cairo, 1951–52; First Sec. at HM Embassy, Baghdad, 1954–58; Counsellor, HM Embassy, Tehran, 1958–62; Imperial Defence Coll., 1963–64; Counsellor, HM Embassy and Consul-Gen., Tel Aviv, 1964–65; Ambassador to Nepal, 1966–70, to Democratic Yemen, 1970–72. Pres., Britain-Nepal Soc., 1975–79. *Publications:* Down to Earth (war memoir of parachute subaltern), 1990; Ready Steady Go (pre-war reminiscences), 1999. *Recreations:* reading, reviewing books. *Address:* Inverockle, Achateny, Acharacle, Argyll PH36 4LG. *T:* (01972) 510265. *Club:* Oxford and Cambridge.

KELLAWAY, (Charles) William; Secretary and Librarian, Institute of Historical Research, University of London, 1971–84; *b* 9 March 1926; *s* of late Charles Halliley Kellaway, FRS; *m* 1952, Deborah, *d* of late Sir Hibbert Alan Stephen Newton; one *s* two *d*. *Educ:* Geelong Grammar Sch.; Lincoln Coll., Oxford. BA Modern History, 1949, MA 1955. FLA, FRHistS. Asst Librarian, Guildhall Library, 1950–60; Sub-Librarian, Inst. of Historical Research, 1960–71. Hon. General Editor, London Record Society, 1964–83. *Publications:* The New England Company, 1649–1776, 1961; (ed jtly) Studies in London History, 1969; Bibliography of Historical Works Issued in UK, 1957–70, 3 vols, 1962, 1967, 1972; (ed jtly) The London Assize of Nuisance 1301–1431, 1973. *Address:* 18 Canonbury Square, N1 2AL. *T:* (020) 7354 0349.

KELLAWAY, Richard Edward; Director General, Commonwealth War Graves Commission, since 2000; *b* 13 Aug. 1946; *s* of late Edward John Kellaway and Elsie May Kellaway (*née* Judd); *m* 1968, Ann Clarke; two *d*. *Educ:* Poole Grammar Sch. Commnd as Officer of Customs and Excise, 1966: Sen. Investigation Officer, 1975-79; Principal, VAT Admin, 1979-80; Asst Chief Investigation Officer, 1980-84; Chief Staff Inspector, 1984-87; Head: Customs Dept, Bermuda, 1987-90; Estates and Security, 1990-94; Chief Investigation Officer, 1994-99; on secondment as Drugs and Serious Crime Advr, FCO, 1999-2000. *Recreations:* industrial archaeology, cooking, gardening. *Address:* c/o Commonwealth War Graves Commission, 2 Marlow Road, Maidenhead, Berks SL6 7DX. *T:* (01628) 507152. *Clubs:* Oriental; Automobile de l'Ouest (France).

KELLEHER, Dame Joan, (Joanna), DBE 1965; Hon. ADC to the Queen, 1964–67; Director, Women's Royal Army Corps, 1964–67; *b* 24 Dec. 1915; *d* of late Kenneth George Henderson, barrister-at-law, Stonehaven; *m* 1970, Brig. M. F. H. Kelleher, OBE, MC, late RAMC. *Educ:* privately at home and abroad. Joined ATS, 1941; commissioned ATS, 1941; WRAC, 1949. *Recreations:* golf, gardening.

KELLENBERGER, Dr Jakob; President, International Committee of the Red Cross, since 2000; *b* 19 Oct. 1944; *s* of Jakob and Klara Kellenberger; *m* 1973, Elisabeth Kellenberger-Jossi; two *d*. *Educ:* Univ. of Zurich (DPhil 1975). Joined Swiss Diplomatic Service, 1974: served Madrid, EU (Brussels), London, 1974–84; Hd, Dept for European Integration, Berne, 1984–92 (Minister, 1984–88; Ambassador, 1988–92); State Sec. for Foreign Affairs, Switzerland, 1992–99. *Publications:* Calderón de la Barca und das Komische, 1975; numerous articles, particularly on Swiss–EU relations. *Recreations:* reading (literature, philosophy), cross country ski-ing, jogging, tennis.

KELLER, Prof. Rudolf Ernst, MA Manchester; DrPhil Zürich; Professor of German Language and Medieval German Literature, University of Manchester, 1960–82, now Emeritus; *b* 3 Feb. 1920; *m* 1947, Ivy Sparrow; two *d*. *Educ:* Kantonsschule Winterthur, Switzerland; University of Zürich. Teacher at Kantonsschule Winterthur, 1944–46; Asst, 1946–47, Asst Lecturer, 1947–49, University of Manchester; Lecturer in German, Royal Holloway College, University of London, 1949–52; Sen. Lecturer, 1952–59, Reader in German, 1959–60, Dean of Faculty of Arts, 1968–70, Pro-Vice-Chancellor, 1976–79, University of Manchester. Corresp. Mem., Inst. für deutsche Sprache, 1969; Goethe Medal, 1981. *Publications:* Die Ellipse in der neuenglischen Sprache als semantisch-syntaktisches Problem, 1944; Die Sprachen der Welt, 1955 (trans. Bodmer: The Loom of

Language); German Dialects, Phonology and Morphology with Selected Texts, 1961; The German Language, 1978; articles in learned periodicals. *Recreations:* reading, travel. *Address:* 8 Wadham Way, Hale, Altrincham, Cheshire WA15 9LJ. *T:* (0161) 980 5237.

KELLETT, Sir Stanley Charles, 7th Bt *cr* 1801; *b* 5 March 1940; *s* of Sir Stanley Everard Kellett, 6th Bt, and of Audrey Margaret Phillips; *S* father, 1983; *m* 1st, 1962, Lorraine May (marr. diss. 1968), *d* of F. Winspear; 2nd, 1968, Margaret Ann (marr. diss. 1974), *d* of James W. Bofinger; 3rd, 1982, Catherine Lorna, *d* of W. J. C. Orr; one *d*. *Heir: uncle* Charles Rex Kellett [*b* 1916; *m* 1940, Florence Helen Bellamy (*d* 1984); two *s* one *d*]. *Address:* 58 Glad Gunson Drive, Eleebana, Newcastle, NSW 2280, Australia.

KELLETT-BOWMAN, Edward Thomas; JP; business and management consultant in private practice, since 1974; *b* 25 Feb. 1931; *s* of late R. E. Bowman and M. Bowman (*née* Mathers); *m* 1st, 1960, Margaret Patricia Blakemore (*d* 1970); three *s* one *d*; 2nd, 1971, (Mary) Elaine Kellett (*see* Dame Elaine Kellett-Bowman). *Educ:* Reed's Sch.; Cranfield Inst. of Technol. MBA, DMS, FIMgt. Technical and management trng in textiles, 1951–53; textile management, 1953–55; pharmaceutical man., 1955–72. Mem. (C) Lancs East, European Parlt, 1979–84; contested same seat, 1984; MEP (C) Hampshire Central, Dec. 1988–1994, Itchen, Test and Avon, 1994–99; contested (C) SE Region, 1999. Liveryman, Worshipful Co. of Wheelwrights, 1979; Freeman, City of London, 1978; Hon. Citizen, New Orleans, 1960. JP Middx, 1966. *Recreations:* shooting, tennis, swimming. *Address:* Endymion, Ampfield, Romsey, Hants SO51 9BD.

KELLETT-BOWMAN, Dame (Mary) Elaine, DBE 1988; MA; *b* 8 July 1924; *d* of late Walter Kay; *m* 1st, 1945, Charles Norman Kellett (decd); three *s* one *d*; 2nd, 1971, Edward Thomas Kellett-Bowman, *qv*. *Educ:* Queen Mary Sch., Lytham; The Mount, York; St Anne's Coll., Oxford; Barnett House, Oxford (post-graduate distinction in welfare diploma). Called to Bar, Middle Temple, 1964. Mem., Denbigh BC, 1952–55; Camden Borough Council: Alderman, 1968–74; Vice-Chm., Housing Cttee, 1968; Chm., Welfare Cttee, 1969. Contested (C): Nelson and Colne, 1955; South-West Norfolk, March and Oct. 1959; Buckingham, 1964, 1966. MP (C) Lancaster, 1970–97. Mem. (C) European Parlt, 1975–84 (Mem. for Cumbria, 1979–84); Mem. Social Affairs, Regional Policy and Development Cttees, Europ. Parlt, 1975–84. Lay Mem., Press Council, 1964–68. Pres., Nat. Assoc. of Widows, 1999–. Governor, Culford Sch., 1963–; Mem. Union European Women, 1956; Delegate to Luxemburg, 1958. No 1 Country Housewife, 1960; Christal MacMillan Law Prize, 1963. *Recreation:* gardening. *Address:* Endymion, Ampfield, Romsey, Hants SO51 9BD.

KELLEY, Joan, CB 1987; Member, Official Side Panel, Civil Service Appeal Board, 1987–96; *b* 8 Dec. 1926; *er d* of late George William Kelley and Dora Kelley. *Educ:* Whalley Range High Sch. for Girls, Manchester; London Sch. of Econs and Polit. Science (BScEcon 1947). Europa Publications Ltd, 1948; Pritchard, Wood & Partners Ltd, 1949; joined Civil Service as Econ. Asst in Cabinet Office, 1949; admin. work in Treasury, 1954; Principal, 1956; Asst Sec., 1968; Under Sec., 1979; on secondment to NI Office, 1979–81; Under Sec., 1979–86, Principal Estabt Officer and Principal Finance Officer, 1984–86, HM Treasury. Mem. Council, Univ. of London Inst. of Educn, 1992–98. *Recreations:* gardening, map reading, drinking wine, foreign travel. *Address:* 21 Langland Gardens, NW3 6QE.

KELLEY, Mrs Joanna Elizabeth, OBE 1973; Assistant Director of Prisons (Women), 1967–74; *b* 23 May 1910; *d* of late Lt-Col William Beadon, 51st Sikhs; *m* 1934, Harper Kelley (*d* 1962); no *c*. *Educ:* Hayes Court; Girton Coll., Cambridge (MA). Souschargé, Dept of Pre-History, Musée de l'Homme, Paris, 1934–39; Mixed Youth Club Leader, YWCA, 1939–42; Welfare Officer, Admiralty, Bath, 1942–47; Prison Service, 1947–74; Governor of HM Prison, Holloway, 1959–66. Member: Council, St George's House, Windsor, 1971–77; Redundant Churches Cttee, 1974–79; Scott Holland Trust, 1978–86; Sponsor, YWCA of GB, 1979–. FSA. Hon. Fellow Girton Coll., Cambridge, 1968. Hon. LLD Hull Univ., 1960. *Publications:* When the Gates Shut, 1967; Who Casts the First Stone, 1978. *Recreation:* reading. *Address:* 31 Westmoreland Terrace, SW1V 4AQ.

KELLGREN, Prof. Jonas Henrik, FRCS, FRCP; Professor of Rheumatology, University of Manchester, 1953–76, now Emeritus; Dean, 1970–73; *b* 11 Sept. 1911; *s* of Dr Harry Kellgren and Vera (*née* Dumelunksen); *m* 1942, Thelma Marian Reynolds; four *d*. *Educ:* Bedales Sch.; University Coll., London. MB, BS, 1934; FRCS 1936; FRCP 1951. Junior clinical appointments, University Coll. Hosp., 1934–42 (Beit Memorial Fellow 1938–39); served War, 1942–46, as surgical and orthopædic specialist, RAMC; Mem. Scientific Staff, Med. Research Council, Wingfield Morris Orthopædic Hosp., Oxford, Chronic Rheumatism, University of Manchester, 1947. Pres. Heberden Soc., 1958–59. *Publications:* numerous articles in medical and scientific jls. *Recreation:* landscape painting. *Address:* Beckside Cottage, Rusland, Ulverston, Cumbria LA12 8JY. *T:* (01229) 84244.

KELLNER, family name of **Baroness Ashton of Upholland**.

KELLOCK, Jane Ursula; JP; Member, Council on Tribunals, 1987–93; *b* 21 Oct. 1925; *d* of late Arthur George Symonds and late Gertrude Frances Symonds; *m* 1967, His Honour Thomas Oslaf Kellock (*d* 1993). *Educ:* Priors Field Sch., Godalming. WRNS, 1943–45. Sec., Africa Bureau, London, 1957–67; Editor, Africa Digest, 1957–75; Member: Bd, Commonwealth Development Corporation, 1965–73; Police Complaints Board, 1977–85. Former Mem., S Metropolitan Conciliation Cttee, Race Relations Bd. JP: Inner London, 1968–77; Nottingham City Bench, 1977–91; Inner London (N Westminster), 1992–95. Editor, Commonwealth Judicial Jl, 1985–89. *Recreation:* travel. *Address:* 4 Pound Lane, Dorchester DT1 1LP.

KELLS, Ronald David, OBE 1999; DL; Group Chief Executive, Ulster Bank Ltd, 1994–98, non-executive Director, since 1998; *b* 14 May 1938; *s* of Robert Kells and Frances Elizabeth Kells; *m* 1964, Elizabeth Anne Kells; one *s* one *d*. *Educ:* Bushmills Grammar Sch.; Sullivan Upper Sch.; Queen's Univ., Belfast (BSc Econ). FCIS 1979; FIB 1985. Joined Ulster Bank, 1964; Investments Manager, 1969–76; Dep. Head, Related Banking Services, 1976–79; Head of Planning and Marketing, 1972–82; seconded to National Westminster Bank, 1982–84; Dir and Head, Retail Services (formerly Branch Banking Div.), 1984–94. Chm., Cunningham Coates Ltd, stockbrokers; Non-exec. Director: United Drug Plc, 1999–; Readymix PLC, 1999–. Pres., Confedn of Ulster Socs. Gov., BFI. DL Belfast, 1998. *Recreations:* golf, ski-ing. *Address:* The Moyle, 10 Upper Knockbreda Road, Belfast BT6 9QA. *T:* (028) 9079 7912. *Clubs:* Ulster Reform (Belfast); Royal County Down Golf, Royal Belfast Golf, Portmarnock Golf.

KELLY, Andrew; *see* Kelly, T. A.

KELLY, Prof. Anthony, CBE 1988; DL; FRS 1973; FREng; Life Fellow, Churchill College, Cambridge, 1985; *b* 25 Jan. 1929; *s* of late Group Captain Vincent Gerald French and Mrs Violet Kelly; *m* 1956, Christina Margaret Dunleavie, BA (*d* 1997); three *s* one *d*. *Educ:* Presentation Coll., Reading; Univ. of Reading (Schol.; BSc 1949); Trinity Coll., Cambridge (PhD 1953, ScD 1968). Research Assoc., Univ. of Illinois, 1953–55; ICI Fellow, Univ. of Birmingham, 1955; Asst, Associate Prof., Northwestern Univ., 1956–59; Univ. Lectr, Cambridge, 1959–67; Founding Fellow, Churchill Coll., 1960; Dir of Studies, Churchill Coll., 1960–67; Supt, Div. of Inorganic and Metallic Structure, 1967–69, Dep. Dir, 1969–75, Nat. Physical Lab. (seconded to ICI, 1973–75); Vice-Chancellor, Univ. of Surrey, 1975–94. Univ. Prof., Univ. of Surrey, 1987. Director: Johnson Wax Ltd, 1981–96; QUO-TEC Ltd, 1984–2000; NPL Management Ltd, 1995–; Chm., Surrey Satellite Technology, 1985–95. Vis. Fellow, Univ. of Göttingen, 1960; Vis. Prof., Carnegie Inst. of Technol., 1967; Prof. invité, Ecole Polytechnique Fédérale de Lausanne, 1977. Chm., Jt Standing Cttee on Structural Safety, Instns of Civil and Structural Engrs, 1988–98; Member: SRC Cttee, 1967–72; Council, Inst. of Metals, 1969–74; Council, British Non-Ferrous Metals Res. Assoc., 1970–73; Engrg Materials Requirements Bd, DoI, 1973–75 (Chm., 1976–80); Adv. Cttee, Community Ref. Bureau of EEC, 1973–75. Pres., Inst. of Materials, 1996–97. Mem., Academia Europaea, 1990; Foreign Associate, Nat. Acad. of Engrg of USA, 1986. Lee Kuan Yew Dist. Visitor to Commonwealth of Singapore, 1999. FRSA 1992. DL Surrey, 1993. Hon. FIL 1988; Hon. FIStructE 1996; Hon. FICE 1997. DUniv Surrey, 1994; Hon. DSc Birmingham, 1997. William Hopkins Prize, Cambridge Philosophical Soc., 1967; Beilby Medal, RIC, 1967; A. A. Griffith Medal, 1974, Platinum Medal, 1992, Inst. of Materials; Medal of Excellence, Univ. of Delaware, 1984; Internat. Gold Medal, Amer. Soc. for Materials, 1991; Acta Metallurgica Gold Medal, 2000. KSG 1992. *Publications:* Strong Solids, 1966, 3rd edn (with N. H. Macmillan) 1986; (with G. W. Groves) Crystallography and Crystal Defects, 1970, rev. edn (with P. Kidd) 1999; many papers in jls of physical sciences. *Recreations:* science of materials, sailing. *Address:* 29 Madingley Road, Cambridge CB3 0EG. *Clubs:* Oxford and Cambridge; Island Sailing (Cowes).

KELLY, Barbara Mary, CBE 1992; DL; Chairman, Architects Registration Board, since 1997; *b* 27 Feb. 1940; *d* of John Maxwell Prentice and Barbara Bain Adam; *m* 1960, Kenneth Archibald Kelly; one *s* two *d* (and two *s* decd). *Educ:* Dalbeattie High Sch.; Kirkcudbright Academy; Moray House Coll., Edinburgh. DipEd. Partner in mixed farming enterprise. Dir, Clydesdale Bank, 1994–98; Member: Scottish Adv. Bd, BP plc, 1990–; Scottish Adv. Bd, BT plc; Scottish PO Bd, 1997–. Chairman: Area Manpower Bd, MSC, 1987–88; Scottish Consumer Council, 1985–90; Rural Forum, 1988–92 (Hon. Pres., 1992–99); Training 2000, 1991–97; Member: Nat. Consumer Council, 1985–90; Scottish Enterprise Bd, 1990–95; Priorities Bd, MAFF, 1990–95; BBC Rural Affairs and Agric. Adv. Cttee, 1991–97; Scottish Econ. Council, 1991–98; Scottish Tourist Bd, 1993–97; Rathbone Community Industry Bd, 1993–98; Scottish Nat. Heritage Bd, 1995–; BBC Broadcasting Council for Scotland, 1997–; Comr, EOC, 1991–95. Convener, Millennium Forest for Scotland Trust, 1995–. Nat. Vice-Chm., Scottish Women's Rural Insts, 1983–86. Hon. Pres., Scottish Conservation Projects Trust. Chm., Scottish Adv. Cttee, and Mem., Nat. Adv. Cttee, Duke of Edinburgh's Award Scheme, 1980–85. Trustee: Scottish Community (formerly Caledonian) Foundn, 1995–; Strathclyde Foundn, 1997–; Crichton Foundn, 1999–. DL Dumfries, 1998. Hon. LLD: Strathclyde, 1995; Aberdeen, 1997. *Recreations:* home and family, music, painting, the pursuit of real food, gardening of necessity. *Address:* Barncleugh, Irongray, Dumfries DG2 9SE. *T:* (01387) 730210.

KELLY, Rt Hon. Sir Basil; *see* Kelly, Rt Hon. Sir J. W. B.

KELLY, Brian; *see* Kelly, H. B.

KELLY, Charles Henry, CBE 1986; QPM 1978; DL; Chief Constable of Staffordshire, 1977–96; *b* 15 July 1930; *s* of Charles Henry Kelly and Phoebe Jane Kelly; *m* 1952, Doris (*née* Kewley) (*d* 1999); one *s* one *d*. *Educ:* Douglas High Sch. for Boys, IOM; London Univ. LLB (Hons). Asst Chief Constable of Essex, 1972; Dep. Chief Constable of Staffordshire, 1976. Associate Prof., Criminal Justice Dept, Michigan State Univ., 1990–2000. Pres., Staffordshire Small Bore Rifle Assoc., 1977–96; Chairman: Staffordshire Police St John Special Centre, 1978–96; ACPO Communications Cttee, 1982–92; No 3 Region, ACPO Cttee, 1985–93. Pres., Stafffordshire Soc., 1997–99. Mem. Court, Keele Univ., 1990–. MUniv Keele, 1991; Hon. LLD Staffordshire Univ., 1996. DL Stafford, 1979. KStJ 1991 (County Pres., Staffordshire, 1996–). *Recreations:* cricket, reading, walking. *Address:* c/o Chief Constable's Office, Cannock Road, Stafford ST17 0QG. *T:* (01785) 257717. *Club:* Special Forces.

KELLY, Sir Christopher (William), KCB 2001; Chairman, National Society for the Prevention of Cruelty to Children, since 2002; *b* 18 Aug. 1946; *s* of late Reginald and of Peggy Kelly; *m* 1970, Alison Mary Collens Durant; two *s* one *d*. *Educ:* Beaumont College; Trinity College, Cambridge (MA); Manchester University (MA (Econ)). HM Treasury, 1970; Private Sec. to Financial Sec., 1971–73; Sec. to Wilson Cttee of Inquiry into Financial Instns, 1978–80; Under Sec., 1987–97; Dir of Fiscal and Monetary Policy, 1994–95; Dir of Budget and Public Finances, 1995; Hd of Policy Gp, DSS, 1995–97; Permanent Sec., DoH, 1997–2000. Mem. Bd, NCC. Gov., Acland Burghley Sch., 1991–98. *Recreations:* narrow-boating, swimming. *Address:* 22 Croftdown Road, NW5 1EH.

KELLY, Sir David (Robert Corbett), Kt 1996; CBE 1991; Chairman, Kelly Packaging Limited, 1962–99 (Managing Director, 1962–85); Chairman, Conservative Party Committee on Candidates, 1995–2000; *b* 10 Dec. 1936; *s* of late Col R. C. Kelly, TD, DL, JP and of Jean Haswell Kelly (*née* Bowran), JP; *m* 1969, Angela Frances Taylor; four *d*. *Educ:* Sedbergh; St John's Coll., Cambridge (Lamor Award; MA). Farm labourer, 1955–56; Nat. Service, 2nd Lt, 2nd Bn, 7th DEO Gurkha Rifles, 1960–61; 17th (later 4th) Bn, Parachute Regt (9 DLI), TA, 1962–69 (Major); Mil. Mem., TA&VRA for N of England, 1969–75. Board Member: Regl Bd, Brit. Technol. Gp, 1980–84; Northumbrian Water Authy, 1983–89; Washington Develt Corp., 1984–88; NE Industrial Develt Bd, 1989–97. Chm., NE Reg., 1966–67, Industrial Relns Cttee, 1968–71, British Box and Packaging Assoc. Confederation of British Industry: Member: Smaller Firms Council, 1977–83; Regl Council, 1979–86; Council, 1981–83; Industrial Policy Cttee, 1981–83; Mem., Lord Chancellor's Adv. Cttee on Tax Comrs, Tyne and Wear, 1981–93. Hon. Advr, Govt-Enterprise Communications Unit, Dept of Politics, Newcastle Univ., 1991–93. Contested (C) Gateshead W, 1979. Chm., Northern Area Conservatives, 1990–93; Vice Pres., 1992–95, Pres., 1995–96, Nat. Union of Cons. and Unionist Assocs; Chm., Cons. Pty Conf., 1995; Chm. Trustees, Cons. Agents Benevolent Fund, 2000–; Trustee, Cons. Agents Superannuation Fund, 2000–. Mem., Gateshead CHC, 1975–77. President: Gateshead Dispensary Housing Assoc., 1992– (Chm., 1982–92 and 1993–); Craigielea Community Nursing Home, 1992– (Chm., 1988–92, 1993–); Chm., Gateshead Dispensary Trust, 1999– (Trustee, 1965–); Trustee, Northbrian Educnl Trust, 1981– (Chm., 1983–93). Exec. Vice Chm., SCF Newcastle City Appeal, 1996–98, Patron, Spirit of Enterprise Appeal, 1997–. Chm. Govs, Westfield Sch., 1983–93. *Recreations:* family, country pursuits, theatre, light adventure (Mount Kilimanjaro, 1994). *Address:* Stanton Fence, Morpeth, Northumberland NE65 8PP. *T:* (01670) 772236. *Club:* Northern Counties (Newcastle upon Tyne).

KELLY, Edward Ronald; journalist and trout farmer; *b* 14 Oct. 1928; *s* of late William Walter Kelly and of Millicent Kelly; *m* 1954, Storm Massada. *Educ:* Honiton Sch. Journalist: Bath Evening Chronicle, 1952; East African Standard, 1953; Sunday Post,

Kenya, 1954; Reuters, 1956; Central Office of Information, 1958–: Editor in Chief, Overseas Press Services Div., 1964; Asst Overseas Controller, 1968; Dir, Publications and Design Services Div., 1970; Home Controller, 1976; Overseas Controller, 1978–84. Chm., Assoc. of Stillwater Game Fishery Managers, 1993–96. *Recreations:* fishing, fly-tying, carpentry. *Address:* Windover House, Runcton Lane, Runcton, near Chichester, West Sussex PO20 6PT. *T:* (01243) 783069. *Club:* Flyfishers'.

KELLY, Prof. Francis Patrick, (Frank), FRS 1989; Professor of the Mathematics of Systems, University of Cambridge, since 1990; Fellow of Christ's College, Cambridge, since 1976; *b* 28 Dec. 1950; *s* of Francis Kelly and Margaret Kelly (*née* McFadden); *m* 1972, Jacqueline Pullin; two *s*. *Educ:* Cardinal Vaughan Sch.; Van Mildert Coll., Durham (BSc 1971); Emmanuel Coll., Cambridge (Knight Prize 1975; PhD 1976). Operational Research Analyst, Scicon, 1971–72; Cambridge University: Asst Lectr in Op. Res., Faculty of Engineering, 1976–78; Lectr in Statistical Lab., 1978–86; Reader in Faculty of Maths, 1986–90; Dir, Statistical Lab., 1991–93; variously Research Fellow, Dir of Studies, Tutor, Mem. College Council and Investments Cttee, Christ's Coll., 1976–. Chm., Lyndewode Research Ltd, 1987–. Clifford Paterson Lectr, Royal Soc., 1995; Blackett Lectr, ORS, 1996. Rollo Davidson Prize, Cambridge Univ., 1979; Guy Medal in Silver, Royal Statistical Soc., 1989; Lanchester Prize, ORS of Amer., 1992; Naylor Prize, London Math. Soc., 1996. *Publications:* Reversibility and Stochastic Networks, 1979; (ed) Probability, Statistics and Optimization, 1994; (ed jtly) Stochastic Networks, 1995; Mathematical Models in Finance, 1995; Stochastic Networks: theory and application, 1996; articles in math. and stat. jls. *Recreations:* golf, ski-ing. *Address:* Statistical Laboratory, Wilberforce Road, Cambridge CB3 0WB. *T:* (01223) 337963.

KELLY, Graham; *see* Kelly, R. H. G.

KELLY, Air Vice-Marshal (Herbert) Brian, CB 1983; LVO 1960; MD, FRCP; RAF, retired; *b* 12 Aug. 1921; *s* of late Surg. Captain James Cecil Kelly and of Meta Matheson (*née* Fraser). *Educ:* Epsom Coll.; St Thomas' Hosp. (MB, BS 1943, MD 1948). MRCP 1945, FRCP 1968; DCH 1966; MFOM 1982. House appts, St Thomas' Hosp., and St Luke's Hosp., Guildford, 1943–45; RNVR, Med. Specialist, RNH Hong Kong, 1945–48; Med. Registrar and Lectr in Medicine, St Thomas' Hosp., 1948–53; joined RAF Medical Br., 1953; Consultant in Medicine at RAF Hosps, Aden, Ely, Nocton Hall, Singapore, Cyprus, Germany, 1953–83; Consultant Adviser in Medicine to RAF, 1974, Senior Consultant, 1979–83. QHS 1978–83. Consultant, CAA, 1974–93. FRSocMed. Liveryman, Worshipful Soc. of Apothecaries, 1978; Freeman, City of London, 1978. *Publications:* papers in BMJ, Lancet, Brit. Heart Jl, and Internat. Jl of Epidemiology. *Recreation:* choir singing. *Address:* 32 Chiswick Quay, Hartington Road, W4 3UR. *T:* (020) 8995 5042; *e-mail:* b-kelly@dircon.co.uk. *Club:* Royal Air Force.

KELLY, Iain Charles MacDonald; HM Diplomatic Service; Ambassador and Consul General, Belarus, since 1999; *b* 5 March 1949; *s* of Walter John Kelly and Doreen Sylvia Wilkins; *m* 1981, Linda Clare McGovern; two *s* (and one *s* decd). *Educ:* Cathays High Sch. for Boys; UCW, Aberystwyth (BSc Econs); UCL (Dip Lib 1974). Joined HM Diplomatic Service, 1974; Russian Wing, Army Sch. of Languages, 1975–76; Moscow, 1976–79; Kuala Lumpur, 1979–82; Istanbul, 1986–88; Los Angeles, 1990–92; Moscow, 1992–95; Amsterdam, 1995–98; Sen. Mem., Jesus Coll., Oxford, 1998–99. FRGS 1999. *Recreations:* early music, privacy. *Address:* c/o Foreign and Commonwealth Office, SW1A 2AH. *T:* (020) 7270 3000. *Clubs:* Oriental, Highland Soc. of London.

KELLY, John Philip, CMG 2000; LVO 1994; MBE 1984; HM Diplomatic Service, retired; Governor, Turks and Caicos Islands, 1996–2000; *b* 25 June 1941; *s* of William Kelly and Norah Kelly (*née* Roche); *m* 1964, Jennifer Anne Buckler; one *s*. *Educ:* Oatlands Coll., Stillorgan, Dublin. Joined Foreign Office, 1959; Leopoldville, 1962–65; Cairo, 1965–68; Bonn, 1968–70; FCO, 1970–73; Canberra, 1973–77; Antwerp, 1977–78; FCO, 1978–81; seconded to Dept of Trade, 1981; Grenada, 1982–86; FCO, 1986–89; Dep. Gov., Bermuda, 1989–94; FCO, 1994–96. *Recreations:* golf, walking, reading. *Address:* The Laurels, 56 Garden Lane, Royston, Herts SG8 9EH.

KELLY, Rt Hon. Sir (John William) Basil, Kt 1984; PC 1984; PC (NI) 1969; a Lord Justice of Appeal, Supreme Court of Judicature, Northern Ireland, 1984–95; a Judge of the High Court of Justice in Northern Ireland, 1973–84; *b* 1920; *o s* of late Thomas William Kelly and late Emily Frances (*née* Donaldson); *m* 1957, Pamela, *o d* of late Thomas Colmer and Marjorie Colthurst. *Educ:* Methodist Coll., Belfast; Trinity Coll., Dublin. BA (Mod.) Legal Science, 1943; LLB (Hons) 1944. Called to Bar: of Northern Ireland, 1944; Middle Temple, 1970; QC (N Ireland) 1958. MP (U) Mid-Down, Parliament of Northern Ireland, 1964–72; Attorney-Gen. for Northern Ireland, 1968–72. Chairman: Council of Legal Educn, NI, 1989–93; Judicial Studies Bd, NI, 1993–95; Mem., Law Adv. Cttee, British Council, 1982–92. *Recreations:* golf, music.

KELLY, Joseph Anthony; Editorial Director, Gabriel Communications, since 1998; Editor, The Universe, since 1995; *b* 10 Aug. 1958; *s* of Terence Christopher Kelly and Catherine Ethel Kelly (*née* Walsh); *m* 1999, Catherine Jane, *d* of William and Margaret Brownlie. *Educ:* Presentation Coll., Reading; Ruskin Coll., Oxford. Associate, Instn of Buyers, 1980. Sen. Buyer, Church & Co., Reading, 1979–81; Buyer, J. Sainsbury, Reading, 1981–82; freelance photo-journalist, 1984–91; Editor: Welsh Arts Council Lit. Rev., 1991–94; Deeside Midweek Leader, 1991–92; Dep. Editor, Wrexham Leader, 1992–93; Ed., Country Quest (mag. for Wales), 1993; Dep. Ed., The Universe, 1994; Ed., Catholic Life Mag., 1995, 1998–. Chm., NW Region, Soc. of Editors, 1999. Gov., RNLI, 1997–. Photo-journalism Award, Irish Post, 1981. *Publications:* From Sulham Head, Collected Poems, 1980; The Pendulum, 1982. *Recreations:* hill-walking, ecclesiastical history, photography. *Address:* c/o Gabriel Communications Ltd, 1st Floor, St James's Buildings, Oxford Street, Manchester M1 6FP. *T:* (office) (0161) 236 8856.

KELLY, Judith Pamela, (Mrs M. Bird), OBE 1997; Artistic Director, since 1988, Chief Executive, since 1993, West Yorkshire Playhouse; *b* 24 March 1954; *d* of John Kelly and Ida Kelly; *m* 1993, Michael Bird (known professionally as Michael Birch); one *s* one *d*. *Educ:* Calder High Sch.; Birmingham Univ. (BA 2nd Cl. Hons). Freelance singer (folk and jazz), 1970–75; actress, Leicester Phoenix Theatre, 1975–76; Founder Dir, Solent People's Theatre, 1976–80; Artistic Dir, Battersea Arts Centre, 1980–85; Dir of Plays, Nat. Theatre of Brent, 1982–85; freelance dir, 1986–88; Festival Dir, York Fest. and Mystery Plays, 1986–88. Major productions include: West Yorkshire Playhouse: Merchant of Venice, 1994; Beatification of Area Boy, 1996 (also NY and Eur. tour); The Seagull, The Tempest, 1998; Singin' in the Rain, 1999 (also RNT, 2000; Olivier Award, 2001); Half a Sixpence, 2000; Sarcophagus, RSC, 1986; When We Are Married, Chichester Fest. Th., transf. Savoy, 1996; Othello, Shakespeare Th., Washington, 1997; The Elixir of Love, ENO, 1997. British Rep. on culture for UNESCO, 1997–. Chair: Common Purpose Charitable Trust, 1997–; QCA, 2001. Vice-Chm., Nat. Adv. Cttee on Creative and Cultural Educn, 1998; Member: Council, RSA, 1998–; ITC, 1999–. Hon. Fellow, Dartington Coll. of Arts, 1999. Hon. DLitt: Leeds Metropolitan, 1995; Bradford, 1996; Hon. Dr Leeds, and York, 2000; DUniv Open, 2001. *Recreation:* wind-surfing. *Address:* West Yorkshire Playhouse, Playhouse Square, Quarry Hill, Leeds LS2 7UP. *T:* (0113) 213 7800.

KELLY, Laurence Charles Kevin; non-executive Director, 1972–93, and Vice-Chairman, 1988–93, Helical Bar PLC (Deputy Chairman, 1981–84; Chairman, 1984–88); *b* 11 April 1933; *s* of late Sir David Kelly, GCMG, MC, and Lady Kelly (*née* Jourda de Vaux); *m* 1963, (Alison) Linda McNair Scott; one *s* two *d*. *Educ:* Downside Sch.; New Coll., Oxford (Beresford Hope Schol.; MA Hons); Harvard Business Sch. Lieut, The Life Guards, 1949–52; served (temp.) Foreign Office, 1955–56; Guest, Keen and Nettlefolds, 1956–72; Director: GKN International Trading Ltd, 1972–77; Morganite International Ltd, 1984–91; KAE, subseq. Mintel, Ltd, 1980–; Chm., Queenborough Steel Co., 1980–89. Member: Northern Ireland Development Agency, 1972–78; Monopolies and Mergers Commn, 1982–89. Chairman, Opera da Camera Ltd (charity), 1981–87; Trustee, Choir of Carmelite Priory, Kensington (charity), 1997–. Vice-Chm., British Iron and Steel Consumers' Council, 1976–85. Sen. Associate Mem., St Antony's Coll., Oxford, 1985–91. FRGS 1972. *Publications:* Lermontov, Tragedy in the Caucasus, 1978 (Cheltenham Literary Prize, 1979); St Petersburg, a Travellers' Anthology, 1981; Moscow, a Travellers' Anthology, 1983; Istanbul, a Travellers' Anthology, 1987; (with Linda Kelly) Proposals, 1989; Diplomacy and Murders in Teheran: Alexander Griboyedov and Imperial Russia's mission to the Shah of Persia, 2001; reviews, TLS, etc. *Recreation:* opera-going. *Address:* 44 Ladbroke Grove, W11 2PA. *T:* (020) 7727 4663; Lorton Hall, Low Lorton, near Cockermouth, Cumbria CA13 9UP. *T:* (01900) 85252. *Clubs:* Beefsteak, Brooks's, Turf; Kildare Street and University (Dublin).

KELLY, Dame Lorna (May) B.; *see* Boreland-Kelly.

KELLY, Mandi; *see* Norwood, M.

KELLY, Matthias John; QC 1999; *b* 21 April 1954; *s* of Ambrose and Annie Kelly; *m* 1979, Helen Holmes; one *s* one *d*. *Educ:* St Patrick's Acad., Dungannon; Trinity Coll., Dublin (BA Mod., LLB). Called to the Bar, Gray's Inn, 1979; in practice as Barrister, 1979–; called to Irish Bar, Belfast and Dublin, 1983; admitted Attorney: NY Bar, 1986; US Federal Bar, 1987; Consultant to EU Commn on UK Health and Safety Law, 1994–96. Vice-Chm., Personal Injuries Bar Assoc., 1999–; Mem., Bar Council (England and Wales), 1998– (Chm., Public Affairs Gp, 2001–; Chm., Policy Gp, 2000). Chairman: End the Vagrancy Act Campaign, 1989–93; Alcohol Recovery Project, 1993–96. FRSocMed 1997. *Publications:* (ed jtly) Personal Injury Manual, 1997, 2001; (contrib.) Munkman Employer's Liability, 2001. *Recreations:* walking, reading, theatre, travel. *Address:* Old Square Chambers, 1 Verulam Buildings, Gray's Inn, WC1R 5LQ. *T:* (020) 7269 0300.

KELLY, Dr Michael, CBE 1983; JP; DL; Managing Director, Michael Kelly Associates, since 1984; Chairman, Children 1st (formerly Royal Scottish Society for the Prevention of Cruelty to Children), 1987–96; *b* 1 Nov. 1940; *s* of David and Marguerite Kelly; *m* 1965, Zita Harkins; one *s* two *d*. *Educ:* Univ. of Strathclyde (BSc(Econ), PhD). FCIM (FInstM 1988). Asst Lectr in Economics, Univ. of Aberdeen, 1965–67; Lectr in Economics, Univ. of Strathclyde, 1967–84. Councillor: Anderston Ward Corp. of Glasgow, 1971–75 (Convener, Schools and Sch. Welfare; Vice-Convener, Transport); Hillington Ward, Glasgow Dist, 1977–84 (Chairman: General Purposes Cttee; Buildings and Property Cttee); Lord Provost of Glasgow, 1980–84 (masterminded "Glasgow's Miles Better" Campaign); Campaign Dir, Edinburgh—Count Me In, 1987–89. Rector, Univ. of Glasgow, 1984–87. Dir, Celtic Football Club, 1990–94. Mem., Scottish Cttee, NACF, 1990–93; ESRC Media Relns Cttee, 2000–. Founding Editor, Jl Economic Studies, 1965. Columnist, Scotsman, 1996–. BBC Radio Scotland News Quiz Champion, 1986, 1987. Presenter, Clyde 2 Talk-In, 1997–. Hon. Mem., Clan Donald, USA; Hon. Mayor, Tombstone, Ariz; Hon. Citizen: Illinois; San José; St Petersburg; Kansas City; Dallas; Fort Worth; Winnipeg. JP Glasgow 1973; DL Glasgow 1984. Hon. LLD Glasgow, 1984. Glasgow Herald Scot of the Year, 1983. OStJ 1983. *Publications:* Studies in the British Coal Industry, 1970; Paradise Lost: the struggle for Celtic's soul, 1994; London Lines, 1996. *Recreations:* photography, ski-ing, golf, philately. *Address:* 50 Aytoun Road, Glasgow G41 5HE. *T:* (0141) 427 1627. *Club:* New (Edinburgh).

KELLY, Prof. Michael Joseph, FRS 1993; FREng; FInstP, FIEE; Head of Advanced Technology Institute, and Director, Centre for Solid State Electronics, University of Surrey, since 2001; *b* New Plymouth, NZ, 14 May 1949; *s* of late Steve and Mary Constance Kelly; *m* 1991, Ann Elizabeth Taylor, BA, *d* of Dr Daniel Brumhall Cochrane Taylor, *qv*; one *d*. *Educ:* Francis Douglas Meml Coll., New Plymouth, NZ; Victoria Univ. of Wellington (BSc Hons 1970; MSc 1971); Gonville and Caius Coll., Univ. of Cambridge (PhD 1974); Trinity Hall, Cambridge (MA 1975; ScD 1994). FInstP 1988; FIEE 1989; FREng (FEng 1998). Fellow, Trinity Hall, Cambridge, 1974–81, 1989–92; IBM Res. Fellow, Univ. of Calif., Berkeley, 1975–76; SRC Advanced Fellow, Cavendish Lab., 1977–81; Mem., Research Staff, GEC Hirst Res. Centre, 1981–92, Co-ordinator, GEC Superlattice Res., 1984–92; University of Surrey: Prof. of Physics and Electronics, 1992–96; Hd of Dept of Electronic and Electrical Engrg, 1996; Hd of Sch. of Electronic Engrg, Inf. Technol. and Maths, then Sch. of Electronics, Computing and Maths, 1997–2001. Vis. Scientist, Cavendish Lab., 1988–92; Royal Soc./SERC Industrial Fellow, 1989–91; Erskine Fellow, Univ. of Canterbury, NZ, 1999. Non-exec. Dir, Surrey Satellite Technol. Ltd, 1997–. Member Council: Univ. of Surrey, 1996–; Inst. of Physics, 1997–2001. Hon. FRSNZ 1999. Royal Soc. Rutherford Meml Lectr, NZ, 2000. Paterson Medal and Prize, Inst. of Physics, 1989; GEC Nelson Gold Medal, 1991; Silver Medal, Royal Acad. Engrg, 1999. *Publications:* (ed jtly) The Physics and Fabrication of Microstructures and Microdevices, 1986; Low Dimensional Semiconductors, 1995; numerous papers and review articles on semiconductor physics-for-devices in scientific jls. *Recreations:* music, literature. *Address:* School of Electronics, Computing and Mathematics, University of Surrey, Guildford, Surrey GU2 4XH. *T:* (01483) 259410.

KELLY, Owen, QPM 1987; Commissioner of Police for City of London, 1985–93; *b* 10 April 1932; *s* of Owen Kelly and Anna Maria (*née* Hamill); *m* 1957, Sheila Ann (*née* McCarthy); five *s*. *Educ:* St Modan's High School, St Ninians, Stirlingshire. National Service, RAF, 1950–52; Metropolitan Police in all ranks from Police Constable to Commander, 1953–82; Asst and Dep. to Comr of Police for City of London, 1982–85; created secure zone in City of London (Ring of Steel) for prevention of terrorist activity, July 1993, and scheme continues. 18th Senior Command Course, Nat. Police Coll., 1981; Mem., 14th Session of Nat. Exec. Inst., FBI, USA, 1991. Mem., Police Disciplinary Appeals Bd, Home Office, 1994–2000. Hon. Sec., Chief Constables' Club, 1989–93. Chm., City of London Br., Leukaemia Res. Fund, 1985–93. Freeman, City of London, 1984. CStJ 1987 (OStJ 1986). Commendation, Order of Civil Merit, Spain, 1986; Ordre du Wissam Alouite Class III, Morocco, 1987; Ordre du Mérite, Senegal, 1988; Ordem do Merito, Class III (Portugal), 1993. *Publications:* contrib. Police Review and Policing. *Recreations:* enjoying the society of a large family, do-it-yourself house and car maintenance, reading.

KELLY, Most Rev. Patrick Altham; *see* Liverpool, Archbishop of, (RC).

KELLY, Peter (John); Under-Secretary for Atomic Energy, United Kingdom Department of Energy, 1980–82; *b* 26 Nov. 1922; *s* of Thomas and Lucy Kelly; *m* 1949,

Gudrun Kelly (*née* Falck); two *s* three *d* (and one *s* decd). *Educ:* Downside; Oxford Univ. (BA). RNVR, 1942–46. 3rd Secretary, Moscow Embassy, 1948–49; journalism, 1950; rejoined public service, 1956; posts in Foreign Office, Defence Dept, Dept of Trade and Industry; Asst Secretary for Internat. Atomic Affairs, 1969–71; Counsellor, Office of UK Permanent Representative to the European Communities, Brussels, 1972–75; Director, Internat. Energy Agency, 1976–79. *Publication:* Safeguards in Europe, 1985. *Recreations:* walking, music. *Address:* 2 The Crouch, Seaford, Sussex BN25 1PX. *T:* (01323) 896881.

KELLY, Philip Charles; Director of Resources and Chief Finance Officer (formerly City Treasurer), Liverpool City Council, 1986–2000; Treasurer, Merseyside Fire and Civil Defence Authority, since 1986; *b* 23 Aug. 1948; *s* of late Charles and of Irene May Kelly; *m* 1971, Pamela (*née* Fagan); one *s* two *d*. *Educ:* Inst. of Science and Technology, Univ. of Wales (BSc Econ). DipM; CIPFA. Market Research, British Steel Corp., 1970–72; Economist, Coventry City Council, 1972–74; Technical Officer, 1974–78, Asst Dir of Finance, 1978–82, Kirklees MDC; Dep. City Treasurer, Liverpool CC, 1982–86. *Recreation:* family. *Address:* Fire Service HQ, Hatton Garden, Liverpool L3 2AD.

KELLY, Philip John; journalist and political consultant; Director, Butler Kelly Ltd, since 1998; *b* 18 Sept. 1946; *s* of late William Kelly and of Mary Winifred Kelly; *m* 1988, Dorothy Margaret Jones; two *s*. *Educ:* St Mary's Coll., Crosby; Leeds Univ. (BA Hons Politics). Freelance journalist and PR consultant, 1970–87; Editor, Tribune, 1987–91; Press Officer to Michael Meacher, MP, 1991–92. Dir, Grandfield Public Affairs, 1995–98. Co-Founder: Leveller, 1976; State Research, 1977; Chair, London Freelance Br., NUJ, 1983. Councillor (Lab) London Borough of Islington, 1984–86, 1990–98 (Chm., Educn Cttee, 1993–97; Dep. Leader, 1997–98). Contested (Lab) Surrey SW, 1992. *Recreations:* railways, model railways, Arsenal FC. *Address:* 56 Windsor Road, N7 6JL. *T:* (020) 7932 2410; *e-mail:* philk@butlerkellyltd.co.uk. *Club:* Red Rose.

KELLY, (Robert Henry) Graham, FCIS; writer and broadcaster; Chief Executive/General Secretary of the Football Association, 1989–98; *b* 23 Dec. 1945; *s* of Thomas John Kelly and Emmie Kelly; *m* 1st, 1970, Elizabeth Anne Wilkinson (marr. diss. 1996); one *s* one *d*; 2nd, 1999, Romayne Armstrong. *Educ:* Baines Grammar Sch., Poulton-le-Fylde. FCIS 1973. Barclays Bank, 1964–68; Football League, 1968–88, Sec., 1979–88. Trustee, Football Grounds Improvement Trust, 1985–88.

KELLY, Rosaline; publishing and industrial relations consultant; Visiting Lecturer in Journalism, London College of Printing, since 1981; *b* 27 Nov. 1922; *d* of Laurence Kelly and Ellen (*née* Fogarty), Drogheda, Co. Louth, Eire. *Educ:* St Louis Convent, Carrickmacross; University Coll., Dublin, NUI. Journalist with Woman magazine, 1958–77; local management, IPC Magazines Ltd, 1977–80. Active in NUJ, 1958–: Mem., National Exec. Council, 1972–78; first woman Pres., 1975–77; Membership of Honour, 1979; Member: NUJ Appeals Tribunal, 1978–; NUJ Standing Orders Cttee, 1978–; Trustee, NUJ Provident Fund Management Cttee, 1977–97 (Chairperson, 1980–82). Mem., Press Council, 1977–80 (first woman to represent Press side). Has been rejected as a catalogue holder by Empire Stores. *Recreations:* language and languages, music, compulsive reader. *Address:* c/o Robert Fleming & Co. Ltd, Hexagon House, 28 Western Road, Romford RM1 3LB; Arash Areesh, 7 Lakeview Road, Wicklow, Eire. *T:* (404) 69596.

KELLY, Ruth Maria, MP (Lab) Bolton West, since 1997; Economic Secretary, HM Treasury, since 2001; *b* 9 May 1968; *d* of Bernard James Kelly and Gertrude Anne Kelly (*née* Murphy); *m* 1996, Derek John Gadd; one *s* two *d*. *Educ:* Queen's Coll., Oxford (BA PPE); London School of Economics (MSc Econs). Economics Writer, The Guardian, 1990–94; Bank of England: Dep. Head, Inflation Report Div., 1994–96; Manager, Special Projects Div., 1997. PPS to Minister of Agric., Fisheries and Food, 1998–2001. Mem., Treasury Select Cttee, 1997–98. *Recreations:* walking, family. *Address:* House of Commons, SW1A 0AA.

KELLY, Susan; *see* Hamilton, S.

KELLY, (Thomas) Andrew; QC 2000; *b* 18 July 1955; *s* of John Kelly and Mary Rea Kelly (*née* McKelvey). *Educ:* Bangor Grammar Sch., NI; Christ Church, Oxford (MA). Called to the Bar: Lincoln's Inn, 1978; NI, 1982; in practice at the Bar, 1981–; res. asst, H of C, 1981–84. *Recreations:* sports, arts, travel, Bristol motor cars, silver, gardening. *Address:* 2 Harcourt Buildings, Temple, EC4Y 9DB. *T:* (020) 7353 8415. *Clubs:* Royal Automobile, Queen's.

KELNER, Simon; Editor-in-Chief, The Independent, since 1998; *b* 9 Dec. 1957; *m* 1988, Karen Bowden (marr. diss. 2001); one *d*. *Educ:* Bury Grammar Sch.; Preston Poly. Trainee reporter, Neath Guardian, 1976–79; sports reporter, Extel, 1979–80; Sports Ed., Kent Evening Post, 1980–83; Asst Sports Ed., Observer, 1983–86; Dep. Sports Ed., Independent, 1986–89; Sports Editor: Sunday Correspondent, 1989–90; Observer, 1990–91; Ed., Observer Mag., 1991–93; Sports Ed., Independent on Sunday, 1993–95; Night Ed., 1995, Features Ed., 1995–96, Independent; Ed., Night & Day mag., Mail on Sunday, 1996–98. Hon. Fellow, Univ. of Central Lancashire, 1999. Ed. of the Year, What the Papers Say Awards, 1999; Edgar Wallace Award, London Press Club, 2000. *Publication:* To Jerusalem and Back, 1996. *Address:* The Independent, Independent House, 191 Marsh Wall, E14 9RS. *Clubs:* Groucho; Swinton Rugby League Supporters.

KELSALL, John Arthur Brooks, MA; Headmaster, Brentwood School, Essex, since 1993; *b* 18 June 1943; *o s* of Joseph Brooks Kelsall and Dorothy Kelsall (*née* Bee); *m* 1965, Dianne Scott Woodward, *o d* of Rev. William James Vaughan Woodward and Jean Ewart Woodward; one *s* one *d*. *Educ:* Royal Grammar Sch., Lancaster; Emmanuel Coll., Cambridge (BA 1965; MA 1969). Head of Economics, King Edward VII Sch., Lytham St Annes, 1965–68; Head of Geography, Whitgift Sch., Croydon, 1968–78; Dep. Headmaster, 1978–81, Headmaster, 1981–87, Bournemouth Sch.; Headmaster, Arnold Sch., Blackpool, 1987–93. Vis. Headmaster, RAF Scholarship Board, RAF Cranwell, 1990–. *Recreations:* golf, fell-walking, opera, ornithology. *Address:* Brentwood School, Essex CM15 8AS. *T:* (01277) 243201. *Clubs:* East India; Royal Lytham St Annes Golf; Thorndon Park Golf.

KELSALL, William, OBE 1971; QPM 1969; DL; Chief Constable of Cheshire, 1974–77; retired; *b* 10 Jan. 1914. DL Cheshire, 1979. CStJ 1983. *Address:* Three Keys Cottage, Quarry Bank, Utkinton, Tarporley, Cheshire CW6 0LA. *T:* (01829) 732328.

KELSEY, Maj.-Gen. John, CBE 1968; Director, Wild Heerbrugg (UK) Ltd, 1978–87; Director of Military Survey, 1972–77; *b* 1 Nov. 1920; *s* of Benjamin Richard Kelsey and Daisy (*née* Powell); *m* 1944, Phyllis Margaret (*d* 1995), *d* of Henry Ernest Smith, Chingford; one *s* one *d*. *Educ:* Royal Masonic Sch.; Emmanuel Coll., Cambridge; Royal Mil. Coll. of Science. BSc. Commnd in RE, 1940; war service in N Africa and Europe; Lt-Col 1961; Col 1965; Dep. Dir Mil. Survey; Brig. Dir Field Survey, Ordnance Survey, 1968; Dir of Mil. Survey, Brig. 1972; Maj.-Gen. 1974. *Recreations:* Rugby football (played for Cambridge Univ., Richmond, Dorset, Wilts; Mem. RFU, 1965–66); sailing.

KELSEY, Linda; Executive Editor, In Style, since 2000; *b* 15 April 1952; *d* of Samuel Cohen and Rhona (*née* Fox); *m* 1972 (marr. diss. 1980); one *s* by Christian Testorf. *Educ:* Woodhouse Grammar Sch., N12. Sub-editor, Good Housekeeping, 1970–72; Features Editor, Cosmopolitan, 1975–78; Deputy Editor: Company, 1978–81; Options, 1981–82; Cosmopolitan, 1983–85, Editor, 1985–89; Editor, She magazine, 1989–95; Editor at Large, Nat. Magazine Co., 1996–98; Consultant Ed., Parkhill Publishing, and freelance writer, 1999–2000. Editor of the Year Award: PPA, 1989, for Cosmopolitan; Brit. Soc. Mag. Editors, 1990, for She. *Recreations:* reading, walking, theatre, film, family. *Clubs:* Groucho, Royal Automobile.

KELSON, Peter John; QC 2001; a Recorder, since 1997; *b* 7 March 1959; *s* of Gordon Charles and Patricia Sylvia Kelson; *m* 1982, Rosalind Margaret Clark; two *s*. *Educ:* Sheffield Univ. (LLB Hons). Called to the Bar, Middle Temple, 1981. *Recreation:* golf, piano playing, vegetable patch. *Address:* Bank House Chambers, Old Bank House, 3 Hartshead, Sheffield S1 2EL. *T:* (0114) 275 1223. *Club:* Sickleholme Golf (Derbys).

KELTZ, Jennie, (Mrs James Keltz); *see* Bond, J.

KELVEDON, Baron *cr* 1997 (Life Peer), of Ongar in the co. of Essex; **Henry Paul Guinness Channon;** PC 1980; *b* 9 Oct. 1935; *o s* of late Sir Henry Channon, MP, and of late Lady Honor Svejdar (*née* Guinness), *e d* of 2nd Earl of Iveagh, KG; *m* 1963, Ingrid Olivia Georgia Guinness (*née* Wyndham); one *s* one *d* (and one *d* decd). *Educ:* Lockers Park, Hemel Hempstead; Eton Coll., Christ Church, Oxford. 2nd Lieut Royal Horse Guards (The Blues), 1955–56. Pres. of Oxford Univ. Conservative Association, 1958. MP (C) Southend W, Jan. 1959–1997; PPS, to Minister of Power, 1959–60, to Home Sec., 1960–62, to First Sec. of State, 1962–63, to the Foreign Sec., 1963–64; Opposition Spokesman on Arts and Amenities, 1967–70; Parly Sec., Min. of Housing and Local Govt, June-Oct. 1970; Parly Under-Sec. of State, DoE, 1970–72; Minister of State, Northern Ireland Office, March-Nov. 1972; Minister for Housing and Construction, DoE, 1972–74; Opposition Spokesman on: Prices and Consumer Protection, March-Sept. 1974; environmental affairs, Oct. 1974–Feb. 1975; Minister of State, CSD, 1979–81; Minister for the Arts, 1981–83; Minister for Trade, 1983–86; Sec. of State for Trade and Industry, 1986–87; Sec. of State for Transport, 1987–89. Chairman: Finance and Services Cttee, H of C, 1992–97; Transport Select Cttee, 1993–97. Dep. Leader, Cons. Delegn to WEU and Council of Europe, 1976–79. Chm., British Assoc. for Central and Eastern Europe, 1992–97. Mem., Gen. Adv. Council to ITA, 1964–66. President: Southend West Cons. Assoc.; Brentwood and Ongar Cons. Assoc.; Old Etonian Assoc., 1999–2000. *Address:* c/o Iveagh Trustees Ltd, 41 Harrington Gardens, SW7 4JU.

KEMBALL, Brig. Humphrey Gurdon, CBE 1971 (OBE 1966); MC 1940; *b* 6 Nov. 1919; *s* of late Brig.-Gen. Alick Gurdon Kemball (late IA) and late Evelyn Mary (*née* Synge); *m* 1945, Ella Margery Emmeline (*née* Bickham) (*d* 1997); no *c*. *Educ:* Trinity Coll., Glenalmond; RMC, Sandhurst. Commissioned 1939, 1st Bn The Prince of Wales's Volunteers. Served War of 1939–45 (MC); Staff Coll., 1943. JSSC, 1956; commanded 1st Bn The Lancashire Regt (PWV), 1961–63; i/c Administration, HQ Federal Regular Army, Aden, 1964–66; Asst Dir, MoD, 1966–68; Mil. Attaché, Moscow, 1968–71; HQ British Forces, Near East, 1971–73; Dep. Comdr, SW District, 1973–74, retired. *Recreations:* fishing, travelling. *Address:* 28 Windsor End, Beaconsfield, Bucks HP9 2JW. *T:* (01494) 671698. *Club:* Naval and Military.

KEMBALL, Air Marshal Sir (Richard) John, KCB 1990; CBE 1981; DL; Co-ordinator of British-American Community Relations, Ministry of Defence, since 1994; Chief Executive, Racing Welfare, since 1995; *b* 31 Jan. 1939; *s* of Richard and Margaret Kemball; *m* 1962, Valerie Geraldine Webster; two *d*. *Educ:* Uppingham; Open Univ. (BA 1990). Commissioned RAF, 1957; OC No 54 Squadron, 1977; OC RAF Laarbruch, 1979; Commandant, CFS, 1983–85; Comdr, British Forces, Falkland Islands, 1985–86; COS and Dep. C-in-C, Strike Command and UK Air Forces, 1989–93. ADC to HM The Queen, 1984–85. Chm., Essex Rivers Healthcare NHS Trust, 1993–95. Hon. Col, 77 Engr Regt (V), 1993–96. Pres., RAFA, 1995–98 (Vice-Pres., 1993–95; Life Vice-Pres., 1998). Gov., Corps of Commissionaires, 1993–. Freeman, City of London. DL Suffolk, 1999. *Recreations:* country pursuits, tennis, cricket, gardening. *Address:* c/o HSBC, 46 Market Hill, Sudbury, Suffolk CO10 6ES. *Club:* Royal Air Force.

KEMBALL-COOK, Brian Hartley, MA Oxon; Headmaster, Bedford Modern School, 1965–77; *b* 12 Dec. 1912; *s* of Sir Basil Alfred Kemball-Cook, KCMG, CB, and Lady (Nancy Annie) Kemball-Cook (*née* Pavitt); *m* 1947, Marian, *d* of R. C. R. Richards, OBE; three *s* one *d*. *Educ:* Shrewsbury Sch. (Sidney Gold Medal for Classics); Balliol Coll., Oxford (Scholar). First Class Classical Honour Mods, 1933; First Class, Litt. Hum., 1935. Sixth Form Classics Master, Repton Sch., 1936–40. Intelligence Corps, 1940–46 (despatches); Regional Intelligence Officer and Political Adviser to Regional Comr, Hanover, 1946; Principal, Min. of Transport, 1946–47. Sen. Classics Master, Repton Sch., 1947–56; Headmaster, Queen Elizabeth's Grammar Sch., Blackburn, 1956–65. Chm., Bedfordshire Musical Festival, 1967–77. Croix de Guerre with Palm, 1946. *Publications:* (ed) Shakespeare, Coriolanus, 1954; (contrib.) Education: Threatened Standards, 1972; translated: Homer, Odyssey, 1994; Homeric Hymn to Hermes, 2000; Homeric Hymn to Demeter, 2001. *Recreations:* mountaineering, music. *Address:* 12 Francis Close, Hitchin, Herts SG4 9EJ. *T:* (01462) 438862. *Club:* Climbers.

KEMBER, Anthony Joseph, MA; Communications Adviser, Department of Health, 1989–92; *b* 1 Nov. 1931; *s* of Thomas Kingsley Kember and May Lena (*née* Pryor); *m* 1957, Drusilla Mary (*née* Boyce); one *s* two *d*. *Educ:* St Edmund Hall, Oxford (MA). MHSM, DipHSM. Deputy House Governor and Secretary to Bd of Governors, Westminster Hospital, 1961–69; Gp Secretary, Hillingdon Gp Hospital Management Cttee, 1969–73; Area Administrator, Kensington and Chelsea and Westminster AHA(T), 1973–78; Administrator, 1978–84, Gen. Man., 1984–89, SW Thames RHA. Mem., Lord Chancellor's Adv. Cttee on JPs for SW London (formerly SW London Area Adv. Cttee on Appointment of JPs), 1994–. Trustee, Disabled Living Foundn, 1981–2000 (Chm., 1993–2000); Founder Trustee, Charity Trust Networks, 1998–2000 (Vice-Chm., 1998–99). Chm., Richmond Art Soc., 1995–97 (Sec., 1992–95); Mem., Richmond upon Thames Arts Council, 2001–. CIMgt (CBIM 1988). *Publications:* The NHS—a Kaleidoscope of Care, 1993; various articles for professional jls. *Recreations:* painting, inside and out; tennis, royal and common-or-garden. *Address:* 16 Orchard Rise, Richmond, Surrey TW10 5BX. *Clubs:* Roehampton; Royal Tennis Court (Hampton Court).

KEMBER, William Percy, FCA; FCT; Group Financial Controller, British Telecommunications, 1981–92; *b* 12 May 1932; *s* of late Percy Kember and Mrs Q. A. Kember, Purley, Surrey; *m* 1982, Lynn Kirkham. *Educ:* Uppingham. Chartered Accountant; Corporate Treasurer. Various posts with Royal Dutch/Shell Group in Venezuela, 1958–63; British Oxygen Co., 1963–67; Coopers & Lybrand, 1967–72; Post Office (Telecommunications), 1972–81. Director: Centel Financial Systems Inc., 1983–86; Marshalls Finance, 1991–98. Visitor, Royal Institution, 1977–79, Chm., 1979. *Recreation:* golf. *Address:* 83 Hillway, N6 6AB. *Clubs:* Royal Automobile; Highgate Golf, Royal Dornoch Golf.

KEMP, family name of **Viscount Rochdale**.

KEMP, Arnold; Foreign News Editor, The Observer, since 1999; *b* 15 Feb. 1939; *s* of Robert Kemp and Meta Strachan; *m* 1963, Sandra Elizabeth Shand (marr. diss.); two *d*. *Educ:* Edinburgh Academy; Edinburgh Univ. (MA). Sub-Editor, Scotsman, 1959–62, Guardian, 1962–65; Production Editor, Scotsman, 1965–70, London Editor, 1970–72, Dep. Editor, 1972–81; Editor, Glasgow Herald, then The Herald, 1981–94; Consultant Editor, Caledonian Publishing, 1994–97; contributor and desk editor, The Observer, 1996–99. Chm., Commn on Future of Voluntary Sector in Scotland, 1995–97. Dr *hc* Edinburgh, 1992; Hon. DLitt Strathclyde, 1993; DUniv Paisley, 1993. *Publication:* The Hollow Drum: Scotland since the war, 1993. *Recreations:* jazz, reading, theatre. *Address:* 8 Buckingham Court, 2 Queen Margaret Drive, Glasgow G12 8DQ. *Club:* Caledonian.

KEMP, Barry John, FBA 1992; Reader in Egyptology and Fellow of Wolfson College, University of Cambridge, since 1990. *Educ:* Liverpool Univ. (MA); MA Cantab 1965. Lectr, Univ. of Cambridge, 1969–90. *Publications:* Amarna Reports, Vols. 1–4, 1984–87; Ancient Egypt: anatomy of a civilisation, 1989; (jtly) Survey of the Ancient City of El-Amarna, 1993. *Address:* Wolfson College, Cambridge CB3 9BB.

KEMP, Charles James Bowring; His Honour Judge Kemp; a Circuit Judge, since 1998; *b* 27 April 1951; *s* of late Michael John Barnett Kemp and of Brigid Ann (*née* Bowring; now Vernon-Smith); *m* 1974, Fenella Anne Herring; one *s* one *d*. *Educ:* Shrewsbury Sch.; University Coll. London (LLB). Called to the Bar, Gray's Inn, 1973; in practice at the Bar, 1974–98; Asst Recorder, 1987–91; a Recorder, 1991–98; South Eastern Circuit. *Recreations:* music, tennis, swimming, golf, country pursuits. *Address:* Law Courts, High Street, Lewes, E Sussex BH7 1YB. *T:* (01273) 480400.

KEMP, David Ashton McIntyre; QC 1973; a Recorder of the Crown Court, 1976–96; *b* 14 Oct. 1921; *s* of late Sir Kenneth McIntyre Kemp and Margaret Caroline Clare Kemp; *m* 1st, 1949, Margaret Sylvia Jones (*d* 1971); 2nd, 1972, Maureen Ann Frances Stevens, *widow*. *Educ:* Winchester Coll.; Corpus Christi Coll., Cambridge. 1st cl. hons Law Cantab. Called to Bar, Inner Temple, 1948, Bencher, 1980. *Publications:* (with M. S. Kemp) The Quantum of Damages, Personal Injuries Claims, 1954 (4th edn 1975); (with M. S. Kemp) The Quantum of Damages, Fatal Accident Claims, 1956 (4th edn 1975). *Recreations:* skiing, tennis, gardening. *Address:* 63 Brixton Water Lane, SW2 1PH. *T:* (020) 7267 3295. *Clubs:* Hurlingham, Ski Club of Great Britain; Kandahar Ski.

KEMP, Sir (Edward) Peter, KCB 1991 (CB 1988); Executive, Foundation for Accountancy and Financial Management, 1993–2000; *b* 10 Oct. 1934; *s* of late Thomas Kemp and Nancie (*née* Sargent); *m* 1961, Enid van Popta; three *s* one *d*. *Educ:* Millfield Sch.; Royal Naval Coll., Dartmouth. FCA (ACA 1959). Principal, later Asst Sec., Min. of Transport, 1967–73; HM Treasury, 1973, Under-Sec., 1978, Dep. Sec., 1983; Second Perm. Sec. and Next Steps Project Manager, Cabinet Office (OMCS), 1988–92. Comr, Audit Commission, 1993–99. Trustee, Action for Blind People, 2001–. Gov., Millfield Sch., 1993–. *Publications:* Beyond Next Steps: a civil service for the twenty-first century, 1993; (with David Walker) A Better Machine: government for the twenty-first century, 1996; articles and pieces. *Address:* 2 Longton Avenue, SE26 6QJ. *Club:* Reform.

KEMP, Rt Rev. Eric Waldram, DD; Bishop of Chichester, 1974–2001; *b* 27 April 1915; *o c* of Tom Kemp and Florence Lilian Kemp (*née* Waldram), Grove House, Waltham, Grimsby, Lincs; *m* 1953, Leslie Patricia, 3rd *d* of late Rt Rev. K. E. Kirk, sometime Bishop of Oxford; one *s* four *d*. *Educ:* Brigg Grammar Sch., Lincs; Exeter Coll., Oxford (MA); St Stephen's House, Oxford. Deacon 1939; Priest 1940; Curate of St Luke, Southampton, 1939–41; Librarian of Pusey House, Oxford, 1941–46; Chaplain of Christ Church Oxford, 1943–46; Actg Chap., St John's Coll., Oxford, 1943–45; Fellow, Chaplain, Tutor, and Lectr in Theology and Medieval History, Exeter Coll., Oxford, 1946–69; Dean of Worcester, 1969–74. Exam. Chaplain: to Bp of Mon, 1942–45; to Bp of Southwark, 1946–50; to Bp of St Albans, 1946–69; to Bp of Exeter, 1949–69; to Bp of Lincoln, 1950–69. Proctor in Convocation for University of Oxford, 1949–69. Bp of Oxford's Commissary for Religious Communities, 1952–69; Chaplain to the Queen, 1967–69. Canon and Prebendary of Caistor in Lincoln Cathedral, 1952; Hon. Provincial Canon of Cape Town, 1960–; Canon of Honour, Chartres Cathedral, 1998. Bampton Lecturer, 1959–60. FRHistS 1951. Hon. DLitt Sussex, 1986; Hon. DD Berne, 1987. *Publications:* (contributions to) Thy Household the Church, 1943; Canonization and Authority in the Western Church, 1948; Norman Powell Williams, 1954; Twenty-five Papal Decretals relating to the Diocese of Lincoln (with W. Holtzmann), 1954; An Introduction to Canon Law in the Church of England, 1957; Life and Letters of Kenneth Escott Kirk, 1959; Counsel and Consent, 1961; The Anglican-Methodist conversations: A Comment from within, 1964; (ed) Man: Fallen and Free, 1969; Square Words in a Round World, 1980; contrib. to English Historical Review, Jl of Ecclesiastical History. *Recreations:* music, travel. *Address:* 5 Alexandra Road, Chichester PO19 4LX. *Club:* National Liberal (Pres., 1994–).

KEMP, Fraser; MP (Lab) Houghton and Washington East, since 1997; an Assistant Government Whip, since 2001; *b* 1 Sept. 1958; *s* of William and Mary Kemp; *m* 1989, Patricia Mary, *d* of Patrick and Patricia Byrne; two *s* one *d*. *Educ:* Washington Comp. Sch. Civil Servant (clerical asst/officer), 1975–81; Labour Party: Agent, Leicester, 1981–84; Asst Regl Organiser, E Midlands, 1984–86; Regl Sec., W Midlands, 1986–94; Nat. Gen. Election Co-ordinator, 1994–96. Mem., Select Cttee on Public Admin, 1997–99. Chm., PLP Cabinet Office Cttee, 1997–. *Recreation:* people. *Address:* House of Commons, SW1A 0AA. *T:* (020) 7219 5181, *T:* (constituency) (0191) 584 9266. *Club:* Usworth and District Working Men's (Washington).

KEMP, Air Vice-Marshal George John, CB 1976; *b* 14 July 1921; *m* 1943, Elspeth Beatrice Peacock; one *s* two *d*. Commnd RAF, 1941; served in night fighter sqdns with spell on ferrying aircraft to Middle East; RAF Staff Coll., 1952; AHQ Iraq, 1953–54; Air Secretary's Dept, Air Ministry, 1955–57; jssc, 1958; MoD Secretariat, 1959; Far East Planning Staff, 1960–61; RAF Staff Coll. Directing Staff, 1962–63; UNISON Planning Staff, MoD, 1964; Dir of Personnel (Policy and Plans), RAF, 1965–67; Stn Comdr RAF Upwood, 1968–69; Dir of Manning (RAF), 1970–72; Dir-Gen. of Personnel Management, RAF, 1973–75. *Recreations:* many and various. *Address:* Old Court, Woolley Street, Bradford on Avon, Wilts BA15 1AE. *T:* (01225) 867832. *Clubs:* Royal Air Force; Bath and County.

KEMP, Hubert Bond Stafford, MS; FRCS, FRCSE; Hon. Consultant Orthopaedic Surgeon, since 1992; Consultant Orthopaedic Surgeon: Royal National Orthopaedic Hospital, London and Stanmore, 1974–92; The Middlesex Hospital, 1984–90; Hon. Consultant Orthopaedic Surgeon, St Luke's Hospital for the Clergy, 1975–90; University Teacher in Orthopaedics; *b* 25 March 1925; *s* of John Stafford Kemp and Cecilia Isabel (*née* Bond); *m* 1967, Moyra Ann Margaret Odgers; three *d*. *Educ:* Cardiff High Sch.; Univ. of South Wales; St Thomas' Hosp., Univ. of London (MB, BS 1949; MS 1969); MRCS, LRCP 1947; FRCSE 1960; FRCS 1970. Robert Jones Gold Medal and Assoc. Prize, 1969 (Proxime Accessit, 1964); Hunterian Prof., RCS, 1969; Hon. Consultant, Royal Nat. Orthopaedic Hosp., London and Stanmore, 1965–74; Sen. Lectr, Inst. of Orthopaedics, 1965–74, Hon. Sen. Lectr, 1974–90. Vis. Professor, VII Congress of Soc. Latino Amer. de Orthopedia y Traumatologica, 1971. Member: MRC Working Party on Tuberculosis of the Spine, 1974–; MRC Working Party on Osteosarcoma, 1985–94. Fellow, Brit. Orthopaedic Assoc., 1972–; Chm., London Bone Tumour Unit, 1985–91; Member: Brit. Orthopaedic Research Soc., 1967–; Internat. Skeletal Soc., 1977–. *Publications:* (jtly) Orthopaedic Diagnosis, 1984; chapter in: A Postgraduate Textbook of Clinical Orthopaedics, 1983, 2nd edn 1995; Baillière's Clinical Oncology, Bone Tumours, 1987; (contrib.) Essential Surgical Practice, 3rd edn, 1995; papers on diseases of the spine, the hip, bone tumours. *Recreations:* fishing, painting. *Address:* 55 Loom Lane, Radlett, Herts WD7 8NX. *T:* and *Fax:* (01923) 854265; 45 Bolsover Street, W1P 8AQ. *T:* (020) 7391 4255, (020) 7387 5070, *Fax:* (020) 7391 4288.

See also Sir G. D. W. Odgers.

KEMP, Prof. Kenneth Oliver, FREng; Emeritus Professor of Civil Engineering and Fellow, University College London, 1984; *b* 19 Oct. 1926; *s* of Eric Austen Kemp; *m* 1952, Josephine Gloria (*née* Donovan); no *c*. *Educ:* University College London (BSc(Eng), PhD). FICE, FIStructE; FREng (FEng 1988). Surveyor, Directorate of Colonial Surveys, 1947–49; Asst Engr, Collins and Mason, Consulting Engrs, 1949–54. University College London: Lectr, Sen. Lectr, Dept of Civil Engrg, 1954–69; Reader in Structural Engrg, 1969–70; Chadwick Prof. of Civil Engrg and Hd of Civil Engrg Dept, 1970–84. *Publications:* papers in: Proc. Instn of Civil Engrs; The Structural Engr; Magazine of Concrete Research; Internat. Assoc. of Bridge and Structural Engrg. *Address:* Rowan Cottage, Brinton, Melton Constable, Norfolk NR24 2QF. *T:* (01263) 860631.

KEMP, Kenneth Reginald; Hon. Life President, Smith & Nephew plc, 1990 (Chairman, 1976–90); *b* 13 Nov. 1921; *s* of Philip R. Kemp and Siew Pukalanan of Thailand; *m* 1949, Florence M. Hetherington (marr. diss.); *m* 1996, Frances M. Kemp-Bell; one *s* one *d*. *Educ:* Bradfield College, Berks. FCA. Joined Leeds Rifles, 1939; commissioned Royal Artillery, 1940–46; served in France, Germany, India, Far East (Captain). Peat, Marwick Mitchell & Co., 1947; qualified CA, 1950; Smith & Nephew: Company Sec., 1953, later Finance Dir; Dir, 1962; Chief Exec., 1968–76. *Recreations:* unlimited. *Address:* Smith & Nephew, Heron House, 15 Adam Street, WC2N 6LA. *T:* (020) 7401 7646.

KEMP, Leslie Charles, CBE 1982; Chairman, Griffiths McGee Ltd, Demolition Contractors, 1982–87; Proprietor, Leslie Kemp Associates, 1976–97; *b* 10 Oct. 1920; *s* of Thomas and Violet Kemp. *Educ:* Hawkhurst Moor Boys' School. Apprentice blacksmith, 1934–39; served War, 1939–46: Infantry, N Africa and Italy. Civil Engrg Equipment Operator, 1947–51; District Organiser, 1951–57, Regional Organiser, 1958–63, Nat. Sec. (Construction), TGWU, 1963–76. Jt Registrar, 1975–76, Dep. Chm., 1976–81, Demolition and Dismantling Industry Registration Council. Member, Nat. Jt Council for Building Industry, 1957–76; Operatives Sec., Civil Engrg Construction Conciliation Bd for GB, 1963–76; Mem., 1964–73, Dep. Chm., 1973–76, Chm., 1976–85, Construction Industry Trng Bd (Chm., Civil Engrg Cttee, 1964–76); Member: EDC for Civil Engrg, 1964–76; Construction Ind. Liaison Gp, 1974–76; Construction Ind. Manpower Bd, 1976; Bragg Adv. Cttee on Falsework, 1973–75; Vice-Pres., Construction Health and Safety Gp. Chm., Corby Develt Corp., 1976–80; Dep. Chm., Peterborough Develt Corp., 1974–82. Member, Outward Bound Trust, 1977–88; Pres., W Norfolk Outward Bound Assoc., 1983–88. Chm., Syderstone Parish Council, 1983–87. Construction News Man of the Year Award, 1973; in recognition of services to trng, Leslie Kemp Europ. Prize for Civil Engrg trainees to study in France, instituted 1973. CompICE; FIMgt. *Recreations:* travel, bird-watching, fishing. *Address:* Lamberts Yard, Syderstone, King's Lynn, Norfolk PE31 8SF. *Clubs:* Lighthouse; Fakenham Golf (Pres., 1985–88).

KEMP, Lindsay; Founder, Artistic Director and Principal Performer, Lindsay Kemp Co., since 1962; painter, designer, teacher; *b* 3 May 1938; *s* of Norman Kemp and Marie (*née* Gilmour). *Educ:* Sunshine Sch. of Dancing, Bradford; Royal Merchant Navy Sch., Bearwood; Bradford Coll. of Art; Sigurd Leeder Sch. of Modern Dance; Ballet Rambert Sch.; studied with Marcel Marceau. Lindsay Kemp Co. productions include: Illuminations, Lyric, Hammersmith, 1965; Turquoise Pantomime; Woyzeck; Salomé; Legends; Flowers, West End, 1974, later Broadway and world tour, 1974–94; Mr Punch's Pantomime; A Midsummer Night's Dream; Duende; Nijinsky; Façade; The Big Parade; Alice; Onnagata; Cinderella: a gothic operetta. Dir, David Bowie's Ziggy Stardust concerts, 1972; created for Ballet Rambert: The Parade's Gone By, 1975; Cruel Garden, 1978; film appearances include: Savage Messiah, 1971; The Lindsay Kemp Circus, 1971; Wicker Man, 1972; Sebastian, 1974; Jubilee, 1977; Italian Postcards, 1986; Travelling Light, 1993. *Publication:* (with D. Haughton) Drawing and Dancing, 1988; *relevant publications:* Lindsay Kemp, by David Haughton, 1982; Flowers, 1987. *Recreation:* interior decorating.

KEMP, Prof. Martin John, FBA 1991; Professor of the History of Art, and Fellow of Trinity College, Oxford University, since 1995; British Academy Wolfson Research Professor, 1993–98; *b* 5 March 1942; *s* of Frederick Maurice Kemp and Violet Anne Tull; *m* 1966, Jill Lightfoot (separated), *d* of Dennis William Lightfoot and Joan Betteridge; one *s* one *d*. *Educ:* Windsor Grammar Sch.; Downing Coll., Cambridge (MA Nat. Scis and Art History; Hon. Fellow, 1999); Courtauld Inst. of Art, London Univ. (Academic Dip.). Lectr in History of Art, Dalhousie Univ., Halifax, NS, Canada, 1965–66; Lectr in History of Fine Art, Univ. of Glasgow, 1966–81; Fellow, Inst. for Advanced Study, Princeton, 1984–85; University of St Andrews: Prof. of Fine Arts, subseq. of Hist. and Theory of Art, 1981–95; Associate Dean of Graduate Studies, Faculty of Arts, 1983–87; Mem. Court, 1988–91; Provost of St Leonard's Coll., 1991–95. Prof. of History and Hon. Mem., Royal Scottish Acad., 1985–; Slade Prof. of Fine Art, Cambridge Univ., 1987–88; Visiting Professor: Benjamin Sonnenberg, Inst. of Fine Arts, New York Univ., 1988; Wiley, Univ. of N Carolina, Chapel Hill, 1993. Co-Founder, Wallace Kemp/Artakt, 2001. Chair, Assoc. of Art Historians, 1989–92; Member: Board, Scottish Museums Council, 1990–95; Res. Awards Adv. Cttee, Leverhulme Trust, 1991–98; Board, Mus. Trng Inst., 1993–99; Board, Interalia, 1993–; Council, British Soc. for History of Sci., 1994–97. Pres., Leonardo da Vinci Soc., 1987–96. Trustee: National Gall. of Scotland, 1982–87; V&A Museum, 1985–89; BM, 1995–. Broadcasts, Radio 3 and TV. For. Mem., American Acad. of Arts and Scis, 1996. FRSA 1983–98; FRSE 1992. Hon. FRIAS 1988. Hon. DLitt Heriot-Watt, 1995. Mitchell Prize for best first book in English on Art History, 1981; Armand Hammer Prize for Leonardo Studies, 1992; President's Prize, Italian Assoc. of America, 1998. *Publications:* Leonardo da Vinci, The Marvellous Works of Nature and Man, 1981; (jtly) Leonardo da Vinci, 1989; (jtly) Leonardo on Painting, 1989; The Science of Art, 1990; Behind the Picture, 1997; (ed) The Oxford History of Western Art, 2000; Visualizations, 2000; (with Marina Wallace) Spectacular Bodies, 2000; articles in Jl of Warburg and Courtauld Insts, Burlington Magazine, Art History, Art Bull., Connoisseur, Procs of British Acad., Jl of RSA, L'Arte, Bibliothèque d'Humanisme et Renaissance, Med. History, TLS, London Rev. of Books, Guardian, Nature, Sunday Times, etc. *Recreations:* hockey, running, avoiding academics. *Address:* Trinity College, Oxford OX1 3BH.

KEMP, Neil Reginald, OBE 1990 (MBE 1980); Director, British Council, Indonesia, since 1995; *b* 18 March 1945; *s* of Harry Reginald Kemp and Ada Mary Kemp (*née* Roberts); *m* 1982, Elizabeth Jacob; two *s*. *Educ:* University College of Wales, Swansea (BSc; PhD Analytical Chem. 1971). Laboratory technician, 1961–63; VSO as Lectr, Gordon Coll., Rawalpindi, Pakistan, 1967–68; joined British Council, 1971: Jakarta, 1971–74; Calcutta, 1976–79; Res. Associate, Univ. of London Inst. of Educn, 1979–80; Head, Sci. and Technol. Dept, London, 1981–85; New Delhi, 1985–89; Colombo, 1990–91; Develt and Trng Services, Manchester, 1991–95. *Recreations:* athletics, cycling, cricket and basketball, travelling, jazz and blues. *Address:* c/o Foreign and Commonwealth Office, King Charles Street, SW1A 2AH; 37 Houndean Rise, Lewes, E Sussex BN7 1EQ.

KEMP, Sir Peter; *see* Kemp, Sir E. P.

KEMP, Richard Geoffrey Horsford, MA; Head Master, Pate's Grammar School, Cheltenham, since 2000; *b* 27 Oct. 1948; *s* of Athole Stephen Horsford Kemp and Alison Kemp (*née* Bostock); *m* 1st, 1970 (marr. diss. 1990); 2nd, 1996, Denise (*née* Fraser); one step *s* one step *d*. *Educ:* Westminster Sch.; Christ Church, Oxford (MA). Marketing and Advertising Manager, Unilever, 1970-73; Teacher: Eton Coll., 1973-74; Henry Box Sch., Witney, 1974-78; Lord Williams's Sch., Thame, 1978-84; res., Dept of Educn, Oxford Univ., 1984-85; Buckinghamshire LEA, 1985-92 (Sen. Educn Advr, 1989-92); Sen. Dep. Head, Actg Headmaster, Aylesbury Grammar Sch., 1992-99. *Publications:* various geography textbooks and atlases. *Recreations:* gardening, wine, travel, military history. *Address:* Lockey House, Langford, Lechlade, Glos GL7 3LF. *T:* (01367) 860176.

KEMP, Robert Thayer; export credit consultant; *b* 18 June 1928; *s* of Robert Kemp and Ada Kemp (*née* Thayer); *m* 1951, Gwendolyn Mabel Minty; three *s*. *Educ:* Bromley Grammar Sch.; London Univ. (BA (Hons) Medieval and Mod. History). Export Credits Guarantee Department: Asst Sec., 1970; Under-Sec., 1975; Head of Project Underwriting Gp, 1981–85; Director: Internat. Gp, 1985–88; Sedgwick Credit, 1989–95. *Publication:* Review of Future Status Options (ECGD), 1989. *Recreations:* cricket, music, theatre. *Address:* 294 Tubbenden Lane South, Farnborough, Orpington, Kent BR6 7DN. *T:* (01689) 853924.

KEMP, Thomas Arthur, MD; FRCP; Physician, St Mary's Hospital, 1947–75, Paddington General Hospital 1950–75; *b* 12 Aug. 1915; *s* of Fred Kemp and Edith Peters; *m* 1942, Ruth May Scott-Keat; one *s* one *d*. *Educ:* Denstone Coll.; St Catharine's Coll., Cambridge (Exhibitioner); St Mary's Hospital, London (Scholar). MB, BChir 1940; MRCP 1941; FRCP 1949; MD 1953. Examiner in Medicine, Universities of London and Glasgow. FRSocMed (Jt Hon. Sec., 1961–67). Served in Middle East, 1944–47; Lt-Col RAMC Officer i/c Medical Division; Hon. Cons. Physician to the Army, 1972–75. Pres. Brit. Student Health Assoc., 1962–63; Chm. Brit. Student Tuberculosis Foundation, 1963–65. Fellow, Midland Div., Woodard Schs, 1962–85; Commonwealth Travelling Fellowship, 1967. *Publications:* papers in medical journals. *Recreations:* games, especially Rugby football (played for Cambridge, 1936, for Barbarians, 1936–49, for St Mary's Hosp., 1937–43, for England, 1937–48 (Captain, 1948, Selector, 1954–61); President: Rugby Football Union, 1971–72; Students' RFU, 1980–97). *Address:* 2 Woodside Road, Northwood, Middx HA6 3QE. *T:* (01923) 821068. *Club:* Hawks (Cambridge).

KEMP-GEE, Mark Norman; Chief Executive, Exeter Investment Group plc, since 1999; *b* 19 Dec. 1945; *s* of late Bernard Kemp-Gee and of Ann Kemp-Gee (*née* Mackilligin); *m* 1980, Hon. Lucy Lyttelton, *d* of 10th Viscount Cobham, KG, GCMG, GCVO, TD, PC; three *s*. *Educ:* Marlborough Coll.; Pembroke Coll., Oxford (MA). Chm., Greig Middleton & Co. Ltd, 1978–99. Director: King & Shaxson Hldgs plc, 1993–96; Gerrard Gp plc, 1996–99. Councillor (C), London Borough of Lambeth, 1982–86. *Recreation:* point-to-pointing. *Address:* Exeter Investment Group plc, 23 Cathedral Yard, Exeter EX1 1HB. *T:* (01392) 256600. *Clubs:* City of London; Oxford Union.

KEMP-WELCH, Sir John, Kt 1999; Director, HSBC Holdings, since 2000; Chairman, London Stock Exchange, 1994–2000 (Director, 1991–2000); *b* 31 March 1936; *s* of Peter Wellesbourne Kemp-Welch, OBE and Peggy Penelope Kemp-Welch; *m* 1964, Diana Elisabeth Leishman; one *s* three *d*. *Educ:* Abberley Hall, Worcs; Winchester Coll. Hoare & Co., 1954–58; Cazenove & Co., 1959–94 (Jt Sen. Partner, 1980–94). Chairman: Scottish Eastern Investment Trust, 1994–99 (Dir, 1993–99); Lowland Investment Co., 1993–97 (Dir, 1963–97); Claridge's Hotel, 1995–97; Martin Currie Portfolio Investment Trust plc, 1999–2000; Director: Savoy Hotel PLC, 1985–98; Royal & Sun Alliance Insurance Gp (formerly Sun Alliance Gp), 1994–99; British Invisibles, 1994–98; Pro Share, 1995–97. Dep. Chm., Financial Reporting Council, 1994–2000; Director: SFA, 1994–97; Accountancy Foundn, 2000–01. Member: City Capital Markets Cttee, 1989–94; Panel on Takeovers and Mergers, 1994–2000. Mem., Stock Exchange, 1959–86. Vice Pres., Fedn of European Stock Exchanges, 1996–98; Mem. Exec. Cttee, Federation Internationale des Bourses de Valeurs, 1994–98; President: Investor Relations Soc., 1994–2000; Securities Industry Mgt Assoc., 1994–. Member: (Lord Mayor of London's) City No 1 Consultancy, 1994–2000; Council, London First, 1994–96. Governor: Ditchley Foundn, 1980–; North Foreland Lodge Sch., 1980–92; Chm., King's Med. Res. Trust, 1991– (Trustee, 1984–); Trustee: KCH Special Trustees, 1997–99; KCH Charitable Trust, 1998–99; Trustee and Mem. Council, Game Conservancy Trust, 1990–94 (Hon. Res. Fellow, 1998–); Mem. Adv. Council, PYBT, 1996–2000; Trustee: Sandford St Martin Trust, 1994–99; Dulverton Trust, 1994– (Dep. Chm. (Finance), 2001–); Chm., Lucy Kemp-Welch Meml Trust, 1965–. Mem., Highland Soc. of London, 1992–. Hon. FSI (MSI 1992; FSI 1996). CIMgt (CBIM 1984); FRSA 1989. Hon. DBA London Guildhall Univ., 1998. Joseph Nickerson Heather Award, Joseph Nickerson Heather Improvement Foundn, 1988. *Recreations:* the hills of Perthshire, country life, cricket, champagne and claret, Impressionist paintings, heather moorland management. *Address:* 12 Tokenhouse Yard, EC2R 7AN. *Clubs:* White's, City of London, Pilgrims, MCC; Essex.

KEMPE, John William Rolfe, CVO 1980; Headmaster of Gordonstoun, 1968–78; *b* 29 Oct. 1917; *s* of late William Alfred Kempe and Kunigunda Neville-Rolfe; *m* 1957, Barbara Nan Stephen, *d* of late Dr C. R. Huxtable, MC, FRCS and of Mrs Huxtable, OAM, Sydney, Australia; two *s* one *d*. *Educ:* Stowe; Clare Coll., Cambridge (Exhibitioner in Mathematics). Served war of 1939–45, RAFVR Training and Fighter Command; CO 153 and 255 Night Fighter Squadrons. Board of Trade, 1945; Firth-Brown (Overseas) Ltd, 1946–47; Head of Maths Dept, Gordonstoun, 1948–51; Principal, Hyderabad Public Sch., Deccan, India, 1951–54; Headmaster, Corby Grammar School, Northants, 1955–67. Chm., Round Square Internat. Service Cttee, 1979–87; Vice-Chm., The European Atlantic Movement, 1982–92 (Vice-Pres., 1992–). Exploration and mountaineering, Himalayas, Peru, 1952–56; Member: Cttee, Mount Everest Foundation, 1956–62; Cttee, Brathay Exploration Group, 1964–73; Foundn Trustee, Univ. of Cambridge Kurt Hahn Trust, 1986–89; Trustee: Thornton Smith Trust, 1981–96; Plevins Charity, 1987–96. *Publications:* A Family History of the Kempes, 1991; articles in Alpine Jl, Geographical Jl, Sociological Review. *Address:* Maple Tree Cottage, 24 Old Leicester Road, Wansford, near Peterborough PE8 6JR. *Clubs:* Royal Air Force, Alpine.

KEMPNER, Prof. Thomas; Principal and Professor of Management Studies, Henley Management College (formerly Administrative Staff College), 1972–90, now Emeritus Professor; Director of Business Studies, Brunel University, 1972–90, now Emeritus Professor; Director, Henley Centre for Forecasting, since 1974 (Chairman, 1974–95); *b* 28 Feb. 1930; *s* of late Martin and Rosa Kempner; *m* 1st, 1958, June Maton (*d* 1980); two *d* (and one *d* decd); 2nd, 1981, Mrs Veronica Ann Vere-Sharp; one step *s* two step *d*. *Educ:* Denstone Coll.; University Coll. London (BSc (Econ)). Asst Administrator, Hyelm Youth Hostels, 1948–49, and part-time, 1951–55; Research Officer, Administrative Staff Coll., Henley, 1954–59; Lectr (later Sen. Tutor) in Business Studies, Sheffield Univ., 1959–63; Prof. of Management Studies, Founder, and Dir of Management Centre, Univ. of Bradford, 1963–72. Chm., Henley Distance Learning Ltd, 1980–95. Member of various cttees, including: Social Studies and Business Management Cttees of University Grants Cttee, 1966–76; Management, Education and Training Cttee of NEDO, 1969–72 (Chm. of its Student Grants Sub-Cttee); Chm., Food Industry Manpower Cttee of NEDO, 1968–71; Jt Chm., Conf. of Univ. Management Schools, 1973–75. Chm. Council, Brunel Univ., 1997–99 (Vice-Chm., 1992–97). Trustee, Greenwich Foundn for RNC, 1997–. CIMgt (FBIM 1971). Hon. DSc Cranfield, 1976; Hon. LLD Birmingham, 1983; DUniv Brunel, 1990. Burnham Gold Medal, 1970. *Publications:* editor, author, and contributor to several books, including: Bradford Exercises in Management (with G. Wills), 1966; Is Corporate Planning Necessary? (with J. Hewkin), 1968; A Guide to the Study of Management, 1969; Management Thinkers (with J. Tillet and G. Wills), 1970; Handbook of Management, 1971, 4th edn 1987; (with K. Macmillan and K. H. Hawkins) Business and Society, 1974; Models for Participation, 1976; numerous articles in management jls. *Recreation:* travel. *Address:* Garden House, Maidensgrove, Henley-on-Thames, Oxon RG9 6EZ. *T:* (01491) 638597.

KEMPSON, Martyn Rex; Strategic Director of Education and Children, London Borough of Barnet, since 1999; *b* 31 July 1947; *s* of Horace and Winifred May Kempson; *m* 1986, Carole J. Kendall; two *s*. *Educ:* Luton Grammar Sch.; North-Western Poly. ALA 1968. Librarian: Luton Public Libraries, 1963–68; Buckinghamshire CC Libraries, 1968–71; London Borough of Sutton Libraries, 1971–91: Borough Librarian, 1987–88; Asst Dir of Leisure, 1988–91; Barnet London Borough Council, 1991–: Controller: Libraries and Arts, 1991–94; Recreation, Leisure and Arts, and Dep. Dir, Educn Services, 1995–98; Dir, Educnl Services, 1998–99. *Publication:* I-Spy Football, 1991. *Recreations:* supporting Luton Town FC, tennis. *Address:* 19 Finchley Park, North Finchley, N12 9JS.

KEMPSON, Rachel, (Lady Redgrave); actress; *b* Devon, 28 May 1910; *d* of Eric William Edward Kempson and Beatrice Hamilton Ashwell Kempson; *m* 1935, Sir Michael Redgrave, CBE (*d* 1985); one *s* two *d*. *Educ:* St Agnes Convent, East Grinstead; Colchester County High Sch.; Oaklea, Buckhurst Hill; RADA. First stage appearance in Much Ado About Nothing, Stratford, 1933; first London appearance in The Lady from Alfaqueque, Westminster, 1933; Stratford season, 1934; Liverpool Playhouse, 1935–36; Love's Labour's Lost, Old Vic, 1936; Volpone, Westminster, 1937; Twelfth Night, Oxford, 1937; The School for Scandal, Queen's, 1937; The Shoemaker's Holiday, Playhouse, 1938; Under One Roof, Richmond, 1940; The Wingless Victory, Phoenix, 1943; Uncle Harry, Garrick, 1944; Jacobowsky and the Colonel, Piccadilly, 1945; Fatal Curiosity, Arts, 1946; The Paragon, Fortune, 1948; The Return of the Prodigal, Globe, 1948; Candida, Oxford, 1949; Venus Observed, Top of the Ladder, St James's, 1950; The Happy Time, St James's, 1952, Shakespeare Meml Theatre Co., 1953; English Stage Co., 1956; The Seagull, St Joan of the Stockyards, Queen's, 1964; Samson Agonistes, Lionel and Clarissa, Guildford, 1965; A Sense of Detachment, Royal Court, 1972; The Freeway, National Theatre, 1974; A Family and a Fortune, Apollo, 1975; The Old Country, Queen's, 1977; Savannah Bay, Royal Court, 1983; Chekhov's Women, Queen's, 1986; The Cocktail Party, Phoenix, 1986; Uncle Vanya, Vaudeville, 1988; Coriolanus, Young Vic, 1989. *Films* include: The Captive Heart, 1945; Georgy Girl; The Jokers; Charge of the Light Brigade; The Virgin Soldiers; Jane Eyre; Out of Africa, 1985; The Understanding, 1985. Frequent *television* appearances include series and serials: Elizabeth R; Jennie; Love for Lydia; The Bell, 1981; The Jewel in the Crown, 1984; The Black Tower, 1985; Small World, 1988; plays: Winter Ladies, Sweet Wine of Youth, 1979; Kate, the Good Neighbour, Getting On, The Best of Everything, and Jude, 1980; Blunt Instrument, Bosom Friends, and The Boxwallah, 1981; World's Beyond, 1986; Boon, She's been away, 1989; Lorna Doone, For the Greater Good, Uncle Vanya, 1990; *radio:* Hester, in The Forsyte Saga, 1990. *Publication:* A Family and its Fortunes (autobiog.), 1986. *Recreations:* gardening, letter writing. *Address:* c/o Creative Artists Management Ltd, 19 Denmark Street, WC2H 8NA.

See also Lynn Redgrave, Vanessa Redgrave.

KEMPSON, Prof. Ruth Margaret, (Mrs M. J. Pinner), FBA 1989; Leverhulme Personal Research Professor, King's College London, since 1999; *b* 26 June 1944; *d* of Edwin Garnett Hone Kempson and Margaret Cecilia Kempson; *m* 1973, Michael John Pinner; two *s*. *Educ:* Univ. of Birmingham (BA (2 ii) Music and English); Univ. of London (MA (with dist.) Mod. English Language 1969; PhD Linguistics 1972). Res. Asst to Survey of English Usage, UCL, 1969–70; School of Oriental and African Studies: Lectr in Linguistics, 1971–85; Reader in Gen. Linguistics, 1985–87, Prof. of Gen. Linguistics, 1987–99, Univ. of London; Head of Linguistics Dept, 1992–96. Vis. Prof. in Semantics, Univ. of Massachusetts, 1982–83. Pres., Linguistics Assoc. of GB, 1986–91. *Publications:* Presupposition and the Delimitation of Semantics, 1975; Semantic Theory, 1977; Mental Representations: the interface between language and reality, 1988; (jtly) Dynamic Syntax: the flow of language understanding, 2000; articles in Linguistics and Philosophy, Jl of Linguistics and edited collections. *Address:* Philosophy Department, King's College London, Strand, WC2R 2LS.

KEMSLEY, 3rd Viscount *cr* 1945, of Dropmore, co. Bucks; **Richard Gomer Berry;** Bt 1928; Baron Kemsley 1936; *b* 17 April 1951; *o s* of Hon. Denis Gomer Berry, 2nd *s* of 1st Viscount Kemsley, GBE and Pamela Berry (*née* Wellesley); *S* uncle, 1999; *m* 1994, Elizabeth Jane Barker; two *s*. *Educ:* Eton. *Heir: s* Hon. Luke Gomer Berry, *b* 2 Feb. 1998. *Address:* Church Hill Farm, Church Lane, Brockenhurst, Hants SO42 7UB.

KENDAL, Felicity Ann, CBE 1995; actress; *d* of late Geoffrey and Laura Kendal; *m* (marr. diss.); one *s*; *m* 1983, Michael Rudman (marr. diss. 1994), *qv*; one *s*. *Educ:* six convents in India. First appeared on stage at age of 9 months, when carried on as the Changeling boy in A Midsummer Night's Dream; grew up touring India and Far East with parents' theatre co., playing pageboys at age of eight and graduating through Puck, at nine, to parts such as Viola in Twelfth Night, Jessica in The Merchant of Venice, and Ophelia in Hamlet; returned to England, 1965; made London debut, Carla in Minor Murder, Savoy, 1967; Katherine in Henry V, and Lika in The Promise, Leicester, 1968; Amaryllis in Back to Methuselah, Nat. Theatre, 1969; Hermia in A Midsummer Night's Dream, and Hero in Much Ado About Nothing, Regent's Park, 1970; Anne Danby in Kean, Oxford, 1970, London, 1971; Romeo and Juliet, 'Tis Pity She's A Whore, and The Three Arrows, 1972; The Norman Conquests, Globe, 1974; Viktosha in Once Upon a Time, Bristol, 1976; Arms and The Man, Greenwich, 1978; Mara in Clouds, Duke of York's, 1978; Constance Mozart in Amadeus, NT, 1979; Desdemona in Othello, NT, 1980; Christopher in On the

Razzle, NT, 1981; Paula in The Second Mrs Tanqueray, NT, 1981; The Real Thing, Strand, 1982; Jumpers, Aldwych, 1985; Made in Bangkok, Aldwych, 1986; Hapgood, Aldwych, 1988; Ivanov, and Much Ado About Nothing, Strand, 1989 (Best Actress Award, Evening Standard); Hidden Laughter, Vaudeville, 1990; Tartuffe, Playhouse, 1991; Heartbreak House, Haymarket, 1992; Arcadia, NT, 1993; An Absolute Turkey, Globe, 1994; Indian Ink, Aldwych, 1995; Mind Millie for Me, Haymarket, 1996; Waste, and The Seagull, Old Vic, 1997; Alarms and Excursions, Gielgud, 1998; Fallen Angels, Apollo, 2000; *Television:* four series of The Good Life, 1975–77; Viola in Twelfth Night, 1979; Solo, 1980, 2nd series 1982; The Mistress, 1985, 2nd series 1986; The Camomile Lawn, 1992; Honey for Tea, 1994; plays and serials. *Films:* Shakespeare Wallah, 1965; Valentino, 1976. Variety Club Most Promising Newcomer, 1974, Best Actress, 1979, 2001; Clarence Derwent Award, 1980; Variety Club Woman of the Year Best Actress Award, 1984. *Publication:* White Cargo (memoirs), 1998. *Recreation:* reading, working. *Address:* c/o Chatto & Linnit, 123A King's Road, SW3 4PL. *T:* (020) 7352 7722.

KENDALL, Prof. David George, DSc, ScD; FRS 1964; Professor of Mathematical Statistics, University of Cambridge, 1962–85 and Fellow of Churchill College, since 1962; *b* 15 Jan. 1918; *s* of Fritz Ernest Kendall and Emmie Taylor, Ripon, Yorks; *m* 1952, Diana Louise Fletcher; two *s* four *d. Educ:* Ripon GS; Queen's Coll., Oxford (MA, 1943; Hon. Fellow 1985); DSc Oxford, 1977; ScD Cambridge, 1988. Fellow Magdalen Coll., Oxford, and Lectr in Mathematics, 1946–62 (Emeritus Fellow, 1989). Visiting Lecturer: Princeton Univ., USA, 1952–53 (Wilks Prize, 1980); Zhong-shan Univ., Guangzhou; Xiangtan Univ.; Changsha Inst. Rlwys; Jiaotong Univ., Xian, 1983. Lectures: Larmor, Cambridge Philos. Soc., 1980; Milne, Wadham Coll., Oxford, 1983; Hotelling, Univ. of N Carolina, 1985; Rietz, Inst. of Math. Stats, 1989; Kolmogorov, Bernoulli Soc., 1990. Member: Internat. Statistical Inst.; Academia Europaea, 1991; Council, Royal Society, 1967–69, 1982–83; President: London Mathematical Soc., 1972–74; Internat. Assoc. Statist. in Phys. Sci., 1973–75; Bernoulli Soc. for Mathematical Stats and Probability, 1975; Section A (Math.) and Section P (Physics), BAAS, 1982. Chm. Parish Reg. Sect., Yorks Archaeol. Soc., 1974–79. Hon. Mem., Romanian Acad., 1992. Hon. D. de l'U Paris (René Descartes), 1976; Hon. DSc Bath, 1986. Guy Medal in Silver, Royal Statistical Soc., 1955; Weldon Meml Prize and Medal for Biometric Science, 1974; Sylvester Medal, Royal Soc., 1976; Whitehead Prize, London Math. Soc., 1980; Guy Medal in Gold, Royal Statistical Soc., 1981; De Morgan Medal, London Math. Soc., 1989. *Publications:* (jt ed) Mathematics in the Archaeological and Historical Sciences, 1971; (jt ed) Stochastic Analysis, 1973; (jt ed) Stochastic Geometry, 1974; (ed) Analytic and Geometric Stochastics, 1986; (jtly) Shape and Shape Theory, 1999. *Address:* 37 Barrow Road, Cambridge CB2 2AR.

KENDALL, David William; Chairman: Celtic Energy Ltd, since 1994; Wagon (formerly Wagon Industrial Holdings) plc, since 1997; *b* 8 May 1935; *s* of William Jack Kendall and Alma May Kendall; *m* 1st, 1960, Delphine Hitchcock (marr. diss.); one *s* one *d*; 2nd, 1973, Elisabeth Rollison; one *s* one *d. Educ:* Enfield Grammar School; Southend High School. FCA. Elles Reeve, Shell-Mex & BP, Irish Shell & BP, 1955–70; British Petroleum Co.: Crude Oil Sales Manager, 1971–72; Manager, Bulk Trading Div., 1973–74; Organisation Planning Cttee, 1975; BP New Zealand: Gen. Manager, 1976–79; Man. Dir and Chief Exec., 1979–82; Chm., BP SW Pacific, 1979–82; BP Oil: Finance and Planning Dir, 1982–85; Man. Dir and Chief Exec., 1985–88; Director: BP Chemicals Internat., 1985–88; BP Oil Internat., 1985–88; Associated Octel Co., 1985–88. Chairman: Bunzl, 1990–93 (Dir, 1988–93); Ruberoid plc, 1993–2000; Whitecroft plc, 1993–2000; Blagden Industries plc, 1994–2000; Meyer Internat., 1994–95; Danka Business Systems plc, 1998–2001 (Dir, 1993–2001); Dep. Chm., British Coal Corp., 1989–91; Director: STC plc, 1988–90; Gowrings plc, 1993–; South Wales Electricity plc, 1993–96; BSI, 2000–. President: UK Petroleum Industries Assoc., 1987–88; Oil Industries Club, 1988. *Recreations:* golf, music, France and its history. *Address:* 41 Albion Street, W2 2AU. *T:* (020) 7258 1955. *Clubs:* Rye Golf, Royal Mid Surrey Golf.

KENDALL, Rev. Frank; Member, Northern Rent Assessment Panels, since 1997; Chairman, Board for Social Responsibility, since 1996, and Licensed Priest, since 1989, Diocese of Liverpool; *b* 15 Dec. 1940; *s* of Norman and Violet Kendall; *m* 1965, Brenda Pickin; one *s* one *d. Educ:* Bradford Grammar School; Corpus Christi College, Cambridge (MA Classics); Southwark Ordination Course (London Univ. Dip. in Religious Studies). MPBW, 1962; DEA, 1967–68; MPBW, DoE and Dept of Transport, 1969–89; Under Secretary 1984; Chief Exec., St Helens MBC, 1989–91; Venue Develt Manager, British Olympic Bid, 1992; Inspector of Schs, 1993–2000. Ordained deacon, 1974, priest, 1975; Hon. Curate: Lingfield, dio. Southwark, 1974–75 and 1978–82; Sketty, dio. Swansea and Brecon, 1975–78; Limpsfield, dio. Southwark, 1982–84; Licensed Preacher, dio. of Manchester, 1984–89. FRSA 1990. *Recreations:* painting: (i) pictures, (ii) decorating. *Address:* 52 Kingsway, Penwortham, Preston PR1 0ED.

KENDALL, Graham; *b* 24 Sept. 1943; *s* of Robert David Kendall and Phillis Margaret Moreton; *m* 1968, Helen Sheila Blackburn; two *s* two *d. Educ:* Helsby Grammar Sch.; Leicester Univ. (BSc); Liverpool Univ. (Post-grad. CertEd). Entered Civil Service as Asst Principal, 1966; DTI; joined Dept of Employment, subseq. DFEE, 1981; Grade 3, 1990; Chief Exec., Sheffield Develt Corp. (on secondment), 1990–97. *Recreations:* running, gardening, family. *Address:* 56 Blackamoor Road, Dore, Sheffield S17 3GJ. *T:* (0114) 236 4533.

KENDALL, Henry Walter George, OBE 1979; Director, British Printing Industries Federation, 1972–81; *b* 21 Dec. 1916; *s* of Henry Kendall and Beatrice (Kerry) Kendall; *m* 1945, Audrey Alison Woodward; two *s* one *d. Educ:* Archbishop Temple's Sch., Lambeth. FCMA. Training with Blades, East & Blades Ltd, 1933–40. War service, RAOC; special duties, War Office, London, 1941; Mil. Coll. of Science, Inspecting Ordnance Officer Western Comd, HQ Allied Land Forces SE Asia, 1940–46. Cost accountant, British Fedn of Master Printers, 1947–55; Chief Cost Accountant, 1955; Head of Management Services, 1967. Mem. Council: CBI, 1972–81; Printing Industry Research Assoc., 1972–81; Inst. of Printing, 1972–81. *Recreations:* theatre, gardening, travel.

KENDALL, Prof. Kevin, FRS 1993; Professor of Formulation Engineering, University of Birmingham, since 2000; *b* 2 Dec. 1943; *s* of Cyril Kendall and Margaret (*née* Swarbrick); *m* 1969, Patricia Jennifer Heyes; one *s* one *d. Educ:* London Univ. (BSc Physics External); PhD Cantab. Joseph Lucas, 1961–66; Cavendish Lab., 1966–69; British Rail Research, 1969–71; Monash Univ., 1972–74 (QEII fellowship); Akron Univ., 1974; ICI Runcorn, 1974–93; Prof. of Materials Science, Keele Univ., 1993–2000. *Publications:* Molecular Adhesion and its Applications, 2001; papers in learned jls on adhesion, fracture, ceramics, material properties. *Recreation:* squash. *Address:* Wycherley, Tower Road, Ashley Heath, Market Drayton, Shropshire TF9 4PY. *T:* (01630) 672665.

KENDALL, Raymond Edward, QPM 1984; Secretary General, International Criminal Police Organization (Interpol), 1985–2000, now Hon. Secretary General; *b* 5 Oct. 1933; *m. Educ:* Simon Langton School, Canterbury; Exeter College, Oxford (MA Hons). RAF, 1951–53 (principally Malaya). Asst Supt of Police, Uganda Police, 1956–62; Metropolitan Police, New Scotland Yard, 1962–86 (principally Special Branch). Mem., Supervisory Cttee, Eur. Anti-Fraud Office. Mem., Forensic Sci. Soc. Editor-in-Chief: Counterfeits and Forgeries; Internat. Criminal Police Review. *Recreations:* shooting, golf. *Address:* BP 202, 69657 Villefranche-Cedex, France. *Clubs:* Special Forces; Chief Constables.

KENDELL, Dr Robert Evan, CBE 1992; FRCP, FRCPE, FRCPsych, FMedSci; FRSE; President, Royal College of Psychiatrists, 1996–99; *b* 28 March 1935; *s* of Robert Owen Kendell and Joan Evans; *m* 1961, Ann Whitfield; two *s* two *d. Educ:* Mill Hill School; Peterhouse, Cambridge. MA, MD. FRCP 1974; FRCPE 1977; FRCPsych 1979; FRSE 1993. KCH Med. School, 1956–59; Maudsley Hosp., 1962–68; Vis. Prof., Univ. of Vermont Coll. of Medicine, 1969–70; Reader in Psychiatry, Inst. of Psychiatry, 1970–74; Prof. of Psychiatry, 1974–91, Dean, Faculty of Medicine, 1986–90, Univ. of Edinburgh; CMO, Scottish Office Home and Health Dept, 1991–96. Chm., WHO Expert Cttee on Alcohol Consumption, 1979; Mem., MRC, 1984–88, 1991–96. Founder FMedSci 1998. Hon. FRCSE 1995; Hon. FRCPSG, 1995. Gaskell Medal, RCPsych, 1967; Paul Hoch Medal, Amer. Psychopathol Assoc., 1988; Medal, Marcé Soc., 1994. *Publications:* The Classification of Depressive Illnesses, 1968; The Role of Diagnosis in Psychiatry, 1975; (ed) Companion to Psychiatric Studies, 3rd edn 1983 to 5th edn 1993. *Recreations:* overeating and walking up hills. *Address:* 3 West Castle Road, Edinburgh EH10 5AT. *T:* (0131) 229 4966, *Fax:* (0131) 228 7547. *Club:* Climbers'.

KENDRICK, Dominic John; QC 1997; *b* 23 Feb. 1955; *m* 1984, Marice Chantal; one *s* two *d. Educ:* St Ambrose Coll.; Trinity Coll., Cambridge (BA Hons, MA); City Univ. (Dip. Law); Inns of Court Sch. of Law. Called to the Bar, Middle Temple, 1981. *Recreations:* old books, old houses, tennis. *Address:* 7 King's Bench Walk, Temple, EC4Y 7DS. *T:* (020) 7583 0404.

KENDRICK, Graham Andrew; song and hymn writer; *b* 2 Aug. 1950; *s* of Maurice and Olive Kendrick; *m* 1976, Jill Gibson; four *d. Educ:* Avery Hill Coll. of Educn (Cert Ed 1972). Music Dir, British Youth for Christ, 1976–80; Kendrick & Stevenson (music and mime duo), 1981–84; Mem., Leadership Team, Ichthus Christian Fellowship, 1984–; Co-founder, March for Jesus, 1987. Songs and hymns sung in many languages worldwide; has recorded numerous albums, incl. the Millennium Chorus, 1971–. Hon. DD Brunel, 2000. *Publications:* Worship, 1984; Ten Worshipping Churches, 1987; March for Jesus, 1992; Shine Jesus Shine, 1992; Awakening our Cities for God, 1993. *Recreations:* family, walking, music. *Address:* c/o Make Way Music, PO Box 263, Croydon, Surrey CR9 5AP. *T:* (020) 8656 0025, *Fax:* (020) 8656 4342.

KENEALLY, Thomas Michael, AO 1983; FRSL; FAAAS; author; *b* 7 Oct. 1935; *s* of Edmond Thomas Keneally; *m* 1965, Judith Mary Martin; two *d.* Studied for NSW Bar. Schoolteacher until 1965; Commonwealth Literary Fellowship, 1966, 1968, 1972; Lectr in Drama, Univ. of New England, 1968–69. Vis. Prof., Dept of English, Univ. of California, Irvine, 1985; Berg Prof., Dept of English, New York Univ., 1988; Distinguished Prof., Dept of English and Comparative Lit., Univ. of Calif, Irvine, 1991–. Chm., Australian Republican Movement, 1991–94. Member: (inaugural) Australia–China Council, 1978–83; Adv. Panel, Australian Constitutional Commn, 1985–88; Literary Arts Bd, Australia, 1985–88; Chm., Aust. Soc. Authors, 1987–90 (Mem. Council, 1985–); Pres., Nat. Book Council Australia, 1985–89. FRSL 1973. Silver City (screenplay, with Sophia Turkiewicz), 1985. Hon. DLitt: Queensland, 1993; NUI, 1994; Fairleigh Dickinson, NJ, 1994. *Publications:* The Place at Whitton, 1964; The Fear, 1965, 2nd edn 1973; Bring Larks and Heroes, 1967, 2nd edn 1973; Three Cheers for the Paraclete, 1968; The Survivor, 1969; A Dutiful Daughter, 1971; The Chant of Jimmie Blacksmith, 1972 (filmed 1978); Blood Red, Sister Rose, 1974; Gossip from the Forest, 1975 (TV film, 1979); The Lawgiver, 1975; Season in Purgatory, 1976; A Victim of the Aurora, 1977; Ned Kelly and the City of the Bees, 1978; Passenger, 1979; Confederates, 1979; Schindler's Ark, 1982, reissued as Schindler's List, 1994 (Booker Prize; LA Times Fiction Prize; filmed as Schindler's List, 1994); Outback, 1983; The Cut-Rate Kingdom, 1984; A Family Madness, 1985; The Playmaker, 1987 (stage adaptation, perf. Royal Court, 1988); Towards Asmara, 1989; Flying Hero Class, 1991 (also screenplay); The Place where Souls are born, 1992; Now and in Time to be, 1992; Woman of the Inner Sea, 1992 (also screenplay); Memoirs from a Young Republic, 1993; Jacko, 1993; The Utility Player (biog.), 1994; A River Town, 1995; Homebush Boy: a memoir, 1995; The Great Shame, 1998; Bettany's Book, 2000. *Recreations:* swimming, crosswords, hiking, cross-country ski-ing. *Address:* c/o Deborah Rogers, 20 Powis Mews, W11 1JN.

KENILOREA, Rt Hon. Sir Peter (Kauona Keninaraiso'ona), KBE 1982; PC 1979; Ombudsman of the Solomon Islands, 1996–2001; Prime Minister of the Solomon Islands, 1978–81 and 1984–86; *b* Takataka, Malaita, 23 May 1943; *m* 1971, Margaret Kwanairara; two *s* two *d. Educ:* Univ. and Teachers' Coll., NZ (Dip. Ed.). Teacher, King George VI Secondary Sch., 1968–70. Asst Sec., Finance, 1971; Admin. Officer, Dist Admin, 1971–73; Lands Officer, 1973–74; Dep. Sec. to Cabinet and to Chief Minister, 1974–75; Dist Comr, Eastern Solomon Is, 1975–76; MLA, subseq. MP, East Are-Are, 1976–91; Chief Minister, Solomon Is, 1976–78; Leader of the Opposition, 1981–84; Dep. Prime Minister, 1987–89; Minister of Foreign Affairs, 1987–89, for Foreign Affairs and Trade Relations, 1990. Dir, Forum Fisheries Agency, 1991–94. Silver Jubilee Medal, 1977; Solomon Is Indep. Medal, 1978. *Publications:* political and scientific, numerous articles. *Address:* (office) Kalala House, PO Box 535, Honiara, Guadalcanal, Solomon Islands.

KENILWORTH, 4th Baron *cr* 1937, of Kenilworth; **(John) Randle Siddeley;** Managing Director, Siddeley Landscapes, since 1976; Director, John Siddeley International Ltd; *b* 16 June 1954; *s* of John Tennant Davenport Siddeley (3rd Baron Kenilworth) and of Jacqueline Paulette, *d* of late Robert Gelpi; *S* father, 1981; *m* 1st, 1983, Kim (marr. diss. 1989), *o d* of Danie Serfontein, Newcastle upon Tyne; 2nd, 1991, Mrs Kiki McDonough; two *s. Educ:* Northease Manor, near Lewes, Sussex; West Dean College (studied Restoration of Antique Furniture); London College of Furniture. Worked at John Siddeley International as interior designer/draughtsman, 1975; formed own company, Siddeley Landscapes, as landscape gardener, 1976; formed Randle Siddeley Associates, as landscape designer, 1994. *Recreation:* ski-ing. *Heir: s* Hon. William Randle John Siddeley, *b* 24 Jan. 1992. *Address:* Randle Siddeley Associates, 2 Palmerston Court, Palmerston Way, SW8 4AJ. *Clubs:* St James's, Annabel's.

KENLIS, Lord; Thomas Rupert Charles Christopher Taylour; *b* 18 June 1989; *s* and *heir* of Earl of Bective, *qv*.

KENNAN, Prof. George Frost; Professor, Institute for Advanced Study, Princeton, NJ, 1956–74, now Professor Emeritus; *b* 16 Feb. 1904; *m* 1931, Annelise Sorensen; one *s* three *d. Educ:* Princeton Univ. (AB); Seminary for Oriental Languages, Berlin. Foreign Service of the USA; many posts from 1926–52; US Ambassador to the USSR, 1952–53; Institute for Advanced Study, Princeton, 1953–61; US Ambassador to Yugoslavia, 1961–63. George Eastman Vis. Prof., Oxford, 1957–58; Reith Lectr, BBC, 1957; Prof., Princeton Univ., 1963 and 1964. Hon. LLD: Dartmouth and Yale, 1950; Colgate, 1951; Notre Dame, 1953; Kenyon Coll., 1954; New School for Social Research, 1955; Princeton, 1956; University of Michigan and Northwestern, 1957; Brandeis, 1958; Wisconsin, 1963; Harvard, 1963; Denison, 1966; Rutgers, 1966; Marquette, 1972; Catholic Univ. of America, 1976; Duke, 1977; Ripon Coll., 1978; Dickinson Coll., 1979; Lake Forest Coll.,

1982; Clark Univ., 1983; Oberlin Coll., 1983; Brown Univ., 1983; New York Univ., 1985; William and Mary Coll., and Columbia Univ., 1986; Rider Coll., 1988; Hon. DCL Oxford, 1969; Dr of Politics *hc* Univ. of Helsinki, 1986. Benjamin Franklin Fellow RSA, 1968. President: Nat. Inst. of Arts and Letters, 1965–68; Amer. Acad. of Arts and Letters, 1968–72; Corresp. FBA, 1983. Pour le Mérite (Germany), 1976. Albert Einstein Peace Prize, Albert Einstein Peace Prize Foundn of Chicago, 1981; Grenville Clark Prize, Grenville Clark Fund at Dartmouth Coll., Inc., 1981; Börsenverein Peace Prize, Frankfurt, 1982; Gold Medal for History, AAIL, 1984; Creative Arts Award for Nonfiction, Brandeis Univ., 1986; Freedom from Fear Award, FDR Foundn, 1987; Physicians for Social Responsibility Award, 1988; Toynbee Prize, 1988; Encyclopeadia Britannica Award 1989; Presidential Medal of Freedom, 1989; Governor's Award of NJ, 1990. *Publications:* American Diplomacy, 1900–50, 1951 (US); Realities of American Foreign Policy, 1954 (US); Amerikanisch Russische Verhältnis, 1954 (Germany); Soviet-American Relations, 1917–20; Vol. I, Russia Leaves the War, 1956 (National Book Award; Pulitzer Prize 1957); Vol. II, The Decision to Intervene, 1958; Russia, the Atom and the West, 1958; Soviet Foreign Policy, 1917–1941, 1960; Russia and the West under Lenin and Stalin, 1961; On Dealing with the Communist World, 1964; Memoirs, vol. 1, 1925–1950, 1967 (National Book Award 1968; Pulitzer Prize 1968); Memoirs, vol. 2, 1950–1963, 1973; From Prague after Munich: Diplomatic Papers 1938–1940, 1968; Democracy and the Student Left, 1968; The Marquis de Custine and his 'Russie en 1839', 1972; The Cloud of Danger, 1977; The Decline of Bismarck's European Order, 1979; The Nuclear Delusion, 1982; The Fateful Alliance: France, Russia and the coming of the First World War, 1985; Sketches from a Life, 1989; Around the Cragged Hill: a personal and political philosophy, 1993; At a Century's Ending: reflections 1982–1995, 1996; *relevant publication:* George F. Kennan and the Origins of Containment 1944–46, 1997. *Club:* Century (New York City).

KENNARD, Prof. Christopher, PhD; FRCP, FMedSci; Professor of Clinical Neurology, and Head, Division of Neuroscience and Psychological Medicine, Imperial College School of Medicine, since 1997; *b* 5 Jan. 1946; *s* of late Keith and Enid Kennard; *m* 1973, Cherry Fay Mortimer; two *d*. *Educ:* St Marylebone Grammar Sch., London; Charing Cross Hosp. Med. Sch., Univ. of London (MB BS Hons 1970; PhD 1978). Research Fellow: NIMR, 1973–76; Neuro-ophthalmology Unit, Univ. of Calif, San Francisco, 1980; Jun. hosp. appts, Charing Cross Hosp. and London Hosp., 1976–81; Consultant Neurologist, Royal London Hosp., 1981–91; Prof. of Clinical Neurology, Charing Cross and Westminster Med. Sch., 1991–97; Clinical Dir, Neuroscis, Hammersmith Hosp. NHS Trust, 1998– (Chief of Service, 1995–98). Non-exec. Mem., W London Mental Health NHS Trust, 2001–. Chm., Cttee on Neurology , RCP, 1997–; Mem., Neuroscience and Mental Health Bd, MRC, 2000–. Pres. elect, Assoc. of British Neurologists, 2001– (Asst Sec., 1990–92; Hon. Sec., 1992–95). FMedSci 2001. Trustee: Migraine Trust; British Brain and Spine Foundn. Ed., Jl Neurology, Neurosurgery and Psychiatry, 1997–. *Publications:* editor, several books on clinical neurology; papers on neuro-ophthalmology. *Recreation:* music. *Address:* Department of Sensorimotor Systems, Division of Neuroscience and Psychological Medicine, Imperial College School of Medicine, Charing Cross Campus, St Dunstan's Road, W6 8RP. *T:* (020) 8846 7598. *Club:* Athenæum.

KENNARD, Dr Olga, (Lady Burgen), OBE 1988; ScD; FRS 1987; Director, Cambridge Crystallographic Data Centre, 1965–97; *b* 23 March 1924; *d* of Joir and Catherina Weisz; *m* 1st, 1948, David William Kennard (marr. diss. 1961); two *d*; 2nd, 1993, Sir Arnold Burgen, *qv*. *Educ:* Cambridge University (MA 1948; ScD 1973). Res. Asst, Cavendish Laboratory, Cambridge, 1944–48; MRC Scientific Staff: Inst. of Ophthalmology, London, 1948–51; Nat. Inst. for Med. Res., London, 1951–61; seconded to University Chemical Laboratory, Cambridge, 1961–71; MRC special appt, 1974–89. Mem. Council, Royal Soc., 1995–97. *Publications:* about 200 pubns in field of X-ray structure determination of organic and bioactive molecules and correlation between structure, chemical properties and biological activity, and technical innovations in X-ray crystallography; ed 20 standard reference books. *Recreations:* music, swimming, architecture. *Address:* Keelson, 8A Hills Avenue, Cambridge CB1 7XA. *T:* (01223) 415381.

KENNAWAY, Sir John (Lawrence); 5th Bt *cr* 1791; *b* 7 Sept. 1933; *s* of Sir John Kennaway, 4th Bt and Mary Felicity (*d* 1991), *yr d* of late Rev. Chancellor Ponsonby; *S* father, 1956; *m* 1961, Christina Veronica Urszenyi, MB, ChB (Cape Town); one *s* two *d*. *Educ:* Harrow; Trinity Coll., Cambridge. *Heir: s* John Michael Kennaway [*b* 17 Feb. 1962; *m* 1988, Lucy Frances, *yr d* of Dr Jeremy Houlton Bradshaw-Smith; two *d*]. *Address:* Escot, Ottery St Mary, Devon EX11 1LU.

KENNEDY, family name of **Marquess of Ailsa**.

KENNEDY OF THE SHAWS, Baroness *cr* 1997 (Life Peer), of Cathcart in the City of Glasgow; **Helena Ann Kennedy;** QC 1991; *b* 12 May 1950; *d* of Joshua Patrick Kennedy and Mary Veronica (*née* Jones); partner, 1978–84, (Roger) Iain Mitchell; one *s*; *m* 1986, Dr Iain Louis Hutchison; one *s* one *d*. *Educ:* Holyrood Secondary Sch., Glasgow; Council of Legal Educn. Called to the Bar, Gray's Inn, 1972, Bencher, 1999; established chambers at: Garden Court, 1974; Tooks Court, 1984; Doughty St, 1990. Member: Bar Council, 1990–93; Cttee, Assoc. of Women Barristers, 1991–; Nat. Bd, Women's Legal Defence Fund, 1989–91; Council, Howard League for Penal Reform, 1989– (Chm., commn of inquiry into violence in penal instns for children, report, 1995); CIBA Commn into Child Sexual Abuse, 1981–83; Exec. Cttee, NCCL, 1983–85; Bd, Minority Access to Legal Profession Project, Poly. of South Bank, 1984–85; British Council Law Adv. Cttee, 1995–; Chairman: British Council, 1998–; Human Genetics Commn, 2000–. Chancellor, Oxford Brookes Univ., 1994–. Chairman: Haldane Soc., 1983–86 (Vice-Pres., 1986–); Charter '88, 1992–97; Standing Cttee for Youth Justice, NACRO, 1993–; Cttee on widening participation of FEFC, 1995–97 (report, Learning Works); Leader of inquiry into health, envmtl and safety aspects of Atomic Weapons Establishment, Aldermaston (report, 1993). Commissioner: BAFTA inquiry into future of BBC, 1990; Hamlyn Nat. Commn on Educn, 1991–. Chm., London Internat. Fest. of Theatre, 1993. Vis. Lectr on Criminal Law, BPMF, 1991–; Advr, Mannheim Inst. on Criminology, LSE, 1992–. Member Board: City Limits Magazine, 1982–84; Counsel Magazine, 1990–; Hampstead Theatre, 1989–. Broadcaster: first female moderator, Hypotheticals (Granada) on surrogate motherhood and artificial insemination; presenter: Heart of the Matter, BBC, 1987; Putting Women in the Picture, BBC2, 1987; The Trial of Lady Chatterley's Lover, Radio 4, 1990; Raw Deal, series of progs on med. negligence, BBC2, 1990; co-producer, Women Behind Bars, Channel 4, 1990; presenter, The Maguires: forensic evidence on trial, BBC2, 1991; creator, drama series, Blind Justice, BBC, 1988; host, After Dark, Channel 4, 1988; presenter, Time Gentlemen Please, BBC Scotland, 1994. FRSA. Hon. Fellow, Inst. of Advanced Legal Studies, Univ. of London, 1997. Holds 12 hon. degrees. UK Woman of Europe Award, 1995. *Publications:* (jtly) The Bar on Trial, 1978; (jtly) Child Abuse Within the Family, 1984; (jtly) Balancing Acts, 1989; Eve was Framed, 1992; lectures; contribs on issues connected with law, civil liberties and women. *Recreations:* theatre, spending time with family and friends. *Address:* House of Lords, SW1A 0PW. *T:* and *Fax:* (01708) 379482.

KENNEDY, Maj.-Gen. Alasdair Ian Gordon, CB 1996; CBE 1991 (OBE); Senior Army Member, Royal College of Defence Studies, 1995–96; retired 1997; *b* 6 Oct. 1945; *m* 1980, Meade Funsten; one *s* one *d*. *Educ:* RMCS. psc. Commnd Gordon Highlanders, 1966; Brig. 1988, Maj.-Gen. 1991. Comdr, HQ 24 Airmobile Bde, 1988–90; Dir Gen., Territorial Army, 1992–95. Hon. Col, Tayforth Univs OTC, 1991–97. Asst Gen. Sec., RAC, 1997.

KENNEDY, A(lfred) James, CBE 1979; DSc (London), PhD (London); FREng, MIEE, FIM, FInstP; consultant; *b* 6 Nov. 1921; *m* 1950, Anna Jordan (*d* 1986); no *c*. *Educ:* Haberdashers' Aske's Hatcham Sch.; University Coll., London (BSc (Physics) 1943; Fellow 1976). Commissioned R Signals, 1944; Staff Major (Telecommunications) Central Comd, Agra, India, 1945–46 and at Northern Comd, Rawalpindi, 1946–47; Asst Lectr in Physics, UCL 1947–50; Res. Fellow, Davy-Faraday Lab. of Royal Institution, London, 1950–51; Royal Society, Armourers' and Brasiers' Research Fellow in Metallurgy (at Royal Institution), 1951–54; Head of Metal Physics Sect., BISRA, 1954–57; Prof. of Materials and Head of Dept. of Materials, Coll. of Aeronautics, Cranfield, 1957–66; Dir, British Non-Ferrous Metals Res. Assoc., later BNF Metals Technol. Centre, Wantage, 1966–78; Dir of Research, Delta Metal Co., and Man. Dir, Delta Materials Research Ltd, 1978–81; Dep. Dir, Technical Change Centre, 1981–86; Dir, BL Technology Ltd, 1979–83. Vis. Prof. in Metallurgy, Imperial Coll. of Science and Technol., London, 1981–86. Institution of Metallurgists: Pres., 1976–77; a Vice Pres., 1971–74, 1975–76; Mem. Council, 1968–76. President: Inst. of Metals, 1970–71 (Mem. Council, 1968–73; Fellow, 1973); Engrg Section, BAAS, 1983; Member: Metallurgy Cttee, CNAA, 1965–71; ARC, 1967–70, 1971–74, 1977–80 (also Mem., ARC cttees); Adv. Council on Materials, 1970–71; Council, The Metals Soc., 1974–84 (Platinum Medallist, 1977); Inst. of Physics, 1968–71; SRC, 1974–78; Metall. and Mat. Cttee, SRC, 1970–75 (Chm. 1973–74); Engrg Bd, 1973–78; Council of Env. Sci. and Eng., 1973–78; Adv. Council for Applied R&D, 1976–80; Mat. and Chem. Res. Requirements Bd, DoI, 1981–83 (Chm., Non-Ferrous Metals Cttee); Chm., Council of Sci. and Tech. Insts, 1983–84. Fellow, Amer. Soc. Met., 1972. Pres., Brit. Soc. of Rheology, 1964–66; a Governor, Nat. Inst. for Agric. Engrg, 1966–74. Hon. DSc Aston, 1980. *Publications:* Processes of Creep and Fatigue in Metals, 1962; The Materials Background to Space Technology, 1964; Creep and Stress Relaxation in Metals (English edn), 1965; (ed) High Temperature Materials, 1968; research papers and articles, mainly on physical aspects of deformation and fracture in crystalline materials, particularly metals. *Recreations:* music, painting. *Address:* Woodhill, Milton under Wychwood, Chipping Norton, Oxford OX7 6EP. *T:* (01993) 830334. *Club:* Athenæum.

KENNEDY, Anthony McLeod; Associate Justice of the Supreme Court of the United States, since 1988; *b* 23 July 1936; *s* of Anthony J. Kennedy and Gladys Kennedy; *m* Mary Davis; two *s* one *d*. *Educ:* Stanford Univ. (AB 1958); LSE; Harvard Univ. (LLB 1961). Mem., Calif. Bar, 1962, US Tax Court Bar, 1971. Associate, Thelen Marrin Johnson & Bridges, San Francisco, 1961–63; sole practice, 1963–67; partner Evans, Jackson & Kennedy, 1967–75. Prof. of Constitutional Law, McGeorge Sch. of Law, Univ. of Pacific, 1965–88; Judge, US Court of Appeals, 9th Circuit, Sacramento, 1976–88. Hon. Fellow: Amer. Bar Assoc.; Amer. Coll. of Trial Lawyers. Hon. Bencher, Inner Temple. *Address:* Supreme Court Building, 1 First Street NE, Washington, DC 20543, USA.

KENNEDY, Prof. Arthur Colville, CBE 1992; FRCPE, FRCPGlas, FRCP; FRSE 1984; Muirhead Professor of Medicine, Glasgow University, 1978–88; *b* 23 Oct. 1922; *s* of Thomas and Johanna Kennedy; *m* 1947, Agnes White Taylor; two *d* (one *s* decd). *Educ:* Whitehill Sch., Glasgow; Univ. of Glasgow. MB ChB 1945; MD 1956. FRCPE 1960; FRCPGlas 1964; FRCP 1977; FRCPI 1988. Hon. Consultant in Medicine, Royal Infirmary, Glasgow, 1959–88; Titular Professor, Univ. of Glasgow, 1969–78. Member: Greater Glasgow Health Bd, 1985–89; GMC, 1989–92 (Chm., Professional and Linguistic Bd, 1987–89). President: RCPSG, 1986–88; BMA, 1991–92; Royal Medico-Chirurgical Soc. of Glasgow, 1971–72; Europ. Dialysis and Transplant Assoc., 1972–75; Scottish Soc. of Physicians, 1983–84; Harveian Soc. of Edinburgh, 1985. Hon. FACP 1987; Hon. FRACP 1988. *Publications:* various papers on renal disease. *Recreations:* gardening, walking, reading, photography. *Address:* 16 Boclair Crescent, Bearsden, Glasgow G61 2AG. *T:* (0141) 942 5326. *Club:* Royal Scottish Automobile (Glasgow).

KENNEDY, Rt Hon. Charles (Peter), PC 1999; MP (Lib Dem) Ross, Skye and Inverness West, since 1997 (MP Ross, Cromarty and Skye, 1983–97, SDP, 1983–88, Lib Dem, 1988–97); Leader of the Liberal Democrats, since 1999; *b* Inverness, 25 Nov. 1959; *yr s* of Ian Kennedy, crofter, and Mary McVarish MacEachen. *Educ:* Lochaber High Sch., Fort William; Univ. of Glasgow (joint MA Hons Philosophy and Politics). President, Glasgow Univ. Union, 1980–81; winner, British Observer Mace for Univ. Debating, 1982. Journalist, BBC Highland, Inverness, 1982; Fulbright Schol. and Associate Instructor in Dept of Speech Communication, Indiana Univ., Bloomington Campus, 1982–83. SDP spokesman on health, social services, social security and Scottish issues, 1983–87; SDP-Liberal Alliance spokesman on social security, 1987; Lib Dem spokesman on trade and industry, 1988–89, on health, 1989–92, on Europe and East-West relations, 1992–97, on agriculture and rural affairs, 1997–99. Member, Select Committee: on Social Services, 1986–87; on Televising of H of C, 1988–90; on Standards and Privileges, 1997–99. Chm., SDP Council for Scotland, 1986–88; Pres., Lib Dems, 1990–94. Occasional journalist, broadcaster and lecturer. *Publication:* The Future of Politics, 2000. *Address:* House of Commons, SW1A 0AA. *T:* (020) 7219 5090. *Club:* National Liberal.

KENNEDY, Danny; *see* Kennedy, T. D.

KENNEDY, David, CMG 1997; Director-General, Commonwealth War Graves Commission, 1993–2000; *b* 7 Nov. 1940; *s* of Lilian Alice Kennedy; *m* 1964, Peta Jennifer Hatton; two *d*. *Educ:* Ryhope Robert Richardson Grammar Sch., Co. Durham; City of London Coll. Exchequer and Audit Dept, 1959–69; Commonwealth War Graves Commission: Higher Exec. Officer, 1969–71; Sen. Exec. Officer, 1971–74; Principal: Dir of Management Services, 1975–79; Dir, Outer Area, 1979–84; Senior Principal: Dir, France Area, 1984–86; Dir of Personnel, 1986–87; Dep. Dir-Gen., Admin, 1987–92; rcds 1992. *Recreations:* tennis, badminton, ski-ing, photography, hill-walking, travel. *Address:* March House, Blands Close, Burghfield Common, Berks RG7 3JY. *T:* (0118) 983 2941.

KENNEDY, Denise Margaret; Her Honour Judge Kennedy; a County Court Judge, Northern Ireland, since 2000; *b* 13 April 1942; *d* of David L. R. Halliday and late Doris Halliday (*née* Molyneaux); *m* 1966, John Andrew Dunn Kennedy; two *s* one *d*. *Educ:* Cheltenham Ladies' Coll.; Exeter Univ. (BA Hons); Queen's Univ. of Belfast. Called to the Bar: NI, 1977; Ireland, 1985; in practice at the Bar, 1977–90; Legal Sec. to Lord Chief Justice of NI, 1990–93; Master, High Court, Supreme Court of Judicature of NI, 1993–2000; Dep. County Court Judge, 1993–2000; Dep. Clerk of Crown for NI, 1993–2000. Part-time Chm., Industrial Tribunals, NI, 1985–90; Mem., Independent Commn for Police Complaints, NI, 1988–90. Mem., Civil Justice Reform Gp for NI,

1998–99. *Recreations:* travel, gardening, cinema. *Address:* c/o Northern Ireland Court Service, Windsor House, Bedford Street, Belfast BT2 7LT.

KENNEDY, Edward Arthur Gilbert; retired; *b* Dublin, 5 May 1920; *s* of Captain Edward H. N. Kennedy, RN, and Frances A. Gosling, Bermuda; *m* 1944, Margarita Dagmara Hofstra; two *s* two *d*. *Educ:* Oundle; Pembroke Coll., Cambridge (BA Mod Langs). Served War, RNVR, 1941–46. Joined Northern Ireland Civil Service, 1947; served mainly in Dept of Commerce until 1970, then in Office of NI Ombudsman (Sen. Dir, 1973–83). Vice-Chm., Music Cttee, N Ireland Arts Council, 1978–83; Hon. Pres., Belfast Ballet Club, 1970–82; Chm., Belfast Picture Borrowing Gp, 1970–84. *Recreation:* interest in the arts. *Address:* 29 Tweskard Park, Belfast BT4 2JZ. *T:* (028) 9076 3638.

KENNEDY, Edward Moore; US Senator (Democrat) from Massachusetts, since 1962; *b* Boston, Mass, 22 Feb. 1932; *y s* of late Joseph Patrick Kennedy and Rose Kennedy (*née* Fitzgerald); *m*; two *s* one *d*; *m* 1992, Victoria Anne Reggie. *Educ:* Milton Acad.; Harvard Univ. (BA 1956); Internat. Law Inst., The Hague; Univ. of Virginia Law Sch. (LLB 1959). Served US Army, 1951–53. Called to Massachusetts Bar, 1959; Asst Dist Attorney, Suffolk County, Mass, 1961–62. Senate majority whip, 1969–71; Chairman: Judiciary Cttee, 1979–81; Labor and Human Resources Cttee, now Health, Educn, Labor and Pensions Cttee, 1987– (Ranking Democrat, 1981–86 and 1995–); Member: Senate Armed Forces Cttee; Senate Jt Economic Cttee. Pres., Joseph P. Kennedy Jr Foundn, 1961–; Trustee: John F. Kennedy Lib.; John F. Kennedy Center for the Performing Arts; Robert F. Kennedy Meml Foundn. Holds numerous hon. degrees, foreign decorations and awards. *Publications:* Decisions for a Decade, 1968; In Critical Condition, 1972; Our Day and Generation, 1979; (with Senator Mark Hatfield) Freeze: how you can help prevent nuclear war, 1982. *Address:* United States Senate, Washington, DC 20510-2101, USA.

KENNEDY, Sir Francis, KCMG 1986; CBE 1977 (MBE 1958); DL; HM Diplomatic Service, retired; Chancellor, University of Central Lancashire, since 1995; *b* 9 May 1926; *s* of late James Kennedy and Alice (*née* Bentham); *m* 1957, Anne O'Malley; two *s* two *d*. *Educ:* Univs of Manchester and London. RN, 1944–46. Min. of Supply, 1951–52; HM Colonial Service, Nigeria, 1953–63; Asst Dist Officer, 1953–56; Dist Officer, 1956–59; Principal Asst Sec. to Premier E Nigeria, 1961–62; Provincial Sec., Port Harcourt, 1962–63; HM Diplomatic Service, 1964; First Sec., Commercial and Economic, Dar-es-Salaam, 1965; First Sec. and Head of Post, Kuching, 1967–69; Consul, Commercial, Istanbul, 1970–73; Consul-Gen., Atlanta, 1973–78; Counsellor later Minister Lagos, 1978–81; Ambassador to Angola, 1981–83; Dir-Gen., British Trade and Investment, and Consul-Gen., NY, 1983–86. Special Advr to Chm. and Bd, 1986–96, Dir, 1987–96, British Airways; Chairman: British Airways Regl, 1993–96 (Dir, 1993–); Fluor Daniel Ltd, 1989–96 (Dir, 1986–96); Director: Leslie & Godwin Ltd, 1986–91; Global Analysis Systems, 1986–88; Hambourne Development Co., 1987–94; Smith & Nephew, 1988–96; Fleming Overseas Investment Trust, 1988–96; Brunner Mond Hldgs, 1992–99; Magadi Soda Co., 1994–; Mem. Bd and Council, Inward, 1986–90; Advr, Brook Lowe Internat., 1999–2000. Chm., Africa Centre, 1999–2000. Mem. Bd, Univ. of Central Lancs (formerly Lancashire Polytechnic), 1989–96. Governor, British Liver Foundn, 1990–93. DL Lancs 1995. *Clubs:* Brooks's; Shaw Hill Golf and Country; Lancashire County Cricket.
See also Rt Rev. Mgr J. Kennedy.

KENNEDY, Hon. Geoffrey Alexander, AO 1994; Judge of the Supreme Court of Western Australia, 1981–2001; *b* 6 Sept. 1931; *s* of Alexander Patrick Kennedy and Dorothy Kennedy (*née* Everington); *m* 1964, Alison King; one *s* two *d*. *Educ:* Scotch College, WA; Univ. of Western Australia (BA, LLB); Wadham Coll., Oxford (Rhodes Scholar, 1955; BCL). Partner, Robinson Cox & Co., Solicitors, 1958–75; Mem., Independent Bar, 1976–80; QC (WA) 1977. Mem., Judicial System Adv. Cttee, Constitutional Commn, Australia, 1986–88; Chm., Royal Commn on Commercial Activities of WA Govt, 1991–92. Chancellor, Univ. of Western Australia, 1990–98; Chairman: Council, Scotch Coll., WA, 1974–83; Nat. Council of Indep. Schs, 1979–81; WA Mus., 1984–91. Hon. LLD Univ. of WA, 1999. *Address:* 32 Keane Street, Peppermint Grove, WA 6011, Australia. *T:* (8) 93845635. *Club:* Weld (Perth).

KENNEDY, (George) Michael (Sinclair), CBE 1997 (OBE 1981); Chief Music Critic, The Sunday Telegraph, since 1989; Staff Music Critic, The Daily Telegraph, since 1950 (Joint Chief Critic, 1987–89); *b* 19 Feb. 1926; *s* of Hew Gilbert Kennedy and Marian Florence Sinclair; *m* 1st, 1947, Eslyn Durdle (*d* 1999); no *c*; 2nd, 1999, Dr Joyce Bourne. *Educ:* Berkhamsted School. Joined Daily Telegraph, Manchester, 1941; served Royal Navy (BPF), 1943–46; rejoined Daily Telegraph, Manchester, serving in various capacities on editorial staff; Asst Northern Editor, 1958; Northern Ed., 1960–86. Gov., Royal Northern Coll. of Music; Mem. Cttee, Vaughan Williams Trust, 1965– (Chm., 1977–); Vice-Pres., Elgar Foundn and Elgar Soc. Hon. Mem., Royal Manchester Coll. of Music, 1971. Hon. MA Manchester, 1975. FJI 1967; FRNCM 1981; CRNCM 1999. *Publications:* The Hallé Tradition, 1960; The Works of Ralph Vaughan Williams, 1964, 2nd edn 1980; Portrait of Elgar, 1968, 4th edn 1993; Portrait of Manchester, 1970; Elgar Orchestral Works, 1970; History of Royal Manchester College of Music, 1971; Barbirolli: Conductor Laureate, 1971; (ed) The Autobiography of Charles Hallé, 1973; Mahler, 1974, 3rd edn 2000 (Japanese edn 1978); Richard Strauss, 1976, 2nd edn 1995; (ed) Concise Oxford Dictionary of Music, 3rd edn, 1980, 4th edn 1996; Britten, 1981, 3rd edn 2000; The Hallé, 1858–1983, 1983; Strauss Tone Poems, 1984; Oxford Dictionary of Music, 1985, 2nd edn 1994; Adrian Boult, 1987; Portrait of Walton, 1989, 2nd edn 1997; Music Enriches All: 21 years of the Royal Northern College of Music, 1994; Richard Strauss: man, musician, enigma, 1999; scripts for BBC, contrib. musical jls. *Recreations:* listening to music, watching cricket. *Address:* The Bungalow, 62 Edilom Road, Manchester M8 4HZ. *T:* (0161) 740 4528, *Fax:* (0161) 720 7171. *Clubs:* Athenæum; Lancashire CC, Middlesex CC.

KENNEDY, Graham Norbert, CVO 1993; Chairman: Walker Crips Weddle Beck, since 2000; Anglo Pacific Resources, 1989–97; Dwyer plc, 1993–97; *b* 21 Oct. 1936; *s* of Ernest Norbert Kennedy and Joan Foster Kennedy; *m* 1960, Dinah Mary Berrill. *Educ:* St Andrews Coll., Grahamstown, S Africa; Millfield. Union Acceptances Ltd, 1964–70; James Capel & Co., 1971–96: Partner, 1974–96; Dir of Moneybroking, 1986–90; Dir, 1990–96; Consultant, 1993–95. Dir, Ockham Hldgs, 1995–. Mem., Council and Bd, London Stock Exchange, 1980–92. *Recreations:* shooting, golf, bridge, ski-ing, music. *Address:* Hatchetts, Church Lane, Worting, Basingstoke, Hants RG23 8PX. *Clubs:* Boodle's, City of London; Rand (Johannesburg); Berkshire Golf, Swinley Forest Golf.

KENNEDY, Sir Ian (Alexander), Kt 1986; Judge of the High Court of Justice, Queen's Bench Division, 1986–2000; *b* 7 Sept. 1930; *s* of late Gerald Donald Kennedy, OBE, and Elizabeth Jane (*née* McBeth); *m* 1962, Susan Margaret, *d* of late Lt-Col Edward John Hatfield, OBE, DL, and of Eileen (*née* Menneer); three *s* one *d*. *Educ:* Wellington Coll., Berks; Pembroke Coll., Cambridge (BA). Called to the Bar, Middle Temple, 1953; Treas., 1999. Dep. Chm., IoW QS, 1971; a Recorder of the Crown Court, 1972; QC 1974. Judge, Employment Appeal Tribunal, 1990–2000. *Recreations:* sailing, theatre, walking, gardening. *Address:* c/o Messrs C. Hoare & Co., 37 Fleet Street, EC4P 4DQ.

KENNEDY, Prof. Ian McColl; Professor of Health Law, Ethics and Policy, School of Public Policy, University College London, since 1997; *b* 14 Sept. 1941; *s* of Robert Charles Kennedy and late Dorothy Elizabeth Kennedy; *m* 1980, Andrea, *d* of Frederick and Barbara Gage, Ventura, Calif; two *s*. *Educ:* King Edward VI Sch., Stourbridge; University Coll. London (1st Cl. Hons LLB; Fellow, 1999); Univ. of Calif, Berkeley (LLM); LLD London. Called to the Bar, Inner Temple, 1974 (Hon. Bencher, 1996). Fulbright Fellow, 1963–65; Lectr in Law, UCL, 1965–71; Ford Foundn Fellow, Yale Univ. and Univ. of Mexico, 1966–67; Vis. Prof., Univ. of Calif, LA, 1971–72; King's College, London: Lectr in Law, 1973–78; Reader in English Law 1978–83; British Acad. Res. Fellow, 1978; Dir, Centre of Law, Medicine and Ethics, subseq. Centre of Med. Law and Ethics, 1978–93; Prof. of Med. Law and Ethics, 1983–97; Hd, Dept of Laws, 1986–89; Hd and Dean of Sch. of Law, 1989–92 and 1993–96; Pres., Centre of Med. Law and Ethics, 1993–97. FKC 1988. Chairman: Sec. of State for Health's Adv. Gp on Ethics of Xeno-transplantation, 1996–97; Minister of Agriculture's Adv. Gp on Quarantine, 1997–98; Public Inquiry into paediatric cardiac surgical services at Bristol Royal Infirmary, 1998–2001; Member: Medicines Commn, 1984–91; GMC, 1984–93; Expert Adv. Gp on AIDS, DHSS, later Dept of Health, 1987–94; Gen. Adv. Council, BBC, 1987–91; Med. Ethics Cttee, BMA, 1990–98; Nuffield Council on Bioethics, 1991– (Chm., 1998–); Archbishop of Canterbury's Adv. Gp on Med. Ethics, 1994–; Register of Ind. Mems, Defence Scientific Adv. Council, MoD, 1997–; Genetics Cttee, ABI, 1997–; Science in Society Cttee, Royal Soc. Mem., Council, Open Section, RSM, 1978–88 (Vice-Pres., 1981–86; FRSocMed 1985). Reith Lectr, 1980. Editor, Medical Law Review, 1993–98. *Publications:* The Unmasking of Medicine, 1981, rev. edn 1983; Treat Me Right, 1988; (with A. Grubb) Medical Law: cases and materials, 1989, 2nd edn as Medical Law: text with materials, 1994, 3rd edn 2000; (with A. Grubb) Principles of Medical Law, 1998. *Club:* Garrick.

KENNEDY, James; *see* Kennedy, A. J.

KENNEDY, Jane Elizabeth; MP (Lab) Liverpool, Wavertree, since 1997 (Liverpool Broadgreen, 1992–97); Minister of State, Northern Ireland Office, since 2001; *b* 4 May 1958; *d* of Clifford and Barbara Hodgson; *m* 1977, Robert Malcolm Kennedy (marr. diss. 1998); two *s*. *Educ:* Haughton Comprehensive Sch.; Darlington; Queen Elizabeth Sixth Form Coll.; Liverpool Univ. Child care residential worker 1979–84, Care Assistant 1984–88, Liverpool Social Services; Area Organiser, NUPE, 1988–92. An Asst Govt Whip, 1997–98; a Lord Comr of HM Treasury (Govt Whip), 1998–99; Parly Sec., LCD, 1999–2001. Mem., Social Security Select Cttee, 1992–94. *Recreation:* dogs. *Address:* House of Commons, SW1A 0AA. *T:* (020) 7219 4523; First Floor, Threlfall Building, Trueman Street, Liverpool L3 2EX. *T:* (0151) 236 1117.

KENNEDY, Joanna Alicia Gore, OBE 1995; FREng, FICE; Director, Ove Arup and Partners, since 1996; *b* 22 July 1950; *d* of late Captain G. A. G. Ormsby, DSO, DSC, RN and Susan Ormsby; *m* 1979, Richard Paul Kennedy, *qv*; two *s*. *Educ:* Queen Anne's School, Caversham; Lady Margaret Hall, Oxford (Scholar, 1969; BA 1st cl. Hons Eng. Sci. 1972; MA 1976; Hon. Mem., Senior Common Room, 1985–87). MICE 1979, FICE 1992; FREng (FEng 1997); MCIArb 2000. Ove Arup and Partners, consulting engineers: Design Engineer, 1972; Asst Resident Engineer (Runnymede Bridge), 1977; Sen. Engr, 1979; Arup Associates, 1987; Arup Project Management, 1990; Associate, 1992; Associate Dir, 1994. Member: Engineering Council, 1984–86 and 1987–90; Council, ICE, 1984–87; Adv. Council, RNEC Manadon, 1988–94; Engrg and Technol. Prog. Adv. Gp, PCFC, 1989–91; Engrg, later Engrg and Technol. Bd, SERC, 1990–94; Tech. Opportunities Panel, EPSRC, 1994–97; Industry and Engrg Adv. Cttee, Royal Commn for the Exhibn of 1851, 1999–. Mem. Bd, PLA, 2000–; Dir, Port of London Properties Ltd, 2001–. Trustee, Nat. Mus. of Science and Industry, 1992–. Mem. Council, Univ. of Southampton, 1996–99; Gov., Channing Sch., 1991–. Hon. DSc Salford, 1994. FRSA 1986. *Address:* Ove Arup & Partners, 13 Fitzroy Street, W1P 6BQ. *T:* (020) 7636 1531; *e-mail:* joanna.kennedy@arup.com.

KENNEDY, Rt Rev. Mgr John; Parish Priest, Holy Family, Southport, since 1991; *b* 31 Dec. 1930; *s* of James Kennedy and Alice Kennedy (*née* Bentham). *Educ:* St Joseph's College, Upholland; Gregorian University, Rome (STL); Oxford University (MPhil). Curate: St John's, Wigan, 1956–63; St Austin's, St Helens, 1963–65; St Edmund's, Liverpool, 1965–68; Lectr in Theology, Christ's College, Liverpool, 1968–84 (Head of Dept, 1976–84); Rector, Ven. English Coll., Rome, 1984–91; Asst Lectr in Theol., Gregorian Univ., Rome, 1984–91. *Recreations:* golf, squash. *Address:* Holy Family Presbytery, 1 Brompton Road, Southport, Merseyside PR8 6AS.
See also Sir Francis Kennedy.

KENNEDY, John Maxwell; Senior Partner, Allen & Overy, 1986–94; *b* 9 July 1934; *s* of George and Betty Gertrude Kennedy; *m* 1958, Margaret Joan (*née* Davies); four *s*. *Educ:* University Coll., London (LLB). Admitted Solicitor, 1957; Partner, Allen & Overy, 1962. Chm., Law Debenture Corp., 1994–2000; Dir, Amlin (formerly Angerstein Underwriting Trust) plc, 1993– (Chm., 1996–98). Mem., FSA (formerly SIB), 1993–98. Dir, Nuclear Generation Decommissioning Fund Ltd, 1996–. Chm., Lloyd's Corporate Capital Assoc., 1995–97. *Recreations:* sport, music, reading. *Address:* 16 Kensington Park Road, W11 3BU. *T:* (020) 7727 6929. *Clubs:* City of London, City Law, Hurlingham; Royal Wimbledon Golf.

KENNEDY, Sir Ludovic (Henry Coverley), Kt 1994; FRSL; writer and broadcaster; *b* Edinburgh, 3 Nov. 1919; *o s* of Captain E. C. Kennedy, RN (killed in action, 1939, while commanding HMS Rawalpindi against German battle-cruisers Scharnhorst and Gneisenau), and Rosalind, *d* of Sir Ludovic Grant, 11th Bt of Dalvey; *m* 1950, Moira Shearer King (*see* Moira Shearer); one *s* three *d*. *Educ:* Eton; Christ Church, Oxford (MA). Served War, 1939–46, RNVR. Priv. Sec. and ADC to Gov. of Newfoundland, 1943–44. Librarian, Ashridge (Adult Education) Coll., 1949; Rockefeller Foundation Atlantic Award in Literature, 1950; Winner, Open Finals Contest, English Festival of Spoken Poetry, 1953; Editor, feature, First Reading (BBC Third Prog.), 1953–54; Lecturer for British Council, Sweden, Finland and Denmark, 1955; Belgium and Luxembourg, 1956. Lectures: Voltaire Meml, 1985; Stevens, RSocMed, 1993. Mem. Council, Navy Records Soc., 1957–60. Contested (L) Rochdale, by-elec., 1958 and Gen. elec., 1959; Pres., Nat. League of Young Liberals, 1959–61; Mem., Lib. Party Council, 1965–67. Pres., Sir Walter Scott Club, Edinburgh, 1968–69; Patron, Russian Convoy Club, 1989–. Pres., Voluntary Euthanasia Soc., 1995–. Columnist: Newsweek International, 1974–75; Sunday Standard, 1981–82. Chm., Royal Lyceum Theatre Co. of Edinburgh, 1977–84. Dir, The Spectator, 1988–90. Chm. of Judges, NCR Book Award, 1990–91. FRSA 1974–76; FRSL 1998. Hon. LLD: Strathclyde, 1985; Southampton, 1993; Dr *hc* Edinburgh, 1990; DUniv Stirling, 1991. Richard Dimbleby BAFTA Award, 1988. Cross, First Class, Order of Merit, Fed. Repub. of Germany, 1979. *TV and radio:* Introd. Profile, ATV, 1955–56; Newscaster, Independent Television News, 1956–58; Introducer of AR's feature On Stage, 1957; Introducer of AR's, This Week, 1958–59; Chm. BBC features: Your Verdict, 1962; Your Witness, 1967–70; Commentator: BBC's Panorama, 1960–63; Television Reporters Internat., 1963–64 (also Prod.); Introducer, BBC's Time Out,

1964–65, World at One, 1965–66; Presenter: Lib. Party's Gen. Election Television Broadcasts, 1966; The Middle Years, ABC, 1967; The Nature of Prejudice, ATV, 1968; Face the Press, Tyne-Tees, 1968–69, 1970–72; Against the Tide, Yorkshire TV, 1969; Living and Growing, Grampian TV, 1969–70; 24 Hours, BBC, 1969–72; Ad Lib, BBC, 1970–72; Midweek, BBC, 1973–75; Newsday, BBC, 1975–76; Tonight, BBC, 1976–78; A Life with Crime, BBC, 1979; Change of Direction, BBC, 1979; Lord Mountbatten Remembers, 1980; Did You See?, 1980–88; Timewatch, 1984; Indelible Evidence, 1987 and 1990; A Gift of the Gab, 1989; Portrait, 1989. *Television films include:* The Sleeping Ballerina; The Singers and the Songs; Scapa Flow; Battleship Bismarck; Life and Death of the Scharnhorst; U-Boat War; Target Tirpitz; The Rise of the Red Navy; Lord Haw-Haw; Coast to Coast; Who Killed the Lindbergh Baby; Elizabeth: the first thirty years; Happy Birthday, dear Ma'am; Consider The End; From Princess to Queen. *Publications:* Sub-Lieutenant, 1942; Nelson's Band of Brothers, 1951; One Man's Meat, 1953; Murder Story (play, with essay on Capital Punishment), 1956; play: Murder Story (Cambridge Theatre), 1954; Ten Rillington Place, 1961; The Trial of Stephen Ward, 1964; Very Lovely People, 1969; Pursuit: the chase and sinking of the Bismarck, 1974; A Presumption of Innocence: the Amazing Case of Patrick Meehan, 1975; Menace: the life and death of the Tirpitz, 1979; The Portland Spy Case, 1979; Wicked Beyond Belief, 1980; (ed) A Book of Railway Journeys, 1980; (ed) A Book of Sea Journeys, 1981; (ed) A Book of Air Journeys, 1982; The Airman and the Carpenter, 1985 (republished in USA as Crime of the Century, 1996; filmed as Crime of the Century, 1996); On My Way to the Club (autobiog.), 1989; Euthanasia: the good death, 1990; Truth to Tell (collected writings), 1991; In Bed with an Elephant: a journey through Scotland's past and present, 1995; All In The Mind: a farewell to God, 1999; Gen. Editor, The British at War, 1973–77. *Address:* c/o Rogers, Coleridge and White, 20 Powis Mews, W11 1JN. *Clubs:* Brooks's, Army and Navy.

KENNEDY, Dr Malcolm William, CBE 2000; FREng, FIEE; Chairman, PB Power (incorporating Merz and McLellan), since 1998 (Executive Chairman, Merz and McLellan, 1995–98); *b* 13 March 1935; *s* of William and Lily Kennedy; *m* 1962, Patricia Ann Forster; one *d. Educ:* Durham Univ. (BSc 1961); Univ. of Newcastle upon Tyne (PhD 1964). FIEE 1974; FREng (FEng 1985). Apprentice, C. A. Parsons, 1951–56; Merz and McLellan, 1964–: Power Systems Design Engr, 1964; Head, Electrical Div., 1976; Sen. Partner, 1988–91; Chm. and Man. Dir, 1991–95. Mem. Electricity Panel, 1993–98, Water and Telecommunications Panel, 1998–, Monopolies and Mergers Commn. Dir, Port of Tyne Authority, 1994–. Pres., IEE, 1999–2000 (Henry Nimmo Premium, 1961; Chm., Power Div., 1986–87; Vice-Pres., 1994–96; Dep. Pres., 1996–99). CIMgt 1992. Methodist local preacher. *Publications:* papers on electricity industry, UK and overseas. *Recreations:* cricket, railways. *Address:* PB Power Ltd, Amber Court, William Armstrong Drive, Newcastle upon Tyne NE4 7YQ. *T:* (0191) 226 1899. *Club:* National.

KENNEDY, Michael; *see* Kennedy, G. M. S.

KENNEDY, Michael Denis, QC 1979; **His Honour Judge Kennedy;** a Circuit Judge, since 1984; *b* 29 April 1937; *s* of Denis George and Clementina Catherine (*née* MacGregor); *m* 1964, Elizabeth June Curtiss; two *s* two *d. Educ:* Downside School; Gonville and Caius College, Cambridge (open Schol., Mod. Langs; MA). 15/19 King's Royal Hussars, 1955–57. Called to the Bar, Inner Temple, 1961; a Recorder, 1979–84; Designated Civil Judge for Sussex, 1999–. *Address:* c/o Lewes Combined Court Centre, Law Courts, High Street, Lewes, E Sussex BN7 1YB. *T.* (01273) 480400.

KENNEDY, Sir Michael Edward; 8th Bt *cr* 1836, of Johnstown Kennedy, Co. Dublin; *b* 12 April 1956; *s* of Sir (George) Ronald Derrick Kennedy, 7th Bt and of Noelle Mona, *d* of Charles Henry Green; *S* father, 1988; *m* 1984, Helen Christine Jennifer, *d* of Patrick Lancelot Rae; one *s* three *d. Heir: s* George Mathew Rae Kennedy; *b* 9 Dec. 1993. *Address:* 48 Telston Lane, Otford, Kent TN14 5LA.

KENNEDY, Moira, (Lady Kennedy); *see* Shearer, M.

KENNEDY, Nigel Paul; solo concert violinist; *b* 28 Dec. 1956; *s* of John Kennedy and Scylla Stoner; partner, Eve Westmore; one *s. Educ:* Yehudi Menuhin School; Juilliard School of Performing Arts, NY. ARCM. Début at Festival Hall with Philharmonia Orch., 1977; regular appearances with London and major orchestras throughout the world, 1978–; Berlin début with Berlin Philharmonic, 1980; Henry Wood Promenade début, 1981; New York début with BBC SO, 1987; tour of Hong Kong and Australia, with Hallé Orch., 1981; foreign tours, 1978–: India, Japan, S Korea, Turkey, USA, Europe, Scandinavia; many appearances as jazz violinist with Stephane Grappelli, incl. Edinburgh Fest., 1974 and Carnegie Hall, 1976; many TV and radio appearances, incl. Vivaldi's Four Seasons with ECO (Golden Rose of Montreux, 1990), and two documentaries. Pop, jazz and classical recordings, incl. Vivaldi's Four Seasons (best-selling album of a complete classical work; No 1 in UK Classical Chart for over one year (Guinness Book of Records, 1990)); Best Classical Record, British Record Industry Awards: for Elgar Violin Concerto, 1985; for Beethoven Violin Concerto, 1991; Best Recording, Gramophone mag., for Elgar Violin Concerto, 1985. Variety Club Showbusiness Personality of the Year, 1991. Sen. Vice-Pres., Aston Villa FC, 1990–. Hon. DLitt Bath, 1991. *Publication:* Always Playing, 1991. *Recreations:* golf, football (watching and playing), cricket. *Address:* Russells, solicitors, Regency House, 1–4 Warwick Street, W1R 5WB.

KENNEDY, Rt Hon. Sir Paul (Joseph Morrow), Kt 1983; PC 1992; **Rt Hon. Lord Justice Kennedy;** a Lord Justice of Appeal, since 1992; Vice-President, Queen's Bench Division, High Court of Justice, since 1997; *b* 12 June 1935; *o s* of late Dr J. M. Kennedy, Sheffield; *m* 1965, Virginia, twin *d* of Baron Devlin, FBA and of Madeleine, *yr d* of Sir Bernard Oppenheimer, 1st Bt; two *s* two *d. Educ:* Ampleforth Coll.; Gonville and Caius Coll., Cambridge (MA, LLB; Hon. Fellow, 1998). Called to Bar, Gray's Inn, 1960, Bencher, 1982 (Vice Treas., 2001; Treas., 2002); a Recorder, 1972–83; QC 1973; Judge, High Court of Justice, QBD, 1983–92; Presiding Judge, N Eastern Circuit, 1985–89. Chm., Criminal Cttee, 1993–96; Mem., Judicial Studies Bd, 1993–96. Hon. LLD Sheffield, 2000. *Address:* Royal Courts of Justice, Strand, WC2A 2LL.

KENNEDY, Prof. Peter Graham Edward, MD, PhD, DSc, FRCP, FRCPath, FMedSci; FRSE; Burton Professor of Neurology, University of Glasgow and Consultant Neurologist, Institute of Neurological Sciences, Southern General Hospital, Glasgow, since 1987; *b* 28 March 1951; *s* of Philip Kennedy and Trudy Sylvia Kennedy (*née* Summer); *m* 1983, Catherine Ann King; one *s* one *d. Educ:* University Coll. Sch.; University College London and UCH Med. Sch. (MB BS, MD, PhD, DSc); Univ. of Glasgow (MLitt, MPhil). FRCP 1988; FRCPath 1997. FRSE 1992. Med. Registrar, UCH and Whittington Hosps, 1977–78; Hon. Res. Asst, MRC Neuroimmunology Project, UCL, 1978–80; Registrar and Res. Fellow, Univ. of Glasgow, 1981; Registrar then Sen. Registrar, Nat. Hosp. for Nervous Diseases, 1982–84; Asst Prof. of Neurology, Johns Hopkins Univ. Hosp., USA, 1985; New Blood Sen. Lectr in Neurology and Virology, Univ. of Glasgow, 1986–87. Chm., Scientist Panel on Infections incl. AIDS, European Fedn of Neurol Socs, 2000–. Vis. Fellow in Medicine, Jesus Coll., Cambridge, 1992; Fogarty Internat. Scholar-in-Residence, NIH, 1993–94. Lectures: Fleming, RCPSG, 1990; Stevens, Univ. of Colorado, 1994; Brain Bursary, KCH, London, 1999. Founder FMedSci 1998. Member: Assoc. of Physicians of GB and Ire.; Assoc. of British Neurologists; Corresp. Mem., Amer. Neurol Assoc., 1989–. Sec., Internat. Soc. for Neurovirology, 2000–. Member Editorial Board: Jl of Neuroimmunology, 1988–; Jl of Neurovirology (Associate Editor), 1994–; Jl of Neurological Scis, 1997–; Brain, 1998–. BUPA Med. Foundn Doctor of the Year Res. Award, 1990; Linacre Medal and Lectr, RCP, 1991; T. S. Srinivasan Gold Medal and Endowment Lectr, 1993. *Publications:* (with R. T. Johnson) Infections of the Nervous System, 1987; (with L. E. Davis) Infectious Diseases of the Nervous System, 2000; numerous papers on neurology, neurobiology and neurovirology. *Recreations:* philosophy, tennis, music, astronomy, walking in the country. *Address:* Glasgow University Department of Neurology, Institute of Neurological Sciences, Southern General Hospital, Glasgow G51 4TF. *T:* (0141) 201 2474, *Fax:* (0141) 201 2993; *e-mail:* p.g.kennedy@clinmed.gla.ac.uk.

KENNEDY, Richard Paul; Head Master of Highgate School, since 1989; *b* 17 Feb. 1949; *e s* of David Clifton Kennedy and Evelyn Mary Hall (*née* Tindale); *m* 1979, Joanna Alicia Gore Ormsby (*see* J. A. G. Kennedy); two *s. Educ:* Charterhouse; New College, Oxford (BA Maths and Phil. 1970; MA 1977). Assistant Master, Shrewsbury Sch., 1971–77, Westminster Sch., 1977–84; Dep. Headmaster, Bishop's Stortford Coll., 1984–89 (Acting Headmaster 1989). Headmasters' Conference: Mem., Sports Cttee, 1992–95; Mem., Cttee, 1995–96; Chm., London Div., 1996. Mem. Council, ISCO, 1995–2000. Governor: The Hall Sch., Hampstead, 1989–; Wycombe Abbey Sch., 1992–. GB internat. athlete (sprints), 1973–76. Mem., Acad. of St Martin-in-the-Fields Chorus, 1977–2000. *Recreations:* choral music, walking in Dorset. *Address:* 12 Bishopswood Road, N6 4NY. *T:* (020) 8340 7626.

KENNEDY, Rosemary; *see* Foot, R. J.

KENNEDY, Thomas Alexander; economist; *b* 11 July 1920; *s* of late Rt Hon. Thomas Kennedy, PC, and Annie S. Kennedy (*née* Michie); *m* 1947, Audrey (*née* Plunkett) (*d* 1991); one *s* two *d. Educ:* Alleyn's Sch., Dulwich; Durham Univ. (BA). Economist: Bd of Trade, 1950–52; Colonial Office, 1952–55; Lecturer in Economics at Makerere Coll., Uganda, 1955–61; Economist: Treasury, Foreign Office, DEA, 1961–67; Economic Director, NEDO, 1967–70; Under-Sec.: DTI, 1970–74; Dept of Energy, 1974–80, resigned. Chief Tech. Adviser (Economist Planner), Min. of Petroleum and Mineral Resources, Bangladesh, 1980–81. Vis. Fellow, Clare Hall, Cambridge, 1981–82. Consultant, World Bank: Uganda, Zambia, Swaziland, 1983–86, retired 1987. *Publication:* Harry Hyndman: an uncommon socialist, 1995. *Address:* 1 Beckside Mews, Staindrop, Darlington, Co. Durham DL2 3PG. *T:* (01833) 660616.

KENNEDY, Thomas Daniel, (Danny); Member (UU) Newry and Armagh, Northern Ireland Assembly, since 1998; *b* 6 July 1959; *s* of John Trevor Kennedy and Mary Ida Kennedy (*née* Black); *m* 1988, Karen Susan McCrum; two *s* one *d. Educ:* Bessbrook Primary Sch.; Newry High Sch. With BTNI, 1978–98. Mem., UU Party, 1974–; Mem., Newry and Mourne DC, 1985– (Chm., 1994–95). Chm., Educn Cttee, NI Assembly, 1999–. Mem., NI Tourist Bd, 1996–98. Clerk of Kirk Session and Sabbath Sch. Superintendent, Bessbrook Presbyterian Church. *Recreations:* family, Church activities, sport (purely spectating), reading. *Address:* Parliament Buildings, Stormont, Belfast BT4 3XX. *T:* (028) 9052 1336; (constituency office) 3 Mallview Terrace, Armagh BT61 9AN. *T:* (028) 3751 1655.

KENNEDY, Air Chief Marshal Sir Thomas Lawrie, (Sir Jock), GCB 1985 (KCB 1980 CB 1978); AFC 1953 and Bar 1960; Lord-Lieutenant of Rutland, since 1997; Royal Air Force, retired; Controller, RAF Benevolent Fund, 1988–93; *b* 19 May 1928; *s* of James Domoné Kennedy and Margaret Henderson Lawrie; *m* 1959, Margaret Ann Parker; one *s* two *d. Educ:* Hawick High Sch. RAF Coll., Cranwell, 1946–49; commissioned, 1949. Sqdn service, 1949–53; exchange service, RAAF, 1953–55; returned to UK, 1955; 27 Sqdn (Canberra), 1955–57; Radar Research Estabt, 1957–60; RAF Coll. Selection Bd, 1960–62; RN Staff Coll., Greenwich, 1962; HQ Middle East, 1962–64; CO, No 99 (Britannia) Sqdn, 1965–67; HQ Air Support Comd, 1967–69; CO, RAF Brize Norton, 1970–71; Dep. Comdt, RAF Staff Coll., 1971–73; Dir of Ops (AS) MoD, 1973–75; Royal Coll. of Defence Studies, 1976; Comdr, Northern Maritime Air Region, 1977–79; Deputy C-in-C, RAF Strike Command, 1979–81; C-in-C, RAF Germany, and Comdr, 2nd Allied Tactical Air Force, 1981–83; Air Mem. for Personnel, 1983–86; Air ADC to the Queen, 1983–86. Dir, Dowty Group, 1987–92. Freeman, City of London, 1987; Hon. Liveryman, Fruiterers' Co., 1987. DL Leics, 1989. *Recreations:* golf, sailing. *Address:* c/o Lloyds TSB, Cox's & King's Branch, PO Box 1190, SW1Y 5NA. *Club:* Royal Air Force.

KENNEDY, William Andrew; His Honour Judge William Kennedy; a Circuit Judge, since 2001; *b* 13 Feb. 1948; *s* of late Sidney Herbert and Kathleen Blanche Kennedy; *m* 1st, 1974, Alice Steen Wilkie (*d* 1987); 2nd, 1988, Lindsey Jane Sheridan; one *s* one *d. Educ:* Buckhurst Hill County High Sch.; College of Law, Lancaster Gate. Articled Clerk, Trotter Chapman & Whisker, Epping, Essex, 1966–72; admitted Solicitor, 1972; Partner 1972–75, Jt Sen. Partner 1975–91, Trotter Chapman & Whisker, later Whiskers; Notary Public, 1981; Metropolitan Stipendiary Magistrate, then Dist Judge (Magistrates' Courts), 1991–2001; Chm., Youth Courts, 1992–2001; an Asst Recorder, 1995–99; a Recorder, 1999–2001; part-time (Plate) Judge Advocate, 1995–2001. Pres., W Essex Law Soc., 1983–84. *Recreations:* golf, gentle domestic pursuits. *Address:* c/o Snaresbrook Crown Court, Snaresbrook, E11 1QW. *Club:* Chigwell Golf.

KENNEDY-GOOD, Sir John, KBE 1983; QSO 1977; JP; Mayor of Lower Hutt, 1970–86; *b* Goulburn, NSW, 8 Aug. 1915; *s* of Charles Kennedy-Good; *m* 1940, June, *d* of Charles Mackay; four *s* three *d. Educ:* Southland Boys' High Sch.; Otago Univ. (BDS). Practised as dentist, 1942–72. Mem., Lower Hutt City Council, 1962–87. Dir, Hutt Milk Corp., 1970–71, 1974–87; Chairman: Hutt Valley Underground Water Authy, 1970–72 (Mem., 1962–72); Wellington Regl Council, 1980–87 (Dep. Chm., 1980–83); NZ Council of Social Services, 1975–82; Member: Wellington Harbour Bd, 1971–80; Hutt Valley Energy Bd, 1970–87. Past Mem., NZ Catchment Authorities' Exec. Pres., NZ Sister Cities Inc. Chm., Dowse Art Mus. Bd, 1971–87; Dep. Chm., Nat. Art Gall. and Mus. Trust Bd (Mem., 1971). Mem., NZ Acad. Fine Arts, 1948. Founder Chm., John Kennedy-Good Human Resources Centre; Chm., Wellington Paraplegic Trust Bd (Vice-Pres., NZ Fed.); past Chm., Council for Dental Health, and past Pres., Wellington Br., NZ Dental Assoc.; Life Patron and Mem. Bd, Hutt Valley Disabled Resources Trust; Pres., Wellington Div., Order of St John; Patron, Wellington Reg. Centre, NZ Red Cross Soc.; patron, pres. or vice-pres. of numerous charity, cultural and sporting orgns. Trustee, Waiwhetu Marae, 1970–; Hon. Elder, Te Atiawa Tribe. JP Lower Hutt, 1970. *Address:* 129 Peninsula Club Resort, 441 Whangaparaoa Road, Hybiscus Coast, Auckland, New Zealand. *Clubs:* Hutt, Hutt Rotary (past Pres.), Hutt Golf.

KENNEDY MARTIN, (Francis) Troy; writer; *b* 15 Feb. 1932; *s* of Frank Martin and Kathleen Flanagan; *m* 1967, Diana Aubrey; one *s* one *d. Educ:* Finchley Catholic Grammar Sch.; Trinity Coll., Dublin (BA (Hons) History). Following nat. service with Gordon

Highlanders in Cyprus, wrote Incident at Echo Six, a TV play, 1959; *television:* The Interrogator, 1961; Z Cars, 1962; Diary of a Young Man, 1964; Man Without Papers, 1965; Reilly, Ace of Spies, 1983; Edge of Darkness, 1985; Hostile Waters, 1998; *films:* The Italian Job, 1969; Kelly's Heroes, 1970. Jt Screenwriters' Guild Award, 1962; BAFTA Scriptwriter's Award, 1962. *Publication:* Beat on a Damask Drum, 1961. *Recreation:* collecting marine models. *Address:* 6 Ladbroke Gardens, W11 2PT.

KENNERLEY, Prof. (James) Anthony (Machell), CEng, CMath; Complaints Commissioner, Channel Tunnel Rail Link, since 1997; *b* 24 Oct. 1933; *s* of William James Kennerley and late Vida May (*née* Machell); *m* 1978, Dorothy Mary (*née* Simpson); one *s* one *d* (twins). *Educ:* Universities of Manchester (BSc; Silver Medallist, 1955) and London (MSc 1967; IMechE James Clayton Fellow). AFIMA, AFRAeS; FCIT; MIMechE. Fourth Engr, Blue Funnel Line, Alfred Holt, 1954; Engineer, A. V. Roe, Manchester, 1955–58; Aerodynamicist, Pratt & Whitney, Montreal, Canada, 1958–59; Jet Pilot, RCAF, 1959–62; Asst Professor of Mathematics, Univ. of New Brunswick, Canada, 1962–67; Director of Graduate Studies, Manchester Business Sch., 1967–69; Associate Professor of Business Studies, Columbia Univ., New York, 1969–70; Director, Executive Programme, London Business Sch., 1970–73; Prof. of Business Admin, and Dir, Strathclyde Business Sch., 1973–83; Dir, InterMatrix Ltd, Management Consultants, 1984–92; Vis. Prof. of Management, 1984–93, Prof. of Health Care Mgt, 1993–97, Univ. of Surrey; Chm., Council for Professions Supplementary to Medicine, 1990–96. Tutor to sen. management courses in the public sector, 1985–. Chairman: W Surrey and NE Hants, then NW Surrey, HA, 1986–95; W Surrey Health Commn, 1995–96. Chairman: Management Res. Gp, Scotland, 1981–82; Scottish Milk Marketing Scheme Arbitration Panel, 1981–83. Member: South of Scotland Electricity Bd, 1977–84; Management Studies Bd, CNAA, 1977–84; BIM Educn Cttee, 1982–92; Competition (formerly Monopolies and Mergers) Commn, 1992–; Adv. Bd, Meta Generics, Cambridge, 1992–95; Council, Inst. of Mgt, 1995–98. Chm., Conf. of Univ. Management Schs, 1981–83; Director: Business Graduates Assoc., 1983–86; First Step Housing Co., Waverley BC, 1990–94. Arbitrator, ACAS, 1976–. Mem., Trans-Turkey Highway World Bank Mission, 1982–83. Founder Mem., Bridgegate Trust, Glasgow, 1982–85. *Publications:* Guide to Business Schools, 1985; Arbitration: cases in industrial relations, 1994; articles, papers on business studies, on Public Sector management, and on applied mathematics. *Recreations:* flying, travelling. *Address:* Complaints Commissioner, 73 Collier Street, N1 9BE; 3 Portside Close, Marchwood, Southampton SO40 4AL. *T:* (023) 8066 9847. *Clubs:* Reform, Caledonian.

KENNET, 2nd Baron *cr* 1935; **Wayland Hilton Young;** author and politician; *b* 2 Aug. 1923; *s* of 1st Baron Kennet, PC, GBE, DSO, DSC, and of Kathleen Bruce (who *m* 1st, Captain Robert Falcon Scott, CVO, RN, and died 1947); *S* father, 1960; *m* 1948, Elizabeth Ann, *d* of late Captain Bryan Fullerton Adams, DSO, RN; one *s* five *d*. *Educ:* Stowe; Trinity Coll., Cambridge. Served in RN, 1942–45. Foreign Office, 1946–47, and 1949–51. Deleg., Parliamentary Assemblies, WEU and Council of Europe, 1962–65; Parly Sec., Min. of Housing and Local Govt, 1966–70; Opposition Spokesman on Foreign Affairs and Science Policy, 1971–74; SDP Chief Whip in H of L, 1981–83; SDP spokesman in H of L on foreign affairs and defence, 1981–90. Co-founder, POST, 1988. Chairman: Adv. Cttee on Oil Pollution of the Sea, 1970–74; Commonwealth Human Ecology Council, 1970–72; CPRE, 1971–72; Internat. Parly Confs on the Environment, 1972–78; Dir, Europe Plus Thirty, 1974–75; Member: Polar Cttee, NERC; Internat. Bioethics Cttee, UNESCO, 1994–98. Member: European Parlt, 1978–79; North Atlantic Assembly, 1997–99; Vice Pres., Parly and Scientific Cttee, 1989–98. Chm., Architecture Club, 1983–94; Mem., Redundant Churches Fund, 1978–84. Hon. FRIBA 1970. Editor of Disarmament and Arms Control, 1962–65. *Publications:* (as Wayland Young): The Italian Left, 1949; The Deadweight, 1952; Now or Never, 1953; Old London Churches (with Elizabeth Young), 1956; The Montesi Scandal, 1957; Still Alive Tomorrow, 1958; Strategy for Survival, 1959; The Profumo Affair, 1963; Eros Denied, 1965; Thirty-Four Articles, 1965; (ed) Existing Mechanisms of Arms Control, 1965; (as Wayland Kennet) Preservation, 1972; The Futures of Europe, 1976; The Rebirth of Britain, 1982; (with Elizabeth Young) London's Churches, 1986; (with Elizabeth Young) Northern Lazio, 1990 (trans. Italian 1993); Parliaments and Screening, 1995; (contrib.) Enciclopedia Treccani (The Italian Encyclopedia), 1998; Fabian and SDP pamphlets on defence, disarmament, environment, multinational companies, etc. *Heir:* *s* Hon. William Aldus Thoby Young [*b* 24 May 1957; *m* 1987, Hon. Josephine, *yr d* of Baron Keyes, *qv*; two *s* one *d*]. *Address:* 100 Bayswater Road, W2 3HJ.

KENNETT, Hon. Jeffrey (Gibb); Chairman, National Depression Initiative, since 2000; Premier of Victoria, 1992–99; *b* 2 March 1948; *m* 1972, Felicity; three *s* one *d*. Founder, KNF Advertising Pty Ltd. Government of Victoria: MLA (L) Burwood, 1976–99; Minister for Aboriginal Affairs, Immigration, Ethnic Affairs and Housing, 1981–82; Leader of the Opposition, 1982–89, 1991–92; Minister for Multicultural Affairs and the Arts, 1996–99. *Address:* (office) Old Treasury Building, Spring Street, Melbourne, Vic 3002, Australia.

KENNETT, Ronald John, FRAeS; Director, Royal Aeronautical Society, 1988–98; *b* 25 March 1935; *s* of William John and Phyllis Gertrude Kennett; *m* 1957, Sylvia Barstow; one *s* three *d*. *Educ:* Bradford Technical College. Lucas Aerospace: joined 1956; Chief Engineer, 1978–86; Quality Assurance Manager, 1986–88. Non-exec. Dir, Beds and Herts Ambulance and Paramedic Service NHS Trust, 2000–. FInstD; AFAIAA. *Recreations:* reading, photography, music, country recreation, golf. *Address:* Greenbanks, Toms Hill Road, Aldbury, Herts HP23 5SA. *Club:* Stocks Golf & Country (Aldbury).

KENNETT BROWN, David; a District Judge (Magistrates' Courts) (formerly Metropolitan Stipendiary Magistrate), since 1982; a Recorder, since 1989; *b* 29 Jan. 1938; *s* of late Thomas Kennett Brown, solicitor, and Vanda Brown; *m* 1966, Wendy Margaret Evans; one *s* two *d*. *Educ:* Monkton Combe Sch.; Lincoln Coll., Oxford. FCIArb 1982. Admitted Solicitor, 1965. Partner, Kennett Brown & Co., 1965–82. Chm., Family Proceedings and Youth Courts, 1983–. Chm., London Rent Assessment Panel, 1979–82; Pres., Central and S Mddx Law Soc., 1982. JP Willesden, 1975–82. *Recreations:* escaping to Cornwall, gardening. *Address:* c/o Marylebone Magistrates' Court, 181 Marylebone Road, NW1 5QJ.

KENNEY, Anthony, FRCS; FRCOG; Consultant Obstetrician and Gynaecologist, St Thomas' Hospital, since 1980; *b* 17 Jan. 1942; *s* of late Eric Alfred Allen Kenney and Doris Winifred Kenney; *m* 1973, Patricia Clare Newbery; four *s* one *d*. *Educ:* Brentwood School; Gonville and Caius College, Cambridge (MA 1967); London Hosp. Med. Coll. MB BChir 1966; FRCS 1970; MRCOG 1972, FRCOG 1987. House appts, London Hosp., Queen Charlotte's Hosp. and Chelsea Hosp. for Women, 1966–72; Registrar and Sen. Registrar, Westminster and Kingston Hosps, 1972–79. Examiner in Obstetrics and Gynaecology, Univ. of London and RCOG; Past Examr, Univs of Liverpool and Cambridge. Mem., Higher Trng Cttee, RCOG, 1997–. Co-founder and Trustee, Tommy's Campaign, 1989–; Trustee, Quit, 1995–. *Publications:* contribs to med. jls. *Recreations:* canal cruising, foreign travel. *Address:* 92 Coombe Lane West, Kingston upon Thames, Surrey KT2 7DB. *T:* (020) 8942 0440. *Clubs:* Royal Society of Medicine, Medical Society of London.

KENNEY, Prof. Edward John, FBA 1968; Kennedy Professor of Latin, University of Cambridge, 1974–82; Fellow of Peterhouse, Cambridge, 1953–91; *b* 29 Feb. 1924; *s* of George Kenney and Emmie Carlina Elfrida Schwenke; *m* 1955, Gwyneth Anne, *d* of late Prof. Henry Albert Harris. *Educ:* Christ's Hospital; Trinity Coll., Cambridge. BA 1949, MA 1953. Served War of 1939–45: Royal Signals, UK and India, 1943–46; commissioned 1944, Lieut 1945. Porson Schol., 1948; Craven Schol., 1949; Craven Student, 1949; Chancellor's Medallist, 1950. Asst Lectr, Univ. of Leeds, 1951–52; University of Cambridge: Research Fellow, Trinity Coll., 1952–53; Asst Lectr, 1955–60, Lectr, 1966–70; Reader in Latin Literature and Textual Criticism, 1970–74; Peterhouse: Director of Studies in Classics, 1953–74; Librarian, 1953–82, Perne Librarian, 1987–91; Tutor, 1956–62; Senior Tutor, 1962–65; Domestic Bursar, 1987–88. James C. Loeb Fellow in Classical Philology, Harvard Univ., 1967–68; Sather Prof. of Classical Literature, Univ. of California, Berkeley, 1968; Carl Newell Jackson Lectr, Harvard Univ., 1980. President: Jt Assoc. of Classical Teachers, 1977–79; Classical Assoc., 1982–83. For. Mem., Royal Netherlands Acad. of Arts and Scis, 1976. Treasurer and Chm., Council of Almoners, Christ's Hosp., 1984–86. Jt Editor, Classical Qly, 1959–65; Jt Gen. Ed., Cambridge Greek and Latin Classics, 1966–. *Publications:* P. Ouidi Nasonis Amores etc (ed), 1961, 2nd edn 1995; (with Mrs P. E. Easterling) Ovidiana Graeca (ed), 1965; (with W. V. Clausen, F. R. D. Goodyear, J. A. Richmond) Appendix Vergiliana (ed), 1966; Lucretius, De Rerum Natura III (ed), 1971; The Classical Text, 1974 (trans. Italian, 1995); (with W. V. Clausen) Latin Literature (ed and contrib.) (Cambridge History of Classical Literature II), 1982; The Ploughman's Lunch (*Moretum*), 1984; introd. and notes to Ovid, Metamorphoses, trans. A. D. Melville, 1986; Ovid, The Love Poems, 1990; Apuleius, Cupid & Psyche (ed), 1990; introd. and notes to Ovid, Sorrows of an Exile (*Tristia*), trans. A. D. Melville, 1992; Ovid, Heroides XVI–XXI (ed), 1996; (trans., with introd. and notes) Apuleius, The Golden Ass, 1998; articles and reviews in classical jls. *Recreations:* cats and books. *Address:* Peterhouse, Cambridge CB2 1RD.

KENNY, Sir Anthony (John Patrick), Kt 1992; FBA 1974; Pro-Vice-Chancellor, Oxford University, 1984–2001 (Pro-Vice-Chancellor for Development, 1999–2001); Warden, Rhodes House, 1989–99; Professorial Fellow, St John's College, Oxford, 1989–99, now Emeritus Fellow; Master of Balliol College, Oxford, 1978–89; *b* Liverpool, 16 March 1931; *s* of John Kenny and Margaret Jones; *m* 1966, Nancy Caroline, *d* of Henry T. Gayley, Jr, Swarthmore, Pa; two *s*. *Educ:* Gregorian Univ., Rome (STL); St Benet's Hall, Oxford; DPhil 1961, DLitt 1980. Ordained priest, Rome, 1955; Curate in Liverpool, 1959–63; returned to lay state, 1963. Asst Lectr, Univ. of Liverpool, 1961–63; University of Oxford: Fellow, 1964–78, Sen. Tutor, 1971–72 and 1976–78, Balliol Coll.; Lectr in Philosophy, Exeter and Trinity Colls, 1963–64; University Lectr, 1965–78; Wilde Lectr in Natural and Comparative Religion, 1969–72; Speaker's Lectureship in Biblical Studies, 1980–83; Mem., Hebdomadal Council, 1981–93; Vice-Chm., Libraries Bd, 1985–88; Curator, Bodleian Library, 1985–88; Deleg., and Mem., Finance Cttee, OUP, 1986–93. Jt Gifford Lectr, Univ. of Edinburgh, 1972–73; Stanton Lectr, Univ. of Cambridge, 1980–83; Bampton Lectr, Columbia Univ., 1983. Visiting Professor: Univs of Chicago, Washington, Michigan, Minnesota and Cornell, Stanford and Rockefeller Univs. Chairman: British Liby Bd, 1993–96 (Mem., 1991–96); Soc. for Protection of Science and Learning, 1989–93; British Nat. Corpus Adv. Bd, 1990–95; British Irish Assoc., 1990–94; Bd, Warburg Inst., Univ. of London, 1996–2000. Pres., British Acad., 1989–93 (Mem. Council, 1985–88; Vice-Pres., 1986–88). MAE 1991; Member: Amer. Phil Soc., 1993; Norwegian Acad. of Scis, 1993. Hon. Fellow, Harris Manchester Coll., Oxford, 1996. Hon. DLitt: Bristol, 1982; Liverpool, 1988; Glasgow, 1990; TCD, 1992; Hull, 1993; Sheffield, Warwick, 1995; Hon. DHumLitt: Denison Univ., Ohio, 1986; Lafayette Univ., Penn, 1990; Hon. DCL: Oxon, 1987; QUB, 1994. Hon. Bencher, Lincoln's Inn, 1999. Editor, The Oxford Magazine, 1972–73. *Publications:* Action, Emotion and Will, 1963; Responsa Alumnorum of English College, Rome, 2 vols, 1963; Descartes, 1968; The Five Ways, 1969; Wittgenstein, 1973; The Anatomy of the Soul, 1974; Will, Freedom and Power, 1975; The Aristotelian Ethics, 1978; Freewill and Responsibility, 1978; Aristotle's Theory of the Will, 1979; The God of the Philosophers, 1979; Aquinas, 1980; The Computation of Style, 1982; Faith and Reason, 1983; Thomas More, 1983; The Legacy of Wittgenstein, 1984; A Path from Rome (autobiog.), 1985; Wyclif, 1985; The Logic of Deterrence, 1985; The Ivory Tower, 1985; A Stylometric Study of the New Testament, 1986; The Road to Hillsborough, 1987; Reason and Religion, 1987; The Heritage of Wisdom, 1987; God and Two Poets, 1988; The Metaphysics of Mind, 1989; The Oxford Diaries of Arthur Hugh Clough, 1990; Mountains: an anthology, 1991; Aristotle on the Perfect Life, 1992; What is Faith?, 1992; Aquinas on Mind, 1993; (ed) Oxford Illustrated History of Western Philosophy, 1994; Frege, 1995; A Life in Oxford (autobiog.), 1997; A Brief History of Western Philosophy, 1998; Essays on the Aristotelian Tradition, 2001. *Address:* The Old Bakery, 1A Larkins Lane, Oxford OX3 9DW. *Club:* Athenæum.

KENNY, Anthony Marriott; His Honour Judge Kenny; a Circuit Judge, since 1987; *b* 24 May 1939; *o s* of late Noel Edgar Edward Marriott Kenny, OBE, and Cynthia Margaret Seton Kenny (*née* Melville); *m* 1969, Monica Grant Mackenzie, *yr d* of late H. B. Grant Mackenzie, Pretoria; three *s*. *Educ:* St Andrew's Coll., Grahamstown, Cape Province; Christ's Coll., Cambridge (MA). Called to the Bar, Gray's Inn, 1963; South Eastern Circuit. A Recorder, 1980–87; Principal Judge in Civil Matters, Berks and Bucks, 1992–98; designated Family Judge: Reading, 1991–2000; Truro, 2000. *Recreations:* music, reading, tennis, ski-ing. *Address:* c/o SE Circuit Administator, 18 Maltravers Street, WC2R 3EU.

KENNY, Gen. Sir Brian (Leslie Graham), GCB 1991 (KCB 1985); CBE 1979; Bath King of Arms, since 1999; *b* 18 June 1934; *s* of late Brig. James Wolfenden Kenny, CBE, and of Aileen Anne Georgina Kenny (*née* Swan); *m* 1958, Diana Catherine Jane Mathew; two *s*. *Educ:* Canford School. Commissioned into 4th Hussars (later Queen's Royal Irish Hussars), 1954; served BAOR, Aden, Malaya and Borneo; Pilot's course, 1961; Comd 16 Recce Flt QRIH; psc 1965; MA/VCGS, MoD, 1966–68; Instructor, Staff Coll., 1971–73; CO QRIH, BAOR and UN Cyprus, 1974–76; Col GS 4 Armd Div., 1977–78; Comd 12 Armd Bde (Task Force D), 1979–80; RCDS 1981; Comdr 1st Armoured Div., 1982–83; Dir, Army Staff Duties, MoD, 1983–85; Comdr 1st (British) Corps, BAOR, 1985–87; Comdr, Northern Army Gp, and C-in-C, BAOR, 1987–89; Dep. SACEUR, 1990–93. Gov., Royal Hosp., Chelsea, 1993–99. Col QRIH, 1985–93; Colonel Commandant: RAVC, 1983–95; RAC, 1988–93. Chm., Army Benevolent Fund, 1993–99. Governor, Canford Sch., 1983–. *Recreations:* ski-ing, cricket, shooting, racing. *Address:* c/o Lloyds TSB, Camberley, Surrey GU15 3SE. *Clubs:* Sloane, MCC, I Zingari, Free Foresters.

KENNY, David John, CBE 1991; Regional General Manager, North West Thames Regional Health Authority, 1984–91 (Regional Administrator, 1982–84); *b* 2 Dec. 1940; *s* of late Gerald Henry Kenny and Ellen Veronica (*née* Crosse); *m* 1964, Elisabeth Ann, *d* of late Robert and of Jean Ferris; three *s*. *Educ:* Royal Belfast Academical Instn; Queen's

Univ., Belfast (LLB). FHSM. Dep. House Governor, Bd of Governors, London Hosp., 1972; Dist Administrator, Tower Hamlets Health Dist, 1974; Area Administrator, Kensington and Chelsea and Westminster AHA, 1978. Mem. Nat. Council, Inst. of Health Service Managers, 1975–86 and 1988–91 (Pres. 1981–82); Chm., Gen. Managers of RHAs, 1989–91. Chm., Data Protection Working Gp, Internat. Med. Informatics Assoc., 1979–87. *Publications:* (jtly) Data Protection in Health Information Systems, 1980; articles on management topics, data protection and ethics. *Recreations:* cinema, theatre, athletics, rugby football. *Address:* 131 Maze Hill, SE3 7UB. *T:* (020) 8858 1545.

KENNY, Yvonne Denise, AM 1989; international opera singer; *b* Australia, 25 Nov. 1950; *d* of late Arthur Raymond Kenny and of Doris Jean (*née* Campbell). *Educ:* Sydney Univ. (BSc). Operatic début in Donizetti's Rosmonda d'Inghilterra, Queen Elizabeth Hall, 1975; joined Royal Opera House, Covent Garden as a principal soprano, 1976; roles include: Pamina in Die Zauberflöte; Ilia in Idomeneo; Marzelline in Fidelio; Susanna, and Countess, in Le Nozze di Figaro; Adina in L'Elisir d'Amore; Liu in Turandot; Aspasia in Mitridate; Alcina; Semele; Cleopatra in Giulio Cesare; Donna Anna in Don Giovanni; Fairy Queen; Countess in Capriccio; Die Feldmarshallin in Der Rosenkavalier; Alice Ford in Falstaff; international appearances include: ENO; Glyndebourne; Berlin Staatsoper; Vienna State Opera; La Scala, Milan; La Fenice, Venice; Paris; Munich; Zurich; Australian Opera, Sydney, etc; regular concert appearances with major orchs and conductors in Europe and USA. Has made numerous recordings. *Recreations:* swimming, walking, gardening. *Address:* c/o Askonas Holt Ltd, Lonsdale Chambers, 27 Chancery Lane, WC2A 1PF.

KENSINGTON, 8th Baron *cr* 1776 (Ire.); **Hugh Ivor Edwardes;** Baron Kensington (UK) 1886; *b* 24 Nov. 1933; *s* of Hon. Hugh Owen Edwardes (*d* 1937) (2nd *s* of 6th Baron) and of Angela Dorothea (who *m* 1951, Lt Comdr John Hamilton, RN retd), *d* of late Lt-Col Eustace Shearman, 10th Hussars; *S* uncle, 1981;; *m* 1961, Juliet Elizabeth Massy Anderson; two *s* one *d*. *Educ:* Eton. *Heir: s* Hon. William Owen Alexander Edwardes [*b* 21 July 1964; *m* 1991, Marie Hélène Anne Véronique, *d* of Jean-Alain Lalouette; one *s* two *d*]. *Address:* Friar Tuck, PO Box 549, Mooi River, Natal 3300, Republic of S Africa. *Clubs:* Boodle's; Durban (Durban).

KENSINGTON, Area Bishop of, since 1996; **Rt Rev. Michael John Colclough;** *b* 29 Dec. 1944; *s* of Joseph and Beryl Colclough; *m* 1983, Cynthia Flora Mary De Sousa; two *s*. *Educ:* Leeds Univ. (BA Hons English and Religious Studies); Cuddesdon Coll., Oxford. Ordained deacon, 1971, priest, 1972; Curate: St Werburgh, Burslem, 1971–75; St Mary, S Ruislip, 1975–79; Vicar, St Anselm, Hayes, 1979–86; Area Dean of Hillingdon, 1985–92; Team Rector, Uxbridge, 1986–92; Archdeacon of Northolt, 1992–94; personal asst to Bp of London (Archdeacon at London House), 1994–96; Priest-in-Charge: St Vedast-alias-Foster, 1994–96; St Magnus the Martyr, London Bridge, 1995–96; Dep. Priest in Ordinary to the Queen, 1995–96. Chm. Mission, Evangelism and Renewal in England Cttee, C of E, 1999–. Vice-Pres., Christian Children's Fund, 1998–. Patron, Micro Loan Foundn, 1999–. *Recreations:* travel, walking in the English countryside, reading, people. *Address:* Dial House, Riverside, Twickenham, Middx TW1 3DT. *T:* (020) 8892 7781, *Fax:* (020) 8891 3969; *e-mail:* bishop.kensington@london.anglican.org.

KENSWOOD, 2nd Baron *cr* 1951; **John Michael Howard Whitfield;** *b* 6 April 1930; *o s* of 1st Baron Kenswood; *S* father, 1963; *m* 1951, Deirdre Anna Louise, *d* of Colin Malcolm Methven, Errol, Perthshire; four *s* one *d*. *Educ:* Trinity Coll. Sch., Ontario, Harrow; Grenoble Univ.; Emmanuel Coll., Cambridge (BA). *Heir: s* Hon. Michael Christopher Whitfield, *b* 3 July 1955.

KENT, Brian Hamilton, FREng, FIEE, FIMechE; Chairman, Wellington Holdings plc, since 1993; President, Institution of Mechanical Engineers, 1994–95; *b* 29 Sept. 1931; *s* of Clarence Kent and Edyth (*née* Mitchell); *m* 1954, Margery Foulds; one *s* two *d*. *Educ:* Hyde Grammar Sch.; Salford Coll. of Technology (BSc Eng). FREng (FEng 1995). Instructor Lieut, RN Short Service Commn, 1954–57. Mather & Platt Ltd: graduate apprentice, 1952–54; Asst Technical Manager, Electrical Gp, then Gen. Manager, Mather & Platt Contracting Ltd, 1957–65; Morgan Crucible Co. Ltd, London, 1965–69; Man. Dir and Chief Exec., Alfa-Laval Ltd, 1969–78; Dir, Staveley Industries Ltd, 1978–80; Staveley Industries plc: Chief Exec., 1980–87; Chm., 1987–93; non-exec. Chm., 1993–94. Chm., British Printing Co. Ltd, 1996–98; Dep. Chm., Industrial Acoustics Corp. Ltd, 2000–. Senator, Engrg Council, 1996–99. Chm., Management Cttee, Industry and Parlt Trust, 1988–90. Gov., Kingston Univ., 1996– (Chm., Finance Bd). FInstD; FRSA. Hon. DSc Salford, 1995. *Recreation:* sailing. *Address:* Wellington Holdings plc, 130 Oldfield Road, Hampton, Middx TW12 2HT. *T:* (020) 8941 3774. *Club:* Royal Automobile.

KENT, Bruce; campaigner for nuclear disarmament; Chairman, Campaign for Nuclear Disarmament, 1987–90 (General Secretary, 1980–85; Vice-Chairman, 1985–87; Hon. Vice President, 1985); *b* 22 June 1929; *s* of Kenneth Kent and Rosemary Kent (*née* Marion); *m* 1988, Valerie Flessati. *Educ:* Lower Canada Coll., Montreal; Stonyhurst Coll.; Brasenose Coll., Univ. of Oxford. LLB. Ordination, Westminster, 1958; Curate, Kensington, North and South, 1958–63; Sec., Archbishop's House, Westminster, 1963–64; Chm., Diocesan Schools Commn, 1964–66; Catholic Chaplain to Univ. of London, 1966–74; Chaplain, Pax Christi, 1974–77; Parish Priest, Somers Town, NW1, 1977–80; retired from active Ministry, Feb. 1987. President: Internat. Peace Bureau, 1985–92; Nat. Peace Council, 1999–2000. Mem., Nat. Exec., UNA, 1993–97. Contested (Lab) Oxford West and Abingdon, 1992. Hon LLD Manchester, 1987. *Publications:* Undiscovered Ends (autobiog.), 1992; essays and pamphlets on disarmament, Christians and peace. *Recreations:* friends, walking. *Address:* 11 Venetia Road, N4 1EJ.

KENT, Michael Harcourt; QC 1996; a Recorder, since 2000; *b* 5 March 1952; *s* of Captain Barrie Harcourt Kent, RN and Margaret Harcourt Kent; *m* 1977, Sarah Ann Ling; two *s*. *Educ:* Nautical Coll., Pangbourne; Sussex Univ. (BA Hons). Called to the Bar, Middle Temple, 1975; SE Circuit; Supplementary Panel, Junior Counsel to the Crown, Common Law, 1988–96. Member: London Common Law and Commercial Bar Assoc.; Admin. Law Bar Assoc. An Asst Recorder, 1999–2000. *Recreation:* sailing. *Address:* Crown Office Chambers, 1 Paper Buildings, Temple, EC4Y 7EP. *T:* (020) 7797 8100.

KENT, Paul Welberry, DSc; FRSC; JP; Student Emeritus of Christ Church, Oxford; *b* Doncaster, 19 April 1923; *s* of Thomas William Kent and Marion (*née* Cox); *m* 1952, Rosemary Elizabeth Boutflower, *y d* of Major C. H. B. Shepherd, MC; three *s* one *d*. *Educ:* Doncaster Grammar Sch.; Birmingham Univ. (BSc 1944, PhD 1947); Jesus Coll., Oxford (MA 1951, DPhil 1953, DSc 1966). Asst Lectr, subseq. ICI Fellow, Birmingham Univ., 1946–50; Vis. Fellow, Princeton Univ., 1948–49; Univ. Demonstrator in Biochem., Oxford, 1950–72; Lectr, subseq. Student, Tutor and Dr Lees Reader in Chem., Christ Church, Oxford, 1955–72; Durham University: Master of Van Mildert Coll. and Dir, Glycoprotein Res. Unit, 1972–82; Mem. of Senate, 1972–82; Mem. of Council, 1976–80. Research Assoc., Harvard, 1967; Vis. Prof., Windsor Univ., Ont, 1971, 1980. Bodleian Orator, 1959. Mem., Oxford City Council, 1964–72; Governor: Oxford Coll. of Technology, subseq. Oxford Polytechnic, 1964–72, 1983–89 (Vice-Chm. 1966–69, Chm. 1969–70); Oxford Polytechnic Higher Educn Corp., 1988–92 (Dep. Chm., 1988–92); Oxford Brookes Univ., 1992–97 (Vice-Chm., 1992–94). Member: Cttee, Biochemical Soc., 1963–67; Chemical Council, 1965–70; Res. Adv. Cttee, Cystic Fibrosis Res. Trust, 1977–82; Commn on Religious Educn in School. Sec., Foster and Wills Scholarships Bd, 1960–72; Pres., Soc. for Maintenance of the Faith, 1974–99; Governor, Pusey House, 1983–2000. JP Oxford, 1972. Hon. Fellow, Canterbury Coll., Ont, 1976. Hon. DLitt Drury, 1973; Hon. DSc CNAA, 1991. Rolleston Prize, 1952; Medal of Société de Chemie Biologique, 1969; Verdienstkreuz (Germany), 1970. *Publications:* Biochemistry of Amino-sugars, 1955; (ed) Membrane-Mediated Information, Vols I and II, 1972; (ed) International Aspects of the Provision of Medical Care, 1976; (ed) New Approaches to Genetics, 1978; (ed with W. B. Fisher) Resources, Environment and the Future, 1982; articles in sci. and other jls. *Recreations:* music, travel. *Address:* 18 Arnolds Way, Cumnor Hill, Oxford OX2 9JB. *T:* (01865) 862087; Briscoe Gate, Cotherstone, Barnard Castle, Co. Durham. *Club:* Athenæum.

KENT, Pendarell Hugh, CBE 1997; Executive Chairman, European Securities Forum, since 2000; *b* 18 Aug. 1937; *s* of Hugh and Ann Kent; *m* 1960, Jill George; one *s* one *d*. *Educ:* University College Sch.; Jesus Coll., Oxford (MA Hons). Intelligence Corps, 2nd Lieut, 1959–61. Bank of England, 1961–97: UK Alternate Exec. Dir, IMF, 1976–79; Head: of Inf. Div., 1984–85; of Internat. Div. (Internat. Financial Instns and Developing Countries), 1985–88; Associate Dir, Finance and Industry, 1988–94; Exec. Dir, 1994–97. Dir, Private Finance Panel, 1993–97. Chm., CRESTCo, 1994–96; non-executive Director: BR Southern Region, 1986–92 (Chm., 1989–92); NatWest Gp, 1997–2000; Strategic Rail Authy, 1999–; Schroder & Co. Ltd, 2001–; CDC (Mem., Commonwealth Develt Corp., 1995–2001); Mem., Technol. Foresight Steering Gp, 1995–97. Dir, City Arts Trust, 1996–2001 (Chm., 1997–2001); Dep. Chm., Heart of the City, 2000–. Trustee, Blind in Business, 1992– (Chm., 1996–); Vice Patron, Missing Persons Helpline, 1994–. Property Award, Coll. of Estate Mgt, 1997. *Publication:* Nursery Schools for All (with Jill Kent), 1970. *Recreations:* art, jazz, ski-ing.

KENT, Peter Humphreys, CMG 2001; Chairman: Starlight Media LLC, New York, since 2000; Starlight Media International Ltd, UK, since 2000; private sector government trade adviser; *b* 21 April 1937; *m* 1964, Noel Mary Curwen; one *s*. *Educ:* Denehurst Prep. Sch.; Royal Grammar Sch., Guildford. Commnd Queen's Royal W Surrey Regt, 1956; seconded RWAFF, 1956; served: 5 Bn Queen's Own Nigeria Regt, 1956-57; 1st Bn Queen's Royal Regt, TA, 1957-60. Union Internat. Co. Ltd, London and Nigeria, 1958-61; I. H. S. Lotinga Ltd, Nigeria, 1961-64; Newton Chambers & Co. Ltd, 1964-73 (Man. Dir, Izal Overseas Ltd, and Dir, Izal Ltd); Mktg Dir, Europe, Sterling Winthrop Ltd, 1973-76; Arthur Guinness & Sons, 1975-78 (Internat. Mktg Dir, Jackel Ltd); Man. Dir, Steinerco (UK) Ltd, 1978-83; Dir, More O'Ferrall Plc, 1983-97. Dir, Taiwan Trade Centre (CETRA) Ltd, 1993-; Chm., Taiwan Advrs Gp, 1997-. Asia Pacific Advr, DTI/BTI/Trade Partners UK, 1985-. FInstD 1968; Fellow, Inst. of Export, 1967. Mem., CBI Internat. Cttee, 1998-2000. Dir, Internat. Shakespeare Globe Centre; 1993-; Trustee, Colchester and Dist Visual Arts Trust, 1993-. Freeman, City of London, 1980; Liveryman, Co. of Launderers, 1980-. Friend of the Foreign Service Medal (Taiwan), 2000. *Recreations:* gardening under direction, overseas shopping, sun bathing, film, theatre, golf lessons. *Address:* Cherry Ground, Holbrook, Suffolk IP9 2PS. *T:* (01473) 328203, *Fax:* (01473) 328472; 202 Marlyn Lodge, Portsoken Street, E1 8RB; *e-mail:* phkent1937@aol.com. *Clubs:* Naval and Military, Academy; Jockey Club Rooms (Newmarket); Hintlesham Golf.

KENT, Roderick David; Managing Director, Close Brothers Group plc, since 1975; *b* 14 Aug. 1947; *s* of Dr Basil Stanley Kent, MB, BS, FFARCS and Vivien Margaret Kent (*née* Baker); *m* 1972, Belinda Jane Mitchell; three *d*. *Educ:* King's Sch., Canterbury; Corpus Christi Coll., Oxford (MA); INSEAD (MBA 1972). MSI. Investment Div., J. Henry Schroder Wagg, 1969–71; Triumph Investment Trust, 1972–74; Dir, 1974–, Chm., 1990–, Close Brothers Ltd. Chm., Grosvenor Ltd, 2000–. Non-executive Director: Wessex Water plc, 1988–98; English and Scottish Investors plc, 1988–98; M & G Gp plc, 1995–99 (non-exec. Chm., 1998–99); Grosvenor Group Hldgs Ltd, 2000–. Trustee, Esmée Fairbairn Foundn, 2001–. Liveryman, Co. of Pewterers, 1976–. *Recreations:* dairy farming, antique furniture restoration, sports. *Address:* (office) 10 Crown Place, EC2A 4FT. *T:* (020) 7426 4000.

KENT, Thomas George, CBE 1979; CEng, MIMechE, FRAeS; aerospace and defence consultant; Director: Third Grosvenor Ltd, since 1987; Grosvenor General Partner, since 1995; *b* 13 Aug. 1925. *Educ:* Borden Grammar School; Medway College of Technology. Joined English Electric Co., 1951; Special Director, British Aircraft Corp., 1967; Dep. Man. Dir, 1974; Man. Dir, 1977; Director, Hatfield/Lostock Division and Stevenage/Bristol Div. of Dynamics Group, British Aerospace, 1977–79; Gp Dep. Chief Exec., BAe Dynamics Gp, 1980–85; Bd Mem., BAe, 1981–85; Director: BAe Australia Ltd, 1980–86 (Chm., 1984–86); Arab British Dynamics, 1980–85; BAJ Vickers Ltd, 1982–87 (non.-exec.); Grosvenor Technol. Ltd, 1984–95; Grosvenor Develt Capital, 1993–95; Mercury Grosvenor Trust PLC, 1995–97. *Address:* Weeamara, Grove Park, Hampton on the Hill, Warwick CV35 8QR.

KENT-JONES, Trevor David, TD; **His Honour Judge Kent-Jones;** a Circuit Judge, since 1991; *b* 31 July 1940; *s* of late David Sandford Kent-Jones and of Madeline Mary Kent-Jones (*née* Russell-Pavier); one *s* one *d*. *Educ:* Bedford Sch.; Liverpool Univ. (LLB; DipIntLaw). Called to the Bar, Gray's Inn, 1962; Mem., NE Circuit, 1963–91, Junior, 1969; a Recorder, 1985–91. Commnd KOYLI TA, 1959; served 4th Bn KOYLI, 5th Bn Light Infantry, HQ NE Dist, 1959–85; Lt-Col 1977. *Recreations:* cricket, travel, fell-walking. *Address:* Leeds Combined Court Centre, 1 Oxford Row, Leeds LS1 3BG. *Club:* Naval and Military.

KENTFIELD, Graham Edward Alfred; Deputy Director, 1994–98, and Chief Cashier, 1991–98, Bank of England; *b* 3 Sept. 1940; *s* of late E. L. H. Kentfield and F. E. M. Kentfield (*née* Tucker); *m* 1965, Ann Dwelley Hewetson; two *d*. *Educ:* Bancroft's Sch., Woodford Green, Essex; St Edmund Hall, Oxford (BA 1st cl. Lit.Hum.). Entered Bank of England, 1963; seconded to Dept of Applied Econs, Cambridge, 1966–67; Editor, Bank of England Qly Bull., 1977–80; Adviser: Financial Stats Div., 1980–84; Banking Dept, 1984–85; Dep. Chief of Banking Dept and Dep. Chief Cashier, 1985–91; Chief of Banking Dept, 1991–94. Member: Bldg Socs Investment Protection Bd, 1991–; Financial Law Panel, 1994–98; Chm., Insolvency Practices Council, 2000–. Trustee: CIB Pension Fund, 1994– (Chm., 2000–); Overseas Bishoprics Fund, 1999–. Vice-Pres., CIB, 2000–. Hon. Treas., Soc. for Promotion of Roman Studies, 1991–. Mem. Council, Univ. of London, 2000–. *Recreations:* Roman history, genealogy, philately.

KENTRIDGE, Sir Sydney (Woolf), KCMG 1999; QC 1984; *b* Johannesburg, 5 Nov. 1922; *s* of Morris and May Kentridge; *m* 1952, Felicia Geffen; two *s* two *d*. *Educ:* King Edward VII Sch., Johannesburg; Univ. of the Witwatersrand (BA); Exeter Coll., Oxford Univ. (MA; Hon. Fellow, 1986). War service with S African forces, 1942–46. Advocate 1949, Senior Counsel 1965, South Africa; called to the English Bar, Lincoln's Inn, 1977, Bencher, 1986. Mem., Ct of Appeal, Botswana, 1981–88; Judge, Cts of Appeal, Jersey and Guernsey, 1988–92; acting Justice, Constitutional Court of S Africa, 1995–96. Roberts

Lectr, Univ. of Pennsylvania, 1979. Hon. Mem., Bar Assoc., NY, 2001. Hon. Fellow, American Coll. of Trial Lawyers, 1999. Hon. LLD: Seton Hall Univ., NJ, 1978; Leicester, 1985; Cape Town, 1987; Natal, 1989; London, 1995; Sussex, 1997; Witwatersrand, 2000. Granville Clark Prize, USA, 1978. *Recreation:* opera-going. *Address:* Brick Court Chambers, 7–8 Essex Street, WC2R 3LD. *T:* (020) 7379 3550. *Club:* Athenæum.

KENWARD, Michael Ronald John, OBE 1990; science writer and editorial consultant; *b* 12 July 1945; *s* of late Ronald Kenward and of Phyllis Kenward; *m* 1969, Elizabeth Rice. *Educ:* Wolverstone Hall; Sussex Univ. Res. scientist, UKAEA, Culham Laboratory, 1966–68; Technical editor, Scientific Instrument Res. Assoc., 1969; various editorial posts, New Scientist, 1969–79, Editor, 1979–90; Science Consultant, The Sunday Times, 1990. Member: Royal Soc. COPUS, 1986–90; Public Affairs Cttee, 1989–93, Sci. and Industry Cttee, 1994–99, BAAS; Bd, Assoc. of British Editors, 1986–90; Royal Instn Task Force, 1995–96; Centre Cttee, Wellcome Centre for Med. Sci., 1997–98; Medicine in Society Panel, Wellcome Trust, 1998–2000; Adv. Cttee, AlphaGalileo electronic news service, 1999–. Internat. Rep., Assoc. of British Sci. Writers, 1993–97. Mem. Editl Cttee, Science and Public Affairs, 1994–97. *Publications:* Potential Energy, 1976; articles on science, technology, and business. *Recreations:* walking, photography, collecting 'middle-aged' books, listening to baroque opera and Texas rock-and-roll, reconfiguring my operating system. *Address:* Grange Cottage, Staplefield, W Sussex RH17 6EL.

KENWAY-SMITH, Wendy Alison, FCA; Assistant Auditor General, National Audit Office, since 2000; *b* 21 Feb. 1959; *d* of Derek Peter Kenway-Smith and Muriel Anne Kenway-Smith (*née* Stevens). *Educ:* Marist Sch., Ascot; Guildford Tech. Coll.; City of London Poly. (BA Hons Accountancy). ACA 1983, FCA 1993. Joined BDO Stoy Hayward, 1980, Partner, 1990–95; Dir, Nat. Audit Office, 1995–99. Freeman, City of London, 1993. *Recreations:* travel, gardening, good food, theatre, classical music. *Address:* National Audit Office, 157-197 Buckingham Palace Road, SW1W 9SP. *T:* (020) 7798 7391.

KENWORTHY, family name of **Baron Strabolgi**.

KENWORTHY, Duncan Hamish, OBE 1999; film producer; Managing Director, Toledo Productions Ltd, since 1995; Co-Chairman, DNA Films Ltd, since 1997; *b* 9 Sept. 1949; *s* of Bernard Ian Kenworthy and Edna Muriel Kenworthy (*née* Calligan). *Educ:* Rydal Sch.; Christ's Coll., Cambridge (MA English 1975); Annenberg Sch., Univ. of Pennsylvania (MA Communications 1973). Children's Television Workshop, NY, 1973–76; Consulting Producer, Arabic Sesame Street, Kuwait, 1977–79; Prod. and Exec., Jim Henson Productions, London, 1979–95. Associate Prod., The Dark Crystal (film), 1980; Producer: *television:* Fraggle Rock, 1982 (Outstanding Children's Programming, Emmy Award, 1983); The Storyteller, 1986–88 (Best Children's Prog., BAFTA, 1989); Living with Dinosaurs, 1988 (Best Children's Prog., Emmy Award, 1990); Monster Maker, 1988; Greek Myths, 1990 (Best Children's Fictional Prog., BAFTA, 1991); Gulliver's Travels, 1996 (Outstanding Mini-series, Emmy Award, 1996); *films:* Four Weddings and a Funeral, 1994 (Best Film, and Lloyd's Bank Peoples' Choice Award, BAFTA, 1994; Best Foreign Film, Cesar Award, 1994); Lawn Dogs, 1997; Notting Hill, 1999 (Orange Audience Award, BAFTA, 2000); The Parole Officer, 2001. Member: Council, BAFTA, 1996– (Dep. Chm., Film, 2000–); Film Policy Review Gp, 1997–99; Film Finance Forum, 1998–; Dir, Film Council, 1999–; Chairman: Film and TV Adv. Cttee, British Council, 1999–; UK-China Forum, 2000–. Trustee, Oscar Moore Foundn, 1997–. British Producer of the Year, London Film Critics, 1994. FRSA 2000. *Address:* DNA Films, 3rd Floor, 75–77 Margaret Street, W1N 7HB. *Clubs:* Oxford and Cambridge, Groucho.

KENWORTHY, Frederick John; Managing Director, Aktus (formerly Align) Consulting (UK) Ltd, since 1997; *b* 6 Dec. 1943; *s* of late Rev. Fred Kenworthy and of Mrs Ethel Kenworthy; *m* 1968, Diana Flintham; one *d*. *Educ:* William Hulme's Grammar Sch., Manchester; Manchester Univ. (BA Econ Hons, Politics). Entered Admin. Class, Home Civil Service, as Asst Principal, MoD (Navy), 1966; Treasury Centre for Admin. Studies, 1968–69; joined BSC, Sheffield, 1969; Principal, MoD, 1972; Royal Commn on the Press Secretariat, 1974; Asst Sec., Dir, Weapons Resources and Progs (Naval), MoD, 1979–83; Head of Resources and Progs (Navy) (formerly DS4), RN Size and Shape Policy, MoD, 1983–86; Dir of Ops (Grade 4), Disablement Services Authy (formerly Div.), DHSS, 1986–88; Dir, IT Systems Directorate (Under Sec.), 1989–90, Chief Exec., IT Services Agency, 1990–93, Dept of Social Security; Management Consultant, ICL (Internat.), 1993–95; Prin. Consultant, Independent Management Consultants, 1996. Interim Dir of Mgt Inf. Services, Univ. of Cambridge, 2001. MInstD. Freeman, Co. of Information Technologists, 1992. *Publications:* contribs on Hungarian revenue collection and on pensions. *Recreations:* music, sport, photography. *Address:* PO Box 20031, NW2 4ZN. *T:* (020) 8208 1043. *Club:* Hendon Golf.

KENWORTHY, Joan Margaret, BLitt, MA; Principal, St Mary's College, University of Durham, 1977–99; *b* Oldham, Lancs, 10 Dec. 1933; *o d* of late Albert Kenworthy and Amy (*née* Cobbold). *Educ:* Girls Grammar Sch., Barrow-in-Furness; St Hilda's Coll., Oxford (BLitt, MA). Henry Oliver Beckit Prize, Oxford, 1955; Leverhulme Overseas Res. Scholar, Makerere Coll., Uganda, and E African Agriculture and Forestry Res. Org., Kenya, 1956–58; Actg Tutor, St Hugh's Coll., Oxford, 1958–59; Tutorial Res. Fellow, Bedford Coll., London, 1959–60; Univ. of Liverpool: Asst Lectr in Geography, 1960–63; Lectr, 1963–73; Sen. Lectr, 1973–77; Warden of Salisbury Hall, 1966–77 and of Morton House, 1974–77. IUC short-term Vis. Lectr, Univ. of Sierra Leone, 1975; Vis. Lectr, Univ. of Fort Hare, Ciskei, 1983. Mem., NE England, Churches Regl Broadcasting Council, 1978–82; Bishop's Selector for ACCM, 1982–87. Member: Council, African Studies Assoc. of UK, 1969–71, 1994–97; Standing Cttee on Univ. Studies of Africa, 1994–98; Council, Inst. of Brit. Geographers, 1976–78; Cttee, Merseyside Conf. for Overseas Students Ltd, 1976–77; Council, RMetS, 1980–83; Treasurer, Assoc. of Brit. Climatologists, 1976–79; Northern Chm., Durham Univ. Soc., 1979–82. Gov., St Anne's Sch., Windermere, 1992–95. *Publications:* (contrib.) Geographers and the Tropics, ed R. W. Steel and R. M. Prothero, 1964; (contrib.) Oxford Regional Economic Atlas for Africa, 1965; (contrib.) Studies in East African Geography and Development, ed S. Ominde, 1971; (contrib.) An Advanced Geography of Africa, ed J. I. Clarke, 1975; (contrib.) Rangeland Management and Ecology in East Africa, ed D. J. Pratt and M. D. Gwynne, 1977; (contrib.) The Climatic Scene: essays in honour of Emeritus Prof. Gordon Manley, ed M. J. Tooley and G. Sheail, 1985; (ed with B. D. Giles) Observatories and Climatological Research, 1994; (ed with J. M. Walker) Colonial Observatories and Observations, 1997; articles in jls, encycs and reports of symposia. *Address:* 3 Satley Plough, Satley, Bishop Auckland, Co. Durham DL13 4JX. *T:* (01388) 730848. *Club:* Royal Commonwealth Society.

KENWORTHY-BROWNE, (Bernard) Peter (Francis); a District Judge (formerly Registrar) of the High Court (Family Division), since 1982; *b* 11 May 1930; *s* of late Bernard Evelyn Kenworthy-Browne and Margaret Sibylla Kenworthy-Browne; *m* 1975, Jane Elizabeth Arthur (marr. diss. 1982); *m* 1989, Elizabeth, *o d* of late Dr J. A. Bowen-Jones. *Educ:* Ampleforth; Oriel Coll., Oxford. MA. 2nd Lieut, Irish Guards, 1949–50. Called to the Bar, Lincoln's Inn, 1955; Oxford, and Midland and Oxford Circuit, 1957–82; a Recorder of the Crown Court, 1981–82. *Recreations:* music, field sports, gardening. *Address:* The Old Vicarage, Staverton, Northants NN11 6JJ. *T:* (01327) 704667. *Club:* Cavalry and Guards.

KENWRIGHT, Prof. John, MD; FRCS; Nuffield Professor of Orthopaedic Surgery, Oxford University, 1992–2001; Professorial Fellow, Worcester College, Oxford, 1992–2001, now Emeritus; *b* 2 May 1936; *s* of Cecil Kenwright and Norah (*née* Langley); *m* 1960, Vivien Mary Curtis; two *s*. *Educ:* University College Sch.; Nottingham High Sch.; St John's Coll., Oxford; University College Hosp. MA Oxon; BM, BCh; MD Stockholm 1972. FRCS 1966. Nuffield Surgical Res. Fellow, Oxford, 1968; Res. Fellow, Karolinska Inst., Stockholm, 1971; Consultant Orthopaedic Surgeon, Nuffield Orthopaedic Centre and John Radcliffe Hosp., Oxford, 1973–. Hunterian Prof., RCS, 1991–92; Robert Jones Lectr, RCS, 1998. President: Girdlestone Orthopaedic Soc., 1993–; Oxford Medico-legal Soc., 1998–; British Limb Reconstruction Soc., 1998–; British Orthopaedic Res. Soc., 1999–. *Publications:* articles in scientific jls on factors which control fracture and soft tissue healing; also on leg lengthening and correction of post traumatic deformity. *Recreation:* sailing. *Address:* Nuffield Orthopaedic Centre, Headington, Oxford OX3 7LD. *T:* (01865) 741155, 227377, *Fax:* (01865) 227354. *Club:* Oxford and Cambridge Sailing Society.

KENWRIGHT, William, (Bill), CBE 2001; theatre producer, since 1970; *b* 4 Sept. 1945; *s* of Albert Kenwright and Hope Kenwright (*née* Jones). *Educ:* Liverpool Inst. Actor, 1964–70; has produced more than 500 plays and musicals, including: Joseph and The Amazing Technicolor Dreamcoat, 1979 (toured for 13 years); The Business of Murder, 1981; A Streetcar Named Desire, 1984; Stepping Out, 1984; Blood Brothers, 1988, transf. NY, 1993; Shirley Valentine, 1989; Travels with My Aunt, 1993; Piaf, 1993; Lysistrata, 1993; Medea, 1993; Pygmalion, 1997; A Doll's House; An Ideal Husband; Passion; *films:* Stepping Out; Don't Go Breaking My Heart, 1999. Dir, Everton FC (Dep. Chm., 1998–). Hon. Prof., Tameside Univ. Hon. Dr Liverpool John Moores, 1994. Has won Tony, Olivier and Evening Standard awards. *Address:* Bill Kenwright Ltd, BKL House, 106 Harrow Road, W2 1RR. *T:* (020) 7446 6200.

KENYON, family name of **Baron Kenyon**.

KENYON, 6th Baron *cr* 1788; **Lloyd Tyrell-Kenyon;** Bt 1784; Baron of Gredington, 1788; *b* 13 July 1947; *s* of 5th Baron Kenyon, CBE and of Leila Mary, *d* of Comdr John Wyndham Cookson, RN and *widow* of Hugh William Jardine Ethelston Peel; *S* father, 1993; *m* 1971, Sally Carolyn, *e d* of J. F. P. Matthews; two *s*. *Educ:* Eton; Magdalene Coll., Cambridge (BA). Mem. (C), Wrexham County (formerly Wrexham Maelor) BC, 1991–. Mem., EU Cttee of the Regions, 1994–97. High Sheriff, Clwyd, 1986. *Heir: s* Hon. Lloyd Nicholas Tyrell-Kenyon, *b* 9 April 1972. *Address:* Gredington, Whitchurch, Shropshire SY13 3DH.

KENYON, Sir George (Henry), Kt 1976; DL; JP; LLD; *b* 10 July 1912; *s* of George Henry Kenyon and Edith (*née* Hill); *m* 1938, Christine Dorey (*née* Brentnall) (*d* 1996); two *s* one *d*. *Educ:* Radley; Manchester Univ. Director: William Kenyon & Sons Ltd, 1942–92 (Chm., 1961–82); Tootal Ltd, 1971–79 (Chm., 1976–79); Manchester Ship Canal, 1972–86; Williams & Glyn's Bank, 1972–83 (Chm., 1978–83); Royal Bank of Scotland, 1978–83; Chm., Vuman Ltd, 1982–88. Gen. Comr, Inland Revenue, 1957–73. Manchester University: Chm. Bldgs Cttee, 1962–70; Treas., 1970–72, 1980–82; Chm. Council, 1972–80. Hon. Treas., Civic Trust, NW, 1962–78, Vice Pres., 1978; Member: NW Adv. Cttee, Civil Aviation, 1967–72; Manchester Reg. Hosp. Bd, 1962–68; NW Reg. Econ. Planning Council, 1970–73. Pres., Arkwright Soc., Cromford, 1995– (Vice-Pres., 1988–94). JP Cheshire, 1959; Chm., S Tameside Bench, 1974–82; DL Chester, 1969, Greater Manchester, 1983. High Sheriff, Cheshire, 1973–74. Hon. LLD Manchester, 1980. *Recreations:* reading, talking, travel. *Address:* Limefield House, Hyde, Cheshire SK14 1DN. *T:* (0161) 368 2012.

KENYON, Ian Roy; HM Diplomatic Service, retired; Executive Secretary, Preparatory Commission for Organisation for Prohibition of Chemical Weapons, The Hague, 1993–97; *b* 13 June 1939; *s* of late S. R. Kenyon and Mrs E. M. Kenyon; *m* 1962, Griselda Rintoul; one *s* one *d*. *Educ:* Lancaster Royal Grammar School; Edinburgh University (BSc Hons). Lever Bros, 1962–68; Birds Eye Foods, 1968–74; First Secretary, FCO, 1974–76; Geneva, 1976–78; Head of Chancery, Bogota, 1979–81; FCO, 1982–83; Head of Nuclear Energy Dept, FCO, 1983–85; Overseas Inspectorate, 1986–88; Dep. Leader, UK Delegn to Conf. on Disarmament, Geneva, 1988–92. Vis. Fellow, Mountbatten Centre for Internat. Studies, Southampton Univ., 1997–. *Recreation:* carriage driving.

KENYON, Margaret; DL; Headmistress, Withington Girls' School, Manchester, 1986–2000; *b* 19 June 1940; *d* of Hugh Richard Parry and Aileen Cole (*née* Morgan); *m* 1962, Christopher George Kenyon; two *s*. *Educ:* Merchant Taylors' Sch. for Girls, Crosby; Somerville Coll., Oxford (MA; Hon. Fellow, 1999). Asst French Mistress, Cheadle Hulme Sch., 1962–63 and 1974–83; Hd of French, Withington Girls Sch., 1983–85. Girls' School Association: Chm., NW Region, 1989–91; Pres., 1993–94. Mem. Adv. Council, Granada Foundn, 1986–. Trustee, Mus. of Science and Industry, Manchester, 1998–. Mem. Court, Univ. of Manchester, 1991–. Gov., Bolton Sch., 2001–. DL Greater Manchester, 1998. *Recreations:* reading, talking, family. *Address:* Westow Lodge, Macclesfield Road, Alderley Edge, Cheshire SK9 7BW.

KENYON, Nicholas Roger, CBE 2001; Controller, BBC Proms, Live Events and TV Classical Music, since 2000 (BBC Proms and Millennium Programmes, 1998–2000); *b* 23 Feb. 1951; *s* of Thomas Kenyon and Kathleen Holmes; *m* 1976, Marie-Ghislaine Latham-Koenig; three *s* one *d*. *Educ:* Balliol College, Oxford (BA Hons 1972). Music critic: The New Yorker, 1979–82; The Times, 1982–85; The Observer, 1985–92; Music Editor, The Listener, 1982–87; Controller, BBC Radio 3, 1992–98; Dir, BBC Promenade Concerts, 1996–. Editor, Early Music, 1983–92. *Publications:* The BBC Symphony Orchestra 1930–80, 1981; Simon Rattle, 1987, 2nd edn 2001; (ed) Authenticity and Early Music, 1988; (ed jtly) The Viking Opera Guide, 1993; (ed jtly) The Penguin Opera Guide, 1995. *Recreation:* family. *Address:* BBC, Broadcasting House, W1A 1AA. *T:* (020) 7765 4928.

KENYON-SLANEY, William Simon Rodolph; JP; Vice Lord-Lieutenant of Shropshire, since 1996; *b* 31 Jan. 1932; *s* of Major R. O. R. Kenyon-Slaney, Grenadier Guards, and Nesta, *d* of Sir George Ferdinand Forestier-Walker, 3rd Bt; *m* 1960, Mary Helena, *e d* of Lt-Col Hon. H. G. O. Bridgeman, DSO, MC, RA, and Joan, *d* of Hon. Bernard Constable Maxwell; three *s*. *Educ:* Eton. FLAS 1964; FRICS 1970. Grenadier Guards, 1950–52; Chartered Land Agent and Surveyor; farmer. Non-exec. Dir, South Staffs Water Holdings, 1988–; Chm., Ludlow Cons. Assoc., 1989–91. Trustee, Ironbridge Gorge Museum, 1995–. Former school governor. Shropshire: JP 1969 (Chm., Shropshire Magistrates' Courts Cttee, 1994–97); CC, 1977–85; High Sheriff, 1979; DL 1986. KStJ 1993 (Mem., Chapter-General, 1990–99, Priory Chapter, 1999–). *Recreations:* gardening, travel, theatre, fishing. *Address:* Chyknell, Bridgnorth, Shropshire WV15 5PP. *T:* (01746) 710210.

KEOHANE, Desmond John, OBE 1991; FIMgt; consultant in education and training, since 1991; *b* 5 July 1928; *s* of William Patrick Keohane and Mabel Margaret Keohane; *m* 1960, Mary Kelliher; two *s* two *d*. *Educ:* Borden Grammar Sch., Sittingbourne; Univ. of Birmingham (BA and Baxter Prize in History, 1949); London Univ. (Postgrad. Cert. in Educn). FIMgt (FBIM 1981). Postgrad. res., 1949–50; Nat. Service, Educn Officer, RAF, 1950–52; sch. teacher and coll. lectr, 1953–64; Head, Dept of Social and Academic Studies, 1964–68, and Vice-Principal, 1969–71, Havering Technical Coll.; Principal, Northampton Coll. of Further Educn, 1971–76; Principal, Oxford Coll. of Further Educn, 1976–90. Part-time Lectr in Educnl Management, Univ. of Leicester, 1990–93; Vis. Fellow (Educn), Oxford Brookes Univ. (formerly Oxford Polytechnic), 1991–94. Member: Council, Southern Regional Council for Further Educn, 1977–90; Secondary Exams Council, 1983–86; Berks and Oxon Area Manpower Board, 1985–88; Special Employment Measures Adv. Gp, MSC, 1986–89; Northampton RC Diocesan Educn Commn, 1991–; E Midlands Panel, Nat. Lottery Charities Bd, 1995–98; Co-opted Mem. Educn Cttee, Northants CC, 1996–. Chm. Trustees, Stress at Work, 1987–. Formerly governor of various educnl instns; Chm. of Govs, Thomas Becket Sch., Northampton, 1983–98. Gen. Ed., series Managing Colleges Effectively, 1994–99. *Recreations:* enjoying family and friends, watching cricket. *Address:* 14 Abington Park Crescent, Northampton NN3 3AD. *T:* (01604) 638829.

KEPA, Sailosi Wai; Ombudsman, Fiji, since 1996 (on secondment); a Judge of the High Court, Fiji, since 1992; *b* 4 Nov. 1938; *m* Adi Teimumu Tuisawau; four *c*. *Educ:* Draiba Fijian Sch.; Lelean Memorial Sch.; Nasinu Training Coll.; Sydney Univ. (Dip. in Teaching of English, 1966). Called to the Bar, Middle Temple, 1972; Barrister and Solicitor, Fiji, 1974. Joined Judicial Dept, as Magistrate, 1969; served Suva, Northern Div., Sigatoka, Nadi; Chief Magistrate, July 1980; Dir of Public Prosecutions, Nov. 1980; High Comr for Fiji in London, 1985–88; Attorney-Gen. and Minister for Justice, Fiji, 1988–92. Chairman: Bd of Legal Educn, Fiji, 1997–; Fiji Human Rights Commn, 1998–. Rugby player (rep. Fiji, Australia 1961), coach, manager, administrator; Life Mem., Fiji Rugby Football Union (Chm., 1983–85); Pres., Suva Rugby Union, 1989–92. *Address:* GPO Box 982, Suva, Fiji. *T:* (office) 211652, (home) 313416, *Fax:* 314756. *Clubs:* Suva Bowling, United Improvement (Suva).

KEPPEL, family name of **Earl of Albemarle**.

KER; *see* Innes-Ker, family name of Duke of Roxburghe.

KERBY, John Vyvyan; UK Director, European Bank for Reconstruction and Development, since 2001; *b* 14 Dec. 1942; *s* of Theo Rosser Fred Kerby and Constance Mary (*née* Newell); *m* 1978, Shirley Elizabeth Pope; one step *s* one step *d*. *Educ:* Eton Coll.; Christ Church, Oxford (MA). Temp. Asst Principal, CO, 1965; Asst Principal, ODM, 1967; Pvte Sec. to Parly Under-Sec. of State, FCO, 1970; Principal, ODA, 1971–74, 1975–77; CSSB, 1974–75; Asst Sec., ODA, 1977; Head of British Develt Div. in Southern Africa, 1983; Under Sec. and Prin. Establishment Officer, ODA, 1986–93; Hd, Asia and Pacific Div., ODA, subseq. Dir, Asia and Pacific, DFID, 1993–97; Dir, Eastern Europe and Western Hemisphere Div., DFID, 1997–2001. Gov., Centre for Internat. Briefing, 1986–. *Recreations:* gardening, cricket, music, entomology. *Address:* c/o Office of UK Delegation to EBRD, 1 Exchange Square, EC2A 2JN. *T:* (020) 7338 6475.

KERDEL-VEGAS, Francisco, Hon. CBE 1973; MD; Venezuelan Ambassador to UNESCO, 1994–99, and to France, 1995–99; *b* 3 Jan. 1928; *s* of Oswaldo F. Kerdel y Sofia Vegas de Kerdel; *m* 1977, Martha Ramos de Kerdel; two *s* four *d*. *Educ:* Liceo Andrés Bello, Caracas (BSc); Univ. Central de Venezuela (MD); Harvard; New York Univ. (MSc). Prof. of Dermatology, Central Univ. of Venezuela, 1954–77; Vis. Scientist, Dept of Experimental Pathology, ARC Inst. of Animal Physiology, Cambridge, 1966–67; Mem., Trinity Coll, Cambridge, 1966–67; Scientific Attaché, Venezuelan Embassy, London, 1966–67; Vice-Chancellor, Simón Bolívar Univ., 1969–70; Venezuelan Ambassador to UK, 1987–92. Mem. Board, Univ. Metropolitana, Caracas, 1970–. Vis. Prof. of Dermatol., UMDS of Guy's and St Thomas' Hosps, 1990. Prosser White Oration, RCP, 1972. A Dir, Internat. Foundn of Dermatol., 1987–. Fellow, Venezuelan Acads of Medicine, 1967–, of Sciences, 1971–; Mem., Nat. Res. Council, Venezuela, 1969–79; President: FUDENA (Nat. chapter of WWF), 1974; Internat. Soc. of Dermatol., 1985–90. Fellow: Amer. Coll. of Physicians; Philadelphia Coll. of Physicians; Amer. Acad. of Dermatology. Foreign Mem., Nat. Academies of Medicine of Brazil, Chile and Paraguay; Hon. Member: RSM; British Assoc. of Dermatologists; German Assoc. of Dermatologists; Socs of Dermatology of France, Austria, Spain, Portugal, Brazil, Argentina, Mexico, Colombia, Ecuador, Peru, Central America, Cuba, Israel, S Africa. Hon. DSc: California Coll. of Podiatric Medicine, 1975; Cranfield, 1991. Venezuelan Orders of: Andrés Bello, 1970; Cecilio Acosta, 1976; Francisco de Miranda, 1978; Diego de Losada, 1985; El Libertador, 1986; Chevalier de la Legion d'Honneur (France), 1972. *Publications:* Tratado de Dermatologia, 1959, 4th edn 1986; chapters of textbooks of Dermatology, UK, USA, Canada, Spain, Mexico. *Recreations:* travelling, swimming, photography. *Address:* c/o Ministry of Foreign Affairs, Torre MRE, Conde a Carmelitas, Caracas 1010, Venezuela. *Clubs:* Oxford and Cambridge, White's; Caracas Country, Camurí Grande (Venezuela).

KERIN, Hon. John Charles, AM 2001; Chairman, Australian Meat and Livestock Corporation, 1994–97; *b* 21 Nov. 1937; *s* of Joseph Sydney Kerin and Mary Louise Fuller; *m* 1st, Barbara Elizabeth Large (marr. diss.); one *d*; 2nd, 1983, Dr June Raye Verrier. *Educ:* Univ. of New England (BA); ANU (BEc). Farmer and businessman, 1952–71; Res. Economist, 1971–72, Principal Res. Economist, 1976–78, Bureau of Agricl Econs. MP (ALP) for Macarthur, NSW, 1972–75, for Werrina, 1978–93; Minister: for Primary Industry, 1983–87; for Primary Industries and Energy, 1987–91; Treas., 1991; Minister: for Transport and Communications, 1991; for Trade and Overseas Develt, 1991–93. Statutory office holder and businessman, 1993–. Chairman: Corporate Investment Australia Funds Management Ltd, 1994–99; John Kerin and Associates, 1994–; Spire Technologies, 1998–; Dep. Chm., Coal Operations Australia Ltd, 1998–2000 (Chm., 1995–98); Mem. Bd, Billiton Coal Australia. Chairman: NSW Water Adv. Council, 1995–; Reef Fisheries Management Adv. Cttee, 1995–; Co-operative Research Centres: Sustainable Plantation Forestry (formerly Temperate Hardwood Forests), 1994–; Tropical Savannas, 1995–; Weed Management Systems, 1995–; Sensor Signals and Information Processing, 1995–. Forestry Comr, NSW, 1998–; Chm., Qld Fisheries Mgt Authy, 1999–2000. Chm. Adv. Cttee, Nat. Quine Johnes Prog., 2000–; Mem., Safe Food Prodn, NSW, 2000–. Dep. Chancellor, and Mem. Bd of Trustees, Univ. of Western Sydney. Fellow, Aust. Inst. of Agricl Sci., 1995. Hon. Dr Rural Sci., New England, 1993; Hon. DLitt Western Sydney, 1995. *Recreations:* live arts, music, reading, walking. *Address:* 26 Harpur Place, Garran, ACT 2605, Australia. *T:* (2) 62852480.

KERMACK, Stuart Ogilvy; Sheriff of Tayside, Central and Fife: at Forfar, 1971–93; at Perth, 1971–75; at Arbroath, 1975–91; at Dundee, 1991–93; *b* 9 July 1934; *s* of late Stuart Grace Kermack, CBE and of Nell P., *y d* of Thomas White, SSC; *m* 1961, Barbara Mackenzie, BSc; three *s* one *d*. *Educ:* Glasgow Academy; Jesus Coll., Oxford; Glasgow Univ.; Edinburgh Univ. BA Oxon (Jurisprudence), 1956; LLB Glasgow, 1959. Called to Scots Bar, 1959. Sheriff Substitute of Inverness, Moray, Nairn and Ross, at Elgin and Nairn, 1965–71. *Publications:* contrib. Pictish Arts Soc. Jl; articles in legal journals. *Address:* 23 South Learmonth Gardens, Edinburgh EH4 1EZ. *T:* (0131) 337 1898; Linshader, Uig, Isle of Lewis HS2 9DR. *T:* (01851) 621201.

KERMAN, Prof. Joseph Wilfred; Professor of Music, University of California at Berkeley, since 1974 (Chambers Professor of Music, 1986–89); *b* 3 April 1924; *m* 1945, Vivian Shaviro; two *s* one *d*. *Educ:* New York Univ. (AB); Princeton Univ. (PhD). Dir of Graduate Studies, Westminster Choir Coll., Princeton, NJ, USA, 1949–51; Music Faculty, Univ. of California at Berkeley, 1951–72, 1974– (Dep. Chm., 1960–63, 1991–93); Heather Prof. of Music, Oxford Univ., and Fellow of Wadham Coll., Oxford, 1972–74. Co-editor, 19th Century Music, 1977–88. Guggenheim, Fulbright and NEH Fellowships; Visiting Fellow: All Souls Coll., Oxford, 1966; Society for the Humanities, Cornell Univ., USA, 1970; Clare Hall, Cambridge, 1971; Walker-Ames Vis. Prof., Univ. of Washington, 1986; Valentine Vis. Prof., Amherst Coll., 1988; Gauss Lectr, Princeton Univ., 1988; Phi Beta Kappa Scholar, 1993; Charles Eliot Norton Prof. of Poetry, Harvard Univ., 1997–98. Fellow, American Academy of Arts and Sciences; Corresp. FBA 1984. Hon. Mem., Amer. Musicol Soc., 1995. Hon. FRAM. Hon. DHL Fairfield Univ., 1970. *Publications:* Opera as Drama, 1956, rev. edn 1988; The Elizabethan Madrigal, 1962; The Beethoven Quartets, 1967; A History of Art and Music (with H. W. Janson), 1968; (ed) Ludwig van Beethoven: Autograph Miscellany, 1786–99 (Kafka Sketchbook), 2 vols, 1970 (Kinkeldey Award); Listen, 1972; The Masses and Motets of William Byrd, 1981 (Kinkeldey Award; Deems Taylor Award); The New Grove Beethoven (with A. Tyson), 1983; (co-ed) Beethoven Studies, vol. 1 1973, vol. 2 1977, vol. 3 1982; Musicology, 1985; (ed) Music at the Turn of the Century, 1990; Write All These Down, 1994 (Deems Taylor Award); Concerto Conversations, 1999; essays, in music criticism and musicology, in: Hudson Review, New York Review, San Francisco Chronicle, etc. *Address:* Music Department, University of California, Berkeley, CA 94720, USA; 107 Southampton Avenue, Berkeley, CA 94707.

KERMODE, Sir (John) Frank, Kt 1991; MA; FBA 1973; *b* 29 Nov. 1919; *s* of late John Pritchard Kermode and late Doris Pearl Kermode; *m* 1947, Maureen Eccles (marr. diss. 1970); twin *s* and *d*. *Educ:* Douglas High Sch.; Liverpool Univ. BA 1940; War Service (Navy), 1940–46; MA 1947; Lecturer, King's Coll., Newcastle, in the University of Durham, 1947–49; Lecturer in the University of Reading, 1949–58; John Edward Taylor Prof. of English Literature in the University of Manchester, 1958–65; Winterstoke Prof. of English in the University of Bristol, 1965–67; Lord Northcliffe Prof. of Modern English Lit., UCL, 1967–74, Hon. Fellow, 1996; King Edward VII Prof. of English Literature, Cambridge Univ., 1974–82; Fellow, King's Coll., Cambridge, 1974–87, Hon. Fellow, 1988. Charles Eliot Norton Prof. of Poetry at Harvard, 1977–78. Co-editor, Encounter, 1966–67. Editor: Fontana Masterguides and Modern Masters series; Oxford Authors. FRSL 1958. Mem. Arts Council, 1968–71; Chm., Poetry Book Soc., 1968–76. For. Hon. Mem., Amer. Acad. of Arts and Scis; Hon. Mem. AAAL. Hon. DHL Chicago, 1975; Hon. DLitt: Liverpool, 1981; Newcastle, 1993; London, 1997; Hon Dr: Amsterdam, 1988; Yale, 1995; Wesleyan, 1997; Sewanee, 1999. Officier de l'Ordre des Arts et des Sciences. *Publications:* (ed) Shakespeare, The Tempest (Arden Edition), 1954; Romantic Image, 1957; John Donne, 1957; The Living Milton, 1960; Wallace Stevens, 1960; Puzzles & Epiphanies, 1962; The Sense of an Ending, 1967; Continuities, 1968; Shakespeare, Spenser, Donne, 1971; Modern Essays, 1971; Lawrence, 1973; (ed, with John Hollander) Oxford Anthology of English Literature, 1973; The Classic, 1975; (ed) Selected Prose of T. S. Eliot, 1975; The Genesis of Secrecy, 1979; Essays on Fiction, 1971–82, 1983; Forms of Attention, 1985; (ed jtly) The Literary Guide to the Bible, 1987; History and Value, 1988; An Appetite for Poetry, 1989; Poetry, Narrative, History, 1990; (ed with Keith Walker) Andrew Marvell, 1990; Uses of Error, 1991; (ed with Anita Kermode) The Oxford Book of Letters, 1995; Not Entitled (memoirs), 1996; Shakespeare's Language, 2000; Pleasing Myself, 2001; contrib. New Republic, Partisan Review, New York Review, New York Times, New Statesman, London Rev. of Books, etc. *Address:* 9 The Oast House, Grange Road, Cambridge CB3 9AP. *T:* (01223) 357931. *Club:* Savile.

KERMODE, Hon. Sir Ronald (Graham Quayle), KBE 1986 (CBE 1975); Judge of the Court of Appeal, Republic of Fiji, 1988–91; *b* 26 June 1919; *s* of George Graham Kermode and Linda Margaret (*née* McInnis); *m* 1945, Amy Rivett Marr; two *s* two *d*. *Educ:* Whangarei High Sch., NZ; Auckland University Coll. (LLB). Served with NZ and Fiji Mil. Forces, 1939–45. In private legal practice, 1945–75; Puisne Judge, Supreme Court of Fiji, 1976–86; Judge of the Court of Appeal: Kiribati, 1983–86; Fiji, 1985–87. Tribunal, Fiji Sugar Industry, 1985–92. Elected European MLC, Fiji, 1958, and served for 15 years as Mem. of Council and Parliament; first elected Speaker of the House of Representatives, 1968–73. *Recreations:* fishing, contract bridge, reading, gardening, bird watching. *Address:* 44A Cook Street, Howick, Auckland, New Zealand. *T:* (9) 5375102.

KERN, Karl-Heinz; Head of Arms Control Department, Ministry of Foreign Affairs, German Democratic Republic, 1987–90; research in international affairs, since 1990; *b* 18 Feb. 1930; *m* 1952, Ursula Bennmann; one *s*. *Educ:* King George Gymnasium, Dresden; Techn. Coll., Dresden (chem. engrg); Acad. for Polit. Science and Law (Dipl. jur., post-grad. History). Leading posts in diff. regional authorities of GDR until 1959; foreign policy, GDR, 1959–62; Head of GDR Mission in Ghana, 1962–66; Head of African Dept, Min. of For. Affairs, 1966–71; Minister and Chargé d'Affaires, Gt Britain, 1973; Ambassador to UK, 1973–80; Dep. Head of Western European Dept, Min. of Foreign Affairs, 1980–82; Ambassador to N Korea, 1982–86. Holds Order of Merit of the Fatherland, etc. *Recreations:* sport, reading, music. *Address:* Karl-Marx-Allee 70a, 10243 Berlin, Germany.

KERNAGHAN, Paul Robert, QPM 1998; Chief Constable, Hampshire Constabulary, since 1999; *b* 27 Dec. 1955; *s* of Hugh Kernaghan and Diane Kernaghan (*née* Herdman); *m* 1983, Mary McCleery; one *d*. *Educ:* Methodist Coll., Belfast; Queen's Univ., Belfast (LLB Hons); Univ. of Ulster (DPM); Univ. of Leicester (MA Public Order). MIPD 1991. Served UDR (part-time), 1974–77; commnd 1976, Second Lieut; served RUC, 1978–91: grad. entrant, Constable, 1978; served Belfast, Londonderry, Strabane and Warrenpoint, operational and staff appts; Superintendent, 1991–92, Detective Superintendent, 1992–95, W Midlands Police; Asst Chief Constable, 1995; Asst Chief Constable (Designated), 1996–99, N Yorks Police; rcds 1997. *Recreations:* family, international security. *Address:* Police Headquarters, West Hill, Winchester, Hants SO22 5DB. *T:* (01962) 841500.

KERNOHAN, Thomas Hugh, CBE 1978 (OBE 1955); Founder, 1959, and Chairman, 1961–80 and 1987–93, Kernohans Joinery Works Ltd (family joinery and plastic firm); *b* 11 May 1922; *s* of Thomas Watson Kernohan and Caroline Kernohan; *m* 1948, Margaret Moore; one *s* one *d*. *Educ:* Carrickfergus Model Sch.; Carrickfergus Technical Sch. On staff (admin), Harland & Wolff Ltd, Belfast, 1940–44; Engineering Employers' NI Association: Asst Sec., 1945; Sec., 1953; Dir, 1966–80; Parly Comr for Admin and Comr for Complaints, NI, 1980–87. *Address:* 103 Maritime Drive, Rodgers Bay, Carrickfergus, Co. Antrim, N Ireland BT38 8GQ.

KERR, family name of **Marquess of Lothian** and **Baron Teviot**.

KERR, Alan Grainger, OBE 2000; FRCS, FRCSE; Consultant Otolaryngologist, Royal Victoria and Belfast City Hospitals, since 1968; *b* 15 April 1935; *s* of Joseph William and Eileen Kerr; *m* 1962, Patricia Margaret M'Neill (*d* 1999); two *s* one *d*. *Educ:* Methodist College, Belfast; Queen's Univ., Belfast (MB). DObst RCOG. Clinical and Res. Fellow, Harvard Med. Sch., 1967; Prof. of Otorhinolaryngology, QUB, 1979–81. Otolaryngology Mem. Council, RCS, 1987–92; President: Otorhinolaryngological Res. Soc., 1985–87; Internat. Otopathology Soc., 1985–88; Otology Sect., RSM, 1989–90; British Assoc. of Otorhinolaryngologists—Head and Neck Surgeons, 1993–96; Irish Otolaryngological Soc., 1997–99; Politzer Soc., 1998–. Lectures, UK, Europe and USA. Prizes: Jobson Horne, BMA; Harrison, RSocMed; Howells, Univ. of London. Gen. Editor, Scott-Brown's Otolaryngology, 1987–. *Publications:* papers on ear surgery. *Recreations:* tennis, ski-ing, hill walking, bowls. *Address:* 6 Cranmore Gardens, Belfast BT9 6JL. *T:* (028) 9066 9181. *Club:* Royal Society of Medicine.

KERR, Prof. Allen, AO 1992; FRS 1986; FAA; Professor of Plant Pathology, University of Adelaide, 1980–91, Professor Emeritus, since 1992; *b* 21 May 1926; *s* of A. B. Kerr and J. T. Kerr (*née* White); *m* 1951, Rosemary Sheila Strachan; two *s* one *d*. *Educ:* George Heriot's Sch., Edinburgh; Univ. of Edinburgh. North of Scotland Coll. of Agric., 1947–51; University of Adelaide: Lectr, 1951–59; Sen. Lectr, 1959–67 (seconded to Tea Research Inst., Ceylon, 1963–66); Reader, 1968–80. For. Associate, Nat. Acad. of Scis, USA, 1991. *Recreation:* golf. *Address:* 419 Carrington Street, Adelaide, SA 5000, Australia. *T:* (8) 82322325.

KERR, Andrew Mark; Partner, Bell & Scott, WS, Edinburgh, 1969–99 (Senior Partner, 1987–96); Clerk to Society of Writers to HM Signet, since 1983; *b* Edinburgh 17 Jan. 1940; *s* of William Mark Kerr and Katharine Marjorie Anne Stevenson; *m* 1967, Jane Susanna Robertson; one *d*. *Educ:* Edinburgh Acad.; Cambridge Univ. (BA); Edinburgh Univ. (LLB). Served RNR, 1961–76. British Petroleum, 1961–62; apprenticeship with Davidson & Syme, WS, Edinburgh, 1964–67; with Bell & Scott, Bruce & Kerr, WS, now Bell & Scott, WS, 1967–99. Vice-Chm., Edinburgh New Town Conservation Cttee, 1972–76; Chm., Edinburgh Solicitors' Property Centre, 1976–81. Chairman: Penicuik House Preservation Trust, 1985–; Arts Trust of Scotland, 1996–; Dunedin Concerts Trust, 1996–; Member: Council, Edinburgh Internat. Fest., 1978–82; Scottish Arts Council, 1988–94 (Chm., Drama Cttee, 1988–91, and 1993–94); Director: Edinburgh Fest. and King's Theatres, 1997–; Edinburgh World Heritage Trust, 1999–; Sec., Edinburgh Fest. Fringe Soc. Ltd, 1969–. Mem. Council, St George's Sch. for Girls, Edinburgh, 1985–93; Gov., New Sch., Butterstone, 1995–. *Recreations:* architecture, hill walking, music, ships, ski-ing, theatre. *Address:* 16 Ann Street, Edinburgh EH4 1PJ. *T:* (home) (0131) 332 9857; (office) (0131) 226 7686. *Club:* New (Edinburgh).

KERR, Andrew Palmer; Member (Lab) East Kilbride, Scottish Parliament, since 1999; *b* 17 March 1962; *s* of William and May Kerr; *m* 1992, Susan Kealy; three *d* (incl. twins). *Educ:* Glasgow Coll. (BA Social Scis). Dep. Pres., Glasgow Coll. Students' Assoc., 1983–85; Convenor, Glasgow Area, NUS, 1985–86; Dep. Pres., NUS (Scotland), 1986–87; R&D Officer, Strathkelvin DC, 1987–90; Man. Dir, Achieving Quality, QA Consultancy, 1990–93; Strategy and Develt Manager, Cleansing Dept, Glasgow CC, 1993–99. *Recreations:* family, football, reading. *Address:* 6 Holm Street, Strathaven ML10 6NB. *T:* (01357) 520816.

KERR, Hon. Sir Brian (Francis), Kt 1993; **Hon. Mr Justice Kerr;** a Judge of the High Court of Justice, Northern Ireland, since 1993; *b* 22 Feb. 1948; *s* of late James William Kerr and Kathleen Rose Kerr; *m* 1970, Gillian Rosemary Owen Widdowson; two *s*. *Educ:* St Colman's College, Newry, Co. Down; Queen's Univ., Belfast (LLB 1969). Called to NI Bar, 1970, to the Bar of England and Wales, Gray's Inn, 1974 (Hon. Bencher, 1997); QC (NI) 1983; Bencher, Inn of Court of NI, 1990; Junior Crown Counsel (Common Law), 1978–83; Sen. Crown Counsel, 1988–93. Chm., Mental Health Commn for NI, 1988. Member: Judicial Studies Bd, NI, 1995–; Franco British Judicial Co-operation Cttee, 1995–. Chm., Distinction and Meritorious Service Awards Cttee, NI, 1997–. Eisenhower Exchange Fellow, 1999. *Recreations:* France, accepting defeat by sons at tennis. *Address:* Royal Courts of Justice, Belfast BT1 3JY.

KERR, Clark; educator; *b* 17 May 1911; *s* of Samuel W. and Caroline Clark Kerr; *m* 1934, Catherine Spaulding; two *s* one *d*. *Educ:* Swarthmore Coll. (AB); Stanford Univ. (MA); Univ. of Calif., Berkeley (PhD). Actg Asst Prof., Stanford Univ., 1939–40; Asst Prof., later Assoc. Prof., Univ. of Washington, 1940–45; Prof., Dir, Inst. of Industrial Relations, Univ. of Calif, Berkeley, 1945–52; Chancellor, Univ. of Calif at Berkeley, 1952–58; Pres., Univ. of Calif, 1958–67, now Emeritus President. Chairman: Carnegie Commn on Higher Educn, 1967–74; Carnegie Council on Policy Studies in Higher Educn, 1974–80; Bd, Work in America Inst., 1975–98; Bd, Global Perspectives in Educn, 1976–85, now Chm. Emeritus. Govt service with US War Labor Board, 1942–45. Mem. Pres. Eisenhower's Commn on Nat. Goals, President Kennedy and President Johnson Cttee on Labor-Management Policy; Program Dir, Strengthening Presidential Leadership Project, Assoc. of Governing Bds of Univs and Colls, 1982–85; Contract Arbitrator for: Boeing Aircraft Co. and Internat. Assoc. of Machinists, 1944–45; Armour & Co. and United Packinghouse Workers, 1945–47, 1949–52; Waterfront Employers' Assoc. and Internat. Longshoremen's and Warehousemen's Union, 1946–47, etc. Member: Amer. Acad. of Arts and Sciences; Royal Economic Society; Amer. Econ. Assoc.; Nat. Acad. of Arbitrators, etc. Phi Beta Kappa, Kappa Sigma. Trustee, Rockefeller Foundation, 1960–75; Chm., Armour Automation Cttee, 1959–79. Hon. Fellow, LSE, 1977. Hon. LLD: Swarthmore, 1952; Harvard, 1958; Princeton, 1959; Notre Dame, 1964; Chinese Univ. of Hong Kong, 1964; Rochester, 1967; Hon. DLitt, Strathclyde, 1965; Hon. Dr, Bordeaux, 1962, etc. Harold W. McGraw, Jr, Prize in Educn, 1990. *Publications:* (jtly) Unions, Management and the Public, 1948, rev. edns 1960, 1967; (jtly) Industrialism and Industrial Man, 1960, rev. edns 1964, 1973; The Uses of the University, 1963, 5th edn 2001; Labor and Management in Industrial Society, 1964, rev. edn 1972; Marshall, Marx and Modern Times, 1969; (jtly) Industrialism and Industrial Man Reconsidered, 1975; Labor Markets and Wage Determination, 1977; Education and National Development, 1979; The Future of Industrial Societies, 1983; (jtly) The Many Lives of Academic Presidents, 1986; (ed jtly) Industrial Relations in a New Age, 1986; (ed jtly) Economics of Labor in Industrial Society, 1986; (jtly) How Labor Markets Work, 1988; (jtly) The Guardians: boards of trustees of American colleges and universities, 1989; The Great Transformation in Higher Education 1960–1980, 1991; Troubled Times for American Higher Education, 1993; Higher Education Cannot Escape History: issues for the twenty-first century, 1993; (ed jtly) Labor Economics and Industrial Relations: markets and institutions, 1994; The Gold and the Blue: a personal memoir of the University of California 1949–67, Vol. I, Academic Triumphs, 2001; contribs to American Economic Review, Review of Economics and Statistics, Quarterly Jl of Economics, etc. *Recreation:* gardening. *Address:* 8300 Buckingham Drive, El Cerrito, CA 94530, USA. *T:* (510) 2339651; (office) Institute of Industrial Relations, University of California, Berkeley, CA 94720-5555, USA. *T:* (510) 6428106, *Fax:* (510) 6435528.

KERR, Prof. David James, MD; DSc; FRCP; FMedSci; Rhodes Professor of Therapeutics, University of Oxford, since 2001; Fellow, Corpus Christi College, Oxford, since 2001; *b* 14 June 1956; *s* of Robert James Andrew Kerr and Sarah Pettigrew Kerr (*née* Hogg); *m* 1980, Anne Miller Young; one *s* two *d*. *Educ:* Univ. of Glasgow (BSc 1st Cl. Hons 1977; MB ChB 1980; MSc 1985; MD 1987; PhD 1990; DSc 1997). FRCPGlas 1995; MRCP 1983, FRCP 1996. Sen. Registrar (Med. Oncol.), Western Infirmary, Glasgow, 1985-89; Sen. Lectr, Glasgow Univ., 1989-92; Prof. of Clinical Oncol., and Clinical Dir, CRC Inst. For Cancer Studies, Univ. of Birmingham, 1992-2001. Visiting Professor: Univ. of Strathclyde, 1991–; Univ. of Nils, Yugoslavia, 1999–. FMedSci 2000. *Publications include:* (ed jtly) Regional Chemotherapy, 1999; contrib. numerous articles to peer reviewed med. and scientific jls. *Recreations:* football, busking. *Address:* Corpus Christi College, Oxford OX1 4JF; 27 Westhill Road, Kings Norton, Birmingham B38 8TL. *T:* (0121) 414 3802. *Clubs:* Reform; Partick Thistle Supporters' (Glasgow).

KERR, Dr David Leigh; *b* 25 March 1923; *s* of Myer Woolf Kerr and Paula (*née* Horowitz); *m* 1st, 1944, Aileen Saddington (marr. diss. 1969); two *s* one *d*; 2nd, 1970, Margaret Dunlop; one *s* two *d*. *Educ:* Whitgift Sch., Croydon; Middlesex Hosp. Med. Sch., London. Hon. Sec., Socialist Medical Assoc., 1957–63; Hon. Vice-Pres., 1963–72. LCC (Wandsworth, Central), 1958–65, and Coun., London Borough of Wandsworth, 1964–68; Mem., Herts CC (Welwyn Garden City S), 1989–2001. Contested (Lab) Wandsworth, Streatham (for Parlt), 1959; MP (Lab) Wandsworth Central, 1964–70; PPS to Minister of State, FCO, 1967–69. Vis. Lectr in Medicine, Chelsea Coll., 1972–82. War on Want: Dir, 1970–77; Vice-Chm., 1973–74; Chm., 1974–77. Family Doctor, Tooting, 1946–82; Chief Exec., Manor House Hosp., London, 1982–87. Member: Inter-departmental Cttee on Death Certification and Coroners; E Herts CHC, 1992–2000 (Vice-Chm., 1998–2000); Med. Assessor, Registered Homes Tribunals, 1986–93. Hon. Vice Pres., Community Practitioners & Health Visitors' Assoc. (formerly Health Visitors' Assoc.), 1969–; Trustee, CPHVA Charitable Trust, 1996–. FRSocMed. Governor, British Film Inst., 1966–71. *Recreations:* reading other people's biographies, refusing to write own. *Address:* 19 Calder Avenue, Brookmans Park, Herts AL9 7AH. *T:* (01707) 653954.

KERR, Prof. David Nicol Sharp, CBE 1992; MSc; FRCP, FRCPE; Professor of Renal Medicine, Royal Postgraduate Medical School, University of London, 1987–93, now Emeritus (Dean, 1984–91); *b* 27 Dec. 1927; *s* of William Kerr and Elsie (Ransted) Kerr; *m* 1960, Eleanor Jones; two *s* one *d*. *Educ:* George Watson's Boys' College; Edinburgh University (MB ChB); University of Wisconsin (MSc); FRCPE 1966; FRCP 1967; House Physician and Surgeon, Royal Infirmary, Edinburgh, 1951–52; Exchange scholar, Univ. of Wisconsin, 1952–53; Surgeon Lieut, RNVR, 1953–55; Asst Lectr, Univ. of Edinburgh, 1956–57; Registrar, Hammersmith Hosp., 1957–59; Lectr, Univ. of Durham, 1959–63; Consultant Physician, Royal Victoria Infirmary, Newcastle upon Tyne, 1962–83; Senior Lectr, 1963–68, Prof. of Medicine, 1968–83, Univ. of Newcastle upon Tyne. Postgrad. Med. Advr, NW Thames RHA, later N Thames Regl Office, NHS Executive, 1991–97. Med. Awards Administrator, Commonwealth Scholarships Commn, 1993–98. Member: Council, Internat. Soc. of Nephrology, 1984–93; Council, British Heart Foundn, 1989–97; NW Thames RHA, 1989–91; Hammersmith and Queen Charlotte's SHA, 1984–91; Ealing Hosp. NHS Trust, 1991–95; Standing Med. Adv. Cttee, DHSS, 1979–90. Sen. Censor and First Vice Pres., RCP, 1990–91. Hon. Fellow, SA Coll. of Medicine, 1992; Hon. Mem., Spanish Soc. of Nephrology, 1992. Trustee, Nat. Kidney Res. Fund, 1999– (Chm. Trustees, 2000–). Editor, Jl of RCP, 1994–98. *Publications:* Short Textbook of Renal Disease, 1968; (ed) Oxford Textbook of Clinical Nephrology, 1992, 2nd edn 1997; chapters in numerous books incl. Cecil-Loeb Textbook of Medicine and Oxford Textbook of Medicine; articles on renal disease in med. jls. *Recreations:* church, walking, theatre, opera. *Address:* 22 Carbery Avenue, W3 9AL. *T:* and *Fax:* (020) 8992 3231. *Club:* Athenæum.

KERR, Deborah Jane, (Deborah Kerr Viertel), CBE 1998; actress; *b* 30 Sept. 1921; *d* of Capt. Arthur Kerr-Trimmer; *m* 1st, 1945, Sqdn Ldr A. C. Bartley, DFC (marr. diss. 1959; he *d* 2001); two *d*; 2nd, 1960, Peter Viertel. *Educ:* Northumberland House, Clifton, Bristol. Open Air Theatre, Regent's Park, 1939, Oxford Repertory, 1939–40; after an interval of acting in films, appeared on West End Stage; Ellie Dunn in Heartbreak House, Cambridge Theatre, 1943; went to France, Belgium, and Holland for ENSA, playing in Gaslight, 1945. *Films:* Major Barbara, 1940; Love on the Dole, 1940–41; Penn of Pennsylvania, 1941; Hatter's Castle, 1942; The Day Will Dawn, 1942; Life and Death of Colonel Blimp, 1942–43; Perfect Strangers, 1944; I See a Dark Stranger, 1945; Black Narcissus, 1946; The Hucksters and If Winter Comes, 1947 (MGM, Hollywood); Edward My Son, 1948; Please Believe Me, 1949 (MGM, Hollywood); King Solomon's Mines, 1950; Quo Vadis, 1952; Prisoner of Zenda, Julius Caesar, Dream Wife, Young Bess (MGM), 1952; From Here to Eternity, 1953; The End of the Affair, 1955; The Proud and Profane, The King and I, 1956; Heaven Knows, Mr Allison, An Affair to Remember, Tea and Sympathy, 1957; Bonjour Tristesse, 1958; Separate Tables, The Journey, Count Your Blessings, 1959; The Sundowners, The Grass is Greener, The Naked Edge, The Innocents, 1961; The Chalk Garden, The Night of the Iguana, 1964; Casino Royale, 1967; Eye of the Devil, Prudence and the Pill, 1968; The Arrangement, 1970; The Assam Garden, 1985. *Stage:* Tea and Sympathy, NY, 1953; The Day After the Fair, London, 1972, tour of US, 1973–74; Seascape, NY, 1975; Candida, London, 1977; The Last of Mrs Cheyney, tour of US, 1978–79; The Day After the Fair, Melbourne and Sydney, 1979; Overheard, Haymarket, 1981; The Corn is Green, Old Vic, 1985. BAFTA Special Award, 1991; Hon. Oscar, Acad. of Motion Picture Arts and Scis, 1994. *Address:* Klosters, 7250 Grisons, Switzerland.

KERR, Dr Edwin, CBE 1986; Chairman, Student Employment Services Ltd, since 1995; *b* 1 July 1926; *e s* of late Robert John Kerr and Mary Elizabeth Kerr (*née* Ferguson); *m* 1949, Gertrude Elizabeth (*née* Turbitt); one *s* two *d*. *Educ:* Royal Belfast Academical Instn; Queen's Univ., Belfast (BSc, PhD). FIMA, FBCS. Asst Lectr in Maths, QUB, 1948–52; Lectr in Maths, Coll. of Technology, Birmingham (now Univ. of Aston in Birmingham), 1952–55; Lectr in Maths, Coll. of Science and Technology, Manchester (now Univ. of Manchester Inst. of Science and Technology), 1956–58; Head of Maths Dept, Royal Coll. of Advanced Technology, Salford (now Univ. of Salford), 1958–66; Principal, Paisley Coll. of Technology, 1966–72; Chief Officer, CNAA, 1972–86; Chm. and Chief Exec., Exam. Bd for Financial Planning, 1987–89; Chief Exec., Coll. for Financial Planning, 1988–96; Chm., Vocational and Academic Bd, Inst. of Health and Care Develts, 1996–99; Academic Dir, Regent's Business Sch., Regent's Coll., London, 1997–2001. Member: Adv. Cttee on Supply and Training of Teachers, 1973–78; Adv. Cttee on Supply and Educn of Teachers, 1980–85; Bd for Local Authority Higher Educn, 1982–85; Bd for Public Sector Higher Educn, 1985–86; Mem. and Vice-Chm., Continuing Educn Standing Cttee, 1985–88. President: Soc. for Res. into Higher Educn, 1974–77; The Mathematical Assoc., 1976–77. Hon. FCP 1984; Hon. Fellow: Coventry Lanchester, Newcastle upon Tyne, Portsmouth and Sheffield Polytechnics, 1986; Huddersfield Polytechnic, and Paisley Coll. of Technol., 1987; Goldsmiths' Coll., London, 1991. DUniv: Open, 1977; Paisley, 1993; Hon. DSc Ulster, 1986; Hon. DEd CNAA, 1989. *Publications:* (with R. Butler) An Introduction to Numerical Methods, 1962; various mathematical and educational. *Recreation:* gardening. *Address:* 59 Craigdarragh Road, Helen's Bay, Co. Down BT19 1UB. *Club:* Travellers.

KERR, Hugh; *b* 9 July 1944; *m*; one *s*. Former Sen. Lectr, Univ, of North London. Former Mem. (Lab) Harlow DC. MEP (Lab 1994–98, Ind. Lab 1998–99), Essex W and Herts E.

KERR, James, QPM 1979; Chief Constable, Lincolnshire Police, 1977–83; *b* 19 Nov. 1928; *s* of William and Margaret Jane Kerr; *m* 1952, Jean Coupland; one *d*. *Educ:* Carlisle Grammar School. Cadet and Navigating Officer, Merchant Navy, 1945–52 (Union Castle Line, 1949–52). Carlisle City Police and Cumbria Constabulary, 1952–74; Asst Director of Command Courses, Police Staff Coll., Bramshill, 1974; Asst Chief Constable (Operations), North Yorkshire Police, 1975; Deputy Chief Constable, Lincs, 1976. Officer Brother, OStJ, 1980. *Recreations:* music, squash. *Address:* 2A Nirvana Crescent, Bulleen, Vic 3150, Australia. *Club:* Royal Automobile (Victoria).

KERR, Adm. Sir John (Beverley), GCB 1993 (KCB 1989); DL; Commander-in-Chief, Naval Home Command, 1991–94; Flag Aide-de-Camp to the Queen, 1991–94; *b* 27 Oct. 1937; *s* late Wilfred Kerr and Vera Kerr (*née* Sproule); *m* 1964, Elizabeth Anne, *d* of late Dr and Mrs C. R. G. Howard, Burley, Hants; three *s*. *Educ:* Moseley Hall County Grammar Sch., Cheadle; Britannia Royal Naval Coll., Dartmouth. Served in various ships, 1958–65 (specialized in navigation, 1964); Staff, BRNC, Dartmouth, 1965–67; HMS Cleopatra, 1967–69; Staff, US Naval Acad., Annapolis, 1969–71; NDC, Latimer, 1971–72; i/c HMS Achilles, 1972–74; Naval Plans, MoD, 1974–75; Defence Policy Staff, MoD, 1975–77; RCDS, 1978; i/c HMS Birmingham, 1979–81; Dir of Naval Plans, MoD, 1981–83; i/c HMS Illustrious, 1983–84; ACNS (Op. Requirements), 1984; ACDS (Op. Requirements) (Sea Systems), 1985–86; Flag Officer First Flotilla/Flotilla One, 1986–88; MoD, 1988–91. Member, Independent Review: of Armed Forces' Manpower, Career and Remuneration Structures, 1994–95; of Higher Educn Pay and Conditions, 1998–99. Mem., Museums and Galls Commn, 1994–2000. Mem., CWGC, 1994–2001 (Vice-Chm., 1998–2001). Cdre, RNSA, 1992–95; Member: Cttee of Management, RNLI, 1993–98; Audit Cttee, 1994–98 (Chm., 1995–98), Council, 1995–98, Lancaster Univ.; Cttee, Manchester Mus., 1994– (Chm., 1996–); Member: Court and Council, Manchester Univ., 1998–; Court, UMIST, 2000–. CIMgt 1993. DL Lancs 1995. *Recreations:* music, sailing, hill walking, history.

KERR, Sir John (Olav), GCMG 2001 (KCMG 1991; CMG 1987); HM Diplomatic Service; Permanent Under-Secretary of State, Foreign and Commonwealth Office, and Head of the Diplomatic Service, 1997–Feb. 2002; *b* 22 Feb. 1942; *s* of late Dr and Mrs J. D. O. Kerr; *m* 1965, Elizabeth, *d* of Mr and Mrs W. G. Kalaugher; two *s* three *d*. *Educ:* Glasgow Academy; Pembroke Coll., Oxford (Hon. Fellow, 1991). Entered Diplomatic Service, 1966; served FO, Moscow, Rawalpindi, FCO; Private Sec. to Permanent Under Secretary, FCO, 1974–79; Head of DM1 Division, HM Treasury, 1979–81; Principal Private Sec. to Chancellor of the Exchequer, 1981–84; Hd of Chancery, Washington, 1984–87; Asst Under-Sec. of State, FCO, 1987–90; Ambassador and UK Perm. Rep. to the EU, Brussels, 1990–95; Ambassador to USA, 1995–97. Hon. LLD: St Andrews, 1996; Glasgow, 1999. *Address:* c/o Foreign and Commonwealth Office, King Charles Street, SW1A 2AH. *Club:* Garrick.

KERR, Rt Hon. Sir Michael (Robert Emanuel), Kt 1972; PC 1981; a Lord Justice of Appeal, 1981–89; *b* 1 March 1921; *s* of Alfred Kerr; *m* 1st, 1952, Julia (marr. diss. 1982), *d* of Joseph Braddock; two *s* one *d*; 2nd, 1983, Diana, *yr d* of H. Neville Sneezum; one *s* one *d*. *Educ:* Aldenham Sch.; Clare Coll., Cambridge (Hon. Fellow, 1986). Served War, 1941–45 (Pilot; Flt-Lt). BA Cantab (1st cl. Hons Law) 1947, MA 1952; called to Bar, Lincoln's Inn, 1948, Bencher 1968, Treas., 1989; QC 1961. Member: Bar Council, 1968–72; Senate, 1969–72. Dep. Chm., Hants QS, 1961–71; Mem. Vehicle and General Enquiry Tribunal, 1971–72; a Judge of the High Court of Justice, Queen's Bench Div., and of the Commercial and Admiralty Cts, 1972–78; Chm., Law Commn of England and Wales, 1978–81. Pres., London Court of Internat. Arbitration, 1985–94, Hon. Pres., 1994; Chm. Comr, UN Compensation Commn, 1996–. Mem. Council of Management: British Inst. of Internat. and Comparative Law, 1973–; Inst. of Advanced Legal Studies, 1979–85; Chairman: Lord Chancellor's inter-deptl cttee on Foreign Judgments, 1974–81; Cttee of Management, Centre of Commercial Law Studies, QMC, 1980–89; Supreme Court Procedure Cttee, 1982–86; Chairman, Appeal Committee: Takeover Panel, 1993–2001; ICAEW (formerly ICA), 1990–; SFA, 1991–; Arbitration Council, WIPO, 1993–; Mem., Internat. Adv. Cttee, British Columbia Internat. Arbitration Centre, 1986–. Vice-Pres., British Maritime Law Assoc., 1977–; President: CIArb, 1983–86; British-German Jurists Assoc., 1986–91; Euro-Arab Assoc. for Internat. Arbitration, 1997–. Hon. Mem., Amer. Law Inst., 1985; Hon. Life Mem., Amer. and Canadian Bar Assocs, 1976. Chorley Lectr, LSE, 1977; Alexander Lectr, CIArb, 1984. Governor, Aldenham Sch., 1959–87. Hon. Fellow, QMC, 1986. Knight Comdr, Grand Cross of Order of Merit (Germany), 1991. *Publications:* McNair's Law of the Air, 1953, 1965; The Macao Sardine Case, 1989; As Far As I Remember, 1995; articles and lectures on commercial law and arbitration. *Recreations:* travel, music, trying to work less, a second edition of children. *Address:* Essex Court Chambers, 24 Lincoln's Inn Fields, WC2A 3AD. *T:* (020) 7813 8000; 10 Peterborough Villas, SW6 2AT. *T:* (020) 7736 2144/6655. *Clubs:* Garrick, Pilgrims.

See also T. J. Kerr.

KERR, Ronald James, CBE 1998; Director of Operations, NHS Executive, Department of Health, since 1998; *b* 2 Feb. 1950; *s* of James Boe Kerr and Margaret Catherine Kerr (*née* Robson); *m* 1st, 1971, Linda Margaret Taylor (marr. diss.); 2nd 1976, Kathryn Mary Pritchard (marr. diss.); one *d*; 3rd, 1988, Lynda Caroline Hamlyn. *Educ:* Sandbach Sch., Cheshire; Cambridgeshire Coll. of Arts and Technol.; London Univ. (BSc Hons Geog. with Econs); London Business Sch. (MSc Business Studies). Sec., S Manchester CHC, 1974–77; Asst Sec., NE Thames RHA, 1977–79; Dep. House Gov., Moorfields Eye Hosp., 1979–80; Hosp. Sec., London Hosp., 1980–85; Dist Gen. Manager, N Herts HA, 1985–88; Dep. Dir of Financial Mgt, NHS Exec., 1988–90; District General Manager: Hounslow and Spelthorne HA, 1990; Lewisham and N Southwark HA and Chief Exec., SE London Commng Agency, 1990–93; Regl Gen. Manager, NW Thames RHA, 1993–94; Regl Dir, N Thames Regl Office, NHS Exec., 1994–98. *Recreations:* travel, reading, restaurants, music, Manchester City FC. *Address:* 41 North Hill, Highgate, N6 4BS. *T:* (020) 8348 6137.

KERR, Rose; Chief Curator (formerly Curator) of the Far Eastern Department (formerly Far Eastern Collections), Victoria and Albert Museum, since 1990; *b* 23 Feb. 1953; *d* of William Antony Kerr and Elizabeth Rendell; *m* 1990. *Educ:* SOAS, Univ. of London (BA Hons 1st Cl., Art and Archaeology of China); Languages Inst., Beijing. Fellow, Percival David Foundn of Chinese Art, 1976–78; joined Far Eastern Dept, V&A, 1978, Keeper, 1987–90. Member: Council, Oriental Ceramic Soc., 1987– (Pres., 2000–); GB-China Educnl Trust, 1995–. *Publications:* (with P. Hughes-Stanton) Kiln Sites of Ancient China, 1980; (with John Larson) Guanyin: a masterpiece revealed, 1985; Chinese Ceramics: porcelain of the Qing Dynasty 1644–1911, 1986; Later Chinese Bronzes, 1990; (ed and contrib.) Chinese Art and Design: the T. T. Tsui Gallery of Chinese Art, 1991; (with Rosemary Scott) Ceramic Evolution in the Middle Ming Period, 1994; England's Victoria and Albert Museum: Chinese Qing Dynasty Ceramics (in Chinese), 1995; articles in Oriental Art, Orientations, Apollo, Craft Magazine, V&A Album. *Recreation:* gardening. *Address:* Garrison House, Church Street, Presteigne, Powys LD8 2BU.

KERR, Thomas Henry, CB 1983; Director, Royal Aircraft Establishment, 1980–84; retired; *b* 18 June 1924; *s* of late Albert Edward Kerr and Mrs Francis Jane Kerr (*née* Simpson); *m* 1946, Myrnie Evelyn Martin Hughes; two *d*. *Educ:* Magnus Grammar, Newark; University Coll., Durham Univ. BSc 1949; CEng, FRAeS; Diplôme Paul Tissendier 1957. RAFVR pilot, 1942–46. Aero Flight, RAE, 1949–55; Head of Supersonic Flight Group, 1955–59; Scientific Adviser to C-in-C Bomber Comd, High Wycombe, 1960–64; Head of Assessment Div., Weapons Dept, RAE, 1964–66; Dep. Dir and Dir of Defence Operational Analysis Estabt, 1966–70; Head of Weapons Research Gp, Weapons Dept, RAE, 1970–72; Dir Gen. Establishments Resources Programmes (C), MoD (PE), 1972–74; Dir, Nat. Gas Turbine Estabt, 1974–80; R&D Dir, Royal Ordnance plc, 1984–86; Dir, Hunting Engineering, 1986–94 (Technical Dir, 1986–88). Consultant, Systems Designers Scientific, 1985–88. Mem. Council, RAeS, 1979, Pres., 1985–86. Freeman, City of London, 1996; Liveryman, GAPAN, 1996–. *Publications:* reports and memoranda of Aeronautical Research Council, lectures to RAeS and RUSI. *Recreations:* bridge, water ski-ing, tennis, badminton. *Address:* Bundu, 013 Kingsley Avenue, Camberley, Surrey GU15 2NA. *T:* (01276) 25961.

KERR, Timothy Julian; QC 2001; *b* 15 Feb. 1958; *s* of Rt Hon. Sir Michael Robert Emanuel Kerr, *qv* and Julia Kerr; one *s*; *m* 1990, Nicola Mary Croucher; two *s*. *Educ:* Westminster Sch.; Magdalen Coll., Oxford (BA 1st Cl. Hons Juris.). Called to the Bar, Gray's Inn, 1983; in practice as barrister, specialising in public law, sport and education law, 1983–. *Publications:* (jtly) Sports Law, 1999; contrib. various articles to learned jls. *Recreations:* music, travel, reading, friends, family, marathon running, supporting Chelsea Football Club. *Address:* (Chambers) 11 King's Bench Walk, Temple, EC4Y 7EQ. *T:* (020) 632 8502.

KERR, William Francis Kennedy, OBE 1984; PhD, CEng, FIMechE; Principal, Belfast College of Technology, 1969–84; *b* 1 Aug. 1923; *m* 1953, H. Adams; two *s*. *Educ:* Portadown Technical Coll. and Queen's Univ., Belfast. BSc (Hons) in Mech. Engineering, MSc, PhD. Teacher of Mathematics, Portadown Techn. Coll., 1947–48; Teacher and Sen. Lectr in Mech. Eng, Coll. of Techn., Belfast, 1948–55; Lectr and Adviser of Studies in Mech. Eng, Queen's Univ. of Belfast, 1955–62; Head of Dept of Mech., Civil, and Prod. Eng, Dundee Coll. of Techn., 1962–67; Vice-Principal, Coll. of Techn., Belfast, 1967–69. Chm., NI Cttee for Educnl Technology, 1973–79; Member: Mech. and Prodn Engrg Subject Panel, CNAA, 1964–67; Council for Educnl Technology, 1973–79; Belfast Educn and Library Bd, 1977–81; NI Council for Educnl Develt, 1980–84; NI Manpower Council, 1981–84; Chm., Assoc. of Principals of Colleges (NI Branch), 1982; Governor, Royal Belfast Academical Instn, 1969–84; Mem. Court, Ulster Univ., 1985–92. *Publications:* contribs on environmental testing of metals, etc. *Recreations:* golf, motoring, reading. *Address:* Apt 1, Avoca House, 83 Princetown Road, Bangor, Co. Down, Northern Ireland BT20 3TD.

KERRIGAN, Greer Sandra; Legal Director (Health) (formerly Principal Assistant Solicitor), Departments of Health and Social Security, since 1991; *b* Port of Spain, Trinidad, 7 Aug. 1948; *d* of Wilfred M. Robinson and Rosina Robinson (*née* Ali); *m* 1974, Donal Brian Mathew Kerrigan; one *s* one *d*. *Educ:* Bishop Anstey High Sch., Trinidad; Coll. of Law, Inns of Court. Called to the Bar, Middle Temple, 1971. Legal Advr, Public Utilities Commn, Trinidad, 1972–74; Department of Health and Social Security, subseq. Department of Social Security, 1974–: Legal Assistant, 1974–77; Sen. Legal Assistant, 1977–85; Asst Solicitor, 1985–91. *Recreations:* reading, music, bridge. *Address:* Departments of Health and Social Security, New Court, 48 Carey Street, WC2A 2LS. *T:* (020) 7412 1341.

KERRIGAN, Herbert Aird; QC (Scot.) 1992; *b* 2 Aug. 1945; *s* of Herbert Kerrigan and Mary Agnes Wallace Hamilton or Kerrigan; one adopted *s*. *Educ:* Whitehill, Glasgow; Univ. of Aberdeen (LLB Hons 1968); Hague Acad. of Internat. Law; Keele Univ. (MA 1970). Admitted Faculty of Advocates, 1970; Lectr in Criminal Law and Criminology, 1969–73, in Scots Law, 1973–74, Edinburgh Univ.; called to the Bar, Middle Temple, 1990; in practice, 1991–. Vis. Prof., Univ. of Southern Calif., 1979–. Mem., Longford Commn, 1972. Church of Scotland: Elder, 1967– (now at Greyfriars Tolbooth and Highland Kirk, Edinburgh); Reader, 1969; Mem., Assembly Council, 1981–85; Sen. Chaplain to Moderator, Gen. Assembly of Church of Scotland, 1999–2000. Pres., Edinburgh Royal Infirmary Samaritan Soc., 1992– (Vice-Pres., 1989–92). *Publications:* An Introduction to Criminal Procedure in Scotland, 1970; (contrib.) Ministers for the 1980s, 1979; (contributing ed.) The Law of Contempt, 1982; (contrib.) Sport and the Law, 2nd edn 1995. *Recreation:* travel. *Address:* c/o Advocates' Library, Parliament House, Edinburgh EH1 4RF. *T:* (0131) 226 5071; 9–12 Bell Yard, WC2 2LF. *T:* (020) 7400 1800, *Fax:* (020) 7400 1405; (home) 20 Edinburgh Road, Dalkeith, Midlothian EH22 1JY. *T:* (0131) 660 3307.

KERRUISH, Sir (Henry) Charles, Kt 1979; OBE 1964; President of Tynwald and of Legislative Council, Isle of Man, since 1990; Speaker, House of Keys, 1962–90; *b* 23 July 1917; *m* 1st, 1944, Margaret Gell; one *s* three *d*; 2nd, 1975, Kay Warriner. *Educ:* Ramsey Grammar Sch. Farmer. Member, House of Keys, 1946–90; Ex-Officio MLC, 1990–. Pres., CPA, 1983–84 (Regional Councillor for British Isles and Mediterranean, 1975–77). Mem. Court, Liverpool Univ., 1974–90. Hon. LLD Lancaster, 1990. *Recreations:* horse breeding, motor cycling. *Address:* Ballafayle, Maughold, Isle of Man. *T:* (01624) 812293. *Club:* Farmers'.

KERRY, Earl of; Simon Henry George Petty-Fitzmaurice; *b* 24 Nov. 1970; *s* and *heir* of Marquess of Lansdowne, *qv*. *Educ:* Eton; Jesus Coll., Cambridge.

KERRY, Knight of; *see* FitzGerald, Sir A. J. A. D.

KERRY, Sir Michael (James), KCB 1983 (CB 1976); QC 1984; *b* 5 Aug. 1923; *s* of Russell Kerry and Marjorie (*née* Kensington); *m* 1951, Sidney Rosetta Elizabeth (*née* Foster); one *s* two *d*. *Educ:* Rugby Sch.; St John's Coll., Oxford (MA; Hon. Fellow 1986). Served with RAF, 1942–46. Called to Bar, Lincoln's Inn, 1949, Bencher 1984. Joined BoT as Legal Asst, 1951; Sen. Legal Asst, 1959; Asst Solicitor, 1964; Principal Asst Solicitor, Dept of Trade and Industry, 1972, Solicitor, 1973–80; HM Procurator Gen. and Treasury Solicitor, 1980–84. Dep. Chm., LAUTRO, 1988–91. *Recreations:* golf, gardening. *Address:* South Bedales, Lewes Road, Haywards Heath, W Sussex RH17 7TE. *T:* (01444) 831303. *Club:* Piltdown Golf.

KERSE, Christopher Stephen, PhD; Second Counsel to Chairman of Committees and Legal Adviser to European Union Committee, House of Lords, since 1995; *b* 12 Dec. 1946; *s* of late William Harold Kerse and Maude Kerse; *m* 1971, Gillian Hanks; one *s* one *d*. *Educ:* King George V Sch., Southport; Univ. of Hull (LLB; PhD 1995). Admitted

Solicitor, 1972. Lecturer in Law: Univ. of Bristol, 1968–72; Univ. of Manchester, 1972–76; Asst Prof., Faculty of Law, Univ. of British Columbia, 1974–75; Sen. Legal Asst, OFT, 1976–81; Department of Trade and Industry: Sen. Legal Asst, 1981–82; Asst Solicitor, 1982–88; Head, Consumer Affairs Div., 1991–93; Under-Sec. (Legal), 1988–95. Vis. Prof., KCL, 1992–. *Publications:* The Law Relating to Noise, 1975; EEC Antitrust Procedure, 1981, 4th edn 1998; (with J. C. Cook) EEC Merger Control, 1991, 3rd edn 2000; articles in various legal jls. *Recreations:* the horn, the double bass, the Vendée.

KERSFELT, Anita Ingegerd; *see* Gradin, A. I.

KERSHAW, family name of **Baron Kershaw**.

KERSHAW, 4th Baron *cr* 1947; **Edward John Kershaw;** Chartered Accountant; Partner in Bartlett Kershaw Trott, Chartered Accountants; *b* 12 May 1936; *s* of 3rd Baron and Katharine Dorothea Kershaw (*née* Staines); *S* father, 1962; *m* 1963, Rosalind Lilian Rutherford; one *s* two *d*. *Educ:* Selhurst Grammar Sch., Surrey. Entered RAF Nov. 1955, demobilised Nov. 1957. Admitted to Inst. of Chartered Accountants in England and Wales, Oct. 1964. Mem., Acad. of Experts, 1995. Lay Governor, The King's Sch., Gloucester, 1986–95. JP Gloucester, 1982–95. *Heir: s* Hon. John Charles Edward Kershaw, *b* 23 Dec. 1971. *Address:* 38 High View, Hempsted, Gloucester GL2 5LN.

KERSHAW, Andrew; broadcaster and journalist, since 1984; *b* 9 Nov. 1959; *s* of John (Jack) Kershaw and Eileen Kershaw (*née* Acton); partner, Juliette Banner; one *s* one *d*. *Educ:* Hulme Grammar Sch., Oldham; Leeds Univ. Joined BBC, 1984: presenter: Whistle Test, 1984–87 (Live Aid, 1985); Andy Kershaw Prog., Radio 1, 1985–2000, Radio 3, 2001–; Andy Kershaw's World of Music, World Service, 1987–2000; occasional foreign news reports for Radio 4, 1990– (incl. Reports from Haiti, Angola, Rwanda, N Korea); Travelog, Channel 4, 1991–97 (incl. first ever film made inside N Korea, 1995); freelance journalist, 1988–; Radio Critic, Independent, 1999. Sony Radio Awards, 1987, 1989 (two), 1996. *Recreations:* music, motorcycle racing, travels to extreme countries, gardening, smoking dope. *Address:* c/o Sincere Management, 6B Bravington Road, W9 3AH. *T:* (020) 8960 4438. *Club:* Academy.

KERSHAW, Sir Anthony; *see* Kershaw, Sir J. A.

KERSHAW, Dame Betty; *see* Kershaw, Dame J. E. M.

KERSHAW, Helen Elizabeth, (Mrs W. J. S. Kershaw); *see* Paling, H. E.

KERSHAW, Prof. Ian, DPhil; FBA 1991; Professor of Modern History, University of Sheffield, since 1989; *b* Oldham, 29 April 1943; *s* of late Joseph Kershaw and of Alice (*née* Robinson); *m* 1966, Janet Elizabeth Murray Gammie (*see* Dame J. E. M. Kershaw); two *s*. *Educ:* St Bede's Coll., Manchester; Univ. of Liverpool (BA 1965); Merton Coll., Oxford (DPhil 1969). FRHistS, 1972–74, 1991. University of Manchester: Asst Lectr in Medieval Hist., 1968–70, Lectr, 1970–74; Lectr in Modern Hist., 1974–79, Sen. Lectr, 1979–87, Reader elect, 1987; Prof. of Modern History, Univ. of Nottingham, 1987–89. Vis. Prof. of Contemporary Hist., Ruhr-Univ., Bochum, 1983–84. Fellow: Alexander von Humboldt-Stiftung, 1976; Wissenschaftskolleg zu Berlin, 1989–90. Bundesverdienstkreuz (Germany), 1994. *Publications:* (ed) Rentals and Ministers' Accounts of Bolton Priory 1473–1539, 1969; Bolton Priory: the economy of a Northern monastery, 1973; Der Hitler-Mythos: Volksmeinung und Propaganda im Dritten Reich, 1980, Eng. trans. 1987; Popular Opinion and Political Dissent in the Third Reich: Bavaria 1933–1945, 1983; The Nazi Dictatorship: problems and perspectives of interpretation, 1985, 3rd edn 1993; (ed) Weimar: why did German democracy fail?, 1990; Hitler: a profile in power, 1991; (ed with M. Lewin) Stalinism and Nazism, 1997; Hitler 1889–1936: hubris, 1998; Hitler 1936–1945: nemesis, 2000 (Wolfson Prize for History, 2001); (ed with David M. Smith) The Bolton Priory Compotus 1286–1325, 2001; articles in learned jls. *Recreations:* Rugby League, cricket, music, real ale, outings in the Yorkshire dales. *Address:* Department of History, University of Sheffield, Sheffield S10 2TN. *T:* (0114) 276 8555.

KERSHAW, Dame Janet Elizabeth Murray, (Dame Betty), DBE 1998; Professor and Dean of the School of Nursing and Midwifery, University of Sheffield, since 1999; *b* 11 Dec. 1943; *d* of Ian U. Gammie and Janet Gammie; *m* 1966, Ian Kershaw, *qv*; two *s*. *Educ:* Crossley and Porter Grammar Sch., Halifax; United Manchester Hosps (SRN; OND); Manchester Univ. (MSc Nursing; RNT). Dir of Educn, Royal Marsden Hosp., 1984–87; Principal, Stockport, Tameside and Glossop Coll. of Nursing, 1987–94; Dir of Nurse Educn, Coll. of Midwifery and Nursing, Manchester, 1994–97; Dir, Centre for Professional Policy Develt, Sch. of Nursing, Midwifery and Health Visiting, Univ. of Manchester, 1997–98. Vis. Prof., Univ. of Northumbria at Newcastle, 1998–. Pres., RCN, 1994–98; Mem. Bd, Commonwealth Nursing Fedn, 1998–. Chief Officer, Nursing and Social Care, St John Ambulance, 1998–. Hon. LLD Manchester, 1995. *Publications:* (with J. Salvage) Models For Nursing, 1986; (with J. Salvage) Models for Nursing 2, 1990; (with Bob Price) The Riehl Model of Care, 1993; (with J. Marr) Caring for Older People, 1998. *Recreations:* theatre, music, travel. *Address:* School of Nursing and Midwifery, University of Sheffield, Winter Street, Sheffield S3 7ND; St John Ambulance National HQ, 27 St John Lane, Clerkenwell, EC1M 4BU.

KERSHAW, Jennifer Christine; QC 1998; a Recorder, since 2000; *b* 1 May 1951. *Educ:* King's Coll., London (LLB 1973). Called to the Bar, Lincoln's Inn, 1974; in practice at the Bar, 1975–; an Asst Recorder, 1996–2000. *Recreations:* horses, gardening, hill walking. *Address:* (office) 6 Park Square, Leeds LS1 2LW. *T:* (0113) 245 9763.

KERSHAW, Sir (John) Anthony, Kt 1981; MC 1943; DL; Barrister-at-Law; *b* 14 Dec. 1915; *s* of Judge J. F. Kershaw, Cairo and London, and of Anne Kershaw, Kentucky, USA; *m* 1939, Barbara, *d* of Harry Crookenden; two *s* two *d*. *Educ:* Eton; Balliol Coll., Oxford (BA). Called to the Bar 1939. Served War, 1940–46: 16th/5th Lancers. Mem. LCC, 1946–49; Westminster City Council, 1947–48. MP (C) Stroud Div. of Gloucestershire, 1955–87. Parly Sec., Min. of Public Building and Works, June-Oct. 1970; Parliamentary Under-Secretary of State: FCO, 1970–73; for Defence (RAF), 1973–74; Chm., H of C Select Cttee on Foreign Affairs, 1979–87; Mem. Exec., 1922 Cttee, 1983–87. Vice-Chm., British Council, 1974–87. DL 1989, Vice Lord-Lieut, 1990–93, Glos. *Address:* West Barn, Didmarton, Badminton, Glos GL9 1DT. *Club:* White's.

KERSHAW, Joseph Anthony; *b* 26 Nov. 1935; *s* of Henry and Catherine Kershaw, Preston; *m* 1959, Ann Whittle; three *s* two *d*. *Educ:* Ushaw Coll., Durham; Preston Catholic Coll., SJ. Short service commn, RAOC, 1955–58; Unilever Ltd, 1958–67; Gp Marketing Manager, CWS, 1967–69; Managing Director: Underline Ltd, 1969–71; Merchant Div., Reed International Ltd, 1971–73; Head of Marketing, Non-Foods, CWS, 1973–74; (first) Director, Nat. Consumer Council, 1975; independent management consultant, 1975–91. Chairman: Antonian Investments Ltd, 1985–87; Organised Business Data Ltd, 1987–89; Director: John Stork & Partners Ltd, 1980–85; Allia (Holdings) Ltd, 1984–88; Associate Director: Foote, Cone & Belding Ltd, 1979–84; Phoenix Advertising, 1984–86. *Recreations:* turning and woodcarving, fishing, cooking, NACF. *Address:* Westmead, Meins Road, Blackburn, Lancs BB2 6QF. *T:* (01254) 55915.

KERSHAW, Michael; *see* Kershaw, P. M.

KERSHAW, (Philip) Michael, QC 1980; **His Honour Judge Kershaw;** a Mercantile Judge (formerly a Circuit Commercial Judge), since 1990; *b* 23 April 1941; *m* 1980, Anne (*née* Williams); one *s*. *Educ:* Ampleforth Coll.; St John's Coll., Oxford (MA). FCIArb 1991. Called to the Bar, Gray's Inn, 1963; in practice, 1963–90; a Recorder, 1980–90. Fellow, Soc. for Advanced Legal Studies, 1999. *Publications:* Fraud and Misrepresentation, and Injunctions, in Atkin's Court Forms; (contrib.) Interests in Goods, 1993. *Address:* Crown Court, Crown Square, Manchester M60 9DJ.

KERSHAW, Stephen Edward; Director, Teachers' Group, Department for Education and Skills (formerly Department for Education and Employment), since 2001; *b* 20 Sept. 1959; *s* of Barry Kershaw, railway signal engr, and Audrey Kathleen (*née* Breadmore). *Educ:* St Peter's C of E Primary Sch., Rickmansworth; William Penn Comprehensive Sch., Rickmansworth, Herts; Wadham Coll., Oxford (Open Schol.; BA 1st Cl. Hons Mod. Hist. 1981; MA; res., 1981–84). Lectr in Mod. Hist., Wadham Coll., Oxford, 1984-85; Cabinet Office, 1985-87 (Private Sec. to Second Perm. Sec., 1986-87); DES, 1987-89; Next Steps Team, Cabinet Office, 1989–92; DFE, later DfEE, 1992–99; on secondment as Hd, Strategic Planning, Manchester LEA, 1999-2000; Actg Dir, Pupil Support and Inclusion Gp, DfEE, 2000-01. *Publications:* (contrib.) The Tudor Nobility, ed G. W. Bernard, 1992; contrib. reviews in various jls. *Recreations:* family history, Spain, Laurel and Hardy, indulging my niece and nephews. *Address:* Department for Education and Skills, Sanctuary Buildings, Great Smith Street, Westminster, SW1P 3BT. *T:* (020) 7925 5000.

KERSLAKE, Robert Walter; Chief Executive, Sheffield City Council, since 1997; *b* 28 Feb. 1955; *m* Anne; one *s* one *d*. *Educ:* Univ. of Warwick (BSc Hons Maths). CPFA. Greater London Council, 1979–85: CIPFA trainee, 1979–82; Transport Finance, 1982–85; with ILEA, 1985–89; Dir of Finance, 1989–90, Chief Exec., 1990–97, London Borough of Hounslow. *Recreations:* music, walking. *Address:* Sheffield City Council, Town Hall, Sheffield S1 2HH. *T:* (0114) 273 4002.

KERWIN, Prof. Larkin, CC 1980 (OC 1977); FRSC; Professor Emeritus, Laval University, since 1991; *b* 22 June 1924; *s* of T. J. Kerwin and Catherine Lonergan-Kerwin; *m* 1950, Maria Guadalupe Turcot; five *s* three *d*. *Educ:* St Francis Xavier Univ. (BSc 1944); MIT (MSc 1946); Université Laval (DSc 1949). Laval University: Asst Prof., 1946; full Prof. of Physics, 1956; Dir, Dept of Physics, 1961–67; Vice-Dean, Faculty of Sciences, 1967–68; Vice-Rector, Academic, 1969–72; Rector, 1972–77. President: Royal Soc. of Canada, 1976–77; National Res. Council of Canada, 1980–89; Canadian Space Agency, 1989–92; IUPAP, 1987–90 (Sec.-Gen., 1972–84; First Vice-Pres., 1984–87). Mem., Académie des Grands Québecois, 1996. Hon. LLD: St Francis Xavier, 1970; Toronto, 1973; Concordia, 1976; Alberta, 1983; Dalhousie, 1983; Hon. DSc: British Columbia, 1973; McGill, 1974; Memorial, 1978; Ottawa, 1981; Royal Military Coll., Canada, 1982; Hon. DCL Bishop's, 1978; DSc (*hc*): Winnipeg, 1983; Windsor, 1984; Moncton, 1985; Montreal, 1991. Médaille de l'Assoc. Canadienne des Physiciens, 1969; Médaille Pariseau, 1965; Laval Alumni Medal, 1978; Gold Medal, Canadian Council of Professional Engineers, 1982; Rousseau Medal, l'ACFAS, 1983. Canadian Centennial Medal, 1967; Kt Comdr with star, Holy Sepulchre of Jerusalem, 1974; Medal of Centenary of Roumania, 1977; Jubilee Medal, 1977; Officier de la Légion d'Honneur, 1989; Académie des Grands Québecois, 1995. *Publications:* Atomic Physics, 1963 (trans. French, 1964, Spanish, 1970); papers in jls. *Recreation:* sailing. *Address:* 2166 Parc Bourbonnière, Sillery, QC G1T 1B4, Canada. *T:* (418) 5277949.

KESSEL, Prof. William Ivor Neil, MD; FRCP, FRCPE, FRCPsych; Professor of Psychiatry, 1965–90, and Dean of Postgraduate Studies, Faculty of Medicine, 1982–90, University of Manchester; *b* 10 Feb. 1925; *s* of Barney Kessel and Rachel Isabel Kessel; *m* 1958, Pamela Veronica Joyce (*née* Boswell); one *s* one *d*. *Educ:* Highgate Sch.; Trinity Coll., Cambridge (MA, MD); UCH Med. Sch.; Inst. of Psychiatry. MSc Manchester. FRCP 1967; FRCPE 1968; FRCPsych 1972. Staff, Inst. of Psych., 1960; scientific staff, MRC Unit for Epidemiol. of Psych. Illness, 1961, Asst Dir 1963; Hon. Sen. Lectr, Edinburgh Univ., 1964; Dean, Faculty of Med., Univ. of Manchester, 1974–76. Member: NW RHA, 1974–77; GMC, 1974–95; Adv. Council on Misuse of Drugs, 1972–80; Health Educn Council, 1979–86; Chm., Adv. Cttee on Alcoholism, DHSS, 1975–78; Cons. Adviser on alcoholism to DHSS, 1972–81, 1983–86. *Publications:* Alcoholism (with Prof. H. J. Walton), 1965, 3rd edn 1975, rev. edn 1989; articles on suicide and self-poisoning, alcoholism, psych. in gen. practice, psychosomatic disorders, psych. epidemiol., genius and mental illness, philosophy of uniform. *Address:* 24 Lees Road, Bramhall, Stockport, Cheshire SK7 1BT. *T:* (0161) 439 5121. *Club:* Athenæum.

KESSLER, James Richard; *b* 6 Sept. 1959; *s* of William and Joanna Kessler; *m* 1983, Jane Marie Pinto; two *s* one *d*. *Educ:* Brasenose Coll., Oxford (MA). FTII 1990. Called to the Bar, Gray's Inn, 1984; in practice at Revenue Bar. Founder, Trusts Discussion Forum, 1999. *Publications:* Tax Planning for the Foreign Domiciliary, 1987, 4th edn 2001; Tax Planning and Fundraising for Charities, 1989, 3rd edn 2000; Drafting Trusts and Will Trusts, 1992, 5th edn 2000. *Recreations:* piano playing, diary writing. *Address:* 24 Old Buildings, Lincoln's Inn, WC2A 3UP. *T:* (020) 7242 2744; *e-mail:* kessler@kessler.co.uk.

KESTELMAN, Sara; actress; *d* of late Morris Kestelman, RA and Dorothy Mary (*née* Creagh). *Educ:* Hampstead Parochial Sch.; Camden Sch. for Girls; Cecchetti ballet trng; Central Sch. of Speech and Drama. Royal Shakespeare Co. includes: A Midsummer Night's Dream, 1970–72, Broadway, 1971; Macbeth, 1982–83; King Lear, 1983; Lear (by Edward Bond), 1983; Moscow Gold, 1990–91; Misha's Party, 1994; National Theatre, subseq. Royal National Theatre, includes: As You Like It, 1979; Love for Love; 3D Opera; American Clock, 1986; Bedroom Farce; Square Rounds, 1992; Copenhagen, 1998, transf. Duchess, 1999; Hamlet, 2000; other productions: The Way of the World, Chichester Festival, 1984; Waste, Lyric, 1985; Three Sisters, Greenwich, transf. Albery, 1987; Lettice and Lovage, Globe, 1989; Another Time, Wyndham's, 1990; The Cabinet Minister, Albery, 1991; The Cherry Orchard, Gate, Dublin, 1992; Cabaret, Donmar, 1993–94 (Olivier Award for best supporting performance in a musical); Fiddler on the Roof, London Palladium, 1994; Three Tall Women, Wyndham's, 1995; A Two Hander (songwriter, jt writer, performer), Hampstead, 1996; Nine, Donmar, 1996–97; *films:* Zardoz, 1973; Lisztomania, 1975; Break of Day, 1976; Lady Jane, 1984; *TV* includes: Caucasian Chalk Circle, 1973; The Cafeteria, 1975; Crown Court; The Last Romantics, 1991; Tom Jones, 1997; Kavanagh QC, 1997; Invasion Earth, 1998; Anna Karenina, 2000; narrations for documentaries; numerous radio appearances. *Publication:* (with Susan Penhaligon) A Two Hander (poems), 1996. *Recreations:* writing – song writer and poet, tapestry, drawing, photography, dance.

KESWICK, Hon. Annabel Thérèse, (Tessa); Director, Centre for Policy Studies, since 1995; *b* 15 Oct. 1942; *d* of 17th Baron Lovat, DSO, MC and of Rosalind, *o d* of Sir Delves Broughton, 11th Bt; *m* 1st, 1964, 14th Lord Reay, *qv* (marr. diss. 1978); two *s* one *d*; 2nd, 1985, Henry Neville Lindley Keswick, *qv*. *Educ:* Convent of the Sacred Heart, Woldingham. Trainee, J. W. Thompson, 1960–62; Dir, Cluff Investments, 1980–95.

Special Advr to Rt Hon. Kenneth Clarke, 1989–95. Mem. (C), Kensington Council, 1982–86 (Member: Housing Cttee; Special Services Cttee). Contested (C), Inverness, Nairn and Lochaber, 1987. Gov., St James' Norland Colville Nursery Sch., and Colville Primary Sch., N Kensington, 1981–86. London Editor, B and E International, 1975–78. *Recreations:* travelling, breeding horses. *Address:* Centre for Policy Studies, 57 Tufton Street, SW1P 3QL. *T:* (020) 7222 4488.

KESWICK, Sir Chippendale; *see* Keswick, Sir J. C. L.

KESWICK, Henry Neville Lindley; Chairman: Matheson & Co. Ltd, since 1975; Jardine, Matheson Holdings Ltd, Hong Kong, 1972–75 and since 1989 (Director, since 1967); Jardine Strategic Holdings, since 1989 (Director, since 1988); *b* 29 Sept. 1938; *e s* of Sir William Keswick and of Mary, *d* of Rt Hon. Sir Francis Lindley, PC, GCMG; *m* 1985, Tessa, Lady Reay (*see* A. T. Keswick). *Educ:* Eton Coll.; Trinity Coll., Cambridge. BA Hons Econs and Law; MA. Commnd Scots Guards, Nat. Service, 1956–58. Director: Sun Alliance and London Insurance, 1975–96; Robert Fleming Holdings Ltd, 1975–2000; Rothmans Internat., 1988–94; Hongkong Land Co., 1988–; Mandarin Oriental Internat., 1988–; Dairy Farm Internat. Hldgs, 1988–; Royal & Sun Alliance (formerly Sun Alliance) Gp, 1989–2000; The Telegraph, 1990–. Member: London Adv. Cttee, Hongkong and Shanghai Banking Corp., 1975–92; 21st Century Trust, 1987–97. Proprietor, The Spectator, 1975–81. Trustee, Nat. Portrait Gall., 1982– (Chm., 1994–). Chm., Hong Kong Assoc, 1988–. *Recreation:* country pursuits. *Address:* Matheson & Co. Ltd, 3 Lombard Street, EC3V 9AQ. *Clubs:* White's, Turf; Third Guards.

See also Sir J. C. L. Keswick, S. L. Keswick.

KESWICK, Sir (John) Chippendale (Lindley), Kt 1993; a Director, Bank of England, since 1993; Director: De Beers Consolidated Mines, since 1993; De Beers Centenary AG, since 1994; *b* 2 Feb.1940; 2nd *s* of Sir William Keswick and of Mary, *d* of Rt Hon. Sir Francis Lindley, PC, GCMG; *m* 1966, Lady Sarah Ramsay, *d* of 16th Earl of Dalhousie, KT, GCVO, GBE, MC; three *s. Educ:* Eton; Univ. of Aix/Marseilles. Glyn Mills & Co., 1961–65; Jt Vice Chm., 1986, Jt Dep. Chm., 1990–97, Gp Chief Exec., 1995–97, Chm., 1997–98, Hambros PLC; Chief Exec., 1985–95, Chm., 1986–98, Hambros Bank. Sen. Banking and Capital Mkts Advr, Société Générale, 1998–2000. Director: Persimmon Plc, 1984–; Edinburgh Investment Trust, 1992–; IMI plc, 1994–; Anglo Amer. plc, 1995–; Investec Bank (UK) Ltd, 2000–. Vice Counsellor, Cancer Research Campaign, 1992–. Mem., Queen's Body Guard for Scotland, Royal Company of Archers, 1976–. *Recreations:* bridge, country pursuits. *Address:* De Beers, 17 Charterhouse Street, EC1N 6RA. *T:* (020) 7430 3553. *Clubs:* White's, Portland.

See also H. N. L. Keswick, S. L. Keswick.

KESWICK, Simon Lindley; Director: Jardine Matheson Holdings Ltd, since 1972 (Chairman, 1983–89); Jardine Strategic Holdings Ltd, since 1987 (Chairman, 1987–89); Matheson & Co. Ltd, since 1982; Jardine International Motor Holdings Ltd, since 1990 (Chairman, 1990–97); Jardine Lloyd Thompson Group plc, since 2001; Chairman: Hongkong Land Holdings Ltd, since 1983; Mandarin Oriental International Ltd, since 1984; Dairy Farm International Holdings Ltd, since 1984; Fleming Mercantile Investment Trust, since 1990 (Director, since 1988); *b* 20 May 1942; *s* of Sir William Keswick and of Mary, *d* of Rt Hon. Sir Francis Lindley, PC, GCMG; *m* 1971, Emma, *d* of Major David Chetwode; two *s* two *d. Educ:* Eton Coll. Director: Hong Kong and Shanghai Banking Corp., 1983–88; Hanson plc, 1991–; Wellcome plc, 1995–96; Chairman: Jardine Matheson Insurance Brokers Ltd, 1978–82; Trafalgar House plc, 1993–96. Trustee, British Museum, 1989–99. Member Council: QMW, 1998–; Cheltenham and Gloucester Coll., 1998–. Patron, RCS, 1998–. *Recreations:* country pursuits, Tottenham Hotspurs. *Address:* May Tower 1, 5–7 May Road, Hong Kong; Rockcliffe, Upper Slaughter, Cheltenham, Glos GL54 2JW. *Clubs:* White's, Portland; Shek O (Hong Kong).

See also H. N. L. Keswick, Sir J. C. L. Keswick.

KESWICK, Hon. Tessa; *see* Keswick, Hon. A. T.

KETTLE, Captain Alan Stafford Howard, CB 1984; Royal Navy (retired); General Manager, HM Dockyard, Chatham, 1977–84; *b* 6 Aug. 1925; *s* of Arthur Stafford Kettle and Marjorie Constance (*née* Clough); *m* 1952, Patricia Rosemary (*née* Gander); two *s. Educ:* Rugby School. CEng, FIMechE. Joined RN, 1943; Comdr, Dec. 1959; Captain, Dec. 1968; retired, Sept. 1977. Entered Civil Service as Asst Under-Sec., Sept. 1977. *Address:* Woodside, 9 Roland Bailey Gardens, Tavistock, Devon PL19 0RB. *T:* (01822) 618721.

KETTLEWELL, Comdt Dame Marion M., DBE 1970 (CBE 1964); General Secretary, Girls' Friendly Society, 1971–78; *b* 20 Feb. 1914; *d* of late George Wildman Kettlewell, Bramling, Virginia Water, Surrey, and of Mildred Frances (*née* Atkinson), Belford, Northumberland. *Educ:* Godolphin Sch., Salisbury; St Christopher's Coll., Blackheath. Worked for Fellowship of Maple Leaf, Alta, Canada, 1935–38; worked for Local Council, 1939–41; joined WRNS as MT driver, 1941; commnd as Third Officer WRNS, 1942; Supt WRNS on Staff of Flag Officer Air (Home), 1961–64; Supt WRNS Training and Drafting, 1964–67; Director, WRNS, 1967–70. Pres., Assoc. of Wrens, 1981–92. *Recreations:* needlework, walking, and country life. *Address:* Flat 2, 9 John Islip Street, SW1P 4PU.

KEVERNE, Prof. Eric Barrington, PhD; FRS 1997; Professor of Behavioural Neuroscience, since 1998, and Fellow of King's College, since 1985, University of Cambridge. *Educ:* London Univ. (BSc, PhD); MA Cantab 1975. University of Cambridge: Lectr, Dept of Anatomy, then of Zoology, until 1990; Reader in Behavioural Neurosci., 1990–98. Former Mem., Animals Res. Cttee, AFRC. Foreign Hon. Fellow, American Acad. of Arts and Scis, 1998. *Address:* Sub-Department of Animal Behaviour, University of Cambridge, Madingley, Cambridge CB3 8AA. *T:* (01954) 210301; King's College, Cambridge CB2 1ST.

KEVILL-DAVIES, Christopher Evelyn, CBE 1973; JP; DL; *b* 12 July 1913; 3rd *s* of William A. S. H. Kevill-Davies, JP, Croft Castle, Herefordshire; *m* 1938, Virginia, *d* of Adm. Ronald A. Hopwood, CB; one *s* one *d. Educ:* Radley College. Served with Suffolk Yeomanry, 1939–43 and Grenadier Gds, 1943–45, France, Belgium and Germany. Mem., Gt Yarmouth Borough Council, 1946–53; Chm., Norfolk Mental Deficiency HMC, 1950–69; Mem., East Anglian Regional Hosp. Bd, 1962 (Vice-Chm. 1967); Vice-Chm., E Anglian RHA, 1974–82. JP 1954, DL 1974–83, Norfolk; High Sheriff of Norfolk, 1965. *Address:* 11 Hale House, 34 De Vere Gardens, Kensington, W8 5AQ. *T:* (020) 7937 5066. *Clubs:* Cavalry and Guards, Royal Automobile; Norfolk (Norwich).

KEY, Brian Michael; Member (Lab) Yorkshire South, European Parliament, 1979–84; *b* 20 Sept. 1947; *s* of Leslie Granville Key and Nora Alice (*née* Haylett); *m* 1974, Lynn Joyce Ambler. *Educ:* Darfield County Primary Sch.; Wath upon Dearne Grammar Sch.; Liverpool Univ. (BA Hons). Careers Officer, West Riding County Council, 1970–73; Sen. Administrative Officer, South Yorkshire CC, 1973–79. *Address:* 25 Cliff Road, Darfield, Barnsley S73 9HR. *Clubs:* Darfield Working Men's; Trades and Labour (Doncaster).

KEY, (Simon) Robert; MP (C) Salisbury, since 1983; *b* 22 April 1945; *s* of late Rt Rev. J. M. Key; *m* 1968, Susan Priscilla Bright Irvine, 2nd *d* of late Rev. T. T. Irvine; one *s* two *d* (and one *s* decd). *Educ:* Salisbury Cathedral Sch.; Forres Sch., Swanage; Sherborne Sch.; Clare Coll., Cambridge. MA; CertEd. Assistant Master: Loretto Sch., Edinburgh, 1967; Harrow Sch., 1969–83. Warden, Nanoose Field Studies Centre, Wool, Dorset, 1972–78; Governor: Sir William Collins Sch., NW1, 1976–81; Special Sch. at Gt Ormond Street Hosp. for Sick Children, 1976–81; Roxeth Sch., Harrow, 1979–82. Founder Chm., ALICE Trust for Autistic Children, 1977–82; Council Mem., GAP Activity Projects, 1975–84. Vice-Chm., Wembley Br., ASTMS, 1976–80. Contested (C) Camden, Holborn and St Pancras South, 1979. Political Sec. to Rt Hon. Edward Heath, 1984–85; PPS: to Minister of State for Energy, 1985–87; to Minister for Overseas Develt, 1987–89; to Sec. of State for the Envmt, 1989–90; Parly Under-Sec. of State, DoE, 1990–92, Dept of Nat. Heritage, 1992–93, Dept of Transport, 1993–94; Opposition front bench spokesman on defence, 1997–2001. Mem., Select Cttee on Educn, Science and the Arts, 1983–86, on Health, 1994–95, on Defence, 1995–97; Sec., Cons. Parly Backbench Cttee on Arts and Heritage, 1983–84; Jt Parly Chm., Council for Educn in the Commonwealth, 1984–87; Vice-Chm., 1988–90, Chm., 1996–97, All-Party Gp on AIDS. Chm., Harrow Central Cons. Assoc., 1980–82; Vice-Chm., Central London Cons. Euro-Constit., 1980–82; Mem., Cons. Party Nat. Union Exec., 1981–83. Member: UK Nat. Commn for UNESCO, 1984–85; MRC, 1989–90 (Mem., AIDS Cttee, 1988–90). Vice-Pres., Haemophilia Soc., 1988–90. Hon. FCollP, 1989. *Recreations:* singing, cooking, country life. *Address:* House of Commons, SW1A 0AA. *T:* (020) 7219 3000.

KEYES, family name of **Baron Keyes**.

KEYES, 2nd Baron *cr* 1943, of Zeebrugge and of Dover; **Roger George Bowlby Keyes;** Bt 1919; RN, retired; *b* 14 March 1919; 2nd *s* of Admiral of the Fleet Baron Keyes, GCB, KCVO, CMG, DSO and Eva Mary Salvin Bowlby (*d* 1973), Red Cross Order of Queen Elisabeth of Belgium, *d* of late Edward Salvin Bowlby, DL, of Gilston Park, Herts, and Knoydart, Inverness-shire; *S* father, 1945; *m* 1947, Grizelda Mary (*d* 1993), 2nd *d* of late Lieut-Col William Packe, DSO; three *s* two *d. Educ:* King's Mead Sch., Seaford; RNC, Dartmouth. Great Officer, Order of Leopold (Belgium), 2000. *Publication:* Outrageous Fortune, 1984 (SE Arts Literary Prize). *Heir: s* Hon. Charles William Packe Keyes, *b* 8 Dec. 1951. *Address:* St George's Lodge, Malling Road, Teston, Kent ME18 5AU.

See also Baron Kennet.

KEYES, Timothy Harold, MA; Headmaster, King's School, Worcester, since 1998; *b* 15 Dec. 1954; *s* of Alfred Edward Keyes and Mary Irene Keyes (*née* Mylchreest); *m* 1979, Mary Anne Lucas; two *s. Educ:* Christ's Hospital, Horsham; Wadham Coll., Oxford (BA 1st cl. Classics, MA, PGCE). Teacher: of classics and rowing, Tiffin Sch., Kingston upon Thames, 1979–83; of classics and hockey, Whitgift Sch., Croydon, 1983–88; Head of Classics, Perse Sch., Cambridge, 1988–93; Dep. Head, Royal Grammar Sch., Guildford, 1993–98. *Recreations:* choral singing, walking, Yorkshire cricket. *Address:* The King's School, Worcester WR1 2LL. *T:* (01905) 721700.

KEYNES, Prof. Richard Darwin, CBE 1984; MA, PhD, ScD Cantab; FRS 1959; Professor of Physiology, University of Cambridge, 1973–87; Fellow of Churchill College, since 1961; *b* 14 Aug. 1919; *e s* of Sir Geoffrey Keynes, MD, FRCP, FRCS, FRCOG, and late Margaret Elizabeth, *d* of Sir George Darwin, KCB; *m* 1945, Anne Pinsent Adrian, *e d* of 1st Baron Adrian, OM, FRS, and Dame Hester Agnes Adrian, DBE, *o d* of Hume C. and Dame Ellen Pinsent, DBE; three *s* (and one *s* decd). *Educ:* Oundle Sch. (Scholar); Trinity Coll., Cambridge (Scholar). Temporary experimental officer, HM Anti-Submarine Establishment and Admiralty Signals Establishment, 1940–45. 1st Class, Nat. Sci. Tripos Part II, 1946; Michael Foster and G. H. Lewes Studentships, 1946; Research Fellow of Trinity Coll., 1948–52; Gedge Prize, 1948; Rolleston Memorial Prize, 1950. Demonstrator in Physiology, University of Cambridge, 1949–53; Lecturer, 1953–60; Fellow of Peterhouse, 1952–60 (Hon. Fellow, 1989); Head of Physiology Dept and Dep. Dir, 1960–64, Dir, 1965–73, ARC Inst. of Animal Physiology. Sec.-Gen., Internat. Union for Pure and Applied Biophysics, 1972–78, Vice-Pres., 1978–81, Pres., 1981–84; Chairman: Internat. Cell Research Orgn, 1981–83; ICSU/Unesco Internat. Biosciences Networks, 1982–93; Pres., Eur. Fedn of Physiol Socs, 1991–94; a Vice-Pres., Royal Society, 1965–68, Croonian Lectr, 1983. Fellow of Eton, 1963–78. Foreign Member: Royal Danish Acad., 1971; American Philosophical Soc., 1977; Amer. Acad. of Arts and Scis, 1978; Amer. Physiolog. Soc., 1994; Acad. Brasileira de Ciencias, 1994. Dr *hc*: Brazil, 1968; Rouen, 1996; Nairobi, 1999. Order of Scientific Merit (Brazil), 1997. *Publications:* The Beagle Record, 1979; (with D. J. Aidley) Nerve and Muscle, 1981, 3rd edn 2001; (ed) Charles Darwin's Beagle Diary, 1988; (ed jtly) Lydia and Maynard: the letters of Lydia Lopokova and John Maynard Keynes, 1989; (ed) Charles Darwin's Zoology Notes and Specimen Lists from HMS Beagle, 2000; papers in Journal of Physiology, Proceedings of Royal Soc., etc. *Recreations:* writing, pre-Columbian antiquities. *Address:* 4 Herschel Road, Cambridge CB3 9AG. *T:* (01223) 353107; Primrose Farm, Wiveton, Norfolk NR25 7TQ. *T:* (01263) 740317.

See also S. D. Keynes, S. J. Keynes.

KEYNES, Prof. Simon Douglas, PhD, LittD; FBA 2000; FSA, FRHistS; Elrington and Bosworth Professor of Anglo-Saxon, University of Cambridge, since 1999; Fellow, Trinity College, Cambridge, since 1976; *b* Cambridge, 23 Sept. 1952; *y s* of Prof. Richard Darwin Keynes, *qv*; one *s* with Tethys Lucy Carpenter. *Educ:* King's Coll. Choir Sch., Cambridge; Leys Sch., Cambridge; Trinity Coll., Cambridge (BA Hons 1973; MA 1977; PhD 1978; LittD 1992). FRHistS 1982; FSA 1985. University of Cambridge: Asst Lectr, Dept of Anglo-Saxon, Norse and Celtic, 1978–82; Lectr, 1982–92; Reader in Anglo-Saxon Hist., 1992–99. British Acad. Res. Reader in Humanities, 1991–93. Member, Editorial Board: Anglo-Saxon England, 1979–; Cambridge Studies in Anglo-Saxon England, 1986–; Early English MSS in Facsimile, 1996–; Associate Ed., New DNB, 1993–. Liveryman, Goldsmiths' Co., 1991–. *Publications:* The Diplomas of King Æthelred 'the Unready' 978–1016, 1980; (with M. Lapidge) Alfred the Great: Asser's Life of King Alfred and other contemporary sources, 1983; Anglo-Saxon History: a select bibliography, 1987, 3rd edn 1998; Facsimiles of Anglo-Saxon Charters, 1991; The Liber Vitae of the New Minster and Hyde Abbey, Winchester, 1996; (ed jtly and contrib.) The Blackwell Encyclopaedia of Anglo-Saxon England, 1999; contrib. articles in books and learned jls, incl. Anglo-Saxon England, Anglo-Norman Studies, English Hist. Rev. and Early Medieval Europe. *Recreation:* research. *Address:* Trinity College, Cambridge CB2 1TQ. *T:* (01223) 338421; Primrose Farm, Wiveton, Norfolk NR25 7TQ. *T:* (01263) 740317.

KEYNES, Stephen John, OBE 1993; Chief Executive, SK Productions, since 1991; *b* 19 Oct. 1927; 4th *s* of Sir Geoffrey Keynes, MD, FRCP, FRCS, FRCOG, and late Margaret Elizabeth, *d* of Sir George Darwin, KCB; *m* 1955, Mary, *o d* of late Senator the Hon. Adrian Knatchbull-Hugessen, QC (Canada), and late Margaret, *o d* of G. H. Duggan; three *s* two *d. Educ:* Oundle Sch.; King's Coll., Cambridge (Foundn Scholar; MA). Royal Artillery, 1949–51. Partner, J. F. Thomasson & Co., Private Bankers, 1961–65; Director:

Charterhouse Japhet Ltd and Charterhouse Finance Corp., 1965–72; Arbuthnot Latham Holdings Ltd, 1973–80; Sun Life Assce Soc. plc, 1965–89; English Trust Co. Ltd, 1980–90; Hawkshead Ltd, 1987–91. Member: IBA (formerly ITA), 1969–74; Cttee and Treas., Islington and North London Family Service Unit, 1956–68; Adv. Cttee, Geffrye Museum, 1964–78; Trustee: Centerprise Community Project, 1971–75; Needham Research Inst. (E Asian Hist. of Science Trust), 1984–; Charles Darwin Trust, 1999–; Chm., English Chamber Theatre, 1986–92; Chairman of Trustees: Whitechapel Art Gallery, 1979–96; William Blake Trust, 1981–; Mark Baldwin Dance Co., 1997–. FLS 1999. *Recreations:* medieval manuscripts, gardening, travelling. *Address:* 14 Canonbury Park South, Islington, N1 2JJ. *T:* and *Fax:* (020) 7226 8170; Lammas House, Brinkley, Newmarket, Suffolk CB8 0SB. *T:* (01638) 507268. *Clubs:* Cranium, Roxburghe, Ad Eundem.

See also R. D. Keynes.

KEYS, Derek Lyle; Director: Billiton plc; Sanlam; *b* 30 Aug. 1931. Exec. Chm., Gencor, 1986–91. Minister of Finance, and of Trade and Industry, S Africa, 1992–94. *Address:* PO Box 61392, Marshalltown 2107, South Africa.

KHABRA, Piara Singh; JP; MP (Lab) Ealing, Southall, since 1992; *b* Punjab, India, 20 Nov. 1924; *m* Beulah Marian. *Educ:* Punjab Univ., India (BA Social Scis, BEd); Whitelands Coll., London (DipEd). Chm., Co-op. Bank and Sarpanch of village Panchayat, Dist Hoshiarpur, Punjab; sch. teacher and later Head of a middle sch.; arrived in UK, 1959; factory work, 1959–61; clerical work, British Oxygen, 1961–64; teacher, ILEA, 1964–78; community worker, 1978–86. Councillor (Lab), London Borough of Ealing, 1978–82; Gen. Cttee Delegate, Ealing/Southall CLP, 1989–90; Member: Exec. Cttee, Ealing, 1989; Local Govt Cttee, Ealing, 1989–90. Mem., Select Cttee on Internat. Develt, 1997–. Founder Mem. and Treas., Ealing CRC (Chm., Finance Cttee); Chairman: Southall Community Law Centre, 1982–; Community Prog. Agency, Southall, 1984–88; Member: Unified Community Action; Community Action Policy Gp, Ealing; Indian Workers' Association, Southall: Educn Sec., 1959–63; Gen. Sec., 1963–65 and 1977–79; Chm., 1979–. Trustee, Dominion Centre, Southall (Vice-Chm., Management Cttee). Gov., various schs in Ealing, incl. Featherstone High Sch. JP Ealing. *Address:* House of Commons, SW1A 0AA.

KHAIR-UD-DIN, Rt Rev.; *see* Ud-Din.

KHALIDI, Prof. Tarif, PhD; Sir Thomas Adams's Professor of Arabic, University of Cambridge, and Fellow of King's College, Cambridge, since 1996; *b* 24 Jan. 1938; *s* of Ahmad Samih Khalidi, MBE and Anbara Salam; *m* 1960, Amal Saidi (decd); one *s* one *d*. *Educ:* Haileybury Coll., Hertford; University Coll., Oxford (BA; MA); Univ. of Chicago (PhD). Prof. of History, American Univ. of Beirut, 1970–96. *Publications:* Islamic Historiography, 1975; (ed) Land Tenure and Social Transformation in the Middle East, 1983; Classical Arab Islam, 1984; Arabic Historical Thought in the Classical Period, 1994. *Recreations:* gliding, admiring trees. *Address:* King's College, Cambridge CB2 1ST. *T:* (01223) 331100.

KHAMENEI, Ayatollah Sayyed Ali; Leader of the Islamic Republic of Iran, since 1989; *b* Mashhad, Khorasan, 1940; *m* 1964; four *s* two *d*. *Educ:* Qom; studied under Iman Khomeini, 1956–64. Imprisoned six times, 1964–78; once exiled, 1978; Mem., Revolutionary Council, 1978 until its dissolution, 1979 (Rep. in Iranian Army and Assistant of Revolutionary Affairs in Min. of Defence); Rep. of First Islamic Consultative Assembly, and of Iman Khomeini in the Supreme Council of Defence, 1980; Comdr, Revolutionary Guards, 1980; Friday Prayer Leader, Teheran, 1980; Sec. Gen., and Pres. of Central Cttee, Islamic Republic Party, 1980–87; survived assassination attempt, June 1981; Pres., Islamic Republic of Iran, 1981–89. *Recreations:* reading, art, literature. *Address:* Office of Religious Leader, Tehran, Islamic Republic of Iran.

KHAN, Geoffrey Allan, PhD; FBA 1998; Reader in Semitic Philology, University of Cambridge, since 1999; *b* 1 Feb. 1958; *s* of Clive and Diana Khan; *m* 1984, Colette Alcock; one *s* one *d*. *Educ:* Acklam Sixth Form Coll.; SOAS, London Univ. (BA Semitic Langs 1980; PhD 1984). Res. Asst, 1983–87, Res. Associate, 1987–93, Taylor-Schechter Genizah Res. Unit, Cambridge Univ. Liby; Lectr in Hebrew and Aramaic, Cambridge Univ., 1993–99. Fellow, Inst. for Advanced Studies, Jerusalem, 1990–91. *Publications:* Studies in Semitic Syntax, 1988; Karaite Bible manuscripts from the Cairo Genizah, 1990; Arabic Papyri: selected material from the Khalili collection, 1992; Arabic Legal and Administrative Documents in the Cambridge Genizah collections, 1993; Bills, Letters and Deeds: Arabic papyri of the 7th–11th centuries, 1993; A Grammar of Neo-Aramaic, 1999; The Early Karaite Tradition of Hebrew Grammatical Thought, 2000; Early Karaite Grammatical Texts, 2000. *Recreations:* mountain-walking, miniature carpentry. *Address:* The Faculty of Oriental Studies, Sidgwick Avenue, Cambridge CB3 9DA. *T:* (01223) 335114.

KHAN, Ghulam Ishaq; President of Pakistan, 1988–93; *b* 20 Jan. 1915; *m* 1950; one *s* five *d*. *Educ:* Islamia Coll., Peshawar; Punjab Univ. Indian Civil Service, 1940–47; NWFP service, 1947–56; Government of West Pakistan: Sec. for Develt and Irrigation, 1956–58; Chm., Water and Power Develt Authy, 1961–66; Chm., Land Reforms Commn, 1978; Sec., Finance, 1966–70; Cabinet Sec., 1970; Sec.-Gen., Ministry of Defence, 1975–77; Sec.-Gen.-in-Chief, Adviser for Planning and Co-ordination, 1977–78; Adviser to Chief Martial Law Administrator, 1978; Minister for Finance and Co-ordination, 1978–79, for Finance, Econ. Affairs, Commerce and Co-ordination, 1979–85; Chairman of Senate, 1985–88. Governor, State Bank of Pakistan, 1971–75; Chm., Jt Ministerial Cttee, Board of Governors of World Bank and IMF, 1982–88. Life Pres., Soc. for Promotion of Engrg Scis and Technology in Pakistan, 1988–; Pres., Bd of Govs, Gulam Ishaq Khan Inst. of Engrg Scis and Technology, 1988–. Millennium Gold Medal, Sarhad Arts Soc., NWFP, Pakistan, 2000. *Address:* 3–B Jamrud Road, University Town, Peshawar, NWFP, Pakistan.

KHAN, Humayun; Director, Commonwealth Foundation, 1993–99; *b* 31 Aug. 1932; *s* of K. B. Safdar Khan and Mumtaz Safdar; *m* 1961, Munawar; three *d*. *Educ:* Bishop Cotton Sch., Simla; Trinity College, Cambridge (MA); Univ. of Southern California (MPA, Dr PA). Called to the Bar, Lincoln's Inn, 1954; joined Pakistan CS, 1955; Sec. to Govt of NWPP, 1970–73; Jt Sec., Pakistan Govt, 1973–74; Minister, Pakistan Embassy, Moscow, 1974–77; Dep. Perm. Rep., UNO, Geneva, 1977–79; Ambassador to Bangladesh, 1979–82; Additional Sec., Min. of Foreign Affairs, Pakistan, 1982–84; Ambassador to India, 1984–88; Foreign Sec. of Pakistan, 1988–89; High Comr in UK, 1990–92. *Recreations:* golf, cricket, shooting, fishing. *Clubs:* Royal Over-Seas League, Royal Automobile; Islamabad.

KHAN, Imran Ahmad; Hilal-e-Imtiaz, Pakistan, 1993; *b* Lahore, 25 Oct. 1952; *m* 1995, Jemima, (Haiqa), *d* of Sir James Goldsmith; two *s*. *Educ:* Aitchison Coll.; Keble Coll., Oxford (BA Hons; cricket blue, 1973, 1974, 1975; Captain, Oxford XI, 1974; Hon. Fellow, 1988). Début for Lahore A, 1969; played first Test for Pakistan, 1970, Captain, 1982–84, 1985–87, 1988–89, 1992; with Worcs CCC, 1971–76 (capped, 1976); with Sussex CCC, 1977–88 (capped, 1978; Hon. Life Mem., 1988). Editor-in-Chief, Cricket Life Internat., 1989–90. Mem., Internat. Cricket Council, 1993–. Special Sports Rep., UNICEF; Founder, Imran Khan Cancer Hosp. Appeal, 1991–. Pride of Performance Award, Pakistan. *Publications:* Imran, 1983; All-Round View (autobiog.), 1988; Indus Journey, 1990; Warrior Race, 1993. *Recreations:* shooting, films, music. *Address:* c/o Shankat Khanum Memorial Trust, 29 Shah Jamal, Lahore 54600, Pakistan. *Clubs:* Tramp; Gymkhana (Lahore).

KHANBHAI, Bashir Yusufali Simba; Member (C) Eastern Region, England, European Parliament, since 1999; *b* 22 Sept. 1945; *s* of Yusufali Simba Khanbhai and Jenambai Khanbhai; *m* 1981, Maria Bashir Khanbhai (*née* Da Silva); one *s*. *Educ:* Sch. of Pharmacy, Univ. of London (BPharm Hons 1966); Balliol Coll., Oxford (MA Hons PPE 1969). Manufg industry, export and finance, 1970–97; Chief Executive Officer: Headlands Chemicals Ltd, 1970–76; Khanbhai Industries Ltd, 1977–84; Teqny Ltd, 1984–99. Mem., Consultative Council, Greenwich Univ. *Publication:* (ed) The Jowett Papers, 1970. *Recreations:* tennis, travel, theatre, music, food. *Address:* (constituency office) 57 Peninsula Cottage, Staitheway Road, Wroxham, Norfolk NR12 8RN.

KHATAMI, Hojjatoleslam Seyed Mohammad; President of the Islamic Republic of Iran, since 1997; *b* 1943; *s* of Ayatollah Sayyid Ruhollah Khatami, religious scholar; *m* 1974, Zohreh Sadeghi; one *s* two *d*. *Educ:* High Sch.; Qom Theol. Sch.; Isfahan Univ. (BA Philosophy); Tehran Univ. (MA); Qom Seminary. Head, Hamburg Islamic Centre, Germany, 1979; Mem. for Ardakan and Maybod, first Islamic Consultative Assembly, 1980–82; Dep. Hd of Jt Comd of Armed Forces, and Chm., War Propaganda HQ, Iran-Iraq War, 1980–88; Dir, Keyhan Newspaper Inst., 1981; Minister of Culture and Islamic Guidance, 1982–92; Advr to Pres. Rafsanjani, 1992–96. Mem., High Council for Cultural Revolution, 1996. Chm., 8th Session, Islamic Summit Conf., 1997–2000. *Publications:* From the World of the City to the City of the World, 1994; Fear of Wave, 1997; Faith and Thought Trapped by Despotism; contrib. articles to Arabic mags and newspapers.

KHAW, Prof. Kay-Tee, (Mrs Kay-Tee Fawcett), FRCP; Professor of Clinical Gerontology, University of Cambridge, since 1989; Fellow, Gonville and Caius College, Cambridge, since 1991; *b* 14 Oct. 1950; *d* of Khaw Kai Boh and Tan Chwee Geok; *m* 1980, Dr James William Fawcett; one *s* one *d*. *Educ:* Girton Coll., Cambridge (BA, MA; MB BChir); St Mary's Hosp. Med. Sch., London; London Sch. of Hygiene and Tropical Med. (MSc). MRCP 1977, FRCP 1993; DCH 1978; MFPHM 1993. LTCL 1969. Wellcome Trust Research Fellow, LSHTM, St Mary's Hosp. and Univ. of California San Diego, 1979–84; Asst Adjunct Prof., Univ. of California Sch. of Med., San Diego, 1985; Sen. Registrar in Community Medicine, Univ. of Cambridge Sch. of Clinical Medicine, 1986–89. Member: NHS Central R&D Cttee, 1991–97; HEFCE, 1992–97. Daland Fellow, Amer. Philosophical Soc., 1984. Trustee, Help the Aged, 1993–. *Publications:* contribs to scientific jls on chronic disease epidemiology. *Address:* Clinical Gerontology Unit, University of Cambridge School of Clinical Medicine, Addenbrooke's Hospital, Cambridge CB2 2QQ.

KHAYAT, Georges Mario; QC 1992; a Recorder, since 1987; *b* 15 Aug. 1941; *s* of Fred Khayat and Julie Germain. *Educ:* Terra Sancta Coll., Nazareth; Prior Park Coll., Bath. Called to the Bar, Lincoln's Inn, 1967. Head of Chambers, 1999–. Chm., Surrey and S London Bar Mess, 1995–98. *Recreations:* horse riding, reading, boating, music. *Address:* 10 King's Bench Walk, Temple, EC4Y 7EB. *T:* (020) 7353 2501.

KHOO, Francis Kah Siang; writer; solicitor and advocate; *b* 23 Oct. 1947; *s* of late Teng Eng Khoo and of Swee Neo Chew; *m* 1977, Dr Swee Chai Ang, MB BS, MSc, FRCS. *Educ:* Univ. of Singapore (LLB (Hons) 1970); Univ. of London (MA 1980). Advocate and Solicitor, Singapore, 1971. Lawyer, Singapore, 1971–77; journalist, South magazine, and Mem., NUJ (UK), 1980–87; Gen. Sec. (Dir), War on Want, 1988–89; Solicitor, England and Wales, 1998–. Founding Mem. and Vice-Chm. of British charity, Medical Aid for Palestinians, 1984–; Trustee and Sec., RADICLE charity. *Publications:* And Bungaraya Blooms All Day: collection of songs, poems and cartoons in exile, UK, 1978; Hang On Tight, No Surrender: tape of songs, 1984; Rebel and the Revolutionary (poems), 1995. *Recreations:* photography, hill-walking, song-writing, camera designing and inventions, swimming. *Address:* 285 Cambridge Heath Road, Bethnal Green, E2 0EL. *T:* and *Fax:* (020) 7729 3994.

KHORANA, Prof. Har Gobind; Sloan Professor of Chemistry and Biology, Massachusetts Institute of Technology, since 1970; *b* Raipur, India, 9 Jan. 1922; *s* of Shri Ganpat Rai and Shrimata Krishna (Devi); *m* 1952, Esther Elizabeth Sibler; one *s* two *d*. *Educ:* Punjab Univ. (BSc 1943; MSc 1945); Liverpool Univ. (PhD 1948; Govt of India Student). Post-doctoral Fellow of Govt of India, Federal Inst. of Techn., Zurich, 1948–49; Nuffield Fellow, Cambridge Univ., 1950–52; Head, Organic Chemistry Group, BC Research Council, 1952–60. Univ. of Wisconsin: Prof. and Co-Dir, Inst. for Enzyme Research, 1960–70; Prof., Dept of Biochemistry, 1962–70; Conrad A. Elvehjem Prof. in the Life Sciences, 1964–70. Visiting Professor: Rockefeller Inst., NY, 1958–60; Stanford Univ., 1964; Harvard Med. Sch., 1966; Andrew D. White Prof.-at-large, Cornell Univ., 1974–80. Has given special or memorial lectures in USA, Poland, Canada, Switzerland, UK and Japan. Fellow: Chem. Inst. of Canada, 1959; Amer. Assoc. for Advancement of Science, 1966; Amer. Acad. of Arts and Sciences, 1967. Overseas Fellow, Churchill Coll., Cambridge, 1967. Member: Nat. Acad. of Sciences, 1966; Deutsche Akademie der Naturforscher Leopoldina, 1968; Pontifical Acad. of Scis, Rome, 1978; Foreign Member: Indian Acad. of Scis, 1976; Royal Society, 1978; RSE, 1982. Various hon. degrees. Merck Award, Chem. Inst. Canada, 1958; Gold Medal for 1960, Professional Inst. of Public Service of Canada; Dannie-Heinneman Preiz, Germany, 1967; Remsen Award, Johns Hopkins Univ., ACS Award for Creative Work in Synthetic Organic Chemistry, Louisa Gross Horwitz Award, Lasker Foundn Award for Basic Med. Research, Nobel Prize for Physiology or Medicine (jtly), 1968; Gairdner Foundn Award, 1980; US Nat. Medal of Science, 1987. Order of San Carlos (Columbia), 1986. *Publications:* Some Recent Developments in the Chemistry of Phosphate Esters of Biological Interest, 1961; numerous papers in Biochemistry, Jl Amer. Chem. Soc., Proc. Nat. Acad. Scis, etc. *Recreations:* hiking, swimming. *Address:* Department of Biology and Chemistry, Massachusetts Institute of Technology, Cambridge, MA 02139, USA.

KHUSH, Dr Gurdev Singh, FRS 1995; Principal Plant Breeder, and Head, Division of Plant Breeding, Genetics and Biochemistry, International Rice Research Institute, Philippines, since 1989; *b* 22 Aug. 1935; *s* of Kartar Singh and Pritam Kaur; *m* 1961, Harwant Kaur Grewal; one *s* three *d*. *Educ:* Punjab Univ., Chandigarh, India (BScAgr); Univ. of Calif, Davis (PhD Genetics 1960). University of California, Davis: Research Asst, 1957–60; Asst Geneticist, 1960–67; International Rice Research Institute, Philippines: Plant Breeder, 1967–72; Head, Dept of Plant Breeding, 1972–89. Hon. DSc: Punjab Agricl, 1987; Tamil Nadu Agricl, 1995; C. S. Azad Univ. of Agric. and Technol., 1995; G. B. Pant Univ. of Agric. and Technol., 1996; De Montfort, 1998; Cambridge, 2000. Borlaug Award in Plant Breeding, Coromandel Fertilizers Ltd, India, 1977; Japan Prize, Japan Sci. and Technol. Foundn, 1987; Fellows Award 1989, Internat. Agronomy Award 1990, Amer. Soc. of Agronomy; Emil M. Mrak Internat. Award, Univ. of California,

Davis, 1990; World Food Prize, World Food Prize Foundn, 1996; Rank Prize, Rank Prize Funds, 1998; Wolf Prize, Wolf Foundn, Israel. *Publications:* Cytogenetics of Aneuploids, 1973; Host Plant Resistance to Insects, 1995; *edited:* Rice Biotechnology, 1991; Nodulation and Nitrogen Fixation in Rice, 1992; Apomix: exploiting hybrid vigor in rice, 1994; Rice Genetics III, 1996; contrib. chapters in books; numerous papers in jls. *Recreation:* reading world history. *Address:* International Rice Research Institute, MCPO Box 3127, Makati City 1271, Philippines. *T:* (2) 8450563.

KIBBEY, Sidney Basil; Under-Secretary, Department of Health and Social Security, 1971–76; *b* 3 Dec. 1916; *y s* of late Percy Edwin Kibbey and Winifred Kibbey, Mickleover, Derby; *m* 1939, Violet Gertrude, (Jane), Eyre; (twin) *s* and *d. Educ:* Derby Sch. Executive Officer, Min. of Health, 1936; Principal, Min. of National Insurance, 1951; Sec., Nat. Insurance Adv. Cttee, 1960–62; Asst Sec., Min. of Pensions and Nat. Insurance, 1962. *Address:* 29 Beaulieu Close, Datchet, Berks SL3 9DD. *T:* (01753) 549101.

KIBBLE, Prof. Thomas Walter Bannerman, CBE 1998; PhD; FRS 1980; Emeritus Professor of Theoretical Physics, and Senior Research Fellow, Imperial College, London, since 1998; *b* 1932; *s* of Walter Frederick Kibble and Janet Cowan Watson (*née* Bannerman); *m* 1957, Anne Richmond Allan; one *s* two *d. Educ:* Doveton-Corrie Sch., Madras; Melville Coll., Edinburgh; Univ. of Edinburgh (MA, BSc, PhD). Commonwealth Fund Fellow, California Inst. of Technology, 1958–59; Imperial College, London: NATO Fellow, 1959–60; Lecturer, 1961; Sen. Lectr, 1965; Reader in Theoretical Physics, 1966; Prof. of Theoretical Physics, 1970–98; Hd, Dept of Physics, 1983–91. Sen. Visiting Research Associate, Univ. of Rochester, New York, 1967–68. Member: Nuclear Physics Bd, SERC, 1982–86; Astronomy, Space and Radio Bd, 1984–86; Physical Sciences Sub-cttee, UGC, 1985–89. Chairman: Scientists Against Nuclear Arms, 1985–91 (Vice-Chm., 1981–85); Martin Ryle Trust, 1985–96. Mem. Council, Royal Soc., 1987–89 (Vice-Pres., 1988–89). (Jtly) Hughes Medal, Royal Soc., 1981; (jtly) Rutherford Medal, 1984, Guthrie Medal, 1993, Inst. of Physics. *Publications:* Classical Mechanics, 1966, 4th edn 1996; papers in Phys. Rev., Proc. Royal Soc., Nuclear Physics, Nuovo Cimento, Jl Physics, and others. *Recreations:* cycling, walking, destructive gardening. *Address:* Blackett Laboratory, Imperial College, Prince Consort Road, SW7 2BW. *T:* (020) 7594 7845.

KIDD, Prof. Cecil; Regius Professor of Physiology, 1984–97, part-time Professor of Physiology, 1997–2000, now Emeritus, Marischal College, University of Aberdeen; *b* 28 April 1933; *s* of Herbert Cecil and Elizabeth Kidd; *m* 1956, Margaret Winifred Goodwill; three *s. Educ:* Queen Elizabeth Grammar School, Darlington; King's College, Newcastle upon Tyne, Univ. of Durham (BSc, PhD). FIBiol; FRSA. Research Fellow then Demonstrator in Physiology, King's Coll., Univ. of Durham, 1954–58; Asst Lectr then Lectr in Physiol., Univ. of Leeds, 1958–68; Res. Fellow in Physiol., Johns Hopkins Univ., 1962–63; Sen. Lectr then Reader in Physiol., 1968–84, Sen. Res. Associate in Cardiovascular Studies, 1973–84, Univ. of Leeds. *Publications:* scientific papers in physiological jls. *Recreations:* opera, walking, food, alpines, gardening. *Address:* c/o Department of Biomedical Sciences, Medical School, University of Aberdeen, Aberdeen AB25 2ZD. *T:* (01224) 273005.

KIDD, Charles William; Editor of Debrett's Peerage, since 1980; *b* 23 May 1952; *yr s* of Charles Vincent Kidd and Marian Kidd, BEM (*née* Foster), Kirkbymoorside. *Educ:* St Peter's Sch., York; Bede Coll., Durham. Assistant Editor: Burke's Peerage, 1972–77; Debrett's Peerage, 1977–80. FSG 2000. *Publications:* Debrett's Book of Royal Children (jtly), 1982; Debrett Goes to Hollywood, 1986. *Recreations:* cinema, researching film and theatre dynasties, tennis.

KIDD, Hon. Douglas Lorimer, DCNZM 2000; List MP (N) New Zealand, since 1999; *b* 12 Sept. 1941; *s* of Lorimer Edward Revington Kidd and Jessie Jean Kidd (*née* Mottershead); *m* 1964, Jane Stafford Richardson; one *s* two *d. Educ:* Ohau Primary Sch.; Horowhenua Coll.; Victoria Univ., Wellington (LLB 1964). Mil. service, Territorial Service, Royal Regt of NZ Artillery, 1960–64. Admitted Barrister and Solicitor, 1964; Partner, Wisheart Macnab & Partners, 1964–78. MP (N) Marlborough, 1978–96, Kaikoura, 1996–99. Minister of Fisheries, and State-Owned Enterprises, 1990–91; Associate Minister of Finance, 1990–94; Minister of Maori Affairs, 1991–94; Minister of Energy, Fisheries, Labour, Accident Rehabilitation and Compensation Insce, 1994–96; Speaker, House of Representatives, 1996–99. Chair, Cabinet Revenue and Expenditure Cttee; Chm., Regulations Rev. Select Cttee, 1999–; Mem., Privileges and Maori Affairs Select Cttee, 1999–. Dir and Partner, plantation forestry, marine farming and wine co. ventures, Marlborough, 1968–94. Hon. Mem., Canterbury/Nelson/Marlborough/W Coast Regt, 1980–94 (Hon. Col, 1997–). CGS's Commendation for outstanding service to NZ Army, 1999. QPSM (NZ Commemoration Medal), 1990. *Recreations:* fishing, reading, travel. *Address:* Parliament House, Wellington, New Zealand. *T:* (4) 4719939. *Club:* Marlborough (Blenheim).

KIDD, Prof. Frank Forrest; Partner, Coopers & Lybrand, Chartered Accountants, 1979–97; *b* 4 May 1938; *s* of Frank F. Kidd and Constance Mary Kidd (*née* Godman); *m* 1961, Beryl Ann (*née* Gillespie); two *s* two *d. Educ:* George Heriot's Sch., Ballards. CA; Mem. Inst. of Taxation. CA apprentice, 1955–60; Partner, Wylie & Hutton, 1962–79; Partner, Coopers & Lybrand, 1979–98 (following merger of Coopers & Lybrand with Wylie & Hutton in 1979). Pres., Inst. of Chartered Accountants of Scotland, 1988–89. Hon. Prof., Dept of Accountancy and Business Law, Univ. of Stirling, 1987–94. Master, Co. of Merchants of City of Edinburgh, 1995–97. *Recreations:* squash, golf, walking. *Address:* 17 Merchiston Park, Edinburgh EH10 4PW. *T:* (0131) 229 3577. *Clubs:* New (Edinburgh); Luffness New Golf (Gullane).

KIDD, Prof. Ian Gray, FBA 1993; Emeritus Professor of Greek, since 1987, Chancellor's Assessor, 1989–98, University of St Andrews; *b* 6 March 1922; *s* of A. H. Kidd and I. Gray; *m* 1949, Sheila Elizabeth Dow; three *s. Educ:* Dundee High Sch.; Univ. of St Andrews (MA, Miller Prize 1947); Queen's Coll., Oxford (BA Greats, MA). Served War of 1939–45: commnd Argyll and Sutherland Highlanders; Sicily, Italy, 1943–44; POW, 1944–45. St Andrews University: Lectr in Greek, 1949–65; Sen. Lectr, 1965–73; Professor: of Ancient Philosophy, 1973–76; of Greek, 1976–87; Vice-Pres., Univ. Court, 1997–98; Provost, St Leonard's Coll., 1978–83 (Hon. Fellow, 1987). Vis. Prof. of Classics, Univ. of Texas at Austin, 1965–66; Mem., Inst. for Advanced Study, Princeton, 1971–72 and 1979–80. General Comr of Inland Revenue, 1982–97. Chm., E Fife Educnl Trust, 1977–89. Gov., Dollar Acad., 1982–91. Hon. Fellow, Inst. for Res. in Classical Philosophy and Sci., Princeton, 1989–. Hon. DLitt St Andrews, 2001. *Publications:* (ed) Posidonius, Works: vol. I, (with L. Edelstein) The Fragments, 1972, 2nd edn 1989; vol. II(i) and (ii), The Commentary, 1988; vol. III, The Translation of the Fragments, 1999; (with R. Waterfield) Plutarch, Essays, 1992; contributions to: Concise Encyclopedia of Western Philosophy and Philosophers, 1960; The Encyclopedia of Philosophy, ed P. Edwards, 1967; Problems in Stoicism, 1971; The Stoics, 1978; Les Stoiciens et leur Logique, 1978; Stoic and Peripatetic Ethics, 1983; Aspects de la Philosophie Hellénistique, 1986; The Criterion of Truth, 1989; Philosophia Togata, 1989; Owls to Athens, 1990; Handbook of Metaphysics and Ontology, 1991; Theophrastus, 1992; Socratic Questions, 1992; Philosophen der Antike, 1996; The Oxford Classical Dictionary, 1996; Polyhistor: studies in the history of ancient philosophy, 1996; Collecting Fragments, 1997; Framentsammlungen philosophischer Texte der Antike, 1998; articles in learned jls. *Recreations:* music, reading, thinking, looking at pictures. *Address:* Ladebury, Lade Braes Lane, St Andrews, Fife KY16 9EP. *T:* (01334) 474367.

KIDD, Sir Robert (Hill), KBE 1979; CB 1975; Head of Northern Ireland Civil Service, 1976–79; *b* 3 Feb. 1918; *s* of Andrew Kidd and Florence Hill, Belfast; *m* 1942, Harriet Moore Williamson; three *s* two *d. Educ:* Royal Belfast Academical Instn; Trinity Coll., Dublin. BA 1940, BLitt 1941. Army, 1941–46: commnd 1942, Royal Ulster Rifles, later seconded to Intell. Corps. Entered Northern Ireland Civil Service, 1947; Second Sec., Dept of Finance, NI, 1969–76. Allied Irish Banks: Dir, 1979–85; Mem., NI Local Bd, 1979–85 (Chm., 1980–85); Mem., NI Adv. Bd, 1985–88. Chairman: Ireland Co-operation North (UK) Ltd, 1982–85 (Bd Mem., 1985–89); Belfast Car Ferries Ltd, 1983–88. Board Mem., Irish Amer. Partnership, 1988–91. Governor, Royal Belfast Academical Inst., 1967–76, 1979–83; a Pro-Chancellor and Chm. Council, New Univ. of Ulster, 1980–84; Pres., TCD Assoc. of NI, 1981–83; Trustee: Scotch-Irish Trust of Ulster, 1980–96; Ulster Historical Foundn, 1981–95 (Chm., 1987–93). Hon. DLitt Ulster, 1985. *Recreation:* gardening. *Address:* 24 Massey Court, Belfast BT4 3GJ. *T:* (028) 9076 8694.

KIDD, Ronald Alexander; HM Diplomatic Service, retired; *b* 19 June 1926; *s* of Alexander and Jean Kidd; *m* 1st, 1954, Agnes Japp Harrower (marr. diss. 1985); two *d*; 2nd, 1985, Pamela Dempster. *Educ:* Robert Gordon's College, Aberdeen; Queens' College, Cambridge; BA Hons 1951, MA 1956. Royal Air Force, 1944–48; Foreign Office, 1951; served at Singapore, Djakarta, Osaka and Macau, 1952–56; FO, 1956–60; Second, later First Sec., Seoul, 1961–62; Djakarta, 1962–63; Tokyo, 1964–68; FCO, 1968–71; Dar Es Salaam, 1971–72; Tokyo, 1972–77; Counsellor, FCO, 1977–81. Jubilee Medal, 1977. *Recreation:* golf. *Address:* 41 Princess Road, NW1 8JS. *T:* (020) 7722 8406; Apdo 159, Lista de Correíos, Sóller, Mallorca, Spain. *Club:* Royal Air Force.

KIDGELL, John Earle; Director of Economic Statistics, Office for National Statistics (formerly Head of Economic Accounts Division, Central Statistical Office), since 1994 (Grade 3, since 1988); *b* 18 Nov. 1943; *s* of Gilbert James Kidgell and Cicely Alice (*née* Earle); *m* 1968, Penelope Jane Tarry; one *s* two *d. Educ:* Eton House Sch., Southend-on-Sea; Univ. of St Andrews (MA); London School of Economics and Political Science (MSc). NIESR, 1967–70; Gallup Poll, 1970–72; Statistician, CSO and Treasury, 1972–79; Chief Statistician, DoE, 1979–86; Hd of Finance Div., PSA, 1986–88; Head of Directorate D, Central Statistical Office, 1989–91. *Publications:* articles in Nat. Inst. Econ. Rev., Econ. Trends, etc. *Recreations:* hill walking, tennis, reading. *Address:* Office for National Statistics, 1 Drummond Gate, SW1V 2QQ.

KIDNEY, David Neil; MP (Lab) Stafford, since 1997; *b* 21 March 1955; *s* of Neil Bernard Kidney and Doris Kidney; *m* 1978, Elaine Dickinson; one *s* one *d. Educ:* Bristol Univ. (LLB). Solicitor in private practice, Kenneth Wainwright & Co., then Wainwrights, subseq. Jewels & Kidney, 1977–97, Partner, 1983–97. Mem. (Lab) Stafford BC, 1987–97. Contested (Lab) Stafford, 1992. *Recreations:* bridge, chess. *Address:* 6 Beechcroft Avenue, Stafford ST16 1BJ.

KIDWELL, Raymond Incledon; QC 1968; a Recorder, 1972–95; a Deputy High Court Judge, 1976–95; *b* 8 Aug. 1926; *s* of late Montague and Dorothy Kidwell; *m* 1st, 1951, Enid Rowe (marr. diss. 1975); two *s*; 2nd, 1976, Carol Evelyn Beryl Maddison, *d* of late Warren G. Hopkins, Ontario. *Educ:* Whitgift Sch.; Magdalen Coll., Oxford. RAFVR, 1944–48. BA (Law) 1st cl. 1950; MA 1951; BCL 1st cl. 1951; Vinerian Law Schol., 1951; Eldon Law Schol., 1951; Arden Law Schol., Gray's Inn, 1952; Birkenhead Law Schol., Gray's Inn, 1955. Called to Bar, 1951; Bencher, 1978. Lectr in Law, Oriel Coll., Oxford, 1952–55; Mem., Winn Commn on Personal Injuries, 1966–68. Member: Bar Council, 1967–71; Senate, 1981–85. *Address:* Sanderstead House, Rectory Park, Sanderstead, Surrey CR2 9JR. *T:* (020) 8657 4161; 2 Crown Office Row, Temple, EC4Y 7HJ. *T:* (020) 7797 8100, *Fax:* (020) 7797 8101.

KIELY, Dr David George; Chief Naval Weapons Systems Engineer (Under Secretary), Ministry of Defence, Procurement Executive, 1983–84; consultant engineer; *b* 23 July 1925; *o s* of late George Thomas and Susan Kiely, Ballynahinch, Co. Down; *m* 1956, Dr Ann Wilhelmina (*née* Kilpatrick), MB, BCh, BAO, DCH, DPH, MFCM, Hillsborough, Co. Down; one *s* one *d. Educ:* Down High Sch., Downpatrick; Queen's Univ., Belfast (BSc, MSc); Sorbonne (DSci). CEng, FIEE; CPhys, FInstP; psc 1961. Appts in RN Scientific Service from 1944; Naval Staff Coll., 1961–62; Head of Electronic Warfare Div., ASWE, 1965–68; Head of Communications and Sensor Dept, ASWE, 1968–72; Dir-Gen., Telecommunications, 1972–74, Dir-Gen., Strategic Electronic Systems, 1974–76, Dir-Gen., Electronics Res., 1976–78, Exec. Officer, Electronics Research Council, 1976–78, Dir, Naval Surface Weapons, ASWE, 1978–83, MoD, PE. Gp Chief Exec. and Dir, Chemring PLC, 1984–85. Chm., R&D Policy Cttee, Gen. Lights Authorities of UK and Eire, 1974–89. Governor: Portsmouth Coll. of Technology, 1965–69; Springfield Sch., Portsmouth, 1993–97. Mem., 1982–89, Chm., 1985–89, Council, Chichester Cathedral. *Publications:* Dielectric Aerials, 1953; Marine Navigational Aids for Coastal Waters of the British Isles, 1987; Naval Electronic Warfare, 1988; Naval Surface Weapons, 1988; Defence Procurement, 1990; The Future for the Defence Industry, 1990; chapter: in Progress in Dielectrics, 1961; in Fundamentals of Microwave Electronics, 1963; in Naval Command and Control, 1989; papers in Proc. IEE and other learned jls, etc. *Recreations:* fly fishing, gardening. *Address:* Cranleigh, 107 Havant Road, Emsworth, Hants PO10 7LF. *T:* (01243) 372250. *Club:* Naval and Military.

KIERNAN, Prof. Christopher Charles; Professor of Behavioural Studies in Mental Handicap, University of Manchester, since 1984 (Director, Hester Adrian Research Centre, 1984–2000); *b* 3 June 1936; *s* of Christopher J. and Mary L. Kiernan; *m* 1962, Diana Elizabeth Maynard; two *s* one *d. Educ:* Nottingham Univ. (BA); London Univ. (PhD); ABPsS. Lecturer in Psychology, Birkbeck Coll., London Univ., 1961–70; Sen. Lectr, Child Development, Univ. of London Inst. of Education, 1970–74; Dep. Director, Thomas Coram Research Unit, Univ. of London Inst. of Education, 1975–84. *Publications:* Behaviour Assessment Battery, 1977, 2nd edn 1982; Starting Off, 1978; Behaviour Modification with the Severely Retarded, 1975; Analysis of Programmes for Teaching, 1981; Signs and Symbols, 1982; Research to Practice, 1993. *Recreation:* survival. *Address:* 29 Edge Lane, Chorlton-cum-Hardy, Manchester M21 1JH.

KILBRACKEN, 3rd Baron *cr* 1909, of Killegar; **John Raymond Godley,** DSC 1945; journalist and author; *b* 17 Oct. 1920; *er s* of 2nd Baron Kilbracken, CB, KC, and Elizabeth Helen Monteith, *d* of Vereker Hamilton and *widow* of Wing Commander N. F. Usborne, RNAS; *S* father, 1950; *m* 1st, 1943, Penelope Anne (marr. diss. 1949), *y d* of Rear-Adm. Sir C. N. Reyne, KBE; one *s* (and one *s* decd); 2nd, 1981, Susan Lee (marr. diss. 1989), *yr d* of N. F. Heazlewood, Melbourne, Australia; one *s. Educ:* Eton; Balliol Coll., Oxford (MA). Served in RNVR (Fleet Air Arm), as pilot, 1940–46; commissioned 1941; Lieut-

Comdr (A) 1945; commanded Nos 835 and 714 Naval Air Sqdns. A reporter for: Daily Mirror, 1947–49; Sunday Express, 1949–51; freelance contributor as writer and photographer to many UK and foreign magazines and newspapers, 1951–. Joined Parly Liberal Party, 1953; transferred to Labour, 1966; Ind., 1999–. Hon. Sec., Connacht Hereford Breeders' Assoc., 1973–76. Pres., British-Kurdish Friendship Soc., 1975–90. *Publications:* Even For An Hour (poems), 1940; Tell Me The Next One, 1950; The Master Forger, 1951; (ed) Letters From Early New Zealand, 1951; Living Like a Lord, 1955; A Peer Behind the Curtain, 1959; Shamrocks and Unicorns, 1962; Van Meegeren, 1967; Bring Back My Stringbag, 1979; The Easy Way to Bird Recognition, 1982 (TES Sen. Information Book Award, 1983); The Easy Way to Tree Recognition, 1983; The Easy Way to Wild Flower Recognition, 1984. TV documentaries: The Yemen, 1965; Morgan's Treasure, 1965; Kurdistan, 1966. *Recreations:* bird-watching, chess. *Heir: s* Hon. Christopher John Godley [*b* 1 Jan. 1945; *m* 1969, Gillian Christine, *yr d* of late Lt-Comdr S. W. Birse OBE, DSC, RN retd, Alverstoke; one *s* one *d. Educ:* Rugby; Reading Univ. (BSc Agric.)]. *Address:* Killegar, Co; Leitrim, Ireland. *T:* and *Fax:* (49) 4334309.

See also Hon. W. A. H. Godley.

KILBY, Michael Leopold; *b* 3 Sept. 1924; *s* of Guy and Grace Kilby; *m* 1952, Mary Sanders; three *s. Educ:* Luton College of Technology. General Motors, 1942–80: Apprentice; European Planning and Govt and Trade Regulations Manager; European Sales, Marketing and Service Ops Manager; Plant Manager; internat. management consultant, 1980–84. Mayor of Dunstable, 1963–64. MEP (C) Nottingham, 1984–89; contested (C) Nottingham, Eur. parly elecn, 1989. Member: SE Economic Planning Council; Industry and Economic Cttee, British Assoc. of Chambers of Commerce. *Publications:* The Man at the Sharp End, 1983, 2nd edn 1991; Mammon's Ladder, 1993; technical and political papers. *Recreations:* all sports; first love cricket; former Minor Counties cricketer. *Address:* Grange Barn, Haversham Village, Milton Keynes, Bucks MK19 7DX. *T:* (01908) 313613.

KILCLOONEY, Baron *cr* 2001 (Life Peer), of Armagh in the County of Armagh; **John David Taylor;** PC (NI) 1970; Member (UU) Strangford, Northern Ireland Assembly, since 1998; *b* 24 Dec. 1937; *er s* of George D. Taylor and Georgina Baird; *m* 1970, Mary Frances Todd; one *s* five *d. Educ:* Royal Sch., Armagh; Queen's Univ. of Belfast (BSc). CEng; AMInstHE, AMICEI. MP (UU) S Tyrone, NI Parlt, 1965–73; Mem. (UU), Fermanagh and S Tyrone, NI Assembly, 1973–75; Mem. (UU), North Down, NI Constitutional Convention, 1975–76; Parly Sec. to Min. of Home Affairs, 1969–70; Minister of State, Min. of Home Affairs, 1970–72; Mem. (UU), North Down, NI Assembly, 1982–86. Mem., Strangford, NI Forum, 1996–98. Mem. (UU) NI, Europ. Parlt, 1979–89. MP (UU) Strangford, 1983–2001 (resigned seat Dec. 1985 in protest against Anglo-Irish Agreement; re-elected Jan. 1986). Mem. Assembly, Council of Europe, 1997–. Partner, G. D. Taylor and Associates, Architects and Civil Engineers, 1966–74; Director: West Ulster Estates Ltd, 1968–; Bramley Apple Restaurant Ltd, 1974–; West Ulster Hotels Co. Ltd, 1976–86; Gosford Housing Assoc. Ltd, 1977–; Tontine Rooms Ltd, 1978–; Ulster Gazette (Armagh) Ltd, 1983–; Cerdac (Belfast) Ltd, 1986–; Tyrone Printing Co. Ltd, 1986–; Tyrone Courier Ltd, 1986–; Sovereign Properties (NI) Ltd, 1989–; Carrickfergus Advertiser Ltd, 1992–; Tyrone Constitution Ltd, 1999–; Outlook Press Ltd, 1999–. *Publication:* (jtly) Ulster—the facts, 1982. *Recreation:* foreign travel. *Address:* Mullinure, Portadown Road, Armagh, Northern Ireland BT61 9EL. *T:* (028) 3752 2409, (020) 7931 7211. *Clubs:* Farmers'; Armagh County (Armagh).

KILDARE, Marquess of; Maurice FitzGerald; landscape and contract gardener; *b* 7 April 1948; *s* and *heir* of 8th Duke of Leinster, *qv*; *m* 1972, Fiona Mary Francesca, *d* of Harry Hollick; two *d* (only *s* Thomas FitzGerald (Earl of Offaly) *d* 1997). *Educ:* Millfield School. Pres., Oxfordshire Dyslexia Assoc. Chm., Thomas Offaly Meml Fund. *Address:* Courtyard House, Oakley Park, Frilford Heath, Oxon OX13 6QW.

KILDARE AND LEIGHLIN, Bishop of, (RC), since 1987; **Most Rev. Laurence Ryan;** DD; *b* 13 May 1931; *s* of Michael Ryan and Brigid Foley. *Educ:* St Patrick's Coll., Maynooth (BA, DD). Lectr in Theology, St Patrick's Coll., Carlow, 1958–80, Pres. 1974–80; Parish Priest of Naas, Co. Kildare, 1980–85; Vicar General of Kildare and Leighlin, 1975–87; Coadjutor Bishop of Kildare and Leighlin, 1984–87. Sec., 1966–71, Chm., 1974–76, Irish Theological Assoc.; Pres., Nat. Conf. of Priests of Ireland, 1976–82. *Publications:* contribs to Irish Theological Qly, The Furrow, Irish Ecclesiastical Record, Christus Rex. *Recreation:* walking. *Address:* Bishop's House, Carlow, Ireland. *T:* (503) 76725.

KILFOIL, Geoffrey Everard; His Honour Judge Kilfoil; a Circuit Judge, since 1987; *b* 15 March 1939; *m* 1962; one *s* one *d. Address:* The Law Courts, Mold, Flints CH7 1AE.

KILFOYLE, Peter; MP (Lab) Liverpool, Walton, since July 1991; *b* 9 June 1946; *s* of Edward and Ellen Kilfoyle; *m* 1968, Bernadette (*née* Slater); two *s* three *d. Educ:* St Edward's Coll., Liverpool; Durham Univ.; Christ's Coll., Liverpool. Building labourer, 1965–70; student, 1970–73; building labourer, 1973–75; teacher/youth worker, 1975–85; Labour Party Organiser, 1985–91. Parly Sec., Cabinet Office, 1997–99 (OPS, 1997–98); Parly Under Sec. of State, MoD, 1999–2000. *Publication:* Left Behind: lessons from Labour's heartlands, 2000. *Recreations:* reading, music, spectator sport, bonsai. *Address:* 6 Heathwood, Sandfield Park, Liverpool L12 2BL; House of Commons, SW1A 0AA. *T:* (020) 7219 3000.

KILGOUR, Dr John Lowell, CB 1987; Occupational Health consultant, since 1994; *b* 26 July 1924; *s* of Ormonde John Lowell Kilgour and Catherine (*née* MacInnes); *m* 1955, Daphne (*née* Tully); two *s. Educ:* St Christopher's Prep. Sch., Hove; Aberdeen Grammar Sch.; Aberdeen Univ. MB, ChB 1947, MRCGP, FFCM. Joined RAMC, 1948; served in: Korea, 1950–52; Cyprus, 1956; Suez, 1956; Singapore, 1961–64 (Brunei, Sarawak); comd 23 Para. Field Amb., 1954–57; psc 1959; ADMS GHQ FARELF, 1961–64; jssc 1964; Comdt, Field Trng Sch., RAMC, 1965–66. Joined Min. of Health, 1968, Med. Manpower and Postgrad. Educn Divs; Head of Internat. Health Div., DHSS, 1971–78; Under-Sec. and Chief Med. Advr, Min. of Overseas Develt, 1973–78; Dir of Co-ordination, WHO, 1978–83; Dir, Prison Medical Services, Home Office, 1983–89; Chairman: CS Commn Recruitment Bds, 1989–91; Industrial Injuries and War Pensions Med. Bds, 1989–94; Med. Examnr, Benefits Agency, DSS, 1989–94. UK Deleg. to WHO and to Council of Europe Public Health Cttees; Chm., European Public Health Cttee, 1976; Mem. WHO Expert Panel on Communicable Diseases, 1972–78, 1983–; Chm., Cttee for Internat. Surveillance of Communicable Diseases, 1976; Consultant, WHO Special Programme on AIDS, 1987–. Vis. Lectr, 1976–89, Governor, 1987–89, LSHTM; Mem. Governing Council, Liverpool Sch. of Tropical Medicine, 1973–87; Mem. Council, 1983–89, Mem. Exec. Cttee, 1987–90, Royal Commonwealth Society for the Blind. Winner, Cons. Constituency Speakers' Competition for London and the SE, 1968. *Publications:* chapter in, Migration of Medical Manpower, 1971; chapter in, The Global Impact of AIDS, 1988; contrib. The Lancet, BMJ, Hospital Medicine, Health Trends and other med. jls. *Recreations:* horse racing, reading, gardening, travel. *Address:* Stoke House, 22 Amersham Road, Chesham Bois, Bucks HP6 5PE. *Clubs:* Hurlingham; Royal Windsor Racing.

KILLALOE, Bishop of, (RC), since 1994; **Most Rev. William Walsh;** *b* 16 Jan. 1935; *s* of Bill Walsh and Ellen Maher. *Educ:* St Flannan's Coll., Ennis; St Patrick's Coll., Maynooth (BSc); Irish Coll., Rome; Lateran Univ., Rome (LTh, DCL); Univ. Coll., Galway (HDipEd). Ordained priest, 1959; postgrad. studies, 1959–63; Teacher of mathematics and physics, St Flannan's Coll., Ennis, 1963–88; Curate at Ennis Cathedral, 1988–94; Priest Dir, 1969–94, Mem. Nat. Exec., 1995–, ACCORD (formerly Catholic Marriage Adv. Council); Mem., Episcopal Social Welfare and Pastoral Commns, 1994–. *Publications:* contrib. Furrow Magazine and other theol jls. *Recreations:* hurling (sometime coach/selector of many teams), golf, walking. *Address:* Bishop's House, Westbourne, Ennis. *T:* (065) 28638. *Clubs:* Eire Og Hurling (Ennis); Ennis, Lahinch and Woodstock Golf.

KILLANIN, 4th Baron *cr* 1900, of Galway, co. Galway; **George Redmond Fitzpatrick Morris;** Bt 1885; film producer; *b* 26 Jan. 1947; *e s* of 3rd Baron Killanin, MBE, TD and of Mary Sheila Cathcart Morris (*née* Dunlop), MBE; *S* father, 1999; *m* 1972, Pauline Horton (marr. diss. 1999); one *s* one *d*; *m* 2000, Sheila Lynch. *Educ:* Ampleforth Coll., York; Trinity Coll., Dublin. Films produced: The Miracle, 1991; Splitting Heirs, 1993; The Butcher Boy, 1998; co-producer: Interview with the Vampire, 1994; Michael Collins, 1996; In Dreams, 1999. *Recreations:* film, theatre, music, Ireland. *Heir: s* Hon. Luke Michael Geoffrey Morris, *b* 22 July 1975. *Address:* 9 Lower Mount Pleasant Avenue, Dublin 6, Ireland. *Club:* Groucho.

KILLEARN, 3rd Baron *cr* 1943, of Killearn, co. Stirling; **Victor Miles George Aldous Lampson;** Bt 1866; Partner, Cazenove & Co., since 1979; *b* 9 Sept. 1941; *s* of 1st Baron Killearn, GCMG, CB, MVO, PC and of his 2nd wife, Jacqueline Aldine Leslie, *o d* of Marchese Count Aldo Castellani; *S* half-brother, 1996; *m* 1971, Melita Amaryllis Pamela Astrid, *d* of Rear Adm. Sir Morgan Morgan-Giles, *qv*; two *s* two *d. Educ:* Eton. Late Captain, Scots Guards. Dir, AMP Ltd, 1999–. *Heir: s* Hon. Miles Henry Morgan Lampson, *b* 10 Dec. 1977. *Clubs:* White's, Pratt's, City of London; Hong Kong.

KILLEN, Hon. Sir (Denis) James, KCMG 1982; LLB; MP (L) Moreton, Queensland, 1955–83; *b* 23 Nov. 1925; *s* of James W. Killen, Melbourne; *m* 1949, Joyce Claire (*d* 2000); two *d. Educ:* Brisbane Grammar Sch.; Univ. of Queensland. Barrister-at-Law. Jackaroo; RAAF (Flight Serjeant); Mem. staff, Rheem (Aust.) Pty Ltd. Minister for the Navy, 1969–71; Opposition Spokesman: on Educn, 1973–74; on Defence, 1975; Minister for Defence, 1975–82; Vice-Pres. of Exec. Council and Leader, House of Representatives, Commonwealth of Australia, 1982–83. Foundn Pres., Young Liberals Movement (Qld); Vice-Pres., Lib. Party, Qld Div., 1953–56. *Recreations:* horseracing, golf. *Address:* 253 Chapel Hill Road, Chapel Hill, Qld 4069, Australia. *Clubs:* Tattersall's, Irish Association, QTC (Brisbane).

KILLEN, Prof. John Tyrrell, PhD; FBA 1995; Professor of Mycenaean Greek, Cambridge University, 1997–99, now Emeritus; Fellow, Jesus College, Cambridge, since 1969; *b* 19 July 1937; *e s* of John Killen and Muriel Caroline Elliott Killen (*née* Bolton); *m* 1964, Elizabeth Ann Ross; one *s* two *d. Educ:* High Sch., Dublin; Trinity Coll., Dublin (1st Foundn Schol. in Classics 1957; 1st Vice-Chancellor's Latin Medallist 1959; BA 1st Cl. 1960); St John's Coll., Cambridge (Gardiner Meml Schol. 1959; PhD 1964). Cambridge University: Asst Lectr in Classics, 1967–70; Lectr, 1970–90; Reader in Mycenaean Greek, 1990–97; Chm., Faculty Bd of Classics, 1984–86; Churchill College: Gulbenkian Res. Fellow, 1961–62; Fellow and Librarian, 1962–69; Jesus College: Lectr, 1965–97; acting Bursar, 1973; Sen. Bursar, 1979–89; Dir, Quincentenary Develt Appeal, 1987–90. *Publications:* (jtly) Corpus of Mycenaean Inscriptions from Knossos, 1986–98; (with J.-P. Olivier) The Knossos Tablets, 1989; articles in learned jls. *Recreations:* golf, watching sport on television, reading the FT, music. *Address:* Jesus College, Cambridge CB5 8BL. *T:* (01223) 339424. *Club:* Gog Magog Golf.

KILLICK, Angela Margaret; Chairman, Mount Vernon and Watford Hospitals NHS Trust, since 1998; *b* 18 May 1943; *o d* of Tom Killick and Dora (*née* Jeffries); *m* 1983, Alec Grezo; one *s. Educ:* Watford Grammar Sch. for Girls. Various posts, incl. voluntary sector and abroad, until 1970; civil servant, incl. Hd, Res. Grants and Council Secretariat, SERC and AFRC; Hd, Radioactive Waste Policy Unit, DoE, 1970–91. Chairman: Hampstead HA, 1990–92; Enfield Community Care NHS Trust, 1992–98. Mem., Radioactive Waste Mgt Adv. Cttee, 1991–98. Mem. (C) Westminster CC, 1974–90. Trustee: Tennant Housing Assoc., 1976–85; Westminster Children's Soc., 1988–95 (Chm., 1993–95). Governor: St Clement Danes Sch., Covent Gdn, 1976–82; St Mary's Sch., Bryanston Sq., 1990–96; Russell Sch., Chorleywood, 1997– (Chm. of Govs, 1998–). Binney Award Certificate for Bravery, Binney Meml Trust, 1985. JP Camberwell, 1983–86. *Publication:* Council House Blues, 1976. *Recreations:* reading, gardening, family history, Private Pilot's licence, 1972. *Address:* Mount Vernon and Watford Hospitals NHS Trust, Vicarage Road, Watford, Herts WD1 8HB. *T:* (01923) 217107. *Club:* English-Speaking Union.

KILLICK, Anthony John, (Tony); Senior Research Associate, Overseas Development Institute, since 1999 (Director, 1982–87; Senior Research Fellow, 1987–99); *b* 25 June 1934; *s* of William and Edith Killick; *m* 1958, Ingeborg Nitzsche; two *d. Educ:* Ruskin and Wadham Colls, Oxford (BA Hons PPE). Lectr in Econs, Univ. of Ghana, 1961–65; Tutor in Econs, Ruskin Coll., Oxford, 1965–67; Sen. Econ. Adviser, Min. of Overseas Develt, 1967–69; Econ. Adviser to Govt of Ghana, 1969–72; Res. Fellow, Harvard Univ., 1972–73; Ford Foundn Vis. Prof., Econs Dept, Univ. of Nairobi, 1973–79; Res. Officer, Overseas Develt Inst., 1979–82. Vis. Fellow, Wolfson Coll., and Vis. Scholar, Dept of Applied Economics, Cambridge Univ., 1987–88. Vis. Prof., Dept of Economics, Univ. of Surrey, 1988–. Member: Commn of Inquiry into Fiscal System of Zimbabwe, 1984–86; Council, Royal Africa Soc. Chm. Bd of Dirs, African Econ. Res. Consortium, 1995–. Former consultant: Govt of Sierra Leone; Govt of Kenya; Govt of Republic of Dominica; Govt of Nepal; Govt of Ethiopia; various internat. orgns. Associate, Inst. of Develt Studies, Univ. of Sussex, 1986–94. Pres., Develt Studies Assoc., 1986–88. Hon. Res. Fellow, Dept of Political Economy, UCL, 1985–. Editorial adviser: Journal of Economic Studies; Eastern Africa Economic Review, Jl of Internat. Develt; World Develt. *Publications:* The Economies of East Africa, 1976; Development Economics in Action: a study of economic policies in Ghana, 1978; Policy Economics: a textbook of applied economics on developing countries, 1981; (ed) Papers on the Kenyan Economy: structure, problems and policies, 1981; (ed) Adjustment and Financing in the Developing World: the role of the IMF, 1982; The Quest for Economic Stabilisation: the IMF and the Third World, 1984; The IMF and Stabilisation: developing country experiences, 1984; The Economies of East Africa: a bibliography 1974–80, 1984; A Reaction Too Far: the role of the state in developing countries, 1989; The Adaptive Economy: adjustment policies in low income countries, 1993; The Flexible Economy: causes and consequences of the adaptability of national economies, 1995; IMF Programmes in Developing Countries, 1995; Aid and the Political Economy of Policy Change, 1998; learned articles and contribs to books on Third World develt and economics. *Recreations:* gardening, photography, music. *Address:* Karibu, Millers Mews, Standard Hill, Ninfield, East Sussex TN33 9JU. *T:* (01424) 892184; *e-mail:* t.killick@odi.org.uk.

KILLICK, Sir John (Edward), GCMG 1979 (KCMG 1971 CMG 1966); HM Diplomatic Service, retired; *b* 18 Nov. 1919; *s* of late Edward William James Killick and Doris Marjorie (*née* Stokes); *m* 1st, 1949, Lynette du Preez (*née* Leach) (*d* 1984); no *c*; 2nd, 1985, Irene M. H. Easton, OBE (*d* 1995). *Educ:* Latymer Upper Sch.; University Coll., London, Fellow 1973; Bonn Univ. Served with HM Forces, 1939–46: Suffolk Regt, W Africa Force and Airborne Forces. Foreign Office, 1946–48; Control Commn and High Commn for Germany (Berlin, Frankfurt and Bonn), 1948–51; Private Sec. to Parly Under-Sec., Foreign Office, 1951–54; British Embassy, Addis Ababa, 1954–57; Canadian Nat. Def. Coll., 1957–58; Western Dept, Foreign Office, 1958–62; Imp. Def. Coll., 1962; Counsellor and Head of Chancery, British Embassy, Washington, 1963–68; Asst Under-Sec. of State, FCO, 1968–71; Ambassador to USSR, 1971–73; Dep. Under-Sec. of State, FCO and Permanent Rep. on Council of WEU, 1973–75; Ambassador and UK Permanent Rep. to NATO, 1975–79. Dir, Dunlop South Africa, 1980–85. Pres., 1985–92, Vice-Pres., 1992–93, GB Atlantic Cttee; Vice-Pres., Atlantic Treaty Assoc., 1992–94. *Recreations:* reading, writing. *Address:* 5 Norstead Gardens, Southborough, Kent TN4 0DE. *Club:* East India.

KILLICK, Tony; *see* Killick, A. J.

KILLIK, Paul Geoffrey; Senior Partner, Killik & Co., since 1989; *b* 24 Dec. 1947; *s* of Guy Frederick Killik and Rita Mildred (*née* Brewer); *m* 1981, Karen Virginia Mayhew; one *s* one *d*. *Educ:* Clayesmore Sch., Dorset. MSI (Dip.) 1992. Hedderwick Borthwick, 1969–71; Killik Haley, 1971–74; Partner, Killik Cassel Haley, 1974–75; joined Quilter Goodison, 1975: Partner, 1977–85, Dir, 1985–88; Head, Private Client Dept, 1983–88. Mem., Stock Exchange, 1973. Chm., The Money Channel plc, 1999–. *Address:* (office) 46 Grosvenor Street, W1K 3HN. *T:* (020) 7337 0400. *Club:* Hurlingham.

KILMAINE, 7th Baron *cr* 1789; **John David Henry Browne;** Bt 1636; Director: Whale Tankers Ltd, since 1974; Fusion (Bickenhill) Ltd, 1969–96; *b* 2 April 1948; *s* of 6th Baron Kilmaine, CBE, and of Wilhelmina Phyllis, *o d* of Scott Arnott, Brasted, Kent; *S* father, 1978; *m* 1982, Linda, *yr d* of Dennis Robinson; one *s* one *d*. *Educ:* Eton. *Heir: s* Hon. John Francis Sandford Browne, *b* 4 April 1983.

KILMARNOCK, 7th Baron *cr* 1831; **Alastair Ivor Gilbert Boyd;** Chief of the Clan Boyd; *b* 11 May 1927; *s* of 6th Baron Kilmarnock, MBE, TD, and Hon. Rosemary Guest (*d* 1971), *er d* of 1st Viscount Wimborne; *S* father, 1975; *m* 1st, 1954, Diana Mary (marr. diss. 1970, she *d* 1975), *o d* of D. Grant Gibson; 2nd, 1977, Hilary Ann, *yr d* of Leonard Sidney and Margery Bardwell; one *s*. *Educ:* Bradfield; King's Coll., Cambridge. Lieutenant, Irish Guards, 1946; served Palestine, 1947–48. Mem. SDP, 1981–92; Chief SDP Whip, House of Lords, 1983–86; Dep. Leader, SDP Peers, 1986–87. Chm., All-Party Parly Gp on AIDS, 1987–96. Gen. Sec., European Public Health Foundn, 1994–98. Editl Consultant, The Social Market Foundn, 1992– (Exec. Dir, 1989–92). *Publications:* Sabbatical Year, 1958; The Road from Ronda, 1969; The Companion Guide to Madrid and Central Spain, 1974, revised edn 2001; (ed) The Radical Challenge: the response of social democracy, 1987; The Essence of Catalonia, 1988; The Sierras of the South, 1992; The Social Market & the State, 1999. *Heir: b* Dr the Hon. Robin Jordan Boyd, MB BS, MRCP, MRCPEd, DCH, *b* 6 June 1941. *Address:* Apartado 445, 29400 Ronda (Málaga), Spain.

KILMISTER, (Claude Alaric) Anthony; Vice President, Prayer Book Society, since 2001 (Chairman, 1989–2001); *b* 22 July 1931; *s* of late Dr Claude E. Kilmister and of Margaret E. Mogford, *d* of Ernest Gee; *m* 1958, Sheila, *d* of Lawrence Harwood. *Educ:* Shrewsbury Sch. National Service (army officer), 1950–52. NCB, 1952–54; Conservative Party Org., 1954–60; Asst Sec. 1960–61, Gen. Sec. 1962–72, Cinema & Television Benevolent Fund; Sec., Royal Film Performance Exec. Cttee, 1961–72; Exec. Dir, Parkinson's Disease Soc. of UK, 1972–91. Founding Cttee Mem., Action for Neurological Diseases, 1987–91; Founder, Prostate Res. Campaign UK, 1994. Founding Mem. and Dep. Chm., Prayer Book Soc. (and its forerunner, BCP Action Gp), 1972–89; Member: Internat. Council for Apostolic Faith, 1987–93; Steering Cttee, Assoc. for Apostolic Ministry, 1989–96; Observer, Council, Forward in Faith, 1997–. *Publications:* The Good Church Guide, 1982; When Will Ye be Wise?, 1983; My Favourite Betjeman, 1985; contribs to jls, etc. *Recreations:* walking, writing. *Address:* 36 The Drive, Northwood, Middlesex HA6 1HP. *T:* (01923) 824278. *Club:* Athenæum.

KILMISTER, Prof. Clive William; Professor of Mathematics, King's College, London, 1966–84; *b* 3 Jan. 1924; *s* of William and Doris Kilmister; *m* 1955, Peggy Joyce Hutchins; one *s* two *d*. *Educ:* Queen Mary Coll., Univ. of London. BSc 1944, MSc 1948, PhD 1950. King's Coll. London: Asst Lectr, 1950; Lectr, 1953; Reader, 1959; FKC 1983. Gresham Prof. of Geometry, 1972–88. President: British Soc. for History of Mathematics, 1973–76; Mathematical Assoc., 1979–80; British Soc. for Philos. of Science, 1981–83. *Publications:* (with G. Stephenson) Special Relativity for Physicists, 1958; (with B. O. J. Tupper) Eddington's Statistical Theory, 1962; Hamiltonian Dynamics, 1964; The Environment in Modern Physics, 1965; (with J. E. Reeve) Rational Mechanics, 1966; Men of Physics: Sir Arthur Eddington, 1966; Language, Logic and Mathematics, 1967; Lagrangian Dynamics, 1967; Special Theory of Relativity, 1970; The Nature of the Universe, 1972; General Theory of Relativity, 1973; Philosophers in Context: Russell, 1984; (ed) Schrödinger: centenary celebration of a polymath, 1987; Eddington's search for a fundamental theory, 1995; (with Ted Bastin) Combinatorial Physics, 1995. *Recreation:* opera going. *Address:* Red Tiles Cottage, High Street, Barcombe, Lewes, East Sussex BN8 5DH.

KILMORE, Bishop of, (RC), since 1998; **Most Rev. Leo O'Reilly;** STD; *b* 10 April 1944; *s* of Terence O'Reilly and Maureen (*née* Smith). *Educ:* St Patrick's Coll., Maynooth (BSc, BD, HDipEd); Gregorian Univ., Rome (STD 1982). Ordained priest, 1969; on staff: St Patrick's Coll., Cavan, 1969–76; Irish Coll., Rome, 1978–81; Chaplain, Bailieborough Community Sch., 1981–88; missionary work, Nigeria: diocese of Minna, 1988–90; staff, St Paul's Seminary, Abuja, 1990–95; Parish Priest, Castletara, Cavan, 1995–97; Coadjutor Bishop of Kilmore, 1997–98. *Publication:* Word and Sign in the Acts of the Apostles: a study in Lucan theology, 1987. *Recreations:* walking, reading, golf. *Address:* Bishop's House, Cullies, Cavan, Co. Cavan, Ireland.

KILMORE, ELPHIN AND ARDAGH, Bishop of, since 2001; **Rt Rev. Kenneth Herbert Clarke;** *b* 23 May 1949; *s* of Herbert and Anne Clark; *m* 1971, Helen Good; four *d*. *Educ:* Holywood Primary Sch.; Sullivan Upper Sch., Holywood, Co. Down; TCD (BA 1971; Div. Testimonium 1972). Ordained deacon, 1972, priest, 1973; Curate: Magheralin, 1972–75; Dundonald, 1975–78; served in Chile with S Amer. Mission Soc., 1978–81; Incumbent: Crinken Ch, Dublin, 1982–86; Coleraine Parish, 1986–2001; Archdeacon of Dalriada, 1998–2001. *Publication:* Called to Minister?, 1990. *Recreations:* walking, reading, golf. *Address:* 48 Carrickfern, Cavan, Co. Cavan, Republic of Ireland. *T:* (49) 437 2759; *e-mail:* bishop@kilmore.anglican.org.

KILMOREY, 6th Earl of; *see* Needham, Rt Hon. Richard Francis.

KILNER, Prof. John Anthony, PhD; CPhys; FIM; Professor of Materials Science, since 1995, and Head, Department of Materials, since 2000, Imperial College of Science, Technology and Medicine, London University; *b* 15 Dec. 1946; *s* of Arnold and Edith Kilner; *m* 1973, Ana Maria del Carmen Sánchez; one *s* one *d*. *Educ:* Univ. of Birmingham (BSc Hons 1968; MSc 1971; PhD 1975). MInstP, CPhys 1987. Res. Fellow and SERC Postdoctoral Res. Fellow, Univ. of Leeds, 1975–79; Department of Materials, Imperial College: Wolfson Res. Fellow, 1979–83; SERC Advanced Res. Fellow, IT, 1983–87; Lectr, 1987–91; Reader in Materials, 1991–95; Dean, RSM, 1998–2000. Member: Polar Solids Discussion Gp, RSC, 1981–; European Materials Res. Soc., 1991–. An Associate Ed., Materials Letters, 1992–. *Publications:* contribs to sci. jls. *Recreations:* travel, walking, food, drink. *Address:* 34 Castle Avenue, Ewell, Surrey KT17 2PQ. *T:* (020) 8224 7959. *Club:* Polish Hearth.

KILNER BROWN, Hon. Sir Ralph; *see* Brown.

KILPATRICK, family name of **Baron Kilpatrick of Kincraig.**

KILPATRICK OF KINCRAIG, Baron *cr* 1996 (Life Peer), of Dysart in the district of Kirkcaldy; **Robert Kilpatrick,** Kt 1986; CBE 1979; President, General Medical Council, 1989–95 (Member, 1972–76 and 1979–95); *b* 29 July 1926; *s* of Robert Kilpatrick and Catherine Sharp Glover; *m* 1950, Elizabeth Gibson Page Forbes; two *s* one *d*. *Educ:* Buckhaven High Sch.; Edinburgh Univ. MB, ChB (Hons) 1949; Ettles Schol.; Leslie Gold Medallist; MD 1960; FRCP(Ed) 1963; FRCP 1975; FRCPSGlas 1991; FRSE 1998. Med. Registrar, Edinburgh, 1951–54; Lectr, Univ. of Sheffield, 1955–66; Rockefeller Trav. Fellowship, MRC, Harvard Univ., 1961–62; Commonwealth Trav. Fellowship, 1962; Prof. of Clin. Pharmacology and Therapeutics, Univ. of Sheffield, 1966–75; Dean, Faculty of Medicine, Univ. of Sheffield, 1970–73; Univ. of Leicester: Prof. and Head of Dept of Clinical Pharmacology and Therapeutics, 1975–83; Dean, Faculty of Medicine, 1975–89; Prof. of Medicine, 1984–89. Chairman: Adv. Cttee on Pesticides, 1975–87; Soc. of Endocrinology, 1975–78; Scottish Hosp. Endowment Res. Trust, 1996–2000. Pres., BMA, 1997–98. Hon. FRCS 1995; Hon. FRCPI 1995; Hon. FRCPath 1996; Hon. FRCSE 1996; Hon. FRCPE 1996. Dr *hc* Edinburgh, 1987; Hon. LLD: Dundee, 1992; Sheffield, 1995; Hon. DSc: Hull, 1994; Leicester, 1994. *Publications:* articles in med. and sci. jls. *Recreation:* golf. *Address:* 12 Wester Coates Gardens, Edinburgh EH12 5LT. *Clubs:* New (Edinburgh); Royal and Ancient (St Andrews).

KILPATRICK, Francesca; *see* Greenoak, F.

KILPATRICK, Prof. (George) Stewart, OBE 1986; MD; FRCP, FRCPE; retired; David Davies Chair of Tuberculosis and Chest Diseases and Head of Department, 1968–92, Vice-Provost, 1987–90, University of Wales College of Medicine, Cardiff; Senior Hon. Consultant Physician to South Glamorgan Health Authority, 1963–90; *b* 26 June 1925; *s* of Hugh Kilpatrick and Annie Merricks Johnstone Stewart; *m* 1954, Joan Askew. *Educ:* George Watson's Coll., Edinburgh; Edinburgh Univ. Med. Sch. (MB ChB 1947, MD 1954). MRCPE 1952, FRCPE 1966; MRCP 1971, FRCP 1975. Medical posts in Edinburgh; Captain RAMC, 1949–51; Mem., Scientific Staff, MRC Pneumoconiosis Research Unit, 1952–54; med. and res. posts, London, Edinburgh and Cardiff; Dean of Clin. Studies, Univ. of Wales Coll. of Medicine, 1970–87. Formerly Chm., Sci. Cttees, Internat. Union Against Tuberculosis (formerly Chm., Treatment Cttee); Chm. Council, Assoc. for Study of Med. Educn, 1981–86; Chm., Assoc. of Medical Deans in Europe, 1982–85. Ext. Examr in Medicine, Queen's Univ. Belfast, 1986–88. Marc Daniels Lectr, RCP 1987. Pres., Cardiff Medical Soc., 1990–91. FRSocMed. Silver Jubilee Medal, 1977. *Publications:* numerous papers to med. and sci. jls; chapters in books on chest diseases, tuberculosis, heart disease, anaemia and med. educn. *Recreations:* travel, reading, photography. *Address:* Millfield, 14 Millbrook Road, Dinas Powys, Vale of Glamorgan CF64 4DA. *T:* (029) 2051 3149.

KILPATRICK, Dame Judith (Ann Gladys), DBE 2000; Headteacher, City of Portsmouth Girls' School, since 1995; *b* 20 Feb. 1952; *d* of James Foxley and late Kathleen Alice Foxley (*née* Kingdon); *m* 1994, Andrew Kelvin Kilpatrick (marr. diss. 1998). *Educ:* Cowley Grammar Sch. for Girls, St Helens; Univ. of Kent (BA Hons); Univ. of Southampton (PGCE). Teacher of History and English and Integrative Studies, 1974–85, Hd of Careers, 1985–86, Regents Park Girls' Sch., Southampton; Schools/Industry Liaison Officer, SE Hants, 1987–89; Dep. Headteacher, King Richard Sch., Portsmouth, 1989–93; Headteacher, The Wavell Sch., Farnborough, 1993–95. *Recreations:* opera, classical music, theatre, reading, travel. *Address:* 2 Rushmere Gate, Green Lane, Hambledon, Hants PO7 4SS. *T:* (023) 9263 2079.

KILPATRICK, Stewart; *see* Kilpatrick, G. S.

KILROY-SILK, Robert; Television Presenter, Kilroy, BBC, since 1987 (Day to Day, 1986–87); Chairman, The Kilroy Television Co., since 1989; *b* 19 May 1942; *s* of William Silk (RN, killed in action, 1943) and Rose O'Rooke; *m* 1963, Jan Beech; one *s* one *d*. *Educ:* Saltley Grammar Sch., Birmingham; LSE (BScEcon). Lectr, Dept of Political Theory and Institutions, Liverpool Univ., 1966–74. Contested (Lab) Ormskirk, 1970. MP (Lab): Ormskirk, Feb. 1974–1983; Knowsley N, 1983–86; PPS to Minister for the Arts, 1974–75; opposition frontbench spokesman on Home Office, 1984–85. Vice-Chairman: Merseyside Gp of MPs, 1974–75; PLP Home Affairs Gp, 1976–86; Chairman: Parly All-Party Penal Affairs Gp, 1979–86; PLP Civil Liberties Gp, 1979–84; Parly Alcohol Policy and Services Group, 1982–83; Mem., Home Affairs Select Cttee, 1979–84. Member: Council, Howard League for Penal Reform, 1979–; Adv. Council, Inst. of Criminology, Cambridge Univ., 1984–; Sponsor, Radical Alternatives to Prison, 1977–; Patron, APEX Trust; Chm., FARE, 1981–84. Governor, National Heart and Chest Hospital, 1974–77. Political columnist: Time Out, 1985–86; Police Review, 1983–; columnist: The Times, 1987–90; Today, 1988–90; Daily Express, 1990–96. TV presenter, Shafted, 2001. *Publications:* Socialism since Marx, 1972; (contrib.) The Role of Commissions in Policy Making, 1973; The Ceremony of Innocence: a novel of 1984, 1984; Hard Labour: the political diary of Robert Kilroy-Silk, 1986; articles in Political Studies, Manchester School of Economic and Social Science, Political Quarterly, Industrial and Labor Relations Review, Parliamentary Affairs, etc. *Recreation:* gardening. *Address:* The Kilroy Programme, BBC Elstree Centre, Hart House, Clarendon Road, Borehamwood, Herts WD6 1JT. *T:* (020) 8228 7465, *Fax:* (020) 8381 5786.

KILVINGTON, Frank Ian; Headmaster of St Albans School, 1964–84; *b* West Hartlepool, 26 June 1924; *e s* of H. H. Kilvington; *m* 1949, Jane Mary, *d* of late Very Rev. Michael Clarke and of Katharine Beryl (*née* Girling); one *s* one *d*. *Educ:* Repton (entrance and foundn scholar); Corpus Christi, Oxford (open class. scholar). 2nd cl. Lit Hum, 1948; MA 1950. Served War of 1939–45: RNVR, 1943–46 (Lt); West Africa Station, 1943–45; RN Intelligence, Germany, 1945–46. Westminster School: Asst Master, 1949–64; Housemaster of Rigaud's House, 1957–64. Chairman: St Albans Marriage Guidance Council, 1968–74; St Albans CAB, 1981–86; Herts Record Soc., 1985–90; St Albans Hospice Care Team, 1988–93. Pres., St Albans and Herts Architectural and Archæological

Soc., 1974–77. *Publication:* A Short History of St Albans School, 1970. *Recreations:* music, local history. *Address:* 122 Marshalswick Lane, St Albans, Herts AL1 4XD.

KILWARLIN, Viscount; Edmund Robin Arthur Hill; *b* 21 May 1996; *s* and *heir* of Earl of Hillsborough, *qv.*

KIM DAE-JUNG; President of Republic of Korea, since 1998; *b* 3 Dec. 1925; *m* Lee Lee Ho. *Educ:* Mokpo Commercial High Sch.; Korea Univ.; Kyung-hee Univ.; Diplomatic Acad. of Foreign Ministry, Russia. Pres., Mokpo Merchant Shipping Co., 1948; arrested by N Korean Communists, escaped from jail, 1950; Pres., Mokpo Daily News, 1950; Dep. Comdr, S Cholla Region, Maritime Defence Force, 1950; Pres., Heungkuk Merchant Shipping Co., 1951; Pres., Dae-yang Shipbldg Co., 1951. Mem., Nat. Assembly of Republic of Korea (S Korea), 1961–72, 1988–97; held posts with Democratic Party, People's Party and New Democratic Party; periods of house-arrest, imprisonment and exile; returned from exile in USA to co-lead New Korea Democratic Party, 1985; Pres., Peace and Democracy Party, 1987; Pres., New Democratic Party, later Democratic Party, 1991; Founder, Nat. Congress for New Politics, 1995, which formed alliance with United Liberal Democrats, 1997. Founder and Chm., Kim Dae-Jung Peace Foundn for Asia-Pacific Region, 1994. Nobel Peace Prize, 2000. *Publications include:* Conscience in Action, 1985; Prison Writings, 1987; Building Peace and Democracy, 1987; Kim Dae- Jung's Views on International Affairs, 1990; In the Name of Justice and Peace, 1991; Korea and Asia, 1994; The Korean Problem: nuclear crisis, democracy and reunification, 1994; Unification, Democracy and Peace, 1994; Mass Participatory Economy: Korea's road to world economic power, 1996. *Address:* (office) Chong Wa Dae, 1 Sejong-no, Chongno-ku, Seoul, Republic of Korea.

KIM, Young Sam; President, Republic of Korea, 1993–98; *b* 20 Dec. 1927; *m* 1951, Sohn Myoung Soon; two *s* three *d.* *Educ:* Coll. of Liberal Arts and Science, Seoul Nat. Univ. (BA). Mem., Nat. Assembly, 1954–93; Member: Liberal Party, 1954–60; Democratic Party, 1960–63; Civil Rule Party, 1963–65; Minjung Party, 1965–67 (also spokesman and floor leader); New Democratic Party, 1967–86 (floor leader, 1967–71, Pres., 1974–76 and 1979); Advr to New Korea Democratic Party, 1986–87; Pres., Reunification Democratic Party, 1987–90; Exec. Chm., 1990–92, Pres., 1992–96, Democratic Liberal Party; Pres., New Korea Party, 1996–97. Candidate for Pres., Republic of Korea, 1987. Chm., Council for the Promotion of Democracy, 1984–86. Averell Harriman Democracy Award, Nat. Democratic Inst. for Internat. Affairs, USA, 1993; Global Leadership Award, UNA, USA, 1995. Grand Order of Mugunghwa (Republic of Korea). *Publications:* We Can Depend on No One but Ourselves, 1964; Why our Country needs Standard-Bearers who are in their 40s, 1971; Government Power is Short, Politics is Long; Hoisting the Flag of Democracy; The True Reality of My Fatherland, 1984; My Resolution, 1987; Democratization, the Way of Salvation of My Country, 1987; Society which wins Honesty and Truth, 1987; New Korea 2000, 1992. *Address:* 7–6 Sangdo 1-dong, Dongjak-ku, Seoul, Korea 156–031.

KIMBALL, family name of **Baron Kimball**.

KIMBALL, Baron *cr* 1985 (Life Peer), of Easton in the County of Leicestershire; **Marcus Richard Kimball,** Kt 1981; DL; *b* 18 Oct. 1928; *s* of late Major Lawrence Kimball; *m* 1956, June Mary Fenwick; two *d.* *Educ:* Eton; Trinity Coll., Cambridge. Dir, Royal Trust Co. of Canada, subseq. Royal Trust Bank, 1970–94. External Mem. Council, Lloyd's, 1982–90. Contested (C) Derby South, 1955; MP (C) Lincs, Gainsborough, Feb. 1956–1983. Privy Council Rep., Council of RCVS, 1969–82, Hon. ARCVS 1982. Jt Master and Huntsman: Fitzwilliam Hounds, 1950–51 and 1951–52; Cottesmore Hounds, 1952–53, 1953–54, 1955–56 (Jt Master, 1956–58). Chm., 1966–82, Pres., 1995–98, British Field Sports Soc.; Dep. Pres., Countryside Alliance, 1999–. Chairman: River Naver Fishing Bd, 1964–92; Firearms Consultative Cttee, 1989–94; British Greyhound Racing Fund, 1993–96. President: Hunters Improvement Soc., 1990; Olympia Internat. Showjumping, 1991–99; British Inst. of Innkeeping, 1992–; Chm., Cambridge Univ. Vet. Sch. Trust, 1989–. Lt Leics Yeo. (TA), 1947; Capt., 1951. Mem. Rutland CC, 1955. DL Leics, 1984. *Address:* Great Easton Manor, Market Harborough, Leics LE16 8TB. *T:* (01536) 770333. *Clubs:* White's, Pratt's.

KIMBER, Sir Charles Dixon, 3rd Bt *cr* 1904; *b* 7 Jan. 1912; *o* surv. *s* of Sir Henry Dixon Kimber, 2nd Bt, and Lucy Ellen, *y d* of late G. W. Crookes; *S* father, 1950; *m* 1st, 1933, Ursula (marr. diss. 1949; she *d* 1981), *er d* of late Ernest Roy Bird, MP; three *s*; 2nd, 1950, Margaret Bonham (marr. diss. 1965), writer; one *d* (one *s* decd). *Educ:* Eton; Balliol Coll., Oxford (BA). Co Founder and Gen. Sec., Federal Union, 1938–41; Market Gardener, 1941–47; Diploma in Social Anthropology, 1948; collaborated in survey of Banbury, 1949–52; small holder, 1952–60; Landlord, Three Pigeons, Drayton St Leonard, 1962–65; apptd to undertake review of Parish Charities in Oxfordshire for Oxfordshire CC, 1967–77. *Heir: s* Timothy Roy Henry Kimber [*b* 3 June 1936; *m* 1960, Antonia Kathleen Brenda (marr. diss. 1974), *d* of Sir Francis Williams, 8th Bt; two *s*; *m* 1979, Susan, *widow* of Richard North, Newton Hall, near Carnforth]. *Address:* Lower End Farm, Great Comberton, Pershore, Worcs WR10 3DU. *T:* (01386) 710230.

KIMBER, Herbert Frederick Sidney; Director, Southern Newspapers Ltd, 1975–82 (Chief Executive, 1980–81); *b* 3 April 1917; *s* of H. G. Kimber; *m* Patricia Boulton (*née* Forfar); one *s.* *Educ:* elementary sch., Southampton. Southern Newspapers Ltd, office boy, 1931. Served War, Royal Navy, 1939–46: commissioned Lieut RNVR, 1941. Manager, Dorset Evening Echo, 1960; Advertisement Manager-in-Chief, Southern Newspapers Ltd, 1961; then Dep. Gen. and Advertisement Manager, 1972; Gen. Manager, 1974. Chairman: Bird Bros, Basingstoke, 1976–81; W. H. Hallett, 1981–82; Southtel, 1981–82. Dir, Regl Newspaper Advertising Bureau, 1980–81. Member: Press Council, 1977–81; Council, Newspaper Soc., 1974–81 (Mem., Industrial Relations Cttee, 1975–81). *Recreations:* reading, travel, gardening under protest. *Address:* 3 Allée de Ste Hélène, Rés. St Gildas, Auray 56400, France.

KIMBERLEY, 4th Earl of, *cr* 1866; **John Wodehouse;** Bt, 1611; Baron Wodehouse, 1797; Lt Grenadier Guards; *b* 12 May 1924; *o s* of 3rd Earl and Margaret (*d* 1950), *d* of late Col Leonard Howard Irby; *S* father, 1941; *m* 1st, 1945; 2nd, 1949; one *s*; 3rd, 1953; two *s*; 4th, 1961; one *s*; 5th, 1970; 6th, 1982, Sarah Jane Hope Consett, *e d* of Colonel Christopher D'Arcy Preston Consett, DSO, MC. *Educ:* Eton; Cambridge. Lieut, Grenadier Guards, 1942–45; Active Service NW Europe. Member: House of Lords All Party Defence Study Gp, 1976–99 (Sec., 1978–92; Pres., 1992–99); House of Lords All Party UFO Study Gp, 1979–99; former Liberal Spokesman on: aviation and aerospace; defence; voluntary community services; left Liberal Party, May 1979, joined Cons. Party. Chm., Foreign Affairs Cttee, Monday Club, 1979–82; Mem. Exec. Cttee, Assoc. of Cons. Peers, 1981–84; Pres., Cricklade and Latton Cons. Assoc., 1988– (Chm., 1986–88). Member: Council, The Air League; Council, British Maritime League; RUSI; IISS; British Atlantic Cttee. Delegate to N Atlantic Assembly, 1981–93. Vice-Pres., World Council on Alcoholism; Chm., Nat. Council on Alcoholism, 1982–85. Mem., British Bobsleigh Team, 1949–58. ARAeS 1977. *Recreations:* shooting, fishing, all field sports, gardening, bridge. *Heir: s* Lord Wodehouse, *qv.* *Address:* Hailstone House, Cricklade, Swindon, Wilts SN6 6JP. *T:* (01793) 750344. *Clubs:* White's, Naval and Military, MCC; House of Lords' Yacht; Falmouth Shark Angling (Pres.).

KIMBLE, Dr David (Bryant), OBE 1962; Editor, Journal of Modern African Studies, 1972–97; *b* 12 May 1921; *s* of John H. and Minnie Jane Kimble; *m* 1st, 1949, Helen Rankin (marr. diss.); three *d* (and one *d* decd); 2nd, 1977, Margareta Westin. *Educ:* Eastbourne Grammar Sch.; Reading Univ. (BA 1942, DipEd 1943, Pres. Students Union, 1942–43); London Univ. (PhD 1961). Lieut RNVR, 1943–46. Oxford Univ. Staff Tutor in Berks, 1946–48, and Resident Tutor in the Gold Coast, 1948–49; Dir, Inst. of Extra-Mural Studies, Univ. of Ghana, 1949–62, and Master of Akuafo Hall, 1960–62; Prof. of Political Science, Univ. Coll., Dar es Salaam, Univ. of E Africa, and Dir, Inst. of Public Admin, Tanzania, 1962–68; Research Advr in Public Admin and Social Sciences, Centre africain de formation et de recherche administratives pour le développement, Tanger, Morocco, 1968–70, and Dir of Research, 1970–71; Prof. of Govt and Admin, Univ. of Botswana, Lesotho, and Swaziland, 1971–75, and Nat. Univ. of Lesotho, 1975–77, Prof. Emeritus, 1978; Tutor in Politics to King Moshoeshoe II, 1975, and Queen 'MaMohato, 1977; Vice-Chancellor, Univ. of Malaŵi, and Chm., Malaŵi Certificate Exam. and Testing Bd, 1977–86. Founder and Joint Editor (with Helen Kimble), West African Affairs, 1949–51, Penguin African Series, 1953–61, and Jl of Modern African Studies, 1963–71; Officier, Ordre des Palmes Académiques, 1982. *Publications:* The Machinery of Self-Government, 1953; (with Helen Kimble) Adult Education in a Changing Africa, 1955; A Political History of Ghana, Vol. I, The Rise of Nationalism in the Gold Coast, 1850–1928, 1963; nine University Congregation Addresses, 1978–86; (with Margareta Kimble) Jl of Modern African Studies: indexed bibliography of contents 1963–97, vols 1–35, 1999. *Recreations:* cricket, photography, editing. *Address:* Huish, Chagford, Devon TQ13 8AR.

See also G. H. T. Kimble.

KIMBLE, George (Herbert Tinley), PhD; retired; *b* 2 Aug. 1908; *s* of John H. and Minnie Jane Kimble; *m* 1935, Dorothy Stevens Berry; one *s* one *d.* *Educ:* Eastbourne Grammar Sch.; King's Coll., London (MA); University of Montreal (PhD). Asst Lecturer in Geography, University of Hull, 1931–36; Lecturer in Geography, University of Reading, 1936–39. Served War as Lt and Lt-Comdr, British Naval Meteorological Service, 1939–44. Prof. of Geography and Chm. Dept of Geography, McGill Univ., 1945–50; Sec.-Treasurer, Internat. Geographical Union, 1949–56; Chm., Commn on Humid Tropics, Internat. Geog. Union, 1956–61. Dir, Amer. Geog. Soc., 1950–53; Dir, Survey of Tropical Africa, Twentieth Century Fund, NY, 1953–60. Chm., Dept of Geography, Indiana Univ., 1957–62; Prof. of Geography, Indiana Univ., 1957–66; Research Dir, US Geography Project, Twentieth Century Fund, 1962–68. Rushton Lecturer, 1952; Borah Lecturer, University of Idaho, 1956; Haynes Foundn Lectr, University of Redlands, 1966; Visiting Prof., University of Calif. (Berkeley), 1948–49; Stanford Univ., 1961; Stockholm Sch. of Economics, 1961. Governor, Eastbourne Sixth Form Coll., 1980–81. FRGS 1931. Hon. Mem., Inst. British Geographers. Editor, Weather Res. Bulletin, 1957–60. *Publications:* Geography in the Middle Ages, 1938; The World's Open Spaces, 1939; The Shepherd of Banbury, 1941; (with Raymond Bush) The Weather, 1943 (Eng.), 1946 (Amer.), (author) 2nd (Eng.) edn, 1951; Military Geography of Canada, 1949; (with Sir Dudley Stamp) An Introduction to Economic Geography, 1949; (with Sir Dudley Stamp) The World: a general geography, 1950; The Way of the World, 1953; Our American Weather, 1955; Le Temps, 1957; Tropical Africa (2 vols), 1960; Ghana, 1960; Tropical Africa (abridged edition), 1962; (with Ronald Steel) Tropical Africa Today, 1966; Hunters and Collectors, 1970; Man and his World, 1972; Herdsmen, 1973; From the Four Winds, 1974; This is our World, 1981; (ed for Hakluyt Soc.) Esmeraldo de Situ Orbis, 1937; (ed for American Geographical Soc. with Dorothy Good) Geography of the Northlands, 1955; articles in: Geog. Jl, Magazine, Review; Canadian Geog. Jl; Bulletin Amer. Meteorological Soc.; The Reporter; Los Angeles Times; The New York Times Magazine. *Recreations:* music, gardening. *Address:* 2 Dymock's Manor, East End Lane, Ditchling, E Sussex BN6 8SX.

See also Dr D. B. Kimble.

KIMMANCE, Peter Frederick, CB 1981; Chief Inspector of Audit, Department of the Environment, 1979–82; Member, Audit Commission for Local Authorities in England and Wales, 1983–87; *b* 14 Dec. 1922; *s* of Frederick Edward Kimmance, BEM, and Louisa Kimmance; *m* 1944, Helen Mary Mercer Cooke. *Educ:* Raines Foundation, Stepney; University of London. Post Office Engineering Dept, 1939; served Royal Signals, 1943; District Audit Service, 1949; District Auditor, 1973; Controller (Finance), British Council, 1973–75; Dep. Chief Inspector of Audit, DoE, 1978. Mem. Council, CIPFA, 1979–83; Hon. Mem., British Council, 1975. *Recreations:* sailing, books, music. *Address:* Herons, School Road, Saltwood, Hythe, Kent CT21 4PP. *T:* (01303) 267921. *Clubs:* Royal Over-Seas League; Medway Yacht (Lower Upnor).

KIMMINS, Simon Edward Anthony, VRD 1967; Lt-Comdr RNR; *b* 26 May 1930; *s* of late Captain Anthony Kimmins, OBE, RN, and Elizabeth Kimmins; *m* 1976, Jonkvrouwe Irma de Jonge; one *s* one *d.* *Educ:* Horris Hill; Charterhouse. Man. Dir, London American Finance Corpn Ltd (originally BOECC Ltd), 1957–73; Dir (non-exec.), Balfour Williamson, 1971–74; Chief Exec., Thomas Cook Gp, 1973–75; Director: Debenhams Ltd, 1972–85; TKM International Trade Finance, 1978–80; Delfinance SA Geneva, 1984–; Aurelian Futures Fund, 1985–87; Chm., Associated Retail Develt Internat. SA Geneva, 1980–85; Pres., Piquet Internat. SA Geneva, 1986–91. Vice-Pres., British Export Houses Assoc., 1974–80 (Chm., 1970–72). Governor, Royal Shakespeare Theatre, 1975–. *Recreations:* cricket (played for Kent), golf, shooting. *Address:* 37 Chemin de Grange Canal, Geneva 1208, Switzerland. *T:* (22) 7356657. *Clubs:* Garrick, MCC, The Pilgrims; Haagseclub.

KINAHAN, Maj.-Gen. Oliver John, CB 1981; Paymaster-in-Chief and Inspector of Army Pay Services, 1979–83; *b* 17 Nov. 1923; *m* 1950, Margery Ellis Fisher (*née* Hill); one *s* two *d.* Commissioned Royal Irish Fusiliers, 1942; served with Nigeria Regt, RWAFF, Sierra Leone, Nigeria, India, Burma, 1943–46; Instr, Sch. of Signals, 1947–49, Sch. of Infantry, 1950–51; transf. to RAPC, 1951; Japan and Korea, 1952–53; psc 1957; Comdt, RAPC Trng Centre, 1974–75; Chief Paymaster, HQ UKLF, 1975–76; Dep. Paymaster-in-Chief (Army), 1977–78. Col Comdt RAPC, 1984–87. FIMgt. *Recreations:* country pursuits. *Address:* c/o Drummonds Branch, Royal Bank of Scotland, 49 Charing Cross, SW1A 2DX.

KINCADE, James, CBE 1988; MA, PhD; Headmaster, Methodist College, Belfast, 1974–88; *b* 4 Jan. 1925; *s* of George and Rebecca Jane Kincade; *m* 1952, Elizabeth Fay, 2nd *d* of J. Anderson Piggot, OBE, DL, JP; one *s* one *d.* *Educ:* Foyle Coll.; Magee University Coll.; Trinity Coll. Dublin (Schol. and Gold Medallist, MA, Stein Research Prize); Oriel Coll., Oxford (MA, BLitt); Edinburgh Univ. (PhD). Served RAF, India and Burma, 1943–47 (commnd, 1944). Senior English Master, Merchiston Castle Sch., 1952–61; Vis. Professor of Philosophy, Indiana Univ., 1959; Headmaster, Royal Sch., Dungannon, 1961–74. Dir, Design Council, NI, 1990–93; Mem., Design Council, UK, 1993–94 (Chm., NI Cttee, 1993–94); Chairman: Fashion Business Centre, NI, 1992–94;

NI Fashion & Design Centre, 1992–94. Nat. Gov. for NI, BBC, 1985–91. President, Ulster Headmasters' Assoc., 1975–77; Vice Pres., Assoc. for Art and Design Educn, 1991–; Mem., Council for Catholic Maintained Schools, 1987–90. Mem. of Senate, and Mem. Standing Cttee, QUB, 1982–98. Trustee, Save the Homeless Fund, 1990–. *Publications:* articles in Mind, Hermathena, Jl of Religion. *Recreations:* reading, writing and arithmetic. *Address:* 10A Harry's Road, Hillsborough BT26 6HJ. *T:* (028) 9268 3865.

KINCH, Christopher Anthony; QC 1999; a Recorder, since 1998; *b* 27 May 1953; *s* of late Anthony Alec Kinch, CBE and Barbara Patricia Kinch; *m* 1994, Carol Atkinson; one *s* one *d*. *Educ:* Bishop Challoner Sch., Shortlands, Bromley; Christ Church, Oxford (MA Modern Hist.). Called to the Bar, Lincoln's Inn, 1976; Stagiaire, EC Commn, 1976–77; in practice at the Bar, 1977–; Asst Recorder, 1994–98. Mem., SE Circuit Cttee, 1992–95 and 1996–99. *Recreations:* travel, wine, cricket, Rugby. *Address:* 23 Essex Street, WC2R 3AS. *T:* (020) 7413 0353; *e-mail:* christopherkinch@23essexstreet.co.uk. *Club:* Beckenham Rugby Football.

KINCHEN, Richard, MVO 1976; HM Diplomatic Service; Ambassador to Lebanon, since 2000; *b* 12 Feb. 1948; *s* of Victor and Margaret Kinchen; *m* 1972, Cheryl Vivienne Abayasekera; one *s* two *d* (and one *d* decd). *Educ:* King Edward VI Sch., Southampton; Trinity Hall, Cambridge (BA). Entered FCO, 1970; attached British Commn on Rhodesian Opinion, 1972; MECAS, 1972; Kuwait, 1973; FCO, 1974; Luxembourg, 1975; Paris, 1977; FCO, 1980; Pvte Sec. to Parly Under-Sec. of State, 1982; Rabat, 1984; Counsellor, UK Mission to UN, 1988–93; Head: Regl Secretariat for British Dependent Territories in Caribbean, 1993–96; Resource Planning Dept, FCO, 1997–2000. Member: UN Adv. Cttee on Admin. and Budgetary Questions, 1991–93; UN Jt Staff Pension Bd, 1992–93. *Address:* c/o Foreign and Commonwealth Office, SW1A 2AH. *T:* (020) 7270 2131.

KINCHIN SMITH, Michael, OBE 1987; Chairman, Banburyshire Community Transport Association Ltd, 1993–98; *b* 8 May 1921; *s* of Francis John Kinchin Smith, Lectr in Classics, Inst. of Educn, London, and Dione Jean Elizabeth, *d* of Sir Francis Henry May, GCMG, sometime Governor of Hong Kong; *m* 1947, Rachel Frances, *er d* of Rt Hon. Sir Henry Urmston Willink, Bt, MC, QC, Master of Magdalene Coll., Cambridge; four *s* two *d*. *Educ:* Westminster Sch. (King's Schol.); Christ Church, Oxford (Schol.). 1st cl. hons Mod. History; Pres. Oxford Union, 1941. Served with 2nd and 3rd Bns, Coldstream Guards in Italian Campaign (Captain; despatches). Commercial and Admin. Trainee, ICI Ltd, 1947; admin. posts with BBC, 1950–78: Asst, Staff Admin, 1950; Admin Officer, Talks (Sound), 1954; Asst Estabt Officer, TV, 1955; Estabt Officer, Programmes, TV, 1961; Staff Admin Officer, 1962; Asst Controller, Staff Admin, 1964; Controller, Staff Admin, 1967; Controller, Development, Personnel, 1976. Lay Assistant to Archbishop of Canterbury, 1979–84; Appointments' Sec. to Archbishops of Canterbury and York, and Sec., Crown Appts Commn, 1984–87. Chm. Exec. Council, RIPA, 1975–77; CIPD; Vice Pres. (Pay and Employment Conditions), IPM, 1978–80; Lay Selector, ACCM, 1963–73 (Mem. Candidates Cttee, 1966–69); Lay Chm., Richmond and Barnes Deanery Synod, 1970–76; Mem. General Synod, C of E, 1975–78. Chm., Diocesan Trustees (Oxford) Ltd, 1991–98. 1st Chm., Mortlake with East Sheen Soc., 1969–71; Chm., Assoc. of Amenity Societies in Richmond-upon-Thames, 1973–77. *Publication:* (jtly) Forward from Victory, 1943. *Recreations:* walking, local history. *Address:* Pitts Orchard, Cumberford, Bloxham, Banbury, Oxon OX15 4QG. *Club:* Oxford and Cambridge.

KINCRAIG, Hon. Lord; Robert Smith Johnston; a Senator of the College of Justice in Scotland, 1972–87; Chairman, Review of Parole and related matters in Scotland, since 1988; *b* 10 Oct. 1918; *s* of W. T. Johnston, iron merchant, Glasgow; *m* 1943, Joan (decd), *d* of late Col A. G. Graham, Glasgow; one *s* one *d*. *Educ:* Strathallan, Perthshire; St John's Coll., Cambridge; Glasgow Univ. BA (Hons) Cantab, 1939; LLB (with distinction) Glasgow, 1942. Mem. of Faculty of Advocates, 1942; Advocate-Depute, Crown Office, 1953–55; QC (Scotland) 1955; Home Advocate Depute, 1959–62; Sheriff Principal of Roxburgh, Berwick and Selkirk, 1964–70; Dean of the Faculty of Advocates of Scotland, 1970–72. Contested (U) Stirling and Falkirk Burghs General Election, 1959. *Recreations:* gardening, golf. *Address:* Westwood Cottage, Longniddry, East Lothian EH32 0PL. *T:* (01875) 853583. *Club:* Hon. Company of Edinburgh Golfers (Edinburgh).
See also A. G. Johnston.

KINDER, Eric; Chairman: Smith & Nephew, 1990–97; Brunner Mond plc, 1992–98; *b* 26 Dec. 1927; *s* of William and Amy Kinder; *m* 1954, Isobel Margaret Barnes; one *s* one *d*. *Educ:* Ashton-under-Lyne and Accrington Grammar Schs. ATI. Joined Textile Div., Smith & Nephew plc, 1957: Divisional Man. Dir, 1969–72; Dir, 1972–97; Chief Exec., 1982–90. Chm., Merchant Retail plc, 1991–94; non-exec. Dir, Intermediate Capital Group plc, 1994–98. Non-exec. Dir, Christie Hosp. NHS Trust, Manchester, 1994–97. *Recreations:* tennis, angling, golf, music. *Address:* Brunner Mond plc, PO Box 4, Northwich, Cheshire CW8 4DT.

KINDERSLEY, family name of **Baron Kindersley**.

KINDERSLEY, 3rd Baron *cr* 1941; **Robert Hugh Molesworth Kindersley;** DL; Chairman, Commonwealth Development Corporation, 1980–89; a Vice-Chairman, Lazard Brothers & Co. Ltd, 1981–85 (Director, 1960–90); *b* 18 Aug. 1929; *s* of 2nd Baron Kindersley, CBE, MC, and Nancy Farnsworth (*d* 1977), *d* of Dr Geoffrey Boyd, Toronto; *S* father, 1976; *m* 1st, 1954, Venice Marigold (Rosie) (marr. diss. 1989), *d* of late Captain Lord (Arthur) Francis Henry Hill; two *s* one *d* (and one *s* decd); 2nd, 1989, Patricia Margaret Crichton-Stuart, *d* of late Hugh Norman. *Educ:* Eton; Trinity Coll., Oxford; Harvard Business Sch., USA. Lt Scots Guards; served Malaya, 1948–49. Chairman: Siam Selective Growth Fund, 1990–2000; Brent Walker Gp, 1991–92; Director: London Assurance, 1957–96; Witan Investment Co. Ltd, 1958–85; Steel Company of Wales, 1959–67; Marconi Co. Ltd, 1963–68; Sun Alliance & London Insurance Gp, 1965–96; English Electric Co. Ltd, 1966–68; Gen. Electric Co. Ltd, 1968–70; British Match Corp. Ltd, 1969–73; Swedish Match Co., 1973–85; Maersk Co. Ltd, 1986–2001; Maersk India, 1988–2001. Financial Adviser to Export Gp for the Constructional Industries, 1961–86; Mem., Adv. Panel, Overseas Projects Gp, 1975–77; Dep. Chm., ECGD Adv. Council, 1975–80; Chm., Exec. Cttee, BBA, 1976–78; Pres., Anglo-Taiwan Trade Cttee, 1976–86. Hon. Treasurer, YWCA, 1965–76. Mem., Institut International d'Etudes Bancaires, 1971–85. Chm., Smith's Charity, 1990–97. Mem. Ct, Fishmongers' Co., 1973–, Prime Warden, 1989–90. DL Kent, 1986. *Recreations:* all country pursuits, including tennis and ski-ing. *Heir:* *s* Hon. Rupert John Molesworth Kindersley [*b* 11 March 1955; *m* 1975, Sarah, *d* of late John D. Warde; one *s* one *d*]. *Address:* West Green Farm, Shipbourne, Kent TN11 9PU. *T:* (01732) 810293. *Clubs:* Pratt's, MCC, All England Lawn Tennis and Croquet, Queen's.

KINDERSLEY, Lydia Helena L. P.; *see* Lopes Cardozo Kindersley.

KINDERSLEY, Peter David; Chairman, Dorling Kindersley, publishers, 1974–2000; *b* 13 July 1941; *s* of late David Kindersley, MBE and of Christine Kindersley; *m* 1965, Juliet Elizabeth Martyn; one *s* one *d*. *Educ:* King Edward VI School, Norwich; Camberwell School of Arts and Crafts. Founding Art Director, Mitchell Beazley, 1969–74. *Recreations:* art, science, biodiversity, work AND WORK.

KING, family name of **Barons King of Bridgwater, King of Wartnaby** and **Earl of Lovelace**.

KING OF BRIDGWATER, Baron *cr* 2001 (Life Peer), of Bridgwater in the County of Somerset; **Thomas Jeremy King,** CH 1992; PC 1979; *b* 13 June 1933; *s* of late J. H. King, JP; *m* 1960, Jane, *d* of late Brig. Robert Tilney, CBE, DSO, TD; one *s* one *d*. *Educ:* Rugby; Emmanuel Coll., Cambridge (MA). National service, 1951–53: commnd Somerset Light Inf., 1952; seconded to KAR; served Tanganyika and Kenya; Actg Captain 1953. Cambridge, 1953–56. Joined E.S. & A. Robinson Ltd, Bristol, 1956; various positions up to Divisional Gen. Man., 1964–69; Chairman: Sale, Tilney Co Ltd, 1971–79 (Dir 1965–79); London Internat. Exhibition Centre Ltd; Dir, Electra Investment Trust. MP (C) Bridgwater, March 1970–2001. PPS to: Minister for Posts and Telecommunications, 1970–72; Minister for Industrial Develt, 1972–74; Front Bench spokesman for: Industry, 1975–76; Energy, 1976–79; Minister for Local Govt and Environmental Services, DoE, 1979–83; Sec. of State for the Environment, Jan.-June 1983, for Transport, June-Oct. 1983, for Employment, 1983–85, for NI, 1985–89, for Defence, 1989–92. Chm., Parly Intelligence and Security Cttee, 1994–2001; Mem., Cttee on Standards in Public Life, 1994–97. *Recreations:* cricket, ski-ing. *Address:* House of Lords, SW1A 0PW.
See also S. R. Clarke.

KING OF WARTNABY, Baron *cr* 1983 (Life Peer), of Wartnaby in the County of Leicestershire; **John Leonard King,** Kt 1979; President Emeritus, British Airways Plc, since 1997 (Chairman, 1981–93; President, 1993–97); President, Babcock International Group plc, since 1994 (Chairman, 1970–94); *yr s* of Albert John King and Kathleen King; *m* 1st 1941, Lorna Kathleen Sykes (*d* 1969); three *s* one *d*; 2nd, 1970, Hon. Isabel Monckton, *y d* of 8th Viscount Galway. Founded Ferrybridge Industries Ltd and Whitehouse Industries Ltd, subseq. Pollard Ball & Roller Bearing Co. Ltd, 1945 (Man. Dir 1945, Chm., 1961–69); Chairman: Dennis Motor Hldgs Ltd, 1970–72; Babcock & Wilcox Ltd, subseq. Babcock International plc, later FKI Babcock plc, then Babcock Internat. Gp, 1970–94; Dir, David Brown Corp. Ltd, 1971–75. Current chairmanships and directorships include: The Daily Telegraph plc; Short Brothers plc; Norman Broadbent International; Wide Range Engineering Services Ltd; The Spectator (1828), 1993–; Gartland Whalley Barker Plc, 1997–; former directorships include: Dick Corp. (USA); Royal Ordnance plc (Dep. Chm.); Clogau Gold Mines; National Nuclear Corp.; British Nuclear Associates Ltd; Tyneham Investments; Babcock (Plant Leasing); 1928 Investment Trust; SKF (UK); Sabena World Airlines; First Union Corp. (USA). Member: Engineering Industries Council, 1975; NEDC Cttee on Finance for Investment, 1976–78; Grand Council and Financial Policy Cttee, CBI, 1976–78; Chairman: City and Industrial Liaison Council, 1973–85; Review Bd for Govt Contracts, 1975–78; British Olympic Appeals Cttee, 1975–78; Macmillan Appeal for Continuing Care, 1977–78; NEB, 1980–81 (Dep. Chm., 1979–80); Alexandra Rose Day Foundn, 1980–85; Mem. Cttee, Ranfurly Library Service; Vice-Pres., Cancer Relief Macmillan Fund (formerly Nat. Soc. for Cancer Relief), 1988; Trustee, Liver Res. Unit Trust, 1988–. Dir, Royal Opera Trust. MFH: Badsworth Foxhounds, 1949–58; Duke of Rutland's Foxhounds (Belvoir), 1958–72; Chm., Belvoir Hunt, 1972. Farms his estate in Leics. Freeman, City of London, 1984. FIMgt (FBIM 1978); FCIT 1982. Hon. CRAeS, 1986. Hon. Dr Gardner-Webb Coll., USA, 1980; Hon. DSc Cranfield Inst. of Technology, 1989. Comdr, Royal Order of Polar Star (Sweden), 1983. Nat. Free Enterprise Award, 1987. *Recreations:* hunting, field sports, racing, painting. *Address:* Berkeley Square House, Berkeley Square, W1X 6BA. *T:* (020) 7930 4915. *Clubs:* White's, Pratts'; Brook (New York).
See also M. Marckus.

KING OF WEST BROMWICH, Baron *cr* 1999 (Life Peer), of West Bromwich in the county of West Midlands; **Tarsem King;** JP; Managing Director, Sandwell Polybags Ltd, since 1990; *b* Kultham, Punjab, 24 April 1937; *s* of Ujagar Singh and Dalip Kaur; *m* 1957, Mohinder Kaur; one *s*. *Educ:* Punjab Univ. (BA); Nat. Foundry Coll., Wolverhampton (Dip. Foundry Technol. and Mgt); Aston Univ. (Dip. Mgt Studies); Teacher Trng Coll., Wolverhampton (CertEd); Essex Univ. (MSc Stats and Operational Res.). Lab. Asst, 1960–62; Foundry Trainee, 1964–65; Teacher, Churchfield Sch., W Bromwich, 1968–74; Dep. Hd, Maths Dept, Great Barr Sch., Birmingham, 1974–90. Formerly non-exec. Dir, Sandwell TEC; non-exec. Dir, Sandwell HA, 1990–. Member: (Lab) Sandwell MDC, 1979– (Leader, 1997–); Sandwell CHC, 1982–83; Sandwell DHA, 1983–89. JP West Bromwich, 1987. *Recreations:* reading, music. *Address:* (office) Unit 3, Thomas Street, West Bromwich B70 6LY; 27 Roebuck Lane, West Bromwich B70 6QP.

KING, Alexander, CMG 1975; CBE 1948; Co-Founder, 1968, and Hon. President, Club of Rome (President, 1984–91); *b* Glasgow, 26 Jan. 1909; *s* of J. M. King; *m* 1933, Sarah Maskell Thompson (*d* 1999); three *d*. *Educ:* Highgate Sch.; Royal College of Science, London (DSc; FIC 1992); University of Munich. Demonstrator, 1932, and later Senior Lecturer, until 1940, in physical chemistry, Imperial Coll. of Science (FIC 1992); Dep. Scientific Adviser, Min. of Production, 1942; Head of UK Scientific Mission, Washington, and Scientific Attaché, British Embassy 1943–47; Head of Lord President's Scientific Secretariat, 1947–50; Chief Scientific Officer, Dept of Scientific and Industrial Research, 1950–56; Dep. Dir, European Productivity Agency, 1956–61; Dir for Scientific Affairs, OECD, 1961–68, Dir-Gen., 1968–74; Chm., Internat. Federation of Insts for Advanced Study, 1974–84. Adviser, Govt of Ontario. Assoc. Fellow, Center for the Study of Democratic Institutions, Santa Barbara, Calif; Vis. Professor: Brandeis Univ., 1978; Univ. of Montréal, 1979. Hon. Sec. Chemical Soc., 1948–50. Leader Imperial Coll. Expedition to Jan Mayen, 1938; Harrison Prize of Chemical Soc., 1938; Gill Memorial Prize, Royal Geographical Society, 1938 (Mem. Council, 1939–41); Erasmus Prize, 1987; Great Medal of Paris, 1988. DSc (*hc*): Ireland, 1974; Guelph, 1987; Bucharest, 1993; DUniv Open, 1976; Hon. LLD Strathclyde, 1982. US Medal of Freedom, 1946. *Publications:* The International Stimulus, 1974; The State of the Planet, 1980; The First Global Revolution, 1991; various chemistry textbooks, and papers in Journal of The Chemical Soc., Faraday Soc.; numerous articles on education, science policy and management. *Address:* 5 Chartwell House, 12 Ladbroke Terrace, W11 3PG; La Negronne, Callian, 83440 Fayence, France. *Club:* Athenæum.
See also C. S. Peckham.

KING, Andrew; MP (Lab) Rugby and Kenilworth, since 1997; *b* 14 Sept. 1948; *s* of late Charles King and Mary King; *m* 1975, Semma Ahmet; one *d*. *Educ:* St John the Baptist Sch., Uddingston; Coatbridge Tech. Coll.; Missionary Inst., London; Hatfield Poly.; Stevenage Coll. (CQSW); Nene Coll., Northants (CMS). Labourer; Postal Officer; apprentice motor vehicle mechanic; Social Work Manager, Northants CC, 1989–97. Member: Warwickshire CC, 1989–98 (Chm., Social Services, 1993–96); Rugby BC, 1995–98. Member: Social Security Select Cttee, 1999–2001; Deregulation Select Cttee, 1999–. Member: Unison (formerly NALGO), 1978–; Co-op. Party, 1995–. *Recreations:*

golf, dominoes. *Address:* House of Commons, SW1A 0AA. *Clubs:* Hillmorton Ex-Servicemen's; Bilton Social; Rugby Golf, Rugby Labour.

KING, Angela Audrey Mary; Founder Director and Joint Co-ordinator, Common Ground, since 1983; *b* 27 June 1944; *d* of Dr George John Graham King and Audrey Thora Dorothee King. *Educ:* Queensmount Sch.; St Christopher Sch., Letchworth; Millfield Sch., Som; Mayer Sch. of Fashion Design, NY. Fashion designer and buyer, NY, 1965–70; Friends of the Earth: wildlife campaigner, 1971–75; campaigned for ban on imports of leopard, cheetah and tiger skins, implemented 1972; (jtly) drafted Wild Creatures and Wild Plants Bill (enacted 1975), and Endangered Species (Import and Export) Act (enacted 1976); Initiator: Save the Whale Campaign, 1972 (campaigned for import ban on baleen whale products, introduced 1973, and Internat. Whaling Commn's 10 year ban on commercial whaling, introduced 1982); (jtly) Otter Project, 1976 (campaigned for ban on otter hunting in England and Wales, introduced 1978); Jt Co-ordinator, Otter Haven Project, 1977–80; Consultant, Earth Resources Res., 1979–80; author of NCC report on wildlife habitat loss, 1981; initiator with Sue Clifford of several projects, including: New Milestones, 1985; Trees, Woods and the Green Man, 1986; Parish Maps Project, 1987; Campaign for Local Distinctiveness, 1990; Confluence, 1998; Orgnr, exhibns which link the arts and the envmt. *Publications:* (ed jtly) Second Nature, 1984; (jtly) Holding Your Ground: an action guide to local conservation, 1987; (ed jtly) Trees Be Company (poetry anthology), 1989, rev. edn 2001; (jtly) The Apple Source Book, 1991; (ed jtly) Local Distinctiveness: place particularity and identity, 1993; (jtly) Celebrating Local Distinctiveness, 1994; (ed jtly) from place to PLACE: maps and Parish Maps, 1996; (ed jtly) Field Days: an anthology of poetry, 1998; (ed jtly) The River's Voice: an anthology of poetry, 2000; (ed jtly) The Common Ground Book of Orchards, 2000; conservation guides, and pamphlets, for Friends of the Earth, Common Ground, etc. *Recreations:* gardening, walking, watching wildlife, reading. *Address:* Common Ground, Gold Hill House, 21 High Street, Shaftesbury, Dorset SP7 8JE. *T:* (01747) 840820, *Fax:* (01747) 850821.

KING, Prof. Anthony Stephen; Professor of Government, University of Essex, since 1969; *b* 17 Nov. 1934; *o s* of late Harold and Marjorie King; *m* 1st, 1965, Vera Korte (*d* 1971); 2nd, 1980, Jan Reece. *Educ:* Queen's Univ., Kingston Ont. (1st Cl. Hons, Hist. 1956); Magdalen Coll., Oxford (Rhodes Schol.; 1st Cl. Hons, PPE, 1958). Student, Nuffield Coll., Oxford, 1958–61; DPhil (Oxon) 1962. Fellow of Magdalen Coll., Oxford, 1961–65; Sen. Lectr, 1966–68, Reader, 1968–69, Essex Univ. ACLS Fellow, Columbia Univ., NY, 1962–63; Fellow, Center for Advanced Study in the Behavioral Scis, Stanford, Calif., 1977–78; Visiting Professor: Wisconsin Univ., 1967; Princeton Univ., 1984. Elections Commentator: BBC; Daily Telegraph. Member: Cttee on Standards in Public Life, 1994–98; Royal Commn on H of L reform, 1999. Hon. Foreign Mem., Amer. Acad. of Arts and Scis, 1993–. *Publications:* (with D. E. Butler) The British General Election of 1964, 1965; (with D. E. Butler) The British General Election of 1966, 1966; (ed) British Politics: People, Parties and Parliament, 1966; (ed) The British Prime Minister, 1969, 2nd edn 1985; (with Anne Sloman) Westminster and Beyond, 1973; British Members of Parliament: a self-portrait, 1974; (ed) Why is Britain becoming Harder to Govern?, 1976; Britain Says Yes: the 1975 referendum on the Common Market, 1977; (ed) The New American Political System, 1978, 2nd edn 1990; (ed) Both Ends of the Avenue: the Presidency, the Executive Branch and Congress in the 1980s, 1983; (ed) Britain at the Polls 1992, 1992; (with Ivor Crewe) SDP: the birth, life and death of the British Social Democratic Party, 1995; Running Scared: why America's politicians campaign too much and govern too little, 1997; (ed) New Labour Triumphs: Britain at the polls, 1997; (ed) British Political Opinion 1937–2000: the Gallup polls, 2001; Does the United Kingdom still have a Constitution?, 2001; frequent contributor to British and American jls and periodicals. *Recreations:* music, theatre, holidays, walking. *Address:* Department of Government, University of Essex, Wivenhoe Park, Colchester, Essex CO4 3SQ. *T:* (01206) 873393; The Mill House, Middle Green, Wakes Colne, Colchester, Essex CO6 2BP. *T:* (01787) 222497.

KING, Anthony William Poole; His Honour Judge Anthony King; a Circuit Judge, since 1993; *b* 18 Aug. 1942; *s* of late Edmund Poole King and Pamela Midelton King (*née* Baker); *m* 1971, Camilla Anne Alexandra Brandreth; two *s* one *d*. *Educ:* Winchester Coll.; Worcester Coll., Oxford (MA Jur.). Called to the Bar, Inner Temple, 1966; a Recorder, 1987–93; Midland and Oxford Circuit. *Recreations:* fishing, other people's gardens. *Address:* Oxford Crown and County Court, St Aldate's, Oxford OX1 1TL. *T:* (01865) 264200.

KING, Prof. Bernard, PhD; FIWSc; CBiol, FIBiol; Vice-Chancellor, University of Abertay Dundee, since 1994 (Principal, Dundee Institute of Technology, 1992–94); *b* 4 May 1946; *s* of Bernard and Cathleen King; *m* 1970, Maura Antoinette Collinge; two *d*. *Educ:* Synge St Christian Brothers Sch., Dublin; Coll. of Technology, Dublin; Univ. of Aston in Birmingham (MSc 1972; PhD 1975). FIWSc 1975; CBiol, FBiol 1987. Research Fellow, Univ. of Aston in Birmingham, 1972–76; Dundee Institute of Technology: Lectr, 1976–79; Sen. Lectr, 1979–83; Head, Dept of Molecular Life Scis, 1983–91; Dean, Faculty of Sci., 1987–89; Asst Principal, Robert Gordon Inst. of Technol., 1991–92. Board Member: Scottish Enterprise Tayside, 1998–; Scottish Knowledge, 2000–; Inst. of Learning and Teaching in Higher Educn, 2001–. Trustee, Tayside Primary Care NHS Trust, 1997–. Governor: Scottish Crop Res. Inst.; Unicorn Preservation Soc. CIMgt 1999. *Publications:* numerous scientific and tech. papers on biodeterioration with particular ref. to biodeterioration and preservation of wood. *Recreations:* reading, music, sailing. *Address:* 11 Dalhousie Place, Arbroath, Angus DD11 2BT.

KING, Billie Jean; tennis player; Chief Executive Officer, Team Tennis, since 1981; *b* 22 Nov. 1943; *d* of Willard J. Moffitt; *m* 1965, Larry King. *Educ:* Los Cerritos Sch.; Long Beach High Sch.; Los Angeles State Coll. Played first tennis match at age of eleven; won first championship, Southern California, 1958; coached by Clyde Walker, Alice Marble, Frank Brennan and Mervyn Rose; won first All England Championship, 1966, and five times subseq., and in 1979 achieved record of 20 Wimbledon titles (six Singles, ten Doubles, four Mixed Doubles); has won all other major titles inc. US Singles and Doubles Championships on all four surfaces, and 24 US national titles in all. Pres., Women's Tennis Assoc., 1980–81. *Publications:* Tennis to Win, 1970; Billie Jean, 1974; (with Joe Hyams) Secrets of Winning Tennis, 1975; Tennis Love (illus. Charles Schulz), 1978; (with Frank Deford) Billie Jean King, 1982; (with Cynthia Starr) We Have Come a Long Way: the story of women's tennis, 1989. *Address:* c/o World Team Tennis, 445 N Wells #404, Chicago, Ill 60610, USA.

KING, Dr Brian Edmund; owner manager, King Innovations, since 1994; *b* 25 May 1928; *s* of Albert Theodore King and Gladys Johnson; *m* 1952 (marr. diss.); two *s*; *m* 1972, Eunice Wolstenholme; one *d*. *Educ:* Pocklington Sch.; Leeds Univ. TMM (Research) Ltd, 1952–57; British Oxygen, 1957–67; Dir, 1967–87, and Chief Exec., 1977–87, Wira Technology Group Ltd (formerly Wool Industries Research Assoc.); Dir and Chief Exec., Barnsley Business and Innovation Centre, 1987–93. *Recreations:* bridge, swimming, travel.

KING, Rt Rev. Brian Franklin Vernon; Bishop of Western Sydney (formerly Bishop in Parramatta) and an Assistant Bishop of Sydney, since 1993; Anglican Bishop to the Australian Defence Force, since 1994; *b* 3 Jan. 1938; *s* of Francis Brindley King and Merle Florence King; *m* 1965, Pamela Diane Gifford; three *s*. *Educ:* Sydney Boys' High Sch.; Univ. of NSW (BComm); Univ. of London (BDiv); Fuller Theol Seminary, Pasadena (DMin); Moore Coll., NSW (Diploma); Aust. Coll. of Theol. (DipRE). ACA (Sydney). Chartered Accountant, 1959–61; theolog. student, 1961–64; Curate, Manly Anglican Church, 1964–67; Rector: Dural, 1967–73; Wahroonga, 1973–87; Manly, 1987–93; Canon, St Andrew's Cathedral, 1989–93. *Recreations:* travel, gardening, sport, family. *Address:* PO Box 1443, Parramatta, NSW 2124, Australia. *T:* (2) 96353186. *Clubs:* Gordon Rugby (Chatswood, Sydney); City Tattersalls (Sydney).

KING, Caradoc; literary agent; Managing Director, 1991–95, Joint Managing Director, since 1996, and Chairman, since 1992, A. P. Watt Ltd; *b* 19 Dec. 1946; *s* of late Joan Bartlett (*née* Richardson); *m* 1975, Jane Grant Morris; one *s* one *d*. *Educ:* Belmont Abbey; Exeter Coll., Oxford (MA). With Associated Book Publishers, 1968–70; Senior Editor: Allen Lane, Penguin Press, 1970–72; Penguin Books, 1970–75; joined A. P. Watt, 1976: Associate, A. P. Watt & Son, 1976–81; Dir, A. P. Watt Ltd, 1981–. *Recreations:* ski-ing, lunch, collecting wine, wind-surfing. *Address:* c/o A. P. Watt Ltd, 20 John Street, WC1N 2DR. *T:* (020) 7405 6774. *Club:* Soho House.

KING, Charles Andrew Buchanan, CMG 1961; MBE 1944; HM Diplomatic Service, retired; *b* 25 July 1915; *s* of late Major Andrew Buchanan King, 7th Argyll and Sutherland Highlanders and of Evelyn Nina (*née* Sharpe). *Educ:* Wellington Coll.; Magdalene Coll., Cambridge (MA). Vice-Consul: Zürich, 1940, Geneva, 1941; Attaché, HM Legation, Berne, 1942; transf. to FO, 1946; 2nd Sec., Vienna, 1950; transf. to FO 1953; to Hong Kong, 1958; to FO 1961; retired, 1967; Head of W European Div., Overseas Dept, London Chamber of Commerce, 1968–70. *Recreation:* travel. *Club:* Naval and Military.

KING, Charles Martin M.; *see* Meade-King.

KING, Prof. Christine Elizabeth, DL; PhD; FRHistS; Vice-Chancellor and Chief Executive, since 1995, and Professor of History, Staffordshire University; *b* 31 Aug. 1944; *d* of William Edwin King and Elizabeth Violet May King (*née* Coates). *Educ:* Birmingham Univ. (BA Hons Hist. and Theol. 1966; MA Theol. 1973; PhD Religious Hist. 1980). FRHistS 1994. Teaching, research and management posts in sch., further and higher educn sectors; Head, Sch. of Histl and Critical Studies, 1985–87, Dean, Faculty of Arts, 1987–90, Lancs Poly.; Staffordshire Polytechnic, subseq. Staffordshire University, 1990–: Prof. of History, 1991–; Dean of Business, Humanities and Social Scis, 1990–92; Pro Vice-Chancellor, 1992–95. Member: Bd, Advantage W Midlands (Regl Develt Agency), 1999–; W Midlands Regl Cultural Consortium, 1999–. Chm., Staffs Learning Partnership, 2000–. DL Staffs, 1999. FRSA; CIMgt 1995 (FIMgt 1993). Hon. Fellow, Univ. of Central Lancs; Hon. DLitt: Birmingham; Portsmouth; DUniv Derby. *Publications:* The Nazi State and the New Religions, 1983; (ed) Through the Glass Ceiling: effective management development for women, 1993; articles and chapters on history of religion in Nazi Germany, women in management, higher educn and on Elvis Presley and his fans. *Address:* Staffordshire University, Beaconside, Stafford ST18 0AD. *T:* (01785) 353202.

KING, Colin Sainthill W.; *see* Wallis-King.

KING, Prof. David Anthony, FRS 1991; FRSC, FInstP; Chief Scientific Adviser to the Government, and Head, Office of Science and Technology, since 2000; 1920 Professor of Physical Chemistry, University of Cambridge, since 1988; Fellow, Queens' College, Cambridge, since 2001; *b* 12 Aug. 1939; *s* of Arnold King and Patricia (*née* Vardy), Durban; *m* Jane Lichtenstein; one *s* one *d*, and two *s* by previous marriage. *Educ:* St John's Coll., Johannesburg; Univ. of the Witwatersrand, Johannesburg (BSc; PhD 1963); ScD E Anglia, 1974; ScD Cantab, 1999. Shell Scholar, Imperial Coll., 1963–66; Lectr in Chemical Physics, Univ. of E Anglia, Norwich, 1966–74; Brunner Prof. of Physical Chemistry, Univ. of Liverpool, 1974–88; Cambridge University: Head, Dept of Chemistry, 1993–2000; Fellow, St John's College, 1988–95; Master, Downing Coll., 1995–2000, Hon. Fellow, 2001. Member: Comité de Direction of Centre de Cinétique Physique et Chimique, Nancy, 1974–81; Nat. Exec., Assoc. of Univ. Teachers, 1970–78 (Nat. Pres., 1976–77); British Vacuum Council, 1978–87 (Chm., 1982–85); Internat. Union for Vacuum Science and Technology, 1978–86; Faraday Div., Council, Chem. Soc., 1979–82; Scientific Adv. Panel, Daresbury Lab., 1980–82; Res. Adv. Cttee, Leverhulme Trust, 1980–92 (Chm., 1995–); Beirat, Fritz Haber Inst., West Berlin, 1981–93. Chairman: Gallery Cttee, Bluecoat Soc. of Arts, 1986–88; Kettle's Yard Gall., Cambridge, 1989–. Miller Vis. Res. Prof., Univ. of Calif, Berkeley, 1996. Lectures: Tilden, Chem. Soc., 1989; Frontiers, Texas A & M Univ., 1993; Dupont Distinguished, Indianapolis Univ., 1993; Dow Chemical Canada, Univ. W Ont, 1994. Member Editorial Board: Jl of Physics C, 1977–80; Surface Science Reports, 1983–98; Surface Science, 2000–; Editor, Chemical Physics Letters, 1989–. Hon. Fellow, Indian Acad. of Scis, 1998. Hon. degrees, UEA, Liverpool and Cardiff, 2001. Chem. Soc. Award for surface and colloid chemistry, 1978; British Vacuum Council medal and prize for research, 1991; Liversidge Lect. and Medal, RSC, 1997. *Publications:* papers on the physics and chemistry of solid surfaces in: Proc. Royal Soc., Surface Science, Science, Jl Chemical Physics, Physical Rev. Letters, etc. *Recreations:* photography, art. *Address:* Office of Science and Technology, Albany House, 94–98 Petty France, SW1H 9ST.

KING, David E., FCCA; Chief Executive, London Metal Exchange Ltd, 1989–2001; *b* 18 Aug. 1945; *m* 1972, Jenny Hall; four *s*. *Educ:* Manchester Poly.; Cranfield Sch. of Mgt (MBA 1984). FCCA 1976. Qualified as Certified Accountant, 1976; sen. financial positions both overseas and in UK, 1976–; joined London Metal Exchange, 1987. *Address:* c/o London Metal Exchange Ltd, 56 Leadenhall Street, EC3A 2DX.

KING, (Denys) Michael (Gwilym), CVO 1989; CEng, FICE, MIMechE; Director, 1986–91, Assistant Chief Executive, 1991, BAA plc, retired (Member, British Airports Authority, 1980–86); *b* 29 May 1929; *s* of William James King, FCIS, and Hilda May King; *m* 1st, 1956, Monica Helen (marr. diss. 1973); three *d*; 2nd, 1985, Ann Elizabeth. *Educ:* St Edmund's Sch., Canterbury; Simon Langton Sch., Canterbury; Battersea Polytechnic, London (BScEng Hons London, 1949). MIMechE 1966; FICE 1977. Engr, J. Laing Construction Ltd, 1961–71, Dir, 1971–74; Engrg Dir, BAA, 1974–77; Dir, 1977–86, Man. Dir, 1986–88, Heathrow Airport; Man. Dir, Airports Div., BAA, 1988–91. *Recreations:* yachting, preserved railways.

KING, Deryk Irving; Managing Director, North America, Centrica plc, since 2000; Chairman and Chief Executive Officer, Direct Energy Marketing Ltd, since 2000; *b* 20 Dec. 1947; *s* of Cyril Montford King and Irene Muriel King (*née* Irving); *m* 1971, Janet Lorraine Amos; one *d*. *Educ:* Arnold Sch., Blackpool; University Coll., Oxford (MA Chem.). Joined Air Products Ltd as sales engr, 1970; with Imperial Chemical Industries PLC, 1973–96: Product Manager, 1973–77; Asst Gen. Manager, Chemicals, ICI Japan Ltd, 1977–79; Sen. Product Manager, 1979–83; Export Sales Manager, Mond Div., 1983–84; Commercial Manager, ICI Soda Ash Products, and Dir, Magadi Soda Co.,

1984–88; Dir, Ellis & Everard (Chemicals) Ltd, 1987–88; Commercial Manager, 1988–91, Gen. Manager, 1991–92, ICI Fertilizers; also Chm., Scottish Agricl Industries and BritAg Industries, and Dir, Irish Fertilizer Industries, 1991–92; Man. Dir, ICI Polyester, 1992–96; Chm., ICI Far Eastern, 1995–96; Gp Man. Dir, PowerGen plc, 1996–98; Dir, Ellis & Everard plc, 1999–2001; Projects Dir, Centrica plc, 1999–2000. Dir, Kvaerner ASA, 1997–; Trustee, Coventry 2000, 1997–2000. Chm., W Midlands Regl Awards Cttee, and Mem., England Cttee, Nat. Lottery Charities Bd, 1998–. FCIM 1992. *Recreations:* travel, wine and food, watching sport. *Address:* Centrica North America, Suite 1500, 25 Sheppard Avenue West, Toronto, ON M2N 6S6, Canada.

KING, Prof. Edmund James, MA, PhD, DLit; Professor of Education, University of London King's College, 1975–79, now Emeritus Professor; *b* 19 June 1914; *s* of James and Mary Alice King; *m* 1939, Margaret Mary Breakell; one *s* three *d*. *Educ:* Univ. of Manchester (BA, MA); Univ. of London (PhD, DLit). Taught in grammar schs, 1936–47; Asst, then Sen. Asst to Dir of Extra-Mural Studies, Univ. of London, 1947–53; Lectr, subseq. Reader, Univ. of London King's Coll., 1953–75, also Dir, Comparative Research Unit, King's Coll., 1970–73. Visiting appts at Amer., Can. and Chinese univs; also in Melbourne, Tokyo, Tehran, etc; lecturing and adv. assignments in many countries. Editor, Comparative Education, 1978–92. *Publications:* Other Schools and Ours, 1958, 5th edn 1979; World Perspectives in Education, 1962, 2nd edn 1965; (ed) Communist Education, 1963; Society, Schools and Progress in the USA, 1965; Education and Social Change, 1966; Comparative Studies and Educational Decision, 1968; Education and Development in Western Europe, 1969; (ed) The Teacher and the Needs of Society, 1970; The Education of Teachers: a comparative analysis, 1970; (with W. Boyd) A History of Western Education, 1972, 12th edn 1995; Post-compulsory Education, vol. I: a new analysis in Western Europe, 1974; vol. II: the way ahead, 1975 (both with C. H. Moor and J. A. Mundy); (ed) Reorganizing Education, 1977; (ed) Education for Uncertainty, 1979; Technological/occupational Challenge, Social Transformation and Educational Response, 1986. *Recreations:* gardening, music, writing. *Address:* 40 Alexandra Road, Epsom, Surrey KT17 4BT.

KING, Eleanor Warwick; *see* Hamilton, E. W.

KING, Francis Henry, CBE 1985 (OBE 1979); FRSL 1948; author; Drama Critic, Sunday Telegraph, 1978–88; *b* 4 March 1923; *o s* of late Eustace Arthur Cecil King and Faith Mina Read. *Educ:* Shrewsbury; Balliol Coll., Oxford. British Council, 1950–63 (Asst Rep., Helsinki, 1957–58; Regl Dir, Kyoto, 1958–63). Chm., Soc. of Authors, 1975–77; Internat. Vice-Pres., PEN, 1989– (Pres., English PEN, 1978–86; Vice-Pres., 1977; Internat. Pres., 1986–89). *Publications: novels:* To the Dark Tower, 1946; Never Again, 1947; An Air That Kills, 1948; The Dividing Stream, 1951 (Somerset Maugham Award, 1952); The Dark Glasses, 1954; The Widow, 1957; The Man on the Rock, 1957; The Custom House, 1961; The Last of the Pleasure Gardens, 1965; The Waves Behind the Boat, 1967; A Domestic Animal, 1970; Flights (two short novels), 1973; A Game of Patience, 1974; The Needle, 1975; Danny Hill, 1977; The Action, 1978; Act of Darkness, 1983; Voices in an Empty Room, 1984; Frozen Music, 1987; The Woman Who Was God, 1988; Punishments, 1989; Visiting Cards, 1990; The Ant Colony, 1991; (with Tom Wakefield and Patrick Gale) Secret Lives, 1991; The One and Only, 1994; Ash on an Old Man's Sleeve, 1996; Dead Letters, 1997; Prodigies, 2001; *short stories:* So Hurt and Humiliated, 1959; The Japanese Umbrella, 1964 (Katherine Mansfield Short Story Prize, 1965); The Brighton Belle, 1968; Hard Feelings, 1976; Indirect Method, 1980; One is a Wanderer, 1985; A Hand at the Shutter, 1996; *poetry:* Rod of Incantation, 1952; *biography:* E. M. Forster and His World, 1978; (ed) My Sister and Myself: the diaries of J. R. Ackerley, 1982; Yesterday Came Suddenly (autobiog.), 1993; *general:* (ed) Introducing Greece, 1956; Japan, 1970; Florence, 1982; (ed) Lafcadio Hearn: Writings from Japan, 1984; Florence: A Literary Companion, 1991. *Address:* 19 Gordon Place, W8 4JE. *T:* (020) 7937 5715; *e-mail:* fhk@dircon.co.uk. *Club:* PEN.

KING, Harold Samuel; dancer and choreographer; Artistic Director, City Ballet of London, 1996–2001; *b* Durban, 13 May 1949. *Educ:* University Ballet Sch., Cape Town. Soloist, Cape Performing Arts Bd Ballet Co., 1968–70; joined Western Th. Ballet, in GB, as dancer and choreographer, 1970; with Opera Ballet, Covent Gdn, 1976–77, incl. seasons with Nat. Ballet of Zimbabwe, as Guest Artist with Cape Performing Arts Bd, and Guest Teacher, Royal Acad. of Dance Summer Sch.; Artistic Co-ordinator, Victor Hochhauser Gala Ballet Season, RFH, 1978; asst, Rudolf Nuryev seasons at London Coliseum, 1978; Dir and toured with, newly-formed London City Ballet, 1978–96; founded City Ballet of London, 1996, produced Dances from Napoli and choreographed Prince Igor, Nutcracker Suite and Carmen; choreographed The Little Princess, 1995 and created Flowers for Mrs Harris, 1998, for London Children's Ballet; choreographed The Lion, the Witch and the Wardrobe for London Studio Centre, 1996.

KING, Henry Edward St Leger; Chairman: Rentokil Initial plc (formerly Rentokil Group), since 1994 (Director, since 1985); GKR Group Ltd, 1995–2000; *b* 11 Oct. 1936; *s* of Robert James King and Dorothy Louisa Marie (*née* Wickert); *m* 1964, Kathleen Bridget Wilcock (marr. diss. 1989); one *d* (one *s* decd); *m* 1996, Margaret Evelyn Empson Cox. *Educ:* Whitgift Middle Sch.; Fitzwilliam Coll., Cambridge (MA, LLB). Solicitor, England, 1964 and Hong Kong, 1977. Nat. Service, 1955–57. Joined Denton Hall, 1964: solicitor, 1964–67; Partner, 1967–96; Chm., 1993–96; Consultant, 1996–. Director: City Centre Restaurants plc, 1986–2001 (Chm., 1996–2001); Brambles Investments PLC, 1988–; TotalFinaElf Exploration UK (formerly Total Oil Marine) plc, 1997–. *Recreations:* travel, theatre, music. *Address:* 1 Fleet Place, EC4M 7WS. *T:* (020) 7245 7015. *Club:* Riverside Racquet.

KING, Hilary William, CBE 1964; HM Diplomatic Service, retired; *b* 10 March 1919; *s* of Dr W. H. King, Fowey, Cornwall; *m* 1947, Dr Margaret Helen Grierson Borrowman; one *s* three *d*. *Educ:* Sherborne; Corpus Christi Coll. Cambridge. Served War of 1939–45; Signals Officer, mission to Yugoslav Partizan GHQ, 1943–45 (MBE 1944). Apptd Mem. Foreign (subseq. Diplomatic) Service, Nov. 1946. A Vice-Consul in Yugoslavia, 1947–48; transferred to Foreign Office, 1949; promoted 1st Sec., 1950; transf. to Vienna as a Russian Sec., 1951; Washington, 1953; transf. Foreign Office, 1958; Commercial Counsellor, Moscow, 1959; acted as Chargé d'Affaires, 1960; Ambassador (and Consul-Gen.) to Guinea, 1962–65; St Antony's Coll., Oxford, Oct. 1965–June 1966; Counsellor of Embassy, Warsaw, 1966–67; Head of UN (Economic and Social) Dept, FCO, 1968–71; Consul-Gen., Hamburg, 1971–74. *Recreations:* sailing, amateur radio. *Address:* Fuaim an Sruth, South Cuan, Oban, Argyll PA34 4TU.

KING, Isobel Wilson; *see* Buchanan, I. W.

KING, Jean Mary; Under Secretary, Chief Executive, Employment Division of the Manpower Services Commission, 1979–82, retired; Member, Civil Service Appeal Board, 1984–93; *b* 9 March 1923; *d* of Edgar and Elsie Bishop; *m* 1st, 1951, Albert Robert Collingridge (*d* 1994); one *d*; 2nd, 1996, John Ernest Agar King (*d* 2000). *Educ:* County High School, Loughton, Essex; University College London (BSc Econ); LSE (Social Science Course). Asst Personnel Officer, C. and J. Clark, 1945–49; Personnel Manager, Pet Foods Ltd, 1949–50; Ministry of Labour/Department of Employment: Personnel Management Adviser and Industrial Relations Officer, 1950–65; Regl Industrial Relations Officer/Sen. Manpower Adviser, 1965–71; Assistant Secretary, Office of Manpower Economics 1971–73, Pay Board 1973–74, Dept of Employment HQ 1974–76; Dep. Chief Exec., Employment Service Div. of Manpower Services Commn, 1976–79. Chm., Kent Area Manpower Bd, 1983–88. Co-ordinator, Fareham Good Neighbours, 1999–. *Publication:* (jtly) Personnel Management in the Small Firm, 1953. *Recreations:* voluntary work with the elderly, ecumenical work with local churches. *Address:* 21 Burnham Wood, Fareham, Hants PO16 7UD. *T:* (01329) 313018.

KING, Jeremy Richard Bruce; restaurateur; *b* 21 June 1954; *s* of Charles Henry King and Molly King (*née* Chinn); *m* 1982, Debra Hauer; one *s* two *d*. *Educ:* Christ's Hosp., Horsham. Co-proprietor (with Christopher Corbin): Caprice Hldgs Ltd, 1982–; Caprice Events Ltd, 1995–; restaurants: Le Caprice, 1981–2000; The Ivy, 1990–2000; J. Sheekey, 1998–2000. Chm., Tate Gall. Restaurants Ltd, 1999–; Mem. Council, Tate Gall. of Modern Art, 1999–; Dir, Royal National Theatre Enterprises Ltd, 1999–2001. Trustee, Artangel Trust, 1994–. Restaurateur of Year, Caterer and Hotelkeeper, 1993. *Recreations:* contemporary art, theatre, solitude. *Clubs:* Garrick, Royal Automobile, Groucho.

KING, John Arthur Charles; Chairman, Analysys Ltd, since 1991; *b* 7 April 1933; *s* of late Charles William King and Doris Frances King; *m* 1958, Ina Solavici; two *s*. *Educ:* Univ. of Bristol. BSc. IBM UK, 1956–70; Managing Director, Telex Computer Products UK Ltd, 1970–73; Dir, DP Div., Metra Consulting Gp, 1974–75; Marketing Dir, UK, later Europe (Brussels), ITT Business Systems, 1976–81; Commercial Dir, Business Communications Systems, Philips (Hilversum), 1981–83; Dir, Marketing and Corporate Strategy, subseq. Corporate Dir and Man. Dir, Overseas Div., BT plc, 1984–88; Man. Dir, Citicorp Information Business Internat., 1988–91; Chm., Quotron Internat., 1988–91; non-executive Director: olsy (formerly Olivetti) UK Ltd, 1991–98 (Chm., 1995–98); Leeds Permanent Building Society, 1991–95 (Vice-Chm., 1994–95); Knowledge Support Systems Ltd, 1997– (non-exec. Chm., 1998–); TTP Capital Partners Ltd, 1999–; non-exec. Chm., Superscape plc, 1998–. Non-exec. Dir, CSA, 1996–97; Mem. Supervisory Bd, FUGRO NV, 1997–. Sec. Gen., Eur. Foundn for Quality Management, 1993–94. Mem., Restrictive Practices Ct, 1995–2000. Freeman, City of London, 1987; Liveryman, Co. of Information Technologists, 1992. FBCS 1968; CIMgt (CBIM 1986); FInstD 1986; FRSA 1993. *Recreations:* golf, bridge, music. *Address:* Analysys Ltd, St Giles Court, 24 Castle Street, Cambridge CB3 0AJ. *T:* (01223) 460600.

KING, Sir John (Christopher), 4th Bt *cr* 1888, of Campsie, Stirlingshire; *b* 31 March 1933; *s* of Sir James Granville Le Neve King, 3rd Bt, TD and of Penelope Charlotte, *d* of late Capt. E. Cooper-Key, CB, MVO, RN; *S* father, 1989; *m* 1st, 1958, Patricia Foster (marr. diss. 1972); one *s* one *d*; 2nd, 1984, Aline Jane Holley (marr. diss. 2000), *d* of Col D. A. Brett, GC, OBE, MC. *Educ:* Eton. Sub Lt, RNVR, 1952–54; Lt, Berks Yeomanry, 1955–60. Mem., Stock Exchange, 1961–73. *Recreations:* sailing, shooting, travelling. *Heir: s* James Henry Rupert King [*b* 24 May 1961; *m* 1995, Elizabeth, *y d* of Richard Ellingworth, *qv*]. *Address:* Wyndham Cottage, Sutton Bingham, Yeovil BA22 9QP. *Club:* Brooks's.

KING, John Edward; Principal Establishment Officer and Under Secretary, Welsh Office, 1977–82; President, Friends of the Welsh College of Music and Drama, since 1992 (Chairman, 1990–92); *b* 30 May 1922; *s* of late Albert Edward and Margaret King; *m* 1st, 1948, Pamela White (marr. diss.); one *d*; 2nd, 1956, Mary Margaret Beaton; two *d*. *Educ:* Penarth County Grammar Sch.; Sch. of Oriental and African Studies, London Univ. Served with Rifle Bde, RWF and Nigeria Regt, 1941–47; Captain, Chindit campaign, Burma (despatches). Cadet, Colonial Admin. Service, N Nigeria, 1947; Permanent Sec., Fed. Govt of Nigeria, 1960; retired from HMOCS, 1963. Principal, CRO, 1963; Navy Dept, MoD, 1966–69; Private Sec. to Sec. of State for Wales, 1969–71; Asst Sec., Welsh Office, 1971–77. CS Mem., 1977–82, External Mem., 1982–86, Final Selection Bd, CS Commn. Consultant, Dept of Educn and Dir, China Studies Centre, UC, Cardiff, 1984–87. *Recreations:* books, swimming, tennis, watercolour painting. *Address:* Fairfields, Fairwater Road, Llandaff, Cardiff CF5 2LF. *T:* (029) 2021 2927. *Clubs:* Civil Service; Cardiff Lawn Tennis, Outer Hebrides Tennis.

KING, Dr John William Beaufoy; Director, Advanced Breeders Ltd, since 1988; Head of AFRC Animal Breeding Liaison Group, 1982–87, retired; *b* 28 June 1927; *s* of late John Victor Beaufoy and Gwendoleen Freda King; *m* 1951, Pauline Margaret Coldicott; four *s*. *Educ:* Marling Sch., Stroud; St Catharine's Coll., Cambridge; Edinburgh Univ. BA Cantab 1947, MA Cantab 1952; PhD Edinburgh 1951; FIBiol 1974; FRSE 1975. ARC Animal Breeding Res. Organisation, 1951–82. Kellogg Foundn Schol. to USA, 1954; Genetics Cons. to Pig Industry Develt Authority, 1959; David Black Award (services to pig industry), 1966; Nuffield Foundn Fellowship to Canada, 1970; Vis. Lectr, Göttingen Univ., 1973. *Publications:* papers in scientific jls. *Recreations:* gardening, dog training. *Address:* Cottage Farm, West Linton, Peeblesshire EH46 7AS. *T:* (01968) 660448.

KING, Dr Julia Elizabeth, CBE 1999; FREng, FIM, FRAeS, FIMarE; Director, Engineering and Technology - Marine, Rolls-Royce plc, since 2000; *b* 11 July 1954; *d* of Derrick Arthur King and Joan Brewer; *m* 1984, Dr Colin William Brown. *Educ:* Godolphin and Latymer Girls' Sch.; New Hall, Cambridge (BA 1975; MA 1978; PhD 1979); FIM, FRAeS, FIMarE. Rolls-Royce Res. Fellow, Girton Coll., Cambridge, 1978–80; Univ. Lectr, Nottingham Univ., 1980–87; Cambridge University: British Gas/FEng Sen. Res. Fellow, 1987–92; Fellow, Churchill Coll., 1987–94; Univ. Lectr, 1992–94; Asst Dir, Univ. Technology Centre for Ni-Base Superalloys, 1993–94; Hd of Materials, Rolls-Royce Aerospace Gp, 1994–96; Dir of Advanced Engrg, Rolls-Royce Industrial Power Gp, 1997–98; Man. Dir, Fan Systems, Rolls-Royce plc, 1998–2000. External Chairs: Univ. of Swansea, 1995–; Univ. of Newcastle, 1997–. Member, Editorial Board: Internat. Jl of Fatigue, 1989–96; Fatigue and Fracture of Engrg Materials and Structures, 1990–97. FREng (FEng 1997); FRSA. Freedom, Co. of Goldsmiths, 1998; Freeman, City of London, 1998. Grunfeld Medal, 1992, (jtly) Bengough Medal, 1995, Inst. of Materials. *Publications:* (ed) Aerospace Materials and Structures, 1997; over 150 papers on fatigue and fracture in structural materials, aeroengine materials and marine propulsion technology. *Recreations:* people, growing orchids, collecting modern prints, gardening, walking. *Address:* Rolls-Royce plc, PO Box 2000, Derby DE21 7XX. *T:* (01332) 622815.

KING, Hon. Leonard James, AC 1987; Chief Justice of South Australia, 1978–95; *b* 1 May 1925; *s* of Michael Owen and Mary Ann King; *m* 1953, Sheila Therese (*née* Keane); two *s* three *d*. *Educ:* Marist Brothers Sch., Norwood, S Aust; Univ. of Adelaide, S Aust (LLB). Admitted to Bar, 1950; QC 1967. Member, House of Assembly, Parlt of S Australia, 1970; Attorney-General and Minister of Community Welfare, 1970; additionally, Minister of Prices and Consumer Affairs, 1972. Judge of Supreme Court of S Aust, 1975. *Address:* 19 Wall Street, Norwood, SA 5067, Australia. *T:* (8) 83317220.

KING, Mark Baxter B.; *see* Barty-King.

KING, Mary Elizabeth; three-day event rider; *b* 8 June 1961; *d* of Lt Comdr Michael Dillon Harding Thomson and Patricia Gillian Thomson; *m* 1995, Alan David Henry King; one *s* one *d*. *Educ:* Manor House Sch., Honiton; King's Sch., Ottery St Mary; Evendine Court, Malvern (Distinction, Cordon Bleu, 1980). British Open Champion, 1990, 1991, 1997; Winner: Windsor Horse Trials, 1988, 1989, 1992; Badminton Horse Trials, 1992, 2000; Mem., Olympic Team, Barcelona, 1992, Atlanta, 1996, Sydney, 2000; Team Gold Medal: European Championships, 1991, 1994, 1997; World Equestrian Games, 1995. *Publications:* Mary Thomson's Eventing Year, 1993; All the King's Horses, 1997; William and Mary, 1998. *Recreations:* tennis, snow and water ski-ing. *Address:* School House, Salcombe Regis, Sidmouth, Devon EX10 0JQ. *T:* (01395) 514882.

KING, Prof. Mervyn Allister, FBA 1992; Director, since 1990, and a Deputy Governor, since 1998, Bank of England; *b* 30 March 1948; *s* of Eric Frank King and Kathleen Alice Passingham. *Educ:* Wolverhampton Grammar School; King's College, Cambridge (BA 1st cl. hons 1969, MA 1973). Research Officer, Dept of Applied Economics, Cambridge, 1969–76; Kennedy Schol., Harvard Univ., 1971–72; Fellow, St John's Coll., Cambridge, 1972–77 (Hon. Fellow, 1997); Lectr, Faculty of Economics, Cambridge, 1976–77; Esmée Fairbairn Prof. of Investment, Univ. of Birmingham, 1977–84; Prof. of Economics, LSE, 1984–95; Chief Economist, Bank of England, 1991–98. Vis. Professor of Economics: Harvard Univ., 1982, 1990; MIT, 1983–84; LSE, 1996–. Co-Dir, LSE Financial Markets Gp, 1987–91. Mem., City Capital Markets Cttee, 1989–91. President: Eur. Econ. Assoc., 1993; Inst. for Fiscal Studies, 1999–. Member: Meade Cttee, 1978; Council and Exec., Royal Economic Soc., 1981–86, 1992–; Fellow, Econometric Soc., 1982. Managing Editor, Review of Economic Studies, 1978–83; Associate Editor: Jl of Public Economics, 1983–99; Amer. Economic Review, 1985–88. Indep. Dir, The Securities Assoc., 1987–89. Trustee, Kennedy Meml Trust, 1990–2000. Sen. Vice-Pres., Aston Villa FC, 1995–. Helsinki Univ. Medal, 1982. *Publications:* Public Policy and the Corporation, 1977; (with J. A. Kay) The British Tax System, 1978, 5th edn 1990; (with D. Fullerton) The Taxation of Income from Capital, 1984; numerous articles in economics jls. *Address:* Bank of England, Threadneedle Street, EC2R 8AH. *Clubs:* Brooks's, Garrick.

KING, Michael; *see* King, D. M. G.

KING, His Honour Michael Gardner; a Circuit Judge, 1972–87; *b* 4 Dec. 1920; *s* of late David Thomson King and late Winifred Mary King, Bournemouth; *m* 1951, Yvonne Mary Lilian, *d* of late Lt-Col M. J. Ambler; two *s* one *d*. *Educ:* Sherborne Sch.; Wadham Coll., Oxford (MA). Served in RN, Lieut RNVR, 1940–46. Called to Bar, Gray's Inn, 1949. Dep. Chm., IoW QS, 1966–72; Dep. Chm., Hants QS, 1968–72. *Recreations:* sailing, shooting, golf. *Clubs:* Royal Naval Sailing Association, Royal Lymington Yacht (Cdre, 1986–88).

KING, Neil Gerald Alexander; QC 2000; *b* 14 Nov. 1956; *s* of Joseph and Leila King; *m* 1978, Matilda Magdalen Grenville (*née* Oppenheimer); four *d*. *Educ:* Harrow Sch.; New Coll., Oxford (MA). Called to the Bar, Inner Temple, 1980. *Publication:* (ed jtly) Ryde on Rating and the Council Tax, 1990–. *Recreations:* classical music, golf, walking, Real tennis. *Address:* The White House, High Street, Whitchurch-on-Thames, Oxon RG8 7HA. *T:* (0118) 984 2915. *Clubs:* Army and Navy, Royal Automobile; Huntercombe Golf.

KING, Vice-Adm. Sir Norman (Ross Dutton), KBE 1989; Chairman, Buckinghamshire Health Authority, 1993–96; President, Safety Centre (Milton Keynes) Ltd, since 1997 (Chairman, 1992–96); *b* 19 March 1933; *s* of Sir Norman King, KCMG and Lady (Mona) King (*née* Dutton); *m* 1967, Patricia Rosemary, *d* of Dr L. B. Furber; two *d*. *Educ:* Fonthill School; RNC Dartmouth; graduate, Naval Command College, Newport, USA, 1969; RCDS 1978. RN Cadet, 1946; served HM Ships Indefatigable, Tintagel Castle, Ceylon, Wild Goose, Hickleton, 1951–57, and Corunna, 1957–59; long TAS course, 1960; BRNC Dartmouth, 1961–63; CO HMS Fiskerton, 1963–64; Jun. Seaman Appointer, Naval Sec's Dept, 1965–66; CO HMS Leopard, 1967–68; Staff Officer (TAS) to CBNS (Washington), 1969–71; XO HMS Intrepid, 1972–73; Staff Warfare TAS Officer, to Dir Naval Warfare, 1974–75; Naval Asst to Second Sea Lord, 1975–77; CO HMS Newcastle and Capt. 3rd Destroyer Sqn, 1979–80; CSO to CBNS (Washington), 1981–82; Dir of Naval Officer Appts (Seaman Officers), 1983–84; Comdr, British Navy Staff and British Naval Attaché, Washington, and UK Nat. Liaison Rep. to SACLANT, 1984–86; Naval Sec., 1987–88; COS to Comdr Allied Naval Forces Southern Europe, 1988–91. Mem., Lord Chancellor's Panel of Independent Inspectors, 1992–. *Publications:* (jointly) All The Queen's Men, 1967, paperback edn as Strictly Personal, 1972. *Recreations:* tennis, golf, music, chess. *Address:* c/o Lloyd's Bank, Secklow Gate West, Milton Keynes MK9 3EH. *Club:* Royal Navy Club of 1765 and 1785.

KING, Oona Tamsyn; MP (Lab) Bethnal Green and Bow, since 1997; *b* 22 Oct. 1967; *d* of Prof. Preston King and Hazel King; *m* 1994, Tiberio Santomarco. *Educ:* Haverstock Comprehensive Secondary Sch.; York Univ. (BA 1st cl. Hons Politics); Univ. of Calif, Berkeley (Scholar). Political Asst to Glyn Ford, MEP, 1991–93; Mem., John Smith's Campaign Team for leadership of Labour Party, 1992; Political Asst to Glenys Kinnock, MEP, 1994–95; Trade Union Organiser, Equality Officer, GMB Southern Region, 1995–97. *Recreations:* cinema, music. *Address:* House of Commons, SW1A 0AA.

KING, Dr Paul Frederick; Transport Consultant, KPMG Passenger Transport Group, since 1997; *b* 4 Jan. 1946; *s* of Cedric Marcus King and Theresa Mary King; *m* 1980, Bertha Ines Avila de King; two *s*. *Educ:* Charterhouse Sch.; Queens' Coll., Cambridge (MA); Univ. of London (MSc, PhD). Lectr, Management Studies, Cambridge Univ., 1970–75; Dir, Special Assignments, TI Group, 1975–79; Sales and Marketing Dir, TI Raleigh, 1979–87; Planning and Marketing Dir, British Shoe Corp, 1987–90; Regional Railways, BR: Planning and Marketing Dir, 1990–93; Man. Dir, 1993–94; Gp Man. Dir, North and West, BRB, 1994–97. Non-executive Director: British Waterways, 1998–; Connex Rail Ltd, 1999–. *Recreation:* canal cruising. *Address:* The Homestead, 65 Swithland Lane, Rothley, Leics LE7 7SG. *T:* (0116) 237 4670.

KING, Paul William; Agent General for British Columbia in the United Kingdom and Europe, since 1995; *b* Srinagar, Kashmir, 6 Sept. 1943; *s* of late Rev. Canon Roderick King and of Kathleen King; *m* 1969, Susan Jane Glenny (*d* 2000); two *s*. *Educ:* Exeter Sch.; Univ. of Alberta (BA). With E. I. du Pont de Nemours, USA, 1964; Kodak Canada Ltd, 1965–77; Dir responsible for trade with Pacific Rim countries, Govt of Alberta, 1977–81; Director: European Ops, Alberta House, London, 1982–90; Trade and Investment, BC House, London, 1990–95. MInstD. Freeman, City of London, 1996. *Recreations:* gardening, travel, motor-racing. *Address:* British Columbia House, 3 Regent Street, SW1Y 4NS. *T:* (020) 7930 6857. *Club:* East India.

KING, Air Vice-Marshal Peter Francis, CB 1987; OBE (mil.) 1964; FRCSE; The Senior Consultant, RAF, 1985–87; Air Vice-Marshal, Princess Mary's RAF Hospital, Halton, 1983–87; Consultant Otorhinolaryngologist, King Edward VII Hospital, Midhurst, since 1988; *b* 17 Sept. 1922; *s* of Sqn Ldr William George King, MBE, RAF, and Florence Margaret King (*née* Sell); *m* 1945, Doreen Maxwell Aaröe, 2nd *d* of Jorgen Hansen-Aaröe; one *s* one *d*. *Educ:* Framlingham Coll.; King's Coll. London, 1940–42; Charing Cross Hosp., 1942–45; Univ. of Edinburgh, 1947. DLO; MRCS, LRCP; MFOM. Kitchener Med. Services Schol. for RAF, 1941; Ho. Phys., Ho. Surg., Charing Cross Hosp., 1945; commnd RAF, 1945; specialist in Otorhinolaryngology, employed Cosford, Ely, Fayid, Halton, CME; Cons. in Otorhinolaryngology, 1955; Hunterian Prof., RCS, 1964; Cons. Adviser in Otorhinolaryngology, 1966; Air Cdre 1976; Reader in Aviation Med., Inst. of Aviation Med., 1977; Whittingham Prof. in Aviation Med., IAM and RCP, 1979; QHS 1979–87; Dean of Air Force Medicine, 1983. Cons. to Herts HA, 1963, and CAA, 1973; Examiner for Dip. in Aviation Med., RCP, 1980. Littler Meml Lectr, British Soc. of Audiology, 2001. Pres., Sect. of Otology, RSocMed, 1977–78 (Sec., 1972–74); Chm., Brit. Soc. of Audiology, 1979–81 (Hon. Life Mem., 1998); Vice-Pres., RNID, 1990 (Vice-Chm., 1980–88); Member: BMA, 1945– (Life Mem., 1996); Scottish Otological Soc., 1955–90; Royal Aeronaut. Soc., 1976– (FRAeS 1998); Council, Brit. Assoc. of Otorhinolaryngologists, 1960–89 (Hon. Life Mem., 1996); Editorial Bd, British Jl of Audiology, 1980–88. Fellow, Inst. of Acoustics, 1977. FRSocMed. CStJ 1987. Lady Cade Medal, RCS, 1967; (jtly) Howells Meml Prize, Univ. of London, 1992. *Publications:* Noise and Vibration in Aviation (with J. C. Guignard), 1972; (with John Ernsting) Aviation Medicine, 1988; (jtly) Assessment of Hearing Disability, 1992; numerous articles, chapters, lectures and papers, in books and relevant jls on aviation otolaryngology, noise deafness, hearing conservation, tympanoplasty, facial paralysis, otic barotrauma, etc. *Recreations:* sculpture, looking at prints. *Address:* 5 Churchill Gate, Oxford Road, Woodstock, Oxon OX20 1QW. *T:* (01993) 813115. *Club:* Royal Air Force.

KING, Rev. Canon Philip David; Secretary, Church of England Board of Mission, 1991–2000 (Secretary, Board for Mission and Unity, 1989–91); *b* 6 May 1935; *s* of Frank Harman King and Gladys Winifred King; *m* 1963, Margaret Naomi Rivers Pitt; two *s* two *d*. *Educ:* Keble College, Oxford (MA Jurisp.); Tyndale Hall, Bristol. Curate, Holy Trinity, Redhill, 1960–63; Minister in charge, St Patrick's, Wallington, 1963–68; Vicar, Christ Church, Fulham, 1968–74; Gen. Sec., S American Missionary Soc., 1974–86; Vicar, Christ Church and St Peter, Harrow, 1986–89. *Publications:* Leadership Explosion, 1987; Making Christ Known, 1992; Good News For A Suffering World, 1996; Leading a Church, 1997. *Recreation:* hill-walking. *Address:* 31 Myrtle Avenue, Ruislip, Middlesex HA4 8SA. *T:* and *Fax:* (020) 8429 0636.

KING, Phillip, CBE 1975; PRA (RA 1991; ARA 1977); sculptor; Professor of Sculpture: Royal College of Art, 1980–90, Emeritus since 1991; Royal Academy Schools, since 1990; President, Royal Academy of Arts, since 1999; *b* 1 May 1934; *s* of Thomas John King and of Gabrielle (*née* Liautard); *m* 1st, 1957, Lilian Odelle (marr. diss. 1987); (one *s* decd); 2nd, 1988, Judith Corballis. *Educ:* Mill Hill Sch.; Christ's Coll., Cambridge Univ. (languages); St Martin's Sch. of Art (sculpture). Teacher at St Martin's Sch. of Art, 1959–78; Asst to Henry Moore, 1959–60. Trustee, Tate Gallery, 1967–69; Mem. Art Panel, Arts Council, 1977–79. Vis. Prof., Berlin Sch. of Art, 1979–81. *One-man exhibitions include:* British Pavilion, Venice Biennale, 1968; European Mus. Tour, 1974–75 (Kroller-Muller Nat. Mus., Holland; Kunsthalle, Düsseldorf; Kunsthalle, Bern; Musée Galliera, Paris; Ulster Mus., Belfast); UK Touring Exhib., 1975–76 (Sheffield, Cumbria, Aberdeen, Glasgow, Newcastle, Portsmouth); Hayward Gall. (retrospective), 1981; Forte di Belvedere, Florence, 1997. Commissions include: Cross Bend, European Patent Office, Munich, 1978; Hiroshima Mus. of Art, 1989. First Prize, Socha Piestanskych Parkov, Piestany, Czechoslovakia, 1969. *Address:* Royal Academy of Arts, Piccadilly, W1J 0BD; c/o Bernard Jacobson Gallery, 14a Clifford Street, W1X 1RF.

KING, Robert George Cecil; Chairman, Social Security Appeal Tribunals, 1987–98; Under Secretary (Legal), HM Customs and Excise, 1985–87; *b* 21 Jan. 1927; *s* of Stanley Cecil and Kathleen Mary King; *m* 1952, Mary Marshall. *Educ:* Nunthorpe Grammar School, York. Called to the Bar, Lincolns Inn, 1965. Army, 1945–48; British Rail, 1948–53; Judicial Dept, Kenya, 1954–61; East African Common Services Organisation, 1962–64; Solicitor's Office, HM Customs and Excise, 1965–87. *Recreations:* golf, bowls, gardening, watching cricket, watching television. *Address:* 181 Greenshaw Drive, Wigginton, York YO32 2SD. *T:* (01904) 765039. *Clubs:* MCC; York Golf, Royal Nairobi Golf.

KING, Robert John Stephen; conductor; harpsichordist; Artistic Director, The King's Consort, since 1980; *b* 27 June 1960; *s* of Stephen King and Margaret Digby. *Educ:* Radley Coll.; St John's Coll., Cambridge (MA). Writer; editor of much music *pre* 1750; broadcaster; conductor, orchestras and choirs, incl. Orq. Sinfonica Euskadi, Orq. di Madrid, Orebro Chamber Orch., Netherlands Chamber Orch. and Chamber Choir, RTL Symphony Orch., Orch. d'Auvergne, English Chamber Orch., Norrköping SO, Atlanta SO, Houston SO, Minnesota SO, Detroit SO, Il Giardino Armonico, Orquesta de Cadaqués, Granada SO, Tölzer Knabenchor, Collegium Vocale Ghent. Artistic Dir, Aldeburgh Easter Fest., 1998–2000. *Publications:* Henry Purcell, 1994; numerous musical edns. *Recreations:* ski-ing, cricket, lupin growing. *Address:* 34 St Mary's Grove, W4 3LN. *T:* (020) 8995 9994, *Fax:* (020) 8995 2115.

KING, Robert Shirley; Under Secretary, Department of Health and Social Security, 1976–80; *b* 12 July 1920; *s* of late Rev. William Henry King, MC, TD, MA, and Dorothy King (*née* Sharpe); *m* 1st, 1947, Margaret Siddall (*d* 1956); two *d*; 2nd, 1958, Mary Rowell (*d* 1996); one *s* two *d*; 3rd, 1998, Daphne Shercliff. *Educ:* Alexandra Road Sch., Oldham; Manchester Grammar Sch.; Trinity Coll., Cambridge (Schol., MA). Served War, RAF, 1940–45. Colonial Service, Tanganyika, 1949–62 (Dist Comr, Bukoba, 1956–58, Geita, 1959–62); Home Office: Principal, 1962–69 (seconded to Civil Service Dept, 1968–69); Asst Sec., 1969–70; transf., with Children's Dept, to DHSS, 1971; Asst Sec., DHSS, 1971–76; Sec., Wkg Party on Role and Tasks of Social Workers, Nat. Inst. for Social Work, 1980–82; part-time Asst Sec., Home Office, 1985–86. Sec., Health Promotion Res, Trust, 1984–89. Member Council: British and Foreign Sch. Soc., 1982–89; Shape, 1982–89. Governor: Cheshunt Foundn, 1976–83; Bell Educnl Trust, 1984–89. *Recreations:* walking, cycling, gardening, African affairs. *Address:* 12 Merton Street, Cambridge CB3 9JD.

KING, Roger Douglas; Chief Executive, Road Haulage Association, since 2000; *b* 26 Oct. 1943; *s* of Douglas and Cecilie King; *m* 1976, Jennifer Susan (*née* Sharpe); twin *s* one *d*. *Educ:* Solihull Sch. Served automobile engrg apprenticeship with British Motor Corp., 1960–66; sales rep., 1966–74; own manufg business, 1974–81; self-employed car product distributor, 1982–83; Dir of Public Affairs, 1992–99, Dep. Chief Exec., 1999–2000, SMMT. Dir, Prince Michael Road Safety Awards Scheme, 1992–. Non-executive Director: Nat. Express Hldgs, 1988–91; Coventry Bldg Soc., 1995–. MP (C) Birmingham, Northfield, 1983–92. PPS to Minister for Local Govt, 1987–88, for Water and Planning, 1988, DoE, to Sec. of State for Employment, 1989–92. Mem., H of C Transport Select Cttee, 1984–87; Vice-Chm., All Party Motor Industry Gp, 1985–92; Jt Sec., Cons. Tourism Cttee, 1985–87. FIMI 1986. Mem., Co. of Carmen, 2001–. *Recreations:* swimming, motoring. *Address:* 241 Tessall Lane, Northfield, Birmingham B31 5EQ. *T:* (0121) 476 6649.

KING, Prof. Roger Patrick; Vice-Chancellor, University of Lincolnshire and Humberside (formerly Humberside), 1992–2000; *b* 31 May 1945; *s* of Timothy Francis

King and Vera May King; *m* 1966, Susan Winifred Ashworth; one *d. Educ:* Wimbledon Coll.; Univ. of London (BSc Hons Econ.); Univ. of Birmingham (MSocSci). HM Civil Service, 1963; Sales Management Trainee, United Glass, 1964; Sales Manager, Marley Tiles, 1965; Lectr and Sen. Lectr in Social Scis, Manchester Polytechnic, 1970–75; Principal Lectr, later Head of Dept of Behavioural Scis, Huddersfield Poly., 1976–85; Dep. Dir, 1985–89, Dir and Chief Exec., 1989–92, Humberside Poly. *Publications:* (with N. Nugent) The British Right, 1977; (with N. Nugent) Respectable Rebels, 1979; The Middle Class, 1981; Capital and Politics, 1983; The State in Modern Society, 1986; (with J. Simmie) The State in Action, 1990. *Recreations:* reading, running, music, Rugby League. *Address:* 43 Sandown Park, Tunbridge Wells, Kent TN2 4RH. *T:* (01892) 823460. *Club:* Reform.

KING, Stephen Edwin; author; *b* Portland, Maine, 21 Sept. 1947; *s* of Donald King and Nellie Ruth King (*née* Pillsbury); *m* 1971, Tabitha Jane Spruce; two *s* one *d. Educ:* Lisbon Falls High Sch.; Univ. of Maine at Orono (BS 1970). Laundry worker, 1970; English Teacher, Hampden Acad., 1971–73; writer in residence, Univ. of Maine at Orono, 1978–79. *Screenplay,* Sleepwalkers, 1991; many of his stories have been filmed; dir., Maximum Overdrive, 1986. *Publications:* Carrie, 1974; 'Salem's Lot, 1975; The Shining, 1976; The Stand, 1978; Night Shift (short stories), 1978; Firestarter, 1980; Danse Macabre, 1981; Cujo, 1981; Different Seasons, 1982; The Dark Tower: vol. 1, The Gunslinger, 1982, vol. 2, The Drawing of the Three, 1987, vol. 3, Waste Lands, 1991, vol. 4, Wizard and Glass, 1997; Christine, 1983; Pet Sematary, 1983; (jtly) The Talisman, 1984; Cycle of the Werewolf, 1985; It, 1986; Skeleton Crew, 1986; The Eyes of the Dragon, 1987; Misery, 1987; The Tommyknockers, 1987; The Dark Half, 1989; The Stand (unabridged edn), 1990; Four Past Midnight, 1990; (jtly) Dark Visions, 1990; Needful Things, 1991; Gerald's Game, 1992; Dolores Claiborne, 1992; Nightmares and Dreamscapes (short stories), 1993; Insomnia, 1994; Desperation, 1996; The Green Mile, 1996; Wizards and Glass, 1997; Bag of Bones, 1998; The Girl Who Loved Tom Gordon, 1999; Hearts In Atlantis, 1999; On Writing: a memoir of the craft, 2000; (as Richard Bachman): Rage, 1977; The Long Walk, 1979; Roadwork, 1981; The Running Man, 1982; Thinner, 1984; The Regulators, 1996. *Address:* c/o Hodder Headline plc, 338 Euston Road, NW1 3BH.

KING, Dame Thea, (Dame Thea Thurston), DBE 2001 (OBE 1985); FRCM, FGSM; freelance musician; Professor, Guildhall School of Music, since 1988; *b* 26 Dec. 1925; *m* Jan. 1953, Frederick John Thurston (*d* Dec. 1953). *Educ:* Bedford High Sch.; Royal College of Music (FRCM 1975; ARCM 1944 and 1947). FGSM 1992. Prof. of Clarinet, RCM, 1961–87. Sadler's Wells Orchestra, 1950–52; Portia Wind Ensemble, 1955–68; London Mozart Players, 1956–84; Member: English Chamber Orchestra, Vesuvius Ensemble, Robles Ensemble. Frequent soloist, broadcaster, recitalist; recordings include Mozart, Brahms, Spohr, Finzi, Bruch, Mendelssohn, Stanford and 20th Century British music. Hon. RAM 1998. *Publications:* clarinet solos, Chester Woodwind series, 1977; arrangement of J. S. Bach, Duets for 2 Clarinets, 1979; Schumann for the Clarinet, 1991; Mendelssohn for the Clarinet, 1993; The Romantic Clarinet, Vol. 1, 1994, Vol. 2, 1995. *Recreations:* cows, pillow lace, painting, ski-ing, piano-playing. *Address:* 16 Milverton Road, NW6 7AS. *T:* (020) 8459 3453.

KING, Timothy Roger Alan; QC 1991; a Recorder, since 1991; *b* 5 April 1949; *s* of late Harold Bonsall King and of Dorothy King; *m* 1986, Bernadette Goodman. *Educ:* Booker Avenue County Primary Sch., Liverpool; Liverpool Inst. High Sch.; Lincoln Coll., Oxford (MA, BCL). Called to the Bar, Lincoln's Inn, 1973 (Bencher, 2000); Mem., Northern Circuit, 1973. *Recreations:* travel, Association football. *Address:* 25 Byrom Street, Manchester M3 4PF. *T:* (0161) 829 2100. *Clubs:* Athenæum (Liverpool); Liverpool Cricket.

KING, Timothy Russell; His Honour Judge King; a Circuit Judge, since 1995; *b* 4 June 1946; *s* of late Charles Albert King and Elizabeth Lily King (*née* Alexander); *m* 1st, 1973, Christine Morison (marr. diss. 1979); two *s*; 2nd, 1989, Rotraud Jane (*née* Oppermann). *Educ:* St Mary's Coll., Bitterne Park, Southampton; Inns of Court Sch. of Law. HM Diplomatic Service (Colonial Office), 1966–67; called to the Bar, Gray's Inn, 1970; in practice, SE Circuit, 1970–86; Dep. Judge Advocate, 1986; AJAG, 1990–95; Asst Recorder, 1989–93; Recorder, 1993–95. Pres., St Leonard's Soc., 1998–. *Recreations:* sailing, ski-ing, classical music, reading, walking, cooking, golf. *Address:* Crown Court at Snaresbrook, Hollybush Hill, E11 1QW. *T:* (020) 8982 5500. *Club:* Royal London Yacht (Cowes).

KING, Prof. Ursula, PhD; Professor of Theology and Religious Studies, University of Bristol, since 1989 (Head of Department, 1989–97); *b* 22 Sept. 1938; *d* of Hedwig and Adolf Brenke; *m* 1963, Prof. Anthony Douglas King; four *d. Educ:* Univs of Bonn, Munich, Paris (STL), Delhi (MA) and London (PhD). Lectr in Divinity, Coloma Coll. of Educn, 1963–65; Visiting Lecturer, 1965–70: Dept of Philosophy, Univ. of Delhi; Indian Inst. of Technology; Indian Social Inst.; Lectr and Sen. Lectr, Dept of Theology and Religious Studies, Univ. of Leeds, 1971–89; S. A. Cook Bye-Fellow, Newnham Coll. and Gonville and Caius Coll., Cambridge, 1976–77. Visiting Professor: in Feminist Theology, Univ. of Oslo, 1999–2001; in Ecumenical Theology, Xavier Univ., Cincinnati, 1999. Bampton Lectr, Oxford Univ., 1996. FRSA. Hon. DD Edinburgh, 1996; Hon. Dr Theol Oslo, 2000. Student awards from Germany and France; Indian Philosophical Congress Gold Medal, 1969. *Publications:* Towards a New Mysticism, 1980; The Spirit of One Earth, 1989; Women and Spirituality, 1989; (ed) Turning Points in Religious Studies, 1990; (ed) Feminist Theology from the Third World, 1994; (ed) Religion and Gender, 1995; Spirit of Fire, 1996; Christ in All Things: exploring spirituality with Teilhard de Chardin, 1997; Christian Mystics: the spiritual heart of the Christian tradition, 1998; (ed) Pierre Teilhard de Chardin: writings selected with an introduction, 1999; (ed) Spirituality and Society in the New Millennium, 2001; contribs to acad. jls. *Recreations:* walking, reading, travelling. *Address:* Department of Theology and Religious Studies, University of Bristol, Bristol BS8 1TB. *T:* (0117) 928 7760.

KING, Sir Wayne Alexander, 8th Bt *cr* 1815; self-employed entrepreneur; *b* 2 Feb. 1962; *s* of Sir Peter Alexander King, 7th Bt, and of Jean Margaret (who *m* 2nd, 1978, Rev. Richard Graham Mackenzie), *d* of Christopher Thomas Cavell, Deal; *S* father, 1973; *m* 1984, Laura Ellen, *d* of Donald James Lea, Almonte, Ontario; one *s. Educ:* Sir Roger Manwood's Sch., Sandwich, Kent; Algonquin Coll., Ottawa, Ont (majored in Accounting and Retail Management). Coach and Head Referee, Almonte Soccer (Canadian Soccer Assoc. Coaching Level I designation); Referee-in-chief, Almonte/ Pakenham Minor Ice Hockey Assoc. *Recreations:* all sports. *Heir: s* Peter Richard Donald King, *b* 4 May 1988. *Address:* 146 High Street, Almonte, ON K0A 1A0, Canada.

KING-HAMILTON, His Honour (Myer) Alan (Barry); QC 1954; an additional Judge of the Central Criminal Court, 1964–79; a Deputy Circuit Judge, 1979–83; *b* 9 Dec. 1904; *o s* of Alfred King-Hamilton; *m* 1935, Rosalind Irene Ellis (*d* 1991); two *d. Educ:* Bishop's Stortford Grammar Sch.; Trinity Hall, Cambridge (BA 1927, MA 1929; President: Cambridge Univ. Law Soc., 1926–27; Cambridge Union Soc., 1927). Called to Bar, Middle Temple, 1929 (Bencher, 1961); served War of 1939–45, RAF, finishing with rank of Squadron Leader; served on Finchley Borough Council, 1938–39 and 1945–50. Recorder of Hereford, 1955–56; Recorder of Gloucester, 1956–61; Recorder of Wolverhampton, 1961–64; Dep. Chm. Oxford County Quarter Sessions, 1955–64, 1966–71; Leader of Oxford Circuit, 1961–64. Elected to General Council of Bar, 1958. Pres., West London Reform Synagogue, 1967–75, 1977–83 (Hon. Life Pres., 1995); Vice-Pres., World Congress of Faiths, 1967–. Legal Member: Med. Practices Cttee, Min. of Health, 1961–64; ABTA Appeal Bd, 1980–95; Mem., Arts and Library Cttee, MCC, 1985–89; first Chm., Pornography and Violence Res. Trust (formerly Mary Whitehouse Res. and Educn Trust), 1986–96 (Mem. Cttee, 1996–). President: Westlon Housing Assoc., 1995–97 (Founder Mem. and first Chm., 1975–95; Hon. Life Pres., 1998); Birnbeck Housing Assoc., 1995–98 (Mem. Cttee, 1982–95; Hon. Life Pres., 1998). Trustee, Barnet Community Trust, 1986–89. Co-founder, Refreshers CC, 1935. Freeman of City of London; Master, Needlemakers' Co., 1969. *Publication:* And Nothing But the Truth (autobiog.), 1982. *Recreations:* cricket, gardening, the theatre. *Clubs:* Royal Air Force, MCC.

KING-HELE, Desmond George, FRS 1966; author; Deputy Chief Scientific Officer, Space Department, Royal Aircraft Establishment, Farnborough, 1968–88, retired; *b* 3 Nov. 1927; *s* of late S. G. and of B. King-Hele, Seaford, Sussex; *m* 1954, Marie Thérèse Newman (separated 1992); two *d. Educ:* Epsom Coll.; Trinity Coll., Cambridge. BA (1st cl. hons Mathematics) 1948; MA 1952. At RAE, Farnborough, 1948–88, working on space research from 1955. Mem., International Academy of Astronautics, 1961. Chairman: Satellite Optical Tracking Cttee, Royal Soc., 1972–97; History of Science Grants Cttee, Royal Soc., 1990–93; British Nat. Cttee for History of Science, Medicine and Technol., 1985–89; Adv. Panel for Culture of Sci., Technol. and Medicine, BL, 1992–2001. Lectures: Symons, RMetS, 1961; Duke of Edinburgh's, Royal Inst. of Navigation, 1964; Jeffreys, RAS, 1971; Halley, Oxford, 1974; Bakerian, Royal Soc., 1974; Sydenham, Soc. of Apothecaries, 1981; H. L. Welsh, Univ. of Toronto, 1982; Milne, Oxford, 1984; Wilkins, Royal Soc., 1997. FIMA; FRAS. Hon. DSc Aston, 1979; DUniv Surrey, 1986. Eddington Medal, RAS, 1971; Charles Chree Medal, Inst. of Physics, 1971; Lagrange Prize, Acad. Royale de Belgique, 1972; Nordberg Medal, Internat. Cttee on Space Res., 1990. Editor, Notes and Records of Royal Soc., 1989–96. *Publications:* Shelley: His Thought and Work, 1960, 3rd edn 1984; Satellites and Scientific Research, 1960; Erasmus Darwin, 1963; Theory of Satellite Orbits in an Atmosphere, 1964; (ed) Space Research V, 1965; Observing Earth Satellites, 1966, 2nd edn 1983; (ed) Essential Writings of Erasmus Darwin, 1968; The End of the Twentieth Century?, 1970; Poems and Trixies, 1972; Doctor of Revolution, 1977; (ed) The Letters of Erasmus Darwin, 1981; (ed) The RAE Table of Earth Satellites, 1981, 4th edn 1990; Animal Spirits, 1983; Erasmus Darwin and the Romantic Poets, 1986; Satellite Orbits in an Atmosphere: theory and applications, 1987; A Tapestry of Orbits, 1992; (ed) John Herschel, 1992; (ed) A Concordance to the Botanic Garden, 1994; Erasmus Darwin: a life of unequalled achievement (Society of Authors' Medical History Prize), 1999; Antic and Romantic (poems), 2000; *radio drama scripts:* A Mind of Universal Sympathy, 1973; The Lunaticks, 1978; 300 papers in Proc. Royal Society, Nature, Keats-Shelley Memor. Bull., New Scientist, Planetary and Space Science, and other scientific and literary jls. *Recreations:* tennis, reading, cross-country running. *Address:* 7 Hilltops Court, 65 North Lane, Buriton, Hants GU31 5RS. *T:* (01730) 261646.

KING MURRAY, Ronald; *see* Murray.

KING-REYNOLDS, Guy Edwin; Head Master, Dauntsey's School, West Lavington, 1969–85; *b* 9 July 1923; *er s* of late Dr H. E. King Reynolds, York; *m* 1st, 1947, Norma Lansdowne Russell (*d* 1949); 2nd, 1950, Jeanne Nancy Perris Rhodes; one *d. Educ:* St Peter's Sch., York; Emmanuel Coll., Cambridge (1944–47). Served RAF, 1942–44. BA 1946, MA 1951. Asst Master, Glenhow Prep. Sch., 1947–48; Head of Geography Dept, Solihull Sch., Warwickshire, 1948–54; family business, 1954–55; Head of Geography, Portsmouth Grammar Sch., 1955–57; Solihull School: Housemaster, 1957–63, Second Master, 1963–69. Part-time Lecturer in International Affairs, Extra-Mural Dept, Birmingham Univ.; Chm., Solihull WEA. Mem., BBC Regl Adv. Council, 1970–73. LRAM (speech and drama) 1968. Governor: St Peter's Sch., York, 1984–97; Dean Close Sch., Cheltenham, 1985–94 (Vice Pres., 1994–99, and Life Gov., 1994); La Retraite, Salisbury, 1985–88. Mem. Cttee, GBA, 1986–89, 1990–97. JP: Solihull, 1965–69; Wiltshire, 1970–91 (Chm., 1982–85, Vice-Chm., 1985–91, Devizes Bench); Avon (Bath), 1991–93. Freeman, City of London, 1988. *Recreations:* drama (director and actor); travel. *Address:* 14 Pulteney Mews, Great Pulteney Street, Bath, Avon BA2 4DS.

KING-SMITH, Ronald Gordon, (Dick); author; *b* 27 March 1922; *s* of Ronald King-Smith and Grace King-Smith; *m* 1943, Myrle England (*d* 2000); one *s* two *d. Educ:* Marlborough; Bristol Univ. (BEd 1975). Served Grenadier Guards, 1941–46. Farmer, 1947–67; teacher, Farmborough Primary Sch., 1975–82. *Publications:* over 110 titles include: The Fox Busters, 1978; Daggie Dogfoot, 1980; The Mouse Butcher, 1982; Magnus Powermouse, 1982; The Queen's Nose, 1983; The Sheep Pig, 1984 (filmed as Babe, 1995); Harry's Mad, 1984; Saddlebottom, 1985; Noah's Brother, 1986; The Hedgehog, 1987; George Speaks, 1988; Martin's Mice, 1988; Sophie's Snail, 1988; The Toby Man, 1989; Dodos are Forever, 1989; Ace, 1990; Paddy's Pot of Gold, 1990; The Water Horse, 1990; The Cuckoo Child, 1991; Sophie's Tom, 1991; Sophie Hits Six, 1991; The Guard Dog, 1991; Find the White Horse, 1991; Lady Daisy, 1992; Pretty Polly, 1992; Dragon Boy, 1993; The Merrythought, 1993; Sophie in the Saddle, 1993; The Schoolmouse, 1994; Harriet's Hare, 1994; Sophie is Seven, 1994; Bobby the Bad, 1994; King Max the Last, 1995; Sophie's Lucky, 1995; The Terrible Trins, 1995; Clever Duck, 1996; Godhanger, 1996; Dick King-Smith's Animal Friends, 1996; Treasure Trove, 1997; Puppy Love, 1997; What Sadie Saw, 1997; The Stray, 1997; The Merman, 1998; How Green Was My Mouse, 1998; A Mouse Called Wolf, 1998; The Crowstarver, 1998; Mr Ape, 1998; Poppet, 1999; The Magic Carpet Slippers, 2000; The Roundhill, 2000. *Recreations:* reading, enjoying the countryside, washing-up. *Address:* Diamond's Cottage, Queen Charlton, Keynsham, Bristol BS31 2SJ.

KING-TENISON, family name of **Earl of Kingston**.

KINGARTH, Hon. Lord; Hon. Derek Robert Alexander Emslie; a Senator of the College of Justice in Scotland, since 1997; *b* 21 June 1949; *s* of Baron Emslie, *qv*; *m* 1974, Elizabeth Jane Cameron Carstairs, *d* of Andrew McLaren Carstairs; one *s* two *d. Educ:* Edinburgh Acad.; Trinity Coll., Glenalmond; Gonville and Caius Coll., Cambridge (Hist. Schol.; BA); Edinburgh Univ. (LLB). Advocate 1974; Standing Jun. Counsel, DHSS, 1979–87; Advocate Depute, 1985–88; QC (Scot.) 1987; part time Chairman: Pension Appeal Tribunal (Scotland), 1988–95; Medical Appeal Tribunal (Scotland), 1990–95. Vice-Dean, Faculty of Advocates, 1995–97. *Recreations:* golf, cinema, wine, watching football. *Address:* 35 Ann Street, Edinburgh EH4 1PL. *T:* (0131) 332 6648. *Clubs:* Hawks (Cambridge); New (Edinburgh); Hon. Co. of Edinburgh Golfers.
See also Hon. G. N. H. Emslie.

KINGDON, Roger Taylor, CBE 1990; FIMechE, FIM; Chief Executive, Davy Corporation, 1987–90; *b* 27 June 1930; *s* of late Fletcher Munroe Kingdon and Laetitia May Kingdon (*née* Wissler); *m* 1956, Gaynor Mary Downs; two *s* one *d. Educ:* Christ's

Hospital; Pembroke College, Cambridge (MA). CEng. Graduate trainee, Woodall Duckham Construction Co., 1954–58; Ashmore Benson Pease & Co., 1958–68 (Dir, 1964–68); Managing Director: Newell Dunford Group, 1968–80; Herbert Morris (Davy Group), 1980–83; Chm., Davy McKee (Stockton), 1983–87; Director: Dunford & Elliot, 1971–80; Peugeot Talbot Motor Co., 1979–92; Davy Corp., 1986–90; Teesside Devel Corp., 1987–98; Carbo plc (formerly Hopkinson Group), 1992–. President: Process Plant Assoc., 1979–80; NE Engineering Employers' Assoc., 1986–89; Chairman: British Metallurgical Plant Constructors' Assoc., 1985–87; Latin American Trade Adv. Group, 1989–90. Vice Chm., South Tees Acute NHS Trust, 1992–95. Mem. Council, Durham Univ., 1995–2000. CIMgt. *Recreations:* fell walking, sailing. *Address:* West End Farm, The Green, Borrowby, Thirsk, North Yorks Y07 4QL. *T:* (01845) 537663. *Club:* Army and Navy.

KINGHAM, Teresa Jane, (Tess); *b* 4 May 1963; *d* of Roy Thomas Kingham and Patricia Ribian Kingham (*née* Murphy); *m* 1991, Mark Luetchford; one *s* two *d* (of whom one *s* one *d* are twins). *Educ:* Dartford Girls' Grammar Sch.; Royal Holloway Coll., Univ. of London (BA Hons German 1984); Univ. of East Anglia (PGCE Mod. Langs 1985). Appeals Dir, War on Want, 1986–90; Mktg and Communications Dir, Blue Cross (animal welfare), 1990–92; Editor, Youth Express, Daily Express, 1992–94; Communications Exec., Oxfam, 1994–96. Contested (Lab) Cotswolds, EP elecn, 1994. MP (Lab) Gloucester, 1997–2001. Chair, All Party Gp on Western Sahara, 1997–2001. Mem., Egypt Exploration Soc. *Recreations:* international travel/affairs, archaeology, walking with family and dog.

KINGHORN, Squadron Leader Ernest; *b* 1 Nov. 1907; *s* of A. Kinghorn, Leeds; *m* 1942, Eileen Mary Lambert Russell (*d* 1980); one *s* (and one *s* one *d* decd). *Educ:* Leeds, Basel and Lille Universities. Languages Master Ashville Coll., Doncaster Grammar Sch. and Roundhay Sch., Leeds. Served in Intelligence Branch, RAF. British Officer for Control of Manpower, SHAEF, and Staff Officer CCG. MP (Lab) Yarmouth Division of Norfolk, 1950–51, Great Yarmouth, 1945–50. *Address:* 59 Queens Avenue, Hanworth, Middx TW13 7NT.

KINGHORN, William Oliver; Chief Agricultural Officer, Department of Agriculture and Fisheries for Scotland, 1971–75; *b* 17 May 1913; *s* of Thomas Kinghorn, Duns, and Elizabeth Oliver; *m* 1943, Edith Johnstone; one *s* two *d*. *Educ:* Berwickshire High Sch.; Edinburgh Univ. BSc (Agr) Hons, BSc Hons. Senior Inspector, 1946; Technical Develt Officer, 1959; Chief Inspector, 1970. SBStJ. *Publication:* contrib. Annals of Applied Biology, 1936. *Address:* 23 Cumlodden Avenue, Edinburgh EH12 6DR. *T:* (0131) 337 1435.

KINGMAN, Sir John (Frank Charles), Kt 1985; FRS 1971; Chairman, Statistics Commission, since 2000; N. M. Rothschild & Sons Professor of Mathematical Sciences, and Director, Isaac Newton Institute for Mathematical Sciences, University of Cambridge, since 2001; Fellow of Pembroke College, Cambridge, 1961–65 and since 2001; *b* 28 Aug. 1939; *er s* of late Dr F. E. T. Kingman, FRSC and Maud (*née* Harley); *m* 1964, Valerie Cromwell, FSA, FRHistS (former Dir, History of Parlt), *d* of late F. Cromwell, OBE, ISO; one *s* one *d*. *Educ:* Christ's Coll., Finchley; Pembroke Coll., Cambridge (MA, ScD; Smith's Prize, 1962; Hon. Fellow, 1988). CStat 1993. Asst Lectr in Mathematics, 1962–64, Lectr, 1964–65, Univ. of Cambridge; Reader in Mathematics and Statistics, 1965–66, Prof. 1966–69, Univ. of Sussex; Prof. of Maths, Univ. of Oxford, 1969–85; Fellow, St Anne's Coll., Oxford, 1978–85, Hon. Fellow, 1985; Vice-Chancellor, Bristol Univ., 1985–2001. Visiting appointments: Univ. of Western Australia, 1963, 1974; Stanford Univ., USA, 1968; ANU, 1978. Chairman: Science Bd, SRC, 1979–81; SERC, 1981–85; Vice-Pres., Parly and Scientific Cttee, 1986–89 (Vice-Chm., 1983–86); Mem. Bd, British Council, 1986–91. Chm., Cttee of Inquiry into the Teaching of English Language, 1987–88. Director: IBM UK Holdings Ltd, 1985–95; Beecham Group plc, 1986–89; SmithKline Beecham plc, 1989–90; British Technology Group plc, 1992 (Mem. Council, British Technol. Gp, 1984–92); SW RHA, 1990–94; Avon HA, 1996–99. Chm., 1973–76, Vice-Pres., 1976–92, Inst. of Statisticians; President: Royal Statistical Soc., 1987–89 (Vice-Pres., 1977–79; Guy Medal in Silver, 1981; Hon. Fellow, 1993); London Math. Soc., 1990–92. Mem., Brighton Co. Borough Council, 1968–71; Chm., Regency Soc. of Brighton and Hove, 1975–81. MAE 1995; AcSS 2000. Hon. Senator, Univ. of Hannover, 1991. Hon. DSc: Sussex, 1983; Southampton, 1985; West of England, 1993; Hon. LLD: Bristol, 1989; Queen's Univ., Kingston, Ontario, 1999; Hon. DPhil Cheltenham and Gloucester, 1998; Dr *hc* St Petersburg Univ. of Humanities and Social Scis, 1994. Royal Medal, Royal Soc., 1983. Officier des Palmes Académiques, 1989. *Publications:* Introduction to Measure and Probability (with S. J. Taylor), 1966; The Algebra of Queues, 1966; Regenerative Phenomena, 1972; Mathematics of Genetic Diversity, 1980; Poisson Processes, 1993; papers in mathematical and statistical jls. *Address:* Isaac Newton Institute for Mathematical Sciences, 20 Clarkson Road, Cambridge CB3 0EH. *Club:* Lansdowne; Savages (Bristol).

KINGSALE, 35th Baron *cr* 1223 (by some reckonings 30th Baron); **John de Courcy;** Baron Courcy and Baron of Ringrone; Premier Baron of Ireland; President, Impex Consultants Ltd, since 1988; Director: Marquis de Verneuil Trust, since 1971; de Courcy, Daunt Professional & Executive Agencies (Australia), since 1987; Kinsale Development Co., since 1989; Chairman, National Association for Service to the Realm; *b* 27 Jan. 1941; *s* of Lieutenant-Commander the Hon. Michael John Rancé de Courcy, RN (killed on active service, 1940), and Joan (*d* 1967), *d* of Robert Reid; *S* grandfather, 1969. *Educ:* Stowe; Universities of Paris and Salzburg. Short service commission, Irish Guards, 1962–65. At various times before and since: law student, property developer, film extra, white hunter, bingo caller, etc. Patron, L'Orchestre du Monde, 1988–. *Recreations:* shooting, food and drink, palaeontology, venery. *Heir: cousin* Nevinson Mark de Courcy, *b* 11 May 1958. *Address:* 15 Dallimore Mead, Nunney, Frome, Somerset BA11 4NB. *Club:* Cavalry and Guards.

KINGSBOROUGH, Viscount; Robert Charles Henry King-Tenison; *b* 20 March 1969; *s* and *heir* of 11th Earl of Kingston, *qv*.

KINGSBURY, Derek John, CBE 1988; FREng, FIEE; Chairman: Fairey Group plc, 1987–96 (Group Chief Executive, 1982–91); David Brown Group plc, 1992–96; Goode Durrant plc, 1992–96; *b* 10 July 1926; *s* of late Major Arthur Kingsbury, BEM, Virginia Water and Gwendoline Mary Kingsbury; *m* 1st, 1959, Muriel June Drake; one *s* (and one *s* decd); 2nd, 1980, Sarah Muriel Morgan; one *s*. *Educ:* Strode's Secondary Sch., City and Guilds Coll. BScEng Hons; DIC. FIEE 1968; FCGI 1977; FREng (FEng 1991). 2nd Lieut, REME, 1947–49. Apprentice, Metropolitan Vickers, 1949–51; Exch. Schol., Univ. of Pennsylvania, 1952–53; Associated Electrical Industries: Manager, E Canada, 1954–61; PA to Chm., 1961–63; Gen. Manager, AEI Distribution Transformers, 1963–66; Gen. Manager, Overseas Manufacturing Develt, 1966–69; Thorn Electrical Industries: Man. Dir, Foster Transformers, 1969–76; Man. Dir, Elect. & Hydr. Div., 1972–76, Exec. Dir, 1973–76; Dowty Group: Dep. Chief Exec., 1976–82. Chm., Ultra Electronics, 1977–82; non-executive Director: Vickers, 1981–91; ACAL plc, 1991–94. Institution of Electrical Engineers: Dir Peter Peregrinus, 1976–81; Mem., Finance Cttee, 1978–80; Confederation of British Industry: Mem. Council, 1980–86; Chm., Overseas Cttee, 1980–84; missions to Japan 1981, 1983, 1985; Defence Manufacturers Association: Mem. Council, 1985–92; Chm., 1987–90; Chm., F and GP Cttee, 1990–92; Vice-Pres., 1993–; Member: Review Bd for Govt Contracts, 1986–94; Engineering Council, 1990–93 (Chm., CET Pilot Scheme Steering Cttee, 1988–90); Council, BEAMA, 1973–75. Freeman, City of London, 1994; Liveryman, Scientific Instrument Makers' Co., 1994. CIMgt; FRSA 1994. President: BHF Horse Show, 1977–98; Aircraft Golfing Soc., 1995–. *Recreations:* golf, swimming, walking. *Address:* Trecaven, Rock, Cornwall PL27 6LB. *T:* (01208) 863608, *Fax:* (01208) 863865. *Clubs:* Royal Automobile, MCC, Lord's Taverners; Beaconsfield Golf, St Enodoc Golf (Vice-Captain, 1997–99; Captain, 1999–2001).

KINGSBURY, Sally Jane; *see* O'Neill, S. J.

KINGSDOWN, Baron *cr* 1993 (Life Peer), of Pemberton in the County of Lancashire; **Robert Leigh-Pemberton, (Robin),** KG 1994; PC 1987; Governor, Bank of England, 1983–93; Lord-Lieutenant of Kent, since 1982 (Vice Lord-Lieutenant, 1972–82); *b* 5 Jan. 1927; *e s* of late Robert Douglas Leigh-Pemberton, MBE, MC, Sittingbourne, Kent; *m* 1953, Rosemary Davina, OBE, *d* of late Lt-Col D. W. A. W. Forbes, MC, and late Dowager Marchioness of Exeter; four *s* (and one *s* decd). *Educ:* St Peter's Court, Broadstairs; Eton; Trinity Coll., Oxford (MA; Hon. Fellow, 1984). Grenadier Guards, 1945–48. Called to Bar, Inner Temple, 1954 (Hon. Bencher, 1983); practised in London and SE Circuit until 1960. National Westminster Bank: Dir, 1972–83; Dep. Chm., 1974; Chm., 1977–83. Director: Birmid Qualcast, 1966–83 (Dep. Chm., 1970; Chm., 1975–77); University Life Assce Soc., 1967–78; Redland Ltd, 1972–83, 1993–98; Equitable Life Assce Soc., 1979–83 (Vice-Pres., 1982–83); Glaxo-Wellcome (formerly Glaxo Holdings), 1993–96; Foreign and Colonial Investment Trust, 1993–98; Hambros, 1993–98. County Councillor (Chm. Council, 1972–75), 1961–77, CA 1965, Kent. Member: SE Econ. Planning Council, 1972–74; Medway Ports Authority, 1974–76; NEDC, 1982–92; Prime Minister's Cttee on Local Govt Rules of Conduct, 1973–74; Cttee of Enquiry into Teachers' Pay, 1974; Cttee on Police Pay, 1977–79. Chm., Cttee of London Clearing Bankers, 1982–83. Trustee: Glyndebourne Arts Trust, 1978–83; RA Trust, 1982–88 (Hon. Trustee Emeritus, 1988–). Pro-Chancellor, Univ. of Kent at Canterbury, 1977–83; Seneschal, Canterbury Cathedral, 1983–. Hon. Colonel: Kent and Sharpshooters Yeomanry Sqn, 1979–92; 265 (Kent and Co. of London Yeo.) Signal Sqn (V), 1979–92; 5th (Volunteer) Bn, The Queen's Regt, 1987–92. Gov., Ditchley Foundn, 1987–. Hon. DCL Kent, 1983; Hon. DLitt: City, 1988; Loughborough, 1990. FRSA 1977; FIMgt (FBIM 1977). JP 1961–75, DL 1970, Kent. KStJ 1983. *Recreation:* country life. *Address:* Torry Hill, Sittingbourne, Kent ME9 0SP. *Clubs:* Brooks's, Cavalry and Guards.

KINGSHOTT, (Albert) Leonard; Director: International Banking Division, Lloyds Bank Plc, 1985–89; Mutual Management Services, since 1993; Member, Monopolies and Mergers Commission, 1990–96; *b* 16 Sept. 1930; *s* of A. L. Kingshott and Mrs K. Kingshott; *m* 1958, Valerie Simpson; two *s* one *d*. *Educ:* London Sch. of Economics (BSc); ACIS 1958, FCIS 1983. Flying Officer, RAF, 1952–55; Economist, British Petroleum, 1955–60; Economist, British Nylon Spinners, 1960–62; Financial Manager, Iraq Petroleum Co., 1963–65; Chief Economist, Ford of Britain, 1965; Treas., Ford of Britain, 1966–67; Treas., Ford of Europe, 1968–70; Finance Dir, Whitbread & Co., 1972; Man. Dir, Finance, BSC, 1972–77; Dir, Lloyds Bank International, responsible for Merchant Banking activities, 1977–80, for European Div., 1980–82, for Marketing and Planning Div., 1983–84; Dep. Chief Exec., Lloyds Bank International, 1985. Exec. Dir, The Private Bank & Trust Co., 1989–91; Director: Bank of London and South America Ltd, 1977–89; Lloyds Bank International, 1977–89; Lloyds Bank (France) Ltd, 1980–89; Lloyd's Bank California, 1985–88; Rosehaugh plc, 1991–92 (Chm.); Shandwick plc, 1993–2000; Newmarket Foods Ltd, 1994–97; Man. Dir, Cypher Science Ltd, 1996–. Mem. Bd, Crown Agents for Oversea Govts and Admin, and Crown Agents Hldg and Realisation Bd, 1989–92. Associate Mem. of Faculty, 1978, Governor, 1980–91, Ashridge Management Coll. Chm., Oakbridge Counselling, 1990–. FCIS. *Publication:* Investment Appraisal, 1967. *Recreations:* golf, chess. *Address:* 4 Delamas, Beggar Hill, Fryerning, Ingatestone, Essex CM4 0PW. *T:* (01277) 352077.

KINGSHOTT, Air Vice-Marshal Kenneth, CBE 1972; DFC 1953; Royal Air Force, retired 1980; *b* 8 July 1924; *s* of Walter James Kingshott and Eliza Ann Kingshott; *m* 1st, 1948, Dorrie Marie (*née* Dent) (*d* 1978); two *s*; 2nd, 1990, Valerie Rosemary Brigden. Joined RAF, 1943; served: Singapore and Korea, 1950; Aden, 1960; Malta, 1965; MoD, London, 1968; OC RAF Cottesmore, 1971; HQ 2 Allied Tactical Air Force, 1973; HQ Strike Command, 1975; Dep. Chief of Staff Operations and Intelligence, HQ Allied Air Forces Central Europe, 1977–79. *Recreations:* golf, fishing, music. *Address:* 9 The Thicket, Penn, Bucks HP10 8JQ. *Club:* Royal Air Force.

KINGSHOTT, Leonard; *see* Kingshott, A. L.

KINGSLAND, Baron *cr* 1994 (Life Peer), of Shrewsbury in the County of Shropshire; **Christopher James Prout,** PC 1994; Kt 1990; TD 1987; QC 1988; DL; barrister-at-law; a Recorder, since 2000; *b* 1 Jan. 1942; *s* of late Frank Yabsley Prout, MC and bar, and Doris Lucy Prout (*née* Osborne). *Educ:* Sevenoaks Sch.; Manchester Univ. (BA); The Queen's Coll., Oxford (Scholar; BPhil, DPhil). TA Officer (Major): OU OTC, 1966–74; 16/5 The Queen's Royal Lancers, 1974–82; 3rd Armoured Div., 1982–88; RARO, 1988–. Called to the Bar, Middle Temple, 1972, Bencher, 1996; Master of the Garden, 2000–. English-Speaking Union Fellow, Columbia Univ., NYC, 1963–64; Staff Mem., IBRD (UN), Washington DC, 1966–69; Leverhulme Fellow and Lectr in Law, Sussex Univ., 1969–79. MEP (C) Shropshire and Stafford, 1979–94; contested (C) Herefordshire and Shropshire, Eur. parly elecns, 1994. Leader, British Cons. MEPs, 1987–94; Dep. Whip, 1979–82, Chief Whip, 1983–87, Chairman and Leader, 1987–92, EDG; Vice Chm., Eur. People's Party Parly Gp, 1992–94; Chm., Parlt Cttee on Legal Affairs, 1987. Rapporteur, Revision of Europ. Parlt's Rules of Procedure, 1987 and 1993. Shadow Lord Chancellor, 1997–. Chm. Sub-Cttee F, H of L Select Cttee on EC, 1996–97. Pres., Shropshire and W Midlands Agricl Show, 1993. Master, Shrewsbury Drapers' Co., 1995. DL Shropshire, 1997. Grande Médaille de la Ville de Paris, 1988; Schuman Medal, EPP, 1995. *Publications:* Market Socialism in Yugoslavia, 1985; (contrib.) vols 8, 51 and 52, Halsbury's Laws of England, 4th edn; various lectures, pamphlets, chapters and articles. *Recreations:* boating, gardening, musical comedy, the turf. *Address:* c/o House of Lords, SW1A 0PW. *Clubs:* White's, Pratt's, Beefsteak, Buck's (Hon. Mem.), Royal Ocean Racing; Royal Yacht Squadron.

KINGSLAND, Sir Richard, Kt 1978; AO 1989; CBE 1967; DFC 1940; idc; psa; Chairman, ACT Health Promotion Fund, 1990–94; *b* Moree, NSW, 19 Oct. 1916; *m* 1943, Kathleen Jewel, *d* of late R. B. Adams; one *s* two *d*. Served War: No 10 Sqdn, Eng., 1939–41; commanded: No 11 Sqdn, New Guinea, 1941–42; RAAF Stn, Rathmines, NSW, 1942–43; Gp Captain 1943; Dir, Intell., RAAF, 1944–45. Dir, Org. RAAF HQ, 1946–48; Manager, Sydney Airport, 1948–49; Airline Pilot, 1949–50; SA Reg. 1950–51, NT Reg. 1951–52, Dept of Civil Aviation; Chief Admin. Asst to CAS, RAAF, 1952–53; IDC 1955; Asst Sec., Dept of Air, Melb., 1954–58; First Asst Sec., Dept of Defence,

1958–63; Secretary: Dept of Interior, 1963–70; Dept of Repatriation, 1970–74; Repatriation and Compensation, 1974–76; Dept of Veterans' Affairs, Canberra, 1976–81. Chairman: Repatriation Commn, 1970–81; ACT Arts Develt Bd (first Chm.), 1981–83; Commonwealth Films Bd of Review, 1982–86; Uranium Adv. Council, 1982–84. Member-at-Large, Nat. Heart Foundn, 1990– (Hon. Nat. Sec., 1976–90); a Dir, Sir Edward Dunlop Med. Res. Foundn, 1995–. A Dir, Arts Council of Aust., 1970–72; first Chairman Council: Canberra Sch. of Music, 1970–74; Canberra Sch. of Art, 1976–83; Mem. Original Council, Australian Conservation Foundn, 1967–69; Member: Canberra Theatre Trust, 1965–75; Aust. Opera Nat. Council, 1983–96; Canberra Festival Cttee, 1988–92; Mem. Bd of Trustees, Aust. War Meml, Canberra, 1966–76; Mem. Council, E. V. Llewellyn Meml Trust, 1982–; a Dir, Aust. Bicentennial Authority, 1983–89. President: Barnardos, Canberra, 1995–; Bd of Management, Goodwin Retirement Villages, 1984–88. Vice Pres., Australia Day in the National Capital Cttee, 1987–91. *Address:* 36 Vasey Crescent, Campbell, ACT 2612, Australia. *Clubs:* Commonwealth, National Press (Canberra).

KINGSLEY, Ben; actor; *b* 31 Dec. 1943; *s* of Rahimtulla Harji Bhanji and Anna Leina Mary Bhanji; *m*; three *s* one *d*. *Educ:* Manchester Grammar Sch. Associate artist, Royal Shakespeare Co.; work with RSC includes, 1970–80; 1985–86: Peter Brook's Midsummer Night's Dream, Stratford, London, Broadway, NY; Gramsci in Occupations; Ariel in The Tempest; title role, Hamlet; Ford in Merry Wives of Windsor; title role, Baal; Squeers and Mr Wagstaff in Nicholas Nickleby; title rôle, Othello, Melons; National Theatre, 1977–78: Mosca in Volponë; Trofimov in The Cherry Orchard; Sparkish in The Country Wife; Vukhov in Judgement; additional theatre work includes: Johnny in Hello and Goodbye (Fugard), King's Head, 1973; Errol Philander in Statements After An Arrest (Fugard), Royal Court, 1974; Edmund Kean, Harrogate, 1981, Haymarket, 1983 (also televised); title role, Dr Faustus, Manchester Royal Exchange, 1981; Waiting for Godot, Old Vic, 1997; *television* 1974–, includes The Love School (series), 1974; Silas Marner (film), 1985, Murderers Amongst Us (mini-series), 1989, and several plays; *films:* title role, Gandhi, 1980 (2 Hollywood Golden Globe awards, 1982; NY Film Critics' Award, 2 BAFTA awards, Oscar, LA Film Critics Award, 1983, Variety Club of GB Best Film Actor award, 1983); Betrayal, 1982; Turtle Diary, 1985; Harem, 1986; Testimony, Maurice, 1987; Pascali's Island, The Train, 1988; Without a Clue, 1989; Bugsy, Sneakers, Dave, 1992; Schindler's List, 1993; Innocent Moves, 1994; Death and the Maiden, Species, 1995; Twelfth Night, 1996; Photographing Fairies, 1997; The Assignment, Weapons of Mass Distraction, Sweeney Todd, Alice in Wonderland, Crime and Punishment, Spookey House, 1998; The Confession, Rules of Engagement, What Planet are you from?, 1999; Sexy Beast, 2001. Best Film Actor, London Standard Award, 1983; Medici Soc. Award, 1989; Simon Wiesenthal Humanitarian Award, 1989; Berlin Golden Camera Award, 1990. Hon. MA Salford, 1984. Padma Shri (India), 1984. *Address:* c/o ICM Ltd, 76 Oxford Street, W1N 0AX.

KINGSLEY, David John; consultant in management, marketing and communications, since 1975; Chairman, Kingsley and Kingsley, since 1974; Director, Francis Kyle Gallery Ltd, since 1978; *b* 10 July 1929; *s* of Walter John Kingsley and Margery Kingsley; *m* 1st, 1954, Enid Sophia Jones; two *d*; 2nd, 1968, Gillian Leech; two *s*; 3rd, 1988, Gisela Reichardt. *Educ:* Southend High Sch.; London School of Economics (BScEcon; Hon. Fellow, 1992). Pres., Students' Union, LSE, 1952; Vice-Pres., Nat. Union of Students, 1953. Served RAF, Personnel Selection, commnd 1948. Prospective Parly Candidate (Lab) E Grinstead, 1952–54; founded Kingsley, Manton and Palmer, advertising agency, 1964; Publicity Advisor to Labour Party and Govt, 1962–70; Publicity and Election advisor to President of Republic of Zambia, 1974–82; Election and Broadcasting advisor to Govt of Mauritius, 1976–81; Publicity advisor to SDP, 1981–87, Advr, London First, 1998–. Mem. Boards, CNAA, 1970–82; Mem., Central Religious Adv. Cttee for BBC and IBA, 1974–82; Governor, LSE, 1966–. Pres., Worldaware, 1992–96; Dir, at Bristol (formerly Bristol 2000), 1993–; Chairman: Children 2000, 1994–; Inter-Action Trust, 1981–90; Design and Industries Assoc., 1994–96; Smart Cities Initiative (Europe), 1996–. Trustee, Royal Philharmonic Orch., 1993–99 (Vice-Chm., 1972–77); Dir, Wren Orch., 1990–98. Mem., Develt Cttee, RCM, 1985–; Vice-Pres., Schumacher Soc. (Trustee, 1980–); Vice-Chm., LSE Communications Cttee, 1999–2000; Hon. Pres., LSE Envmtl Network, 1998; Trustee, British American Arts Assoc., 1980–94; Chm., Cartoon Arts Trust, 1994–2001; Chm., Creative Summit, 1999. FIPA; FRSA; MCSD. Hon. RCM. Hon. Fellow, Soka Univ., Tokyo, 1990. *Publications:* Albion in China, 1979; contribs to learned jls; various articles. *Recreations:* politics, creating happy national events, music, travel, art and any books. *Address:* 81 Mortimer Road, N1 5AR. *Club:* Reform.

KINGSLEY, Roger James, OBE 1992; FREng, FIChemE; Director, Kingsley Process & Management, retired 2000; Consultant and Director, CAPCIS Ltd, retired 1999; *b* 2 Feb. 1922; *s* of Felix and Helene Loewenstein; changed name to Kingsley, 1942; *m* 1949, Valerie Marguerite Mary (*née* Hanna); one *s* two *d*. *Educ:* Manchester Grammar Sch.; Faculty of Technol., Manchester Univ. (BScTech); Harvard Business Sch. (Internat. Sen. Managers Program). Served War, Royal Fusiliers, 1940–46; Commando service, 1942–45; Captain; mentioned in despatches, 1946. Chemical Engr, Petrocarbon Ltd, 1949–51; technical appts, ultimately Tech. Dir, Lankro Chemicals Ltd, 1952–62; gen. management appts, Lankro Chemicals Group Ltd, 1962–77; Man. Dir, Lankro Chemicals Group Ltd, 1972–77; Director: ICI-Lankro Plasticisers Ltd, 1972–77; Fallek-Lankro Corp., Tuscaloosa, Ala, 1976–77; Dep. Chm., Diamond Shamrock Europe, 1977–82; Chairman: Duolite Internat., 1978–84; LMK Engrg, to 1989; UMIST Ventures, to 1994; Freeman Process Systems, to 1992. Pres., IChemE, 1974–75. Member: Court of Governors, UMIST, 1969–79, 1985–. Hon. DEng UMIST, 1998. *Publications:* contrib. Chem. Engr, and Proc. IMechE. *Recreations:* ski-ing, riding, music. *Address:* Fallows End, Wicker Lane, Hale Barns, Cheshire WA15 0HQ. *Club:* Royal Anglo-Belgian.

KINGSMILL, Denise Patricia Byrne, CBE 2000; a Deputy Chairman, Competition (formerly Monopolies and Mergers) Commission, since 1997; Chairman, Optimum Health Services NHS Trust, since 1991; *b* 24 April 1947; *d* of Patrick Henry Byrne and Hester Jean Byrne; *m* 1970, David Gordon Kingsmill; one *s* one *d*. *Educ:* Girton Coll., Cambridge. Admitted Solicitor, 1980. With ICI Fibres, then Internat. Wool Secretariat, 1968–75; Robin Thompson & Partners, 1979–82; Russell Jones and Walker, 1982–85; Denise Kingsmill & Co., 1985–90; Partner, D. J. Freeman, 1990–93; Consultant, Denton Hall, 1994–2000. Non-executive Director: Rainbow UK, 1993–94; MFI Furniture Gp, 1997– (Dep. Chm.); Norwich and Peterborough Bldg Soc., 1997–2001. Chm., Women's Employment and Pay Review, 2001. Trustee, Design Mus. Gov., Coll. of Law. Hon. Fellow, Univ. of Wales, Cardiff. *Recreation:* trying to stay fit. *Address:* c/o Competition Commission, New Court, 48 Carey Street, WC2A 2JT. *Club:* Riverside Racquet.

KINGSTON, 11th Earl of, *cr* 1768; **Barclay Robert Edwin King-Tenison;** Bt 1682; Baron Kingston, 1764; Viscount Kingsborough, 1766; Baron Erris, 1800; Viscount Lorton, 1806; formerly Lieutenant, Royal Scots Greys; *b* 23 Sept. 1943; *o s* of 10th Earl of Kingston and Gwyneth, *d* of William Howard Evans (she *m* 2nd, 1951, Brig. E. M. Tyler (marr. diss.), DSO, MC, late RA and 3rd, 1963, Robert Woodford); *S* father, 1948; *m* 1st, 1965, Patricia Mary (marr. diss. 1974), *o d* of E. C. Killip, Llanfairfechan, N Wales; one *s* one *d*; 2nd, 1974, Victoria (marr. diss. 1979), *d* of D. C. Edmonds; 3rd, 1990, Corleen Jennifer Rathbone; 4th, 2000, Jane Sutherland. *Educ:* Winchester. *Heir:* *s* Viscount Kingsborough, *qv*.

KINGSTON (Ontario), Archbishop of, (RC), since 1982; **Most Rev. Francis John Spence;** *b* Perth, Ont., 3 June 1926; *s* of William John Spence and Rose Anna Spence (*née* Jordan). *Educ:* St Michael's Coll., Toronto (BA 1946); St Augustine's Seminary, Toronto; St Thomas Univ., Rome (JCD 1955). Ordained priest, 1950; Bishop, 1967; Auxiliary to Mil. Vicar, Canadian Forces, 1967–82; Bishop of Charlottetown, PEI, 1970–82; Mil. Vicar, 1982–88. Pres., Canadian Conf. of Catholic Bishops, 1995–97. *Address:* 390 Palace Road, Kingston, ON K7L 4T3, Canada.

KINGSTON, (William) Martin; QC 1992; a Recorder, 1991–99; *b* 9 July 1949; *s* of William Robin Kingston and Iris Edith Kingston; *m* 1972, Jill Mary Bache; one *s* two *d*. *Educ:* Middlewich Secondary Modern Sch.; Hartford Coll. of Further Educn; Liverpool Univ. (LLB). Called to the Bar, Middle Temple, 1972; Asst Recorder, 1987. Dep. Chm., Agricl Lands Tribunal, 1985–. Asst Comr, Parly Boundary Commn for England, 1992–. *Recreations:* ski-ing, fishing, reading, going on holiday. *Address:* (chambers) 5 Fountain Court, Steelhouse Lane, Birmingham B4 6DR; Bevere Green, Bevere, Worcester WR3 7RG; 25–27 Old Queen Street, SW1H 9JA.

KINGSTON-upon-THAMES, Area Bishop of, since 1997; **Rt Rev. Peter Bryan Price;** *b* 17 May 1944; *s* of Alec Henry Price and Phyllis Evelyn Mary Price; *m* 1967, Edith Margaret Burns; four *s*. *Educ:* Redland Coll., Bristol (Cert Ed 1966); Oak Hill Theol Coll. (Dip. in Pastoral Studies, 1974). Asst Master, Ashton Park Sch., Bristol, 1966–70; Tutor, Lindley Lodge, Nuneaton, 1970; Head of Religious Studies, Cordeaux Sch., Louth, 1970–72; ordained, 1974; Community Chaplain, Crookhorn, Portsmouth and Asst Curate, Christ Church, Portsdown, 1974–78; Chaplain, Scargill House, Kettlewell, 1978–80; Vicar, St Mary Magdalene, Addiscombe, Croydon, 1980–88; Canon Residentiary and Chancellor, Southwark Cathedral, 1988–91, Canon Emeritus, 1992–97; Gen. Sec., USPG, 1992–97. *Publications:* The Church as Kingdom, 1987; Seeds of the Word, 1996; Telling it as it is, 1998; Living Faith in the World through Word and Action, 1998; To Each their Place, 1999; Mark 2000, 1999; Jesus Manifesto: reflections on St Luke's gospel, 2000. *Recreations:* painting, swimming, walking, conversation. *Address:* 24 Albert Drive, SW19 6LS. *T:* (020) 8789 3218.

KINGTON, Miles Beresford; humorous columnist; *b* 13 May 1941; *s* of William Beresford Nairn Kington and Jean Anne Kington; *m* 1st, 1964, Sarah Paine (marr. diss. 1987); one *s* one *d*; 2nd, 1987, Mrs Hilary Caroline Maynard; one *s*. *Educ:* Trinity College, Glenalmond; Trinity College, Oxford (BA Mod Langs). Plunged into free-lance writing, 1963; took up part-time gardening while starving to death, 1964; jazz reviewer, The Times, 1965; joined staff of Punch, 1967, Literary Editor, 1973, left 1980; free-lance, 1980–; daily Moreover column in The Times, 1981–86; columnist, The Independent, 1986–; ex-member, musical group Instant Sunshine on double bass; jazz player, 1970–; *television:* various programmes incl. Three Miles High (Great Railway Journeys of the World series), 1980, Steam Days, 1986, and The Burma Road, 1989; In Search of the Holy Foreskin, 1996; writer and presenter, Fine Families, 1998; *radio:* co-presenter with Edward Enfield, Double Vision, 1996–. Stage play, Waiting for Stoppard, Bristol New Vic, 1995; stage shows with Simon Gilman, Edinburgh Festival: Bizarre, 1995; Death of Tchaikovsky–a Sherlock Holmes Mystery, 1996. *Publications:* World of Alphonse Allais, 1977, repr. as A Wolf in Frog's Clothing, 1983; 4 Franglais books, 1979–82; Moreover, 1982; Miles and Miles, 1982; Nature Made Ridiculously Simple, 1983; Moreover, Too …, 1985; The Franglais Lieutenant's Woman, 1986; Welcome to Kington, 1989; Steaming Through Britain, 1990; (ed) Jazz: an anthology, 1992; Motorway Madness, 1998; (ed) The Pick of Punch, 1998. *Recreations:* mending punctures, rehabilitating Clementi's piano works, falsifying personal records to mystify potential biographers. *Address:* Lower Hayes, Limpley Stoke, Bath BA3 6HR. *T:* (01225) 722262. *Clubs:* 100, Ronnie Scott's.

KINKEAD-WEEKES, Prof. Mark, FBA 1992; Professor of English and American Literature, University of Kent at Canterbury, 1974–84, now Professor Emeritus; *b* 26 April 1931; *s* of Lt-Col Alfred Bernard Kinkead-Weekes, MC and Vida May Kinkead-Weekes; *m* 1959, Margaret Joan Irvine; two *s*. *Educ:* Potchefstroom Boys' High Sch.; Univ. of Cape Town (BA); Brasenose Coll., Oxford (BA, MA). University of Edinburgh: Asst Lectr in English, 1956–58; Lectr, 1958–65; University of Kent at Canterbury: Lectr, 1965–66; Sen. Lectr, 1966–74; Pro-Vice-Chancellor, 1974–77. Rhodes Scholarship (Cape Province), 1951; Woodrow Wilson Fellow, Smithsonian Instn, 1993–94. Former Governor: Christ Church Coll., Canterbury; King's Coll., Rochester; Contemp. Dance Trust. Chm., Friends of St George, Ramsgate. *Publications:* William Golding, a Critical Study (with Ian Gregor), 1967, 2nd edn 1984; Samuel Richardson: dramatic novelist, 1973; (ed) D. H. Lawrence: The Rainbow, 1989; D. H. Lawrence: triumph to exile 1912–1922, 1996; articles, mainly on fiction. *Recreations:* walking, music, travel. *Address:* 5 Albion Place, Ramsgate, Kent CT11 8HQ. *T:* (01843) 593168.

KINKEL, Dr Klaus; Member (FDP) Bundestag, since 1994; Minister of Foreign Affairs, Germany, 1992–98; *b* 17 Dec. 1936; *m* 1961, Ursula Vogel; one *s* three *d*. *Educ:* Bonn, Cologne and Tubingen univs. LLD. State Sec., Ministry of Justice, 1982–83, and 1987–91; Head of External Intelligence Service, 1983–87; Minister of Justice, 1991–92. Leader, FDP, 1993–95. *Address:* Bundestag, Platz der Republik, 11011 Berlin, Germany.

KINLOCH, Prof. Anthony James, PhD, DSc; FREng, CEng; CChem, FRSC; FIM; Professor of Adhesion and Director of Postgraduate Research, Imperial College, London, since 1990; *b* 7 Oct. 1946; *s* of Nathan and Hilda May Kinloch; *m* 1969, Gillian Patricia Birch; two *s* one *d*. *Educ:* London Nautical Sch.; Queen Mary Coll., London (PhD 1972); DSc London 1989. CChem 1982; FRSC 1982; FIM 1982; FREng (FEng 1997). RARDE, MoD, 1972–84; Reader, Imperial Coll., London, 1984–89. Visiting Professor: EPFL, Lausanne, 1986; Univ. of Utah, 1988. Lectures: C&G Centenary, 1995; Thomas Hawksley, IMechE, 1996. Mem. Council, Inst. Materials, 1997–; Chm., Soc. for Adhesion and Adhesives, 2000–. Fellow, US Adhesion Soc., 1995. Adhesion Soc. of Japan Award, 1994; Griffith Medal and Prize, Inst. of Materials, 1996; Thomas Hawksley Gold Medal, IMechE, 1997. *Publications:* Adhesion and Adhesives: science and technology, 1987; (with R. J. Young) Fracture Behaviour of Polymers, 1983; (ed) Durability of Structural Adhesives, 1983; (ed jtly) Toughened Plastics: I 1993, II 1996; over 150 papers in learned jls. *Recreations:* opera, tennis, walking. *Address:* Imperial College of Science, Technology and Medicine, Department of Mechanical Engineering, Exhibition Road, SW7 2BX.

KINLOCH, Sir David, 13th Bt *cr* 1686, of Gilmerton; *b* 5 Aug. 1951; *s* of Sir Alexander Davenport Kinloch, 12th Bt and of Anna, *d* of late Thomas Walker, Edinburgh; *S* father, 1982; *m* 1st, 1976, Susan Middlewood (marr. diss. 1986); one *s* one *d*; 2nd, 1987, Maureen Carswell; two *s*. *Educ:* Gordonstoun. Career in research into, and recovery and replacement of underground services. *Recreation:* treasure hunting. *Heir:* *s* Alexander

Kinloch, *b* 31 May 1978. *Address:* Gilmerton House, North Berwick, East Lothian EH39 5LQ. *T:* (01620) 880207.

KINLOCH, Sir David Oliphant, 5th Bt *cr* 1873, of Kinloch, co. Perth; CA; Director, Caledonia Investments PLC, since 1988; *b* 15 Jan. 1942; *s* of Sir John Kinloch, 4th Bt and Doris Ellaline (*d* 1997), *e d* of C. J. Head; *S* father, 1992; *m* 1st, 1968, Susan Minette Urquhart (marr. diss. 1979), *y d* of Maj.-Gen. R. E. Urquhart, CB, DSO; three *d*; 2nd, 1983, Sabine Irene, *o d* of Philippe de Loës; one *s* one *d*. *Educ:* Charterhouse. *Heir: s* Alexander Peter Kinloch, *b* 30 June 1986. *Address:* House of Aldie, Kinross KY13 0QH; 29 Walpole Street, SW3 4QS.

KINLOCH, Henry, (Harry); Chairman, Quartermaine & Co., since 1989; *b* 7 June 1937; *s* of William Shearer Kinloch and Alexina Alice Quartermaine Kinloch; *m* 1st, 1966, Gillian Anne Ashley (marr. diss. 1979); one *s* one *d*; 2nd, 1987, Catherine Elizabeth Hossack. *Educ:* Queen's Park Sch., Glasgow; Univs of Strathclyde, Birmingham and Glasgow. MSc, PhD, ARCST, CEng, FIMechE. Lecturer in Engineering: Univ. of Strathclyde, 1962–65; Univ. of Liverpool, 1966; Vis. Associate Prof. of Engrg, MIT, 1967; Sen. Design Engr, CEGB, 1968–70; PA Management Consultants, 1970–73; Chief Exec., Antony Gibbs (PFP) Ltd, 1973–74; Chm. and Chief Exec., Antony Gibbs Financial Services Ltd, 1975–77; Man. Dir, British Shipbuilders, 1978–80; Dep. Man. Dir and Chief Exec., Liberty Life Assce Co., 1980–83; Chm. and Chief Exec., Ætna Internat. (UK), 1984–89. Chm., Helm Investments Ltd, 1995–98; Gp Man. Dir, Ultraseal Internat. Ltd, 1997–98. *Publications:* many publications on theoretical and applied mechanics, financial and business studies. *Recreations:* reading book reviews, opera, political biography, ostling. *Address:* Oasis Europe Ltd, The Linen Hall, Regent Street, W1R 5TB. *Club:* Athenæum.

KINLOSS, Lady (12th in line, of the Lordship *cr* 1602); **Beatrice Mary Grenville Freeman-Grenville;** (surname changed by Lord Lyon King of Arms, 1950); *b* 18 Aug. 1922; *e d* of late Rev. Hon. Luis Chandos Francis Temple Morgan-Grenville, Master of Kinloss; *S* grandmother, 1944; *m* 1950, Dr Greville Stewart Parker Freeman-Grenville, FSA, FRAS (name changed from Freeman by Lord Lyon King of Arms, 1950), Capt. late Royal Berks Regt, *er s* of late Rev. E. C. Freeman; one *s* two *d*. Cross-bencher; Mem., EC Sub-Cttee C (Social and Consumer Affairs), 1993–95; has served on numerous select cttees. FRAS 1997. *Heir: s* Master of Kinloss, *qv*. *Address:* North View House, Sheriff Hutton, York YO60 6ST. *T:* (01347) 878447. *Club:* Civil Service.

KINLOSS, Master of; Hon. Bevil David Stewart Chandos Freeman-Grenville; *b* 20 June 1953; *s* of Dr Greville Stewart Parker Freeman-Grenville, FSA, Capt. late Royal Berks Regt, and of Lady Kinloss, *qv*; m 2001, Marie-Thérèse, d of late William Driscoll, and *widow* of Stuart Sturrock. *Educ:* Redrice Sch. *Address:* North View House, Sheriff Hutton, York YO60 6ST.

KINMONTH, Prof. Ann-Louise, MD; FRCP, FRCPCH, FRCGP, FMedSci; Professor of General Practice, and Fellow of St John's College, University of Cambridge, since 1997; *b* 8 Jan. 1951; *d* of Maurice Henry Kinmonth and Gwendolyn Stella (*née* Phillipps). *Educ:* New Hall, Cambridge (MA); St Thomas' Hosp. Med. Sch. (MB, BChir, MSc, MD 1984). FRCGP 1992; FRCP 1994; FRCPCH 1997. House Officer, Lambeth and Salisbury Hosps, 1975–76; SHO, Oxford Hosps, 1976–78; Res. Fellow in Paediatrics, Oxford Univ., 1978–80; Oxfam MO, Somalia, 1981; general practice trng, Oxford, 1981–82; Principal, Aldermoor Health Centre, Southampton, 1983–96; University of Southampton: Lectr, 1983–84; Sen. Lectr, 1984–91; Reader, 1991–92; Prof., 1992–96. Founder FMedSci 1998. *Publications:* (ed with J. D. Baum) Care of the Child with Diabetes Mellitus, 1986; (ed with R. Jones) Critical Reading for Primary Care, 1995; contrib. papers on diabetes care and prevention of cardio-vascular disease in peer reviewed jls. *Address:* 1 Cambridge Road, Great Shelford, Cambridge CB2 5JE. *T:* (01223) 843316.

KINNEAR, Ian Albert Clark, (Tim), CMG 1974; HM Diplomatic Service, retired; *b* 23 Dec. 1924; *s* of late George Kinnear, CBE and Georgina Lilian (*née* Stephenson), Nairobi; *m* 1966, Rosemary, *d* of late Dr K. W. D. Hartley, Cobham; two *d*. *Educ:* Marlborough Coll.; Lincoln Coll., Oxford (MA). HM Forces, 1943–46 (1st E Africa Reconnaissance Regt). Colonial Service (later HMOCS): Malayan Civil Service, 1951–56: District Officer, Bentong, then Alor Gajah, Asst Sec. Econ. Planning Unit; Kenya, 1956–63: Asst Sec., then Sen. Asst Sec., Min. of Commerce and Industry; 1st Sec., CRO, later Commonwealth Office, 1963–66; 1st Sec. (Commercial), British Embassy, Djakarta, 1966–68; 1st Sec. and Head of Chancery, British High Commn, Dar-es-Salaam, 1969–71; Chief Sec., later Dep. Governor, Bermuda, 1971–74; Senior British Trade Comr, Hong Kong, 1974–77; Consul-Gen., San Francisco, 1977–82. *Recreation:* painting. *Address:* Castle Hill Cottage, Crook Road, Brenchley, Tonbridge, Kent TN12 7BN. *T:* (01892) 723782.

KINNEAR, Tim; *see* Kinnear, I. A. C.

KINNELL, Ian; QC 1987; professional arbitrator; *b* 23 May 1943; *o s* of Brian Kinnell and Grace Madeline Kinnell; *m* 1970, Elizabeth Jane Ritchie; one *s* one *d*. *Educ:* Sevenoaks Sch., Kent. Called to the Bar, Gray's Inn, 1967. A Recorder, 1987–89; Immigration Appeal Adjudicator, 1990–91; part-time Chm., Immigration Appeal Tribunal, 1991–97. Mem., London Maritime Arbitrator's Assoc., 1991. *Recreations:* rural pursuits. *Address:* Woodside House, The Maypole, Monmouth NP25 5QH. *T:* (01600) 713077, *Fax:* (01600) 772880.

KINNOCK, Glenys Elizabeth; Member (Lab) Wales, European Parliament, since 1999 (South Wales East, 1994–99); *b* 7 July 1944; *m* 1967, Rt Hon. Neil Kinnock, *qv*; one *s* one *d*. *Educ:* Holyhead Comprehensive Sch.; University College of Wales, Cardiff. Teacher in secondary and primary schools, and special sch., 1966–93. Vice-Pres., Univ. of Wales, Cardiff, 1988–95; Pres., Coleg Harlech, 1998–. Mem. Council, VSO; Pres., One World Action. FRSA. Hon. Fellow, Univ. of Wales Coll., Newport, 1998. Hon. LLD Thames Valley, 1994; Hon. Dr: Brunel, 1997; Kingston, 2001. *Publications:* Eritrea: images of war and peace, 1988; (ed) Voices for One World, 1988; Namibia: birth of a nation, 1990; By Faith and Daring, 1993. *Recreations:* reading, cinema, theatre. *Address:* (office) 16 Sachville Avenue, Cardiff CF14 3NY. *T:* (02920) 618337, *Fax:* (02920) 618226; *e-mail:* gkinnock@europe-wales.new.labour.org.uk.

KINNOCK, Rt Hon. Neil Gordon, PC 1983; Member, since 1995, and a Vice President, since 1999, European Commission; *b* 28 March 1942; *s* of Gordon Kinnock, labourer, and Mary Kinnock (*née* Howells), nurse; *m* 1967, Glenys Elizabeth Parry (*see* G. E. Kinnock); one *s* one *d*. *Educ:* Lewis Sch., Pengam; University Coll., Cardiff. BA in Industrial Relations and History, UC, Cardiff (Chm. Socialist Soc., 1963–66; Pres. Students' Union, 1965–66; Hon. Fellow, 1982). Tutor Organiser in Industrial and Trade Union Studies, WEA, 1966–70; Mem., Welsh Hosp. Bd, 1969–71. MP (Lab) Bedwellty, 1970–83, Islwyn, 1983–95. PPS to Sec. of State for Employment, 1974–75; Chief Opposition spokesman on educn, 1979–83; Leader of the Labour Party, and Leader of the Opposition, 1983–92. Member: Nat. Exec. Cttee, Labour Party, 1978–94 (Chm., 1987–88); Parly Cttee of PLP, 1980–92. Chm. Internat. Cttee, Labour Party, 1993–94; Vice-Pres., Socialist Internat., 1984–. Hon. Prof., Thames Valley Univ., 1993–; Pres., Univ. of Cardiff, 1998–. Hon. FIHT 1997. Hon. LLD: Wales, 1992; Glamorgan, 1996. *Publications:* Making Our Way, 1986; Thorns and Roses, 1992; contribs to various jls. *Recreations:* music esp. opera and male choral, Rugby football, theatre, being with family. *Address:* European Commission, Rue de la Loi 200, 1049 Brussels, Belgium.

KINNOULL, 15th Earl of, *cr* 1633; **Arthur William George Patrick Hay;** Viscount Dupplin and Lord Hay, 1627, 1633, 1697; Baron Hay (Great Britain), 1711; *b* 26 March 1935; *o surv. s* of 14th Earl and Mary Ethel Isobel Meyrick (*d* 1938); *S* father, 1938; *m* 1961, Gay Ann, *er d* of Sir Denys Lowson, 1st Bt; one *s* three *d*. *Educ:* Eton. Chartered Land Agent, 1960; Mem., Agricultural Valuers' Assoc., 1962; Fellow, Chartered Land Agents' Soc., 1964; FRICS 1970. Pres., National Council on Inland Transport, 1964–76. Mem. of Queen's Body Guard for Scotland (Royal Company of Archers), 1965. Junior Cons. Whip, House of Lords, 1966–68; Cons. Opposition Spokesman on Aviation, House of Lords, 1968–70. Mem., British Delegn, Council of Europe, 1985–. Chairman: Property Owners' Building Soc., 1976–87 (Dir, 1971–87); Woolwich Homes, 1994–97; Dir, Woolwich Equitable Building Soc., 1987–97. Mem., Air League Council, 1972; Council Mem., Deep Sea Fishermen's Mission, 1977 (Chm., 1997). Vice-Pres., Nat. Assoc. of Local Councils (formerly Nat. Assoc. of Parish Councils), 1970–80. Gov., St John's Sch., Leatherhead, 1978–. *Heir: s* Viscount Dupplin, *qv*. *Address:* 15 Carlyle Square, SW3 6EX; Pier House, Seaview, Isle of Wight. *Clubs:* Turf, Pratt's, White's, MCC.

KINROSS, 5th Baron *cr* 1902; **Christopher Patrick Balfour;** Partner in Taylor Kinross, Solicitors, since 1997; *b* 1 Oct. 1949; *s* of 4th Baron Kinross, OBE, TD, and Helen Anne (*d* 1969), *d* of A. W. Hog; *S* father, 1985; *m* 1974, Susan Jane (separated 1999), *d* of I. R. Pitman, WS; two *s*. *Educ:* Belhaven Hill School, Dunbar; Eton College; Edinburgh Univ. (LLB). Mem., Law Soc. of Scotland, 1975; WS 1975. Partner, Shepherd & Wedderburn, WS, Solicitors, 1977–97. UK Treas., James IV Assoc. of Surgeons, 1981– (Hon. Mem., 1985–); Treas., Edinburgh Gastro-intestinal Res. Fund, 1981–. Member, Queen's Body Guard for Scotland, Royal Company of Archers, 1980–. Member: Mil. Vehicle Trust; Scottish Land Rover Owners' Club. KLJ 1996. *Recreations:* rifle and shotgun shooting, stalking, motorsport. *Heir: s* Hon. Alan Ian Balfour, *b* 4 April 1978. *Address:* 27 Walker Street, Edinburgh EH3 7HX. *T:* (0131) 225 3476. *Club:* New (Edinburgh).

KINSELLA, Thomas; poet; *b* 4 May 1928; *m* 1955, Eleanor Walsh; one *s* two *d*. Entered Irish Civil Service, 1946; resigned from Dept of Finance, 1965. Artist-in-residence, 1965–67, Prof. of English, 1967–70, Southern Illinois Univ.; Prof. of English, Temple Univ., Philadelphia, 1970–90. Elected to Irish Academy of Letters, 1965. J. S. Guggenheim Meml Fellow, 1968–69, 1971–72. Hon. PhD NUI, 1984. *Publications: poetry:* Poems, 1956; Another September, 1958; Downstream, 1962; Nightwalker and other poems, 1968; Notes from the Land of the Dead, 1972; Butcher's Dozen, 1972, 2nd edn 1992; A Selected Life, 1972; Finistère, 1972; New Poems, 1973; Selected Poems 1956 to 1968, 1973; Vertical Man and The Good Fight, 1973; One, 1974; A Technical Supplement, 1976; Song of the Night and Other Poems, 1978; The Messenger, 1978; Fifteen Dead, 1979; One and Other Poems, 1979; Poems 1956–73, 1980; Peppercanister Poems 1972–78, 1980; One Fond Embrace, 1981, 2nd edn 1988; Songs of the Psyche, 1985; Her Vertical Smile, 1985; St Catherine's Clock, 1987; Out of Ireland, 1987; Blood and Family, 1988; Personal Places, 1990; Poems from Centre City, 1990; Madonna, 1991; Open Court, 1991; From Centre City, 1994; Collected Poems 1956–1994, 1996; The Pen Shop, 1997; The Familiar, 1999; Godhead, 1999; Citizen of the World, 2000; Littlebody, 2000; *translations and general:* (trans.) The Táin, 1969; contrib. essay in Davis, Mangan, Ferguson, 1970; (ed) Selected Poems of Austin Clarke, 1976; An Duanaire—Poems of the Dispossessed (trans. Gaelic poetry, 1600–1900), 1981; (ed) Our Musical Heritage: lectures on Irish traditional music by Seán Ó Riada, 1982; (ed, with translations) The New Oxford Book of Irish Verse, 1986; The Dual Tradition: an essay on poetry and politics in Ireland, 1995.

KINSEY, Thomas Richard Moseley, FREng; Chairman, Delcam International (formerly Deltacam Systems), since 1989; *b* 13 Oct. 1929; *s* of late Richard Moseley Kinsey and Dorothy Elizabeth Kinsey; *m* 1953, Ruth (*née* Owen-Jones); two *s*. *Educ:* Newtown Sch.; Trinity Hall, Cambridge (MA). FIMechE; FREng (FEng 1982). ICI Ltd, 1952–57; Tube Investments,1957–65; joined Delta plc, 1965: Director, 1973–77; Jt Man. Dir, 1977–82; Dir, 1980, Dep. Chief Exec., 1982–87, Mitchell Cotts plc, 1980–87. Chm., Birmingham Battery & Metal Co., 1984–89; Director: Gower Internat., 1984–89; Telcon, 1984–89; Unistrut Europe, 1989–92. CIMgt. *Recreations:* golf, travel. *Address:* Sutton Lodge, Solihull, W Midlands B91 1NB. *T:* (0121) 704 2592. *Clubs:* Athenæum; Edgbaston Golf.

KINSMAN, Surgeon Rear-Adm. Francis Michael, CBE 1982 (OBE 1972); Surgeon Rear Admiral (Ships and Establishments), 1980–82, retired; *b* 5 May 1925; *s* of Oscar Edward Kinsman and Margaret Vera Kinsman; *m* 1st, 1949, Catherine Forsyth Barr; one *s*; 2nd, 1955, Margaret Emily Hillier; two *s*. *Educ:* Rydal Sch., Colwyn Bay; St Bartholomew's Hosp. MRCS, LRCP, MFCM; DA. Joined RN, 1952; served, 1952–66: HMS Comus, HMS Tamar, HMS Centaur; RN Hosp. Malta, RN Air Med. Sch., RNAS Lossiemouth; Pres., Central Air Med. Bd, 1966–69; Jt Services Staff Coll., 1969; Staff, Med. Dir Gen. (Naval), 1970–73; Dir, Naval Med. Staff Trng, 1973–76; Comd MO to C-in-C Naval Home Comd, 1976–79; MO i/c RN Hosp. Gibraltar, 1979–80. QHP 1980–82. OStJ 1977. *Recreations:* music, painting, fishing, woodwork. *Address:* Pound House, Meonstoke, Southampton, Hants SO32 3NP.

KINSMAN, Rodney William, RDI 1990; FCSD; Chairman and Managing Director, OMK Design, since 1966; *b* 9 April 1943; *s* of John Thomas Kinsman and Lilian Kinsman (*née* Bradshaw); *m* 1966, Lisa Sai Yuk; one *s* two *d*. *Educ:* Mellow Lane Grammar Sch.; Central Sch. of Art (NDD 1965). FCSD 1983. Founded: OMK Design Ltd, 1966; Kinsman Associates, 1981. Mem., British Furniture Council, 1995 (Exec. Mem., RDI Cttee). Numerous internat. exhibns; work in permanent collections incl. Omstak Chair and other designs, in V&A, museums in USA, Spain, Germany. Broadcasts on TV and radio. Vis. Prof., London Inst., 1996–; former Vis. Prof. and Ext. Examr, RCA. Gov., London Inst. Hon. FRCA 1988; FRSA. Many internat. awards. *Recreations:* polo, ski-ing. *Address:* OMK Design, Stephen Building, 30 Stephen Street, W1T 1QR. *T:* (020) 7631 1335. *Clubs:* Reform, Institute of Directors, Groucho, Chelsea Arts, Royal Berkshire.

KINTORE, 13th Earl of, *cr* 1677 (Scot.); **Michael Canning William John Keith;** Lord Keith of Inverurie and Keith Hall, 1677 (Scot.); Bt 1897; Baron 1925; Viscount Stonehaven 1938; *b* 22 Feb. 1939; *s* of 12th Earl of Kintore, and of Delia Virginia, *d* of William Loyd; assumed surname of Keith in lieu of Baird, 1967; *S* father, 1989; *m* 1972, Mary Plum, *d* of late Sqdn Leader E. G. Plum, Rumson, NJ, and of Mrs Roy Hudson; one *s* one *d*. *Educ:* Eton; RMA Sandhurst. Lately Lieutenant, Coldstream Guards. President: Westminster Exams plc, 1996–; Inst. of Certified Book-Keepers, 1997–. ACII. Hon. Fellow, Internat. Assoc. of Book-Keepers, 1994– (Pres., 1994–96). Hon. LLD Aberdeen, 1993. *Heir: s* Lord Inverurie, Master of Kintore, *qv*. *Address:* The Stables, Keith Hall, Inverurie, Aberdeenshire AB51 0LD. *T:* (01467) 620495.

KINVIG, Maj.-Gen. Clifford Arthur; Director, Educational and Training Services (Army) (formerly Director of Army Education, Ministry of Defence), 1990–93, retired; *b* 22 Nov. 1934; *s* of Frank Arthur Kinvig and Dorothy Maud (*née* Hankinson); *m* 1954, Shirley Acklam; two *s* one *d*. *Educ:* Waterloo Grammar Sch., Liverpool; Durham Univ. (BA 1956); King's Coll., London (MA War Studies 1969). Commnd, RAEC, 1957; educnl and staff appts in Lichfield, Beaconsfield and York, 1957–65; served FE, 1965–68; Sen. Lectr, RMA, Sandhurst, 1969–73; SO2 Educn, UKLF, 1973–75; Chief Educn Officer, W Midland Dist, 1976–79; SO1 Educn, MoD, 1979–82; Sen. Lectr and Head of Econs, Politics and Social Studies Br., RMCS, Shrivenham, 1982–86; Col AEd1, MoD, 1986; Comdt, RAEC Centre, 1986–90. Dep. Col Comdt, AGC, 1997–2000. Mem., Management Bd, NFER, 1990–93. Trustee and Sec., Gallipoli Meml Lect. Trust, 1990–92. *Publications:* Death Railway, 1973; River Kwai Railway, 1992; (contrib.) The Forgotten War, 1992; Scapegoat: General Percival of Singapore, 1996; (contrib.) Japanese Prisoners of War, 2000; contribs to jls on mil. hist. topics. *Recreations:* writing, gardening, reading, walking. *Address:* c/o Lloyds TSB, Castle Street, Cirencester, Glos GL7 1QJ.

KIPKULEI, Benjamin Kipkech; Chairman, Harmonisation Commission, Office of the President, Kenya, since 1998; *b* 5 Jan. 1946; *s* of Mr and Mrs Kipkulei Chesoro; *m* 1972, Miriam; three *s* two *d*. *Educ:* BAEd Nairobi; DipEd Scotland; MEd London. Local Government, 1964 and 1965; Teacher, 1970; Education Officer, 1974; Under Secretary, 1982; High Comr for Kenya in UK, and Ambassador to Italy and Switzerland, 1984–86; Permanent Secretary: Min. of Educn, 1987–92; Min. of Finance, 1993–97. Alternate Gov. for Kenya, World Bank, 1993; Alternate Dir, IMF, 1993; Director: Central Bank of Kenya; Kenya Commercial Bank, 1993. *Recreations:* swimming, photography.

KIRBY, Prof. Anthony John, PhD; FRS 1987; CChem, FRSC; Professor of Bioorganic Chemistry, since 1995, and Fellow, Gonville and Caius College, since 1962, Cambridge University; *b* 18 Aug. 1935; *s* of Samuel Arthur Kirby and Gladys Rosina Kirby (*née* Welch); *m* 1962, Sara Sophia Benjamina Nieweg; one *s* two *d*. *Educ:* Eton College; Gonville and Caius College, Cambridge (MA, PhD 1962). NATO postdoctoral Fellow: Cambridge, 1962–63; Brandeis Univ., 1963–64; Cambridge University: Demonstrator, 1964–68, Lectr, 1968–85, Reader, 1985–95, in Organic Chemistry; Gonville and Caius College: Dir of Studies in Natural Scis and Coll. Lectr, 1968–; Tutor, 1966–74. Visiting Professor/Scholar: Paris (Orsay), 1970; Groningen, 1973; Cape Town, 1987; Paris VI, 1987; Haifa, 1991; Queen's, Kingston, Ont, 1996; Toronto, 1997; Western Ontario, 1997. Co-ordinator, European Network on Catalytic Antibodies, 1993–96, on Gemini Surfactants, 1997–, on Artificial Nucleases, 2000–. Fellow, Japan Soc. for Promotion of Science, 1986; Royal Society of Chemistry: Fellow, 1980; Award in Organic Reaction Mechanisms, 1983; Tilden Lectr, 1987; Chm., Organic Reaction Mechanisms Gp, 1986–90; Ingold Lectr, 1996–97. *Publications:* The Organic Chemistry of Phosphorus (with S. G. Warren), 1967; The Anomeric Effect and Related Stereoelectronic Effects at Oxygen, 1983; Stereoelectronic effects, 1996; papers in Jls of RSC and Amer. Chem. Soc. *Recreations:* chamber music, walking. *Address:* University Chemical Laboratory, Cambridge CB2 1EW. *T:* (01223) 336370; 14 Tenison Avenue, Cambridge CB1 2DY. *T:* (01223) 359343.

KIRBY, David Donald, CBE 1988; formerly railway manager and transport consultant; Chairman, Halcrow Transmark (formerly Transmark), 1994–97; *b* 12 May 1933; *s* of Walter Donald Kirby and Margaret Irene (*née* Halstead); *m* 1955, Joan Florence (*née* Dickins); one *s* one *d*. *Educ:* Royal Grammar Sch., High Wycombe; Jesus Coll., Oxford (MA). FCIT. British Rail and its subsidiaries: Divisional Shipping Manager, Dover, 1964; Operations Manager, Shipping and Continental, 1965; Asst Gen. Man., Shipping and International Services, 1966; Continental Traffic Man., BR, 1968; Gen. Man., Shipping and Internat. Services, 1974; Man. Dir, Sealink UK Ltd, 1979; Dir, London and SE, 1982–85; Mem., 1985–89, Jt Man. Dir (Rlys), 1985–87, Vice-Chm., 1987–89, BRB. *Recreations:* painting, choral singing. *Address:* Penrose, Tresarrett, Blisland, Bodmin, Cornwall PL30 4QY.

KIRBY, Dennis, MVO 1961; MBE 1955; Hon. Manager, European Investment Bank, Luxembourg; *b* 5 April 1923; *s* of William Ewart Kirby and Hannah Kirby; *m* 1st, 1943, Mary Elizabeth Kilby (*d* 1994); 2nd, 1994, Ava Robertson. *Educ:* Hull Grammar Sch.; Queens' Coll., Cambridge. Lt (A) RNVR (fighter pilot), 1940–46. Colonial Service, Sierra Leone, 1946–62 (District Comr, 1950; Perm. Sec., 1961–62); 1st Sec., UK Diplomatic Service, 1962; Managing Director: East Kilbride Development Corp., 1963–68; Irvine Development Corp., 1967–72; Industrial Dir, Scotland, DTI, 1972–74; European Investment Bank, 1974–87: Conseiller Principal, 1974; Dir Adjoint, 1976; Dir Associé, 1984; Dir, NM UK Ltd, 1988–93. *Recreations:* shooting, golf, bridge. *Address:* 74 Westgate, Chichester, W Sussex PO19 3HH. *Clubs:* Oxford and Cambridge, Royal Commonwealth Society; Wisley Golf (Dir, 1991–95).

KIRBY, Dame Georgina (Kamiria), DBE 1994; QSO 1981; JP; Director, Maori Women's Development Fund, since 1978; *b* 31 Jan. 1936; *d* of William Tawhiri Matea Smith and Tuhe Nga Tukemata Christie (*née* Thompson); *m* 1961, Brian Ian Kirby; two *s* one *d*. *Educ:* Horohoro Sch., Rotorua; Rotorua High Sch.; Auckland Univ. Cert. Book-keeping; Cert. Practical Accounting. Jun. Asst Teacher, Rotorua, 1953–55; NZ PO Trng Officer, 1955–63; managed and partnered husband in service businesses, 1966–70; Personnel Officer, Stock & Station, 1971–76. Estabd Te Taumata Art Gall., 1991. Mem., Maori Women's Welfare League Inc., 1976– (Nat. Pres., 1983–87). NZ Vice Pres., Commonwealth Countries League, London, 1988–. JP NZ, 1987. Commemoration Medal (NZ), 1988; Women's Suffrage Medal (NZ), 1993. *Publications:* Liberated Learning, 1993; Vision Aotearoa Kaupapa New Zealand, 1994; contrib. NZ Maori Artists and Writers Mag., Koru. *Recreations:* reading, badminton, horse-riding. *Address:* 11A Northland Street, Grey Lynn, Auckland 1, New Zealand. *T:* (9) 3767032, *T:* and *Fax:* (9) 3077014. *Club:* Zonta International (Auckland).

KIRBY, Prof. Gordon William, ScD, PhD; FRSC; FRSE; Regius Professor of Chemistry, 1972–96, Professor of Chemistry, 1997, now Emeritus, University of Glasgow; *b* 20 June 1934; *s* of William Admiral Kirby and Frances Teresa Kirby (*née* Townson); *m* 1964, Audrey Jean Rusbridge (marr. diss. 1983), *d* of Col C. E. Rusbridge; two *s*. *Educ:* Liverpool Inst. High Sch.; Gonville and Caius Coll., Cambridge (Schuldham Plate 1956; MA, PhD, ScD); FRIC 1970; FRSE 1975. 1851 Exhibn Senior Student, 1958–60, Asst Lectr, 1960–61, Lectr, 1961–67, Imperial Coll. of Science and Technology; Prof. of Organic Chemistry, Univ. of Technology, Loughborough, 1967–72; Mem., Chem. Cttee, SRC, 1971–75. Chm., Jls Cttee, Royal Soc. of Chemistry, 1981–84. Corday-Morgan Medal, Chem. Soc., 1969; Tilden Lectr, Chem. Soc., 1974–75. *Publications:* Co-editor: Elucidation of Organic Structures by Physical and Chemical Methods, vol. IV, parts I, II, and III, 1972; Fortschritte der Chemie organischer Naturstoffe, subseq. entitled Progress in the Chemistry of Organic Natural Products, 1971–; (ed) Comprehensive Organic Functional Group Transformations, vol. IV, 1995; contributor to Jl Chem. Soc., etc. *Address:* c/o Chemistry Department, The University, Glasgow G12 8QQ.

KIRBY, Gwendolen Maud, LVO 1969; Matron, The Hospital for Sick Children, Great Ormond Street, 1951–69; *b* 17 Dec. 1911; 3rd *d* of late Frank M. Kirby, Gravesend, Kent. *Educ:* St Mary's Sch., Calne, Wilts. State Registered Nurse: trained at Nightingale Training Sch., St Thomas' Hosp., SE1. 1933–36; The Mothercraft Training Soc., Cromwell House, Highgate, 1936; State Certified Midwife: trained at General Lying-in Hosp., York Road, Lambeth, 1938–39; Registered Sick Children's Nurse: trained at the Hospital for Sick Children, Great Ormond Street, WC1, 1942–44. Awarded Nightingale Fund Travelling Scholarship, 1948–49, and spent 1 year in Canada and United States. Member: RCN, 1936–; Gen. Nursing Council, 1955–65. *Address:* Brackenfield, Winsford, Minehead, Som TA24 7JL.

KIRBY, Louis; Editor, UK Mail, since 1993; *b* 30 Nov. 1928; 2nd *s* of late William Kirby and Anne Kirby; *m* 1st, 1952, Marcia Teresa Lloyd (marr. diss. 1976); two *s* three *d*; 2nd, 1976, Heather Veronica (*née* Nicholson); one *s* one *d*; 3rd, 1983, Heather McGlone; two *d*. *Educ:* Coalbrookdale High Sch. Daily Mail: Gen. Reporter, subseq. Courts Corresp., and Polit. Corresp., 1953–62; Daily Sketch: Chief Reporter, subseq. Leader Writer and Polit. Editor, Asst Editor, Exec. Editor, and, Actg Editor, 1962–71; Daily Mail (when relaunched): Dep. Editor, 1971–74; Editor, Evening News, 1974–80; Vice-Chm., Evening News Ltd, 1975–80; Editor, Evening Standard, 1980–86; Editl Dir, Mail Newspapers plc, 1986–88; Political Consultant, Daily Mail, 1988–93. *Recreations:* theatre, reading. *Address:* Northcliffe House, Derry Street, W8 5TT. *Clubs:* Reform, Special Forces.

KIRBY, Michael Donald, AC 1991; CMG 1983; **Hon. Justice Kirby;** Justice of the High Court of Australia, since 1996; *b* 18 March 1939; *s* of Donald Kirby and late Jean Langmore Kirby; partner, since 1969, Johan van Vloten. *Educ:* Fort Street Boys' High Sch.; Univ. of Sydney (BA, LLM, BEc). Admitted Solicitor, 1962; called to the Bar of NSW, 1967; Mem., NSW Bar Council, 1974; Judge, Federal Court of Australia, 1983–84; President, Court of Appeal: NSW, 1984–96; Solomon Is, 1995–96; Actg Chief Justice of NSW, 1988, 1990, 1993. Dep. Pres., Aust. Conciliation and Arbitration Commn, 1974–83; Chairman: Australian Law Reform Commn, 1975–84; OECD Inter-govtl Gp on Privacy and Internat. Data Flows, 1978–80; OECD Inter-govtl Gp on Security of Information Systems, 1991–92; Member: Admin. Review Council of Australia, 1976–84; Council of Aust. Acad. of Forensic Scis, 1978–89 (Pres., 1987–89); Aust. National Commn for Unesco, 1980–83, 1996–; Aust. Inst. of Multi-cultural Affairs, 1981–84; Exec., CSIRO, 1983–86. Deleg., Unesco Gen. Conf., Paris, 1983; Chm., Unesco Expert Gp on Rights of Peoples, 1989 (Rapporteur, Budapest, 1991); Member: Unesco Expert Gps on Self-Determination and Rights of Peoples, 1984; Perm. Tribunal of Peoples, Rome, 1992–; ILO Fact Finding and Conciliation Commn on S Africa, 1991–92; Ethics Cttee, Human Genome Orgn 1995–; Internat. Bioethics Cttee, UNESCO, 1996–; Internat. Jury, UNESCO Prize for Teaching of Human Rights, 1994–96; Special Rep. of UN Sec.-Gen., for Human Rights in Cambodia, 1993–96; Indep. Chm., Malaŵi Constitl Conf., 1994, Chm. Constitl Seminar, 1997. International Commission of Jurists: Comr, 1984–; Mem. Exec. Cttee, 1989–95, Chm., 1992–95; Pres., 1995–; Pres., Aust. Section, 1989–96. Internat. Consultant, Commn for Transborder Data Flow Develt, Intergovtl Bureau of Informatics, Rome, 1985–86; Mem., Bd, Internat. Trustees, Internat. Inst. for Inf. and Communication, Montreal, 1986–; President: Criminology Sect., ANZAAS, 1981–82; Law Sect., ANZAAS, 1984–85. Granada Guildhall Lectr, 1985; Acting Prof., Fac. of Salzburg Seminar, Salzburg, 1985; Hon. Prof., Nat. Law Sch. of India Univ., Bangalore, 1995–; Sen. Anzac Fellow, NZ Govt, 1981; Fellow, NZ Legal Res. Foundn, 1985. Pres., Nat. Book Council of Australia, 1980–83; Member: Library Council of NSW, 1976–85; NSW Ministerial Adv. Cttee on AIDS, 1987; Trustee, AIDS Trust of Australia, 1987–93; Comr, Global Commn on AIDS, WHO, Geneva, 1989–91. Mem. Council, Australian Opera, 1983–89; Patron, RSPCA, Australia. Fellow, Senate, Sydney Univ., 1964–69; Dep. Chancellor, Univ. of Newcastle, NSW, 1978–83; Chancellor, Macquarie Univ., Sydney, 1984–93. Mem. Bd of Governors, Internat. Council for Computer Communications, Washington, 1984–. Hon. Mem., Amer. Law Inst., 2000; Hon. FASSA 1997. Hon. DLitt: Newcastle, NSW, 1987; Ulster, 1998; Hon. LLD: Macquarie, 1994; Sydney, 1996; Nat. Law Sch. of India Univ., 1997; Buckingham, 2000; DUniv S Australia, 2001. Australian Human Rights Medal, 1991; UNESCO Prize for Human Rights Educn, 1998. *Publications:* Industrial Index to Australian Labour Law, 1978, 2nd edn 1983; Reform the Law, 1983; The Judges (Boyer Lectures), 1983; (ed jtly) A Touch of Healing, 1986; Through the World's Eye, 2000; essays and articles in legal and other jls. *Recreation:* work. *Address:* High Court of Australia, Canberra, ACT 2600, Australia. *T:* (2) 92308202, *Fax:* (2) 92308626.

KIRBY, Maj.-Gen. Norman George, OBE 1971; FRCS; Consultant Accident and Emergency Surgeon, Guy's Nuffield House, since 1994; Consultant Accident and Emergency Surgeon, 1982–93, Director, Clinical Services, Accidents and Emergencies, 1985–93, Guy's Hospital; *b* 19 Dec. 1926; *s* of George William Kirby and Laura Kirby; *m* 1949, Cynthia Bradley; one *s* one *d*. *Educ:* King Henry VIII Sch., Coventry; Univ. of Birmingham (MB, ChB). FRCS 1964, FRCSE 1980; FICS 1980; FFAEM 1993; DMCC 1997. Surgical Registrar: Plastic Surg. Unit, Stoke Mandeville Hosp., 1950–51; Birmingham Accident Hosp., 1953–55; Postgraduate Med. Sch., Hammersmith, 1964. Regt MO 10 Parachute Regt, 1950–51; OC 5 Parachute Surgical Team, 1956–59 (Suez Landing, 5 Nov. 1956); Officer i/c Surg. Div., BMH Rinteln, 1959–60; OC and Surg. Specialist, BMH Tripoli, 1960–62; OC and Consultant Surgeon, BMH Dhekelia, 1967–70; Chief Cons. Surgeon, Cambridge Mil. Hosp., 1970–72; Cons. Surg. HQ BAOR, 1973–78; Dir of Army Surgery, Cons. Surg. to the Army and Hon. Surgeon to the Queen, 1978–82; Hon. Cons. Surgeon, Westminster Hosp., 1979–. Examnr in Anatomy, RCSE, 1982–90; Mem., Court of Examiners, RCS, 1988–94. Chm., Army Med. Dept Working Party Surgical Support for BAOR, 1978–80; Member: MoD Med. Bds, 1978–82; Med. Cttee, Defence Scientific Adv. Council, 1979–82. Hon. Colonel: 308 (Co. of London) Gen. Hosp. RAMC, TA, 1982–87; 144 Para Field Sqdn (formerly Field Ambulance) RAMC (Volunteers), TA, 1985–96; Col Comdt, RAMC, 1987–92. Member: Council, Internat. Coll. of Surgeons; Airborne Med. Soc.; British Assoc. for Accident and Emergency Medicine (formerly Casualty Surgeons Assoc.), 1981–94 (Vice-Pres., 1988; Pres., 1990–93); Pres., Med. Soc. of London, 1992–93 (FMS 1981); Vice-Pres., British Assoc. of Trauma in Sport, 1982–88; Chm., Accidents & Emergencies Cttee, SE Thames RHA, 1984–88. Mem. Council, TAVRA, Gtr London, 1990–97. Liveryman, Soc. of Apothecaries of London, 1983–; Mem., HAC, 1988. Fellow, British Orthopaedic Assoc., 1967. Hon. Mem., Amer. Coll. of Emergency Physicians, 1993. McCombe Lectr, RCSE, 1979. Mem., Editl Bd, Brit. Jl Surg. and Injury, 1979–82. Mem., Surgical Travellers Club, 1979–. OStJ 1977 (Mem. Council, London, 1990–). Mitchener Medal, RCS, 1982. *Publications:* (ed) Field Surgery Pocket Book, 1981; Pocket Reference, Accidents and Emergencies, 1988, 2nd edn 1991; contrib. Brit. Jl Surg., Proc. RSocMed, etc. *Recreations:* travel, motoring, reading, archaeology. *Address:* 12 Woodsyre, Sydenham Hill, Dulwich, SE26 6SS. *T:* (020) 8670 5327.

KIRBY, Hon. Sir Richard (Clarence), Kt 1961; AC 1985; Chairman, Advertising Standards Council, 1973–88; *b* 22 Sept. 1904; *s* of Samuel Enoch Kirby and Agnes Mary Kirby, N Queensland; *m* 1st, 1937, Hilda Marie Ryan (*d* 1991); two *d*; 2nd, 1998, Joyce

Sidaway. *Educ:* The King's Sch., Parramatta; University of Sydney (LLB). Solicitor, NSW, 1928; called to Bar, 1933; served AIF, 1942–44; Mem. Adult Adv. Educl Council to NSW Govt, 1944–46; Judge, Dist Court, NSW, 1944–47; Mem. Austr. War Crimes Commn, 1945, visiting New Guinea, Morotai, Singapore, taking evidence on war crimes; Australia Rep. on War Crimes, Lord Mountbatten's HQ, Ceylon, 1945; Royal Commissioner on various occasions for Federal, NSW and Tasmanian Govts, 1945–47; Acting Judge Supreme Court of NSW, 1947; Chief Judge, Commonwealth Court of Conciliation and Arbitration, 1956–73; Austr. Rep., UN Security Council's Cttee on Good Offices on Indonesian Question, 1947–48, participating in Security Council Debates, Lake Success, USA; Chm. Stevedoring Industry Commn, 1947–49; (first) Pres., Commonwealth Conciliation and Arbitration Commn, 1956–73. Chm., Nat. Stevedoring Conf., 1976–77. Pres., H. V. Evatt Meml Foundn, 1979–85. Mem. Council, Wollongong Univ., 1979–84. Hon. DLitt Wollongong Univ., 1984. Bintag Jasa Ultama (Indonesia), 1995. *Recreation:* encouraging good will in industry. *Address:* Unit 60, Bayview Gardens Village, Cabbage Tree Road, Bayview, NSW 2104, Australia. *T:* (2) 99972096. *Club:* Athenæum (Melbourne).

KIRCHNER, Prof. Emil Joseph, PhD; Professor of European Studies, Department of Government, University of Essex, since 1992; *b* 19 March 1942; *m* 1975, Joanna Bartlett; two *s. Educ:* Case Western Reserve Univ. (BA Econ 1970; MA 1971; PhD 1976, Pol. Sci.). Essex University: Lectr and Sen. Lectr, Dept of Govt, 1974–92; Mem., Senate, 1992–. Dir, Inst. for European Community Policy Making, Brussels, 1981–86. Visiting Professor: Dept of Pol. Sci., Univ. of Connecticut, 1986–87; Centre for Econ. Res. and Grad. Educn, Charles Univ., Prague, 1997–2000; External Assessor, Poly. of W London, 1991. Member: Human Rights Steering Gp, Helsinki Conf. on Security Co-operation in Europe, 1991; Exec. Cttee, Univ. Assoc. for Contemporary European Studies, 1989; Exec. Cttee, Assoc. for Study of German Politics, 1989–90. Gen. Series Editor, Europe in Change (Manchester Univ. Press), 1993; Exec. Ed., Jl of European Integration, 1997–. *Publications:* Decision Making in the European Community, 1992; (jtly) The Federal Republic of Germany and NATO: 40 years after, 1992; (jtly) The Future of European Security, 1994; (jtly) The Recasting of the European Order: security architectures and economic co-operation, 1996; (jtly) The New Europe: east, west, centre, 1997; Decentralization and Transition in the Visegrad, 1999; (jtly) Committee Governance in the EU, 2000. *Recreations:* music, sports, travel. *Address:* University of Essex, Centre for European Studies, Wivenhoe Park, Colchester CO4 3SQ. *T:* (01206) 872749.

KIRCHNER, Peter James, MBE 1970; HM Diplomatic Service, retired; Consul General, Berlin, 1978–80; *b* 17 Sept. 1920; *s* of late William John Kirchner and Winifred Emily Homer (*née* Adams); *m* 1952, Barbro Sarah Margareta (*née* Klockhoff); one *s* two *d. Educ:* St Brendan's Coll., Clifton, Bristol; BA Open, 1991, BA Hons 1996. Served War, RA, 1939–41. Timber production, UK and Germany, 1941–48; FO, Germany, 1948; Home Office Immigration Dept, 1952–64; Head of UK Refugee Missions in Europe, 1960–63; FCO (formerly FO): Barbados, 1965; Nairobi, 1968; Ankara, 1970; Vienna, 1973; Jerusalem, 1976. Chm., Bd of Trustees, Retirement Trust, 1995–. Freeman, City of London, 1963. *Recreations:* golf, croquet, modern European history, northern baroque architecture, travel in Europe. *Address:* 86 York Mansions, Prince of Wales Drive, SW11 4BN. *T:* (020) 7622 7068.

KIRK, Anthony James Nigel; QC 2001; *b* 3 May 1958; *s* of late James Brian Kirk and of Lavinia Mary Kirk (*née* Kellow). *Educ:* Ipswich Sch.; King Edward VII Sch., Lytham St Anne's; King's Coll., London (LLB Hons; AKC). Called to the Bar, Gray's Inn, 1981 (Stuart Cunningham Macaskie and Lord Justice Holker Schol.); in practice as barrister, 1982–. Member: Family Law Bar Assoc. (Nat. Sec., 1999–); Bar Council, 1996–99 (Mem., Professional Conduct and Complaints Cttee, 1999–); Bd, Family Mediators' Assoc., 1999–. Mem., RCO. *Publication:* (contrib.). Jackson & Davies Matrimonial Finance and Taxation, 6th edn 1996. *Recreation:* classical music. *Address:* (chambers) 1 King's Bench Walk, Temple, EC4Y 7DB. *T:* (020) 7936 1500.

KIRK, Prof. Geoffrey Stephen, DSC 1945; LittD; FBA 1959; Regius Professor of Greek, University of Cambridge, 1974–82, now Emeritus; Fellow of Trinity College, Cambridge, 1974–82; *b* 3 Dec. 1921; *s* of Frederic Tilzey Kirk, MC, and Enid Hilda (*née* Pentecost); *m* 1st, 1950, Barbara Helen Traill (marr. diss. 1975); one *d*; 2nd, 1975, Kirsten Ricks (*née* Jensen). *Educ:* Rossall Sch.; Clare Coll., Cambridge. LittD Cambridge, 1965. Served War in Royal Navy, 1941–45; commissioned 1942; Temp. Lt, RNVR, 1945. Took Degree at Cambridge, 1946; Research Fellow, Trinity Hall, 1946–49; Student, Brit. Sch. at Athens, 1947; Commonwealth Fund Fellow, Harvard Univ., 1949–50; Fellow, Trinity Hall, 1950–70; Cambridge University: Asst Lecturer in Classics, 1951; Lecturer in Classics, 1952–61; Reader in Greek, 1961–65; Prof. of Classics, Yale Univ., 1965–70; Prof. of Classics, Bristol Univ., 1971–73. Visiting Lecturer, Harvard Univ., 1958; Sather Prof. of Classical Literature, University of California, Berkeley, 1968–69; Mellon Prof., Tulane Univ., 1979. Pres., Soc. for Promotion of Hellenic Studies, 1977–80. Corresp. Mem., Acad. of Athens, 1993. MA (Yale) 1965. *Publications:* Heraclitus, the Cosmic Fragments, 1954; (with J. E. Raven) The Presocratic Philosophers, 1958; The Songs of Homer, 1962 (abbrev., as Homer and the Epic, 1965); Euripides, Bacchae, 1970; Myth, 1970; The Nature of Greek Myths, 1974; Homer and the Oral Tradition, 1977; The Iliad: a commentary, Vol.1, books 1–4, 1985, Vol. 2, books 5–8, 1990; Towards the Aegean Sea, 1997; articles in classical, archæological and philosophical journals. *Recreations:* writing, 18th century architecture. *Address:* 12 Sion Hill, Bath BA1 2UH.

KIRK, Rt Hon. Herbert Victor; PC (N Ireland) 1962; Member (U) for South Belfast, Northern Ireland Assembly, 1973–75; *b* 5 June 1912; *s* of Alexander and Mary A. Kirk; *m* 1944, Gladys A. Dunn; three *s. Educ:* Queen's Univ., Belfast (BComSc). FCA 1940. MP Windsor Div. of Belfast, NI Parlt, 1956–72; Minister of Labour and Nat. Insce, Govt of N Ireland, 1962–64; Minister of Education, 1964–65; Minister of Finance, 1965–72, Jan.–May 1974, resigned. *Recreation:* golf. *Address:* 38 Massey Avenue, Belfast, Northern Ireland BT4 2JT. *Clubs:* Royal Portrush Golf, Belvoir Park Golf.

KIRK, Raymond Maurice, FRCS; Consulting Surgeon, Royal Free Hospital, since 1989; part-time Lecturer in Anatomy, Royal Free and University College Medical School (formerly Royal Free Hospital School of Medicine), since 1989; *b* 31 Oct. 1923; *m* 1952, Margaret Schafran; one *s* two *d. Educ:* Mundella Sch., Nottingham; County Secondary Sch., West Bridgford; King's College London; Charing Cross Hosp. MB BS, MS, London; LRCP. RN 1942–46; Lieut RNVR. Charing Cross Hosp., 1952–53; Lectr in Anatomy, King's Coll. London, 1953–54; Hammersmith Hosp., 1954–56; Charing Cross Hosp., 1956–60; Senior Surgical Registrar, Royal Free Hosp., 1961; Consultant Surgeon, Willesden Gen. Hosp., 1962–74, Royal Free Hosp. Group, 1964–89. Dir, Overseas Doctors' Trng Scheme, RCS, 1990–; Examiner: Univ. of London; formerly Mem. Court of Examrs, RCS; formerly Examr to RCPSG, Univs of Liverpool, Bristol, Khartoum, Colombo, Kuwait; Mem. Council, RCS, 1983–91; Pres., Medical Soc. of London, 1988; FRSocMed (Pres., Surgical Section, 1986–87). Member: British Soc. of Gastroenterol.; Surg. Res. Soc.; BMA; Med. Soc. of London; Hunterian Soc. (Pres., 1995–96); Soc. of Authors. Hon. Editor, Annals of RCS, 1983–92. *Publications:* Manual of Abdominal Operations, 1967; Basic Surgical Techniques, 1973, 4th edn 1995; (jtly) Surgery, 1974; General Surgical Operations, 1978, 4th edn 2000; Complications of Upper Gastrointestinal Tract Surgery, 1987; (jtly) Clinical Surgery in General, 1993, 3rd edn 1999; A Career in Medicine, 1998; (jtly) Essential General Surgical Operations, 2001; papers in sci. jls and chapters in books on peptic ulcer, oesophageal, gastric and general abdominal surgery and surgical trng. *Recreations:* opera, theatre, squash, cycling. *Address:* 10 Southwood Lane, Highgate Village, N6 5EE. *T:* (020) 8340 8575; *e-mail:* kirk@rfc.ucl.ac.uk. *Club:* Royal Society of Medicine.

KIRK, Richard Stanley; Chief Executive, Peacock's Stores, since 1996; *b* 16 Nov. 1945; *s* of Charles Kirk and Margaret (*née* Green); *m* 1st, 1969 (marr. diss. 1988); two *s*; 2nd, 1995, Barbara Mount. *Educ:* Chesterfield Grammar Sch. Store Manager, then Area Manager, F. W. Woolworth, 1966–77; Iceland Frozen Foods, subseq. Iceland Gp, PLC, 1977–96: Stores Dir, 1982–86; Man. Dir, 1986–96. *Recreations:* ski-ing, shooting, travel. *Address:* Faddiley Hall, Faddiley, Nantwich, Cheshire CW5 8JW.

KIRK-GREENE, Anthony Hamilton Millard, CMG 2001; MBE 1963; FRHistS; Emeritus Fellow, St Antony's College, Oxford, since 1992; *b* 16 May 1925; *e s* of late Leslie and Helen Kirk-Greene; *m* 1967, Helen Margaret Martyn Sellar. *Educ:* Rugby Sch.; Clare Coll., Cambridge (MA); Edinburgh Univ. Served Indian Army, 8th Punjab Regt, 1943–47. Colonial Admin. Service, Northern Nigeria, 1950–66; Supervisor, Admin. Service Trng, 1957–60; Sen. Dist Officer, 1960–66; Reader in Govt, Ahmadu Bello Univ., 1962–66; Sen. Res. Fellow in African Studies, St Antony's Coll., Oxford, 1967–80; Special Lectr in Modern Hist. of Africa, Oxford Univ., 1981–92; Director: Oxford Colonial Records Project, 1980–84; Oxford Univ. Foreign Service Prog., 1986–90. ODA Consultant, E African Staff Coll., 1972; UK Election Supervisor, Rhodesia/Zimbabwe, 1980. Harkness Fellow, Northwestern Univ. and UCLA, 1958; Hans Wolff Lectr, Indiana Univ., 1973. Killam Vis. Prof., Calgary Univ., 1985; Leverhulme Emeritus Fellow, 1993; Adjunct Prof., Stanford Univ. in Oxford, 1992–99. Mem. Council, Britain-Nigeria Assoc., 1984–; Pres., African Studies Assoc., UK, 1988–90; Vice-Pres., Royal African Soc., 1990–. Associate Ed., New DNB, 1996–. *Publications:* Adamawa Past and Present, 1958; Barth's Travels in Nigeria, 1962; Principles of Native Administration in Nigeria, 1965; (with S. J. Hogben) Emirates of Northern Nigeria, 1966; Hausa Proverbs, 1967; Crisis and Conflict in Nigeria 1966-1970, 1971; (with C. Kraft) Teach Yourself Hausa, 1975; A Biographical Dictionary of the British Colonial Governor, 1980; 'Stay by Your Radios': the military in Africa, 1981; (with D. Rimmer) Nigeria since 1970, 1981; A Biographical Dictionary of the British Colonial Service, 1991; The Diplomatic Academic Annual Conference: a Jubilee history, 1994; (with J. H. Vaughan) Hamman Yaji: diary of a Nigerian Chief, 1995; On Crown Service, 1999; (with D. Rimmer) Britain's Intellectual Engagement with Africa, 2000; Britain's Imperial Administrators, 2000; Glimpses of Empire, 2001; numerous monographs, chapters and articles on African and Imperial history. *Recreations:* reading, travel, controlled walking, wine tasting. *Address:* St Antony's College, Oxford OX2 6JF. *T:* (01865) 284700. *Clubs:* Royal Commonwealth Society; Hawks (Cambridge).

KIRKBRIDE, Julie; MP (C) Bromsgrove, since 1997; *b* 5 June 1960; *d* of late Henry Raymond Kirkbride and of Barbara (*née* Bancroft); *m* 1997, A. J. MacKay, *qv*; one *s. Educ:* Highlands Sch., Halifax; Girton Coll., Cambridge. Researcher, Yorkshire TV, 1983–86; Producer: BBC news and current affairs, 1986–89; ITN, 1989–92; Political Correspondent: Daily Telegraph, 1992–96; also Social Affairs Ed., Sunday Telegraph, 1996. Rotary Foundn Scholar, Yorkshire Area, 1982–83. *Recreations:* walking, travelling, opera. *Address:* House of Commons, SW1A 0AA.

KIRKBY, Emma, OBE 2000; freelance classical concert singer; soprano; *b* 26 Feb. 1949; *d* of late Capt. Geoffrey Kirkby, CBE, DSC, RN and of Daphne Kirkby; one *s* by Anthony Rooley, *qv. Educ:* Hanford School; Sherborne School for Girls; Somerville College, Oxford (BA Classics). FGSM 1991. Private singing lessons with Jessica Cash. Regular appearances with Taverner Choir and Players, 1972–; Member: Consort of Musicke, 1973–; Academy of Ancient Music, 1975–; numerous radio broadcasts, gramophone recordings, appearances at the Proms, 1977–. Hon. DLitt Salford, 1985; Hon. DMus: Bath, 1994; Sheffield, 2000.

KIRKE, Rear-Adm. David Walter, CB 1967; CBE 1962 (OBE 1945), retired; *b* 13 March 1915; *s* of late Percy St George Kirke and late Alice Gertrude, *d* of Sir James Gibson Craig, 3rd Bt; *m* 1st, 1936, Tessa O'Connor (marr. diss., 1950); one *s*; 2nd, 1956, Marion Margaret Gibb; one *s* one *d. Educ:* RN Coll., Dartmouth. China Station, 1933–35; Pilot Training, 1937; served War of 1939–45, Russian Convoys, Fighter Sqdns; loaned RAN, 1949–50; Chief of Naval Aviation, Indian Navy, New Delhi, 1959–62; Rear-Adm. 1965; Flag Officer, Naval Flying Training, 1965–68. MBIM 1967. *Recreation:* golf. *Address:* Lismore House, Pluckley, Kent TN27 0QZ. *T:* (01233) 840439. *Club:* Army and Navy.

KIRKHAM, family name of **Baroness Berners**.

KIRKHAM, Baron *cr* 1999 (Life Peer), of Old Cantley in the county of South Yorkshire; **Graham Kirkham,** Kt 1996; CVO 2001; Chairman, DFS Furniture Company plc, since 1983. Sen. Party Treas., Conservative Party, 1997–98. *Address:* (office) Bentley Moor Lane, Adwick-le-Street, Doncaster, S Yorkshire DN6 7BD.

KIRKHAM, Donald Herbert, CBE 1996; FCIS, FCIB; Group Chief Executive, Woolwich Building Society, 1991–95 (Chief Executive, 1986–90); *b* 1 Jan. 1936; *s* of Herbert and Hettie Kirkham; *m* 1960, Kathleen Mary Lond; one *s* one *d. Educ:* Grimsby Technical Sch. Woolwich Equitable Building Society, later Woolwich Building Society: Representative, 1959; Branch Manager, 1963; Gen. Manager's Asst, 1967; Business Planning Manager, 1970; Asst Gen. Manager, 1972; Gen. Manager, 1976; Mem. Local Board, 1979; Dep. Chief Gen. Manager, 1981; Mem. Board, 1982; non-exec. Dir, 1996–97; Dir, Gresham Insurance Co. Ltd, 1995–96. President: Banque Woolwich SA, 1995–; Banca Woolwich SpA, 1995–. Director: Horniman Museum and Public Park Trust, 1989– (Chm., 1996–); Building Socs Investor Protection Bd, 1995–97; Bexley and Greenwich HA, 1996–98 and 1999–2001. Chartered Building Societies Institute: Mem. Council, 1976; Dep. Pres., 1980; Pres., 1981; Vice-Pres., 1986–93, then Vice-Pres., CIB, 1993–98; Institute of Chartered Secretaries and Administrators: Mem. Council, 1979; Vice-Pres., 1985; Sen. Vice-Pres., 1990; Pres., 1991; Building Societies Assocation: Mem. Council, 1991–95; Dep. Chm., 1993–94; Chm., 1994–95. MInstD 1984. Hon. DBA Thames Poly., 1991. *Recreations:* boating, sea fishing. *Address:* 2 Chaundrye Close, The Court Yard, Eltham, SE9 5QB. *T:* (020) 8859 4295. *Club:* Royal Over-Seas League.

KIRKHAM, Frances Margaret; Her Honour Judge Kirkham, FCIArb; a Circuit Judge, Technology and Construction Court, Birmingham, since 2000; Chartered Arbitrator; *b* 29 Oct. 1947; *d* of Brian Llewellyn Morgan Davies and Natalie May Davies (*née* Stephens); *m* 1971, Barry Charles Kirkham. *Educ:* King's Coll. London (BA Hons 1969; AKC 1969). FCIArb 1991. Bank of England, 1969–73; Lloyds Bank Internat., 1973–74; admitted solicitor, 1978; Pinsent & Co., 1976–84; Bettinsons, 1984–87; Edge & Ellison, 1987–95; Dibb Lupton Alsop, 1995–2000. Parly Boundary Comr, 2000. Member:

Wkg Party on Civil Justice Reform, Law Soc. and Bar Council, 1992–93; Civil Litigation Cttee, 1988–92, Litigation Casework Cttee, 1990–92, Law Soc. Civil Litigation Cttee, Birmingham Law Soc., 1992–93; Council, CIArb, 1992–97, 2000 (Chm., W Midlands Br., 1994–97). Founder Chm., W Midlands Assoc. Women Solicitors. Mem., Adv. Bd, Centre for Advanced Litigation, Nottingham Law Sch., 1992–97. Gov., Heathfield Sch., Harrow, 1981–91 (Chm., 1984–91). *Recreations:* time with friends, sailing, ski-ing, walking, music, theatre, gardening. *Address:* Priory Courts, 33 Bull Street, Birmingham B4 6DW. *T:* (0121) 681 3181. *Club:* Bank of England Sailing.

KIRKHAM, Rt Rev. John Dudley Galtrey; Assistant Bishop, Diocese of Salisbury, since 2001; *b* 20 Sept. 1935; *s* of late Rev. Canon Charles Dudley Kirkham and Doreen Betty Galtrey; *m* 1986, Mrs Hester Gregory. *Educ:* Lancing Coll.; Trinity Coll., Cambridge (BA 1959, MA 1963). Commnd, Royal Hampshire Regt, seconded to 23 (K) Bn, King's African Rifles, 1954–56. Trinity Coll., Cambridge, 1956–59; Westcott House, 1960–62; Curate, St Mary-le-Tower, Ipswich, 1962–65; Chaplain to Bishop of Norwich, 1965–69; Priest in Charge, Rockland St Mary w. Hellington, 1967–69; Chaplain to Bishop of New Guinea, 1969; Asst Priest, St Martin-in-the-Fields and St Margaret's, Westminster, 1970–72; Domestic Chaplain to Archbishop of Canterbury, and Canterbury Diocesan Director of Ordinands, 1972–76; Bp Suffragan, later Area Bp, of Sherborne, 1976–2001; Canon and Preb., Salisbury Cath., 1977–2001; Bp to the Forces, 1992–2001. Archbishop of Canterbury's Advr to HMC, 1990–92. Commissary to Bp of Polynesia and Archbp of PNG. ChStJ 1991; Chaplain to the Guild of the Nineteen Lubricators. Croix d'Argent de Saint-Rombaut, 1973. *Recreations:* running, cross-country ski-ing. *Address:* Flamston House, Flamstone Street, Bishopstone, Salisbury, Wilts SP5 4BZ. *Clubs:* Army and Navy, Kandahar.

KIRKHAM, Keith Edwin, OBE 1987; PhD; Administrative Director, Clinical Research Centre, Medical Research Council, 1988–94; *b* 20 Oct. 1929; *s* of Thomas Kirkham and Clara Prestwich Willacy; *m* 1953, Dorothea Mary Fisher; two *s*. *Educ:* Kirkham Grammar Sch.; Birmingham Univ. (BSc); Fitzwilliam House, Cambridge (DipAgSci; T. H. Middleton Prize); MA, PhD Cantab. National Service, 2nd Lieut RA, 1955–57. Asst in Res., Cambridge, 1951–54; Univ. Demonstr, Cambridge, 1954–60; Sci. Staff, Clin. Endocrinology Res. Unit, MRC, 1960–73; Asst Dir (Admin), Clin. Res. Centre, MRC, 1973–88. Sec., Soc. for Endocrinology, 1975–79. Governor: Harrow Coll. of Higher Educn, 1983–90 (Chm. of Govs, 1986–90); Univ. of Westminster (formerly Poly. of Central London), 1990–2000. Hon. DSc Westminster, 1999. *Publications:* contribs to sci. jls on endocrinology. *Recreations:* cruising, sport (watching). *Address:* Spring Drive, Eastcote, Pinner, Middx HA5 2ES.

KIRKHILL, Baron *cr* 1975 (Life Peer), of Kirkhill, Aberdeen; **John Farquharson Smith;** *b* 7 May 1930; *s* of Alexander F. Smith and Ann T. Farquharson; *m* 1965, Frances Mary Walker Reid; one step-*d*. Lord Provost of the City and Royal Burgh of Aberdeen, 1971–75. Minister of State, Scottish Office, 1975–78. Chm., N of Scotland Hydro-Electric Bd, 1979–82. Deleg. to Parly Assembly of Council of Europe and WEU, 1987– (Chm., Council of Europe Cttee on Legal Affairs and Human Rights, 1991–95). Hon. LLD Aberdeen, 1974. *Address:* 3 Rubislaw Den North, Aberdeen AB15 4AL. *T:* (01224) 314167.

KIRKHOPE, Timothy John Robert; Member (C) Yorkshire and the Humber Region, European Parliament, since 1999; solicitor; *b* 29 April 1945; *s* of late John Thomas Kirkhope and Dorothy Buemann Kirkhope (*née* Bolt); *m* 1969, Caroline (*née* Maling); four *s*. *Educ:* Royal Grammar School, Newcastle upon Tyne; College of Law, Guildford. Conservative Party: joined 1961 (N Area Vice-Chm of YC and Mem., Nat. Cttee); Hexham Treasurer, 1982–85; Exec., N Area, 1975–87; Mem., Nat. Exec., 1985–87. County Councillor, Northumberland, 1981–85. Mem., Newcastle Airport Bd, 1982–85; Mem., Northern RHA, 1982–86; Founder Lawyer Mem., Mental Health Act Commn, 1983–86. Contested (C): Durham, Feb. 1974; Darlington, 1979. MP (C) Leeds North East, 1987–97; contested (C) same seat, 1997. PPS to Minister of State for the Envmt and Countryside, 1989–90; an Asst Govt Whip, 1990–92; a Lord Comr of HM Treasury (Govt Whip), 1992–95; Vice Chamberlain, HM Household, 1995; Parly Under-Sec. of State, Home Office, 1995–97. Mem., Select Cttee on Statutory Instruments, 1987–90; Vice Chm., Backbench Legal Cttee, 1988–89; Jt Hon. Sec., Cons. Backbench Envmt Cttee, 1988–89. European Parliament: Chief Whip, UK Conservatives, 1999–; Cons. spokesman on justice and home affairs, 1999–; Mem., Culture, Media, Arts, Youth and Educn Cttee, 1999–. Dir, Bournemouth and W Hampshire Water Co., 1999–. Dep. Chm., GBA, 1990–98. Gov., Royal Grammar Sch., Newcastle upon Tyne, 1989–99. MInstD 1998. *Recreations:* flying (holds private pilot's licence), tennis, swimming, watching TV quiz shows. *Address:* 7 Dewar Close, Collingham, Wetherby, West Yorks LS22 5JR; European Parliament, Rue Wiertz, Brussels 1047, Belgium. *Clubs:* Northern Counties (Newcastle upon Tyne); Dunstanburgh Castle Golf (Northumberland).

KIRKMAN, William Patrick, MBE 1993; Secretary: University of Cambridge Careers Service, 1968–92; Cambridge Society, since 1992; Administrator, American Friends of Cambridge University, 2000–01; Fellow, Wolfson College, (formerly University College), Cambridge, 1968–2000, now Emeritus; *b* 23 Oct. 1932; *s* of late Geoffrey Charles Aylward Kirkman and Bertha Winifred Kirkman; *m* 1959, Anne Teasdale Fawcett; two *s* one *d*. *Educ:* Churcher's Coll., Petersfield, Hants; Oriel Coll., Oxford. 2nd cl. hons, mod. langs, 1955; MA 1959; MA (Cantab) by incorporation, 1968. National Service, 1950–52, RASC (L/Cpl); TA, 1952–59, Intell. Corps (Lieut). Editorial staff: Express & Star, Wolverhampton, 1955–57; The Times, 1957–64 (Commonwealth staff, 1960–64, Africa Correspondent, 1962–64). Asst Sec., Oxford Univ. Appointments Cttee, 1964–68. Chm., Standing Conf. of University Appointments Services, 1971–73; Member: Management Cttee, Central Services Unit for Univ. Careers and Appointments Services, 1971–74, 1985–87; British Cttee, Journalists in Europe, 1985–97; Cambridge Univ. PR Co-ordinating Cttee, 1987–96; Trng Bd, ESRC, 1990–93; Non-service Mem., Home Office Extended Interview Bds, 1993–. Member: BBC South and East Regl Adv. Council, 1990–92, Midlands and E Regl Adv. Council, 1992–93, E Regl Adv. Council, 1994–96; Chm., BBC Radio Cambridgeshire Adv. Council, 1992–96. Wolfson College: Vice-Pres., 1980–84; Mem. Council, 1969–73, 1976–80, 1988–92, 1994–95; Dir, Press Fellowship Programme, 1982–96. Churchwarden, St Mary and All Saints Willingham, 1978–85, 1996–97. Vice-Chm., Assoc. of Charitable Foundns, 1994–97; Mem. Regl Cttee, RSA, 1997–. Trustee: Sir Halley Stewart Trust, 1969– (Hon. Sec., 1978–82, Vice-Chm., 1998–); Willingham British Sch. Trust, 1974–91; Homerton Coll., 1980–89; Lucy Cavendish Coll., 1989–97; Mem. Cttee, Cambridge Soc., 1979–83. Editor: Cambridge, 1992–; CRAC Newsletter, 1997–98. *Publications:* Unscrambling an Empire, 1966; contrib.: Policing and Social Policy, 1984; Models of Police/Public Consultation in Europe, 1985; Managing Recruitment, 4th edn 1988; Graduate Recruitment: a 25-year retrospective, 1993; contributor to journals incl.: Commonwealth, International Affairs, Africa Contemporary Record, Financial Times, Cambridge Rev., The Higher, The Hindu (Chennai), and to BBC. *Recreations:* broadcasting, gardening, church activities, writing. *Address:* 19 High Street, Willingham, Cambridge CB4 5ES. *T:* (01954) 260393; *e-mail:* wpk1000@cam.ac.uk. *Clubs:* Royal Commonwealth Society, Oxford and Cambridge.

KIRKNESS, Donald James, CB 1980; Deputy Secretary, Overseas Development Administration, 1977–80; *b* 29 Sept 1919; *s* of Charles Stephen and Elsie Winifred Kirkness; *m* 1947, Monica Mary Douch; one *d*. *Educ:* Harvey Grammar Sch., Folkestone. Exchequer and Audit Dept, 1938. Served War: RA and Royal Berkshire Regt, 1939–46. Colonial Office, 1947 (Asst Principal); Financial and Economic Adviser, Windward I, 1955–57; Dept of Economic Affairs, 1966; Civil Service Dept, 1970–73; ODA/ODM, 1973. UK Governor, Internat. Fund for Agricultural Develt, 1977–81; Mem., Exec. Bd, UNESCO, 1978–83.

KIRKPATRICK, Gavin Alexander Yvone, FCIPD, FBCS; Chief Executive, The British Computer Society, 1991–95; *b* 8 July 1938; *s* of late Yvone Kirkpatrick, OBE, TD, MA and Margaret (*née* Sclanders); *m* 1961, Susan Ann Frances Parselle; two *s* one *d*. *Educ:* Cheltenham Coll. Nat. Service, RN, 1957–59. John Trundell & Partners, Publishers, 1959–61; International Computers Ltd: Technical Sales, Personnel Officer, 1961–67; Personnel Manager Internat., 1967–70; Sperry Univac Division of Sperry Rand Corporation: Personnel Dir, Europe, 1970–76; Dir, Worldwide Personnel, Planning and Develt (USA), 1976–78; International Computers Plc, 1978–91: Gp Personnel Manager, 1978–81; Ops Personnel Manager, HQ, 1981–92; on secondment to Brit. Computer Soc. as Programme Dir, Europe, 1989–91. Member: European Movement, 1990– (Vice Chm., Outer London Europe Gp, 1994–95; Sec., 1996–99, Chm., 1999–, Central & W Dorset Branch; Vice Chm., Branches Assoc., 1997–99; Mem. Mgt Bd, 1998–2000; Chm., Branches Council, 1999–2000); British-German Assoc., 1992–. Friend, London Bach Soc., 1989– (Mem. Cttee, 1996–2001). MInstD 1970. FRSA 1992. Liveryman, Co. of Information Technologists, 1994–. *Recreations:* music, sailing, travel, photography, other Europeans. *Address:* West Walks House, Dorchester, Dorset DT1 1RE. *T:* (01305) 269946, *Fax:* (01305) 269986; *e-mail:* gkirkpatrick@bcs.org.uk.

KIRKPATRICK, Sir Ivone Elliott, 11th Bt *cr* 1685; *b* 1 Oct. 1942; *s* of Sir James Alexander Kirkpatrick, 10th Bt and Ellen Gertrude, *o d* of Captain R. P. Elliott, late RNR; *S* father, 1954. *Educ:* Wellington Coll., Berks; St Mark's Coll., University of Adelaide. *Heir:* *b* Robin Alexander Kirkpatrick, *b* 19 March 1944. *Address:* c/o ANZ Bank, 81 King William Street, Adelaide, SA 5000, Australia.

KIRKPATRICK, John Lister, CBE 1981; chartered accountant, retired; *b* 27 June 1927; *s* of late Dr Henry Joseph Rodway Kirkpatrick and Dr Nora Kirkpatrick (*née* Lister); *m*; one *s* one *d*; *m* 1977, Gay Elmslie (*née* Goudielock) (*d* 1995); *m* 1996, Mary-Alex (*née* Daly). *Educ:* Inverness Royal Acad. Served RNVR, 1944–47. Thomson McLintock & Co., subseq. KMG Thomson McLintock, then Peat Marwick McLintock, later KPMG: apprentice, 1948; qual. CA 1952; Partner, 1958; Joint Senior Partner, Glasgow and Edinburgh, 1974–80; Co-Chm., UK Policy Council, 1974–83; Sen. Partner, Scotland, 1980–87; UK Dep. Chm., 1983–87; Consultant, 1987–90; McLintock Main Lafrenz (MML), subseq. Klynveld Main Goerdeler (KMG): Partner, 1974–87; Mem. Bd of Mgt, and Chm., Eastern Hemisphere Exec. Cttee, 1974–79; Mem., Central Mgt Cttee, and Chm., Region 1 (Europe, Africa, ME, India, Pakistan), 1979–85; Chm., ME, 1985–87. Institute of Chartered Accountants of Scotland: Vice Pres., 1975–77; Pres., 1977–78; Member: Examg Bd, Parly and Law Cttee (Chm.), Acctg and Auditing Standards Cttee (Chm.), and F and GP Cttee (Chm.), 1964–75; Council, 1970–75. Mem. (rep. GB and Ireland), 1978–85, Chm., 1985–87, Internat. Acctg Standards Cttee; Lay Mem., Scottish Solicitors' Discipline Tribunal, 1981–96. Member: BoT Accountants' Adv. Cttee, 1967–72; Exam. Supervisory Bd, Arab Soc. of Certified Accountants, 1988–96 (Hon. FASCA 1997); Rev. Body on Doctors' and Dentists' Remuneration, 1983–89; Panel for Financial Services Tribunal, 1988–95; Audits Jt Cttee, Securities Assoc., 1990–95. Member: Royal Glasgow Inst. of Fine Arts; Merchants House of Glasgow; RSPB; Saints and Sinners Club of Scotland. Trustee, Highland Fund Foundn, 1983–90. FRSA 1989. Addresses and TV presentations to nat. and internat. audiences. *Publications:* various prof. papers and articles. *Recreations:* fishing, gardening, painting (watercolour), protection of precious environment of rural and island Scotland. *Address:* 1 Letham Drive, Newlands, Glasgow G43 2SL. *T:* (0141) 633 1407; The Bungalow, Daliburgh, Isle of South Uist HS8 5SS. *T:* (01878) 700652. *Club:* New (Edinburgh).

KIRKPATRICK, William Brown, OBE 1998; Member: Gaming Board for Great Britain, 1990–99; National Lottery Charities Board, 1994–98; *b* 27 April 1934; *s* of late Joseph and Mary Kirkpatrick, Thornhill, Dumfriesshire; *m* 1990, Joan L. Millar. *Educ:* Morton Acad., Thornhill; George Watson's Coll., Edinburgh; Univ. of Strathclyde (BScEcon); Columbia Business Sch., NY (MS and McKinsey Scholar); Stanford Executive Program. After three years in manufacturing industry in Glasgow, Dundee and London, served 3i, 1960–85, latterly at director level, and worked in London, Scotland and Australia in investment capital, corporate finance, fixed interest capital markets, on secondment as Industrial Director of Industry Department for Scotland, in shipping finance and as a nominee director; company dir and corporate advr with various cos, 1985–95 (incl. appt within DoE on water privatisation). JP Inner London, 1985–92. *Recreations:* Scottish paintings, porcelain pigs, current affairs. *Address:* Roughhills, Sandyhills, Dalbeattie, Kirkcudbrightshire DG5 4NZ. *T:* (01387) 780239. *Club:* Caledonian.

KIRKUP, James; travel writer, poet, novelist, playwright, translator, broadcaster; *b* 23 April 1918; *o s* of James Harold Kirkup and Mary Johnson. *Educ:* South Shields High Sch.; Durham Univ. (BA; Hon. Fellow, Grey Coll., 1992). FRSL 1962. Gregory Fellow in Poetry, University of Leeds, 1950–52; Visiting Poet and Head of English Dept, Bath Academy of Art, Corsham Court, Wilts, 1953–56; Lectr in English, Swedish Ministry of Education, Stockholm, 1956–57; Prof. of Eng. Lang. and Lit., University of Salamanca, 1957–58, of English, Tohoku Univ., Sendai, Japan, 1958–61; Lecturer in English Literature, University of Malaya in Kuala Lumpur, 1961–62; Literary Editor, Orient/West Magazine, Tokyo, 1963–64; Prof., Japan Women's Univ., 1964–; Poet in Residence and Visiting Prof., Amherst Coll., Mass, 1968–; Prof. of English Literature, Nagoya Univ., 1969–72; Arts Council Fellowship in Creative Writing, Univ. of Sheffield, 1974–75; Morton Vis. Prof. of Internat. Literature, Ohio Univ., 1975–76; Playwright in Residence, Sherman Theatre, University Coll., Cardiff, 1976–77; Prof. of English Lit., Kyoto Univ. of Foreign Studies, Kyoto, Japan, 1977–89. President: Poets' Soc. of Japan, 1969; British Haiku Soc., 1990; Sponsor, Inst. of Psychophysical Res., 1970. Atlantic Award in Literature (Rockefeller Foundn), 1950; Mabel Batchelder Award, 1968; Keats Prize for Poetry, 1974; Scott-Moncrieff Prize for Translation, 1997. *Plays performed:* Upon this Rock (perf. Peterborough Cathedral), 1955; Masque, The Triumph of Harmony (perf. Albert Hall), 1955; The True Mistery of the Nativity, 1957; Dürrenmatt, The Physicists (Eng. trans.), 1963; Dürrenmatt, The Meteor (Eng. trans.); Dürrenmatt, Play Strindberg (Eng. trans.), 1972; The Magic Drum, children's play, 1972, children's musical, 1977; Dürrenmatt, Portrait of a Planet, 1972; Dürrenmatt, The Conformer, 1974; Schiller, Don Carlos, 1975; Cyrano de Bergerac, 1975; *operas:* An Actor's Revenge, 1979; Friends in Arms, 1980; The Damask Drum, 1982; *television plays performed:* The Peach Garden, Two

Pigeons Flying High, The Prince of Homburg, etc. Contributor to BBC, The Listener, The Spectator, Times Literary Supplement, The Independent, Modern Poetry in Translation, Time and Tide, New Yorker, Botteghe Oscure, London Magazine, Japan Qly, English Teachers' Magazine (Tokyo), etc. *Publications:* The Drowned Sailor, 1948; The Cosmic Shape, 1947; The Creation, 1950; The Submerged Village, 1951; A Correct Compassion, 1952; A Spring Journey, 1954; Upon This Rock, 1955; The True Mistery of the Nativity, 1957; The Descent into the Cave, 1957; Sorrows, Passions and Alarms, 1959; These Horned Islands, A Journal of Japan, 1962; frères Gréban, The True Mistery of the Passion, 1962; Refusal to Conform, 1963; Tropic Temper: a Memoir of Malaya, 1963; Japan Industrial, 1964–65 (2 vols); Daily Life in the French Revolution, 1964; Tokyo, 1965; England, Now, 1965; Japan, Now, 1966; Frankly Speaking, I-II, 1968; Bangkok, 1968; One Man's Russia, 1968; Filipinescas, 1968; Streets of Asia, 1969; Japan Physical, 1969; Aspects of the Short Story, 1969; Hong Kong, 1970; Japan Behind the Fan, 1970; Heaven, Hell and Hara-Kiri, 1974; (with Birgit Skiöld) Zen Gardens, 1974; Scenes from Sesshu, 1977; Zen Contemplations, 1979; (with Birgit Skiöld) The Tao of Water, 1980; Folktales Japanesque, 1982; Modern American Myths, 1982; I Am Count Dracula, 1982; I Am Frankenstein's Monster, 1983; Miniature Masterpieces of Kawabata Yasunari, 1983; When I was a Child: a study of nursery-rhymes, 1983; My Way-USA, 1984; The Glory that was Greece, 1984; The Mystery & Magic of Symbols, 1987; The Cry of the Owl: Native Folktales & Legends, 1987; (ed) A Certain State of Mind: an anthology of modern and contemporary Japanese haiku poets, 1995; (ed) Burning Giraffes: modern and contemporary Japanese poets, 1995; *poems:* The Prodigal Son, 1959; Paper Windows: Poems from Japan, 1968; Shepherding Winds (anthol.), 1969; Songs and Dreams (anthol.), 1970; White Shadows, Black Shadows: Poems of Peace and War, 1970; The Body Servant; poems of exile, 1971; A Bewick Bestiary, 1971; Modern Japanese Poetry (anthol.), 1978; Dengonban Messages (one-line poems), 1980; To the Ancestral North: poems for an autobiography, 1983; The Sense of the Visit: new poems, 1984; The Guitar-Player of Zuiganji, 1985; Fellow Feelings, 1986; Shooting Stars (haiku), 1992; First Fireworks (haiku), 1992; Short Takes (one-line poems), 1993; Words for Contemplation, 1993; Look at it this way! (for children), 1993; Blue Bamboo: haiku, senryu and tanka, 1994; Formulas for Chaos, 1994; Strange Attractors, 1995; An Extended Breath: collected longer poems, 1995; Selected Shorter Poems, vol. 1 Omens of Disaster, vol. 2 Once and for All, 1995; Noems, Koans and a Navel Display, 1995; Counting to 9,999: haiku and tanka, 1995; Utsusemi: tanka, 1996; The Patient Obituarist: new poems, 1996; A Book of Tanka (Japan Fest. Foundn Award), 1997; Figures in a Setting, 1997; He Dreamed he was a Butterfly: tanka, 1997; One-Man Band: poems without words, 1999; A Crack in the Wall: an anthology of modern Arab poetry, 2000; Tokonoma, 2000; TankAlphabet, 2001; A Tiger in your Tanka, 2001; *poems and translations:* Ecce Homo: My Pasolini, 1982; No More Hiroshimas, 1982; *autobiography:* vol. 1, The Only Child, 1957 (trans. Japanese, 1986, reprinted with vol. 2 as A Child of the Tyne, 1997); vol. 2, Sorrows, Passions and Alarms, 1987 (trans. Japanese); vol. 3, I, of All People: an Autobiography of Youth, 1990; vol. 4, A Poet could not But be Gay: some Legends of my Lost Youth, 1991; vol. 5, Me All Over: memoirs of a misfit, 1993; Throwback: poems towards an autobiography, 1992; *novels:* The Love of Others, 1962; Insect Summer (for children), 1971; The Magic Drum (for children), 1973; Gaijin on the Ginza, 1991; Queens have Died Young and Fair, 1993; *essays:* Eibungaku Saiken, 1980; The Joys of Japan, 1985; Lafcadio Hearn (biog.), 1985; James Kirkup's International Movie Theatre, 1985; Trends and Traditions, 1986; Portraits & Souvenirs (biog.), 1987; *opera:* The Damask Drum, 1982; An Actor's Revenge, 1989; The Genius of Haiku: essays on R. H. Blyth, 1994; *translations:* Camara Laye, The Dark Child, 1955; Ancestral Voices, 1956; Camara Laye, The Radiance of the King, 1956; Simone de Beauvoir, Memoirs of a Dutiful Daughter, 1958; The Girl from Nowhere, 1958; It Began in Babel, 1961; The Captive, 1962; Sins of the Fathers, 1962; The Gates of Paradise, 1962; The Heavenly Mandate, 1964; Daily Life of the Etruscans, 1964; Erich Kästner, The Little Man, 1966; Erich Kästner, The Little Man and The Little Miss, 1969; Heinrich von Kleist, Michael Kohlhaas, 1966; E. T. A. Hoffmann, Tales of Hoffmann, 1966; Camara Laye, A Dream of Africa, 1967; The Eternal Virgin (Eng. trans. of Valéry's La Jeune Parque), 1970; (with C. Fry) The Oxford Ibsen, vol III, Brand and Peer Gynt, 1972; Selected Poems of Kyozo Takagi, 1973, rev. edn as How to Cook Women, 1997; Camara Laye, The Guardian of the Word, 1980; Cold Mountain Poems (trans. Han Shan), 1980; Petru Dimitriu, To the Unknown God, 1982; Michel Kpomassié, An African in Greenland, 1982; Tierno Monénembo, The Bush Toads, 1982; Margherita Guidacci, This Little Measure, 1990; Patrick Drevet, A Room in the Woods, 1991; Marc Rigaudis, Ito-san, 1991; Jean-Baptiste Niel, Painted Shadows, 1991; Jean-Noël Pancrazi, Vagabond Winter, 1992; Pascal Quignard, All the World's Mornings, 1992; Patrick Drevet, My Micheline, 1993; Hervé Guibert, The Man in the Red Hat, The Compassion Protocol, 1993; Georges-Arthur Goldschmidt, Worlds of Difference, 1993; Hervé Guibert, Blindsight, Paradise, 1995; Tahar Ben Jelloun, State of Absence, 1995; Marcelle Lagesse, Isabelle, 1995; Patrick Drevet, Auvers-sur-Oise, 1997; *festschrift:* Diversions: Festschrift for James Kirkup's 80th Birthday, 1998. *Recreation:* standing in shafts of moonlight. *Address:* British Monomarks-Box 2780, London WC1N 3XX.

KIRKUP, William, FRCOG, FFPHM; Regional Director of Public Health and Healthcare, Northern and Yorkshire, NHS Executive, Department of Health, since 1999; *b* 29 April 1949; *s* of late William Kirkup and Patience Kirkup (*née* Wilford); *m* 1972 (marr. diss. 1983); three *d*; *m* 1991, Evelyn May Watson. *Educ:* Newcastle Royal Grammar Sch.; Worcester Coll., Oxford (MA, BM BCh 1974). MRCOG 1979, FRCOG 1993; MFPHM 1986, FFPHM 1994. Obstetrics and gynaecology posts, Oxford, Sheffield and Newcastle, 1975–82; public health trng, 1982–86; Consultant, Newcastle, 1986–87; Sen. Lectr, Newcastle Univ., 1986–91; Dir of Public Health, N Tyneside, 1987–91; Dir posts, (Performance Review, Healthcare Devlt, NHS Trusts Div.), Northern Reg. and NHS Exec., 1991–99. *Publications:* contribs to learned jls. *Recreations:* Newcastle United FC, music, playing with computers. *Address:* NHS Executive, Northern and Yorkshire, John Snow House, Durham DH1 3YG. *T:* (0191) 301 1300.

KIRKWOOD, family name of **Baron Kirkwood**.

KIRKWOOD, 3rd Baron *cr* 1951, of Bearsden; **David Harvie Kirkwood;** Senior Lecturer in Metallurgy, 1976–87, Hon. Senior Lecturer and Metallurgical Consultant, since 1987, Sheffield University; *b* 24 Nov. 1931; *s* of 2nd Baron Kirkwood and Eileen Grace (*d* 1999), *d* of Thomas Henry Boalch; *S* father, 1970; *m* 1965, Judith Rosalie, *d* of late John Hunt; three *d*. *Educ:* Rugby; Trinity Hall, Cambridge (MA, PhD); CEng. Lectr in Metallurgy, Sheffield Univ., 1962; Warden of Stephenson Hall, Sheffield Univ., 1974–80. Mem., Select Cttee on Sci. and Technology, H of L, 1987–92, 1996–99. *Heir:* *b* Hon. James Stuart Kirkwood [*b* 19 June 1937; *m* 1965, Alexandra Mary, *d* of late Alec Dyson; two *d*]. *Address:* 56 Endcliffe Hall Avenue, Sheffield S10 3EL. *T:* (0114) 266 3107.

KIRKWOOD, Rt Hon. Lord; Ian Candlish Kirkwood; PC 2000; a Senator of the College of Justice in Scotland, since 1987; *b* 8 June 1932; *o s* of late John Brown Kirkwood, OBE, and Mrs Constance Kirkwood, Edinburgh; *m* 1970, Jill Ingram Scott; two *s*. *Educ:* George Watson's Boys' Coll., Edinburgh; Edinburgh Univ.; Univ. of Michigan, USA. MA (Edin) 1952; LLB (Edin) 1954; LLM (Mich) 1956. Called to Scottish Bar, 1957; apptd Standing Junior Counsel to Scottish Home and Health Dept, 1963; QC (Scot.) 1970. Member: Rules Council (Court of Session); Parole Bd for Scotland, 1994–97. Formerly Pres., Wireless Telegraphy Appeal Tribunal in Scotland. Chm., Med. Appeal Tribunal in Scotland. *Recreations:* fishing, golf, chess, tennis. *Address:* 58 Murrayfield Avenue, Edinburgh EH12 6AY. *T:* (0131) 477 1994; Knockbrex House, near Borgue, Kirkcudbrightshire. *Club:* New (Edinburgh).

KIRKWOOD, Hon. Sir Andrew (Tristram Hammett), Kt 1993; **Hon. Mr Justice Kirkwood;** a Judge of the High Court of Justice, Family Division, since 1993; *b* 5 June 1944; *s* of Maj. T. G. H. Kirkwood, RE (killed in action, 1944) and late Lady Faulks; *m* 1968, Penelope Jane (*née* Eaton); two *s* one *d*. *Educ:* Radley Coll., Abingdon, Oxon; Christ Church, Oxford (MA). Called to the Bar, Inner Temple, 1966, Bencher, 1993; QC 1989; a Recorder, 1987–93; a Judge, Employment Appeal Tribunal, 1996–98; Liaison Judge, Family Div., Midland and Oxford Circuit, 1999–. Chm., Leics Inquiry, 1992. Mem., Judicial Studies Bd, 1994–99 (Co-Chm., Civil and Family Cttee, 1994–98; Chm., Family Cttee, 1998–99). *Address:* Royal Courts of Justice, Strand, WC2A 2LL. *Club:* MCC.

KIRKWOOD, Archibald Johnstone, (Archy); MP Roxburgh and Berwickshire, since 1983 (L/Alliance 1983–88, Lib Dem since 1988); *b* 22 April 1946; *s* of David Kirkwood and Jessie Barclay Kirkwood; *m* 1972, Rosemary Chester; one *d* one *s*. *Educ:* Cranhill School; Heriot-Watt University. BSc Pharmacy. Notary Public; Solicitor. Lib Dem convenor and spokesman on welfare, 1988–92, on social security, 1992–94, and 1997–2001, on community care, 1994–97; Chief Whip, 1992–97. Chairman: Social Security Select Cttee, 1997–2001; Work and Pensions Select Cttee, 2001–. Trustee, Joseph Rowntree Reform Trust, 1985– (Chm., 1999–). *Address:* House of Commons, SW1A 0AA. *T:* (020) 7219 3000.

KIRKWOOD, Ian Candlish; *see* Kirkwood, Rt Hon. Lord.

KIRKWOOD, Dr James Kerr; Chief Executive and Scientific Director, Universities Federation for Animal Welfare and of Humane Slaughter Association, since 2000; *b* 8 Nov. 1951; *s* of late Andrew Kerr Kirkwood and of Patricia Mary Kirkwood (*née* Brown); *m* 1983, Julia Mary Christine Brittain; two *s* one *d*. *Educ:* Bradfield Coll., Berks; Bristol Univ. (BVSc 1975; PhD 1982). CBiol, FIBiol 1997; MRCVS. Research Associate, later Res. Fellow, Dept of Pathology, Bristol Univ., 1981–84; Sen. Vet. Officer, Zoological Soc. of London, and Head of Vet. Sci. Gp, Inst. of Zoology, 1984–96; specialist in zoo and wildlife medicine, 1992–2000; Scientific Dir, UFAW, and Hon. Dir, Humane Slaughter Assoc., 1996–2000. Ed.-in-Chief, Animal Welfare, 1996–. Dir, Master's Course in Wild Animal Health, RVC/Inst. of Zoology, 1994–96; Vis. Prof., Dept of Pathology and Infectious Diseases, RVC, 1997–; Hon. Research Fellow: UCL, 1996–; Inst. of Zoology, 1997–. Member: IUCN Vet. Specialist Gp, 1990–; Zoos Forum, 1999–; Trustee, Zebra Foundn for Vet. Zool Educn, 1990–; Pres., British Vet. Zool Soc., 1994–96. Mem. Companion, Animal Welfare Council, 2000–. *Publications:* (with K. Stathatos) Biology, Rearing and Care of Young Primates, 1992; sundry publications on biology, diseases, veterinary care, conservation and welfare of captive and free-living wild animals. *Recreations:* wind surfing, surfing. *Address:* Universities Federation for Animal Welfare and Humane Slaughter Association, The Old School, Wheathampstead, Herts AL4 8AN. *T:* (01582) 831818.

KIRKWOOD, Prof. Thomas Burton Loram, PhD; Professor of Medicine, and Head of Department of Gerontology, University of Newcastle upon Tyne, since 1999; *b* 6 July 1951; *s* of late Kenneth Kirkwood; *m* 1973, Betty Rosamund Bartlett (marr. diss. 1995); one *s* one *d*; *m* 1995, Jane Louise Bottomley. *Educ:* Dragon Sch., Oxford; Magdalen Coll. Sch., Oxford; St Catharine's Coll., Cambridge (MA; PhD 1983); Worcester Coll., Oxford (MSc). Scientist, Nat. Inst. for Biol Standards and Control, 1973–81; National Institute for Medical Research: Sen. Scientist, 1981–88; Head, Lab. of Mathematical Biol., 1988–93; Prof. of Biol Gerontology, Univ. of Manchester, 1993–99. Various distinguished lectures incl. Reith Lectures, 2001. Chm., Brit. Soc. for Research on Ageing, 1992–99; Dir, Jt Centre on Ageing, Univs of Manchester and Newcastle upon Tyne, 1996–; Gov., 1998–2001, and Chm., Res. Adv. Council, 1999–2000, Research into Ageing; Chm., Foresight Task Force on Health Care of Older People, 1999–2001; Member: WHO Expert Adv. Panel on Biol Standardization, 1985–; UK Human Genome Mapping Project Cttee, 1991–93; Basic Scis Interest Gp., Wellcome Trust, 1992–97; BBSRC, 2001–. Co-Ed., Mechanisms of Ageing and Devolt, 2000–. Pres., Internat. Biometric Soc. (British Reg.), 1998–2000. Fellow, Inst. for Advanced Study, Budapest, 1997. FMedSci 2001. Heinz Karger Prize, 1983; Fritz Verzár Medal, 1996; Dhole-Eddlestone Prize, British Geriatrics Soc., 2001. *Publications:* (jtly) Accuracy in Molecular Processes: its control and relevance to living systems, 1986; Time of Our Lives: the science of human ageing, 1999; (with C. E. Finch) Chance, Development and Aging, 2000; The End of Age, 2001; (jtly) Sex and Longevity: sexuality, gender, reproduction, parenthood; many scientific articles. *Recreations:* hill-walking, running, pottery, gardening. *Address:* Institute for Ageing and Health, Wolfson Research Centre, Newcastle General Hospital, Westgate Road, Newcastle upon Tyne NE4 6BE. *T:* (0191) 256 3319, *Fax:* (0191) 219 5074; *e-mail:* Tom.Kirkwood@newcastle.ac.uk.

KIRNER, Hon. Joan Elizabeth, AM 1980; Chairman, Australian Centre for Equity through Education, since 1996; Co-Convenor, EMILY's List, Australia, since 1996; *b* 20 June 1938; *d* of J. K. and B. E. Hood; *m* 1960, Ronald Kirner; two *s* one *d*. *Educ:* University High Sch.; Melbourne Univ. (BA, Dip. Educn). English and Social Studies Teacher, Ballarat Tech. Sch., 1959–60; positions with Vic. Fedn of State Schs Parents' Clubs, Aust. Council of State Schs Orgns and Tech. and Further Educn Councils, to 1982. Joined ALP 1979; MLC Melbourne West, 1982–88; MLA (ALP) Williamstown, Victoria, 1988–94; Minister for: Conservation, Forests and Lands, 1985–88; Education, 1988–90; Ethnic Affairs, 1990–91; Women's Affairs, 1990–92; Dep. Premier, 1989–90; Premier of Victoria, 1990–92; Leader of the Opposition, 1992–94; Shadow Minister for Ethnic Affairs, and for Women's Affairs, 1992–93. Chairman: Employment Services Regulatory Authy, 1994–97; Adv. Cttee, Centenary of Federation, 1994–96. Fellow, Aust. Coll. of Educn, 1983. *Recreations:* films, walking, music. *Address:* Old Treasury Building, Spring Street, Melbourne, Vic 3000, Australia. *T:* (3) 96516510.

KIRSHBAUM, Ralph; cellist; *b* Texas, 4 March 1946; *m* 1982, Antoinette Reynolds; one *s*. Founder and Artistic Dir, RNCM Manchester Internat. Cello Fest., 1988–. Has performed with major orchestras including: BBC Symphony; Boston Symphony; Cleveland Orch.; London Symphony; Orchestre de Paris; Pittsburgh Symphony; San Francisco Symphony; Chicago Symphony; Tonhalle; Berlin Radio Symphony; Royal Danish; Stockholm Philharmonic. Festival appearances at Aspen, Bath, Edinburgh, Lucerne, New York and Ravinia. Chamber music collaboration with Gyorgy Pauk, Peter Frankl and Pinchas Zukerman. Recordings include: concertos: Barber; Elgar; Haydn D major; Tippett Triple; Walton; Beethoven Triple; Brahms Double; Ravel, Shostakovich and Brahms Trios, complete Bach suites. *Address:* c/o Ingpen & Williams, 26 Wadham Road, SW15 2LR.

KIRTON, Muriel Elizabeth; Director, Yugoslavia, British Council, since 2001; *b* 4 July 1950; *d* of William Waddell Kirton and Belle Jane Kirton (*née* Barnett). *Educ:* Glasgow Univ. (MA Hons Eng. and French 1974); Kent Univ. (MA TEFL 1979); Edinburgh Univ. (DipEd 1975); Moray House Coll. of Educn (PGCE 1975). Teacher of French and English, Cornwall Coll., Montego Bay, Jamaica, 1975–77; teacher of French, Dane Court Tech. High Sch., Broadstairs, 1977–78; Lectr in ELT, Hilderstone Coll., Kent, 1978–79; Sen. Lectr in ELT, Nonington Coll., Kent, 1979–82; joined British Council, 1982: Project Manager, ELT, China, 1982–85; Projects Dir, Hong Kong, 1985–89; Educn Officer, Egypt, 1990–93; Director: Vietnam, 1993–96; Commonwealth Relations, 1996–2000; Cyprus, 2000–01. *Recreations:* scuba diving, alternative/complementary healing therapies, reading, cinema, theatre. *Address:* British Council, 10 Spring Gardens, SW1A 2BN. *T:* (020) 7389 4441.

KIRUI, Nancy Chepkemoi; High Commissioner for Kenya in the United Kingdom, since 2000; *b* 4 June 1957; *d* of Isaiah Cheluget and Rael Cheluget; *m* 1993, Nicholas Kirui; two *d*, and three step *s* one step *d*. *Educ:* Alliance Girls' Sch., Kikuyu, Kenya; Univ. of Nairobi (LLB); Kenya Sch. of Law (Postgrad. Dip. Law). Legal Officer: Min. of Foreign Affairs, Nairobi, 1985–88; Perm. Mission of Kenya to UN, Geneva, 1988–91; Min. of Foreign Affairs, 1991–94; Kenya High Commn, London, 1994–98; Hd of Legal Div., then Hd, Americas Div., Min. of Foreign Affairs, 1998–2000. *Recreations:* sketching, painting, cooking. *Address:* Kenya High Commission, 45 Portland Place, W1N 4AS. *T:* (020) 7636 2371.

KIRYA, Prof. George Barnabas; High Commissioner for Uganda in the United Kingdom, since 1990, and Ambassador to Ireland, since 1995 (Senior High Commissioner at the Court of St James's, 1997); Dean of the Diplomatic Corps, since 1999; *b* 9 Feb. 1939; *m*; five *s* one *d*. *Educ:* Univ. of E Africa (MB ChB 1966); Birmingham Univ. (MSc Gen. Virology 1971); Manchester Univ. (Dip. Bacteriology 1974). Med. House Officer, Mulago Hosp., Uganda, 1966–67; Sen. House Officer, Dept of Paediatrics and Child Health, Makerere Fac. of Medicine, 1967; East Africa Virus Res. Inst., Entebbe: Virologist, 1967; Sen. Med. Res. Officer, 1968; Principal Med. Res. Officer and Head, Dept of Arbovirology, 1969; Hon. Lectr, Dept of Med. Microbiol., Makerere Univ., 1970; Consultant on Yellow Fever Epidemics, WHO, 1970; Department of Microbiology, Faculty of Medicine, Makerere University: Sen. Lectr, 1973–75; Associate Prof. and Hd of Dept, 1975–78; Prof. and Hd of Dept, 1978; Makerere University: Mem. Senate, 1977–90; Mem. Univ. Council, 1981–90; Vice Chancellor, 1986–90. Chairman: Commonwealth Finance Cttee, 1993–; OAU Heads of Mission Gp, London, 1997–; Commonwealth Heads of Mission Gp, 1997–; Commonwealth Africa Gp, 1997–. Mem., WHO Scientific and Technical Adv. Gp, serving as WHO Temp. Advr, 1990–93. Dir, Central Public Health Labs in Uganda supported by WHO, UNICEF and Min. of Health; Chm., Disease Surveillance Sub-Cttee, Min. of Health; Member: Nat. Cttee for Prevention of Blindness in Uganda; Adv. Cttee for Res. of Viruses in Uganda; E and Central African Physicians Assoc. Uganda Medical Association: Treas., 1978–82; Pres., 1982–86. Teaching and supervising undergrad. and post-grad. med. students, med. lab. technologists, nurses and midwives and health visitors. Internal examnr and external examnr for several univs incl. Univ. of Ibadan, Lagos Univ. and Univ. of Nairobi. Member, Editorial Bd: E African Jl for Med. Res.; Uganda Med. Jl. Hon. LLD Birmingham, 2001. *Address:* Uganda House, 58/59 Trafalgar Square, WC2N 5DX. *T:* (020) 7839 5783; 30 Ingram Avenue, Hampstead, NW11. *Club:* Africa Cricket (Kampala).

KISSIN, Evgeny Igorevich; concert pianist; *b* 10 Oct. 1971; *s* of Igor Kissin and Emilia Kissina. *Educ:* Gnessin Special Sch. of Music, Moscow; Gnessin Russian Acad. of Music, Moscow. Début, Moscow State Philharmonic Orch., conducted by Dmitry Kitaenko, Great Hall, Moscow Conservatoire, 1984; toured Japan, 1986; European début with Berlin Radio Orch., 1987; UK début with BBC Manchester Orch., Lichfield Fest., 1987; USA début with NY Philharmonic Orch., 1990. Has made numerous recordings. Musician of the Year, Chigiana Music Acad., Italy, 1991; Instrumentalist of the Year, Musical America mag., 1994; Triumph Award for outstanding contrib. to Russian culture, Triumph Ind. Charity Foundn, 1997; various awards for recordings in UK, France, Holland. *Recreations:* reading, long and fast walks, getting together with friends. *Address:* c/o Askonas Holt Ltd, Lonsdale Chambers, 27 Chancery Lane, WC2A 1PF. *T:* (020) 7400 1700.

KISSINGER, Henry Alfred; Hon. KCMG 1995; Bronze Star (US); Chairman, Kissinger Associates Inc., since 1982; Counselor to Center for Strategic and International Studies, since 1977 and Trustee, since 1987; *b* Germany, 27 May 1923; *s* of late Louis Kissinger and Paula (*née* Stern); *m* 1st, 1949, Anne Fleischer (marr. diss. 1964); one *s* one *d*; 2nd, 1974, Nancy Maginnes. *Educ:* George Washington High Sch., NYC; Harvard Univ., Cambridge, Mass (BA 1950, MA 1952, PhD 1954). Emigrated to United States, 1938; naturalised, 1943. Served Army, 1943–46. Teaching Fellow, Harvard Univ., 1950–54; Study Director: Council on Foreign Relations, 1955–56: Rockefeller Bros Fund, 1956–58; Associate Professor of Govt, Harvard Univ., 1958–62, Prof. of Govt, 1962–71, and Faculty Mem., Center for Internat. Affairs, Harvard; Director: Harvard Internat. Seminar, 1951–69; Harvard Defense Studies Program, 1958–69; Asst to US President for Nat. Security Affairs, 1969–75; Secretary of State, USA, 1973–77. Chm., Nat. Bipartisan Commn on Central America, 1983–84; Member: President's Foreign Intelligence Adv. Bd, 1984–90; Commn on Integrated Long-Term Strategy of the National Security Council and Defense Dept, 1986–88; Dir, Internat. Rescue Cttee, 1987–; Hon. Gov., Foreign Policy Assoc., 1985–. Chm., Internat. Adv. Bd, American Internat. Group, Inc., 1988–; Counselor and Mem., Internat. Adv. Cttee, Chase Manhattan Corp. (formerly Chase Manhattan Bank), 1977–; Advr to Bd of Dirs, American Express Co.; Director: Continental Grain Co.; Freeport-McMoRan; Hollinger Internat. Inc. Trustee, Metropolitan Mus. of Art, 1977–. Syndicated writer, Los Angeles Times, 1984–. (Jtly) Nobel Peace Prize, 1973; Presidential Medal of Freedom, 1977; Medal of Liberty, 1986. *Publications:* A World Restored: Castlereagh, Metternich and the Restoration of Peace, 1957; Nuclear Weapons and Foreign Policy, 1957 (Woodrow Wilson Prize, 1958; citation, Overseas Press Club, 1958); The Necessity for Choice: Prospects of American Foreign Policy, 1961; The Troubled Partnership: a reappraisal of the Atlantic Alliance, 1965; Problems of National Strategy: A Book of Readings (ed), 1965; American Foreign Policy: three essays, 1969, 3rd edn 1977; White House Years (memoirs), 1979; For the Record: selected statements 1977–1980, 1981; Years of Upheaval (memoirs), 1982; Observations: selected speeches and essays 1982–1984, 1985; Diplomacy, 1994; Years of Renewal, 1999; Does America Need a Foreign Policy?, 2001. *Address:* Suite 400, 1800 K Street, NW, Washington, DC 20006, USA; 350 Park Avenue, New York, NY 10022, USA. *Clubs:* Century, River, Brook (New York); Metropolitan (Washington); Bohemian (San Francisco).

KISZELY, Maj.-Gen. John Panton, MC 1982; Deputy Commander, NATO Force, Bosnia, since 2001; *b* 2 April 1948; *s* of Dr John Kiszely and Maude Kiszely; *m* 1984, Hon. Arabella Jane, *d* of Baron Herschell, *qv*; three *s*. *Educ:* Marlborough Coll.; RMA Sandhurst. Commnd into Scots Guards, 1969; Co. Comdr, 2nd Bn Scots Guards, 1981–82; Bde Major, 7 Armd Bde, 1982–85; CO 1st Bn Scots Guards, 1986–88; Comdr, 22 Armd Bde, 1991–92; Comdr, 7 Armd Bde, 1993; Dep. Comdt, Staff Coll., Camberley, 1993–96; GOC 1st (UK) Armd Div., 1996–98; ACDS (Progs), MOD, 1998–2000. Regtl Lt-Col, Scots Guards, 1995–2001. *Recreations:* sailing, fishing, music, chess. *Address:* c/o Headquarters Scots Guards, Wellington Barracks, Birdcage Walk, SW1E 6HQ. *Clubs:* Cavalry and Guards; Royal Yacht Squadron, Royal Solent Yacht.

KITAJ, R. B., RA 1991 (ARA 1984); artist; *b* Ohio, 29 Oct. 1932; *m* (wife decd); two *c*; *m* 1983, Sandra Fisher (*d* 1994); one *s*. *Educ:* Cooper Union Inst., NY; Acad. of Fine Art, Vienna; Ruskin Sch. of Art, Oxford; RCA (ARCA). Part-time teacher: Camberwell Sch. of Art, 1961–63; Slade Sch., 1963–67; Visiting Professor: Univ. of Calif. at Berkeley, 1968; UCLA, 1970. Lives in Los Angeles and London. *One-man Exhibitions:* Marlborough New London Gall., 1963, 1970; Marlborough Gall., NY, 1965, 1974; Los Angeles County Museum of Art, 1965; Stedelijk Mus., Amsterdam, 1967; Mus. of Art, Cleveland, 1967; Univ. of Calif, Berkeley, 1967; Kestner Gesellschaft, Hanover, 1970; Boymans-van-Beuningen Mus., Rotterdam, 1970; Cincinnati Art Mus., Ohio, 1973; Marlborough Fine Art, 1977, 1980, 1985. *Retrospective Exhibitions:* Hirshhorn Museum, Washington, 1981; Cleveland Museum of Art, Ohio, 1981; Kunsthalle, Düsseldorf, 1982; Tate Gall. and LA County Mus., 1994; Metropolitan Mus., NY, 1994–95. Member: US Acad. (formerly Inst.) of Arts and Letters, NY, 1982; Nat. Acad. of Design, NY, 1982. Hon. DLit London, 1982; Hon. DLitt Durham, 1996; Hon. Dr: RCA, 1991; Calif Coll. of Art, 1995. Grand Prize for Painting (Golden Lion), Venice Biennale, 1995. Order of Arts & Letters (France), 1996. *Publication:* First Diasporist Manifesto, 1989; *relevant publication:* R. B. Kitaj by M. Livingstone, 1985. *Address:* c/o Marlborough Fine Art (London) Ltd, 6 Albemarle Street, W1X 3HF.

KITAMURA, Hiroshi; Japanese Ambassador to the Court of St James's, 1991–94; Corporate Advisor to Mitsubishi Corporation, since 1994; President, Shumei University, since 1998; *b* 20 Jan. 1929; *s* of Teiji and Fusako Kitamura; *m* 1953, Sachiko Ito; two *d*. *Educ:* Univ. of Tokyo (LLB 1951); Fletcher School of Law and Diplomacy, Medford, USA, 1952. Joined Min. of Foreign Affairs, Tokyo, 1953; postings to Washington DC, New York, New Delhi, London; Dir, Policy Planning Div., Res. and Planning Dept, Tokyo, 1974; Private Sec. to Prime Minister, 1974–76; Dep. Dir-Gen., Amer. Affairs Bureau, 1977–79; Consul-Gen., San Francisco, 1979–82; Dir-Gen., American Affairs Bureau, 1982–84; Dep. Vice Minister for Foreign Affairs, 1984–87; Dep. Minister, 1987–88; Ambassador to Canada, 1988–90. *Publication:* Psychological Dimensions of US-Japanese Relations, 1977. *Recreations:* traditional Japanese music, culinary arts, golf. *Address:* c/o Mitsubishi Corporation, 6–3 Marunouchi 2–chome, Chiyoda-ku, Tokyo 100–86, Japan.

KITCATT, Sir Peter (Julian), Kt 1992; CB 1986; Speaker's Secretary, House of Commons, 1986–93; *b* 5 Dec. 1927; *s* of late Horace Wilfred Kitcatt and Ellen Louise Kitcatt (*née* Julian); *m* 1952, Audrey Marian Aylen; three *s* two *d*. *Educ:* Borden Grammar Sch., Sittingbourne; King's Coll., Cambridge (Scholar). RASC (2nd Lt) 1948. Asst Principal, Colonial Office, 1950–53; Asst Private Sec. to Sec. of State for the Colonies, 1953–54; Principal, Colonial Office, 1954–64; Sec. to HRH The Princess Royal on Caribbean Tour, 1960; Sec., E African Econ. and Fiscal Commn, 1960; HM Treasury: Principal, 1964; Asst Sec., 1966; RCDS, 1972; Under Sec., 1973, seconded to DHSS, 1975–78. *Recreation:* golf. *Club:* Croham Hurst Golf (Croydon).

KITCHEN, Michael; actor; *b* 31 Oct. 1948; *s* of Arthur and Betty Kitchen; partner, Rowena Miller; two *s*. *Educ:* City of Leicester Boys' Grammar School. Entered acting profession, 1970; *stage includes:* seasons at Belgrade Theatre, Coventry, National Youth Theatre; Royal Court, 1971–73; Big Wolf, Magnificence, Skyvers; Young Vic, 1975: Othello, Macbeth, As You Like It, Charley's Aunt; National Theatre: Spring Awakening, 1974; Romeo and Juliet, 1974; State of Revolution, 1977; Bedroom Farce, 1977; No Man's Land, 1977; The Homecoming, 1978; Family Voices, 1981; On the Razzle, 1981; The Provok'd Wife, 1981; Rough Crossing, 1984; Royal Shakespeare Co: Romeo and Juliet, Richard II, 1986; The Art of Success, 1987; *films include:* The Bunker; Breaking Glass; Towards the Morning; Out of Africa; Home Run; The Russia House; Fools of Fortune; The Dive; Goldeneye; Mrs Dalloway; The Last Contract; The World is not Enough; *television series:* Steven Hind; Divorce; Freud, 1983; The Justice Game, 1989; The Guilty, 1992; To Play the King, 1993; Dandelion Dead, 1994; The Hanging Gale, 1995 (Best Actor Award, Internat. Fest. of Audiovisual Progs, Biarritz, 1996); Reckless, 1997; Oliver Twist (serial), 1999; *television films and plays include:* Caught on a Train; Benefactors; Ball-Trap; Pied Piper; The Enchanted April; Hostage; numerous other TV and radio performances. *Recreations:* piano, guitar, flying, writing, tennis, riding. *Address:* c/o ICM, Oxford House, 76 Oxford Street, W1R 1RB.

KITCHENER OF KHARTOUM, 3rd Earl *cr* 1914, and of Broome, in the county of Kent; **Henry Herbert Kitchener,** TD; DL; Viscount Kitchener of Khartoum; and of the Vaal, Transvaal, and of Aspall, Suffolk, 1902; Viscount Broome, 1914; Baron Denton, 1914; late Major, Royal Corps of Signals; *b* 24 Feb. 1919; *er s* of Viscount Broome (*d* 1928) and Adela Mary Evelyn (*d* 1986), *e d* of late J. H. Monins, Ringwould House, near Dover; *S* grandfather, 1937. *Educ:* Sandroyd Sch.; Winchester Coll.; Trinity Coll., Cambridge. President: Lord Kitchener Nat. Meml Fund, 1950–; Henry Doubleday Res. Assoc. DL Cheshire, 1972. *Heir:* none. *Address:* Westergate Wood, Eastergate, Chichester, W Sussex PO20 6SB. *T:* (01243) 545797. *Club:* Brooks's.

KITCHIN, David James Tyson; QC 1994; *b* 30 April 1955; *s* of late Norman Tyson Kitchin and of Shirley Boyd Kitchin (*née* Simpson); *m* 1989, Charlotte Anne Cadbury, *d* of Comdr David Jones; one *s* one *d*. *Educ:* Oundle Sch. (schol.); Fitzwilliam Coll., Cambridge (MA). Called to the Bar, Gray's Inn, 1977; pupilled to Robin Jacob, 1978; entered chambers of Thomas Blanco White, 1979. A Dep. High Ct Judge, 2001–; apptd to hear Trade Mark Appeals, 2001–. Chm., Vet. Code of Practice Cttee, Nat. Office of Animal Health, 1995–. *Publications:* (ed jtly) Patent Law of Europe and the United Kingdom, 1979; (ed jtly) Kerly's Law of Trade Marks and Trade Names, Supplement to 12th edn 1994, 13th edn, 2001; (jtly) The Trade Marks Act 1994 (text and commentary), 1995. *Recreations:* golf, tennis. *Address:* 8 New Square, Lincoln's Inn, WC2A 3QP. *T:* (020) 7405 4321. *Clubs:* Hawks (Cambridge); Leander (Henley); Walton Heath Golf.

KITCHIN, Prof. Laurence Tyson; university teacher, translator and critic; *b* 21 July 1913; *s* of James Tyson Kitchin, MD Edin, and Eliza Amelia Kitchin (*née* Hopps); *m* 1955, Hilary Owen, artist; one step *s*. *Educ:* Bootham Sch.; King's Coll., London Univ. (BA 1934); Central Sch. of Speech and Drama (Acting Cert., 1st cl.). Served War, RAMC and briefly, RAEC, 1941–46. Mem., univ. debates team, USA, 1933; acted in Housemaster on stage and screen, 1936, and in films, incl. Pimpernel Smith; wrote extensively for BBC Third Prog., 1948–55; The Times corresp. and drama critic, 1956–62; numerous BBC talks on literature and drama, 1962–66; UK rep., Théâtre dans le Monde, UNESCO, 1961–66; Lectr, Bristol Univ. and Tufts, London, 1966–70; Vis. Prof. of Drama, Stanford Univ., Calif, 1970–72; Vis. Prof. of Liberal Arts, City Univ. of NY, 1972–73, Prof., 1973–76; Vis. Prof. of Shakespeare Studies, Simon Fraser Univ., Canada, 1976–77. Renaissance verse translations from Italian, French and Spanish, BBC, 1978–79. Selected as one of Outstanding Educators of America, 1973. *Publications:* Len Hutton, 1953; Three on Trial: Byron, Bowdler and Machiavelli, 1959; Mid-Century Drama, 1960, 2nd edn 1962; Drama in the Sixties, 1966; Love Sonnets of the Renaissance (trans. from Italian, French, Spanish and Portuguese), 1990; radio scripts, incl.: The Trial of Lord Byron, 1948, Canada 1978; The Trial of Machiavelli, 1957; The Court Lady (trans. from Castiglione), 1954; The Elizabethan, Canada 1978; The Flaming Heart (Crashaw), 1981; contrib. Shakespeare Survey, Confronto Letterario, Mod. Lang. Rev., TLS, Encounter, Observer, Listener, THES. *Recreations:* tennis, televised soccer. *Address:* c/o National Westminster Bank, St James's & Piccadilly Branch, W1A 2DG. *Club:* Athenæum.

KITCHING, Alan, RDI 1994; Art Director and Proprietor, The Typography Workshop, since 1989; *b* 29 Dec. 1940; *s* of Walter Kitching and Kathleen (*née* Davies); *m* 1962, Rita Haylett (*d* 1984); two *s.* Apprentice compositor, 1955–61; Asst, Exptl Printing Workshop, Watford Coll. of Technol. Sch. of Art, 1963–68; Vis. Tutor in Typography, Central Sch. of Art and Design, 1968–72; Established freelance design practice, working in magazine, book and exhibition design, 1971; Partner, Omnific Studios (Graphic Design), 1977–88; Vis. Tutor in Typography, RCA, 1988–. AGI 1994. *Publication:* Typography Manual, 1970. *Recreations:* accordion, snooker. *Address:* 19 Cleaver Street, SE11 4DP. *T:* (020) 7735 8525, *Fax:* (020) 7820 8098. *Club:* Chelsea Arts.

KITCHING, Christopher John, PhD; FSA, FRHistS; Secretary, Royal Commission on Historical Manuscripts, since 1992; *b* 5 Aug. 1945; *s* of Donald Walton Kitching and Vera (*née* Mosley); *m* 1976, Hilary Mary Ruth Horwood; two *s.* *Educ:* Durham Univ. (BA Mod. Hist. 1967; PhD 1970). Registered Mem., Soc. of Archivists, 1987. Asst Keeper, PRO, 1970–82; Asst Sec., Royal Commn on Historical MSS, 1982–92. Asst Editor, Archivum, 1984–92. Hon. Treasurer, RHistS, 1980–85; Council Mem., Canterbury and York Soc., 1974–. Chm., Trustees, St Mary-the-Virgin, Primrose Hill, 1998–; Trustee, Miss E. M. Johnson's Charitable Trust, 1997–. Mem. Editl Bd, Jl of Soc. of Archivists, 1992–. Alexander Prize, RHistS, 1973. *Publications:* The Royal Visitation of 1559, 1975; Survey of the Central Records of the Church of England, 1976; London and Middlesex Chantry Certificate 1548, 1980; Surveys of historical manuscripts in the United Kingdom: a select bibliography, 1989, 3rd edn 1997; The impact of computerisation on archival finding aids, 1990; Archive Buildings in the United Kingdom 1977–1992, 1993; Archives: the very essence of our heritage, 1996; articles and reviews. *Recreations:* singing, writing choral music, reading, cycling. *Address:* 11 Creighton Road, NW6 6EE. *T:* (020) 8969 6408.

KITNEY, Prof. Richard Ian, OBE 2001; PhD, DSc(Eng); FRCPE; FREng; Professor of Biomedical Systems Engineering, and Head of Department of Biological and Medical Systems, Imperial College of Science, Technology and Medicine, since 1997; *b* 13 Feb. 1945; *s* of Leonard Walter Richard Kitney and Gladys Simpson Kitney; *m* 1977, Vera Baraniecka; two *s.* *Educ:* Enfield Grammar Sch.; Univ. of Surrey (DipEE, MSc); Imperial Coll., London Univ. (PhD, DIC 1972; DSc(Eng) 1993). FRCPE 1996; FREng 1999. Electronics Engr, Thorn Electrical Industries, 1963–72; Lectr in Biophysics, Chelsea Coll., London Univ., 1972–78; Imperial College, London: Lectr, 1975–85; Reader, 1985–89; Dir, Centre for Biol and Med. Systems, 1991–97; Gov., 1995–98; Gov., RPMS, 1995–98. Visiting Professor: Georgia Inst. of Technology, 1981–90; MIT, 1991–. Tech. Dir, Intravascular Res. Ltd, 1987–94; Dir, St Mary's Imaging plc, 1991–96; Dep. Chm. and Tech. Dir, comMedica Ltd, 1999–; Trustee, Smith and Nephew Foundn, 1996–. Mem., Adv. Cttee on Technology in Medicine, DTI, 1995. FRSocMed 1994. Freeman, City of London, 1996; Liveryman, Co. of Engineers, 1995. Regular contributor, BBC Radio. Nightingale Prize, Internat. Fedn of Biol Engrg Socs, 1975. *Publications:* (jtly) Recent Advances in the Study of Heart Rate Variability, 1980; (jtly) The Beat-by-Beat Investigation of Cardiac Function, 1987; (jtly) The Coming of the Global Healthcare Industry, 1998; conf. proceedings, papers in learned jls. *Recreations:* history, cooking, France. *Address:* Department of Biological and Medical Systems, Imperial College of Science, Technology and Medicine, Exhibition Road, SW7 2BX. *T:* (020) 7594 6226. *Club:* Athenæum.

KITSON, Gen. Sir Frank (Edward), GBE 1985; (CBE 1972; OBE 1968; MBE 1959); KCB 1980; MC 1955 and Bar 1958; DL; *b* 15 Dec. 1926; *s* of late Vice-Adm. Sir Henry Kitson, KBE, CB and Lady (Marjorie) Kitson (*née* de Pass); *m* 1962, Elizabeth Janet, *d* of late Col C. R. Spencer, OBE, DL; three *d.* *Educ:* Stowe. 2nd Lt Rifle Bde, 1946; served BAOR, 1946–53; Kenya, 1953–55; Malaya, 1957; Cyprus, 1962–64; CO 1st Bn, Royal Green Jackets, 1967–69; Defence Fellow, University Coll., Oxford, 1969–70; Comdr, 39 Inf. Bde, NI, 1970–72 (CBE for gallantry); Comdt, Sch. of Infantry, 1972–74; RCDS, 1975; GOC 2nd Division, later 2nd Armoured Division, 1976–78; Comdt, Staff College, 1978–80; Dep. C-in-C, UKLF, and Inspector-Gen., TA, 1980–82; C-in-C, UKLF, 1982–85. ADC Gen. to the Queen, 1983–85. 2nd Bn, The Royal Green Jackets: Col Comdt, 1979–87; Rep. Col Comdt, 1982–85; Hon. Col, Oxford Univ. OTC, 1982–87. DL 1989. *Publications:* Gangs and Counter Gangs, 1960; Low Intensity Operations, 1971; Bunch of Five, 1977; Warfare as a Whole, 1987; Directing Operations, 1989; Prince Rupert: portrait of a soldier, 1994; Prince Rupert: Admiral and General-at-sea, 1998. *Address:* c/o Lloyds TSB, Farnham, Surrey GU9 7LT. *Club:* Boodle's.

KITSON, George McCullough; Principal, Central School of Speech and Drama, London, 1978–87; *b* Castlegore, Ireland, 18 May 1922; *s* of George Kitson and Anna May McCullough-Kitson; *m* 1951, Jean Evelyn Tyte; four *s.* *Educ:* early educn in Ireland; London Univ. (Dip. in Child Develt, 1947); Trent Park Coll. (Teachers' Cert., 1949). Associate, Cambridge Inst. of Educn, 1956; MEd Leicester, 1960. Served War, RAF, 1940–45; Navigator, Coastal Comd. Asst Master, schs in Herts, 1949–54; Dep. Headmaster, Broadfield Sch., Hemel Hempstead, Herts, 1954–56; Lectr in Educn, Leicester Coll. of Educn, 1956–66; Tutor i/c Annexe for Mature Teachers, Northampton, 1966–71; Dep. Principal, Furzedown Coll., London, 1971–76; Vice-Principal, Philippa Fawcett and Furzedown Coll., 1976–78. Member: Nat. Council for Drama Trng, 1978–88; Conference of Drama Schs, 1980– (Chm., 1980–87; Pres., 1999–); Hon. Mem., GSMD, 1998. *Publications:* (contrib.) Map of Educational Research, 1969; articles on educn, social psychol., and interprofessionalism in Forum, New Era, Educn for Teaching, and Brit. Jl of Educnl Psychol. *Recreations:* book collecting (first editions), sailing, walking, music, theatre. *Address:* 11 Bates Close, Burnmill Grange, Market Harborough, Leics LE16 7NT. *Club:* Arts.

KITSON, Sir Timothy (Peter Geoffrey), Kt 1974; Chairman: Fishers International plc, since 1992; London Clubs International plc, since 1995; *b* 28 Jan. 1931; *s* of late Geoffrey H. and of Kathleen Kitson; *m* 1959, Diana Mary Fattorini; one *s* two *d.* *Educ:* Charterhouse; Royal Agricultural College, Cirencester. Farmed in Australia, 1949–51. Chm., Provident Financial Gp, later Provident Financial plc, 1983–95; Dir, SIG plc, 1995–. Member: Thirsk RDC, 1954–57; N Riding CC, 1957–61. MP (C) Richmond, Yorks, 1959–83; PPS to Parly Sec. to Minister of Agriculture, 1960–64; an Opposition Whip, 1967–70; PPS to the Prime Minister, 1970–74, to Leader of the Opposition, 1974–75. Chm., Defence Select Cttee, 1982–83. *Recreations:* shooting, hunting, racing. *Address:* Ulshaw Farm, Middleham, Leyburn, N Yorks DL8 4PU.

KITZINGER, Sheila Helena Elizabeth, MBE 1982; author, social anthropologist and birth educator; *b* 29 March 1929; *d* of Alec and Clare Webster; *m* 1952, Uwe Kitzinger, *qv*; five *d.* *Educ:* Bishop Fox's Girls' Sch., Taunton; Ruskin Coll., Oxford; St Hugh's Coll., Oxford; motherhood; educn continuing. Res. Asst, Dept of Anthropology, Univ. of Edinburgh, 1952–53 (MLitt 1954; thesis on race relations in Britain). Course Team Chm., Open Univ., 1981–83. Mem. Editl Bd, Midwives Information and Resource Service; Chairperson, Foundation for Women's Health Res. and Develt, 1985–87; Consultant, Internat. Childbirth Educn Assoc.; Adviser: Baby Milk Coalition; Maternity Alliance. Pres., Oxford Br., Royal Coll. of Midwives; Patron, Seattle Sch. of Midwifery. Co-founder (with Uwe Kitzinger), Lentils for Dubrovnik, 1991 (relief agency sending aid to women and children in Croatia). MRSocMed. Hon. Prof., Thames Valley Univ., 1994. Joost de Blank Award, to do research on problems facing West Indian mothers in Britain, 1971–73. *Publications:* The Experience of Childbirth, 1962, 6th edn 1987; Giving Birth, 1971, rev. and expanded edn 1987; Education and Counselling for Childbirth, 1977; Women as Mothers, 1978; (ed with John Davis) The Place of Birth, 1978; Birth at Home, 1979; The Good Birth Guide, 1979; The Experience of Breastfeeding, 1979, 2nd edn 1987; Pregnancy and Childbirth, 1980; Sheila Kitzinger's Birth Book, 1981; (with Rhiannon Walters) Some Women's Experiences of Episiotomy, 1981; Episiotomy: physical and emotional aspects, 1981; Birth over Thirty, 1982; The New Good Birth Guide, 1983; Woman's Experience of Sex, 1983; (ed with Penny Simkin) Episiotomy and the Second Stage of Labor, 1984; Being Born, 1986; Celebration of Birth, 1987; Freedom and Choice in Childbirth (US edn Your Baby Your Way), 1987; Giving Birth: how it really feels, 1987; Some Women's Experiences of Epidurals, 1987; (ed) The Midwife Challenge, 1988; The Crying Baby, 1989; The New Pregnancy and Childbirth, 1989; Breastfeeding Your Baby, 1989; (with Celia Kitzinger) Talking With Children About Things That Matter, 1989; (contrib.) Ethnography of Fertility and Birth, 1982; (contrib.) The Management of Labour, 1985; (contrib.) Effective Care in Pregnancy and Childbirth, 1989; (with Vicky Bailey) Pregnancy Day by Day, 1990; Homebirth, 1991; (contrib.) Women's Health Matters, 1991; Ourselves as Mothers, 1992; The Year After Childbirth, 1994; Birth Over Thirty-Five, 1994; The New Pregnancy and Childbirth, 1997; Becoming a Grandmother, 1997; (contrib.) Childbirth and Authoritative Knowledge, 1997; Breastfeeding, 1998; Rediscovering Birth, 2000. *Recreations:* painting, talking. *Address:* The Manor, Standlake, Oxfordshire OX29 7RH. *T:* (01865) 300266, *Fax:* (01865) 300438.

See also David Webster.

KITZINGER, Uwe, CBE 1980; President: International Association of Macro-Engineering Societies, since 1996 (Founding President, 1987–92); Fédération Britannique des Alliances Françaises, since 1999; Visiting Scholar, Harvard University, since 1993; Founding President, Templeton College, Oxford, 1984–91 (sabbatical, 1991–93; Hon. Fellow); *b* 12 April 1928; *o s* of late Dr G. and Mrs L. Kitzinger, Abbots Langley, Herts; *m* 1952, Sheila Helena Elizabeth Webster (*see* S. H. E. Kitzinger); five *d.* *Educ:* Watford Grammar Sch.; Balliol Coll. and New Coll. (Foundn Schol.), Oxford. 1st in Philosophy, Politics and Economics, MA, MLitt; Pres., Oxford Union, 1950. Economic Section, Council of Europe, Strasbourg, 1951–58; Nuffield College, Oxford: Research Fellow, 1956–62, Official Fellow, 1962–76, Emeritus Fellow, 1976; Acting Investment Bursar, 1962–64; Investment Bursar, 1964–76; Mem., Investment Cttee, 1962–88; Assessor of Oxford University, 1967–68. Visiting Professor: of Internat. Relations, Univ. of the West Indies, 1964–65; of Government, at Harvard, 1969–70; at Univ. of Paris (VIII), 1970–73. Leave of absence as Adviser to Sir Christopher (later Lord) Soames, Vice-Pres. of the Commn of the European Communities, Brussels, 1973–75; Dean, INSEAD (European Inst. of Business Admin), Fontainebleau, 1976–80 (Mem. Board, 1976–83); Dir, Oxford Centre for Management Studies, 1980–84. Sen. Res. Fellow, Atlantic Council, 1993–. Member: ODM Cttee for University Secondment, 1966–68; British Universities Cttee of Encyclopædia Britannica, 1967–98; Nat. Council of European Movement, 1974–76; Council, RIIA, 1973–85; Court, Cranfield Inst. of Technology, 1984–85. Founding Chm., Cttee on Atlantic Studies, 1967–70. Co-Founder, Lentils for Dubrovnik, 1991–. Member: Oxfam Council, 1981–84; Major Projects Assoc., 1981–91 (Founding Chm., 1981–86); Adv. Bd, Pace Univ., NY, 1982–92; Berlin Science Centre, 1983–90; Acad. Adv. Bd, World Management Council, 1989–; Bd, Jean Monnet Foundn, Lausanne, 1990–; Adv. Bd, Asian Disaster Preparedness Center, Bangkok, 2000–. Trustee: European Foundn for Management Educn, Brussels, 1978–80; Oxford Trust for Music and the Arts, 1986–91. Chm., Oxford Radio Consortium, 1988. Founding Editor, Jl of Common Market Studies, 1962–. Hon. LLD Buena Vista, 1986. Order of the Morning Star (Croatia), 1997. *Publications:* German Electoral Politics, 1960 (German edn, 1960); The Challenge of the Common Market, 1961 (Amer. edn, The Politics and Economics of European Integration, 1963, et al); Britain, Europe and Beyond, 1964; The Background to Jamaica's Foreign Policy, 1965; The European Common Market and Community, 1967; Commitment and Identity, 1968; The Second Try, 1968; Diplomacy and Persuasion, 1973 (French edn, 1974); Europe's Wider Horizons, 1975; (with D. E. Butler) The 1975 Referendum, 1976, 2nd edn 1996; (ed with E. Frankel) Macro-Engineering and the Earth, 1998. *Recreations:* sailing, travel, old buildings. *Address:* Standlake Manor, near Witney, Oxon OX29 7RH. *T:* (01865) 300266, *Fax:* (01865) 300438; 519 Lowell House, Cambridge, MA 02138, USA. *T:* and *Fax:* (617) 4953495; La Rivière, 11100 Bages, France. *T:* and *Fax:* (4) 68417013; *e-mail:* kitzing@fas.harvard.edu. *Clubs:* Royal Thames Yacht, Oxford and Cambridge.

KLARE, Hugh John, CBE 1967; *b* Berndorf, Austria, 22 June 1916; *yr s* of F. A. Klare; *m* 1946, Eveline Alice Maria, *d* of Lieut-Col J. D. Rankin, MBE. *Educ:* privately. Came to England, 1932. Served war in Middle East and Europe; Major. Dep. Dir, Economic Organisation Br., Brit. Control Commn for Germany, 1946–48; Sec., Howard League for Penal Reform, 1950–71; seconded to Coun. of Europe as Dep. Head, Div. of Crime Problems, 1959–61; Head of Div., 1971–72; Member of Council: Internat. Soc. of Criminology, 1960–66; Inst. for Study and Treatment of Delinquency, 1964–66; Nat. Assoc. for Care and Resettlement of Offenders, 1966–71. Chm. Planning Cttee, Brit. Congress on Crime, 1966. Member: Bd of Visitors, Long Lartin Prison, 1972–76; Gloucestershire Probation and Aftercare Cttee, 1972–85; Parole Board, 1972–74. Founder and Trustee, Cheltenham and N Cotswold Eye Therapy Trust, 1976–; Chm. of Trustees, Gloucestershire Arthritis Trust, 1987– (Trustee, 1984). A Governor, British Inst. of Human Rights, 1974–80. *Publications:* Anatomy of Prison, 1960; (ed and introd) Changing Concepts of Crime and its Treatment, 1966; (ed jtly) Frontiers of Criminology, 1967; People in Prison, 1972; contribs on crime and penology to Justice of the Peace. *Address:* 34 Herriots Court, St George's Crescent, Droitwich, Worcs WR9 8HJ. *T:* (01905) 773332.

KLAUS, Prof. Václav; Member, and President, Chamber of Deputies, since 1998, Czech Parliament; Chairman, Civic Democratic Party, Czech Republic, since 1991; *b* 19 June 1941; *s* of Václav Klaus and Marie Klausová; *m* 1968, Livia Klausová; two *s.* *Educ:* Prague Sch. of Economics (Hon. Dr 1994); Cornell Univ. Researcher, Inst. of Econs, Czechoslovak Acad of Scis, to 1970; Czechoslovak State Bank, 1971–86 (Head, Dept of Macroeconomic Policy); Inst. of Forecasting, Czechoslovak Acad. of Scis, 1987; founder,

Civic Forum Movement (Chm., 1990–91); Minister of Finance, 1989–92; Dep. Prime Minister, 1991–92; Prime Minister, 1992–97. Vice-Chm., European Democratic Union, 1996–. Prof. of Finance, Prague Sch. of Economics, 1994–. Hon. doctorates from Univs in USA, Canada, Guatemala, Mexico, Argentina, France, UK, Czech Republic, Germany; numerous awards from USA, Germany, France, Denmark, Austria, Switzerland, Czech Republic. *Publications:* A Road to Market Economy, 1991; Tomorrow's Challenge, 1991; Economic Theory and Economic Reform, 1991; Signale aus dem Herzen Europas, 1991; I Do Not Like Catastrophic Scenarios, 1991; Dismantling Socialism, 1992; Why Am I a Conservative?, 1992; The Year: how much is it in the history of the country?, 1993; The Czech Way, 1994; Rebirth of a Country, 1994; Summing Up to One, 1995; Tschechische Transformation & Europäische Integration, 1995; Economic Theory and Reality of Transformation Processes, 1995; Between the Past and the Future, 1996; Renaissance, 1997; The Defence of Forgotten Ideas, 1997; Thus Spoke Václav Klaus, 1998; Why I Am not a Social Democrat, 1998; The Country without Governing, 1999; The Way out of the Trap, 1999; From the Opposition Treaty to the Tolerance Patent, 2000. *Recreations:* tennis, ski-ing. *Address:* Office of the President, Chamber of Deputies, Sněmovní 4, 11826 Prague 1, Czech Republic. *T:* (2) 57173007, *Fax:* (2) 57320160.

KLEEMAN, Harry, CBE 1984; Chairman: Kleeman Plastics group of companies, 1968–94; Kleeman Management Ltd, since 1990; *b* 2 March 1928; *s* of Max Kleeman and Lottie Bernstein; *m* 1955, Avril Lees; two *s* two *d*. *Educ:* Westminster Sch.; Trinity Coll., Cambridge. FIM (FPRI 1980). Director, O. & M. Kleemann Ltd, 1951–65. President, British Plastics Fedn, 1979–80; Chairman: Polymer Engineering Directorate, SERC, 1980–84; Plastics Processing EDC, NEDO, 1980–85; Small Firms Cttee, OFTEL, 1985–88; Council, Plastics & Rubber Inst., 1985–87; Adv. Bd, London Sch. of Polymer Technology, 1988–94; Member: CBI Smaller Firms Council, 1982–91 (Vice-Chm., 1987–88, Chm., 1988–90); CBI Council, 1984–94. Chairman: Central British Fund for World Jewish Relief, 1991–96 (Treasurer, 1969–91); Hampstead and Highgate Conservative Parly Club, 1991–95. Member: Zoological Soc., 1950–; Royal Society of Arts, 1978–; Worshipful Co. of Horners, 1954– (Master, 1992). *Recreations:* horse riding, amateur radio, tennis, sculpture. *Address:* 41 Frognal, NW3 6YD. *T:* (020) 7794 3366; *e-mail:* harry@kleeman.net.

KLEIN, Bernat, CBE 1973; FCSD (FSIAD 1974); Chairman and Managing Director, Bernat Klein Ltd, 1973–93; *b* 6 Nov. 1922; *s* of Lipot Klein and Serena Weiner; *m* 1951, Margaret Soper; one *s* two *d*. *Educ:* Senta, Yugoslavia; Bezalel Sch. of Arts and Crafts, Jerusalem; Leeds Univ. Designer to: Tootal, Broadhurst, Lee, 1948–49; Munrospun, Edinburgh, 1949–51; Chm. and Man. Dir, Colourcraft, 1952–62; Man. Dir of Bernat Klein Ltd, 1962–66; Chm. and Man. Dir, Bernat Klein Design Ltd, 1966–81. Member: Council of Industrial Design, Scottish Cttee, 1965–71; Royal Fine Art Commn for Scotland, 1980–87. Exhibitions of paintings: E-SU, 1965; Alwyn Gall., 1967; O'Hana Gall., 1969; Assoc. of Arts Gall., Capetown, Goodman Gall., Johannesburg, and O'Hana Gall., 1972; Laing Art Gall., Newcastle upon Tyne, 1977; Manchester Polytechnic, 1977. Hon. FRIAS, 1990. *Publications:* Eye for Colour, 1965; Design Matters, 1976. *Recreations:* reading, tennis, walking. *Address:* High Sunderland, Galashiels, Selkirkshire TD1 3PL. *T:* (01750) 20730.

KLEIN, Calvin Richard; fashion designer; *b* 19 Nov. 1942; *s* of Leo Klein and Flore (*née* Stern); *m* 1st, 1964, Jayne Centre (marr. diss. 1974); one *d*; 2nd, 1986, Kelly Rector. *Educ:* Fashion Inst. of Technology, NY; High Sch. of Art and Design. Started own fashion business, 1968; Vice Chm., Calvin Klein Inc., 1969–. Dir, Fashion Inst. of Technology, 1975–. Numerous awards. *Address:* Calvin Klein Industries Inc., 205 West 39th Street, New York, NY 10018, USA.

KLEIN, Prof. Dan Victor; International Executive Director, Phillips International Auctioneers, since 1998; Research Professor in Glass, University of Sunderland, since 1996; *b* 4 Nov. 1938; *s* of Frederick Klein and Bianka Breitmann. *Educ:* Westminster Sch.; Wadham Coll., Oxford (BA Hons Greats). Guest soloist, Sadler's Wells Opera, 1966; Member, English Opera Group, 1968–73; freelance singer performing in operas and recitals, also founded and perf. with own ensemble, 1973–77; owner, 20th Century Decorative Arts Gall., Belgravia, 1978–84; Dir, 20th Century Decorative Arts, Christie's, London, 1985–95; Vice-Pres., Christie's, Switzerland, 1990–95. Partner, @DKA (formerly Dan Klein Associates), consultants in contemp. glass, 1994–. Regular lectr in Britain, USA, Switzerland, Sweden and Australia; orgnr, Venezia Aperto Vetro, first Internat. Biennale of Contemporary Glass, Venice, 1996. Mem. Bd, Pilchuck Glass Sch., USA, 1985–. *Publications:* All Colour Book of Art Deco, 1974; (ed jtly) The History of Glass, 1985; (jtly) Decorative Arts from 1880 to the Present Day, 1986; (jtly) In the Deco Style, 1986; Glass: a contemporary art, 1989; (contrib.) L'Art Décoratif en Europe, vol. III, 1994; (ed jtly) Venezio Aperto Vetro (catalogue), 1996; articles in jls. *Recreations:* collecting 20th Century Decorative Arts, contemporary British glass. *Address:* 43 Hugh Street, SW1V 1QJ. *T:* (020) 7821 6040.

KLEIN, Prof. Jacob, PhD; Professor, Weizmann Institute of Science, Israel, since 1987; Dr Lee's Professor of Physical Chemistry, and Head, Department of Physical Chemistry, University of Oxford, since 2000; *b* 20 Aug. 1949; *s* of Moshe Klein and Edna Klein (*née* Lipper); *m* 1974, Michele Castle; two *s* two *d*. *Educ:* in Israel; Whittinghame Coll., Brighton; St Catharine's Coll., Cambridge (BA 1st Cl. Hons Physics 1973; MA, PhD 1977). Mil. Service, Israel, 1967–70; Post-doctoral res., Weizmann Inst., Israel, 1977–80; Demonstrator, Cavendish Lab., and Fellow of St Catharine's Coll., Cambridge, 1980–84; Weizmann Institute, Israel: Sen. Scientist, 1980–84; Associate Prof., 1984–87; Chm., Polymer Res. Dept, 1989–91. Somach Sacks Prize, Weizmann Inst., 1983; Charles Vernon Boys Prize, Inst. Physics (GB), 1984; Jeanett and Samuel Lubel Prize, 1989; Internat. Kao Fellow (Japan), 1994; Ford Prize for Polymer Physics, APS, 1995. *Publications:* contrib. numerous papers to scientific jls, etc. *Recreations:* reading, family holidays, hiking. *Address:* 1 Ruppin Street, Rehovot 76353, Israel; Materials & Interfaces Department, Weizmann Institute of Science, Rehovot 76100, Israel; Physical and Theoretical Chemistry Laboratory, South Parks Road, Oxford OX1 3QZ.

KLEIN, Jonathan David; Co-Founder and Chief Executive Officer, Getty Images Inc., since 1995; *b* 13 May 1960; *s* of Louis and Hilda Klein; *m* 1988, Deborah Ann Hunter; three *s*. *Educ:* Trinity Hall, Cambridge (MA). Hambros Bank Ltd, 1983–98: Dir, 1989–93; non-exec. Dir, 1993–98. *Recreations:* all sports, travel, the environment, movies. *Address:* 3815 East John Street, Seattle, WA 98112, USA. *T:* (206) 268 1900.

KLEIN, Prof. Lawrence Robert; economist; Benjamin Franklin Professor, University of Pennsylvania, 1968–91, Emeritus 1991; *b* Omaha, 14 Sept. 1920; *s* of Leo Byron Klein and Blanche Monheit; *m* 1947, Sonia Adelson; one *s* three *d*. *Educ:* Univ. of Calif at Berkeley (BA); MIT (PhD 1944); Lincoln Coll., Oxford (MA 1957). Chicago Univ., 1944–47; Nat. Bureau of Econ. Res., NY, 1948–50; Michigan Univ., 1949–54; Oxford Inst. of Stats, 1954–58; Prof., 1958, University Prof., 1964, Univ. of Pennsylvania. Consultant: UNCTAD, 1966, 1967, 1975; UNIDO, 1973–75; Congressional Budget Office, 1977–; Council of Econ. Advisers, 1977–80. Mem., Commn on Prices, Fed. Res. Bd, 1968–70. Member: Adv. Bd, Strategic Studies Center, Stanford Res. Inst., 1974–76; Adv. Council, Inst. for Advanced Studies, Vienna, 1977–; Director: Nat. Bureau of Econ. Res., Inc., 1989–; Inst. for East-West Security Studies, 1989–; W. P. Carey & Co., 1984–. Corresp. FBA, 1991; Fellow: Econometric Soc. (past Pres.); Amer. Acad. of Arts and Scis; Member: Nat. Acad. of Scis; Amer. Philosophical Soc.; Amer. Economic Assoc. (Past Pres.; J. B. Clark Medal, 1959). William F. Butler Award, NY Assoc. of Business Economists, 1975; Nobel Prize for Economics, 1980. *Publications:* The Keynesian Revolution, 1947; Textbook of Econometrics, 1953; An Econometric Model of the United States 1929–52, 1955; Wharton Econometric Forecasting Model, 1967; Essay on the Theory of Economic Prediction, 1968; (ed) Econometric Model Performance, 1976; (ed) Comparative Performance of US Econometric Models, 1991. *Address:* 1317 Medford Road, Wynnewood, PA 19096, USA; University of Pennsylvania, Philadelphia, PA 19104, USA.

KLEIN, Hon. Ralph Phillip; MLA (Progressive C) for Calgary-Elbow, since 1989; Premier of Alberta, Canada, since 1992; *b* Calgary, 1 Nov. 1942; *m* Colleen; one *d*. *Educ:* Calgary Business Coll. Teacher, later Principal, Calgary Business Coll.; PR with Alberta Div. of Red Cross and United Way of Calgary and Dist, 1963–69; Sen. Civic Affairs reporter, CFCN TV and Radio, 1969–80; Mayor of Calgary, 1980–89; Minister of Envmt, 1989–92; Leader, Progressive Cons. Party, 1992–. OStJ 1986. *Address:* Office of the Premier, 307 Legislature Building, Edmonton, AB T5K 2B6, Canada.

KLEIN, Prof. Rudolf Ewald, CBE 2001; Professor of Social Policy, University of Bath, 1978–98, now Emeritus; *b* 26 Aug. 1930; *o s* of Robert and Martha Klein; *m* 1957, Josephine Parfitt (*d* 1996); one *d*. *Educ:* Bristol Grammar Sch.; Merton Coll., Oxford (Postmaster) (Gibbs Schol. 1950; MA). Leader Writer, London Evening Standard, 1952–62; Editor, 'The Week', Leader Writer, Home Affairs Editor, The Observer, 1962–72; Research Associate, Organisation of Medical Care Unit, London Sch. of Hygiene and Tropical Medicine, 1972–73; Sen. Fellow, Centre for Studies in Social Policy, 1973–78; Professorial Fellow, then Sen. Associate, King's Fund, 1995–. Visiting Professor: LSE, 1996; LSHTM, 2001–. Member: Wiltshire AHA, 1980–82; Bath DHA, 1982–84. Jt Editor, Political Quarterly, 1981–87. Hon. DArts Oxford Brookes, 1998. Margaret E. Mahoney Award, Commonwealth Fund, NY, 1999. *Publications:* Complaints Against Doctors, 1973; (ed) Social Policy and Public Expenditure, 1974; (ed) Inflation and Priorities, 1975; (with Janet Lewis) The Politics of Consumer Representation, 1976; The Politics of the NHS, 1983; (ed with Michael O'Higgins) The Future of Welfare, 1985; (with Patricia Day) Accountabilities, 1987; (with Linda Challis *et al*) Joint Approaches to Social Policy, 1988; (with Patricia Day) Inspecting the Inspectorates, 1990; (with Neil Carter and Patricia Day) How organisations measure success, 1991; (with Patricia Day and David Henderson) Home Rules, 1993; The New Politics of the NHS, 1995; (with Patricia Day and Sharon Redmayne) Managing Scarcity, 1996; papers on public policy, health policy and public expenditure in various jls. *Recreations:* opera, cooking, football. *Address:* 12A Laurier Road, NW5 1SG. *T:* (020) 7428 9767.

KLEINPOPPEN, Prof. Hans Johann Willi, FRSE; Professor of Experimental Physics, 1968–96, now Emeritus, and Head, Unit of Atomic and Molecular Physics, 1982–96, University of Stirling; *b* Duisburg, Germany, 30 Sept. 1928; *m* 1958, Renate Schröder. *Educ:* Univ. of Giessen (Dipl. Physics 1955); Univ. of Tübingen. Dr re.nat. 1961. Habilitation, Tübingen, 1967. Head, Physics Dept, 1971–73, Dir, Inst. of Atomic Physics, 1975–81, Univ. of Stirling. Vis. Fellow, Univ. Colorado, 1967–68; Vis. Associate Prof., Columbia Univ., 1968; Fellow, Center for Theoretical Studies, Univ. of Miami, 1972–73; Bielefeld University: Guest Prof., 1978–79; Vis. Fellow, Zentrum für interdisziplinäre Forschung, 1979–80; Sen. Res. Fellow, 1980–98; Res. Visitor, Fritz Haber Inst., Berlin, 1991–; Leverhulme Emeritus Fellow, 1998–2000. Chairman: Internat. Symposium on Physics of One- and Two-Electron Atoms (Arnold Sommerfeld Centennial Meml Meeting, Munich 1968); Internat. Symposium on Electron and Photon Interactions with Atoms, in honour of Ugo Fano, Stirling, 1974; Internat. Workshop on Coherence and Correlation in Atomic Collisions, dedicated to Sir Harrie Massey, UCL, 1978; Internat. Symp. on Amplitudes and State Parameters in Atomic Collisions, Kyoto, 1979; Orgng Cttee on Workshops on Polarized Electron and Polarized Photon Physics, SERC, 1993, 1994; Co-Chm., Peter Farago Symposium on Electron Physics, RSE, 1995; Co-Dir, Advanced Study Inst. on Fundamental Processes in Energetic Atomic Collisions, Maratea, Italy, 1982; Dir, Advanced Study Inst. on Fundamental Processes in Atomic Collision Physics, S Flavia, Sicily, 1984; Co-Dir, Advanced Study Inst. on Fundamental Processes on Atomic Dynamics, Maratea, Italy, 1987. FInstP 1969; Fellow Amer. Physical Soc. 1969; FRAS 1974; FRSE 1987; FRSA 1990. *Publications:* edited: (with F. Bopp) Physics of the One- and Two-Electron Atoms, 1969; (with M. R. C. McDowell) Electron and Photon Interactions with Atoms, 1976; Progress in Atomic Spectroscopy, (with W. Hanle) Vol. A 1978 and Vol. B 1979, (with H.-J. Beyer) Vol. C 1984 and Vol. D 1987; (with J. F. Williams) Coherence and Correlations in Atomic Collisions, 1980; (with D. J. Fabian and L. H. Watson) Inner-Shell and X-Ray Physics of Atoms and Solids, 1981; (with J. S. Briggs and H. O. Lutz): Fundamental Processes in Energetic Atomic Collisions, 1983; Fundamental Processes in Atomic Collision Physics, 1985; Fundamental Processes in Atomic Dynamics, 1988; (with W. R. Newell) Polarized Electron/Polarized Photon Physics, 1995; (with D. M. Campbell) Selected Topics on Electron Physics, 1996; (with P. G. Burke) series editor, Physics of Atoms and Molecules; about 200 papers in Zeitschr. f. Physik, Z. f. Naturf., Z. f. Angew Physik, Physikalische Blätter, Physical Review, Physical Review Letters, Jl of Physics, Physics Letters, Internat. Jl of Quantum Chemistry, Physics Reports, Advances of Atomic and Molecular Physics, Applied Physics, Physica; *festschrift* (for 60th birthday) (ed H.-J. Beyer, K. Blum and R. Hippler) Coherence in Atomic Collision Physics, 1988; (for 70th birthday) Hans Kleinpoppen–Symposium on Complete Scattering Experiments, 1998. *Address:* Orberstrasse 12, 14195 Berlin, Germany.

KLEINWORT, Sir Richard (Drake), 4th Bt *cr* 1909, of Bolnore, Cuckfield, Sussex; Head of Financial Public Relations, Ogilvy Public Relations Worldwide, since 2000; *b* 4 Nov. 1960; *s* of Sir Kenneth Drake Kleinwort, 3rd Bt and his 1st wife, Lady Davina Pepys (*d* 1973), *d* of 7th Earl of Cottenham; *S* father, 1994; *m* 1989, Lucinda, *d* of William Shand Kydd; three *s* one *d*. *Educ:* Stowe; Exeter Univ. (BA). Kleinwort Benson, Geneva, 1979; Banco General de Negocios, Buenos Aires, 1984; Deutsche Bank AG, Hamburg and Frankfurt, 1985–88; Biss Lancaster plc, 1988–89; Grandfield Rork Collins Financial, 1989–91; Partner, 1991–2000, Dir, 1994–2000, Cardew & Co. President: Haywards Heath Hospital, 1991–97; The Little Black Bag Housing Assoc., 1991–. Dir, Steppes East Gp. Life Mem., British Field Sports Soc., 1981; Member: WWF (1001) Club, 1979–; S of England Agricl Soc., 1988–; RHS, 1991–. Chm., Knepp Castle Polo Club, 1997–. Fellow, World Scout Foundn, Geneva, 1989. Mem., Instn of King Edward VII Hosp., Midhurst, 1992–; Patron: Cuckfield Soc., 1995–; Ackroyd Trust, 1995–; Vice Pres., Chichester Cathedral Millennium Endowment Trust, 1998–. Ambassador, The Prince's Trust, 1998–. Gov., Stowe Sch. (Chm., Foundn Appeal), 1999–. *Recreations:* travel, my family, laughter, shooting, gardening, farming, watching England winning any sport. *Heir:* *s* Rufus Drake Kleinwort, *b* 16 Aug. 1994. *Clubs:* Turf, Royal Automobile, White's.

KLEMPERER, Prof. Paul David, PhD; FBA 1999; Edgeworth Professor of Economics, University of Oxford, since 1995; Fellow, Nuffield College, Oxford, since 1995; *b* 15 Aug. 1956; *s* of late Hugh G. Klemperer and Ruth M. M. Klemperer (*née* Jordan); *m* 1989, Margaret Meyer; two *s* one *d*. *Educ:* King Edward's Sch., Birmingham; Peterhouse, Cambridge (BA Engrg, 1st Cl. Hons with Dist., 1978); Stanford Univ. (MBA 1982 (Top Student Award); PhD Econs 1986). Sen. Consultant, Arthur Andersen & Co., 1978–80; Harkness Fellow, Commonwealth Fund, 1980–82; Oxford University: Univ. Lectr in Operations Res. and Mathematical Econs, 1985–90; Reader in Econs, 1990–95; John Thomson Fellow and Tutor, St Catherine's Coll., 1985–95. Visiting positions: MIT, 1987; Berkeley, 1991, 1993; Stanford, 1991, 1993; Yale, 1994; Princeton, 1998. Consultant: DTI, 1997–2000; US Federal Trade Commn, 1999–; OFT, 2000–; Nat. Audit Office, 2000; private firms. Fellow, Econometric Soc., 1994. Editor, RAND Jl of Econs, 1993–99; Associate Editor or Member, Editorial Board: Rev. of Econ. Studies, 1989–97; Jl of Industrial Econs, 1989–96; Oxford Econ. Papers, 1986–2000; Internat. Jl of Industrial Orgn, 1993–; Eur. Econ. Rev., 1997–; Rev. of Econ. Design, 1997–2000; Econ. Policy, 1998–99; Econ. Jl, 2000–; Frontiers in Econs, 2000–; BEJl of Econ. Analysis and Policy, 2001. *Publications:* The Economic Theory of Auctions, 2000; articles in econs jls on industrial organization, auction theory, and other econ. theory. *Address:* Nuffield College, Oxford OX1 1NF. *T:* (01865) 278588.

KLEPSCH, Dr Egon Alfred; President, European Parliament, 1992–94; *b* 30 Jan. 1930; *m* 1952, Anita Wegehaupt; three *s* three *d*. *Educ:* Marburg Univ. (DPhil 1954). Mem., CDU, 1951– (Mem. of Bureau, 1977–94); Fed. Chm., Young Christian Democrats, 1963–69; Chm., European Young Christian Democrats, 1964–70; Mem. for Koblenz-St Goar, Bundestag, 1965–80; European Parliament: Member, 1973–79, elected Mem. (EPP/CDU), 1979–94; Vice-Pres., 1982–84; Mem., Political Affairs and other Cttees, 1989–92; Vice-Pres., EPP, 1977–92; Chm., EPP Gp, 1977–82, 1984–92; Mem. Bureau, EPP, 1992–94. Chm., Europa-Union Deutschland, 1989–97 (Hon. Chm., 1997–); Vice-Chm., German Council of Eur. Movement, 1990–99 (Hon. Mem., 1999–). Hon. LLD Sunderland; Dr *hc* Buenos Aires. Grosses Verdienstkreuz mit Stern und Schulterband (Germany), 1986; orders from Italy, Luxembourg, Argentina and Chile. *Publications:* Die Deutsche Russlandpolitik unter dem Reichsminister des Auswärtigen Dr Gustav Stresemann, 1955; Der Kommunismus in Deutschland, 1964; Der Europäische Abgeordnete, 1978; Programme für Europa, 1978; Die Abgeordneten Europas, 1984.

KLESTIL, Thomas; President of Austria, since 1992; *b* 4 Nov. 1932; *m*; two *s* one *d*. *Educ:* Economic Univ., Vienna. Mem., Austrian Delegn to OECD, Paris, 1959–62; with Austrian Embassy, Washington, 1962–66; Sec. to Chancellor, 1966–69; Consul-Gen., Los Angeles, 1969–74; Rep. of Austria to UN, 1978–82; Ambassador to Washington, 1982–87; Sec.-Gen. for Foreign Affairs, 1987–92. *Address:* Präsidentschaftskanzlei, Hofburg, 1014 Vienna, Austria.

KLEVAN, Hon. Sir Rodney (Conrad), Kt 1998; **Hon. Mr Justice Klevan;** a Judge of the High Court, Queen's Bench Division, since 1998; *b* 23 May 1940; *s* of late Sidney Leopold Klevan and Florence Klevan (*née* Eaton); *m* 1968, Susan Rebecca (*née* Lighthill) (*d* 1991); two *s* one *d*. *Educ:* Temple Primary School; Manchester Central Grammar School; Birmingham Univ. (LLB Hons 1962). Pres., Birmingham Univ. Guild of Undergraduates, 1962–63. Called to the Bar, Gray's Inn, 1966, Bencher, 1992; Deputy Circuit Judge, 1977; a Recorder, 1980–98; QC 1984; Leader, Northern Circuit, 1992–95. *Recreations:* theatre, art, following the fortunes of Lancashire CCC. *Address:* Royal Courts of Justice, Strand, WC2A 2LL.

KLIBANSKY, Raymond, GOQ 1999; MA, PhD; FRSC; FRHistS; Frothingham Professor of Logic and Metaphysics, McGill University, Montreal, 1946–75, now Emeritus Professor; Fellow of Wolfson College, Oxford, 1981–95 (Hon. Fellow, 1995); *b* Paris, 15 Oct. 1905; *s* of late Hermann Klibansky. *Educ:* Paris; Odenwald Sch.; Univs of Kiel, Hamburg, Heidelberg. PhD, 1928; MA Oxon by decree, 1936. Asst, Heidelberg Acad., 1927–33; Lecturer in Philosophy: Heidelberg Univ., 1931–33; King's Coll., London, 1934–36; Oriel Coll., Oxford, 1936–48; Forwood Lectr in Philosophy of Religion, Univ. of Liverpool, 1938–39. Political Warfare Exec., FO, 1941–46. Dir of Studies, Warburg Inst., Univ. of London, 1947–48. Vis. Prof. of History of Philosophy, Université de Montréal, 1947–68; Mahlon Powell Prof., Indiana Univ., 1950; Cardinal Mercier Prof. of Philosophy, Univ. of Louvain, 1956; Vis. Prof. of Philosophy, Univ. of Rome, 1961, Univ. of Genoa, 1964, Univ. of Tokyo, 1971; Prof. Emeritus, Heidelberg Univ., 1975–, Hon. Senator, 1986–. President: Inst. Internat. de Philosophie, Paris, 1966–69 (Hon. Pres. 1969–); Société Internationale pour l'étude de la Philos. Médiévale, Louvain, 1968–72 (Hon. Pres., 1972–); Canadian Soc. for History and Philosophy of Science, 1959–72 (Pres. Emeritus, 1972–); Centro Studi di Civiltà del Medioevo e del Rinascimento, Parma 1990–. Fellow: Accademia Nazionale dei Lincei, Rome; Acad. of Athens; Académie Internationale d'Histoire des Sciences, Paris; Iranian Acad. of Philosophy, Teheran; Acad. dei Dafnici e degli Zelanti; Acireale; Corresponding Fellow: Mediaeval Acad. of America; Heidelberg Acad. of Scis; Deutsche Akad. für Sprache und Dichtung, Darmstadt; Braunschweigische Wissenschaftliche Gesellschaft. Hon. Member: Allgemeine Gesellsch. für Philosophie in Deutschland; Assoc. des Scientifiques de Roumanie, Bucarest; Foreign Hon. Mem., Amer. Acad. of Arts and Scis. Hon. Fellow: Oriel Coll., Oxford; Warburg Inst., Univ. of London; Accad. Ligure delle Scienze, Genoa; Canadian Mediterranean Inst., Athens, Rome, Cairo. Guggenheim Foundation Fellow, 1954 and 1965; Vis. Fellow, Wolfson Coll., Oxford, 1976–78. Dir, Canadian Academic Centre in Italy, Rome, 1980. Mem. Exec. Council, Union Académique Internationale, 1978–80. Comité Directeur, Fedn Internat. des Socs de Philosophie, 1958–83. DPhil *hc*: Bologna; Marburg; Ottawa; Reconnaissance de Mérite Scientifique, Québec à Montréal, 1991. Gauss Medal, Brunswick, 1990; Lessing Prize, Hamburg, 1994. Grand Cross, Order of Merit (Germany), 1994; Medal, City of Paris, 1999. Gen. Editor, Corpus Platonicum Medii Aevi, (Plato Latinus and Plato Arabus), Union Académique Internat., 1937–; Joint Editor and contributor to: Magistri Eckardi Opera Latina, 1933–36; Philosophy and History, 1936; Mediaeval and Renaissance Studies, 1941–68; Editor: Philosophical Texts, 1951–62; Philosophy and World Community, 1957–95; Philosophy in the Mid-Century, 1958–59; Contemporary Philosophy, 1968–71; Dir, Bibliographie de la Philosophie, 45 vols, 1954–99. *Publications:* Ein Proklos-Fund und seine Bedeutung, 1929; Heidelberg Acad. edn of Opera Nicolai de Cusa, 5 vols, 1929–82; The Continuity of the Platonic Tradition, 1939, enlarged 4th edn incl. Plato's Parmenides in the Middle Ages and the Renaissance, 1982; (with E. Panofsky and F. Saxl) Saturn and Melancholy, 1964 (enlarged French, German and Spanish edns, 1989–92); (with F. Regen) Überlieferungsgeschichte der philosophischen Werke des Apuleius, 1993; (ed and contrib.) La Philosophie en Europe, 1993; Le Philosophe et la Mémoire du siècle, 1998; articles in Jahresberichte d. Heidelberger Akademie, Proceedings of British Acad., Enciclopedia Italiana, and elsewhere. *Address:* Wolfson College, Oxford OX2 6UD; Leacock Building, McGill University, Montreal, QC H3A 2T7, Canada.

KLOOTWIJK, Jaap; Director, Grove Holdings Ltd, since 1991; *b* 16 Nov. 1932; *s* of J. L. Klootwijk and W. J. Boer. *Educ:* Rotterdam Grammar Sch.; Technological Univ., Delft (MSc Mech. Eng, 1956). Lieut Royal Netherlands Navy, 1956–58. Joined Royal Dutch/Shell Gp, 1958; worked in various capacities in Holland, UK, France, Switzerland, Sweden, Algeria, Kenya; Area Co-ordinator, SE Asia, 1976–79; Man. Dir, Shell Internat. Gas Ltd, 1979–82; Jt Man. Dir, Shell UK, 1983–88; Man. Dir, Shell UK Oil, 1983–88; Chm., UK Oil Pipelines, 1983–88. Dir, The Flyfishers' Co. Ltd, 1985–94. Pres., UK Petroleum Industry Assoc., 1985–87. *Recreations:* shooting, fishing, reading. *Address:* 26 Manor House Court, Warwick Avenue, W9 2PZ. *T:* (020) 7289 4276. *Club:* Flyfishers' (Pres., 1985–87).

KLOSE, Hans-Ulrich; Member (SPD), since 1983, Chairman, Committee of Foreign Affairs, since 1998, Bundestag, Germany; *b* 14 June 1937; *m* 1992, Dr Anne Steinbeck-Klose; two *s* two *d* by former marriages. *Educ:* Bielefeld; Clinton, Iowa; Freiburg Univ. (Law graduate 1965). Joined SDP 1964; Dep. Chm., Young Socialists, 1966; Dep. Chm., SPD, 1968; Mayor of Hamburg, 1974–81; Treasurer, SPD, 1987–91. Bundestag: Leader of the Opposition, 1991–94; Vice-Pres., 1994–98. *Publications:* Altern der Gesellschaft, 1993; Altern hat Zukunft, 1993. *Address:* c/o Bundeshaus, 11011 Berlin, Germany.

KLUG, Sir Aaron, OM 1995; Kt 1988; ScD (Cantab); FRS 1969; Director, Medical Research Council Laboratory of Molecular Biology, Cambridge, 1986–96 (member of staff, since 1962, Joint Head, Division of Structural Studies, 1978–86); President, Royal Society, 1995–2000; Hon. Fellow of Peterhouse, since 1993 (Fellow, 1962–93); *b* 11 Aug. 1926; *s* of Lazar Klug and Bella Klug (*née* Silin); *m* 1948, Liebe, *o d* of Alexander and Annie Bobrow, Cape Town, SA; one *s* (and one *s* decd). *Educ:* Durban High Sch.; Univ. of the Witwatersrand (BSc); Univ. of Cape Town (MSc). Junior Lecturer, Cape Town, 1947–48; 1851 Exhibn Overseas Fellow from SA to Cambridge; Research Student, Cavendish Laboratory, Cambridge, 1949–52; Rouse-Ball Research Studentship, Trinity Coll., Cambridge, 1949–52; Colloid Science Dept, Cambridge, 1953; Nuffield Research Fellow, Birkbeck Coll., London, 1954–57; Head, Virus Structure Research Group, Birkbeck Coll., 1958–61. Mem., Council for Sci. and Technology, 1993–2000. Hon. Prof., Univ. of Cambridge, 1989. Lectures: Carter-Wallace, Princeton, 1972; Leeuwenhoek, Royal Soc., 1973; Dunham, Harvard Medical Sch., 1975; Harvey, NY, 1979; Lane, Stanford Univ., 1983; Silliman, Yale Univ., 1985; Nishina Meml, Tokyo, 1986; Pauli, ETH Zürich, 1986; Cetus, Univ. of California, Berkeley, 1987; Konrad Bloch, Harvard, 1988; Steenbock, Univ. of Wisconsin, 1989; National, US Biophysical Soc., Washington, 1993; William and Mary, Leiden, 1996. Founder FMedSci 1998. For. Associate, Nat. Acad. of Scis, USA, 1984; For. Mem., Max Planck Soc., Germany, 1984; For. Hon. Mem., Amer. Acad. of Arts and Scis, 1969; For. Associate, Acad. des Scis, Paris, 1989. Hon. FRCP 1987; Hon. FRCPath 1991. Hon. Fellow: Trinity Coll., Cambridge, 1983; Amer. Phil Soc., 1996. Hon. DSc: Chicago, 1978; Columbia Univ., 1978; Witwatersrand, 1984; Hull, 1985; St Andrews, 1987; Western Ontario, 1991; Warwick, 1994; Cape Town, 1997; Weizmann Inst., 1997; Stirling, 1998; London, 2000; Oxford, 2000; Dr *hc* Strasbourg, 1978; Hon. PhD Jerusalem, 1984; Hon. Dr Fil. Stockholm, 1980; Hon. LittD Cantab, 1998. Heineken Prize, Royal Netherlands Acad. of Science, 1979; Louisa Gross Horwitz Prize, Columbia Univ., 1981; Nobel Prize in Chemistry, 1982; Gold Medal of Merit, Univ. of Cape Town, 1983; Copley Medal, Royal Soc., 1985; Harden Medal, Biochem. Soc., 1985; Baly Medal, RCP, 1987; William Bate Hardy Prize, Cambridge Phil. Soc., 1996. *Publications:* papers in scientific jls. *Recreations:* reading, ancient history. *Address:* MRC Laboratory of Molecular Biology, Hills Road, Cambridge CB2 2QH. *T:* (01223) 248011.

KLYBERG, Rt Rev. Mgr Charles John; *b* 29 July 1931; *s* of late Captain Charles Augustine Klyberg, MN and Ivy Lilian Waddington, LRAM; unmarried. *Educ:* Eastbourne College. Eaton Hall OCS, 1953; 2nd Lieut, 1st Bn The Buffs, Kenya Emergency, 1953–54; Lieut 1955. ARICS. Asst Estates Manager, Cluttons, 1954–57. Lincoln Theological Coll., 1957–60. Curate, S John's, East Dulwich, 1960–63; Rector of Fort Jameson, Zambia, 1963–67; Vicar, Christ Church and S Stephen, Battersea, 1967–77; Dean of Lusaka Cathedral, Zambia, and Rector of the parish, 1977–85, Dean Emeritus, 1985; Vicar General, 1978–85; Bishop Suffragan of Fulham, 1985–96; first Archdeacon of Charing Cross, 1989–96. Received into RC Ch and ordained priest, 1996; Prelate of Honour, 2000. UK Commissary for Anglican Church in Zambia, 1985–89. Chairman: Church Property Development Gp, 1978–85; Fulham Palace Museum Trust, 1991–96. Pres., Guild of All Souls, 1988–95. Guardian, Shrine of Our Lady of Walsingham, 1991–96. Warden, Quainton Hall Sch., Harrow, 1992–96. *Recreations:* reading, music, travel. *Club:* Athenæum.

KLYNE, Dame Barbara Evelyn; *see* Clayton, Dame B. E.

KNAGGS, Kenneth James, CMG 1971; OBE 1959; formerly overseas civil servant; *b* 3 July 1920; *e s* of late James Henry Knaggs and Elsie Knaggs (*née* Walton); *m* 1945, Barbara, *d* of late Ernest James Page; two *s*. *Educ:* St Paul's Sch., London. Served War, 1939–46. Northern Rhodesia Civil Service, 1946; Sec. to Govt, Seychelles, 1955 (Actg Governor, 1957–58); Northern Rhodesia: Asst Sec., 1960; Under Sec., 1961; Permanent Sec., Min. of Finance and subseq. the same in Zambia, 1964; retd 1970. European Rep. and Manager, Zambia Airways, 1970–72; Consultant, Commonwealth Develt Corp., 1974–87. *Recreations:* walking, gardening, cooking. *Address:* High House Farm, Earl Soham, near Framlingham, Suffolk IP13 7SN. *T:* (01728) 685416.

KNAPMAN, Dr Paul Anthony, FRCP, FRCS; HM Coroner for Westminster, since 1980 (Jurisdiction of Inner West London); *b* 5 Nov. 1944; *s* of Frederick Ethelbert and Myra Knapman; *m* 1970, Penelope Jane Cox; one *s* three *d*. *Educ:* Epsom Coll.; King's Coll., London; St George's Hosp. Med. Sch. (MB, BS 1968). MRCS, LRCP 1968; DMJ 1975; FRCP 1998; FRCS 1999. Called to the Bar, Gray's Inn, 1972. Dep. Coroner for Inner W London, 1975–80. Hon. Lectr in Med. Jurisprudence, St George's Hosp. Med. Sch., 1978–; Hon. Clinical Teacher (Forensic Medicine), Royal Free and UC (formerly Middlesex and UCH) Med. Sch., 1981–; Hon. Clinical Sen. Lectr, ICSTM (formerly Westminster and Charing Cross Med. Sch.), 1987–. President: S Eastern England Coroners' Soc., 1980; Sect. of Clinical Forensic Medicine, RSocMed, 1995–97; Vice-Pres., Coroners' Soc. of England and Wales, 2000. Gov., London Nautical Sch., 1981–99 (Chm., 1995–99); Pres., Old Epsomian Club, 1999–2000. Liveryman, 1982–, and Mem., Ct of Assistants, 1993–, Soc. of Apothecaries. Mem., Lodge of Friendship (No 6). Specialist Editor (Coroners Law), JP Reports, 1990–. *Publications:* (jtly) Coronership: the law and practice on coroners, 1985; Medicine and the Law, 1989; Casebook on Coroners, 1989; Sources of Coroners' Law, 1999; contributor to: Medical Negligence, 1990, 3rd edn 2000; Atkin's Court Forms, vol. 13, 1992, 3rd edn 2000; papers on medico-legal subjects. *Recreations:* boating, beagling. *Address:* Westminster Coroner's Court, Horseferry Road, SW1P 2ED. *T:* (020) 7834 6515. *Clubs:* Athenæum, Garrick; Royal Torbay Yacht.

KNAPMAN, Roger Maurice; Political Adviser, UK Independence Party, since 2000; *b* 20 Feb. 1944; *m* 1967, Carolyn Trebell (*née* Eastman); one *s* one *d*. *Educ:* Royal Agricl Coll., Cirencester. FRICS 1967. MP (C) Stroud, 1987–97; contested (C) same seat, 1997. PPS to Minister of State for Armed Forces, 1991–93; an Asst Govt Whip, 1995–96; a Lord Comr of HM Treasury (Govt Whip), 1996–97. Vice-Chm., Cons. backbench European Affairs Cttee, 1989–90; Mem., Select Cttee on Agric., 1994–95. Mem., AFRC, 1991–94. *Address:* Coryton House, Coryton, Okehampton, Devon EX20 4PA.

KNAPP, David; *see* Knapp, J. D.

KNAPP, Edward Ronald, CBE 1979; Managing Director, Timken Europe, 1973–85, retired; *b* 10 May 1919; *s* of Percy Charles and Elsie Maria Knapp; *m* 1942, Vera Mary Stephenson; two *s* two *d*. *Educ:* Cardiff High Sch.; St Catharine's Coll., Cambridge (MA 1940); Harvard Business Sch. (AMP 1954). Served RNVR, Special Branch, Lt-Comdr, 1940–46: HMS Aurora, 1941–44; US Naval Research, Anacostia, 1944–46. Joined British Timken, 1946, Man. Dir, 1969; Dir, Timken Co., USA, 1976. Technical and Management Educnl Governor, Nene Coll., 1953–. Pres., Northampton RFC, 1986–88. *Recreations:* gardening, golf; played Rugby for Wales, 1940, Captain of Cambridge Univ. 1940 and Northampton RFC, 1948. *Address:* The Elms, 1 Millway, Duston, Northampton NN5 6ER. *T:* (01604) 584737. *Clubs:* East India, Devonshire, Sports and Public Schools; Northants County Golf; Hawks (Cambridge).

KNAPP, (John) David, OBE 1986; Director of Conservative Political Centre, 1975–88; an Assistant Director, Conservative Research Department, 1979–88; *b* 27 Oct. 1926; *s* of late Eldred Arthur Knapp and Elizabeth Jane Knapp; *m* 1st, 1954, Dorothy Ellen May (*née* Squires) (marr. diss.); one *s*; 2nd, 1980, Daphne Monard, OBE, *widow* of Major S. H. Monard. *Educ:* Dauntsey's Sch., Wilts; King's Coll., London (BA Hons). Dir, Knapp and Bates Ltd, 1950–54. Vice-Chm., Fedn of University Conservative and Unionist Assoc., 1948–49; Conservative Publicity and Political Educn Officer, Northern Area, 1952–56; Political Educn Officer, NW Area, 1956–61, and Home Counties N Area, 1961; Dep. Dir, Conservative Political Centre, 1962–75. Member (C), Hampshire CC, 1989–93. *Recreations:* philately, walking cavalier spaniels. *Address:* Greenway, Yaverland Road, Yaverland, Isle of Wight PO36 8QP. *T:* (01983) 401045.

KNAPP, Trevor Frederick William Beresford; Director, KADE, since 1997; *b* 26 May 1937; *s* of Frederick William Knapp and Linda Knapp (*née* Poffley); *m* 1964, Margaret Fry; one *s* one *d*. *Educ:* Christ's Hospital; King's College London (BSc 1958). ARIC 1960. Ministry of Aviation, 1961; Sec., Downey Cttee, 1965–66; Sec., British Defence Research and Supply Staff, Canberra, 1968–72; Asst Sec., MoD, 1974; GEC Turbine Generators Ltd, 1976; Central Policy Review Staff, 1977–79; Ministry of Defence: Under-Sec., 1983; Dir Gen. (Marketing), 1983–88; Asst Under Sec. of State (Supply and Organisation) (Air), 1988–91; Asst Under-Sec. of State (Infrastructure and Logistics), 1992–96. Member Board: Waltham Abbey Royal Gunpowder Mills Co., 1997– (Chm., 1998–); Waltham Abbey Trust, 1997–; Trustee, Bromley Volunteer Sector Trust, 1999–. *Address:* c/o National Westminster Bank, Charing Cross, WC2H 0PD.

KNAPP-FISHER, Rt Rev. Edward George; Hon. Assistant Bishop, diocese of Chichester, since 1987; *b* 8 Jan. 1915; *s* of late Rev. George Edwin and Agatha Knapp-Fisher; *m* 1965, Joan, *d* of late R. V. Bradley. *Educ:* King's School, Worcester; Trinity College, Oxford (MA). Assistant Curate of Brighouse, Yorks, 1939; Chaplain, RNVR, 1942; Chaplain of Cuddesdon College, 1946; Chaplain of St John's College, Cambridge, 1949; Vicar of Cuddesdon and Principal of Cuddesdon Theological College, 1952–60; Bishop of Pretoria, 1960–75; Canon and Archdeacon of Westminster, 1975–87; Sub-Dean, 1982–87; Asst Bishop, Dio. Southwark 1975–87, Dio. London 1976–87; Custos, St Mary's Hosp., Chichester, 1987–2001. Member, Anglican Roman-Catholic Preparatory Commission, 1967–68; Member, Anglican-Roman Catholic Internat. Commn, 1969–81. *Publications:* The Churchman's Heritage, 1952; Belief and Prayer, 1964; To be or not to be, 1968; Where the Truth is Found, 1975, (ed jtly and contrib.) Towards Unity in Truth, 1981; Eucharist, Many-Sided Mystery, 1988. *Recreations:* walking, theatre, gardening. *Address:* 2 Vicars' Close, Canon Lane, Chichester, West Sussex PO19 1PT. *T:* (01243) 789219.

KNARESBOROUGH, Bishop Suffragan of, since 1997; **Rt Rev. Frank Valentine Weston;** *b* 16 Sept. 1935; *s* of William Valentine Weston and Gertrude Hamilton Weston; *m* 1963, Penelope Brighid, *d* of Marmaduke Carver Middleton Athorpe, formerly of Dinnington, Yorks and Hilda Bridget (*née* Waterfall); one *s* two *d*. *Educ:* Christ's Hospital; Queen's Coll., Oxford (BA 1960; MA 1964); Lichfield Theological Coll. Curate, St John the Baptist, Atherton, Lancs, 1961–65; Chaplain, 1965–69, Principal, 1969–76, College of the Ascension, Selly Oak, Birmingham; Vice-Pres., Selly Oak Colls, 1973–76; Principal and Pantonian Prof., Edinburgh Theological Coll., 1976–82; Archdeacon of Oxford, 1982–97; Canon of Christ Church, Oxford, 1982–97, Emeritus Student, 1998. Court of Assistants, Salters' Co., 1984– (Master, 1992–93). Governor: St Augustine's Upper Sch., Oxford, 1983–97; Christ's Hosp., 1988– (Almoner, 1996–); Tudor Hall Sch., 1988–97. Provost, Northern Div., Woodard Corp., 1998–. *Publications:* (contrib.) Quel Missionnaire, 1971; (contrib.) Gestalten der Kirchengeschichte, 1984. *Recreations:* wine, persons and song; exploring the countryside. *Address:* 16 Shaftesbury Avenue, Leeds LS8 1DT. *T:* (0113) 266 4800.
See also Rev. Canon D. W. V. Weston.

KNATCHBULL, family name of **Baron Brabourne** and **Countess Mountbatten of Burma**.

KNEALE, George Victor Harris, CBE 1989; Speaker, House of Keys, Isle of Man, 1990–91; retired; *b* 12 Jan. 1918; *s* of James Kneale and Ellen (*née* Harris); *m* 1940, Thelma Eugenie Creer; two *d*. *Educ:* Demesne Road Elementary Sch.; Douglas High Sch. for Boys. Served RHA, 1940–46, ME and Italy. Photo-process engraver, 1935–40 and 1946–57. Mem., IOM Educn Authy, 1951–62; Chm., Bd of Educn, 1962–72, 1981–86; Minister for Educn, 1986–90; Member: House of Keys, 1962–74, 1981–91; Legislative Council, 1974–81; Founder Chm., IOM PO Authy, 1972–81. President: IOM Art Soc.; IOM Br., Royal Artillery Assoc.; former President: IOM Scout Assoc.; Manx Gateway Club. Hon. MA Salford, 1990. Boy Scouts Awards: Medal of Merit; Silver Acorn; Silver Wolf. *Recreations:* drawing, painting, photography, Boy Scouts. *Address:* Carrmyers, 15 Cronkbourne Avenue, Douglas, Isle of Man IM2 3LA. *T:* (01624) 676996.

KNEALE, (Robert) Bryan (Charles), RA 1974 (ARA 1970); sculptor; Professor of Drawing, Royal College of Art, 1990–95; *b* 19 June 1930; *m* 1956, Doreen Lister (*d* 1998); one *d* (one *s* decd). *Educ:* Douglas High Sch.; Douglas Sch. of Art, IOM; Royal Academy Schools: Rome prize, 1949–51; RA diploma. Tutor, RCA Sculpture Sch., 1964–; Head of Sculpture Sch., Hornsey, 1967; Assoc. Lectr, Chelsea Sch. of Art, 1970. Fellow RCA, 1972, Sen. Fellow, 1995; Head of Sculpture Dept, RCA, 1985–90 (Sen. Tutor, 1980–85); Royal Academy: Master of Sculpture, 1982–85; Prof. of Sculpture, 1985–90; Trustee, 1995–. Member: Fine Art Panels, NCAD, 1964–71, Arts Council, 1971–73, CNAA, 1974–82; Chm., Air and Space, 1972–73. *Organised:* Sculpture '72, RA, 1972; Battersea Park Silver Jubilee Sculpture, 1977 (also exhibited); Sade Exhbn, Cork, 1982. *Exhibitions:* Redfern Gallery, 1954, 1956, 1958, 1960, 1962, 1964, 1967, 1970, 1976, 1978, 1981; 1983; John Moores, 1961; Sixth Congress of Internat. Union of Architects, 1961; Art Aujourd'hui, Paris, 1963; Battersea Park Sculpture, 1963, 1966; Profile III Bochum, 1964; British Sculpture in the Sixties, Tate Gall., 1965; Whitechapel Gall. 1966 (retrospective), 1981; Structure, Cardiff Metamorphis Coventry, 1966; New British Painting and Sculpture, 1967–68; City of London Festival, 1968; Holland Park, Sculpture in the Cities, Southampton, and British Sculptors, RA, 1972; Holland Park, 1973, 2000; Royal Exchange Sculpture Exhibition, 1974; New Art, Hayward Gallery, 1975; Sculpture at Worksop, 1976; Taranman Gall., 1977, 1981; Serpentine Gall., 1978; Compass Gall., Glasgow, 1981; 51 Gall., Edinburgh, 1981; Bath Art Fair, 1981; Henry Moore Gall., RCA (retrospective), 1986; Fitzwilliam Mus., 1987; Sala Uno, Rome, 1988; Chichester Fest., 1988; New Art Centre, 1990; Nat. History Mus., 1991; Manx Mus., 1992; RWA (retrospective), 1995; Angela Flowers Gall., 1998; 70th Birthday Exhibn, Roche Court, 2000; Eye of the Storm, Turin, 2000; *commissions:* LCC, Fenwick Place, 1961; Loughborough campus, 1962; Camberwell Beauty Liby, Old Kent Rd, 1964; Hall Caine Meml, Douglas, 1971; King Edward Sch., Totnes, 1972; Woodside Sculpture, Gloversville, NY, 1972–73; Monumental Sculpture for Manx Millenium, Ronaldsway, IOM, 1979; Wall Sculpture for Govt Bldgs, Douglas, IOM, 1996; Sculpture at Goodwood Sculpture Park, 1996; Bronze doors, Portsmouth Cathedral, 1997; Relief Sculpture for Westminster Cath., 1999. Arts Council Tours, 1966–71. *Collections:* Arts Council of GB; Contemp. Art Soc.; Manx Museum; Leics Educn Authority; Nat. Galls of Victoria, S Australia and New Zealand; City Art Galls, York, Nottingham, Manchester, Bradford and Leicester; Tate Gall.; Beaverbrook Foundn, Fredericton; Museum of Modern Art, São Paulo, Brazil; Bahia Museum, Brazil; Oriel Coll., Oxford; Museum of Modern Art, New York; City Galleries, Middlesbrough, Birmingham, Wakefield; Fitzwilliam Museum, Cambridge; W Riding Educn Authority; Unilever House Collection; Walker Art Gallery; Nat. History Mus., Taiwan; Nat. History Mus., London. *Address:* 10A Muswell Road, N10 2BG. *T:* (020) 8444 7617; New Art Centre, Roche Court, East Winterslow, Wilts. *T:* (01980) 862447.

KNEBWORTH, Viscount; Philip Anthony Scawen Lytton; *b* 7 March 1989; *s* and *heir* of Earl of Lytton, *qv*.

KNELLER, Sir Alister (Arthur), Kt 1996; Chief Justice of Gibraltar, 1986–95; *b* 11 Nov. 1927; *s* of Arthur Kneller and Hester (*née* Farr). *Educ:* King's Sch., Canterbury; Corpus Christi Coll., Cambridge (MA 1954; LLM 1985). Kenya: Resident Magistrate, 1955; Sen. State Counsel, 1962; Registrar of the High Court, 1965; Puisne Judge, 1969, Judge of the Court of Appeal, 1982. Hon. Bencher, Gray's Inn, 1995. *Recreations:* music, reading. *Club:* Oxford and Cambridge.

KNIBB, Prof. Michael Anthony, PhD; FBA 1989; Samuel Davidson Professor of Old Testament Studies, 1997–2001, now Emeritus, and Head, School of Humanities, 2000–01, King's College London; *b* 14 Dec. 1938; third *s* of Leslie Charles Knibb and Christian Vera Knibb (*née* Hoggar); *m* 1972, Christine Mary Burrrell. *Educ:* Wyggeston Sch., Leicester; King's Coll. London (BD, PhD; FKC 1991); Union Theol Seminary, NY (STM); Corpus Christi Coll., Oxford. King's College London: Lectr in OT Studies, 1964–82; Reader, 1982–86; Prof. of OT Studies, 1986–97; Head, Dept of Theology and Religious Studies, 1989–93, 1998–2000; Dep. Head, Sch. of Humanities, 1992–97. British Academy: Res. Reader, 1986–88; Schweich Lectr, 1995; Mem., Humanities Res. Bd, 1995–98 (Chm., Postgrad. Cttee, 1996–98). Editor: Book List of SOTS, 1980–86; Guides to the Apocrypha and Pseudepigrapha, 1995–. Hon. Sec., Palestine Exploration Fund, 1969–76. *Publications:* The Ethiopic Book of Enoch: a new edition in the light of the Aramaic Dead Sea Fragments, 2 vols, 1978; Het Boek Henoch, 1983; Cambridge Bible Commentary on 2 Esdras, 1979; (ed jtly) Israel's Prophetic Tradition: essays in honour of P. R. Ackroyd, 1982; The Qumran Community, 1987; (ed with P. W. van der Horst) Studies on the Testament of Job, 1989; Translating the Bible: the Ethiopic version of the Old Testament, 1999; reviews and articles in books and learned jls. *Recreation:* hill walking. *Address:* 6 Shootersway Park, Berkhamsted, Herts HP4 3NX. *T:* (01442) 871459. *Club:* Athenæum.

KNIGHT, family name of **Baroness Knight of Collingtree**.

KNIGHT OF COLLINGTREE, Baroness *cr* 1997 (Life Peer), of Collingtree in the co. of Northamptonshire; **Joan Christabel Jill Knight,** DBE 1985 (MBE 1964); *m* 1947, Montague Knight (*d* 1986); two *s*. *Educ:* Fairfield Sch., Bristol; King Edward Grammar Sch., Birmingham. Mem., Northampton County Borough Council, 1956–66. MP (C) Birmingham, Edgbaston, 1966–97. Member: Select Cttee on Race Relations and Immigration, 1969–72; Select Cttee for Home Affairs, 1980–83, 1992–97; Chairman: Lords and Commons All-Party Child and Family Protection Gp, 1978–97; Cons. Back Bench Health and Social Services Cttee, 1982–97; Member: Exec. Cttee, 1922 Cttee, 1979–97 (Sec., 1983–87; Vice-Chm., 1987–88, 1992–97); Council of Europe, 1977–88, 1999–; WEU, 1977–88, 1999– (Chm., Cttee for Parly and Public Relations, 1984–88); Exec. Cttee, IPU, 1991–97 (Chm., 1994–97). Mem., Select Cttee on EU, 1999–. Pres., West Midlands Conservative Political Centre, 1980–83. Vice-Pres., Townswomen's Guilds, 1986–95. Director: Computeach International plc, 1991–; Heckett Multiserv, 1999–. Hon. DSc Aston, 1999. Kentucky Colonel, USA, 1973; Nebraska Admiral, USA, 1980. *Publication:* About the House, 1995. *Recreations:* music, reading, tapestry work, theatre-going, antique-hunting. *Address:* c/o House of Lords, SW1A 0PW.

KNIGHT, Prof. Alan Sydney, DPhil; Professor of the History of Latin America, and Fellow of St Antony's College, Oxford, since 1992; *b* 6 Nov. 1946; *s* of William Henry Knight and Eva Maud Crandon; *m* 1st, 1969, Carole Jones (marr. diss. 1979); one *d*; 2nd, 1985, Lidia Lozano; two *s*. *Educ:* Balliol Coll., Oxford (BA Modern Hist. 1968); Nuffield Coll., Oxford (DPhil 1974). Research Fellow, Nuffield Coll., Oxford, 1971–73; Lectr in Hist., Essex Univ., 1973–85; Worsham Centennial Prof. of History, Univ. of Texas at Austin, 1986–92. *Publications:* The Mexican Revolution (2 vols), 1986; US-Mexican Relations 1910–40, 1987; contrib. Jl of Latin American Studies, Bull. of Latin American Res., etc. *Recreation:* kayaking. *Address:* St Antony's College, Oxford OX2 6JF. *T:* (01865) 274486.

KNIGHT, Very Rev. Alexander Francis; Dean of Lincoln, since 1998; *b* 24 July 1939; *s* of late Rev. Benjamin Edward Knight and of Dorothy Mary Knight; *m* 1962, Sheelagh Elizabeth (*née* Faris); one *s* three *d*. *Educ:* Taunton Sch.; St Catharine's Coll., Cambridge (MA). Curate, Hemel Hempstead, 1963–68; Chaplain, Taunton Sch., 1968–74; Dir, Bloxham Project, 1975–81; Dir of Studies, Aston Training Scheme, 1981–83; Priest-in-charge, Easton and Martyr Worthy, 1983–90; Archdeacon of Basingstoke and Canon Residentiary of Winchester Cathedral, 1990–98. *Publications:* contrib. SPCK Taleteller series. *Recreations:* hill walking, theatre, reading, gardening. *Address:* The Deanery, 12 Eastgate, Lincoln LN2 1QG.

KNIGHT, Andrew Stephen Bower, farmer in Warwickshire and Dannevirke; *b* 1 Nov. 1939; *s* of late M. W. B. Knight and S. E. F. Knight; *m* 1st, 1966, Victoria Catherine Brittain (marr. diss.); one *s*; 2nd, 1975, Sabiha Rumani Malik (marr. diss. 1991); two *d*. Editor, The Economist, 1974–86; Chief Exec., 1986–89, Editor-in-Chief, 1987–89, Daily Telegraph plc; Chairman: News Internat. plc, 1990–94; Times Newspapers Hldgs, 1990–94 (Dir, 1990–). Director: The News Corporation Ltd, 1991–; Rothschild Investment Trust CP, 1996–; Dep. Chm., Home Counties Newspapers Hldgs, 1996–98. Member: Steering Cttee, Bilderberg Meetings, 1980–98; Adv. Bd, Center for Economic Policy Research, Stanford Univ., 1981–; Adv. Council, Inst. of Internat. Studies, Stanford Univ., 1990–. Trustee, Harlech Scholars' Trust. Governor and Mem. Council of

Management, Ditchley Foundn, 1982–. Chm., Shipston Home Nursing, 1997–. *Clubs:* Beefsteak, Brooks's, Royal Automobile; Tadmarton Heath Golf (Tadmarton).

KNIGHT, Angela Ann; Chief Executive, Association of Private Client Investment Managers and Stockbrokers, since 1997; *b* 31 Oct. 1950; *d* of Andrew McTurk Cook and late Barbara Jean (*née* Gale); *m* 1981, David George Knight (marr. diss.); two *s*. *Educ:* Penrhos Coll., N Wales; Sheffield Girls' High Sch.; Bristol Univ. (BSc Hons Chem. 1972). Management posts with Air Products Ltd, 1972–77; Man. Dir and Chm., Cook & Knight (Metallurgical Processors) Ltd, 1977–84; Chm., Cook & Knight (Process Plant), 1984–91. Non-exec. Director: PEP and ISA (formerly PEP) Managers Assoc., 1997–99; Scottish Widows, 1997–; Saur Water Services and South East Water plc (formerly Saur Water Services), 1997–; Mott MacDonald, 1998–2001; Logica, 1999–. MP (C) Erewash, 1992–97; contested (C) same seat, 1997. PPS to Minister for Industry, 1993–94, to Chancellor of the Exchequer, 1994–95; Econ. Sec. to HM Treasury, 1995–97. Governor: Gayhurst Sch., 2000–; Bradfield Coll., 2001–. *Recreations:* walking, ski-ing, music, books. *Address:* Association of Private Client Investment Managers and Stockbrokers, 112 Middlesex Street, E1 7HY. *Clubs:* Carlton, Capital.

KNIGHT, Sir Arthur (William), Kt 1975; Chairman, National Enterprise Board, 1979–80; Chairman, Courtaulds Ltd, 1975–79; *b* 29 March 1917; *s* of Arthur Frederick Knight and Emily Scott; *m* 1st, 1945, Beatrice Joan Osborne (*née* Oppenheim) (*d* 1968); one *s* three *d*; 2nd, 1972, Sheila Elsie Whiteman. *Educ:* Tottenham County Sch.; London Sch. of Economics (evening student) (BCom; Hon. Fellow 1984). J. Sainsbury, Blackfriars, 1933–38; LSE, Dept of Business Admin (Leverhulme Studentship), 1938–39; Courtaulds, 1939. Served War, Army, 1940–46. Courtaulds, 1946–79: apptd Dir, 1958; Finance Dir, 1961. Non-exec. Director: Pye Holdings, 1972–75; Rolls-Royce (1971), 1973–78; Richard Thomas & Baldwin, 1966–67; Dunlop Holdings, 1981–84. Member: Council of Manchester Business Sch., 1964–71; Cttee for Arts and Social Studies of Council for Nat. Academic Awards, 1965–71; Commn of Enquiry into siting of Third London Airport, 1968–70; Council of Industry for Management Educn, 1970–73; Finance Cttee, RIIA, 1971–75; Council, RIIA, 1975–85; Court of Governors, London Sch. of Economics, 1971–94; Economic Cttee, CBI, 1965–72; Cairncross (Channel Tunnel) Cttee, 1974–75; NIESR Exec. Cttee, 1976–96; BOTB, 1978–79; The Queen's Award Adv. Cttee, 1981–86; Cttee on Fraud Trials, 1984–85. *Publications:* Private Enterprise and Public Intervention: the Courtauld experience, 1974; various papers. *Recreations:* walking, music, reading. *Address:* Charlton End, Singleton, West Sussex PO18 0HX. *Club:* Reform.

KNIGHT, Prof. Bernard Henry, CBE 1993; MD, FRCPath; novelist; consultant in forensic medicine; Consultant Pathologist to Home Office, 1965–96; Professor of Forensic Pathology, University of Wales College of Medicine, 1980–96, now Emeritus; *b* 3 May 1931; *s* of Harold Ivor Knight and Doris (*née* Lawes); *m* 1955, Jean Gwenllian Ogborne; one *s*. *Educ:* Univ. of Wales (BCh, MD); MRCPath 1964, FRCPath 1966; DMJ (Path) 1967; MRCP 1983. Called to the Bar, Gray's Inn, 1967. Captain RAMC, Malaya, 1956–59. Lecturer in Forensic Medicine: Univ. of London, 1959–61; Univ. of Wales, 1961–65; Sen. Lectr, Forensic Med., Univ. of Newcastle, 1965–68; Sen. Lectr, then Reader of Forensic Pathology, Univ. of Wales Coll. Med., 1968–80. Hon. Consultant Pathologist, Cardiff Royal Infirmary, 1968–96. Vis. Prof., Univs of Hong Kong, Kuwait, Malaya and Guangzhou (China). Mem., Home Office Policy Adv. Cttee in Forensic Pathology; Chm., Forensic Sub-Cttee and Bd Examnrs, RCPath, 1990–93; Mem., GMC, 1979–94. President: Brit. Assoc. Forensic Med., 1991–93; Forensic Science Soc., 1988–90; Vice-Pres., Internat. Acad. Legal Med., 1980–. Hon. FRSocMed 1994. Hon. Mem., German, Finnish and Hungarian Socs of Forensic Med. Hon. DSc Glamorgan, 1995; Hon. LLD Wales, 1998; Hon. MD Turku, Finland, 2000; Hon. PhD Tokyo, 2000. GSM Malaya, 1956. *Publications: fiction:* The Lately Deceased, 1961; The Thread of Evidence, 1963; Russian Roulette, 1968; Policeman's Progress, 1969; Tiger at Bay, 1970; Deg y Dragwyddoldeb (Welsh), 1972; Edyfyn Brau (Welsh), 1973; Lion Rampant, 1973; The Expert, 1975; Prince of America, 1977; The Sanctuary Seeker, 1998; The Poisoned Chalice, 1998; Crowner's Quest, 1999; The Awful Secret, 2000; The Tinner's Corpse, 2000; The Grim Reaper, 2001; *biography:* Autopsy: the memoirs of Milton Helpern, 1977; *non-fiction:* Murder, Suicide or Accident, 1965; Discovering the Human Body, 1980; *medical textbooks:* Legal Aspects of Medical Practice, 1972, 5th edn 1992; Forensic Radiology, 1982; Sudden Infant Death, 1982; Post-mortem Technician's Handbook, 1983; Forensic Medicine for Lawyers, 1984, 2nd edn 1998; Forensic Medicine, 1985; (ed) Simpson's Forensic Medicine, 9th edn 1985, 11th edn 1996; Coroner's Autopsy, 1985; Forensic Pathology, 1991, 2nd edn 1996; Estimation of the Time of Death, 1995, 2nd edn 2001. *Recreation:* writing. *Address:* 26 Millwood, Llysfaen, Cardiff CF14 0TL. *T:* (029) 2075 2798.

KNIGHT, Brian Joseph; QC 1981; **His Honour Judge Knight;** a Circuit Judge, since 1998; Business List Judge, Central London County Court, since 1998; *b* 5 May 1941; *s* of Joseph Knight and Vera Lorraine Knight (*née* Docksey); *m* 1967, Cristina Karen Wang Nobrega de Lima. *Educ:* Colbayns High Sch., Clacton; University Coll. London. LLB 1962, LLM 1963. FCIArb 1995. Called to the Bar, Gray's Inn, 1964, *ad eundem* Lincoln's Inn, 1979; called to the Bar of Hong Kong, 1978, of Northern Ireland, 1979; a Recorder, 1991–98. Asst Parly Boundary Comr, 1992. *Address:* Central London County Court, 26–29 Park Crescent, W1N 4HT. *T:* (020) 7917 7889. *Club:* Garrick.

KNIGHT, Edmund Alan; Commissioner of Customs and Excise, 1971–77; *b* 17 June 1919; *s* of Arthur Philip and Charlotte Knight; *m* 1953, Annette Ros Grimmitt (*d* 1998); one *d*. *Educ:* Drayton Manor Sch.; London Sch. of Economics. Entered Exchequer and Audit Dept, 1938; HM Customs and Excise, 1948; Asst Sec., 1957; Sec. to Cttee on Turnover Taxation, 1963–64; seconded to Inland Revenue, 1969–71; returned to Customs and Excise, 1971; Eur. Affairs Adviser to BAT Co., 1978–85; consultant on indirect taxation, 1985–87. Mem., SITPRO Bd, 1971–76. *Recreations:* local history and environment, gardening. *Address:* 40 Park Avenue North, Harpenden, Herts AL5 2ED. *Club:* Royal Commonwealth Society.

KNIGHT, Dr Geoffrey Wilfred; retired; Regional Medical Officer, North West Thames Regional Health Authority, 1973–76; *b* 10 Jan. 1920; *s* of Wilfred Knight and Ida Knight; *m* 1944, Christina Marion Collins Scott; one *s* one *d*. *Educ:* Leeds Univ. Med. Sch. MB, ChB, MD, DPH (Chadwick Gold Medal). County Med. Officer of Health, Herts, 1962–73. Formerly: Governor, Nat. Inst. of Social Work; Member: Personal Social Services Council; Central Midwives Bd; Exec. Cttee, Child Health Bureau; Adv. Panel, Soc. for Health Educn; formerly Mem., Govt Techn. and Sci. Cttee on Disposal of Toxic Wastes. *Recreations:* painting, golf. *Address:* 114 20655 88th Avenue, Langley, BC V1M 2M5, Canada.

KNIGHT, Rt Hon. Gregory; PC 1995; MP (C) Yorkshire East, since 2001; writer, business consultant and solicitor; *b* 4 April 1949; *s* of George Knight and late Isabella Knight (*née* Bell). *Educ:* Alderman Newton's Grammar School, Leicester; College of Law, Guildford. Self employed solicitor, 1973–83. Member: Leicester City Council, 1976–79; Leicestershire County Council, 1977–83 (Chm., Public Protection Cttee). MP (C) Derby North, 1983–97; contested (C) same seat, 1997. PPS to the Minister of State: Home Office, 1987; Foreign Office, 1988–89; an Asst Govt Whip, 1989–90; a Lord Comr of HM Treasury, 1990–93; Dep. Govt Chief Whip and Treas. of HM Household, 1993–96; Minister of State, DTI, 1996–97. Vice Chm., Cons. Candidates' Assoc., 1998–. Dir, Leicester Theatre Trust, 1979–85 (Chm., Finance Cttee, 1982–83). *Publications:* (jtly) Westminster Words, 1988; Honourable Insults: a century of political insult, 1990; Parliamentary Sauce: more political insults, 1992; Right Honourable Insults, 1998; pamphlets and articles for law publications. *Recreation:* driving and collecting classic cars. *Club:* Bridlington Conservative.

KNIGHT, Sir Harold (Murray), KBE 1980; DSC 1945; *b* 13 Aug. 1919; *s* of W. H. P. Knight, Melbourne; *m* 1951, Gwenyth Catherine Pennington; four *s* one *d*. *Educ:* Scotch Coll., Melbourne; Melbourne Univ. Commonwealth Bank of Australia, 1936–40. AIF (Lieut), 1940–43; RANVR (Lieut), 1943–45. Commonwealth Bank of Australia, 1946–55; Asst Chief, Statistics Div., Internat. Monetary Fund, 1957–59; Reserve Bank of Australia: Research Economist, 1960–62; Asst Manager, Investment Dept, 1962–64, Manager, 1964–68; Dep. Governor and Dep. Chm. of Board, 1968–75; Governor and Chm. of Bd, 1975–82. Chairman: Mercantile Mutual Hldgs, 1985–89; IBJ Australia Bank Ltd, 1985–92; Dir, Western Mining Corp., 1982–91. Mem., Police Bd of NSW, 1988–89, 1991–93. Mem. Council, Macquarie Univ., 1990–92. Pres., Scripture Union, NSW, 1983–. *Publication:* Introducción al Analisis Monetario (Spanish), 1959. *Address:* 4 Tunks Street, Waverton, NSW 2060, Australia.

KNIGHT, James Philip, (Jim); MP (Lab) Dorset South, since 2001; *b* 6 March 1965; *s* of Philip Knight and Hilary Howlett; *m* 1989, Anna Wheatley; one *s* one *d*. *Educ:* Eltham Coll., London; Fitzwilliam Coll., Cambridge (BA Hons Geog. and Social and Pol Sci.). Worker, Works Theatre Co-operative Ltd, 1986–88; Manager, Central Studio Arts Centre, 1988–90; Dir, W Wilts Arts Centre Ltd, 1990–91; Dentons Directories Ltd: Sales Exec., 1991–96; Gen. Manager, 1997–98; Dir, 1998–2000; Prodn Manager, 2000–01. *Recreations:* cooking, tennis, watching Arsenal and Weymouth Football Clubs, literature. *Address:* (constituency office) Winfrith Technology Centre, Dorset DT2 8DU. *T:* (01305) 853408.

KNIGHT, Jeffrey Russell, FCA; Chief Executive, The Stock Exchange, 1982–89; *b* 1 Oct. 1936; *s* of Thomas Edgar Knight and Ivy Cissie Knight (*née* Russell); *m* 1959, Judith Marion Delver Podger; four *d*. *Educ:* Bristol Cathedral Sch.; St Peter's Hall, Oxford (MA). Chartered Accountant, 1966; The Stock Exchange, subseq. Internat. Stock Exchange, 1967–90: Head of Quotations Dept, 1973; Dep. Chief Executive, 1975. Member: City Company Law Cttee, 1974–80; Dept of Trade Panel on Company Law Revision, 1980–84; Accounting Standards Cttee, 1982–89; Special Adviser to Dept of Trade, 1975–81; Adviser to Council for the Securities Industry, 1978–85; UK Delegate: to EEC Working Parties; to Internat. Fedn of Stock Exchanges, 1973–90 (Chm., Task Force on Transnational Settlement, 1987–91); to Fedn of Stock Exchanges in EEC, 1974–90 (Chm., Wking Cttee, 1980–90); to Internat. Orgn of Securities Commns, 1987–91 (Chm. Wkg Party on Capital Adequacy). *Recreations:* cricket, music. *Address:* Lordsmeade, Hurtmore Road, Godalming, Surrey GU7 2DY. *T:* (01483) 424399. *Clubs:* Brooks's, MCC.

KNIGHT, Maureen R.; *see* Rice-Knight.

KNIGHT, Sir Michael (William Patrick), KCB 1983 (CB 1980); AFC 1964; Chairman, Cranfield Aerospace Ltd, since 2000; *b* 23 Nov. 1932; *s* of William and Dorothy Knight; *m* 1967, Patricia Ann (*née* Davies); one *s* two *d*. *Educ:* Leek High Sch.; Univ. of Liverpool (BA Hons 1954; Hon. DLitt 1985). MBIM 1977; FRAeS 1984. Univ. of Liverpool Air Sqn, RAFVR, 1951–54; commnd RAF, 1954; served in Transport and Bomber Comds, and in Middle and Near East Air Forces, 1956–63; Comd No 32 Sqn, RAF Akrotiri, 1961–63; RAF Staff Coll., 1964; Min. of Aviation, 1965–66; Comd Far East Strike Wing, RAF Tengah, 1966–69; Head of Secretariat, HQ Strike Comd, 1969–70; Mil. Asst to Chm., NATO Mil. Cttee, 1970–73; Comd RAF Laarbruch, 1973–74; RCDS, 1975; Dir of Ops (Air Support), MoD, 1975–77; SASO, HQ Strike Command/DCS (Ops & Intelligence) HQ UK Air Forces, 1977–80; AOC No 1 Gp, 1980–82; Air Mem. for Supply and Organisation, 1983–86; UK Military Rep. to NATO, 1986–89; Air ADC to the Queen, 1986–89 (ADC, 1973–74); retd in rank of Air Chief Marshal, 1989; commnd Flying Officer, RAFVR (Trng Br.), 1989. Adjunct Prof., Internat. Peace and Security, Carnegie Mellon Univ., Pittsburgh, 1989–95. Dep. Chm., 1994–95, Chm., 1995–2001, Cobham plc; Chm., Page Gp Hldgs Ltd, 1996–2000; Director: Craigwell Research, 1990–; RAFC Co. Ltd, 1993–; SBAC (Farnborough) Ltd, 1996–; non-executive Director: FR Group plc, 1990–94; Page Aerospace Gp, 1991–96; Smiths Industries Aerospace and Defence Systems Group, 1992–95; Network Orgn Ltd, 2001–; Assoc., JGW Associates Ltd, 1989–; Chm., Northern Devon Healthcare NHS Trust, 1991–94. Mem., Internat. Adv. Bd, British/Amer. Business Council, 1995–. Mem., IISS, 1968–; Member Council: RUSI, 1984–87; The Air League, 1990– (Chm., 1992–98; Pres., 1998–); SBAC, 1995–99; Pres., Council, NAAFI, 1984–86; Vice-Pres., Atlantic Council of UK, 1994–. Chm., N Devon Family Support Service, Leonard Cheshire Foundn, 1989–91; Mem., Management Cttee, Westmead Cheshire Home, 1989–92; Devon County Rep., RAF Benev. Fund, 1990–; RAF Pres., 1991–97, Sen. Pres., 1997–2000, Officers' Assoc.; President: Aircrew Assoc., 1992–97; Buccaneer Aircrew Assoc., 1994–; No 32 (The Royal) Sqn Assoc., 1997–; Vice-President: Royal Internat. Air Tattoo, 1991–; The Youth Trust, 1994–98; Guild of Aviation Artists, 1997–; Patron: Bournemouth Red Arrows Assoc., 1997–; Vulcan Restoration Appeal, 2000–; Vice-Patron, Yorks Air Mus., 1997–; Trustee: RAF Central Fund, 1983–86; RAF Mus., 1983–86; Exmoor Calvert Trust, 1999– (Chm., 2000–). Gov. and Council Mem., Taunton Sch., 1987–2000; Mem., Univ. of Liverpool Develt Team, 1986–. Rugby Football Union: Mem. Cttee, 1977–92; Mem. Exec. Cttee, 1989–92; Chm., Internat. Sub Cttee, 1987–90; Chm., Forward Planning Sub Cttee, 1990–92. President: RAF Rugby Union, 1985–89 (Chm., 1975–78); Combined Services RFC, 1987–89 (Chm., 1977–79); RAF Lawn Tennis Assoc., 1984–86; Vice-President: Leek RUFC, 1959–; Crawshay's Welsh RFC, 1997–; Penguin Internat. RFC, 2001–; Mem., Staffs Co. Rugby Union, 1969–. FRGS 1994 (Mem. Council, 1995–97); FRSA 1994. Liveryman, GAPAN, 1993– (Upper Freeman, 1990–93); Freeman, City of London, 1989. *Publications:* (contrib.) War in the Third Dimension, 1986; Strategic Offensive Air Power and Technology, 1989; articles in prof. pubns, 1975–. *Recreations:* Rugby football, lesser sports, music, writing, after-dinner speaking. *Address:* c/o National Westminster Bank, Leek, Staffs. *Clubs:* Royal Air Force (Vice-Pres., 1983–), Colonels (founder); Saunton Golf.

KNIGHT, Nicholas David Gordon; photographer; Director, N. K. Image Ltd, since 1998; *b* 24 Nov. 1958; *s* of Michael A. G. Knight and Beryl Rose Knight; *m* 1995, Charlotte Esme Wheeler; one *s* two *d*. *Educ:* Hinchingbrooke Comprehensive Sch., Huntingdon; Chelsea Coll., London Univ.; Bournemouth and Poole Coll. of Art (PQE Dip. in Art and Design (Distinction) 1982; Hon. Fellow, 1998). Commissioning Picture Editor, ID magazine, 1990; Photographer, Vogue, 1995–. *Publications:* Skinhead, 1982; Nicknight, 1994; Flora, 1997. *Recreations:* architecture, natural history. *T:* (020) 8940 1086.

KNIGHT, Dr Peter Clayton, CBE 1995; Vice-Chancellor, University of Central England in Birmingham, since 1992 (Director, Birmingham Polytechnic, 1985–92); *b* 8 July 1947; *s* of Norman Clayton Knight and Vera Catherine Knight; *m* 1977, Catherine Mary (*née* Ward); one *s* one *d*. *Educ:* Bishop Vesey's Grammar Sch., Sutton Coldfield; Univ. of York (BA 1st cl. Hons Physics; DPhil). SRC Studentship, 1968; Asst Teacher, Plymstock Comprehensive Sch., 1971; Plymouth Polytechnic: Lectr, 1972; Sen. Lectr, 1974; Head of Combined Studies, 1981; Dep. Dir, Lancashire Polytechnic, 1982–85. Nat. Pres., NATFHE, 1977; Chm., SRHE, 1987–89; Member: Burnham Cttee of Further Educn, 1976–81; Working Party on Management of Higher Educn, 1977; Nat. Adv. Body on Public Sector Higher Educn, 1982–85; PCFC, 1989–93; Polytechnic and Colleges Employers Forum, 1989–94; Teacher Training Agency, 1994–2000. Mem., Focus Housing Assoc., 1991–; Chm., Focus Housing Gp, 1996–. DUniv York, 1991; Hon. DSc Aston, 1997. *Publications:* articles, chapters and reviews in learned jls on educnl policy, with particular ref. to higher educn. *Recreations:* middle-distance running, flying light aircraft. *Address:* Sandy Lodge, Sandy Lane, Brewood, Staffs ST19 9ET. *T:* (01902) 851339.

KNIGHT, Prof. Peter Leonard, DPhil; FRS 1999; FInstP; Professor of Quantum Optics, since 1988, and Head of the Quantum Optics and Laser Science (formerly Laser Optics and Spectroscopy) Group, since 1992, Physics Department, Imperial College of Science, Technology and Medicine, University of London; *b* 12 Aug. 1947; s of Joseph and Eva Knight; *m* 1965, Christine Huckle; two *s* one *d*. *Educ:* Bedford Modern Sch.; Sussex Univ. (BSc, DPhil). FInstP 1991. Research Associate, Univ. of Rochester, NY, 1972–74; SRC Res. Fellow, Sussex Univ., 1974–76; Jubilee Res. Fellow, RHC, 1976–78; SERC Advanced Fellow: RHC, 1978–79; Imperial Coll., 1979–83; Lectr, 1983–87, Reader, 1987–88, Imperial Coll. Mem., SERC Atomic and Molecular Physics Sub Cttee, 1987–90; Co-ordinator, SERC Nonlinear Optics Initiative, 1989–92 (Chm., Prog. Adv. Gp, 1992–95). Chm., Quantum Electronics Div., European Physical Soc., 1988–92; Pres., Physics Sect., BAAS, 1994–95; Dir, Optical Soc. of America, 1999– (Fellow 1996). MAE 2001; Corresp. Mem., Mexican Acad. of Scis, 2000. Hon. DSc: Nat. Inst. for Astronomy, Optics and Electronics, Mexico, 1998; Slovak Acad. of Scis, 2000. Parsons Meml Lectr, Royal Soc. and Inst. of Physics, 1991; Humboldt Res. Award, Alexander von Humboldt Foundn, 1993; Einstein Medal and Prize for Laser Science, Soc. of Optical and Quantum Electronics and Eastman Kodak Co., 1996; Thomas Young Medal and Prize, Inst. of Physics, 1999. Editor: Jl of Modern Optics, 1987–; Contemporary Physics, 1993–. *Publications:* Concepts of Quantum Optics, 1983; papers in Phys. Rev., Phys. Rev. Letters and other jls. *Recreations:* traditional music, walking. *Address:* Blackett Laboratory, Imperial College of Science, Technology and Medicine, SW7 2BZ. *T:* (020) 7594 7727.

KNIGHT, Roger David Verdon; Secretary and Chief Executive, Marylebone Cricket Club, since 1994; *b* 6 Sept. 1946; *s* of late David Verdon Knight and Thelma Patricia Knight; *m* 1971, Christine Ann McNab (*née* Miln); one *s* one *d*. *Educ:* Dulwich Coll.; St Catharine's Coll., Cambridge (BA Modern and Medieval Langs 1969; MA 1972; DipEd 1970). Assistant Master: Eastbourne Coll., 1970–78; Dulwich Coll., 1978–83; Housemaster, Cranleigh Sch., 1983–90; Headmaster, Worksop Coll., 1990–93. Professional cricketer (summers only): Gloucestershire, 1971–75; Sussex, 1976–77; Surrey, 1978–84 (Captain, 1978–83). Vice-Chm., SE Region, Sports Council, 1985–90; Chm. Management Cttee, SE Region, Centres of Excellence, 1987–90; Member: Cricket Cttee, Surrey CCC, 1987–90; MCC Cttee, 1989–92; HMC Sports Sub-Cttee, 1991–93; ICC Develt Cttee, 1996–; Mgt Bd, ECB, 1997–; Council, London Playing Fields Soc., 1998–; Pres., European Cricket Fedn, 1994–97. Governor: TVS Trust, 1987–92; Rendcomb Coll., 1995–99; King's Sch., Taunton, 1998–. *Recreations:* cricket, tennis, bridge, piano music, 17th Century French literature. *Address:* MCC, Lord's Ground, NW8 8QN.

KNIGHT, Dr Roger John Beckett; Visiting Professor of Naval History, University of Greenwich, since 2000; *b* 11 April 1944; *s* of John Beckett Knight and Alyson Knight (*née* Nunn); *m* 1st, 1968, Elizabeth Magowan (marr. diss. 1980); two *s*; 2nd, 1998, Jane Hamilton-Eddy. *Educ:* Tonbridge Sch.; Trinity Coll., Dublin (MA); Sussex Univ. (PGCE); University Coll. London (PhD). Asst Master, Haberdashers' Aske's Sch., Elstree, 1972–73; National Maritime Museum: Dep. Custodian of Manuscripts, 1974–77, Custodian, 1977–80; Dep. Head, Printed Books and Manuscripts Dept, 1980–84; Head, Inf. Project Gp, 1984–86; Head, Documentation Div., 1986–88; Chief Curator, 1988–93; Dep. Dir, 1993–2000. Member: Council, Soc. for Nautical Research, 1977–81 (Vice-Pres., 1993–); Council, Navy Records Soc., 1974– (Vice-Pres., 1980–84). *Publications:* Guide to the Manuscripts in the National Maritime Museum, vol. 1, 1977, vol. 2, 1980; (with Alan Frost) The Journal of Daniel Paine 1794–1797, 1983; Portsmouth Dockyard Papers 1774–1783: the American War, 1987; (ed jtly) British Naval Documents 1204–1960, 1993; articles, reviews in jls. *Recreations:* sailing, cricket, music. *Address:* Greenwich Maritime Institute, University of Greenwich, Old Royal Naval College, Greenwich, SE10 9LS. *T:* (020) 8331 7688. *Clubs:* Athenæum; West Wittering Sailing.

KNIGHT, Terence Gordon, FRICS; Partner, Weatherall Green & Smith, since 1976 (Senior Partner, 1992–98); *b* 1 June 1944; *s* of Albert Henry and Eileen Doris Knight; *m* 1968, Gillian Susan West; two *s*. *Educ:* St Paul's Sch. FRICS 1976. Weatherall Green & Smith, Chartered Surveyors, 1962–. Liveryman, Chartered Surveyors' Co., 1988. *Recreations:* golf, walking. *Address:* Weatherall Green & Smith, Norfolk House, 31 St James's Square, SW1Y 4JR. *T:* (020) 7338 4200. *Clubs:* Naval and Military; Worplesdon Golf.

KNIGHT, Warburton Richard, CBE 1987; Director of Educational Services, Bradford Metropolitan District Council, 1974–91; *b* 2 July 1932; *s* of late Warburton Henry Johnston and Alice Gweneth Knight; *m* 1961, Pamela Ann (*née* Hearmon); two *s* one *d*. *Educ:* Trinity Coll., Cambridge (MA). Teaching in Secondary Modern and Grammar Schs in Middlesex and Huddersfield, 1956–62; joined West Riding Educn Authority, 1962; Asst Dir for Secondary Schs, Leics, 1967; Asst Educn Officer for Sec. Schs and later for Special and Social Educn in WR, 1970. Hon. DLitt Bradford, 1992. *Recreations:* walking, choral music, travel. *Address:* Thorner Grange, Sandhills, Thorner, Leeds LS14 3DE. *T:* (0113) 289 2356. *Club:* Royal Over-Seas League.

KNIGHT, William John Langford; Senior Partner, Simmons & Simmons, 1996–2001; *b* 11 Sept. 1945; *s* of William Knight and Gertrude Alice Knight; *m* 1973, Stephanie Irina Williams; one *s* one *d*. *Educ:* Sir Roger Manwood's Sch., Sandwich; Bristol Univ. (LLB). Admitted solicitor, 1969; joined Simmons & Simmons, 1967; Partner, 1973; i/c Hong Kong Office, 1979–82; Head, Corporate Dept, 1994–96. Mem. Council, Lloyd's, 2000–. Liveryman, City of London Solicitors' Co. FRSA. *Publication:* The Acquisition of Private Companies and Business Assets, 1975, 7th edn 1997. *Recreations:* riding, photography, Arsenal FC. *Clubs:* Travellers; Hong Kong (Hong Kong).

KNIGHT SMITH, Ian; *see* Smith.

KNIGHTLEY; *see* Finch-Knightley.

KNIGHTLEY, Sharman; *see* Macdonald, S.

KNIGHTON, Dr Tessa Wendy; writer; Editor, Early Music, since 1992 (Assistant Editor, 1988–91); Fellow, Clare College, Cambridge, since 1996; *b* 31 March 1957; *d* of Geoffrey Morris Knighton and (Margaret) Wendy Knighton; *m* 1984, Ivor Bolton, *qv*; one *s*. *Educ:* Felixstowe Coll., Suffolk; Clare Coll., Cambridge (MA 1980; PhD 1984). Jun. Res. Fellow, Lady Margaret Hall, Oxford, 1982–84; freelance writer and editor, 1984–; Lectr, Faculty of Music, Cambridge Univ., 1991–93; Res. Associate, RHBNC, Univ. of London, 1993–99; Leverhulme Res. Asst, Faculty of Music, Univ. of Cambridge, 2000–. Artistic Dir, Lufthansa Fest. of Baroque Music, 1986–97; Early Music Critic: Gramophone, 1988–; The Times, 1995–; radio broadcasts. *Publications:* (ed jtly) Companion to Medieval and Renaissance Music, 1992; Música y Músicos en la Corte de Fernando de Aragón 1474–1516, 2000; (jtly) Felipe II y la Música, 2001; articles in Early Music History, Early Music, Plainsong and Medieval Music, Revista de Musicología, Renaissance Studies, Artigrama, etc. *Recreations:* wine, walking, whippets, song. *Address:* Clare College, Cambridge CB2 1TL. *T:* (01223) 333243.

KNIGHTON, William Myles, CB 1981; Principal Establishment and Finance Officer, Department of Trade and Industry, 1986–91; *b* 8 Sept. 1931; *s* of late George Harry Knighton, OBE, and Ella Knighton (*née* Stroud); *m* 1957, Brigid Helen Carrothers; one *s* one *d*. *Educ:* Bedford School; Peterhouse, Cambridge (MA). Asst Principal, Min. of Supply, 1954; Principal, Min. of Aviation, 1959; Cabinet Office, 1962–64; Principal Private Sec. to Minister of Technology, 1966–68; Asst Sec., Min. of Technology, subseq. DTI and Dept of Trade, 1967–74; Under Sec., 1974–78, Dep. Sec., 1978–83, Dept of Trade; Dep. Sec., Dept of Transport, 1983–86. *Publication:* (with D. E. Rosenthal) National Laws and International Commerce, 1982. *Recreations:* gardening, hill-walking, music, reading. *Address:* Court Green, St Anne's Hill, Midhurst, W Sussex GU29 9NN. *T:* (01730) 817860. *Club:* Oxford and Cambridge.

KNIGHTS, family name of **Baron Knights**.

KNIGHTS, Baron *cr* 1987 (Life Peer), of Edgbaston in the County of West Midlands; **Philip Douglas Knights;** Kt 1980; CBE 1976 (OBE 1971); QPM (Dist. Service) 1964; DL; Chief Constable, West Midlands Police, 1975–85; *b* 3 Oct. 1920; *s* of Thomas James Knights and Ethel Knights; *m* 1945, Jean Burman. *Educ:* King's Sch., Grantham. Lincolnshire Constabulary: Police Cadet, 1938–40; Constable, 1940. Served War, RAF, 1943–45. Sergeant, Lincs Constab., 1946; seconded to Home Office, 1946–50; Inspector, Lincs Constab., 1953, Supt 1955, Chief Supt 1957. Asst Chief Constable, Birmingham City Police, 1959; seconded to Home Office, Dep. Comdt, Police Coll., 1962–66; Dep. Chief Constable, Birmingham City Police, 1970; Chief Constable, Sheffield and Rotherham Constab., 1972–74; Chief Constable, South Yorks Police, 1974–75. Winner of Queen's Police Gold Medal Essay Competition, 1965. Mem., Lord Devlin's Cttee on Identification Procedures, 1974–75. Pres., Assoc. of Chief Police Officers, 1978–79. Member: Council, Univ. of Aston, 1985–98; Adv. Council, Cambridge Univ. Inst. of Criminology, 1986–. CIMgt. DL W Midlands, 1985. Hon. DSc Aston, 1996. *Recreations:* sport, gardening. *Address:* House of Lords, SW1A 0PW. *Club:* Royal Over-Seas League.

KNIGHTS, Laurence James W.; *see* West-Knights.

KNIGHTS, Rosemary Margaret; Chief Executive, Warrington Hospital NHS Trust, 1993–98; *b* 2 Nov. 1945; *d* of Donald and Margaret Robson; *m* 1983, Michael A. Knights. *Educ:* Houghton-le-Spring Grammar School; Coll. of Nursing, Sunderland AHA. RGN, OND. Clinical nursing career, 1962–75 (Ward Sister posts, Sunderland and Harrogate); Nursing Officer, Harrogate, 1975–78; Sen. Nursing Officer, North Tees, Stockton, 1978–80; Dir of Nursing, Central Manchester HA, 1981–85; Unit Gen. Manager and Dist Nursing Officer, Manchester Royal Eye Hosp., 1985–88; Regl Nursing Officer, 1988–90, Dep. Chief Exec., 1989–91, Mersey RHA; Exec. Dir, NHS Mgt Exec. Trust Monitoring Unit (NW), 1991–93. Mem., S Manchester HA, 1983–88; Sec. and Chief Exec., Ophthalmic Nursing Bd, 1983–88. *Publications:* articles in nursing and health service papers. *Recreations:* music (piano; Friends of Hallé), fashion. *Address:* 21 Crossfield Drive, Worsley, Manchester M28 1GP. *Club:* Soroptomist International (Manchester).

KNILL, Sir John (Lawrence), Kt 1994; PhD, DSc; FREng, FICE; Chairman, SAUL Trustee Co., since 1997; Professor of Engineering Geology, Imperial College of Science, Technology and Medicine, University of London, 1973–93, now Emeritus, and Senior Research Fellow, since 1993; *b* 22 Nov. 1934; *s* of late William Cuthbert Knill and Mary (*née* Dempsey); *m* 1957, Diane Constance Judge; one *s* one *d*. *Educ:* Whitgift Sch.; Imperial Coll. of Science and Technol. (BSc, ARCS 1955; PhD, DIC 1957; DSc 1981). FIGeol 1985; FICE 1981; FHKIE 1982; FREng (FEng 1991). Geologist, Sir Alexander Gibb & Partners, 1957; Imperial College, London: Asst Lectr, 1957; Lectr, 1959; Reader in Engrg Geology, 1965; Dean of Royal Sch. of Mines, 1980–83; Head of Dept of Geology, 1979–88; Chm., Centre for Remote Sensing, 1984–88; Chm. and Chief Exec., NERC, 1988–93. Member: Council, Nat. Stone Centre, 1984–91; Nature Conservancy Council, 1985–91; Jt Nature Conservation Cttee, 1991–96; Radioactive Waste Management Adv. Cttee, 1985–95 (Chm., 1987–95); Univs Cttee for Non-Teaching Staffs, 1987–88; Resources Bd, BNSC, 1988–93; ABRC, 1988–93; Council, Royal Acad. of Engrg, 1992–95. President: Instn of Geologists, 1981–84; Geologists' Assoc., 1982–84 (Hon. Mem., 1990); Section C, BAAS, 1988–89. Chm., UK Coordinating Cttee for UN Decade for Natural Disaster Reduction, 1992–95. Vis. Prof. in Engrg Hydrogeology, Royal Holloway, Univ. of London, 1996–. Lectures: Manuel Rocha, Lisbon, 1991; F. H. Moore, Sheffield, 1991; Wilson Campbell, Newcastle, 1992; Royal Acad. of Engrg, Southampton, 1992. Membre Correspondant, Société Geologique de Belgique, 1976. Hon. FCGI 1988. Hon. DSc: Kingston, 1992; Exeter, 1995; Hon. DTech: Nottingham Trent, 1996; East London, 1999. Whitaker Medal, IWEM, 1969; Aberconway Medal, Instn of Geologists, 1989; William Smith Medal, Geol Soc., 1995. *Publications:* Industrial Geology, 1978; Geological and Landscape Conservation, 1994; articles on geology of Scotland and engrg geology. *Recreation:* viticulture. *Address:* Highwood Farm, Long Lane, Shaw-cum-Donnington, Newbury, Berks RG14 2TB. *Clubs:* Athenæum, Chaps.

KNILL, Sir Thomas (John Pugin Bartholomew), 5th Bt *cr* 1893, of The Grove, Blackheath, Kent; *b* 23 Aug. 1952; *er s* of Sir John Kenelm Stuart Knill, 4th Bt and Violette Maud Florence Martin (*née* Barnes; *d* 1983); *S* father, 1998; *m* 1977, Kathleen Muszynski. *Heir:* *b* Jenkyn Martin Benedict Stuart Knill, *b* 19 Jan. 1954. *Address:* 6 Jessie Hughes Court, Lower Swainswick, Bath, Somerset BA1 7BE.

KNOLLYS, family name of **Viscount Knollys**.

KNOLLYS, 3rd Viscount *cr* 1911, of Caversham; **David Francis Dudley Knollys;** Baron *cr* 1902; *b* 12 June 1931; *s* of 2nd Viscount Knollys, GCMG, MBE, DFC, and Margaret (*d* 1987), *o d* of Sir Stuart Coats, 2nd Bt; *S* father, 1966; *m* 1959, Hon. Sheelin Virginia Maxwell (granted, 1959, title, rank and precedence of a baron's *d*; which would have been hers had her father survived to succeed to barony of Farnham), *d* of late Lt-Col Hon. Somerset Maxwell, MP and late Mrs Remington Hobbs; three *s* one *d*. *Educ:* Eton. Lt,

Scots Guards, 1951. *Heir:* *s* Hon. Patrick Nicholas Mark Knollys [*b* 11 March 1962; *m* 1998, Mrs Sarah Wright, *o d* of Michael Petch; one *s*]. *Address:* The Bailiff's House, Bramerton Hall Farm, Norwich, Norfolk NR14 7DN.

KNORPEL, Henry, CB 1982; QC 1988; Counsel to the Speaker, House of Commons, 1985–95; *b* 18 Aug. 1924; 2nd *s* of late Hyman and Dora Knorpel; *m* 1953, Brenda Sterling; two *d*. *Educ:* City of London Sch.; Magdalen Coll., Oxford. BA 1945, BCL 1946, MA 1949. Called to Bar, Inner Temple, 1947, Entrance Scholar, 1947–50, Bencher, 1990; practised 1947–52; entered Legal Civil Service as Legal Asst, Min. of Nat. Insce, 1952; Sen. Legal Asst, Min. of Pensions and Nat. Insce, 1958; Law Commn, 1965; Min. of Social Security, 1967; Dept of Health and Social Security: Asst Solicitor, 1968; Principal Asst Solicitor (Under-Sec.), 1971; Solicitor (also to OPCS and Gen. Register Office), 1978–85. Vis. Lecturer: Kennington Coll. of Commerce and Law, 1950–58; Holborn Coll. of Law, Languages and Commerce, 1958–70; Univ. of Westminster (formerly Polytechnic of Central London), 1970–. *Publications:* articles on community law. *Recreation:* relaxing. *Address:* Conway, 32 Sunnybank, Epsom, Surrey KT18 7DX. *T:* (01372) 721394.

KNOTT, Prof. John Frederick, ScD; FRS 1990; FREng; Feeney Professor of Metallurgy and Materials, University of Birmingham, since 1990 (Head, School of Metallurgy and Materials, 1990–96, and Dean of Engineering, 1995–98); *b* Bristol, 9 Dec. 1938; *s* of Fred Knott and Margaret (*née* Chesney); *m* 1st, 1963, Christine Mary Roberts (marr. diss. 1986); two *s*; 2nd, 1990, Susan Marilyn Cooke (*née* Jones); two step *s*. *Educ:* Queen Elizabeth's Hosp., Bristol; Sheffield Univ. (BMet 1st cl. Hons 1959); Cambridge Univ. (PhD 1963; ScD 1991). FIM 1974; FWeldI 1985; FREng (FEng 1988); FIMechE 1994. Res. Officer, Central Electricity Res. Labs, Leatherhead, 1962–67; Cambridge University: Lectr, Dept of Metallurgy, 1967–81; Reader in Mechanical Metallurgy, 1981–90; Churchill College: Goldsmiths' Fellow, Coll. Lectr and Dir of Studies in Metallurgy and Materials Sci., 1967–90; Tutor, 1969–79; Tutor for Advanced Students, 1979–81; Vice-Master, 1988–90; Extra-Ordinary Fellow, 1991–. Member: Nuclear Safety Adv. Cttee, HSE; Technical Adv. Gp on Structural Integrity, Nuclear Power Industries; Materials and Processing Adv. Bd, Rolls-Royce plc; Res. Bd, Welding Inst. Pres., Internat. Congress on Fracture, 1993–97. FRSA. Hon. Professor: Beijing Univ. of Aeronautics and Astronautics, 1992; Xian Jiaotong Univ., 1995. Mem. Governing Body, Shrewsbury Sch., 1996–. Foreign Mem., Acad. of Scis of the Ukraine, 1993. L.B. Pfeil Prize, 1973, Rosenhain Medal, 1978, Metals Soc.; Leslie Holliday Prize, Materials Sci. Club, 1978; Griffith Medal, 1999. *Publications:* Fundamentals of Fracture Mechanics, 1973, 2nd edn 1979; (with P. A. Withey) Fracture Mechanics: worked examples, 1993; many scientific papers in Acta Met., Metal Sci., Met. Trans, Engrg Fracture Mechanics, etc. *Recreations:* bridge, cryptic crosswords, traditional jazz, playing the tenor recorder with enthusiasm rather than skill. *Address:* 54 Evesham Road, Stratford-upon-Avon, Warwickshire CV37 9BA.

KNOTT, Air Vice-Marshal Ronald George, CB 1967; DSO 1944; DFC 1943; AFC 1955 and Bar, 1958; retired 1972; *b* 19 Dec. 1917; *s* of late George and Edith Rose Knott; *m* 1941, Hermione Violet (*née* Phayre); three *s* one *d*. *Educ:* Borden Grammar Sch., Sittingbourne, Kent. No 20 Sqdn RAF, 1938–40; No 5 Flight IAFVR, 1940–41; HQ Coast Defence Wing, Bombay, 1942; No 179 Sqdn, 1943–44; No 524 Sqdn, 1944–45; RAF, Gatow (Ops), 1949–50; OC, RAF Eindhoven, 1950–51; HQ 2nd TAF, 1951–52; RAF Staff Coll., 1952; Flying Trng Comd, 1953–55; Chief Flying Instructor, Central Flying Sch., 1956–58; Air Plans, Air Min., 1959; OC, RAF Gutersloh, 1959–61; ACOS Plans, 2 ATAF, 1962–63; Defence Res. Policy Staff, Min. of Def. 1963; DOR2 (RAF), Min. of Def., 1963–67; SASO, HQ NEAF Cyprus, 1967–70; AOA, HQ Air Support Comd, RAF, 1970–72. *Recreations:* gardening, wine growing. *Address:* Pilgrims Cottage, Charing, Kent TN27 0DR. *T:* (01233) 712723.

KNOWLAND, Raymond Reginald, CBE 1992; Managing Director, British Petroleum, 1990–92; *b* 18 Aug. 1930; *s* of Reginald George Knowland and Marjorie Doris Knowland (*née* Alvis); *m* 1956, Valerie Mary Higgs; three *s*. *Educ:* Bristol Grammar Sch.; Sir John Cass College London. CChem, FRSC 1972. BP Chemicals: specialty plastics and PVC Plant Management, Barry Works, 1957–69; Works Gen. Manager, Barry Works, 1969–75, Baglan Bay Works, 1975–78; Man. Dir, Belgium, 1978–80; Dir, London, 1980–90; Chief Exec. Officer, London, 1983–90. Non-exec. Dir, BSI plc, 1992–99. President: British Plastics Fedn, 1983–84; Assoc. of Petrochemical Producers in Europe, 1985–88; CIA, 1990–92; Vice Pres., SCI, 1993–96. Chm., European Chemical Industry Ecology and Toxicology Centre, 1986–90. Liveryman, Horners' Co., 1987 (Master, 2000, Dep. Master, 2001). *Recreations:* sailing, photography, Rugby football (spectator). *Address:* Heron's Wake, Flowers Hill, Pangbourne, Reading RG8 7BD. *T:* (0118) 984 4576. *Club:* Athenæum.

KNOWLES, Ann; *see* Knowles, P. A.

KNOWLES, Ben; Editor, New Musical Express, since 2000; *b* 29 Aug. 1973; *s* of John and Pat Knowles. *Educ:* Beverley Grammar Sch.; Hertford Coll., Oxford (BA Hons Hist.). Writer: Daily Mirror, 1994–95; Smash Hits, 1995–97; Melody Maker, 1998–2000. *Recreations:* Fulham FC, pubs, horse-racing, rock 'n' roll. *Address:* New Musical Express, 25th Floor, King's Reach Tower, Stamford Street, SE1 9LS. *T:* (020) 7261 6472.

KNOWLES, Sir Charles (Francis), 7th Bt *cr* 1765; architect in private practice, since 1984; *b* 20 Dec. 1951; *s* of Sir Francis Gerald William Knowles, 6th Bt, FRS, and of Ruth Jessie, *d* of late Rev. Arthur Brooke-Smith; *S* father, 1974; *m* 1979, Amanda Louise Margaret, *d* of Lance Bromley, *qv*; two *s*. *Educ:* Marlborough Coll.; Oxford Sch. of Architecture (DipArch 1977; RIBA 1979). Director: Charles Knowles Design Ltd (architects); Richmond Knowles Architects; works include: new Battersea Dogs Home, London and Old Windsor; refurbishment of Bank of England, historic country houses and listed London properties. FRSA. *Recreations:* shooting, travel, piloting light aircraft. *Heir:* *s* (Charles) William (Frederick Lance) Knowles, *b* 27 Aug. 1985. *Address:* Wyndham Croft, Turners Hill, W Sussex RH10 4PS.

KNOWLES, Colin George, PhD; Director of Development and Public Relations, University of Bophuthatswana, 1985–95; Secretary and Trustee, University of Bophuthatswana Foundation, 1985–95; *b* 11 April 1939; *s* of late George William Knowles, Tarleton, Lancs; *m* 1998, Dr Rosalie Marion Lander (*née* Turner); three *d* by former marriages. *Educ:* King George V Grammar Sch., Southport; CEDEP, Fontainebleau, France; Trinity Coll., Delaware, USA (MA 1991; PhD 1994). MInstM 1966; MIPR 1970; Mem. BAIE 1972; FIMgt (FBIM 1972); FPRISA 1993 (MPRISA 1983); APR 1987; AAArb 1991; MSAAIE 1993. Appointed Comr of Oaths, 1991. Joined John Player & Sons, 1960; sales and marketing management appts; Head of Public Relations, 1971–73; joined Imperial Tobacco Ltd, 1973; Hd of Public Affairs, 1973–80; Company Sec., 1979–80. Chairman: Griffin Associates Ltd, 1980–84; Concept Communications (Pty) Ltd (S Africa), 1983–84; Dir, TWS Public Relations (Pty) Ltd (S Africa), 1984–85. Mem. Council, Tobacco Trade Benevolent Assoc., 1975–80; Chm., Bophuthatswana Reg., PRISA, 1988–91. Dir, Bophuthatswana Council for Consumer Affairs, 1991–94. Director: Nottingham Festival Assoc. Ltd, 1969–71; English Sinfonia Orchestra, 1972–80; Midland Sinfonia Concert Soc. Ltd, 1972–80; (also co-Founder) Assoc. for Business Sponsorship of The Arts Ltd, 1975–84 (Chm., 1975–80); Bristol Hippodrome Trust Ltd, 1977–81; Bath Archaeological Trust Ltd, 1978–81; The Palladian Trust Ltd, 1979–82; Mem., Chancellor of Duchy of Lancaster's Cttee of Honour on Business and the Arts, 1980–81. Arts sponsorship initiatives include responsibility for: Internat. Cello Competition (with Tortelier), Bristol, 1975 and 1977; Internat. Conductors Awards, 1978; Pompeii Exhibn, RA, 1976–77; new prodns at Royal Opera House, Covent Garden, at Glyndebourne, and at National Theatre. Governor: Manning Grammar Sch., Nottingham, 1972–73; Clayesmore Sch., Dorset, 1975–85. Chm., St John Ambulance Foundn in Bophuthatswana, 1989–94; Mem. Chapter, Priory of St John, S Africa, 1992–99. Liveryman, Worshipful Co. of Tobacco Pipe Makers and Tobacco Blenders, 1973; Freeman, City of London, 1974. FRSA 1975; FRCSoc 1976. KStJ 1995 (CStJ 1991; OStJ 1977). *Recreations:* reading, travel, country pursuits. *Address:* 15 Standen Park House, Lancaster LA1 3FF; *e-mail:* oakfields@smpanet.com. *Clubs:* Carlton, MCC.

KNOWLES, Sir Durward (Randolph), Kt 1996; OBE 1964; OM (Bahamas) 1996; President, Caribbean Towing Company, since 1982; *b* 2 Nov. 1917; *s* of late Harry Knowles and Charlotte Knowles; *m* 1947, Holly; one *s* two *d*. *Educ:* Queen's Coll., Nassau, Bahamas. Captain of freighters plying in Caribbean, 1942–46; various Captain appts, 1946–52; Harbour Pilot, Nassau, 1952–96. Pres., Island Sand; Vice-Pres., Island Shipping. Bronze Medal for Yachting, 1956 Olympics, Gold Medal, 1964 Olympics. *Relevant Publication:* Driven by the Stars: the story of Durward Knowles, by Douglas Hanks, Jr, 1992. *Recreation:* yachting. *Address:* Winton Highway, PO Box N-1216, Nassau, Bahamas. *Clubs:* Nassau Yacht; Coral Reef Yacht (Coconut Grove, Florida).

KNOWLES, George Peter; Registrar of the Province and Diocese of York, and Archbishop of York's Legal Secretary, 1968–87; *b* 30 Dec. 1919; *s* of Geoffrey Knowles and Mabel Bowman; *m* 1948, Elizabeth Margaret Scott; one *s* two *d*. *Educ:* Clifton Coll., Bristol; Queens' Coll., Cambridge. MA, LLM. Served war, Royal Artillery, 1939–46 (Lieut). Admitted a solicitor, 1948; Chm., York Area Rent Tribunal, 1959; Mem., Mental Health Review Tribunal for Yorkshire Regional Health Authority Area, 1960. *Recreations:* gardening, fishing, wildlife. *Address:* 11 Lang Road, Bishopthorpe, York YO23 2QJ. *T:* (01904) 706443. *Club:* Yorkshire (York).

KNOWLES, Very Rev. Graeme Paul; Dean of Carlisle, since 1999; *b* 25 Sept. 1951; *s* of Grace and Stanley Knowles; *m* 1973, Susan Gail Knowles. *Educ:* Dunstable Grammar Sch., 1963–70; King's Coll. London, 1970–73 (AKC). Ordained deacon, 1974, priest, 1975; Asst Curate, St Peter in Thanet, 1974–79; Precentor and Sen. Curate, Leeds Parish Church, 1979–81; Chaplain and Precentor, 1981–87, Chapter Clerk, 1985–87, Portsmouth Cathedral; Vicar of Leigh Park, 1987–93; Rural Dean of Havant, 1990–93; Archdeacon of Portsmouth, 1993–99. *Recreations:* Victorian and Edwardian songs, the books of E. F. Benson, wine and food. *Address:* The Deanery, Carlisle, Cumbria CA3 8TZ. *T:* (01228) 523335. *Club:* Naval and Military.

KNOWLES, Prof. Jeremy Randall, CBE 1993; FRS 1977; Amory Houghton Professor of Chemistry and Biochemistry (formerly of Chemistry), since 1974, Dean of Faculty of Arts and Sciences, since 1991, Harvard University; *b* 28 April 1935; *s* of late Kenneth Guy Jack Charles Knowles and of Dorothy Helen Swingler; *m* 1960, Jane Sheldon Davis; three *s*. *Educ:* Magdalen College Sch.; Balliol Coll. (Hon. Fellow 1984), Merton Coll. and Christ Church, Oxford (MA, DPhil). Sir Louis Stuart Exhibr, Balliol Coll., Oxford, 1955–59; Harmsworth Schol., Merton Coll., Oxford, and Research Lectr, Christ Church, Oxford, 1960–62; Research Associate, Calif. Inst. of Technology, 1961–62; Fellow of Wadham Coll., Oxf., 1962–74 (Hon. Fellow 1990); Univ. Lectr, Univ. of Oxford, 1966–74. Visiting Prof., Yale Univ., 1969, 1971; Sloan Vis. Prof., Harvard Univ., 1973; Newton-Abraham Vis. Prof., Oxford Univ., 1983–84. Fellow, Amer. Acad. of Arts and Scis, 1982; Foreign Associate, Nat. Acad. of Scis, USA, 1988; Mem., Amer. Philosophical Soc., 1988. Hon. FRSC 1993. Dr *hc* Edinburgh, 1992. Charmian Medal, RSC, 1980; Prelog Medal, ETH, 1989; Bader Award and Cope Scholar Award, 1989, Repligen Award, 1993, Nakanishi Award, 1999, Amer. Chemical Soc.; Davy Medal, Royal Soc., 1991; Robert A. Welch Award in Chemistry, Robert A. Welch Foundn, USA, 1995. *Publications:* research papers and reviews in learned jls. *Address:* 7 Bryant Street, Cambridge, MA 02138, USA. *T:* (617) 8768469.

KNOWLES, Rev. John Geoffrey; Rector, Hutchesons' Grammar School, since 1999; *b* 12 June 1948; *s* of Geoffrey and Jean Knowles; *m* 1974, Roey Wills; three *d*. *Educ:* St Bees Sch.; Univ. of Manchester (BSc Physics); Worcester Coll., Oxford (CertEd); Univ. of London (MSc Nuclear Physics); W Midlands Ministerial Trng Course. Assistant Master: Mill Hill Sch., 1970–75; Wellington Coll., 1975–76; Head of Physics, Watford GS, 1976–84; Vice Master, Queen Elizabeth's GS, Blackburn, 1984–90; Headmaster, King Edward VI Five Ways Sch., Birmingham, 1990–99; ordained deacon 1998, priest 1999; Non-Stipendiary Curate, Holy Trinity, The Lickey, 1998–99. Chief Examr, A-Level Physics (Nuffield), 1990–99. Vice-Chm., 1996–98, Chm., 1998–99, Assoc. Heads of Grant Maintained Schools. Chm. Governors, Kingsmead Sch., 1986–92. Treas., 1976–84, Vice-Chm., 1991–95, Elgar Soc. *Publications:* Elgar's Interpreters on Record, 1978, 2nd edn 1985; (contrib.) Elgar Studies, 1988; (contrib.) This is the Best of Me, 1999. *Recreation:* music. *Address:* Hutchesons' Grammar School, 21 Beaton Road, Glasgow G41 4NW. *T:* (0141) 423 2933.

KNOWLES, Michael; independent political consultant, since 1992; *b* 21 May 1942; *s* of Martin Christopher and Anne Knowles; *m* 1965, Margaret Isabel Thorburn; three *d*. *Educ:* Clapham Coll. RC Grammar Sch. Sales Manager, Export & Home Sales. Mem. (C), 1971–83, Leader, 1974–83, Kingston upon Thames Borough Council. MP (C) Nottingham East, 1983–92; PPS to Minister for Planning and Regional Affairs, 1986, to Minister for Housing and Planning, 1987–88, DoE; Member: Select Cttee on European Legislation, 1984; Select Cttee on Defence, 1990. *Recreations:* walking, history. *Address:* 2 Ditton Reach, Portsmouth Road, Thames Ditton, Surrey KT7 0XB.

KNOWLES, Dr Michael Ernest, CChem, FRSC; FIFST; Director, Scientific and Regulatory Affairs, Greater Europe, Coca-Cola, Brussels, since 1997 (Director, Scientific and Regulatory Affairs (Europe, Middle East and Africa), Coca-Cola International, Brussels, 1992–97); *b* 6 May 1942; *s* of late Ernest Frederick Walter Knowles and Lesley (*née* Lambert); *m* 1st, 1965, Rosalind Mary Griffiths (marr. diss. 1975); two *s*; 2nd, 1994, Alexandra Knowles (*née* Hadjiyianni). *Educ:* Nottingham Univ. (BPharm 1st cl. Hons; PhD). CChem 1969; FRSC 1982; FIFST 1983. ICI Postdoctoral Fellow, Nottingham Univ., 1967–69; Ministry of Agriculture, Fisheries and Food: Food Sci. Unit, Norwich, 1969–74; Scientific Advr, Food Sci. Div., 1974–79; Head, Food Sci. Lab., 1979–85; Head, Food Sci. Div., 1985–89; Chief Scientist (Fisheries and Food), 1989–91. FRSA. *Publications:* series of papers on chemical aspects of food safety in learned jls. *Recreations:* target shooting, walking. *Address:* Avenue du Faucon 28, Rhode-St-Genèse 1640, Belgium. *T:* (2) 3584029. *Clubs:* Strangers (Norwich); Château St Ann (Brussels).

KNOWLES, (Patricia) Ann, (Mrs P. A. Knowles-Foster); North West Regional Development Worker, Marriage Care, since 1997; *b* 31 Oct. 1944; *d* of John and Margaret Miller; *m* 1st, 1964, Leslie John Knowles (*d* 1996); two *s* one *d*; 2nd, 2000, Malcolm Foster. *Educ:* Our Lady's Prep. Sch., Barrow-in-Furness; Our Lady's Convent Sch.; Open Univ. (BA). Reporter: North Western Evening Mail, Barrow, 1962–68; North Somerset Mercury, Clevedon, 1969–70; Western Daily Press, Bristol, 1970–72; Theatre Critic, Evening Star, Burnley, 1973–77; Sub-Editor, Dep. Chief Sub-Editor, News Editor, Burnley Express, 1977–84; Asst Editor, Citizen Publications, Blackburn, 1985–87; Sub-Editor, Keighley News, 1987–89; Group Editor, Herald and Post, Burnley, 1989–90; Editor, The Universe, 1990–95. Member: Nat. Assoc. of Tangent Clubs, 1984–; Soroptimists International, Burnley, 1990–92; Catholic Union of GB, 1991–99; Nat. Bd of Catholic Women, 1994–98. *Publication:* (with Mgr John Furnival) Archbishop Derek Worlock—His Personal Journey, 1997. *Recreations:* gardening, interior decoration, family interests, travel. *Address:* 34 Ball Grove Drive, Colne, Lancs BB8 7HY.

KNOWLES, Peter Francis Arnold, CB 1996; Parliamentary Counsel, since 1991; *b* 10 July 1949; *s* of Sidney Francis Knowles and Patricia Anette Knowles; *m* 1972, Patricia Katharine Clifford; two *s*. *Educ:* Whitgift School, Croydon; University College, Oxford (MA). Called to the Bar, Gray's Inn, 1971. In practice at Chancery Bar, 1973–75; joined Parliamentary Counsel Office, 1975; with Law Commission, 1979–81, 1993–96. *Publications:* (contrib.) Halsbury's Laws of England; The Giulia Coupes 1963–1976. *Recreations:* music, sailing, ski-ing, surfing, classic car restoration. *Address:* Parliamentary Counsel Office, 36 Whitehall, SW1A 2AY.

KNOWLES, Sir Richard (Marchant), Kt 1989; Lord Mayor of Birmingham, 1994–95; Member, Birmingham City Council, 1972–74 and 1978–2000 (Leader, 1984–93); Chairman, Northfield Area Regeneration Initiative, since 1993; *b* 20 May 1917; *s* of William and Charlotte Knowles; *m* 1st, 1941, Dorothy Forster (*d* 1979); one *s*; 2nd, 1981, Anne Little (*née* Macmenemey). *Educ:* village schools in Kent; WEA; technical school. Building industry, 1931–39; served RE, 1940; building and shipbuilding, 1941–50; Labour Organiser, Sevenoaks, Dover, Leeds and Birmingham, 1950–72; Nat. Organiser, Co-op Party, 1971–83. Mem., W Midlands County Council, 1973–77; Chm., Planning Cttee, Birmingham CC, 1972–74, 1980–82. Mem., Policy Cttee, 1974–77, 1984–2000, Sec., Lab Gp, 1992–94, AMA. Dir, Nat. Exhibition Centre Ltd, 1982–. Member: Partnership Adv. Univ. Hosp., 2000–; Council, Birmingham Univ., 1996–; Bd, S Birmingham Coll., 2001–. Hon. LLD Birmingham, 1996. *Publications:* UNIP Election Manual, 1964; ABC of Organisation, 1977; A Voice for your Neighbourhood, 1977; contribs to local govt jls, planning and political pamphlets. *Recreations:* cycling, travel, rough gardening. *Address:* 64 Woodgate Lane, Bartley Green, Birmingham B32 3QY. *T:* (0121) 422 8061.

KNOWLES, Robin St John; QC 1999; a Recorder, since 2000; *b* 7 April 1960; *s* of Norman Richard Knowles and Margaret Mary Knowles (*née* Robinson); *m* 1987, Gill Adams; one *d*. *Educ:* Sir Roger Manwood's Grammar Sch.; Trinity Coll., Cambridge (MA). Called to the Bar, Middle Temple, 1982, Gray's Inn (*ad eundem*); in practice at the Bar, 1983–; Asst Recorder, 1998–2000. Member: Mgt Cttee, Bar Pro Bono Unit, 1996–; Cttee (co-opted), S Eastern Circuit, 1998–; Exec., Commercial Bar Assoc., 1999–; various Bar Council and Commercial Bar Assoc. working parties. *Recreations:* the East End of London, and being with friends and family. *Address:* 3–4 South Square, Gray's Inn, WC1R 5HP. *T:* (020) 7696 9900.

KNOWLES, Timothy; Director, Welsh Water, then Hyder, plc, 1989–99; *b* 17 May 1938; *s* of Cyril William Knowles and Winifred Alice Knowles (*née* Hood); *m* 1967, Gaynor Hallett; one *d*. *Educ:* Bishop Gore Grammar Sch., Swansea. Chartered Accountant. Company Sec./Accountant, Louis Marx & Co. Ltd, 1960–68; Controller, Modco Valenite, 1968–69; HTV Ltd: Company Sec., 1969–78; Financial Dir, 1975–81; Asst Man. Dir, 1981–86; HTV Group plc: Financial Dir, 1976–86; Gp Man. Dir, 1986–88; Finance Dir, Insurance Services Gp, ECGD (for privatisation), 1990–91; Dir, Frost & Reed (Holdings) Ltd, 1985–88. Member: S Wales Electricity Bd, 1981–82; Welsh Water Authority, 1982–89; Disciplinary Cttee, ICAEW, 1993– (Chm. Tribunals, 1996–). Dir, University Hosp. of Wales Healthcare NHS Trust, 1995–99. Chm., CG90, 1994–97. Contested (C) Swansea East, 1966. Mem., Welsh Livery Guild, 1994– (Treas., 2001–). *Recreations:* travel, watching cricket, golf. *Address:* Cae Ffynnon, 12 Ger-y-Llan, St Nicholas, Cardiff CF5 6SY. *T:* (01446) 760726. *Clubs:* Cardiff and County (Cardiff); Glamorgan CC; Cottrell Park Golf.

KNOWLES, Wyn; Editor, Woman's Hour, BBC, 1971–83; *b* 30 July 1923; *d* of Frederick Knowles and Dorothy Ellen Knowles (*née* Harrison). *Educ:* St Teresa's Convent, Effingham; Convents of FCJ in Ware and Switzerland; Polytechnic Sch. of Art, London. Cypher Clerk, War Office, 1941–45. Secretarial work, 1948–57; joined BBC, 1951; Asst Producer, Drama Dept, 1957–60; Woman's Hour: Producer, Talks Dept, 1960–65; Asst Editor, 1965–67; Dep. Editor, 1967–71. *Publication:* (ed with Kay Evans) The Woman's Hour Book, 1981. *Recreations:* travel, cooking, writing, painting.

KNOWLES-FOSTER, (Patricia) Ann; *see* Knowles, P. A.

KNOWLTON, Richard James, CBE 1983; QFSM 1977; HM Chief Inspector of Fire Services (Scotland), 1984–89; *b* 2 Jan. 1928; *s* of Richard John Knowlton and Florence May Humby; *m* 1949, Pamela Vera Horne; one *s*. *Educ:* Bishop Wordsworth's Sch., Salisbury. FIFE. Served 42 Commando RM, 1945. Southampton Fire Bde, 1948; Station Officer, Worcester City and County Fire Bde, 1959; London Fire Brigade: Asst Divl Officer, 1963; Divl Officer, 1965; Divl Comdr, 1967; Winston Churchill Travelling Fellowship, 1969; Firemaster: SW Area (Scotland) Fire Bde, 1971; Strathclyde Fire Bde, 1975–84. Mem., later Chm., Bds, Fire Service Coll. Extended Interview, 1970–81; Mem., Fire Service Coll. Bd, 1978–82; Mem., later Chm., Scottish Fire Services Examinations Panel, 1971–75; Mem., Scottish Fire Service Examinations Bd, 1974–75; Fire Adviser: to Scottish Assoc. of CCs, 1974; to Convention of Scottish Local Authorities, 1975–81; Sec. to Appliances and Equipment Cttee of Chief and Asst Chief Fire Officers Assoc., 1974–81, Pres. of the Assoc., 1980; Chm., Scottish Dist Chief and Asst Chief Fire Officers Assoc., 1977–81; Zone Fire Comdr (Designate), CD for Scotland, 1975–84; Member: Scottish Central Fire Bdes Adv. Council, 1977–81 (Uniform and Personal Equipment Cttee, 1974–82); Jt Cttee on Design and Develt, 1978–82; England and Wales Central Fire Bdes Adv. Council, 1979–81; Chairman: London Branch, Instn of Fire Engineers, 1969; Scottish Assoc., Winston Churchill Fellows, 1979–81; Hazfile Cttee, 1979–81; Vice-Pres., Fire Services Nat. Benevolent Fund, 1981– (Chm. 1980). Mem., Nat. Jt Council for Chief Fire Officers, 1980–82; Mem., later Chm., Management Structures Working Gp of Nat. Jt Council for Local Authority Fire Bdes, 1980–83; British Mem., Admin. Council of European Assoc. of Professional Fire Bde Officers, 1981–85 (Vice Pres., 1984–85). *Address:* 5 Potters Way, Laverstock, Salisbury, Wilts SP1 1PY. *T:* (01722) 326487.

KNOX, family name of **Earl of Ranfurly**.

KNOX, (Alexander) David; CMG 1988; Vice President, International Bank for Reconstruction and Development, 1980–87, retired; *b* 15 Jan. 1925; *s* of James Knox and Elizabeth Maxwell Knox; *m* 1950, Beatrice Lily (*née* Dunell); one *s* two *d*. *Educ:* Univ. of Toronto (BA); London School of Economics and Political Science (Hon. Fellow, 1982). LSE, 1949–63, Reader in Economics, 1955–63; International Bank for Reconstruction and Development (World Bank), 1963–87: Vice President: W Africa, 1980–84; Latin America, 1984–87. Chm., Task Force on Project Quality, African Develt Bank, 1993–94. Member: Bd of Dirs, Liverpool Associates in Tropical Health, 1990–99; Prog. Adv. Panel, SCF, 1993–99; Council, Worldaware, 1994–. *Publications:* Latin American Debt: facing facts, 1990; articles in Economica, OECF Res. Qly (Japan), etc. *Recreations:* opera, walking. *Address:* Knights Barn, Manor Farm Lane, East Hagbourne, Oxon OX11 9ND. *T:* (01235) 817792.

KNOX, Bryce Harry, CB 1986; a Deputy Chairman, and Director General, Internal Taxation Group, Board of Customs and Excise, 1983–88, retired; *b* 21 Feb. 1929; *e s* of late Brice Henry Knox and Rose Hetty Knox; *m* Norma, *d* of late George and Rose Thomas; one *s*. *Educ:* Stratford Grammar Sch.; Nottingham Univ. BA(Econ). Asst Principal, HM Customs and Excise, 1953; Principal, 1958; on loan to HM Treasury, 1963–65; Asst Sec., HM Customs and Excise, 1966; seconded to HM Diplomatic Service, Counsellor, Office of UK Perm. Rep. to European Communities, 1972–74; Under-Sec., 1974, Comr, 1975, HM Customs and Excise. *Address:* 9 Manor Way, Blackheath, SE3 9EF. *T:* (020) 8852 9404. *Clubs:* Reform, MCC.

KNOX, Col Sir Bryce (Muir), KCVO 1990; MC 1944 and Bar, 1944; TD 1947; Lord-Lieutenant of Ayrshire and Arran (formerly County of Ayr), 1974–91 (Vice-Lieutenant, 1970–74); Vice-Chairman, Lindustries Ltd, 1979 (Director, 1953–79); *b* 4 April 1916; *s* of late James Knox, Kilbirnie; *m* 1948, Patricia Mary Dunsmuir (*d* 1989); one *s* one *d*. *Educ:* Stowe; Trinity Coll., Cambridge. Served with Ayrshire (ECO) Yeomanry, 1939–45, N Africa and Italy; CO, 1953–56; Hon. Col, 1969–71; Hon. Col, The Ayrshire Yeomanry Sqdn, Queen's Own Yeomanry, T&AVR, 1971–77; Pres., Lowlands T&AVR, 1978–83. Member, Queen's Body Guard for Scotland, Royal Company of Archers. Pres., RHAS, 1990–91. CStJ. *Publication:* The History of the Eglinton Hunt, 1984. *Recreation:* country sports. *Address:* Martnaham Lodge, by Ayr KA6 6ES. *T:* (01292) 560204.

KNOX, David; *see* Knox, A. D.

KNOX, Sir David (Laidlaw), Kt 1993; *b* 30 May 1933; *s* of late J. M. Knox, Lockerbie and Mrs C. H. C. Knox (*née* Laidlaw); *m* 1980, Mrs Margaret Eva Maxwell, *d* of late A. McKenzie. *Educ:* Lockerbie Academy; Dumfries Academy; London Univ. (BSc (Econ) Hons). Management Trainee, 1953–56; Printing Executive, 1956–62; O&M Consultant, 1962–70. Contested (C): Stechford, Birmingham, 1964 and 1966; Nuneaton, March 1967. MP (C) Leek Div. of Staffs, 1970–83, Staffordshire Moorlands, 1983–97. PPS to Ian Gilmour, Minister of State for Defence, 1973, Sec. of State for Defence, 1974. Member: Select Cttee on European Legislation, 1976–97; House of Commons Chairmen's Panel, 1983–97; Secretary: Cons. Finance Cttee, 1972–73; Cons. Trade Cttee, 1974; Vice-Chm., Cons. Employment Cttee, 1979–80; Chairman: W Midlands Area Young Conservatives, 1963–64; W Midlands Area Cons. Political Centre, 1966–69; a Vice Chairman: Cons. Party Organisation, 1974–75; Cons. Gp for Europe, 1984–87. Editor, Young Conservatives National Policy Group, 1963–64. Chm., London Union of Youth Clubs, 1998–99; Dep. Chm., Fedn of London Youth Clubs, 1999–. Vice Pres., Commercial Travellers' Benevolent Instn, 1998–. *Recreations:* watching association football and cricket, reading, theatre, walking. *Address:* The Mount, Alstonefield, Ashbourne, Derbys DE6 2FS.

KNOX, Prof. Henry Macdonald; Professor of Education, The Queen's University of Belfast, 1951–82, now Emeritus Professor; *b* 26 Nov. 1916; *e s* of Rev. R. M. Knox, Edinburgh, and J. E. Church; *m* 1945, Marian, *yr d* of N. Starkie, Todmorden; one *s* one *d*. *Educ:* George Watson's Coll., Edinburgh; University of Edinburgh. MA 1938; MEd 1940; PhD 1949. Served as Captain, Intelligence Corps, commanding a wireless intelligence section, Arakan sector of Burma, and as instructor, War Office special wireless training wing, 1940–46. Lecturer in Education, University Coll. of Hull, 1946; Lecturer in Education, University of St Andrews, 1949; former Dean of Faculty of Education, and acting Dir, Inst. of Educn, 1968–69, QUB. Assessor in Educn, Univ. of Strathclyde, 1984–89; sometime Examiner in Educn, Universities of Durham, Leeds, Sheffield, Aberdeen, Glasgow, Strathclyde, Wales and Ireland (National); occasional Examiner, Universities of Edinburgh, Belfast, Dublin and Bristol. Chm., N Ireland Council for Educn Research, 1979–82; Member: Advisory Council on Educn for N Ireland, 1955–58, 1961–64; Senior Certificate Examination Cttee for N Ireland, 1962–65; Adv. Bd for Postgraduate Studentships in Arts Subjects, Ministry of Educn for N Ireland, 1962–74; Adv. Cttee on Supply and Training of Teachers for NI, 1976–82; NI Council for Educnl Develt, 1980–82. Mem. Governing Body: Stranmillis Coll. of Educn, Belfast, 1968–82 (Vice-Chm., 1975–82); St Joseph's Coll. of Educn, Belfast, 1968–82. *Publications:* Two Hundred and Fifty Years of Scottish Education, 1696–1946, 1953; John Dury's Reformed School, 1958; Introduction to Educational Method, 1961; Schools in Europe (ed W. Schultze): Northern Ireland, 1969; (contrib.) Chambers Scottish Biographical Dictionary, 1992; numerous articles in educational journals. *Address:* 9 Elliot Gardens, Colinton, Edinburgh EH14 1EH. *T:* (0131) 441 6283.

KNOX, John; Under-Secretary, Department of Trade and Industry, retired, 1974; Head of Research Contractors Division, 1972–74; *b* 11 March 1913; *s* of William Knox and May Ferguson; *m* 1942, Mary Blackwood Johnston, *d* of late Rt Hon. Thomas Johnston, CH; one *s* one *d*. *Educ:* Lenzie Acad.; Glasgow Univ. (Kitchener's Schol.; MA). Business Management Trng, 1935–39; joined RAE, 1939; Op. Research with RAF, 1939–45; Asst Chief Scientific Adviser, Min. of Works, 1945–50; Dep. Dir and Dir, Intelligence Div., DSIR, 1950–58; Dep. Dir (Industry), DSIR, 1958–64; Min. of Technology, later DTI: Asst Controller, 1964–65; CSO, Head of External Research and Materials Div., 1965–68; Head of Materials Div., 1968–71; Head of Res. Div., 1971–73. *Publications:* occasional articles on management of research, development and industrial innovation. *Recreation:* golf. *Address:* 6 Mariners Court, Victoria Road, Aldeburgh, Suffolk IP15 5EH. *T:* (01728) 453657.

KNOX, John, (Jack), RSA 1979 (ARSA 1972); RGI 1980; RSW 1987; Head of Painting Studios, Glasgow School of Art, 1981–92; *b* 16 Dec. 1936; *s* of Alexander and Jean Knox; *m* 1960, Margaret Kyle Sutherland; one *s* one *d*. *Educ:* Lenzie Acad.; Glasgow Sch. of Art (DA). On the Drawing and Painting Staff at Duncan of Jordanstone Coll. of Art, Dundee, 1965–81. Work in permanent collections: Scottish Nat. Gallery of Modern Art; Arts Council; Contemporary Arts Soc.; Scottish Arts Council; Otis Art Inst., Los Angeles; Olinda Museum, São Paulo; Aberdeen, Dundee and Manchester art galleries; Hunterian Museum, Glasgow; Scottish Nat. Portrait Gall.; Kelvingrove Art Galls and Mus. Retrospective exhibn, Knox 1960–83, Scottish Arts Council, 1983. Member: Scottish Arts Council, 1974–79; Trustees Cttee, Scottish Nat. Gallery of Modern Art, 1975–81; Bd of Trustees, Nat. Galls of Scotland, 1982–87. Sec., Royal Scottish Acad., 1990–91. Member: Bd of Governors, Duncan of Jordanstone Coll. of Art, Dundee, 1980–82; Bd of

Governors, Glasgow Sch. of Art, 1985–88. Hon. FRIAS 1997. *Address:* 31 North Erskine Park, Bearsden, Glasgow G61 4LY.

KNOX, John Andrew; Board Member, Criminal Cases Review Commission, since 1997; *b* 22 July 1937; *s* of late James Telford Knox and Mary Knox; *m* 1964, Patricia Mary Martin; one *s* one *d*. *Educ:* Dame Allan's Sch., Newcastle upon Tyne; Merton Coll., Oxford (MA). ACA 1964, FCA 1974. Cooper Brothers & Co. Chartered Accountants, 1961–65; Vickers Ltd, 1966–72; entered CS as a Sen. Accountant, 1972; Chief Accountant, 1973; Asst Sec., 1976; Head of Accountancy Services Div., 1977–85; Grade 3, 1979–96; Hd of Industrial Financial Appraisal Div, DTI, 1985–87; Chief Accountant, 1987–90, and Dep. Dir, 1990–96, Serious Fraud Office. Leonard Shaw Award for Management Accountancy, Leonard Shaw Meml Fund, 1973.

KNOX, Prof. John Henderson, FRS 1984; FRSE 1971; University Fellow and Emeritus Professor of Physical Chemistry, University of Edinburgh, since 1984; *b* 21 Oct. 1927; *s* of John Knox and Elizabeth May Knox (*née* Henderson); *m* 1957, Josephine Anne Wissler; four *s*. *Educ:* George Watson's Boys' Coll.; Univ. of Edinburgh (BSc 1949, DSc 1963); Univ. of Cambridge (PhD 1953). University of Edinburgh: Lectr in Chemistry, 1953–66; Reader in Physical Chemistry, 1966–74; Director of Wolfson Liquid Chromatography Unit, 1972–92; Personal Prof. of Phys. Chem., 1974–84. Sen. Vis. Research Scientist Fellow, Univ. of Utah, 1964. *Publications:* Gas Chromatography, 1962; Molecular Thermodynamics, 1971, 2nd edn 1978; Applications of High Speed Liquid Chromatography, 1974; High Performance Liquid Chromatography, 1978, 3rd edn 1983. *Recreations:* ski-ing, sailing, hill walking. *Address:* 67 Morningside Park, Edinburgh EH10 5EZ. *T:* (0131) 447 5057; *e-mail:* j.h.knox@ed.ac.uk.

KNOX, Sir John (Leonard), Kt 1985; a Judge of the High Court of Justice, Chancery Division, 1985–96; *b* 6 April 1925; *s* of Leonard Needham Knox and Berthe Hélène Knox; *m* 1st, 1953, Anne Jacqueline Mackintosh (*d* 1991); one *s* three *d*; 2nd, 1993, Benedicta Eugenie Cooksey. *Educ:* Radley Coll.; Worcester Coll., Oxford (Hon. Mods, 1st Cl.; Jurisprudence, 1st Cl.). Called to the Bar, Lincoln's Inn, 1953, Bencher, 1977; Member, Senate of the Inns of Court, 1975–78. QC 1979; Junior Treasury Counsel: in *bona vacantia*, 1971–79; in probate, 1978–79; Attorney-Gen., Duchy of Lancaster, 1984–85. Member: Lord Chancellor's Law Reform Cttee, 1978–; Council of Legal Educn, 1975–79; Chm., Chancery Bar Assoc., 1985. Dep. Chm., Parly Boundary Commn, 1987–95.

KNOX, John Robert, FSA; Keeper, Department of Oriental Antiquities, British Museum, since 1994; *b* Port Alberni, BC, Canada, 4 June 1946; *s* of John Arthur Knox and Rosalind Knox (*née* Kingscote); *m* 1981, Helen Elizabeth Irène Zarb; three *d*. *Educ:* Univ. of Victoria, BC (BA Hons); Emmanuel Coll., Cambridge (MA). Asst Keeper, 1978, Dep. Keeper, 1992, Dept of Oriental Antiquities, British Museum. Member Council: Percival David Foundn, 1998–; Oriental Ceramic Soc., 1998–. Trustee, Gurkha Mus., 2000–. FSA 1991 (Vice Pres., 1994–97). *Publications:* Ancient China, 1978; (jtly) India: past into present, 1982; (jtly) Explorations and Excavations in Bannu District, North-West Frontier Province, Pakistan 1985–88, 1991; Amaravati, Buddhist Sculpture from the Great Stupa, 1992; (jtly) Akra, the First Capital of Bannu (NWFP Pakistan), 2000; articles in learned jls on archaeol. of India and Pakistan. *Recreations:* walking, music, theatre, 78s, France. *Address:* Department of Oriental Antiquities, British Museum, Great Russell Street, WC1B 3DG. *T:* (020) 7323 8000.

KNOX, Hon. Sir William Edward, Kt 1979; FCIT, FAIM; Leader of Parliamentary Liberal Party, Queensland, 1983–88; *b* 14 Dec. 1927; *s* of E. Knox, Turramurra; *m* 1956, Doris Ross; two *s* two *d*. *Educ:* Melbourne High School. State Pres., Qld Young Liberals, 1953–56; Vice-Pres., Qld Div., Liberal Party, 1956–57, Mem. Exec., 1953–58, 1962–65; Sec., Parly Lib. Party, 1960–65. MLA (L) Nundah, Qld, 1957–89; Minister for Transport, Qld, 1965–72; Minister for Justice and Attorney-Gen., Qld, 1971–76; Dep. Premier and Treasurer of Qld, 1976–78; Leader, State Parly Liberal Party, 1976–78 and 1983–88; Minister for Health, Qld, 1978–80; Minister for Employment and Labour Relations, Qld, 1980–83. Chm., Qld Road Safety Council and Mem., Aust. Transport Adv. Council, 1965–72. Mem., Nat. Exec. Aust. Jnr Chamber of Commerce, 1961–62; Senator Jnr Chamber Internat., 1962–. State Pres., Father and Son Movement, 1965; Pres., Assoc. of Independent Schs, Qld, 1991–97. Chm., St John Council for Qld, 1983–95. KStJ 1995. *Address:* 1621 Sandgate Road, Nundah, Queensland 4012, Australia.

KNOX-JOHNSTON, Sir William Robert Patrick, (Sir Robin), Kt 1995; CBE 1969; RD (and bar) 1983; Marina Consultant since 1974; *b* 17 March 1939; *s* of late David Robert Knox-Johnston and Elizabeth Mary Knox-Johnston (*née* Cree); *m* 1962, Suzanne (*née* Singer); one *d*. *Educ:* Berkhamsted School. Master Mariner; FRGS; MRIN. Merchant Navy, 1957–67. First person to sail single-handed non-stop Around the World, 14 June 1968 to 22 April 1969, in yacht Suhaili; won Sunday Times Golden Globe, 1969; won Round Britain Race, Ocean Spirit, 1970; won round Britain Race, British Oxygen, 1974; set British transatlantic sailing record, from NY to the Lizard, 11 days 7 hours 45 mins, 1981; established new record of 10 days 14 hours 9 mins, 1986; set world sailing record for around Ireland, 76 hours 5 mins 34 secs, May 1986; World Class II Multihull Champion, 1985; completed Guardian Columbus voyage, 1989; with Peter Blake, set non-stop around the world sailing record, 74 days, 22 hours, 17 mins 22 secs, 1994. Man. Dir, St Katharine's Yacht Haven Ltd, 1975–76; Director: Mercury Yacht Harbours Ltd, 1970–73; Rank Marine International, 1973–75; Troon Marina Ltd, 1976–83; National Yacht Racing Centre Ltd, 1979–86; Knox-Johnston Insurance Brokers Ltd, 1983–; St Katherine's Dock, 1975– (Man. Dir, 1991–93); Chm., Clipper Ventures plc, 1997–. Pres., British Olympic Yachting Appeal, 1977–; Pres. (formerly Chm.), STA, 1993–; Member: Cttee of Management, RNLI, 1983–; Sports Council Lottery Panel, 1995–; Sport England Council, 1999–. Trustee: Nat. Maritime Mus., Greenwich, 1993; Nat. Maritime Mus., Cornwall, 1997–. Freeman, Borough of Bromley, Kent, 1969; Younger Brother, Trinity House, 1973. Freeman, City of London, 1992. Liveryman, Co. of Master Mariners, 1975. Lt-Comdr RNR 1971, retired. Hon. DSc Maine Maritime Acad., 1989; Hon. DTech Nottingham, 1993. Yachtsman of the Year, 1969; Silk Cut Seamanship Award, 1990; Seamanship Foundn Trophy, RYA, 1991; Gold Medal, RIN, 1992; Yachtsman of the Year, Yachting Journalists Assoc., 1994; Internat. Yacht Racing Union Sailor of the Year, 1994. *Publications:* A World of my Own, 1969; Sailing, 1975; Twilight of Sail, 1978; Last but not Least, 1978; Bunkside Companion, 1982; Seamanship, 1986; The BOC Challenge 1986–1987, 1988; The Cape of Good Hope, 1989; History of Yachting, 1990; The Columbus Venture, 1991 (Book of the Sea Award); Sea, Ice and Rock, 1992; Cape Horn, 1994; Beyond Jules Verne, 1995; Running Free (autobiog.), 1998. *Recreation:* sailing. *Address:* St Francis Cottage, Torbryan, Newton Abbot, Devon TQ12 5UR. *Clubs:* Little Ship (Pres.); Royal Yacht Squadron (Hon. Mem.) (Cowes); Royal Harwich Yacht (Hon. Mem.); Royal Irish Yacht (Hon. Life Mem., 1969) (Dublin).

KNOX-LECKY, Maj.-Gen. Samuel, CB 1979; OBE 1967; BSc(Eng); CEng, FIMechE; Director-General, Agricultural Engineers Association, 1980–88; *b* 10 Feb. 1926; *s* of late J. D. Lecky, Coleraine; *m* 1947, Sheila Jones; one *s* two *d*. *Educ:* Coleraine Acad.; Queen's Univ., Belfast (BSc). Commnd REME, 1946; served Egypt, 1951–52; Kenya, 1953–54; jssc 1964; AA&QMG HQ 1(BR) Corps, 1965–66; CREME 4 Div., 1966–68; Sec., Principal Personnel Officers, MoD, 1968–70; RCDS, 1971; Comdt, SEME, 1972–74; DEME, BAOR, 1975; Dir, Military Assistance Office, MoD, 1976–77; Minister (DS), British Embassy, Tehran, 1977–79. Hon. Col, QUB OTC, 1978–83; Col Comdt, REME, 1980–86. *Recreations:* fishing, sailing.

KNOX-MAWER, Ronald; retired; *b* 3 Aug. 1925; *s* of George Robert Knox-Mawer and Clara Roberts; *m* 1951, June Ellis; one *s* one *d*. *Educ:* Grove Park Sch. (Denbighshire County Exhibnr); Emmanuel Coll., Cambridge (Exhibitioner; MA). Royal Artillery, 1943–47. Called to Bar, Middle Temple; Wales and Chester Circuit, 1947–52; Chief Magistrate and Actg Chief Justice, Aden, 1952–58; Sen. Magistrate, Puisne Judge, Justice of Appeal, Actg Chief Justice, Fiji, and conjointly Chief Justice, Nauru and Tonga, 1958–71; Northern Circuit, 1971–75; Metropolitan Stipendiary Magistrate, 1975–84; Dep. Circuit Judge, London, 1979–84. Various series of humorous reminiscences broadcast on BBC Radio: Tales from a Palm Court, 1984; Islands of Hope and Glory, 1985; Wretchedness in Wrexham, 1986; More Tales from a Palm Court, 1987–88; Tales of a Man called Father, 1989; The Queen Goes West, 1990; A Case of Bananas, 1992; Family Failings, 1994; Tales from Land of My Father, 1998; A Man Called Father (new series), 1999. *Publications:* Palm Court, 1979 (as Robert Overton); Tales from a Palm Court, 1986; Tales of a Man Called Father, 1989; A Case of Bananas and other South Sea Trials, 1992; Land of My Father, 1994; Are You Coming or Going?, 1999; (contrib.) Wales: a celebration, 2000; short stories and features (under different pseudonyms) in Punch, Cornhill, Argosy, The Times, Sunday Express, Blackwoods, Listener, Weekend Telegraph, Times Saturday Review, Sunday Telegraph; various contribs to legal jls. *Recreation:* countryside. *Address:* c/o HSBC, Ruabon, N Wales LL14 6AA.

KNUSSEN, (Stuart) Oliver, CBE 1994; composer and conductor; Music Director, London Sinfonietta, since 1998; *b* Glasgow, 12 June 1952; *s* of Stuart Knussen and Ethelyn Jane Alexander; *m* 1972, Susan Freedman; one *d*. *Educ:* Watford Field Sch.; Watford Boys Grammar Sch.; Purcell Sch. Private composition study with John Lambert, 1963–68; Countess of Munster Awards, 1964, 1965, 1967; Peter Stuyvesant Foundn Award, 1965; début conducting Symph. no 1 with LSO, 1968; Watney-Sargent award for Young Conductors, 1969; Fellowships to Berkshire Music Center, Tanglewood, 1970, 1971, 1973; Caird Trav. Schol., 1971; Margaret Grant Composition Prize (Symph. no 2), Tanglewood, 1971; study with Gunther Schuller in USA, 1970–73; Koussevitzky Centennial Commn, 1974; Composer-in-residence: Aspen Fest., 1976; Arnolfini Gall., 1978; Instr in composition, RCM Jun. Dept, 1977–82; BBC commn for Proms 1979 (Symph. no 3); Co-Artistic Dir, Aldeburgh Fest., 1983–98; Berkshire Music Center, Tanglewood: Guest Teacher, 1981; Composer-in-residence, 1986; Co-ordinator of Contemporary Music Activities, 1986–90. Arts Council Bursaries, 1979, 1981; winner, first Park Lane Gp Composer award (suite from Where the Wild Things Are), 1982; BBC commn for Glyndebourne Opera, 1983. Frequent guest conductor, Philharmonia Orch., many other ensembles, UK and abroad, 1981–; Associate Guest Conductor, BBC SO, 1989–; Dir, Almeida Ensemble, 1986–. Mem. Exec. Cttee, SPNM, 1978–85; Member: Leopold Stokowski Soc.; International Alban Berg Soc., New York; Hon. Mem., AAAL, 1994. *Publications* include: Symphony no 1 op. 1, 1966–67; Symphony no 2 op. 7, 1970–71; Symphony no 3 op. 18, 1973–79; Where the Wild Things Are—opera (Maurice Sendak), op. 20, 1979–83 (staged, Glyndebourne at NT, 1984); Higglety Pigglety Pop!—opera (Sendak), op. 21, 1983–85 (staged Glyndebourne, 1984 and 1985); Horn Concerto, 1994 (commnd for Barry Tuckwell); numerous orchestral, chamber, vocal works; articles in Tempo, The Listener, etc. *Recreations:* cinema, record collecting, record producing, visual arts. *Address:* c/o Faber Music Ltd, 3 Queen Square, WC1N 3AR; c/o Harrison Parrott Ltd, 12 Penzance Place, W11 4PA.

KNUTSFORD, 6th Viscount *cr* 1895; **Michael Holland-Hibbert;** Bt 1853; Baron 1888; DL; *b* 27 Dec. 1926; *s* of Hon. Wilfrid Holland-Hibbert (*d* 1961) (2nd *s* of 3rd Viscount) and of Audrey, *d* of late Mark Fenwick; *S* cousin, 1986; *m* 1951, Hon. Sheila, *d* of 5th Viscount Portman; two *s* one *d*. *Educ:* Eton College; Trinity Coll., Cambridge (BA). Welsh Guards, 1945–48. SW Regional Director, Barclays Bank, 1956–86. National Trust: Chm. Cttee for Devon and Cornwall, 1973–86; Mem. Exec. Cttee, 1973–86; Mem. Council, 1979–85; Mem. Finance Cttee, 1986–99. DL 1977, High Sheriff 1977–78, Devon. *Heir: er s* Hon. Henry Thurstan Holland-Hibbert [*b* 6 April 1959; *m* 1988, Katherine, *d* of Sir John Ropner, Bt, *qv*; two *s* two *d*]. *Address:* Broadclyst House, Exeter, Devon EX5 3EW. *T:* (01392) 461244. *Club:* Brooks's.

KNUTTON, Maj.-Gen. Harry, CB 1975; MSc, CEng, FIEE; Director-General, City and Guilds of London Institute, 1976–85; *b* Rawmarsh, Yorks, 26 April 1921; *m* 1958, Pamela Brackley, E Sheen, London; three *s* one *d*. *Educ:* Wath-upon-Dearne Grammar Sch.; RMCS. Commnd RA, 1943; served with 15th Scottish and 1st Airborne Divs, NW Europe, 1944–45; India, 1945–47; Instructor in Gunnery, 1946–49; Project Officer, Min. of Supply, 1949–51; served Middle East, 1953–55; Directing Staff, RMCS, 1955–58; jssc 1958; various staff appts, MoD, 1958–60, 1962–64, 1966–67; Comdr Missile Regt, BAOR, 1964–66; Comdr Air Defence Bde, 1967–69; Fellow, Loughborough Univ. of Technology, 1969–70; Dir-Gen. Weapons (Army), 1970–73; Dir, Royal Ordnance Factories and Dep. Master-Gen. of Ordnance, 1973–75. Col Comdt, RA, 1977–82. Teacher, Whitgift Foundn, 1975–76. Member: Associated Examining Bd, 1976–85; Dep. Chm., Standing Conf. on Schools' Science and Technology, 1983–90. Governor, Imperial Coll., London, 1976–91. FCollP 1983. FCGI 1985. Liveryman, Engineers' Co. *Address:* 85 Hayes Lane, Kenley, Surrey CR8 5JR.

KOCH, Edward Irving; Partner, Robinson Silverman Pearce Aronsohn & Berman, New York, since 1990; Mayor, City of New York, 1978–89; *b* 12 Dec. 1924; *s* of Louis Koch and Joyce Silpe. *Educ:* Southside High School, Newark, NJ; City Coll. of NY; NY Univ. Law Sch. Served US Army, 1943–46, USA, France, Rhineland. Mem., NY State Bar, 1949; private law practice, 1949–64; Senior Partner, Koch, Lankenau, Schwartz & Kovner, 1965–69. Democratic dist. leader, Greenwich Village, 1963–65; Mem., NY City Council, 1967–68; NY Congressman, 1969–77. *Publications:* Mayor, 1983; Politics, 1985; (jtly) His Eminence and Hizzoner, 1989; All the Best, 1990; Citizen Koch (autobiog.), 1992; Ed Koch on Everything, 1994; Murder at City Hall, 1995; Murder on Broadway, 1996; Murder on 34th Street, 1997; The Senator Must Die, 1998; Giuliani: nasty man, 1999; I'm not done yet, 1999. *Address:* 2 Fifth Avenue, New York, NY 10011, USA.

KOCIENSKI, Prof. Philip Joseph, PhD; FRS 1997; FRSE; FRSC; Professor and Head of Department of Organic Chemistry, University of Leeds, since 2000; *b* 23 Dec. 1946; *s* of Philip Joseph Kocienski and Marian Edyth (*née* Peters); *m* 1st, 1967, Anna Petruso (marr. diss. 1987); one *s* one *d*; 2nd, 1987, Joanna Davie. *Educ:* Brown Univ., Providence, RI (PhD 1973). FRSC 1995; FRSE 1998. Lectr, Leeds Univ., 1979–85; Prof. of Chemistry, Southampton Univ., 1985–97. Regius Prof. of Chemistry, Glasgow Univ., 1997–2000. Mem., EPSRC, 1999–. Marie Sklowdowska Curie Medal, Polish Chem. Soc., 1997. *Publications:* Protecting Groups, 1994; numerous res. papers in learned jls. *Recreations:* Russian and Eastern European music, violin. *Address:* Department of Chemistry, Leeds University, Leeds LS2 9JT. *T:* (0113) 233 6555.

KOENIGSBERGER, Prof. Helmut Georg, MA, PhD; FBA 1989; Professor of History, King's College London, 1973–84, now Emeritus; *b* 24 Oct. 1918; *s* of late Georg Felix Koenigsberger, chief architect, borough of Treptow, Berlin, Germany, and of late Käthe Koenigsberger (*née* Born); *m* 1961, Dorothy M. Romano; two *d* (twins). *Educ:* Adams' Grammar Sch., Newport, Shropshire; Gonville and Caius Coll., Cambridge. Asst Master: Brentwood Sch., Essex, 1941–42; Bedford Sch., 1942–44. Served War of 1939–45, Royal Navy, 1944–45. Lecturer in Economic History, QUB, 1948–51; Senior Lecturer in Economic History, University of Manchester, 1951–60; Prof. of Modern History, University of Nottingham, 1960–66; Prof. of Early Modern European History, Cornell, 1966–73. Visiting Lecturer: Brooklyn Coll., New York, 1957; University of Wisconsin, 1958; Columbia University, 1962; Cambridge Univ., 1963; Washington Univ., St Louis, 1964; Fellow, Historisches Kolleg, Munich, 1984–85. Sec., 1955–75, Vice-Pres., 1975–80, Pres., 1980–85, Internat. Commn for the History of Representative and Parliamentary Institutions; Vice-Pres., RHistS, 1982–85. Hon. FKC 1999. Encomienda, Order of Isabel the Catholic (Spain), 1997. *Publications:* The Government of Sicily under Philip II of Spain, 1951, new edn, as The Practice of Empire, 1969; The Empire of Charles V in Europe (in New Cambridge Modern History II), 1958; Western Europe and the Power of Spain (in New Cambridge Modern History III), 1968; Europe in the Sixteenth Century (with G. L. Mosse), 1968, 2nd edn (with G. L. Mosse and G. Q. Bowler) 1989; Estates and Revolutions, 1971; The Habsburgs and Europe, 1516–1660, 1971; (ed) Luther: a profile, 1972; Politicians and Virtuosi, 1986; Medieval Europe, 1987; Early Modern Europe, 1987; (ed) Republiken und Republikanismus im Europa der frühen Neuzeit, 1988; Monarchies, States Generals and Parliaments, 2001; contrib. to historical journals. *Recreations:* playing chamber music, sailing, travel. *Address:* 116 Waterfall Road, N14 7JN. *T:* (020) 8886 6416.

KOFFMANN, Pierre; chef; Proprietor, La Tante Claire, since 1977; *b* 21 Aug. 1948; *s* of Albert and Germaine Koffmann; *m* 1972, Annie Barrau; one *d*. *Educ:* Ecole Jean Jacques Rousseau, Tarbes. Mil. Service, 1967–69. Commis: L'Aubette, Strasbourg, 1966; Grand Hôtel Palais, Juan les Pins, 1967; Le Provençal, La Ciotat, 1969–70; La Voile d'Or, Lausanne, 1970; Le Gavroche, 1970–71; Chef: Brasserie Benoist, London, 1971; Waterside Inn, Bray, 1971–77. *Publications:* Memories of Gascony, 1990; La Tante Claire: recipes from a master chef, 1992. *Address:* La Tante Claire Restaurant Ltd, Wilton Place, SW1X 7RL. *T:* (020) 7823 2003.

KOGAN, Prof. Maurice; Professor of Government and Social Administration, 1969, now Emeritus, and Director, Centre for the Evaluation of Public Policy, since 1990, Brunel University; *b* 10 April 1930; *s* of Barnett and Hetty Kogan; *m* 1960, Ulla Svensson; two *s*. *Educ:* Stratford Grammar Sch.; Christ's Coll., Cambridge (MA). Entered Civil Service, admin. cl. (1st in open examinations), 1953. Secretary: Secondary Sch. Exams Council, 1961; Central Advisory Council for Educn (England), 1963–66; Harkness Fellow of Commonwealth Fund, 1960–61; Asst Sec., DES, 1966. Brunel University: Head of Sch. of Social Scis, 1971–74; Dean, Faculty of Soc. Scis, 1987–89; Acting Vice-Chancellor, 1989–90. Member: Educn Sub-Cttee, Univ. Grants Cttee, 1972–75; SSRC, 1975–77; Davies Cttee on Hosp. Complaints' Procedure, 1971; Houghton Cttee on Teachers' Pay, 1974; Genetic Manipulation Adv. Gp, 1979–80; Chm., Adv. Gp, Cttee of award, Harkness Fellowship, 1989–. George A. Miller Vis. Prof., Univ. of Illinois, 1976; Vis. Scholar, Univ. of Calif, Berkeley, 1981; Leverhulme Emeritus Fellow, 1996–98. Founder AcSS 2000. Hon. DSc (Econ) Hull, 1987; DUniv Brunel, 1991. *Publications:* The Organisation of a Social Services Department, 1971; Working Relationships within the British Hospital Service, 1971; The Government of Education, 1971; The Politics of Education, 1971; (ed) The Challenge of Change, 1973; County Hall, 1973; Advisory Councils and Committees in Education, 1974; Educational Policy-Making, 1975; The Politics of Educational Change, 1978; The Working of the National Health Service, 1978; (with T. Becher) Process and Structure in Higher Education, 1980, 2nd edn 1992; The Government's Commissioning of Research, 1980; (with T. Bush) Directors of Education, 1982; (with D. Kogan) The Battle for the Labour Party, 1982; (with M. Henkel) Government and Research, 1983; (with D. Kogan) The Attack on Higher Education, 1983; (with T. Husen) Educational Research and Policy: how do they relate?, 1984; (with D. Johnson and others) School Governing Bodies, 1984; Education Accountability, 1986; (jtly) The Use of Performance Indicators in Higher Education, 1988, 2nd edn 1990; (jtly) Higher Education and Employment, 1988; (ed) Evaluating Higher Education, 1989; (jtly) Directors of Education Facing Reform, 1989; (jtly) Evaluation as Policy Making, 1990; (jtly) Encyclopaedia of Government and Politics, 1992; (jtly) In Support of Education: the functioning of local government, 1993; (jtly) Graduate Education in Britain, 1994; (jtly) Making Use of Clinical Audit, 1995; Advancing Quality, 1995; Higher Education and Work, 1995; Reforming Higher Education, 2000; contribs to TES, THES, Jl of Social Policy. *Recreations:* reading, listening to music. *Address:* 48 Duncan Terrace, Islington, N1 8AL. *T:* (020) 7226 0038.

KOHL, Dr Helmut; Grosskreuz Verdienstorden, 1979; Member, Bundestag, since 1976; Chancellor, Federal Republic of Germany, 1982–98 (re-elected, 1991, as Chancellor of reunited Germany); *b* 3 April 1930; *s* of Hans and Cäcilie Kohl; *m* 1960, Hannelore Renner (*d* 2001); two *s*. *Educ:* Frankfurt Univ.; Heidelberg Univ. (Dr phil 1958 Heidelberg). On staff of a Trade Assoc., 1958–59; Mem., Parlt of Rhineland Palatinate, 1959–76; Leader, CDU Parly Party in Rhineland Palatinate Parlt, 1963–69; Mem., Federal Exec. Cttee of CDU at federal level, 1964–98; Chairman: CDU, Rhineland Palatinate, 1966–74; CDU, 1973–98; Minister-President, Rhineland Palatinate, 1969–76; Leader of the Opposition, Bundestag, 1976–82. Numerous foreign decorations. *Publications:* Die politische Entscheidung in der Pfalz und das Wiedererstehen der Parteien nach 1945, 1958; Hausputz hinter den Fassaden, 1971; Zwischen Ideologie und Pragmatismus, 1973; Die CDU: Porträt einer Volkspartei, 1981; Der Weg zur Wende, 1983; Reden 1982–1984, 1984; Die Deutsche Einheit, 1992; Der Kurs der CDU, 1993; Mein Tagebuch 1998–2000, 2000. *Address:* Marbacher Strasse 11, 67071 Ludwigshafen (Rhein), Germany.

KÖHLER, Dr Horst; Managing Director, International Monetary Fund, since 2000; *b* 22 Feb. 1943; *s* of Eduard and Elisa Köhler; *m* 1969, Eva Luise Bohnet; one *s* one *d*. *Educ:* Tübingen Univ. (PhD Econs and Pol Sci. 1977). Inst. for Applied Econ. Res., 1969–76; economist, German Federal Min. of Econs, 1976–80; Advr to Ministerpräsident, Chancellery, Schleswig-Holstein, 1981–82; German Federal Min. of Finance, 1982–93 (Permanent Under Sec., 1990–93); Pres., German Savings Banks Assoc., 1993–98; Pres., EBRD, 1998–2000. *Address:* International Monetary Fund, 700 19th Street NW, Washington, DC 20431, USA.

KOHLHAUSSEN, Martin; Chairman, Supervisory Board, Commerzbank AG, since 2001; *b* 6 Nov. 1935; *m*; three *c*. *Educ:* Univs of Frankfurt (Main), Freiburg, Marburg (Law). Worked domestically in banking, Frankfurt and Hanau (Br. Man.), 1965–76; worked internationally in banking (Br. Man.), Tokyo and New York, 1976–81. Mem., 1982–2001, Chm., 1991–2001, Bd of Man. Dirs, Commerzbank AG. *Address:* Commerzbank AG, 60261 Frankfurt, Germany. *T:* (69) 13620.

KOHN, Dr Ralph, FRPharmS; Chairman, Harley Street Holdings Ltd, since 1998; baritone; *b* Leipzig, 9 Dec. 1927; *s* of Marcus Kohn and Lena Kohn (*née* Aschheim); *m* 1963, Zahava Kanarek; three *d*. *Educ:* primary sch., Amsterdam; Manchester Univ. (BSc, MSc; PhD 1954). FRPharmS (FPS 1952). Charter Travelling Fellow, 1954–56, Paterno Fellow, 1956–57, Inst. of Health, Rome; Riker Fellow, Albert Einstein Coll. of Medicine, NY, 1957–58; Head, exploratory pharmacology, Smith Kline & French Labs, UK, 1958–65; Man. Dir, UK subsid. of Robapharm AG, 1965–71; estabd Adv. Services (Clinical and Gen.) Ltd, first co. in Adv. Services Hldgs Gp, 1971; Man. Dir, Adv. Services Hldgs Gp, 1971–98 (Queen's Award for Export Achievement, to Gp, 1990). Med. Advr, Nat. Osteoporosis Soc., 1986–; Mem. Exec. Cttee, Brit. Digestive Foundn, 1997–. Chm. Cttee, Sir John Eliot Gardiner's Millennium Bach Cantata Pilgrimage. Member: President's Circle, Royal Soc., 1997–; RSocMed; RPSGB; Brit. Pharmacol Soc.; RSH. Has given numerous recitals and performances with orchestras in UK and abroad, incl. concerts at Wigmore Hall, Purcell Room, St John's, Smith Sq., Queen Elizabeth Hall and Royal Albert Hall; orchestral broadcasts for radio; has made numerous recordings; lectures on medical, scientific and musical topics. Chm. Cttee, Wigmore Hall Internat. Song Comp., 1997–. Founder Mem., Jewish Music Inst., 2000–. Chm. Trustees, Kohn Foundn, 1991–; Trustee, Rudolf Kempe Soc., 1998–. *Recreations:* music, chess, literature. *Address:* 50 West Heath Road, NW3 7UR. *T:* (020) 8458 2037, (office) (020) 7436 6001. *Club:* Athenæum.

KOHN, Prof. Walter, PhD; Professor of Physics, 1984–91, now Emeritus, and Research Professor, since 1991, University of California at Santa Barbara; *b* Vienna, 9 March 1923; *s* of Salomon and Gittel Kohn; *m* 1st, 1948, Lois Mary Adams; three *d*; 2nd, 1978, Maia Schiff. *Educ:* Univ. of Toronto (BA Math. and Physics 1945; MA Applied Math. 1946); Harvard Univ. (PhD Physics 1948; Lehman Fellow). Indust. Physicist (pt-time), Sutton Horsley Co., 1941–43; Geophysicist (pt-time), Koulomzine, Quebec, 1944–46; Instr, Dept of Physics, Harvard Univ., 1948–50; Asst Prof., 1950–53, Associate Prof., 1953–56, Prof., 1956–60, Dept of Physics, Carnegie Mellon Univ.; Prof., 1960–79, and Chm., 1961–63, Dept of Physics, UCSD; Dir, Inst. of Theoretical Physics, UCSB, 1979–84. Consultant: Westinghouse Res. Lab., 1953–57; Bell Telephone Labs, 1953–66; Gen. Atomic, 1960–72; IBM, 1978. Oersted Fellow, Copenhagen, 1951–52; Sen. NSF Fellow, Imperial Coll., London, 1958; Guggenheim Fellow, Paris, 1963. Member: Amer. Acad. of Arts and Scis, 1963–; NAS, 1969–; Reactor Div., Nat. Inst. of Sci. and Technol., 1946–98; Bd of Govs, Tel Aviv Univ.; Bd of Govs, Weizmann Inst., 1996–. Numerous hon. doctorates. Buckley Medal, 1960, Davisson-Germer Prize, 1977, APS; Feenberg Medal, 1991; Nobel Prize for Physics, 1998; Niels Bohr Medal, UNESCO, 1998. *Publications:* more than 200 articles and reviews in Phys. Review, Phys. Review Letters, Review of Modern Phys., etc. *Recreations:* listening to classical music, reading, going for walks, roller blading. *Address:* Department of Physics, University of California at Santa Barbara, Santa Barbara, CA 93106, USA. *T:* (805) 8933061.

KOHNSTAMM, Max; Groot Officier, Order of Orange Nassau, 1988; Comdr of the Order of House of Orange, 1949; Hon. Secretary-General, Action Committee for Europe, since 1989 (Sec.-Gen., 1985–88); Senior Fellow, European Policy Centre, Brussels, since 1991; *b* 22 May 1914; *s* of Dr Philip Abraham Kohnstamm and Johanna Hermana Kessler; *m* 1944, Kathleen Sillem; two *s* three *d*. *Educ:* Univ. of Amsterdam (Hist. Drs); American Univ., Washington. Private Sec. to Queen Wilhelmina, 1945–48; subseq. Head of German Bureau, then Dir of European Affairs, Netherlands FO; Sec. of High Authority, 1952–56; 1st Rep. of High Authority, London, 1956; Sec.-Gen. (later Vice-Pres.), Action Cttee for United States of Europe, 1956–75; Pres., European Community Inst. for Univ. Studies, 1958–75; Principal, Eur. Univ. Inst. of Florence, 1975–81. Co-Chm., Cttee on Soc. Develt and Peace, World Council of Churches and Pontifical Commn for Justice and Peace, 1967–75; European Pres., Trilateral Commn, 1973–75. Grande Ufficiale dell' Ordine Al Merito della Repubblica Italiana, 1981; Grosse Verdienstkreuz, 1982, mit Stern, 1989, Bundesrepublik Deutschland. *Publications:* The European Community and its Role in the World, 1963; (ed jtly) A Nation Writ Large?, 1972; (jtly) Europe: l'impossible statu quo, 1996. *Recreation:* walking. *Address:* 20 Fenffe, 5560 Houyet, Belgium. *T:* (84) 377183, *Fax:* (84) 377113.

KOHT, Paul; Ambassador of Norway to Denmark, 1975–82; *b* 7 Dec. 1913; *s* of Dr Halvdan Koht and Karen Elisabeth (*née* Grude); *m* 1938, Grete Sverdrup; two *s* one *d*. *Educ:* University of Oslo. Law degree, 1937. Entered Norwegian Foreign Service, 1938; held posts in: Bucharest, 1938–39; London, 1940–41; Tokyo, 1941–42; New York, 1942–46; Lisbon, 1950–51; Mem. Norwegian Delegn to OEEC and NATO, Paris, and Perm. Rep. to Coun. of Europe, 1951–53; Dir General of Dept for Econ. Affairs, Min. of For. Affairs, Oslo, 1953–56; Chargé d'Affaires, Copenhagen, 1956–58; Ambassador to USA, 1958–63; Ambassador to Fed. Republic of Germany, 1963–68; Ambassador to the Court of St James's, 1968–75. Comdr, Order of St Olav; Grand Cross, Order of Dannebrog; Grand Cross, Order of Merit (Federal Republic of Germany). *Address:* Lille Frogner Allé 4b, 0263 Oslo, Norway.

KOK, William, (Wim); Prime Minister and Minister for General Affairs, the Netherlands, since 1994; *b* 29 Sept. 1938. *Educ:* Nijenrode Business Sch. Mil. Service, 1959–60. Netherlands Federation of Trade Unions: Asst Internat. Officer, Construction Div., 1961–65; Mem. for Econ. Affairs, 1965–67; Union Sec., 1967–69; Sec., 1969–72; Dep. Chm., 1972–73; Chm., 1973–85. Leader, Parly Labour Party, and Mem., Lower House, Netherlands, 1986–89, re-elected 1994, and 1998; Dep. Prime Minister and Minister of Finance, 1989–94. Vice Chm. of Bd, Netherlands Bank. Chm., ETUC, 1979–82; Dep. Chm., Socialist Internat., 1989. Advr to EC. *Address:* Office of the Prime Minister, Binnenhof 20, PO Box 20001, 2500 EA The Hague, Netherlands.

KOLAKOWSKI, Leszek, PhD; FBA 1980; Senior Research Fellow, All Souls College, Oxford, 1970–95; *b* 23 Oct. 1927; *s* of Jerzy and Lucyna (*née* Pietrusiewicz); *m* 1949, Dr Tamara Kołakowska (*née* Dynenson); one *d*. *Educ:* Łódź Univ., Poland 1945–50; Warsaw Univ. (PhD 1953). Asst in Philosophy: Łódź Univ., 1947–49; Warsaw Univ., 1950–59; Prof. and Chm., Section of History of Philosophy, Warsaw Univ., 1959–68, expelled by authorities for political reasons; Visiting Professor: McGill Univ., 1968–69; Univ. of California, Berkeley, 1969–70; Yale Univ., Conn, 1975; Univ. of Chicago, 1981–94. McArthur Fellowship, 1983. MAE; Member: Internat. Inst. of Philosophy, 1969; Académie Universelle des Cultures, 1993; Polish Acad. of Scis, 1997; Foreign Mem., Amer. Academy of Arts and Science, 1997; Mem.-correspondent, Bayerische Akademie des Künste, 1977. Hon. Dr Lit. Hum Bard Coll., 1984; Hon. LLD Reed Coll., 1985; Hon. DHum: Adelphi, and NY State, USA; Hon. DPhil: Łódź, and Gdansk, Poland. Friedenpreis des Deutschen Buchhandels, 1977; Jurzykowski Foundn award, 1968; Charles Veillou Prix Européen d'Essai, 1980; (jtly) Erasmus Prize, 1984; Jefferson Award, 1986; Prix Tocqueville, Assoc. Alexis de Tocqueville, 1993. *Publications:* about 30 books, some of them only in Polish; trans. of various books in 14 languages; *in English:* Marxism and Beyond, 1968; Conversations with the Devil, 1972; Positivist Philosophy, 1972; Husserl and the Search for Certitude, 1975; Main Currents of Marxism, 3 vols, 1978; Religion, 1982; Bergson, 1985; Metaphysical Horror, 1988; God Owes Us Nothing; Freedom, Fame, Lying and Betrayal (essays), 1999; *in French:* Chrétiens sans Eglise, 1969;

in German: Traktat über die Sterblichkeit der Vernunft, 1967; Geist und Ungeist christlicher Traditionen, 1971; Die Gegenwärtigkeit des Mythos, 1973; Der revolutionäre Geist, 1972; Leben trotz Geschichte Lesebuch, 1977; Zweifel um die Methode, 1977. *Address:* 77 Hamilton Road, Oxford OX2 7QA. *T:* (01865) 558790.

KOLBERT, His Honour Colin Francis; Chairman of Disciplinary Tribunal, Securities and Futures Authority, since 1995 (Independent Board Member, 1995–2000); Assistant Surveillance Commissioner, since 2001; *b* 3 June 1936; *s* of late Arthur Richard Alexander Kolbert and Dorothy Elizabeth Kolbert (*née* Fletcher); *m* 1959, Jean Fairgrieve Abson; two *d. Educ:* Queen Elizabeth's, Barnet; St Catharine's Coll., Cambridge (Harold Samuel Schol., 1959; BA 1959; PhD 1962; MA 1963). FCIArb 1997. RA, 1954–56. Called to the Bar, Lincoln's Inn, 1961; a Recorder, SE Circuit, 1985–88; a Circuit Judge, 1988–95. Oxford University: Fellow and Tutor in Jurisprudence, St Peter's Coll., 1964–68 (MA, DPhil (Oxon) by incorp., 1964); CUF Lectr, Faculty of Law, 1965–68; Cambridge University: Fellow, Magdalene Coll., 1968– (Tutor, 1969–88); Univ. Lectr in Law, Dept of Land Economy, 1969–88; Sec., Faculty of Music, 1969–75; Coll. Rugby Administrator, CURUFC, 1982–88 (Trustee, 1989–); Mem. CUCC Cttee, 1996–. Vis. Prof. and Moderator, Univs of Ife, Lagos, Enugu, and Ahmadu Bello, Nigeria, 1970–80. Mem., Cambridge City Council, 1970–74. Member: Istituto di Diritto Agrario Internazionale e Comparato, Florence, 1964–; Secretariat, World Conf. on Agrarian Reform and Rural Develt, FAO Rome, 1978–79 (Customary Land Tenure Consultant, 1974–80). Freeman, City of London, 1998; Liveryman, Wax Chandlers' Co., 1999–. Governor: Wellingborough Sch., 1970–80; Cranleigh Sch., 1970–88; Glenalmond Coll., 1978–89; Hurstpierpont Coll., 1978–89; Feoffee, Chetham's Hosp. and Library, 1993–. Violin music critic, Records and Recording, 1972–78. *Publications:* (trans. and ed) The Digest of Justinian, 1979, 4th edn 1993; various legal and musical. *Recreations:* music (especially playing the violin), cricket, Rugby, military history, cooking, walking in London and Yorkshire. *Address:* Magdalene College, Cambridge CB3 0AG; 35 Essex Street, Temple, WC2R 3AR. *Clubs:* MCC, Farmers'; Leeds; Hawks (Cambridge); Cambridge University Rugby Union Football; Colonsay Golf.

KOLTAI, Ralph, CBE 1983; RDI 1984; freelance stage designer; designer for Drama, Opera and Dance, since 1950; Associate Designer, Royal Shakespeare Company, 1963–66 and since 1976; *b* 31 July 1924; Hungarian-German; *s* of Dr(med) Alfred Koltai and Charlotte Koltai (*née* Weinstein); *m* 1956, Annena Stubbs. *Educ:* Central Sch. of Art and Design (Dip. with Dist.). Early work entirely in field of opera. First production, Angelique, for London Opera Club, Fortune Theatre, 1950. Designs for The Royal Opera House, Sadler's Wells, Scottish Opera, National Welsh Opera, The English Opera Group. First of 7 ballets for Ballet Rambert, Two Brothers, 1958. Head , Sch. of Theatre Design, Central Sch. of Art & Design, 1965–72. *Productions:* RSC: The Caucasian Chalk Circle, 1962; The Representative, 1963; The Birthday Party, Endgame, The Jew of Malta, 1964; The Merchant of Venice, Timon of Athens, 1965; Little Murders, 1967; Major Barbara, 1970; Too True To Be Good, 1975; Old World, 1976; Wild Oats, 1977; The Tempest, Love's Labour's Lost, 1978; Hippolytus, Baal, 1979; Romeo and Juliet, Hamlet, 1980; The Love Girl and the Innocent, 1981 (London Drama Critics Award); Much Ado About Nothing, Molière, 1982; Custom of the Country, Cyrano de Bergerac (SWET Award), 1983; Troilus and Cressida, Othello, 1985; They Shoot Horses, Don't They?, 1987; for National Theatre: an "all male" As You Like It, 1967; Back to Methuselah, 1969; State of Revolution, 1977; Brand (SWET Award), The Guardsman, 1978; Richard III, The Wild Duck, 1979; Man and Superman, 1981; *other notable productions include: opera:* for Sadler's Wells/English National Opera: The Rise and Fall of the City of Mahagonny, 1963; From the House of the Dead, 1965; Bluebeard's Castle, 1972; Wagner's (complete) Ring Cycle, 1973; Seven Deadly Sins, 1978; Anna Karenina, 1981; Pacific Overtures, 1987; for The Royal Opera House: Taverner, 1972; The Ice Break, 1977; Tannhäuser, Sydney, 1973; Wozzeck, Netherlands Opera, 1973; Fidelio, Munich, 1974; Verdi's Macbeth, Edinburgh Festival, 1976; Les Soldats, Lyon Opera, 1983; Italian Girl in Algiers, 1984, Tannhäuser, 1986, Geneva; (also dir.) Flying Dutchman, Hong Kong, 1987; La Traviata, Hong Kong, 1990, Stockholm, 1993; The Makropulas Affair, Oslo, 1991; Otello, Essen, 1994; Madam Butterfly, Tokyo, 1995; Simon Boccanegra, WNO, and Carmen, Royal Albert Hall, 1997; Dalibor, Scottish Opera and Nabucco, Chorégie Orange, 1998; Don Giovanni, Kirov, 1999; Genoveva, Prague, 2000; *theatre:* Pack of Lies, Lyric, 1983; Across from the Garden of Allah, Comedy, 1986; Twelfth Night, Theatre Royal, Copenhagen, 1996; Midsummer Night's Dream, and Macbeth, Teater Gladsaxe, Copenhagen, 1998; (also dir.) Suddenly Last Summer, Nottingham Playhouse, 1998; for Aalborg Theatre, Denmark: Threepenny Opera, 1979; The Love Girl and the Innocent, 1980; Terra Nova, 1981; The Carmelites, 1981; Mahagonny, 1984; *musicals:* Billy, Drury Lane, 1974; Bugsy Malone, Her Majesty's, 1983; Dear Anyone, Cambridge Theatre, 1983; Carrie, Stratford, NY, 1988; Metropolis, Piccadilly, 1989; My Fair Lady, NY, 1993; *ballet:* The Planets, Royal Ballet, 1990; Cruel Garden, 1992; has worked in most countries in Western Europe, also Bulgaria, Argentine, USA, Canada, Australia. Retrospective exhibition, London, Beijing, HK, Taipei, Prague, 1997–99. Fellow: Acad. of Performing Art, Hong Kong, 1994; London Inst., 1996; Rose Bruford Coll.; FRSA. London Drama Critics Award, Designer of the Year, 1967 (for Little Murders and As You Like It); (jtly) Gold Medal, Internat. Exhibn of Stage Design, Prague Quadriennale, 1975, 1979; Individual Silver Medal, Prague Quadriennale, 1987. *Publication:* Ralph Koltai: designer for the stage, 1997. *Recreation:* wildlife photography. *Address:* c/o London Management, 2–4 Noel Street, W1V 3RB. *T:* (020) 7287 9000.

KOMANSKY, David H.; Chief Executive Officer, since 1996, Chairman, since 1997, Merrill Lynch & Co. Inc.; *b* 27 April 1939; *m* Phyllis; two *d. Educ:* Univ. of Miami; Harvard Univ. (AMP 1990). Joined Merrill Lynch & Co. Inc., 1968: Financial Consultant, 1968–75, Sales Manager, 1975, Forest Hills, NY office; Sales Manager, Garden City, NY office, 1975–77; Office Manager, Manhasset, NY office, 1977–81; Private Client Group: Regional Director: Mideast Reg., 1981–83; Metropolitan Reg., 1983–85; Pres. and CEO, Merrill Lynch Realty Inc., 1985–88; Dir, Nat. Sales, 1988–93; Executive Vice President: Global Equity Mkts Gp, 1990–92; Debt Mkts Gp, 1992–93; Debt and Equity Mkts Gp, 1993–95. Member, Board of Directors: NY Stock Exchange; Business Council of NY State Inc.; NYC Investment Fund; Associates of Harvard Business Sch. *Address:* c/o Merrill Lynch & Co. Inc., World Headquarters, North Tower, World Financial Center, New York, NY 10080, USA.

KOMISARENKO, Prof. Sergiy Vassiliovych, MD; PhD; Director, Palladin Institute of Biochemistry, since 1998; President, Ukrainian Institute for Peace and Democracy, since 1999; *b* 9 July 1943; *s* of late Prof. Vassiliy Komisarenko and Lubov Drosovska-Komisarenko; *m* 1970, Natalia Ignatiuk; one *d. Educ:* Ukrainian-English Sch., Kiev; Kiev Med. Inst. (MD with dist. 1966); Kiev Univ.; Inst. of Biochem., Kiev (PhD 1970); Inst. of Molecular Biology, Kiev (DSc 1989). Palladin Institute of Biochemistry, Ukrainian Academy of Sciences, Kiev: Jun., then Sen. Scientific Researcher, 1969–75; Scientific Sec., 1972–74; Hd of Dept, 1975–92; Prof. of Biochem., 1989; Dir, 1989–92; Dep. Prime Minister, Ukraine, 1990–92; Ambassador of Ukraine to UK, 1992–98, and to Ireland, 1995–98. Visiting Scientist: Pasteur Inst., Paris, 1974–75; Sloan-Kettering Cancer Inst., NY, 1981. Pres., Ukranian Biochem. Soc., 1999–. Member: Ukrainian Nat. Acad. of Scis, 1991; Ukrainian Acad. of Med. Scis, 1993. Mem., Rotary Club, London, 1995–. Ukrainian State Award, 1979; Ukrainian State Order of Merit, 1996. *Publications:* Radiation and Human Immunity, 1994; numerous articles on biochem. and immunology; also articles on Ukrainian culture and politics. *Recreations:* music, ski-ing, clay pigeon shooting, lawn tennis, wind-surfing. *Address:* Institute of Biochemistry, 9 Leontovicha Street, Kiev 30, Ukraine. *T:* (44) 2245974; *e-mail:* SVK@biochem.KIEV.ua. *Club:* Royal Automobile.

KOMOROWSKI, Dr Stanislaw Jerzy; Ambassador of the Republic of Poland to the Court of St James's, since 1999; *b* 18 Dec. 1953; *s* of Henryk Komorowski and Helena Komorowska (*née* Krokowska); *m* 1st, 1976, Irena Kwiatkowska (marr. diss. 1987); two *s*; 2nd, 1989, Maria Wegrzecka (marr. diss. 1997); one *s. Educ:* Inst. of Physics, Univ. of Warsaw (MSc 1978); Inst. of Physical Chem., Polish Acad. of Scis (PhD 1985). Research Fellow, Physical Chem. Inst., Polish Acad. of Scis, 1978–90; Post-doctoral Fellow, Univ. of Utah, Salt Lake City, 1986–87; Adjunct, Physical Chem. Inst., 1987–89; Asst Prof., Univ. of Utah, 1989–90; Ministry for Foreign Affairs, Poland: Head of Section and Asst Head, Personnel Dept, 1991; Asst Head, 1991–92, Head, 1992–94, Eur. Dept; Ambassador to the Netherlands, 1994–98; Head, Office of Minister for Foreign Affairs, 1998–99. Grand Cross, Order of Orange Nassau (Netherlands), 1998. *Publications:* articles in American, French and Dutch physical chemistry jls. *Recreations:* tennis, ski-ing, photography. *Address:* Embassy of the Republic of Poland, 47 Portland Place, W1B 1JH. *T:* (020) 7580 4324. *Clubs:* Garrick, Rotary, Travellers, Army and Navy, Beefsteak.

KONIGSBERG, Allen Stewart; *see* Allen, Woody.

KONSTANT, Rt Rev. David Every; *see* Leeds, Bishop of, (RC).

KOOPS, Hon. Dame Mary Claire; *see* Hogg, Hon. Dame M. C.

KOOTENAY, Archbishop of, since 1994; **Most Rev. David Perry Crawley;** Metropolitan of British Columbia and Yukon, since 1994; *b* 26 July 1937; *s* of Rev. Canon George Antony Crawley, LTh and Lucy Lillian Crawley (*née* Ball); *m* 1st, 1959, Frances Mary Louise Wilmot; two *d*; 2nd, 1986, Joan Alice Bubbs; one *d* (and one *d* decd). *Educ:* Univ. of Manitoba (BA 1958); St John's Coll., Winnipeg (LTh 1961; DD 1990); Univ. of Kent at Canterbury (MA 1967). Ordained Deacon 1961, Priest 1962. Incumbent, St Thomas', Sherwood Park, Edmonton, 1961–66; Canon Missioner, All Saints Cathedral, Edmonton, 1967–70; Rector, St Matthew's, Winnipeg, 1971–77; Archdeacon of Winnipeg, 1974–77; Archdeacon of Rupert's Land, 1977–81; Lectr, St John's College, Winnipeg, 1981–82; Rector, St Michael and All Angels, Regina, 1982–85; Rector, St Paul's, Vancouver, 1985–90; Bishop of Kootenay, 1990–. *Recreations:* ski-ing, hiking. *Address:* 1876 Richter Street, Kelowna, BC V1Y 2M9, Canada.

KOPELOWITZ, Dr (Jacob) Lionel (Garstein), JP; General Medical Practitioner, since 1953; *b* 9 Dec. 1926; *s* of Maurice and Mabel Kopelowitz; *m* 1980, Sylvia Waksman (*née* Galler). *Educ:* Clifton Coll., Bristol; Trinity Coll., Cambridge (MA 1947); University Coll. Hosp. London. MRCS, LRCP 1951; MRCGP 1964. Resident MO, London Jewish Hosp., 1951–52; Flying Officer, RAF Med. Branch, 1952–53. Member: General Medical Council, 1984–94; General Optical Council, 1979–93; Standing Med. Adv. Cttee, DHSS, 1974–78; British Medical Association: Fellow, 1980; Mem. Council, 1982–94; Chm., Newcastle Div., 1968–69; Pres., Northern Regional Council, 1984–88; Mem., Gen. Med. Services Cttee, 1971–90 (Past Chm., Maternity Services Sub-Cttee); Chm., Central Adv. Cttee, Deputising Services, 1980–; Dep. Chm., Private Practice Cttee, 1972–89; Chairman: St Marylebone and Bloomsbury Div., 1992–; London Regl Council, 2001–. Chm., Newcastle upon Tyne FPC, 1979–85; Pres., Soc. of FPCs of England and Wales, 1978–79; Mem. Council, RCGP, 1995–. Vice-Pres., Trades Adv. Council, 1988–. President: Board of Deputies of British Jews, 1985–90; Nat. Council for Soviet Jewry, 1985–91; European Jewish Congress, 1986–91; Vice President: Conf. on Jewish Material Claims Against Germany, 1988–; Conf. on Jewish Material Claims Against Austria, 1988–. Member: Exec. Cttee, Meml Foundn for Jewish Culture, 1988–; United Synagogue, 1991–96. Vice-Pres., Assoc. of Baltic Jews, 1995–; Mem., Chm., Pres., numerous med. bodies and Jewish organisations, UK and overseas. Vice-Pres., British Council, Share Zedek Med. Centre, 1990–. Mem. Bd of Govs, Clifton Coll., Bristol, 1988–; Pres., Old Cliftonian Soc., 1991–93. Liveryman, Apothecaries' Co., 1969. JP Northumberland, 1964. Grand Cross, Order of Merit (Germany), 1993. *Publications:* articles in med. jls; contrib. to Med. Annual. *Recreations:* foreign travel, contract bridge. *Address:* 10 Cumberland House, Clifton Gardens, W9 1DX. *T:* (020) 7289 6375; Little Jesmond, 145 Barrack Lane, Aldwick, W Sussex PO21 4ED. *T:* (01243) 268134. *Club:* Athenæum.

KORAB-KARPINSKI, Marek Romuald, FRCS, FRCSE; Consultant Orthopaedic and Spinal Surgeon, East Yorkshire Hospitals NHS Trust, since 1987; *b* 29 Jan. 1950; *s* of Lt Col Marian Korab-Karpinski, MC, VM and Zofia Korab-Karpinska; *m* 1999, Dr Malgorzata Szymanska, orthopaedic surgeon; two *s* one *d* by previous marriage. *Educ:* Univ. of Nottingham (BMedSci 1977; BM BS); Univ. of Liverpool (MChOrth 1985). FRCS 1981; FRCSE 1981 (FRCSE (Orth) 1985). Higher surgical orthopaedic trng, Birmingham, 1981–83, Nottingham, 1983–87. Hon. Vis. Prof., Poznan Acad. of Orthopaedics, Poland, 1997. Fellow, Brit. Orthopaedic Assoc., 1985. Patron, PPA Internat., 1997. Hon. Fellow, Univ. of Hull, 1996. Computer Assisted Operative Surgery Prize, BCS, 1996. Designated co-inventor, Computer Assisted Robotic Surgery Technique, 1997. *Publications:* Posterior Lumbar Interbody Fusion and Cages, 1977; (contrib.) Current Concepts in Lumbar Spine Disorders, Vol. 2, 1997; various articles related to orthopaedics and computers, incl. robotic surgery; res. papers. *Recreations:* tennis, snow ski-ing, travel, charity work of a surgical nature. *Address:* 10 Harley Street, W1N 1AA. *T:* (020) 7436 5252. *Club:* Kandahar.

KORALEK, Paul George, CBE 1984; RA 1991 (ARA 1986); RIBA; RIAI; Founding Partner, 1961 and Director, Ahrends Burton and Koralek, architects; *b* 7 April 1933; *s* of late Ernest and Alice Koralek; *m* 1958, Jennifer Chadwick; one *s* two *d. Educ:* Aldenham School; Architectural Assoc. School of Architecture. RIBA 1957; AA Dip. Hons. Architect: with Powell & Moya, London, 1956–57; with Marcel Breuer, New York, 1959–60. Part-time teaching, Sch. of Arch., Leicester Polytechnic, 1982–84. *Major projects include: public buildings:* Redcar Library, 1971; Maidenhead Libr., 1972; Roman Catholic Chaplaincy, Oxford, 1972; Nucleus Low Energy Hosp., IoW, 1982; winning entry, Nat. Gall. Extension Hampton Site Comp., 1982; Dover Heritage Centre, 1988–90 (Civic Trust Award, 1992); British Embassy, Moscow, 1993–99; Dublin Dental Hosp., Trinity Coll., 1994–98 (RIBA Arch. Award; RIAI Award); Techniquest Science Centre, Cardiff, 1995 (RIBA Arch. Award); Offaly County Council offices, 1999–; County Offices, Neneagh, Tipperary, 2000; *educational buildings:* Chichester Theol Coll., 1965; Berkeley Liby, TCD, 1967 (1st Prize, Internat. Comp., 1961); Templeton Coll., Oxford, 1967; Arts Faculty Bldg, TCD, 1975–79; Portsmouth Poly. Liby, 1975–79; Residential bldg, Keble Coll., Oxford, 1976 (RIBA Arch. Award, 1978); Selly Oak Colls Learning Resources Centre, 1997; Insts of Technol. at Tralee, Waterford and Blanchardstown, 1997–; Loughborough Univ. Business Sch., 1998; Innovation Centre, TCD, 2001; *residential* *buildings:* houses, Dunstan Rd, Oxford, 1969; Nebenzahl House, Jerusalem, 1972; Chalvedon Housing, 1975–77; Whitmore Court Housing, Basildon, 1975 (RIBA Good Design in Housing Award, 1977); Felmore Housing, 1975–80; *commercial/industrial buildings:* Habitat Warehouse, Showroom and Offices, Wallingford, 1974 (Financial Times Indust. Arch. Award, and Structl Steel Design Award (Warehouse), 1976); factory bldgs and refurbishment, Cummins Engine Co., Shotts, Scotland, 1975–83 (Structl Steel Design Award, 1980); J. Sainsbury supermarket, Canterbury, 1984 (Structl Steel Design Award, 1985; FT Arch. at Work Award Commendation, 1986); W. H. Smith Offices, Greenbridge, 1985 and 1996 (FT Arch. at Work Award Commendation, 1987); John Lewis Dept Store, Kingston-upon-Thames, 1987 (Civic Trust Commendation, 1991). *Exhibitions of drawings and works:* RIBA Heinz Gall., 1980; Douglas Hyde Gall. Dublin, 1981; Technical Univ. of Braunschweig and Tech. Univ. of Hanover, Germany, Mus. of Finnish Arch., Helsinki, Univ. of Oulu, and Alvar Aalto Mus., Jvasklya, Finland, 1982; HQ of AA, Oslo, 1983. Member: Develt Adv. (formerly Design and Architectural Rev.) Panel, Cardiff Bay Develt Corp., 1988; ARCUK Bd of Architectural Educn, 1987–93; Trustee, Bldg Industry Youth Trust, 1981–95. External Examiner: Sch. of Arch., Univ. of Manchester, 1981–85; Plymouth Poly, 1988; Assessor: RIBA competitions, incl. Toyota UK HQ, 1997; Irish Dept of Educn Schs competition; Civic Trust Awards; Advr, Cardiff Bay Opera House, 1994–95. Papers and lectures, UK and abroad, 1964–. *Publications:* paper and articles in RIBA and other prof. jls. *Recreations:* drawing, walking, gardening. *Address:* Unit 1, 7 Chalcot Road, NW1 8LH. *T:* (020) 7586 3311, *Fax:* (020) 7722 5445; *e-mail:* abk@abklondon.com.

KORNBERG, Prof. Arthur; Professor of Biochemistry, Stanford University, since 1959; *b* Brooklyn, 3 March 1918; *m*; three *s*. *Educ:* College of the City of New York (BSc 1937); University of Rochester, NY (MD 1941). Strong Memorial Hospital, Rochester, 1941–42; National Insts of Health, Bethesda, Md, 1942–52; Professor of Microbiology, Washington Univ., and Head of Dept of Microbiology, 1953–59; Head of Dept of Biochemistry, Stanford Univ., 1959–69. MNAS; MAAS; Mem. Amer. Phil Soc. Foreign Mem., Royal Soc., 1970. Many honours and awards, including: Paul Lewis Award in Enzyme Chemistry, 1951; Nobel Prize (joint) in Medicine, 1959; Nat Medal of Science, 1979. *Publications:* DNA Synthesis, 1974; DNA Replication, 1980 (Suppl., 1982); articles in scientific jls. *Address:* Stanford University Medical Center, Palo Alto, CA 94305–5307, USA.

KORNBERG, Prof. Sir Hans (Leo), Kt 1978; MA, DSc, ScD, PhD; FRS 1965; FIBiol 1965; University Professor and Professor of Biology, Boston University, since 1995; Sir William Dunn Professor of Biochemistry, University of Cambridge, 1975–95, and Fellow of Christ's College, since 1975 (Master, 1982–95); *b* 14 Jan. 1928; *o s* of Max Kornberg and Margarete Kornberg (*née* Silberbach); *m* 1st, 1956, Monica Mary King (*d* 1989); twin *s* two *d*; 2nd, 1991, Donna, *d* of William B. Haber and Ruth Haber. *Educ:* Queen Elizabeth Grammar Sch., Wakefield; University of Sheffield (BSc, PhD); MA 1958, DSc 1961, Oxon; ScD Cantab 1961. Commonwealth Fund Fellow of Harkness Foundation, at Yale University and Public Health Research Inst., New York, 1953–55; Mem. of scientific staff, MRC Cell Metabolism Res. Unit, University of Oxford, 1955–60; Lectr, Worcester Coll., Oxford, 1958–61 (Hon. Fellow 1980); Prof. of Biochemistry, Univ. of Leicester, 1960–75. Visiting Instructor, Marine Biological Lab., Woods Hole, Mass, 1964–66, 1981–95, Trustee, 1982–93. Dir, UK Nirex Ltd, 1986–95. Member: SRC, 1967–72 (Chm., Science Bd, 1969–72); UGC Biol. Sci. Cttee, 1967–77; NATO Adv. Study Inst. Panel, 1970–76 (Chm., 1974–75); Kuratorium, Max-Planck Inst., Dortmund, 1979–90 (Chm., Sci. Adv. Cttee); AFRC (formerly ARC), 1980–84; Priorities Bd for R & D in Agriculture, 1984–90; BP Venture Res. Council, 1981–91; ACARD, 1982–85; Adv. Council on Public Records, 1984–86; UK Cttee on Eur. Year of the Environment, 1986–88; Vice-Chm., EMBO, 1978–81; Chairman: Royal Commn on Environmental Pollution, 1976–81; Adv. Cttee on Genetic Modification, 1986–95; Co-ordinating Cttee on Environmental Res., Res. Councils, 1986–88; Sci. Adv. Cttee, Inst. for Mol. Biol. and Medicine, Monash Univ., 1987–; President: BAAS, 1984–85; Biochemical Soc., 1990–95; IUBMB, 1991–94; Assoc. for Science Educn, 1991–92; Vice-Pres., Inst. of Biol., 1971–73. A Managing Trustee, Nuffield Foundn, 1973–93; Trustee, 1990–92, Gov., 1992–95, Wellcome Trust; Academic Governor, Hebrew Univ. of Jerusalem, 1976–97 (Hon. Gov., 1997–); Governor: Weizmann Inst., 1980–97 (Hon. Gov., 1997–); Lister Inst., 1990–95. Hon. Fellow: Brasenose Coll., Oxford, 1983; Wolfson Coll., Cambridge, 1990. FRSA 1972. Fellow, Amer. Acad. of Microbiol., 1992. For. Associate, Nat. Acad. of Sciences, USA, 1986; Foreign Member: Amer. Philosoph. Soc., 1993; Accademia Nazionale dei Lincei, 1997; Hon. For. Mem., Amer. Acad. of Arts & Scis, 1987; Member: Leopoldina German Acad. of Scis, 1982; Acad. Europaea, 1989; Hon. Member: Amer. Soc. Biol Chem., 1972; Biochem. Soc., FRG, 1973; Japanese Biochem. Soc., 1981; Phi Beta Kappa, 1996; Hon. FRCP 1989. Hon. ScD Cincinnati, 1974; Hon. DSc: Warwick, 1975; Leicester, 1979; Sheffield, 1979; Bath, 1980; Strathclyde, 1985; South Bank, 1994; Leeds, 1995; La Trobe, 1997; DUniv Essex, 1979; Dr med Leipzig, 1984; LLD Dundee, 1999. Colworth Medal of Biochemical Soc., 1965; Otto Warburg Medal, Biochem. Soc. of Federal Republic of Germany, 1973. *Publications:* (with Sir Hans Krebs) Energy Transformations in Living Matter, 1957; articles in scientific jls. *Recreations:* cooking and conversation. *Address:* The University Professors, 745 Commonwealth Avenue, Boston, MA 02215, USA; (home) 134 Sewall Avenue, # 2, Brookline, MA 02446, USA.

KORNER, Joanna Christian Mary; QC 1993; a Recorder, since 1995; *b* 1 July 1951; *d* of John Hugh George Korner and Martha (*née* Tupay von Isertingen). *Educ:* Queensgate Sch.; Inns of Court Sch. of Law. Called to the Bar, Inner Temple, 1974, Bencher, 1996. Member: Bar Council, 1994–97; Crown Court Rules Cttee, 1994–2000. Sen. Prosecutor, UN War Crimes Tribunal, The Hague, 1999–. *Recreations:* collecting books and porcelain, cinema, tennis. *Address:* 6 King's Bench Walk, Temple, EC4Y 7DR. *T:* (020) 7583 0410.

KORNICKI, Peter Francis, DPhil; FBA 2000; Reader in Japanese History and Bibliography, since 1995, and Fellow of Robinson College, since 1986, University of Cambridge; *b* 1 May 1950; *er s* of Sqn Leader Franciszek Kornicki and Patience Ceridwen Kornicka (*née* Williams); *m* 1st, 1975, Catharine Olga Mikolaski (*d* 1995); one *s* one *d*; 2nd, 1998, Francesca Orsini. *Educ:* St George's Coll., Weybridge; Lincoln Coll., Oxford (BA 1972; MSc 1975); St Antony's Coll., Oxford (DPhil 1979). Lectr, Univ. of Tasmania, 1978–82; Associate Prof., Kyoto Univ., 1982–84; Cambridge University: Lectr, 1985–95; Chm., Faculty Bd of Oriental Studies, 1993–95. Pres., European Assoc. for Japanese Studies, 1997–2000. Special Prize, Japan Foundn, 1992. *Publications:* The Reform of Fiction in Meiji Japan, 1982; Early Japanese Books in Cambridge University Library, 1991; (jtly) Cambridge Encyclopedia of Japan, 1993; The Book in Japan: a cultural history, 1998; Early Japanese Books in the Russian State Library, 1999; numerous articles and reviews in jls. *Recreations:* travel, cooking, languages. *Address:* Faculty of Oriental Studies, Sidgwick Avenue, Cambridge CB3 9DA. *T:* (01223) 335106.

KOSSOFF, David; actor; author; illustrator; *b* 24 Nov. 1919; *s* of Louis and Anne Kossoff, both Russian; *m* 1947, Margaret, (Jennie), Jenkins (*d* 1995); one *s* (and one *s* decd). *Educ:* elementary sch.; Northern Polytechnic. Commercial Artist, 1937; Draughtsman, 1937–38; Furniture Designer, 1938–39; Technical Illustrator, 1939–45. Began acting, 1943; working as actor and illustrator, 1945–52, as actor and designer, 1952–. BBC Repertory Company, 1945–51. Took over part of Colonel Alexander Ikonenko in the Love of Four Colonels, Wyndham's, 1952; Sam Tager in The Shrike, Prince's, 1953; Morry in The Bespoke Overcoat, and Tobit in Tobias and the Angel, Arts, 1953; Prof. Lodegger in No Sign of the Dove, Savoy, 1953; Nathan in The Boychik, Embassy, 1954 (and again Morry in The Bespoke Overcoat); Mendele in The World of Sholom Aleichem, Embassy, 1955, and Johannesburg, 1957; one-man show, One Eyebrow Up, The Arts, 1957; Man on Trial, Lyric, 1959; Stars in Your Eyes, Palladium, 1960; The Tenth Man, Comedy, 1961; Come Blow Your Horn, Prince of Wales, 1962; one-man show, Kossoff at the Prince Charles, 1963, later called A Funny Kind of Evening (many countries); Enter Solly Gold, Mermaid, 1970; Cinderella, Palladium, 1971; Bunny, Criterion, 1972; own Bible storytelling programmes on radio and TV, as writer and teller, 1964–66; solo performance (stage), 'As According to Kossoff', 1970–. Has appeared in many films. Won British Acad. Award, 1956. Elected MSIA 1958. FRSA 1969. Hon. DLitt, Hatfield Poly., 1990. *Play:* Big Night for Shylock, 1968. *Publications:* Bible Stories retold by David Kossoff, 1968; The Book of Witnesses, 1971; The Three Donkeys, 1972; The Voices of Masada, 1973; The Little Book of Sylvanus, 1975; You Have a Minute, Lord?, 1977; A Small Town is a World, 1979; Sweet Nutcracker, 1985. *Recreations:* conversation, working with the hands. *Address:* 45 Roe Green Close, Hatfield, Herts AL10 9PD.

KOTCH, Laurie, (Mrs J. K. Kotch); *see* Purden, R. L.

KOTSOKOANE, Hon. Joseph Riffat Larry; Commander, Order of Ramatseatsana, 1982; development consultant (agriculture and rural development, formerly human and natural resources), since 1986; Minister of Education, Sports and Culture, Lesotho, 1984–86; *b* 19 Oct. 1922; *s* of Basotho parents, living in Johannesburg, South Africa; *m* 1947, Elizabeth (*née* Molise); two *s* three *d*. BSc (SA); BSc Hons (Witwatersrand); Cert. Agric. (London). Development Officer, Dept of Agric., Basutoland, 1951–54; Agric. Educn Officer i/c of Agric. Sch. for junior field staff, 1955–62; Agric. Extension Officer i/c of all field staff of Min. of Agric., 1962–63; Prin. Agric. Off. (Dep. Dir), Min. of Agric., 1964–66; High Comr for Lesotho, in London, 1966–69; Ambassador to Germany, Holy See, Rome, France, and Austria, 1968–69; Permanent Sec. and Hd of Diplomatic Service, Lesotho, 1969–70; Permanent Sec. for Health, Educn and Social Welfare, Lesotho, 1970–71; High Comr for Lesotho in East Africa, Nigeria and Ghana, 1972–74; Minister: of Foreign Affairs, Lesotho, 1974–75; of Education, 1975–76; of Agriculture, 1976–78; Perm. Rep. to UN, 1978; Sec. to the Cabinet and Head of CS (Sen. Perm. Sec.), 1978–84. Guest of Min. of Agric., Netherlands, 1955; studied agric. educn, USA (financed by Carnegie Corp. of NY and Ford Foundn), 1960–61; FAO confs in Tunisia, Tanganyika and Uganda, 1962 and 1963; Mem. Lesotho delegn to 24th World Health Assembly, 1971; travelled extensively to study and observe methods of agric. administration, 1964; meetings on nutrition, Berlin and Hamburg, 1966; diplomatic trainee, Brit. Embassy, Bonn, 1966. Hon. PhD Fort Hare, S Africa, 2001. Gold Medal, Fertilizer Soc. of SA, 1998; Merit Award, Nat. African Farmers' Union of SA, 1998; Medal, ARC of SA, 1999. *Recreations:* swimming, amateur dramatics, photography, debating, reading, travelling. *Address:* PO Box 1015, Maseru 100, Lesotho, Southern Africa. *T:* 312913, *Fax:* 311769.

KOUMI, Margaret, (Maggie); Joint Editor, 1988–93, Editor, 1993–2001, Hello! magazine; *b* 15 July 1942; *d* of Yiasoumi Koumi and Melexidia Paraskeva; *m* 1980, Ramon Sola. *Educ:* Buckingham Gate Sch., London. Sec., Thomas Cook Travel, 1957–60; Sub-Editor and writer, Boyfriend and Trend magazines, 1960–66; Sub-Editor, TV World, 1967–68; Production Editor, 1968–70, Editor, 1970–86, 19 magazine; Man. Editor, Practical Parenting and Practical Health, 1986–87. Hello! magazine has won several awards. *Recreation:* reading. *Address:* c/o Hello! magazine, Wellington House, 69–71 Upper Ground, SE1 9PQ. *T:* (020) 7667 8721.

KOVACEVICH, Stephen; pianist and conductor; *b* 17 Oct. 1940; *s* of Nicholas Kovacevich and Loreta (*née* Zuban, later Bishop). *Educ:* studied under Lev Shorr and Myra Hess. Solo and orchestral debut, San Francisco, USA 1951; London debut, Nov. 1961. First known professionally as Stephen Bishop, then as Stephen Bishop-Kovacevich, and since 1991 as Stephen Kovacevich. Concert tours: in England, Europe and USA, with many of the world's leading orchestras, incl. New York Philharmonic, Los Angeles Philharmonic, Israel Philharmonic, Amsterdam Concertgebouw, London Symphony, London Philharmonic, and BBC Symphony. Has appeared at Edinburgh, Bath, Berlin and San Sebastian Festivals. Gave 1st performance of Richard Rodney Bennett's Piano Concerto, 1969 (this work is dedicated to and has been recorded by him, under Alexander Gibson). Performed all Mozart Piano concertos, 1969–71. Principal Guest Conductor: Australian Chamber Orch., 1987–91; Zagreb Philharmonic Orch.; Music Dir, Irish Chamber Orch., 1990–93. Edison Award for his recording of Bartok's 2nd Piano Concerto and Stravinsky's Piano Concerto, with BBC Symphony Orchestra, under Colin Davis; Gramophone Award, 1993 and Stereo Review Record of the Year for Brahms' Piano Concerto No 1 with LPO, under Wolfgang Sawallisch. *Recreations:* snooker, chess, films, tennis. *Address:* c/o Van Walsum Management, 4 Addison Bridge Place, W14 8XP. *T:* (020) 7371 4343.

KOWALSKI, Gregor; Deputy Parliamentary Counsel, since 2001; *b* 7 Oct. 1949; *s* of Mieczyslaw Kowalski and Jeanie Hutcheson Kowalski (*née* MacDonald); *m* 1974, Janet McFarlane Pillatt; two *s*. *Educ:* Airdrie Academy; Strathclyde Univ. (LLB 1971). Apprentice, then Asst Solicitor, Levy & McRae, Glasgow, 1971–74; Procurator Fiscal Depute, Glasgow, 1974–78; Asst, later Deputy Parly Draftsman for Scotland and Asst Legal Sec. to Lord Advocate, 1978–87; seconded to Govt of Seychelles as Legal Draftsman, 1982–83; Scottish Parly Counsel and Asst Legal Sec. to Lord Advocate, 1987–99; Scottish Parly Counsel to UK Govt, 1999–2001. Founding Mem. and Sec., Soc. of Scottish Lawyers in London, 1987–89 (Vice Pres., 1989–91; Pres., 1991–92). *Recreations:* singing, music. *Address:* 36 Whitehall, SW1A 2AY. *T:* (020) 7210 6622.

KRAEMER, (Thomas Whilhelm) Nicholas; conductor; *b* 7 March 1945; *s* of William Paul Kraemer and Helen Bartrum; *m* 1984, Elizabeth Mary Anderson; two *s* two *d* (and one *s* decd). *Educ:* Edinburgh Acad.; Lancing Coll.; Dartington Coll. of Arts; Nottingham Univ. (BMus 1967). ARCM. Harpsichordist with Acad. of St Martin in the Fields, 1972–80, with Monteverdi Choir and Orchestra, 1970–80; Musical Director: Unicorn Opera, Abingdon, 1971–75; West Eleven Children's Opera, 1971–88; Founder and Dir, Raglan Baroque Players, 1978–; Principal Conductor, Divertimenti, 1979–; Principal Guest Conductor, Manchester Camerata, 1995– (Principal Conductor, 1992–95); Conductor, Glyndebourne, 1980–82; Musical Dir, Opera 80, 1980–83; Associate Conductor, BBC Scottish SO, 1983–85; Artistic Director: London Bach Orch., 1985–; Irish Chamber Orch., 1985–90 (now Guest Conductor); Guest Conductor: CBSO, Scottish Chamber Orch., Orch. of Age of Enlightenment, Northern Sinfonia, Israel Chamber Orch., Stadt Orch. Winterthur, Nord Nederlands Orch., BBC Nat. Orch. of Wales, City of London Sinfonia, Hallé Orch., St Paul Chamber Orch. (USA), Music of the Baroque (Chicago). Prog. Dir, Bath Fest., 1994. Recordings include works by Vivaldi,

Locatelli, Mozart, Handel. *Recreation:* keeping fit. *Address:* c/o Caroline Phillips Management, Tailor House, 63–65 High Street, Whitwell, Herts SG4 8AH. *T:* (01438) 871828, *Fax:* (01438) 871838.

KRAMER, Prof. Ivor Robert Horton, OBE 1984; MDS; DSc (Med); FDSRCS, FFDRCSI, Hon. FRACDS, FRCPath; Emeritus Professor of Oral Pathology, University of London; *b* 20 June 1923; *yr s* of late Alfred Bertie and Agnes Maud Kramer; *m* 1st, 1946, Elisabeth Dalley (*d* 1978); one *s*; 2nd, 1979, Mrs Dorothy Toller (*d* 1985); 3rd, 1991, Mrs Virginia Webster. *Educ:* Royal Dental Hosp. of London Sch. of Dental Surgery; MDS 1955; DSc (Med) London 1993. FDSRCS 1960 (LDSRCS 1944); FRCPath 1970 (MRCPath 1964); FFDRCSI 1973. Asst to Pathologist, Princess Louise (Kensington) Hosp. for Children, 1944–48; Wright Fleming Inst. of Microbiol., 1948–49; Instr in Dental Histology, Royal Dental Hosp. Sch. of Dental Surgery, 1944–50; Asst Pathologist, Royal Dental Hosp., 1950–56; Institute of Dental Surgery: Lectr in Dental Path., 1949–50, Sen. Lectr, 1950–57; Reader in Oral Path., 1957–62; Prof. of Oral Path., 1962–83; Sub-dean, 1950–70; Dean and Dir of Studies, 1970–83; Head, Dept of Path., Eastman Dental Hosp., 1950–83. Civilian Cons. in Dental Path., RN, 1967–83. Member: WHO Expert Adv. Panel on Dental Health, 1975–97; Bd of Faculty of Dental Surgery, RCS, 1964–80, Council, RCS, 1977–80; GDC, 1973–84; Mem., Council for Postgrad. Med. Educn in Eng. and Wales, 1972–77 (Chm., Dental Cttee, 1972–77); Pres., Odontological Section, RSocMed, 1973–74; Pres., British Div., Internat. Assoc. for Dental Res., 1974–77. Hon. Pres. of the Assoc., 1974–75. Editor, Archives of Oral Biology, 1959–69. Lectures: Wilkinson, Manchester, 1962; Charles Tomes, 1969, Webb Johnson, 1981, RCS; Holme, UCH, 1969; Elwood Meml, QUB, 1970; Hutchinson, Edinburgh, 1971; Wilkinson, IDS, 1987. Hon. FRACDS 1978. Howard Mummery Prize, BDA, 1966; Maurice Down Award, Brit. Assoc. of Oral Surgeons, 1974; Colyer Gold Medal, FDS, RCS, 1985. Dr *hc* Helsinki, 2000. *Publications:* (with R. B. Lucas) Bacteriology for Students of Dental Surgery, 1954, 3rd edn 1966; (with J. J. Pindborg and H. Torloni) World Health Organization International Histological Classification of Tumours: Odontogenic Tumours, Jaw Cysts and Allied Lesions, 1972 (2nd edn, with J. J. Pindborg and M. Shear, as World Health Organisation Histological Typing of Odontogenic Tumours, 1992); (with B. Cohen) Scientific Foundations of Dentistry, 1976; numerous papers in med. and dental jls. *Address:* 11 Sheepcote Close, Beaconsfield, Bucks HP9 1SX. *T:* (01494) 680306.

KRAMER, Prof. Dame Leonie (Judith), AC 1993; DBE 1983 (OBE 1976); DPhil; Professor of Australian Literature, University of Sydney, 1968–89, now Professor Emeritus; Chancellor, University of Sydney Senate, since 1991 (Deputy Chancellor, 1989–91); *b* 1 Oct. 1924; *d* of Alfred and Gertrude Gibson; *m* 1952, Harold Kramer (*d* 1988); two *d*. *Educ:* Presbyterian Ladies Coll., Melbourne; Univ. of Melbourne (BA 1945); St Hugh's Coll., Oxford Univ. (DPhil 1953; Hon. Fellow, 1994); MA Sydney, 1989. FAHA; FACE. Tutor and Lectr, Univ. of Melb., 1945–49; Tutor and Postgrad. Student, St Hugh's Coll., Oxford, 1949–52; Lectr, Canberra University Coll., 1954–56; Lectr, subseq. Sen. Lectr and Associate Prof., Univ. of NSW, 1958–68. Chm., Quadrant Mag., 1986–99. Member: Univs Council, 1974–86; NSW Bd of Studies, 1990–; Adv. Bd, World Book Encyclopaedia, 1989–99; Internat. Adv. Cttee, Encyc. Brit., 1991–98. Director: Australia and NZ Banking Gp, 1983–94; Western Mining Corp., 1984–96. Mem., NSW Council, Aust. Inst. of Co. Dirs, 1992–. Comr, Electricity Commn, NSW, 1988–95. Chairman: ABC, 1982–83; Operation Rainbow Aust. Ltd, 1996–; Dep. Chm. Bd of Dirs, Nat. Inst. of Dramatic Art, 1992–95 (Chm., 1987–92). Dir, St Vincent's Hosp., Sydney, 1988–93. Mem. Council, Nat. Roads & Motorists Assoc., 1984–95; Nat. Pres., Australia–Britain Soc., 1984–93; Member Council: Asia Soc., 1991–2000; Foundn for Young Australians, 1989–. Sen. Fellow, Inst. of Public Affairs, 1988–96. Hon. DLitt: Tasmania, 1977; Queensland, 1991; New South Wales, 1992; Hon. LLD: Melbourne, 1983; ANU, 1984. Britannica Award, 1986. *Publications:* as L. J. Gibson: Henry Handel Richardson and Some of Her Sources, 1954; as Leonie Kramer: A Companion to Australia Felix, 1962; Myself when Laura: fact and fiction in Henry Handel Richardson's school career, 1966; Henry Handel Richardson, 1967, repr. as contrib. to Six Australian Writers, 1971; (with Robert D. Eagleson) Language and Literature: a synthesis, 1976; (with Robert D. Eagleson) A Guide to Language and Literature, 1977; A. D. Hope, 1979; (ed and introd) The Oxford History of Australian Literature, 1981; (ed with Adrian Mitchell) The Oxford Anthology of Australian Literature, 1985; (ed and introd) My Country: Australian poetry and short stories—two hundred years, 1985; (ed and introd) James McAuley, 1988; (ed) Collected Poems of David Campbell, 1989; (ed) Collected Poems of James McAuley, 1995. *Recreations:* gardening, music. *Address:* 12 Vaucluse Road, Vaucluse, NSW 2030, Australia. *T:* (2) 93514164.

KRAMER, Stephen Ernest; QC 1995; a Recorder, since 1991; *b* 12 Sept. 1947; *s* of Frederic Kramer and Lotte Karoline Kramer (*née* Wertheimer); *m* 1978, Miriam Leopold; one *s* one *d*. *Educ:* Hampton Grammar Sch.; Keble Coll., Oxford (BA 1969; MA 1987); Université de Nancy. Called to the Bar, Gray's Inn, 1970; Standing Counsel to HM Customs and Excise (Crime), S Eastern Circuit, 1989–95. Chairman: Liaison Cttee, Bar Council/Inst. of Barristers' Clerks, 1996–99; Criminal Bar Assoc., 2000–2001 (Vice-Chm., 1998–2000). Contested (L), Twickenham, Feb. and Oct. 1974. *Recreations:* swimming, walking, theatre, still attempting to be computer literate. *Address:* 2 Hare Court, Temple, EC4Y 7BA. *T:* (020) 7353 5324.

KREBS, Prof. Edwin Gerhard, MD; Professor, Departments of Pharmacology and Biochemistry, University of Washington, Seattle, 1983–88, now Professor Emeritus (Professor and Chairman, Department of Pharmacology, 1977–83); *b* 6 June 1918, Iowa; *m* 1945, Virginia French; one *s* two *d*. *Educ:* Univ. of Illinois (AB Chem. 1940); Washington Univ. Sch. of Med., St Louis, Mo (MD 1943). Intern and Asst Resident in Internal Med., Barnes Hosp., St Louis, Mo, 1944–45; Res. Fellow, Washington Univ. Sch. of Med., St Louis, 1946–48; University of Washington, Seattle: Asst Prof. of Biochem., 1948–52; Associate Prof., 1952–57; Prof., 1957–68; Asst Dean for Planning, Sch. of Med., 1966–68; Prof. and Chm., Dept of Biol Chem., Sch. of Med., Univ. of Calif, Davis, 1968–76; Howard Hughes Medical Institute: Investigator, 1977–80; Sen. Investigator, 1980–90, Emeritus, 1991–. Member: Editl Bd, Jl Biol Chem., 1965–70 (Associate Ed., 1972–93); Editl Adv. Bd, Biochem., 1971–76; Editl and Adv. Bd, Molecular Pharmacol., 1972–77; Editl Advr, Molecular and Cellular Biochem., 1987–. Member: Amer. Soc. for Biochem. and Molecular Biol., 1951–; Amer. Acad. Arts and Scis, 1971–; Nat. Acad. Scis, 1973–; Amer. Soc. Pharmacology and Exptl Therapeutics, 1980–. Hon. DSc Geneva, 1979. Numerous awards; (jtly) Nobel Prize in Physiology or Medicine, 1992. *Address:* Department of Pharmacology and Biochemistry, Box 357370, University of Washington, Seattle, WA 98195, USA.

KREBS, Prof. Sir John (Richard), Kt 1999; DPhil; FRS 1984; Chairman, Food Standards Agency, since 2000; Royal Society Research Professor, Department of Zoology, Oxford University, since 1988 (on leave of absence, 1994–99); Fellow, Pembroke College, Oxford, since 1981 (E. P. Abraham Fellow, 1981–88); *b* 11 April 1945; *s* of Sir Hans Adolf Krebs, FRCP, FRS and Margaret Cicely Krebs; *m* 1968, Katharine Anne Fullerton; two *d*. *Educ:* City of Oxford High School; Pembroke College, Oxford. BA 1966; MA 1970; DPhil 1970. Asst Prof., Univ. of British Columbia, 1970–73; Lectr in Zoology, UCNW, 1973–75; Univ. Lectr in Zoology, Oxford Univ., 1976–88. Dir, AFRC Unit of Ecology and Behaviour, NERC Unit of Behavioural Ecology, 1989–94; Chief Exec., NERC, 1994–99. Storer Lectr, Univ. of Calif, 1985. Mem., AFRC, 1988–94 (Animals Res. Cttee, 1990–94; sen. scientific consultant, 1991–94). President: Internat. Soc. for Behavioral Ecology, 1988–90; Assoc. for the Study of Animal Behaviour, 1993–94. Scientific Member: Max Planck Soc., 1985–; Council, Zoological Soc. of London, 1991–92; Academia Europæa, 1995. Hon. Mem., British Ecol Soc., 1999; Foreign Mem., Amer. Philosophical Soc., 2000; Hon. Foreign Mem., Amer. Acad. Arts and Scis, 2000. Hon. Fellow, Cardiff Univ., 1999. Hon. DSc: Sheffield, 1993; Wales, Birmingham, 1997; Exeter, 1998; Warwick, 2000; Cranfield, Kent, 2001; DUniv Stirling, 2000. Scientific Medal, Zool Soc., 1981; Bicentenary Medal, Linnaean Soc., 1983; Frink Medal, Zool Soc., 1997; Elliot Coues Award, Amer. Ornithol Union, 1999; Medal, Assoc. for Study of Animal Behaviour, 2000. *Publications:* Behavioural Ecology, 1978, 4th edn 1997; Introduction to Behavioural Ecology, 1981, 3rd edn 1993; Foraging Theory, 1986; Behavioural and Neural Aspects of Learning and Memory, 1991; articles in Animal Behaviour, Jl of Animal Ecology. *Recreations:* gardening, violin, running, walking, cooking. *Address:* Food Standards Agency, Aviation House, 125 Kingsway, WC2B 6NH. *T:* (020) 7274 8010; *e-mail:* john.krebs@foodstandards.gsi.gov.uk.

KREISEL, Prof. Georg, FRS 1966; Professor Emeritus of Logic and the Foundations of Mathematics, Stanford University, Stanford, California, USA; *b* 15 Sept. 1923. *Address:* Institut für Wissenschaftstheorie, Internationales Forschungszentrum, Mönchsberg 2, 5020 Salzburg, Austria.

KREMER, Gidon; violinist; *b* 27 Feb. 1947. *Educ:* Riga Sch. of Music; Moscow Conservatory. First Prize, Internat. Tchaikovsky Competition, Moscow, 1970. Has played with most major internat. orchestras including: Berlin Philharmonic; Boston Symphony; Concertgebouw; London Philharmonic; LA Philharmonic; NY Philharmonic; Philadelphia; Royal Philharmonic; Vienna Philharmonic. Founded Lockenhaus Fest., Austria, 1981. *Address:* c/o ICM Artists, 40 West 57th Street, New York, NY 10019, USA.

KRETZMER, Herbert; journalist and lyricist; *b* Kroonstad, S Africa, 5 Oct. 1925; *s* of William and Tilly Kretzmer; *m* 1st, 1961, Elisabeth Margaret Wilson (marr. diss., 1973); one *s* one *d*; 2nd, 1988, Sybil Sever. *Educ:* Kroonstad High Sch.; Rhodes Univ., Grahamstown. Entered journalism, 1946, writing weekly cinema newsreel commentaries and documentary films for African Film Productions, Johannesburg. Reporter and entertainment columnist, Sunday Express, Johannesburg, 1951–54; feature writer and columnist, Daily Sketch, London, 1954–59; Columnist, Sunday Dispatch, London, 1959–61; feature writer and theatre critic, Daily Express, 1962–78; TV critic, Daily Mail, 1979–87. TV Critic of the Year, Philips Industries Award, 1980; commended in British Press Awards, 1981. As lyric writer, contributed weekly songs to: That Was The Week…, Not So Much A Programme…, BBC 3, That's Life. Wrote lyrics of Goodness Gracious Me, 1960 (Ivor Novello Award) and Yesterday When I was Young, 1969 (ASCAP award); Gold record for She, 1974; Our Man Crichton, Shaftesbury Theatre, 1964 (book and lyrics); The Four Musketeers, Drury Lane, 1967 (lyrics); Les Misérables, RSC, 1985 (lyrics (Tony Award, 1987; Grammy Award, 1988)); *film:* Can Heironymus Merkin Ever Forget Mercy Humppe And Find True Happiness?, 1969 (lyrics); has also written lyrics for other films, and for TV programmes. Hon. Dr of Letters, Richmond Coll., Amer. Internat. Univ. in London, 1996. Jimmy Kennedy Award, British Acad. of Songwriters, Composers and Authors, 1989. Chevalier de l'Ordre des Arts et des Lettres, 1988. *Publications:* Our Man Crichton, 1965; (jointly) Every Home Should Have One, 1970. *Address:* c/o London Management, Noel House, 2/4 Noel Street, W1V 3RB. *Club:* Royal Automobile.

KRIER, Léon; architect; *b* Luxembourg, 7 April 1946. *Educ:* Univ. of Stuttgart. Asst to James Stirling, London, 1968–70, 1973–74; Project Partner, J. P. Kleihues, Berlin, 1971–72; private architectl practice, London, 1974–. Lecturer: Architectl Assoc. Sch., 1973–76; Princeton Univ., 1974–77; RCA, 1977; Jefferson Prof. of Architecture, Univ. of Virginia, 1982; Davenport Prof., Yale Univ., 1990–91. *Projects* include: Spitalfields Market, 1987; Poundbury Farm devélt, 1989; Justice Palace, Luxembourg, 1994; Village Hall, Windsor, Fla, 1997; Archaeol Mus., Sintra, Portugal, 1999; Heueberg Urban Devélt, Knokke, Belgium, 1998; Urban Centre Alessandria, Italy, 1999; furniture designs for Giorgetti, Italy, 1991–. *Exhibitions* include: Triennale, Milan, 1973; Inst. for Architecture and Urban Studies, NY, 1978; Walker Art Center, Minn and US tour, 1980; Verona, 1980; Drawings, Max Protetch Gall., NY, 1981; ICA, 1983; Max Protetch Gall, NY, 1984; solo exhibn, MOMA, NY, 1985. Jefferson Meml Medal, 1985; Chicago AIA Award, 1987; City of Berlin Architecture Prize, 1987; Eur. Culture Prize, 1995; Silver Medal, Acad. Française, 1997. *Publications* include: (ed) James Stirling: Buildings and Projects, 1974; (ed) Cities Within the City, 1977; Rational Architecture, 1978; Houses, Palaces, Cities, 1984; Albert Speer: architecture 1932–42, 1985; The Completion of Washington DC, 1986; Atlantis, 1987; New Classicism, 1990; Architecture and Urban Design 1967–1992, 1992; Architecture: choice or fate, 1997; articles in jls. *Address:* 8 rue des Chapeliers, 83830 Claviers, France.

KRIKLER, Dennis Michael, MD; FRCP; Consultant Cardiologist, Hammersmith Hospital, and Senior Lecturer in Cardiology, Royal Postgraduate Medical School, 1973–94, now Emeritus; *b* 10 Dec. 1928; *s* of late Barnet and Eva Krikler; *m* 1955, Anne (*née* Winterstein); one *s* one *d*. *Educ:* Muizenberg High Sch.; Univ. of Cape Town, S Africa. Ho. Phys. and Registrar, Groote Schuur Hosp., 1952–55; Fellow, Lahey Clinic, Boston, 1956; C. J. Adams Meml Travelling Fellowship, 1956; Sen. Registrar, Groote Schuur Hosp., 1957–58; Consultant Physician: Salisbury Central Hosp., Rhodesia, 1958–66; Prince of Wales's Hosp., London, 1966–73; Consultant Cardiologist, Ealing Hosp., 1973–89. Expert Clinicien en Cardiologie, Ministère des Affaires Sociales, Santé, France, 1983. Visiting Professor: Baylor, Indiana and Birmingham Univs, 1985; Boston, Los Angeles and Kentucky, 1988; Lectures: Internat., Amer. Heart Assoc., 1984 (Paul Dudley White Citation for internat. achievement); George Burch Meml, Assoc. of Univ. Cardiologists, 1989; Joseph Welker Meml, Univ. of Kansas, 1989; Denolin, Eur. Soc. of Cardiology, 1990; Hideo Ueda, Japanese Soc. of Electrocardiology, 1990; Howard Burchell, Univ. of Minnesota, 1991. Member, British Cardiac Soc., 1971– (Treasurer, 1976–81); Hon. Member: Soc. Française de Cardiologie, 1981–; Soc. di Cultura Medica Vercellese, Italy; Soc. de Cardiologia de Levante, Spain. Editor, British Heart Journal, 1981–91; Member, Editorial Committee: Cardiovascular Res., 1975–91; Archives des Maladies du Coeur et des Vaisseaux, 1980–; Revista Latina de Cardiologia, 1980–; ACCEL Audiotape Jl, 1987–2000. Mem. Scientific Council, Revista Portuguesa de Cardiologia, 1982–. FACC 1971; Fellow, Eur. Soc. of Cardiology, 1989 (Medal of Honour, 1990). Hon. Fellow, Council on Clin. Cardiol., Amer. Heart Assoc., 1984. Freeman: Soc. of Apothecaries, 1989; City of London, 1990. McCullough Prize, 1949; Sir William Osler Award, Miami Univ., 1981; Silver Medal, British Cardiac Soc., 1992. Chevalier, Legion of Honour (France), 1999. *Publications:* Cardiac Arrhythmias (with J. F. Goodwin), 1975; (with A. Zanchetti) Calcium antagonism in cardiovascular therapy,

1981; (with D. A. Chamberlain and W. J. McKenna) Amiodarone and arrhythmias, 1983; (with P. G. Hugenholtz) Workshop on calcium antagonists, 1984; papers on cardiology in British, American and French jls. *Recreations:* reading (and also writing), especially history (contemporary and cardiological); photography. *Address:* 55 Wimpole Street, W1G 8YL. *T:* (020) 7935 2098.

KRIKLER, His Honour Leonard Gideon; a Circuit Judge, 1984–2001; *b* 23 May 1929; *s* of late Major James Harold Krikler, OBE, ED, and Tilly Krikler; *m* 1st, 1955, Dr Thilla Krikler (*d* 1973); four *s*; 2nd, 1975, Lily Appleson; one *s*, and one step *s* two step *d*. *Educ:* Milton Sch., Bulawayo, S Rhodesia (Zimbabwe). Called to Bar, Middle Temple, 1953. Crown Counsel, Court Martial Appeals Court, 1968; Dep. Circuit Judge, 1974; a Recorder, 1980–84. Head of Chambers, London and Cambridge, 1975–84. *Recreations:* cartooning, carpentry, painting. *Club:* Cressbrook.

KRIKORIAN, Gregory, CB 1973; Solicitor for the Customs and Excise, 1971–78; *b* 23 Sept. 1913; *s* of late Kevork and late Christine Krikorian; *m* 1943, Seta Mary (*d* 1995), *d* of Souren Djirdjirian; one *d*. *Educ:* Polytechnic Secondary Sch.; Lincoln Coll., Oxford (BA). Called to Bar, Middle Temple, 1939; practised at Bar, 1939; BBC Overseas Intell. Dept, 1940; served in RAF as Intell. Officer, Fighter Comd, 1940–45 (despatches); practised at Bar, 1945–51, Junior Oxford Circuit, 1947; joined Solicitor's Office, HM Customs and Excise, 1951. *Publication:* (jtly) Customs and Excise, in Halsbury's Laws of England, 1975. *Recreations:* gardening, bird-watching. *Address:* The Coach House, Hawkchurch, Axminster, Devon EX13 5TX. *T:* (01297) 678414. *Clubs:* Reform, Civil Service.

KRISH, Tanya, (Mrs Felix Krish); *see* Moiseiwitsch, T.

KRISTIANSEN, Erling (Engelbrecht), Grand Cross, Order of Dannebrog; Hon. GCVO 1974; Director, East Asiatic Co., 1978–90, and other companies; *b* 31 Dec. 1912; *s* of Kristian Engelbrecht Kristiansen, Chartered Surveyor, and Andrea Kirstine (*née* Madsen); *m* 1st, 1938, Annemarie Selinko (*d* 1986), novelist; 2nd, 1996, Harriet Thrige Laursen (*née* Lund Jensen). *Educ:* Herning Gymnasium; University of Copenhagen (degree awarded equiv. of MA Econ). Postgraduate Studies, Economics and Internat. Relations, Geneva, Paris, London, 1935–37. Sec.-Gen., 1935, Pres. 1936, of the Fédération Universitaire Internationale pour la Société des Nations. Danish Civil Servant, 1941; served with: Free Danish Missions, Stockholm, 1943; Washington, 1944; London, 1945; joined Danish Diplomatic Service and stayed in London until 1947; Danish Foreign Ministry, 1947–48; Head of Denmark's Mission to OEEC, Paris, 1948–50; Sec. to Economic Cttee of Cabinet, 1950–51; Asst Under-Sec. of State, 1951; Dep. Under-Sec. of State (Economic Affairs), Danish For. Min., 1954–64; Ambassador to UK, 1964–77 (concurrently accredited to Republic of Ireland, 1964–73); Doyen of the Diplomatic Corps, 1973–77; retd 1977. Dir, S. G. Warburg & Co. International Holdings Ltd, 1980–84; Mem., Internat. Adv. Bd, S. G. Warburg & Co., 1984–86, Mercury Internat. Gp, 1986–90; Nordic Investment Bank: Dir, 1977–86; Vice-Chm., 1977–78; Chm., 1978–80. Co-founder and Bd Mem., CARE, Denmark, 1987–91. Grand Officier, Légion d'Honneur; Kt Comdr: Order of St Olav; Order of White Rose of Finland; Star of Ethiopia; Knight Grand Cross, Icelandic Falcon; Comdr, Order of Northern Star of Sweden. *Publication:* Folkeforbundet (The League of Nations), 1938. *Recreations:* ski-ing, fishing and other out-door sports, modern languages. *Address:* Kratkrogen 8, 2920, Charlottenlund, Denmark. *Clubs:* MCC; Special Forces *et al.*

KRIWET, Dr Heinz; Member, Supervisory Board, ThyssenKrupp (formerly Thyssen) AG, Düsseldorf (Chairman, Executive Board, 1991–96; Chairman, Supervisory Board, 1996–2001); *b* Bochum, 2 Nov. 1931. *Educ:* Univs of Köln and Freiburg (Masters degree 1957; Dr rer. pol. 1959). Trainee, German Iron and Steel Fedn, 1960–61; Hüttenwerk Rheinhausen (Krupp), 1962–67; Gen. Manager, Sales, 1968, Mem. Exec. Bd i/c Sales, Friedrich Krupp Hüttenwerke AG, Bochum, 1969–72; Mem. Exec. Bd i/c Sales, Thyssen AG, Düsseldorf, 1973–83; Chm. Exec. Bd, Thyssen Stahl AG, Duisburg, 1983–91. *Address:* c/o ThyssenKrupp AG, August Thyssen-Strasse 1, 40211 Düsseldorf, Germany. *T:* (211) 8241.

KROHN, Dr Peter Leslie, FRS 1963; Professor of Endocrinology, University of Birmingham, 1962–66; *b* 8 Jan. 1916; *s* of Eric Leslie Krohn and Doris Ellen Krohn (*née* Wade); *m* 1941, Joanna Mary French; two *s*. *Educ:* Sedbergh; Balliol Coll., Oxford. BA 1st Cl. Hons Animal Physiol, 1937; BM, BCh Oxon, 1940. Wartime Research work for Min. of Home Security, 1940–45; Lectr, then Reader in Endocrinology, University of Birmingham, 1946–53; Nuffield Sen. Gerontological Research Fellow and Hon. Prof. in University, 1953–62. *Publications:* contrib. to scientific jls on physiology of reproduction, transplantation immunity and ageing. *Recreations:* scuba diving, mountain walking. *Address:* Coburg House, New St John's Road, St Helier, Jersey, Channel Islands JE2 3LD. *T:* (01534) 874870.

KROLL, Natasha, RDI 1966; FCSD; freelance television and film designer; *b* Moscow, 20 May 1914; *d* of Dr (phil.) Hermann Kroll and Sophie (*née* Rabinovich). *Educ:* Berlin. Teacher of window display, Reimann Sch. of Art, London, 1936–40; Display Manager: Messrs Rowntrees, Scarborough and York, 1940–42; Simpson Piccadilly Ltd, 1942–55; Sen. Designer, BBC TV, 1955–66: programmes include: Monitor, Panorama, science programmes, Lower Depths, Death of Danton, The Duel, Ring Round the Moon, La Traviata, Day by the Sea, The Sponge Room and many others; freelance designer, 1966–; TV designs include: The Seagull, 1966; Family Reunion, 1966; Eugene Onegin, 1967; The Soldier's Tale, 1968; La Vida Breve, 1968; Mary Stuart, 1968; Doll's House, 1969; Three Sisters, Cherry Orchard, Rasputin, Wild Duck, 1971; Summer and Smoke, Hedda Gabler, 1972; The Common, 1973; Lady from the Sea, 1974; Love's Labour's Lost, 1975; Very Like a Whale, 1980; production-designer of: The Music Lovers, 1970; The Hireling, 1973 (FTA Film award for best Art Direction); Summer Rag-time, 1976; Absolution, 1978. *Publication:* Window Display, 1954. *Recreations:* painting, family, entertaining. *Address:* 5 Ruvigny Gardens, SW15 1JR. *T:* (020) 8788 1556.

KROLL, Nicholas James; Director, Corporate Services Group, and Principal Establishment and Finance Officer, Department for Culture, Media and Sport, since 2000; *b* 23 June 1954; *s* of Alexander Kroll and Maria Kroll (*née* Wolff); *m* 1981, Catherine Askew; one *s* one *d* (and one *d* decd). *Educ:* St Paul's Sch.; Corpus Christi Coll., Oxford. Entered Civil Service, 1977: DoE/Dept of Transport, 1977–86; HM Treasury, 1986–93; DNH, then DCMS, 1993–: Dir, Creative Industries Media and Broadcasting Gp, 1996–2000. *Recreation:* music. *Address:* Department for Culture, Media and Sport, 2–4 Cockspur Street, SW1Y 5DH.

KROLL, Rev. Dr Una (Margaret Patricia), CJC; writer and broadcaster, since 1970; *b* 15 Dec. 1925; *d* of George Hill, CBE, DSO, MC, and Hilda Hill; *m* 1957, Leopold Kroll (*d* 1987); one *s* three *d*. *Educ:* St Paul's Girls' Sch.; Malvern Girls' Coll.; Girton Coll., Cambridge; The London Hosp. MB, BChir (Cantab) 1951; MA 1969. MRCGP 1967. House Officer, 1951–53; Overseas service (Africa), 1953–60; General Practice, 1960–81; Clinical MO, 1981–85, Sen. Clinical MO, 1985–88, Hastings Health Dist. Theological trng, 1967–70; worker deaconess, 1970–88; ordained deacon, 1988, priest, 1997, Church in Wales; Sister, Soc. of the Sacred Cross, 1991–94; political work as a feminist, with particular ref. to status of women in the churches in England and internationally, 1970–89. Mem., Provincial Validating Bd, Church in Wales, 1989–. *Publications:* Transcendental Meditation: a signpost to the world, 1974; Flesh of My Flesh: a Christian view on sexism, 1975; Lament for a Lost Enemy: study of reconciliation, 1976; Sexual Counselling, 1980; The Spiritual Exercise Book, 1985; Growing Older, 1988; In Touch with Healing, 1991; Vocation to Resistance, 1995; Trees of Life, 1997; Forgive and Live, 2000; Anatomy of Survival, 2001; contrib. Cervical Cytology (BMJ), 1969. *Recreation:* doing nothing. *Address:* St Mary's Lodge, Priory Street, Monmouth NP5 3BR.

KROTO, Sir Harold (Walter), Kt 1996; FRS 1990; Royal Society Research Professor, University of Sussex, since 1991 (Professor of Chemistry, 1985–91); *b* 7 Oct. 1939; *s* of Heinz and Edith Kroto; *m* 1963, Margaret Henrietta Hunter; two *s*. *Educ:* Bolton Sch.; Univ. of Sheffield (BSc, PhD). Res. in fullerenes, spectroscopy, radioastronomy, clusters and nanotechnology; Res. student, Sheffield Univ., 1961–64; Postdoctoral Fellow, NRCC, 1964–66; Res. scientist, Bell Telephone Labs, NJ, 1966–67; Tutorial Fellow, 1967–68, Lectr, 1968–77, Reader, 1977–85, Univ. of Sussex. Visiting Professor: UBC 1973; USC 1981; UCLA, 1988–92; Univ. of Calif, Santa Barbara, 1996–. Chm., Vega Sci. Trust, 1995–. (Jtly) Nobel Prize for Chemistry, 1996. *Publications:* Molecular Rotation Spectra, 1975, 2nd edn 1983; 300 papers in chemistry, chem. physics and astronomy jls. *Recreations:* graphic design, tennis. *Address:* School of Chemistry, Physics and Environmental Science, University of Sussex, Brighton BN1 9QJ. *T:* (01273) 678329.

KRUGER, Prudence Margaret, (Mrs Rayne Kruger); *see* Leith, P. M.

KUBIŠ, Ján; Secretary General, Organisation for Security and Co-operation in Europe, since 1999 (with title of Ambassador); *b* Bratislava, 12 Nov. 1952; *m*; one *d*. *Educ:* Jura Hronca High Sch., Bratislava; Moscow State Inst. for Internat. Affairs. Internat. Econ. Orgns Dept, Min. of Foreign Affairs, Prague, 1976–77; Office of the Minister, 1978–80; Attaché and Third Sec., Addis Ababa, 1980–85; Second Sec., 1985–87, Hd of Section, Security and Arms Control, 1987–88, Main Political Questions Dept, Min. of Foreign Affairs, Prague; First Sec. and Counsellor, Moscow, 1989–90; Dep. Hd of Embassy and Hd of Political Section, Moscow, 1990–91; Dir-Gen., Euro-Atlantic Section, Min. of Foreign Affairs, Prague, and Ambassador-at-large, 1991–92; Chm., Cttee of Sen. Officials, CSCE, 1992; Perm. Rep. of Czechoslovakia, 1992, of Slovak Republic, 1993–94, to UN and GATT, Geneva; Special Ministerial Envoy and Slovak Chief Negotiator on Pact for Stability in Europe, 1994; Dir, Conflict Prevention Centre, OSCE, 1994–98; Special Rep. of UN Sec.-Gen. for Tajikistan and Head, UN Mission of Observers to Tajikistan, 1998–99. OSCE Medal, 1998. *Publications:* Contrib. learned jls. *Address:* OSCE, Kärntner Ring 5–7, 1010 Vienna, Austria.

KUCHMA, Leonid Danylovych; President of Ukraine, since 1994; *b* 1938. *Educ:* Dnipropetrovsk State Univ. Constructor, Research-Production Union, Yuzhny Mashinostroitelny Zavod, 1960–75; Sec., Party Cttee, 1975–82; Dep. Dir Gen., 1982–86; Dir Gen., 1986–92; Chm., Ukrainian Union of Industrialists and Entrepreneurs, 1993–94. Deputy, Ukraine Parlt, 1991–94; Prime Minister, Ukraine, 1992–93. Mem., Central Cttee, Ukraine Communist Party, 1981–91; Mem., CPSU, 1960–91. *Address:* Office of the President, Bankova Street 11, 01220 Kyiv, Ukraine. *T:* 2915152.

KUENSSBERG, Nicholas Christopher Dwelly; Principal, Horizon Co-Invest, since 1995; *b* 28 Oct. 1942; *s* of late Ekkehard von Kuenssberg, CBE; *m* 1965, Sally Robertson; one *s* two *d*. *Educ:* Edinburgh Acad.; Wadham Coll., Oxford (BA Hons). FCIS. Worked overseas, 1965–78; Dir, J. & P. Coats Ltd, 1978–91; Chm., Dynacast International Ltd, 1978–91; Director: Coats Patons Plc, 1985–91; Coats Viyella plc, 1986–91; Chief Exec., Dawson Premier Brands, 1991–94; Man. Dir, Dawson International PLC, 1994–95. Chairman: David A. Hall Ltd, 1996–98; GAP Gp Ltd, 1996–; Stoddard Internat. PLC, 1997–2000; Bio-Logic Remediation Ltd, 1999–2000 (non-exec. Dir, 1997–99); Canmore Partnership Ltd, 1999–; Iomart, 2000–; Mindwarp Pavilion, 2001–; Director: Scottish Power plc (formerly S of Scotland Electricity Bd), 1984–97; W of Scotland Bd, Bank of Scotland, 1984–88; Standard Life Assce Co., 1988–97; Baxi Partnership, 1996–99; Sanmex International plc, 1998–; Chamberlin & Hill plc, 1999–; Citizens Theatre Glasgow Ltd, 2000–. Member: Scottish Legal Aid Bd, 1996–; SEPA, 1999–. Hon. Res. Fellow, 1986–88, Vis. Prof., 1988–91, Strathclyde Business Sch. Ext. Examr, Aberdeen Business Sch., 1998–. Chm., Assoc. of Mgt Educn & Trng in Scotland, 1996–98. Chm., Scottish Internat. Resource Prog., 2001–. Mem., Scottish Cttee, British Council, 1999–. Dir, Glasgow Sch. of Art, 2001–; Gov., Queen's Coll., Glasgow, 1989–91. CIMgt; FInstD (Chm., Scotland, 1997–99); FRSA. *Recreations:* sport, travel, opera, languages. *Address:* 6 Cleveden Drive, Glasgow G12 0SE. *T:* (0141) 339 8345. *Clubs:* New (Edinburgh); Vincent's (Oxford); Muirfield Golf.

KUHN, Prof. Karl Heinz, FBA 1987; Professor of Coptic, Durham University, 1982–84, now Emeritus Professor; *b* 2 Aug. 1919; *s* of Max Kuhn and Gertrud Kuhn (*née* Hiller); *m* 1949, Rachel Mary Wilkinson; one *s* one *d*. *Educ:* school in Germany; St John's Coll., Univ. of Durham (BA 1949, PhD 1952). Scarbrough Research Studentship, Durham Univ. and abroad, 1949–53; Univ. of Durham: Research Fellow in Arts, 1953–55; Lectr, later Sen. Lectr in Hebrew and Aramaic, 1955–77; Reader in Coptic, 1977–82; Prof. of Coptic, 1982–84. Mem., editl bd, Corpus Scriptorum Christianorum Orientalium, Louvain, 1970–2000. *Publications:* Letters and Sermons of Besa, 1956; Pseudo-Shenoute: on Christian behaviour, 1960; A Panegyric on John the Baptist attributed to Theodosius, Archbishop of Alexandria, 1966; A Panegyric on Apollo, Archimandrite of the Monastery of Isaac by Stephen, Bishop of Heracleopolis Magna, 1978; (contrib.) Sparks, The Apocryphal Old Testament, 1984; (with W. J. Tait) Thirteen Coptic Acrostic Hymns from Manuscript M574 of the Pierpont Morgan Library, 1996; (contrib.) English trans. of Foerster, Gnosis, 1974, and Rudolph, Gnosis, 1983; articles in Jl of Theol Studies, Le Muséon and other learned jls. *Recreations:* music. *Address:* 28 Nevilledale Terrace, Durham DH1 4QG. *T:* (0191) 384 2993.

KÜHNL, Karel; Member (Civic Democratic Alliance) Chamber of Deputies, Czech Republic, since 1997; Minister of Industry and Trade, 1997–98; *b* 12 Sept. 1954; *s* of Karel Kühnl and Marie Kühnlova (*née* Větrovcová); *m* 1983, Daniela Kusin; one *s* one *d*. *Educ:* Charles Univ., Prague (BA Law 1978); Univ. of Vienna (BA Econs 1983). Left Czechoslovakia in 1980 for political reasons; free-lance journalist, Vienna and Munich, 1983–87; editor and analyst, Radio Free Europe, Munich (Czech and Slovak broadcasting), 1987–91; returned to Czechoslovakia, 1991, after fall of communism in 1989; Sen. Lectr, Law Faculty, Charles Univ., Prague, 1991–93; Chief Advr to Prime Minister of Czech Republic, 1991–93; Ambassador to UK, 1993–97. Hd of Bd, Czech TV, 1992–93. *Publications:* numerous articles in Czech, German and Austrian newspapers and jls. *Recreations:* family, history, archaeology, architecture. *Address:* Chamber of Deputies, Snemovni 14, 11826 Prague 1, Czech Republic.

KUHRT, Prof. Amélie Thekla Luise, FBA 2001; Professor of Ancient Near Eastern History, University College London, since 1997; *b* 23 Sept. 1944; *d* of Edith Woodger and

Ernest Woodger (adoptive father); *m* 1965, David Alan Kuhrt (marr. diss. 1977); two *d*. *Educ:* King's Coll., London; University Coll. London; Sch. of Oriental and African Studies (BA Hons Ancient Hist.). Lectr in Near Eastern Hist., 1979–89, Reader, 1989–97, UCL. James Henry Breasted Prize, Amer. Historical Assoc., 1997. *Publications:* (with A. Cameron) Images of Women in Antiquity, 1983, 2nd edn 1993; (with H. Sancisi-Weerdenburg) Archaemenid History II-IV, 1987–90, VI, 1991, VIII, 1994; (with S. Sherwin-White) Hellenism in the East, 1987; From Samarkhand to Sardis, 1992; The Ancient Near East, 2 vols, 1995 (trans. Spanish). *Recreations:* music, literature. *Address:* Department of History, University College London, Gower Street, WC1E 6BT. *T:* (020) 7679 3634.

KUHRT, Ven. Gordon Wilfred; Director of Ministry, Archbishops' Council, Church of England, since 1999; Archdeacon Emeritus, diocese of Southwark, since 1996; *b* 15 Feb. 1941; *s* of Wilfred and Doris Kuhrt; *m* 1963, Olive Margaret Powell; three *s*. *Educ:* Colfe's Grammar School; London Univ. (BD Hons); Oak Hill Theol Coll. Religious Education teacher, 1963–65; Curate: Illogan, Cornwall, 1967–70; Wallington, Surrey, 1970–74; Vicar: Shenstone, Staffs, 1974–79; Emmanuel, South Croydon, Surrey, 1979–89; RD, Croydon Central, 1981–86; Hon. Canon, Southwark Cathedral, 1987–89; Archdeacon of Lewisham, 1989–96; Chief Sec., ABM, Gen. Synod of C of E, 1996–98. Mem., C of E Gen. Synod, 1986–96 (Mem., Bd of Ministry, 1991–96). Fellow, Coll. of Preachers (Mem. Council, 1992–). Theological Lectr, London Univ. Extra-Mural Dept, 1984–89. *Publications:* A Handbook for Council and Committee Members, 1985; Believing in Baptism, 1987; (contrib.) The Church and its Unity, 1992; (ed and contrib.) Doctrine Matters, 1993; (contrib.) Growing in Newness of Life: Christian initiation in Anglicanism today, 1993; (ed) To Proclaim Afresh, 1995; (contrib.) Church Leadership, 1997; Issues in Theological Education and Training, 1997; Clergy Security, 1998; An Introduction to Christian Ministry, 2000. *Address:* Ministry Division, Church House, Great Smith Street, SW1P 3NZ. *T:* (020) 7898 1390; 6 Layzell Walk, Mottingham, SE9 4QD. *T:* (020) 8857 3476.

KUIPERS, John Melles; *b* 7 July 1918; *s* of late Joh Kuipers and Anna (*née* Knoester); *m* 1947, Joan Lilian Morgan-Edwards; one *s* three *d*. *Educ:* Royal Masonic Sch., Bushey. Served RA, 1939–46 (Lt-Col). Ford Motor Co. Ltd, 1947–51; Treasurer, Canadian Chemical Co. Ltd, Montreal, 1951–55; Gp Manager, Halewood, and Dir, Stamping and Assembly Gp, Ford Motor Co. Ltd, 1955–67; EMI Ltd, 1967–80: Chief Exec. Electronic and Industrial Ops, 1969–72; Chm. and Chief Exec., EMI (Australia) Ltd, 1974–77; Man. Dir and Vice-Chm., 1977–79; Dir, Thames TV Ltd, 1977–81; Chairman: Huntleigh Gp PLC, 1980–83; ATT Ltd, 1984–91. Dir, Gowrings, 1980–89. *Address:* 2 Bell Lane, Henley-on-Thames, Oxon RG9 2HP. *T:* (01491) 574760.

KULKARNI, Prof. Shrinivas Ramachandra, PhD; FRS 2001; Professor of Astronomy and Planetary Science, California Institute of Technology, Pasadena, since 1996; *b* 4 Oct. 1956; *s* of Dr Ramachandra H. Kulkarni and Vimala Kulkarni; *m* 1985, Dr Hiromi Komiya; two *d*. *Educ:* Indian Inst. of Technology, New Delhi (MS Physics 1978); Univ. of California at Berkeley (PhD Astronomy 1983). Post-doctoral Fellow, Radio Astronomy Lab., Univ. of California at Berkeley, 1983–85; California Institute of Technology: Robert A. Millikan Fellow in Radio Astronomy, 1985–87; Asst Prof. of Astronomy, 1987–90; Associate Prof. of Astronomy, 1990–92; Prof. of Astronomy, 1992–95; Exec. Officer, Astronomy, 1997–2000; Sen. Fellow, Mount Wilson Inst., Pasadena, 1998–. John D. and Catherine T. MacArthur Prof. of Astronomy and Planetary Sci., 2001. Helen B. Warner Prize, 1991, Alan T. Waterman Prize, 1992, NSF. *Publications:* (contrib.) Interstellar Processes, 1987; contrib. Nature in fields of pulsers, brown dwarfs and gamma-ray bursters. *Address:* Mail Stop 105–24, Astronomy, California Institute of Technology, Pasadena, CA 91125, USA. *T:* (626) 395 4010; *e-mail:* srk@astro.caltech.edu.

KULUKUNDIS, Sir Eddie, Kt 1993; OBE 1988; Chairman, Ambassadors Theatre Group, since 1992; Director, Rethymnis & Kulukundis Ltd, since 1964; Member of Lloyd's, since 1964 (Member Council, 1983–89); *b* 20 April 1932; *s* of late George Elias Kulukundis and Eugénie (*née* Diacakis); *m* 1981, Susan Hampshire, *qv*. *Educ:* Collegiate Sch., New York; Salisbury Sch., Connecticut; Yale Univ. Mem., Baltic Exchange, 1959–2001. Chairman: Sports Aid Foundn Ltd, 1988–93 (Gov., 1977–); London Coaching Foundn, 1990–; British Athletics Charitable Trust (formerly British Athletics Field Events Charitable Trust), 1996–; Athletics Youth Foundn, 1997–; Midland Coaching Foundn, 2000–; Vice-Pres., UK Athletics, 1998–. Governor: Royal Shakespeare Theatre, 1976– (Mem. Council of Mgt); The Raymond Mander and Joe Mitchenson Theatre Collection Ltd, 1981–; Vice-President: Greenwich Theatre Ltd, 1988–; Traverse Theatre, 1988–; Director: Royal Shakespeare Theatre Trust, 1968– (Mem. Council of Mgt; Vice-Chm., 1983–); Hampstead Theatre Ltd, 1969–; Hampstead Theatre Trust, 1980–. Mem., Richmond Theatre Trust, 2001–. Mem. Bd, SOLT. Trustee: Theatres Trust, 1976–95; Salisbury Sch., Connecticut, 1983–; Sports Aid Foundn Trust, 1987–. FRSA. Theatrical Producer, 1969–96; London productions include (some jtly): Enemy, 1969; The Happy Apple, Poor Horace, The Friends, How the Other Half Loves, Tea Party and The Basement (double bill), The Wild Duck, 1970; After Haggerty, Hamlet, Charley's Aunt, Straight Up, 1971; London Assurance, Journey's End, 1972; Small Craft Warnings, A Private Matter, Dandy Dick, 1973; The Waltz of the Toreadors, Life Class, Pygmalion, Play Mas, The Gentle Hook, 1974; A Little Night Music, Entertaining Mr Sloane, The Gay Lord Quex, What the Butler Saw, Travesties, Lies, The Sea Gull, A Month in the Country, A Room With a View, Too True to Be Good, The Bed Before Yesterday, 1975; Dimetos, Banana Ridge, Wild Oats, 1976; Candida, Man and Superman, Once A Catholic, 1977; Privates on Parade, Gloo Joo, 1978; Bent, Outside Edge, Last of the Red Hot Lovers, 1979; Beecham, Born in the Gardens, 1980; Tonight At 8.30, Steaming, Arms and the Man, 1981; Steafel's Variations, 1982; Messiah, Pack of Lies, 1983; Of Mice and Men, The Secret Diary of Adrian Mole Aged 13¾, 1984; Camille, 1985; The Cocktail Party, 1986; Curtains, 1987; Separation, South Pacific, Married Love, 1988; Over My Dead Body, 1989; Never the Sinner, 1990; The King and I, Carmen Jones, 1991; Noël and Gertie, A Slip of the Tongue, Shades, Making it Better, 1992; The Prime of Miss Jean Brodie, 1994; New York productions (jtly): How the Other Half Loves, 1971; Sherlock Holmes, London Assurance, 1974; Travesties, 1975; The Merchant, 1977; Players, 1978; Once a Catholic, 1979. *Address:* c/o Rethymnis & Kulukundis Ltd, 21 New Fetter Lane, EC4A 1JJ. *T:* (020) 7583 2266; c/o Ambassadors Theatre Group, Duke of York's Theatre, 104 St Martin's Lane, WC2N 4BG. *T:* (020) 7854 7000. *Club:* Garrick.

KUMAR, Dr Ashok; MP (Lab) Middlesbrough South and Cleveland East, since 1997; *b* 28 May 1956; *s* of Jagat Ram Saini and late Santosh Kumari. *Educ:* Univ. of Aston in Birmingham (BSc ChemEng 1978; MSc Process Control 1980; PhD Fluid Mechanics 1982). Res. Officer, British Steel Research, 1978–79; Res. Fellow, Imperial Coll. of Science and Technology, 1982–85; Sen. Res. Investigator, Teeside Labs, British Steel, 1985–91; Res. Officer, British Steel Technical, 1992–97. Mem., Middlesbrough BC, 1987–97: Chair, Equal Opportunities Sub-Cttee, 1995–97; Vice Chair, Educn Cttee, 1995–97. MP (Lab) Langbaurgh, Nov. 1991–1992; contested (Lab) Langbaurgh, 1992. Member: Sci. and Technol Select Cttee, 1997–2001; Trade and Industry Select Cttee, 2001–. Jt Sec., All Party Parly Gp for Chemical Industry, 1997–; Chairman: Parly Gp for Energy Studies, 1999–; All Party Parly British–Bahrain Gp, 1999–; All Party Parly Gp for Chemical Industry, 2001–; Sec., All Party British-Indo Parly Gp, 1999–. Chairman: Chem. Eng. Soc., 1981–82; Labour Club, Univ. of Aston, 1980–81. *Publications:* articles in scientific and mathematical jls. *Recreations:* reading, listening to music, cricket, badminton. *Address:* House of Commons, SW1A 0AA. *Clubs:* Reform; Easterside and Beechwood Social; Marton Cricket.

KUMARATUNGA, Chandrika Bandaranaike; President of Sri Lanka, since 1994; *b* 29 June 1945; *d* of late Solomon W. R. D. Bandaranaike and Sirimavo R. D. Bandaranaike, former Prime Minister of Sri Lanka; *m* 1978, Wijaya Kumaratunga (*d* 1988); one *s* one *d*. *Educ:* St Bridget's Convent, Colombo; Inst. of Pol Studies, Paris; Ecole Pratique des Hautes Etudes, Paris. Chm. and Man. Dir, Dinakara Sinhala, 1975–85; Chief Minister, W Province Council, 1993–94; Prime Minister of Sri Lanka, Aug.–Nov. 1994; Minister of Finance and Planning, of Ethnic Affairs and Nat. Integration, of Defence, and of Buddha Sasana, 1994–. Sri Lanka Freedom Party: Member: Exec. Cttee, and Women's League, 1974; Exec. Cttee and Wkg Cttee, 1980; Central Cttee, 1992; Dep. Leader, 1992; Vice-Pres., 1984, Pres., 1986, Sri Lanka Mahajana Party; Leader, People's Alliance, 1988. *Publications:* research papers on agrarian and land reforms and food policies. *Address:* President's Secretariat, Republic Square, Colombo 1, Sri Lanka. *T:* (1) 24801.

KUME, Yutaka; President, 1985–92, Chairman, 1992, Nissan Motor Co.; *b* 20 May 1921; *s* of Kinzaburo Kume and Chiyo Kume; *m* 1947, Aya Yamamoto; one *s* one *d*. *Educ:* Univ. of Tokyo (BE aircraft engineering). Joined Nissan Motor Co., 1946; General Manager: Production control and Engineering Dept, Zama Plant, 1964; Yoshiwara Plant, 1971; Tochigi Plant, 1973–78; Dir and Mem. Bd, 1973; Managing Dir, 1977; Exec. Managing Dir, 1982; Exec. Vice-Pres. and Gen. Manager, Quality Admin Div., 1983. Blue Ribbon Medal from Emperor of Japan, 1986; Commander, Order of Orange Nassau (Holland), 1986; Order of Cruz de San Jordi (Catalonia, Spain), 1990; Commander, Order of the Crown (Belgium), 1991. *Recreations:* photography, haiku (Japanese short poems), reading. *Address:* Nissan Motor Co. Ltd, 17–1 Ginza 6-chome, Chuo-ku, Tokyo 104, Japan. *T:* (3) 5435523.

KUNCEWICZ, Eileen, (Mrs Witold Kuncewicz); *see* Herlie, E.

KUNDERA, Milan; writer; *b* Brno, 1 April 1929; *s* of Dr Ludvik Kundera and Milada Kunderova-Janosikova; *m* 1967, Věra Hrabánková. *Educ:* Film Faculty, Acad. of Music and Dramatic Arts, Prague, later Asst Prof. and Prof. there, 1958–69; Prof., Univ. of Rennes, 1975–80; Prof., Ecole des hautes études en sciences sociales, Paris, 1980. Mem., Union of Czechoslovak Writers, 1963–69. Member: Editl Bd, Literárni noviny, 1963–67, 1968; Editl Bd, Listy, 1968–69. Czechoslovak Writers' Publishing House Prize, 1969; Commonwealth Award, 1981; Prix Europa-Littérature, 1982; Jerusalem Prize, 1985; Nelly Sachs Preis, 1987; Österreichische Staatspreis, 1988; London Independent Prize, 1991. *Publications:* The Joke, 1967; Laughable Loves (short stories), 1970; Jacques et son maître (drama), 1971–81; Life is Elsewhere, 1973 (Prix Médicis); The Farewell Party, 1976 (Prem. lett. Mondello); The Book of Laughter and Forgetting, 1979; The Unbearable Lightness of Being, 1984 (LA Times Prize); The Art of the Novel, 1987; Immortality, 1990; Les testaments trahis, 1993; Slowness, 1996; Francis Bacon, 1996; Identity, 1998.

KÜNG, Prof. Dr Hans; Ordinary Professor of Ecumenical Theology, 1980–96 and Director of Institute for Ecumenical Research, 1963–96, University of Tübingen, now Professor Emeritus; *b* Sursee, Lucerne, 19 March 1928. *Educ:* schools in Sursee and Lucerne; Papal Gregorian Univ., Rome (LPhil, LTh); Sorbonne; Inst. Catholique, Paris. DTheol 1957. Further studies in Amsterdam, Berlin, Madrid, London. Ordained priest, 1954. Pastoral work, Hofkirche, Lucerne, 1957–59; Asst for dogmatic theol., Univ. of Münster, 1959–60; Ord. Prof. of fundamental theol., 1960–63, Ord. Prof. of dogmatic and ecumenical theol., 1963–80, Univ. of Tübingen. Official theol. consultant (peritus) to 2nd Vatican Council, 1962–65; Guest Professor: Union Theol. Seminary, NYC, 1968; Univ. of Basle, 1969; Univ. of Chicago Divinity Sch., 1981; Univ. of Michigan, 1983; Toronto Univ., 1985; Rice Univ., Texas, 1987, 1989; guest lectures at univs in Europe, America, Asia and Australia; Hon. Pres., Edinburgh Univ. Theol Soc., 1982–83. President: Foundn Global Ethic, Germany, 1995, Switzerland, 1997. Editor series, Theologische Meditationen; co-Editor series, Ökumenische Forschungen and Ökumenische Theologie; Associate Editor, Jl of Ecum. Studies. Mem., Amer. and German Pen Clubs. Holds hon. doctorates. *Publications:* (first publication in German) The Council and Reunion, 1961; That the World may Believe, 1963; The Living Church, 1963; The Changing Church, 1965; Justification: the doctrine of Karl Barth and a Catholic reflection, 1965; Structures of the Church, 1965; (contrib.) Theologische Meditationen, 1965 (Amer. edn as Freedom Today, 1966); The Church, 1967; (contrib.) Christian Revelation and World Religions, ed J. Neuner, 1967; Truthfulness: the future of the Church, 1968; Infallible? an enquiry, 1971 (paperback 1972); Why Priests?, 1972; 20 Thesen zum Christsein, 1975; On Being a Christian, 1977 (abridged as The Christian Challenge, 1979); Was ist Firmung?, 1976; Jesus im Widerstreit: ein jüdisch-christlicher Dialog (with Pinchas Lapide), 1976; Brother or Lord?, 1977; Signposts for the Future, 1978; Freud and the Problem of God, 1979; The Church—Maintained in Truth?, 1980; Does God Exist?, 1980; Art and the Question of Meaning, 1981; Eternal Life?, 1984; (jtly) Christianity and World Religions, 1986; The Incarnation of God, 1986; Church and Change: the Irish experience, 1986; Why I am still a Christian, 1987; Theology for the Third Millennium: an ecumenical view, 1988; (with Julia Ching) Christianity and Chinese Religions, 1989; Reforming the Church Today: keeping hope alive, 1990; Global Responsibility: in search of a new world ethic, 1991; Judaism: the religious situation of our time, 1992; Mozart: traces of transcendence, 1992; Credo: the Apostles' Creed explained for today, 1993; Great Christian Thinkers, 1994; Christianity: essence and history, 1995; (jtly) A Dignified Dying: a plea for personal responsibility, 1995; Yes to a Global Ethic, 1996; A Global Ethic for Global Politics and Economics, 1997; (ed with Helmut Schmidt) A Global Ethic and Global Responsibilities: two declarations, 1998; The Catholic Church: a short history, 2001. *Address:* Waldhäuserstrasse 23, 72076 Tübingen, Germany.

KUNKEL, Edward Thomas; Director, President and Chief Executive Officer, Foster's Brewing Group Ltd, since 1992; *b* 22 May 1943; *s* of Francis James Kunkel and Doris Kunkel (*née* Baulcombe). *Educ:* Auckland Univ. (BSc Chem. and Zool.). Joined Carlton & United Breweries, Melbourne, 1968 as Asst Brewer; sen. positions throughout Group, 1968–84; Gen. Manager, NSW, 1985–87; Pres. and Chief Exec. Officer, Carling O'Keefe Breweries of Canada Ltd, 1987–89; Exec. Chm., Molson Breweries, N America, 1989–92; Chm., Molson Breweries, Canada, 1996–98. *Recreations:* golf, fitness. *Address:* Foster's Brewing Group Ltd, 77 Southbank Boulevard, Melbourne, Vic 3006, Australia. *T:* (3) 96332001, *Fax:* (3) 96332004. *Clubs:* Melbourne (Melbourne); Huntingdale Golf (Victoria); Sanctuary Cove Country (Qld).

KUPER, Prof. Adam Jonathan, PhD; FBA 2000; Professor of Social Anthropology, Brunel University, since 1985; *b* 29 Dec. 1941; *s* of Simon Meyer Kuper and Gertrude (*née* Hesselson); *m* 1966, Jessica Sue Cohen; two *s* one *d*. *Educ:* Univ. of Witwatersrand

(BA 1961); King's Coll., Cambridge (PhD 1966). Lecturer: in Social Anthropol., Makerere Univ., Kampala, 1967–70; in Anthropol., UCL, 1970–76; Prof. of African Anthropol. and Sociol., Univ. of Leiden, 1976–85. MAE 1993. Hon. DFil Gothenburg, 1978. Rivers Meml Medal, RAI, 2000. *Publications:* Kalahari Village Politics: an African democracy, 1970; (ed with A. Richards) Councils in Action, 1971; Anthopologists and Anthropology: the British School 1922–1972, 1973, 3rd edn 1996; Changing Jamaica, 1976; (ed) The Social Anthopology of Radcliffe-Brown, 1977; Wives for Cattle: bridewealth and marriage in Southern Africa, 1982; (ed with J. Kuper) The Social Science Encyclopedia, 1985, 2nd edn 1996; South Africa and the Anthopologist, 1987; The Invention of Primitive Society: transformations of an illusion, 1988; (ed) Conceptualising Society, 1992; The Chosen Primate: human nature and cultural diversity, 1994; Culture: the anthropologists' account, 1999; Among the Anthropologists: history and context in anthropology, 1999. *Address:* 16 Muswell Road, N10 2BG. *T:* (020) 8883 0400. *Club:* Pretenders Cricket.

KUREISHI, Hanif; writer; *b* 5 Dec. 1954; *s* of Rafiushan Kureishi and Audrey Buss. *Educ:* King's College London. *Filmscripts:* My Beautiful Laundrette, 1984; Sammy and Rosie Get Laid, 1987; (also dir.) London Kills Me, 1991; My Son the Fanatic, 1998. *Publications: plays:* Outskirts, 1981; Borderline, 1981; Birds of Passage, 1983; Outskirts and Other Plays, 1992; Sleep With Me, 1999; *novels:* The Buddha of Suburbia, 1990 (televised 1993); The Black Album, 1995; Intimacy, 1998; Gabriel's Gift, 2001; *short stories:* Love in a Blue Time, 1997; Midnight All Day, 1999; (ed jtly) The Faber Book of Pop, 1995. *Recreations:* pop music, cricket, sitting in pubs. *Address:* c/o Deborah Rogers, Rogers, Coleridge & White Ltd, 20 Powis Mews, W11 1SN.

KURIA, Most Rev. Manasses; Executive Chairman, Jehovah Jireh Christian Homes for Street Children and Families, since 1995; Archbishop of Kenya and Bishop of Nairobi, 1980–94; *b* 22 July 1929; *s* of John Njoroge Kuria; *m* 1947, Mary Kuria; two *s* four *d*. *Educ:* locally. Teaching, 1944–53; Deacon, 1955; ordained Priest, 1957; Archdeacon of Eldoret, 1965–70; Asst Bishop of Nakuru, 1970–75; Bishop of Nakuru, 1976–79. *Publication:* Uwakili Katika Kristo (Stewardship of Christ), 1969. *Address:* Jehovah Jireh Christian Homes, PO Box 20050, Nairobi, Kenya.

KUSHNER, Lindsey Joy; QC 1992; **Her Honour Judge Kushner;** a Circuit Judge, since 2000; *b* 16 April 1952; *d* of Harry Kushner and Rita Kushner (*née* Alexander); *m* 1976, David Norman Kaye; one *s* one *d*. *Educ:* Manchester High Sch. for Girls; Liverpool Univ. (LLB). Called to the Bar, Middle Temple, 1974; part time Chm., Medical Appeal Tribunal, 1989–2000, Disablement Appeal Tribunal, 1992–99; Asst Recorder, 1989–93; a Recorder, 1993–2000. Mem., Ethnic Adv. Cttee, Lord Chancellor's Dept, 1994–99. *Recreations:* cooking, cinema. *Address:* c/o Northern Circuit Administrator, 15 Quay Street, Manchester M60 9FD.

KUSTOW, Michael David; writer, producer and director; *b* 18 Nov. 1939; *m* 1973, Orna (marr. diss. 1998), *d* of Jacob and Rivka Spector, Haifa, Israel. *Educ:* Haberdashers' Aske's; Wadham Coll., Oxford (BA Hons English). Festivals Organiser, Centre 42, 1962–63; Royal Shakespeare Theatre Company: Dir, RSC Club, Founder of Theatregoround, Editor of Flourish, 1963–67; Dir, Inst. of Contemporary Arts, 1967–70; Associate Dir, National Theatre, 1973–81; Commissioning Ed. for Arts progs, Channel Four TV, 1981–89; Dir, Michael Kustow Productions, 1990–; Co-Dir, The Greek Collection, 1990–. Lectr in Dramatic Arts, Harvard Univ., 1980–82. Chevalier de l'Ordre des Arts et des Lettres, République Française, 1980. *Productions:* Punch and Judas, Trafalgar Square, 1963; I Wonder, ICA, 1968; Nicholas Tomalin Reporting, 1975; Brecht Poetry and Songs, 1976; Larkinland, Groucho Letters, Robert Lowell, Audience, 1977–78; Miss South Africa, Catullus, A Nosegay of Light Verse, The Voice of Babel, Anatol, 1979; Iris Murdoch's Art and Eros, Shakespeare's Sonnets, Stravinsky's Soldier's Tale, 1980; Charles Wood's Has Washington Legs, Harold Pinter's Family Voices, 1981; The Mahabharata, 1989; The War that Never Ends, 1991; The Last Bolshevik, 1993; ABC of Democracy, 1994; A Maybe Day in Kazakhstan, 1994; Fireworks, 1994; Shakespeare Workshops, 1994; Everybody's Shakespeare Festival, 1994; Hiroshima, 1995; Jerusalem, Between Heaven and Hell, 1996; Dionysus and the Mighty Mouse, Prometheus, 1998; Pandaemonium, 1999; Tantalus, 2000. *Exhibitions:* Tout Terriblement Guillaume Apollinaire, ICA, 1968; AAARGH! A Celebration of Comics, ICA, 1971. *Publications:* Punch and Judas, 1964; The Book of US, 1968; Tank: an autobiographical fiction, 1975; One in Four, 1987; theatre@risk, 2000. *Recreations:* painting, jazz. *Address:* 17 Haslemere Road, N8 9QB. *T:* (020) 8347 8967.

KWAPONG, Alexander Adum, MA, PhD Cantab; Director, African Programmes, Teacher Education, Research and Evaluation, The Commonwealth of Learning, Vancouver, 1991–93; *b* Akropong, Akwapim, 8 March 1927; *s* of E. A. Kwapong and Theophilia Kwapong; *m* 1956, Evelyn Teiko Caesar, Ada; six *d*. *Educ:* Presbyterian junior and middle schools, Akropong; Achimota Coll.; King's Coll., Cambridge (Exhibr, Minor Schol. and Foundn Schol.). BA 1951, MA 1954, PhD 1957, Cantab. 1st cl. prelims, Pts I and II, Classical Tripos, 1951; Sandys Res. Student, Cambridge Univ.; Richards Prize, Rann Kennedy Travel Fellowship, King's Coll., Cambridge. Lectr in Classics, UC Gold Coast, 1953, Sen. Lectr in Classics 1960; Vis. Prof., Princeton Univ., 1961–62; Prof. of Classics, Univ. of Ghana, 1962; Dean of Arts, Pro-Vice-Chancellor, Univ. of Ghana, 1962–65, Vice-Chancellor 1966–75; Vice-Rector for Instl Planning and Resource Develt, UN Univ., 1976–88 (Sen. Advr to Rector, 1988–); Lester B. Pearson Prof. in Develt Studies, Dalhousie Univ., Halifax, Canada, 1988–91. Chairman: Educn Review Cttee, Ghana Govt, 1966–67; Smithsonian Instn 3rd Internat. Symposium, 1969; Assoc. of Commonwealth Univs, 1971. Sir Samuel Manuwa Meml Lectr, W African Coll. of Surgeons, 1990. Member: Admin. Bd, Internat. Assoc. Univs, Paris, 1970–80; Exec. Bd, Assoc. African Univs, 1967–74; Bd of Trustees, Internat. Council for Educnl Develt, NY; Aspen Inst. for Humanistic Studies, 1972–85; Board of Directors: Internat. Assoc. for Cultural Freedom, Paris, 1967–75; Internat. Cttee for the Study of Educnl Exchange; Aspen Berlin Inst., 1975–; IDRC; Harold Macmillan Trust, 1986–; Internat. Foundn for Educn and Self Help, Phoenix, Arizona, 1988–; African Leadership Forum. Consultant, World Bank, 1988–89. Fellow, Ghana Academy of Arts and Sciences. Hon. DLitt: Warwick; Ife; Ghana; Hon. LLD Princeton. Order of Volta, Ghana. *Publications:* The Role of Classical Studies in Africa Today, 1969; Higher Education and Development in Africa Today: a reappraisal, 1979; Underdevelopment and the Challenges of the 1980's: the role of knowledge, 1980; The Relevance of the African Universities to the Development Needs of Africa, 1980; What Kind of Human Beings for the 21st Century—a second look, 1981; The Humanities and National Development: a second look, 1984; The Crisis of Development: education and identity, 1985; Medical Education and National Development, 1987; Culture, Development and African Unity, 1988; African Scientific and Technical Institution—Building and the Role of International Co-operation, 1988; The Challenge of Education in Africa, 1988; (ed with B. Lesser) Capacity Building and Human Resource Development in Africa, 1990; (ed with B. Lesser) Meeting the Challenge: the African Capacity Building Initiative, 1992; *contribs to:* Grecs et Barbars, 1962; Dawn of African History (ed R. Oliver); Man and Beast: Comparative Social Behaviour (ed J. F. Eisenberg and W. S. Dillon), 1971; Pearson Notes, 1988–89; The Role of Service-Learning in International Education (procs of Wingspread conf.) (ed S. W. Showalter), 1989; Culture, Development and Democracy: role of intellectuals in Africa, 1991; Recent Trends in Governance in African Universities: the challenge of scientific and intellectual leadership, 1992; various articles in classical jls, especially on Ancient and Greco-Roman Africa; various addresses and lectures on internat. higher educn in ICED pubns. *Recreations:* tennis, billiards, music and piano-playing, learning Japanese. *Address:* 19 Highfield Avenue, Golders Green, NW11 9EU. *T:* (020) 8209 0878. *Club:* Athenæum.

KYDD, Ian Douglas; HM Diplomatic Service; Consul General, Vancouver, since 1998; *b* 1 Nov. 1947; *s* of late Alexander Henry John Kydd and Sheila Doreen Riley Kydd (*née* Kinnear); *m* 1968, Elizabeth Louise Pontius; one *s* one *d*. *Educ:* Melville Coll., Edinburgh. DSAO, later FCO, 1966; Attaché, New Delhi, 1970–74; Dep. Dir, later Dir, Radio and TV Div., British Inf. Services, NY, 1974–79; FCO, 1979; Press Officer to Prime Minister, 1981–83; First Sec., Lagos, 1984–88, Ottawa, 1988–92; Dep. Head, News Dept and Head of Newsroom, FCO, 1993–95; Consul-Gen. and Counsellor (Mgt), Moscow, 1995–98. *Recreations:* all sport, esp. downhill ski-ing, squash, sailing, golf. *Address:* c/o Foreign and Commonwealth Office, SW1A 2AH. *Club:* Vancouver.

KYLE, Barry Albert; freelance director, since 1991; Hon. Associate Director, Royal Shakespeare Company, since 1991 (Associate Director, 1978–91); *b* 25 March 1947; *s* of Albert Ernest Kyle and Edith Ivy Bessie Gaskin; *m* 1st, 1971, Christine Susan Iddon (marr. diss. 1988); two *s* one *d*; 2nd, 1990, Lucy Joy Maycock; one *d*. *Educ:* Birmingham Univ. (BA, MA). Associate Dir, Liverpool Playhouse, 1970–72; joined RSC as Asst Dir, 1973; first Artistic Dir, Swan Theatre, Stratford-upon-Avon, 1987; numerous RSC productions and directing abroad, incl. Australia, Israel, USA, Czechoslovakia; founding Artistic Dir, Swine Palace Productions, La, USA; Dir, Theatre for a New Audience, NYC, 1995–96. Vis. Dir, Czechoslovak Nat. Theatre, Prague (first Briton to direct there). *Publications:* Sylvia Plath: a dramatic portrait, 1976; contribs to Literary Review. *Recreations:* foreign travel, reading, physical activities. *Address:* Flat 5, 20 Charing Cross Road, WC2H 0HR. *T:* (020) 7836 5911.

KYLE, David William; Member, Criminal Cases Review Commission, since 1997; *b* 30 March 1951; *s* of William and Judy Kyle; *m* 1975, Rosemary Elizabeth Bazire; two *d*. *Educ:* Monkton Combe Sch.; Queens' Coll., Cambridge (BA). Called to the Bar, Inner Temple, 1973; Office of Director of Public Prosecutions: Legal Asst, 1975–79; Sen. Legal Asst, 1979–86; Crown Prosecution Service: Branch Crown Prosecutor, 1986–89; Head of Div., HQ Casework, 1989–93; Head of HQ Casework, then Chief Crown Prosecutor, Central Casework, 1993–97. *Recreations:* music, walking, amateur dramatics. *Address:* Alpha Tower, Suffolk Street, Queensway, Birmingham B1 1TT. *T:* (0121) 633 1800.

KYLE, James, CBE 1989; FRCSE; FRCSI; FRCS; Chairman, Raigmore Hospital NHS Trust, 1993–97; *b* 26 March 1925; *s* of John Kyle and Dorothy Frances Kyle; *m* 1950, Dorothy Elizabeth Galbraith; two *d*. *Educ:* Queen's Univ., Belfast. MB BCh BAO 1947 (Gold Medal in Surgery); MCh 1956 (Gold Medal); DSc 1972. FRCSI 1953; FRCS 1954; FRCSE 1964. Mayo Clinic, USA, 1950; Tutor in Surgery, QUB, 1952; Lectr in Surgery, Univ. of Liverpool, 1957; Aberdeen University: Sen. Lectr, Surgery, 1959; Mem., Univ. Senatus, 1970; Consultant Surgeon, Aberdeen Royal Infirmary, 1959–89; Chm., Grampian Health Bd, 1989–93 (Mem., 1973). Mem., GMC, 1979–94; Chairman: Scottish Cttee for Hosp. Med. Services, 1977–81; Rep. Body, BMA, 1984–87; Scottish Jt Consultants' Cttee, 1984–89. Ext. Examr, Belfast, Dublin, Dundee, Edinburgh, Sydney, West Indies. Pres., Aberdeen Medico-Surgical Soc. Bicentenary, 1989–90; Member: Council, Surgical Res. Soc., 1972–74; Internat. Soc. of Surgery, 1971–84; Cons. Med. Soc., 1988–93. MInstD. FRPSL. Burgess of Aberdeen, 1990. *Publications:* Peptic Ulceration, 1960; Pye's Surgical Handicraft, 21st edn, 1962; Scientific Foundations of Surgery, 3rd edn, 1967; Crohn's Disease, 1973; papers on surgery, history, philately. *Recreations:* amateur radio (callsign GM4 CHX), philately. *Address:* Grianan, 7 Fasaich, Gairloch, Ross-shire IV21 2DB. *T:* and *Fax:* (01445) 712398. *Club:* Royal Northern (Aberdeen).

KYLE, (James) Terence; Chief Executive, Linklaters & Alliance, since 1998; *b* 9 May 1946; *s* of James Kyle and Elizabeth Kyle (*née* Cinnamond); *m* 1975, Diana Jackson; one *s* two *d*. *Educ:* Royal Belfast Academical Instn; Christ's Coll., Cambridge (MA). Linklaters & Paines: Articled Clerk, 1970–72; Solicitor, 1972–79; Partner, 1979–89; Head, Internat. Finance, 1989–95; Managing Partner, 1995–98. *Recreations:* cricket, tennis, golf.

KYLE, Peter William; Director-General, International Shakespeare Globe Centre, since 1998; *b* 21 Nov. 1948; *s* of late Robert Kyle and Evelyn Kyle (*née* Palliser-Bosomworth); *m* Kathryn Anna Grundy; two *d*. *Educ:* Rambert Sch. of Ballet; Bretton Hall Coll., Yorks; Inst. fur Buhnentanz, Cologne. Former ballet dancer; soloist: Northern Ballet Theatre, 1971–73; Royal New Zealand Ballet, 1973–75; Dance Advr, Leics Educn Authy, 1975–81; Dance Officer, Arts Council of GB, 1981–83; Artistic Dir, Queen's Hall Arts Centre, Hexham, 1983–88; Chief Exec., Scottish Ballet, 1988–95; arts consultant and choreographer, 1995–97; Dean, Arts Educational Sch., London, 1997–98. *Address:* International Shakespeare Globe Centre, New Globe Walk, SE1 9DT.

KYLE, Air Vice-Marshal Richard Henry, CB 1997; MBE 1977; Air Officer Commanding Maintenance Units, RAF Logistics Command, 1993–97; *b* 4 Jan. 1943; *s* of Air Chief Marshal Sir Wallace Hart Kyle, GCB, KCVO, CBE, DSO, DFC and Lady (Molly) Kyle; *m* 1971, Anne Weatherup; two *s* two *d*. *Educ:* Cranbrook Sch., Kent; RAF Tech. College, Henlow; Southampton Univ. (BSc Eng 1964). CEng 1971. FRAeS 1993. Served RAF stations: Syerston, 1965–67; Acklington, 1967–68; Ternhill, 1968–69; Changi, 1969–71; MoD, 1971–73; No 1 (F) Sqn, RAF Wittering, 1973–76; MoD, 1976–78; RAF Staff Coll., 1978; RAF Gütersloh, 1979–81; MoD, 1982–84; RAF Halton, 1984–86; RCDS, 1987; MoD, 1988–89; RAF St Athan, 1990–92; Dir Gen. Support Services (RAF), 1992–93. *Recreations:* squash, orienteering, golf, offshore sailing, hill walking. *Club:* Royal Air Force.

KYLE, Terence; *see* Kyle, J. T.

KYLIÁN, Jirí; Resident Choreographer and Adviser, Nederlands Dans Theater, since 1999 (Artistic Director, 1975–99); *b* Prague, 21 March 1947; *s* of Vaclav Kylián and Marketá Pestová. *Educ:* Ballet Sch., Nat. Theatre, Prague; Prague Conservatory; Royal Ballet Sch., London. Stuttgarter Ballett, Germany; Guest Choreographer, Nederlands Dans Theater, 1973–75; *works choreographed include:* Viewers, 1973; Stoolgame, 1974; La cathédrale engloutie, 1975; Return to a Strange Land, 1975; Sinfonietta, 1978; Symphony of Psalms, 1978; Forgotten Land, 1981; Svadebka, 1982; Stamping Ground, 1983; L'Enfant et les Sortilèges, 1984; No More Play, 1988; Falling Angels, 1989; Sweet Dreams, 1990; Sarabande, 1990; Petite Mort, 1991; As If Never Been, 1992; No Sleep Till Dawn of Day, 1992; Whereabouts Unknown, 1993; Double You, 1994; Arcimboldo, 1995; Tears of Laughter, 1996; Wings of Wax, 1997; A Way a Lone, 1998; Indigo Rose, 1998; Half Past, 1999; Doux Mensonges, 1999. Has worked with numerous cos, incl. Royal Swedish Ballet, Royal Danish Ballet, Royal Ballet, London, Finnish Nat. Ballet, Aust. Ballet, Nat. Ballet of Canada, Amer. Ballet Theatre, Wiener Staatsoper, Tokyo Ballet,

Opéra de Paris, Rambert Dance Co. Hon. Dr, Juilliard Sch., NY, 1997. Critics' Award for Dance, Edinburgh Fest., 1996, 1997; Joost van den Vondel Preis, 1997. Officier: Ordre des arts et des lettres (France); Order of Oranje Nassau (Netherlands), 1995; Golden Medal for Outstanding Merits (Czech Republic). *Address:* c/o Nederlands Dans Theater, Schedeldoekshaven 60, 2511 En Den Haag, Netherlands. *T:* (70) 3609931; Kylián Foundation, Antonie Duyckstr. 115, 2582 TG Den Haag, Netherlands.

KYME, Rt Rev. Brian Robert; Episcopal Assistant to Primate of Australia, since 2000; *b* 22 June 1935; *s* of John Robert Kyme and Ida Eileen Benson; *m* 1961, Doreen Muriel Williams; one *s* one *d*. *Educ:* Melbourne High School; Ridley Theological Coll., Melbourne; WA Coll. of Advanced Educn. (BA 1989); Aust. Coll. of Theology (ThL 1956); Melbourne Coll. of Divinity (Dip RE 1958). MACE 1991. Deacon, 1958; priest, 1960; Curate: St John's, E Malvern, 1958–60; Glenroy and Broadmeadows, 1960–61; Morwell, 1961–63; Vicar, St Matthew's, Ashburton, 1963–69; Dean, Holy Cross Cathedral, Geraldton, WA, 1969–74; Rector, Christ Church, Claremont, Perth, 1974–82; Archdeacon of Stirling, 1977–82; Asst Bishop of Perth, 1982–93; Nat. Dir, Australian Bd of Missions, later Anglican Bd of Mission-Australia, 1993–2000. ChLJ, WA, 1985–93; ChLJ, NSW, 1998–. *Recreations:* reading, music. *Address:* 153 Carr Street, West Perth, WA 6005, Australia. *T:* (office) (8) 93257455, (home) (8) 93286065, *Fax:* (8) 93256741. *Club:* Rotary.

KYNASTON, Nicolas; freelance organist, since 1971; Organist, Athens Concert Hall, since 1995; *b* 10 Dec. 1941; *s* of late Roger Tewkesbury Kynaston and Jessie Dearn Caecilia Kynaston (*née* Parkes); *m* 1st, 1961, Judith Felicity Heron (marr. diss. 1989); two *s* two *d*; 2nd, 1989, Susan Harwood Styles. *Educ:* Westminster Cathedral Choir Sch.; Downside; Accademia Musicale Chigiana, Siena; Conservatorio Santa Cecilia, Rome; Royal Coll. of Music. Organist of Westminster Cathedral, 1961–71; concert career, 1971–, travelling throughout Europe, North America, Asia and Africa. Début recital, Royal Festival Hall, 1966; Recording début, 1968. Artistic Dir, Athens Organ Fest., 1997, 1999. Consultant, J. W. Walker & Sons Ltd, 1982–83 (Artistic Dir, 1978–82); Organ Consultant: Bristol Cathedral, 1986–91; St Chad's Cathedral, Birmingham, 1989–94; Bath Abbey, 1989–97; Tewkesbury Abbey, 1993–97; City of Halle, Germany, 1997–2000; Rugby Sch., 1998–2001. Mem., Westminster Abbey Fabric Commn, 2000–. Jury member: Grand Prix de Chartres, 1971; St Albans Internat. Organ Festival, 1975. Pres., Incorp. Assoc. of Organists, 1983–85; Chm., Assoc. of Ind. Organ Advrs, 1997–2000. Chm., Nat. Organ Teachers' Encouragement Scheme, 1993–95. Hon. FRCO 1976. Records incl. 6 nominated Critic's Choice; EMI/CFP Sales Award, 1974; MTA nomination Best Solo Instrumental Record of the Year, 1977; Deutscher Schallplattenpreis, 1978; Preis der Deutschen Schallplattenkritik, 1988. *Publication:* Transcriptions for Organ, 1997. *Recreations:* walking, church architecture. *Address:* 28 High Park Road, Kew Gardens, Richmond-upon-Thames, Surrey TW9 4BH. *T:* (020) 8878 4455, *Fax:* (020) 8392 9314.

KYNOCH, George Alexander Bryson; Drumduan Associates, since 1997; *b* 7 Oct. 1946; *s* of late Lt Col Gordon Bryson Kynoch, CBE and Nesta Alicia Janet Thora (*née* Lyon); *m* 1971, Dr Rosslyn Margaret McDevitt; one *s* one *d*. *Educ:* Cargilfield Sch., Edinburgh; Glenalmond Coll., Perthshire; Univ. of Bristol (BSc Hons Mech. Engrg). Plant Engr Silicones Plant, ICI Ltd, Nobel Div., 1968–71; G. and G. Kynoch, subseq. Kynoch Group, 1971–92; Finance Dir, then Jt Man. Dir; Chief Exec., 1981–90; Gp Exec. Dir, 1990–92; non-exec. Dir, 1992–95. Non-executive Director: Aardvark Holdings Ltd, 1992–95; PSL Holdings, 1998; Premisys Technologies (formerly WML Gp, then Premisys Gp) plc, 1998–; non-executive Chairman: Silvertech Internat., 1997–2000; London Marine Gp, 1998–; Muir Matheson, 1998–; Benson Gp, 1998–; Jetcam Internat. Hldgs, 1999–. Chm., Scottish Woollen Publicity Council, 1983–90; Pres., Scottish Woollen Industry, 1990–91; Mem., Aberdeen and Dist MMB, 1988–92; Dir, Moray Badenoch and Strathspey Local Enterprise Co. Ltd, 1991–92. MP (C) Kincardine and Deeside, 1992–97; contested (C) Aberdeenshire West and Kincardine, 1997. Parliamentary Private Secretary: to Minister of State, FCO, 1992–94; to Sec. of State for Educn, 1994–95; Parly Under Sec. of State, Scottish Office (Minister for Industry and Local Govt), 1995–97. Mem., Scottish Affairs Select Cttee, 1992–95. Chm., Moray and Banff Cons. and Unionist Assoc., 1990–92; Vice-Chm., Northern Area, Scottish Cons. and Unionist Assoc., 1991–92. *Recreations:* golf, ski-ing, travel. *Address:* Newton of Drumduan, Dess, Aboyne, Aberdeenshire AB34 5BD. *Club:* Carlton.

KYPRIANOU, Spyros; Grand Cross of the Order of George I of Greece, 1962; Grand Cross, Order of the Saviour, Greece, 1983; President of the Republic of Cyprus, 1977–88; President, Democratic Party of Cyprus, since 1976; *b* Limassol, 1932; *s* of Achilleas and Maria Kyprianou; *m* Mimi Kyprianou; two *s*. *Educ:* Greek Gymnasium, Limassol; City of London Coll. Called to the Bar, Gray's Inn, 1954 (Hon. Bencher, 1985); Dip. Comparative Law. Founded Cypriot Students' Union in England (first Pres. 1952–54). Sec. of Archbp Makarios, in London, 1952; Sec. of Cyprus Ethnarchy in London, 1954; left Britain for Greece, 1956, to work for world projection of Cyprus case; later in 1956, rep. Cyprus Ethnarchy, New York, until 1957; resumed London post until signing of Zürich and London Agreements, returning to Cyprus with the Archbp in 1959. On declaration of Independence, 16 Aug. 1960, following brief appt as Minister of Justice, became Foreign Minister, accompanying the Pres. on visits to countries world-wide, 1961–71; rep. Cyprus at UN Security Council and Gen. Assembly sessions, notably during debates on the Cyprus question; signed Agreement in Moscow for Soviet Military Aid to Cyprus, 1964; had several consultations with Greek Govt on Cyprus matter. Mem. Cttee of Ministers of Council of Europe at meetings in Strasburg and Paris (Pres. Cttee, April-Dec. 1967). Resigned post of Foreign Minister, 1972, after dispute with military régime in Athens. Practised law, withdrawing from politics until the coup and Turkish invasion of Cyprus, 1974; travelled between Athens, London and New York, where he led Cyprus delegn during debate on Cyprus in Gen. Assembly of UN, 1974; participated in talks between Greek Govt and Pres. Makarios, 1974; an *ad hoc* member of Cyprus delegn at Security meeting in New York, 1975. Announced estabt of Democratic Party in Cyprus, 1976, becoming Pres. of House of Reps on the party's victory in parly elections. On death of Archbp Makarios, Aug. 1977, became Actg Pres. of Republic, until elected Pres. in same month; re-elected Pres., unopposed, in Feb. 1978 for a full five-year term; re-elected for further five-year term, 1983. Holds numerous foreign decorations. *Recreations:* literature, music, sport. *Address:* Antistaseos 1, Engomi, Nicosia, Cyprus.

KYRIAZIDES, Nikos Panayis; Comdr, Order of George I of Greece; Deputy Minister, Ministry of Finance, Greece, 1994–96; *b* 3 Sept. 1927; *m* 1960, Ellie Kyrou; one *s* one *d*. *Educ:* Exeter Coll., Oxford Univ. (MA); Chicago Univ. Min. of Co-ordination, 1949; Head, Monetary Policy Div., 1950–51; Dir, External Payments and Trade, 1951–54; Alternate Economic Advr, Bank of Greece, 1956–60; Mem., Greek Delegn, negotiations for EFTA and assoc. of Greece to EEC, 1957–61; seconded to Min. of Co-ordination as Dir Gen., relations with EEC, 1962–64; Economic Advr, Nat. Bank of Greece, 1964–67; Sen. Economist, IMF, 1968–70; Advr to Cyprus Govt, negotiations for assoc. of Cyprus to EEC, 1971–72; Dep. Governor, Bank of Greece, 1974–77; Head of Greek delegn to Accession negotiations to the EEC, 1974–77; Advr to Cyprus Govt on relations with EEC, 1979–82; Ambassador to UK, and to Republic of Iceland, 1982–85; Alternate Exec. Dir, IMF, 1986–92. Knight Commander: Order of Merit (Italy); Order of Leopold II (Belgium); Comdr, Order of Merit (FRG). *Address:* 28 Loukianou Street, Athens 10675, Greece. *Club:* Athens (Athens).

KYRLE POPE, Rear-Adm. Michael Donald, CB 1969; MBE 1946; DL; *b* 1 Oct. 1916; *e s* of late Comdr R. K. C. Pope, DSO, OBE, RN retd, and of Mrs A. J. Pope (*née* Macdonald); *m* 1947, Angela Suzanne Layton; one *s* one *d*. *Educ:* Wellington Coll., Berks. Joined RN, 1934; Submarine Service, 1938; HMS Vanguard, 1946–47; BJSM, Washington, 1951–53; Naval Intelligence: Germany, 1955–57, FE, 1958–60; Sen. Naval Off., Persian Gulf, 1962–64; MoD (Naval Intell.), 1965–67; Chief of Staff to C-in-C Far East, 1967–69; retd 1970. Comdr 1951; Capt. 1958; Rear-Adm. 1967. Gen. Manager, Middle East Navigation Aids Service, Bahrain, 1971–77. Dean's Administrator, St Alban's Abbey, 1977–80. Dir, Jerusalem and East Mission Trust, 1978–92. County Pres., Royal British Legion, 1987–95. DL Herts 1983. *Recreations:* country pursuits, sailing. *Address:* Mayfield House, 2 Tidcombe Lane, Tiverton EX16 4DZ. *T:* (01884) 259852. *Club:* Army and Navy.

See also J. Leigh.

KYTE, Peter Eric; QC 1996; a Recorder, since 1991; *b* 8 May 1945; *s* of Eric Frank Kyte and Cicely Evelyn Leslie Kyte; *m* 1969, Virginia Cameron Cornish-Bowden; one *s* one *d*. *Educ:* Wellington Coll.; Trinity Hall, Cambridge (MA Law). Called to the Bar, Gray's Inn, 1970; in business, 1970–74; Asst Recorder, 1988. *Recreations:* tennis, motorcycling, scuba diving, watching son and England perform on the sports field. *Address:* Queen Elizabeth Building, Temple, EC4Y 9BS. *T:* (020) 7583 5766. *Club:* Aula (Cambridge).

L

LABOUISSE, Eve, (Mrs H. R. Labouisse); *see* Curie, E.

LABOVITCH, Neville, LVO 1993; MBE 1977; *b* Leeds; *s* of late Mark and Anne Labovitch; *m* 1958, Sonia Deborah Barney (marr. diss. 1986); two *d*. *Educ:* Brasenose College, Oxford (MA). Treasurer, Oxford Union, 1945. Dir, 1954–82, Man. Dir, 1966–82, Darley Mills. Chairman: Brenta Construction, 1987–91 (Dir, 1985–91); Brenta Cogifar-Impresit, 1990–91; Brenta AB, 1993–; CP Carpets, Kidderminster, 1991–93. Chairman: Trafalgar Square Assoc., 1974–76; Knightsbridge Assoc., 1978–98 (Hon. Pres., 1998); Cleaner London Campaign, 1978–; Piccadilly Tourist Trust, 1978–82; Great Children's Party for IYC, 1979; London Environmental Campaign, 1983; Westminster Quatercentenary Cttee, 1984; Prince of Wales Royal Parks Tree Appeal, 1987–; Mem., Royal Parks Ministerial Adv. Bd, 1994–99; Mem., London Celebrations Cttee for Queen's Silver Jubilee, and Chm., Silver Jubilee Exhibn, Hyde Park, 1977; Pres., Jubilee Walkway Trust, 2001– (Vice-Chm., 1978–95; Chm., 1995–2001); Chairman: Organizing Cttee, Queen's 60th Birthday Celebrations, 1986; Queen's Anniv. Cttee, Hampton Court Palace 1952–1992, 1992. Mem., Vis. Cttee, RCA, 1983–90. Director: Nat. Children's Charities Fund, 1979–; Spitalfields Market Opera Ltd, 1994–2000. Trustee, Albert Memorial Trust, 1994–. FRSA. Cavaliere Ufficiale, Order of Merit (Italy), 1991. *Recreations:* reading and ruminating. *Club:* Brooks's.

LACEY, George William Brian; Keeper, Department of Transport, Science Museum, London, 1971–86; *b* 15 Nov. 1926; *m* 1956, Lynette (*née* Hogg); two *s*. *Educ:* Brighton, Hove and Sussex Grammar Sch., 1938–44; Brighton Technical Coll., 1944–47. BSc(Eng) 2nd Cl. Hons (External, London). National Service, REME, 1947–49. Rolls-Royce Ltd, Derby: Grad. Apprentice, Tech. Asst, Mechanical Develt and Performance Analysis, 1949–54. Asst Keeper, Science Museum, London, SW7, 1954. Chm., Historical Gp, Royal Aeronautical Soc., 1971–78; Vice-Pres., Assoc. British Transport Museums, 1990– (Chm., 1973–83); Mem. Council, Transport Trust, 1978–89. *Recreations:* golf, genealogy. *Address:* Hurst Grange Cottage, Albourne Road, Hurstpierpoint, W Sussex BN6 9ES. *T:* (01273) 833914.

LACEY, Prof. Richard Westgarth, MD, PhD; FRCPath; Professor of Medical Microbiology, University of Leeds, 1983–98, now Emeritus; Consultant to Leeds Health Authority, 1983–98; *b* 11 Oct. 1940; *s* of Jack and Sybil Lacey; *m* 1972, Fionna Margaret Stone; two *d*. *Educ:* Felsted Sch., Essex; Cambridge Univ. (BA, MB, BChir; MD 1969); London Hosp.; Univ. of Bristol (PhD 1974). FRCPath 1985; DCH 1966. House Officer, London and Eastbourne, 1964–66; Sen. House Officer, 1966–67, Registrar, 1967–68, Bristol Royal Infirmary; Lectr, 1968–73, Reader in Clinical Microbiology, 1973–74, Univ. of Bristol; Consultant in Microbiology, 1974–83, and Consultant in Chemical Pathology, 1975–83, Queen Elizabeth Hosp., King's Lynn; Consultant in Chem. Path., E Anglian RHA, 1974–83. Consultant, WHO, 1983–. Evian Health Award, 1989; Caroline Walker Award, 1989; Freedom of Information Award, 1990. *Publications:* Safe Shopping, Safe Cooking, Safe Eating, 1989; Unfit for Human Consumption, 1991; Hard to Swallow, 1994; Mad Cow Disease: a history of BSE in Britain, 1994; Poison on a Plate, 1998; 210 contribs to learned scientific jls. *Recreations:* antique furniture, gardening, chess, sleeping, walking, eating (not recently). *Address:* Carlton Manor, near Yeadon, Leeds LS19 7BE.

LACEY, Stephen Charles David Lloyd; gardener, author, journalist and broadcaster; *b* 6 May 1957; *s* of Charles Leslie Lacey and Myra Lloyd Lacey (*née* Lloyd Williams). *Educ:* Trearddur House Prep. Sch.; Shrewsbury Sch.; Trinity Coll., Oxford (MA Mod. Langs). Early career in property investment; gardening columnist, Daily Telegraph, 1989–; a presenter, Gardeners' World, BBC TV, 1992–; freelance horticultural lectr in UK, USA and Canada. *Publications:* The Startling Jungle, 1986; Scent in Your Garden, 1991; Lawns and Ground Cover, 1991; Gardens of the National Trust, 1996. *Recreations:* adventurous travel, tropical birdwatching, collecting, ski-ing. *Address:* 2 Queen's Gate Place, SW7 5NS. *T:* (020) 7584 8410.

LACHMANN, Prof. Peter Julius, FRCP, FRCPath; FRS 1982; PMedSci; Sheila Joan Smith Professor of Immunology (formerly Tumour Immunology), University of Cambridge, 1977–99, now Emeritus Professor; Fellow of Christ's College, Cambridge, 1962–71 and since 1976; Head, Microbial Immunology Group, Centre for Veterinary Science, Cambridge, 1997–2001; *b* 23 Dec. 1931; *s* of late Heinz Lachmann and Thea (*née* Heller); *m* 1962, Sylvia Mary, *d* of Alan Stephenson; two *s* one *d*. *Educ:* Christ's Coll., Finchley; Trinity Coll., Cambridge; University College Hosp. MA, MB BChir, PhD, ScD (Cantab). FRCP 1973; FRCPath 1981. John Lucas Walker Student, Dept of Pathology, Cambridge, 1958–60; Vis. Investigator, Rockefeller Univ., New York, 1960–61; Empire Rheumatism Council Res. Fellow, Dept of Pathology, Cambridge, 1962–64; Asst Dir of Res. in Pathology, Univ. of Cambridge, 1964–71; Prof. of Immunology, Royal Postgraduate Med. Sch., 1971–75; Hd, 1976–77, Hon. Hd, 1977–80, MRC Gp on Mechanisms in Tumour Immunity; Hon. Dir, MRC Mechanisms in Tumour Immunity Unit, later MRC Molecular Immunopathology Unit, 1980–96; Hon. Clin. Immunologist, Cambridge HA, 1976–99. Member: Systems Bd, MRC, 1982–86; Med. Adv. Cttee, British Council, 1983–97; Council, RCPath, 1982–85, 1989–93 (Pres., 1990–93); Gene Therapy Adv. Cttee, 1993–96; UNESCO Internat. Bioethics Cttee, 1993–98; Med. Educn Res. Co-ordinating Cttee, 1994–; Scientific Adv. Bd, SmithKline Beecham, 1995–; Chm. Scientific Adv. Bd, and Dir, Adprotech plc, 1997–. Chairman: Med. Res. Cttee, Muscular Dystrophy Gp, 1987–91; Sci. Cttee, Assoc. Medical Res. Charities, 1988–92. Trustee, Darwin Trust, 1991–. Vis. Investigator, Scripps Clinic and Research Foundn, La Jolla, 1966, 1975, 1980, 1986, 1989; Vis. Scientist, Basel Inst. of Immunology, 1971; RSM Vis. Prof. in USA (various centres), 1983; Smith Kline & French Vis. Prof. in Australia (various centres), 1987; Vis. Prof., Dept of Medicine, RPMS, London, 1986–89 (Fellow, 1995; FIC 1999). Meyerhoff Vis. Prof., Weizmann Inst., Rehovoth, 1989; Prof., Collège de France, 1993; RCS Sir Arthur Sims Travelling Prof., India, 1994; Lectures: Foundn, RCPath, 1983; Langdon-Brown, RCP, 1986; first R. R. Porter Meml, 1986; Heberden Oration, 1986; Prathap Meml, Malaysia, 1991; Charnock Bradley Meml, Royal (Dick) Vet. Sch., Edinburgh, 1994; Frank May Med. Scis, Univ. of Leicester, 1994; Vanguard Medica, Univ. of Surrey, 1998; Lloyd Roberts, Med. Soc. of London, 1999. Biological Sec., and a Vice-Pres., Royal Soc., 1993–98; Founder FMedSci 1998 (Pres., 1998–). Foreign Fellow, Indian Nat. Sci. Acad., 1997; Foreign Member: Norwegian Acad. of Science and Letters, 1991; Academia Europea, 1992. Hon. Fellow, Faculty of Pathology, RCPI, 1993; Hon. Mem., Assoc. of Physicians, 1998. Gold Medal, Eur. Complement Network, 1997. Associate Editor, Clinical and Experimental Immunology, 1989–2001. *Publications:* co-ed, Clinical Aspects of Immunology, 3rd edn 1975, 4th edn 1982, 5th edn 1993; papers in sci. jls on complement and immunopathology. *Recreations:* walking in mountains, keeping bees. *Address:* Conduit Head, 36 Conduit Head Road, Cambridge CB3 0EY. *T:* (01223) 354433. *Club:* Athenæum.

LACKEY, Mary Josephine, CB 1985; OBE 1966; former Under Secretary, Department of Trade and Industry; *b* 11 Aug. 1925; *d* of William and Winifred Lackey. *Educ:* King Edward VI High Sch., Birmingham; Lady Margaret Hall, Oxford (MA). Board of Trade, 1946; Asst Principal, Central Land Bd, 1947–50; BoT, 1950–61; UK Delegn to EFTA and GATT, 1961–66; BoT, subseq. DTI and Dept of Trade, 1966–85; Asst Sec., 1968; Under Sec., 1974. *Club:* Oxford and Cambridge.

LACLOTTE, Michel René; Commandeur de la Légion d'honneur; Commandeur de l'ordre national du Mérite; Hon. CBE 1994; Director, The Louvre Museum, Paris, 1987–94; *b* 27 Oct. 1929; *s* of Pierre Laclotte, advocate, and Huguette (*née* de Kermabon). *Educ:* Lycée Pasteur, Neuilly; Institut d'art et d'archéologie, l'Université de Paris; Ecole du Louvre. Inspector, Inspectorate General of provincial museums, 1955–66; Chief Conservator: Dept of Paintings, Louvre Mus., 1966–87; Collections of Musée d'Orsay, 1970–86. *Publications:* works on history of art, catalogues, articles in art reviews, esp. on Italian paintings of 14th and 15th centuries and French primitives. *Address:* 10 bis rue du Pré-aux-Clercs, 75007 Paris, France.

LACOME, Myer; professional artist/designer; Principal, Duncan of Jordanstone College of Art, Dundee, 1978–87; *b* 13 Nov. 1927; *s* of Colman Lacome and Sara (*née* Sholl); *m* 1954, Jacci Edgar; one *s* two *d*. *Educ:* Regional Coll. of Art, Liverpool. MSIAD, MSTD, MInstPkg; FRSA. National Service, RAF, 1946–48. Post-grad. course, 1948–49; designer, New York, 1949–51; consultant designer, London, 1951–59; Head of Sch. of Design, Duncan of Jordanstone Coll. of Art, Dundee, 1962–77. Vis. Fellow, Royal Melbourne Inst. of Technol., 1979. Chm., Visual Art Cttee, Scottish Arts Council, 1986–93; Member: Council, CNAA, 1979–84; Higher Educn Cttee, Scottish Design Council, 1984–86; Governor, Scottish Film Council, 1982–. One-man exhibitions include: Paris: paintings and collages, French Cultural Inst., Edin., Paperpoint Gall., Covent Gdn, and Univ. of Dundee, 1992; Holocaust and After?, Chessel Gall., Edinburgh, 1995, Mackintosh Mus. Sch., Glasgow, 1996, Manchester Jewish Mus., 1997; Scottish Exec., 2000; work in permanent collection of Nat. Museums of Scotland, 1999. *Publications:* papers on crafts in Scotland and on Scandinavian design and crafts. *Recreations:* enjoying: no longer sitting on committees or quangos, not wearing a tie, painting in my studio, listening to Bach, Glenn Gould, Miles Davis and Thelonius Monk. *Address:* 4 Campbells Close, off Royal Mile, Edinburgh EH8 8JJ.

LACON, Sir Edmund (Vere), 8th Bt *cr* 1818; Company Secretary, S.A.K. Ventures Ltd, since 1992; *b* 3 May 1936; *s* of Sir George Vere Francis Lacon, 7th Bt, and of Hilary Blanche (now Mrs J. D. Turner), *d* of late C. J. Scott, Adyar, Walberswick; *S* father, 1980; *m* 1963, Gillian, *d* of J. H. Middleditch, Wrentham, Suffolk; one *s* one *d*. *Educ:* Taverham Hall, Norfolk; Woodbridge School, Suffolk. RAF Regiment, 1955–59. *Recreations:* golf, water-skiing, being politically incorrect. *Heir:* *s* (Edmund) Richard (Vere) Lacon [*b* 2 Oct. 1967; *m* 1997, Natalie, *o d* of Joginder Shinh]. *Club:* Naval and Military.

LACOSTE, Prof. Paul, OC 1977; DUP; Rector, Université de Montréal, 1975–85, Professor Emeritus since 1987; Chairman, Federal Environmental Assessment Review of the Great Whale Project, 1991–98; *b* 24 April 1923; *s* of Emile Lacoste and Juliette Boucher Lacoste; *m* 1973 (marr. diss.); one *s* two *d*. *Educ:* Univ. de Montréal (BA, MA, LPh, LLL). DUP 1948. Fellow, Univ. of Chicago, 1946–47; Univ. de Montréal: Prof., Faculty of Philosophy, 1948; Full Prof., 1958; Vice-Rector, 1968–75; Vis. Prof., Faculty of Law, 1962–70 and 1985–87. Practising lawyer, 1964–66. Pres., Assoc. des universités partiellement ou entièrement de langue française, 1978–81. Hon. LLD: McGill, 1975; Toronto, 1978; Hon DU Laval, 1986. Chevalier de la Légion d'Honneur, 1985. *Publications:* (jtly) Justice et paix scolaire, 1962; A Place of Liberty, 1964; Le Canada au seuil du siècle de l'abondance, 1969; Principes de gestion universitaire, 1970; (jtly) Education permanente et potentiel universitaire, 1977. *Address:* Université de Montréal, PO Box 6128, succursale Centre-Ville, Pavillon 2910, Montréal, QC H3C 3J7, Canada. *T:* (514) 3437727.

LACROIX, Christian Marie Marc; Commandeur des Arts et des Lettres, France, 1998; designer; *b* 16 May 1951; *s* of Maxime Lacroix and Jeannette Bergier; *m* 1989, Françoise Roesenstiehl. *Educ:* Paul Valéry Univ., Montpellier; Sorbonne. History of Art degree. Assistant at Hermès, 1978; Asst for Guy Paulin, 1980; designer for Patou, 1981–86. Golden Thimble Award, 1986 and 1988; CFDA Award, NY, 1987; Prix Balzac, 1989; Goldene Spinnrad, Kneffeld RFA, 1990; Molière Theatre Award, 1996. *Publications:* Pieces of a Pattern (autobiog.), 1992; The Diary of a Collection, 1996. *Address:* 73 Faubourg St Honoré, 75008 Paris, France. *T:* (1) 42657900.

LACROIX, Prof. Robert, PhD; Rector, University of Montreal, since 1998; *b* 15 April 1940; *s* of Léo Lacroix and Léonne Galarneau; *m* 1962, Ginette Teasdale; three *d*. *Educ:* Univ. of Montreal (BA, BSc, MA Econs); Univ. of Louvain, Belgium (PhD Econs 1970). University of Montreal: Asst Prof., 1970, Prof., 1979, Dept of Econs; Chm., Dept of Econs, 1977–83; Dir, Centre for R&D in Econs, 1985–87; Dean, Faculty of Arts and Scis, 1987–93; Pres. and CEO, Centre for Interuniv. Res. and Analysis on Orgns, 1994–98. Project Dir, Econ. Council of Canada, 1976–. Member, Board of Directors: Assoc. of Univs and Colls of Canada, 1998– (Vice-Pres. and Mem., Finance Cttee, 2000–); Conf. of Rectors and Principals of Quebec Univs, 1998–; Ecole Polytechnique de Montréal, 1998–; Ecole des Hautes Etudes Commerciales, 1998–; Mem., Academic Adv. Cttee, Inst. of Canadian Bankers, 1999–. *Publications:* (with J. M. Cousineau) Wage Determination in Major Collective Agreements in the Private and Public Sectors, 1977; (with Y. Rabeau) Politiques nationales, Conjonctures régionales: la stabilisation économique, 1981; (with F. Martin) Les conséquences de la décentralisation régionale des activités de R&D, 1987; (with M. Huberman) Le partage de l'Emploi: solution au chômage ou frein à l'emploi, 1996. *Address:* Cabinet du Recteur, Université de Montréal, PO Box 6128, Station Centre-Ville, Montreal, QC H3C 3J7, Canada. *T:* (514) 3436776. *Clubs:* Mount Royal, Saint-Denis (Montreal).

LACY, Sir John (Trend), Kt 1992; CBE 1983; General Director of Party Campaigning, Conservative Central Office, 1989–92; *b* 15 March 1928; *s* of Rev. Hubert Lacy and Mrs Gertrude Lacy (*née* Markham); *m* 1956, Pamela Guerin; one *s*. *Educ:* King's Sch., Ely, Cambs. Served RN, 1945–48. Harvey & Clark (Manufrs), 1948–50; Conservative Party: London, 1950–56; Aylesbury, 1956–61; W Midlands area, 1961–64; Northern area, 1964–71; S Eastern area, 1971–85; Dir of Campaigning, 1985–89. *Recreations:* racing, fishing, philately. *Address:* 18 Windmill Close, Milford-on-Sea, Hants SO41 0SX. *T:* (01590) 643984. *Clubs:* Carlton, St Stephen's Constitutional (Vice Chm., 1988–93).

LACY, Sir Patrick Bryan Finucane, 4th Bt *cr* 1921, of Ampton, co. Suffolk; *b* 18 April 1948; *s* of Sir Maurice John Pierce Lacy, 2nd Bt and of his 2nd wife, Nansi Jean (*née* Evans); *S* brother, 1998; *m* 1971, Phyllis Victoria James; one *s* one *d*. *Educ:* Downside. *Heir: s* Finian James Pierce Lacy, *b* 24 Sept. 1972.

LADDIE, Hon. Sir Hugh Ian Lang, Kt 1995; **Hon. Mr Justice Laddie;** Judge of the High Court of Justice, Chancery Division, since 1995; *b* 15 April 1946; *s* of late Bertie Daniel Laddie and of Rachel Laddie; *m* 1970, Stecia Elizabeth (*née* Zamet); two *s* one *d*. *Educ:* Aldenham Sch.; St Catharine's Coll., Cambridge (MA). Called to the Bar, Middle Temple, 1969 (Blackstone Pupillage Award; Bencher, 1993); Jun. Counsel to HM Treasury in Patent Matters, 1981–86; QC 1986. Jun. Bar Rep., Patents Procedure Cttee, 1976. Sec., 1971–75, Chm., 1993–94, Patent Bar Assoc.; Mem. Cttee, Chancery Bar Assoc., 1991–92. Chm., Vet. Code of Practice Cttee, Nat. Office of Animal Health; Dep. Chm., Copyright Tribunal, 1993–95; Dep. Ind. Chm., London Theatre Council and Provincial Theatre Council, 1993–95. Asst Ed.-in-Chief, Annual of Industrial Property Law, 1975–79; UK Correspondent, European Law Rev., 1978–83; Editor, Supreme Court Practice, 1995–; Ed.-in-Chief, In Context, 1998. *Publications:* (jtly) Patent Law of Europe and the United Kingdom, 1978; (jtly) The Modern Law of Copyright, 1980, 2nd edn 1995. *Recreations:* music, gardening, fishing.

LADDS, Rt Rev. Robert Sidney; *see* Whitby, Bishop Suffragan of.

LADE, Hilary Jane; Chairman, Royal Parks Advisory Board, since 1999; *b* 11 June 1957; *d* of Herbert Alfred Lade and Margaret (*née* Clark). *Educ:* Selwyn Coll., Cambridge (MA Oriental Studies (Chinese)); Harvard Univ. (MA E Asian Langs and Civilisations); Univ. of Calif, Berkeley (MA Internat. Relns). Oil trader, Shell Internat., 1984–87; Man. Dir, Shell Gas Ltd, Shell UK, 1987–91; Estate Manager, Fountains Abbey and Studley Royal, NT, 1991–93; Dir of Historic Properties, English Heritage, 1993–97; Hd of Business Improvement, Shell, 1997–99. Director: Nat. Forest Co., 1998–; Southern Arts Bd, 1998–; YHA, 1999–; BTA, 2000–; Nat. Trust, 2001–. Winston Churchill Travelling Fellow, 1978; Harkness Fellow, 1980. *Recreations:* music (violin player), travel, ski-ing, mountaineering. *Address:* 2 Victoria Terrace, Dyers Hill, Charlbury, Oxford OX7 3QF; *e-mail:* hilary.lade@virgin.net.

LADENIS, Nicholas Peter; Chef Patron, Chez Nico, 1973–99; Owner, Chez Nico Restaurants, since 1985; *b* 22 April 1934; *s* of Peter and Constandia Ladenis; *m* 1963, Dinah-Jane Zissu; two *d*. *Educ:* Prince of Wales Sch., Nairobi; Regent Street Poly.; LSE; Hull Univ. (BSc Econs 1958). Appts with various cos, incl. Caltex, Ford Motor Co., Sunday Times, up to 1970; entered catering trade, 1971; opened restaurants (with wife and business partner): Chez Nico, 1973; Simply Nico, 1986; Nico Central, 1989; Chez Nico at Ninety Park Lane, 1992; Incognico, 2000. Hon. DSc(Econ) Hull, 1997. *Publications:* My Gastronomy, 1987; Nico, 1996. *Recreations:* food, family, home, travel, expensive cars. *Address:* 90 Park Lane, W1K 7TN. *T:* (020) 7409 1290.

LADER, Prof. Malcolm Harold, OBE 1996; MD, PhD, DSc; FRCPsych, FMedSci; Professor of Clinical Psychopharmacology, Institute of Psychiatry, University of London, since 1978; *b* 27 Feb. 1936; *s* of Abe and Minnie Lader; *m* 1961, Susan Ruth Packer; three *d*. *Educ:* Univ. of Liverpool (BSc 1956; MB ChB 1959; MD 1964); University Coll. London (PhD 1963; DSc 1976); DPM 1966. FRCPsych 1976. Res. Asst, UCL, 1960–63; Registrar in Psychiatry, 1963–66, Hon. Consultant, 1970–2001, Maudsley Hosp.; Mem., MRC External Staff, 1966–2001. FRSocMed 1963; FMedSci 1999. Hon. Fellow: Amer. Coll. of Psychiatrists, 1993; Soc. for Study of Addiction, 1998; British Assoc. for Psychopharmacology, 1994. *Publications:* Psychiatry on Trial, 1978; (ed jtly) Psychiatry and General Practice, 1982; (jtly) Role of Neurotransmitter Systems in Anxiety Modulation, 1984; (contrib.) Patterns of Improvement in Depressed In-patients, 1987; (ed) Psychopharmacology of Addiction, 1988; Biological Treatments in Psychiatry, 1990, 2nd edn 1996; (ed jtly) Nature of Alcohol and Drug-related Problems, 1992; (jtly) Anxiety, Panic and Phobias, 1997; 640 articles in scientific jls. *Recreations:* antiques, eating too much. *Address:* 11 Kelsey Way, Beckenham, Kent BR3 3LP. *T:* (020) 8650 0366.

LADER, Philip, JD; Chairman, WPP Group, since 2001; *b* 17 March 1946; *s* of Phil and Mary Tripoli Lader; *m* 1980, Linda LeSourd; two *d*. *Educ:* Duke Univ. (BA 1966); Univ. of Michigan (MA History 1967); Pembroke Coll., Oxford (Hon. Fellow); Harvard Law Sch. (JD). Admitted to Bar: Florida, 1972; District of Columbia, 1973; S Carolina, 1979; Associate, Sullivan & Cromwell, 1972; Law Clerk to US Circuit Judge, 1973; President: Sea Pines Co., 1979–83; Winthrop Univ., 1983–86; GOSL Land Assets Mgt, 1986–88; 1st Southern Corp., 1989–91, 1997–; Business Execs for Nat. Security, 1990; Pres. and Vice Chancellor, Bond Univ., Australia, 1991–92; Dep. Dir for Mgt, Office of Mgt and Budget, US Govt, 1993; White House Dep. Chief of Staff and Asst to the Pres., 1993–94; Adminr, Small Business Admin, and Mem., President's Cabinet, 1994–97; Ambassador of the USA to the UK, 1997–2001. Trustee, British Museum, 2001–. Mem., Council on Foreign Relns, Chief Execs' Orgn. John C. Whitehead Lecture, RIIA, 1998. Various hon. doctorates. *Recreations:* walking, tennis. *Address:* WPP Group, 27 Farm Street, W1X 6RD. *Clubs:* Harvard (New York); Metropolitan (Washington).

LADYMAN, Dr Stephen John; MP (Lab) South Thanet, since 1997; *b* 6 Nov. 1952; *s* of Frank Ladyman and Winifred Ladyman; *m* 1st, 1975 (marr. diss. 1994); 2nd, 1995, Janet Ann Baker; one *d*, and two step *s* one step *d*. *Educ:* Liverpool Poly. (BSc Hons Applied Biol. 1975); Strathclyde Univ. (PhD 1982). Res. scientist, MRC Radiobiol. Unit, 1979–84; Head: of Computing, Mathilda and Terence Kennedy Inst. of Rheumatology, 1984–90; of Computer-User Support, Pfizer Central Res., 1990–97. Mem. (Lab) Thanet DC, 1995–99 (Chm., Finance and Monitoring, 1995–97). Contested (Lab) Wantage, 1987. PPS to Minister for the Armed Forces, 2001–. Mem., Select Cttee on Envmt, Transport and the Regs, 1999–2001 (Mem., Transport Sub-Cttee, 1999–2001). Chm., All Party Parly Gp on Autism, 2000–. *Publications:* Natural Isotopic Abundances in Soil Studies, 1982; various learned articles. *Recreations:* occasional golf, walking the dog, watching soccer. *Address:* House of Commons, SW1A 0AA; Chilton Farmhouse, Chilton Lane, Ramsgate, Kent CT11 0LQ. *T:* (01843) 850315.

LAFITTE, Prof. François; Professor of Social Policy and Administration, University of Birmingham, 1959–80, now Emeritus; *b* 3 Aug. 1913; *s* of John Armistead Collier and Françoise Lafitte and adopted *s* of late Havelock Ellis; *m* 1938, Eileen (*née* Saville) (*d* 1996); (one *s* decd). *Educ:* Collège Municipal, Maubeuge; George Green's Sch., Poplar; St Olave's Grammar Sch., Southwark; Worcester Coll., Oxford. Research and translating for Miners' Internat. Fed., 1936–37; on research staff, and subseq. Dep. Sec., PEP, 1938–43; on editorial staff of The Times, as special writer on social questions, 1943–59; Chm. of PEP research groups on health services, 1943–46, on housing policy, 1948–51. Dean of Faculty of Commerce and Social Science, Birmingham, Univ., 1965–68. Member: Home Office Advisory Council on the Treatment of Offenders, 1961–64; Adv. Cttees Social Science Research Council, 1966–69; Redditch New Town Corp., 1964–75; Chm., British Pregnancy Adv. Service, 1968–88. *Publications:* The Internment of Aliens, 1940, repr. 1988; Britain's Way to Social Security, 1945; Family Planning in the Sixties, 1964; (part author) Socially Deprived Families in Britain, 1970; many PEP Planning monographs; many papers on abortion and related issues; contributed to British Journal of Delinquency, Eugenics Review, Chambers's Encyclopædia. etc. *Address:* 77 Oakfield Road, Birmingham B29 7HL. *T:* (0121) 472 2709. *Club:* University Staff (Birmingham).

LAFONTAINE, Oskar; Member of Bundestag, 1990–94 and 1998–99; Minister of Finance, Germany, 1998–99; *b* 16 Sept. 1943; *m* 1993, Christa Müller; one *s*; one *s* by a former marriage. *Educ:* Bonn Univ.; Saarbrücken Univ. Social Democratic Party (SPD), Germany: joined, 1966; officer, Saarland, 1970–75; Chm., Saarland Reg., 1977–96; Mem., Nat. Exec., 1994–; Chm., SPD, 1995–99. Mem., 1970–75 and 1985–98, Premier, 1985–98, Saarland Regl Parlt; Mayor, 1974–76, Lord Mayor, 1976–85, Saarbrücken; Pres., Bundesrat, 1995–96; Chm., Jt Cttee of Bundesrat and Bundestag, 1995–96. *Publications:* Angst vor den Freunden: die Atomwaffen-Strategie der Supermächte Zerstört die Bündnisse, 1983; Der andere Fortschritt: Verantwortung statt Verweigerung, 1985; Die Gesellschaft der Zukunft, 1988; Das Lied vom Teilen, 1989; Deutsche Wahrheiten, 1990; The Heart Beats on the Left (autobiog.), 1999. *Address:* SPD Parteivorstand, Willy-Brandt-Haus, Wilhelmstrasse 140, 10963 Berlin, Germany. *T:* (30) 259910, *Fax:* (30) 25991410.

LA FRENAIS, Ian; writer, screenwriter and producer; *b* 7 Jan. 1937; *s* of Cyril and Gladys La Frenais; *m* 1984, Doris Vartan; one step *s*. *Educ:* Dame Allan's School, Northumberland. *Television:* writer or co-writer (with Dick Clement): The Likely Lads, 1965–68; The Adventures of Lucky Jim, 1968; Whatever Happened to the Likely Lads, 1971–73; Seven of One, 1973; Thick as Thieves, 1974; Comedy Playhouse, 1975; Porridge, 1974–77; Going Straight, 1978; Further Adventures of Lucky Jim, 1983; Auf Wiedersehen Pet, 1983–84; Mog, 1985; Lovejoy, 1986; Spender, 1990; Freddie and Max, 1990; Old Boy Network, 1991; Full Stretch, 1993; Over the Rainbow, 1993; *US television:* On The Rocks, 1976–77; Billy, 1979; Sunset Limousine, 1983; Tracy Ullman Special, 1993; Tracy Takes On, 1995–99; *films:* writer or co-writer (with Dick Clement): The Jokers, 1967; The Touchables, 1968; Otley, 1968; Hannibal Brooks, 1969; The Virgin Soldiers, 1969; Villain, 1970; Catch Me a Spy, 1971; The Likely Lads, 1975; Porridge, 1979; To Russia with Elton, 1979; Prisoner of Zenda, 1981; Water, 1984; writer-producer (with Dick Clement): Vice Versa, 1987; The Commitments, 1991; Excess Baggage, 1997; Still Crazy, 1998; Honest, 2000; *stage:* writer, Billy, 1974; co-producer, Anyone for Denis?, 1982. Partner (with Dick Clement and Allan McKeown), Witzend Productions; producer, co-producer, director, numerous productions. Awards from BAFTA, Broadcasting Guild, Evening News, Pye, Screen Writers' Guild, Soc. of TV Critics, Writers' Guild of America, London Film Critics' Circle, Acad. of Television Arts and Scis. *Publications:* novelisations of The Likely Lads, Whatever Happened to the Likely Lads, Porridge, Auf Wiedersehen Pet. *Recreations:* music, films, sports, wine, driving.

LAGACOS, Eustace P.; *b* 4 June 1921; one *d*. *Educ:* Univ. of Athens (Graduate of Law). Embassy Attaché, 1949; served Athens, Paris, Istanbul, Nicosia, London; Minister, 1969; Foreign Ministry, Athens, 1970; Ambassador to Nicosia, 1972; Dir Gen., Economic Affairs, Foreign Ministry, Athens, 1974; Permanent Representative to NATO, Brussels, 1976; Ambassador to UK, 1979–82. Mem., Eur. Parlt, 1989–94. Grand Officer of Order of the Phoenix, Greece; Commander of Order of George I, Greece; Grand Cordon of Order of Manuel Amadoi Guerrero, Panama; Commander of Legion of Honour, France; Kt Commander of Order of Queen Isabella I, Spain; Grand Officer of Order of the Republic, Egypt. *Publications:* The Cyprus Question, 1987; Populism in Foreign Affairs Issues, 1996. *Address:* 7 Kapsali Street, Athens 10674, Greece.

LAGOS, Archbishop of, (RC), since 1973 (and Metropolitan); **Most Rev. Anthony Olubunmi Okogie,** CON 1999; DD; *b* Lagos, 16 June 1936. *Educ:* St Gregory's Coll., Lagos; St Theresa's Minor Seminary, Ibadan; St Peter and St Paul's Seminary, Ibadan; Urban Univ., Rome. Priest, 1966; appointments include: Acting Parish Priest, St Patrick's Church, Idumagbo, 1967–71; Asst Priest, and Master of Ceremonies, Holy Cross Cathedral, Lagos, 1967–71; Religious Instructor, King's Coll., Lagos, 1967–71; Director of Vocations, Archdiocese of Lagos, 1968–71; Manager, Holy Cross Group of Schools, Lagos, 1969–71; Auxiliary Bishop of Oyo, 1971–72; Auxiliary Bishop to Apostolic Administrator, Archdiocese of Lagos, 1972–73. Vice-Pres., 1983–88, Pres., 1988–94, Catholic Bishops Conf. of Nigeria; Roman Catholic Trustee of Christian Assoc. of Nigeria, 1974–; Member: State Community Relns Cttee, 1984–; Prerogative of Mercy, 1986–; Adv. Council on Religious Affairs, 1987–; Chm., Christian Assoc. of Nigeria, 1989–97. *Address:* Holy Cross Cathedral, PO Box 8, Lagos, Nigeria. *T:* (1) 2635729 and (1) 2633841, *Fax:* 2633841.

LAGOS, Bishop of; *see* Nigeria, Metropolitan Archbishop and Primate of.

LAHNSTEIN, Manfred; Member, Supervisory Board, Bertelsmann Corporation, since 1994 (Executive Board, 1983–94); President, Electronic-Media Division, since 1985; *b* 20 Dec. 1937; *s* of Walter and Hertha Lahnstein; one *s* one *d*. *Educ:* Cologne Univ. (Dipl. Kfm). German Trade Union Fedn, Dusseldorf, 1962–64; European Trade Union Office, Brussels, 1965–67; European Commn, 1967–73; German Govt service, 1973–82: served in Finance Min. and as Head of Chancellor's Office; Minister of Finance, April–Oct. 1982.

Pres., Bertelsmann printing and manufacturing gp, 1983–85. *Publications:* various articles. *Recreation:* classical music. *Address:* Herrengraben 3, 20459 Hamburg, Germany.

LAÏDI, Ahmed; Algerian Ambassador to Mexico, 1988–89; *b* 20 April 1934; *m* 1964, Aicha Chabbi-Lemsine; one *s* one *d* (and one *s* decd). *Educ:* Algiers Univ. (BA); Oran Univ. (LLB). Counsellor to Presidency of Council of Algerian Republic, 1963; Head of Cabinet of Presidency, 1963–64; Dir. Gen. of Political and Economic Affairs, Min. of Foreign Affairs, 1964–66; Chm., Prep. Cttee, second Afro-Asian Conf., 1964–65; Special Envoy to Heads of States, Senegal, Mali, Ivory Coast and Nigeria, 1966; Ambassador to Spain, 1966–70; Head, Delegn to Geneva Conf. of non-nuclear countries, 1968; Wali (Governor): province Médea, 1970–74; province Tlemcen, 1975–78; Ambassador to Jordan, 1978–84; Special Envoy to Heads of States and govts, Zambia, Malaŵi, Botswana, Zimbabwe, 1985; Ambassador to UK, 1984–88, and to Ireland, 1985–88. Member: Algerian Football Fedn, 1964–66; Algerian Nat. Olympic Cttee, 1965–72. Foreign Orders: Liberia, 1963; Bulgaria, 1964; Yugoslavia, 1964; Spain, 1970; Jordan, 1984. *Recreations:* theatre, cinema, football.

LAIDLAW, Sir Christophor (Charles Fraser), Kt 1982; Chairman: BP Oil, 1977–81; BP Oil International, 1981; *b* 9 Aug. 1922; *m* 1952, Nina Mary Prichard; one *s* three *d*. *Educ:* Rugby Sch.; St John's Coll., Cambridge (MA; Hon. Fellow, 1996). Served War of 1939–45: Europe and Far East, Major on Gen. Staff; Intelligence Corps, 1941–46. Joined British Petroleum, 1948: BP Rep. in Hamburg, 1959–61; Gen. Manager, Marketing Dept, 1963–67; Dir, BP Trading, 1967; Dir (Ops), 1971–72; a Man. Dir, 1972–81, and Dep. Chm., BP, 1980–81; Dir, Soc. Française BP, 1964–85; President, BP: Belgium, 1967–71; Italiana, 1972–73; Deutsche BP, 1972–83; Chm., Boving & Co. Ltd, 1984–86. Chm., ICL plc, 1981–84; Pres., ICL France, 1983; Chm., Bridon, 1985–90. Director: Commercial Union Assurance, 1978–83; Barclays Bank International, 1980–87; Barclays Bank plc, 1981–88; Barclays Merchant Bank Ltd, 1984–86; Equity Capital for Industry Ltd, 1983–86; Amerada Hess Corp., 1983–94; Amerada Hess Ltd, 1986–99; Dalgety, 1984–92; Redland, 1984–92; TWIL Ltd, 1985–89; Mercedes-Benz (UK) Ltd, 1986–93; Daimler-Benz (UK) Ltd, 1994–99; Daimler-Chrysler (UK) Hldgs Ltd, 1999–2001. Pres., German Chamber of Industry and Commerce, 1983–86; Vice Pres., British–German Assoc., 1996–; Mem., Internat. Council, 1980–, Chm. UK Adv. Bd, 1984–91, Dir, 1987–94, INSEAD. Trustee, Internat. Spinal Res. Trust, 1991–. FRSA 1996. Master, Tallow Chandlers' Co., 1988–89. *Address:* 49 Chelsea Square, SW3 6LH. *Clubs:* Buck's, Garrick.

See also W. S. H. Laidlaw.

LAIDLAW, (Henry) Renton; golf correspondent, Evening Standard, 1973–98; *b* 6 July 1939; *s* of late Henry Renton Laidlaw and of Margaret McBeath Laidlaw (*née* Raiker). *Educ:* James Gillespie's Boys' School, Edinburgh; Daniel Stewart's College, Edinburgh. Golf corresp., Edinburgh Evening News, 1957–67; news presenter and reporter, Grampian Television, Aberdeen, 1968–69; BBC news presenter, Edinburgh, 1970–72; BBC Radio golf reporter, 1976–90; presenter: BBC Radio Sport on 2, 1986, 1987; ITV Eurosport, 1988; golf presenter: BSB, 1989–91; Golf Channel, US, 1995–; Chief Commentator, PGA European Tour Prodns, 1988–. *Publications:* Play Golf (with Peter Alliss), 1977; Jacklin—the first 40 years, 1984; (ed) Johnnie Walker Ryder Cup '85, 1985; Play Better Golf, 1986; (ed) Johnnie Walker Ryder Cup '87, 1987; Ten Years—the history of the European Open, 1988; Golf Heroes, 1989; (ed) Johnnie Walker Ryder Cup '89, 1989; (with Bernard Gallacher) Captain at Kiawah, 1991; Wentworth: a host of happy memories, 1993; (ed) The Royal and Ancient Golfer's Handbook, annually, 1998–; (ed) The Golfers' Guide to Scotland, 2000–. *Recreations:* theatre, golf. *Address:* c/o Mrs Kay Clarkson, Flat 4, 82 Lupus Street, SW1V 3EL. *T:* and *Fax:* (020) 7932 0996. *Clubs:* Caledonian; Royal & Ancient (St Andrews); Sunningdale Golf, Wentworth, Royal Burgess Golf, Ballybunion Golf.

LAIDLAW, William Samuel Hugh, (Sam); Chief Executive, Enterprise Oil plc, since 2001; *b* 3 Jan. 1956; *s* of Sir Christophor Charles Fraser Laidlaw, *qv*; *m* 1989, Deborah Margaret Morris-Adams; three *s* one *d*. *Educ:* Eton College; Gonville and Caius College, Cambridge (MA); MBA. Admitted Solicitor, 1980; Insead, Fontainbleau, 1981. Soc. Françaises Petroles BP, 1980; Amerada Hess: Manager, corporate planning, NY, 1981–83; Vice-Pres., London, 1983–85, Sen. Vice-Pres., 1986–90, Man. Dir, 1986–95, London; Exec. Vice-Pres., NY, 1990–95; Pres. and CEO, NY, 1995–2001; Chm., London, 1995–2001. Director: Premier Oil, 1995–; Yes Television plc. Mem., Govt Energy Adv. Panel, 1994–98. Chm., Petroleum Sci. and Tech. Inst., 1993–94; NEL, 1993–95. Pres., UKOOA, 1991. FInstPet (Vice-Pres., 1994–95). *Address:* (office) Grand Buildings, Trafalgar Square, WC2N 5EJ. *Club:* Royal Thames Yacht.

LAIGHT, Barry Pemberton, OBE 1970; Eur Ing; FREng, FIMechE, FRAeS; Consultant to: Design Council, since 1983; VAWT Ltd, since 1983; RES Ltd, since 1983; Production Engineering Research Association, since 1986; Department of Trade and Industry, 1988–90; *s* of Donald Norman Laight and Nora (*née* Pemberton); *m* 1951, Ruth Murton; one *s* one *d*. *Educ:* Johnston Sch., Durham; Birmingham Central Tech. Coll.; Merchant Venturers' Tech. Coll., Bristol; Bristol Univ. (MSc). FREng (FEng 1981). SBAC Scholar, apprentice, Bristol Aeroplane Co., 1937; Chief Designer, 1952, Technical Dir, 1960, Blackburn & General Aircraft (develt of Beverley and design of Buccaneer, 1953, for RN service, 1960); Chief Engineer Kingston, 1963, Dir for Military Projects, 1968, Hawker Siddeley Aviation (Harrier develt to RAF service; introd. Hawk Trainer); Exec. Dir Engineering, Short Brothers, 1977–82 (develt SD360 and Blowpipe); Sec., RAeS, 1983–85. Mem. Council, RAeS, 1955–90 (Pres., 1974–75; British Silver Medal in Aeronautics, 1963); Chairman: Educn Cttee, SBAC, 1962–67; Tech. Board, SBAC, 1967–82; Member: Aircraft Res. Assoc. Board, 1972–77 (Chm., Tech. Cttee); ARC, 1973–76; Air Educn and Recreational Organisation Council, 1969–72; CBI: Mem., Res. and Tech. Cttee; Educn Cttee; Chm., Transport Technology Panel, SRC, 1969–73; Hon. Treasurer, Internat. Council of Aero. Scis, 1978–84; AGARD Nat. Delegate, 1968–73; Sec., Bristol Gliding Club, 1949–52; Mem., Mensa, 1945. AFAIAA; FInstD. *Publications:* papers in RAeS jls. *Recreations:* reading on any subject, house and car maintenance, music. *Address:* 5 Littlemead, Esher, Surrey KT10 9PE. *T:* (01372) 463216.

LAINÉ, Christopher Norman; Chairman, Allied Textile Companies plc, 1999–2001 (Director, 1998–2001); Partner, Coopers & Lybrand, 1971–98; President, Institute of Chartered Accountants in England and Wales, 1997–98; *b* 12 Oct. 1936; *s* of James Norman Balliol Lainé and Sybil Mary Lainé (*née* Fuge); *m* 1967, Sally Outhwaite; one *s* one *d*. *Educ:* King's Sch., Canterbury (Scholar); Trinity Coll., Oxford (Exhibnr; MA). FCA. Nat. Service, RA, 1955–57; commnd 1956. Cooper Brothers & Co., later Coopers & Lybrand: joined 1960; Partner i/c S Coast, 1971–90; Sen. Partner, S Coast, 1990–98. Pres., Southern Soc. of Chartered Accountants, 1986–87; Institute of Chartered Accountants in England and Wales: Mem. Council, 1990–2000; Chm., 1999–2000; Chm., Dist Socs Cttee, 1991–95; Exec., 1993–; Vice-Pres., 1995–96; Dep. Pres., 1996–97. Gov., Canford Sch., 1990–. *Recreations:* cricket, golf, classical music, painting. *Address:* Woodlands Cottage, Lower Common Road, West Wellow, Romsey, Hants SO51 6BT. *T:* (01794) 322247. *Clubs:* Hampshire CC; Stoneham Golf; Hampshire Hogs Cricket, Forty.

LAINE, Dame Clementine Dinah, (Dame Cleo), DBE 1997 (OBE 1979); vocalist, actress; *b* 28 Oct. 1927; British; *m* 1st, 1947, George Langridge (marr. diss. 1957); one *s*; 2nd, 1958, John Philip William Dankworth, *qv*; one *s* one *d*. Joined Dankworth Orchestra, 1953; with John Dankworth estabd Performing Arts Centre, Wavendon Stables, 1969. Melody Maker and New Musical Express Top Girl Singer Award, 1956; Moscow Arts Theatre Award for acting role in Flesh to a Tiger, 1958; Top place in Internat. Critics Poll by Amer. Jazz magazine, Downbeat, 1965. Lead, in Seven Deadly Sins, Edinburgh Festival and Sadler's Wells, 1961; acting roles in Edin. Fest., 1966, 1967, Cindy-Ella, Garrick, 1968; film, Last of the Blonde Bombshells, 2000. Many appearances with symphony orchestras performing Façade (Walton), Pierrot Lunaire and other compositions; played Julie in Show Boat, Adelphi, 1971; title role in Colette, Comedy, 1980; Hedda Gabler; Valmouth; A Time to Laugh; The Women of Troy; The Mystery of Edwin Drood, 1986; Into the Woods (US nat. tour), 1989; Noyes Fludde (Proms), 1990. Frequent TV appearances. Woman of the Year, 9th annual Golden Feather Awards, 1973; Edison Award, 1974; Variety Club of GB Show Business Personality Award (with John Dankworth), 1977; TV Times Viewers Award for Most Exciting Female Singer on TV, 1978; Grammy Award for Best Female Jazz Vocalist, 1985; Theatre World Award, 1986; NARM Presidential Lifetime Achievement Award, 1990; British Jazz Awards Vocalist of the Year, 1990; Distinguished Artists Award, Internat. Soc. for the Performing Arts, 1999; Gold Discs: Feel the Warm; I'm a Song; Live at Melbourne; Platinum Discs: Best Friends; Sometimes When We Touch. Hon. MA Open, 1975; Hon. DMus: Berklee Sch. of Music, 1982; York, 1993. *Publications:* Cleo (autobiog.), 1994; You Can Sing If You Want To, 1997. *Recreation:* painting. *Fax:* (01908) 584414.

LAING, family name of **Baron Laing of Dunphail**.

LAING OF DUNPHAIL, Baron *cr* 1991 (Life Peer), of Dunphail in the District of Moray; **Hector Laing,** Kt 1978; Life President, United Biscuits (Holdings) plc, 1990 (Director, 1953; Managing Director, 1964; Chairman, 1972–90); *b* 12 May 1923; *s* of Hector Laing and Margaret Norris Grant; *m* 1950, Marian Clare, *d* of Maj.-Gen. Sir John Laurie, 6th Bt, CBE, DSO; three *s*. *Educ:* Loretto Sch., Musselburgh, Scotland; Jesus Coll., Cambridge (Hon. Fellow, 1988). Served War, Scots Guards, 1942–47 (American Bronze Star, despatches, 1944); final rank, Captain. McVitie & Price: Dir, 1947; Chm., 1963. Mem. Bd, Royal Insurance Co., 1970–78; Director: Allied-Lyons, 1979–82; Exxon Corp. (USA), 1984–94. A Dir, Bank of England, 1973–91. Chairman: Food and Drink Industries Council, 1977–79; Scottish Business in the Community, 1982–91; Business in the Community, 1987–91; Dir, Grocery Manufrs of America, 1984–90; President: Eur. Catering Assoc., 1990–93; Inst. of Business Ethics, 1991–94. Treas., Cons. Party, 1988–93. Chm. Trustees, Lambeth Fund, 1983–97; Trustee: The Duke of Edinburgh's Commonwealth Study Conf., 1986–93; Royal Botanic Gardens Kew Foundn, 1990–94. Mem., St George's Council, Windsor, 1989–93 and 1995–; Gov., Wycombe Abbey Sch., 1981–94. FRSE 1989. DUniv Stirling, 1985; Hon. DLitt Heriot-Watt, 1986. Businessman of the Year Award, 1979; National Free Enterprise Award, 1980. *Recreations:* gardening, walking. *Address:* High Meadows, Windsor Road, Gerrards Cross, Bucks SL9 8ST. *T:* (01753) 882437. *Club:* White's.

LAING, Alastair David, FSA; Adviser on Pictures and Sculpture, National Trust, since 1986; *b* 5 Aug. 1944; *s* of Malcolm Strickland Laing and Margaret Clare Laing (*née* Briscoe); *m* 1979, Hana Novotná; one *s*. *Educ:* Chafyn Grove Sch.; Bradfield Coll.; Corpus Christi Coll., Oxford (BA Hons 1966; Dip. Hist. Art 1967); Courtauld Inst. of Art, Univ. of London. FCO, 1967–68; translator, 1969–76; Night Operator, Internat. Telephone Exchange, 1973–76; Researcher, Heim Gall., 1976–83; Researcher and Jt Curator, François Boucher exhibn, NY, Detroit and Paris, 1983–85; Area Editor, Macmillan Dictionary of Art, 1985–86. Chevalier, l'Ordre des Arts et des Lettres (France), 1988. *Publications:* (with Anthony Blunt) Baroque & Rococo, 1978; Lighting, 1982; exhibn catalogues incl. François Boucher, 1986, and In Trust for the Nation, 1995; articles in Country Life, Apollo, Burlington Mag., Umění, etc. *Recreation:* church- and tomb-crawling. *Address:* 24 Aberdeen Road, N5 2UH. *Club:* Travellers.

LAING, Alastair Stuart, CBE 1980; MVO 1959; *b* 17 June 1920; *s* of Captain Arthur Henry Laing and Clare May Laing (*née* Ashworth); *m* 1946 Audrey Stella Hobbs, MCSP, *d* of Dr Frederick Hobbs and Gladys Marion Hobbs (*née* George); one *s* decd. *Educ:* Sedbergh School. Served Indian Army, 10th Gurkha Rifles, 1940–46, Captain; seconded to Civil Administration, Bengal, 1944–46. Commonwealth War Graves Commission, 1947–83 (Dep. Dir Gen., 1975–83). Chm., Vale of Aylesbury Hunt, 1981–87. *Publications:* various articles. *Recreations:* gardening, foxhunting, racing, history. *Address:* Wagtails, Lower Wood End, Marlow, Bucks SL7 2HN. *T:* (01628) 484481.

LAING, Dr Douglas Rees; consultant on agricultural and environmental issues in the American tropics, since 1995; Director General, CAB International, 1993–94; *b* 31 Aug. 1936; *s* of Douglas Harvey Laing and Jessie Hilda Laing; *m* 1st, 1966, Rosemary Isabel Whiting; one *s* one *d*; 2nd, 1992, Olga Lucia Villa. *Educ:* Univ. of Queensland (BAgrSc Hons); Iowa State Univ. (PhD 1966). Fulbright Scholar, 1962. Lectr, then Sen. Lectr, Dept of Agronomy, Univ. of Sydney, 1966–73; International Center for Tropical Agriculture, Colombia: Physiologist, 1974–79; Dir, Crop Research, 1979–84; Dep. Dir General, 1984–92. FAIAS 1993. *Publications:* Ornamental Gardening in the American Tropics, 2001; contrib. chaps in books; numerous pubns and workshop and conference contribs on crop physiology, and internat. agriculture. *Recreations:* natural history, scuba diving, reading. *Address:* Apartado Aereo 25470, Cali, Colombia; *e-mail:* drlaing99@hotmail.com.

LAING, Eleanor Fulton; MP (C) Epping Forest, since 1997; *b* 1 Feb. 1958; *d* of Matthew and Betty Pritchard; *m* 1983, Alan Laing; one *s*. *Educ:* St Columba's Sch., Kilmacolm; Edinburgh Univ. (Pres., Union, 1980–81; BA, LLB 1982). Solicitor, Edinburgh and London, 1983–89; Special Advr to Rt Hon. John MacGregor, MP, 1989–94. Contested (C) Paisley N, 1987. An Opposition Whip, 1999–2000; frontbench opposition spokesman on constitutional affairs, 2000–. *Recreations:* theatre, music, golf, Agatha Christie Society. *Address:* House of Commons, SW1A 0AA.

LAING, Gerald O.; *see* Ogilvie-Laing.

LAING, James Findlay; Under Secretary, Scottish Office Environment Department (formerly Scottish Development Department), 1988–93; *b* 7 Nov. 1933; *s* of Alexander Findlay Laing and Jessie Ross; *m* 1969, Christine Joy Canaway; one *s*. *Educ:* Nairn Academy; Edinburgh Univ. MA (Hons History). Nat. Service, Seaforth Highlanders, 1955–57. Asst Principal and Principal, Scottish Office, 1957–68; Principal, HM Treasury, 1968–71; Asst Sec., Scottish Office, 1972–79; Under Sec., Scottish Econ. Planning Dept, later Industry Dept for Scotland, 1979–88. *Recreations:* squash, chess. *Address:* 6 Barnton Park Place, Edinburgh EH4 6ET. *T:* (0131) 336 5951. *Club:* Edinburgh Sports.

LAING, Jennifer Charlina Ellsworth; Chairman and Chief Executive Officer, North American Operations, Saatchi & Saatchi, 1997–2000; *b* 1947; *d* of late James Ellsworth Laing, FRCS, and of Mary McKane (*née* Taylor); *m* John Henderson (marr. diss.). Joined Garland-Compton, 1969; Dir, Saatchi & Saatchi Garland-Compton, 1977; Dep. Chm., 1983, Jt Chm., 1987, Saatchi & Saatchi Advertising UK; Chm. and CEO, Aspect Hill Holiday (later Laing Henry Ltd), 1988, which merged with Saatchi & Saatchi Advertising UK, 1995; Chm., Saatchi & Saatchi Advertising UK, 1995–96. Mem. Exec. Bd, Saatchi & Saatchi Worldwide, 1996–2000. Former non-executive Director: Remploy; Great Ormond Street Hosp. for Children NHS Trust.

LAING, Prof. John Archibald, PhD; Professor Emeritus, University of London, since 1984 (Courtauld Professor of Animal Husbandry and Hygiene, at Royal Veterinary College, University of London, 1959–84); *b* 27 April 1919; *s* of late John and Alexandra Laing; *m* 1946, June Margaret Lindsay Smith, *d* of Hugh Lindsay Smith, Downham Market; one *s* two *d*. *Educ:* Johnston Sch., Durham; Royal (Dick) School of Veterinary Studies, Edinburgh University (BSc); Christ's Coll., Cambridge. (PhD). CBiol, FIBiol. Aleen Cust Scholar, Royal Coll. of Veterinary Surgeons. Research Officer, 1943–46, Asst Veterinary Investigation Officer, 1946–49, Ministry of Agriculture; Univ. of Bristol, 1949–59 (Reader in Veterinary Science, 1957–59). Anglo-Danish Churchill Fellowship, Univ. of Copenhagen, 1954; Visiting Professor, Univs of: Munich, 1967; Mexico, 1967; Queensland, 1970 (and John Thompson Memorial Lectr); Ankara, 1977; Assiut, 1980; Consultant to FAO, UN, 1955–57; Representative of FAO in Dominican Republic, 1957–58; Consultant to UNESCO in Central America, 1963–65; Mem., British Agricultural Mission to Peru, 1970. Member: EEC Veterinary Scientific Cttee, 1981–84; Dairy Product Quota Tribunal for England and Wales, 1984. Hon. Mem., Internat. Congress on Animal Reproduction, 1988 (Sec., 1961–80; Pres., 1980–84). Chm., Melrose Meml Trust, 1984–91; Member: Governing Body, Houghton Poultry Research Station, 1968–74; Council, Royal Veterinary Coll., 1975–84; Vice-Pres., University Fedn for Animal Welfare, 1977–84 (Treasurer, 1969–75; Chm., 1975–77). Pres., World Assoc. for Transport Animal Welfare Studies, 1996–98. Hon. Fellow Veterinary Acad., Madrid. Editor, British Veterinary Journal, 1960–84. *Publications:* Fertility and Infertility in the Domestic Animals, 1955, 4th edn 1988; papers on animal breeding and husbandry in various scientific journals. *Address:* Ayot St Lawrence, Herts AL6 9BW. *T:* (01438) 820413. *Club:* Athenæum.

LAING, Sir (John) Martin (Kirby), Kt 1997; CBE 1991; DL; Chairman, John Laing, since 1985; *b* 18 Jan. 1942; *s* of Sir (William) Kirby Laing, *qv*; *m* 1965, Stephanie Stearn Worsdell; one *s* one *d*. *Educ:* St Lawrence College, Ramsgate; Emmanuel College, Cambridge (MA). FRICS. Joined Laing Group 1966; Dir, John Laing, 1980. Chairman: BOTB, 1995–99; Construction Industry Employers Council, 1995–2000; Vice-Chm., British Trade Internat., 1999; Member: Major Contractors Gp, 1985 (Chm., 1991–92); CBI Council, 1986–; CBI Overseas Cttee, 1983–96 (Chm., 1989–96); CBI Task Force on Business and Urban Regeneration, 1987–88; Cttee for Middle East Trade, 1982–86; SE Asia Trade Adv. Group, 1985–89; UK Adv. Cttee, British American Chamber of Commerce, 1985–; Council, World Economic Forum, 1986–; NEDO Construction Industry Sector Gp, 1988–93; Business in the Community, 1986– (Mem. Bd, 1995–2000); World Business Council for Sustainable Develt, 1991–; UK–Japan 2000 Gp, 1988–; British Council, 1997–; Council, BESO, 1999–; Chm., British Urban Develt, 1988–90; Dep. Chm., Building Experience Trust, 1992–95. Chm., Americas Advrs, Trade Partners UK, 2000–. Mem. Council, London First, 1992–. Member: Home Office Parole Review Cttee, 1987–88; Archbishop's Council, Church Urban Fund, 1987–94; Trilateral Commn, 1993–99. Pres., Construction Confedn, 1997–2000. Dir, City of London Sinfonia, 1988–95. Dir, Herts Groundwork Trust, 1986–91; Trustee: Nat. Energy Foundn, 1988–99; WWF Internat., 1991–97; Marine Stewardship Council, 1998–; Trustee Emeritus, WWF (UK), 1998– (Trustee, 1988–97; Chm., 1990–97). Crown Mem., Court of Univ. of London, 1987–95; Member: Council, United World Coll. of the Atlantic, 1996–; Board of Governors, Papplewick School, Ascot, 1983–93; Governor: St Lawrence Coll., Ramsgate, 1988–95; NIESR, 1999–. Trustee, RICS Foundn, 2001–. Master, Paviors' Co., 1995–96. CIMgt (CBIM 1985); CIEx 1987; FCIM 1987; FRSA 1988; FICE 1993; FIHT 1995; FCIOB 1995. DL Hertford, 1987. Hon. DSc City, 1996; Hon. DEng UWE, 1997. *Recreations:* gardening, music, travel. *Address:* John Laing plc, Page Street, NW7 2ER.

LAING, Sir (John) Maurice, Kt 1965; Director, 1939–88, and Life President, since 1988, John Laing plc (formerly John Laing & Son Ltd) (Deputy Chairman, 1966–76, Chairman, 1976–82); *b* 1 Feb. 1918; *s* of Sir John Laing, CBE, and late Beatrice Harland; *m* 1940, Hilda Violet Richards; one *s*. *Educ:* St Lawrence Coll., Ramsgate. RAF, 1941–45. Dir, Bank of England, 1963–80. Member: UK Trade Missions to Middle East, 1953, and to Egypt, Sudan and Ethiopia, 1955; Economic Planning Bd, 1961; Export Guarantees Adv. Council, 1959–63; Min. of Transport Cttee of Inquiry into Major Ports of Gt Brit. (Rochdale Cttee), 1961–62; NEDC, 1962–66. First Pres., CBI, 1965–66; President: British Employers Confederation, 1964–65; Export Group for the Constructional Industries, 1976–80; Fedn of Civil Engrg Contractors, 1977–80. Visiting Fellow, Nuffield Coll., 1965–70; Governor: Administrative Staff Coll., 1966–72; Nat. Inst. of Economic and Social Research, 1964–82. Pres., London Bible Coll., 1993–99. Admiral, Royal Ocean Racing Club, 1976–82; Rear-Cdre, Royal Yacht Squadron, 1982–86 (Trustee, 1996–); Pres., Royal Yachting Assoc., 1983–87. Hon. FCGI 1978; Hon. FCIOB 1981. Hon. LLD Strathclyde, 1967; Hon. DSc Exeter, 1996. Winner, Aims of Industry Free Enterprise Award, 1979. Has keen interest in Church activities at home and abroad. *Recreations:* sailing, swimming. *Address:* John Laing plc, Page Street, NW7 2ER. *Clubs:* Royal Ocean Racing; Royal Yacht Squadron.

See also Sir W. K. Laing.

LAING, (John) Stuart; HM Diplomatic Service; High Commissioner to Brunei, 1998–2002; Ambassador to Oman, from April 2002; *b* 22 July 1948; *s* of late Dr Denys Laing and Dr Judy Laing (*née* Dods); *m* 1972, Sibella Dorman, *d* of Sir Maurice Dorman, GCMG, GCVO; one *s* two *d*. *Educ:* Rugby Sch.; Corpus Christi Coll., Cambridge. Joined HM Diplomatic Service, 1970; FCO, 1970–71; MECAS, Lebanon, 1971–72; 2nd Sec., Jedda, 1973–75; First Secretary: UK Perm. Rep. to EC, 1975–78; FCO, 1978–83; Cairo, 1983–87; FCO, 1987–89; Counsellor, Prague, 1989–92; Dep. Hd of Mission and HM Consul-Gen., British Embassy, Riyadh, 1992–95; Hd, Know How Fund for Central Europe, FCO, later DFID, 1995–98. *Recreations:* music, hill-walking, desert travel. *Address:* c/o Foreign and Commonwealth Office, King Charles Street, SW1A 2AH.

LAING, Sir Kirby; *see* Laing, Sir W. K.

LAING, Sir Martin; *see* Laing, Sir J. M. K.

LAING, Sir Maurice; *see* Laing, Sir J. M.

LAING, Peter Anthony Neville Pennethorne; Founding Director, ActionAid Spain, since 1982; *b* 12 March 1922; *s* of late Lt-Col Neville Ogilvie Laing, DSO, 4th QO Hussars, and Zara Marcella (*née* Pennethorne), Fleet, Hants; *m* 1958, Penelope Lucinda, *d* of Sir William Pennington-Ramsden, 7th Bt; two *d*. *Educ:* Eton; Paris Univ. Served War: volunteer, French Army, 1939–40, Free French Forces, 1942–44; Grenadier Guards, 1944–46. Attaché, British Embassy, Madrid, 1946; internat. marketing consultant in Western Europe, USA, Caribbean and Latin America; UN, 1975–: Dir of ITC proj. for UNDP in the Congo; Dir, Help the Aged internat. charity, 1976–82. Advr, European Affairs, Internat. Centre of Social Gerontology, 1982–87. Creator, Mediterranean Retirement Inc. (wardened housing villages for ageing Europeans of ind. means), 1985–. *Recreations:* people, foreign travel, riding any horse, fine arts. *Address:* Turweston Manor, near Brackley, Northants NN13 5JX. *T:* (01280) 703498, 700049. *Club:* Turf.

LAING, Sophie Henrietta T.; *see* Turner Laing.

LAING, Stuart; *see* Laing, J. S.

LAING, (William James) Scott; special assignments for United Nations and other international agencies, 1977–98; *b* 14 April 1914; *er s* of late William Irvine Laing and Jessie C. M. Laing (*née* Scott); *m* 1952, Isabelle Mary Durrant-Fox (*d* 1990); one *s*. *Educ:* George Watson's Coll.; Edinburgh Univ. Appointed to Dept of Overseas Trade, 1937; Asst to Commercial Counsellor, British Embassy, Buenos Aires, 1938; Second Sec. (Commercial), Buenos Aires, 1944; First Sec. (Commercial), Helsinki, 1947; Consul, New York, 1950; Consul-Gen. (Commercial), New York, 1954; Counsellor (Commercial), Brussels and Luxembourg, 1955; Consultant to UN Secretariat, Financial Policies and Institutions Section, 1958, African Training Programme, 1960; Editor, UN Jl, 1964; Chief, Publications Sales Section, UN Secretariat, 1969–76; consultant to motor industry pubns, EIU, 1977–92. *Publications:* The US Market for Motor Vehicle Parts and Accessories, 1977; Concentration and Diversification of the Self-Propelled Heavy Machinery Industries in USA, 1979; (jtly) Financial Assessment of the US Automotive Industry, 1982; (jtly) Foreign Outsourcing by US Auto Manufacturers, 1983. *Address:* 1016 Chantilly Road, Bel-Air, CA 90077, USA. *Club:* Caledonian.

LAING, Sir (William) Kirby, Kt 1968; JP; DL; MA; FREng, FICE; Chairman, Laing Properties plc, 1978–87, President, 1987–90; *b* 21 July 1916; *s* of Sir John Laing, CBE, and Lady Laing (*née* Beatrice Harland); *m* 1st, 1939, Joan Dorothy Bratt (*d* 1981); three *s*; 2nd, 1986, Dr (Mary) Isobel Lewis, *yr d* of late Edward C. Wray. *Educ:* St Lawrence Coll., Ramsgate; Emmanuel Coll., Cambridge (Hon. Fellow, 1983). FREng (FEng 1977). Served with Royal Engineers, 1943–45. Dir, John Laing plc (formerly John Laing & Son Ltd), 1939–80 (Chm., 1957–76). President: London Master Builders Assoc., 1957; Reinforced Concrete Assoc., 1960; Nat. Fedn of Building Trades Employers (later Building Employers' Confedn) 1965, 1967 (Hon. Mem., 1975); ICE, 1973–74 (a Vice-Pres., 1970–73); Construction Industry Res. and Inf. Assoc., 1984–87 (Chm., 1978–81); Chm., Nat. Jt Council for Building Industry, 1968–74. Member, Board of Governors: St Lawrence Coll. (Chm., 1977–89, Pres., 1977–); Princess Helena Coll., 1984–87; Member: Court of Governors, The Polytechnic of Central London, 1963–82; Council, Royal Albert Hall, 1970–92 (Pres., 1979–92). Hon. Mem., Amer. Assoc. of Civil Engineers. Master, Paviors' Co., 1987–88. DL Greater London, 1978–91. Hon. Fellow, UCNW, 1988. Hon. DTech, Poly. of Central London, 1990; Dr *hc* Edinburgh, 1991. *Publications:* papers in Proc. ICE and other jls concerned with construction. *Recreations:* flyfishing, travelling, listening to music. *Address:* 133 Page Street, NW7 2ER. *Clubs:* Naval and Military; Royal Fowey Yacht.

See also Sir J. M. K. Laing.

LAINSON, Prof. Ralph, OBE 1996; FRS 1982; Director, Wellcome Parasitology Unit, Instituto Evandro Chagas, Belém, Pará, Brazil, 1965–92; *b* 21 Feb. 1927; *s* of Charles Harry Lainson and Anne (*née* Denyer); *m* 1st, 1957, Anne Patricia Russell; one *s* two *d*; 2nd, 1974, Zeá Constante Lins. *Educ:* Steyning Grammar Sch., Sussex; London Univ. (BSc, PhD, DSc). Lecturer in Medical Protozoology, London Sch. of Hygiene and Tropical Medicine, London Univ., 1955–59; Officer-in-Charge, Dermal Leishmaniasis Unit, Baking-Pot, Cayo Dist, Belize, 1959–62; Attached Investigator, Dept of Medical Protozoology, London Sch. of Hygiene and Tropical Medicine, 1962–65. Career devoted to research in Medical Protozoology in the Tropics. Hon. Fellow, LSHTM, 1982; Hon. Professor, Federal Univ. of Pará, Brazil, 1982; Associate Fellow, Third World Acad. of Scis, 1989; Hon. FRSTM&H 1997; Hon. Member: British Soc. of Parasitology, 1984; Soc. of Protozoologists, 1997. Chalmer's Medal, Royal Soc. of Tropical Medicine and Hygiene, 1971; Oswaldo Cruz Medal, Conselho Estadual de Cultura do Pará, 1973; Manson Medal, Royal Soc. of Tropical Medicine and Hygiene, 1983; Commemorative medals: 10th anniv., Health Council for State of Pará, Brazil, 1983; 30th anniv., Fed. Univ. of Pará, Brazil, 1988. *Publications:* author, or co-author, of approximately 300 pubns in current scientific jls and text-books, on protozoal parasites of man and animals. *Recreations:* fishing, swimming, collecting South American Lepidoptera, music, philately. *Address:* Avenida Visconde de Souza Franco, 1237 (Edificio 'Visconti'), Apartamento 902, 66053–000 Belém, Pará, Brazil. *T:* (91) 2232382.

LAIRD, family name of **Baron Laird**.

LAIRD, Baron *cr* 1999 (Life Peer), of Artigarvan in the county of Tyrone; **John Dunn Laird;** Chairman, John Laird Public Relations Ltd, since 1976; *b* Belfast, 23 April 1944; *s* of late Dr Norman Davidson Laird, OBE, sometime NI MP, and Margaret Laird; *m* 1971, Caroline Ethel Ferguson; one *s* one *d*. *Educ:* Royal Belfast Academical Institution. Bank Official, 1963–67; Bank Inspector, 1967–68; Computer Programmer, 1968–73. MP (UU) St Anne's, Belfast, NI Parlt, 1970–73; Member (UU) West Belfast: NI Assembly, 1973–75; NI Constitutional Convention, 1975–76. Vis. Prof. of Public Relns, Univ. of Ulster, 1993–. FIPR 1991. *Recreations:* history, railways, travel. *Address:* (office) 104 Holywood Road, Belfast BT4 1NU. *T:* (028) 9047 1282.

LAIRD, David Logan, OBE 2000; JP, DL; WS; FRICS; solicitor; Partner, Thorntons WS, since 1985; chartered surveyor; *b* 13 April 1937; *s* of William Twaddle Laird and Janet Nicolson (*née* MacDonald); *m*; two *s* one *d*. *Educ:* Bell Baxter Sch., Cupar. Chartered surveyor and land agent, 1963; Partner, Clark Oliver Dewar & Webster, SSC, 1971–85. Mem., and Chm. NE Region, NCC Scotland, now Scottish Natural Heritage, 1990– (Chm., E Area Bd, 1997–2000); Chm. Bd, Cairngorms Partnership, 1994–97. JP 1968, DL 1989, Angus. *Recreations:* stalking, gardening, shooting, fishing. *Address:* West Memus, Forfar, Angus DD8 3TY. *T:* (01307) 860251. *Club:* New (Edinburgh).

LAIRD, Endell Johnston; Director and Editor in Chief, Scottish Daily Record and Sunday Mail, 1988–94; Editor in Chief, The Glaswegian, 1988–94; *m* 1958, June Keenan; one *s* two *d*. *Educ:* Forfar Academy. Served RAF, 1952–54. Journalist: Dundee Courier, 1954–56; Scottish Daily Express, 1956–58; Evening Times, 1958–60; Sunday Mail, 1960–71; Daily Record, 1971–81; Editor, Sunday Mail, 1981–88. Edtl Dir (SDR), Mirror Gp Newspapers, 1991–94. Chm., Scottish Editors Cttee, 1986–88; Mem., D-Notice Cttee, 1986–94. Mem. Bd, Children's Hospice Assoc. Scotland, 1994–. *Recreations:* walking, golf, bridge. *Clubs:* Bishopbriggs Golf; Bishopbriggs Bridge.

LAIRD, Sir Gavin (Harry), Kt 1995; CBE 1988; General Secretary, AEU Section, Amalgamated Engineering and Electrical Union, 1992–95; Chairman, Greater Manchester Buses North, 1994–97; *b* 14 March 1933; *s* of James and Frances Laird; *m* 1956, Catherine Gillies Campbell; one *d*. *Educ:* Clydebank High School. Full-time Trade Union Official, 1972–95; Mem. Exec. Council, 1975–95, Gen. Sec., 1982–94, AUEW, subseq. AEU, then AEEU. Mem., TUC Gen. Council, 1979–82; Mem. Exec., CSEU, 1975–95. Director: BNOC, 1976–86; Bank of England, 1986–94; non-exec. Director: Scottish Media Group plc (formerly Scottish TV), 1986–99; FS Assurance, then Britannia Life, 1988–99; GEC Scotland, 1991–99; Edinburgh Investment Trust, 1994–; Britannia, then Britannic, Investment Managers, 1996–; Chm., Murray VCT 4, 2000–; Mem. Adv. Cttee, Murray Johnstone Pvte Equity Partnerships 1 & 2, 1995–. Pt-time Mem., SDA, 1987–92. Member: Arts Council of GB, 1983–86; London Cttee, Scottish Council for Devel t and Industry, 1984–95; President's Cttee, Business in the Community, 1988–90; Forestry Commn, 1991–94; Envmtl Council, BNFL, 1993–96; Adv. Bd, Know How Fund, 1988–95; Armed Forces Pay Review Body, 1995–98; Employment Appeal Tribunal, 1996–. Chm., Trade Union Friends of Israel, 1980–. Dir, Westminster Foundn for Democracy, 1992–96. Mem. Governing Council, 1987–91, Gov., 1991–97, Atlantic Coll.; Trustee, Anglo-German Foundn, 1994–. Pres., Kent Active Retirement Assoc., 1996–. Fellow, Paisley Coll. of Technol., 1991. Hon. DLitt: Keele, 1994; Heriot-Watt, 1994. *Recreations:* hill walking, reading, music. *Address:* 9 Clevedon House, Holmbury Park, Bromley BR1 2WG. *T:* and *Fax:* (020) 8460 8998.

LAIRD, Margaret Heather, OBE 1999; Third Church Estates Commissioner, 1989–99; *b* 29 Jan. 1933; *d* of William Henry Polmear and Edith Polmear; *m* 1961, Rev. Canon John Charles Laird; two *s*. *Educ:* High Sch., Truro; Westfield College, London (BA Hons Mediaeval History, 1954); King's College London (Cert. in Religious Knowledge, 1955). Divinity Mistress: Grey Coat Hospital, SW1, 1955–59; Newquay Grammar Sch., 1959–60; St Albans High Sch., 1960–62; Head of Religious Studies, Dame Alice Harpur Sch., Bedford, 1969–89. Member: Gen. Synod of C of E, repr. Dio. St Albans, 1980–90 (ex officio, 1990–99); Panel of Assessors, Dio. St Albans, 1988–. Dep. Chm., English Clergy Assoc., 2001–. Vice-Pres., Soc. for Maintenance of the Faith, 1995–. Trustee: Lambeth Palace Library, 1993–99; Kentish's Educnl Foundn, 2001–; Cleaver Ordination Candidates Foundn, 2001–; Member: Allchurches Trust Ltd, 1994–; Exec., Open Churches Trust, 1995–. Mem., Royal Instn of Cornwall, 1997–. Governor, Pusey House, Oxford, 1993–. FRSA 1996. *Publication:* From Now to Eternity, 2001. *Recreations:* mediaeval art, architecture, pilgrims' routes. *Address:* The Chaplaincy, Fore Street Lodge, Hatfield Park, Hatfield, Herts AL9 5NQ. *Club:* Oxford and Cambridge.

LAIRD, Hon. Melvin R.; Consultant, Reader's Digest Association, since 1999 (Senior Counsellor for National and International Affairs, 1974–99); *b* 1 Sept. 1922; *s* of Melvin R. Laird and Helen Laird (*née* Connor); *m* 1945, Barbara Masters (*d* 1992); two *s* one *d*. *Educ:* Carleton Coll., Northfield, Minn (BA 1944). Enlisted, US Navy, 1942, commissioned, 1944; served in Third Fleet and Task Force 58 (Purple Heart and other decorations). Elected: to Wisconsin State Senate, 1946 (re-elected, 1948); to US Congress, Nov. 1952 (83rd through 90th; Chm., House Republican Conf., 89th and 90th); Sec. of Defense, 1969–73; Counsellor to President of the US, 1973–74. Chm., Communications Satellite Corp., 1992–96 (Dir, 1974–96); Director: Metropolitan Life Insurance Co., 1974–; Northwest Airlines, 1974–93; IDS Mutual Fund Gp Inc., 1974–97; Phillips Petroleum Co., 1976–98; Science Applications Internat. Corp., 1978–97; Martin Marietta Corp., 1981–95; Public Oversight Bd, 1984– (SEC Practice Sect., AICPA); DeWitt Wallace, and Lila Wallace, Reader's Digest Funds (for the promotion of the arts and humanities), 1990–98; Reader's Digest Assoc. Inc., 1990–98. Member Board of Trustees: George Washington Univ.; Kennedy Center. Various awards from Assocs, etc (for med. research, polit. science, public health, nat. educn); many hon. memberships and hon. degrees. *Publications:* A House Divided: America's Strategy Gap, 1962; Editor: The Conservative Papers, 1964; Republican Papers, 1968. *Recreations:* golf, fishing. *Address:* Suite 212, 1730 Rhode Island Avenue NW, Washington, DC 20036, USA. *Clubs:* Burning Tree (Washington, DC); Augusta National Golf.

LAIT, Jacqui; MP (C) Beckenham, since Nov. 1997; *b* 16 Dec. 1947; *d* of Graham Harkness Lait and Margaret Stewart (*née* Knight); *m* 1974, Peter Jones. *Educ:* Paisley Grammar Sch.; Univ. of Strathclyde. Public relations posts: jute trade, Dundee; Visnews, internat. TV news agency; with Govt Inf. Service, in Scottish Office, Privy Council Office and Dept of Employment, 1974–80; Parly Advr, Chemical Inds Assoc., 1980–84; Parly Consultancy, 1984–92. Contested (C): Strathclyde W, Euro-election, 1984; Tyne Bridge, Dec. 1985. MP (C) Hastings and Rye, 1992–97; contested (C) same seat, 1997. An Asst Govt Whip, 1996–97; Opposition Whip, 1999–2000; Opposition spokesman on pensions, 2000–01; Shadow Scottish Sec., 2001–. Chm., City and E London FHSA, 1988–91. Chm., British Section, European Union of Women, 1990–92; Vice-Chm., Cons. Women's Nat. Cttee, 1990–92. *Recreations:* walking, theatre, food and wine. *Address:* House of Commons, SW1A 0AA.

LAIT, Leonard Hugh Cecil, (Josh); His Honour Judge Lait; a Circuit Judge, since 1987; *b* 15 Nov. 1930; *m* 1967, Cheah Phaik Teen; one *d*. *Educ:* John Lyon School, Harrow; Trinity Hall, Cambridge (BA). Called to the Bar, Inner Temple, 1959; Mem., SE circuit; a Recorder, 1985–87. *Recreations:* music, gardening.

LAITHWAITE, John, FIMechE, FInstPet; engineering consultant; Director, Capper Neill Ltd, 1965–83 (Vice-Chairman, 1972–82); *b* 29 Nov. 1920; *s* of Tom Prescott Laithwaite and Mary Anne Laithwaite; *m* 1943, Jean Chateris; one *s* two *d*. *Educ:* Manchester Univ. (BSc Hons Mech. Eng). FIMechE 1974; FInstPet 1960; MInstW 1950. Wm Neill & Son (St Helens) Ltd, 1942–43; Dartford Shipbuilding & Engineering Co., 1943–44; Dir, Wm Neill & Son (St Helens) Ltd, 1955–58, Man. Dir, 1958–64; Man. Dir, Capper Neill Ltd, 1968–72. Mem. Council, NW Regional Management Centre. Chm., Process Plant Assoc., 1975–77, Hon. Vice-Pres., 1980–. *Publications:* articles on process plant industry and pressure vessel standardisation. *Recreations:* shooting, golf. *Address:* Gwydd Gwyllt, Malltraeth, Anglesey LL62 5AW. *T:* (01407) 840586. *Clubs:* Royal Automobile; Anglesey Golf.

LAITTAN, James S.; *see* Smith-Laittan.

LAITY, Mark Franklin; Deputy Spokesman and Personal Adviser to Secretary General, NATO, since 2000; *b* 18 Dec. 1955; *s* of Frank and Pamela Laity; *m* 1990, Lisa Parker-Gomm. *Educ:* Redruth Co. Grammar Sch.; Univ. of York (BA Hons Hist./Politics; MA Southern African Studies). Reporter, Western Mail, 1978–81; BBC Radio: Producer, Radio Wales and Today prog., 1981–86; Sen. Producer, Analysis prog., 1986–88; Dep. Ed., The World This Weekend, 1988–89; Defence Corresp., BBC TV, 1989–2000. Sen. Associate Res. Fellow, Centre for Defence Studies, KCL. *Recreations:* sailing, reading. *Address:* NG 144, NATO, 1110 Brussels, Belgium. *T:* (2) 7075035; (4) 75777739; 35 Cherry Orchard Road, Molesey, Surrey KT8 1QZ; *e-mail:* markflaity@hotmail.com. *Clubs:* Royal Air Force; Thames Sailing; Royal Cornwall Yacht (Falmouth).

LAKE, Sir (Atwell) Graham, 10th Bt *cr* 1711; Senior Technical Adviser, Ministry of Defence, retired 1983; *b* 6 Oct. 1923; *s* of Captain Sir Atwell Henry Lake, 9th Bt, CB, OBE, RN, and Kathleen Marion, *d* of late Alfred Morrison Turner; *S* father, 1972; *m* 1983, Mrs Katharine Margaret Lister, *d* of late D. W. Last and M. M. Last. *Educ:* Eton. British High Commission, Wellington, NZ, 1942; Gilbert and Ellice Military Forces, 1944; Colonial Administrative Service, 1945 (Secretary to Govt of Tonga, 1950–53); Norris Oakley Bros, 1957; Min. of Defence, 1959; British High Commission, New Delhi, 1966; attached Foreign and Commonwealth Office, 1969–72. Chm., Abbeyfield Epping Soc., 1995–97 (Hon. Sec., 1987–96). *Recreations:* golf, bridge, chess. *Heir:* *b* Edward Geoffrey Lake [*b* 17 July 1928; *m* 1965, Judith Ann, *d* of John Fox; one *s* one *d*]. *Club:* Lansdowne.

LAKE, (Charles) Michael, CBE 1996; Director General, Help the Aged, since 1996; *b* 17 May 1944; *s* of Stanley Giddy and late Beryl Giddy (*née* Heath); step *s* of late Percival Redvers Lake; *m* 1970, Christine Warner; three *d*. *Educ:* Humphry Davy Grammar Sch., Penzance; RMA, Sandhurst. FILog 1995. Commnd RCT, 1965; Regtl appts, Germany, Hong Kong, NI, Oman; attached Commandant-Gen., RM, 1977–78; Directing Staff, Staff Coll., 1982–83; Comd, 1st Div. Transport Regt, 1983–86; Comdr Transport, HQ British Forces Riyadh, Gulf War, 1990–91; Regtl Col., RLC, 1992–96; retired 1997. External Advr, RBL, 1999. Mem., Central Panel, Pensions Adv. Service, 1999. Dir, Chelsea Arts Club, 1997–. Member, Board: HelpAge Internat., 1996–; Network Housing Assoc., 2000–. Freeman: City of London, 1995; Carmen's Co., 1995. *Recreations:* sports, avid golfer, declining cricketer, Rugby; Post Impressionism, Penzance and Newlyn school. *Address:* Help the Aged, St James's Walk, Clerkenwell Green, EC1R 0BE. *T:* (020) 7250 4428; c/o Holt's Bank, Royal Bank of Scotland, Farnborough, Hants GU14 7NR. *Clubs:* Army and Navy; Fadeaways, Walkers Cricket Circus.

LAKE, Robert Andrew; Director of Social Services, Staffordshire County Council, since 1996; *b* 14 April 1948; *s* of Rev. William Henry Lake and Ruth Lake (*née* Hammond); *m* 1975, Celia Helen Probert; one *s* two *d*. *Educ:* Hull Grammar Sch.; Univ. of Coventry (CQSW). Welfare Asst, Bolton Welfare Dept, 1968–70; various posts, Coventry Social Services Dept, 1972–80; Area Manager, 1980–82, Principal Asst, 1982–84, Newcastle upon Tyne Social Services; Asst Dir, 1984–91, Dir, 1991–96, Humberside Social Services Dept. Vis. Fellow, Keele Univ., 1997. *Recreations:* music, D-I-Y, the family. *Address:* Staffordshire Social Services Department, St Chad's Place, Stafford ST16 2LR. *T:* (01785) 277001.

LAKER, Sir Freddie, (Sir Frederick Alfred Laker), Kt 1978; Chairman and Managing Director, Laker Airways (Bahamas) Ltd, since 1992; *b* 6 Aug. 1922; British. *Educ:* Simon Langton Sch., Canterbury. Short Brothers, Rochester, 1938–40; General Aircraft, 1940–41; Air Transport Auxiliary, 1941–46; Aviation Traders, 1946–65; Man. Dir, British United Airways, 1960–65; Chm. and Man. Dir, Laker Airways Ltd, 1966–82; Dir, Freddie Laker's Skytrain Ltd, 1982–83; creator of Skytrain Air Passenger Service to USA; Partner, Laker Airways Inc., 1995–98. Hon. Fellow Univ. of Manchester Inst. of Science and Technol., 1978; Hon. DSc: City, 1979; Cranfield Inst. of Technol., 1980; Hon. LLD Manchester, 1981. *Recreations:* horse breeding, racing, sailing. *Address:* Princess Tower, West Sunrise, Box F40207, Freeport, Grand Bahama, Bahamas. *Clubs:* Eccentric, Little Ship, Jockey.

LAKES, Major Gordon Harry, CB 1987; MC 1951; Deputy Director General, Prison Service, 1985–88; *b* 27 Aug. 1928; *s* of Harry Lakes and Annie Lakes; *m* 1950, Nancy (*née* Smith) (*d* 1992); one *d*. *Educ:* Army Technical School, Arborfield; RMA Sandhurst. Commissioned RA 1948; service in Tripolitania, Korea, Japan, Hong Kong, Gold Coast (RWAFF), Ghana (Major), 1949–60. Middle Temple, 1960–61. Prison Service College, 1961–62; HM Borstal Feltham, 1962–65; Asst Principal, Officers' Training Sch., Leyhill, 1965–68; Governor, HM Remand Centre, Thorp Arch, 1968–70; Prison Service HQ, 1970–74; HM Prisons: Pentonville, 1974–75; Gartree, 1975–77; Prison Service HQ, 1977–82; HM Dep. Chief Inspector of Prisons, 1982–85. Mem., Parole Bd, 1989–92; Comr, Mental Health Act, 1991– (Mem. Mgt Bd, 1996–, Actg Chm. 1998–99). Non-exec. Dir, HM Prison, Buckley Hall, 2000–. Chm., Nat. AIDS and Prisons Forum, 1989–98. Consultant to 8th UN Congress on Prevention of Crime and Treatment of Offenders, 1989–90; Assessor to Lord Justice Woolf's Inquiry into Prison Disturbances, 1990–91; Consultant on prison staffing and ops, Min. of Justice, Dublin, 1998–. Council of Europe: Mem., Cttee for Co-operation in Prison Affairs, 1986–91; Expert Witness, Cttee for Prevention of Torture, 1990–2000; Advr, Themis Plan (Prisons Proj.), 1993–2000; Co-Chm., Nord-Balt Prison Project, 1996–; Chm., Steering Cttee for Reform of Ukranian Prison System, 1997–. *Recreations:* golf, photography.

LAKEY, Prof. John Richard Angwin, PhD; CEng, FInstE; CPhys, FInstP; radiological protection consultant; founder, John Lakey Associates, 1989–2000; *b* 28 June 1929; *s* of late William Richard Lakey and Edith Lakey (*née* Hartley); *m* 1955, Dr Pamela Janet, *d* of late Eric Clifford Lancey and Florence Elsie Lancey; three *d*. *Educ:* Morley Grammar Sch.; Sheffield Univ. BSc (Physics) 1950, PhD (Fuel Technology) 1953. R&D posts with Simon Carves Ltd, secondment to AERE Harwell and GEC, 1953–60; Royal Naval College, Greenwich: Asst Prof., 1960–80; Prof. of Nuclear Sci. and Technol., 1980–89; Dean, 1984–86, 1988–89. Reactor Shielding Consultant, DG Ships, 1967–89; Radiation Consultant, WHO, 1973–74; Mem. and Vice-Chm., CNAA Physics Board, 1973–82; Mem., Medway Health Authy, 1981–90; Chm., UK Liaison Cttee for Scis Allied to Medicine and Biology, 1984–87. University of Surrey: External Examr, 1980–86; Hon. Vis. Prof., 1987–94; Vis. Lectr, Harvard Univ., 1984–; Vis. Prof., Univ. of Greenwich, 1998–. President: Internat. Radiation Protection Assoc., 1988–92 (Publications Dir, 1979–88); Instn of Nuclear Engrs, 1988–90 (Vice-Pres., 1983–87); Vice-President: London Internat. Youth Science Forum, 1988–; European Nuclear Soc., 1989–95. Liveryman, Engineers' Co., 1988–. Eur. Ing. 1989. Hon. FSRP 1992. Mem. Editorial Bd, Physics in Medicine and Biology, 1980–83; News Editor, Health Physics, 1980–88. *Publications:* Protection Against Radiation, 1961; Radiation Protection Measurement: philosophy and implementation, 1975; (ed) ALARA principles and practices, 1987; (ed) IRPA Guidelines on Protection Against Non-Ionizing Radiation, 1991; (ed) Off-site Emergency Response to Nuclear Accidents, 1993; (jtly) Radiation and Radiation Protection: a course for primary and secondary schools, 1995; Radiation Protection for Emergency Workers, 1997; papers on nuclear safety, radiological protection and management of emergencies. *Recreations:* photography, conversation. *Address:* 5 Pine Rise, Meopham, Gravesend, Kent DA13 0JA. *T:* (01474) 812551. *Clubs:* Athenæum; Royal Naval Sailing Association.

LAKHANI, Kamlesh, (Mrs N. Lakhani); *see* Bahl, K.

LAKIN, Sir Michael, 4th Bt *cr* 1909; *b* 28 Oct. 1934; *s* of Sir Henry Lakin, 3rd Bt, and Bessie (*d* 1965), *d* of J. D. Anderson, Durban; *S* father, 1979; *m* 1st, 1956, Margaret Wallace (marr. diss. 1963); 2nd, 1965, Felicity Ann Murphy; one *s* one *d*. *Educ:* Stowe. *Heir:* *s* Richard Anthony Lakin [*b* 26 Nov. 1968; *m* 1997, Lara Maryanne Rose]. *Address:* Little Sherwood Hill, Tunley, near Cirencester, Glos GL7 6DN.

LAKIN, Peter Maurice; His Honour Judge Lakin; a Circuit Judge, since 1995; *b* 21 Oct. 1949; *s* of late Ronald Maurice Lakin and of Dorothy Kathleen Lakin (*née* Cowlishaw); *m* 1971, Jacqueline Jubb; one *s* one *d*. *Educ:* King Henry VIII Sch., Coventry; Manchester Univ. (LLB). Articled Clerk, Conn Goldberg, solicitors, Manchester, 1971–74; Goldberg Blackburn, solicitors, Manchester (later Pannone & Partners): Asst Solicitor, 1974–76; Partner i/c of Corporate Defence and Forensic Unit, 1976–95; Asst Recorder, 1989–93; Recorder, 1993–95. Hon. Sec., Manchester and Dist Medico-Legal Soc., 1989–95. *Recreations:* fell-walking, opera, gardening, local history. *Address:* Manchester Crown Court, Crown Square, Manchester M3 3FL.

LAKING, Sir George (Robert), KCMG 1985 (CMG 1969); Chief Ombudsman, New Zealand, 1977–84, retired; *b* Auckland, NZ, 15 Oct. 1912; *s* of R. G. Laking; *m* 1940, Patricia, *d* of H. Hogg; one *s* one *d*. *Educ:* Auckland Grammar Sch.; Auckland Univ.; Victoria Univ. of Wellington (LLB). Prime Minister's and Ext. Affairs Depts, 1940–49; New Zealand Embassy, Washington: Counsellor, 1949–54; Minister, 1954–56; Dep. Sec. of Ext. Affairs, Wellington, NZ, 1956–58; Acting High Comr for NZ, London, 1958–61, and NZ Ambassador to European Economic Community, 1960–61; New Zealand Ambassador, Washington, 1961–67; Sec. of Foreign Affairs and Permanent Head, Prime Minister's Dept, NZ, 1967–72; Ombudsman, 1975–77; Privacy Comr, 1977–78. Member: Human Rights Commn, 1978–84; Public and Administrative Law Reform Cttee, 1980–85. Chairman: NZ-US Educnl Foundn, 1976–78; NZ Oral History Archive Trust, 1985–90; Wellington Civic Trust, 1985–86; Legislation Adv. Cttee, 1986–91; Pres., NZ Inst. of Internat. Affairs, 1980–84. Mem. Internat. Council, Asia Soc., NY, 1985–92. *Address:* 3 Wesley Road, Wellington 1, New Zealand. *T:* (4) 4728454.

LAL, Prof. Devendra, PhD; FRS 1979; Professor, Geological Research Division, Scripps Institution of Oceanography, University of California, La Jolla, since 1967; Fellow: Physical Research Laboratory, Ahmedabad, since 1990 (Director, 1972–83; Senior Professor, 1983–89); Tata Institute of Fundamental Research, Bombay, since 1996; *b* 14 Feb. 1929; *s* of Radhekrishna Lal and Sita Devi; *m* 1955, Aruna L. Damany (*d* 1993). *Educ:* Banaras Hindu Univ. (BSc; MSc); Univ. of Bombay (PhD). Fellow, Indian Acad. of Sciences, 1964. Tata Inst. of Fundamental Research, Bombay: Res. Student, 1949–50; Res. Asst, 1950–53; Res. Fellow, 1953–57; Fellow, 1957–60; Associate Prof., 1960–63; Prof., 1963–70; Sen. Prof., 1970–72. Res. Geophysicist, UCLA-IGPP, 1965–66. Vis. Prof., UCLA, 1983–84. K. S. Krishnan Meml Lect., INSA, 1981. Foreign Sec., Indian Nat. Sci. Acad., 1981–84 (Fellow, 1971); Founder Mem., Third World Acad. of Scis, Trieste, 1983; President: Internat. Assoc. of Physical Scis of the Ocean, 1979–83; Internat. Union of Geodesy & Geophysics, 1983–87. Fellow: Nat. Acad. of Scis, Allahabad, 1988; Physical Res. Lab., Ahmedabad, 1996; Tata Inst. of Fundamental Res., Bombay, 1996; FAAAS 1997; Foreign Associate, Nat. Acad. of Sciences, USA, 1975; For. Mem., Amer. Acad. of Arts and Scis, 1989; Associate, RAS, 1984; Mem., Internat. Acad. Astronautics, 1985. Mem., Sigma Xi, USA, 1984. Hon. Fellow, Geol Soc. of India, 1992. Hon. DSc Banaras Hindu Univ., 1981. Krishnan Medal for Geochemistry and Geophysics, Indian Geophysical Union, Hyderabad, 1965; Shanti Swarup Bhatnagar Award for Physical Sciences, CSIR, 1967; Outstanding Scientist Award, Fedn of Indian Chambers of Commerce and Industry, 1974; Pandit Jawaharlal Nehru Award for Scis, Madhya Pradesh Govt, 1986; C. V. Raman Birth Centenary Award, Indian Sci. Congress Assoc., 1996–97; V. M. Goldschmidt Medal, and Fellow, Geochem. Soc., USA, 1997. Padma Shri, 1971. *Publications:* (ed) Early Solar System Processes and the Present Solar System, 1980; (ed) Biogeochemistry of the Arabian Sea, 1994; *contributed:* Earth Science and Meteoritics, 1963; International Dictionary of Geophysics, 1968; The Encyclopedia of Earth Sciences: vol. IV, Geochemistry and Environmental Sciences, 1972; Further Advances in Lunar Research: Luna 16 and 20 samples, 1974; McGraw Hill Encyclopedia of Science and Technology, 1992; jt author of chapters in books; scientific papers to learned jls; proc. confs. *Recreations:* music, puzzles, painting, photography. *Address:* Scripps Institution of Oceanography, University of California at San Diego, La Jolla, CA 92093–0244, USA. *T:* (office) (858) 5342134, (home) (858) 5871535; *e-mail:* dlal@ucsd.edu.

LALANDI-EMERY, Lina, (Mrs Ralph Emery), OBE 1975; Director, English Bach Festival, since 1962; *b* Athens; *d* of late Nikolas Kaloyeropoulos (former Dir of Byzantine Museum, Athens, and Dir of Beaux Arts, Min. of Educn, Athens) and Toula Gelekis. *Educ:* Athens Conservatoire (grad. with Hons in Music); privately, in England (harpsichord and singing studies). International career as harpsichordist in Concert, Radio and TV. Founded English Bach Festival Trust, 1962; now specialising in presentation of baroque opera perfs at ROH, Covent Gdn and numerous music fests. Officier, l'Ordre des Arts et des Lettres, 1978. *Recreations:* astrophysics, reading, knitting. *Address:* 15 South Eaton Place, SW1W 9ER. *T:* (020) 7730 5925, *Fax:* (020) 7730 1456; *e-mail:* info@english-bachfestival.org.uk.

LALANNE, Bernard Michel L.; *see* Loustau-Lalanne.

LALLY, Patrick James; JP; DL; Lord Provost and Lord-Lieutenant of Glasgow, 1995–99; *s* of Patrick James Lally and Sarah Joyce Lally; *m* 1967, Margaret Beckett McGuire; two *s*. Former Dir, Retail Clothing Co. Member: Glasgow Corp., 1966–75 (Dep. Leader, 1972–75); Glasgow DC, 1975–77, 1980–96 (Treas., 1984–86; Leader, 1986–92, 1994–96). Chairman: Gtr Glasgow Tourist Bd, 1989–96; Gtr Glasgow and Clyde Valley Tourist Bd, 1996–99; Director: Glasgow Internat. Jazz Fest. (Chm., 1989–99); Glasgow Develt Agency, 1990–92; Scottish Exhibn Centre Ltd, 1994–99; Glasgow 1999 Co. Ltd, 1996–99. JP Glasgow, 1970, DL Glasgow, 1986. Hon. Citizen, Dalian, China, 1995. OStJ 1997. Comdr, Ordre Nat. du Mérite (France), 1996. *Publication:* Lazarus Only Done it Once (autobiog.), 1999. *Recreations:* enjoying the arts, reading, watching TV, football. *Address:* 2 Tanera Avenue, Simshill, Glasgow G44 5BU. *Clubs:* Caledonian; Royal Scottish Automobile, Cathcart Labour Party Social (Hon. Life Mem.) (Glasgow).

LALONDE, Hon. Marc; PC (Can.) 1972; OC 1989; QC 1971; Law Partner, Stikeman, Elliott, Montreal, since 1984; *b* 26 July 1929; *s* of late J. Albert Lalonde and Nora (*née* St Aubin); *m* 1955, Claire Tétreau; two *s* two *d*. *Educ:* St Laurent Coll., Montreal (BA 1950); Univ. of Montreal (LLL 1954; MA Law 1955); Oxford Univ. (Econ. and Pol. Science; MA 1957); Ottawa Univ. (Dip. of Superior Studies in Law, 1960). Prof. of Commercial Law and Econs, Univ. of Montreal, 1957–59; Special Asst to Minister of Justice, Ottawa, 1959–60; Partner, Gelinas, Bourque Lalonde & Benoit, Montreal, 1960–68; Lectr in Admin. Law for Doctorate Students, Univ. of Ottawa and Univ. of Montreal, 1961–62; Policy Advisor to Prime Minister, 1967; Principal Sec. to Prime Minister, 1968–72; MP (L) Montreal-Outremont, 1972–84; Minister of National Health and Welfare, 1972–77; Minister of State for Federal-Provincial Relations, 1977–78; Minister resp. for Status of Women, 1975–78; Minister of Justice and Attorney-Gen., 1978–79; Minister of Energy, Mines and Resources, 1980–82; Minister of Finance, 1982–84. *Ad hoc* Judge, Internat. Court of Justice, 1985–. Counsel before several Royal Commns inc. Royal Commn on Great Lakes Shipping and Royal Commn on Pilotage. Mem., Cttee on Broadcasting, 1964; Dir, Canadian Citizenship Council, 1960–65; Member, Bd of Directors: Inst. of Public Law, Univ. of Montréal, 1960–64; Citibank Canada, 1985–; O&Y Properties, 1993–; Sherritt Power Inc., 1998–; Oxbow Equities Corp., 2000–. Dr *hc* Univ. of Limburg, Maastricht, 1992. Dana Award, Amer. Public Health Assoc., 1978. *Publications:* The Changing Role of the Prime Minister's Office, 1971; New Perspectives on the Health of Canadians (working document), 1974. *Recreations:* tennis, squash, skiing, jogging, sailing, reading. *Address:* 5440 Légaré, Montréal, QC H3T 1Z4, Canada.

LALUMIÈRE, Catherine; French politician; Member, since 1994, a Vice-President, since 2001, European Parliament; President, European Radical Alliance Group, since 1994; *b* Rennes, 3 Aug. 1935. Dr in Public Law; degree in Pol Scis and History of Law. Asst, Univ. of Bordeaux I, and Bordeaux Inst. of Pol Studies, 1960–71; Sen. Lectr, Univ. of Paris I, 1971–81. Mem., National Assembly for Gironde, 1981, and 1986–89: Vice-Pres., Cttee of For. Affairs; Vice-Pres., Delegn to EC. Sec. of State i/c Public Service, 1981; Minister of Consumer Affairs, 1981–84; Sec. of State, resp. for Eur. Affairs, Min. of For. Affairs, 1984–86; Mem., Parly Assembly, Council of Europe, 1987–89; Sec. Gen., Council of Europe, 1989–94. Regl Councillor, Ile de France, 1998–. *Recreation:* walking. *Address:* European Parliament, Rue Wiertz, 1047 Brussels, Belgium.

LAM, Martin Philip; *b* 10 March 1920; *m* 1953, Lisa Lorenz; one *s* one *d*. *Educ:* University College Sch.; Gonville and Caius Coll., Cambridge (Scholar). Served War of 1939–45, Royal Signals and Special Ops Mediterranean. Asst Principal, Board of Trade, 1947; Nuffield Fellowship (Latin America), 1952–53; Asst Sec., 1960; Counsellor, UK Delegn to OECD, 1963–65, Advr, Commercial Policy, 1970–74, Leader UNCTAD Delegn, 1972; Under-Sec. (Computer Systems and Electronics), DoI, 1974–78; Associate of BIS Mackintosh, and of General Technology Systems, 1979–90; on contract to Directorate-Gen. XIII, European Commn, 1986–88; consultant: Scaneurope, 1989–90; KCL, 1991–92. *Publication:* (jtly) Kanji from the Start, 1995. *Address:* 22 The Avenue, Wembley, Middlesex HA9 9QJ. *T:* (020) 8904 2584.

LAMB, family name of **Baron Rochester**.

LAMB, Sir Albert Thomas, (Sir Archie), KBE 1979 (MBE 1953); CMG 1974; DFC 1945; HM Diplomatic Service, retired; *b* 23 Oct. 1921; *s* of R. S. Lamb and Violet Lamb (*née* Haynes); *m* 1944, Christina Betty Wilkinson; one *s* two *d*. *Educ:* Swansea Grammar Sch. Served RAF 1941–46. FO 1938–41; Embassy, Rome, 1947–50; Consulate-General, Genoa, 1950; Embassy, Bucharest, 1950–53; FO 1953–55; Middle East Centre for Arabic Studies, 1955–57; Political Residency, Bahrain, 1957–61; FO 1961–65; Embassy, Kuwait, 1965; Political Agent in Abu Dhabi, 1965–68; Inspector, 1968–70, Sen. Inspector, 1970–73, Asst Under-Sec. of State and Chief Inspector, FCO, 1973–74; Ambassador to Kuwait, 1974–77; Ambassador to Norway, 1978–80. Mem., BNOC, 1981–82; Dir, Britoil plc, 1982–88; Member Board: British Shipbuilders, 1985–87; Nat. Bank of Kuwait (Internat.), 1994–; Sen. Associate, Conant and Associates Ltd, Washington DC, 1985–93; Adviser, Samuel Montagu and Co. Ltd, 1986–88. Clerk to Parish Councils of Zeals and Stourton with Gasper, 1991–97. *Address:* White Cross Lodge, Zeals, Wilts BA12 6PF. *T:* (01747) 840321. *Club:* Royal Air Force.

LAMB, Prof. Christopher John, PhD; Director, John Innes Centre, and John Innes Professor of Biology, University of East Anglia, since 1999; *b* 19 March 1950; *s* of John Mungall Lamb and late Eileen Blanche Lamb (*née* Marley); *m* 1970, Jane Susan Wright; two *s* one *d*. *Educ:* Fitzwilliam Coll., Cambridge (BA 1972, PhD 1976, in Biochemistry). Oxford University: ICI Postdoctoral Fellow, Sch. of Botany, 1975–77; Deptl Demonstr., Dept of Biochemistry, 1977–82; Browne Res. Fellow, Queen's Coll., 1977–82; Dir and Prof., Plant Biology Lab., Salk Inst. for Biol Studies, Calif, 1982–98; Adjunct Prof., UCSD, 1988–98; Regius Prof. of Plant Sci., Univ. of Edinburgh, 1999. Founder, Akkadix Inc., 1998. FAAAS 1992. McKnight Schol., 1983, Herman Frasch Award, 1986, ACS. *Publications:* numerous articles in Nature, Science, Cell and other learned jls. *Recreations:* fell walking, swimming, wine, sushi. *Address:* John Innes Centre, Norwich Research Park, Colney, Norwich NR4 7UH. *T:* (01603) 450000.

LAMB, Air Vice-Marshal George Colin, CB 1977; CBE 1966; AFC 1947; Chairman, Yonex (UK) Ltd, 1995–97 (Managing Director, 1990–95); *b* 23 July 1923; *s* of late George and Bessie Lamb, Hornby, Lancaster; *m* 1st, 1945, Nancy Mary Godsmark; two *s*; 2nd, 1981, Mrs Maureen Margaret Mepham. *Educ:* Lancaster Royal Grammar School. War of 1939–45: commissioned, RAF, 1942; flying duties, 1942–53; Staff Coll., 1953; Air Ministry, special duties, 1954–58; OC No 87 Sqdn, 1958–61; Dir Admin. Plans, MoD, 1961–64; Asst Comdt, RAF Coll., 1964–65; Dep. Comdr, Air Forces Borneo, 1965–66; Fighter Command, 1966; MoD (Dep. Command Structure Project Officer), 1967; HQ, Strike Command, 1967–69; OC, RAF Lyneham, 1969–71; RCDS, 1971–72; Dir of Control (Operations), NATS, 1972–74; Comdr, Southern Maritime Air Region, RAF Mount Batten, 1974–75; C of S, No 18 Gp Strike Comd, RAF, 1975–78. RAF Vice-Pres., Combined Cadet Forces Assoc., 1978–94. Chief Exec., Badminton Assoc. of England, 1978–89; Gen. Sec., London Inst. of Sports Medicine, 1989–90. Consultant, Television, Sport and Leisure Ltd, 1989–90. Chairman: Lilleshall National Sports Centre, 1984–; British Internat. Sports Develt Aid Trust, 1995–; Member: Sports Council, 1983–88 (Mem., Drug Abuse Adv. Gp, 1988–92); Sports Cttee, Prince's Trust, 1985–88; Privilege Mem. of RFU, 1985– (Mem., RFU Cttee, 1973–85); British Internat. Sports Cttee, 1989–. Dir (non-exec.), Castle Care-Tech. Security, 1993–. President: St George's Day Club, 1994–; Assoc. of Lancastrians in London, 1999. FIMgt. *Recreations:* international Rugby football referee, cricket (former Pres., Adastrian Cricket Club). *Address:* Hambledon, 17 Meadway, Berkhamsted HP4 2PN. *T:* (01442) 862583. *Club:* Royal Air Force.

LAMB, Prof. Joseph Fairweather, PhD; FRCPE; FRSE; Chandos Professor of Physiology, St Leonard's College, University of St Andrews, 1969–93, now Professor Emeritus; *b* 18 July 1928; *s* of Joseph and Agnes May Lamb; *m* 1st, 1955, Olivia Janet Horne (marr. diss. 1989); three *s* one *d*; 2nd, 1989, Bridget Cecilia Cook; two *s*. *Educ:* Brechin High School; Edinburgh Univ. (MB ChB, BSc, PhD). FRCPE 1985. National Service, RAF, 1947–49. House Officer, Dumfries and Edinburgh, 1955–56; Hons Physiology Course, 1956–57; Univ. Junior Res. Fellow, 1957; Lectr in Physiology, Royal (Dick) Vet. Sch., 1958–61; Lectr, Sen. Lectr in Physiol., Glasgow, 1961–69. Sec., Physiol. Soc., 1982–85; Chm., Save British Science Soc., 1986–97; Chm./Organiser, Gas Greed Campaign, 1994–95. Gov., Rowett Res. Inst., Aberdeen, 1998–. Editor: Jl of Physiol., 1968–74; Amer. Jl of Physiol., 1985–88. FRSA; FRSE 1985. *Publications:* Essentials of Physiology, 1980, 3rd edn 1991; articles in learned jls. *Recreations:* sailing, boatbuilding, reading. *Address:* Kenbrae, Millbank, Cupar, Fife KY15 5DP. *T:* (01334) 652791. *Club:* Royal Society of Medicine.

LAMB, Juliet; *see* Warkentin, J.

LAMB, Norman Peter; MP (Lib Dem) Norfolk North, since 2001; *b* 16 Sept. 1957; *s* of late Hubert Horace Lamb and of Beatrice Moira Lamb; *m* 1984, Mary Elizabeth Green; two *s*. *Educ:* Wymondham Coll., Norfolk; Leicester Univ. (LLB). Sen. Asst Solicitor, Norwich CC, 1984–86; Solicitor, 1986–87, Partner, 1987–2001, Steele & Co. *Publication:* Remedies in the Employment Tribunal, 1998. *Recreations:* football, walking. *Address:* House of Commons, SW1A 0AA. *T:* (020) 7219 8480; (office) 15 Market Place, North Walsham NR28 9BP. *Club:* National Liberal.

LAMB, Hon. Timothy Michael; Chief Executive, England and Wales (formerly Test and County) Cricket Board, since 1996; *b* 24 March 1953; *s* of Baron Rochester, *qv*; *m* 1978, Denise Ann Buckley; one *s* one *d*. *Educ:* Shrewsbury Sch.; Queen's Coll., Oxford (MA Modern Hist.). Professional cricketer: with Middx CCC, 1974–77; with Northants CCC, 1978–83; Sec. and Gen. Manager, Middx CCC, 1984–88; Cricket Sec., 1988–96, Dep. Chief Exec., May–Oct. 1996, TCCB. *Recreations:* golf, travel, walking. *Address:* England and Wales Cricket Board, Lord's Ground, NW8 8QZ. *T:* (020) 7432 1200.

LAMB, Timothy Robert; QC 1995; a Recorder, since 2000; *b* 27 Nov. 1951; *s* of Stephen Falcon Lamb and Pamela Elizabeth Lamb (*née* Coombes); *m* 1978, Judith Anne Ryan; one *s* one *d*. *Educ:* Brentwood Sch.; Lincoln Coll., Oxford (MA Jurisp.). Called to the Bar, Gray's Inn, 1974. An Asst Recorder, 1998–2000. *Recreations:* family, travel, water sports, gliding. *Address:* 3 Paper Buildings, EC4Y 7EU. *T:* (020) 7583 8055. *Club:* Lasham Gliding Soc.

LAMB, Prof. Trevor David, FRS 1993; Professor of Neuroscience, University of Cambridge, since 1994; Fellow, Darwin College, Cambridge, since 1985; *b* 20 Sept. 1948; *s* of Arthur and Margaret Lamb; *m* 1979, (Janet) Clare Conway; two *s* one *d*. *Educ:* Melbourne Grammar Sch.; Univ. of Melbourne (BE 1st Cl. Hons 1969); Univ. of Cambridge (PhD 1975; ScD 1988). Physiological Laboratory, University of Cambridge: Wellcome Sen. Res. Fellow, 1978–80; Royal Soc. Locke Res. Fellow, 1980–84; Univ. Lectr in Physiol., 1984–91; Reader in Neuroscience, 1991–94. *Publications:* articles on photoreceptors and sensory transduction in Jl Physiol. and other learned jls. *Address:* Physiological Laboratory, University of Cambridge, Downing Street, Cambridge CB2 3EG. *T:* (01223) 333856, *Fax:* (01223) 333840; *e-mail:* tdl1@cam.ac.uk.

LAMB, Prof. Willis E(ugene), Jr; Professor of Physics and Optical Sciences, University of Arizona, since 1974, and Regents' Professor, since 1990; *b* Los Angeles, California, USA, 12 July 1913; *s* of Willis Eugene Lamb and Marie Helen Metcalf; *m* Ursula Schaefer (*d* 1996); *m* 1996, Bruria Kaufman. *Educ:* Los Angeles High Sch.; University of California (BS, PhD). Columbia Univ.: Instructor in Physics, 1938–43, Associate, 1943–45, Assistant Professor, 1945–47, Associate Professor, 1947–48, Professor of Physics, 1948–52; Professor of Physics, Stanford Univ., California, 1951–56; Wykeham Prof. of Physics and Fellow of New Coll., University of Oxford, 1956–62; Yale University: Ford Prof. of Physics, 1962–72; Gibbs Prof. of Physics, 1972–74. Morris Loeb Lectr, Harvard Univ., 1953–54; Lectr, University of Colorado, Summer, 1959; Shrum Lectr, Simon Fraser Univ., 1972; Visiting Professor, Tata Institute of Fundamental Research, Bombay, 1960; Guggenheim Fellow, 1960–61; Visiting Professor, Columbia Univ., 1961; Fulbright Lecturer, University of Grenoble, Summer, 1964. MNAS, 1954. Hon. Mem., Optical Soc. of Amer., 2000; Hon. Fellow, Institute of Physics and Physical Society, 1962; Hon. FRSE 1981. Hon. DSc: Pennsylvania, 1954; Gustavus Adolphus Coll., 1975; Columbia, 1990; MA (by decree), Oxford, 1956; Hon. MA Yale, 1961; Hon. LHD Yeshiva, 1965; Dr rer. nat. *hc* Ulm, 1997. Res. Corp Award, 1954; Rumford Medal, American Academy of Arts and Sciences, 1953; (jointly) Nobel Prize in Physics, 1955; Guthrie Award, The Physical Society, 1958; Yeshiva University Award, 1962. *Publications:* (with M. Sargent and M. O. Scully) Laser Physics, 1974; contributions to The Physical Review, Physica, Science, Journal of Applied Physics, etc. *Address:* Optical Sciences Center, University of Arizona, Tucson, AZ 85721, USA.

LAMBART, family name of **Earl of Cavan.**

LAMBECK, Prof. Kurt, DPhil, DSc; FRS 1994; FAA; Professor of Geophysics, Australian National University, since 1977; *b* 20 Sept. 1941; *s* of Jacob and Johanna Lambeck; *m* 1967, Bridget Marguerite Nicholls; one *s* one *d*. *Educ:* Univ. of NSW (BSurv. Hons); Hertford Coll., Oxford (DPhil, DSc). Geodesist, Smithsonian Astrophysical Observatory and Harvard Coll. Observatory, Cambridge, Mass, 1967–70; Directeur Scientifique, Observatoire de Paris, 1970–73; Prof. of Geophysics, Univ. of Paris, 1973–77; Dir, Res. Sch. of Earth Scis, ANU, 1984–93. Tage Erlander Prof., Swedish Res. Council, 2001. Vice Pres., 1998–2000, Foreign Sec., 2000–, Aust. Acad. Sci. Fellow, Amer. Geophysical Union, 1976; FAA 1984. Foreign Member: Royal Netherlands Acad. of Arts and Scis, 1993; Norwegian Acad. of Science and Letters, 1994. Foreign MAE, 1999. Hon. Mem., European Geophysical Soc., 1987. Hon. DEng Nat. Tech. Univ., Athens, 1994; Hon. DSc NSW, 1999. Mcelwane Medal, 1976, Whitten Medal, 1993, Amer. Geophysical Union; Jaeger Medal, Aust. Acad. of Sci., 1995; Alfred Wegener Medal, Eur. Union of Geoscis, 1997. *Publications:* The Earth's Variable Rotation, 1980; Geophysical Geodesy: the slow deformations of the earth, 1988; numerous articles in fields of geodesy, geophysics and geology. *Address:* Research School of Earth Sciences, Australian National University, Canberra, ACT 0200, Australia; 31 Brand Street, Hughes, ACT 2605, Australia.

LAMBERT, Anne; *see* Lambert, G. M. A.

LAMBERT, Sir Anthony (Edward), KCMG 1964 (CMG 1955); HM Diplomatic Service, retired; *b* 7 March 1911; *o s* of late R. E. Lambert, Pensbury House, Shaftesbury, Dorset; *m* 1948, Ruth Mary (*d* 1998), *d* of late Sir Arthur Fleming, CBE; two *d*. *Educ:* Harrow; Balliol Coll., Oxford (scholar). Entered HM Foreign (subseq. Diplomatic) Service, 1934, and served in: Brussels, 1937; Ankara, 1940; Beirut and Damascus, 1942; Brussels, 1944; Stockholm, 1949; Athens, 1952; HM Minister to Bulgaria, 1958–60; HM Ambassador to: Tunisia, 1960–63; Finland, 1963–66; Portugal, 1966–70.

LAMBERT, David Arthur Charles; General President, National Union of Knitwear, Footwear and Apparel Trades, 1991–94 (General Secretary, 1975–82, General President, 1982–90, National Union of Hosiery and Knitwear Workers); President, International Textile, Garment and Leather Workers' Federation, Brussels, 1992–96 (Vice-President, 1984–92); *b* 2 Sept. 1933; *m* Beryl Ann (*née* Smith); two *s* one *d*. *Educ:* Hitchin Boys' Grammar Sch., Herts. Employed as production worker for major hosiery manufr; active as lay official within NUHKW; full-time official, NUHKW, 1964–90. Member: Employment Appeal Tribunal, 1978–; TUC Gen. Council, 1984–94; CRE, 1987–93.

LAMBERT, David George; Legal Adviser, Office of the Presiding Officer, National Assembly for Wales, since 2000; Registrar of Diocese of Llandaff, since 1986; *b* 7 Aug. 1940; *s* of George and Elsie Lambert; *m* 1966, Diana Mary Ware; one *s* one *d*. *Educ:* Barry Grammar Sch.; UCW, Aberystwyth (LLB). Notary Public; Solicitor in private practice, 1965; Welsh Office: Legal Officer, 1966–74; Asst Legal Adviser, 1974–91; Solicitor and Legal Advr, 1991–99. Tutor, Univ. of Wales Coll. of Cardiff (formerly UC, Cardiff), 1972–99; Res. Fellow, Univ. of Wales, Cardiff, 1999. Dep. Chapter Clerk, Llandaff Cath., 1980–. *Recreations:* ecclesiastical law, Baroque music. *Address:* 9 The Chantry, Llandaff, Cardiff CF5 2NN. *T:* (029) 2056 8154.

LAMBERT, (Gillian Mary) Anne; Deputy Director General, Office of Telecommunications, since 1998; *b* 11 July 1956; *d* of Roy and Joyce Lambert. *Educ:* St Anne's Coll., Oxford (BA Hons Exptl Psychol. 1977). Joined Department of Trade and Industry, 1977: Telecommunications Div., 1982–84; Industrial Policy Div. (Grade 7), 1984–86; Insce Div., 1986–88; Personnel Div. (Grade 6), 1989–90; Insce Div. (Grade 5), 1990–93; on secondment to FCO as Counsellor (Industry), UK Perm. Repn to EU, Brussels, 1994–98. *Recreations:* theatre, squash, tennis, walking. *Address:* OFTEL, 50 Ludgate Hill, EC4M 7JJ.

LAMBERT, Harold George; *b* 8 April 1910; *s* of late Rev. David Lambert; *m* 1934, Winifred Marthe, *d* of late Rev. H. E. Anderson, Farnham, Surrey; two *s*. *Educ:* King Edward's Sch., Birmingham; Corpus Christi Coll., Cambridge (MA); Imperial College of Science, London. Entered Ministry of Agriculture and Fisheries, 1933; Private Secretary to Parliamentary Secretary, 1938–39; Sec., Agricultural Machinery Develt Bd, 1942–45; Assistant Secretary, 1948; Under-Sec., MAFF, 1964–70, retired. Mem., panel of indep. inspectors for local enquiries, DoE and DoT, 1971–80. *Recreations:* music, art. *Address:* 74 Chichester Drive West, Saltdean, Brighton BN2 8SF.

LAMBERT, Henry Uvedale Antrobus; Chairman: Sun Alliance Insurance Group, 1985–93; Agricultural Mortgage Corporation PLC, 1985–93; *b* 9 Oct. 1925; *o s* of late Roger Uvedale Lambert and Muriel, *d* of Sir Reginald Antrobus, KCMG, CB; *m* 1951, Diana, *y d* of Captain H. E. Dumbell, Royal Fusiliers; two *s* one *d*. *Educ:* Winchester College (Scholar); New College, Oxford (Exhibitioner; MA). Served War of 1939–45, Royal Navy, in HM Ships Stockham and St Austell Bay in Western Approaches and Mediterranean, subseq. RNR; Lt-Comdr (retired). Entered Barclays Bank 1948; a Local Dir at Lombard Street, 1957, Southampton, 1959, Birmingham, 1969; Vice-Chm., Barclays Bank UK Ltd, 1972; Vice-Chm., Barclays Bank Ltd, 1973; Chm., Barclays Bank Internat., 1979–83; Dep. Chm., 1979–85, Dir, 1966–91, Barclays Bank PLC; Agricultural Mortgage Corporation: Dir, 1966; Dep. Chm., 1977–85; Sun Alliance Insurance Group: Dir, 1972; Vice-Chm., 1978–83; Dep. Chm., 1983–85. Dir, British Airways, 1985–89. Mem. Council, RASE, 1985– (Vice Pres., 1994–96; Hon. Vice Pres., 1996–2000). Trustee: Imperial War Graves Endowment Fund, 1987–94 (Chm., 1989–94); Nat. Maritime Mus., 1990–95. Vice-Pres., Navy Records Soc., 1985–89, 1992–96, 2001– (Hon. Treas., 1974–85); Mem., Council, White Ensign Assoc., 1982– (Chm., 1992–96). Fellow, Winchester Coll., 1979–91. Hon. Mem., RICS, 1993. *Recreations:* fishing, gardening, golf, naval history. *Address:* Lowton Manor, Taunton, Somerset TA3 7SX. *Clubs:* Brooks's, MCC.

LAMBERT, Jean Denise; Member (Green) London Region, European Parliament, since 1999; *b* 1 June 1950; *d* of Frederick John and Margaret Archer; *m* 1977, Stephen Lambert; one *s* one *d*. *Educ:* Palmers Grammar Sch. for Girls, Grays, Essex; University Coll., Cardiff (BA Modern Langs); St Paul's Coll., Cheltenham (PGCE). ADB(Ed). Secondary sch. teacher, Waltham Forest, 1972–89 (exmnr in spoken and written English, 1983–88). Green Party: joined 1977 (then Ecology Party); London Area Co-ordinator, 1977–81; Co-Chm. Council, 1982–85, 1986–87; Rep. to European Green Parties, 1985–86, 1988–89; UK rep. to Green Gp in European Parlt, 1989–94; Green Party Speaker, 1988–, Jt Principal Speaker, 1992–93; Chair of Executive, 1993–94. Contested (Green Party): GLC, 1981; local Council, 1986; London NE, European Parlt, 1984, 1989, 1994; Walthamstow, gen. elec., 1992. Founder Member: Ecology Building Soc., 1981 (Bd, 1981–84; Chm., 1982–83; now Patron); Play for Life, 1984; Member: Council, Charter 88, 1990–; Cttee, Voting Reform Gp, 1995–. Trustee, London Ecology Centre, 1995–97. Radio and TV broadcaster. *Publications:* (contrib.) Into the 21st Century, 1988; No Change? No Chance!, 1996; articles to magazines. *Recreations:* reading (esp. detective fiction), cooking, dance. *Address:* Unit 56–59, Hop Exchange, 24 Southwark Street, SE1 1TY. *T:* (020) 7407 6269; *e-mail:* jeanlambert@greenmeps.org.uk.

LAMBERT, Sir John (Henry), KCVO 1980; CMG 1975; HM Diplomatic Service, retired; Vice-President, Heritage of London Trust, since 1996 (Director, 1981–96); *b* 8 Jan. 1921; *s* of Col R. S. Lambert, MC, and Mrs H. J. F. Mills; *m* 1950, Jennifer Ann (*née* Urquhart); one *s* two *d*. *Educ:* Eton Coll.; Sorbonne; Trinity Coll., Cambridge. Grenadier Guards, 1940–45 (Captain). Appointed 3rd Secretary, HM Embassy, The Hague, 1945; Member of HM Foreign Service, 1947; FO, 1948; 2nd Secretary, Damascus, 1951; 1st Secretary, 1953; FO, 1954; Dep. to UK Representative on International Commn for Saar Referendum, 1955; Belgrade, 1956; Head of Chancery, Manila, 1958; UK Delegation to Disarmament Conference, Geneva, 1962; FO, 1963; Counsellor, Head of Chancery, Stockholm, 1964–67; Head of UN (Political) Dept, FCO, 1967–70; Commercial Counsellor and Consul-Gen. Vienna, 1971–74; Minister and Dep. Comdt, Berlin, 1974–77; Ambassador to Tunisia, 1977–81. Chm., Channel Tunnel Investments plc, 1986–92. *Recreations:* the arts, music, tennis, golf. *Address:* 103 Rivermead Court, SW6 3SB. *T:* (020) 7731 5007. *Clubs:* MCC; Hurlingham, Royal St George's Golf.

LAMBERT, John Sinclair; Consultant in leadership and partnership development; *b* 8 April 1948; *s* of late Norman Lambert and of Doris Lambert; *m* 1971, Ann Dowzell; two *s*. *Educ:* Denstone Coll.; Selwyn Coll., Cambridge (MA). Department of Employment, subseq. Department for Education and Employment, 1970–2000: Private Sec. to Perm. Sec., 1973–74; on secondment to Marconi Space and Defence Systems, 1977–78; Dep. Chief Conciliation Officer, ACAS, 1982–83; Head of European Communities Branch, 1983–85; Dir of Field Ops, MSC, 1987–90; Dir of Ops (N and W), 1990–92; Dir, Adult Learning Div., 1992–93; Dir, Sheffield First Partnership, 1993–97 (on secondment); Regl Dir, Govt Office for Eastern Reg., 1997–98; Dir, Learning Ops, Univ. for Industry, 1998–99. *Recreations:* birdwatching, music, mountain walking. *Address:* Bar Cottage, Bar Road, Baslow, Derbys DE45 1SF.

LAMBERT, Nigel Robert Woolf; QC 1999; a Recorder, since 1996; *b* 5 Aug. 1949; *s* of Dr E. Vivian Lambert, MB BS, MRCS, LRCP, and Sadie Lambert (*née* Woolf); *m* 1975, Roamie Elisabeth Sado; one *s* one *d*. *Educ:* Cokethorpe Sch., Oxford; Coll. of Law, London. Called to the Bar, Gray's Inn, 1974; *ad eundem* Mem., Inner Temple, 1986. Asst Recorder, 1992–96. Member: Bar Council, 1993–2000 (Member: Professional Standards Cttee, 1993–95, 1997–99; Public Affairs Cttee, 1994; Finance Cttee, 1994; Legal Aid and Fees Cttee, 1996); S Eastern Circuit Cttee, 1992– (Mem. Exec. Cttee, 2001–; Chm., S Eastern Circuit/Inst. of Barristers' Clerks Cttee, 2001–); Criminal Bar Assoc. (Mem., Cttee, 1993–2000); Justice. Chm., N London Bar Mess, 2001–. Gov., Cokethorpe Sch., 1971–78 (Life Vice Pres., Cokethorpe Old Boys' Assoc.). *Recreations:* supervising, organising, gossiping. *Address:* (Chambers) 2–4 Tudor Street, EC4Y 0AA.

LAMBERT, Patricia, OBE 1981; Member, Consumer Panel, Personal Investment Authority, 1995–96; retired; *b* 16 March 1926; *d* of Frederick and Elsie Burrows; *m* 1949, George Richard Lambert (marr. diss. 1983); one *s* one *d*. *Educ:* Malet Lambert High Sch., Hull; West Bridgford Grammar Sch., Nottingham; Nottingham and Dist Technical Coll. Served Royal Signals, Germany, 1944–46; medical technician, 1946–49. British Standards Institution: Member: BSI Bd, 1980–86; Quality Assce Bd, 1986–91; Chm., Consumer Standards Adv. Council, 1980–86; chm. of several technical cttees; Public Interest Dir, Lautro, 1986–94. Member: National Consumer Council, 1978–82; National House Bldg Council, 1980–91; Consumer Affairs Panel, Unit Trust Assoc., 1981–96; Direct Mail Services Standards Bd, 1983–96; Consumer Cttee, PIA, 1994–96. Dir and Vice-Chm., Invest in Britain, 1983–94. Local Govt Councillor, 1959–78. *Recreations:* driving, music, glass engraving. *Address:* 100 Wolds Drive, Keyworth, Nottingham NG12 5FS.

LAMBERT, Sir Peter John Biddulph, 10th Bt *cr* 1711, of London; teacher; *b* 5 April 1952; *s* of John Hugh Lambert (*d* 1977) (*g s* of 5th Bt) and of Edith May, *d* of late James Bance; *S* kinsman, Sir Greville Foley Lambert, 9th Bt, 1988; *m* 1989, Leslie Anne, *d* of R. W. Lyne; one *s* one *d*. *Educ:* Upper Canada Coll., Toronto; Trent Univ. (BSc 1975); Univ. of Manitoba (MA 1980); Univ. of Toronto (BEd). *Heir: s* Thomas Hugh John Lambert, *b* 14 March 1999.

LAMBERT, Captain Richard Edgar, CBE 1982; RN; Vice Lord-Lieutenant, County of Powys, since 1997; *b* 24 Oct. 1929; *s* of Joseph Edgar Hugo Lambert and Mildred Lambert (*née* Mason); *m* 1954, Eleanor Ruth Owen; two *s* one *d*. *Educ:* RNC, Dartmouth; BA Hons Open 1994. RN 1943–82; RCDS 1977; CO, HMS Raleigh, 1978–79. Marconi Underwater Systems, 1982–88. Non-exec. Dir, S and E Wales Ambulance NHS Trust, 1993–97. Dir, Machynlleth Tabernacle Trust, 1986–. President: Côr Meibion Powys, 1989–; Montgomeryshire Area Scout Council, 1997–. DL Powys, 1993. *Recreations:* gardening, music, art, ornithology. *Address:* Garthgwynion, Glaspwll, Machynlleth, Powys SY20 8TX. *T:* (01654) 702128. *Club:* Army and Navy.

LAMBERT, Richard Peter; Editor, Financial Times, 1991–2001; *b* 23 Sept. 1944; *s* of Peter and Mary Lambert; *m* 1973, Harriet Murray-Browne; one *s* one *d*. *Educ:* Fettes Coll.; Balliol Coll., Oxford (BA). Staff of Financial Times, 1966–2001; Lex Column, 1972; Financial Editor, 1978; New York Correspondent, 1982; Dep. Editor, 1983. *Address:* c/o Financial Times, Number One, Southwark Bridge, SE1 9HL.

LAMBERT, Stephen; Director of Programmes, RDF Media, since 1998; *b* 22 March 1959; *s* of Roger Lambert and Monika Lambert (*née* Wagner); *m* 1988, Jenni Russell; one *s* one *d*. *Educ:* Univ. of East Anglia; Nuffield Coll., Oxford. Joined BBC Television, 1983; Producer and Dir, BBC Documentary Features Dept, 1986–94, prog. series incl. 40 Minutes (East Side Story, Dolebusters, Greenfinches, Who'll win Jeanette?, Crack Doctors, Hilary's in Hiding, Malika's Hotel), Inside Story (Children of God, The Missing, Suicide Killers, Dogs of War), and True Brits; Exec. Producer, BBC Documentaries Dept, 1994–99, progs incl. The System (Best Factual Series, RTS), Mersey Blues, The Clampers, Lakesiders, 42 Up, Born in the USSR, Premier Passions, The Day the Guns Fell Silent, The Mayfair Set, The Hunt, The Terror and The Truth, Love Town, Seeking Pleasure, Health Farm; Editor: Modern Times, BBC TV, 1994–98; Real Life, ITV, 1998–2001; Exec. Producer, RDF Media, 1999–, progs incl. Royal Wedding Bells, The Hip Hop Years, Shipwrecked, Love and Money, Together Again, Faking It, Going Native, Dynasties, Tony's People. Mem. Council, BAFTA, 1996–98. Best Commissioning Editor, Broadcast Production Awards, 1996. *Publication:* Channel Four: television with a difference?, 1982. *Recreations:* ski-ing, sailing, walking, cinema, my children. *Address:* RDF Media, 140 Kensington Church Street, W8 4BN. *T:* (020) 7313 6718; *e-mail:* stephen.lambert@rdfmedia.com.

LAMBERT, Susan Barbara, (Mrs J. D. W. Murdoch); Chief Curator, Department of Prints, Drawings and Paintings, Victoria and Albert Museum, since 1989; *b* 24 Jan. 1944; *d* of Alan Percival Lambert and Barbara May Lambert (*née* Herbert); *m* 1990, John Derek Walter Murdoch, *qv*. *Educ:* Downe House; Courtauld Inst. of Art, London Univ. (BA). Department of Prints and Drawings, Victoria and Albert Museum: Res. Asst, 1968–75; Asst Keeper, 1975–79; Dep. Keeper, 1979–89. *Publications:* Printmaking, 1983; Drawing, Technique and Purpose, 1984; The Image Multiplied, 1987; Form Follows Function?, 1993; Prints, Art and Technique, 2001. *Address:* 14 South End Row, W8 5BZ. *T:* (020) 7938 2003.

LAMBERT, Verity Ann; independent film and television producer; Director, Cinema Verity Productions Ltd, since 1985; *b* 27 Nov.; *d* of Stanley Joseph Lambert and Ella Corona Goldburg. *Educ:* Roedean; La Sorbonne, Paris. Joined BBC Television as drama producer, 1963; first producer of Dr Who; also produced: The Newcomers, Somerset Maugham Short Stories (BAFTA Award, 1969), Adam Adamant, Detective; joined LWT as drama producer, 1970: produced Budgie and Between the Wars; returned to BBC, 1973: produced and co-created Shoulder to Shoulder; joined Thames Television as Controller of Drama Dept, 1974 (Dir of Drama, 1981–82; Dir, Thames Television, 1982–85): responsible for: Rock Follies, Rooms, Rumpole of the Bailey, Edward and Mrs Simpson, The Naked Civil Servant (many awards), Last Summer, The Case of Cruelty to Prawns, No Mama No; made creatively responsible for Euston Films Ltd, 1976 (Chief Executive, 1979–82): developed series which included Out and Danger UXB; responsible for: Minder (three series), Quatermass, Fox, The Flame Trees of Thika, Reilly: ace of spies; single films include: Charlie Muffin, Stainless Steel and the Star Spies, The Sailor's Return, The Knowledge; Dir of Prodn, THORN EMI Screen Entertainment, 1982–85: responsible for: Morons from Outer Space, Dreamchild, Restless Natives, Link, Clockwise. Executive Producer: American Roulette, 1987; May to December (5 series, 1989–); So Haunt Me (3 series), 1992–; Producer: A Cry in the Dark, 1988; Coasting, 1990; GBH, 1991; The Boys from the Bush, 1991, 1992; Sleepers, 1991; Comics, 1993; Class Act, 1994, Class Act II, 1995; She's Out, 1995; Heavy Weather, 1995; A Perfect State, 1996; Jonathan Creek, series II, 1998 and III, 1999; (jtly) The Cazalets, 2001. McTaggart Lect., Edinburgh TV Fest., 1990. Governor: BFI, 1981–86 (Fellow, 1998; Chairperson, Prodn Bd, 1981–82); Nat. Film and Television Sch., 1984–. Hon. LLD Strathclyde, 1988. Veuve-Clicquot Businesswoman of 1982; Woman's Own Woman of Achievement, 1983. *Recreations:* reading, eating. *Address:* 11 Addison Avenue, W11 4QS.

LAMBETH, Archdeacon of; *see* Baines, Ven. N.

LAMBIE, David; *b* 13 July 1925; *m* 1954, Netta May Merrie; one *s* four *d*. *Educ:* Kyleshill Primary Sch.; Ardrossan Academy; Glasgow University; Geneva University. BSc, DipEd. Teacher, Glasgow Corp., 1950–70. Chm., Glasgow Local Assoc., Educnl Inst. for Scotland, 1958–59; Chm., Scottish Labour Party, 1964; Chief Negotiator on behalf of Scottish Teachers in STSC, 1969–70; Sec., Westminster Branch, Educnl Inst. for Scotland, 1985–88, 1991–92. MP (Lab) Ayrshire Central, 1970–83, Cunninghame South, 1983–92. Chm., Select Cttee on Scottish Affairs, 1981–87; Sec., Parly All-Party Cttee for Energy Studies, 1980–92; Chm., PLP Aviation Cttee, 1990–92. Chm., Saltcoats Labour Party, 1993–95; Mem., Cunninghame N Constituency Labour Party, 1993–. Chm. Develt Cttee, Cunninghame Housing Assoc., 1992–. Dir, Galloway Training Ltd, 1997–. Member: Council of Europe, 1987–92; WEU, 1987–92. FEIS 1970. *Recreation:* watching football. *Address:* 11 Ivanhoe Drive, Saltcoats, Ayrshire KA21 6LS. *T:* (01294) 464843. *Club:* Cunninghame North Constituency Labour Social (Saltcoats).

LAMBIE-NAIRN, Martin John, RDI 1987; FCSD; Founder, and Creative Director, Lambie-Nairn, Corporate Identity Specialists (formerly Lambie-Nairn and Co.), since 1976 (Chairman, 1976–97); *b* 5 Aug. 1945; *s* of Stephen John and Joan Lois Lambie-Nairn; *m* 1970, Cordelia Margot Summers; one *s* two *d*. *Educ:* King Ethelbert Sch., Birchington, Kent; Canterbury Coll. of Art. NDD. Asst Designer, Graphic Design Dept, BBC, 1965; Designer, Rediffusion, 1966; freelance graphic designer, 1967; Art Dir, Conran Associates, 1968; Dep. to Sen. Designer, ITN, overseeing changeover from black and white to colour tv, 1968; Designer, LWT, working on light entertainment, drama and current affairs progs, 1970; formed Robinson Lambie-Nairn Ltd, design consultancy producing film and TV graphics, corporate identity, packaging and financial lit., 1976; work includes Channel 4 TV corporate identity, 1982, develt of original idea for Spitting Image, 1984, Anglia TV corporate identity, 1988, TFI (France) corporate identity, 1989, BBC1 and BBC2 channel identities, 1991, Carlton Television corporate identity, 1993, Orange (Sky NZ) channel identity, and ARTE corporate identity, 1995, BBC corporate identity, 1997–, New Millennium Experience corporate identity, 1998, BAE SYSTEMS corporate identity, 1999. Creative Dir, NTL, 2001–. Mem. Cttee, D & AD, 1985– (Pres., 1990–91; Chm., Corporate Identity Jury, 2000); Chm., Graphics Jury, BBC Design Awards, 1987. FCSD (FSIAD 1982). Hon. Fellow, Kent Inst. of Art and Design, 1994. Jt winner, BAFTA Craft Awards (for excellence in craft of graphics), 1991; RTS Judges' Award, 1996; President's Award, D&AD, 1997; Prince Philip Designers' Prize, 1998. *Publication:* Brand Identity for Television with Knobs On, 1997. *Recreations:* opera, family, France. *Address:* Lambie-Nairn, Greencoat House, Francis Street, SW1P 1DH.

LAMBIRTH, Mark Nicholas; Director of Local Government Finance, Department for Transport, Local Government and the Regions (formerly Local Government Finance Policy, Department of the Environment, Transport and the Regions), since 1998; *b* 30 May 1953; *s* of Peter Mabson Lambirth and Jean Margaret Lambirth; *m* 1986, Anne Catherine Wood. *Educ:* St Albans Sch.; Queens' Coll., Cambridge. Price Commn, 1975; entered Civil Service, 1977; Department of Transport, 1983–95: Ministerial speechwriter and Dep. Head, Inf. Div., 1988–89; Asst. Sec., 1989; Head, Public Transport in London Div., 1989–92; Head, Central Finance Div., 1992–95; Under-Sec., 1995; Dir of Planning and Transport, Govt Office for London, 1995–98. *Recreations:* poetry, cooking, wine. *Address:* Local and Regional Government Group, Department for Transport, Local Government and the Regions, Eland House, Bressenden Place, SW1E 5DU. *T:* (020) 7890 4060. *Club:* MCC.

LAMBO, Prof. Thomas Adeoye, NNOM 1979; CON 1979; OBE 1962; MD, DPM; FRCP; JP; Deputy Director-General, World Health Organization, 1973–88 (Assistant Director-General, 1971–73); Executive Director, Lambo Foundation, since 1988; *b* 29 March 1923; *s* of Chief D. B. Lambo, The Otunbade of Igbore, Abeokuta, and Madam F. B. Lambo, The Iyalode of Egba Christians; *m* 1945, Dinah Violet Adams; three *s*. *Educ:* Baptist Boys' High Sch., Abeokuta; Univs of Birmingham and London. From 1949, served as House Surg. and House Phys., Birmingham, England; Med. Officer, Lagos, Zaria and Gusau; Specialist, Western Region Min. of Health, 1957–60; Consultant Psychiatrist, UCH Ibadan, 1956–63; Sen. Specialist, Western Region Min. of Health, Neuro-Psychiatric Centre, 1960–63; Prof. of Psychiatry and Head of Dept of Psychiatry and Neurology, Univ. of Ibadan, 1963–71; Dean, Medical Faculty, Univ. of Ibadan, 1966–68; Vice-Chancellor, Univ. of Ibadan, 1968–71. Member: Scientific Council for Africa (Chm., 1965–70); Expert Adv. Panel on Mental Health, WHO, 1959–71; UN Perm. Adv. Cttee on Prevention of Crime and the Treatment of Offenders (Chm. 1968–71); Exec. Cttee, World Fedn for Mental Health, 1964–; Scientific Adv. Panel, Ciba Foundn, 1966–; WHO Adv. Cttee on Med. Research, 1970–71; Scientific Cttee on Advanced Study in Developmental Sciences, 1967–; Nigeria Medical Council, 1969–; Scientific Council of the World Future Studies Fedn, 1975–; World Soc. for Ekistics (Pres., 1979–81); Adv. Bd, Earthscan, 1975–; Bd of Dirs, Internat. Inst. for Envmt and Develt, 1986–; Vice-Chm., UN Adv. Cttee on Application of Science and Technology to Development, 1970–71; Co-Chm., Internat. Soc. for Study of Human Development, 1968–; Chairman: West African Examinations Council, 1969–71, co-ordinating Bd, African Chairs of Technology in Food Processing, Biotechnologies and Nutrition and Health, 1986–, etc. Founding Member: Third World Acad. of Scis, 1986–; African Acad. of Scis, 1986–. Member: Pontifical Acad. of Sciences, 1974– (first African Life Mem., 1982); Internat. Inst. for World Resources, Washington. Patron, Nigerian Assoc. of Gen. and Pvte Med. Practitioners, 1999. Hon. Fellow: RCPsych, 1970 (Founding Fellow); Royal Australian and NZ Coll. of Psychiatrists. JP Western State, 1968. Hon. LLD: Kent State, Ohio, 1969; Birmingham 1971; Pennsylvania, Philadelphia; Hon. DSc: Ahmadu Bello, Nigeria; Long Island, NY, 1975; McGill, Canada, 1978; Jos, Nigeria, 1979; Nigeria, Nsukka, 1979; Hacettepe, Ankara, 1980; Hahnemann, Philadelphia, 1984; Dr *hc* Benin, 1973; Aix-Marseille, France, 1974; Louvain, Belgium, 1976. Haile Selassie African Res. Award, 1970; Leader of Psychiatry Award, World Psychiatric Assoc., 1999. *Publications:* (jtly) Psychiatric Disorders Among the Yorubas, 1963; monographs, and contribs to medical and other scientific jls. *Recreation:* tennis. *Address:* Lambo Foundation, 15 Olatunbosun Street, PO Box 702, Maryland Estate, Ikeja, Lagos State, Nigeria. *T:* (1) 4976110, *T:* and *Fax:* (home) (1) 4976110; *e-mail:* talambo@beta.linkserve.com.

LAMBTON, family name of **Earldom of Durham.**

LAMBTON, Viscount; Antony Claud Frederick Lambton; *b* 10 July 1922; *s* of 5th Earl of Durham (*d* 1970) and Diana (*d* 1924), *o d* of Granville Farquhar; disclaimed peerages for life, 1970 but allowed by Mr Speaker Lloyd to continue to sit in Parliament using courtesy title; *m* 1942, Belinda, *d* of Major D. H. Blew-Jones, Westward Ho!, North Devonshire; one *s* five *d*. MP (C) Berwick upon Tweed Div. of Northumberland, 1951–73; Parly Under-Sec. of State, MoD, 1970–May 1973; PPS to the Foreign Secretary, 1955–57. *Publications:* Snow and Other Stories, 1983; Elizabeth and Alexandra, 1985; The Abbey in the Wood, 1986; The Mountbattens, 1989; Pig and Other Stories, 1990. *Heir to disclaimed peerages: s* Hon. Edward Richard Lambton (Baron Durham) [*b* 19 Oct. 1961; *m* 1st, 1983, Christabel (marr. diss.), *y d* of late Rory McEwen and of Mrs McEwen, Bardrochat; one *s*; 2nd, 1995, Catherine, *e d* of D. J. V. Fitz-Gerald, *qv*]. *Address:* Villa Cetinale, Sovicille, Siena, Italy; Biddick Hall, Chester-le-Street, Co. Durham.

See also L. Lambton, Sir P. V. Naylor-Leyland, Bt, Sir P. G. Worsthorne.

LAMBTON, Prof. Ann Katharine Swynford, OBE 1942; FBA 1964; Professor of Persian, University of London, 1953–79, now Emeritus; *b* 8 Feb. 1912; *d* of late Hon. George Lambton. PhD London, 1939; DLit London, 1953. Press Attaché, British Embassy (formerly Legation), Tehran, 1939–45; Senior Lecturer in Persian, School of Oriental and African Studies, 1945–48; Reader in Persian, University of London, 1948–53. Hon. Fellow: New Hall, Cambridge, 1973; SOAS, Univ. of London, 1983. Hon. DLit Durham, 1971; Hon. LittD Cambridge, 1973. Reader Emeritus, dio. of Newcastle, 1988. *Publications:* Three Persian Dialects, 1938; Landlord and Peasant in Persia, 1953; Persian Grammar, 1953; Persian Vocabulary, 1964; The Persian Land Reform 1962–66, 1969; (ed, with others) The Cambridge History of Islam, vols 1–11, 1971; Theory and Practice in Medieval Persian Government, 1980; State and Government in Medieval Islam, 1981; Qajar Persia, 1987; Continuity and Change in Medieval Persia, 1988. *Address:* Gregory, Kirknewton, Wooler, Northumberland NE71 6XE.

LAMBTON, Lucinda; photographer and writer, since 1960; broadcaster, since 1983; *b* 10 May 1943; *e d* of Viscount Lambton, *qv*; *m* 1st, 1965, Henry Mark Harrod (marr. diss. 1973); two *s*; 2nd, 1986, Sir Edmund Fairfax-Lucy, *qv* (marr. diss. 1989); 3rd, 1991, Sir Peregrine Worsthorne, *qv*. *Educ:* Queensgate Sch., London. Television series include: Hurray for Today, 1989; Hurray for Today, USA, 1990; Lucinda Lambton's Alphabet of Britain (3 series), 1990; Old New World, 2001. Lectures throughout Britain on subjects researched for broadcasts and publications. Hon. FRIBA 1997. *Publications:* Vanishing

Victoriana, 1976; Temples of Convenience, 1978, 2nd edn 1995; Chambers of Delight, 1983; Beastly Buildings, 1985; An Album of Curious Houses, 1988; (ed) Magnificent Menagerie (anthology), 1992; Lucinda Lambton's Alphabet of Britain, 1996; Old New World, 2000. *Recreations:* talking to dogs and taking them for walks, pre-1960s movies. *Address:* The Old Rectory, Hedgerley, Bucks SL2 3UY. *T:* (01753) 646167.

LAMBURN, Patricia, (Mrs Donald Derrick), CBE 1985; Editorial Director, IPC Magazines Ltd, 1981–86; Director, IPC,1968–86; *er d* of Francis John Lamburn and Nell Winifred (*née* Kennedy); *m* 1949, Donald G. E. Douglas Derrick, DDS, LDSRCS, FRCD(Can.), FACD, FICD; one *s* one *d. Educ:* Queen's Gate Sch., S Kensington. Amalgamated Press, 1943–49; Curtis Publishing Co., USA, 1949–50; joined George Newnes Ltd, 1950; during ensuing yrs, edited, developed and was associated creatively with wide range of women's and teenage magazines; Dir, George Newnes Ltd, 1966–68; Gp Dir, Young Magazines Gp, 1968–71; Publishing Dir, Women's Magazines Gp, 1971–76, Asst Man. Dir (Editorial), 1976–81. Mem., Interim Licensing Authority for In Vitro Fertilisation and Embryology, 1986–91. Chm., Gen. Adv. Council, IBA, 1982–85 (Mem., 1980–82); Member: Health Educn Council, 1973–78; Editl Cttee, PPA, 1975–87; Information Cttee, British Nutrition Foundn, 1979–85; Periodical Publishing Trng Cttee, PPITB, 1980–82; Public Relations Cttee, RCP, 1981–88; Press Council, 1982–87; HFEA Inspectorate, 1991–94. Trustee, CancerBACUP, 1993–2000 (Mem. Exec. Cttee, 1986–93). Mem., Chelsea Crime Prevention Panel, 1990–95. *Address:* Chelsea, London.

LAMER, Rt Hon. Antonio; PC (Can.) 1990; CC; Chief Justice of Canada, 1990–2000; with Stikeman Elliott, Barristers and Solicitors, since 2000; *b* 8 July 1933; *m*; one *s*; *m* 1987, Danièle Tremblay; one step *s* one step *d. Educ:* Univ. of Montreal. Called to the Bar, Quebec, 1957; private practice, Cutler, Lamer, Bellemare & Associates; Prof., Faculty of Law, Univ. of Montreal; Judge, Superior Court and Queen's Bench, Province of Quebec, 1969–78; Chm., Law Reform Commn of Canada, 1976 (Vice-Chm., 1971); Justice, Quebec Court of Appeal, 1978–80; Justice, Supreme Court of Canada, 1980–90. Associate Prof. of Law, Univ. of Montreal, 2000–. Dir, Canadian Human Rights Foundn, 1974. Pres., Soc. de Criminologie, Québec, 1974. Chairman: Adv. Council, Historica Foundn; Bd of Dirs, Les Rendez-vous de la francophonie. Hon. Col, 2nd Field Regt of Canada; Vice-Pres., Nat. Council of Hon. Cols and Lt-Cols (Pres., Land Force, Quebec Area). DU Saint Paul, 2001. KStJ 1993. Order of Merit, Univ. of Montreal, 1991. Silver Jubilee Medal, 1977; Canadian Confedn 125th Anniv. Medal, 1992. *Address:* Stikeman Elliott, 50 O'Connor Street, Suite 1600, Ottawa, ON K1P 6L2, Canada.

LAMFALUSSY, Baron Alexandre; President, European Monetary Institute, 1994–97; *b* 26 April 1929; *cr* Baron, 1993; *m* 1957, Anne-Marie Cochard; two *s* two *d. Educ:* Catholic Univ., Louvain (economics degree); Nuffield Coll., Oxford (PhD). Banque de Bruxelles: economist, 1955–61; Economic Advr, 1962; Exec. Dir, later Chm., Exec. Bd, 1965–76; Bank for International Settlements, Basle: Economic Advr, 1976–80; Asst Gen. Manager, 1981; Gen. Manager, 1985–93. Vis Lectr, Yale, 1961–62. Hon. doctorates: Univ. Lumière-Lyon, 1987; Inst. d'Etudes Politiques, Paris, 1993. *Publications:* Investment and Growth in Mature Economies, 1961; The UK and the Six, 1963; Les marchés financiers en Europe, 1968; The Restructuring of the Financial Industry, 1992; The Per Jacobsson Lecture, 1994. *Recreations:* hiking, sailing. *Address:* c/o European Monetary Institute, Eurotower, Kaiserstrasse 29, 60311 Frankfurt, Germany. *T:* (69) 272270.

LAMFORD, (Thomas) Gerald, OBE 1979; ASVU Representative, Cyprus, 1985–88; Commandant, Police Staff College, 1976–79; *b* Carmarthen, 3 April 1928; *s* of late Albert and Sarah Lamford; *m* 1952, Eira Hale; one *s* one *d. Educ:* Technical Coll., Swansea; London Univ. (LLB 1969); Police Coll. (Intermed. Comd Course, 1969; Sen. Comd Course, 1973). Radio Officer, Merchant Navy, 1945; Wireless Operator, RAF, 1946–48, Aden. Carmarthenshire Constab. (now Dyfed Powys Police), 1949; reached rank of Chief Inspector, CID, Crime Squad; Force Trng Officer, 1965–69; Supt, Haverfordwest, 1970; Chief Supt, Llanelli, 1971–74; Asst Chief Constable, Greater Manchester Police, 1974–79; Investigating Officer, FCO, 1981–84. Vis. Prof. of Police Science, John Jay Coll. of Criminal Justice, City Univ. of New York, 1972; sometime Vis. Lecturer: Southern Police Inst., Univ. of Louisville, Ky; N Eastern Univ., Boston; NY Univ. Sch. of Law; Rutgers Univ., NJ; Mercy Coll., Detroit. County Comr, St John Amb. Bde, Pembrokeshire, 1970; SBStJ. Mem., Probus Club, Ammanford (Pres., 1996). *Publications:* The Defence of Lucy Walter, 2001; articles in Police Studies, Internat. Rev. of Police Devel t, Police Rev., Bramshill Jl, World Police. *Recreations:* photography, genealogy. *Address:* 11 Llwyn y Bryn, Ammanford SA18 2ES.

LAMING, Baron *cr* 1998 (Life Peer), of Tewin in the co. of Hertfordshire; **William Herbert Laming,** Kt 1996; CBE 1985; DL; Chief Inspector, Social Services Inspectorate, Department of Health, 1991–98; *b* 19 July 1936; *s* of William Angus Laming and Lillian Laming (*née* Robson); *m* 1962, Aileen Margaret Pollard. *Educ:* Univ. of Durham (Applied Social Scis); Rainer House (Home Office Probation Trng, 1960–61); LSE (Mental Health Course, 1965–66). Notts Probation Service: Probation Officer, 1961–66; Sen. Probation Officer, 1966–68; Asst Chief Probation Officer, Nottingham City and Co. Probation Service, 1968–71; Dep. Dir, 1971–75, Dir, 1975–91, Social Services, Herts CC. Pres., Assoc. of Dirs Social Services, 1982–83. DL Hertford, 1999. *Publications:* Lessons from America: the balance of services in social care, 1985; contribs to professional jls. *Address:* 1 Firs Walk, Tewin Wood, Welwyn, Herts AL6 0NY. *T:* (01438) 798574.

LAMMIMAN, Surg. Rear Adm. David Askey, CB 1993; LVO 1978; FFARCS; Medical Director General (Naval), 1990–93; Deputy Surgeon General: Health Services, 1990–91; Operations and Plans, 1991–93; *b* 30 June 1932; *s* of Herbert Askey Lammiman and Lilian Elsie (*née* Park); *m* 1st, 1957, Sheila Mary Graham (marr. diss. 1984); three *s* one *d*; 2nd, 1984, Caroline Dale Brooks. *Educ:* Wyggeston Sch., Leicester; St Bartholomew's Hosp. (MB, BS 1957). DA 1962; DObstRCOG 1962; FFARCS 1969. Resident House Officer, Redhill County Hosp. and St Bartholomew's Hosp., 1957–58; joined RN, 1959; gen. service and hosp. appts at home and abroad; Clinical Asst, Southampton Gp of Hosps, Alder Hey Children's Hosp., Liverpool, and Radcliffe Infirmary, Oxford, 1966–69; served in: HMS Chaplet, 1959; HMS Eagle, 1967–68; HMY Britannia, 1976–78; Consultant Anaesthetist, RN Hospital: Malta, 1969–71; Haslar, 1971–73; Gibraltar, 1973–75; Plymouth, 1975–76; Haslar, 1978–82; Dir of Med. Personnel, MoD, 1982–84; Medical Officer i/c RN Hospital: Plymouth, 1984–86; Haslar, 1986–88; Surg. Rear Adm. (Support Med. Services), 1989–90. QHS 1987–93. *Recreations:* fly fishing, golf, tennis. *Club:* Flyfishers'.

LAMMY, David Lindon; MP (Lab) Tottenham, since June 2000; *b* 19 July 1972; *s* of David and Rosalind Lammy. *Educ:* King's Sch., Peterborough; SOAS, London Univ. (LLB Hons 1993); Harvard Law Sch. (LLM 1997). Called to the Bar, Lincoln's Inn; Attorney, Howard Rice, Calif, 1997–98; with D. J. Freeman, 1998–2000. Mem. (Lab), London Assembly, GLA, May–June 2000. PPS to Sec. of State for Educn and Skills, 2001–. Member: Procedure Cttee, 2001; Public Admin Cttee, 2001. Member: Gen. Synod, C of E, 1999–; Archbishops' Council, 1999–. Trustee, Actionaid, 2001–. *Recreations:* film, live music, Spurs FC, watching Match of the Day. *Address:* c/o House of Commons, SW1A 0AA. *T:* (020) 7219 0767. *Club:* Home House.

LAMOND, James Alexander; JP, DL; *b* Burrelton, Perthshire, 29 Nov. 1928; *s* of Alexander N. G. Lamond and Christina Lamond (*née* Craig); *m* 1954, June Rose Wellburn; three *d. Educ:* Burrelton Sch.; Coupar Angus Sch. Draughtsman. Mem., Aberdeen City Council, 1959–71; Lord Provost of Aberdeen, 1970–71; Lord Lieutenant of the County of the City of Aberdeen, 1970–71. MP (Lab) Oldham East, 1970–83, Oldham Central and Royton, 1983–92; Mem., Chairmen's Panel, 1979–92. Member (Lab): Grampian Regl Council, 1994–96; Aberdeen CC, 1995– (Convenor: Planning and Strategic Develt Cttee, 1995–99; Standards and Scrutiny Cttee, 1999–). Chm., Aberdeen Exhibition and Conf. Centre Ltd, 1996–. Mem., MSF (formerly TASS), 1944– (Chm., No 1 Divisional Council of DATA, 1965–70); Sec., Aberdeen Trades Council, 1994–98 (Pres., 1969). JP Aberdeen, 1967; DL Aberdeen, 1995. *Recreations:* golf, travel, reading, thinking. *Address:* 15 Belvidere Street, Aberdeen AB25 2QS. *T:* (01224) 638074.

LAMONT, family name of **Baron Lamont of Lerwick**.

LAMONT OF LERWICK, Baron *cr* 1998 (Life Peer), of Lerwick in the Shetland Islands; **Norman Stewart Hughson Lamont;** PC 1986; politician, writer and company director; *b* Lerwick, Shetland, 8 May 1942; *s* of late Daniel Lamont and of Helen Irene; *m* 1971, Alice Rosemary White; one *s* one *d. Educ:* Loretto Sch. (scholar); Fitzwilliam Coll., Cambridge (BA). Chm., Cambridge Univ. Conservative Assoc., 1963; Pres., Cambridge Union, 1964. PA to Rt Hon. Duncan Sandys, MP, 1965; Conservative Research Dept, 1966–68; Merchant Banker, N. M. Rothschild & Sons, 1968–79; Dir, Rothschild Asset Mgt, 1978. Non-exec. Dir, N. M. Rothschild & Sons, 1993–95; Director: Balli Gp Plc, 1995–; Cie Internat. de Participations Bancaires et Financières, 1999–; Banca Commerciala Robank, 2000–; European Growth and Income Trust, 2000–; Chairman: E European Food Fund; Archipelago Fund, 1995–2000. Advr, Monsanto Corp., 1994–99. Contested (C) East Hull, Gen. Election, 1970. MP (C) Kingston-upon-Thames, May 1972–97; contested (C) Harrogate and Knaresborough, 1997. PPS to Norman St John-Stevas, MP, Minister for the Arts, 1974; an Opposition Spokesman on: Prices and Consumer Affairs, 1975–76; Industry, 1976–79; Parly Under Sec. of State, Dept of Energy, 1979–81; Minister of State, DTI (formerly DoI), 1981–85; Minister of State for Defence Procurement, 1985–86; Financial Sec. to HM Treasury, 1986–89; Chief Sec. to HM Treasury, 1989–90; Chancellor of the Exchequer, 1990–93. Chairman: G7 Gp of Finance Ministers, 1991; EU Finance Ministers, 1992; Advr to Romanian Govt on privatisation, 1995–97. Mem., H of L Select Cttee on EU, 1999–. Chairman: Coningsby Club, 1970–71; Bow Group, 1971–72; Conservatives Against a Federal Europe, 1998–99; Vice-Pres., Bruges Gp, 1994–. *Publications:* Sovereign Britain, 1995; In Office, 1999. *Recreations:* books, ornithology, music, theatre. *Address:* c/o Balli Group Plc, 5 Stanhope Gate, W1K 1AH. *T:* (020) 7306 2000. *Clubs:* Garrick, Beefsteak, White's.

LAMONT, Donald Alexander; HM Diplomatic Service; Governor, Falkland Islands, and Commissioner for South Georgia and South Sandwich Islands, since 1999; *b* 13 Jan. 1947; *s* of Alexander Lamont and Alexa Lee Lamont (*née* Will); *m* 1981, Lynda Margaret Campbell; one *s* one *d. Educ:* Aberdeen Grammar Sch.; Aberdeen Univ. (MA Russian Studies). British Leyland Motor Corp., 1970; Second Sec., subseq. First Sec., FCO, 1974; First Sec., UNIDO/IAEA, Vienna, 1977; First Sec. (Commercial), Moscow, 1980; First Sec., FCO, 1982; Counsellor on secondment to IISS, 1988; Political Advr and Head of Chancery, British Mil. Govt, Berlin, 1988–91; Ambassador to Uruguay, 1991–94; Hd of Republic of Ireland Dept, FCO, 1994–97; COS and Dep. High Rep., Sarajevo, 1997–99. *Address:* c/o Foreign and Commonwealth Office, SW1A 2AH. *Clubs:* Caledonian, Royal Commonwealth Society.

LAMONT, Johann MacDougall; Member (Lab) Glasgow Pollok, Scottish Parliament, since 1999; *b* 11 July 1957; *y d* of Archie Lamont and Effie Lamont (*née* Macleod); *m* Archie Graham; one *s* one *d. Educ:* Univ. of Glasgow (MA Hons); Jordanhill Coll. of Educn (postgrad. secondary teaching qualification). Secondary School teacher, 1979–99. Mem., EIS, 1979–. *Recreations:* running, watching football, doing crosswords, enjoying time with my children. *Address:* Scottish Parliament, Edinburgh EH99 1SP.

LAMONTAGNE, Hon. (J.) Gilles, OC 1991; CD 1980; PC (Can.); Lieutenant-Governor of Quebec, 1984–90; *b* 17 April 1919; *s* of Trefflé Lamontagne and Anna Kieffer; *m* 1949, Mary Katherine Schaefer; three *s* one *d. Educ:* Collège Jean-de-Brébœuf, Montréal, Québec (BA). Served RCAF, 1941–45 (despatches, 1945). Businessman in Québec City, 1946–66. Alderman, Québec City, 1962–64, Mayor, 1965–77. MP (L) Langelier, 1977–84; Parly Sec. to Minister of Energy, Mines and Resources, 1977; Minister without Portfolio, Jan. 1978; Postmaster Gen., Feb. 1978–1979; Actg Minister of Veterans Affairs, 1980–81; Minister of National Defence, 1980–83. Dir, Québec City Chamber of Commerce and Industry; Member: Econ. Council of Canada; Br. 260, Royal Canadian Legion (Grand Pres., 1991–94). Consultant, GPC Relations gouvernementales (formerly GPC Consilium), 1992–. Mem. Bd, Canadian Centre of Substance Abuse, 1991–95. Chm. Bd, Royal Mil. Coll., Kingston, Canada, 1996–2000. Hon. Col, Tactical Aviation Wing (Montreal), 1987. KStJ 1985. Hon. LLD Kingston Royal Mil. Coll., 1986; Hon. DAdmin St Jean Royal Mil. Coll., 1989. UN Medal 1987. Croix du Combattant de l'Europe. *Address:* 8 Jardins Mérici # 1405, QC G1S 4N9, Canada. *Clubs:* Cercle de la Garrison de Québec, Royal Québec Golf.

LAMPERT, Catherine Emily; Director, Whitechapel Art Gallery, 1988–2001; *b* 15 Oct. 1946; *d* of Emily F. Schubach and Chester G. Lampert; *m* 1971, Robert Keith Mason (marr. diss. 1994); one adopted *d. Educ:* Brown Univ. (BA); Temple Univ. (MFA). UCL, 1966–67; Asst Curator, RI Sch. of Design, Mus. of Art, 1968–69; Studio Internat., 1971–72; Sen. Exhibn Organiser, Hayward Gall., 1973–88. Curator, Frank Auerbach: painting and drawing 1954–2001, RA, Paris and tour, 2001–02. *Publications:* Rodin: sculpture and drawings, 1986; Lucian Freud: recent work, 1993; numerous catalogue essays on Frank Auerbach, Barry Flanagan, Tony Cragg, Francisco Toledo and other subjects of Twentieth Century art. *Address:* 92 Lenthall Road, E8 3JN. *T:* (020) 7249 7650.

LAMPL, Sir Frank (William), Kt 1990; Executive Director, Peninsular and Oriental Steam Navigation Company, 1985–99; Chairman, Bovis Construction Group, 1989–2000; President, Bovis Lend Lease Holding, since 2000 (Chairman, 1999–2000); *b* Czechoslovakia, 6 April 1926; adopted British nationality, 1974; *s* of Dr Otto Lampl and Olga (*née* Jelinek); *m* 1948, Blanka (*née* Kratochvílová); one *s. Educ:* Univ. of Brno, Czechoslovakia (Dip Eng, Faculty of Architecture and Engineering). Emigrated from Czechoslovakia to UK, 1968, after Russian invasion, Exec. Dir, Bovis Construction, 1974; Man. Dir, Bovis International, 1978; Dir, Bovis, 1979; Chm., Bovis Construction and Bovis International, 1985; Dep. Chm., Lehrer MacGovern-Bovis, NY, 1987. First Chancellor, Kingston Univ., 1994–2000. FCIOB 1973 (Pres.'s Gold Medal, 1993); FAPM 1973; CIMgt. Hon. DEng Technical Univ., Brno, 1993; Dr *hc* Kingston, 1994; Hon. DSc Reading Univ., 1995. *Recreation:* reading. *Address:* Bovis Lend Lease, 127 Sloane Street, SW1X 9BA. *T:* (020) 8422 3488. *Clubs:* Athenæum, Royal Automobile.

LAMPL, Peter, OBE 2000; Chairman, Sutton Trust, since 1997; *b* 21 May 1947; *s* of Frederick and Margaret Lampl; *m* 1st, 1976, Janet Clowes (marr. diss. 1980); 2nd, 1994,

Karen Gordon; one *s* two *d*. *Educ:* Reigate Grammar Sch.; Cheltenham Grammar Sch.; Corpus Christi Coll., Oxford (BA, MA; Hon. Fellow, 1998); London Business Sch. (MBA). Mktg Exec., Beecham Gp, London, 1970–71; Mgt Consultant, Boston Consulting Gp, Boston, Paris, Munich, 1973–77; Dir, Planning and Business Develt, Internat. Paper, NY, then Pres., Internat. Paper Realty, 1977–83; Founder, Pres., then Chm., Sutton Co. (private equity firm), NY, London, Munich, 1983–97; Sutton Trust, 1997– (provides educnl opportunities for bright young people from non-privileged backgrounds). Ind. Advr to govt on access to higher educn, 2000–. Hon. DSc Nottingham, 1999; Hon Dr jur Bristol, 2001. *Recreations:* golf, tennis, ski-ing, swimming, body surfing, opera. *Address:* The Sutton Trust, Heritage House, 21 Inner Park Road, Wimbledon, SW19 6ED. *T:* (020) 8788 3223. *Clubs:* Queen's, Hurlingham, Royal Automobile, Roehampton; Wisley Golf (Surrey); Westchester Country (NY).

LAMPORT, Stephen Mark Jeffrey, CVO 1999; HM Diplomatic Service; Private Secretary and Treasurer to the Prince of Wales, since 1996; *b* 27 Nov. 1951; *s* of Eric and Jeanne Lamport; *m* 1979, Angela Vivien Paula Hervey; two *s* one *d*. *Educ:* Dorking Co. Grammar Sch.; Corpus Christi Coll., Cambridge (Schol., MA); Sussex Univ. (MA). Entered HM Diplomatic Service, 1974: UK Mission to UN, 1974; Tehran, 1975–79; FCO, 1979–84; Private Secretary to Minister of State, 1981–84; First Sec., Rome, 1984–88; FCO, 1988–93; Dep. Private Sec. to the Prince of Wales, 1993–96. *Publication:* (with D. Hurd) The Palace of Enchantments, 1985. *Address:* St James's Palace, SW1A 1BS. *Clubs:* Royal Automobile, Grillion's.

LAMPSON, family name of **Baron Killearn**.

LAMY, Pascal Lucien Fernand; Member, European Commission, since 1999; *b* 8 April 1947; *s* of Jacques Lamy and Denise (*née* Dujardin); *m* 1972, Geneviève Luchaire; three *s*. *Educ:* Ecole des Hautes Etudes Commerciales; Inst d'Etudes Politiques, Paris; Ecole Nat. d'Admin. Inspector-Gen. of Finances, 1975–79; French Treasury, 1979–81; Advr to Minister for Econ. Affairs and Finance, 1981–83; Dep. Hd, Prime Minister's Pvte Office, 1983–84; Head, Pvte Office of Pres. of EC, 1985–94; with Crédit Lyonnais, 1994–, Dir Gen., 1999. Mem. Steering Cttee, Socialist Party of France, 1985–94. Officier, Légion d'Honneur, 1999. *Address:* European Commission, 200 rue de la Loi, 1049 Brussels, Belgium.

LANCASTER, Bishop Suffragan of, since 1998; **Rt Rev. (Geoffrey) Stephen Pedley;** *b* 13 Sept. 1940; *s* of Geoffrey Heber Knight and Muriel Pedley; *m* 1970, Mary Frances Macdonald; two *s* one *d*. *Educ:* Marlborough College; Queens' College, Cambridge (MA); Cuddesdon Theological College. Curate: Liverpool Parish Church, 1966; Holy Trinity, Coventry, 1969; Rector of Kitwe, Zambia, 1971–77; Vicar of St Peter's, Stockton, 1977–88; Rector, Whickham, 1988–93; Residentiary Canon, Durham Cathedral, 1993–98. Chaplain to the Queen, 1984–98. *Recreations:* architecture, English literature, travel. *Address:* The Vicarage, Shireshead, Forton, Preston PR3 0AE. *T:* (01524) 799900.

LANCASTER, Bishop of, (RC), since 2001; **Rt Rev. Patrick O'Donoghue;** *b* 4 May 1934; *s* of Daniel O'Donoghue and Sheila O'Donoghue (*née* Twomey). *Educ:* St Edmund's Coll., Ware, Herts. Ordained priest, 1967; Asst priest, Willesden, 1967–70; Mem., Diocesan Mission Team, Westminster, 1970–73; Pastoral Dir, Allen Hall, 1973–78; Asst Administrator, Westminster Cathedral, 1978–85; Rector, Allen Hall, 1985–91; Administrator, Westminster Cathedral, 1991–93; Auxiliary Bishop of Westminster (Bishop in W London), 1993–2001. *Recreations:* football, theatre, country walking, the Arts. *Address:* Bishop's House, Cannon Hill, Lancaster LA1 5NG.

LANCASTER, Archdeacon of; *see* Williams, Ven. C. H.

LANCASTER, Margaret Elizabeth; *see* Douglas, M. E.

LANCASTER, Patricia Margaret; Headmistress, Wycombe Abbey School, 1974–88; a Church Commissioner, 1989–98; *b* 22 Feb. 1929; *d* of Vice-Adm. Sir John Lancaster, KBE, CB. *Educ:* Univs of London (BA) and Southampton (Certif. Educn). English Mistress, St Mary's Sch., Calne, 1951–58; Housemistress, St Swithun's Sch., Winchester, 1958–62; Headmistress, St Michael's, Burton Park, Petworth, 1962–73. Pres., Girls' Schools' Assoc., 1979–80. Governor: Berkhamsted Sch., 1989–97; Marlborough Coll., 1989–96; Repton Sch., 1989–95; St Mary's Sch., Calne, 1989–97; St Swithun's Sch., Winchester, 1989–96. *Recreations:* theatre, art galleries, gardening. *Address:* 8 Vectis Road, Alverstoke, near Gosport, Hants PO12 2QF.

LANCE, Seán Patrick; Chairman and Chief Executive, Chiron Corporation, 1998–99; *b* 4 Aug. 1947; *s* of James Lance and Kathleen (*née* Carmody); *m* 1st, 1969, Pamela Joan Gray (marr. diss. 1990); two *s* two *d*; 2nd, 1990, Patricia Anne (*née* Bungay). *Educ:* Christian Brothers Coll., Pretoria. Noristan Gp, S Africa, 1967–82; Chm., Boots Co., S Africa, 1982–85; Man. Dir, Glaxo, S Africa, 1985–87; Regl Dir (London), Glaxo Hldgs plc, 1987–89; Man. Dir, Glaxo Pharms UK Ltd, 1989–93; Dir, Glaxo Hldgs plc, 1993–97; Chief Operating Officer, Glaxo Wellcome plc, 1997. President: Proprietary Assoc. of S Africa, 1983–84; Pharmaceutical Manufacturers Assoc. of S Africa, 1987–88; Internat. Fedn of Pharmaceut. Manufacturers Assoc., 1996–; Vice-Pres., Assoc. of British Pharmaceutical Industry, 1993–94. Special Forces, S Africa, 1965–76. *Recreations:* hockey, golf, football, cricket, Kyukoshin karate (2nd Dan). *Clubs:* Special Forces; Harlequins, Pretoria Country (Pretoria); Richmond Hockey.

LANCELOT, James Bennett, FRCO; Master of the Choristers and Organist, Durham Cathedral, since 1985; *b* 2 Dec. 1952; *s* of late Rev. Roland Lancelot; *m* 1982, Sylvia Jane (*née* Hoare); two *d*. *Educ:* St Paul's Cathedral Choir Sch.; Ardingly Coll., Royal College of Music (ARCM); King's Coll., Cambridge (Dr Mann Organ Student; MA; BMus). Asst Organist, St Clement Danes and Hampstead Parish Ch., 1974–75; Sub-Organist, Winchester Cath., 1975–85; Asst Conductor, Winchester Music Club, 1983–85; Conductor, Durham Univ. Choral Soc., 1987–. Member: Council, RCO, 1988–99; Cathedrals Liturgy Gp, 1993–. Has played or conducted premières, incl. Mathias' Berceuse, Tavener's Ikon of St Cuthbert, Josephs' Mass for St Cuthbert. Organ recitals and broadcasts in UK; concerts in Germany, Denmark, France, Norway, Sweden, Poland, Belgium, Russia, Brazil, Canada, USA, NZ. Recordings with choirs of King's Coll., Cambridge, Winchester Cath., Durham Cath., and as soloist. *Publications:* (with R. Hird) Durham Cathedral Organs, 1991; (contrib.) The Sense of the Sacramental, 1993. *Recreations:* railways, the works of John Buchan. *Address:* 6 The College, Durham DH1 3EQ. *T:* (0191) 3864766.

LANCHBERY, John Arthur, OBE 1990; FRAM; conductor; *b* London, 15 May 1923; *s* of William Lanchbery and Violet (*née* Mewett); *m* 1951, Elaine Fifield (marr. diss. 1960); one *d*. *Educ:* Alleyn's Sch., Dulwich; Royal Academy of Music. Henry Smart Composition Scholarship, 1942. Served, Royal Armoured Corps, 1943–45. Royal Academy of Music, 1945–47; Musical Director, Metropolitan Ballet, 1948–50; Sadler's Wells Theatre Ballet, 1951–57; Royal Ballet, 1957–72 (Principal Conductor, 1959–72); Musical Director: Australian Ballet, 1972–77; American Ballet Theatre, 1978–80. ARAM 1953. Bolshoi Theatre Medal, Moscow, 1961; Queen Elizabeth II Coronation Award, Royal Acad. of Dancing, 1989; Carina Ari Medal, Stockholm, 1989. *Film scores* include: The Turning Point, 1977; Nijinsky, 1980; Evil Under the Sun, 1983; The Birth of a Nation, 1993; The Iron Horse, 1994; Orphans of the Storm, 2001. *Arrangements and compositions* of ballets include: Pleasuredrome, 1949; Eve of St Agnes (BBC commission), 1950; House of Birds, 1955; La Fille Mal Gardée, 1960; The Dream, 1964; Don Quixote, 1966; Giselle, 1968; La Sylphide, 1970; Tales of Beatrix Potter, 1971; Tales of Hoffman, 1972; Merry Widow, 1975; Month in the Country, 1976; Mayerling, 1978; Rosalinda, 1978; Papillon, 1979; La Bayadère, 1980; Peer Gynt, 1980; The Devil to Pay, 1982; The Sentimental Bloke, 1985; Le Chat Botté, 1985; Midsummer Night's Dream, 1985; Hunchback of Notre Dame, 1988; Figaro, 1992; Madame Butterfly, 1995; The Highwaymen, 1996; Dracula, 1997; The Snow Maiden, 1998; Cleopatra, and Toad, 2000. *Recreations:* walking, reading. *Address:* 71 Park Street, St Kilda West, Vic 3182, Australia. *T:* (3) 95370520, *Fax:* (3) 95370521.

LANCHIN, Gerald, OBE 2001; consultant; a Vice-President, National Federation of Consumer Groups, since 1984; Member, Data Protection Tribunal, 1985–98; *b* 17 Oct. 1922; *o s* of late Samuel Lanchin, Kensington; *m* 1951, Valerie Sonia Lyons; one *s* two *d*. *Educ:* St Marylebone Grammar Sch.; London Sch. of Economics. BCom 1st cl. hons 1951; Leverhulme Schol. 1950–51. Min. of Labour, 1939–51; served with Army, RAOC and REME, 1942–46; Board of Trade (subseq. DTI and Dept of Trade): Asst Principal, 1952; Principal 1953; 1st Sec., UK Delegn to OEEC, Paris, 1955–59; Principal, Estabt and Commercial Relations and Exports Divs, 1959–66; Asst Sec., Finance and Civil Aviation Divs, 1966–71; Under-Sec., Tariff, Commercial Relations and Export, Shipping Policy, General and Consumer Affairs Divs, 1971–82. Chairman: Packaging Council, 1983–84; Direct Mail Services Standards Bd, 1983–89; Member: Council, Consumers' Assoc., 1983–88; Consumer Panel, PIA, 1994–98; Financial Services Consumer Panel, 1998–2000. *Publication:* Government and the Consumer, 1985. *Recreations:* photography, reading, music. *Address:* 28 Priory Gardens, Berkhamsted, Herts HP4 2DS. *T:* (01442) 875283.

LAND, Gillian; *see* Lynne, Gillian.

LAND, Prof. Michael Francis, FRS 1982; PhD; Professor of Neurobiology, University of Sussex, since 1984; *b* 12 April 1942; *s* of late Prof. Frank William Land and of Nora Beatrice Channon; *m* 1980, Rosemary (*née* Clarke); one *s* two *d*. *Educ:* Birkenhead Sch., Cheshire; Jesus Coll., Cambridge (MA); University Coll. London (PhD). Asst Lectr in Physiology, UCL, 1966–67; Miller Fellow, 1967–79, and Asst Prof. of Physiology-Anatomy, 1979–81, Univ. of Calif, Berkeley; Lectr in Biol Sciences, 1971–77, Reader, 1977–84, Univ. of Sussex. Vis. Prof., Univ. of Oregon, 1980; Sen. Res. Fellow, ANU, 1982–84. Frink Medal, Zool Soc. of London, 1994; Rank Prize for Optoelectronics, 1998. *Publications:* numerous papers on animal vision in learned jls. *Recreations:* photography, music. *Address:* White House, Cuilfail, Lewes, East Sussex BN7 2BE. *T:* (01273) 476780.

LAND, Nicholas Charles Edward, FCA; Chairman, Ernst & Young, since 1995; *b* 6 Feb. 1948; *s* of Charles and Norma Land; *m* 1975, Sonia Tan; one *s*. *Educ:* Steyning Grammar Sch. FCA 1971. Articled Spain Brothers Dalling & Co., 1967–71; joined Turquand Young, later Ernst & Young, 1971: Partner, 1978–; Managing Partner, London Office, 1986–92; Managing Partner, 1992–95. *Recreations:* gardening, opera. *Address:* (office) Becket House, 1 Lambeth Palace Road, SE1 7EU. *T:* (020) 7951 3002.

LANDA, Lynda; *see* Baroness Chalker of Wallasey.

LANDALE, Sir David (William Neil), KCVO 1993; DL; company director; *b* 7 May 1934; *s* of David Fortune Landale and Louisa (*née* Forbes); *m* 1961, Melanie Roper; three *s*. *Educ:* Eton Coll.; Balliol Coll., Oxford (MA Hist. 1958). Served Black Watch, RHR, 1952–54. Director: Jardine Matheson & Co. Ltd (served in Hong Kong, Thailand, Taiwan and Japan), 1959–75; Matheson & Co. Ltd, 1975–; Pinneys of Scotland, Annan, 1982–87; Duchy Originals Ltd, 1992–95. Chm., T. C. Farries & Co. Ltd, 1982–97. Regl Chm., Timber Growers, Scotland, 1983–85; Chm., Timber Growers UK Ltd, 1985–87. Chairman: Scottish Forestry Trust, 1995–; Ingliston Develt Trust, 1996–; N Dist. Fisheries Bd, 2000–. Member: Exec. Cttee and Council, NT for Scotland, 1980–85; Exec. Cttee, Scottish Landowners Fedn, 1980–87. Sec. and Keeper of Records, Duchy of Cornwall, 1987–93. Chairman: Sargent Cancer Care, Scotland (formerly Cttee for Scotland, Malcolm Sargent Cancer Fund for Children), 1994–96; Crichton Foundn (formerly Crichton Coll. Endowment Trust), 1998–. Mem., Royal Co. of Archers, Queen's Body Guard for Scotland, 1966–. FRSA 1990. DL Nithsdale/Annandale Dumfries, 1988. *Recreations:* all countryside pursuits, theatre, reading, history. *Address:* Dalswinton, Dumfries DG2 0XZ. *T:* (01387) 740208. *Clubs:* Boodle's, Pratt's; New (Edinburgh).

LANDAU, Dr David; Chairman, Saffron Hill Ventures, since 2000; *b* 22 April 1950; *s* of Aharon Landau and Evelyne Conti; *m* 2001, Rosi Kahane. *Educ:* Univ. of Pavia, Italy (MD 1978); Wolfson Coll., Oxford (MA 1979). Print Curator, The Genius of Venice, RA, 1983; Chm., Steering Cttee, Andrea Mantegna exhibn, RA and Metropolitan Mus. of Art, NY, 1992. Founder and Jt Man. Dir, Loot, 1985–95; Chm., Loot Gp of Cos, 1995–2000. Founder and Editor, Print Qly, 1984–; Founder, FAPIA (Free-ad Papers Internat. Assoc.), 1986, Chm., 1990–91; Dir, Nat. Gall. Co. (formerly Nat. Gall. Pubns), 1995– (Chm., 1998–). Trustee: British Friends of Art Museums of Israel, 1995–; Nat. Gall. Trust, 1996–; NACF, 1996–; Nat. Gall., 1996–; Venice in Peril Fund, 1996– (Treas., 1997–). Supernumerary Fellow, Worcester Coll., Oxford, 1980–. *Publications:* Georg Pencz, 1978; Federica Galli, 1982; (with Prof. P. Parshall) The Renaissance Print, 1994; articles in Print Qly, Master Drawings, Burlington Mag., etc. *Recreations:* looking at and collecting art, opera, Venice. *Address:* 80 Carlton Hill, NW8 0ER. *T:* (020) 7624 5544.

LANDAU, Sir Dennis (Marcus), Kt 1987; Chief Executive, Co-operative Wholesale Society Ltd, 1980–92 (Deputy Chief Executive Officer, 1974–80); *b* 18 June 1927; *s* of late Michael Landau, metallurgist; *m* 1992, Mrs Pamela Garlick; two step *s*. *Educ:* Haberdashers' Aske's Hampstead Sch. Schweppes Ltd, 1952; Man. Dir, Schweppes (East Africa) Ltd, 1958–62; Chivers-Hartley: Prodn Dir, 1963; Man. Dir, 1966–69; Chm., Schweppes Foods Div., 1969; Dep. Chm. and Man. Dir, Cadbury Schweppes Foods, 1970; Controller, Food Div., Co-operative Wholesale Society Ltd, 1971. Chairman: CWS (India) Ltd, 1980–92; Unity Trust Bank plc, 1992–2000 (Dir, 1984–2000); Dep. Chm., Co-operative Bank plc, 1989–92; Vice-Chm., Lancashire Enterprises plc, 1989–97; Director: Co-operative Retail Services Ltd, 1980–91; CWS (NZ Hldgs) Ltd, 1980–91; Co-operative Insce Soc. Ltd, 1980–92. Chm., Social Economy Forum, 1993–2001; Member: Metrication Bd, 1972–80; Exec. Cttee, Food & Drink Fedn (formerly Food Manufacturers' Fedn Inc.), 1972–92. Member: Council, Manchester Business Sch., 1982–93 (Chm., 1991–93); Court, Manchester Univ., 1992–2000. FIGD 1977 (Pres. 1982–85); CIMgt (CBIM 1980). FRSA 1992. *Recreations:* Rugby, cricket, music. *Clubs:* Royal Over-Seas League; Lancashire CC (Hon. Treas., 1997–).

LANDELS, William, (Willie); painter; *b* Venice, 14 June 1928; *s* of late Reynold Landels and Carla Manfredi; *m* 1958, Angela Ogden; two *d. Educ:* privately. Apprentice stage designer at La Scala, Milan, 1947; Art Director: J. Walter Thompson, 1950; Queen Magazine, 1965; Editor, Harpers & Queen, 1970–86; Art Dir, 1986–89, Editor, 1989–90, Departures. One-man Exhibitions: Hamburg, 1992; Rebecca Hossack Gall., London, 1993, 1995, 1998; Olsen-Carr Gall., Sydney, 1994; Gallery 482, Brisbane, 1997. *Publication:* (with Alistair Burnet) The Best Years of Our Lives, 1981. *Recreation:* cooking. *Address:* 292 South Lambeth Road, SW8 1UJ.

LANDEN, Dinsdale (James); actor; *b* 4 Sept. 1932; *s* of Edward James Landen and Winifred Alice Landen; *m* 1959, Jennifer Daniel. *Educ:* King's Sch., Rochester; Hove County Grammar Sch. *Stage:* Dead Secret, Piccadilly, 1957; Auntie Mame, Adelphi; Provok'd Wife, Vaudeville; Philanthropist, May Fair, 1970; London Assurance, New, 1972; Alphabetical Order, May Fair, 1975; Bodies, Ambassadors, 1980; Taking Steps, Lyric, 1980; Loot, Lyric, 1984; Sufficient Carbohydrate, Albery, 1984; Wife Begins at Forty, Ambassadors, 1985; Selling the Sizzle, Hampstead, 1986; Dangerous Obsession, Apollo, then Fortune, 1987; Thark, Lyric, Hammersmith, 1989; Bookends, Apollo, 1990; Twelfth Night, Playhouse, 1991; Chatsky, Almeida, 1993; School for Scandal, 1995, Racing Demon, 1998, Chichester Fest. *National Theatre:* Plunder; The Philanderer; On the Razzle, 1981; Uncle Vanya, 1982. *Films:* The Valiant; Every Home Should Have One; Digby the Biggest Dog in the World; Mosquito Squadron; Morons from Outer Space; The Steal; *television:* Great Expectations; Mickey Dunne; The Spies; Glittering Prizes; Devenish; Two Sundays; Fathers and Families; Pig in the Middle; Radio Pictures; Absent Friends; Events in a Museum; What the Butler Saw; Some Other Spring; Fighting Against Slavery; Arms and the Man; The Buccaneers; The Wingless Bird. *Recreations:* walking, golf. *Address:* 48 Ashlone Road, SW15 1LR. *Club:* Stage Golfing Society.

LANDER, Sir Stephen (James), KCB 2000 (CB 1995); Director General, Security Service, since 1996; *b* 1947; *s* of John N. B. Lander and (Eleanor) Tessa Lander (*née* Heanley); *m* 1972, Felicity Mary Brayley; one *s* one *d. Educ:* Bishops Stortford Coll.; Queens' Coll., Cambridge (BA, MA, PhD). Inst. of Historical Research, Univ. of London, 1972–75; Security Service, 1975–. *Address:* PO Box 3255, SW1P 1AE.

LANDERER, John, CBE 1997; AM 1990; lawyer; Senior Partner, Landerer & Co., since 1979; *b* 3 May 1947; *s* of William and Felicia Landerer; *m* 1986, Michelle H. Sugar; one *s* one *d. Educ:* Sydney Univ. (LLB 1969). Chairman: FAI Insurances Ltd, 1989–99 (Actg Chm., 1988); Tiger Investment Co. Ltd, 1994–99; Goldsearch Ltd, 1995–; Nat. Hire Gp Ltd, 1997–; Terrace Tower Gp, 1998–; Director: Internat. Distillers Hldgs Ltd, 1986–99; D. W. Gp of Cos, 1996–; formerly dir, several other cos. Chm., NSW Govt Home Purchase Assistance Authy, 1994–. University of Sydney: Hon. Fellow, 1990; Hon. Gov., Law Sch. Foundn, 1990–; Mem. Bd, Asia Pacific Law Centre, 1994–; Macquarie University: Chm., Adv. Bd, Business Law Dept, 1994–; Vis. Prof., 1998–. Trustee, WWF Australia, 1992–. Councillor, Sydney Conservatorium of Music Foundn, 1993–. Member: Victor Chang Cardiac Centre Appeal Cttee, St Vincent's Hosp., 1990–; Red Shield Appeal Cttee, Salvation Army, 1994–. Hon. LLD Macquarie, 1999. *Recreations:* reading, walking, swimming. *Address:* (office) Level 31, 133 Castlereagh Street, Sydney, NSW 2000, Australia. *T:* (612) 92614242, *Fax:* (612) 92618523. *Clubs:* Carlton; American, Tattersalls (Sydney).

LANDERS, Brian James; Chief Operating Officer, Pearson Education, since 2000 (Group Finance Director, 2000); *b* 21 April 1949; *s* of James Jocelyn Landers, OBE and Beatrice Edith Landers (*née* Western); *m* 1st, 1975, Elsa Louise Dawson (marr. diss.); 2nd, 1986, Thérèse Doumit (marr. diss.); one *s*; 3rd, 1993, Sarah Catherine Cuthbert; two *d. Educ:* Univ. of Exeter (BA); London Business Sch. (MSc). With Commercial Union, 1973–79; Internat. Planned Parenthood Fedn, 1979–82; Tenneco Automotive, 1982–83; Chief Internal Auditor, then Retail Financial Controller, J. Sainsbury plc, 1985–88; Price Waterhouse, 1988–90; UK Finance Dir, then Gp Finance Dir, Habitat, 1990–93; Finance Director: HM Prison Service, 1993–96; W. H. Smith Retail, 1996–97; with Waterstones Ltd, 1997–98. Dep. Chm., Financial Ombudsman Service, 1999–. Trustee, Royal Armouries, 1999–. *Address:* Pearson Education, Edinburgh Gate, Harlow, Essex CM21 2JE.

LANDON, Prof. David Neil; Professor of Neurocytology, University of London, since 1991; Dean, and Member Committee of Management, Institute of Neurology, London, 1987–95; *b* 15 May 1936; *er s* of Christopher Guy Landon and Isabella Catherine (*née* Campbell); *m* 1960, Karen Elizabeth, *yr d* of late John Copeland and Else Margrethe Poole, Bolney, Sussex; two *s* one *d. Educ:* Lancing Coll.; Guy's Hospital Med. Sch. (BSc Hons Anat.; MB BS 1960). LRCP, MRCS 1959. Ho. Officer, Guy's Hosp., 1959–60; Lectr in Anatomy, Guy's Hosp. Med. Sch., 1961–64; Lectr, later Sen. Lectr, in Neurobiology, MRC Res. Gp in Applied Neurobiology, 1964–77; Reader in Neurocytology, Inst. of Neurology, 1977–91. Hon. Cons. in Morbid Anatomy, National Hosps, Queen Square, 1974–. University of London: Member: Senate and Academic Council, 1992–94; Univ. Council, 1996–2001; Mem., Med. Cttee, 1996–98; Convenor, Subject Panel in Anatomy, 1996–2001. Vis. Prof., Coll. of Medicine, Lagos, 1975. Gov., National Hosps for Nervous Diseases SHA, 1988–95; Appointed Mem., GMC, 1988–94. Member: Res. Cttee, World Fedn of Neurology, 1987–; Cttees of Management, Inst. of Child Health, 1987–96, Inst. of Dental Surgery, 1993–95; Chm., Med. Res. Ethics Cttee, 1987–93, Chm., Med. Cttee, 1998–2000, Nat. Hosp. for Neurology and Neurosurgery; Hon. Fellow, Inst. of Child Health, London Univ., 1996. Editorial Cttee, Jl of Anatomy, 1981–94; Associated Editor: Jl of Neurocytol., 1980–83; Neuromuscular Disorders, 1990–94; Muscle and Nerve, 1997–2001. *Publications:* The Peripheral Nerve, 1976; contribs to learned jls on the fine structure, develt and pathology of nerve and muscle. *Recreations:* gardening, travel. *Address:* Woodmans, Wallcrouch, Wadhurst, East Sussex TN5 7JG. *T:* (01580) 200833.

LANDON, Howard Chandler Robbins; author and music historian; *b* 6 March 1926; *s* of late William Grinnell Landon and Dorothea LeBaron Robbins; *m* 1957, Else Radant. *Educ:* Aiken Preparatory Sch.; Lenox Sch.; Swarthmore Coll.; Boston Univ., USA (BMus). European rep. of Intercollegiate Broadcasting System, 1947; founded Haydn Soc. (which recorded and printed music of Joseph Haydn), 1949; became a Special Correspondent of The Times, 1957 and contrib. to that newspaper until 1961. Visiting Prof., Queen's Coll., NYC, 1969; Regents Prof. of Music, Univ. of California (Davis), 1970, 1975, 1979; John Bird Prof. of Music, UC Cardiff, 1978–; Christian Johnson Prof. of Music, Middlebury Coll., Vermont, USA, 1980 . Advr, Prague Mozart Foundn, 1992–. Hon. Professorial Fellow, University Coll., Cardiff, 1971–79; Hon. Fellow, Lady Margaret Hall, Oxford, 1979–. Hon. DMus: Boston Univ., 1969; Queen's Univ., Belfast, 1974; Bristol, 1982. Verdienstkreuz für Kunst und Wissenschaft from Austrian Govt, 1972; Gold Medal, City of Vienna, 1987; Haydn Prize, Govt of Burgenland, Austria, 1990. Co-editor, The Haydn Yearbook, 1962–. *Publications:* The Symphonies of Joseph Haydn, 1955; The Mozart Companion (co-ed with Donald Mitchell), 1956; The Collected Correspondence and London Notebooks of Joseph Haydn, 1959; Essays on Eighteenth-Century Music, 1969; Ludwig van Beethoven: a documentary study, 1970; critical edn of the 107 Haydn Symphonies, (completed) 1968; five-vol. biog. of Haydn: vol. 3, Haydn in England, 1976; vol. 4, Haydn: The Years of The Creation, 1977; vol. 5, Haydn: The Late Years, 1977; vol. 1, Haydn: The Early Years, and vol. 2, Haydn in Eszterhaza, 1978–80; Haydn: a documentary study, 1981; Mozart and the Masons, 1982; Handel and his World, 1984; 1791: Mozart's Last Year, 1988; (with David Wyn Jones) Haydn: his life and music, 1988; Mozart: the golden years, 1989; (ed) The Mozart Compendium, 1990; Mozart and Vienna, 1991; Five Centuries of Music in Venice, 1991; Vivaldi: voice of the Baroque, 1993; The Mozart Essays, 1995; Horns in High C: a memoir of musical discoveries and adventures, 1999; scholarly edns of eighteenth-century music (various European publishing houses). *Recreations:* swimming, cooking, walking. *Address:* Anton Frankgasse 3, Vienna 1180, Austria. *T:* (1) 4796383; Château de Foncoussières, 81800 Rabastens (Tarn), France. *T:* 563406145.

LANDRETH, Rev. Canon Derek, TD 1963; Vicar of Icklesham, Diocese of Chichester, 1983–89 (Priest-in-charge, 1982–83), also Priest-in-charge of Fairlight, 1984–86; Chaplain to the Queen, 1980–90; Rural Dean of Rye, 1984–89; *b* 7 June 1920; *s* of Rev. Norman Landreth and Muriel Landreth; *m* 1st, 1943, Myra Joan Brown; one *s* three *d*; 2nd, 1986, Dss Mavis Isabella White. *Educ:* Kingswood School, Bath; King's College, Cambridge (MA); Bishops' College, Cheshunt. Commissioned, Royal Artillery, 1942–46 (service India and Burma); CF (TA), 1951–67, (TAVR) 1967–70; Asst Curate, St George, Camberwell, 1948–53; Vicar, St Mark, Battersea Rise, 1953–59; Deputy Chaplain, HM Prison, Wandsworth, 1954–59; Vicar of Richmond, Surrey, and Chaplain, Star and Garter Home for Disabled Soldiers, Sailors and Airmen, 1959–70; Rector of Sanderstead, Surrey, 1970–77; Hon. Chaplain to Bishop of Southwark, 1962–80; Hon. Canon of Southwark Cathedral, 1968–77; Canon Residentiary and Librarian, Southwark Cathedral, 1977–82; Canon Emeritus, 1982–. Proctor in Convocation, 1980–83. Indep. Mem., Richmond Borough Council, 1961–65. *Recreations:* gardening, fishing. *Address:* Gossamer Cottage, Slindon, near Arundel, W Sussex BN18 0QT. *T:* (01243) 814224.

LANDSHOFF, Prof. Peter Vincent, PhD; Professor of Mathematical Physics, University of Cambridge, since 1994; Fellow, since 1963, Vice-Master, since 1999, Christ's College, Cambridge; *b* 22 March 1937; *m* 1962, Pamela Carmichael; three *s. Educ:* City of London Sch.; St John's Coll., Cambridge (MA, PhD). FInstP 1999. Cambridge University: Fellow, St John's Coll., 1961–63; Reader in Mathematical Physics, 1974–94. Instructor, Princeton Univ., 1961–62; Scientific Associate, CERN, Geneva, 1975–76, 1984–85, 1991–92. Editor, Physics Letters B (Elsevier Science), 1982–. FRSA. *Publications:* (jtly) The Analytic S-matrix, 1966; (jtly) Simple Quantum Physics, 1979, 2nd edn 1997; research papers on theoretical high-energy physics. *Address:* Department of Applied Mathematics and Theoretical Physics, Centre for Mathematical Sciences, Wilberforce Road, Cambridge CB3 0WA. *T:* (01223) 337880; pvl@damtp.cam.ac.uk.

LANDY, John Michael, AC 2001; MBE 1955; Governor of Victoria, Australia, since 2001; *b* 12 April 1930; *s* of Clarence Gordon Landy and Elva Katherine Ashton; *m* 1971, Lynne (*née* Fisher); one *s* one *d. Educ:* Malvern Grammar Sch.; Geelong Grammar; Univ. of Melbourne (BAgSc). Holder: 1500m World Record, 1954–55; one mile World Record, 1954–57; Olympic and Commonwealth Games medals; second man to run the mile in under 4 mins. ICI Australia, 1962–82, R&D Manager, Biological Gp, 1971–82. Chairman: Wool R&D Corp., 1989–94; Clean-up Australia, 1990–94; Australia Day Cttee (Victoria), 1990–93; Coode Is. (major chemical spill) Review Panel, 1991–92; Athletics Task Force, 1992–93; Meat Res. Corp., 1995–98; Dir, Australian Sports Drug Agency, 1998–2000. Chairman: Bd Governors, Australian Nat. Insect Collection, 1995–2000; AWTA Ltd Wool Educn Trust, 1997–2000; Athletics Internat. Trust, 1997–2000; Pres., Greening Australia (Victoria), 1998–2000; Member: Land Conservation Council of Victoria, 1971–79; Reference Areas Cttee, Victoria's system of Scientific Reference Areas, 1979–86; Bd Dirs, Australian Inst. of Sport, 1985–87; ASTEC External Earnings Review Working Party, 1993–94. Hon. LLD Victoria, BC; Hon. D Rural Sci. New England. *Publications:* Close to Nature, 1985 (C. J. Dennis Award); A Coastal Diary, 1993. *Address:* Government House, Melbourne, Vic 3004, Australia. *T:* (3) 96554211.

LANE, family name of **Baron Lane** and **Baron Lane of Horsell**.

LANE, Baron *cr* 1979 (Life Peer), of St Ippollitts; **Geoffrey Dawson Lane;** PC 1974; Kt 1966; AFC 1943; Lord Chief Justice of England, 1980–92; *b* 17 July 1918; *s* of late Percy Albert Lane, Lincoln; *m* 1944, Jan, *d* of Donald Macdonald; one *s. Educ:* Shrewsbury; Trinity Coll., Cambridge (Hon. Fellow 1981). Served in RAF, 1939–45; Sqdn-Leader, 1942. Called to Bar, Gray's Inn, 1946; Bencher 1966. QC 1962. Dep. Chm., Beds. QS, 1960–66; Recorder of Bedford, 1963–66; a Judge of the High Court of Justice, Queen's Bench Div., 1966–74; a Lord Justice of Appeal, 1974–79; a Lord of Appeal in Ordinary, 1979–80. Mem., Parole Board, 1970–72 (Vice-Chm., 1972). Hon. Bencher, Inner Temple, 1980. Hon. LLD Cambridge, 1984. *Address:* Royal Courts of Justice, Strand, WC2A 2LL.

LANE OF HORSELL, Baron *cr* 1990 (Life Peer), of Woking in the County of Surrey; **Peter Stewart Lane,** Kt 1984; JP; FCA; Senior Partner, Binder Hamlyn, Chartered Accountants, 1979–92; Deputy Chairman, More O'Ferrall, later More Group, 1985–97; *b* 29 Jan. 1925; *s* of late Leonard George Lane; *m* Doris Florence (*née* Botsford) (*d* 1969); two *d. Educ:* Sherborne Sch., Dorset. Served RNVR (Sub-Lieut), 1943–46. Qualified as chartered accountant, 1948; Partner, Binder Hamlyn or predecessor firms, 1950–92. Chairman: Brent Internat., 1985–95; Elswick, 1993–94; Attwoods, 1994; Automated Security (Hldgs), 1994–96. National Union of Conservative Associations: Vice Chairman, 1981–83; Chairman, 1983–84; Chm., Exec. Cttee, 1986–91; Vice President, 1984–. Chm., Nuffield Hosps, 1993–96 (Dep. Chm., 1990–93). Chm., Action on Addiction, 1991–94. JP Surrey, 1976–; Freeman, City of London. *Address:* c/o House of Lords, SW1A 0PW. *Clubs:* Boodle's, Beefsteak, MCC.

See also Baron Trefgarne.

LANE, Dr Anthony John, FRCP, FFPHM; Regional Medical Officer, North Western Regional Health Authority, 1974–86, retired; *b* 6 Feb. 1926; *s* of John Gill Lane and Marian (*née* Brumfield); *m* 1948, Hannah Holečková; one *s* two *d. Educ:* St Christopher's Sch., Letchworth; Emmanuel Coll., Cambridge. MA, MB, BChir. House posts in surgery, medicine, obstetrics, and paediatrics, London area, 1949–51; MO with Methodist Missionary Soc., Andhra State, India, 1951–57; Registrar: Tropical Diseases, UCH, 1958; Gen. Med., St James' Hosp., Balham, 1958–61; Infectious Diseases, Western Hosp., Fulham, 1961–63; MO (Trainee), Leeds RHB, 1963–64; Asst Sen. MO, Leeds RHB, 1964–66; Principal Asst Sen. MO, Leeds RHB, 1966–70; Dep. Sen. Admin. MO, SW Metrop. RHB, 1970–71; Sen. Admin. MO, Manchester RHB, 1971–74. Hon. MD Manchester, 1986. *Publications:* contrib. Positions, Movements and Directions in Health Services Research, 1974; contrib. Proc. Royal Soc. Med. *Recreations:* music, competitive indoor games, walking, gardening. *Address:* 4 Queens Road, Wilmslow, Cheshire SK9 5HS. *T:* (01625) 523889.

LANE, Anthony John, CB 1990; consultant on public policy issues; Deputy Secretary, Department of Trade and Industry, 1987–96; *b* 30 May 1939; *s* of late Eric Marshall Lane and Phyllis Mary Lane; *m* 1967, Judith Sheila (*née* Dodson); two *s* one *d*. *Educ:* Caterham Sch.; Balliol Coll., Oxford (BA PPE, MA). Investment Analyst, Joseph Sebag & Co., 1964–65; joined Civil Service as Asst Principal, 1965; various appts in DTI, Dept of Transport, DoE and OFT; Prin. Pvte Sec. to several Ministers; Asst Sec., 1975; Under Sec., 1980; Head of Internat Trade Policy, DTI, 1984–87; Dep. Dir Gen., OFT, 1987–90; Dir Gen. for Industry, DTI, 1990–94; Chief Exec., PSA, 1994–96. Brighton University: Mem., Bd of Govs, 1997– (Dep. Chm., 1999–); Chm., Univ. Property Cttee, 1998–99. *Recreations:* music, gardens, travel. *Address:* Foxbury, East Grinstead, Sussex RH19 3SS.

LANE, Dr Anthony Milner, FRS 1975; Deputy Chief Scientific Officer, Atomic Energy Research Establishment, Harwell, 1976–89; *b* 27 July 1928; *s* of Herbert William Lane and Doris Ruby Lane (*née* Milner); *m* 1st, 1952, Anne Sophie Zissman (*d* 1980); two *s* one *d*; 2nd, 1983, Jill Valerie Parvin; five step *d*. *Educ:* Trowbridge Boys' High Sch.; Selwyn Coll., Cambridge. BA Maths, PhD Theoretical Physics. Joined Harwell, 1953. *Publications:* Nuclear Theory, 1963; numerous research articles in Review of Modern Physics, Phys. Review, Nuclear Physics, etc. *Recreations:* gardening, bird-watching. *Address:* 6 Walton Street, Oxford OX1 2HG. *T:* (01865) 556565.

LANE, Maj.-Gen. Barry Michael, CB 1984; OBE 1974 (MBE 1965); Chief Executive, Cardiff Bay Development Corporation, 1987–92; *b* 10 Aug. 1932; *m* 1st, 1956, Eveline Jean (*d* 1986), *d* of Vice-Adm. Sir Harry Koelle, KCB and Enid (*née* Corbould-Ellis); one *s* one *d*; 2nd, 1987, Shirley Ann, *d* of E. V. Hawtin. *Educ:* Dover Coll. Commissioned, 1954; served Somerset LI, 1954–59, Somerset and Cornwall LI, 1959–68, LI, 1968–75; Instructor, Staff Coll. Camberley, 1970–72; CO, 1st Bn, LI, 1972–75; Comd, 11 Armoured Bde, 1977–78; RCDS, 1979; Dep. Dir, Army Staff Duties, MoD, 1980–81; Dir, Army Quartering, 1981–82; VQMG, 1982–83; GOC SW Dist, 1984–87. Col, The LI, 1982–87. Hon. Colonel: 6th Bn, LI, 1987–97; Bristol Univ., OTC, 1988–99. Pres. of Council, and Chm. of Govs, Taunton Sch., 1997–2001. *Club:* Army and Navy.

LANE, David Goodwin; QC 1991; a Recorder of the Crown Court, since 1987; *b* 8 Oct. 1945; *s* of James Cooper Lane and Joyce Lilian Lane; *m* 1991, Jacqueline Elizabeth Cocks. *Educ:* Crypt Sch., Gloucester; King's College London (LLB, AKC). Lord Justice Holker Junior Exhibnr; Lee Essay Prizeman, H. C. Richard Ecclesiastical Law Prizeman; Albion Richardson Scholar. Called to the Bar, Gray's Inn, 1968; Asst Recorder, 1982. Freeman, City of London. *Address:* Phoenix Chambers, Gray's Inn Chambers, Gray's Inn, WC1R 5JA. *T:* (020) 7404 7888; Queen Square Chambers, 56 Queen Square, Bristol BS1 4PR. *T:* (0117) 921 1966.

LANE, Rev. David John; Principal, College of the Resurrection, Mirfield, 1990–97; *b* 12 June 1935; *s* of late Rex Clayphen Fox Lane and Constance Mary Lane. *Educ:* Hurstpierpoint Coll. (Scholar); Magdalen Coll., Oxford (BA Theol 1958; Oriental Studies 1960; Pusey and Ellerton Schol., 1959; Hall Houghton Syriac Prize, 1961; MA 1962; BD 1989). Nat. Service, Royal Signals, 1953–55. Coll. of the Resurrection, Mirfield, 1960–61; Codrington Coll., Barbados, 1961–62. Deacon and Priest, Barbados, 1962; Lectr, 1961, Sen. Tutor, 1963, Codrington Coll., Barbados; Curate, St Peter's, Wolvercote, 1965–66; Associate Chaplain, and Kennicott Hebrew Fellow, 1966–68, Lectr in Theol., 1968–71, Pembroke Coll., Oxford; Lectr and Tutor, St Stephen's House, Oxford, 1968–71; Asst Prof., Near Eastern Studies, Univ. of Toronto, 1971, Associate Prof., 1974–83; Sen. Fellowship, Trinity Coll., Toronto, 1977–82; College of the Resurrection: Lectr and Tutor, 1983; Dir of Studies, 1984; Vice-Principal, 1987–90. Hon. Lectr, Dept of Theology and Religious Studies, Univ. of Leeds, 1983–2001. *Publications:* The Old Testament in Syriac: Part II, fasc. 5 ((ed) Ecclesiastes; (ed with J. A. Emerton) Wisdom of Solomon and Song of Songs), 1979, Part I, fasc. 2 ((ed) Leviticus), 1991; The Peshitta of Leviticus, 1994; articles in learned jls. *Recreations:* gardening, reading, photography. *Club:* Royal Over-Seas League.

LANE, David Neil, CMG 1983; HM Diplomatic Service, retired; *b* 16 April 1928; *er s* of late Clive and Hilda Lane, Bath; *m* 1968, Sara, *d* of late Cecil Nurcombe, MC; two *d*. *Educ:* Abbotsholme Sch.; Merton Coll., Oxford. Army, 1946–48; Foreign (later Foreign and Commonwealth) Office: 1951–53, 1955–58, 1963–68, 1972–74; British Embassy, Oslo, 1953–55; Ankara, 1959–61, 1975–78; Conakry, 1961–63; UK Mission to the United Nations, New York, 1968–72, 1979; High Comr in Trinidad and Tobago, 1980–85; Ambassador to the Holy See, 1985–88. Pres., UN Trusteeship Council, 1971–72; UK Delegate, Internat. Exhibns Bureau, 1973–74. Asst Sec.-Gen., 1989–92, Sec., 1990–92, Order of St John; OStJ 1990. Chm., Anglo-Turkish Soc., 1995–2001. *Composition:* Three Carols (for chorus and orch.). *Recreations:* music, walking, travel. *Address:* 6 Montagu Square, W1H 2LB. *T:* (020) 7486 1673.

LANE, Sir David (Philip), Kt 2000; PhD; FRCPath, FMedSci; FRS 1996; FRSE; Professor of Molecular Oncology, University of Dundee, since 1990; *b* 1 July 1952; *s* of John Wallace Lane and Cecelia Frances Evelyn Lane (*née* Wright); *m* 1975, Ellen Birgitte Muldal; one *s* one *d*. *Educ:* John Fisher Sch., Purley; University College London (BSc, PhD). FRCPath 1996. FRSE 1992. Res. Fellow, ICRF, 1976–77; Lectr, Imperial Coll., 1977–85; Staff Scientist, ICRF, 1985–90. Vis. Fellow, Cold Spring Harbor Labs, NY, 1978–80; Gibb Fellow, CRC, 1990–. Mem., EMBO, 1990–. Founder FMedSci 1998. Hon. DSc Abertay Dundee, 1999. Prize, Charles Rodolphe Brupbacher Foundn, 1993; Prize, Joseph Steiner Foundn, 1993; Howard Hughes Internat. Scholar, Howard Hughes Med. Inst., 1993; Yvette Mayent Prize, Inst. Curie, 1994; Medal, Swedish Soc. of Oncology, 1994; Prize, Meyenberg Foundn, 1995; Black Prize, Jefferson Hosp., 1995; Silvanus Thompson Medal, British Inst. of Radiol., 1996; Henry Dryerre Prize, 1996; Paul Ehrlich Prize, 1998; Tom Connors Prize, 1998. *Publications:* Antibodies: a laboratory manual, 1988; numerous papers in learned jls. *Recreations:* tennis, motor cycles, walking. *Address:* CRC Laboratories, Department of Biochemistry, The University, Dundee DD1 4HN. *T:* (01382) 344982.

LANE, David Stuart, PhD, DPhil; Reader in Sociology, 1992–2000, and Official Fellow of Emmanuel College, 1974–80 and 1990–2000, Senior Research Associate, since 2001, University of Cambridge; *b* Monmouthshire (now Gwent), 24 April 1933; *s* of Reginald and Mary Lane; *m* 1962, Christel Noritzsch; one *s* one *d*. *Educ:* Univ. of Birmingham (BSocSc); Univ. of Oxford (DPhil). PhD Cantab. Graduate student, Nuffield Coll., Oxford, 1961–62, 1964–65. Formerly engrg trainee, local authority employee, sch. teacher; univ. teacher, Birmingham, Essex (Reader in Sociology) and Cambridge Univs; Prof. of Sociology, Univ. of Birmingham, 1981–90; Lectr in Sociology, Cambridge Univ., 1990–92. Visiting Professor: Lund Univ., 1985; Cornell Univ., 1987; Univ. of Graz, 1991, 1996; Harvard Univ., 1993, 2001; Kennan Inst., Washington, 1986, 1996; Sabanci Univ., 2000–01. Member: Exec. Cttee, British Sociol Assoc., 1987–92; Exec. Cttee, European Social Assoc., 1999–2001; Co-Chair, first European Conf. of Sociology, 1992. Vice-Chm., Birmingham Rathbone, 1986–90; Vice-Chm., Down's Children's Assoc., 1981–82; Chm., W Midlands Council for Disabled People, 1983–86. ESRC res. award to study Soviet and Russian political elites, 1991–95, econ. elites, 1996–98, and financial business elite, 1999–. Member, Editorial Boards: Sociology, 1985–88; Disability, Handicap and Society, 1987–90. *Publications:* Roots of Russian Communism, 1969, 2nd edn 1975; Politics and Society in the USSR, 1970, 2nd edn 1978; The End of Inequality?, 1971; (with G. Kolankiewicz) Social Groups in Polish Society, 1973; The Socialist Industrial State, 1976; (with F. O'Dell) The Soviet Industrial Worker, 1978; The Work Needs of Mentally Handicapped Adults, 1980; Leninism: a sociological interpretation, 1981; The End of Social Inequality?: class status and power under state socialism, 1982; State and Politics in the USSR, 1985; Soviet Economy and Society, 1985; (ed jtly and contrib.) Current Approaches to Down's Syndrome, 1985; (ed) Employment and Labour in the USSR, 1986; Soviet Labour and the Ethic of Communism, 1987; (ed and contrib.) Political Power and Elites in the USSR, 1988; Soviet Society under Perestroika, 1990, 2nd edn 1992; (ed and contrib.) Russia in Flux, 1992; (ed and contrib.) Russia in Transition, 1995; The Rise and Fall of State Socialism, 1996; (with C. Ross) The Transition from Communism to Capitalism: ruling elites from Gorbachev to Eltsin, 1998; (ed and contrib.) Political Economy of Russian Oil, 1999; (ed and contrib.) The Legacy of State Socialism and the Future of Transformation, 2001; (ed and contrib.) Russian Banking: evolution, problems and prospects, 2002; contribs to jls incl. Communist and Post-Communist Studies, Pol Studies, Europe-Asia Studies, Sociology, and Jl of Communist and Transition Politics. *Recreations:* soccer, squash, films, TV. *Address:* Emmanuel College, Cambridge CB2 3AP. *T:* (01223) 334202, *Fax:* (01223) 334426; *e-mail:* dsl10@cus.cam.ac.uk.

LANE, Denis Joseph; Editor in Chief, The Universe, since 1994; Managing Director and Editor in Chief, Gabriel Communications, since 1994; *b* 20 Nov. 1960; *s* of Richard and Annie Lane; *m* 1991, Fiona Fahey; one *s* one *d*. *Educ:* University Coll., Cork (BComm). Sen. Auditor, Peat Marwick Mitchell, 1981–83; Gp Accountant, James A. Barry, 1983–87; Manager of Finance, Princeton Gp, 1987–91; Financial Controller, 1991–93, Chief Exec., 1993–94, Gabriel Communications. Member: Grouse Shooting Ground Club, 1994–; British Assoc. for Shooting and Conservation, 1993–. *Recreations:* shooting, fell walking, chess. *Address:* Gabriel Communications, 1st Floor, St James's Buildings, Oxford Street, Manchester M1 6FP. *T:* (0161) 236 8856.

LANE, Jane; *see* Tewson, J.

LANE, Rev. John Ernest, OBE 1994; charity consultant; Director, Corporate Affairs, St Mungo Community Housing Association Ltd, 1996–2001; *b* 16 June 1939; *s* of Ernest William Lane and Winifred (*née* Lloyd); *m* 1st, 1962, Eileen Williams (marr. diss. 1988); three *d*; 2nd, 2001, Ishbel, *d* of William and Jean Curr. *Educ:* Burnley Grammar Sch.; Handsworth Coll., Birmingham; City of London Polytechnic (DMS); Cranfield Inst. of Technol. (MSc). Methodist Minister: Llanharan, 1962–64; Great Harwood, 1964–67; Lewisham and Peckham, 1967–72; Dir, Peckham Settlement, 1972–77; Nat. Public Relns Officer, YWCA of GB, 1977–80; Dir and Sec., St Mungo Community Housing Assoc. Ltd, 1980–96; Sec., 1980–96, Dir, 1994–96, St Mungo Assoc. Charitable Trust. Ordained deacon and priest, 1980; Hon. Curate, St John and St Andrew, Peckham, 1980–95; permission to officiate, dio. of Southwark, 1995–98; NSM, St Alfege with St Peter, Greenwich, 1998–2000. Administrator, European Fedn of Nat. Orgns Working with the Homeless, 1991–95. Dir, Nat. Sleep Out Week, 1990–94. *Publication:* (ed) Homelessness in Industrialised Countries, 1987. *Recreations:* cooking, washing up, cricket, travel, arts, persuading Yvonne not to support Arsenal, vetting Vanessa's boyfriends, following Alison around the world. *Address:* 2 Tregony Rise, Lichfield, Staffs WS14 9SN.

LANE, Kenneth Frederick; former mining consultant; Director, RTZ Consultants, 1988–97; *b* 22 March 1928; British; *m* 1950, Kathleen Richards; one *s* two *d*. *Educ:* Emanuel Coll., Cambridge. Degree in Maths. Steel Industry in Sheffield, 1951–59; North America, 1959–61; Rio Tinto-Zinc Corp., 1961–65; Man. Dir, RTZ Consultants Ltd, 1965–70; Dir, RTZ Corp., 1970–75. Dir, Energy Management & Finance, 1988–89. Advisor to Civil Service, 1970–74. Vis. Prof., RSM, 1979–85. *Publication:* The Economic Definition of Ore, 1988. *Recreations:* bridge, boat building, sailing. *Address:* 4 Towerdene, 16 Tower Road, Poole, Dorset BH13 6HZ. *T:* (01202) 751958.

LANE, Hon. Dame Miriam; *see* Rothschild, Hon. Dame M. L.

LANE, Dr Nancy Jane, OBE 1994; CBiol, FIBiol; FZS; Project Director, Women in Science, Engineering and Technology Initiative, University of Cambridge, since 1999; Senior Research Associate, Zoology Department, University of Cambridge, since 1990; Fellow, and Lecturer, Girton College, Cambridge, since 1970; *d* of Temple Haviland Lane and Frances de Forest Gilbert Lane; *m* 1969, Prof. Richard Nelson Perham, *qv*; one *s* one *d*. *Educ:* Dalhousie Univ., Nova Scotia (BSc, MSc); Lady Margaret Hall, Oxford (DPhil 1963); Girton Coll., Cambridge (PhD 1968; ScD 1981). CBiol 1991, FIBiol 1991; FZS 1986. Res. Asst Prof., Albert Einstein Coll. of Medicine, NY, 1964–65; Res. Staff Biologist, Yale Univ., 1965–68; University of Cambridge: SSO, 1968–73, PSO, 1973–82, SPSO, 1982–90, AFRC Unit, Zoology Dept; Tutor, Girton Coll., 1975–98. Editor-in-Chief, Cell Biol. Internat., 1995–98. Non-executive Director: Smith & Nephew plc, 1991–2000; Peptide Therapeutics plc, 1995–98. Member: PM's Adv. Panel for Citizen's Charter, 1991–93; Chairman: BTEC's Adv. Bd for Sci. and Caring, 1991–94; Wkg Party for Women in Sci. and Engrg (OST), Cabinet Office, 1993–94. Member: Forum UK, 1994–; All Souls Gp, Oxford, 1994–; CVCP's Commn on Univ. Career Opportunities (CUCO), 1996–2000; UNESCO's Sci. Cttee for Women, Sci. and Technol., 1997–; Dep. Chm., Steering Cttee for CUCO/OST/HEFCE Athena Project, 1998–. Pres., Inst. of Biology, April 2002–. Mem. Council, Zool Soc. of London, 1998–2001 (Vice-Pres., 1999–); Mem., Brit. Soc. Cell Biol, 1980– (Sec., 1982–90). FRSA 1992; MInstD 1991. Hon. LLD Dalhousie, 1985; Hon. ScD Salford, 1994. *Publications:* contrib. numerous scientific papers and chapters on cell-cell junctions, cellular structures and interactions, in field of cell biology, in a range of learned scientific jls. *Recreations:* theatre and opera, 20th century art, travelling. *Address:* Department of Zoology, University of Cambridge, Downing Street, Cambridge CB2 3EJ. *T:* (01223) 330116/336600/363752, *Fax:* (01223) 330116/336676; *e-mail:* njl1@cam.ac.uk. *Club:* Oxford and Cambridge.

LANE, Dr Richard Paul; Programme Director, The Wellcome Trust, since 1997; *b* 16 May 1951; *s* of Alfred George Lane and Patricia Ann Lane (*née* Trotter); *m* 1972, Maureen Anne Grogan; two *s* one *d*. *Educ:* Imperial Coll., Univ. of London (BSc, ARCS, DIC, PhD). Dept of Entomology, British Museum (Natural History), 1974–85, Head of Med. Insects Sect., 1983–85; Sen. Lectr, LSHTM, Univ. of London, 1985–92, Head of Vector Biology and Transmission Dynamics Unit, 1989–92; Keeper of Entomology, Natural History Mus., 1992–97. Member: Council, RSTM&H, 1985–89, 1999–; Biological Council, 1985–89; Wellcome Trust Panels, 1986–97; Expert Adv. Panel on Parasitic Diseases, WHO, 1988–; Steering Cttee on Leishmaniasis, WHO, 1988–93; Bd of Trustees, Biosis, Philadelphia, 1993–98. Royal Entomological Society: Mem. Council, 1980–83, 1989–92; Vice-Pres., 1991–92; Pres., 1994–96; Mem. Council, Internat. Congress of Entomology, 1992–2000. *Publications:* (ed jtly) Medical Insects and Arachnids, 1993; papers on insects of medical importance in sci. jls, esp. on sandflies and transmission of leishmaniasis. *Recreation:* sailing. *Address:* The Wellcome Trust, 183 Euston Road, NW1 2BE. *T:* (020) 7611 8888.

LANE, Ronald Anthony Stuart, CMG 1977; MC 1945; Deputy Chairman, Chartered Trust Ltd, 1979–83; *b* 8 Dec. 1917; 2nd *s* of late Wilmot Ernest Lane and F. E. Lane (*née* Blakey); *m* 1948, Anne Brenda, 2nd *d* of E. Walsh; one *s* one *d*. *Educ:* Lancing College.

FIB. Served War, 1940–45, 7th Light Cavalry, Indian Army, India and Burma (Major). Joined Chartered Bank of India, Australia & China, 1937; served in Far East, 1939–60; Gen. Manager, 1961, Chief Gen. Manager, 1972, Man. Dir, 1973–77, Vice-Chm., 1977–83, Standard Chartered Bank Ltd. Mem., Export Guarantees Adv. Council, 1973–78 (Dep. Chm., 1977–78). *Recreations:* sailing, gardening. *Address:* West Hold, By the Church, West Mersea, Essex CO5 8QD. *T:* (01206) 382563. *Clubs:* East India, MCC; West Mersea Yacht.

LANE FOX, Robin James, FRSL; Fellow, New College, Oxford, since 1977; Reader in Ancient History, Oxford, since 1990; *b* 5 Oct. 1946; *s* of James Henry Lane Fox and Anne (*née* Loyd); *m* 1970, Louisa Caroline Mary (marr. diss. 1993), *d* of Charles and Lady Katherine Farrell; one *s* one *d*. *Educ:* Eton; Magdalen Coll., Oxford (Craven and de Paravicini scholarships, 1966; Passmore Edwards and Chancellors' Latin Verse Prize, 1968). FRSL 1974. Fellow by examination, Magdalen Coll., Oxford, 1970–73; Lectr in Classical Lang. and Lit., 1973–76, Res. Fellow, Classical and Islamic Studies, 1976–77, Worcester Coll., Oxford; Lectr in Ancient Hist., Oxford Univ., 1977–90. Weekly gardening correspondent, Financial Times, 1970–. *Publications:* Alexander the Great, 1973, 3rd edn 1978 (James Tait Black, Duff Cooper, W. H. Heinemann Awards, 1973–74); Variations on a Garden, 1974, rev. edn 1986; Search for Alexander, 1980; Better Gardening, 1982; Pagans and Christians, 1986; The Unauthorized Version, 1991. *Recreations:* gardening, hunting, poetry, rough travel. *Address:* New College, Oxford OX1 3BN. *Club:* Beefsteak.

LANE-FOX-PITT-RIVERS, Valerie; *see* Pitt-Rivers, V.

LANE-NOTT, Rear Adm. Roger Charles, CB 1996; Secretary, British Racing Drivers' Club, since 1999; *b* 3 June 1945; *s* of John Henry Lane-Nott, MBE and Kathleen Mary Lane-Nott; *m* 1968, Roisin MacQuillan; one *s* two *d*. *Educ:* Pangbourne Coll.; BRNC, Dartmouth. Joined RN, 1963: qualified submarines, 1966; served in HM Submarines: Andrew, Opossum, Otus, Revenge (Starboard), Conqueror, Aeneas, 1966–74; commanded HM Submarines: Walrus, 1974–76; Swiftsure, 1979; Splendid, 1979–82 (mentioned in despatches, Falklands, 1982); US Naval War Coll., 1983; Captain SM, Third Submarine Sqdn, 1985–86; Asst Dir, Defence Concepts, MoD, 1986–89; RCDS 1989; Captain First Frigate Sqdn and in comd HMS Coventry, 1990–91; Sen. Naval Officer, ME, 1991; Chief of Staff to Flag Officer Submarines, 1992–93; Flag Officer Submarines, and Comdr Submarines (NATO), Eastern Atlantic and Northwest, 1993–96; COS (Ops) to C-in-C Fleet, 1994–96; RN retd, 1996. Chief Exec., Centre for Marine and Petroleum Technol., 1997–99. Formula One Race Dir and Safety Delegate, Fédn Internat. de l'Automobile, 1996–. MRIN 1976; MNI 1991; FIMgt 1983; MInstPet 1997. *Recreations:* watching sport (Rugby, cricket, motor racing), unusual stationery. *Address:* British Racing Drivers' Club, Silverstone Circuit, Silverstone, Northants NN12 8TN.

LANE-SMITH, Roger; Senior Partner, DLA (formerly Dibb Lupton Alsop), Solicitors, since 1998; *b* 19 Oct. 1945; *s* of Harry Lane-Smith and Dorothy Lane-Smith; *m* 1969, Pamela; one *s* one *d*. *Educ:* Stockport Grammar Sch.; Guildford Coll. of Law. Admitted Solicitor, 1969; founded Lee Lane-Smith, 1977; Lee Lane-Smith merged with Alsop Stevens, 1983; Alsop Stevens merged with Wilkinson Kimbers to form Alsop Wilkinson, 1988; Chm. and Sen. Partner, Alsop Wilkinson, 1993–96; Alsop Wilkinson merged with Dibb Lupton to form Dibb Lupton Alsop, 1996; Dep. Sen. Partner, Dibb Lupton Alsop, 1996–98. *Recreations:* golf, tennis, shooting. *Address:* (office) 2 Noble Street, EC2V 7EE. *T:* (020) 7796 6090. *Clubs:* Mark's; St James' (Manchester).

LANG, family name of **Baron Lang of Monkton**.

LANG OF MONKTON, Baron *cr* 1997 (Life Peer), of Merrick and the Rhinns of Kells in Dumfries and Galloway; **Ian Bruce Lang;** PC 1990; DL; company chairman and director; *b* 27 June 1940; *y s* of late James Fulton Lang, DSC, and of Maude Margaret (*née* Stewart); *m* 1971, Sandra Caroline *e d* of late John Alastair Montgomerie, DSC; two *d*. *Educ:* Lathallan Sch., Kincardineshire; Rugby Sch.; Sidney Sussex Coll., Cambridge (BA 1962). Insurance Broker, 1962–79. Chairman: Murray Ventures Investment Trust, now Murray tmt, plc, 1998–; Thistle Mining Inc. (Can.), 1998–; China Internet Ventures Ltd, 2000–; BFS US Special Opportunities Trust plc; Dep. Chm., European Telecom, 1997–; Director: CGU (formerly General Accident) plc, 1997–2000; Marsh & McLennan Cos Inc., 1997–; Second Scottish Nat. Trust plc, 1997–; Lithgows Ltd, 1997–; Automobile Assoc., 1998–99. Trustee: Savings Bank of Glasgow, 1969–74; West of Scotland Trustee Savings Bank, 1974–83. Member, Queen's Body Guard for Scotland (Royal Company of Archers), 1974–. Contested (C): Central Ayrshire, 1970; Glasgow Pollok, Feb. 1974; MP (C) Galloway, 1979–83, Galloway and Upper Nithsdale, 1983–97; contested (C) Galloway and Upper Nithsdale, 1997. An Asst Govt Whip, 1981–83; a Lord Comr of HM Treasury, 1983–86; Parliamentary Under Secretary of State: Dept of Employment, 1986; Scottish Office, 1986–87; Minister of State, Scottish Office, 1987–90; Sec. of State for Scotland and Lord Keeper of the Great Seal of Scotland, 1990–95; Pres., Board of Trade, and Sec. of State for Trade and Industry, 1995–97. Mem., Constitution Cttee, H of L. Chm., Patrons of Nat. Galls of Scotland, 1999–. Gov., Rugby Sch., 1997–. DL Ayrshire and Arran, 1998. OStJ 1974. *Address:* House of Lords, SW1A 0PW. *Clubs:* Pratt's; Prestwick Golf.

LANG, Alistair Laurie, MBE 1970; Chief Executive, Canine Partners for Independence, since 2000; *b* 9 Sept. 1943; *s* of Comdr John Robert Lang, RN (retd) and late Jennifer Douglas Lang; *m* 1979, Ilona Augusta Avery; one *s* one *d*. *Educ:* Hurstpierpoint Coll.; BRNC; University Coll., Oxford (BA 1979); Internat. Management Inst., Geneva (MBA 1989). Served Royal Navy, 1962–75: in HM Ships Wizard, Salisbury, Devonshire, Malcolm, Plymouth and Kent; loan service to: Kenya Navy (Kenya Navy Ship Chui), 1966; Royal Malaysian Navy (i/c Kapel di-Raja Sri Sarawak and Fleet Ops Officer), 1968–70; Imperial Iranian Navy, 1974. Hong Kong Civil Service, 1979–90: Asst Sec. for Security, 1980–82; City Dist Officer, Kowloon City, 1982–83; support to Governor during negotiation with China on future of Hong Kong, 1983–85; Clerk of Councils (Sec. to Exec. and Legislative Councils), 1985–88; attached British Embassy, Beijing (on secondment), 1989; UK Rep., Hong Kong Exec. and Legislative Councils, 1990–92. Clerk to Drapers' Co., 1993–2000. Mem., Trollope Soc. *Recreations:* swimming, walking, reading, theatre. *Address:* Little Mead, Home Lane, Sparsholt, Winchester, Hants SO21 2NN. *T:* (01962) 776204.

See also Rear-Adm. J. S. Lang.

LANG, Prof. Andrew Richard, FRS 1975; Professor of Physics, University of Bristol, 1979–87, now Emeritus; Senior Research Fellow, University of Bristol, since 1995; *b* 9 Sept. 1924; *s* of late Ernest F. S. Lang and late Susannah (*née* Gueterbock); unmarried. *Educ:* University College of South-West, Exeter, (BSc Lond. 1944; MSc Lond. 1947); Univ. of Cambridge (PhD 1953). Research Dept, Lever Bros, Port Sunlight, 1945–47; Research Asst, Cavendish Laboratory, 1947–48; North American Philips, Irvington-on-Hudson, NY, 1952–53; Instructor, Harvard Univ., 1953–54; Asst Professor, Harvard Univ., 1954–59; Lectr in Physics, 1960–66, Reader, 1966–79, Univ. of Bristol. FInstP. Mem. Geol Assoc.; Mem. Soc. Sigma Xi. Foreign Associate, RSSAf 1996. Hon. DSc Exeter, 1994. Charles Vernon Boys Prize, Inst. of Physics, 1964; Hughes Medal, Royal Soc., 1997. *Publications:* contribs to learned jls. *Address:* 1B Elton Road, Bristol BS8 1SJ. *T:* (0117) 973 9784.

LANG, Beverley Ann Macnaughton; QC 2000; *b* 13 Oct. 1955; *d* of William Macnaughton Lang and Joan Margaret Mantua Lang (*née* Utting); one *d*. *Educ:* Wycombe Abbey Sch., Bucks; Lady Margaret Hall, Oxford (BA Hons Jurisprudence 1977). Called to the Bar, Inner Temple, 1978; Lectr, UEA, 1978–81; in practice at the Bar, 1981–; Chm. (pt-time), Employment Tribunals, 1995–2001. *Address:* Blackstone Chambers, Blackstone House, Temple, EC4Y 9BW. *T:* (020) 7583 1770.

LANG, Dr Brian Andrew; Principal and Vice-Chancellor, University of St Andrews, since 2001; *b* 2 Dec. 1945; *s* of Andrew Ballantyne Lang and Mary Bain Lang (*née* Smith); *m* 1st, 1975 (marr. diss. 1982); one *s*; 2nd, 1983 (marr. diss. 2000); one *s* one *d*. *Educ:* Royal High Sch., Edinburgh; Univ. of Edinburgh (MA, PhD). Social anthropological field research, Kenya, 1969–70; Lectr in social anthropology, Aarhus Univ., 1971–75; Scientific Staff, SSRC, 1976–79; Scottish Office (Sec., Historic Buildings Council for Scotland), 1979–80; Sec., Nat. Heritage Meml Fund, 1980–87; Dir of Public Affairs, Nat. Trust, 1987–91; Chief Exec. and Dep. Chm., British Library, 1991–2000; Chairman: Eur. Nat. Libraries Forum, 1993–2000; Heritage Image Partnership, 2000–. Member: Liby and Inf. Services Council (England), 1991–94; Liby and Inf. Commn, 1995–2000. Vis. Prof., Napier Univ., Edin., 1999–; Vis. Scholar, Getty Inst., Calif, 2000. Pforzheimer Lecture, Univ. of Texas, 1998. Trustee, 21st Century Learning Initiative, 1995–99. Mem. Council, St Leonard's Sch. Pres., Inst. of Information Scientists, 1993–94 (Hon. Fellow, 1994); Hon. FLA 1997. *Publications:* numerous articles, contribs etc to professional jls. *Recreations:* music, museums and galleries, pottering. *Address:* University of St Andrews, College Gate, St Andrews, Fife KY16 9AJ. *T:* (01334) 462545. *Club:* Royal & Ancient (St Andrews).

LANG, Rt Rev. Declan; *see* Clifton, Bishop of, (RC).

LANG, Hugh Montgomerie, CBE 1978; Chairman, Acertec Holdings Ltd, since 1999; *b* Glasgow, 7 Nov. 1932; *s* of John Montgomerie Lang and Janet Allan (*née* Smillie); *m* 1st, 1959, Marjorie Jean Armour (marr. diss. 1981); one *s* one *d*; 2nd, 1981, Susan Lynn Hartley (*née* Russell). *Educ:* Shawlands Acad., Glasgow; Glasgow Univ. (BSc). ARCST 1953; CEng 1967; FIEE (FIProdE 1976); FIMC 1970. Officer, REME, 1953–55 (National Service). Colvilles Ltd, 1955–56; Glacier Metal Co. Ltd, 1956–60; L. Sterne & Co. Ltd, 1960–61; P-E Consulting Group, 1961–92: Manager for ME, 1965–68; Scottish Reg. Manager, 1968–72; Man. Dir, 1974–77; Chm., P-E Internat., 1980–92 (Dir, 1972–92; Chief Exec., 1977–92). Chairman: Brammer plc, 1990–98; Manganese Bronze Hldgs, 1992–2000; Victaulic, 1995; Albion Automotive, 1997–98; Director: Redman Heenan Internat., 1981–86 (Chm., 1982–86); Fairey Holdings Ltd, 1978–82; UKO International, 1985–86; B. Elliott, 1986–88; Siebe, 1987–91; Strong & Fisher (Hldgs), 1988–90; Co-ordinated Land and Estates, 1988–93; OGC International, 1993–94; Ericsson Ltd, 1993–99. Chairman: Food, Drink and Packaging Machinery Sector Working Party, 1976–81; Technology Transfer Services Adv. Cttee, 1982–85 (Mem., 1978–85); Member: Business Educn Council, 1980–81; CBI Industrial Policy Cttee, 1980–83; Design Council, 1983–90 (Dep. Chm., 1986–90); Engrg Council, 1984–86. *Recreations:* fishing, gardening, golf, reading. *Address:* Welders Wood, Chalfont St Peter, Bucks SL9 8TT. *Clubs:* Brooks's; Denham Golf.

LANG, Jack Mathieu Emile, Chevalier de la Légion d'Honneur; Hon. GCVO 1992; Minister for Education, since 2000; Mayor of Blois, since 1989; *b* 2 Sept. 1939; *s* of Roger Lang and Marie-Luce Lang (*née* Bouchet); *m* 1961, Monique Buczynski; two *d*. *Educ:* Inst. d'Etudes Politiques; Dr of Public Law. Founder and Producer, World Fest. Univ. Theatre, Nancy, 1963–72; Dir, Nancy Univ. Theatre, 1963–72; Dir, Palais de Chaillot Théâtre, 1972–74; Prof. of Internat. Law, 1971–81; Dir, teaching and research unit in legal and econ. scis, Nancy, 1977–80; Prof., Univ. of Paris X, 1986–88. Paris councillor, 1977–89; nat. deleg. for cultural affairs, Socialist Party, 1979–81; Minister of Culture, 1981–83 and 1984–86; Deputy, Loir-et-Cher, 1986–88 and 1997–2000; Minister of Culture and Communication, 1988–92; Govt Spokesman, 1991–92; Minister of State, and Minister of Nat. Educn and Culture, 1992–93. Pres., Foreign Affairs Cttee, French Nat. Assembly, 1997–. Conseiller Général de Blois, 1992–. Order of Orange Nassau (Netherlands), 1991; Order of the Crown of Belgium, 1992. *Publications:* L'Etat et le Théâtre, 1968; Le plâteau continental de la mer du nord, 1970; Les politiques culturelles comparée en Europe; La jonction au fond des exceptions préliminaires devant la cour, 1971; Demain les femmes, 1995; Lettre à Malraux, 1996; François 1er ou le rêve italien, 1997; contribs to newspapers. *Address:* Mairie de Blois, 9 place Saint-Louis, 41012 Blois, France.

LANG, Jacqueline Shelagh; Headmistress, Walthamstow Hall, Sevenoaks, 1984–Aug. 2002; *b* 17 June 1944; *d* of James Wicks and Mary Mills Wicks (*née* Green); *m* 1965, Andrew Lang; two *d*. *Educ:* Walthamstow Hall; St Anne's Coll., Oxford (Schol.; MA). Res., mediaeval French literature, KCL, 1964–66; Ursuline Convent School, Wimbledon: Asst Mistress, 1970–76; Head of Langs, 1976–83; Foundn Gov., 1984–93. Chairman: London and SE Region, ISIS, 1991–95; Assisted Places Cttee, ISC, 1998–; Pres., GSA, 1997. *Recreations:* history of architecture, gardens, visiting archaeological sites. *Address:* (until Aug. 2002) Walthamstow Hall, Sevenoaks, Kent TN13 3UL. *T:* (01732) 451334; (from Aug. 2002) 82 Richmond Road, SW20 0PD. *Club:* University Women's.

LANG, Very Rev. John Harley; Dean of Lichfield, 1980–93, now Emeritus; Chaplain to HM the Queen, 1976–80; Member, Broadcasting Standards Commission, 1997–98 (Broadcasting Standards Council, 1994–97); *b* 27 Oct. 1927; *e s* of Frederick Henry Lang and Eileen Annie Lang (*née* Harley); *m* 1972, Frances Rosemary Widdowson; three *d*. *Educ:* Merchant Taylors' Sch.; King's Coll., London (BD); MA Cantab; MST Oxon 1999; LRAM. Subaltern, XII Royal Lancers, 1951–52; Asst Curate, St Mary's Portsea, 1952–57; Priest Vicar, Southwark Cathedral, 1957–60; Chaplain, Emmanuel Coll., Cambridge, 1960–64; Asst Head of Religious Broadcasting, BBC, 1964–67; Head of Religious Programmes, Radio, 1967–71; Head of Religious Broadcasting, BBC, 1971–80. Mem., English Heritage Cathedrals and Churches Adv. Cttee, 1994–99. Trustee, Historic Churches Preservation Trust, 1994–2000. President: Staffordshire Soc., 1993–95; Lichfield Festival, 1994–. Mem., Kellogg Coll., Oxford, 1997–. Freeman, Goldsmiths' Co., 1994. Hon. DLitt Keele, 1988. *Recreations:* books, music. *Address:* South Barn, Stanton, Broadway, Worcs WR12 7NQ. *T:* (01386) 584251.

LANG, Rear-Adm. John Stewart, FNI, FRIN; Royal Navy, retired; Chief Inspector of Marine Accidents, Marine Accident Investigation Branch, Department for Transport, Local Government and the Regions (formerly Department of Transport, then Department of the Environment, Transport and the Regions), 1997–July 2002; *b* 18 July 1941; *s* of Comdr John Robert Lang, RN and late Jennifer Douglas Lang; *m* 1971, Joanna Judith Pegler; two *d*. *Educ:* Cheltenham Coll. Jun. Sch.; Nautical Coll., Pangbourne. FNI 1986; FRIN 1997. Navigating Officer Apprentice, P&OSN Co., 1959–62; RN 1962; served HM Ships Chilcompton, Totem, Auriga, Oberon, Revenge, Opossum, 1964–71; qualified Submarine Command, 1971; commanded: HMS Walrus, 1971–72; HMS Renown, 1976–78; HMS Beaver, 1983–85; Captain, Royal Naval Presentation Team,

1986–87; ACOS (Ops) to C-in-C Fleet, 1987–89; Dir, Naval Ops and Trade, 1989–91; Dep. Chief of Defence Intelligence, 1992–95. *Recreations:* sailing, photography, oil painting, travel, pharology, international affairs. *Address:* Wangfield House, Martyr Worthy, Winchester, Hants SO21 1AT.

See also A. L. Lang.

LANG, Rear-Adm. William Duncan, CB 1981; retired; *b* 1 April 1925; *s* of James Hardie Lang and Elizabeth Foggo Paterson Lang (*née* Storie); *m* 1947, Joyce Rose Weeks; one *s* one *d. Educ:* Edinburgh Acad. Entered Royal Navy, 1943; trained as Pilot; served in 800, 816 and 825 Sqdns and as Flying Instr and Test Pilot; comd 802 Sqdn, 1958–59; Commander (Air): RNAS Culdrose, 1962–63; HMS Eagle, 1964–65; Fleet Aviation Officer, Far East Fleet, 1966–68; Captain 1969; comd RNAS Lossiemouth, 1970–72; Dep. Comdt, Jt Warfare Estabt, 1973–74; COS to Flag Officer, Naval Air Comd, 1975–76; Mil. Dep. to Hd of Defence Sales, 1978–81; Dir, Naval Security, MoD, 1981–86. Naval ADC to the Queen, 1978; Rear-Adm. 1978. *Recreation:* golf (Pres., RN Golf Soc., 1979–85). *Address:* c/o HSBC, 19 High Street, Haslemere, Surrey GU27 2HQ. *Club:* Army and Navy.

LANGAN, Peter St John Hevey; QC 1983; **His Honour Judge Langan;** a Circuit Judge, since 1991; Senior Circuit Judge, Mercantile and Chancery Court, North Eastern Circuit, since 2001; *b* 1 May 1942; *s* of late Frederick Hevey Langan and of Myrrha Langan (*née* Jephson), Mount Hevey, Hill of Down, Co. Meath; *m* 1976, Oonagh May Winifred McCarthy. *Educ:* Downside School; Trinity College, Dublin (MA, LLB); Christ's College, Cambridge (PhD). Lectr in Law, Durham Univ., 1966–69. In practice at the Bar, 1970–91; a Recorder, 1989–91; Designated Civil Judge, Norwich and Cambridge, 1998–2001. Legal Assessor: GMC, 1990–91; GDC, 1990–91. Mem., Legal Commn, Caritas Internationalis, Rome, 1991–93; Trustee, CAFOD, 1993–99 (Mem., Management Cttee, 1984–91). *Publications:* Maxwell on Interpretation of Statutes, 12th edn, 1969; Civil Procedure and Evidence, 1st edn, 1970, 3rd edn (with L. D. J. Henderson) as Civil Procedure, 1983; (with P. V. Baker) Snell's Principles of Equity, 28th edn, 1982, 29th edn, 1990. *Address:* Court House, 1 Oxford Row, Leeds LS1 3BG. *T:* (0113) 283 0040.

LANGDALE, Simon John Bartholomew; Director of Grants and Special Projects (formerly Educational and General Grants), The Rank Foundation, since 1988; *b* 26 Jan. 1937; *s* of late Geoffrey Ronald Langdale and Hilda Joan Langdale (*née* Bartholomew); *m* 1962, Diana Marjory Hall; two *s* one *d. Educ:* Tonbridge Sch.; St Catharine's Coll., Cambridge. Taught at Radley Coll., 1959–73 (Housemaster, 1968–73); Headmaster: Eastbourne Coll., 1973–80; Shrewsbury Sch., 1981–88. *Recreations:* reading, gardening, golf. *Address:* Park House, Culworth, Banbury, Oxon OX17 2AP. *T:* (01295) 760222. *Clubs:* East India; Hawks (Cambridge); Free Foresters, Jesters.

See also T. J. Langdale.

LANGDALE, Timothy James; QC 1992; a Recorder, 1996–99; *b* 3 Jan. 1940; *m* twice; two *d. Educ:* Sevenoaks Sch.; St Andrews Univ. (MA). Called to the Bar, Lincoln's Inn, 1966. Res. Assistant, Community Justice Center, Watts, Los Angeles, 1969–70; Jun. Prosecuting Counsel to the Crown, 1979–87, Sen. Prosecuting Counsel, 1987–92, CCC. *Recreations:* reading, opera, theatre, cinema. *Address:* Queen Elizabeth Building, Temple, EC4Y 9BS. *T:* (020) 7583 5766.

See also S. J. B. Langdale.

LANGDON, Anthony James; Deputy Under Secretary of State, Home Office, 1989–95; *b* 5 June 1935; *s* of Dr James Norman Langdon and Maud Winifred Langdon; *m* 1969, Helen Josephine Drabble, *y d* of His Honour J. F. Drabble, QC; one *s* one *d. Educ:* Kingswood Sch., Bath; Christ's Coll., Cambridge. Entered Home Office, 1958; Office of Minister for Science, 1961–63; Treasury, 1967–69; Under Sec., Cabinet Office, 1985–89. *Publication:* (with Ian Dunbar) Tough Justice, 1998.

LANGDON, David, OBE 1988; FRSA; cartoonist, illustrator and caricaturist; contributor to Punch, since 1937, The New Yorker, since 1952, and The Spectator, since 1997; *b* 24 Feb. 1914; *er s* of late Bennett and Bess Langdon; *m* 1955, April Sadler-Phillips; two *s* one *d. Educ:* Davenant Gram. Sch., London. Architect's Dept, LCC, 1931–39; Executive Officer, London Rescue Service, 1939–41; served in Royal Air Force, 1941–46; Squadron Leader, 1945. Editor, Royal Air Force Jl, 1945–46. Creator of Billy Brown of London Town for LPTB. Official Artist to Centre International Audio-Visuel d'Etudes et de Recherches, St Ghislain, Belgium, 1970–75. Cartoonist to Sunday Mirror, 1948–93. Caricatures: of High Court Judges for Sweet and Maxwell, 1956; of racing celebrities for Ladbrokes Racing Calendar, 1959–94. Exhibitions: Ottawa, Oxford, New York, Lille, London. *Publications:* Home Front Lines, 1941; All Buttoned Up, 1944; Meet Me Inside, 1946; Slipstream (with R. B. Raymond), 1946; The Way I See It, 1947; Hold Tight There!, 1949; Let's Face It, 1951; Wake Up and Die (with David Clayton), 1952; Look at You, 1952; All in Fun, 1953; Laugh with Me, 1954; More in Fun, 1955; Funnier Still, 1956; A Banger for a Monkey, 1957; Langdon At Large, 1958; I'm Only Joking, 1960; Punch with Wings, 1961; How to Play Golf and Stay Happy, 1964; David Langdon's Casebook, 1969; How To Talk Golf, 1975; Punch in the Air, 1983; Soccer—It's a Funny Old Game, 1998. *Recreation:* golf. *Address:* Greenlands, Honor End Lane, Great Missenden, Bucks HP16 9QY. *T:* (01494) 862475. *Club:* Royal Air Force.

LANGDON, Janet Mary; Director and Secretary, Water Services Association of England and Wales, 1992–98; *b* 5 March 1940; *d* of late Geoffrey Harry Langdon and Iris Sarah Langdon. *Educ:* St Hilda's Coll., Oxford (BSc, MA). Asst Lectr, Wellesley Coll., Mass, 1962–63; Distillers' Co. Ltd, 1963–68; NEDO, 1968–71; Shell Chemicals UK Ltd and Shell Internat. Chemical Co. Ltd, 1971–82; Projects and Export Policy Div., DTI, 1982–85; Director: Asia, Gp Exports, GEC PLC, 1985–89; Export Div., GEC ALSTHOM Ltd, 1989–92. Member: Sch. Teachers' Rev. Body, 1996–; POUNC, 1998–2000. *Recreations:* walking, tennis, travel, theatre. *Address:* 43 Fairfax Place, NW6 4EJ. *T:* (020) 7624 3857.

LANGDON, Jonathan Bertram Robert Louis; His Honour Judge Langdon; a Circuit Judge, since 1991; *b* 1 Nov. 1939; *s* of Captain John Edward Langdon, RN and Nancy Langdon; *m* 1962, Hilary Jean Fox Taylor; twin *s* one *d. Educ:* Hurstpierpoint Coll.; RNC Dartmouth. Entered RN, 1958; served HM Ships Bermuda, Lincoln and London, 1960–64; Supply Officer, HMS Daring, 1965–68; legal trng, 1968–70; called to the Bar, Gray's Inn, 1970; Staff Legal Advr to FO Plymouth, 1970–73; RN FE Legal Advr, Hong Kong, 1973–75; Comdr, 1977; Supply Officer, HMS Norfolk, 1977–79; various MoD and staff appts, 1980–86; Captain, 1986; Chief Naval Judge Advocate, 1987–90; Sec. to C-in-C Naval Home Command, 1990–91; retired voluntarily from RN, 1991. Hon. Recorder, City of Canterbury, 2000–. *Recreations:* sailing, gardening, croquet, travel. *Address:* The Law Courts, Chaucer Road, Canterbury, Kent CT1 1ZA.

LANGDON, Richard Norman Darbey, FCA; Senior Partner, Spicer and Pegler, 1978–84; *b* 19 June 1919; *s* of Norman Langdon and Dorothy Langdon; *m* 1944, June Dixon; two *s. Educ:* Shrewsbury Sch. Officer, RA, 1939–46. Admitted Mem. Inst. of Chartered Accountants in England and Wales, 1947; joined Spicer and Pegler, 1949, Partner 1953, Managing Partner, 1971–82. Chairman: Hammond and Champness Ltd, 1966–89; Aspinall Hldg, 1983–89; Finlay Packaging PLC, 1984–93; First National Finance Corp., 1985–92; Beeson Gregory, 1989–95; Director: Time Products PLC, 1984–93 (Chm., 1984–92); Rockware Group PLC, 1985–91; Chemring Gp PLC, 1985–96 (Dep. Chm., 1985–92). Treasurer, CGLI, 1982–90. Mem. Council, Univ. of Surrey, 1988–90. *Recreation:* gardening. *Address:* Whitedale House, Hambledon, Hants PO7 4RZ. *T:* (023) 9263 2457. *Club:* Old Salopian.

LANGDON-DOWN, Antony Turnbull; Volunteer Consultant, Sevenoaks Citizens' Advice Bureau, since 1995; Clerk to Merchant Taylors Company, 1980–85; *b* 31 Dec. 1922; *s* of Dr Reginald Langdon-Down and Ruth Langdon-Down (*née* Turnbull); *m* 1954, Jill Elizabeth Style (*née* Caruth) (*d* 2001); one *s* one *d. Educ:* Harrow School. Member of Lincoln's Inn, 1940–60, called to the Bar, 1948; enrolled as a solicitor, 1960; practised as solicitor, 1961–80. Pt-time Chm., Social Security Appeals Tribunal, 1985–95. Pilot, Royal Air Force, 1942–47 (finally Flt Lieut). Master of Merchant Taylors Company, 1979–80. *Recreations:* sailing, tennis, bridge, music, art. *Address:* Drumard, The Street, Plaxtol, Sevenoaks, Kent TN15 0QP. *T:* (01732) 810720. *Clubs:* Savile, MCC; Bough Beech Sailing.

LANGE, Rt Hon. David Russell, CH 1990; PC 1984; *b* 4 Aug. 1942; *s* of late Eric Roy Lange and Phoebe Fysh Lange; *m* 1st, 1968, Naomi Joy Crampton; two *s* one *d*; 2nd, 1992, Margaret Forsyth Pope; one *d. Educ:* Univ. of Auckland (LLM Hons). Called to the Bar of NZ and admitted Solicitor, 1966. MP (Lab) Mangere, NZ, 1977–96; Dep. Leader of the Opposition, 1979–83, Leader 1983–84; Minister of Foreign Affairs, 1984–87; Prime Minister, and Minister in charge of Security Intelligence Service, 1984–89, and Minister of Education, 1987–89; Attorney Gen., and Minister of State, 1989–90. *Publications:* Nuclear-Free—the New Zealand Way, 1990; Broadsides, 1992; Cuttings, 1994. *Address:* PO Box 59–120, Mangere Bridge, New Zealand.

LANGER, Bernhard; golfer; *b* Germany, 27 Aug. 1957; *m* Vikki Lopez; two *s* two *d.* Major championships include: US Masters, 1985, 1993; German Open 5 times; 9 Ryder Cup appearances for Europe, 1981–94. *Publication:* (with Bill Elliott) While the Iron is Hot (autobiog.), 1988. *Address:* c/o IMG, Pier House, Strand on the Green, Chiswick, W4 3NN.

LANGFORD, 9th Baron *cr* 1800; **Colonel Geoffrey Alexander Rowley-Conwy,** OBE 1943; DL; RA, retired; Constable of Rhuddlan Castle and Lord of the Manor of Rhuddlan; *b* 8 March 1912; *s* of late Major Geoffrey Seymour Rowley-Conwy (killed in action, Gallipoli, 1915), Bodrhyddan, Flints, and Bertha Gabrielle Rowley-Conwy, JP (*d* 1984), *d* of late Lieutenant Alexander Cochran, Royal Navy, Ashkirk, Selkirkshire; *S* kinsman, 1953; *m* 1st, 1939, Ruth St John (marr. diss. 1956; she *d* 1991), *d* of late Albert St John Murphy, The Island House, Little Island, County Cork; 2nd, 1957, Grete (*d* 1973), *d* of late Col E. T. C. von Freiesleben, formerly Chief of the King's Adjutants Staff to the King of Denmark; three *s*; 3rd, 1975, Susan Winifred Denham, *d* of C. C. H. Denham, Chester; one *s* one *d. Educ:* Marlborough; RMA Woolwich. Served War of 1939–45, with RA (2nd Lieut, 1932; Lieut, 1935; Captain, 1939; Major 1941); Singapore, (POW escaped) and with Indian Mountain Artillery in Burma (Arakan, Kohima), 1941–45 (despatches, OBE); Staff Coll., Quetta, 1945; Berlin Airlift, Fassberg, 1948–49; GSOI 42 Inf. Div., TA, 1949–52; Lt-Col 1945; retired 1957; Colonel (Hon.), 1967. Freeman, City of London, 1986–. DL Clwyd, 1977. *Heir: s* Hon. Owain Grenville Rowley-Conwy [*b* 27 Dec. 1958; *m* 1986, Joanna (marr. diss. 1993), *d* of Jack Featherstone; one *s* one *d*]. *Address:* Bodrhyddan, Rhuddlan, Denbighshire LL18 5SB. *Club:* Army and Navy.

LANGFORD, Anthony John, CB 1996; FRICS; Chief Executive, Valuation Office Agency, 1994–96; *b* 25 June 1936; *s* of Freeman and Ethel Langford; *m* 1958, Joan Winifred Barber; one *s* one *d. Educ:* Soham Grammar School. FRICS 1978. Joined Valuation Office, Inland Revenue, 1957; District Valuer, Camden, 1976; Superintending Valuer, Northern Region, 1981; Asst Chief Valuer, 1983; Dep. Chief Valuer, then Dep. Chief Exec., Valuation Office Agency, 1988–94. *Recreations:* walking, gardening, bowls.

LANGFORD, Prof. Paul, DPhil; FRHistS; FBA 1993; Professor of Modern History, University of Oxford, since 1996; Fellow, and Tutor in Modern History, since 1970, and Rector, since 2000, Lincoln College, Oxford; *b* 20 Nov. 1945; *s* of Frederick Wade Langford and Olive Myrtle Langford (*née* Walters); *m* 1970, Margaret Veronica Edwards; one *s. Educ:* Monmouth Sch.; Hertford Coll., Oxford (MA, DPhil; Hon. Fellow, 2000). FRHistS 1979. Jun. Res. Fellow, Lincoln Coll., Oxford, 1969–70; Reader in Modern History, Oxford Univ., 1994–96. Ford's Lectr in English History, Oxford Univ., 1990; Raleigh Lectr, British Acad., 1996. Mem., Humanities Res. Bd, British Acad., 1995–98. Chm. and Chief Exec., AHRB, 1998–2000. Sen. Fellow, RCA, 2001. General Editor: The Writings and Speeches of Edmund Burke, 1974–; Oxford History of the British Isles, 1996–. *Publications:* The First Rockingham Administration 1765–66, 1973; The Excise Crisis: society and politics in the age of Walpole, 1975; (ed) Writings and Speeches of Edmund Burke, vol. II: Party, Parliament and The American Crisis 1766–74, 1981; A Polite and Commercial People 1727–83, 1989 (New Oxford History of England series); Public Life and the Propertied Englishman 1689–1789, 1991; Englishness Identified: manners and character 1650–1850, 2000. *Recreation:* gardening. *Address:* Lincoln College, Oxford OX1 3DR; Valpys, Noakes Hill, Ashampstead, Berks RG8 8RY. *T:* (01635) 578181. *Club:* Athenæum.

LANGHAM, Sir James (Michael), 15th Bt *cr* 1660; TD 1965; *b* 24 May 1932; *s* of Sir John Charles Patrick Langham, 14th Bt, and Rosamond Christabel (MBE 1969) (*d* 1992), *d* of late Arthur Rashleigh; *S* father, 1972; *m* 1959, Marion Audrey Eleanor, *d* of O. H. Barratt, Gararagua Estate, Tanzania; two *s* one *d. Educ:* Rossall School, Fleetwood. Served as Captain, North Irish Horse, 1953–67. *Heir: s* John Stephen Langham [*b* 14 Dec. 1960; *m* 1991, Sarah Jane, *d* of late J. D. Verschoyle-Greene]. *Address:* Claranagh, Tempo, Co. Fermanagh BT94 3FJ. *T:* (028) 6654 1247.

LANGHORNE, Prof. Richard Tristan Bailey, FRHistS; Professor of Political Science, and Director of Center for Global Change and Governance, Rutgers University, New Jersey, since 1996; *b* 6 May 1940; *s* of late Eadward John Bailey Langhorne and of Rosemary Scott-Foster; *m* 1971, Helen Logue, *o d* of William Donaldson, CB and Mary Donaldson; one *s* one *d. Educ:* St Edward's Sch., Oxford; St John's Coll., Cambridge (Exhibr). BA Hist. Tripos, 1962; Certif. in Hist. Studies, 1963; MA 1965. Tutor in History, Univ. of Exeter, 1963–64; Research Student, St John's Coll., Cambridge, 1964–66; Lectr in History, 1966–74 and Master of Rutherford Coll., 1971–74, Univ. of Kent at Canterbury; St John's College, Cambridge: Steward, 1974–79; Junior Bursar, 1974–87; Fellow, 1974–93; Dir, Centre of Internat. Studies, Univ. of Cambridge, 1987–93; Dir and Chief Exec., Wilton Park, FCO, 1993–96. Vis. Prof., Univ. of Southern Calif, 1986; Hon. Prof. of Internat. Relns, Univ. of Kent at Canterbury, 1994–97. Freeland K. Abbott Meml Lectr, Tufts Univ., 1990; Queen Beatrix Lectr, Royal Foundn, Amsterdam, 1998. *Publications:* The Collapse of the Concert of Europe, 1890–1914, 1980;

(ed) Diplomacy and Intelligence during the Second World War, 1985; (with K. Hamilton) The Practice of Diplomacy, 1994; The Coming of Globalization, 2000; chapters in: The Twentieth Century Mind, 1971; British Foreign Policy under Sir Edward Grey, 1977; reviews and articles in Historical Jl, History, Review of International Studies, and Diplomacy and Statecraft. *Recreations:* music, railways. *Address:* Rutgers University, 123 Washington Street, Suite 510, Newark, NJ 07102–1895, USA; 6 Carleton Court, Maplewood, NJ 07040, USA; 14 Love Lane, Canterbury, Kent CT1 1TZ. *Club:* Athenæum.

LANGLANDS, Sir (Robert) Alan, Kt 1998; Principal and Vice-Chancellor, Dundee University, since 2000; *b* 29 May 1952; *s* of James Langlands and May Langlands (*née* Rankin); *m* 1977, Elizabeth McDonald; one *s* one *d. Educ:* Allan Glen's Sch.; Univ. of Glasgow (BSc Pure Sci); MHSM, DipHSM. Grad. Trainee, NHS Scotland, 1974–76; Argyll and Clyde Health Bd, 1976–78; Simpson Meml Maternity Pavilion, Elsie Inglis Hosp., 1978–81; Unit Administrator, Middx and University Coll. Hosps and Hosp. for Women, Soho, 1981–85; Dist Gen. Manager, Harrow HA, 1985–89; Practice Leader, Health Care, Towers Perrin, 1989–91; Gen. Manager, NW Thames RHA, 1991–92; Dep. Chief Exec., 1993–94, Chief Exec., 1994–2000, NHS Executive. Member: Central R&D Cttee, NHS, 1991–92; Nat. Forum R&D, 1994–99; Health Sector Gp, BOTB, 1998–2000. Hon. Prof., 1996, and Mem. Bd, Univ. of Warwick Business Sch., 1999–2000; Mem. Council and Court, Univ. of York, 1998–2000. Hon. FFPHM 1994; FIA 1999; FCGI 2000; CIMgt 2000; FRCGP 2001; Hon. FRCP 2001. *Recreation:* living and walking in Scotland and Yorkshire. *Address:* University of Dundee, Dundee DD1 4HN.

LANGLANDS, Prof. Robert Phelan, FRS 1981; Professor of Mathematics, Institute for Advanced Study, Princeton, New Jersey, since 1972; *b* 6 Oct. 1936; *s* of Robert Langlands and Kathleen Johanna (*née* Phelan); *m* 1956, Charlotte Lorraine Cheverie; two *s* two *d. Educ:* Univ. of British Columbia (BA 1957, MA 1958); Yale Univ. (PhD 1960). FRSC 1972. Princeton University: Instructor, 1960–61; Lectr, 1961–62; Asst Prof., 1962–64; Associate Prof., 1964–67; Prof., Yale Univ., 1967–72. Associate Prof., Ortadoğu Teknik Universitesi, 1967–68; Gast Prof., Universität Bonn, 1980–81. Mem., Nat. Acad. of Scis, USA, 1993. Hon. DSc: British Columbia, 1985; McMaster, 1985; CUNY, 1985; Paris VII, 1989; McGill, 1991; Toronto, 1993; Montreal, 1997; Hon. DMath Waterloo, 1988. Wilbur L. Cross Medal, Yale Univ., 1975; Cole Prize, Amer. Math. Sec., 1982; Common Wealth Award, Sigma Xi, 1984; Maths Award, Nat. Acad. of Scis, 1988; Wolf Prize in Maths, Wolf Foundn of Israel, 1996; Grande Médaille d'Or, Acad. des Scis, 2000. *Publications:* Automorphic Forms on GL(2) (with H. Jacquet), 1970; Euler Products, 1971; On the Functional Equations satisfied by Eisenstein Series, 1976; Base Change for GL(2), 1980; Les débuts d'une formule des traces stable, 1983; contrib. Canadian Jl Maths, Proc. Amer. Math. Soc. Symposia, Springer Lecture Notes. *Address:* Institute for Advanced Study, School of Mathematics, Princeton, NJ 08540, USA. *T:* (609) 7348106.

LANGLEY, Sir Desmond; *see* Langley, Sir H. D. A.

LANGLEY, Hon. Sir Gordon; *see* Langley, Hon. Sir J. H. G.

LANGLEY, Maj.-Gen. Sir (Henry) Desmond (Allen), KCVO 1983; MBE 1967; Governor and Commander-in-Chief of Bermuda, 1988–92; *b* 16 May 1930; *s* of late Col Henry Langley, OBE, and Winsome Langley; *m* 1950, Felicity Joan, *d* of Lt-Col K. J. P. Oliphant, MC; one *s* one *d. Educ:* Eton; RMA Sandhurst. Commissioned The Life Guards, 1949; Adjt, Household Cavalry Regt, 1953–54; GSO3 HQ 10th Armoured Div., 1956–57; Regtl Adjt, Household Cavalry, 1959–60; psc 1961; GSO2(Ops) HQ Far East Land Forces, 1963–65; Bde Major, Household Bde, 1965–67; Comdg Officer, The Life Guards, 1969–71; Asst Sec., Chiefs of Staff Secretariat, 1971–72; Lt-Col Comdg Household Cavalry and Silver Stick-in-Waiting, 1972–75; Comdr 4th Guards Armoured Bde, 1976–77; RCDS 1978; BGS HQ UK Land Forces, 1979; GOC London District and Maj.-Gen. Comdg Household Div., 1979–83; Administrator, Sovereign Base Areas and Comdr, British Forces, Cyprus, 1983–85; retired, 1986. Gov., Church Lads' and Church Girls' Brigade, 1986–. Freeman, City of London, 1983. KStJ 1989.

LANGLEY, Hon. Sir (Julian Hugh) Gordon, Kt 1995; **Hon. Mr Justice Langley;** a Judge of the High Court, Queen's Bench Division, since 1995; *b* 11 May 1943; *s* of late Gordon Thompson Langley and of Marjorie Langley; *m* 1968, Beatrice Jayanthi Langley; two *d. Educ:* Westminster School; Balliol College, Oxford (MA, BCL). Called to the Bar, Inner Temple, 1966, Bencher, 1996; QC 1983; a Recorder, 1986–95. *Recreations:* music, sport. *Address:* Royal Courts of Justice, Strand, WC2A 2LL. *Club:* Travellers.

LANGLEY, Ven. Robert; Archdeacon of Lindisfarne, since 2001; *b* 25 Oct. 1937; *s* of Maurice and Kathleen Langley; *m* 1961, Elisabeth Hart; one *s* two *d. Educ:* Worksop Coll.; St Catherine's Coll., Oxford (BA Maths 1961). Ordained deacon, 1963, priest, 1964; Asst Curate, Aston cum Aughton, Sheffield, 1963–68; Midlands and HQ Sec., Christian Educn Movt, 1968–74; Principal: Ian Ramsay Coll., Brasted, 1974–77; St Albans Dio. Ministerial Trng Scheme, 1977–85; Canon Missioner, Newcastle Dio., 1985–98; Dir, Ministry and Trng, Newcastle Dio., 1998–2001. *Recreations:* cycling, walking, music. *Address:* 4 Acomb Close, Stobhill Manor, Morpeth, Northumberland NE61 2YH.

LANGLEY, Prof. Robin Stewart, PhD; Professor of Mechanical Engineering, since 1998, and Deputy Head (Graduate Studies), Department of Engineering, since 1999, Cambridge University; Fellow of Fitzwilliam College, Cambridge, since 1998; *b* 5 April 1957; *s* of Robert Langley and Marie Langley (*née* Lewins); *m* 1982, Pamela Heath (marr. diss. 1997). *Educ:* Univ. of Leicester (BSc 1978); Cranfield Univ. (MSc 1981; PhD 1983). CMath, FIMA 1989; CEng, MRAeS 1990. Accountant, Armitage and Norton, 1978–79; Teaching Associate, 1983–84, Lectr in Structural Dynamics, 1984–91, Cranfield Univ.; Sen. Lectr in Aerospace Structures, 1991–95, Prof. of Structural Dynamics, 1995–98, Southampton Univ. Fellow, Acoustical Soc. of Amer., 2000. *Publications:* articles in academic jls, mainly on random vibration, structural dynamics, and acoustics. *Recreations:* walking, literature, family and friends. *Address:* Department of Engineering, University of Cambridge, Trumpington Street, Cambridge CB2 1PZ. *T:* (01223) 766385.

LANGMAN, Prof. Michael John Stratton, MD; Hon. Professor of Medicine, University of Birmingham, since 2000 (William Withering Professor of Medicine, 1987–2000, and Dean, Faculty of Medicine and Dentistry, 1992–97); *b* 30 Jan. 1935; *s* of John A. H. and E. Margaret Langman; *m* 1960, Rosemary A. Hempton; two *s* two *d. Educ:* St Paul's Sch.; Guy's Hosp. Med. Sch., Univ. of London (BSc, MB (Hons), MD). FRCP 1973; FFPM (by distinction) 1989. House Physician and Surg., Guy's Hosp., 1958–59; House Physician, Brompton, Hammersmith and Queen Square Hosps, 1959–61; Registrar, Central Middlesex Hosp., 1961–63; Lectr in Medicine, Guy's Hosp., 1963–68; Mem., Scientific Staff, MRC Statistical Res. Unit, UCH, 1963–68; Consultant Physician and Sen. Lectr, 1968–70, Reader, 1970–74, in Medicine, Nottingham Hosps and Univ.; Boots Prof. of Therapeutics, Univ. of Nottingham, 1974–87. Non-exec. Dir, Birmingham HA, 1992–98. Hon. Sen. Res. Fellow, European Inst. of Oncology, Milan, 1996–; Hon. Consultant, WHO, 1996–. Lectures: Avery Jones, Central Middx Hosp., 1977; Melrose, Caledonian Soc. of Gastroenterology, 1987; William Withering Prize, RCP, 1988; Honeyman Gillespie, Edinburgh Univ., 1989; Barany, Swedish Soc. of Gastroenterology, 1992. Chairman: Adv. Expert Gp on Vitamins and Minerals, MAFF, 1999–; Jt Cttee on Vaccination and Immunization UK, 2000–; Member: Cttee on Review of Medicines, 1980–87; Cttee on Safety of Medicines, 1987– (Chm., Subcttee on Pharmacovigilance, 1992–95). Chm., Warwicks Ambulance NHS Trust, 2000–. Pres., British Soc. of Gastroenterology, 1997–99. Gov., St Martin's Sch., Solihull, 1997–. Founder FMedSci 1998. *Publications:* Concise Textbook of Gastroenterology, 1973; various papers on chronic digestive disease. *Recreations:* tennis, music, cricket. *Address:* Department of Medicine, Queen Elizabeth Hospital, Birmingham B15 2TH. *T:* (0121) 627 2380. *Clubs:* Athenæum, MCC; Claverdon Lawn Tennis.

LANGRIDGE, Philip Gordon, CBE 1994; FRAM, FRCM; concert and opera singer (tenor), since 1964; *b* 16 Dec. 1939; *m* 1981, Ann Murray, *qv*; one *s* (and one *s* two *d* by former marriage). *Educ:* Maidstone Grammar Sch.; Royal Academy of Music, London. ARAM 1977; FRAM 1985; FRCM 1997. Glyndebourne Festival début, 1964; BBC Promenade Concerts, 1970–; Edinburgh Fest., 1970–; Netherlands Opera, Scottish Opera, Handel Opera etc. Covent Garden: L'Enfant et les Sortilèges, Rossignole, Boris, Jenufa, Idomeneo, Peter Grimes, Death in Venice, Rheingold, Palestrina; ENO: Turn of the Screw, Osud (Olivier Award, Outstanding Individual Performer in a New Opera Production, 1984), The Mask of Orpheus, Billy Budd, Beatrice and Benedict, Makropoulos Case; Peter Grimes; Glyndebourne, 1977–: Don Giovanni, Idomeneo, Fidelio, Jenufa, La Clemenza di Tito; The Second Mrs Kong; La Scala, 1979–: Rake's Progress, Wozzeck, Boris Godunov, Il Sosia, Idomeneo, Oberon, Peter Grimes; Frankfurt Opera: Castor and Pollux, Rigoletto, Die Entführung; Bavarian State Opera: Peter Grimes, Midsummer Marriage, La Clemenza di Tito, Rheingold; Zurich Opera: Poppea, Lucio Silla; Don Giovanni; La Fenice: Janacek's Diary; Palermo: Otello (Rossini); Pesaro: La Donna del Lago; Aix en Provence: Alcina, Les Boriades; Metropolitan Opera, NY: Così fan Tutte, Boris Godunov, Das Rheingold, Billy Budd, Peter Grimes, Moses und Aron; Vienna State Opera: Wozzeck; Salzburg Festival: Moses und Aron, Idomeneo, From the House of the Dead, Poppea, Boris Godunov; Amsterdam: Poppea, Idomeneo, Il Barbieri di Seviglia, Dorian Gray, Pelléas et Mélisande; Los Angeles: Peter Grimes; Barcelona: Billy Budd. Concerts with major, international orchestras and conductors including: Berlin Phil. (Abbado, Ozawa), Boston (Previn), Chicago (Solti, Abbado), Los Angeles (Christopher Hogwood), Sydney (Mackerras), Vienna Phil. (Previn), Orchestre de Paris (Barenboim, Mehta), and all major British orchestras; recitals with Pollini, Schiff, Donohoe, Norris. Many first performances of works, some dedicated to and written for him. Master classes on communication through singing. Has made over 100 records of early, baroque, classical, romantic and modern music (Grammy Awards: for Schönberg's Moses und Aron, 1985; for Peter Grimes, 1996). Mem., Music Panel, Arts Council of GB, 1983–86. Singer of the Year, RPS/Heidsieck Award, 1989; Santay Award, Co. of Musicians; Making Music/Sir Charles Groves Award, 2001. *Recreation:* collecting water colour paintings and Victorian postcards. *Address:* c/o Allied Artists Agency, 42 Montpelier Square, SW7 1JZ. *T:* (020) 7589 6243.

LANGRIDGE, Richard James, CVO 1992; HM Diplomatic Service, retired; Consul-General, Bordeaux, 1990–92; *b* 29 Oct. 1932; *m* 1965, Jeannine Louise Joosen; one *d.* HM Forces, 1951–53; joined FO 1953; served NY, Leopoldville, Athens, Dakar, Paris and FCO; Ambassador to Madagascar, 1979–84; FCO, 1985; Dep. High Comr, Colombo, 1985–89.

LANGRISH, Rt Rev. Michael Laurence; *see* Exeter, Bishop of.

LANGRISHE, Sir James Hercules, 8th Bt *cr* 1777, of Knocktopher Abbey, Kilkenny; *b* 3 March 1957; *o s* of Sir Hercules Ralph Hume Langrishe, 7th Bt and of Hon. Grania Sybil Enid Wingfield, *o d* of 9th Viscount Powerscourt; *S* father, 1998; *m* 1985, Gemma Mary Philomena, *e d* of Patrick O'Daly; one *s* one *d. Heir: s* Richard James Hercules Langrishe, *b* 8 April 1988. *Address:* Arlonstown, Dunsany, Co. Meath, Ireland.

LANGSDALE, Philip Richard, CEng; Director, Distribution and Technology (formerly Technology), British Broadcasting Corporation, since 1998; *b* 23 Dec. 1955; *s* of Reginald Eric Langsdale and Dorothy May Langsdale; *m* 1984, Vanessa Gabrielle Marsland; two *d. Educ:* King's Coll., Cambridge (MA Maths). CEng 1993. Systems Engr, IBM UK, 1979–82; IT Consultant, Nolan Norton & Co., 1982–85; Associate Dir, Coopers & Lybrand, 1985–88; Dir, IT Planning, Midland Bank, 1988–92; IT Director: Asda Gp, 1992–97; Cable & Wireless Communications, 1997–98. Mem., Exec. Cttee, BBC, 2000–. *Recreations:* opera, music, mountain-climbing. *Address:* 25 Highbury Place, N5 1QP.

LANGSHAW, George Henry; Managing Director, UK Regions, British Gas, 1992; *b* 6 Dec. 1939; *s* of George Henry and Florence Evelyn Langshaw; *m* 1962, Maureen Cosgrove; one *s* two *d. Educ:* Liverpool Inst. High Sch. FCMA; ACIS. Various accountancy appts, Wm Crawford & Sons, 1957–63, Littlewoods Orgn, 1963–67; British Gas: Accountant, NW, 1967–70; Develt Accountant, Southern, 1970–73; Prin. Financial Analyst, HQ, 1973–76; Chief Accountant, Wales, 1976–78; Dir of Finance, Southern, 1978–82; Dep, Chm., NW, 1982–87; Regional Chm., British Gas (Wales), 1987–89; Gp Dir of Personnel, 1989–90; Man. Dir, Global Gas, 1990–92. Chm., BG Corporate Ventures, 1990. Director: British Gas Deutschland GmbH, 1991; British Gas Holdings (Canada), 1992; BG Holdings Inc., 1992. Dir, Bd of Gas Consumers, Canada, 1990. CIGasE 1988; CIMgt (CBIM 1991). *Recreations:* soccer, reading, golf.

LANGSLOW, Derek Robert, CBE 2000; PhD; Member, Agriculture and Environment Biotechnology Commission, since 2000; *b* 7 Feb. 1945; *s* of Alexander Frederick Langslow and Beatrice Bibby Langslow (*née* Wright); *m* 1969, Helen Katherine (*née* Addison); one *s* one *d. Educ:* Ashville College, Harrogate; Queens' College, Cambridge (MA, PhD). Post-Doctoral Fellow, Cambridge and Univ. of Kansas; Lectr, Univ. of Edinburgh, 1972–78; Nature Conservancy Council: Senior Ornithologist, 1978–84; Asst Chief Scientist, 1984–87; Dir, Policy and Planning, 1987–90; Chief Scientist, 1990; Chief Exec., English Nature, 1990–2000. Chm., Rail Passenger Cttee for Eastern England, 2000–; Director: British Waterways, 2000–; Harwich Haven Authy, 2001–; Mem., Wetlands Internat. Asia Pacific, 1996–. *Publications:* numerous papers in learned jls. *Recreations:* badminton, walking, bird watching, music. *Address:* 4 Engaine, Orton Longueville, Peterborough PE2 7QA. *T:* (01733) 232153.

LANGSTAFF, Brian Frederick James; QC 1994; a Recorder, since 1995; a Judge, Employment Appeal Tribunal, since 2000; *b* 30 April 1948; *s* of Frederick Sidney Langstaff and Muriel Amy Maude Langstaff (*née* Griffin); *m* 1975, Deborah Elizabeth Weatherup; one *s* one *d. Educ:* George Heriot's Sch.; St Catharine's Coll., Cambridge (BA); Inns of Court Sch. of Law. VSO, Sri Lanka, 1966–67. Called to the Bar, Middle Temple, 1971 (Harmsworth Schol., 1975); called to the Bar of NI, 1999. Lectr and Sen. Lectr in Law, Mid-Essex Technical Coll. and Sch. of Art, Chelmsford, 1971–75; Asst Recorder, SE Circuit, 1991–95. Leading Counsel, Bristol Royal Infirmary Inquiry, 1998–. Chairman: Personal Injury Bar Assoc., 1999–; Exec. Cttee, Industrial Law Soc., 1997–; Law Reform Cttee, Bar Council, 2001– (Vice-Chm., 1999–2001). Gov., local primary sch., 1986–

(Chm. Govs, 1991–98). Adv. Editor, Occupational Health, Safety & Environment, 1997–. *Publications:* Concise College Casenotes: equity and trusts, 1975; Health and Safety at Work: Halsbury's Laws vol. 20, 4th edn 1994; Computing Special Damages, 1999; (ed and contrib.) Personal Injury Handbook, 2000; (adv. ed.) Bullen, Leake and Jacobs, Precedents of Pleading, 2001; (contrib.) Munkman's Employers' Liability, 2001; legal articles. *Recreations:* sport, politics, mowing the lawn, bell-ringing. *Address:* Cloisters, 1 Pump Court, Temple, EC4Y 7AA. *T:* (020) 7827 4000.

LANGSTON, Group Captain John Antony S.; *see* Steff-Langston.

LANGTON; *see* Temple-Gore-Langton, family name of Earl Temple of Stowe.

LANGTON, Lord; James Grenville Temple-Gore-Langton; *b* 11 Sept. 1955; *er s* and *heir* of Earl Temple of Stowe, *qv*.

LANGTON, Bryan David, CBE 1988; Director, Bass plc, 1985–96; Chairman and Chief Executive Officer, Holiday Inn Worldwide, 1990–96; *b* 6 Dec. 1936; *s* of Thomas Langton and Doris (*née* Brown); *m* 1960, Sylva Degenhardt; two *d*. *Educ:* Accrington Grammar Sch.; Westminster Tech. Coll. (Hotel Operation Dip.); Ecole Hotelière de la SSA, Lausanne (Operations Dip.). Dep. Manager, Russell Hotel, London, 1959–63; General Manager: Victoria Hotel, Nottingham, 1964–66; Grand Hotel, Manchester, 1966–71; Crest Hotels: Divl Manager, 1971–73; Ops Dir UK, 1973–75; Ops Dir Europe, 1975–77; Divl Managing Dir, Europe, 1977–81; Managing Dir, Ops, 1981–82; Man. Dir, 1982–88; Chairman, 1985–90. Chairman: Holiday Inns International, 1988–90; Toby Restaurants, 1988–90; Fairfield Communities Inc., 1999– (non-exec. Dir, 1996–99); Dir, Caribiner Internat. Inc., 1996–; Member: Adv. Bd, Mote Marine Sarasota, 1997–; Bd, Florida West Coast Symphony, 1997–. Vice Pres., Internat. Hotel Assoc., 1990. Trustee, Educnl Inst., Amer. Hotel and Motel Assoc., 1990–97. Member, Board of Trustees: Woodruff Arts Center, Atlanta, 1990–97; Northside Hosp. Foundn Bd, 1990–97; YMCA, Sarasota, Fla, 1999–. Trustee, Bd of Visitors, Emory Univ., 1990–97. Hon. Fellow, Manchester Poly., later Manchester Metropolitan Univ., 1990–99. *Recreations:* golf, cricket, reading, theatre. *Address:* 3632 Fair Oaks Place, Longboat Key, FL 34228, USA. *T:* (941) 3835046, *Fax:* (941) 3834862; *e-mail:* blangton@mindspring.com.

LANGTRY, (James) Ian; Education Officer, Association of County Councils, 1988–96; *b* 2 Jan. 1939; *s* of late Rev. H. J. Langtry and I. M. Langtry (*née* Eagleson); *m* 1959, Eileen Roberta Beatrice (*née* Nesbitt) (*d* 1999); one *s* one *d*. *Educ:* Coleraine Academical Instn; Queen's Univ., Belfast (Sullivan Schol.; BSc 1st Cl., Physics). Assistant Master, Bangor Grammar Sch., 1960–61; Lectr, Belfast College of Technology, 1961–66; Asst Director of Examinations/Recruitment, Civil Service Commission, 1966–70; Principal, Dept of Educn and Science, 1970–76, Asst Sec., 1976–82, Under Sec., 1982–87; Under Sec., DHSS, 1987–88. *Recreation:* golf. *Address:* 5 Marke Close, Keston Park, Keston, Kent BR2 6EX. *T:* (01689) 860761. *Clubs:* Royal Portrush Golf; West Kent Golf.

LA NIECE, Rear-Adm. Peter George, CB 1973; CBE 1967; *b* 23 July 1920; *s* of late George David Nelson La Niece and Gwynneth Mary (*née* Morgan); *m* 1948, Evelyn Mary Wrixon Babington (*d* 1982); two *s* one *d*. *Educ:* Whitgift Sch., Croydon. Entered RN, 1937; served War of 1939–45 in battleships, cruisers and destroyers; Gunnery Specialist 1945; Comdr 1953; Captain 1961; comd HMS Rame Head, 1962; Senior UK Polaris Rep., Washington, 1963–66; comd HMS Triumph, 1966–68; Cdre Clyde in Comd Clyde Submarine Base, 1969–71; Rear-Adm. 1971; Flag Officer Spithead and Port Admiral, Portsmouth, 1971–73; retired 1973. Dir in Exco Gp of Cos, 1976–85. *Address:* 31 Crittles Court, Townlands Road, Wadhurst, E Sussex TN5 6BY. *T:* (01892) 782161. *Club:* Army and Navy.

LANKESTER, Richard Shermer; Clerk of Select Committees, House of Commons, 1979–87; Registrar of Members' Interests, 1976–87; *b* 8 Feb. 1922; *s* of late Richard Ward Lankester; *m* 1950, Dorothy, *d* of late Raymond Jackson, Worsley; two *s* one *d* (and one *s* decd). *Educ:* Haberdashers' Aske's Hampstead Sch.; Jesus Coll., Oxford (MA). Served Royal Artillery, 1942–45. Entered Dept of Clerk of House of Commons, 1947; Clerk of Standing Cttees, 1973–75; Clerk of Expenditure Cttee, 1975–79. Co-Editor, The Table, 1962–67. *Address:* The Old Farmhouse, The Green, Boughton Monchelsea, Maidstone, Kent ME17 4LT. *T:* (01622) 743749.

LANKESTER, Sir Timothy Patrick, (Sir Tim), KCB 1994; President, Corpus Christi College, Oxford, since 2001; *b* 15 April 1942; *s* of late Preb. Robin Prior Archibald Lankester and of Jean Dorothy (*née* Gilliat); *m* 1968, Patricia Cockcroft; three *d*. *Educ:* Monkton Combe Sch.; St John's Coll., Cambridge (BA; Hon. Fellow, 1995); Jonathan Edwards Coll., Yale (Henry Fellow, MA). Teacher (VSO), St Michael's Coll., Belize, 1960–61; Fereday Fellow, St John's Coll., Oxford, 1965–66; Economist, World Bank, Washington DC, 1966–69; New Delhi, 1970–73; Principal 1973, Asst Sec. 1977, HM Treasury; Private Secretary to Rt Hon. James Callaghan, 1978–79; to Rt Hon. Margaret Thatcher, 1979–81; seconded to S. G. Warburg and Co. Ltd, 1981–83; Under Sec., HM Treasury, 1983–85; Economic Minister, Washington and Exec. Dir, IMF and World Bank, 1985–88; Dep. Sec., HM Treasury, 1988–89; Perm. Sec., ODA, FCO, 1989–94; Perm. Sec., Dept for Educn, 1994–95; Dir, SOAS, London Univ., 1996–2000. Director: Smith and Nephew plc, 1996–; London Metal Exchange, 1997–. Dep. Chm., British Council, 1999– (Mem., Bd, 1989–). Gov., Asia-Europe Foundn, 1997–; Mem., UK Nat. Cttee, Aga Khan Foundn, 2000–. *Address:* Corpus Christi College, Oxford OX1 4JF. *T:* (01865) 276740, *Fax:* (01865) 276769; *e-mail:* tim.lankester@ccc.ox.ac.uk.

LANSBURY, Angela Brigid, CBE 1994; actress; *b* London, England, 16 Oct. 1925; *d* of Edgar Lansbury and late Moyna Macgill (who *m* 1st, Reginald Denham); *m* 1st, Richard Cromwell; 2nd, 1949, Peter Shaw; one *s* one *d* and one step *s*. *Educ:* South Hampstead High Sch. for Girls; Webber Douglas Sch. of Singing and Dramatic Art, Kensington; Feagin Sch. of Drama and Radio, New York. With Metro-Goldwyn-Mayor, 1943–50; *films:* Gaslight, 1944; National Velvet, 1944; The Picture of Dorian Gray, 1945; The Harvey Girls, 1946; The Hoodlum Saint, 1946; Till the Clouds Roll By, 1946; The Private Affairs of Bel-Ami, 1947; If Winter Comes, 1948; Tenth Avenue Angel, 1948; State of the Union, 1948; The Three Musketeers, 1948; The Red Danube, or Storm over Vienna, or Vespers in Vienna, 1949; Samson and Delilah, 1949; Kind Lady, 1951; Mutiny, 1952; Remains to be Seen, 1953; A Life at Stake, or Key Man, 1955; The Purple Mask, 1956; The Court Jester, 1956; A Lawless Street, 1956; Please Murder Me, 1956; The Long Hot Summer, 1958; The Reluctant Debutante, 1958; Breath of Scandal, 1960; The Dark at the Top of the Stairs, 1960; Season of Passion, 1961; Blue Hawaii, 1961; All Fall Down, 1962; The Manchurian Candidate, 1962; In the Cool of the Day, 1963; The World of Henry Orient, 1964; Dear Heart, 1964; The Greatest Story Ever Told, 1965; Harlow, 1965; The Amorous Adventures of Moll Flanders, 1965; Mister Buddwing, or Woman Without a Face, 1966; Something for Everyone, or Black Flowers for the Bride, 1970; Bedknobs and Broomsticks, 1971; Death on the Nile, or Murder on the Nile, 1978; The Lady Vanishes, 1980; The Mirror Crack'd, 1980; The Pirates of Penzance, 1982; The Company of Wolves, 1983; Beauty and the Beast, 1991; *plays:* appearances include: Hotel Paradiso (Broadway debut), 1957; Helen, in A Taste of Honey, Lyceum Theatre, New York, 1960; Anyone Can Whistle (Broadway musical), 1964; Mame (Tony Award for best actress in a Broadway musical), Winter Garden, NYC, 1966–68; Dear World (Broadway), 1969 (Tony Award); Pretty Belle, 1971; All Over, RSC, 1971; Gypsy (Broadway Musical), Piccadilly, 1973, US tour, 1974 (Tony Award; Chicago, Sarah Siddons Award, 1974); Gertrude, in Hamlet, Nat. Theatre, 1975; Anna, in The King and I (Broadway), 1978; Mrs Lovett, in Sweeney Todd (Broadway), 1979 (Tony Award); A Little Family Business, 1983; *television includes:* series, Murder She Wrote, 1984–95 (Golden Globe Award, 1984, 1986, 1991, 1992); Little Gloria, Happy At Last, 1982; The Gift of Love: a Christmas Story, 1983; A Talent for Murder (with Laurence Olivier), 1984; Lace, 1984; The First Olympico-Athens 1896, 1984; Rage of Angels II, 1986; Shootdown, 1988; The Shell Seekers, 1989; The Love She Sought, 1990; Mrs Arris Goes to Paris, 1992; Mrs Santa Claus, 1996; South by Southwest, 1997; The Unexpected Mrs Pollifax, 1998; A Story to Die for, 2000. NY Drama Desk Award, 1979; Sarah Siddons Award, 1980 and 1983; inducted Theatre Hall of Fame, 1982; Silver Mask for Lifetime Achievement, BAFTA, 1991; Lifetime Achievement Award, Screen Actors' Guild, 1997; Nat. Medal of the Arts, USA, 1997. *Address:* Corymore Productions, 100 Universal City Plaza, Universal City, CA 91608, USA.

LANSDOWN, Gillian Elizabeth, (Mrs Richard Lansdown); *see* Tindall, G. E.

LANSDOWNE, 9th Marquess of, *cr* 1784 (GB); **Charles Maurice Petty-Fitzmaurice;** 30th Baron of Kerry and Lixnaw, 1181; Viscount Clanmaurice and Earl of Kerry, 1722; Baron Dunkeron and Viscount Fitzmaurice, 1751; Earl of Shelburne, 1753; Baron Wycombe (GB), 1760; Viscount Calne and Calston and Earl of Wycombe (GB), 1784; DL; *b* 21 Feb. 1941; *s* of 8th Marquess of Lansdowne, PC and Barbara, *d* of Harold Stuart Chase; *S* father, 1999; *m* 1st, 1965, Lady Frances Eliot, *o d* of 9th Earl of St Germans; two *s* two *d*; 2nd, 1987, Fiona Merritt, *d* of Lady Davies and Donald Merritt. *Educ:* Eton. Page of Honour to The Queen, 1956–57. Served with Kenya Regt, 1960–61; with Wiltshire Yeomanry (TA), amalgamated with Royal Yeomanry Regt, 1963–73. Pres., Wiltshire Playing Fields Assoc., 1965–74; Wiltshire County Councillor, 1970–85; Mem., South West Economic Planning Council, 1972–77; Chairman: Working Committee Population & Settlement Pattern (SWEPC), 1972–77; North Wiltshire DC, 1973–76; Mem., Calne and Chippenham RDC, 1964–73. Mem., Historic Bldgs and Monuments Commn, 1983–89; Pres., HHA, 1988–93 (Dep. Pres., 1986–88). Mem., Prince's Council, 1990–; President: Wiltshire Assocs Boys Clubs and Youth Clubs, 1976–; North-West Wiltshire District Scout Council, 1977–88; N Wilts Cons. Assoc., 1986–. Contested (C) Coventry North East, 1979. DL Wilts, 1990. *Heir: s* Earl of Kerry, *qv*. *Address:* Bowood House, Calne, Wiltshire SN11 0LZ. *T:* (01249) 813343. *Clubs:* Turf, Brooks's.

LANSLEY, Andrew David, CBE 1996; MP (C) Cambridgeshire South, since 1997; *b* 11 Dec. 1956; *s* of Thomas and Irene Lansley; *m* 1985, Marilyn Jane Biggs (marr. diss. 2001); three *d*; *m* 2001, Sally Ann Low. *Educ:* Univ. of Exeter (BA). Administration trainee, Dept of Industry, 1979; Private Sec. to Sec. of State for Trade and Industry, 1984–85; Principal Private Sec. to Chancellor of Duchy of Lancaster, 1985–87; Dir, Policy, 1987–89, Dep. Dir-Gen., 1989–90, ABCC; Director: Cons. Res. Dept, 1990–95; Public Policy Unit, 1995–97. Shadow Minister for the Cabinet and Shadow Chancellor of the Duchy of Lancaster, 1999–2001. Mem., Select Cttee on Health, 1997–98. A Vice-Chm., Cons. Party, 1998–99. *Publications:* A Private Route?, 1988; Conservatives and the Constitution, 1997. *Recreations:* travel, bridge, cricket, films, political biography. *Address:* House of Commons, SW1A 0AA. *T:* (020) 7219 3000.

LANYON, (Harry) Mark, CEng; Regional Director, Government Office for East Midlands, 1994–98; *b* 15 July 1939; *s* of late Henry Lanyon and Heather Gordon (*née* Tyrrell); *m* 1970, Elizabeth Mary Morton; one *s* one *d*. *Educ:* Ardingly Coll.; St Andrews Univ. (BSc Hons 1962). CEng 1965; MIMechE 1965. Ministry of Aviation: Engr Cadet, 1963–65; Aeronautical Inspectorate, 1965–68; Concorde Div., Min. of Technol., 1968–75; Department of Trade and Industry: Shipbuilding Policy Div., 1975–77; Dep. Dir, SW Region, 1977–82; Regl Dir, W Midlands, 1982–85; Hd of Br., Mechanical and Electrical Engrg Div., 1985–90; Asst Dir, Consumer Affairs, OFT, 1990–93; Regl Dir, Yorks and Humberside, DTI, 1993–94.

See also L. E. Lanyon.

LANYON, Prof. Lance Edward, CBE 2001; Principal, Royal Veterinary College, since 1989; Pro-Vice-Chancellor, University of London, 1997–99; *b* 4 Jan. 1944; *s* of late Henry Lanyon and Heather Gordon (*née* Tyrrell); *m* 1972, Mary Kear (marr. diss. 1997); one *s* one *d*. *Educ:* Christ's Hospital; Univ. of Bristol (BVSC, PhD, DSc). MRCVS. Lectr, 1967, Reader in Vet. Anatomy, 1967–79, Univ. of Bristol; Associate Prof., 1980–83, Prof., 1983–84, Tufts Sch. of Vet. Medicine, Boston, Mass; Prof. of Vet. Anatomy, Royal Vet. Coll., Univ. of London, 1984–89, personal title, 1989– (Head, Dept of Vet. Anatomy, 1984–87, of Vet. Basic Scis, 1987–88). Founder FMedSci 1998. *Publications:* chapters in books on orthopaedics, osteoporosis, and athletic training; articles in professional jls. *Recreations:* building, home improvements, sailing. *Address:* Royal Veterinary College, Royal College Street, NW1 0TU. *T:* (020) 7387 2898.

See also H. M. Lanyon.

LANYON, Mark; *see* Lanyon, H. M.

LAPIDGE, Prof. Michael, PhD, LittD; FBA 1994; Notre Dame Professor of English, University of Notre Dame, Indiana, since 1999; Fellow of Clare College, Cambridge, since 1990; *b* 8 Feb. 1942; *s* of Rae H. Lapidge and Catherine Mary Lapidge (*née* Carruthers). *Educ:* Univ. of Calgary (BA 1962); Univ. of Alberta (MA 1965); Univ. of Toronto (PhD 1971); LittD Cantab 1988. Cambridge University: Lectr, 1974–88; Reader in Insular Latin Literature, 1988–91; Elrington and Bosworth Prof. of Anglo-Saxon, 1991–98. Corresp. Fellow, Bayerische Akademie der Wissenschaften, 1997. *Publications:* Aldhelm: the prose works, 1979; Alfred the Great, 1983; Aldhelm: the poetic works, 1985; A Bibliography of Celtic Latin Literature 400–1200, 1985; Wulfstan of Winchester: the life of St Ethelwold, 1991; Anglo-Saxon Litanies of the Saints, 1991; Anglo-Latin Literature 900–1066, 1993; Biblical Commentaries from the Canterbury School of Theodore and Hadrian, 1994; Archbishop Theodore, 1995; Byrhtferth's Enchiridion, 1995; Anglo-Latin Literature 600–899, 1996; articles in learned jls. *Recreation:* mountaineering. *Address:* 143 Sturton Street, Cambridge CB1 2QH. *T:* (01223) 363768.

LA PLANTE, Lynda; writer and producer; Founder and Chairman, La Plante Productions, since 1994; *m* Richard La Plante (marr. diss.). *Educ:* RADA (schol.). Former actress. Writer: *television: series:* Widows, 1983; Prime Suspect, 1991, series 3, 1993; Civvies, 1992; Seekers, 1993; The Lifeboat, 1994; The Governor, 1995, series 2, 1996; The Prosecutors (US); Supply and Demand, 1996, series 2, 1998; Trial and Retribution, 1997, series 2, 1998, series 3, 1999, series 4, 2000; Killer Net, 1998; Mind Games, 2000; *play:* Seconds Out. *Publications:* The Legacy, 1988; The Talisman, 1989; Bella Mafia, 1991 (televised, US); Entwined, 1992; Framed, 1993; Seekers, 1993; Widows, 1994; Cold Shoulder, 1994; Prime Suspect, 1995; Prime Suspect 3, 1995; She's Out, 1995; The Governor, 1995; Cold Blood, 1986; Cold Heart, 1998; Trial and Retribution, no 1, 1997, no 2, 1998, no 3, 1999, no 4, 2000; Sleeping Cruelty, 2000. *Address:* La Plante Productions Ltd, Paramount House, 162–170 Wardour Street, W1V 3AT.

LAPLI, Sir John Ini, GCMG 1999; Governor General, Solomon Islands, since 1999; baptized 24 June 1955; *s* of Christian Mekope and Ellen Lauai; *m* 1985, Helen; three *s* one *d*. *Educ:* Nabakaenga Jun. Primary Sch., Solomon Is; Lueslemba Sen. Primary Sch., Solomon Is; Selwyn Coll., Guadalcanal; Bp Patterson Theol Coll., Guadalcanal (Cert. Theol.); St John's Theol Coll., Auckland (LTh, Dip. and Licentiate in Theol.). Tutor, Theol Coll., 1982–83; teacher, Catechist Sch., Rural Trng Centre, 1985; parish priest, 1986; Bible translator, 1987–88; Premier, Tembtu Province, Solomon Is, 1988–99. *Recreation:* gardening, before taking up the current office. *Address:* Government House, PO Box 252, Honiara, Solomon Islands. *T:* 22222, 21777.

LAPOINTE, Paul André; Ambassador for Fisheries Conservation, Canada, 1994–96; *b* 1 Nov. 1934; *s* of Henri and Regina Lapointe; *m* 1965, Iris Donati; one *d*. *Educ:* Université Laval. BA, LLL. Called to the Bar, Québec, 1958. Journalist, Le Soleil, 1959–60; joined Canadian Foreign Service, 1960; served Vietnam and Laos, 1961–62, NATO, Paris, 1962–64, Geneva, 1968–72, New Delhi, 1975–76, New York, 1976–79; Dep. Perm. Rep. to UN Security Council, 1977–78; Dep. High Comr in UK, 1981–85; Consul Gen., Marseille, France, 1985–87; Sen. Negotiator, Canada-France Maritime Affairs, Dept of External Affairs, Canada, 1987–90; Canadian Ambassador to Turkey, 1990–93. *Club:* Travellers.

LAPOTAIRE, Jane Elizabeth Marie; actress; *b* 26 Dec. 1944; *d* of unknown father and Louise Elise Lapotaire; *m* 1st, 1965, Oliver Wood (marr. diss. 1967); 2nd, 1974, Roland Joffé (marr. diss. 1982); one *s*. *Educ:* Northgate Grammar Sch., Ipswich; Old Vic Theatre Sch., Bristol. Bristol Old Vic Co., 1965–67; Nat. Theatre Co., 1967–71, incl. Measure for Measure, Flea in Her Ear, Dance of Death, Way of the World, Merchant of Venice, Oedipus, The Taming of the Shrew; freelance films and TV, 1971–74; RSC, 1974–75 (roles included Viola in Twelfth Night, and Sonya in Uncle Vanya); Prospect Theatre Co., West End, 1975–76 (Vera in A Month in the Country, Lucy Honeychurch in A Room with a View); freelance films and TV, 1976–78; Rosalind in As You Like It, Edin. Fest., 1977; RSC, 1978–81: Rosaline in Love's Labours Lost, 1978–79; title role in Piaf, The Other Place 1978, Aldwych 1979, Wyndhams 1980, Broadway 1981 (SWET Award 1979, London Critics Award and Variety Club Award 1980, and Broadway Tony Award 1981); National Theatre: Eileen, Kick for Touch, 1983; Belvidera, Venice Preserv'd, Antigone, 1984; Saint Joan (title rôle), Compass Co., 1985; Double Double, Fortune Theatre, 1986; RSC, 1986–87: Misalliance, 1986; Archbishop's Ceiling, 1986; Greenland, Royal Court, 1988; Shadowlands, Queen's, 1989–90 (Variety Club Best Actress Award); RSC, 1992–94: Gertrude in Hamlet, 1992; Mrs Alving in Ghosts, 1993; Katharine of Aragon in Henry VIII, RSC, UK and USA tour, 1996–98 (Helen Hayes Award, USA, 1998); one-woman show, Shakespeare as I knew her, Bristol, 1996, Stratford and USA, 1997; *television:* Marie Curie (serial), 1977; Antony and Cleopatra, 1981; Macbeth, 1983; Seal Morning (series), 1985; Napoleon and Josephine, 1987; Blind Justice (serial), 1988 (British Press Guild Best Actress Award); The Dark Angel, 1989; Love Hurts (series), 1992, 1993; The Big Battalions (series), 1992; Johnny and the Dead (series), 1994; *films* include: Eureka, 1983; Lady Jane, 1986; Surviving Picasso, 1996; There's Only One Jimmy Grimble, 2000. Vis. Fellow, Sussex Univ., 1986–. Mem., Marie Curie Meml Foundn Appeals Cttee, 1986–88. Pres., Bristol Old Vic Theatre Club, 1985–; Hon. Pres., Friends of Southwark Globe, 1986–. Hon. Associate Artist, RSC, 1992. Hon. DLitt: Bristol, 1997; East Anglia, 1998; Warwick, 2000. *Publications:* Grace and Favour (autobiog.), 1989; Out of Order: a haphazard journey through one woman's year, 1999. *Recreation:* walking. *Address:* Storm Artists Management, 47 Brewer Street, W1R 3FD.

LAPPER, Maj.-Gen. John; Medical Director, International Hospitals Group, 1984–1988; *b* 24 July 1921; *s* of late Col Wilfred Mark Lapper, OBE, Legion of Merit (USA), late RE, and Agnes Lapper (*née* Powner); *m* 1948, Dorothy, *d* of late Roland John and Margaret Simpson (*née* Critchlow); three *s*. *Educ:* Wolverhampton Grammar Sch.; King Edward VI Sch., Birmingham; Birmingham Univ. MB, ChB 1946; DLO 1952. House appts, Queen Elizabeth and Children's Hosp., Birmingham, and Ronkswood Hosp. and Royal Infirm., Worcester; Registrar, Royal Berks Hosp., Reading. Commnd RAMC, 1950; ENT specialist, Mil. Hosps in UK, Libya, Egypt, Germany, Singapore, Malaya; CO 14 Field Amb., BAOR, 1958; CO BMH Rinteln, BAOR, 1964; Asst Comdt, Royal Army Med. Coll., 1965–68; ADMS Hong Kong, 1969–71; CO Queen Alexandra's Mil. Hosp., Millbank, 1971–73; ADMS 3 Div., 1973; DDMS HQ UKLF, 1974–77; Dir, Med. Supply, MoD, 1977; Dir, Med. Policy and Plans, MoD, 1978–80, retired; QHS 1977–80. Hospital and Medical Dir, Nat. Guard Saudi Arabia, 1981–83. Hudson-Evans Lectr, W Kent Medico-Chirurgical Soc., 1980; Mem. Sands Cox Med. Soc., Birmingham Univ. FFPHM (FFCM 1980); FIMgt (FBIM 1980); FRSocMed; FMedSoc London; Mem. BMA; Pres. Med. Soc., Hong Kong, 1970–71; Mem., RUSI; Chm. Council, Yateley Industries for the Disabled, 1983–95. OStJ 1959. *Publications:* articles in professional jls. *Recreations:* travel, militaria, DIY. *Address:* The Chimes, 4 Manor Fields, Alrewas, Burton-upon-Trent, Staffs DE13 7DA. *T:* (01283) 791628; Rocas Del Mar, Mijas Costa, (Malaga), Spain.

LAPPERT, Prof. Michael Franz, FRS 1979; Research Professor of Chemistry, University of Sussex, since 1997 (Professor of Chemistry, 1969–97); *b* 31 Dec. 1928; *s* of Julius Lappert and Kornelie Lappert (*née* Beran); *m* 1980, Lorna McKenzie. *Educ:* Wilson's Grammar School; Northern Polytechnic, London. BSc, PhD, DSc (London). FRSC. Northern Polytechnic, London: Asst Lecturer, 1952–53; Lecturer, 1953–55; Sen. Lectr, 1955–59. UMIST: Lectr, 1959–61; Sen. Lectr, 1961–64; Reader, Univ. of Sussex, 1964–69. SERC Sen. Res. Fellow, 1980–85. Pres., Dalton Div., RSC, 1989–91. Tilden Lectr, Chem. Soc., 1972–73; Nyholm Lectr, 1994, Frankland Lectr, 1999, RSC. Hon. Dr rer. nat. München, 1989. First recipient of (London) Chemical Soc. Award in Main Group Metal Chemistry, 1970; Award in Organometallic Chemistry, 1978; F. S. Kipping Award of American Chem. Soc., 1976. *Publications:* (ed jtly) Developments in Inorganic Polymer Chemistry, 1962; (jtly) Metal and Metalloid Amides, 1980; (jtly) Organo-zirconium and -hafnium Compounds, 1986; approx. 700 papers in Jl Chem. Soc., etc. *Recreations:* theatre, opera, tennis, walking. *Address:* 4 Varndean Gardens, Brighton BN1 6WL. *T:* (01273) 503661; John Dalton Cottage, Eaglesfield, Cumbria CA13 0SD.

LAPPING, Anne Shirley Lucas; independent television producer; Director, Brook Lapping Productions (formerly Brook Associates), since 1982; Vice Chairman, Brent, Kensington, Chelsea and Westminster NHS Trust, since 1999; *b* 10 June 1941; *d* of late Frederick Stone and of Dr Freda Lucas Stone; *m* 1963, Brian Michael Lapping, *qv*; three *d*. *Educ:* City of London Sch. for Girls; London Sch. of Econs. New Society, 1964–68; London Weekend TV, 1970–73; writer on The Economist, 1974–82. Other writing and broadcasting. Director: Channel Four, 1989–94; NW London Mental Health NHS Trust, 1992–99; Scott Trust, 1994–. Member: SSRC, 1977–79; Nat. Gas Consumers' Council, 1978–79. Gov., LSE, 1994–. *Recreations:* literature, cooking. *Address:* 61 Eton Avenue, NW3 3ET. *T:* (020) 7586 1047.

LAPPING, Brian Michael; television producer; Director, Brook Lapping Productions Ltd (formerly Brian Lapping Associates), since 1988; *b* 13 Sept. 1937; *s* of Max and Doris Lapping; *m* 1963, Anne Shirley Lucas Stone (*see* A. S. L. Lapping); three *d*. *Educ:* Pembroke Coll., Cambridge (BA). Reporter, Daily Mirror, 1959–61; reporter and Dep. Commonwealth Corresp., The Guardian, 1961–67; Ed., Venture (Fabian Soc. monthly jl), 1963–68; feature writer, Financial Times, 1967–68; Dep. Ed., New Society, 1968–70; Granada TV, 1970–88: Producer: What the Papers Say; Party confs; This is Your Right; Executive Producer: World in Action; Hypotheticals; End of Empire; Apartheid; Breakthrough at Reykjavik, etc; as independent producer, 1988–: Countdown to War, 1989; The Second Russian Revolution, 1991; Question Time, 1991–94; Watergate, 1993; The Death of Yugoslavia, 1995; Fall of the Wall, Death of Apartheid, 1996; The 50 Years' War—Israel and the Arabs, 1998; Hostage, Playing the China Card, Finest Hour, 1999. Awards include: RTS Awards, 1978, 1991, 1995; Emmy Award, 1994; BPG Awards, 1986, 1991, 1995; Gold Medal, NY Internat. Film and TV Fest., 1986, 1990, 1995; The Indie, Producers Alliance for Cinema and Television, 1996. *Publications:* (with G. Radice) More Power to the People, 1962; The Labour Government 1964–70, 1970; End of Empire, 1985; Apartheid: a history, 1987. *Recreation:* tending vines. *Address:* 61 Eton Avenue, NW3 3ET. *T:* (020) 7586 1047.

LAPPING, Peter Herbert; Headmaster of Sherborne, 1988–2000; *b* 8 Aug. 1941; *s* of late Dr Douglas James Lapping, MBE and Dorothy Lapping (*née* Horrocks) of Nhlangano, Swaziland; *m* 1967, Diana Dillworth, *d* of late Lt-Col E. S. G. Howard, MC, RA; one *s* one *d*. *Educ:* St John's College, Johannesburg; Univ. of Natal, Pietermaritzburg (BA Hons *cum laude*); Lincoln College, Oxford (MA). Asst Master, Reed's Sch., Cobham, 1966–67; Head of History, Loretto Sch., 1967–79 (Housemaster, Pinkie House, 1972–79); Headmaster, Shiplake Coll., Oxon, 1979–88. Member: Cttee, Ind. Schs GBA; Chartered Accountants Investigation Cttee. *Recreations:* cricket and other games, cooking, walking, basking in the beauty of the Cotswolds. *Address:* Lower Bubblewell, Minchinhampton, Glos GL6 9DL. *Clubs:* East India, Devonshire, Sports and Public Schools, MCC; Vincent's (Oxford).

LAPSLEY, Peter Michael; Chief Executive, Skin Care Campaign, since 2001; *b* 19 June 1943; *s* of Air Marshal Sir John Hugh Lapsley, KBE, CB, DFC, AFC and Jean Margaret (*née* McIvor); *m* 1st, 1970, Jennifer Mary Blockley (marr. diss. 1985); one *s* one *d*; 2nd, 1986, Elizabeth Ann Wyatt. *Educ:* Aldenham Sch., Elstree; RMA, Sandhurst. Served Army, King's Own Royal Border Regt, 1962–73: served Germany, UK, British Guyana, Aden, Trucial States (UAE), NI; Principal, then Sen. Principal, MoD, 1973–80; Co-owner/Manager, Rockbourne Trout Fishery, 1980–84; Sen. Principal, MoD, 1984–87; Chief Exec., Nat. Back Pain Assoc., 1987–90; Dept of Transport, 1990–96 (HM Chief Inspector of Aviation Security, 1991–96); Chief Exec., Nat. Eczema Soc., 1997–2001. FRGS 1996. *Publications:* The Bankside Book of Stillwater Trout Flies, 1978, 2nd edn 1983; Trout From Stillwaters, 1981; River Trout Flyfishing, 1988; (ed) The Complete Fly Fisher, 1990; (jtly) Fly Fishing by J. R. Hartley, 1991; Fly Fishing for Trout, 1992; (jtly) J. R. Hartley Casts Again, 1992; Fishing for Falklands Sea Trout, 2000. *Recreations:* fly fishing, writing, photography, travel. *Address:* 27 Lillian Avenue, W3 9AN. *T:* (020) 8993 7453. *Club:* Flyfishers'.

LAPTHORNE, Richard Douglas, CBE 1997; Chairman: Morse Holdings plc, since 1998; Avecia Ltd, since 1999; Nycomed Amersham, since 1999 (Deputy Chairman, 1997–99); Tunstall Ltd, since 2000; TI Automotive Systems plc, since 2001; *b* 25 April 1943; *s* of Eric Joseph Lapthorne and Irene Ethel Lapthorne; *m* 1967, Valerie Waring; two *s* two *d*. *Educ:* Calday Grange GS, West Kirby; Liverpool Univ. (BCom). FCMA, FCCA, FCT. Unilever plc: Audit, 1965–67; Lever Brothers, Zambia, 1967–69; Central Pensions Dept, 1969–71; Food Industries, 1971–75; Synthetic Resins, 1975–77; Sheby, Paris, 1978–80; Crosfield Chemicals, 1980–83; Gp Financial Controller, 1983–86, Gp Finance Dir, 1986–92, Courtaulds plc; Gp Finance Dir, 1992–98, Vice Chm., 1998–99, British Aerospace plc. Director: Oasis Internat. Leasing (Abu Dhabi), 1998–; Orange plc, 2001–. Ext. Advr, Navy Bd, 2000–. Trustee: Royal Botanic Gdns, Kew, 1998– (Chm., Foundn and Friends, 1997–); Calibre, 1999–. CIMgt. *Recreations:* gardening, opera, tennis, travel.

LAPUN, Sir Paul, Kt 1974; *b* 1923; *m* 1951, Lois; two *s* one *d*. *Educ:* Catholic Mission, Vunapope. Teacher, Catholic Mission, 1947–61. Under-Secretary for Forests, Papua and New Guinea, 1964–67. Founder Mem., for S Bougainville, PNG House of Assembly, 1964; Founder, Pangu Party, 1967 (Leader, 1967–68; Dep. Parly Leader, 1968); Minister: for Mines and Energy, 1972–75; for Health, 1975–77. Hon. Mem., Internat. Mark Twain Soc., USA. *Address:* Bougainville, N Solomons Province, Papua New Guinea.

LAQUEUR, Walter; Chairman, Research Council, Center for Strategic and International Studies, Washington, since 1975; Director, Institute of Contemporary History and Wiener Library, London, 1964–92; *b* 26 May 1921; *s* of late Fritz Laqueur and late Else Laqueur; *m* 1st, 1941, Barbara (*d* 1995), *d* of Prof. Richard Koch and Maria Koch (*née* Rosenthal); two *d*; 2nd, 1996, Christa Susi Wichmann (*née* Genzen). Agricultural labourer during War, 1939–44. Journalist, free lance author, 1944–55; Editor of Survey, 1955–65; Co-editor of Journal of Contemporary History, 1966–. Prof., History of Ideas, Brandeis Univ., 1967–71; Prof. of Contemporary History, Tel Aviv Univ., 1970–; Vis. Professor: Chicago Univ.; Johns Hopkins Univ.; Harvard Univ. Hon. Dr: Hebrew Union Coll., NY, 1988; Adelphi Univ., 1990; Brandeis Univ., 1991. Grand Cross of Merit, FRG, 1986. *Publications:* Communism and Nationalism in the Middle East, 1956; Young Germany, 1961; Russia and Germany, 1965; The Road to War, 1968; Europe Since Hitler, 1970; Out of the Ruins of Europe, 1971; Zionism, a History, 1972; Confrontation: the Middle East War and World Politics, 1974; Weimar: a Cultural History, 1918–33, 1974; Guerrilla, 1976; Terrorism, 1977; The Missing Years, 1980; (ed jtly) A Reader's Guide to Contemporary History, 1972; (ed) Fascism: a reader's guide, 1978; The Terrible Secret, 1980; Farewell to Europe, 1981; Germany Today: a personal report, 1985; World of Secrets: the uses and limits of intelligence, 1986; The Long Road to Freedom, 1989; Stalin: the glasnost revelations, 1991; Europe in Our Time, 1992. *Recreations:* swimming, motor-boating.

LARCOM, Sir (Charles) Christopher (Royde), 5th Bt, *cr* 1868; *b* 11 Sept. 1926; *s* of Sir Philip Larcom, 4th Bt, and Aileen Monica Royde (*née* Colbeck); *S* father, 1967; *m* 1956, Barbara Elizabeth, *d* of Balfour Bowen; four *d*. *Educ:* Radley; Clare Coll., Cambridge. (Wrangler, 1947; BA, 1947; MA, 1951). Served RN (Lieutenant), 1947–50. Articled to Messrs Spicer and Pegler (Chartered Accountants), 1950–53; ACA 1954; FCA 1965; joined Grieveson, Grant and Co., 1955, Partner, 1960, retired, 1986. Member, The Stock Exchange, London, 1959 (Mem. Council, 1970–80). *Recreations:* sailing, music. *Address:* 8 The Postern, Barbican, Wood Street, EC2Y 8BJ. *T:* (020) 7920 0388; 4 Village Cay Marina, PO Box 145, Roadtown, Tortola, BV1. *T:* 42485.

LARCOMBE, Brian Paul; Chief Executive, 3i Group plc, since 1997; *b* 27 Aug. 1953; *s* of John George Larcombe and Joyce Lucille Larcombe (*née* Westwood); *m* 1983, Dr Catherine Bullen. *Educ:* Bromley Grammar Sch.; Univ. of Birmingham (BCom). Joined 3i Gp, 1974: Local Dir, 1982; Regl Dir, 1988; Finance Dir, 1992–97. Member: Council, British Venture Capital Assoc., 1989–96 (Chm., 1994–95); UK Council, INSEAD,

1997–; Singapore British Business Council, 1997–; Exchange Markets GP, London Stock Exchange, 2001–. *Recreations:* golf, biographies, modern paintings. *Address:* 3i Group plc, 91 Waterloo Road, SE1 8PX. *T:* (020) 7928 3131.

LARGE, Sir Andrew (McLeod Brooks), Kt 1996; a Deputy Chairman, Barclays Bank, since 1998 (Director, since 1998); *b* 7 Aug. 1942; *s* of late Maj.-Gen. Stanley Eyre Large, MBE and of Janet Mary Large (*née* Brooks); *m* 1967, Susan Mary Melville; two *s* one *d*. *Educ:* Winchester Coll.; Corpus Christi Coll., Cambridge (BA Hons Econ; MA); INSEAD, Fontainebleau (MBA). BP, 1964–71; Orion Bank, 1971–79; Swiss Bank Corp., 1980–89; Large, Smith & Walter, 1990–92; Chm., SIB, 1992–97. Chm., Euroclear, 1998–2000, now Dir Emeritus; non-executive Director: Nuclear Electric, 1990–94; Rank Hovis McDougall, 1990–92; Phoenix Securities, 1990–92; Dowty Gp, 1991–92; English China Clays, 1991–96; London Fox, 1991–92 (Chm.); Luthy Baillie Dowsett Pethick, 1990–92 (Chm.). Chm., Securities Assoc., 1986–87; Member: Council, Stock Exchange, 1986–87; Panel on Takeovers and Mergers, 1987–88; Lloyds Council, 1992–93; Bd of Banking Supervision, 1996–97. Member Board: Inst. of Internat. Finance, Washington, 1998–; INSEAD, 1998– (Chm. UK Council, 1997–). Governor: Abingdon Sch., 1991–98; Winchester Coll., 1998–; Christ Coll., Brecon, 1998–. *Recreations:* ski-ing, walking, photography, music, old apple trees. *Address:* Barclays PLC, 54 Lombard Street, EC3P 3AH. *Club:* Brooks's.

LARGE, Sir Peter, Kt 1993; CBE 1987 (MBE 1974); President, Joint Committee on Mobility for Disabled People (formerly Mobility for the Disabled), since 1997 (Chairman, 1971–97); *b* 16 Oct. 1931; *s* of Ethel May Walters and Rosslyn Victor Large; *m* 1st, 1962, Susy Fisher (*d* 1982); one step *s* two step *d*; *m* 2nd, 1992, Sheenah McCaffrey. *Educ:* Enfield Grammar Sch.; University Coll. London. BSc Civil Eng. 1953. National Service, HM Submarines, 1953–55 (Sub Lt (E)). Joined Shell International, 1956; West Africa, 1957; Ghana, 1957–60; South East Arabia, 1960–61; Indonesia, 1961–62; paralysed by poliomyelitis, 1962; Civil Service, 1966–91. Chm., Assoc. of Disabled Professionals, 1971–93 (Parly Advr, 1993–); Governor, Motability, 1978–; Mem., Disabled Persons Transport Adv. Cttee, 1986–; Vice-Chm., Disablement Income Group, 1985–93 (Parly Advr, 1973–93); Chairman: Silver Jubilee Cttee on Improving Access for Disabled People, 1977–79; Cttee on Restrictions against Disabled People, 1979–82; Member: Exec. Cttee, British Council for Rehabilitation of the Disabled, 1966–77; Exec. Cttee, RADAR, 1977– (Vice Chm., 1995–99); Access Cttee for England, 1984–94; Nat. Adv. Council on Employment of People with Disabilities (formerly Disabled People), 1987–98; Disability Living Allowance Adv. Bd, 1991–99. FRSA 1993. Field-Marshal Lord Harding of Petherton Award, Action Res. and RADAR, 1992. *Recreation:* conversing with Siamese cats. *Address:* 14 Birch Way, Warlingham, Surrey CR6 9DA.

LARKEN, Comdt Anthea, CBE 1991; Director and Company Secretary, Operational Command Training Organisation Ltd, 1991–96; *b* 23 Aug. 1938; *d* of Frederick William Savill and Nance (*née* Williams); *m* 1987 (marr. diss. 1997). *Educ:* Stafford Girls' High Sch. Joined WRNS as Range Assessor, 1956; commnd, 1960; qualified: as Photographic Interpreter, 1961; as WRNS Secretarial Officer, 1967; Staff Officer in Singapore, 1964–66; i/c WRNS Officers' Training, BRNC Dartmouth, 1976–78; NATO Military Agency for Standardisation, Brussels, 1981–84; CSO (Admin) to Flag Officer Plymouth, 1985–86; RCDS, 1987; Dir, WRNS, 1988–91. ADC to the Queen, 1988–91. *Recreations:* theatre, music, reading, home, family and friends. *Club:* Army and Navy.

LARKEN, Rear Adm. (Edmund Shackleton) Jeremy, DSO 1982; Managing Director, OCTO Ltd, since 1991; advisory consultant in crisis/emergency management and leadership to major-hazard industries and organisations; *b* 14 Jan. 1939; *s* of Rear Adm. Edmund Thomas Larken, CB, OBE and Eileen Margaret (*née* Shackleton); *m* 1st, 1963, Wendy Nigella Hallett (marr. diss. 1987); two *d*; 2nd, 1987, Anthea Savill (*see* Comdt Anthea Larken) (marr. diss. 1997); 3rd, 1997, Helen Shannon; one *s*. *Educ:* Bryanston Sch.; BRNC, Dartmouth. Joined RN as Cadet, 1957; qualified: in Submarines, 1960; in Navigation, 1965; in Submarine Comd, 1960; served HMS Tenby, Finwhale, Tudor, Ambush and Narwhal; Navigation Officer, HMS Valiant; First Lieut, HMS Otus; commanded HMS Osiris, Glamorgan and Valiant, Third Submarine Sqn, and HMS Fearless (including Falklands Campaign, 1982); exchange with USN (Submarines), 1971–73; Naval Plans; Dir, Naval Staff Duties, 1985; Cdre Amphibious Warfare, 1985–87; ACDS (Overseas), 1988–90. Dir, OCSYS Ltd, 1998–. MInstD 1996; Member: RUSI, 1970; Inst. of Petroleum, 1983. Governor, Bryanston Sch., 1988–99. *Publications:* papers and articles in professional books and periodicals. *Recreations:* maritime and aviation interests, strategy, theatre, reading, home, family and friends. *Address:* c/o Lloyds TSB, 5 The Square, Petersfield, Hants GU32 3HL.

LARMINIE, (Ferdinand) Geoffrey, OBE 1971; Director, British Geological Survey, 1987–90; *b* 23 June 1929; *s* of late Ferdinand Samuel Larminie and of Mary Larminie (*née* Willis); *m* 1956, Helena Elizabeth Woodside Carson; one *s* one *d*. *Educ:* St Andrews Coll., Dublin; Trinity Coll., Dublin (BA 1954, MA 1972; Hon. Fellow, 1989). Asst Lectr in Geology, Univ. of Glasgow, 1954–56; Lectr in Geology, Univ. of Sydney, 1956–60; joined British Petroleum Co. Ltd, 1960: Exploration Dept in Sudan, Greece, Canada, Libya, Kuwait, California, New York, Thailand and Alaska, 1960–74; Scientific Advr, Inf. Dept, London, 1974–75; Gen. Manager, Public Affairs and Inf. Dept, London, 1975–76; Gen. Manager, Environmental Control Centre, London, 1976–84; External Affairs Co-ordinator, Health, Safety and Environmental Services, BP plc, 1984–87. Chm., Cambridge Arctic Shelf Prog., 1996–98 (Vice-Chm., 1993–96). Member: Royal Commn on Environmental Pollution, 1979–83; NERC, 1983–87. Council Mem., RGS, 1984–90, Vice-Pres., 1987–90. President: Alaska Geol Soc., 1969; Soc. of Underwater Technol., 1987–89 (Hon. Fellow, 1992). Trustee, Bermuda Biological Station 1978–91, Life Trustee, 1991; Member: Bd of Management, Inst. of Offshore Engrg, Heriot-Watt Univ., 1981–90; Polar Res. Bd, Nat. Res. Council, Washington, DC, 1984–88. Mem., IBA Gen. Adv. Council, 1980–85. Mem. of numerous scientific and professional socs. *Publications:* papers in scientific and technical jls on oil ind., and occasional reviews. *Recreations:* archaeology, natural history, reading, shooting. *Address:* Lane End, Lanes End, Tring, Herts HP23 6LF. *T:* (01296) 624907.

LaROCQUE, Judith Anne, CVO 1992; Secretary to the Governor General of Canada, since 1990; Secretary General, Order of Canada and Order of Military Merit, and Herald Chancellor of Canada, since 1990; *b* Hawkesbury, Ontario, 27 Sept. 1956; *d* of Olier LaRocque and Elizabeth (*née* Murray); *m* 1991, André Roland Lavoie. *Educ:* Carleton Univ. (BA Pol Sci. 1979; MA Public Admin 1992). Admin. Asst, Internal Audit Directorate, Public Service Commn, 1979; writer/researcher, Prime Minister's Office, 1979; Special Asst, Office of Leader of Opposition, 1980–82; Cttee Clerk, Cttees and Private Legislation Br., H of C, 1982–84; Legislative Asst to Govt House Leader, 1984–85; Head of House Business, Office of Govt House Leader, Pres. Queen's Privy Council for Canada and Minister Responsible for Regulatory Affairs, 1985–86; Exec. Asst to Minister of Justice and Attorney Gen. of Canada, 1986–89; COS to Govt Leader in Senate and Minister of State for Federal-Provincial Relns, 1989–90. OStJ 1990. *Recreations:* gardening, cross-country ski-ing. *Address:* Government House, Rideau Hall, 1 Sussex Drive, Ottawa, ON K1A 0A1, Canada. *T:* (613) 9938200.

LAROSIÈRE de CHAMPFEU, Jacques Martin Henri Marie de; *see* de Larosière de Champfeu.

LARPENT, Andrew Lionel Dudley de H.; *see* de Hochepied Larpent.

LARRY; *see* Parkes, T.

LARSEN, Prof. Henning; architect; founder and owner, Henning Larsens Tegnestue, architectural practice; Professor of Architecture, Royal Academy of Fine Arts, Copenhagen, since 1968; *b* 20 Aug. 1925; *s* of Erik Peter Larsen and Johanne Mary Gøbel; *m* Lone Backe. *Educ:* Royal Acad. of Fine Arts, Copenhagen (Dip. 1952); Sch. of Architecture, London; MIT, USA. Major projects include: Copenhagen Business Sch., 1988; Nation Centre, Nairobi, 1992; Physics Res. Centre, Stockholm, 1994–; Roskilde Univ. Centre, 1996–; NeuroSearch Co. HQ, 1997; Ferring Co. HQ, 1998–; housing and commercial develts in Denmark and Sweden. Founder: architectural magazine Skala; Gallery Skala, 1986–94. Guest Professor: Yale, 1964, Princeton, 1965. Member: Royal Danish Acad. of Fine Arts; Royal Swedish Acad. of Fine Arts, Hon. mem. of Arch. Insts in England, Scotland, Germany, USA. Awards in competitions include: Kammergericht, Berlin, 1979; Min. of Foreign Affairs, Riyadh, 1980; Compton Verney Opera House, 1989; Conf. Centre, Cambridge, 1989; Extension of Ny Carlsberg Glyptotek, Copenhagen, 1992; New Concert Hall, Copenhagen, 1993; City Library, Malmö, 1993; Danish Design Centre, Copenhagen, 1994; Max Planck Inst., Rostock, 1996; Terminal 2, Copenhagen Airport, 1997; Kunsthalle Adolf Würth, Germany, 1997; architectural prizes include: Internat. Design Award, UK, 1987; Domino's 30 Architects, USA, 1988; Aga Khan Award, 1989; Marble Architectural Award, Carrara, 1990 and 1999; Europa Nostra Diploma of EC, 1998. *Address:* Vimmelskaftet 49, 1161 Copenhagen K, Denmark. *T:* 33134557.

LARSON, Gary; cartoonist; *b* 14 Aug. 1950; *s* of Vern and Doris Larson; *m* 1988. *Educ:* Washington State Univ. (BA Communications). Cartoonist: Far Side syndicated panel (1900 newspapers worldwide), 1981–95 (Best Syndicated Panel Award, 1985); Far Side syndicated panel (syndicated internationally in 40 countries), 1995–. *Films:* Gary Larson's Tales From The Far Side, 1994; Gary Larson's Tales From The Far Side II, 1997. Reuben Award for Outstanding Cartoonist of Year, 1991 and 1994; Max Moritz Prize, Best Internat. Cartoon, 1993; Grand Prix, Annecy Film Fest., 1995; Internat. Comics Fest. Award, for French lang. edn of Hound of The Far Side, 1997. *Publications:* The Far Side, 1982; Beyond The Far Side, 1983; Hound of The Far Side, 1984; In Search of The Far Side, 1984; Valley of The Far Side, 1985; Bride of The Far Side, 1985; It Came From The Far Side, 1986; The Far Side Observer, 1987; Night of The Crash-Test Dummies, 1988; Wildlife Preserve, 1989; Wiener Dog Art, 1990 (Wheatley Medals Award, Liby Assoc., 1991); Unnatural Selections, 1991; Cows of Our Planet, 1992; The Chickens are Restless, 1993; The Curse of Madame C, 1994; Last Chapter and Worse, 1996; There's a Hair in My Dirt! A Worm's Story, 1998; *anthologies:* The Far Side Gallery, 1, 2, 3, 4, 5; The Pre-History of The Far Side, 1989. *Recreations:* jazz guitar, pick-up basketball. *Address:* c/o Creators Syndicate, Suite 700, 5777 W Century Boulevard, Los Angeles, CA 90045, USA. *T:* (310) 3377003; c/o Andrews McMeel Publishers, 4520 Main Street, Kansas City, MO 64111–7701, USA. *T:* (816) 9326700.

LARSSON, Comr John; Chief of the Staff, Salvation Army International Headquarters, since 1999; *b* 2 April 1938; *s* of Sture and Flora Larsson; *m* 1969, Freda Turner; two *s*. *Educ:* London Univ. (BD). Commnd as Salvation Army Officer, 1957, in corps, youth and trng work; Chief Sec., S America West, 1980–84; Principal, William Booth Meml Trng Coll., 1984–88; Admin. Planning, 1988–90; Territorial Commander: UK and Republic of Ireland, 1990–93; NZ and Fiji, 1993–96; Sweden and Latvia, 1996–99. *Publications:* Doctrine Without Tears, 1974; Spiritual Breakthrough, 1983; The Man Perfectly Filled with the Spirit, 1986; How Your Corps can Grow, 1988. *Recreations:* music, walking. *Address:* Salvation Army International Headquarters, 101 Queen Victoria Street, EC4P 4EP.

LASCELLES, family name of **Earl of Harewood**.

LASCELLES, Viscount; David Henry George Lascelles; freelance film and television producer; *b* 21 Oct. 1950; *s* and *heir* of 7th Earl of Harewood, *qv*; *m* 1979, Margaret Rosalind Messenger; three *s* one *d*; *m* 1990, Diane Jane Howse. *Educ:* The Hall Sch.; Westminster; Bristol Univ. Productions include: *films:* Tibet–a Buddhist Trilogy, 1977; Richard III, 1995; The Wisdom of Crocodiles, 1998; *television:* Inspector Morse IV and V, 1990 (BAFTA Best TV Series award); Wide-Eyed & Legless, 1992; Moll Flanders, 1996; Second Sight, 1999. Mem Bd, Yorkshire Arts. Chm., Harewood House Trust Ltd, 1993–; Trustee: Orient Foundn, 1983–; Yorks Media Consortium, 1998–. *Address:* Harewood, Leeds, West Yorks LS17 9LG.

LASH, Prof. Nicholas Langrishe Alleyne, DD; Norris-Hulse Professor of Divinity, University of Cambridge, 1978–99, now Emeritus; Fellow, Clare Hall, Cambridge, since 1988; *b* 6 April 1934; *s* of late Henry Alleyne Lash and Joan Mary Lash (*née* Moore); *m* 1976, Janet Angela Chalmers; one *s*. *Educ:* Downside Sch.; Oscott Coll.; St Edmund's House, Cambridge. MA, PhD, BD, DD. Served RE, 1952–57. Oscott Coll., 1957–63; Asst Priest, Slough, 1963–68; Fellow, 1969–85, Dean, 1971–75, St Edmund's House, Cambridge; Univ. Asst Lectr, Cambridge, 1974–78. *Publications:* His Presence in the World, 1968; Change in Focus, 1973; Newman on Development, 1975; Voices of Authority, 1976; Theology on Dover Beach, 1979; A Matter of Hope, 1982; Theology on the Way to Emmaus, 1986; Easter in Ordinary, 1988; Believing three ways in one God, 1992; The Beginning and End of 'Religion', 1996. *Address:* 4 Hertford Street, Cambridge CB4 3AG.

LASKEY, Prof. Ronald Alfred, FRS 1984; Charles Darwin Professor of Animal Embryology, since 1983 and Fellow of Darwin College, since 1982, University of Cambridge; *b* 26 Jan. 1945; *s* of Thomas Leslie and Bessie Laskey; *m* 1971, Margaret Ann Page; one *s* one *d*. *Educ:* High Wycombe Royal Grammar Sch.; Queen's Coll., Oxford. MA, DPhil 1970. Scientific Staff: Imperial Cancer Research Fund, 1970–73; MRC Lab. of Molecular Biology, 1973–83; Co-Dir, Molecular Embryology Group, Cancer Research Campaign, 1983–91; CRC Dir, Wellcome CRC Inst., 1991–. Hon. Dir, MRC Cancer Cell Unit, 1999–. Pres., British Soc. of Cell Biology, 1996–99. Mem., Academia Europaea, 1989; Founder FMedSci 1998. Trustee, Strangeways Res. Lab., 1993–. Colworth Medal, Biochem. Soc., 1979; CIBA Medal, Biochem. Soc., 1997; Feldberg Foundn Prize, 1998; Louis Jeantet Prize for Medicine, Jeantet Foundn, Geneva, 1998. *Publications:* Songs for Cynical Scientists and More Songs for Cynical Scientists; articles on cell biology in scientific jls. *Recreations:* music, mountains. *Address:* Wellcome Trust/Cancer Research Campaign Institute for Cancer and Developmental Biology, Tennis Court Road, Cambridge CB2 1QR. *T:* (01223) 334106.

LASKO, Prof. Peter Erik, CBE 1981; FBA 1978; Professor of the History of Art, Courtauld Institute, University of London, 1974–85; Director, Courtauld Institute, 1974–85; *b* 5 March 1924; *s* of Leo Lasko and Wally Lasko (*née* Seifert); *m* 1948, Gwendoline Joan Norman; three *d. Educ:* Courtauld Institute, Univ. of London (BA Hons 1949). Asst Keeper, British Museum, 1950–65; Prof. of the Visual Arts, Univ. of East Anglia, 1965–73. Member: Cathedrals Adv. Commn, 1981–91; Royal Commn on Historical Monuments (England), 1984–91; Cathedrals Fabric Commn, 1991–96; Trustee: British Mus., 1981–95; Royal Armouries, 1984–91. Hon. DLitt East Anglia, 1997. *Publication:* Ars Sacra 800–1200 (Pelican History of Art), 1972, 2nd edn 1994. *Address:* 1 Hawke Lane, Bloxham, Oxon OX15 4PY.

LASKY, Melvin Jonah, MA; Editor, Encounter Magazine, 1958–90; *b* New York City, 15 Jan. 1920; *s* of Samuel Lasky and Esther Lasky (*née* Kantrowitz); *m* 1947, Brigitte Newiger (marr. diss. 1974); one *s* one *d. Educ:* City Coll. of New York (BSS); Univ. of Michigan (MA); Columbia Univ. Literary Editor, The New Leader (NY), 1942–43; US Combat Historian in France and Germany, 1944–45; Capt., US Army, 1946; Foreign Correspondent, 1946–48; Editor and Publisher, Der Monat (Berlin), 1948–58 and 1978–83; Editorial Director, Library Press, NY, 1970–80; Publisher, Alcove Press, London, 1972–82. Regular television broadcaster, Cologne, Zürich and Vienna, 1955–. Fellow, Inst. of Advanced Study, Berlin, 1988–89. Hon. PhD York (Canada), 1990. Univ. of Michigan, Sesquicentennial Award, 1967; Distinguished Alumnus Award, City Univ., NY, 1978. *Publications:* (ed) The Hungarian Revolution, 1957; Reisenotizen und Tagebücher, 1958; Africa for Beginners, 1962; Utopia and Revolution, 1976 (Spanish edn 1982; German edn 1989); On the Barricades, and Off, 1989; Voices in a Revolution, 1991 (also German edn); The Language of Journalism, vol I: newspaper culture, 2001; contributor to: America and Europe, 1951; New Paths in American History, 1965; Sprache und Politik, 1969; Festschrift for Raymond Aron, 1971; Koestler, Orwell *et al*, 1999; Ein Fenster zur Welt, 2000. *Address:* Mommsenstrasse 67, 10629 Berlin, Germany; 37 Godfrey Street, Chelsea, SW3 3SX. *Club:* Garrick.

LASLETT, (Thomas) Peter (Ruffell), CBE 1997; FBA 1979; Reader in Politics and the History of Social Structure, Cambridge University, 1966–83; Co-Founder and Director, Cambridge Group for the History of Population and Social Structure, since 1964; Fellow of Trinity College, Cambridge, since 1953; *b* 18 Dec. 1915; *s* of Rev. G. H. R. Laslett and E. E. Laslett (*née* Alden); *m* 1947, Janet Crockett Clark; two *s. Educ:* Watford Grammar Sch.; St John's Coll., Cambridge. Served War, Royal Navy, 1940–45: Lieut RNVR, Japanese Naval Intelligence. Producer, BBC, 3rd Programme Talks, 1946–60; Fellow: St John's Coll., Cambridge, 1948–51; Inst. for Advanced Study, Princeton, 1959. With Michael Young and others developed plans for Open Univ. in the 1960s, and for univs of the Third Age in the 1970s; Mem., govt cttee on foundn of Open Univ., 1965; oversaw instn of first Univ. of the Third Age, 1981. Visiting Professor: Johns Hopkins Univ., 1972; Collège de France, Paris, 1976; Yale Univ., 1977; Nihon Univ., Tokyo, 1992. DUniv: Open, 1980; Keele, 1993; Tulane, 2000. Founder and Chief Ed., series, Philosophy, Politics and Society, 1957 (6th series 1992). *Publications:* Sir Robert Filmer, 1949; Locke's Two Treatises of Government, 1960, 3rd edn 1988; The World We Have Lost, 1965, 3rd edn 1983; (with R. Wall) Household and Family in Past Time, 1972; Family Life and Illicit Love in Earlier Generations, 1977; (with R. M. Smith and others) Bastardy and its Comparative History, 1980; (jtly) Family Forms in Historic Europe, 1983; A Fresh Map of Life, 1989, 2nd edn 1996; (with J. Fishkin) Justice between Age Groups and Generations, 1992; (with D. Kertzer) Ageing in the Past, 1995. *Recreations:* book collecting, gardening. *Address:* Trinity College, Cambridge CB2 1TQ; Cambridge Group, 27 Trumpington Street, Cambridge CB2 1QA. *T:* (01223) 333181.

LASOK, (Karol) Paul (Edward), PhD; QC 1994; a Recorder, since 2000; *b* 16 July 1953; *s* of Prof. Dominik Lasok, QC; *m* 1991, Karen Bridget Morgan Griffith; two *d. Educ:* St Mary's Sch., Clyst St Mary; Jesus Coll., Cambridge (MA); Exeter Univ. (LLM, PhD). Called to the Bar, Middle Temple, 1977; Legal Sec., Court of Justice of the EC, 1980–84 and (*locum tenens*) 1985; private practice, 1985–. Consultant Editor, Butterworths European Court Practice; Jt Editor, Common Market Law Reports, 1996–. *Publications:* The European Court of Justice: practice and procedure, 1984, 2nd edn 1994; contribs to: Halsbury's Laws of England, 4th edn, vols 51 and 52; Law of European Communities (ed D. Vaughan); Lasok and Bridge's Law and Institutions of the European Union, 6th edn, 1994, 7th edn 2000; (with J. Lever) Weinberg and Blank on Takeovers and Mergers; legal periodicals. *Recreation:* amusing daughters. *Address:* 4 Raymond Buildings, Gray's Inn, WC1R 5BP. *T:* (020) 7405 7211.

LAST, Maj.-Gen. Christopher Neville, CB 1990; OBE 1976; health management consultant, 1998; *b* 2 Sept. 1935; *s* of Jack Neville Last, MPS, FSMC, FBOA and Lorna (*née* Goodman), MPS; *m* 1961, Pauline Mary Lawton, BA; two *d. Educ:* Culford Sch.; Brighton Tech. Coll. psc†, ndc. Commnd Royal Signals, 1956; Germany, Parachute Bde, Borneo, Singapore, 1956–67; OC 216 Para. Signal Sqdn, 1967; RMCS and Staff Coll., Logistics Staff 1 (BR) Corps, 1968–71; NDC, 1972; Lt-Col, Signal Staff HQ, BAOR, 1973; CO Royal Signals NI, 1974; Staff, MoD Combat Develt, 1976, Mil. Ops, 1977; Col, Project Manager MoD (PE) for Army ADP Comd and Control, 1977; CO (Col) 8 Signal Regt Trng, Royal Signals, 1980; Brig., Comd 1 Signal Bde 1 (BR) Corps, 1981; Dir, Mil. Comd and Control Projects, MoD (PE), 1984; Head of Defence Procurement Policy (Studies Team), on Chief of Defence Procurement Personal Staff, MoD (PE), 1985; Maj.-Gen. 1986; Vice Master Gen. of the Ordnance, 1986–88; Mil. Dep. to Head of Defence Export Services, 1988–90; Chief Exec., Clwyd FHSA, 1990–96; Dir of Business Management, Clwyd and Oswestry Tissue Bank, 1996–97. Col Comdt, RCS, 1990–96. Chairman: Royal Signals Instn, 1994–98; Bd of Trustees, Royal Signals Mus., 1996–. Mem., TA&VRA for Wales, 1996–. Pres., BRCS N Wales, 1996–; Vice-Pres., BRCS Wales, 2000–. Chm., Kigezi Foundn, 2001–. Liveryman, Co. of Information Technologists, 1988 (Chm., Med. and Health Panel, 1998–); Freeman, City of London, 1988. *Recreations:* travel, theatre, ballet, sailing, ski-ing, shooting and country pursuits, hockey (Army and Combined Services). *Address:* c/o National Westminster Bank, 34 North Street, Lancing, Sussex BN15 9AB. *Clubs:* Special Forces, Fadeaways.

LAST, John William, CBE 1989; Director, Public Affairs, United Utilities plc (formerly North West Water Group), 1993–98; Chairman, Museums Training Institute, 1990–97; *b* 22 Jan. 1940; *s* of late Jack Last (sometime Dir of Finance, Metrop. Police) and Freda Last (*née* Evans); *m* 1967, Susan Josephine, *er d* of late John and Josephine Farmer; three *s. Educ:* Sutton Grammar Sch., Surrey; Trinity Coll., Oxford (MA 1965). Littlewoods Organisation, Liverpool, 1969–93. Chm., Dernier Properties Ltd, 1996–; Director: Boom, 1990–93; Inward, investment agency for NW, 1992–96; sparesFinder.com Ltd, 1999–. Mem., Merseyside CC, 1973–86 (Chm., Arts Cttee, 1977–81); contested (C) Liverpool, West Derby, Feb. and Oct. 1974, Stockport N, 1979. Vis. Prof., City Univ., London, 1987–. Bd Mem., Royal Liverpool Philharmonic Soc., 1973–93 (Chm., 1977–81, 1986–92); Founder Chairman: Merseyside Maritime Museum, 1977; Empire Theatre (Merseyside) Trust, 1979–81 (Bd Mem., 1986–); Chairman: Walker Art Gall., Liverpool, 1977–81; Library Assoc./Arts Council Wkg Party on Art in Libraries, 1982–84; Wkg Party to form Merseyside TEC, 1989–90; Nat. Chm., Area Museums Councils of GB, 1979–82; Vice-Pres., NW Museum and Art Gall. Service, 1992– (Chm., 1977–82, 1987–92); Vice-Chm., Merseyside Arts, 1985–88; Member: Museums Assoc. Council, 1978–86 (Vice-Pres., 1983); Arts Council of GB, 1980–84 (Chm., Housing the Arts Cttee, 1981–84; Chm., Regional Cttee, 1981–84); Museums and Galleries Commn, 1983–95 (Mem., Scottish Wkg Pty, 1984–85); Enquiry into Tyne and Wear Service, 1988–89; Chm., Enquiry into Local Authorities and Museums, 1989–91; Bd, Northern Ballet Theatre, 1986–98 (Vice Chm., 1986–88); Merseyside Tourism Bd, 1986–92; NW Industrial Council, 1985–98; Council, NE Wales Inst., 1999–; Court, Liverpool Univ., 1973–96 (Mem. Council, 1977–81, 1986–96); Calcutt Cttee on Privacy and Intrusion by the Press, 1989–90; Lay Mem., Press Council, 1980–86; Advr on Local Govt to Arts Council, 1984–91; Chm., Arts, Initiative and Money Cttee, Gulbenkian Foundn, 1980–83. Mem. Bd, Charities Trust, 1990–94; Trustee: Norton Priory Museum, 1983–87; V&A Museum, 1984–86 (Mem., Adv. Council, 1978–84; Mem., Theatre Museum Cttee, 1983–86); Nat. Museums and Galls on Merseyside, 1986–99; Governor: NYO, 1985–93; Nat. Mus. of Wales, 1994–97. Patron, N Wales Music Festival, 1994–. Chm., Centenary Develt Trust, Sutton Grammar Sch. FRSA 1988. Hon. FMA, 1987. Hon. Fellow, Liverpool John Moores Univ. (formerly Liverpool Polytechnic), 1989. Freedom of City of London, 1985; Barber Surgeons' Co.: Freeman, 1985; Liveryman, 1987–; Mem., Ct of Assts, 1999–. Hon. DLitt City, 1995. Hon. Mem., Amer. Chapter, Order of King Charles the Martyr, 1996. Merseyside Gold Medal for Achievement, 1991. *Publications:* A Brief History of Museums and Galleries, 1986; The Last Report on Local Authorities and Museums, 1991; reports: (jtly) Arts: the way forward, 1978; (jtly) A Future for the Arts, 1987. *Recreations:* swimming, music, memorabilia of Edward VIII. *Address:* Llannerch Hall, near St Asaph, Denbighshire LL17 0BD; 106 Waterloo Dock, Liverpool L3 0BQ. *Club:* Royal Automobile.

LATCHMAN, Prof. David Seymour; Professor of Human Genetics, and Dean, Institute of Child Health, University College London and Great Ormond Street Hospital for Children, since 1999; *b* 22 Jan. 1956; *s* of Emanuel Latchman and Ella Latchman (*née* Wohl). *Educ:* Haberdashers' Aske's Sch.; Queens' Coll., Cambridge (BA 1978; MA 1981; PhD 1981); DSc London 1994. FRCPath 1999. Lectr in Molecular Genetics, Dept of Biology, UCL, 1984–88; Dir, Med. Molecular Biology Unit and Reader in Molecular Biology, Dept of Biochemistry, UCL and Middlesex Sch. of Medicine, 1988–91; University College London: Prof. of Molecular Pathology, 1991–99; Head, Div. of Pathol., 1995–99; Dir, Windeyer Inst of Med. Scis, 1996–99; Dep. Hd, UCL Graduate Sch., 1998–99. Chm., Sci. Expert Adv. Cttee, Univ. of London, 1988–97. External Examiner: Brunel Univ., 1993–97; Nottingham Univ., 1999–; Mem., Examng Panel in Genetics, RCPath, 1999–. Member: Med. Adv. Panel, Parkinson's Disease Soc., 1995– (Dep. Chm., 1997–); MRC Adv. Bd, 1997–; Project Grants Cttee, BHF, 1998–; Sci. Policy Adv. Cttee, Nat. Inst. for Biol Standards and Control, 1998–. Haldane Lectr, 1994, Crabtree Orator, 1997, UCL. Dep. Chm., Editl Bd, Biochemical Jl, 1995–97. *Publications:* Gene Regulation, 1990, 3rd edn 1998; Eukaryotic Transcription Factors, 1991, 3rd edn 1998; (ed) Transcription Factors: a practical approach, 1993, 2nd edn 1999; (ed) From Genetics to Gene Therapy, 1994; (ed) PCR applications in Pathology, 1995; (ed) Genetic Manipulation of the Nervous System, 1995; (ed) Basic Molecular and Cell Biology, 1997; (ed) Landmarks in Gene Regulation, 1997; (ed) Stress Proteins, 1999. *Recreations:* book collecting, opera. *Address:* Institute of Child Health, 30 Guilford Street, WC1N 1EH. *Club:* Athenæum.

LATHAM, family name of **Baron Latham.**

LATHAM, 2nd Baron *cr* 1942, of Hendon; **Dominic Charles Latham;** Senior Structural Engineer with Gerard Barry Associates, since 1992; *b* 20 Sept. 1954; *s* of Hon. Francis Charles Allman Latham (*d* 1959) and Gabrielle Monica (*d* 1987), *d* of Dr S. M. O'Riordan; *S* grandfather, 1970. *Educ:* Univ. of New South Wales, Australia (BEng (civil), 1977, Hons I; MEngSc 1981). Civil Engr, Electricity Commn, NSW, 1979–88; Structl Engr, Rankine & Hill, Consulting Engrs, 1988–91. Teacher, Rock around the Clock Dancing, 1993–. *Recreations:* rock-'n'-roll/ballroom dancing, electronics, personal computing, sailboarding. *Heir:* yr twin *b* Anthony Michael Latham; *b* 20 Sept. 1954. *Address:* PO Box 355, Kensington, NSW 2033, Australia.

LATHAM, Arthur Charles; Member (Lab), Havering Council (formerly Romford Borough Council), 1952–78 and 1986–98; *b* Leyton, 14 Aug. 1930; *m* 1951, Margaret Latham; one *s* one *d. Educ:* Romford Royal Liberty Sch.; Garnett Coll. of Educn. Lectr in Further Educn, Southgate Technical Coll., 1967–. Havering Council (formerly Romford Borough Council): Leader, Labour Gp, 1962–70 and 1986–98; Leader of the Opposition, 1986–90; Leader of Council, 1990–96; Alderman, 1962–78. Mem., NE Regional Metropolitan Hosp. Bd, 1966–72; part-time Mem., July-Nov. 1983, Mem., 1983–84, LTE. MP (Lab) Paddington N, Oct. 1969–1974, City of Westminster, Paddington, 1974–79; Founder, and Jt Chm., All Party Gp for Pensioners, 1971–79; Chm., Tribune Gp, 1975–76 (Treasurer, 1977–79). Contested (Lab): Woodford, 1959; Rushcliffe, Notts, 1964; City of Westminster, Paddington, 1979; Westminster N, 1983. Chm., Greater London Lab. Party, 1977–86; Vice-Chm., Nat. Cttee, Labour League of Youth, 1949–53; Vice-President: Labour Action for Peace; AMA; Treasurer, Liberation (Movement for Colonial Freedom), 1969–79; Member: British Campaign for Peace in Vietnam; Campaign for Nuclear Disarmament. Vegetarian. *Recreations:* bridge, chess, cricket. *Address:* 17 Tudor Avenue, Gidea Park, Romford RM2 5LB.

LATHAM, Cecil Thomas, OBE 1976; Stipendiary Magistrate, Greater Manchester (sitting at Salford), 1976–94; *b* 11 March 1924; *s* of Cecil Frederick James Latham and Elsie Winifred Latham; *m* 1945, Ivy Frances (*née* Fowle); one *s* one *d. Educ:* Rochester Cathedral Choir Sch.; King's Sch., Rochester. Solicitor. War Service, 1942–45. Asst Clerk, Magistrates' Courts: Chatham, 1939–42; Maidstone, 1945; Leicester, 1948–54; Bromley, 1954–63; Dep. Justices' Clerk, Liverpool, 1963–65; Justices' Clerk, Manchester, 1965–76. Member: Magistrates' Courts Rule Cttee, 1966–94; Royal Commn on Criminal Procedure, 1978–81; Criminal Law Revision Cttee, 1981–94. Hon. MA Manchester, 1984. *Publications:* (ed) Stone's Justices' Manual, 101st-109th edns; How Much?: determining maintenance in magistrates' courts, 1976; Care Proceedings, 1989; (ed) Family Law Reports, 1980–86; specialist editor, Justice of the Peace Reports, 1986–93; founder editor, Family Court Reporter, 1987–99; contrib. Criminal Law Rev., Justice of Peace, Family Law. *Recreation:* music. *Address:* 12 Oakside Way, Oakwood, Derby DE21 2UH. *T:* (01332) 544338.

LATHAM, Christopher George Arnot; Chairman, James Latham PLC, 1988–95; *b* 4 June 1933; *s* of late Edward Bryan Latham and Anne Arnot Duncan; *m* 1963, Jacqueline Cabourdin; three *s. Educ:* Stowe Sch.; Clare Coll., Cambridge (MA). FCA. Articled Fitzpatrick Graham, chartered accountants, 1955; joined James Latham Ltd, timber importers, 1959, Dir 1963. A Forestry Comr, 1973–78. Dir, CILNTEC, 1991–97. Pres., Inst. of Wood Sci., 1977–79; Chairman: Timber Res. and Develt Assoc., 1972–74; Commonwealth Forestry Assoc., 1975–77; Psychiatric Rehabilitation Assoc., 1983–91. Mem., Co. of Builders Merchants, 1985– (Master, 1999–2000). FRGS 1995. *Recreations:* forestry, classic cars. *Address:* Quarry Court, Quarry Wood, Marlow SL7 1RF.

LATHAM, Rt Hon. Sir David (Nicholas Ramsay), Kt 1992; PC 2000; **Rt Hon. Lord Justice Latham;** a Lord Justice of Appeal, since 2000; *b* 18 Sept. 1942; *s* of Robert Clifford Latham, CBE, FBA and late Eileen (*née* Ramsay); *m* 1967, Margaret Elizabeth (*née* Forrest); three *d*. *Educ:* Bryanston Sch.; Queens' Coll., Cambridge (MA). Called to the Bar, Middle Temple, 1964, Bencher, 1989; QC 1985; one of the Junior Counsel to the Crown, Common Law, 1979–85; Junior Counsel to Dept of Trade in export credit matters, 1981–85; a Recorder, 1983–92; a Judge of the High Court, QBD, 1992–2000; Presiding Judge, Midland and Oxford Circuit, 1995–99. Vice-Chm., Council of Legal Educn, 1992–97 (Mem., 1988–97); Member: Gen. Council of the Bar, 1987–92; Judicial Studies Bd, 1988–91. *Recreations:* reading, music, travel. *Address:* Royal Courts of Justice, Strand WC2A 2LL. *Clubs:* Travellers; Leander.

LATHAM, Sir Michael (Anthony), Kt 1993; DL; Director, since 1996 and Chairman, since 1999, Willmott Dixon Ltd; Deputy Chairman: J. R. Knowles (Holdings) plc, since 1997; Building Information Warehouse Ltd, since 2000; Chairman: Knowles Management Ltd (formerly PPSL), since 1998; Partnership Sourcing, since 2000; *b* 20 Nov. 1942; *m* 1969, Caroline Terry; two *s*. *Educ:* Marlborough Coll.; King's Coll., Cambridge; Dept of Educn, Oxford. BA Cantab 1964, MA Cantab 1968, CertEd Oxon 1965. Housing and Local Govt Officer, Conservative Research Dept, 1965–67; Parly Liaison Officer, Nat. Fedn of Building Trades Employers, 1967–73; Dir, House-builders Fedn, 1971–73. Westminster City Councillor, 1968–71. Contested (C) Liverpool, West Derby, 1970; MP (C) Melton, Feb. 1974–1983, Rutland and Melton, 1983–92. Member: House of Commons Expenditure Cttee, 1974–79; Jt Cttee on Statutory Instruments, 1974–75; Jt Ecclesiastical Cttee of both Houses of Parliament, 1974–92; Select Cttee on Energy, 1979–82; Public Accounts Cttee, 1983–92; H of C Chairmen's Panel, 1987–92. Chm., British-Israel Parly Gp, 1981–90; Vice Pres., Anglo-Israel Assoc., 1994– (Pres., 1990–94; Chm. Exec. Cttee, 1986–90). Dir, Lovell Homes Ltd, 1975–85; Housing Adviser, Y. J. Lovell PLC, 1985–89; Dir, Lovell Partnerships, 1989–92; Dir, Building (Publications) Ltd, 1988–91; Corporate Affairs Dir, Builder Group, 1992–93; Director: Ansoll Estates Ltd, 1993–96; Streamline Hldgs plc, 1997–98; Public Affairs Consultant: Bldg Employers Confedn, 1992–93; House Builders Fedn, 1992–95. Chairman: Construction Industry Bd, 1995–96; Jt Major Contractors Gp, 1996–; Jt Industry Bd for Electrical Contracting Industry, 1998–; Dep. Chm., Roofing Industry Alliance, 1997–; President: British Flat Roofing Council, 1996–99; Flat Roofing Alliance, 1999–. Chm., Jt Govt/Industry Rev. of Procurement and Contractual Problems in Construction Industry, 1993–94. Mem., Adv. Council on Public Records, 1985–91. Vice-Pres., Building Socs Assoc., 1981–91. Mem. Exec. Cttee, 1987–2000, Dir, 1992, Jt Hon. Treas., 1996–2000, Vice-Pres., 2000–, CCJ. Visiting Professor: Northumbria Univ., 1995–2000; Bartlett Sch. of Architecture, UCL, 1997–. C of E Lay Reader, 1988–. Trustee, Oakham Sch., 1987–. FRSA 1992. Hon. Mem. RICS, 1996; Hon. FCIPS 1994; Hon. FCIOB 1995; Hon. FICE 1995; Hon. FASI 1995; Hon. Fellow, Inst. of Building Control, 1995; Hon. FREng (Hon. FEng 1997); Hon. FLI 1997; Hon. FRIAS 1998. DL Leics, 1994. Hon. LLD Nottingham Trent, 1995; Hon. DEng Birmingham, 1998; Hon. DCL Northumbria, 1999. *Publications:* articles on housing, land, town planning and building. *Recreations:* gardening, fencing, listening to classical music, cricket. *Address:* 508 Hood House, Dolphin Square, SW1V 3NH. *Club:* Carlton.

LATHAM, Air Vice-Marshal Peter Anthony, CB 1980; AFC 1960; *b* 18 June 1925; *s* of late Oscar Frederick Latham and Rhoda Latham; *m* 1953, Barbara Mary; two *s* six *d*. *Educ:* St Phillip's Grammar Sch., Birmingham; St Catharine's Coll., Cambridge. psa 1961. Joined RAF, 1944; 1946–69: served No 26, 263, 614, and 247 Sqdns; CFE; Air Min.; Comd No 111 Sqdn; RAF Formation Aerobatic Team (Leader of Black Arrows, 1959–60); MoD Jt Planning Staff; Comd NEAF Strike and PR Wing; Coll. of Air Warfare; Ops No 38 Gp; Comd RAF Tengah, 1969–71; MoD Central Staff, 1971–73; Comd Officer and AOC, Aircrew Selection Centre, Biggin Hill, 1973–74; SASO No 38 Gp, 1974–76; Dir Def. Ops, MoD Central Staff, 1976–77; AOC No 11 Group, 1977–81. Principal, Oxford Air Trng Sch., and Dir, CSE Aviation Ltd, 1982–85; Sen. Air Advr, Short Bros, 1985–90. Cdre, RAF Sailing Assoc., 1974–80; Pres., Assoc. of Service Yacht Clubs, 1978–81. Pres., British Horological Inst., 1996. Liveryman, Clockmakers' Co., 1987 (Mem., Ct of Assts, 1990–; Master, 1996). *Recreations:* sailing, horology. *Address:* c/o Lloyds TSB, PO Box 61, The Rotunda, 149 New Street, Birmingham B2 4NZ. *Club:* Royal Air Force.

LATHAM, Peter Heaton; His Honour Judge Latham; a Circuit Judge, since 1997; *b* 3 June 1938; *s* of Tom Heaton Latham and Dorothy Latham (*née* Williams). *Educ:* The Grammar Sch., Ashton-in-Makerfield, Lancs; Pembroke Coll., Oxford (BA Juris 1962). Nat. Service, 2nd Lieut, RA, 1957–59. Instructor, Univ. of Pennsylvania Law Sch., 1962–64; called to the Bar Gray's Inn, 1965 (James Mould Schol., 1965; Lee Essay Prize, 1965); in practice, 1965–97. *Address:* Barnet County Court, Regent's Park Road, Finchley Central, N3 1BQ. *T:* (020) 8343 4272.

LATHAM, Richard Brunton; QC 1991; a Recorder, since 1987; *b* 16 March 1947; *s* of Frederick and Joan Catherine Latham; *m* 1972, Alison Mary Goodall; three *s*. *Educ:* Farnborough Grammar School; Univ. of Birmingham (LLB 1969). Called to the Bar, Gray's Inn, 1971; Bencher, 2000; practice on Midland and Oxford Circuit; Standing Prosecuting Counsel to Inland Revenue, Midland and Oxford Circuit, 1987–91. *Recreations:* sailing, opera. *Address:* 7 Bedford Row, WC1R 4BU. *T:* (020) 7242 3555.

LATHAM, Sir Richard Thomas Paul, 3rd Bt *cr* 1919, of Crow Clump; *b* 15 April 1934; *s* of Sir (Herbert) Paul Latham, 2nd Bt, and Lady Patricia Doreen Moore (*d* 1947), *o d* of 10th Earl of Drogheda; *S* father, 1955; *m* 1958, Marie-Louise Patricia, *d* of Frederick H. Russell, Vancouver, BC; two *d*. *Educ:* Eton; Trinity Coll., Cambridge. *Address:* 2125 Birnam Wood Drive, Santa Barbara, CA 93108, USA.

LATHAM, Roger Alan; County Treasurer, Nottinghamshire County Council, since 1991; *b* 3 May 1950; *s* of Edward and Florrie Latham; *m* 1973, Angela Judith Warwick (*née* Pearce); one *s*. *Educ:* Bristol Univ. (BSc Econs with Stats); Birmingham Univ. (MSocSc); Liverpool Polytechnic. CPFA; CStat. Economic Assistant, National Westminster Bank, 1972–76; Economist, 1976–85, Asst Chief Finance Officer, 1985–90, Dudley MBC; Dep. County Treasurer, Notts CC, 1990–91. Methodist Local Preacher. *Recreations:* photography, gardening, computers, reading, dinosaurs, Japanese films. *Address:* 25 Potters Lane, East Leake, Loughborough, Leics LE12 6NQ. *T:* (01509) 856562.

LATHE, Prof. Grant Henry; Professor of Chemical Pathology, University of Leeds, 1957–77, now Emeritus Professor; *b* 27 July 1913; *s* of Frank Eugene and Annie Smith Lathe; *m* 1st, 1938, Margaret Eleanore Brown; one *s*; 2nd, 1950, Joan Frances Hamlin; one *s* two *d*. *Educ:* McGill Univ.; Oxford Univ. ICI Research Fellow: Dept. of Biochemistry, Oxford Univ., 1946; Dept. of Chemical Pathology, Post Graduate Medical School of London, 1948; Lecturer in Chemical Pathology, Guy's Hospital Medical School, 1948; Biochemist, The Bernhard Baron Memorial Research Laboratories, Queen Charlotte's Maternity Hospital, London, 1949. John Scott Award (with C. R. J. Ruthven), 1971, for invention of gel filtration. *Publications:* papers in medical and biochemical journals. *Recreations:* fell-walking, campaigning against nuclear weapons. *Address:* 12A The Avenue, Leeds LS8 1EH. *T:* (0113) 266 1507.

See also R. F. Lathe.

LATHE, Prof. Richard Frank; Research Professor, University of Edinburgh, since 1989; *b* 23 April 1952; *s* of Grant Henry Lathe, *qv*; one *s* four *d*. *Educ:* Univ. of Edinburgh (BSc Molecular Biol. 1973); Free Univ. of Brussels (DésSc 1976). Research Scientist: Univ. of Heidelberg, 1977–79; Univ. of Cambridge, 1979–81; Asst Sci. Dir, Transgene SA, Strasbourg, 1981–84; Principal Sci. Officer, Animal Breeding Res. Orgn, 1984–85; Prof. of Genetics and Genetic Engrg, Lab. of Eukaryotic Molecular Genetics, and Co-Dir, Ecole Supérieure de Biotechnologie, Univ. of Strasbourg, 1985–89. *Address:* Centre for Genome Research, University of Edinburgh, King's Buildings, West Mains Road, Edinburgh EH9 3JQ. *T:* (0131) 650 5890.

LATIMER, Sir (Courtenay) Robert, Kt 1966; CBE 1958 (OBE 1948); *b* 13 July 1911; *er s* of late Sir Courtenay Latimer, KCIE, CSI; *m* 1st, 1944, Elizabeth Jane Gordon (*née* Smail) (*d* 1989); one *s* one *d*; 2nd, 1990, Frederieka Jacoba Blankert (*née* Witteween). *Educ:* Rugby; Christ Church, Oxford. ICS, 1934 (Punjab); IPS, 1939; Vice-Consul, Bushire, 1940–41; Sec. Foreign Publicity Office, Delhi, 1941–42; Sec. Indian Agency Gen., Chungking, 1944; in NW Frontier Prov., as Asst Political Agent N Waziristan, Dir of Civil Supplies, Sec. to Governor and District Comr, Bannu, 1942–43 and 1945–47. HM Overseas Service, 1948; served in Swaziland, 1948–49; Bechuanaland Protectorate, 1951–54; Office of High Comr for Basutoland, the Bechuanaland Protectorate and Swaziland, as Asst Sec., 1949–51; Sec. for Finance, 1954–60; Chief Sec., 1960–64; Minister, British Embassy, Pretoria, 1965–66; Registrar, Kingston Polytechnic, 1967–76. *Recreations:* golf, photography. *Address:* Benedicts, Old Avenue, Weybridge, Surrey KT13 0PS.

LATIMER, Sir Graham (Stanley), KBE 1980; President, New Zealand Maori Council, since 1972 (Delegate, 1964; Vice-President, 1969–72); *b* Waiharara, N Auckland, 7 Feb. 1926; *s* of Graham Latimer and Lillian Edith Latimer (*née* Kenworthy); *m* 1948, Emily Patricia Moore; two *s* two *d*. *Educ:* Pukenui and Kaitaia District High School. Dairy farmer, 1961–. Chairman: Aotearoa Fisheries, 1991–; Crown Forestry Rental, 1991–; Moana Pacific, 1991–98; Dep. Chm., Maori Fisheries Commn, 1989–90; Negotiator, NZ Maori Fisheries. Member: Tai Tokerau Dist Maori Council, 1962– (Sec. 1966–75; Chm., 1976–); Otamatea Maori Exec., 1959– (Sec. Treas. 1962–72, Chm. 1975–); Otamatea Maori Cttee, 1955–62; Arapaoa Maori Cttee, 1962– (Chm. 1962–69 and 1972–); N Auckland Power Bd, 1977–; Waitangi Tribunal, 1976–. Chairman: (since inception) Northland Community Coll.; Tai Tokerau Maori Trust Bd, 1979– (Mem., 1975–); Pacific Foundn, 1990–; Trustee: Kohanga Reo Nat. Trust, 1979–; Maori Education Foundn; Member: Ngatikahu Trust Bd, 1976–; Cttee, Nat. Art Gall. Museum and War Memorial; NZ Maori Arts and Crafts Inst., 1980–; Tourist Adv. Council; Northland Regional Develt Council, 1980–; Alcoholic Liquor Adv. Council, 1980–. Lay Canon, Auckland Anglican Cathedral, 1978; Mem. Gen. Synod. JP. *Recreations:* Rugby football, tennis. *Address:* PO Box 661, Kaitaia, New Zealand.

LATIMER, Sir Robert; *see* Latimer, Sir C. R.

LATNER, Stephen; Managing Director, Warburg Dillon Read, 1998–99; *b* 23 July 1946; *s* of late Julius Latner and of Anita Latner; *m* 1971, Jennifer Keidan; three *s*. *Educ:* Grocers' Sch.; Queen Mary Coll., London (BSc); Manchester Business Sch. (MBA). With ICL, 1968–71; joined S. G. Warburg, 1973: Dir, 1983–96; Dep. Chm., 1993–96; UK Country Hd, SBC Warburg, then Warburg Dillon Read, 1996–98. Mem. Council, Bobath Centre for Children with Cerebral Palsy, 1999–. *Recreations:* music, cinema, theatre, reading, sport.

LATOUR-ADRIEN, Hon. Sir (Jean François) Maurice, Kt 1971; Chief Justice of Mauritius, 1970–77; Chairman, Mauritius Union Assurance Co. Ltd, since 1982 (Director since 1978); *b* 4 March 1915; 2nd *s* of late Louis Constant Emile Adrien and late Maria Ella Latour. *Educ:* Royal Coll., Mauritius; Univ. Coll., London; Middle Temple, London. LLB 1940. Called to the Bar, Middle Temple, 1940. Mauritius: Dist Magistrate, 1947; Crown Counsel, 1950; Additl Subst. Procureur and Advocate-Gen., 1954; Sen. Crown Counsel, 1958; Asst Attorney-Gen., 1960; Solicitor-Gen., 1961; Dir of Public Prosecutions, 1964; Puisne Judge, 1966–70; Acting Governor-Gen., Feb. 1973, July–Aug. 1974, Jan.–Feb. and June–Aug. 1975, July–Sept. 1976. Pres., Mauritius Red Cross Soc., 1978–; Vice-Pres., Inst. Internat. de Droit d'Expression Française (IDEF). Pres., Mauritius Commercial Bank Ltd, 1993–94 (Dir, 1980–83, 1984–87, 1988–91, 1992–95, 1996–99, 2000–; Vice-Pres., 1992–93, 1996–97); Legal Consultant: Mauritius Commercial Bank Ltd, 1983–; Promotion and Development Ltd, 1985–; Mauritius Commercial Bank Finance Corp., 1991–94; Mauritius Commercial Bank Registry and Securities, 1991–; Caudan Development Co. Ltd, 1991–; Fincorp Investment Ltd, 1994–. President: Mental Health Assoc., 1985– (Vice-Pres., 1978–84); Mauritius Red Cross, 1978–. Mem., War Meml Bd of Trustees, 1978–84 (Vice Pres., 1985–). KLJ 1969. *Address:* Vacoas, Mauritius; c/o Mauritius Union Assurance Co. Ltd, 4 Léoville l'Homme Street, Port Louis, Mauritius.

LA TROBE-BATEMAN, Richard George Saumarez; structures designer/maker; *b* 17 Oct. 1938; *s* of late John La Trobe-Bateman and of Margaret (*née* Schmid); *m* 1969, Mary Elizabeth Jolly (OBE 2000); one *s* two *d*. *Educ:* Westminster Sch.; St Martin's Sch. of Art; Royal Coll. of Art (MDesRCA). Set up workshop, 1968. Member: Council of Management, British Crafts Centre, 1975–86; Council, Contemporary Applied Arts, 1987–94; Crafts Council: Mem., 1984–86; Index Selector, 1972–73; Chm., Index Selection Cttee, 1980–82. Work in: V&A Collection, 1979; Crafts Council Collection, 1981 and 1984; Keble Coll., Oxon, 1981; Temple Newsam Collection, 1983; Southern Arts Collection, 1983; Pembroke Coll., Oxon, 1984; Crafts Study Centre Collection, Bath, 1985; Northern Arts Collection, 1988; Royal Soc. of Arts, 1994; work presented by Crafts Council to the Prince of Wales, 1982; Longlands footbridge, Cumbria, 1995; Nat. Pinetum footbridge, Kent, 1999. Vis. Prof., San Diego State Univ., 1986–87. *Publications:* articles in Crafts, American Crafts. *Recreations:* listening to music, hill-walking. *Address:* Elm House, Batcombe, Shepton Mallet, Somerset BA4 6AB. *T:* (01749) 850442. *Club:* Contemporary Applied Arts.

LATTER, Henry James Edward; a Vice President, Immigration Appeal Tribunal, since 2001; *b* 19 April 1950; *s* of Henry Edward Latter and Hilda Bessie Latter; *m* 1978, Penelope Jane Morris; one *s* one *d*. *Educ:* Reigate Grammar Sch.; Trinity Hall, Cambridge (BA 1971; MA 1974). Called to the Bar, Middle Temple, 1972; in practice as Barrister, 1972–95; full-time Immigration Adjudicator, 1995–96; Regl Adjudicator, Hatton Cross, 1996–98; Dep. Chief Adjudicator, 1998–2001. *Address:* Immigration Appeal Tribunal, Field House, Bream's Buildings, Chancery Lane, EC4 1DZ.

LATTER, Michèle Brigitte; *see* Roberts, M. B.

LATYMER, 8th Baron *cr* 1431; **Hugo Nevill Money-Coutts;** *b* 1 March 1926; *s* of 7th Baron Latymer and Patience (*d* 1982), *d* of late William Courtenay-Thompson; *S* father,

1987; *m* 1st, 1951, Hon. Penelope Ann Clare (marr. diss. 1965), *yr d* of late T. A. Emmet and Baroness Emmet of Amberley; two *s* one *d*; 2nd 1965, Jinty, *d* of late Peter George Calvert; one *s* two *d*. *Educ:* Eton. *Heir: s* Hon. Crispin James Alan Nevill Money-Coutts [*b* 8 March 1955; *m* 1st, 1978, Hon. Lucy Rose (marr. diss. 1995), *y d* of Baron Deedes, *qv*; one *s* two *d*; 2nd, 1995, Mrs Shaunagh Heneage]. *Address:* Vivero Hortus, Santa Maria, Mallorca, Spain.

LAUDER, Desmond Michael Frank Scott; Director, Hong Kong, British Council, since 1997; *b* 28 July 1947; *s* of late Col Philip Lauder and of Frances Lauder; *m* 1975, Xanthe Aristidou Theodosiadou; one *s* one *d*. *Educ:* Magdalene Coll., Cambridge (BA, MA); Inst. of Education, Univ. of London (PGCE). Teacher: Royal Grammar School, Guildford, 1970–72; Saint Ignatius Coll., Enfield, 1972–73; British Council: Asst Dir, Salonika, Greece, 1973–76; Asst Dir, Rio de Janeiro, Brazil, 1976–79; Asst Sec., CNAA, 1979–83; British Council: service in Czechoslovakia and Singapore, 1983–87; Dir, Ecuador, 1991–93; Regl Dir, Asia Pacific, 1994–97. *Recreations:* tennis, walking, music. *Address:* British Council, 10 Spring Gardens, SW1A 2BN.

LAUDER, Sir Piers Robert Dick-, 13th Bt *cr* 1688; *S* father, 1981.

LAUDERDALE, 17th Earl of, *cr* 1624; **Patrick Francis Maitland;** Baron Maitland, 1590; Viscount Lauderdale, 1616; Viscount Maitland, Baron Thirlestane and Boltoun, 1624; Bt of Nova Scotia, 1680; Hereditary Bearer of the National Flag of Scotland, 1790 and 1952; Chief of the Clan Maitland; *b* 17 March 1911; *s* of Reverend Hon. Sydney G. W. Maitland and Ella Frances (*née* Richards); *S* brother, 1968; *m* 1936, Stanka, *d* of Professor Milivoje Lozanitch, Belgrade Univ.; two *s* two *d*. *Educ:* Lancing Coll., Sussex; Brasenose Coll., Oxford. BA Hons Oxon, 1933; Journalist 1933–59. Appts include: Balkans and Danubian Corresp., The Times, 1939–41; Special Corresp. Washington, News Chronicle, 1941; War Corresp., Pacific, Australia, New Zealand, News Chronicle, 1941–43. Foreign Office, 1943–45. MP (U) for Lanark Div. of Lanarks, 1951–Sept. 1959 (except for period May-Dec. 1957 when Ind. C). Founder and Chairman, Expanding Commonwealth Group, House of Commons, 1955–59; re-elected Chairman, Nov. 1959. Chm., Sub-Cttee on Energy, Transport and Res., House of Lords Select Cttee on EEC Affairs, 1974–79; Vice Chm. and Co-founder, Parly Gp for Energy Studies, 1980–99. Dir, Elf Petroleum (UK). Editor of The Fleet Street Letter Service, and of The Whitehall Letter, 1945–58. Mem., Coll. of Guardians of National Shrine of Our Lady of Walsingham, Norfolk, 1955–82 (Guardian Emeritus, 1982–). President, The Church Union, 1956–61. FRGS. *Publications:* European Dateline, 1945; Task for Giants, 1957. *Heir: s* The Master of Lauderdale, Viscount Maitland, *qv*. *Address:* 10 Ovington Square, SW3 1LH. *T:* (020) 7589 7451, (020) 7219 5452; 12 St Vincent Street, Edinburgh EH3 6SH. *T:* (0131) 556 5692. *Club:* New (Edinburgh).
See also R. W. P. H. Hay, Lady H. O. Maitland.

LAUDERDALE, Master of; *see* Maitland, Viscount.

LAUENER, Peter Rene; Director, Learning Delivery and Standards Group, Department for Education and Skills (formerly Department for Education and Employment), since 2000; *b* 29 Sept. 1954; *s* of Rene George Lauener and Anne McLean Lauener (*née* Ross); *m* 1976, Angela Margaret Mulliner; one *s* two *d*. *Educ:* George Watson's Coll., Edinburgh; Univ. of Durham (BA Hons Econs 1975). Economic Assistant, Scottish Office, 1975–82; Economic Advr, 1982–85, Hd of Strategy, Evaluation and Res., 1986–87, MSC; Dept of Employment, 1988–92, 1995–96; Dir, Skills & Enterprise, Govt Office for E Midlands, 1992–95; Head of Resources & Budget Mgt, DfEE, 1996–2000. Gov., Dobcroft Jun. Sch., Sheffield. Treas., Holy Trinity C of E, Millhouses, Sheffield. *Recreations:* reading, walking, wine. *Address:* 82 Pingle Road, Sheffield S7 2LL. *T:* (office) (0114) 259 3735; (home) (0114) 236 2188.

LAUGHARNE, Albert, CBE 1983; QPM 1978; Deputy Commissioner, Metropolitan Police, 1983–85; *b* 20 Oct. 1931; *s* of Reginald Stanley Laugharne and Jessica Simpson Laugharne; *m* 1st, 1954, Barbara Thirlwall (*d* 1994); two *d*; 2nd, 1999, Margaret Ann Blackmore; four step *s*. *Educ:* Baines' Grammar Sch., Poulton-le-Fylde; Manchester Univ. Detective Inspector, Manchester City Police, 1952–66; Supt, Cumbria Constab., 1966–70; Chief Supt, W Yorks Constab., 1970–73; Asst Chief Constable, Cheshire Constab., 1973–76; Chief Constable: Warwicks, 1977–78; Lancashire, 1978–83. RCDS, 1975. *Publication:* Seaford House Papers, 1975. *Recreations:* gardening, painting.

LAUGHLAND, His Honour (Graham Franklyn) Bruce; QC 1977; a Circuit Judge, 1989–96, at the Central Criminal Court; *b* 18 Aug. 1931; 3rd *s* of late Andrew and late Constance Laughland; *m* 1st, 1969, Victoria Nicola Christina Jarman (*d* 1994); one *s*; 2nd, 1999, Jacqueline Marie Bakes-Bradbury. *Educ:* King Edward's Sch., Birmingham; Christ Church, Oxford (MA). Stick of Honour, Mons Officer Cadet Sch., 1954; Lieut 8th RTR, 1954–56. Called to Bar, Inner Temple, 1958, Bencher, 1985; Dep. Chm., Bucks QS, 1971; Standing Counsel to the Queen's Proctor, 1968; a Recorder, 1972–89; First Prosecuting Counsel to the Inland Revenue (Midland and Oxford Circuit), 1973–77; actg Judge of the Supreme Court of the Falkland Is, 1985. Mem., Gen. Council of the Bar, 1970; Treas., Midland and Oxford Circuit, 1986–89. Chm., Westminster Assoc. for Youth, 1984–89. Liveryman, Curriers' Co., 1992–. *Address:* 30 Monmouth Road, W2 4UT. *T:* (020) 7229 5045. *Club:* Garrick.

LAUGHLIN, Prof. Robert Betts, PhD; Anne T. and Robert M. Bass Professor of Physics, School of Humanities and Sciences, Stanford University, since 1992; *b* 1 Nov. 1950; *s* of David H. and Margaret B. Laughlin; *m* 1979, Anita R. Perry; two *s*. *Educ:* Univ. of Calif, Berkeley (AB Maths 1972); Massachusetts Inst. of Technol. (PhD Physics 1979). Post-doctoral res., Bell Telephone Labs, 1979–81; post-doctoral res., then Res. Physicist, Lawrence Livermore Nat. Lab., 1981–84; Associate Prof. of Physics, 1984–89, Prof., 1989–92, Stanford Univ. Member: Amer. Acad. Arts and Scis, 1990–; NAS, 1994–. E. O. Lawrence Award for Physics, US Dept of Energy, 1985; Oliver E. Buckley Prize, APS, 1986; Franklin Medal for Physics, 1998; (jtly) Nobel Prize for Physics, 1998. *Publications:* contrib. numerous articles in Physical Rev. Letters, Physical Rev., Advances in Physics, etc. *Recreations:* hiking, ski-ing, computers, music. *Address:* Department of Physics, Stanford University, Stanford, CA 94305, USA. *T:* (650) 7234563, *Fax:* (650) 72565411; *e-mail:* rbl@large.stanford.edu.

LAUGHLIN, Prof. Simon Barry, PhD; FRS 2000; Rank Research Professor in Opto-electronics, Department of Zoology, University of Cambridge, since 1999; Fellow, Churchill College, Cambridge, since 1991; *b* 19 Dec. 1947; *s* of Peter and Margaret Laughlin; *m* 1980, Barbara Frances Howard; two *s* one *d*. *Educ:* Clare Coll., Cambridge (BA, MA); Australian Nat. Univ. (PhD Neurobiol. 1974). Fellow, Res. Sch. of Biol Scis, ANU, 1976–84; Lectr in Zool., 1984–96, Reader in Sensory Neuroscience, 1996–99, Univ. of Cambridge. *Publications:* contribs on vision, neural processing and insects to learned jls. *Recreations:* classical bassoon, sailing. *Address:* Department of Zoology, Downing Street, Cambridge CB2 3EJ. *T:* (01223) 336608.

LAUGHTON, Sir Anthony Seymour, Kt 1987; FRS 1980; oceanographic consultant; Director, Institute of Oceanographic Sciences, 1978–88; *b* 29 April 1927; *s* of Sydney Thomas Laughton and Dorothy Laughton (*née* Chamberlain); *m* 1st, 1957, Juliet Ann Chapman (marr. diss. 1962); one *s*; 2nd, 1973, Barbara Clare Bosanquet; two *d*. *Educ:* Marlborough Coll.; King's Coll., Cambridge (MA, PhD). RNVR, 1945–48. John Murray Student, Columbia Univ., NY, 1954–55; Nat. Inst. of Oceanography, later Inst. of Oceanographic Sciences, 1955–88: research in marine geophysics in Atlantic and Indian Oceans, esp. in underwater photography, submarine morphology, ocean basin evolution, midocean ridge tectonics; Principal Scientist of deep sea expedns. Member: Co-ordinating Cttee for Marine Sci. and Technol., 1987–91; nat. and internat. cttees on oceanography and geophysics. President: Challenger Soc. for Marine Sci., 1988–90; Soc. for Underwater Technol., 1995–97 (Mem. Council, 1986–92; President's Award, 1998); Hydrographic Soc., 1997–99. Member Council: Royal Soc., 1986–87; Marine Biology Assoc., 1980–83, 1988–92. Member: Governing Body, Charterhouse Sch., 1981–2000 (Chm., 1995–2000); Council, University Coll. London, 1983–93; Adv. Council, Ocean Policy Inst., Hawaii, 1991–93. Trustee, Natural Hist. Mus., 1990–94. Pres., Haslemere Musical Soc., 1997–. Silver Medal, RSA, 1958; Cuthbert Peek grant, RGS, 1967; Prince Albert 1er Monaco Gold Medal for Oceanography, 1980; Founders Medal, RGS, 1987; Murchison Medal, Geol. Soc., 1989. *Publications:* papers on marine geophysics and oceanography. *Recreations:* music, gardening, sailing. *Address:* Okelands, Pickhurst Road, Chiddingfold, Surrey GU8 4TS. *T:* (01428) 683941.

LAUGHTON, Prof. Michael Arthur, PhD, DSc (Eng); FREng, FIEE; Professor of Electrical Engineering, Queen Mary and Westfield (formerly Queen Mary) College, University of London, 1977–2000, now Emeritus; *b* 18 Dec. 1934; *s* of William Arthur Laughton and Laura (*née* Heap); *m* 1960, Margaret Mary Coleman (marr. diss. 1994); two *s* two *d*. *Educ:* King Edwards Five Ways Sch., Birmingham; Etobicoke Collegiate Inst., Toronto; Toronto Univ. (BASc 1957); Univ. of London (PhD 1965; DSc(Eng) 1976). CEng, FREng (FEng 1989); FIEE 1977. GEC, Witton, 1957–61; Queen Mary, later Queen Mary and Westfield, College, London University: Res. Student, Dept of Elect. Engrg, 1961–64; Lectr, 1964–72; Reader, 1972–77; Dean, Faculty of Engrg, 1983–85; Pro-Principal, 1985–89; Dean of Engrg, London Univ., 1990–94. Visiting Professor: Purdue Univ., USA, 1966; Tokyo Univ., 1977. Sec. and Dir, Unicom Ltd, 1971–74; Dir, QMC Industrial Res. Ltd, 1979–91 (Chm., 1988–91); Chm., Tower Shakespeare Co. Ltd, 1985–93. Organising Sec., 1963–81, Chm., 1981–, Power Systems Computation Confs; Science and Engineering Research Council: Chm., Machines and Power Educn and Trng Cttee, 1983–86; Member: Elect. Engrg Cttee, 1982–84; Wind Energy Panel, 1985–86; Institution of Electrical Engineers: Chm., Wkg Gp on New Electronic Technol. in Publishing, 1983–87; Member: Council, 1990–94; Governing Cttee, Benevolent Fund, 1990–93; Mem. Exec., Watt Cttee on Energy, 1986– (Chm., Wkg Gp on Renewable Energy Sources, 1986–88); Mem., Inf. Cttee, Royal Soc., 1988–92. Specialist Adviser: Sub-Cttee B (Energy, Transport and Technol.), H of L Select Cttee on Eur. Communities, 1987–89; H of C Select Cttee on Welsh Affairs, 1993–94. Member: Fulbright Commn Scholarships Cttee, 1991–; Council, Cranfield Inst of Technol., 1991–96. Freeman: City of London, 1990; Barbers' Co., 1990 (Liveryman, 1995). Founder and Jt Ed., Internat. Jl of Electrical Power and Energy Systems, 1978–; Ed., Procs of Power System Computation Confs 5–8, 1975–84. *Publications:* edited: Energy Policy Planning, 1979; Electrical Engineers Reference Book, 14th edn 1985, 15th edn 1993, 16th edn 2002; Renewable Energy Sources, 1990; Expert System Applications in Power Systems, 1990; over one hundred papers and contribs in the fields of control systems, electrical power systems, energy economics, electrical machines, computational techniques and modelling theory. *Recreations:* music, cricket, Rugby. *Address:* 28 Langford Green, Champion Hill, SE5 8BX. *T:* (020) 7326 0081; *e-mail:* m.a.laughton@elec.qmul.ac.uk. *Club:* Athenæum.

LAUGHTON, Roger Froome, CBE 2000; Head, Media School, Bournemouth University, since 1999; *b* 19 May 1942; *s* of late Eric Laughton and Elizabeth Laughton (*née* Gibbons); *m* 1967, Suzanne Elizabeth Taylor; one *d*. *Educ:* King Edward VII Sch., Sheffield; Merton Coll., Oxford (Postmaster; BA 1st Cl. Hons Modern Hist.); Inst. of Educn, Oxford Univ. (DipEd (Dist)). Royal Insce Co. Fellow, Stanford Univ., USA, 1964–65; BBC, 1965–90: Producer, 1965–77; Editor, Features, Manchester, 1977–80; Head: Network Features, 1980–85 (Jt Series Producer, River Journeys (BAFTA Award for best documentary series), 1984); Daytime Programmes, 1985–87; Dir, Co-prodns and BBC Enterprises, 1987–90; Man. Dir, MAI Media, 1990–96; Chief Executive: Meridian Broadcasting, 1991–96; United Broadcasting and Entertainment, 1996–99. Chm., ITV Broadcast Bd, 1995–97; Director: ITV, 1992–99; United News and Media, 1996–2000; ITN, 1997–99. Chm., DCMS/Skillset Audio-Visual Industries Trng Gp, 1999–2001. Mem., Internat. TV Acad., 1994; FRTS 1994 (Gold Award, 1999). *Recreations:* walking, cricket, reading. *Address:* The Roof House, Windmill Lane, Avon Castle, Ringwood BH24 2DQ. *T:* (01425) 470578. *Clubs:* Royal Automobile; Hampshire County Cricket.

LAUNDER, Prof. Brian Edward, FRS 1994; FREng, FIMechE, FRAeS; UMIST Research Professor, Department of Mechanical Engineering, University of Manchester Institute of Science and Technology, since 1998; *b* 20 July 1939; *s* of Harry Edward Launder and Elizabeth Ann Launder (*née* Ayers); *m* 1967, Dagny Simonsen; one *s* one *d*. *Educ:* Enfield Grammar Sch.; Imperial Coll., London (BScEng Mech Engrg 1961); MIT (SM 1963; ScD 1965 Mech Engrg). Res. Asst, MIT, 1961–64; Lectr, 1964–71, Reader in Fluid Mechanics, 1971–76, Imperial Coll.; Prof. of Mech. Engrg, Univ. of California, Davis, 1976–80; University of Manchester Institute of Science and Technology: Prof. of Mech. Engrg, 1980–98; Head, Thermo-Fluids Div., 1980–90; Head, Dept of Mech. Engrg, 1983–85 and 1993–95. Hon. Prof., Nanjing Aeronautics Inst., 1993. FREng (FEng 1994); FASME. Dr *hc* Institut National Polytechnique de Toulouse, 1999. *Publications:* (with D. B. Spalding) Mathematical Models of Turbulence, 1972; (ed) Turbulent Shear Flows, vol. 1, 1978–vol. 9, 1994; numerous articles on turbulent flow in learned jls. *Recreations:* vacationing in France, photography, country walking, gentle bicycling. *Address:* Department of Mechanical Engineering, UMIST, PO Box 88, Manchester M60 1QD. *T:* (0161) 200 3701.

LAURANCE, Anthony John; Regional Director, South West, NHS Executive, Department of Health, since 1995; *b* 11 Nov. 1950; *s* of Dr Bernard Laurance and Margaret Audrey Laurance (*née* Kidner); *m* 1981, Judith Allen; two *d*. *Educ:* Bryanston Sch.; Clare Coll., Cambridge (MA). Drum Publications, Zambia, 1973–74; News Training Scheme, BBC, 1975; joined DHSS, 1975; Admin. Trainee, subseq. HEO(D), 1975–80; Mgt Services, 1980–81; Policy Strategy Unit, 1981–83; Finance Div., 1983–85; Prin. Private Sec. to Sec. of State for Social Services, 1985–87; Newcastle Central Office, 1987–90; Territorial Dir, Benefits Agency, 1990–95; Regl Gen. Manager/Regl Dir, South and West RHA, 1995. *Recreations:* modern fiction, poker, walking the dog. *Address:* NHS Executive South West, Westward House, Lime Kiln Close, Stoke Gifford, Bristol BS34 6SR. *T:* (0117) 984 1851.

LAUREN, Ralph; fashion designer; Chairman, Polo Ralph Lauren Corporation; *b* 14 Oct. 1939; *s* of Frank and Frieda Lifschitz; changed name to Lauren, 1955; *m* 1964, Ricky Beer;

three *s*. Salesman, New York: Bloomingdale's; Brooks Bros; Asst Buyer, Allied Stores; Rep., Rivetz Necktie Manufrs; Neckwear Designer, Polo Div., Beau Brummel, 1967–69; creator of designer and ready-to-wear clothing, accessories, fragrances, home furnishings, etc; Founder: Polo Menswear Co., 1968; Ralph Lauren's Women's Wear, 1971; Polo Leathergoods, 1978; Polo Ralph Lauren Luggage, 1982; Ralph Lauren Home Collection, 1983. Numerous fashion awards. *Address:* Polo Ralph Lauren Corporation, 650 Madison Avenue, New York, NY 10022, USA.

LAURENCE, Ven. Christopher; *see* Laurence, Ven. J. H. C.

LAURENCE, Dan Hyman; Literary and Dramatic Advisor, Estate of George Bernard Shaw, 1973–90; *b* 28 March 1920. *Educ:* New York City public schs; Hofstra Univ. (BA 1946); New York Univ. (MA 1950). First went on the stage as child actor, 1932; radar specialist with Fifth Air Force, USA, in S Pacific, 1942–45; wrote and performed for Armed Forces Radio Service in New Guinea and the Philippines during World War II, and subseq. for radio and television in USA and Australia; began teaching in 1950 as graduate asst, New York Univ.; Instr of English, Hofstra Univ., 1953–58; Editor, Readex Microprint Corp., 1959–60; Associate Prof. of English, New York Univ., 1962–67, Prof., 1967–70. Vis. Professor: Indiana Univ., 1969; Univ. of Texas at Austin, 1974–75; Tulane Univ., 1981 (Mellon Prof. in the Humanities); Univ. of BC, Vancouver, 1984; Adjunct Prof. of Drama, Univ. of Guelph, 1986–91 (Dist. Vis. Prof. of Drama, 1983); Vis. Fellow, Inst. for Arts and Humanistic Studies, Pennsylvania State Univ., 1976. John Simon Guggenheim Meml Fellow, 1960, 1961 and 1972; Montgomery Fellow, Dartmouth Coll., 1982. Literary Advr, 1982–90, Associate Dir, 1987–, Shaw Fest., Ont. Associate Mem., RADA, 1979. Phi Beta Kappa (hon.), 1967. President's Medal, Hofstra Univ., 1990. *Publications:* Henry James: a bibliography (with Leon Edel), 1957 (3rd edn 1981); Robert Nathan: a bibliography, 1960; (ed) Collected Letters of Bernard Shaw, vol. 1, 1874–1897, 1965, vol. 2, 1898–1910, 1972, vol. 3, 1911–1925, 1985, Vol. 4, 1926–1950, 1988; (ed) Bernard Shaw, Collected Plays with their Prefaces, 1970–74; Shaw, Books, and Libraries, 1976; Shaw: an exhibit, 1977; (dramatization) The Black Girl in Search of God, 1977; (ed) Shaw's Music, 1981, 2nd edn 1989; Bernard Shaw: a bibliography, 1983; A Portrait of the Author as a Bibliography (Engelhard Lecture on the Book, L of C, 1982), 1983; (Uncollected Writings of Shaw): How to Become a Musical Critic, 1960 (2nd edn 1968); Platform and Pulpit, 1961; (ed with David H. Greene) The Matter with Ireland, 1962, 2nd edn 2001; (ed with Daniel J. Leary) Flyleaves, 1977; (Gen. Editor) Bernard Shaw: Early Texts, Play Manuscripts in Facsimile, 12 vols, 1981; (with James Rambeau) Agitations: letters to the Press 1875–1950, 1985; (with Martin Quinn) Shaw on Dickens, 1985; (with Nicholas Grene) Shaw, Lady Gregory, and the Abbey, 1993; (ed with Daniel J. Leary) Shaw, Complete Prefaces, vol. I, 1993, vol. II, 1995, vol. III, 1997; (ed) Bernard Shaw, Theatrics, 1995; (ed with Margot Peters) Unpublished Shaw, 1996; (ed with Fred D. Crawford) Bibliographical Shaw, 2000. *Recreations:* theatre-going, music, mountain climbing. *Address:* 102 West Rampart Road (Apt Q106), San Antonio, TX 78216–6708, USA.

LAURENCE, George Frederick; QC 1991; a Recorder, since 2000; *b* 15 Jan. 1947; *s* of Dr George Bester Laurence and Anna Margaretha Laurence; *m* 1st, 1976, (Ann) Jessica Chenevix Trench (*d* 1999); one *s* one *d*, and one step *s*; 2nd, 2000, (Anne) Jacqueline Baker; one *d*. *Educ:* Pretoria High Sch. for Boys; Univ. of Cape Town (Smuts Meml Scholarship; BA); University College, Oxford (Rhodes Scholar; MA). Called to the Bar, Middle Temple, 1972 (Harmsworth Law Scholar; Bencher, 1999); Asst Recorder, 1993–2000; a Dep. High Court Judge, Chancery Div., 1996–. Mem. Council, S African Inst. of Race Relns, 1998–. Fellow, Soc. for Advanced Legal Studies, 1998. *Publications:* articles in Jl of Planning and Envmt Law and Rights of Way Law Review. *Recreations:* theatre, access to the countryside, cricket, tennis. *Address:* 12 New Square, Lincoln's Inn, WC2A 3SW. *T:* (020) 7419 8050.

LAURENCE, Ven. (John Harvard) Christopher; Archdeacon of Lindsey, Diocese of Lincoln, 1985–94, now Archdeacon Emeritus; *b* 15 April 1929; *s* of Canon H. P. Laurence and Mrs E. Laurence; *m* 1952, E. Margaret E. Chappell; one *s* one *d*. *Educ:* Christ's Hospital; Trinity Hall, Cambridge (MA); Westcott House, Cambridge. Nat. service commn, Royal Lincolnshire Regt, 1948–50. Asst Curate, St Nicholas, Lincoln, 1955–59; Vicar, Crosby St George, Scunthorpe, 1959–73; St Hugh's Missioner, Lincoln Diocese, 1974–79; Bishops' Director of Clergy Training, London Diocese, 1979–85. *Recreation:* sculpture. *Address:* 5 Haffenden Road, Lincoln LN2 1RP. *T:* (01522) 531444.

LAURENCE, Sir Peter (Harold), KCMG 1981 (CMG 1976); MC 1944; DL; HM Diplomatic Service, retired; Vice-President of Council, British Institute of Archaeology, Ankara, since 1995 (Chairman, 1984–95); *b* 18 Feb. 1923; *s* of late Ven. George Laurence, MA, BD and late Alice (*née* Jackson); *m* 1948, Elizabeth Aïda Way; two *s* (one *d* decd). *Educ:* Radley Coll.; Christ Church, Oxford. 60th Rifles, 1941–46 (Major). Entered Foreign Service, 1948; Western Dept, FO, 1948–50; Athens, 1950–53; Asst Political Adviser, Trieste, 1953–55; 1st Sec., Levant Dept, FO, 1955–57; Prague, 1957–60; Cairo, 1960–62; North and East African Dept, FO, 1962–65; Personnel Dept, DSAO, 1965–67; Counsellor, 1965; Political Adviser, Berlin, 1967–69; Visiting Fellow, All Souls Coll., 1969–70; Counsellor (Commercial), Paris, 1970–74; Chief Inspector, HM Diplomatic Service (Asst Under-Sec. of State), 1974–78; Ambassador to Ankara, 1980–83. Chairman: Foreign Anglican Church and Educnl Assoc. Ltd, 1976–; Community Council of Devon, 1986–92; Fellow, Woodard Corp. (W Div.), 1985. Mem. Council, Univ. of Exeter, 1989–99. Chm. of Governors, Grenville Coll., Bideford, 1988–95. DL Devon, 1989. *Address:* Trevilla, Beaford, Winkleigh, N Devon EX19 8NS. *Club:* Army and Navy.

LAURENCE, Commodore Timothy James Hamilton, MVO 1989; RN; Assistant Commandant (Maritime), Joint Services Command and Staff College, Shrivenham, since 1999; *b* 1 March 1955; *s* of Guy Stewart Laurence and Barbara Alison Laurence (*née* Symons); *m* 1992, HRH The Princess Royal. *Educ:* Sevenoaks Sch.; Durham Univ. (BSc Geog.). Joined RN, 1973; in command: HMS Cygnet, 1979–80; HMS Boxer, 1989–91; MoD, 1992–95; in command: HMS Cumberland, 1995–96; HMS Montrose and 6th Frigate Sqdn, 1996–97; MoD, 1997–98; Hudson Vis. Fellow, St Antony's Coll., Oxford, 1999. *Recreations:* most sporting and outdoor activities. *Address:* c/o Buckingham Palace, SW1A 1AA.

See also under Royal Family.

LAURENS, André; Editor-in-Chief of Le Monde, 1982–84; *b* 7 Dec. 1934; unmarried. Journalist: L'Eclaireur méridional, Montpellier, 1953–55; l'Agence centrale de la presse, Paris, 1958–62; joined Le Monde, 1963; Home Affairs reporter, 1969; Associate Editor, Home Affairs, 1979. Vice-Pres., Société des Rédacteurs. *Publications:* Les nouveaux communistes, 1972; D'une France à l'autre, 1974; Le métier politique, 1980.

LAURENSON, James Tait; Managing Director, Hillhouse Investments Ltd, since 1993; *b* 15 March 1941; *s* of James Tait Laurenson, FRCS and Vera Dorothy Kidd; *m* 1969, Hilary Josephine Thompson; one *s* three *d*. *Educ:* Eton; Magdalene College, Cambridge (MA). FCA. Ivory & Sime, investment managers, 1968–83, Partner 1970, Dir 1975; Tayburn Design Group: Man. Dir, 1983–84; Chm., 1984–89. Adam & Company Group: founder Dir and Dep. Chm., 1983; first Man. Dir, 1984–93. Chm., Govett European Enhanced Investment Trust, 1999–; Director: Alvis, 1971–95; I & S UK Smaller Companies Trust, 1983–; The Life Association of Scotland, 1991–93; Roberts & Hiscox, 1992–; Fidelity Special Values, 1994–; Frizzell Bank, 1996–. Chairman: Hopetoun House Preservation Trust, 1998–; Governing Council, Erskine Stewart's Melville, 1994–99. *Recreations:* spending time with the family, gardening. *Address:* Hill House, Kirknewton, Midlothian EH27 8DR. *T:* (01506) 883947. *Clubs:* New (Edinburgh); Hon. Company of Edinburgh Golfers.

LAURIE, (James) Hugh (Calum); actor, comedian, writer; *b* 1959; *s* of late Dr (William George) Ranald (Mundell) Laurie; *m* 1989, Jo; two *s* one *d*. *Educ:* Dragon Sch., Oxford; Eton Coll.; Selwyn Coll., Cambridge (Rowing Blue; Pres., Footlights). *TV series:* Alfresco, 1982–84; Blackadder II, 1985; Blackadder the Third, 1987; Blackadder Goes Forth, 1989; A Bit of Fry and Laurie, 1989–95; Jeeves and Wooster, 1990–92; All or Nothing at All; *films:* Plenty, 1985; Peter's Friends, 1992; Sense and Sensibility, 1996; 101 Dalmatians, 1996; Cousin Bette, 1998; Maybe Baby, 2000; Stuart Little, 2000; Dir, From a View to Death, 1995; *theatre*, Gasping, Theatre Royal, Haymarket, 1990. *Publication:* The Gun Seller, 1996. *Address:* Hamilton Asper Ltd, Ground Floor, 24 Hanway Street, W1P 9DD. *T:* (020) 7636 1221.

LAURIE, Sir (Robert) Bayley (Emilius), 7th Bt *cr* 1834; Chairman, C. T. Bowring & Co. Ltd, 1985–89; *b* 8 March 1931; *s* of Maj.-Gen. Sir John Emilius Laurie, 6th Bt, CBE, DSO, and Evelyn Clare, (*d* 1987), *d* of late Lt-Col Lionel James Richardson-Gardner; *S* father, 1983; *m* 1968, Laurelie, *d* of Sir Reginald Lawrence William Williams, 7th Bt, MBE, ED; two *d*. *Educ:* Eton. National Service, 1st Bn Seaforth Highlanders, 1949–51; Captain, 11th Bn Seaforth Highlanders (TA), 1951–67. Lloyd's, 1951–92, Mem., 1955–; with C. T. Bowring & Co. Ltd, 1958–89; Chief Exec., Bowring Members' Agency Ltd, 1974. *Heir: cousin* Andrew Ronald Emilius Laurie [*b* 20 Oct. 1944; *m* 1970, Sarah Anne, *e d* of C. D. Patterson; two *s*]. *Address:* The Old Rectory, Little Tey, Colchester, Essex CO6 1JA. *T:* (01206) 210410.

LAURIE, Robert Peter, OBE 1994; JP; DL; farmer, 1958–89, retired; Vice-Lord Lieutenant, Essex, 1985–92; *b* 20 Aug. 1925; *s* of late Col Vernon Stewart Laurie, CBE, TD, DL, and Mary, 2nd *d* of Selwyn Robert Pryor; *m* 1952, Oonagh Margaret Faber Wild, 3rd *d* of W. P. Wild, Warcop Hall, Westmorland; three *s* one *d*. *Educ:* Eton College. Served Coldstream Guards, 1943–47, Hon. Captain. Member of Stock Exchange, 1953; Partner, Heseltine, Powell & Co., then Heseltine, Moss & Co., 1953–80, Consultant, 1980–86; Director, British Empire Securites & General Trust Ltd, 1954–95 (Chm., 1973–84). Governor: Brentwood Sch., 1974–95; Alleyn's Sch., 1984–95; Chm., 1977–86, Pres., 1986–, Essex Assoc. of Boys' Clubs; a Vice-Pres., NABC-CYP (formerly NABC), 1986–; President: Essex Agricl Soc., 1986–87; Essex Shire Horse Assoc., 1987–2001; Essex Home Workers, 1986–2000; Chelmsford and Mid Essex Samaritans, 1986–92. Member: Ct, Essex Univ., 1979–; Council, CGLI, 1984–97. Master, Saddlers' Co., 1981–82. Chm., Essex Co. Cttee, TAVRA, 1987–91; Hon. Col. Essex, ACF, 1994–98. JP 1974, High Sheriff 1978–79, DL 1979, Essex. *Recreations:* foxhunting and field sports, gardening, reading. *Address:* The Old Vicarage, Cornish Hall End, Braintree, Essex CM7 4HF. *Club:* City Livery.

LAURIE, Robin; His Honour Judge Laurie; a Circuit Judge, South Eastern Circuit, since 1986; *b* 26 Jan. 1938; *s* of J. R. Laurie and Dr W. Metzner; *m* 1965, Susan Jane (*neé* Snelling); two *d*. *Educ:* Fettes Coll.; Geneva Univ.; Jesus Coll., Oxford (MA). Called to the Bar, Inner Temple, 1961; practice at the Bar (South Eastern Circuit), 1961–86. *Recreations:* mountaineering, mycology. *Address:* c/o 4 Paper Buildings, Temple, EC4Y 7EX. *Club:* Alpine.

LAURISTON, His Honour Alexander Clifford; QC 1972; a Circuit Judge, 1976–93; a Deputy Circuit Judge, since 1993; Chairman, Registered Homes Appeals Tribunal, 1994–98; *b* 2 Oct. 1927; *s* of Alexander Lauriston and Nellie Lauriston (*née* Ainsworth); *m* 1954, Inga Louise Cameron; two *d*. *Educ:* Coatham Sch., Redcar, Yorks; Trinity Coll., Cambridge (MA). National Service: Army, Green Howards and RAPC, 2nd Lieut, 1948–50. Called to Bar, Inner Temple, 1952. A Recorder of the Crown Court, 1972–76. Mem., Loriners' Co., 1969; Freeman, City of London, 1969. *Recreations:* outdoor activities, painting, music. *Address:* 199 Strand, WC2R 1DR. *Clubs:* Oxford and Cambridge; Berkshire Golf.

See also R. B. Lauriston.

LAURISTON, Richard Basil; a Permanent Chairman of Industrial Tribunals, 1976–89; formerly Senior Partner, Alex Lauriston & Son, Solicitors, Middlesbrough; *b* 26 Jan. 1917; *s* of Alexander Lauriston, MBE, and Nellie Lauriston; *m* 1944, Monica, *d* of Wilfred Leslie Deacon, BA, Tonbridge, and Dorothy Louise Deacon; three *s*. *Educ:* Sir William Turner's Sch., Redcar; St John's Coll., Cambridge (MA, LLM). Solicitor, 1948; a Recorder of the Crown Court, 1974–82. Commnd and served in War of 1939–45, Royal Corps of Signals. *Recreations:* fishing, travelling. *Address:* Auchlochan House, 19 The Courtyard, New Trows Road, Lesmahagow, Lanarks ML11 0JS.

See also A. C. Lauriston.

LAUTERPACHT, Sir Elihu, Kt 1998; CBE 1989; QC 1970; Fellow of Trinity College, Cambridge, since 1953; Director, Research Centre for International Law, 1983–95, now Director Emeritus, and Hon. Professor of International Law, since 1994, University of Cambridge; practising international lawyer and arbitrator; *b* 13 July 1928; *o s* of late Sir Hersch Lauterpacht, QC and Rachel Steinberg; *m* 1955, Judith Maria (*d* 1970), *er d* of Harold Hettinger; one *s* two *d*; *m* 1973, Catherine Daly; one *s*. *Educ:* Phillips Acad., Andover, Mass; Harrow; Trinity Coll., Cambridge (Entrance Schol.). 1st cl. Pt II of Law Tripos and LLB; Whewell Schol. in Internat. Law, 1950; Holt Schol. 1948 and Birkenhead Schol. 1950, Gray's Inn; called to Bar, 1950, Bencher, 1983. Joint Sec., Interdepartmental Cttee on State Immunity, 1950–52; Cambridge University: Asst Lectr in Law, 1953; Lecturer, 1958–81; Reader in Internat. Law, 1981–88. Founding Sec., Internat. Law Fund, 1955–85; Dir of Research, 1959–60, Lectr 1976 and 1996, Hague Academy of Internat. Law; Vis. Prof. of Internat. Law, Univ. of Delhi, 1960. Chm., East African Common Market Tribunal, 1972–75; Consultant to Central Policy Review Staff, 1972–74, 1978–81; Legal Adviser, Australian Dept of Foreign Affairs, 1975–77; Consultant on Internat. Law, UN Inst. for Training and Res., 1978–79; mem. arbitration panel, Internat. Centre for Settlement of Investment Disputes; Chm., North Atlantic Free Trade Area Dispute Settlement Panels, 1996 and 1997–; Panel Chm., UN Compensation Commn, 1998–99; Deputy Leader: Australian Delegn to UN Law of the Sea Conf., 1975–77; Australian Delegn to UN Gen. Assembly, 1975–77. Judge *ad hoc*, Internat. Court of Justice (Bosnia *v* Yugoslavia), 1993–. Pres., Eastern Reg., UNA, 1991–; Pres., World Bank Admin. Tribunal, 1996–98 (Mem., 1980–98; Vice-Pres., 1995–96); Chm., Asian Develt Bank Admin. Tribunal, 1991–95; Member: Social Sciences Adv. Cttee, UK Nat. Commn for Unesco, 1980–84; Panel of Arbitrators, Internat. Energy Agency Dispute Settlement Centre; Panel of Arbitrators, UN Law of the Sea Convention, 1998–; Inst. of Internat. Law; Trustee, Internat. Law Fund, 1983. Editor: British Practice in International Law, 1955–68; International Law Reports, 1960–. Hon. Fellow, Hebrew Univ. of

Jerusalem, 1989. Hon. Mem., Amer. Soc. of Internat. Law, 1993. Comdr, Order of Merit, Chile, 1969; awarded Annual Cert. of Merit, Amer. Soc. Internat. Law, 1972. *Publications:* Jerusalem and the Holy Places, 1968; (ed) International Law: the collected papers of Sir Hersch Lauterpacht, vol I, 1970, vol. II, 1975, vol. III, 1977, vol. IV, 1978; The Development of the Law of International Organization, 1976; (ed) Individual Rights and the State in Foreign Affairs, 1977; Aspects of the Administration of International Justice, 1991; various articles on international law. *Address:* Research Centre for International Law, 5 Cranmer Road, Cambridge CB3 9BL. *T:* (01223) 335358; 20 Essex Street, WC2R 3AL. *T:* (020) 7583 9294, *Fax:* (020) 7583 1341. *Club:* Garrick.

LAUTI, Rt Hon. Sir Toaripi, GCMG 1990; PC 1979; Governor-General of Tuvalu, 1990–95; *b* Papua New Guinea, 28 Nov. 1928; *m;* three *s* two *d. Educ:* Tuvalu; Fiji; Wesley Coll., Paerata, NZ; St Andrew's Coll., Christchurch, NZ; Christchurch Teachers' Coll., NZ. Taught in KGV, Tarawa, Kiribati, 1953–62; Labour Relations and Trng Officer, Nauru and Ocean Islands, engaged by British Phosphate Comrs; returned to Tuvalu, 1974, and entered politics; MP, elected unopposed to House of Assembly, May 1975; elected Chief Minister, Tuvalu, upon separation of Ellice Islands (Tuvalu) from Kiribati, Oct. 1975, re-elected Chief Minister in Sept. 1977; First Prime Minister, Tuvalu, 1978–81; Leader of the Opposition, 1981–90. Chm., 18th South Pacific Conference, Noumea, Oct. 1978. *Address:* PO Box 84, Funafuti, Tuvalu, Central Pacific.

LAVAN, Hon. Sir John Martin, Kt 1981; retired 1981 as Senior Puisne Judge of the Supreme Court of Western Australia; *b* 5 Sept. 1911; *s* of late M. G. Lavan, KC; *m* 1st, 1939, Leith Harford (decd); one *s* three *d;* 2nd, 1984, Dorothy Bell (decd). *Educ:* Aquinas Coll., Perth; Xavier Coll., Melbourne. Barrister in private practice, 1934–69; a Judge of the Supreme Court of WA, 1969–81. Chm., Parole Bd, WA, 1969–79. Mem., Barristers' Bd, WA, 1960–69; Pres., Law Soc. of WA, 1964–66. KStJ. *Address:* Unit 1, 8 Philip Road, Dalkeith, WA 6009, Australia. *Club:* Weld (Perth).

LAVELLE, Roger Garnett, CB 1989; financial executive; Hon. Vice-President, European Investment Bank, since 1993 (Vice-President, 1989–93); *b* 23 Aug. 1932; *s* of Henry Allman Lavelle and Evelyn Alice Garnett; *m* 1956, Elsa Gunilla Odeberg; three *s* one *d. Educ:* Leighton Park; Trinity Hall, Cambridge (BA, LLB). Asst Principal, Min. of Health, 1955; Principal, HM Treasury, 1961; Special Assistant (Common Market) to Lord Privy Seal, 1961–63; Private Sec. to Chancellor of the Exchequer, 1965–68; Asst Secretary, 1968, Under Sec., 1975, Dep. Sec., 1985, HM Treasury; Dep. Sec., Cabinet Office, 1987. Dir, EBRD, 1993–2000. *Recreations:* music and gardening. *Address:* 36 Cholmeley Crescent, Highgate, N6 5HA. *T:* (020) 8340 4845.

LAVENDER, Rt Rev. Mgr Gerard; Parish Priest, Holy Family, Darlington, since 1993; *b* 20 Sept. 1943; *s* of Joseph and Mary Lavender. *Educ:* Ushaw Coll., Durham. Ordained, 1969; Asst Priest, St Mary Cath., Newcastle upon Tyne, 1969–75; loaned to Royal Navy as Chaplain, 1975; completed All Arms Commando Course, 1976; served with RM, 1976–79; sea going, 1979–80, 1987–89; Exchange Chaplain to San Diego, with US Navy, 1981–83; Chaplain in: Scotland (Rosyth), 1983–85; Portsmouth, 1985–87; Plymouth, 1989–90. GSM, NI, 4 visits 1977–79; Prin. RC Chaplain (Navy), MoD, 1990–93, retired. *Recreations:* golf, tennis, hill walking. *Address:* Holy Family Presbytery, 60 Cockerton Green, Darlington, Co. Durham DL3 9EU.

LAVER, Frederick John Murray, CBE 1971; Member, Post Office Corporation, 1969–73, retired; *b* 11 March 1915; *er s* of late Clifton F. Laver and Elsie Elizabeth Palmer, Bridgwater; *m* 1948, Kathleen Amy Blythe; one *s* two *d. Educ:* Plymouth Coll. BSc London. Entered PO Engrg Dept, 1935; PO Research Stn, 1935–51; Radio Planning, 1951–57; Organization and Efficiency, 1957–63; Asst Sec., HM Treasury, 1963–65; Chief Scientific Officer, Min. of Technology, 1965–68; Director, National Data Processing Service, 1968–70; Mem., NRDC, 1974–80. Vis. Prof., Computing Lab., Univ. of Newcastle upon Tyne, 1975–79. Mem. Council: IEE, 1966–69, 1972–73; British Computer Soc., 1969–72; Nat. Computing Centre, 1966–68, 1970–73; IEE Electronic Divl Bd, 1966–69, 1970–73. Mem. Council, 1979–87, Chm., 1985–87, Pro-Chancellor, 1981–87, Exeter Univ. Pres., Devonshire Assoc., 1990–91. CEng, FIEE; Hon. FBCS. Hon. DSc Exeter, 1988. *Publications:* nine introductory books on physics and computing; several scientific papers. *Recreations:* reading, writing, and watching the sea. *Address:* 2 Park Lane, Budleigh Salterton, Devon EX9 6QT.

LAVER, Prof. John David Michael Henry, CBE 1999; FBA 1990; FRSE; Research Professor of Speech Sciences, Queen Margaret University College, since 2001; *b* 20 Jan. 1938; *s* of Harry Frank Laver and Mary Laver (*née* Brearley); *m* 1st, 1961, Avril Morna Anel Macqueen Gibson; two *s* one *d;* 2nd, 1974, Sandra Traill; one *s. Educ:* Churcher's Coll., Petersfield; Univ. of Edinburgh (MA Hons; Postgrad. Dip. in Phonetics; PhD; DLitt). Asst Lectr and Lectr in Phonetics, Univ. of Ibadan, 1963–66; University of Edinburgh: Lectr, Sen. Lectr, Reader in Phonetics, 1966–85; Prof. of Phonetics, 1985–2000; Dir, 1984–89, Chm., 1989–94, Centre for Speech Technology Research; Associate Dean, Faculty of Arts, 1989–92; Vice-Principal, 1994–97. Pres., Internat. Phonetic Assoc., 1991–95 (Mem. Council, 1986–); Member: Board, European Speech Communication Assoc., 1988–92; Council, Philological Soc., 1994–97; Council, British Acad., 1998–2001 (Chm., Humanities Res. Bd, 1994–98); Board of Governors: Edinburgh Univ. Press, 1999–2000; Caledonian Res. Foundn, 1999–. FRSE 1994 (Vice-Pres., 1996–99; Fellowship Sec., 1999–Oct. 2002); FRSA 1995; Fellow, Inst. of Acoustics, 1988. Hon. DLitt: Sheffield, 1999; De Montfort, 1999. *Publications:* Communication in Face to Face Interaction, 1972; Phonetics in Linguistics, 1973; The Phonetic Description of Voice Quality, 1980; The Cognitive Representation of Speech, 1981; Aspects of Speech Technology, 1988; The Gift of Speech, 1991; Principles of Phonetics, 1994; The Handbook of Phonetic Sciences, 1997. *Recreations:* travel, reading, birdwatching. *Address:* Faculty of Health Sciences, Queen Margaret University College, Corstorphine Campus, Edinburgh EH12 8TS. *T:* (0131) 317 3500. *Club:* New (Edinburgh).

LAVER, Patrick Martin; HM Diplomatic Service, retired; Director of Research, Foreign and Commonwealth Office, 1980–83; *b* 3 Feb. 1932; *s* of late James Laver, CBE, RE, FRSL, and late Veronica Turleigh; *m* 1st, 1966, Marianne Ford (marr. annulled); one *d;* 2nd, 1979, Dr Elke Maria Schmitz, *d* of Thomas and Anneliese Schmitz. *Educ:* Ampleforth Coll., Yorks; New Coll., Oxford. Third Sec., Foreign Office, 1954; Second Sec., Djakarta, 1956; FO, 1957; Paris, 1958; Yaoundé, 1961; UK Delegn to Brussels Conf., 1962; First Sec., FO, 1963; UK Mission to UN, New York, 1964; Diplomatic Service Admin., 1965; Commercial Sec., Nairobi, 1968; FCO, 1970; Counsellor (Economic), Pretoria, 1973; UK Delegn to Conf. on Security and Co-operation in Europe, Geneva, 1974; Head of Rhodesia Dept, FCO, 1975–78; Counsellor, Paris, 1979–80. *Address:* The Coach House, Keldholme Priory, Keldholme, N Yorks YO62 6LZ. *T:* (01751) 432648. *Club:* Athenæum.

LAVER, William Graeme, PhD; FRS 1987; Head, Influenza Research Unit, Australian National University, since 1983; *b* 3 June 1929; *s* of Lawrence and Madge Laver; *m* 1954, Judith Garrard Cahn; one *s* two *d. Educ:* Ivanhoe Grammar Sch., Melbourne; Univ. of Melbourne (BSc, MSc); Univ. of London (PhD). Technical Asst, Walter & Eliza Hall Inst. of Med. Res., Melbourne, 1947–52; Res. Asst, Dept of Biochemistry, Melbourne Univ., 1954–55; Res. Fellow, 1958–62, Fellow, 1962–64, Senior Fellow, 1964–90, Special Prof., 1990–, John Curtin Sch. of Med. Res., ANU. International Meetings: Rougemont, Switzerland, 1976; Baden, Vienna, 1977; Thredbo, Australia, 1979; Beijing, China, 1982; Banbury Center, Cold Spring Harbor, NY, 1985; Kona, Hawaii, 1989. (Jtly) Australia Prize, 1996. *Publications:* papers on structure of influenza virus antigens and molecular mechanisms of antigenic shift and drift in type A influenza viruses; numerous research articles. *Recreations:* raising beef cattle, viticulture, wine-making, ski-ing, climbing volcanoes. *Address:* John Curtin School of Medical Research, PO Box 334, Canberra, ACT 2601, Australia. *T:* (2) 61252397; Barton Highway, Murrumbateman, NSW 2582, Australia. *T:* (2) 62275633.

LAVERCOMBE, Dr Brian James; Honorary Member, British Council, since 1997 (Regional Director for the Americas, 1994–96); *b* 17 Dec. 1938; *s* of Ralph Lavercombe and Doris (*née* Hawkins); *m* 1966, Margaret Jane Chambers; one *s* one *d. Educ:* Barnstaple Grammar Sch.; Imperial Coll., London (BSc Hons Physics, ARCS, MSc, DIC; PhD 1966). Post-doctoral Fellow and Asst Prof. in Residence, UCLA, 1966–68; British Council: Science Officer: Chile, 1968–72; Spain, 1972–77; Israel, 1977–80; Projects Officer, Science and Technol. Div., 1980–81; Dir, Science Dept, 1981–84; Rep., Colombia, 1984–87; Dep. Controller, Sci., Technol. and Educn Div., 1987–90; Dir, Mexico, 1990–94. Advr, Earthwatch, 1997–. *Publications:* papers on scientific co-operation and technology transfer; research papers in Nature and Accoustica; articles on ornithology. *Recreations:* cricket, ornithology, painting, mediaeval history. *Address:* 37 Playfield Road, Kennington, Oxford OX1 5RS. *T:* (01865) 739659. *Club:* Whiteditch Wanderers Cricket (Basingstoke).

LAVERICK, Elizabeth, OBE 1993; PhD, CEng, FIEE; CPhys, FInstP, FIEEE (US); Project Director, Advanced Manufacturing in Electronics, 1985–88; *b* 25 Nov. 1925; *d* of William Rayner and Alice Garland; *m* 1946 (marr. diss. 1960); no *c. Educ:* Dr Challoner's Grammar Sch., Amersham; Durham Univ. Research at Durham Univ., 1946–50; Section Leader at GEC, 1950–53; Microwave Engineer at Elliott Bros, 1954; Head of Radar Research Laboratory of Elliott-Automation Radar Systems Ltd, 1959; Jt Gen. Manager, Elliott-Automation Radar Systems Ltd, 1968–69, Technical Dir, 1969–71; Dep. Sec., IEE, 1971–85; Electronics CADMAT (Computer Aided Design, Manufacture and Test) Project Dir, 1982–85. Mem. Electronics Divisional Bd, 1967–70, Mem. Council, 1969–70, IEE. Chm., Engrg Careers Co-ordinating Cttee, 1983–85; Member: DE Adv. Cttee on Women's Employment, 1970–82; Adv. Cttee for Electronic and Electrical Engrg, Sheffield Univ., 1984–87; Nat. Electronics Council, 1986–98; Chm., Ninth Internat. Conf. of Women Engrs and Scientists, 1989–91; Hon. Sec., Women's Engrg Soc., 1991–95 (Pres., 1967–69). Member Council: Inst. of Physics, 1970–73 (Chm., Women in Physics Cttee, 1985–90); City and Guilds of London Inst., 1984–87 (Hon. Mem., 1991; Fellow, 1998); Member Court: Brunel Univ., 1985–88; City Univ., 1991–95. Mem. Ct of Govs, IEE Benevolent Fund, 1991–99. Liveryman, Co. of Engrs, 1985–88. FRSA 1991; FCGI. Hon. Fellow, UMIST, 1969. Editor, Woman Engr (Jl of Women's Engrg Soc.), 1984–90. *Publications:* contribs to IEE and IEEE Jls. *Recreations:* music, gardening, tapestry. *Address:* Lynwood, Brays Lane, Hyde Heath, Amersham, Bucks HP6 5RU.

LAVERS, Patricia Mae, (Mrs H. J. Lavers); Executive Director, Bond Street Association, 1961–76, and Regent Street Association, 1972–76; *b* 12 April 1919; *d* of Edric Allan Jordan and May Holdcraft; *m* 1st, 1945, Frederick Handel Hayward (*d* 1965); one *s;* 2nd, 1966, John Harold Ellen, OBE; 3rd, 1976, Lt-Comdr Herbert James Lavers. *Educ:* Sydenham High School. Clerk, Securities Dept, National Provincial Bank, 1938–45; Export Dir, Perth Radios, 1955–60. Alderman, St Pancras Council, 1960–66 (Libraries/Public Health). Elected to Executive of Westminster Chamber of Commerce, 1971, Chm. City Affairs Cttee, 1971–75. Chm., Sandwich Soc., 1983–. FZS. *Recreations:* swimming, collecting first editions and press books, walking. *Address:* Horse Pond Sluice, Delf Street, Sandwich, Kent CT13 9HD. *Clubs:* Arts, Lansdowne, Naval.

LAVERS, Richard Douglas; HM Diplomatic Service; Ambassador to Guatemala, since 2001; *b* Nairobi, 10 May 1947; *s* of Douglas Arthur Lavers and Edyth Agnes (*née* Williams); *m* 1986, Brigitte Anne Julia Maria Moers, *e d* of late Robert Moers, Turnhout, Belgium; two *s. Educ:* Hurstpierpoint Coll.; Exeter Coll., Oxford (MA). Joined HM Diplomatic Service, 1969; Third Sec., Buenos Aires, 1970–72; Second, later First Sec., Wellington, 1973–76; FCO, 1976–81; First Sec., Pol and Econ., Brussels, 1981–85; on secondment to Guinness Mahon, 1985–87; FCO, 1987–89; NATO Defence Coll., Rome, 1989; Dep. Hd of Mission and HM Consul General, Santiago, 1990–93; Ambassador to Ecuador, 1993–97; Counsellor, 1997–2001, Hd of Research Analysts, 1999–2001, FCO. *Recreations:* books, pictures, travel, fishing. *Address:* c/o Foreign and Commonwealth Office, King Charles Street, SW1A 2AH. *Club:* Oxford and Cambridge.

LAVERTY, Ashley; *see* Page, A.

LAVERY, (Charles) Michael; QC (NI) 1971; Chairman, Standing Advisory Commission on Human Rights, 1995–99; *b* 10 June 1934; *s* of Charles Lavery and Winifred (*née* McCaffrey); *m* 1962, Anneliese Gisela Lehmann; three *s* two *d. Educ:* Queen's Univ., Belfast (LLB 1954); Trinity Coll., Dublin (BA 1956). Member of the Bar: NI, 1956– (Bencher, 1974, Treas., 1987, Inn of Court); Ireland, 1974–. Chm., Gen. Council of Bar, NI, 1987–89. *Recreations:* walking, reading, cooking. *Address:* The Bar Library, Royal Courts of Justice, Belfast.

LAVIGNE, Marc T.; *see* Tessier-Lavigne.

LAVIN, Deborah Margaret; Principal-elect of new college, and Co-Director, Research Institute for the Study of Change, University of Durham, 1995–97; Hon. Fellow, Department of History, University of Durham, since 1998; *b* 22 Sept. 1939. *Educ:* Roedean Sch., Johannesburg, SA; Rhodes Univ., Grahamstown, SA; Lady Margaret Hall, Oxford (MA, DipEd). Asst Lectr, Dept of History, Univ. of the Witwatersrand, 1962–64; Lectr, 1965–78, Sen. Lectr, 1978–80, Dept of Mod. Hist., The Queen's Univ. of Belfast; Principal, Trevelyan College, Durham Univ., 1980–95 (Hon. Fellow, 1997); Pres., Howlands Trust, Univ. of Durham, 1993–97. Trustee, Westlakes Research Ltd, 1995–. Mem. Council, Benenden Sch., 1998–. Assoc. Fellow, RIIA, 1997–2000. FRSA 1996. *Publications:* South African Memories, 1979; The Making of the Sudanese State, 1990; The Transformation of the Old Order in the Sudan, 1993; From Empire to International Commonwealth: a biography of Lionel Curtis, 1995; articles in learned jls. *Recreations:* the arts, gardening, some sport. *Address:* Hickmans Cottages, Cat Street, East Hendred, Oxon OX12 8JT. *T:* (01235) 833408. *Club:* Reform.

LAVOIE, Judith Anne, (Mrs A. R. Lavoie); *see* LaRocque, J. A.

LAW, family name of **Barons Coleraine** and **Ellenborough**.

LAW, Prof. Colin Nigel, PhD; Head of Laboratory, Cambridge Laboratory, Institute of Plant Science Research, John Innes Centre, Norwich, 1989–92; *b* 18 Nov. 1932; *s* of

Joseph and Dorothy Mildred Law; *m* 1964, Angela Patricia Williams; three *d*. *Educ:* Queen Elizabeth's Grammar Sch., Blackburn; Univ. of Birmingham (BSc Hons Genetics); UCW, Aberystwyth (PhD). Nat. Service, RA, 1955–57. Res. worker, Plant Breeding Inst., Cambridge, 1960–87, Head of Cytogenetics Dept, 1972–87; Divl Head, Plant Genetics and Breeding, Inst. of Plant Sci. Res., 1987–89. Sen. Foreign Res. Fellow, Nat. Sci. Foundn, N Dakota State Univ., 1969. Hon. Prof., Univ. of East Anglia, 1990–. Prix Assinsel, Assoc. Internationale des Sélectionneurs, 1982. *Publications:* papers and articles on chromosome manipulation techniques to identify genes of agric. importance in crop plants, esp. wheat; genetic control of cereal plant responses to envmtl stress, particularly salinity. *Recreations:* fishing, painting. *Address:* 41 Thornton Close, Girton, Cambridge CB3 0NF. *T:* (01223) 276554.

LAW, Francis Stephen, (Frank Law), CBE 1981; Chairman, Varta Group UK, since 1971; *b* 31 Dec. 1916; *s* of Henry and Ann Law-Lowensberg; *m* 1959, Nicole Vigne (*née* Fesch); one *s* (one *d* by previous *m*). *Educ:* on the Continent. War service, 1939–45. Wills Law & Co., 1947; Truvox Engrg, 1960, subseq. Dir of Controls and Communications; Dep. Chm., NFC, 1982–85 (Dir, Consortium and its predecessors, 1969–87). Chairman: Rubis Investment & Cie, 1990–; Aegis (formerly WRCS) Gp plc, 1992–2000 (Dir, 1988–2000); Director: B. Elliott Plc, 1968–86; BMW (GB) Ltd, 1978–88; Siemens, 1984–98; NFC Internat. Hldgs, 1985–92; Celab Ltd, 1991–2001; Mem. Adv. Bd, Berliner Bank, 1988–92. Chm., Social Responsibilities Council, NFC, 1988–92; Member: Org. Cttee, NFC, 1968; Economic and Social Cttee, EEC, 1978–86. Governor, RSC, 1985–. *Recreations:* music, reading, theatre, ski-ing, swimming. *Address:* 43 Lennox Gardens, SW1X 0DF. *T:* (020) 7225 2142. *Clubs:* Boodle's; Pilgrims.

LAW, George Llewellyn; Vice Chairman, Morgan Grenfell Group plc, 1987–89; *b* 8 July 1929; *s* of late George Edward Law and Margaret Dorothy Law, OBE (*née* Evans); *m* 1960, Anne Stewart, *d* of late Arthur Wilkinson and Ness Wilkinson (*née* Muir); one *d*. *Educ:* Westminster Sch. (Schol.); Clare Coll., Cambridge (Schol.; BA). ACIArb. Solicitor. Slaughter and May, Solicitors, 1952–67, Partner 1961–67; Dir, Morgan Grenfell & Co. Ltd, 1968–91; Dir, Morgan Grenfell Gp plc, 1971–89. Deputy Chairman: Baker Perkins plc, 1986–87 (Dir, 1981–87); Blackwood Hodge plc, 1988–90 (Dir, 1968–90); Director: Bernard Sunley Investment Trust, 1968–75; Sidlaw Group, 1974–82; APV, 1987–90. Mem., Arbitration Panel, SFA Consumer Arbitration Scheme, 1988–. Member of Council: Furniture Hist. Soc., 1978–85; Ancient Monuments Soc., 1992–; British-Italian Soc., 1994–97. Mem. Council of Management, Hon. Life Patron and Chm. Patrons' Cttee, Spitalfields Fest., 1995–. Trustee and Hon. Treas., Nat. Assoc. for Gambling Care, Educnl Resources and Trng, 1998–. FRSA. *Recreations:* history of furniture and decorative arts, opera, reading, swimming, cricket. *Address:* 6 Phillimore Gardens Close, W8 7QA. *T:* (020) 7937 3061. *Clubs:* Brooks's, MCC, Surrey County Cricket.

LAW, Adm. Sir Horace (Rochfort), GCB 1972 (KCB 1967; CB 1963); OBE 1950; DSC 1941; retired 1972; Chairman, R. & W. Hawthorn Leslie & Co., 1973–81; *b* 23 June 1911; *s* of S. Horace Law, MD, FRCSI, and Sybil Mary (*née* Clay); *m* 1941, Heather Valerie Coryton (*d* 1996); two *s* two *d*. *Educ:* Sherborne Sch. Entered Royal Navy, 1929; gunnery specialist, 1937. Served War of 1939–45 (DSC): AA Cruisers: Cairo, 1939; Coventry, 1940; Cruiser Nigeria, 1942; Comdr 1946; Capt. 1952; comd HMS Centaur, 1958 and Britannia, RN Coll., 1960; Rear-Adm. 1961; Vice-Adm. 1965; Flag Officer Sea Training, 1961–63; Flag Officer, Submarines, 1963–65; Controller of the Navy, 1965–70; C-in-C, Naval Home Comd, and Flag Officer, Portsmouth Area, 1970–72; First and Principal Naval Aide-de-Camp to the Queen, 1970–72. Mem., Security Commn, 1973–82. President: RINA, 1975–77; Officers' Christian Union, 1976–86; Chm., Church Army Bd, 1980–87. Grand Cross, Order of the Crown (Netherlands), 1972. *Recreations:* walking, gardening. *Address:* West Harting, Petersfield, Hants GU31 5NT.

LAW, Peter John; JP; Member (Lab) Blaenau Gwent, National Assembly for Wales, since 1999; *b* 1 April 1948; *s* of John Law and Rita Mary Law; *m* 1976, Patricia Bolter; two *s* three *d*. *Educ:* Llanfoist Primary Sch.; Grofield Secondary Sch. Self-employed grocer, 1965–80; retail develt, 1980–90; self-employed consultant in local govt and public authorities, 1990–99. Chm., Gwent Healthcare NHS Trust, 1999. Mem. (Lab) Blaenau Gwent CBC, 1974–99. Envmt and Local Govt Sec., Nat Assembly for Wales, 1999–2000. MIPR 1997. Mem., Welsh Lang. Bd, 1990–95. JP Gwent, 1985. *Recreations:* walking, Land Rovers, countryside. *Address:* (office) 1A Bethcar Street, Ebbw Vale, Blaenau Gwent NP23 6HH. *T:* (01495) 304569. *Clubs:* Nant-y-glo Rugby Football, Ebbw Vale Rugby Football.

LAW, Phillip Garth, AC 1995 (AO 1975); CBE 1961; MSc, FAIP, FTSE, FAA; *b* 21 April 1912; *s* of Arthur James Law and Lillie Lena Chapman; *m* 1941, Nellie Isabel Allan; no *c*. *Educ:* Hamilton High Sch.; Ballarat Teachers' Coll.; Melbourne Univ. FAIP 1948; FTSE 1976; FAA 1978. Science master, State secondary schs, Vic., 1933–38; Tutor in Physics, Newman Coll., Melbourne Univ., 1940–47; Lectr in Physics, 1943–48. Research Physicist and Asst Sec. of Scientific Instrument and Optical Panel of Austr. Min. of Munitions, 1940–45. Sen. Scientific Officer, ANARE, 1947–48; cosmic ray measurements in Antarctica and Japan, 1948; Dir, Antarctic Div., Dept of External Affairs, Aust., and Leader, ANARE, 1949–66; Expedition relief voyages to Heard I. and Macquarie I., 1949, 1951, 1952, 1954. Australian observer with Norwegian-British-Swedish Antarctic Exped., 1950; Leader of expedition: to establish first permanent Australian station in Antarctica at Mawson, MacRobertson Land, 1954; which established second continental station at Davis, Princess Elizabeth Land, 1957; which took over Wilkes station from USA, 1959; to relieve ANARE stations and to explore coast of Australian Antarctic Territory, annually, 1955–66. Chm., Australian Nat. Cttee for Antarctic Research, 1966–80. Exec. Vice-Pres., Victoria Inst. of Colls, 1966–77; Pres., Victorian Inst. of Marine Scis, 1978–80. Member: Council of Melbourne Univ., 1959–78; Council, La Trobe Univ., 1964–74; Chm., RMIT Foundn, 1995–98; President: Royal Soc. of Victoria, 1967, 1968; Aust. and NZ Schs Exploring Soc., 1977–82. Dep. Pres., Science Museum of Victoria, Melbourne, 1979–82 (Trustee, 1968–83). Pres., Grad. Union, Melbourne Univ., 1972–77. Patron, British Schs Exploring Soc. Fellow: Aust. Acad. of Sci.; Aust. Inst. of Physics; ANZAAS; Foundn Fellow, Royal Soc. of Victoria, 1996. Hon. Fellow, Royal Melbourne Inst. of Technology. Hon. DAppSc Melbourne, 1962; Hon. DEd Victoria Inst. of Colls, 1978; Hon. DSc La Trobe, 1995. Founder's Gold Medal, RGS, 1960; Gold Medal, Aust. Geographic Soc., 1988; Clunies Ross Nat. Sci. and Technol. Award, 2001. *Publications:* (with John Béchervaise) ANARE, 1957; Antarctic Odyssey, 1983; The Antarctic Voyage of HMAS Wyatt Earp, 1995; You Have to be Lucky, 1995; chapters in: It's People that Matter, ed Donald McLean, 1969; Search for Human Understanding, ed M. Merbaum and G. Stricker, 1971; ed series of ANARE scientific reports; numerous papers on Antarctica and education. *Recreations:* tennis, ski-ing, music, photography. *Address:* 16 Stanley Grove, Canterbury, Vic 3126, Australia. *Clubs:* Melbourne, Kelvin, Melbourne Cricket, Royal South Yarra Lawn Tennis (Melbourne).

LAW, Prof. Robin Christopher Charles, PhD; FRHistS; FBA 2000; Professor of African History, Stirling University, since 1993; *b* 7 Aug. 1944. *Educ:* Balliol Coll., Oxford (BA 1st cl. Hons Lit.Hum. 1966); PhD (Hist. and African Studies) Birmingham 1971. Res. Asst to Dir of African Studies, Lagos Univ., 1966–69; Res. Fellow, Centre of W African Studies, Birmingham Univ., 1970–72; Stirling University: Lectr in Hist., 1972–78; Sen. Lectr, 1978–83; Reader, 1983–93. Visiting posts: Ilorin Univ., Nigeria, 1978; Leiden Univ., Netherlands, 1993–94; York Univ., Canada, 1996–97; Hebrew Univ. of Jerusalem, 2000–01. FRHistS 1997. *Publications:* The Oyo Empire *c*1600–*c*1836, 1977; The Horse in West African History, 1980; The Slave Coast of West Africa 1550–1750, 1991; (ed) From Slave Trade to Legitimate Commerce: the commercial transition in 19th century West Africa, 1995. *Address:* Department of History, Stirling University, Stirling FK9 4LA. *T:* (01786) 46583.

LAW, Roger, RDI 2000; artist in residence, National Art School, Sydney, 1998; *b* 6 Sept. 1941; *m* 1959, Deirdre Amsden; one *s* one *d*. *Educ:* Littleport Secondary Mod. Sch.; Cambridge Sch. of Art (expelled 1960). Acquitted of malicious damage, 1959; fined £5 for rioting, 1960; cartoonist and illustrator, The Observer, 1962–65; voluntary probation for assault, 1963; illustrator, Sunday Times, 1965–67; probation for theft, 1967; Artist in Residence, Reed Coll., Oregon, and first puppet film, 1967; freelance illustrator, Pushpin Studios, NY, 1968–69; deported voluntarily from USA, 1969; caricaturist and features editor, Sunday Times, 1971–75; with Peter Fluck: formed Luck & Flaw, 1976; founder, Spitting Image, 1982 (first series televised, 1984, 18th series, 1996); Creative Dir, Spitting Image Productions Ltd, 1984–97; first American show for NBC TV, 1986; TV series: The Winjin' Pom, 1991; Crapston Villas, 1995, 2nd series 1997; deported from China, 1998; film, Potshots, 1999. Major installation for Barbican art gall., 1992; ceramic exhibitions with Janice Tchalenko: V&A, 1993; Richard Dennis Gall., 1996; puppet installation, RA, 1997; one-man exhibn, Aussie Stuff, Hossack Gall., 2000. Mem., AGI, 1993; Fellow, Internat. Specialised Skills, Melbourne, 1997. Hon. DLitt Loughborough, 1999. D & AD Award, 1967; Assoc. of Illustrators Award (to Luck & Flaw), 1982; BPG TV Award for Best Light Entertainment Prog., 1984; D & AD Award (to Luck and Flaw), 1984; Internat. Emmy Award (for Spitting Image), 1986; Grammy Award, 1987; Emmy Award (for Peter and the Wolf), 1994; Lifetime Achievement Award, Cartoon Art Trust, 1998. *Publications:* The Appallingly Disrespectful Spitting Image Book, 1985; Spitting Images, 1987; The Spitting Image Giant Komic Book, 1988; (with L. Chester) A Nasty Piece of Work, 1992; Goodbye, 1992; Thatcha: The real Maggie memoirs, 1993; illustrator with Peter Fluck: A Christmas Carol, 1979; Treasure Island, 1986. *Recreation:* making mischief.

LAW, Sylvia, OBE 1977; *b* 29 March 1931; *d* of late Reginald Howard Law and late Dorothy Margaret Law. *Educ:* Lowther Coll.; Girton Coll., Cambridge (MA); Regent Street Polytechnic (DipTP). MRTPI. Teaching, Benenden Sch., 1952–55; market research, Unilever Ltd, 1955–58; town and country planning and policy studies and research, Kent CC and GLC, 1959–86. Royal Town Planning Institute: Mem. Council, 1965–78; Chm. of Educn Cttee, 1970–73; Vice-Pres., 1972–74; Pres., 1974–75. Mem. Planning Cttee, SSRC, 1977–79. Volunteer Advr, CAB, 1986–98. Member: Cambridge Soc., 1981–; Bury St Edmunds Univ. of Third Age, 1999–. *Publications:* (contrib.) Recreational Economics and Analysis, 1974; (ed) Planning and the Future, 1976; articles in RTPI Jl, Official Architecture and Planning, Planning Outlook, Town Planning Rev., Greater London Intelligence Qly, etc. *Recreations:* music, photography, gardening.

LAW, Dr Vivien Anne, (Lady Shackleton), FBA 1999; Fellow, Trinity College, Cambridge, since 1997; Reader in the History of Linguistic Thought, University of Cambridge, since 1998; *b* 22 March 1954; *d* of John Ernest and Anne Elizabeth Law; *m* 1986, Nicholas John Shackleton (*see* Sir N. J. Shackleton). *Educ:* Trafalgar Sch. for Girls, Montreal; McGill Univ. (BA 1974); Girton Coll., Cambridge (PhD 1979). MIL 1979. University of Cambridge: Res. Fellow, Jesus Coll., 1977–80; David Thomson Sen. Res. Fellow, 1980–84, Fellow, 1984–97, Sidney Sussex Coll.; Lectr in Hist. of Linguistics, 1984–98; Co-Founder, Post Soviet States in Transition Res. Prog., Sidney Sussex Coll., 1993–97. Invited Lectr, Hungarian Acad. Scis, 1995; O'Donnell Meml Lectr, Toronto, 1998. Associate Ed., Beiträge zur Geschichte der Sprachwissenschaft, 1991–. Mem. Council, Philological Soc., 1990–95 and 1996–2000; Chm., Cambridge Regl Soc., Inst. Linguists, 1994–2001; Henry Sweet Society for the History of Linguistic Ideas: Membership Sec., 1987–90; Conf. Sec., 1990–93; Chm., 2000–; Mem. Editl Bd, Studies in Hist. of Linguistics, 1995–. Co-founder and Jt Leader, Humanities Res. Gp and Humanities Section in GB, Sch. of Spiritual Sci., 1997–. Fellow, Soc. Internazionale per lo Studio del Medioevo Latino, 1996– (Corresp. Mem., 1981–96); Comité Internat., Soc. d'Histoire et d'Epistémologie des Sciences du Langage, 1998. *Publications:* The Insular Latin Grammarians, 1982; (ed) History of Linguistic Thought in the Early Middle Ages, 1993; Wisdom, Authority and Grammar in the Seventh Century: decoding Virgilius Maro Grammaticus, 1995; (ed jtly) Dionysius Thrax and the Techné Grammatiké, 1995; (ed jtly) Linguists and Their Diversions, 1996; Grammar and Grammarians in the Early Middle Ages, 1997; (jtly) Nation-Building in the Post-Soviet Borderlands: the politics of national identities, 1998; contrib. articles and book chapters. *Recreations:* orchestral flute and piccolo playing, rollerblading. *Address:* Trinity College, Cambridge CB2 1TQ. *T:* (01223) 338549.

LAWES, Glenville Richard; Chief Executive, Ironbridge Gorge Museum Trust, since 1991; *b* 28 May 1945; *s* of Eric Lawes and Phyllis (*née* Witchalls); *m* 1969, Isobel Prescott Thomas; one *s* two *d*. *Educ:* Univ. of Birmingham (BSc Eng). Technol. Editor, New Scientist, 1967–70; HM Diplomatic Service, 1970–80: served Moscow, Geneva and Paris; First Sec., FCO, 1976; with British Petroleum Co. plc, 1980–91; Sen. Analyst, BP Internat., 1980–86; Gen. Manager, BP Middle East, 1986–90; Regl Manager, BP Oil Internat., 1990–91. FRSA. *Recreations:* music, reading, theatre, renovating old houses. *Address:* c/o IGMT, 7 The Wharfage, Ironbridge, Telford, Shropshire TF8 7AW. *T:* (01952) 433522.

LAWLER, Geoffrey John; Managing Director, The Public Affairs Company (formerly Lawler Associates), since 1987; Vice-President, International Access Inc., since 1987; *b* 30 Oct. 1954; *s* of Major Ernest Lawler (RAEC retd) and late Enid Lawler; *m* 1989, Christine (marr. diss. 1998), *d* of Carl Roth, Cheyenne, Wyoming. *Educ:* Richmond Sch., N Yorks; Hull Univ. (BSc (Econ); Pres., Students' Union, 1976–77). Trainee chartered accountant, 1977–78. Community Affairs Dept, 1978–80, Research Dept, 1980–82, Cons. Central Office; Public Relations Exec., 1982–83; Dir, publicity co., 1983. Contested (C) Bradford N, 1987. MP (C) Bradford N, 1983–87. EC Observer for Russian elections, 1993, 1995, 1996, for Liberian election, 1997; UN Observer for S African elections, 1994. Dir, Democracy Internat. Ltd, 1995–. Mem. Council, UKIAS, 1987–93. Hon. Pres., British Youth Council, 1983–87; Pres., W Yorks Youth Assoc., 1995– (Vice-Pres., 1986–95). *Recreations:* cricket, music, travel. *Address:* 1 Moorland Leys, Leeds LS17 5BD. *T:* (0113) 266 0583; *e-mail:* geoff@legend.co.uk.

LAWLER, Sir Peter (James), Kt 1981; OBE 1965; retired 1987; Australian Ambassador to Ireland and the Holy See, 1983–86; *b* 23 March 1921; *m*; six *s* two *d*. *Educ:* Univ. of Sydney (BEc). Prime Minister's Dept, Canberra, 1949–68 (British Cabinet Office, London, 1952–53); Dep. Secretary: Dept of the Cabinet Office, 1968–71; Dept of the Prime Minister and Cabinet, 1972–73; Secretary: Dept of the Special Minister of State,

1973–75; Dept of Admin. Services, Canberra, 1975–83. *Recreation:* writing. *Address:* 32 Eucumbene Drive, Duffy, ACT 2611, Australia. *T:* (2) 62889253. *Clubs:* Melbourne (Melbourne); University House, Wine and Food (Canberra).

LAWLER, Simon William; QC 1993; a Recorder, since 1989; *b* 26 March 1949; *s* of Maurice Rupert Lawler and Daphne Lawler (*née* Elkins); *m* 1985, Josephine Sallie Day; two *s*. *Educ:* Winchester County Secondary Sch.; Peter Symonds, Winchester; Univ. of Hull (LLB Hons). Called to the Bar, Inner Temple, 1971; in practice at the Bar, 1972–; Asst Recorder, 1983–89. *Recreations:* cricket, gardening, opera, wine. *Address:* 6 Park Square, Leeds LS1 2LW. *T:* (0113) 245 9763; 11 King's Bench Walk, Temple, EC4Y 7EQ. *T:* (020) 7535 3337.

LAWLEY, Dr Leonard Edward; Director of Kingston Polytechnic, 1969–82; *b* 13 March 1922; *yr s* of late Albert Lawley; *m* 1944, Dorothy Beryl Round; one *s* two *d*. *Educ:* King Edward VI Sch., Stourbridge; Univs of Wales and Newcastle upon Tyne. BSc, PhD; FInstP, CPhys. Served with RAF, 1941–46; Lectr, Univ. of Newcastle upon Tyne, 1947–53; Sen. Lectr, The Polytechnic, Regent Street, 1953–57; Kingston Coll. of Technology: Head of Dept of Physics and Maths, 1957–64; Vice-Principal, 1960–64; Principal, 1964–69. *Publications:* various papers in scientific jls on transmission ultrasonic sound waves through gases and liquids and on acoustic methods for gas analysis.

LAWLEY, Susan, (Sue), OBE 2001; broadcaster, since 1970; *b* 14 July 1946; *d* of Thomas Clifford and Margaret Jane Lawley; *m* 1st, 1975, David Ashby (marr. diss. 1985); one *s* one *d*; 2nd, 1987, Hugh Williams. *Educ:* Dudley Girls' High Sch., Worcs; Bristol Univ. (BA Hons Modern Languages). Thomson Newspapers' graduate trainee, Western Mail and South Wales Echo, Cardiff, 1967–70; BBC Plymouth: sub-editor/reporter/presenter, 1970–72; presenter, BBC Television: Nationwide, 1972–75; Tonight, 1975–76; Nationwide, 1977–83; Nine O'Clock News, 1983–84; Six O'Clock News, 1984–88; Here and Now, 1995–97; Presenter, Desert Island Discs, BBC Radio Four, 1988–; other programmes, 1977–97, including general elections and budgets. Board Member: English Tourism Council, 2000–; ENO, 2001–. Hon. LLD Bristol, 1989; Hon. MA Birmingham, 1989; Hon. DLitt CNAA, 1991. *Publication:* Desert Island Discussions, 1989. *Recreations:* family, walking, ski-ing, bridge. *Address:* c/o BBC, Broadcasting House, W1A 1AA.

LAWRANCE, Cynthia; *see* Lawrance, J. C.

LAWRANCE, John Ernest; Under Secretary, Director, Technical Division 1, Inland Revenue, 1982–88, retired; *b* 25 Jan. 1928; *s* of Ernest William and Emily Lewa Lawrance; *m* 1956, Margaret Elsie Ann Dodwell; two *s* one *d*. *Educ:* High School for Boys, Worthing; Southampton Univ. (BA Hons Modern History). Entered Inland Revenue as Inspector of Taxes, 1951; Principal Inspector, 1968; Senior Principal Inspector on specialist technical duties, 1974. *Address:* 71A Alderton Hill, Loughton, Essex IG10 3JD. *T:* (020) 8508 7562.

LAWRANCE, Mrs (June) Cynthia; Headmistress of Harrogate Ladies' College, 1974–93; *b* 3 June 1933; *d* of late Albert Isherwood and of Ida Emmett; *m* 1957, Rev. David Lawrance, MA, BD (*d* 1999); three *d*. *Educ:* St Anne's Coll., Oxford (MA). Teaching appts: Univ. of Paris, 1954–57; Cyprus, 1957–58; Jordan, 1958–61; Oldham, Lancs, 1962–70; Headmistress, Broughton High Sch., Salford, 1971–73. *Recreations:* music, French literature, chess. *Address:* Kinver House, The Green, Kirklington, Bedale DL8 2NQ.

LAWRANCE, Keith Cantwell; Deputy Chairman, Civil Service Appeal Board, 1981–89 (Member 1980–89); Vice-President, Civil Service Retirement Fellowship, since 1988 (Chairman, 1982–88); *b* 1 Feb. 1923; *s* of P. J. Lawrance; *m* 1952, Margaret Joan (*née* Scott); no *c*. *Educ:* Latymer Sch., N9. Clerical Officer, Admiralty, 1939. Served War, RNVR, 1942–46; Sub-Lt (A), 1945. Exec. Officer, Treasury, 1947; Asst Principal, Post Office, 1954; Principal, Post Office, 1959; Asst Sec., Dept of Economic Affairs, Dec. 1966; Under-Sec., Civil Service Dept, 1971–79. Vice-Chm., Inst. of Cancer Research, 1989–95. *Recreations:* model engineering, music. *Address:* White Gables, 35 Fairmile Avenue, Cobham, Surrey KT11 2JA. *T:* (01932) 863689.

LAWRENCE, family name of **Baron Lawrence** and of **Baron Trevethin and Oaksey**.

LAWRENCE, 5th Baron *cr* 1869; **David John Downer Lawrence;** Bt 1858; *b* 4 Sept. 1937; *s* of 4th Baron Lawrence and Margaret Jean (*d* 1977), *d* of Arthur Downer, Kirdford, Sussex; *S* father, 1968. *Educ:* Bradfield College. *Address:* c/o Bird & Bird, 90 Fetter Lane, EC4A 1JP.

LAWRENCE, Prof. Andrew, PhD; FRAS; Regius Professor of Astronomy, University of Edinburgh, since 1994; Head, Institute for Astronomy, Edinburgh, since 1994; *b* 23 April 1954; *s* of Jack Lawrence and Louisa Minnie (*née* Sandison); partner, Debbie Ann Capel; three *s* one *d*. *Educ:* Chatham House Grammar Sch., Ramsgate; Univ. of Edinburgh (BSc Hons 1976); Univ. of Leicester ((PhD 1980). FRAS 1983. Exchange scientist, MIT, 1980–81; Sen. Res. Fellow, Royal Greenwich Observatory, 1981–84; PDRA, QMC, 1984–87; Queen Mary and Westfield College, London: SERC Advanced Fellow, 1987–89; Lectr, 1989–94. Mem., various res. councils and internat. cttees, panels, etc, 1983–99; Mem., PPARC, 2000–. FRSE 1997. *Publications:* (ed) Comets to Cosmology, 1987; numerous contribs to professional astronomy jls. *Recreations:* acting, painting electrons, teasing publishers. *Address:* Edinburgh Institute for Astronomy, University of Edinburgh, Royal Observatory Edinburgh, Blackford Hill, Edinburgh EH9 3HJ. *T:* (0131) 668 8346.

LAWRENCE, Rt Rev. Caleb James; *see* Moosonee, Bishop of.

LAWRENCE, Hon. Carmen (Mary), PhD; MP (ALP) Fremantle, since 1994; *b* 2 March 1948; *d* of Ern and Mary Lawrence; *m* (marr. diss.); one *s*. *Educ:* Univ. of Western Australia (BPsych 1st cl. Hons 1968; PhD 1983). Univ. lectr, tutor, researcher, consultant, 1968–83; Research Psychologist, Psychiatric Services Unit, Health Dept, 1983–86. MLA (ALP): Subiaco, WA, 1986–89; Glendalough, WA, 1989–94; Minister for Education, 1988–90; Premier of WA, 1990–93; Leader of the Opposition, WA, 1993–94; Minister for Human Services and Health, and Minister assisting the Prime Minister for the Status of Women, Australia, 1994–96; Shadow Minister: for the Envmt, for the Arts, and assisting the Leader of the Opposition on the Status of Women, Australia, 1996–97; for Industry, Innovation and Technol., and for Status of Women, 2000–. *Publications:* psychological papers. *Recreations:* literature, theatre, music. *Address:* Parliament House, Canberra, ACT 2600, Australia.

LAWRENCE, Christopher Nigel, NDD, FTC; FIPG; goldsmith, silversmith; modeller, medallist, industrial and graphic designer; *b* 23 Dec. 1936; *s* of late Rev. William W. Lawrence and Millicent Lawrence; *m* 1958, Valerie Betty Bergman; two *s* two *d*. *Educ:* Westborough High Sch.; Central School of Arts and Crafts. Apprenticed, C. J. Vander Ltd; started own workshops, 1968. *One man exhibitions:* Galerie Jean Renet, 1970, 1971; Hamburg, 1972; Goldsmiths' Hall, 1973; Ghent, 1975; Hasselt, 1977. Major commissions from Royalty, British Govt, City Livery cos, banks, manufacturing cos; official silversmith to Bank of England. Judge and external assessor for leading art colleges; specialist in symbolic presentation pieces and limited edns of decorative pieces, *eg* silver mushrooms. Chm., Goldsmiths, Craft and Design Council, 1976–77; Liveryman, Goldsmiths' Co., 1978–; television and radio broadcaster. Jacques Cartier Meml award for Craftsman of the Year, 1960, 1963, 1967 (unique achievement). *Recreations:* badminton, tennis, bowls, carpentry, painting. *Address:* 20 St Vincent's Road, Westcliff-on-Sea, Essex SS0 7PR. *T:* (01702) 338443, (workshop) (01702) 344897.

LAWRENCE, Prof. Clifford Hugh, FRHistS; Professor of Medieval History, 1970–87, now Emeritus (Head of the Department of History, Bedford College, Royal Holloway and Bedford New College (formerly at Bedford College), University of London, 1981–85); *b* 28 Dec. 1921; *s* of Ernest William Lawrence and Dorothy Estelle; *m* 1953, Helen Maud Curran; one *s* five *d*. *Educ:* Stationers' Co.'s Sch.; Lincoln Coll., Oxford (BA 1st Cl. Hons Mod. Hist. 1948; MA 1953; DPhil 1956). FRHistS 1960; FSA 1984. War service in RA and Beds and Herts: 2nd Lieut 1942, Captain 1944, Major 1945. Asst Archivist to Co. of Gloucester, 1949. Bedford Coll., London: Asst Lectr in History, 1951; Lectr, 1953–63; Reader in Med. History, 1963–70. External Examr, Univ. of Newcastle upon Tyne, 1972–74, Univ. of Bristol, 1975–77, Univ. of Reading, 1977–79; Chm., Bd of Examnrs in History, London Univ., 1981–83. Mem., Press Council, 1976–80; Vice-Chm. of Govs, Governing Body, Heythrop Coll., Univ. of London; Mem. Council, Westfield Coll., Univ. of London, 1981–86. *Publications:* St Edmund of Abingdon, History and Hagiography, 1960; The English Church and the Papacy in the Middle Ages, 1965, 2nd edn 1999; Medieval Monasticism, 1984, 3rd edn 2000; The Friars: the impact of the early mendicant movement on western society, 1994; (trans. with biog.) Matthew Paris, The Life of St Edmund, 1996; contribs to: Pre-Reformation English Spirituality, 1967; The Christian Community, 1971; The History of the University of Oxford, Vol. I, 1984; The Oxford Companion to Christian Thought, 2000; articles and reviews in Eng. Hist. Review, History, Jl Eccles. Hist., Oxoniensia, Encycl. Brit., Lexicon für Theol u Kirche, etc. *Recreations:* gardening, painting. *Address:* 11 Durham Road, SW20 0QH. *T:* (020) 8946 3820.

LAWRENCE, Sir David (Roland Walter), 3rd Bt *cr* 1906; late Captain, Coldstream Guards, 1951; *b* 8 May 1929; *er s* of Sir Roland Lawrence, 2nd Bt, MC, and Susan, 3rd *d* of late Sir Charles Addis, KCMG; *S* father, 1950; *m* 1955, Audrey, Duchess of Leeds, *yr d* of Brig. Desmond Young, OBE, MC. *Educ:* Radley; RMC Sandhurst. *Heir:* *b* Clive Wyndham Lawrence [*b* 6 Oct. 1939; *m* 1966, Sophia Annabel Stuart, *d* of late (Ian) Hervey Stuart Black, TD; three *s*]. *Address:* 28 High Town Road, Maidenhead, Berks SL6 1PB.

LAWRENCE, Dennis George Charles, OBE 1963; Director, 1978–82, Board Member, 1981–84, Cooperative Development Agency; retired; *b* 15 Aug. 1918; *s* of George Herbert and Amy Frances Lawrence; *m* 1946, Alida Jantine, *d* of Willem van den Berg, The Netherlands. *Educ:* Haberdashers' Aske's Hatcham School. Entered Civil Service as Clerical Officer, Min. of Transport, 1936; served RA, 1939–46; Exec. Officer 1946; Asst Principal, Central Land Board, 1947; Principal, 1949; GPO, 1953; Asst Sec. 1960; Sec., Cttee on Broadcasting, 1960–62; Asst Sec., GPO, 1962; Under-Secretary: GPO, 1969; Min. of Posts and Telecommunications, 1969–74; Dept of Industry, 1974–78. Chm., Working Group on a Cooperative Develt Agency, 1977. *Publications:* Democracy and Broadcasting (pamphlet), 1986; The Third Way, 1988. *Recreations:* walking, painting, travel. *Address:* Little London Farmhouse, Cann, Shaftesbury, Dorset SP7 0PZ.

LAWRENCE, Sir Henry (Peter), 7th Bt *cr* 1858, of Lucknow; Head of Dosimetry Radiotherapy Physics Unit, Bristol Oncology Centre, since 1991; *b* 2 April 1952; *s* of late George Alexander Waldemar Lawrence and of Olga Lawrence (*née* Schilovsky); *S* uncle, 1999; *m* 1979, Penny Maureen Nunan (marr. diss. 1993); one *s* one *d*. *Educ:* Eton Coll.; Hackney Coll. BSc Physics with Astronomy, MSc Radiation Physics, London Univ. Builder and scaffolder, 1970–79; Physicist, Royal London Hosp., 1981–86; Sen. Physicist, Cheltenham Gen. Hosp., 1986–90. Author of computer programs for Europlan and Szplug radiotherapy treatment planning systems which are used in hospitals worldwide. Mem., Inst. of Physics and Engineering in Medicine. Hon. Mem., Romanian Assoc. of Medical Physics. *Publication:* Physics in Medicine and Biology, 1990. *Recreations:* music (folk), juggling, cycling, football. *Heir:* *s* Christopher Cosmo Lawrence, *b* 10 Dec. 1979. *Address:* The Mall House, Brockham End, Lansdown, Bath BA1 9BZ. *T:* (01225) 481185.

LAWRENCE, (Henry) Richard (George); writer and lecturer on music; *b* 16 April 1946; *s* of late George Napier Lawrence, OBE, and Peggy Neave (*née* Breay). *Educ:* Westminster Abbey Choir Sch.; Haileybury (music schol.); Worcester Coll., Oxford (Hadow Schol.; BA 1967). Overseas Dept, Ginn & Co., educational publishers, 1968–73; Music Officer, 1973–83, Music Dir, 1983–88, Arts Council of GB; Chief Exec., RSCM, 1990–94; Acting Ed., 1994–95, Ed., 1995–96, Early Music News; Ed., Leading Notes, 1997–99. Tutor: Wandsworth Adult Coll., 1997–; Morley Coll., 1998–. Lectr, Martin Randall Travel Ltd, 2000–. Occasional broadcaster, 1989–. Chm., Arts Council Staff Assoc., 1974–76. Voluntary work, Friends of the Earth Trust, 1989–90. *Publications:* (contrib.) Collins Classical Music Encyclopedia, 2000; revs and articles in TLS, Church Times, Opera Now, BBC Music Mag, Jl of RAS, Amadeus (Milan). *Recreations:* travelling in Asia, pre-1914 Baedekers. *Address:* 15 Hugh Street, SW1V 1QJ. *T:* (020) 7834 9846.

LAWRENCE, Sir Ivan (John), Kt 1992; QC 1981; barrister-at-law; a Recorder, since 1987; *b* 24 Dec. 1936; *o s* of late Leslie Lawrence and Sadie Lawrence, Brighton; *m* 1966, Gloria Hélène; one *d*. *Educ:* Brighton, Hove and Sussex Grammar Sch.; Christ Church, Oxford (MA). Nat. Service with RAF, 1955–57. Called to Bar, Inner Temple, 1962 (Yarborough-Anderson Schol.; Bencher, 1991); S Eastern Circuit; Asst Recorder, 1983–87; Hd of Chambers, 1 Essex Ct, 1997–2000. Contested (C) Peckham (Camberwell), 1966 and 1970. MP (C) Burton, Feb. 1974–1997; contested (C) same seat, 1997. Mem., Select Cttee on Foreign Affairs, 1983–92; Chm., Select Cttee on Home Affairs, 1992–97; Chairman: Cons. Parly Legal Cttee, 1987–97; Cons. Parly Home Affairs Cttee, 1988–97; All-Party Parly Anti-Fluoridation Cttee; All-Party Parly Barristers Gp, 1987–97; Member: Parly Expenditure Select Sub-Cttee, 1974–79; Jt Parly Cttee on Consolidation of Statutes, 1974–87. Mem. Exec., 1922 Cttee, 1988–89, 1992–97. Chm., Exec. Cttee, UK CPA, 1994–97 (Mem., 1989–97). Member: Council of Justice, 1989–95; Council, Statute Law Soc., 1985–95; Exec., Soc. of Conservative Lawyers, 1989–97 (Chm., Criminal Justice Cttee, 1997–). Vice-Pres., Fed. of Cons. Students, 1980–82; Mem., W Midlands Cons. Council, 1985–97. Vice Chm., Cons. Friends of Israel, 1994–97; Mem. Bd of Deputies of British Jews, 1979–. Chm., Burton Breweries Charitable Trust, 1979–97. Freeman, City of London, 1993. *Publications:* pamphlets (jointly): Correcting the Scales; The Conviction of the Guilty; Towards a New Nationality; Financing Strikes; Trial by Jury under attack; newspaper articles on law and order topics and foreign affairs. *Recreations:* piano, squash, football, travel. *Address:* 2 Paper Buildings, Temple, EC4Y 7ET. *T:* (020) 7556 5500. *Clubs:* Carlton, Pratt's; Burton (Burton-on-Trent).

LAWRENCE, Jacqueline Rita, (Jackie); MP (Lab) Preseli Pembrokeshire, since 1997; *b* 9 Aug. 1948; *d* of Sidney and Rita Beale; *m* 1968, David Lawrence; two *s* one *d*. *Educ:* Upperthorpe Sch., Darlington, Co. Durham; Upperthorpe Coll.; Open Univ. With TSB

Bank plc; Asst to Nicholas Ainger, MP, 1992–96. *Address:* House of Commons, SW1A 0AA.

LAWRENCE, John, OBE 1974; Director, Africa and Middle East Division, British Council, 1990–93; *b* 22 April 1933; *s* of William and Nellie Lawrence. *Educ:* Queens' College, Cambridge (BA 1956, Cert. Ed. 1957, MA 1961); Indiana University (MA 1959). Teaching posts in USA and UK, 1957–60; British Council headquarters appts, 1961; Regional Representative, Sabah, 1965; Representative, Zambia, 1968, Sudan, 1974, Malaysia, 1976; Dir, South Asia Dept, 1980; Controller, America, Pacific and S Asia Div., 1982–87; Rep., Brazil, 1987–90. *Recreations:* walking and talking, simultaneously or otherwise. *Address:* Scroggs Fold, Brow Lane, Staveley, Kendal, Cumbria LA8 9PH.

LAWRENCE, Sir (John) Patrick (Grosvenor), Kt 1988; CBE 1983; DL; Chairman, Enterprise Venture Capital Trust plc, since 1996; *b* 29 March 1928; *s* of Ernest Victor Lawrence and Norah Grosvenor Lawrence (*née* Hill); *m* 1954, Anne Patricia (*née* Auld); one *d* (one *s* decd). *Educ:* Denstone Coll., Staffs. Served RNVR, 1945–48. Admitted Solicitor 1954; Partner, Wragge & Co., Solicitors, Birmingham 1959–93 (Sen. Partner, 1982–93). Chm., Midland Rent Assessment Panels, 1971–98. Chm., Kidderminster Healthcare NHS Trust, 1993–96. Mem., Bromsgrove RDC, 1967–74. Chm., Nat. Union of Conservative and Unionist Assocs, 1986–87; Pres., W Midlands Conservative Council, 1988–91 (Chm., 1979–82). Chm., British Shooting Sports Council, 1996– (Vice-Chm., 1985–96). Member of Council: Denstone Coll., Staffs, 1989–98; Birmingham Chamber of Industry and Commerce, 1989–93; ABCC, 1990–93; Aston Univ., 1990– (Vice-Chm. Council, 1999–); White Ensign Assoc. Ltd, 1996–. Chm., Birmingham Cathedral in Need Appeal, 1990; Mem., Admin. Chapter, Birmingham Cathedral, 1995–2000. Freeman, City of London, 1991; Liveryman, Gunmakers' Co., 1991. DL West Midlands, 1993. Hon. DSc Aston, 1996. *T:* (0121) 454 1093. *Clubs:* Royal Over-Seas League; Bean (Birmingham); Law Society's Yacht.

LAWRENCE, Air Vice-Marshal John Thornett, CB 1975; CBE (mil.) 1967 (OBE (mil.) 1961); AFC 1945; *b* 16 April 1920; *s* of late T. L. Lawrence, JP, and Mrs B. M. Lawrence; *m* 1951, Hilary Jean (*née* Owen); three *s* one *d*. *Educ:* The Crypt School, Gloucester. RAFVR 1938. Served War of 1939–45 in Coastal Command (235, 202 and 86 Squadrons); Directing staff, RAF Flying Coll., 1949–53; CO 14 Squadron, 1953–55; Group Captain Operations, HQ AFME, 1962–64; CO RAF Wittering, 1964–66; AOC, 3 Group, Bomber Command, 1967; Student, IDC, 1968; Dir of Organisation and Admin Plans (RAF), 1969–71; Dir-Gen. Personnel Management (RAF), 1971–73; Comdr N Maritime Air Region and AOC Scotland and NI, 1973–75, retired 1975. Corporate Mem., Cheltenham Ladies' Coll., 1977–. Vice-Pres., Glos County SSAFA, 1990– (Chm., 1980–90); Mem., Nat. Council, SSAFA, 1987–90. Order of Leopold II, Belgium, 1945; Croix de Guerre, Belgium, 1945. *Recreations:* golf, bridge. *Address:* The Coach House, Wightfield Manor, Apperley, Glos GL19 4DP. *Club:* Royal Air Force.

LAWRENCE, John Wilfred, RE 1987; book illustrator and wood engraver; *b* 15 Sept. 1933; *s* of Wilfred James Lawrence and Audrey Constance (*née* Thomas); *m* 1957, Myra Gillian Bell; two *d*. *Educ:* Salesian Coll., Cowley, Oxford; Hastings Sch. of Art; Central Sch. of Art. Visiting Lecturer in Illustration: Brighton Polytech., 1960–68; Camberwell Sch. of Art, 1960–; Vis. Prof. in Illustration, London Inst., 1994–; External Assessor in Illustration: Bristol Polytech., 1978–81; Brighton Polytech., 1982–85; Duncan of Jordanstone Coll. of Art, 1986–89; Exeter Coll. of Art, 1986–89; Kingston Polytechnic, 1989–93; Edinburgh Coll. of Art, 1991–94. Member: Art Workers Guild, 1972 (Master, 1990); Soc. of Wood Engravers, 1984. Work represented in Ashmolean Mus., V&A Mus., Nat. Mus. of Wales, and collections abroad. *Publications:* The Giant of Grabbist, 1968; Pope Leo's Elephant, 1969; Rabbit and Pork Rhyming Talk, 1975 (Francis Williams Book Illustration Award, 1977); Tongue Twisters, 1976; George, His Elephant and Castle, 1983; A Selection of Wood Engravings, 1986; Good Babies, Bad Babies, 1987; *illustrated:* more than 100 books, incl.: Colonel Jack, 1967 (Francis Williams Book Illustration Award, 1971); Diary of a Nobody, 1969; The Blue Fairy Book, 1975; The Illustrated Watership Down, 1976; Everyman's Book of English Folk Tales, 1981; The Magic Apple Tree, 1982; Mabel's Story, 1984; Entertaining with Cranks, 1985; Emily's Own Elephant, 1987; Christmas in Exeter Street, 1989; A New Treasury of Poetry, 1990; The Sword of Honour trilogy, 1990; Treasure Island, 1990; Shades of Green, 1991 (Signal Prize for Poetry); Poems for the Young, 1992; King of King's, 1993; The Twelve Days of Christmas, 1994; The Christmas Collection, 1994; Memoirs of a Georgian Rake, 1995; Robin Hood, 1995; Poems for Christmas, 1995; Collected Poems for Children by Charles Causley, 1996; (with Allan Ahlberg) The Mysteries of Zigomar, 1997; A Year and a Day, 1999; This Little Chick, 2002. *Address:* 6 Worts Causeway, Cambridge CB1 8RL.

LAWRENCE, Michael Hugh, CMG 1972; Head of the Administration Department, House of Commons, 1972–80; retired 1980; *b* 9 July 1920; *s* of late Hugh Moxon Lawrence and Mrs. L. N. Lawrence; *m* 1948, Rachel Mary (MA Cantab), *d* of late Humphrey Gamon, Gt Barrow, Cheshire; one *s* two *d*. *Educ:* Highgate (Scholar); St Catharine's Coll., Cambridge (Exhibnr; MA). Served Indian Army, 1940–45. Indian Civil Service, 1945–46; Asst Clerk, House of Commons, 1947; Senior Clerk, 1948; Deputy Principal Clerk, 1962; Clerk of the Overseas Office, 1967–72; Clerk Administrator, H of C Services Cttee, 1972–76; Mem., Bd of Management, House of Commons, 1979–80. Sec., History of Parliament Trust, 1959–66. *Recreations:* beagling, looking at churches, gardening. *Address:* 22 Stradbroke Road, Southwold, Suffolk IP18 6LQ. *T:* (01502) 722794.

LAWRENCE, Michael John, PhD; FCA; Chief Executive, London Stock Exchange, 1994–96; *b* 25 Oct. 1943; *s* of Geoffrey Frederick Lawrence and Kathleen Bridge Lawrence; *m* 1967, Maureen Joy Blennerhassett; two *s* one *d*. *Educ:* Exeter Univ. (BSc 1st Cl. Hons Physics); Bristol Univ. (PhD Mathematical Physics). FCA 1972. With Price Waterhouse, 1969–87, Partner 1978; Finance Dir, Prudential Corp., 1988–93. Non-executive Director: PLA, 1983–89; London Transport, 1994–99; Yattendon Investment Trust, 1998–. Ext. Mem., Council, DERA, 1990–. Chm., 100 Gp of Finance Dirs, 1991–93. Mem. (C), Royal Borough of Windsor and Maidenhead Unitary Council (Leader, 2000–). Freeman, City of London, 1974; Liveryman, Tin Plate Workers' Co., 1974– (Master, 2000–01). *Recreations:* sailing, bridge, tennis, opera. *Address:* Springmead, Bradcutts Lane, Cookham Dean, Berks SL6 9AA.

LAWRENCE, Murray; see Lawrence, W. N. M.

LAWRENCE, Sir Patrick; see Lawrence, Sir J. P. G.

LAWRENCE, Peter Anthony, PhD; FRS 1983; Staff Scientist, Medical Research Council Laboratory of Molecular Biology, Cambridge, since 1969; *b* 23 June 1941; *s* of Ivor Douglas Lawrence and Joy Lawrence (*née* Liebert); *m* 1971, Birgitta Haraldson. *Educ:* Wennington Sch., Wetherby, Yorks; Cambridge Univ. (MA, PhD). Harkness Fellowship, 1965–67; Dept of Genetics, Univ. of Cambridge, 1967–69. *Publications:* Insect Development (ed), 1976; The Making of a Fly, 1992; scientific papers. *Recreations:* Ascalaphidae, fungi, gardening, golf, theatre, trees. *Address:* MRC Laboratory of Molecular Biology, Hills Road, Cambridge CB2 2QH.

LAWRENCE, Richard; see Lawrence, H. R. G.

LAWRENCE, Timothy; His Honour Judge Lawrence; a Circuit Judge, since 1986; *b* 29 April 1942; *s* of late A. Whiteman Lawrence, MBE, and of Phyllis G. Lawrence (*née* Lloyd-Jones). *Educ:* Bedford School; Coll. of Law. Admitted Solicitor, 1967; with Solicitor's Dept, New Scotland Yard, 1967–70; Partner with Claude Hornby & Cox, Solicitors, 1970–86 (Sen. Partner, 1977–86). An Asst Recorder, 1980; a Recorder, 1983–86; Pres., Industrial Tribunals for Eng. and Wales (as Sen. Circuit Judge), 1991–97. Legal Mem., Mental Health Review Tribunals, 1989–; Mem., Parole Bd, 1998–; Chm., No 14 Area, Regional Duty Solicitor Cttee, 1984–86; Mem., No 13 Area, Legal Aid Cttee, 1983–86. Pres., London Criminal Courts Solicitors' Assoc., 1984–86 (Sec., 1974–84); Member: Law Society's Criminal Law Cttee, 1980–86; Council, Westminster Law Soc., 1979–82; Judicial Studies Bd, 1984–88, 1991–96; British Academy of Forensic Sciences, 1972– (Pres., 1992–93). Legal Assessor: Professions Supplementary to Medicine, 1976–86; Insurance Brokers Registration Council, 1983–86. Jt Editor, Medicine, Science and the Law, 1996–. FRSA 1991. *Publications:* various articles in legal jls. *Recreations:* walking, wine, travel. *Address:* 8 Slaidburn Street, SW10 0JP; Hill Cottage, Great Walsingham, Norfolk NR22 6DR. *Clubs:* Reform, Hurlingham.

LAWRENCE, Vanessa Vivienne; Director General and Chief Executive, Ordnance Survey, since 2000; *b* 14 July 1962; *d* of Leonard Walter Sydney Lawrence and Margaret Elizabeth Lawrence. *Educ:* St Helen's Sch., Northwood, Middx; Sheffield Univ. (BA (Soc. Sci.) Hons Geography); Dundee Univ. (MSc Remote Sensing, Image Processing and Applications). Longman Group UK Ltd: Publisher, 1985–89; Sen. Publisher, 1989–91; Publishing Manager, 1991–92; Tech. Dir, GeoInformation Internat. (Pearson Gp), 1993–96; Regl Business Develt Manager, UK, ME, Africa, GIS Solutions Div., Autodesk Ltd, 1996–2000; Global Manager, Strategic Mktg and Communications, GIS Solutions Div., Autodesk Inc., 2000. Hon. Res. Associate, Manchester Univ., 1990–; Vis. Prof., Southampton Univ., 2000–. Member: RGS, 1987–; Assoc. for Geographic Inf., 1992– (Mem. Council, 1995–2000; Chm., 1999). Hon. DSc Sheffield, 2000. *Publications:* contrib. many books and jls on Geographical Inf. Systems. *Recreations:* scuba diving, sailing, tennis, collecting antique maps. *Address:* Ordnance Survey, Romsey Road, Southampton SO16 4GU. *Club:* Rickmansworth Sailing.

LAWRENCE, Vernon John; freelance television producer; *b* 30 April 1940; *m* 1960, Jennifer Mary Drewe; two *s* one *d*. *Educ:* Dulwich Coll.; Kelham Coll. BBC Studio Manager, 1958; BBC Radio Producer, 1964; BBC TV Producer and Dir, 1967; Yorkshire Television: Exec. Producer, 1973; Controller, Entertainment, 1985; Controller, Network Drama and Entertainment, ITV, 1993–95; Man. Dir, MAI Prodns, 1995–97; Man. Dir, 1995–97, Chm., 1997–2000, United Film & TV Prodns, subseq. United Prodns. FRTS 1995. *Recreations:* oil painting, fishing, walking, gardening.

LAWRENCE, (Walter Nicholas) Murray; Chairman of Lloyd's, 1988–90 (a Deputy Chairman 1982, 1984–87; Member: Committee of Lloyd's, 1979–82; Council of Lloyd's, 1984–91); Chairman, Murray Lawrence Holdings Ltd, 1988–94; *b* 8 Feb. 1935; *s* of Henry Walter Neville Lawrence and Sarah Schuyler Lawrence (*née* Butler); *m* 1961, Sally Louise O'Dwyer; two *d*. *Educ:* Winchester Coll.; Trinity Coll., Oxford (BA, MA). C. T. Bowring & Co. (Ins.) Ltd, 1957–62; Asst Underwriter, H. Bowring & Others, 1962–70, Underwriter, 1970–84; Director: C. T. Bowring (Underwriting Agencies) Ltd, 1973–84; C. T. Bowring & Co. Ltd, 1976–84; Murray Lawrence Members Agency Ltd, 1988–94 (Chm., 1988–93); Murray Lawrence & Partners Ltd, 1989–95 (Sen. Partner, 1985–89; Chm., 1989–92); Chm., Fairway (Underwriting Agencies) Ltd, 1979–85. Mem., Lloyd's Underwriters Non-Marine Assoc., 1970–84 (Dep. Chm., 1977; Chm., 1978). *Recreations:* golf, opera, travelling. *Clubs:* Boodle's, MCC; Royal & Ancient (St Andrews), Swinley, Royal St George's (Sandwich), Rye, New Zealand.

LAWRENCE, Sir William (Fettiplace), 5th Bt *cr* 1867, of Ealing Park, Middlesex; General Manager, Newdawn & Sun Ltd, since 1981; *b* 23 Aug. 1954; *s* of Sir William Lawrence, 4th Bt and of Pamela, *yr d* of J. E. Gordon; *S* father, 1986. *Educ:* King Edward VI School, Stratford-upon-Avon. Assistant Accountant, Wilmot Breeden Ltd/W. B. Bumpers Ltd, 1973–81. Member: Stratford-on-Avon District Council, 1982– (Chm., 1990–91); S Warwickshire CHC, 1983–84; S Warwickshire HA, 1984–92; S Warwickshire Gen. Hosps NHS Trust, 1993–; Cttee, Employment of People with Disabilities, Coventry and Warwickshire, 1994–97; Rural Develt Commn, Warwickshire, 1995–; Dir, S Warwickshire Business Partnership, 1995–. Chm., Heart of England Tourist Bd, 1991– (Mem. Bd, 1989–); Mem., W Midlands Arts, 1989–91 (Mem., Management Council, 1984–89); Director: Unicorn Tourism Ltd, 1994–; Stratford-upon-Avon and Dist Marketing Ltd, 1995–; Midland Music Fests, 1996–; Stratford-upon-Avon Crossroads Care Attendant Scheme Ltd, 1996–. President: Stratford and District Mencap, 1990–; Stratford-upon-Avon Chamber Music Soc., 1991–; Stratford Town FC, 1992–94; Pres., and Chm. of Trustees, Action Unlimited Trust, 1991– (Trustee, 1988–). Consultant Trainer, Insite Consultancy, Edinburgh, 1995–. Mem. Court, Univ. of Birmingham, 1990–. Mem., Corp. of Stratford-upon-Avon Coll., 1996–; Gov., King Edward VI GS, Stratford-upon-Avon, 1987–. Gov., Royal Shakespeare Theatre, 1991–. *Heir: cousin* Peter Stafford Hayden Lawrence [*b* 9 Feb. 1913; *m* 1940, Helena Francis, *d* of late Hon. George William Lyttelton; two *s* four *d*]. *Address:* The Knoll, Walcote, near Alcester, Warwickshire B49 6LZ. *T:* (01789) 488303.

LAWRENCE-JONES, Sir Christopher, 6th Bt *cr* 1831; *S* uncle, 1969; *m* 1967, Gail Pittar, Auckland, NZ; two *s*. *Educ:* Sherborne; Gonville and Caius Coll., Cambridge; St Thomas' Hospital. MA Cantab 1964; MB, BChir Cantab 1964; DIH Eng. 1968. MFOM 1979, FFOM 1987; FRCP 1991. Medical adviser to various orgns, 1967–94; CMO, Imperial Chemical Industries PLC, 1985–93; Chm., Medichem, 1986–92. Pres., Section of Occupational Medicine, RSM, 1990–91; Mem. Management Cttee, British Occupational Health Res. Foundn, 1991–94. *Recreation:* cruising under sail (yacht Mermerus). *Heir: s* Mark Christopher Lawrence-Jones, *b* 28 Dec. 1968. *Club:* Royal Cruising.

LAWRENSON, Prof. Peter John, DSc; FRS 1982; FREng, FIEE, FIEEE; Founder Chairman, Switched Reluctance Drives Ltd, 1981–97 (Managing Director, 1986–94; Director, since 1997); Professor of Electrical Engineering, Leeds University, 1966–91, now Emeritus; *b* 12 March 1933; *s* of John Lawrenson and Emily (*née* Houghton); *m* 1958, Shirley Hannah Foster; one *s* three *d*. *Educ:* Prescot Grammar Sch.; Manchester Univ. (BSc, MSc; DSc 1971). FIEE 1974; FIEEE 1975; FREng (FEng 1980). Duddell Scholar, IEE, 1951–54; Res. Engr, Associated Electrical Industries, 1956–61; University of Leeds: Lectr, 1961–65; Reader, 1965–66; Head, Dept of Electrical and Electronic Engrg, 1974–84; Chm., Faculty of Science and Applied Science, 1978–80; Chm., Shadow Faculty of Engrg, 1981. Science and Engineering Research Council: Mem., Electrical and Systems Cttee, 1971–77; Chm., Electrical Engrg Sub-Cttee, 1981–84; Mem., Machines and Power Cttee, 1981–84; Mem., Engrg Bd, 1984–87; Organiser, National Initiative,

Integrated Drive Systems, 1984–86. Director: Allenwest Ltd, 1988–91; Dale Electric Internat., 1988–94; Consultant: Emerson Electric Co., 1994–97; Rolls-Royce, 2000–. Institution of Electrical Engineers: Mem. Council, 1966–69 and 1981–98; Chm., Accreditation Cttee, 1979–83; Chm., Power Divisional Bd, 1985–86; Dep. Pres., 1990–92; Pres., 1992–93. Mem. of cttees, Engrg Council, 1983–89 and 1997–; Mem. Council, Buckingham Univ., 1987–93. IEE Awards: Premia-Crompton, 1957 and 1967; John Hopkinson, 1965; The Instn, 1981; Faraday Medal, 1990. James Alfred Ewing Medal, ICE and Royal Soc., 1983; Royal Soc. Esso Energy Award, 1985. *Publications:* (with K. J. Binns) Analysis and Computation of Electromagnetic Field Problems, 1963, 2nd edn 1973; (with M. R. Harris and J. M. Stephenson) Per Unit Systems, 1970; (with K. J. Binns and C. W. Trowbridge) The Analytical and Numerical Solution of Electric and Magnetic Fields, 1992; papers and patents in areas of electromagnetism, electromechanics and control. *Recreations:* lawn tennis, squash, chess, bridge, jewelry making. *Address:* Switched Reluctance Drives Ltd, East Park House, Harrogate HG3 1PR.

LAWREY, Keith; JP; Learned Societies' Liaison Officer, Foundation for Science and Technology, since 1997; *b* 21 Aug. 1940; *s* of George William Bishop Lawrey and Edna Muriel (*née* Gass); *m* 1969, Helen Jane Marriott, BA; two *s* two *d*. *Educ:* Colfe's Sch.; Birkbeck Coll., Univ. of London (MSc Econ; LLB); Heythrop Coll., Univ. of London (MA). Barrister-at-Law; called to Bar, Gray's Inn, 1972. Education Officer, Plastics and Rubber Inst., 1960–68; Lectr and Sen. Lectr, Bucks Coll. of Higher Educn, 1968–74; Head of Dept of Business Studies, Mid-Kent Coll. of Higher and Further Educn, 1974–78; Sec.-Gen., Library Assoc., 1978–84; Dean, Faculty of Business and Management, Harrow Coll. of Higher Educn, subseq. Head, Sch. of Business and Management, Polytechnic of Central London/Harrow Coll., 1984–90; Sec. and Registrar, RCVS, 1990–91; Headmaster, Cannock Sch., 1992–95; Clerk to Corp. of S Kent Coll., 1996–99. Mem., Social Security Appeal Tribunal, 1996–99. FCollP (Hon. Treas., 1987–); FCIS. Gov., Cannock Sch., 1976–92. Mem., Orpington Rotary Club (Pres., 1999–2000; Hon. Treas., 2000–); Trustee, Carers Support and Inf. Service, 2001–. Mem., Worshipful Co. of Chartered Secretaries and Administrators; Hon. Clerk, Guild of Educators, 1997–. JP Inner London, 1974. *Publications:* papers in Law Soc. Gazette, Educn Today, Jl Assoc. of Law Teachers, Trans and Jl of Plastics Inst. *Recreations:* preaching, sailing, swimming, theatre, gardening. *Address:* c/o College of Teachers, Room 310, 33 John Street, WC1N 2AT. *Clubs:* Old Colfeians; Dell Quay Sailing.

LAWS, David Anthony; MP (Lib Dem) Yeovil, since 2001; *b* 30 Nov. 1965; *s* of David Anthony, (Tony), Laws and Maureen Teresa Laws. *Educ:* St George's Coll., Weybridge (Observer Mace Schs Debating Champion 1984); King's Coll., Cambridge (schol.; Double 1st Cl. Hons Econs 1987). Vice Pres., Treasury Dept, J. P. Morgan and Co., 1987–92; Man. Dir, Hd of Sterling and US Dollar Treasury, Barclays de Zoete Wedd, 1992–94; Econs Advr, Lib Dem Parly Party, 1994–97; Dir of Policy and Res., Lib Dems, 1997–99; drafted first Partnership Agreement for Lib Dem-Lab Coalition in Scottish Parlt, 1999. Mem., Treasury Select Cttee, 2001–. Contested (Lib Dem) Folkestone and Hythe, 1997. *Recreations:* running, watching Rugby, visiting desert regions. *Address:* House of Commons, SW1A 0AA; (constituency office) 94 Middle Street, Yeovil, Somerset BA20 1LT.

LAWS, Frederick Geoffrey; Vice-Chairman, Commission for Local Administration in England, 1984–94; *b* Blackpool, 1 Aug. 1928; *s* of Frederick and Annetta Laws. *Educ:* Arnold School; Manchester Univ.; London Univ. (LLB); solicitor 1952. Asst Solicitor, Blackpool Corp., 1952–54, Bournemouth Corp., 1954–59; Southend-on-Sea Corporation: Asst Sol., 1959–62; Dep. Town Clerk and Clerk of the Peace, 1962–71; Town Clerk, 1971–74; Chief Exec., Southend-on-Sea Borough Council, 1974–84. Pres., Southend-on-Sea Law Soc., 1981. Hon. Freeman, Southend-on-Sea Borough Council, 1985.

LAWS, Rt Hon. Sir John (Grant McKenzie), Kt 1992; PC 1999; **Rt Hon. Lord Justice Laws;** a Lord Justice of Appeal, since 1999; *b* 10 May 1945; *s* of late Dr Frederic Laws and Dr Margaret Ross Laws, *d* of Prof. John Grant McKenzie; *m* 1973, Sophie Susan Sydenham Cole Marshall, BLitt, MA; one *d*. *Educ:* Durham Cathedral Choir Sch.; Durham Sch. (King's Scholar); Exeter Coll., Oxford (Sen. Open Classical Scholar; BA 1967, Hon. Sch. of Lit. Hum. 1st Cl.; MA 1976; Hon. Felllow, 2000). Called to the Bar, Inner Temple, 1970, Bencher, 1985; practice at Common Law Bar, 1971–92; First Junior Treasury Counsel, Common Law, 1984–92; Asst Recorder, 1983–85; Recorder, 1985–92; a Judge of the High Court of Justice, QBD, 1992–98; admitted to Bar: New South Wales, 1987; Gibraltar, 1988. Pres., Bar European Gp, 1994–. An Hon. Vice-Pres., Administrative Law Bar Assoc., 1992. Judicial Visitor, UCL, 1997–. Hon. Fellow, Robinson Coll., Cambridge, 1992. *Publications:* contributor to: Halsbury's Laws of England, 4th edn 1973; Dict. of Medical Ethics, 1977; Supperstone and Goudie, Judicial Review, 1992, 2nd edn 1997; Importing the First Amendment, 1998; The Golden Metwand and the Crooked Cord, 1998; Cicero the Advocate; reviews for Theology, Law & Justice; contribs to legal jls. *Recreations:* Greece, living in London, philosophy. *Address:* Royal Courts of Justice, WC2A 2LL. *Club:* Garrick.

LAWS, Richard Maitland, CBE 1983; PhD, ScD; FRS 1980; Director, British Antarctic Survey, 1973–87; Master, St Edmund's College, Cambridge, 1985–96; *b* 23 April 1926; *s* of Percy Malcolm Laws and Florence May (*née* Heslop); *m* 1954, Maureen Isobel Winifred (*née* Holmes); three *s*. *Educ:* Dame Allan's Sch., Newcastle-on-Tyne; St Catharine's Coll., Cambridge (Open Scholar, 1944–47; BA 1947, MA 1952; Res. Scholar, 1952–53; PhD 1953; ScD 1994; Hon. Fellow, 1982). FIBiol 1973. Biologist and Base Leader, Falkland Is Dependencies Survey, 1947–53; Biologist and Whaling Inspector, F/F Balaena, 1953–54; Principal Sci. Officer, Nat. Inst. of Oceanography, 1954–61; Dir, Nuffield Unit of Tropical Animal Ecology, Uganda, 1961–67; Dir, Tsavo Research Project, Kenya, 1967–68; Smuts Meml Fund Fellowship, 1968–69; Leverhulme Research Fellowship, 1969; Head, Life Sciences Div., British Antarctic Survey, 1969–73. Dir, NERC Sea Mammal Res. Unit, 1977–87; Scientific Committee for Antarctic Research: Member: Gp of Specialists on Seals, 1972–98 (Convener, 1972–88); Biology Working Gp, 1972–90 (Chm., 1980–86); UK Delegate, 1984–93 and 1998; Pres., 1990–94; Hon. Mem., 1996. Food and Agriculture Organization: Mem., 1974–77, Chm., 1976–77, Working Party on Marine Mammals; Chm., Scientific Consultation on Conservation and Management of Marine Mammals and their Environment, 1976. Zoological Society of London: Mem. Council, 1982–84; Vice-Pres., 1983–84; Sec., 1984–88. University of Cambridge: Mem., Financial Bd, 1988–91; Mem., Council of Senate, 1989–92; Chm., Local Examinations Syndicate, 1990–94. Vice-Pres., Inst. Biol., 1984–85. Mem., Soc. of Wildlife Artists, 1965–75. Hon. Mem., Soc. for Marine Mammalogy, 1994. Foreign Mem., Norwegian Acad. of Sci. and Letters, 1998. Hon. Lectr, Makerere Univ., 1962–66; Lectures: 36th annual Lectr, CIBA Foundn, 1984; Cranbrook Meml, Mammal Soc.; 4th DICE (Durrell Inst. Conservation and Ecol.), Univ. of Kent, 1997. Hon. Warden, Uganda Nat. Parks, 1996. Hon. Fellow, St Edmund's Coll., Cambridge, 1996. Hon. DSc Bath, 1991. Bruce Medal, RSE, 1954; Scientific Medal, Zool Soc. London, 1965; Polar Medal, 1976. *Publications:* (with I. S. C. Parker and R. C. B. Johnstone) Elephants and their Habitats, 1975; (ed) Scientific Research in Antarctica, 1977; (ed) Antarctic Ecology, 1984; (ed jtly) Antarctic Nutrient Cycles and Food Webs, 1985; Antarctica: the last frontier, 1989; (ed jtly) Life at Low Temperatures, 1990; (ed jtly) Antarctica and Environmental Change, 1992; (ed) Antarctic Seals: research methods and techniques, 1993; (ed jtly) Elephant Seals: aspects of population, ecology, behaviour and physiology, 1994; papers in biol and other jls. *Recreations:* gardening, photography, painting. *Address:* 3 The Footpath, Coton, Cambridge CB3 7PX. *T:* (01954) 210567.

LAWS, Stephen Charles, CB 1996; Parliamentary Counsel, since 1991; *b* 28 Jan. 1950; *s* of late Dennis Arthur Laws and of Beryl Elizabeth Laws (*née* Roe); *m* 1972, Angela Mary Deardon (*d* 1998); two *s* three *d*; *m* 2001, Elizabeth Ann Owen (*née* Williams). *Educ:* St Dunstan's College, Catford; Bristol Univ. (LLB Hons 1972). Called to the Bar, Middle Temple, 1973. Asst Lectr, Univ. of Bristol, 1972; Legal Asst, Home Office, 1975; Asst, Sen. Asst, then Dep. Parly Counsel, 1976–91. *Publications:* (with Peter Knowles) Statutes title in Halsbury's Laws of England, 4th edn, 1983. *Address:* Office of the Parliamentary Counsel, 36 Whitehall, SW1A 2AY. *T:* (020) 7210 6611.

LAWSON, family name of **Barons Burnham** and **Lawson of Blaby**.

LAWSON OF BLABY, Baron *cr* 1992 (Life Peer), of Newnham in the County of Northamptonshire; **Nigel Lawson;** PC 1981; *b* 11 March 1932; *o s* of Ralph Lawson and Joan Elisabeth Lawson (*née* Davis); *m* 1st, 1955, Vanessa Salmon (marr. diss. 1980; she *d* 1985); one *s* two *d* (and one *d* decd); 2nd, 1980, Thérèse Mary Maclear; one *s* one *d*. *Educ:* Westminster; Christ Church, Oxford (Scholar; 1st class hons PPE, 1954). Served with Royal Navy (Sub-Lt RNVR), 1954–56. Mem. Editorial Staff, Financial Times, 1956–60; City Editor, Sunday Telegraph, 1961–63; Special Assistant to Prime Minister (Sir Alec Douglas-Home), 1963–64; Financial Times columnist and BBC broadcaster, 1965; Editor of the Spectator, 1966–70; regular contributor to: Sunday Times and Evening Standard, 1970–71; The Times, 1971–72; Fellow, Nuffield Coll., Oxford, 1972–73; Special Pol Advr, Cons. Party HQ, 1973–74. Contested (C) Eton and Slough, 1970; MP (C) Blaby, Leics, Feb. 1974–1992; An Opposition Whip, 1976–77; an Opposition Spokesman on Treasury and Economic Affairs, 1977–79; Financial Sec. to the Treasury, 1979–81; Sec. of State for Energy, 1981–83; Chancellor of the Exchequer, 1983–89. Chm., Coningsby Club, 1963–64. Vice-Chm., Cons. Political Centre Nat. Adv. Cttee, 1972–75. Chm., Central Europe Trust Co., 1990–; Dir, Barclays Bank, 1990–98. Mem., Bd of Dirs, Inst. for Internat. Econs, Washington, 1991–; Pres., British Inst. of Energy Econs, 1995–. Mem., Adv. Council, Prince's Youth Business Trust, 1994–. Mem., Governing Body, Westminster Sch., 1999–. Hon. Student, Christ Church, Oxford, 1996. *Publications:* (with Jock Bruce-Gardyne) The Power Game, 1976; The View from No 11: memoirs of a Tory radical, 1992; (with Thérèse Lawson) The Nigel Lawson Diet Book, 1996. *Address:* House of Lords, SW1A 0PW. *Clubs:* Garrick, Pratt's, Political Economy.

See also Hon. D. R. C. Lawson, N. L. Lawson.

LAWSON, Sir Christopher (Donald), Kt 1984; management consultant; Director, Communications Centre, since 1984; *b* 31 Oct. 1922; *s* of James Lawson and Ellen de Verrine; *m* 1945, Marjorie Bristow; two *s* one *d*. *Educ:* Magdalen Coll., Oxford. Served RAF, 1941–49: Pilot, Sqdn Leader. Thomas Hedley (Proctor and Gamble), 1949–57; Cooper McDougal Robertson, 1958–61; Managing Dir, TMC, 1961–63; Director: Mars Ltd, 1965–81; Mars Inc., USA, 1975–82; Pres., Mars Snackmaster, USA, 1977–82; Chm. and Man. Dir, Goodblue Ltd, 1981–; Chm., Spearhead Ltd, 1983–; Dir of Marketing, 1982–83, Dir of Special Services, 1986–87, Cons. and Unionist Party. *Recreations:* collecting antiques and new artists' work; all sport, particularly golf, cricket, hockey. *Address:* Pound Cottage, Buckland, Oxon SN7 8QN. *Clubs:* Royal Air Force, Carlton, MCC; Lillybrook Golf (Cheltenham); Doublegate Country (Ga, USA).

LAWSON, Prof. David Hamilton, CBE 1993; Consultant Physician, Glasgow Royal Infirmary, since 1973; *b* 27 May 1939; *s* of David Lawson and Margaret Harvey Lawson (*née* White); *m* 1963, Alison Diamond (*d* 1996); three *s*. *Educ:* High Sch. of Glasgow; Univ. of Glasgow. MB, ChB 1962; MD 1973. FRCPE 1975; FRCPGlas 1986; FFPM 1989; FRCPL 2001; FFPHM 2001. Junior medical posts in Royal Infirmary and Western Infirmary, Glasgow; Boston Collaborative Drug Surveillance Prog., Boston, Mass, 1970–72; Attending Physician, Lemuel Shattuck Hosp., Boston, 1971; Adviser on Adverse Drug Reactions, Wellcome Foundn, 1975–87; Vis. Prof., Faculty of Sci., Univ. of Strathclyde, 1976–; Hon. Prof. of Medicine, Univ. of Glasgow, 1993–. Chm., Medicines Commn, 1994–; Member: Health Services Res. Cttee of Chief Scientist Office, SHHD, 1984–88; Cttee on Safety of Medicines, Dept of Health (formerly DHSS), 1987–93; Mem., 1979–91, Chm., 1987–91, Cttee on Review of Medicines, Dept of Health (formerly DHSS). Mem. Council, RCPE, 1992– (Vice-Pres., 1997–99). Examiner, Final MB, Univs of Glasgow, Dundee, Birmingham, London, Kota Bharu, Malaysia. Hon. DSc: Hertfordshire, 2000; Strathclyde, 2001. *Publications:* Clinical Pharmacy and Hospital Drug Management (ed with R. M. E. Richards), 1982; Current Medicine 2, 1990; (ed jtly) Risk Factors for Adverse Drug Reactions: epidemiological approaches, 1990; Current Medicine 3, 1991; Current Medicine 4, 1994; papers on clinical pharmacol, haematol and renal topics. *Recreations:* hill-walking, photography, bird-watching. *Address:* 25 Kirkland Avenue, Blanefield, Glasgow G63 9BY. *T:* (01360) 770081. *Club:* Royal Commonwealth Society.

LAWSON, Hon. Dominic Ralph Campden; Editor, The Sunday Telegraph, since 1995; *b* 17 Dec. 1956; *s* of Baron Lawson of Blaby, *qv* and late Vanessa Mary Addison Lawson (*née* Salmon); *m* 1st, 1982, Jane Whytehead (marr. diss.); 2nd, 1991, Hon. Rosamond Mary, *o d* of Viscount Monckton of Brenchley, *qv*; two *d*. *Educ:* Westminster Sch.; Christ Church, Oxford (exhibnr; Hons PPE). Researcher, BBC TV and radio, 1979–81; Financial Times: joined 1981; energy corresp., 1983–86; columnist (Lex), 1986–87; The Spectator: Dep Editor, 1987–90; Editor, 1990–95; columnist: Sunday Correspondent, 1990; Financial Times, 1991–94; Daily Telegraph, 1994–95; Sunday Telegraph, 1995–. FRSA 1993. Harold Wincott Prize for financial journalism, 1987. *Publications:* (with Raymond Keene) Kasparov-Korchnoi, the London Contest, 1983; (jtly) Britain in the Eighties, 1989; The Inner Game, 1993. *Recreation:* chess. *Address:* The Sunday Telegraph, 1 Canada Square, Canary Wharf, E14 5DT. *Clubs:* Garrick, MCC.

LAWSON, Prof. Donald Douglas; Professor of Veterinary Surgery, University of Glasgow, 1974–86; *b* 25 May 1924; *s* of Alexander Lawson and Jessie Macnaughton; *m* 1949, Barbara Ness (*d* 1998); one *s* one *d* (and one *s* one *d* decd). *Educ:* Whitehill Sch., Glasgow; Glasgow Veterinary Coll. MRCVS, BSc, DVR. Asst in Veterinary Practice, 1946–47; Asst, Surgery Dept, Glasgow Vet. Coll., 1947–49; Glasgow Univ.: Lectr, Vet. Surgery, 1949–57; Sen. Lectr, 1957–66; Reader, 1966–71; Titular Prof., 1971–74. *Publications:* many articles in Veterinary Record and Jl of Small Animal Practice. *Recreations:* gardening, motoring. *Address:* 5 Hewlings Place, Temuka 8752, New Zealand.

LAWSON, Edmund James; QC 1988; *b* 17 April 1948; *s* of Donald and Veronica Lawson; *m* 1973, Jennifer Cleary; three *s*. *Educ:* City of Norwich Sch.; Trinity Hall, Cambridge (BA Hons, Law). Called to the Bar, Gray's Inn, 1971, Bencher, 1998; in chambers of: Dr F. Hallis, 1971–76; Sir Arthur Irvine, QC, subseq. Gilbert Gray, QC,

1976–; Head of Chambers, 1990–98. *Recreations:* music, Rugby. *Address:* 9–12 Bell Yard, WC2A 2LF. *T:* (020) 7400 1800.

LAWSON, Elizabeth Ann; QC 1989; a Recorder, since 1998; *b* 29 April 1947; *d* of Alexander Edward Lawson, FCA, and Helen Jane Lawson (*née* Currie). *Educ:* Croydon High School for Girls (GPDST); Nottingham Univ. (LLB). Called to Bar, Gray's Inn, 1969, Bencher, 1999. Chm., Family Law Bar Assoc., 1995–97. Chm., Leeways Enquiry for London Borough of Lewisham, 1985; Chm., Liam Johnson Review for Islington Area Child Protection Cttee, 1989. *Recreations:* knitting, reading, cake decoration. *Address:* 1 Pump Court, Temple, EC4Y 7AB.

LAWSON, Rear-Adm. Frederick Charles William, CB 1971; DSC 1942 and Bar, 1945; Chief Executive, Royal Dockyards, Ministry of Defence, 1972–75; *b* 20 April 1917; *s* of M. L. Lawson, formerly of Public Works Dept, Punjab, India; *m* 1945, Dorothy (*née* Norman) (*d* 1986), Eastbourne; one *s* three *d. Educ:* Eastbourne Coll.; RNEC. Joined RN, 1935; specialised in engrg; Cmdr 1949; Captain 1960; Cdre Supt Singapore, 1965–69; Rear-Adm. 1969; Flag Officer, Medway and Adm. Supt, HM Dockyard, Chatham, 1969–71, retired. *Address:* Weaverhoult, 20 Woolley Street, Bradford-on-Avon, Wilts BA15 1AF.

See also Vice-Adm. Sir M. A. C. Moore.

LAWSON, Prof. Gerald Hartley; Professor of Business Finance, Manchester Business School, University of Manchester, 1969–88, now Emeritus; financial and economic consultant; *b* 6 July 1933; of English parents; *m* 1957, Helga Elisabeth Anna Heine; three *s. Educ:* King's Coll., Univ. of Durham. BA (Econ), MA (Econ); MBA, PhD Manchester; FCCA. Accountant in industry, 1957–59; Lectr in Accountancy and Applied Economics, Univ. of Sheffield, 1959–66; Prof. of Business Studies, Univ. of Liverpool, 1966–69. Prof., Univ. of Augsburg, Germany, 1971–72; Prof., Univ. of Texas, 1977, 1981; Prof., Ruhr Univ., Bochum, 1980; British Council Scholar, Hochschule für Welthandel, Vienna, 1967, and Univ. of Louvain, 1978. Visiting Professor: Southern Methodist Univ., Dallas, 1989–93; Nanyang Technological Univ., Singapore, 1989; Martin Luther Univ., Halle-Wittenberg, 1993–96; Otto-von-Guericke-Univ. of Magdeburg, 1998–2001; Vis. Erskine Fellow, Univ. of Canterbury, NZ, 1997. Dir, Dietsmann (UK), 1984–89. *Publications:* (with D. W. Windle): Tables for Discounted Cash Flow, etc, Calculations, 1965 (5th repr. 1978); Capital Budgeting in the Corporation Tax Regime, 1967; (with M. Schweitzer and E. Trossman) Break-Even Analyses: basic model, variants, extensions, 1991; Studies in Cash Flow Accounting, 1992; Aspects of the Economic Implications of Accounting, 1997; many articles and translations. *Recreations:* cricket, ski-ing, opera. *Address:* 1702 Woodcreek Drive, Richardson, TX 75082, USA. *Club:* Manchester Business School.

LAWSON, James Robert; Regional Nursing Officer, Mersey, 1985–89, retired; *b* 29 Dec. 1939; *s* of James and Grace Lawson; *m* 1962, Jean; two *d. Educ:* Keswick High School; Royal Albert Hosp. (Registered Nurse of Mentally Handicapped); Cumberland Infirmary (Registered Gen. Nurse). Chief Nurse, 1972; Area Nurse, Personnel, 1974; Divl Nursing Officer, 1976; District Nursing Officer, 1982–85. *Recreations:* fellwalking, caravaning, active sports. *Address:* 11 Hazelgarth, Church Road, Allithwaite, Grange-over-Sands, Cumbria LA11 7RS.

LAWSON, John Alexander Reid, OBE 1979; FRCGP; General Medical Practitioner, 1948–86, retired; Regional Adviser in General Practice, Tayside Region, 1972–82; *b* 30 Aug. 1920; *s* of Thomas Reid Lawson and Helen Scrimgour Lawson; *m* 1944, Pat Kirk; two *s* two *d. Educ:* High Sch. of Dundee; Univ. of St Andrews (MB, ChB). RAMC, 1944–47 (Major). Surgical Registrar, Royal Infirmary, Dundee, 1947–48. Royal College of General Practitioners: Mem., 1952; Fellow, 1967; Chm. Council, 1973–76; Pres., 1982–85. Mem. Cttee of Enquiry into Competence to Practice, 1974–76; Chairman: Jt Cttee on Postgraduate Training for General Practice, 1975–78; Armed Service Gen. Practice Approval Bd, 1979–87. *Recreations:* shooting, fishing, golf, gardening. *Address:* The Ridges, 458 Perth Road, Dundee DD2 1NG. *T:* (01382) 566675. *Club:* Royal and Ancient Golf (St Andrews).

LAWSON, Col Sir John Charles Arthur Digby, 3rd Bt *cr* 1900; DSO 1943; MC 1940; Colonel 11th Hussars, retired; former Chairman, Fairbairn Lawson Ltd, Leeds; *b* 24 Oct. 1912; *e s* of Sir Digby Lawson, Bt, TD, JP, and late Mrs Gerald Wallis (*née* Iris Mary Fitzgerald); *S* father, 1959; *m* 1st, 1945, Rose (marr. diss. 1950; she *d* 1972), *widow* of Pilot Officer William Fiske, RAF, and *er d* of late D. C. Bingham and late Lady Rosabelle Brand; 2nd, 1954, Tresilla Ann Elinor (de Pret Roose) (*d* 1985), *d* of late Major E. Buller Leyborne Popham, MC; one *s. Educ:* Stowe; RMC, Sandhurst; commissioned 11th Hussars (PAO), 1933; Palestine, 1936–37; Transjordan Frontier Force, 1938; Western Desert, 1940–43 (despatches twice, MC, DSO); Armoured Adviser to Gen. Patton, N Africa, 1943; Staff Coll., 1943; US Marines Staff Course, 1944; Special Liaison Officer to Gen. Montgomery, NW Europe, 1944; Comd Inns of Court Regt, 1945–47; retired, 1947. Colonel, 11th Hussars (PAO), 1965–69; Col, The Royal Hussars (PWO), 1969–73. Legion of Merit (US). *Heir: s* Charles John Patrick Lawson [*b* 19 May 1959; *m* 1987, Lady Caroline Lowther, *d* of Earl of Lonsdale, *qv*; three *s* one *d. Educ:* Harrow; Royal Agricl Coll., Cirencester. With Jackson-Stops & Staff]. *Clubs:* Cavalry and Guards, MCC.

LAWSON, John David, ScD; FRS 1983; Deputy Chief Scientific Officer, Rutherford Appleton Laboratory, Science and Engineering Research Council, Chilton, Oxon, 1978–87, retired, now Hon. Scientist; *b* 4 April 1923; *s* of Ronald L. Lawson and Ruth (*née* Houseman); *m* 1949, Kathleen (*née* Wyllie); two *s* one *d. Educ:* Wolverhampton Grammar Sch.; St John's Coll., Cambridge (BA, ScD). FInstP. TRE Malvern, Aerials group, 1943; AERE Malvern Br., Accelerator gp, 1947; AERE Harwell, Gen. Physics Div., 1951–62; Microwave Laboratory, Stanford, USA, 1959–60; Rutherford Laboratory (later Rutherford Appleton Laboratory), Applied Phys. Div., and later Technology Div., 1962–87, except, Vis. Prof., Dept of Physics and Astronomy, Univ. of Maryland, USA, 1971; Culham Lab., Technology Div., 1975–76. *Publications:* The Physics of Charged Particle Beams, 1977, 2nd edn 1988; papers on various topics in applied physics in several jls. *Recreations:* travel, walking, collecting old books, bookbinding. *Address:* 7 Clifton Drive, Abingdon, Oxon OX14 1ET. *T:* (01235) 521516.

LAWSON, Sir John Philip H.; *see* Howard-Lawson.

LAWSON, Lesley, (Twiggy); actress and singer; *b* 19 Sept. 1949; *y d* of late (William) Norman Hornby and of Nell (Helen) Hornby (*née* Reeman); *m* 1st, 1977, Michael Whitney Armstrong (*d* 1983); one *d*; 2nd, 1988, Leigh Lawson. Started modelling in London, 1966; toured USA and Canada, 1967; world's most famous model, 1966–71. *Films:* The Boy Friend, 1971 (most promising newcomer and best actress in a musical or comedy, Golden Globe Awards); W, 1973; There Goes the Bride, 1979; Blues Brothers, 1981; The Doctor and the Devils, 1986; Club Paradise, 1986; Madame Sousatzka, 1989; Harem Hotel, Istanbul, 1989; Woundings, 1998; *stage:* Cinderella, 1976; Captain Beaky, 1982; My One and Only, 1983, 1984; Blithe Spirit, Chichester, 1997; Noel and Gertie, NY, 1998; If Love Were All, NY, 1999; *television:* numerous appearances and series, UK and USA; numerous recordings. Many awards and honours including Hon. Col, Tennessee Army, 1977. *Publications:* Twiggy, 1975; An Open Look, 1985; Twiggy in Black and White (autobiog.), 1997. *Recreations:* daughter Carly, music, design. *Address:* c/o Peters, Fraser & Dunlop, Drury House, 34–43 Russell Street, WC2B 5HA. *T:* (020) 7344 1010, *Fax:* (020) 7836 9544.

LAWSON, Mark Gerard; journalist, broadcaster and author; *b* 11 April 1962; *s* of Francis Lawson and Teresa Lawson (*née* Kane); *m* 1990, Sarah Bull; two *s* one *d. Educ:* St Columba's Coll., St Albans; University College London (BA Hons English). Junior reporter and TV critic, The Universe, 1984–85; TV previewer, Sunday Times, 1985–86; TV critic and parly sketchwriter, The Independent, 1986–89; feature writer, Independent Magazine, 1988–95; columnist, The Guardian, 1995–; writer and presenter for radio and TV, 1990–, incl. Late Review, (later Review, then Newsnight Review) (BBC2), Never Ending Stories (BBC2), A Brief History of the Future, The People's God, Front Row (Radio 4). British Press Award, 1987; TV critic of the Year, 1989, 1990. *Publications:* Bloody Margaret, 1991; The Battle for Room Service, 1993; Idlewild, 1995; John Keane, 1995; Going Out Live, 2001. *Recreations:* theatre, cricket, tennis, wine, reading. *Address:* c/o The Guardian, 119 Farringdon Road, EC1R 3ER. *T:* (020) 7239 9959.

LAWSON, Ven. Michael Charles; Archdeacon of Hampstead, since 1999; *b* 23 May 1952; *s* of Gerald Simon Lawson and Myrtle Helena Lawson; *m* 1978, Claire Mary MacClelland; three *d. Educ:* Hove Grammar Sch.; Guildhall Sch. of Music; Ecoles d'Art Américaines, Fontainebleau; Univ. of Sussex (BA); Trinity Coll., Bristol (BCTS). Composer and pianist, 1970–75. Deacon 1978, priest 1979; Curate, St Mary the Virgin, Horsham, 1978–81; Dir of Pastoring, All Souls, Langham Place, W1, 1981–86; Vicar, Christ Church, Bromley, 1987–99. *Publications:* Sex and That, 1985, 2nd edn 1992; Facing Anxiety and Stress, 1986, 2nd edn 1995; The Unfolding Kingdom, 1987; Facing Depression, 1989, 2nd edn 1997; Facing Conflict, 1990; The Better Marriage Guide, 1998; Conflict, 1999; Living by God's Masterplan, 2000. *Recreations:* my wife and children, friends, music, writing, video production, photography, computers, theatre, cookery, lots of things. *Address:* 1 Regent's Park Terrace, NW1 7EE.

LAWSON, Michael Henry; QC 1991; a Recorder, since 1987; *b* 3 Feb. 1946; *s* of Dr Richard Pike Lawson, MC and late Margaret Haines (*née* Knight); *m* 1969, Ann Pleasance Symons Brisker; two *d. Educ:* Monkton Combe School, Bath; London Univ. (LLB). Called to the Bar, Inner Temple, 1969, Bencher, 1993. Leader, SE Circuit, 1997–2000. Mem., Bar Council, 1997–. *Publications:* (jtly) Professional Conduct (Inns of Court School of Law Manual), annually, 1989–; (contrib.) Refocus on Child Abuse, 1994. *Recreations:* opera, music, wine. *Address:* 23 Essex Street, WC2R 3AS. *T:* (020) 7413 0353.

LAWSON, Nigella Lucy; freelance journalist and broadcaster, since 1982; *b* 6 Jan. 1960; *d* of Baron Lawson of Blaby, *qv* and late Vanessa (*née* Salmon); *m* 1992, John Diamond (*d* 2001); one *s* one *d. Educ:* Lady Margaret Hall, Oxford (BA (Hons) Medieval and Mod. Langs). Presenter, television series: Nigella Bites, 2000; Nigella Bites II, 2001. *Publications:* How to Eat, 1998; How to be a Domestic Goddess, 2000; Nigella Bites, 2001. *Address:* c/o Ed Victor Ltd, 6 Bayley Street, Bedford Square, WC1B 3HB. *T:* (020) 7304 4100.

See also Hon. D. R. C. Lawson.

LAWSON, Gen. Sir Richard (George), KCB 1980; DSO 1962; OBE 1968; Commander-in-Chief, Allied Forces Northern Europe, 1982–86; *b* 24 Nov. 1927; *s* of John Lawson and Florence Rebecca Lawson; *m* 1956, Ingrid Lawson; one *s. Educ:* St Alban's Sch.; Birmingham Univ. CO, Independent Squadron, RTR (Berlin), 1963–64; GSO2 MoD, 1965–66; CofS, South Arabian Army, 1967; CO, 5th RTR, 1968–69; Comdr, 20th Armoured Bde, 1972–73; Asst Military Deputy to Head of Defence Sales, 1975–77; GOC 1st Armoured Div., 1977–79; GOC Northern Ireland, 1980–82. Col Comdt, RTR, 1980–82. Leopold Cross (Belgium), 1963; Knight Commander, Order of St Sylvester (Vatican), 1964. *Publications:* Strange Soldiering, 1963; All the Queen's Men, 1967; Strictly Personal, 1972. *Address:* c/o Drummonds, 49 Charing Cross, SW1A 2DX. *Club:* Army and Navy.

LAWSON, Richard Henry, CBE 1994; Chairman: Greenwell Montagu, Stockbrokers, 1987–91; Securities and Futures Authority, 1991; *b* 16 Feb. 1932; *s* of Sir Henry Brailsford Lawson, MC, and Lady (Mona) Lawson; *m* 1958, Janet Elizabeth Govier; three *s* (one *d* decd). *Educ:* Lancing College. ICI, 1952–54; W. Greenwell & Co. (now Greenwell Montagu & Co.), 1954–91; Jt Sen. Partner, 1980–86. Deputy Chairman: Stock Exchange, 1985–86; Securities Assoc., 1986–91. Chm., Investors Compensation Scheme, 1993–96 (Dir, 1989–96); Dir, Securities Institute, 1992–93. *Recreations:* golf, tennis, walking, birdwatching, skiing.

LAWSON, Roger Hardman; Director, 3i plc, since 1987; *b* 3 Sept. 1945; *s* of Harold Hardman Lawson and Mary Doreen Lawson (*née* Buckley); *m* 1974, Jenniferjane Grey; three *d. Educ:* Bedford School. CA 1967; FCA. Articled Wilson de Zouche & Mackenzie, 1963–67; joined ICFC, subseq. 3i, 1968; Manager, Regions, 1968–84; Dir, 3i International (USA, Asia and Pacific), 1984–92; Dir Resource (handling substantial investments), 3i plc, 1993–; Director: Banner Homes Gp; several unquoted trading cos. Mem., Takeover Panel, 1994–95. Chairman: London Soc. of Chartered Accountants, 1985–86; Bd for Chartered Accountants in Business, 1990–91; CCAB Ltd, 1994–95; Pres., ICAEW, 1994–95 (Vice-Pres., 1992–93; Dep.-Pres., 1993–94). *Recreations:* food, family, golf. *Address:* 3i plc, 91 Waterloo Road, SE1 8XP. *T:* (020) 7928 3131. *Clubs:* Royal Wimbledon Golf; Rye Golf.

LAWSON, Sonia, RA 1991 (ARA 1982); RWS 1988 (ARWS 1985); artist; Visiting Lecturer, Royal Academy Schools; *b* 2 June 1934; *d* of Frederick Lawson and Muriel (*née* Metcalfe), artists; *m* 1969, C. W. Congo; one *d. Educ:* Leyburn; Southwick Girls' Sch.; Doncaster Sch. of Art; Royal Coll. of Art (ARCA 1st cl. 1959). Postgraduate year, RCA; Travelling Scholarship, France, 1960. *Solo exhibitions:* Zwemmer, London, 1960; New Arts Centre, London, 1963; Queen's Sq. Gall., Leeds, 1964; Trafford Gall., London, 1967; Bradford New Liby, 1972; Middlesbrough and Billingham, 1977; Open Univ., Darlington and Harrogate Art Galls, 1979; Harrogate Northern Artists, 1980; Manchester City Art Gall., 1987; Wakefield City Art Gall., 1988; Cartwright Hall, Bradford, 1989; Boundary Gall., London, 1989, 1995, 1998, 2000; Univ. of Birmingham, 1994; retrospective, Shrines of Life, toured 1982–83, Sheffield (Mappin), Hull (Ferens), Bradford (Cartwright), Leicester Poly., Milton Keynes (Exhibn Gall); retrospective, Dean Clough Gall., Halifax, 1996; Shire Hall, Stafford, 1999; RWA, 2000; Carlow Arts Fest., Ireland, 2001; *mixed exhibitions:* Arts Council of GB Touring Exhibns (Fragments against Ruin, The Subjective Eye); Tolly Cobbold National Exhibns; Moira Kelly Fine Art; Hayward Annual; Soho, New York (8 in the 80s); Fruitmarket Gall., Edinburgh; London Gp; RCA (Exhibition Road, to celebrate 150 years of RCA), 1988; Smith Gall., London, 1988, 1989; Faces of Britain, China (British Council Touring Exhibn), 1989–90; Glasgow Royal Inst. of Fine Art, 1990; Galerie zur alten deutschen Schule, Thun, Switzerland, 1990; Royal Academy (The Infernal Method, etchings by Academicians), 1991; John Moores, Liverpool, 1991; Bonnington Gall., Nottingham Trent Univ. (Representing Lives), 1997; RWS annual (featured artist), 2001. Works in public collections: Arts Council of GB; Graves Art Gall.,

Sheffield; Huddersfield, Bolton, Carlisle, Belfast, Middlesbrough, Bradford, Dewsbury, Rochdale, Wakefield, and Harrogate Art Galls; Imperial War Mus.; Min. of Educn; Min. of Works; Leeds Univ.; Open Univ.; Cranfield Inst. of Technol.; RCA; St Peter's Coll., Oxford; Nuffield Foundn; Augustine (commissioned), presented by Archbishop of Canterbury to Pope John Paul II, Vatican Collection, Rome, 1989; private collections in UK, Germany, Australia, USA. BBC TV, Monitor, 1960, John Schlesinger's doc. "Private View". Visual records of preparations for Exercise Lionheart, BAOR, 1984 (Imperial War Mus. commn). Rowney Prize, Royal Acad., 1984; Gainsborough House Drawing Prize, Eastern Arts, 1984; Lorne Scholarship, Slade Sch. of Fine Art, 1986; Lady Evershed Drawing Prize, Eastern Arts Open, 1990. *Address:* c/o Royal Academy of Arts, Burlington House, Piccadilly, W1V 0DS. *T:* (020) 7300 5680; *e-mail:* art@sonialawson.co.uk. *Club:* Royal Over-Seas League.

LAWSON JOHNSTON, family name of **Baron Luke**.

LAWSON JOHNSTON, Hon. Hugh de Beauchamp, TD 1951; DL; *b* 7 April 1914; *yr s* of 1st Baron Luke, KBE and Hon. Edith Laura (*d* 1941), *d* of 16th Baron St John of Bletsoe; *m* 1946, Audrey Warren, *d* of late Colonel F. Warren Pearl and late Mrs A. L. Pearl; three *d*. *Educ:* Eton; Chillon Coll.; Corpus Christi, Cambridge. BA 1934, MA (Cantab), 1938. With Bovril Ltd, 1935–71, finally as Chm. Territorial Service with 5th Bn Beds and Herts Regt, 1935–; Captain, 1939, and throughout War. Chm., Tribune Investment Trust Ltd, 1951–86; Chm., Pitman Ltd, 1973–81. Chm. of Cttees, United Soc. for Christian Literature, 1949–82. High Sheriff of Bedfordshire, 1961–62; DL Beds, 1964. *Recreations:* walking, gardening, photography. *Address:* Woodleys Farm House, Melchbourne, Bedfordshire MK44 1AG. *T:* (01234) 708282.

LAWSON-ROGERS, (George) Stuart; QC 1994; a Recorder, since 1990; *b* 23 March 1946; *s* of late George Henry Roland Rogers, CBE, sometime MP and Mary Lawson; *m* 1969, Rosalind Denise Leach; one *s* one *d*. *Educ:* LSE (LLB Hons). Called to the Bar, Gray's Inn, 1969; Asst Recorder, 1987–89. Asst Comr, Parly and Local Govt Boundary Commns, 1981, 1983; Chm., Structure Plan Exams in Public, DoE, 1984; Legal Assessor, GMC and GDC, 1988–; Standing Counsel (Crime, SE Circuit) to HM Customs and Excise, 1989–94; DTI Inspector, Insider Dealing, 1989; Dept of Transport Inspector, Merchant Shipping Act 1988, 1989–90. Dir, Watford AFC Ltd, 1990–96. *Recreations:* theatre, music, opera, reading, gardening. *Address:* 23 Essex Street, WC2R 3AS. *T:* (020) 7413 0353, (020) 7836 8366, *Fax:* (020) 7413 0374; *e-mail:* clerks@essexstreet23.demon.co.uk. *Club:* Athenæum.

LAWSON-TANCRED, Sir Henry, 10th Bt *cr* 1662; JP; *b* 12 Feb. 1924; *e surv. s* of Major Sir Thomas Lawson-Tancred, 9th Bt, and Margery Elinor (*d* 1961), *d* of late A. S. Lawson, Aldborough Manor; *S* father, 1945; *m* 1st, 1950, Jean Veronica (*d* 1970), 4th and *y d* of late G. R. Foster, Stockeld Park, Wetherby, Yorks; five *s* one *d*; 2nd, 1978, Mrs Susan Drummond, *d* of Sir Kenelm Cayley, 10th Bt. *Educ:* Stowe; Jesus Coll., Cambridge. Served as Pilot in RAFVR, 1942–46. JP West Riding, 1967. *Heir:* s Andrew Peter Lawson-Tancred, *b* 18 Feb. 1952. *Address:* 17 Hungate, Brompton-by-Sawdon, Scarborough, Yorks YO13 9DW. *T:* (01723) 859419.

LAWTHER, Prof. Patrick Joseph, CBE 1978; DSc; FRCP; Professor of Environmental and Preventive Medicine, University of London, at St Bartholomew's Hospital Medical College, 1968–81, also at London Hospital Medical College, 1976–81, now Professor Emeritus; Member, Medical Research Council Scientific Staff, 1955–81; *b* 9 March 1921; *s* of Joseph and Winefride Lawther; *m* 1944, Kathleen May Wilkowski, MB BS (*d* 1998); two *s* one *d*. *Educ:* Carlisle and Morecambe Grammar Schs; King's Coll., London; St Bartholomew's Hosp. Med. Coll. MB BS 1950; DSc London 1971. FRCP 1963 (MRCP 1954); FFOM 1981 (MFOM 1980). St Bartholomew's Hospital: Ho. Phys., Med. Professorial Unit, 1950; Cooper & Coventson Res. Schol., 1951–53; Associate Chief Asst, 1952–62; Hon. Cons. and Phys.-in-Charge, Dept of Envir. and Prev. Med., 1962–81; Consulting Physician, 1981–. Director, MRC Air Pollution Unit (later Envir. Hazards Unit), 1955–77; Head of Clinical Sect., MRC Toxicology Unit, 1977–81. Cons. Expert, WHO, 1960–; Civilian Cons. in Envir. Medicine, RN, 1975–90, now Emeritus. Chairman: DHSS Cttee on Med. Aspects of Contamination of Air and Soil, 1973–83; DHSS Working Party on Lead and Health, 1978–80; Environmental Dirs Gp, MRC, 1981–85; Cttee on Environmental and Occupational Health, MRC, 1985–89; Assessor, Inquiry on Lorries, People and Environment, (Armitage Inquiry), 1979–80. Pres., Nat. Soc. for Clean Air, 1975–77. Sir Arthur Thomson Vis. Prof., Univ. of Birmingham, 1975–76; RCP Marc Daniels Lectr, 1970; Harben Lectr, RIPH&H, 1970; Guymer Meml Lectr, St Thomas' Hosp., 1979. RSA Silver Medal, 1964; Acad. Nat. de Médecine Bronze Medal, 1972; RCP Bissett Hawkins Medal, 1974; RSM Edwin Stevens Gold Medal, 1975. *Publications:* various papers and chapters in books relating to environmental and occupational medicine. *Recreations:* almost everything. *Address:* 13 The Ridge, Purley, Surrey CR8 3PF. *T:* (020) 8660 6398. *Club:* Surrey CC.

LAWTON, Prof. Denis; Academic Secretary, Universities Council for the Education of Teachers, since 2000; *b* 5 April 1931; *s* of William Benedict Lawton and Ruby (*née* Evans); *m* 1953, Joan Weston; two *s*. *Educ:* St Ignatius Coll.; Univ. of London Goldsmiths' Coll. (BA); Univ. of London Inst. of Education (PhD). Asst Master, Erith Grammar Sch., 1958–61; Head of English/Housemaster, Bacon's Sch., SE1, 1961–63; University of London Institute of Education: Research Officer, 1963–64; Lectr in Sociology, 1964–67; Sen. Lectr in Curriculum Studies, 1967–72; Reader in Education, 1972–74; Professor of Education, 1974; Dep. Dir, 1978–83; Dir, 1983–89. Chairman: Univ. of London Sch. Exams Bd, subseq. Sch. Exams and Assessment Council, 1984–96; Consortium for Assessment and Testing in Schools, 1989–91; Jt Council for GCSE, 1996–99. Hon. Fellow, College of Preceptors, 1983. *Publications:* Social Class, Language and Education, 1968; Social Change, Education Theory and Curriculum Planning, 1973; Class, Culture and the Curriculum, 1975; Social Justice and Education, 1977; The Politics of the School Curriculum, 1980; An Introduction to Teaching and Learning, 1981; Curriculum Studies and Educational Planning, 1983; (with P. Gordon) HMI, 1987; Education, Culture and the National Curriculum, 1989; Education and Politics in the 1990s, 1992; The Tory Mind on Education, 1994; Beyond the National Curriculum, 1996; Royal Eduction Past, Present and Future, 1999. *Recreations:* walking German Shepherd dogs, photographing bench-ends, sampling real ale, music. *Address:* Laun House, Laundry Lane, Nazeing, Essex EN9 2DY.

LAWTON, Harold Walter, MA; Docteur de l'Université de Paris; Officier d'Académie; Emeritus Professor, University of Sheffield, since 1964; *b* Stoke-on-Trent, 27 July 1899; *y s* of late William T. C. and Alice Lawton; *m* 1933, Bessie (*d* 1991), *y d* of T. C. Pate; one *d* (and two *s* decd). *Educ:* Middle Sch., Newcastle under Lyme; Rhyl Grammar Sch.; Universities of Wales and Paris. BA Hons (Wales) 1921; MA (Wales) 1923; Fellow University of Wales, 1923–26; Docteur de l'Univ. de Paris, 1926. University College, Southampton: Lecturer in French, 1926–37; Professor of French, 1937–50; Dean of Faculty of Arts, 1945–49; first Warden of New, later Connaught, Hall, 1930–33; University of Sheffield: Professor of French, 1950–64; Warden of Ranmoor House, 1957–63; Deputy Pro-Vice-Chancellor, 1958–61; Pro-Vice-Chancellor, 1961–64. Transcriber, the Gladstone Diaries, 1933–36. Médaille d'Argent de la Reconnaissance Française, 1946; Officier d'Académie, 1948. Chevalier, Légion d'Honneur (France), 1999. *Publications:* Térence en France au XVIe Siècle: éditions et traductions (Paris), 1926; repr. 1970; Handbook of French Renaissance Dramatic Theory, 1950, repr. 1972; J. du Bellay, Poems, selected with introduction and notes, 1961; Térence en France au XVIe Siècle: imitation et influence, 1972; articles and reviews to British and French periodicals. *Address:* Oak House, Pond Lane, Greetham, Rutland LE15 7NW.

LAWTON, Prof. John Hartley, CBE 1997; FRS 1989; Chief Executive, Natural Environment Research Council, since 1999; *b* 24 Sept. 1943; *s* of Frank Hartley Lawton and Mary Lawton; *m* 1966, Dorothy (*née* Grimshaw); one *s* one *d*. *Educ:* Balshaw's Grammar Sch., Leyland, Lancs; University Coll. and Dept of Zoology, Univ. of Durham (BSc, PhD). Res. Student, Univ. of Durham, 1965–68; Deptl Demonstrator in Animal Ecology, Oxford Univ., 1968–71; College Lectr in Zoology, St Anne's and Lincoln Colls, Oxford, 1970–71; University of York: Lectr, 1971–78; Sen. Lectr, 1978–82; Reader, 1982–85; Personal Chair, 1985–89; Dir, NERC Centre for Population Biology, ICSTM, 1989–99. Member: Royal Commn on Envmtl Pollution, 1989–96; NERC, 1995–99. Hon. Vis. Res. Fellow, Nat. Hist. Mus., 1990–; Adjunct Scientist, Inst. of Ecosystem Studies, NY Botanic Garden, 1991–2000. Vice-President: RSPB, 1999– (Chm. Council, 1993–98); British Trust for Ornithology, 1999–. Hon. DSc Lancaster, 1993. *Publications:* Insects on Plants: community patterns and mechanisms (with D. R. Strong and T. R. E. Southwood), 1984; (ed jtly) The Evolutionary Interactions of Animals and Plants, 1991; (ed jtly) Extinction Rates, 1996; (ed jtly) Linking Species and Ecosystems, 1996; Community Ecology in a Changing World, 2000; over 300 sci. papers in specialist jls. *Recreations:* bird watching, natural history photography, travel, gardening, walking. *Address:* 18 Gartons Road, Middleleaze, Swindon SN5 5TR.

LAXTON, Robert; MP (Lab) Derby North, since 1997; *b* 7 Sept. 1944; *s* of Alan and Elsie Laxton; *m* (marr. diss.); one *s*. *Educ:* Woodlands Secondary Sch.; Derby Coll. of Art and Technology. Branch Officer, CWU, 1974–97; Telecommunications Engr, BT plc, 1961–97. Mem., Derby CC, 1979–97 (Leader, 1986–88, 1994–97). Mem., Trade and Industry Select Cttee, 1997–. Vice Chairman: Trade Union Gp of Lab. MPs; PLP DTI Deptl Cttee. Chm., E Midlands Local Govt Assoc., 1995–97; Vice Pres., LGA. *Address:* House of Commons, SW1A 0AA.

LAY, Richard Neville, CBE 2001; Chairman: DTZ (formerly Debenham Tewson & Chinnocks) Holdings plc, 1987–2000; DTZ Debenham Tie Leung, 1999–2000; President, Royal Institution of Chartered Surveyors, 1998–99; *b* 18 Oct. 1938; *s* of late Edward John Lay and Nellie Lay; *m* 1st, 1964; one *s* one *d*; 2nd, 1991. *Educ:* Whitgift School. FRICS. Partner, Debenham Tewson & Chinnocks, 1965–87. Vice Chm., 1992–2001, Chm., 2001–, Central London Board, Royal and Sun Alliance (formerly Sun Alliance and London) Insurance Group. Chairman: cttee advising RICS on market requirements of the profession, 1991; Commercial Property Panel, RICS, 1992–95; Member: Council, British Property Fedn, 1992–99; General Council, RICS, 1994–2000; Bank of England Property Forum, 1994–99; Mem., Adv. Panel on Standards in Planning Inspectorate, 1983–2000. Dir and Trustee, Portman Estate, 1999–. Trustee, Tate Gall. Foundn, 1989–94. Renter Warden, Armourers' and Brasiers' Co., 2001–July 2002 (Surveyor, 1983–98; Mem., Ct of Assts, 1998–). Governor, Belmont Sch., Surrey, 1983–88; Mem. Bd, Coll. of Estate Mgt, 2000–. Property Person of the Year, Property Week, 1999. *Recreations:* gardening, walking. *Address:* One Curzon Street, W1A 5PZ. *T:* (020) 7643 6040. *Club:* Royal Automobile.

LAYARD, Baron *cr* 2000 (Life Peer), of Highgate in the London Borough of Haringey; **Peter Richard Grenville Layard;** Director, Centre for Economic Performance, London School of Economics, since 1990 (Professor of Economics, 1980–99, now Emeritus); *b* 15 March 1934; *s* of Dr John Layard and Doris Layard; *m* 1991, Molly Meacher. *Educ:* Eton Coll.; King's Coll., Cambridge (BA); London School of Economics (MScEcon). History Master: Woodberry Down Sch., 1959–60; Forest Hill Sch., 1960–61; Senior Research Officer, Robbins Cttee on Higher Educn, 1961–63; London School of Economics: Dep. Director, Higher Educn Research Unit, 1964–74 (part-time from 1968); Lectr in Economics, 1968–75; Reader in the Economics of Labour, 1975–80; Hd, Centre for Labour Econs, 1974–90. Chm., Employment Inst., 1987–92. Mem., UGC, 1985–89. Econ. Consultant to Russian Govt, 1991–97; Consultant, DfEE, 1997–. *Publications:* (jtly) The Causes of Graduate Unemployment in India, 1969; (jtly) The Impact of Robbins: Expansion in Higher Education, 1969; (jtly) Qualified Manpower and Economic Performance: An Inter-Plant Study in the Electrical Engineering Industry, 1971; (ed) Cost-Benefit Analysis, 1973, 2nd edn 1994; (jtly) Microeconomic Theory, 1978; (jtly) The Causes of Poverty, 1978; More Jobs, Less Inflation, 1982; How to Beat Unemployment, 1986; (jtly) Handbook of Labour Economics, 1986; (jtly) The Performance of the British Economy, 1988; (jtly) Unemployment: Macroeconomic Performance and the Labour Market, 1991; (jtly) Reform in Eastern Europe, 1991; (jtly) East-West Migration: the alternatives, 1992; (jtly) Post-Communist Reform: pain and progress, 1993; Macroeconomics: a text for Russia, 1994; (jtly) The Coming Russian Boom, 1996; What Labour Can Do, 1997; Tackling Unemployment, 1999; Tackling Inequality, 1999. *Recreations:* walking, tennis, the clarinet. *Address:* 45 Cholmeley Park, N6 5EL. *T:* (020) 7955 7281.

LAYARD, Adm. Sir Michael (Henry Gordon), KCB 1993; CBE 1982; Second Sea Lord, and Chief of Naval Personnel (Member of Admiralty Board, Defence Council), 1993–95; Commander-in-Chief Naval Home Command, 1994–95; Flag Aide-de-Camp to the Queen, 1994–95; *b* Sri Lanka, 3 Jan. 1936; *s* of late Edwin Henry Frederick and Doris Christian Gordon (*née* Spence); *m* 1966, Elspeth Horsley Fisher; two *s*. *Educ:* Pangbourne Coll.; RN Coll., Dartmouth. Joined RN, 1954; specialised in aviation, 1958; Fighter Pilot, 1960–72; Air Warfare Instructor, 1964; Commanded: 899 Naval Air Sqn, in HMS Eagle, 1970–71; HMS Lincoln, 1971–72; ndc, 1974–75; Directorate, Naval Air Warfare, MoD, 1975–77; Comdr (Air), HMS Ark Royal, 1977–78; CSO (Air), FONAC, 1979–82; Sen. Naval Officer, SS Atlantic Conveyor, Falklands conflict, 1982 (CBE); Commanded: RNAS Culdrose, 1982–84; HMS Cardiff, 1984–85; Task Gp Comdr, Persian Gulf, 1984; Dep. Dir, Naval Warfare (Air), MoD, 1985–88; Flag Officer Naval Aviation (formerly Air Comd), 1988–90; Dir Gen., Naval Manpower and Trng, 1990–92; Leader of RN Officers Study Gp, MoD, 1992–93; Adm. Pres., RNC, Greenwich, 1993–94. Gentleman Usher to the Sword of State, 1997–. Non-exec. Dir, Taunton & Somerset NHS Trust, 1996–2000. Trustee, FAA Mus., 1995–. Mem., FAA Officers' Assoc., 1964–; Member Council: White Ensign Assoc., 1996– (Chm., 1996–99); Royal Patriotic Fund, 1995–. Governor: Pangbourne Coll., 1995–; King's Coll., Taunton, 1997–; King's Hall, Taunton, 1997–. Chevalier Bretvin, 1984. Freeman, City of London, 1994. *Recreations:* painting, sailing, music, history, collecting experiences. *Address:* Harwood House, Aller, Somerset TA10 0QN. *Clubs:* Royal Navy of 1765 and 1785; Royal Naval Sailing Association; Royal Navy Golfing Society (Pres, 1988–94).

LAYCRAFT, Hon. James Herbert; Chief Justice of Alberta, 1985–92; *b* 5 Jan. 1924; *s* of George Edward Laycraft and Hattie Cogswell Laycraft; *m* 1948, Helen Elizabeth

Bradley; one *s* one *d*. *Educ:* University of Alberta (BA, LLB 1951). Admitted to Bar, 1952; law practice, 1952–75; Trial Div. Judge, Supreme Court of Alberta, 1975; Judge, Court of Appeal, Alberta, 1979–85. Hon. LLD Calgary, 1986. *Publications:* articles in Canadian Bar Review and Alberta Law Review. *Recreations:* outdoor activities. *Address:* 200 Lincoln Way SW, Apt 419, Calgary, AB T3E 7G7, Canada. *Club:* Ranchman's (Calgary).

LAYDEN, Anthony Michael; HM Diplomatic Service; Ambassador to Morocco and (non-resident) to Mauritania, since 1999; *b* 27 July 1946; *s* of Sheriff Michael Layden, SSC, TD and Eileen Mary Layden; *m* 1969, Josephine Mary McGhee; three *s* one *d*. *Educ:* Holy Cross Academy, Edinburgh; Edinburgh Univ. (LLB Hons Law and Econ. 1968). Lieut, 15th (Scottish Volunteer) Bn, Parachute Regt, 1966–69. Foreign Office, 1968; MECAS, Lebanon, 1969; Jedda, 1971; Rome, 1973; FCO, Middle East, Rhodesia, Personnel Ops Depts, 1977–82; Head of Chancery, Jedda, 1982–85; Hong Kong Dept, FCO, 1985–87; Counsellor and Head of Chancery, Muscat, 1987–91; Counsellor (Economic and Commercial), 1991–95, and Dep. Hd of Mission, 1994–95, Copenhagen; Head of Western European Dept, FCO, 1995–98. *Recreations:* sailing, walking, music, bridge. *Address:* c/o Foreign and Commonwealth Office, SW1A 2AH. *Club:* Travellers.

See also P. J. Layden.

LAYDEN, Patrick John, TD 1981; QC (Scot.) 2000; Legal Secretary to the Lord Advocate, since 1999; *b* 27 June 1949; *s* of Sheriff Michael Layden, SSC, TD and Eileen Mary Layden; *m* 1984, Patricia Mary Bonnar; three *s* one *d*. *Educ:* Holy Cross Acad., Edinburgh; Edinburgh Univ. (LLB Hons). Called to the Scottish Bar, 1973; Lord Advocate's Department: Dep. Scottish Parly Counsel and Asst Legal Sec., 1977–87; Scottish Parly Counsel and Sen. Asst Legal Sec., 1987–99. Univ. of Edinburgh OTC, 1967–71; 2/52 Lowland Vol., TA, 1971–77; 1/51 Highland Vol., 1977–81 (OC London Scottish, 1978–81); OC 73 Ord. Co. (V), 1981–84. *Recreations:* reading, walking. *Address:* Legal Secretariat to the Lord Advocate, 25 Chambers Street, Edinburgh EH1 1LA.

See also A. M. Layden.

LAYMAN, Rear-Adm. Christopher Hope, CB 1991; DSO 1982; LVO 1977; Consultant in Communications and Information Systems and Maritime Affairs, since 1991; *b* 9 March 1938; *s* of late Captain H. F. H. Layman, DSO, RN and Elizabeth Hughes; *m* 1964, Katharine Romer Ascherson; one *s* one *d*. *Educ:* Winchester. Joined Royal Navy, 1956; specialised Communications and Electronic Warfare, 1966; commanded HM Ships: Hubberston, 1968–70; Lynx, 1972–74; Exec. Officer, HM Yacht Britannia, 1976–78; Captain, 7th Frigate Sqn, 1981–83; commanded HM Ships: Argonaut, 1981–82; Cleopatra, 1982–83; Invincible, 1984–86; Commander, British Forces Falkland Islands, 1986–87; Asst Dir (Communications and Information Systems), IMS, NATO HQ, Brussels, 1988–91, retd. Gentleman Usher of the Green Rod, Order of the Thistle, 1997–. *Publications:* Man of Letters, 1990; The Falklands and the Dwarf, 1995. *Recreations:* fishing, archaeology. *Club:* New (Edinburgh).

LAYTON, family name of **Baron Layton**.

LAYTON, 3rd Baron *cr* 1947, of Danehill; **Geoffrey Michael Layton;** Director: Imperial Aviation Group, since 1992; Historical Aviation Group, since 1992; Wellington International Ltd, since 1992; Historical Aviation Mail Order Ltd, since 1996; *b* 18 July 1947; *s* of 2nd Baron Layton and Dorothy Rose (*d* 1994), *d* of Albert Luther Cross; *S* father, 1989; *m* 1st, 1969, Viviane Cracco (marr. diss. 1971); 2nd, 1989, Caroline Jane Soulis. *Educ:* St Paul's School; Stanford Univ., California; Univ. of Southern California. Director: The Toxbox Co. Ltd, 1986–93; Westminster and Whitehall Environmental Consultants Ltd, 1990–92. Trustee, Historical Aviation Foundn, 1995–. *Recreation:* riding. *Heir: uncle* Hon. David Layton, MBE [*b* 5 July 1914; *m* 1st, 1939, Elizabeth (marr. diss. 1972; she *d* 2000), *d* of Robert Gray; two *s* one *d*; 2nd, 1972, Joy Parkinson].

See also Hon. C. W. Layton.

LAYTON, Alexander William; QC 1995; barrister; a Recorder, since 2000; *b* 23 Feb. 1952; *s* of Paul Henry Layton and Frances Evelyn Layton (*née* Weekes); *m* 1988, Sandy Forshaw (*née* Matheson); two *d*. *Educ:* Marlborough Coll.; Brasenose Coll., Oxford (MA); Ludwig-Maximillian Univ., Munich. Called to the Bar, Middle Temple, 1976 (Astbury Law Scholar); Asst Recorder, 1998–2000. Chm., British-German Jurists Assoc., 1988–93. FCIArb 2000. *Publications:* (contrib.) The Bar on Trial, 1977; (jtly) European Civil Practice, 1989; (contrib.) Practitioners' Handbook of EC Law, 1998. *Recreation:* family. *Address:* 20 Essex Street, WC2R 3AL. *T:* (020) 7842 1200, *Fax:* (020) 7583 1341; *e-mail:* alayton@20essexst.com.

LAYTON, Hon. Christopher Walter; Founder Member, Grimstone Community, since 1990; *b* 31 Dec. 1929; *s* of 1st Baron Layton; *m* 1st, 1952, Anneliese Margaret, *d* of Joachim von Thadden, Hanover (marr. diss. 1957); one *s* one *d*; 2nd, 1961, Margaret Ann, *d* of Leslie Moon, Molesey, Surrey (marr. diss. 1995); two *d* (and one *d* decd); 3rd, 1995, Wendy Daniels, *d* of Kenneth Bartlett, Hemel Hempstead; one *d*. *Educ:* Oundle; King's Coll., Cambridge. Intelligence Corps, 1948–49; ICI Ltd, 1952; The Economist Intelligence Unit, 1953–54; Editorial writer, European affairs, The Economist, 1954–62; Economic Adviser to Liberal Party, 1962–69; Dir, Centre for European Industrial Studies, Bath Univ., 1968–71; Commission of European Communities: Chef de Cabinet to Commissioner Spinelli, 1971–73; Dir, Computer Electronics, Telecomms and Air Transp. Equipment Manufg, Directorate-Gen. of Internal Market and Industrial Affairs, 1973–81, now Hon. Dir-Gen.; Editor, Alliance, 1982–83, Associate Editor, New Democrat, 1983–85. Dir, World Order Project, Federal Trust, 1987–90. Contested: (L) Chippenham, Nov. 1962, 1964, 1966; (SDP) London W, European Parly Elecn, 1984. *Publications:* Transatlantic Investment, 1966; European Advanced Technology, 1968; Cross-frontier Mergers in Europe 1970; (jtly) Industry and Europe, 1971; (jtly) Ten Innovations: International Study on Development Technology and the Use of Qualified Scientists and Engineers in Ten Industries, 1972; Europe and the Global Crisis, 1987; A Step Beyond Fear, 1989; The Healing of Europe, 1990. *Recreations:* painting, sculpture, healing. *Address:* Grimstone Manor, Jordan Lane, Horrabridge, near Yelverton, Devon PL20 7QY.

LAYTON, Stephen David, FRCO; conductor; Director of Music and Organist, Temple Church, London, since 1997; *b* 23 Dec. 1966; *s* of David Layton and Hazel Layton (*née* Bestwick). *Educ:* Pilgrim's Sch., Winchester; Eton Coll. (Music Schol.); King's Coll., Cambridge (A. H. Mann Organ Schol.; BA 1988; MA 1991). FRCO 1985. Asst Organist, Southwark Cathedral, 1988–97; Founder and Music Dir, Polyphony, 1986–; Music Dir, Holst Singers, 1993–; Dep. Chorusmaster, Philharmonia Chorus, 1993–97. Conductor, BBC Promenade Concerts and Aldeburgh Fest., 1995–2001; Guest Conductor, BBC Singers, 1997–; Chief Guest Conductor, Danish Nat. Radio Choir, 1999–; Chief Conductor, Netherlands Kammerchor, 2001 (Guest Conductor, 1998–2001); début, ENO, 2000; *tours* as conductor include: USA, 1989, 1994, 1996; Bournemouth Sinfonietta, Brazil, 1995; Estonian Choirs, Estonia, 1993, 1995; Danish Nat. Radio Choir, Denmark, 1996; Polyphony, Italy, 1996; Istanbul SO, 2000; Australian Chamber Orch., 2000; Irish Chamber Orch., 2000. Recordings incl. premières of Grainger, Britten, Holst, Gretchaninov and Rutter. *Recreations:* food, cyberspace, kite flying, gadgets. *Address:* 13 King's Bench Walk, Temple, EC4Y 7EN.

LAZARE, Philippe Henri; Chief Executive Officer, Eurotunnel, since 2001 (Managing Director, 2000–01); *b* Neuilly-sur-Seine, 30 Oct. 1956; *s* of Robert Lazare and Suzanne (*née* Legallo); *m* 1995, Sophie Muth; two *s*, and two *s* from previous marriage. *Educ:* Lycée Marcel Roby, Saint-Germain-en-Laye; École Supérieure d'architecture, Paris-la-Défense (Architect Govt Dip.). Industrial buyer, 1983–87; Project Manager for 605 Peugeot, 1987–89; Peugeot Planning Manager, Soc. Gén. d'achats PSA gp, 1989–90; Groupe Sextant Avionique: Industrial sub-contracting Manager, 1990–91; Site Industrial Manager, 1991–93; Site Dir at Chatellerault, 1993–94; Manager, Peat Marwick Consultants, 1994–95; Air France: Dir, Maintenance Result Centre, 1995–96; Man. Dir, Industries Profit Centre, and Dep. Manager i/c industrial logistics, 1996; Chm., Servair Gp and Cie de réparation de moteurs d'avion (CRMA), 1997–98; Man. Dir, Lucien Barrière Gp, 1998–2000. *Recreations:* sports: Rugby, show jumping. *Address:* Eurotunnel, UK Terminal, PO Box 2000, Folkestone, Kent CT18 8XY; (home) King's Cross House, High Street, Eastry, Kent CT13 0HF; *email:* philippe.lazare@eurotunnel.com.

LAZAREV, Alexander Nikolaevich; Principal Conductor, Royal Scottish National Orchestra, since 1997; *b* 5 July 1945; *m* Tamara Lazareva; one *d*. *Educ:* St Petersburg Conservatory; Moscow Conservatory. Bolshoi Theatre: Founder, Ensemble of Soloists, 1978; Chief Conductor and Artistic Dir, 1987–95; UK début with Liverpool Philharmonic Orch., 1987; Principal Guest Conductor: BBC SO, 1992–95; Royal Scottish Nat. Orch., 1994–97. 1st Prize and Gold Medal, Karajan Comp., Berlin, 1972; People's Artist of Russia, 1982; Glinka Prize, 1986. *Address:* c/o Tennant Artists, Unit 2, 39 Tadema Road, SW10 0PZ.

LAZARIDIS, Stefanos; freelance opera, ballet and theatre designer and director in UK and abroad, since 1967; *b* Ethiopia, 28 July 1942; *s* of Nicholas Lazaridis and Alexandra Cardovillis. *Educ:* Greek Sch., Addis Ababa; Ecole Internationale, Geneva; Byam Shaw Sch. of Art; Central Sch. of Speech and Drama. Professional début, Eccentricities of a Nightingale, Yvonne Arnaud Theatre, Guildford, 1967; *ballet:* El Amor Brujo, 1969, Knight Errant, 1975, Royal Ballet, Covent Garden; *theatre:* London (Almeida, Barbican and West End), Stratford-upon-Avon, Chichester Fest., Oxford, Guildford, Watford, Milan, Bologna, Paris, Athens, 1967–95; *opera:* prodns for ENO incl. Doctor Faust, The Mikado (SWET Award, for Doctor Faust and The Mikado, 1986), Hansel and Gretel, and Lady Macbeth of Mtsensk (Laurence Olivier Award); directed and designed: Oedipus Rex, Opera North; Duke Bluebeard's Castle, Oedipus Rex, Maria Stuarda, Scottish Opera; Orphée et Eurydice, Australian Opera, 1994; The Ark of Life, by Dimitriadis, world première, Athens, 1995; *arena prodn:* Carmen, Earl's Court, 1988, also internat. tour; *rock show:* Duran Duran, US tour, 1993; designs for opera houses of Paris, Berlin, Frankfurt, Munich, Stuttgart, Brussels, Zurich, La Scala Milan, Florence, Bologna, Venice, Tel Aviv, Amsterdam, Moscow, St Petersburg, Tokyo, Vancouver, Sydney, Melbourne, Houston, Los Angeles and San Francisco; also Bregenz, Rossini, and Bayreuth Festivals. Laurence Olivier and Evening Standard Awards for Most Outstanding Achievement in Opera, 1987; German Critics' Award, Designer of the Year, 1998; Diploma of Honour, Internat. Exhibn of Stage Design, Prague Quadrennial, 1999; Martinu Foundn Medal, for outstanding services to Martinu's operas, 2000. *Recreations:* reading, travel. *Address:* c/o English National Opera, London Coliseum, St Martin's Lane, WC2N 4ES. *T:* (020) 7836 0111.

LAZAROWICZ, Marek Jerzy, (Mark); MP (Lab) Edinburgh North and Leith, since 2001; *b* 8 Aug. 1953. *Educ:* Univ. of St Andrews (MA); Univ. of Edinburgh (LLB; Dip. Legal Practice). Member (Lab): City of Edinburgh DC, 1980–96; City of Edinburgh Council, 1999–2001. *Publications:* (jtly) The Scottish Parliament: an introduction, 1999, 2nd edn 2000; various articles and papers on legal and political matters. *Address:* c/o House of Commons, SW1A 0AA; (constituency office) 274 Leith Walk, Edinburgh EH6 5EL. *T:* (0131) 555 0598.

LAZENBY, Prof. Alec, AO 1988; FTSE, FIBiol, FAIAST; Principal Consultant, International Development Program of Australian Universities (consultant on agricultural research and development and higher education), since 1991; *b* 4 March 1927; *s* of G. and E. Lazenby; *m* 1957, Ann Jennifer, *d* of R. A. Hayward; one *s* two *d*. *Educ:* Wath on Dearne Grammar Sch.; University Coll. of Wales, Aberystwyth. BSc 1949, MSc 1952, Wales; MA 1954, PhD 1959, ScD 1985, Cantab. Scientific Officer, Welsh Plant Breeding Station, 1949–53; Demonstr in Agricultural Botany, 1953–58, Lectr in Agricultural Botany, 1958–65, Univ. of Cambridge; Fellow and Asst Tutor, Fitzwilliam Coll., Cambridge, 1962–65; Foundation Prof. of Agronomy, Univ. of New England, NSW, 1965–70, now Professor Emeritus; Vice-Chancellor, Univ. of New England, Armidale, NSW, 1970–77; Dir, Grassland Res. Inst., 1977–82; Vice-Chancellor, Univ. of Tasmania, 1982–91. Vis. Prof., Reading Univ., 1978; Hon. Professorial Fellow, Univ. of Wales, 1979; Hon. Prof., Victoria Univ. of Technol., 1992–97. Hon DRurSci New England, NSW, 1981; Hon. LLD Tasmania, 1992. *Publications:* (ed jtly) Intensive Pasture Production, 1972; (ed jtly) Australian Field Crops, vol. I, 1975, vol. II, 1979; Australia's Plant Breeding Needs, 1986; (ed jtly) The Grass Crop, 1988; (jtly) The Story of IDP, 1999; papers on: pasture plant breeding; agronomy; weed ecology, in various scientific jls. *Recreation:* golf. *Address:* International Development Program, GPO Box 2006, Canberra, ACT 2601, Australia.

LEA OF CRONDALL, Baron *cr* 1999 (Life Peer), of Crondall in the county of Hampshire; **David Edward Lea,** OBE 1978; Assistant General Secretary of the Trades Union Congress, 1977–99; *b* 2 Nov. 1937; *s* of Edward Cunliffe Lea and Lilian May Lea. *Educ:* Farnham Grammar Sch.; Christ's Coll., Cambridge (MA). Pres., CU Liberal Club, 1960; Nat. Pres., Union of Liberal Students, 1961; Inaugural Chair, Cambridge Univ. Students' Representative Council, 1961. Nat. Service, RHA, 1955–57. Economist Intelligence Unit, 1961; Economic Dept, TUC, 1964, Asst Sec., 1967, Sec. 1970. Jt Sec., TUC-Labour Party Liaison Cttee, 1972–86; Secretary: TUC Cttee on European Strategy, 1989–99; Envmt Action Gp, 1989–99; Task Force on Representation at Work, 1994–99; Chm., Econ. Cttee, 1980–91, Mem. Steering Cttee, 1991–99, Vice Pres., 1997–98, ETUC; Member: Royal Commn on the Distribution of Income and Wealth, 1974–79; Adv. Gp on Channel Tunnel and Cross-Channel Services, 1974–75; Cttee of Inquiry on Industrial Democracy, 1975–77; Energy Commn, 1977–79; Retail Prices Index Adv. Cttee, 1977–99; Delors Cttee on Economic and Social Concepts in the Community, 1977–79; NEDC Cttee on Finance for Investment, 1978–92; Kreisky Commn on Unemployment in Europe, 1986–89; Franco-British Council, 1982–99; EU Steering Cttee on Social Dialogue, 1992–99; Sub Cttee A, EU Cttee, H of L, 1999–; Central Arbitration Cttee, 2000–; UK Round Table on Sustainable Develt, 1995–99; Chm., Round Table Gp on Greening Business, 1997–98; Expert Adviser, UN Commn on Transnational Corporations, 1977–81; Hon. Mem., UK Delegn, Earth Summit on Envmt and Develt, Rio, 1992. Governor, NIESR, 1981–; Trustee, Employment Policy Inst., 1992–99. Chm., Farnham Roads Action, 1986–; Mem. Cttee, Tilford Bach Soc., 1995–99; Patron, Third Age Trust, 1991–97. FRSA 1993. Mem. Editl Bd, New

Economy (IPPR review), 1993–2000. *Publications:* Trade Unionism, 1966; contrib. The Multinational Enterprise, 1971; Industrial Democracy (TUC), 1974; Keynes Plus: a participatory economy (ETUC), 1979. *Address:* South Court, Crondall, Hants GU10 5QF. *T:* (01252) 850711; 17 Ormonde Mansions, 106 Southampton Row, WC1B 4BP. *T:* (020) 7405 6237. *Club:* Bourne (Farnham).

LEA, Rev. His Honour Christopher Gerald, MC; Assistant Curate (non-stipendiary), parish of Stratfield Mortimer, since 1992; a Circuit Judge, 1972–90; *b* 27 Nov. 1917; *y s* of late George Percy Lea, Franche, Kidderminster, Worcs; *m* 1952, Susan Elizabeth Dorrien Smith, *d* of Major Edward Pendarves Dorrien Smith, Greatwood, Restronguet, Falmouth, Cornwall; two *s* one *d* (and one *d* decd). *Educ:* Charterhouse; RMC, Sandhurst; St Stephen's House, Oxford. Commissioned into XX The Lancashire Fusiliers, 1937, and served with Regt in UK until 1939. Served War of 1939–45 (despatches, MC): with Lancashire Fusiliers, No 2 Commando, 11th SAS Bn, and Parachute Regt in France, Italy and Malaya. Post-war service in Indonesia, Austria and UK; retired, 1948. Called to Bar, Inner Temple, 1948; Oxford Circuit. Mem. Nat. Assistance Bd Appeal Tribunal (Oxford Area), 1961–63; Mem. Mental Health Review Tribunal (Oxford Region), 1962–68, 1983–92. A Metropolitan Magistrate, 1968–72; Dep. Chm., Berks QS, 1968–71. Ordained deacon, 1992, priest, 1993. *Address:* Simms Farm House, Mortimer, Berks RG7 2JP. *T:* (0118) 933 2360. *Club:* English-Speaking Union.
See also J. A. Harvie.

LEA, Vice-Adm. Sir John (Stuart Crosbie), KBE 1979; retired; Director General, Naval Manpower and Training, 1977–80; *b* 4 June 1923; *m* 1947, Patricia Anne Thoseby; one *s* two *d*. *Educ:* Boxgrove Sch., Guildford; Shrewsbury Sch.; RNEC, Keyham. Entered RN, 1941; Cruisers Sheffield and Glasgow, 1943; RNEC, 1942–45; HMS Birmingham, 1945; entered Submarines, 1946; HMS/Ms Talent, Tireless, Aurochs, Explorer; Sen. Engr, HMS Forth (Depot Ship), 1952–53; on Staff, RNEC, 1954–57; psc 1958; Sqdn Engr Officer, 2nd Destroyer Sqdn and HMS Daring, 1959–61; Staff of CinC Portsmouth, 1961–62; Naval Staff in Ops Div., 1963–65; Engr Officer, HMS Centaur, 1966; Staff of Flag Officer Submarines; Dep. Supt, Clyde Submarine Base, 1967–68; idc 1969; Dir of Naval Admin. Planning, 1970–71; Cdre HMS Nelson, 1972–75; Asst Chief of Fleet Support, 1976–77. Comdr 1957; Captain 1966; Rear-Adm. 1976; Vice-Adm. 1978. Chm., 1980–86, Dir, 1986–88, GEC Marine & Industrial Gears Ltd. Chairman: Portsmouth Naval Heritage Trust, 1983–87; Regular Forces Employment Assoc., 1986–89; RN and RM Br. and Special Duties Officers Benevolent Fund, 1993–98. President: Hayling Island Horticultural Soc., 1994– (Chm., 1980–94); Hants Autistic Soc., 1988–95. Trustee: Hayling Island Community Centre, 1981–; Plumbers Museum and Workshop, Singleton, 1993–. Master, Worshipful Co. of Plumbers, 1988–89. *Recreations:* walking, woodwork, gardening. *Address:* Springfield, Brights Lane, Hayling Island, Hants PO11 0JX.

LEA, Ruth Jane; Head of Policy Unit, Institute of Directors, since 1995; *b* 22 Sept. 1947; *d* of Thomas Lea and Jane (*née* Brown). *Educ:* Lymm Grammar Sch.; York Univ. (BA); Bristol Univ. (MSc). FSS 1996. Asst Statistician, later Sen. Economic Assistant, HM Treasury, 1970–73; Lectr in Econs, Thames Poly., 1973–74; Statistician: CS Coll., 1974–77; HM Treasury, 1977–78; CSO, 1978–84; Statistician, 1984–87, Dep. Dir, Invest in Britain Bureau, 1987–88, DTI; Sen. Economist, 1988–90, Chief Economist, 1990–93, Mitsubishi Bank; Chief UK Economist, Lehman Bros, 1993–94; Econs Ed., ITN, 1994–95. Member: Retail Prices Adv. Cttee, 1992–94; NCC, 1993–96; Nurses' Pay Rev. Body, 1994–98; Bd, ESRC Res. Priorities (formerly ESRC Res. Centres), 1996–97. ONS Stats Adv. Cttee, 1996–97. Member Council: REconS, 1995–2000; Business for Sterling, 1999–. Trustee, New Europe Res. Trust, 1999–. Mem., Oxford and Cambridge Musical Club. FRSA 1993. Hon. DBA Greenwich, 1997. *Publications:* numerous research papers and articles on economic issues. *Recreations:* music (singing), philately. *Address:* 25 Redbourne Avenue, N3 2BP. *T:* (020) 8346 3482. *Club:* Reform.

LEA, Sir Thomas (William), 5th Bt *cr* 1892, of The Larches, Kidderminster and Sea Grove, Dawlish; *b* 6 Sept. 1973; *s* of Sir Julian Lea, 4th Bt and of Gerry Valerie, *d* of late Captain Gibson C. Fahnestock; *S* father, 1990. *Educ:* Uppingham Sch. *Heir: b* Alexander Julian Lea, *b* 28 Oct. 1978.

LEACH, Allan William, FLA; Director-General and Librarian, National Library for the Blind, 1982–95; *b* 9 May 1931; *yr s* of Frank Leach, MBE and Margaret Ann Bennett; *m* 1962, Betty, *e d* of William George Gadsby and Doris Cree; one *s* one *d*. *Educ:* Watford Grammar Sch.; Loughborough Coll. BA Open; DPA London. Various posts with Hertfordshire County Library, 1948–59; Librarian, RAF Sch. of Educn, 1949–51; Regional Librarian, Warwickshire County Libr., 1959–65; County Librarian, Bute County Libr., 1965–71; Librarian and Curator, Ayr Burgh, 1971–74; Dir of Library Services, Kyle and Carrick District, 1974–82. Vice-Chm., UK Assoc. of Braille Producers, 1994–96 (Chm., 1991–94); Member: Standing Cttee, Section of Libraries for the Blind, IFLA, 1983–95 (Chm., 1985–87; Ed., Newsletter, 1985–92); Nat. Steering Cttee, Share the Vision, 1992–95. Chm., Ulverscroft Foundn, 1999– (Trustee, 1993–). Editor: Rickmansworth Historian, 1961–66; Ayrshire Collections, 1973–82. *Publications:* Begin Here, 1966; Rothesay Tramways, a brief history, 1969; Round old Ayr (with R. Brash and G. S. Copeland), 1972; Libraries in Ayr, 1975; Looking Ahead, 1987; articles on libraries, local history, literature, braille and educn. *Recreations:* music, the countryside, books, people. *Address:* 4 Windsor Road, Hazel Grove, Stockport, Cheshire SK7 4SW. *T:* (0161) 285 1287.

LEACH, (Charles Guy) Rodney, MA; Director, Jardine Matheson Holdings Ltd, since 1984; Deputy Chairman, Jardine Lloyd Thompson Group plc, since 1997; *b* 1 June 1934; *s* of late Charles Harold Leach and Nora Eunice Ashworth; *m* 1993, Mrs Jessica Douglas-Home; two *s* three *d* from a previous marriage to Felicity Ballantyne. *Educ:* Harrow; Balliol Coll., Oxford (1st Cl. Hon. Mods, 1st Cl. Lit. Hum.). N. M. Rothschild & Sons, 1963–76: Partner, 1968; Dir, 1970; Director: Trade Development Bank, 1976–83; Matheson & Co., 1983–; Hongkong Land, 1985–; Dairy Farm, 1987–; Mandarin Oriental, 1987–; Robert Fleming Hldgs Ltd, 1999–2000. Mem. Bd, British Library, 1996–. *Publication:* Europe: a concise encyclopedia of the European Union, 1998. *Recreations:* the humanities, sport, bridge. *Address:* 3 Lombard Street, EC3V 9AQ. *T:* (020) 7528 4000. *Clubs:* White's, Portland, Queen's, Vanderbilt.

LEACH, Clive William, CBE 2000; Chairman: Yorkshire Enterprise Ltd, since 1995; Gabriel Communications Ltd, since 1997; *b* 4 Dec. 1934; *s* of Stanley and Laura Leach; *m* 1st, 1958, Audrey (*née* Parker) (*d* 1978); three *s*; 2nd, 1980, Stephanie (*née* McGinn); one *s*. *Educ:* Sir John Leman Grammar Sch., Beccles, Suffolk. Gen. Sales Manager, Tyne Tees Television, 1968–74; Sales Dir, 1974–79, Dir of Sales and Marketing, 1979–82, Trident Television; Man. Dir, Link Television, 1982–85; Dir of Sales and Marketing, 1985–88, Man. Dir, 1988–93, Yorkshire Television; Man. Dir, 1985–88, Chm., 1988–93, Yorkshire Television Enterprises. Chairman: Yorkshire Television Internat., 1988–93; Yorkshire–Tyne Tees Television Holdings, 1993 (Gp Chief Exec., 1992–93); Dir, ITN, 1988–93. Chm., Yorkshire Fund Managers Ltd, 1996–; Dir, British Small Cos Venture Capital Trust plc, 1996–. Dep. Chm., Regl Chamber for Yorks and Humber. Chairman: Leeds TEC, 1991–; Leeds HA, 1996–2000; W Yorks Learning and Skills Council, 2000–; Yorks Cultural Consortium, 2001–; Dir, Opera North Ltd. FRSA; MCIM 1994. *Recreations:* golf, cricket, travel. *Address:* The White House, Barkston Ash, Tadcaster, N Yorks LS24 9TT. *Clubs:* Reform, MCC; Alwoodley Golf.

LEACH, David Andrew, OBE 1987; potter, designer, lecturer; *b* 7 May 1911; *e s* of Bernard Leach, CH, CBE, and Edith Muriel, *o d* of Dr William Evans Hoyle; *m* 1938, Mary Elizabeth Facey; three *s*. *Educ:* Prep. Sch., Bristol; Dauntsey's Sch., Wilts. At age of 19, began to work in his father's pottery at St Ives, Cornwall (tuition from him and associates); Manager and Partner, 1946–55; took Manager's course, N Staffs Technical Coll., Stoke-on-Trent, to 1937; taught pottery at Dartington Hall Progressive Sch., 1933. Served War, DCLI, 1941–45. Taught at Penzance Sch. of Art and St Ives, 1945. Designed and made David Leach Electric Kiln, 1950; helped to start a pottery in Norway, 1951; in charge of Ceramic Dept, and taught, at Loughborough Coll. of Art, 1953 (later Vis. Lectr); started pottery for Carmelite Friars at Aylesford, 1954; started workshop at Bovey Tracey, 1956; researched into glazes and changed from slipware to stoneware, 1961; now makes a large percentage of porcelain. Late Mem. Council, Craftsmen Potters Assoc. of GB (Past Chm.), late Mem. Grants Cttee of the Crafts Adv. Commn; Mem. Council, Crafts Council, 1977; Chm., Devon Guild of Craftsmen, 1986–87; Adviser, Dartington Pottery Trng Workshop. Has exhibited in Europe, USA and Far East; first major one-man show, CPA, 1966; Internat. Ceramics Exhibn, 1972, and Craftsmen's Art, 1973, V&A Mus., 1973; major one-man show, NY, 1978; exhibitions in Germany (Darmstadt, Munich, Deidesheim, Sandhausen-bei-Heidelberg, and Hanover), Holland (Amsterdam), Belgium (Brussels), USA (San Francisco), Japan (Osaka) and Norway (Oslo); Joint Exhibitions: New Ashgate Gall., Farnham, 1982, 1983, (3 Generations Leach) 1986; Beaux Arts Gall., Bath, 1984; (with John Leach) Peter Dingley Gall., Stratford, 1985; Solus Exhibitions: NY, and lecture tour, USA, 1978; Washington DC, and 2nd lecture tour, USA, 1979; British Crafts Centre, London, 1979. Galerie St Martin, Cologne, 1982; St Paul's Sch., Barnes, 1982; Robert Welch Gall., Chipping Campden, 1982; Frontroom Gall., Dallas, 1983; Chestnut Gall., Bourton-on-the-Water, 1984; Century Gall., Henley-on-Thames, 1984; Castle Mus., Norwich, 1985; Galerie F15, Oslo, 1986; Elaine Potter Gall., San Francisco, 1986; Greenwich House Gall., NY, 1987; New Ashgate Gall., Farnham, 1988; Lecture at Setagaya Mus., Tokyo, 1989; Lecture demonstration tours: in USA, 1985, 1986, 1987 and 1988; in Caracas, Venezuela, 1987, 1991 (with exhbn). Craft of the Potter, BBC, 1976. Gold Medal, Istanbul, 1967. *Publications:* David Leach: A Potter's Life, with Workshop Notes (introd. by Bernard Leach), 1977. *Address:* Lowerdown Pottery, Bovey Tracey, Devon TQ13 9LE. *T:* (01626) 833408.

LEACH, Prof. Donald Frederick, CBE 1996; Principal, 1985–96, and Vice Patron, 1993–96, Queen Margaret College, Edinburgh; *b* 24 June 1931; *s* of Frederick John Mansell Leach and Annie Ivy Foster; *m* 1st, 1952, June Valentine Reid (*d* 1997); two *s* one *d*; 2nd, 1999, Marilyn Annette Jeffcoat. *Educ:* John Ruskin Grammar Sch., Croydon; Norwood Tech. Coll.; Dundee Tech. Coll.; Univ. of London (Ext. Student, BSc); Jordanhill Coll. of Educn, MInstP, CPhys, 1960; FIMA, CMath, 1969; MBCS, CEng, 1968. Pilot Officer, RAF, 1951–53. Physicist, British Jute Trade Res. Assoc., Dundee, 1954–65; Tech. Dir, A. R. Bolton & Co., 1965–66; Napier College: Lectr and Sen. Lectr in Maths, 1966–68; Head, Dept of Maths and Computing, 1968–74; Asst Principal/Dean, Faculty of Science, 1974–85. Interim Chief Exec., Edinburgh's Lifelong Learning Partnership, 1998. Chairman: Creative Edge Software Ltd, 1999–; D. M. Vaughan & Co. Ltd, 1999–. Member: Council for Professions Supplementary to Medicine, 1985–97; Exec. Cttee, Scottish Council Develt and Indust., 1987–96; Boards of: Edinburgh Chamber of Commerce and Manufactures, 1991–98 (Sen. Vice-Pres., 1996; Pres., 1996–98); Leith Chamber of Commerce, 1991–96 (Pres., 1994–96); British Chambers of Commerce, 1997–99; Higher Educn Quality Council, 1992–96; The Capital Enterprise Trust, 1993–98. Dir, Businessweb Ltd, 1999–. Vice Convenor, One Parent Families Scotland, 1998–. Contested: (L) W Edinburgh, 1959; (L) E Fife by-election, 1961; (Lab) Kinross and W Perthshire, 1970. Hon. Prof., Queen Margaret Coll., 1993. Hon. Fellow, Soc. of Chiropodists and Podiatrists, 1994. FRSA. *Publications:* Future Employment and Technological Change (jtly), 1986; papers in sci., tech. and eductl jls on textile physics, electronic instrumentation, maths and statistics, higher educn. *Recreations:* badminton, walking, ski-ing, cooking. *Address:* 18 Rothesay Terrace, Edinburgh EH3 7RY. *T:* (0131) 226 7166. *Clubs:* New, Scottish Arts (Edinburgh).

LEACH, Admiral of the Fleet Sir Henry (Conyers), GCB 1978 (KCB 1977); DL; *b* 18 Nov. 1923; 3rd *s* of Captain John Catterall Leach, MVO, DSO, RN and Evelyn Burrell Leach (*née* Lee), Yarner, Bovey Tracey, Devon; *m* 1958, Mary Jean (*d* 1991), *yr d* of Adm. Sir Henry McCall, KCVO, KBE, CB, DSO; two *d*. *Educ:* St Peter's Court, Broadstairs; RNC Dartmouth. Cadet 1937; served in: cruiser Mauritius, S Atlantic and Indian Ocean, 1941–42; battleship Duke of York, incl. Scharnhorst action, 1943–45; destroyers in Mediterranean, 1945–46; spec. Gunnery, 1947; various gunnery appts, 1948–51; Gunnery Officer, cruiser Newcastle, Far East, 1953–55; staff appts, 1955–59; comd destroyer Dunkirk, 1959–61; comd frigate Galatea as Captain (D) 27th Sqdn and Mediterranean, 1965–67; Dir of Naval Plans, 1968–70; comd Commando Ship Albion, 1970; Asst Chief of Naval Staff (Policy), 1971–73; Flag Officer First Flotilla, 1974–75; Vice-Chief of Defence Staff, 1976–77; C-in-C, Fleet, and Allied C-in-C, Channel and Eastern Atlantic, 1977–79; Chief of Naval Staff and First Sea Lord, 1979–82. First and Principal Naval ADC to the Queen, 1979–82. psc 1952; jssc 1961. Chm., St Dunstan's, 1983–98 (Hon. Vice Pres., 1999–); President: RN Benevolent Soc., 1983–95; Sea Cadet Assoc., 1984–93; Royal Bath and West of England Soc., 1993 (Vice-Pres., 1994–); Patron: Meridian Trust Assoc., 1993–; Hampshire RBL, 1994–. Chm. Council, King Edward VII Hosp., 1987–98 (Hon. Vice-Pres., 1998–). Gov., Cranleigh Sch., 1983–93. Freeman: City of London; Shipwrights' Co.; Hon. Freeman, Merchant Taylors' Co. DL Hampshire, 1992. *Publications:* Endure no Makeshifts (autobiog.), 1993; Anecdotage, 1996. *Recreations:* fishing, shooting, gardening, antique furniture repair. *Address:* Wonston Lea, Wonston, Winchester, Hants SO21 3LS.

LEACH, Paul Arthur; General Consultant to The Law Society, 1980–81, retired; *b* 10 July 1915; *s* of Rev. Edward Leach and Edith Swannell Leach; *m* 1st, 1949, Daphne Copeland (marr. diss. 1957); one *s* one *d*; 2nd, 1958, Rachel Renée Lachmann. *Educ:* Marlborough Coll.; Keble Coll., Oxford (1st Cl. Hons BA Mod. Hist., 1937; MA 1945); Birmingham Univ. (2nd Cl. Hons LLB 1940). Law Soc. Finals, 1940; admitted Solicitor, 1946. Served War, RA, 1940–45: Staff Captain 1st AA Bde; attached SO II, RAEC, 1945–46. Private practice as solicitor, 1946–48; Talks Producer, BBC Home Talks, 1949; joined Law Soc. staff, 1950; Clerk and later Sec., Professional Purposes Cttee, 1950–71; Secretary: Future of the Profession Cttee, 1971–80; Internat. Relations Cttee, 1975–80; Dep. Sec.-Gen., 1975–80; removed from Roll of Solicitors, at own request, 1991. Secretary: UK Delegn to Commn Consultative des Barreaux de la Communauté Européenne, 1975–81; Inter-Professional Gp, 1978–81; UK Vice-Pres., Union Internationale des Avocats, 1978–81. *Publications:* (ed) Guide to Professional Conduct of Solicitors, 1974; articles in Law Society's Gazette. *Recreations:* foreign travel, history, listening to classical music. *Address:* 19 Lavant Court, Charles Street, Petersfield, Hants GU32 3EQ; 5333 Myrtlewood, The Meadows, Sarasota, FL 34235, USA.

LEACH, Penelope, PhD; psychologist and writer on childcare; *b* 19 Nov. 1937; *d* of late Nigel Marlin Balchin and Elisabeth Balchin; *m* 1963, Gerald Leach; one *s* one *d. Educ:* Newnham Coll., Cambridge (BA Hons 1959); LSE (Dip. in Soc. Sci. Admin 1960; MA Psychol. 1962; PhD Psychol. 1964). Home Office, 1960–61; Lectr in Psychol., LSE, 1965–67; Res. Officer and Res. Fellow, MRC, 1967–76; Ext Med. Ed., Penguin Books, 1970–78; Founder and Dir, Lifetime Productions (childcare videos), 1985–87; Res. Consultant, Internat. Centre for Child Studies, 1984–90. Dir, Families, Children and Child Care Project, 1997–, and Hon. Sen. Res. Fellow, 1997–, Royal Free and UCL Med. Sch., Univ. of London. Mem., Voluntary Licensing Authy on IVF, 1985–89; Comr, Commn on Social Justice, 1993–95; Mem., Commn on Children and Violence, 1993–95. Founder and Parent-Educn Co-ordinator, End Physical Punishment for Children, 1989–; Chm., Child Develt Soc., 1993–95 (Pres., 1992–93); Pres., Nat. Child Minders' Assoc., 1999–; Vice-President: Pre-School Playgroups Assoc., 1977; Health Visitors Assoc., 1982–99. Mem. Adv. Council, Amer. Inst. for Child, Adolescent and Family Studies, 1993–. Mem., professional socs and assocs; FBPsS 1988; Hon. Fellow, Dept of Mental Health, Bristol Univ., 1988. Hon. DEd Kingston, 1996. *Publications:* Babyhood, 1974; Baby and Child, 1977, 2nd edn 1989; Who Cares?, 1979; The Parents' A–Z, 1984; The First Six Months, 1987; The Babypack, 1990; Children First, 1994; Your Baby and Child, 1997. *Recreations:* cooking, family and friends, gardening, travel. *Address:* 3 Tanza Road, NW3 2UA. *T:* (020) 7435 9025.

LEACH, Rodney; *see* Leach, C. G. R.

LEACH, Rodney, PhD; CEng; FRINA; FIMgt; FCIM; company director; Chief Executive and Managing Director, VSEL Consortium plc, 1986–88; Chief Executive, 1985–88, and Chairman, 1986–88, Vickers Shipbuilding and Engineering Ltd; Chairman, Cammell Laird Shipbuilders Ltd, 1985–88; *b* 3 March 1932; *s* of Edward and Alice Leach; *m* 1958, Eira Mary (*née* Tuck); three *s* one *d. Educ:* Baines Grammar Sch., Poulton Le Fylde, Lancs; Birmingham Univ. (BSc, PhD). CEng, FRINA 1987; FCIM (FInstM 1972); FIMgt (FIIM 1987). Radiation Physicist, Nuclear Power Plant Co. Ltd, 1957; Physicist, UKAEA, 1960; Sen. Physicist, South of Scotland Electricity Board, 1963; Associate, McKinsey & Co. Inc., 1965, Partner, 1970; Peninsular & Oriental Steam Navigation Co.: Hd of European and Air Transport Div., 1974; Dir, 1978–85; Chairman: P&O European Transport Services Ltd, 1979–83; P&O Cruises Ltd, 1980–85. Director: Jasmin plc, 1989–97; United Utilities (formerly North West Water Group plc), 1989–99; Mem., NW Water Authority, 1989; Vice-Chm. and Dir, S Cumbria Community and Mental Health NHS Trust, 1993–97. Member: Gen. Council, Cumbria Tourist Bd, 1986–92; Northern Council for Sport and Recreation, 1991–95. Dir, 1989–93, Vice-Chm., 1991–94, Renaissance Arts Theatre Trust Ltd. Pres., Lakeland Sinfonia Concert Soc., 1998–. Conseiller Spécial, Chambre de Commerce et d'Industrie de Boulogne-sur-Mer et de Montreuil, 1989–94. Mem., RYA, 1977–. Gov., St Anne's Sch., Windermere, 1991–97. Liveryman: Worshipful Company of Carmen, 1976; Worshipful Company of Shipwrights, 1988–; Freeman, City of London, 1976. FRSA 1989. *Publications:* (jtly) Containerization: the key to low cost transport, 1965; frequent papers in scientific and technical jls, 1965–72. *Recreations:* fell-walking, sailing, gardening, literature. *Address:* Dockwray Cottage, Grasmere, Cumbria LA22 9QD. *T:* (01539) 435288. *Club:* Royal Automobile.

LEADBETTER, Alan James, CBE 1994; DSc; Directeur Adjoint, Institut Laue Langevin, Grenoble, France, 1994–99; *b* 28 March 1934; *s* of Robert and Edna Leadbetter; *m* 1957, Jean Brenda Williams; one *s* one *d. Educ:* Liverpool Univ. (BSc 1954; PhD 1957); Bristol Univ. (DSc 1971). CPhys 1972; FInstP 1972; CChem 1980; FRSC 1980. Fellow, NRCC, 1957–59; Res. Asst, Lectr and Reader, Univ. of Bristol, 1959–74; Prof. of Phys. Chem., Univ. of Exeter, 1975–82; Associate Dir, Science, Rutherford Appleton Lab., SERC, 1982–88; Dir, Daresbury Lab., SERC, 1988–94. Member: Divl Review Cttee, Los Alamos Nat. Lab., 1999–; Technical Adv. Cttee, Australian Nuclear Sci. and Technol. Orgn, 2000–. Hon. Professor: Univ. of Hull, 1992–; Univ. of Manchester, 1989–94; Vis. Prof., De Montfort Univ., 1994–2001; Hon. Univ. Fellow, Univ. of Exeter, 1999–. *Publications:* res. papers in chem. and phys in learned jls. *Recreations:* gardening, walking, cooking. *Address:* 23 Hillcrest Park, Exeter EX4 4SH.

See also M. Leadbetter.

LEADBETTER, David Hulse, CB 1958; Assistant Under-Secretary of State, Department of Education and Science, 1964–68 (Under Secretary, Ministry of Education, 1953–64); *b* 14 Aug. 1908; *s* of late Harold Leadbetter; *m* 1933, Marion (*d* 1995), *d* of late Horatio Ballantyne, FRIC, FCS; two *s* two *d* (and one *d* decd.). *Educ:* Whitgift; Merton Coll., Oxford (Classical Postmaster). Entered Board of Education, 1933. *Recreations:* photography, gardening. *Address:* The Old Vicarage, Leigh, Sherborne, Dorset DT9 6HL. *T:* (01935) 874020.

LEADBETTER, Michael; Director of Social Services, Essex, since 1993; *b* 25 July 1946; *s* of Robert Leadbetter and Edna (*née* Garlic); *m* Pamela Corti; two *s. Educ:* Ladybarn Secondary Mod. Sch.; Manchester Coll. of Sci. and Technol.; Manchester Coll., of Art and Design (DA); Manchester Univ. Extra Mural Dept (CQSW); MA (Econ) Manchester Univ. 1982. Works and prodn manager, 1971–72; Manchester Social Services: Social Worker, then Sen. Social Worker, 1972–82; Residential and Day Care Services Manager, 1982–86; Dir of Social Services, Tameside, 1986–92. NW Association of Directors of Social Services: Chm., Gtr Manchester Dirs Gp, 1987–92; Chm., Regl Trng Unit, 1987–92; Chm., 1989–90; Pres., Assoc. of Dirs of Social Services, 2001–Sept. 2002. Founder Mem., British Inst. of Transactional Analysis, 1974. FIMgt (FBIM 1990). England International, Rugby Union, 1970; 35 appearances for Lancs, 1968–74; Rugby League professional, Rochdale Hornets, 1974–76. *Recreations:* weight training, ski-ing, food, wine, opera. *Address:* Essex County Council, Social Services Department, PO Box 297, County Hall, Chelmsford, Essex CM1 1YS. *T:* (01245) 492211; The Laurels, Station Road, Wakes Colne, Essex CO6 2DS. *Club:* England Internationals.

See also A. J. Leadbetter.

LEADLAY, Prof. Peter Francis, DPhil, PhD; FRS 2000; Professor of Molecular Enzymology, University of Cambridge, since 1999; Fellow of Clare College, Cambridge, since 1979; Co-Founder and Chairman, BIOTICA Technology Ltd, since 1996; *b* 13 Dec. 1949; *s* of late Kenneth Rupert Simpson Leadlay, RN and Ellen Theresa Leadlay (*née* Coleman); *m* 1974, Christina Maria Peake; three *d. Educ:* St Joseph's Coll., London; New Coll., Oxford (Gibbs Schol.; BA 1971); Corpus Christi Coll., Oxford (Sen. Schol.; DPhil 1974; MA 1974); Clare Coll., Cambridge (PhD 1979). Royal Soc. European Res. Fellow, ETH, Zürich, 1974–76; Demonstr, Dept of Biochemistry, and Jun. Res. Fellow, Wolfson Coll., Univ. of Oxford, 1976–79; University of Cambridge: Demonstr in Biochemistry, 1979–84; Lectr, 1984–95; Reader in Molecular Enzymology, 1995–99; Sen. Res. Fellow, BBSRC, 1999–. *Publications:* Enzyme Chemistry, 1969; articles in scientific jls, particularly on enzymes and antibiotic biosynthesis. *Recreations:* reading, walking, gardening. *Address:* Department of Biochemistry, 80 Tennis Court Road, Cambridge CB2 1TL. *T:* (01223) 333656.

LEAHY, Helen Blodwen; *see* Rees, H. B.

LEAHY, Sir John (Henry Gladstone), KCMG 1981 (CMG 1973); HM Diplomatic Service, retired; *b* 7 Feb. 1928; *s* of late William Henry Gladstone and late Ethel Leahy; *m* 1954, Elizabeth Anne, *d* of late J. H. Pitchford, CBE; two *s* two *d. Educ:* Tonbridge Sch.; Clare Coll., Cambridge; Yale University. RAF, 1950–52; FO, 1952–54 (Asst Private Sec. to Minister of State, 1953–54); 3rd, later 2nd Sec., Singapore, 1955–57; FO, 1957–58; 2nd, later 1st Sec., Paris, 1958–62; FO, 1962–65; Head of Chancery, Tehran, 1965–68; Counsellor, FCO, 1969; Head of Personnel Services Dept, 1969–70; Head of News Dept, FCO, 1971–73; Counsellor and Head of Chancery, Paris, 1973–75; seconded as Under Sec., NI Office, 1975–76; Asst Under-Sec. of State, FCO, 1977–79; Ambassador to South Africa, 1979–82; Dep. Under- Sec. of State, FCO, 1982–84; High Comr, Australia, 1984–88. Chm., Lonrho, 1994–97 (Dir, 1993–98; Vice-Chm, 1994); Dir, The Observer, 1989–93. Chm., Urban Foundn (London), 1991–94 (Exec. Dir, 1989–91). Pro-Chancellor, City Univ., 1991–97. Chm., British-Australia Soc., 1994–97. Mem., Franco-British Council (Chm., 1989–93). Master, Skinners' Co., 1993–94. Hon. DCL City, 1997. Officier, Légion d'Honneur (France), 1996. *Recreations:* canal boating, golf. *Address:* 16 Ripley Chase, The Goffs, Eastbourne, East Sussex BN21 1HB. *T:* (01323) 725368.

LEAHY, Michael James; General Secretary, Iron and Steel Trades Confederation, since 1999; *b* 7 Jan. 1949; *s* of Michael James Cyril Leahy, ISM, and Iris Jarrett Leahy; *m* 1974, Irene Powell; two *s. Educ:* Twmpath Secondary Modern Sch., Pontypool. Chargehand, Cold Rolling Dept, Panteg Works, Richard Thompson & Baldwins Ltd, 1965–77; Iron and Steel Trades Confederation: Mem., 1965–; Organiser, 1977–86; Sen. Organiser, 1986–92; Asst Gen. Sec. Elect, 1992–93; Asst Gen. Sec., 1993–98; Gen. Sec. Elect, 1998–99. Various posts, British Steel/Corus Gp plc, 1995– (Employees' Sec., Eur. Works Council, 1998–). Mem., 1992–, Chm., 1998–, Steel Co-ordinating Cttee, Nat. Trades Union; Mem. Exec. Council, CSEU, 1994–99; Mem., 1995–, Mem., Sub-cttee for Mkts and Forward Studies, 1995–, Consultative Cttee, ECSC; General Federation of Trade Unions: Mem., Exec. Council, 1996–; Mem., Educnl Trust, 1996- (Trustee, 1999–); Vice Pres., 1999–2001; Pres., 2001–; Mem. Gen. Council, 1999–, Mem., Exec. Cttee, 2000–, TUC. Hon. Sec., British Section, 1999–, Pres., Iron, Steel and Non-Ferrous Metals Dept, 1999–, Internat. Metalworkers Fedn; European Metalworkers' Federation: Member: Exec. Cttee, 1999–; Industrial Policy Cttee, 1999–; Steel Cttee, 1999–. Labour Party: Mem., 1966–; Member: NEC, 1996; Nat. Policy Forum, 1996-99. Chm., Bevan Foundn, 2000–. *Recreations:* golf, Rugby. *Address:* Iron and Steel Trades Confederation, Swinton House, 324 Gray's Inn Road, WC1X 8DD. *T:* (020) 7239 1228.

LEAHY, Terence Patrick; Chief Executive, Tesco plc, since 1997; *s* of Terence and Elizabeth Leahy; *m* Alison; two *s* one *d. Educ:* St Edward's Coll., Liverpool; UMIST (Bsc Hons Mgt Scis). Joined Tesco, 1979, as Mktg Exec.; Marketing Dir, 1984–86; Dir, 1992–; Dep. Man. Dir, 1995–97. *Recreations:* sport, reading, theatre, architecture. *Address:* Tesco plc, Tesco House, PO Box 18, Delamare Road, Cheshunt, Waltham Cross, Herts EN8 9SL. *T:* (01992) 632222.

LEAKE, Prof. Bernard Elgey, PhD, DSc, FRSE, FGS; Hon. Research Fellow, Department of Earth Sciences, Cardiff University, since 1998; Leverhulme Emeritus Fellow, 2000–June 2002; Professor of Geology, Department of Geology and Applied Geology, and Keeper of Geological Collections in Hunterian Museum, University of Glasgow, 1974–97, now Professor Emeritus (Head, Department of Geology and Applied Geology, 1974–92); *b* 29 July 1932; *s* of late Norman Sidney Leake and Clare Evelyn (*née* Walgate); *m* 1955, Gillian Dorothy Dobinson; five *s. Educ:* Wirral Grammar Sch., Bebington, Cheshire; Liverpool Univ. (1st Cl. Hons BSc, PhD); Bristol Univ. (DSc 1974); Glasgow Univ. (DSc 1998). Leverhulme post-doctoral Res. Fellow, Liverpool Univ., 1955–57; Asst Lectr, subseq. Lectr in Geology, Bristol Univ., 1957–68, Reader in Geol., 1968–74. Res. Associate, Berkeley, Calif, 1966; Gledden Sen. Vis. Fellow, Univ. of W Australia, 1986; Erskine Vis. Res. Fellow, Univ. of Canterbury, NZ, 1999. Chm., Cttee on amphibole nomenclature, Internat. Mineral Assoc., 1982– (Sec., 1968–79); Member: NERC, 1978–84 (Chm., Vis. Gp to Brit. Geol Survey, formerly Inst. of Geological Sciences, 1982–84; Chm., Isotope Facilities Prog. Cttee, 1981–85, 1987–91); Council, Mineral Soc., 1965–68, 1978–80, 1996–99 (Vice-Pres., 1979–80, 1996–97; Pres., 1998–99; Managing Trustee, 1997–98, 2000–); Council, Geol Soc., 1971–74, 1979–85, 1989–96 (Vice-Pres., 1980; Treasurer, 1981–85, 1989–96; Pres., 1986–88; Lyell Medal, 1977); Council, RSE, 1988–90; publication cttees, Mineral Soc., 1970–85, Geol Soc., 1970–85, and 1986–96; Geol Soc. Publication Bd, 1987– (Chm., 1987–96); Treas., Geologists' Assoc., 1997–. FRSE 1978. Sodic amphibole mineral, leakeite, named by Internat. Mineral Assoc., 1992. Editor: Mineralogical Magazine, 1970–83; Jl of Geol Soc., 1973 and 1974. *Publications:* A Catalogue of analysed calciferous and sub-calciferous amphiboles, 1968; The Geology of South Mayo, 1989; The Geology of the Dalradian and associated rocks of Connemara, W Ireland, 1994; over 100 papers in geol, mineral and geochem. jls on geol. of Connemara, study of amphiboles, X-ray fluorescence anal. of rocks and use of geochem. in identifying origins of highly metamorphosed rocks; geological maps: Connemara, 1982; South Mayo, 1985; Slyne Head, 1985; Errismore, 1990; Clifden, 1997. *Recreations:* walking, reading, theatre, museums, genealogy, study of railway and agricultural development. *Address:* Department of Earth Sciences, Cardiff University, PO Box 914, Cardiff CF1 3YE. *T:* (029) 2087 4573; The Chippings, Bridge Road, Llanblethian, Cowbridge, Vale of Glamorgan CF71 7JG. *Club:* Geological Society.

LEAKE, Rt Rev. David; *see* Argentina, Bishop of.

LEAKEY, Dr David Martin, FREng; Group Technical Adviser, British Telecom, 1990–92; independent consultant, David Leakey Consultancy in telecommunication services, systems and networks, since 1992; *b* 23 July 1932; *s* of Reginald Edward and Edith Doris Leakey; *m* 1957, Shirley May Webster; one *s* one *d. Educ:* Imperial College, Univ. of London (BScEng, PhD, DIC). FCGI 1976; FIEE 1969; FREng (FEng 1979). GEC Coventry, 1953–57; GEC Hirst Research Centre, 1957–63; Tech. Manager, Public Exchange Div., GEC Coventry, 1963–66; Head, Elect. Eng. Dept, Lanchester Polytechnic, 1966–67; Advanced Product Planning Manager, 1967–69, Technical Dir, 1969–84, GEC Coventry; Dep. E-in-C, 1984–86, Chief Scientist, 1986–90, British Telecom. Director: Fulcrum Ltd, 1985–92; Mitel Corp., 1986–92. Vis. Prof., Univ. of Bristol, 1987–. Vice-Pres., IEE, 1984–87. Liveryman, Worshipful Co. of Engineers, 1985–. Hon. DEng Bristol, 1995. *Publications:* papers to professional journals. *Recreations:* horticulture, wine. *Address:* Rocheberie, Grassy Lane, Sevenoaks, Kent TN13 1PW.

LEAKEY, Richard Erskine Frere; Permanent Secretary, Secretary to the Cabinet and Head of the Public Service, Kenya, 1999–2001; *b* 19 Dec. 1944; *s* of late Louis Seymour Bazett Leakey, FBA, and Mary Douglas Leakey, FBA; *m* 1970, Dr Meave (*née* Epps); three *d. Educ:* Nairobi Primary Sch.; Lenana (formerly Duke of York) Sch., Nairobi. Self employed tour guide and animal trapper, 1961–65; Dir, Photographic Safaris in E Africa, 1965–68; Administrative Dir, 1968–74, Dir, 1974–89, Nat. Museums of Kenya; Dir, Wildlife and Conservation Management Service, Kenya, 1989–90; Chm., 1989–93, Dir, 1993–94 and 1998–99, Kenya Wildlife Service; Man. Dir, Richard Leakey and Associates, wildlife consultancy, 1994–98; Sec. Gen. SAFINA, 1995–98. MP Kenya, 1998. Co-leader, palaeontol expedn to Lake Natron, Tanzania, 1963–64; expedn to Lake Baringo,

Kenya, in search of early man, 1966; Co-leader, Internation Omo River Expedn, Ethiopia, in search of early man, 1967; Leader, E Turkana (formerly E Rudolf) Res. Proj. (multi-nat., interdisciplinary sci. consortium investigation of Plio/Pleistocene, Kenya's northern Rift Valley), 1968–. Chairman: Foundn for Res. into Origin of Man (FROM), 1974–81; E African Wild Life Soc., 1984–89 (Vice-Chm., 1978–84); Kenya Cttee, United World Colls, 1987; Bd of Governors and Council, Regent's Coll., London, 1985–90; Nat. Museums of Kenya, 1999–; Trustee: Nat. Fund for the Disabled; Wildlife Clubs of Kenya, 1980–; Rockford Coll., Illinois, 1983–85. Presenter: The Making of Mankind, BBC TV series, 1981; Earth Journal, US TV series, 1991. Mem., Selection Cttee, Beyond War Award, 1985–; Juror: Kalinga Prize, Unesco, 1986–88; Rolex Awards, 1990. Hon. Mem., Bd of Dirs, Thunderbird Res. Corp., USA, 1988–. Hon. degrees from Wooster Coll., Rockford Coll., SUNY, Univs of Kent, Ohio, Aberdeen, Washington and Bristol. Golden Ark Medal for Conservation, 1989. *Publications:* (contrib.) General History of Africa, vol. 1, 1976; (with R. Lewin) Origins, 1978; (with R. Lewin) People of the Lake, 1979; (with M. G. Leakey) Koobi Fora Research Project, vol. I, 1979; The Making of Mankind, 1981; Human Origins, 1982; One Life, 1984; (with R. Lewin) Origins Reconsidered, 1992; (with R. Lewin) The Origins of Humankind, 1995; (with R. Lewin) The Sixth Extinction: biodiversity and its survival, 1996; articles on palaeontol. in Nature, Jl of World Hist., Science, Amer. Jl of Phys. and Anthropol. *Address:* PO Box 24926, Nairobi, Kenya.

LEAN, Geoffrey; Environment Editor, Independent on Sunday, since 2000; *b* 21 April 1947; *s* of late Garth Dickinson Lean and Margaret Mary Lean (*née* Appleyard); *m* 1972, Judith Eveline Wolfe; one *s* one *d*. *Educ:* Sherborne Sch.; St Edmund Hall, Oxford (BA (Hons) Mod. Hist). Grad. Trainee, Yorkshire Post Newspapers, 1969–72; reporter, Goole Times, 1969; Yorkshire Post: reporter, 1969–72; Feature Writer, 1972–77; Envmt Correspondent, 1973–77; Reporter, 1977–79, Envmt Correspondent, 1979–93, The Observer; Dir, Central Observer, 1990–93; Envmt Correspondent, Independent on Sunday, 1993–2000. External Editor, Our Planet (UNEP), 1994–; Mem., Exec. Cttee, UNED Forum (formerly UNED-UK), 1989–. Trustee, European Sect., Internat. Inst. of Energy Conservation, 1995–98; UK rep. to Commn IV, Gen. Conf. of UNESCO, 1997; Mem. Bd, Leadership in Envmt and Develt Internat., 1998–; Trustee, LEAD UK, 2000–. Consultancies for UNEP, UNDP, UNICEF, World Bank, FAO and WMO. Clerk, Yorkshire Post and Yorkshire Evening Post jt chapels, NUJ, 1975–77; Vice Chm., Leeds Branch, NUJ, 1977. Chair of Judges, Andrew Lees Meml Award, 1994–; Juror, Goldman Envmtl Prize, 1996–. Yorkshire Council for Social Press Award, 1972; Glaxo Science Fellowship, 1972; World Envmt Fest. Rose Award, 1986; Communication Arts Award of Excellence, 1986; UN Global 500, 1987; Awareness Award, 1991, Journalist of the Year, 1993, British Envmt and Media Awards; Schumacher Award, 1994; Foundn Award to launch IUCN/Reuters press awards, 1998; Scoop of the Year, London Press Club Awards, 2000, British Press Awards, 2001. *Publications:* Rich World, Poor World, 1978; (jtly) The Worst Accident in the World, 1986; (jtly) Chernobyl: the end of the nuclear dream, 1987; (gen. ed.) Atlas of the Environment, 1990, revd edn 1994; (ed) Radiation: doses, effects, risks, 1985; (ed) Action on Ozone, 1988, revd edn 1990; (contrib. ed.) Dimensions of Need: a world atlas of food and agriculture, 1995; (ed) Down to Earth, 1995; (ed) Human Development Report, 1998; (ed) Progress of Nations Report, 1999; (ed) A Sea of Troubles, 2001; (ed) Protecting the Oceans from Land-Based Activities, 2001. *Recreations:* family, garden, West Cork, bad puns. *Address:* c/o Independent on Sunday, 191 Marsh Wall, E14 9RS. *T:* (020) 7005 2000.

LEANING, Very Rev. David; Dean (formerly Provost) and Rector of Southwell, since 1991; *b* 18 Aug. 1936. *Educ:* Keble Coll., Oxford, 1957–58; Lichfield Theological Coll. Deacon 1960, priest 1961, dio. Lincoln; Curate of Gainsborough, 1960–65; Rector of Warsop with Sookholme, 1965–76; Vicar of Kington and Rector of Huntington, Diocese of Hereford, 1976–80; RD of Kington and Weobley, 1976–80; Archdeacon of Newark, 1980–91; Warden, Community of St Laurence, Belper, 1984–96. Mem., Bd of Selectors, ABM (formerly ACCM), 1988–96, 2000–. MA Lambeth, 2001. *Address:* The Residence, Southwell, Notts NG25 0HP. *T:* (01636) 812593, *Fax:* (01636) 812782.

LEAPER, Prof. Robert Anthony Bernard, CBE 1975; Professor of Social Administration, University of Exeter, 1970–86, Professor Emeritus 1987; *b* 7 June 1921; *s* of William Bambrick Leaper and Gertrude Elizabeth (*née* Taylor); *m* 1950, Elizabeth Arno; two *s* one *d*. *Educ:* Ratcliffe Coll., Leicester; St John's Coll., Cambridge (MA); Balliol Coll., Oxford (MA). Dipl. Public and Social Admin. (Oxon). Coal miner, 1941–44. Warden, St John Bosco Youth Centre, Stepney, 1945–47; Cadet officer, Civil Service, 1949–50; Co-operative Coll., Stanford Hall, 1950–56; Principal, Social Welfare Trng Centre, Zambia, 1956–59; Lectr, then Sen. Lectr, then Acting Dir, Social Admin., UC, Swansea, 1960–70. Vis. Lectr, Roehampton Inst., Univ. of Surrey, 1986–98; Vis. Prof., Post-grad. Med. Sch., Univ. of Exeter, 1996–2001. Exec., later Vice-Chm., Nat. Council of Social Service, 1964–80; Pres., European Region, Internat. Council on Social Welfare, 1971–79; Chm., Area Bd, MSC, 1975–86; Governor, Centre for Policy on Ageing, 1982–88; Trustee, Age Concern England, 1993–98. Editor, Social Policy and Administration, 1973–93. DUniv Surrey, 1992; Dr *hc* Univ. de Rennes, 1987. Médaille de l'Ecole Nationale de Santé, France, 1975. *Publications:* Communities and Social Change, 1966; Community Work, 1969, 2nd edn 1972; Health, Wealth and Housing, 1980; Change and Continuity, 1984; At Home in Devon, 1986; Age Speaks for Itself, 1988; Age Speaks for Itself in Europe, 1993; Employment Post 50, 1998. *Recreations:* walking, railways, wine. *Address:* Birchcote, New North Road, Exeter EX4 4AD. *T:* (01392) 272565.

LEAR, Joyce, (Mrs W. J. Lear); *see* Hopkirk, J.

LEAR, Peter; *see* Lovesey, P. H.

LEARMONT, Gen. Sir John (Hartley), KCB 1989; CBE 1980 (OBE 1975); Quarter Master General, Ministry of Defence, 1991–94, retired; *b* 10 March 1934; *s* of Captain Percy Hewitt Learmont, CIE, RIN and Doris Orynthia Learmont; *m* 1957, Susan (*née* Thornborrow); three *s*. *Educ:* Fettes College; RMA Sandhurst. Commissioned RA, 1954; Instructor, RMA, 1960–63; student, Staff Coll., 1964; served 14 Field Regt, Staff Coll. and 3 RHA, 1965–70; MA to C-in-C BAOR, 1971–73; CO 1 RHA, 1974–75 (despatches 1974); HQ BAOR, 1976–78; Comdr, 8 Field Force, 1979–81; Dep. Comdr, Commonwealth Monitoring Force, Rhodesia, Nov. 1979–March 1980; student RCDS, 1981; Chief of Mission, British Cs-in-C Mission to Soviet Forces in Germany, 1982–84; Comdr Artillery, 1 (British) Corps, 1985–87; COS, HQ UKLF, 1987–88; Comdt, Staff Coll. Camberley, 1988–89; Mil. Sec., MoD, 1989–91. Conducted review (Learmont Inquiry) of Prison Service security in Eng. and Wales, 1995. Colonel Commandant: Army Air Corps, 1988–94; RA, 1989–March 1999; RHA, 1990–March 1999; Hon. Colonel: 2nd Bn Wessex Regt (Vols), 1990–95; 2nd (Vol.) Bn, Royal Gloucestershire, Berkshire and Wiltshire Regt, 1995–97. Patron: Glider Pilot Regtl Assoc., 1996–; Air OP Officers' Assoc., 2000–. *Recreations:* fell walking, golf, theatre. *Club:* Naval and Military.

LEARY, Brian Leonard; QC 1978; *b* 1 Jan. 1929; *o s* of late A. T. Leary; *m* 1965, Myriam Ann Bannister, *d* of Kenneth Bannister, CBE, Mexico City. *Educ:* King's Sch. Canterbury; Wadham Coll., Oxford. MA Oxon. Called to the Bar, Middle Temple, 1953; Harmsworth Scholar; Bencher, 1986. Senior Prosecuting Counsel to the Crown at Central Criminal Court, 1971–78. Chm., British-Mexican Soc., 1989–92. *Recreations:* travel, sailing, growing herbs. *Address:* 5 Paper Buildings, Temple, EC4Y 7HB. *T:* (020) 7583 6117.

LEASK, Maj.-Gen. Anthony de Camborne Lowther, CB 1996; CBE 1990 (OBE 1984; MBE 1979); Director, National Association of Almshouses, since 1996; *b* 4 Jan. 1943; *s* of Lt-Gen. Sir Henry Leask, *qv*, and Zoe Leask (*née* Paynter); *m* 1974, Heather Catherine Moir; one *s* two *d*. *Educ:* Wellington Coll.; RMA, Sandhurst. Comnd Scots Guards, 1963; mentioned in despatches, 1974; CO Bn, 1981–83; attached US Army, 1983–85; Col Mil. Ops 2, MoD, 1986–89; in Comd, 15 Inf. Bde, 1989–91; rcds 1992; Dir, Defence Commitments, Far East and Western Hemisphere, 1993–94; Maj.-Gen. 1994; retd 1996. Dir, Corps of Commissionaires Mgt Ltd, 1999–. Mem., Queen's Bodyguard for Scotland, Royal Co. of Archers, 1976–. *Recreations:* wildlife, country pursuits. *Address:* c/o Bank of Scotland, Aberfoyle, by Stirling.

LEASK, Lt-Gen. Sir Henry (Lowther Ewart Clark), KCB 1970 (CB 1967); DSO 1945; OBE 1957 (MBE 1945); GOC Scotland and Governor of Edinburgh Castle, 1969–72, retired; *b* 30 June 1913; *s* of Rev. James Leask, MA; *m* Zoë de Camborne, *d* of Col W. P. Paynter, DSO, RHA; one *s* two *d*. 2nd Lt Royal Scots Fusiliers, 1936. Served War of 1939–45 in Mediterranean and Italy; Staff College Camberley, 1942; GSO 1942; Bde Major Inf. Bde 1943; 2nd in Comd and CO, 8 Bn Argyll and Sutherland Highlanders, 1944–45; Comd 1st Bn London Scottish, 1946–47; RAF Staff College, 1947; Gen. Staff Mil. Ops, WO, 1947–49; Instr Staff Coll., 1949–51; Comd 1st Bn The Parachute Regt, 1952–54; Asst Military Sec. to Sec. of State for War, 1955–57; Comdt, Tactical Wing Sch. of Inf., 1957–58; Comd Infantry Bde, 1958–61; idc 1961; Dep. Mil. Sec. to Sec. of State for War, 1962–64; GOC 52 Lowland Div., 1964–66; Dir of Army Training, MoD (Army), 1966–69. Brig. 1961, Maj.-Gen. 1964, Lt-Gen. 1969. Col of the Royal Highland Fusiliers, 1964–69; Col Comdt, Scottish Div. of Infantry, 1968–72. Chm., Army Benevolent Fund, Scotland, 1972–88. *Recreation:* field sports. *Clubs:* Carlton, Hurlingham.

See also Maj.-Gen. A. de C. L. Leask.

LEASOR, (Thomas) James; author; *b* 20 Dec. 1923; *s* of late Richard and Christine Leasor, Erith, Kent; *m* 1951, Joan Margaret Bevan, BA, LLB, Barrister-at-law, *o d* of late Roland and Dora Bevan, Crowcombe, Somerset; three *s*. *Educ:* City of London Sch.; Oriel Coll., Oxford. Kentish Times, 1941–42. Served in Army in Burma, India, Malaya, 1942–46, Capt. Royal Berks Regt. Oriel Coll., Oxford, 1946–48, BA 1948; MA 1952; edited The Isis. On staff Daily Express, London, 1948–55, as reporter, foreign correspondent, feature writer. Contrib. to many American and British magazines, newspapers and periodicals; scriptwriter for TV series The Michaels in Africa. FRSA. OStJ. *Publications: novels:* Not Such a Bad Day, 1946; The Strong Delusion, 1951; NTR-Nothing to Report, 1955; Passport to Oblivion, 1964; Spylight, 1966; Passport in Suspense, 1967; Passport for a Pilgrim, 1968; They Don't Make Them Like That Any More, 1969; A Week of Love, 1969; Never had a Spanner on Her, 1970; Love-all, 1971; Follow the Drum, 1972; Host of Extras, 1973; Mandarin Gold, 1973; The Chinese Widow, 1974; Jade Gate, 1976; Love and the Land Beyond, 1979; Open Secret, 1982; Ship of Gold, 1984; Tank of Serpents, 1986; Frozen Assets, 1989; Love Down Under, 1991; *as Andrew MacAllan:* Succession, 1989; Generation, 1990; Diamond-Hard, 1991; Fanfare, 1992; Speculator, 1993, Traders, 1994; *non-fiction:* Author by Profession, The Monday Story, 1951; Wheels to Fortune, The Serjeant Major, 1954; The Red Fort; (with Kendal Burt) The One That Got Away, 1956; The Millionth Chance, 1957; War at the Top, 1959; (with Peter Eton) Conspiracy of Silence, 1959; Bring Out Your Dead, 1961; Rudolf Hess: The Uninvited Envoy, 1961; Singapore: The Battle that Changed the World, 1968; Green Beach, 1975; Boarding Party, 1977; The Unknown Warrior, 1980; Who Killed Sir Harry Oakes?, 1983; The Marine from Mandalay, 1988; Rhodes & Barnato: the Premier and the prancer, 1997. *Recreation:* vintage sports cars. *Address:* Swallowcliffe Manor, Salisbury, Wilts SP3 5PB. *Club:* Garrick.

LEATES, Margaret; freelance parliamentary draftsman, since 1990; *b* 30 March 1951; *d* of Henry Arthur Sargent Rayner and Alice (*née* Baker); *m* 1973, Timothy Philip Leates; one *s* one *d*. *Educ:* Lilley and Stone Girls' High Sch., Newark; King's Coll., London (LLB 1st cl. hons, LLM distinction; undergrad. and postgrad. schol.; AKC); MA (Theol) distinction, Univ. of Kent. Admitted Solicitor, 1975; joined Office of Parliamentary Counsel, 1976; seconded to Law Commn, 1981–83 and 1987–89; Dep. Parly Counsel, 1987–90. *Publication:* When I'm 64: a guide to pensions law. *Recreations:* hermeneutics, junk, other people's gardens. *Address:* Crofton Farm, 161 Crofton Lane, Orpington, Kent BR6 0BP. *T:* (01689) 820192; Nyanza, 87 Bennell's Avenue, Whitstable, Kent CT5 2HR. *T:* (01227) 272335; Mumford House, Church Hill, Kingsnorth, Ashford, Kent TN23 3EG. *T:* (01223) 610269; *e-mail:* mleates@cwcom.net.

LEATHAM, Dr Aubrey (Gerald), FRCP; cardiologist; Hon. Consulting Physician: St George's Hospital, London; National Heart Hospital; King Edward VII Hospital, London; *b* 23 Aug. 1920; *s* of Dr H. W. Leatham (*d* 1973), Godalming and Kathleen Pelham Burn (*d* 1971), Nosely Hall, Leicester; *m* 1954, Judith Augustine Savile Freer; one *s* three *d*. *Educ:* Charterhouse; Trinity Hall, Cambridge; St Thomas' Hospital. BA Cambridge 1941; MB, BChir 1944; MRCP 1945; FRCP 1957. House Phys., St Thomas' Hosp., 1944; RMO, Nat. Heart Hosp., 1945; Phys., RAMC, 1946–47; Sherbrook Research Fellow, Cardiac Dept, and Sen. Registrar, London Hosp., 1948–50; Asst Dir, Inst. of Cardiology, 1951–54, Dean, 1962–69. Goulstonian Lectr, RCP, 1958. R. T. Hall Travelling Prof., Australia and NZ, 1963. Member: Brit. Cardiac Soc.; Sociedad Peruana de Cardiologia, 1966; Sociedad Colombiana de Cardiologia, 1966. Hon. FACC 1986. Royal Order of Bhutan, 1966. *Publications:* Auscultation of the Heart and Phonocardiography, 1970; (jtly) Lecture Notes in Cardiology, 1990; articles in Lancet, British Heart Jl, etc, on auscultation of the heart and phonocardiography, artificial pacemakers, coronary artery disease, etc. *Recreations:* ski-ing and ski-touring, mountain walking, tennis, racquets, gardening, photography. *Address:* 27 Sulivan Road, SW6 3DT. *T:* (020) 7736 2237; The Heart Hospital, 47 Wimpole Street, W1M 7DG. *T:* (020) 7573 8899; Rookwood Farmhouse, West Wittering, Sussex PO20 8QH. *T:* (01243) 514649.

LEATHAM, Dorian; Chief Executive, London Borough of Hillingdon, since 1998; *b* 2 Aug. 1949; *s* of Robert Clement Leatham and Anna Ismay Leatham; partner, Janet Patrick; one *s* one *d*. *Educ:* High Wycombe Coll. of Technol. (BSc Sociol. (ext.) London); Brunel Univ. (MA Public and Social Admin). Various posts, 1970–75; Allocations Manager, Lambeth, 1975–77; District Housing Manager: City of Westminster, 1977–83; Camden, 1983–87; Dep. Dir of Housing, Brent, 1987–92; Dir, Housing Mgt, Circle 33 Housing Trust, 1992–93; Asst Dir of Housing, Hounslow, 1993–95; Dir of Housing, Croydon, 1995–98. *Recreations:* watching cricket, going to cinema and theatre, cooking, reading, supporting voluntary groups. *Address:* London Borough of Hillingdon, Civic Centre, Uxbridge UB8 1UW. *T:* (01895) 250569.

LEATHER, Sir Edwin (Hartley Cameron), KCMG 1974; KCVO 1975; Kt 1962; Governor and C-in-C of Bermuda, 1973–77; writer and broadcaster; *b* 22 May 1919; *s* of

Harold H. Leather, MBE, Hamilton, Canada, and Grace C. Leather (*née* Holmes); *m* 1940, Sheila A. A. (CStJ) (*d* 1994), *d* of Major A. H. Greenlees, Hamilton; two *d*. *Educ:* Trinity College Sch., Canada; Royal Military Coll., Kingston, Canada (BMilSc 1994). Commnd RCHA; served War of 1939–45 with Canadian Army, UK and in Europe, 1940–45. Contested (C) South Bristol, 1945; MP (C) N Somerset, 1950–64. Mem., Exec. Cttee, British Commonwealth Producers Organisation, 1960–63; Chairman: Bath Festival Soc., 1960–65; Horder Centre for Arthritics, 1962–65; Cons. and Unionist Assocs, 1969–70 (Mem. Nat. Exec. Cttee, 1963–70); Mem. Cons. Party Bd of Finance, 1963–67; Mem., Bd of Dirs, Yehudi Menuhin Sch., 1967–; Dir, N. M. Rothschild (Bermuda), 1978–91, and other cos. Canadian Legion rep. on Exec. Cttee of Brit. Commonwealth Ex-Servicemen's League, 1954–63; Pres., Institute of Marketing, 1963–67. Lay Reader, in Anglican Church, 1950–97. Chm., Bermuda Cttee, United World Colls, 1975–91; Mem. Council, Imp. Soc. of Knights Bachelor, 1969–; Nat. Gov., Shaw Fest., Niagara-on-the-Lake, Ontario, 1990–; Trustee, Menuhin Foundn of Bermuda, 1975–96, now Emeritus; Hon. Patron, Bermuda Fest., 1975–; Hon. Mem. Cttee, Canada Meml Foundn, 1991–. Freemason, 1942– (Past Grand Warden, Grand Lodge of England; Past Grand Registrar, Grand Lodge of Canada in Ontario). Grand Senechal Confrerie des Chevaliers du Tastevin, 1990–95. FRSA 1969; Hon. LLD: Bath, 1975; McMaster, 1999. KStJ 1974. Hon. Citizen: Kansas City, USA, 1957; S Carolina, 1995. Gold Medal, Nat. Inst. Social Sciences, NY, 1977. Medal of Merit, Royal Canadian Legion, 1963. *Publications:* The Vienna Elephant, 1977; The Mozart Score, 1978; The Duveen Letter, 1980. *Address:* 23 Inwood Drive, Paget, Bermuda PG05. *Clubs:* Carlton; Hamilton (Ontario); Royal Bermuda Yacht.

LEATHER, Ted; *see* Leather, Sir E. H. C.

LEATHERS, family name of **Viscount Leathers**.

LEATHERS, 3rd Viscount *cr* 1954, of Purfleet, Co. Essex; **Christopher Graeme Leathers;** Baron Leathers, 1941; with Department of Transport, since 1988; *b* 31 Aug. 1941; *er s* of 2nd Viscount Leathers and his 1st wife, Elspeth Graeme Stewart (*d* 1985); *S* father, 1996; *m* 1964, Maria Philomena, *yr d* of Michael Merriman, Charlestown, Co. Mayo; one *s* one *d*. *Educ:* Rugby Sch.; Open Univ. (BA Hons). New Zealand Shipping Co. Ltd, 1961–63; Wm Cory & Son Ltd, 1963–84; Mostyn Docks Ltd, 1984–88. MICS 1965; MIMgt 1987. Liveryman, Shipwrights' Co., 1969–. JP Clwyd, 1993. *Heir: s* Hon. James Frederick Leathers, *b* 27 May 1969. *Address:* Lime Cottage, High Street, Burwash, Etchingham, E Sussex TN19 7EL. *T:* (01435) 882530.

LEATHWOOD, Barry, OBE 1998; National Secretary, Rural, Agricultural and Allied Workers National Trade Group, Transport and General Workers' Union, since 1987; *b* 11 April 1941; *s* of Charles and Dorothy Leathwood; *m* 1963, Veronica Ann Clarke; one *d*. Apprentice Toolmaker, 1956–62; Toolmaker/Fitter, 1962–73; District Organiser, Nat. Union of Agric. and Allied Workers, 1973–83; Regional Officer, TGWU Agric. Group, 1983–87. FRSA 1996. *Recreations:* socialist politics, reading, photography. *Address:* (office) 128 Theobalds Road, WC1X 8TN. *T:* (020) 7611 2615.

LEAVER, Sir Christopher, GBE 1981; JP; director of private and public companies; Vice Chairman, Thames Water Plc, 1994–2000 (Deputy Chairman, 1989–93; Chairman, 1993–94); *b* 3 Nov. 1937; *s* of Dr Robert Leaver and Mrs Audrey Kerpen; *m* 1975, Helen Mireille Molyneux Benton; one *s* two *d*. *Educ:* Eastbourne Coll. Commissioned (Army), RAOC, 1956–58. Member, Retail Foods Trades Wages Council, 1963–64. JP Inner London, 1970–83, City, 1974–92; Member: Council, Royal Borough of Kensington and Chelsea, 1970–73; Court of Common Council (Ward of Dowgate), City of London, 1973; Alderman (Ward of Dowgate), City of London, 1974; Sheriff of the City of London, 1979–80; Lord Mayor of London, 1981–82; one of HM Lieutenants, City of London, 1982–. Chm., London Tourist Bd, 1983–89; Dep. Chm., Thames Water Authority, 1983–89; Chm., Thames Line Plc, 1987–89; Director: Bath & Portland Gp, 1983–85; Thermal Scientific plc, 1986–88; Unionamerica Holdings Plc, 1994–97. Advr on Royal Parks to Sec. of State for Nat. Heritage, 1993–96. Member: Bd of Brixton Prison, 1975–78; Court, City Univ., 1978– (Chancellor, 1981–82); Council of the Missions to Seamen, 1983–95; Council, Wine and Spirit Benevolent Soc., 1983–88; Finance Cttee, London Diocesan Fund, 1983–86; Transitional Council, St Paul's Cathedral, 1999; Trustee: Chichester Festival Theatre, 1982–97; LSO, 1983–91; Vice-President: Bridewell Royal Hosp., 1982–89; NPFA, 1983–99; Governor: Christ's Hospital Sch., 1975–; City of London Girls' Sch., 1975–78; City of London Freemen's Sch., 1980–81; Chm., Council, Eastbourne Coll., 1989– (Mem., 1988–); Almoner Trustee, St Paul's Cathedral Choir Sch. Foundn, 1986–90. Trustee, Music Therapy Trust, 1981–89; Chairman, Young Musicians' Symphony Orch. Trust, 1979–81; Hon. Mem., Guildhall Sch. of Music and Drama, 1982–. Church Warden, St Olave's, Hart Street, 1975–90 (Patronage Trust, 1990–96); Church Comr, 1982–93, 1996–99. Mem., Ct of Assistants, Carmen's Co., 1973 (Master, 1987–88); Hon. Liveryman: Farmers' Company, 1980; Water Conservators' Co., 2000 (Hon. Freeman, 1995); Freeman, Co. of Watermen and Lightermen, 1988; Hon. Mem., Co. of Environmental Cleaners, 1983–; Hon. Col, 151 (Greater London) Tpt Regt RCT (V), 1983–88; Hon. Col Comdt, RCT, 1988–91. Hon. DMus City, 1981. KStJ 1982. Order of Oman Class II. *Recreations:* gardening, music.

LEAVER, Prof. Christopher John, CBE 2000; FRS 1986; FRSE; Sibthorpian Professor of Plant Sciences, since 1990, and Head, Department of Plant Sciences, since 1991, University of Oxford; Fellow, St John's College, since 1989; *b* 31 May 1942; *s* of Douglas Percy Leaver and Elizabeth Constance Leaver; *m* 1971, Anne (*née* Huggins); one *s* one *d*. *Educ:* Imperial College, University of London (BSc, ARCS, DIC, PhD); MA (Oxon) 1990. Fulbright Scholar, Purdue Univ., 1966–68; Scientific Officer, ARC Plant Physiology Unit, Imperial Coll., 1968–69; University of Edinburgh: Lectr, Dept of Botany, 1969–80; Reader, 1980–86; SERC Sen. Res. Fellow, 1985–89; Prof. of Plant Molecular Biol., 1986–89. Member: AFRC, 1990–94; Priorities Bd for R&D to advise MAFF, 1990–94 (Chm., Arable Crops Adv. Sectoral Gp, 1990–94); Council, EMBO, 1991–97 (Chm., 1996–97); ACOST, 1992–93; Council, Royal Soc., 1992–94; BBSRC, 2000–; Chm., Adv. Bd, IACR, Rothamsted, 1995–2000. Curator, Oxford Botanic Garden, 1991–98. Trustee: John Innes Foundn, 1987–; Nat. History Mus., 1997–. FRSE 1987; MAE 1988. T. H. Huxley Gold Medal, Imperial Coll., 1970; Tate & Lyle Award, Phytochem. Soc. of Europe, 1984; Humboldt Prize, Alexander von Humboldt Foundn, Bonn, 1997. *Publications:* numerous papers in internat. sci. jls. *Recreations:* walking and talking in Upper Coquetdale. *Address:* Department of Plant Sciences, University of Oxford, South Parks Road, Oxford OX1 3RB. *T:* (01865) 275143, *Fax:* (01865) 275144; *e-mail:* chris.leaver@plants.ox.ac.uk.

LEAVER, Elaine Kildare; *see* Murray, E. K.

LEAVER, Peter Lawrence Oppenheim; QC 1987; a Recorder, since 1994; *b* 28 Nov. 1944; *er s* of Marcus Isaac Leaver and Lena Leaver (*née* Oppenheim); *m* 1969, Jane Rachel, *o d* of Leonard and Rivka Pearl; three *s* one *d*. *Educ:* Aldenham Sch., Elstree; Trinity Coll., Dublin. Called to the Bar, Lincoln's Inn, 1967, Bencher, 1995. Chairman: Bar Cttee, 1989; Internat. Practice Cttee, 1990; Member: Gen. Council of the Bar, 1987–90; Cttee on the Future of the Legal Profession, 1986–88; Council of Legal Educn, 1986–91. Chief Exec., FA Premier League, 1997–99. Dir, IMRO Ltd, 1994–2000. *Recreations:* sport, theatre, wine. *Address:* 1 Essex Court, Temple, EC4Y 9AR. *T:* (020) 7583 2000; 5 Hamilton Terrace, NW8 9RE. *T:* (020) 7286 0208. *Clubs:* Garrick, Groucho, MCC.

LEAVETT, Alan; Chairman, Long Ashton Parish Council, 1997–99; *b* 4 May 1924; *s* of George and Mabel Dorothy Leavett; *m* 1948, Jean Mary Wanford; three *d*. *Educ:* Gosport County Sch.; UC, Southampton. BA Hons 1943. MAP (RAE), 1943; HM Customs and Excise, 1947; HM Foreign Service, 1949; Rio de Janeiro, 1950–53; Bangkok, 1955–59; UK Perm. Delegate to ECAFE, 1958; Cabinet Office, 1961; Min. of Housing and Local Govt, 1963; Sec., Noise Adv. Council, 1970; Under-Sec., Civil Service Selection Bd, 1973, Dept of Environment, 1974–81. Gen. Sec., Avon Wildlife Trust, 1981–84; Member: Rural Develt Commn, 1982–91; Council, World Wildlife Fund UK, 1983–86; Clifton Suspension Bridge Trust, 1991–95; Vice-Pres., ACRE, 1987–92; Vice-Chm., Avon Community Council, 1981–89. Mem., Woodspring DC, 1986–95. *Publication:* Historic Sevenoaks, 1969. *Recreations:* book-collecting, music. *Address:* Darenth House, St Martins, Long Ashton, Som BS41 9HP. *T:* (01275) 392876.

LEAVEY, Thomas Edward, PhD; Director General, International Bureau of Universal Postal Union, since 1995; *b* Kansas City, 10 Nov. 1934; *s* of Leonard J. Leavey and Mary (*née* Horgan); *m* 1968, Anne Roland. *Educ:* Josephinium Coll., Columbus, Ohio (BA 1957); Institut Catholique, Paris; Princeton Univ. (MA 1967; PhD 1968). Sch. administrator and teacher, Kansas City, Mo, 1957–63; Prof., Fairleigh Dickinson Univ., NJ and George Washington Univ., Washington, 1968–70; United States Postal Service: Prof., Trng and Develt Inst., Bethesda, Md, 1970–72; Dir, Postal Service Trng and Develt Mgt Trng Center, LA, 1973–75; Gen. Manager, Employment and Placement Div., HQ, 1976–78; Dir, Postal Career Exec. Service, HQ, 1979; Postmaster/Sectional Manager, Charlottesville, Va, 1980; Regl Dir of Human Resources, Central Reg., Chicago, 1981; Controller, HQ, 1982; Gen. Manager, Internat. Mail Processing Div., HQ, 1982–87; Asst PMG and Sen. Dir, Internat. Postal Affairs, HQ, 1987–94. Universal Postal Union: Chairman: Customs Co-operation Council Contact Cttee, 1987–89; Private Operators Contact Cttee, 1991–94; Postal Develt Action Gp, 1991–94; Provident Scheme Mgt Bd, Internat. Bureau, 1989–94; Exec. Council, 1989–94. USPS Special Achievement Awards for Distinguished Service, 1970–90; John Wanamaker Award, USPS, 1991. *Publications:* numerous articles on business and postal matters in postal and trade jls. *Recreations:* golf, tennis, ski-ing. *Address:* International Bureau of the Universal Postal Union, Weltpoststrasse 4, 3000 Berne 15, Switzerland. *T:* (31) 3503101.

LE BAILLY, Vice-Adm. Sir Louis (Edward Stewart Holland), KBE 1972 (OBE 1952); CB 1969; DL; Director-General of Intelligence, Ministry of Defence, 1972–75; *b* 18 July 1915; *s* of Robert Francis Le Bailly and Ida Gaskell Le Bailly (*née* Holland); *m* 1946, Pamela Ruth Berthon; three *d*. *Educ:* RNC Dartmouth. HMS Hood, 1932; RNEC, 1933–37; HMS Hood, 1937–40; HMS Naiad, 1940–42; RNEC, 1942–44; HMS Duke of York, 1944–46; Admiralty, 1946–50 (Sec. to Lord Geddes' Admiralty Oil Cttee); HMS Bermuda, 1950–52; Dept of Second Sea Lord, 1952–55; RNEC, 1955–58; Admiralty: Staff Officer to Dartmouth Review Cttee, 1958; Asst Engineer-in-Chief, 1958–60; Naval Asst to Controller of the Navy, 1960–63; IDC, 1963; Dep. Dir of Marine Engineering, 1963–67; Naval Attaché, Washington, DC, and Comdr, British Navy Staff, 1967–69; Min. of Defence, 1970–72; Vice-Adm. 1970, retired 1972. Chm., civil service, police and fire service selection bds, 1976–82. Mem. Council, Research Inst. for Study of Conflict and Terrorism, 1976–. Chm. of Govs, Rendcomb Coll., 1979–85. DL Cornwall, 1982. FIMechE; FInstPet; FIMarE. Hon DSc Plymouth, 1994. *Publications:* The Man Around the Engine, 1990; From Fisher to the Falklands, 1991; Old Loves Return, 1993. *Address:* Garlands House, St Tudy, Bodmin, Cornwall PL30 3NN. *Club:* Naval.

LeBLANC, Rt Hon. Roméo; PC (Can.) 1974; CC 1995; CMM 1995; CD 1995; Governor General and Commander-in-Chief of Canada, 1995–99; *b* 18 Dec. 1927; *s* of Philias and Lucie LeBlanc; *m* Diana Fowler. *Educ:* Université St-Joseph, Memramcook (BA 1948; BEd 1951); Paris Univ. Teacher, New Brunswick, 1951–59; corresp. for Radio-Canada, in Ottawa, UK and US, 1960–67; Press Sec. to Prime Minister of Canada, 1967–71; Asst to Pres. and Dir of Public Relns, Moncton Univ., 1971–72. MP (L) Westmorland-Kent, 1972–84; Minister of State, Fisheries, 1974–76; Minister of: Fisheries and the Envmt, 1976–79; Fisheries and Oceans, 1980–82; Public Works, 1982–84; served on various Cabinet cttees; Mem., Senate, 1984–94; served on various Senate cttees; Speaker, 1993–94. Hon. DCL Mt Allison, 1977; Hon. Dr in Public Admin Moncton, 1979; Hon. LLD: Sainte-Anne, 1995; St Thomas, 1997; Meml, 1997; McGill, 1997; Hon. DLitt Ryerson, 1996; DUniv Ottawa, 1996. *Address:* PO Box 5254, Shediac, NB E4P 8T9, Canada.

LEBLOND, Prof. C(harles) P(hilippe), CC 1999 (OC 1977); MD, PhD, DSc; FRSC 1951; FRS 1965; Professor of Anatomy, McGill University, Canada, since 1948; *b* 5 Feb. 1910; *s* of Oscar Leblond and Jeanne Desmarchelier; *m* 1936, Gertrude Elinor Sternschuss; three *s* one *d*. *Educ:* Sch. St Joseph, Lille, France; Univs. of Lille, Paris, Montreal. L-ès-S, Nancy 1932; MD Paris 1934; PhD Montreal 1942; DSc Sorbonne 1945. Asst in Histology, Med. School, Univ. of Paris, 1934–35; Rockefeller Fell., Sch. of Med., Yale Univ., 1936–37; Asst, Laboratoire de Synthèse Atomique, Paris, 1938–40; McGill University: Lectr in Histology and Embryology, 1941–42; Asst Prof. of Anatomy, 1942–43; Assoc. Prof. of Anatomy, 1946–48; Chm. of Dept of Anatomy, 1957–75. Mem. Amer. Assoc. of Anatomists; Fellow, Amer. Acad. of Arts and Scis. Hon. DSc: Acadia, 1972; McGill, 1982; Montreal, 1985; York, 1986. *Publications:* over 300 articles, mainly on radio-autography and cell dynamics, in anatomical journals. *Recreation:* country. *Address:* (home) 68 Chesterfield Avenue, Westmount, Montreal, QC H3Y 2M5, Canada. *T:* (514) 4864837; (office) Department of Anatomy and Cell Biology, McGill University, 3640 University Street, Montreal, QC H3A 2B2, Canada. *T:* (514) 3986340.

LEBRECHT, Andrew John; Director General, Food, Farming and Fisheries, Department for Environment, Food and Rural Affairs, since 2001; *b* 13 Dec. 1951; *s* of late Heinz Martin Lebrecht and of Margaret (*née* Cardis); *m* 1976, Judit Catan; two *d*. *Educ:* De La Salle Coll., Hove; Leeds Univ. (BA Econs); Reading Univ. (MSc Agricl Econs). Ministry of Agriculture, Fisheries and Food, 1977–2001: Private Sec. to Parly Sec., 1980–82; on secondment to HM Diplomatic Service as First Sec. (Fisheries and Food), UK Rep. Brussels, 1985–89; Principal Private Sec. to Minister of Agriculture, 1989–91; Head: Sheep and Livestock Subsidies Div., 1991–93; Review of Animal Health and Veterinary Gp, 1993–94; EU Div., 1994–98; EU and Internat. Policy, 1998–2001. *Recreations:* family life, the countryside, reading. *Address:* 10 Bulmershe Road, Reading, Berks RG1 5RJ. *T:* (0118) 966 7048.

LE BRETON, David Francis Battye, CBE 1978; HM Diplomatic Service, retired; Secretary, Overseas Service Pensioners Association and Benevolent Society, since 1992; *b* 2 March 1931; *e s* of late Lt-Col F. H. Le Breton, MC, and Elisabeth, (Peter), Le Breton (*née* Trevor-Battye), Endebess, Kenya; *m* 1961, Patricia June Byrne; one *s* two *d*. *Educ:* Winchester; New Coll., Oxford. Colonial Administrative Service, Tanganyika, 1954; Private Sec. to Governor, 1959–60; Magistrate, 1962; Principal, CRO, 1963; HM

Diplomatic Service, 1965; First Sec., Zanzibar, 1964; Lusaka, 1964–68; FCO, 1968–71; Head of Chancery, Budapest, 1971–74; HM Comr in Anguilla, 1974–78; Counsellor and Head of Chancery, Nairobi, 1978–81; High Comr in The Gambia, 1981–84; Head of Commonwealth Co-ordination Dept, FCO, 1984–86; Head of Nationality and Treaty Dept, FCO, 1986–87. Financial Advr/Sales Associate, Allied Dunbar Assurance, 1987–91. *Recreations:* country living, garden-clearing, African and colonial affairs. *Address:* Brackenwood, French Street, near Westerham, Kent TN16 1PN.

le BROCQUY, Louis, FCSD (FSIAD 1960); HRHA 1983; painter since 1939; *b* Dublin, 10 Nov. 1916; *s* of late Albert le Brocquy, MA, and late Sybil Staunton; *m* 1st, 1938, Jean Stoney (marr. diss., 1948); one *d*; 2nd, 1958, Anne Madden Simpson; two *s*. *Educ:* St Gerard's Sch., Wicklow, Ireland. Self-taught. Founder-mem. of Irish Exhibn of Living Art, 1943; Visiting Instructor, Central Sch. of Arts and Crafts, London, 1947–54; Visiting Tutor, Royal Coll. of Art, London, 1955–58. Member: Irish Council of Design, 1963–65; Adv. Council, Guinness Peat Awards, 1980–85. Director: Kilkenny Design Workshops, 1965–77; Irish Mus. of Modern Art, 1989–. Represented Ireland, Venice Biennale (awarded internat. prize), 1956. Work exhibited in: "50 Ans d'Art Moderne", Brussels, 1958; Painting since World War II, Guggenheim Mus., New York, 1987–88; Olympiad of Art, Seoul, 1988; L'Europe des Grands Maîtres 1870–1970, Inst. de France, 1989; Internat. Art Fest., Seoul, 1991; Premiers Chefs d'Oeuvres des Grands Maîtres, Museums of Art, Tokyo, Osaka, Kyoto, 1992. One Man Shows: Leicester Galleries, London, 1948; Gimpel Fils, London, 1947, 1949, 1951, 1955, 1956, 1957, 1959, 1961, 1966, 1968, 1971, 1974, 1978, 1983, 1988, 1991, 1993, 1997, 2001; Waddington, Dublin, 1951; Robles Gallery, Los Angeles, 1960; Gallery Lienhard, Zürich, 1961; Dawson/Taylor Gallery, Dublin, 1962, 1966, 1969, 1971, 1973, 1974, 1975, 1981, 1985, 1986, 1988, 1991, 1992, 1993, 1996, 1999, 2000; Municipal Gallery of Modern Art, Dublin, 1966, 1978, 1992; Ulster Mus., Belfast, (retrospective) 1967, 1987, 1993; Gimpel-Hanover, Emmerich Zürich, 1969, 1978, 1983; Gimpel, NY, 1971, 1978, 1983; Fondation Maeght, 1973; Bussola, Turin, 1974; Arts Council, Belfast, 1975, 1978; Musée d'Art Moderne, Paris, 1976; Giustiniani, Genoa, 1977; Waddington, Montreal, Toronto, 1978; Maeght, Barcelona, Madrid, Granada, 1978–79; Jeanne Bucher, Paris, 1979, 1982; NY State Mus., 1981; Boston Coll. 1982; Westfield Coll., Mass, 1982; Palais des Beaux Arts, Charleroi, 1982; Art 13, Internat. Basel (Börjeson), 1982; Chicago Internat. Expo (Brownstone Gall.), 1986; Arts Council, Dublin, 1987; Nat. Gall. of Vic, Melbourne, Festival Centre, Adelaide, and Mus. of Contemp. Art, Brisbane, 1988; Musée Picasso, Antibes, 1989; Kerlin, Dublin, 1991; Mus. of Modern Art, Kamakura, 1991; Itami City Mus. of Art, Osaka, 1991; City Mus. of Contemp. Art, Hiroshima, 1991; Carré Davidson, Tours, 1995; Irish Mus. of Modern Art, 1996; Espace Ricard, Paris, 1996; Galerie Maeght, Paris, 1996; Château Musée de Tours, 1997; Municipal Gall. of Modern Art, Ljubljana, 1998; Museo de Arte Contemporaneo, Instituto de Artes Gráficas, Oaxaca, 2000; Agnew's, 2001. Public Collections possessing work include: Albright Museum, Buffalo; Arts Council, London; Carnegie Inst., Pittsburgh; l'Etat Français; Chicago Arts Club; Columbus Mus., Ohio; Detroit Inst. of Art; Dublin Municipal Gallery; Fort Worth Center, Texas; Foundation of Brazil Museum, Bahia; Gulbenkian Mus., Lisbon; Guggenheim Museum, NY; J. H. Hirshhorn Foundation, Washington; Ho-Am Mus., Seoul; Irish Mus. of Modern Art, Dublin; Itami Mus., Osaka; Kunsthaus, Zürich; Fondation Maeght, St Paul; Leeds City Art Gallery; Musée d'Art Moderne, Paris; Musée Picasso, Antibes; Mus. of Contemp. Art, Hiroshima; Mus. of Modern Art, Kamakura; NY State Mus.; San Diego Mus., Calif.; Tate Gallery; Uffizi, Florence; Ulster Museum, Belfast; Vatican Mus.; V&A Museum. RHA 1950–69. Film, An Other Way of Knowing, RTE, 1986. Hon. DLitt Dublin, 1962; Hon. LLD NUI, 1988; Hon. DPh Dublin City, 1999. Saoi, Aosdána, Irish Arts Council, 1993. Commandeur du Bontemps de Médoc et des Graves, 1969. Chevalier de la Légion d'Honneur, 1975; Officier, l'Ordre des Arts et des Lettres, 1996. *Illustrated work:* The Táin, trans. Thomas Kinsella, 1969; The Playboy of the Western World, Synge, 1970; The Gododdin O'Grady, 1978; Dubliners, Joyce, 1986; Stirrings Still, Samuel Beckett, 1988. *Relevant publications:* Louis le Brocquy by D. Walker, introd. John Russell, Ireland 1981, UK 1982; The Irish Landscape, by G. Morgan, 1992; Seeing his Way, by A. Madden le Brocquy, 1994; Procession, by G. Morgan, 1994; The Head Image: interviews by G. Morgan and M. Peppiatt, 1996. *Address:* c/o Gimpel Fils, 30 Davies Street, W1Y 1LG.

LE BRUN, Christopher Mark, RA 1997; artist; Professor of Drawing, Royal Academy, since 2000; *b* 20 Dec. 1951; *s* of late John Le Brun, BEM and of Eileen Betty (*née* Miles); *m* 1979, Charlotte Eleanor Verity; two *s* one *d*. *Educ:* Portsmouth Southern Grammar Sch.; Slade Sch. of Fine Art (DFA); Chelsea Sch. of Art (MA). Lecturer: Brighton Coll. of Art, 1975–82; Wimbledon Coll. of Art, 1982–84; Vis. Lectr, Slade Sch. of Fine Art, 1984–90. Deutsche Akademische Austauschdienste Fellowship, Berlin, 1987–88. Designer, Ballet Imperial, Royal Opera Hse, Covent Gdn, 1984. One man exhibitions include: Nigel Greenwood Gall., London, 1980, 1982, 1985, 1989; Gillespie-Laage-Salomon, Paris, 1981; Sperone Westwater, NY, 1983, 1986, 1988; Fruitmarket Gall., Edinburgh, 1985; Arnolfini Gall., Bristol, 1985; Kunsthalle, Basel, 1986; Daadgalerie, Berlin, 1988; Galerie Rudolf Zwirner, Cologne, 1988; Art Center, Pasadena, Calif, 1992; LA Louver Gall., Venice, Calif, 1992; Marlborough Fine Art, 1994, 1998, 2001; Galerie Fortlaan 17, Ghent, 1994; Astrup Fearnley Mus. of Modern Art, Oslo, 1995; Fitzwilliam Mus., Cambridge, 1995; group exhibitions include: Milan, 1980; Berlin, 1982; Tate Gall., 1983; Mus. Modern Art, NY, 1984; The British Show, toured Australia and NZ, 1985; Oxford, Budapest, Prague, Warsaw, 1987; LA County Mus., 1987; Cincinatti Mus. and American tour, 1988–89; Setagaya Art Mus. and Japanese tour, 1990–91; Scottish Nat. Gall. Modern Art, 1995; Yale Center for British Art, New Haven, 1995; Nat. Gall., 2000; work in public collections includes: Arts Council of GB, British Council, BM, NY Mus. Modern Art, Scottish Nat. Gall. Modern Art, Tate Gall., Walker Art Gall., Liverpool, Whitworth Art Gall., Manchester and Fitzwilliam Mus., Cambridge. Trustee: Tate Gall., 1990–95; Nat. Gall., 1996–; Dulwich Picture Gall., 2000–; Member: Slade Cttee, 1992–95; Develt Cttee, Tate Gall. of British Art, 1995–97. Prizewinner, John Moores Liverpool Exhibns, 1978 and 1980; Gulbenkian Foundn Printmakers Award, 1983. *Publication:* Christopher Le Brun, 2001. *Address:* c/o Marlborough Fine Art, 6 Albemarle Street, W1X 4BY. *T:* (020) 7629 5161.

LE CARRÉ, John; *see* Cornwell, David John Moore.

LE CHEMINANT, Peter, CB 1976; Director-General, General Council of British Shipping, 1985–91; consultant on government administration; *b* 29 April 1926; *s* of William Arthur Le Cheminant and Agnes Ann Le Cheminant (*née* Wilson); *m* 1959, Suzanne Elisabeth Horny; three *s*. *Educ:* Holloway Sch.; London Sch. of Economics. Sub Lt, RNVR, 1944–47. Min. of Power, 1949; Cabinet Office, 1950–52 and 1964–65; UK Delegn to ECSC, 1962–63; Private Sec. to Prime Minister, 1965–68; Min. of Power, later Min. of Technology, 1968–71; Under-Sec., DTI, 1971–74; Deputy Secretary: Dept of Energy, 1974–77; Cabinet Office, 1978–81; CSD, subseq. HM Treas., 1981–83; Second Perm. Sec., Cabinet Office (MPO), 1983–84. Member, Council: Inst. of Employment Studies (formerly Manpower), 1983–97; King George's Fund for Sailors, 1987–. Freeman, City of London, 1987; Liveryman, Worshipful Co. of Shipwrights, 1987. CIMgt (CBIM 1984); FCIT 1987. *Publication:* Beautiful Ambiguities, 2001. *Recreations:* reading, walking, history. *Club:* Reform.

LE CHEMINANT, Air Chief Marshal Sir Peter (de Lacey), GBE 1978; KCB 1972 (CB 1968); DFC 1943, and Bar, 1951; Lieutenant-Governor and Commander-in-Chief of Guernsey, 1980–85; *b* 17 June 1920; *s* of Lieut-Colonel Keith Le Cheminant and Blanche Etheldred Wake Le Cheminant (*née* Clark); *m* 1940, Sylvia (*d* 1998), *d* of J. van Bodegom; one *s* two *d*. *Educ:* Elizabeth Coll., Guernsey; RAF Coll., Cranwell. Flying posts in France, UK, N Africa, Malta, Sicily and Italy, 1940–44; comd No 223 Squadron, 1943–44; Staff and Staff Coll. Instructor, 1945–48; Far East, 1949–53; comd No 209 Sqn, 1949–51; Jt Planning Staff, 1953–55; Wing Comdr, Flying, Kuala Lumpur, 1955–57; jssc 1958; Dep. Dir of Air Staff Plans, 1958–61; comd RAF Geilenkirchen, 1961–63; Dir of Air Staff Briefing, 1964–66; SASO, HQ FEAF, 1966–67, C of S, 1967–68; Comdt Joint Warfare Estabt, MoD, 1968–70; Asst Chief of Air Staff (Policy), MoD, 1971–72; UK Mem., Perm. Mil. Deputies Gp, CENTO, Ankara, 1972–73; Vice-Chief of Defence Staff, 1974–76; Dep. C-in-C, Allied Forces, Central Europe, 1976–79. FRUSI 2001. KStJ 1980. *Publications:* The Royal Air Force - A Personal Experience, 2001; *as Desmond Walker:* Bedlam in the Bailiwicks, 1987; Task Force Channel Islands, 1989. *Recreations:* golf, writing, reading. *Address:* La Madeleine De Bas, Ruette de la Madeleine, St Pierre du Bois, Guernsey, CI. *Club:* Royal Air Force.

LECHÍN-SUÁREZ, General Juan; Condor de los Andes (Bolivia), 1966; *b* 8 March 1921; *s* of Juan Alfredo Lechín and Julia Suárez; *m* 1947, Ruth Varela; one *s* three *d*. *Educ:* Bolivian Military College. Chief of Ops, Bolivian Army HQ, 1960–61; Military and Air Attaché, Bolivian Embassy, Bonn, 1962–63; Comdr, Bolivian Army Fifth Inf. Div., 1964; Pres., Bolivian State Mining Corp. (with rank of Minister of State), 1964–68; Comdr, Bolivian Army Third Inf. Div., 1969; Bolivian Ambassador to the UK and to the Netherlands, 1970–74; Minister for Planning and Co-ordination, 1974–78; Chm., Nat. Adv. and Legislation Council, 1980–81. Guerrillero José Miguel Lanza, Mérito Aeronautico, and Mérito Naval, 1966, Bolivia. Das Grosse Verdienstkreuz (FRG), 1975. *Publications:* La Estrategia del Altiplano Boliviano, 1975; La Batalla de Villa Montes, 1989; Historia Trágica de un Camino Inexistente, 2000. *Recreations:* tennis, swimming. *Address:* Casilla 4405, La Paz, Bolivia.

LECHMERE, Sir Reginald Anthony Hungerford, 7th Bt *cr* 1818, of The Rhydd, Worcestershire; *b* 24 Dec. 1920; *s* of Anthony Hungerford Lechmere, 3rd *s* of 3rd Bt, and Cicely Mary Lechmere; *S* cousin, 2001; *m* 1956, Anne Jennifer Dind; three *s* one *d*. *Educ:* Charterhouse; Trinity Hall, Cambridge. Served Army, 1940–47, 5th Royal Inniskilling Dragoon Guards, HQ6 Armoured Div. Publicity Manager, Penguin Books, 1950–51; journalist, 1952–56. *Heir:* *s* Nicholas Anthony Hungerford Lechmere [*b* 24 April 1960; *m* 1991, Caroline Gahan; two *s* one *d*]. *Address:* Primeswell, Colwall, near Malvern, Worcs WR13 6DT. *T:* (01684) 540340.

LECKY, (Arthur) Terence, CMG 1968; HM Diplomatic Service, retired; *b* 10 June 1919; *s* of late Lieut-Colonel M. D. Lecky, DSO, late RA, and late Bertha Lecky (*née* Goss); *m* 1946, Jacqualine (*d* 1974), *d* of late Dr A. G. Element; three *s*. *Educ:* Winchester Coll.; Clare Coll., Cambridge (1938–39). Served RA, 1939–46. FO (Control Commission for Germany), 1946–49; FO, 1950–54; Vice-Consul, Zürich, 1954–56; FO, 1957–61; First Secretary, The Hague, 1962–64, FCO (formerly FO), 1964–70, retired. Mem., Hants CC, 1981–89. Vice-Chm., Hants Police Authority, 1988–89. *Address:* 1 Old Blackmore Museum, St Ann Place, Salisbury, Wilts SP1 2SU. *T:* (01722) 338937.

LECKY, Maj.-Gen. Samuel K.; *see* Knox-Lecky.

LECKY, Terence; *see* Lecky, A. T.

LECONFIELD; Baron; *see* Egremont.

LECOURT, Robert; Commandeur, Legion of Honour; Croix de Guerre; Rosette de la Résistance; Member, Constitutional Council of the French Republic, 1979–89; *b* 19 Sept. 1908; *s* of Léon Lecourt and Angéle Lépron; *m* 1932, Marguerite Chabrerie; one *d*. *Educ:* Rouen; Univ. de Caen (DenDroit). Advocate, Court of Appeal: Rouen, 1928; Paris, 1932. Served with French Air Force, 1939–40; Mem. Resistance Movt, 1942–44; Deputy for Paris, 1945–58 and for Hautes Alpes, 1958–61, National Assembly; Pres., Parly Gp, MRP, 1945–48 and 1952–57; Minister of Justice, 1948–49 and 1957–58; Minister of State responsible for co-operation with Africa, 1958–61. Judge, Court of Justice, European Community, 1962, President 1967–76; Hon. Bencher, Gray's Inn, 1972; DUniv Exeter, 1975. Holds numerous foreign decorations. *Publications:* Nature juridique de l'action en réintégrande, 1931; Code pratique du travail, Responsabilité des architectes et entrepreneurs, etc, 1932–39; Le Juge devant le marché commun, 1970; L'Europe des juges, 1976; Concorde sans concordat 1952–57, 1978. *Address:* 11 Boulevard Suchet, 75016 Paris, France.

LEDERBERG, Prof. Joshua, PhD; Sackler Scholar, Rockefeller University, since 1995 (President, 1978–90; University Professor, 1990–95); consultant; *b* Montclair, NJ, USA, 23 May 1925; *s* of Zwi H. and Esther Lederberg (*née* Goldenbaum); *m* 1968, Marguerite Stein Kirsch, MD; one *d*; one step *s*. *Educ:* Stuyvesant High Sch., NYC; Columbia Coll. (BA); Yale Univ. (PhD). Assistant Professor of Genetics, University of Wisconsin, 1947; Associate Professor, 1950; Professor, 1954; Fulbright Vis. Prof. of Bacteriology, Univ. of Melbourne, Aust., 1957; Prof. and Exec. Head, Dept of Genetics, Sch. of Medicine, Stanford Univ., 1959–78. Shared in discoveries concerning genetic re-combination, and organization of genetic material of bacteria, contributing to cancer research; discovered a method of artificially introducing new genes into bacteria in investigation of hereditary substance. Chm., President's Cancer Panel (US), 1980–81. Member: Adv. Cttee for Med. Res., WHO, 1971–76; Defense Sci. Bd, USA, 1979–; Chief of Naval Ops Exec. Panel, USN, 1981–; Tech. Assessment Adv. Cttee, Office of Technology Assessment, US Congress, 1988–; Adv. Cttee to Dir, NIH, 1993–; Ellison Med. Foundn, 1997–; Member Board: Chemical Industry Inst. for Toxicology, 1980–; Dreyfus Foundn, 1983–; Revson Foundn, 1986–93; Proctor and Gamble Co., Cincinnati, 1984–95; Carnegie Corp., NYC, 1985–93. Columnist, Science and Man (Washington Post Syndicate), 1966–71. Mem., National Academy of Sciences, United States, 1957. For. Mem., Royal Society, 1979. Hon. degrees include: ScD: Yale Univ.; Columbia Univ.; Univ. of Wisconsin; Rockefeller Univ.; MD Tufts Univ. (Jointly) Nobel Prize in Medicine, 1958. US Nat. Medal of Science, 1989. *Publications:* (ed) Emerging Infections, 1992; (ed) Biological Weapons: containing the threat, 1999; (Ed. in Chief) Encyclopedia of Microbiology; contribs to learned journals on genetics, bacteria and general biological problems. *Address:* Rockefeller University, 1230 York Avenue, New York, NY 10021, USA. *T:* (212) 3277809.

LEDERMAN, David; QC 1990; a Recorder, since 1987; *b* 8 Feb. 1942; *s* of Eric Kurt Lederman and Marjorie Alice Lederman; *m* 1974, Georgina Anne Rubin; one *s* two *d*. *Educ:* Clayesmore School, Dorset; Gonville and Caius College, Cambridge. Called to the Bar, Inner Temple, 1966; criminal practice, fraud, murder, etc. *Recreations:* tennis, horses, France, family.

LEDERMAN, Dr Leon Max, FInstP; Director, Fermi National Accelerator Laboratory, 1979–89, Director Emeritus, since 1989; Pritzker Professor of Science, Illinois Institute of Technology, since 1992; *b* 15 July 1922; *s* of Minnie Rosenberg and Morris Lederman; *m* 1st, Florence Gordon; one *s* two *d*; 2nd, 1981, Ellen. *Educ:* City College of New York (BS 1943); Columbia Univ. (AM 1948; PhD 1951). FInstP 1998. US Army, 1943–46. Columbia University: Research Associate, Asst Prof., Associate Prof., 1951–58; Prof. of Physics, 1958–89; Associate Dir, Nevis Labs, 1953, Director, 1962–79. Resident Scholar, Ill Maths and Sci. Acad., 1998–. Ford Foundn Fellow, 1958–59; John Simon Guggenheim Foundn Fellow, 1958–59; Ernest Kempton Adams Fellow, 1961. Fellow, Amer. Physical Soc.; Mem., Nat. Acad. of Scis, 1965. Numerous hon. degrees. Nat. Medal of Science, 1965; (jtly) Nobel Prize in Physics, 1988; Enrico Fermi Prize, DOE, US, 1992. *Publications:* From Quartz to the Cosmos, 1989; The God Particle, 1992; papers and contribs to learned jls on high energy physics. *Recreations:* mountain hiking, ski-ing, jogging, piano, riding, gardening. *Address:* Fermi National Accelerator Laboratory, PO Box 500, Batavia, IL 60510, USA. *T:* (630) 8402856; (312) 5678920.

LEDGER, Frank, CBE 1992 (OBE 1985); FREng; Deputy Chairman, Nuclear Electric plc, 1990–92, retired; *b* 16 June 1929; *s* of Harry and Doris Ledger; *m* 1953, Alma Moverley; two *s*. *Educ:* Leeds College of Technology (BSc Eng). FREng (FEng 1990); FIMechE; FIEE. Student Apprentice, Leeds Corp. Elect. Dept, 1947; appts in power station construction and generation operation in CEA then CEGB, 1955–65; Station Manager, Cottam Power Station, 1965; Central Electricity Generating Board: Group Manager, Midlands Region, 1968; System Operation Engineer, 1971; Dir, Resource Planning, Midlands Region, 1975; Dir of Computing, 1980; Dir of Operations, 1981; Exec. Bd Mem. for Prodn, 1986. Sen. Associate, Nichols Associates Ltd, 1992–98. Member: Council, IEE, 1987–92; British Nat. Cttee, UNIPEDE, 1981–90; Council, British Energy Assoc., 1990–92; Vice-Pres., Energy Industries Club, 1988–92. *Publication:* (jtly) Crisis Management in the Power Industry: an inside story, 1994. *Recreations:* music, photography, gardening, walking. *Address:* 3 Barns Dene, Harpenden, Herts AL5 2HH. *T:* (01582) 762188.

LEDGER, Sir Philip (Stevens), Kt 1999; CBE 1985; Principal, Royal Scottish Academy of Music and Drama, 1982–2001; *b* 12 Dec. 1937; *s* of Walter Stephen Ledger and Winifred Kathleen (*née* Stevens); *m* 1963, Mary Erryl (*née* Wells); one *s* one *d*. *Educ:* Bexhill Grammar Sch.; King's Coll., Cambridge (Maj. Schol.); John Stewart of Rannoch Schol. in Sacred Music; 1st Cl. Hons in Pt I and Pt II, of Music Tripos; MA, MusB. FRCO (Limpus and Read prizes); FRCM 1983; FRNCM 1989; FRSE 1990. Master of the Music, Chelmsford Cathedral, 1962–65; Dir of Music, Univ. of East Anglia, 1965–73 (Dean of Sch. of Fine Arts and Music, 1968–71); Dir of Music and Organist, King's Coll., Cambridge, 1974–82; Conductor, CU Musical Soc., 1973–82. Artistic Dir, 1968–89, Vice-Pres., 1989–, Aldeburgh Festival of Music and the Arts. Hon. Prof., Univ. of Glasgow, 1993–98. President: RCO, 1992–94; ISM, 1994–95; Chm., Cttee of Principals of Conservatoires, 1994–98. Hon. RAM 1984; Hon. GSM 1989. Hon. LLD Strathclyde, 1987; DUniv UCE, 1998; Hon. DMus: Glasgow, 2001; RSAMD, 2001. *Publications:* (ed) Anthems for Choirs 2 and 3, 1973; (ed) The Oxford Book of English Madrigals, 1978; other edns of Byrd, Handel and Purcell; carol arrangements. *Recreations:* swimming, theatre, membership of Sette of Odd Volumes. *Address:* 2 Lancaster Drive, Upper Rissington, Cheltenham, Glos GL54 2QZ.

LEDGER, Ronald Joseph; Casino Proprietor and Manager; *b* 7 Nov. 1920; *s* of Arthur and Florence Ledger; brought up by Dr Barnardo's, 1923–37; *m* 1946, Madeleine Odette de Villeneuve; three *s* one *d*. *Educ:* Skinners Grammar Sch., Tunbridge Wells; Nottingham Univ. Toolroom Engineer, 1938–42. Served RAF, 1942–47, fitter, Leading Aircraftsman; India three years. Univ. of Nottingham, 1947–49 (Diploma in Social Science); Staff Training Officer, Enfield Highway Co-op. Society, 1949; Business Partner, 1950, Company Director, 1953, Employment Specialists. Mem. Herts CC, 1952–54. Contested (Lab) Rushcliffe Div. of Nottingham, 1951; MP (Lab and Co-op) Romford, 1955–70. Director: Enfield Electronics (CRT) Ltd, 1958; London Co-operative Society Ltd, 1961. Chairman, Hairdressing Council, 1966–79. *Recreations:* tennis, cricket, golf, snooker. *Address:* Lisbon, Heath Gardens, Lake, Isle of Wight PO36 8PQ. *Club:* Shanklin and Sandown Golf.

LEDINGHAM, Prof. John Gerard Garvin, DM; FRCP; May Reader in Medicine, 1974–95, Professor of Clinical Medicine, 1989–95, and Director of Clinical Studies, 1977–82 and 1991–95, University of Oxford; Fellow of New College, Oxford, 1974–95, Emeritus, 1995–2000, Hon. Fellow, since 2000; Hon. Clinical Director, Biochemical and Clinical NMR Unit, Medical Research Council, Oxford, 1988–95; *b* 1929; *s* of late John Ledingham, MB BCh, DPH, and late Una Ledingham, MD, FRCP, *d* of J. L. Garvin, CH, Editor of The Observer; *m* 1961, Elaine Mary, *d* of late R. G. Maliphant, MD, FRCOG, and of Dilys Maliphant, Cardiff; four *d*. *Educ:* Rugby Sch.; New Coll., Oxford; Middlesex Hosp. Med. Sch. (1st Cl. Physiol.; BM BCh; DM 1966). FRCP 1971 (MRCP 1959). Junior appts, Middlesex, London Chest, Whittington, and Westminster Hospitals, London, 1957–64; Travelling Fellow, British Postgraduate Med. Fedn, Columbia Univ., New York, 1965–66; Consultant Physician, Oxford AHA(T), 1966–82, Hon. Consultant Physician, Oxfordshire HA, 1982–. Chm., Medical Staff Council, United Oxford Hosps, 1970–72. Chm., Medical Res. Soc., 1988–92; Hon. Sec., Assoc. of Physicians of Gt Britain and Ireland 1977–82, Hon. Treas., 1982–88; Pro-Censor, RCP, 1983–84, Censor, 1984–85. Member: Commonwealth Scholarship Commn, ACU, 1993–98; Nuffield Council on Bioethics, 2000–. Governing Trustee, Nuffield Trust (formerly Nuffield Provincial Hosps Trust), 1978–; Trustee, Beit Trust, 1989–. Osler Meml Medal, 2000. *Publications:* (ed jtly) Oxford Textbook of Medicine, 1982, 3rd edn 1995; contribs to med. books and scientific jls in the field of hypertension and renal diseases. *Recreations:* music, golf. *Address:* 22 Hid's Copse Road, Cumnor Hill, Oxford OX2 9JJ. *T:* (01865) 862023. *Club:* Vincent's (Oxford).

LEDLIE, John Kenneth, CB 1994; OBE 1977; Partnership Secretary, Linklaters (formerly Linklaters & Paines), since 1995; *b* 19 March 1942; *s* of late Reginald Cyril Bell Ledlie and Elspeth Mary Kaye; *m* 1965, Rosemary Julia Allan; three *d*. *Educ:* Westminster School (Hon. Schol.); Brasenose Coll., Oxford (Triplett Exbnr; MA Lit Hum). Solicitor of the High Court; articles with Coward Chance, 1964–67; Min. of Defence, 1967; Asst Private Sec. to Minister of State for Equipment and Sec. of State for Defence, 1969–70; First Sec., UK Delegn to NATO, Brussels, 1973–76; Dep. Chief, Public Relations, 1977–79; NI Office and Cabinet Office, 1979–81; Procurement Exec., MoD, 1981–83; Head, Defence Secretariat 19, MoD, 1983; Regional Marketing Dir, Defence Sales Orgn, 1983–85; Chief of PR, MoD, 1985–87; Fellow, Center for Internat. Affairs, Harvard Univ., 1987–88; Asst Under-Sec. of State, MoD, 1988–90; Dep. Sec., NI Office, 1990–93; Dep. Under Sec. of State (Personnel and Logistics), MoD, 1993–95. *Recreations:* ornithology, cricket, tennis, golf, theatre, opera. *Address:* c/o Linklaters, One Silk Street, EC2Y 8HQ. *T:* (020) 7456 3722. *Club:* Oxford and Cambridge.

LEDSOME, Neville Frank, CB 1988; Deputy Chairman, Civil Service Appeal Board, 1994–99; Under Secretary, Personnel Management Division, Department of Trade and Industry, 1983–89, retired; *b* 29 Nov. 1929; *s* of late Charles Percy Ledsome and Florence Ledsome; *m* 1953, Isabel Mary Lindsay; three *s*. *Educ:* Birkenhead Sch. Exec. Officer, BoT, 1948; Monopolies Commn, 1957; Higher Exec. Officer, BoT, 1961; Principal, 1964; DEA, 1967; HM Treasury, 1969; DTI, 1970; Asst Sec., 1973; Under Sec., 1980. *Recreations:* gardening, theatre.

LEDWITH, Prof. Anthony, CBE 1995; FRS 1995; Professor and Head of Department of Chemistry, University of Sheffield, 1996–99, now Emeritus Professor; Chairman, Engineering and Physical Sciences Research Council, since 1999 (Member, 1994–97); *b* 14 Aug. 1933; *s* of Thomas Ledwith and Mary (*née* Coghlan); *m* 1960, Mary Clare Ryan; one *s* three *d*. *Educ:* BSc (external) London 1954; PhD 1957, DSc 1970, Liverpool Univ. FRSC 1986. Liverpool University: Lectr, 1959, Prof., 1976, Campbell Brown Prof. of Industrial Chem., 1980, Dept of Inorganic Physical and Industrial Chem.; Dean, Faculty of Sci., 1980–83; Dep. Dir, Group R&D, 1984–88, Dir, Group Res., 1988–96, Pilkington plc. Member: DSAC, 1988–; SERC, 1990–94. Pres., RSC, 1998–2000. *Publications:* (with A. D. Jenkins) Reactivity, Mechanism and Structure in Polymer Chemistry, 1974; (with A. M. North) Molecular Behaviour and the Development of Polymeric Materials, 1975; (with S. J. Moss) The Chemistry of the Semiconductor Industry, 1987; (ed jtly) Comprehensive Polymer Science, 7 vols, 1989. *Recreations:* squash, tennis, golf. *Address:* 193 Wigan Road, Standish, Wigan WN6 0AE.

LEE, Alan Peter; racing correspondent, The Times, since 1999; *b* 13 June 1954; *s* of Peter Alexander Lee and Christina Carmichael; *m* 1980, Patricia Drury; one *s* one *d*. *Educ:* Cavendish Grammar Sch., Hemel Hempstead. With Watford Observer, 1970–74; Hayters Agency, 1974–78; freelance, 1978–82; cricket correspondent: Mail on Sunday, 1982–87; The Times, 1988–99. *Publications:* A Pitch in Both Camps, 1979; Diary of a Cricket Season, 1980; Lambourn, Village of Racing, 1983; *biographies:* (with Tony Greig) My Story, 1978; (with David Gower) With Time to Spare, 1980; (with Graham Gooch) Out of the Wilderness, 1985; Fred (biog. of Fred Winter), 1991; (with Pat Eddery) To Be A Champion, 1992; Lord Ted, 1995; Raising the Stakes, 1996. *Recreations:* National Hunt racing (has owned or part-owned ten horses), tennis, wine. *Address:* 8 The Courtyard, Montpellier Street, Cheltenham, Glos GL50 1SR. *T:* (01242) 572637. *Club:* Cricketers'.

LEE, Hon. Allen; *see* Lee Peng-Fei, A.

LEE, Dr Anne Mary Linda; educational and business adviser; Headmistress, Malvern Girls' College, 1994–96; *b* 14 Oct. 1953; *d* of Cecil and Eugenie Covell; *m* 1973, Anthony Mervyn Lee, *qv*; one *s* one *d*. *Educ:* Shenfield High Sch.; Open Univ. (BA); Univ. of Surrey (PhD). FIPD. Inf. Officer, Unilever, 1972–74; Trng Officer, G. D. Searle & Co., 1974–76; Management and Trng Advr, Industrial Soc., 1976–78; Head of Trng, Morgan Guaranty Trust Co., 1978–81; Dir, Anne M. Lee (Training) Ltd, 1983–94. Dir, Next Chapter Ltd, 1998–. Governor: Queenswood Sch., 1996–; Sarum Hall Sch., 1997–. FRSA. *Publications:* contribs to personnel and management jls and The Times. *Recreations:* singing, walking, friendship, words and music. *Address:* The Post House, West Clandon, Guildford, Surrey GU4 7ST. *T:* (01483) 222610. *Club:* Reform.

LEE, Anthony Mervyn; Executive Director, Muscular Dystrophy Campaign, since 1998; *b* 21 Feb. 1949; *s* of Sydney Ernest Lee and Evelyn May Lee; *m* 1973, Anne Mary Linda Lee, *qv*; one *s* one *d*. *Educ:* Romford Sch.; Cranfield Sch. of Mgt (MBA). FCCA 1971; FCMA 1975. Financial trng, Eastern Electricity Bd, 1967–72; Finance Manager, ITT SemiConductors, 1972–74; Financial Controller, Mars Confectionery, 1974–77; Managing Director: Am Bruning Ltd, 1978–82; Citibank Trust, 1982–86; Chief Exec., Access (JCCC Ltd), 1987–91; Ops Dir, Natwest Card Services, 1991–97. *Recreations:* keep fit, gardening, politics. *Address:* The Post House, The Street, West Clandon, Surrey GU4 7SJ. *T:* (01483) 222610.

LEE, Sir Arthur (James), KBE 1966 (CBE 1959); MC and Bar (1939–45); Company Director; National President, Returned Services League, Australia, 1960–74 (State President, 1954–60); *b* 30 July 1912; *s* of Arthur James and Kathleen Maud Lee; *m* 1945, Valerie Ann Scanlan; three *s* one *d*. *Educ:* Collegiate School of St Peter, Adelaide. Chm., War Veterans Home, SA, 1967–91. Trustee, Aust. War Meml, 1960–74. *Recreation:* golf. *Clubs:* Naval and Military, Royal Adelaide Golf (Adelaide).

LEE, Christopher Frank Carandini, CBE 2001; actor; entered film industry, 1947; *b* 27 May 1922; *s* of Geoffrey Trollope Lee (Lt-Col 60th KRRC), and Estelle Marie Carandini; *m* 1961, Birgit, *d* of Richard Emil Kroencke; one *d*. *Educ:* Wellington Coll. RAFVR, 1941–46 (Flt Lieut; mentioned in despatches, 1944). Films include: Moulin Rouge; Tale of Two Cities; Dracula; Rasputin; The Devil Rides Out; Private Life of Sherlock Holmes; The Wicker Man; The Three Musketeers; The Four Musketeers; The Man with the Golden Gun; To the Devil, a Daughter; Airport '77; The Passage; Bear Island; 1941; The Serial; The Last Unicorn; Safari 3000, The Salamander; Goliath Awaits; An Eye for an Eye; Charles and Diana; The Return of Captain Invincible; The House of the Long Shadows; The Far Pavilions; The Disputation; Mio My Mio; The Return of the Musketeers; The French Revolution; Gremlins II; Treasure Island; The Rainbow Thief; Sherlock Holmes—the Golden Years; Death Train; A Feast at Midnight; The Stupids; Jinnah; Sleepy Hollow; The Lord of the Rings; Star Wars - Episode II; television includes: Young Indy; Moses; Tales of Mystery and Imagination; Gormenghast. CStJ 1997 (OStJ 1986). Officier des Arts et des Lettres, France, 1973. *Publications:* Christopher Lee's 'X' Certificate, 1975 (2nd edn 1976); Christopher Lee's Archives of Evil, USA 1975 (2nd edn 1976); Tall, Dark and Gruesome (autobiog.), 1977, new edn 1997. *Recreations:* travel, opera, golf, cricket. *Address:* c/o London Management, 2–4 Noel Street, W1V 3RB. *Clubs:* Buck's, MCC; Honourable Company of Edinburgh Golfers; Travellers (Paris).

LEE, David John, CBE 1989; FREng; Consultant: G. Maunsell and Partners, Consulting Engineers, since 1994 (Partner, 1966–94; Chairman, 1984–94); Maunsell Structural Plastics Ltd, since 1994; Director of Maunsell Group cos; *b* 28 Aug. 1930; *s* of Douglas and Mildred Lee; *m* 1957, Helga Bass; one *s* one *d*. *Educ:* Manchester Univ. (BSc Tech 1950); Imperial Coll. of Science and Technol. (DIC 1954). MICE 1957, FICE 1966; MIStructE 1960, FIStructE 1968; FREng (FEng 1980). National Service, RE, 1950–52. Engr, Reinforced Concrete Steel Co. Ltd, 1952–53 and 1954–55; G. Maunsell and Partners, Consulting Engineers: Resident Engr, 1955–59; Sen. Engr, 1960–65; Associate, 1965–66. Vis. Prof., Imperial College, London, 1987–94. OC Engr and Logistic (formerly Transport) Staff Corps, RE (TA), 1977–95 (Col). Pres., IStructE, 1985–86; Mem. Council, Concrete Soc., 1968–71, Vice Pres. 1977–78. Chm., Council, CIRIA, 1989–92; Mem., Overseas Project Bd, DTI, 1989–94; Hon. Mem., Internat. Assoc. for Bridge and Structural Engrg. FCGI. George Stephenson Medal, ICE, 1969; Medal, 1974, and Hon. Pres., Fedn Internationale de la Précontrainte. *Publications:* The Theory and Practice of Bearings and Expansion Joints for Bridges, 1971, 2nd edn as Bridge Bearings and Expansion Joints, 1993; (contrib. chapter on bridges) The Civil Engineer's Reference Book, 3rd edn 1975, 4th edn 1989; (contrib. chapter on bridges) Developments in Prestressed Concrete, vol. 2 1978; papers in Proc. ICE and Proc. IStructE. *Recreations:* art, music. *Address:* 26 Paget Gardens, Chislehurst, Kent BR7 5RX. *T:* (020) 8325 0942. *Club:* East India.

LEE, Air Chief Marshal Sir David (John Pryer), GBE 1969 (KBE 1965; CBE 1947; OBE 1943); CB 1953; retired, 1971; *b* 4 Sept. 1912; *s* of late John Lee, Byron Crescent, Bedford; *m* 1938, Denise, *d* of late Louis Hartoch; one *s* one *d. Educ:* Bedford Sch.; RAF Coll., Cranwell. NWFP, India, 1933–36; Central Flying Sch., Upavon, 1937; RAF Examining Officer, Supt. of Reserve, 1938–39; Bomber Command, Hemswell, 1939–40; RAF Staff Coll. (student), 1942; Deputy Director Plans, Air Ministry, 1943–44; OC 904 Fighter Wing, Batavia, Java, 1945–46; Directing Staff, RAF Staff Coll., 1948–50; Deputy Director Policy, Air Ministry, 1951–53; OC RAF Scampton, Lincs, 1953–55; Secretary, Chiefs of Staff Cttee, Ministry of Defence, 1956–59; AOC, AFME (Aden), 1959–61; Comdt, RAF Staff Coll., 1962–65; Air Member for Personnel, MoD, 1965–68; UK Military Rep. to NATO, 1968–71. Vice-Pres., RAF Benevolent Fund, 1988–; Chm., Governing Trustees, Nuffield Trust for Armed Forces, 1975–96; Dir, Utd Services Trustee, 1971–88; Pres., Corps of Commissionaires, 1984–88. *Publications:* Flight from the Middle East, 1981; Never Stop the Engine When It's Hot, 1983; Eastward: a history of the Royal Air Force in the Far East 1945–1972, 1984; Wings in the Sun, 1989; And We Thought the War was Over, 1990. *Address:* The Garden House, Catherine Close, Shrivenham, Swindon SN6 8ER. *T:* (01793) 784264. *Club:* Royal Air Force.

LEE, Prof. David Morris, FInstP; Professor of Physics, Cornell University, since 1968; *b* 20 Jan. 1931; *s* of Marvin and Annette Lee; *m* 1960, Dana Thorangkul; two *s. Educ:* Harvard Univ. (AB 1952); Connecticut Univ. (MS 1955); Yale Univ. (PhD Physics 1959). FInstP 1998. US Army, 1952–54. Cornell University: Instructor in Physics, 1959–60; Asst Prof., 1960–63; Associate Prof., 1963–68. Guggenheim Fellow, 1966, 1974; Fellow, Japan Soc. for Promotion of Science, 1977. Member: Amer. Acad. Arts and Scis, 1987; Nat. Acad. of Scis, 1991. Sir Francis Simon Meml Prize, British Inst. of Physics, 1976; Oliver Buckley Prize, APS, 1981; (jtly) Nobel Prize for Physics, 1996. *Publications:* articles in learned jls. *Recreations:* hiking in the mountains, fishing, boating, running. *Address:* Cornell University Physics Department, Clark Hall, Ithaca, NY 14853, USA. *T:* (607) 2555286.

LEE, Derek William, FCIB; Chairman, Friendly Societies Commission, 1992–98; *b* 11 April 1935; *s* of Richard William Lee and Ivy Elizabeth Lee; *m* 1960, Dorothy Joan Preece; one *d. Educ:* St Dunstan's Coll.; London Univ. (LLB Hons external). FCIB 1973. Nat. Service, REME, Malaya, 1953–55. Lloyds Bank, 1955–73, Manager, Threadneedle St Br., 1970–73; Asst Gen. Manager, 1973–77, Gen. Manager, 1977–87, Mercantile Credit Co. Ltd; Man. Dir, H & H Factors, 1988–89; Registrar, Friendly Societies, 1989–95. Freeman, City of London, 1999. *Recreations:* tennis, clarinet, art, golf. *Address:* Birchleys, 8 Bennetts Copse, Chislehurst, Kent BR7 5SG. *Clubs:* Sundridge Park Lawn Tennis; High Elms Golf.

LEE, Edward, MSc, PhD; Director, Admiralty Research Laboratory, Teddington, 1971–74, retired; *b* 2 March 1914; *s* of Thomas and Florence Lee; *m* 1942, Joan Pearson; three *d. Educ:* Consett Grammar Sch.; Manchester Univ.; Pembroke Coll., Cambridge. Admiralty Research Laboratory, 1939–46; Ministry of Defence, 1946–48; Dept of Physical Research, Admiralty, 1948–51; Admiralty Research Laboratory, 1951–55; Dir of Operational Research, Admty, 1955–58; Dep. Dir, Nat. Physical Laboratory, 1958–60; Director, Stations and Industry Div., DSIR, 1960–65; Dep. Controller (R), Min. of Technology, 1965–70; Head of Res. Services, Dept of Trade and Industry, 1970–71. *Publications:* scientific papers. *Address:* 17 Farington Acres, Vale Road, Weybridge, Surrey KT13 9NH. *T:* (01932) 841114.

LEE, (Edward) Stanley, FRCS; Consulting Surgeon Westminster Hospital; formerly Civilian Consultant in Surgery of Neoplastic Diseases, Queen Alexandra Military Hospital; Surgeon Emeritus, Guildford Radiotherapy Centre; *b* 10 Sept. 1907; *m* 1951, Elizabeth Priestnall (*d* 2001); one *s* two *d. Educ:* Westminster Hospital. MB, BS 1931; FRCS 1933; MS London, 1936. Member of Court of Examiners, Royal College of Surgeons, England, 1953–59; Member: Grand Council British Empire Cancer Campaign; Internat. Union against Cancer; Assoc. of Head and Neck Oncologists of GB. FRSocMed; Sen. Fellow, Assoc. of Surgeons. Hon. Mem. Royal College of Radiologists. *Publications:* contributions to medical literature, etc. *Address:* Ingram, The Grand, Folkestone, Kent CT20 2LR.

LEE, George Ranson, CVO 1980; CBE 1983; HM Diplomatic Service, retired; *b* 26 Sept. 1925; *s* of late Wilfred Lee and Janet (*née* Ranson); *m* 1955, Anne Christine Black; one *d.* Served Indian Army, 6th Gurkha Rifles, NW Frontier Prov., 1945–47; TA, W Yorks Regt, 1948–53. Employed in Trng Dept, Min. of Food, 1948–53; joined CRO, 1954; Karachi, 1955–58; First Sec., Madras, 1959–63; CRO, 1964; Head of Chancery: Singapore, 1965–69; Santiago, 1969–72; FCO, 1972–74; Dep. UK Perm. Rep. to Council of Europe, Strasbourg, 1974–78; Counsellor, Berne, 1978–83. Council of Europe Medal, *pro merito*, 1978. *Address:* Garthmynd, Trevor Hill, Church Stretton, Shropshire SY6 6JH. *Club:* Royal Commonwealth Society.

LEE, Brig. Sir Henry; *see* Lee, Brig. Sir L. H.

LEE, Prof. Hermione, FRSL; FBA 2001; Goldsmiths' Professor of English Literature, University of Oxford, since 1998; Fellow of New College, Oxford, since 1998; *b* 29 Feb. 1948; *d* of Dr Benjamin Lee and Josephine Lee (*née* Anderson); *m* 1991, Prof. John Michael Barnard, *qv. Educ:* St Hilda's Coll., Oxford (MA; Hon. Fellow, 1998); St Cross Coll., Oxford (MPhil; Hon. Fellow, 1998). Instructor, Coll. of William and Mary, Williamsburg, Va, 1970–71; Lectr, Dept of English, Univ. of Liverpool, 1971–77; Department of English and Related Literature, University of York: Lectr. 1977–87; Sen. Lectr, 1987–90; Reader, 1990–93; Prof., 1993–98. Presenter, Book Four, Channel 4, 1982–86. FRSL 1992. *Publications:* The Novels of Virginia Woolf, 1977; Elizabeth Bowen, 1981, 2nd edn 1999; Philip Roth, 1982; (ed) The Mulberry Tree: writings of Elizabeth Bowen, 1986; Willa Cather: a life saved up, 1989, US edn as Willa Cather: double lives, 1991; (ed) The Selected Stories of Willa Cather, 1989; Virginia Woolf, 1996. *Recreations:* reading, music, countryside. *Address:* New College, Oxford OX1 3BN.

LEE, James Giles; Principal, Lee & Company, since 1992; Chairman, Scottish Screen, since 1998; *b* 23 Dec. 1942; *s* of John Lee, CBE and Muriel Giles; *m* 1966, Linn Macdonald; one *s* two *d. Educ:* Trinity Coll., Glenalmond; Glasgow Univ.; Harvard Univ., USA. Consultant, McKinsey & Co., 1969–80; Mem., Central Policy Review Staff, 1972. Dep. Chm. and Chief Exec., Pearson Longman, 1980–83; Chairman: Penguin Publishing Co., 1980–84; Longman Gp, 1980–84; Direct Broadcasting by Satellite Consortium, 1986–87; Deputy Chairman: Westminster Press, 1980–84; Financial Times, 1980–84; Yorkshire TV, 1982–85; Dir, S. Pearson & Son, 1981–84; Chm., 1981–85, Chief Exec., 1983–85, Goldcrest Films and Television; Dir, Boston Consulting Gp, 1987–92. Non-executive Director: Pearson Television, 1993–; Phoenix Pictures Inc., 1996–. Chm., Performing Arts Labs Trust, 1989–99; Dir, Film Council, 1999–. *Publications:* Planning for the Social Services, 1978; The Investment Challenge, 1979. *Recreations:* photography, travelling, sailing. *Address:* Meadow Wood, Penshurst, Kent TN11 8AD. *T:* (01892) 870309. *Clubs:* Reform; Harvard (New York, USA).

LEE, Hon. James Matthew; PC (Can.) 1982; Chairman, PEI Workers Compensation Board, since 1998; Leader, Progressive Conservative Party, Prince Edward Island, 1981–96; *b* Charlottetown, 26 March 1937; *s* of late James Matthew Lee and of Catherine Blanchard Lee; *m* 1960, Patricia, *d* of late Ivan Laurie; one *s* two *d. Educ:* Queen's Square Sch.; St Dunstan's Univ. Architectural draftsman. Elected MLA (PC) for 5th Queens Riding, by-election, 1975; former Minister: of Health and Social Services; of Tourism, Parks and Conservation; Premier and Pres. Exec. Council, PEI, 1981–86. Comr, Canadian Pension Commn, 1986–97. Jaycee Internat. Senator, 1983. *Address:* Stanhope Bay Road, York RR1, PE C0A IP0, Canada. *T:* (902) 6722870.

LEE, Maj.-Gen. (James) Stuart, CB 1990; MBE 1970; Director of Army Education, 1987–90; *b* 26 Dec. 1934; *s* of George Lee and Elizabeth (*née* Hawkins); *m* 1960, Alice Lorna; one *s. Educ:* Normanton Grammar Sch.; Leeds Univ. (BA Hons); King's Coll., London (MA War Studies, 1976). Pres., Leeds Univ. Union, 1958–59. Educn Officer in UK Trng Units, Catterick, Taunton, Bovington, 1959–64; Mil. Trng Officer, Beaconsfield, 1964; RMCS and Staff Coll., 1964–65; DAQMG HQ Cyprus Dist, 1966 and HQ NEARELF, 1967; SO2 MoD (Army Educn 1), 1968–70; DAA&QMG HQ FARELF, 1970 and GSO2 HQ FARELF, 1970–71; OC Officer Wing, Beaconsfield, 1971–74; Gp Educn Officer, 34 AEC, Rheindahlen, 1974–75; Chief Educn Officer, HQ NE Dist, 1976–78; Hd, Officer Educn Br., 1978–79; SO1 Trng HQ UKLF, 1979; Chief Inspector of Army Educn and Col Res., 1980–82; Res. Associate, IISS, 1982–83; Comdr Educn, HQ BAOR, 1983–87. Dep. Col Comdt, AGC, 1993–97. Pres., RAEC Assoc., 1993–97. Dep. Comr, British Scouts Western Europe, 1983–87; Mem., Management Bd, NFER, 1987–90. Non-exec. Dir, Exhibition Consultants Ltd, 1990–99. Dir and Trustee, Assessment and Qualifications Alliance, 1998–. Member: Nat Adv. Bd, Duke of Edinburgh Award Scheme, 1987–90; Council, Scout Assoc., 1988–. City and Guilds of London Institute: Mem. Council, 1989–; Jt Hon. Sec., 1993–; Chm., Sen. Awards Cttee, 1990–99; Chm., Inst. Affairs and Awards Cttee, 1999–. Trustee and Sec., Gallipoli Meml Lecture Trust, 1987–90. Gov., 1991–99, Mem. Court, 1999, Imperial Coll.; Mem. Court, Univ. of Leeds, 1994–. FRSA 1987; FIPD (FITD 1991); Hon. FCGI 1996. *Publication:* contrib. Arms Transfers in Third World Development, 1984. *Recreations:* theatre, boats.

LEE, John Michael Hubert; Barrister-at-Law; *b* 13 Aug. 1927; *s* of late Victor Lee, Wentworth, Surrey, and late Renee Lee; *m* 1960, Margaret Ann, *d* of late James Russell, ICS, retired, and late Kathleen Russell; one *s* one *d. Educ:* Reading Sch.; Christ's Coll., Cambridge (Open Exhibnr Modern Hist.; 2nd Cl. Hons Pts I and II of Hist. Tripos; MA). Colonial Service: Administrative Officer, Ghana, 1951–58; Principal Assistant Secretary, Min. of Communications, Ghana, 1958. On staff of BBC, 1959–65. Called to the Bar, Middle Temple, 1960; practising, Midland and Oxford Circuit, 1966–; Dep. Circuit Judge, 1978–81; Assistant Recorder, 1981–87. MP (Lab) Reading, 1966–70; MP (Lab) Birmingham, Handsworth, Feb. 1974–1979; Chm., W Midland Gp of Labour MPs, 1974–75. *Recreations:* watching tennis, watching cricket, walking, studying philosophy. *Address:* Bell Yard Chambers, 116–118 Chancery Lane, WC2A 1PP. *Club:* Royal Over-Seas League.

LEE, John Robert Louis; DL; FCA; company director, investor and financial journalist; *b* 21 June 1942; *s* of late Basil and Miriam Lee; *m* 1975, Anne Monique Bakirgian; two *d. Educ:* William Hulme's Grammar Sch., Manchester. Accountancy Articles, 1959–64; Henry Cooke, Lumsden & Co., Manchester, Stockbrokers, 1964–66; Founding Dir, Chancery Consolidated Ltd, Investment Bankers; non-executive Director: Paterson Zochonis (UK) Ltd, 1974–75, 1990–99; Paterson Zochonis PLC; Emerson Developments (Hldgs), 2000–; Manchester and London Investment Trust, 2000–; Trustee, Refuge Assurance Pension Funds. Contested (C) Manchester, Moss Side, Oct. 1974; MP (C) Nelson and Colne, 1979–83, Pendle, 1983–92; contested (C) Pendle, 1992. PPS to Minister of State for Industry, 1981–83, to Sec. of State for Trade and Industry, 1983; Parly Under Sec. of State, MoD, 1983–86, Dept of Employment, 1986–89 (Minister for Tourism, 1987–89). Chm., All-Party Tourism Cttee, 1991–92. Jt Sec., Conservative Back Benchers' Industry Cttee, 1979–80. Chm., Christie Hosp. NHS Trust, 1992–98. Chairman: ALVA, 1990–; Mus. of Sci. and Industry in Manchester; Mem., English Tourist Bd, 1992–99. Vice-Chm., NW Conciliation Cttee, Race Relations Bd, 1976–77; Chm. Council, Nat. Youth Bureau, 1980–83. Mem. Ct, and Mem. Investment Cttee, 2000–, Univ. of Manchester. DL 1995, High Sheriff 1998, Greater Manchester. *Recreations:* golf, fly fishing, collecting. *Address:* Bowdon Old Hall, 49 Langham Road, Bowdon, Altrincham, Cheshire WA14 3NS.

LEE KUAN YEW; Prime Minister, Singapore, 1959–90; Senior Minister, Prime Minister's Office, since 1990; *b* 16 Sept. 1923; *s* of Lee Chin Koon and Chua Jim Neo; *m* 1950, Kwa Geok Choo; two *s* one *d. Educ:* Raffles Coll., Singapore; Fitzwilliam Coll., Cambridge (class 1 both parts of Law Tripos). Called to Bar, Middle Temple, 1950, Hon. Bencher, 1969. Advocate and Solicitor, Singapore, 1951. Formed People's Action Party, 1954, Sec.-Gen., 1954–92; People's Action Party won elections, 1959; became PM, 1959, re-elected 1963, 1968, 1972, 1976, 1980, 1984, 1988; MP Fed. Parlt of Malaysia, 1963–65. Hon. Freeman, City of London, 1982. Hon. CH 1970; Hon. GCMG 1972. *Publications:* The Singapore Story (memoirs), 1998; From Third World to First: the Singapore Story 1965–2000 (memoirs), 2000. *Recreation:* swimming. *Address:* Prime Minister's Office, Istana Annexe, Singapore 238823.

LEE, Brig. Sir (Leonard) Henry, Kt 1983; CBE 1964 (OBE 1960); Deputy Director, Conservative Board of Finance, 1970–92; *b* 21 April 1914; *s* of late Henry Robert Lee and Nellie Lee; *m* 1949, Peggy Metham (*d* 2000). *Educ:* Portsmouth Grammar Sch.; Southampton Univ. (Law). Served War, 1939–45; with BEF in France, ME and NW Europe (despatches, 1945); Royal Scots Greys, Major; Staff Lt-Col 1954: Chief of Intelligence to Dir of Ops, Malaya, 1957–60; Mil. and Naval Attaché, Saigon, S Vietnam, 1961–64; Chief of Personnel and Admin, Allied Land Forces Central Europe, France, 1964–66; Chief of Intelligence, Allied Forces Central Europe, Netherlands, 1966–69; retd 1969. Chm. Trustees, Royal Cambridge Home for Soldiers' Widows, 1972–. *Recreation:* gardening. *Address:* Fairways, Sandy Lane, Kingswood, Surrey KT20 6ND. *T:* (01737) 832577.

LEE, Martin; *see* Lee Chu-Ming, M.

LEE, Michael Charles M.; *see* Malone-Lee.

LEE, Maj.-Gen. Patrick Herbert, CB 1982; MBE 1964; CEng, FIMechE; Director: Road Haulage Association, 1988–98 (Chairman, 1994–96; Vice-Chairman, 1990–94); Wincanton Ltd (formerly Wincanton Transport, subseq. Wincanton Distribution Services, Ltd), 1983–98; *b* 15 March 1929; *s* of Percy Herbert and Mary Dorothea Lee; *m* 1952, Peggy Eveline Chapman; one *s* one *d. Educ:* King's Sch., Canterbury; London Univ. (BSc (Gen.), BSc (Special Physics)). Commnd RMA Sandhurst, 1948; Staff Coll., 1960; WO Staff Duties, 1961–63; CO, Parachute Workshop, 1964–65; JSSC, 1966; Military Asst to Master General of Ordnance, 1966–67; Directing Staff, Staff Coll., 1968–69; Commander, REME 2nd Div., 1970–71; Col AQ 1 British Corps, 1972–75; Dep. Comdt, Sch. of Electrical and Mechanical Engrg, 1975–77; Comdt, REME Trng Centre,

1977–79; Dir Gen., Electrical and Mechanical Engrg (Army), 1979–83. Col Comdt, REME, 1983–89. Mem., Wessex Water Authy, 1983–88. Confederation of British Industry: Mem. Council, 1991–98; Vice-Chm., 1992–94, Chm., 1994–96, SW Region. Gov., Wellington Sch., Som, 1992– (Chm., 2000–). FIMgt; MIEMA. *Recreations:* gardening, railways, Roman history, industrial archaeology. *Club:* Army and Navy.

LEE, Rt Rev. Patrick Vaughan, DD; Bishop of Rupert's Land, 1994–99; *b* 20 June 1931; *s* of William Samuel Lee and Elizabeth Miriam (*née* Struthers); *m* 1958, Mary Thornton; four *d*. *Educ:* Univ. of Manitoba (BA 1953); St John's Coll., Winnipeg (LTh 1957; DD 1978). Missioner, Interlake/Eriksdale, Manitoba, 1956–59; Rector: St Bartholomew, Winnipeg, 1959–67; St Mary la Prairie, Portage la Prairie, Manitoba, 1967–75; District Dean, Portage and Pembina Deaneries, 1970–75; Dean of Cariboo and Rector, St Paul's Cathedral, Kamloops, BC, 1975–84; Dean of Training and Educn Sec., Dio. of W Buganda, 1984–90; Exec. Archdeacon of Rupert's Land, 1990–94. *Recreations:* cross country ski-ing, cycling, woodworking, reading, stamp collecting. *Address:* 28 Ramblewood Road, Winnipeg, MB R3X 1Z4, Canada. *T:* (204) 2571570.

LEE, Rt Rev. Paul Chun Hwan, Hon. CBE 1974; Bishop of Seoul, 1965–83; *b* 5 April 1922; unmarried. *Educ:* St Michael's Theological Seminary, Seoul; St Augustine's College, Canterbury. Deacon, 1952 (Pusan Parish); Priest, 1953 (Sangju and Choungju Parish). Director of Yonsei University, Seoul, 1960–, Chm., Bd of Trustees, 1972–, Hon. DD 1971. Chairman: Christian Council of Korea, 1966–67; Christian Literature Soc. of Korea, 1968–83; Korean Bible Soc., 1972–83 (Vice-Pres., 1969–72); Nat. Council of Churches in Korea, 1976–78. Hon. LLD Korea, 1978. *Recreation:* reading. *Address:* 104–401 Dae Woo Apt, Bang Bae 3 Dong, 981, So'cho-Ku, Seoul 137–063, Korea.

LEE, Peter Gavin; DL; FRICS; Senior Partner, Strutt & Parker, 1979–96; *b* 4 July 1934; *s* of late Mr and Mrs J. G. Lee; *m* 1963, Caroline Green; two *s* one *d*. *Educ:* Midhurst Grammar School; College of Estate Management; Wye College. FRICS 1966. Joined Strutt & Parker, 1957. Chm., Prince's Trust for Essex, 2000–. High Sheriff, 1990, DL 1991, Essex. *Recreations:* the restoration and enjoyment of vintage cars and aircraft, flying, country pursuits. *Address:* Fanners, Great Waltham, Chelmsford, Essex CM3 1EA. *T:* (01245) 360470.

LEE, Peter Wilton, CBE 1994; Vice Lord-Lieutenant of South Yorkshire, since 1997; Director, since 1987, Chairman, since 1994, Edward Pryor & Son Ltd; *b* 15 May 1935; *s* of Sir (George) Wilton Lee, TD and late Bettina Stanley Lee (*née* Haywood); *m* 1962, Gillian Wendy Oates; three *s* one *d*. *Educ:* Uppingham Sch.; Queens' Coll., Cambridge (MA). Lieut, RE, 1956. Grad. Engr, Davy & United Engrg Co. Ltd, 1958–62; Arthur Lee & Sons plc: Engr, Works Manager, 1962–67; Works Dir, 1967–70; Jt Man. Dir, 1970–72; Man. Dir, 1972–79; Chm. and Man. Dir, 1979–92; Chm., 1992–93; Dep. Chm., 1993–95, Dir, 1995–, Carclo Engrg Gp PLC. Dir, Sanderson Gp (formerly Sanderson Electronics) PLC, 1994–2000. Dir, Sheffield Enterprise Agency Ltd, 1987–. President: Brit. Independent Steel Producers' Assoc., 1981–83; Engrg Employers' Sheffield Assoc., 1994–96. Confederation of British Industry: Member: Nat. Council, 1992–95; Nat. Mfg Council, 1992–94; Chm., Yorks and Humberside Regl Council, 1993–95. University of Sheffield: Mem. Council, 1965– (Chm., 1996–); Pro Chancellor, 1987–. Trustee: Sheffield Church Burgesses Trust, 1977–; S Yorks Community Foundn, 1986–99 (Vice-Pres., 1999–); Dir, Sheffield Royal Soc. for Blind, 1997– (Chm., 1998–). Chm. Council, Sheffield & Dist YMCA, 1972–81. CIMgt 1976. Chm. Govs, Monkton Combe Sch., 1996– (Gov., 1982–). Master, Co. of Cutlers in Hallamshire, 1985–86. DL 1978, High Sheriff, 1995–96, S Yorks. *Recreations:* family, music and the arts, walking. *Address:* Mayfield House, 48 Canterbury Avenue, Sheffield S10 3RU. *T:* (0114) 230 5555. *Club:* Royal Automobile.

LEE, Rowland Thomas Lovell; a Recorder of the Crown Court, 1979–92; *b* 7 March 1920; *s* of late Ronald Lovell Lee and of Jessie Maude Lee; *m* 1944, Marjorie Betty, *d* of late William Holmes and Clare Johnston Braid Holmes; two *d*. *Educ:* Bedford Modern School. Served Royal Navy, 1939–48; POW, Sept. 1942–March 1943. Bedfordshire Constabulary, 1948–52; Articles with E. A. S. Barnard, Dunstable, 1954; qualified as solicitor, 1957; Principal, Wynter Davies & Lee, Hertford, 1959–89. Chairman: Medical Services Cttee, Hertfordshire Family Practitioners Cttee, 1970–77; N Herts HA (formerly Herts AHA), 1977–84. *Publications:* poetry: Scarecrow Galabieh, 1998; Small Lazarus, 2000; Each Different Beauty, 2001; Your Face at the Window, 2002. *Address:* Culpepers, 5 Letty Green, Hertford, Herts SG14 2NZ. *T:* (01707) 261445.

LEE, Seng Tee; Director: Singapore Investments (Pte) Ltd, since 1951; Lee Rubber Co. (Pte) Ltd, since 1951; Lee Pineapple Co. (Pte) Ltd, since 1951; Lee Foundation, since 1952; *b* April 1923; *s* of Lee Kong Chian and Alice Lee; *m* 1950, Betty Wu; two *s* one *d*. *Educ:* Anglo-Chinese Sch, Singapore; Wharton Business Sch., Univ. of Pennsylvania. Member: Singapore Preservation of Monuments Bd, 1971–88; Bd, Singapore Art Mus., 1995– (Mem., Adv. Cttee, 1992–94). Member Council: Univ. of Malaya in Singapore, 1959–61; Univ. of Singapore, 1962–63; Hon. Advr, Xiamen Univ., China, 1993–; Member: Bd of Advrs, Nat. Univ. of Singapore Endowment Fund, 1997–; Adv. Cttee, E Asia Inst., Cambridge Univ., 1998–. Mem., Chancellor's Court of Benefactors, Oxford, 1996–. Hon. Trustee, Royal Botanic Gardens, Kew, 1996. Hon. Foreign Mem., American Acad. of Arts and Scis, 2001. Hon. FBA 1998; Hon. Fellow: Wolfson Coll., Cambridge, 1986; Needham Res. Inst., Cambridge, 1992; Oriel Coll., Oxford, 1992; SOAS, London Univ., 2001. Hon. DTech Asian Inst. of Technol., Thailand, 1998. Distinguished Service Award, Wharton Sch., Univ. of Penn., 1995. *Recreations:* reading, natural history. *Address:* GPO Box 1892, Singapore 903742, Republic of Singapore. *Club:* Executive (Singapore).

LEE, Prof. Simon Francis; Rector and Chief Executive, Liverpool Hope University College, since 1995; *b* 29 March 1957; *s* of Norman John Lee and Mary Teresa Lee (*née* Moran); *m* 1982, Patricia Mary, *d* of Bernard Anthony McNulty and Maud Catherine McNulty (*née* Kenny); one *s* two *d*. *Educ:* Balliol Coll., Oxford (Scholar, BA 1st Cl. Jurisp); Yale Law Sch. (Harkness Fellow, LLM). Lecturer in Law: Trinity Coll., Oxford, 1981–82; KCL, 1982–88; Queen's University, Belfast: Prof. of Jurisprudence, 1989–95; Dean, Faculty of Law, 1992–94; Prof. Emeritus, 1995. Gresham Prof. of Law, 1995–98; Hon. Prof., Univ. of Liverpool, 1995. Mem., Standing Adv. Commn on Human Rights, 1992–96. Mem., Nat. Standards Task Force, DFEE, 1997–2001. Non-exec. Dir, S & E Belfast Health and Social Services NHS Trust, 1994–95. Chairman: Merseyside Rapid Transit Project Bd, 1997–; Netherley-Valley Partnership, 1998–. Co-founder, Initiative '92, 1992. *Publications:* Law and Morals, 1986; Judging Judges, 1988; (with Peter Stanford) Believing Bishops, 1990; The Cost of Free Speech, 1990; (with Marie Fox) Learning Legal Skills, 1991; (ed) Freedom from Fear, 1992. *Recreations:* family, sport, broadcasting, hope. *Address:* Liverpool Hope University College, Hope Park, Liverpool L16 9JD. *T:* (0151) 291 3000, *Fax:* (0151) 291 3100; Vale House Farm, 77 Langham Road, Bowdon, Cheshire WA14 3NT, *T:* (0161) 929 1571, *Fax:* (0161) 929 6821.

LEE, Stanley; *see* Lee, (Edward) S.

LEE, Maj.-Gen. Stuart; *see* Lee, Maj.-Gen. J. S.

LEE, Timothy John B.; *see* Berners-Lee.

LEE, Tsung-Dao; Enrico Fermi Professor of Physics, since 1964, and University Professor, since 1984, Columbia University, USA; *b* 25 Nov. 1926; 3rd *s* of C. K. and M. C. Lee; *m* 1950, Jeannette H. C. Chin; two *s*. *Educ:* National Chekiang Univ., Kweichow, China; National Southwest Associated Univ., Kunming, China; University of Chicago, USA. Research Associate: University of Chicago, 1950; University of California, 1950–51; Member, Inst. for Advanced Study, Princeton, 1951–53. Columbia University: Asst Professor, 1953–55; Associate Professor, 1955–56; Professor, 1956–60; Member, Institute for Advanced Study, Princeton, 1960–63; Columbia Univ.: Adjunct Professor, 1960–62; Visiting Professor, 1962–63; Professor, 1963–. Hon. Professor: Univ. of Sci and Technol. of China, 1981; Jinan Univ., China, 1982; Fudan Univ., China, 1982; Qinghua Univ., 1984; Peking Univ., 1985; Nanjing Univ., 1985; Nankai Univ., 1986; Shanghai Jiao Tong and Suzhou Univs, 1987; Zhejiang Univ., 1988; Northwest Univ., Xian, 1993. Member: Acad. Sinica, 1957; Amer. Acad. of Arts and Scis, 1959; Nat. Acad of Scis, 1964; Amer. Philosophical Soc., 1972; Acad. Nazionale dei Lincei, Rome, 1982; Chinese Acad. of Scis, Beijing, 1994. Hon. DSc: Princeton, 1958; City Coll., City Univ. of NY, 1978; Bard Coll., 1984; Peking, 1985; Bologna, 1988; Columbia, 1990; Adelphi, 1991; Tsukuba, 1992; Rockefeller, 1994; Hon. LLD Chinese Univ. of Hong Kong, 1969; Hon. LittD Drexel Univ., 1986; Dip. di Perfezionamento in Physics, Scuola Normale Superiore, Pisa, 1982. Nobel Prize for the non-conservation of parity (with C. N. Yang), 1957; Albert Einstein Award in Science, 1957; Ettore Majorana-Erice Sci. for Peace Prize, 1990. Grand'Ufficiale, Order of Merit (Italy), 1986. *Publications:* Particle Physics: an introduction to field theory, 1981; papers mostly in Physical Review, and Nuclear Physics. *Address:* Department of Physics, Columbia University, New York, NY 10027, USA.

LEE, Most Rev. William; *see* Waterford and Lismore, Bishop of, (RC).

LEE YONG LENG, Dr; Professor of Geography, National University of Singapore, 1977–90, retired; *b* 26 March 1930; *m* Wong Loon Meng; one *d*. *Educ:* Univs of Oxford, Malaya and Singapore. BLitt (Oxon), MA (Malaya), PhD (Singapore). Research Asst, Univ. of Malaya, 1954–56; University Lectr/Sen. Lectr, Univ. of Singapore, 1956–70; Associate Prof., Univ. of Singapore, 1970–71; High Comr for Singapore in London, 1971–75; Ambassador to Denmark, 1974–75, and Ireland, 1975; Min. of Foreign Affairs, Singapore, 1975–76. Mem., Govt Parly Cttee on Defence and For. Affairs, 1987–90. Chm., Singapore Nat. Library Bd, 1978–80. Dir, Centre for Advanced Studies, National Univ. of Singapore, 1983–85. *Publications:* North Borneo, 1965; Sarawak, 1970; Southeast Asia and the Law of the Sea, 1978; The Razor's Edge: boundaries and boundary disputes in Southeast Asia, 1980; Southeast Asia: essays in political geography, 1982; articles in: Population Studies; Geog. Jl; Erdkunde; Jl Trop. Geog., etc. *Recreations:* swimming, tennis, travelling, reading.

LEE, Prof. Yuan Tseh; President, Academia Sinica, Taiwan, since 1994; *b* 29 Nov. 1936; *s* of Tse Fan Lee and Pei Tsai; *m* 1963, Bernice Chinli Wu; two *s* one *d*. *Educ:* Nat. Taiwan Univ. (BSc 1959); Nat. Tsinghua Univ., Taiwan (MSc 1961); Univ. of California (PhD 1965). Military service, 1961–62. University of California, Berkeley: Postdoctoral Fellow, 1965–67; Research Fellow, 1967–68; James Franck Inst. and Dept of Chemistry, Univ. of Chicago: Asst Prof. of Chemistry, 1968–71; Associate Prof. of Chemistry, 1971–72; Prof. of Chemistry, 1973–74; University of California, Berkeley: Prof. of Chemistry, 1974–91; Univ. Prof. of Chemistry, 1991–94; Principal Investigator, Materials and Molecular Research Div., Lawrence Berkeley Lab., 1974–94. Vis Lectr, US and overseas univs. Mem., edtl boards, chem. and sci. jls. Mem., Nat. Acad. of Sciences, 1979, and other learned bodies. Nobel Prize in Chemistry (jtly), 1986; numerous awards from US and foreign instns. *Publications:* papers on molecular chemistry and related subjects. *Recreations:* sports (baseball, ping pong, tennis), classical music. *Address:* Academia Sinica, Nankang, Taipei 11529, Taiwan.

LEE CHU-MING, Martin, (Martin Lee); QC (Hong Kong) 1979; JP; Chairman, Democratic Party, Hong Kong, since 1994; Member, Hong Kong Legislative Council, 1985–97 and since 1998; *b* 8 June 1938; *m* 1969, Amelia Lee; one *s*. *Educ:* Wah Yan College, Kowloon; Univ. of Hong Kong (BA 1960). Called to the Bar, Lincoln's Inn, 1966. Member: Hong Kong Law Reform Commn, 1985–91; Hong Kong Fight Crime Cttee, 1986–92; Basic Law Drafting Cttee, 1985–89; numerous groups and cttees advising on Govt, law, nationality and community matters. Chm., United Democrats of Hong Kong, 1990–94. JP Hong Kong, 1980. *Publication:* The Basic Law: some basic flaws (with Szeto Wah), 1988. *Address:* Admiralty Centre, Room 704A, Tower I, 18 Harcourt Road, Hong Kong. *T:* 25290864. *Clubs:* Hong Kong; Hong Kong Golf, Hong Kong Jockey.

LEE PENG-FEI, Allen, (Allen Lee), CBE 1988 (OBE 1982); JP; Chairman, Pacific Dimensions Consultants Ltd, since 1998; *b* 24 April 1940; *m* Maria Lee; two *s* one *d*. *Educ:* Univ. of Michigan (BSc Engineering Maths). Test Engineer Supervisor, Lockheed Aircraft International, 1966–67; Engineering Ops Manager, Fabri-teck, 1967; Test Engineer Manager, Lockheed Aircraft International, 1968–70; Test Manager, Ampex Ferrotec, 1970–72; Gen. Manager, Dataproducts HK, 1972–74; Managing Dir, Ampex Ferrotec, 1974–79; Gen. Manager, Ampex World Operations, 1979–83; Managing Dir, Ampex Far East Operations, 1983–84; Pres., Meadville, 1984–95. Appointed Mem., Hong Kong Legislative Council, 1978–98; MEC, Hong Kong, 1985–92; Dep. for HKSAR, 9th Nat. People's Congress, China, 1997–; Chm., HK Liberal Party, 1993. Mem., Commn on Strategic Develt, HKSAR, 1998–. Chm., Bd of Overseers, Hong Kong Inst. of Biotechnol., 1990–. JP Hong Kong, 1980. FHKIE, 1985. Hon. DEng Hong Kong Poly., 1990; Hon. LLD Chinese Univ. of Hong Kong, 1990. Nat. Award, Asian Productivity Organization, 1986; Outstanding Young Persons Award, Hong Kong, 1977. *Recreations:* swimming, tennis. *Address:* Room 1208, Tower 1, New World Tower, 18 Queen's Road Central, Hong Kong. *T:* 21368787, *Fax:* 21368782. *Clubs:* Hong Kong Jockey, Hong Kong Country, Dynasty (Hong Kong).

LEE-POTTER, Jeremy Patrick, FRCPath; Vice-President, since 1998, and Chairman, Audit Committee, since 1999, British Medical Association; Consultant Haematologist, Poole General Hospital, 1969–95; *b* 30 Aug. 1934; *s* of Air Marshal Sir Patrick Lee Potter, KBE, MD, QHS and Audrey Mary (*née* Pollock); *m* 1957, Lynda Higginson; one *s* two *d*. *Educ:* Epsom Coll.; Guy's Hosp. Med. Sch. MB BS 1958; MRCS, LRCP 1958; DTM&H 1963; DCP 1965; FRCPath 1979. Specialist in Pathology, 1960, Sen. Specialist, 1965, RAF (Sqn Ldr); in charge of Haematology Dept, RAF Inst. of Pathology and Tropical Medicine; Lectr in Haematology, St George's Hosp. Med. Sch., 1968–69. British Medical Association: Chm. Council, 1990–93 (Mem. Council, 1988–95); Dep. Chm., Central Consultants and Specialists Cttee, 1988–90 (Chm., Negotiating Cttee). Member: Standing Med. Adv. Cttee, 1990–93; GMC, 1994–99 (Dep. Chm., Professional Conduct Cttee, 1996–99); Clinical Disputes Forum, 1999. Consultant Surveyor, King's Fund Orgnl Audit, 1993–95. Engineering Council: Mem. Senate, 2000–; Mem., Bd for Engrs' Regulation, 2001–. *Publication:* A Damn Bad Business: the NHS deformed, 1997. *Recreations:* printing, printmaking, visual arts. *Address:* Icen House, Stoborough, Wareham,

Dorset BH20 5AN. *T:* (01929) 556307; 23 Palmerston House, Kensington Place, W8 7PU. *T:* (020) 7727 9393. *Clubs:* Athenæum; Parkstone Golf.

LEE-STEERE, Sir Ernest (Henry), KBE 1977 (CBE 1963); JP; Lord Mayor of Perth, Western Australia, 1972–78; company director, pastoralist and grazier; *b* Perth, 22 Dec. 1912; *s* of Sir Ernest Lee-Steere, JP, KStJ; *m* 1942, Jessica Margaret, *d* of Frank Venn; two *s* three *d*. *Educ:* Hale Sch., Perth; St Peter's Coll., Adelaide. Served War: Captain Army/Air Liaison Group, AIF; SW Pacific Area, 1944–45 (Philippine Liberation Medal, 1996). President (for WA): Pastoralists and Graziers Assoc., 1959–72; Boy Scout Assoc., 1957–64; National Trust, 1969–72. Vice-Pres., Council of Royal Flying Doctor Service of WA, 1954–59 and 1962–74. Chairman: State Adv. Cttee, CSIRO, 1962–71 (Councillor, Fed. Adv. Council, 1960–71); WA Soil Conservation Adv. Cttee, 1955–72; Aust. Capital Cities Secretariat, 1975–76; WA Turf Club, 1963–84 (Vice-Chm., 1959–63). Member: Nat. Council of Aust. Boy Scouts Assoc., 1959–64; Exec. Cttee of WA State Cttee, Freedom from Hunger Campaign; WA State Adv. Cttee, Aust. Broadcasting Commn, 1961–64; Aust. Jubilee Cttee for the Queen's Silver Jubilee Appeal for Young Australians, 1977; Aust. Wool Industry Conf., 1971–74 (also Mem. Exec. Cttee). Councillor: Aust. Wool Growers and Graziers Council (Pres., 1972–73); St George's Coll., Univ. of WA, 1945–81. Chm. and dir of several cos. Leader, Trade Mission to India, 1962. JP Perth, 1965. *Publication:* Be Fair & Fear Not (autobiog.), 1995. *Recreation:* polo (played in WA Polo Team in Australasian Gold Cup). *Address:* Dardanup, 26 Odern Crescent, Swanbourne, WA 6010, Australia. *T:* (9) 3842929. *Club:* Weld (Perth).

LEE-STEERE, Gordon Ernest; Vice Lord-Lieutenant of Surrey, since 1996; *b* 26 Dec. 1939; *s* of Charles Augustus Lee-Steere and Patience Hargreaves Lee-Steere; *m* 1966, Mary Katharine Stuart; one *s* three *d*. *Educ:* Eton; Trinity Coll., Cambridge (MA). Computer consultant, 1966–74; self-employed farmer, 1960–. Pres., CLA, 1987–89. *Recreations:* shooting, walking. *Address:* Jayes Park, Ockley, Surrey RH5 5RR. *T:* (01306) 621223. *Club:* Boodle's.

LEECH, Prof. Geoffrey Neil, FBA 1987; Research Professor of English Linguistics, University of Lancaster, since 1996; *b* 16 Jan. 1936; *s* of Charles Richard Leech and Dorothy Eileen Leech; *m* 1961, Frances Anne Berman; one *s* one *d*. *Educ:* Tewkesbury Grammar School; University College London (BA 1959; MA 1963; PhD 1968). Asst Lectr, UCL, 1962–64; Harkness Fellow, MIT, 1964–65; Lectr, UCL, 1965–69; University of Lancaster: Reader, 1969–74; Prof. of Linguistics and Modern English Lang., 1974–96. Visiting Professor: Brown Univ., 1972; Kobe Univ., 1984; Kyoto Univ., 1991; Meikai Univ., 1999, 2000. Hon. Fil Dr Lund, 1987. *Publications:* English in Advertising, 1966; A Linguistic Guide to English Poetry, 1969; Towards a Semantic Description of English, 1969; Meaning and the English Verb, 1971, 2nd edn 1987; (with R. Quirk, S. Greenbaum and J. Svartvik) A Grammar of Contemporary English, 1972; Semantics, 1974, 2nd edn 1981; (with J. Svartvik) A Communicative Grammar of English, 1975, 2nd edn 1994; Explorations in Semantics and Pragmatics, 1980; (ed with S. Greenbaum and J. Svartvik) Studies in English Linguistics: for Randolph Quirk, 1980; (with M. Short) Style in Fiction, 1981; (with R. Hoogenraad and M. Deuchar) English Grammar for Today, 1982; Principles of Pragmatics, 1983; (with R. Quirk, S. Greenbaum, and J. Svartvik) A Comprehensive Grammar of the English Language, 1985; (ed with C. N. Candlin) Computers in English Language Teaching and Research, 1986; (ed with R. Garside and G. Sampson) The Computational Analysis of English: a corpus-based approach, 1987; An A–Z of English Grammar and Usage, 1989, 2nd edn (with B. Cruickshank and R. Ivanic) 2001; Introducing English Grammar, 1992; (ed with E. Black and R. Garside) Statistically-driven Computer Grammars of English, 1993; (ed with G. Myers and J. Thomas) Spoken English on Computer, 1995; (ed with R. Garside and T. McEnery) Corpus Annotation: linguistic information from computer text corpora, 1997; (jtly) Longman Grammar of Spoken and Written English, 1999; (with P. Rayson and A. Wilson) Word Frequencies in Written and Spoken English, 2001. *Recreations:* music, esp. playing the piano in chamber music groups, walking. *Address:* Department of Linguistics, University of Lancaster, Bailrigg, Lancaster LA1 4YT.

LEECH, John, (Hans-Joachim Freiherr von Reitzenstein); Head of External Relations and Member of Management Board, Commonwealth Development Corporation, 1981–85; Chairman, Farm Services Co. BV, 1988–2000; Deputy Chairman, Rural Investment Overseas Ltd, 1990–2000 (Chairman, 1985–90); *b* 21 April 1925; *s* of Hans-Joachim and Josefine von Reitzenstein; *m* 1st, 1949, Mair Eiluned Davies (marr. diss. 1958); one *d*; 2nd, 1963, Noretta Conci, concert pianist. *Educ:* Bismarck Gymnasium, Berlin; Whitgift, Croydon. L. G. Mouchel & Partners, Consulting Civil Engineers, 1942–52; Bird & Co. Ltd, Calcutta, 1953–57; Dir, Europe House, London, and Exec. Mem. Council, Britain in Europe Ltd, 1958–63; Pres., Internat. Fedn of Europe Houses, 1961–65; Dir, Joint Industrial Exports Ltd, 1963–65; with Commonwealth Develt Corp., London and overseas, 1965–85; Co-ordinator, Interact Gp of European develt finance instns, 1973–85; Europ. Co-ordinator, West-West Agenda, 1987–. Asst Dir, NATO Parliamentarians' Conf., 1959–60. Vice-Chm., Indian Concrete Soc., 1953–57; Member: Council, Federal Trust for Educn and Research, 1985–; Adv. Council (formerly Exec. Cttee), London Symphony Orch., 1979–96; Council, Royal Commonwealth Soc. for the Blind, 1983–99; Internat. Council, Duke of Edinburgh's Award Internat. Assoc., 1993–98. Chm., Keyboard Charitable Trust for Young Professional Performers, 1991–. Liveryman, Worshipful Co. of Paviors, 1968– (Mem. Court of Assts, 1992–). FRSA. *Publications:* The NATO Parliamentarians' Conference 1955–59, 1960; Europe and the Commonwealth, 1961; Aid and the Community, 1972; Halt! Who Goes Where?: the future of NATO in the new Europe, 1991; contrib. to jls on aspects of overseas develt, European matters and arts subjects. *Recreations:* music, travel, Italy. *Address:* 8 Chester Square Mews, SW1W 9DS. *T:* (020) 7730 2307. *Club:* Travellers.

LEECH, Rev. Kenneth; M. B. Reckitt Urban Fellow, St Botolph's Church, Aldgate, since 1991; *b* 15 June 1939; *s* of late John and Annie Leech; *m* 1970, Rheta Wall (marr. diss. 1993); one *s*. *Educ:* King's College London (BA Hons Mod. History, AKC 1961); Trinity Coll., Oxford (BA Hons Theol. 1961, MA 1968); St Stephen's House, Oxford. Deacon 1964, priest 1965; Curate: Holy Trinity, Hoxton, N1, 1964–67; St Anne, Soho, W1, 1967–71; Sec., Soho Drugs Group, 1967–71; Dir, Centrepoint, Soho, 1969–71; Chaplain and Tutor, St Augustine's Coll., Canterbury, 1971–74; Rector of St Matthew, Bethnal Green, 1974–80; Field Work Sec., BCC, 1980; Race Relations Field Officer, C of E Bd for Social Responsibility, 1981–87; Dir, Runnymede Trust, 1987–90. Visiting Lecturer: St Stephen's House, Chicago, 1978–90; Brent House, Chicago, 1990–. DD Lambeth, 1998. *Publications:* Pastoral Care and the Drug Scene, 1970; A Practical Guide to the Drug Scene, 1972; Keep the Faith, Baby, 1972; Youthquake, 1973; Soul Friend, 1977; True Prayer, 1980; The Social God, 1981; True God, 1984; Spirituality and Pastoral Care, 1986; Struggle in Babylon: Racism in the Cities and Churches of Britain, 1988; Care and Conflict, 1990; Subversive Orthodoxy, 1992; The Eye of the Storm, 1992 (HarperCollins Religious Book Award, 1993); We Preach Christ Crucified, 1994; The Sky is Red, 1997; Drugs and Pastoral Care, 1998; Through Our Long Exile, 2001. *Recreations:* cartoon drawing, Lancashire dialect poetry, pubs. *Address:* St Botolph's Church, Aldgate, EC3N 1AB. *T:* (020) 7377 0721.

LEECH, Kevin Ronald; Founder and Chairman, ML Laboratories plc, 1987–2000; Chairman, Queensborough Holdings plc, 1994–2000; *b* 18 Aug. 1943; two *s* one *d* from former marriage. *Educ:* St Bede's Coll., Manchester. Accountancy, until 1964; built up family business, R. T. Leech & Sons Ltd, into UK's largest private funeral dir, 1964–82; entrepreneur, business manager, and venture capitalist, 1982–; non-executive Chairman: Top Jobs on the Net, 1999; CI4Net.Com Ltd, 1999–. FIMgt 1983; FInstD 1984; FRSA 1997. Hon. LLD Manchester, 1998. *Recreations:* Manchester United, football generally, ski-ing, sailing, fishing. *Address:* La Vignette, Rue de la Vignette, St Saviour, Jersey JE2 7NY.

LEECH, Prof. Rachel Mary, DPhil; Professor of Biology, University of York, 1978–99, now Emeritus; *b* 3 June 1936; *d* of Alfred Jack Leech and Frances Mary Ruth Leech (*née* Cowley). *Educ:* Prince Henry's Grammar Sch., Otley, W Yorks; St Hilda's Coll., Oxford (MA, DPhil 1961; Christopher Welch Scholar). Naples Biol Scholar, Stazione Zoologica, Naples, 1957–60; Professorial Res. Fellow, 1960–63, Lectr in Analytical Cytology, 1963–66, Imperial Coll., London; University of York: Lectr in Biology, 1966–69; Sen. Lectr, 1969–75; Reader, 1975–78. Leverhulme Emeritus Fellow, 2001–02. Mem., BBSRC, 1994–96. *Publications:* (with R. A. Reid) The Biochemistry and Structure of Subcellular Organelles, 1980; articles in Plant Physiology, Nature, The Biochemical Jl, The Plant Jl, Proc. of NAS, NY. *Recreations:* gardening, walking, enjoying the company of friends. *Address:* Department of Biology, University of York, Heslington, York YO1 5DD. *T:* (01904) 430000.

LEECH, His Honour Robert Radcliffe; a Circuit Judge (formerly Judge of County Courts), 1970–86; *b* 5 Dec. 1919; *s* of late Edwin Radcliffe Leech; *m* 1951, Vivienne Ruth, *d* of A. J. Rickerby, Carlisle; two *d*. *Educ:* Monmouth Sch.; Worcester Coll., Oxford (Open Classics Exhibnr 1938). Served War, 1940–44, Border Regt (despatches twice). Called to Bar, Middle Temple, 1949 (Harmsworth Law Scholar); Dep. Chm., Cumberland QS, 1966–71; Hon. Recorder of Carlisle, 1985–86. *Recreations:* sailing, golf. *Address:* Scaur House, Cavendish Terrace, Stanwix, Carlisle, Cumbria CA3 9ND. *Club:* Oriental.

LEEDER, Prof. Michael Robert, PhD; Professor of Environmental Sciences, University of East Anglia, since 1999; *b* 22 Nov. 1947; *s* of Norman George Leeder and Evelyn (*née* Patterson); *m* 1st, 1974, Susan Frances Green (marr. diss.); 2nd, 1980, Catherine Margaret Johnston (marr. diss.); 3rd, 1999, Marta Peréz-Arlucea. *Educ:* Univ. of Durham (BSc 1st Cl. Hons Geology); Univ. of Reading (PhD 1972). University of Leeds: Lectr in Earth Scis, 1972–85; Reader, 1985–91; Prof., 1991–99. Lyell Medal, Geol Soc., 1992; Phillips Medal, Geol Soc. of Yorks, 1990. *Publications:* Dynamic Stratigraphy of the British Isles, 1979; Sedimentology, 1982; Sedimentology and Sedimentary Basins, 1999; Fire Over East Anglia, 1999; contrib. various scientific papers. *Recreation:* living generally. *Address:* School of Environmental Sciences, University of East Anglia, Norwich NR4 7TJ.

LEEDHAM, Carol Jean; *see* Mountford, C. J.

LEEDS, Bishop of, (RC), since 1985; **Rt Rev. David Every Konstant;** *b* 16 June 1930; *s* of Antoine Konstant and Dulcie Marion Beresford Konstant (*née* Leggatt). *Educ:* St Edmund's College, Old Hall Green, Ware; Christ's College, Cambridge (MA); Univ. of London Inst. of Education (PGCE). Priest, dio. Westminster, 1954; Cardinal Vaughan School, Kensington, 1959; Diocesan Adviser on Religious Education, 1966; St Michael's School, Stevenage, 1968; Director, Westminster Religious Education Centre, 1970; Auxiliary Bishop of Westminster (Bishop in Central London) and Titular Bishop of Betagbara, 1977–85. Chm., Dept for Catholic Education and Formation (formerly Dept for Christian Doctrine and Formation), 1984–99, Dept for Internat. Affairs, 1999–, Bishops' Conf. of Eng. and Wales; Chm., Catholic Educn Service, 1991–99. FRSA 1996. Freeman, City of London, 1984. *Publications:* various books on religious education and liturgy. *Recreation:* music. *Address:* Bishop's House, 13 North Grange Road, Headingley, Leeds LS6 2BR. *T:* (0113) 230 4533, *Fax:* (0113) 278 9890; *e-mail:* dakons@aol.com.

LEEDS, Archdeacon of; *see* Oliver, Ven. J. M.

LEEDS, Sir Christopher (Anthony), 8th Bt *cr* 1812; Visiting Research Fellow, University of Kent at Canterbury; *b* 31 Aug. 1935; *s* of Geoffrey Hugh Anthony Leeds (*d* 1962) (*b* of 6th Bt) and Yoland Thérèse Barré (*d* 1944), *d* of James Alexander Mitchell; *S* cousin, 1983; *m* 1974, Elaine Joyce (marr. diss. 1981), *d* of late Sqdn Ldr C. H. A. Mullins. *Educ:* King's School, Bruton; LSE, Univ. of London (BSc Econ. 1958); Univ. of Southern California (Fulbright Travel Award; Sen. Herman Fellow in Internat. Relations, MA 1966). Assistant Master: Merchant Taylors' School, Northwood, 1966–68; Christ's Hospital, 1972–75; Stowe School, 1978–81. Publisher, 1975–78. Sen. Lectr, Univ. of Nancy 2, 1982–2000; Vis. Lectr, Univ. of Strasbourg I, 1983–87. *Publications include:* Political Studies, 1968, 3rd edn 1981; European History 1789–1914, 1971, 2nd edn 1980; Italy under Mussolini, 1972; Unification of Italy, 1974; Historical Guide to England, 1976; (with R. S. Stainton and C. Jones) Management and Business Studies, 1974, 3rd edn 1983; Basic Economics Revision, 1982; Politics in Action, 1986; World History—1900 to the present day, 1987; Peace and War, 1987; English Humour, 1989. *Recreations:* hill-walking, modern art, travel. *Heir: cousin* Antony Hildyard Leeds [*b* 15 Dec. 1937; *m* 1966, Elizabeth Helen Cornell (marr. diss. 1973)]. *Address:* 6 Hurlingham Mews, 14 Manor Road, Eastcliff, Bournemouth BH1 3EY; 7 rue de Turique, 54000 Nancy, France. *Club:* Lansdowne.

LEEMING, Cheryl Elise Kendall, (Mrs J. C. Leeming); *see* Gillan, C. E. K.

LEEMING, Geraldine Margaret; *see* Coleridge, G. M.

LEEMING, Ian; QC 1988; a Recorder, since 1989; *b* Preston, Lancs, 10 April 1948; *s* of late Thomas Leeming (Bombing Leader, RAF), and of Lilian (*née* Male); *m* 1973, Linda Barbara Cook; one *s* two *d*. *Educ:* The Catholic Coll., Preston; Manchester Univ. (LLB 1970). Called to the Bar: Gray's Inn, 1970; Lincoln's Inn (*ad eundem*), 1981. In practice at Chancery and Commercial Bars, 1971–. Dep. Deemster, Manx High Court, 1998; Mem., Court of Appeal, IOM, 1998. Lectr in Law (part-time), Manchester Univ., 1971–75. Formerly Counsel to Attorneys, Malcolm A. Hoffmann & Co., NY. Dir of limited cos. Vice-Chm., Northern Soc. of Cons. Lawyers, 1985–88. Fellow, Soc. for Advanced Legal Studies, 1998. Member: Chancery Bar Assoc.; Professional Negligence Bar Assoc.; Technol. and Construction Court Bar Assoc. *Publications:* (with James Bonney) Observations upon the Insolvency Bill, 1985; articles, notes and reviews in legal jls and specialist periodicals. *Recreations:* squash, real tennis. *Address:* Lamb Chambers, Lamb Building, Temple EC4Y 7AS. *T:* (020) 7797 8300.

LEEMING, John Coates; space consultant; Director General, British National Space Centre, 1987–88 (Director, Policy and Programmes, 1985–87); *b* 3 May 1927; *s* of late James Arthur Leeming and Harriet Leeming; *m* 1st, 1949 (marr. diss. 1974); two *s*; 2nd, 1985, Cheryl Elise Kendall Gillan, *qv*. *Educ:* Chadderton Grammar Sch., Lancs; St John's Coll., Cambridge (Schol.). Teaching, Hyde Grammar Sch., Cheshire, 1948. Asst Principal, HM Customs and Excise, 1950 (Private Sec. to Chm.); Principal: HM Customs and Excise, 1954; HM Treasury, 1956; HM Customs and Excise, 1958; Asst Sec., HM Customs and Excise, 1965; IBRD (World Bank), Washington, DC, 1967; Asst Sec., 1970, Under Sec., 1972, CSD; a Comr of Customs and Excise, 1975–79; Dept of Industry (later DTI), 1979–85. *Recreation:* golf. *Club:* Royal Automobile.

LEES, Sir Antony; *see* Lees, Sir W. A. C.

LEES, His Honour C(harles) Norman; a Circuit Judge, 1980–96; Designated Family Judge, Greater Manchester, 1991–96; *b* 4 Oct. 1929; *s* of late Charles Lees, Bramhall, Cheshire; *m* 1961, Stella (*d* 1987), *d* of late Hubert Swann, Stockport; one *d. Educ:* Stockport Sch.; Univ. of Leeds. LLB 1950. Called to Bar, Lincoln's Inn, 1951. Dep. Chm., Cumberland County QS, 1969–71; a Recorder of the Crown Court, 1972–80; Chm., Mental Health Review Tribunal, Manchester Region, 1977–80 (Mem., 1971–80; Pres. (restricted patients), 1983–98). *Recreations:* tennis, music, history. *Address:* 24 St John Street, Manchester M3 4ES. *T:* (0161) 214 6000. *Clubs:* Lansdowne; Northern Lawn Tennis.

LEES, Sir David (Bryan), Kt 1991; FCA; Chairman: GKN plc, since 1988 (Director, since 1982); Tate & Lyle plc, since 1998; a Director, Bank of England, 1991–99; *b* 23 Nov. 1936; *s* of late Rear-Adm. D. M. Lees, CB, DSO, and C. D. M. Lees; *m* 1961, Edith Mary Bernard; two *s* one *d. Educ:* Charterhouse. Qualified as a chartered accountant, 1962. Chief Accountant, Handley Page Ltd, 1964–68; GKN Sankey Ltd: Chief Accountant, 1970–72; Dep. Controller, 1972–73; Director, Secretary and Controller, 1973–76; Guest Keen and Nettlefolds, later GKN plc: Group Finance Executive, 1976–77; General Manager Finance, 1977–82; Finance Dir, 1982–87; Man. Dir, 1987–88. Chm., Courtaulds plc, 1996–98 (Dir, 1991–98). Mem. Council, CBI, 1988– (Chm., Economic Affairs (formerly Economic and Financial Policy) Cttee, 1988–94); Pres., EEF, 1990–92; Member: Audit Commission, 1983–90; Listed Cos Adv. Cttee, 1990–97; European Round Table, 1995–; Nat. Defence Industries Council, 1995–. Dir, Inst. for Manufacturing, 1998–. Pres., Soc. of Business Economists, 1994–99. Dir, Royal Opera House, 1998–. Mem. Governing Body, Shrewsbury Sch., 1986–; Gov., Suttons Hosp., Charterhouse, 1995–. Founding Societies Centenary Award for Chartered Accountants, 1999. Officer's Cross, Order of Merit (Germany), 1996. *Recreations:* walking, golf, opera, music. *Address:* Tate & Lyle plc, Sugar Quay, Lower Thames Street, EC3R 6DQ. *Club:* MCC.

See also Rear-Adm. R. B. Lees.

LEES, Prof. Dennis Samuel, CBE 1980; Emeritus Professor of Industrial Economics, University of Nottingham, since 1983 (Professor, 1968–82); *b* 20 July 1924; *s* of late Samuel Lees and Evelyn Lees (*née* Withers), Borrowash, Derbyshire; *m* 1950, Elizabeth Bretisch, London (*d* 1992); two *s* one *d. Educ:* Derby Technical Coll.; Nottingham Univ. BSc(Econ), PhD. Lecturer and Reader in Economics, Keele Univ., 1951–65; Prof. of Economics, University Coll., Swansea, 1965–67. Exchange Lectr, Reed Coll., Portland, Ore, 1958–59; Visiting Prof. of Economics: Univ. of Chicago, 1963–64; Univ. of California, Berkeley, 1971; Univ. of Sydney, 1975. Chairman: Nat. Ins. Advisory Committee, 1972–80; Industrial Injuries Advisory Council, 1973–78; Mem., Adv. Council, Inst. of Econ. Affairs, 1974–93 (Hon. Fellow, 1994). Freeman, City of London, 1973. *Publications:* Local Expenditure and Exchequer Grants, 1956; Health Thru Choice, 1961; Economic Consequences of the Professions, 1966; Economics of Advertising, 1967; Financial Facilities for Small Firms, 1971; Impairment, Disability, Handicap, 1974; Economics of Personal Injury, 1976; Solicitors' Remuneration in Ireland, 1977; articles on industrial and social policy in: Economica, Jl of Political Economy, Amer. Econ. Rev., Jl of Law and Econ., Jl Industrial Econ., Jl Public Finance. *Recreations:* cricket and pottering. *Address:* 8 Middleton Crescent, Beeston, Nottingham NG9 2TH. *T:* (0115) 925 8730.

LEES, Geoffrey William; Headmaster, St Bees School, 1963–80; *b* 1 July 1920; *o s* of late Mr and Mrs F. T. Lees, Manchester; *m* 1949, Joan Needham, *yr d* of late Mr and Mrs J. Needham, Moseley, Birmingham. *Educ:* King's Sch., Rochester; Downing Coll., Cambridge. Royal Signals, 1940–46 (despatches): commissioned 1941: served in NW Europe and Middle East, Captain. 2nd Class Hons English Tripos, Pt I, 1947; History Tripos, Part II, 1948; Asst Master, Brighton Coll., 1948–63. Leave of absence in Australia, Asst Master, Melbourne Church of England Gram. Sch., 1961–62. *Recreations:* reading, lepidoptera, walking. *Address:* 10 Merlin Close, Upper Drive, Hove, Sussex BN3 6NU. *Clubs:* Hawks, Union (Cambridge).

LEES, Capt. Nicholas Ernest Samuel; Clerk of the Course and Managing Director, Leicester Racecourse, since 1972 (Assistant Manager, 1970–71); Chairman, Stratford on Avon Racecourse Co. Ltd, since 2001 (Director, since 1990); *b* 3 May 1939; *s* of Ernest William Lees and Marjorie May Lees; *m* 1st, 1969, Elizabeth Helen Spink (marr. diss. 1985); one *d*; 2nd, 1985, Jocelyn Kosina; one *d. Educ:* Abbotsholme Sch., Rocester, Staffs. Shell Oil, 1956–59; commnd 17/21 Lancers, 1959; retd from Army, 1967; studied for Chartered Surveyors exams, 1967–69 (passed final exams but never practised); auctioneer, Warner, Sheppard & Wade Ltd, Leicester, 1969–73; Clerk of the Course: Teesside Park, 1972–73; Great Yarmouth, 1977–91; Chief Exec., 1974–97, Clerk of the Course, 1974, and Dir of Racing, 1998–2000, Newmarket. Dir, Racecourse Assoc. Ltd, 1988–93. *Recreations:* horse racing, point to pointing, antique furniture, silver, sporting art. *Address:* Capers End, Bradfield St George, Bury St Edmunds, Suffolk IP30 0AY. *T:* (01284) 386651.

LEES, Norman; *see* Lees, C. N.

LEES, Robert Ferguson, CBE 1999; Regional Procurator Fiscal for Lothian and Borders, 1991–98; *b* 15 Sept. 1938; *s* of William Lees and Martha Lees (*née* McAlpine); *m* 1966, Elizabeth (Elsie) Loughridge. *Educ:* Bellshill Acad.; Strathclyde Univ. (LLB). Joined Procurator Fiscal Service, 1972; Legal Asst, Paisley, 1972–75; Legal Asst, 1975–76, Sen. Legal Asst, 1976–78, and Sen. Depute Fiscal, 1978–81, Glasgow; Asst Procurator Fiscal, Dundee, 1982–88; Regl Procurator Fiscal for N Strathclyde, 1989–91. Vis. Scholar, Valdosta State Univ., Ga, 1999–2000. *Publication:* (jtly) Criminal Procedure, 1990. *Recreations:* music, travel, languages, photography.

LEES, Air Vice-Marshal Robin Lowther, CB 1985; MBE 1962; Air Officer in charge of Administration, RAF Support Command, 1982–85, and Head of Administration Branch, RAF, 1983–85, retired; *b* 27 Feb. 1931; *e s* of late Air Marshal Sir Alan Lees, KCB, CBE, DSO, AFC, and Norah Elizabeth (*née* Thompson); *m* 1966, Alison Mary Benson, *o d* of late Col C. B. Carrick, MC, TD, JP; three *s. Educ:* Wellington Coll.; RAF Coll., Cranwell. Commissioned RAF, 1952; served AAFCE Fontainebleau, 1953–56; Waterbeach, 1956–58; UKSLS Ottawa, 1958–61; DGPS(RAF) Staff MoD, 1962–66; Wyton, 1966–68; HQ Far East Comd, 1968–70; Directing Staff RAF Staff Coll., 1971–74; RAF PMC, 1974–76; Dir of Personnel (Ground) MoD, 1976; Dir of Personal Services (2) (RAF) MoD, 1976–80; RCDS 1980; Dir of Personnel Management (Policy and Plans) (RAF) MoD, 1981–82. Chief Exec., BHA, 1986–96. Mem. Council, CBI, 1990–93. Vice-Pres., HOTREC, 1991–93; Mem. Bd, Internat. Hotel and Restaurant Assoc., 1994–95. Gov., Wellington Coll., 1990–2001. Protocol Dir, Wentworth Golf Club, 1996–. FBIM, 1974–94; FIPM, 1976–94. *Recreations:* real tennis, lawn tennis, golf. *Address:* c/o Barclays Bank, 6 Market Place, Newbury, Berks RG14 5AY. *Clubs:* Royal Air Force (Chairman, 1977–82); Jesters', All England Lawn Tennis and Croquet.

LEES, Rear-Adm. Rodney Burnett, CVO 2001; Defence Services Secretary to the Queen, and Director General of Reserve Forces and Cadets, 1998–2001; Chief Naval Supply Officer, 1998–2000; *b* 31 Dec. 1944; *s* of Rear-Adm. Dennis Marescaux Lees, CB, DSO and Daphne Lees; *m* 1st, 1969, Rosemary Elizabeth Blake (marr. diss. 1978); two *s*; 2nd, 1982, Molly McEwen. *Educ:* Charterhouse. Called to Bar, Gray's Inn, 1976. Joined RN 1962; HMS Devonshire, 1966–68; Captain SM10, 1968–70; HMS Apollo, 1972–74; legal training, 1974–77; Staff Legal Adviser to FO Portsmouth and Command Legal Adviser to C-in-C Naval Home Comd, 1977–79; Dep. Supply Officer, HM Yacht Britannia, 1980; DCSO (Pay), MoD 1980–82; Supply Officer, HMS Illustrious, 1982–83; Fleet Legal and Admin Officer, 1984–86; Sec. to Chief of Fleet Support, 1986–88; Dep. Comd Sec. to C-in-C Fleet, 1988–90; Sec. to First Sea Lord, 1990–92; Dir, Defence Personnel, 1992–95; Dir Gen., Naval Personnel Strategy and Plans, COS to Second Sea Lord and C-in-C Naval Home Comd, 1995–98. *Recreations:* horse racing, soccer, golf, country and folk music. *Address:* Langham House, Langham, Norfolk NR25 7BX. *Club:* Army and Navy.

See also Sir D. B. Lees.

LEES, Sir Thomas (Edward), 4th Bt *cr* 1897; landowner; *b* 31 Jan. 1925; 2nd *s* of Sir John Victor Elliott Lees, 3rd Bt, DSO, MC, and Madeline A. P. (*d* 1967), *d* of Sir Harold Pelly, 4th Bt; *S* father, 1955; *m* 1st, 1949, Faith Justin (*d* 1996), *d* of G. G. Jessiman, OBE, Great Durnford, Wilts; one *s* three *d*; 2nd, 1998, Ann Christine, *d* of Major Cyril Thomas Kelleway, Auckland, NZ. *Educ:* Eton; Magdalene Coll., Cambridge. Served War in RAF; discharged 1945, after losing eye. Magdalene, Cambridge, 1945–47; BA Cantab 1947 (Agriculture). Since then has farmed at and managed South Lytchett estate. Chm., Post Green Community Trust Ltd. Mem., General Synod of C of E, 1970–90. JP 1951, CC 1952–74, High Sheriff 1960, Dorset. Hon. DLitt Bournemouth, 1992. *Recreation:* sailing. *Heir: s* Christopher James Lees [*b* 4 Nov. 1952; *m* 1st, 1977, Jennifer (marr. diss. 1987), *d* of John Wyllie; 2nd, 1989, Clare, *d* of Austen Young, FRCS, Aberystwyth; two *s* three *d*]. *Address:* Post Green, Lytchett Minster, Poole, Dorset BH16 6AP. *T:* (01202) 622048. *Club:* Royal Cruising.

LEES, Sir Thomas Harcourt Ivor, 8th Bt *cr* 1804 (UK), of Black Rock, County Dublin; *b* 6 Nov. 1941; *s* of Sir Charles Archibald Edward Ivor Lees, 7th Bt, and Lily, *d* of Arthur Williams, Manchester; *S* father, 1963. *Heir: kinsman* John Cathcart d'Olier-Lees [*b* 12 Nov. 1927; *m* 1957, Wendy Garrold, *yr d* of late Brian Garrold Groom; two *s*].

LEES, Dr William, CBE 1970; TD 1962; FRCOG; Medical Manpower Consultant to South West Thames Regional Health Authority, 1981–87, retired; *b* 18 May 1924; *s* of William Lees and Elizabeth Lees (*née* Massey); *m* 1947, Winifred Elizabeth (*née* Hanford); three *s. Educ:* Queen Elizabeth's, Blackburn; Victoria Univ., Manchester. MB ChB; LRCP; MRCS; MRCOG, FRCOG; DPH; MFCM. Obstetrics and Gynaecology, St Mary's Hosps, Manchester, 1947–58; Min. of Health, later DHSS, 1959–81; Under Sec., (SPMO) 1977–81. QHP, 1969–72. Col, 10th, later no 257, Gen. Hosp., TAVR RAMC, 1966–71; Col Comdt, NW London Sector, ACF, 1971–76; Mem. for Greater London, TA&VRA, 1966–. OStJ 1967. *Publications:* numerous contribs on: intensive therapy, progressive patient care, perinatal mortality, day surgery, district general hospital. *Recreations:* music, golf, travel. *Address:* 13 Hall Park Hill, Berkhamsted, Herts HP4 2NH. *T:* (01442) 863010. *Clubs:* Athenæum, St John's.

LEES, Sir (William) Antony Clare, 3rd Bt *cr* 1937; *b* 14 June 1935; *s* of Sir (William) Hereward Clare Lees, 2nd Bt, and of Lady (Dorothy Gertrude) Lees, *d* of F. A. Lauder; *S* father, 1976; *m* 1986, Joanna Olive Crane. *Educ:* Eton; Magdalene Coll., Cambridge (MA). *Heir:* none.

LEESE, Richard Charles, CBE 2001; Member (Lab), since 1984, and Leader, since 1996, Manchester City Council; *b* 21 April 1951; *s* of Samuel and Hilda Leese; *m* 1982, Michal Evans (marr. diss. 2000); one *s* one *d. Educ:* Warwick Univ. (BSc Maths). Teacher of Maths, Sidney Stringer Sch. and Community Coll., Coventry, 1974–78, with one year at Washington Jun. High School, Duluth, Minn; youth worker, 1979–82; researcher, 1983–84; community worker, 1984–88. Manchester City Council: Chair: Educn Cttee, 1986–90; Finance Cttee, 1990–95; Dep. Leader, 1990–96. *Recreations:* swimming, football, cricket, political campaigning, the Labour Party, travel, friends, family, music. *Address:* Manchester City Council, Town Hall, Albert Square, Manchester M60 2LA. *T:* (0161) 234 3004.

LE FANU, Sir (George) Victor (Sheridan), KCVO 1987; Serjeant at Arms, House of Commons, 1982–89; *b* 1925; *s* of late Maj.-Gen. Roland Le Fanu, DSO, MC, and Marguerite (*née* Lumsden); *m* 1956, Elizabeth, *d* of late Major Herbert Hall and Kitty (*née* Gauvain); three *s. Educ:* Shrewsbury School. Served Coldstream Guards, 1943–63; Asst-Adjt, Royal Military Academy, Sandhurst, 1949–52; Adjt 2nd Bn Coldstream Guards, 1952–55; sc Camberley, 1959; Staff Captain to Vice-Quartermaster-General to the Forces, War Office, 1960–61; GSO2, Headquarters London District, 1961–63; Dep. Asst Serjeant at Arms, House of Commons, 1963–76; Asst Serjeant at Arms, 1976–81; Deputy Serjeant at Arms, 1981–82. Chm., Morley Coll., 1992–2000. Trustee, Wall Trust, 1991–. *Address:* 29 Cranmer Court, Whitehead's Grove, SW3 3HN.

LE FANU, Mark, OBE 1994; General Secretary, The Society of Authors, since 1982; *b* 14 Nov. 1946; *s* of Admiral of the Fleet Sir Michael Le Fanu, GCB, DSC and Prudence, *d* of Admiral Sir Vaughan Morgan, KBE, CB, MVO, DSC; *m* 1976, Lucy Cowen; three *s* one *d. Educ:* Winchester; Univ. of Sussex. Admitted Solicitor, 1976. Served RN, 1964–73; McKenna & Co., 1973–78; The Society of Authors, 1979–. Vice Chm., British Copyright Council, 1992–98; Mem., Literature Adv. Cttee, British Council, 1989–; Chairman: Strachey Trust, 1995–; W11 Opera, 1997–2000. *Recreations:* sailing, travel, golf. *Address:* 25 St James's Gardens, W11 4RE. *T:* (020) 7603 4119; The Society of Authors, 84 Drayton Gardens, SW10 9SB. *T:* (020) 7373 6642. *Clubs:* PEN; Thorney Island Sailing.

LeFANU, Prof. Nicola Frances; composer; Professor of Music, University of York, since 1994 (Head of Department of Music, 1994–2001); *b* 28 April 1947; *d* of late William Richard LeFanu and Dame Elizabeth Violet Maconchy, DBE; *m* 1979, David Newton Lumsdaine; one *s. Educ:* St Mary's Sch., Calne; St Hilda's Coll., Oxford (BA Hons 1968, MA 1972; Hon. Fellow, 1993); Royal Coll. of Music; DMus London, 1988. Cobbett Prize for chamber music, 1968; BBC Composers' Competition, 1st Prize, 1971; Mendelssohn Scholarship, 1972; Harkness Fellowship for composition study, Harvard, 1973–74. Dir of Music, St Paul's Girls' Sch., 1975–77; Composer in Residence (jtly with David Lumsdaine), NSW Conservatorium of Music, Sydney, 1979; Sen Lectr in Music, 1977–93, Prof. of Musical Composition, KCL, 1993–94. Deleg. to Moscow Internat. New Music Festival, 1984. FRCM 1995. Hon. DMus Durham, 1995. Leverhulme Res. Award, 1989. *Publications:* numerous compositions, incl. opera, orchestral works, chamber music with and without voice, choral music and solo pieces; *major works include:* The Same Day Dawns (for soprano and ensemble), 1974; Columbia Falls (for symphony orch.), 1975; Dawnpath (chamber opera), 1977; The Old Woman of Beare (for soprano and ensemble), 1981; The Story of Mary O'Neill (radio opera), 1986; The Green Children (children's opera), 1990; Blood Wedding (opera), 1992; The Wildman (opera), 1995; Duo Concertante (for violin, viola and orch.), 1999. *Recreations:* natural history, and therefore conservation; peace movement, women's movement. *Address:* 5 Holly Terrace, York YO10 4DS. *T:* (01904) 651759, *Fax:* (01904) 610467.

LE FANU, Sir Victor; *see* Le Fanu, Sir G. V. S.

LEFEBVRE, Prof. Arthur Henry, FREng; Distinguished Reilly Professor of Combustion Engineering, School of Mechanical Engineering, Purdue University, 1979–93, now Emeritus Professor (Professor and Head of School, 1976–80); *b* 14 March 1923; *s* of Henri and May Lefebvre; *m* 1952, Elizabeth Marcella Betts; two *s* one *d*. *Educ:* Long Eaton Grammar Sch; Nottingham Univ.; Imperial Coll., London (DSc (Eng), DIC, PhD). FREng (FEng 1994); FIMechE, FRAeS. Ericssons Telephones Ltd: Engrg apprentice, 1938–41; Prodn Engr, 1941–47; res. work on combustion and heat transfer in gas turbines, Rolls Royce, Derby, 1952–61; Prof. of Aircraft Propulsion, Coll. of Aeronautics, 1961–71; Prof. and Hd of Sch. of Mechanical Engrg, Cranfield Inst. of Technol., 1971–76. Mem., AGARD Combustion and Propulsion Panel, 1957–61; Mem., AGARD Propulsion and Energetics Panel, 1970–76; Chm., Combustion Cttee, Aeronautical Res. Council, 1970–74. Hon. DSc Cranfield Inst. of Technology, 1989. Gas Turbine Award, ASME, 1982; R. Tom Sawyer Award, ASME, 1984; inaugural AIAA Propellants and Combustion Award, 1990; Marshall Award, Instn for Liquid Atomization and Spray Systems, 1993; Internat. Gas Turbine Inst. Scholar Award, ASME, 1995; Aircraft Engine Technology Award, ASME, 1996. *Publications:* Gas Turbine Combustion, 1983; Selected Papers on Fundamentals of Gas Turbine Combustion, 1988; Atomization and Sprays, 1989; papers on combustion and heat transfer in Proc. Royal Soc., internat. symposium vols on combustion, combustion and flame, combustion science and technology. *Recreations:* music, reading. *Address:* Low Furrow, Pebworth, Stratford-upon-Avon, Warwicks CV37 8XW. *T:* (01789) 721429.

LEFEVER, Kenneth Ernest, CB 1974; Deputy Chairman, Civil Service Appeal Board, 1978–80 (Official Side Member, 1976–78); *b* 22 Feb. 1915; *s* of E. S. Lefever and Mrs E. E. Lefever; *m* 1939, Margaret Ellen Bowley; one *s* one *d*. *Educ:* County High Sch., Ilford. Board of Customs and Excise: joined Dept as Officer, 1935; War Service, 1942–46 (Captain, RE); Principal Inspector, 1966; Dep. Chief Inspector, 1969; Collector, London Port, 1971; Chief Inspector, 1972; Dir of Organisation and Chief Inspector, 1974; Comr, Bd of Customs and Excise, 1972–75, retd. *Recreations:* gardening, walking, cricket. *Address:* Trebarwith, 37 Surman Crescent, Hutton Burses, Brentwood, Essex CM13 2PW. *T:* (01277) 212110. *Clubs:* MCC, Civil Service.

LEFF, Prof. Gordon; Professor of History, University of York, 1969–88, now Emeritus; *b* 9 May 1926; *m* 1953, Rosemary Kathleen (*née* Fox) (marr. diss 1980); one *s*. *Educ:* Summerhill Sch.; King's Coll., Cambridge. BA 1st Cl. Hons, PhD, LittD. Fellow, King's Coll., Cambridge, 1955–59; Asst Lectr, Lectr, Sen. Lectr, in History, Manchester Univ., 1956–65; Reader in History, Univ. of York, 1965–69. Carlyle Vis. Lectr, Univ. of Oxford, 1983. *Publications:* Bradwardine and the Pelagians, 1957; Medieval Thought, 1958; Gregory of Rimini, 1961; The Tyranny of Concepts, 1961; Richard Fitzralph, 1963; Heresy in the Later Middle Ages, 2 vols, 1967; Paris and Oxford Universities in 13th and 14th Centuries, 1968; History and Social Theory, 1969; William of Ockham: the metamorphosis of scholastic discourse, 1975; The Dissolution of the Medieval Outlook, 1976. *Recreations:* walking, gardening, watching cricket, listening to music. *Address:* The Sycamores, 12 The Village, Strensall, York Y032 5XS. *T:* (01904) 490358.

LEFF, Prof. Julian Paul, MD; FRCPsych; Professor of Social and Cultural Psychiatry, Institute of Psychiatry, University of London, since 1987; *b* 4 July 1938; *s* of Samuel Leff and Vera Miriam (*née* Levy); *m* 1975, Joan Lillian Raphael; three *s* one *d*. *Educ:* University Coll. London (BSc, MB BS); MD London 1972. FRCPsych 1979; MRCP; MFPHM. House Officer: University Coll. Hosp., 1961–62; Whittington Hosp., 1962–63; career scientist, MRC, 1972–; Dir, Team for Assessment of Psychiatric Services, 1985–; Dir, MRC Social and Community Psychiatry Unit, 1989–95. Starkey Prize, Royal Coll. of Health, 1976; Burghölzli Award, Univ. of Zürich, 1999. *Publications:* Psychiatric Examination in Clinical Practice, 1978, 3rd edn 1990; Expressed Emotion in Families, 1985; Psychiatry around the Globe, 1981, 2nd edn 1988; Family Work for Schizophrenia, 1992; Principles of Social Psychiatry, 1993; Care in the Community: illusion or reality?, 1997; The Unbalanced Mind, 2001. *Recreations:* piano, squash, croquet, swimming. *Address:* Institute of Psychiatry, De Crespigny Park, SE5 8AF. *T:* (020) 7708 3235.

le FLEMING, Sir David (Kelland), 13th Bt *cr* 1705, of Rydal, Westmorland; *b* 12 Jan. 1976; *s* of Sir Quentin John le Fleming, 12th Bt and of Judith Ann le Fleming (*née* Peck); *S* father, 1995. *Educ:* Queen Elizabeth Coll., Palmerston North; Wairarapa Polytech. Coll. Studying at Wellington Polytech. Coll. for Visual Communications Design Degree. *Heir:* *b* Andrew John le Fleming, *b* 4 Oct. 1979. *Address:* 147 Stanford Street, Ashhurst, Manawatu, North Island, New Zealand. *T:* (6) 3268406.

le FLEMING, Morris John; DL; Chief Executive, Hertfordshire County Council, and Clerk to the Lieutenancy, Hertfordshire, 1979–90; *b* 19 Aug. 1932; *s* of late Morris Ralph le Fleming and Mabel le Fleming; *m* 1960, Jenny Rose Weeks; one *s* three *d*. *Educ:* Tonbridge Sch.; Magdalene Coll., Cambridge (BA). Admitted Solicitor, 1958. Junior Solicitor, Worcester CC, 1958–59; Asst Solicitor: Middlesex CC, 1959; Nottinghamshire CC, 1959–63; Asst Clerk, Lindsey (Lincolnshire) CC, 1963–69; Hertfordshire CC: Second Dep. Clerk, 1969–74; County Secretary, 1974–79; Clerk, Magistrates' Courts Cttee, 1979–90; Sec., Probation Care Cttee, 1979–90. Dir, Herts TEC, 1989–90. Chm., Stansted Airport Consultative Cttee, 1991–; Mem., N Wales Child Abuse Tribunal of Enquiry, 1996–99. Dir, Herts Groundwork Trust, 1990–98; Trustee, Herts Community Trust, 1991–96. Pres., Herts Scouts, 1997– (Chm., 1991–97). DL Herts, 1991. Hon. LLD Hertfordshire, 1994. *Address:* Swangleys Lane, Knebworth, Herts SG3 6AA. *T:* and *Fax:* (01438) 813152. *Club:* Royal Over-Seas League.

LE FLEMING, Peter Henry John; health management consultant, since 1988; Regional General Manager, South East Thames Regional Health Authority, 1984–88; *b* 25 Oct. 1923; *s* of late Edward Ralph Le Fleming and Irene Louise Le Fleming (*née* Adams); *m* 1st, 1949, Gudrun Svendsen (marr. diss. 1981); two *s*; 2nd, 1987, Jean, *yr d* of Edgar and Alice Price, Llangenny, Wales. *Educ:* Addison Gardens Sch., Hammersmith; Pembroke Coll., Cambridge. MA; FHSM. Served 1942–47, RTR and Parachute Regt, MEF, CMF, Palestine; commnd 1943. Sudan Political Service, Equatoria, Kassala, Blue Nile Provinces, 1949–55; NHS, 1955–: Redevelt Sec., St Thomas's Hosp., London, 1955–57; Hosp. Sec., The London Hosp., 1957–61; Dep. Clerk to the Governors, Guy's Hosp., 1961–69; Gp Sec., Exeter and Mid Devon Hosp. Management Cttee, 1969–74; Area Administrator, Kent AHA, 1974–81; Regional Administrator, SE Thames RHA, 1981–84. Mem., Health Service Supply Council, 1982–86. Clerk to Special Trustees, Guy's Hosp., 1988–97; Chm., Evelina Family Trust, 1996–98. Freeman, City of London, 1992. *Recreations:* long distance fell walking, horse riding, trad jazz and serious music. *Address:* Lilacs, Leys Road, Tostock, near Bury St Edmunds, Suffolk IP30 9PN. *T:* (01359) 271015.

LEGARD, Sir Charles Thomas, 15th Bt *cr* 1660; *S* father, 1984. *Heir:* *s* Christopher John Charles Legard [*b* 19 April 1964; *m* 1986, Miranda, *d* of Maj. Fane Gaffney; one *s*].

LÉGER, Most Rev. Ernest Raymond; *see* Moncton, Archbishop of (RC).

LEGG, Barry Charles, FCCA; *b* 30 May 1949; *s* of Henry and Elfreda Legg; *m* 1974, Margaret Rose; one *s* two *d*. *Educ:* Sir Thomas Rich's Grammar Sch., Gloucester; Manchester Univ. (BA Hons Hist.). ATII. Courtaulds Ltd, 1971–76; Coopers & Lybrand, 1976–78; Hillsdown Holdings plc, 1978–92. MP (C) Milton Keynes South West, 1992–97; contested (C) same seat, 1997. Member: Treasury and Civil Service Select Cttee, 1992–96; Treasury Select Cttee, 1996–97 (Chm.). *Publications:* Maintaining Momentum: a radical tax agenda for the 1990s, 1992; Who Benefits?—Reinventing Social Security, 1993; Civil Service Reform, a Case for More Radicalism, 1994. *Recreation:* watching cricket. *Address:* 22 Chapel Street, SW1X 7BY. *Clubs:* United and Cecil; Gloucestershire CC.

LEGG, Prof. Brian James, FIBiol; FREng; Director, NIAB (formerly National Institute of Agricultural Botany), since 1999; *b* 20 July 1945; *s* of Walter and Mary Legg; *m* 1972, Philippa Whitehead; one *s* one *d*. *Educ:* Balliol Coll., Oxford (BA Physics 1966); Imperial Coll. London (PhD 1972). FInstP, FIAgrE, FIBiol, CPhys, FREng (FEng 1994). Voluntary Service Overseas, The Gambia, 1966–67; Res. Scientist, Rothamsted Exptl Station, 1967–83; Head, Res. Divs, Silsoe Res. Inst., 1983–90; Dir, Silsoe Res. Inst., BBSRC (formerly AFRC), 1990–99. Vis. Scientist, CSIRO Div. of Envtl Mechanics, Canberra, 1980–82; Vis. Prof., Silsoe Coll., Cranfield Inst. of Technology, 1990–. *Publications:* contribs to learned jls. *Recreations:* sailing, ski-ing, music. *Address:* NIAB, Huntingdon Road, Cambridge CB3 0LE.

LEGG, Cyrus Julian Edmund; Blue Arrow Personnel Services, since 1997; *b* 5 Sept. 1946; *s* of Cyrus and Eileen Legg; *m* 1967, Maureen Jean (*née* Lodge); two *s*. *Educ:* Tiffin School. Agricultural and Food Research Council, 1967–83; HM Treasury, 1983–87; Sec., BM (Natural Hist.) subseq. Natural History Mus., 1987–97. *Recreation:* gardening. *Address:* c/o Blue Arrow, 82 High Street, Bedford MK40 1NN. *T:* (01234) 270575.

LEGG, Keith (Leonard Charles), OBE 1981; PhD, MSc (Eng); CEng, FIMechE, FRAeS, FCIT, FILT; FHKIE; Hon. Professor and Advisor to Xian Jiaotung University, Shanghai Polytechnic University and South China Institute of Technology, China; consultant on aerospace engineering and on higher education; *b* 24 Oct. 1924; *s* of E. H. J. Legg; *m* 1947, Joan, *d* of H. E. Green; two *s*. *Educ:* London Univ. (External); Cranfield Inst. of Technology. Engineering apprenticeship, 1940–45; Dep. Chief Research and Test Engr, Asst Chief Designer, Chief Project and Structural Engr, Short Bros & Harland Ltd, Belfast, 1942–56; Chief Designer and Prof., Brazilian Aeronautical Centre, São Paulo, 1956–60; Head of Dept, 1960–72, and Prof., 1965–72, Loughborough Univ. of Technology (Sen. Pro Vice-Chancellor, 1967–70); Dir, Lanchester Polytechnic, 1972–75; Dir, Hong Kong Polytechnic, 1975–84. Chm., Internat. Directing Cttee, CERI/OECD Higher Educn Institutional Management, 1973–75; Member: Road Transport Industrial Trng Bd, 1966–75 (former Chm.); Hong Kong Bd of Educn, 1975–84; World Council for Co-operative Educn, 1979–84; Adv. Cttee on Environmental Protection, 1977–84 (Chm., Noise Cttee); Hong Kong Management Assoc. Council, 1982–84; Environmental and Pollution Council of Hong Kong; Indust. Develt Bd, 1982–84. Royal Aeronautical Society: Member: Council, 1967–75; Educn Cttee, 1990–; Grading Cttee, 1991–. Adviser to OECD in Paris; mem. various nat. and professional cttees. Member: Council of City Polytechnic of Hong Kong, 1984; Court, Cranfield Inst. of Technology (now Univ.), 1987– (Hon. Vice-Pres. of Convocation, 1987–); Court, Loughborough Univ., 1993–. JP Hong Kong, 1978–84. Fellow, Hong Kong Management Assoc. Hon. DTech Loughborough, 1982; Hon. LLD: Hong Kong Univ., 1984, Hong Kong Poly., 1992. *Publications:* numerous: on aerospace structures and design, transport systems, higher educn, educnl analytical models and on Hong Kong/China. *Recreations:* most sports, classical music, theatre, walking, aid to the handicapped, public lectures on Hong Kong and China. *Address:* 408 Hardaker Court, 317–323 Clifton Drive South, St Anne's-on-Sea, Lancs FY8 1HN. *T:* (01253) 725387.

LEGG, Sir Thomas (Stuart), KCB 1993 (CB 1985); QC 1990; Permanent Secretary, Lord Chancellor's Department, and Clerk of the Crown in Chancery, 1989–98; *b* 13 Aug. 1935; *e s* of Stuart Legg and Margaret Legg (*née* Amos); *m* 1st, 1961, Patricia Irene Dowie (marr. diss.); two *d*; 2nd, 1983, Marie-Louise, *e d* of late Humphrey Jennings. *Educ:* Horace Mann-Lincoln Sch., New York; Frensham Heights Sch., Surrey; St John's Coll., Cambridge (MA, LLM). 2nd Lieut, Royal Marines (45 Commando), 1953–55. Called to the Bar, Inner Temple, 1960, Bencher, 1984; joined Lord Chancellor's Dept, 1962; Private Secretary to Lord Chancellor, 1965–68; Asst Solicitor, 1975; Under Sec., 1977–82; SE Circuit Administrator, 1980–82; Dep. Sec., 1982–89; Dep. Clerk of the Crown in Chancery, 1986–89; Sec. of Commns, 1989. Conducted Sierra Leone Arms Investigation, 1998. Hon. Sen. Res. Fellow, Sch. of Public Policy, UCL, 1999–; Vis. Fellow, Constitution Unit, 1999–. Consultant, Clifford Chance, 1998–. Chm., Hammersmith Hosps NHS Trust, 2000–. Trustee, Civil Service Benevolent Fund, 1998–2000 (Chm., 1993–98). Mem. Bd, Inst. of Advanced Legal Studies, 1989–98; Visitor, Brunel Univ., 2001– (Mem. Council, 1993–2000). Hon. Mem., SPTL, 1991. *Address:* c/o National Westminster Bank, PO Box 1, 1 Stoke Road, Guildford, Surrey GU1 3ZR. *Club:* Garrick.

LEGGATT, Rt Hon. Sir Andrew (Peter), Kt 1982; PC 1990; Chief Surveillance Commissioner, since 1998; a Lord Justice of Appeal, 1990–97; *b* 8 Nov. 1930; *er s* of late Captain William Ronald Christopher Leggatt, DSO, RN and Dorothea Joy Leggatt (*née* Dreyer); *m* 1953, Gillian Barbara Newton; one *s* one *d*. *Educ:* Eton; King's Coll., Cambridge (Exhibr). MA 1957. Commn in Rifle Bde, 1949–50; TA, 1950–59. Called to the Bar, Inner Temple, 1954, Bencher, 1976. QC 1972; a Recorder of the Crown Court, 1974–82; Judge, High Court of Justice, QBD, 1982–90. Mem., Top Salaries Review Body, 1979–82; conducted review, Tribunals for Users, 2000–01. Mem., Judges' Council, 1988–97. Pres., Council of Inns of Court, 1995–97; Member: Bar Council, 1971–82; Senate, 1974–83; Chm. of the Bar, 1981–82. Hon. Member: American Bar Assoc.; Canadian Bar Assoc.; non-resident mem., American Law Inst.; Hon. Fellow, Amer. Coll. of Trial Lawyers, 1996. *Recreations:* listening to music, personal computers. *Clubs:* MCC, Pilgrims.

See also *G. A. M. Leggatt.*

LEGGATT, George Andrew Midsomer; QC 1997; *b* 12 Nov. 1957; *s* of Rt Hon. Sir Andrew Peter Leggatt, *qv* and Gillian Barbara Leggatt (*née* Newton); *m* 1987, Dr Stavia Brigitte Blunt; one *s* one *d*. *Educ:* Eton (King's Schol.); King's Coll., Cambridge (MA); Harvard (Harkness Fellow); City Univ. (Dip. Law). Bigelow Teaching Fellow, Univ. of

Chicago Law Sch., 1982–83; called to the Bar, Middle Temple, 1983; Associate, Sullivan & Cromwell, New York, 1983–84. *Publication:* (contrib.) Halsbury's Laws of England, 4th edn 1989. *Recreations:* wine, philosophy. *Address:* Brick Court Chambers, 7-8 Essex Street, WC2R 3LD. *T:* (020) 7379 3550.

LEGGATT, Sir Hugh (Frank John), Kt 1988; art dealer, retired; *b* 27 Feb. 1925; 2nd *s* of late Henry and Beatrice Leggatt; *m* 1st, 1953, Jennifer Hepworth (marr. diss. 1990); two *s*; 2nd, 1991, Gaynor, *yr d* of late W. L. Tregoning, CBE and D. M. E. Tregoning. *Educ:* Eton; New Coll., Oxford. RAF, 1943–46. Joined Leggatt Bros, 1946; Partner, 1952; Sen. Partner, 1962–92. Hon. Rep., Nat. Portrait Galls of London and Edinburgh, 1946–92. Pres., Fine Art Provident Instn, 1960–63; Chm., Soc. of London Art Dealers, 1966–70; Mem., Museums and Galleries Commn, 1983–92. Hon. Sec., Heritage in Danger, 1974–. *Address:* 21 Rue du Lac, 1800 Vevey, Switzerland. *T:* and *Fax:* (21) 9236810.

LEGGE, family name of **Earl of Dartmouth**.

LEGGE, (John) Michael, CB 2001; CMG 1994; Secretary and Director of Administration, Royal Hospital, Chelsea, since 2001; *b* 14 March 1944; *s* of Alfred John Legge and Marion Frances Legge (*née* James); *m* 1971, Linda (*née* Bagley); two *s*. *Educ:* Royal Grammar Sch., Guildford; Christ Church Oxford (BA, MA). Ministry of Defence: Asst Principal, 1966; Asst Private Sec. to Sec. of State for Defence, 1970; Principal, 1971; 1st Sec., UK Delegn to NATO, 1974–77; Asst Sec., MoD, 1979–87; Rand Corp., Santa Monica, California, 1982; Asst Under Sec. of State (Policy), MoD, 1987–88; Asst Sec. Gen. for Defence Planning and Policy, NATO, 1988–93; Deputy Under-Secretary of State: NI Office, 1993–96; MoD, 1996–2000. *Publication:* Theatre Nuclear Weapons and the NATO Strategy of Flexible Response, 1983. *Recreations:* golf, gardening. *Address:* Royal Hospital, Chelsea, SW3 4SR.

LEGGE, Rt Rev. William Gordon, DD; *b* 20 Jan. 1913; *s* of Thomas Legge and Jane (*née* Gill); *m* 1941, Hyacinth Florence Richards; one *s* one *d*. *Educ:* Bishop Feild and Queen's Colls, St John's, Newfoundland. Deacon 1938, priest 1939; Curate, Channel, 1938–41; Incumbent of Botwood, 1941–44; Rector, Bell Island, 1944–55; Sec., Diocesan Synod, 1955–68; Archdeacon of Avalon, 1955–68; Canon of Cathedral, 1955–76; Diocesan Registrar, 1957–68; Suffragan Bishop, 1968; Bishop of Western Newfoundland, 1976–78. DD *hc*, Univ. of King's College, Halifax, NS, 1973. *Address:* 52 Glenhaven Boulevard, Corner Brook, NF A2H 4P6, Canada.

LEGGE-BOURKE, Hon. (Elizabeth) Shân (Josephine), LVO 1988; Lord-Lieutenant of Powys, since 1998; *b* 10 Sept. 1943; *o c* of 3rd Baron Glanusk, DSO and of Margaret (*née* Shoubridge, now Dowager Viscountess De L'Isle); *m* 1964, William Legge-Bourke, DL; one *s* two *d*. Lady-in-waiting to HRH Princess Anne, now HRH Princess Royal, 1978–. President: Royal Welsh Agricl Soc., 1997; Nat. Fedn of Young Farmers Clubs of England and Wales, 1998–2000; Save the Children Fund (Wales), 1983–; former Chief Pres. and Chief Cadet Officer (Wales), St John's Ambulance Bde. High Sheriff of Powys, 1991–92. Gov., Christ's Coll., Brecon, 1997–. *Address:* Penmyarth, Glanusk Park, Crickhowell, Powys NP8 1LP. *T:* (01873) 810414.

LEGGE-SCHWARZKOPF, Dame Elisabeth; *see* Schwarzkopf.

LEGGETT, Sir Clarence (Arthur Campbell), Kt 1980; MBE (mil.) 1943; FRACS, FACS; Surgeon; Hon. Consulting Surgeon, Princess Alexandra Hospital, Brisbane, since 1968; *b* 24 July 1911; *s* of late A. J. Leggett; *m* 1939, Avril, *d* of late R. L. Bailey; one *s* two *d*. *Educ:* Sydney Univ. (MA, MB BS; 1st cl. Hons, Univ. Medallist, 1936); Queensland Univ. (MS). RMO, Royal Prince Alfred Hosp., Sydney, 1937–38; Asst Dep. Med. Supt, 1939. Major, AAMC, 1941–46. Asst Surgeon, Royal Brisbane Hosp., 1941–51; Junior Surg., 1951–56; Senior Surg., Princess Alexandra Hosp., Brisbane, 1956–68. University of Queensland: Hon. Demonstrator and Examiner, Anatomy Dept, 1941–47; Chief Asst, Dept of Surgery, 1947–51; Mem. Faculty Bd, 1947–51; Special Lectr, 1951–68. Member of Council: Queensland Inst. for Med. Research, 1948–65; RACS, 1966–75 (Gordon Craig Schol.; Chm. Court of Examiners, 1971–75; Junior Vice-Pres., 1973–75; Mem. Ct of Honour). FAMA 1985; Hon. FRCS 1983. *Publications:* numerous surgical and historical papers, orations and theses. *Recreations:* breeding Arabian horses and Hereford cattle; univ. blue, and mem., Australian hockey team, 1934. *Address:* Craigston, 217 Wickham Terrace, Brisbane, Queensland 4000, Australia. *T:* (7) 38310031. *Club:* Queensland (Brisbane).

LEGH; *see* Cornwall-Legh, family name of Baron Grey of Codnor.

LEGH, family name of **Baron Newton**.

LEGH-JONES, (Piers) Nicholas; QC 1987; *b* 2 Feb. 1943; *s* of late John Herbert Legh-Jones and Elizabeth Anne (*née* Halford). *Educ:* Winchester College; New College, Oxford (MA Hist. 1964, Jurisp. 1966). Legal Instructor, Univ. of Pennsylvania, 1966–67; Lectr in Law, New College, Oxford, 1967–71; Eldon Law Scholar, Univ. of Oxford, 1968. Called to the Bar, Lincoln's Inn, 1968. Vis. Prof., King's Coll., London, 1998–. *Publications:* (ed) MacGillivray and Parkington on Insurance Law, 6th edn, to 8th edn 1988; (gen. ed.) MacGillivray on Insurance Law, 9th edn, 1997; contribs to Modern Law Review and Cambridge Law Jl. *Recreations:* vintage motorcars, modern history. *Address:* 20 Essex Street, WC2R 3AL. *T:* (020) 7583 9294.

LEGHARI, Farooq Ahmed Khan; President of Pakistan, 1993–97; *b* 2 May 1940; *s* of Nawab Sardar Muhammad Khan Leghari; *m*; two *s* two *d*. *Educ:* Aitchison Coll., Lahore; Punjab Univ. (BA Hons); St Catherine's Coll., Oxford (BA Hons PPE, MA). Civil Servant, 1964–73; Mem., Pakistan People's Party, 1973–93; Senate of Pakistan, 1975; Mem. for Dera Ghazi Khan, Nat. Assembly, 1977; Minister for Production, 1977; jailed on numerous occasions, 1977–88; Sec.-Gen. and Mem. Exec. Cttee, Pakistan People's Party, 1978–83; Mem., Nat. Assembly, and Minister for Water and Power, 1989–90; re-elected 1990 and 1993; Dep. Leader of Opposition, 1990–93; Finance Minister, later Minister for Foreign Affairs, 1993. Chief, Baluchi Leghari Tribe.

LEGON, Prof. Anthony Charles, PhD, DSc; FRS 2000; Professor of Physical Chemistry, 1984–89, and since 1990, and EPSRC Senior Fellow, 1997–Sept. 2002, University of Exeter; *b* 28 Sept. 1941; *s* of George Charles Legon and late Emily Louisa Florence Legon (*née* Conner); *m* 1963, Deirdre Anne Rivers; two *s* one *d*. *Educ:* Coopers' Co. Sch., London (Gibson Exhibnr); UCL (BSc 1963; PhD 1967; DSc 1981). FRSC 1978. Turner & Newall Fellow, Univ. of London, 1968–70; University College London: Lectr, 1970–83, Reader, 1983–84, in Chemistry; Thomas Graham Prof. of Chemistry, 1989–90. Vis. Res. Associate Prof., Univ. of Illinois, 1980; Hassel Lectr, Univ. of Oslo, 1997; Prof. Invité, Univ. de Lille, 2000. Mem., Physical Chemistry Sub Cttee, 1984–87, NATO Postdoctoral Fellowships (Chemistry) Cttee, 1987, 1988, 1991–93, Advanced Fellowships (Chemistry) Cttee, 1991–92 (Chm., 1991), SERC; Royal Society of Chemistry: Chairman: Peninsula Section, 1988–89; High Resolution Spectroscopy Gp, 1998–2000; Tilden Lectr and Medallist, 1990; Mem. Council, 1996–99, Vice-Pres., 2001–, Faraday Div.; Associate Ed., Chem. Communications, 1996–98; Spectroscopy Award, 1999. Member Editorial Board: Chemical Physics Letters, 1988–; Spectrochimica Acta, 1989–97; Jl of Molecular Structure, 1990–; Jl Chem. Soc. Faraday Trans, 1994–98. *Publications:* Principles of Molecular Recognition, 1993; more than 300 res. papers in learned jls. *Recreations:* watching soccer (Exeter City AFC), and cricket (Somerset CCC). *Address:* School of Chemistry, University of Exeter, Stocker Road, Exeter EX4 4QD. *T:* (01392) 263488, *Fax:* (01392) 263434; *e-mail:* a.c.legon@exeter.ac.uk.

LE GOY, Raymond Edgar Michel, FCIT, FILT; a Director General, Commission of the European Communities, now European Union, since 1981; *b* 1919; *e s* of J. A. S. M. N. and May Le Goy; *m* 1960, Ernestine Burnett, Trelawny, Jamaica; two *s*. *Educ:* William Ellis Sch.; Gonville and Caius Coll., Cambridge (BA 1st cl. hons Hist. Tripos, 1939, 1940; MA). Sec. Cambridge Union; Chm., Union Univ. Liberal Socs. Served Army, 1940–46: Staff Captain, HQ E Africa, 1944; Actg Major, 1945. LPTB, 1947; Min. of Transport, 1947; UK Shipping Adviser, Japan, 1949–51; Far East and SE Asia, 1951; Dir, Goeland Co., 1952; Asst Secretary: MoT, 1958; Min. of Aviation, 1959; BoT and DEA, 1966; Under-Sec., 1968, BoT, later DTI; Dir Gen. for Transport, EEC, 1973–81. FCIT 1974; FILT 1999. *Publication:* The Victorian Burletta, 1953. *Recreations:* theatre, music, race relations. *Address:* c/o Fortis Banque, Agence Schuman, Rond Point Schuman 10, 1040 Brussels, Belgium.

LE GREW, Daryl John; Vice-Chancellor, University of Canterbury, New Zealand, since 1998; *b* Melbourne, 17 Sept. 1945; *s* of A. J. and N. M. R. Le Grew; *m* 1971, Josephine de Tarczynska; one *s* two *d*. *Educ:* Trinity Grammar Sch., Kew; Univ. of Melbourne (BArch, MArch). University of Melbourne: Lectr, Dept of Town and Regl Planning, 1969–73; Lectr, then Sen. Lectr, Dept of Architecture and Bldg, 1973–85; Deakin University: Prof. of Architecture, 1986–98; Dean, Faculty of Design and Technol., 1992–93; Chm., Acad. Bd, 1992–98; Pro-Vice-Chancellor (Acad.), 1993–94; Dep. Vice-Chancellor and Vice-Pres. (Acad.), 1994–98. Life Fellow, Mus. of Victoria, 1997. *Recreations:* swimming, music, poetry, philosophy. *Address:* University of Canterbury, Private Bag 4800, Christchurch 1, New Zealand.

LEHANE, Maureen, (Mrs Peter Wishart); concert and opera singer; *d* of Christopher Lehane and Honor Millar; *m* 1966, Peter Wishart (*d* 1984), composer. *Educ:* Queen Elizabeth's Girls' Grammar Sch., Barnet; Guildhall Sch. of Music and Drama. Studied under Hermann Weissenborn, Berlin (teacher of Fischer Dieskau); also under John and Aida Dickens (Australian teachers of Joan Sutherland); gained Arts Council award to study in Berlin. Speciality is Handel; has sung numerous leading roles (operas inc. Ezio, Ariadne and Pharamondo) with Handel opera societies of England and America, in London, and in Carnegie Hall, New York, also in Poland, Sweden and Germany; gave a number of master classes on the interpretation of Handel's vocal music (notably at s'Hertogenbosch Festival, Holland, July 1972; invited to repeat them in 1973); masterclasses on Handel and Purcell, The Hague and Maastricht, 1991; Vocal Dept, WCMD, 1997. Debut at Glyndebourne, 1967. Festival appearances include: Stravinsky Festival, Cologne; City of London; Aldeburgh; Cheltenham; Three Choirs; Bath; Oxford Bach; Göttingen Handel Festival, etc; has toured N America; also 3–month tour of Australia at invitation of ABC and 2–month tour of Far East and ME, 1971; sang in Holland, and for Belgian TV, 1978; visits also to Berlin, Lisbon, Poland and Rome, 1979–80, to Warsaw, 1981. Title and lead rôles in: Purcell's Dido and Aeneas, Netherlands Opera, 1976; Peter Wishart's operas, Clytemnestra and The Lady of the Inn; Mozart's Marriage of Figaro, Cologne Opera; Rossini's La Cenerentola; 13 of Handel's operas. Cyrus in first complete recording of Handel's Belshazzar. Appeared regularly on BBC; also in promenade concerts. Has made numerous recordings (Bach, Haydn, Mozart, Handel, etc). Mem. Jury, Internat. Singing Comp., s'Hertogenbosch Fest., Holland, 1982–; Adjudicator, Llangollen Internat. Eisteddfod 1991–93 and 1997. Founder and Music Dir, Great Elm Music Festival, 1987–98; Founder and Artistic Dir, Jackdaws Educnl Trust, 1993–. *Publication:* (ed with Peter Wishart) Songs of Purcell. *Recreations:* cooking, gardening, reading. *Address:* Bridge House, Great Elm, Frome, Somerset BA11 3NY. *T:* (01373) 812383.

LEHMAN, Prof. Meir, (Manny), DSc, PhD; FREng, FBCS, FIEE, FIEEE, FACM; Managing and Technical Director, Lehman Software Technology Associates Ltd, since 1985; Professor of Computing Science, Imperial College of Science and Technology, University of London, 1972–84, now Emeritus Professor, Senior Research Fellow, since 1989 and Senior Research Investigator, since 1998; *b* 24 Jan. 1925; *s* of late Benno and Theresa Lehman; *m* 1953, Chava Robinson; three *s* two *d*. *Educ:* Letchworth Grammar Sch.; Imperial Coll. of Science and Technol. (BSc Hons, PhD, ARCS, DIC); DSc (London) 1987. FIEE 1972 (StuIEE 1947); FBCS 1968 (MBCS 1956); FIEEE 1985 (MIEEE 1974); FREng (FEng 1989); FACM 1994 (MACM 1953). Murphy Radio, 1941–50; Imperial Coll., 1950–56; London Labs, Ferranti, 1956–57; Scientific Dept, Israeli Defence Min., 1957–64; Res. Div., IBM, 1964–72; Department of Computing, Imperial College: 1972–84 (part-time 1984–87); Hd of Dept, 1979–84; Principal Investigator, Feedback Evolution and Software Technology, EPSRC Project, 1996–98 and 1999–2001; Imperial Software Technology Ltd: Founder, 1982; Chm., 1982–84; Dir, 1984–87; Exec. Dir, 1987–88. Vice-Chm. of Exec., Kisharon Day Sch. for Special Educn, 1976–2000 (Vice-Chm. of Trustees and Gov., 1976–2000). *Publications:* Software Evolution—Processes of Program Change, 1985; over 190 refereed pubns and some 14 book chapters. *Recreations:* family, Talmudic studies, classical orchestral music, gardening, DIY. *Address:* 5 Elm Close, NW4 2PH; Department of Computing, Imperial College of Science, Technology and Medicine, SW7 2BZ. *T:* (office) (020) 7594 8214, *Fax:* (020) 7594 8215; *e-mail:* mml@doc.ic.ac.uk.

LEHMANN, Prof. Andrew George; Emeritus Professor, University of Buckingham; *b* 17 Feb. 1922; *m* 1942, Alastine Mary (*d* 2000), *d* of late K. N. Bell; two *s* one *d*. *Educ:* Dulwich Coll.; The Queen's Coll., Oxford. MA, DPhil Oxon. Served with RCS and Indian Army, 6th Rajputana Rifles (invalided). Fenced for England (Sabre), 1939. Asst lecturer and lecturer, Manchester Univ., 1945–51; Prof. of French Studies, 1951–68, Dean of Faculty of Letters and Soc. Scis, Univ. of Reading, 1960–66. Hon. Prof., Univ. of Warwick, 1968–78; various industry posts, 1968–78; Dir, Inst. of European Studies, Hull Univ., 1978–83; Rank Foundn Prof. of European Studies, and Dean, Sch. of Humanities, Univ. of Buckingham, 1983–88. Mem., Hale Cttee on University Teaching Methods, 1961–63; Chm., Industrial Council for Educnl and Trng Technology, 1974–76 (Pres., 1979–81, Vice-Pres., 1981–85); Mem., Anglo-French Permanent Mixed Cultural Commission, 1963–68. Adviser: Chinese Univ. of Hong Kong, 1964; Haile Sellassie I Univ., Ethiopia, 1965. Member: Hong Kong Univ. Grants Cttee, 1966–73; Academic Planning Board and Academic Adv. Cttee, New Univ. of Ulster, 1966–77; Planning Bd, 1970–72, Acad. Adv. Cttee, 1974–83, UC at Buckingham; Court and Council, Bedford Coll., London Univ., 1971–78; British Library Adv. Cttee (Reference), 1975–78; Princeton Univ. Academic Adv. Council, 1975–81. Shakespeare Prize Cttee, FVS Foundn, Hamburg, 1984–90. Governor, Ealing Tech. Coll., 1974. *Publications:* The Symbolist Aesthetic in France, 1950 and 1967; Sainte-Beuve, a portrait of the Critic, 1962; The European Heritage, 1984; articles in various periodicals and learned reviews. *Recreations:* music, travel, gardening. *Address:* Westway Cottage, West Adderbury, Banbury, Oxon OX17 3EU. *T:* (01295) 810272.

LEHN, Prof. Jean-Marie; Officier, Ordre National du Mérite, 1993 (Chevalier, 1976); Commandeur, Légion d'Honneur, 1996 (Chevalier, 1983; Officier, 1988); Professor of Chemistry, Collège de France, Paris, since 1979; *b* Rosheim, Bas-Rhin, 30 Sept. 1939; *s* of Pierre Lehn and Marie Lehn (*née* Salomon); *m* 1965, Sylvie Lederer; two *s*. *Educ:* Univ. of Strasbourg (PhD); Research Fellow, Harvard, 1964. CNRS, 1960–66; Asst Prof., Univ. of Strasbourg, 1966–69; University Louis Pasteur, Strasbourg: Associate Prof., 1970; Prof. of Chemistry, 1970–79. Visiting Professor, 1972–: Harvard, Zürich, Cambridge, Barcelona, Frankfurt. Mem. or Associate, and hon. degrees from professional bodies in Europe and USA; Hon. FRSC 1987; For. Mem., Royal Soc., 1993. Nobel Prize for Chemistry (jtly), 1987, and numerous awards from sci. instns. Orden pour le mérite für Wissenschaften und Künste (FRG), 1990. *Publications:* many chapters in books and contribs to learned jls on supramolecular chemistry, physical organic chemistry and photochemistry. *Recreation:* music. *Address:* Institut de Science d'Ingénierie Supramoléculaires, Université Louis Pasteur, 4 rue Blaise Pascal, 67000 Strasbourg, France. *T:* (3) 90241369, *Fax:* (3) 90241117; *e-mail:* lehn@chimie.u-strasbg.fr; Collège de France, 11 place Marcelin Berthelot, 75005 Paris, France. *T:* 144271360, *Fax:* 144271356.

LEHRER, Thomas Andrew; writer of songs since 1943; *b* 9 April 1928; *s* of James Lehrer and Anna Lehrer (*née* Waller). *Educ:* Harvard Univ. (AB 1946, MA 1947); Columbia Univ.; Harvard Univ. Student (mathematics, especially probability and statistics) till 1953. Part-time teaching at Harvard, 1947–51. Theoretical physicist at Baird-Atomic, Inc., Cambridge, Massachusetts, 1953–54. Entertainer, 1953–55, 1957–60. US Army, 1955–57. Lecturer in Business Administration, Harvard Business Sch., 1961; Lecturer: in Education, Harvard Univ., 1963–66; in Psychology, Wellesley Coll., 1966; in Political Science, MIT, 1962–71; Lectr, Univ. of Calif, Santa Cruz, 1972–. *Publications:* Tom Lehrer Song Book, 1954; Tom Lehrer's Second Song Book, 1968; Too Many Songs by Tom Lehrer, 1981; contrib. to Annals of Mathematical Statistics, Journal of Soc. of Industrial and Applied Maths. *Recreation:* piano. *Address:* 11 Sparks Street, Cambridge, MA 02138, USA. *T:* (617) 3547708.

LEICESTER, 7th Earl of, *cr* 1837; **Edward Douglas Coke;** Viscount Coke 1837; *b* 6 May 1936; *er s* of 6th Earl of Leicester and his 1st wife, Moyra Joan (*d* 1987), *d* of Douglas Crossley; *S* father, 1994; *m* 1st, 1962, Valeria Phyllis (marr. diss. 1985), *e d* of late L. A. Potter; two *s* one *d*; 2nd, 1986, Mrs Sarah de Chair. *Educ:* St Andrew's, Grahamstown, CP, S Africa. Mem., King's Lynn and W Norfolk BC, 1973–91 (Leader, 1980–85; Chm. Planning Cttee, 1987–91). Pres., HHA, 1998–. Chm. Trustees, de Montfort Univ. Global Educn Trust. President: Wells, Norfolk Br., RNLI; League of Friends, Wells, Norfolk Cottage Hosp.; Royal Norfolk Show, 1995; Assoc. of Drainage Authorities. Mem. Council, Royal Norfolk Agricl Assoc. DL Norfolk, 1981–85. *Recreations:* history, conservation of the built heritage, wildlife matters, reading, shooting. *Heir: s* Viscount Coke, *qv*. *Address:* Holkham, Wells-next-the-Sea, Norfolk NR23 1AB. *Clubs:* Brooks's, White's, Farmers'.

LEICESTER, Bishop of, since 1999; **Rt Rev. Timothy John Stevens;** *b* 31 Dec. 1946; *s* of Ralph and Jean Ursula Stevens; *m* 1973, Wendi Kathleen; one *s* one *d*. *Educ:* Chigwell Sch.; Selwyn Coll., Cambridge (BA 1968; MA 1972); Ripon Hall, Oxford (Dip Th). BOAC, 1968–72; FCO, 1972–73. Ordained priest, 1976; Curate, East Ham, 1976–79; Team Vicar, Upton Park, 1979–80; Team Rector, Canvey Island, 1980–88; Bp of Chelmsford's Urban Officer, 1988–91; Archdeacon of West Ham, 1991–95; Bishop Suffragan of Dunwich, 1995–99. Hon. Canon of Chelmsford, 1987–95. *Recreations:* golf, cricket. *Address:* Bishop's Lodge, 10 Springfield Road, Leicester LE2 3BD. *T:* (0116) 270 8985, *Fax:* (0116) 270 3288.

LEICESTER, Dean of; *see* Faull, Very Rev. V. F.

LEICESTER, Archdeacon of; *see* Edson, Ven. M.

LEIFLAND, Leif, Hon. GCVO 1983; Ambassador of Sweden to the Court of St James's, 1982–91; *b* 30 Dec. 1925; *s* of Sigfrid and Elna Leifland; *m* 1954, Karin Abard; one *s* two *d*. *Educ:* Univ. of Lund (LLB 1950). Joined Ministry of Foreign Affairs, 1952; served: Athens, 1953; Bonn, 1955; Stockholm, 1958; Washington, 1961; Stockholm, 1964; Washington, 1970; Stockholm, 1975. Secretary, Foreign Relations Cttee, Swedish Parliament, 1966–70; Under Secretary for Political Affairs, 1975–77; Permanent Under-Secretary of State for Foreign Affairs, 1977–82; Chm. Bd, Swedish Inst. of Internat. Affairs, 1991–. *Publications:* books and articles on foreign policy and national security questions. *Address:* Nybrogatan 77, 11440 Stockholm, Sweden.

LEIGH, family name of **Baron Leigh**.

LEIGH, 5th Baron *cr* 1839; **John Piers Leigh;** *b* 11 Sept. 1935; *s* of 4th Baron Leigh, TD and Anne (*d* 1977), *d* of Ellis Hicks Beach; *S* father, 1979; *m* 1st, 1957, Cecilia Poppy (marr. diss. 1974), *y d* of late Robert Cecil Jackson; one *s* one *d* (and one *d* decd); 2nd, 1976, Susan (marr. diss. 1982), *d* of John Cleave, Whitnash, Leamington Spa; one *s*; 3rd, 1982, Mrs Lea Hamilton-Russell (marr. diss. 1998), *o d* of Col Noel Wild. *Educ:* Eton; Oxford and London Universities. *Recreations:* horses, hunting, racing, sport, country pursuits. *Heir: s* Hon. Christopher Dudley Piers Leigh [*b* 20 Oct. 1960; *m* 1990, Sophy-Ann, *d* of Richard Burrows; one *s* one *d*].

LEIGH, Christopher Humphrey de Verd; QC 1989; **His Honour Judge Leigh;** a Circuit Judge, since 2001; *b* 12 July 1943; *s* of late Wing Commander Humphrey de Verd Leigh and of Johanna Leigh; *m* 1970, Frances Powell. *Educ:* Harrow. Called to the Bar, Lincoln's Inn, 1967, Bencher, 1999. A Recorder, 1985–2001. *Recreations:* ski-ing, travel. *Address:* Southampton Combined Court Centre, London Road, Southampton SO15 2XQ. *T:* (023) 8021 3200.

LEIGH, David, PhD; Executive Director, United Kingdom Institute for Conservation, since 2001; *b* 11 Jan. 1943; *s* of Jacques Leigh and Gwendoline (*née* Bright); *m* 1969, Judith Mary Latham; one *s* two *d*. *Educ:* Univ. of Durham (BSc Physics 1966); Inst. of Archaeology, Univ. of London (Dip. Archaeol Conservation 1968); UC, Cardiff (PhD 1980). Experimental Officer (Conservation), Dept of Archaeology, Univ. of Southampton, 1968–74; Lectr in Archaeol Conservation, UC, Cardiff, 1975–87; Head of Conservation Unit, Museums and Galls Commn, 1987–93; Dir, Mus. Training Inst., 1993–95; Principal, West Dean Coll., 1995–2000. Member: Internat. Inst. for Conservation, 1970–75; Sci. and Conservation Panel, 1984–94, Ancient Monuments Adv. Cttee, 1988–90, English Heritage; Rescue. FSA; FIIC; ACR. *Publications:* (ed) First Aid for Finds, 1976; articles on Anglo-Saxon artefacts, especially early Anglo-Saxon jewellery, conservation and restoration, training and educn. *Recreations:* family, music, walking. *Address:* United Kingdom Institute for Conservation, 109 The Chandlery, 50 Westminster Bridge Road, SE1 7QY.

LEIGH, Edward Julian Egerton; MP (C) Gainsborough, since 1997 (Gainsborough and Horncastle, 1983–97); *b* 20 July 1950; *s* of Sir Neville Egerton Leigh, KCVO; *m* 1984, Mary Goodman; three *s* three *d*. *Educ:* St Philip's Sch., Kensington; Oratory Sch., Berks; French Lycée, London; UC, Durham Univ. (BA Hons). Called to the Bar, Inner Temple, 1977. Mem., Cons. Res. Dept, seconded to office of Leader of Opposition, GLC, 1973–75; Prin. Correspondence Sec. to Rt Hon. Margaret Thatcher, MP, 1975–76. Member (C): Richmond Borough Council, 1974–78; GLC, 1977–81. Contested (C) Teesside, Middlesbrough, Oct. 1974. PPS to Minister of State, Home Office, 1990; Parly Under-Sec. of State, DTI, 1990–93. Sec., Conservative backbench Cttees on agric., defence and employment, 1983–90; Vice Chm., Conservative Back bench Cttees on foreign affairs and social security, 1997–2001. Chm., Nat. Council for Civil Defence, 1980–82; Dir, Coalition for Peace Through Security, 1982–83. Kt of Honour and Devotion, SMO Malta, 1994. *Publications:* Right Thinking, 1979; Responsible Individualism, 1994. *Recreations:* walking, reading. *Address:* House of Commons, SW1A 0AA.

LEIGH, Sir Geoffrey (Norman), Kt 1990; Chairman, Allied London Properties, 1987–98 (Managing Director, 1970–87); Arrow Property Investments Ltd, since 2000; *b* 23 March 1933; *s* of late Rose Leigh and Morris Leigh; *m* 1st, 1955, Valerie Lennard (marr. diss. 1975; she *d* 1976); one *s* two *d*; 2nd, 1976, Sylvia Pell; one *s* one *d*. *Educ:* Haberdashers' Aske's Hampstead Sch.; Univ. of Michigan. Man. Dir, 1965, Chm., 1980–98, Sterling Homes. Founder and First Pres., Westminster Junior Chamber of Commerce, 1959–63; Underwriting Mem., Lloyd's, 1973–97. Special Advisor, Land Agency Bd, Commn for the New Towns, 1994–96; Member: Cttee, Good Design in Housing for Disabled, 1977; Cttee, Good Design in Housing, 1978–79; British ORT Council, 1979–80; Internat. Adv. Bd, American Univ., Washington, 1983–97; Adv. Council, Prince's Youth Business Trust, 1985–; Main Finance Bd, NSPCC, 1985– (Hon. Mem. Council, 1995–); Governing Council, Business in the Community, 1987–; Somerville Coll. Appeal, 1987–; Royal Fine Art Commn Art and Arch. Educn Trust, 1988–99; Per Cent Club, 1988–2000; Council, City Technology Colls Trust, 1988–; City Appeal Cttee, Royal Marsden Hosp., 1990–93; Review Body on Doctors' and Dentists' Remuneration, 1990–93; Wellbeing Council, 1994–; Chancellor's Ct of Benefactors, Oxford Univ., 1991–; Emmanuel Coll., Cambridge, Develt Campaign, 1994–96; Chm., St Mary's Hosp. 150th Anniversary Appeal, 1995–. Comr and Trustee, Fulbright Commn, 1991–99 (Chm., Fulbright US-UK. Adv. Bd, 1995–); Sponsor, Leigh City Technology Coll., Dartford (Chm. of Govs, 1988–); Founder/Sponsor, Friends of British Liby, 1987– (Vice-Pres., 2000–); Founder, Margaret Thatcher Centre, Somerville Coll., Oxford, 1991; Treasurer: Commonwealth Jewish Council, 1983–89; Commonwealth Jewish Trust, 1983–89; a Treas., Cons. Party, 1995–97; Vice President: Hampstead and Highgate Cons. Assoc., 1997– (Patron, 1991–94; Pres., 1994–97); Conservatives Abroad, 1995–; Treas. and Trustee, Action on Addiction, 1991–; Trustee: Margaret Thatcher Foundn, 1991–; Industry in Educn, 1993–98; Philharmonia, 1992–99. Governor: Royal Sch., Hampstead, 1991–; City Lit. Inst., 1991–98. Hon. Mem., Emmanuel Coll., Cambridge, 1995; Foundn Fellow, Somerville Coll., Oxford, 1998. Hon. Life Mem., Cons. Med. Soc., 1998. Freeman, City of London, 1976; Liveryman: Haberdashers' Co., 1992–; Furniture Makers' Co., 1987 (Mem., Court of Assistants, 1992–94). FRSA; FICPD. Presidential Citation, The American Univ., 1987. *Recreations:* photography, reading, golf. *Address:* 38 Belgrave Square, SW1X 8NT. *T:* (020) 7235 9548. *Clubs:* Carlton, United and Cecil, Pilgrims, Royal Automobile; Wentworth.

LEIGH, Prof. Irene May, MD; DSc; FRCP, FMedSci; Professor of Cellular and Molecular Medicine, since 1999, and Assistant Warden (Research), Barts and the London, Queen Mary's School of Medicine and Dentistry (formerly St Bartholomew's and Royal London School of Medicine and Dentistry, Queen Mary and Westfield College, London University); *b* 25 April 1947; *d* of Archibald and May Lilian Allen; *m* 1st, P. Nigel Leigh (marr. diss. 1999); one *s* three *d*; 2nd, 2000, John E. Kernthaler. *Educ:* London Hosp. Med. Coll. (BSc 1968; MB BS 1971; MD 1992; DSc 1999). FRCP 1987. Consultant Dermatologist and Sen. Lectr, 1983–92, Prof. of Dermatol., 1992–97, Royal London Hosp. and London Hosp. Med. Coll. FMedSci 1999. *Publications:* contrib. numerous articles on keratinocyte biol., genodermatoses and skin carcinogenesis to peer-reviewed jls. *Recreations:* music, film, opera, theatre. *Address:* Centre for Cutaneous Research, 2 Newark Street, E1 2AT. *T:* (020) 7882 7170.

LEIGH, Jonathan; Head Master, Blundell's School, since 1992; *b* 17 June 1952; *s* of Rupert M. Leigh and Isabel A. Leigh (*née* Villiers); *m* 1976, Emma Mary, *d* of Rear-Adm. M. D. Kyrle Pope, *qv*; one *s* one *d*. *Educ:* Eton Coll.; Corpus Christi Coll., Cambridge (MA History). Cranleigh School: Asst Master, 1976–82; Housemaster, 1982–88; Head of History, 1987; Second Master, 1988–92. Mem., Devon County Residential Care Standards Adv. Cttee (Chm., 1994–98); Vice Pres., Devon Playing Fields Assoc., 1998–. Member: Council, ISIS South-West, 1995–2001; Cttee, Belgian Sect., Assoc. Européene des Enseignants, 1994–; Admiralty Interview Bd, 1994–; Interviewing Panel, ESU, 1996–; Sec., SW Div., HMC, 2000– (Chm., 2001). Trustee: Tiverton Adventure Playground Assoc., 1992–; Inner Cities Young People's Project, 1996–. FRSA 1994. Governor: St Petroc's Sch., Bude, 1993–; Wolborough Hill Sch., Newton Abbot, 1998–2000; Abbey Sch., Tewkesbury, 2000–; Dir, Highfield Sch., Liphook, 2000–. Dir, Devon and Exeter Steeplechases, 2000–. *Recreations:* singing, horse racing, opera, labradors, late 19th century African history, the Charente. *Address:* Blundell House, Blundell's Avenue, Tiverton, Devon EX16 4DL. *T:* (01884) 252543. *Club:* East India.

LEIGH, Prof. Leonard Herschel; Professor of Criminal Law in the University of London, at the London School of Economics and Political Science, 1982–97; Board Member, Criminal Cases Review Commission, since 1997; *b* 19 Sept. 1935; *s* of Leonard William and Lillian Mavis Leigh; *m* 1960, Jill Diane Gale; one *s* one *d*. *Educ:* Univ. of Alberta (BA, LLB); Univ. of London (PhD 1966). Admitted to Bar: Alberta, 1959; NW Territories, 1961; Inner Temple, 1993. Private practice, Province of Alberta, 1958–60; Dept of Justice, Canada, 1960–62; London School of Economics: Asst Lectr in Law, 1964–65; Lectr, 1965–71; Reader, 1971–82. Vis. Prof., Queen's Univ., Kingston, Ont, 1973–74; Bowker Vis. Prof., Univ. of Alberta, 1999. British Council Lecturer: Univ. of Strasbourg, 1978; National Univ. of Mexico, 1980; UN Asia and Far East Inst., Tokyo, 1986; South India, 1989, 1991. Mem., Canadian Govt Securities Regulation Task Force, 1974–78; UK Convenor, Université de l'Europe Steering Cttee, 1987–90; Chm., English Nat. Section, 1988–, Mem., Conseil de Direction, 1989–, Internat. Assoc. of Penal Law. Mem., Exec. Cttee, Canada-UK Colloquia, 1993–. Member, Council of Europe Training Missions: Hungary, 1990; Poland, 1991; Albania, 1992; Mem., Council of Europe Wkg Party on Reform of Russian Penal Law, 1994–95. UK Rep., Internat. Penal and Penitentiary Foundn, 1994–. *Publications:* The Criminal Liability of Corporations in English Law, 1969; (jtly) Northey and Leigh's Introduction to Company Law, 1970, 4th edn 1987; Police Powers in England and Wales, 1975, 2nd edn 1986; Economic Crime in Europe, 1980; (jtly) The Companies Act 1981, 1981; (jtly) The Management of the Prosecution Process in Denmark, Sweden and the Netherlands, 1981; The Control of Commercial Fraud, 1982; Strict and Vicarious Liability, 1982; (jtly) A Guide to the Financial Services Act, 1986; articles in British, European, Amer. and Canadian jls. *Recreations:* music, walking. *Address:* Criminal Cases Review Commission, 21st Floor, Alpha Tower, Suffolk Street, Queensway, Birmingham B1 1TT. *T:* (0121) 633 1820; (chambers) 2 Pump Court, Temple, EC4Y 7AH. *T:* (020) 7353 5597.

LEIGH, Mike, OBE 1993; dramatist; theatre and film director; *b* 20 Feb. 1943; *s* of late Alfred Abraham Leigh, MRCS, LRCP and of Phyllis Pauline Leigh (*née* Cousin); *m* 1973, Alison Steadman, *qv*; two *s*. *Educ:* North Grecian Street County Primary Sch.; Salford Grammar Sch.; RADA; Camberwell Sch. of Arts and Crafts; Central Sch. of Art and Design (Theatre Design Dept); London Film Sch. Sometime actor, incl. Victoria Theatre, Stoke-on-Trent, 1966; Assoc. Dir, Midlands Arts Centre for Young People, 1965–66; Asst Dir, RSC, 1967–68; Drama Lectr, Sedgley Park and De La Salle Colls, Manchester, 1968–69; Lectr, London Film Sch., 1970–73. Arts Council of GB: Member: Drama Panel, 1975–77; Dirs' Working Party and Specialist Allocations Bd, 1976–84; Member: Accreditation Panel, Nat. Council for Drama Trng, 1978–91; Gen. Adv. Council, IBA, 1980–82. NFT Retrospective, 1979; BBC TV Retrospective (incl. Arena: Mike Leigh Making Plays), 1982. Hon. MA Salford, 1991. George Devine Award, 1973; Michael Balcon Award, 1995; Alexander Korda Award, 1996. Productions of own plays and films; *stage plays:* The Box Play, 1965, My Parents Have Gone To Carlisle, The Last Crusade Of The Five Little Nuns, 1966, Midlands Arts Centre; Nenaa, RSC Studio, Stratford-upon-Avon, 1967; Individual Fruit Pies, E15 Acting Sch., 1968; Down Here And Up There, Royal Ct Th. Upstairs, 1968; Big Basil, 1968, Glum Victoria And The Lad With Specs, Manchester Youth Theatre, 1969; Epilogue, Manchester, 1969; Bleak Moments, Open Space, 1970; A Rancid Pong, Basement, 1971; Wholesome Glory, Dick Whittington and his Cat, Royal Ct Th. Upstairs, 1973; The Jaws of Death, Traverse, Edinburgh Fest., 1973; Babies Grow Old, Other Place, 1974, ICA, 1975; The Silent Majority, Bush, 1974; Abigail's Party, Hampstead, 1977; Ecstasy, Hampstead, 1979; Goose-Pimples, Hampstead, Garrick, 1981 (Standard Best Comedy Award); Smelling a Rat, Hampstead, 1988; Greek Tragedy, Sydney, 1989, Edinburgh Fest. and Theatre Royal, Stratford East, 1990; It's A Great Big Shame!, Theatre Royal, Stratford East, 1993. *BBC radio play:* Too Much Of A Good Thing, 1979; *feature films:* Bleak Moments, 1971 (Golden Hugo, Chicago Film Fest., 1972; Golden Leopard, Locarno Film Fest., 1972); High Hopes, 1989 (Critics' Award, Venice Film Fest., 1988; Evening Standard Peter Sellers Comedy Award, 1989); Life is Sweet, 1991; Naked, 1993 (Best Dir, Cannes Film Fest., 1993); Secrets and Lies, 1996 (Palme d'Or, Cannes Film Fest., 1996); Career Girls, 1997; Topsy-Turvy, 1999 (Evening Standard Best Film Award, 2001); *BBC TV plays and films:* A Mug's Game, 1972; Hard Labour, 1973; The Permissive Society, Afternoon, A Light Snack, Probation, Old Chums, The Birth Of The 2001 FA Cup Final Goalie, 1975; Nuts in May, Knock For Knock, 1976; The Kiss Of Death, Abigail's Party, 1977; Who's Who, 1978; Grown-Ups, 1980; Home Sweet Home, 1982; Four Days In July, 1984; *Channel Four films:* Meantime, 1983; The Short and Curlies, 1987. *Relevant publications:* The Improvised Play: the work of Mike Leigh, by Paul Clements, 1983; The World According to Mike Leigh, by Michael Coveney, 1996. *Address:* c/o Peters, Fraser & Dunlop, Drury House, 34–43 Russell Street, WC2B 5HA. *T:* (020) 7344 1000.

LEIGH, Peter William John, FRICS; chartered surveyor and property consultant; *b* 29 June 1929; *s* of John Charles Leigh and Dorothy Grace Leigh; *m* 1956, Mary Frances (*née* Smith); two *s* one *d*. *Educ:* Harrow Weald County Grammar Sch.; Coll. of Estate Management (ext.). National Service, Royal Signals, 1947–49. Private surveying practice, 1949–53; Valuation Asst, Mddx CC, 1953–60; Commercial Estates Officer, Bracknell Develt Corp., 1960–66; sen. appts, Valuation and Estates Dept, GLC, 1966–81; Dir of Valuation and Estates, GLC, 1981–84; Dir of Property Services, Royal County of Berks, 1984–88. Member: Gen. Council, RICS, 1984–86; RICS Gen. Practice Divl Council, 1993–96; Govt Property Adv. Gp, 1984–88. Exec. Mem., Local Authority Valuers Assoc., 1981–88. Editor, Old Wealden Newsletter, 1978–. *Recreations:* exploring Cornwall, drawing, gardening (therapy). *Address:* 41 Sandy Lane, Wokingham, Berks RG41 4SS. *T:* (0118) 978 2732.

LEIGH, Sir Richard (Henry), 3rd Bt *cr* 1918, of Altrincham, Cheshire; *b* 11 Nov. 1936; *s* of Eric Leigh (*d* 1982), 2nd *s* of Sir John Leigh, 1st Bt, and his 1st wife, Joan Lane Fitzgerald (*d* 1973), *e d* of M. C. L. Freer, South Africa; *S* uncle, 1992; *m* 1st, 1962, Barbro Anna Elizabeth (marr. diss. 1977), *e d* of late Stig Carl Sebastian Tham, Sweden; 2nd, 1977, Cherie Rosalind, *e d* D. D. Dale, Cherval, France and *widow* of Alan Reece, RMS. *Educ:* England and Switzerland. *Recreations:* fishing, gardening. *Heir:* half *b* Christopher John Leigh [*b* 6 April 1941; *m* 1963, Gillian Ismay, *o d* of W. K. Lowe; one *s* one *d*]. *Address:* Trythall Vean, Madron, Cornwall TR20 8SY. *T:* (01736) 366604; (020) 7266 5512.

LEIGH, Prof. Roger Allen, PhD; FIBiol; Professor of Botany, University of Cambridge, since 1998; Professorial Fellow, Girton College, Cambridge, since 1998; *b* 7 Feb. 1949; *s* of Harry Leigh and Catherine Leigh (*née* O'Neill); *m* 1974, Beatrice Katherine Halton (marr. diss. 1999). *Educ:* Ellesmere Port Boys' GS; UCNW, Bangor (BSc 1970; PhD 1974). FIBiol 1991. Maria Moors Cabot Fellow in Botanical Res., Harvard Univ., 1974–76; Royal Society Pickering Res. Fellow, Botany Sch., Univ. of Cambridge, 1976–79; Scientist, Rothamsted Experimental Station, Harpenden, 1979–98; Head of Crop Production Dept, 1987–89; Head of Biochemistry and Physiology Dept, 1989–98; Head of Soils and Crop Scis Div., 1989–94; Dep. Dir, 1994–98. *Publications:* (jtly) Long-Term Experiments in Agricultural and Ecological Sciences, 1994; (jtly) Membrane Transport in Plants and Fungi: molecular mechanisms and control, 1994; scientific papers in learned jls, incl. Plant Physiology, Planta, Jl of Exptl Botany. *Recreations:* sports of all kinds, bird watching, photography. *Address:* Department of Plant Sciences, University of Cambridge, Downing Street, Cambridge CB2 3EA. *T:* (01223) 333958; *e-mail:* RL225@cam.ac.uk.

LEIGH-HUNT, Barbara; actress; *b* 14 Dec. 1935; *d* of Chandos A. Leigh-Hunt and Elizabeth Leigh-Hunt; *m* 1967, Richard Edward Pasco, *qv*. *Educ:* Bath, Som; Kensington High Sch.; Bristol Old Vic Theatre Sch. (Most Promising Student, Bristol Evening Post Award, 1953). Began broadcasting for BBC at age 12 in Children's Hour, and has continued to do so regularly on Radios 3 and 4. *Theatre:* début in Midsummer Night's Dream, London Old Vic tour to USA and Canada, 1954–55; subseq. also Twelfth Night and Merchant of Venice, Old Vic and tours, 1957–60; seasons at Nottingham and Guildford, 1960–62; Bristol Old Vic and tours, 1961–68; The Seagull, Hedda Gabler, She Stoops to Conquer, Much Ado About Nothing, Blithe Spirit, Love's Labour's Lost, Hamlet, and Macbeth; A Severed Head, Criterion, 1963; Mrs Mouse, are you within?, Duke of York's, 1968; Venice Preserv'd, Prospect Th. Co. tour, 1970; Royal Shakespeare Company: Sherlock Holmes, Travesties, 1974; A Winter's Tale, Richard III, 1975; King Lear, Troilus and Cressida, 1976; That Good Between Us, Every Good Boy Deserves Favour, 1977; Richard III, Hamlet, 1980; The Forest, La Ronde, 1981; Pack of Lies, Lyric 1983; Barnaby and the Old Boys, Theatr Clwyd, 1987; Royal National Theatre: Cat on a Hot Tin Roof, 1988; Bartholomew Fair, The Voysey Inheritance, 1989; Racing Demon, 1990 and Los Angeles, 1995; An Inspector Calls, 1992 (Best Supporting Actress, Olivier Award, 1993); Absence of War, 1993; A Woman of No Importance, RSC, Haymarket and Fortune Ths, 1992; The Importance of Being Earnest, Old Vic, 1995; frequent appearances in poetry and prose anthology progs in UK and abroad; works as speaker with Medici String Quartet. *Films:* Frenzy, 1972, Henry VIII and his Six Wives, 1972; A Bequest to the Nation, 1973; Oh, Heavenly Dog, 1978; Paper Mask, 1990; Keep the Aspidistra Flying, 1997; Billy Elliott, 2000; The Martins, 2000; Iris, 2001. *Television* includes: Search for the Nile, 1971; Loves Lies Bleeding; The Voysey Inheritance; Macbeth; Wagner, 1984; The Siegfried Idyll; All for Love; Tumbledown, 1988; A Perfect Hero; Cold Feet; Pride and Prejudice, 1995; The Echo, 1998; Sunburn, Wives and Daughters, 1999; Longitude, 2000; Kavanagh QC. Gov. and Associate Actor, RSC; Pres., Friends of the Other Places, 1993–97; Vice-Pres., Royal Theatrical Fund, 1995; Vice-Pres., Theatrical Ladies Guild of Charity, 1983; Patron: Soc. of Teachers of Speech and Drama, 1995; Orch. of The Swan, 1997. *Recreation:* book collecting. *Address:* c/o Whitehall Artists, 10 Lower Common South, SW15 1BP. *T:* (020) 8785 3737, *Fax:* (020) 8788 2340; *e-mail:* mwhitehall@email.man.com.

LEIGH-PEMBERTON, family name of **Baron Kingsdown**.

LEIGHFIELD, John Percival, CBE 1998; FBCS; Chairman: RM plc, since 1994; Synstar plc, since 1998; Director, KnowledgePool Ltd, since 2000; *b* 5 April 1938; *s* of Henry Tom Dainton Leighfield and Patricia Zilpha Maud Leighfield (*née* Baker); *m* 1963, Margaret Ann Mealin; one *s* one *d*. *Educ:* Magdalen Coll. Sch., Oxford (State Scholarship); Exeter Coll., Oxford (MA Lit.Hum.). FIDPM 1990; FBCS 1991. Mgt trainee, Ford Motor Co., 1962–65; Systems Manager, EDP Exec., Plessey Telecomms, 1965–69; Systems Planning, EDP Exec., Plessey Co. Ltd, 1969–72; British Leyland: Systems Planning Manager, 1972–75; Systems Dir, 1975–79; Man. Dir, BL Systems Ltd, 1979–84; Man. Dir and Chm. ISTEL Ltd, 1984–89; AT&T ISTEL: Chm., 1989–93; Dir, 1993–97; Officer and Sen. Vice-Pres., AT&T, 1989–93; Director: Birmingham Midshires Bldg Soc., 1993–99 (Chm., 1996–99); RM Ltd, 1993–94; ICom Solutions Ltd, 1997–98; Halifax plc, 1999–2001. Dir, Central England TEC, 1991–97. Mem., Alvey Prog. Steering Cttee, 1983–87. President: BCS, 1993–94; Computing Services and Software Assoc., 1995–96; Inst. Data Processing Mgt, 2000–. Hon. Prof., 1992, Chm., Adv. Bd, 1997–, Warwick Business Sch.; Mem. Council, Warwick Univ., 1991–96, 1997–; Gov., Magdalen Coll. Sch., Oxford, 1993– (Chm. 1996–). Liveryman, Co. of Information Technologists, 1992–. FInstD 1989; FRSA 1996. DUniv Central England, 1993; Hon. DTech De Montfort, 1994. *Publications:* various papers on information technology. *Recreations:* historical cartography, music, walking, computing. *Address:* 91 Victoria Road, Oxford OX2 7QG. *T:* (01865) 559055. *Clubs:* Royal Automobile; Royal Fowey Yacht.

LEIGHTON OF ST MELLONS, 3rd Baron *cr* 1962, of St Mellons, co. Monmouth; **Robert William Henry Leighton Seager;** Bt 1952; *b* 28 Sept. 1955; *er s* of 2nd Baron Leighton of St Mellons and Elizabeth Rosita (*née* Hopgood; *d* 1979); *S* father, 1998.

LEIGHTON, Prof. Angela, FBA 2000; Professor of English, University of Hull, since 1997; *b* 23 Feb. 1954; *d* of Kenneth Leighton and Lydia Leighton (*née* Vignapiano). *Educ:* St Hugh's Coll., Oxford (BA Hons 1976; MLitt 1981). Lectr in English, 1979–93, Sen. Lectr, 1993–95, Reader, 1995–97, Univ. of Hull. *Publications:* Shelley and the Sublime, 1984; Elizabeth Barrett Browning, 1986; Victorian Women Poets: writing against the heart, 1992; Victorian Women Poets: a critical anthology, 1995; A Cold Spell, 2000. *Address:* English Department, University of Hull, Hull HU6 7RX.

LEIGHTON, Jane; Project Director, Virtuall (formerly London Mental Health Learning Partnership), since 2000; Deputy Chair, Broadcasting Standards Commission, 1997–2001; *b* 17 March 1944. Administrator, British Pregnancy Adv. Service, 1971–74; Sec., Liverpool CHC, 1974–79; reporter, World in Action, Granada TV, 1979–85; Producer, Channel 4, 1985–88; Independent Consultancy, Littlewoods Orgn, 1985–88; Exec. Dir, Mersey TV, 1988–90; Hd of Public Affairs, Granada TV Ltd, 1990–92; Industrial Relns Consultant, Liverpool HAT, 1992–96; Hd of Organisational Develt, Tate Gall., 1995–97. Chair: Mental Health Services, Salford NHS Trust, 1993–95; Camden and Islington Area Mental Health Cttee, 1998–2000; non-exec. Dir, Camden and Islington NHS Community Trust, 1998–. Mem., Broadcasting Complaints Commn, 1993–96 (Chm., 1996–97). Non-executive Director: City of London Sinfonia, 1992–97; Hallé Concerts Soc., 1992–95; Royal Liverpool Philharmonic Orch., 1990–92. Mem., NW Arts Bd. Gov., UC, Salford, 1992–95. FRSA 1997. RTS Award for best internat. current affairs programme, 1981; BMA Award for medical progs, 1983; Equal Opportunities Award, Women in Mgt Award, 1987. *Address:* 56 Thomas More House, Barbican, EC2Y 8BT; *e-mail:* jane.leighton@virgin.net.

LEIGHTON, Leonard Horace; Under Secretary, Department of Energy, 1974–80; *b* 7 Oct. 1920; *e s* of Leonard and Pearl Leighton, Bermuda; *m* 1945, Mary Burrowes; two *s*. *Educ:* Rossall Sch.; Magdalen Coll., Oxford (MA). FInstF. Royal Engrs, 1940–46; Nat. Coal Bd, 1950–62; Min. of Power, 1962–67; Min. of Technology, 1967–70; Dept of Trade and Industry, 1970–74. *Publications:* papers in various technical jls. *Address:* Hither Mickley, Lower Grinsty Lane, Callow Hill, Worcs B97 5PJ.

LEIGHTON, Sir Michael (John Bryan), 11th Bt *cr* 1693; *b* 8 March 1935; *o s* of Colonel Sir Richard Tihel Leighton, 10th Bt, and Kathleen Irene Linda (*d* 1993), *o d* of Major A. E. Lees, Rowton Castle, Shrewsbury; *S* father, 1957; *m* 1st, 1974 (marr. diss. 1980); 2nd, 1991, Diana Mary Gamble (marr. diss. 1998); one *d*. *Educ:* Stowe; Tabley House Agricultural Sch.; Cirencester Coll. *Address:* Loton Park, Shrewsbury, Salop SY5 9AJ.

LEIGHTON WILLIAMS, John; *see* Williams.

LEINSTER, 8th Duke of, *cr* 1766; **Gerald FitzGerald;** Baron of Offaly, 1205; Earl of Kildare, 1316; Viscount Leinster (Great Britain), 1747; Marquess of Kildare, 1761; Earl of Offaly, 1761; Baron Kildare, 1870; Premier Duke, Marquess, and Earl, of Ireland; Major late 5th Royal Inniskilling Dragoon Guards; *b* 27 May 1914; *o s* of 7th Duke of Leinster and May (*d* 1935), *d* of late Jesse Etheridge; *S* father, 1976; *m* 1st, 1936, Joane (who obtained a divorce, 1946), *e d* of late Major McMorrough Kavanagh, MC, Borris House, Co. Carlow; two *d*; 2nd, 1946, Anne Eustace Smith; two *s*. *Educ:* Eton; Sandhurst. *Heir:* *s* Marquess of Kildare, *qv*. *Recreations:* fishing, shooting. *Address:* Kilkea House, Ramsden, Chipping Norton, Oxfordshire OX7 3BA.

LEINSTER, Dr Paul, CChem; Director of Pollution Prevention and Control, Environment Agency, since 1999; *b* 20 Feb. 1953; *s* of Victor and Eva Leinster; *m* 1976, Felicity Lawrence; two *s* one *d*. *Educ:* Imperial Coll., London (BSc Chemistry 1974; PhD Envmtl Engrg 1977); Cranfield Sch. of Management (MBA 1991). FIOH 1991; CChem, FRSC 1998. BP International plc: Analytical Support and Res. Div., Res. Centre, 1977–79; Health, Safety and Envmt Directorate, 1979–85; Schering Agrochemicals, 1985–88; Thomson-MTS Ltd: Head of Res. and Consultancy, 1988–90; Man. Dir, 1990–94; Dir, Envmtl Services, SmithKline Beecham, 1994–98; Dir of Envmtl Protection, EA, 1998–99. *Publications:* technical papers, articles and contribs to books. *Recreations:* sports (mainly supporting and transporting now), local church, reading, walking. *Address:* 36 Brockwell, Oakley, Bedford MK43 7TD. *T:* (01234) 823401.

LEISER, Helen; Director, Nuclear Industries, Department of Trade and Industry, since 1998; *b* 3 July 1947; *d* of George and Audrey Leiser. *Educ:* Twickenham County Grammar Sch.; LSE (BScEcon). Economic Dept, TUC, 1968–73; Employment Dept, 1974; seconded to Cabinet Office, Machinery of Govt Div., 1983–85; Asst Sec., HSE, 1986–93; seconded to Dept of Energy, Offshore Safety Directorate, 1991; Dir of Business Develt and Mem., Exec. Bd, Employment Service, 1993; Head, Industrial Relations Div., Dept of Employment, 1994; Hd of Industrial Relns Policy, then Dir, Employment Relns Policy, DTI, 1995–98. *Recreations:* travel, reading, films. *Address:* Department of Trade and Industry, 1 Victoria Street, SW1H 0ET.

LEISHMAN, Frederick John, CVO 1957; MBE 1944; *b* 21 Jan. 1919; *s* of Alexander Leishman and Freda Mabel (*née* Hood); *m* 1945, Frances Webb, Evanston, Illinois, USA; two *d. Educ:* Oundle; Corpus Christi, Cambridge. Served RE, 1940–46, and with Military Government, Germany, 1945–46; Regular Commission, 1945; resigned 1946. Joined Foreign Service, 1946; FO, 1946–48; Copenhagen, 1948–51; CSSB, 1951; Asst Private Sec. to Foreign Sec., 1951–53; First Sec., Washington, 1953–58; First Sec. and Head of Chancery, Teheran, 1959–61; Counsellor, 1961; HM Consul-General, Hamburg, 1961–62; FO, 1962–63. Dir, Hill Samuel & Co. Ltd, 1965–80; Dep. Chm. and Chief Exec., Hill Samuel Gp (SA) Ltd, 1969–72; Partner and Chm., Hill Samuel & Co. oHG, Germany, 1975–77; Dir and Exec. Vice-Pres., Saehan Merchant Banking Corp., Seoul, 1977–80. Vice-Pres., The Friends of the Bowes Museum, 1992– (Chm., 1985–90). FRSA. *Recreations:* golf, fishing, hill walking. *Address:* Saltoun House, Cotherstone, Barnard Castle, Co. Durham DL12 9PF. *T:* (01833) 650671. *Clubs:* Hawks (Cambridge); Cambridge University Rugby Union Football; London Scottish Football; Barnard Castle Rugby (Pres., 1987–99); Royal Ashdown Forest Golf, Barnard Castle Golf.

LEITCH, Alexander Park; Chief Executive, Zurich Financial Services (UKISA) Ltd, since 1998; *b* 20 Oct. 1947; *s* of late Donald Leitch, Blairhall, Dunfermline, and of Agnes Smith; *m*; three *d. Educ:* Dunfermline High Sch. MBCS 1966. Chief Systems Designer, Nat. Mutual Life, then Hambro Life, 1969–88; Allied Dunbar Plc, 1988–96 (Dep. Chm., 1990; Chief Exec., 1993–96); Chm., Allied Dunbar Assce Plc, 1996–2001; Chief Exec., British American Financial Services (UK and Internat.) Ltd, 1996–98; Chairman: Dunbar Bank, 1994–2001; Eagle Star Hldgs Plc, 1996–; Threadneedle Asset Mgt, 1996–; Dir, BAT Industries Plc, 1997–98. Mem. Bd, 1996–98, Dep. Chm., 1997–98, Chm., 1998–2000, ABI. Dep. Chm., BITC, 1996–. Chm., SANE, 1999–2000. Trustee, Nat. Galls Scotland, 1999. *Recreations:* football, tennis, antiquarian books. *Address:* Zurich Financial Services Ltd, 22 Arlington Street, SW1A 1RW. *T:* (020) 7495 5563.

LEITCH, David Alexander; Under Secretary, Social Work Services Group, Scottish Education Department, 1983–89; *b* 4 April 1931; *s* of Alexander and Eileen Leitch; *m* 1954, Marie (*née* Tain); two *s* one *d. Educ:* St Mungo's Acad., Glasgow. Min. of Supply, 1948–58; Dept of Agriculture and Fisheries for Scotland: Asst Principal, 1959; Principal, 1963; Asst Sec., 1971; Asst Sec., Local Govt Finance, Scottish Office (Central Services), 1976–81, Under Sec., 1981–83. Part-time Mem., Scottish Legal Aid Bd, 1989–97. *Recreations:* climbing, hill-walking. *Address:* 3 The Glebe, Cramond, Edinburgh EH4 6NW.

LEITCH, Sir George, KCB 1975 (CB 1963); OBE 1945; retired; *b* 5 June 1915; *er s* of late James Simpson and Margaret Leitch; *m* 1942, Edith Marjorie Maughan; one *d. Educ:* Wallsend Grammar Sch.; King's Coll., University of Durham. Research and teaching in mathematics, 1937–39. War Service in Army (from TA), 1939–46 (despatches, OBE): Lieut-Colonel in charge of Operational Research in Eastern, then Fourteenth Army, 1943–45; Brigadier (Dep. Scientific Adviser, War Office), 1945–46; entered Civil Service, as Principal, 1947; Ministry of Supply, 1947–59 (Under-Secretary, 1959); War Office, 1959–64; Ministry of Defence: Asst Under-Secretary of State, 1964–65; Dep. Under-Sec. of State, 1965–72; Procurement Executive, MoD: Controller (Policy), 1971–72; 2nd Permanent Sec., 1972–74; Chief Exec. (Permanent Sec.), 1974–75; Chm., Short Brothers Ltd, 1976–83. Chm., Adv. Cttee on Trunk Rd Assessment, 1977–80. Commonwealth Fund Fellow, 1953–54. Hon. DSc Durham, 1946. *Address:* 10 Elmfield Road, Gosforth, Newcastle upon Tyne NE3 4AY. *T:* (0191) 2846559.

LEITH, family name of **Baron Burgh**.

LEITH, Sir George Ian David F.; *see* Forbes-Leith.

LEITH, Prudence Margaret, (Mrs Rayne Kruger), OBE 1989; DL; Chairman, Leith's Ltd, 1992–96; Deputy Chairman, Royal Society of Arts, since 1998 (Council Member, since 1992; Chairman, 1995–97); *b* 18 Feb. 1940; *d* of late Sam Leith and of Margaret Inglis; *m* Rayne Kruger; one *s* one *d. Educ:* Hayward's Heath, Sussex; St Mary's, Johannesburg; Cape Town Univ.; Sorbonne, Paris; Cordon Bleu, London. French studies at Sorbonne, and preliminary cooking apprenticeship with French families; Cordon Bleu sch. course; small outside catering service from bedsitter in London, 1960–65; started Leith's Good Food (commercial catering co.), 1965, and Leith's (restaurant), 1969 (Michelin star, 1994); Man. Dir, Prudence Leith Ltd, 1972; Cookery Corresp., Daily Mail, 1969–73; opened Leith's Sch. of Food and Wine, 1975; added Leith's Farm, 1976; Cookery Corresp., Sunday Express, 1976–80; Cookery Editor, 1980–85, Columnist, 1986–90, The Guardian. Board Member: British Transport Hotels, 1977–83; Halifax plc (formerly Leeds Permanent, then Halifax, Bldg Soc.), 1992–99; Whitbread plc, 1995–; Triven VCT, 1999–; pt-time Mem., BRB, 1980–85. Member: Food from Britain Council, 1983–86; Leisure Industries EDC, NEDO, 1986–90; Nat. Trng Task Force, 1989–90; NCVQ, 1992–96; Bd, UK Skills, 1993–; Chm., 3E's Enterprises, 1997–. Chm., Restaurateurs' Assoc. of GB, 1990–94; Mem. Council, Museum of Modern Art, Oxford, 1984–90. Governor: Ashridge Management Coll., 1992–; City Technology Coll., 1994–. Chm. Govs, Kings Coll., Guildford, 1999–. Trustee, Food Foundn, 1996–; Chairman: British Food Trust, 1997–; Forum for the Future, 2000–. FRSA 1984–90; FCGI 1992. DL Greater London, 1998. Business Woman of the Year, 1990. *Publications:* Leith's All-Party Cook Book, 1969; Parkinson's Pie (in aid of World Wild Life Fund), 1972; Cooking For Friends, 1978; The Best of Prue Leith, 1979; (with J. B. Reynaud) Leith's Cookery Course (3–part paperback), 1979–80, (comp. hardback with C. Waldegrave), 1980; The Cook's Handbook, 1981; Prue Leith's Pocket Book of Dinner Parties, 1983; Dinner Parties, 1984; (with Polly Tyrer) Entertaining with Style, 1986; Confident Cooking (52 issue part-work), 1989–90; (with Caroline Waldegrave): Leith's Cookery School, 1985; Leith's Cookery Bible, 1991; Leith's Complete Christmas, 1992; Leith's Book of Baking, 1993; Leith's Vegetarian Cookery, 1993; *novels:* Leaving Patrick, 1999; Sisters, 2001. *Recreations:* riding, tennis, walking, old cookbooks and kitchen antiques. *Address:* (office) 94 Kensington Park Road, W11 2PN. *T:* (020) 7221 5282.

LEITH-BUCHANAN, Sir Charles (Alexander James), 7th Bt *cr* 1775; President, United Business Machines Inc., Alexandria, Va, since 1978; *b* 1 Sept. 1939; *s* of John Wellesley MacDonald Leith-Buchanan (*g s* of 4th Bt) (*d* 1956) and Jane Elizabeth McNicol (*d* 1955), *d* of Ronald McNicol; *S* cousin, 1973; *m* 1962, Mary Anne Kelly (marr. diss. 1987); one *s* one *d*; *m* 1988, Janice J., *d* of Robert Granger Jenkins. *Heir: s* Gordon Kelly McNicol Leith-Buchanan, *b* 18 Oct. 1974.

le JEUNE d'ALLEGEERSHECQUE, Susan Jane; HM Diplomatic Service; Deputy Head of Mission, Caracas, since 1999; *b* 29 April 1963; *d* of Gerald Miller, FCA, and Judith Anne Miller (*née* Rolfe); *m* 1991, Stéphane Hervé Marie le Jeune d'Allegeerschecque; two *s. Educ:* Ipswich High Sch. for Girls, GPDST; Univ. of Bristol (BA Hons 1985). Licentiate, CIPD 1999. Joined HM Diplomatic Service, 1985: FCO, 1985–87; Third, later Second Sec., UK Perm. Representation to EC, 1987–90; FCO, 1990–92; Second Sec. (Press/Econ.), Singapore, 1992–95; FCO, 1995–99. *Recreations:* art, music, France. *Address:* c/o Foreign and Commonwealth Office, King Charles Street, SW1A 2AH.

LELLO, Walter Barrington, (Barry); Deputy Director, North-West Region, Department of Trade and Industry, 1988–91; *b* 29 Sept. 1931; *o s* of Walter Joseph Lello and Louisa (*née* McGarrigle); *m* 1959, Margaret, *o d* of Alexander and Alice McGregor. *Educ:* Liverpool Institute High School. Nat. Service, RN, 1950–52. Open Exec. Comp. to Civil Service, 1949; Min. of Supply, later Aviation, 1952–64; Asst British Civil Aviation Rep., Far East, Hong Kong, 1964–67; BoT, later Dept of Trade, 1967–71; Civil Air Attaché, Middle East, Beirut, 1971–76; DTI, 1976–78; Dir Gen., Saudi–British Economic Co-operation Office, Riyadh, 1978–81; seconded to British Electricity International as Dir, Middle East Ops, 1981–83; DTI, 1983; Commercial Counsellor, Cairo, 1984–88. *Recreations:* mountaineering, reading, theatre, furniture restoration. *Address:* 15 Long Meadow, Gayton, Wirral, Merseyside L60 8QQ.

LE MARCHANT, Sir Francis (Arthur), 6th Bt *cr* 1841, of Chobham Place, Surrey; artist and farmer; *b* 6 Oct. 1939; *s* of Sir Denis Le Marchant, 5th Bt and of Elizabeth Rowena, *y d* of late Arthur Hovenden Worth; *S* father, 1987. *Educ:* Gordonstoun; Royal Academy Schools. Principal one-man shows include: Agnews; Sally Hunter Fine Art; Roy Miles; Mus. of Arts and Sci., Evansville, USA; group shows include: Leicester Galls; RA Summer Exhibns; Spink; work in public collections includes: Govt Art Collection; FT; Mus. of Arts and Sci., Evansville, USA; Univ. of Evansville, In, collection of late Mrs Anne Kessler. *Recreations:* landscape conservation, garden design, music. *Heir: cousin* Michael Le Marchant [*b* 28 July 1937; *m* 1st, 1963, Philippa Nancy (marr. diss.), *er d* of late R. B. Denby; two *s* two *d*; 2nd, 1981, Sandra Elisabeth Champion (*née* Kirby) (separated)]. *Address:* c/o HSBC, 88 Westgate, Grantham, Lincs NG31 6LF.

LE MARECHAL, Robert Norford, CB 1994; Deputy Comptroller and Auditor General, National Audit Office, 1989–2000; *b* 29 May 1939; *s* of late Reginald Le Marechal and of Margaret Le Marechal; *m* 1963, Linda Mary (*née* Williams); two *d. Educ:* Taunton's School, Southampton. Joined Exchequer and Audit Dept, 1957; Nat. Service, RAEC, 1958–60; Senior Auditor, Exchequer and Audit Dept, 1971; Chief Auditor, 1976; Dep. Dir of Audit, 1980; Dir of Audit, 1983; Dir of Policy and Planning, 1984–86, Asst Auditor General, 1986–89, Nat. Audit Office. *Recreations:* reading, gardening. *Address:* 62 Woodcote Hurst, Epsom, Surrey KT18 7DT. *T:* (01372) 721291.

LEMKIN, James Anthony, CBE 1986; Consultant, Field Fisher Waterhouse, Solicitors, 1990–91 (Senior Partner, 1985–90); *b* 21 Dec. 1926; *s* of late William Lemkin, CBE, and Rachel Irene (*née* Faith); *m* 1960, Joan Dorothy Anne Casserley, FFARCS, MRCPsych; two *s* two *d. Educ:* Charterhouse; Merton Coll., Oxford (MA). Admitted solicitor, 1953; RN, 1945–47. Greater London Council: Additional Mem., 1970–73, Mem. for Hillingdon, Uxbridge, 1973–86; Chm., Legal and Parly Cttee, 1977–78; Chm., Scrutiny Cttee, 1978–81; Cons. spokesman on police, 1981–82; Opposition Chief Whip, 1982–86. Contested: (C and NL) Chesterfield, 1959; (L) Cheltenham, 1964. Chm., Bow Gp, 1952, 1956, 1957 (Founder Chm., Crossbow, 1957–60); a Vice-Pres., Soc. of Cons. Lawyers. Member: NW Thames RHA, 1980–84; Royal Marsden Hosp. SHA, 1982–89; Appeal Cttee, Cancer Res. Campaign, 1967–81; Chm., Barnet FPC, 1985–90. Governor: Westfield Coll., London Univ., 1970–83; Commonwealth Inst., 1985–92. Trustee, Whitechapel Art Gall., 1983 93; Chm., Hampstead Wells and Campden Trust, 1995–98. Co-founder, Africa Confidential, 1960. High Sheriff, Gtr London, 1992–93. *Publication:* (ed) Race and Power, 1956. *Recreation:* umpiring cricket. *Address:* 4 Frognal Close, NW3 6YB. *T:* (020) 7435 6499. *Club:* Athenæum.

LEMLEY, Jack Kenneth; Chairman and Chief Executive Officer, American Ecology Corporation, Boise, Idaho, since 1995; *b* 2 Jan. 1935; *s* of Kenneth Clyde Lemley and Dorothy Whitsitte; *m* 1st, 1961, Georgia Marshall (marr. diss. 1978); two *s* one *d*; 2nd, 1983, Pamela (*née* Hroza). *Educ:* Coeur d'Alene High Sch., Idaho; Univ. of Idaho (BA Architecture 1960). Asst Project Engineer, Guy F. Atkinson Co., 1960–69; Pres., Healthcare, 1969–70; Manager, Indust. and Power Construction Div., Guy F. Atkinson Co., 1971–77; Sen. Vice-Pres., Constr. Div., Morrison-Knusden Co., 1977–87; Pres. and Chief Exec., Blount Construction Gp, 1987–88; Management Consultant, Lemley & Associates, 1988–89; Chief Exec. Officer, Transmanche-Link, Channel tunnel contractors, 1989–93. *Publications:* numerous papers on underground construction projects and international tunnelling. *Recreations:* snow ski-ing, sailing, white water rafting, reading. *Address:* 1508 N 13th Street, Boise, ID 83702, USA. *T:* (208) 3455226; 2045 Table Rock Road, Boise, ID 83712, USA. *T:* (208) 3839253. *Club:* Arid (Boise, Idaho).

LEMMON, Rt Rev. George Colborne; Bishop of Fredericton, 1989–2000; *b* 20 March 1932; *m* 1957, Lois Jean Foster; two *s* one *d. Educ:* Univ. of New Brunswick (BA 1959); Wycliffe Coll., Toronto (LTh 1962; BD 1965). Linotype operator, Globe Print, Telegraph Jl, Toronto Telegram, 1949–62. Deacon 1962, priest 1963; Incumbent, Canterbury with Benton, 1962; Rector of: Wilmot with Wicklow and Peel, 1965; Renforth, 1969; Sackville with Dorchester, dio. of Fredericton, 1972–84; Christ Church, Fredericton, 1984–89; Canon of Fredericton, 1983–89. Hon. DD: King's Coll., Halifax, 1990; Wycliffe Coll., Toronto, 1991. *Recreation:* golfing. *Address:* 16 Riverside Court, Fredericton, NB E3B 5P1, Canada.

LE MOIGNAN, Rev. Christina; President, Methodist Conference, 2001–June 2002; Chairman, Birmingham Methodist District, since 1996; *b* 12 Oct. 1942; *d* of Edward Frank Le Moignan and (Winifred) Muriel Le Moignan. *Educ:* Somerville Coll., Oxford (MA; Dip. Public and Social Admin); Univ. of Ibadan, Nigeria (PhD 1970); Wesley House, Cambridge (MA). Ordained, 1976; Methodist minister, Huntingdon, Southampton, Portchester, 1976–1989; Tutor, Queen's Coll., Birmingham, 1989–94; Principal, W Midlands Ministerial Trng Course (Queen's Coll., Birmingham), 1994–96. *Publication:* Following the Lamb: a reading of Revelation for the new millennium, 2000. *Recreation:* music. *Address:* 36 Amesbury Road, Moseley, Birmingham B13 8LE.

LEMON, Sir (Richard) Dawnay, Kt 1970; CBE 1958; QPM 1964; Chief Constable of Kent, 1962–74; *b* 29 May 1912; *o s* of late Lieut-Colonel F. J. Lemon, CBE, DSO, and of Mrs Laura Lemon; *m* 1939, Sylvia Marie Kentish; one *s* one *d* (and one *d* decd). *Educ:* Uppingham Sch.; RMC, Sandhurst. Joined West Yorks Regt, 1932; retired 1934. Metropolitan Police, 1934–37; Leicestershire Constabulary, 1937–39; Chief Constable of East Riding of Yorkshire, 1939–42; Chief Constable of Hampshire and Isle of Wight, 1942–62. *Recreations:* cricket, golf. *Address:* 9 Milchester House, Staveley Road, Eastbourne BN20 7JX. *T:* (01323) 649441. *Clubs:* Royal Yacht Squadron (Cowes (hon.)); Royal St Georges Golf (Sandwich).

LEMOS, Gerard Anthony, CMG 2001; writer, social researcher; Partner, Lemos & Crane, since 1990; *b* 26 Feb. 1958; *s* of late Ronald Lemos and Cynthia (*née* Mitchell). *Educ:* Dulwich Coll.; Univ. of York. Dir, ASRA Housing Assoc., 1982–85; Area Manager and Dir of Devel, Circle 33 Housing Trust, 1985–90; Dir of Studies, Sch. for Social Entrepreneurs, 1997–99. Director: Mortgage Code Compliance Bd, 2000–; Banking

Code Standards Bd, 2000–; Mem., Audit Commn, 2000–; Civil Service Comr, 2001–. Member of Board: London Internat. Fest. of Theatre, 1993–; British Council, 1999–. *Publications:* Interviewing Perpetrators of Racial Harassment, 1994; Fair Recruitment and Selection, 1995; Safe as Houses: supporting people experiencing racial harassment, 1996; (jtly) The Communities We Have Lost and Can Regain, 1997; Urban Village, Global City: the regeneration of Colville, 1998; A Future Foretold: new approaches to meeting the long-term needs of single homeless people, 1999; Racial Harassment: action on the ground, 2000. *Recreations:* literature, cricket. *Address:* (office) 20 Pond Square, N6 6BA. *T:* (020) 8348 8263.

LENDRUM, Christopher John; Group Executive Director and Chief Executive, Corporate Banking, Barclays plc, since 1998; *b* 15 Jan. 1947; *s* of Herbert Colin Lendrum and Anne Margaret (*née* Macdonell); *m* 1970, Margaret Patricia Parker; one *s* one *d*. *Educ:* Felsted Sch., Essex; Durham Univ. (BA Econs). FCIB 1992. Joined Barclays Bank plc, 1969: Regl Dir, 1991–93; Dep. Man. Dir of Banking Div., 1993–95; Man. Dir of UK Business Banking, 1995–98. Adv. Bd, CAB, 2001–. Gov., Kent Coll., Pembury, 2000–. Liveryman, Woolmen's Co., 1999–. *Recreations:* gardening, travel, restoring neglected motor cars. *Address:* (office) 54 Lombard Street, EC3P 3AH. *T:* (020) 7699 2959.

LENG, Christopher Anthony William, OBE 1987; Vice Lord-Lieutenant, Tweeddale, 1994–97; *b* 5 April 1922; *s* of Douglas Christopher Leng and Marcia Mary Leng (*née* Maxwell Stuart); *m* 1953, Patricia Lillywhite; two *s* two *d*. *Educ:* Downside Sch.; Hertford Coll., Oxford (MA); Royal Agricl Coll. (MRAC). Royal Armoured Corps, 1940–43; Special Ops Executive, 1943–46. Overseas Develt Corp., 1947–50; farmer, 1952–91. *Recreations:* gardening, fishing, reading. *Address:* Juniper Bank, Walkerburn, Peeblesshire EH43 6DE. *T:* (01896) 870230. *Club:* Special Forces.

LENG, James William; Chief Executive, Laporte, since 1995; *b* 19 Nov. 1945; *m* 1974, Carole Ann Guyll. John Waddington, 1967–84; Low & Bonar: Man. Dir, Bonar & Flotex, 1984–86; Chief Exec., Plastics Div., 1986–88; Chief Exec., European Ops, 1988–92; Dir, 1989–; Group Chief Exec., 1992–95. Non-exec. Dir, Pilkington plc, 1998. Vice-Pres., CIA, 1999. Gov., NIESR, 1999. *Recreations:* sport, music. *Address:* Laporte plc, Nations House, 103 Wigmore Street, W1U 1QS; Glenuyll, Caledonian Crescent, Gleneagles, Perth PH3 1NG. *Club:* Royal Automobile.

LENG, Gen. Sir Peter (John Hall), KCB 1978 (CB 1975); MBE 1962; MC 1945; Master-General of the Ordnance, 1981–83, retired; *b* 9 May 1925; *s* of J. Leng; *m* 1st, Virginia Rosemary Pearson (marr. diss. 1981); three *s* two *d*; 2nd, 1981, Mrs Flavia Tower, *d* of late Gen. Sir Frederick Browning and Lady Browning (Dame Daphne du Maurier, DBE). *Educ:* Bradfield Coll. Served War of 1939–45: commissioned in Scots Guards, 1944; Guards Armoured Div., Germany (MC). Various post-war appts; Guards Independent Parachute Company, 1949–51; commanded: 3rd Bn Royal Anglian Regt, in Berlin, United Kingdom and Aden, 1964–66; 24th Airportable Bde, 1968–70; Dep. Military Sec., Min. of Defence, 1971–73; Comdr Land Forces, N Ireland, 1973–75; Dir, Mil. Operations, MoD, 1975–78; Comdr 1 (Br) Corps, 1978–80. Colonel Commandant: RAVC, 1976–83; RMP, 1976–83. Fund Raising Dir, Jubilee Sailing Trust, 1984–85. Chm., Racecourse Assoc., 1985–89. *Recreations:* fishing, gardening. *Address:* c/o Barclays Bank, 1 Brompton Road, SW3 1EB.

See also V. H. A. Elliot.

LENG, Virginia Helen Antoinette; *see* Elliot, V. H. A.

LENNARD, Rev. Sir Hugh Dacre B.; *see* Barrett-Lennard.

LENNIE, Douglas; *b* 30 March 1910; *e s* of Magnus S. Lennie; *m* 1941, Rhona Young Ponsonby; two *s*. *Educ:* Berkhamsted Sch.; Guy's Hospital, LDS, RCS, 1934; Northwestern University, Chicago, DDS, 1938. Served War of 1939–45, Temporary Surg. Lt-Comdr (D) RNVR; formerly Surgeon Dentist to Queen Mary. *Address:* 72 Chiltley Way, Liphook, Hants GU30 7HE.

LENNOX; *see* Gordon-Lennox and Gordon Lennox.

LENNOX, Lionel Patrick Madill; Registrar of the Province and Diocese of York, and Registrar of the Convocation of York, since 1987; Partner, Denison Till, Solicitors, York and Leeds, since 1987; *b* 5 April 1949; *s* of Rev. James Lennox and late May Lennox; *m* 1979, Barbara Helen Firth; two *s* one *d*. *Educ:* St John's Sch., Leatherhead; Univ. of Birmingham (LLB). Admitted Solicitor, 1973; Ecclesiastical Notary, 1987; Notary Public, 1992. Solicitor in private practice, 1973–81; Asst Legal Advr to Gen. Synod, 1981–87. Secretary: Archbishop of Canterbury's Gp on Affinity, 1982–84; Legal Adv. Commn, Gen. Synod of C of E, 1986–. Sec., Yorks Mus. of Farming, 1991–94. Trustee: Yorks Historic Churches Trust, 1988–; St Leonard's Hospice, York, 2000–. *Address:* Stamford House, Piccadilly, York YO1 9PP. *T:* (01904) 623487.

LENNOX, Robert Smith, CBE 1978; JP; Lord Provost of Aberdeen, 1967–70 and 1975–77; *b* 8 June 1909; *m* 1963, Evelyn Margaret; no *c*. *Educ:* St Clement Sch., Aberdeen. Hon. LLD Aberdeen, 1970. JP Aberdeen. *Address:* 7 Gillespie Crescent, Ashgrove, Aberdeen AB2 5AX. *T:* (01224) 483862.

LENNOX-BOYD, family name of **Viscount Boyd of Merton**.

LENNOX-BOYD, Hon. Sir Mark (Alexander), Kt 1994; *b* 4 May 1943; 3rd *s* of 1st Viscount Boyd of Merton, CH, PC and of Lady Patricia Guinness, 2nd *d* of 2nd Earl of Iveagh, KG, CB, CMG, FRS; *m* 1974, Arabella Lacloche; one *d*. *Educ:* Eton Coll.; Christ Church, Oxford. Called to the Bar, Inner Temple, 1968. MP (C) Morecambe and Lonsdale, 1979–83, Morecambe and Lunesdale, 1983–97; contested (C) Morecambe and Lunesdale, 1997. Parliamentary Private Secretary: to Sec. of State for Energy, 1981–83; to the Chancellor of the Exchequer, 1983–84; Asst Govt Whip, 1984–86; a Lord Comr of HM Treasury (Govt Whip), 1986–88; PPS to Prime Minister, 1988–90; Parly Under-Sec. of State, FCO, 1990–94. *Recreation:* travel. *Address:* Gresgarth Hall, Caton, Lancashire LA2 9NB. *Clubs:* White's, Pratt's, Beefsteak.

LENON, Barnaby John, MA; Head Master, Harrow School, since 1999; *b* 10 May 1954; *s* of Philip John Fitzmaurice Lenon and Jane Alethea Lenon (*née* Brooke); *m* 1983, Penelope Anne Thain, BA; two *d*. *Educ:* Eltham Coll.; Keble Coll., Oxford (schol.; BA 1st Cl. Hons 1976; MA); St John's, Cambridge (PGCE; Univ. Prize for Educn 1978). Assistant Master: Eton Coll., 1977; Sherborne Sch., 1978–79; Eton Coll., 1979–90; Teacher, Holland Park Sch., 1988; Dep. Head Master, Highgate Sch., 1990–95; Headmaster, Trinity Sch. of John Whitgift, 1995–99. Governor: John Lyon Sch., 1999–; Hale Sch., 1999–; Swanbourne Sch., 1999–; Orley Farm Sch., 1999–; Wellesley House Sch., 1999–; Beacon Sch., 2000–. FRGS 1987 (Mem. Council, 1987–90 and 1998–2000; Chm., Educn Sub-Cttee, 1996–99). *Publications:* Techniques and Fieldwork in Geography, 1983; London, 1988; London in the 1990s, 1993; Fieldwork Techniques and Projects in Geography, 1994; The United Kingdom: geographical case studies, 1995; (ed jtly) Directory of University Geography Courses, 1995, 2nd edn 1997; contribs to geographical jls. *Recreations:* oil painting, athletics, deserts. *Address:* Harrow School, Harrow-on-the-Hill, Middlesex HA1 3HW. *T:* (020) 8872 8000. *Clubs:* East India, Lansdowne.

LEON, Sir John (Ronald), 4th Bt *cr* 1911; actor (stage name, **John Standing**); *b* 16 Aug. 1934; *er s* of 3rd Bt and late Kay Hammond; *S* father, 1964; *m* 1961, Jill (marr. diss. 1972), *d* of Jack Melford; one *s*; *m* 1984, Sarah, *d* of Bryan Forbes, *qv*; one *s* two *d*. *Educ:* Eton. Late 2nd Lt, KRRC. *Plays include:* Darling Buds of May, Saville, 1959; leading man, season, Bristol Old Vic, 1960; The Irregular Verb to Love, Criterion, 1961; Norman, Duchess, 1963; So Much to Remember, Vaudeville, 1963; The Three Sisters, Oxford Playhouse, 1964; See How They Run, Vaudeville, 1964; Seasons at Chichester Theatre, 1966, 1967; The Importance of Being Earnest, Haymarket 1968; Ring Round the Moon, Haymarket, 1968; The Alchemist, and Arms and the Man, Chichester, 1970; Popkiss, Globe, 1972; A Sense of Detachment, Royal Court, 1972; Private Lives, Queen's and Globe, 1973, NY and tour of USA, 1974; Jingo, Aldwych, 1975; Plunder, The Philanderer, NT, 1978; Close of Play, NT, 1979; Tonight at 8.30, Lyric, 1981; The Biko Inquest, Riverside, 1984; Rough Crossing, National, 1984; Hay Fever, Albery, 1992; A Month in the Country, Albery, 1994; Son of Man, RSC, 1995; A Delicate Balance, Haymarket, 1997. *Films:* The Wild and the Willing, 1962; Iron Maiden, 1962; King Rat, 1964; Walk, Don't Run, 1965; Zee and Co., 1973; The Eagle has Landed, 1976; The Class of Miss MacMichael, 1977; The Legacy, 1977; The Elephant Man, 1979; The Sea Wolves, 1980; (TV film) The Young Visiters, 1984; Nightflyers; 8½ Women, Rogue Trader, 1999. Television appearances incl.: for British TV: Arms and the Man; The First Churchills; Charley's Aunt; Rogue Male; The Sinking of HMS Victoria; Home and Beauty; Tinker, Tailor, Soldier, Spy; The Other 'Arf; Old Boy Network; Tonight at 8.30; Count of Solar; Gulliver's Travels; for American TV: Lime Street; Hotel; Flap Jack Floozie; Visitors; Murphy's Law; The Endless Game; Murder She Wrote; LA Law; Windmills of the Gods; Drovers' Gold; A Dance to The Music of Time. *Recreation:* painting. *Heir: s* Alexander John Leon, *b* 3 May 1965. *Address:* c/o ICM Ltd, Oxford House, 76 Oxford Street, W1N 0AX.

LEONARD, Anthony James; QC 1999; a Recorder, since 2000; *b* 21 April 1956; *s* of Sir (Hamilton) John Leonard, *qv* and late Doreen Enid (*née* Parker); *m* 1983, Shara Jane Cormack; two *d*. *Educ:* Hurstpierpoint Coll., Sussex; Council of Legal Educn. Short Service Limited Commn, Queen's Regt, 1975–76; Major, 6/7 Queen's (TA), 1976–85. Called to the Bar, Inner Temple, 1978; Standing Counsel to Inland Revenue, S Eastern Circuit, 1993–99. Liveryman, Plaisterers' Co. *Recreations:* opera, wine, reading. *Address:* 6 King's Bench Walk, Temple, EC4Y 7DR. *Club:* Garrick.

LEONARD, Brian Henry; Head of Regions, Tourism, Millennium and International Group, Department for Culture, Media and Sport, since 1998; *b* 6 Jan. 1948; *s* of William Henry Leonard and Bertha Florence Leonard (*née* Thomas); *m* 1975, Margaret Meade-King; two *s*. *Educ:* Dr Challoner's Grammar Sch., Amersham; LSE (BSc Econ 1969). Heal & Son, 1969–73; Price Commn, 1973–74; joined DoE, 1974; Circle 33 Housing Trust, 1982–83; Fellow, Hubert H. Humphrey Inst., Minneapolis, 1987–88; Regl Dir, N Reg., DoE and Dept of Transport, 1993–94; Regl Dir, Govt Office for SW, 1994–97; Dir, Envmt Protection Strategy, DETR, 1997–98. *Recreations:* friends, games, pottering about. *Address:* (office) 2–4 Cockspur Street, SW1Y 5DH. *Club:* MCC.

LEONARD, David Charles; Group Chief Executive, BPB plc, 1999–2000 (non-executive Director, since 2000); *b* 26 June 1938; *s* of Charles and Audrey Leonard; *m* 1961, Jennifer Capes; two *s* one *d*. *Educ:* Hellesdon Secondary Sch., Norwich. FCMA, ACIS. Managing Dir, food and other manufacturing industries; BPB plc: Man. Dir, British Gypsum, 1990–94; Dir, New Business Develt, 1993–97; Mem. Main Bd, 1995; Dep. Chm., Gypsum, 1996; Chm., British Gypsum, 1996–; Chief Operating Officer, all building products, 1997; Dir, BMP, 1999–. FRSA. *Recreations:* reading, music, opera, an interest in most sports, tennis, walking, golf. *Address:* BPB plc, Park House, 15 Bath Road, Slough SL1 3UF. *T:* (01753) 898800.

LEONARD, David John, TD 1974; Judge, Supreme Court of Hong Kong, 1991–97; *b* 18 Sept. 1937; *s* of Jeremiah Leonard and Rosaleen Oonagh Leonard (*née* Mellett); *m* 1966, Frances Helen Good; two *s*. *Educ:* Hendon Grammar Sch.; Magdalene Coll., Cambridge (MA). Admitted solicitor, 1967; admitted solicitor and barrister, Victoria, Australia, 1982. Solicitors' Dept, New Scotland Yard, 1966–71; Batten & Co., Solicitors, Yeovil, 1971–77; Hong Kong: Permanent Magistrate, 1977–81; Dist Judge, 1981–91; Judicial Comr, High Court, Brunei Darussalam, 2001. Chm., Judicial Studies Bd, Hong Kong, 1994–97. Served in TA: HAC, RA, Intelligence Corps, 1960–77, Maj. (retd) Intelligence Corps; Royal Hong Kong Regt (Volunteers), 1977–91, Maj. (retd). Part-time Immigration Adjudicator, 1997–98. Member: Acad. of Experts, 1995– (Vice-Chm., 1997–98); Arbitration Panel, Hong Kong Internat. Arbitration Centre, 1996–; Panel of Arbitrators, China Internat. Economic and Trade Arbitration Commn, 1997–. Mem. Cttee, Wilts TAVRA, 1997. FCIArb 1995 (Professional Conduct Cttee, 2000). Fellow: Singapore Inst. of Arbitrators, 1996; Hong Kong Inst. of Arbitrators, 1997. Freeman and Liveryman, Painter-Stainers' Co., 1996–. *Recreations:* travel, reading, walking. *Address:* Hill Cottage, Chapel Plaister, Box, Corsham, Wilts SN13 8HZ. *Clubs:* Cavalry and Guards; Bath & County (Bath); Hong Kong (Hong Kong).

LEONARD, Dick; *see* Leonard, Richard Lawrence.

LEONARD, Rt Rev. Mgr and Rt Hon. Graham Douglas, KCVO 1991; PC 1981; *b* 8 May 1921; *s* of late Rev. Douglas Leonard, MA; *m* 1943, Vivien Priscilla, *d* of late M. B. R. Swann, MD, Fellow of Gonville and Caius Coll., Cambridge; two *s*. *Educ:* Monkton Combe Sch.; Balliol Coll., Oxford (Hon. Fellow, 1986). Hon. Sch. Nat. Science, shortened course. BA 1943, MA 1947. Served War, 1941–45; Captain, Oxford and Bucks Light Infantry; Army Operational Research Group (Ministry of Supply), 1944–45. Westcott House, Cambridge, 1946–47. Deacon 1947, Priest 1948; Vicar of Ardleigh, Essex, 1952–55; Director of Religious Education, Diocese of St Albans, 1955–58; Hon. Canon of St Albans, 1955–57; Canon Residentiary, 1957–58; Canon Emeritus, 1958; General Secretary, Nat. Society, and Secretary, C of E Schools Council, 1958–62; Archdeacon of Hampstead, Exam. Chaplain to Bishop of London, and Rector of St Andrew Undershaft with St Mary Axe, City of London, 1962–64; Bishop Suffragan of Willesden, 1964–73; Bishop of Truro, 1973–81; Bishop of London, 1981–91; received into RC Ch and ordained priest *sub conditione*, 1994. Dean of the Chapels Royal, 1981–91; Prelate of the Order of the British Empire, 1981–91; Prelate of the Imperial Soc. of Knights Bachelor, 1986–91. Chairman: C of E Cttee for Social Work and the Social Services, 1967–76; C of E Board for Social Responsibility, 1976–83; Churches Main Cttee, 1981–91; C of E Board of Education, 1983–88; BBC and IBA Central Religious Adv. Cttee, 1984–89. Member: Churches Unity Commn, 1977–78, Consultant 1978; Churches Council for Covenanting, 1978–82; PCFC, 1989–93. An Anglican Mem., Commn for Anglican Orthodox Jt Doctrinal Discussions, 1974–81; one of Archbp of Canterbury's Counsellors on Foreign Relations, 1974–81. Pres., Path to Rome Internat. Convention (Miles Jesu), 1997–2001. Elected delegate, 5th Assembly WCC, Nairobi, 1975. House of Lords, 1977–91. Select Preacher to University of Oxford, 1968, 1984 and

1989; Hensley Henson Lectr, Univ. of Oxford, 1991–92. Lectures: John Findley Green Foundn, Fulton, Missouri, 1987; Earl Mountbatten Meml, Cambridge Union, 1990. Freeman, City of London, 1970. President: Middlesex Assoc., 1970–73; Corporation of SS Mary and Nicholas (Woodard Schools), 1973–78, Hon. Fellow, 1978. Fellow, Sion Coll., 1991–. Member Court of City Univ., 1981–91. Hon. Bencher, Middle Temple, 1982. Hon. DD: Episcopal Seminary, Kentucky, 1974; Westminster Coll., Fulton, Missouri, 1987; Hon. DCnL Nashotah, USA, 1983; STD Siena Coll., USA, 1984; Hon. LLD, Simon Greenleaf Sch. of Law, USA, 1987; Hon. DLitt CNAA, 1989. Episcopal Canon of Jerusalem, 1982–91; Prelate of Honour to the Pope, 2000. *Publications:* Growing into Union (Jt author), 1970; The Gospel is for Everyone, 1971; God Alive: Priorities in Pastoral Theology, 1981; Firmly I Believe and Truly, 1985; Life in Christ, 1986; (jtly) Let God be God, 1990; contrib. to: The Christian Religion Explained, 1960; Retreats Today, 1962; Communicating the Faith, 1969; A Critique of Eucharistic Agreement, 1975; Is Christianity Credible?, 1981; The Price of Peace, 1983; The Cross and the Bomb, 1983; Unholy Warfare, 1983; Synod of Westminster, 1986; After the Deluge, 1987; (ed) Faith and the Future, 1988; Tradition and Unity, 1991; Families for the Future, 1991; Challenge: spreading the faith, 1997; The Path to Rome, 1999. *Recreations:* reading, especially biographies; music. *Address:* 25 Woodlands Road, Witney, Oxon OX28 2DR. *Club:* Garrick.

LEONARD, Sir (Hamilton) John, Kt 1981; a Judge of the High Court, Queen's Bench Division, 1981–93; Presiding Judge, Wales and Chester Circuit, 1982–86; *b* 28 April 1926; *s* of late Arthur and Jean Leonard, Poole, Dorset; *m* 1948, Doreen Enid (*d* 1996), *yr d* of late Lt-Col Sidney James Parker, OBE, and May Florence Parker, Sanderstead, Surrey; one *s* one *d*. *Educ:* Dean Close Sch., Cheltenham; Brasenose Coll., Oxford (MA). Coldstream Guards (Captain), 1944–47. Called to Bar, Inner Temple, 1951; Master of the Bench, 1977; practised on South-Eastern Circuit; 2nd Junior Prosecuting Counsel to the Crown at Central Criminal Court, 1964–69; QC 1969; Dep. Chm., Surrey QS, 1969–71; Comr, CCC, 1969–71; a Recorder of the Crown Court, 1972–78; a Circuit Judge, 1978–81; Common Serjeant in the City of London, 1979–81. Member: General Council of the Bar, 1970–74, Senate, 1971–74, Senate of Four Inns and the Bar, 1974–77. Chm., Criminal Bar Assoc., 1975–77. Member: Home Sec.'s Adv. Bd on Restricted Patients, 1973–78; Deptl Cttee to Review Laws on Obscenity, Indecency and Censorship, 1977–79; Judicial Studies Bd, 1979–82. Mem. Council, Hurstpierpoint Coll., 1975–83; Gov., Dean Close Sch., Cheltenham, 1986–2000. Liveryman, Plaisterers' Co.; HM Lieutenant, City of London, 1980–81. *Recreations:* books, music, painting. *Address:* Royal Courts of Justice, WC2A 2LL. *Club:* Garrick.

See also A. J. Leonard.

LEONARD, Hugh, (John Keyes Byrne); playwright since 1959; Programme Director, Dublin Theatre Festival, since 1978; Literary Editor, Abbey Theatre, 1976–77; *b* 9 Nov. 1926; *m* 1955, Paule Jacquet; one *d*. *Educ:* Presentation College, Dun Laoghaire. Hon. DHL Rhode Island, 1980; Hon. DLitt TCD, 1988. *Stage plays:* The Big Birthday, 1956; A Leap in the Dark, 1957; Madigan's Lock, 1958; A Walk on the Water, 1960; The Passion of Peter Ginty, 1961; Stephen D, 1962; The Poker Session, and Dublin 1, 1963; The Saints Go Cycling In, 1965; Mick and Mick, 1966; The Quick and the Dead, 1967; The Au Pair Man, 1968; The Barracks, 1969; The Patrick Pearse Motel, 1971; Da, 1973; Thieves, 1973; Summer, 1974; Times of Wolves and Tigers, 1974; Irishmen, 1975; Time Was, 1976; A Life, 1977; Kill, 1982; Scorpions (3 stage plays), 1983; The Mask of Moriarty, 1985; Moving, 1991; Senna for Sonny, 1994; The Lily Lally Show, 1994; Chamber Music (2 plays), 1994; Magic, 1997; Love in the Title, 1998; Fillums, 1999; Colquhoun and MacBryde, 2000; *adaptations:* Great Expectations, 1995; A Tale of Two Cities, 1996. *TV plays:* Silent Song (Italia Award, 1967); The Last Campaign, 1978; The Ring and the Rose, 1978; A Life, 1986; Hunted Down, 1989; The Celadon Cup, 1993. *TV serials:* Nicholas Nickleby, 1977; London Belongs to Me, 1977; Wuthering Heights, 1978; Strumpet City, 1979; The Little World of Don Camillo, 1980; Good Behaviour, 1983; O'Neill, 1983; The Irish RM, 1985; Troubles, 1987; Parnell and the Englishwoman, 1991. *Films:* Herself Surprised, 1977; Da, 1988; Widows' Peak, 1994; Banjaxed, 1995. *Publications:* Home Before Night (autobiog.), 1979; Out After Dark (autobiog.), 1988; Parnell and the Englishwoman (novel), 1990; Rover and other cats (memoir), 1992; The Off-Off-Shore Island (novel), 1993; The Mogs (for children), 1995; A Wild People (novel), 2000. *Recreations:* travel (esp. French canals and waterways), vintage films, lunch, dinner, friendships. *Address:* 6 Rossaun, Pilot View, Dalkey, Co. Dublin. *T:* 2809590.

LEONARD, His Honour James Charles Beresford Whyte, MA Oxon; a Circuit Judge (formerly Deputy Chairman of Quarter Sessions, Inner London and Middlesex), 1965–79; Judge of the Mayor's and City of London Court, 1972–79; *b* 1905; *s* of Hon. J. W. Leonard, Middle Temple, KC (S Africa); *m* 1939, Barbara Helen (*d* 1989), *d* of late Capt. William Incledon-Webber; two *s* one *d*. *Educ:* Clifton Coll.; Christ Church, Oxford. Called to the Bar, Inner Temple, 1928, Bencher 1961. Served 1940–45, with RAF (Sqdn Ldr). Recorder of Walsall, Staffs, 1951–64; Junior Counsel to Ministry of Agriculture, Fisheries and Food, Forestry Commission and Tithe Redemption Commission, 1959–64; Deputy Chairman of QS: Co. of London, 1964–65; Oxfordshire, 1962–71. Chairman: Disciplinary Cttee, Pharmaceutical Soc. of GB, 1960–64; Adv. Cttee dealing with internment under Civil Authorities (Special Powers) Act (NI) 1962, April–Nov. 1972; Comr under Terrorism (N Ireland) Order 1972, 1972–74; Dep. Chm., Appeal Tribunal, 1974–75. *Address:* Cross Trees, Sutton Courtenay, Oxon OX14 4AD. *T:* (01235) 848230.

See also Earl of Westmeath.

LEONARD, Hon. Sir John; *see* Leonard, Hon. Sir H. J.

LEONARD, Richard Lawrence, (Dick Leonard); writer and journalist; *b* 12 Dec. 1930; *s* of late Cyril Leonard, Pinner, Middx, and Kate Leonard (*née* Whyte); *m* 1963, Irène, *d* of late Dr Ernst Heidelberger and Dr Gertrud Heidelberger, Bad Godesberg, Germany; one *s* one *d*. *Educ:* Ealing Grammar Sch.; Inst. of Education, London Univ.; Essex Univ. (MA). School teacher, 1953–55; Dep. Gen. Sec., Fabian Society, 1955–60; journalist and broadcaster, 1960–68; Sen. Research Fellow (Social Science Research Council), Essex Univ., 1968–70. Mem., Exec. Cttee, Fabian Soc., 1972–80 (Chm., 1977–78); Chm., Library Adv. Council, 1978–81. Trustee, Assoc. of London Housing Estates, 1973–78. Vis. Prof., Free Univ. of Brussels, 1988–96. European Advr, Publishers Assoc., 1987–94; Sen. Advr, Centre for European Policy Studies, 1994–99. Contested (Lab) Harrow W, 1955; MP (Lab) Romford, 1970–Feb. 1974; PPS to Rt Hon. Anthony Crosland, 1970–74; Mem., Speaker's Conf. on Electoral Law, 1972–74. Introduced Council Housing Bill, 1971; Life Peers Bill, 1973. Asst Editor, The Economist, 1974–85; Brussels and EU correspondent, The Observer, 1989–97; Brussels correspondent, Europe magazine, 1992–. *Publications:* Guide to the General Election, 1964; Elections in Britain, 1968; (ed jtly) The Backbencher and Parliament, 1972; Paying for Party Politics, 1975; BBC Guide to Parliament, 1979; (ed jtly) The Socialist Agenda, 1981; (jtly) World Atlas of Elections, 1986; Pocket Guide to the EEC, 1988; Elections in Britain Today, 1991; The Economist Guide to the European Community, 1992, 4th edn as The Economist Guide to the European Union, 1997, 7th edn 2000 (French, German, Polish, Bulgarian, Georgian, Spanish and Portuguese edns); Replacing the Lords, 1995; (jtly) Eminent Europeans, 1996; (ed) Crosland and New Labour, 1999; (ed jtly) The Pro-European Reader, 2001; contrib.: Guardian, Financial Times, TLS, The Bulletin, Prospect, and leading newspapers in USA, Canada, Japan, India, Australia and New Zealand. *Recreations:* walking, book-reviewing, family pursuits. *Address:* 32 rue des Bégonias, 1170 Brussels, Belgium. *T:* (2) 6602662. *Clubs:* Reform; Brussels Croquet.

LEORO-FRANCO, Dr Galo Alberto; Gran Cruz, National Order Al Mérito of Ecuador, 1970; Minister of Foreign Affairs, Ecuador, 1994–97; Member, Consultative Board, Ministry of Foreign Affairs, since 1997; *s* of José Miguel Leoro and Albertina Franco de Leoro; *m* 1957, Aglae Monroy de Leoro; one *s* two *d*. *Educ:* Central Univ., Quito. Licenciado in Political and Soc. Scis, 1949; Dr in Jurisprudence, Faculty of Law, 1951. Third Sec., Washington, 1955–56, Second Sec., 1956–58; First Sec., Ministry of Foreign Affairs, 1960; Counsellor, Mexico, 1961, Chargé d'Affaires, 1962; Counsellor, Alternate Rep. of Ecuador to OAS, Washington, DC, 1962–64, Minister, 1964–68; Ambassador, 1968–; Chief Legal Advisor to Ministry of Foreign Affairs, 1969–70; Undersec. Gen., Ministry of Foreign Affairs, 1970–71; Ambassador to the Dominican Republic, 1971–72; Perm. Rep. of Ecuador to OAS, 1972–79; Advisor on Internat. Orgns, Ministry of Foreign Affairs, 1979–81; Advisor on Nat. Sovereignty, Ministry of Foreign Affairs, and Rep. of the Ministry in Nat. Congress, 1981–83; Ambassador to UK, 1983–84; Ambassador and Permanent Rep. to Office of UN, Geneva, 1984–91; Chief Legal Advr, Ministry of Foreign Affairs, 1991–92; Ambassador to Holy See, 1993–94. Chairman: OAS Permanent Council, 1972–78 (Chm. of several Cttees of OAS Council and Gen. Assembly); Cttee II, Special Commn for Study of Interamerican System, Economic Co-operation problems, Washington, DC, 1973–75; INTELSAT Panel of Jurisexperts, Washington, DC, 1983–85; Rapporteur, Interamerican Conf. for Revision of TIAR; elected mem., Interamerican Juridical Cttee, Rio de Janeiro, 1981–84, Vice-Chm., 1982–83, Chm., 1985–96; Conciliator, Internat. Center for Settlement of Investment Disputes, IMF, Washington, DC, 1986–; Ecuadorian Mem., National Gp of Arbiters, Internat. Court of Arbitration, The Hague, 1987. Representative of Ecuador at over 100 internat. conferences and Chm. of the Delegation at various of them. Gran Cruz: Iron Cross, Fed. Repub. of Germany, 1970; Order of Duarte, Sánchez and Mella, Dominican Repub., 1972; Order of the Sun, Perú, 1976; 1st Class, Order of Francisco de Miranda, Venezuela, 1976; Order of Piana, Holy See; Order of San Carlos, Colombia; Order of Bernardo O'Higgins, Chile; 1st Class, Al Merito, Korea. *Publications:* contrib. Interamerican Law Year Book and Courses of Internat. Law of the OAS, Washington; various papers for Ecuadorean Year Book of Internat. Law. *Recreations:* chess, tennis. *Address:* González Suárez Avenida, N33–12 Quito, Ecuador. *Club:* Quito Tennis and Golf.

LÉOTARD, François Gérard Marie; Member: National Assembly, 1978–86, 1988–92 and since 1995; Regional Council, Provence; *b* Cannes, 26 March 1942; *s* of André Léotard and Antoinette (*née* Tomasi); *m* 1992, Ysabel Duret. *Educ:* Paris Law Univ.; Institut d'Etudes Politiques de Paris; Ecole Nationale d'Administration. Various appts in French admin, 1968–76; Mayor of Fréjus, 1977–; Minister of Culture and Communication, 1986–88; Minister of Defence, 1993–95; Mem., General Council, Var, 1980–88. Republican Party (Parti Républicain): Gen. Sec., 1982–88; Pres., 1988–90 and 1995–97; Hon. Pres., 1990–95; Pres., UDF, 1996–98. *Publications:* A Mots Découverts, 1987; Culture: les chemins de printemps, 1988; La Ville Aimée: mes chemins de Fréjus, 1989; Pendant la Crise, le Spectacle Continue, 1989; Adresse au Président des Républiques Françaises, 1991; Place de la République, 1992; Ma Liberté, 1995; Pour l'honneur, 1997; Je vous hais tous avec douceur, 2000. *Address:* Assemblée Nationale, 126 rue de l'Université, 75007 Paris, France.

LEPAGE, Robert, OC 1995; OQ 1999; Director and President, RLI, since 1988; Founder, President and Artistic Director: Ex Machina Theatre Company, since 1994; In Extremis Images Inc., since 1995; *b* 12 Dec. 1957; *s* of Fernand and Germaine Lepage. *Educ:* Ecole Joseph-François Perreault, Quebec City; Conservatoire d'Art Dramatique de Québec. Joined Théâtre Repère, as actor, 1980, also Jt Artistic Dir and writer, 1987–89; Artistic Dir, Théâtre Français, Ottawa Nat. Arts Theatre, 1989–93; Artistic Dir, La Caserne, 1997–. *Stage* includes: *joint writer, director and actor:* Théâtre Repère: Circulations, 1984; La Trilogie des dragons, 1985; Vinci (one-man show), 1986; Le polygraphe, 1987; Les plaques tectoniques, 1988–91; Les aiguilles et l'opium (one-man show), 1991; La face cachée de la lune (one-man show), 2000–02; *director:* Carmen, Théâtre d'Bon'Humeur, 1983; Le songe d'une nuit d'été, Théâtre du Nouveau Monde, Montreal, 1988; A Midsummer Night's Dream, RNT, London, 1992; Le Cycle William Shakespeare, Quebec City, Maubeuge, Frankfurt and Paris, 1992; Macbeth and La tempête, Tokyo Globe Theatre, Tokyo, 1993; Les Sept branches de la rivière Ota (also jt writer), 1994; Elseneur (one-man show, also adapter and actor), 1995; La géométrie des miracles (world tour; also jt writer), 1998; Zulu Time, Zulu Timie Ltd, 1999–; La damnation de Faust, Japan, 1999, France, 2001; TV advertisements; *films include: writer and director:* Le confessionnal, 1995; Le polygraphe, 1996; Nô, 1998; Possible Worlds, 2000. Chevalier de l'Ordre des Arts et des Lettres (France), 1990. *Address:* c/o Lynda Beaulieu, 103 Dalhousie Street, Quebec City, QC G1K 4B9, Canada.

LE POER, Baron; Richard John Beresford; *b* 19 Aug. 1987; *s* and *heir* of Earl of Tyrone, *qv*.

LE POER TRENCH, family name of **Earl of Clancarty**.

LE PORTZ, Yves; Comdr Légion d'Honneur 1978; Grand Officier de l'Ordre National du Mérite; French financial executive; Inspector-General of Finances, 1971; *b* Hennebont, 30 Aug. 1920; *m* 1946, Bernadette Champetier de Ribes; five *c*. *Educ:* Univ. de Paris à la Sorbonne; Ecole des Hautes Etudes Commerciales; Ecole Libre des Sciences Politiques. Attached to Inspection Générale des Finances, 1943; Directeur Adjoint du Cabinet, Président du Conseil, 1948–49; Sous-Directeur, then Chef de Service, Min. of Finance and Economic Affairs, 1949–51; Directeur du Cabinet: Sec. of State for Finance and Economic Affairs, 1951–52; Minister for Posts, Telegraphs and Telephones (PTT), 1952–55; Minister for Reconstruction and Housing, 1955–57; French Delegate to UN Economic and Social Council, 1957–58; Dir-Gén., Finance, Algeria, 1958–62; Administrateur-Gén., Development Bank of Algeria, 1959–62. European Investment Bank: Vice-Pres. and Vice-Chm., Bd of Dirs, 1962–70; Pres. and Chm. Bd of Dirs, 1970–84; Hon. Pres., 1984. Chairman: Commn des Opérations de Bourse, Paris, 1984–88; Investment Funds Supervisory Cttee, Principality of Monaco, 1988–; Statutory Auditors' Ethics Cttee, 1999–. *Address:* 127 avenue de Wagram, 75017 Paris, France.

LEPPARD, Captain Keith André, CBE 1977; RN; Secretary, Institute of Brewing, 1977–90; Director Public Relations (Royal Navy), 1974–77; *b* 29 July 1924; *s* of Wilfred Ernest Leppard and Dora Gilmore Keith; *m* 1954, Betty Rachel Smith; one *s* one *d*. *Educ:* Purley Grammar Sch. MRAeS 1973; FBIM 1973; FSAE 1985. Entered RN, FAA pilot duties, 1943; Opnl Wartime Service, Fighter Pilot, N Atlantic/Indian Oceans, 1944–45; Fighter Pilot/Flying Instr, Aircraft Carriers and Air Stns, 1946–57; CO 807 Naval Air

Sqdn (Aerobatic Display Team, Farnborough), 1958–59; Air Org./Flying Trng Staff appts, 1959–63; Comdr (Air), HMS Victorious, 1963–64; Jt Services Staff Coll., 1964–65; Dir, Naval Officer Appts (Air), 1965–67; Chief Staff Officer (Air), Flag Officer Naval Air Comd, 1967–69; Chief Staff Officer (Ops/Trng), Far East Fleet, 1969–71; CO, Royal Naval Air Stn, Yeovilton, and Flag Captain to Flag Officer Naval Air Comd, 1972–74. Naval ADC to the Queen, 1976–77. *Recreations:* country life, tennis, golf. *Address:* Little Holt, Kingsley Green, Haslemere, Surrey GU27 3LW. *T:* (01428) 642797.

LEPPARD, Raymond John, CBE 1983; conductor, harpsichordist, composer; Music Director, Indianapolis Symphony Orchestra, 1987–2001; *b* 11 Aug. 1927; *s* of A. V. Leppard. *Educ:* Trinity Coll., Cambridge. Fellow of Trin. Coll., Cambridge, Univ. Lecturer in Music, 1958–68. Hon. Keeper of the Music, Fitzwilliam Museum, 1963–82. Conductor: Covent Garden, Sadler's Wells, Glyndebourne, and abroad; Principal Conductor, BBC Northern Symphony Orchestra, 1972–80; Prin. Guest Conductor, St Louis SO, 1984–93. Hon. RAM 1972; Hon. GSM 1983; Hon. FRCM 1984. Hon. DLitt Univ. of Bath, 1972. Commendatore al Merito della Repúbblica Italiana, 1974. *Publications:* realisations of Monteverdi: Il Ballo delle Ingrate, 1958; L'Incoronazione di Poppea, 1962; L'Orfeo, 1965; Il Ritorno d'Ulisse, 1972; realisations of Francesco Cavalli: Messa Concertata, 1966; L'Ormindo, 1967; La Calisto, 1969; Magnificat, 1970; L'Egisto, 1974; L'Orione, 1983; realisation of Rameau's Dardanus, 1980; Authenticity in Music, 1988; Raymond Leppard on Music, 1993; British Academy Italian Lecture, 1969, Procs Royal Musical Assoc. *Recreations:* music, theatre, books, friends. *Address:* c/o Clarion/Seven Muses, 47 Whitehall Park, N19 3TW. *T:* (020) 7272 8448, *Fax:* (020) 7281 9687.

LEPPER, David; MP (Lab and Co-op) Brighton Pavilion, since 1997; *b* 15 Sept. 1945; *s* of late Henry George Lepper and Maggie Lepper (*née* Osborne); *m* 1966, Jeane Stroud; one *s* one *d*. *Educ:* St John's C of E Primary Sch., Richmond; Gainsborough Secondary Sch., Richmond; Wimbledon Co. Secondary Sch.; Univ. of Kent (BA Hons); Univ. of Sussex (PGCE); PCL (Dip. Film); Univ. of Sussex (Dip. Media). Teacher: Westlain GS, Brighton, 1968–73; Falmer Sch., Brighton, 1973–96. Mem. (Lab), Brighton BC, 1980–97 (Leader, 1986–87; Mayor, 1993–94). *Publications:* John Wayne, 1986; various articles in film and media jls. *Recreations:* cinema, music, books, watching professional cycling. *Address:* (office) John Saunders House, 179 Preston Road, Brighton BN1 6AG. *T:* (01273) 551532. *Club:* Brighton Trades and Labour.

LEPPING, Sir George (Geria Dennis), GCMG 1988; MBE 1981; Governor-General of the Solomon Islands, 1988–94; *b* 22 Nov. 1947; *e s* of Chief Dionisio Tanutanu, BEM and Regina Suluki; *m* 1972, Margaret Kwalea Teioli; two *s* four *d* (incl. twins) and one adopted *d*. *Educ:* St John's and St Peter's Primary Schs; King George VI Secondary Sch.; Agricl Coll., Vudal, PNG (Dip. Tropical Agric.); Reading Univ. (Dip. Agric.; MSc). Joined Solomon Is Public Service as Field Officer, Dept of Agric. and Rural Economy, 1968; Sen. Field Officer, then Under-Sec. (Agricl), Min. of Agric., 1979–80; Permanent Secretary: Min. of Home Affairs and Nat. Devolt, 1981–84; Special Duties, as Project Dir, Rural Services Project (Develt), 1984–87; Min. of Finance, 1988. Sometime Dir, Chm. or Mem., various govt cos and authorities; Chm., Nat. Disaster Council, 1981–84. Pres., Solomon Is Amateur Athletics Union, 1970–73, 1981–82 (first Solomon Is athlete to win internat. sports medals). KStJ 1991. *Recreations:* reading, swimming, lawn tennis, snooker, snorkelling, high-speed boat driving, fishing. *Address:* PO Box 1431, Honiara, Solomon Islands.

LEPSCHY, Prof. Giulio Ciro, FBA 1987; Emeritus Professor of Italian, University of Reading, since 2000 (Professor, 1975–97; part-time Professor, 1997–2000); *b* 14 Jan. 1935; *s* of Emilio Lepschy and Sara Castelfranchi; *m* 1962, Anna Laura Momigliano. *Educ:* Univ. of Pisa (Dott. Lett.); Scuola Normale Superiore, Pisa (Dip. Lic. and Perf.). Lib. Doc., Italy. Research, 1957–64, at Univs of Zurich, Oxford, Paris, London, Reading; Lectr 1964, Reader 1967, Univ. of Reading. Mem. Council, Philological Soc., 1984–89, 1992–96; Pres., MHRA, 2001. Corr. Mem., Accademia della Crusca, 1991. Hon. Prof., UCL, 1998. Member editorial boards: The Italianist; Lingua e Stile. Hon. Dr, Univ. of Turin, 1998. Serena Medal, British Acad., 2000. *Publications:* A Survey of Structural Linguistics, 1970, new edn 1982; (jtly) The Italian Language Today, 1977, 2nd edn 1988; Saggi di linguistica italiana, 1978; Intorno a Saussure, 1979; Mutamenti di prospettiva nella linguistica, 1981; Nuovi saggi di linguistica italiana, 1989; Sulla linguistica moderna, 1989; Storia della linguistica, 1990; La linguistica del Novecento, 1992; History of Linguistics, 1994; (jtly) L'amanuense analfabeta e altri saggi, 1999; contribs to learned jls. *Address:* 335 Latymer Court, Hammersmith Road, W6 7LH. *T:* and *Fax:* (020) 8748 7780.

LE QUESNE, Caroline; *see* Lucas, C.

LE QUESNE, Sir (Charles) Martin, KCMG 1974 (CMG 1963); HM Diplomatic Service, retired; *b* 10 June 1917; *s* of C. T. Le Quesne, QC; *m* 1948; three *s*. *Educ:* Shrewsbury; Exeter Coll., Oxford (Hon. Fellow, 1990). Served in Royal Artillery, 1940–45. Apptd HM Foreign Service, 1946; 2nd Sec. at HM Embassy, Baghdad, 1947–48; 1st Secretary: Foreign Office, 1948–51, HM Political Residency, Bahrain, 1951–54; attended course at NATO Defence Coll., Paris, 1954–55; HM Embassy, Rome, 1955–58; Foreign Office, 1958–60; apptd HM Chargé d'Affaires, Republic of Mali, 1960, subsequently Ambassador there, 1961–64; Foreign Office, 1964–68; Ambassador to Algeria, 1968–71; Dep. Under-Sec. of State, FCO, 1971–74; High Comr in Nigeria, 1974–76. Mem., States of Jersey, 1978–90 (Dep. for St Saviour's parish). Hon. Vice-Pres., Royal African Soc. Mem. Council, Southampton Univ. *Recreations:* gardening, books. *Address:* Beau Désert, St Saviour, Jersey, Channel Islands. *T:* (01534) 22076. *Clubs:* Reform (Chairman 1973–74), MCC; Victoria, United (Jersey); Royal Channel Islands Yacht.

See also Sir J. G. Le Quesne, L. P. Le Quesne.

LE QUESNE, Sir (John) Godfray, Kt 1980; QC 1962; Judge of Courts of Appeal of Jersey, 1964–97, and Guernsey, 1964–95; a Recorder, 1972–97; *b* 18 Jan. 1924; 3rd *s* of late C. T. Le Quesne, QC; *m* 1963, Susan Mary Gill; two *s* one *d*. *Educ:* Shrewsbury Sch.; Exeter Coll., Oxford (MA). Pres. of Oxford Union, 1943. Called to Bar, Inner Temple, 1947; Master of the Bench, Inner Temple, 1969, Reader, 1988, Treasurer, 1989; admitted to bar of St Helena, 1959. Dep. Chm., Lincs (Kesteven) QS, 1963–71. Chm., Monopolies and Mergers Commn, 1975–87 (a part-time Mem., 1974–75). Chm. of Council, Regent's Park Coll., Oxford, 1958–87. *Publication:* Jersey and Whitehall in the Mid-Nineteenth Century, 1992. *Recreations:* music, walking. *Address:* 3 Hare Court, Temple, EC4Y 7BJ. *T:* (020) 7415 7800.

See also Sir C. M. Le Quesne, L. P. Le Quesne.

LE QUESNE, Prof. Leslie Philip, CBE 1984; DM, MCh, FRCS; Medical Administrator, Commonwealth Scholarship Commission, 1984–91; *b* 24 Aug. 1919; *s* of late C. T. Le Quesne, QC; *m* 1969, Pamela Margaret (*d* 1999), *o d* of late Dr A. Fullerton, Batley, Yorks; two *s*. *Educ:* Rugby; Exeter Coll., Oxford; Middlesex Hosp. Med. Sch. Jun. Demonstrator, Path. and Anat., 1943–45; House Surgeon, Southend Hosp. and St Mark's Hosp., 1945–47; Appointments at Middlesex Hospital: Asst, Surgical Professorial Unit, 1947–52; Asst Dir, Dept of Surgical Studies, 1952–63; Surgeon, 1960–63; Prof. of Surgery, Med. Sch., and Dir, Dept of Surgical Studies, 1963–84; Dep. Vice-Chancellor and Dean, Fac. of Medicine, Univ. of London, 1980–84. Sir Arthur Sims Commonwealth Travelling Prof., 1975. Mem. GMC, 1979–84. Arris and Gale Lectr, RCS, 1952; Baxter Lectr, Amer. Coll. Surgs, 1960. Mem., Ct of Examrs, RCS, 1971–77. Formerly Chm., Assoc. of Profs of Surgery; Pres., Surgical Res. Soc. Chm., The British Jl of Surgery. Hon. FRACS, 1975; Hon. FACS, 1982; Hon. Fellow RPMS, 1985. Moynihan Medal, 1953. *Publications:* medical articles and contribs to text books; Fluid Balance in Surgical Practice, 2nd edn, 1957. *Recreations:* fishing, reading. *Address:* Flat 1, 10 Strathray Gardens, NW3 4NY.

See also Sir C. M. Le Quesne, Sir J. G. Le Quesne.

LE QUESNE, Sir Martin; *see* Le Quesne, Sir C. M.

LEREGO, Michael John; QC 1995; *b* 6 May 1949; *s* of late Leslie Ivor Lerego and Gwendolen Frances Lerego; *m* 1972, Susan Northover; three *d* (one *s* decd). *Educ:* Manchester Grammar Sch.; Haberdashers' Aske's Sch., Elstree; Keble Coll., Oxford (Open Schol.; Dist. Law Mods 1968; Gibbs Prize in Law 1969; BA Jurisp. 1st Cl. 1970; BCL 1st Cl. 1971; MA Oxon 1978). Called to the Bar, Inner Temple, 1972; in practice, 1972–. Weekender, Queen's Coll., Oxford, 1972–78. Member: Jt Working Party of Law Soc. and Bar on Banking Law, 1987–91; Law Soc's Sub-Cttee on Banking Law, 1991–96; an Arbitrator: Lloyd's Modified Arbitration Scheme, 1988–92; Lloyd's Arbitration Scheme, 1993–. Governor: Wroxham Sch., Potters Bar, 1995–. FCIArb 1997. *Publications:* (contrib.) The Law of Bank Payments, 2nd edn 1999; (ed jtly) Commercial Court Procedure, 2000. *Recreation:* watching sport. *Address:* Fountain Court, Temple, EC4Y 9DH. *T:* (020) 7583 3335.

LERENIUS, Bo Åke; Group Chief Executive, Associated British Ports Holdings plc, since 1999; *b* 11 Dec. 1946; *s* of Åke Lerenius and Elisabeth Lerenius; *m* (marr. diss.); one *s* one *d*. *Educ:* Malmö, Sweden; Westchester High Sch., LA; Univ. of Lund, Sweden (BA Business Admin). Div. Dir, Tarkett (part of Swedish Nobel Gp), 1983–85; Gp Pres. and CEO, Emstromgruppen, 1985–92; Gp Chief Exec., Stena Line, 1992–98; Vice Chm., Stena Line and Dir, New Business Investments, Stena AB, 1998–99. *Recreations:* golf, shooting. *Address:* Associated British Ports Holdings plc, 150 Holborn, EC1N 2LR. *Clubs:* East India; Wentworth Golf; Royal Bachelors (Gothenburg); Falsterbo Golf (Sweden).

LE ROY LADURIE, Prof. Emmanuel Bernard; Commandeur de la Légion d'Honneur, 1996; Commandeur de l'Ordre des Arts et des Lettres; Professor of History of Modern Civilisation, Collège de France, since 1973; *b* 19 July 1929; *s* of Jacques Le Roy Ladurie and Léontine (*née* Dauger); *m* 1956, Madeleine Pupponi; one *s* one *d*. *Educ:* Univ. of Sorbonne (agrégé d'histoire); DèsL 1952. Teacher, Lycée de Montpellier, 1955–57; Res. Assistant, CNRS, 1957–60; Assistant, Faculté des Lettres de Montpellier, 1960–63; Asst Lectr, 1963, Dir of Studies, 1965–, Ecole Pratique des Hautes Etudes; Lectr, Faculté des Lettres de Paris, 1969; Prof., Sorbonne, 1970; UER Prof. of Geography and Social Sci., Univ. de Paris VII, 1971–. General Administrator, Bibliothèque Nationale, 1987–94 (Pres., Conseil scientifique, 1994–). Mem. de l'Institut, Acad. des Scis morales et politiques, 1993–. Foreign Member: Amer. Philosophical Soc., 2000; Polish Acad. of Scis, 2000; For. Hon. Mem., American Acad. of Scis, 1984; Hon. FBA 1985. Hon. doctorate: Geneva, 1978; Michigan, 1981; Leeds, 1982; East Anglia, 1985; Leicester, York, 1986; Carnegie Mellon, Pittsburgh, 1987; Durham, 1987; Hull, 1990; Dublin, 1992; Albany, Haifa, Montréal, Oxford, 1993; Pennsylvania, 1995; HEC, Paris, 1999. *Publications:* Les Paysans du Languedoc, 1966; Histoire du climat depuis l'an mil, 1967, 2nd edn 1983; Le Territoire de l'historien, vol. 1 1973, vol. 2 1978; Montaillou: village occitan 1294–1324, 1975; (jtly) Histoire économique et sociale de la France, vol. 1 1450–1660, vol. 2 Paysannerie et Croissance, 1976; Le Carnaval de Romans 1579–1580 (Prix Pierre Lafue), 1980; L'Argent, l'Amour et la Mort en pays d'Oc, 1980; (jtly) Inventaire des campagnes, 1980; (jtly) L'Histoire urbaine de la France, vol. 3, 1981; Parmi les historiens, 1983; Pierre Prion: scribe, 1987; L'Histoire de France: l'état royal 1460–1610, 1987; (ed) Monarchies, 1987; L'Ancien Régime, 1991; Le siècle des Platter 1499–1628, vol. 1 Le mendiant et le professeur, 1995, vol. 2 Le voyage de Thomas Platter 1595–1599, 2000; (ed jtly) Mémoires de Jacques Le Roy Ladurie, 1997; Saint-Simon et le système de la cour, 1997; L'Historien, le chiffre et le texte, 1997. *Address:* Collège de France, 11 place Marcelin Berthelot, 75231 Paris cedex 05, France; (home) 88 rue d'Alleray, 75015 Paris, France.

LeROY-LEWIS, David Henry, FCA; Director, Touche, Remnant & Co., 1974–88 (Deputy Chairman, 1981–88); Chairman, Henry Ansbacher Holdings plc, 1982–88; *b* 14 June 1918; *er s* of late Stuyvesant Henry LeRoy-Lewis and late Bettye LeRoy-Lewis; *m* 1953, Cynthia Madeleine, *er d* of late Comdr John C. Boldero, DSC, RN (Retd); three *d*. *Educ:* Eton. FCA 1947. Chairman: TR North America Trust PLC (formerly Continental Union Trust Ltd) 1974–88 (Dir, 1948–88); R. P. Martin plc, 1981–85; Hill Martin, 1989–93; Director: TR Industrial & General Trust PLC, 1967–88; Akroyd & Smithers Ltd, 1970–81 (Chm., 1976–81); TR Trustees Corp. PLC, 1973–88; TR Energy PLC, 1981–88. Mem., 1961–81, a Dep. Chm., 1973–76, Stock Exchange Council. *Recreation:* fishing. *Address:* Stoke House, Stoke, Andover, Hants SP11 0NP. *T:* (01264) 738548. *Club:* MCC.

LESCHLY, Jan; Chairman and Chief Executive Officer, Care Capital LLC, since 2000; *b* 11 Sept. 1940; *m* 1963, Dr Lotte Engelbredt; four *s*. *Educ:* Copenhagen Coll. of Pharmacy (MSc Pharmacy); Copenhagen Sch. of Econs and Business Admin (BS Business Admin). Pharmaceutical industry, 1972–2000: Exec. Vice Pres. and Pres., Pharmaceutical Div., Novo Industries A/S, Denmark, 1972–79; Squibb Corporation: joined 1979; Vice-Pres., Commercial Develt, 1979–81; US Pres., 1981–84; Gp Vice-Pres. and Dir, 1984–86; Exec. Vice-Pres., 1986–88; Pres. and Chief Operating Officer, 1988–90; Chm., SmithKline Beecham Pharmaceuticals, 1990–94; Chief Exec., SmithKline Beecham, 1994–2000. Member, Board of Directors: Amer. Express Co.; Viacom Corp.; Ventro Corp.; Maersk Gp; Mem. Internat. Adv. Bd, DaimlerChrysler. Member: British Pharma Group; Bd of Dirs, Pharmaceutical Res. and Manufrs of America; Pharmaceutical Res. and Manufrs Foundn; Bd of Trustees, Nat. Foundn for Infectious Diseases; Dean's Adv. Council, Emory Univ. Business Sch. *Address:* Care Capital LLC, Princeton Overlook I, 100 Overlook Center and Route 1, Princeton, NJ 08540, USA.

LESCOEUR, Bruno Jean; Chairman and Chief Executive, London Electricity Group plc, since 1999; *b* 19 Nov. 1953; *m* 1976, Janick Dreyer; two *s* one *d*. *Educ:* Ecole Polytechnique, Paris. Electricité de France (EDF): responsible for pricing, 1978–87, for distribn of gas and electricity, Mulhouse, France, 1987–89; Rep., as Founder Mem., Electricity Pool in London, 1990; Head, Distribution Unit, EDF and GDF, South of France, 1991–93; Dep. Chief Financial Officer, 1994–98. FRSA. *Recreation:* sailing. *Address:* (office) Templar House, 81–87 High Holborn, WC1V 6NU; 48 Little Boltons, SW10 9LN; 28 rue Washington, 75008 Paris, France.

LESITER, Ven. Malcolm Leslie; Archdeacon of Bedford, since 1993; *b* 31 Jan. 1937; *m*; four *d*. *Educ:* Cranleigh Sch.; Selwyn Coll., Cambridge (BA 1961; MA 1965); Cuddesdon Coll., Oxford. Ordained deacon, 1963, priest, 1964; Curate, Eastney, 1963–66; Curate, 1966–71, Team Vicar, 1971–73, St Paul, Hemel Hempstead; Vicar: All Saints, Leavesden,

1973–88; Radlett, 1988–93. RD, Watford, 1981–88. *Address:* 17 Lansdowne Road, Luton, Beds LU3 1EE. *T:* (01582) 730722, *Fax:* (01582) 877354.

LESLIE, family name of **Earl of Rothes**.

LESLIE, Lord; James Malcolm David Leslie; *b* 4 June 1958; *s* and *heir* of 21st Earl of Rothes, *qv*. *Educ:* Eton. Graduated Parnham House, 1990. *Address:* Littlecroft, West Milton, Bridport, Dorset DT6 3SL.

LESLIE, Sir Alan; *see* Leslie, Sir C. A. B.

LESLIE, (Alison) Mariot; HM Diplomatic Service; Minister and Deputy Head of Mission, Rome, since 1998; *b* Edinburgh, 25 June 1954; *d* of Stewart Forson Sanderson and Alison Mary Sanderson; *m* 1978, Andrew David Leslie; two *d*. *Educ:* George Watson's Ladies' Coll., Edinburgh; Leeds Girls' High Sch.; St Hilda's Coll., Oxford (BA 1975). Scottish Office, 1975; joined HM Diplomatic Service, 1977: Singapore, 1978–81; Bonn, 1982–86; Paris (on secondment to Quai d'Orsay), 1990–92; Head, Envmt, Sci. and Energy Dept, FCO, 1992–93; Scottish Office Industry Dept, 1993–95; Head, Policy Planning Staff, FCO, 1996–98. *Recreations:* food, travel, argument. *Address:* c/o Foreign and Commonwealth Office, King Charles Street, SW1A 2AH.

LESLIE, Dr Andrew Greig William, FRS 2001; Senior Staff Scientist, MRC Laboratory of Molecular Biology, Cambridge, since 1991 (Staff Scientist, 1988–91); *b* 26 Oct. 1949; *s* of John and Margaret Leslie; *m* 1977, Catherine Alice Fuchs; two *s* one *d* (and one *d* decd). *Educ:* Jesus Coll., Cambridge (BA, MA); Univ. of Manchester (PhD 1974). Res. Asst, Purdue Univ., Indiana, 1974–79; Res. Asst, 1979–83, MRC Sen. Fellow, 1983–88, ICSTM. *Publications:* numerous contribs to scientific jls incl. Nature, Science, Cell, Molecular Cell. *Recreations:* walking, cycling, swimming, films, music. *Address:* MRC Laboratory of Molecular Biology, Hills Road, Cambridge CB2 2QH. *T:* (01223) 248011.

LESLIE, Ann Elizabeth Mary, (Mrs Michael Fletcher); journalist and broadcaster; *b* Pakistan; *d* of Norman Leslie and Theodora (*née* McDonald); *m* 1969, Michael Fletcher; one *d*. *Educ:* Presentation Convent, Matlock, Derbyshire; Convent of the Holy Child, Mayfield, Sussex; Lady Margaret Hall, Oxford (BA). Daily Express, 1962–67; freelance, 1967–: regular contributor to Daily Mail. Variety Club Women of the Year Award for journalism and broadcasting, 1981; British Press Awards Feature Writer of the Year, 1981, 1989; British Press Awards Commendation, 1980, 1983, 1985, 1987, 1991, 1996, 1999; Feature Writer of the Year Award, What the Papers Say, Granada Television, 1991; Lifetime Achievement Award, Media Soc., 1997; James Cameron Meml Award, James Cameron Meml Trust, 1999. *Recreation:* family life. *Address:* c/o Daily Mail, Northcliffe House, 2 Derry Street, Kensington, W8 5TS. *T:* (020) 7938 6000, *Fax:* (020) 7267 0117.

LESLIE, Christopher Michael; MP (Lab) Shipley, since 1997; Parliamentary Secretary, Cabinet Office, since 2001; *b* 28 June 1972; *s* of Michael N. Leslie and Dania K. Leslie. *Educ:* Bingley Grammar Sch.; Univ. of Leeds (BA Hons Pol. and Parly Studies 1994; MA Indust. and Labour Studies 1996). Research Assistant: Rep. Bernie Sanders, US Congress, 1992; Gordon Brown, MP, 1993; Adminr, Bradford Labour Party, 1995–97; Researcher, Barry Seal, MEP, 1997. PPS to Minister of State, Cabinet Office, 1998–2001. Mem. (Lab), Bradford MDC, 1994–98. *Recreations:* music, tennis, golf, travel. *Address:* House of Commons, SW1A 0AA. *T:* (020) 7219 3000.

LESLIE, Sir (Colin) Alan (Bettridge), Kt 1986; Commissioner, Foreign Compensation Commission, 1986–90; *b* 10 April 1922; *s* of Rupert Colin Leslie and Gladys Hannah Leslie (*née* Bettridge); *m* 1st, 1953, Anne Barbara (*née* Coates) (*d* 1982); two *d*; 2nd, 1983, Jean Margaret (Sally), widow of Dr Alan Cheatle. *Educ:* King Edward VII School, Lytham; Merton College, Oxford (MA Law). Solicitor. Commissioned, The Royal Scots Fusiliers, 1941–46. Legal practice, Stafford Clark & Co., Solicitors, 1948–60; Head of Legal Dept and Company Secretary, British Oxygen Co., later BOC International, then BOC Group, 1960–83. Law Society: Vice-Pres., 1984–85; Pres., 1985–86. Adjudicator, Immigration Appeals, 1990–94. *Recreation:* fishing. *Address:* Tye Cottage, Alfriston, E Sussex BN26 5TD. *T:* (01323) 870518; 36 Abingdon Road, W8 6AS. *T:* (020) 7937 2874. *Club:* Oxford and Cambridge.

LESLIE, Rt Rev. (Ernest) Kenneth, OBE 1972; *b* 14 May 1911; *s* of Rev. Ernest Thomas Leslie and Margaret Jane Leslie; *m* 1941, Isabel Daisy Wilson (*d* 1994); two *s* one *d* (and one *s* decd). *Educ:* Trinity Gram. Sch., Kew, Vict.; Trinity Coll., University of Melbourne (BA); Aust. Coll. of Theology (ThL, 2nd Cl. 1933, Th Schol. 1951, 2nd Cl. 1952). Deacon, 1934; priest, 1935; Asst Curate, Holy Trinity, Coburg, 1934–37; Priest-in-Charge, Tennant Creek, Dio. Carpentaria, 1937–38; Alice Springs with Tennant Creek, 1938–40; Rector of Christ Church, Darwin, 1940–44; Chaplain, AIF, 1942–45; Rector of Alice Springs with Tennant Creek, 1945–46; Vice-Warden, St John's Coll., Morpeth, NSW, 1947–52; Chap. Geelong Church of Eng. Gram. Sch., Timbertop Branch, 1953–58; Bishop of Bathurst, 1959–81. Hon. DLitt Charles Sturt, 1996. *Recreations:* walking, woodwork. *Address:* 54 Alcheringa Road, Kelso, NSW 2795, Australia.

LESLIE, (Harman) John; Master, Queen's Bench Division, High Court of Justice, since 1996; *b* 8 April 1946; *s* of Percy Leslie and Sheila Mary Leslie (*née* Harris); *m* 1st, 1971, Alix Helen Cohen (marr. diss. 1980); two *s*; 2nd, 1986, Valerie Gibson. *Educ:* Dover Coll.; Clare Coll., Cambridge (BA 1968). Called to the Bar, Middle Temple, 1969, Bencher, 2001; in practice at the Bar, 1969–96. Member: Civil Procedure Rule Cttee, 1997–; Vice-Chancellor's Wkg Party on Civil Procedure Practice Directions, 1997–2000. Gov., Dover Coll., 1974– (Mem. Council, 1975–84). *Publications:* (contrib.) Halsbury's Laws of England, 4th edn, 1999; (ed jtly) Civil Court Practice, 1999–; Civil Court Manual, 1999. *Recreations:* France, bridge, woodworking. *Address:* Royal Courts of Justice, Strand, WC2A 2LL. *Club:* Royal Automobile.

LESLIE, Prof. Ian Malcolm, PhD; Professor of Computer Science, since 1998 and Head of Department, since 1999, University of Cambridge Computer Laboratory; Fellow of Christ's College, Cambridge, since 1985; *b* 11 Feb. 1955; *s* of Douglas Alexander Leslie and Phyllis Margaret Leslie; *m* 1986, Patricia Valerie Vyoral (marr. diss. 2000); one *s* one *d*; *m* 2001, Celia Mary Denton. *Educ:* Univ. of Toronto (BASc 1977; MASc 1979); Darwin Coll., Cambridge (PhD 1983). Asst Lectr, 1983–86, Lectr, 1986–98, Univ. of Cambridge Computer Lab. *Publications:* guest ed. and contrib. on selected areas in communication to IEEE Jl. *Address:* Christ's College, Cambridge CB2 3BU.

LESLIE, James Bolton, AC 1993 (AO 1984); MC 1944; ED 1966; Chancellor, Deakin University, 1987–96; *b* 27 Nov. 1922; *s* of Stuart Deacon Leslie and Dorothy Clare (*née* Murphy); *m* 1955, Alison Baker three *s* one *d*. *Educ:* Trinity Grammar Sch., Melbourne; Harvard Business Sch., Boston, USA. Served war, Australian Infantry, Pacific Theatre, 1941–46. Mobil Oil Australia Ltd: joined, 1946; Manager, Fiji, 1947–50; various postings, Australia, 1950–59; Mobil Corp., New York, 1959–61; Gen. Manager, New South Wales, 1961–66; Director, Mobil Australia, 1966–68; Chm. and Chief Exec., Mobil New Zealand, 1968–72; Chairman: Mobil Australia and Pacific, 1972–80; Qantas Airways, 1980–89; Christies Australia Ltd, 1990–95; Boral Ltd, 1991–94. Chm., Corps of Commissionaires Aust Ltd, 1991–; Dep. Chm., Equity Trustees, 1990–97. Hon. LLD Deakin, 1997. *Recreations:* golf, gardening, art collecting. *Address:* 42 Grey Street, East Melbourne, Victoria 3002, Australia. *T:* (3) 94196149. *Clubs:* Melbourne, Melbourne Cricket, Beefsteak, Victoria Racing (Melbourne).

LESLIE, John; *see* Leslie, H. J.

LESLIE, Sir John (Norman Ide), 4th Bt *cr* 1876; *b* 6 Dec. 1916; *s* of Sir (John Randolph) Shane Leslie, 3rd Bt and Marjorie (*d* 1951), *y d* of Henry C. Ide, Vermont, USA; *S* father, 1971. *Educ:* Downside; Magdalene College, Cambridge (BA 1938). Captain, Irish Guards; served War of 1939–45 (prisoner-of-war). Kt of Honour and Devotion, SMO Malta, 1947; KCSG 1958. *Recreations:* ornithology, ecology. *Heir: nephew* Shaun Rudolph Christopher Leslie [*b* 4 June 1947; *m* 1987, Charlotte Bing (marr. diss. 1989)]. *Address:* Glaslough, Co. Monaghan, Ireland. *Clubs:* Travellers; Circolo della Caccia (Rome).

LESLIE, Rt Rev. Kenneth; *see* Leslie, Rt Rev. E. K.

LESLIE, Mariot; *see* Leslie, A. M.

LESLIE, Sir Peter (Evelyn), Kt 1991; Chairman, Commonwealth Development Corporation, 1989–95; *b* 24 March 1931; *s* of late Patrick Holt Leslie, DSc and Evelyn (*née* de Berry); *m* 1975, Charlotte, former wife of W. N. Wenban-Smith, *qv* and *d* of Sir Edwin Chapman-Andrews, KCMG, OBE and of Lady Chapman-Andrews; two step *s* two step *d*. *Educ:* Dragon Sch., Oxford; Stowe Sch.; New Coll., Oxford (Exhibnr; MA). Commnd Argyll and Sutherland Highlanders, 1951; served 7th Bn (TA), 1952–56. Entered Barclays Bank DCO, 1955; served in Sudan, Algeria, Zaire, Kenya and the Bahamas, 1956–71; Gen. Manager, Barclays Bank and Barclays Bank Internat., 1973–81, Sen. Gen. Manager, 1981–84; Dir, 1980–91, Chief Gen. Man., 1985–87, Man. Dir, 1987–88, Dep. Chm., 1987–91, Barclays Bank plc. Dep. Chm., Midland Bank plc, 1991–92; Chm., NCM Credit Insurance Ltd, 1995–98; Mem., Supervisory Bd, NCM Holding NV, 1995–2000. Mem., Bd of Banking Supervision, Bank of England, 1989–94. Chm., Export Guarantees Adv. Council, 1987–92 (Mem., 1978–81, Dep. Chm., 1986–87); Mem., Matthews Cttee on ECGD, 1983. Chairman: Exec. Cttee, British Bankers Assoc., 1978–79; Cttee, London and Scottish Clearing Bankers, 1986–88; Overseas Develt Inst., 1988–95. Member: Council for Ind. and Higher Educn, 1987–91; CARE Britain Bd, 1988–95; Council, RIIA, 1991–97; Ranfurly Liby Service, 1991–94. Chm. Council, Queen's Coll., London, 1989–94; Curator of Univ. Chest, Oxford, 1990–95; Chm., Audit Cttee, Oxford Univ., 1992–2001. Governor: Stowe Sch., 1983–2001 (Chm., 1994–2001); National Inst. of Social Work, 1973–83. *Recreations:* natural history, historical research.

LESLIE, Stephen Windsor; QC 1993; *b* 21 April 1947; *s* of Leslie Leonard Leslie and Celia Leslie (*née* Schulsinger); *m* 1st, 1974, Bridget Caroline Oldham (marr. diss. 1989); two *d*; 2nd, 1989, Amrit Kumari Mangra; one *s*. *Educ:* Brighton Coll.; King's Coll. London (LLB). Called to the Bar, Lincoln's Inn, 1971. Liveryman, Feltmakers' Co., 1998–. *Publications:* articles in The Times and New Law Jl. *Recreations:* Spanish sun, gardening, haggling for a bargain, the telephone. *Address:* 32 Furnival Street, EC4A 1JQ. *Clubs:* Carlton; Thunderers'.

LESLIE MELVILLE, family name of **Earl of Leven and Melville**.

LESOURNE, Jacques François; Officier de la Légion d'Honneur, 1993; Commandeur de l'ordre National de Mérite, 1981; Officier des Palmes Académiques, 1995; Directeur-gérant, Le Monde, 1991–94; Professor of Economics, Conservatoire National des Arts et Métiers, since 1974; *b* 26 Dec. 1928; *s* of André Lesourne and Simone Guille; *m* 1961, Odile Melin; one *s* two *d* (and one *s* decd). *Educ:* Ecole Polytechnique; Ecole Nationale Supérieure des Mines, Paris. Head, Econ. Dept, French Coal Mines, 1954–57; Directeur général, later Pres., SEMA, 1958–75; Dir, Interfutures Project, OECD, 1976–79. Pres., Internat. Fedn of OR Socs, 1986–88; Vice-President: Internat. Inst. for Applied Systems Analysis, 1973–79; Centre for European Policy Studies, 1987–93; Member Council: Inst. of Management Science, 1976–79; Eur. Econ. Assoc., 1984–89; Mem., Applications Cttee, Acad. des Scis, Paris, 1999–. Harold Lander Prize, Canadian OR Soc., 1991. *Publications:* Technique économique et gestion industrielle, 1958 (Economic Technique and Industrial Management, 1962); Le Calcul économique, 1964; Du bon usage de l'étude économique dans l'entreprise, 1966; (jtly) Matière grise année O, 1970 (The Management Revolution, 1971); Le Calcul économique, théorie et applications, 1972 (Cost-Benefit Analysis and Economic Theory, 1975); Modèles économiques de croissance de l'entreprise, 1972; (jtly) Une Nouvelle industrie: la matière grise, 1973; Les Systèmes de destin, 1976; A Theory of the Individual for Economic Analysis, 1977; (jtly) L'Analyse des décisions d'aménagement regional, 1979; Demain la France dans le monde, 1980; Les Mille Sentiers de l'avenir, 1982 (World Perspectives—a European Assessment, 1982); (jtly) Facilitating Development in a Changing Third World, 1983; Soirs et lendemains de fête: journal d'un homme tranquille, 1981–84 (autobiog.), 1984; (jtly) La gestion des villes, analyse des décisions d'économie urbaine, 1985; (jtly) La Fin des habitudes, 1985; L'Entreprise et ses futurs, 1985; L'après-Communisme, de l'Atlantique à l'Oural, 1990 (After-communism, from the Atlantic to the Urals, 1991); L'economie de l'ordre et du désordre, 1991 (The Economics of Order and Disorder, 1992); Vérités et mensonges sur le chômage, 1995; Le modèle français, grandeur et décadence, 1998; Un homme de notre siècle, 2000. *Recreation:* piano. *Address:* 52 rue de Vaugirard, 75006 Paris, France.

LESSELS, Norman, CBE 1993; Chairman, Cairn Energy PLC, since 1991 (Director, since 1988); *b* 2 Sept. 1938; *s* of John Clark Lessels and Gertrude Margaret Ellen Lessels (*née* Jack); *m* 1st, 1960, Gillian Durward Lessels (*née* Clark) (*d* 1979); one *s* (and one *s* one *d* decd); 2nd, 1981, Christine Stevenson Lessels (*née* Hitchman). *Educ:* Melville Coll.; Edinburgh Acad. CA (Scotland) 1961. CA apprentice with Graham Smart & Annan, Edinburgh, 1955–60; with Thomson McLintock & Co., London, 1960–61; Partner, Wallace & Somerville, Edinburgh, merged with Whinney Murray & Co., 1969, latterly Ernst & Whinney, 1962–80; Partner, 1980–93, Sen. Partner, 1993–98, Chiene & Tait, CA. Director: Standard Life Assurance Co., 1978–2002 (Dep. Chm., 1982–88; Chm., 1988–98); Scottish Eastern Investment Trust, 1980–99; Bank of Scotland, 1988–97; Havelock Europa, 1989–98 (Chm., 1993–98); Robert Wiseman Dairies, 1994–; Martin Currie Portfolio Investment Trust, 1999–2001. Pres., Inst. of Chartered Accountants of Scotland, 1987–88. *Recreations:* golf, bridge, music. *Address:* 11 Forres Street, Edinburgh EH3 6BJ. *T:* (0131) 225 5596. *Clubs:* New (Edinburgh); Hon. Company of Edinburgh Golfers, Royal & Ancient Golf.

LESSING, Charlotte; Editor of Good Housekeeping, 1973–87; freelance writer; *b* 14 May; *m* 1948, Walter B. Lessing (*d* 1989); three *d*. *Educ:* Henrietta Barnet Sch.; evening classes. Univ. of London Dipl. Eng. Lit. Journalism and public relations: New Statesman and Nation; Royal Society of Medicine; Lilliput (Hulton Press); Notley Public Relations; Good Housekeeping: Dep. Editor, 1964–73; Editor, 1973–87; Editor-in-Chief, Country Living, 1985–86. PPA Editor of the Year, 1982; Wine Writer of the Year, Wine Guild/Taittinger, 1995. Chevalier, Ordre du Mérit Agricole (France), 1996. *Publications:* short stories, travel and feature articles; monthly wine page in The Lady. *Address:* 2 Roseneath Road, SW11 6AH.

LESSING, Mrs Doris (May), CH 2000; CLit 2001; author; *b* Persia, 22 Oct. 1919; *d* of Captain Alfred Cook Tayler and Emily Maude McVeagh; lived in Southern Rhodesia, 1924–49; *m* 1st, 1939, Frank Charles Wisdom (marr. diss. 1943); one *s* one *d*; 2nd, 1945, Gottfried Anton Nicholas Lessing (marr. diss. 1949); one *s*. Associate Member: AAAL, 1974; Nat. Inst. of Arts and Letters (US), 1974. Mem., Inst. for Cultural Res., 1974. Hon. Fellow, MLA (Amer.), 1974. Hon. DLitt: Princeton, 1989; Durham, 1990; Warwick, 1994; Bard Coll., NY State, 1994; Harvard, 1995; London, 1999. Austrian State Prize for European Literature, 1981; Shakespeare Prize, Hamburg, 1982; Grinzane Cavour Award, Italy, 1989; Premio Internacional, Cataluña, 1999; David Cohen British Lit. Prize, 2001; Prince of Asturias Prize, 2001. *Publications:* The Grass is Singing, 1950 (filmed 1981); This Was the Old Chief's Country, 1951; Martha Quest, 1952; Five, 1953 (Somerset Maugham Award, Soc. of Authors, 1954); A Proper Marriage, 1954; Retreat to Innocence, 1956; Going Home, 1957; The Habit of Loving (short stories), 1957; A Ripple from the Storm, 1958; Fourteen Poems, 1959; In Pursuit of the English, 1960 (adapted for stage, 1990); The Golden Notebook, 1962 (Prix Médicis 1976 for French trans., Carnet d'or); A Man and Two Women (short stories), 1963; African Stories, 1964; Landlocked, 1965; The Four-Gated City, 1969; Briefing for a Descent into Hell, 1971; The Story of a Non-Marrying Man (short stories), 1972; The Summer Before the Dark, 1973; The Memoirs of a Survivor, 1975 (filmed 1981); Collected Stories: Vol. I, To Room Nineteen, 1978; Vol. II, The Temptation of Jack Orkney, 1978; Canopus in Argos: Archives: Re Planet 5, Shikasta, 1979; The Marriages Between Zones Three, Four and Five, 1980; The Sirian Experiments, 1981; The Making of the Representative for Planet 8, 1982 (libretto, 1988); The Sentimental Agents in the Volyen Empire, 1983; The Diaries of Jane Somers, 1984 (Diary of a Good Neighbour, 1983; If the Old Could . . . , 1984; published under pseudonym Jane Somers); The Good Terrorist, 1985 (W. H. Smith Literary Award, 1986; Palermo Prize and Premio Internazionale Mondello, 1987); The Fifth Child, 1988; Doris Lessing Reader, 1990; London Observed (short stories), 1992; Love, Again, 1996; Playing the Game, 1996; Mara and Dann: an adventure, 1999; Ben, in the World, 2000; The Sweetest Dream, 2001; *non-fiction:* Going Home, 1957; Particularly Cats, 1966, rev. edn as Particularly Cats and More Cats, 1990; Prisons We Choose to Live Inside, 1986; The Wind Blows Away Our Words, 1987; African Laughter: four visits to Zimbabwe, 1992; Under My Skin: volume one of my autobiography to 1949, 1994 (James Tait Black Meml Prize, 1995; LA Times Book Prize, 1995); A Small Personal Voice, 1994; Walking in the Shade: volume two of my autobiography 1949–1962, 1997; *play:* play with a Tiger, 1962. *Address:* c/o Jonathan Clowes Ltd, Iron Bridge House, Bridge Approach, NW1 8BD.

LESSOF, Leila, OBE 2000; FRCP, FFPHM; Chairman, Moorfields Eye Hospital NHS Trust, 1998–2001; *b* 4 June 1932; *d* of Lionel Liebster and Renée (*née* Segalov); *m* 1960, Maurice Hart Lessof, *qv*; one *s* two *d*. *Educ:* Queen's Coll., Harley St; Royal Free Hosp. Sch. of Medicine (MB BS; DMRD). FFPHM 1986; FRCP 2000. Jun. posts, Royal Free Hosp., London Hosp. and UCH; Consultant Radiologist and Clinical Tutor, Hackney Hosp., 1964–78; Registrar in Public Health Medicine, KCH and Guy's Hosp., 1978–82; Director of Public Health: Islington HA, 1982–90; Kensington, Chelsea and Westminster HA, 1990–95; Chm., Westminster Assoc. for Mental Health, 1995–98. *Recreations:* opera, theatre, travel. *Address:* 8 John Spencer Square, N1 2LZ. *T:* (020) 7226 0919.

LESSOF, Prof. Maurice Hart, MD; FRCP; Professor of Medicine, University of London at United Medical and Dental Schools (Guy's Hospital), 1971–89, now Emeritus; *b* 4 June 1924; *s* of Noah and Fanny Lessof; *m* 1960, Leila Liebster (*see* L. Lessof); one *s* two *d*. *Educ:* City of London Sch.; King's Coll., Cambridge (MA 1945; MD 1956). Appts on junior staff of Guy's Hosp., Canadian Red Cross Memorial Hosp., Johns Hopkins Hosp., etc; Clinical Immunologist and Physician, Guy's Hosp., 1967. Chairman: SE Thames Regl Med. Audit Cttee, 1990–91; Lewisham NHS Trust, 1993–97 (Dep. Chm., Guy's and Lewisham NHS Trust, 1991–93); Royal Hospitals NHS Trust, 1998–99. Adviser on Allergy, DHSS, 1982–91. Vice-Pres. and Sen. Censor, RCP, 1987–88; Past Pres., British Soc. for Allergy. Mem. Senate, London Univ., 1981–85. Mem., Johns Hopkins Soc. of Scholars, 1991. *Publications:* (ed) Immunological Aspects of Cardiovascular Diseases, 1981; (ed) Immunological and Clinical Aspects of Allergy, 1984 (Spanish and Portuguese edns, 1987); (ed) Clinical Reactions to Food, 1983; (ed) Allergy: an international textbook, 1987; Food Intolerance, 1992 (Spanish edn 1996); Food Allergy: issues for the food industry, 1997. *Recreations:* sculpting, painting. *Address:* 8 John Spencer Square, Canonbury, N1 2LZ. *T:* (020) 7226 0919, *Fax:* (020) 7354 8913. *Club:* Athenæum.

LESTER, family name of **Baron Lester of Herne Hill**.

LESTER OF HERNE HILL, Baron *cr* 1993 (Life Peer), of Herne Hill in the London Borough of Southwark; **Anthony Paul Lester;** QC 1975; QC (NI); a Recorder, 1987–93; *b* 3 July 1936; *e s* of Harry and Kate Lester; *m* 1971, Catherine Elizabeth Debora Wassey; one *s* one *d*. *Educ:* City of London Sch.; Trinity Coll., Cambridge (Exhibnr) (BA); Harvard Law Sch. (Harkness Commonwealth Fund Fellowship) (LLM). Served RA, 1955–57, 2nd Lieut. Called to Bar, Lincoln's Inn, 1963 (Mansfield scholar), Bencher, 1985; called to Bar of N Ireland, 1984; Irish Bar, 1983. Special Adviser to: Home Secretary, 1974–76; Standing Adv. Commn on Human Rights, 1975–77; UK Legal Expert, Network Cttee on Equal Pay and Sex Discrimination, EEC, 1983–93. Mem., H of L Sub-Cttees on European Law and Institutions, Inter-Govtl Conf. 1996–, Procedure, and Social Affairs, Educn and Home Affairs; Mem., Parly Jt Human Rights Commn, 2001–. Hon. Vis. Prof., UCL, 1983–. Lectures: Owen J. Roberts, Univ. of Pennsylvania Law Sch., 1976; F. A. Mann, London, 1983; Rubin, Columbia Law Sch., 1988; Street, Manchester, 1993; Lionel Cohen, Hebrew Univ. of Jerusalem, 1994; Stephen Lawrence, London, 2000; Thomas More, and Denning Soc., Lincoln's Inn, 2000. Mem., Bd of Overseers, Univ. of Pennsylvania Law Sch., 1978–89. Pres., Interights, 1991–; Chm., Runnymede Trust, 1991–93 (Trustee, 1969–); Member: Internat. Law Assoc. Cttee on Human Rights; Amer. Law Inst., 1985–; Bd of Dirs, Salzburg Seminar; Internat. Adv. Bd, Open Soc. Inst., 2000–; Co-Chm., Exec. Bd, European Roma Rights Center, Budapest, 1999–; Council and Exec. Cttee, Justice; Adv. Bd, Inst. of European Public Law, Hull Univ. Governor, British Inst. of Human Rights. Mem. Adv. Cttee, Centre for Public Law, Univ of Cambridge, 1999–; Mem., Bd of Govs, James Allen's Girls' Sch., 1984–94 (Chm., 1987–91); Governor, Westminster Sch., 1998–. Mem. Editl Bd, Public Law. *Publications:* Justice in the American South, 1964 (Amnesty Internat.); (co-ed.) Shawcross and Beaumont on Air Law, 3rd edn, 1964; (co-author) Race and Law, 1972; (ed) Constitutional Law and Human Rights, 1996; (co-ed) Human Rights Law and Practice, 1999; contributor to: British Nationality, Immigration and Race Relations, in Halsbury's Laws of England, 4th edn, 1973, repr. 1992; The Changing Constitution (ed Jowell and Oliver), 1985, 3rd edn 1994. *Address:* Blackstone Chambers, Blackstone House, Temple, EC4Y 9BW. *T:* (020) 7583 1770.

LESTER, Sir James Theodore, (Sir Jim), Kt 1996; adviser on parliamentary and government affairs; *b* 23 May 1932; *s* of Arthur Ernest and Marjorie Lester; *m* (marr. diss. 1989); two *s*; *m* 1989. *Educ:* Nottingham High School. Mem. Notts CC, 1967–74. MP (C) Beeston, Feb. 1974–1983, Broxtowe, 1983–97; contested (C) Broxtowe, 1997. An Opposition Whip, 1976–79; Parly Under-Sec. of State, Dept of Employment, 1979–81. Mem., Select Cttee on Foreign affairs, 1982–97; Vice-Chm., All Party Gp on overseas devolt, 1983–97. Deleg. to Council of Europe and WEU, 1975–76. *Recreations:* reading, music, motor racing, travelling. *Address:* 4 Trevose House, Orsett Street, SE11 5PN.

LESTER, Paul John; Group Managing Director, Balfour Beatty plc, since 1997; *b* 20 Sept. 1949; *s* of John Trevor Lester and late Joyce Ethel Lester; *m* 1973, Valerie Osbourn (separated); one *s* one *d*; partner, Karen Lester (*née* White); one *d*. *Educ:* Trent Poly. (BSc (Hons) Mech. Engrg; Dip Mgt Studies (Distinction)). Sen. Management, Dowty Group, 1968–80; Gen. Management, Schlumberger, UK, France, USA, 1980–87; Man. Dir, Defense & Air Systems, Dowty Gp, 1987–90; Chief Exec., Graseby plc, 1990–97. Chm., A & P Gp, 1993–99; Dir, Vosper Thornycroft, 1998–. Mem., Adv. Bd, Alchemy Partners Ltd, 1997–. Pres., EEF, 2000– (Sen. Dep. Pres., 1999–2000; Chm., Economic Policy Cttee, 1993–2000). Gov., Barnet Coll. of Further Educn, 1993–. *Recreations:* tennis, weight training, running, football; life-long West Bromwich Albion supporter. *Address:* Balfour Beatty plc, 130 Wilton Road, SW1V 1LQ.

LESTER, Richard; film director; *b* 19 Jan. 1932; *s* of Elliott and Ella Young Lester; *m* 1956, Deirdre Vivian Smith; one *s* one *d*. *Educ:* Wm Penn Charter Sch.; University of Pennsylvania (BSc). Television Director: CBS (USA), 1951–54; AR (Dir TV Goon Shows), 1956. Directed The Running, Jumping and Standing Still Film (Acad. Award nomination; 1st prize San Francisco Festival, 1960). *Feature Films directed:* It's Trad, Dad, 1962; Mouse on the Moon, 1963; A Hard Day's Night, 1964; The Knack, 1964 (Grand Prix, Cannes Film Festival); Help, 1965 (Best Film Award and Best Dir Award, Rio de Janeiro Festival); A Funny Thing Happened on the Way to the Forum, 1966; How I won the War, 1967; Petulia, 1968; The Bed Sitting Room, 1969 (Gandhi Peace Prize, Berlin Film Festival); The Three Musketeers, 1973; Juggernaut, 1974 (Best Dir award, Teheran Film Fest.); The Four Musketeers, 1974; Royal Flash, 1975; Robin and Marian, 1976; The Ritz, 1976; Butch and Sundance: the early days, 1979; Cuba, 1979; Superman II, 1981; Superman III, 1983; Finders Keepers, 1984; The Return of the Musketeers, 1989; Get Back, 1991. *Recreations:* music, tennis. *Address:* Twickenham Film Studios, St Margaret's, Twickenham, Mddx TW1 2AW.

LESTER SMITH, Ernest; *see* Smith, E. L.

L'ESTRANGE, Michael Gerard; High Commissioner for Australia in the United Kingdom, since 2000; *b* 12 Oct. 1952; *m* 1983, Jane Allen; five *s*. *Educ:* St Aloysius Coll., Sydney; Univ. of Sydney (BA Hons); Oxford Univ. (NSW Rhodes Schol., 1976–79; BA 1st Cl. Hons, MA). Dept of Prime Minister and Cabinet, Canberra, 1981–89; Harkness Fellow, Georgetown Univ. and Univ. of Calif, Berkeley, 1987–89; Sen. Advr, Office of Leader of Opposition, 1989–95; Exec. Dir, Menzies Res. Centre, Canberra, 1995–96; Sec. to Cabinet, and Hd, Cabinet Policy Unit, 1996–2000. *Recreations:* cricket, Rugby, golf. *Address:* Australian High Commission, Australia House, Strand, WC2B 4LA. *T:* (020) 2887 5220.

LETH, Air Vice-Marshal David Richard H.; *see* Hawkins-Leth.

LETHBRIDGE, Sir Thomas (Periam Hector Noel), 7th Bt *cr* 1804; *b* 17 July 1950; *s* of Sir Hector Wroth Lethbridge, 6th Bt, and of Evelyn Diana, *d* of late Lt-Col Francis Arthur Gerard Noel, OBE; *S* father, 1978; *m* 1976, Susan Elizabeth Rocke (marr. diss. 1998); four *s* two *d*. *Educ:* Milton Abbey. Studied farming, Cirencester Agricultural Coll., 1969–70; Man. Dir, Art Gallery, Dorset and London, 1972–77; also fine art specialist in sporting paintings and engravings. *Recreations:* shooting, swimming. *Heir:* *s* John Francis Buckler Noel Lethbridge, *b* 10 March 1977.

LETTS, Anthony Ashworth; President, Charles Letts Group, 1994–96 (Chairman, Charles Letts Holdings Ltd, 1977–94); *b* 3 July 1935; *s* of Leslie Charles Letts and Elizabeth Mary (*née* Gibson); *m* 1962, Rosa Maria Ciarrapico; one *s* one *d*. *Educ:* Marlborough Coll.; Cambridge Univ. (MAEcon); Yale Univ. (Industrial Admin). National Service, RE, 2 Lieut, 1954–56. Joined Charles Letts & Co. Ltd, 1960; Man. Dir, 1965 (Charles Letts family business founded by John Letts (g g g grandfather), 1796). Director: Cambridge Market Intelligence, 1994–; Accademia Club Ltd, 1996–; EA Restaurart Ltd, 1999–. Gov., Westminster Kingsway (formerly Westminster) Coll., London, 1993–. *Recreations:* tennis, sailing, hill walking, theatre. *Address:* 2 The Towers, Soberton, Hants SO32 3PS. *T:* (01489) 877684. *Club:* Hurlingham.

LETTS, John Campbell Bonner, OBE 1980; Founder and Chairman, Trollope Society, since 1987; *b* 18 Nov. 1929; *s* of C. Francis C. Letts and Ereleen F. C. Letts; *m* 1957, Sarah, *d* of E. Brian O'Rorke, RA; three *s* one *d*. *Educ:* Oakley Hall, Cirencester; Haileybury Coll.; Jesus Coll., Cambridge (English Schol.; BA 1953). Trainee, S. H. Benson, 1954–59; Publicity Manager, Penguin Books, 1959; Copywriter, J. Walter Thompson, 1960–64; General Manager: Sunday Times Publications, 1964–66; Book Club Associates, 1966–69; Mktg Dir, Hutchinsons, 1969–71; Jt Chm. (Editorial and Mktg), Folio Soc., 1971–87. Founder Trustee, Empire Mus., 1987–; Founder and Dir, Earth Centre, Doncaster, 1988–; Chairman: Nat. Heritage, 1971–98 (Life Pres., 1999); Empire Museum Ltd, 1989–; European Museums Trust, 1994–. FRSA. *Publication:* A Little Treasury of Limericks, 1975. *Recreations:* buying plants, walking in Scotland, listening to music, reading, keeping in touch with the past. *Address:* 83 West Side, Clapham Common, SW4 9AY. *T:* (020) 7228 9448. *Club:* Reform.

LETTS, Melinda Jane Frances; charity and health policy consultant, since 1998; *b* 6 April 1956; *d* of Richard Letts and Jocelyn (*née* Adami); *m* 1991, Neil Scott Wishart McIntosh, *qv*; one *s* one *d*. *Educ:* Wycombe Abbey; Cheltenham Coll.; St Anne's Coll., Oxford (BA Hons, Lit Hum Cl. I). Theatre Jobs, 1978–80; Res. Asst, Brunel Univ., 1980–81; Head of Admin, CND, 1982–84, VSO, 1985–87; Prog. Funding Manager, 1987, Regl Prog. Manager, ME and S Asia, 1987–89, VSO; Staffing Manager, McKinsey & Co., 1989–91; Dep. Dir, 1991–92, Dir, later Chief Exec., 1992–98, Nat. Asthma Campaign. Chm., Long Term Medical Conditions Alliance, 1998–; Member: Commn for Health Improvement, 1999–; NHS Modernisation Bd, 2000–. Trustee: NCVO, 1997–; Comic Relief, 1998–; Member: Exec. Cttee, Tobacco Control Alliance, 1997–98; Bd, New Opportunities Fund, 1998–2001. Mem. Council, Cheltenham Coll., 1990–93; Governor, Oakley Hall Sch., Cirencester, 1993–94. Mem., ACENVO, 1992–98. MIMgt 1992. *Recreations:* reading, knitting, tapestry, photography. *Address:* *e-mail:* melindaletts@dial.pipex.com.

LETTS, Quentin Richard Stephen; freelance journalist; Parliamentary Sketchwriter, Daily Mail, since 2000; *b* 6 Feb. 1963; *s* of Richard Francis Bonner Letts and Jocelyn Elizabeth Letts (*née* Adami); *m* 1996, Lois Henrietta, *d* of Patrick and Marion Rathbone; one *s* one *d*. *Educ:* Haileybury; Bellarmine Coll., Kentucky; Trinity Coll., Dublin (BA); Jesus Coll., Cambridge (Dip. Classical Archaeol.). Writer, specialist pubns, Cardiff, 1987; Daily Telegraph, 1988–95: City Diarist, 1989–90; NY Corresp., 1991; Ed., Peterborough Column, 1991–95; NY Bureau Chief, The Times, 1995–97; Parly Sketchwriter, Daily

Telegraph, 1997–2000. *Recreations:* gossip, character defenestration. *Address:* Scrubs' Bottom, Bisley, Glos GL6 7BU. *T:* (01452) 813899. *Club:* Savile.
See also M. J. F. Letts.

LETWIN, Dr Oliver; MP (C) West Dorset, since 1997; *b* 19 May 1956; *s* of Prof. William Letwin, *qv*; *m* 1984, Isabel Grace Davidson; one *s* one *d*. *Educ:* Eton Coll.; Trinity Coll., Cambridge (BA, MA, PhD 1982). Vis. Fellow, Princeton Univ., 1981; Research Fellow, Darwin Coll., Cambridge, 1982–83; Special Advr, DES, 1982–83; Mem., Prime Minister's Policy Unit, 1983–86; with N. M. Rothschild & Sons Ltd, 1986– (Dir, 1991–). Opposition front-bench spokesman on constitutional affairs, 1998–99, on Treasury affairs, 1999–2000; Shadow Chief Sec. to HM Treasury, 2000–01; Shadow Home Sec., 2001–. FRSA 1991. *Publications:* Ethics, Emotion and the Unity of the Self, 1984; Aims of Schooling, 1985; Privatising the World, 1987; Drift to Union, 1990; The Purpose of Politics, 1999; numerous articles in learned and popular jls. *Recreations:* ski-ing, tennis, walking. *Address:* House of Commons, SW1A 0AA. *T:* (020) 7219 3000. *Club:* St Stephen's Constitutional.

LETWIN, Prof. William; Professor Emeritus, London School of Economics, since 1988; *b* 14 Dec. 1922; *s* of Lazar and Bessie Letwin; *m* 1944, Shirley Robin (*d* 1993); one *s*. *Educ:* Univ. of Chicago (BA 1943, PhD 1951); London Sch. of Economics (1948–50). Served US Army, 1943–46. Postdoctoral Fellow, Economics Dept, Univ. of Chicago, 1951–52; Research Associate, Law Sch., Univ. of Chicago, 1953–55; Asst. Prof. of Industrial History, MIT, 1955–60; Associate Prof. of Economic History, MIT, 1960–67; Reader in Political Science, 1966–76, Prof. of Pol Science, 1976–88, LSE. Senior Advisor: Putnam, Hayes & Bartlett, 1988–96; Spectrum Strategy Consultants, 1996–97. Chm., Bd of Studies in Economics, Univ. of London, 1971–73. *Publications:* (ed) Frank Knight, on The History and Method of Economics, 1956; Sir Josiah Child, 1959; Documentary History of American Economic Policy, 1961, 2nd edn 1972; Origins of Scientific Economics 1660–1776, 1963; Law and Economic Policy in America, 1965; (ed) Against Equality, 1983; Freeing the Phones, 1991; articles in learned jls. *Address:* 255 Kennington Road, SE11 6BY.
See also O. Letwin.

LEUCHARS, Maj.-Gen. Peter Raymond, CBE 1966; Chief Commander, St John Ambulance, 1980–89 (Commissioner-in-Chief, 1978–80 and 1985–86); *b* 29 Oct. 1921; *s* of late Raymond Leuchars and Helen Inez Leuchars (*née* Copland-Griffiths); *m* 1953, Hon. Gillian Wightman Nivison, *d* of 2nd Baron Glendyne; one *s*. *Educ:* Bradfield College. Commnd in Welsh Guards, 1941; served in NW Europe and Italy, 1944–45; Adjt, 1st Bn Welsh Guards, Palestine, 1945–48; Bde Major, 4 Guards Bde, Germany, 1952–54; GSO1 (Instr.), Staff Coll., Camberley, 1956–59; GSO1 HQ 4 Div. BAOR, 1960–63; comd 1st Bn Welsh Guards, 1963–65; Principal Staff Off. to Dir of Ops, Borneo, 1965–66; comd 11 Armd Bde BAOR, 1966–68; comd Jt Operational Computer Projects Team, 1969–71; Dep. Comdt Staff Coll., Camberley, 1972–73; GOC Wales, 1973–76. Col, The Royal Welch Fusiliers, 1974–84. Pres., Guards' Golfing Soc., 1977–2001. Chairman: St John Fellowship, 1989–95 (Vice-Pres., 1996–); Lady Grover's Fund for Officers' Families, 1991–98. FRGS 1996. BGCStJ 1989. Order of Istiqlal (Jordan), 1946. *Recreations:* golf, shooting, travel, photography. *Address:* 5 Chelsea Square, SW3 6LF. *T:* (020) 7352 6187. *Clubs:* Royal and Ancient Golf; Royal Wimbledon Golf; Sunningdale Golf (Captain 1975).

LEUNG Kin Pong, Andrew; Director-General, Government Office of Hong Kong Special Administrative Region in United Kingdom, since 2000; *b* 13 Nov. 1945; *m* 1974, Peggy Fung Lin Tong; one *s* one *d*. *Educ:* BA (ext.) London; Wolfson Coll., Cambridge (postgrad. Dip. in Develt Studies); Harvard Univ. (PMD); Solicitor's qualifying certs, England and Hong Kong. Hong Kong Civil Service: Exec. Officer, then Sen. Exec. Officer, 1967–73; Asst Sec. for Security, 1973–75; Council Office, 1976–77; Asst Financial Sec., 1979–82; on secondment to Standard Chartered Bank, 1982–83; Counsellor (Hong Kong Affairs), Brussels, 1983–87; Dep. Dir-Gen. of Industry, 1987–91; Dep. Sec. for Transport, 1991–92; Police Admin Officer, 1994–96; Dir-Gen. of Social Welfare, 1996–2000. JP Hong Kong, 1989. *Recreations:* tennis, swimming, jogging, horse-riding, travelling, singing, reading, Chinese calligraphy. *Address:* 19 Cowley Street, SW1P 3LZ. *T:* (020) 7222 0635; (office) (020) 7290 8201; *e-mail:* andrewkpleung@hotmail.com. *Clubs:* Hurlingham; Hong Kong Jockey.

LEVEN, 14th Earl of, **AND MELVILLE,** 13th Earl of, *cr* 1641; **Alexander Robert Leslie Melville;** Baron Melville, 1616; Baron Balgonie, 1641; Earl of Melville, Viscount Kirkcaldie, 1690; Lord-Lieutenant of Nairn, 1969–99; *b* 13 May 1924; *e s* of 13th Earl and Lady Rosamond Sylvia Diana Mary Foljambe (*d* 1974), *d* of 1st Earl of Liverpool; *S* father, 1947; *m* 1953, Susan, *er d* of Lieut-Colonel R. Steuart-Menzies of Culdares, Arndilly House, Craigellachie, Banffshire; two *s* one *d*. *Educ:* Eton. ADC to Governor General of New Zealand, 1951–52. Formerly Capt. Coldstream Guards; retired, 1952. Vice-Pres., Highland Dist TA. Pres., British Ski Fedn, 1981–85. DL, County of Nairn, 1961; Convener, Nairn CC, 1970–74. Chm. Governors, Gordonstoun Sch., 1971–89. *Heir: s* Lord Balgonie, *qv*. *Address:* Raith, Old Spey Bridge, Grantown-on-Spey, Morayshire PH26 3NQ. *T:* (01479) 872908. *Club:* New (Edinburgh).

LEVENE, family name of **Baron Levene of Portsoken**.

LEVENE OF PORTSOKEN, Baron *cr* 1997 (Life Peer), of Portsoken, in the City of London; **Peter Keith Levene,** KBE 1989; JP; Vice Chairman, Deutsche Bank, since 2001 (Chairman, Investment Banking Europe, 1999–2001); *b* 8 Dec. 1941; *s* of late Maurice Levene and Rose Levene; *m* 1966, Wendy Ann (*née* Fraiman); two *s* one *d*. *Educ:* City of London School; Univ. of Manchester (BA Econ). Joined United Scientific Holdings, 1963; Man. Dir, 1968–85; Chm., 1982–85; Chief of Defence Procurement, MoD, 1985–91; UK Nat. Armaments Dir, 1988–91; Chm., European Nat. Armaments Dirs, 1989–90. Member: SE Asia Trade Adv. Group, 1979–83; Council, Defence Manufacturers' Assoc., 1982–85 (Vice-Chm., 1983–84; Chm., 1984–85); Citizen's Charter Adv. Panel, 1992–93; Personal Adviser to: Sec. of State for Defence, 1984; Sec. of State for the Envmt, 1991–92; Chancellor of the Exchequer on Competition and Purchasing, 1992; Pres. of BoT, 1992–95; Prime Minister on Efficiency and Effectiveness, 1992–97. Chairman: Docklands Light Railway Ltd, 1991–94; Bankers Trust Internat. plc, 1998–99; IFSL (formerly British Invisibles), 2000–; Dep. Chm., Wasserstein Perella & Co. Ltd, 1991–94; Chm. and Chief Exec., Canary Wharf Ltd, 1993–96; Director: Haymarket Gp Ltd, 1997–; J. Sainsbury plc, 2001–. Sen. Advr, Morgan Stanley & Co. Ltd, 1996–98. Member: Bd of Management, London Homes for the Elderly, 1984–93 (Chm., 1990–93); Internat. Adv. Bd, Singapore Govt Nat. Labs, 1998–99; Chairman's Council, Alcatel, 2000–. Governor: City of London Sch. for Girls, 1984–85; City of London Sch., 1986–; Sir John Cass Primary Sch., 1985–93 (Dep. Chm., 1990–93). Mem. Court, HAC, 1984–; Mem., Court of Common Council, City of London, 1983–84 (Ward of Candlewick); Alderman (Ward of Portsoken), 1984–; Sheriff, City of London, 1995–96; Lord Mayor of London, 1998–99; Liveryman, Carmen's Co., 1984– (Master, 1992–93). Hon. Col Comdt, RCT, 1991–93, RLC, 1993–. Fellow, QMW, 1995. CIMgt; FCIT; FCIPS. JP City of London, 1984. Hon. DSc City, 1998. KStJ 1998. Commandeur, Ordre National du Mérite (France), 1996; Kt Comdr, Order of Merit (Germany), 1998; Middle Cross, Order of Merit (Hungary), 1999. *Recreations:* ski-ing, watching association football, travel. *Address:* Deutsche Bank, 1 Great Winchester Street, EC2N 2DB. *Clubs:* Guildhall, City Livery, Royal Automobile.

LEVENE, Ben, RA 1986 (ARA 1975); painter; *b* 23 Dec. 1938; *s* of late Mark Levene and Charlotte (*née* Leapman); *m* 1st; two *d*; 2nd, 1978, Susan M. Williams. *Educ:* Slade School (DFA). Boise Scholarship, 1961; lived in Spain, 1961–62. Exhibited at: Thackeray Gall., 1973–81 (one man shows, 1973, 1975, 1978, 1981); Browse & Darby, London, 1986– (one man shows, 1986, 1988, 1993, 2001). Works in private and public collections. Curator, Royal Academy Schs, 1995–98. *Address:* c/o Royal Academy of Arts, Piccadilly, W1V 0DS.

LEVENE, Prof. Malcolm Irvin, MD; FRCP; Professor of Paediatrics and Child Health, since 1989, Chairman, Division of Paediatrics, since 1992, University of Leeds; *b* 2 Jan. 1951; *s* of Maurice Levene and Helen Levene (*née* Kutner); *m* 1st, 1972, Miriam Bentley (marr. diss. 1990); three *d*; 2nd, 1991, Susan Anne Cave; one *s* one *d*. *Educ:* Varndean Grammar Sch., Brighton; Guy's Hosp. Med. Sch., London Univ. (MB BS 1972); MD 1981. MRCS, LRCP, 1972; MRCP 1978; FRCP 1988. Junior posts at Royal Sussex, Northampton General and Charing Cross Hosps, 1974–77; Registrar, Derby Children's and Charing Cross Hosps, 1977–79; Res. Lectr, RPMS, Hammersmith Hosp., 1979–82; Sen. Lectr and Reader, Dept of Paediatrics, Univ. of Leicester, 1982–88; Med. Dir, Women's and Children's Subsidiary, Univ. of Leeds Teaching Hosp. NHS Trust, 1998–. Mem., DoH Nat. Adv. Body, Confidential Enquiry into Stillbirths and Deaths in Infancy, 1991. Chm., Scientific Adv. Cttee, Action Res., 1994–97. Hancock Prize, RCS, 1974; British Paediatric Association: Donald Paterson Prize, 1982; Michael Blecklow Meml Prize, 1982; Guthrie Medal, 1987; Ronnie MacKeith Prize, British Paed. Neurology Assoc., 1984; BUPA Res. Prize, 1988. *Publications:* (with H. Nutbeam) A Handbook for Examinations in Paediatrics, 1981; (jtly) Ultrasound of the Infant Brain, 1985; (jtly) Essentials of Neonatal Medicine, 1987, 2nd edn 1993; (ed jtly) Fetal and Neonatal Neurology and Neurosurgery, 1988, 2nd edn 1995; Diseases of Children, 6th edn, 1990; Paediatrics and Child Health, 1999; chapters in books and articles in learned jls on paed. topics, esp. neurology of new-born. *Recreations:* music, occasional gentle golf and gardening. *Address:* Acacia House, Acacia Park Drive, Apperley Bridge, W Yorks BD10 0PH. *T:* (0113) 250 9959.

LEVENSON, Howard; Social Security Commissioner and Child Support Commissioner, since 1997; *b* 4 Dec. 1949; *s* of Albert and Marlene Levenson; *m* 1971, Ros Botsman; one *s* one *d*. *Educ:* Tottenham Grammar Sch.; Univ. of Sheffield (BJur Hons 1970; LLM 1972); Coll. of Law, London. Admitted solicitor, 1974; Legal Officer, NCCL, 1974–77; Law Lectr, Poly., then Univ., of E London, 1977–92; Consultant, Nash and Dowell (Solicitors), 1981–91; part-time Chm., Tribunals, 1986–92; Chm., Independent Tribunal Service, 1993–97. Chm., Haldane Soc., 1980–83. *Publications:* The Price of Justice, 1981; (jtly) Social Welfare Law: Legal Aid and Advice, 1985; (jtly) Police Powers, 1985, 3rd edn 1996; contrib. vols of Atkin's Court Forms on Child Support, Judicial Review, Personal Rights, Social Security; contrib. to Modern Law Rev., Criminal Law Rev., New Law Jl, etc. *Address:* (office) Harp House, 83–86 Farringdon Street, EC4A 4DH. *Club:* Leyton Orient Football.

LEVENTHAL, Colin David; Director, HAL Films Ltd, since 2000; *b* 2 Nov. 1946; *s* of Morris and Olga Leventhal. *Educ:* Carmel Coll., Wallingford, Berks; King's Coll., Univ. of London (BA Philosophy). Solicitor of Supreme Court of England and Wales. Admitted Solicitor, 1971; BBC, 1974–81, Head of Copyright, 1978; Head of Prog. Acquisition, Channel Four TV, 1981–87; Dir of Acquisition and Sales, Channel Four TV Co., 1987–92 (Dir, 1988–92); Dir of Acquisition, Channel Four TV Corp., 1993–97; Man. Dir, Channel Four Internat. Ltd, 1993–97; Jt Chief Exec., Miramax HAL Films Ltd, 1998–2000. Mem., Film Council, 1999–. *Recreations:* theatre, film. *Address:* 10 Well Walk, Hampstead, NW3 1LD. *T:* (020) 7435 3038.

LEVER, Hon. Bernard Lewis; His Honour Judge Lever; a Circuit Judge, since 2001; *b* 1 Feb. 1951; *s* of Baron Lever and of Ray Rosalia, Lady Lever; *m* 1985, Anne Helen Ballingall, only *d* of Patrick Chandler Gordon Ballingall, MBE; two *d*. *Educ:* Clifton; Queen's Coll., Oxford (Neale Exhibnr; MA). Called to the Bar, Middle Temple, 1975; in practice, Northern Circuit, 1975–2001; Standing Counsel to Inland Revenue, 1997–2001. Co-founder, SDP in NW, 1981. Contested (SDP) Manchester Withington, 1983. *Recreations:* walking, music, fishing, picking up litter. *Address:* Manchester Crown Court, Minshull Street, Manchester M1 3FS. *T:* (0161) 954 7500. *Club:* Vincent's (Oxford).

LEVER, Sir Christopher; *see* Lever, Sir T. C. A. L.

LEVER, Jeremy Frederick; QC 1972; QC (NI) 1988; *b* 23 June 1933; *s* of late A. Lever. *Educ:* Bradfield Coll.; University Coll., Oxford; Nuffield Coll., Oxford. Served RA, 1951–53. 1st cl. Jurisprudence, 1956, MA Oxon; Pres., Oxford Union Soc., 1957, Trustee, 1972–77 and 1988–. Fellow, All Souls Coll., Oxford, 1957– (Sub-Warden, 1982–84; Sen. Dean, 1988–). Called to Bar, Gray's Inn, 1957, Bencher, 1985. Chairman: Oftel Adv. Body on Fair Trading in Telecommunications, 1996–2000; Appeals Panel, PRS, 1997–. Mem. Council, British Inst. of Internat. and Comparative Law, 1987–. Director (non-exec.): Dunlop Holdings Ltd, 1973–80; Wellcome plc, 1983–94. Mem., Arbitral Tribunal, US/UK Arbitration concerning Heathrow Airport User Charges, 1989–94. Vis. Prof., Wissenschaftszentrum, Berlin, für Sozialforschung, 1999. Lectures: Hamlyn, Hamlyn Trust, 1991; Lord Fletcher Meml, Law Soc., 1997; Grotius, British Inst. of Internat. and Comparative Law, 1998. Governor, Berkhamsted Schs, 1985–95. FRSA. *Publications:* The Law of Restrictive Practices, 1964; other legal works. *Recreations:* ceramics, music. *Address:* 26 John Street, WC1N 2BW. *T:* (020) 7831 0351, *Fax:* (020) 7405 1675; *e-mail:* chambers@monckton.co.uk. *Club:* Garrick.

LEVER, John Darcy, MA; Headmaster, Canford School, since 1992; *b* 14 Jan. 1952; *s* of Prof. Jeffrey Darcy Lever; *m* 1981, Alisoun Margaret Yule; one *s* two *d*. *Educ:* Westminster Sch.; Trinity Coll., Cambridge (MA); Christ Church, Oxford (Cert Ed). St Edward's Sch., Oxford, 1974–76; Winchester Coll., 1976–92. *Recreations:* walking, clocks, maps, visiting country houses. *Address:* Canford School, Wimborne, Dorset BH21 3AD. *T:* (01202) 882411.

LEVER, His Honour (John) Michael; QC 1977; a Circuit Judge, 1981–97; *b* 12 Aug. 1928; *s* of late John and Ida Donaldson Lever; *m* 1964, Elizabeth Marr (*d* 1998); two *s*. *Educ:* Bolton Sch.; Gonville and Caius Coll., Cambridge (Schol.). BA (1st cl. hons Law Tripos), 1949. Flying Officer, RAF, 1950–52. Called to Bar, Middle Temple, 1951 (Blackstone Schol.); practised Northern Circuit from 1952; Asst Recorder, Salford, 1969–71; a Recorder of the Crown Court, 1972–81. Vice-Chm., Governors, Bolton Sch. *Recreations:* theatre, books (watching) sport of all kinds. *Address:* Lakelands, Rivington, near Bolton, Lancs BL6 7RT. *T:* (01204) 468189.

LEVER, Sir Paul, KCMG 1998 (CMG 1991); HM Diplomatic Service; Ambassador to the Federal Republic of Germany, since 1997; *b* 31 March 1944; *s* of John Morrison Lever and Doris Grace (*née* Battey); *m* 1990, Patricia Anne, *d* of John and Anne Ramsey. *Educ:* St Paul's Sch.; The Queen's Coll., Oxford (MA). 3rd Secretary, Foreign and Commonwealth Office, 1966–67; 3rd, later 2nd Secretary, Helsinki, 1967–71; 2nd, later 1st Secretary, UK Delegn to NATO, 1971–73; FCO, 1973–81; Asst Private Sec. to Sec. of State for Foreign and Commonwealth Affairs, 1978–81; Chef de Cabinet to Christopher Tugendhat, Vice-Pres. of EEC, 1981–85; Head of UN Dept, FCO, 1985–86; Head of Defence Dept, 1986–87; Head of Security Policy Dept, FCO, 1987–90; Ambassador and Hd, UK Delegn to Conventional Arms Control Negotiations, Vienna, 1990–92; Asst Under-Sec. of State, FCO, 1992–94; Dep. Sec., Cabinet Office, and Chm., Jt Intelligence Cttee, 1994–96; Dep. Under-Sec. of State (Dir for EU and Economic Affairs), FCO, 1996–97. *Recreations:* walking, art deco pottery. *Address:* c/o Foreign and Commonwealth Office, SW1A 2AH.

LEVER, Sir (Tresham) Christopher (Arthur Lindsay), 3rd Bt *cr* 1911; *b* 9 Jan. 1932; *s* of Sir Tresham Joseph Philip Lever, FRSL, 2nd Bt, and Frances Yowart (*d* 1959), *d* of Lindsay Hamilton Goodwin; step *s* of Pamela Lady Lever, *d* of late Lt-Col Hon. Malcolm Bowes Lyon; *S* father, 1975; *m* 1st, 1970; 2nd, 1975, Linda Weightman McDowell, *d* of late James Jepson Goulden, Tennessee, USA. *Educ:* Eton; Trinity Coll., Cambridge (BA 1954, MA 1957). FLS. Commissioned, 17th/21st Lancers, 1950. Peat, Marwick, Mitchell & Co., 1954–55; Kitcat & Aitken, 1955–56; Dir, John Barran & Sons Ltd, 1956–64. Consultant: Zoo Check Charitable Trust, 1984–91; Born Free Foundn, 1991–; Chairman: African Fund for Endangered Wildlife (UK), 1987–90; UK Elephant Gp, 1991–92; Mem., IUCN Species Survival Commn, 1988–; Trustee: Internat. Trust for Nature Conservation, 1980–92 (Vice-Pres. 1986–91; Pres., 1991–92); Rhino Rescue Trust, 1986–91 (Patron 1985–); Chm. and Patron, Tusk Trust, 1990–; Chm., Ruaha Trust, 1990–95; Member Council: Soc. for Protection of Animals in N Africa, 1986–88; British Trust for Ornithology, 1988–91 (Chm., Nat. Centre Appeal, 1987–92); SOS Sahel Internat. (UK), 1995–; Dir, WSPA, 1998–; Mem., Council of Ambassadors, WWF-UK, 1999–; Patron: Lynx Educnl Trust for Animal Welfare, 1991–; Respect for Animals, 1995–. Hon. Life Mem., Brontë Soc., 1988. *Publications:* Goldsmiths and Silversmiths of England, 1975; The Naturalized Animals of the British Isles, 1977; (contrib.) Wildlife '80: the world conservation yearbook, 1980; (contrib.) Evolution of Domesticated Animals, 1984; Naturalized Mammals of the World, 1985; Naturalized Birds of the World, 1987; (contrib.) Beyond the Bars: the zoo dilemma, 1987; (contrib.) For the Love of Animals, 1989; The Mandarin Duck, 1990; They Dined on Eland: the story of the acclimatisation societies, 1992; (contrib.) The New Atlas of Breeding Birds in Britain and Ireland: 1988–1991, 1993; Naturalized Animals: the ecology of successfully introduced species, 1994; (contrib.) The Introduction and Naturalisation of Birds, 1996; Naturalized Fishes of the World, 1996; (contrib.) Stocking & Introduction of Fish, 1997; (contrib.) The EBCC Atlas of European Breeding Birds: their distribution and abundance, 1997; The Cane Toad: the history and ecology of a successful colonist, 2001; (contrib.) The Migration Atlas: movements of the birds of Britain and Ireland, 2001; contribs to art, scientific and general publications. *Recreations:* watching and photographing wildlife, golf, fishing. *Heir:* none. *Address:* Newell House, Winkfield, Berks SL4 4SE. *T:* (01344) 882604, *Fax:* (01344) 891744. *Clubs:* Boodle's; Swinley Forest Golf.

LEVERTON, Colin Allen H.; *see* Hart-Leverton.

LEVERTON, Roger Frank, FCA; Chairman: Haden MacLellan Holdings plc, since 1997; Infast Group plc, since 1997; Renold plc, since 1998; Betts Group Holdings Ltd, since 1998; *b* 22 April 1939; *s* of Frank Arthur Leverton and Lucia Jean Leverton (*née* Harden); *m* 1st, 1962, Patricia Jones (marr. diss.); one *s* one *d* (and one *d* decd); 2nd, 1992, Marilyn Williams. *Educ:* Haberdashers' Askes Sch. FCA 1962. Black & Decker Manufacturing Co., 1968–84: European Dir and Gen. Manager, France, 1978–81; Gp Vice-Pres., Southern Europe, 1981–84; Chief Exec., MK Electric Gp, subseq. Pillar Electrical plc, 1984–89; Pres. and Chief Exec., Indal Ltd (RTZ Corp. plc), 1989–92; Chief Exec., Pilkington plc, 1992–97. *Recreations:* tennis, golf, ski-ing, theatre. *Address:* Willow Park, 1 Westminster Avenue, Chester CH4 8JB.

LEVESON, Lord; George James Leveson Gower; *b* 22 July 1999; *s* and *heir* of Earl Granville, *qv*.

LEVESON, Hon. Sir Brian (Henry), Kt 2000; **Hon. Mr Justice Leveson;** a Judge of the High Court, Queen's Bench Division, since 2000; Presiding Judge, Northern Circuit, since 2002; *b* 22 June 1949; *er s* of late Dr Ivan Leveson and Elaine Leveson, Liverpool; *m* 1981, Lynne Rose (*née* Fishel); two *s* one *d*. *Educ:* Liverpool College, Liverpool; Merton College, Oxford (MA; Hon. Fellow, 2001). Called to the Bar, Middle Temple, 1970, Bencher, 1995; Harmsworth Scholar, 1970; practised Northern Circuit, 1971; University of Liverpool: Lectr in Law, 1971–81; Mem. Council, 1983–92; QC 1986; a Recorder, 1988–2000; a Dep. High Court Judge, 1998–2000. Mem., Parole Bd, 1992–95. Mem. Council, UCS, Hampstead, 1998–. *Recreation:* golf. *Address:* Royal Courts of Justice, Strand, WC2A 2LL.

LEVESON GOWER, family name of **Earl Granville**.

LEVEY, Sir Michael (Vincent), Kt 1981; LVO 1965; MA Oxon and Cantab; FRSL; FBA 1983; Director of the National Gallery, 1973–87 (Deputy Director, 1970–73); *b* 8 June 1927; *s* of O. L. H. Levey and Gladys Mary Milestone; *m* 1954, Brigid Brophy (*d* 1995), FRSL; one *d*. *Educ:* Oratory Sch.; Exeter Coll., Oxford, Hon. Fellow, 1973. Served with Army, 1945–48; commissioned, KSLI, 1946, and attached RAEC, Egypt. National Gallery: Asst Keeper, 1951–66, Dep. Keeper, 1966–68, Keeper, 1968–73. Slade Professor of Fine Art, Cambridge, 1963–64; Supernumerary Fellow, King's Coll., Cambridge, 1963–64; Slade Professor of Fine Art, Oxford, 1994–95; Hon. Fellow, Royal Acad., 1986; Foreign Mem., Ateneo Veneto, 1986. Hon. DLitt Manchester, 1989. *Publications:* Six Great Painters, 1956; National Gallery Catalogues: 18th Century Italian Schools, 1956; The German School, 1959; Painting in 18th Century Venice, 1959, 3rd. edn 1994; From Giotto to Cézanne, 1962; Dürer, 1964; The Later Italian Paintings in the Collection of HM The Queen, 1964, rev. edn 1991; Canaletto Paintings in the Royal Collection, 1964; Tiepolo's Banquet of Cleopatra (Charlton Lecture, 1962), 1966; Rococo to Revolution, 1966; Bronzino (The Masters), 1967; Early Renaissance, 1967 (Hawthornden Prize, 1968); Fifty Works of English Literature We Could Do Without (co-author), 1967; Holbein's Christina of Denmark, Duchess of Milan, 1968; A History of Western Art, 1968; Painting at Court (Wrightsman Lectures), 1971; 17th and 18th Century Italian Schools (Nat. Gall. catalogue), 1971; The Life and Death of Mozart, 1971, 2nd edn 1988; The Nude: Themes and Painters in the National Gallery, 1972; (co-author) Art and Architecture in 18th Century France, 1972; The Venetian Scene (Themes and Painters Series), 1973; Botticelli (Themes and Painters Series), 1974; High Renaissance, 1975; The World of Ottoman Art, 1976; Jacob van Ruisdael (Themes and Painters Series), 1977; The Case of Walter Pater, 1978; Sir Thomas Lawrence (Nat. Portrait Gall. exhibn), 1979; The Painter Depicted (Neurath Lect.), 1981; Tempting Fate (fiction), 1982; An Affair on the Appian Way (fiction), 1984; (ed) Pater's Marius the Epicurean, 1985; Giambattista Tiepolo, 1986 (Banister Fletcher Prize, 1987); The National Gallery Collection: a selection, 1987; Men at Work (fiction), 1989; (ed) The Soul of the Eye: anthology of painters and painting, 1990; Painting and Sculpture in France 1700–1789, 1992; Florence: a portrait, 1996; The Chapel is on Fire (memoir), 2000; contributions Burlington Magazine, etc. *Address:* 36 Little Lane, Louth, Lincs LN11 9DU.

LEVI, Renato, (Sonny), RDI 1987; freelance powerboat designer; *b* 3 Sept. 1926; *s* of Mario Levi and Eleonora Ciravegna; *m* 1954, Ann Watson; two *s* one *d*. *Educ:* Collège de Cannes; St Paul's, Darjeeling. Over 30 years contributing to development of fast planing craft. *Publications:* Dhows to Deltas, 1971; Milestones in my Designs, 1992. *Recreation:* the Far East. *Address:* Sandhills, Porchfield, Isle of Wight PO30 4LH.

LEVI-MONTALCINI, Prof. Rita; research scientist; *b* 22 April 1909; *d* of Adamo Levi and Adele Montalcini. *Educ:* Turin Univ. Med. Sch. Neurological research, Turin and Brussels, 1936–41, Piemonte, 1941–43; in hiding in Florence, 1943–44; worked among war refugees, Florence, 1944–45; Univ. of Turin, 1945; with Prof. Viktor Hamburger, St Louis, USA, at Washington Univ., 1947–77 (Associate Prof., 1956, Prof., 1958–77); Dir, Inst. of Cell Biology, Italian Nat. Council of Research, Rome, 1969–79, Guest Prof., 1979–. For. Mem., Royal Soc., 1995. (Jtly) Nobel Prize for Physiology or Medicine, 1986. *Publications:* In Praise of Imperfection: my life and work (autobiog.), 1988; articles in learned jls on chemical growth factors controlling growth and development of different cell lines. *Address:* Institute of Neurobiology, CNR, Viale Marx 15, 00137 Rome, Italy.

LÉVI-STRAUSS, Claude; Grand Croix de la Légion d'Honneur, 1991; Commandeur, Ordre Nationale du Mérite, 1971; Member of French Academy, since 1973; Professor, Collège de France, 1959–82, Hon. Professor, since 1983; *b* 28 Nov. 1908; *s* of Raymond Lévi-Strauss and Emma Lévy; *m* 1st, 1932, Dina Dreyfus; 2nd, 1946, Rose-Marie Ullmo; one *s*; 3rd, 1954, Monique Roman; one *s*. *Educ:* Lycée Janson-de-Sailly, Paris; Sorbonne. Prof., Univ. of São Paulo, Brazil, 1935–39; Vis. Prof., New School for Social Research, NY, 1941–45; Cultural Counsellor, French Embassy, Washington, 1946–47; Associate Curator, Musée de l'Homme, Paris, 1948–49. Corresp. Member: Royal Acad. of Netherlands; Norwegian Acad.; British Acad.; Nat. Acad. of Sciences, USA; Amer. Acad. and Inst. of Arts and Letters; Amer. Philos. Soc.; Royal Anthrop. Inst. of Great Britain; London Sch. of African and Oriental Studies. Hon. Dr: Brussels, 1962; Oxford, 1964; Yale, 1965; Chicago, 1967; Columbia, 1971; Stirling, 1972; Univ. Nat. du Zaïre, 1973; Uppsala, 1977; Johns Hopkins, 1978; Laval, 1979; Mexico, 1979; Visva Bharati, India, 1980; Harvard, 1986; Montreal, 1998. *Publications:* La Vie familiale et sociale des Indiens Nambikwara, 1948; Les Structures élémentaires de la parenté, 1949 (The Elementary Structures of Kinship, 1969); Race et histoire, 1952; Tristes Tropiques, 1955 (A World on the Wane, 1961; complete English edn as Tristes Tropiques, 1973); Anthropologie structurale, Vol. 1, 1958, Vol. 2, 1973 (Structural Anthropology, Vol. 1, 1964, Vol. 2, 1977); Le Totémisme aujourd'hui, 1962 (Totemism, 1963); La Pensée sauvage, 1962 (The Savage Mind, 1966); Le Cru et le cuit, 1964 (The Raw and the Cooked, 1970); Du Miel aux cendres, 1967 (From Honey to Ashes, 1973); L'Origine des manières de table, 1968 (The Origin of Table Manners, 1978); L'Homme nu, 1971 (The Naked Man, 1981); La Voie des masques, 1975 (The Way of the Masks, 1982); Le Regard éloigné, 1983 (The View from Afar, 1985); Paroles Données, 1984 (Anthropology and Myth, 1987); La Potière Jalouse, 1985 (The Jealous Potter, 1988); (with D. Eribon) De Près et de loin, 1988 (Conversations with Claude Lévi-Strauss, 1991); Histoire de Lynx, 1991 (The Story of Lynx, 1995); Regarder écouter lire, 1993 (Look, Listen, Read, 1997); Saudades do Brasil, 1994 (A Photographic Memoir, 1995); *relevant publications:* Entretiens avec Lévi-Strauss (ed G. Charbonnier), 1962; Claude Lévi-Strauss and the Making of Structural Anthropology, by Marcel Henaff, 1998; by Octavio Paz: On Lévi-Strauss, 1970; Claude Lévi-Strauss: an introduction, 1972. *Address:* 2 rue des Marronniers, 75016 Paris, France. *T:* 142883471.

LEVICK, William Russell, FRS 1982; FAA; Professor, John Curtin School of Medical Research, Australian National University, 1983–96, now Emeritus Professor; *b* 5 Dec. 1931; *s* of Russell L. S. Levick and Elsie E. I. (*née* Nance); *m* 1961, Patricia Jane Lathwell; two *s* one *d*. *Educ:* Univ. of Sydney (BSc 1st Cl. Hons, MSc, MB, BS 1st Cl. Hons). Registered Medical Practitioner, State of NSW. FAA 1973. RMO, Royal Prince Alfred Hosp., Sydney, 1957–58; National Health and Med. Res. Council Fellow, Univ. of Sydney, 1959–62; C. J. Martin Travelling Fellow, Cambridge Univ. and Univ. of Calif, Berkeley, 1963–64; Associate Res. Physiologist, Univ. of Calif, Berkeley, 1965–66; Sen. Lectr in Physiol., Univ. of Sydney, 1967; Professorial Fellow of Physiology, John Curtin Sch. of Medicine, ANU, 1967–83. Fellow, Optical Soc. of America, 1977. *Publications:* articles on neurophysiology of the visual system in internat. scientific jls. *Address:* Division of Psychology, Australian National University, Canberra, ACT 0200, Australia. *T:* (2) 62492525.

LEVIEN, Robin Hugh, RDI 1995; owner, Studio Levien, since 1999; *b* 5 May 1952; *s* of John Blomefield Levien and Louis Beryl Levien; *m* 1978, Patricia Anne Stainton. *Educ:* Bearwood Coll., Wokingham; Central Sch. of Art and Design (BA Hons 1973); Royal Coll. of Art (MA 1976). MCSD. Joined Queensberry Hunt, 1977; Partner, Queensberry Hunt, later Queensberry Hunt Levien, 1982–99. Designer of mass market products for manufrs and retailers, incl. Thomas China, Wedgwood, Ideal Standard, American Standard, Habitat, Dartington Crystal; *major products designed:* Trend (for Thomas China), 1981 (Die Gute Industrieform, Hanover, 1982; Golden Flame Award, Valencia, 1983); Studio bathroom range (for Ideal Standard), 1986; Domi bathroom taps, 1989; Symphony range of bathtubs (for American Standard), 1990 (Winner, Interior Design Product Award, Amer. Soc. of Interior Designers, 1991); Kyomi bathroom range (for Ideal Standard), 1996 (Winner, Design Week Awards, 1997); Space bathroom range (for Ideal Standard) (D&AD Silver Award; Winner, FX Internat. Interior Design Award), 1999. Vis. Prof., London Inst., 1997–. Mem. Council, RCA, 2001–. FRSA 1991 (Chm., Product Design, Student Design Awards, 1991–98; Paul Reilly Meml Lectr, 1998). *Publications:* articles in Design mag. *Recreations:* Fulham farmer on 1952 Ferguson tractor, tennis, softball, films, cooking. *Address:* Cooks Farm, North Brewham, Som BA10 0JQ. *T:* (01749) 850610.

LEVIN, Bernard; *see* Levin, H. B.

LEVIN, David Roger; Headmaster, City of London School, since 1999; *b* 2 Oct. 1949; *s* of Jack Levin, Cape Town and Isobel Elizabeth Levin (*née* Robinson), Norfolk, England; *m* 1977, Jean Isobel, *d* of Major J. A. P. Hall. *Educ:* Kearsney Coll., Natal; Univ. of Natal (BEcon); Univ. of Sussex (MA). Gen. Manager, Cutty Sark Hotel, Scottburgh, S Africa (family business), 1972–73; Asst Master, Whitgift Sch., Croydon, 1974–75; Articled Clerk, Radcliffes & Co., Solicitors, 1976–78; Asst Master, Portsmouth Grammar Sch., 1978–80; Head of Economics, 1980–93 and Second Master, 1987–93, Cheltenham Coll.; Headmaster, Royal Grammar Sch., High Wycombe, 1993–99. Mem., Economic Res. Council, 1991. Trustee: Lomans Trust, 1999–; Student Partnership Worldwide, 1999–. FRSA. Gov., Canford School, 1995–. *Recreations:* long distance swimming, Rugby football coaching, theatre, hill walking, opera, economic history. *Address:* Malden Court, Cheltenham, Glos GL52 2BL. *T:* (01242) 521692; City of London School, Queen Victoria Street, EC4V 3AL. *T:* (020) 7489 0291.

LEVIN, David Saul; Chief Executive Officer, Psion plc, since 1999; *b* 28 Jan. 1962; *s* of late Archie Z. Levin and of Leah S. Levin, OBE; *m* 1992, Lindsay Caroline White; three *s*. *Educ:* Wadham Coll., Oxford (MA 1983); Stanford Grad. Sch. of Business (MBA 1987). Served Army, SSLC, 2nd Lieut, 1st Bn RRF, 1980. Manager, Bain & Co., 1983–89; Associate Dir, Apax Partners & Co., 1990–94; Man. Dir, Unicorn Abrasives Ltd, 1992–94; Chief Operating Officer, Euromoney Pubns plc, 1994–99. *Address:* 12 Park Crescent, W1B 1PH; *e-mail:* david.levin@psion.com.

LEVIN, Gerald Manuel; Chief Executive Officer, AOL Time Warner Inc., since 2001; *b* 6 May 1939; *m* Barbara J. Riley. *Educ:* Haverford Coll. (BA 1960); Univ. of Pennsylvania Law Sch. (LLB 1963). Attorney, Simpson Thacher & Bartlett, NYC, 1963–67; Develt and Resources Corp., 1967–71 (Gen. Manager and Chief Operating Officer, 1969–71); Rep., Internat. Basic Economy Corp., Tehran, 1971–72; joined Time Inc., 1972: Vice-Pres., Programming, 1972–73, Pres. and CEO, 1973–76, Chm., 1976–79, Home Box Office; Gp Vice-Pres., Video, 1979–84; Exec. Vice-Pres., 1984–88; Vice-Chm. and Dir, 1988–90; merger with Warner Communications Inc. to form Time Warner, 1990: Chief Operating Officer, Vice-Chm. and Dir, 1991–92; Pres. and Co-CEO, Feb.–Dec. 1992; CEO, 1992–2001; Chm., 1993–2001; merger with AOL to form AOL Time Warner, 2001. Dir, NY Stock Exchange Inc. Member: Council on Foreign Relns; Trilateral Commn. Member, Board: NY City Partnership; Nat. Cable TV Center and Mus.; Aspen Inst.; Mus. of Jewish Heritage. Dir and Treas., NY Philharmonic. Hon. LLD: Texas Coll., 1985; Middlebury Coll., 1994; Haverford Coll.; Hon. LHD Denver, 1995. *Address:* AOL Time Warner Inc., 75 Rockefeller Plaza, New York, NY 10019–6908, USA. *T:* (212) 4848000.

LEVIN, (Henry) Bernard, CBE 1990; journalist and author; *b* 19 Aug. 1928; *s* of late Phillip Levin and Rose (*née* Racklin). *Educ:* Christ's Hospital; LSE, Univ. of London. BSc (Econ.). Has written regularly or irregularly for many newspapers and magazines in Britain and abroad, 1953–, principally The Times, Sunday Times, Observer, Manchester Guardian, Truth, Spectator, Daily Express, Daily Mail, Newsweek, International Herald-Tribune; has written and broadcast for radio and television, 1952–, incl. BBC and most ITV cos. Sir Dorab Tata Trust Lectr, India, 1990. Pres., English Assoc., 1984–85, Vice-Pres., 1985–88. Various awards for journalism. Hon. Fellow, LSE, 1977–. Mem., Order of Polonia Restituta (by Polish Government-in-Exile), 1976. *Publications:* The Pendulum Years, 1971; Taking Sides, 1979; Conducted Tour, 1981; Speaking Up, 1982; Enthusiasms, 1983; The Way We Live Now, 1984; A Shakespeare Mystery (English Assoc. Presidential address), 1985; Hannibal's Footsteps, 1985; In These Times, 1986; To The End Of The Rhine, 1987; All Things Considered, 1988; A Walk Up Fifth Avenue, 1989; Now Read On, 1990; If You Want My Opinion, 1992; A World Elsewhere, 1994; I Should Say So, 1995; Enough Said, 1998. *Address:* The Times, 1 Pennington Street, E1 9XN.

LEVIN, Prof. Richard Charles, PhD; Frederick William Beinecke Professor of Economics, since 1992, President, since 1993, Yale University; *b* San Francisco, 7 April 1947; *s* of D. Derek Levin and Phylys (*née* Goldstein); *m* 1968, Jane Ellen Aries; two *s* two *d*. *Educ:* Stanford Univ. (BA 1968); Merton Coll., Oxford (LittB 1971; Hon. Fellow, 1996); Yale Univ. (PhD 1974). Yale University, 1974–: Chm., Econs Dept, 1987–92; Dean, Grad. Sch., 1992–93; Res. Associate, Nat. Bureau of Econ. Res., Cambridge, Mass, 1985–90; Program Dir, Internat. Inst. Applied System Analysis, Vienna, 1990–92. Dir, Yale–New Haven Health Services Corp. Inc., 1993–. Consultant, numerous law and business firms. Trustee: Yale–New Haven Hosp., 1993–; Tanner Lectures on Human Values, 1993–. Member: Univs Res. Assoc., 1994–; Nat. Res. Council Bd on Sci., Technol. and Econ. Policy, 1998–. Member: Amer. Econ. Assoc.; Econometric Soc. Hon. LLD: Princeton, 1993; Harvard, 1994; Hon. DCL Oxford, 1998. *Recreations:* hiking, basket-ball. *Address:* Yale University, 105 Wall Street, New Haven, CT 06511, USA.

LEVINE, James; American conductor and pianist; Principal Conductor, since 1973, Music Director, since 1976, and Artistic Director, since 1986, Metropolitan Opera, New York; Chief Conductor, Munich Philharmonic, since 1999; *b* 23 June 1943; *s* of Lawrence Levine and Helen Levine (*née* Goldstein). *Educ:* Walnut Hills High Sch.; Juilliard Sch. of Music. Asst Conductor, Cleveland Orch., 1964–70; Music Director: Ravinia Fest., 1973–93; Cincinnati May Fest., 1974–78; Conductor: Salzburg Fest., 1975–93; Bayreuth Fest., 1982–98. Piano début with Cincinnati SO, 1953; conducting début, Aspen Music Fest., 1961; has conducted many major orchestras throughout US and Europe, incl. Vienna Philharmonic, Berlin Philharmonic, Chicago Symphony, NY Philharmonic, Dresden Staatskapelle, Israel Philharmonic, Philharmonia, London Symphony, Boston Symphony, Philadelphia, etc. Has made numerous recordings. Smetana Medal (Czechoslovakia), 1987; nine Grammy awards. *Address:* Metropolitan Opera Association Inc., Metropolitan Opera House, Lincoln Center, New York, NY 10023, USA.

LEVINE, Sir Montague (Bernard), Kt 1979; FRCGP, FRCPI; general practitioner, 1956–87; HM Coroner, Inner South District, Greater London, 1987–97; Clinical Tutor in General Practice, St Thomas' Hospital, 1972–97; *b* 15 May 1922; *s* of late Philip Levine and of Bessie Levine; *m* 1959, Dr Rose Gold; one *s* one *d*. *Educ:* Royal Coll. of Surgeons in Ireland (LRCSI); Royal Coll. of Physicians in Ireland (MRCPI, LRCPI, LM). DMJ Clin.; FRCGP 1988; FRCPI 2000. Licentiate of Rubber Industry, 1944. Industrial physicist, rubber industry, 1939–45; House Surgeon: Royal Victoria Hosp., Bournemouth, 1955; Meath Hosp., Dublin, 1955; Metrop. Police Surg., 1960–66; Asst Dep. Coroner, Inner South London, 1974. Hon. Lectr in Coroners' Law, St Thomas' Hosp. and Guy's Hosp., 1987–97. President: British Acad. of Forensic Sciences, 1993–94; Hunterian Soc., 1997–98. Fellow, Hunterian Soc., 1990. Freeman, Borough of Southwark, 1997. Hon. DSc City, 1997. Royal College of Surgeons in Ireland: Stoney Meml Gold Medal in Anatomy, 1951; Silver Medallist, Medicine, 1953, Pathology, 1953, and Medical Jurisprudence, 1954; Macnaughton Gold Medal in Obs and Gynae., 1955; Lectr in Anat., 1956. *Publications:* Inter-parental Violence and its Effect on Children, 1975; Levine on Coroners' Courts, 1999. *Recreations:* fishing, photography, painting. *Address:* Gainsborough House, 120 Ferndene Road, Herne Hill, SE24 0AA. *T:* (020) 7274 9196. *Club:* Organon.

LEVINE, Sydney; a Recorder, North-Eastern Circuit, 1975–95; *b* 4 Sept. 1923; *s* of Rev. Isaac Levine and Mrs Miriam Levine; *m* 1959, Cécile Rona Rubinstein; three *s* one *d*. *Educ:* Bradford Grammar Sch.; Univ. of Leeds (LLB). Called to the Bar, Inner Temple, 1952; Chambers in Bradford, 1953–98. *Recreations:* music, gardening, amateur theatre, learning to use a computer. *Address:* 2A Primley Park Road, Leeds LS17 7HS. *T:* (0113) 268 3769.

LEVINGE, Sir Richard (George Robin), 12th Bt *cr* 1704; farming since 1968; *b* 18 Dec. 1946; *s* of Sir Richard Vere Henry Levinge, 11th Bt, MBE, TD, and Barbara Mary (*d* 1997), *d* of late George Jardine Kidston, CMG; *S* father, 1984; *m* 1st, 1969, Hilary (marr. diss. 1978), *d* of Dr Derek Mark; one *s*; 2nd, 1978, Donna Maria d'Ardia Caracciolo; one *s* one *d*. *Educ:* Brook House, Bray, Co. Wicklow; Hawkhurst Court, West Sussex; Mahwah High School, New York; Craibstone Agricultural Coll. *Heir: s* Richard Mark Levinge, *b* 15 May 1970. *Address:* Clohamon House, Bunclody, Co. Wexford, Ireland. *T:* (54) 77253.

LEVINSON, Prof. Stephen Curtis, PhD; FBA 1988; Director, Max Planck Institute for Psycholinguistics, since 1994 (Managing Director, 1998–2001); Professor, Catholic University, Nijmegen, since 1995; *b* 6 Dec. 1947; *s* of Dr Gordon A. Levinson and Dr Mary C. Levinson; *m* 1976, Dr Penelope Brown; one *s*. *Educ:* Bedales Sch.; King's Coll., Cambridge (Sen. Schol.; 1st Cl. Hons. Archaeology and Anthropology Tripos 1970); PhD Linguistics Anthropology, Calif., 1977. Asst Lectr, 1975–78, Lectr, 1978–91, Reader, 1991–94, Linguistics Dept, Cambridge; Hd, Res. Gp for Cognitive Anthropol., Max Planck Inst. for Psycholinguistics, 1991–97. Vis. Res. Fellow, ANU, 1980–82; Vis. Associate Prof., Stanford Univ., 1987–88. *Publications:* Pragmatics, 1983; (with Dr P. Brown) Politeness, 1987; (with J. Gumperz) Rethinking Linguistic Relativity, 1996; Presumptive Meanings: the theory of generalized conversational implicature, 2000; (ed with M. Bowerman) Language Acquisition and Conceptual Development, 2001; articles in books and jls. *Recreations:* Sunday painting, hiking. *Address:* Payensweg 7, 6523 MB Nijmegen, The Netherlands; Max Planck Institute for Psycholinguistics, PB 310, 6500 AH Nijmegen, The Netherlands.

LEVISON, Rev. Mary Irene; an Extra Chaplain to the Queen in Scotland, since 1993 (Chaplain, 1991–93); *b* 8 Jan. 1923; *d* of late Rev. David Colville Lusk and Mary Theodora Lusk (*née* Colville); *m* 1965, Rev. Frederick Levison (*d* 1999). *Educ:* St Leonard's Sch., St Andrews; Lady Margaret Hall, Oxford (BA); Univ. of Edinburgh (BD). Deaconess in the parish of Inveresk, Musselburgh, 1954–58; Tutor, St Colm's Coll., Edinburgh, 1958–61; Asst Chaplain, Univ. of Edinburgh, 1961–64; Asst Minister, St Andrew's and St George's Church, Edinburgh and Chaplain to the retail trade, 1978–83. Moderator of the Presbytery of Edinburgh, 1988. Vice-Pres., St Leonard's Sch., 1996–. Hon. DD Edinburgh, 1994. *Publication:* Wrestling with the Church, 1992. *Recreations:* music, gardening. *Address:* 2 Gillsland Road, Edinburgh EH10 5BW. *T:* (0131) 228 3118.

LEVITT, Tom; MP (Lab) High Peak, since 1997; *b* 10 April 1954; *s* of John and Joan Levitt; *m* 1983, Teresa Sledziewska; one *d*. *Educ:* Lancaster Univ. (BSc Hons 1975); New Coll., Oxford (PGCE 1976). Biology teacher: Wootton Bassett Sch., 1976–79; Cirencester Sch., 1980–81; Brockworth Sch., Glos., 1981–91; supply Teacher, Staffs, 1991–95; freelance res. consultant, 1993–97. Member (Lab): Cirencester Town Council, 1983–87; Stroud DC, 1990–92; Derbys CC, 1993–97. Contested (Lab): Stroud, 1987; Cotswold, EP elecn, 1989; High Peak, 1992. PPS to Minister of State, Home Office, 1999–2001, Cabinet Office, 2001–. Mem., Standards and Privileges Select Cttee, 1997–. Trustee, RNID, 1998–. *Publications:* Sound Practice, 1995; Clear Access, 1997; pubns on local govt access issues for people with disabilities. *Recreations:* cricket, theatre, walking, travel. *Address:* 3 The Square, Buxton, Derbys SK17 6AZ. *T:* (01298) 26366; (office) 20 Hardwick Street, Buxton, Derbys SK17 6DH. *T:* (01298) 71111.

LEVVY, (Clinton) George; Chief Executive, Motor Neurone Disease Association, since 1995; *b* 30 Nov. 1953; *s* of late Guildford Albert Levvy and of Averil Clinton Levvy (*née* Chance); *m* 1st, 1984, Irené M. Young (marr. diss. 1989); 2nd, 1991, Bethe R. Alpert; one *s* one *d*. *Educ:* Robert Gordon's Coll., Aberdeen; Univ. of Edinburgh (MB ChB). Jun. hosp. doctor, 1977–84; Med. Dir and Consultant, Excerpta Medica, Tokyo, 1984–88; Commercial Manager, Countrywide Communications Gp Ltd, 1988–91; Hd, Mktg and Communications, BRCS, 1991–94. Member: Appraisal Cttee, NICE, 2000–; Adv. Cttee, New and Emerging Applications of Technol., DoH, 2000–. Trustee, Haemophilia Soc., 1999–. *Publications:* contribs to jls and ed vols. *Recreations:* walking, sailing, reading, cricket. *Address:* Motor Neurone Disease Association, PO Box 246, Northampton NN1 2PR. *T:* (01604) 250505.

LEVY, family name of **Baron Levy**.

LEVY, Baron *cr* 1997 (Life Peer), of Mill Hill in the London Borough of Barnet; **Michael Abraham Levy;** Chairman: Wireart Ltd, since 1992; Chase Music Ltd (formerly M & G Music Ltd), since 1992; *b* 11 July 1944; *s* of Samuel and Annie Levy; *m* 1967, Gilda (*née* Altbach); one *s* one *d*. *Educ:* Fleetwood Primary Sch. (Head Boy); Hackney Downs Grammar Sch. FCA 1966. Lubbock Fine (Chartered Accountants), 1961–66; Principal, M. Levy & Co., 1966–69; Partner, Wagner Prager Levy & Partners, 1969–73; Chairman: Magnet Group of Cos, 1973–88; D & J Securities Ltd, 1988–92; M & G Records, 1992–97; Vice Chairman: Phonographic Performance Ltd, 1979–84; British Phonographic Industry Ltd, 1984–87. Chm., British Music Industry Awards Cttee, 1992–95; Patron, British Music Industry Awards, 1995–. Nat. Campaign Chm., United Jt Israel Appeal, 1982–85 (Hon. Vice Pres., 1994–2000; Hon. Pres., 2000–); Chairman: Jewish Care, 1991–97 (Pres., 1998–); Jewish Care Community Foundn, 1995–; Vice Chm., Central Council for Jewish Community Services, 1994–. Chairman: Chief Rabbinate Awards for Excellence, 1992–; Foundn for Educn, 1993–; Member: Jewish Agency World Bd of Governors, 1990–95 (World Chm., Youth Aliyah Cttee, 1991–95); Keren Hayesod World Bd of Trustees, 1991–95; World Commn on Israel-Diaspora Relns, 1995–; Internat. Bd of Governors, Peres Center for Peace, 1997–; Adv. Council, Foreign Policy Centre, 1997–; FCO Panel 2000, 1998–2000; NCVO Adv. Cttee, 1998–; Community Legal Service Champions Panel, 1999–; Hon. Cttee, Israel, Britain and the Commonwealth Assoc., 2000–. Personal Envoy for Prime Minister to Middle East. Pres., CSV, 1998–; Trustee: Holocaust Educnl Trust, 1997–; Policy Network Foundn, 2000–; Patron: Ben Uri Art Soc., 1997–2000; Prostate Cancer Charitable Trust, 1997–; Friends of Israel Educnl Trust, 1997–; Save a Child's Heart Foundn, 2000–. Governor, Jewish Free Sch., 1990–95 (Hon. Pres., 1995–). Hon. Dr Middlesex Univ., 1999. B'nai B'rith First Lodge Award, 1994; Scopus Award, Hebrew Univ. of Jerusalem, 1998. *Recreations:* tennis, swimming. *Address:* House of Lords, SW1A 0PW.

LEVY, Rabbi Dr Abraham; Spiritual Head, Spanish and Portuguese Jews' Congregation in UK, since 1983; *b* 16 July 1939; *s* of Isaac Levy and Rachel (*née* Hassan); *m* 1963, Estelle Nahum; one *s*. *Educ:* Carmel Coll.; Jews' Coll.; UCL (PhD 1978). Minister, Spanish and Portuguese Jews' Congregation, 1962–80; Communal Rabbi, 1980–. (With Chief Rabbi) Ecclesiastical Authy, Bd of Deputies of British Jews, 1980–. Dir, Young Jewish Leadership Inst., 1970–86; Founder and Principal, Naima Jewish Prep. Sch., 1983–; Dep. Pres., London Sch. of Jewish Studies (formerly Jews' Coll.), 1985–. Pres., Union Anglo-Jewish Preachers, 1973–75; Vice President: Anglo-Jewish Assoc., 1984–; Jewish Care, 1993–; Norwood Ravenswood, 2000–. Patron, Centre for Jewish-Christian Relations, Cambridge, 2001–. Kt Comdr (Encomienda), Order of Merit (Spain), 1993. *Publications:* The Sephardim: a problem of survival, 1972; (jtly) Ages of Man, 1985; (jtly) The Sephardim, 1992. *Recreation:* collecting antique Judaica. *Address:* 2 Ashworth Road, W9 1JY. *T:* (020) 7289 2573.

LEVY, Allan Edward; QC 1989; a Recorder, since 1993 (an Assistant Recorder, 1990–93); barrister; author; *b* 17 Aug. 1942; *s* of Sidney Levy and Mabel (*née* Lewis). *Educ:* Bury Grammar Sch.; Hull Univ. (LLB Hons); Inns of Court Law School. Called to the Bar, Inner Temple, 1969, Bencher, 1993. Member: Family Law Bar Assoc. Cttee, 1987–97; Council, Justice, 1988–; Bar Council Law Reform Cttee, 1989–90; Council,

Medico-Legal Soc., 1990–; Bar Council, 1995–97. Speaker at seventh Internat. Congress on Child Abuse, Rio de Janeiro, 1988; Keynote speaker, Australasian child abuse conf., Melbourne, 1995; Chm., Staffordshire Pindown Child Care Inquiry, 1990; Member: Gulbenkian Foundn Commn on children and violence, 1994–95; Howard League Commn of Inquiry into violence in penal instns for young people, 1994–95. Hon. Legal Advr, Nat. Children's Bureau, 1990–. Vis. Prof., Washburn Law Sch., Kansas, 2001. Sidgwick Meml Lectr, Newnham Coll., Cambridge, 2001. Chm., Intercountry Adoption Lawyers' Assoc., 1991–95. Internat. Bar Assoc. Observer, Hague Conf. on Private Internat. Law (special commn on intercountry adoption), 1992. Patron: Children's Legal Centre, 1999; Bar Cttee on Rights of the Child, 1999–. Fellow: Internat. Acad. of Matrimonial Lawyers, 1992; Soc. for Advanced Legal Studies, 1998. FRSocMed 1993. Broadcaster on legal topics. *Publications:* Wardship Proceedings, 1982, 2nd edn 1987; Custody and Access, 1983; (with J. F. Josling) Adoption of Children, 10th edn 1985; (ed and contrib.) Focus on Child Abuse, 1989; (with B. Kahan) The Pindown Experience and the Protection of Children, 1991; (contrib.) One Scandal Too Many: the case for comprehensive protection for children in all settings, 1993; (ed and contrib.) Re-Focus on Child Abuse, 1994; (contrib.) Medico-Legal Essentials in Health Care, 1996; (contrib.) Children Who Kill, 1996; (contrib.) Whistleblowing in the Social Services, 1998; (contrib.) Consent, Rights and Choices in Health Care for Children and Young People, 2000; Family Law and the Human Rights Act, 2001; (contrib.) Legal Concepts of Childhood, 2001; contrib. legal jls and nat. newspapers. *Recreations:* travel, writing, watching sport. *Address:* 17 Bedford Row, WC1R 4EG. *T:* (020) 7831 7314, *Fax:* (020) 7831 0061. *Club:* Reform.

LEVY, Dennis Martyn; QC 1982; **His Honour Judge Levy;** a Circuit Judge, since 1991; *b* 20 Feb. 1936; *s* of late Conrad Levy and Tillie (*née* Swift); *m* 1967, Rachel Jonah; one *s* one *d. Educ:* Clifton Coll.; Gonville and Caius Coll., Cambridge (MA). Called to the Bar, Gray's Inn, 1960, Hong Kong, 1985, Turks and Caicos Is, 1987. Granada Group Ltd, 1960–63; Time Products Ltd, 1963–67; in practice at the Bar, 1967–91; a Recorder, 1989–91. Member: Employment Appeal Tribunal, 1996–; Lands Tribunal, 1998. *Recreations:* living in London and travelling abroad. *Address:* c/o 24 Old Buildings, Lincoln's Inn, WC2A 3UJ. *T:* (020) 7404 0946, *Fax:* (020) 7289 2079.

LEVY, Prof. John Court, (Jack), OBE 1984; FREng; FIMechE, FRAeS; FCGI; engineering consultant, since 1990; Director, Engineering Profession, Engineering Council, 1983–90 and 1997; *b* London, 16 Feb. 1926; *s* of Alfred and Lily Levy; *m* 1952, Sheila Frances Krisman; two *s* one *d. Educ:* Owens Sch., London; Imperial Coll., Univ. of London (BScEng, ACGI, PhD); Univ. of Illinois, USA (MS). Stressman, Boulton-Paul Aircraft, 1945–47; Asst to Chief Engr, Fullers Ltd, 1947–51. Asst Lectr, Northampton Polytechnic, London, 1951–53; Fulbright Award to Univ. of Illinois, for research into metal fatigue, 1953–54; Lectr, Sen. Lectr, Reader, Northampton Polytechnic (later City Univ.), 1954–66; also a Recognised Teacher of the Univ. of London, 1958–66; Head of Department of Mechanical Engineering, 1966–83 (now Prof. Emeritus), and Pro-Vice-Chancellor, 1975–81, City Univ. Consultant to Shell International Marine, 1963–85; Chairman, 1st Panel on Marine Technology, SRC, 1971–73; Chm., Chartered Engr Section, Engineers Registration Bd, CEI, 1978–82; non-exec. Dir, City Technology Ltd, 1980–91. Vice Chm., Bd of Govs, Middlesex Univ., 1997–2000; Chm., Mus. of Domestic Design and Architecture, 1999–. Freeman, City of London, 1991; Liveryman, Co. of Engineers, 1991. FREng (FEng 1988). Hon. DTech CNAA, 1990; DUniv Leeds Metropolitan, 1992; Hon DSc City, 1994. Internat. Gold Medal for contribs to engrg educn, WFEO, 1999. *Publications:* The Engineering Dimension in Europe, 1991; papers on metal fatigue, marine technology, engrg educn, in jls of IMechE, RAeS, IEE, etc. *Recreations:* theatre, chess, exploring cities. *Address:* 18 Woodberry Way, Finchley, N12 0HG. *T:* (020) 8445 5227. *Club:* Island Sailing (Cowes, IoW).

LEVY, Paul, PhD; FRSL; author and broadcaster; Senior Contributor, Europe Leisure and Arts, Wall Street Journal, since 1993; Wine and Food Writer, You Magazine, The Mail on Sunday, since 1993; *b* 26 Feb. 1941; *er s* of late H. S. Levy and Mrs Shirley Meyers (*née* Singer), Lexington, Ky, USA; *m* 1977, Penelope, *o c* of late Clifford and Ruby Marcus; two *d. Educ:* Univ. of Chicago (AB); University Coll. London; Harvard Univ. (PhD 1979); Nuffield Coll., Oxford. FRSL 1980. Teaching Fellow, Harvard, 1966–68; lapsed academic, 1971–; freelance journalist, 1974–80; Food Correspondent, 1980–82, Food and Wine Ed., 1982–92, The Observer; frequent radio and television broadcasting. Member: Soc. of Authors; PEN; Location Register of Manuscripts Panel, SCONUL. Trustee: Strachey Trust, 1972–; Jane Grigson Trust, 1990–. Corning Award for food writing, 1980, 1981; Glenfiddich Food Writer of the Year, 1980, 1983; Glenfiddich Restaurant Critic of the Year, 1983; Specialist Writer Commendation, British Press Awards, 1985, 1987; Wine Journalist of the Year, Wine Guild of the UK, 1986. Confrèrie des Mousquetaires, 1981; Chevalier du Tastevin, 1987; Chevalier de l'ordre des Dames du Vin et de la Table, 1989; Chevalier de la Commanderie des Dindes de Lique, 1991. *Publications:* (ed) Lytton Strachey: the really interesting question, 1972; The Bloomsbury Group, in Essays on John Maynard Keynes, ed Milo Keynes, 1975; G. E. Moore and the Cambridge Apostles, 1979, 3rd edn 1989; (ed with Michael Holroyd) The Shorter Strachey, 1980, 2nd edn 1989; (with Ann Barr) The Official Foodie Handbook, 1984; Out to Lunch, 1986 (Seagrams/ Internat. Assoc. of Cookery Professionals Award, USA, 1988); Finger-Lickin' Good: a Kentucky childhood (autobiog.), 1990; The Feast of Christmas, 1992 (also TV series); (ed) The Penguin Book of Food and Drink, 1996; contribs to New York Times, TLS, Independent. *Recreations:* being cooked for, drinking better wine, trying to remember. *Address:* PO Box 35, Witney, Oxon OX29 8YT. *T:* (01993) 883477. *Club:* Groucho.

LEVY, Prof. Philip Marcus, PhD; CPsychol, FBPsS; Professor of Psychology, University of Lancaster, 1972–94, now Professor Emeritus; *b* 4 Feb. 1934; *s* of late Rupert Hyam Levy and of Sarah Beatrice Levy; *m* 1958, Gillian Mary (*née* Harker); two *d. Educ:* Leeds Modern School; Univ. of Leeds (BA 1955); Univ. of Birmingham (PhD 1960). Res. Fellow, Birmingham Univ., 1955–59; Psychologist, RAF, 1959–62; Sen. Res. Fellow, Lectr, Sen. Lectr, Birmingham Univ., 1962–72. Economic and Social Research Council (formerly Social Science Research Council): Mem. Council, 1983–86; Mem., Psychol. Cttee, 1976–82 (Chm., 1979–82); Chm., Educn and Human Develt Cttee, 1982–87; Chm., Human Behaviour and Develt R&D Gp, 1987–89 (Mem. Council, 1987–89). British Psychological Society: Mem. Council, 1973–80; Pres., 1978–79. Editor, Brit. Jl of Mathematical and Statistical Psychology, 1975–80. *Publications:* (jtly) Tests in Education, 1984; (jtly) Cognition in Action, 1987; numerous in psychol jls.

LEVY, Prof. Raymond, FRCPE, FRCPsych; Professor of Old Age Psychiatry, University of London at Institute of Psychiatry, 1984–96, now Emeritus Professor; Hon. Consultant, Bethlem Royal and Maudsley Hospitals, since 1984; *b* 23 June 1933; *o s* of late Gaston Levy and Esther Levy (*née* Bigio); *m* 1956, Katherine Margaret Logie (marr. diss. 1982); two *d. Educ:* Victoria Coll., Cairo; Edinburgh Univ. (MB, ChB 1957; PhD 1961); Univ. of London (DPM 1964). Jun. hosp. appts, Royal Infirmary, Northern Gen., Leith, Bethlem Royal and Maudsley Hosps, to 1966; Sen. Lectr and Hon. Consultant Psychiatrist, Middx Hosp. Med. Sch., 1966–71; Consultant Psychiatrist, Bethlem Royal and Maudsley Hosps, 1971–84. Mem., Med. Adv. Commn on Res. into Ageing. Pres., Internat. Psychogeriatric Assoc., 1995–98 (Mem., Bd of Dirs, 1998–); Vice-Pres., Eur. Assoc. Geriatric Psych.; Foundn Mem., RCPsych, 1971. Asst Editor, Internat. Jl Geriatric Psych. *Publications:* (all jtly) The Psychiatry of Late Life, 1982; Diagnostic and Therapeutic Assessment in Alzheimer's Disease, 1991; Delusions and Hallucinations in Old Age, 1992; Clinical diversity in late onset of Alzheimer's Disease, 1992; Treatment and Care in Old Age Psychiatry, 1993; Dementia, 1993; contribs to learned jls. *Recreations:* looking at pictures, drinking good wine, travelling, playing tennis. *Address:* Institute of Psychiatry, de Crespigny Park, Denmark Hill, SE5 8AF. *T:* (020) 7703 5411; 52 Westminster Palace Gardens, Artillery Row, SW1P 1RR. *Clubs:* Reform; Campden Hill Lawn Tennis.

LEVY-LANG, André; Légion d'Honneur; Chairman: Compagnie Financière de Paribas, 1990–99; Banque Paribas, 1991–99; *b* 26 Nov. 1937. *Educ:* Ecole Polytechnique; Stanford Univ. (PhD Business Admin; Harkness Fellow, 1963–65). Res. physicist, French Atomic Energy Commn, 1960–62; Schlumberger Gp, 1962–74; Compagnie Bancaire: joined 1974; Mem. Bd, 1979; Chm., 1982; Chm., Adv. Bd, 1993. Director: AGF; Schlumberger; Dexia; Mem. Exec. Cttee, Pargesa Holding. Bd mem., banking and employers' assocs. *Address:* 48 boulevard Emile Augier, 75116 Paris, France.

LEW, Jonathan Michael; Chief Executive, United Synagogue, 1986–98; *b* 23 Nov. 1937; *s* of Rabbi Maurice A. Lew and Rachel Lew; *m* 1963, Linda Samad; one *s* one *d. Educ:* Univ. of Witwatersrand (BCom). ACMA. Finance Director: Dorland Advertising, 1973–79; Dancer Fitzgerald Sample Internat., 1979–83; MWK Advertising, 1984–85. Hon. Officer, United Synagogue, 1984–86. Lay Mem., Marylebone Duty Solicitors' Cttee, 1987–; Gen. Comr for Income Taxes, 1992–; Member: Central London Valuation Tribunal, 1998–; Adv. Gp on Religion in Prisons, 1998–; Ind. Review Panels, London Region, NHS Exec., DoH, 1999–; London Regl Cttee, Duty Solicitors' Scheme, 2000–. *Recreations:* bridge, travel, family. *Address:* 41 Eyre Court, St John's Wood, NW8 9TU.

LEWANDO, Sir Jan (Alfred), Kt 1974; CBE 1968; *b* 31 May 1909; *s* of Maurice Lewando and Eugenie Lewando (*née* Goldsmid); *m* 1948, Nora Slavouski; three *d. Educ:* Manchester Grammar Sch.; Manchester University. Served War of 1939–45, British Army: British Army Staff, Washington DC and British Min. of Supply Mission, 1941–45 (Lt-Col, 1943). Marks & Spencer Ltd, 1929–70 (Dir 1954–70); Chairman: Carrington Viyella Ltd, 1970–75; Consolidated Textile Mills Ltd, Canada, 1972–75; Penn Consultants Ltd, 1975–99; Pres., Carrington Viyella Inc. (USA), 1971–75; Director: Carrington Tesit (Italy), 1971–75; Heal and Son Holdings, 1975–82 (Dep. Chm., 1977–82); Bunzl PLC (formerly Bunzl Pulp & Paper Ltd), 1976–86; W. A. Baxter & Sons Ltd, 1975–99; Johnston Group Inc. (USA) (formerly Johnston Industries Inc.), 1976–85; Edgars Stores Ltd (South Africa), 1976–82; Royal Worcester Spode Ltd, 1978–79; Bunzl and Biach AG (Austria), 1979–80; Johnston Industries Ltd, 1980–85; Chm., Gelvenor Textiles Ltd, S Africa, 1973–75. Vice Chm., Clothing Export Council, 1966–70; Pres., British Textile Confedn, 1972–73; Vice Pres., Comitextil, Brussels, 1972–73; Member: British Overseas Trade Bd, 1972–77; British Overseas Trade Adv. Council, 1975–77; BNEC, 1969–71; Council, UK-S Africa Trade Assoc., 1973–92; Export Council for Europe, 1965–69; European Steering Cttee, CBI, 1968–71; Grand Council, CBI, 1971–75. Vice Pres., Transport Trust, 1973–88 and 1991– (Pres., 1989–91). Chm., Appeal Cttee, British Inst. of Radiology, 1979–84. CIMgt (CBIM 1980; FBIM 1972); FRSA 1973. Companion, Textile Inst., 1972. Order of Legion of Merit (USA), 1946.

LEWEN, John Henry, CMG 1977; HM Diplomatic Service, retired; Ambassador to the People's Republic of Mozambique, 1975–79; *b* 6 July 1920; *s* of Carl Henry Lewen and Alice (*née* Mundy); *m* 1945, Emilienne Alette Julie Alida Galant; three *s. Educ:* Christ's Hospital; King's Coll., Cambridge. Royal Signals, 1940–45. HM Foreign (subseq. Diplomatic) Service, 1946; HM Embassy: Lisbon, 1947–50; Rangoon, 1950–53; FO, 1953–55; HM Embassy: Rio de Janeiro, 1955–59; Warsaw, 1959–61; FO, 1961–63; Head of Chancery, HM Embassy, Rabat, 1963–67; Consul-General, Jerusalem, 1967–70; Inspector of HM Diplomatic Estabts, 1970–73; Dir, Admin and Budget, Secretariat-Gen. of Council of Ministers of European Communities, 1973–75. OStJ 1969. *Recreations:* singing, history. *Address:* 1 Brimley Road, Cambridge CB4 2DQ. *T:* (01223) 359101.

LEWER, Michael Edward; QC 1983; a Recorder of the Crown Court, 1983–98; a Deputy High Court Judge, 1989–98; *b* 1 Dec. 1933; *s* of late Stanley Gordon Lewer and Jeanie Mary Lewer; *m* 1965, Bridget Mary Gill; two *s* two *d. Educ:* Tonbridge Sch.; Oriel Coll., Oxford (MA). Called to Bar, Gray's Inn, 1958, Bencher, 1992. Territorial Army: Captain, 300 LAA Regt, RA, 1955–64; APIS, Intelligence Corps, 1964–67. Chm., Home Secretary's Adv. Cttee on Local Govt Electoral Arrangements for England, 1971–73; Comr, Parly Boundary Commn for England, 1997– (Asst Comr, 1965–69, 1976–88, 1992–96). Chm., Criminal Injuries Compensation Appeals Panel, 1994–; Mem., Criminal Injuries Compensation Bd, 1986–2000. Mem., European Parly Constituency Cttee for England, 1993–94. Member: Bar Council, 1978–81; Bar Council Professional Conduct Cttee, 1993–95 (Vice Chm., 1995). *Address:* 11th Floor, Cardinal Tower, 12 Farringdon Road, EC1M 3HS. *T:* (020) 7549 4666. *Club:* Western (Glasgow).

LEWERS, Very Rev. Benjamin Hugh; Provost of Derby, 1981–97; *b* 25 March 1932; *s* of late Hugh Bunnett Lewers, DSO, OBE and Coral Helen Lewers; *m* 1957, Sara Blagden; three *s. Educ:* Sherborne School; Selwyn Coll., Cambridge (MA); Lincoln Theological Coll. Employee, Dunlop Rubber Co., 1953–57. Curate, St Mary, Northampton, 1962–65; Priest-in-charge, Church of the Good Shepherd, Hounslow, 1965–68; Industrial Chaplain, Heathrow Airport, 1968–75; Vicar of Newark, 1975–80, Rector 1980–81. A Church Commissioner, 1985–97. *Recreations:* cricket, music, gardening, wine and rug making, photography. *Address:* Thimble Cottage, Marshwood, Bridport, Dorset DT6 5QF. *T:* (01297) 678515.

LEWES, Suffragan Bishop of, since 1997; **Rt Rev. Wallace Parke Benn;** *b* 6 Aug. 1947; *s* of William and Lucinda Jane Benn; *m* 1978, Lindsay Develing; one *s* one *d. Educ:* St Andrew's Coll., Dublin; UC, Dublin (BA); Trinity Coll., Bristol (external DipTheol London Univ.). Ordained deacon, 1972, priest, 1973; Assistant Curate: St Mark's, New Ferry, Wirral, 1972–76; St Mary's, Cheadle, 1976–82; Vicar: St James the Great, Audley, Stoke-on-Trent, 1982–87; St Peter's, Harold Wood, and part-time Chaplain, Harold Wood Hosp., 1987–97. *Publications:* The Last Word, 1996; Jesus our Joy, 2000; articles in theol jls. *Recreations:* reading, walking with my wife, Rugby, motor sports. *Address:* Bishop's Lodge, 16a Prideaux Road, Eastbourne, E Sussex BN21 2NB. *T:* (01323) 648462. *Club:* London Irish Rugby Football.

LEWES AND HASTINGS, Archdeacon of; *see* Reade, Ven. N. S.

LEWINGTON, Richard George; HM Diplomatic Service; Ambassador to Kazakhstan and Kyrgyzstan (resident in Almaty), since 1999; *b* 13 April 1948; *s* of late Jack and Ann Lewington; *m* 1972, Sylviane Paulette Marie Cholet; one *s* one *d. Educ:* Orchard Secondary Modern Sch., Slough; Slough Grammar Sch. Joined HM Diplomatic Service, 1967; Ulaan Baatar, 1972–75; Lima, 1976–80; FCO, 1980–82; Moscow, 1982–83; First Sec. (Commercial), Tel Aviv, 1986–90; FCO, 1991–95; Dep. High Comr, Malta,

1995–99. *Recreations:* Dorset, Dvořák. *Address:* c/o Foreign and Commonwealth Office, King Charles Street, SW1A 2AH. *T:* (020) 7270 3000. *Club:* Royal Over-Seas League.

LEWINGTON, (Thomas) Charles, OBE 1997; Managing Director, Media Strategy Ltd, since 1998; *b* 6 April 1959; *s* of Maurice Lewington and late Sheila Lewington; *m* 1995, Philippa Jane Kelly; one *d. Educ:* Sherborne Sch., Dorset; Univ. of Bath (BSc Econs). Reporter, Bath Evening Chronicle, 1981–86; Western Daily Press: Asst News Editor, 1986–88; Political Corresp., 1988–90; Political Corresp., Daily Express, 1990–92; Political Editor, Sunday Express, 1992–95; Dir of Communications, Cons. Party, 1995–97. *Recreations:* reading, playing the piano, Brittany, France. *Address:* (office) 8 Hanover Street, W1S 1YE. *T:* (020) 7290 2700; 203 Broomwood Road, SW11 6JX. *T:* (020) 7228 8091. *Club:* Soho House.

LEWINTON, Sir Christopher, Kt 1993; FREng; Chairman: TI Group plc, 1989–2000 (Deputy Chairman, 1986–89; Chief Executive, 1986–97); Dowty Group PLC, since 1992; *b* 6 Jan. 1932; *s* of Joseph and Elizabeth Lewinton; *m* 1st, Jennifer Alcock (marr. diss.); two *s*; 2nd, 1979, Louise Head; two step *s. Educ:* Acton Technical College. CEng, FREng (FEng 1994); FIMechE; FRAeS. Army Service, Lieut REME. Pres., Wilkinson Sword, N America, 1960–70; Chm., Wilkinson Sword Group, 1970–85; Pres., Internat. Gp, Allegheny International, 1976–85 (Exec. Vice-Pres., Mem. Board). Non-executive Director: Young & Rubicam, NY, 1999–2001; WPP, 2001–; Video Networks, 2000–; J F Lehman & Co., 2000– (Chm., Europe). *Recreations:* golf, tennis, travel, reading. *Address:* 63 Curzon Street, W1J 8PD. *T:* (020) 7758 8090. *Clubs:* Buck's; Sunningdale Golf; University (New York); Everglades (Palm Beach).

LEWIS; *see* Day-Lewis.

LEWIS, family name of **Baron Lewis of Newnham** and of **Barony of Merthyr**.

LEWIS OF NEWNHAM, Baron *cr* 1989 (Life Peer), of Newnham in the County of Cambridgeshire; **Jack Lewis,** Kt 1982; FRS 1973; FRSC; (first) Warden of Robinson College, Cambridge, 1975–2001; Professor of Chemistry, University of Cambridge, 1970–95; Hon. Fellow of Sidney Sussex College (Fellow, 1970–77); *b* 13 Feb. 1928; *m* 1951, Elfreida Mabel (*née* Lamb); one *s* one *d. Educ:* Barrow Grammar Sch. BSc London 1949; PhD Nottingham 1952; DSc London 1961; MSc Manchester 1964; MA Cantab 1970; ScD Cantab 1977. Lecturer: Univ. of Sheffield, 1954–56; Imperial Coll., London, 1956–57; Lecturer-Reader, University Coll., London, 1957–61; Prof. of Chemistry: Univ. of Manchester, 1961–67; UCL, 1967–70. Firth Vis. Prof., Univ. of Sheffield, 1967; Vis. Prof., UCL, 1996–; Lectures: Frontiers of Science, Case/Western Reserve, 1963; Tilden, RIC, 1966; Miller, Univ. of Illinois, 1966; Shell, Stanford Univ., 1968; Venables, Univ. of N Carolina, 1968; A. D. Little, MIT, 1970; Boomer, Univ. of Alberta, 1971; AM, Princeton, 1974; Baker, Cornell, 1974; Nyholm, Chem. Soc., 1974; Chini, Italian Chem. Soc., 1980; Bailar, Illinois Univ., 1981; Dwyer, NSW Inst. of Tech., 1982; Power, Queensland Univ., 1982; Mond, Chem. Soc., 1984; Leeumaker, Wesleyan Univ., 1984; Pettit May, Texas, 1985; Nieuwland, Notre Dame, 1986; Wheeler, Dublin, 1987; Bakerian, Roy. Soc., 1989; Sir Jesse Boot Foundn, Nottingham, 1989; Garner, 1993; Gordon Stone, 1993; Shell, Edinburgh, 1994. Member: CNAA Cttee, 1964–70; Exec. Cttee, Standing Cttee on Univ. Entry, 1966–76; Schs Council, 1966–70; SERC (formerly SRC): Polytechnics Cttee, 1973–79; Chemistry Cttee (Chm., 1975–82); Science Bd, 1975–79; Council, 1979–84; SERC/SSRC Jt Cttee, 1979–84; UGC (Phy. Sci.), 1973–79; Council, Royal Soc., 1982–84 (a Vice-Pres., 1984); Vis. Cttee, Cranfield Inst. of Tech., 1982–92 (Chm., 1985–92); Royal Commn on Environmental Pollution, 1985–92 (Chm., 1986–92); Chairman: Standing Cttee on Structural Safety, 1998–; ESART Bd, 1998–. Mem., H of L European Communities Select Cttee, 1993–95, 1997– (Chm. Sub-Cttee C, 1993–95). Pres., Royal Soc. of Chemistry, 1986–88 (Hon. Fellow, 1998); Sci. Rep. for UK on NATO Sci. Cttee, 1986–98. Trustee: Kennedy Meml Trust, 1989–; Croucher Foundn, 1989–98. Dir, BOC Foundn, 1990–. Pres., Arthritis Res. Campaign, 1998–. Hon. Pres., Envmtl Industries Commn, 1996–. Patron, Student Community Action Develt Unit, 1985–. Hon. Mem., SCI, 1996. Chm. Govs, Leys Sch., 1997–. Foreign Member: Amer. Acad. of Arts and Science, 1983; Amer. Philos. Soc., 1994; Accademia Nazionale dei Lincei, Italy, 1995; Polish Acad. of Arts and Scis, 1996; Fellow, Indian Nat. Sci. Acad., 1985; For. Fellow, Bangladesh Acad. of Scis, 1992; For. Associate, Nat. Acad. of Sciences, USA, 1987. FNA 1980 (For. Fellow 1986); Hon. Fellow: UCL, 1990; UMIST, 1990; Central Lancs, 1993. Dr *hc* Rennes, 1980; DUniv: Open, 1982; Kingston, 1993; Hon. DSc: East Anglia, 1983; Nottingham, 1983; Keele, 1984; Leicester, 1988; Birmingham, 1988; Waterloo, Canada, 1988; Manchester, 1990; Wales (Swansea), 1990; Sheffield, 1992; Cranfield, 1993; Edinburgh, 1994; Bath, 1995; Durham, 1996; Hong Kong, 1998; NUI, 1999. American Chem. Soc. Award in Inorganic Chemistry, 1970; Transition Metal Award, Chem. Soc., 1973; Davy Medal, Royal Soc., 1985; Mallinckrodt Award in Inorganic Chemistry, American Chem. Soc., 1986; Gold Medal, Apothecaries Soc., 1993; Paracelsus Prize and Gold Medal, New Swiss Chemical Soc., 1996; Sir Geoffrey Wilkinson Prize, Elsevier Science SA, 1997; August Wilhelm von Hofmann Denkmünze Meml Medal, German Chemical Soc., 1999. Chevalier, Ordre des Palmes Académiques, 1993; Commander, Cross of the Order of Merit (Poland), 1996. *Publications:* papers, mainly in Jl of Chem. Soc. *Address:* Robinson College, Grange Road, Cambridge CB3 9AN. *Clubs:* Royal Over-Seas League, Oxford and Cambridge.

LEWIS, Adam Anthony Murless, FRCS, FRCSE; Surgeon to the Royal Household, since 1991; Consultant Surgeon, Royal Free Hospital, since 1975; Surgeon: St John and Elizabeth Hospital, London; King Edward VII Hospital for Officers, London; *s* of late Bernard S. Lewis, CBE, DSC and of Mary Lewis (*née* Murless); *m* 1964, Margaret Catherine Ann Surgey; two *s* two *d. Educ:* St Bartholomew's Hosp. Med. Coll. (MB, BS London 1963); FRCSE 1968; FRCS 1969. Formerly: Sen. Registrar (Surg.), Royal Free Hosp.; Post Doctoral Fellow, Stanford Univ.; Sen. Lectr (Surg.), Univ. of Benin. *Publications:* papers on general and gastro-intestinal surgery. *Address:* Private Mail Box, Department of Surgery, Royal Free Hospital, NW3 2QG.

LEWIS, Maj.-Gen. Alfred George, CBE 1969; *b* 23 July 1920; *s* of Louis Lewis; *m* 1946, Daye Neville, *d* of Neville Greaves Hunt; two *s* two *d. Educ:* St Dunstan's Coll.; King's Coll., London. Served War of 1939–45, India and Burma. Commanded 15th/19th Hussars, 1961–63; Dir, Defence Operational Requirements Staff, MoD, 1967–68; Dep. Comdt, Royal Mil. Coll. of Science, 1968–70; Dir Gen., Fighting Vehicles and Engineer Equipment, 1970–72, retired 1973. Man. Dir, 1973–80, Dep. Chm., 1980–81, Alvis Ltd; Dep. Chm., Self Changing Gears Ltd, 1976–81; Company Secretary: Leyland Vehicles, 1980–81; Bus Manufacturers (Hldgs), 1980–84; Staff Dir, BL plc, 1981–84. Hon. Col, Queen's Own Mercian Yeomanry, 1977–82. Mem., St John Council for Warwickshire, 1973–97; OStJ 1996. *Recreations:* gardening, writing, making things, croquet.

LEWIS, (Alun) Kynric; QC 1978; QC (NI) 1988; a Recorder of the Crown Court, 1979–97; *b* Harlech, 23 May 1928; 3rd *s* of late Rev. Cadwaladr O. Lewis and Ursula Lewis; *m* 1955, Bethan, *er d* of late Prof. Edgar Thomas, CBE, and Eurwen Thomas; one *s* two *d. Educ:* The Grammar School, Beaumaris; University Coll. of N Wales (BSc); London School of Economics (LLB). Barrister, Middle Temple, 1954, Bencher, 1988; Gray's Inn, 1961; in practice in intellectual property law chambers, 1955–98. Asst Comr, Parly Boundary Commn for Wales, 1996–99. Member: Cttees of Investigation for GB and England and Wales under Agricl Marketing Act, 1979–88; Parole Bd, 1982–85; Welsh Arts Council, 1986–92. Hon. Counsel, Welsh Books Council, 1989–. *Recreations:* walking, fishing, tending vines. *Address:* Penrallt, Llys-faen, Caerdydd CF4 5TG; 8 New Square, Lincoln's Inn, WC2A 3QP. *Clubs:* Reform; Caerdydd a'r Sir.

LEWIS, Ann Walford, CMG 2000; HM Diplomatic Service, retired; *b* 2 May 1940; *d* of Dr Gwyn Walford Lewis and Winifred Marguerite Emma Lewis; one *s. Educ:* Allerton High Sch., Leeds; Leeds Univ. (BA). Teacher, translator and journalist, Finland, 1962–66; HM Diplomatic Service, 1966–2000: Research Dept, FCO, 1966–70; Second Secretary: Moscow, 1970–71; Res. Dept, FCO, 1971–72; Helsinki, 1972–74; Res. Dept, FCO, 1974–79; on secondment as Mem., Assessments Staff, Cabinet Office, 1979–82; Head of Chancery, E Berlin, 1982–85; Eastern Eur. Dept, FCO, 1985–91 (Dep. Head, 1988–91); Dep. Head, 1991–96, Head, 1996–2000, Cultural Relns Dept, FCO. Founder Dir, 1992, Dep. Chm., 1998–, English Coll. Foundn; Governor: English Coll., Prague, 1995–; St Clare's, Oxford, 2000–. Trustee, BEARR Trust, 1999–. *Publication:* (ed) The EU and Ukraine, 2001. *Recreations:* theatre, gardening, travel. *Address:* 16 Townley Road, SE22 8SR. *T:* (020) 8693 6418.

LEWIS, Anthony; *see* Lewis, J. A.

LEWIS, Anthony Meredith; Director, Mentmore Abbey plc (formerly Birkby plc), since 1992 (Chairman, 1995–97); *b* 15 Nov. 1940; *s* of Col Glyndwr Vivian Lancelot Lewis and Gillian Lewis (*née* Fraser); *m* 1970, Mrs Ewa Maria Anna Strawinska, former Social Editor of Tatler; one *s* one *d. Educ:* Rugby School; St Edmund Hall, Oxford (MA Law). Freshfields, 1964–70; Partner, Joynson-Hicks, 1970–86, Senior Partner, 1986–89; Jt Sen. Partner, Taylor Joynson Garrett, 1989–94. Chief Exec., City & Thames Gp, 1994–; Dir, South Thames Properties Ltd, 1994–. Panel Mem., The Prince's Trust, 1996–. *Recreations:* opera, tennis, ski-ing, golf.

LEWIS, Anthony Robert, (Tony Lewis); DL; writer and broadcaster; Consultant: World Sport Group; British Tourist Authority (Sport); *b* 6 July 1938; *s* of Wilfrid Llewellyn Lewis and Florence Marjorie Lewis (*née* Flower); *m* 1962, Joan (*née* Pritchard); two *d. Educ:* Neath Grammar Sch.; Christ's Coll., Cambridge (MA). Double Blue, Rugby football, 1959, cricket, 1960–62, Captain of cricket, 1962, Cambridge Univ. Glamorgan CCC: cricketer, 1955–74; Captain, 1967–72; Chm., 1988–93; Pres., 1999–April 2002; 9 Tests for England, 1972–73 (Captain of 8); Captained MCC to India, Ceylon and Pakistan, 1972–73. Presenter: sports and arts magazine programmes, HTV, 1971–82; Sport on Four, BBC Radio, 1977–86; BBC TV presenter of cricket and commentator, 1974–98; Cricket Correspondent, Sunday Telegraph, 1974–93; freelance sports contributor, Sunday Telegraph, 1993–99. Chm. Cttee, Assoc. of Business Sponsorship of the Arts (Wales), 1988–90; Member: Bd, Sports Council for Wales, 1967–69; Welsh Economic Council, 1994–96; Tourism Action Gp, CBI, 1994–; Bd, BTA, 1992–2000; Chm., Wales Tourist Bd, 1992–2000. DL, 1994, High Sheriff, 1998–99, Mid Glam. Hon. Fellow: St David's Univ. Coll., Lampeter, 1993; Glamorgan Univ., 1995; Univ. of Wales, Swansea, 1996; Cardiff Univ., 1999. *Publications:* A Summer of Cricket, 1976; Playing Days, 1985; Double Century, 1987; Cricket in Many Lands, 1991; MCC Masterclass, 1994. *Recreations:* classical music, golf. *Address:* Castellau, near Llantrisant, Mid Glamorgan CF72 8LP. *Clubs:* East India, MCC (Pres., 1998–2000); Cardiff and County; Royal Porthcawl Golf, Royal Worlington & Newmarket Golf, Royal & Ancient Golf.

LEWIS, Prof. Barry, MD, PhD; FRCP; FRCPath; Consultant Physician and Professor Emeritus, University of London; *b* 16 March 1929; *s* of George Lewis and Pearl Lewis; *m* 1972, Eve Simone Rothschild; three *c. Educ:* Rondebosch School, Cape Town; University of Cape Town. PhD, MD. Training posts, Groote Schuur Hosp., Cape Town, 1953; lectureship and fellowships, St George's Hosp., 1959; MRC, 1963; Consultant Pathologist, St Mark's Hosp., 1967; Sen. Lectr in Chemical Pathology, hon. consultant chem. pathologist and physician, Hammersmith Hosp., 1971; Chm., Dept of Chem. Path. and Metabolic Disorders, St Thomas' Hosp., and Dir of Lipid Clinic, 1976–88. Recent research interests: causes, prevention and regression of atherosclerosis. Chm., Internat. Taskforce for Prevention of Coronary Heart Disease, 1987–94. Heinrich Wieland Prize, 1980. *Publications:* The Hyperlipidaemias: clinical and laboratory practice, 1976; (with Eve Lewis) The Heart Book, 1980; (with N. Miller) Lipoproteins, Atherosclerosis and Coronary Heart Disease, 1981; (jtly) Metabolic and Molecular Bases of Acquired Disease, 1990; Handbook on Prevention of Coronary Heart Disease, 1990; (with G. Assmann) Social and Economic Contexts of Coronary Disease Prevention, 1990; (jtly) Prevention of Coronary Heart Disease in the Elderly, 1991; (jtly) Prevention of Coronary Heart Disease: scientific background and clinical guidelines, 1993; (jtly) Low Blood Cholesterol: health implications, 1993; Paradise Regained: insights into coronary heart disease prevention, 1997; numerous papers on heart disease, nutrition and lipoproteins in med. and sci. jls. *Recreations:* music, travel, reading. *Address:* 14 Wimpole Street, W1M 7AB. *T:* (020) 7636 9901.

LEWIS, Bernard, BA, PhD; FBA 1963; FRHistS; Cleveland E. Dodge Professor of Near Eastern Studies, Princeton University, 1974–86, now Emeritus; Director of Annenberg Research Institute, Philadelphia, 1986–90; *b* London, 31 May 1916; *s* of H. Lewis, London; *m* 1947, Ruth Hélène (marr. diss. 1974), *d* of late Overretsagfrer M. Oppenhejm, Copenhagen; one *s* one *d. Educ:* Wilson Coll.; The Polytechnic; Universities of London and Paris (Fellow UCL 1976). Derby Student, 1936. Asst Lecturer in Islamic History, Sch. of Oriental Studies, University of London, 1938; Prof. of History of Near and Middle East, SOAS, London Univ., 1949–74 (Hon. Fellow, 1986). Served RAC and Intelligence Corps, 1940–41; attached to a dept of Foreign Office, 1941–45. Visiting Professor: UCLA, 1955–56; Columbia Univ., 1960; Indiana Univ., 1963; Collège de France, 1980; Ecoles des Hautes Etudes, Paris 1983–86; A. D. White Prof.-at-Large, Cornell Univ., 1984–90; Hon. Incumbent, Kemal Atatürk Chair in Ottoman and Turkish Studies, 1992–93. Vis. Mem., 1969, Long-term Mem., 1974–86, Inst. for Advanced Study, Princeton, New Jersey; Lectures: Class of 1932, Princeton Univ., 1964; Gottesman, Yeshiva Univ., 1974; Exxon Foundn, Chicago, 1986; Tanner, Brasenose Coll., Oxford, 1990; Jefferson, NEH, 1990; Il Mulino, Bologna, 1991; Weizman, Rehovot, Israel, 1991; Henry M. Jackson Meml, Seattle, 1992; Merle Curti, Wisconsin, 1993. Mem., Amer. Acad. of Arts and Scis, 1983; Membre Associe, Institut d'Egypte, Cairo, 1969; For. Mem., Amer. Philosophical Soc., 1973; Corresp. Mem., Institut de France, 1994; Hon. Mem., Turkish Acad. of Scis, 1997. Hon. Fellow, Turkish Historical Soc., Ankara, 1972; Hon. Dr: Hebrew Univ., Jerusalem, 1974; Tel Aviv Univ., 1979; State Univ. of NY, Univ. of Penn, Hebrew Union Coll., 1987; Haifa, 1991; Yeshiva, 1991; Bar-Ilan, 1992; Brandeis, 1993; Ben-Gurion Univ., 1996; Ankara, 1996. Certificate of Merit for services to Turkish Culture, Turkish Govt, 1973. Harvey Prizewinner, 1978. *Publications:* The Origins of Ismā'īlism, 1940; Turkey Today, 1940; British contributions to Arabic Studies, 1941; Handbook of Diplomatic and Political Arabic, 1947, 1956; (ed) Land of Enchanters, 1948; The Arabs in History, 1950, 6th rev. edn 1993; Notes and Documents from the Turkish Archives, 1952; The Emergence of Modern Turkey, 1961 (rev. edn, 1968); The Kingly Crown (translated from Ibn Gabirol), 1961; co-ed. with P. M. Holt, Historians of the Middle East, 1962; Istanbul and the Civilization of the Ottoman Empire, 1963; The Middle East and the West, 1964; The Assassins, 1967; Race and Colour in Islam, 1971; Islam in History, 1973, rev. edn 1993; Islam from the Prophet Muhammad to the Capture of Constantinople, 2 vols, 1974; History, Remembered, Recovered, Invented, 1975; (ed) The World of Islam: Faith, People, Culture, 1976; Studies in Classical and Ottoman Islam, 7th-16th centuries, 1976; (with Amnon Cohen) Population and Revenue in the Towns of Palestine in the Sixteenth Century, 1978; The Muslim Discovery of Europe, 1982; The Jews of Islam, 1984; Le Retour de l'Islam, 1985; (ed, with others) As Others See Us: mutual perceptions East and West, 1985; Semites and Anti-Semites, 1986, rev. edn 1999; The Political Language of Islam, 1988; Race and Slavery in the Middle East, 1990; (ed jtly) Muslims in Europe, 1992; (ed jtly) Religionsgerspräche im Mittelalter, 1992; Islam and the West, 1993; The Shaping of the Modern Middle East, 1994; Cultures in Conflict: Christians, Muslims and Jews in the Age of Discovery, 1994; The Middle East: two thousand years of history from the rise of Christianity to the present day, 1995; The Future of the Middle East, 1997; The Multiple Identities of the Middle East, 1998; A Middle East Mosaic: fragments of life, letters and history, 2000; co-ed, Encyclopaedia of Islam, 1956–87; (ed, with others) The Cambridge History of Islam, vols 1–11, 1971; articles in learned journals. *Address:* Near Eastern Studies Department, Jones Hall, Princeton University, Princeton, NJ 08544-1008, USA. *Club:* Athenæum.

LEWIS, Very Rev. Bertie; Vicar of Nevern with Eglwyswrw, Meline, Eglwyswen and Llanfair Nant-gwyn, 1994–96; *b* 24 Aug. 1931; *m* 1958, Rayann Pryce; one *s* three *d. Educ:* St David's Coll., Lampeter (BA); St Catherine's Coll., Oxford (MA); Wycliffe Hall, Oxford. Deacon 1957; priest 1958; Curate: Cwmaman, 1957–60; Aberystwyth St Michael, 1960–62; Vicar: Llanddewibrefi, 1962–65; Henfynyw with Aberaeron, 1965–75; Lampeter, 1975–80; Canon, St Davids Cathedral, 1978–86; Rector, Rectorial Benefice of Aberystwyth, 1980–88; Archdeacon of Cardigan, 1986–90; Vicar of Nevern, 1988–90; Dean of St David's Cathedral, 1990–94, Hon. Canon, 1994–96. *Recreations:* rugby, music, books. *Address:* Bryn Golau, Llanfarian, Aberystwyth, Ceredigion SY23 4BT.

LEWIS, Brian William; His Honour Judge Brian Lewis; a Circuit Judge, since 1997; *b* 23 July 1949; *o s* of Gilbert Pryce Lewis and Mary Williamson Lewis (now Sharples); *m* 1981, Maureen O'Hare; one *s. Educ:* Sale Co. GS for Boys; Univ. of Hull (LLB Hons). Called to the Bar, Inner Temple, 1973; Lectr, Barnet Coll., 1973–74; in practice at the Bar, Cardiff, 1974–75, Liverpool, 1976–97; Asst Recorder, 1989–93; a Recorder, 1993–97. *Recreations:* family life, sport, reading, military history. *Address:* Queen Elizabeth II Law Courts, Derby Square, Liverpool L2 1XA. *T:* (0151) 473 7373.

LEWIS, Carl; *see* Lewis, F. C.

LEWIS, Very Rev. Christopher Andrew, PhD; Dean of St Albans, since 1994; *b* 4 Feb. 1944; *s* of Adm. Sir Andrew Lewis, KCB and late Rachel Elizabeth (*née* Leatham); *m* 1970, Rhona Jane Martindale; two *s* one *d. Educ:* Marlborough Coll.; Bristol Univ. (BA 1969); Corpus Christi Coll., Cambridge (PhD 1974); Westcott House, Cambridge. Served RN, 1961–66; ordained deacon, 1973, priest, 1974; Asst Curate, Barnard Castle, 1973–76; Tutor, Ripon Coll., Cuddesdon, 1976–81; Dir, Oxford Inst. for Church and Soc., 1976–79; Priest-in-charge, Aston Rowant and Crowell, 1978–81; Vice Principal, Ripon Coll., Cuddesdon, 1981–82; Vicar of Spalding, 1982–87; Canon Residentiary, Canterbury Cathedral, 1987–94; Dir of Ministerial Trng, dio. of Canterbury, 1989–94. Chm., Assoc. of English Cathedrals, 2000–. *Recreations:* guinea fowl, bicycles. *Address:* The Deanery, St Albans, Herts AL1 1BY. *T:* (01727) 890202, *Fax:* (01727) 890227; *e-mail:* dean@stalbanscathedral.org.uk.

LEWIS, Claire; *see* Curtis-Thomas, C.

LEWIS, Clive Hewitt, FRICS; President, Royal Institution of Chartered Surveyors, 1993–94; *b* 29 March 1936; *s* of Thomas Jonathan Lewis, OBE and Marguerite Eileen Lewis; *m* 1961, Jane Penelope White; two *s* one *d. Educ:* St Peter's Sch., York. FRICS 1963; FSVA 1979. With Goddard & Smith, 1957–62; Founder and Sen. Partner, Clive Lewis & Partners, 1963–92, when merged with Edward Erdman; Jt Chm., Colliers Erdman Lewis, 1993–95. Non-executive Director: St Modwen Properties, 1983–; Town Centre Securities, 1994–; Freeport Leisure, 1997–. Dep. Chm., Merseyside Develt Corp., 1989–98. Chm., Bank of England Property Forum, 1994–. Mem. Council, Internat. Year of Shelter for the Homeless, 1985–88. Mem., Gen. Council, RICS, 1987–95 (Pres., Gen. Practice Div., 1989–90); President: Eur. Council of Real Estate Professionals, 1990; UK, 1976–77, World, 1984–85, Internat. Real Estate Fedn (Mem. Exec. Cttee, 1977–92). Pres., Land Aid Charitable Trust, 1986–. Freeman, City of London, 1983; Liveryman, Chartered Surveyors' Co., 1983–. Hon. DLitt S Bank, 1993. *Recreations:* bridge, dogs, golf, cricket. *Address:* Oakhurst, 7 Totteridge Common, N20 8LL. *T:* (020) 8445 5109. *Clubs:* MCC; S Herts Golf.

LEWIS, Prof. Dan, PhD; DSc; FRS 1955; Quain Professor of Botany, London University, 1957–78, now Emeritus; Hon. Research Fellow, University College, London, since 1978; *b* 30 Dec. 1910; *s* of Ernest Albert and Edith J. Lewis; *m* 1933, Mary Phœbe Eleanor Burry; one *d. Educ:* High Sch., Newcastle-under-Lyme, Staffs; Reading University (BSc); PhD, DSc (London). Research Scholar, Reading Univ., 1935–36; Scientific Officer, Pomology Dept, John Innes Hort. Inst., 1935–48; Head of Genetics Dept, John Innes Horticultural Institution, Bayfordbury, Hertford, Herts, 1948–57. Rockefeller Foundation Special Fellowship, California Inst. of Technology, 1955–56; Visiting Prof. of Genetics, University of Calif, Berkeley, 1961–62; Royal Society Leverhulme Visiting Professor: University of Delhi, 1965–66; Singapore, 1970; Vis. Prof., QMC, 1978–. Pres., Genetical Soc., 1968–71; Mem., UGC, 1969–74. *Publications:* Sexual Incompatibility in Plants, 1979; Editor, Science Progress; scientific papers on Genetics and Plant Physiology. *Recreations:* swimming, gardening, music. *Address:* Flat 2, 56/57 Myddelton Square, EC1R 1YA. *T:* (020) 7278 6948.

LEWIS, Sir David Courtenay M.; *see* Mansel Lewis.

LEWIS, David Henry L.; *see* LeRoy-Lewis.

LEWIS, (David) Ralph; QC 1999; a Recorder, since 2000; *b* 29 June 1956; *s* of David Ieuan Lewis and (Annie Mary) Eunice Lewis (*née* Evans); *m* Elizabeth Shelley; two *s* one *d. Educ:* Dudley Grammar Sch.; Jesus Coll., Oxford (MA). Called to the Bar, Middle Temple, 1978; an Asst Recorder, 1996–2000. Mem., Bar Council, 1999–. *Recreations:* shooting, travel, ski-ing. *Address:* 5 Fountain Court, Steelhouse Lane, Birmingham B4 6DR. *T:* (0121) 606 0500. *Club:* Oxford and Cambridge.

LEWIS, David Robert; Secretary, Royal Commission on Environmental Pollution, 1992–2001; *b* 27 Nov. 1940; *o c* of William Lewis, Pembroke Dock and Kate Lewis (*née* Sperring); *m* 1965, Christine, *o d* of Leslie and Maud Tye; three *s. Educ:* Stoneleigh W Co. Primary Sch.; Tiffin Sch.; New Coll., Oxford (Classical Exhibn; MA; DPhil 1970). Editor: Breakthrough, 1960–61; New Directions, 1964–66; joined Min. of Housing and Local Govt, 1965; Sec., Central Adv. Water Cttee, 1969–73; HM Treasury, 1973–75; Asst Sec., Central Unit on Envmtl Pollution, DoE, 1975–77; Dir, Public Admin and Social Policy, CS Coll., 1978–80; Asst Sec., DoE, 1981–89; Hd, Water Services Div., DoE, 1990–92. Chm. Govs, Ernest Bevin Sch., later Coll., 1988–99; Chm., Sir Walter St John's Educnl Charity, 1997–. *Publications:* The Electrical Trades Union and the Growth of the Electrical Industry, 1970; (ed jtly) Policies into Practice, 1984. *Recreations:* exploring new places, 17th and 18th century literature. *Club:* Powysland (Welshpool).

LEWIS, David Thomas Rowell; Senior Partner, Norton Rose, since 1997; *b* 1 Nov. 1947; *s* of Thomas Price Merfyn Lewis; *m* 1970, Theresa Susan Poole; one *s* one *d. Educ:* Dragon Sch., Oxford; St Edward's Sch., Oxford; Jesus Coll., Oxford (MA 1969; Hon. Fellow 1998). Admitted solicitor, 1972, Hong Kong, 1977; joined Norton Rose, 1969: articled, 1969–72; Asst Solicitor, 1972–76; Partner, 1977; Managing Partner, Hong Kong Office, 1979–82; Head: Corporate Finance, 1989–94; Professional Resources, 1994–99. Trustee: Oxford Univ. Law Foundn, 1997–; Oxford Inst. of Legal Practice, 2001–. Director and Governor: Dragon Sch., Oxford, 1987–; Oxford Brookes Univ., 1995–; Mem., Law Soc. Legal Practice Course Bd, 1995–2000. Pres., St Edward's Sch. Soc., 1995–96. *Publications:* contrib. articles in jls. *Recreations:* keeping fit, spoiling my dogs, collecting maps, travel, supporting Welsh Rugby. *Address:* Norton Rose, Kempson House, Camomile Street, EC3A 7AN. *T:* (020) 7283 6000. *Clubs:* Achilles; Hong Kong (Hong Kong).

LEWIS, David Whitfield, RDI 1995; freelance design consultant, since 1967; *b* 19 Feb. 1939; *s* of John Whitfield Lewis and Joan Lewis; *m* 1964, Marianne Mygind; one *s* one *d. Educ:* Central Sch. of Design, London. Employed by Danish design consultancy, working on radio and television equipment designs, incl. designs for Beolab 5000 Series Hi-Fi music systems for Bang & Olufsen, and invented slide rule motif, 1960–68; collaborated with Henning Moldenhawer on television equipment for Bang & Olufsen, and industrial processing machinery and marine products, 1968–80; work included in Design Collection, Mus. of Modern Art, NY. ID Prize, Danish Design Centre, 1976 (marine folding propeller), 1982 (dental tools), 1986 (television set), 1990 (push button system), 1994 (audio system); Design Prize, EC, 1988; MITI, G-Mark Grand Prix, 1991 (audio hi-fi system); Internat. Design Prize, Badenwurttemberg, 1993 (audio hi-fi system). *Address:* David Lewis Industrial Design Aps, Store Kongensgade 110c, 1264 Copenhagen, Denmark. *T:* 33139635; Piniehøj 2, 2960 Rungsted Kyst, Denmark.

LEWIS, Dr Dennis Aubrey, BSc; Director, Aslib, the Association for Information Management, 1981–89; *b* 1 Oct. 1928; *s* of Joseph and Minnie Lewis; *m* 1956, Gillian Mary Bratby; two *s. Educ:* Latymer Upper Sch.; Univ. of London (BSc 1st Cl. Hons Chemistry, 1953; PhD 1956). FIInfSc 1984. Res. Chemist, 1956–68, Intelligence Manager, 1968–81, ICI Plastics Div. Member: Adv. Council, British Library, 1976–81; Library Adv. Cttee, British Council, 1981–. Member: Welwyn Garden UDC, 1968–74; Welwyn Hatfield DC, 1974– (Chm., 1976–77). *Publications:* Index of Reviews in Organic Chemistry, annually 1963–; (ed jtly) Great Information Disasters, 1991; pubns on information management in Aslib Procs and other journals. *Recreations:* music, old churches, 'futurology'. *Address:* c/o National Westminster Bank, Welwyn Garden City, Herts.

LEWIS, Derek (Compton); Chairman, Patientline Ltd, since 1998 (Chief Executive, 1998–2001); *b* 9 July 1946; *s* of Kenneth Compton Lewis and Marjorie Lewis; *m* 1969, Louise (*née* Wharton); two *d. Educ:* Wrekin Coll., Telford; Queens' Coll., Cambridge (MA); London Business Sch. (MSc). Ford Motor Co., 1968–82, Dir of Finance, Ford of Europe, 1978–82; Dir of Corporate Develt and Gp Planning Man., Imperial Gp, 1982–84; Granada Group: Finance Dir, 1984–87; Man. Dir, 1988–89; Gp Chief Exec., 1990–91; Dir, Courtaulds Textiles, 1990–93; Chief Exec. and Dir Gen., HM Prison Service, 1993–95. Chairman: UK Gold Television Ltd, 1992–97; Sunsail International, 1997–99. Trustee, Patients Assoc., 1999–. Mem. Council, Univ. of Essex, 1999–. *Publication:* Hidden Agendas, 1997. *Address:* (office) Monarch House, 1A Herschel Street, Slough, Bucks SL1 1SY. *Club:* Caledonian.

LEWIS, (Derek) Trevor; Vice-Chairman, Bradford & Bingley plc (formerly Bradford & Bingley Building Society), since 1995 (Director, since 1990); *b* 21 Oct. 1936; *s* of Lionel Lewis and Mabel (*née* Clare); *m* 1961, Pamela Jean Ratcliffe; one *s* one *d. Educ:* Bradford Grammar Sch.; Leeds Univ. (LLB); 2nd Cl. Hons Solicitors' Final Exam., 1960. With A. V. Hammond & Co., subseq. Hammond Suddards: articled to Sir Richard Denby, 1955–60; Asst Solicitor, 1960–63; Partner 1964–87; Jt Sen. Partner, 1987–95. Dir, W Yorks Independent Hosp., 1979–85 (Chm., 1985–88); Chairman: Little Germany Urban Village Co. Ltd, 1999–; Arts and Business Yorkshire Ltd, 2000–. *Address:* PO Box 88, Croft Road, Crossflatts, Bingley, W Yorks BD16 2UA. *T:* (01274) 555555.

LEWIS, Dr Dewi Meirion, FInstP; Vice President Physics, Nycomed Amersham plc, since 1999; *b* Chester, 4 Sept. 1948; *s* of Hugh and Mair Lewis; *m* 1972, Elizabeth Mary Williams; two *s* one *d. Educ:* Ysgol Ardudwy Harlech, Gwynedd; UCW, Swansea (BSc 1969; PhD 1972). FInstP 1995. Res. Fellow, CERN, Geneva, 1973–74; Engr i/c, CERN ISR accelerator, 1974–79; Cyclotron Project Leader, TRC Ltd, 1979–83; Amersham International plc: Hd, Cyclotron Dept, 1983–88; Business Manager, Cyclotron and Reactor Pharmaceuticals, 1988–91; Mfg Strategy Manager, 1991–94; R&D Strategy Manager, 1994–99. Vis. Prof. of Physics, Liverpool Univ., 1997–2001. Non-exec. Dir, Reviss Services Ltd, 1992–95. Member: OECD/NEA Expert Panel on Isotopes, 1997–99; Measurement Adv. Cttee, DTI, 2001–. Member: Council, PPARC, 2000– (Chm., Audit Cttee, 2001–); EPSRC Coll., 2000–. Chm., Tech. Cttee, ARPES, Brussels, 1993–; Scientific Advr, EC DG XII, 1994–; Mem., EMIR Network, Brussels, 2001– (Chm., Isotopes Cttee, 2001–). Mem., British Astronomical Soc., 2001. Member: Amer. Assoc. Physicists in Medicine, 2001; Eur. Assoc. Nuclear Medicine, 2001. *Publications:* contrib. articles to res. jls. *Recreations:* ski-ing, Alpine walking, golf, Rugby coaching, choral music, astronomy. *Address:* Solaise, Kiln Road, Prestwood, Bucks HP16 9DG. *T:* (01494) 543065; Nycomed Amersham plc, Amersham Laboratories, White Lion Road, Amersham, Bucks HP7 9LL. *Club:* Harewood Downs (Bucks).

LEWIS, Donald Gordon, OBE 1988; Director, National Exhibition Centre, 1982–84; *b* 12 Sept. 1926; *s* of late Albert Francis Lewis and Nellie Elizabeth Lewis; *m* 1950, Doreen Mary (*née* Gardner); one *d. Educ:* King Edward's Sch., Birmingham; Liverpool Univ. Dairy Industry, 1947–91; Gen. Sales Manager, Birmingham Dairies, 1961–91. Councillor (C) Birmingham CC, Selly Oak Ward, 1959, Alderman 1971–74; past Chairman, Transport and Airport Committees; West Midlands County Council: Mem., 1974–81; Chm., 1980–81; Chairman, Airport Cttee, 1974–80; Sec., Conservative Group, 1974–80; City of Birmingham District Council: Mem., 1982–95; Hon. Alderman, 1995–; Chm., Nat. Exhibn Centre Cttee, 1982–84; Chm., Birmingham Housing Cttee, 1983–84. Mem., W Midlands PTA, 1984–95; Director: Birmingham International Airport plc, 1994–96; Community Transport Ltd, 1997–; Broader Choices for Old People, 1999–. Chm., Selly Oak (Birmingham) Constituency Conservative Assoc., 1975–80, Pres., 1980; Vice-Pres., Birmingham Cons. Assoc., 1987– (Chm., 1984–87). Gov., Selly Park Girls' Sch., 1980–. *Recreation:* eating out. *Address:* 25 Albany Gardens, Hampton Lane, Solihull B91 2PT. *T:* (0121) 705 7661.

LEWIS, Prof. Edward B., PhD; Thomas Hunt Morgan Professor of Biology, California Institute of Technology, 1966–88, now Emeritus; *b* 20 May 1918; *s* of Edward B. Lewis and Laura H. Lewis; *m* 1946, Pamela H. Harrah; two *s* (and one *s* decd). *Educ:* Univ. of Minnesota (BA Biostats 1939); California Inst. of Technol. (PhD Genetics 1942; MS Meteorology 1943). Served USAAF (Capt.), 1942–46. Instructor, CIT, 1946–48; Rockefeller Foundn Fellow, Cambridge Univ., 1947–48; California Institute of Technology: Asst Prof. of Biol., 1948–49; Associate Prof., 1949–56; Prof. of Biol., 1956–66. Guest Prof., Inst. of Genetics, Univ. of Copenhagen, 1975–76. Hon. PhD Umeå, Sweden, 1981; Hon. DSc Minnesota, 1993. Nat. Medal of Sci., USA, 1990; (jtly) Nobel Prize in Physiology or Medicine, 1995. *Publications:* (ed) Genetics and Evolution: selected papers of A. H. Sturtevant, 1961; contrib. chapters in books; contrib. numerous papers and articles in Proc. Nat. Acad. Sci., Genetics, Jl Heredity, Nature, Science, Genes and Develt, and others. *Recreations:* flute, swimming, jogging, marine biology. *Address:* California Institute of Technology, Division of Biology 156–29, Pasadena, CA 91125, USA. *Fax:* (626) 5649685.

LEWIS, Ernest Gordon, (Toby), CMG 1972; OBE 1958; HM Diplomatic Service, retired; *b* New Zealand, 26 Sept. 1918; *s* of George Henry Lewis; *m* 1949, Jean Margaret, *d* of late A. H. Smyth. *Educ:* Otago Boys' High Sch.; Otago Univ., NZ. Served War, Army, with 2nd NZ Div., Middle East, 1939–46 (Lt-Col; despatches, MBE); Staff Coll., Haifa, 1943. Joined Colonial Service, Nigeria, 1947; Administrator, Turks and Caicos Is, 1955–59; Permanent Sec., to Federal Govt of Nigeria, 1960–62; First Sec., Pakistan, 1963–66; Foreign and Commonwealth Office, 1966–69; Kuching, Sarawak, 1969–70; Governor and C-in-C, Falkland Islands, and High Comr, British Antarctic Territory, 1971–75; Head of Gibraltar and General Dept, FCO, 1975–77. *Address:* 5 Smith Street, Chelsea, SW3 4EE.

LEWIS, His Honour Esyr ap Gwilym; QC 1971; a Circuit Judge (Official Referee), 1984–98; Senior Official Referee, 1994–98; *b* 11 Jan. 1926; *s* of late Rev. T. W. Lewis, BA, and Mary Jane May Lewis (*née* Selway); *m* 1957, Elizabeth Anne Vidler Hoffmann, 2nd *d* of O. W. Hoffmann, Bassett, Southampton; four *d*. *Educ:* Salford Grammar Sch.; Mill Hill Sch.; Trinity Hall, Cambridge (MA, LLM). Served in Intelligence Corps, 1944–47. Exhibitioner, 1944, Scholar, 1948, at Trinity Hall (Dr Cooper's Law Studentship, 1950); 1st cl. hons, Law Tripos II, 1949, 1st cl. LLB, 1950, Cambridge. Holker Sen. Schol., Gray's Inn, 1950; Called to Bar, Gray's Inn, 1951 (Bencher, 1978; Treas., 1997). Law Supervisor, Trinity Hall, 1950–55; Law Lectr, Cambridgeshire Technical Coll., 1949–50. A Recorder, 1972–84; a Dep. High Court Judge, 1978–84; Leader, Wales and Chester Circuit, 1978–81. Member: Bar Council, 1965–68; Council of Legal Education, 1967–73; Criminal Injuries Compensation Bd, 1977–84. Contested (L) Llanelli, 1964. *Publication:* contributor to Newnes Family Lawyer, 1963. *Recreations:* reading, gardening, watching Rugby football. *Address:* 2 South Square, Gray's Inn, WC1R 5HP. *T:* (020) 7405 5918. *Clubs:* Garrick; Old Millhillians.
See also M. ap G. Lewis.

LEWIS, Frederick Carlton, (Carl); athlete; *b* 1 July 1961; *s* of Bill and Evelyn Lewis. *Educ:* Univ. of Houston. Winner, 100m, 200m, and long jump, US National Athletics Championships, 1983; *Olympic Games:* Gold medals, 100m and 200m, long jump and 4×100m, 1984; Gold medals, 100m and long jump, Silver medal, 200m, 1988; Gold medals, long jump and 4×100m, 1992; Gold medal long jump, 1996; *World Championships:* Gold medals, 100m, long jump, 4×100m, 1983; Gold medals, long jump, 4×100m, 1987; Gold medals, 100m, 4×100m, 1991. World Record: long jump (8.79m), 1983; 100m (9.86 seconds), 1991. James E. Sullivan Meml Award, Amateur Athletic Union of US, 1981; Athlete of the Century, IAAF, 1999.

LEWIS, Prof. Geoffrey Lewis, CMG 1999; FBA 1979; Professor of Turkish, University of Oxford, 1986, now Emeritus; Fellow, St Antony's College, Oxford, 1961, now Emeritus; *b* 19 June 1920; *s* of Ashley Lewis and Jeanne Muriel (*née* Sintrop); *m* 1941, Raphaela Rhoda Bale Seideman; one *s* (one *d* decd). *Educ:* University Coll. Sch.; St John's Coll., Oxford (MA 1945, DPhil 1950; James Mew Arabic Scholar, 1947; Hon. Fellow, 2000). Lectr in Turkish, 1950–54, Sen. Lectr in Islamic Studies, 1954–64, Sen. Lectr in Turkish, 1964–86, Oxford Univ. Vis. Professor: Robert Coll., Istanbul, 1959–68; Princeton Univ., 1970–71, 1974; UCLA, 1975; British Acad. Leverhulme Vis. Prof., Turkey, 1984. Vice-Pres., Anglo-Turkish Soc., 1972–; Mem., British-Turkish Mixed Commn, 1975–95; Pres., British Soc. for Middle Eastern Studies, 1981–83. Corresp. Mem., Turkish Language Soc., 1953–. DUniv: Univ. of the Bosphorus, Istanbul, 1986; Univ. of Istanbul, 1992. Turkish Govt Cert. of Merit, 1973; Turkish Min. of For. Affairs Exceptional Service Plaque, 1991; Order of Merit (Turkish Republic), 1998. *Publications:* Teach Yourself Turkish, 1953, rev. edn 1989; Modern Turkey, 1955, 4th edn 1974; (trans., with annotations) Katib Chelebi, The Balance of Truth, 1957; Plotiniana Arabica, 1959; (with Barbara Hodge) A Study in Education for International Misunderstanding (Cyprus School History Textbooks), 1966; Turkish Grammar, 1967, rev. edn 2000; (with M. S. Spink) Albucasis on Surgery and Instruments, 1973; The Book of Dede Korkut, 1974; The Atatürk I Knew, 1981; Thickhead and other Turkish Stories, 1988; Just a Diplomat, 1992; Turkish Language Reform: a catastrophic success, 1999; articles on Turkish language, history and politics, and on Arab alchemy. *Recreations:* bodging, etymology. *Address:* St Antony's College, Oxford OX2 6JF; 93 Woodstock Road, Oxford OX2 6HL. *T:* (01865) 557150.

LEWIS, Gillian Marjorie, FMA, FIIC; heritage consultant, since 1994; *b* 10 Oct. 1945; *d* of late William Lewis and of Marjorie Lewis (*née* Pargeter). *Educ:* Tiffin Sch., Kingston upon Thames; Univ. of Newcastle upon Tyne (BA 1967); DCP, Gateshead Tech. Coll., 1969; Birkbeck Coll., London (Cert. Ecology, 1991). FIIC 1977; FMA 1988. Shipley Art Gallery, Co. Durham, 1967–69; free-lance conservator, 1969–73; Nat. Maritime Mus., 1973–94; Keeper of Conservation, 1978; Hd, Div. of Conservation and Technical Services, 1978–88; Asst Dep. Dir, 1982–86; Hd of Conservation and Registration, 1988–91; Head of Collection Projects, 1991–92; Head of External Affairs, 1992–94. Vice-Chm., UK Inst. for Conservation, 1983–84 (Mem. Cttee, 1978–80). Member: Technical Cttee, City and Guilds of London Sch. of Art, 1981–; Cttee, Dulwich Picture Gall., 1983–92; Wallpaintings Conservation Panel, Council for Care of Churches, 1985–88; Volunteer Steering Cttee, Office of Arts and Libraries, 1988–90; Adv. Cttee, Museums and Galleries Commn, 1988–96; Trng Standards Panel, Museums Trng Inst., 1990–93; Council, Leather Conservation Centre, 1991–92; Fabric Adv. Cttee, Southwark Cathedral, 1997–; Preservation Advr to Dean and Chapter, Peterborough Cathedral, 1994–; Advr, Heather Trust for the Arts, 1997–2000. Examiner, London Inst., Camberwell Sch. of Art, 1991–93; Assessor, Clore Small Grants Prog., 1998–. Trustee: Whatmore Trust, 1988–; Southwark Cathedral Millennium Trust, 1998–; Cathedral Camps, 1998–; Edward James Foundn, 1999–. UN50 UK Ambassador, 1995. FRSA 1987. *Address:* 28 Trinity Church Square, SE1 4HY. *Club:* Architecture.

LEWIS, Prof. Glyn Hywel, PhD; FRCPsych; Professor of Community and Epidemiological Psychiatry, University of Wales College of Medicine, since 1996; *b* 6 Dec. 1956; *s* of Jeffrey and Marion Lewis; *m* 1982, Priscilla Hall; one *s*. *Educ:* University Coll., Oxford (MSc 1980; MA 1983); University Coll. London (MB BS 1982); Inst. of Psychiatry, London Univ. (PhD 1991). FRCPsych 1998. Registrar, Bethlem and Maudsley Hosp., 1983–86; Res. Fellow, 1986–91, Sen. Lectr, 1991–95, Inst. of Psychiatry, London Univ.; on secondment to DoH, 1991–94; Res. Fellow, LSHTM, 1993–95. *Address:* Division of Psychological Medicine, University of Wales College of Medicine, Heath Park, Cardiff CF4 4XN.

LEWIS, Graham D.; *see* Dixon-Lewis.

LEWIS, Prof. Graham Pritchard; Dean, Hunterian Institute (formerly Institute of Basic Medical Sciences), 1982–89, Vandervell Professor of Pharmacology, 1974–89, now Emeritus, Royal College of Surgeons; *b* 5 Aug. 1927; *s* of George Henry and Ruth Lewis; *m* Averil Priscilla Myrtle; two *s* two *d*. *Educ:* Monkton House School, Cardiff; University College Cardiff (BPharm, PhD). Mem., Scientific Staff, Nat. Inst. for Med. Research, MRC, 1953–63; Dep. Dir, Research, and Dir, Biological Research, Ciba-Geigy Pharmaceuticals, 1964–73. Mem., Horserace Scientific Adv. Cttee, Jockey Club, 1989–97. Hon. Mem., British Pharmacol. Soc., 1994. *Publications:* 5-Hydroxytryptamine, 1958; The Role of Prostaglandins in Inflammation, 1976; Mechanisms of Steroid Action, 1981; Mediators of Inflammation, 1986; numerous contribs to British and overseas sci. jls, esp. Jl Physiol., BJ Pharmacol. *Recreations:* writing unfathomable stories, painting indescribable paintings and cooking excruciating dishes.

LEWIS, Prof. Gwynne, DPhil; Professor of History, 1984–97, and Director, Centre for Social History, 1992–97, University of Warwick; *b* 4 Nov. 1933; *s* of Rev. Dewi Emlyn Lewis and Elizabeth May Lewis; *m* 1960, Madeline Ann Rosser; two *s* one *d*. *Educ:* Pontypridd Grammar Sch.; UCW, Aberystwyth (BA); Univ. of Manchester (MA); DPhil Oxford. Asst Lectr, 1963–65, Lectr, 1965–68, UCW, Aberystwyth; Lectr, 1968–74, Sen. Lectr, 1974–80, Reader, 1980–84, Univ. of Warwick. Hon. Vis. Fellow, Southampton Univ., 1997–. *Publications:* Life in Revolutionary France, 1971; The Second Vendee, 1978; The Advent of Modern Capitalism in France 1770–1840, 1993; The French Revolution: rethinking the debate, 1993. *Recreations:* music, Rugby, walking, Paris. *Address:* 26 Marley Avenue, New Milton, Hants BH25 5LJ.

LEWIS, Henry Nathan; director of companies; *b* 29 Jan. 1926; *m* 1953, Jenny Cohen; one *s* two *d*. *Educ:* Hollywood Park Council Sch., Stockport; Stockport Sch.; Manchester Univ. (BA Com); LSE. Served RAF (Flt Lt), 1944–48. Joined Marks & Spencer, 1950; Dir, 1965; Jt Man. Dir responsible for textiles, 1973–76, 1983–85, for foods, 1976–83; retired 1985. Chm., Primrose Care Ltd, 1992–97; Dep. Chm., S&W Berisford, subseq. Berisford Internat., 1987–90; Director: Dixons Group, 1985–95; Hunter Saphir, 1987–91; Porter Chadburn (formerly LDH Group), 1987–; Delta Galil, 1988–; Gabicci, 1992–93; Cupid, 1993–94; Oasis, 1994–; Value Retail, 1994–; Electronics Boutique plc (formerly Rhino), 1995–; Uno plc, 1996–99. *Address:* Flat 15, Pavilion Court, Frognal Rise, NW3 6PZ.

LEWIS, H(erbert) J(ohn) Whitfield, CB 1968; *b* 9 April 1911; *s* of Herbert and Mary Lewis; *m* 1963, Pamela (*née* Leaford); one *s* three *d*. *Educ:* Monmouth Sch.; Welsh Sch. of Architecture. Associate with Norman & Dawbarn, Architects and Consulting Engineers; in charge of housing work, 1945–50; Principal Housing Architect, Architects Dept, London County Council, 1950–59; County Architect, Middlesex County Council, 1959–64; Chief Architect, Ministry of Housing and Local Govt, 1964–71. FRIBA; DisTP 1957. *Recreations:* music, electronics. *Address:* 8 St John's Wood Road, NW8 8RE.

LEWIS, Rt Rev. (Hurtle) John, AM 1990; Bishop of North Queensland, 1971–96; *b* 2 Jan. 1926; *s* of late Hurtle John Lewis and late Hilda Lewis. *Educ:* Prince Alfred Coll.; London Univ. (BD). ThL of ACT. Royal Australian Navy, 1943–46; Student, St Michael's House, S Aust., 1946–51; Member, SSM, 1951–; Provincial Australia, SSM, 1962–68; Prior, Kobe Priory, Japan, 1969–71. *Recreations:* rowing, horse riding. *Address:* Unit 1, 4 Stuart Street, North Ward, Townsville 4810, Australia.

LEWIS, Huw George; Member (Lab) Merthyr Tydfil and Rhymney, National Assembly for Wales, since 1999; *b* 17 Jan. 1964; *m* 1996, Lynne Neagle, *qv*. *Educ:* Edinburgh Univ. (BSc Hons Chemistry). Teacher, N Berwick High Sch., and Bathgate Acad., 1987–90; House of Commons Researcher, 1990–91; Teacher, Afon Taf High Sch., 1991–94; Asst Gen. Sec., Wales Labour Party, 1994–99. *Address:* National Assembly for Wales, Cardiff Bay, Cardiff CF99 1NA.

LEWIS, Ian Talbot; Under Secretary (Legal), Treasury Solicitor's Office, 1982–90; *b* 7 July 1929; *s* of late Cyril Frederick Lewis, CBE and Marjorie (*née* Talbot); *m* 1st, 1962, Patricia Anne (*née* Hardy) (marr. diss. 1978); two *s*; 2nd, 1986, Susan Lydia Sargant. *Educ:* Marlborough Coll. Admitted Solicitor, 1951. National Service, 3rd The King's Own Hussars, 1952–53. Solicitor, private practice, London, 1954–57; Treasury Solicitor's Office: Legal Asst, 1957; Sen. Legal Asst, 1963; Asst Treasury Solicitor, 1977. Liveryman, Merchant Taylors' Co., 1966–. Chm., Penshurst Parish Council, 1994–96. Chm., Fordcombe Soc., 1990–94; Trustee, Fordcombe Village Hall, 1997–. Gov., Fordcombe C of E Primary Sch., 1991–93. Trustee, Penshurst Retreat Charity, 1993–. *Recreations:* sport, natural history, modern first editions, theatre. *Address:* Gables, Fordcombe, near Tunbridge Wells, Kent TN3 0RY. *T:* (01892) 740413. *Clubs:* Cavalry and Guards, MCC; Blackheath Football (Rugby Union) (Past Pres.); Blackheath Cricket (Hon. Vice Pres.); Piltdown Golf.

LEWIS, Prof. Ioan Myrddin, DPhil; FBA 1986; Professor of Anthropology, London School of Economics and Political Science, 1969–93, now Emeritus; Consultative Director, International African Institute, since 1988 (Hon. Director, 1981–88); *b* 30 Jan. 1930; *s* of John Daniel Lewis and Mary Stevenson Scott (*née* Brown); *m* 1954, Ann Elizabeth Keir; one *s* three *d*. *Educ:* Glasgow High Sch.; Glasgow Univ. (BSc 1951); Oxford Univ. (Dip. in Anthrop., 1952; BLitt 1953; DPhil 1957). Res. Asst to Lord Hailey, Chatham House, 1954–55; Colonial SSRC Fellow, 1955–57; Lectr in African Studies, University Coll. of Rhodesia and Nyasaland, 1957–60; Lectr in Social Anthrop., Glasgow Univ., 1960–63; Lectr, then Reader in Anthrop., UCL, 1963–69. Hitchcock Prof., Univ. of Calif at Berkeley, 1977; Vis. Professor: Univ. of Helsinki, Finland, 1982; Univ. of Rome, 1983; Univ. of Malaya, 1986; Univ. of Kyoto, 1986; Univ. of Naples, 1989; Univ. of Addis Ababa, 1992; CNRS, Marseille, 1993. Malinowski Meml Lectr, London, 1966; Blackwood Lectr, Oxford, 1994. Hon. Sec., Assoc. of Social Anthropologists of the Commonwealth, 1964–67; Member: Council and Standing Cttee of Council, Royal Anthropol Inst., 1965–67 and 1981–84 (Vice-Pres., 1992–96); Court of Governors and Standing Cttee, LSE, 1984–88; Internat. Cttee, Centro di Ricerca e Documentazione Febbraio '74, 1980–; Chm., African Educn Trust, 1993 (Trustee, 1992). Editor, Man (Jl of RAI), 1969–72. *Publications:* Peoples of the Horn of Africa, 1955, 3rd edn 1994; A Pastoral Democracy: pastoralism and politics among the Northern Somali of the Horn of Africa, 1961, 3rd edn 1999 (trans. Italian); (with B. W. Andrzejewski) Somali Poetry, 1964, 2nd edn 1968; The Modern History of Somaliland: from nation to state, 1965, 3rd rev. edn 1988; Ecstatic Religion, 1971, 4th rev. edn 1989 (trans. Dutch, Italian, French, Portuguese and Japanese); Social Anthropology in Perspective, 1976, 4th edn 1990 (trans.

Italian and Chinese); Religion in Context: cults and charisma, 1986 (trans. German and Italian), rev. edn 1996; (ed and introd): Islam in Tropical Africa, 1966, 3rd edn 1980; History and Anthropology, 1968 (trans. Spanish); Symbols and Sentiments: cross-cultural studies in symbolism, 1977; (co-ed with Fred Eggan and C. von Fürer-Haimendorf), Atlas of Mankind, 1982; Nationalism and Self-Determination in the Horn of Africa, 1983; (co-ed with Gustav Jahoda) Acquiring Culture: cross cultural studies in child development, 1988; (ed jtly) Women's Medicine: the Zar-Bori Cult in Africa and beyond, 1991; Understanding Somalia, 1993; Blood and Bone: the call of Kinship in Somali society, 1994; (co-ed with R. J. Hayward) Voice and Power: the culture of language in North-East Africa, 1996; Saints and Somalis: Islam in a clan-based society, 1998; Arguments with Ethnography: comparative approaches to history, politics and religion, 1999; contrib. learned jls. *Recreations:* travel, fishing. *Address:* 26 Bramshill Gardens, NW5 1JH. *T:* (020) 7272 1722.

LEWIS, Ivan; MP (Lab) Bury South, since 1997; Parliamentary Under-Secretary of State, Department for Education and Skills, since 2001; *b* 4 March 1967; *s* of Joel and Gloria Lewis; *m* 1990, Juliette, *d* of Leslie and Joyce Fox; two *s*. *Educ:* William Hulme Grammar Sch.; Stand Coll.; Bury Coll. of FE. Co-ordinator, Contact Community Care Gp, 1986–89; Jewish Social Services: Social Worker, 1989–91; Community Care Manager, 1991–92; Chief Exec., 1992–97. Mem., Bury MBC, 1990–98. PPS to Sec. of State for Trade and Industry, 1999–2001. Member: H of C Deregulation Select Cttee, 1997–99; Health Select Cttee, 1999; Sec., All Party Parly Gp on Parenting, 1998–2001; Dep. Chm., Labour Friends of Israel, 1997–; Vice Chm., Inter-Parly Council Against Anti-Semitism, 1998–2001. Trustee, Holocaust Educnl Trust. *Recreation:* supporter of Manchester City FC. *Address:* House of Commons, SW1A 0AA. *T:* (020) 7219 6404; 513 Bury New Road, Prestwich, Manchester M25 3AJ. *T:* (0161) 773 5500.

LEWIS, Prof. Jane Elizabeth, PhD; Barnett Professor of Social Policy, University of Oxford, since 2000, and Fellow of St Cross College, Oxford, since 2000; *b* 14 April 1950; *d* of Hedley Lewis and Dorothy Lewis (*née* Beck); *m* 1971, Mark Shrimpton. *Educ:* Reading Univ. (BA Hons 1971); Univ. of Western Ontario (PhD 1979). Department of Social Policy and Administration, London School of Economics: Lectr, 1979–87; Reader, 1987–91; Prof., 1991–96; Fellow of All Souls Coll., and Dir, Wellcome Unit for the Hist. of Medicine, Oxford, 1996–98; Prof. of Social Policy, Nottingham Univ., 1998–2000. Mem., RSCan, 1995. *Publications:* The Politics of Motherhood: child and maternal welfare in England 1900–1939, 1980; (ed) Women's Welfare/Women's Rights, 1983; Women in England, 1870–1950: sexual divisions and social change, 1984; (ed) Labour and Love: women's experience of home and family 1850–1950, 1986; (ed jtly) Women and Offshore Oil in Britain, Canada and Norway, 1987; (ed) Before the Vote was Won, 1987; (jtly) Daughters Who Care: daughters looking after mothers at home, 1988; (ed jtly) The Goals of Social Policy, 1989; Women and Social Action in Victorian and Edwardian England, 1991; Women in Britain since 1945: women, family and work in the post-war years, 1992; (jtly) Whom God Hath Joined: marriage and the marital agencies 1930–1990, 1992; (ed) Women and Social Policies in Europe, 1993; The Voluntary Sector, the State and Social Work in Britain, 1995; (ed jtly) Comparing Social Welfare Systems in Europe, vol. I, 1995; (ed jtly) Protecting Women: labor legislation in Europe, the United States and Australia 1880–1920, 1995; (jtly) Implementing the New Community Care, 1996; (ed) Lone Mothers in European Welfare Regimes, 1998; (jtly) Lone Motherhood in Twentieth-Century Britain, 1998; The End of Marriage?, 2001; articles in jls. *Address:* Department of Social Policy and Social Work, Barnett House, 32 Wellington Square, Oxford OX1 2ER.

LEWIS, Rt Rev. John; *see* Lewis, Rt Rev. H. J.

LEWIS, Ven. John Arthur; Archdeacon of Cheltenham, 1988–98, now Archdeacon Emeritus; *b* 4 Oct. 1934; *s* of Lt-Col Harry Arthur Lewis and Evaline Helen Ross Lewis; *m* 1959, Hazel Helen Jane Morris; one *s* one *d*. *Educ:* Jesus College, Oxford (MA); Cuddesdon College. Assistant Curate: St Mary, Prestbury, Glos, 1960–63; Wimborne Minster, 1963–66; Rector, Eastington with Frocester, 1966–70; Vicar of Nailsworth, 1970–78; Vicar of Cirencester, 1978–88; RD of Cirencester, 1984–88. Hon. Canon, 1985–88, Canon, 1988–98, Canon Emeritus, 1998–, Gloucester Cathedral. Hon. Chaplain, Glos Constabulary, 1988–98. Chairman: Diocesan Stewardship Cttee, 1988–96; Diocesan Redundant Church Uses Cttee, 1988–98; Diocesan Bd of Educn, 1990–98. Mem. Council, Cheltenham Ladies' Coll., 1992–97. *Recreations:* travel, music, walking, gardening. *Address:* 5 Vilverie Mead, Bishops Cleeve, Cheltenham, Glos GL52 7YY. *T:* (01242) 678425.

LEWIS, John Elliott, MA; Head Master, Eton College, 1994–Aug. 2002; *b* 23 Feb. 1942; *s* of John Derek Lewis and Margaret Helen (*née* Shaw); *m* 1968, Vibeke Lewis (*née* Johansson). *Educ:* King's College, Auckland, NZ; Corpus Christi Coll., Cambridge (Girdlers' Company Schol.; MA Classics). Assistant Master, King's Coll., Auckland, 1964, 1966–70; Jun. Lecturer in Classics, Auckland Univ., 1965; Asst Master, 1971–80, Master in College, 1975–80, Eton College; Head Master, Geelong Grammar Sch., Australia, 1980–94. *Address:* Eton College, Windsor, Berks SL4 6DL.

LEWIS, Rt Rev. (John Hubert) Richard; *see* St Edmundsbury and Ipswich, Bishop of.

LEWIS, Very Rev. John Thomas; Dean of Llandaff, since 2000; *b* 14 June 1947; *s* of Rev. David Islwyn Lewis and Eleanor Tranter Lewis; *m* 1976, Dr Cynthia Sheelagh McFetridge; two *s*. *Educ:* Dyffryn Grammar Sch., Port Talbot; Jesus Coll., Oxford (scholar; BA (Maths) 1969; Dip. Applied Stats 1970; MA 1973); St John's Coll., Cambridge (BA (Theol.) 1972; MA 1992); Westcott House, Cambridge. Ordained deacon, 1973, priest, 1974. Assistant Curate: Whitchurch, 1973–77; Lisvane, 1977–80; Chaplain, Cardiff Univ., 1980–85; Warden of Ordinands, Llandaff, 1981–85; Vicar, Brecon St David with Llanspyddid and Llanilltyd, 1985–91; Vicar, then Rector, Bassaleg, 1991–2000. Sec., Provincial Selection Panel, Church in Wales, 1987–94; Bishop of Monmouth's Chaplain for Continuing Ministerial Educn, 1998–2000. *Recreations:* hill walking, swimming, music, sport, family life. *Address:* The Deanery, The Cathedral Green, Llandaff, Cardiff CF5 2YF. *T:* (029) 2056 1545.

LEWIS, (Joseph) Anthony; Chief London Correspondent, New York Times, 1965–72, editorial columnist, since 1969; Lecturer in Law, Harvard Law School, 1974–89; James Madison Visiting Professor, Columbia University, since 1983; *b* 27 March 1927; *s* of Kassel Lewis and Sylvia Lewis (*née* Surut), NYC; *m* 1st, 1951, Linda (marr. diss. 1982), *d* of John Rannells, NYC; one *s* two *d*; 2nd, 1984, Margaret, *d* of Bernard Charles Marshall, Osterville, Mass. *Educ:* Horace Mann Sch., NY; Harvard Coll. (BA). Sunday Dept, New York Times, 1948–52; Reporter, Washington Daily News, 1952–55; Legal Corresp., Washington Bureau, NY Times, 1955–64; Nieman Fellow, Harvard Law Sch., 1956–57. Governor, Ditchley Foundation, 1965–72. Mem., Amer. Acad. of Arts and Scis, 1991. Pulitzer Prize for Nat. Correspondence, 1955 and 1963; Heywood Broun Award, 1955; Overseas Press Club Award, 1970. Hon. DLitt: Adelphi Univ. (NY), 1964; Rutgers Univ., NJ, 1973; NY Med. Coll., 1976; Williams Coll., Mass, 1978; Clark Univ., Mass, 1982; Hon. LLD: Syracuse, 1979; Colby Coll., 1983; Northeastern Univ., Mass, 1987. *Publications:* Gideon's Trumpet, 1964; Portrait of a Decade: The Second American Revolution, 1964; Make No Law: the Sullivan case and the First Amendment, 1991; articles in American law reviews. *Recreation:* dinghy sailing. *Address:* 2 Faneuil Hall Marketplace, Boston, MA 02109, USA. *Club:* Tavern (Boston).

LEWIS, Dr Julian Murray; MP (C) New Forest East, since 1997; *b* 26 Sept. 1951; *s* of Samuel Lewis, tailor and designer, and late Hilda Lewis. *Educ:* Dynevor Grammar Sch., Swansea; Balliol Coll., Oxford (MA 1977); St Antony's Coll., Oxford (DPhil 1981). Sec., Oxford Union, 1972. Seaman, RNR, 1979–82. Res. in defence studies, 1975–77, 1978–81; Sec., Campaign for Representative Democracy, 1977–78; Res. Dir and Dir, Coalition for Peace Through Security, 1981–85; Dir, Policy Res. Associates, 1985–; Dep. Dir, Cons. Res. Dept, 1990–96. Contested (C) Swansea W, 1983. Member: Select Cttee on Welsh Affairs, 1998–; Select Cttee on Defence, 2000; Sec., Cons. Parly Defence Cttee, 1997–; Vice-Chairman: Cons. Parly Foreign Affairs Cttee, 2000–; Cons. Parly European Affairs Cttee, 2000–. Mem., Armed Forces Parly Scheme (RAF), 1998 (RAF Graduate Course, 2000). Trustee, British Military Powerboat Trust, 1998–. *Publications:* Changing Direction: British military planning for post-war strategic defence 1942–47, 1988; Who's Left?: an index of Labour MPs and left-wing causes 1985–1992, 1992; Labour's CND Cover-up, 1992; political pamphlets; contrib. to Encounter, Wall Street Jl (Eur.), Salisbury Rev., etc. *Recreations:* history, fiction, films, music, photography. *Address:* House of Commons, SW1A 0AA. *T:* (020) 7219 3000. *Clubs:* Athenæum; Totton Conservative.

LEWIS, Keith William, AO 1994; CB 1981; Director General and Engineer in Chief, Engineering and Water Supply Department, South Australia, 1974–87; *b* 10 Nov. 1927; *s* of Ernest John and Alinda Myrtle Lewis; *m* 1958, Alison Bothwell Fleming; two *d*. *Educ:* Adelaide High Sch.; Univ. of Adelaide (BE Civil); Imperial Coll., Univ. of London (DIC). FTS. Engineer for Water and Sewage Treatment, Engrg and Water Supply Dept, SA, 1968–74. Chm., Pipelines Authy of SA, 1987–94; Dep. Chm., Electricity Trust of SA, 1994–95. Chairman: S Australian Water Resources Council, 1976–87; Australian Water Res. Adv. Council, 1985–90; Murray-Darling Basin Freshwater Res. Centre, 1986–91; Energy Planning Exec., 1987–93; SA Urban Land Trust, 1990–94; Member: Standing Cttee, Australian Water Resources Council, 1974–87; Electricity Trust of S Australia, 1974–84; State Planning Authority, 1974–82; Golden Grove Jt Venture Cttee, 1984–97; Bd, Amdel Ltd, 1987–94. River Murray Commissioner, representing SA, 1982–87. Hon. FIEAust 1993. Silver Jubilee Medal, 1977. *Recreations:* reading, ornithology, golf, tennis. *Address:* 24 Delamere Avenue, Netherby, SA 5062, Australia. *T:* (8) 83381507, *Fax:* (8) 83382431. *Clubs:* Adelaide, Kooyonga Golf (South Australia).

LEWIS, Kynric; *see* Lewis, A. K.

LEWIS, Leigh Warren, CB 2000; Chief Executive, Employment Service, Department for Work and Pensions (formerly Department for Education and Employment), 1997–April 2002; Chief Executive, Jobcentre Plus, Department for Work and Pensions, from April 2002; *b* 17 March 1951; *s* of Harold and Ray Rene Lewis; *m* 1973, Susan Evelyn Gold; two *s*. *Educ:* Harrow County Grammar Sch. for Boys; Liverpool Univ. (BA Hons 1973). MIPD. Dept of Employment, 1973; Private Sec. to Parly Under Sec. of State, 1975–76; Incomes and Indust. Relations Divs, 1978–84; Principal Private Sec. to Minister without Portfolio and Sec. of State for Employment, 1984–86; Asst Sec., EC Br., 1986–87; Dir of Ops, Unemployment Benefit Service, 1987–88; Group Dir of Personnel, Cable and Wireless plc, 1988–91 (on secondment); Dir, Internat. Div., 1991–94; Dir, Finance and Resource Mgt Div., 1994–95; Dir, Finance, DFEE, 1995–96. *Recreations:* tennis, Watford Football Club. *Address:* Employment Service (from April 2002, Jobcentre Plus), Caxton House, Tothill Street, SW1H 9NA.

LEWIS, Lennox Claudius, MBE 1998; professional boxer, since 1989; *b* 2 Sept. 1965; *s* of Violet Blake. World jun. heavyweight champion, 1983; Olympic heavyweight champion (rep. Canada), 1988; European heavyweight champion, 1990; British heavyweight champion, 1991; WBC world heavyweight champion, 1993, 1997; undisputed world heavyweight champion, 1999; world heavyweight champion, 2000; Founder, Lennox Lewis Coll., Hackney, London, 1994. DUniv N London, 1999. *Publication:* Lennox Lewis (autobiog.), 1993, 2nd edn 1997. *Recreations:* chess, golf, reading, listening to music. *Address:* (office) Shelana House, 31–32 Eastcastle Street, W1N 8NL. *T:* (020) 7636 4563.

LEWIS, Martyn John Dudley, CBE 1997; journalist and broadcaster; Co-Founder and Chairman: Global Intercasting Ltd, since 1999; Global Factory Ltd, since 2000; Teliris Ltd, since 2001; *b* 7 April 1945; *s* of late Thomas John Dudley Lewis and of Doris (*née* Jones); *m* 1970, Elizabeth Anne Carse; two *d*. *Educ:* Dalriada High Sch., Ballymoney, NI; Trinity Coll., Dublin (BA 1967). Reporter: BBC, Belfast, 1967–68; HTV, Cardiff, 1968–70; Independent Television News: reporter, 1970–86; Head, Northern Bureau, 1971–78; presenter, News at Ten, 1981–86; Presenter: BBC One O'Clock News, 1986–87; BBC Nine O'Clock News, 1987–94; BBC TV Six O'Clock News, 1994–99; Today's the Day, BBC2, 1993–99; Crimebeat, 1996–98. Documentaries include: Battle for the Falklands; The Secret Hunters; Fight Cancer; Living with Dying; Great Ormond Street—a Fighting Chance; Health UK; A Century to Remember; series for ITV: Bethlehem–Year Zero, 1999; Dateline Jerusalem, 2000; News 40, 2000; Ultimate Questions, 2000–. Dir, Drive for Youth, 1986–99 (Chm., 1990–99); Chm. and Founder, YouthNet UK, 1995–. Advr, Ogden Educnl Trust, 2000–. Member: Policy Adv. Cttee, Tidy Britain Gp, 1988–98; Volunteer Partnership (govt cttee), 1995–97; Director: Hospice Arts, 1989–97; CLIC UK, 1990–96; Adopt-A-Student, 1988–96; Inst. for Citizenship Studies, 1993–97; Friends of Nelson Mandela Children's Fund, 1997–; President: United Response, 1989–; George Thomas Centre for Hospice Care, 1996–; Vice-President: Macmillan Cancer Relief (formerly Cancer Relief Macmillan Fund), 1988– (Dir, 1990–96); Marie Curie Cancer Care, 1990–; Help the Hospices, 1990–; British Soviet Hospice Soc., 1990–96; Demelza House Children's Hospice, 1996–; Voices for Hospices, 1996–; Barrett's Oesophagus Foundn, 2000–; Trustee, Windsor Leadership Trust, 2001–; Patron: London Lighthouse, 1990–99; SW Children's Hospice, 1991–; Internat. Sch. for Cancer Care, 1991–99; Children's Hosp. SW, 1992–; Hope House Children's Hospice, 1992–; Cities in Schools, 1995–97 (Dir, 1989–95); Tomorrow Project, 1996–; Dementia Relief Trust, 1998–; James Powell (UK) Trust, 1998–; Mildmay Mission Hosp., 1998–; Nat. Centre for Volunteering, 1998–; E Anglia Children's Hospices, 1999– (Cambridge Children's Hospice, 1989–99; Quidenham Children's Hospice, 1996–99). Freeman, City of London, 1989; Liveryman, Pattenmakers' Co., 1989–. FRSA 1990. Hon. DLitt Ulster, 1994. *Publications:* And Finally, 1983; Tears and Smiles—the Hospice Handbook, 1989; Cats in the News, 1991 (trans. Japanese, 1994); Dogs in the News, 1992 (trans. Japanese, 1996); Go For It: Martyn Lewis's essential guide to opportunities for young people (annual), 1993–97, as Book of the Site, 1998–99; Reflections on Success, 1997; Seasons of our Lives, 1999. *Recreations:* tennis, photography, piano, good food, keeping fit, after-dinner speaking. *Address:* c/o Capel & Land, 29 Wardour Street, W1V 3HB. *T:* (020) 7734 2414, *Fax:* (020) 7734 8101. *Clubs:* Annabel's, Vanderbilt.

LEWIS, Michael ap Gwilym; QC 1975; a Recorder of the Crown Court, 1976–97; *b* 9 May 1930; *s* of Rev. Thomas William Lewis and Mary Jane May Selway; *m* 1988, Sarah

Turvill; two *d*, and one *d* three *s* by a previous marriage. *Educ:* Mill Hill; Jesus Coll., Oxford (Scholar). MA (Mod. History). 2nd Royal Tank Regt, 1952–53. Called to Bar, Gray's Inn, 1956, Bencher, 1986; Mem., Senate, 1979–82; South Eastern Circuit. Mem., Criminal Injuries Compensation Bd, 1993–. *Address:* 2 Bedford Row, WC1R 4BU. *T:* (020) 7440 8888.

See also E. ap G. Lewis.

LEWIS, Rt Rev. Michael Augustine Owen; *see* Middleton, Bishop Suffragan of.

LEWIS, Michael David; Controller, Radio Sports Rights, BBC Sport, since 1996; *b* 5 June 1947; *s* of late David Lloyd Lewis and of Gwendoline Lewis; *m* 1992, Hilary Anne East; two *d*. *Educ:* Erith Grammar Sch., Kent. Dartford Reporter newspaper, 1966–70; Brighton Evening Argus, 1970–73; LBC/Independent Radio News, 1973–82; BBC Radio Sport: Duty Editor, 1982–83; Dep. Editor, 1983–84; Editor, 1984–91; Head of Sport and Outside Broadcasts, 1991–93. *Recreations:* watching Arsenal, bringing up two daughters, reading newspapers. *Address:* BBC Sport, Room 5106, Television Centre, Wood Lane, W12 7TS. *T:* (020) 8624 8947, *Fax:* (020) 8624 8939.

LEWIS, Naomi, FRSL; author, critic and broadcaster; *b* coastal Norfolk. Contributor at various times to Observer, New Statesman, New York Times, Listener, Encounter, TLS, TES, etc. *Publications:* A Visit to Mrs Wilcox, 1957; A Peculiar Music, 1971; Fantasy, 1977; The Silent Playmate, 1979; Leaves, 1980; Come With Us (poems), 1982; Once upon a Rainbow, 1981; A Footprint on the Air (poems), 1983; Messages (poems), 1985; A School Bewitched, 1985; Arabian Nights, 1987; Cry Wolf!, 1988; Proud Knight, Fair Lady, 1989; Johnny Longnese, 1989; The Mardi Gras Cat, 1994; Classic Fairy Tales, 1996; *translations* include: Hans Andersen's Fairy Tales, 1981; The Snow Queen, 1988; The Frog Prince, 1990; The Emperor's New Clothes, 1997. *Recreation:* trying in practical ways to alleviate the lot of horses, camels, bears, sheep, wolves, cows and other ill-used mortals of the animal kind. *Address:* 13 Red Lion Square, WC1R 4QF. *T:* (020) 7405 8657.

LEWIS, Norman; author; *s* of Richard and Louise Lewis. *Educ:* Enfield Grammar Sch. Served War of 1939–45, in Intelligence Corps. DU Essex, 1987. *Publications:* Sand and Sea in Arabia, 1938; Samara, 1949; Within the Labyrinth, 1950, new edn 1985; A Dragon Apparent, 1951, new edn 1982; Golden Earth, 1952, repr. 1983; A Single Pilgrim, 1953; The Day of the Fox, 1955, new edn 1985; The Volcanoes Above Us, 1957; The Changing Sky, 1959, repr. 1984; Darkness Visible, 1960; The Tenth Year of the Ship, 1962; The Honoured Society, 1964, rev. edn 1984; A Small War Made to Order, 1966; Every Man's Brother, 1967; Flight from a Dark Equator, 1972; The Sicilian Specialist, 1974, new edn 1985; The German Company, 1979; Cuban Passage, 1982; A Suitable Case for Corruption, 1984; A View of the World, 1986; The March of the Long Shadows, 1987; To Run Across the Sea, 1989; A Goddess in the Stones: travels in India, 1991; An Empire of the East, 1993; The Norman Lewis Omnibus, 1995; The Happy Ant Heap and Other Pieces, 1998; In Sicily, 2000; *autobiography:* Naples '44, 1978, repr. 1983; Voices of the Old Sea, 1984, new edn 1996; Jackdaw Cake, 1985, rev. edn as I Came, I Saw, 1994; The Missionaries, 1988; The World, The World, 1996. *Address:* c/o Jonathan Cape, 20 Vauxhall Bridge Road, SW1V 2SA.

LEWIS, Paul Keith; QC 2001; a Recorder; *b* 26 May 1957; *s* of John Keith Lewis and Susan Patricia Lewis (*née* Cronin); *m* 1983, Siân Price; one *s* one *d*. *Educ:* Pontypridd Grammar Sch. for Boys; Univ. of Leicester (LLB Hons); Inns of Court Sch. of Law. Called to the Bar, Gray's Inn, 1981; in practice, Cardiff, 1981–. *Recreations:* sport, travel, music. *Address:* Chapel Mill, Chain Road, Abergavenny, Monmouthshire NP7 7HH. *T:* (01873) 858441; 30 Park Place, Cardiff, S Glamorgan CF10 3BS. *T:* (029) 2039 8421, *Fax:* (029) 2039 8725; *e-mail:* clerk@30parkplace.law.co.uk. *Club:* Monmouthshire Golf (Abergavenny).

LEWIS, Peter; Director, Policy Co-ordination Unit, 1994–96, and the Tax Simplification Project, 1995–96, Inland Revenue; *b* 24 June 1937; *s* of Reginald George and Edith Lewis; *m* 1962, Ursula Brigitte Kilian; one *s* one *d*. *Educ:* Ealing Grammar School; St Peter's Hall, Oxford. Royal Navy, 1955–57. Inland Revenue Inspector of Taxes, 1960–69; Inland Revenue Policy and Central Divs, 1969–85; Director: Personal Tax Div., 1986–91; Company Tax Div., 1991–95. *Address:* Glyndavas, 9 Waterloo Close, St Mawes, Cornwall TR2 5BD.

LEWIS, Peter Ronald; Director General, Bibliographic Services, British Library, 1980–89; *b* 28 Sept. 1926; *s* of Charles Lewis and Florence Mary (née Kirk); *m* 1952, June Ashley; one *s* one *d*. *Educ:* Royal Masonic Sch.; Belfast Univ. (MA). FLA; Hon. FLA 1989. Brighton, Plymouth, Chester public libraries, 1948–55; Head, Bibliographic Services, BoT Library, 1955–65; Lectr in Library Studies, QUB, 1965–69; Librarian: City Univ., 1969–72; Univ. of Sussex, 1972–80. Vice-Pres., 1979–85 and Hon. Treasurer, 1980–82, Library Assoc. (Chm., Bd of Fellowship, 1979–87); Mem., IFLA Professional Bd, 1985–87. Chm., LA Publishing Co., 1983–85. *Publications:* The Literature of the Social Sciences, 1960; The Fall and Rise of National Bibliography (Bangalore), 1982; numerous papers on librarianship and bibliography, 1963–91. *Recreations:* acting, choral singing. *Address:* Wyvern, Blackheath Road, Wenhaston, Suffolk IP19 9HD.

LEWIS, Peter Tyndale; Chairman, John Lewis Partnership, 1972–93; *b* 26 Sept. 1929; *s* of Oswald Lewis and Frances Merriman Lewis (*née* Cooper); *m* 1961, Deborah Anne, *d* of late Sir William (Alexander Roy) Collins, CBE and Priscilla Marian, *d* of late S. J. Lloyd; one *s* one *d*. *Educ:* Eton; Christ Church, Oxford (MA 1953). National service, Coldstream Guards, 1948–49; called to Bar (Middle Temple) 1956; joined John Lewis Partnership, 1959. Member: Council, Industrial Soc., 1968–79; Design Council, 1971–74; Chm., Retail Distributors' Assoc., 1972. Member: Southampton Univ. Develt Trust, 1994–; Council, Queen's Coll., Harley St, 1994–99. Trustee, Jt Educnl Trust, 1985–87. Governor: NIESR, 1983; Windlesham Hse Sch., 1979–95; The Bell Educnl Trust, 1987–97. CIMgt; FRSA. *Address:* 34 Victoria Road, W8 5RG.

LEWIS, Ralph; *see* Lewis, D. R.

LEWIS, Rhodri Price; QC 2001; a Recorder, since 1998; *b* 7 June 1952; *s* of George and Nansi Lewis; *m* 1983, Barbara Sinden; two *d*. *Educ:* Ysgol Cymraeg Ynyswen; Cowbridge Grammar Sch.; Pembroke Coll., Oxford (MA); Sidney Sussex Coll., Cambridge (Dip. Criminol.). Called to the Bar, Middle Temple, 1975. *Publications:* Environmental Law, 2000; contrib. to Jl Planning and Envmt Law. *Recreations:* Rugby, playing the guitar, enjoying the company, coast and country of Pembrokeshire. *Address:* Eldon Chambers, Falcon Court, 30–32 Fleet Street, EC4Y 1AA. *T:* (020) 7583 1355. *Clubs:* Farmers', London Welsh Rugby Football.

LEWIS, Rt Rev. Richard; *see* Lewis, Rt Rev. J. H. R., Bishop of St Edmundsbury and Ipswich.

LEWIS, Very Rev. Richard; Dean of Wells, since 1990; *b* 24 Dec. 1935; *m* 1959, Jill Diane Wilford; two *s*. *Educ:* Royal Masonic Sch.; Fitzwilliam House, Cambridge (BA 1958; MA 1961); Ripon Hall, Oxford. Asst Curate, Hinckley, Leicester, 1960–63; Priest-in-Charge, St Edmund, Riddlesdown, 1963–66; Vicar: All Saints, South Merstham, 1966–72; Holy Trinity and St Peter, Wimbeldon, 1972–79; St Barnabas, Dulwich and Foundation Chaplain of Alleyn's College of God's Gift at Dulwich, 1979–90. *Publication:* (contrib.) Cathedrals Now, 1996. *Recreations:* music of all sorts, walking, gardening, reading. *Address:* The Dean's Lodging, 25 The Liberty, Wells, Somerset BA5 2SZ. *T:* (01749) 72192.

LEWIS, Rev. Canon Robert Hugh Cecil; Chaplain to the Queen, 1987–95; *b* 23 Feb. 1925; *s* of Herbert Cecil and Olive Frances Lewis; *m* 1948, Joan Dorothy Hickman; one *s* one *d*. *Educ:* Manchester Grammar School; New Coll., Oxford (BA 1950, MA 1950); Westcott House, Cambridge. Deacon 1952, priest 1953; Curate: St Mary, Crumpsall, 1952–54; New Bury, 1954–56; Incumbent, Bury St Peter, 1956–63; Vicar, Poynton, dio. of Chester, 1963–91; RD of Stockport, 1972–85, of Cheadle, 1985–87. Diocesan Ecumenical Officer, 1987–91; County Ecumenical Officer for Cheshire, 1987–91; Hon. Canon, Chester Cathedral, 1975–91, Canon Emeritus, 1991–. *Recreations:* gardening, poetry. *Address:* 78 Dean Drive, Wilmslow, Cheshire SK9 2EY. *T:* (01625) 524761.

LEWIS, Roger Charles; Managing Director and Programme Controller, Classic FM, since 1998; Director, since 1998, and Chairman of Commercial Board, since 2000, GWR plc; *b* 24 Aug. 1954; *s* of late Griffith Charles Job Lewis and Dorothy Lewis (*née* Russ); *m* 1980, Dr Christine, *d* of Leslie Trollope; two *s*. *Educ:* Cynffig Comprehensive Sch., Bridgend; Univ. of Nottingham (BMus Hons 1976). Musician, 1976–80: Avon Touring Th. Co., 1977–79; Birmingham Rep. Th. Studio, 1978; Ludus Dance in Educn Co., 1979; Scottish Ballet Workshop Co., 1979; Music Officer, Darlington Arts Centre, 1980–82; Dir, Cleveland Arts Ltd, 1982–84; Presenter, Radio Tees, 1981–84; Producer: Capital Radio, 1984–85; BBC Radio 1, 1985–87; Hd of Music, Radio 1, 1987–90; Dir, 1990–95, Man. Dir, 1995, Classical Div., EMI Records; Man. Dir, EMI Premier, 1995–97; Pres., Decca Record Co., 1997–98. Dir, The Radio Corp. Ltd, 1999–; non-exec. Dir, Barchester Adv. Ltd, 2001–. Chairman: Classical Cttee, British Phonographic Industry Ltd, 1996–98; Music and Ballet Scheme Adv. Gp, DFEE, 2000–. Trustee: Masterprize (Internat. Composers' Competition), 1995–; Masterclass Charitable Trust, 2000–; Chairman: Trustees, Ogmore Centre, 1996–; Classic FM Charitable Trust, 2000–. Pres., Bromley Youth Music Trust, 2000–; Mem., WNO Develt Circle, 2001–. FRSA. Sony Radio Award, 1987, 1988, 1989; Grand Award Winner and Gold Medal, NY Radio Fest., 1987; One World Broadcasting Trust Award, 1989. *Recreations:* Rugby football, wine (Mem., Wine Soc.), walking, ski-ing. *Address:* Classic FM House, 7 Swallow Place, W1R 7AA. *T:* (020) 7344 2781. *Club:* Bridgend Rugby Football.

LEWIS, Roland Swaine, FRCS; Honorary Consultant Surgeon to the ENT Department, King's College Hospital, since 1973 (Consultant Surgeon, 1946–65, Senior Consultant Surgeon, 1965–73); Honorary Consultant ENT Surgeon: to Mount Vernon Hospital and The Radium Institute; to Norwood and District Hospital; *b* 23 Nov. 1908; *s* of Dr William James Lewis, MOH, and Constance Mary Lewis, Tyrwaun, Ystalyfera; *m* 1936, Mary Christianna Milne (Christianna Brand) (*d* 1988); one adopted *d*. *Educ:* Epsom Coll.; St John's Coll., Cambridge; St George's Hospital. BA Cantab 1929; FRCS 1934; MA Cantab 1945; MB BCh Cantab 1945. Surgical Chief Asst, St George's Hospital, 1935. Major, RAMC (ENT Specialist), 1939–45. *Publications:* papers to medical journals. *Recreations:* ornithology, fishing. *Address:* 88 Maida Vale, W9 1PR. *T:* (020) 7624 6253; Aberdar, Cwrt y Cadno, Llanwrda, Dyfed.

LEWIS, Sean Michael, PhD; Director, British Council, Canada, 1997–2000, retired; *b* 23 Oct. 1943; *s* of Leonard Leon Lewis and Margaret Lewis (*née* Moore); *m* 1971, Jennifer M. Williams; one *s*. *Educ:* Univ. of Liverpool (BSc 1967; PhD 1971). British Council: London, 1970, 1973–75, 1978–89, 1992–97; Nigeria, 1971–73; Sri Lanka, 1975–78; Sweden, 1989–92. *Documentary films:* (co-prod.) There We Are John, 1993; (prod.) Lucky Man, 1995. *Recreations:* minimal effort downhill ski-ing, pyrotechnics, films, landscape gardening, real ale, country pubs. *Address:* 38 Ninehams Road, Caterham on the Hill, Surrey CR3 5LD. *T:* (020) 8763 1644.

LEWIS, Simon David; Director, International Development, Centrica plc, since 2000; *b* 8 May 1959; *s* of David Lewis and Sally Lewis (*née* Valentine); *m* 1985, Claire Elizabeth Anne Pendry; two *s* one *d*. *Educ:* Whitefield Comprehensive, London; Brasenose Coll., Oxford (MA); Univ. of Calif, Berkeley (Fulbright Scholar; MA). FIPR 1998. PR Consultant, Shandwick Consultants, 1983–86; Head: of Communications, SDP, 1986–87; of PR, S. G. Warburg Gp plc, 1987–92; Director, Corporate Affairs: NatWest Gp, 1992–96; Centrica plc, 1996–98; on secondment as Communications Sec., Buckingham Palace, 1998–2000. Mem., Fulbright Commn, 2001–. Pres., IPR, 1997. Trustee and Dir, Crime Concern, 1996. Hon. Prof., Cardiff Sch. of Journalism, 2000. FRSA. *Recreations:* family, sport, current affairs, cinema. *Address:* Centrica plc, Charter Court, 50 Windsor Road, Slough, Berks SL1 2HA. *Club:* Reform.

LEWIS, Susan; HM Chief Inspector of Education and Training in Wales (formerly Chief Inspector of Schools in Wales), since 1997; *b* 7 Nov. 1947; *d* of Kenneth A. L. Lewis and Elsie (*née* Woods). *Educ:* Univ. of Newcastle upon Tyne (BSc Hons); Univ. of Sheffield (DipEd). Asst teacher, Bradfield Sch., WR Yorks, 1970–74; Hd of Dept and Asst Hd of Sixth Form, Shelley High Sch., Kirklees, 1974–80; Dep. Head, later Actg Head, Wisewood Sch., Sheffield, 1980–86; HM Inspector of Schools, 1986–95; Staff Inspector, Office of HM Chief Inspector, 1995–97. *Recreations:* gardening, walking, genealogy. *Address:* Estyn, Anchor Court, Keen Road, Cardiff CF24 5JW. *T:* (029) 2044 6475, *Fax:* (029) 2044 6448.

LEWIS, Terence; MP (Lab) Worsley, since 1983; *b* 29 Dec. 1935; *s* of Andrew Lewis; *m* 1958, Audrey, *d* of William Clarke; one *s* (and one *s* decd). *Educ:* Mt Carmel Sch., Salford. Nat. service, RAMC, 1954–56. Personnel Officer. Member: Kearsley UDC, 1971–74; Bolton BC, 1975– (Chm., Educn Cttee, 1982–83). Mem., Standards and Privileges Select Cttee, 1997–2001. *Address:* House of Commons, SW1A 0AA; 54 Greenmount Park, Kearsley, Bolton, Lancs BL4 8NS. *Labour Clubs:* Astley, Higher Folds, Little Hulton, Walkden.

LEWIS, Sir Terence (Murray), Kt 1986; OBE 1979; GM 1960; QPM 1977; Commissioner of Police, Queensland, 1976–89; *b* 29 Feb. 1928; *s* of late George Murray Lewis and of Monica Ellen Lewis (*née* Hanlon); *m* 1952, Hazel Catherine Lewis (*née* Gould); three *s* two *d*. *Educ:* Univ. of Queensland (DPA 1974; BA 1978). Queensland Police Force, 1948; Criminal Investigation Br., 1950–63; Juvenile Aid Bureau, 1963–73; Inspector of Police, 1973. Member: Royal Aust. Inst. of Public Admin, 1964; Internat. Police Assoc., 1968; Internat. Assoc. of Chiefs of Police, 1977. Churchill Fellow, 1968; FAIM 1978. Hon. Correspondent for Royal Humane Soc. of Australasia, 1981. Patron, Vice-Patron, Pres., Trustee, or Mem., numerous Qld organisations. Queensland Father of the Year, 1980. Silver Jubilee Medal, 1977. *Recreation:* reading. *Address:* 12 Garfield Drive, Paddington Heights, Qld 4064, Australia.

LEWIS, Thomas Loftus Townshend, CBE 1979; FRCS; Consultant Obstetric and Gynæcological Surgeon at Guy's Hospital, Queen Charlotte's Maternity Hospital and

Chelsea Hospital for Women, 1948–83; Hon. Consultant in Obstetrics and Gynaecology, to the Army, 1973–83; *b* 27 May 1918; *e s* of late Neville Lewis and his first wife, Theodosia Townshend; *m* 1946, Kathleen Alexandra Ponsonby Moore; five *s*. *Educ:* Diocesan Coll., Rondebosch, S Africa; St Paul's Sch.; Cambridge Univ.; Guy's Hospital. BA Cantab (hons in Nat. Sci. Tripos), 1939; MB, BChir Cantab, 1942. FRCS 1946; MRCOG 1948; FRCOG 1961. House Appointments Guy's Hospital, 1942–43; Gold Medal and Prize in Obstetrics, Guy's Hospital, 1942. Volunteered to join South African Medical Corps, 1944; seconded to RAMC and served as Capt. in Italy and Greece, 1944–45. Returned to Guy's Hospital; Registrar in Obstetrics and Gynæcology, 1946, Obstetric Surgeon, 1948; Surgeon, Chelsea Hosp. for Women, 1950; Surgeon, Queen Charlotte's Maternity Hosp., 1952. Examiner in Obstetrics and Gynæcology: University of Cambridge, 1950; University of London, 1954; Royal College of Obstetricians and Gynæcologists, 1952; London Soc. of Apothecaries, 1955; University of St Andrews, 1960. Hon. Sec. and Mem. Council, Royal College of Obstetricians and Gynæcologists, 1955–68, 1971–, Vice-Pres., 1976–78; Mem. Council Obstetric Section, Royal Society of Med., 1953– (Pres. 1981); co-opted Mem. Council, RCS, 1978–81. Guest Prof. to Brisbane, Australia, Auckland, New Zealand, 1959, Johns Hopkins Hosp., Baltimore, 1966; Litchfield Lectr, University of Oxford, 1968; Sims-Black Prof. to Australia, NZ and Rhodesia, 1970. *Publications:* Progress in Clinical Obstetrics and Gynæcology, 2nd edn 1964; (ed jtly and contrib.) Obstetrics by Ten Teachers, 11th edn 1966 to 16th edn 1995; (jtly) Queen Charlotte's Textbook of Obstetrics, 12th edn 1970; (ed jtly and contrib.) Gynaecology by Ten Teachers, 12th edn 1970 to 16th edn 1995; (contrib.) French's Index of Differential Diagnosis, 10th edn 1973 to 12th edn 1984; contributions to: Lancet, BMJ, Practitioner, Proc. Roy. Soc. Med., Encyclopædia Britannica Book of the Year (annual contrib.), etc. *Recreations:* ski-ing, sailing, tennis, golf, croquet, wind-surfing, underwater swimming, photography, viniculture on the Isle of Elba. *Address:* 13 Copse Hill, Wimbledon, SW20 0NB. *T:* (020) 8946 5089. *Clubs:* Old Pauline; Royal Wimbledon Golf; Guy's Hospital Rugby Football (ex-Pres.).

LEWIS, Tony; *see* Lewis, A. R.

LEWIS, Trevor; *see* Lewis, D. T.

LEWIS, Dr Trevor, CBE 1992; Director, AFRC Institute of Arable Crops Research, 1989–93; Head, 1987–93, Lawes Trust Senior Fellow, since 1993, Rothamsted Experimental Station; Visiting Professor in Invertebrate Zoology, University of Nottingham, since 1977; *b* 8 July 1933; *s* of Harold and Maggie Lewis; *m* 1959, Margaret Edith Wells; one *s* one *d*. *Educ:* Univ. of Nottingham (DSc 1986); Imperial Coll. of Science and Technol., Univ. of London (PhD, DIC 1958); MA Cambridge, 1960. University Demonstr in Agricl Zoology, Sch. of Agriculture, Cambridge, 1958–61; scientific staff, Rothamsted Experimental Station, 1961–; seconded to ODA as Sen. Res. Fellow, Univ. of WI, Trinidad, 1970–73; Head, Entomology Dept, 1976–83; Dep. Dir, 1983–87; Hd of Crop and Envmt Protection Div., 1983–89. Special Lectr in Invertebrate Zool., Univ. of Nottingham, 1968–69 and 1973–75. AFRC Assessor to MAFF Adv. Cttee on Pesticides, 1984–89; Member: Management Bd, British Crop Protection Council, 1985–94; Bd, British Crop Protection Enterprises, 1994–; R&D Cttee, Potato Marketing Bd, 1985–89. Mem. Council, British Ecological Soc., 1982–84; Pres., Royal Entomol Soc. of London, 1985–87; Pres., Agric. and Forestry Sect., BAAS, 1997. Huxley Gold Medal, Imperial Coll. of Science and Technol., Univ. of London, 1977. *Publications:* (with L. R. Taylor) Introduction to Experimental Ecology, 1967; Thrips—their biology, ecology and economic importance, 1973; (ed) Insect Communication, 1984; Thrips as Crop Pests, 1997; contribs to scientific jls on topics in entomology. *Recreations:* music, gardening.

LEWIS, Trevor Oswin, CBE 1983; DL; *b* 29 Nov. 1935; *s* of 3rd Baron Merthyr, PC, KBE, TD, and of Violet, *y d* of Brig.-Gen. Sir Frederick Charlton Meyrick, 2nd Bt, CB, CMG; *S* father, 1977, as 4th Baron Merthyr, but disclaimed his peerage for life; also as 4th Bt (*cr* 1896) but does not use the title; *m* 1964, Susan Jane, *yr d* of A. J. Birt-Llewellin; one *s* three *d*. *Educ:* Downs Sch.; Eton; Magdalen Coll., Oxford; Magdalene Coll., Cambridge. Member: Landscape Adv. Cttee, Dept of Transport, 1968–92 (Chm., 1991–92); Countryside Commn, 1973–83 (Dep. Chm., 1980–83); Chm., Countryside Commn's Cttee for Wales, 1973–80. JP Pembs, then Dyfed, 1969–94; DL Dyfed, 1994. *Heir:* (*to disclaimed peerage*): *s* David Trevor Lewis, *b* 21 Feb. 1977. *Address:* Hean Castle, Saundersfoot SA69 9AL. *T:* (01834) 812222.

LEWIS, Dame Vera Margaret; *see* Lynn, Dame Vera.

LEWIS-BOWEN, His Honour Thomas Edward Ifor; a Circuit Judge, 1980–98; *b* 20 June 1933; *s* of late Lt-Col J. W. Lewis-Bowen and K. M. Lewis-Bowen (*née* Rice); *m* 1965, Gillian, *d* of late Reginald Brett, Puckington, Som; one *s* two *d*. *Educ:* Ampleforth; St Edmund Hall, Oxford. Called to Bar, Middle Temple, 1958. A Recorder of the Crown Court, 1974–80.

LEWISHAM, Archdeacon of; *see* Hardman, Ven. C. E.

LEWISOHN, His Honour Anthony Clive Leopold; a Circuit Judge, 1974–90; *b* 1 Aug. 1925; *s* of John Lewisohn and Gladys (*née* Solomon); *m* 1957, Lone Ruthwen Jurgensen; two *s*. *Educ:* Stowe; Trinity Coll., Oxford (MA). Royal Marines, 1944–45; Lieut, Oxf. and Bucks LI, 1946–47. Called to Bar, Middle Temple, 1951; S Eastern Circuit.

LEWISOHN, Neville Joseph; Director of Dockyard Manpower and Productivity (Under Secretary), Ministry of Defence, 1979–82; *b* 28 May 1922; *s* of Victor and Ruth Lewisohn; *m* 1944, Patricia Zeffertt; two *d* (and one *d* decd). *Educ:* Sutton County Sch., Surrey. Entered Admiralty as Clerical Officer, 1939; promoted through intervening grades to Principal, 1964; Dir of Resources and Progs (Ships), 1972 (Asst Sec.); Head of Civilian Management (Specialists), 2 Div., 1976. *Recreations:* music, drama. *Address:* 20 Ragleth Grove, Trowbridge, Wilts BA14 7LE. *T:* (01225) 776046.

LEWISON, Jeremy Rodney Pines; Director of Collections, Tate Gallery, since 1998; *b* 13 Jan. 1955; *s* of late Anthony Frederick Lewison and of Dinora Pines; *m* 1993, Caroline Maria Aviva Schuck; one step *s* one step *d*. *Educ:* Westminster Sch.; Magdalen Coll., Oxford (MA; Dip Hist. of Art). Curator, Kettle's Yard, Univ. of Cambridge, 1977–83; Tate Gallery: Asst Keeper, Print Collection, 1983–86; Asst Keeper, 1986–90, Dep. Keeper, 1990–97, Modern Collection. *Publications:* Anish Kapoor Drawings, 1990; Ben Nicholson, 1991; David Smith Medals for Dishonour, 1991; Brice Marden Prints 1961–91, 1992; Ben Nicholson, 1993; Shirazeh Houshiary, 1995; Karl Weschke, 1998; Interpreting Pollock, 1999. *Recreations:* tennis, ski-ing, mountain walking. *Address:* Tate Gallery, Millbank, SW1P 4RG. *T:* (020) 7887 8000.
See also *K. M. J. Lewison.*

LEWISON, Kim Martin Jordan; QC 1991; a Recorder, since 1997; a Deputy High Court Judge, since 2000; *b* 1 May 1952; *s* of late Anthony Frederick Lewison and of Dinora Lewison (*née* Pines); *m* 1979, Helen Mary Janecek (marr. diss. 1998); one *s* one *d*. *Educ:* St Paul's Sch., London; Downing Coll., Cambridge (MA 1973); Council of Legal Education. Called to the Bar, Lincoln's Inn, 1975, Bencher, 1998; Asst Recorder, 1994–97. Mem. Council, Liberal Jewish Synagogue, 1990–96. Mem. Council, Leo Baeck Coll., 1997–; Gov., Anglo-American Real Property Inst., 1996–2000 (Chm. elect, 2000). *Publications:* Development Land Tax, 1978; Drafting Business Leases, 1979, 5th edn 1996; Lease or Licence, 1985; The Interpretation of Contracts, 1989, 2nd edn 1997; (Gen. Editor) Woodfall on Landlord and Tenant, 1990–. *Recreations:* visiting France, avoiding tsores. *Address:* Falcon Chambers, Falcon Court, EC4Y 1AA. *T:* (020) 7353 2484.
See also *J. R. P. Lewison.*

LEWITH, Dr George Thomas, FRCP; Senior Research Fellow in University Medicine and Hon. Consultant Physician, Southampton Medical School, University of Southampton, since 1995; Partner, Centre for Study of Complementary Medicine, Southampton, since 1982; *b* 12 Jan. 1950; *s* of Frank and Alice Lewith; *m* 1977, Nicola Rosemary Bazeley; two *s* one *d*. *Educ:* Queen's Coll., Taunton; Trinity Coll., Cambridge (MA); Westminster Hosp. Med. Sch. (MB BChir); DM Soton 1994. MRCGP 1980; FRCP 1999. Lectr in Primary Med. Care, Southampton Univ., 1979–82. *Publications:* contribs to numerous academic books and papers in field of complementary medicine. *Recreations:* the theatre, ski-ing, sport, sailing, gardening. *Address:* Sway Wood House, Mead End Road, Sway, Lymington, Hants SO41 6EE. *T:* (01590) 682129.

LEWITTER, Prof. Lucjan Ryszard; Professor of Slavonic Studies, 1968–84, and Fellow of Christ's College, since 1951, University of Cambridge; *b* 1922. *Educ:* schools in Poland; Perse Sch., Cambridge; Christ's Coll., Cambridge (BA; PhD 1951). Cambridge University: Asst Lectr in Polish, 1948; Univ. Lectr in Slavonic Studies (Polish), 1953–68; Christ's College: Dir of Studies in Modern Languages, 1951–64; Tutor, 1960–68; Vice-Master, 1977–80. *Publications:* (ed with A. P. Vlasto) Ivan Pososhkov, The Book of Poverty and Wealth, 1987; articles, mostly on Russo-Polish relations, in learned jls. *Address:* Christ's College, Cambridge CB2 3BU. *T:* (01223) 357320. *Club:* Oxford and Cambridge.

LEWSLEY, Patricia; Member (SDLP) Lagan Valley, Northern Ireland Assembly, since 1998; *b* 3 March 1957; *d* of Patrick and Mary Killen; *m* 1976, Hugh Lewsley (marr. diss. 1998); three *s* two *d*. *Educ:* St Dominic's High Sch.; Univ. of Ulster. Contested (SDLP) Lagan Valley, 2001. *Recreations:* reading, travel. *Address:* 34 Alina Gardens, Dunmurry, Belfast BT17 0QJ.

LEWTHWAITE, Brig. Sir Rainald Gilfrid, 4th Bt *cr* 1927, of Broadgate, Thwaites, Co. Cumberland; CVO 1975; OBE 1974; MC 1943; *b* 21 July 1913; 2nd *s* of Sir William Lewthwaite, 2nd Bt of Broadgate, Cumberland, and Beryl Mary Stopford Hickman; *S* brother, 1993; *m* 1936, Margaret Elizabeth Edmonds, MBE 1942 (*d* 1990), 2nd *d* of late Harry Edmonds and Florence Jane Moncrieffe Bolton, High Green, Redding, Conn, USA; one *s* (and one *s* two *d* decd). *Educ:* Rugby Sch.; Trinity Coll., Cambridge. BA (Hons) Law 1934. Joined Scots Guards, 1934. Served War of 1939–45 (MC, despatches twice). Retired as Defence and Military Attaché, British Embassy, Paris, 1968. Dir of Protocol, Hong Kong, 1969–76. French Croix-de-Guerre with Palm, 1945. *Recreation:* country life. *Heir:* *s* David Rainald Lewthwaite [*b* 26 March 1940; *m* 1969, Diana Helena, twin *d* of W. R. Tomkinson, TD; two *d*]. *Address:* Broadgate, Millom, Cumbria LA18 5JY. *T:* (01229) 716295. *Club:* Cavalry and Guards.

LEWTY, (David) Ian; HM Diplomatic Service, retired; *b* 27 July 1943; *s* of late Harry Lewty and Ruby Lewty (*née* Buck); *m* 1968, Mary Law; two *d*. *Educ:* Lancing Coll.; Magdalen Coll., Oxford (MA). Third Sec., FO, 1965; MECAS, Lebanon, 1966; Third, later Second Sec., Ottawa, 1967–71; Hd, British Interests Section, Baghdad, 1971–72; First Sec., FCO, 1972–76; Hd of Chancery, Jedda, 1976–79; (on secondment) L'Ecole Nationale d'Administration, Paris, 1979–81; UK Delegn to OECD, Paris, 1981–84; FCO, 1984–87; Counsellor and Dep. Hd of Mission, Khartoum, 1987–89; Diplomatic Service Inspector, 1989–92; Hd, Migration and Visa Dept, FCO, 1992–95; Ambassador to Bahrain, 1996–99. *Address:* 38 Burlington Avenue, Richmond, Surrey TW9 4DH.

LEY, Sir Ian (Francis), 5th Bt *cr* 1905, of Epperstone, Nottingham; *b* 12 June 1934; *o s* of Sir Francis Douglas Ley, 4th Bt, MBE and Violet Geraldine Ley (*née* Johnson) (*d* 1991); *S* father, 1995; *m* 1957, Caroline Margaret (*née* Errington); one *s* one *d*. *Educ:* Eton Coll. Dep. Chm., 1972–80, Chm., 1981–82, Ley's Foundries and Engineering plc. High Sheriff, Derbyshire, 1985. *Recreation:* shooting. *Heir:* *s* Christopher Ian Ley [*b* 2 Dec. 1962; *m* 1999, Henrietta, *yr d* of David Nicholls]. *Address:* Fauld Hall, Tutbury, Staffordshire DE13 9HR. *T:* (01283) 812266. *Club:* White's.

LEY, Prof. Steven Victor, FRS 1990; BP (1702) Professor of Organic Chemistry, and Fellow of Trinity College, University of Cambridge, since 1992; *b* 10 Dec. 1945; *s* of Mary Ley (*née* Hall) and Ralph Gilbert Ley; *m* 1970, Rosemary Ann Jameson; one *d*. *Educ:* Loughborough Univ. of Technology (BSc 1st cl. Hons 1969; DIS 1969; PhD 1972); DSc London 1983; MA 1997, ScD 1999, Cantab. Res. Fellow, Ohio State Univ., 1972–74; Imperial College, London: Res. Asst, 1974–75; Lectr, 1975–83; Prof. of Organic Chemistry, 1983–92; Head of Chemistry Dept, 1989–92. Royal Soc. Bakerian Lectr, 1997. Hon. DSc Loughborough, 1994. Royal Society of Chemistry: Hickinbottom Res. Fellow, 1981–83 (1st recipient); Corday Morgan Medal and Prize, 1982; Tilden Lectr and Medal, 1988; Award for Synthetic Chem., 1989; Pedlar Lectr and Medal, 1992; Simonsen Lectr and Medal, 1993; Award for Natural Products Chemistry, 1994; Flintoff Medal, 1996; Rhône-Poulenc Lectureship Medal and Prize, 1998; Pres., 2000–02. Pfizer Res. Award, Pfizer Central Research, 1983 (1st recipient); Adolf Windaus Medal, German Chem. Soc., 1994; Dr Paul Janssen Prize for Creativity in Organic Synthesis, 1996. *Publications:* over 400 papers in internat. jls of chemistry. *Recreations:* ski-ing, listening to opera. *Address:* Department of Chemistry, Lensfield Road, Cambridge CB2 1EW.

LEYLAND, Sir Philip Vyvian N.; *see* Naylor-Leyland.

LEYLAND, Ronald Arthur; Chief Executive, North Yorkshire County Council, 1990–94; *b* 23 Aug. 1940; *s* of Arthur and Lucy Leyland; *m* 1962, Joan Virginia Sinclair; three *s*. *Educ:* Merchant Taylors' Sch., Crosby; Liverpool Univ. (LLB Hons 1961). Solicitor (Hons 1964). Assistant Solicitor: Bootle CBC, 1964–65; Nottingham City Council, 1965–68; Sen. Asst Solicitor, then Dir of Admin, Leeds MDC, 1968–75; County Sec., Hampshire CC, 1975–90. Dir, N Yorks TEC, 1990–94. Chm., Soc. of County Secretaries, 1986–87. *Recreations:* walking, family history. *Address:* White House, Maunby, near Thirsk YO7 4HG. *Club:* Rotary.

LI, David Kwok Po, OBE 1990; FCIB; FCA; Chairman, since 1997, and Chief Executive, since 1986, Bank of East Asia Ltd; *b* 13 March 1939; *s* of Li Fook Shu and Woo Tze Ha; *m* 1971, Penny Poon; two *s*. *Educ:* Univ. of Cambridge (MA). FCIB 1988; FCA 1977. Bank of East Asia Ltd: Chief Accountant, 1969–72; Asst Chief Manager, 1973–76; Dep. Chief Manager, 1977–81; Dir, 1981–; Dep. Chm., 1995–97. Hon. Fellow: Robinson Coll., Univ. of Cambridge, 1989; Selwyn Coll., Cambridge, 1992. Hon. LLD: Cantab, 1993; Warwick, 1994; Hong Kong, 1996. *Recreations:* tennis, art, antiques, reading. *Address:* Bank of East Asia Ltd, 22nd Floor, 10 Des Voeux Road Central, Hong Kong. *T:* 28423206. *Clubs:* Wentworth; Hong Kong Country, Hong Kong Golf, Hong Kong Yacht (Hong Kong); Waialae Country (Hawaii).

LI, Fook Kow, CMG 1975; JP; Chairman, Public Service Commission, Hong Kong, 1980–87, retired; *b* 15 June 1922; *s* of Tse Fong Li; *m* 1946, Edith Kwong Li (*d* 1992); four *c*. *Educ:* Massachusetts Inst. of Technology (BSc, MSc). Mem. Hong Kong Admin. Service; Teacher, 1948–54; various departmental posts and posts in the Government Secretariat, 1955–60; Asst Financial Sec., Asst Estabt Officer, Dep. Financial Sec. and Estabt Officer, 1961–69; Dep. Dir of Commerce and Industry, 1970; Dep. Sec. for Home Affairs, 1971–72; Dir of Social Welfare, 1972; Sec. for Social Services, 1973; Sec. for Home Affairs, 1977–80. JP Hong Kong, 1959. *Address:* H22 Celeste Court, 12 Fung Fai Terrace, Hong Kong. *Clubs:* Hong Kong Jockey, Hong Kong Country.
See also K. N. A. Li.

LI Ka-shing, Sir, KBE 2000 (CBE 1989); Chairman: Cheung Kong (Holdings) Ltd, since 1971; Hutchison Whampoa Ltd, since 1981; *b* 1928; *m* Chong Yuet-Ming (decd); two *s*. Moved from mainland China to Hong Kong, 1940; took first job as salesman, 1943; promoted to gen. manager, 1948; founded Cheung Kong Industries, 1950; Man. Dir, Cheung Kong (Holdings) Ltd, 1971–98; took over Hongkong Electric Hldgs Ltd, 1985; business interests in China, UK, Canada, Hong Kong and many other parts of the world including all G7 countries except Italy. Adviser to Beijing Govt, 1992–97; Member: Drafting Cttee for Basic Law, HKSAR, 1985–90; Preparatory Cttee to oversee 1997 handover of Hong Kong, 1993–97; Selection Cttee for first govt of HKSAR, 1996. Hon. Citizen: Shantou, Guangzhou, Shenzhen, Nanhai, Foshan, Jiangmen, Choazhou, Beijing. JP. Hon. LLD: Hong Kong, 1986; Calgary, 1989; Chinese Univ. of Hong Kong, 1997; Cantab, 1999; Hon. Dr Beijing, 1992; Hon. DSocSci: Hong Kong Univ. of Sci. and Technology, 1995; City Univ. of Hong Kong, 1998; Open Univ. of Hong Kong, 1999. *Recreations:* golf, boating. *Address:* Cheung Kong (Holdings) Ltd, 70/F Cheung Kong Center, 2 Queen's Road Central, Hong Kong. *Club:* Hong Kong Jockey.

LI Kwok Nang, Andrew, CBE 1993; JP; Chief Justice, and President of the Court of Final Appeal, Hong Kong, since 1997; *b* 12 Dec. 1948; *s* of Li Fook Kow, *qv*; *m* 1973, Judy M. Y. Woo; two *d*. *Educ:* St Paul's Primary Sch., Hong Kong; St Paul's Co-Educnl Coll., Hong Kong; Repton Sch.; Fitzwilliam Coll., Cambridge (MA, LLM; Hon. Fellow, 1999). Called to the Bar: Middle Temple, 1970 (Hon. Bencher, 1997); Hong Kong, 1973; QC (Hong Kong) 1988. JP Hong Kong, 1985. Hon. DLitt Hong Kong Univ. of Sci. and Technol., 1993; Hon. LLD: Baptist Univ., Hong Kong, 1994; Open Univ., Hong Kong, 1997; Univ. of Hong Kong, 2001. *Recreations:* the turf, tennis. *Address:* Court of Final Appeal, No 1 Battery Path, Central, Hong Kong. *T:* 21230011. *Clubs:* Athenæum; Hong Kong Jockey (Hon. Steward), Hong Kong Country, Shek O Country (Hong Kong).

LI, Simon Fook Sean, GBM 1997; Director, The Bank of East Asia Ltd, Hong Kong, since 1987; *b* 19 April 1922; 3rd *s* of late Koon Chun Li and Doy Hing Tam Li; *m* Marie Veronica Lillian Yang; four *s* one *d*. *Educ:* King's Coll., Hong Kong; Hong Kong Univ.; Nat. Kwangsi Univ.; University Coll., London Univ. (LLB 1950; Fellow, 1991). Barrister-at-Law, Lincoln's Inn, 1951. Crown Counsel, Attorney-General's Chambers, Hong Kong, 1953; Senior Crown Counsel, 1962; District Judge, 1966–71, Puisne Judge, 1971–80, Justice of Appeal, 1980–84, Vice-Pres., Court of Appeal, 1984–87, Hong Kong. Chm., Insce Claims Complaints Bd, 1990–94; Mem., Hong Kong Special Admin. Region Basic Law Drafting Cttee, 1985–90. PR China: Hong Kong Affairs Advr, 1992–97; Dep. Dir, Preliminary Working Cttee, 1993–95, and HK Special Admin. Region Prep. Cttee, 1996–97. Hon. LLD Chinese Univ., Hong Kong, 1986. *Recreations:* hiking, swimming. *Address:* 3/F Shun Pont Comm. Bldg, 5–11 Thomson Road, Wanchai, Hong Kong. *T:* 28668680. *Clubs:* Royal Commonwealth Society; Hong Kong (Chm., 1995–96), Chinese, Hong Kong Jockey (Hon. Steward) (Hong Kong).

LIANG, Prof. Wei Yao, PhD; Professor of Superconductivity, University of Cambridge, since 1994; Fellow and Lecturer, Gonville and Caius College, Cambridge, since 1971; *b* 23 Sept. 1940; *s* of late Tien Fu Liang and of Po Seng Nio Lie; *m* 1968, Lian Choo (*née* Choong); three *d*. *Educ:* Pah Chung Chinese High Sch., Jakarta; Portsmouth Coll. of Technology; Imperial Coll., London (BSc, ARCS 1st Class Hons Theoretical Physics); Univ. of Cambridge (PhD). Gonville and Caius College, Cambridge: Comyns Berkeley Unofficial Fellow, 1969–71; Dir of Studies in Natural Scis, 1975–89; University of Cambridge: Demonstrator, 1971–75; Lectr in Physics, 1975–92; Reader in high temperature superconductivity, 1992–93; Co-Dir, 1988–89, Dir, 1989–98, Interdisciplinary Res. Centre in Superconductivity. Vis. Scientist, Xerox Palo Alto Res. Centre, 1975, 1976; Visiting Professor: EPF Lausanne, 1978; Inst. of Semiconductors, Beijing, 1983; Sci. Univ. of Tokyo, 2000; Univ. of Tokyo, 2001. *Publications:* (ed with A. S. Alexandrov and E. K. H. Salje) Polarons and Bipolarons in High Tc Superconductors and Related Materials, 1995; (ed with W. Zong) Fundamental Research in High Tc Superconductivity, 1999. *Recreations:* music, photography. *Address:* Gonville and Caius College, Cambridge CB2 1TA. *T:* (01223) 337077.

LIAO Poon-Huai, Donald, CBE 1983 (OBE 1972); company director; *b* 29 Oct. 1929; *s* of late Liao Huk-Koon and Yeo Tsai-Hoon; *m* 1963, Christine Yuen Ching-Me; two *s* one *d*. *Educ:* Univ. of Hong Kong (BArch Hons); Univ. of Durham (Dip. Landscape Design). Architect, Hong Kong Housing Authority, 1960, Housing Architect, 1966; Commissioner for Housing and Member, Town Planning Board, 1968; Director of Housing and Vice-Chm., Hong Kong Housing Authority, 1973; Sec. for Housing and Chm., Hong Kong Housing Authority, 1980; Sec. for Dist Admin, Hong Kong, 1985. Chm., HSBC China Fund, 1992–; Dir, TCC Internat. Hldgs Ltd, 1997–. MLC, Hong Kong, 1980; MEC, 1985. Mem., Sino-British Jt Liaison Gp, 1987–89. Fellow, Hong Kong Inst. of Architects. Hon. FIH. *Recreations:* golf, skiing, riding. *Address:* (residence) 95A Kadoorie Avenue, Kowloon, Hong Kong. *T:* 27155822; (office) 1515 Ocean Centre, Canton Road, Kowloon, Hong Kong. *T:* 23020820. *Clubs:* Athenæum; Hong Kong Golf, Hong Kong Jockey (Hong Kong).

LIARDET, Rear-Adm. Guy Francis, CB 1990; CBE 1985; *b* 6 Dec. 1934; *s* of Maj.-Gen. Henry Maughan Liardet, CB, CBE, DSO; *m* 1962, Jennifer Anne O'Hagan; one *s* two *d*. *Educ:* Royal Naval Coll., Dartmouth; Southampton Univ. (BA Hons 1999). Trng Comdr, BRNC, Dartmouth, 1969–70; comd HMS Aurora, 1970–72; Exec. Officer, HMS Bristol, 1974–76; Defence Policy Staff, MoD, 1978–79; RCDS, 1980; CSO (Trng), C-in-C Naval Home Comd, 1981–82; comd HMS Cleopatra and Seventh Frigate Sqn, 1983–84; Dir of Public Relations (Navy), MoD, 1984–86; Flag Officer Second Flotilla, 1986–88; Comdt, JSDC, 1988–90, retd. Dir of Public Affairs, CIA, 1990–93. Mem., RNSA, 1970–. *Publications:* contrib. Naval Review. *Recreation:* sailing. *Address:* The Downs Cottage, New Road, Meonstoke, Southampton SO32 3NN. *Club:* Royal Yacht Squadron (Cowes).

LIBBY, Donald Gerald, PhD; Under Secretary, Office of Science and Technology, Cabinet Office, and Secretary, Advisory Board for the Research Councils, 1991–94; *b* 2 July 1934; *s* of late Herbert Lionel Libby and Minnie Libby; *m* 1st, 1961, Margaret Elizabeth Dunlop McLatchie (*d* 1979); one *d*; 2nd, 1982, June Belcher. *Educ:* RMA, Sandhurst; London Univ. (BSc, PhD Physics). CEng, FIEE. Department of Education and Science: Principal Scientific Officer, 1967–72; Principal, 1972–74; Asst Sec., 1974–80; Under Sec., 1980–91 (Planning and Internat. Relations Br., 1980–82, Architects, Bldg and Schs Br., 1982–86, Further and Higher Educn Br. 2, 1986–91). Adviser, Logica UK Ltd, 1995–96. *Recreations:* music, rowing, golf. *Address:* Lygon Cottage, 26 Wayneflete Tower Avenue, Esher, Surrey KT10 8QG.

LIBESKIND, Daniel; Architect, Architectural Studio Libeskind, Berlin, since 1995; *b* Łodz, Poland, 12 May 1946; *s* of Nachman Libeskind and Dora Libeskind (*née* Blaustein); *m* 1969, Nina Lewis; two *s* one *d*. *Educ:* in Poland and Israel; Bronx High Sch. of Sci., NYC; Cooper Union Sch. of Architecture, NYC (BArch 1970); Sch. of Comparative Studies, Univ. of Essex (MA Hist. and Theory of Architecture 1971). Architectural trng in The Hague, NYC and Helsinki; Inst. for Architecture and Urban Studies, NY, 1971–72; Irving Grossman Associates, Toronto, 1972–73; Project Planners Associates, Toronto, 1973; Asst Prof. of Architecture, Univ. of Ky, 1973–75; Unit Master, AA, London, 1975–77; Sen. Lectr, Poly. of Central London, and Critic in Architecture, Centre of Advanced Studies in Architecture, 1975–77; Associate Prof. of Architecture, Univ. of Toronto, 1977–78; Hd, Sch. of Architecture, and Architect-in-Residence, Cranbrook Acad. of Art, Bloomfield Hills, Mich, 1978–85; Founder and Dir, *Architecture Intermundium*, Milan, 1986–89; Architect, Berlin, 1989–94, LA, 1994–95. Vis. Critic in Architecture, Houston, Lund, London, Harvard and Helsinki, 1981–84; Visiting Professor, Europe, US and Canada, 1985–, including: Bannister Fletcher Architecture Prof., Univ. of London, 1990–91; Hochschule Weissensee, Berlin, 1993–95; Sch. of Architecture and Urban Planning, UCLA, 1994–98; Hochschule für Gestaltung, Karlsruhe; First Louis Kahn Prof., Yale Univ. Sch. of Architecture. Ext. Examr, Bartlett Sch. of Architecture, Univ. of London, 1993. Major works include: Uozu Mt Pavilion, Japan, 1997; Polderland Gdn, Netherlands, 1997; Felix Nussbaum Haus, Osnabruk, 1998; Berlin Mus. with Jewish Mus., 1999. DU Essex, 1999. Numerous awards, including: Award for Architecture, AAAL; Berlin Cultural Prize, 1996. *Publications:* numerous monographs. *Recreations:* meditation, listening to music. *Address:* Architectural Studio Libeskind, Windscheidstrasse 18, 10627 Berlin, Germany. *T:* (30) 3249963.

LICHFIELD, 5th Earl of, *cr* 1831; **Thomas Patrick John Anson;** Viscount Anson and Baron Soberton, 1806; DL; *b* 25 April 1939; *s* of Viscount Anson (Thomas William Arnold) (*d* 1958) and Princess Anne of Denmark (*née* Anne Fenella Ferelith Bowes-Lyon) (*d* 1980); *S* grandfather, 1960; *m* 1975, Lady Leonora Grosvenor (LVO 1997) (marr. diss. 1986), *d* of 5th Duke of Westminster, TD; one *s* two *d*. *Educ:* Harrow Sch.; RMA, Sandhurst. Joined Regular Army, Sept. 1957, as Officer Cadet; Grenadier Guards, 1959–62 (Lieut). Now photographer (known professionally as Patrick Lichfield). FBIPP; FRPS. Freeman, City of London, 1981. DL Stafford 1996. *Publications:* The Most Beautiful Women, 1981; Lichfield on Photography (also video cassettes), 1981; A Royal Album, 1982; Patrick Lichfield's Unipart Calendar Book, 1982; Patrick Lichfield Creating the Unipart Calendar, 1983; Hot Foot to Zabriskie Point, 1985; Lichfield on Travel Photography, 1986; Not the Whole Truth (autobiog.), 1986; (ed) Courvoisier's Book of the Best, 1986, 5th edn 1994; Lichfield in Retrospect, 1988; (ed) Queen Mother: the Lichfield selection, 1990; (ed) Elizabeth R: a photographic celebration of 40 years, 1991. *Heir: s* Viscount Anson, *qv*. *Address:* Lichfield Studios, 133 Oxford Gardens, W10 6NE. *T:* (020) 8969 6161; (seat) Shugborough Hall, Stafford. *T:* (01889) 881454. *Club:* White's.

LICHFIELD, Bishop of, since 1984; **Rt Rev. Keith Norman Sutton;** *b* 23 June 1934; *s* of Norman and Irene Sutton; *m* 1963, Edith Mary Jean Geldard (*d* 2000); three *s* one *d*. *Educ:* Jesus College, Cambridge (MA 1959). Curate, St Andrew's, Plymouth, 1959–62; Chaplain, St John's Coll., Cambridge, 1962–67; Tutor and Chaplain, Bishop Tucker Coll., Mukono, Uganda, 1968–73; Principal of Ridley Hall, Cambridge, 1973–78; Bishop Suffragan of Kingston-upon-Thames, 1978–83. General Synod: Chairman: Bd for Mission and Unity, 1989–91; Bd of Mission, 1991–94; Member: Standing Cttee, 1989–94; Theol Gp, House of Bishops, 1989–. Select Preacher, Univ. of Cambridge, 1987. Pres., Queen's Coll., Birmingham, 1986–94. Entered House of Lords, 1989. Episcopal Visitor, Simon of Cyrene Theol Inst., 1992–. Hon. Vice-Pres., CMS, 1995–. Patron: Russian Poets Fund, Keele Univ., 1995–; New Art Gall., Walsall, 1998–. DUniv Keele, 1992; Hon. DLitt Wolverhampton, 1994. *Publication:* The People of God, 1983. *Recreations:* Russian literature, third world issues, music. *Address:* Bishop's House, 22 The Close, Lichfield, Staffs WS13 7LG.

LICHFIELD, Dean of; *see* Yorke, Very Rev. M. L.

LICHFIELD, Archdeacon of; *see* Liley, Ven. C. F.

LICHFIELD, Prof. Nathaniel; Professor Emeritus, University of London, since 1978; Partner, Dalia and Nathaniel Lichfield Associates, urban and environmental planners and economists, since 1992; *b* 29 Feb. 1916; 2nd *s* of Hyman Lichman and Fanny (*née* Grecht); *m* 1st, 1942, Rachel Goulden (*d* 1968); two *d*; 2nd, 1970, Dalia Kadury; one *s* one *d*. *Educ:* Raines Foundn Sch.; University of London. BSc (EstMan), PhD (Econ); PPRTPI, FRICS. Sen. Partner, 1962–89, Chm., 1989–92, Nathaniel Lichfield & Partners Ltd, planning, develt, urban design and econ. consultants; from 1945 has worked continuously in urban and regional planning, specialising in econs of planning from 1950, with particular reference to social cost-benefit in planning, impact assessment, land policy and urban conservation; worked in local and central govt depts and private offices. Consultant commns in UK and all continents. Special Lectr, UCL, 1950; Prof. of Econs of Environmental Planning, UCL, 1966–79. Visiting Professor: Univ. of California, 1976–78; Univ. of Tel Aviv, 1959–60, 1966; Technion—Israel Inst. of Technol., 1972–74; Hebrew Univ., Jerusalem, 1980–; Univ. of Naples, 1986–; Special Prof., Univ. of Nottingham, 1989–. Chm., Econs Cttee, ICOMOS, 1988–95 (Conservation Econs Cttee report published 1993); Member: Exec. Cttee, Internat. Centre for Land Policy Studies, 1975–85; Council, Tavistock Inst. of Human Relations, 1968–93 (Vice Pres., 1993–); formerly Member: SSRC; CNAA; SE Econ. Planning Council; Chairman: Economics of Urban Villages Cttee, Urban Villages Forum (report published 1995); Land Assembly Cttee, DETR/Urban Villages Forum, 1998–99 (summary report 2001). Hon. Fellow, Centre for Social and Econ. Res. on Global Envmt, 1992–. *Publications:* Economics of Planned Development, 1956; Cost Benefit Analysis in Urban Redevelopment, 1962; Cost Benefit Analysis in Town Planning: a Case Study of Cambridge, 1966; Israel's New Towns: a Development Strategy, 1971; (with Prof. A. Proudlove) Conservation and Traffic: a case study of York, 1975; (with Peter Kettle and Michael Whitbread) Evaluation in the Planning Process, 1975; (with Haim Darin-Drabkin) Land Policy in Planning, 1980; (with Leslie Lintott) Period Buildings: evaluation of development–conservation options, 1985; (with Prof. J. Schweid) Conservation of the Built Heritage, 1986; Economics in Urban Conservation, 1988; Community Impact Evaluation, 1996; (with Owen Cannellan) Land Value Taxation in Britain: past, current and prospective, 2002; papers in Urban Studies, Regional Studies, Land Economics, Town Planning Review, Restauro, Built Environment, Project Appraisal, Planning and Envmtl Law, Chartered Surveyor, Planner, Envmt and Planning, Transport and Econ.

Policy. *Recreations:* finding out less and less about more and more, countering advancing age, singing. *Address:* 13 Chalcot Gardens, England's Lane, NW3 4YB. *T:* (020) 7586 0461. *Club:* Reform.

LICHFIELD, Patrick; *see* Lichfield, 5th Earl of.

LICHTER, Dr Ivan, ONZ 1997; FRCS, FRACS; Medical Director, Te Omanga Hospice, Lower Hutt, New Zealand, 1986–94; *b* 14 March 1918; *s* of Goodman Lichter and Sarah (*née* Mierowsky); *m* 1951, Heather Lloyd; three *s* one *d. Educ:* Univ. of Witwatersrand, Johannesburg (MB BCh). FRCS 1949; FRACS 1964. Capt, SAMC in Madagascar, Egypt, Italy and Hosp. Ship Amra, 1942–45. Postgrad. Registrar, Guy's Hosp., London, 1946; Resident Surgical Officer: Queen Mary's Hosp., London, 1947; Wembley Hosp., Middx, 1948; Registrar, and Chief Asst, Thoracic Surgical Unit, Harefield Hosp., Middx, 1948–51; Thoracic Surgeon: Johannesburg, SA, 1952–60; Otago Hosp. Bd, and Associate Prof. of Surgery, Univ. of Otago, Dunedin, 1961–84. NZ Postgrad. Travelling Fellow, 1976. Examr in Cardio-Thoracic Surgery, RACS, 1974–84. Estabd and developed palliative care services in NZ and undertook teaching and research in palliative medicine, 1974–94. *Publications:* Communication in Cancer Care, 1987; (contrib.) Oxford Textbook of Palliative Medicine, 1993, 2nd edn 1997; numerous contribs to learned jls, esp. on aspects of palliative care. *Recreations:* reading, music, walking. *Address:* 41 Kitchener Road, Milford, Auckland, New Zealand. *T:* (9) 4895340.

LICKISS, Sir Michael (Gillam), Kt 1993; Chairman: The Edexcel Foundation (formerly Business and Technology Education Council), 1994–2000; South West of England Regional Development Agency, since 1998; *b* 18 Feb. 1934; *s* of Frank Gillam and Elaine Rheta Lickiss; *m* 1st, 1959, Anita (marr. diss. 1979); two *s* two *d*; 2nd, 1987, Anne; one *s. Educ:* Bournemouth Grammar Sch.; LSE, London Univ. (BSc Econ 1955). FCA. Articled, Bournemouth, 1955–58; commissioned, Army, 1959–62; practised Bournemouth, 1962–68; Partner, Thornton Baker, Bournemouth, 1968–73, London, 1973–94: Exec. Partner, 1975; Managing Partner, 1985–89; firm's name changed to Grant Thornton, 1986; Sen. Partner, 1989–94. DTI Inspector, jtly with Hugh Carlisle, QC, 1986–88; Lectr, UK and overseas. Chairman: Accountancy Television Ltd, 1992–94; Somerset Economic Partnership, 1994–99; West of England Develt Agency, 1994–97; Director: MAI plc, 1994–96; United News and Media plc, 1996–97, and other cos. Institute of Chartered Accountants: Mem. Council, 1971–81, 1983–95; Vice-Pres., 1988–89; Dep. Pres., 1989–90; Pres., 1990–91; Past Chairman: Educn and Training, Tech. Cttee and Ethics Cttee; Professional Conduct Directorate; Chm., Somerset Rural Youth Project, 1997–99; Dir, British Trng Internat., 1998–2000. Chm., CCAB, 1990–91; Dep. Chm., Financial Reporting Council, 1990–91; Member: Council, BTEC (Chm., Finance Cttee, 1985–93); FEFCE, 1992–96; Copyright Tribunal, 1994–99; Senate, Engrg Council, 1996–99; Learning and Skills Nat. Council, 2000–; Industrial Develt Adv. Bd, DTI, 2000–. Founder President, Assoc. of Accounting Technicians, 1980–82. Trustee, Parnham Trust, 1992–96. Mem., Court of Govs, LSE, 1992–; Vice Chm., Court of Govs, Plymouth Univ., 1995–98; Mem. Council, London Univ., 1997–. *Publications:* articles in learned jls. *Recreations:* gardening in Somerset, walking in the Lake District. *Address:* Old Vicarage, Drayton, near Langport, Som TA10 0JX. *Club:* Royal Automobile.

LICKLEY, Gavin Alexander Fraser, CA; Head of Structured Finance, Global Corporates and Institutions Division, Deutsche Bank AG (formerly Head of Structured Finance, Deutsche Morgan Grenfell), 1995–99; *b* 14 Aug. 1946; *s* of Alexander Thompson Lickley and Gladys Ann Fraser (*née* Smith); *m* 1973, Anne Muir Forrester; two *d. Educ:* Univ. of Edinburgh (LLB Hons 1967). CA 1970. Corporate Finance Exec., GKN plc, 1971–72; with Morgan Grenfell & Co. Ltd, 1972–95 (Head of Banking, 1991–95); Chm., Morgan Grenfell and Co. Ltd, 1996–98. *Recreations:* golf, ski-ing. *Address:* 6 Westmoreland Road, SW13 9RY. *T:* (020) 8748 7618. *Clubs:* City of London, Roehampton; Royal Wimbledon Golf.

LICKORISH, Leonard John, CBE 1975; *b* 10 Aug. 1921; *s* of Adrian J. and Josephine Lickorish; *m* 1945, Eileen Maris Wright (*d* 1983); one *s. Educ:* St George's Coll., Weybridge; University Coll., London (BA). Served RAF, 1941–46. British Travel Assoc., 1946–70; Dir-Gen., BTA, 1970–86. Vis. Prof., Univ. of Strathclyde, 1989–96. Chm., European Travel Commn, 1984–86 (Hon. Vice-Chm., 1986); Chm., Exhibition Industry Federation, 1987–89; Vice Chm., European Tourism Action Group, 1997– (Sec., 1986–97). Officer of Crown of Belgium, 1967. *Publications:* The Travel Trade, 1955; The Statistics of Tourism, 1975; Tourism Marketing, 1989; Developing Tourism Destinations, 1991; An Introduction to Tourism, 1997; numerous for nat. and internat. organisations on internat. travel. *Recreations:* gardening, walking, fishing. *Address:* 46 Hillway, Highgate, N6 6EP. *Club:* Royal Over-Seas League.

LICKORISH, Prof. William Bernard Raymond, ScD; Fellow, Pembroke College, Cambridge, since 1964; Professor of Geometric Topology, since 1996, Head, Department of Pure Mathematics and Mathematical Statistics, since 1997, University of Cambridge; *b* 19 Feb. 1938; *s* of William Percy Lickorish and Florence Lickorish; *m* 1962, Margaret Ann Russell; one *s* two *d. Educ:* Merchant Taylors' Sch.; Pembroke Coll., Cambridge (ScD 1991). Asst Lectr in Maths, Univ. of Sussex, 1963–64; University of Cambridge: Asst Lectr, 1964–69; Lectr, 1969–90; Reader, 1990–96; Asst Dir, then Dir of Studies in Maths, Pembroke Coll., 1964–91. Visiting Professor: Univ. of Wisconsin, 1967–68; Univ. of Calif, Berkeley, 1974, Santa Barbara, 1979–80 and 1996–97; Univ. of Texas, 1989; UCLA, 1990. Sen. Whitehead Prize, London Mathematical Soc., 1991. *Publications:* An Introduction to Knot Theory, 1997; contrib. many articles on topology. *Recreations:* gardening, to walk, to bathe. *Address:* Pembroke College, Cambridge CB2 1RF.

LIDDELL, family name of **Baron Ravensworth**.

LIDDELL, Alasdair Donald MacDuff, CBE 1997; Director, Government Services, Impower plc, since 2000; *b* 15 Jan. 1949; *s* of late Donald Liddell and of Barbara Liddell (*née* Dixon); *m* 1976, Jennifer Abramsky, *qv*; one *s* one *d. Educ:* Balliol College, Oxford (BA Hons Jurisp. 1970); DMS Thames Polytechnic; LHA. King's College and Royal Free Hosps, 1972–77; Administrator (Planning and Policy), Tower Hamlets HA, 1977–79; Area Gen. Administrator, Kensington and Chelsea and Westminster AHA (T), 1979–82; District Administrator, Hammersmith and Fulham HA, 1982–84; District Administrator later District Gen. Manager, Bloomsbury HA, 1984–88; Regl Gen. Manager, E Anglian RHA, 1988–94; Dir of Planning, DoH, 1994–2000. Dir, Enlighten UK Ltd, 2000–. King's Fund Internat. Fellow, 1987–88. Trustee: Public Management Foundn, 1999– (Chm., 1990–94); Cambodia Trust, 1999–; Jt Chm. and Founder, Assoc. for Public Health, 1992–94. *Publications:* contrib. to In Dreams Begins Responsibility: a tribute to Tom Evans, 1987; Towards an Effective NHS, 1993. *Recreations:* ski-ing, playing with computers, buying French wine. *Address:* 3 Brookfield Park, NW5 1ES. *T:* (020) 7485 7465.

LIDDELL, Rt Hon. Helen (Lawrie); PC 1998; MP (Lab) Airdrie and Shotts, since 1997 (Monklands East, July 1994–1997); Secretary of State for Scotland, since 2001; *b* 6 Dec. 1950; *d* of Hugh Reilly and late Bridget Lawrie Reilly; *m* 1972, Dr Alistair Henderson Liddell; one *s* one *d. Educ:* St Patrick's High Sch., Coatbridge; Strathclyde Univ. Head, Econ. Dept, 1971–75, and Asst Sec., 1975–76, Scottish TUC; Econ. Correspondent, BBC Scotland, 1976–77; Scottish Sec., Labour Party, 1977–88; Dir, Personnel and Public Affairs, Scottish Daily Record and Sunday Mail (1986) Ltd, 1988–92; Chief Exec., Business Venture Prog., 1993–94. Contested (Lab) Fife E, Oct. 1974. Opposition spokeswoman on Scotland, 1995–97; Economic Sec., HM Treasury, 1997–98; Minister of State, Scottish Office, 1998–99; Minister of Transport, 1999; Minister of State, DTI, 1999–2001. *Publication:* Elite, 1990. *Recreations:* cooking, hill-walking, music, writing. *Address:* House of Commons, SW1A 0AA.

LIDDELL, Jennifer, (Mrs Alasdair Liddell); *see* Abramsky, Jennifer.

LIDDELL, Air Vice-Marshal Peter, CEng, FIEE, FRAeS; Director General, Equipment Support (Air), Defence Logistics Organisation, since 2000; *b* 9 Oct. 1948; *s* of Stanley Liddell and Mary Elizabeth Liddell (*née* Underwood); *m* 1979, Jennifer Marion, *d* of late Lt-Col Jack Prichard, DSO, MC and Eilleen Patricia Prichard; two *s* one *d. Educ:* Keswick Sch.; Manchester Univ. (BSc). FIEE 1996; FRAeS 1996. Commnd (Univ. Cadet), 1966; served No 20 Sqn, Wildenrath, 1970–73; St Mawgan, 1973–75; Swanton Morley, 1975–77; MoD, 1978–80; Marham, 1981–82; sc 1983; OC Engrg Wing, Brize Norton, 1984–85; Cranwell, 1986–88; HQ Support Comd, 1989–90; Stn Comdr, Sealand, 1991–92; rcds 1993; HQ Logistics Comd, 1994–96; HQ Strike Comd, 1997–98; AO Communications Inf. Systems and Support Services, 1999–2000. *Recreations:* golf, hill walking, theatre. *Address:* Cranswick House, RAF Wyton, Huntingdon, Cambs PE28 2EA. *T:* (01480) 52451. *Club:* Royal Air Force.

LIDDELL-GRAINGER, Ian Richard Peregrine; MP (C) Bridgwater, since 2001; *b* 23 Feb. 1959; *s* of David Ian Liddell-Grainger of Ayton and Anne Mary Sibylla Liddell-Grainger (*née* Smith); *m* Jill Nesbitt; one *s* two *d. Educ:* Wellesley House Sch., Kent; Millfield Sch., Somerset; S of Scotland Agricl Coll., Edinburgh (NCA). Farmer, Berwicks, 1980–85; Man. Dir, property mgt and develt co., 1985–. Mem., Tynedale DC, 1989–95. Contested (C) Torridge and Devon West, 1997. Major, Queen's Div., TA (formerly with 6th (Vol.) Bn), RRF. *Address:* (office) 16 Northgate, Bridgwater, Somerset TA6 3EU; c/o House of Commons, SW1A 0AA.

LIDDIARD, Ronald; aviation, management and social work consultant; commercial flying instructor; *b* 26 July 1932; *s* of Tom and Gladys Liddiard; *m* 1957, June Alexandra (*née* Ford); two *d. Educ:* Canton High Sch., Cardiff; Colleges of Commerce and Technology, Cardiff; Inst. of Local Govt Studies, Birmingham Univ.; Oxford Air Training Sch. Dip. Municipal Admin, Certif. Social Work; ATPL. Health Administrator, 1958–60; Social Worker, 1960–64; Sen. Welfare Administrator, 1964–70; Dir of Social Services: Bath, 1971–74; Birmingham, 1974–85; airline pilot, 1987–97. Hon. Kentucky Col, 1977. *Publications:* How to Become an Airline Pilot, 1989; chapters in: Innovations in the Care of the Elderly, 1984; Self-Care and Health in Old Age, 1986; articles in social work, aviation, management and health jls. *Recreations:* travel, reading, wines. *Address:* Whitefriars, Portway, Worcs B48 7HP. *T:* (01564) 826235.

LIDDIMENT, David; Director of Programmes, ITV Network Ltd, since 1997. Benton and Bowles, Advertising Agency, 1974–75; Granada TV: Promotions Scriptwriter, 1975; researcher, dir, prod. and journalist; Exec. Prod., Children's Progs, 1986–88; Head of Entertainment, 1988–92; Dir of Progs, 1992–93; Head of Light Entertainment Gp, BBC TV, 1993–95; Dep. Man. Dir and Dir of Progs, 1995–96, Dep. Chm., 1997, LWT; Man. Dir, Granada UK Broadcasting, 1996–97. Gov., W Yorks Playhouse. *Address:* ITV Network Ltd, 200 Gray's Inn Road, WC1X 8HF.

LIDDINGTON, Sir Bruce, Kt 2000; Professional Adviser, City Academies Unit, Department for Education and Skills, since 2001; *b* 4 Sept. 1949; *s* of Gordon Philip Liddington and Joan Liddington; *m* 1978, Carol Jane Tuttle; two *s* one *d. Educ:* Queen Mary Coll., London Univ. (BA 1971); King's Coll., Cambridge (PGCE 1972); Washington State Univ., USA (MA 1977). Teacher: Northcliffe Sch., Conisbrough, 1972–75; Westfield Sch., Wellingborough, 1975–76; Head of English, Westwood High Sch., Leek, 1977–81; Dep. Head, Ousedale Sch., Newport Pagnell, 1981–86; Headteacher, Northampton Sch. for Boys, 1986–2000. Ministerial Advr, Quality Assce Unit, 1999–2001, Project Broker, City Academies Unit, 2000–01, DfEE. *Recreations:* opera, reading, music, films, travel, food. *Address:* 2 The Elms, 1A Green Lane, Wolverton, Milton Keynes MK12 5HB. *T:* (01908) 310710.

LIDDLE, Caroline; *see* Thomson, C.

LIDINGTON, David Roy, PhD; MP (C) Aylesbury, since 1992; *b* 30 June 1956; *s* of Roy N. and Rosa Lidington; *m* 1989, Helen Mary Farquhar Parry; four *s* (incl. twins). *Educ:* Haberdashers' Aske's Sch., Elstree; Sidney Sussex Coll., Cambridge (MA, PhD). British Petroleum plc, 1983–86; RTZ plc, 1986–87; Special Adviser to: Home Sec., 1987–89; Foreign Sec., 1989–90; Consultant, PPU Ltd, 1991–92. PPS to Leader of the Opposition, 1997–99; Opposition front-bench spokesman on home affairs, 1999–2001; Opposition front-bench spokesman on HM Treasury affairs, 2001–. *Publications:* articles on Tudor history. *Recreations:* history, choral singing. *Address:* House of Commons, SW1A 0AA. *T:* (020) 7219 3000; 100 Walton Street, Aylesbury, Bucks HP21 7QP.

LIEBERMAN, Joseph I.; Member (Democrat) for Connecticut, US Senate, since 1989; *b* 24 Feb. 1942; *s* of Henry Lieberman and Marcia Lieberman; *m* 1983, Hadassah Freilich; one *d*; one *s* one *d* from a previous marriage. *Educ:* Yale Univ. (BA 1964; JD 1967). Called to the Bar, Conn, 1967; Partner, Lieberman, Segaloff & Wolfson, New Haven, 1972–83. Mem. (Democrat), State Senate of Connecticut, 1971–81 (Majority Leader, 1975–81); Attorney-Gen., Conn, 1983–89. Democratic candidate for US Vice-President, 2000. *Publications:* The Power Broker, 1966; The Scorpion and the Tarantula, 1970; The Legacy, 1981; Child Support in America, 1986; In Praise of Public Life, 2000. *Address:* US Senate, 706 Hart Senate Office Building, Washington, DC 20510, USA.

LIEBESCHUETZ, Prof. (John Hugo) Wolfgang (Gideon), PhD; FSA; FBA 1991; Professor of Classical and Archaeological Studies, Nottingham University, 1979–92, now Professor Emeritus; *b* Hamburg, 22 June 1927; *s* of Prof. H. Liebeschuetz and Dr E. A. R. Liebeschuetz (*née* Plaut); *m* 1955, Margaret Rosa Taylor; one *s* three *d. Educ:* UCL (BA 1951; Fellow 1997); PhD London 1957. Schoolteacher, 1957–63; Leicester University: Lectr in Classics, 1963–74; Sen. Lectr, 1974–78; Reader, 1978–79. FSA 1999. Mem., Princeton Inst. for Advanced Study, 1993. Corresp. Mem., German Archaeol Inst., 1994. *Publications:* Antioch: city and imperial administration in the later Roman Empire, 1972; Continuity and Change in Roman Religion, 1979; Barbarians and Bishops: army, church and state in the age of Arcadius and Chrysostom, 1990; From Diocletian to the Arab Conquest: change in the late Roman Empire, 1990; The Decline and Fall of the Roman City, 2001; contribs to learned jls. *Address:* 1 Clare Valley, The Park, Nottingham NG7 1BU.

LIESNER, Hans Hubertus, CB 1980; Member, 1989–97, Deputy Chairman, 1989–95, Monopolies and Mergers Commission; *b* 30 March 1929; *e s* of Curt Liesner, lawyer, and

Edith L. (*née* Neumann); *m* 1968, Thelma Seward; one *s* one *d*. *Educ:* German grammar schs; Bristol Univ. (BA); Nuffield Coll., Oxford; MA Cantab. Asst Lectr, later Lectr, in Economics, London Sch. of Economics, 1955–59; Lectr in Economics, Univ. of Cambridge; Fellow, Dir of Studies in Economics and some time Asst Bursar, Emmanuel Coll., Cambridge, 1959–70; Under-Sec. (Economics), HM Treasury, 1970–76; Dep. Sec., and Chief Econ. Advr, DTI (formerly Industry, Trade and Prices and Consumer Protection), 1976–89. Standing Mem., Adv. Bd on Fair Trading in Telecoms, 1997–2000; Mem. Council of Mgt, NIESR, 1989–; Chm. Adv. Gp, ESRC Centre for Economic Learning and Social Evolution, 1996–. Mem. Council, Friends of British Library, 2001–. *Publications:* The Import Dependence of Britain and Western Germany, 1957; Case Studies in European Economic Union: the mechanics of integration (with J. E. Meade and S. J. Wells), 1962; Atlantic Harmonisation: making free trade work, 1968; Britain and the Common Market: the effect of entry on the pattern of manufacturing production (with S. S. Han), 1971; articles in jls, etc. *Recreations:* ski-ing, walking, gardening. *Address:* 32 The Grove, Brookmans Park, Herts AL9 7RN. *T:* (01707) 653269. *Club:* Reform.

LIEVEN, Prof. Dominic Christophe Bogdan, PhD; FBA 2001; Professor of Russian Government and History, since 1993, and Convenor, Department of Government, since 2001, London School of Economics and Political Science, University of London; *b* 19 Jan. 1952; *s* of Prince Alexander Lieven and Veronica Lieven (*née* Monahan); *m* 1985, Mikiko Fujiwara; one *s* one *d*. *Educ:* Downside Sch.; Christ's Coll., Cambridge (BA); SSEES, London Univ. (PhD 1978). Kennedy Schol., Harvard Univ., 1973–74; FCO, 1974–75; Lectr, LSE, 1978–93. Humboldt Fellow, 1986; Visiting Professor: Univ. of Tokyo, 1992–94; Harvard Univ., 1993. Member, Editorial Board: Jl Contemporary Hist., 1994–; Slavonic Rev., 2000–. *Publications:* Russia and the Origins of the First World War, 1983; Russia's Rulers under the Old Regime, 1989; The Aristocracy in Europe 1815–1914, 1992; Nicholas II, 1993; Empire: the Russian Empire and its rivals, 2000; books trans. German, Japanese and Russian. *Recreation:* collecting Russian regimental models. *Address:* Department of Government, London School of Economics, Houghton Street, WC2A 2AE. *T:* (020) 7955 7184. *Club:* Travellers.

LIEW Foo Yew, PhD, DSc; FRCPath; FRSE; Gardiner Professor and Head of Department of Immunology, University of Glasgow, since 1991; *b* 22 May 1943; *s* of Liew Soon and Chai Man Ngon; *m* 1973, Dr Woon Ling Chan; one *s*. *Educ:* Monash Univ., Australia (BSc 1st cl. Hons); ANU (PhD; DSc). MRCPath 1990, FRCPath 1996. FRSE 1995. Lectr, Univ. of Malaya, 1972–77; Sen. Scientist, 1977–84, Head, Dept of Immunology, 1984–91, Wellcome Res. Lab., Beckenham. Mem., Nat. Biol Standards Bd, 1996–. FMedSci 1999. *Publications:* Vaccination Strategies of Tropical Diseases, 1989; Immunology of intracellular parasitism, 1998; more than 250 papers in learned jls. *Recreations:* reading classical Chinese, gardening. *Address:* Department of Immunology, University of Glasgow, Glasgow G11 6NT; 37 Elwill Way, Beckenham, Kent BR3 3AB; 556 Crow Road, Glasgow G13 1NP. *T:* (0141) 211 2695.

LIFFORD, 9th Viscount *cr* 1781 (Ire.); **Edward James Wingfield Hewitt;** Director, Rathbones plc, since 1996; *b* 27 Jan. 1949; *s* of 8th Viscount Lifford and of Alison Mary Patricia, *d* of T. W. Ashton; *S* father, 1987; *m* 1976, Alison Mary, *d* of Robert Law; one *s* two *d*. *Educ:* The Old Malthouse, Dorset; Aiglon College, Switzerland. Mem., Stock Exchange. Chairman: Basepoint plc; TPN Hldgs plc. *Recreations:* country sports. *Heir: s* Hon. James Thomas Wingfield Hewitt, *b* 29 Sept. 1979. *Address:* Field House, Hursley, Hants SO21 2LE. *T:* (01962) 775203. *Clubs:* Boodle's, Pratt's; St Moritz Tobogganing.

LIFSCHUTZ, Alexander Joseph; Director, Lifschutz Davidson, architects, since 1986; *b* 11 Feb. 1952; *s* of late Simon Lifschutz and of Hanna Lifschutz; *m* 1978, Monique Charlesworth; one *s* one *d*. *Educ:* St Paul's Sch.; Univ. of Bristol (BSc Jt Hons Sociology and Psychology 1974); Architectural Assoc. Foster Associates, 1981–86. *Projects* include: office extension for Richard Rogers and Partners, Thames Wharf Studios, 1991 (RIBA Award, 1992; British Steel Award of Merit, 1992); Broadwall Community Housing, 1994 (Royal Fine Arts Commn/Sunday Times Building of the Year, 1995; RIBA Award, 1995; Nat. Housing Design Award, DoE, 1996; Civic Trust Housing Award, 1996); mixed use develt, Oxo Tower Wharf, 1996 (Urban Regeneration Award, Royal Fine Art Commn, 1997; RIBA Award, 1997; Civic Trust Award, 1998); Harvey Nichols 8th Floor Restaurant, 1997 (RIBA Award); Royal Victoria Dock Bridge, 1999 (AJ/Bovis/Royal Acad. Award, 1997; ICE Merit Award, 1998; Millennium Award, 1999); refurbishment of Piper Building, London, 1998 (Housing Design Award, 1999); *current projects* include: office develt for Derwent Valley Hldgs; River Thames Hungerford footbridge; new facilities for Old Vic Theatre. *Recreations:* tennis, travel, family. *Address:* Lifschutz Davidson Ltd, Thames Wharf Studios, Rainville Road, W6 9HA.

LIGETI, Prof. György Sándor; Member, Order of Merit, Germany, 1975; music composer; Professor for Composition, Hamburg Academy of Music, 1973–89; *b* 28 May 1923; *s* of Dr Sándor Ligeti and Dr Ilona Somogyi; *m* 1957, Dr Vera Spitz; one *s*. *Educ:* Budapest Academy of Music (Dipl. in composition). Lecturer for harmony and counterpoint, Budapest Acad. of Music, 1950–56; Guest Prof., Stockholm Acad. of Music, 1961–71; composer in residence, Stanford Univ., Calif, 1972. Member: Swedish Royal Acad. of Music, 1964; Acad. of Arts, Berlin, 1968; Free Acad. of Arts, Hamburg, 1971; Bavarian Acad. of Fine Arts, Munich, 1978. Hon. Mem., Amer. Acad. and Inst. of Arts and Letters, 1984. Dr *hc* Hamburg, 1988. Grawemeyer Award, 1986. *Main compositions:* Apparitions, for orch., 1959; Atmosphères, for orch., 1961; Aventures, for 3 singers and 7 instrumentalists, 1962; Requiem, for 2 soli, chorus and orch., 1965; Cello concerto, 1966; Chamber concerto, 1970; Melodien, for orch., 1971; Le Grand Macabre, opera, 1977; Trio, for violin, horn, piano, 1982; Piano études, 1985; Piano concerto, 1986; Nonsense madrigals, 1988; Violin concerto, 1991; Viola sonata, 1996. *Address:* Himmelhofgasse 34, 1130 Vienna, Austria; Beim Schlump 27, Haus 3, 20144 Hamburg, Germany.

LIGGINS, Sir Graham (Collingwood), Kt 1991; CBE 1983; FRCSE, FRACS, FRCOG; FRS 1980; FRSNZ 1976; Professor of Obstetrics and Gynaecological Endocrinology, University of Auckland, New Zealand, 1968–87, now Professor Emeritus (formerly Senior Lecturer); Consultant to National Women's Hospital, Auckland. *Educ:* Univ. of NZ. MB, ChB, Univ. NZ, 1949; PhD, Univ. of Auckland, 1969. MRCOG 1956; FRCSE 1958; FRACS 1960. Is distinguished for his work on the role of foetal hormones in the control of parturition. Hon. FAGS, 1976; Hon. FACOG, 1978. Hon. MD Lund, 1983; Hon. DSc Edinburgh, 1996. Hector Medal, RSNZ, 1980. *Publications:* approx. 200 published papers. *Recreations:* forestry, sailing, fishing. *Address:* Postgraduate School of Obstetrics and Gynaecology, National Women's Hospital, Claude Road, Auckland 3, New Zealand. *T:* (9) 3775127; 3/38 Awatea Road, Parnell, Auckland 1, New Zealand.

LIGHT, (Sidney) David; a Civil Service Commissioner, 1978–79; Member, Civil Service Commission's Panel of Selection Board Chairmen, 1980–89; *b* 9 Dec. 1919; *s* of late William Light; *m* Edna Margaret Honey; one *s*. *Educ:* King Edward VI Sch., Southampton. RAF, 1940–46. HM Customs and Excise, 1938; HM Treasury, 1948–68; Asst Sec., CS Commn, 1969–75; Under Sec., CSD, 1975–78. *Recreations:* bricolage, watching cricket, travel. *Address:* Church House Cottage, Bentley, Hampshire GU10 5HY. *Clubs:* Royal Commonwealth Society; Hampshire Cricket.

LIGHTBODY, Ian (Macdonald), CMG 1974; Chairman, Public Services Commission, Hong Kong, 1978–80; *b* 19 Aug. 1921; *s* of Thomas Paul Lightbody and Dorothy Marie Louise Lightbody (*née* Cooper); *m* 1954, Noreen, *d* of late Captain T. H. Wallace, Dromore, Co. Down; three *s* one *d*. *Educ:* Queens Park Sch., Glasgow; Glasgow Univ. (MA). War service, Indian Army, India and Far East, 1942–46 (Captain); Colonial Admin. Service, Hong Kong, 1945; various admin. posts; District Comr, New Territories, 1967–68; Defence Sec., 1968–69; Coordinator, Festival of Hong Kong, 1969; Comr for Resettlement, 1971; Sec. for Housing and Chm., Hong Kong Housing Authority, 1973–77; Sec. for Admin, Hong Kong, 1977–78. MLC 1971; MEC 1977; retd from Hong Kong, 1980. Mem., Arun DC, 1983–91. *Recreations:* walking, tennis. *Address:* 29 Henty Gardens, Chichester, Sussex PO19 3DL. *Clubs:* Hong Kong, Hong Kong Jockey.

LIGHTBOWN, Ronald William, MA; FSA, FRAS; art historian and author; Keeper of the Department of Metalwork, Victoria and Albert Museum, 1985–89; *b* Darwen, Lancs, 2 June 1932; *s* of late Vincent Lightbown and of Helen Anderson Lightbown (*née* Burness); *m* 1962, Mary Dorothy Webster; one *s*. *Educ:* St Catharine's Coll., Cambridge (MA). FSA, FRAS. Victoria and Albert Museum: Asst Keeper, Library, 1958–64; Asst Keeper, Dept of Metalwork, 1964–73; Dep. Keeper, 1973–76, Keeper, 1976–85, Library. Fellow, Inst. for Res. in the Humanities, Wisconsin Univ., 1974. Pres., Jewellery History Soc., 1990–93; a Vice-Pres., Soc. of Antiquaries, 1986–90 (Sec., 1979–86); Associate Trustee, Soane Mus., 1981–98. Socio dell' Ateneo Veneto, for contrib. to study of culture of Venice and the Veneto, 1987; Socio dell' Accademia Clementina, Bologna, for contribns to study of Italian art, 1988. *Publications:* French Secular Goldsmiths' work of the Middle Ages, 1978; Sandro Botticelli, 1978, 2nd edn, 1989 (Prix Vasari, 1990); (with M. Corbett) The Comely Frontispiece, 1978; (ed and trans. with A. Caiger-Smith) Piccolpasso: the art of the potter, 1980; Donatello and Michelozzo, 1980; Andrea Mantegna, 1986; Piero della Francesca, 1992 (Prix de Mai des Libraires de France, 1992); Viaggio in un capolavoro di Piero della Francesca, 1992; (with J. Delumeau) Histoire de l'art: la Renaissance, 1995; (ed and introd) History of Art in 18th Century England (series of source-books on 18th century British art), 14 vols, 1970–71; V&A Museum catalogues and publications: (pt author) Italian Sculpture, 1964; Tudor Domestic Silver, 1970; Scandinavian and Baltic Silver, 1975; French Silver, 1979; (with M. Archer) India Observed, 1982; Medieval European Jewellery, 1992; contrib. to books, and many articles in learned jls, incl. Burlington Magazine, Warburg Jl and Art Bulletin. *Recreations:* reading, travel, music, conversation. *Address:* Barrowmount House, Goresbridge, Co. Kilkenny, Ireland.

LIGHTFOOT, His Honour George Michael; a Circuit Judge, 1986–2001; *b* 9 March 1936; *s* of Charles Herbert Lightfoot and Mary Lightfoot (*née* Potter); *m* 1963, Dorothy (*née* Miller); two *s* two *d*. *Educ:* St Michael's Catholic College, Leeds; Exeter College, Oxford (MA). Schoolmaster, 1962–66. Called to the Bar, Inner Temple, 1966; practised on NE circuit. A Recorder, 1985–86. Mem., Home Farm Trust, 1980–; President: Leeds Friends of Home Farm Trust, 1987–; Mencap, Leeds, 1987–. Vice-Pres., Hunslet Hawks Rugby League Football Club, 1999–. *Recreations:* cricket and sport in general, gardening (labourer), learning to listen to music, reading. *Clubs:* Catenian Association (City of Leeds Circle); Yorkshire CC; Northern Cricket Society.

LIGHTMAN, Hon. Sir Gavin (Anthony), Kt 1994; **Hon. Mr Justice Lightman;** a Judge of the High Court of Justice, Chancery Division, since 1994; *b* 20 Dec. 1939; *s* of Harold Lightman, QC and of Gwendoline Joan (*née* Ostrer); *m* 1965, Naomi Ann Claff; one *s* two *d*. *Educ:* Univ. of London (LLB 1st cl. Hons); Univ. of Michigan (LLM). Called to the Bar, Lincoln's Inn, 1963, Bencher 1987; QC 1980. Vice Pres., Anglo Jewish Assoc., 1995– (Dep. Pres., 1986–92); Chairman: Educn Cttee, Anglo Jewish Assoc., 1986–94; Educn Cttee, Hillel House, 1992–96 (Vice-Pres., 1996–); Legal Friends, Haifa Univ., 1990– (Gov., 1994). Patron: Jewish Commonwealth Council, 1994–; Hammerson Home, 1996–. *Publications:* (with G. Battersby) Cases and Statutes on Real Property, 1965; (with G. Moss) The Law Relating to the Receivers of Companies, 1986, 2nd edn 1994; A Report on the National Union of Miners, 1990. *Recreations:* reading, cricket, walking, travel. *Address:* Royal Courts of Justice, Strand, WC2A 2LL. *Club:* Royal Automobile.
See also S. L. Lightman.

LIGHTMAN, Ivor Harry, CB 1984; Chairman, Cardiff University of Third Age, since 2001; *b* 23 Aug. 1928; *s* of late Abraham and Mary Lightman; *m* 1950, Stella Doris Blend; one *s*. *Educ:* Abergele Grammar Sch. Clerical Officer, Min. of Food, 1946; Officer of Customs and Excise, 1949–56; Asst Principal, then Principal, Ministry of Works, 1957–65; HM Treasury, 1965–67; Assistant Secretary: MPBW, 1967–70; CSD, 1970–73; Under Secretary: Price Commn, 1973–76; Dept of Prices and Consumer Protection, 1976–78; Dept of Industry, 1978–81; Dep. Sec., Welsh Office, 1981–88, retd; Co-ordinator, Cardiff Charter 88, 1998–2000. Mem., Parole Bd, 1990–94. Chm., First Choice Housing Assoc., 1989–94; Vice Chm., United Welsh Housing Assoc., 1994–; Chm., All-Wales Adv. Panel on Services for Mentally Handicapped People, 1990–96. *Address:* 6 Clos Coedydafarn, Lisvane, Cardiff CF14 0ER.

LIGHTMAN, Lionel; Lay Observer attached to Lord Chancellor's Department, 1986–90; *b* 26 July 1928; *s* of late Abner Lightman and late Gitli Lightman (*née* Szmul); *m* 1952, Helen, *y d* of late Rev. A. Shechter and late Mrs Shechter; two *d*. *Educ:* City of London Sch.; Wadham Coll., Oxford (MA). Nat. Service, RAEC, 1951–53 (Temp. Captain). Asst Principal, BoT, 1953; Private Sec. to Perm. Sec., 1957; Principal 1958; Trade Comr, Ottawa, 1960–64; Asst Sec. 1967; Asst Dir, Office of Fair Trading, 1973–75; Under Sec., Dept of Trade, 1975–78, DoI, 1978–81; Dir of Competition Policy, OFT, 1981–84. *Address:* 73 Greenhill, NW3 5TZ. *T:* (020) 7435 3427.

LIGHTMAN, Prof. Stafford Louis, PhD; FRCP, FMedSci; Professor of Medicine, University of Bristol, since 1993; *b* 7 Sept. 1948; *s* of Harold Lightman, QC and of Gwendoline Joan (*née* Ostrer); *m* 1977, Susan Louise Stubbs (*see* Susan Lightman) (marr. diss. 1995); three *s* one *d*. *Educ:* Repton Sch.; Gonville and Caius Coll., Cambridge (MA, MB BChir, PhD); Middlesex Hosp. Med. Sch. Vis. Sen. Scientist, MRC Neuro. Pharm. Unit, Cambridge, 1980–81; Wellcome Trust Sen. Lectr, St Mary's Hosp. Med. Sch. and Hon. Consultant Physician and Endocrinologist, St Mary's Hosp., 1981–82; Charing Cross and Westminster Medical School: Reader in Medicine, 1982–88; Prof. of Clinical Neuroendocrinology, 1988–92; Consultant Physician and Endocrinologist to Charing Cross and Westminster Hosps, 1988–92; Hon. Sen. Res. Fellow, Inst. of Neurology and Consultant Endocrinologist to Nat. Hosp. for Neurology and Neurosurgery, 1988–. Chm., Pituitary Foundn, 1995–. Founder FMedSci 1998. Editor-in-Chief, Jl of Neuroendocrinology, 1989–96. *Publications:* (ed with B. J. Everitt) Neuroendocrinology, 1986; (with Michael Powell) Pituitary Tumours: a handbook on management, 1996; (ed) Horizons in Medicine Vol. 7, 1996; (with A. Levy) Core Endocrinology, 1997; (with Graham Rook) Steroid Hormones and the T cell Cytokine Profile, 1997. *Recreations:* squash, ski-ing, hill walking, scuba diving, music, theatre, anthropology. *Address:* University of Bristol, Department of Medicine, Marlborough Street, Bristol BS2 8HW.

T: (0117) 928 2871.
See also Hon. Sir G. A. Lightman.

LIGHTMAN, Prof. Susan Louise, PhD; FRCP, FRCOphth; Professor of Clinical Ophthalmology, Institute of Ophthalmology and Moorfields Eye Hospital, since 1993; *b* 2 Sept. 1952; *d* of John and Valerie Stubbs; *m* 1st, 1977, Prof. Stafford Louis Lightman, FRCP (marr. diss. 1995); three *s* one *d*; 2nd, 1995, Hamish Towler; one *s*. *Educ:* St Paul's Girls' Sch.; Middlesex Hosp., Univ. of London (MB BS Hons 1975); PhD London 1987. MRCP 1978, FRCP 1992; FRCOphth 1988. Wellcome Training Fellowship: in Ophthalmology, Inst. of Ophthalmol. and Moorfields Eye Hosp., 1979–83; in Immunology, NIMR, 1983–85; MRC Travelling Fellowship and Vis. Scientist, NIH, 1985–87; MRC Sen. Clinical Fellow, 1988–90; Duke Elder Prof. of Ophthalmology, BPMF, 1990–93. FMedSci 2000. *Publications:* Immunology of Eye Diseases, 1989; Diagnosis and Management of Uveitis, 1998; HIV and the Eye, 1999; numerous papers in peer reviewed jls. *Recreations:* walking, music, sewing, reading. *Address:* Institute of Ophthalmology, Moorfields Eye Hospital, City Road, EC1V 2PD. *T:* (020) 7566 2266.

LIGHTON, Sir Thomas (Hamilton), 9th Bt *cr* 1791 (Ire.), of Merville, Dublin; Chairman, Society of London Art Dealers, 1993–95 and 1998–2000; *b* 4 Nov. 1954; *o s* of Sir Christopher Robert Lighton, 8th Bt, MBE and his 2nd wife, Horatia Edith (*d* 1981), *d* of A. T. Powlett; *S* father, 1993; *m* 1990, Belinda, *d* of John Fergusson; twin *s* one *d* (and one *s* decd). *Educ:* Eton. *Heir: s* James Christopher Hamilton Lighton, *b* 20 Oct. 1992.

LIIKANEN, Erkki Antero; a Member, European Commission, since 1995; *b* 19 Sept. 1950; *m* 1971, Hanna-Liisa Issakainen; two *d*. *Educ:* Helsinki Univ. MP (SDP), Finland 1972–90; Minister of Finance, 1987–90; Ambassador to EU, 1990–95. Gen. Sec., SDP, 1981–87. *Address:* European Commission, 200 rue de la Loi, 1049 Brussels, Belgium.

LIKIERMAN, Sir (John) Andrew, Kt 2001; Head of Government Accountancy Service and Chief Accountancy Adviser to HM Treasury, since 1993; Managing Director (formerly Director), Financial Management, Reporting and Audit, HM Treasury, since 1995 (Principal Finance Officer, 1995–2000); *b* 30 Dec. 1943; *s* of Dolek and Olga Likierman; *m* 1987, Dr Meira, *d* of Joshua and Miriam Gruenspan; one step *s* one step *d*. *Educ:* Stowe Sch.; Univ. of Vienna; Balliol Coll., Oxford (MA). FCMA, FCCA. Divl Management Accountant, Tootal Ltd, 1965–68; Asst Lectr, 1968–69, Lectr, 1972–74, Dept of Management Studies, Leeds Univ.; Qualitex Ltd, 1969–72 (Man. Dir, Overseas Div., 1971–72); Vis. Fellow, Oxford Centre for Management Studies, 1972–74; Chm., Ex Libris Ltd, 1973–74; London Business Sch., 1974–76 and 1979–: Dir, Part-time Masters Programme, 1981–85; Dir, Inst. of Public Sector Management, 1983–88; Chm., Faculty Bd, 1986–89; Prof. of Accounting and Financial Control, 1987–97; Vis. Prof., 1997–; Dean of External Affairs, 1989–92; Dep. Principal, 1990–92; Elected Governor, 1986–89, *ex officio* Governor, 1990–93. Asst Sec., Cabinet Office (Mem., Central Policy Review Staff), 1976–79, Advr, 1979–82; Advisor, H of C Select Committees: Treasury and CS, 1981–90; Employment, 1985–89; Transport, 1981, 1987–90; Social Services, 1988; Social Security, 1991; Mem., various govt inquiries including: North Sea Oil Costs, 1975; Power Plant Industry, 1976; Post Office Internat. Comparisons, 1981; Accounting for Econ. Costs (Byatt Cttee), 1986; Professional Liability (Chm.), 1989. Member: Finance Cttee, Oxfam, 1974–84; Cttee on med. costs, London Univ., 1980–81; Current Affairs Adv. Gp, Channel 4, 1986–87; Audit Commn, 1988–91; Financial Reporting Council, 1990– (Observer, 1993–); Exec. Cttee, British Acad. of Management, 1988–90; Auditing Practices Bd, 1991–92; Cttee on Financial Aspects of Corporate Governance (Cadbury Cttee), 1991–95 (Chm., Monitoring Cttee, 1993–95); Council: RIPA, 1982–88; Consumers' Assoc., 1983–85; Chartered Inst. of Management Accountants, 1985–94 (Pres., 1991–92); Civil Service Coll., 1989–94; Scientific Council, Eur. Inst. of Public Admin, 1990–93; Defence Operational Analysis Centre, 1992–93; Bd, Tavistock and Portman NHS Trust, 2000–. Chm. Editl Bd, Public Money and Management, 1988–93; non-exec. Dir, Economists' Bookshop, 1981–91 (non-exec. Chm., 1987–91). Hon. DBA Southampton Business Sch., 1997; Hon. DPhil London Guildhall, 1999. *Publications:* The Reports and Accounts of Nationalised Industries, 1979; Cash Limits and External Financing Limits, 1981; (jtly) Public Sector Accounting and Financial Control, 1983, 4th edn 1992; (with P. Vass) Structure and Form of Government Expenditure Reports, 1984; Public Expenditure, 1988; (jtly) Accounting for Brands, 1989; contribs to academic and professional jls. *Recreations:* tennis, cycling, choral singing, architecture, wine. *Address:* 5 Downshire Hill, NW3 1NR. *T:* (020) 7435 9888. *Club:* Reform.

LILEY, Ven. Christopher Frank; Archdeacon of Lichfield, and Treasurer and Canon Residentiary of Lichfield Cathedral, since 2001; *b* 1947. *Educ:* Nottingham Univ. (BEd 1970); Lincoln Theol Coll. Ordained deacon, 1974, priest, 1975; Curate, Holy Trinity, Kingswinford, 1974–79; Team Vicar, Stafford, 1979–84; Vicar, Norton, 1984–96; RD Hitchin, 1989–94; Vicar, St Chad and St Mary, and Priest i/c St Alkmund, Shrewsbury, 1996–2001. Chm., Lichfield Diocesan Bd of Ministry, 2001–. *Address:* 24 The Close, Lichfield, Staffs WS13 7LD.

LILFORD, 7th Baron *cr* 1797; **George Vernon Powys;** *b* 8 Jan. 1931; *s* of late Robert Horace Powys (*g g grandson* of 2nd Baron) and of Vera Grace Bryant, Rosebank, Cape, SA; *S* kinsman, 1949; *m* 1st, 1954, Mrs Eve Bird (marr. diss.); 2nd, 1957, Anuta Merritt (marr. diss. 1958); 3rd, 1958, Norma Yvonne Shell (marr. diss. 1961); 4th, 1961, Mrs Muriel Spottiswoode (marr. diss. 1969); two *d*; 5th, 1969, Margaret Penman (marr. diss. 1991); one *s* two *d*. *Educ:* St Aidan's Coll., Grahamstown, SA; Stonyhurst Coll. *Recreations:* golf, cricket. *Heir: s* Hon. Mark Vernon Powys, *b* 16 Nov. 1975. *Address:* Le Grand Câtelet, St John, Jersey, Channel Islands JE3 4FL.

LILFORD, Prof. Richard James, PhD; FRCP, FRCOG; Director of Research and Development, West Midlands Regional Office, NHS Executive, Department of Health, since 1996; Professor of Health Services Research, University of Birmingham, since 1996; *b* Cape Town, 22 April 1950; *m* 1982, Victoria Lomax; one *s* two *d*. *Educ:* St John's Coll., Johannesburg; Univ. of Witwatersrand (MB BCh 1973); PhD London 1984. MRCOG 1979, FRCOG 1996; MRCP 1981, FRCP 1998; MFPHM 1995. House officer in Medicine, Johannesburg Gen. Hosp., 1974; house officer in Surgery, Tygerberg Hosp., Cape Town, 1974–75; GP in S African Army, 1975; Groote Schuur Hospital, Cape Town: SHO in Obstetrics and Gynaecol., 1976; Registrar, 1977–78; Lecturer and Senior Registrar: Royal Free Hosp., London, 1979–80; St Bartholomew's Hosp. and Med. Coll., 1980–83; Sen. Lectr and Consultant in Obstetrics and Gynaecol., Queen Charlotte's Hosp. for Women and Inst. of Obstetrics and Gynaecol., 1983–85; University of Leeds: Prof. of Obstetrics and Gynaecol., 1985–95; Chm., Inst. of Epidemiology and Health Services Res., 1991–95; Dir of Res., United Leeds Teaching Hosps NHS Trust, 1993–95. Hon. Prof., Univ. of Warwick. Mem., Internat. Editl Adv. Bd, Jl RSocMed, 1974–. Mem., Leeds E HA, 1989–90. Advr, NHS Nat. Clinical Trials, 1996–. Chm. and Mem., numerous cttees incl. DoH adv. cttees and working parties. Royal College of Obstetricians and Gynaecologists: Mem. Council, 1989–92 and 1992–95; Chm., Audit Cttee, 1992–95; Member: Scientific Adv. Cttee, 1992–95; Educn Bd, 1992–94. *Publications:* (with T. Chard) Basic Sciences for Obstetricians and Gynaecologists, 1983, 4th edn 1995; (with M. Setchell) Multiple Choice Questions in Gynaecology and Obstetrics: with answers and explanatory comments, 1985, 2nd edn 1991; Prenatal Diagnosis and Prognosis, 1990; Computing and Decision Support in Obstetrics and Gynaecology, 1990; (with T. Chard) Multiple Choice Questions in Obstetrics and Gynaecology, 1993; (with M. Levine) Fetal and Neonatal Neurology and Neurosurgery, 1994; contrib. chapters in books and numerous articles to medical and professional jls. *Address:* NHS Executive, Bartholomew House, 142 Hagley Road, Birmingham B16 9PA.

LILL, John Richard, OBE 1978; concert pianist; Professor at Royal College of Music; *b* 17 March 1944; *s* of George and Margery Lill. *Educ:* Leyton County High Sch.; Royal College of Music. FRCM; Hon. FTCL; FLCM; Hon. RAM 1988. Gulbenkian Fellowship, 1967. First concert at age of 9; Royal Festival Hall debut, 1963; Promenade Concert debut, 1969. Numerous broadcasts on radio and TV; has appeared as soloist with all leading British orchestras. Recitals and concertos throughout Great Britain, Europe, USA, Canada, Scandinavia, USSR, Japan and Far East, Australia, New Zealand, etc. Overseas tours as soloist with many orchestras including London Symphony Orchestra and London Philharmonic Orchestra. Complete recordings of Beethoven sonatas and concertos, Prokofiev sonatas, Brahms concertos and Rachmaninov piano music; complete Beethoven cycle, London, 1982, 1986, and Tokyo, 1988. Chappell Gold Medal; Pauer Prize; 1st Prize, Royal Over-Seas League Music Competition, 1963; Dinu Lipatti Medal in Harriet Cohen Internat. Awards; 1st Prize, Internat. Tchaikovsky Competition, Moscow, 1970. Hon. DSc Aston, 1978; Hon. DMus Exeter, 1979. *Recreations:* amateur radio, chess, walking. *Address:* c/o Askonas Holt Ltd, Lonsdale Chambers, 27 Chancery Lane, WC2A 1PF. *T:* (020) 7400 1700.

LILLEY, Prof. David Malcolm James, PhD; FRSE; Professor of Molecular Biology, since 1989, and Director, CRC Nucleic Acid Structure Research Group, since 1993, University of Dundee; *b* 28 May 1948; *s* of Gerald Albert Thomas Lilley and Betty Pamela Lilley; *m* 1981, Patricia Mary Biddle; two *d*. *Educ:* Univ. of Durham (BSc 1st Cl. Hons Chemistry 1969; PhD Physical Chemistry 1973); Imperial Coll., London (MSc Biochem. 1973). Lectr, 1981–84, Reader, 1984–89, in Biochem., Univ. of Dundee. Mem., EMBO, 1984. FRSE 1988. Colworth Medal, British Biochemical Soc., 1982; Gold Medal of G. J. Mendel, Czech Acad. Scis, Prague, 1994; Prelog Gold Medal in Stereochemistry, ETH, Zürich, 1996. *Publications:* ed. numerous books, incl. DNA-proteins: structural interactions, 1995; (with Dr F. Eckstein) Nucleic Acids and Molecular Biology series, 1987–98; contrib. numerous scientific papers. *Recreation:* foreign languages. *Address:* Biochemistry Department, University of Dundee, Dundee DD1 5EH. *T:* (01382) 344243; *e-mail:* dmjlilley@bad.dundee.ac.uk.

LILLEY, Prof. Geoffrey Michael, OBE 1981; CEng, FRSA, FRAeS, MIMechE, FIMA; Professor of Aeronautics and Astronautics, University of Southampton, 1964–82, now Emeritus Professor; Director, Hampshire Technology Centre, since 1985; *b* Isleworth, Mddx, 16 Nov. 1919; *m* 1948, Leslie Marion Wheeler (*d* 1996); one *s* two *d*. *Educ:* Isleworth Grammar Sch.; Battersea and Northampton Polytechnics; Imperial Coll. BSc(Eng) 1944, MSc(Eng) 1945, DIC 1945. RAF, 1935–36. Gen. engrg trg, Benham and Kodak, 1936–40; Drawing Office and Wind Tunnel Dept, Vickers Armstrong Ltd, Weybridge, 1940–46; Coll. of Aeronautics: Lectr, 1946–51; Sen. Lectr, 1951–55; Dep. Head of Dept of Aerodynamics, 1955, and Prof. of Experimental Fluid Mechanics, 1962–64. Visiting Professor: Stanford Univ., 1977–78; ME Technical Univ., Ankara, Turkey, 1983–90; Univ. of the Witwatersrand, 1990; Visiting Scientist: Inst. of Computer Applications in Sci. and Engrg, NASA Langley Res. Center, 1992–94, 1997–; Center for Turbulence Res., Stanford Univ., 1995–96. Past Member: Aeronautical Res. Council (past Mem. Council and Chm. Aerodynamics, Applied Aerodynamics, Noise Res., Fluid Motion and Performance Cttees); Noise Advisory Council (Chm., Noise from Air Traffic Working Group); Past Chm., Aerodynamics Cttee, Engrg Sci. Data Unit. Consultant to: Rolls Royce, 1959–61, 1967–84; AGARD, 1959–63 and 1988–89; OECD, 1969–71. Gold Medal for Aeronautics, RAeS, 1983; Aerodynamic Noise Medal, AIAA, 1985. *Publications:* (jt editor) Proc. Stanford Conf. on Complex Turbulent Flows; articles in reports and memoranda of: Aeronautical Research Council; Royal Aeronautical Soc., and other jls. *Recreations:* music, chess, walking. *Address:* Highbury, Pine Walk, Chilworth, Southampton SO16 7HQ. *T:* (023) 8076 9109. *Club:* Athenæum.

LILLEY, Rt Hon. Peter Bruce; PC 1990; MP (C) Hitchin and Harpenden, since 1997 (St Albans, 1983–97); *b* 23 Aug. 1943; *s* of Arnold Francis Lilley and Lilian (*née* Elliott); *m* 1979, Gail Ansell. *Educ:* Dulwich Coll.; Clare Coll., Cambridge. MA; FInstPet 1978. Economic consultant in underdeveloped countries, 1966–72; investment advisor on energy industries, 1972–84. Chm., London Oil Analysts Gp, 1979–80; Partner, 1980–86, Dir, 1986–87, W. Greenwell & Co., later Greenwell Montagu. Consultant Dir, Cons. Res. Dept, 1979–83. Chm., Bow Group, 1972–75. Contested (C) Tottenham, Oct. 1974. PPS to Ministers for Local Govt, Jan.–Oct. 1984, to Chancellor of the Exchequer, 1984–87; Economic Sec. to HM Treasury, 1987–89, Financial Sec., 1989–90; Secretary of State: for Trade and Industry, 1990–92; for Social Security, 1992–97; front bench Opposition spokesman on HM Treasury, 1997–98. Dep. Leader, Cons. Party, 1998–99. *Publications:* Do You Sincerely Want to Win?, 1972, 2nd edn 1973; Lessons for Power, 1974; (with S. Brittan) Delusion of Incomes Policy, 1977; (contrib.) Skidelsky: End of the Keynesian Era, 1980; Thatcherism: the next generation, 1990; Winning the Welfare Debate, 1996; Patient Power, 2000; Common Sense on Cannabis, 2001. *Address:* House of Commons, SW1A 0AA. *T:* (020) 7219 3000. *Clubs:* Carlton, Beefsteak.

LILLEYMAN, Prof. John Stuart, DSc; FRCP, FRCPE, FRCPath, FRCPCH; Professor of Paediatric Oncology, Barts and the London, Queen Mary's School of Medicine and Dentistry (formerly St Bartholomew's and the Royal London School of Medicine and Dentistry, Queen Mary and Westfield College), University of London, since 1995; President, Royal College of Pathologists, 1999–Nov. 2002; *b* 9 July 1945; *s* of Ernest Lilleyman and Frances Lilleyman (*née* Johnson); *m* 1st, 1970, Patricia Ann Traylen (marr. diss. 1996); one *s*; 2nd, 1998, Elizabeth Anne Lawrence. *Educ:* Oundle Sch.; St Bartholomew's Hosp. Med. Coll. (MB BS 1968; DSc Med. 1996). FRCP 1983; FRCPath 1984; FRCPCH 1997; FRCPE 2000. Jun. Posts at St Bartholomew's Hosp. and United Sheffield Hosps, 1968–72; Res. Fellow, Welsh Nat. Sch. of Medicine, 1972–74; Consultant Haematologist, Sheffield Children's Hosp., 1975–95; Prof. of Paediatric Haematology, Univ. of Sheffield Med. Sch., 1993–95. Pres., UK Assoc. of Clinical Pathologists, 1998–99. Vice Chm., Acad. of Med. Royal Colls, 2000–02. Hon. Fellow, Inst. Biomed. Sci., 1996. *Publications:* (Chief Ed.) Pediatric Hematology, 1992, 2nd edn 2000; Childhood Leukaemia: the facts, 1994, 2nd edn 2000; contrib. articles on childhood leukaemia and blood diseases. *Recreations:* theatre, long distance walking. *Address:* Strathmore, Pertenhall Road, Keysoe, Beds MK44 2HR. *T:* (01234) 708697.

LILLFORD, Prof. Peter John, CBE 1998; PhD; Chief Scientist (Foods), Unilever Research, 1999–2001; *b* 16 Nov. 1944; *s* of John Leslie Lillford and Ethel Ruth Lillford (*née* Wimlett); *m* 1969, Elisabeth Rosemary Avery; two *s*. *Educ:* King's Coll., London (BSc Hons Chemistry; PhD 1968); Cornell Univ. Res. Fellow, Cardio Vascular Res. Inst., San Francisco, 1970–71; Res. Scientist, 1971–87, Principal Scientist, 1987–99, Unilever. Special Prof. of Biophysics, Nottingham Univ., 1988–; Hon. Prof., Stirling Univ.,

1989–2000; Vis. Prof., York Univ., 2000–. Chairman: Foresight Food and Drink Panel, OST, 1993–97; Agri-Food Cttee, BBSRC, 1997–2000. Pres., Inst. Food Sci. and Technology, 2001–. FRSA 1996. Hon. DEng Birmingham 1999. Sen. Medal, RSC, 1991. *Publications:* Foods Structure and Behaviour, 1987; Feeding and the Texture of Food, 1991; Glassy States in Foods, 1993; (ed) Technology Foresight, Food and Drink, 1995. *Recreations:* old houses, old cars, old whisky. *Address:* The Firs, 20 Pavenham Road, Carlton, Beds MK43 7LS. *T:* (01234) 720869.

LILLINGSTON, George David I. I.; *see* Inge-Innes-Lillingston.

LIM FAT, Sir (Maxime) Edouard (Lim Man), Kt 1991; Professor Emeritus, University of Mauritius, since 1975; company director; *s* of V. Lim Fat and S. Lifo; *m* 1952, Y. H. Chan Wah Hak; two *s* one *d. Educ:* Univ. of London (BSc Chem. Eng.); Univ. of Newcastle (MSc Agric. Eng.). AEE Harwell, 1950–51; Engineer, Min. of Agriculture, Mauritius, 1951–63; Principal, Mauritius Coll. of Agriculture, 1963–68; Head, Sch. of Industrial Technology, Univ. of Mauritius, 1968–80; Director: Bank of Mauritius, 1980–92; NEDC, 1991–; two factories; Chm., Mauritius Freeport, 1992–. *Publications:* numerous articles, mainly on industrial develt and educn. *Recreations:* golf, economics, music. *Address:* 19 Rev. Lebrun Street, Rose-hill, Mauritius. *T:* (home) 4547680, (office) 4548288, *Fax:* 4545656. *Clubs:* Gymkhana, Vacoas.

LIM PIN, Professor, MD; FRCP, FRCPE, FRACP, FACP; University Professor and Professor of Medicine, National University of Singapore, since 2000; Senior Consultant, National University Hospital, since 2000; *b* 12 Jan. 1936; *s* of late Lim Lu Yeh and of Choo Siew Kooi; *m* 1964, Shirley Loo; two *s* one *d. Educ:* Queens' Coll., Cambridge (Queen's Schol., 1957; MA; MD 1970). FRCP 1976; FRCPE 1981; FRACP 1978; FACP 1981. MO, Min. of Health, Singapore, 1965–66; Univ. of Singapore: Lectr in Medicine, 1966–70; Sen. Lectr in Medicine, 1971–73; Associate Prof. of Medicine, 1974–77; Prof. and Head, Dept of Medicine, 1978–81; Dep. Vice-Chancellor, 1979–81; Vice-Chancellor, Nat. Univ. of Singapore, 1981–2000. Eisenhower Fellow, USA, 1982. Founder Pres., Endocrine and Metabolic Soc. of Singapore. Chairman: Nat. Wages Council; Bio-ethics Adv. Cttee. Chm., Mgt Bd, Tropical Marine Sci. Inst. Member, Board of Governors: Inst. of Policy Studies, 1988–; Singapore Internat. Foundn, 1991–; Chinese Heritage Centre, 1995–. Member, Board of Directors: Overseas Union Bank, 1991–; PharmBio Growth Fund Pte Ltd, 1997–; Raffles Medical Gp. Hon. Fellow: Coll. of Gen. Practitioners of Singapore, 1982; Internat. Coll. of Dentists, USA, 1999; (Dental Surgery), RCSE, 1999; Hon FRACOG 1992; FRCPSGlas 1997; Hon. FRCSE 1997. Hon. DSc Hull, 1999. Public Administration Medal (Gold), Singapore, 1984; Meritorious Service Medal, Singapore, 1990; Friend of Labour Award, NTUC, 1995. DSO (Singapore), 2000; Officier, Ordre des Palmes Académiques (France), 1988. *Publications:* articles in New England Jl of Medicine, Med. Jl of Australia, BMJ, Qly Jl of Medicine, and Tissue Antigens. *Recreations:* swimming, badminton. *Address:* Department of Medicine, National University of Singapore, 5 Lower Kent Ridge Road, Singapore 119074, Republic of Singapore. *Club:* Singapore Island Country.

LIMBU; *see* Rambahadur Limbu.

LIMERICK, 6th Earl of, *cr* 1803 (Ire.); **Patrick Edmund Pery,** KBE 1983; Hon. AM 2001; DL; MA, CA; Baron Glentworth, 1790 (Ire.); Viscount Limerick, 1800 (Ire.); Baron Foxford, 1815 (UK); Chairman, Pirelli UK, since 1989; Chancellor, London Guildhall University, since 1999; *b* 12 April 1930; *e s* of 5th Earl of Limerick, GBE, CH, KCB, DSO, TD, and Angela Olivia, Dowager Countess of Limerick, GBE, CH (*d* 1981); *S* father, 1967; *m* 1961, Sylvia Rosalind Lush (*see* Countess of Limerick); two *s* one *d. Educ:* Eton; New Coll., Oxford. CA 1957. Chairman: Mallinson–Denny Ltd, 1979–81; Polymeters Response Internat., 1988–93; AMP Asset Management plc, 1992–98; De La Rue plc, 1993–97 (Dir, 1983–); Dep. Chm., Henderson plc, 1998–2000; Director: Kleinwort Benson Ltd, 1967–87 (Vice Chm., 1983–85; Dep Chm., 1985–87); Kleinwort Benson Gp, 1982–90; Kleinwort Benson Australian Income Fund Inc., subseq. Dresdner RCM Global Strategic Fund Inc., 1986–2000; Commercial Bank of Australia Ltd (London Adv. Bd), 1969–72; TR Pacific Investment Trust, 1987–92; Brooke Bond Gp, 1981–84. Parly Under-Sec. of State for Trade, DTI, 1972–74; Chairman: BOTB, 1979–83 (Mem., 1975–91); BIEC, subseq. British Invisibles, 1984–91; Pres., Inst. of Export, 1983–95; Vice-Pres., Assoc. of British Chambers of Commerce, 1977– (Pres., 1974–77); Member: Cttee for ME Trade, 1968–79 (Chm., 1975–79); Council, London Chamber of Commerce, 1968–79. Pres., Canning House, 1994–97. Chairman: Ct of Govs, London Guildhall Univ. (formerly City of London Poly.), 1984–99; Cttee of Univ. Chairmen, 1995–97; Trustees, City Parochial Foundn, 1992–96 (Trustee, 1971–). Pres., South of England Agricl Soc., 1993. Chairman: Britain-Australia Soc., 1997–99 (Vice-Pres., 2000–); European-Atlantic Gp, 1999–; Sussex Heritage Trust, 2000–. Master, Guild of World Traders, 1991. President: Anglo-Swiss Soc., 1984–2000; Ski Club of GB, 1974–81; Alpine Ski Club, 1985–87 (Vice-Pres., 1975–77); Vice-Pres., Alpine Club, 1989–91. Hon. Colonel: 71st (Yeomanry) Signal Regt (Volunteers), 1993–98; Inns of Court and City Yeomanry (Volunteers), 1993–. Kt Pres., Soc. of Knights of the Round Table, 1999–. DL W Sussex, 1988. *Recreations:* skiing, mountaineering. *Heir: s* Viscount Glentworth, *qv. Address:* Chiddinglye, West Hoathly, East Grinstead, West Sussex RH19 4QT. *T:* (01342) 810214; 30A Victoria Road, W8 5RG. *T:* (020) 7937 0573. *Club:* Cavalry and Guards.

LIMERICK, Countess of; Sylvia Rosalind Pery, CBE 1991; President, Community Practitioners' and Health Visitors' Association (formerly Health Visitors' Association), since 1984 (a Vice President, 1978–84); Vice-Chairman, Foundation for the Study of Infant Deaths, since 1971; Chairman, Eastman Foundation for Oral Research and Training, since 1999; *b* 7 Dec. 1935; *e d* of Maurice Stanley Lush, CB, CBE, MC; *m* 1961, Viscount Glentworth (now 6th Earl of Limerick, *qv*); two *s* one *d. Educ:* St Swithun's, Winchester; Lady Margaret Hall, Oxford (MA). Research Asst, Foreign Office, 1959–62. British Red Cross Society: Nat. HQ Staff, 1962–66; Pres., Kensington and Chelsea Div., 1966–72; a Vice-Pres., London Br., 1972–85; Vice-Chm., Council, 1984–85; Chm., 1985–95 (Chm. Emeritus, 1995–97); Hon. Vice-Pres., 1999–; a Vice-Pres., Internat. Fedn of Red Cross Red Crescent Socs, 1993–97. Mem., Bd of Governors, St Bartholomew's Hosp., 1970–74; Vice-Chm., CHC, S District of Kensington, Chelsea, Westminster Area, 1974–77; Chm., Eastman Dental Inst., 1996–99; Member: Kensington, Chelsea and Westminster AHA, 1977–82; Eastman Dental Hosp. SHA, 1990–96. Non-exec. Dir, UCL Hosps NHS Trust, 1996–97. Vice President: UK Cttee for UN Children's Fund, 1979–99 (Pres., 1972–79); Nat. Assoc. for Maternal and Child Welfare, 1985–90 (Pres., 1973–84). Member: Cttee of Management, Inst. of Child Health, 1976–96; Council, King Edward's Hospital Fund, 1977– (Mem., Cttee of Management, 1977–81, 1985–89); Maternity Services Adv. Cttee, DHSS, 1981–84; CS Occupational Health Service Adv. Bd, 1989–92; Chm., CMO's Expert Gp to investigate Cot Death Theories, 1994–98. Trustee: Child Accident Prevention Trust, 1979–87; Voluntary Hosp. of St Bartholomew, 1993–; Child Health Res. Trust, 1996–; Eastman Dental Res. Foundn, 1996–98. Reviewed National Association of Citizens Advice Bureaux, 1983. FRSocMed 1977. Hon. FRCP 1994 (Hon. MRCP 1990); Hon. FRCPCH (Hon. Mem., BPA, 1986); Hon. Fellow, Inst. of Child Health, 1996. Hon. DLitt CNAA, 1990; Hon. LLD Bristol, 1998. Hon. Freeman, Salters' Co., 1992. *Publication:* (jtly) Sudden Infant Death: patterns, puzzles and problems, 1985. *Recreations:* music, mountaineering, ski-ing. *Address:* 30A Victoria Road, W8 5RG. *T:* (020) 7937 0573; Chiddinglye, West Hoathly, East Grinstead, W Sussex RH19 4QT. *T:* (01342) 810214.

LIMERICK AND KILLALOE, Bishop of, since 2000; **Rt Rev. Michael Hugh Gunton Mayes;** *b* 31 Aug. 1941; *s* of Thomas David Dougan Mayes and Hilary Gunton; *m* 1966, Elizabeth Annie Eleanor Irwin; one *s* two *d. Educ:* The Royal Sch., Armagh; Trinity Coll., Dublin (BA); Univ. of London (BD). Ordained, 1964; Assistant Curate: St Mark's, Portadown, 1964–67; St Columba's, Portadown, 1967–68; Missionary, Japan, 1968–74; Incumbent: St Michael's, Cork, 1975–86; Moviddy, Cork, 1986–88; Rathcooney, Cork, 1988–93; Archdeacon of Cork, Cloyne and Ross, 1986–93; Bishop of Kilmore, Elphin and Ardagh, 1993–2000. *Recreations:* reading, music, photography, walking. *Address:* Bishop's House, North Circular Road, Limerick, Ireland. *T:* (61) 451532, *Fax:* (61) 451100; *e-mail:* bishop@limerick.anglican.org.

LIMON, Sir Donald (William), KCB 1997 (CB 1993); Clerk of the House of Commons, 1994–97; *b* 29 Oct. 1932; *s* of late Arthur and Dora Limon; *m* 1987, Joyce Beatrice Clifton. *Educ:* Durham Cathedral Chorister Sch.; Durham Sch.; Lincoln Coll., Oxford (MA). A Clerk in the House of Commons, 1956–97: Sec. to House of Commons Commn, 1979–81; Clerk of Financial Cttees, 1981–84; Principal Clerk, Table Office, 1985–89; Clerk of Cttees, 1989–90; Clerk Asst, 1990–94. *Publication:* (ed jtly) Erskine May's Parliamentary Practice, 22nd edn 1997. *Recreations:* cricket, golf, singing. *Address:* West Barn, Kingsdon, Somerton TA11 7LL. *T:* (01935) 840450.

LINACRE, Sir (John) Gordon (Seymour), Kt 1986; CBE 1979; AFC 1943; DFM 1941; CIMgt; Deputy Chairman, United Newspapers plc, 1981–91 (Director, 1969–91; Joint Managing Director, 1981–83; Chief Executive, 1983–88); President, Yorkshire Post Newspapers Ltd, since 1990 (Managing Director, 1965–83; Deputy Chairman, 1981–83; Chairman, 1983–90); *b* 23 Sept. 1920; *s* of John James Linacre and Beatrice Barber (*née* Seymour); *m* 1943, Irene Amy (*née* Gordon); two *d. Educ:* Firth Park Grammar Sch., Sheffield. CIMgt (FBIM 1973). Served War, RAF, 1939–46, Sqdn Ldr. Journalistic appts, Sheffield Telegraph/Star, 1937–47; Kemsley News Service, 1947–50; Dep. Editor: Newcastle Journal, 1950–56; Newcastle Evening Chronicle, 1956–57; Editor, Sheffield Star, 1958–61; Asst Gen. Man., Sheffield Newspapers Ltd, 1961–63; Exec. Dir, Thomson Regional Newspapers Ltd, London, 1963–65. Chairman: United Provincial Newspapers Ltd, 1983–88; Sheffield Newspapers Ltd, 1981–88; Lancashire Evening Post Ltd, 1982–88; Northampton Mercury Co. Ltd, 1983–88; The Reporter Ltd, 1970–88; Blackpool Gazette & Herald Ltd, 1984–88; Chameleon Television, 1992–; Dep. Chm., Express Newspapers, 1985–88; Director: United Newspapers (Publications) Ltd, 1969–88; Trident Television Ltd, 1970–84; Yorkshire Television Ltd, 1967–90. Dir, INCA/FIEJ Res. Assoc., Darmstadt, Germany, 1971–79 (Pres., 1974–77); Pres. FIEJ, 1984–88 (Mem. Bd, 1971–90). Dir, ASA, 1991–94; Member: Newspaper Soc. Council, 1966–90 (Pres., Newspaper Soc., 1978–79); Press Assoc., 1967–74 (Chm., 1970–71); Reuters Ltd, 1970–74 (Trustee, 1974–98); Evening Newspaper Advertising Bureau Ltd, 1966–78 (Chm., 1975–76); N Eastern Postal Bd, 1974–80; Adv. Bd, Yorks and Lincs, BIM, 1973–75; Health Educn Council, 1973–77; Leeds TEC, 1989–91 (Chm.). Mem., ENO, 1978–81, Chm., 1978–98, Pres., 1998–, Opera North (formerly English Nat. Opera North). Governor, Harrogate Festival of Arts and Sciences Ltd, 1973– (Pres., 1992–). Trustee, Yorks and Lincs Trustee Savings Bank, 1972–78; Mem. Council, 1985–93, and Court, 1995–2000, Chm. Foundation, 1989–2000, Leeds Univ. Kt, Order of White Rose (Finland), 1987; Grande Ufficiale al Merito della Repubblica Italiana, 1988 (Commendatore, 1973). *Recreations:* golf, fishing, walking. *Clubs:* Alwoodley Golf; Yorkshire Fly; Huby Angling.

LINAKER, Lawrence Edward, (Paddy); Deputy Chairman and Chief Executive, M&G Group, 1987–94; *b* 22 July 1934; *s* of late Lawrence Wignall and Rose Linaker; *m* 1963, Elizabeth Susan Elam; one *s. Educ:* Malvern College. FCA. Esso Petroleum, 1957–63; joined M&G Group, 1963; Man. Dir, 1972, Chm., 1987–94, M&G Investment Management. Chairman: Fisons, 1994–95; Marling Industries, 1996–97; Fleming Technol. Investment Trust plc, 1997–2001; Director: Fleming Mercantile Investment Trust, 1994–; TSB Gp, 1994–95; Lloyds TSB Gp, 1995–2001; Wolverhampton & Dudley Breweries plc, 1996–. Chm., Institutional Fund Managers' Assoc., 1992–94; Dir, Securities Inst., 1992–94. Trustee, Lloyds TSB Foundn for Eng. and Wales, 1995–2001; Life Trustee, Carnegie UK Trust, 1995. Chm., YMCA Nat. Coll., 1992–2000; Treas., Childline, 1994–2000; Member: Council, RPMS, 1977–88; Governing Body, SPCK, 1976–95; Council, Malvern College, 1988– (Treas., 1993–); Governing Body, Canterbury Christ Church Coll., 1993–98; Court, ICSTM, 1999–. *Recreations:* music, wine, gardening. *Clubs:* Athenæum, Brooks's.

LINCOLN, 19th Earl of, *cr* 1572; **Robert Edward Fiennes-Clinton;** *b* 17 June 1972; *s* of Hon. Edward Gordon Fiennes-Clinton and Julia (*née* Howson); *S* grandfather, 2001. *Heir: b* William Roy Fiennes-Clinton, *b* 1980.

LINCOLN, Bishop of, since 2001; **Rt Rev. John Charles Saxbee,** PhD; *b* 7 Jan. 1946; *s* of Charles Albert Saxbee and Florence Violet Saxbee (*née* Harris); *m* 1965, Jacqueline Margaret Carol Skym; one *d. Educ:* Cotham Grammar Sch., Bristol; Bristol Univ. (BA 1968); Durham Univ. (DipTh 1969; PhD 1976); Cranmer Hall, Durham. Ordained deacon, 1972, priest, 1973; Asst Curate, Emmanuel with St Paul, Plymouth, 1972–77; Vicar of St Philip, Weston Mill, Plymouth, 1977–81; Team Vicar, Central Exeter Team Ministry, 1981–87; Dir, SW Ministry Training Course, 1981–92; Priest-in-Charge of Holy Trinity, Wistanstow with St Michael, Cwm Head and St Margaret, Acton Scott, 1992–94; Archdeacon of Ludlow, 1992–2001, Bishop Suffragan of Ludlow, 1994–2001. Prebendary: of Exeter Cathedral, 1988–92; of Hereford Cathedral, 1992–2001. Pres., Modern Churchpeople's Union, 1997–. Religious Advr, Central TV, 1997–. Member: Exec., Springboard, 1998–; Coll. of Evangelists, 1999–. *Publication:* Liberal Evangelism: a flexible response to the decade, 1994. *Recreations:* Wisty the cat, televised sport, most kinds of music. *Address:* Bishop's House, Eastgate, Lincoln LN2 1QQ. *T:* (01522) 534701.

LINCOLN, Dean of; *see* Knight, Very Rev. A. F.

LINCOLN, Archdeacon of; *see* Hawes, Ven. A. J.

LINCOLN, Prof. Dennis William, PhD; FRSE; Deputy Vice-Chancellor (Research), Griffith University, since 1996; *b* 21 July 1939; *s* of late Ernest Edward Lincoln and Gertrude Emma Holmes; one *s* one *d. Educ:* Bracondale Sch., Norwich; Essex Inst. of Agriculture; Univ. of Nottingham (BSc 1964); Corpus Christi Coll., Cambridge (MA 1966; PhD 1967); Univ. of Bristol (DSc 1974). FRSE 1992. Agricl labourer, 1955–57; Research Technician, Univ. of Nottingham, 1957–59; Res. Fellow, Corpus Christi Coll., Cambridge, 1966–67; Lectr, 1967–74, Reader, 1974–81, Prof., 1981–82, Univ. of Bristol; Dir, MRC Reproductive Biology Unit, Edinburgh, 1982–96; Hon. Prof., Edinburgh Univ., 1984–96. Short-term appts in Switzerland, The Netherlands, USA, Australia;

numerous nat. and internat. duties related to promotion of reproductive health. *Publications:* papers on reproductive biology, esp. on neural mechanisms in control of lactation and fertility. *Recreations:* ornithology, international travel, wildlife photography. *Address:* Griffith University, Nathan, Qld 4111, Australia. *T:* (7) 38756427, *Fax:* (7) 38757507.

LINCOLN, Paul Arthur; Director of Learning Services, Essex County Council, since 1997; *b* 11 April 1946. *Educ:* Clare Coll., Cambridge (BA (Hons) History; PGCE 1969; MA 1971). Various teaching posts in secondary schools in Sussex and Essex, 1969–82; Sen. Dep. Head, William de Ferrers Sch., Essex, 1982–88; Essex County Council Education Department: Sen. Inspector, 1988–89; Principal Inspector, 1989–91; Head of Strategic Planning, 1991–92; Principal Educn Officer, Quality, 1992–93; Dep. County Educn Officer, 1994–95; Dir of Educn, 1995–97. *Publications:* The Learning School, 1987; Supporting Improving Primary Schools, 1999. *Recreations:* reading, walking, gardening. *Address:* Learning Services Directorate, Essex County Council, PO Box 47, County Hall, Chelmsford, Essex CM2 6WN. *T:* (01245) 492211.

LIND, Per; Swedish Ambassador to the Court of St James's, 1979–82, retired; *b* 8 Jan. 1916; *s* of Erik and Elisabeth Lind; *m* 1942, Eva Sandström; two *s* two *d. Educ:* Univ. of Uppsala. LLB 1939. Entered Swedish Foreign Service as Attaché, 1939; served in Helsinki, 1939–41; Berlin, 1942–44; Second Sec., Stockholm Foreign Ministry, 1944–47; First Sec., Swedish Embassy, Washington, 1947–51; Personal Asst to Sec.-General of UN, 1953–56; re-posted to Swedish Foreign Ministry: Chief of Div. of Internat. Organisations, 1956–59; Dep. Dir Political Affairs, 1959–64; Ambassador with special duties (*ie* disarmament questions) and actg Chm., Swedish Delegation in Geneva, 1964–66; Ambassador to Canada, 1966–69; Under-Sec. of State for Administration at Foreign Ministry, Stockholm, 1969–75; Chm. Special Political Cttee of 29th Session of Gen. Assembly of UN, 1974; Ambassador to Australia, 1975–79. *Recreation:* golf. *Address:* Gyllenstiernsgatan 7, 11526 Stockholm, Sweden.

LINDAHL, Tomas Robert, MD; FRS 1988; Director, Clare Hall Laboratories, Imperial Cancer Research Fund, since 1983; *b* 28 Jan. 1938; *s* of Robert and Ethel Lindahl; *m* 1967, Alice Adams (marr. diss. 1979); one *s* one *d. Educ:* Karolinska Inst., Stockholm (MD). Research Fellow, Princeton Univ., 1964–67; Helen Hay Whitney Fellow, 1967–69, Asst Prof., 1968–69, Rockefeller Univ.; Asst Prof., 1969–75, Associate Prof., 1975–77, Karolinska Inst.; Prof. of Medical Biochemistry, Univ. of Gothenburg, 1978–81; Imperial Cancer Research Fund: Staff Scientist, 1981–83; Asst Dir of Research, 1985–89; Associate Dir of Research, 1989–91; Dep Dir, Res., 1991–96; Dir, Res., 1996–98; Dep. Dir, Res., 1998–. Member: EMBO; Royal Swedish Acad. of Scis; Norwegian Acad. of Sci. and Letters; Academia Europaea. Founder FMedSci 1998. *Publications:* res. papers in biochem. and molecular biol. *Recreations:* piano, wine, modern art. *Address:* ICRF Clare Hall Laboratories, South Mimms, Herts EN6 3LD.

LINDBLOM, Keith John; QC 1996; a Recorder, since 2001; *b* 20 Sept. 1956; *s* of John Eric Lindblom and June Elizabeth Lindblom (*née* Balloch); *m* 1991, Fiona Margaret Jackson; one *s* three *d. Educ:* Whitgift Sch.; St John's Coll., Oxford (MA). Called to the Bar, Gray's Inn, 1980; in practice as barrister, 1981–. An Asst Parly Boundary Comr, 2000–. *Recreations:* music, reading, walking. *Address:* 2 Harcourt Buildings, Temple, EC4Y 9DB. *T:* (020) 7353 8415. *Club:* Caledonian.

LINDEN, Anya, (Lady Sainsbury of Preston Candover); Ballerina, Royal Ballet, 1958–65, retired; *b* 3 Jan. 1933; English; *d* of George Charles and Ada Dorothea Eltenton; *m* 1963, John Davan Sainsbury (*see* Baron Sainsbury of Preston Candover); two *s* one *d. Educ:* Berkeley, Calif; Sadler's Wells Sch., 1947. Entered Sadler's Wells Co. at Covent Garden, 1951; promoted Soloist, 1952; Ballerina, 1958. Principal rôles in the ballets: Coppelia; Sylvia; Prince of Pagodas; Sleeping Beauty; Swan Lake; Giselle; Cinderella; Agon; Solitaire; Noctambules; Fête Etrange; Symphonic Variations; The Invitation; Firebird; Lady and the Fool; Antigone; Ondine; Seven Deadly Sins. Ballet coach: Royal Ballet Sch., 1989–; Rambert Sch., 1989–. Member: Nat. Council for One-Parent Families, 1978–90 (Hon. Vice-Pres., 1985–90; Mem. Appeal Cttee, 1966–87); Adv. Council, British Theatre Museum, 1975–83; Drama and Dance Adv. Cttee, British Council, 1981–83; Theatre Museum Assoc., 1984–86. Dep.-Chm. and Dir, Rambert Dance Co. (formerly Ballet Rambert), 1975–89; Governor: Royal Ballet Sch., 1977–; Rambert Sch. of Ballet Charitable Trust Ltd, 1983–; Dep. Chm. and Mem. Council of Management, Benesh Inst. of Choreology (formerly Benesh Inst. of Movement Notation), 1986–97. Chm., Linbury Prize for Theatre Design, 1987–. Dir, Anvil Trust, 1992–98; Trustee, Galitzine—St Petersburg Library, 1993–; Patron, Landlife 1993–. DUniv Brunel, 1995. *Recreations:* gardening, painting, photography.

LINDEN, Ian, CMG 2000; PhD; Executive Director, Catholic Institute for International Relations, 1986–2001; *b* 18 Aug. 1941; *s* of Henry Thomas William Linden and Edna Jessie Linden; *m* 1963, Jane Winder; two *s* two *d. Educ:* Southend High Sch. for Boys; St Catharine's Coll., Cambridge (MA 1966); PhD London Univ. (Middx Hosp. Med. Sch., 1966, SOAS 1975). Asst Lectr in Zoology, Nat. Univ. of Ireland, 1965–66; Res. Associate, Rockefeller Univ., NY, 1966–68; Lectr in Biology, Univ. of Malaŵi, 1968–71; Lectr, subseq. Sen. Lectr, in History, Ahmadu Bello Univ., 1973–76; Researcher, Arbeitskreis Entwicklung und Frieden, 1977–79; Prof. of African History, Univ. of Hamburg, 1979–80; Southern Africa Desk Officer and Co-ordinator of Policy Dept, Catholic Inst. for Internat. Relns, 1980–86. Hon. LLD Southampton, 1998. *Publications:* Catholics, Peasants and Chewa Resistance in Nyasaland, 1974; Church and Revolution in Rwanda, 1977; The Catholic Church and the Struggle for Zimbabwe, 1980; (jtly) Islam in Modern Nigeria, 1984; Christianisme et pouvoirs au Rwanda 1900–1990, 1999. *Recreations:* swimming, theology, walking. *Address:* 31 Royal Close, Manor Road, N16 5SE.

LINDESAY-BETHUNE, family name of **Earl of Lindsay**.

LINDISFARNE, Archdeacon of; *see* Langley, Ven. R.

LINDLEY, Bryan Charles, CBE 1982; Chairman and Chief Executive, Lord Lindley Associates, since 1990; Director, J & B Imaging, since 1998; *b* 30 Aug. 1932; *m* 1987; one *s* by former *m. Educ:* Reading Sch.; University Coll. London (Fellow 1979). BSc (Eng) 1954; PhD 1960; FIMechE 1968; FIEE 1968; FInstP 1968; FInstD 1968; FPRI 1984. National Gas Turbine Establishment, Pyestock, 1954–57; Hawker Siddeley Nuclear Power Co. Ltd, 1957–59; C. A. Parsons & Co. Ltd, Nuclear Research Centre, Newcastle upon Tyne, 1959–61; International Research and Development Co. Ltd, Newcastle upon Tyne, 1962–65; Man., R&D Div., C. A. Parsons & Co. Ltd, Newcastle upon Tyne, 1965–68; Electrical Research Assoc. Ltd: Dir, 1968–73; Chief Exec. and Man. Dir, ERA Technology Ltd, 1973–79; Dir, ERA Patents Ltd, 1968–79; Chm. and Man. Dir, ERA Autotrack Systems Ltd, 1971–79. Director: Dunlop Ltd, 1982–85; Soil-Less Cultivation Systems, 1980–85; Chm. and Dir, Thermal Conversions (UK), 1982–85; Dir of Technology, Dunlop Holdings, 1979–85; Director: BICC Cables Ltd, 1985–88; BICC Research and Engineering Ltd, 1985–88; Thomas Bolton & Johnson Ltd, 1986–88; Settle-Carlisle Railway Develt Co., 1992–94; Chairman: Optical Fibres, 1985–87; Linktronic Systems Ltd, 1990–92; Wetheriggs Pottery Ltd, 1992–94; SKAND Systems Ltd, 1995–97; Chief Exec., Nat. Advanced Robotics Res. Centre, 1989–90. Chm., N Lakeland Healthcare NHS Trust, 1993–97. Vis. Prof., Univ. of Liverpool, 1989–. Chairman: Materials, Chemicals and Vehicles Requirements Bd, DTI, 1982–85; RAPRA Council, 1984–85; Dir, RAPRA Technology Ltd, 1985–97; Member: Nat. Electronics Council, 1969–79; Res. and Technol. Cttee, CBI, 1974–80; Design Council, 1980–86 (Mem., Design Adv. Cttee, 1980–86); Cttee of Inquiry into Engineering Profession, 1977–80; Adv. Council for Applied Research and Develt, 1980–86; Adv. Cttee for Safety of Nuclear Installations, 1987–90; Chm., Sci. Educn and Management Div., IEE, 1974–75; Dep. Chm., Watt Cttee on Energy Ltd, 1976–80. Mem., SAE, 1984. *Publications:* articles on plasma physics, electrical and mechanical engineering, management science, impact of technological innovation, etc, in learned jls. *Recreations:* music, photography, ski-ing, walking, sailing. *Address:* Lindenthwaite, Beacon Edge, Penrith, Cumbria CA11 8BN.

LINDLEY, Prof. Dennis Victor; Professor and Head of Department of Statistics and Computer Science, University College London, 1967–77; *b* 25 July 1923; *s* of Albert Edward and Florence Louisa Lindley; *m* 1947, Joan Armitage; one *s* two *d. Educ:* Tiffin Boys' Sch., Kingston-on-Thames; Trinity Coll., Cambridge. MA Cantab 1948. Min. of Supply, 1943–45; Nat. Physical Lab., 1945–46 and 1947–48; Statistical Lab., Cambridge Univ., 1948–60 (Dir, 1957–60); Prof. and Head of Dept of Statistics, UCW, Aberystwyth, 1960–67, Hon. Professorial Fellow, 1978–. Hon. Prof., Univ. of Warwick, 1978–96. Vis. Professor: Chicago and Stanford Univs, 1954–55; Harvard Business Sch., 1963; Univ. of Iowa, 1974–75; Univ. of Bath, 1978–81. Wald Lectr, Inst. Math. Statistics, 1988. Guy Medal (Silver), Royal Statistical Soc., 1968. Fellow, Inst. Math. Statistics; Fellow, American Statistical Assoc. *Publications:* (with J. C. P. Miller) Cambridge Elementary Statistical Tables, 1953; Introduction to Probability and Statistics (2 vols), 1965; Making Decisions, 1971, rev. edn 1985; Bayesian Statistics, 1971; (with W. F. Scott) New Cambridge Elementary Statistical Tables, 1985, rev. edn as New Cambridge Statistical Tables, 1995; contribs to Royal Statistical Soc., Biometrika, Annals of Math. Statistics. *Address:* Woodstock, Quay Lane, Minehead, Somerset TA24 5QU. *T:* (01643) 705189.

LINDLEY, Simon Geoffrey; Master of the Music, Leeds Parish Church, since 1975; Leeds City Organist, since 1976; Senior Assistant Music Officer (formerly Music and Special Projects Officer), Leeds Leisure Services Department, Leeds City Council, since 1988; *b* 10 Oct. 1948; *s* of Rev. Geoffrey Lindley and Jeanne Lindley (*née* Cammaerts); *m*; three *s* one *d. Educ:* Magdalen Coll. Sch., Oxford; Royal Coll. of Music. FRCO(CHM), FTCL, GRSM (Lond), ARCM, LRAM, ARSCM 1987. Studies with Richard Silk, David Carver, Dr Bernard Rose, Vincent Packford, Dr Philip Wilkinson and, principally, Dr John Birch. Dir of Music, St Anne & St Agnes and St Olave, London, 1968–70; Asst Master of Music, St Alban's Abbey, 1970–75; Dir of Music, St Alban's Sch., 1971–75; Sen. Lectr, Leeds Poly., 1976–88. Chorus Master: Leeds Phil. Soc., 1975–83; Halifax Choral Soc., 1975–87 (Vice-Pres., 1988–); Conductor: St Peter's Singers and Chamber Orch., 1977–; Univ. of Huddersfield Chamber Choir, 1997–98; LCM Choral Soc., 1999–; Chief Guest Conductor, Yorkshire Evening Post Band, 1998– (Resident Conductor, 1995–98); Music Dir, Overgate Hospice Choir, Halifax, 1997–. Organist, London Festival Players; Special Comr, RSCM, 1975–; Centre Chm., ISM, 1976–82; Mem. Council, RCO, 1977–98 (Pres., 2000–Sept. 2002); Sec., Church Music Soc., 1991–. Dir, English Hymnal Co. Ltd. Advr, Yorks TV Religious and Educl Progs, 1981–; Artistic Advr, Leeds Summer Heritage Festivals, biennially, 1989–. Trustee: Sir George Thalben-Ball Meml Trust; Ecclesiastical Music Trust, 1998–; Pilling Trust, 1999–. Concert Organist début, Westminster Cathedral, 1969; tours of USA, France, Germany, Far East, USSR. Numerous recordings as organist and as conductor. Hon. FGMS 1996; Hon. FGCM 2000; Hon. Fellow, Leeds Coll. of Music, 2000. DUniv Leeds Metropolitan, 2001. *Compositions:* Anthems for Unison and 2 part singing, vol. 2, 1979; Ave Maria, 1980; Matthew, Mark, Luke and John, 1986; *carols:* Come, sing and dance, 1977; How far is it to Bethlehem?, Jacob's Ladder, Now the Green Blade riseth, On Easter Morn, 1995. *Publications:* contribs to Musical Times, Choir and Organ, Organists' Review, The Dalesman, The Organ. *Recreations:* churches, cathedrals, Victorian architecture, food. *Address:* 17 Fulneck, Pudsey LS28 8NT. *T:* and *Fax:* (0113) 255 6143; Leeds Leisure Services, Leeds Town Hall, The Headrow, Leeds LS1 3AD. *T:* (0113) 247 8334, *Fax:* (0113) 247 8397; *e-mail:* slg@simonlindley.org.uk. *Club:* Leeds (Leeds).

LINDOP, Sir Norman, Kt 1973; DL; MSc; CChem, FRSC; Chairman, Hertfordshire County Council, 1997–99 (Member (Lab), since 1993); Director, Hatfield Polytechnic, 1969–82; *b* 9 March 1921; *s* of Thomas Cox Lindop and May Lindop, Stockport, Cheshire; *m* 1974, Jenny C. Quass; one *s. Educ:* Northgate Sch., Ipswich; Queen Mary Coll., Univ. of London (BSc, MSc). Various industrial posts, 1942–46; Lectr in Chemistry, Queen Mary Coll., 1946; Asst Dir of Examinations, Civil Service Commn, 1951; Sen. Lectr in Chemistry, Kingston Coll. of Technology, 1953; Head of Dept of Chemistry and Geology, Kingston Coll. of Technology, 1957; Principal: SW Essex Technical Coll. and Sch. of Art, 1963; Hatfield Coll. of Technology, 1966; Principal, British Sch. of Osteopathy, 1982–90. Chairman: Cttee of Dirs of Polytechnics, 1972–74; Council for Professions Supplementary to Medicine, 1973–81; Home Office Data Protection Cttee, 1976–78; Cttee of Enquiry into Public Sector Validation, DES, 1984–85; British Library Adv. Council, 1986–94; Herts Area Manpower Bd, 1986–88; Res. Council for Complementary Medicine, 1989–90; Member: CNAA, 1974–81; US-UK Educn (Fulbright) Commn, 1971–81; SRC, 1974–78; GMC, 1979–84. Chm. Council, Westfield Coll., London Univ., 1983–89. FCP 1980; Fellow: QMC, 1976; Hatfield Polytechnic, 1983; Hon. Fellow, Brighton Polytechnic, 1990. FRSA. DL Hertford, 1989. Hon. DEd CNAA, 1982; Hon. DSc: Ulster, 1994; Hertfordshire, 1997. *Recreations:* mountain walking, music (especially opera). *Address:* 36 Queens Road, Hertford, Herts SG13 8AZ. *Club:* Athenæum.

LINDOP, Prof. Patricia Joyce, (Mrs G. P. R. Esdale); Professor of Radiation Biology, University of London, 1970–84, now Emeritus; Chairman, Thames Liquid Fuels (Holdings) Ltd, since 1992; *b* 21 June 1930; 2nd *c* of Elliot D. Lindop and Dorothy Jones; *m* 1957, Gerald Paton Rivett Esdale (*d* 1992); one *s* one *d. Educ:* Malvern Girls' Coll.; St Bartholomew's Hospital Med. Coll.; BSc (1st cl. Hons), MB, BS, PhD; DSc London 1974; MRCP 1956; FRCP 1977. Registered GP, 1954. Research and teaching in physiology and medical radiobiology at Med. Coll. of St Bartholomew's Hosp., 1955–84. UK Mem., Council of Pugwash Confs on Science and World Affairs, 1982–87 (Asst Sec. Gen., 1961–71); Mem., Royal Commn on Environmental Pollution, 1974–79; Chm. and Trustee, Soc. for Education in the Applications of Science, 1968–91; Member: Cttee 10 of ICRU, 1972–79; ESRO-NASA, 1970–74; Soc. for Radiol Protection, 1987–. Member Council: Science and Society, 1975–90; Soc. for Protection of Science and Learning, 1974–86; formerly Mem. Council, British Inst. of Radiology; Chairman: Univ. of London Bd of Studies in Radiation Biology, 1979–81; Interdisciplinary Special Cttee for the Environment, 1979–81. Governor, St Bartholomew's Hosp. Med. Coll., 1984–. Hon. Member: RCR, 1972; ARR, 1984. Ciba Award, 1957; Leverhulme Res. Award, 1984. *Publications:* in field of radiation effects. *Address:* 58 Wildwood Road, NW11 6UP. *T:* (020) 8455 5860. *Club:* Royal Society of Medicine.

LINDSAY, family name of **Earl of Crawford** and **Baron Lindsay of Birker**.

LINDSAY, 16th Earl of, *cr* 1633 (Scot.); **James Randolph Lindesay-Bethune;** Lord Lindsay of The Byres, 1445; Lord Parbroath, 1633; Viscount of Garnock, Lord Kilburnie, Kingsburn and Drumry, 1703; *b* 19 Nov. 1955; *s* of 15th Earl of Lindsay and of Hon. Mary Clare Douglas-Scott-Montagu, *y d* of 2nd Baron Montagu of Beaulieu; *S* father, 1989; *m* 1982, Diana, *er d* of Major Nigel Chamberlayne-Macdonald, Cranbury Park, Winchester; two *s* three *d* (of whom one *s* one *d* are twins). *Educ:* Eton; Univ. of Edinburgh (MA Hons); Univ. of Calif, Davis. A Lord in Waiting (Govt Whip), 1995; Parly Under-Sec. of State, Scottish Office, 1995–97; elected Mem., H of L, 1999. Chairman: Assured British Meat, 1997–2001; Aquaculture Scotland, 1998–2000; Scottish Quality Salmon, 1998–; Director: UA Group plc (formerly United Auctions (Scotland) Ltd), 1998–; Mining (Scotland) Ltd, 2001–; Bd Mem., Cairngorms Partnership, 1998–. Mem., UK Round Table on Sustainable Develt, 1998–2000. Trustee, Gardens for the Disabled Trust, 1984–98. Chm., Landscape Foundn, 1991–95; Pres., Internat. Tree Foundn, 1995– (Vice-Pres., 1994–95); Mem., Adv. Council, World Resource Foundn, 1994–98. Chm., RSPB Scotland, 1998– (Mem., UK Council, 1998–). Chm., Elmwood Coll. of Mgt, 2001–. Vice-Pres., Royal Smithfield Club, 1999–. ARAgS 2000. *Publications:* (jtly) Garden Ornament, 1989; Trellis, 1991. *Heir: s* Viscount Garnock, *qv*. *Address:* Lahill, Upper Largo, Fife KY8 6JE.

See also Sir G. R. B. Wrey, Bt.

LINDSAY OF BIRKER, 3rd Baron *cr* 1945, of Low Ground, Co. Cumberland; **James Francis Lindsay;** Deputy High Commissioner, Australian High Commission, Nairobi, Kenya, 1996–2000; *b* 29 Jan. 1945; *s* of 2nd Baron Lindsay of Birker and of Li Hsiao-li, *d* of Col Li Wen-chi; *S* father, 1994; *m* 1969 (marr. diss. 1985); no *c*. *Educ:* Univ. of Keele (BSc 1966); Univ. of Liverpool (Post-grad. Dip. in transport design). Lectr in physics, Tunghai Univ., Taichung, Taiwan, 1967–68; exploration geophysicist, Darwin, Australia, 1969–70; Australian Foreign Service, 1972–2000; served in Chile, 1973–76; Laos, 1980–81; Bangladesh, 1982–84; Venezuela, 1987–90; Dep. High Comr, Pakistan, 1993–96. *Recreations:* hiking, tennis. *Heir: cousin* Alexander Sebastian Lindsay, *b* 27 May 1940.

LINDSAY, Master of; Alexander Thomas Lindsay; *b* 5 Aug. 1991; *s* and *heir* of Lord Balniel, *qv*.

LINDSAY, Maj.-Gen. Courtenay Traice David, CB 1963; Director-General of Artillery, War Office, 1961–64, retired; *b* 28 Sept. 1910; *s* of late Courtenay Traice Lindsay and Charlotte Editha (*née* Wetenhall); *m* 1934, Margaret Elizabeth, *d* of late William Pease Theakston, Huntingdon; two *s*. *Educ:* Rugby Sch.; RMA Woolwich. 2nd Lt RA, 1930. Mem., Ordnance Board (Col), 1952; Dir of Munitions, British Staff (Brig.), Washington, 1959; Maj.-Gen. 1961. *Address:* Huggits Farm, Stone-in-Oxney, Tenterden, Kent TN30 7JT. *Club:* Rye Golf.

LINDSAY, Crawford Callum Douglas; QC 1987; **His Honour Judge Lindsay;** a Circuit Judge, since 1998; *b* 5 Feb. 1939; *s* of Douglas Marshall Lindsay, FRCOG and Eileen Mary Lindsay; *m* 1963, Rosemary Gough; one *s* one *d*. *Educ:* Whitgift Sch., Croydon; St John's Coll., Oxford. Called to the Bar, Lincoln's Inn, 1961, Bencher, 1994. A Recorder, 1982–98. Mem., Criminal Injuries Compensation Bd, 1988. *Clubs:* Garrick, MCC.

LINDSAY, Donald Dunrod, CBE 1972; *b* 27 Sept. 1910; *s* of Dr Colin Dunrod Lindsay, Pres. BMA 1938, and Mrs Isabel Baynton Lindsay; *m* 1936, Violet Geraldine Fox; one *s* one *d*. *Educ:* Clifton Coll., Bristol; Trinity Coll., Oxford. Asst Master, Manchester Gram. Sch., 1932; Asst Master, Repton Sch., 1935; temp. seconded to Bristol Univ. Dept of Education as lecturer in History, 1938; Senior History Master, Repton Sch., 1938–42; Headmaster: Portsmouth Gram. Sch., 1942–53; Malvern Coll., 1953–71. Dir, Independent Schs Information Service, 1972–77. Chm., Headmasters' Conference, 1968. Governor, Harrow Sch., 1977–82. *Publications:* A Portrait of Britain Between the Exhibitions, 1952; A Portrait of Britain, 1688–1851, 1954; A Portrait of Britain Before 1066, 1962; Authority and Challenge, Europe 1300–1600, 1975; Europe and the World, 1979; Friends for Life: a portrait of Launcelot Fleming, 1981; Forgotten General, 1986; Sir Edmund Bacon: a Norfolk life, 1988; A Form of Gratitude: the life of Angela Limerick, 1992. *Recreations:* walking, theatre, music. *Address:* 29 Teme Avenue, Malvern, Worcs WR14 2XA.

LINDSAY, Rt Rev. Hugh; Bishop (RC) of Hexham and Newcastle, 1974–92; *b* 20 June 1927; *s* of William Stanley Lindsay and Mary Ann Lindsay (*née* Warren). *Educ:* St Cuthbert's Grammar Sch., Newcastle upon Tyne; Ushaw Coll., Durham. Priest 1953; Assistant Priest: St Lawrence's, Newcastle upon Tyne, 1953; St Matthew's, Ponteland, 1954; Asst Diocesan Sec., 1953–59, Diocesan Sec., 1959–69, Hexham and Newcastle; Chaplain, St Vincent's Home, West Denton, 1959–69; Auxiliary Bishop of Hexham and Newcastle and Titular Bishop of Chester-le-Street, 1969–74. *Recreations:* walking, swimming. *Address:* Boarbank Hall, Grange-over-Sands, Cumbria LA11 7NH. *T:* (015395) 35591.

LINDSAY, Sir James Harvey Kincaid Stewart, Kt 1966; Chairman, Kanbay Resources International (UK) Ltd, 1994–98; *b* 31 May 1915; *s* of Arthur Harvey Lindsay and Doris Kincaid Lindsay; *m* Marguerite Phyllis Boudville (one *s* one *d* by previous marriage). *Educ:* Highgate Sch. Joined Metal Box Co. Ltd, 1934; joined Metal Box Co. of India Ltd, 1937; Man. Dir, 1961; Chm., 1967–69; Dir of Internat. Programmes, Admin. Staff Coll., Henley-on-Thames, 1970–79. Vis. Lectr, Univ. of Buckingham, 1984–89. President: Bengal Chamber of Commerce and Industry; Associated Chambers of Commerce and Industry of India, 1965; Rotary Club of Calcutta, 1965. Director: Indian Oxygen Co., 1966; Westinghouse, Saxby Farmer Ltd, Hindusthan Pilkington, 1966. Pres., Calcutta Management Association, 1964; Pres. (and elected Life Mem., 1984), All India Management Assoc., 1964–69; Mem. of Governing Body: Indian Inst. of Management, Calcutta, 1964; Administrative Staff Coll. of India, 1965; Indian Institutes of Technology, 1966; National Council of Applied Economic Research, 1966; All-India Board of Management Studies, 1964; Indian Inst. of Foreign Trade, 1965; Member: BoT, Central Adv. Council of Industries, Direct Taxes Adv. Cttee, 1966; National Council on Vocational and Allied Trades, 1963. Convener, Internat. Exposition of Rural Develt, 1981–85; Pres., Inst. of Cultural Affairs Internat., Brussels, 1982–89. Trustee, Inst. of Family and Environmental Research, 1971–92. Mem. Council, Inst. of Organizational Mgt, 1988–92. FInstD; FCIM (FInstM 1975); CIMgt (FBIM 1971). *Recreation:* music. *Address:* Christmas Cottage, Lower Shiplake, near Henley-on-Thames, Oxon RG9 3JT. *T:* (0118) 940 2859; *e-mail:* peglindsay@aol.com. *Club:* Institute of Directors.

LINDSAY, Hon. Sir John (Edmund Fredric), Kt 1992; **Hon. Mr Justice Lindsay;** a Judge of the High Court of Justice, Chancery Division, since 1992; *b* 16 Oct. 1935; *s* of late George Fredric Lindsay and Constance Mary Lindsay (*née* Wright); *m* 1967, Patricia Anne Bolton; three *d*. *Educ:* Ellesmere Coll.; Sidney Sussex Coll., Cambridge (BA 1959; MA). Fleet Air Arm, 1954–56; Sub-Lt, RNVR. Called to the Bar, Middle Temple, 1961, Bencher, 1987; joined Lincoln's Inn (*ad eundem*); Junior Treasury Counsel, *bona vacantia*, 1979–81; QC 1981; a Judge of the Employment Appeals Tribunal, 1996–99; Pres., Employment Appeal Tribunal, 1999–. Member: Senate of Inns of Court and Bar, 1979–82; Legal Panel, Insolvency Law Review Cttee (Cork Report), 1980–82; Insolvency Rules Adv. Cttee, 1985–92. *Address:* Royal Courts of Justice, Strand, WC2A 2LL. *Club:* Athenæum.

LINDSAY, (John) Maurice, CBE 1979; TD 1946; Consultant, The Scottish Civic Trust, since 1983 (Director, 1967–83); *b* 21 July 1918; *s* of Matthew Lindsay and Eileen Frances Brock; *m* 1946, Aileen Joyce Gordon; one *s* three *d*. *Educ:* Glasgow Acad.; Scottish National Acad. of Music (now Royal Scottish Acad. of Music, Glasgow). Drama Critic, Scottish Daily Mail, Edinburgh, 1946–47; Music Critic, The Bulletin, Glasgow, 1946–60; Prog. Controller, 1961–62, Prodn Controller, 1962–64, and Features Exec. and Chief Interviewer, 1964–67, Border Television, Carlisle. Mem., Historic Buildings Council for Scotland, 1976–87; Pres., Assoc. for Scottish Literary Studies, 1988–91; Trustee: National Heritage Meml Fund, 1980–84; New Lanark Conservation Trust, 1987–94; Hon. Vice-Pres., Scottish Envmtl Educn Council, 1984–; Hon. Sec.-Gen., Europa Nostra, 1983–91. Hon. FRIAS 1985. Hon. DLitt Glasgow, 1982. Atlantic Rockefeller Award, 1946. Editor: Scots Review, 1949–50; The Scottish Review, 1975–85. *Publications: poetry:* The Advancing Day, 1940; Perhaps To-morrow, 1941; Predicament, 1942; No Crown for Laughter: Poems, 1943; The Enemies of Love: Poems 1941–1945, 1946; Selected Poems, 1947; Hurlygush: Poems in Scots, 1948; At the Wood's Edge, 1950; Ode for St Andrews Night and Other Poems, 1951; The Exiled Heart: Poems 1941–1956, 1957; Snow Warning and Other Poems, 1962; One Later Day and Other Poems, 1964; This Business of Living, 1969; Comings and Goings: Poems, 1971; Selected Poems 1942–1972, 1973; The Run from Life, 1975; Walking Without an Overcoat, Poems 1972–76, 1977; Collected Poems, 1979; A Net to Catch the Winds and Other Poems, 1981; The French Mosquitoes' Woman and Other Diversions and Poems, 1985; Requiem for a Sexual Athlete and Other Poems and Diversions, 1988; Collected Poems 1940–1990, 1990; On the Face of It: Collected Poems, vol. 2, 1993; News of the World: last poems, 1995; Speaking Likenesses: a postscript, 1997; Worlds Apart, 2000; *prose:* A Pocket Guide to Scottish Culture, 1947; The Scottish Renaissance, 1949; The Lowlands of Scotland: Glasgow and the North, 1953, 3rd edn, 1979; Robert Burns: The Man, His Work, The Legend, 3rd edn, 1980; Dunoon: The Gem of the Clyde Coast, 1954; The Lowlands of Scotland: Edinburgh and the South, 1956, 3rd edn, 1979; Clyde Waters: Variations and Diversions on a Theme of Pleasure, 1958; The Burns Encyclopedia, 1959, 3rd edn, 1980; Killochan Castle, 1960; By Yon Bonnie Banks: A Gallimaufry, 1961; Environment: A Basic Human Right, 1968; Portrait of Glasgow, 1972, rev. edn, 1981; Robin Philipson, 1977; History of Scottish Literature, 1977, rev. edn 1992; Lowland Scottish Villages, 1980; Francis George Scott and the Scottish Renaissance, 1980; (with Anthony F. Kersting) The Buildings of Edinburgh, 1981, 2nd edn 1987; Thank You For Having Me: a personal memoir, 1983; (with Dennis Hardley) Unknown Scotland, 1984; The Castles of Scotland, 1986, rev. edn 1994; Count All Men Mortal—A History of Scottish Provident 1837–1987, 1987; Victorian and Edwardian Glasgow, 1987; Glasgow 1837, 1989; (with David Bruce) Edinburgh Past and Present, 1990; (with Joyce Lindsay) Chambers Guide to Good Scottish Gardens, 1995; Glasgow: fabric of a city, 2000; *editor:* Poetry Scotland One, Two, Three, 1943, 1945, 1946, (with Hugh MacDiarmid) Scottish Poetry Four, 1949; Sailing Tomorrow's Seas: An Anthology of New Poems, 1944; Modern Scottish Poetry: An Anthology of the Scottish Renaissance 1920–1945, 1946, 4th edn, 1986; (with Fred Urquhart) No Scottish Twilight: New Scottish Stories, 1947; Selected Poems of Sir Alexander Gray, 1948; Poems, by Sir David Lyndsay, 1948; (with Hugh MacDiarmid) Poetry Scotland Four, 1949; (with Helen Cruickshank) Selected Poems of Marion Angus, 1950; John Davidson: A Selection of His Poems, 1961; (with Edwin Morgan and George Bruce) Scottish Poetry One to Six 1966–72; (with Alexander Scott and Roderick Watson) Scottish Poetry Seven to Nine, 1974, 1976, 1977; (with R. L. Mackie) A Book of Scottish Verse, 1967, 3rd edn 1983; The Discovery of Scotland: Based on Accounts of Foreign Travellers from the 13th to the 18th centuries, 1964, 2nd edn 1979; The Eye is Delighted: Some Romantic Travellers in Scotland, 1970; Scotland: An Anthology, 1974, 2nd edn 1989; As I Remember, 1979; Scottish Comic Verse 1425–1980, 1980; (with Alexander Scott) The Comic Poems of William Tennant, 1990; Thomas Hamilton, The Youth and Manhood of Cyril Thornton, 1991; with Joyce Lindsay: The Scottish Dog, 1989; The Scottish Quotation Book, 1991; A Pleasure of Gardens, 1991; The Music Quotation Book, 1992; The Theatre and Opera Lovers' Quotation Book, 1993; A Mini-Guide to Scottish Gardens, 1994; The Robert Burns Quotation Book, 1994. *Recreations:* enjoying and adding to compact disc collection, cooking. *Address:* Park House, 104 Dumbarton Road, Bowling, Dunbartonshire G60 5BB. *T:* (01389) 606662.

LINDSAY, Maurice; *see* Lindsay, J. M.

LINDSAY, Most Rev. and Hon. Orland Ugham, OJ 1997; OD (Antigua) 1996; Archbishop of the West Indies, 1986–98; Bishop of the North-Eastern Caribbean and Aruba (formerly Antigua), 1970–98; *b* 24 March 1928; *s* of Hubert and Ida Lindsay; *m* 1959, Olga Daphne (*née* Wright); three *s*. *Educ:* Culham Coll., Oxon (Teachers' Cert.); St Peter's Coll., Jamaica; McGill Univ. BD (London) 1957. RAF, 1944–47. Teacher, Franklyn Town Govt School, Jamaica, 1949–52; Asst Master, Kingston College, 1952–53. Deacon 1956, priest 1957; Asst Curate, St Peter's Vere, Jamaica, 1956–57; Asst Master, Kingston Coll., 1958–67, Chaplain 1962–63; Priest-in-Charge, Manchioneal Cure, Jamaica, 1960; Chaplain, Jamaica Defence Force, 1963–67; Principal, Church Teachers' Coll., Mandeville, 1967–70. Sec. to Jamaica Synod, 1962–70. Hon. DD: Berkeley Divinity School at Yale, 1978; St Paul's Coll., Va, 1998; Hon. STD, Montreal Diocesan Theol Coll., 1997. *Recreations:* jazz music, photography. *Address:* Flagstaff, Crosbies, PO Box 3456, St John's, Antigua.

LINDSAY of Dowhill, Sir Ronald Alexander, 2nd Bt *cr* 1962, of Dowhill; 23rd Representer of Baronial House of Dowhill; *b* 6 Dec. 1933; *er s* of Sir Martin Lindsay of Dowhill, 1st Bt, CBE, DSO, and Joyce Lady Lindsay (*d* 1998), *d* of late Major Hon. Robert Lindsay, Royal Scots Greys; *S* father, 1981; *m* 1968, Nicoletta, *yr d* of late Captain Edgar Storich, Royal Italian Navy and late Mrs Storich; three *s* one *d*. *Educ:* Eton College; Worcester Coll., Oxford (MA). National service in Grenadier Guards (Lieut), 1952–54. Insurance broker, 1958– (chiefly Hogg Robinson, and Minets); gen. manager, UK Br., Ocaso SA, Madrid, 1980–84; Lloyd's Members' Agent, 1984–; Director: AHJ Members Agency, 1984–88; Sturge Hldgs members' agencies, 1989–93. Mem., Standing Council of the Baronetage, 1978– (Chm., 1987–89); Trustee, Baronets Charitable Trust, 1986–95 (Chm., 1990–92); Vice-Pres., Anglo-Spanish Soc., 1993– (Vice-Chm., 1985–93). Member of Queen's Body Guard for Scotland (Royal Company of Archers), 1963. FCII 1963. Encomienda, Orden de Isabel la Católica (Spain), 1988. *Heir: s* James Martin Evelyn Lindsay [*b* 11 Oct. 1968; *m* 2000, Annabel, *yr d* of Dr Peter Knight]. *Address:* 104 Edith Road, W14 9AP. *T:* (020) 7603 0278.

LINDSAY-HOGG, Sir Michael Edward, 5th Bt *cr* 1905, of Rotherfield Hall, Rotherfield, Sussex; film and theatre director; *b* 5 May 1940; *o s* of Sir Edward William Lindsay-Hogg, 4th Bt and of Geraldine Mary, *d* of E. M. Fitzgerald; *S* father, 1999; *m*

1967, Lucy Mary (marr. diss. 1971), *o d* of Donald Davies. *Films* include: Let It Be, 1970; Nasty Habits, 1977; Dr Fischer of Geneva, 1983; The Object of Beauty, 1992; Frankie Starlight, 1996; *theatre* includes: Whose Life Is It Anyway?, Mermaid, 1978, transf. NY, 1979; *television* includes: Electra, 1962; Professional Foul, 1977; (co-dir) Brideshead Revisited, 1981. *Heir:* none.

LINDSAY-SMITH, Iain-Mór; Deputy Managing Director, 1987–90, Chief Executive and Managing Director, 1991–97, and Executive Deputy Chairman, 1997–98, Lloyd's of London Press Ltd, later LLP Group Ltd; Chairman, Lloyds List, 1990–98 (Publisher, 1984–98); *b* 18 Sept. 1934; *s* of Edward Duncanson Lindsay-Smith and Margaret Wilson Anderson; *m* 1960, Carol Sara Paxman (marr. diss. 1997); one *s. Educ:* High Sch. of Glasgow; London Univ. (diploma course on Internat. Affairs). Scottish Daily Record, 1951–57; Commissioned 1st Bn Cameronians (Scottish Rifles), 1953–55; Daily Mirror, 1957–60; Foreign Editor, subseq. Features Editor, Daily Mail, 1960–71; Dep. Editor, Yorkshire Post, 1971–74; Editor, Glasgow Herald, 1974–77; Exec. Editor, The Observer, 1977–84. Lloyd's of London Press, subseq. LLP Ltd: Exec. Dir, 1984–87; Chm. and Chief Exec., Lloyd's, then LLP, Information Services Ltd, 1990–98; Chm., LLP Business Publishing Ltd, 1990–98; Director: LLP Incorporated, USA, 1985–97 (Chm., 1992–97); LLP Asia, 1989–98; LLP GmbH, Germany, 1989–96; Lloyd's Maritime Information Services Ltd, 1990–97 (Chm., 1993–97); Lloyd's Maritime Information Services Inc., USA, 1990–97 (Chm., 1992–97); Lutine Publications Ltd, 1984–97 (Chm., 1992–97); Internat. Art & Antique Loss Register Ltd, 1990–97; PPA, 1992–98; DYP Gp Ltd, 1995–98; IBJ Associates Ltd, 1995–98; Cotton Investments Ltd, 1995–98. Dir, Mercury Th., Colchester, 1990–95. Member: Little Horkesley Parish Council, 1987–91; PCC, 1985–92. FRSA 1992. *Publication:* article in Electronics and Power. *Recreations:* shooting (game and clay), playing Highland bagpipe, the outdoors. *Address:* Park View, Gardner Road, Southwold, Suffolk IP18 8HJ. *Club:* Travellers.

LINDSEY, 14th Earl of, *cr* 1626, **AND ABINGDON,** 9th Earl of, *cr* 1682; **Richard Henry Rupert Bertie;** Baron Norreys, of Rycote, 1572; *b* 28 June 1931; *o s* of Lt-Col Hon. Arthur Michael Bertie, DSO, MC (*d* 1957) and Aline Rose (*d* 1948), *er d* of George Arbuthnot-Leslie, Warthill, Co. Aberdeen, and *widow* of Hon. Charles Fox Maule Ramsay, MC; *S* cousin, 1963; *m* 1957, Norah Elizabeth Farquhar-Oliver, *yr d* of late Mark Oliver, OBE; two *s* one *d. Educ:* Ampleforth. Late Lieut, Royal Norfolk Regt. Insurance broker and underwriting agent at Lloyd's, 1958–92. Chm., Dawes and Henderson (Agencies) Ltd, 1988–92. Chm., Anglo-Ivory-Coast Soc., 1974–77. High Steward of Abingdon, 1963–. *Heir: s* Lord Norreys, *qv. Address:* Gilmilnscroft House, Sorn, Mauchline, Ayrshire KA5 6ND. *Clubs:* Turf, Pratt's.

LINE, Frances Mary, (Mrs James Lloyd), OBE 1996; Controller, BBC Radio 2, 1990–96; *b* 22 Feb. 1940; *d* of Charles Edward Line and Leoni Lucy Line (*née* Hendriks); *m* 1972, James Richard Beilby Lloyd. *Educ:* James Allen's Girls' Sch., Dulwich. Joined BBC as clerk/typist, 1957; Sec. in TV and Radio, 1959–67; Radio 2 producer, 1967–73; senior producer, 1973–79; Chief Assistant: Radio 2, 1979–83; Radio 4, 1983–85; Head, Radio 2 Music Dept, 1985–89. Vice-President: Eastbourne Soc.; Eastbourne Br., Age Concern. Hon. Fellow, Radio Acad., 1996. *Recreations:* visual arts, travel, happy snaps. *Address:* 13 Naomi Close, Eastbourne, E Sussex BN20 7UU. *Club:* Royal Commonwealth Society.

LINE, Matthew John Bardsley; Editor, Homes & Gardens, since 1997; *b* 22 April 1958; *s* of John Line and Jill Line (*née* Rowland); *m* 1987, Elinor Jane Fairhurst; two *d. Educ:* Chiswick Sch.; Exeter Univ. (BA Hons Drama). Actor, 1982; Asst Publisher, Shepheard-Walwyn Publishers, 1984–87; Production Dir, Concertina Publications, 1988; freelance journalist, 1987–92; Editor: Up Country, 1992–93; Dialogue, 1993–95; Launch Editor, Colour, 1995; Gp Editor, home interest titles, Redwood Publishing, 1996–97. *Recreations:* family, gardening, philosophy. *Address:* IPC, King's Reach Tower, Stamford Street, SE1 9LS. *T:* (020) 7261 5678.

LINE, Maurice Bernard, MA; FRSA; FLA, FIInfSc; CIMgt; Director General (Science, Technology and Industry), British Library, 1985–88 (Deputy Director General, 1973–74, Director General, 1974–85, Lending Division); *b* 21 June 1928; *s* of Bernard Cyril and Ruth Florence Line; *m* 1954, Joyce Gilchrist; one *s* one *d. Educ:* Bedford Sch.; Exeter Coll., Oxford (MA). Library Trainee, Bodleian Library, 1950–51; Library Asst, Glasgow Univ., 1951–53; Sub-Librarian, Southampton Univ., 1954–65; Dep. Librarian, Univ. of Newcastle upon Tyne, 1965–68; Librarian, Univ. of Bath, 1968–71; Librarian, Nat. Central Library, 1971–73; Project Head, DES Nat. Libraries ADP Study, 1970–71. Prof. Associate, Sheffield Univ., 1977–; External Prof., Loughborough Univ., 1986–92. Member: Library Adv. Council for England, 1972–75; British Library Board, 1974–88; Pres., Library Assoc., 1990. Editor, Alexandria, 1988–; Gen. Editor, Librarianship and Information Work Worldwide, 1990–2000. Mem. Bd of Dirs, Engineering Information Inc., 1990–98. Fellow, Birmingham Polytech., 1992. Hon. DLitt Heriot Watt, 1980; Hon. DSc Southampton, 1988. *Publications:* A Bibliography of Russian Literature in English Translation to 1900, 1963; Library Surveys, 1967, 2nd edn 1982; (ed jtly) Essays on Information and Libraries, 1975; (ed with Joyce Line) National Libraries, 1979; (jtly) Universal Availability of Publications, 1983; (jtly) Improving the Availability of Publications, 1984; (ed) The World of Books and Information, 1987; (ed with Joyce Line) National Libraries II, 1987; (jtly) The Impact of New Technology on Document Availability and Access, 1988; Line on Interlending, 1988; A Little Off Line, 1988; (ed) Academic Library Management, 1990; (ed with Joyce Line) National Libraries III, 1995; contribs to: Jl of Documentation; Aslib Proc.; Jl of Librarianship and Information Science, etc. *Recreations:* music, walking, other people. *Address:* 10 Blackthorn Lane, Burn Bridge, Harrogate, North Yorks HG3 1NZ. *T:* (01423) 872984.

LINEHAN, Anthony John; President, Construction Health & Safety Group, since 1993; *b* 27 June 1931; *s* of Daniel and Ada Linehan; *m* 1955, Oonagh Patricia FitzPatrick; two *s* two *d. Educ:* Bristol Univ. (BA Hons 1952). Short Service Commission, RN, 1953–57. HM Factory Inspectorate: joined 1958; HM District Inspector, 1969; Labour Adviser, Hong Kong Govt, 1973–76; Health and Safety Executive: HQ, 1976–79; Area Dir, Wales, 1979–84; HM Dep. Chief Inspector of Factories, 1984–88; Chief Inspector of Factories, 1988–92; Dir of Field Ops, 1990–92. *Recreations:* walking, reading, watching Rugby. *Address:* 2 Brookside Manor, Leigh Road, Wimborne, Dorset BH21 2BZ. *T:* (01202) 848597.

LINEHAN, Stephen; QC 1993; a Recorder, since 1990; *b* 12 March 1947; *s* of Maurice Gerald Linehan and Mary Joyce (*née* Norrish); *m* 1976, Victoria Maria Rössler; one *s. Educ:* Mount St Mary's Coll., Spinkhill, Derbys; King's Coll., London (LLB Hons). Called to the Bar, Lincoln's Inn, 1970, Bencher, 1999. *Address:* 5 Fountain Court, Steelhouse Lane, Birmingham B4 6DR. *T:* (0121) 606 0500.

LINEKER, Gary Winston, OBE 1992; journalist and broadcaster; professional footballer, 1976–94; *b* 30 Nov. 1960; *s* of Barry and Margaret Lineker; *m* 1986, Michelle Cockayne; four *s.* Football Clubs played for: Leicester City, 1976–85; Everton, 1985–86; Barcelona, 1986–89; Tottenham Hotspur, 1989–92; Nagoya Grampus 8, 1993–94; England team, 1984–92: Captain, 1990–92; 80 appearances, 48 goals. Freeman, City of Leicester, 1995. Hon. MA: Loughborough, 1992; Leicester, 1992. *Recreations:* golf, cricket, snooker. *Address:* c/o SFX Sports Group, 35/36 Grosvenor Street, W1K 4QX. *T:* (020) 7529 4300. *Clubs:* Groucho, MCC.

LINES, (Walter) Moray, CBE 1969; Chairman, Lines Brothers Ltd, 1962–71 (Joint Managing Director, 1962–70); *b* 26 Jan. 1922; *er s* of late Walter Lines; *m* 1955, Fiona Margaret Denton; three *s* one *d. Educ:* Gresham Sch. Joined Board of Lines Bros Ltd, 1946; Chm., British Toy Manufacturers Assoc., 1968–70. *Address:* Stable Cottage, Shirwell, near Barnstaple, N Devon EX31 4JU. *T:* (01271) 850265.

LINFORD, Alan C.; *see* Carr Linford.

LING, Jeffrey, CMG 1991; HM Diplomatic Service, retired; Chairman and Chief Executive, Dean & Drysdale Ltd, since 1999; *b* 9 Sept. 1939; *s* of Frank Cecil Ling and Mary Irene Nixon; *m* 1967, Margaret Anne Tatton; one *s. Educ:* Bristol Univ. BSc (Hons); FInstP; FIMgt; FBCS. FCO, 1966–69; Private Sec. to HM Ambassador, Washington, 1969–71; First Sec., Washington, 1971–73; Perm. Delegn to OECD, Paris, 1973–77; FCO, 1977–79; on secondment as Special Adviser to HM the Sultan of Brunei, 1979–82; Counsellor (Technology), Paris, 1982–86; Dir of Res., FCO, 1986–89; Asst Under-Sec. of State and Dir of Communications, subseq. of Information Systems, FCO, 1989–96; Dir Gen., Trade and Inward Investment in US, and Consul-Gen., NY, 1996–99. Dir (non-exec.), RTZ Borax and Minerals, 1991–96; Mem., Internat. Adv. Bd, Buchanan Ingersoll, 2000–; Special Advr to Chm. and CEO, Maxim Pharmaceuticals, 2000–; Advisor: to CEO of Basepoint plc; Cedar Gp plc; Bd, E-Lynxx Corp.; Chm., Soho 4 Associates. Chm., London New York City Alliance, 2000–01. *Recreations:* travel, old cars. *Address:* 26 The Ridings, Epsom, Surrey KT18 5JJ.

LING, John de Courcy; *see* de Courcy Ling.

LING, Norman Arthur; HM Diplomatic Service; High Commissioner to Malaŵi, since 2001; *b* 12 Aug. 1952; *s* of late William Arthur Ling and of Helma Ling (*née* Blum); *m* 1979, Selma Osman. *Educ:* Sheffield Univ. (BA Hons German and Econ. Hist.). British Commercial Transport, 1975–76; Ocean Transport and Trading, 1976–78; joined Diplomatic Service, 1978; FCO, 1978–80; Second Sec., Tripoli, 1980–81; Second, later First, Sec., British Interests Section, Tehran, 1981–84; FCO, 1984–88; Dep. Consul Gen., Johannesburg, 1988–92; Dep. Head of Mission, Ankara, 1993–97; Head, Aviation, Maritime Sci. and Energy Dept, FCO, 1997–2001. *Recreations:* travel, walking, organic farming. *Address:* c/o Foreign and Commonwealth Office, King Charles Street, SW1A 2AH.

LING, Prof. Roger John, PhD; FSA; Professor of Classical Art and Archaeology, University of Manchester, since 1992; *b* 13 Nov. 1942; *s* of Leslie James Ling and Kathleen Clara Ling (*née* Childs); *m* 1967, Lesley Ann Steer. *Educ:* Watford Grammar Sch.; St John's Coll., Cambridge (BA 1964; MA 1969; PhD 1970). FSA 1979. Lectr in Classics, UC of Swansea, 1967–71; University of Manchester: Lectr in History of Art, 1971–75; Sen. Lectr, 1975–83; Reader, 1983–92; Head of Dept of Hist. of Art, 1988–91. British Acad. Res. Reader, 1991–93; Balsdon Sen. Res. Fellow, British Sch. at Rome, 1994–95. *Publications:* The Greek World, 1976, 2nd edn as Classical Greece, 1988; (jtly) Wall Painting in Roman Britain, 1982; (ed) Cambridge Ancient History, vol. VII.1, 1984; Romano-British Wall Painting, 1985; Roman Painting, 1991; The Insula of the Menander at Pompeii I: the structures, 1997; Ancient Mosaics, 1998; Stuccowork and Painting in Roman Italy, 1999; (ed) Making Classical Art: process and practice, 2000; numerous articles in learned jls. *Recreations:* playing squash, watching football. *Address:* Department of Art History and Archaeology, University of Manchester, Manchester M13 9PL. *T:* (0161) 275 3320.

LINGARD, Joan Amelia, MBE 1998; author, since 1963; *b* 1932; *d* of Henry James Lingard; *m* Martin Birkhans; three *d. Educ:* Bloomfield Collegiate Sch., Belfast; Moray House Coll. of Educn (Gen. Teaching Cert.). *Publications: novels:* Liam's Daughter, 1963; The Prevailing Wind, 1964; The Tide Comes In, 1966; The Headmaster, 1967; A Sort of Freedom, 1968; The Lord on Our Side, 1970; The Second Flowering of Emily Mountjoy; Greenyards; Reasonable Doubts, 1979; The Women's House, 1981; Sisters by Rite, 1984; After Colette, 1993 (Scottish Arts Council Award); Dreams of Love and Modest Glory, 1995; *children's novels:* The Twelfth Day of July, 1970; Frying as Usual, 1971; Across the Barricades, 1972 (Buxtehude Bülle, 1986); Into Exile, 1973; The Clearance, 1973; A Proper Place; The Resettling; Hostages to Fortune; The Pilgrimage, 1975; The Reunion, 1977; Snake among the Sunflowers, 1977; The Gooseberry, 1978; The File on Fraulein Berg, 1980; Strangers in the House, 1981; The Winter Visitor, 1983; The Freedom Machine, 1986; The Guilty Party, 1987; Rags and Riches, 1988; Tug of War, 1989; Glad Rags, 1990; Between Two Worlds, 1991; Secrets and Surprises, 1991; Hands off Our School, 1992; Night Fires, 1993; Clever Clive and Loopy Lucy, 1993; Slo Flo and Boomerang Bill, 1994; Sulky Suzy and Jittery Jack, 1995; Lizzie's Leaving, 1996; Morag and the Lamb, 1996; Dark Shadows, 1998; A Secret Place, 1998; Tom and the Tree House, 1998 (Scottish Arts Council Award); Can You Find Sammy the Hamster?, 1998; The Egg Thieves, 1999; River Eyes, 2000; Natasha's Will, 2000; The Same Only Different, 2000. *Recreations:* reading, walking, travelling. *Address:* c/o David Higham Associates, 5/8 Lower John Street, Golden Square, W1R 4HA. *T:* (020) 7437 7888. *Club:* Lansdowne.

LINGARD, (Peter) Anthony, CBE 1977; TD; Director General, St John Ambulance Association, 1978–82; *b* 29 Feb. 1916; *s* of late Herbert Arthur Lingard and Kate Augusta Burdett; *m* 1946, Enid Nora Argile; two *d. Educ:* Berkhamsted Sch.; London Univ. (BCom). Served RA, 1939–46; Major, 1941 (despatches twice). Co. of London Electric Supply Gp, 1936; Area Manager Lambeth and Camberwell, County Group, 1947; Commercial Officer, S Western Sub-Area, 1948, Chief Commercial Officer, 1959–62, London Electricity Board; Commercial and Development Adviser, Electricity Council, 1962–65; Mem., Electricity Council, 1965–77; Chm., E Midlands Electricity Bd, 1972–77. Member: CEGB, 1972–75; Directing Cttee, Internat. Union of Producers and Distributors of Electrical Energy, 1973–77. County Dir, Suffolk, St John Ambulance, 1982–85. Member until 1977: Ct of Governors, Admin. Staff Coll.; Council, IEE; Council of Industrial Soc.; E Midlands Econ. Planning Council; Mem. Nottingham Univ. Ct, 1975–77. CompIEE 1967. FIMgt (FBIM 1973). KStJ. *Recreations:* photography, painting, golf, fly-fishing, reading. *Address:* The Dumble, High Street, Orford, Woodbridge, Suffolk IP12 2NW. *T:* (01394) 450622. *Clubs:* Army and Navy; Orford Sailing (Pres.); Aldeburgh Yacht, Aldeburgh Golf.

LINGARD, Robin Anthony; owner/manager, Kinnairdie Consulting, since 1997; *b* 19 July 1941; *s* of late Cecil Lingard and Lucy Lingard; *m* 1968, Margaret Lucy Virginia Elsden; two *d. Educ:* Felsted School; Emmanuel College, Cambridge (Exhibnr, MA). Min. of Aviation, 1963–66; Min. of Technology, 1966–70 (Private Sec. to Jt Parly Sec., 1966–68); DTI, 1971–74; DoI, 1974–83, Asst Sec., 1976; Under Sec., DTI, 1984, Cabinet Office (Enterprise Unit), 1984–85; Hd, Small Firms and Tourism Div., Dept of

Employment, 1985–87; Mem. Bd, Highlands and Islands Develt Bd, 1988–91; Dir of Trng and Social Develt, 1991–93, Dir of Highlands and Is Univ. Project, 1993–97, Highlands and Islands Enterprise. Member: NEDC Sector Gp for Tourism and Leisure Industries, 1987–92; Scottish Tourist Bd, 1988–92; Management Bd, Prince's Trust and Royal Jubilee Trusts, 1989–95; Chairman: Highlands, Orkney and Western Isles Cttee, Prince's Trust, 1992–98; YouthLink Scotland, 1997–; BBC Scotland Appeals Adv. Cttee, 1998–. FTS 1988. *Recreations:* reading, walking, watching birds, aviation history, dinghy sailing. *Address:* Kinnairdie House, Dingwall, Ross-shire IV15 9LL. *T:* (01349) 861044.

LINGS, Dr Martin; Keeper Emeritus of Oriental Manuscripts and Printed Books, British Library; *b* 24 Jan. 1909; *e s* of late George Herbert Lings and late Gladys Mary Lings (*née* Greenhalgh), Burnage, Lancs; *m* 1944, Lesley, 3rd *d* of late Edgar Smalley. *Educ:* Clifton Coll.; Magdalen Coll., Oxford; Sch. of Oriental and African Studies, Univ. of London. Class. Mods 1930, BA English 1932, MA 1937, Oxon; BA Arabic 1954, PhD 1959, London. Lectr in Anglo-Saxon and Middle English, Univ. of Kaunas, 1935–39; Lectr in English Lit., Univ. of Cairo, 1940–51; Asst Keeper, Dept of Oriental Printed Books and Manuscripts, British Museum, 1955–70; Deputy Keeper, 1970; Keeper, 1971; seconded to the British Library, 1973. FRAS. *Publications:* The Book of Certainty, 1952 (trans. Spanish, Turkish and French); (with A. S. Fulton) Second Supplementary Catalogue of Arabic Printed Books in the British Museum, 1959; A Moslem Saint of the Twentieth Century, 1961 (trans. French and Arabic); Ancient Beliefs and Modern Superstitions, 1965 (trans. Turkish, Portuguese, French, German and Greek); Shakespeare in the Light of Sacred Art, 1966; The Elements and Other Poems, 1967; The Heralds and Other Poems, 1970; A Sufi Saint of the Twentieth Century, 1971 (trans. Urdu, Persian, Spanish, Turkish, German and French); What is Sufism?, (trans. French, Italian, Spanish, German, Portuguese and Bosnian); (with Y. H. Safadi) Third Supplementary Catalogue of Arabic Printed Books in the British Library, 1976; (with Y. H. Safadi) The Qur'ān, Catalogue of an Exhibition at the British Library, 1976; The Quranic Art of Calligraphy and Illumination, 1977 (trans. Persian); Muhammad: his life based on the earliest sources, 1983 (trans. French, Urdu, Tamil, Spanish, Arabic, Dutch, Bosnian, German and Italian); The Secret of Shakespeare, 1984 (trans. Italian, Spanish, Persian, Greek and French); The Eleventh Hour, 1987 (trans. German and French); Collected Poems, 1987; Symbol and Archetype: studies in the meaning of existence, 1990 (trans. French); The Sacred Art of Shakespeare, 1998; Summits of Qur'ān Calligraphy and Illumination, 2001 (trans. German and French); contrib. Encycl. Britannica, Encycl. Islam, Studies in Comparative Religion, Cambridge History of Arabic Literature, etc. *Recreations:* walking, gardening, music. *Address:* 3 French Street, Westerham, Kent TN16 1PN. *T:* (01959) 562855.

LINKIE, William Sinclair, CBE 1989; Controller, Inland Revenue (Scotland), 1983–90; *b* 9 March 1931; *s* of late Peter Linkie and of Janet Black Linkie (*née* Sinclair; she *m* 2nd, John McBryde); *m* 1955, Elizabeth Primrose Marion (*née* Reid); one *s* one *d*. *Educ:* George Heriot's Sch., Edinburgh. Dept of Agriculture and Fisheries for Scotland, 1948; Inland Revenue (Scotland), 1952–90: HM Inspector of Taxes, 1961; Dist Inspector, Edinburgh 6, 1964; Principal Inspector i/c Centre I, 1975; Dist Inspector, Edinburgh 5, 1982. Pres., Inland Revenue Sports Assoc. (Scotland), 1983–90. Elder, Church of Scotland. *Recreations:* golf, painting, choral singing.

LINKLATER, family name of **Baroness Linklater of Butterstone**.

LINKLATER OF BUTTERSTONE, Baroness *cr* 1997 (Life Peer), of Riemore in Perth and Kinross; **Veronica Linklater;** Founder and Executive Chairman, The New School, Butterstone, since 1991; *b* 15 April 1943; *d* of late Lt-Col A. M. Lyle, OBE, and Hon. Elizabeth Lyle, *y d* of 1st Viscount Thurso, KT, CMG, PC; *m* 1967, Magnus Duncan Linklater, *qv*; two *s* one *d*. *Educ:* Cranborne Chase Sch.; Univ. of Sussex; Univ. of London (DipSoc). Child Care Officer, LB of Tower Hamlets, 1967–68; Governor, three Islington schs, 1970–85; Co-Founder, Visitors' Centre, Pentonville Prison, 1971–77; Winchester prison project, Prison Reform Trust, 1981–82; Founder, Administrator, then Consultant, The Butler Trust, 1983–87 (Trustee, 1987–); Trustee: Esmée Fairbairn Charitable Trust, 1991–; Young Musicians Trust, 1993–97; Develt Trust, Univ. of Highlands and Is, 1999–; Dir, Maggie Keswick Jencks Cancer Caring Centres Trust, 1997–. Member: Children's Panel, Edinburgh S, 1989–97; Beattie Cttee on post-sch. provision for young people with special needs in Scotland, 1998–99. Co-ordinator, Trustee and Vice Chm., Pushkin Prizes (Scotland), 1989–; Mem. Cttee, Gulliver Award for Performing Arts in Scotland, 1990–96. Pres., Soc. of Friends of Dunkeld Cathedral, 1989–. Patron: Sutherland Trust, 1993–; Airborne Initiative, 1998–; Nat. Schizophrenia Fellowship Scotland, 2000–; Foundn Patron, Queen Margaret UC, Edinburgh, 1998–; Appeal Patron, Hopetoun House Preservation Trust, 2001–. Contested (Lib Dem) Perth and Kinross, May 1995. JP Inner London, 1985–88. *Recreations:* music, theatre, gardening. *Address:* 5 Drummond Place, Edinburgh EH3 6PH. *T:* (0131) 557 5705, *Fax:* (0131) 557 9757; *e-mail:* v.linklater@talk21.com.

LINKLATER, Magnus Duncan; journalist; Chairman, Scottish Arts Council, 1996–2001; *b* 21 Feb. 1942; *s* of late Eric Robert Linklater, CBE, TD, and Marjorie MacIntyre; *m* 1967, Veronica Lyle (*see* Baroness Linklater of Butterstone); two *s* one *d*. *Educ:* Eton Coll.; Freiburg Univ.; Sorbonne; Trinity Hall, Cambridge (BA 2nd Cl. Hons (Mod. Lang.)). Reporter, Daily Express, Manchester, 1965–66; Diary Reporter, London Evening Standard, 1966–67; Editor: Londoner's Diary, Evening Standard, 1967–69; 'Spectrum', Sunday Times, 1969–72; Sunday Times Colour Magazine, 1972–75; Assistant Editor: News, Sunday Times, 1975–79; Features, Sunday Times, 1979–81; Exec. Editor (Features), Sunday Times, 1981–83; Man. Editor (News), The Observer, 1983–86; Editor: London Daily News, 1987; The Scotsman, 1988–94; columnist: The Times, 1994–; Scotland on Sunday, 1998–; broadcaster, Radio Scotland, 1994–97. Mem., Scottish Cultural Strategy Gp, 1999–2000. Chm., Edinburgh Book Fest., 1995–96. Hon. DArts Napier, 1994; Hon. LLD Aberdeen, 1997; Hon. DLitt Glasgow, 2001. *Publications:* (with Stephen Fay and Lewis Chester) Hoax—The Inside Story of the Howard Hughes/Clifford Irving Affair, 1972; (with Lewis Chester and David May) Jeremy Thorpe: a secret life, 1979; Massacre: the story of Glencoe, 1982; (with the Sunday Times Insight Team) The Falklands War, 1982; (with Isabel Hilton and Neal Ascherson) The Fourth Reich—Klaus Barbie and the Neo-Fascist Connection, 1984; (with Douglas Corrance) Scotland, 1984; (contrib.) A Scottish Childhood, 1985; (with David Leigh) Not With Honour: inside story of the Westland Scandal, 1986; (with Christian Hesketh) For King and Conscience: the life of John Graham of Claverhouse, Viscount Dundee, 1989; (ed jtly) Anatomy of Scotland, 1992; (with Colin Prior) Highland Wilderness, 1993; People in a Landscape, 1997. *Recreations:* cricket, fishing, book-collecting. *Address:* 5 Drummond Place, Edinburgh EH3 6PH. *T:* (0131) 557 5705. *Club:* MCC.

LINLEY, Viscount; David Albert Charles Armstrong-Jones; *b* 3 Nov. 1961; *s* and *heir* of 1st Earl of Snowdon, *qv*, and *s* of HRH the Princess Margaret; *m* 1993, Hon. Serena Alleyne Stanhope, *o d* of Viscount Petersham, *qv*; one *s*. *Educ:* Bedales; Parnham School for Craftsmen in Wood. Designer and Cabinet maker; Chairman: David Linley Furniture Ltd, 1985–; David Linley & Company Ltd, 1998–. Vogue-Sotheby's Cecil Beaton Award for portrait photograph, 1983. *Publications:* Classical Furniture, 1993, 2nd edn 1998; Extraordinary Furniture, 1996; Design and Detail in the Home, 2000. *Heir: s* Hon. Charles Patrick Inigo Armstrong-Jones, *b* 1 July 1999. *Address:* Linley, 60 Pimlico Road, SW1W 8LP.

See under Royal Family.

LINLITHGOW, 4th Marquess of, *cr* 1902; **Adrian John Charles Hope;** Bt (NS) 1698; Baron Hope, Viscount Aithrie, Earl of Hopetoun 1703 (Scot.); Baron Hopetoun 1809 (UK); Baron Niddry 1814 (UK); Stockbroker; *b* 1 July 1946; *s* of 3rd Marquess of Linlithgow, MC, TD, and Vivienne (*d* 1963), *d* of Capt. R. O. R. Kenyon-Slaney and of Lady Mary Gilmour; *S* father, 1987; *m* 1st, 1968, Anne (marr. diss. 1978), *e d* of A. Leveson, Hall Place, Hants; two *s*; 2nd, 1980, Peta C. Binding (marr. diss. 1997); one *s* one *d*; 3rd, 1997, Auriol Mackeson-Sandbach, former wife of Sir John Ropner, *qv*. *Educ:* Eton. Joined HM Navy, 1965. *Heir: s* Earl of Hopetoun, *qv*. *Address:* Hopetoun House, South Queensferry, West Lothian EH30 9SL. *T:* (0131) 331 1169. *Club:* White's.

LINNANE, Prof. Anthony William, AM 1995; FAA; FRS 1980; FTSE; Director, Centre for Molecular Biology and Medicine, since 1983; Professor of Biochemistry, Monash University, Australia, 1965–94, Emeritus Professor, since 1996; *b* 17 July 1930; *s* of late W. Linnane, Sydney; *m* 1956, Judith Neil (marr. diss. 1980); one *s* one *d*; *m* 1980, Daryl, *d* of A. Skurrie. *Educ:* Sydney Boys' High School; Sydney Univ. (PhD, DSc); Univ. of Wisconsin, USA. Lecturer, then Senior Lectr, Sydney Univ., 1958–62; Reader, Monash Univ., Aust., 1962–65. Visiting Prof., Univ. of Wisconsin, 1976. President: Aust. Biochemical Soc., 1974–76; Fedn of Asian and Oceanic Biochemical Socs, 1975–77; 12th Internat. Congress of Biochemistry, 1982; Treasurer, Internat. Union of Biochemistry and Molecular Biol., 1988–97; Founder and Dir, Australian Soc. for Cellular and Molecular Gerontology. Work concerned especially with the biogenesis and genetics of mitochondria, mucinous cancers and the human ageing process. Editor-in-Chief, Biochemistry and Molecular Biol. Internat., 1988–97. *Publications:* Autonomy and Biogenesis of Mitochondria and Chloroplasts, 1971; over 300 contributions to learned journals. *Address:* Centre for Molecular Biology and Medicine, Epworth Hospital, 2nd Floor, 185–187 Hoddle Street, Richmond, Vic 3121, Australia. *T:* (3) 94264200, *Fax:* (3) 94264201; *e-mail:* tlinnane@cmbm.com.au; 24 Myrtle Road, Canterbury, Vic 3126, Australia. *Clubs:* Athenæum; Moonee Valley Race; VRC; VATC.

LINNARD, Robert Wynne; Director of Railways, Department for Transport, Local Government and the Regions (formerly of the Environment, Transport and the Regions), since 1999; *b* 18 June 1953; *s* of late John Adrian Linnard and Gwenita Linnard (*née* Johns); *m* 1974, Sally Judith Gadsden; three *s* three *d*. *Educ:* Dulwich Coll. Entered Civil Service, DoE, 1973; Principal, Dept of Transport, 1984–91; Asst Sec., 1991–99. *Recreations:* family, labradors, walking. *Address:* Department for Transport, Local Government and the Regions, Great Minster House, 76 Marsham Street, SW1P 4DR.

LINNELL, Andrew John, FRGS; Head Master, Reading School, since 1997; *b* 28 June 1956; *s* of Cyril Barrie Linnell and Maureen (*née* Goodyear); *m* 1989, Juliet, *d* of Prof. Oswald Hanfling and Helga Hanfling; one *s* one *d*. *Educ:* Wolstanton Grammar Sch., Staffs; Univ. of Salford (BSc); Univ. of Keele (PGCE). FRGS 1983; ACP 1988. Teacher, Howard Sch., Gillingham, Kent, 1979–86; Educn Officer, Kent CC, 1986–92; Dep. Headteacher, St Joseph Williamson's Mathematical Sch., Rochester, 1992–97. *Recreations:* jogging, swimming, cycling, travelling. *Address:* Reading School, Reading, Berks RG1 5LW. *T:* (0118) 901 5600.

LINNELL, David George Thomas, CBE 1987; Chairman, 1993–96, Deputy Chairman, 1996–98, Hiscox Dedicated Insurance Fund plc, later Hiscox plc; *b* 28 May 1930; *s* of George and Marguerite Linnell; *m* 1953, Margaret Mary Paterson; one *s* one *d*. *Educ:* Leighton Park School, Reading. Managing Dir, Thomas Linnell & Sons, 1964–75; Chief Exec., Linfood Holdings, 1975–79; Chm., Spar Food Holdings, 1975–81; Chm., Eggs Authority, 1981–86; Chairman: Neighbourhood Stores, 1983–87; Birkdale Group, 1987–95; Kendell, 1994–97. Pres., Inst. of Grocery Distribution, 1980–82. Gov., St Andrew's Hosp., Northampton, 1992–. *Address:* The Old Rectory, Titchmarsh, Kettering, Northants NN14 3DG. *Club:* Carlton.

LINSTEAD, Stephen Guy; Director, Department of Trade and Industry, West Midlands Region, 1990–94; *b* 23 June 1941; *s* of late George Frederick Linstead and of May Dorothy Linstead (*née* Griffiths); *m* 1st, 1971 (marr. diss.); two *s*; 2nd, 1982, Rachael Marian Feldman; two *d*. *Educ:* King Edward VII Sch., Sheffield; Corpus Christi Coll., Oxford (MA Mod. Hist.; Dip. Public and Social Admin.); Carleton Univ., Ottawa (MA Political Sci.). Board of Trade, 1964–76 (Private Sec. to Minister of State, 1967–69); Principal, 1969; Asst Sec., Dept of Prices and Consumer Protection, 1976–79; Dept of Trade, 1979–82; Office of Fair Trading, 1982–90; Under-Sec., DTI, 1990–94. Mem. Steering Gp, Industry '96, 1994–96. Vice-Chm., Assoc. of First Div. Civil Servants, 1982–84. Member: Exec. Cttee, Solihull Chamber of Commerce and Industry, 1996– (Vice-Pres., 2000–); Oversight Cttee, United Coll. of the Ascension, Selly Oak, 1996–. Reader, dio. of Birmingham, 1991–. *Publication:* contrib. Ottawa Law Review. *Recreations:* biblical criticism, swimming, travel, entertainment. *Address:* 20 Silhill Hall Road, Solihull, W Midlands B91 1JU. *T:* and *Fax:* (0121) 705 1376. *Club:* Royal Over-Seas League.

LINTON, Alan Henry Spencer, LVO 1969; HM Diplomatic Service, retired; Consul-General, Detroit, USA, 1976–79; *b* Nottingham, 24 July 1919; *s* of Rt Rev. James Henry Linton, DD and Alicia Pears (*née* Aldous); *m* 1959, Kaethe Krebs (*d* 1990); four *d*. *Educ:* St Lawrence, Ramsgate; Magdalen Coll., Oxford (MA). Served War, RA, 1940–46. HM Overseas Civil Service, Tanganyika, 1947–62; FO, 1963–65; First Sec. (Inf.), Vienna, 1965–69; Head of Chancery, Lusaka, Zambia, 1970–73; First Sec. (Commercial), Kingston, Jamaica, 1973–75; Dep. High Comr, Kingston, 1975–76. *Recreations:* walking, photography. *Address:* 29 The Avenue, Poole BH13 6LH.

LINTON, (John) Martin; MP (Lab) Battersea, since 1997; *b* 11 Aug. 1944; *s* of Sydney and Karin Linton; *m* 1975, Kathleen Stanley (*d* 1995); two *d*. *Educ:* Christ's Hosp.; Pembroke Coll., Oxford (MA). Journalist: Daily Mail, 1966–71; Labour Weekly, 1971–79; Daily Star, 1979–81; The Guardian, 1981–97. Mem. (Lab), Wandsworth LBC, 1971–82. PPS to Minister for the Arts, 2001–. Member: Home Affairs Select Cttee, 1997–2001; Admin Cttee, 2001–. *Publications:* The Swedish Road to Socialism, 1974; Guardian Guide to the House of Commons, 1992; Money and Votes, 1994; Was It the Sun Wot Won It?, 1995; Guardian Election Guide, 1997; Making Votes Count, 1998; Beyond 2002: long-term policies for Labour, 1999. *Recreations:* playing music, watching football. *Address:* (office) 177 Lavender Hill, Battersea, SW11 5TE. *T:* (020) 7223 5306; House of Commons, SW1A 0AA. *T:* (020) 7219 4619.

LINTOTT, Robert Edward, FInstPet; Chief Executive, Coverdale Organisation, 1987–91; *b* 14 Jan. 1932; *s* of Charles Edward and Doris Mary Lintott; *m* 1958, Mary Alice Scott; three *s*. *Educ:* Cambridgeshire High School; Trinity College, Cambridge. BA Nat. Scis 1955, MA. Served RAF, 1950–52 (Flying Officer); joined Esso Petroleum Co. Ltd, 1955; Corporate Planning Dept, Exxon Corp., 1975–78; Exec. Asst to Chm., Exxon Corp., 1978–79; Director: Esso Petroleum Co. Ltd, 1979–84; Esso Pension Trust,

1979–87; Esso Exploration & Production UK, 1984–87; Esso UK plc, Esso Petroleum, 1984–87 (Man. Dir, 1984–86); Matthew Hall Engineering Holdings Ltd, 1987–89; CSM Parly Consultants Ltd, 1995–; MLD (Hong Kong) Ltd, 1995–; Chairman: Irish Refining Co., 1979–82; Esso Teoranta, 1982–84. Vice-Pres., UK Petroleum Industry Assoc., 1985–86; Pres., Oil Industries Club, 1986–88. Mem., Standards Bd, BSI, 1991–2000. Council Mem., 1979–, and Chm. Exec. Cttee, 1987–, Foundn for Management Educn; Member: Council for Management Educn and Develt, 1989–2000; Steering Cttee, Oxford Summer Business Sch., 1979–94 (Chm., 1987–91); Council, Manchester Business Sch., 1985–92. Councillor, Royal Bor. of Windsor and Maidenhead, 1987–91. Chm. of Govs, Queen's Coll. Taunton, 1994–. *Recreations:* cricket, vintage and modern motoring. *Address:* Huish Barton, Watchet, Somerset TA23 0LU. *T:* (01984) 640208. *Clubs:* Royal Air Force, MCC.

LION, Jacques Kenneth, OBE 1979; President, The London Metal Exchange Ltd, 1987–91; *b* 18 Dec. 1922; *s* of Felix J. Lion and Ethel (*née* Myers); *m* 1947, Jean Elphinstone (*née* Mackenzie); two *s* one *d*. *Educ:* St Paul's Sch. Sen. Partner, 1969–86, Chm., 1986–90, Philipp & Lion (Holdings) Ltd. Pres., Non-Ferrous Div., Bureau Internationale de la Récupération, 1970–74; Mem. Council, British Secondary Metals Assoc., 1956–77 (Pres., 1959 and 1964). Dir, 1972, Chm., 1984–91, Metal Market & Exchange Co. Ltd. *Recreations:* music, gardening, golf. *Address:* Nore, Hascombe, near Godalming, Surrey GU8 4BT. *Club:* City of London.

LIPKIN, Miles Henry J.; *see* Jackson-Lipkin.

LIPMAN, Maureen Diane, (Mrs J. M. Rosenthal), CBE 1999; actress; *b* 10 May 1946; *d* of Maurice and Zelma Lipman; *m* 1973, Jack Morris Rosenthal, *qv*; one *s* one *d*. *Educ:* Newland High Sch. for Girls, Hull; London Acad. of Music and Dramatic Art. Professional début in The Knack, Watford, 1969; Stables Theatre, Manchester, 1970; National Theatre (Old Vic), 1971–73: The Front Page; Long Day's Journey into Night; The Good Natur'd Man; *West End:* Candida, 1976; Outside Edge, 1978; Meg and Mog, 1982; Messiah, 1983; Miss Skillen, in See How They Run, 1984 (Laurence Olivier Award; Variety Club of GB Award); Wonderful Town, Queen's, 1986; Re: Joyce!, Fortune, 1988, Vaudeville, 1989 and 1991, Long Wharf, Conn, USA, 1990; The Cabinet Minister, Albery, 1991; Lost in Yonkers, Strand, 1992 (Variety Club Best Stage Actress, 1993); Live and Kidding, Duchess, 1997; Peggy For You, Comedy, 2000; other plays include: Celia, in As You Like It, RSC, 1974; Jenny, in Chapter Two, Hammersmith, 1981; Kitty McShane, in On Your Way, Riley, Stratford East, 1983; The Sisters Rosenweig, Old Vic, 1994; The Rivals, Manchester Royal Exchange, 1996; Oklahoma!, RNT, 1998, transf. Lyceum, 1999; Sitting Pretty, Th. Royal, Bath, 2001; Dir, The Sunshine Boys, Royal Lyceum, Edinburgh, 1993; *television:* plays, series and serials include: The Evacuees; Smiley's People; The Knowledge; Rolling Home; Outside Edge; Princess of France, in Love's Labour's Lost; Absurd Person Singular; Shift Work; Absent Friends; Jane Lucas, in 4 series of Agony; All at No 20 (TV Times Award, 1989); About Face, 1989 and 1990; Re: Joyce; Enid Blyton, in Sunny Stories, 1992; Eskimo Day, 1996; Cold Enough for Snow, 1997; *films:* Up the Junction, 1969; Educating Rita, 1983; Captain Jack, 1998; Solomon and Gaenor, 1999; Oklahoma! (video), 1999; Discovery of Heaven, 2001; The Pianist, 2001; *radio:* The Lipman Test (2 series), 1996, 1997; Choice Grenfell, 1998. BAFTA Award, for BT Commercials, 1992. Magazine columnist: Options, 1983–88; She, 1988–91 (PPA Columnist of the Year, 1991); Good Housekeeping, 1993–. Hon. DLitt: Hull, 1994; Sheffield, 1999; Hon. MA Salford, 1995. *Publications:* How Was it for You?, 1985; Something to Fall Back On, 1987; You Got an 'Ology?, 1989; Thank You for Having Me, 1990; When's It Coming Out?, 1992; You Can Read Me Like a Book, 1995; Lip Reading, 1999. *Recreation:* reading and trying to remember what I've read!

LIPPIETT, Rear-Adm. Richard John, MBE 1979; Commandant, Joint Services Command and Staff College, since 2002; *b* 7 July 1949; *s* of late Rev. Canon Vernon Kingsbury Lippiett and Katharine F. I. S. Lippiett (*née* Langston-Jones); *m* 1976, Jennifer Rosemary Wratislaw Walker; two *s* one *d*. *Educ:* Brighton, Hove and Sussex Grammar Sch.; BRNC, Dartmouth. Joined RN 1967; served HM Ships Appleton, Eagle, Yarmouth, Achilles, Fife, Ambuscade and ashore at HMS Raleigh and Fleet HQ; Flag Lieut to C-in-C Fleet, 1973–74; Comd, HMS Shavington, 1975–77 and HMS Amazon, 1986–87; jsdc 1987; Naval Asst to First Sea Lord, 1988–90; Comd, HMS Norfolk and 9th Frigate Sqdn, 1991–92; rcds, 1993; COS Surface Flotilla, 1993–95; Comd, HMS Dryad and Sch. of Maritime Ops, 1995–97; Flag Officer Sea Trng, 1997–99; COS to Comdr Allied Naval Forces Southern Europe, and Sen. British Officer Southern Region, 1999–2001. Younger Brother of Trinity House, 1993. *Publication:* The Type 21 Frigate, 1990. *Recreations:* family, classical music, gardening, sailing. *Address:* c/o Naval Secretary, Victory Building, HM Naval Base, Portsmouth PO1 3LS. *Club:* Royal Navy of 1765 and 1785.

LIPPINCOTT, Dr Kristen Clarke; Deputy Director, National Maritime Museum, since 2000; *b* 18 Nov. 1954; *d* of Lt-Col Clifford Ellwood Lippincott and Maureen Virginia Lippincott (*née* O'Brien); *m* 1992, Gordon Stephen Barrass, *qv*. *Educ:* Bennington Coll., Vermont, USA (BA); Univ. of Chicago (MA, PhD). Fellowships in Italy and at Warburg Inst., 1982–90; National Maritime Museum: Curator of Astronomy, 1990 and Head of Navigational Scis, 1991–94, Old Royal Observatory; Mus. Planner and Strategist, 1994–95; Director: Display Div., 1995–96; Millennium Project, Old Royal Observatory, Greenwich, 1996–2000; Royal Observatory Greenwich, 1998–2001. Council Mem., Scientific Instruments Soc., 1994–96; Trustee, Cubitt Gall., 1996–. Freeman, Clockmakers' Co., 2000–. FRSA 1997. *Publications:* Eyewitness Science: Astronomy, 1994; The Story of Time, 1999; numerous articles on Italian Renaissance and on history of art, of science, of scientific instruments, in learned jls. *Recreations:* travelling, sleeping. *Address:* National Maritime Museum, Greenwich, SE10 9NF. *T:* (020) 8858 4422.

LIPPONEN, Paavo Tapio; Prime Minister, Republic of Finland, since 1995; MP (SDP) Helsinki, 1983–87 and since 1991; *b* 23 April 1941; *s* of Orvo and Hilkka Lipponen; *m* 1998, Paivi Hertzberg; two *d*, and one *d* from former marriage. *Educ:* Kuopio; Univ. of Helsinki (MScSoc 1971); Dartmouth Coll., USA. Journalist, 1963–67; SDP Res. and Internat. Affairs Sec. and Head, political section, 1967–79; Prime Minister's Sec. (Special Political Advr), 1979–92; Head, Finnish Inst. Internat. Affairs, 1989–91; Mem., Helsinki City Council, 1985–95; Speaker of Parliament, 1995. Social Democratic Party: Chm., Helsinki Dist, 1985–92; Member: Exec. Cttee, 1987–90; Party Council, 1990–93; Chm., 1993–. Man. Dir, Viestinta Teema Oy, 1988–95; Chm., Supervisory Bd, Outokumpo Oy, 1989–90. Member: Exec. Cttee, Internat. Commn on Employment, 1987–89; Gp of Experts on Internat. Politics of Sec.-Gen., Council of Europe, 1989–91. Hon. LLD Dartmouth Coll., USA, 1997. Grand Cross, Order of White Rose (Finland). Holds several foreign decorations. *Publications:* Muutoksen Suunta, 1986; articles in Finnish, Swedish, English and German in domestic and foreign books, newspapers and periodicals. *Recreations:* sports activities – swimming, architecture, literature, music. *Address:* Office of the Prime Minister, Snellmaninkatu 1A, 00170 Helsinki, Finland. *Club:* Finnish (Helsinki).

LIPSCOMB, Prof. William Nunn; Abbott and James Lawrence Professor of Chemistry, Harvard University, 1971–90, now Emeritus; Nobel Laureate in Chemistry, 1976; *b* 9 Dec. 1919; *s* of late William Nunn Lipscomb Sr, and of Edna Patterson Porter; *m* 1983, Jean Craig Evans; one *d*, and one *s* one *d* by previous marriage. *Educ:* Univ. of Kentucky (BS); California Inst. of Technology (PhD). Univ. of Minnesota, Minneapolis: Asst Prof. of Physical Chem., 1946–50; Associate Prof., 1950–54; Actg Chief, Physical Chem. Div., 1952–54; Prof. and Chief of Physical Chem. Div., 1954–59; Harvard Univ.: Prof. of Chemistry, 1959–71 (Chm., Dept of Chem., 1962–65). Member: Bd of Dir's, Dow Chemical Co., USA, 1982–89; Scientific Adv. Bd, Robert A. Welch Foundn, 1982–. Member: Amer. Chemical Soc. (Chm., Minneapolis Section, 1949); Amer. Acad. of Arts and Sciences, 1959–; Nat. Acad. of Sciences, USA, 1961–; Internat. Acad. of Quantum Molecular Science, 1980; Académie Européenne des Scis, des Arts et des Lettres, Paris, 1980; Foreign Mem., Netherlands Acad. of Arts and Sciences, 1976; Hon. Member: Internat. Assoc. of Bioinorganic Scientists, 1979; RSC, 1983. MA (hon.) Harvard, 1959; Hon. DSc: Kentucky, 1963; Long Island, 1977; Rutgers, 1979; Gustavos Adolphus, 1980; Marietta, 1981; Miami, 1983; Dr *hc* Munich, 1976. *Publications:* Boron Hydrides, 1963 (New York); (with G. R. Eaton) Nuclear Magnetic Resonance Studies of Boron and Related Compounds, 1969 (New York); chapters in: The Aesthetic Dimensions of Science, ed D. W. Curtin, 1982; Crystallography in North America, ed D. McLachlan and J. Glusker, 1983; contribs to scientific jls concerning structure and function of enzymes and natural products in inorganic chem. and theoretical chem. *Recreations:* tennis, chamber music. *Address:* Department of Chemistry and Chemical Biology, Harvard University, 12 Oxford Street, Cambridge, MA 02138, USA. *T:* (617) 4954098.

LIPSEY, family name of **Baron Lipsey**.

LIPSEY, Baron *cr* 1999 (Life Peer), of Tooting Bec in the London Borough of Wandsworth; **David Lawrence Lipsey;** *b* 21 April 1948; *s* of Lawrence and Penelope Lipsey; *m* 1982, Margaret Robson; one *d*. *Educ:* Bryanston Sch.; Magdalen Coll., Oxford (1st Cl. Hons PPE). Research Asst, General and Municipal Workers' Union, 1970–72; Special Adviser to Anthony Crosland, MP, 1972–77 (Dept of the Environment, 1974–76; FCO, 1976–77); Prime Minister's Staff, 10 Downing Street, 1977–79; Journalist, New Society, 1979–80; Sunday Times: Political Staff, 1980–82; Economics Editor, 1982–86; Editor, New Society, 1986–88; Co-founder and Dep. Editor, The Sunday Correspondent, 1988–90; Associate Ed., The Times, 1990–92; journalist, The Economist, 1992–99 (Political Ed., 1994–98). Vis. Prof. in Public Policy, Univ. of Ulster, 1993–. Member: Royal Commn on Long Term Care of the Elderly, 1997–99; Ind. Commn on the Voting System, 1997–98; Licence Fee Rev. Panel (Davies Inquiry), 1999; Council, ASA, 1999–. Secretary, Streatham Labour Party, 1970–72; Chm., Fabian Soc., 1981–82; Mem., Exec. Cttee, Charter for Jobs, 1984–86. A public interest Dir, PIA, 1994–; non-exec. Dir, Horserace Totalisator Bd, 1998–. *Publications:* Labour and Land, 1972; (ed, with Dick Leonard) The Socialist Agenda: Crosland's Legacy, 1981; Making Government Work, 1982; The Name of the Rose, 1992; The Secret Treasury: how Britain's economy is really run, 2000. *Recreations:* golf, racing, opera. *Address:* 94 Drewstead Road, SW16 1AG. *T:* (020) 8769 9043. *Club:* Soho House.

LIPSEY, Prof. Richard George, OC 1991; FRSC; Professor of Economics, Simon Fraser University, Burnaby, BC, 1989–97, now Emeritus; Fellow, Canadian Institute for Advanced Research, since 1989; *b* 28 Aug. 1928; *s* of R. A. Lipsey and F. T. Lipsey (*née* Ledingham); *m* 1960, Diana Louise Smart; one *s* two *d*. *Educ:* Univ. of British Columbia (BA 1st Cl. Hons 1950); Univ. of Toronto (MA 1953); LSE (PhD 1957). Dept of Trade and Industry, British Columbia Provincial Govt, 1950–53; LSE: Asst Lectr, 1955–58; Lectr, 1958–60; Reader, 1960–61; Prof. 1961–63; Univ. of Essex: Prof. of Economics, 1963–70; Dean of School of Social Studies, 1963–67; Sir Edward Peacock Prof. of Econs, Queen's Univ., Kingston, Ont, 1970–87. Vis. Prof., Univ. of California at Berkeley, 1963–64; Simeon Vis. Prof., Univ. of Manchester, 1973; Irving Fisher Vis. Prof., Yale Univ., 1979–80. Economic Consultant, NEDC, 1961–63; Sen. Econ. Advr, C. D. Howe Inst., Toronto, 1984–89. Member of Council: SSRC, 1966–69; Royal Economic Soc., 1968–71. President: Canadian Economics Assoc., 1980–81; Atlantic Economic Assoc., 1986–87. Editor, Review of Economic Studies, 1960–64. Fellow, Econometric Soc., 1972. FRSC 1980. Hon. LLD: McMaster, 1984; Victoria, 1985; Carleton, 1987; Queen's Univ. at Kingston, 1990; Guelph, 1993; Western Ontario, 1994; Essex, 1996; British Columbia, 1999; Hon. DSc Toronto, 1992. *Publications:* An Introduction to Positive Economics, 1963, 9th edn 1999; (with P. O. Steiner) Economics, 1966, 12th edn 1999; (with G. C. Archibald) An Introduction to a Mathematical Treatment of Economics, 1967, 3rd edn 1977; The Theory of Customs Unions: a general equilibrium analysis, 1971; (with G. C. Archibald) An Introduction to Mathematical Economics, 1975; (with C. Harbury) An Introduction to the UK Economy, 1983, 5th edn 1993; (with F. Flatters) Common Ground for the Canadian Common Market, 1984; (with M. Smith): Canada's Trade Options in a Turbulent World, 1985; Global Imbalance and US Policy Response, 1987; (with R. York) A Guided Tour through the Canada—US Free Trade Agreement, 1988; (with C. Harbury) First Principles of Economics, 1988, 2nd edn 1992; (jtly) The NAFTA: what's in, what's out, what's next, 1994; (with K. Carlaw) A Structuralist Assessment of Innovation Policies, 1998; articles in learned jls on many branches of theoretical and applied economics. *Recreations:* skiing, sailing, rambling. *Address:* Economic Growth and Policy Program, Simon Fraser University at Harbour Centre, 515 W Hastings Street, Vancouver, BC V6B 5K3, Canada; *e-mail:* rlipsey@sfu.ca.

LIPSTEIN, Prof. Kurt; Professor of Comparative Law, Cambridge University, 1973–76; Fellow of Clare College, Cambridge, since 1956; *b* 19 March 1909; *e s* of Alfred Lipstein, MD and Hilda (*née* Sulzbach); *m* 1944, Gwyneth Mary Herford (*d* 1998); two *d*. *Educ:* Goethe Gymnasium, Frankfurt on Main; Univs of Grenoble and Berlin; Trinity Coll., Cambridge. Gerichtsreferendar 1931; PhD Cantab 1936; LLD 1977. Called to Bar, Middle Temple, 1950, Hon. Bencher, 1966. Univ. Lectr, Cambridge, 1946; Reader in Conflict of Laws, Cambridge Univ., 1962–73. Dir of Research, Internat. Assoc. Legal Science, 1954–59. Vis. Professor: Univ. of Pennsylvania, 1962; Northwestern Univ., Chicago, 1966, 1968; Paris I, 1977. Mem., Inst. de Droit Internat., 1999. Hon. QC 1998. Hon. Fellow, Wolfson Coll., Cambridge, 2000. Hon. Dr jur. Würzburg, 1995. Humboldt Prize, Alexander von Humboldt Stiftung, Bonn, 1981. *Publications:* The Law of the EEC, 1974; Principles of the Conflict of Laws, National and International, 1981; joint editor and contributor: Dicey's Conflict of Laws, 6th edn, 1948—8th edn, 1967; Leske-Loewenfeld, Das Eherecht der europäischen Staaten, 1963; (ed) International Encyclopaedia of Comparative Law, vol. Private International Law, 1972; Harmonization of Private International Law by the EEC, 1978; contrib. English and foreign legal periodicals. *Address:* Clare College, Cambridge CB2 1TL. *T:* (01223) 333200; 7 Barton Close, Cambridge CB3 9LQ. *T:* (01223) 357048; 13 Old Square, Lincoln's Inn, WC2A 3UA. *T:* (020) 7404 4800.

LIPTON, Prof. Peter, DPhil; Professor of the History and Philosophy of Science, since 1997, and Fellow of King's College, since 1994, Cambridge University; *b* NYC, 9 Oct. 1954; *s* of Louis Lipton and Lini Lipton (*née* Strauss); *m* 1984, Diana Warner; two *s*. *Educ:* Fieldston Sch., NY; Wesleyan Univ., Connecticut (BA 1976); New Coll., Oxford (BPhil

1978; DPhil 1985). Asst Res. Prof., Clark Univ., Mass, 1982–85; Asst Prof., Williams Coll., Mass, 1985–91; Univ. Asst Lectr, 1991–94, Univ. Lectr, 1994–97, Cambridge Univ. *Publications:* Inference to the Best Explanation, 1991; (ed) Theory, Evidence and Explanation, 1995; contribs to philosophical jls. *Recreation:* pilpul. *Address:* King's College, Cambridge CB2 1ST; *e-mail:* peter.lipton@kings.cam.ac.uk.

LIPTON, Sir Stuart (Anthony), Kt 2000; Chief Executive, Stanhope PLC, since 1995; Chairman, Commission for Architecture and the Built Environment, since 1999; *b* 9 Nov. 1942; *s* of Bertram Green and Jeanette Lipton; *m* 1966, Ruth Kathryn Marks; two *s* one *d*. *Educ:* Berkhamsted Sch. Director: Sterling Land Co., 1971–73; First Palace Securities Ltd, 1973–76; Man. Dir, Greycoat PLC, 1976–83; Chief Exec., Stanhope Properties PLC, 1983–95. Advr to Hampton Site Co. for Sainsbury Bldg, Nat. Gall., 1985–91; Advr, new Glyndebourne Opera House, 1988–94; Member: Adv. Bd, Dept of Construction Management, Reading Univ., 1983–91; Property Adv. Gp, DoE, 1986–96; Mil. Bldgs Cttee, MoD, 1987–98; Barbican Centre Adv. Council, 1997–. Mem. Council, British Property Fedn, 1987–99. Mem., Royal Fine Art Commn, 1988–99. Dir, Nat. Gall. Trust Foundn, 1998–. Trustee: Whitechapel Art Gall., 1987–94; Architecture Foundn, 1992–99 (Dep. Chm., 1992–99); Urban Land Inst., Washington, 1996–; Millennium Bridge Trust, 1998–; Member: English Partnerships Millennium Housing Trust Jury, 1998–; Jury, RIBA Gold Medal Award, 1998–99. Member of Board: Royal Nat. Theatre, 1988–98; Royal Opera House, 1998–. Member, Governing Body: Imperial Coll., 1987– (FIC 1998); LSE, 2000–. Liveryman, Goldsmiths' Co., 1997–. Hon. RIBA 1986. Bicentenary Medal, RSA. *Recreations:* architecture, crafts, art and technology, wine. *Address:* (office) 26 Mount Row, W1Y 5DA. *T:* (020) 7495 7575.

LIPWORTH, Sir (Maurice) Sydney, Kt 1991; Trustee, International Accounting Standards Committee Foundation, since 2000; Chairman, Financial Reporting Council, 1993–2001; *b* 13 May 1931; *s* of Isidore and Rae Lipworth; *m* 1957, Rosa Liwarek; two *s*. *Educ:* King Edward VII Sch., Johannesburg; Univ. of the Witwatersrand, Johannesburg (BCom, LLB). Admitted Solicitor, Johannesburg, 1955; called to the South African Bar, 1956; called to Bar, Inner Temple, 1991. Barrister, Johannesburg, 1956–64; Non-Exec. Dir, Liberty Life Assoc. of Africa Ltd, 1956–64; Director: private trading/financial gps, 1965–67; Abbey Life Assurance Gp, 1968–70; Allied Dunbar Assurance plc (formerly Hambro Life Assurance), 1971–88 (Jt Man. Dir, 1980–84; Dep. Chm., 1984–87); Chairman: Dunbar Bank, 1983–88; Allied Dunbar Unit Trusts, 1985–88 (Man. Dir, 1983–85); ZENECA Group, 1995–99 (Dir, 1994–99); Dep. Chm., Nat. Westminster Bank, 1993–2000; Director: J. Rothschild Holdings plc, 1984–87; BAT Industries plc, 1985–88; Carlton Communications plc, 1993–; Centrica plc, 1999–. Mem., 1981–93, Chm., 1988–93, Monopolies and Mergers Commn; Member: Sen. Salaries Review Body, 1994–; Cttee on Financial Aspects of Corporate Governance, 1994–95. Mem. Adv. Panel, BreakThrough Breast Cancer Res. Trust, 1990–; Trustee: Allied Dunbar Charitable Trust, 1971–94; Philharmonia Orchestra, 1982– (Dep. Chm., 1986–93, Chm., 1993–, of Trustees); Royal Acad. Trust, 1988–; South Bank Foundn Ltd, 1996–; Chairman: NatWest Gp Charitable Trust, 1994–2001; Marie Curie Cancer Care 50th Anniversary Appeal, 1997–; Governor: Contemp. Dance Trust, 1981–87; Sadler's Wells Foundn, 1987–90. Chm., Bar Assoc. for Commerce, Finance and Industry, 1991–92. Mem., Gen. Council of the Bar, 1992–94. Hon. Bencher, Inner Temple, 1989; Hon. QC 1993. *Publications:* chapters and articles on investment, life insurance, pensions and competition law. *Recreations:* tennis, music, theatre. *Address:* International Accounting Standards Board, 30 Cannon Street, EC4M 6XH. *Clubs:* Reform, Queen's.

LISBURNE, 8th Earl of, *cr* 1776; **John David Malet Vaughan;** DL; Viscount Lisburne and Lord Vaughan, 1695; barrister-at-law; *b* 1 Sept. 1918; *o s* of 7th Earl of Lisburne; *S* father, 1965; *m* 1943, Shelagh, *er d* of late T. A. Macauley, 1266 Redpath Crescent, Montreal, Canada; three *s*. *Educ:* Eton; Magdalen Coll., Oxford (BA, MA). Called to Bar, Inner Temple, 1947. Captain, Welsh Guards. Director: British Home Stores Ltd, 1964–87; S Wales Regional Bd, Lloyds Bank Ltd, 1978–; Divisional Dir for Wales, Nationwide Building Soc., 1982–. Chm., then Pres., Wales Council for Voluntary Action (formerly Council of Social Service for Wales), 1976–97; Hon. Life Mem., AA (Mem. Exec. Cttee, 1981–88). DL Dyfed, 1992. *Heir: s* Viscount Vaughan, *qv*. *Address:* Manor House, Hopton Wafers, Kidderminster, Worcs DY14 0NA. *Clubs:* Beefsteak, Turf.

LISHMAN, (Arthur) Gordon, OBE 1993; Director General, Age Concern, since 2000; *b* 29 Nov. 1947; *s* of Dr Arthur Birkett Lishman and Florence May Lishman; *m* 1st, 1968, Beverley Ann Witham (marr. diss. 1972); 2nd, 1973, Stephanie Margaret Allison-Beer (marr. diss. 1984); one *s* one *d*; 3rd, 1988, Margaret Ann Brodie-Browne (*née* Long); one step *d*. *Educ:* Univ. of Manchester (BA Econ 1968). Age Concern England, 1974–: Field Officer, 1974–77; Head of Fieldwork, 1977–87; Ops Dir, 1987–2000; Dir, Age Concern Enterprises, 1995–. Mem. Steering Cttee, Better Govt for Old People, 1997–; Sec.-Gen., Eurolink Age, 2001–; Bd Mem. and Sec. Adjoint, AGE– the Eur. Older People's Platform, 2001–; Bd Mem., Internat. Fedn on Ageing, 2001–. Mem., Liberal, later Liberal Democrat, Party, 1963–. *Address:* Age Concern, Astral House, 1268 London Road, SW16 4ER. *T:* (020) 8765 7701. *Club:* National Liberal.

LISHMAN, Prof. William Alwyn, MD, DSc; FRCP, FRCPsych; Professor of Neuropsychiatry, Institute of Psychiatry, University of London, 1979–93, now Professor Emeritus; Consultant Psychiatrist, Bethlem Royal and Maudsley Hospitals, 1967–93; *b* 16 May 1931; *s* of George Hackworth Lishman and Madge Scott (*née* Young); *m* 1966, Marjorie Loud; one *s* one *d*. *Educ:* Houghton-le-Spring Grammar Sch.; Univ. of Birmingham (BSc Hons Anatomy and Physiology, 1953; MB, ChB Hons 1956; MD 1965). DPM London, 1963; DSc London, 1985. MRCP 1958, FRCP 1972; FRCPsych 1972. House Phys. and House Surg., Queen Elizabeth Hosp., Birmingham, 1956–57; MO Wheatley Mil. Hosp., 1957–59 (Major, RAMC); Registrar, United Oxford Hosps, 1959–60; Registrar, later Sen. Registrar, Maudsley Hosp., London, 1960–66; Consultant in Psychol Medicine, Nat. Hosp. and Maida Vale Hosp., London, 1966–67; Sen. Lectr in Psychol Medicine, Hammersmith Hosp. and RPMS, 1967–69; Consultant Psychiatrist, Bethlem Royal and Maudsley Hosps, 1967–74; Reader in Neuropsychiatry, Inst. of Psychiatry, 1974–79. Vis. Fellow, Green Coll., Oxford, 1983. Advisor to Bermuda Hosps Bd, 1971; Scientific Advisor, DHSS, 1979–82; Civilian Consultant, RAF, 1987–93. Member: Neurosciences Bd, MRC, 1976–78 (Dep. Chm., 1976–77); Scientific Adv. Panel, Brain Res. Trust, 1986–93; Adv. Cttee, Mason Med. Res. Trust, 1986–93. Examiner: Univ. of Oxford (also Mem. Bd of Examrs), 1975–79; Univ. of Birmingham, 1984–87; Nat. Univ. of Malaysia, 1989. Chm., British Neuropsychiatry Assoc., 1987–93; (Hon. Life Pres., 1993); Member: Experimental Psychology Soc., 1975–; Assoc. of British Neurologists, 1979–95; Court of Electors, and Exams Subcttee, RCPsych, 1991–96. Trustee, Psychiatry Res. Trust, 1999–. Gaskell Gold Medal, Royal Medico-Psychol Assoc., 1965. Member, Editorial Boards: Psychological Medicine, 1970–93; Neuropsychiatry, Neuropsychology and Behavioral Neurology, 1988–95; Cognitive Neuropsychiatry, 1996–. Guarantor of Brain, 1984–99. *Publications:* Organic Psychiatry: the psychological consequences of cerebral disorder, 1978, 3rd edn 1998; physiol and psychol papers on brain maturation, cerebral dominance, organisation of memory; clinical papers on head injury, dementia, epilepsy, neuroimaging, and alcoholic brain damage. *Recreations:* organ, piano, harpsichord, travelling. *Address:* 9 Elwill Way, Beckenham, Kent BR3 3AB.

LISLE; *see* Orchard-Lisle.

LISLE, 8th Baron *cr* 1758 (Ire.), of Mount North, co. Cork; **Patrick James Lysaght;** *b* 1 May 1931; *s* of Horace James William Lysaght (*d* 1977), *yr b* of 7th Baron Lisle, and Joanna Mary (*née* Nolan; *d* 1985); *S* uncle, 1997; *m* 1957, Mrs Mary Louise Shaw-Stuart (marr. diss.); two *s* one *d*. *Educ:* Shrewsbury. Late Lieut, Grenadier Guards. *Heir: s* Hon. John Nicholas Geoffrey Lysaght, *b* 20 May 1960. *Address:* 30 Springhurst House, Greenham, Newbury, Berks RG14 7UD.

LISS, Prof. Peter Simon, PhD; Professor, School of Environmental Sciences, University of East Anglia, since 1985; *b* 27 Oct. 1942; *s* of Michael and Gertrude Liss; *m* 1967, Ruth Adler; three *s*. *Educ:* University College, Durham (BSc); Marine Science Labs, Univ. of Wales (PhD). NERC Post-doctoral Res. Fellow, Dept. of Oceanography, Southampton Univ., 1967–69; Lectr, 1969–77, Reader, 1977–85, Sch. of Envmtl Scis, UEA. Vis. Prof., Univ. of Washington, Seattle, 1977; Visiting Scientist: Ocean Chem. Lab., Canada, 1975; Grad. Sch. of Oceanography, Univ. of Rhode Island, 1989, 1990; Guest Prof., Ocean Univ., Qingdao, China, 1997–. Envmtl Chemistry Dist. Lectr, RSC, 2002. Scientific Advisor, CEGB, London, 1979–82. Mem., NERC, 1990–95; Treasurer, 1990–93, Chm., 1993–97, Sci. Cttee for Internat. Geosphere-Biosphere Prog. Challenger Medal, Challenger Soc. for Marine Sci., 2000. *Publications:* Estuarine Chemistry, 1976; Environmental Chemistry, 1980; Man-Made Carbon Dioxide and Climatic Change, 1983; Quimica Ambiental, 1983; Air-Sea Exchange of Gases and Particles, 1983; Power Generation and the Environment, 1990; An Introduction to Environmental Chemistry, 1996; The Sea Surface and Global Change, 1997. *Recreations:* reading, music, house renovation. *Address:* 5 Chester Place, Norwich, Norfolk NR2 3DG. *T:* (01603) 623815; *e-mail:* p.liss@uea.ac.uk.

LISSACK, Richard Antony; QC 1994; a Recorder, since 1999; *b* 7 June 1956; *s* of late Victor Jack Lissack and of Antoinette Rosalind Lissack; *m* 1986, Carolyn Dare Arscott; three *d* (incl. twins). *Educ:* UCS, Hampstead. Called to the Bar, Inner Temple, 1978; an Asst Recorder, 1993–99. Chairman: S & W Wilts Hunt, 1996–; Kilmington Internat. Horse Trials, 1997–; Disciplinary Cttee, British Horse Trials, 2000–. *Recreations:* breeding, competing and falling off thoroughbred horses, farming. *Address:* 35 Essex Street, Temple, WC2A 3AR. *T:* (020) 7353 6381. *Clubs:* Babbington House; Rock Sailing.

LISTER; *see* Cunliffe-Lister, family name of Earl of Swinton.

LISTER, Geoffrey Richard, CBE 1994; FCA; FCIB; Joint Vice Chairman, 1996–97, Director, 1988–97, Bradford & Bingley Building Society; *b* 14 May 1937; *s* of Walter and Margaret Lister; *m* 1962, Myrtle Margaret (*née* Cooper); one *s* two *d*. *Educ:* St Bede's Grammar Sch., Bradford. Articled clerk, J. Pearson & Son, 1955–60, qual. chartered accountant, 1960; Computer and Systems Sales, Burroughs Machines Ltd, 1961–63; Audit Man., Thos Gardner & Co., 1963–65; Bradford & Bingley Building Society: Asst Accountant, 1965–67; Computer Man., 1967–70; Chief Accountant, 1970–73; Asst Gen. Man., 1973–75; Dep. Gen. Man., 1975–80; Gen. Man., 1980–84; Dep. Chief Exec., 1984–85; Chief Exec., 1985–95. Director: NHBC, 1992–97; PIA, 1994–95; Anchor Trust, 1997–99. Building Societies' Association: Mem. Council, 1984–97; Dep. Chm., 1992–93; Chm., 1993–94. CIMgt. *Recreations:* walking, gardening. *Address:* Harbeck House, Harbeck Drive, Harden, Bingley, W Yorks BD16 1JG. *T:* (01535) 272350. *Clubs:* Carlton; Bradford and Bingley Sports (Bingley, W Yorks).

LISTER, Prof. James, MD, FRCS; Professor of Paediatric Surgery, University of Liverpool, 1974–86, now Emeritus; *b* 1 March 1923; *s* of Thomas and Anna Rebecca Lister; *m* 1946, Greta Redpath; three *d*. *Educ:* St Paul's Sch., London; Edinburgh Univ. (MB, ChB 1945; MD 1972). FRCS 1975, FRCSE 1950, FRCSGlas 1969. Surg. Lieut, RNVR, 1945–48. Surgical training posts, Edinburgh and Dundee, 1948–58; Halstead Res. Fellow, Colorado Univ., 1959; Sen. Lectr in Paediatric Surgery and Consultant Surgeon, Hosp. for Sick Children, Great Ormond St, and Queen Elizabeth Hosp., Hackney Rd, 1960–63; Consultant Paediatric Surgeon, Sheffield Children's Hosp., 1963–74. Civil Consultant in Paediatric Surgery to RN, 1979–86. Past Examiner: Univs of Glasgow and Sheffield (in paediatric surgery); DCH London; Part I and Part II FRCSE. Mem. Council, RCSE, 1977–91 (Convenor of Examinations Cttee, 1986–90; a Vice-Pres., 1988–91); Mem., St Helens & Knowsley DHA, 1983–86. Chm., European Union of Paediatric Surgical Assocs, 1983–86; Hon. Member: British Assoc. of Paediatric Surgeons (Pres., 1975–76); Paediatric Surgical Assocs of Austria, Brazil, Chile, Germany, Greece, Hungary, Peru, Poland, Scandinavia, Yugoslavia. Hon. Fellow: Amer. Acad. of Paediatrics, 1976; Assoc. of Surgeons of India, 1985. Former Member of Editorial Board: Jl of RCSEd; Jl of Paediatric Surgery; Annals of Tropical Paediatrics; Consultant Ed., Eur. Jl of Pediatric Surgery, 1991–2000. *Publications:* Neonatal Surgery, ed jtly 2nd edn 1978 and 3rd edn, 1990; Complications in Paediatric Surgery, 1986; papers on neonatal surgery and myelomeningocele. *Recreations:* gardening, hill walking. *Address:* Kailheugh, Hownam, Kelso, Roxburghshire TD5 8AL. *T:* (01573) 440224.

LISTER, Very Rev. John Field, MA; *b* 19 Jan. 1916; *s* of Arthur and Florence Lister. *Educ:* King's Sch., Worcester; Keble Coll., Oxford; Cuddesdon Coll., Oxford. Asst Curate, St Nicholas, Radford, Coventry, 1939–44; Asst Curate, St John Baptist, Coventry, 1944–45; Vicar of St John's, Huddersfield, 1945–54; Asst Rural Dean of Halifax, 1955–61; Archdeacon of Halifax, 1961–72; Vicar of Brighouse, 1954–72; Provost of Wakefield, 1972–82. Examng Chaplain to Bishop of Wakefield, 1972–78. Hon. Canon of Wakefield Cathedral, 1961, Canon, 1968; RD of Wakefield, 1972–80. Chaplain to The Queen, 1966–72. *Address:* 5 Larkcliff Court, The Parade, Birchington, Kent CT7 9NB.

LISTER, Prof. (Margot) Ruth (Aline), CBE 1999; Professor of Social Policy, Loughborough University, since 1994; *b* 3 May 1949; *d* of Dr Werner Bernard Lister and Daphne (*née* Carter). *Educ:* Univ. of Essex (BA Hons Sociology); Univ. of Sussex (MA Multi-Racial Studies). Child Poverty Action Group: Legal Res. Officer, 1971–75; Asst Dir, 1975–77; Dep. Dir, 1977–79; Dir, 1979–87; Prof. of Applied Social Studies, Univ. of Bradford, 1987–93. Vice-Chair, NCVO, 1991–93. Member: Opsahl Commn, 1992–93; Commn for Social Justice, 1992–94; Commn on Poverty, Participation and Power, 1999–2000. Eleanor Rathbone Meml Lecture, Univ. of Leeds, 1989. Founding Academician, Acad. of Social Scis, 1999. Hon. LLD Manchester, 1987. *Publications:* Supplementary Benefit Rights, 1974; Welfare Benefits, 1981; The Exclusive Society, 1990; Women's Economic Dependency and Social Security, 1992; Citizenship: feminist perspectives, 1997; pamphlets, articles, and contrib. to many books on poverty, social security and women's citizenship. *Recreations:* relaxing—with friends, music, and through walking, meditation and Tai Chi; reading. *Address:* Loughborough University, Loughborough, Leics LE11 3TU; 45 Quayside Close, Nottingham NG2 3BP.

LISTER, Patrick; *see* Lister, R. P.

LISTER, Raymond (George), MA, LittD Cantab; President, Royal Society of Miniature Painters, Sculptors and Gravers, 1970–80; Chairman, Board of Governors, Federation of British Artists, 1976–80 (Governor, 1972–80); *b* 28 March 1919; *s* of late Horace Lister and Ellen Maud Mary Lister (*née* Arnold); *m* 1947, Pamela Helen, *d* of late Frank Bishop Brutnell; one *s* one *d*. *Educ:* St John's Coll. Choir Sch., Cambridge; Cambridge and County High Sch. for Boys. Served apprenticeship in family firm (architectural metalworking), 1934–39; specialised war service (engrg), 1939–45; Dir of family firm, 1941–94; Man. Editor, Golden Head Press, 1952–72; Dir, John P. Gray and Son, craft bookbinders, 1978–82. Hon. Senior Mem., University Coll., subseq. Wolfson Coll., Cambridge, 1971–75, Mem. Coll. Council, 1983–85, Emeritus Fellow, 1986 (Fellow, 1975–86); a Syndic, Fitzwilliam Mus., Cambridge, 1981–89. Liveryman, Blacksmiths' Co., 1957, Mem. Ct of Assistants, 1980, Prime Warden, 1989–90. Associate Mem. 1946, Mem. 1948, Royal Soc. of Miniature Painters; Pres., Private Libraries Assoc., 1971–74; Vice-Pres., Architectural Metalwork Assoc., 1970–75, Pres., 1975–77. *Publications:* Decorative Wrought Ironwork in Great Britain, 1957; Decorative Cast Ironwork in Great Britain, 1960; Edward Calvert, 1962; Beulah to Byzantium, 1965; Victorian Narrative Paintings, 1966; William Blake, 1968; Hammer and Hand, 1969; Samuel Palmer and his Etchings, 1969; A Title to Phoebe, 1972; British Romantic Art, 1973; Samuel Palmer: a biography, 1974; (ed) The Letters of Samuel Palmer, 1974; Infernal Methods: a Study of William Blake's art techniques, 1975; Apollo's Bird, 1975; For Love of Leda, 1977; Great Images of British Printmaking, 1978; (jtly) Samuel Palmer: a vision recaptured, 1978; Samuel Palmer in Palmer Country, 1980; George Richmond, 1981; Bergomask, 1982; There was a Star Danced, 1983; Prints and Printmaking, 1984; Samuel Palmer and 'The Ancients', (catalogue of exhibn at Fitzwilliam Mus., Cambridge, also selected by R. Lister), 1984; The Paintings of Samuel Palmer, 1985; The Paintings of William Blake, 1986; Samuel Palmer, his Life and Art, 1987; Catalogue Raisonné of the Works of Samuel Palmer, 1988; British Romantic Painting, 1989; trans., A. M. St Léon, Stenochoreography, 1992; With My Own Wings (autobiog.), 1994; contrib. Climbers' Club Jl, The Irish Book, Blake Studies, Blake Quarterly, Gazette des Beaux-arts, Connoisseur, Studies in Romanticism, Book Collector and TLS. *Recreations:* mountaineering in the fens, merels. *Address:* 9 Sylvester Road, Cambridge CB3 9AF. *T:* (01223) 324443. *Club:* Sette of Odd Volumes (Pres. 1960, 1982).

LISTER, (Robert) Patrick, CBE 1993; retired; *b* 6 Jan. 1922; *s* of Robert B. Lister; *m* 1942, Daphne Rosamund, *d* of Prof. C. J. Sisson; three *s* one *d* (and one *s* decd). *Educ:* Marlborough College; Cambridge University (MA); Harvard Business School (MBA). Captain Royal Engineers, 1942–46; Massey Harris, Toronto, 1949–51; joined Coventry Climax Ltd, 1951, Managing Director, 1971–80, Deputy Chairman, 1980–81; Dir, Climax Fork Trucks, 1981–83; Dir and Chief Exec., Engrg Employers W Midlands Assoc., 1983–84. President: Fedn Européenne de la Manutention, 1978–80; Coventry and Dist Engineering Employers' Assoc., 1979–80 and 1983; British Indust. Truck Assoc., 1980–81; Vice-Pres., Inst. of Materials Handling, later Inst. of Materials Management, 1982–93 (FILog Emeritus, 1993). Mem., 1984–97, Chm., 1986–97, Bd of Govs, and Pro-Chancellor, 1997–, Coventry Univ.; Gov., Coventry Technical Coll., 1984–. Hon. DBA Coventry, 1997. KSS 1992. *Recreations:* pastoral work, travel, gardening, DIY. *Address:* 35 Warwick Avenue, Coventry CV5 6DJ. *T:* (024) 7667 3776.

LISTER, Ruth; *see* Lister, M. R. A.

LISTER, Tom, CBE 1978; QFSM 1977; Chief Fire Officer, West Midlands County Council, 1975–81, retired; *b* 14 May 1924; *s* of late T. Lister and Mrs E. Lister; *m* 1954, Linda, *d* of late T. J. and Mrs H. Dodds; one *d*. *Educ:* Charter House, Hull. Hull Fire Service, 1947–60; divisional officer, Lancs, 1960–62; Asst Chief Fire Officer, Warwicks, 1962–68; Chief Fire Officer, Glos, 1968–71, Bristol and Avon, 1972–75.

LISTER-KAYE, Sir John (Phillip Lister), 8th Bt *cr* 1812, of Grange, Yorks; Director of the Aigas Trust, since 1979; *b* 8 May 1946; *s* of Sir John Christopher Lister Lister-Kaye, 7th Bt and Audrey Helen (*d* 1979), *d* of E. J. Carter; *S* father, 1982; direct linear descendant of Kaye Btcy *cr* 1641, of Woodsome (ext 1809); *m* 1st, 1972, Sorrel Deirdre Bentinck (marr. diss. 1987), *d* of 11th Earl of Portland; one *s* two *d*; 2nd, 1989, Lucinda Anne (formerly Hon. Mrs Evan Baillie), *d* of Robin Law, Withersfield; one *d*. *Educ:* Allhallows School. Naturalist, author, farmer, lecturer. Created first field studies centre in Highlands of Scotland, 1970; Founder Director of Scottish conservation charity, the Aigas Trust, 1979; Dir, Aigas Quest Ltd, 1997–. Mem., Internat. Cttee, World Wilderness Foundn, 1983–; Chairman: Scottish Adv. Cttee, RSPB, 1986–92; Cttee for Scotland, NCC, 1989–91; NW Region, NCC for Scotland, 1991–92; NW Region, Scottish Natural Heritage, 1992–96. Pres., Scottish Wildlife Trust, 1996–; Vice-Pres., Council for Protection of Rural Scotland, 1998–. *Publications:* The White Island, 1972; Seal Cull, 1979; The Seeing Eye, 1980; One for Sorrow, 1994; Ill Fares The Land, 1995. *Recreations:* breeding and showing pedigree highland cattle. *Heir: s* John Warwick Noel Lister-Kaye, *b* 10 Dec. 1974. *Address:* House of Aigas, Beauly, Inverness-shire IV4 7AD. *T:* (01463) 782729, *Fax:* (01463) 782097. *Club:* Caledonian.

LISTOWEL, 6th Earl of, *cr* 1822 (Ire.); **Francis Michael Hare;** Baron Ennismore (Ire.), 1800; Viscount Ennismore and Listowel (Ire.), 1816; Baron Hare (UK), 1869; *b* 28 June 1964; *s* of 5th Earl of Listowel, GCMG, PC and of his 3rd wife, Pamela Reid (*née* Day); *S* father, 1997. Elected Mem., H of L, 1999; Treas., All-Party Parly Gp for Children. *Heir: b* Hon. Timothy Patrick Hare, *b* 23 Feb. 1966.

LITCHFIELD, Dame Ruby (Beatrice), DBE 1981 (OBE 1959); Director, Festival City Broadcasters Ltd, 1975–86, retired (first woman appointed); Trustee, Adelaide Festival Centre, 1971–82, retired (first woman to be appointed to this position) (Life Member, 1982); *b* 5 Sept. 1912; *d* of Alfred John Skinner and Eva Hanna (*née* Thomas); *m* 1940, Kenneth Lyle Litchfield (*d* 1976); one *d*. *Educ:* North Adelaide Primary Sch.; Presbyterian Girls' Coll., Glen Osmond. Bd Mem., Kidney Foundn, 1968–; Chairperson: Carclew Youth Performing Arts Centre, 1972–88 (Life Patron, 1988); Families, Religion, Cultural Cttee, S Aust. Jubilee 150th, 1980–86. First woman Mem., Bd of S Aust. Housing Trust, 1962–70; Life Member: Queen Victoria Maternity Hosp., 1972 (Mem. Bd and Vice-Pres., 1953–72); Adelaide Rep. Th., 1967 (Mem. Bd, 1951–68); Hon. Life Mem., Spastic Paralysis Welfare Assoc. Inc. Mayoress of Prospect, 1954–57; Pres., Sportswomen's Assoc., 1969–74; Mem., Divl Council, Red Cross Soc., SA, 1955–71; Councillor, Royal Dist Bush Nursing Soc., 1957–64; Member: S Aust. Davis Cup Cttee, 1952, 1963, 1968; SA Cttee of Royal Acad. of Dancing, 1961–66; Bd, Telethon Channel 9, 1969–86; Mem. Cttee, Adelaide Festival of Arts, 1960 (Mem. Bd of Govs, 1966–90); Council, Sudden Infant Death Syndrome Res. Foundn, 1979–; Bd, Mary Potter Foundn (Chair, Hospice Appeal Cttee, 1988–; Life Mem., 1992); Mem. Bd, Crippled Children's Assoc., 1976–; First Life Mem., Telethon, 1992; Patron: Adelaide Chamber Orch., 1992–; State Theatre Co. Friends Cttee, 1993–; SA Div., Internat. AIDS Meml Fund, 1993–. Silver Jubilee Medal, 1977; Advance Australia Award, 1985; S Australia Great Award, 1987. *Recreation:* tennis (SA Hardcourt Champion, 1932–35). *Address:* 33 Hallett Road, Burnside, SA 5066, Australia. *Club:* Royal Commonwealth Society (Adelaide).

LITHERLAND, Prof. Albert Edward, (Ted), FRS 1974; FRSC 1968; University Professor, 1979–93, now Emeritus, and Professor of Physics, 1966–93, University of Toronto; Director, Isotrace Laboratory, University of Toronto, since 1982; *b* 12 March 1928; *e s* of Albert Litherland and Ethel Clement; *m* 1956, (Elizabeth) Anne Allen; two *d*. *Educ:* Wallasey Grammar Sch.; Univ. of Liverpool (BSc, PhD). State Scholar to Liverpool Univ., 1946; Rutherford Memorial Scholar to Atomic Energy of Canada, Chalk River, Canada, 1953; Scientific Officer at Atomic Energy of Canada, 1955–66. Guggenheim Fellow, Toronto Univ., 1986–87. Hon. DSc Toronto, 1998. Canadian Assoc. of Physicists Gold Medal for Achievement in Physics, 1971; Rutherford Medal and Prize of Inst. of Physics (London), 1974; JARI Silver Medal, Pergamon Press, 1981; Henry Marshall Tory Medal, RSC, 1993. Izaac Walton Killam Memorial Scholarship, 1980. *Publications:* numerous, in scientific jls. *Address:* Apt #801, 120 Rosedale Valley Road, Toronto, ON M4W 1P8, Canada. *T:* (416) 9235616; *e-mail:* ted.litherland@utoronto.ca.

LITHERLAND, Robert Kenneth; *b* 23 June 1930; *s* of Robert Litherland and Mary (*née* Parry); *m* 1953, Edna Litherland; one *s* one *d*. *Educ:* North Manchester High Sch. for Boys. Formerly sales representative for printing firm. Mem., Manchester City Council, 1971 (Dep. Chm., Housing Cttee, 1979; Chm., Manchester Direct Works Cttee, 1974–78); Dep. Chm., Public Works Cttee, Assoc. of Municipal Authorities, 1977–78. MP (Lab) Manchester Central, Sept. 1979–1997. Member: Council of Europe, 1987–97; WEU, 1987–97. *Address:* 32 Darley Avenue, Didsbury, Manchester M20 8YD.

LITHERLAND, Ted; *see* Litherland, A. E.

LITHGOW, Sir William (James), 2nd Bt *cr* 1925, of Ormsary; DL; CEng; industrialist and farmer; Vice-Chairman and Director, Lithgows Ltd, since 1956 (Chairman, 1959–84 and 1988–99); *b* 10 May 1934; *o s* of Colonel Sir James Lithgow, 1st Bt of Ormsary, GBE, CB, MC, TD, DL, JP, LLD, and Gwendolyn Amy, *d* of late John Robinson Harrison of Scalesceugh, Cumberland; *S* father, 1952; *m* 1964, Valerie Helen (*d* 1964), 2nd *d* of late Denis Scott, CBE and Mrs Laura Scott; *m* 1967, Mary Claire, (DL Argyll and Bute), *d* of Colonel F. M. Hill, CBE and Mrs Hill; two *s* one *d*. *Educ:* Winchester Coll. CEng; FRINA; CBIM 1980 (FBIM 1969). Chm., Scott Lithgow Drydocks Ltd, 1967–78; Vice-Chm., Scott Lithgow Ltd, 1968–78; Chairman: Western Ferries (Argyll) Ltd, 1972–85; Hunterston Develt Co. Ltd, 1987– (Dir, 1971–); Director: Bank of Scotland, 1962–86; Campbeltown Shipyard Ltd, 1970–96; Lithgows Pty Ltd, 1972–; Landcatch, 1981–96. Member: Council, Shipbuilding Employers Fedn, 1961–62; British Cttee, Det Norske Veritas, 1966–92; Exec. Cttee, Scottish Council Develt and Industry, 1969–85; Scottish Regional Council of CBI, 1969–76; Clyde Port Authority, 1969–71; Bd, National Ports Council, 1971–78; West Central Scotland Plan Steering Cttee, 1970–74; General Board (Royal Soc. nominee), Nat. Physical Lab., 1963–66; Greenock Dist Hosp. Bd, 1961–66; Scottish Milk Marketing Bd, 1979–83. Chm., Iona Cathedral Trustees Management Bd, 1979–83; Mem. Council, Winston Churchill Meml Trust, 1979–83. Hon. President: Mid Argyll Agricl Soc., 1976–99; Inverclyde and Dist Bn, Boys' Brigade, 1998–2000 (Vice Hon. Pres., 2000–); former Hon. Pres., W Renfrewshire Bn Boys' Brigade. Hon. Pres., Students Assoc., and Mem. Court, Univ. of Strathclyde, 1964–69. Petitioner in case of Lithgow and others *v* UK, at Eur. Court of Human Rights, 1986. Member, Queen's Body Guard for Scotland (Royal Company of Archers), 1964. Fellow: Scottish Council, 1988; Bishop Mus., Hawaii, 1969. FRSA 1990. DL Renfrewshire, 1970. Hon. LLD Strathclyde, 1979. *Publications:* lectures and papers. *Recreations:* rural life, invention, photography. *Heir: s* James Frank Lithgow [*b* 13 June 1970; *m* 1997, Claire, *yr d* of Nicholas du Cane Wilkinson; one *s* one *d*]. *Address:* Ormsary House, by Lochgilphead, Argyllshire PA31 8PE. *T:* (01880) 770252; Drums, Langbank, Renfrewshire PA14 6YH. *T:* (01475) 540606; RMB 125A, Karridale, WA 6288, Australia. *T:* (8) 97582261; (office) PO Box 7, Lochgilphead, Argyllshire PA31 8JH. *T:* (01880) 770711. *Clubs:* Oriental; Western, Royal Scottish Automobile (Glasgow).

LITHIBY, John Grant; Director, Panmure Gordon & Co. Ltd, since 1958 (Chairman, 1986–95); *b* 1 Dec. 1930; *s* of John Stewart Lithiby and Dorothy (*née* Schwartz); *m* 1961, Sarah Branch; two *s* one *d*. *Educ:* Eton Coll. Nat. Service, 1950–53; commnd Life Guards, 1950. Carl M. Loeb Rhoades, 1953–57; joined Panmure Gordon & Co. Ltd, 1957. *Recreations;* bridge, gardening, tennis. *Address:* Panmure Gordon & Co. Ltd, New Broad Street House, New Broad Street, EC2M 1NH. *Clubs:* White's, Hurlingham.

LITHMAN, Nigel Mordecai Lloyd; QC 1997; a Recorder, since 2000; *b* 9 March 1952; *s* of Dr Leslie Henry Lithman, FFARCS, and Ethel Imber Lithman. *Educ:* Bancroft's Sch., Woodford Green; Mid Essex Coll., Chelmsford (LLB Hons). Called to the Bar, Inner Temple, 1976; in practice at the Bar, 1976–; Asst Recorder, 1996–2000. *Recreations:* fresh air, the arts. *Address:* Highgate, London; Stanbrook Mead, Stanbrook, Thaxted, Essex CM6 2NQ. *Club:* Lansdowne.

LITTLE, Alastair; *see* Little, R. A.

LITTLE, Anthony Richard Morrell; Headmaster, Oakham School, 1996–Aug. 2002; Head Master, Eton College, from Sept. 2002; *b* 7 April 1954; *s* of Edward Little and Rosemary Margaret Little (*née* Morrell); *m* 1978, Jennifer Anne Greenwood; one *d*. *Educ:* Eton Coll.; Corpus Christi Coll., Cambridge (MA English); Homerton Coll., Cambridge (PGCE). FCollP 1990. Asst Master, Tonbridge Sch., 1977–82; Hd of English and Boarding Housemaster, Brentwood Sch., 1982–89; Headmaster, Chigwell Sch., 1989–96. Governor: Northwood Coll., 1990–98; St Albans Sch., 1994–; five prep schs. FRSA 1991. *Recreations:* films, theatre, music, Norfolk. *Address:* (until Aug. 2002) Chapel Close, Oakham, Rutland LE15 6DT. *T:* (01572) 722487; (from Sept. 2002) Eton College, Windsor, Berks SL4 6DL. *Club:* East India.

LITTLE, Ian Malcolm David, CBE 1997; AFC 1943; FBA 1973; Professor of Economics of Underdeveloped Countries, University of Oxford, 1971–76; *b* 18 Dec. 1918; *s* of Brig.-Gen. M. O. Little, CB, CBE, and Iris Hermione Little (*née* Brassey); *m* 1st, 1946, Doreen Hennessey (*d* 1984); one *s* one *d*; 2nd, 1991, Lydia Segrave. *Educ:* Eton; New Coll., Oxford (MA, DPhil; Hon. Fellow, 1999). RAF Officer, 1939–46. Fellow: All Souls Coll., Oxford, 1948–50; Trinity Coll., Oxford, 1950–52; Nuffield Coll., Oxford, 1952–76, Emeritus Fellow, 1976. Dep. Dir, Economic Section, Treasury, 1953–55; Mem., MIT Centre for Internat. Studies, India, 1958–59 and 1965; Vice-Pres., OECD Develt Centre, Paris, 1965–67. Dir, Investing in Success Ltd, 1960–65; Bd Mem., British Airports Authority, 1969–74. Dir, Gen. Funds Investment Trust, 1974–76; Special Adviser, IBRD, 1976–78. Hon. DSc(SocSci) Edinburgh, 1976. *Publications:* A Critique of Welfare Economics, 1950; The Price of Fuel, 1953; (jtly) Concentration in British Industry, 1960; Aid to Africa, 1964; (jtly) International Aid, 1965; (jtly) Higgledy-Piggledy Growth Again, 1966; (jtly) Manual of Industrial Project Analysis in Developing Countries, 1969; (jtly) Industry and Trade in Some Developing Countries, 1970; (jtly) Project Analysis and Planning, 1974; Economic Development: theory, policy and international relations, 1982; (jtly) Small Manufacturing Enterprises, 1987; (jtly) Boom, Crisis and Adjustment, 1993; (jtly) India: macroeconomics and political economy 1964–1991, 1994; (jtly) India's Economic Reforms 1991–2001, 1996; (ed jtly) India's Economic Reforms and Development: essays for Manmohan Singh, 1998; many articles in learned jls.

LITTLE, John Philip Brooke B.; *see* Brooke-Little.

LITTLE, (Robert) Alastair; chef and restaurant proprietor; *b* 25 June 1950; *s* of Robert Geoffrey Little and Marion Irving Little; one *s* one *d*; *m* 2000, Sharon Jacob. *Educ:* Kirkham Grammar Sch., Lancs; Downing Coll., Cambridge (MA). Chef proprietor: Le Routier, Suffolk, 1976; Simpson's, Putney, 1979; L'Escargot, Soho, 1981; 192, London, 1983; Alastair Little, Soho, 1985; Alastair Little, Lancaster Road, 1995; proprietor, La Cacciata, Orvieto, Italy, 1994. *Publications:* (with Richard Whittington) Keep it Simple, 1993; (with Richard Whittington) Food of the Sun, 1995; Alastair Little's Italian Kitchen, 1996; Soho Cooking, 1999. *Recreations:* reading, mycology. *Address:* 49 Frith Street, W1V 5TE. *T:* (020) 7437 6733. *Club:* Groucho.

LITTLE, Dr Robert Clement; Head of Chemistry Division, Agricultural Science Service, Ministry of Agriculture, Fisheries and Food, 1979–85; *b* 8 Nov. 1925; *s* of Ernest William Little and Hannah Little; *m* 1950, Margaret Isobel Wilson; two *d*. *Educ:* Carlisle Grammar Sch.; Manchester Univ. (BScTech); Glasgow Univ. (PhD). W of Scotland Agricultural Coll., 1946–55; Agricultural Develt and Adv. Service (formerly National Agricl Adv. Service), MAFF, 1955–85. *Recreations:* golf, gardening, fell walking. *Address:* 9 Ashcroft Close, Harpenden, Herts AL5 1JJ. *T:* (01582) 715613.

LITTLE, Tasmin, (Mrs M. Hatch); violinist; *b* 13 May 1965; *d* of George Villiers Little and Gillian (*née* Morris); *m* 1993, Michael Hatch; one *d*. *Educ:* Yehudi Menuhin Sch.; Guildhall Sch. of Music (DipGSM 1986). ARCM 1984. Has performed as soloist in UK, Europe, USA, Scandinavia, S America, Hong Kong, Oman, Zimbabwe and SA. Concerto performances with leading orchestras including: Leipzig Gewandhaus; Berlin Symphony; LSO; Philharmonia; Royal Philharmonic; Hallé; Bournemouth; Royal Liverpool Philharmonic; EC Chamber Orch.; Royal Danish; Stavanger Symphony; NY Philharmonic; Cleveland; acknowledged interpreter of music of Delius. TV appearances, radio broadcasts; recordings. FGSM. Hon. DLitt Bradford, 1996. *Publication:* contrib. Delius Soc. Jl. *Recreations:* theatre, cinema, swimming, cooking, languages. *Address:* c/o Askonas Holt Ltd, Lonsdale Chambers, 27 Chancery Lane, WC2A 1PF. *T:* (020) 7400 1700.

LITTLE, Most Rev. Thomas Francis, KBE 1977; DD, STD; Archbishop of Melbourne (RC), 1974–96; *b* 30 Nov. 1925; *s* of Gerald Thompson Little and Kathleen McCormack. *Educ:* St Patrick's Coll., Ballarat; Corpus Christi Coll., Werribee; Pontifical Urban Coll., Rome. STD Rome, 1953. Priest 1950; Asst Priest, Carlton, 1953–55; Secretary, Apostolic Deleg. to Aust., NZ and Oceania, 1955–59; Asst Priest, St Patrick's Cathedral, Melbourne, 1959–65; Dean, 1965–70; Episcopal Vicar for Lay Apostolate, 1969; Pastor, St Ambrose, Brunswick, 1971–73; Auxiliary Bishop, Archdiocese of Melbourne, 1973. STD *hc*, Melbourne Coll. of Divinity, 1992; DU Australian Catholic Univ., 1997. OM (Poland), 1999. *Address:* 21 Trafalgar Road, Camberwell, Vic 3124, Australia. *T:* (3) 98130291, *Fax:* (3) 98130296.

LITTLE, Dr Thomas William Anthony, CBE 2001; FIBiol; Director and Chief Executive, Veterinary Laboratories Agency (formerly Central Veterinary Laboratory), Ministry of Agriculture, Fisheries and Food, 1990–2000; *b* 27 June 1940; *s* of late Thomas Lowden Little and Marjorie Annie Little; *m* 1st, 1963 (marr. diss.); one *s* one *d*; 2nd, 1985, Sally Anne Headlam; two *s*. *Educ:* Dame Allan's Sch., Newcastle upon Tyne; Edinburgh Univ. (BVMS); London Univ. (Dip. Bact., PhD). MRCVS 1963. General veterinary practice, March, Cambs, 1963–66; joined MAFF, 1966; Central Vet. Lab., Weybridge, 1966–82, Sen. Res. Officer 1973–82; Dep. Regl Vet. Officer, 1982–85, Vet. Head of Section, 1985–86, Tolworth; Dep. Dir, Central Vet. Lab., 1986–90. Vice-Pres., BVA. FRSA. *Publications:* contribs to veterinary jls and text books. *Recreations:* outdoor activities. *Address:* 10 Fox Close, Pyrford, Woking, Surrey GU22 8LP.

LITTLECHILD, Prof. Stephen Charles; international consultant on privatisation, competition and regulation, since 1999; Principal Research Fellow, Judge Institute of Management Studies, University of Cambridge, since 2000; *b* 27 Aug. 1943; *s* of Sidney F. Littlechild and Joyce M. Littlechild (*née* Sharpe); *m* 1974, Kate Crombie (*d* 1982); two *s* one *d*. *Educ:* Wisbech Grammar Sch.; Univ. of Birmingham (BCom); Univ. of Texas (PhD). Temp. Asst Lectr in Ind. Econs, Univ. of Birmingham, 1964–65; Harkness Fellow, Stanford Univ., 1965–66; Northwestern Univ., 1966–68; Univ. of Texas at Austin, 1968–69; ATT Post-doctoral Fellow, UCLA and Northwestern Univ., 1969; Sen. Res. Lectr in Econs, Graduate Centre for Management Studies, Birmingham, 1970–72; Prof. of Applied Econs and Head of Econs, Econometrics, Statistics and Marketing Subject Gp, Aston Management Centre, 1972–75; Prof. of Commerce and Hd of Dept of Industrial Econs and Business Studies, Univ. of Birmingham, 1975–89; Dir Gen., Electricity Supply, 1989–98. Vis. Scholar, Dept of Econs, UCLA, 1975; Vis. Prof., New York, Stanford and Chicago Univs, and Virginia Polytechnic, 1979–80; Hon. Prof., Sch. of Business, Univ. of Birmingham, 1994–. Member: Monopolies and Mergers Commn, 1983–89; Sec. of State for Energy's Adv. Council on R&D, 1987–89. Hon. DSc Birmingham, 2001. Zale Award, Stanford Univ., 1999; Pace Catalyst Award, UMS Gp, 2000. *Publications:* Operational Research for Managers, 1977, 2nd edn (with M. F. Shutler) as Operations Research in Management, 1991; The Fallacy of the Mixed Economy, 1978, 2nd edn 1986; Elements of Telecommunications Economics, 1979; Energy Strategies for the UK, 1982; Regulation of British Telecommunications' Profitability, 1983; Economic Regulation of Privatised Water Authorities, 1986; Privatization, Competition and Regulation in the British Electricity Industry, with Implications for Developing Countries, 2000; over 60 articles in econs and ops res. jls. *Recreations:* football, genealogy. *Address:* White House, The Green, Tanworth-in-Arden B94 5AL; *e-mail:* sclittlechild@tanworth.mercianet.co.uk.

LITTLEJOHN, Alan Morrison; Director, Shipbuilders and Shiprepairers Association (formerly Shiprepairers and Shipbuilders Independent Association), 1977–90; Secretary General, UK Land and Hydrographic Survey Association Limited, 1980–90; retired; *b* 17 Oct. 1925; *s* of Frank Littlejohn and (Ethel) Lucy (*née* Main); *m* 1955, Joy Dorothy Margaret (*née* Till); one *d*. *Educ:* Dame Allan's Boys' Sch., Newcastle upon Tyne; King's Coll., Durham Univ. (BScAgric); Lincoln Coll. and Agricultural Economics Res. Inst., Oxford Univ. (BLitt, DipAgEcon). Asst Agric. Economist: King's Coll., Durham Univ., 1945–47; Wye Coll., London Univ., 1950–51; Agric. Chemical Div., Shell Internat. Chemical Co., London, 1951–67; Economist, Agric. Engineers Assoc., 1968–73; Dir Gen., Clay Pipe Develt Assoc., 1973–77; Dir, Assoc. of High Pressure Water Jetting Contractors, 1980–87. Chm., Catherine Place Personnel Services Ltd, 1981–89. Member: Chorleywood Parish Council, 1979–91 (Vice-Chm., 1984–85, 1987–88; Chm., 1985–87); (C) Three Rivers Dist Council, 1988–96 (Chm., Resources Cttee, 1990–91; Dep. Leader, 1990–91, Leader, 1991–95, Cons. Gp; Leader, 1992–94, Chm., 1995–96, Council). Hon. Life Vice-President: Chorleywood Cons. Assoc., 1998; SW Herts Cons. Assoc., 1999. *Recreation:* current affairs. *Address:* 5 The Readings, Chorleywood, Herts WD3 5SY. *T:* (01923) 284420.

LITTLEJOHN, Bel; *see* Brown, C. E. M.

LITTLEJOHN, Doris, CBE 1998; JP; retired as President, Industrial Tribunals (Scotland); *b* 19 March 1935; *m* 1958, Robert White Littlejohn; three *d*. *Educ:* Univ. of Glasgow (BL). Chm., Forth Valley Primary Care NHS Trust. Mem., Govt Human Genetics Adv. Commn, until 1999. Chm. Ct, Univ. of Stirling, 1999–. JP Stirlingshire, 1970. DUniv Stirling, 1993. *Address:* 125 Henderson Street, Bridge of Allan, Stirlingshire FK9 4RQ. *T:* (01786) 832032.

LITTLEJOHN, William Hunter, RSA 1973 (ARSA 1966); Head of Fine Art Department, 1982–85, Head of Drawing and Painting Department, 1970–85, Gray's School of Art, Aberdeen, (Lecturer, 1966–70); *b* Arbroath, 16 April 1929; *s* of late William Littlejohn and Alice Morton King. *Educ:* Arbroath High Sch.; Dundee Coll. of Art (DA). National Service, RAF, 1951–53; taught Art at Arbroath High Sch. until 1966. *One man exhibitions:* The Scottish Gallery, Edinburgh, 1962, 1967, 1972, 1977, 1984, 1989; Bohun Gall., Henley-on-Thames, 1991. Exhibits in RA, RSA, SSA, etc. *Address:* 43 Viewfield Road, Arbroath, Angus, Scotland DD11 2DW. *T:* (01241) 874402.

LITTLER, Sir (James) Geoffrey, KCB 1985 (CB 1981); Director, Montanaro UK Smaller Companies Investment Trust plc, 1995–2000; *b* 18 May 1930; *s* of late James Edward Littler and Evelyn Mary Littler (*née* Taylor); *m* 1958, Shirley Marsh (*see* Shirley Littler); one *s*. *Educ:* Manchester Grammar Sch.; Corpus Christi Coll., Cambridge (MA; Hon. Fellow, 1994). Asst Principal, Colonial Office, 1952–54; transf. to Treasury, 1954; Principal 1957; Asst Sec. 1966; Under-Sec. 1972; Dep. Sec., 1977; Second Permanent Sec. (Overseas Finance), 1983–88. Chairman: EC Monetary Cttee Deputies, 1974–77; Working Party 3, OECD, 1985–88; EC Monetary Cttee, 1987–88. Chairman: TR European Growth Trust plc, 1990–98; County NatWest Group Ltd, 1991–92; Director: NatWest Investment Bank, 1989–91; National Westminster Bank PLC, 1991–92; Chm., Israel Fund plc, 1994–99; Dir, Maritime Transport Services Ltd, 1990–93; Sen. Advr, BZW Ltd, 1993–98. *Recreation:* music. *Club:* Reform.

LITTLER, Shirley, (Lady Littler); Chairman, Gaming Board for Great Britain, 1992–98; *b* 8 June 1932; *d* of late Sir Percy William Marsh, CSI, CIE, and late Joan Mary Beecroft; *m* 1958, Sir (James) Geoffrey Littler, *qv*; one *s*. *Educ:* Headington Sch., Oxford; Girton Coll., Cambridge (MA; Hon. Commoner, 1998). Assistant Principal, HM Treasury, 1953; Principal: HM Treasury, 1960; Dept of Trade and Industry, 1964; HM Treasury, 1966; Asst Secretary, National Board for Prices and Incomes, 1969; Secretary, V&G Tribunal, 1971; transf. to Home Office, 1972, Asst Under-Sec. of State, 1978–83. Joined IBA, 1983; Dep. Dir Gen., 1986–89; Dir Gen., 1990. Chm., Gaming Regulators Eur. Forum, 1996–98. Chm., Nat. Adv. Body for Health Depts' Confidential Enquiry into Stillbirths and Deaths in Infancy, 1992–99. Trustee, Police Foundn, 1992–2001. *Recreations:* history, reading.

LITTLETON, family name of **Baron Hatherton**.

LITTLEWOOD, Joan (Maud); theatre artist; *b* 6 Oct. 1914. *Educ:* London. Dir, Theatre of Action, Manchester (street theatre), 1931–37; founder, Theatre Union, Manchester, introducing individual work system, 1937–39; freelance writer, 1939–45 (banned from BBC and ENSA for political opinions); founded Theatre Workshop with Gerry Raffles, 1945; touring in GB, Germany, Norway, Sweden with original works, 1945–50; moved to Theatre Royal, Stratford, London, with classics, 1953; invited to Theatre of the Nations, Paris, 1955, then yearly (Best Production of the Year three times); Centre Culturel, Hammamet, Tunisia, 1965–67; Image India, Calcutta, 1968; creation of Children's Environments, Bubble Cities, learn and play areas around Theatre Royal, Stratford, 1968–75. Left England to work in France, 1975; Seminar Relais Culturel, Aix-en-Provence, 1976. Productions include: Lysistrata, 1958 (Gold Medal, East Berlin, 1958; Olympic Award, Taormina, 1959), transferred to London from Stratford, 1960–61; Sparrers Can't Sing (film), 1962; Oh What a Lovely War (with Gerry Raffles and the Company), 1963; Vildrosen, Stockholm, 1995. Mem., French Academy of Writers, 1964. SWET Special Award, 1983. Women of Achievement in the Arts Award, Arts Council of GB, 1993; Lifetime's Achievement Award, Director's Guild, 1995. Dr *hc* Univ. of the Air, 1977; DUniv: Flinders, SA, 1995; Open, 1995. Commandeur de l'Ordre des Arts et des Lettres (France), 1986. *Publications:* Milady Vine: biography of Philippe de Rothschild, 1984; Joan's Book (autobiog.), 1994. *Recreation:* theatre. *Address:* c/o Theatre Royal Stratford East, Gerry Raffles Square, Newham, E15 1BN.

LITTLEWOOD, Prof. Peter Brent, PhD; Professor of Physics, Cavendish Laboratory, University of Cambridge, since 1997; Fellow, Trinity College, Cambridge, since 1997; *b* 18 May 1955; *s* of Horace Victor Littlewood and Edna May Littlewood; *m* 1978, Elizabeth Lamb; one *s* one *d*. *Educ:* St Olave's Sch., Orpington; Trinity Coll., Cambridge (BA 1976); Massachusetts Inst. of Technol. (Kennedy Schol.); Clare Coll., Cambridge (Denman Baynes Student; PhD 1980). Bell Laboratories, Murray Hill, New Jersey: Mem., Technical Staff, 1980–97; Hd, Theoretical Physics Res. Dept, 1992–97. Fellow, APS, 1988. *Publications:* numerous contribs to learned jls on theoretical condensed matter physics. *Recreations:* squash, music. *Address:* Cavendish Laboratory, Cambridge University, Madingley Road, Cambridge CB3 0HE. *T:* (01223) 339991.

LITTMAN, Mark; QC 1961; Director: Granada Group PLC, 1977–93; Burton Group plc, 1983–93; *b* 4 Sept. 1920; *s* of Jack and Lilian Littman; *m* 1965, Marguerite Lamkin, USA. *Educ:* Owen's Sch.; London Sch. of Economics; The Queen's Coll., Oxford. BScEcon. (first class hons) 1939; MA Oxon 1941. Served RN, Lieut, 1941–46. Called to Bar, Middle Temple, 1947, Bencher, 1970, Treas., 1988; practised, as Barrister-at-law, 1947–67 and 1979–; Member: General Council of the Bar, 1968–72; Senate of Inns of Court and the Bar, 1968. Dep. Chm., BSC, 1970–79. Mem. Royal Commn on Legal Services, 1976–79. Director: Rio Tinto-Zinc Corp. PLC, 1968–91; Commercial Union Assurance Co. Ltd, 1970–81; Amerada Hess Corp. (US), 1973–86; British Enkalon Ltd, 1976–80; Envirotech Corp. (US), 1974–78. Mem., Internat. Council for Commercial Arbitration, 1978–. Mem., Ct of Governors, LSE, 1980–. *Address:* 79 Chester Square, SW1W 9DU. *Clubs:* Garrick, Reform, Oxford and Cambridge, Royal Automobile; Century Association (New York).

LITTON, Andrew; conductor and pianist; Principal Conductor, Dallas Symphony Orchestra, since 1994; *b* New York, 16 May 1959; *m*; one *c*. *Educ:* Fieldston Sch., NYC; Juilliard Sch. of Music, NYC (piano with Nadia Reisenberg; Bruno Walter Meml Conducting Scholar). Rehearsal pianist, La Scala, Milan,1980–81; Staff Conductor, 1983–85, Associate Conductor, 1985–86, National SO, Washington; sometime Principal Conductor, Virginia Chamber Orch.; Principal Guest Conductor, 1986–88, Principal Conductor and Artistic Advr, 1988–94, Bournemouth SO, now Conductor Laureate. Début piano recital, Carnegie Hall, NY, 1979; conducting débuts include: Henry Wood Promenade Concert, 1983; RPO, 1983; Royal Opera House, Covent Garden, 1992. Winner: William Kapell Piano Comp., 1978; BBC/Rupert Foundn Internat. Conductors Comp., 1982. *Address:* c/o IMG Artists, 616 Chiswick High Road, W4 5RX.

LITTON, Peter Stafford; Under Secretary, Department of Education and Science, 1978–81; a General Commissioner of Income Tax, Epsom Division, 1983–96; *b* 26 Oct.

1921; *s* of late Leonard Litton and Louisa (*née* Horn); *m* 1942, Josephine Peggy Bale; one *d. Educ:* Barnstaple Grammar School. Clerical Officer, Board of Education, 1938. Served in Royal Corps of Signals, 1941–46. Min. of Education, 1946; Principal Private Sec. to Secretary of State for Educn and Science, 1965–66. *Recreations:* gardening, armchair astronomy. *Address:* 14 Guillards Oak, Midhurst, W Sussex GU29 9JZ. *T:* (01730) 815491.

LIU, Hon. Tsz-Ming, Benjamin; a Justice of Appeal, Court of Appeal of the High Court (formerly Supreme Court), Hong Kong, 1994–99; *b* 17 May 1931; *s* of late Dr Y. T. Liu and of Dorothy Mei-Kow (*née* Kwok); *m* 1954, Annemarie Marent; one *s* one *d. Educ:* Wah Yan College. Called to the Bar, Lincoln's Inn, 1957, Hong Kong, 1959; QC (Hong Kong) 1973; Judge of the District Court, Hong Kong, 1973–79; Judicial Comr, Supreme Ct, State of Brunei, 1978–89; a Judge of the High Court, Hong Kong, 1980–94. Panel Mem., Inland Revenue Bd of Review, Hong Kong, 1972; Chairman: Sub-Cttee on Bail in Criminal Proceedings, Law Reform Commn, 1985–89; Working Party on appropriate safeguards for execution of Anton Piller Orders, 1992–94. Pres., Hong Kong Local Judicial Officers' Assoc., 1992–99. Hong Kong Expert, China Foreign Experts Bureau, 2000; Hon. Pres., Hong Kong Soc. of Experts, 2001. *Publications:* How Are We Judged?, 2000; The Triad Societies Before and After the 1997 Change-over, 2001. *Address:* 18 22 Kennedy Road, Hong Kong. *T:* 28495803. *Clubs:* Hong Kong, Chinese, Hong Kong Country, Correctional Services Officers' (Hong Kong).

LIVELY, Penelope Margaret, OBE 1989; writer; *b* 17 March 1933; *d* of Roger Low and Vera Greer; *m* 1957, Jack Lively (*d* 1998); one *s* one *d. Educ:* St Anne's Coll., Oxford (BA Mod. History). Member: Soc. of Authors, 1973–; PEN, 1985–; British Library Bd, 1993–99; Bd, British Council, 1998–. FRSL 1985. *Publications: children's books:* Astercote, 1970; The Whispering Knights, 1971; The Wild Hunt of Hagworthy, 1971; The Driftway, 1972; The Ghost of Thomas Kempe, 1973 (Carnegie Medal); The House in Norham Gardens, 1974; Going Back, 1975; Boy Without a Name, 1975; A Stitch in Time, 1976 (Whitbread Award); The Stained Glass Window, 1976; Fanny's Sister, 1976; The Voyage of QV66, 1978; Fanny and the Monsters, 1979; Fanny and the Battle of Potter's Piece, 1980; The Revenge of Samuel Stokes, 1981; Fanny and the Monsters (three stories), 1983; Uninvited Ghosts and other stories, 1984; Dragon Trouble, 1984; Debbie and the Little Devil, 1987; A House Inside Out, 1987; The Cat, the Crow and the Banyan Tree, 1994; Staying with Grandpa, 1997; In Search of a Homeland: the story of the Aeneid, 2001; *non-fiction:* The Presence of the Past: an introduction to landscape history, 1976; Oleander, Jacaranda: a childhood perceived, 1994; A House Unlocked (memoir), 2001; *fiction:* The Road to Lichfield, 1976; Nothing Missing but the Samovar and other stories, 1978 (Southern Arts Literature Prize); Treasures of Time, 1979 (National Book Award); Judgement Day, 1980; Next to Nature, Art, 1982; Perfect Happiness, 1983; Corruption and other stories, 1984; According to Mark, 1984; Pack of Cards, collected short stories 1978–86, 1986; Moon Tiger, 1987 (Booker Prize); Passing On, 1989; City of the Mind, 1991; Cleopatra's Sister, 1993; Heat Wave, 1996; Beyond the Blue Mountains, 1997; Spiderweb, 1998; (ed with George Szirtes) New Writing 10, 2001; television and radio scripts. *Recreations:* gardening, landscape history, talking and listening. *Address:* c/o David Higham Associates, 5–8 Lower John Street, Golden Square, W1R 4HA. *T:* (020) 7437 7888.

LIVERMAN, John Gordon, CB 1973; OBE 1956; Deputy Secretary, Department of Energy, 1974–80; *b* London, 21 Oct. 1920; *s* of late George Gordon Liverman and Hadassah Liverman. *Educ:* St Paul's Sch.; Trinity Coll., Cambridge (BA). Served with RA, 1940–46. Civil servant in various government departments, 1947–80. *Address:* 24 Graces Mews, Camberwell, SE5 8JF. *T:* (020) 7708 5017.

LIVERPOOL, 5th Earl of, *cr* 1905 (2nd creation); **Edward Peter Bertram Savile Foljambe;** Baron Hawkesbury, 1893; Viscount Hawkesbury, 1905; Joint Chairman, Melbourns Brewery Ltd, since 1975 (Managing Director, 1970–87); Chairman and Managing Director, Rutland Properties Ltd, since 1987 (Director, since 1986); Chairman, Rutland Group, since 1996; *b* posthumously, 14 Nov. 1944; *s* of Captain Peter George William Savile Foljambe (killed in action, 1944) and of Elizabeth Joan (who *m* 1947, Major Andrew Antony Gibbs, MBE, TD), *d* of late Major Eric Charles Montagu Flint, DSO; *S* great uncle, 1969; *m* 1st, 1970, Lady Juliana Noel (marr. diss. 1994), *e d* of Earl of Gainsborough, *qv;* two *s;* 2nd, 1995, Marie-Ange, *e d* of Comte Géraud Michel de Pierredon. *Educ:* Shrewsbury School; Univ. for Foreigners, Perugia. Director: Rutland Properties Ltd, 1985–; Hart Hambleton Plc, 1986–92; J. W. Cameron & Co., 1987–90; Hilstone Developments Ltd, 1987–91; Rutland Management Ltd, 1989–. Elected Mem., H of L, 1999. *Heir: s* Viscount Hawkesbury, *qv. Address:* House of Lords, SW1A 0PW. *Clubs:* Turf, Pratt's, Air Squadron.

LIVERPOOL, Archbishop of, (RC), and Metropolitan of the Northern Province with Suffragan Sees, Hallam, Hexham, Lancaster, Leeds, Middlesbrough and Salford, since 1996; **Most Rev. Patrick Altham Kelly;** *b* 23 Nov. 1938; *s* of John Joseph Kelly and Mary Ann Kelly (*née* Altham). *Educ:* St Mary's Primary School, Morecambe; Preston Catholic Coll.; English College and Gregorian Univ., Rome (STL, PhL). Curate, Lancaster Cathedral, 1964–66; Lectr in Theology, 1966–79 and Rector, 1979–84, St Mary's Coll., Oscott; RC Bishop of Salford, 1984–96. *Address:* Archbishop's House, Lowood, Carnatic Road, Liverpool L18 8BY. *T:* (0151) 724 6398.

LIVERPOOL, Bishop of, since 1998; **Rt Rev. James Stuart Jones;** *b* 18 Aug. 1948; *s* of Major James Stuart Anthony Jones and Helen Jones; *m* 1980, Sarah Caroline Rosalind Marrow; three *d. Educ:* Duke of York's Royal Mil. Sch., Dover; Exeter Univ. (BA Hons Theol.); Wycliffe Hall, Oxford. Teacher, Sevenoaks Sch., 1970–74; Producer, Scripture Union, 1975–81; ordained deacon, 1982, priest, 1983; Curate, Christ Church, Clifton, 1982–90; Vicar, Emmanuel Church, S Croydon, 1990–94; Bishop Suffragan of Hull, 1994–98. Hon. DD Hull, 1999. *Publications:* Finding God, 1987; Why do people suffer?, 1993; The Power and the Glory, 1994; A Faith that touches the World, 1994; People of the Blessing, 1999. *Recreations:* opera, planning family holidays in France, swimming. *Address:* The Bishop's Lodge, Woolton Park, Woolton, Liverpool L25 6DT. *T:* (0151) 421 0831, *Fax:* (0151) 428 3055.

LIVERPOOL, Auxiliary Bishop of, (RC); *see* Malone, Rt Rev. Vincent.

LIVERPOOL, Dean of; *see* Hoare, Rt Rev. R. W. N.

LIVERPOOL, Archdeacon of; *see* Metcalf, Ven. R. L.

LIVERSIDGE, Pamela Edwards, OBE 1999; DL; DSc; FREng, FIMechE; Managing Director, Quest Investments Ltd, since 1997; President, Institution of Mechanical Engineers, 1997–98; *b* 23 Dec. 1949; *d* of William H. Humphries and Dorothy Humphries; *m* 1st, 1971, Dr Dale S. Edwards (marr. diss. 1980); 2nd, 1991, Douglas B. Liversidge; two step *s* one step *d. Educ:* Aston Univ. (BSc Hons 1971; DSc 1998). CEng 1980; FIMechE 1988; FCGI 1997; FREng 1999. Graduate trainee and project engr, GKN plc, 1971–73; Thornton Precision Forgings: Asst Technical Manager, 1973–78; Prodn Control Manager, 1978–81; Aerofoils Product Manager, 1981–86; Sales and Mkting Dir, 1986–89; Strategic Planning Manager, E Midlands Electricity plc, 1989–93; Man. Dir, Scientific Metal Powders Ltd, 1993–97. Dir, Sheffield TEC, 1997–; Chm., Sheffield Business Link, 1998–. Vis. Prof., Sheffield Univ., 1996–. Gov., Sheffield Hallam Univ., 1994–. FRSA 1996. DL S Yorks, 1999. DUniv UCE, 1998; DEng Bradford, 2000. *Recreations:* golf, public speaking at specialist events. *Address:* 309 Ecclesall Road South, Sheffield S11 9PW. *T:* (0114) 296 2009, *Fax:* (0114) 220 9371.

LIVESAY, Adm. Sir Michael (Howard), KCB 1989; Chief of Naval Personnel, Second Sea Lord and Admiral President, Royal Naval College, Greenwich, 1991–93; *b* 5 April 1936; *s* of William Lindsay Livesay and Margaret Eleanor Chapman Steel; *m* 1959, Sara House; two *d. Educ:* Acklam Hall Grammar Sch.; Britannia Royal Naval Coll. Joined RN, 1952; training appts, 1954–57; commnd 1957; qual. Aircraft Direction Specialist, 1959; Direction Officer, HMS Hermes, HMS Aisne, Fighter Direction Sch., and 893 Sqdn, 1959–66; i/c HMS Hubberston, 1966–68, HMS Plymouth, 1970–72; Captain Fishery Protection/Captain Mine Counter Measures, 1975–77; 1st CO HMS Invincible, 1979–82; Dir of Naval Warfare, 1982–84; Flag Officer Sea Training, 1984–85; ACNS, 1986–88; Flag Officer Scotland and NI, 1989–91. Director: Scottish Nuclear, 1993–98; ICM (formerly Inter Exec) Scotland Ltd, 1994–98. Comr, Northern Lighthouse Bd, 1994– (Chm., 1997–2001). Pres., RBL, Scotland, 1996–. *Recreations:* sailing, ski-ing, fishing, golf. *Address:* c/o The Naval Secretary, Victory Building, HM Naval Base, Portsmouth PO1 3LS. *Clubs:* Army and Navy, Royal Navy of 1765 and 1785; Royal Perth; Royal Yacht Squadron.

LIVESEY, Bernard Joseph Edward; QC 1990; a Recorder, since 1987; a Deputy High Court Judge, since 1998; *b* 21 Feb. 1944; *s* of Joseph Augustine Livesey and Marie Gabrielle Livesey (*née* Caulfeild); *m* 1971, Penelope Jean Harper; two *d. Educ:* Cardinal Vaughan Sch., London; Peterhouse, Cambridge (MA, LLB). Called to the Bar, Lincoln's Inn, 1969. Fellow, Internat. Acad. of Trial Lawyers, 1993. *Recreations:* music, gardening, ski-ing, bellringing. *Address:* 4–5 New Square, Lincoln's Inn, WC2A 3RJ. *T:* (020) 7822 2000.

LIVESEY, David Anthony, PhD; Secretary General of Faculties, University of Cambridge, since 1992; Fellow, Emmanuel College, Cambridge, since 1974; *b* 30 May 1944; *s* of Vincent Livesey and Marie Livesey (*née* Parr); *m* 1967, Sally Anne Vanston; one *s* two *d. Educ:* Derby Sch.; Imperial Coll., Univ. of London (ACGI; BSc Eng); Christ's Coll., Cambridge (PhD 1971). University of Cambridge: Res. Officer in Applied Econs, 1969–75; Lectr in Engrg, 1975–91; Cambridge Dir, Cambridge-MIT Inst., 1999–2000; Res. Fellow, Peterhouse, 1971–74; Tutor, 1975–83, Bursar, 1983–91, Emmanuel Coll. Mem., HM Treasury Cttee on Policy Optimisation, 1976–78. Dir, Cambridge Econometrics Ltd, 1981–84 (Chm., 1982–84). Non-exec. Dir, Addenbrooke's NHS Trust, 1993–99. Gov., St Albans RC Primary Sch., 1977–92 (Chm., 1984–92). *Recreations:* books, swimming, trying to learn Welsh. *Address:* The Old Schools, Cambridge CB2 1TT. *T:* (01223) 765929.

LIVESEY, Ronald John Dearden; QC 1981; **His Honour Judge Livesey;** a Circuit Judge, since 1992; Senior Judge, Sovereign Base Areas, Cyprus, since 1996 (Deputy Senior Judge, 1983–96); *b* 11 Sept. 1935; *s* of John William and Una Florence Livesey; *m* 1965, Elizabeth Jane Coutts; one *s* one *d. Educ:* Malvern Coll.; Lincoln Coll., Oxford (MA). Called to the Bar, Lincoln's Inn, 1962, Bencher, 1989; a Recorder, 1981–92. *Recreation:* golf. *Address:* Preston Crown Court, Openshaw Way, Preston PR1 2LL. *Club:* Union (Southport).

LIVESLEY, Prof. Brian, MD; FRCP; Professor in the Care of the Elderly, University of London at Imperial College School of Medicine (formerly Charing Cross and Westminster Medical School), 1988–2001; Director-General, St John Ambulance, 1994–96 (Assistant Director-General, 1993–94); *b* 31 Aug. 1936; *s* of late Thomas Clement Livesley and Stella Livesley; *m* 1st, 1963, Beryl Hulme (*d* 1966); one *s;* 2nd, 1969, Valerie Anne Nuttall; two *d. Educ:* King George V Grammar Sch., Southport; Leeds Univ. Med. Sch. (MB, ChB 1960); Univ. of London (MD 1979). MRCP 1971, FRCP 1989. DHMSA 1973. Hospital appointments: Leeds Gen. Infirmary, 1961–62; Dist and Univ. Hosps, Leeds, Manchester and Liverpool, 1963–68; Harvey Res. Fellow, KCH, 1969–72; Cons. Physician in Geriatric Medicine, Lambeth, Southwark and Lewisham HA, 1973–87. Clinical Examnr in Medicine, Univ. of London, 1980–94 (Sen. Examnr, 1990–94); External Examnr, Royal Free and UC Med. Sch., 1998–; Examiner: for Dip. in Geriatric Medicine, RCP, 1987–93; in Medicine, Soc. of Apothecaries, 1987–93; Mem., United Examng Bd for England and Scotland, 1993–96. NW Thames Regl Advr on Medicine for the Elderly, 1990–; Chm., N Thames Regl Trng Commn, 1993–. Mem., Med. Commn on Accident Prevention, 1984–89 (Chm., Home and Family Safety Commn, 1988–89). Freeman, City of London, 1975; Liveryman, Soc. of Apothecaries, 1980– (Yeoman, 1975; Mem. Ct of Assts, 1990–; Chm., Futures Cttee, 1999–; Chm., Acad. Cttee, 2000–). JP SE London, 1983–96. KStJ 1994. *Publications:* monographs and investigations on scientific, historical, educnl and forensic problems of medicine in our ageing soc. *Recreations:* family, Christian culture study, encouraging people to think. *Address:* Chelsea and Westminster Hospital, Fulham Road, SW10 9NH. *T:* (020) 8746 8063, *Fax:* (020) 8746 8183; PO Box 295, Oxford OX2 9GD.

LIVINGSTON, Air Vice-Marshal Graham; consultant occupational health physician; *b* 2 Aug. 1928; *s* of late Neil Livingston and Margaret Anderson (*née* Graham); *m* 1970, Carol Judith Palmer; one *s* one *d* (and one *s* one *d* (and one *d* decd) of former marriage). *Educ:* Bo'ness Academy; Edinburgh Univ. (MB ChB 1951, DPH 1963); DIH (Conjoint) 1963; MFPHM (MFCM 1974); MFOM 1981. Joined RAF 1952; served N Ireland and Egypt, 1952–55; civilian GP and obst., 1956–57; rejoined RAF 1958; served Lindholme and Honington, 1958–62; post grad. study in public and indust. health, Edinburgh Univ., 1962–63; SMO, RAF Laarbruch, 1963–66; RAF Coll., Cranwell, 1966–70; served Cosford, Halton and Akrotiri, 1970–74; OC RAF Hosps, Cosford, 1974–76, Wegberg, 1976–79; Dep. Dir. Med. Personnel and Dep. Dir Med. Orgn, MoD, 1979–80; Dep. PMO, Strike Command, 1981–83; Principal Medical Officer: RAF Germany, 1983–84; RAF Support Comd, 1984–89; QHS 1985–89. Consultant in community medicine, 1984; Consultant Occupational Health Physician: NW Herts HA, 1989–94; Wycombe HA, 1991–94. Freeman, City of London, 1982. FIMgt (FBIM 1986). *Recreations:* golf, gardening, dog walking. *Address:* c/o Lloyds TSB, Cox's and King's Branch, PO Box 1190, 7 Pall Mall, SW1Y 5NA. *Clubs:* Royal Air Force; Ashridge Golf.

LIVINGSTONE, Prof. David Noel, PhD; FBA 1995; MRIA; Professor of Geography and Intellectual History, Queen's University of Belfast, since 1997 (Professor of Geography, 1993–97); *b* 15 March 1953; *s* of Robert Livingstone and Winifred (*née* Turkington); *m* 1977, Frances Allyson Haugh; one *s* one *d. Educ:* Queen's Univ. of Belfast (BA; PhD; DipEd). Queen's University, Belfast: Curator of Maps, 1984–89; Lectr, 1989–91; Reader, 1991–93; British Acad. Res. Reader, 1999–2001. Visiting Professor: Calvin Coll., Michigan, 1989–90; Univ. of Notre Dame, Indiana, 1995; Regent Coll., Vancouver, 1997, 2000; Vis. Noted Scholar, Univ. of BC, 1999. Lectures: Charles Lyell, BAAS, 1994–95; Hettner, Univ. of Heidelberg, 2001. Mem. Ct, Univ. of Ulster,

1996–2000, 2001–. MRIA 1998 (Mem., Nat. Cttee for Hist. and Philosophy of Sci., 1988–96, for Geography, 1996–; Mem. Council, 2001–02); FRSA 2001. Adm. Back Award, RGS, 1997; Centenary Medal, RSGS, 1998; Templeton Foundn Lect. Award, 1999. *Publications:* Nathaniel Southgate Shaler and the Culture of American Science, 1987; Darwin's Forgotten Defenders, 1987; The Preadamite Theory, 1992; The Geographical Tradition, 1992; (ed jtly) The Behavioural Environment, 1989; (ed jtly) Charles Hodge, What is Darwinism, 1994; (ed jtly) Human Geography: an essential anthology, 1996; (jtly) Them and Us, 1997; (jtly) Ulster-American Religion, 1999; (ed jtly) Evangelicals and Science in Historical Perspective, 1999; (ed jtly) Geography and Enlightenment, 1999; articles in learned jls. *Recreations:* music, photography. *Address:* School of Geosciences, Queen's University of Belfast, Belfast BT7 1NN. *T:* (028) 9033 5145.

LIVINGSTONE, Ian Lang, CBE 1998 (OBE 1993); Chairman: Lanarkshire Health Board, since 1993 (Member, since 1989); Scottish Enterprise Lanarkshire (formerly Lanarkshire Development Agency), 1991–2000; *b* 23 Feb. 1938; *s* of John Lang Livingstone and Margaret Steele Livingstone (*née* Barbour); *m* 1967, Diane Hales; two *s*. *Educ:* Hamilton Acad.; Glasgow Univ. (BL). NP 1960. Qualified as solicitor, 1960; apprentice, Alex L. Wright & Co., Solicitors, 1957–60, legal asst, 1960–62; Ballantyne & Copland, Solicitors: Partner, 1962–70; Sen. Partner, 1970–86; Consultant, 1986–; Chm. and Dir, Bowmere Properties Ltd, 1967–; Chairman: New Lanarkshire Ltd; Clan FM Ltd. Chm., Motherwell Coll. Bd, 1991–98. Chm., Motherwell FC, 1975–88. *Recreations:* football, walking, travelling, music. *Address:* Roath Park, 223 Manse Road, Motherwell, Strathclyde ML1 2PY. *T:* (01698) 253750.

LIVINGSTONE, Kenneth Robert, (Ken); Mayor of London, since 2000; *b* 17 June 1945; *s* of late Robert Moffat Livingstone and Ethel Ada Livingstone; *m* 1973, Christine Pamela Chapman (marr. diss. 1982). *Educ:* Tulse Hill Comprehensive Sch.; Philippa Fawcett Coll. of Educn (Teacher's Cert.). Technician, Chester Beatty Cancer Res. Inst., 1962–70. Joined Labour Party, 1969; Reg. Exec., Greater London Lab. Party, 1974–86; Lambeth Borough Council: Councillor, 1971–78; Vice-Chm., Housing Cttee, 1971–73; Camden Borough Council: Councillor, 1978–82; Chm., Housing Cttee, 1978–80; Greater London Council: Mem. for Norwood, 1973–77, for Hackney N, 1977–81, for Paddington, 1981–86; Lab. Transport spokesman, 1980–81; Leader of Council and of Lab. Gp, 1981–86. Mem., NEC, Labour Party, 1987–89, 1997–98. Contested (Lab) Hampstead, 1979. MP (Lab) Brent East, 1987–2001. Mem., NI Select Cttee, 1997–99. Mem. Council, Zoological Soc. of London, 1994–98 and 1999– (Vice-Pres., 1996–98). *Publications:* If voting changed anything they'd abolish it, 1987; Livingstone's Labour, 1989. *Recreations:* cinema, science fiction, gardening, natural history. *Address:* Greater London Authority, Romney House, 43 Marsham Street, SW1P 3PY.

LIVSEY, family name of **Baron Livsey of Talgarth**.

LIVSEY OF TALGARTH, Baron *cr* 2001 (Life Peer), of Talgarth in the County of Powys; **Richard Arthur Lloyd Livsey,** CBE 1994; *b* 2 May 1935; *s* of Arthur Norman Livsey and Lilian Maisie (*née* James); *m* 1964, Irene Martin Earsman; two *s* one *d*. *Educ:* Talgarth County Primary Sch.; Bedales Sch.; Seale-Hayne Agricl Coll.; Reading Univ. (MSc Agric.). Develt Officer, Agric. Div., ICI, 1961–67; Farm Manager, Blairdrummond, 1967–71; farmer at Llanon; Sen. Lectr in Farm Management, Welsh Agricl Coll., Aberystwyth, 1971–85; Develt Manager, ATB Landbase Wales, 1992–95. Joined Liberal Party, 1960, contested (L): Perth and E Perth, 1970; Pembroke, 1979; Brecon and Radnor, 1983; MP (L July 1985–1988, Lib Dem 1988–92) Brecon and Radnor; MP (Lib Dem) Brecon and Radnorshire, 1997–2001. Liberal Party spokesman on agric., 1985–87; Alliance spokesman on the countryside and on agric. in Wales, and on Wales, 1987; Leader, Welsh Liberal Democrats and Party Spokesman on Wales, 1988–92 and 1997–2001. Chm., Brecon Jazz Fest., 1993–96; Mem., Talgarth Male Voice Choir, 1993–. Pres., Brecon and Dist Disabled Club, 1986–. *Recreations:* cricket, fishing. *Address:* House of Lords, SW1A 0PW.

LLANDAFF, Bishop of, since 1999; **Rt Rev. Barry Cennydd Morgan,** PhD; *b* 31 Jan. 1947; *s* of Rees Haydn Morgan and Mary Gwyneth Morgan; *m* 1969, Hilary Patricia Lewis; one *s* one *d*. *Educ:* Ystalyfera Grammar Sch.; University Coll. London (BA Hons History 1969); Selwyn Coll., Cambridge (BA Hons Theol. 1971); Westcott House, Cambridge. MA Cantab 1974; PhD Wales 1986. Priest, Llandaff, 1973; Curate, St Andrew's Major, Dinas Powis, 1972–75; Chaplain, Bryn-y-Don Community Sch., 1972–75; Chaplain and Lectr, St Michael's Coll., Llandaff, 1975–77; Lectr, University Coll., Cardiff, 1975–77; Warden of Church Hostel, Bangor, Anglican Chap., UCNW and Lectr in Theology, UCNW, 1977–84; Rector of Wrexham, 1984–86; Archdeacon of Merioneth and Rector of Criccieth, 1986–92; Bishop of Bangor, 1993–99. Editor, Welsh Churchman, 1975–82. Exam. Chaplain to Abp of Wales, 1978–82, to Bp of Bangor, 1983; Diocese of Bangor: In-Service Trng Officer, 1979–84; Warden of Ordinands, 1982–84; Canon of Bangor Cathedral, 1983–84. Mem., Archbishop's Doctrinal Commn, 1982–93 (Chm. 1989–93); Chm., Div. of Stewardship, Provincial Bd of Mission, 1988–95. Vice-Chairman: Nat. Soc., 1999; Bible Soc., 1999. *Publications:* O Ddydd i Ddydd, Pwyllgor Darlleniadau Beiblaidd Cyngor Eglwysi Cymru, 1980; History of the Church Hostel and Anglican Chaplaincy at University College of North Wales, Bangor, 1986; Concepts of Mission and Ministry in Anglican University Chaplaincy Work, 1988. *Recreation:* golf. *Address:* Llys Esgob, The Cathedral Green, Llandaff, Cardiff CF5 2YE.

LLANDAFF, Dean of; *see* Lewis, Very Rev. J. T.

LLEWELLIN, Rt Rev. John Richard Allan; Head of the Archbishop of Canterbury's staff (with title of Bishop at Lambeth), since 1999; *b* 30 Sept. 1938; *s* of John Clarence Llewellin and Margaret Gwenllian Llewellin; *m* 1965, Jennifer Sally (*née* House); one *s* two *d*. *Educ:* Clifton College, Bristol; Westcott House and Fitzwilliam Coll., Cambridge (MA). Solicitor, 1960. Ordained deacon, 1964; priest, 1965; Curate at Radlett, Herts, 1964–68; Curate at Johannesburg Cathedral, 1968–71; Vicar of Waltham Cross, 1971–79; Rector of Harpenden, 1979–85; Suffragan Bishop: of St Germans, 1985–92; of Dover, 1992–99. Chm., USPG, 1994–97. *Recreations:* sailing, DIY. *Address:* Lambeth Palace, SE1 7JU. *T:* (020) 7898 1200, *Fax:* (020) 7898 1210; *e-mail:* richard.llewellin@lampal.c-of-e.org.uk.

LLEWELLYN, Bryan Henry; Director, Granada Travel PLC, 1989–92; *s* of Nora and Charles Llewellyn; *m* 1983, Joanna (*née* Campbell); two *s*. *Educ:* Charterhouse; Clare Coll., Cambridge (BA). Commissioned, The Queen's, 1946. Research Asst, Dept of Estate Management, Cambridge, 1954; joined Fisons Ltd, 1955; Marketing Manager, Greaves & Thomas Ltd, 1960; Regional Marketing Controller, Thomson Regional Newspapers Ltd, 1962; Marketing Dir, TRN Ltd, 1966; Managing Director: Thomson Holidays Ltd, 1969; Thomson Travel Ltd, 1972 (Chm., 1977–78); Exec. Dir, Thomson Organisation Ltd, 1972–80; Man. Dir and Chief Exec., Thomson Publications Ltd, 1977–80; Man. Dir, The Kitchenware Merchants Ltd, 1985–88. Non-exec. Dir, Orion Insurance Ltd, 1976–92. *Club:* Reform.

LLEWELLYN, Sir David St Vincent, (Sir Dai), 4th Bt *cr* 1922, of Bwllfa, Aberdare, co. Glamorgan; impresario, writer and broadcaster; *b* 2 April 1946; *er s* of Sir Harry Llewellyn, 3rd Bt, CBE and Hon. Christine Saumarez, 2nd *d* of 5th Baron de Saumarez; *S* father, 1999; *m* 1980, Vanessa Mary Theresa Hubbard (marr. diss. 1987); two *d*. *Educ:* Eton; Univ. d'Aix-Marseille. Chevalier, l'Ordre des Côteaux de Champagne, 1992. KLJ 2000 (CLJ 1995). *Recreations:* equestrian sports, wildlife conservation. *Heir: b* Roderic Victor Llewellyn [*b* 9 Oct. 1947; *m* 1981, Tatiana Manora Caroline Soskin; three *d*]. *Address:* Studio Two, 2 Lansdowne Row, W1X 8HL. *T:* (020) 7413 9533.

LLEWELLYN, Prof. David Thomas; Professor of Money and Banking, and Chairman of the Banking Centre, Loughborough University, since 1976; Public Interest Director, Personal Investment Authority, since 1994; Director, Personal Investment Authority Ombudsman Bureau Ltd, since 1994; *b* 3 March 1943; *s* of Alfred George Llewellyn and Elsie Alexandria Frith; *m* 1970, Wendy Elizabeth James; two *s*. *Educ:* William Ellis Grammar Sch., London; London Sch. of Econs and Pol Science (BSc Econ). FCIB. Economist: Unilever NV, Rotterdam, 1964; HM Treasury, London, 1965–67; Lectr in Econs, Nottingham Univ., 1967–73; Economist, IMF, Washington, 1973–76. Consultant Economist to: Harlow Butler Ueda, 1981–99; Garban Intercapital plc; Mem., London Bd of Dirs, Halifax Building Soc., 1988–93; at various times Consultant to World Bank, Building Societies Assoc., bldg socs and banks in UK and overseas. Member: Bank of England Panel of Academic Consultants; Internat. Adv. Bd, Italian Bankers' Assoc., 1994–; Exec. Bd, European Financial Management Assoc., 1994–; Internat. Adv. Bd, NCR Financial Solutions (formerly NCR Financial Systems) Gp, 1997–; Financial Services Panel, DTI Technology Foresight Prog., 1997–. Special Advr, H of C and H of L Jt Cttee on Financial Services and Markets, 1999–. Pres., Société Universitaire Européenne Recherches Financières, 2000–. TV and radio broadcasts on financial issues. FRSA. *Publications:* International Financial Integration, 1980; Framework of UK Monetary Policy, 1984; The Evolution of the British Financial System, 1985; Prudential Regulation and Supervision of Financial Institutions, 1986; Reflections on Money, 1989; (ed) Recent Developments in International Monetary Economics, 1991; (ed) Surveys in Monetary Economics, vols 1 and 2, 1991; Competition or Credit Controls?, 1991; (jtly) Financial Regulations: why, how and where now?, 1998; Economic Rationale of Financial Resulation, 1998; The New Economics of Banking, 1999; articles in academic and professional jls and books on monetary policy and instns, and on internat. finance. *Recreations:* DIY, culinary arts, travel, boating. *Address:* 8 Landmere Lane, Ruddington, Notts NG11 6ND. *T:* (0115) 921 6071; Economics Department, Loughborough University, Loughborough, Leics LE11 3TU. *T:* (01509) 222700.

LLEWELLYN, David Walter, CBE 1983; Director, Walter Llewellyn & Sons Ltd, and other Companies in the Llewellyn Group, since 1953; *b* 13 Jan. 1930; *s* of late Eric Gilbert and Florence May Llewellyn; *m* 1st, 1955, Josephine Margaret Buxton (marr. diss. 1985); three *s*; 2nd, 1985, Tessa Caroline Sandwith. *Educ:* Radley College. FCIOB. Commissioned Royal Engineers, 1952. Industrial Adviser to Minister of Housing and Local Govt, 1967–68; Mem., Housing Corp., 1975–77; Pres., Joinery and Timber Contractors' Assoc., 1976–77; Chm., Nat. Contractors' Gp of Nat. Fedn of Building Trades Employers (now Building Employers Confedn), 1977; Chm., Building Regulations Adv. Cttee, 1977–85 (Mem. 1966–74); Dep. Chm., Nat. Building Agency, 1977–82 (Dir. 1968–82). Pres., CIOB, 1986–87. Master, Worshipful Co. of Tin Plate Workers alias Wireworkers, 1985. Governor, St Andrew's Sch., Eastbourne, 1966–70, Trustee, Queen Alexandra Cottage Homes, Eastbourne, 1973–94. Provincial Grand Master, Sussex, United Grand Lodge of Freemasons of England, 1989–97. *Recreation:* the use, restoration and preservation of historic vehicles. *Address:* (office) 16/20 South Street, Eastbourne BN21 4XE; (home) Cooper's Cottage, Chiddingly, near Lewes, East Sussex BN8 6HD. *Clubs:* Reform; Devonshire (Eastbourne), Eastbourne.

LLEWELLYN, Sir Donald Rees, (Sir Don), KNZM 1999; CBE 1992; JP; Foundation Vice-Chancellor, University of Waikato, 1964–85; *b* 20 Nov. 1919; *s* of late R. G. Llewellyn, Dursley; *m* 1943, Ruth Marian, *d* of late G. E. Blandford, Dursley; one *s* one *d*. *Educ:* Dursley Grammar Sch.; Univ. of Birmingham, 1939–41, BSc 1st cl. hons Chem. 1941, DSc 1957; Oxford 1941–44, DPhil 1943. Research Fellow, Cambridge Univ., 1944–46; Lectr in Chemistry, UC of N Wales, 1946–49; ICI Research Fellow, UCL, 1949–52; Lectr in Chemistry, UCL, 1952–57; Prof. of Chemistry and Dir of Labs, Univ. of Auckland, 1957–64; Asst Vice-Chancellor, Univ. of Auckland, 1962–64. Mem., NZ Atomic Energy Cttee, 1958–85. Pres., NZ Inst. Chemistry, 1967 and 1988 (Vice-Pres., 1965–67, 1986–88). Member: Council, Hamilton Teachers Coll., 1965–85; Council, Waikato Tech. Inst., 1968–85; Pres., NZ Nat. Fieldays Soc., 1969–75 and 1978–81 (Life Mem., 1981); Patron, Waikato Med. Res. Foundn, 1990–99. Paul Harris Fellow, Rotary Foundn. Hon. Mem., Golden Key Internat. Honor Soc., 2001. JP Waikato, 1971. Freeman, City of Hamilton, 1985. CChem, FRSC (FRIC 1952); FNZIC 1957 (Hon. FNZIC 1985); FRSA 1960. Hon. Dr Waikato, 1985. Waikato Business Pioneer, 1990; Thomson Medal, Royal Soc. of NZ, 1994. *Publications:* numerous papers on application of stable isotopes in Jl Chem. Soc. and others. *Recreations:* showjumping (FEI Judge), photography, travel. *Address:* RD4, Hamilton, New Zealand. *T:* (7) 8569172. *Club:* Hamilton (NZ).

LLEWELLYN, Rear-Adm. Jack Rowbottom, CB 1974; Assistant Controller of the Navy, 1972–74; retired; *b* 14 Nov. 1919; *s* of Ernest and Harriet Llewellyn, Ashton under Lyne, Lancs; *m* 1944, Joan Isabel, *d* of Charles and Hilda Phillips, Yelverton, Devon; one *s*. *Educ:* Purley County Sch. Entered RN, 1938; RNEC, Keyham, 1939. Served War of 1939–45: HMS Bermuda, 1942; RNC, Greenwich, 1943; HMS Illustrious, 1945. Engr in Chief's Dept, Admlty, 1947; HMS Sluys, 1949; HMS Thunderer, 1951; HMS Diamond, 1953; Comdr, 1953; Asst Engr in Chief, on loan to Royal Canadian Navy, 1954; in charge Admty Fuel Experimental Station, Haslar, 1958; HMS Victorious, 1960; Asst Dir, Marine Engrg, MoD (N), 1963; Captain, 1963; in command, HMS Fisgard, 1966; Dep. Dir, Warship Design, MoD (N), 1969; Rear-Adm., 1972. *Recreations:* travel, gardening. *Address:* 3 Jubilee Terrace, Chichester, W Sussex PO19 1XL. *T:* (01243) 780180.

LLEWELLYN, His Honour John Desmond S.; *see* Seys-Llewellyn.

LLEWELLYN, Rev. Richard Morgan, CB 1992; OBE 1979 (MBE 1976); Director, Christ College, Brecon Foundation, since 2001; *b* 22 Aug. 1937; *s* of Griffith Robert Poyntz Llewellyn and Bridget Margaret Lester Llewellyn (*née* Karslake); *m* 1964, Elizabeth Lamond (Polly) Sobey; three *s* one *d* (and one *d* decd). *Educ:* Haileybury; Imperial Service College; rcds, psc; Salisbury and Wells Theol Coll. Enlisted Royal Welch Fusiliers (Nat. Service), 1956; active service, Malaya and Cyprus, 1957–59; Instructor, Army Outward Bound Sch., 1962–63; Staff Coll., 1970; MA to CGS, 1971–72; Brigade Major, 1974–76; CO, 1st Bn RWF, 1976–79; Directing Staff, RCDS, 1979–81; Comdr, Gurkha Field Force, 1981–84; Dir, Army Staff Duties, 1985–87; GOC Wales, 1987–90; C of S, HQ UKLF, 1990–91; retired in rank of Maj.-Gen. Ordained deacon, 1993, priest, 1994; Minor Canon, Brecon Cathedral and Asst Curate, Brecon with Battle and Llandew, 1993–95; Chaplain, Christ Coll., Brecon, 1995–2001. Regtl Col, Gurkha Transport Regt, subseq. Queen's Own Gurka Transport Regt, 1984–94; Col, RWF, 1990–97. Chm., Army Mountaineering Assoc., 1988–91; Vice-Pres., Soldiers' and Airmen's Scripture Readers Assoc. Welsh Patron, Friends of War Memls, 1999–. FIMgt. *Recreations:* most outdoor pursuits, gardening, reading. *Address:* Christ College, Brecon, Powys LD3 8AG. *Club:* Army and Navy.

LLEWELLYN, Timothy David; Director, Henry Moore Foundation, since 1994; *b* 30 May 1947; *s* of late Graham David Llewellyn and of Dorothy Mary Driver; *m* 1st, 1970, Irene Sigrid Mercy Henriksen (marr. diss.); one *s*; 2nd, 1978, Elizabeth Hammond. *Educ:* St Dunstan's College; Magdalene College, Cambridge. Sotheby's: Old Master Painting Dept, 1969; Director, 1974; Man. Dir, 1984–91; Chief Exec., 1991–92; Dep. Chm., Europe, 1992–94. Chm., Friends of the Courtauld Inst. of Art, 1986–. Mem. Council, Harvard Univ. Center for Italian Renaissance Studies, Villa I Tatti, 1996– (Mem., Internat. Council, 1990–96). Co-Chm., Elgar Birthplace Appeal, 1992–99; Trustee: Elgar Foundn, 1992–99; Bd, Courtauld Inst. of Art, 1992–; Gilbert Collection Trust, 1998–; Chm., Henry Moore Sculpture Trust, 1994–99; Member: Council, Walpole Soc., 1994–99; Visual Arts Adv. Cttee, British Council, 1995–; Council, British Sch. at Rome, 2000–. Fellow, Ateneo Veneto, 1992. Hon. DLitt Southampton Inst., 1998. Order of Cultural Merit, Min. of Culture and Fine Arts, Poland, 1986. *Recreations:* music, fishing, travel. *Address:* 3 Cranley Mansion, 160 Gloucester Road, SW7 4QF. *T:* (020) 7373 2333, *Fax:* (020) 7244 0126; Henry Moore Foundation, Dane Tree House, Perry Green, Much Hadham, Herts SG10 6EE. *T:* (01279) 843333, *Fax:* (01279) 843647; *e-mail:* director@henry-moore-fdn.co.uk. *Club:* Brooks's.

LLEWELLYN-JONES, His Honour Ilston Percival; a Circuit Judge, 1978–88; *b* 15 June 1916; *s* of Rev. L. Cyril F. Jones and Gertrude Anne Jones; *m* 1963, Mary Evelyn; one *s* (by a former *m*). *Educ:* prep. schs; St John's Sch., Leatherhead. Admitted Solicitor, Nov. 1938; practised privately until served Sussex Yeomanry RA and 23rd Field Regt RA (commnd), 1939–42; Solicitors Dept, Metropolitan Police, New Scotland Yard, 1942–48; private practice, Torquay, 1948–52; Devon County Prosecuting Solicitor, 1952–56; Clerk to N Devon Justices, 1956–62; private practice, 1962–77; a Recorder of the Crown Court, 1972–78. *Recreations:* golf, swimming. *Address:* Calle Toni Llido, 3–4° pta. 11, 03730 Javea (Alicante), Spain. *T:* (96) 5795584.

LLEWELLYN SMITH, Prof. Sir Christopher Hubert, (Sir Chris), Kt 2001; FRS 1984; Provost and President of University College London, since 1999; *b* 19 Nov. 1942; *s* of late J. C. and of M. E. F. Llewellyn Smith; *m* 1966, Virginia Grey; one *s* one *d*. *Educ:* Wellington College; New College, Oxford (Scholar; BA 1964; DPhil 1967; full Blue for cross-country running, 1961–63, Captain 1963; full Blue for Athletics, 1963). Royal Society Exchange Fellow, Lebedev Inst., Moscow, 1967; Fellow, CERN, Geneva, 1968; Research Associate, SLAC, Stanford, Calif, 1970; Staff Mem., CERN, 1972; Oxford University: Lectr, 1974; Reader in Theoretical Physics, 1980; Prof. of Theoretical Physics, 1987–98 (on leave of absence, 1994–98); Chm. of Physics, 1987–92; Fellow, St John's Coll., 1974–98 (Hon. Fellow, 2000); Dir-Gen., CERN, 1994–98. Mem. of various policy and programme cttees for CERN (Chm., Scientific Policy Cttee, 1990–92), SLAC, Deutsches Elektronen-Synchrotron Hamburg and SERC, 1972–92; Mem., ACOST, 1989–92. MAE 1989; Fellow, APS, 1994; For. Fellow, INSA, 1998. Hon. Fellow, Cardiff Univ., 1998. Hon. DSc: Bristol, 1997; Shandong, 1997; Hon. DCien Granada, 1997. Maxwell Prize and Medal, Inst. of Physics, 1979; Medal, Japanese Assoc. of Med. Scis, 1997; Gold Medal, Slovak Acad. of Scis, 1997; Glazebrook Medal, Inst. of Physics, 1999; Distinguished Associate Award, US Dept of Energy, 1998; Distinguished Service Award, US Nat. Sci. Foundn, 1998. *Publications:* numerous articles in Nuclear Physics, Physics Letters, Phys. Rev., etc. *Recreations:* books, travel, opera. *Address:* University College London, Gower Street, WC1E 6BT.

See also E. M. Llewellyn-Smith, Sir M. J. Llewellyn Smith.

LLEWELLYN-SMITH, Elizabeth Marion, CB 1985; Principal, St Hilda's College Oxford, 1990–2001; *b* 17 Aug. 1934; *d* of late John Clare Llewellyn Smith and of Margaret Emily Frances (*née* Crawford). *Educ:* Christ's Hospital, Hertford; Girton Coll., Cambridge (MA; Hon. Fellow, 1992). Joined Board of Trade, 1956; various appointments in Board of Trade, Cabinet Office, Dept of Trade and Industry, Dept of Prices and Consumer Protection, 1956–76; Royal Coll. of Defence Studies, 1977; Under Sec., Companies Div., Dept of Trade, later DTI, 1978–82; Dep. Dir Gen., OFT, 1982–87; Dep. Sec., DTI, 1987–90. UK Dir, EIB, 1987–90. Member: Hebdomadal Council, Oxford Univ., 1993–2000; Res. Ethical Cttee, HSE, 1993–; Business Appointments Panel, DTI, 1996–. Trustee, Jacqueline du Pré Meml Fund, 1991–2001. Mem., Governing Body, Rugby Sch., 1991–. Hon. Fellow, St Mary's Coll., Univ. of Durham, 1999. *Recreations:* travel, books, entertaining. *Address:* Brook Cottage, Taston, near Charlbury, Oxon OX7 3JL. *T:* (01608) 811874.

See also Sir C. H. Llewellyn Smith, Sir M. J. Llewellyn Smith.

LLEWELLYN SMITH, Sir Michael (John), KCVO 1996; CMG 1989; HM Diplomatic Service, retired; Ambassador to Greece, 1996–99; *b* 25 April 1939; *s* of late J. C. Llewellyn Smith and of M. E. F. Crawford; *m* 1967, Colette Gaulier; one *s* one *d*. *Educ:* Wellington Coll.; New Coll., Oxford; St Antony's Coll., Oxford. BA, DPhil. FCO, 1970; Cultural Attaché, Moscow, 1973; Paris, 1976; Royal Coll. of Defence Studies, 1979; Counsellor and Consul Gen., Athens, 1980–83; Hd of Western European Dept, FCO, 1984–85; Hd of Soviet Dept, FCO, 1985–87; Minister, Paris, 1988–91; Ambassador to Poland, 1991–96. Non-exec. Dir, Coca-Cola HBC SA, 2000–. Vice-Chm., Cathedrals Fabric Commn for England, 1999–. Chm., British Inst. in Paris, 2000–. *Publications:* The Great Island: a study of Crete, 1965, 2nd edn 1973; Ionian Vision: Greece in Asia Minor 1919–22, 1973, 2nd edn 1998; The British Embassy Athens, 1998. *Recreations:* music, walking, wine. *Address:* 25 Home Park Road, SW19 7HP. *Club:* Oxford and Cambridge.

See also Sir C. H. Llewellyn Smith, E. M. Llewellyn-Smith.

LLEWELYN, Sir John Michael Dillwyn V.; *see* Venables-Llewelyn.

LLOWARCH, Martin Edge, FCA; Chairman (part-time): Transport Development Group plc, 1992–2000; Firth Rixson (formerly Johnson & Firth Brown) plc, 1993–2001; *b* 28 Dec. 1935; *s* of Wilfred and Olga Llowarch; *m* 1965, Ann Marion Buchanan; one *s* two *d*. *Educ:* Stowe Sch., Buckingham. FCA 1973. Coopers & Lybrand, 1962–68; British Steel Corporation, subseq. British Steel plc: Hd of Special Projects, 1968; Man. Dir (S Africa), 1971; Dir, Finance and Admin (Internat.), 1973; Finance Dir, Tubes Div., 1975; Finance Controller, Strip Products Gp, 1980; Man. Dir, Finance, 1983; Mem., Main Bd, 1984–91; Dep. Chief Exec., 1986; Chief Exec., 1986–91. Dep. Chm., Abbey National plc, 1994–99; non-exec. Dir, Hickson Internat., 1992–99. Mem., Accounting Standards Cttee, 1985–87. CIMgt (CBIM 1985). Chm. Govs, Stamford Endowed Schs, 1998–. *Recreations:* most forms of sport, music, gardening, reading.

LLOYD OF BERWICK, Baron *cr* 1993 (Life Peer), of Ludlay in the County of East Sussex; **Anthony John Leslie Lloyd,** Kt 1978; PC 1984; DL; a Lord of Appeal in Ordinary, 1993–98; Chairman, Security Commission, 1992–99 (Vice-Chairman, 1985–92); *b* 9 May 1929; *o s* of late Edward John Boydell Lloyd and Leslie Johnston Fleming; *m* 1960, Jane Helen Violet, *er d* of C. W. Shelford, Chailey Place, Lewes, Sussex. *Educ:* Eton (Schol.); Trinity Coll., Cambridge (Maj. Schol.). 1st cl. Classical Tripos Pt I; 1st cl. with distinction Law Tripos Pt II. National Service, 1st Bn Coldstream Guards, 1948. Montague Butler Prize, 1950; Sir William Browne Medal, 1951. Choate Fellow, Harvard, 1952; Fellow of Peterhouse, 1953 (Hon. Fellow, 1981); Fellow of Eton, 1974–86. Called to Bar, Inner Temple, 1955 (Bencher, 1976; Treasurer, 1999); QC 1967; Attorney-General to HRH The Prince of Wales, 1969–77; Judge of the High Court of Justice, Queen's Bench Div., 1978–84; a Lord Justice of Appeal, 1984–93. Vice-Chm., Parole Bd, 1984–85 (Mem., 1983); Mem., Criminal Law Revision Cttee, 1981. Chm., Sussex Assoc. for Rehabilitation of Offenders, 1985–91; Pres., Sussex Downsmen, 1995–; Vice-Pres., British Maritime Law Assoc., 1983–. Mem., Top Salaries Review Body, 1971–77. Trustee: Smiths Charity, 1971–94; Glyndebourne Arts Trust, 1973–94 (Chm., 1975–94); Dir, RAM, 1979– (Hon. FRAM 1985); Chm., Chichester Diocesan Bd of Finance, and Mem., Bishop's Council, 1972–76. Hon. Mem., Salters' Co., 1988 (Master, 2000–01). DL E Sussex, 1983. *Recreations:* music, carpentry; formerly running (ran for Cambridge in Mile, White City, 1950). *Address:* 68 Strand-on-the-Green, Chiswick, W4 3PF. *T:* (020) 8994 7790; Ludlay, Berwick, East Sussex BN26 6TE. *T:* (01323) 870204. *Club:* Brooks's.

LLOYD OF HIGHBURY, Baroness *cr* 1996 (Life Peer), of Highbury in the London Borough of Islington; **June Kathleen Lloyd,** DBE 1990; FRCP, FRCPE; FRCGP; Nuffield Professor of Child Health, British Postgraduate Medical Federation, London University, 1985–92, now Emeritus Professor; *b* 1 Jan. 1928; *d* of Arthur Cresswell Lloyd and Lucy Bevan Lloyd. *Educ:* Royal School, Bath; Bristol Univ. (MD); Durham Univ. (DPH). FRCP 1969; FRCPE 1989; FRCGP 1990. Junior Hosp. appts, Bristol, Oxford and Newcastle, 1951–57; Res. Fellow and Lectr in Child Health, Univ. of Birmingham, 1958–65; Sen. Lectr, Reader in Paediatrics, Inst. of Child Health, 1965–73; Prof. of Paediatrics, London Univ., 1973–75; Prof. of Child Health, St George's Hosp. Med. Sch., London Univ., 1975–85. Vis. Examr in Paediatrics in Univs in UK and abroad. Scientific Advr, AMRC, 1990–95. Chm., DoH Adv. Cttee on Gene Therapy, 1990–95; Member: Council, RCP, 1982–85, 1986–88 (Paediatric Vice Pres., 1992–95); MRC, 1984–88; ABRC, 1989–90. Pres., British Paediatric Assoc., 1988–91; Mem., Finnish, French, Swiss, German, Amer. and Sri Lankan Paediatric Assocs; Hon. Mem., Paediatric Res. Soc. of Australia. Hon. DSc: Bristol, 1991; Birmingham, 1993. *Publications:* research articles, reviews and leading articles in sci. jls. *Recreations:* cooking, gardening, walking. *Address:* 37 Allingham Street, N1 8NX.

LLOYD, Rev. (Albert) Kingsley; President of the Conference of the Methodist Church, 1964; *b* 2 Nov. 1903; *s* of Rev. Albert Lloyd; *m* 1926, Ida Marian (*née* Cartledge) (*d* 1969); one *s* one *d*; 2nd, 1972, Katharine G. (*d* 1999), *d* of late A. G. L. Ives, CVO. *Educ:* Kingswood Sch., Bath; Richmond Coll., Surrey (University of London). Methodist Circuit Minister: London, Bedford, Cambridge, 1926–52; Chm., London N Dist, 1951–53. Secretary, Dept of Connexional Funds of the Methodist Church, 1952–69. Wesley Historical Soc. Lectr, 1968. *Address:* 13 High Street, Orwell, Royston, Herts SG8 5QN.

LLOYD, Anthony Joseph; MP (Lab) Manchester Central, since 1997 (Stretford, 1983–97); *b* 25 Feb. 1950; *s* of late Sydney and Ciceley Beaumont Lloyd; *m* 1974, Judith Ann Tear; one *s* three *d*. *Educ:* Stretford Grammar Sch.; Nottingham Univ. (BSc Hons); Manchester Business Sch. (DipBA). Lectr, Dept of Business and Administration, Salford Univ., 1979–83. Opposition spokesman: on transport, 1988–89; on employment, 1988–92, 1993–94; on education, 1992–94; on the environment, 1994–95; on foreign and commonwealth affairs, 1995–97; Minister of State, FCO, 1997–99. *Address:* House of Commons, SW1A 0AA.

LLOYD, Ven. (Bertram) Trevor; Archdeacon of Barnstaple, since 1989; *b* 15 Feb. 1938; *s* of Bertram and Gladys Lloyd; *m* 1962, Margaret Eldey; two *s* one *d* (and one *s* decd). *Educ:* Highgate School; Hertford Coll., Oxford (schol; BA History 1960, Theology 1962; MA 1962); Clifton Theol Coll., Bristol. Curate, Christ Church, Barnet, 1964–69; Vicar, Holy Trinity, Wealdstone, 1970–84; Priest-in-charge, St Michael and All Angels, Harrow Weald, 1980–84; Vicar, Trinity St Michael, Harrow, 1984–89; Area Dean of Harrow, 1977–82; Prebendary of Exeter Cathedral, 1991–. Member: C of E Liturgical Commn, 1981–; Gen. Synod of C of E, 1990– (Mem., Standing Cttee, 1996–98); Central Bd of Finance, C of E, 1990–98; Council for the Care of Churches, 1992–2001; Churches' Main Cttee, 1996–. *Publications:* Informal Liturgy, 1972; Institutions and Inductions, 1973; The Agape, 1973; Liturgy and Death, 1974; Ministry and Death, 1974; Lay Presidency at the Eucharist?, 1977; Evangelicals, Obedience and Change, 1977; (ed) Anglican Worship Today, 1980; Ceremonial in Worship, 1981; Introducing Liturgical Change, 1984; Celebrating Lent, Holy Week and Easter, 1985; Celebrating the Agape today, 1986; The Future of Anglican Worship, 1987; A Service of the Word, 1999; Dying and Death Step by Step, 2000; (consultant ed.) Common Worship Today, 2001. *Recreations:* hill walking, photography, swimming, caravanning, making things from wood. *Address:* Stage Cross, Whitemoor Hill, Bishop's Tawton, Barnstaple, Devon EX32 0BE. *T:* (01271) 375475, *Fax:* (01271) 377934; *e-mail:* archdeacon.of.barnstaple@exeter.anglican.org.

LLOYD, Dr Brian Beynon, CBE 1983; Director, International Nutrition Foundation, 1990–95; Chairman of Directors, Oxford Gallery, 1967–97; Chairman, Trumedia Study Oxford Ltd, since 1985; *b* 23 Sept. 1920; *s* of David John Lloyd, MA Oxon and Olwen (*née* Beynon); *m* 1949, Reinhild Johanna Engeroff; four *s* three *d* (inc. twin *s* and twin *d*). *Educ:* Newport High Sch.; Winchester Coll. (Schol.); Balliol Coll., Oxford (Domus and Frazer Schol.). Special Certif. for BA (War) Degree in Chem., 1940; took degrees BA and MA, 1946; Theodore Williams Schol. and cl. I in Physiology, 1948; DSc 1969. Joined Oxford Nutrition Survey after registration as conscientious objector, 1941; Pres., Jun. Common Room, Balliol Coll., 1941–42; Chm., Oxford Univ. Undergraduate Rep. Council, 1942; Biochemist: SHAEF Nutrition Survey Team, Leiden, 1945; Nutrition Survey Group, Düsseldorf, 1946. Fellow of Magdalen by exam. in Physiology, 1948–52, by special election, 1952–70; Senior Tutor, 1963–64; Vice-Pres., 1967 and 1968; Emeritus Fellow, 1970–; Chemist, Laboratory of Human Nutrition, later Univ. Lectr in Physiology, Univ. of Oxford, 1948–70; Senior Proctor, 1960–61; Dir, Oxford Polytechnic, 1970–80 (Hon. Fellow, 1991; opened Lloyd Bldg, 1984). Chairman: CNAA Health and Med. Services Bd, 1975–80; Health Educn Council, 1979–82 (Mem., 1975–82); Mem., Adv. Council on Misuse of Drugs, 1978–81. Vis. Physiologist, New York, 1963. Pres., Section I, 1964–65, Section X, 1980, British Assoc. for the Advancement of Science. Chm. of Govs, Oxford Coll. of Technology, 1963–69. Chairman: Oxford-Bonn Soc., 1973–81; Oxford Management Club, 1979–80; Pullen's Lane Assoc., 1985–95; Pres., Oxford Polytechnic Assoc., 1984–90 (Hon. Mem., 1992). *Publications:* Gas Analysis Apparatus, 1960; (jt ed) The Regulation of Human Respiration, 1962; Cerebrospinal Fluid and the Regulation of Respiration, 1965; (jt ed) Sinclair (biog.), 1990; articles in physiological and biochemical jls. *Recreations:* Klavarskribo, Correggio, round tables, the analysis of athletic records, slide rules, ready reckoners, soldering irons, home computing, collecting pictures. *Address:* High Wall, Pullen's Lane, Oxford OX3 0BX. *T:* (01865) 763353.

LLOYD, Christopher, OBE 2000; VMH 1979; MA, BSc (Hort.); writer on horticulture; regular gardening correspondent, Country Life, since 1963; *b* 2 March 1921; *s* of late Nathaniel Lloyd and Daisy (*née* Field). *Educ:* Wellesley House, Broadstairs, Kent; Rugby

Sch.; King's Coll., Cambridge (MA Mod Langs); Wye Coll., Univ of London (BSc Hort.). Asst Lectr in Decorative Horticulture, Wye Coll., 1950–54. Then returned to family home at Great Dixter and started Nursery in clematis and uncommon plants. DUniv Open, 1996. *Publications:* The Mixed Border, 1957; Clematis, 1965, rev. edn (with Tom Bennett), 1989; Shrubs and Trees for Small Gardens, 1965; Hardy Perennials, 1967; Gardening on Chalk and Lime, 1969; The Well-Tempered Garden, 1970, rev. edn 1985; Foliage Plants, 1973, rev. edn 1985; The Adventurous Gardener, 1983; The Well-Chosen Garden, 1984; The Year at Great Dixter, 1987; (with Richard Bird) The Cottage Garden, 1990; (with Graham Rice) Garden Flowers from Seed, 1991; Christopher Lloyd's Flower Garden, 1993; In My Garden, 1993; Other People's Gardens, 1995; Gardener Cook, 1997; (with Beth Chatto) Dear Friend and Gardener, 1998; Christopher Lloyd's Gardening Year, 1999; Lloyd's Garden Flowers, 2000; Colour for Adventurous Gardeners, 2001; regular gardening contributor to The Guardian, American Horticulture, Country Life. *Recreations:* walking, entertaining and cooking for friends. *Address:* Great Dixter, Northiam, Rye, East Sussex TN31 6PH. *T:* (01797) 253107.

LLOYD, Christopher Hamilton, LVO 1996; Surveyor of The Queen's Pictures, since 1988; *b* 30 June 1945; *s* of Rev. Hamilton Lloyd and Suzanne Lloyd (*née* Moon); *m* 1967, Christine Joan Frances Newth; four *s*. *Educ:* Marlborough Coll.; Christ Church, Oxford (BA 1967; MA 1971; BLitt 1972). Asst Curator of Pictures, Christ Church, Oxford, 1967–68; Dept of Western Art, Ashmolean Museum, 1968–88. Fellow of Villa I Tatti, Florence (Harvard Univ.), 1972–73; Vis. Res. Curator of Early Italian Painting, Art Inst., Chicago, 1980–81. *Publications:* (ed) Studies on Camille Pissarro, 1986; The Royal Collection: a thematic exploration of the paintings in the collection of HM the Queen, 1992; *catalogues of permanent collections:* Catalogue of Earlier Italian Paintings in the Ashmolean Museum, 1977; (with Richard Brettell) Catalogue of Drawings by Camille Pissarro in the Ashmolean Museum, 1980; (introd. and ed) Catalogue of Old Master Drawings at Holkham Hall, by A. E. Popham, 1986; Early Italian paintings in the Art Institute of Chicago, 1993; *exhibition catalogues:* Art and its Images, 1975; Camille Pissarro, 1980; (with Richard Thomson) Impressionist Drawings from British Collections, 1986; (with Simon Thurley) Henry VIII—images of a Tudor King, 1990; The Queen's Pictures: Royal collectors through the centuries, 1991; (contrib.) Alfred Sisley, ed M. A. Stevens, 1992; Gainsborough and Reynolds: contrasts in Royal patronage, 1994; (with Vanessa Remington) Masterpieces in Little: portrait miniatures from the collection of Her Majesty Queen Elizabeth II, 1996; The Quest for Albion: monarchy and the patronage of British painting, 1998; reviews and contribs to learned jls. *Recreations:* books, theatre, cinema, music, real tennis. *Address:* Apartment 29B, St James's Palace, SW1A 1BG. *T:* (020) 7839 5902. *Club:* Garrick.

LLOYD, Clive Hubert, AO 1985; CBE 1992; OJ 1985; OB 1986; Executive Promotion Officer, Project Fullemploy, since 1987; *b* Georgetown, Guyana, 31 Aug. 1944; *er s* of late Arthur Christopher Lloyd and of Sylvia Thelma Lloyd; *m* 1971, Waveney Benjamin; one *s* two *d*. *Educ:* Chatham High Sch., Georgetown (schol.). Clerk, Georgetown Hosp., 1960–66. Began cricket career, Demarara CC, Georgetown, 1959; début for Guyana, 1963; first Test Match, 1966; played for Haslingden, Lancs League, 1967; Lancashire County Cricket Club: Mem., 1968–86, capped 1969; Captain, 1981–84 and 1986; Captain, WI cricket team, 1974–78 and 1979–85; World Series Cricket in Australia, 1977–79. Made first 1st class century, 1966; passed total of 25,000 runs (incl. 69 centuries), 1981; captained WI teams which won World Cup, 1975, 1979; Manager, WI cricket tour in Australia, 1988–89; WI Team Manager, 1996–99. First Pres., WI Players' Assoc., 1973. Former Dir, Red Rose Radio. Mem. (part-time), Commn for Racial Equality, 1987–90. Hon. Fellow: Manchester Polytechnic, 1986; Lancashire Polytechnic, 1986. Hon. MA: Manchester; Hull; Hon. Dr of Letters, Univ. of West Indies, Mona. Golden Arrow of Achievement (Guyana), 1975; Cacique Crown of Honours, Order of Rorima (Guyana), 1985. *Publications:* (with Tony Cozier) Living for Cricket, 1980; *relevant publication:* Clive Lloyd, by Trevor McDonald, 1985. *Address:* c/o Harefield, Harefield Drive, Wilmslow, Cheshire SK9 1NJ.

LLOYD, Air Vice-Marshal Darrell Clive Arthur, CB 1980; Commander, Northern Maritime Air Region, 1981–83; retired; *b* 5 Nov. 1928; *s* of Cecil James Lloyd and Doris Frances Lloyd; *m* 1957, Pamela (*née* Woodside); two *s*. *Educ:* Stowe; RAF Coll., Cranwell. Commnd 1950; ADC to C-in-C, ME Air Force, 1955–57; Instr, Central Flying Sch., 1958–60; Personal Air Sec. to Sec. of State for Air, 1961–63; CO, RAF Bruggen, 1968–70; RCDS, 1972; Dir of Defence Policy, UK Strategy Div., 1973–75; Dep. Comdr, RAF Germany, 1976–78; ACAS (Ops), 1978–81. FBIM 1972. *Recreations:* travel, golf, painting. *Address:* c/o Lloyds TSB, 7 Pall Mall, SW1Y 5NA. *Clubs:* Royal Air Force; Royal Cinque Ports Golf (Deal); Tandridge Golf (Oxted).

LLOYD, David Alan; Chairman, David Lloyd Associates, since 1980; Chief Executive, Next Generation Clubs, since 1998; *b* 3 Jan. 1948; *s* of Dennis and Doris Lloyd; *m* 1972, Veronica Jardine; one *s* two *d*. *Educ:* Southend High Sch. Tennis player; mem., British Davis Cup team, 1973–82; ranked in Britain's top ten, 1970–81; semi-finalist, Wimbledon Championship doubles, 1973; British Wightman Cup coach, 1981; non-playing Captain, British Davis Cup team, 1995–2000. Chm., David Lloyd Leisure, 1981–96; Chm. and owner, Hull City AFC, 1997–. Freeman, City of London, 1985. Entrepreneur of the Year, PLC Awards, 1994. *Publications:* Improve Your Tennis Skills, 1989; Successful Tennis, 1989; Winning Tennis Fitness, 1991; How to Succeed in Business by Really Trying, 1995. *Recreations:* National Hunt racing, golf, swimming, tennis, football. *Address:* David Lloyd Associates Ltd, 12 Leys Road, Oxshott, Surrey KT22 0QE. *Clubs:* All England Lawn Tennis; Wisley Golf.

LLOYD, David Andrew, OBE 1993; HM Diplomatic Service, retired; Director of Information Services, Middle East Association, since 2001; *b* 24 Dec. 1940; *s* of John Owen Lloyd and Ellen Marjorie Howard Lloyd; *m* 1st, 1965, Janet Elizabeth Rawcliffe; one *s* one *d*; 2nd, 1979, Patricia Villa (marr. diss.); 3rd, 1987, Katharine Jane Smith; three *d*. *Educ:* Lancing Coll.; Clare Coll., Cambridge (BA Hons Arabic). Entered Foreign Office, 1964; served Kuwait, Bogotá, FCO and Madrid; First Sec., FCO, 1983–88; Head, British Trade Office, Al Khobar, Saudi Arabia, 1988–93; FCO, 1994–96; Ambassador to Slovenia, 1997–2000. *Recreations:* squash, tennis, theatre, concerts. *Address:* New Thorntons, 150 North Road, Hertford SG14 2BZ. *T:* (01992) 583795.

LLOYD, David Bernard; Secretary, Royal College of Physicians, 1986–98; *b* 14 Jan. 1938; *s* of George Edwards and Lilian Catherine Lloyd; *m* 1968, Christine Vass; three *d*. *Educ:* Presteigne Grammar Sch.; Hereford High Sch. FCCA. Early posts in local govt, UCL, UCH Med. Sch.; Royal College of Obstetricians and Gynaecologists: Accountant, 1971–76; Secretary, 1976–82; Secretary, Nat. Inst. of Agricultural Engineering, 1982–86. Chm., Management Cttee, St Albans CAB, 1990–94 (Mem., 1985–94); Co. Sec., Harpenden Day Centre Assoc., 2000–. Member (C): Harpenden Town Council, 1992–99, 2001–; Herts CC, 1997– (Chm., Protection Cttee, 1999–2000). Chm., Harpenden Trust, 1995–96. Governor: Sir John Lawes Sen. Sch., 1986–87 (also Chm.); Roundwood Jun. Sch., 1980–89 (Chm., 1985–88). Hon. FRCP 1998; Hon. FFPM 1998. *Recreations:* local charity, garden. *Address:* 16 Hartwell Gardens, Harpenden, Herts AL5 2RW. *T:* (01582) 761292, *Fax:* (01582) 467177.

LLOYD, David Graham, PhD; FRS 1992; FRSNZ; Professor of Plant Science, University of Canterbury, Christchurch, New Zealand, 1986–93, now Emeritus; *b* 20 June 1937; *m* 1st, 1973, Jacqueline Mary Renouf (marr. diss. 1985); two adopted *s* one adopted *d*; 2nd, 1994, Linda Eileen Newstrom. *Educ:* Univ. of Canterbury, NZ (BSc 1st Cl. Hons 1959); Harvard Univ. (PhD 1964). University of Canterbury: Postdoctorate Fellow, 1964–67; Lectr, 1967–71; Sen. Lectr, 1971–75; Reader, 1975–86. FRSNZ 1984. Foreign Mem., Amer. Acad. of Arts and Scis, 1993. *Publications:* (ed jtly) Floral Biology, 1996; numerous res. papers. *Recreation:* reading.

LLOYD, David Mark; Head of News, Current Affairs and Business, Channel Four Television, since 1997; *b* 3 Feb. 1945; *s* of late Maurice Edward and Roma Doreen Lloyd; *m* 1982, Jana Tomas; one *s* one *d* and one step *s*. *Educ:* Felsted Sch.; Brentwood Sch.; Brasenose Coll., Oxford (MA 1967). Joined BBC as Gen. Trainee, 1967: Dep. Ed., Nationwide, 1978; Editor: Money Prog., 1980; Newsnight, 1982; Sixty Minutes, 1983; Breakfast Time, 1984; Sen. Commng Editor, News and Current Affairs, Channel 4, 1988–97. Shell Film and TV Award, 1982. *Recreations:* cricket, golf, music, travel. *Address:* Channel Four Television Co. Ltd, 124 Horseferry Road, SW1P 2TX. *T:* (020) 7396 4444.

LLOYD, David Rees; Member (Plaid Cymru) South Wales West, National Assembly for Wales, since 1999; *b* 2 Dec. 1956; *s* of Aneurin Rees Lloyd and Dorothy Grace Lloyd; *m* 1982, Dr Catherine Jones; two *s* one *d*. *Educ:* Lampeter Comprehensive Sch.; Welsh Nat. Sch. of Medicine, Cardiff (MB BCh 1980; Dip. in Therapeutics, 1995). MRCGP 1989. Jun. hosp. med. posts, 1980–84; GP, 1984–99. Shadow Health Sec., Nat. Assembly for Wales, 1999–. *Recreation:* lay preacher. *Address:* National Assembly for Wales, Cardiff Bay, Cardiff CF99 1NA; 76 Pastoral Way, Tycoch, Swansea SA2 9LY. *T:* (01792) 201797.

LLOYD, Rev. David Richard, (Rev. Denys Lloyd); Parish Priest, Our Lady's, Stowmarket, since 1996; *b* 28 June 1939; *s* of Richard Norman Lloyd and Grace Enid Lloyd. *Educ:* Brighton College (George Long Scholar); Trinity Hall, Cambridge (Exhibitioner; BA 1961, MA 1965); Leeds Univ. (MA 1969). Asst Curate, St Martin's, Rough Hills, Wolverhampton, 1963–67; professed as Mem. of Community of Resurrection, 1969 (taking name Denys); Tutor, Coll. of Resurrection, 1970–75, Vice-Principal, 1975–84; Principal, 1984–90; Associate Lecturer, Dept of Theology and Religious Studies, Univ. of Leeds, 1972–90. Received into Roman Catholic Church at Quarr Abbey, 1990; Missionary Inst., London, 1993–94; ordained priest, 1994; Asst Priest, St Mark's, Ipswich, and RC Chaplain, Ipswich Hosp., 1994–96. *Publications:* contribs to theolog. jls. *Address:* The Presbytery, 29 Lockington Road, Stowmarket, Suffolk IP14 1BQ. *T:* (01449) 612946.

LLOYD, Rev. Denys; *see* Lloyd, Rev. David Richard.

LLOYD, Eve, (Lady Lloyd); *see* Pollard, E.

LLOYD, Frances Mary, (Mrs James Lloyd); *see* Line, F. M.

LLOYD, Frederick John, CBE 1977; FIA; Chairman, Road Transport Industry Training Board, 1978–83; *b* 22 Jan. 1913; *m* 1942, Catherine Johnson (*née* Parker); one *s* one *d*. *Educ:* Ackworth Sch., Yorks; Liverpool Univ. (BSc). FIA 1947; FIS 1949; FCIT 1968. War Service, Operational Research, Bomber Comd, 1942–45. Royal Insurance Co., 1933–47; London Passenger Transport Bd, 1947–69: Staff Admin Officer, 1952; Divl Supt (South), 1957; Chief Operating Manager (Central Buses), 1961; Chief Commercial and Planning Officer, 1965–69; Dir Gen., West Midlands Passenger Transport Exec., 1969–78. *Publications:* contribs to actuarial and transport jls. *Recreations:* golf, gardening. *Address:* 8 Cliveden Coppice, Sutton Coldfield, West Midlands B74 2RG. *T:* (0121) 308 5683. *Clubs:* Birmingham Rotary; Whittington Heath Golf (Lichfield, Staffs).

LLOYD, Sir Geoffrey (Ernest Richard), Kt 1997; PhD; FBA 1983; Professor of Ancient Philosophy and Science, University of Cambridge, 1983–2000, now Emeritus; Master of Darwin College, Cambridge, 1989–2000 (Hon. Fellow, 2000); *b* 25 Jan. 1933; *s* of William Ernest Lloyd and Olive Irene Neville Lloyd; *m* 1956, Janet Elizabeth Lloyd; three *s*. *Educ:* Charterhouse; King's Coll., Cambridge (BA 1954; MA 1958; PhD 1958). Cambridge University: Asst Lectr in Classics, 1965–67; Lectr, 1967–74; Reader in Ancient Philosophy and Science, 1974–83; Fellow, 1957–89 (Hon. Fellow, 1990), and Sen. Tutor, 1969–73, King's Coll. Bonsall Prof., Stanford Univ., 1981; Sather Prof., Berkeley, 1983–84; A. D. White Prof.-at-large, Cornell Univ., 1990–97. Chm., E Asian Hist. of Sci. Trust, 1992–. Fellow, Japan Soc. for the Promotion of Science, 1981. Hon. For. Mem., Amer. Acad. of Arts and Scis, 1995. Sarton Medal, History of Science Soc., USA, 1987. *Publications:* Polarity and Analogy, 1966; Aristotle: the growth and structure of his thought, 1968; Early Greek Science: Thales to Aristotle, 1970; Greek Science after Aristotle, 1973; (ed) Hippocratic Writings, 1978; (ed) Aristotle on Mind and the Senses, 1978; Magic, Reason and Experience, 1979; Science, Folklore and Ideology, 1983; Science and Morality in Greco-Roman Antiquity, 1985; The Revolutions of Wisdom, 1987; Demystifying Mentalities, 1990; Methods and Problems in Greek Science, 1991; Adversaries and Authorities, 1996; Aristotelian Explorations, 1996; (ed) Le Savoir grec, 1996 (English edn, Greek Thought, 2000); contribs to classical and philosophical jls. *Recreation:* travel. *Address:* 2 Prospect Row, Cambridge CB1 1DU; Needham Research Institute, Sylvester Road, Cambridge CB3 9AF.

LLOYD, (George) Peter, CMG 1965; CVO 1983; Governor, Cayman Islands, 1982–87, retired; *b* 23 Sept. 1926; *er s* of late Sir Thomas Ingram Kynaston Lloyd, GCMG, KCB; *m* 1957, Margaret Harvey; two *s* one *d*. *Educ:* Stowe Sch.; King's Coll., Cambridge. Lieut, KRRC, 1945–48; ADC to Governor of Kenya, 1948; Cambridge, 1948–51 (MA; athletics blue); District Officer, Kenya, 1951–60; Principal, Colonial Office, 1960–61; Colonial Secretary, Seychelles, 1961–66; Chief Sec., Fiji, 1966–70; Defence Sec., Hong Kong, 1971–74; Dep. Governor, Bermuda, 1974–81. Chm., Bermuda Fest., 1987–99; Trustee, Bermuda Maritime Mus., 1987–97. *Address:* Watch house, 13 Fort Hamilton Drive, Pembroke HM 19, Bermuda.

LLOYD, Graham; *see* Lloyd, J. G.

LLOYD, Humphrey John; QC 1979; **His Honour Judge Humphrey Lloyd;** a Judge of the Technology and Construction Court (formerly an Official Referee) of the High Court, since 1993; *b* 16 Nov. 1939; *s* of Rees Lewis Lloyd of the Inner Temple, barrister-at-law, and Dorothy Margaret Ferry (*née* Gibson); *m* 1969, Ann Findlay; one *s* one *d*. *Educ:* Westminster; Trinity Coll., Dublin (BA (Mod), LLB; MA). Called to the Bar, Inner Temple, 1963, Bencher, 1985. A Recorder, 1990–93. Mem., Architects' Registration Bd, 2001–. Pres., Soc. of Construction Law, 1985–88. Hon. Senior Vis. Fellow, QMC, 1987; Hon. Fellow, Amer. Coll. of Construction Law, 1997. Editor-in-chief: Building Law Reports, 1977–93 (Consultant Editor, 1993–98); The Internat. Construction Law Rev., 1983–; Consultant Editor: Emden's Construction Law, 1993–; Technology and

Construction Law Reports, 1999–. *Publications:* (ed) The Liability of Contractors, 1986; (contrib.) Halsbury's Laws of England, 4th edn, 1992. *Address:* St Dunstan's House, 133–137 Fetter Lane, EC4A 1HD. *Club:* Reform.

LLOYD, Sir Ian (Stewart), Kt 1986; *b* 30 May 1921; *s* of late Walter John Lloyd and Euphemia Craig Lloyd; *m* 1951, Frances Dorward Addison, *d* of late Hon. W. Addison, CMG, OBE, MC, DCM; three *s*. *Educ:* Michaelhouse; University of the Witwatersrand; King's Coll., Cambridge (President, Cambridge Union, and Leader, Cambridge tour of USA, 1947; MA 1951; MSc 1952). Served War of 1939–45, Flying Instructor, then No 7 Sqdn, SAAF; RAFVR (Cambridge Univ. Air Sqdn), 1945–49. Econ. Adviser, Central Mining and Investment Corporation, 1949–52; Member, SA Board of Trade and Industries, 1952–55; Director, Acton Soc. Trust, 1956; Dir of Res., 1956–64, Economic Advr, 1956–83, British and Commonwealth Shipping. Chairman, UK Cttee and Vice-Chairman, International Exec., International Cargo Handling Co-ordination Assoc., 1961–64. MP (C): Portsmouth, Langstone, 1964–74; Havant and Waterloo, 1974–83; Havant, 1983–92. Chairman: Cons. Parly Shipping and Shipbuilding Cttee, 1974–77; Select Cttee on Sci. Sub-Cttee, 1975–77; Select Cttee on Sci. Sub-Cttee on Technological Innovation, 1977–79; Select Cttee on Energy, 1979–89; All-Party Cttee on Information Technology, 1979–87; Pres., Parly and Scientific Cttee, 1990–92 (Vice-Pres., 1983–87; Vice-Chm., 1988–90); Chm. Bd, Parly Office of Science and Technology. Member, UK Delegation, Council of Europe, Western European Union, 1968–72; UK rep., Internat. Parly Conf., Bucharest, 1975; Leader: UK Delegn, OECD Conf. on Energy, 1981; Parly and Scientific Cttee delegn to China, 1991. Member of Council: Save British Sci., 1992; Sci. Policy Support Gp, 1992–2000 (Chm., 2000–). Trustee: Kasanka Trust, 1986–96; New Era Schs Trust, 1990–97. *Publications:* Rolls-Royce, 3 vols, 1978; contribs to various journals on economics, politics and information technology. *Recreations:* genealogy, good music. *Clubs:* Army and Navy, Royal Yacht Squadron.

LLOYD, Illtyd Rhys; HM Chief Inspector of Schools (Wales), 1982–90, retired; *b* 13 Aug. 1929; *s* of John and Melvina Lloyd; *m* 1955, Julia Lewis; one *s* one *d*. *Educ:* Port Talbot (Glan-Afan) County Grammar Sch.; Swansea UC (Hon. Fellow, Univ. of Wales, 1987). BSc, MSc; DipStat, DipEd. Commnd Educn Br., RAF, 1951–54 (Flt Lieut). Second Maths Master, Howardian High Sch. for Boys, Cardiff, 1954–57; Hd of Maths Dept, Pembroke Grammar Sch., 1957–59; Dep. Headmaster, Howardian High Sch., 1959–63; Welsh Office: HM Inspector of Schs, 1964–70; Staff Inspector (Secondary Educn), 1971–82. Chm., Educn Resources Centre, Aberystwyth Univ., 1991–; Vice-Chm., S Glam FHSA, 1993–96 (Mem., 1990–96); Member: Indep. Schs Tribunal Educn Panel, 1990–; Exec. Cttee, Council for Educn in World Citizenship–Cymru, 1990– (Chm., 1997–). Churches Together in Wales: Mem. Council, 1991–; Treas., 1999–; Mem., Finance Cttee, 1990– (Vice Chm., 1995–98; Chm., 1999–); Baptist Union of Wales: Mem. Council, 1990–; Treas., 1992–; Vice-Pres., 1995–96; Pres., 1996–97; Member: Educn Cttee, Free Churches Council, 1993–; Finance Cttee, CTBI, 1994–. Member, Council: Cardiff Theol Coll., 1990– (Chm., 1995–); Univ. of Wales, Lampeter, 1999–; Gov., Swansea Inst. of Higher Educn, 1990–95. Chairman: Mgt Cttee, Glyn Nest Christian Home, 1992–; Bryn Llifon Baptist Home, 1999–. Trustee, Churches Counselling Service, 1994–2000. Hon. Mem., Gorsedd of Bards, 1990. *Publications:* Geirfa Mathemateg, 1956; Secondary Education in Wales 1965–85, 1991; Gwyr y Gair, 1993; Yr Hyn a Ymddiriedwyd i'n Gofal, 1996. *Recreation:* walking. *Address:* 134 Lake Road East, Roath Park, Cardiff CF23 5NQ. *T:* (029) 2075 5296.

LLOYD, (John) Graham; consultant, 1994–96; Director of Property Services, Commission for the New Towns, 1992–94; *b* Watford, 18 Feb. 1938; *s* of late Richard and Edith Lloyd; *m* 1st, 1960, Ann (*née* Plater) (marr. diss. 1989); three *s*; 2nd, 1989, Monica (*née* Barlow). *Educ:* City of London Sch.; College of Estate Management, London Univ. (BSc Estate Management). FRICS. In private practice, London and Leamington Spa, 1959–75. Commission for the New Towns: Commercial and Industrial Manager, 1975–78, Manager, 1978–81, Hemel Hempstead; Exec. Officer/Commercial Surveyor, Corby, 1981–91; Head of Estate Management Services, 1991–92. *Recreations:* soccer, motor racing, jazz and popular music, gardening. *Address:* 4 Fairway, Kibworth Beauchamp, Leics LE8 0LB.

LLOYD, John Nicol Fortune; journalist; Associate Editor, New Statesman (formerly New Statesman & Society), since 1996; *b* 15 April 1946; *s* of Joan Adam Fortune and Christopher Lloyd; *m* 1983, Marcia Levy (marr. diss. 1997); one *s*. *Educ:* Waid Comprehensive School; Edinburgh Univ. (MA Hons). Editor, Time Out, 1972–73; Reporter, London Programme, 1974–76; Producer, Weekend World, 1976–77; industrial reporter, labour corresp., industrial and labour editor, Financial Times, 1977–86; Editor, New Statesman, 1986–87; re-joined Financial Times, 1987; E European Editor, 1987–90; Moscow Correspondent, 1991–95; columnist, The Times, 1997–98. Director: East-West Inst., NY, 1997–; Foreign Policy Centre, 1999–. Sen. Associate Fellow, Kennedy Sch., Harvard Univ., 1995; Sen. Associate Mem., St Antony's Coll., Oxford, 1996–99. Journalist of the Year, Granada Awards, 1984; Specialist Writer of the Year, IPC Awards, 1985; Rio Tinto David Watt Meml Prize, 1997. *Publications:* (with Ian Benson) The Politics of Industrial Change, 1982; (with Martin Adeney) The Miners' Strike: loss without limit, 1986; (with Charles Leadbeater) In Search of Work, 1987; (contrib.) Counterblasts, 1989; Rebirth of a Nation: an anatomy of Russia, 1998; Re-engaging Russia, 2000. *Recreations:* opera, hill walking. *Address:* c/o New Statesman, Victoria Station House, 191 Victoria Street, SW1E 5NE.

LLOYD, Prof. John Raymond; *see* Lloyd, M. R.

LLOYD, John Wilson, CB 1992; Clerk and Head of the Office of the Presiding Officer, National Assembly for Wales, 1999–2001; *b* 24 Dec. 1940; *s* of late Dr Ellis Lloyd and of Mrs Dorothy Lloyd; *m* 1967, Buddug Roberts (*d* 1996); two *s* one *d*. *Educ:* Swansea Grammar Sch.; Clifton Coll., Bristol; Christ's Coll., Cambridge (MA). Asst Principal, HM Treasury, 1962–67 (Private Sec. to Financial Sec., 1965–67); Principal, successively HM Treasury, CSD and Welsh Office, 1967–75 (Private Sec. to Sec. of State for Wales, 1974–75); Welsh Office: Asst Sec., 1975–82; Under Sec., 1982–88; Principal Establishment Officer, 1982–86; Hd, Housing, Health and Social Servs Policy Gp, 1986–88; Dep. Sec., 1988; Dir, Social Policy and Local Govt Affairs, 1988–98. *Recreations:* golf, walking, swimming. *Address:* c/o National Assembly for Wales, Cardiff Bay, Cardiff CF99 1NA. *T:* (029) 2082 5111. *Club:* Oxford and Cambridge.

LLOYD, Jonathan Bruce; composer; writer; *b* 30 Sept. 1948; *s* of Geoffrey and Nancy Lloyd; *m* 1st, 1970, Poppy Holden (marr. diss. 1975); one *s*; 2nd, 1981, Katherine Bones; two *s*. *Educ:* Royal Coll. of Music. Mendelssohn Scholar, 1969; Fellow, Berkshire Music Centre, Tanglewood, USA, 1973 (Koussevitzky Composition Prize); Composer-in-residence, Dartington Coll., 1978–79. *Principal works:* Cantique, 1968; Till the Wind Blows, 1969; Scattered Ruins, 1973; Everything Returns, 1977; Viola Concerto, 1979; Toward the Whitening Dawn, 1980; Waiting for Gozo, 1981; Three Dances, 1982; Mass, 1983; 5 Symphonies, 1983–89; The Shorelines of Certainty, 1984; The Adjudicator, 1985; Almeida Dances, 1986; Revelation, 1990; Wa Wa Mozart, 1991; Ballad for the Evening of a Man, 1992; Blackmail, 1993; Tolerance, 1994; Violin Concerto, 1995; And Beyond, 1996; A Dream of a Pass, 1997; Shadows of our Future Selves, 1998; The Beggar's Opera (musical adaptation), 1999; Inventing Bach, Summon the Spirit, 2000; Music to Maze, Songs, 2001. *Recreations:* tennis, walking, cycling. *Address:* c/o Boosey & Hawkes Music Publishers, 295 Regent Street, W1R 8JH. *T:* (020) 7580 2060.

LLOYD, Rev. Kingsley; *see* Lloyd, Rev. A. K.

LLOYD, Leslie, CBE 1981; FCIT; General Manager, Western Region, British Rail, 1976–82; *b* 10 April 1924; *s* of Henry Lloyd and Lilian Wright; *m* 1953, Marie Snowden; one *s* two *d*. *Educ:* Hawarden Grammar Sch. RAF, 1943–47. British Rail: Management Trainee, Eastern Reg., 1949–52; Chief Controller, Manchester, 1953–56; Freight Officer, Sheffield, 1956–59; Modernisation Asst, King's Cross, 1959–61; Dist Manager, Marylebone, 1961–63; Movements Supt, Great Northern Line, 1963–64; Ops Officer, Eastern Reg., 1964–67; Man., Sundries Div., 1967; Movements Man., Western Reg., 1967–69; Chief Ops Man., British Rail HQ, 1969–76. *Recreations:* golf, gardening. *Address:* 73 The Fairway, Burnham, Bucks SL1 8DY. *Club:* Burnham Beeches Golf (Burnham).

LLOYD, Prof. Michael Raymond; Professor, Oslo School of Architecture, 1993–96; Executive Architect/Planner, Norconsult International, Oslo, 1981–93; *b* 20 Aug. 1927; *s* of W. R. Lloyd; *m* 1957, Berit Hansen; one *s* two *d*. *Educ:* Wellington Sch., Somerset; AA School of Architecture. AA Dipl. 1953; ARIBA 1954; MNAL 1960. Private practice and Teacher, State School of Arts and Crafts, Oslo, 1955–60 and 1962–63; First Year Master, AA School of Architecture, 1960–62; Dean, Faculty of Arch., and Prof. of Arch., Kumasi Univ. of Science and Technology, 1963–66; Principal, AA Sch. of Architecture, 1966–71; Consultant, Land Use Consultants (Internat.) Lausanne, 1971–72; Senior Partner, Sinar Associates, Tunbridge Wells, 1973–78; Consultant Head, Hull Sch. of Architecture, 1974–77; Technical Officer, ODA, Central America, 1979–81. Prof., Bergen Sch. of Architecture, 1986–92. Leverhulme Sen. Res. Fellow, UCL, 1976–78. *Publications:* (as J. R. Lloyd) Tegning og Skissing; ed World Architecture, Vol. I Norway, Vol. III Ghana; Norwegian Laftehus; Environmental Impact of Development Activities. *Recreations:* sailing, ski-ing. *Address:* Balcon de Aguas 11, Aguas de Busot, 03569 Alicante, Spain.

LLOYD, Sir Nicholas (Markley), Kt 1990; MA; Chairman, Brown Lloyd James, since 1997; *b* 9 June 1942; *s* of Walter and Sybil Lloyd; *m* 1st, 1968, Patricia Sholliker (marr. diss. 1978); two *s* one *d*; 2nd, 1979, Eve Pollard, *qv*; one *s*. *Educ:* Bedford Modern Sch.; St Edmund Hall, Oxford (MA Hons History); Harvard Univ., USA. Reporter, Daily Mail, 1964; Educn Correspondent, Sunday Times, 1966; Dep. News Editor, Sunday Times, 1968; News Editor, The Sun, 1970; Asst Editor, News of the World, 1972; Asst Editor, The Sun, 1976; Dep. Editor, Sunday Mirror, 1980; Editor: Sunday People, 1982–83; News of the World, 1984–85; Daily Express, 1986–95. Presenter, LBC, 1997–99. *Recreations:* Arsenal, golf, books, theatre. *Address:* 25 Lower Belgrave Street, SW1W 0NR.

LLOYD, Peter, CBE 1957; Director, Booth International Holdings Ltd, 1973–79 (Consultant, 1980–83); *b* 26 June 1907; *s* of late Godfrey I. H. Lloyd and late Constance L. A. Lloyd; *m* 1st, 1932, Nora K. E. Patten; one *s* one *d*; 2nd, 1951, Joyce Evelyn Campbell. *Educ:* Gresham's Sch.; Trinity Coll., Cambridge (MA). Industrial Research in Gas Light and Coke Co., London, 1931–41; Royal Aircraft Establishment, 1941–44; Power Jets (Research and Development), 1944–46. National Gas Turbine Establishment, Pyestock, 1946–60, Deputy Director, 1950; Dir-Gen. Engine R&D, Mins of Aviation and Technology, 1961–69; Head of British Defence Research and Supply Staff, Canberra, 1969–72. Chm., Gas Turbine Collaboration Cttee, 1961–68. CEng, FRAeS, SFInstE. Pres., Cambridge Univ. Mountaineering Club, 1928–29; Chm., Mount Everest Foundn, 1982–84 (Vice Chm., 1980–82). Himalayan expeditions: Nanda Devi, 1936; Everest, 1938; Langtang Himal, 1949; Kulu, 1977. *Publications:* various papers in scientific and technical journals. *Recreations:* mountaineering, fishing, gardening. *Address:* 121 Tourist Road, Toowoomba, Qld 4350, Australia. *Clubs:* Alpine (Vice-Pres., 1961–63, Pres., 1977–80); Himalayan (Hon. Mem., 1992); Queensland (Brisbane).

See also T. A. Evans.

LLOYD, Peter; *see* Lloyd, G. P.

LLOYD, Peter Gordon, CBE 1976 (OBE 1965); retired; British Council Representative, Greece, 1976–80; *b* 20 Feb. 1920; *s* of Peter Gleave Lloyd and Ellen Swift; *m* 1952, Edith Florence (*née* Flurey); two *s* one *d*. *Educ:* Royal Grammar Sch., Newcastle upon Tyne; Balliol Coll., Oxford (Horsley Exhibnr, 1939; BA, MA 1948). RA (Light Anti-Aircraft), subseq. DLI, 1940–46, Captain. British Council, 1949–: Brit. Council, Belgium and Hon. Lector in English, Brussels Univ., 1949–52; Reg. Dir, Mbale, Uganda, 1952–56; Dep. Dir Personnel, 1956–60; Representative: Ethiopia, 1960–68; Poland, 1969–72; Nigeria, 1972–76. *Publications:* (introd) Huysmans, A Rebours, 1946; The Story of British Democracy, 1959; Perspectives and Identities, 1989; critical essays on literature in periodicals. *Recreations:* literature, music, travel. *Address:* 111 Sussex Road, Petersfield, Hants GU31 4LB. *T:* (01730) 262007. *Club:* Oxford and Cambridge.

LLOYD, Rt Hon. Sir Peter (Robert Cable), Kt 1995; PC 1994; *b* 12 Nov. 1937; *s* of late David and Stella Lloyd; *m* 1967, Hilary Creighton; one *s* one *d*. *Educ:* Tonbridge Sch.; Pembroke Coll., Cambridge (MA). Formerly Marketing Manager, United Biscuits Ltd. MP (C) Fareham, 1979–2001. Sec., Cons. Parly Employment Cttee, 1979–81; Vice-Chm., Cons. European Affairs Cttee, 1980–81; PPS to Minister of State, NI Office, 1981–82, to Sec. of State for Educn and Sci., Sir Keith Joseph, 1983–84; Asst Govt Whip, 1984–86; a Lord Comr of HM Treasury (Govt Whip), 1986–88; Parly Under-Sec. of State, Dept of Social Security, 1988–89, Home Office, 1989–92; Minister of State, Home Office, 1992–94. Mem., Treasury Select Cttee, 1997–99; Chm., All Party Penal Affairs Cttee, 1997–2001. Chairman, Bow Group, 1972–73; Editor of Crossbow, 1974–76. Chm., New Bridge, 1994–. *Recreations:* theatre, gardening.

LLOYD, Phyllida Christian; freelance theatre director; *b* 17 June 1957; *d* of Patrick Lloyd and Margaret (*née* Douglas-Pennant). *Educ:* Birmingham Univ. (BA English and Drama 1979). Arts Council trainee dir, Wolsey Theatre, Ipswich, 1985. Productions include: The Comedy of Errors, A Streetcar Named Desire, Dona Rosita the Spinster, Oliver Twist, Bristol Old Vic, 1989; The Winter's Tale, The School for Scandal, Death and the King's Horseman, Medea, Manchester Royal Exchange, 1990–91; The Virtuoso, Artists and Admirers, RSC, 1991–92; L'Etoile, La Bohème, Gloriana, Medea, Opera North, 1991–96; Six Degrees of Separation, Hysteria, Royal Court, 1992, 1993; Pericles, What the Butler Saw, The Way of the World, RNT, 1994–95; Threepenny Opera, Donmar Warehouse, 1994; Doña Rosita, Almeida, 1997; The Prime of Miss Jean Brodie, RNT, 1998; Carmen, Opera North, 1998; Macbeth, Paris Opera, 1999; The Carmelites, 1999, Verdi's Requiem, 2000, ENO; Mamma Mia!, Prince Edward, 1999, Canada and USA, 2000, Australia, 2001; The Handmaid's Tale, Royal Danish Opera, 2000; Gloriana (BBC TV film), 2000; Boston Marriage, Donmar Warehouse, 2001. *Address:* c/o Annette Stone, 2nd Floor, 22 Great Marlborough Street, W1V 1AF. *T:* (020) 7734 0626.

LLOYD, Sir Richard (Ernest Butler), 2nd Bt *cr* 1960, of Rhu, Co. Dunbarton; Chairman: Vickers plc, 1992–97 (Director, 1978–97; Deputy Chairman, 1989–92); Argos plc, 1995–98; *b* 6 Dec. 1928; *s* of Major Sir (Ernest) Guy Richard Lloyd, 1st Bt, DSO, and Helen Kynaston (*d* 1984), *yr d* of Col E. W. Greg, CB; *S* father, 1987; *m* 1955, Jennifer Susan Margaret, *e d* of Brigadier Ereld Cardiff, CB, CBE; three *s*. *Educ:* Wellington Coll.; Hertford Coll., Oxford (MA). Nat. Service (Captain, Black Watch), 1947–49. Joined Glyn, Mills & Co., 1952; Exec. Dir, 1964–70; Chief Executive, Williams & Glyn's Bank Ltd, 1970–78; Hill Samuel & Co. Ltd: Dep. Chm., 1978–87, 1991–95; Chief Exec., 1980–87; Chm., 1987–91. Member: CBI Council, 1978–96; Industrial Develt Adv. Bd, 1972–77; Nat. Econ. Develt Council, 1973–77; Cttee to Review the Functioning of Financial Institutions, 1977–80; Overseas Projects Bd, 1981–85; Advisory Bd, Royal Coll. of Defence Studies, 1987–95; Chm., Business and Industry Adv. Cttee, OECD, 1998–99. Pres., British Heart Foundn, 1995–; Gov., Ditchley Foundn, 1974–. *Recreations:* walking, fly-fishing, gardening. *Heir: s* Richard Timothy Butler Lloyd [*b* 12 April 1956; *m* 1989, Wilhelmina, *d* of Henri Schut]. *Address:* Sundridge Place, Sundridge, Sevenoaks, Kent TN14 6DD. *T:* (01959) 563599. *Club:* Boodle's.

LLOYD, Richard Hey; *b* 25 June 1933; *s* of Charles Yates Lloyd and Ann Lloyd (*née* Hey); *m* 1962, Teresa Morwenna Willmott; four *d*. *Educ:* Lichfield Cathedral Choir Sch.; Rugby Sch. (Music Scholar); Jesus Coll., Cambridge (Organ Scholar). MA, FRCO, ARCM. Asst Organist, Salisbury Cath., 1957–66; Organist and Master of the Choristers, Hereford Cath., 1966–74; Conductor, Three Choirs Festival, 1966–74 (Chief Conductor 1967, 1970, 1973); Organist and Master of the Choristers, Durham Cathedral, 1974–85; Dep. Headmaster, Salisbury Cathedral Choir Sch., 1985–88. Examiner, Associated Bd of Royal Schs of Music, 1967–. Mem. Council, RCO, 1974–93. *Publications:* church music. *Recreations:* cricket, theatre, travel, reading. *Address:* Refail Newydd, Pentraeth, Anglesey LL75 8YF. *T:* (01248) 450220.

LLOYD, Robert Andrew, CBE 1991; freelance opera singer, broadcaster and writer; *b* 2 March 1940; *s* of William Edward Lloyd and May (*née* Waples); *m* 1st, 1964, Sandra Dorothy Watkins (marr. diss. 1990); one *s* three *d*; 2nd, 1992, Lynda Anne Hazell (*née* Powell). *Educ:* Southend-on-Sea High Sch.; Keble Coll., Oxford (MA Hons Mod. History; Hon. Fellow, 1990). Instructor Lieut RN (HMS Collingwood), 1963–66; Civilian Tutor, Police Staff Coll., Bramshill, 1966–68; studied at London Opera Centre, 1968–69; début in Leonore, Collegiate Theatre, 1969; Principal Bass: Sadler's Wells Opera, Coliseum, 1969–72; Royal Opera House, 1972–82; Parsifal, Covent Garden, 1988; Flying Dutchman, La Scala, 1988; début at Metropolitan Opera, NY, in Barber of Seville, 1988; début at Vienna State Opera in La Forza del Destino. Guest appearances in Amsterdam, Berlin, Hamburg, Aix-en-Provence, Milan (La Scala), San Francisco, Florence, Paris, Munich, Nice, Boston, Toronto, Salzburg, Tokyo; soloist with major orchestras; over 70 recordings; associated with rôles of King Philip, Boris Godunov (first British bass to sing this rôle at Kirov Opera), Gurnemanz (opened 1991 season, La Scala), Fiesco, Banquo, King Henry; created rôle of Tyrone in Tower (opera by Hoddinott), 1999; film, Parsifal; TV productions: Six Foot Cinderella, 1988; Bluebeard's Castle (opera), 1988; 20 progs for BBC Radio 3, Opera in Action, 2000–01. Vis. Prof., RCM, 1996–. President: British Youth Opera, 1989–94; Southend Choral Soc., 1996–; Member: Exec. Cttee, Musicians Benevolent Fund, 1988–94; Conservatoires Adv. Gp, HEFCE, 1993–97; Patron: Abertillery Orpheus Choir, 1990–; Carl Rosa Trust, 1993–. Hon. RAM 1999. Sir Charles Santley Award, Musicians' Co., 1997; Foreign Artist of the Year Medal, Buenos Aires, 1997; Chaliapin Commem. Medal, St Petersburg, 1998. *Publications:* contrib. miscellaneous jls. *Recreations:* sailing, straight theatre. *Address:* c/o Askonas Holt Ltd, 27 Chancery Lane, WC2A 1PF. *Club:* Garrick.

LLOYD, Stephen Harris; His Honour Judge Stephen Lloyd; a Circuit Judge, since 1995; *b* 16 Sept. 1938; *s* of Thomas Richard Lloyd and Amy Irene Lloyd; *m* 1972, Joyce Eileen Baxter; two step *d*. *Educ:* Ashville Coll., Harrogate; Leeds Univ. (LLB). Dale & Newbery, solicitors: articled, 1962; admitted solicitor, 1965; Partner, 1968–85; Sen. Partner, 1985–95; Asst Recorder, 1989–93; Recorder, 1993–95. Chairman: Nat. Council for One Parent Families, 1975–83; Mediation in Divorce, 1986–90. Vice-Chm., St Peter's NHS Trust, Chertsey, 1991–95. Chm., Bd of Govs, Manor House Sch., 1987–95. Member: Morris Register, 1985–; Post Vintage Humber Club, 1992–. *Recreations:* two 1936 motor cars, cottages in Yorkshire National Park, charity and committee work, walking, arts. *Address:* Brighton County Court, Family Centre, 1 Edward Street, Brighton BN2 2JD. *T:* (01273) 811333, *Fax:* (01273) 607638.

LLOYD, Thomas Owen Saunders, DL; FSA; Chairman, Historic Buildings Council for Wales, since 1992; *b* 26 Feb. 1955; *s* of John Audley Lloyd, MC and Mary Ivy Anna Lloyd (*née* Owen); *m* 1987, Christabel Juliet Anne Harrison-Allen (*d* 1996). *Educ:* Radley; Downing Coll., Cambridge (MA Law). FSA 1992. Solicitor, in private practice, London, 1978–87; Dir and Co. Sec., Golden Grove Book Co., Carmarthen, 1987–89; non-executive Director: Dyfed FHSA, 1990–95 (also Chm., Patients' Complaints Cttees); Wales Tourist Bd, 1995–99. Consultant (Wales), Sotheby's, 1999–. Chairman: Pembrokeshire Historical Soc., 1991–94; Buildings at Risk Trust, 1992–; Carmarthenshire Antiquarian Soc., 1999–. DL Dyfed, 2001. Hon. Fellow, Soc. of Architects in Wales, 1993. *Publications:* The Lost Houses of Wales, 1986, 2nd edn 1989; contribs to jls of various Welsh historical socs. *Recreation:* old books and bookplates. *Address:* Freestone Hall, Cresselly, Kilgetty, Pembrokeshire SA68 0SX. *T:* (01646) 651493.

LLOYD, Hon. Sir Timothy (Andrew Wigram), Kt 1996; **Hon. Mr Justice Lloyd;** a Judge of the High Court of Justice, Chancery Division, since 1996; *b* 30 Nov. 1946; *s* of late Thomas Wigram Lloyd and of Margo Adela Lloyd (*née* Beasley); *m* 1978, Theresa Sybil Margaret Holloway. *Educ:* Winchester College; Lincoln College, Oxford. MA. Called to the Bar, Middle Temple, 1970, Bencher, 1994; QC 1986; Mem., Middle Temple and Lincoln's Inn. Attorney Gen., Duchy of Lancaster, 1993–96. *Publication:* (ed) Wurtzburg & Mills, Building Society Law, 15th edn 1989. *Recreations:* music, travel. *Address:* Royal Courts of Justice, Strand, WC2A 2LL.

LLOYD, Ven. Trevor; *see* Lloyd, Ven. B. T.

LLOYD-DAVIES, Andrew; Social Security and Child Support Commissioner, since 1998; *b* 18 June 1948; *s* of late Martyn Howard Lloyd-Davies and Penelope Catherine (*née* Vevers); *m* 1989, Lucy Laetitia Anne, *d* of late Christopher William Trelawny Morshead, MC, and Hope (*née* Rodd); one *s* one *d*. *Educ:* Haileybury; St John's Coll., Oxford (BA Lit. Hum.). Called to the Bar, Lincoln's Inn, 1973; in practice at Chancery Bar, 1975–98; Dep. Social Security Comr, 1996–98. *Address:* Office of the Social Security and Child Support Commissioners, Harp House, 83–85 Farringdon Street, EC4A 4DH. *Club:* MCC.

LLOYD-EDWARDS, Captain Norman, RD 1971 and Bar 1980, RNR; JP; Lord-Lieutenant of South Glamorgan, since 1990 (Vice Lord-Lieutenant, 1986–90); *b* 13 June 1933; *s* of Evan Stanley Edwards and Mary Leah Edwards. *Educ:* Monmouth School for Boys; Quaker's Yard Grammar School; Univ. of Bristol (LLB). Joined RNVR 1952, RN 1958–60; RNR 1960–86; CO S Wales Div., RNR, 1981–84; Naval ADC to the Queen, 1984. Partner, Cartwrights, later Cartwrights, Adams & Black, Solicitors, Cardiff, 1960–93, Consultant, 1993–98. Cardiff City Councillor, 1963–87; Dep. Lord Mayor, 1973–74; Lord Mayor, 1985–86. Member: Welsh Arts Council, 1983–89; BBC Adv. Council (Wales), 1987–90. Chapter Clerk, Llandaff Cathedral, 1975–90. Chm. of Wales, 1981–96, Pres., 1996–, Duke of Edinburgh's Award; Nat. Rescue Training Council, 1983–95. Chm., Glamorgan TAVRA, 1987–90; President: Utd Services Mess, Cardiff, 1986–; S Glam Scouts, 1989–; Cardiff Assoc., National Trust, 1990–; King George's Fund for Sailors, 1990–; Christian Aid (Cardiff and Dist), 1992–; SE Wales Community Foundn, 1993–; Pres., RFCA Wales, 1999–. Vice-Pres., WCMD, 1995–. Founder Master, Welsh Livery Guild, 1992–95. Patron, British Red Cross (S Glam), 1991–. Hon. Colonel: 2 Bn (TA), Royal Regt of Wales, 1996–99; Royal Welsh Regt, 1999–. DL S Glamorgan 1978; JP 1990. GCStJ 1996 (KStJ 1988, Prior of Wales, 1989–). *Recreations:* music, gardening, table talk. *Address:* Hafan Wen, Llantrisant Road, Llandaff CF5 2PU. *Clubs:* Army and Navy; Cardiff and County, United Services Mess (Cardiff).

LLOYD GEORGE, family name of **Earl Lloyd George of Dwyfor**.

LLOYD-GEORGE, family name of **Viscount Tenby**.

LLOYD GEORGE OF DWYFOR, 3rd Earl, *cr* 1945; **Owen Lloyd George;** Viscount Gwynedd, 1945; DL; *b* 28 April 1924; *s* of 2nd Earl Lloyd George of Dwyfor, and Roberta Ida Freeman, 5th *d* of Sir Robert McAlpine, 1st Bt; *S* father, 1968; *m* 1st, 1949, Ruth Margaret (marr. diss. 1982), *o d* of Richard Coit; two *s* one *d*; 2nd, 1982, Cecily Josephine, *d* of late Sir Alexander Gordon Cumming, 5th Bt, MC, and of Elizabeth Countess Cawdor, *widow* of 2nd Earl of Woolton and former wife of 3rd Baron Forres. *Educ:* Oundle. Welsh Guards, 1942–47. Italian Campaign, 1944–45. Formerly Captain Welsh Guards. An Underwriting Member of Lloyd's. Carried the Sword at Investiture of HRH the Prince of Wales, Caernarvon Castle, 1969. Mem., Historic Buildings Council for Wales, 1971–94. DL Dyfed 1993. *Publication:* A Tale of Two Grandfathers, 1999. *Heir: s* Viscount Gwynedd, *qv*. *Recreations:* shooting, gardening. *Address:* Ffynone, Boncath, Pembrokeshire SA37 0HQ; 47 Burton Court, SW3 4SZ. *Clubs:* White's, Pratt's.

LLOYD-HUGHES, Sir Trevor Denby, Kt 1970; author; former consultant in Government/industry relations, now retired; Chairman, Lloyd-Hughes Associates Ltd, International Consultants in Public Affairs, 1970–89; *b* 31 March 1922; *er s* of late Elwyn and Lucy Lloyd-Hughes, Bradford, Yorks; *m* 1st, 1950, Ethel Marguerite Durward (marr. diss. 1971), *o d* of late J. Ritchie, Dundee and Bradford; one *s* one *d*; 2nd, 1971, Marie-Jeanne, *d* of Marcel and late Helene Moreillon, Geneva; one *d* (and one adopted *d*— a Thai girl). *Educ:* Woodhouse Grove Sch., Yorks; Jesus Coll., Oxford (MA). Commissioned RA, 1941; served with 75th (Shropshire Yeomanry) Medium Regt, RA, in Western Desert, Sicily and Italy, 1941–45. Asst Inspector of Taxes, 1948; freelance journalist, 1949; joined staff of Liverpool Daily Post, 1949; Political Corresp., Liverpool Echo, 1950, Liverpool Daily Post, 1951. Press Secretary to the Prime Minister, 1964–69; Chief Information Adviser to Govt, 1969–70. Dir, Trinity International Holdings plc (formerly Liverpool Daily Post and Echo Ltd), 1978–91. Member of Circle of Wine Writers, 1961, Chm., 1972–73. *Recreations:* yoga, gardening, reading, walking, travel. *Address:* 52 Glen Road, Castle Bytham, Grantham, Lincs NG33 4RJ. *T:* (01780) 410001. *Clubs:* Reform, Mosimann's, Wellington.

LLOYD-JACOB, David Oliver, CBE 1984; Executive Chairman, Fibaflo Ltd, since 1999; *b* 30 March 1938; *s* of Sir George and Lady Lloyd-Jacob; *m* 1st, 1961, Clare Bartlett; two *d*; 2nd, 1982, Carolyn Howard. *Educ:* Westminster; Christ Church, Oxford. Pres., Azcon Corp., USA, 1974–79; Man. Dir, Consolidated Gold Fields plc, 1979–81; Chm., Amcon Group Inc., USA, 1979–82; Chm. and Chief Exec. Officer, Levinson Steel Co., Pittsburgh, 1983–90; Chm., Butte Mining plc, 1991–2000. Chm., Britain Salutes NY, 1981–83. *Recreations:* opera, theatre, restoring old houses. *Address:* 28 Lewes Crescent, Brighton BN2 1GB. *T:* (office) (01202) 624141. *Clubs:* Garrick; Leander (Henley-on-Thames).

LLOYD JONES, Charles Beynon; *see* Jones.

LLOYD-JONES, David Mathias; freelance conductor; *b* 19 Nov. 1934; *s* of late Sir Vincent Lloyd-Jones, and Margaret Alwena, *d* of late G.H. Mathias; *m* 1964, Anne Carolyn Whitehead; two *s* one *d*. *Educ:* Westminster Sch.; Magdalen Coll., Oxford (BA). Repetiteur, Royal Opera House, Covent Garden, 1959–60; Chorus Master, New Opera Co., 1961–64; conducted at: Bath Fest., 1966; City of London Fest., 1966; Wexford Fest., 1967–70; Scottish Opera, 1968; WNO, 1968; Royal Opera House, 1971; ENO (formerly Sadler's Wells Opera), 1969 (Asst Music Dir, 1972–78); Artistic Dir, Opera North, 1978–90; Leeds and Edinburgh Fests; also conductor of BBC broadcasts, TV operas (Eugene Onegin, The Flying Dutchman, Hansel and Gretel), and operas and concerts in France, Holland, Russia, Germany, Italy, Switzerland, Bulgaria, Poland, Chile, Canada, Argentina, Ireland, Norway and Australia; has appeared with most British symph. orchs. Numerous recordings with LPO, RSNO, Bournemouth Sinfonietta and English Northern Philharmonia (Founder Conductor). Chm., Delius Trust, 1997–. Gen. Ed., William Walton Edition, 1996–. FGSM 1992. Hon. DMus Leeds, 1986. *Publications:* (trans.) Boris Godunov (vocal score), 1968; (trans.) Eugene Onegin (vocal score), 1971; Boris Godunov (critical edn of original full score), 1975; The Gondoliers, 1986; contrib. 6th edn Grove's Dictionary of Music and Musicians, 1981; contrib. Musik in Geschichte und Gegenwart, Music and Letters, and The Listener. *Recreations:* theatre, old shrub roses, travel. *Address:* 94 Whitelands House, Cheltenham Terrace, SW3 4RA. *T:* and *Fax:* (020) 7730 8695.

LLOYD JONES, John; *see* Jones.

LLOYD-JONES, Sir (Peter) Hugh (Jefferd), Kt 1989; FBA 1966; Regius Professor of Greek in the University of Oxford and Student of Christ Church, 1960–89, now Emeritus Professor and Emeritus Student; *b* 21 Sept. 1922; *s* of Major W. Lloyd-Jones, DSO, and Norah Leila, *d* of F. H. Jefferd, Brent, Devon; *m* 1st, 1953, Frances Elisabeth Hedley (marr. diss. 1981); two *s* one *d*; 2nd, 1982, Mary Lefkowitz (Andrew W. Mellon Professor in the Humanities, Wellesley College, Mass), *d* of Harold and Mena Rosenthal, New York. *Educ:* Lycée Français du Royaume Uni, S Kensington; Westminster Sch.; Christ Church, Oxford. Served War of 1939–45, 2nd Lieut, Intelligence Corps, India, 1942; Temp. Captain, 1944. 1st Cl. Classics (Mods), 1941; MA 1947; 1st Cl., LitHum, 1948; Chancellor's Prize for Latin Prose, 1947; Ireland and Craven Schol., 1947; Fellow of Jesus Coll., Cambridge, 1948–54; Asst Lecturer in Classics, University of Cambridge, 1950–52, Lecturer, 1952–54; Fellow and E. P. Warren Praelector in Classics, Corpus Christi Coll., Oxford, 1954–60; J. H. Gray Lecturer, University of Cambridge, 1961; Visiting Prof., Yale Univ., 1964–65, 1967–68; Sather Prof. of Classical Literature, Univ. of California at Berkeley, 1969–70; Alexander White Vis. Prof., Chicago, 1972; Vis. Prof., Harvard Univ., 1976–77. Fellow, Morse Coll., Yale Univ. Hon. Mem., Greek Humanistic Soc., 1968; Corresponding Member: Acad. of Athens, 1978 (Fellow, 2001); Nordrhein-Westfälische Akad. der Wissenschaften, 1983; Accademia di Archeologia Lettere e Belle Arti, Naples, 1984; Bayerische Akad. der Wissenschaften, 1992; Hon. Foreign Mem.,

Amer. Acad. of Arts and Scis, 1978; Mem., Amer. Philos. Soc., 1992. Hon. DHL Chicago, 1970; Hon. DPhil Tel Aviv, 1984; Hon. PhD Thessalonica, 1999. *Publications:* Appendix to Loeb Classical Library edn of Aeschylus, 1957; Menandri Dyscolus (Oxford Classical Text), 1960; (trans.) Paul Maas, Greek Metre, 1962; (ed) The Greeks, 1962; Tacitus (in series The Great Historians), 1964; (trans.) Aeschylus: Agamemnon, The Libation-Bearers, and The Eumenides, 1970, 2nd edn 1979; The Justice of Zeus, 1971, 2nd edn 1983; (ed) Maurice Bowra, 1974; Females of the Species: Semonides of Amorgos on Women, 1975; (with Marcelle Quinton) Myths of the Zodiac, 1978; (with Marcelle Quinton) Imaginary Animals (US edn as Mythical Beasts), 1979; Blood for the Ghosts, 1982; Classical Survivals, 1982; (with P. J. Parsons) Supplementum Hellenisticum, 1983; (with N. G. Wilson) Sophoclis Fabulae, 1990; (with N. G. Wilson) Sophoclea, 1990; Academic Papers (2 vols), 1990; Greek in a Cold Climate, 1991; Sophocles I–II, 1994; Sophocles III, 1996; (with N. G. Wilson) Sophocles: second thoughts, 1997; contribs to periodicals. *Recreations:* cats, remembering past cricket. *Address:* 15 West Riding, Wellesley, MA 02482, USA. *T:* (617) 2372212, *Fax:* (617) 2372246; Christ Church, Oxford OX1 1DP. *T:* (01865) 791063. *Club:* Oxford and Cambridge.

LLOYD JONES, Sir Richard (Anthony), KCB 1988 (CB 1981); Permanent Secretary, Welsh Office, 1985–93; Chairman, Arts Council of Wales, 1994–99; *b* 1 Aug. 1933; *s* of Robert and Anne Lloyd Jones; *m* 1955, Patricia Avril Mary Richmond; two *d*. *Educ:* Long Dene Sch., Edenbridge; Nottingham High Sch.; Balliol Coll., Oxford (MA). Entered Admiralty, 1957; Asst Private Sec. to First Lord of the Admiralty, 1959–62; Private Sec. to Secretary of the Cabinet, 1969–70; Asst Sec., Min. of Defence, 1970–74; Under Sec., 1974–78, Dep. Sec. 1978–85, Welsh Office. Chairman: Civil Service Benevolent Fund, 1987–93 (Trustee, 1993–2000); Adv. Cttee on local govt staff transfers (Wales), 1993–94; Local Govt Staff Commn for Wales, 1994–97. Member: BBC Gen. Adv. Council, 1994–96; Commn for Local Democracy, 1994–95. President: Welsh Council, Ramblers' Assoc., 1993–; Groundwork Merthyr and Rhondda Cynon Taff, 1996–; Chm., Age Concern Cymru, 1999– (Pres., 1996–99); Vice-Chm., Prince of Wales' Cttee, 1993–96; Vice-Chm., Prince's Trust Bro, 1996–99. Vice Pres., Univ. of Wales, Cardiff, 1993–; Member: Ct, Univ. of Wales, 1995–2000; Ct, Nat. Mus. of Wales, 1996–99. Hon. Fellow: UCW Aberystwyth, 1990; Trinity Coll., Carmarthen, 1996. Hon. Dr Glamorgan, 1996. *Recreations:* music, railways, swimming, walking. *Address:* Radyr, Cardiff. *Clubs:* Oxford and Cambridge; Cardiff and County.

LLOYD MOSTYN, family name of **Baron Mostyn**.

LLOYD-NEWSTROM, Prof. David Graham; *see* Lloyd, D. G.

LLOYD WEBBER, family name of **Baron Lloyd-Webber**.

LLOYD-WEBBER, Baron *cr* 1997 (Life Peer), of Sydmonton in the co. of Hampshire; **Andrew Lloyd Webber,** Kt 1992; composer; *b* 22 March 1948; *s* of late William Southcombe Lloyd Webber, CBE, DMus, FRCM, FRCO, and Jean Hermione Johnstone; *m* 1st, 1971, Sarah Jane Tudor (*née* Hugill) (marr. diss. 1983); one *s* one *d*; 2nd, 1984, Sarah Brightman (marr. diss. 1990); 3rd, 1991, Madeleine Astrid Gurdon; two *s* one *d*. *Educ:* Westminster Sch.; Magdalen Coll., Oxford; Royal Coll. of Music (FRCM 1988). Composer: (with lyrics by Timothy Rice): Joseph and the Amazing Technicolor Dreamcoat, 1968, rev. 1973 and 1991; Jesus Christ Superstar, 1970, rev. 1996; Evita, 1976 (stage version, 1978); (with lyrics by Alan Ayckbourn) Jeeves, 1975, revived as By Jeeves, 1996; (with lyrics by Don Black) Tell Me on a Sunday, 1980; Cats, 1981 (based on poems by T. S. Eliot); (with lyrics by Don Black) Song & Dance, 1982; (with lyrics by Richard Stilgoe) Starlight Express, 1984; (with lyrics by Richard Stilgoe and Charles Hart) The Phantom of the Opera, 1986; (with lyrics by Don Black and Charles Hart) Aspects of Love, 1989; (with lyrics by Christopher Hampton and Don Black) Sunset Boulevard, 1993; (with lyrics by Jim Steinman) Whistle Down the Wind, 1996; (with lyrics by Ben Elton) The Beautiful Game, 2000. Producer: Joseph and the Amazing Technicolor Dreamcoat, 1973, 1974, 1978, 1980, 1991; Jeeves Takes Charge, 1975; Cats, 1981; Song and Dance, 1982; Daisy Pulls It Off, 1983; The Hired Man, 1984; Starlight Express, 1984; On Your Toes, 1984; The Phantom of the Opera, 1986; Café Puccini, 1986; The Resistable Rise of Arturo Ui, 1987; Lend Me a Tenor, 1988; Aspects of Love, 1989; Shirley Valentine, 1989 (Broadway); La Bête, 1992; Sunset Boulevard, 1993; By Jeeves, 1996; Jesus Christ Superstar, 1996, 1998; Whistle Down the Wind, 1996, 1998, and others. Film scores: Gumshoe, 1971; The Odessa File, 1974. Composed "Variations" (based on A minor Caprice No 24 by Paganini), 1977, symphonic version, 1986; Requiem Mass, 1985. Awards include Acad. Award (Oscar), Golden Globe, Tony, Drama Desk, and Grammy. *Publications:* (with Timothy Rice) Evita, 1978; Cats: the book of the musical, 1981; (with Timothy Rice) Joseph and the Amazing Technicolor Dreamcoat, 1982; The Complete Phantom of the Opera, 1987; The Complete Aspects of Love, 1989; Sunset Boulevard: from movie to musical, 1993. *Recreations:* architecture, art, food critic (Daily Telegraph, 1996–). *Address:* 22 Tower Street, WC2H 9NS.
See also J. Lloyd Webber.

LLOYD WEBBER, Julian, FRCM; 'cellist; *b* 14 April 1951; *s* of late William Southcombe Lloyd Webber, CBE, DMus, FRCM, FRCO, and Jean Hermione Johnstone; *m* 1st, 1974, Celia Mary Ballantyne (marr. diss. 1989); 2nd, 1989, Princess Zohra Mahmud Ghazi (marr. diss. 1999); one *s*; 3rd, 2001, Kheira Bourahla. *Educ:* University College Sch., London; Royal College of Music. ARCM 1967, FRCM 1994. Studied 'cello with: Douglas Cameron, 1965–68; Pierre Fournier, Geneva, 1972. Début, Queen Elizabeth Hall, 1972; USA début, Lincoln Center, NY, 1980. Has performed with the world's major orchestras; toured: USA, Germany, Holland, Africa, Bulgaria, S America, Spain, Belgium, France, Scandinavia, Portugal, Denmark, Australasia, Singapore, Japan, Korea, Czechoslovakia, Austria, Canada, Hong Kong and Taiwan. Has made first recordings of works by Benjamin Britten, Frank Bridge, Gavin Bryars, Michael Nyman, Delius, Rodrigo, Holst, Vaughan Williams, Haydn, Philip Glass, Sullivan, John McCabe, Malcolm Arnold; recorded: Elgar Cello Concerto (cond. Menuhin), 1985 (British Phonographic Industry Award for Best Classical Recording, 1986); Dvořák Cello Concerto with Czech Philharmonic Orchestra, 1988; also concertos by Britten, Delius, Haydn, Honegger, Lalo, Miaskovsky, Saint-Saëns, Walton and Tchaikovsky Rococo Variations. Crystal Award, World Economic Forum, Switzerland, 1998. *Publications:* Travels with My Cello, 1984; Song of the Birds, 1985; Married to Music, 2001; edited: series, The Romantic 'Cello, 1978, The Classical 'Cello, 1980, The French 'Cello, 1981; Frank Bridge 'Cello Music, 1981; Young Cellist's Repertoire, Books 1, 2, 3, 1984; Holst, Invocation, 1984; Vaughan Williams, Fantasia on Sussex Folk Tunes, 1984; Recital Repertoire for Cellists, 1987; Short, Sharp Shocks, 1990; The Great 'Cello Solos, 1992; contribs to music jls and national Press in UK, US, Canada and Australia. *Recreations:* countryside (especially British), Leyton Orient FC. *Address:* c/o IMG Artists Europe, Lovell House, 616 Chiswick High Road, W4 5RX. *T:* (020) 8233 5800.
See also Baron Lloyd-Webber.

LLWYD, Elfyn; MP (Plaid Cymru) Meirionnydd Nant Conwy, since 1992; *b* 26 Sept. 1951; *s* of late Huw Meirion Hughes and of Hefina (*née* Roberts); surname Hughes abandoned by deed poll, 1970; *m* 1974, Eleri Llwyd; one *s* one *d*. *Educ:* Ysgol Dyffryn Conwy Llanrwst; Univ. of Wales, Aberystwyth (LLB Hons); Coll. of Law, Chester. Admitted solicitor, 1977; called to the Bar, 1997. Plaid Cymru Parly Whip, 1995–. Pres., Gwynedd Law Soc., 1990–91. Mem. Nat. Council, NSPCC Wales, 1993–. Mem. Ct, Univ. of Wales, Aberystwyth, 1993–. *Recreations:* pigeon breeding, Rugby, choral singing, fishing. *Address:* Ty Glyndwr, Heol Glyndwr, Dolgellau, Gwynedd LL40 1BD. *T:* (01341) 422661; Glandwr, Llanuwchllyn, Y Bala, Gwynedd LL23 7TW.

LLWYD MORGAN, Derec; *see* Morgan.

LOACH, Kenneth; television and film director; *b* 17 June 1936; *s* of late John Loach and of Vivien Loach (*née* Hamlin); *m* 1962, Lesley Ashton; two *s* two *d* (and one *s* decd). *Educ:* King Edward VI School, Nuneaton; St Peter's Hall, Oxford (Hon. Fellow, St Peter's Coll., 1993). BBC Trainee, Drama Dept, 1963. *Television:* Diary of a Young Man, 1964; 3 Clear Sundays, 1965; The End of Arthur's Marriage, 1965; Up The Junction, 1965; Coming Out Party, 1965; Cathy Come Home, 1966; In Two Minds, 1966; The Golden Vision, 1969; The Big Flame, 1969; After A Lifetime, 1971; The Rank and File, 1972; Days of Hope, 1975; The Price of Coal, 1977; The Gamekeeper, 1979; Auditions, 1980; A Question of Leadership, 1981; Questions of Leadership, 1983 (banned from TV); The Red and the Blue, 1983; Which Side Are You On?, 1985; The View from the Woodpile, 1988; Dispatches, 1991; Flickering Flame, 1996; Another City, 1998. *Films:* Poor Cow, 1968; Kes, 1970; In Black and White, 1970; Family Life, 1972; Black Jack, 1979; Looks and Smiles, 1981; Fatherland, 1987; Hidden Agenda, 1990; Riff-Raff, 1991; Raining Stones, 1993; Ladybird, Ladybird, 1994; Land and Freedom, 1995; Carla's Song, 1996; My Name is Joe, 1998; Bread and Roses, 2000; The Navigators, 2001. *Address:* c/o Parallax Pictures, 7 Denmark Street, WC2H 8LS.

LOADER, Sir Leslie (Thomas), Kt 1987; CBE 1980; retired company chairman; *b* 27 April 1923; *s* of Edward Robert Loader and Ethel May Loader (*née* Tiller); *m* 1957, Jennifer (marr. diss.); three *d*. *Educ:* Bitterne Park; Bournemouth Municipal Coll.; London Sch. of Economics and Political Science (occasional student). Served War of 1939–45; commnd Hampshire Regt (now Royal Hampshire Regt); saw active service in Italy. Mem., Southampton Borough Council, 1947–59 (first to propose sale of council houses to tenants, 1949); contested (C) Southampton, Itchen, 1955; Chairman: Southampton Young Conservatives, 1947; Southampton Itchen Cons. Assoc., 1964–70; Wessex Area Cons. Party, 1972–75; Euro-Cons. Council for Wight and Hants E, 1979–82 (Hon. Treas., 1984–87); Mem. Exec., Nat. Union of Cons. and Unionist Assocs, 1967–76 (Mem., Standing Adv. Cttee on Parly Cands; Hon. Life Vice Pres., Wessex Area, 1990); Pres., Eastleigh Cons. Assoc., 1985–98; Founder Chairman: Southern Parishes Cons. Club, Eastleigh; Cosham Cons. Club, Portsmouth N. Founded: Rotary Club of Bitterne, 1962; Woolston Housing Assoc., 1962 (Chm., 1962–83; Pres., 1983–98); Pres., Swaythling Housing Soc. Ltd, 1983–92 (Chm., 1976–83); Chm., Wessex Body Scanner Appeal, 1980–83; Member: Southampton Harbour Bd, 1951–56; Southampton and SW Hampshire HA, 1981–86; Trustee, Wessex Med. Sch. Trust, 1983–86. Formerly Mem. Ct of Governors, UC Southampton, later Univ. of Southampton. Founder, S Hampshire Aviation Historical Soc., 1980. Freeman, City of London; Liveryman, Painter-Stainers' Co. *Publications:* booklets and articles on housing and political matters. *Recreation:* social history research. *Club:* Carlton.

LOADES, Prof. Ann Lomas, CBE 2001; PhD; Professor of Divinity, Durham University, since 1995; *b* 21 Sept. 1938; *d* of Gerard Joseph Glover and Amy Lomas. *Educ:* Durham Univ. (BA Theol. 1960; PhD 1975); McMaster Univ. (MA 1965). Durham University: Lectr in Theology, 1975–81; Sen. Lectr, 1981–90; Reader, 1990–95; Chm., Bd of Studies in Theol., 1989–91. Arts and Humanities Research Board: Convenor, assessment panel for postgrad. awards in philosophy, law and religious studies, 1999–; Mem., Postgrad. Cttee, 1999–; Mem., Res. Centres Scheme Cttee, 1999–. Lay Mem., Durham Cathedral Chapter, 2001–. Editor, Theology, 1991–97. *Publications:* (ed) W. A. Whitehouse, The Authority of Grace, 1981; (ed with J. C. Eaton) For God and Clarity, 1983; Kant and Job's Comforters, 1985; Searching for Lost Coins (Scott Holland Lectures), 1987; (ed) Feminist Theology, 1990; (ed with M. McLain) Hermeneutics, the Bible and Literary Criticism, 1992; (ed with L. Rue) Contemporary Classics in Philosophy of Religion, 1991; (ed) Dorothy L. Sayers, Spiritual Writings, 1993; (ed with D. W. Brown) The Sense of the Sacramental, 1995; (ed) Spiritual Classics from the late Twentieth Century, 1995; (ed with D. W. Brown) Christ: the sacramental word, 1996; Evelyn Underhill, 1997; Feminist Theology: voices from the past, 2001. *Recreations:* going to the theatre, cooking, swimming. *Address:* Theology Department, Abbey House, Palace Green, Durham DH1 3RS. *T:* (0191) 374 2052.

LOADES, David Henry, CB 1996; FIA; Directing Actuary (Under Secretary), Government Actuary's Department, 1983–97; *b* 16 Oct. 1937; *s* of John Henry Loades and Evelyn Clara Ralph; *m* 1962, Jennifer Glenys Stevens; one *s* two *d*. *Educ:* Beckenham and Penge County Grammar Sch. for Boys. BA. FIA 1961. Govt Actuary's Dept, 1956–97. Medal of Merit for services to the Scout Assoc., 1986. *Publications:* papers in actuarial jls. *Recreations:* painting, visiting art galleries.

LOANE, Most Rev. Marcus Lawrence, KBE 1976; DD; *b* 14 Oct. 1911; *s* of K. O. A. Loane; *m* 1937, Patricia Evelyn Jane Simpson Knox; two *s* two *d*. *Educ:* The King's School, Parramatta, NSW; Sydney University (MA). Moore Theological College, 1932–33; Australian College of Theology (ThL, 1st Class, 1933; Fellow, 1955). Ordained Deacon, 1935, Priest, 1936; Resident Tutor and Chaplain, Moore Theological College, 1935–38; Vice-Principal, 1939–53; Principal, 1954–59. Chaplain AIF, 1942–44. Canon, St Andrew's Cathedral, 1949–58; Bishop-Coadjutor, diocese of Sydney, 1958–66; Archbishop of Sydney and Metropolitan of Province of NSW, 1966–82; Primate of Australia, 1978–82. Hon. DD Wycliffe College, Toronto, 1958. *Publications:* Oxford and the Evangelical Succession, 1950; Cambridge and the Evangelical Succession, 1952; Masters of the English Reformation, 1955; Life of Archbishop Mowll, 1960; Makers of Religious Freedom, 1961; Pioneers of the Reformation in England, 1964; Makers of Our Heritage, 1966; The Hope of Glory, 1968; This Surpassing Excellence, 1969; They Were Pilgrims, 1970; Hewn from the Rock, 1976; Men to Remember, 1987. *Address:* 18 Harrington Avenue, Warrawee, NSW 2074, Australia. *T:* (2) 94892975.

LOASBY, Prof. Brian John, FBA 1994; Professor of Management Economics, University of Stirling, 1971–84, Emeritus and Hon. Professor of Economics, since 1984; *b* 2 Aug. 1930; *s* of Frederick Thomas Loasby and Mabel Phyllis Loasby; *m* 1957, Judith Ann Robinson; two *d*. *Educ:* Kettering GS; Emmanuel Coll., Cambridge (BA 1952; MLitt 1958; MA 1998). Assistant in Pol Economy, Aberdeen Univ., 1955–58; Bournville Res. Fellow, Birmingham Univ., 1958–61; Tutor in Management Studies, Bristol Univ., 1961–67; Stirling University: Lectr in Econs, 1967–68; Sen. Lectr, 1968–71. Management Fellow, Arthur D. Little Inc., Cambridge, Mass, 1965–66; Vis. Fellow, Oxford Centre for Management Studies, 1974. Pres., Scottish Economic Soc., 1987–90. DUniv Stirling, 1998. *Publications:* The Swindon Project, 1973; Choice, Complexity and Ignorance, 1976; The Mind and Method of the Economist, 1989; Equilibrium and Evolution, 1991; (ed with N. J. Foss) Economic Organization, Capabilities and Co-ordination: essays in honour of G. B. Richardson, 1998; Knowledge, Institutions and Evolution in Economics, 1999;

contrib. books, and econs and management jls. *Recreation:* gardening. *Address:* Department of Economics, University of Stirling, Stirling FK9 4LA. *T:* (01786) 467470; 8 Melfort Drive, Stirling FK7 0BD. *T:* (01786) 472124.

LOBO, António C.; *see* Costa-Lobo.

LOBO, Sir Rogerio Hyndman, (Sir Roger), Kt 1985; CBE 1978 (OBE 1972); JP; Chairman, P. J. Lobo & Co. Ltd, Hong Kong, since 1960; Chairman, Broadcasting Authority of Hong Kong, 1989–97; *b* 15 Sept. 1923; *s* of Dr P. J. Lobo and Branca Helena (*née* Hyndman); *m* 1947, Margaret Mary (*née* Choa); five *s* five *d*. *Educ:* Escola Central, Macao; Seminario de S Jose, Macao; Liceu Nacional Infante Dom Henrique, Macao; La Salle Coll., Hong Kong. Director: Kjeldsen & Co. (HK) (formerly Danish Fancy Food Gp), 1982–; Shun Tak Hldgs Ltd, 1994–; Pacific Century CyberWorks Ltd, 1999–; dir of 4 other cos. Unofficial MLC, Hong Kong, 1972–85 (Sen. Mem., 1980–85); Unofficial MEC, 1978–85. Member: Urban Council, 1965–78; Housing Authority, 1967–83; Chm., Adv. Cttee on Post-Retirement Employment, 1987–98; Comr, Civil Aid Services, 1977–92 (Mem., 1955–). Hon. LLD Univ. of Hong Kong, 1982. JP Hong Kong, 1963. Silver Jubilee Medal, 1977; Civil Aid Services Long Service Medal, 1970; Civil Defence Long Service Clasp, 1982. Comdr, Order of St Gregory the Great, The Vatican, 1969. *Recreation:* golf. *Address:* Woodland Heights, E1, 2 Wongneichong Gap Road, Hong Kong. *T:* 25740779; (business) 28/F Aon Insurance Tower, 3 Lockhart Road, Wanchai, Hong Kong. *T:* 25269418/25378697. *Clubs:* Dynasty, Hong Kong, Rotary, Hong Kong Jockey, Hong Kong Golf, Hong Kong Country (Hong Kong).

LOCHHEAD, Richard Neilson; Member (SNP) North East Scotland, Scottish Parliament, since 1999; *b* 24 May 1969; *s* of Robert William Lochhead and Agnes Robertson Cloughley. *Educ:* Williamwood High Sch., Clarkston, Glasgow; Univ. of Stirling (BA Hons Political Studies, 1994). SSEB, 1987–89; Office Manager for Alex Salmond, MP, 1994–98; Develt Officer, Dundee CC, 1998–99. Contested (SNP) Gordon, 1997. *Recreations:* travelling, reading novels and history books, cinema, squash, five-a-side football. *Address:* (office) 70 Rosemount Place, Aberdeen AB25 2XJ.

LOCHORE, Sir Brian (James), KNZM 1999; OBE 1970; farmer; Chairman, Hillary Commission, since 1998 (Member, since 1995); *b* 3 Sept. 1940; *s* of James Denniston Lochore and Alma Joyce Lochore (*née* Wyeth); *m* 1963, Pamela Lucy, *d* of David and Nancy Young; one *s* twin *d*. *Educ:* Opaki Primary Sch.; Wairarapa Coll. Farmer of own property, 1961–. Tennis Rep., 1957–65 and 1973–84, Rugby Rep., 1959–71, Wairarapa; Mem., NZ All Black Rugby Team, 1963–71 (Capt., 1966–70); Rugby Coach: Wairarapa Bush team, 1980–82 (Life Mem., 1988); NZ team, 1985–87 (incl. inaugural World Cup); World XV, IRB Centennial, 1986; NZ Rugby Selector, 1983–87; Manager and Selector, World XV, 1992; Campaigns Manager, All Blacks World Cup, 1995. Member: Electoral Coll., Meat & Wool Bd, 1972–73; Romney Breeders' Council, 1993–97. Bd Mem., Sports Foundn, 1996–98 (Chm., High Perf. Funding Cttee, 1997–98). Trustee: Masterton Charitable Trust, 1989–90; Halberg Trust, 1992–. Member: Mauriceville Sch. Cttee, 1973–79 (Chm., 1975–79); Masterton Secondary Schs Bd, 1980–86 (Chm., 1987–88); Comr, Kuranui Coll., 1994–95. *Recreations:* golf, tennis, thoroughbred horse breeding. *Address:* Riverlands, Paierau Road, Masterton, New Zealand. *T:* (6) 3770195.

LOCK, David Anthony; barrister; *b* 2 May 1960; *s* of John Kirby Lock and Jeannette Mary Lock (*née* Bridgewater); *m* 1985, Dr Bernadette Clare Gregory; one *s* two *d*. *Educ:* Jesus Coll., Cambridge (MA 1982); Central London Poly. (Dip. Law 1984). Mgt Trainee, GEC Telecommuncations, 1982–83; called to the Bar, Gray's Inn, 1985 (Wilson Schol.); started practice at the Bar, 1987. Mem. (Lab), Wychavon DC, 1995–97 (Chairman: Amenities and Economic Develt Cttee, 1995; Community and Leisure Cttee, 1995–97). MP (Lab) Wyre Forest, 1997–2001; contested (Lab) same seat, 2001. PPS, Lord Chancellor's Dept, 1997–98, to Lord Chancellor and Minister of State, Lord Chancellor's Dept, 1998–99; Parly Sec., Lord Chancellor's Dept, 1999–2001. Secretary: All-Party Occupational Pensions Gp, 1997–99; All Party Cycling Gp, 1998–99; Vice Chm., Textiles, Carpets and Footwear Industry Gp, 1998–99. *Recreations:* cycling, family, wine and friends. *Address:* Woodeaves, Pleasant Harbour, Bewdley, Worcs DY12 1AD. *T:* (01299) 403494.

LOCK, David Peter; Chief Planning Adviser, Department of the Environment, 1994–97; Chairman, David Lock Associates Ltd, since 1988; *b* 12 March 1948; *s* of Arthur Lovering Lock and late Kathleen Barbara (*née* Nash); *m* 1970, Jeanette Anita Jones; three *d*. *Educ:* Sir Roger Manwood's Grammar Sch., Sandwich, Kent; Nottingham Coll. of Art and Design/Trent Poly. (DipT&CP). MRTPI 1975. Area Planning Officer, Leicester CC, 1970–73; Planning Aid Officer, TCPA, 1973–78; Planning Manager, Milton Keynes Develt Corp., 1978–81; Associate Dir, Conran Roche Ltd, 1981–88. Chm., DLA Architects Ltd, 1998–; Director: City Discovery Centre Ltd, 1987–; City Discovery Centre (Trading) Ltd, 1997–; non-exec. Dir, Rapid Transport Internat. plc, 1997–. Vis Prof., Univ. of Central England in Birmingham, 1988–98. Trustee and Vice-Chm., TCPA. *Publications:* (contrib.) People and their Settlements, 1976; (contrib.) Growth and Change in the Future City Region, 1976; (contrib.) New Towns in National Development, 1980; Riding the Tiger: planning the South of England, 1989; (jtly) Alternative Development Patterns: new settlements, 1993. *Recreations:* history, geography, reading, research. *Address:* David Lock Associates Ltd, 50 North Thirteenth Street, Central Milton Keynes, Bucks MK9 3BP. *T:* (01908) 666276.

LOCK, (George) David; Managing Director, Private Patients Plan Ltd, 1975–85; *b* 24 Sept. 1929; *s* of George Wilfred Lock and Phyllis Nita (*née* Hollingworth); *m* 1965, Ann Elizabeth Biggs; four *s* one *d*. *Educ:* Haileybury and ISC; Queens' Coll., Cambridge (MA). British Tabulating Machine Co. Ltd (now ICL), 1954–59; Save & Prosper Group Ltd, 1959–69; American Express, 1969–74; Dir, Plan for Active Retirement, Frizzell Insce and Financial Services Ltd (formerly New Business Ventures, Frizzell Consumer Services Ltd), 1986–89. Director: Priplan Investments Ltd, 1979–85; Priplan Services Ltd, 1979–85; PPP Medical Centre Ltd (incorp. Cavendish Medical Centre), 1981–85. Director: Home Concern for the Elderly, 1985–87, 1989–96; The Hosp. Management Trust, 1985–92; Bd of Management, St Anthony's Hosp., Cheam, 1986–; HMT Hospitals Ltd, 1993–; Gainsborough Clinic Ltd, 2000–; Sec., Frizzell Foundn, 1989–93. Sec., Friends of Children of Great Ormond Street, 1986. Trustee, Eynsham Trust, 1975–83; Gov., PPP Medical Trust Ltd (Dir, 1983–89). Member: Nuffield Nursing Homes Trust, 1979–; Exec. Cttee, Assoc. of Independent Hosps, 1981–87. Mem., RSocMed., 1979–92. Freeman, Barbers' Co., 1982–. *Recreations:* bridge, golf, music, family activities, entertaining. *Address:* Buckhurst Place, Horsted Keynes, Sussex RH17 7AH. *T:* (01825) 790599.

LOCK, Graham; *see* Lock, T. G.

LOCK, John Arthur, QPM 1975; Deputy Assistant Commissioner, Metropolitan Police, and National Co-ordinator, Regional Crime Squads of England and Wales, 1976–79, retired; *b* 20 Oct. 1922; *s* of Sidney George Lock and Minnie Louise Lock; *m* 1950, Patricia Joyce Lambert; two *d*. *Educ:* George Palmer Central School, Reading. Royal Air Force, 1941–46; Wireless Operator/Air Gunner; Flying Officer. Joined Metropolitan Police, 1946. *Recreation:* golf. *Club:* St Mellion Golf and Country.

LOCK, Ven. Peter Harcourt D'Arcy; Archdeacon of Rochester and Residentiary Canon of Rochester Cathedral, since 2000; *b* 2 Aug. 1944; *s* of Edward and Ruth Lock; *m* Susan; one *s* one *d*. *Educ:* King's College, London (AKC 1967). Ordained deacon, 1968, priest, 1969; Curate: Meopham, 1968–72; Wigmore with Hempstead, 1972; S Gillingham, 1972–77; Rector: Hartley, 1977–83; Fawkham and Hartley, 1983–84; Vicar: Holy Trinity, Dartford, 1984–93; St Peter and St Paul, Bromley, 1993–2000; RD Bromley, 1996–2000. *Address:* The Archdeaconry, King's Orchard, The Precinct, Rochester, Kent ME1 1TG.

LOCK, Stephen Penford, CBE 1991; MA, MD; FRCP; Research Associate in History, Wellcome Trust (formerly Wellcome Institute for the History of Medicine), 1992–2000; Editor, British Medical Journal, 1975–91; *b* 8 April 1929; *er s* of Wallace Henry Lock, Romford, Essex; *m* 1955, Shirley Gillian Walker, *d* of E. W. Walker, Bridlington, Yorks; one *d* (one *s* decd). *Educ:* City of London Sch.; Queens' Coll., Cambridge; St Bartholomew's Hosp., London. MA 1953; MB 1954; MD 1987; MRCP 1963; FRCP 1974; FACP 1989; FRCPE 1989. Jun. hosp. appts, 1954–63; Asst Editor, British Med. Jl, 1964–69, Sen. Asst Editor, 1969–74, Dep. Editor, 1974–75. Consulting Editor: Encyclopaedia Britannica Year Book of Medicine, 1992–99; Med. Jl of Australia, 1994–96; an Associate Ed., DNB, 1995–. Organiser and/or participant in numerous Postgrad. Courses in Med. Writing and confs in scientific editing worldwide, 1971–. Mem., Res. Ethics Cttee, KCH Medical Sch., 1992–96. Mem. Council, Harveian Soc., 1992–96 (Pres., 1994); Founder Pres., 1982–85, Mem. Council, 1985–91, European Assoc. of Sci. Editors. Vis. Prof. in Medicine, McGill Univ., 1978; Visitor, Acad. Dept of Medicine, Monash Univ., 1982; Rockefeller Scholar, Villa Serbelloni, Bellagio, 1985; Foundn Vis. Prof. in Medicine, RCSI, 1986; Vis. Prof. in Epidemiology and Biostatistics, McGill Univ., 1992; Vis. Lectr, Erasmus Summer Sch., Rotterdam, 1993–. Lectures: Wade, Keele Univ., 1980; Morgan, Royal Cornwall Hosp., 1984; Rock Carling, Nuffield Provincial Hosps Trust, 1985; Maurice Bloch, Glasgow Univ., 1986; Wolfson, Wolfson Coll., Oxford, 1986; Estelle Brodman, Washington Univ., St Louis, 1989; Sarah Davies, TCD, 1990; William Hey, Leeds Univ., 1990; George McGovern, Med. Library Assoc. of America, San Francisco, 1991; College, RCP, 1996; Carmichael, RCSI, 1999. Chairman: Friends of Dulwich Picture Gall., 1993–96; Aldeburgh Soc., 1998–2001 (Mem., Cttee, 1997–; Acting Sec., 2001–). Hon. FRCPI 1987; Hon. Fellow, Amer. Med. Writers Assoc., 1994; Hon. Founder Fellow, RCPCH, 1997 (Hon. Mem., BPA, 1991). Hon. MSc Manchester, 1985. Donders Medal, Ned. Tijdsch. Geneesk, 1981; Internat. Medal, Finnish Med. Soc. Duodecim, 1981; Medal of Honour, Finnish Med. Jl, 1987; Fothergillian Medal, Med. Soc., London, 1992; Meritorious Award, Council of Biol. Eds, 1993. Officer, first cl., White Rose of Finland, 1982. *Publications:* An Introduction to Clinical Pathology, 1965; Health Centres and Group Practices, 1966; The Enemies of Man, 1968; Better Medical Writing, 1970; Family Health Guide, 1972; Medical Risks of Life, 1976; Thorne's Better Medical Writing, 2nd edn 1977; (ed) Adverse Drug Reactions, 1977; (ed) Remembering Henry, 1977; (contrib.) Oxford Companion to Medicine, 1983; A Difficult Balance: editorial peer review in medicine, 1985; (ed) The Future of Medical Journals, 1991; Medical Journals and Medical Progress, 1992; (ed) Fraud and Misconduct in Medical Research, 1993, 3rd edn 2001; (ed jtly) The Oxford Medical Companion, 1995; (contrib.) Oxford Illustrated History of Medicine, 1996; (ed) Ashes to Ashes, 1998; (contrib.) Our NHS, 1998; (ed) Oxford Illustrated Companion to Medicine, 2001. *Recreation:* reading reviews of operas I can't afford to see. *Address:* 3 Alde House, Alde House Drive, Aldeburgh, Suffolk IP15 5EE. *T:* (01728) 452411. *Club:* Royal Air Force.

LOCK, (Thomas) Graham; Chief Executive, Amalgamated Metal Corporation plc, 1983–91; *b* 19 Oct. 1931; *s* of Robert Henry Lock and Morfydd Lock (*née* Thomas); *m* 1954, Janice Olive Baker Lock (*née* Jones) (marr. diss. 1992; she *d* 1995); two *d*. *Educ:* Whitchurch Grammar School; University College of South Wales and Monmouthshire (BSc Metall); College of Advanced Technology, Aston; Harvard Business School. CEng, FIM, CBIM. Instructor Lieut, RN, 1953–56; Lucas Industries and Lucas Electrical, 1956–61; Dir, Girling Bremsen GmbH, 1961–66; Gen. Man. and Overseas Ops Dir, Girling Ltd, 1966–73; Gen. Man. and Dir, Lucas Service Overseas Ltd, 1973–79; Man. Dir, Industrial Div., Amalgamated Metal Corp., 1979–83; non-exec. Director: Marshall's Universal plc, 1983–86; Evode Gp plc, 1985–91. Liveryman, Co. of Gold and Silver Wyre Drawers, 1988–. Freeman, City of London, 1987. *Recreations:* sailing, music, skiing. *Address:* Parolas Villa, 4520 Parekklisia, near Limassol, Cyprus. *Clubs:* Army and Navy; Royal Naval Sailing Association (Portsmouth), Royal Southern Yacht (Hamble).

LOCKE, John Christopher, FRICS; Chief Executive, Property Advisers to the Civil Estate, 1997–2000; *b* 4 March 1947; *s* of late Comdr Cyril Frederick Locke, RN, CEng, FIEE and Marjorie Alice Batt Locke (*née* Collins); *m* 1st, 1969 (marr. diss. 1989); two *s*; 2nd, 1990, Maria Patricia, *d* of Eileen Rogers. *Educ:* Pangbourne Coll.; Regent Street Poly.; Brixton Sch. of Building; Northern Poly. ARICS 1971 (Prizewinner), FRICS 1981. Prudential Assurance Co. Ltd, 1964–88 (Dir, Estate Management, 1987–88); Divl Dir, Estate Management, Prudential Portfolio Managers Ltd, 1989–91; Director: Southbank Technopark Ltd, 1985–91 (Chm., 1989–90); City Aviation Insurance Tenancies Ltd, 1989–90; Chm., Briggait Co. Ltd, 1987–90; Surveyor, Watling Street Properties, 1989–90; Chief Exec., NHS Estate Mgt and Health Bldg Agency, 1991–97. Member: Commercial Property Cttee, RICS, 1983–89; Central Govt Support Panel, RICS, 1997–2000 (Chm., 1999–2000); Mgt Consultancy Practice Panel, RICS, 1997–2000; Govt Construction Client Panel, HM Treasury, 1997–2000 (Chm. of Strategy, Dialogue with Industry Gp, 1998–2000); Bd of Mgt, British Council for Offices, 1997–2000 (Mgt Exec., 1999–2000). Mem. Editl Adv. Bd, Property Week, 2000. Hon. FIHEEM (Hon. FIHospE 1992). *Recreations:* opera, theatre, music, film, travel, family, home. *Address:* 11 Shrewsbury Road, Beckenham, Kent BR3 4DB.

LOCKE, Patrick, CBE 1998; Secretary to Church Commissioners, 1992–98; *b* 17 March 1934; *s* of Roy Albert Locke and Nora Katherine Locke (*née* Taylor); *m* 1959, Iris Constance Cory; one *s* one *d*. *Educ:* Bristol Cathedral Sch.; Wadham Coll., Oxford (Schol.; MA). Nat. Service, 1952–54. Church Commissioners Office, 1957–98: Dep. Sec., 1985–92. Mem. Court, Corp. of Sons of Clergy, 1989–. Trustee, Pollen Estate, 1991–. Gov., Pusey House, 1999–. *Recreations:* 18th and 19th century literature, theatre, opera. *Address:* Romans, Beggars Lane, Winchester, Hants SO23 0HE. *T:* (01962) 866386. *Club:* Athenæum.

LOCKETT, His Honour Reginald; a Circuit Judge, 1981–99, a Senior Circuit Judge, 1997–99; *b* 24 June 1933; *s* of George Alfred Lockett and Emma (*née* Singleton); *m* 1959, Edna (*née* Lowe); one *s* one *d*. *Educ:* Ashton-in-Makerfield Grammar Sch.; Manchester Univ.; London Univ. (LLB 1954). Solicitor, 1955. Asst Coroner for Wigan, 1963–70; Dist Registrar and County Court Registrar, Manchester, 1970–81; a Recorder of the Crown Court, 1978–81. Hon. Recorder, Borough of Preston, 1996–99. Pres., Manchester Law Students' Soc., 1975–77. Pres., The Boys' Bde, 1999– (Vice Pres., 1978–99; Dist Pres., NW Dist, 1973–90). Reader, Anglican Church, 1970–. Editor, Butterworths Family Law

Service, 1983–90; Consultant Editor, Sweet-Maxwell's High Court Litigation Manual, 1990. *Recreations:* music, photography. *Address:* 7 Blandford Rise, Lostock, Bolton BL6 4JH. *T:* (01204) 699791.

LOCKHART; *see* Bruce Lockhart and Bruce-Lockhart.

LOCKHART, Brian Alexander; Sheriff in Glasgow and Strathkelvin, since 1981 (in North Strathclyde, 1979–81); *b* 1 Oct. 1942; *s* of John Arthur Hay Lockhart and Norah Lockhart; *m* 1967, Christine Ross Clark; two *s* two *d. Educ:* Glasgow Academy; Glasgow Univ. (BL). Qualified as solicitor, 1964; Partner in Robertson Chalmers & Auld, Solicitors, Glasgow, 1966–79. Mem., Parole Bd for Scotland, 1997–. Sec., Sheriffs' Assoc, 1997–. *Recreations:* fishing, golf, family. *Address:* 18 Hamilton Avenue, Glasgow G41 4JF. *T:* (0141) 427 1921.

LOCKHART, Brian Robert Watson; Headmaster, Robert Gordon's College, Aberdeen, since 1996; *b* 19 July 1944; *s* of George Watson Lockhart and Helen Lockhart (*née* Rattray); *m* 1970, Fiona Anne Sheddon, MA; one *s* two *d. Educ:* Leith Acad.; George Heriot's Sch.; Aberdeen Univ. (MA); Edinburgh Univ. (DipEd). History Teacher, 1968–72, Principal History Teacher, 1972–81, George Heriot's Sch.; Dep. Rector, High Sch. of Glasgow, 1981–96. Council Mem., 1988–, Asst Sec. and Exec. Mem., 1989–94, Headteachers' Assoc. of Scotland; Mem., Higher Still Implementation Gp, 1997–2000; Chm., UCAS Scottish Standing Cttee, 2001 (Mem., 1994–99; Co-Chm., 1998–99); Mem., HMC Univs Working Party, 1999–. *Publication:* History of the Architecture of George Heriot's Hospital and School 1628–1978, 1978. *Recreations:* architecture, reading biographies, sport, films, politics. *Address:* 80 Gray Street, Aberdeen AB10 6JE. *T:* (01224) 315776. *Club:* Royal Northern and University (Aberdeen).

LOCKHART, Frank Roper; His Honour Judge Lockhart; a Circuit Judge, since 1988; *b* 8 Dec. 1931; *s* of Clement and Betsy Lockhart; *m* 1958, Brenda Harriett Johnson; one *s* one *d. Educ:* King Edward VI Sch., Retford; Doncaster Grammar Sch.; Univ. of Leeds (LLB Hons). Asst Town Clerk, Southend-on-Sea, 1960–65; Partner, Jefferies, Solicitors, 1965–87. Chairman: Industrial Tribunal, 1983–87; Social Security Tribunal, 1970–87; a Recorder, 1985–88. *Recreations:* golf, Rack II. *Address:* Southend Crown Court, The Court House, Southend SS2 6EG. *Clubs:* Thorpe Hall Golf, Hazards Golf.

LOCKHART, Harry Eugene, (Gene), CPA; President and Chief Executive Officer, The New Power Company; *b* 4 Nov. 1949; *s* of Harry Eugene Lockhart, Sen., Austin, Texas, and Gladys Cummings Lockhart; *m* 1974, Terry Lockhart; one *s* three *d. Educ:* Univ. of Virginia (MechEng degree); Darden Graduate Bus. Sch. (MBA). CPA 1976. Sen. Cons., Arthur Anderson & Co., 1974–77; Man. Principal, Europe, Nolan Norton & Co., 1977–82; Gp Dir, Management Services, C. T. Bowring & Co., 1982–85; Vice Pres., First Manhattan Consulting Gp, 1985–87; Chief Exec., IT, 1987–88, Gp Ops, 1988–92, UK Banking, 1990–92, Midland Bank; Pres., First Manhattan Consulting Internat., 1992–94; Pres. and CEO, Mastercard International, 1994. *Recreations:* tennis, golf, running, ski-ing, photography, riding, classical music, ballet. *Address:* (office) 10 Glenville Street, Greenwich, CT 06831, USA. *Clubs:* Blind Brook; Indian Harbor Yacht; Mill Reef.

LOCKHART, James Lawrence, FRCM, FRCO(CHM); Director of Opera, London Royal Schools' Vocal Faculty, 1992–96 (Opera Consultant, 1996–98); *b* 16 Oct. 1930; *s* of Archibald Campbell Lockhart and Mary Black Lawrence; *m* 1954, Sheila Margaret Grogan; two *s* one *d. Educ:* George Watson's Boys' College; Edinburgh Univ. (BMus); Royal College of Music (ARCM, FRCM). Yorkshire Symphony Orchestra, 1954–55; Münster City Opera, 1955–56; Bavarian State Opera, 1956–57; Glyndebourne Festival Opera, 1957, 1958, 1959; Opera Workshop, Univ. of Texas, 1957–59; Royal Opera House, Covent Garden, 1959–60; BBC Scottish Orchestra, 1960–61; Scottish Opera, 1960–61; Conductor, Sadler's Wells Opera, 1961–62; Conductor and Repetiteur, Royal Opera House, Covent Garden, 1962–68; Music Dir, Welsh National Opera, 1968–73; Generalmusikdirektor: Staatstheater, Kassel, 1972–80; Koblenz Opera, 1981–88; Rheinische Philharmonie, 1981–91 (Ehrendirigent, 1991); Dir of Opera, RCM, 1986–92. Guest Prof. of Conducting, Tokyo Nat. Univ. of Fine Arts and Music (Tokyo Geidai), 1998–2001, now Prof. Emeritus. Hon. RAM 1993. *Recreations:* swimming, hill-walking, travel, languages. *Address:* 105 Woodcock Hill, Harrow, Middx HA3 0JJ. *T:* and *Fax:* (020) 8907 2112. *Club:* Savage.

LOCKHART, Sir Simon John Edward Francis S.; *see* Sinclair-Lockhart.

LOCKHART-MUMMERY, Christopher John; QC 1986; a Recorder, since 1994; a Deputy High Court Judge, since 1995; *b* 7 Aug. 1947; *s* of Sir Hugh Lockhart-Mummery, KCVO, MD, MChir, FRCS and late Elizabeth Jean Crerar, *d* of Sir James Crerar, KCSI, CIE; *m* 1st, 1971, Elizabeth Rosamund (marr. diss. 1992), *d* of N. P. M. Elles, *qv* and of Baroness Elles, *qv*; one *s* two *d*; 2nd, 1993, Mary Lou Putley. *Educ:* Stowe; Trinity College, Cambridge (BA). Called to the Bar, Inner Temple, 1971 (Bencher, 1991). Specialist Editor, Hill and Redman's Law of Landlord and Tenant, 1974–89. *Recreations:* fishing, listening to music, opera, walking the dog. *Address:* 4 Bream's Buildings, EC4A 1AQ. *T:* (020) 7353 5835; 78 Lansdowne Road, W11 2LS. *T:* (020) 7221 8628. *Clubs:* Garrick, Royal Automobile.

LOCKLEY, Andrew John Harold; Head of Public Law (formerly Professional Services and Public Law), Irwin Mitchell, Solicitors, since 1996; Chairman, Special Educational Needs Tribunal, since 1996; *b* 10 May 1951; *s* of Ven. Harold Lockley, *qv*; *m* 1974, Ruth Mary Vigor; two *s* one *d. Educ:* Marlborough Coll.; Oriel Coll., Oxford (BA Lit. Hum. 1973; MA 1982). Admitted a Solicitor, 1979. Res. Fellow, World Council of Churches, 1973–75; Solicitor in private practice, 1979–82; Law Society: Asst Sec., 1982–85, Sec., 1985–87, Contentious Business Dept; Dir, Legal Practice, 1987–95; Dir, Corporate and Regl Affairs, 1995–96. Non-exec. Chm., Solicitors Property Centres Ltd, 1998–2000 (Dir, 1997–98). Mem., Commn on Efficiency in the Criminal Courts, 1986–93. Mem., IT and Courts Cttee, 1990–95. Gov., William Austin Sch., Luton, 1992–96. Hon. Fellow, Univ. of Sheffield, 1999. *Publications:* Christian Communes, 1976; (ed) The Pursuit of Quality: a guide for lawyers, 1993; contribs to legal periodicals. *Recreations:* growing fruit and vegetables, swimming, walking, cooking. *Address:* Irwin Mitchell, St Peter's House, Hartshead, Sheffield S1 2EL. *T:* (0114) 276 7777, *Fax:* (0114) 275 3306; *e-mail:* lockleya@irwinmitchell.co.uk.

LOCKLEY, Ven. Harold; Archdeacon of Loughborough, 1963–86, Archdeacon Emeritus since 1986; *b* 16 July 1916; *s* of Harry and Sarah Elizabeth Lockley; *m* 1947, Ursula Margaret, JP (*d* 1990), *d* of Rev. Dr H. Wedell and Mrs G. Wedell (*née* Bonhoeffer); three *s. Educ:* Loughborough Coll. (Hons Dip. Physical Education); London University (BA Hons 1937; BD Hons 1943; MTh 1949); Westcott House, Cambridge; PhD Nottingham 1955; Emmanuel Coll., Cambridge (MLitt 1990). Served RN, 1940–45. Chaplain and Tutor, Loughborough Coll., 1946–51; Vicar of Glen Parva and South Wigston, 1951–58; Canon Chancellor of Leicester Cathedral, 1958–63; Vicar of All Saints, Leicester, 1963–78. Postgrad. res student, Emmanuel Coll., Cambridge, 1986–88. OCF Royal Leics Regt, 1951–58; Chaplain, Leics Yeomanry Assoc., 1968–; Chaplain, Leicester Royal Infirmary Maternity Hospital, 1967–74; Proctor in Convocation of Canterbury, 1960–80. Sen. Examining Chaplain to Bishop of Leicester, 1951–79; part-time Lectr in Divinity, Univ. of Leicester, 1953–86; Mem., Leics Educn Cttee, 1973–85. Chm., Anglican Young People's Assoc., 1966–86. Founder Governor, Leicester Grammar Sch., 1981–. Editor, Leicester Cathedral Quarterly, 1960–63. *Publications:* Leicester Grammar School: the first ten years, 1992; Dietrich Bonhoeffer: his 'Ethics' and its value for today, 1993; numerous reviews and theological articles. *Recreations:* walking and foreign travel. *Address:* 21 Saxon Close, Market Harborough, Leics LE16 7PR. *T:* (01858) 465605. *Club:* Leicestershire (Leicester).

See also Prof. E. A. O. G. Wedell, A. J. H. Lockley.

LOCKLEY, Stephen Randolph, FCIT; transport consultant; *b* 19 June 1943; *s* of Randolph and Edith Lockley; *m* 1968, Angela; two *d. Educ:* Manchester Univ. (BScCivEng, 1st Cl. Hons). MICE; MIHT; FCIT 1987, FILT. Lancashire County Council: North West Road Construction Unit, Highway Engrg and Planning, 1964–72; Highway/Transportation Planning, 1972–75; Lanarkshire CC, Strathclyde Regional Council: Prin. Engr (Transportation), 1975–77; Depute Dir of Policy Planning, 1977–80; Prin. Exec. Officer, 1980–86; Dir Gen., Strathclyde PTE, 1986–97. *Address:* 64 Townhead Street, Strathaven ML10 6DJ. *T:* (01357) 521774.

LOCKWOOD, Baroness *cr* 1978 (Life Peer), of Dewsbury, W Yorks; **Betty Lockwood;** DL; President, Birkbeck College, London, 1983–89; a Deputy Speaker, House of Lords, since 1989; *b* 22 Jan. 1924; *d* of Arthur Lockwood and Edith Alice Lockwood; *m* 1978, Lt-Col Cedric Hall (*d* 1988). *Educ:* Eastborough Girls' Sch., Dewsbury; Ruskin Coll., Oxford. Chief Woman Officer and Asst Nat. Agent of Labour Party, 1967–75; Ed., Labour Woman, 1967–71; Chm., Equal Opportunities Commn, 1975–83. Vice-Chm., Internat. Council of Social Democratic Women, 1969–75; Chm., Adv. Cttee to European Commn on Equal Opportunities for Women and Men, 1982–83. Chm., Mary Macarthur Educnl Trust, 1971–94; Pres., Mary Macarthur Holiday Trust, 1990– (Chm., 1971–90). Member: Dept of Employment Adv. Cttee on Women's Employment, 1969–83; Adv. Council on Energy Conservation, 1977–80; Council, Advertising Standards Authority, 1983–93; Leeds Urban Develt Corp., 1988–95. Pres., Hillcroft Coll., 1987–95. Chancellor, Bradford Univ., 1997– (Mem. Council, 1983–; a Pro-Chancellor, 1988–97); Leeds Univ., 1985–91; Vice Pres., UMIST, 1992–95. Chm. Bd of Trustees, Nat. Coal Miners Mus., 1995–. DL W Yorks, 1987. Hon. Fellow: UMIST, 1986; Birkbeck Coll., 1987. Hon. DLitt Bradford, 1981; Hon. LLD Strathclyde, 1985; DUniv Leeds Metropolitan, 1999. *Recreations:* walking and country pursuits, music. *Address:* 6 Sycamore Drive, Addingham, Ilkley LS29 0NY. *Club:* Soroptomist.

LOCKWOOD, Prof. David, CBE 1998; FBA 1976; Professor of Sociology, University of Essex, 1968–2001 (Pro-Vice-Chancellor, 1989–92); *b* 9 April 1929; *s* of Herbert Lockwood and Edith A. (*née* Lockwood); *m* 1954, Leonore Davidoff; three *s. Educ:* Honley Grammar Sch.; London Sch. of Economics. BSc(Econ) London, 1st Cl. Hons 1952; PhD London, 1957. Trainee, textile industry, 1944–47; Cpl, Intell. Corps, Austria, 1947–49. Asst Lectr and Lectr, London Sch. of Economics, 1953–60; Rockefeller Fellow, Univ. of California, Berkeley, 1958–59; Univ. Lectr, Faculty of Economics, and Fellow, St John's Coll., Cambridge, 1960–68. Visiting Professor: Dept of Sociology, Columbia Univ., 1966–67; Delhi Univ., 1975; Stockholm Univ., 1989; Vis. Fellow, ANU, 1993. Mem., SSRC (Chm., Sociol. and Soc. Admin Cttee), 1973–76; Chm., ESRC Rev. of Govt Social Classifications, 1994–98. Mem., Academia Europaea, 1990. DU Essex, 2001. *Publications:* The Blackcoated Worker, 1958, 2nd edn 1989; (jtly) The Affluent Worker in the Class Structure, 3 vols, 1968–69; Solidarity and Schism, 1992; numerous articles in jls and symposia. *Address:* 82 High Street, Wivenhoe, Essex CO7 9AB. *T:* (01206) 823530.

LOCKWOOD, Robert; General Director, Overseas Planning and Project Development, General Motors Corporation, 1982–85, retired; *b* 14 April 1920; *s* of Joseph A. Lockwood and Sylvia Lockwood; *m* 1947, Phyllis M. Laing; one *s* one *d. Educ:* Columbia Univ. (AB); Columbia Law Sch. (LLB). Attorney, Bar of New York, 1941; US Dist of New York and US Supreme Court, 1952. Pilot, USAAF (8th Air Force), 1944–45. Attorney: Ehrich, Royall, Wheeler & Holland, New York, 1941 and 1946–47; Sullivan & Cromwell, New York, 1947–54; Sec. and Counsel, Cluett, Peabody & Co., Inc., New York, 1955–57; Man. Dir, Cluett, Peabody & Co., Ltd, London, 1957–59; General Motors: Overseas Ops, Planning and Develt, 1960–61; Asst to Man. Dir, GM Argentina, Buenos Aires, 1962; Asst to Man. Dir, and Manager, Parts, Power and Appliances, GM Continental, Antwerp, 1964–66; Branch Man., Netherlands Br., GM Continental, Rotterdam, 1967–68; Man., Planning and Develt, GM Overseas Ops, New York, 1969–73; Vice Pres., GM Overseas Corp., and Gen. Man., Japan Br., 1974–76; Exec. Vice Pres., Isuzu Motors Ltd, Tokyo, 1976; Chm., GM European Adv. Council, 1977–82. Mem., Panel of Arbitrators, Amer. Arbitration Assoc., 1989–. *Recreations:* tennis, bridge, reading. *Address:* 126 Littlefield Road, Monterey, CA 93940, USA. *Clubs:* Monterey Peninsula Country, Spanish Bay, Beach and Tennis (Pebble Beach); Marines' Memorial (San Francisco).

LOCKWOOD, Rear Adm. Roger Graham; Chief of Staff to Second Sea Lord, and Commander in Chief Naval Home Command, since 2000; *b* 26 June 1950; *s* of Eric Garnett Lockwood and Nunda Lockwood (*née* Doak); *m* 1984, Susan Jane Cant; three *s* two *d. Educ:* Kimbolton Sch., Cambs; Univ. of Warwick (BA Maths). BRNC Dartmouth, 1971; Sub Lieut, HMS Fearless, 1972; Lieut, HMS Soberton, 1973; Supply Officer (Cash), HMS Tiger, 1974–76; Captain's Sec., 2nd Submarine Sqn, 1976–78; Supply Officer, HMS Naiad, 1979–81; Flag Lieut to CDS, 1981–82; Captain's Sec., RNAS Culdrose, 1982–84; jsdc 1985; Comdr, 1985; Base Supply Officer, HMS Dolphin, 1985–87; Comdr, RN Supply Sch., 1987–89; Supply Officer, HMS Ark Royal, 1989–91; Captain, 1991; Dep. Dir, Naval Service Conditions (Pay), 1991–93; rcds 1994; Secretary to: Second Sea Lord, 1995–96; First Sea Lord, 1996–98; Cdre, 1998; Cdre, HMS Raleigh, 1998–2000; Rear Adm., 2000. Gov., Kimbolton Sch., 2001–. *Recreations:* family, studying the history of the SOE in France. *Address:* Victory Building, HM Naval Base, Portsmouth PO1 3LS. *T:* (023) 9272 7101.

LOCKYER, Rear-Adm. (Alfred) Austin, LVO 1973; Chief Staff Officer (Engineering) to Commander-in-Chief Fleet, 1982–84, retired; Director General, Timber Trade Federation, 1985–92; *b* 4 March 1929; *s* of late Austin Edmund Lockyer and Jane Russell (*née* Goldman); *m* 1965, Jennifer Ann Simmons; one *s. Educ:* Frome County School; Taunton School; Royal Naval Engineering College. Entered RN 1947; Comdr 1965; Staff of Commander Far East Fleet, 1965–67; jssc, 1968–69; Ship Dept, 1969–71; HMY Britannia, 1971–73; Captain 1973; sowc, 1973–74; Naval Ship Production Overseer, Scotland and NI, 1974–76; Dep. Dir, Fleet Maintenance, 1976–78; Dir, Naval Officers Appointments (Engrg), 1978–80; HMS Sultan in Comd, 1980–82; ADC to the Queen, 1981; Rear-Adm. 1982. Governor: Forres Sch., Swanage, 1980–92 (Chm., 1983–92); Sherborne Sch., 1981–97. *Recreations:* gardening, golf, listening to good music. *Address:* 8 Darlington Place, Bath BA2 6BX.

LOCKYER, Lynda; Director, Corporate Development and Services, Home Office, since 2000; *b* 17 Aug. 1946; *d* of Donald Lockyer and Gwendoline Lockyer (*née* Fulcher); *m* 1984, John Anthony Thompson; one *s. Educ:* Bromley High Sch.; Newnham Coll.,

Cambridge (MA Classics). Press Officer: Shell-Mex, BP Ltd, 1968–73; Sperry Univac, 1974; DHSS, later DoH, 1974–96; Home Office, 1996–; Head of Police Resources Unit, 1996–99; Dir, Corporate Resources, 1999–2000. *Recreations:* films, theatre, opera, Europe. *Address:* Corporate Development Services Group, Home Office, Clive House, Petty France, SW1H 9HD.

LODDER, Peter Norman; QC 2001; a Recorder, since 2000; *b* 3 Feb. 1958; *s* of Norman George Lodder and Ann Lodder; *m* 1992, Elizabeth Gummer, two *c. Educ:* King's Sch., Gloucester; Portsmouth Grammar Sch.; Univ. of Birmingham (LLB). Called to the Bar, Middle Temple, 1981 (Jules Thorn Major Schol. 1982); specialist in fraud and criminal law; Asst Recorder, 1998–2000. *Address:* 2 Bedford Row, WC1R 4BU. *T:* (020) 7440 8888.

LODER, family name of **Baron Wakehurst**.

LODER, Sir Edmund Jeune, 4th Bt *cr* 1887, of Whittlebury, Northamptonshire, and of High Beeches, Slaugham, Sussex; *b* 26 June 1941; *er s* of Sir Giles Rolls Loder, 3rd Bt and of Marie Violet Pamela Loder (*née* Symons-Jeune); *S* father, 1999; *m* 1st, 1966, Penelope Jane Forde (marr. diss. 1971); one *d*; 2nd, 1992, Susan Warren Pearl. *Address:* Eyrefield Lodge, The Curragh, Co. Kildare, Ireland.

LODGE, Anton James Corduff; QC 1989; a Recorder, since 1985; *b* 17 April 1944; *s* of Sir Thomas Lodge and Aileen (*née* Corduff). *Educ:* Ampleforth College; Gonville and Caius College, Cambridge (MA). Called to the Bar, Gray's Inn, 1966, Bencher, 1998. *Recreations:* cricket, tennis, ski-ing, music, theatre. *Address:* Park Court Chambers, 16 Park Place, Leeds LS1 2SJ. *T:* (0113) 243 3277. *Club:* Yorkshire (York).

LODGE, Prof. David John, CBE 1998; MA, PhD; FRSL; writer; Emeritus Professor of English Literature, University of Birmingham, since 2001 (Professor of Modern English Literature, 1976–87, Hon. Professor, 1987–2000); *b* 28 Jan. 1935; *s* of William Frederick Lodge and Rosalie Marie Lodge (*née* Murphy); *m* 1959, Mary Frances Jacob; two *s* one *d. Educ:* St Joseph's Acad., Blackheath; University College, London (Hon. Fellow, 1982). BA hons, MA (London); PhD (Birm). FRSL 1976. National Service, RAC, 1955–57. British Council, London, 1959–60. Univ. of Birmingham: Asst Lectr in English, 1960–62; Lectr, 1963–71; Sen. Lectr, 1971–73; Reader in English, 1973–76. Harkness Commonwealth Fellow, 1964–65; Visiting Associate Prof., Univ. of California, Berkeley, 1969; Henfield Writing Fellow, Univ. of E Anglia, 1977. Hon. Fellow, Goldsmiths' Coll., London, 1992. Hon. DLitt: Warwick, 1997; Birmingham, 2001. Yorkshire Post Fiction Prize, 1975; Hawthornden Prize, 1976; Whitbread Book of the Year Award, 1980; Sunday Express Book of the Year Award, 1988. Chevalier, l'Ordre des Arts et des Lettres (France), 1997. Stage plays: The Writing Game, Birmingham Rep., 1990 (adapted for television, 1996); Home Truths, Birmingham Rep., 1998. Adaptation of Dickens, Martin Chuzzlewit, for television, 1994. *Publications: novels:* The Picturegoers, 1960; Ginger, You're Barmy, 1962; The British Museum is Falling Down, 1965; Out of the Shelter, 1970, rev. edn 1985; Changing Places, 1975; How Far Can You Go?, 1980; Small World, 1984 (televised 1988); Nice Work, 1988 (adapted for television, 1989); Paradise News, 1991; Therapy, 1995; Home Truths: a novella, 1999; Thinks..., 2001; *plays:* The Writing Game, 1991; Home Truths, 1999; *criticism:* Language of Fiction, 1966; The Novelist at the Crossroads, 1971; The Modes of Modern Writing, 1977; Working with Structuralism, 1981; Write On, 1986; After Bakhtin (essays), 1990, The Art of Fiction, 1992; The Practice of Writing, 1996; *edited:* Jane Austen's Emma: a casebook, 1968; Twentieth Century Literary Criticism, 1972; Modern Criticism and Theory, 1988, 2nd edn 1999. *Recreations:* tennis, television, cinema, theatre. *Address:* c/o Department of English, University of Birmingham, Birmingham B15 2TT. *T:* (0121) 414 3344.

LODGE, Prof. Geoffrey Arthur, BSc, PhD, FIBiol; FRSE 1986; Professor of Animal Science, Sultan Qaboos University, Muscat, 1986–90, retired; *b* 18 Feb. 1930; *m* 1956, Thelma (*née* Calder); one *s* two *d. Educ:* Durham University (BSc). PhD Aberdeen. Formerly Reader in Animal Production, Univ. of Nottingham School of Agriculture, and Principal Research Scientist, Animal Research Inst., Ottawa; Strathcona-Fordyce Prof. of Agriculture, Univ. of Aberdeen, and Principal, North of Scotland Coll. of Agriculture, 1978–86. *Publications:* (ed jointly) Growth and Development of Mammals, 1968; contribs to journals and books. *Recreations:* food, malt whisky, travelling, farming. *Address:* RR3, Almonte, ON K0A 1A0, Canada.

LODGE, Oliver Raymond William Wynlayne; Regional Chairman of Industrial Tribunals, London South Region, 1980–92; *b* Painswick, Glos, 2 Sept. 1922; *e s* of Oliver William Foster Lodge and Winifred, (Wynlayne), *o d* of Sir William Nicholas Atkinson, ISO, LLD; *m* 1953, Charlotte (*d* 1990), *o d* of Col Arthur Davidson Young, CMG; one *s* two *d. Educ:* Bryanston Sch.; King's Coll., Cambridge. BA 1943, MA 1947. Officer-cadet, Royal Fusiliers, 1942. Called to the Bar, Inner Temple, 1945; admitted *ad eundem*, Lincoln's Inn, 1949 (Bencher, 1973; Treas., 1995); practised at Chancery Bar, 1945–74; Permanent Chairman of Industrial Tribunals, 1975–92, part-time Chm., 1992–94. Member: Bar Council, 1952–56, 1967–71; Supreme Court Rules Cttee, 1968–71. Gen. Comr of Income Tax, Lincoln's Inn, 1983–91. *Publications:* (ed) Rivington's Epitome of Snell's Equity, 3rd edn, 1948; (ed) Fraudulent and Voidable Conveyances, article in Halsbury's Laws of England, 3rd edn, 1956; contribs to legal periodicals. *Recreations:* freemasonry, walking, reading history, formerly sailing. *Address:* Southridge House, Hindon, Salisbury, Wilts. SP3 6ER. *T:* (01747) 820238. *Clubs:* Garrick; Bar Yacht.

LOEHNIS, Anthony David, CMG 1988; Director, St James's Place Capital plc, since 1993; *b* 12 March 1936; *s* of Sir Clive Loehnis, KCMG; *m* 1965, Jennifer Forsyth Anderson; three *s. Educ:* Eton; New Coll., Oxford (MA); Harvard Sch. of Public Administration. HM Diplomatic Service, 1960–66; J. Henry Schroder Wagg & Co. Ltd, 1967–80 (on secondment to Bank of England, 1977–79); Bank of England: Associate Dir (Overseas), 1980–81; Exec. Dir, 1981–89; Dir, S. G. Warburg Group plc, 1989–92; a Vice-Chm., S. G. Warburg & Co., 1989–92. Chairman: Henderson (formerly HTR) Japanese Smaller Companies Trust, 1993–; Knox D'Arcy Trust, 1996–; Director: Alpha Bank London, 1994–; Tokyo-Mitsubishi Internat., 1996–; AGCO Corp. (US), 1997–. A Public Works Loan Comr, 1994– (Chm., 1997–). Exec. Dir, UK-Japan 21st Century (formerly UK-Japan 2000) Gp, 1999– (Dir, 1990–). Member: Council: Ditchley Foundn, 1992– (Chm., F & G P Cttee, 1993–); Baring Foundn, 1994–. Gov., British Assoc. for Central and Eastern Europe, 1994–. *Address:* 11 Cranleigh, 139 Ladbroke Road, W11 3PX. *Club:* Garrick.

LOFTHOUSE, family name of **Baron Lofthouse of Pontefract**.

LOFTHOUSE OF PONTEFRACT, Baron *cr* 1997 (Life Peer), of Pontefract in the co. of West Yorkshire; **Geoffrey Lofthouse,** Kt 1995; JP; *b* 18 Dec. 1925; *s* of Ernest and Emma Lofthouse; *m* 1946, Sarah Lofthouse (*d* 1985); one *d. Educ:* Featherstone Primary and Secondary Schs; Leeds Univ. FIPD (MIPM 1984). Haulage hand in mining industry at age of 14. Personnel Manager, NCB Fryston, 1970–78. Member: Pontefract Borough Council, 1962–74 (Mayor, 1967–68); Wakefield Metropolitan District Council, 1974–79 (Chm., Housing Cttee). MP (Lab) Pontefract and Castleford, Oct. 1978–1997. Dep. Chm. of Ways and Means, and Dep. Speaker, H of C, 1992–97; Dep. Speaker, H of L, 1998–. Mem., NUM, 1939–64, APEX, 1970–. JP Pontefract, 1970. *Publications:* A Very Miner MP (autobiog.), 1986; Coal Sack to Woolsack (autobiog.), 1999. *Recreations:* Rugby League, cricket. *Address:* 67 Carleton Crest, Pontefract, West Yorkshire WF8 2QR.

LOFTHOUSE, John Alfred, (Jack), OBE 1967; Member, British National Oil Corporation, 1980–82; *b* 30 Dec. 1917; *s* of John Duncan Lofthouse and Clara Margaret Smith; *m* 1950, Patricia Ninette Mann (*d* 1956); one *d. Educ:* Rutlish Sch., Merton; St Catharine's Coll., Cambridge (BA Hons, MA). Joined ICI Ltd as engr, 1939; Engrg Manager, Petrochemicals Div., 1958; Technical Dir, Nobel Div., 1961; Chm., Petrochems Div., 1967; Dir, Main Bd of ICI Ltd, 1970–80: responsibilities included Personnel Dir, Petrochems, Oil, and Explosives businesses, and Chm., ICI Americas Ltd; Dir, Britoil, 1983–88. *Publications:* contrib. Geographical Jl and engrg jls. *Recreations:* gardening, hill-walking, music. *Address:* 10 Westley Court, Austcliffe Lane, Cookley, near Kidderminster, Worcs DY10 3RT.

LOFTHOUSE, Reginald George Alfred, FRICS; Member, Advisory Committee, Centre for Agricultural Strategy, Reading University, 1980–98 (Chairman, 1982–92); Convener, 1978–88, Vice-Chairman, 1988–98, Standing Conference on Countryside Sports; *b* Workington, 30 Dec. 1916; *m* 1939, Ann Bernardine Bannan; two *d* (and one *d* decd). *Educ:* Workington Secondary Sch.; with private land agent, Cockermouth. Chartered Surveyor and Land Agent (Talbot-Ponsonby Prizeman). Asst District Officer, Penrith, 1941–42; District Officer, Carlisle, for Cumberland War Agric. Exec. Cttee, 1942–43; Asst Land Comr, West Riding, 1943–46; Land Commissioner: N and E Ridings, 1946–48; Derbys, Leics, Rutland, Northants, 1948–50; Somerset and Dorset, 1950–52; Regional Land Comr, Hdqtrs, 1952–59, and SE Region, 1959–71; Regional Officer, SE Region, Agric., Develt and Adv. Service, 1971–73; Chief Surveyor, MAFF, 1973–76. Chairman: UK Jt Shelter Res. Cttee, 1958–71; Statutory Cttee on Agricl Valuations, 1973–76. Mem., Farming and Wildlife Adv. Gp, 1966–81. Adviser to: Lord Porchester's Exmoor Study, 1977; Nature Conservancy Council, 1978–82; Council for Environmental Conservation, 1980–81. Vis. Lectr in Rural Estate Management and Forestry, Regent Street Polytechnic, 1954–62. Member: Bd of Governors, Coll. of Estate Management, 1963–85 (Chm., 1972–77; Research Fellow, 1982–85, Hon. Fellow 1985; Chm., Centre for Advanced Land Use Studies, 1972–81); Court and Council, Reading Univ., 1973–; Delegacy for Nat. Inst. for Res. in Dairying, Shinfield, 1974–80; Gen. Council, RICS, 1974–76; RICS Land Agency and Agric. Div. Council, 1974–77. Hon. Life Mem., Cambridge Univ. Land Soc.; Chm. Farm Bldgs Cttee 1973–80, Mem. Engrg and Bldgs Res. Bd 1973–80, ARC Jt Consultative Organisation. Liveryman, Loriners' Co., 1976; Freeman, City of London, 1976. *Publications:* The Berwyn Mountains Area of Wales, 1979; Some countryside policy conflicts, 1997; contrib. professional, techn. and countryside jls. *Clubs:* Athenæum, MCC.

LOFTUS, Viscount; Charles John Tottenham; Director of Admissions (formerly Head of French Department), Strathcona-Tweedsmuir School, Calgary; *b* 2 Feb. 1943; *e s* and *heir* of 8th Marquess of Ely, *qv*; *m* 1969, Judith Marvelle, *d* of Dr J. J. Porter, FRS, Calgary, Alberta; one *s* one *d. Educ:* Trinity Coll. Sch., Port Hope, Ont; Ecole Internationale de Genève; Univ. of Toronto (MA). *Address:* 23 Suncanyon Park SE, Calgary, AB T2X 2Z2, Canada.

LOFTUS, Simon Pierse Dominic; Chairman, Adnams plc, since 1996; *b* 5 Aug. 1946; *s* of Nicholas Alastair Ayton Loftus and Prudence Loftus (*née* Wootten); *m* 1980, Irène Yamato; one *d. Educ:* Ampleforth; Trinity Coll., Cambridge (MA). Joined Adnams, 1968, Dir, 1973. Dir, Aldeburgh Productions, 1998–. *Publications:* Anatomy of the Wine Trade, 1985; A Pike in the Basement, 1987; Puligny Montrachet, 1992; (ed) Guides to the Wines of France series, 1988–90; numerous articles in jls. *Recreations:* cooking, Anglo-Irish history, writing. *Address:* Bulcamp House, Halesworth, Suffolk IP19 9LG. *T:* (01502) 727200. *Club:* Groucho.

LOGAN, Sir David (Brian Carleton), KCMG 2000 (CMG 1991); HM Diplomatic Service, retired; Director, Centre for Studies in Security and Diplomacy, and Hon. Professor, School of Social Sciences, University of Birmingham, since 2002; *b* 11 Aug. 1943; *s* of late Captain Brian Ewen Weldon Logan, RN (Retd) and Mary Logan (*née* Fass); *m* 1967, Judith Margaret Walton Cole; one *s* one *d* (and one *s* decd). *Educ:* Charterhouse; University College, Oxford (MA). Foreign Office, 1965; served Istanbul, Ankara and FCO, 1965–70; Private Sec. to Parly Under Sec. of State for Foreign and Commonwealth Affairs, 1970–73; First Sec., 1972; UK Mission to UN, 1973–77; FCO, 1977–82; Counsellor, Hd of Chancery and Consul-Gen., Oslo, 1982–86; Hd of Personnel Ops Dept, FCO, 1986–88; Sen. Associate Mem., St Antony's Coll., Oxford, 1988–89; Minister and Dep. Head of Mission, Moscow, 1989–92; Asst Under Sec. of State (Central and Eastern Europe), 1992–94, (Defence Policy), 1994–95, FCO; Minister, Washington, 1995–97; Ambassador to Turkey, 1997–2001. *Recreations:* music, reading, sailing. *Clubs:* Royal Ocean Racing, Hurlingham.

LOGAN, Sir Donald (Arthur), KCMG 1977 (CMG 1965); HM Diplomatic Service, retired; *b* 25 Aug. 1917; *s* of late Arthur Alfred Logan and Louise Anne Bradley; *m* 1957, Irène Jocelyne Angèle, *d* of Robert Everts (Belgian Ambassador at Madrid, 1932–39) and Alexandra Comnène; one *s* two *d. Educ:* Solihull. Fellow, Chartered Insurance Institute, 1939. War of 1939–45: Major, RA; British Army Staff, Washington, 1942–43; Germany, 1945. Joined HM Foreign (subseq. Diplomatic) Service, Dec. 1945; Foreign Office, 1945–47; HM Embassy, Tehran, 1947–51; Foreign Office, 1951–53; Asst Political Agent, Kuwait, 1953–55; Asst Private Sec. to Sec. of State for Foreign Affairs, 1956–58; HM Embassy, Washington, 1958–60; HM Ambassador to Guinea, 1960–62; Foreign Office, 1962–64; Information Counsellor, British Embassy, Paris, 1964–70; Ambassador to Bulgaria, 1970–73; Dep. Permanent UK Rep. to NATO, 1973–75; Ambassador and Permanent Leader, UK Delegn to UN Conf. on Law of the Sea, 1976–77. Leader, UK delegn to Conf. on Marine Living Resources of Antarctica, Buenos Aires and Canberra, 1978–80. Dir, GB/E Europe Centre, 1980–87. Gov., St Clare's Coll., Oxford, 1982–2000 (Chm., 1984–93). Chairman: Jerusalem and the East Mission Trust Ltd, 1981–93; Brompton Assoc., 1986–97; Friends of Bulgaria, 1991–. Vice-Pres., Internat. Exhibitions Bureau, Paris, 1963–67. *Address:* 6 Thurloe Street, SW7 2ST. *Clubs:* Brooks's, Royal Automobile.

See also J. C. S. M. Brisby.

LOGAN, Sir Douglas; *see* Logan, Sir R. D.

LOGAN, (James) Fergus (Graeme); Chief Executive, Arthritis Research Campaign, since 1998; *b* 20 June 1950; *s* of James John Forbes Moffat, (Hamish), Logan and late Lorna Jane Logan; *m* 1977, Wendy Elizabeth Plaskett, *d* of Maj.-Gen. F. J. Plaskett, *qv*; three *s* one *d. Educ:* Monmouth Sch. Gen. Sec., Nat. Youth Theatre, 1969–80; Head of Appeals, MENCAP, 1981–86; Head of Ops, UNICEF UK, 1986–88; Develt Dir, Bath Internat. Fest. of the Arts, 1988–90; Dir, Meml Fund for Disaster Relief, 1990; Exec. Dir, Muscular

Dystrophy Gp, 1990–97. Founder and Chm., "Batteries not included" (250 charity consortium), 1992–96; Chairman: Exec. Cttee, European Neuromuscular Centre, Baarn, Netherlands, 1992–98; AMRC, 1995–99 (Mem. Exec. Council, 1992–95); Res. for Health Charities Gp, 1996–98. Trustee, Neuromuscular Centre, Winsford, Ches., 1991–97. *Recreations:* family, sport, books, beer. *Address:* Tideswell Lodge, Tideswell, near Buxton, Derbys SK17 8LH. *T:* (01298) 871919.

LOGAN, Joseph Andrew; Chairman, Hay & Kilner, Solicitors, Newcastle, Wallsend and Gosforth, since 1998; *b* 5 Nov. 1942; *s* of late Joseph Baird Logan and of Hellen Dawson Logan; *m* 1964, Heather Robertson; one *s* one *d. Educ:* Hilton Acad., Aberdeen. Sales Manager: Aberdeen Journals, 1958–69; Newcastle Evening Chronicle, 1969–77; Newcastle Chronicle and Journal: Exec. Asst, 1976–77; Asst Man. Dir, 1979–82; Dir, 1984–89; Man. Dir, 1985–89; Asst Man. Dir, Evening Post, Luton and Evening Echo, Watford, 1977–79; Man. Dir, Peter Reed and Co., 1982; Dep. Man. Dir, Aberdeen Journals, 1982–83 (Dir, 1984); Man. Dir, Scotsman Publications, 1989–94; Pres. and Chief Exec., Thomson Newspaper Corp., Western USA, 1994–97. Director: Weekly Courier Ltd, 1971–89; Thomson Regional Newspapers, 1984–94; Thomson Scottish Organisation Ltd, 1989–94; Northern Rock Building Soc. Scotland, 1989–94 (Dep. Chm., Northern Rock Foundn, 1989–2000). Pres., Scottish Daily Newspaper Soc., 1990–92 (Vice Pres., 1989–90); Trustee, NE Civic Trust, 1984–89; Member: British Airways Consumer Council, 1986–89; Bd, BITC, 1985–89; ScotBIC, 1989–94; Dir, Prince's Scottish Youth Business Trust, 1989–94. Mem. Council, Univ. of Newcastle upon Tyne, 1985–89. *Address:* 2 Bishops Hill, Acomb, Hexham, Northumberland NE46 4NH. *T:* (01434) 600369; *e-mail:* joe@jalogan.freeserve.co.uk.

LOGAN, Prof. Malcolm Ian, AC 1996; PhD; Chairman, Education Gateway Holdings Ltd, since 1998; *b* 3 June 1931; *m* 1954, Antoinette, *d* of F. Lalich; one *d. Educ:* Univ. of Sydney (BA Hons 1951, DipEd 1952, PhD 1965). Lectr in Geography, Sydney Teachers Coll., 1956–58; Lectr in Geog., 1959–64, Sen. Lectr, 1965–67, Univ. of Sydney; Prof. of Geog. and of Urban and Regional Planning, Univ. of Wisconsin, Madison, USA, 1967–71; Monash University: Prof. of Geog., 1971–81; Pro Vice-Chancellor, 1982–85; Dep. Vice-Chancellor, 1986; Vice-Chancellor, 1987–96. Visiting Professor: Univ. of Ibadan, Nigeria, 1970–71; LSE, 1973; Nanyang Univ., Singapore, 1979. Chm., Open Learning Agency, Australia Pty Ltd, 1993–96. Australian Newspaper Australian of the Year, 1996. *Publications:* (jtly) New Viewpoints in Economic Geography, 1966; Studies in Australian Geography, 1968; New Viewpoints in Urban and Industrial Geography, 1971; Urban and Regional Australia, 1975; Urbanisation, the Australian Experience, 1980; (jtly) The Brittle Rim, 1989; contribs to Aust. Geographical Studies, Regional Studies, Land Econs, and Econ. Geography. *Address:* 1/50 Bourke Street, Melbourne, Vic 3000, Australia. *Clubs:* Athenæum, Melbourne (Melbourne).

LOGAN, Sir (Raymond) Douglas, Kt 1983; grazier (sheep and cattle), since 1944; *b* 31 March 1920; *s* of Raymond Hough Logan and Agnes Eleanor Logan; *m* 1944, Florence Pearl McGill (MBE 1975); one *s* one *d* (and one *s* decd). *Educ:* Thornburgh College, Charters Towers. Served RAAF, 1941–44 (Flying Officer, pilot; trained EATS, Australia, 1941–42; served with 66 Sqdn RAF, 1942–44). Member: Qld Govt Beef Cttee of Enquiry, 1975–77; Qld Meat Industry Orgn and Marketing Authority (now Livestock and Meat Authority of Qld), 1978–87; United Graziers Assoc. of Qld; Cattlemen's Union, Qld. *Recreations:* tennis, horse riding, sailing, flying. *Address:* PO Box 200, Dobson Road, Malanda, Qld 4885, Australia.

LOGAN, Rt Rev. Vincent; *see* Dunkeld, Bishop of, (RC).

LOGAN, William Philip Dowie, MD, PhD, BSc, DPH, FRCP; epidemiological consultant to various national and international organisations, 1974–89; Director, Division of Health Statistics, WHO, 1961–74; *b* 2 Nov. 1914; *s* of late Frederick William Alexander Logan and late Elizabeth Jane Dowie; *m* 1st, Pearl (*née* Piper) (marr. diss.); four *s* two *d* (and one *s* decd); 2nd, Barbara (*née* Huneke). *Educ:* Queen's Park Sch., Glasgow; Universities of Glasgow and London. RAF Med. Branch, 1940–46 (Squadron Leader). Hospital appointments in Glasgow, 1939–40 and 1946. Gen. practice in Barking, Essex, 1947–48; General Register Office, 1948–60 (Chief Medical Statistician, Adviser on Statistics to Ministry of Health, Head of WHO Centre for Classification of Diseases, and Member, WHO panel of experts on Health Statistics). *Publications:* contribs on epidemiology, vital and health statistics in official reports and medical jls. *Address:* 16 Southview Road, Bognor Regis, West Sussex PO22 7JA.

LOGSDAIL, (Christopher) Nicholas (Roald); Managing Director, Lisson Gallery, since 1967; *b* 21 June 1945; *s* of late John Logsdail and Else Logsdail (*née* Dahl); *m* 1st, 1968, Fiona McLean; one *s*; 2nd, 1985, Caroline Mockett; two *s* one *d. Educ:* Bryanston Sch.; Slade Sch., University College London. Opened Lisson Gallery, 1967; organised over 300 exhibns with contemporary artists, Lisson Gall. and elsewhere, representing work of British and internat. artists; instrumental in introducing new generation of British sculptors and contemporary artists, 1979–; Mem., Soc. of London Art Dealers. *Publications:* monographs and artists books, 1970–. *Recreations:* collecting 20th century art and furniture, books, palaeoanthropology. *Address:* Lisson Gallery, 67 Lisson Street, NW1 5DA. *T:* (020) 7724 2739.

LOGUE, Christopher; *b* 23 Nov. 1926; *s* of John Logue and Molly Logue (*née* Chapman); *m* 1985, Rosemary Hill. *Educ:* Prior Park Coll., Bath; Portsmouth Grammar Sch. Mem., Equity. *Screen plays:* Savage Messiah (dir Ken Russell), 1972; (with Walon Green) Crusoe (based on Defoe's novel), 1989. *Broadcast:* The Arrival of the Poet in the City: a melodrama for narrator and seven musicians (music by George Nicholson), 1985; Strings (melodrama for voice and 14 musicians, with music by Jason Osborn), 1988. *Recordings:* (with Tony Kinsey and Bill Le Sage) Red Bird (poetry and jazz), 1960; Songs from The Establishment (singer Annie Ross), 1962; The Death of Patroclus (with Vanessa Redgrave, Alan Dobie and others), 1963; Audiologue (readings of own poetry set to music), 2001. *Film roles:* Swinburne, in Ken Russell's Dante's Inferno, 1966; John Ball, in John Irvin's The Peasants' Revolt, 1969; Cardinal Richelieu, in Ken Russell's The Devils, 1970; TV and stage roles. Wilfred Owen Award (first), for poetry concerning warfare, 1998. Trans. Baal, by Brecht, perf. 1985. *Publications: verse:* Wand & Quadrant, 1953; Devil, Maggot & Son, 1956; Songs, 1959; Patrocleia, 1962; ABC, 1966; Pax, 1967; New Numbers, 1969; Twelve Cards, 1972; The Crocodile (illus. Binette Schroeder), 1976; Abecedary (illus. Bert Kitchen), 1977; War Music, 1981; Ode to the Dodo, 1981; Kings, 1991; The Husbands, 1995; Selected Poems, 1996; *prose:* Ratsmagic (illus. Wayne Anderson), 1976; The Magic Circus (illus. Wayne Anderson), 1979; The Bumper Book of True Stories (illus. Bert Kitchen), 1980; *plays:* The Trial of Cob & Leach, 1959; (with Harry Cookson) The Lilywhite Boys, 1959; trans. Hugo Claus, Friday, 1971; trans. Brecht and Weill, The Seven Deadly Sins, 1986; *anthologies:* The Children's Book of Comic Verse, 1979; London in Verse, 1982; Sweet & Sour, 1983; The Oxford Book of Pseuds, 1983; The Children's Book of Children's Rhymes, 1986; *autobiography:* Prince Charming: a memoir, 1999; contrib. Private Eye, The Times, The Sunday Times, etc; *as Count Palmiro Vicarion:* Lust, a pornographic novel, 1957; (ed) Count Palmiro Vicarion's Book of Limericks, 1957; (ed) Count Palmiro Vicarion's Book of Bawdy Ballads, 1957; *relevant publication:* Christopher Logue: a bibliography 1952–1997, by George Ramsden, 1998. *Address:* 41 Camberwell Grove, SE5 8JA.

LOISELLE, Hon. Gilles; PC 1990; Adviser to the Chairman, Executive Committee, Power Corporation of Canada, since 1994; *b* 20 May 1929; *s* of Arthur Loiselle and Antoinette Lethiecq; *m* 1962, Lorraine Benoît; one *s* one *d. Educ:* Sacred-Heart Coll., Sudbury, Ont. BA Laval. Tafari Makonnen Sch., Addis Ababa, 1951–53; Journalist, Le Droit, Ottawa, 1953–56; Haile Selassie First Day Sch., Addis Ababa, 1956–62; Dir, Behrane Zarie Néo Inst., Addis Ababa, 1958–62; Canadian Broadcasting Corporation: Editor, TV French Network, 1962–63; Quebec and Paris correspondent, French Radio and TV Network, 1963–67; Counsellor, Quebec House, Paris, 1967–72; Dir Gen. of Quebec Govt Communications, 1972–76; Pres., Intergovtl Deptl Cttee for Olympic Year, 1976; Dir, Interparly Relations, Quebec Nat. Assembly, 1977; Agent General for Quebec in London, with responsibility for Scandinavian countries, Iceland, and Ireland, 1977–83; Dep. Minister for federal provincial relations, 1983–84, for Cultural Affairs, Quebec, 1984–85; Agent Gen. for Quebec in Rome, 1985–88. MP (PC) Langelier, 1988–93; Minister of State for Finance, 1989–93; Pres., Treasury Bd of Canada, 1990–93; Minister of Finance, 1993. Founder Mem., Assoc. France-Québec, 1969–72; Member: Council, Office franco-québécois pour la Jeunesse, 1973–76. Hon. Col, 55th Bde. *Recreations:* reading, gardening. *Address:* Power Corporation of Canada, 751 Victoria Square, Montreal, QC H2Y 2J3, Canada.

LOKOLOKO, Sir Tore, GCMG 1977; GCVO 1982; OBE; Chairman, Indosuez Niugini Bank, 1983–89; *b* 21 Sept. 1930; *s* of Loko Loko Tore and Kevau Sarufa; *m* 1950, Lalahaia Meakoro; four *s* six *d. Educ:* Sogeri High Sch., PNG. Dip. in Cooperative, India. Chm., PNG Cooperative Fedn, 1965–68; MP, 1968–77 (two terms); Minister for Health, and Dep. Chm. of National Exec. Council, 1968–72. Rep. PNG: Co-op. Conf., Australia, 1951; S Pacific Conf., Lae, 1964; attended UN Gen. Assembly, 1969, and Trusteeship Council, 1971. Governor-General of Papua New Guinea, 1977–82. KStJ 1979. *Address:* PO Box 5622, Boroko, NCD, Papua New Guinea.

LOLE, Simon Richard Anthony; Director of Music and Master of the Choristers, Salisbury Cathedral, since 1997; *b* 23 Dec. 1957; *s* of Margaret and Dennis Lole. *Educ:* St Paul's Cathedral Choir Sch.; King's Coll., London (BMus 1978); Guildhall Sch. of Music. ARCO(CHM). Organist and Choirmaster: Barking Parish Church, 1978–80; Croydon Parish Church, 1980–85; Dir of Music, St Mary's Collegiate Church, Warwick, 1985–94; Master of the Music, Sheffield Cathedral, 1994–97. *Publications:* many church compositions. *Recreations:* walking, reading, sport. *Address:* 5 The Close, Salisbury, Wilts SP1 2EF. *T:* (01722) 331436.

LOMAS, Alfred; *b* 30 April 1928; *s* of Alfred and Florence Lomas; one *s* one *d. Educ:* St Paul's Elem. Sch., Stockport; various further educnl estabs. Solicitor's clerk, 1942–46; Radio Telephony Operator, RAF, 1946–49; various jobs, 1949–51; railway signalman, 1951–59; Labour Party Sec./Agent, 1959–65; Polit. Sec., London Co-op., 1965–79. MEP (Lab) London NE, 1979–99; Leader, British Lab Gp, EP, 1985–87. *Publication:* The Common Market—why we should keep out, 1970. *Recreations:* chess, jogging, arts, sport. *Address:* 28 Brookway, SE3 9BJ. *T:* (020) 8852 6689. *Club:* Hackney Labour.

LOMAS, Prof. David Arthur, PhD; FRCP, FMedSci; Professor of Respiratory Biology, University of Cambridge, since 1998; Hon. Consultant Physician, Addenbrooke's and Papworth Hospitals, since 1995; *b* 19 Feb. 1962; *s* of Peter Harry Lomas and Margaret Lomas (*née* Halsall); *m* 1987, Judith Amanda Glasbey; three *s. Educ:* Univ. of Nottingham (BMedSci 1983; BM BS Hons 1985); Trinity Coll., Cambridge (PhD 1993). MRCP 1988, FRCP 1997; ILTM 2000. SHO, Central Birmingham HA, 1986–88; Registrar, Gen. Hosp., Birmingham, 1988–90; MRC Trng Fellow, and Mem., Trinity Coll., Cambridge, 1990–93; MRC Clinician Scientist Fellow, Cambridge, 1993–95; Lectr in Medicine, Univ. of Cambridge, 1995–98. FMedSci 2001. Res. Award, BUPA Foundn, 1996; Oon Internat. Prize in Preventative Medicine, Downing Coll., Cambridge, 1996. *Publications:* res. on α_1-antitrypsin deficiency and conformational diseases in med. jls. *Recreations:* family life, cricket, walking, modern literature. *Address:* Respiratory Medicine Unit, Department of Medicine, Wellcome Trust Centre for the Study of Molecular Mechanisms in Disease, Cambridge Institute for Medical Research, Wellcome Trust/MRC Building, Hills Road, Cambridge CB2 2XY. *T:* (01223) 762818.

LOMAS, Eric George; Managing Director, Gatwick Airport, 1994–97; *b* 26 June 1938; *s* of Arthur Edward Lomas and Florence Lomas; *m* 1959, Carol Letitia Davies; two *d. Educ:* Willesden County Grammar School. FCIT. PLA, 1954–69; Associated Container Transportation, 1969–70; BAA, 1970–86, BAA plc, 1986–97; Man. Dir, Stansted Airport, 1989–94. Dir, Sussex TEC, 1995–97. Mem., SE Reg., CBI, 1995–97. *Recreation:* motor boat cruising. *Address:* 207 Petersham Road, Richmond, Surrey TW10 7AW. *Club:* British Motor Yacht.

LOMAS, Julia Carole; Consultant, Irwin Mitchell, Solicitors, since 2000; *b* 9 Dec. 1954; *d* of Charles James Lomas and Sadie Lomas; *m* (marr. diss.); one *s. Educ:* Lanchester Poly. (BA Business Law). Admitted solicitor, 1980. Articled clerk, London Borough of Islington, 1977–80; Dep. Borough Solicitor, London Borough of Waltham Forest, 1980–89; Borough Solicitor, London Borough of Haringey, 1989–94; Public Trustee, and Chief Exec., Public Trust Office, 1994–99. FIMgt 1994. *Recreations:* theatre, crosswords, dining out. *Address:* Irwin Mitchell, 150 Holborn, EC1N 2NS.

LOMAX, (Janis) Rachel; Permanent Secretary, Department for Work and Pensions (formerly Department of Social Security), since 1999; *b* 15 July 1945; *d* of William and Dilys Salmon; *m* 1967, Michael Acworth Lomax (marr. diss. 1990); two *s. Educ:* Cheltenham Ladies' Coll.; Girton Coll., Cambridge (MA); LSE (MSc). HM Treasury: Econ. Assistant, 1968; Econ. Advr, 1972; Sen. Econ. Advr, 1978; Principal Pvte Sec. to Chancellor of the Exchequer, 1985–86; Under-Sec., 1986–90; Dep. Chief Econ. Advr, 1990–92; Dep. Sec. (Financial Instns and Markets), 1992–94; Dep. Sec., Cabinet Office, 1994–95; Vice Pres. and Chief of Staff, World Bank, 1995–96; Permanent Sec., Welsh Office, 1996–99. Chm., UK Selection Cttee, Harkness Fellowships, 1995–97. Mem. Council, REconS, 1989–94. Governor: De Montfort Univ., 1997–; London Inst., 1998–; Henley Coll. of Mgt, 2000–. *Address:* Department for Work and Pensions, Richmond House, 79 Whitehall, SW1A 2NS.

LOMAX, Kevin John; Executive Chairman, Misys plc, since 1985; *b* 8 Dec. 1948; *s* of Brig. Kenneth John Lomax and Mary Lomax (*née* Foley); *m* 1975, Penelope Frances Flynn; one *s* two *d. Educ:* Ampleforth Coll.; Manchester Univ. (BSc Hons 1970). Advanced Project Manager, J & S Pumps Ltd, 1970–73; Asst to Divl Chm., Allied Polymer Gp, 1973–75; Managing Director: British Furnaces Ltd, 1975–77; Wellman Incandescent Ltd, 1977–80; Dir and Divl Chm., Caparo Industries (CMT) Ltd, 1980–83; Dir and Divl CEO, Electronic Components Div., STC plc, 1983–85. Non-exec. Dir, Marks & Spencer, 2000–. Trustee, Royal Opera House, 1999–. *Recreations:* golf, shooting, fishing, horse-racing, military history, music. *Address:* Hawling Manor, Hawling, Cheltenham, Glos GL54 5TA.

LOMAX, Rachel; *see* Lomax, J. R.

LOMBARD, Rt Rev. Charles F.; *see* Fitzgerald-Lombard.

LOMBE, Hon. Sir Edward Christopher E.; *see* Evans-Lombe.

LOMER, Dennis Roy, CBE 1984; Member, Central Electricity Generating Board, 1977–83; *b* 5 Oct. 1923; *s* of Bertie Cecil Lomer and Agnes Ellen Coward; *m* 1949, Audrey May Bick; one *s* one *d*. With Consulting Engineers, 1948–50; joined Electricity Supply Industry, 1950; Project Engr, Transmission Div., 1961; Asst Chief Transmission Engr, 1965; Generation Construction Div. (secondment at Dir level), 1972; Dep. Dir-Gen. (Projects), 1973; Dir-Gen., Transmission Div., 1975; Mem., Technical Review Gp for Eurotunnel, 1988–92. Dir, Davidson Gp Ltd, 1983–88. Pres., 1985–87, Non-Exec. Dir, 1988–94, Welding Inst; Hon. FWeldI. FIEE; CIMgt. *Recreations:* golf, sailing. *Address:* Henley House, Heathfield Close, Woking, Surrey GU22 7JQ. *T:* (01483) 764656. *Club:* West Hill Golf (Surrey).

LOMER, Geoffrey John, CBE 1985; MA; FREng; FIEE; Chairman, Satellite Information Services Ltd, 1993–96; Director (non-executive), Vodafone Group plc, 1992–97; *b* 5 Jan. 1932; *s* of Frederick John Lomer and Dorothy Lomer; *m* 1st, 1955, Pauline Helena May (*d* 1974); one *s* one *d*; 2nd, 1977, Antoinette Ryall; one step *s* one step *d*. *Educ:* St Austell Grammar School; Queens' College, Cambridge (MA). FREng (FEng 1984). Research Engineer, EMI Research Laboratories, 1953–57; Head of Radio Frequency Div., Broadcast Equipment Dept, EMI Electronics, 1957–63; Head of Transmitter Lab., Racal Communications, 1963–68; Technical Dir, Racal Mobilcal, 1968–70; Dir in Charge, Racal Communications Equipment, 1970–76; Dep. Man. Dir, Racal Tacticom, 1976–77; Technical Dir, Racal Electronics plc, 1977–92. Vice Pres., IEE, 1991–94; Hon. FIEE 1998. *Recreations:* music, theatre. *Address:* Ladiko, Little Croft Road, Goring-on-Thames, Reading RG8 9ER.
See also W. M. Lomer.

LOMER, William Michael, PhD; Director, Culham Laboratory, United Kingdom Atomic Energy Authority, 1981–90, retired; *b* 2 March 1926; *s* of Frederick John Lomer and Dorothy Lomer; *m* 1952, Pamela Anne Wakelin; one *s* two *d*. *Educ:* St Austell County School; University College of the South West, Exeter (MSc London); Queens' College, Cambridge (MA, PhD). Research Scientist, UKAEA, 1952; AERE Harwell: Divison Head, Theory Div., 1958–62; Division Head, Solid State Physics, 1962–68; Research Director, 1968–81; Dep. Dir, Inst. Laue Langevin, Grenoble, 1973–74. Hon. Treasurer, Inst. of Physics, 1980–82. Chm., Oxford CAB, 1994–97. Trustee, Oxford Trust, 1991–. FInstP. *Publications:* papers in physics and metallurgical jls. *Recreations:* gardening, walking, painting. *Address:* 7 Hids Copse Road, Cumnor Hill, Oxford OX2 9JJ. *T:* (01865) 862173.
See also G. J. Lomer.

LONDESBOROUGH, 9th Baron *cr* 1850; **Richard John Denison;** *b* 2 July 1959; *s* of John Albert Lister, 8th Baron Londesborough, TD, AMICE, and Elizabeth Ann (*d* 1994), *d* of late Edward Little Sale, ICS; *S* father, 1968; *m* 1987, Rikki Morris, *d* of J. E. Morris, Bayswater; one *s* one *d*. *Educ:* Wellington College; Exeter Univ. *Heir: s* Hon. James Frederick Denison, *b* 4 June 1990. *Address:* Edw Cottage, Aberedw, Builth Wells, Powys LD2 3UR.

LONDON, Bishop of, since 1995; **Rt Rev. and Rt Hon. Richard John Carew Chartres;** PC 1995; Prelate of the Order of the British Empire, since 1995; Dean of the Chapels Royal, since 1995; *b* 11 July 1947; *s* of Richard and Charlotte Chartres; *m* 1982, Caroline Mary (*née* McLintock); two *s* two *d*. *Educ:* Hertford Grammar Sch.; Trinity Coll., Cambridge (BA 1968; MA 1973); Cuddesdon Theol Coll., Oxford; Lincoln Theol Coll. Ordained: deacon, 1973; priest, 1974; Asst Curate, St Andrew's, Bedford, dio. of St Albans, 1973–75; Bishop's Domestic Chaplain, St Albans, 1975–80; Archbishop of Canterbury's Chaplain, 1980–84; Vicar, St Stephen with St John, Westminster, 1984–92; Director of Ordinands for London Area, 1985–92; Area Bishop of Stepney, 1992–95. Chairman: Churches Main Cttee, 1998–; C of E Heritage Forum, 1998–. Gresham Prof. of Divinity, 1986–92. Six Preacher, Canterbury Cathedral, 1991–96. Hon. Bencher, Middle Temple, 1998. Liveryman, Merchant Taylors' Co., 1997; Hon. Freeman: Weavers' Co., 1998; Leathersellers' Co., 1999; Woolmen's Co., 2000. FSA 1999. BD Lambeth, 1983. Hon. DLitt London Guildhall, 1998; Hon. DD: London, 1999; City, 1999; Brunel, 1999. *Publication:* The History of Gresham College 1597–1997, 1998. *Address:* The Old Deanery, Dean's Court, EC4V 5AA. *T:* (020) 7248 6233.

LONDON, Archdeacon of; *see* Delaney, Ven. P. A.

LONDONDERRY, 9th Marquess of, *cr* 1816; **Alexander Charles Robert Vane-Tempest-Stewart;** Baron Londonderry, 1789; Viscount Castlereagh, 1795; Earl of Londonderry, 1796; Baron Stewart, 1814; Earl Vane, Viscount Seaham, 1823; *b* 7 Sept. 1937; *s* of 8th Marquess of Londonderry and Romaine (*d* 1951), *er d* of Major Boyce Combe, Great Holt, Dockenfield, Surrey; *S* father, 1955; *m* 1st, 1958, Nicolette (marr. diss. 1971; she *d* 1993), *d* of Michael Harrison, Netherhampton, near Salisbury, Wilts; two *d*; 2nd, 1972, Doreen Patricia Wells, *qv* (marr. diss. 1989); two *s*. *Educ:* Eton. *Heir: s* Viscount Castlereagh, *qv*. *Address:* PO Box No 8, Shaftesbury, Dorset SP7 0LR.

LONDONDERRY, Doreen, Marchioness of; *see* Wells, D. P.

LONG, family name of **Viscount Long**.

LONG, 4th Viscount *cr* 1921, of Wraxall; **Richard Gerard Long,** CBE 1993; *b* 30 Jan. 1929; *s* of 3rd Viscount and Gwendolyn (*d* 1959), *d* of Thomas Reginald Hague Cook; *S* father, 1967; *m* 1957, Margaret Frances (marr. diss. 1984), *d* of late Ninian B. Frazer; one *s* one *d* (and one *d* decd); *m* 1984, Catherine Patricia Elizabeth Mier-Woolf (marr. diss. 1990); *m* 1990, Helen Fleming-Gibbons. *Educ:* Harrow. Wilts Regt, 1947–49. Opposition Whip, 1974–79; a Lord in Waiting (Govt Whip), 1979–97. Vice-Pres. and formerly Vice-Chm., Wilts Royal British Legion; Pres., Bath Gliding Club. Freeman, City of London, 1991. *Heir: s* Hon. James Richard Long, *b* 31 Dec. 1960. *Address:* Owles Hall, Buntingford, Herts SG9 9PL. *Club:* Pratt's.

LONG, Athelstan Charles Ethelwulf, CMG 1968 CBE 1964 (MBE 1959); Chairman, International Management Group, since 1988; Chairman and Director of some twelve companies; Chairman, Public Service Commission, since 1987; Deputy Chairman, Public Service Pensions Board, since 1992; *b* 2 Jan. 1919; *s* of Arthur Leonard Long and Gabrielle Margaret Campbell (historical writer and novelist, Marjorie Bowen); *m* 1948, Edit Majken Zadie Harriet Krantz, *d* of late Erik Krantz, Stockholm; two *s*. *Educ:* Westminster Sch.; Brasenose Coll., Oxford. Served War of 1939–45: commnd into RA, 1940; seconded 7th (Bengal) Battery, 22nd Mountain Regt, IA, 1940; served Malaya; POW as Capt., 1942–45; appointed to Indian Political Service, 1946. Cadet, Burma Civil Service, 1947–48; Colonial Admin. Service (N Nigeria), 1948; Sen. District Officer, 1958; Resident, Zaria Province, 1959; Perm. Sec., Min. of Animal Health and Forestry, 1959; started new Min. of Information as Perm. Sec., 1960; Swaziland: appointed Govt Sec., 1961; Chief Sec., 1964; Leader of Govt business in Legislative Council and MEC, 1964–67; HM Dep. Comr, 1967–68; Administrator, later Governor, of the Cayman Is, 1968–71; Comr of Anguilla, March–July 1972; Admin. Sec., Inter-University Council, 1972–73. Man. Dir, Anegada Corp. Ltd, 1973–74; Pres., United Bank Internat., Cayman Is, 1976–96; Dir and Chm., Cayman Airways, 1977–81. Chairman: Planning Appeals Tribunal, 1982–84; Coastal Works Adv. Cttee, 1986–91. Chm. Governing Council, Waterford Sch., Swaziland, 1963–68. FRAS; FRGS. *Recreations:* travel, tropical farming, reading. *Address:* Box 131, Savannah, Grand Cayman, Cayman Islands, West Indies.

LONG, Christopher William, CMG 1986; HM Diplomatic Service, retired; Director, Foreign Service Programme, University of Oxford, since 1999; *b* 9 April 1938; *s* of late Eric and May Long; *m* 1972, Patricia, *d* of late Dennis and May Stanbridge; two *s* one *d*. *Educ:* King Edward's Sch., Birmingham; Balliol Coll., Oxford (Deakin Scholar); Univ. of Münster, W Germany. Served RN, 1956–58. HM Diplomatic Service, 1963–98: FO, 1963–64; Jedda, 1965–67; Caracas, 1967–69; FCO, 1969–74; Budapest, 1974–77; Belgrade (CSCE), 1977; Counsellor, Damascus, 1978–80; Counsellor and Dep. Perm. Rep., UKMIS, Geneva, 1980–83; Head, Near East and N Africa Dept, FCO, 1983–85; Asst Under-Sec. of State (Dep. Chief Clerk and Chief Inspector), FCO, 1985–88; Ambassador: to Switzerland, 1988–92 and also to Liechtenstein, 1992; to Egypt, 1992–95; to Hungary, 1995–98. Non-executive Director: Gideon Richter plc, Budapest, 1998–; KFKI Computer Systems Corp., Budapest, 2001–. Gov., Prior Park Coll., Bath, 2000–. *Address:* 7 Old Pye Street, SW1P 2LD. *Club:* Athenæum.

LONG, Hubert Arthur, CBE 1970; Deputy Secretary, Exchequer and Audit Department, 1963–73; *b* 21 Jan. 1912; *s* of Arthur Albert Long; *m* 1937, Mary Louise Parker; three *s*. *Educ:* Taunton's Sch., Southampton. Entered Exchequer and Audit Department, 1930. *Address:* 2A Hawthorndene Road, Hayes, Kent BR2 7DY. *T:* (020) 8462 4373.

LONG, John Richard, CBE 1987; freelance consultant on National Health Service management and state regulation of medicines; *b* 9 March 1931; *s* of late Thomas Kendall Long and Jane Long; *m* 1952, Margaret (*née* Thistlethwaite); one *s* two *d*. *Educ:* Kirkham Grammar School; Dip. in EU Law, KCL, 1993. Clerical Officer, Customs and Excise, 1947; Exec. Officer, Min. of Pensions, subseq. DHSS, 1949; various posts on health functions; Asst Sec., 1978 (posts on regulation and pricing of medicines, maternity and child health, and communicable diseases); Under Sec., 1987 (NHS Personnel Div.), resigned 1988; Mem., professional disciplinary cttees, Lambeth, Southwark and Lewisham HA (formerly FHSA), 1992–. *Publications:* co-author, articles on regulation of medicines. *Recreations:* golf, vegetable growing, wild life, foreign travel. *Address:* 77 Prospect Road, Farnborough, Hants GU14 8NT. *T:* (01252) 548525.

LONG, Ven. John Sanderson, MA; Archdeacon of Ely, Hon. Canon of Ely and Rector of St Botolph's, Cambridge, 1970–81; Archdeacon Emeritus, 1981; *b* 21 July 1913; *s* of late Rev. Guy Stephenson Long and Ivy Marion Long; *m* 1948, Rosamond Mary (*d* 1999), *d* of Arthur Temple Forman; one *s* three *d*. *Educ:* St Edmund's Sch., Canterbury; Queens' Coll., Cambridge; Cuddesdon Theological Coll. Deacon, 1936; Priest, 1937; Curate, St Mary and St Eanswythe, Folkestone, 1936–41. Chaplain, RNVR, 1941–46. Curate, St Peter-in-Thanet, 1946; Domestic Chaplain to the Archbishop of Canterbury, 1946–53, Vicar of Bearsted, 1953–59; Petersfield with Sheet, 1959–70; Rural Dean of Petersfield, 1962–70. *Recreations:* walking, gardening. *Address:* 23 Thornton Road, Girton, Cambridge CB3 0NP. *T:* (01223) 276421.

LONG, Olivier; Ambassador; President, Graduate Institute of Public Administration, Lausanne, 1981–89; *b* 1915; *s* of Dr Edouard Long and Dr Marie Landry; *m* 1946, Francine Roels; one *s* two *d*. *Educ:* Univ. de Paris, Faculté de Droit et Ecole des Sciences Politiques; Univ. de Genève. PhD Law, 1938; Rockefeller Foundn Fellow, 1938–39; PhD Pol. Sc., 1943. Swiss Armed Forces, 1939–43; International Red Cross, 1943–46; Swiss Foreign Affairs Dept, Berne, 1946–49; Washington Embassy, 1949–54; Govt Delegate for Trade Agreements, 1955–66; Head of Swiss Delegn to EFTA, 1960–66; Ambassador to UK and Malta, 1967–68; Dir-Gen., GATT, 1968–80. Prof., Graduate Inst. of Internat. Studies, Geneva, 1962–85. Hon. Mem., Internat. Red Cross Cttee, 1985– (Mem., 1980–85). Trustee, Foundn for Internat. Conciliation, Geneva, 1984–96. *Publications:* Law and its Limitations in the GATT Multilateral Trade System, 1985; Le dossier secret des Accords d'Evian—une mission suisse pour la paix en Algérie, 1988. *Address:* 6 rue Constantin, 1206 Geneva, Switzerland.

LONG, Captain Rt Hon. William Joseph, OBE 1985; PC (N Ireland) 1966; JP; Minister of Education, Northern Ireland, 1969–72; MP (Unionist) Ards, Parliament of Northern Ireland, 1962–72; *b* 23 April 1922; *s* of James William Long and Frederica (Walker); *m* 1942, Dr Elizabeth Doreen Mercer; one *s*. *Educ:* Friends' Sch., Great Ayton, Yorks; Edinburgh Univ.; RMC, Sandhurst. Served Royal Inniskilling Fusiliers, 1940–48. Secretary: NI Marriage Guidance Council, 1948–51; NI Chest and Heart Assoc., 1951–62. Parliamentary Secretary, Min. of Agriculture, NI, 1964–66; Sen. Parliamentary Secretary, Min. of Development, NI, Jan.–Oct. 1966; Minister of Educn, 1966–68; Minister of Home Affairs, Dec. 1968–March 1969; Minister of Develt, March 1969–May 1969. *Recreations:* cricket, horticulture, angling, sailing, model engineering, aviation. *Address:* Lisvarna, Warren Road, Donaghadee, Co. Down.

LONGAIR, Deborah Janet; *see* Howard, D. J.

LONGAIR, Prof. Malcolm Sim, CBE 2000; PhD; FRSE 1981; Jacksonian Professor of Natural Philosophy, since 1991, and Head of Department of Physics, Cavendish Laboratory, since 1998, University of Cambridge; Professorial Fellow, Clare Hall, Cambridge, since 1991; *b* 18 May 1941; *s* of James Sim Longair and Lily Malcolm; *m* 1975, Dr Deborah Janet Howard, *qv*; one *s* one *d*. *Educ:* Morgan Acad., Dundee; Queen's Coll., Dundee, Univ. of St Andrews (BSc Electronic Physics, 1963); Cavendish Lab., Univ. of Cambridge (MA, PhD 1967). Res. Fellow, Royal Commn for Exhibn of 1851, 1966–68; Royal Soc. Exchange Fellow to USSR, 1968–69; University of Cambridge: Res. Fellow, 1967–71, and Official Fellow, 1971–80, Clare Hall; Univ. Demonstrator in Phys., 1970–75; Univ. Lectr in Phys., 1975–80; Astronomer Royal for Scotland, Regius Prof. of Astronomy, Univ. of Edinburgh, and Dir, Royal Observatory, Edinburgh, 1980–90. Visiting Professor: of Radio Astronomy, Calif Inst. of Technol., 1972; of Astronomy, Inst for Advanced Study, Princeton, 1978; Space Telescope Sci. Inst., 1997; Regents' Fellow, Carnegie Inst., Harvard Univ., 1990. Pres., RAS, 1996–98 (Editor, Monthly Notices, 1974–78). Hon. LLD Dundee, 1982. Britannica Award, 1986. *Publications:* (ed) Confrontation of Cosmological Theories with Observational Data, 1974; (ed with J. Einasto) The Large-Scale Structure of the Universe, 1978; (with J. E. Gunn and M. J. Rees) Observational Cosmology, 1978; (ed with J. Warner) The Scientific Uses of the Space Telescope, 1980; High Energy Astrophysics: an informal introduction, 1980, rev. edn as High Energy Astrophysics, vol. 1: Particles, Photons and their Detection, 1992; High Energy Astrophysics, vol. 2: Stars, the Galaxy and the Interstellar Medium, 1994; (ed with H. A. Brück and G. Coyne) Astrophysical Cosmology, 1982; Theoretical Concepts in Physics, 1984; Alice and the Space Telescope, 1989; The Origins of Our Universe,

1991; (with A. R. Sandage and R. G. Kron) The Deep Universe, 1995; Our Evolving Universe, 1996; Galaxy Formation, 1998; over 200 papers, mostly in Monthly Notices of RAS. *Recreations:* music, art, architecture, mountain walking. *Address:* c/o Cavendish Laboratory, Madingley Road, Cambridge CB3 0HE. *T:* (01223) 337429.

LONGBOTHAM, Tom; His Honour Judge Longbotham; a Circuit Judge, since 1999; *b* 9 Aug. 1942; *s* of George Ferrand Longbotham and Elizabeth Ann Longbotham; *m* 1964, Eirlys Thomas; one *s* (and one *s* decd). *Educ:* Rossall Sch.; Bristol Univ. (LLB). Admitted Solicitor, 1966; Sen. Litigation Partner, Bishop Longbotham & Bagnall, Solicitors, until 1999; Asst Recorder, 1990–95; a Recorder, 1995–99. *Recreations:* golf, gardening, hill walking, theatre. *Club:* West Wiltshire Golf.

LONGBOTTOM, Charles Brooke; Trustee, Acorn Christian Foundation (formerly Acorn Christian Healing Trust), since 1983 (Chairman, 1988–2001); *b* 22 July 1930; *s* of late William Ewart Longbottom, Forest Hill, Worksop; *m* 1962, Anita, *d* of G. Trapani and Mrs Basil Mavroleon; two *d.* *Educ:* Uppingham. Contested (C) Stockton-on-Tees, 1955; MP (C) York, 1959–66; Parly Private Secretary to Mr Iain Macleod, Leader of the House, 1961–63. Barrister, Inner Temple, 1958; Chairman: Austin & Pickersgill, Shipbuilders, Sunderland, 1966–72; A&P Appledore International Ltd, 1970–79; Seascope Holdings Ltd, 1970–82; Seascope Sale & Purchase, 1970–87; Seascope Shipping Ltd, 1982–87; Seascope Insurance Holdings Ltd, 1984–86; Seascope Insurance Services Ltd, 1984–87; Illingworth Morris Pension Trustees Ltd, 1990–94; Director: Henry Ansbacher Hldgs Ltd, 1982–87; Henry Ansbacher & Co., 1982–87; Ansbacher (Guernsey) Ltd, 1982–87; British Shipbuilders, 1986–; Kelt Energy plc, 1988–95; MC Shipping Inc., 1989–; Newman Martin & Buchan, 1992–2000. Member: General Advisory Council, BBC, 1965–75; Community Relations Commn, 1968–70. *Recreations:* shooting, golf, travel. *Address:* 66 Kingston House North, Princes Gate, SW7 1LN. *Clubs:* White's, Carlton; Wentworth; Berkshire.

LONGDEN, Wilson; JP; industrial relations consultant; *b* 26 May 1936; *s* of late Harold and Doris Longden; *m* 1st, 1966 (marr. diss. 1982); two *s*; 2nd, 1985, Olga Longden (marr. diss. 1993). *Educ:* Chesterfield Grammar Sch.; Univ. of Hull (BA Hons, Dip Ed); Univ. of Bradford (MSc). National service, RAF, 1955–57; Teacher, Northmount High Sch., Canada, 1961–62; Lecturer: Matthew Boulton Tech. Coll., Birmingham, 1962–66; Bingley Coll. of Educn, 1966–67; Margaret McMillan Coll. of Educn, 1967–68; Hatfield Polytechnic, 1968–69; Coventry (Lanchester) Polytechnic, 1969–73; Vice-Principal, Barnfield College, Luton, 1973–87. Sec., Assoc. of Vice-Principals of Colleges, 1986–87 (Pres., 1982–84). Comr, MSC, 1983–85. JP Luton, 1980; Mem., Beds Magistrates' Courts Cttee, 1998–. *Publications:* The School Manager's and the School Governor's Handbook, 1977; Meetings, 1977, 2nd edn, 1997; Making Secondments Work, 1990. *Recreations:* music, playing the piano. *Address:* 311 Turnpike Drive, Luton LU3 3RE. *T:* (01582) 573905.

LONGFIELD, Anne Elizabeth, OBE 2000; Director, Kids' Clubs Network, since 1994; *b* 5 July 1960; *d* of James Vincent Longfield and Jean Elizabeth Longfield; partner, Richard Reeve; one *s.* *Educ:* Prince Henry's Grammar Sch., Otley; Univ. of Newcastle upon Tyne (BA Hons History). Researcher, Save the Children Fund, 1982–83; community develt with children's and women's orgns in London, 1983–87; Develt, Kids' Clubs Network, 1987–93. FRSA 1998. *Publications:* articles in jls on childcare and community develt. *Recreations:* family, gardening, interior design. *Address:* c/o Kids' Clubs Network, Bellerive House, 3 Muirfield Crescent, E14 9SZ. *T:* (020) 7512 2112.

LONGFIELD, Dr Michael David; Vice-Chancellor, University of Teesside, 1992 (Director, Teesside Polytechnic, 1980–92), retired; *b* 28 April 1928; *s* of late Edric Douglas Longfield and Dorothy Longfield (*née* Hennessey); *m* 1st, 1952, Ann McDonnell; two *s* two *d*; 2nd, 1970, June Shirley, *d* of late Levi and Esther Beman; two *s.* *Educ:* Prince Henry's Grammar Sch., Otley; Leeds Univ. BSc, PhD; CEng, MIMechE. Lectr in Mech. Engrg, Univ. of Leeds, 1960–68; Manager, Leeds Univ. Industrial Unit of Tribology, 1968–70; Head of Dept of Mech., Marine and Production Engrg, Liverpool Polytechnic, 1970–72; Asst Dir, Teesside Poly., 1972–80. Hon. DSc Teesside, 1996. *Recreation:* the genealogy of not only the Longfields but also the Langfields. *Address:* 16 Firs Road, Harrogate HG2 8HA.

LONGFORD, Earldom of, *cr* 1785; title not used by 8th Earl (*see* Pakenham, T. F. D.)

LONGFORD, Countess of; Elizabeth Pakenham, CBE 1974; *b* 30 Aug. 1906; *d* of late N. B. Harman, FRCS, 108 Harley Street, W1, and of Katherine (*née* Chamberlain); *m* 1931, Hon. F. A. Pakenham (later 7th Earl of Longford, KG, PC, he *d* 2001); four *s* three *d* (and one *d* decd). *Educ:* Headington Sch., Oxford; Lady Margaret Hall, Oxford (MA). Lectr for WEA and Univ. Extension Lectr, 1929–35. Contested (Lab) Cheltenham, 1935, Oxford, 1950; candidate for King's Norton, Birmingham, 1935–43. Mem., Rent Tribunal, Paddington and St Pancras, 1947–54; Trustee, National Portrait Gall., 1968–78; Member: Adv. Council, V&A Museum, 1969–75; Adv. Bd, British Library, 1976–80; Hon. Life Pres., Women Writers and Journalists, 1979. Hon. DLitt Sussex 1970. *Publications:* (as Elizabeth Pakenham): Points for Parents, 1956; Catholic Approaches (ed), 1959; Jameson's Raid, 1960, new edn 1982; (as Elizabeth Longford): Victoria RI, 1964 (James Tait Black Memorial Prize for Non-Fiction, 1964); Wellington: Years of the Sword, 1969 (Yorkshire Post Prize); Wellington: Pillar of State, 1972; The Royal House of Windsor, 1974; Churchill, 1974; Byron's Greece, 1975; Life of Byron, 1976; A Pilgrimage of Passion: the life of Wilfrid Scawen Blunt, 1979; (ed) Louisa: Lady in Waiting, 1979; Images of Chelsea, 1980; The Queen Mother, a biography, 1981; Eminent Victorian Women, 1981; Elizabeth R, 1983; The Pebbled Shore (autobiog.), 1986; The Oxford Book of Royal Anecdotes, 1989; Darling Loosy: Letters to Princess Louise 1856–1939, 1991; Wellington (abridged), 1992; Poet's Corner: an anthology, 1992; Royal Throne: the future of the Monarchy, 1993; Queen Victoria, 1999. *Recreation:* audio books. *Address:* Bernhurst, Hurst Green, East Sussex TN19 7QN. *T:* (01580) 860248; 18 Chesil Court, Chelsea Manor Street, SW3 5QP. *T:* (020) 7352 7794.

See also Lady Rachel Billington, Lady Antonia Fraser, Hon. M. A. Pakenham, T. F. D. Pakenham.

LONGFORD, Elizabeth; *see* Longford, Countess of.

LONGHURST, Andrew Henry, FCIB; FBCS; Deputy Chairman, Royal London Mutual Insurance Society Ltd, since 2000; *b* 23 Aug. 1939; *s* of Henry and Connie Longhurst; *m* 1962, Margaret; one *s* two *d.* *Educ:* Nottingham University (BSc Hons). FBCS 1968; FCIB (FCBSI 1990); CIMgt (CBIM 1989). Computer systems consultancy, 1961; Cheltenham & Gloucester Building Society: Data Processing Manager, 1967; Asst Gen. Man. (Admin), 1970; Dep. Gen. Man., 1977; Chief Exec. and Dir, 1982–95; Cheltenham & Gloucester plc: Chief Exec., 1995–96; Dir, 1995–98; Chm., 1997–98; Gp Dir Customer Finance, and Dir, Lloyds TSB Group plc, 1997–98; Chm., United Assurance Gp plc, 1998–2000. Director: Lloyds Bank plc, 1995–98; TSB Bank plc, 1995–98; Chairman, 1997–98: Lloyds UDT Ltd; Lloyds Bowmaker Ltd; United Dominions Trust Ltd; Dir, Cardnet Merchant Services Ltd, 1997–98. Non-executive Director: Hermes Lens Asset Management, 1998–; Thames Water Plc, 1998–2000. FRSA. Chm., Council of Mortgage Lenders, 1994. *Recreation:* golf. *Address:* 53 Sandy Lane, Charlton Kings, Cheltenham, Glos GL53 9DG.

LONGLEY, Mrs Ann Rosamund; Head Mistress, Roedean School, 1984–97; *b* 5 March 1942; *d* of late Jack Gilroy Dearlove and of Rhoda E. M. Dearlove (*née* Billing); *m* 1964, Stephen Roger Longley (*d* 1979); one *s* two *d.* *Educ:* Walthamstow Hall School, Sevenoaks; Edinburgh University (MA 1964); PGCE Bristol University, 1984. Wife and mother, 1964–; Teacher, Toorak Coll., Victoria, Australia, 1964–65; Asst Housemistress, Peninsula C of E Sch., Victoria, 1966–67; Residential Teacher, Choate School, Conn, USA, 1968–73; Teacher, Webb School, Calif, 1975–78; Headmistress, Vivian Webb School, Calif, 1981–84. FRSA 1987. DUniv Sussex, 1991. *Recreations:* film, theatre, fishing, walking.

LONGLEY, Clifford Edmund; JP; journalist; *b* 6 Jan. 1940; *s* of Harold Anson Longley and Gladys Vera (*née* Gibbs); *m* 1980, Elizabeth Anne Holzer; one *s* two *d.* *Educ:* Trinity Sch., Croydon; Univ. of Southampton (BSc Eng.). Reporter: Essex and Thurrock Gazette, 1961–64; Portsmouth Evening News, 1964–67; The Times, 1967–92 (Asst Ed. (Leaders) and Religious Affairs Ed., 1990–92); leader writer and columnist, Daily Telegraph, 1992–95; leader writer and columnist, The Tablet, 1996– (Actg Ed., 1996); columnist, Daily Telegraph, 1995–2000; freelance broadcaster and author. Consultant, RC Bishops' Conf. of England and Wales, 1996–. Mem. Adv. Council, Three Faiths Forum, 1995–. Select Preacher, Oxford Univ., 1988; lectures: Hugh Kay Meml, Christian Assoc. of Business Execs, 1990; Cardinal Bea Meml, CCJ, 1994. Hon. Fellow, St Mary's UC Strawberry Hill, Surrey Univ., 1999. Specialist Writer of the Year, British Press Awards, 1986. JP Bromley, 1999. *Publications:* The Times Book of Clifford Longley, 1991; The Worlock Archive, 1999; numerous articles and book chapters. *Recreations:* classical music (piano), grandchildren, reading, theology, musicology. *Address:* 24 Broughton Road, Orpington, Kent BR6 8EQ. *T:* (01689) 853189; *e-mail:* clongley@cwcom.net.

LONGLEY, Dr Michael George; freelance writer, since 1991; *b* 27 July 1939; *s* of Richard Cyril Longley and Constance Evelyn (*née* Longworth); *m* 1964, Edna Mary Broderick; one *s* two *d.* *Educ:* Royal Belfast Academical Instn; Trinity Coll., Dublin (BA). Teacher, secondary schs in Dublin, Belfast and London, 1963–69; Combined Arts Dir, Arts Council of NI, 1970–91. Hon. LLD: QUB, 1995; TCD, 1999. Literary prizes include: Eric Gregory Award, 1966; Cholmondeley Award, 1991; Whitbread Prize, 1991; Queen's Gold Medal for Poetry, 2001. *Publications:* Poems 1963–1983, 1985; Gorse Fires, 1991; Selected Poems, 1995; The Ghost Orchid, 1995; The Weather in Japan (Hawthornden Prize, T. S. Eliot Prize), 2000. *Recreations:* jazz, classical music, ornithology, botany, cooking. *Address:* c/o Lucas Alexander Whitley, 14 Vernon Street, W14 0RJ. *T:* (020) 7471 7900.

LONGMAN, Gary Leslie; Headteacher, King's Cathedral School, Peterborough, since 1994; *b* 14 April 1954; *s* of late Bernard Longman and of Betty Longman; *m* 1977, Alison Mary Shepherd; one *s* one *d.* *Educ:* Univ. of Nottingham (BSc Hons Botany). FCollP 1994. Assistant science teacher: Dayncourt Sch., Nottingham, 1977–79; Queen Elizabeth's Sch., Mansfield, 1979–82; Hd of Biology, 1982–85, Hd of Sci., 1985–88, Toot Hill Sch., Bingham, Notts; Dep. Head Teacher, Heysham High Sch., Morecambe, Lancs, 1988–94. *Recreations:* travel, wine-tasting, home and garden, my family. *Address:* The Ridings, Station Road, Barnack, Stamford, Lincs PE9 3DW.

LONGMAN, Peter Martin; Director, The Theatres Trust, since 1996 (Trustee, 1991–95); *b* 2 March 1946; *s* of Denis Martin Longman and Mary Joy Longman (*née* Simmonds); *m* 1976, Sylvia June Prentice; two *d.* *Educ:* Huish's School, Taunton; University College, Cardiff; Univ. of Manchester. Finance Dept and Housing the Arts Officer, Arts Council, 1968–78; Dep. Dir, Crafts Council, 1978–83; Dep. Sec., 1983–84, Dir, 1984–95, Museums and Galleries Commn. Dir, Caryl Jenner Productions Ltd, 1983–87. A Director: Scottish Museums Council, 1986–95; Walpole Foundn, 1997–; Member: Council, Textile Conservation Centre Ltd, 1983– (Chm., 1998–2000; Mem., Exec. Cttee, 1983–85, 1996–99); BTA Heritage Cttee, 1991–95; Exec., Council for Dance Educn and Trng, 1996–97; Adv. Council, Art in Churches, 1996–98; Chichester Fest. Theatre Trust, 1998–; Develt Cttee, ENO, 1999–. FRSA 1989. Hon. FMA 1995. *Publications:* Working Party Reports: Training Arts Administrators, Arts Council, 1971; Area Museum Councils and Services, HMSO, 1984; Museums in Scotland, HMSO, 1986; articles on theatre, the arts, museums. *Recreations:* discovering Britain, listening to music. *Address:* The Theatres Trust, 22 Charing Cross Road, WC2H 0QL. *T:* (020) 7836 8591, *Fax:* (020) 7836 3302.

LONGMORE, Rt Hon. Sir Andrew (Centlivres), Kt 1993; PC 2001; **Rt Hon. Lord Justice Longmore;** a Lord Justice of Appeal, since 2001; *b* 25 Aug. 1944; *s* of John Bell Longmore and Virginia Longmore (*née* Centlivres); *m* 1979, Margaret Murray McNair; one *s.* *Educ:* Winchester College; Lincoln College, Oxford (MA; Hon. Fellow, 2001). Called to the Bar, Middle Temple, 1966, Bencher, 1990. QC 1983; a Recorder, 1992–93; a Judge of the High Court, QBD, 1993–2001. Chm., Law Reform Cttee, Bar Council, 1987–90. *Publications:* (co-editor) MacGillivray and Parkington, Law of Insurance, 6th edn 1975, 9th edn 1997. *Recreation:* fell-walking. *Address:* Royal Courts of Justice, Strand, WC2A 2LL.

LONGRIGG, Anthony James, CMG 1992; HM Diplomatic Service; Governor, Montserrat, since 2001; *b* 21 April 1944; *m* 1967, Jane Rosa Cowlin; three *d.* Joined FCO, 1972; Second, later First, Sec., Moscow, 1975; FCO 1978; Brasilia, 1981; First Sec., FCO, 1985; Counsellor, Moscow, 1987; Counsellor, Madrid, 1991; Head, S Atlantic and Antarctic Dept, FCO, 1995–97; Minister, Moscow, 1997–2000. *Address:* c/o Foreign and Commonwealth Office, SW1A 2AH.

LONGRIGG, John Stephen, CMG 1973; OBE 1964; HM Diplomatic Service, retired; *b* 1 Oct. 1923; *s* of late Brig. Stephen Hemsley Longrigg, OBE; *m* 1st, 1953, Lydia Meynell (marr. diss. 1965); one *s* one *d*; 2nd, 1966, Ann O'Reilly; one *s* decd. *Educ:* Rugby Sch.; Magdalen Coll., Oxford (BA). War Service, Rifle Bde, 1942–45 (despatches). FO, 1948; Paris, 1948; Baghdad, 1951; FO, 1953; Berlin, 1955; Cabinet Office, 1957; FO, 1958; Dakar, 1960; Johannesburg, 1962; Pretoria, 1962; Washington, 1964; FO, 1965–67; Bahrain, 1967–69; FCO, 1969–73; seconded to HQ British Forces, Hong Kong, 1974–76; FCO, 1976–82; Administrator, Common Law Inst. of Intellectual Property, 1983–88. *Recreation:* golf. *Address:* 45A Blackheath Park, Blackheath, SE3 9SQ. *T:* (020) 8852 4007. *Clubs:* Reform; Royal Blackheath Golf, Littlestone Golf.

LONGSTRETH THOMPSON, Francis Michael; *see* Thompson.

LONGUET-HIGGINS, Prof. Hugh Christopher, DPhil (Oxon); FRS 1958; Professor Emeritus, University of Sussex, 1989 (Royal Society Research Professor, 1974–88); *b* 11 April 1923; *e s* of late Rev. H. H. L. Longuet-Higgins. *Educ:* Winchester (schol.); Balliol Coll., Oxford (schol., MA). Research Fellow of Balliol Coll., 1946–48; Lecturer and Reader in Theoretical Chemistry, University of Manchester, 1949–52; Prof. of

Theoretical Physics, King's Coll., University of London, 1952–54; FRSE; John Humphrey Plummer Professor of Theoretical Chemistry, University of Cambridge, 1954–67; Royal Soc. Res. Prof., Univ. of Edinburgh, 1968–74; Fellow of Corpus Christi Coll., 1954–67, Life Fellow 1968; Hon. Fellow: Balliol Coll., Oxford, 1969; Wolfson Coll., Cambridge, 1977. A Governor, BBC, 1979–84. Warden, Leckhampton House, 1961–67. Editor of Molecular Physics, 1958–61. For. Mem., Amer. Acad. of Arts and Scis, 1961; Foreign Associate, US National Academy of Sciences, 1968. DUniv York, 1973; DU Essex, 1981; Hon. DSc: Bristol, 1983; Sussex, 1989; Hon. DMus Sheffield, 1995. Harrison Meml Prize, Chemical Soc., 1950; Naylor Prize, London Mathematical Soc., 1981. *Publications:* co-author, The Nature of Mind (Gifford Lectures), 1972; Mental Processes, 1987; papers on theoretical physics, chemistry and biology in scientific journals. *Recreations:* music and arguing. *Address:* Laboratory of Experimental Psychology, University of Sussex, Falmer, Brighton BN1 9QY. *T:* (01273) 678341.

LONGUET-HIGGINS, Michael Selwyn, FRS 1963; Senior Research Physicist, University of California at San Diego, and Adjunct Professor, Scripps Institution of Oceanography, La Jolla, California, since 1989; Fellow, Trinity College, Cambridge, since 1969; *b* 8 Dec. 1925; *s* of late Henry Hugh Longuet and Albinia Cecil Longuet-Higgins; *m* 1958, Joan Redmayne Tattersall; two *s* two *d.* *Educ:* Winchester Coll. (Schol.); Trinity Coll., Cambridge (Schol.). (BA). Admiralty Research Lab., Teddington, 1945–48; Res. Student, Cambridge, 1948–51; PhD Cambridge, 1951; Rayleigh Prize, 1951; Commonwealth Fund Fellowship, 1951–52; Res. Fellow, Trinity Coll., Cambridge, 1951–55; Nat. Inst. of Oceanography, 1954–69; Royal Soc. Res. Prof., Univ. of Cambridge, 1969–89. Visiting Professor: MIT, 1958; Institute of Geophysics, University of California, 1961–62; Univ. of Adelaide, 1964; Prof. of Oceanography, Oregon State Univ., 1967–69. Foreign Associate, US Nat. Acad. of Sci., 1979. Hon. DTech Tech. Univ. of Denmark, 1979; Hon. LLD Glasgow, 1979. Sverdrup Gold Medal, Amer. Meteorolog. Soc., 1983; Internat. Coastal Engrg Award, Amer. Soc. of Civil Engineers, 1984; Oceanography Award, Soc. for Underwater Technol., 1990. *Publications:* papers in applied mathematics, esp. physical oceanography, dynamics of sea waves and currents. *Recreations:* music, mathematical toys. *Address:* Gage Farm, Comberton, Cambridge CB3 7DH.

LONGWORTH, Ian Heaps, CBE 1994; PhD; FSA, FSAScot; Keeper of Prehistoric and Romano-British Antiquities, British Museum, 1973–95; *b* 29 Sept. 1935; *yr s* of late Joseph Longworth and Alice (*née* Heaps); *m* 1967, Clare Marian Titford; one *s* one *d.* *Educ:* King Edward VII, Lytham; Peterhouse, Cambridge. Open and Sen. Scholar, Matthew Wren Student, 1957, MA, PhD, Cantab. Temp. Asst Keeper, Nat. Museum of Antiquities of Scotland, 1962–63; Asst Keeper, Dept of British and Medieval Antiquities, Brit. Mus., 1963–69; Asst Keeper, Dept of Prehistoric and Romano-British Antiquities, Brit. Mus., 1969–73. Member: Ancient Monuments Bd for England, 1977–84; Ancient Monuments Adv. Cttee, Historic Buildings and Monuments Commn, 1991–94. Chm., Area Archaeol. Adv. Cttee for NW England, 1978–79. Hon. Sec., Prehistoric Soc., 1966–74, Vice-Pres., 1976–80; Sec., Soc. of Antiquaries of London, 1974–79, Vice-Pres., 1985–89. *Publications:* Yorkshire (Regional Archaeologies Series), 1965; (with G. J. Wainwright) Durrington Walls—excavations 1966–68, 1971; Collared Urns of the Bronze Age in Great Britain and Ireland, 1984; Prehistoric Britain, 1985; (with I. A. Kinnes) Catalogue of the Excavated Prehistoric and Romano-British Material in the Greenwell Collection, 1985; (ed with J. Cherry) Archaeology in Britain since 1945, 1986; (with A. Ellison and V. Rigby) Excavations at Grimes Graves, Norfolk, 1972–76, Fasc. 2, 1988, (*et al.*) Fasc. 3, 1991, Fasc. 4, 1992, Fasc. 5, 1996, Fasc. 6, 2002; articles in various learned jls on topics of prehistory. *Address:* 2 Hurst View Road, South Croydon, Surrey CR2 7AG. *T:* (020) 8688 4960. *Club:* MCC.

LONGWORTH, Peter, CMG 2001; HM Diplomatic Service, retired; High Commissioner, Zimbabwe, 1998–2001; *b* 26 May 1942; *y s* of late Frank Longworth and of Edith E. (*née* Robinson); *m* 1975, Christina Margareta, *d* of late Folke Wallin and Gun Wallin, Växjö. *Educ:* Chislehurst and Sidcup Grammar Sch.; Univ. of Sheffield (BA). Journalist, 1963–74: Labour and Ind. Corresp., Bristol Evening Post, 1964–66; Lobby Corresp., Western Daily Press., 1966–68; Diplomatic Corresp., Westminster Press., 1968–74; joined FCO, 1974; First Secretary: FCO, 1974–77; (Econ.), Bonn, 1977–81; Head of Chancery and HM Consul, Sofia, 1981–84; FCO, 1984–87; Counsellor (Econ. and Commercial), Copenhagen, 1987–91; Dep. Hd of Mission, Counsellor (Econ. and Commercial) and Consul Gen., Seoul, 1991–94; Consul-Gen., Johannesburg, and Dir of UK Trade Promotion and Investment, S Africa, 1994–98. *Club:* Reform.

LONGWORTH, Wilfred Roy, AM 1986; MSc, PhD; FRSC, FRACI; Principal Director (formerly Director), Swinburne Institute of Technology and College of Technical and Further Education, 1970–86, retired; *b* 13 Dec. 1923; *s* of Wilfred Arnold Longworth and Jessie Longworth; *m* 1951, Constance Elizabeth Dean; two *d.* *Educ:* Bolton Sch.; Manchester Univ. (BSc, MSc, PhD). FRIC 1963; FRACI 1970; FACE 1976. Works Manager and Chief Chemist, Blackburn & Oliver, 1948–56; postgrad. res., Univ. of Keele, 1956–59; Lectr in Physical Chemistry, Huddersfield Coll. of Technol., 1959–60; Sen. Lectr in Phys. Chem., Sunderland Technical Coll., 1960–64; Head, Dept of Chem. and Biol., Manchester Polytechnic, 1964–70. Pres., World Council on Co-op. Educn, 1983–85. *Publications:* articles on cationic polymerisation in learned jls. *Recreations:* lawn bowls, gardening. *Address:* Unit 28, Fountain Court Village, 100 Station Street, Burwood, Vic 3125, Australia. *T:* (3) 98080346.

LÖNNGREN, Thomas; Executive Director, European Agency for the Evaluation of Medicinal Products, since 2001; *b* Sweden, 16 Dec. 1950; *m* 1988, Ann-Charlotte Fondelius; one *s* one *d.* *Educ:* Univ. of Uppsala (MSc Social Pharmacy 1976); Stockholm Sch. of Econs (Advanced Course in Health Econ. 1999). Pharmacist, 1976; Lectr, Pharmaceutical Faculty, Uppsala Univ., 1976–78; Sen. Pharmaceutical Officer, Dept of Drugs, Nat. Bd of Health and Welfare, Sweden, 1978–90; Sen. Pharmaceutical Consultant for Swedish health co-operation prog. in Vietnam, 1982–94; Dir of Ops, 1990–98, Dep. Dir Gen., 1998–2000, Med. Products Agency, Sweden. *Address:* EMEA, 7 Westferry Circus, Canary Wharf, E14 4HB. *T:* (020) 7418 8406, *Fax:* (020) 7418 8409; *e-mail:* thomas.lonngren@emea.eudra.org.

LONSDALE, 7th Earl of, *cr* 1807 (UK); **James Hugh William Lowther,** Viscount and Baron Lowther, 1797; Bt 1764; *b* 3 Nov. 1922; *er s* of Anthony Edward, Viscount Lowther (*d* 1949), and Muriel Frances, Viscountess Lowther (*d* 1968), 2nd *d* of late Sir George Farrar, Bt, DSO, and Lady Farrar; *S* grandfather, 1953; *m* 1975, Caroline, *y d* of Sir Gerald Ley, 3rd Bt, TD; one *s* one *d* (and three *s* three *d* of previous marriages). *Educ:* Eton. Armed Forces, 1941–46; RAC and East Riding Yeo. (despatches, Captain). Retired. CIMgt; FRSA 1984. *Heir:* *s* Viscount Lowther, *qv.* *Address:* Askham Hall, Penrith, Cumbria CA10 2PF. *T:* (01931) 712208. *Clubs:* Brooks's, Turf.

LONSDALE, Anne Mary; President, New Hall, Cambridge, since 1996; Pro-Vice-Chancellor, Cambridge University, since 1998; *b* 16 Feb. 1941; *d* of Dr Alexander Menzies and Mabel Menzies; *m* 1st, 1962, Geoffrey Griffin (*d* 1962); 2nd, 1964, Roger Harrison Lonsdale, *qv* (marr. diss. 1994); one *s* one *d.* *Educ:* St Anne's Coll., Oxford (BA Hons Lit. Hum. 1962; BA Hons Chinese (Oriental Studies) 1965; MA 1965). Oxford University: Davis Sen. Schol. and Lectr in Chinese, St Anne's Coll., 1965–74; Univ. Adminr, 1974–90; Dir, External Relations, 1990–93; Sec.-Gen., Central European Univ., Budapest, Prague, and Warsaw, 1994–96. Chairman: Conf. of Univ. Admin, UK and Ireland, 1991–93; Interdisciplinary Envmtl Studies Cttee, 1996–; Jt Chm., Assoc. of Univ. Admin, 1993–94; Member: Commonwealth Scholarships Commn, 1996–; Council of Senate, Cambridge Univ., 1997–. Trustee: Inter-Univ. Foundn, 1988–; Cambridge Commonwealth Trust, 1995–; Cambridge Overseas Trust, 1996–; Cambridge European Trust, 1998–; Newton Trust, 1999–; Moscow Sch. of Social and Econ. Scis, 1999–; Univ. of Silicon Lake, Shanghai, 2000–. Cavaliere, Order of Merit (Italy), 1988. *Recreation:* travelling. *Address:* New Hall, Cambridge CB3 0DF. *T:* (01223) 762201, *Fax:* (01223) 762217.

LONSDALE, Maj.-Gen. Errol Henry Gerrard, CB 1969; MBE 1942; Transport Officer-in-Chief (Army) 1966–69; *b* 26 Feb. 1913; 2nd *s* of Rev. W. H. M. Lonsdale, Arlaw Banks, Barnard Castle; *m* 1944, Muriel Allison, *d* of E. R. Payne, Mugswell, Chipstead; one *s* one *d.* *Educ:* Westminster Sch.; St Catharine's Coll., Cambridge (MA). 2nd Lt, RASC, 1934; Bt Lt-Col 1952; Col 1957; Brig. 1961; Maj.-Gen. 1965. Sudan Defence Force, 1938–43 (despatches); Chief Instr, RASC Officers Trng Centre, 1944–45; AQMG FARELF, 1945–47; CRASC 16 Airborne Div., 1947–48; GSOI, 1948–51; AA & QMG, War Office, 1951–53; Korea, 1953–54; Malaya, 1954–56 (despatches); ACOS, G4 Northern Army Group, 1957–60; DDST, 1st Corps, 1960–62; Comdt RASC Trng Centre, 1962–64; Inspector, RASC, 1964–65; ADC to the Queen, 1964–66; Inspector, RCT, 1965–66; psc; jssc. Col Comdt, RCT, 1969–74. Hon. Colonel: 160 Regt RCT(V), 1967–74; 562 Para Sqdn RCT(V), 1969–78. FCIT (MInstT) 1966. Vice-President: Transport Trust, 1969; Internat. Union for Modern Pentathlon and Biathlon, 1976–80; Pres., Modern Pentathlon Assoc. of Great Britain, 1977–88, Hon. Pres., 1988– (Chm., 1967); Chm., Inst. of Advanced Motorists, 1971–79, Vice-Pres., 1979. *Recreations:* modern pentathlon, photography, driving. *Address:* Windleys, Podgers Lane, Ilton, Ilminster, Somerset TA19 9HE.

LONSDALE, Robert Henry H.; *see* Heywood-Lonsdale.

LONSDALE, Prof. Roger Harrison, DPhil; FBA 1991; Fellow and Tutor in English, Balliol College, Oxford, 1963–2000, now Fellow Emeritus; Professor of English Literature, University of Oxford, 1992–2000; *b* 6 Aug. 1934; *s* of Arthur John Lonsdale and Phebe (*née* Harrison); *m* 1st, 1964, Anne Mary Menzies (*see* A. M. Lonsdale) (marr. diss. 1994); one *s* one *d*; 2nd, 1999, Nicoletta Momigliano. *Educ:* Hymers Coll., Hull; Lincoln Coll., Oxford (BA 1st class Hons 1957); DPhil (Oxon) 1962. National Service, RAF, commnd as Navigator, 1952–54. English Dept, Yale Univ., 1958–60; Oxford University: Bradley Jun. Res. Fellow, Balliol Coll., 1960–63; Reader in English Literature, 1990–92. *Publications:* Dr Charles Burney: a literary biography, 1965; *edited:* The Poems of Gray, Collins and Goldsmith, 1969; Vathek, by William Beckford, 1970; Dryden to Johnson, 1971; The New Oxford Book of Eighteenth-century Verse, 1984; The Poems of John Bampfylde, 1988; Eighteenth-century Women Poets: an Oxford anthology, 1989. *Recreations:* music, book-collecting. *Address:* c/o Balliol College, Oxford OX1 3BJ. *T:* (01865) 277777.

LONZARICH, Prof. Gilbert George, PhD; FRS 1989; Professor of Condensed Matter Physics, since 1997, and Fellow of Trinity College, since 1977, University of Cambridge. *Educ:* Univ. of California (BA); Univ. of Minnesota (MS); PhD British Columbia; MA Cantab 1977. University of Cambridge: Demonstrator, Physics Dept, 1976; Lectr in Physics until 1990; Reader in Physics, 1990–97. *Address:* Department of Physics, Cavendish Laboratory, Madingley Road, Cambridge CB3 0HE. *T:* (01223) 337351; Trinity College, Cambridge CB2 1TQ; 6 Hicks Lane, Girton, Cambridge CB3 0JS. *T:* and *Fax:* (01223) 277570.

LOOP, Bernadine P., (Mrs Floyd Loop); *see* Healy, B. P.

LOOSLEY, Brian; a District Judge (Magistrates' Courts) (formerly Metropolitan Stipendiary Magistrate), since 1989; *b* 20 Dec. 1948; *s* of late Bernard Allan Loosley and of Barbara Clara Randle; *m* 1971, Christine Mary Batt; one *s* one *d.* *Educ:* Sir William Borlase Grammar Sch., Marlow; Leeds Univ. (LLB 1971). Admitted Solicitor 1974; Prosecuting Solicitor, Thames Valley Police, 1975–78; practised privately, 1978–89. *Recreations:* history, foreign travel. *Address:* West London Magistrates' Court, 181 Talgarth Road, W6 8DN. *T:* (020) 8700 9302.

LOPES, family name of **Baron Roborough.**

LOPES CARDOZO KINDERSLEY, Lydia Helena, (Lida); owner, Cardozo Kindersley Workshop, since 1981 (co-owner, 1981–95 and since 1998); *b* 22 July 1954; *d* of Prof. Dr Paul Lopes Cardozo and Ottoline Barones van Hemert tot Dingshof; *m* 1st, 1986, David Kindersley, MBE (*d* 1995); three *s*; 2nd, 1998, Graham F. Beck. *Educ:* Royal Acad. of Fine Arts, Den Haag, Holland. David Kindersley's Workshop: Lettercutter, 1976; Partner, 1981; Founder Editor, Cardozo Kindersley Editions, 1989. Associate Mem., Clare Hall, Cambridge, 1999. Member: Assoc. Typographique Internationale, 1974; Wynkyn de Worde Soc., 1978 (Chm., 1988). Patron, Michaelhouse Project, Cambridge, 1999–. Gov., Impington Village Coll., 1997–2000. *Publications:* Glass & Engraver, 1983; (with David Kindersley) Letters Slate Cut, 1981, 2nd edn 1990; (with R. McKitterick) Lasting Letters, 1992; Oxford Handwriting Practice, 1993; The Cardozo Kindersley Workshop: a guide to commissioning work, 1996; (with Emma Lloyd-Jones) Letters for the Millennium, 1999; (with W. Graham Cannon) Kindersley at Addenbrooke's Hospital, 2000. *Recreations:* letter writing, religion. *Address:* Cardozo Kindersley Workshop, 152 Victoria Road, Cambridge CB4 3DZ. *T:* (01223) 362170. *Club:* Double Crown.

LOPPERT, Max Jeremy; writer; Associate Editor, Opera, 1986–97; *b* Johannesburg, 24 Aug. 1946; *m* 1972, Delayne Aarons. *Educ:* Univ. of Witwatersrand, Johannesburg (BA 1966); Univ. of York (BA Music 1971). Chief Music Critic, FT, 1980–96. Vis. Music Schol., Univ. of Natal, 1998–99. *Publications:* contrib. to: Opera on Record (ed Alan Blyth), 3 vols, 1979, 1983, 1984; The New Grove Dictionary of Music and Musicians, 1980; The New Grove Dictionary of Opera, 1992; Who's Who in Hollywood, 1993. *Recreations:* cinema, cooking, pottery. *Address:* Via Molinetto 12, Refrontolo (TV), 31020, Italy.

LORAINE-SMITH, Nicholas George Edward; Senior Treasury Counsel, Central Criminal Court, since 1999; a Recorder, since 2000; *b* 24 Jan. 1953; *s* of Maj. Bernard Lawson Loraine-Smith, MC, and Rachel Anne Loraine-Smith; *m* 1980, Annabelle Catherine Schicht; two *d.* *Educ:* Eton Coll.; Oriel Coll., Oxford (BA English). Called to the Bar, Inner Temple, 1977; Jun. Treasury Counsel, Central Criminal Court, 1994–99; Asst Recorder, 1997–2000. *Address:* 2 Harcourt Buildings, Temple, EC4Y 9DB. *T:* (020) 7353 2112. *Clubs:* MCC; Chelsea Football.

LORAM, Vice-Adm. Sir David (Anning), KCB 1979; CVO 1994 (LVO 1957); Deputy Supreme Allied Commander Atlantic, 1977–80, retired; Gentleman Usher to The

Queen, 1982–94, Extra Gentleman Usher, since 1994; *b* 24 July 1924; *o* surv. *s* of late Mr and Mrs John A. Loram; *m* 1st, 1958, Fiona Beloe (marr. diss. 1981); three *s*; 2nd, 1983, Diana Keigwin (marr. diss. 1990); 3rd, 1996, Sara Stead-Ellis (*née* Strickland Goodall). *Educ:* Royal Naval Coll., Dartmouth (1938–41). Awarded King's Dirk. Served War: HMS Sheffield, Foresight, Anson, Zealous, 1941–45. ADC to Governor-Gen. of New Zealand, 1946–48; specialised in Signal Communications, 1949; served in HMS Chequers, 1951; Equerry to the Queen, 1954–57; qualified helicopter pilot, 1955; commanded HMS Loch Fada, 1957; Directing Staff, JSSC, 1959–60; served in HMS Belfast, 1961; Naval Attaché, Paris, 1964–67; commanded HMS Arethusa, 1967; Dir, Naval Ops and Trade, 1970–71; commanded HMS Antrim, 1971; ADC to The Queen, 1972–73; Comdr British Forces, FO Malta, and NATO Comdr SE Mediterranean, 1973–75; Comdt, Nat. Defence Coll., 1975–77. Mem., RN Cresta Team, 1954–59. *Recreation:* fishing. *Address:* Grange End House, Oborne, Sherborne, Dorset DT9 4LA. *T:* (01935) 813891. *Club:* Chesapeake.

LORD, Alan, CB 1972; Deputy Chairman and Chief Executive, Lloyd's of London, 1986–92; *b* 12 April 1929; *er s* of Frederick Lord and Anne Lord (*née* Whitworth), Rochdale; *m* 1953, Joan Ogden; two *d*. *Educ:* Rochdale; St John's Coll., Cambridge (BA 1950 (1st Cl. Hons); MA 1987). Entered Inland Revenue, 1950; Private Sec. to Dep. Chm. and to Chm. of the Board, 1952–54; HM Treasury, 1959–62; Principal Private Sec. to First Secretary of State (then Rt Hon. R. A Butler), 1962–63; Comr of Inland Revenue, 1969–73, Dep. Chm. Bd, 1971–73; Principal Finance Officer to DTI, subseq. to Depts of Industry, Trade, and Prices and Consumer Protection, 1973–75; Second Permanent Sec. (Domestic Econ.), HM Treasury, 1975–77. Man. Dir, 1980, Chief Exec., 1982–84, Dunlop Hldgs plc; formerly: Exec. Dir, Dunlop Hldgs; Man. Dir, Dunlop Internat. AG, 1978. Director: Allied-Lyons plc, 1979–86; Bank of England, 1983–86; Johnson Matthey Bankers, 1985–86. Chm., CBI Taxation Cttee, 1979–81. Mem. Council of Management, Henley Centre for Forecasting, 1977–82. Governor, NIESR. Pres., Johnian Soc., 1985–86. *Publications:* A Strategy for Industry (Sir Ellis Hunter Meml Lecture, Univ. of York), 1976; Earning an Industrial Living (1985 Johnian Society Lecture). *Recreations:* reading, gardening, rough-shooting. *Address:* Mardens, Hildenborough, Tonbridge, Kent TN11 8PA. *Club:* Reform.

LORD, Geoffrey, OBE 1989; Founder Trustee, since 1989, and Vice President, since 2000, Adapt Trust (Founder Director, 1989–96); *b* 24 Feb. 1928; *s* of Frank Lord and Edith Lord; *m* 1955, Jean; one *s* one *d*. *Educ:* Rochdale Grammar Sch.; Univ. of Bradford (MA Applied Social Studies). AIB. Midland Bank Ltd, 1946–58; Probation and After-Care Service, 1958–76: Dep. Chief Probation Officer, Greater Manchester, 1974–76; Sec. and Treas., Carnegie UK Trust, 1977–93. Chairman: Unemployed Voluntary Action Fund (Scotland), 1990–95; Pollock Meml Missionary Trust, 1985–; Pres., Centre for Envmtl Interpretation, 1984–97. Member, Scottish Arts Lottery Bd, 1994–98; Council, NYO of Scotland, 1998–. Trustee, Home-Start (formerly Home-Start Consultancy) UK, 1993–98; Sec. and Trustee, Edin. Vol. Orgns' Trusts, 1996–. FRSA 1985. Hon. Fellow, Manchester Metropolitan Univ. (formerly, Manchester Poly.), 1987. *Publication:* The Arts and Disabilities, 1981. *Recreations:* philately, walking, appreciation of the arts. *Address:* 9 Craigleith View, Ravelston, Edinburgh EH4 3JZ. *T:* (0131) 337 7623. *Club:* New (Edinburgh).

LORD, Sir Michael (Nicholson), Kt 2001; MP (C) Central Suffolk and North Ipswich, since 1997 (Suffolk Central, 1983–97); Second Deputy Chairman of Ways and Means and a Deputy Speaker, since 1997; *b* 17 Oct. 1938; *s* of John Lord and Jessie Lord (*née* Nicholson); *m* 1965, Jennifer Margaret (*née* Childs); one *s* one *d*. *Educ:* Christ's College, Cambridge. MA. FArborA. Arboricultural consultant. PPS: to Minister of State, MAFF, 1984–85; to Chief Secretary to the Treasury, 1985–87. Member: Select Cttee on Parly Comr for Admin, 1990–97; Council of Europe, 1987–91; WEU, 1987–91. *Recreations:* golf, sailing, gardening, trees. *Address:* House of Commons, SW1A 0AA.

LORD, Peter Duncan Fraser; Co-founder (with D. Sproxton), owner and Creative Director, Aardman Animations, since 1972; *b* 4 Nov. 1953; *s* of Peter and Margaret Lord; *m* 1976, Karen Jane Bradshaw; two *s* one *d*. *Educ:* Univ. of York (BA 1976). Films directed include: The Amazing Adventures of Morph, 1981–83; Conversation Pieces, 1982–83; Wat's Pig, 1996; Chicken Run, 2000. Hon Dr Design UWE, 1995. Chevalier, Ordre des Arts et des Lettres (France), 2001. *Publication:* Cracking Animation, 1999. *Recreations:* cricket, comic books, walking. *Address:* Aardman Animations, Gas Ferry Road, Bristol BS1 6UN. *T:* (0117) 984 8485. *Clubs:* Soho House, MCC; Babington House (Somerset).

LORD, Peter Herent, OBE 1991; FRCS; Consultant Surgeon, Wycombe General Hospital, High Wycombe, 1964–90; *b* 23 Nov. 1925; *s* of Sir Frank Lord, KBE, JP, DL and Rosalie Jeanette Herent; *m* 1952, Florence Shirley Hirst; two *s* two *d*. *Educ:* Manchester Grammar Sch.; St John's Coll., Cambridge (MA, MChir). St George's Hosp., Salford Royal Hosp., Christie Hosp., Manchester, St Margaret's, Epping, St George's Hosp., 1949–63 (Captain, RAMC, 1952–53). Royal College of Surgeons: H. N. Smith Research Fellow, 1964; Penrose May Teacher, 1970; Mem. Council, 1978–90; Vice-Pres., 1986–88. *Publications:* Cardiac Pacemakers, 1964; Pilonidal Sinus, 1964; Wound Healing, 1966; Haemorrhoids, 1969; Hydrocoele, 1972, Surgery in Old Age, 1980. *Recreations:* sailing, fishing. *Address:* Holly Tree House, 39 Grove Road, Beaconsfield, Bucks HP9 1PE. *T:* (01494) 674488, *Fax:* (01494) 675188; Bucklebury, Solva, Pembs SA62 6TB.

LORD, Stuart; Director, Service Strategy and Commercial Partnerships, Department for Work and Pensions (formerly of Social Security), since 2000; *b* 10 Feb. 1951; *yr s* of William Ughtred Lord and Sybil Lord (*née* Greenhalgh); *m* 1970, Dwynwen Williams; one *s* one *d*. *Educ:* Manchester Grammar Sch.; University Coll. of Swansea (BScEcon Hons). DHSS, later DSS, now Department for Work and Pensions, 1972–; Principal Private Sec. to Sec. of State, 1988–91; Asst Sec. seconded to DoE, 1991; seconded to Prudential Life and Pensions, 1993; Head of Security, Benefits Agency, 1993–94; Head of Planning and Finance Divisions, and Prin. Finance Officer, 1994–98; Head of Transport and Corporate Directorate, Govt Office for London (on secondment), 1998–2000. *Publication:* (contrib.) Economics of Unemployment, 1981. *Recreations:* holidays and other family time, observing the technological advances in consumer electronics. *Address:* Service Strategy and Commercial Partnerships, Department for Work and Pensions, The Adelphi, 1–11 John Adam Street, WC2N 6HT.

LORD, William Burton Housley, CB 1979; scientist; *b* 22 March 1919; *s* of Arthur James Lord and Elsie Lord (*née* Housley); *m* 1942, Helena Headon Jaques; two *d*. *Educ:* King George V Sch., Southport; Manchester Univ.; London Univ. (External MSc); Trinity Coll., Cambridge (MA). Enlisted Royal Fusiliers, commn S Lancs Regt (served Middle East and N Africa), 1941–46. Cambridge Univ., 1946. Entered Civil Service, 1949; joined Atomic Weapons Res. Estab., 1952; Head of Metallurgy Div., AWRE, 1958; moved to MoD, 1964; Asst Chief Scientific Adviser (Research), 1965; Dep. Chief Scientist (Army), 1968–71; Dir Gen., Establishments, Resources and Programmes (B), MoD, 1971–76; Dir, RARDE, 1976–79. Award for wartime invention of radio proximity fuse, 1952. *Recreations:* amateur radio, hill-walking, swimming. *Address:* c/o Barclays Bank, 2 Victoria Street, SW1H 0ND.

LOREN, Sophia; film actress; *b* 20 Sept. 1934; *d* of Ricardo Scicolone and Romilda Villani; *m* 1957, Carlo Ponti, film producer (marriage annulled in Juarez, Mexico, Sept. 1962; marriage in Paris, France, April 1966); two *s*. *Educ:* parochial sch. and Teachers' Institute, Naples. First leading role in, Africa sotto i Mari, 1952; acted in many Italian films, 1952–55; subsequent films include: The Pride and the Passion, Boy on a Dolphin, Legend of the Lost, 1957; The Key, Desire under the Elms, Houseboat, 1958; The Black Orchid (Venice Film Festival Award, 1958), That Kind of Woman, 1959; It Started in Naples, Heller in Pink Tights, The Millionairess, A Breath of Scandal, 1960; Two Women (Cannes Film Festival Award, 1961), Madame sans Gêne, El Cid, 1961; Boccaccio 70, 1962; Five Miles to Midnight, 1963; Yesterday, Today and Tomorrow, The Fall of the Roman Empire, Marriage, Italian Style, 1964; Operation Crossbow, Lady L, 1965; Judith, Arabesque, 1996; A Countess from Hong Kong, 1967; Sunflower, 1970; The Priest's Wife, 1971; Man of La Mancha, 1972; The Voyage, 1973; The Verdict, 1974; A Special Day, 1977; Firepower, Blood Feud, 1979; Running Away, 1989; Saturday, Sunday and Monday, 1990; Prêt-à-Porter. Chevalier, Legion of Honour (France), 1991. *Publications:* Eat with Me, 1972; Sophia Loren on Woman and Beauty, 1984; *relevant publication:* Sophia: living and loving, by A. E. Hotcher, 1979. *Address:* Case Postale 430, 1211 Geneva 12, Switzerland.

LORENZ, Andrew Peter Morrice; Business Editor, The Sunday Times, since 1995; *b* 22 June 1955; *s* of Hans Viktor Lorenz and Catherine Jesse Cairns Lorenz (*née* James); *m* 1988, Helen Marianne Alway; two *s*. *Educ:* Stamford Sch., Lincs; Worcester Coll., Oxford (MA Mod. Hist.). The Journal, Newcastle: News Reporter, 1978–80; Educn Correspondent, 1980–81; Industrial Correspondent, 1981–82; Business Correspondent, The Scotsman, 1982–86; City Correspondent, 1986–88, Dep. City Editor, 1988–89, Sunday Telegraph; Industrial Editor, Sunday Times, 1989–95. Business Journalist of the Year, UK Press Awards, 1999; Business Journalist of the Year, Corp. of London, 2000. *Publications:* A Fighting Chance: British manufacturing industry in the 1980s, 1989; BZW: the first ten years, 1996; The Powerhouse: the story of Warwick Manufacturing Group, 2001. *Recreations:* film, music, sport. *Address:* Redwood House, Queen Anne's Road, Windsor SL4 2BJ.

LORIMER, Prof. (Andrew) Ross, MD; FRCP, FRCPE, FRCPGlas, FMedSci; President, Royal College of Physicians and Surgeons of Glasgow, since 2000; *b* 5 May 1937; *s* of James Lorimer and Katherine Lorimer (*née* Ross); *m* 1963, Fiona Marshall; three *s*. *Educ:* Uddingston Grammar Sch.; High Sch. of Glasgow; Univ. of Glasgow (MD Hons 1976). FRCPGlas 1972; FRCP 1978; FRCPE 1981; FFPHM. Res. Fellow in Medicine, Vanderbilt Univ., Nashville, 1961–63; Registrar in Medicine, Royal Infirmary, Glasgow; Lectr in Cardiol., Glasgow Univ., 1966–71; Consultant Cardiologist, Royal Infirmary, Glasgow, 1971–91; Hon. Prof. of Medicine, Glasgow Univ., 1991–2001. FMedSci 1998. *Publication:* Preventive Cardiology, 1988. *Recreations:* golf, cricket, hill-walking. *Address:* 6 Homeston Avenue, Bothwell, Glasgow G71 8PL. *T:* (01698) 852156.

LORIMER, Sir Desmond; *see* Lorimer, Sir T. D.

LORIMER, Prof. George Huntly, FRS 1986; Professor, Department of Chemistry and Biochemistry, University of Maryland, since 1998; *b* 14 Oct. 1942; *s* of late Gordon and Ellen Lorimer; *m* 1970, Freia (*née* Schulz-Baldes); one *s* one *d*. *Educ:* George Watson's College, Edinburgh; Univ. of St Andrews (BSc); Univ. of Illinois (MS); Michigan State Univ. (PhD). Scientist, Max-Planck Society, Berlin, 1972–74; Research Fellow, Inst. for Advanced Studies, ANU, Canberra, 1974–77; Scientist, Society for Radiation and Environmental Research, Munich, 1977; Prin. Investigator, then Res. Leader, E. I. Du Pont de Nemours & Co., 1978–91; Dupont Fellow, Central Res. Dept, Dupont Co., Delaware, 1991–97. Adjunct Prof., Dept of Biochemistry, Univ. of Pennsylvania, 1992. Member: Amer. Soc. of Biochemistry and Molecular Biology; NAS, USA, 1997. Editor, Biochimica et Biophysica Acta, 1995; Mem Editl Bd, Jl of Biol Chem., 1998. Res. Award, Alexander von Humboldt Foundn, 1997. *Publications:* contribs to Biochemistry, Jl of Biological Chemistry, Nature, Science. *Recreations:* music, political history. *Address:* 7705 Lake Glen Drive, Glenn Dale, MD 20769–2028, USA. *T:* (home) (301) 3523679, (office) (301) 4051828, *Fax:* (home) (301) 3525539, (office) (301) 3149121; *e-mail:* GL48@umail.umd.edu.

LORIMER, Ross; *see* Lorimer, A. R.

LORIMER, Sir (Thomas) Desmond, Kt 1976; Chairman, Northern Bank Ltd, 1986–97 (Director, 1983–97; Deputy Chairman, 1985); *b* 20 Oct. 1925; *s* of Thomas Berry Lorimer and Sarah Ann Lorimer; *m* 1957, Patricia Doris Samways; two *d*. *Educ:* Belfast Technical High Sch. Chartered Accountant, 1948; Fellow, Inst. of Chartered Accountants in Ireland, 1957. Practised as chartered accountant, 1952–74; Sen. Partner, Harmood, Banner, Smylie & Co., Belfast, Chartered Accountants, 1960–74; Chairman: Lamont Holdings PLC, 1973–96; Northern Ireland Electricity, 1991–94; Dir, Irish Distillers PLC, 1986–98. Chm., Industrial Develt Bd for NI, 1982–85; Pres., Inst. of Chartered Accountants in Ireland, 1968–69; Chairman: Ulster Soc. of Chartered Accountants, 1960; NI Housing Exec., 1971–75; Mem., Rev. Body on Local Govt in NI, 1970. *Recreations:* gardening and golf. *Address:* Windwhistle Cottage, 6A Circular Road West, Cultra, Holywood, Co. Down BT18 0AT. *T:* (028) 9042 3323. *Clubs:* Royal Belfast Golf, Royal Co. Down Golf (Co. Down).

LOSINSKA, Kathleen Mary, (Kate), OBE 1986; Senior Vice-President, Civil and Public Services Association, 1986–88 (President, 1979–82 and 1983–86, a Vice-President, 1982–83); *b* Croydon, Surrey, 5 Oct. 1924; *d* of late James Henry Conway, Border Regt and Dorothea Marguerite Hill; *m* 1942, Stanislaw Losinski (formerly serving Officer, Polish Air Force, subseq. 301 Bomber Sqdn, RAF, retd with rank of Sqdn Leader; awarded Polish Virtuti Militari Cross, Croix de Guerre, Cross of Lorraine, Yugoslav Cross of Valour, etc); one *s*. *Educ:* Selhurst Grammar Sch., Croydon (matriculation); university of life generally. Entered Civil Service, 1939; with Office of Population Censuses and Surveys. Delegate Mem., Council of Civil Service Unions, 1970–87 (Chm. 1980–81); Vice-Chm., CS Retirement Fellowship, 1988–; Management Cttee, CS Benevolent Fund, 1991–. Commissioner: Trade Union TUC Nuclear Energy Review; CS Appeals Bd, 1988. Founder Mem. and Vice-Chm., Trade Union Cttee for European and Transatlantic Understanding. Chairman: White Eagle Trust, 1985; Solidarnosc Foundn. Has held all honorary positions, CPSA. Founder Mem., Resistance Internat., 1983. Governor, Ruskin Coll., 1976, 1979–86. Silver Jubilee Medal, 1977. Kt Comdr, Order of Polonia Restituta, 1987. *Recreations:* journalism, reading, music, history, travel; work for the Christian Trade Union and Moderate Trade Union Movements. *Address:* Loretto, Baggottstown West, Bruff, Co. Limerick, Ireland. *T:* (61) 382225. *Club:* Civil Service.

LOSOWSKY, Prof. Monty Seymour, FRCP; Professor of Medicine and Head of University Department of Medicine, St James's University Hospital, Leeds, 1969–96, now Emeritus Professor; *b* 1 Aug. 1931; *s* of Dora and Myer Losowsky; *m* 1971, Barbara Malkin; one *s* one *d*. *Educ:* Coopers' Company's Sch., London; Univ. of Leeds (Hons MB, ChB; MD). House appts, Leeds Gen. Infirmary, 1955–56; Registrar in Medicine, Epping, 1957–59; Asst, Externe Hôpital St Antoine, Paris, 1960; Research Fellow, Harvard Med.

Unit, 1961–62; Lectr, Sen. Lectr, Reader in Medicine, 1962–69, Dean, Faculty of Medicine, 1989–94, Univ. of Leeds. Member: Leeds Eastern Health Authy, 1981–89; Specialist Adv. Cttee on General (Internal) Medicine, 1984–88; Systems Bd Grants Cttee B, MRC, 1984–88; Panel of Studies Allied to Medicine, UGC, 1982–89; British Digestive Foundn Sci. and Res. Awards Cttee, 1987–90; Yorks RHA, 1989–90; Working Gp, France Steering Gp on Undergrad. Medical and Dental Educn, DoH, 1990–94; Council, British Nutrition Foundn, 1991– (Mem. Scientific Adv. Cttee, 1987–91; Scientific Governor, 1991–); GMC, 1991–96; CVCP Rep., Acad. and Res. Staff Cttee of DoH Jt Planning and Adv. Cttee, 1990–94 (Mem., General Purposes Working Gp, 1989–94); Chm., Other Studies and Professions Allied to Medicine Panel, HEFCE, 1995–97. Lectures: Watson Smith, RCPE, 1995; Simms, RCP, 1996. Pres., British Soc. of Gastroenterol., 1993–94. Chm., Coeliac Trust, 1983–95; Governor: Coeliac Soc., 1995– (Chm., Med. Adv. Council, 1995–); British Liver Trust, 1999– (Chm., Med. Adv. Cttee, 1999–). Examr for Membership, RCP, 1982–96; Academic Observer and Ext. Examr, Utd Examining Bd, 1994–96. Trustee, Thackray Med. Mus., 1995–. Gov., Leeds GS, 1988– (Chm., 2000–). *Publications:* (jtly) Malabsorption in Clinical Practice, 1974; (ed) The Gut and Systemic Disease, 1983; (ed jtly) Advanced Medicine, 1983; (jtly) The Liver and Biliary System, 1984; (jtly) Clinical Nutrition in Gastroenterology, 1986; (jtly) Gut Defences in Clinical Practice, 1986; (jtly) Gastroenterology, 1988; Consensus in Clinical Nutrition, 1994; papers relating to hepatology and gastroenterology. *Recreations:* golf, watching cricket, walking, DIY, medical biography. *Address:* Southview, Ling Lane, Scarcroft, Leeds LS14 3HT. *T:* (0113) 289 2699. *Club:* Royal Society of Medicine.

LOSTY, Howard Harold Walter, FREng, FIEE; Secretary, Institution of Electrical Engineers, 1980–89; *b* 1 Aug. 1926; *s* of Patrick J. Losty and Edith E. Wilson; *m* 1950, Rosemary L. Everritt; two *d. Educ:* Harvey Grammar Sch, Folkestone; Sir John Cass Coll., London. BSc. GEC Research Laboratories, 1942–53; GEC Nuclear Power Programme, 1953–66; Head of Engineering Div., GEC Research Centre, 1966–71; Dir, GEC Hirst Research Centre, 1971–77; Man. Dir, GEC Electronic Devices Ltd, 1977–80. Hon. DEng Bradford, 1986. *Publications:* (co-author) Nuclear Graphite, 1962; some forty technical papers. *Recreations:* walking, listening to music (opera), reading history. *Address:* Shandon, 14 Wyatts Road, Chorleywood, Herts WD3 5TE. *T:* (01923) 283568.

LOTEN, Alexander William, CB 1984; FCIBSE; Under Secretary, Department of the Environment, and Director, Mechanical and Electrical Engineering Services, Property Services Agency, 1981–85, retired; *b* 11 Dec. 1925; *s* of late Alec Oliver Loten and Alice Maud Loten; *m* 1954, Mary Diana Flint; one *s* one *d. Educ:* Churcher's Coll., Petersfield; Corpus Christi Coll., Cambridge Univ. (BA). CEng, FIMechE 1980; FCIBSE 1970. Served War, RNVR, 1943–46 (Air Engr Officer). Engineer: Rolls-Royce Ltd, Derby, 1950–54; Benham & Sons, London, 1954–58; Air Min. Work Directorate, 1958–64; Sen. Engr, 1964–70, Superintending Engr (Mechanical Design), 1970–75, MPBW; Dir of Works, Civil Accommodation, PSA, 1975–81. Pres., CIBS, 1976–77. Lt-Col, Engr and Railway Staff Corps RE, T&AVR, 1979–97. *Recreations:* walking, gardening, bridge. *Address:* Hockridge House, London Road, Maresfield, E Sussex TN22 2EH.

LOTEN, Graeme Neil; HM Diplomatic Service; Ambassador to Mali, since 2001; *b* 10 March 1959; *s* of Richard Maurice Loten and Brenda Ivy Elizabeth Loten. *Educ:* Portsmouth Grammar Sch.; Liverpool Univ. (BA). Entered Diplomatic Service, 1981; Private Sec. to Ambassador to NATO, 1983–86; Third Sec., Khartoum, 1986–87; Second Sec., The Hague, 1988–92; Dep. Head of Mission, Almaty, 1993–97; Ambassador to Rwanda and (non-resident) to Burundi, 1998–2001. *Recreations:* travel, tennis, rabbit breeding. *Address:* c/o Foreign and Commonwealth Office, SW1A 2AH. *Club:* Royal Commonwealth Society.

LOTHIAN, 12th Marquess of, *cr* 1701; **Peter Francis Walter Kerr,** KCVO 1983; DL; Lord Newbattle, 1591; Earl of Lothian, 1606; Baron Jedburgh, 1622; Earl of Ancram, Baron Kerr of Nisbet, Baron Long-Newton and Dolphingston, 1633; Viscount of Brien, Baron Kerr of Newbattle, 1701; Baron Ker (UK), 1821; Lord Warden of the Stannaries and Keeper of the Privy Seal of the Duke of Cornwall, 1977–83; *b* 8 Sept. 1922; *s* of late Captain Andrew William Kerr, RN, and Marie Constance Annabel, *d* of Capt. William Walter Raleigh Kerr; *S* cousin, 1940; *m* 1943, Antonella (OBE 1997), *d* of late Maj.-Gen. Sir Foster Newland, KCMG, CB, and Donna Agnese Carr; two *s* four *d. Educ:* Ampleforth; Christ Church, Oxford. Lieut, Scots Guards, 1943. Mem. Brit. Delegation: UN Gen. Assembly, 1956–57; European Parliament, 1973; UK Delegate, Council of Europe and WEU, 1959. PPS to Foreign Sec., 1960–63; a Lord in Waiting (Govt Whip, House of Lords), 1962–63, 1972–73; Joint Parliamentary Sec., Min. of Health, April-Oct. 1964; Parly Under-Sec. of State, FCO, 1970–72. Chm., Scottish Council, British Red Cross Soc., 1976–86. Mem., Queen's Body Guard for Scotland (Royal Company of Archers). Mem., Prince of Wales Council, 1976–83. DL, Roxburgh, 1962. Kt, SMO Malta. *Heir: s* Earl of Ancram, *qv. Address:* Ferniehirst Castle, Jedburgh, Roxburghshire TD8 6NX. *T:* (01835) 864021; 177 Cranmer Court, Whiteheads Grove, SW3 3HF. *Clubs:* Boodle's; New (Edinburgh).

See also Col Sir D. H. Cameron of Lochiel, Earl of Dalkeith, Earl of Euston.

LOTHIAN, Prof. Niall; Professor, Graduate Business School, Heriot-Watt University, since 1996; President, Institute of Chartered Accountants of Scotland, 1995–96; *b* 27 Feb. 1948; *s* of Revd Thomas Lothian and Jean Morgan Lothian (*née* Henderson); *m* 1971, Carol Miller; one *s* one *d. Educ:* Daniel Stewart's Coll.; Heriot-Watt Univ. (BA 1971). CA 1972. Lectr, Sen. Lectr, 1973–88, Prof. of Accounting, 1988–96, Director, 1991–93, Business School, Heriot-Watt Univ. Visiting Professor: IMEDE, Lausanne, 1979–80; Univ. of Witwatersrand, 1984; Mem., internat. vis. faculty, INSEAD, Fontainebleau, 1984–; Consultant: UNIDO, China, 1980; NZ Soc. of Accountants, 1992. Mem., Internat. Exec. Adv. Bd, Coll. of Finance and Accountancy, Budapest; Gov., George Watson's Coll., 1991– (Chm., 1999–). Non-exec. Dir, Stoddard Internat. plc, 1998–. Trustee, Lloyds TSB Charitable Foundn for Scotland, 1997–99. FRSA. *Publications:* How Companies Manage R&D, 1984; Measuring Corporate Performance, 1987; (jtly) Accounting, 1991; (contrib.) Ernst and Young Manager's Handbook, 2nd edn 1992; articles in professional jls. *Recreations:* graveyards, golf. *Address:* 30 Granby Road, Edinburgh EH16 5NL. *T:* (0131) 667 4429. *Clubs:* New (Edinburgh); Royal & Ancient Golf; Luffness New Golf.

LOTON, Brian Thorley, AC 1989; FTS; Chairman: Broken Hill Proprietary Co. Ltd, 1992–97; Atlas Copco Australia Pty Ltd, 1996–2001; Director, Australian Foundation Investment Co. Ltd, since 1993; *b* Perth, WA, 17 May 1929; *s* of Sir (Ernest) Thorley Loton and Grace (*née* Smith); *m* 1956, Joan Kemelfield; two *s* two *d. Educ:* Hale Sch., Perth; Trinity Coll., Melbourne Univ. (BMetEng 1953). Joined BHP as Cadet 1954; Technical Asst, 1959; Asst Chief Engr, 1961; Gen. Manager Planning and Develt, 1969, Gen. Manager Newcastle Steel Works, 1970; Exec. Gen. Manager Steel Div., 1973; Dir, 1976; Chief Gen. Manager, 1977; Man. Dir, 1982; Chief Exec. Officer, 1984, Dep. Chm., 1991. Director: Nat. Australia Bank, 1988–99 (Vice Chm., 1992–99); Amcor Ltd, 1992–99. President: Aust. Inst. of Mining and Metallurgy, 1982 (Mem. Council); Australian Mining Industry Council, 1983–84; Business Council of Aust., 1990–92; Vice-Chairman: Internat. Iron and Steel Inst., 1988, 1992–94 (Chm., 1991–92); Defence Industry Cttee, 1976–88; Member: Aust. Sci. and Technol. Council, 1977–80; Aust. Manufg Council, 1977–81; Vict. Govt Long Range Policy Planning Cttee, 1980–82; Aust. Council on Population and Ethnic Affairs, 1980–82. Internat. Counsellor, The Conf. Bd, 1984–. Pres., Vic. Br., Scout Assoc. of Australia, 1997–99. Mem. Faculty Engrg, Melbourne Univ., 1980–83. FIE (Aust) 1984 (Hon. Fellow); FAIM 1973; FIDA 1980. *Address:* c/o GPO Box 86A, Melbourne, Vic 3001, Australia. *Clubs:* Melbourne, Australian (Melbourne).

LOTT, (Chester) Trent, JD; US Senator from Mississippi, since 1989; *b* 9 Oct. 1941; *s* of Chester P. Lott and Iona Lott (*née* Watson); *m* 1964, Patricia E. Thompson; one *s* one *d. Educ:* Univ. of Mississippi (BPA 1963; JD 1967). Admitted to Mississippi Bar, 1967; Associate, Bryan & Gordon, 1967; Admin. Asst to Congressman William M. Colmer, 1968–72; Mem., US Congress, 1973–89; Leader, US Senate, 1996–2001. Mem., Senate Republican Policy Cttee. *Address:* Russell Senate Office Building, Washington, DC 20510, USA.

LOTT, Dame Felicity (Ann Emwhyla), DBE 1996 (CBE 1990); soprano; *b* 8 May 1947; *d* of John Albert Lott and Whyla (*née* Williams); *m* 1st, 1973, Robin Mavesyn Golding (marr. diss. 1982); 2nd, 1984, Gabriel Woolf; one *d. Educ:* Pate's Grammar Sch. for Girls, Cheltenham; Royal Holloway Coll., Univ. of London (BA Hons French; Hon. Fellow, 1995); Royal Acad. of Music (LRAM; ARAM 1976; FRAM 1986). Début: ENO, 1975; Covent Garden, 1976; Glyndebourne, 1977. Particularly associated with Mozart and Richard Strauss, whose operas she has sung in Glyndebourne, Covent Garden, Cologne, Hamburg, Brussels, Paris, Vienna, Munich, Dresden, Milan, NY, Chicago and Japan; gives recitals worldwide; many recordings. Founder Mem., The Songmakers' Almanac. Dr *hc* Sussex, 1989; Hon. DLitt Loughborough, 1996; Hon. DMus: London, 1997; RSAMD 1998; Leicester, 2000; Oxford, 2001. Officier, Ordre des Arts et des Lettres (France), 2000 (Chevalier, 1993). *Recreations:* reading, annoying the family, singing. *Address:* c/o Askonas Holt Ltd, Lonsdale Chambers, 27 Chancery Lane, WC2A 1PF. *T:* (020) 7400 1700.

LOTT, Trent; *see* Lott, C. T.

LOTZ, Prof. Dr Kurt; German business executive; *b* 18 Sept. 1912; *m* Elizabeth Lony; two *s* one *d. Educ:* August-Vilmar-Schule, Homberg. Joined Police Service, 1932; Lieut 1934. Served Luftwaffe (Gen. Staff; Major), 1942–45. Employed by Brown Boveri & Cie, Dortmund, 1946; Head of Business Div., Mannheim, 1954; Dir 1957; Chm. 1958–67; Mem. Board of Directors in parent company, Baden, Switzerland, 1961; Managing Director, 1963–67. Dep. Chm., 1967–68, Chm., 1968–71, Volkswagenwerk AG. Chm., Deutscher Rat für Landespflege, 1984–91 (Mem., 1973; Hon. Mem., 1991); Founder Chm., 1984–97, Hon. Chm., 1997, WWF, World Wildlife Fund, Germany. Mem., Rotary Internat. Mem., Stiftung Univ., Heidelberg; Hon. Senator, Heidelberg Univ., 1963; Hon. Prof., Technische Universität Carolo Wilhelmina, Brunswick, 1970. Dr rer. pol. *hc* Mannheim, 1963. *Publication:* Lebenserfahrungen: Worüber man in Wirtschaft und Politik auch sprechen sollte, 1978.

LOUDEN, Rt Rev. Mgr Stephen Henry, PhD; Research Associate, Centre for Theology and Education, University of Wales, Bangor; *b* 18 Nov. 1941; *s* of late Joseph Henry Louden and Sarah (*née* McNaughten). *Educ:* Upholland Coll. BA Open 1975; DipTh CNAA 1991; MTh Oxon 1993; PhD Wales 1998. Ordained priest, dio. Liverpool, 1968; Curate: All Saints, Anfield, 1968–73; St John's, Kirkdale, 1973–75; Our Lady's, Formby, 1975–78; Royal Army Chaplains' Department: TA Commn, 1973–78; Regular Army Commn, 1978; Dortmund Garrison, 1978–79; 8 Inf. Bde, 1979–80; Munster Garrison, 1980–82; Dhekelia Garrison, 1982–84; RC Chaplain, RMA Sandhurst, 1984–86; Berlin Inf. Bde, 1986–88; HQ NI, 1988; Hong Kong, 1988–90; Senior Chaplain RC: HQ BAOR, 1990–92; HQ NI, 1992–93; Principal RC Chaplain and VG (Army), 1993–97. Prelate of Honour, 1993. *Publications:* Chaplains in Conflict, 1996; contrib. to learned jls. *Recreations:* horology, photography, history. *Address:* Wesley House, Jesus Lane, Cambridge CB5 8BJ. *Club:* Army and Navy.

LOUDON, George Ernest; Chairman, Helix Associates Ltd, since 1993; *b* 19 Nov. 1942; *m* 1968, Angela Mary Goldsbrough; one *s* one *d. Educ:* Christelijk Lyceum, Zeist; Balliol Coll., Oxford (BA); Johns Hopkins Univ., Washington (MA). Lazard Frères & Cie, Paris, 1967–68; Ford Foundn, New York and Jakarta, 1968–71; McKinsey & Co., Amsterdam, 1971–76; Amro Bank, Amsterdam: Gen. Man., 1976–83; Mem., Bd of Man. Dirs, 1983–88; Dir, Midland Group, 1988–92; Chief Exec., 1988–92, Chm., 1991–92, Midland Montagu. Dir, M&G Group, 1993–94; non-executive Director: Arjo-Wiggins Appleton, 1993–2000; Harrison/Parrott Ltd, 1993–; Global Asset Management, 1994–99; CMG plc, 1998–. Trustee, Tate Foundn, 1992–. *Address:* Suite B, Bristol House, 67 Lower Sloane Street, SW1W 8DD.

LOUDON, John Duncan Ott, OBE 1988; FRCSE, FRCOG; retired; Consultant Obstetrician and Gynaecologist, Eastern General Hospital, Edinburgh, 1960–87; Senior Lecturer, University of Edinburgh, 1962–93; *b* 22 Aug. 1924; *s* of late James Alexander Law Loudon and Ursula (*née* Ott); *m* 1953, Nancy Beaton (*née* Mann); two *s. Educ:* John Watson's Sch., Edinburgh; Wyggeston Sch., Leicester; Univ. of Edinburgh (MB, ChB 1947). FRCSE 1954; FRCOG 1973 (MRCOG 1956). National Service, RAF, 1948–50. House appts, Edinburgh and Cambridge, 1948–52; Registrar, Sen. Registrar and Consultant Obstetrician and Gynaecologist, Simpson Maternity Pavilion and Royal Infirm., Edinburgh, 1954–66. Formerly Examiner in Obstetrics and Gynaecology: Univs of Cardiff, Manchester, Leeds, Dundee, Glasgow, Aberdeen, Newcastle upon Tyne, Cape Town, RCSI, RCSE, RCOG and RACOG. Adviser in Family Welfare to Govt of Malta, 1976–81. Vice Pres., RCOG, 1981–84 (Mem. Council, 1966–72 and 1976–81). Member: Interim Licensing Authority for IVF, 1985–91; GMC, 1986–92. *Publications:* papers to obstetric and gynaecol jls. *Recreations:* gardening, golf, travel, food and wine. *Address:* Ardbeg, 4 Kinnear Road, Edinburgh EH3 5PE. *T:* (0131) 552 1327. *Clubs:* Royal Air Force; Bruntsfield Links Golfing Society (Edinburgh).

LOUDON, Prof. Rodney, FRS 1987; Professor of Physics, Essex University, since 1967; *b* 25 July 1934; *s* of Albert Loudon and Doris Helen (*née* Blane); *m* 1960, Mary Anne Philips; one *s* one *d. Educ:* Bury Grammar Sch.; Brasenose Coll., Oxford (MA, DPhil). Postdoctoral Fellow, Univ. of California, Berkeley, 1959–60; Scientific Civil Servant, RRE Malvern, 1960–65; Member, Technical Staff: Bell Labs, Murray Hill, NJ, 1965–66, 1970; RCA Labs, Zurich, 1975; Essex University: Reader in Physics, 1966–67; Dean of Sch. of Physical Scis, 1972–74; Chm. of Physics Dept, 1976–79 and 1988–89. Visiting Professor: Yale Univ., 1975; Univ. of California, Irvine, 1980; Ecole Polytechnique, Lausanne, 1985; Univ. of Rome, 1988 and 1996; Chm., Bd of Editors of Optica Acta, 1984–87. Fellow, Optical Soc. of America, 1994. Thomas Young Medal and Prize, Inst. of Physics, 1987; Max Born Award, Optical Soc. of Amer., 1992; Alexander von Humboldt Prize, 1998. *Publications:* The Quantum Theory of Light, 1973, 3rd edn 2000; (with W. Hayes) Scattering of Light by Crystals, 1978; (ed with V. M. Agranovich) Surface Excitations, 1984; (with D. J. Barber) An Introduction to the Properties of

Condensed Matter, 1989; papers in Nature, Phys. Rev., JL Mod. Opt., Jl Phys., etc. *Recreation:* music, particularly choral singing. *Address:* 3 Gaston Street, East Bergholt, Colchester, Essex CO7 6SD. *T:* (01206) 298550.

LOUDOUN, Countess of (13th in line) *cr* 1633; **Barbara Huddleston Abney-Hastings;** Lady Campbell Baroness of Loudoun, 1601; Lady Tarrinzean and Mauchline, 1638; the 3 English baronies of Botreaux 1368, Stanley 1456, and Hastings 1461, which were held by the late Countess, are abeyant, the Countess being a *co-heiress* (with her sister, nephew and nieces); *b* 3 July 1919; assumed by deed poll, 1955, the surname of Abney-Hastings in lieu of that of Griffiths; *S* mother, 1960; *m* 1st, 1939 (marr. diss., 1945), Capt. Walter Strickland Lord; one *s*; 2nd, 1945, Capt. Gilbert Frederick Greenwood (*d* 1951); one *s* one *d*; 3rd, 1954, Peter Griffiths (who assumed by deed poll the surname of Abney-Hastings in lieu of his patronymic, 1958); three *d*. *Heir: s* Lord Mauchline, *qv*. *Address:* Mount Walk, Ashby-de-la-Zouch, Leics LE65 1BG. *T:* (01530) 415844.

LOUGHBOROUGH, Lord; Jamie William St Clair-Erskine; *b* 28 May 1986; *s* and *heir* of Earl of Rosslyn, *qv*.

LOUGHBOROUGH, Archdeacon of; *see* Stanes, Ven. I. T.

LOUGHEED, Hon. (Edgar) Peter, CC 1987; PC (Can.) 1982; QC (Can.) 1972; Counsel, Bennett Jones, barristers and solicitors, Calgary and Edmonton; *b* Calgary, 26 July 1928; *s* of late Edgar Donald Lougheed and Edna Bauld; *m* 1952, Jeanne Estelle Rogers, Edmonton; two *s* two *d*. *Educ:* public and secondary schs, Calgary; Univ. of Alberta (BA, LLB); Harvard Grad. Sch. of Business (MBA). Read law with Calgary firm of lawyers; called to Bar of Alberta, 1955, and practised law with same firm, 1955–56. Joined Mannix Co. Ltd, as Sec., 1956 (Gen. Counsel, 1958, Vice-Pres., 1959, Dir, 1960). Entered private legal practice, 1962. Chairman: Luscar Ltd; Quorum Funding Corp.; Director: Princeton Developments; Aon Reed Stenhouse Cos Ltd; Bechtel Canada Inc.; Canadian Hunter Exploration Ltd. Elected: Provincial Leader of Progressive Conservative Party of Alberta, also Member for Calgary West, 1965; Leader of the Official Opposition, 1967; Premier of Alberta, 1971–85 (re-elected 1975, 1979 and 1982). Mem., Trilateral Commn. Chancellor, Queen's Univ., Ontario, 1996–. Hon. LLD: St Francis Xavier, 1983; Alberta, 1986; Calgary, 1986; Windsor, Lethbridge, 1988; Dalhousie, 1995; Queen's, 1996; Toronto, 1997. *Recreations:* golf, ski-ing. *Address:* (office) 4500 Bankers Hall East, 855 2nd Street SW, Calgary, AB T2P 4K7, Canada.

LOUGHRAN, James; Chief Conductor, Aarhus Symphony Orchestra, Denmark, since 1996; *b* 30 June 1931; *s* of James and Agnes Loughran; *m* 1st, 1961, Nancy Coggon (marr. diss. 1983; she *d* 1996); two *s*; 2nd, 1985, Ludmila (*née* Navratil). *Educ:* St Aloysius' Coll., Glasgow; Bonn, Amsterdam and Milan. FRNCM 1976; FRSAMD 1983. 1st Prize, Philharmonia Orchestra's Conducting Competition, 1961. Associate Conductor, Bournemouth Symphony Orchestra, 1962–65; Principal Conductor: BBC Scottish Symphony Orchestra, 1965–71; Bamberg Symphony Orchestra, 1979–83; Prin. Conductor and Musical Advr, 1971–83, Conductor Laureate, 1983–91, Hallé Orchestra; Musical Dir, English Opera Gp, 1966 (Festivals of Drottningholm, Versailles and Aldeburgh). Guest conductor of principal orchestras of Europe, America, Australasia and Japan; Permanent Guest Conductor, Japan Philharmonic Symphony Orch., 1993–. Internat. festivals and tours with Bamberg and Hallé orchestras, as well as Munich Philharmonic, BBC Symphony, Stockholm Philharmonic, London Philharmonic and Scottish Chamber orchestras. Many recordings, including complete Beethoven and Brahms symphonies. Gold Disc, EMI, 1983. Freeman, City of London, 1991; Liveryman, Musicians' Co., 1992. Hon. DMus Sheffield, 1983. *Address:* 34 Cleveden Drive, Glasgow G12 0RX.

LOUGHRAN, Rear-Adm. Terence William, CB 1997; Chief Executive, Sabrage Enterprises, since 1998; *b* Newcastle-upon-Tyne, 27 March 1943; parents decd; *m* (marr. diss. 1988); one *s* two *d*; *m* 1995, Philippa Mary Vernon. *Educ:* Devonport High Sch.; Britannia Royal Naval Coll. MNI 1993; FRAeS 1997. Qualified as: rotary wing pilot, 1967; flying instructor, 1971; graduated Canadian Forces Comd and Staff Coll., 1976; i/c 706 Naval Air Sqdn, 1976–77; Comdr 1979; i/c HMS Phoebe, 1980–81; Executive Officer: HMS Bristol, 1983–84; HMS Intrepid, 1984–85; Captain 1986; i/c HMS Gloucester and Comdr Armilla Patrol, Arabian Gulf Task Unit, 1986–88; Dep. Dir, Internat. Affairs in Naval Staff Duties, 1988–90; Dir, Naval Manpower Planning, 1990–92; i/c HMS Ark Royal and Comdr, Grapple Adriatic Task Gp, 1993–94; Rear-Adm., 1995; Flag Officer, Naval Aviation, 1995–98. Mem., Rona Trust, 1991–; Gov., Countess Gytha Sch., 1996–. *Publications:* (contrib.) Royal United Services Inst. Jl. *Recreations:* sailing, motor cycling, spinning yarns. *Address:* Court Lodge, St Margarets Road, Tintinhull, Somerset BA22 8PL. *T:* and *Fax:* (01935) 824298; *e-mail:* twl@sabrage.com. *Clubs:* Naval; Travellers (Newcastle).

LOUGHREY, (Stephen) Patrick (Victor); Director, Nations and Regions, BBC, since 2000; *b* 29 Dec. 1955; *s* of Eddie Loughrey and Mary Loughrey (*née* Griffin); *m* 1978, Patricia Kelly; one *s* two *d*. *Educ:* Loretto Coll., Milford; Univ. of Ulster (BA); Queen's Univ. (MA). Res. student, Trent Univ., Canada, 1977; teacher, St Colm's Draperstown, 1978–84; BBC: Producer, Educn, 1984–88; Hd, Educnl Broadcasting, 1988–91; Hd of Progs, NI, 1991–94; Controller, NI, 1994–2000. Jt Editor, Ulster Local Studies, 1988–91. *Publication:* People of Ireland, 1988. *Recreations:* walking, talking. *Address:* BBC Broadcasting House, Portland Place, W1A 1AA. *T:* (020) 7765 1536.

LOUGHTON, David Clifford; Chief Executive, University Hospitals Coventry and Warwickshire NHS Trust (formerly Walsgrave Hospitals NHS Trust), since 1986; *b* 28 Jan. 1954; *s* of late Clifford Loughton and of Hazel Loughton; *m* 1986, Deborah Wellington; one *s* one *d*. *Educ:* Roxet Manor Sch., Harrow; tech. colls in Harrow, Watford and Southall. MIHospE 1974; MIPlantE 1976; TEng (CEI) 1978; MHSM 1993. Asst hosp. engr, Hillingdon AHA, 1974–76; hosp. engr, Herts AHA, 1976–78; Dir and Gen. Manager, Ducost Ltd, 1978–83; Divl Manager, GEC Electrical Projects, 1984–86. Chm., Coventry and Warwicks Educn and Trng Consortium, 1996–2001. *Recreations:* home improvements, walking, sport. *Address:* University Hospitals Coventry and Warwickshire NHS Trust, Walsgrave Hospital, Clifford Bridge Road, Coventry CV2 2DX; Blacon Cottage, Norton Lindsey, Warwick CV35 8JN. *T:* (01926) 842070.

LOUGHTON, Timothy Paul; MP (C) East Worthing and Shoreham, since 1997; *b* 30 May 1962; *s* of Rev. Michael Loughton and Pamela Dorothy Loughton (*née* Brandon); *m* 1992, Elizabeth Juliet MacLauchlan; one *s* two *d*. *Educ:* Priory Sch., Lewes; Univ. of Warwick (BA 1st cl. Hons); Clare Coll., Cambridge. Joined Montagu Loebl Stanley, then Fleming Private Asset Mgt, 1984, Dir 1992–2000. Formerly: Member: Wandsworth CHC; Substance Misuse Cttee, Wandsworth HA; Battersea Sector Policing Gp; Vice-Chm., Wandsworth Alcohol Gp. Joined Conservative Party, 1977; various posts in local assocs in Lewes, Warwick Univ., Cambridge Univ. and Battersea, 1978–91; Dep. Chm., Battersea Cons. Assoc., 1994–96. Contested (C) Sheffield Brightside, 1992. Mem., Envmtl Audit Select Cttee, 1997–. Member: Finance Bill Standing Cttee, 1997–98; Jt House Cttee on Financial Services and Markets Bill, 1999; Sec., Parly Animal Welfare Gp; Vice Chm., All Party Parly Small Business Gp; Chm., Cons. Disability Gp; Treas., British Parly Maritime Gp, 1997–. Member: Sussex Archaeol Soc.; BM Soc. *Recreations:* archaeology, classics, English wine, ski-ing, tennis, hockey. *Address:* House of Commons, SW1A 0AA. *Club:* Carlton.

LOUIS, Prof. William Roger, Hon. CBE 1999; DLitt; FBA; Kerr Professor of English History and Culture, since 1985, Distinguished Teaching Professor, since 1998, University of Texas at Austin; Supernumerary Fellow, St Antony's College, Oxford, 1986–96 (Hon. Fellow, since 1996); *b* 8 May 1936; *s* of Henry Edward and Bena May Louis; *m* 1st, 1960, Patricia Ann Leonard; one *s* one *d*; 2nd, 1983, Dagmar Cecilia Friedrich. *Educ:* Univ. of Oklahoma (Phi Beta Kappa, BA 1959); Harvard (Woodrow Wilson Fellow; MA 1960); St Antony's Coll., Oxford (Marshall Scholar; DPhil 1962); DLitt Oxon 1979. FRHistS 1984; Corresp. FBA 1993. Asst and Associate Prof., Yale, 1962–70; Humanities Research Center, University of Texas: Prof. of History and Curator, Historical Collections, 1970–85; Dir, British Studies, 1975–; Teaching Awards, 1984, 1992, 1993, 1998; National Endowment Humanities: Sen. Fellow, 1974–75; Dir, Seminars, 1985–2000. Guggenheim Fellow, 1979–80; Vis. Fellow, 1979–80, Chichele Lectr, 1990, All Souls Coll., Oxford; Fellow/Lecturer: Churchill Coll., Cambridge, 1985; Brookings Instn, 1989; LSE, 1992; Woodrow Wilson Internat. Center for Scholars, 1994–95, 2000; lectures: Cust, Univ. of Nottingham, 1995; British Acad. Inaugural Elie Kedourie Meml, 1996; Churchill Meml, Westminster Coll., Fulton, Mo, 1998; Dist. Vistor, Dept of Hist., Univ. of Peking, 1998; Dist. Vis. Prof., Amer. Univ. in Cairo, 2001. Pres., Amer. Historical Assoc., 2001. Editor, British Documents on the End of Empire, 1988–; Editor-in-Chief, Oxford History of the British Empire, 1992–99. Hon. DPhil Westminster Coll., 1998. *Publications:* Ruanda-Urundi, 1963; Germany's Lost Colonies, 1967; (ed with P. Gifford) Britain and Germany in Africa, 1967; (with J. Stengers) Congo Reform Movement, 1968; British Strategy in the Far East, 1971; (ed with P. Gifford) France and Britain in Africa, 1971; (ed) Nationalism Security and International Trusteeship in the Pacific, 1972; (ed) A. J. P. Taylor and his Critics, 1972; (ed) Imperialism: the Robinson and Gallagher controversy, 1976; Imperialism at Bay, 1977; (ed with W. S. Livingston) Australia, New Zealand and the Pacific Islands, 1979; (ed with P. Gifford) The Transfer of Power in Africa, 1982; The British Empire in the Middle East 1945–51, 1984 (Amer. Hist. Assoc. Prize); (ed with R. Stookey) The End of the Palestine Mandate, 1986; (ed with H. Bull) The Special Relationship, 1986; (ed with P. Gifford) Decolonization in Africa, 1988; (ed with J. A. Bill) Musaddiq, Nationalism and Oil, 1988; (ed with R. Owen) Suez 1956, 1989; (ed with R. Fernea) The Iraqi Revolution, 1991; In the Name of God Go! Leo Amery and the British Empire, 1992; (ed with R. Blake) Churchill, 1993; (ed) Adventures with Britannia: personalities, politics and culture in Britain, 1995; (ed) More Adventures with Britannia, 1998; (ed with Michael Howard) The Oxford History of the Twentieth Century, 1998; (ed with J. M. Brown) The Oxford History of the British Empire, vol. IV: the twentieth century, 1999; (ed with Roger Owen) A Revolutionary Year: the Middle East in 1958, 2002; *festschrift:* (ed Robert King and Robin Kilson) The Statecraft of British Imperialism: essays in honor of Wm Roger Louis, 1999. *Recreation:* a German wife. *Address:* Department of History, University of Texas, Austin, TX 78712, USA. *Clubs:* Reform; Century (NY), Metropolitan (Washington).

LOUISY, Dame (Calliopa) Pearlette, Grand Cross, Order of St Lucia, 1997; GCMG 1999; Governor General, St Lucia, since 1997; *b* 8 June 1946; *d* of Rita Louisy. *Educ:* St Joseph's Convent; Univ. of West Indies (BA); Université Laval, Quebec (MA); Univ. of Bristol (PhD 1994). Principal, St Lucia A-Level Coll., 1981–86; Sir Arthur Lewis Community College: Dean, 1986–94; Vice Principal, 1994–95; Principal, 1996–97. Hon. LLD Bristol, 1999. *Recreations:* horticulture, performing arts, reading. *Address:* Government House, Morne Fortune, Castries, St Lucia. *T:* 4522481.

LOUSTAU-LALANNE, Bernard Michel; barrister; international business and copyright consultant; *b* 20 June 1938; *s* of Michel Loustau-Lalanne, OBE, and Madeleine (*née* Boullé); *m* 1974, Debbie Elizabeth Grieve (*née* Temple-Brown) (marr. diss. 1982); one *d*. *Educ:* Seychelles Coll.; St Mary's Coll., Southampton; Imperial Coll., London. Called to the Bar, Middle Temple, London, 1969. Assistant Inspector, Northern Rhodesia Police, 1962–64; Crown Counsel, Seychelles, 1970–72; Sen. State Counsel and Official Notary, 1972–76; Attorney-General, Seychelles, 1976–78; High Comr for Seychelles, in London, 1978–80; concurrently Seychelles Ambassador to USA, and Seychelles Perm. Rep. to UN; Internat. Rep., PRS, 1980–90; Sec.-Gen., Eur. Fedn of Mgt Consulting Assocs, 1991–92. *Recreations:* international affairs, French literature, theatre, tennis. *Address:* Holborn Chambers, 6 Gate Street, WC2A 3HP.

LOUTH, 16th Baron *cr* 1541, **Otway Michael James Oliver Plunkett;** *b* 19 Aug. 1929; *o s* of Otway Randal Percy Oliver Plunkett, 15th Baron, and Ethel May, *d* of Walter John Gallichen, Jersey, Channel Islands; *S* father, 1950; *m* 1951, Angela Patricia Cullinane, Jersey; three *s* two *d*. *Heir: s* Hon. Jonathan Oliver Plunkett, BSc, AMIEE [*b* 4 Nov. 1952; *m* 1981, Jennifer, *d* of Norman Oliver Hodgetts, Weston-super-Mare; one *s* one *d*]. *Address:* 4A Temple Court, St John, Jersey JE3 4BJ.

LOVAT, 18th Lord (S) *cr* 1458–1464 (*de facto* 16th Lord, 18th but for the attainder); **Simon Fraser;** Baron (UK) 1837; *b* 13 Feb. 1977; *er s* of Hon. Simon Augustine Fraser, Master of Lovat (*d* 1994) and of Virginia Fraser (who *m* F. R. Johnson, *qv*), *d* of David Grose; *S* grandfather, 1995. *Educ:* Harrow; Edinburgh Univ. *Heir: b* Jack Fraser, Master of Lovat, *b* 22 Aug. 1984.

LOVE, Andrew; MP (Lab and Co-op) Edmonton, since 1997; *b* 21 March 1949; *s* of late James Love and Olive Love (*née* Mills); *m* 1983, Ruth, *d* of late Jack and Esther Rosenthal. *Educ:* Strathclyde Univ. (BSc Hons). ACIS. Parly Officer, Co-operative Party, 1993–97. Mem. (Lab), Haringey LBC, 1980–86 (Chairman: Finance, 1984–85; Housing, 1985–86). Mem., NE Thames RHA, 1988–90. Contested (Lab and Co-op) Edmonton, 1992. Member: Public Accounts Cttee, H of C, 1997–; Deregulation Select Cttee, 1999–. Chairman: All Party Building Socs Gp, 1997–; All Party Homelessness and Housing Needs Gp; Sec., All Party Small Businesses Gp; Vice-Chm., All Party Opera Gp. Trustee, Industrial Common Ownership Finance, 1991–. *Recreations:* golf, opera, reading. *Address:* House of Commons, SW1A 0AA. *T:* (020) 7219 5497, (office) (020) 8803 0574, *Fax:* (020) 7219 6623; *e-mail:* lovea@parliament.uk.

LOVE, Prof. Philip Noel, CBE 1983; DL; Vice Chancellor, University of Liverpool, 1992–Aug. 2002; *b* 25 Dec. 1939; *o s* of Thomas Isaac and Ethel Violet Love; *m* 1st, 1963, Isabel Leah (*d* 1993), *yr d* of Innes Taylor and Leah Wallace Mearns; three *s*; 2nd, 1995, Isobel, *widow* of David Pardey. *Educ:* Aberdeen Grammar Sch.; Aberdeen Univ. (MA 1961, LLB 1963). Admitted Solicitor in Scotland, 1963; Advocate in Aberdeen, 1963–; Partner, Campbell Connon, Solicitors, Aberdeen, 1963–74, Consultant, 1974–. University of Aberdeen: Prof. of Conveyancing and Professional Practice of Law, 1974–92; Dean, Faculty of Law, 1979–82, 1991–92; Vice Principal, 1986–90. Law Society of Scotland: Mem. Council, 1975–86; Examr, 1975–83 (Chm. Examrs, 1977–80); Vice-Pres., 1980–81; Pres., 1981–82. Local Chm., Rent Assessment Panel for Scotland, 1972–92; Chairman: Sec. of State for Scotland's Expert Cttee on house purchase and sale, 1982–84; Scottish Conveyancing and Executry Services Bd, 1991–96; Vice-Pres., Scottish

Law Agents Soc., 1970; Member: Jt Standing Cttee on Legal Educn in Scotland, 1976–85 (Chm., 1976–80); Rules Council, Court of Session, 1968–92; Council, Internat. Bar Assoc., 1983–87 (Vice-Chm., Legal Educn Div., 1983–87); Jt Ethical Cttee, Grampian Health Bd, 1984–92 (Vice-Chm., 1985; Chm., 1986–92); Scottish Law Commn, 1986–95; Council, CVCP, then UUK, 1996–2002. Chm., Aberdeen Home for Widowers' Children, 1971–92. Pres., Aberdeen Grammar Sch. Former Pupils' Club, 1987–88. Chm., Univs and Colls Employers Assoc., 1995–2002. Hon. Sheriff of Grampian, Highland and Islands, 1978–. Chm., Registers of Scotland Customer Adv. Gp, 1990–92. Trustee: Grampian and Islands Family Trust, 1988–92; St George's Hall Trust, 1996–. Chm., Mersey Partnership, 1995–98. Gov., Inst. of Occupational Medicine Ltd, 1990–. Mem., Editl Consultative Bd for Scotland, Butterworth & Co. (Publishers) Ltd, 1990–95. DL Merseyside, 1997. Hon. LLD: Abertay Dundee, 1996; Aberdeen, 1997. *Address:* (until Aug. 2002) Vice-Chancellor's Lodge, 12 Sefton Park Road, Liverpool L8 3SL. *T:* (0151) 794 2003; 1 Mayfield Court, Victoria Road, Formby, Merseyside L37 7JL. *T:* (01704) 832427. *Clubs:* Athenæum; New (Edinburgh); Aberdeen Grammar School Former Pupils' Club Centre (Aberdeen); Formby Golf, Royal Aberdeen Golf.

LOVEDAY, Alan (Raymond); solo violinist; *b* 29 Feb. 1928; *s* of Leslie and Margaret Loveday; *m* 1952, Ruth Stanfield; one *s* one *d*. *Educ:* privately; Royal College of Music (prizewinner). Made debut at age of 4; debut in England, 1946; has given many concerts, broadcasts, and made TV appearances, in this country and abroad, playing with all leading conductors and orchestras; repertoire ranges from Bach (which he likes to play on an unmodernised violin), to contemporary music. Prof., RCM, 1955–72. Formerly full-time Mem. and Soloist, Acad. of St Martin-in-the-Fields. *Recreations:* chess, bridge.

LOVEDAY, Mark Antony; Senior Partner, Cazenove & Co., 1994–2001; *b* 22 Sept. 1943; *s* of George Arthur Loveday and Sylvia Mary Loveday; *m* 1981, Mary Elizabeth Tolmie; one *s* one *d*. *Educ:* Winchester Coll.; Magdalen Coll., Oxford (MA). Cazenove & Co., 1966–2001; Partner, 1974–2001. Dir, Foreign & Colonial Investment Trust PLC, 2001–. Dir, Metropolitan Hosp. Sunday Fund, 1972–; Council of Mgt, British Kidney Patient Assoc., 2001–. Trustee: Magdalen Coll. Develt Trust, 1982–; Grosvenor Estate, 1999–. Liveryman, Skinners' Co., 1972. *Recreation:* golf. *Address:* 42 Royal Avenue, SW3 4QF. *T:* (020) 7730 4031, (office) (020) 7588 2828. *Clubs:* Boodle's, City University, Hurlingham, MCC; Royal St George's Golf.

LOVEGROVE, His Honour Geoffrey David; QC 1969; a Circuit Judge (formerly County Court Judge), 1971–92; *b* 22 Dec. 1919; *s* of late Gilbert Henry Lovegrove; *m* 1959, Janet, *d* of John Bourne; one *s* two *d*. *Educ:* Haileybury; New College, Oxford (MA). Army, 1940–46. Called to the Bar, Inner Temple, 1947; Dep. Chairman, W Sussex Quarter Sessions, 1965–71. Master, Innholders' Company, 1980–81.

LOVEJOY, Joseph Reginald; Football Correspondent, Sunday Times, since 1994; *b* 23 June 1951; *s* of Reginald Henry Lovejoy and Ivy May Lovejoy; *m* 1st, 1973, Cynthia Turner (marr. diss. 1990); one *s* one *d*; 2nd, 1995, Lesley Griffiths. *Educ:* Bancrofts Sch., Woodford Green; Portsmouth Tech. Coll. (NCTJ Proficiency). Reporter: Kentish Observer, 1969–73; Doncaster Evening Post, 1973; Derby Evening Telegraph, 1973–77; South Wales Echo, 1977–83; Mail on Sunday, 1983–86; Independent, 1986–94. *Publication:* Bestie: portrait of a legend, 1998. *Recreations:* darts, gym. *Address:* Rushbrook, Forge Road, Tintern, Monmouthshire NP16 6TH. *Club:* St Pierre Golf (Chepstow).

LOVELACE, 5th Earl of, *cr* 1838; **Peter Axel William Locke King;** Baron King and Ockham, 1725; Viscount Ockham, 1838; *b* 26 Nov. 1951; *s* of 4th Earl of Lovelace and Manon Lis (*d* 1990), *d* of Axel Sigurd Transo, Copenhagen, Denmark; *S* father, 1964; *m* 1994, Kathleen Anne Smolders, Melbourne, Aust. *Address:* Torridon House, Torridon, Ross-shire IV22 2HA.

LOVELL, Sir (Alfred Charles) Bernard, Kt 1961; OBE 1946; FRS 1955; Founder and Director of Jodrell Bank Experimental Station, Cheshire, subseq. Nuffield Radio Astronomy Laboratories, 1951–81 (renamed Jodrell Bank Observatory, 2000); Professor of Radio Astronomy, University of Manchester, 1951–80, now Emeritus Professor; *b* 31 Aug. 1913; *s* of G. Lovell, Oldland Common, Gloucestershire; *m* 1937, Mary Joyce Chesterman (*d* 1993); two *s* three *d*. *Educ:* Kingswood Grammar Sch., Bristol; University of Bristol. Asst Lectr in Physics, Univ. of Manchester, 1936–39; Telecommunication Res. Establishment, 1939–45; Physical Laboratories, Univ. of Manchester and Jodrell Bank Experimental Station, Cheshire; Lectr, 1945, Sen. Lectr, 1947, Reader, 1949, in Physics. Reith Lectr, 1958; Lectures: Condon, 1962; Guthrie, 1962; Halley, 1964; Queen's, Berlin, 1970; Brockington, Kingston, Ont, 1970; Bickley, Oxford, 1977; Crookshank, RCR, 1977; Angel Meml, Newfoundland, 1977; Blackett Meml, Operational Res. Soc., 1987. Vis. Montague Burton Prof. of Internat. Relations, Univ. of Edinburgh, 1973. Member: Air Navigation Cttee, 1953–56 (Vice-Chm., 1955–56); Air Warfare Cttee, 1954–60; ARC, 1955–58; Radar & Signals Adv. Bd, 1956–59; Sci. Adv. Council, 1957–60; Guided Weapons Adv. Bd, 1958–60; SRC, 1965–70; Amer. Philosophical Soc., 1974–. Pres., RAS, 1969–71; Vice-Pres., Internat. Astronomical Union, 1970–76; Pres., British Assoc., 1975–76. Pres., Guild of Church Musicians, 1976–89; Jun. Warden, 1984–85, Sen. Warden, 1985–86, Master, 1986–87, Musicians' Co. Hon. Freeman, City of Manchester, 1977. Hon. Fellow, Society of Engineers, 1964; Hon. Foreign Member American Academy of Arts and Sciences, 1955; Hon. Life Member, New York Academy, 1960; Hon. Member: Royal Swedish Academy, 1962; RNCM, 1981; Manchester Lit. & Philos. Soc., 1988. Hon. LLD: Edinburgh, 1961; Calgary, 1966; Liverpool, 1999; Hon. DSc: Leicester, 1961; Leeds, 1966; London, 1967; Bath, 1967; Bristol, 1970; DUniv Stirling, 1974; DUniv Surrey, 1975; Hon. FIEE, 1967; Hon. FInstP, 1976. Duddell Medal, 1954; Royal Medal, 1960; Daniel and Florence Guggenheim International Astronautics Award, 1961; Ordre du Mérite pour la Recherche et l'Invention, 1962; Churchill Gold Medal, 1964; Maitland Lecturer and Silver Medallist, Institution of Structural Engineers, 1964; Second RSA American Exchange Lectr, Philadelphia, 1980; Benjamin Franklin Medal, RSA, 1980; Gold Medal, Royal Astronomical Soc., 1981; Rutherford Meml Lectr, Royal Soc., 1984. Commander's Order of Merit, Polish People's Republic, 1975. *Publications:* Science and Civilisation, 1939; World Power Resources and Social Development, 1945; Radio Astronomy, 1951; Meteor Astronomy, 1954; The Exploration of Space by Radio, 1957; The Individual and The Universe, (BBC Reith Lectures, 1958); The Exploration of Outer Space (Gregynog Lectures, 1961); Discovering the Universe, 1963; Our Present Knowledge of the Universe, 1967; (ed with T. Margerison) The Explosion of Science: The Physical Universe, 1967; The Story of Jodrell Bank, 1968; The Origins and International Economics of Space Exploration, 1973; Out of the Zenith, 1973; Man's Relation to the Universe, 1975; P. M. S. Blackett: a biographical memoir, 1976; In the Centre of Immensities, 1978; Emerging Cosmology, 1981; The Jodrell Bank Telescopes, 1985; Voice of the Universe, 1987; (with Sir Francis Graham Smith) Pathways to the Universe, 1988; Astronomer by Chance (autobiog.), 1990; Echoes of War, 1991; many publications in Physical and Astronomical journals. *Recreations:* cricket, gardening, music. *Address:* The Quinta, Swettenham, Cheshire CW12 2LD. *T:* (01477) 571254. *Clubs:* Athenæum, MCC; Lancashire County Cricket (Pres., 1995–96).

LOVELL, Kenneth Ernest Walter; Treasurer to the Greater London Council, 1977–80, retired; *b* 25 Oct. 1919; *s* of Ernest John and Alice Lovell; *m* 1946, Vera Mary Pithouse; one *s* two *d*. *Educ:* Ashford County Grammar School. Mem. Chartered Inst. of Public Finance and Accountancy. Middlesex County Council (Finance Dept): Computer Manager, 1961; Asst County Treasurer, 1963. Greater London Council: Asst Treasurer, 1965; Finance Officer, ILEA, 1972. *Recreations:* gardening, cricket, hockey, photography; study of social and economic development of British Isles; study of landscape of British Isles. *Address:* 15 Meadway Close, Staines, Mddx TW18 2PR. *T:* (01784) 452806.

LOVELL-BADGE, Dr Robin Harcourt, FRS 2001; Head, Division of Developmental Genetics, MRC National Institute for Medical Research, since 1993; *b* 14 June 1953; *s* of Don Lovell-Badge and Eileen Betty Cator (*née* Daniels). *Educ:* Norwich Sch. (King Edward VI); University Coll. London (BSc Hons Zool. 1975; PhD Embryol. 1978). Postdoctoral research: Dept of Genetics, Univ. of Cambridge, 1978–81; EMBO Long Term Fellow, Institut Jacques Monod, Univ. Paris VII, 1981–82; Member: Scientific Staff, MRC Mammalian Develt Unit, UCL, 1982–88; MRC Scientific Staff, NIMR, 1988–. Hon. Sen. Res. Fellow, Dept of Anatomy and Develtl Biol., UCL, 1994–; Vis. Prof., Dept Biochem., Univ. of Hong Kong, 1996–. Mem., EMBO, 1993. FMedSci 1999. Louis Jeantet Prize for Medicine, 1995; Amory Prize, Amer. Acad. Arts and Scis, 1996. *Publications:* contribs to learned jls. *Recreations:* drawing, painting, sculpture, cooking, good food and wine. *Address:* Laboratory of Developmental Genetics, MRC National Institute for Medical Research, The Ridgeway, Mill Hill, NW7 1AA. *T:* (020) 8913 8696.

LOVELL-PANK, Dorian Christopher; QC 1993; a Recorder, since 1989; *b* 15 Feb. 1946; *s* of late Christopher Edwin Lovell-Pank, Madrid and Jean Alston de Oliva-Day (*née* McPherson), Cape Town and Buenos Aires; *m* 1983, Diana, *d* of late Michael Cady Byford and of Sonia Byford, Claret Hall, Clare, Suffolk; one *s* one *d*. *Educ:* Downside; Colegio Sarmiento, Buenos Aires; LSE; Inns of Court Sch. of Law. Called to the Bar, Inner Temple, 1971, Bencher, 1998; in practice SE Circuit; Asst Recorder, 1985–89. Mem., Panel of Chairmen, Police Discipline Appeal Tribunals, 1991–; Member: Cttee, Criminal Bar Assoc., 1989– (Chm., Internat. Relations Sub-Cttee, 1993–); Gen. Council of Bar, 1989–92, 1998– (Vice-Chm., Internat. Relations Cttee, 1998–); Chm., Bar Conf., 1999. Member: Internat. Bar Assoc., 1993–; Human Rights Inst., 1996– (Mem. Council, 2000–); Chm., Bar Conf., 1999. Mem., Council of Mgt, British Inst. of Internat. and Comparative Law, 2001–. Associate Mem., ABA, 1997. *Recreations:* travel, reading, things latin, swimming. *Address:* 6 King's Bench Walk, Temple, EC4Y 7DR. *T:* (020) 7583 0410. *Clubs:* Garrick, Hurlingham, Riverside, Annabel's; Aldeburgh Yacht, RNVR Yacht.

LOVELOCK, Sir Douglas (Arthur), KCB 1979 (CB 1974); First Church Estates Commissioner, 1983–93; Chairman, Central Board of Finance of the Church of England, 1983–92; *b* 7 Sept. 1923; *s* of late Walter and Irene Lovelock; *m* 1961, Valerie Margaret (*née* Lane); one *s* one *d*. *Educ:* Bec Sch., London. Entered Treasury, 1949; Min. of Supply, 1952; Private Sec. to Permanent Sec., 1953–54; Principal, 1954; Private Sec. to successive Ministers of Aviation (Rt Hon. Peter Thorneycroft and Rt Hon. Julian Amery), 1961–63; Asst Sec., 1963; Under-Sec. (Contracts), Min. of Technology, subseq. Min. of Aviation Supply, 1968–71; Asst Under-Sec. of State (Personnel), MoD, 1971–72; Dep. Sec., DTI, 1972–74, Depts of Trade, Industry, Prices and Consumer Protection, 1974–77, Chm., Bd of Customs and Excise, 1977–83. Chm., Civil Service Benevolent Fund, 1980–83. Chm., Review of Citizens' Advice Bureaux Service, 1983–84. Gov., 1986–, Chm., 1993–, Whitgift Foundn (Whitgift Sch., Trinity Sch., Old Palace Sch.). *Publication:* While I Remember, 1998. *Recreations:* walking, gardening, outdoor activities generally. *Address:* The Old House, 91 Coulsdon Road, Old Coulsdon, Surrey CR3 2LD. *T:* (01737) 555211.

LOVELOCK, Prof. James Ephraim, CBE 1990; FRS 1974; independent scientist, since 1964; Hon. Visiting Fellow, Green College, Oxford, since 1994; *b* 26 July 1919; *s* of Tom Arthur Lovelock and Nellie Ann Elizabeth (*née* March); *m* 1st, 1942, Helen Mary Hyslop (*d* 1989); two *s* two *d*; 2nd, 1991, Sandra Jean Orchard. *Educ:* Strand Sch., London; Manchester and London Univs. BSc, PhD, DSc, ARIC. Staff Scientist, Nat. Inst. for Med. Research, 1941–61; Rockefeller Fellow, Harvard Univ., 1954–55; Yale Univ., 1958–59; Prof. of Chemistry, Baylor Univ. Coll. of Medicine, Texas, 1961–64. Vis. Prof., Univ. of Reading, 1967–90. Pres., Marine Biol Assoc., 1986–90. Mem. Sigma Xi, Yale Chapter, 1959. Hon. ScD East Anglia, 1982; Hon. DSc: Exeter, 1988; Plymouth Univ. (formerly Plymouth Poly.), 1988; Edinburgh, 1993; Kent, 1996; Univ. of E London, 1996; Colorado, 1997; Hon. DSci Stockholm, 1991. Amsterdam Prize, Roy. Netherlands Acad. of Arts and Scis, 1990; Prize, Volvo Envmt Prize Foundn, 1996; Nonino Prize, Italy, 1996; Blue Planet Prize, Asahi Glass Foundn, Tokyo, 1997. *Publications:* Gaia, 1979; (with Michael Allaby) The Great Extinction, 1983; (with Michael Allaby) The Greening of Mars, 1984; The Ages of Gaia, 1988; Gaia: the practical science of planetary medicine, 1991; Homage to Gaia: the life of an independent scientist (autobiog.), 2000; numerous papers and patents. *Recreations:* walking, digital photography, reading. *Address:* Coombe Mill, St Giles on the Heath, Launceston, Cornwall PL15 9RY.

LOVELUCK, Paul Edward, CBE 1993; JP; Chief Executive, Countryside Council for Wales, since 1995; *b* 3 Feb. 1942; *s* of Edward Henry Loveluck and Elizabeth Loveluck (*née* Treharne); *m* 1965, Lynne Gronow; one *s* one *d*. *Educ:* Maesteg Grammar Sch.; UCW, Cardiff (BA). Board of Trade, 1963–69; Welsh Office, 1969–84 (Asst Sec., 1975–84); Chief Exec., Wales Tourist Bd, 1984–95. President: Maesteg Male Voice Choir, 1990–; Drama Assoc. of Wales, 1996–; Chm., Welsh Chamber Orch., 1999–. JP Cardiff, 1982. *Recreations:* hillwalking, music. *Address:* (office) Plas Penrhos, Ffordd Penrhos, Bangor, Gwynedd LL57 2LQ. *T:* (01248) 385500; Tudor Cottage, 38 Rhiwbina Hill, Cardiff CF4 6UQ.

LOVEMAN, Stephen Charles Gardner; Under Secretary, Department of Employment, then Department for Education and Employment, 1989–96; *b* 26 Dec. 1943; *s* of Charles Edward Loveman and Edith Mary Gardner; *m* 1972, Judith Pamela Roberts; one *s* one *d*. *Educ:* Arnold Sch., Blackpool; Emmanuel College, Cambridge (BA). Dept of Employment, 1967; Private Sec. to Minister of State for Employment, 1972–74; Health and Safety Exec., 1974–77; Dept of Employment, 1977–80; Manpower Services Commn, 1980–87; Dept of Employment, 1987–88; Cabinet Office, 1988–89. *Recreations:* TV, cinema, theatre, reading, keeping fit, voluntary work (witness support). *Address:* 24 Brincliffe Crescent, Sheffield S11 9AW.

LOVERANCE, Rowena Kathryn; Head of Outreach and Learning Resources, British Museum, since 2001; *b* 4 Sept. 1952; *d* of Maurice and Wilfreda Loverance. *Educ:* Manchester High Sch. for Girls; Somerville Coll., Oxford (BA Hons Modern History; Dip. Archaeol.). Res. Fellow, Univ. of Birmingham, 1979–80; Lectr, Dept of Ancient History and Classical Archaeology, Univ. of Sheffield, 1980–83; Education Officer, 1985–98, Head of Educnl IT, 1998–2001, BM. Pres., Churches Together in England, 1998–2001. *Publication:* Byzantium, 1988. *Recreations:* Byzantine studies, archaeology. *Address:* Education Department, British Museum, Great Russell Street, WC1B 3DG.

LOVERIDGE, Sir John (Warren), Kt 1988; JP; senior partner of family businesses in agriculture, education and property; *b* 9 Sept. 1925; *s* of C. W. Loveridge and Emily (Mickie), *d* of John Malone; *m* 1954, Jean Marguerite, *d* of E. J. Chivers; three *s* two *d*. *Educ:* St John's Coll., Cambridge (MA). Mem., Hampstead BC, 1953–59. Contested (C) Aberavon, 1951, Brixton (LCC), 1952. MP (C) Hornchurch, 1970–74, Upminster, 1974–83. Member: Parly Select Cttee on Expenditure (Mem. General Purposes Sub-Cttee); Procedure Cttee; Chm., Cons. Smaller Business Cttee, 1979–83). Treasurer/Trustee, Hampstead Conservative Assoc., 1959–74; President: Hampstead and Highgate Conservative Assoc., 1986–91; Upminster Conservative Assoc., 1992–; Vice-Pres., Greater London Area Conservatives, 1984–93 and 1996– (Pres., 1993–96). Vice-Pres., Nat. Council for Civil Protection (formerly Civil Defence), 1980–. Pres., Dinosaurs Club (former Cons. MPs), 1999– (Chm., 1993–98). JP West Central Division, 1963. FRAS; FRAgS; MRIIA. Liveryman, Girdlers' Co.; Mem., Guild of Freemen of City of London. *Publications:* (jtly) Moving Forward: small businesses and the economy, 1983; *poems:* God Save the Queen: Sonnets of Elizabeth I, 1981; Hunter of the Moon, 1983; Hunter of the Sun, 1984. *Recreations:* painter, sculptor, writer; historic houses, shooting. *Address:* c/o The Private Office, 2 Arkwright Road, NW3 6AD. *Clubs:* Buck's, Carlton, Hurlingham.

LOVERING, John David; Executive Chairman, Homebase Ltd, since 2001; Chairman: Birthdays Group Ltd, since 1996; Peacock Group Ltd, since 1997; Fired Earth Ltd, since 1998; Odeon Cinemas Ltd, since 2000; *b* 11 Oct. 1949; *s* of John George and Ruby Beatrice Lovering; *m* 1971, Brenda Joan Wotherspoon; two *s* one *d*. *Educ:* Dulwich Coll.; Exeter Univ. (BA Hons); Manchester Business Sch. (MBA). Planning Manager, Spillers Internat. Div., 1975–78; Corporate Strategy Manager, Lex Service plc, 1978–83; Grand Metropolitan plc, Commercial Dir Express Dairy Ltd, 1983–85; Head of Gp Finance and Planning, Imperial Gp plc, 1985–86; Finance Dir, Sears plc, 1986–93; Chief Operating Officer, Tarmac plc, 1993–95. Trustee and Dir, SCF, 1990–96. *Recreations:* sport, walking. *Club:* Alleyn (Dulwich).

LOVERING, Prof. John Francis, AO 1993; FAA; FTSE; Chairman, Environment Conservation Council of Victoria, since 1998; *b* 27 March 1930; *s* of George Francis Lovering and Dorothy Irene Mildwater; *m* 1954, Jennifer Kerry FitzGerald; two *s* one *d*. *Educ:* Canterbury High Sch., Sydney; Univ. of Sydney (MSc); Univ. of Melbourne (MSc); California Inst. of Technology (PhD). FAA 1982; FTSE (FTS 1993). Asst Curator of Minerals, Australian Museum, 1951–55; Research Fellow, Fellow and Sen. Fellow, Dept of Geophysics and Geochemistry, ANU, 1956–69; University of Melbourne: Prof. of Geology, 1969–87; Dean of Science, 1983–85; Dep. Vice-Chancellor (Research), 1985–87; Vice-Chancellor and Prof. of Geology, Flinders Univ. of SA, 1987–95. Chairman of Directors: Comlabs Ltd, 1985–93; Geotrack International Pty Ltd, 1987–93; Open Learning Technology Corp., 1992–96. Pres., Murray-Darling Basin Commn, 1994–99. Hon. DSc Flinders Univ., 1995. Chevalier des Palmes Académiques, 1981. *Publications:* Last of Lands: Antarctica (with J. R. V. Prescott), 1979; contribs to learned jls. *Recreations:* music, wine, food. *Address:* 66a Molesworth Street, Kew, Vic 3101, Australia. *Clubs:* Adelaide (Adelaide); Commonwealth (Canberra); Antarctic, Banool Ski, Melbourne, Wallaby (Melbourne).

LOVESEY, Peter Harmer; crime writer, since 1970; *b* 10 Sept. 1936; *s* of Richard Lear Lovesey and Amy Lovesey (*née* Strank); *m* 1959, Jacqueline Ruth Lewis; one *s* one *d*. *Educ:* Hampton Grammar Sch.; Reading Univ. (BA Hons 1958). Flying Officer, RAF, 1958–61; Lectr, Thurrock Technical Coll., 1961–69; Head of Gen. Educn Dept, Hammersmith & West London Coll., 1969–75. Crime Writers' Association: Chm., 1991–92; Cartier Diamond Dagger, 2000; Grand Prix de Littérature Policière (French Crime Writers' Assoc.), 1985. *Publications:* The Kings of Distance, 1968; (jtly) The Guide to British Track and Field Literature, 1969; Wobble to Death, 1970 (televised 1980); The Detective Wore Silk Drawers, 1971 (televised 1980); Abracadaver, 1972 (televised 1980); Mad Hatter's Holiday, 1973 (televised 1981); Invitation to a Dynamite Party, 1974 (televised 1981); A Case of Spirits, 1975 (televised 1980); Swing, Swing Together, 1976 (televised 1980); Waxwork (Silver Dagger), 1978 (televised 1979); The Official Centenary History of the Amateur Athletic Association, 1979; The False Inspector Dew (Gold Dagger), 1982; Keystone, 1983; Rough Cider, 1986; Bertie and the Tinman, 1987; On the Edge, 1989; Bertie and the Seven Bodies, 1990; The Last Detective, 1991; Diamond Solitaire, 1992; Bertie and the Crime of Passion, 1993; The Summons (Silver Dagger), 1995; Bloodhounds (Silver Dagger), 1996; Upon a Dark Night, 1997; The Vault, 1999; The Reaper, 2000; (jtly) An Athletics Compendium: an annotated guide to the UK literature of track and field, 2001; *short stories:* Butchers and Other Stories of Crime, 1985; The Crime of Miss Oyster Brown and Other Stories, 1994; Do Not Exceed the Stated Dose, 1998; *as Peter Lear:* Goldengirl, 1977 (filmed 1979); Spider Girl, 1980; The Secret of Spandau, 1986. *Recreations:* researching athletics history, visiting teashops. *Address:* c/o Vanessa Holt Ltd, 59 Crescent Road, Leigh-on-Sea, Essex SS9 2PF. *Club:* Detection.

LOVILL, Sir John (Roger), Kt 1987; CBE 1983; DL; Chairman, Sloane Square Investments, 1980–99; *b* 26 Sept. 1929; *s* of Walter Thomas Lovill and Elsie Lovill (*née* Page); *m* 1958, Jacqueline (*née* Parker); two *s* one *d*. *Educ:* Brighton Hove and Sussex Grammar School. S. G. Warburg, 1951–55; Dep. Gen. Manager, Securicor Ltd, 1955–60; Dir, Municipal Gen. Insce Co., 1984–95; Managing Trustee, Municipal Mutual Insce, 1988– (Chm., 1993–); Chm., Nationwide Small Business Property Trust, 1988–96; Chm., Prime Health Ltd, 1992–94. Contested (C) Ebbw Vale, 1966; Mem., East Sussex CC, 1967–89, Leader, 1973–77; Chairman: Sussex Police Authority, 1976–79; Local Authority Conditions of Service Adv. Bd, 1978–83; ACC, 1983–86; Pres., Sussex Assoc. of Local Councils, 1987–97; Vice Pres., Nat. Assoc. of Local Councils, 1991–93; Leader, Conservative Assoc. of County Councils, 1981–83. DL E Sussex 1983. *Recreations:* opera, politics, marine paintings. *Address:* Hampden House, Glynde, Lewes, Sussex BN8 6TA. *T:* (01273) 858212.

LOW, family name of **Baron Aldington**.

LOW, Brian Buik, CBE 1994; HM Diplomatic Service, retired; High Commissioner to Papua New Guinea, 1994–97; *b* 15 Nov. 1937; *s* of Robert James Low and Helen Duncan Low; *m* 1960, Anita Joan Allum; three *d*. *Educ:* Arbroath High Sch. Served RAF, 1956–61. Joined Diplomatic Service, 1962; FO, 1962–65; Sofia, 1965–67; Sydney, 1967–69; Kuala Lumpur, 1969–73; Moscow, 1973–74; FCO, 1974–78; Singapore, 1978–81; Commercial Consul, British Trade Develt Office, NY, 1981–84; First Sec., FCO, 1984–88; Head of Chancery, Lima, 1988–91; Ambassador to Estonia, 1991–94. *Recreations:* music, reading, golf, watching sport. *Address:* 63 Carlogie Road, Carnoustie, Angus DD7 6EX. *Clubs:* Carnoustie Golf; Singapore Cricket.

LOW, Prof. Donald Anthony, DPhil, LittD; FRHistS, FAHA, FASSA; President of Clare Hall, 1987–94, Smuts Professor of the History of the British Commonwealth, 1983–87, and Deputy Vice-Chancellor, 1990–94, University of Cambridge; *b* 22 June 1927; *o s* of late Canon Donald Low and Winifred (*née* Edmunds); *m* 1952, Isobel Smails; one *s* two *d*. *Educ:* Haileybury and ISC; Exeter Coll., Oxford (Open Scholar in Modern History, 1944; Amelia Jackson Sen. Student, 1948; MA, DPhil; Hon. Fellow, 1992); PhD 1983, LittD 1998, Cantab. Lectr, subseq. Sen. Lectr, Makerere Coll., University Coll. of E Africa, 1951–58; Uganda corresp., The Times, 1952–58; Fellow, subseq. Sen. Fellow in History, Res. Sch. of Social Sciences, ANU, 1959–64; Founding Dean of Sch. of African and Asian Studies, and Prof. of Hist., Univ. of Sussex, 1964–72; Australian National University: Prof. of History, 1973–83; Dir, Res. Sch. of Pacific Studies, 1973–75; Vice Chancellor, 1975–82; University Fellow, 1997–2000; University of Cambridge: Fellow, Churchill Coll., 1983–87; Dir, Centre of Internat. Studies, 1985–87; Mem., Council of Senate, 1985–88. Sen. Visitor Nuffield Coll., Oxford, 1956–57; Smuts Fellow and Vis. Fellow, Clare Hall, Cambridge, 1971–72 (Hon. Fellow, 1999). Chm., Educn Adv. Cttee, Aust. Develt Assistance Bureau, 1979–82; Mem. Exec., 1976–82, Dep. Chm., 1980, Aust. Vice-Chancellors' Cttee; Member: Council, Univ. of Papua New Guinea, 1974–82; Standing Cttee, Aust. Univs Internat. Develt Program, 1975–82; Council, ACU, 1980–82; Cttee, Australian Studies Centre, London Univ., 1983–94; Governing Body: Inst. of Develt Studies, Sussex Univ., 1966–72 and 1984–91; SOAS, 1983–94; Haileybury, 1985–94; Chm., Cttee of Management, Inst. of Commonwealth Studies, London Univ., 1984–94. Hon. Fellow: Inst. of Develt Studies, UK, 1972; University House, ANU 1983. President: African Studies Assoc. of Aust. and Pacific, 1979–82; Asian Studies Assoc. of Aust., 1980–82; British Australian Studies Assoc., 1984–86; Chm., Co-ordinating Council, Area Studies Assoc., 1988–91; Vice-Pres., Australian Acad. of Humanities, 1996–98. Chm., Round Table Moot, 1992–94. Commander of the Order of Civil Merit (Spain), 1984. *Publications:* Buganda and British Overrule, 1900–1955 (with R. C. Pratt), 1960; (ed) Soundings in Modern South Asian History, 1968; (with J. C. Iltis and M. D. Wainwright) Government Archives in South Asia, 1969; Buganda in Modern History, 1971; The Mind of Buganda, 1971; Lion Rampant, 1973; (ed) Congress and the Raj 1917–1947, 1977; Oxford History of East Africa: (contrib.) Vol. I, 1963 and Vol. II, 1965; (contrib. and ed jtly) Vol. III, 1976; (ed) Constitutional Heads and Political Crises, 1988; (ed) The Indian National Congress, 1988; (ed jtly) Sovereigns and Surrogates, 1990; Eclipse of Empire, 1991; (ed) Political Inheritance of Pakistan, 1991; The Egalitarian Moment: Asia and Africa 1950–80, 1996; Britain and Indian Nationalism, 1997; articles on internat. history in jls. *Address:* 18/36 Shackleton Park, Mawson, Canberra, ACT 2607, Australia.

LOW, Dr (George) Graeme (Erick), CBE 1989; Member, 1986–91, Managing Director, Site Operations, 1990–91, United Kingdom Atomic Energy Authority; *b* Palmerston North, NZ, 29 Nov. 1928; *s* of George Eric Low and Evelyn Edith Low (*née* Gillman); *m* 1st, 1952, Marion Townsend (marr. diss. 1977); two *d*; 2nd, 1985, Joan Kathleen Swinburne. *Educ:* New Plymouth Boys' High Sch., NZ; Canterbury Coll., Univ. of NZ (BSc, MSc); Univ. of Reading (PhD, DSc). FInstP. Special Branch, RNZN, 1952–58; Research Scientist, 1958–68, Head of Materials Physics Div., 1968–70, AERE Harwell; Special Asst to Dir, UKAEA Research Gp, 1970–73; Programme Dir (Applied Nuclear), 1973–76, Research Dir (Industry), 1976–81, Dir of Environmental Research, 1981–83, AERE Harwell; Dir, AEE, Winfrith, 1983–86; Dir, AERE Harwell, 1986–87; Mem. for Estabts, UKAEA, 1987–90. Dir, UK Nirex Ltd, 1986–91. *Publications:* papers on semi-conductors, neutron beam studies of the solid state, magnetism and management. *Recreations:* reading, walking, family and friends. *Address:* 21 New Road, Reading RG1 5JD.

LOW, Sir James (Richard) Morrison-, 3rd Bt *cr* 1908; DL; DFH, CEng, MIEE; Director, Osborne & Hunter Ltd, Glasgow, 1956–89 (Electrical Engineer with firm, since 1952); *b* 3 Aug. 1925; *s* of Sir Walter John Morrison-Low, 2nd Bt and Dorothy Ruth de Quincey Quincey (*d* 1946); *S* father, 1955; *m* 1953, Ann Rawson Gordon; one *s* three *d*. *Educ:* Ardvreck; Harrow; Merchiston. Served Royal Corps of Signals, 1943–47; demobilised with rank of Captain. Faraday House Engineering Coll., 1948–52. Chm., Scottish Cttee, Nat. Inspection Council for Electrical Installation Contracting, 1982–88; Pres., Electrical Contractors Assoc. of Scotland, 1982–84. Chm., Fife Area Scout Council, 1966–84. Hon. Pipe-Major, Royal Scottish Pipers Soc., 1981–83. Eur Ing, 1990. DL Fife, 1978. *Recreations:* shooting, piping. *Heir: s* Richard Walter Morrison-Low, *b* 4 Aug. 1959. *Address:* Kilmaron House, Cupar, Fife KY15 4NE. *T:* (01334) 652248. *Clubs:* New, Royal Scottish Pipers Society (Edinburgh).

LOW, Prof. Martin Geoffrey, PhD; FRS 1996; Professor of Physiology and Cellular Biophysics, Columbia University, New York, since 1994; *b* 27 July 1950; *s* of Kenneth Douglas Low and Joan Elizabeth Low; *m* 1979, Eileen Ann Whalen; two *s*. *Educ:* Univ. of Newcastle upon Tyne (BSc Biochem.); Univ. of Birmingham (PhD Biochem. 1975). Postdoctoral Research Fellow: Univ. of Birmingham, 1974–77; Cornell Univ., 1977–79; Instructor, Med. Coll. of Va, 1979–81; Oklahoma Medical Research Foundation: Asst Mem., 1981–86; Associate Mem., 1986–87; Associate Prof., Columbia Univ., NY, 1987–94. *Publications:* contrib. original research and review articles in scientific jls incl. Science, Nature, Jl Biol Chem., Biochem. Jl. *Recreations:* reading, listening to music, fell walking, gardening. *Address:* Department of Physiology and Cellular Biophysics, Columbia University, 630 W 168th Street, New York, NY 10032, USA. *T:* (212) 3051707.

LOWCOCK, Andrew Charles; His Honour Judge Lowcock; a Circuit Judge, since 2001; *b* 22 Nov. 1949; *s* of Eric and Elizabeth Lowcock; *m* 1st, 1976, Patricia Anne Roberts (marr. diss. 1985); 2nd, 1985, Sarah Elaine Edwards; two *s*. *Educ:* Malvern Coll.; New Coll., Oxford (MA). Called to the Bar, Middle Temple, 1973; barrister, specialising in criminal and family law, Northern Circuit, 1974–2001; Asst Recorder, 1993–97; Recorder, 1997–2001. *Recreations:* music, theatre, watching cricket and football. *Address:* The Crown Court, Crown Square, Manchester M3 3HA. *Clubs:* Lancashire County Cricket, Nefyn Golf.

LOWDEN, Gordon Stuart; President, Institute of Chartered Accountants of Scotland, 1989–90 (Senior Vice-President, 1988–89); Chairman, Dundee Port Authority, 1979–92; *b* 22 May 1927; *s* of James Soutar Lowden and Jean Lowden; *m* 1953, Kathleen Arnot; two *s* one *d*. *Educ:* Dundee High Sch.; Strathallan Sch.; St John's Coll., Cambridge (MA); Univ. of St Andrews (LLB). CA. Moody Stuart & Robertson, later Peat Marwick McLintock: training, 1949–53; Partner, 1959; Office Managing Partner, 1985; retired 1988. University of Dundee: Lectr, Sen. Lectr, 1955–83; Hon. Vis. Prof., Dept of Accountancy and Business Finance, 1987. *Recreations:* golf, watching sport, bridge. *Address:* 169 Hamilton Street, Barnhill, Dundee DD5 2RE. *T:* (01382) 778360. *Club:* Royal and Ancient Golf.

LOWDEN, Richard Purdie; His Honour Judge Lowden; a Circuit Judge, North Eastern Circuit, since 1994; *b* 23 April 1948; *s* of Thomas Geoffrey Lowden, FRCS and Margaret Lowden (*née* Purdie); *m* 1973, Patricia; one *s* two *d*. *Educ:* Sedbergh Sch.; Keble Coll., Oxford (MA). Called to the Bar, Inner Temple, 1971; a Recorder of the Crown Court, 1988–94. *Recreations:* fishing, fell walking, theatre. *Address:* Newcastle upon Tyne Combined Court Centre, Quayside, Newcastle upon Tyne NE1 2LA.

LOWE, Prof. (Alan) Vaughan, PhD; Chichele Professor of Public International Law, and Fellow of All Souls College, Oxford University, since 1999; *b* 1952; *m* Sally. *Educ:* UWIST (LLB 1973; LLM 1978; PhD 1980); MA Cantab 1991; MA Oxon 1999. Called to the Bar, Gray's Inn, 1993; in practice at the Bar, 1993–. Lectr, Cardiff Law Sch.,

1973–79; Lectr, 1979–86, Sen. Lectr, 1986–88, Manchester Univ.; Cambridge University: Lectr, 1988–94; Reader in Internat. Law, 1994–99; Fellow of Corpus Christi Coll., 1988–99; Warden of Leckhampton, 1998–99. Visiting Professor: Duke Law Sch., USA, 1990; Tulane Law Sch., USA, 2000. *Publications:* Extraterritorial Jurisdiction, 1983; (jtly) The Law of the Sea, 1983, 3rd edn 1999; (jtly) Fifty Years of the International Court of Justice, 1996; (jtly) The Settlement of International Disputes, 1999; papers in jls. *Recreations:* hill walking, music. *Address:* All Souls College, Oxford OX1 4AL. *T:* (01865) 279379.

LOWE, Prof. Christopher Robin, PhD; Fellow, Trinity College, Cambridge, since 1984; Director of Biotechnology, since 1984, Director, Institute of Biotechnology, since 1988, and Professor of Biotechnology, since 1999, University of Cambridge; *b* 15 Oct. 1945; *s* of late Thomas Lowe and of Hilda Lowe (*née* Moxham); *m* 1974, Patricia Margaret Reed; one *s* one *d*. *Educ:* Univ. of Birmingham (BSc 1967; PhD Biochem, 1970). Postdoctoral Research Associate: Dept of Biochem., Univ. of Liverpool, 1970–73; Pure and Applied Biochem., Univ. of Lund, Sweden, 1973–74; Lectr in Biochem., 1975–82, Sen. Lectr, 1982–84, Univ. of Southampton. Visiting Professor: Univ. of Lund, 1995–; Univ. of Bath, 1996–. *Publications:* Affinity Chromatography, 1974; An Introduction to Affinity Chromatography, 1979; numerous contribs to learned jls; 34 patents. *Recreations:* antiques, travel. *Address:* Institute of Biotechnology, University of Cambridge, Tennis Court Road, Cambridge CB2 1QT. *T:* (01223) 334160; The Limes, Hempstead, Saffron Walden, Essex CB10 2PW. *T:* (01799) 599307.

LOWE, David Alexander; QC 1984; *b* Kilbirnie, Ayrshire, 1 Nov. 1942; *o s* of late David Alexander Lowe and of Rea Sadie Aitchison Lowe (*née* Bridges); *m* 1972, Vivian Anne Langley; three *s* two *d*. *Educ:* Pocklington Sch., York; St John's Coll., Cambridge (schol.; MA; MacMahon Law Student). Called to Bar, Middle Temple, 1965 (Harmsworth Schol.; Bencher, 1992), *ad eundem*; Lincoln's Inn, 1975. In practice at the Chancery Bar, 1966–. *Address:* Wilberforce Chambers, 8 New Square, Lincoln's Inn, WC2A 3QP. *T:* (020) 7306 0102.

LOWE, His Honour David Bruce Douglas; a Circuit Judge, 1983–98; *b* 3 April 1935; *o s* of late Douglas Gordon Arthur Lowe, QC, and of Karen, *e d* of Surgeon Einar Thamsen; *m* 1978, Dagmar, *o d* of Horst and Anneliese Bosse; one *s* three *d* (and one *s* one *d* by a previous marriage). *Educ:* Winchester College; Pembroke Coll., Cambridge (MA). National service, RN, 1953–55. Profumo Scholar, Inner Temple. Called to the Bar, Inner Temple, 1960; Midland and Oxford Circuit (formerly Midland); Prosecuting Counsel to Dept of Trade, 1975–83; a Recorder of the Crown Court, 1980–83. *Recreations:* music, tennis, gardening (formerly rackets and real tennis). *Address:* Marsh Green Cottage, Marsh, Aylesbury, Bucks HP17 8SP. *Club:* Hawks (Cambridge).

LOWE, Hon. Douglas Ackley, AM 2000; Executive Officer, Tasmanian Branch, Australian Medical Association, since 1992; *b* 15 May 1942; *s* of Ackley Reginald Lowe and Dulcie Mary Lowe (*née* Kean); *m* 1963, Pamela June (*née* Grant); two *s* two *d*. *Educ:* St Virgil College, Hobart. Mem. Tasmanian House of Assembly, for Franklin, 1969–86: ALP, 1969–82; Ind., 1982–86. Minister for Housing, 1972; Chief Secretary, 1974; Deputy Premier, 1975–77; Chief Sec. and Minister for Planning and Reorganisation, 1975; Premier, 1977–81; Treasurer, 1980–81; Minister for: Industrial Relations, Planning and the Environment, 1976; Industrial Relations and Health, Aug. 1976; Industrial Relations and Manpower Planning, 1977–79; Economic Planning and Development, 1979–80; Energy, 1979–81; MLC (Ind.) Buckingham, Tas., 1986–92; Dep. Leader for Govt, Legislative Council, 1989–92. Australian Labor Party: State Sec. 1965–69, State Pres. 1974–75, Tasmanian Section. Tasmanian Deleg. to Aust. Constitutional Convention, 1973–85. Senator, Jaycees Internat. State Pres., Tasmanian Swimming Inc., 1990–98; Mem. Panel, Australian Swimming Disciplinary Tribunal, 1996–98. Silver Jubilee Medal, 1977; Australian Sports Medal, 2000. *Publication:* The Price of Power, 1984. *Address:* (home) 1 Michele Court, Berriedale, Tas 7011, Australia; (office) AMA House, 2 Gore Street, Hobart, Tas 7001, Australia. *T:* (3) 62232047.

LOWE, Air Chief Marshal Sir Douglas (Charles), GCB 1977 (KCB 1974; CB 1971); DFC 1943; AFC 1946; *b* 14 March 1922; *s* of John William Lowe; *m* 1944, Doreen Elizabeth (*née* Nichols); one *s* one *d*. *Educ:* Reading School. Joined RAF, 1940; No 75 (NZ) Sqdn, 1943; Bomber Comd Instructors' Sch., 1945; RAF Coll., Cranwell, 1947; Exam. Wing CFS, 1950; Air Min. Operational Requirements, 1955; OC No 148 Sqdn, 1959; Exchange Officer, HQ SAC, USAF, 1961; Stn Comdr Cranwell, 1963; idc 1966; DOR 2 (RAF), MoD (Air), 1967; SASO, NEAF, 1969–71; ACAS (Operational Requirements), 1971–73; AOC No 18 Group, RAF, 1973–75; Controller, Aircraft, MoD Procurement Executive, 1975–82; Chief of Defence Procurement, MoD, Sept. 1982–June 1983. Air ADC to the Queen, 1978–83. Chairman: Mercury Communications Ltd, 1984–85; Band III Hldgs, 1986–91; Director: Royal Ordnance plc, 1984–7; Rolls Royce, 1984–92. Mem. Council, St John's Sch., Leatherhead, 1984–94. CRAeS 1982; CIMgt (CBIM 1984). *Recreations:* gardening, domestic odd-jobbing, photography, theatre, music. *Club:* Royal Air Force.

See also Baron Glanusk.

LOWE, Sir Frank (Budge), Kt 2001; Founder, 1981, and Chairman of The Lowe Group; Director, Interpublic, USA, since 1990; *b* 23 Aug. 1941; *s* of Stephen and Marion Lowe; two *s* one *d*. *Educ:* Westminster School. Founder, 1997, and Chm., Octagon. Vis. Prof., UCL, 1990–. *Address:* The Lowe Group, 4 Eaton Gate, SW1W 9BJ.

LOWE, Geoffrey Colin; aviation consultant, 1980–88; *b* 7 Sept. 1920; *s* of late Colin Roderick and late Elsie Lowe; *m* 1948, Joan Stephen (*d* 1985); one *d*; *m* 1988, Jean Marion Bailey (*née* Wigginton). *Educ:* Reigate Grammar Sch. GPO, 1937; Exchequer and Audit Dept, 1939. Served War, RAFVR, 1941–46 (Flt-Lt). Asst Principal, Min. of Civil Aviation, 1947; Private Sec. to Permanent Sec., MCA, 1950; Principal, 1950; Colonial Office, 1954–57; Min. of Transport and Civil Aviation, 1957–61; Civil Air Attaché, SE Asia, 1961–64; Asst Sec., Overseas Policy Div., Min. of Aviation, 1964–68; Investment Grants Div., Bd of Trade, 1968–71; Counsellor (Civil Aviation), British Embassy, Washington, 1971–73, Counsellor (Civil Aviation and Shipping), Washington, 1973–74; Under Sec. (Management Services and Manpower), Depts of Industry and Trade, 1974–80. *Recreations:* theatre, crossword puzzles. *Address:* 13 Highwood, Sunset Avenue, Woodford Green, Essex IG8 0SZ. *T:* (020) 8504 7035. *Club:* Civil Service.

LOWE, Prof. Gordon, FRS 1984; CChem, FRSC; Professor of Biological Chemistry, University of Oxford, 1989–2000; Supernumerary Fellow, Lincoln College, Oxford since 2000 (Fellow and Tutor, 1962–99, Embling Fellow, 1995–99, Professorial Fellow, 1999–2000); *b* 31 May 1933; *s* of Harry Lowe and Ethel (*née* Ibbetson); *m* 1956, Gwynneth Hunter; two *s*. *Educ:* Imperial Coll. of Science and Technol., Univ. of London (Governors Prize and Edmund White Prize, 1954; Edmund White Prize, 1957; BSc 1954; ARCS 1954; PhD 1957; DIC 1957); MA 1960, DSc Oxon 1985 . CChem, FRSC 1981. University of Oxford: Pressed Steel Res. Fellow, 1957–59; Deptl Demonstrator, 1959–65; Weir Jun. Res. Fellow, University Coll., 1959–61; Lectr, Organic Chemistry, 1965–88; Aldrichian Praelector in Chemistry, 1988–89; Sub-Rector, Lincoln Coll., 1986–89. Irvine Lectr, Univ. of St Andrews, 1984; Upper Rhine Lectr, Univs of Basle, Mulhouse, Strasbourg, Freiburg and Karlsruhe, 1989; Liversidge Lectr, Univ. of Sydney, 1990. Member: Biochemistry and Biophysics Cttee, SERC, 1979–82; Molecular Enzymology Cttee, Biochemical Soc., 1978–84; Editorial Adv. Panel, Biochemical Jl, 1981–99; Editorial Bd, Bio-organic Chemistry, 1983–. FRSA 1986. Charmian Medal, 1983, Stereochemistry Medal, 1992, RSC. *Publications:* reports on the cysteine proteinases, β-Lactam antibiotics, chiral phosphate and sulphate esters, antitumour and antimalarial agents, and combinatorial chemistry; articles in primary chemical and biochemical jls. *Address:* 17 Norman Avenue, Abingdon, Oxon OX14 2HQ. *T:* (01235) 523029.

LOWE, Dr John; Head, Country Educational Policy Reviews, Education and Training Division, OECD, 1973–87; *b* 3 Aug. 1922; *s* of John Lowe and Ellen (*née* Webb); *m* 1949, Margaret James (*d* 1982); two *s* one *d*. *Educ:* Univ. of Liverpool (BA Hons 1950); Univ. of London (CertEd 1951, PhD 1960). Served War of 1939–45 and Control Commn for Germany, 1945–47 (Captain). Lectr, subseq. Sen. Lectr, Univ. of Liverpool, 1955–63; Dir, Extra-Mural Studies, Univ. of Singapore, 1963–64; Dir, Dept of Adult Educn and Extra-Mural Studies, subsequently Head, Dept of Educnl Studies, Univ. of Edinburgh, 1964–72; Consultant in field, 1964–. Sec./Treas., Internat. Congress of Univ. Adult Educn, 1972–76. Hon. Prof., Warwick Univ., 1990–2000. *Publications:* On Teaching Foreign Languages to Adults (ed jtly), 1965; Adult Education in England and Wales, 1970; (ed) Adult Education and Nation-Building, 1970; (ed) Education and Nation-Building in the Third World, 1971; The Education of Adults: a world perspective, 1975, rev. edn, 1982; (ed) The Clanricarde Letter Book, 1983; Compulsory Schooling in a Changing World, 1983; (jtly) Schools and Quality, 1989; (jtly) Reviews of National Policies for Education: Ireland, 1991; Educational Trends and Prospects in OECD Countries, 1991; The Pursuit of Literacy, 1997; articles in educnl and hist. jls. *Recreations:* reading, music. *Address:* 3 Rue Ribera, 75016 Paris, France. *T:* 45202515.

LOWE, John Evelyn, MA, FSA, FRSA; cultural consultant and author, since 1978; foreign travel specialist, journalist and photographer; *b* 23 April 1928; *s* of late Arthur Holden Lowe; *m* 1st, 1956, Susan Helen Sanderson (marr. diss. 1981); two *s* one *d*; 2nd, 1989, Yukiko Nomura; one *d*. *Educ:* Wellington Coll., Berks; New Coll., Oxford. Served in RAEC, 1947–49 (Sgt Instructor). Victoria and Albert Museum, Dept of Woodwork, 1953–56; Deputy Story Editor, Pinewood Studios, 1956–57; Victoria and Albert Museum: Dept of Ceramics, 1957–61; Assistant to the Director, 1961–64; Dir, City Museum and Art Gall., Birmingham, 1964–69; Dir, Weald and Downland Open Air Museum, 1969–74; Principal, West Dean College, Chichester, West Sussex, 1972–78. Vis. Prof. in British Cultural Studies, Doshisha Univ., Japan, 1979–81; Vis. Prof., Internat. Res. Centre for Japanese Studies, Kyoto, 2001–02. Literary Editor, Kansai Time Out, 1983–88. Hofer-Hecksher Bibliographical Lectr, Harvard, 1974. Pres., Midlands Fedn of Museums, 1967–69. Member: Exec. Cttee, Midland Arts Centre for Young People, 1964–69; Council of the British School at Rome, 1968–70; Crafts Adv. Cttee, 1973–78. Consultant to: Seibu Ltd, Tokyo, 1968–72; Specialtours, London, 1969–74. Trustee: Sanderson Art in Industry Fund, 1968–; Edward James Foundn, 1972–73; Idlewild Trust, 1972–78. Hon. Fellow, RCA, 1988. Asst Ed., Collins Crime Club, 1953–54; Founding Ed., Faber Furniture Series, 1954–56. Eponymous collection of Japanese arts and crafts presented to Pitt Rivers Mus., 1996. *Publications:* Thomas Chippendale, 1955; Cream Coloured Earthenware, 1958; Japanese Crafts, 1983; Into Japan, 1985; Into China, 1986; Corsica: a traveller's guide, 1988; A Surrealist Life—Edward James—Poet, Patron & Eccentric, 1991; Glimpses of Kyoto Life, 1996; The Warden: a portrait of John Sparrow, 1998; Old Kyoto, 1999; major contribs to Encylopædia Britannica and OUP Junior Encyclopedia; articles on applied arts, foreign travel, social history and Japan. *Recreations:* Japan, music, reading, book-collecting, travel. *Address:* 2 rue Jean Guiton, 47300 Villeneuve sur Lot, France. *T:* 0553417253.

LOWE, Prof. (Joseph) John, PhD; Professor of Geography and Quaternary Science, Royal Holloway, University of London, since 1992; *b* 12 June 1946; *s* of Joseph Lowe and Margaret (*née* Rooney); *m* 1969, Jeanette P. Bell; two *s*. *Educ:* Univ. of St Andrews (MA 1st Cl. Hons Geog. 1970); Univ. of Edinburgh (PhD 1977). City of London Polytechnic: Lectr, 1973–77; Sen. Lectr, 1977–85; Principal Lectr and Reader, 1985–88; Prof. and Hd, Dept of Geog., 1988–89; Royal Holloway and Bedford New College, University of London: Sen. Lectr, 1989–90; Reader, 1990–92; Dean of Sience, 1997–2000; Dir, Centre for Quaternary Res., Univ. of London, 1989–97. Vice-Pres., UK Quaternary Res. Assoc., 1992–97; Chm., Earth Scis Cttee, NERC, 1993–96. Univ. of Helsinki Medal, 1996. *Publications:* Studies in the Scottish Lateglacial Environment, 1977; Studies in the Lateglacial Environment of North-West Europe, 1980; (with M. J. C. Walker) Reconstructing Quaternary Environments, 1984, 2nd edn 1997; contrib. to Nature, Jl Geol Soc., Jl Ecology, Proc. Prehist. Soc. and others. *Recreations:* music, hill-walking, soccer (training). *Address:* Department of Geography, Royal Holloway, University of London, Egham, Surrey TW20 0EX. *T:* (01784) 443672; *e-mail:* j.lowe@rhul.ac.uk.

LOWE, Prof. Kenneth Gordon, CVO 1982; MD; FRCP, FRCPE, FRCPGlas; Physician to the Queen in Scotland, 1971–82; Formerly Consultant Physician, Royal Infirmary and Ninewells Hospital, Dundee; Hon. Professor of Medicine, Dundee University, since 1969; *b* 29 May 1917; *s* of Thomas J. Lowe, MA, BSc, Arbroath, and Flora MacDonald Gordon, Arbroath; *m* 1942, Nancy Young, MB, ChB (*d* 1999), twin *d* of Stephen Young, Logie, Fife; two *s* one *d*. *Educ:* Arbroath High Sch.; St Andrews Univ. (MD Hons). Served with RAMC, 1942–46; Registrar, Hammersmith Hosp., Royal Postgrad. Med. Sch., 1947–52; Sen. Lectr in Medicine, St Andrews Univ., 1952–61. *Publications:* (jtly) Regional Anatomy Illustrated, 1983; contribs to med. and scientific jls, mainly on renal, metabolic and cardiac disorders. *Recreations:* reading, fishing. *Address:* 36 Dundee Road, West Ferry, Dundee DD5 1HY. *T:* (01382) 778787. *Club:* Flyfishers'.

LOWE, (Nicholas) Mark; QC 1996; a Recorder, since 2000; *b* 17 June 1947; *s* of late John Lancelot Lowe, solicitor, and of Margaret Janet Lowe (*née* Hucklesby); *m* 1975, Felicity Anne Parry-Williams; two *s* one *d*. *Educ:* Colchester Royal Grammar Sch.; Leicester Univ. (LLB 1969). Called to the Bar, Gray's Inn, 1972; in practice at the Bar, 1973–. *Recreations:* fishing (occasional), tennis (erratic), gardening, sheepkeeping, school sports from the touchline. *Address:* 2–3 Gray's Inn Square, WC1R 5JH. *T:* (020) 7242 4986.

LOWE, Philip Martin; Chef de Cabinet to Vice-President, Neil Kinnock, European Commission, since 2000; *b* 29 April 1947; *s* of late Leonard Ernest Lowe and Marguerite Helen Lowe (*née* Childs); *m* 1st, 1967, Gillian Baynton Forge (marr. diss. 1980); two *s*; 2nd, 1984, Nora Mai O'Connell. *Educ:* Leeds Grammar Sch.; Reading Sch.; St John's Coll., Oxford (MA in PPE); London Business Sch. (MSc Business Studies). Tube Investments, 1968–73; Commission of the European Communities, later European Commission: Directorate-Gen. for Credit and Investments, Luxembourg, 1973–82; Mem., Cabinet of President Gaston Thorn, 1982–85, of Alois Pfeiffer, 1985–86; Directorate-Gen. for Co-ordination of Structural Instruments, 1986–89; Chef de Cabinet to Rt Hon. Bruce Millan, Comr for regl policy, 1989–91; Dir, Rural Develt, 1991–93; Dir, Merger Task Force, 1993–94; Chef de Cabinet to Rt Hon. Neil Kinnock, 1995–97;

Dir-Gen., Develt, 1997–2000. *Recreations:* music, running, hillwalking. *Address:* avenue Michel-Ange 18, 1000 Brussels, Belgium. *T:* (office) 2965040; (home) 7349665; *e-mail:* philip.lowe@cec.eu.int.

See also Bishop Suffragan of Hulme.

LOWE, Dr Robert David; Medical Research Consultant, National Heart Foundation of Australia, 1986–89, retired; *b* 23 Feb. 1930; *s* of John Lowe and Hilda Althea Mead; *m* 1952, Betty Irene Wheeler; one *s* three *d. Educ:* Leighton Park Sch.; Emmanuel Coll., Cambridge; UCH Medical School. BCh, MB, MA, MD, PhD Cantab; FRCP, LMSSA. Medical Specialist, RAMC, 1955–59; Research Asst, UCH Med. Sch., 1959–61; St George's Hosp. Med. Sch.: MRC Res. Fellow, 1961–62; Wellcome Sen. Res. Fellow in Clinical Science, 1963–64; Sen. Lectr in Medicine, St Thomas' Hosp. Med. Sch., 1964–70; Hon. Consultant to St Thomas' Hosp., 1966–70; Dean, St George's Hosp. Med. Sch., 1971–82. AUCAS: Exec. Mem., 1967–; Chm., 1972–78. *Publications:* (with B. F. Robinson) A Physiological Approach to Clinical Methods, 1970; papers on peripheral circulation, hypertension, adrenergic mechanisms, central action of angiotensin, control of cardiovascular system. *Recreations:* bridge, squash, hill-walking, sailing. *Address:* Waipapa Road, RD2 Kerikeri, New Zealand. *T:* (9) 4077911.

LOWE, Rt Rev. Stephen Richard; *see* Hulme, Bishop Suffragan of.

LOWE, Sir Thomas (William Gordon), 4th Bt *cr* 1918, of Edgbaston, City of Birmingham; *b* 14 Aug. 1963; *s* of Sir Francis Reginald Gordon Lowe, 3rd Bt and of Franziska Cornelia, *d* of Siegfried Steinkopf; *S* father, 1986; *m* 1996, Mozhgan, *d* of Hassan Asilzadeh. *Educ:* Stowe School; London School of Economics (LLB 1984); Jesus Coll., Cambridge (LLM 1986). Called to the Bar, Inner Temple, 1985. *Publications:* articles in various legal periodicals. *Heir: b* Christopher Colin Francis Lowe, *b* 25 Dec. 1964. *Address:* 45 Limerston Street, SW10 0BL; 8 New Square, Lincoln's Inn, WC2A 3QP.

LOWE, Vaughan; *see* Lowe, A. V.

LOWE, Veronica Ann; Head of Legal Services, Oxford Brookes University, since 2000; *b* 29 June 1951; *d* of late Arthur Ernest Bagley and Agatha (*née* Blackham); *m* 1977, Ian Stanley Lowe; one *d. Educ:* King Edward VI Grammar Sch. for Girls, Handsworth, Birmingham; St Hugh's Coll., Oxford (MA); Oxford Polytechnic (MIL Exams); City of Birmingham Polytechnic. Articled Clerk, Ryland, Martineau & Co., Birmingham, 1976–78; Lectr in Labour Law, Univ. of Aston in Birmingham, 1978–80; admitted solicitor, 1979; solicitor in private practice, 1979–86; Asst Area Dir, Legal Aid Area No 8, 1986–88; Area Dir (W Midlands), Legal Aid Area No 6, 1988–89; Gp Manager (Midlands), Legal Aid Bd, 1989–90; Dir, Solicitors' Complaints Bureau, 1990–95; Chief Exec., Valuation Office Agency, 1996–97; mgt consultant, 1998–99; solicitor, Pinsent Curtis, 1999–2000. *Publications:* contribs to publications on law for accountants and businessmen. *Recreations:* cooking, eating and drinking, reading, writing unfinished novels, listening to music, travel, talking, current affairs, being with my daughter, all historical subjects. *Address:* Phoenix Cottage, 6 Rugby Road, Dunchurch, Warwicks CV22 6PE. *Club:* Oxford and Cambridge.

LOWEN, Jonathan Andrew Michael; His Honour Judge Lowen; a Circuit Judge, since 2000; *b* 16 Aug. 1943; *s* of George Lowen, QC and Vera Fanny Lowen; *m* 1974, Eve Susan Karpf; two *s. Educ:* Christ Church, Oxford (MA); Witwatersrand Univ., Johannesburg (BA). Called to the Bar, Gray's Inn, 1972; a Recorder, 1995–2000. *Recreations:* art and design, horticulture. *Address:* Isleworth Crown Court, 36 Ridgeway Road, Isleworth, TW7 5LP.

LOWENTHAL, Prof. David, PhD; FBA 2001; Professor of Geography, University College London, 1972–85, now Professor Emeritus (Hon. Research Fellow, 1986); *b* 26 April 1923; *s* of Max and Eleanor (Mack) Lowenthal; *m* 1970, Mary Alice Lamberty; two *d. Educ:* Harvard (BS Hist. 1943); Univ. of Calif, Berkeley (MA Geog. 1950); Univ. of Wisconsin (PhD Hist. 1953). Served US Army (infantry, OSS, Europe), 1943–45. US State Dept, 1945–46; Asst Prof. of Hist. and Hd, Dept of Geog., Vassar Coll., 1952–56; Consultant, Inst. of Social and Econ. Studies, Dept of Hist., Univ. of WI, 1956–70; Inst. Race Relns, UK, 1961–72. Regents Prof., UC Davis, Calif, 1973; Katz Dist. Prof. of Humanities, Univ. of Washington, 1988; Visiting Professor: Univs of Calif, Berkeley, Minn, Washington, Clark and Harvard; CUNY; MIT; West Dean Coll.; St Mary's UC, Strawberry Hill; Lectures: Dist., Center of Humanities and Arts, Univ. of Georgia, 1998; A. W. Franks, BM, 1999; H. Harvey Dist., Univ. of Newfoundland, 1999; Dist., Pinchot Conservation Inst., US, 2001. Member, Editorial Boards, including: Envmt and Behaviour, 1969–76; Geog. Rev., 1973–95; London Jl, 1974–86; Progress in Geog., 1976–90; Internat. Jl Cultural Property, 1989–. Member: Council, AAAS, 1964–71; Council, Assoc. Amer. Geographers, 1968–71; US Nat. Res. Council, 1968–71; SSRC Ethnic Relns Cttee, 1972–77; Bd, Insts of Latin American Studies and Commonwealth Studies, Univ. of London, 1972–87; Landscape Res. Gp, 1984–89 (Chair). Advisor to various organisations, including: US Peace Corps on the Caribbean; UNESCO, IGU on envmtl perception; English Heritage, V&A, Sci. Mus., BM, ICOMOS, UNESCO, etc on heritage. Fellowships: Fulbright, 1956–57; Guggenheim, 1965; Res. Inst. for Study of Man, Landes (US), 1992–93; Leverhulme, 1992–94. Victoria Medal, RGS, 1997; Cullum Medal, Amer. Geog. Soc., 1999. *Publications:* George Perkins Marsh: versatile Vermonter, 1958 (Assoc. Amer. Geographers Award); West Indies Federation, 1961; West Indian Societies, 1972; (with M. J. Bowden) Geographies of the Mind, 1975; (with M. Binney) Our Past Before Us, 1981; The Past is a Foreign Country, 1985 (Historic Preservation (US) Book Prize); (with E. C. Penning-Rowsell) Landscape Meanings and Values, 1986; (with P. Gathercole) Politics of the Past, 1989; Heritage Crusade and the Spoils of History, 1997; George Perkins Marsh: prophet of conservation, 2000 (J. B. Jackson Book Prize, Assoc. Amer. Geographers). *Address:* 1401 LeRoy Avenue, Berkeley, CA 94708, USA.

LOWES, Peter Donald; Director, Anti-Slavery Society for Protection of Human Rights, 1987–89; *b* 13 Sept. 1926; *s* of Col J. H. Lowes and Queenie Frances Lowes (*née* Bowyer); *m* 1954, Linnea Newton (marr. diss. 1980); one *s* two *d. Educ:* Bradfield Coll.; Emmanuel Coll., Cambridge (MA); Univ. of British Columbia (LLB); Geneva Univ. (PhD). Served with Royal Engineers, 1946–48. Master, Wanganui Collegiate Sch., NZ, 1949, Upper Canada Coll., Toronto, 1950–51; practised law, Vancouver, 1953–55; UNRWA, Jordan, 1955–58; journalist, Canadian Broadcasting Corp., 1958; UN Narcotic Drugs, Geneva, 1959–65; External Aid, Canadian Govt, Ottawa, 1965–66; Resident Representative, United Nations Development Programme: Lesotho, 1966–68; Swaziland, 1968–71; Malawi, 1971–74; HQ, NY, 1974–75; Morocco, 1975–79; Co-ordinator, Internat. Drinking Water Supply and Sanitation Decade, Geneva, 1979–86. Mem. Bd, 1980–86, Consultant, 1987, Internat Reference Centre, The Hague; UNDP and World Bank Consultant, 1987–97. Adviser: CARE (UK), 1987–93; Help the Aged, 1987–93; Crisis at Christmas, 1989–99; St Ethelburga's Project, 1995–99. *Publication:* The Genesis of International Narcotics Control, 1965. *Recreations:* walking, mountaineering, history. *Address:* Apartment 34, 4 Clos Belmont, Geneva 1208, Switzerland. *T:* 7350313. *Clubs:* Alpine, Climbers'.

LOWMAN, Ven. David Walter; Archdeacon of Southend, since 2001; *b* 27 Nov. 1948; *s* of Cecil Walter Lowman and Queenie Norah Lowman. *Educ:* Crewkerne Sch., Somerset; City of London Coll. (Dip. in English Civil Law 1970); King's Coll. London (BD 1973; AKC 1973). Estate Duty Office, Inland Revenue, 1966–70. Ordained deacon, 1975, priest, 1976; Curate: Notting Hill Team Ministry, 1975–78; St Augustine, Kilburn, 1978–81; Vocations Adviser and Selection Sec., ACCM, and Chaplain, Church House, Westminster, 1981–86; Team Rector, Wickford and Runwell, Dio. Chelmsford, 1986–93; Diocesan Dir of Ordinands, and Non-residentiary Canon of Chelmsford Cathedral, 1993–2001. Mem. Wkg Pty, House of Bishops (reported on marriage in church after divorce), 1999. *Recreations:* cricket, travel (France, Italy, USA, Cyprus), opera, red wine. *Address:* The Archdeacon's Lodge, 136 Broomfield Road, Chelmsford, Essex CM1 1RN. *T:* (01245) 258257.

LOWNIE, His Honour Ralph Hamilton; a Circuit Judge, 1986–95; *b* 27 Sept. 1924; *yr s* of James H. W. Lownie and Jesse H. Aitken; *m* 1960, Claudine Therese, *o d* of Pierre Lecrocq, Reims; one *s* one *d. Educ:* George Watson's Coll.; Edinburgh Univ. (MA, LLB, Dip. Admin. Law and Practice); Univ. of Kent (PhD). Royal Engineers, 1943–47, NW Europe. WS 1952; enrolled as solicitor, 1953; Mem. Faculty of Advocates 1959; called to Bar, Inner Temple, 1962. Dep. Registrar, Supreme Court of Kenya, 1954–56; Resident Magistrate, 1956–61, Sen. Resident Magistrate, 1961–63, Dep. Registrar-Gen., Kenya, 1963–65; Sen. Magistrate, Bermuda, 1965–72; a Metropolitan Stipendiary Magistrate, 1974–86; a Deputy Circuit Judge, 1976–82; a Recorder, 1983–86. Chm. of Juvenile Courts, 1976–85. Lectr, Kenya Sch. of Law, 1963–65. *Recreation:* historical research. *Address:* 57 Greenhill Road, Otford, Kent TN14 5RR.

LOWRY, Her Honour Noreen Margaret, (Nina); a Circuit Judge, 1976–95; *b* 6 Sept. 1925; *er d* of late John Collins, MC, and Hilda Collins; *m* 1st, 1950, Edward Lucas Gardner, QC (marr. diss., 1962); one *s* one *d*; 2nd, 1963, His Honour Richard John Lowry, QC; one *d. Educ:* Bedford High Sch.; Birmingham Univ. LLB Birmingham, 1947. Called to the Bar, Gray's Inn, 1948, Bencher, 1995. Criminal practice on S Eastern Circuit, Central Criminal Court, Inner London Sessions, etc., practising as Miss Nina Collins; Metropolitan Stipendiary Magistrate, 1967–76. Member: Criminal Law Revision Cttee, 1975–; Criminal Injuries Compensation Bd, 1995–2000. Freeman, City of London, 1985. Hon. LLD Birmingham, 1992. *Recreations:* theatre, travel.

LOWRY-CORRY, family name of **Earl of Belmore**.

LOWSON, Ven. Christopher; Archdeacon of Portsdown, since 1999; *b* 3 Feb. 1953; *s* of George Frederick Lowson, CEng, FIMarE and Isabella Annie Lowson (*née* Spence); *m* 1976, Susan Mary Osborne, RGN, RSCN, MSc; one *s* one *d. Educ:* Newcastle Cathedral Sch.; Consett Grammar Sch.; King's Coll. London (AKC 1975); St Augustine's Coll., Canterbury; Pacific Sch. of Religion, Berkeley, Calif (STM 1978); Heythrop Coll., Univ. of London (MTh 1996). Deacon 1977, priest 1978; Asst Curate, Richmond, Surrey, 1977–82; Priest in charge, 1982–83, Vicar 1983–91, Holy Trinity, Eltham; Chaplain: Avery Hill Coll., 1982–85; Thames Poly., 1985–91; Vicar of Petersfield and Rector of Buriton, Hants, 1991–99; RD of Petersfield, 1995–99; Archdeacon of Portsmouth, 1999. Chm., Portsmouth Diocesan Bd of Ministry, 1999–; Bp of Portsmouth's Liaison Officer for Prisons, 1999–. Vis. Lectr, Portsmouth Univ., 1998–; Dir, Portsmouth Educn Business Partnership, 2000–. Foundn Trustee, Gallipoli Meml Lecture Trust, 1985–91. *Recreations:* watching cricket, the theatre. *Address:* 5 Brading Avenue, Southsea, Hants PO4 9QJ. *T:* (023) 9243 2693, *Fax:* (023) 9229 8788; *e-mail:* lowson@surfaid.org. *Clubs:* Athenæum, MCC.

LOWSON, Sir Ian (Patrick), 2nd Bt *cr* 1951; *b* 4 Sept. 1944; *s* of Sir Denys Colquhoun Flowerdew Lowson, 1st Bt and of Patricia, OStJ, *yr d* of 1st Baron Strathcarron, PC, KC; *S* father, 1975; *m* 1979, Mrs Tanya Du Boulay, *d* of R. F. A. Judge; one *s* one *d. Educ:* Eton; Duke Univ., USA. OStJ. *Heir: s* Henry William Lowson, *b* 10 Nov. 1980. *Address:* 23 Flood Street, SW3 5ST. *Clubs:* Boodle's, Pilgrims; Brook (NY).

LOWSON, Prof. Martin Vincent, FREng; FRAeS; Sir George White Professor of Aerospace Engineering, University of Bristol, since 1986; *b* 5 Jan. 1938; *s* of Alfred Vincent Lowson and Irene Gertrude Lowson; *m* 1961, Ann Pennicutt; one *s* one *d. Educ:* King's Sch., Worcester; Univ. of Southampton (BScEng, PhD). Apprentice, Vickers Armstrong (Aircraft), 1955; Res. student and Assistant, Univ. of Southampton, 1960; Head, Applied Physics, Wyle Labs, Huntsville, USA, 1964; Rolls-Royce Reader, Loughborough Univ., 1969; Westland Helicopters: Chief Scientist, 1973; Div. Dir, Corporate Develt, 1979. Chairman: Flow Solutions Ltd, 1986–97; Advanced Transport Systems Ltd, 1995–. Fellow, Acoustical Soc. of America, 1969; FREng (FEng 1991); FAIAA 1996. *Publications:* numerous papers in learned jls, and patents. *Recreations:* research, squash, bluegrass music. *Address:* Alpenfels, North Road, Leigh Woods, Bristol BS8 3PJ. *T:* (0117) 973 6497.

LOWSON, Robert Campbell; Director of Communications, Department for Environment, Food and Rural Affairs (formerly Ministry of Agriculture, Fisheries and Food), since 1999; *b* 7 March 1949; *s* of late George Campbell Lowson and Betty Lowson (*née* Parry); *m* 1973, Hilary Balsdon; one *s* one *d. Educ:* Gravesend Grammar Sch.; Brasenose Coll., Oxford (BA History 1970). Joined Ministry of Agriculture, Fisheries and Food, 1970: UK Mission, Geneva, 1977; Principal Private Sec. to Minister of Agric., Fisheries and Food, 1982; successively Head of Cereals, Milk, Animal Health, and Agric. Resource Policy Divs, 1983–94; Under Sec., 1994; Minister, UK Repn Brussels, on loan to FCO, 1995–99. *Recreations:* all the usual things. *Address:* Department for Environment, Food and Rural Affairs, Nobel House, 17 Smith Square, SW1P 3JR.

LOWTHER, family name of **Earl of Lonsdale** and **Viscount Ullswater**.

LOWTHER, Viscount; Hugh Clayton Lowther; *b* 27 May 1949; *s* and *heir* of 7th Earl of Lonsdale, *qv*, and Tuppina Cecily, *d* of late Captain G. H. Bennet; *m* 1971, Pamela Middleton; *m* 1986, Angela M., *d* of Captain Peter J. Wyatt, RN and Mrs Christine Wyatt; one *d*.

LOWTHER, Col Sir Charles (Douglas), 6th Bt *cr* 1824; farmer, company director; *b* 22 Jan. 1946; *s* of Lt-Col Sir William Guy Lowther, 5th Bt, OBE, and of Grania Suzanne, *d* of late Major A. J. H. Douglas Campbell, OBE; *S* father, 1982; *m* 1975, Florence Rose, *y d* of Colonel Alexander James Henry Cramsie, O'Harabrook, Ballymoney, Co. Antrim; one *s* one *d. Educ:* Winchester College. Commissioned, Queen's Royal Irish Hussars, 1966; Regimental Duty UK and BAOR, 1974–76; Army Staff College, Camberley, 1978–79; Staff appointment, 1981; CO, QRIH, 1986–89; Officer i/c, Household Cavalry and RAC Manning and Record Office, 1989–93. Mem., HM Body Guard, Hon. Corps of Gentlemen-at-Arms, 1997–. High Sheriff, Clwyd, 1997. Racing Mem., Jockey Club, 1999. *Recreations:* fieldsports, travel. *Heir: s* Patrick William Lowther, *b* 15 July 1977. *Club:* Cavalry and Guards.

LOWTHER, Sir John (Luke), KCVO 1997; CBE 1983; JP; Lord Lieutenant for Northamptonshire, 1984–98; *b* 17 Nov. 1923; *s* of Col J.G. Lowther, CBE, DSO, MC, TD and the Hon. Mrs Lowther; *m* 1952, Jennifer Jane Bevan; one *s* two *d. Educ:* Eton;

Trinity College, Oxford. MA 1949. Served King's Royal Rifle Corps, 1942–47; worked for Singer Sewing Co., USA, 1949–51; Managing Dir, own manufacturing Co., 1951–60; farmer, 1960–. CC Northants, 1970–84 (Leader of Council, 1977–81); High Sheriff 1971, DL 1977, JP 1984, Northants. Hon. Colonel: Royal Anglian Regt (Northamptonshire), TA, 1986–89; Northants ACF, 1991–96. *Recreations:* shooting, countryman. *Address:* Nortoft Grange, Guilsborough, Northants NN6 8QB. *T:* (01604) 740289. *Club:* Boodle's.

LOWTHER, Merlyn Vivienne; Deputy Director and Chief Cashier, Bank of England, since 1999; *b* 3 March 1954; *d* of Norman Edward Douglas Humphrey and Joan Margaret Humphrey (*née* Hewitt); *m* 1975, David John Lowther; one *s* one *d*. *Educ:* Manchester High Sch. for Girls; Univ. of Manchester (BSc Hons Maths 1975); London Business Sch. (MSc Econs 1981). FCIB 1999. Bank of England, 1975–: Sen. Dealer, Gilt Edged Div., 1985–87; Head, Banking Div. and Dep. Chief Cashier, 1991–96; Personnel Dir, 1996–98. Mem. Adv. Gp, Manchester Federal Sch. of Business and Mgt, 1999–. FRSA 1996. Hon. LLD Manchester, 1999. *Recreations:* theatre, singing, reading, family. *Address:* Bank of England, Threadneedle Street, EC2R 8AH. *T:* (020) 7601 4444.

LOY, Francis David Lindley, CBE 1997; Stipendiary Magistrate at Leeds, 1974–97; a Recorder of the Crown Court, 1983–96; *b* 7 Oct. 1927; *s* of late Archibald Loy and late Sarah Eleanor Loy; *m* 1954, Brenda Elizabeth Walker; three *d*. *Educ:* Repton Sch.; Corpus Christi Coll., Cambridge. BA Hons (Law) 1950. Royal Navy, 1946–48. Called to the Bar, Middle Temple, 1952; practised North-Eastern Circuit, 1952–72; Recorder (Northern Circuit), 1972; Stipendiary Magistrate of Leeds, 1972–74. Hon. Sec., Soc. of Provincial Stipendiary Magistrates, 1980–89, Chm., 1990–96. *Recreations:* reading, English History, walking, travel. *Address:* 4 Wedgewood Drive, Roundhay, Leeds LS8 1EF; 14 The Avenue, Sheringham, Norfolk NR26 8DG. *T:* (01263) 822697. *Club:* Leeds (Leeds).

LOYD, Christopher Lewis, MC 1943; *b* 1 June 1923; 3rd and *o* surv. *s* of late Arthur Thomas Loyd, OBE, JP, Lockinge, Wantage, Berks, and Dorothy, *d* of late Paul Ferdinand Willert, Headington, Oxford; *m* 1957, Joanna, *d* of Captain Arthur Turberville Smith-Bingham, Milburn Manor, Malmesbury, Wilts; two *s* one *d*. *Educ:* Eton; King's Coll., Cambridge (MA). Served 1942–46, with Coldstream Guards, Captain. ARICS 1952, FRICS 1955. Mem., Jockey Club. Trustee, Wallace Collection, 1973–90. JP 1950, DL 1954, Oxfordshire (formerly Berks); High Sheriff of Berkshire, 1961. *Address:* Lockinge, Wantage, Oxfordshire OX12 8QL. *T:* (01235) 833265. *Club:* Boodle's.

LOYD, Sir Francis Alfred, KCMG 1965 (CMG 1961); OBE 1954 (MBE 1951); *b* 5 Sept. 1916; *s* of Major A. W. K. Loyd, Royal Sussex Regt; *m* 1st, 1946, Katharine Layzell (*d* 1981), *d* of Lt Col S. C. Layzell, MC, Mwatati, Kenya; two *d*; 2nd, 1984, Helen Monica, *widow* of Lt Col C. R. Murray Brown, DSO, Worlington, Suffolk. *Educ:* Eton; Trinity Coll., Oxford (MA). District Officer, Kenya, 1939; Mil. Service, E Africa, 1940–42; Private Secretary to Governor of Kenya, 1942–45; HM Consul, Mega, Ethiopia, 1945; District Comdr, Kenya, 1947–55; Commonwealth Fund Fellowship to USA, 1953–54; Provincial Commissioner, 1956; Permanent Secretary, Governor's Office, 1962–63; HM Commissioner for Swaziland, 1964–68. Dir, London House for Overseas Graduates, 1969–79; Chm., Oxfam Africa Cttee, 1979–85. *Recreations:* golf, gardening. *Address:* 53 Park Road, Aldeburgh, Suffolk IP15 5EN. *T:* (01728) 452478. *Club:* Vincent's (Oxford).

LOYD, His Honour John Anthony Thomas; QC 1981; a Circuit Judge, assigned to Official Referees' business, London, 1990–97; *b* 18 July 1933; *e s* of Leslie William Loyd and Joan Louisa Loyd; *m* 1963, Rosaleen Iona Ward; one *d* (and one *d* decd). *Educ:* Wycliffe Coll.; Gonville and Caius Coll., Cambridge (BA 1956, MA 1959). RAF Regt, 1951–53. Called to the Bar, Gray's Inn, 1958, Bencher, 1994; a Recorder, 1985–90. *Recreation:* viticulture. *Address:* 31 Swan Street, Boxford, Suffolk CO10 5NZ; Segos, 46800 Le Boulvé, France.

LOYD, Sir Julian (St John), KCVO 1991 (CVO 1979); DL; FRICS; Land Agent to HM The Queen, Sandringham Estate, 1964–91; *b* 25 May 1926; *s* of General Sir Charles Loyd, GCVO, KCB, DSO, MC and Lady Moyra Loyd; *m* 1960, Mary Emma, *d* of Sir Christopher Steel, GCMG, MVO and Lady Steel; one *s* two *d*. *Educ:* Eton Coll.; Magdalene Coll., Cambridge (MA). FRICS 1955. Coldstream Guards, 1944–45. Partner in Savills, Norwich, 1955–64. DL Norfolk, 1983. *Recreation:* fishing. *Address:* Perrystone Cottage, Burnham Market, King's Lynn PE31 8HA. *T:* (01328) 730168. *Club:* Army and Navy.

LOYDEN, Edward; *b* 3 May 1923; *s* of Patrick and Mary Loyden; *m* 1944, Rose Ann (*d* 1986); one *s* two *d* (and one *d* decd). *Educ:* Friary RC Elem. School. Shop boy, margarine factory, 1937; Able-Seaman, MN, 1938–46; Seaman Port Worker, Mersey Docks & Harbour Co., 1946–74. Transport and General Workers' Union: Shop Steward, 1954; Branch Chm. 1959; Mem. District Cttee, Docks and Waterways, 1967; Mem. Nat. Cttee, 1968; Chm., Parly Gp of MPs, 1991–97. Member: Liverpool City Council, 1960 (Dep. Leader, 1983); Liverpool District Council, 1973; Merseyside Met. CC, 1973; Liverpool Met. Dist Council (St Mary's Ward), 1980–83. MP (Lab) Liverpool, Garston, Feb. 1974–1979 and 1983–97. Member: PLP Transport Cttee, 1983–97; For. Affairs Cttee, 1983–97; Health Cttee, 1983–97. President: Liverpool Trades Council, 1967; Merseyside Trades Council, 1974. *Recreations:* full-time political. *Address:* 456 Queens Drive, Liverpool L4 8UA. *T:* (0151) 226 4478. *Clubs:* Gillmoss Labour, Woolton Labour.

LUBA, Jan Michael Andrew; QC 2000; a Recorder (part-time), since 2000; *b* 12 Feb. 1957; *s* of Zenon and Marlene Luba; *m* 1978, Adriana; two *d*. *Educ:* London Sch. of Economics (LLB); Univ. of Leicester (LLM). Called to the Bar, Middle Temple, 1980; Legal Officer, CPAG, 1987–89; Nat. Housing Law Service, 1990–92; private practice at the Bar, England and Wales, 1992–. *Publications:* (with Stephen Knafler) Repairs: Tenant's Rights, 3rd edn 1999; (with Nic Madge and Derek McConnell) Defending Possession Proceedings, 5th edn 2001. *Recreations:* spending time with my family, walking. *Address:* 2 Garden Court, Temple, EC4Y 9BL.

LUBBERS, Rudolphus Frans Marie, (Ruud); UN High Commissioner for Refugees, since 2001; *b* Rotterdam, 7 May 1939; *s* of Paulus J. Lubbers and Wilhelmine K. Van Laack; *m* 1962, Maria E. J. Hoogeweegan; two *s* one *d*. *Educ:* Erasmus Univ., Rotterdam. Sec. to Mgt Bd, 1963–65, Co-Dir, 1965, Lubbers Hollandia Engrg Works; Minister of Econ. Affairs, Netherlands, 1973–77; Mem., Second Chamber of States-Gen.; Sen. Dep. Leader, then Leader, Christian Democratic Alliance, 1977–82; Prime Minister of the Netherlands, 1982–94. Prof., Faculty of Econs and Business Admin, Tilburg Univ.; Vis. Prof., John F. Kennedy Sch. of Govt, Harvard Univ. Kt, Order of the Lion (Netherlands). *Address:* (office) Centre William Rappard, 154 rue de Lausanne, PO Box 2500, 1211 Geneva 2, Switzerland.

LUBBOCK, family name of **Baron Avebury**.

LUCAN, 7th Earl of, *cr* 1795; **Richard John Bingham;** Bt 1632; Baron Lucan, 1776; Baron Bingham (UK), 1934; *b* 18 Dec. 1934; *e s* of 6th Earl of Lucan, MC; *S* father, 1964; *m* 1963, Veronica, *d* of late Major C. M. Duncan, MC, and of Mrs J. D. Margrie; one *s* two *d*. *Educ:* Eton. Lieut (Res. of Officers) Coldstream Guards. *Heir: s* Lord Bingham, *qv*.

[The Earl has been missing since Nov. 1974 and was 'presumed deceased' in Chambers on 11 Dec. 1992.]

LUCAS, family name of **Baron Lucas of Chilworth**.

LUCAS OF CHILWORTH, 2nd Baron *cr* 1946, of Chilworth; **Michael William George Lucas;** *b* 26 April 1926; *er s* of 1st Baron and Sonia (*d* 1979), *d* of Marcus Finkelstein, Libau, Latvia; *S* father, 1967; *m* 1st, 1955, Ann-Marie (marr. diss. 1989), *o d* of Ronald Buck, Southampton; two *s* one *d*; 2nd, 1998, Jill Mary MacKean. *Educ:* Peter Symond's Sch., Winchester; Luton Technical Coll. Served with Royal Tank Regt. A Lord in Waiting (Govt Whip), 1983–84; Parly Under-Sec. of State, DTI, 1984–87. Mem., House of Lords Select Cttee on Science and Technol., 1980–83, on European Communities, 1988–94; UK deleg., N Atlantic Assembly, 1981–83, 1988–98. TEng(CEI); FIMI (Mem. Council, 1972–76; Vice Pres., 1993–); FInstTA; LAE. President: League of Safe Drivers, 1976–80; Inst. of Transport Administration, 1980–83; Vice-Pres., RoSPA, 1980; Mem., Public Policy Cttee, RAC, 1981–83, 1988–98. Governor, Churcher's Coll., Petersfield, 1985–96. Hon. FIHT. *Heir: s* Hon. Simon William Lucas, late Capt. RE [*b* 6 Feb. 1957; *m* 1993, Fiona, *yr d* of Thomas Mackintosh, Vancouver. *Educ:* Churcher's Coll., Petersfield; Leicester Univ. (BSc). Geophysicist, Canada].

See also Hon. I. T. M. Lucas.

LUCAS OF CRUDWELL, 11th Baron *cr* 1663, **AND DINGWALL,** 14th Lord *cr* 1609; **Ralph Matthew Palmer;** *b* 7 June 1951; *s* of 10th Baroness Lucas of Crudwell and 13th Lady Dingwall and of Maj. the Hon. Robert Jocelyn Palmer, MC, 3rd *s* of 3rd Earl of Selborne, PC, CH; *S* mother, 1991; *m* 1st, 1978, Clarissa Marie (marr. diss. 1995), *d* of George Vivian Lockett, TD; one *s* one *d*; 2nd, 1995, Amanda Atha (*d* 2000). *Educ:* Eton; Balliol Coll., Oxford (BA (Hons) Physics). BDO Binder Hamlyn, 1972–76; S. G. Warburg & Co. Ltd, 1976–88. A Lord in Waiting (Govt Whip), 1994–97; Govt spokesman on educn, 1994–95, social security and Wales, 1994–97, agric. and envmnt, 1995–97; Opposition spokesman on internat. develt, 1997–98; elected Mem., H of L, 1999. *Heir: s* Hon. Lewis Edward Palmer, *b* 7 Dec. 1987. *Address:* House of Lords, SW1A 0PW. *T:* (020) 7219 4177; *e-mail:* lucasr@parliament.uk.

LUCAS, Adrian Paul, FRCO(CHM); Organist and Master of the Choristers, Worcester Cathedral, since 1996; *b* 14 March 1962; *s* of Kenneth David Lucas and Kathleen Lucas (*née* Mash); *m* 1986, Joanna Louise Harrison; one *s* one *d*. *Educ:* St John's Coll., Cambridge (Organ Schol.; MA). FRCO(CHM) 1990. Actg Asst Organist, Salisbury Cathedral, 1980; Asst Organist, Norwich Cathedral, 1983–90; Tutor, UEA, 1985–90; Organist, Portsmouth Cathedral, 1990–96. Musical Director: Worcester Fest. Choral Soc., 1997–; Worcs SO, 2000–; City of Birmingham Choir, June 2002–. Guest Conductor, Philharmonia Orch., 2000–. Examr, Associated Bd, RSM, 1989–. Freelance recitalist, broadcaster and conductor, incl. Three Choirs Fest. Recordings incl. 3 solo organ discs and choral works with Portsmouth and Worcester Cathedral Choirs, and Choirs of Three Choirs Fest. *Publications:* various musical compositions, incl. Noël for boys' voices, harp and organ (also recorded); contrib. to musical training books. *Recreations:* bread making, wine, gardening. *Address:* 13 College Green, Worcester WR1 2LH. *T:* (01905) 28854.

LUCAS, Prof. Alan, MD; FRCP, FMedSci; MRC Clinical Research Professor, and Director, MRC Childhood Nutrition Research Centre, since 1996, and concurrently Professor of Paediatric Nutrition, since 2001, Institute of Child Health, University College London; Fellow, Clare College, Cambridge, since 1982; *b* 30 June 1946; *s* of late Dr Saul H. Lucas, Maj., RAMC, and Dr Sophia Lucas; *m* 1st, 1967, Sally Wedeles (marr. diss.); 2nd, 1978, Penny Hodgson; one *s* two *d*. *Educ:* Bedales Sch., Hants; Clare Coll., Cambridge (Foundn Schol.; BA Med. & Natural Sci. Tripos 1st Cl. Hons 1968; BChir 1971, MB 1972; MA 1985); MD Cantab 1991; Oxford Univ. Med. Sch. FRCP 1991; FRCPCH 1997. Jun. posts, Radcliffe Infirmary, Oxford and Addenbrooke's Hosp., Cambridge, 1971–77; Lector, Trinity Coll., Cambridge, 1972–76; University of Oxford: Wellcome Res. Fellow, Dept of Paediatrics, 1977–79; Lectr, St Edmund Hall, 1977–80; University of Cambridge: Clinical Lectr, 1980–82, Hon. Consultant, 1982–96, Dept of Paediatrics; Dir, Med. Studies, Peterhouse, 1980–86; Dir, Studies in Medicine and in Anatomy, Clare Coll., 1982–97; Hd, Infant and Child Nutrition, MRC Dunn Nutrition Unit, Cambridge, 1982–96; Hon. Consultant, Gt Ormond St Hosp. for Children, 1996–. Member: Panel on Child Nutrition, DHSS, 1988–96; Wkg Gp on Infant Formula, EEC, 1988; Standing Cttee on Nutrition, BPA, subseq. RCPCH, 1988–2000 (Mem., Acad. Bd, 1989–94); Physiol Medicine and Infections Bd, 1992–96, Wkg Gp on Fluoride and Osteoporosis, 1994 (Chm.) and Health Services Res. Bd, 1995–96, MRC. FMedSci 2000. Hon. Citizen, Georgia, USA (for educnl services), 1994. Guthrie Medal, RCPCH, 1982. *Publications:* over 300 scientific papers and articles, and contrib. to books, on child health, nutrition and metabolism, notably long term health effects of early nutrition. *Recreations:* art, art history, music, sports. *Address:* Institute of Child Health, 30 Guilford Street, WC1N 1EH. *T:* (020) 7905 2389.

LUCAS, Andrew, FRCO; Master of the Music, Cathedral and Abbey Church of St Alban, since 1998; *b* 19 Aug. 1958; *s* of Richard John Lucas and Vera Mary Lucas (*née* Lawrence). *Educ:* Wakeman Sch., Shrewsbury; Royal Coll. of Music (GRSM 1979; BMus (London) 1981); Sweelinck Conservatoire, Amsterdam. FRCO 1979. Dir of Music, St James', Sussex Gardens, London, 1981–85; St Paul's Cathedral: organ student, 1980–84; Asst Sub-Organist, 1985–89; Sub-Organist and Asst Dir of Music, 1990–98; Acting Organist and Master of Choristers, St Andrew's Cathedral, Sydney, Aust., 1997. Conductor, St Albans Bach Choir, 1998–; Artistic Dir, St Albans Internat. Organ Fest., 1999–. Chm., Asst Cathedral Organists' Assoc., 1993–98; Mem. Council, RCO, 1997–. Liveryman, Co. of Musicians, 1998–. *Recreations:* theatre, travel, architecture, gardens, good food and coffee. *Address:* Cathedral and Abbey Church of St Alban, St Albans, Herts AL1 1BY. *T:* and *Fax:* (01727) 851810; *e-mail:* andrewl01@aol.com; 31 Abbey Mill Lane, St Albans, Herts AL3 4HA.

LUCAS, Prof. Arthur Maurice, PhD; Professor of Science Curriculum Studies, since 1980, and Principal, since 1993, King's College, London; Deputy Vice-Chancellor, London University, since 1997; *b* 26 Oct. 1941; *s* of Joseph Alfred Percival Lucas and May Queen Lucas (*née* Griffin); *m* 1970, Paula Jean Williams; one *s* one *d*. *Educ:* Univ. of Melbourne (BSc 1963; BEd 1968); Ohio State Univ. (PhD 1972; Fulbright Award). FIBiol 1981. Appts at Yallourn and Newborough High Schs, 1964–66; Flinders Univ. of SA, 1967–70; Ohio State Univ., 1970–72; Warrnambool Inst. of Advanced Educn, 1973; Flinders University: Lectr in Sci. Educn, 1974–80; Sen. Lectr, 1976; Vice-Chm., 1976, Chm., 1977–79, Sch. of Educn; King's College, London: Asst Principal, 1987–89; Vice-Principal, 1991–93; Actg Principal, 1992; London University: Chm., Bd of Educnl Studies, 1986–88; Mem. Council, 1995–; Chm., Mgt Bd, Marine Biol. Stn, Millport, 1995–; Dep. Vice Chancellor, 1997–. Member, Council: Commonwealth Assoc. for Sci., Maths and Technol. Educn, 1981–89; Zoological Soc. of London, 1992–93 (Vice Pres., 1993); Royal Instn, 1998–; British Soc. for History of Sci., 1999–; Member: Exec. Cttee, Field Studies Council, 1986–92, 1994–; COPUS, 1993–95; Bd, Univs and Colls

Employers Assoc., 1996–. Chm., Medicine and Soc. Panel, Wellcome Trust, 1998–. Mem., SE Thames RHA, 1993–94. FACE. *Publications:* Review of British Science Curriculum Projects (with D. G. Chisman), 1973; Environment and Environmental Education, 1979; (ed jtly) New Trends in Biology Education, 1987; (ed with P. J. Black) Children's Informal Ideas in Science, 1993; (ed jtly) Regardfully Yours: selected correspondence of Ferdinand von Mueller, vol. 1 1840–1859, 1998; numerous articles in learned jls. *Recreation:* reading. *Address:* Principal's Office, King's College London, James Clerk Maxwell Building, 57 Waterloo Road, SE1 8WA. *T:* (020) 7872 3434. *Club:* Athenæum.

LUCAS, Ven. Brian Humphrey, CB 1993; Rector of Caythorpe, Fulbeck, and Carlton Scroop with Normanton, Diocese of Lincoln, since 2000 (Priest-in-charge, 1996–2000); *b* 20 Jan. 1940; *s* of Frederick George Humphrey Lucas and Edith Mary Lucas; *m* 1966, Joy Penn; two *s* one *d. Educ:* St David's Coll., Lampeter (BA); St Stephen's House, Oxford. Ordained deacon 1964, priest 1965; Curate: Llandaff Cathedral, 1964–67; Parish of Neath, 1967–70; Royal Air Force: Chaplain, 1970–87; Asst Chaplain-in-Chief, 1987–91; Chaplain-in-Chief, and Archdeacon of the RAF, 1991–95, Archdeacon Emeritus, 1996; Canon and Prebendary of Lincoln Cathedral, 1991–95, now Emeritus; Priest-in-charge, St Clement Danes, 1991–95. QHC, 1989–95. Mem., Gen. Synod of C of E, 1991–95. Vice-Pres., Clergy Orphan Corp., 1991–95; Visitor, Soldiers' and Airmen's Scripture Readers Assoc., 1991–95; Mem. Council, Bible Reading Fellowship, 1992–95. Mem. Council, RAF Benevolent Fund, 1991–95. FRSA 1993. *Recreations:* archaeology of the Near East, travel (excluding tourist areas), watching Welsh Rugby football. *Address:* Pen-y-Coed, 6 Arnhem Drive, Caythorpe, Lincs NG32 3DQ; *e-mail:* brian.lucas@savageclub.com. *Clubs:* Savage (Hon. Sec., 1998–); Royal Air Force.

LUCAS, Dr Caroline; Member (Green) South East Region, England, European Parliament, since 1999; *b* 9 Dec. 1960; *d* of Peter and Valerie Lucas; *m* 1991, Richard Le Quesne Savage; two *s.* Oxfam: Press Officer, 1989–91; Communications Officer for Asia, 1991–93; Policy Adviser on trade and envmt, 1993–97; on secondment to Trade Team, DFID, 1997–98; Team Leader, Trade and Investment Policy Team, 1998–99. Mem., Oxford CC, 1993–97. European Parliament: Mem., Cttee on Industry, Ext. Trade, Energy and Res., 1999–; Subst. Mem., Regl Policy and Transport Cttee, 1999–; Vice Chm., ACP Delegn, 1999–. Green Party: Mem., 1986–; Nat. Press Officer, 1987–89; Co-Chair, 1989–90. *Publications* (as Caroline Le Quesne): Writing for Women, 1989; Reforming World Trade: the social and environmental priorities, 1996. *Recreations:* gardening, walking, piano playing. *Address:* 58 The Hop Exchange, 24 Southwark Street, SE1 1TY. *T:* (020) 7407 6281.

LUCAS, (Charles) Vivian; Chief Executive, Devon County Council, 1974–79; solicitor; *b* 31 May 1914; *s* of Frank and Mary Renshaw Lucas, Malvern, Worcs; *m* 1941, Oonah Holderness; two *s* two *d. Educ:* Malvern Coll.; abroad; London Univ. (LLB). Clerk, Devon County Council, 1972–74; Clerk to the Lieutenancy of Devon, 1972–79. *Recreations:* sport, bridge. *Address:* Highfield Lodge, 7 Salterton Road, Exmouth EX8 2BR. *Club:* Golf and Country (Exeter).

LUCAS, Christopher Charles; Under Secretary, Community and International Policy Division, Department of Energy, 1977–80, retired; *b* 5 June 1920; *s* of Charles Edwin Lucas and Mabel Beatrice Read; *m* 1945, Beryl June Vincent; two *d. Educ:* Devonport High Sch.; Balliol Coll., Oxford (Newman Exhibnr). Min. of Fuel, 1946; Central Econ. Planning Staff, 1948; HM Treasury, 1950–70; Cabinet Office, 1970–72; Sec., NEDC, 1973–76; Under-Sec., Dept of Energy, 1976–80. *Recreation:* riding. *Address:* Orchard Croft, Withycombe, near Minehead, Somerset TA24 6PT. *T:* (01643) 821551.

LUCAS, Christopher Tullis, CBE 1994; Project Director, Animarts, since 1999; *b* 20 Dec. 1937; *s* of late Philip Gaddesden Lucas, GM and Maise Lucas; *m* 1962, Tina Colville; two *d. Educ:* Winchester Coll. Apprenticeship with Thomson McLintock & Co.; CA 1965; Chief Exec., ICEM Ltd, 1966–72; Sen. Radio Officer, IBA, 1972–74; first Man. Dir, Radio Forth, Edinburgh, 1974–77; Dir and Sec., RSA, and Sec., Faculty of Royal Designers for Industry, 1977–94; Project Dir, RSA Project 2001, 1994–98. *Recreations:* carpenter, walking, ski-ing, theatre, Suffolk. *Address:* 24 Montpelier Row, Twickenham TW1 2NQ. *T:* (020) 8892 6584.

LUCAS, Dr Colin Renshaw, FRHistS; Vice-Chancellor, University of Oxford, since 1997; Master of Balliol College, Oxford, 1994–2001 (Hon. Fellow, 2001); *b* 25 Aug. 1940; *s* of Frank Renshaw Lucas and Janine (*née* Charpentier); *m* 1st, 1964, Christiane Berchon de Fontaine Goubert (marr. diss. 1975); one *s*; 2nd, 1990, Mary Louise Hume. *Educ:* Sherborne Sch.; Lincoln Coll., Oxford (MA, DPhil). FRHistS 1974. Asst Lectr, then Lectr, Sheffield Univ., 1965–69; Vis. Asst Prof., Indiana Univ., 1969–70; Lectr, Manchester Univ., 1970–73; Fellow, Balliol Coll., Oxford, and Lectr in Modern History, Oxford University, 1973–90; Prof., 1990–94, and Dean, Div. of Social Scis, 1993–94, Chicago Univ. Trustee, Rhodes Trust, 1995–. Hon. DLitt: Lyon, 1989; Sheffield, 2000; Western Australia, 2000; Hon. LLD Glasgow, 2001. Officier, Ordre des Arts et des Lettres (France), 1989; Chevalier: Ordre du Mérite (France), 1994; Légion d'Honneur (France), 1998. *Publications:* The Structure of the Terror, 1973; (with G. Lewis) Beyond the Terror, 1983; (ed) The Political Culture of the French Revolution, 1988; numerous articles. *Address:* University Offices, Wellington Square, Oxford OX1 2JD. *T:* (01865) 270242.

LUCAS, Sir Cyril (Edward), Kt 1976; CMG 1956; FRS 1966; Director of Fisheries Research, Scotland (Department of Agriculture and Fisheries for Scotland) and Director Marine Laboratory Aberdeen, 1948–70; *b* Hull, Yorks, 30 July 1909; *o s* of late Archibald and Edith Lucas, Hull; *m* 1934, Sarah Agnes (*d* 1974), *o d* of late Henry Alfred and Amy Rose; two *s* one *d. Educ:* Grammar Sch., Hull; University Coll., Hull. BSc (London) 1931, DSc (London) 1942. FRSE 1939; Vice-Pres., 1962–64; Neill Prize, 1960. Research Biologist, University Coll., Hull, 1931; Head of Dept of Oceanography, University Coll., Hull, 1942. UK Expert or Delegate to various internat. confs on Marine Fisheries and Conservation, 1948–80, and Chm. of research cttees in connexion with these; Chm., Consultative and Liaison Cttees, Internat. Council for Exploration of Sea, 1962–67; Member: Adv. Cttee on Marine Resources Research, FAO, 1964–71 (Chm. 1966–71); Council for Scientific Policy, 1968–70; Nat. Environmental Res. Council, 1970–78. Hon. DSc Hull, 1975; Hon. LLD Aberdeen, 1977. *Publications:* various scientific, particularly on marine plankton and fisheries research in Bulletins of Marine Ecology (Joint Editor), Jl of Marine Biological Assoc., etc and various international jls. *Address:* 16 Albert Terrace, Aberdeen AB10 1XY. *T:* (01224) 645568.

LUCAS, Geoffrey Haden; Secretary, Headmasters' and Headmistresses' Conference, since 2000; *b* 1 Sept. 1951; *s* of Alfred Philip Lucas and Joyce Lucas; *m* 1974, Elaine Jean Helsby; two *s* one *d. Educ:* Northgate Grammar Sch. for Boys, Ipswich; Univ. of Birmingham (BA Hons); Univ. of Leeds (MEd Dist.); Trinity and All Souls Coll., Leeds (PGCE). Asst teacher, then Hd of Dept, George Dixon Sch., Birmingham, 1974–80; Sen. Lectr, then Principal Lectr and Dir, PGCE Secondary Course, Trinity and All Souls Coll., Leeds, 1980–89; Professional Officer, Modern Langs/Teacher Educn, Nat. Curriculum Council, York, 1989–93; Asst Chief Exec., SCAA, 1993–97; Hd, Corporate Policy and Dir, Special Projects, QCA, 1997–2000. *Recreations:* golf, gardening, cooking, family holidays. *Address:* 4 The Haydens, Tonbridge, Kent TN9 1NS. *T:* (01732) 353345. *Club:* East India.

LUCAS, George; film director, producer and screenwriter; Chairman, Lucasfilm, since 1974; *b* 14 May 1944; *s* of George and Dorothy Lucas. *Educ:* Univ. of Southern California (Bachelor of Fine Arts, 1966). Asst to Francis Ford Coppola on The Rain People, 1967 (winner, Grand Prize, Nat. Student Film Festival for short film, THX-1138, 1967); director, co-author of screenplays: THX-1138, 1970; American Graffiti, 1973; director, author: Star Wars, 1977; Star Wars: the Phantom Menace, 1999; executive producer, author: More American Graffiti, 1979; The Empire Strikes Back, 1980; Return of the Jedi, 1983; Indiana Jones and the Temple of Doom, 1984; Willow, 1988; The Young Indiana Jones Chronicles (TV series), 1992–93; co-executive producer: Raiders of the Lost Ark (and co-author), 1981; Land Before Time, 1988; Indiana Jones and the Last Crusade, 1989; executive producer: Mishima, 1985; Howard the Duck, 1986; Labyrinth, 1986; Tucker, the Man and his Dream, 1988; Radioland Murders, 1994. *Publication:* Star Wars, 1976. *Address:* Lucasfilm Ltd, PO Box 2009, San Rafael, CA 94912, USA. *T:* (415) 6621800.

LUCAS, Prof. Ian Albert McKenzie, CBE 1977; Principal of Wye College, 1977–88, Professor, 1988, University of London, now Professor Emeritus, and Fellow since 1992; *b* 10 July 1926; *s* of Percy John Lucas and Janie Inglis (*née* Hamilton); *m* 1950, Helen Louise Langerman; one *s* two *d. Educ:* Clayesmore Sch.; Reading Univ.; McGill Univ. BSc, MSc; CBiol, FIBiol; FRAgS. Lectr, Harper Adams Agricl Coll., 1949–50; pig nutrition res., Rowett Res. Inst., Aberdeen, 1950–57 and 1958–61; Res. Fellow, Ruakura Res. Station, New Zealand, 1957–58; Prof. of Agriculture, UCNW, Bangor, 1961–77. Chm., Agricl and Vet. Cttee, British Council, 1978–87. Member: Jt Cttee on use of antibiotics in animal husbandry and vet. medicine, 1967–69; MAFF Adv. Council for Agric. and Hortic., 1969–79; Agric. and Vet. Sub-Cttee, UGC, 1972–77; CVCP, 1985–88; Cttee, Internat. Co-operation in Higher Educn, British Council, 1986–90. President: Sect. M, BAAS, 1983; Agricl Educn Assoc., 1987; Rural Educn and Develt Assoc., 1994. Member Governing Body: Grassland Res. Inst., 1970–79; Rydal Sch., 1975–77; RVC, 1978–88; E Malling Res. Station, 1978–87; Hadlow Agric. Coll., 1978–88; Inst. for Grassland and Animal Production Research, 1987–89. Hon. Life Mem., British Council, 1987. Hon. DSc McGill, 1996. *Publications:* scientific papers in Jl Agricl Science, Animal Production, Brit. Jl Nutrition and others. *Recreations:* sailing. *Address:* Valley Downs, Brady Road, Lyminge, Folkestone, Kent CT18 8DU. *T:* (01303) 863053. *Clubs:* Farmers'; Hollowshore Cruising (Oare, Kent).

LUCAS, Ian Colin; MP (Lab) Wrexham, since 2001; *b* 18 Sept. 1960; *s* of Colin and Alice Lucas; *m* 1986, Norah Anne (*née* Sudd); one *s* one *d. Educ:* New Coll., Oxford (BA Jurisprudence). Articled Clerk, then Solicitor, Russell-Cooke, Potter and Chapman Solicitors, Putney and Kingston, 1983–85; Solicitor: Percy, Hughes and Roberts, Chester, 1985–86; Lees, Moore and Price, Birkenhead, 1986–87; Kirwan Nicholas Jones, then Roberts Moore Nicholas Jones, Birkenhead and Wrexham, 1987–92; D. R. Crawford, Oswestry, 1992–97; Sole Principal, Crawford Lucas, Oswestry, 1997–2000; Partner, Stevens Lucas, Oswestry and Chirk, 2001. Contested (Lab) N Shropshire, 1997. Non-exec. Dir, Robert Jones and Agnes Hunt Hosp., Gobowen, Shropshire, 1997–2001. *Recreations:* history, sport, art. *Address:* (office) 67 Regent Street, Wrexham LL11 1PG. *T:* (01978) 355743.

LUCAS, Hon. Ivor Thomas Mark, CMG 1980; HM Diplomatic Service, retired; Assistant Secretary-General, Arab–British Chamber of Commerce, 1985–87; *b* 25 July 1927; 2nd *s* of George William Lucas, 1st Baron Lucas of Chilworth, and Sonia Lucas; *m* 1954, Christine Mallorie Coleman; three *s. Educ:* St Edward's Sch., Oxford; Trinity Coll., Oxford (MA). Served in Royal Artillery, 1945–48 (Captain). BA Oxon 1951. Entered Diplomatic Service, 1951; Middle East Centre for Arab Studies, Lebanon, 1952; 3rd, later 2nd Sec., Bahrain, Sharjah and Dubai, 1952–56; FO, 1956–59; 1st Sec., Karachi, 1959–62; 1st Sec. and Head of Chancery, Tripoli, 1962–66; FO, 1966–68; Counsellor, Aden, 1968–69 (Chargé d'Affaires, Aug. 1968–Feb. 1969); Dep. High Comr, Kaduna, Nigeria, 1969–71; Counsellor, Copenhagen, 1972–75; Head of Middle East Dept, FCO, 1975–79; Ambassador to Oman, 1979–81, to Syria, 1982–84. Fellow in Internat. Politics of ME, Centre of Internat. Studies, Cambridge, 1991–94. Mem., Central Council, Royal Over-Seas League, 1988–94, 1996–; Chm., Anglo-Omani Soc., 1990–95 (Vice Pres., 1996–); Mem. Council, RSAA, 1988–94; Chm. Editl Bd, Asian Affairs, 1995–. Chm. Adv. Bd, Centre of Near and Middle Eastern Studies, SOAS, 1987–90. Trustee, Commonwealth Linking Trust, 1996–. *Publications:* A Road to Damascus: mainly diplomatic memoirs from the Middle East, 1997; chapters in: Politics and the Economy in Syria, 1987; The Middle East: a handbook, 1988; various articles and reviews. *Recreations:* music, crosswords, scrabble. *Clubs:* Royal Over-Seas League, Royal Commonwealth Society.

LUCAS, John Randolph, FBA 1988; Fellow and Tutor of Merton College, Oxford, 1960–96; *b* 18 June 1929; *s* of late Rev. E. de G. Lucas, sometime Archdeacon of Durham and Joan Mary Lucas; *m* 1961, Morar Portal, *er d* of Sir Reginald Portal, KCB, DSC; two *s* two *d. Educ:* St Mary's Coll., Winchester; Balliol Coll., Oxford (John Locke Schol., 1952; MA). Jun. Res. Fellow, Merton Coll., Oxford, 1953–56; Fellow and Asst Tutor, Corpus Christi Coll., Cambridge, 1956–59; Reader in Philosophy, Oxford Univ., 1990–96. Jane Eliza Procter Vis. Fellow, Princeton Univ., 1957–58; Leverhulme Res. Fellow, Leeds Univ., 1959–60. Chm., Oxford Consumers' Gp, 1961–63, 1965. Member: Archbishops' Commn on Christian Doctrine, 1967–76; Lichfield Commn on Divorce and Remarriage, 1975–78. Pres., British Soc. for the Philosophy of Sci., 1991–93. Lectures: (jtly) Gifford, Univ. of Edinburgh, 1971–73; Margaret Harris, Univ. of Dundee, 1981; Harry Jelema, Calvin Coll., Grand Rapids, 1987; Darwin, Cambridge Univ., 2000. *Publications:* Principles of Politics, 1966, 2nd edn 1985; The Concept of Probability, 1970; The Freedom of the Will, 1970; (jtly) The Nature of Mind, 1972; (jtly) The Development of Mind, 1973; A Treatise on Time and Space, 1973; Essays on Freedom and Grace, 1976; Democracy and Participation, 1976 (trans. Portuguese, 1985); On Justice, 1980; Space, Time and Causality, 1985; The Future, 1989; (jtly) Space, Time and Electromagnetism, 1990; Responsibility, 1993; (jtly) Ethical Economics, 1997; The Conceptual Roots of Mathematics, 1999; various articles in learned jls. *Recreation:* walking and talking. *Address:* Lambrook House, East Lambrook, South Petherton, Som TA13 5HW. *T:* (01460) 240413; *e-mail:* john.lucas@merton.oxford.ac.uk.

LUCAS, Keith Stephen; artist; *b* 28 Aug. 1924; *m* 1969, Rona Stephanie Lucas (*née* Levy); two *s* one *d* (and two step *s*). *Educ:* Royal Coll. of Art (ARCA). London Press Exchange, 1956–64; Prof. of Film and Television, Royal Coll. of Art, 1964–72 (first holder of Chair); Dir, British Film Institute, 1972–78; Television Consultant, BFI, 1979–84; Hd of Radio, Film and Television Studies, Christ Church Coll., Canterbury, 1984–89. Artistic Dir, Commonwealth Film and TV Fest. and supporting arts prog., Cyprus, 1980. Exhibitions: retrospective 1956–86, Poor Priests Hosp., Canterbury, 1986; John Nevill Gall., Canterbury, 1988; Royal Mus., Canterbury, 1990; Anna Mei Chadwick Gall., 1993, 1995; Cleary Gall., Canterbury, 1993. Chairman: Canterbury New Theatre Ltd, 1979–83;

Canterbury Theatre and Festival Trust, 1983–86 (Pres., 1986); Vice-Pres., Centre Internat. de Liaison des Ecoles de Cinéma et de Télévision, 1970–72. Governor: North East London Poly., 1971–72; Canterbury Coll. of Art (formerly Canterbury Sch. of Art), 1971–74, 1981–87; Maidstone Coll. of Art, 1982–87; Kent Inst. of Art and Design, 1987–89. Hon. Fellow, Royal Coll. of Art, 1972. *Recreations:* writing, listening to music. *Address:* The Penthouse, 88 Valiant House, Vicarage Crescent, SW11 3LX. *T:* (020) 7228 5289. *Club:* Chelsea Arts.

LUCAS, Prof. Raleigh Barclay; Professor of Oral Pathology, University of London, 1954–79, now Emeritus; Consultant Pathologist, Royal Dental Hospital of London, 1950–79; *b* 3 June 1914; *s* of H. Lucas; *m* 1942, Violet Sorrell; one *d* (one *s* decd). *Educ:* George Watson's Coll.; Univ. of Edinburgh. MB, ChB (Edinburgh) 1937; DPH 1939; MD 1945; MRCP 1946; FRCPath 1963; FRCP 1974; FDS RCS 1974. Asst Bacteriologist, Edinburgh Royal Infirmary, 1939–40; Pathologist, Stoke Mandeville Hosp. and Royal Buckinghamshire Hospital, 1947–49; Reader in Pathology, University of London, 1950–54; Dean, Sch. of Dental Surgery, Royal Dental Hospital of London, 1958–73. Examiner in Pathology and Bacteriology for dental degrees, Univs of London, Glasgow, Birmingham, Sheffield, Liverpool and Wales. Served War of 1939–45, Major RAMC. FRSocMed; Fellow and Past Pres., Royal Medical Society; Mem. Pathological Soc. of Great Britain and Ireland; Mem. BMA. *Publications:* (jtly) Bacteriology for Students of Dental Surgery, 1954; Pathology of Tumours of the Oral Tissues, 1964; (jtly) Tumors of the Major Salivary Glands, 1974; (jtly) Atlas of Oral Pathology, 1985; various articles in medical and scientific journals.

LUCAS, Prof. Robert Emerson, PhD; John Dewey Distinguished Service Professor of Economics, University of Chicago, since 1980; *b* 15 Sept. 1937; *s* of Robert Emerson Lucas and Jane Templeton Lucas; *m* 1959, Rita Cohen (marr. diss.); two *s*. *Educ:* Roosevelt High Sch., Seattle; Univ. of Chicago (BA 1959; PhD 1964). Lectr, Dept of Econs, Univ. of Chicago, 1962–63; Asst Prof. of Econs, Carnegie Inst. of Technol., 1963–67; Associate Prof., 1967–70, Prof. of Econs, 1970–74, Carnegie-Mellon Univ.; University of Chicago: Ford Foundn Vis. Res. Prof., 1974–75; Prof. of Econs, 1975–80; Vice-Chm, 1975–83, Chm., 1986–88, Dept of Econs. Fellow, Amer. Acad. of Arts and Scis, 1980; Mem., NAS, USA, 1981. Nobel Prize for Economics, 1995. *Publications:* Studies in Business-cycle Theory, 1981; (with T. J. Sargent) Rational Expectations and Econometric Practice, 1981; Models of Business Cycles, 1987; (with N. L. Skokey) Recursive Methods in Economic Dynamics, 1989; Customer Service: skills and concepts for business, 1996; papers on growth theory, public finance and monetary theory. *Address:* Department of Economics, University of Chicago, 1126 East 59th Street, Chicago, IL 60637, USA.

LUCAS, Sir Thomas (Edward), 5th Bt *cr* 1887; MA; scientist, executive coach, author, management consultant, lecturer and healer; Chairman, Olafield Technologies PLC; *b* 16 Sept. 1930; *s* of late Ralph John Scott Lucas (killed in action, Libya, 1941), and Dorothy (*d* 1985), *d* of late H. T. Timson, Tatchbury Mount, Hants; *S* cousin, 1980; *m* 1st, 1958, Charmian (*d* 1970), *d* of late Col J. S. Powell; one *s*; 2nd, 1980, Ann Graham Moore. *Educ:* Wellington College; Trinity Hall, Cambridge. Chm., EmDI Ltd.; Dir, Digital Health Research Ltd. Consultant to European Commn DG XIII, The Hale Clinic, and to other orgns; formerly Director: SGF Properties plc; Columbia Industrial Gp; Vacuum Metallizing Processes Inc., and other cos. Senior Trustee: Inlight Trust; Truemark Trust. Mem., Scientific & Medical Network. *Heir: s* Stephen Ralph James Lucas [*b* 11 Dec. 1963; *m* 1993, Charlotte Johnson; one *s* one *d*]. *Address:* Shermans Hall, Dedham, Colchester, Essex CO7 6DE. *T:* (01206) 323506.

LUCAS, Vivian; *see* Lucas, C. V.

LUCAS-TOOTH, Sir (Hugh) John, 2nd Bt *cr* 1920, of Bught; *b* 20 Aug. 1932; *s* of Sir Hugh Vere Huntly Duff Munro-Lucas-Tooth of Teananich, 1st Bt and Laetitia Florence, OBE (*d* 1978), *er d* of Sir John Ritchie Findlay, 1st Bt, KBE; *S* father, 1985; *m* 1955, Hon. Caroline, *e d* of 1st Baron Poole, PC, CBE, TD; three *d*. *Educ:* Eton College; Balliol Coll., Oxford. *Heir: cousin* James Lingen Warrand [*b* 6 Oct. 1936; *m* 1960, Juliet Rose, *yr d* of late T; A. Pearn; two *s* one *d*]. *Address:* Parsonage Farm, East Hagbourne, Didcot, Oxon OX11 9LN; 41 Lancaster Road, W11 1QJ. *Clubs:* Brooks's, Beefsteak.

LUCE, family name of **Baron Luce**.

LUCE, Baron *cr* 2000 (Life Peer), of Adur in the co. of West Sussex; **Richard Napier Luce,** GCVO 2000; Kt 1991; PC 1986; DL; Lord Chamberlain of HM Household, since 2000; *b* 14 Oct. 1936; *s* of late Sir William Luce, GBE, KCMG, and Margaret, *d* of late Adm. Sir Trevylyan Napier, KCB; *m* 1961, Rose, *d* of Sir Godfrey Nicholson, 1st Bt; two *s*. *Educ:* Wellington Coll.; Christ's Coll., Cambridge. 2nd cl. History. Nat. Service officer, 1955–57, served in Cyprus. Overseas Civil Service, served as District Officer, Kenya, 1960–62; Brand Manager, Gallaher Ltd, 1963–65; Marketing Manager, Spirella Co. of GB; Dir, National Innovations Centre, 1968–71; Mem. European Adv. Bd, Corning Glass International, 1975–79; Director: Booker Tate, 1991–96; Meridian Broadcasting, 1991–96. Vice-Chancellor, Univ. of Buckingham, 1992–96. Contested (C) Hitchin, 1970. MP (C) Arundel and Shoreham, Apr. 1971–74, Shoreham, 1974–92. PPS to Minister for Trade and Consumer Affairs, 1972–74; an Opposition Whip, 1974–75; an Opposition spokesman on foreign and commonwealth affairs, 1977–79; Parly Under Sec. of State, 1979–81, Minister of State, 1981–82 and 1983–85, FCO; Minister of State, Privy Council Office (Minister for the Arts), 1985–90. Governor and C-in-C, Gibraltar, 1997–2000. Chairman: Commonwealth Foundn, 1992–96; Atlantic Council of the UK, 1993–96. Mem., Royal Mint Adv. Cttee. Pres., Voluntary Art Network, 1993–. Gov., RSC, 1994–. Member, Board of Trustees: Historic Royal Palaces; Royal Collection Trust; Trustee, Geographers' A–Z Map Trust, 1993–; Emeritus Trustee, RA: DL W Sussex, 1991. *Recreations:* painting, piano. *Address:* House of Lords, SW1A 0PW. *Club:* Royal Automobile.

LUCE, Thomas Richard Harman, CB 1996; public policy consultant; Chairman, Home Office Review of Coroners, since 2001; *b* 11 July 1939; *s* of late Air Cdre Charles Luce, DSO, and Joyce Marjorie Elizabeth Luce (*née* Johnson); *m* 1991, Virginia Manson Hunt; two step *s*. *Educ:* Clifton Coll.; Christ's Coll., Cambridge (BA Hons); Indiana Univ., USA. HM Inspector of Taxes, 1965–67; Asst Principal, Ministries of Aviation and Technology, 1967–69; Principal, CSD, 1969–72; Department of Health and Social Security: Principal, 1972–75; Asst Sec., 1975–84; Under Sec., 1984, seconded to HM Treasury (Head of Management Policy and Running Costs Gp), 1987–90; Dep. Dir, NHS Finance, 1990; Under Sec., Community Services Div., 1990–94, Hd of Social Care Policy, 1995–99, DoH. Trustee, Hampstead and Highgate Fest., 1997– (Chm., 1997–2000). *Publications:* occasional music criticism. *Recreations:* music, reading, walking, swimming. *Address:* 6 Morpeth Mansions, Morpeth Terrace, SW1P 1ER. *T:* (020) 7834 6835; *e-mail:* tom.luce@btinternet.com. *Club:* Athenæum.

LUCIE-SMITH, (John) Edward (McKenzie); poet, art critic and photographer; *b* Kingston, Jamaica, 27 Feb. 1933; *s* of John Dudley Lucie-Smith and Mary (*née* Lushington); unmarried. *Educ:* King's Sch., Canterbury; Merton Coll., Oxford (MA). Settled in England, 1946. Education Officer, RAF, 1954–56; subseq. worked in advertising and as free-lance journalist and broadcaster. Curator of a number of exhibns, UK and USA, 1977–. Mem., Acad. de Poésie Européenne. FRSL. *Publications:* A Tropical Childhood and other poems, 1961 (jt winner, John Llewellyn Rhys Mem. Prize; winner, Arts Coun. Triennial Award); (ed, with Philip Hobsbaum) A Group Anthology, 1963; Confessions and Histories, 1964; (with Jack Clemo, George MacBeth) Penguin Modern Poets 6, 1964; (ed) Penguin Book of Elizabethan Verse, 1965; What is a Painting?, 1966; (ed) The Liverpool Scene, 1967; (ed) A Choice of Browning's Verse, 1967; (ed) Penguin Book of Satirical Verse, 1967; Thinking about Art, 1968; Towards Silence, 1968; Movements in Art since 1945, 1969; (ed) British Poetry Since 1945, 1970; (with Patricia White) Art in Britain 69–70, 1970; (ed) A Primer of Experimental Verse, 1971; (ed with S. W. Taylor) French Poetry: the last fifteen years, 1971; A Concise History of French Painting, 1971; Symbolist Art, 1972; Eroticism in Western Art, 1972; The First London Catalogue, 1974; The Well Wishers, 1974; The Burnt Child (autobiog.), 1975; The Invented Eye (early photography), 1975; World of the Makers, 1975; (with Celestine Dars) How the Rich Lived, 1976; Joan of Arc, 1976; (with Celestine Dars) Work and Struggle, 1977; Fantin-Latour, 1977; The Dark Pageant (novel), 1977; Art Today, 1977, revd edn 1999; A Concise History of Furniture, 1979; Super Realism, 1979; Cultural Calendar of the Twentieth Century, 1979; Art in the Seventies, 1980; The Story of Craft, 1981; The Body, 1981; A History of Industrial Design, 1983; Art Terms: an illustrated dictionary, 1984; Art in the Thirties, 1985; American Art Now, 1985; Lives of the Great Twentieth Century Artists, 1986; Sculpture since 1945, 1987; (ed) The Essential Osbert Lancaster, 1988; (with Carolyn Cohen, Judith Higgins) The New British Painting, 1988; Art in the Eighties, 1990; Art Deco Painting, 1990; Fletcher Benton, 1990; Jean Rustin, 1991; Harry Holland, 1992; Art and Civilisation, 1992; (ed) The Faber Book of Art Anecdotes, 1992; Andres Nagel, 1992; Wendy Taylor, 1992; Alexander, 1992; British Art Now, 1993; Race, Sex and Gender: issues in contemporary art, 1994; (with Elisabeth Frink) Elisabeth Frink: a portrait, 1994; American Realism, 1994; Art Today, 1995; Visual Arts in the Twentieth Century, 1996; Ars Erotica: an arousing history of erotic art, 1997; Adam, 1998; Zoo, 1998; (with Judy Chicago) Women and Art: contested territory, 1999; Judy Chicago: an American vision, 2000; Flesh and Stone (photographs), 2000; contribs to Times, Sunday Times, Independent, Mail-on-Sunday, Listener, Spectator, New Statesman, Evening Standard, Encounter, London Magazine, Illustrated London News, etc. *Recreation:* the Internet. *Address:* c/o Rogers, Coleridge & White, 20 Powis Mews, W11 1JN.

LUCIER, Pierre; President, University of Quebec, since 1996; *b* 15 Oct. 1941. *Educ:* Univ. of Montreal (BA 1963; LRelSc 1970); Jesuit Coll. Maximum (MA Philosophy 1965; MA Theology 1971); Univ. des Sciences Humaines, Strasbourg (Dr d'Etat (Phil.) 1975). Prof., Faculty of Theology, Univ. of Montreal, 1970–75; Sen. Researcher, Center for Res. in Educn, Montreal, 1975–78; Sen. Counselor, Cultural and Scientific Develt Secretariat, Exec. Council, Quebec, 1978–80; Asst Dep. Minister of Educn, Quebec, 1980–84; President: Superior Council for Educn, Quebec, 1984–89; Council of Univs, Quebec, 1989–90; Dep. Minister of Higher Educn and Sci., Quebec, 1990–93; Dep. Minister of Educn, Quebec, 1993–96. Canadian Member: Centre for Educnl Res. and Innovation, OECD, Paris, 1984–86; Cttee of Educn, OECD, Paris, 1996–97; Chm., Council of Canadian Dep. Ministers of Educn, 1993–95; Member: Sci. and Technology Council of Quebec, 1990–96; Bd of Dirs and Council of Govs, Agence Universitaire de la Francophonie, 1998–; Standing Adv. Cttee for Univ. Res., Assoc. of Univs and Colls of Canada, 1998–; Vice Pres., Conf. of Univ. Rectors and Principals of Quebec, 1997–. *Publications:* approx. 150 pubns, incl. a treatise on logical empiricism, and papers and articles on culture, epistemology, educn, educnl systems, instnl evaluation and higher learning. *Recreations:* reading, travelling, cinema. *Address:* (office) 475 rue de l'Eglise, Quebec, QC G1V 9H7, Canada.

LUCK, Keith Frank; Director of Resources, Metropolitan Police Service, since 2000; *b* 18 July 1960; *s* of Jack Luck and Mauree Luck (*née* Campbell); *m* 1987, Michelle Susan Harris; one *s* one *d*. *Educ:* Sidney Sussex Coll., Cambridge (BA Hons 1981; MA 1985). ACMA 1986, FCMA 1993; Associate Mem., ACT, 1994. Internal audit, then financial, mgt and systems accounting, BT, 1981–85 (CIMA Inst. Prize and Harold Wilmot Prize, 1985); BT Schol., RAPC, Worthy Down, 1983–85; Head of Financial Training, BT Mgt Coll., 1986–87; Consultant, Deloitte, Haskins & Sells, 1987–89; Business Systems Manager, 1989–90, Project Dir, 1990–91, Financial Controller, 1991–93, Midland Bank; Head of Corporate Finance, 1993–94, Asst Dir (Corporate Finance and Property) and Chief Internal Auditor, 1994–97, Tower Hamlets LBC; Dir of Finance and Support Services, Lewisham LBC, 1997–99; Dir, Support Services, Accord plc, 1999. Member: Strategic Planning Soc., 1996–99; Soc. of London Treasurers, 1997–99; London Financial Adv. Cttee, 1998–99; Steering Gp, Review of Organised Fraud, 1999; Founder Mem., UK Chapter, Assoc. of Fraud Examrs, 1997–; Local Authy Rep., Review of Revenue Grant Distribution (England and Wales), DETR, 1999; Sec., London Team for Action against Fraud, 1998–99. FIMgt 1987; FRSA 2000. *Recreations:* family, motorcycling, local history, historical geography, archaeology. *Address:* New Scotland Yard, Broadway, SW1H 0BG; *e-mail:* keith.luck@btinternet.com. *Clubs:* Central London Golf, Lyneham Golf and Country.

LUCKETT, Dr Richard; Fellow, since 1978, and Pepys Librarian, since 1982, Magdalene College, Cambridge; *b* 1 July 1945; *s* of late Rev. Canon Gerald Archer Luckett and of Margaret Mary Luckett (*née* Chittenden). *Educ:* St John's Sch., Leatherhead; St Catharine's Coll., Cambridge (MA, PhD). Lectr, RMA, Sandhurst, 1967–69; Cambridge University: Res. Fellow, 1970–72, Fellow, 1972–78, Dean, 1974–78, St Catharine's Coll.; Univ. Asst Lectr in English, 1973–78; Lectr, 1978–2001; Precentor, Magdalene Coll., 1982–94. *Publications:* The White Generals, 1971, 2nd edn 1988; The Fabric of Dryden's Verse (Chatterton Lect.), 1981; (ed with C. Hogwood) Music in Eighteenth Century England, 1983; (contrib.) The Pepys Companion, 1983; Handel's Messiah: a celebration, 1992; (ed) The Cryes of London, 1994. *Address:* Magdalene College, Cambridge CB3 0AG. *T:* (01223) 332100. *Club:* Army and Navy.

LUCY, Sir Edmund John William Hugh Cameron-Ramsay F.; *see* Fairfax-Lucy.

LUDDINGTON, Sir Donald (Collin Cumyn), KBE 1976; CMG 1973; CVO 1974; retired; *b* 18 Aug. 1920; *s* of late F. Norman John Luddington, Ceylon Civil Service, and late M. Myrtle Amethyst Payne; *m* 1945, Garry Brodie Johnston; one *s* one *d*. *Educ:* Dover Coll.; St Andrews Univ. (MA). Served War, Army, 1940–46, KOYLI and RAC, Captain. Hong Kong Govt, 1949–73; Sec. for Home Affairs, 1971–73; Governor, Solomon Islands, 1973–76. Chm., Public Services Commn, Hong Kong, 1977–78; Comr, Indep. Commn against Corruption, Hong Kong, 1978–80. *Recreation:* walking. *Address:* The Firs, Little Lane, Easingwold, York YO61 3AQ. *Clubs:* Royal Commonwealth Society; Hong Kong (Hong Kong).

LUDER, (Harold) Owen, CBE 1986; President, Royal Institute of British Architects, 1981–83 and 1995–97; Vice-Chairman, Architects Registration Board, since 1997;

architect and construction industry consultant; Principal, Owen Luder Consultancy, Communication in Construction Ltd, since 1987; *b* London, 7 Aug. 1928; *s* of late Edward Charles and Ellen Clara Luder; *m* 1st, 1951, Rose Dorothy (Doris) Broadstock (marr. diss. 1988); four *d* (one *s* decd); 2nd, 1989, Jacqueline Ollerton. *Educ:* Deptford Park Primary Sch.; Peckham Sch. for Girls; Brixton Sch. of Building; Regent St Polytechnic Sch. of Architecture. ARIBA 1954, FRIBA 1967. Private practice in architecture, 1957–87; Founder and Sen. Partner, Owen Luder Partnership, 1958–78, when it became one of the first architectural partnerships to convert to an unlimited co., Chm. and Man. Dir, 1978–87; on withdrawal from architectural practice, set up Owen Luder Consultancy (specialising in communication in construction), 1987; Director: Communication in Construction Ltd, 1990–; Jarvis PLC, 1995–. Principal architectural works in commercial and industrial architecture and environmental and urban planning in UK and abroad; consultant: to NCB for Vale of Belvoir coal mining project, 1975–87; to BR for re-use of Engrg Works, Shildon and Swindon, 1985–86; Consultant Architect, RCS, 1974–87; Architect/Planning Consultant, Marine Soc., 1990–. Royal Institute of British Architects: Mem. Council, 1967–89, 1993–; Hon. Treasurer, 1975–78; Vice-Pres., Membership Communications, 1989–90; Hon. Sec./Treasurer, Commonwealth Assoc. of Architects, 1985–87; Chm. Organising Cttee, IUA Congress 1987. Pres., Norwood Soc., 1981–92. Columnist: Building magazine, 1969–78, 1983–90; Building Design magazine, 1978–81, 1994–95; Editor and Presenter, Architectural Practice Video Magazine, 1987–90; Consultant and Presenter: RIBA Technical Seminar Prog., 1985–93; Building Design Update Seminars, 1994–. Occasional radio and TV broadcaster, UK and USA. British Kart Racer, 1961–63; survivor, Lakonia cruise-liner disaster, 1963. FRSA 1984. Mem., British Acad. of Experts, 1991 (Vice Chm., 1997–99). Trustee, Children Nationwide, 1997–. RIBA Architecture Bronze Medal (for Eros House, Catford), 1963; various Civic Trust architectural and housing awards and commendations; Silver Jubilee Medal, for Housing Strategy for the 80s, Town Planning Assoc., 1981; Business Columnist of the Year, Publisher magazine, 1985. Arkansas Traveller, USA, 1971. *Publications:* Sports Stadia after Hillsborough, 1990; Keeping out of Trouble, 1999; contribs on architectural, planning and building matters to various jls. *Recreations:* writing, swimming, photography, theatre, playing golf badly, supporting Arsenal FC avidly. *Address:* (office) 2 Smith Square, SW1P 3HS. *Club:* Royal Automobile.

LUDFORD, Baroness *cr* 1997 (Life Peer), of Clerkenwell in the London Borough of Islington; **Sarah Ann Ludford;** Member (Lib Dem) London Region, European Parliament, since 1999; *b* 14 March 1951. *Educ:* Portsmouth High Sch.; London Sch. of Economics (BSc Econ; MSc Econ); Inns of Court Sch. of Law. Called to the Bar, Gray's Inn, 1979. With European Commn, 1979–85; European Advr, Lloyd's of London, 1985–87; Vice Pres., Corporate External Affairs, American Express Europe, 1987–90. Mem. (Lib Dem) Islington LBC, 1991–99. Mem., Lib Dem Federal Policy Cttee, 1990– (Vice Chm., 1992–98); Vice Chm., London Lib Dems, 1990–94. Contested: (L) Wight and Hampshire E, 1984, (Lib Dem) London Central, 1989 and 1994, EP elections; (Lib Dem) Islington N, 1992, Islington S and Finsbury, 1997. *Address:* 36 St Peter's Street, N1 8JT. *T:* (020) 7288 2526.

LUDLOW, Bishop Suffragan of; *no new appointment at time of going to press.*

LUDLOW, Archdeacon of; *see* Ludlow, Bishop Suffragan of.

LUDLOW, Caroline Mary; Her Honour Judge Ludlow; a Circuit Judge, since 1997; Designated Judge, Chelmsford County Court, since 2000; *b* 25 Sept. 1947; *d* of William George Hughes Woodward and Mary Josephine Woodward; *m* 1st, 1970, Brian Ludlow (marr. diss. 1976); 2nd, 1987, John Warwick Everitt; one *d. Educ:* Hillingdon Court; St Mary's Grammar Sch.; Queen Mary Coll., London Univ. (LLM). Called to the Bar, Inner Temple, 1970; practised on South Eastern Circuit, 1979–97; a Recorder, 1995–97. Mem., Law Sch. Adv. Cttee, 1992–, Court, 1999–, Essex Univ. (Bar Co-ordinator, Law in Action course, 1992–97). *Recreations:* reading, gardening. *Address:* East Anglian Chambers, 52 North Hill, Colchester CO1 1PY. *T:* (01206) 572756.

LUDLOW, (Ernest John) Robin, TD 1979; career consultant, since 1996; *b* 2 May 1931; *s* of late Donald Ernest Ludlow, Blandford, Dorset, and Buxted, Sussex; *m* 1st, 1970, Sonia Louise Hatfeild (marr. diss. 1993); one *s* one *d*; 2nd, 1996, Mrs Primrose June King (*née* Palmer). *Educ:* Framlingham Coll., Suffolk. RMA Sandhurst, 1949–52; commissioned RASC, 1952; Staff, RMA Sandhurst, 1954–57; retd 1957. J. Lyons & Co. Ltd, 1957–59; The Economist, 1959–72; Press Sec. to the Queen, 1972–73; Dep. Dir, Aims of Industry, 1973–77; Head of Publicity, Strutt and Parker, 1977; Man. Dir, Kiernan and Co. Ltd (Exec. Search), 1977–79; Partner, Boyden Internat. (Exec. Search), 1979–81; Managing Director: Robin Ludlow & Associates (Exec. Search), 1981–89; Management Search Internat., 1985–89; Managing Consultant, Euro Management Search, 1990–95. Governor: Clergy Orphan Corp. (St Edmund's Sch. Canterbury, St Margaret's Sch. Bushey), 1973–83; Royal Star and Garter Home for Disabled Servicemen, 1987–91; Chairman: The Yeomanry Benevolent Fund, 1981–90 (Mem. Cttee, 1975–2000); Sharpshooters Yeomanry Assoc., 1973–83 (Mem. Cttee, 1972–2000). Kent and Co. of London Yeomanry (Sharpshooters), TA, 1959–69; The Queen's Regt, TA, 1971–78 (Maj.). Vice Chm., SE, TA&VRA, 1988–91 (Mem., F and GP Cttee, 1973–86; Mem., 1973–86, Chm., 1988–91, Kent Cttee). *Recreations:* shooting, gardening, conservation. *Address:* 19 North Row, Warminster, Wilts BA12 9AD. *T:* and *Fax:* (01985) 213025; *e-mail:* robin.ludlow@btinternet.com.

LUDMAN, Harold, FRCS; Consultant Surgeon in Neuro-otology, National Hospital for Neurology and Neurosurgery, 1967–98; Consultant Surgeon to Ear, Nose and Throat Department, King's College Hospital, 1965–94; *b* 23 Feb. 1933; *s* of Nathan Ludman and Fanny Dinah Jerome; *m* 1957, Lorraine Israel; one *s* one *d. Educ:* Bradford Grammar Sch.; Sidney Sussex Coll., Cambridge (BA 1954; MB, BChir 1957; MA 1958). FRCS 1961. House Physician, UCH, 1957; House Surgeon: Royal Ear Hosp., UCH, 1957; Edgware Gen. Hosp., 1958; Royal Marsden Hosp., 1958–59; Registrar and Sen. Registrar, Ear, Nose and Throat Dept, KCH, 1960–65. President: British Assoc. Otolaryngology, 1990–93; Section of Otology, RSocMed, 1985; Chm., Soc. Audiology Technicians, 1967–75. Chm., Specialist Adv. Cttee in Otolaryngology, Jt Cttee Higher Surgical Trng, 1988–91; Mem., Intercollegiate Bd in Otolaryngology, RCS (formerly Mem. Court of Examiners); Chm., working party on deafness, MRC, 1973–77; formerly Mem., Hearing Aid Council. W. J. Harrison Prize, RSocMed, 1987; W. Jobson Horne Prize, BMA, 1990. *Publications:* (jtly) Diseases of the Ear, 1963, 6th edn 1997; (contrib.) Scott-Brown's Diseases of the Ear, Nose and Throat, 4th edn 1979, 5th edn 1987, 6th edn 1996; contribs to books on ear diseases; numerous papers to learned jls on diseases of the ear. *Recreations:* photography, computers, reading, theatre, bird watching.

LUDWIG, Christa; singer; *b* Berlin, 16 March; *d* of Anton Ludwig, singer, stage director and opera general manager and Eugenie (*née* Besalla), singer; *m* 1st, 1957, Walter Berry (marr. diss. 1970), baritone; one *s*; 2nd, 1972, Paul-Emile Deiber, actor and stage-director. *Educ:* Matura. Staedtische Buehnen, Frankfurt; Landestheater Darmstadt; Landestheater, Hannover; Vienna State Opera; guest appearances in New York, Chicago, London, Berlin, Munich, Tokyo, Milan, Rome, Lucerne, Salzburg, Epidauros, Zürich, Holland, Los Angeles, Cleveland, Saratoga, Bayreuth, Copenhagen, Gent, Montreal, Prague, Budapest and others. Kammersängerin, Austria, 1962; Grand Prix du Disque, 1966; Grammy Award, 1967; Mozart Medal, Mozartgemeinde, Vienna, 1969; First Class Art and Science, Austria, 1969; Deutscher Schallplattenpreis, 1970; Orphée d'Or, 1970; Prix des Affaires Culturelles, 1972; Vienna Philharmonic Silver Rose, 1980; Hugo Wolf Medal, 1980; Gustav Mahler Medal, 1980; Ehrenring, Staatsoper Vienna, 1980, Hon. Mem., 1981, Fidelio Medal, 1991; Golden Medal, City of Salzburg, 1988, and Vienna, 1988; Echo Prize, Germany, 1994; Musician of the Year, Musical America, 1994. Commandeur des Arts et des Lettres (France), 1988; Chevalier, Légion d'Honneur (France), 1989; Grosses Ehrenzeichen (Austria), 1994; Commandeur, Ordre pour le Mérite (France), 1997. *Publication:* Und ich wäre so gern Primadonna gewesen (autobiog.), 1994 (French edn 1996, US edn 1999). *Recreations:* listening to music, theatre, concerts, reading. *Address:* c/o Heidrun Artmüller, Goethegasse 1, 1010 Wien, Austria.

LUE, Dr Abraham Sek-Tong, CMG 1998; MBE 1984; *b* 7 Jan. 1939; *s* of Lue Phang and Chin Choy Keow; *m* 1985, Dr Adaline Mang-Yee Ko. *Educ:* King George V Sch., Hong Kong; University Coll. London (BSc); King's Coll. London (PhD 1965; FKC 1993). King's College London: Lectr and Sen. Lectr in Maths, 1962–86; Asst Principal, 1986–92. Dir, Fleming Chinese Investment Trust PLC, 1993–. Dir, Chelsea and Westminster NHS Healthcare Trust, 1994–96. Mem., Home Sec.'s Adv. Cttee on Race Relns, 1979–86; Chm., 1988–92, Hon. Vice Pres., 1992–, Westminster Race Equality Council. Founder and Chm., Chinese Community Centre, London, 1980–96; GB/China Centre: Mem., Exec. Cttee, 1992–; Hon. Treas., 1994–95; Vice Chm., 1996–. European Rep., K.C. Wong Educn Foundn, Hong Kong, 1987–96. Chm., British Liby Internat. Dunhuang Project, 1994–. *Publications:* Basic Pure Mathematics II, 1974; mathematical papers on homological algebra in learned jls. *Recreation:* reading. *Address:* 27 Magazine Gap Road, Hong Kong. *T:* 28492880, *Fax:* 28492881; 18 Randolph Road, W9 1AN. *Clubs:* Athenæum, Hurlingham; Hong Kong Jockey (Hong Kong).

LUETCHFORD, Teresa Jane; *see* Kingham, T. J.

LUFF, Rev. Canon Alan Harold Frank; Canon Residentiary of Birmingham Cathedral, 1992–96, Canon Emeritus, 1996; *b* 6 Nov. 1928; *s* of late Frank Luff and Elsie Lilian Luff (*née* Down), Bristol; *m* 1956, Enid Meirion, *d* of late Robert Meirion Roberts and Daisy Harker Roberts; three *s* one *d. Educ:* Bristol Grammar School; University Coll., Oxford (BA 1951, Dip. Theol. 1952, MA 1954); Westcott House, Cambridge. ARCM 1977. Deacon, 1956; priest, 1957; Assistant Curate: St Mathew, Stretford, Manchester, 1956–59; St Peter, Swinton, Manchester (with charge of All Saints, Wardley), 1959–61; Precentor of Manchester Cathedral, 1961–68; Vicar of Dwygyfylchi (otherwise Penmaenmawr), Gwynedd, dio. Bangor, 1968–79; Precentor, 1979–92, also Sacrist, 1979–86, Westminster Abbey; licensed to officiate, dio. Llandaff, 1996–. Chm., Hymn Soc. of Great Britain and Ireland, 1987–93 (Hon. Sec., 1973–86); Vice Pres., Internat. Arbeitsgemeinschaft für Hymnologie, 1999–. Chm., Pratt Green Trust, 1988–. Hon. FGCM 1993 (Warden, 1984–97; Vice Pres., 1997–); ARSCM 2000. *Publications:* Hymns and Psalms (composer and author), 1981; Welsh Hymns and their tunes, 1990; (ed) Story Song, 1993; (ed) Sing His Glory, 1997; (ed and trans.) Ann Griffiths, Hymns and Letters, 1999; contribs to New Christian, Musical Times, Choir and Organ, etc. *Recreations:* singing, conducting, cooking. *Address:* 12 Heol Tyn y Cae, Rhiwbina, Cardiff CF14 6DJ.

LUFF, Geoffrey Shadrack, IPFA; County Treasurer, Nottinghamshire County Council, 1984–91; *b* 12 July 1933; *s* of Shadrack Thomas Luff and Rosie Winifred Luff (*née* Lister); *m* 1st, 1956, Gloria Daphne Taylor (*d* 1992); one *s* one *d*; 2nd, 1997, Brenda Wilson. *Educ:* Mundella Grammar Sch., Nottingham; BA Hons Open, 1998. Various posts in City Treasury, Nottingham CC, 1949–67; Sen. Technical Asst and Asst Bor. Treasurer, Derby CBC, 1967–73; Asst County Treasurer, Derbyshire CC, 1973–78; Dep. County Treasurer, Nottinghamshire CC, 1978–84. *Recreations:* bowls, gardening, birdwatching, photography.

LUFF, Peter James; MP (C) Mid Worcestershire, since 1997 (Worcester, 1992–97); *b* 18 Feb. 1955; *s* of Thomas Luff and Joyce (*née* Mills); *m* 1982, Julia Jenks; one *s* one *d. Educ:* Windsor Grammar Sch.; Corpus Christi Coll., Cambridge (MA Econs). Research Asst to Rt Hon. Peter Walker, 1977–80; Head of Private Office to Rt Hon. Edward Heath, 1980–82; Dir, Good Relations Public Affairs, 1982–87; Special Advr to Rt Hon. Lord Young of Graffham, 1987–89; Sen. Consultant, Lowe Bell Communications, 1989–90; Asst Man. Dir, Good Relations Ltd, 1990–92. PPS to Minister for Industry and Energy, 1993–96, to Lord Chancellor, 1996–97, to Minister of State, Home Office, 1996–97; Chm., Agriculture Select Cttee, 1997–2000; an Opposition Whip, 2000–. Patron, Conservative Students, 1995–98. Vice-Pres., Severn Valley Railway, 1997–. FIPR 1998. *Recreations:* performing arts, steam railways. *Address:* House of Commons, SW1A 0AA. *T:* (01905) 763952; *e-mail:* luffpj@parliament.uk. *Clubs:* Royal Automobile; Worcestershire CC.

LUFFINGHAM, Prof. John Kingley, FDSRCSE; Professor of Orthodontics, University of Glasgow, 1976–93; *b* 14 Aug. 1928; *s* of Alfred Hulbert Carr Luffingham and Frances Tugby; *m* 1968, Elizabeth Margaret Anderson; two *s* one *d. Educ:* Haileybury; London Hosp. Med. Coll. (BDS, PhD London); Dip. Orth RCSE. House Surgeon, London Hosp. Med. Coll., 1957–58; Registrar, KCH, 1959–61; Clinical Research Fellow, MRC, 1961–64; Sen. Registrar, Guy's Hosp., 1965–67; Sen. Lectr, Glasgow Univ., 1968–76; Consultant Orthodontist, Greater Glasgow Health Board, 1968–76. *Publications:* articles in dental jls, incl. British Jl of Orthodontics, European Jl of Orthodontics, Archives of Oral Biology. *Recreations:* sailing, skiing.

LUFT, His Honour Arthur Christian, CBE 1988; Member, Legislative Council, Isle of Man, 1988–98; *b* 21 July 1915; *e s* of late Ernest Christian Luft and late Phoebe Luft; *m* 1950, Dorothy, *yr d* of late Francis Manley; two *s. Educ:* Bradbury Sch., Cheshire. Served Army, 1940–46. Admitted to Manx Bar, 1940; Attorney-Gen., IOM, 1972–74; Second Deemster, 1974–80; HM's First Deemster, Clerk of the Rolls, and Dep. Governor, IOM, 1980–88. Chairman: IOM Criminal Injuries Compensation Tribunal, 1974–80; Prevention of Fraud (Unit Trust) Tribunal, 1974–80; IOM Licensing Appeal Court, 1974–80; Wireless Telegraphy Appeal Bd for IOM, 1974–80; IOM Income Tax Appeal Comrs, 1980–88; IOM Gaming Control Comrs, 1988–90; Rivers Pollution Cttee, 1989–92; Data Protection Tribunal, 1990–92; IOM Arts Council, 1992–98; Member: Dept of Local Govt and Envmt, IOM, 1988–93; Dept of Agric., Fisheries and Forestry, IOM, 1993–98; Public Accounts Cttee, 1988–98; Ecclesiastical Cttee of Tynwald, 1992–98; Standing Orders Cttee of Legislative Council, 1995–98. Chm., Legislative Cttee, Diocesan Synod., 1989–98. Pres., Youth Adv. Gp, 1991–94. Pres., Manx Deaf Soc., 1975–. Pres., IOM Cricket Club, 1980–98. *Recreations:* theatre, watching cricket, gardening. *Address:* Leyton, Victoria Road, Douglas, Isle of Man IM2 6AQ. *T:* (01624) 621048. *Clubs:* Ellan Vannin, Manx Automobile (Douglas).

LUKE, 3rd Baron *cr* 1929, of Pavenham, Co. Bedford; **Arthur Charles St John Lawson Johnston;** DL; fine art dealer, since 1972; an Opposition Whip, House of Lords, since 1997; *b* 13 Jan. 1933; *e s* of 2nd Baron Luke and of Barbara, *d* of Sir FitzRoy Hamilton

Anstruther-Gough-Calthorpe, 1st Bt; *S* father, 1996; *m* 1st, 1959, Silvia Maria (marr. diss. 1971), *yr d* of Don Honorio Roigt; one *s* two *d*; 2nd, 1971, Sarah Louise, *d* of Richard Hearne, OBE; one *s*. *Educ:* Eton; Trinity Coll., Cambridge (BA Hons). Elected Mem., H of L, 1999. Mem., Beds CC, 1965–70 (Chm., Staffing Cttee, 1967–70). President: Nat. Assoc. of Warehousekeepers, 1962–78; Internat. Assoc. of Book-Keepers, 1997–. Comdr, St John Ambulance, Beds, 1985–90 (Comr, 1972–85). Member Court: Corp. of Sons of the Clergy, 1980–; Drapers' Co., 1993– (Master Warden, 2000–01). High Sheriff, Beds, 1969–70, DL Beds, 1989. KStJ 1988. *Recreations:* shooting, fishing. *Heir: s* Hon. Ian James St John Lawson Johnston [*b* 3 Oct. 1963; *m* 1998, Rowena Jane, *y d* of John Aldington; one *s*]. *Address:* Odell Manor, Bedfordshire MK43 7BB. *T:* (01234) 720416.

LUKE, Iain M.; JP; MP (Lab) Dundee East, since 2001; *b* 8 Oct. 1951; *m*. *Educ:* Univ. of Dundee (MA 1980); Univ. of Edinburgh; Jordanhill Teacher Trng Coll. Asst Collector of Taxes, Inland Revenue, 1969–74; Lectr, then Sen. Lectr, Dundee Coll. of Further Educn, 1983–2001. Member (Lab): Dundee DC, 1984–96; Dundee CC, 1995–. *Address:* (office) 18b Market Gait, Dundee DD1 1QR; c/o House of Commons, SW1A 0AA.

LUKES, Prof. Steven Michael, DPhil; FBA 1987; Professor of Sociology, New York University, since 2000 (autumn trimester); Visiting Centennial Professor, London School of Economics and Political Science, since 2001; *b* 8 March 1941; *o s* of S. Lukes; *m* 1977, Nina Vera Mary Stanger (*d* 1999); two *s* one *d*. *Educ:* Royal Grammar School, Newcastle upon Tyne; Balliol Coll., Oxford (MA 1965; DPhil 1968). Student, 1962–64, Res. Fellow, 1964–66, Nuffield Coll., Oxford; Fellow of Balliol Coll., Oxford, 1966–88; Lectr in Politics, Oxford Univ., 1967–88; Prof. of Political and Social Theory, European Univ. Inst., Florence, 1987–95; Prof. of Moral Philosophy, Univ. of Siena, 1995–2000. *Publications:* (ed jtly) The Good Society, 1972; Emile Durkheim: his life and work, 1972; Individualism, 1973; Power: a radical view, 1974; Essays in Social Theory, 1976; (ed) Durkheim: Rules of Sociological Method, 1982; (ed jtly) Rationality and Relativism, 1982; (ed jtly) Durkheim and the Law, 1984; Marxism and Morality, 1985; (jtly) No Laughing Matter: a collection of political jokes, 1985; (ed) Power, 1986; Moral Conflict and Politics, 1991; Isaiah Berlin: tra filosofia e storia delle idee, 1994; The Curious Enlightenment of Professor Caritat: a comedy of ideas, 1995. *Recreation:* playing jazz piano. *Address:* Department of Sociology, London School of Economics and Political Science, Houghton Street, WC2A 2AE; (Sept.–Dec.) Department of Sociology, New York University, 269 Mercer Street, New York, NY 10003, USA; 25d Cannon Place, NW3 1EH. *T:* and *Fax:* (020) 7435 2408; *e-mail:* s.lukes@lse.ac.uk.

LUMET, Sidney; film director; *b* Philadelphia, 25 June 1924; *o s* of Baruch and Eugenia Lumet; *m* Rita Gam (marr. diss.); *m* 1956, Gloria Vanderbilt (marr. diss. 1963); *m* 1963, Gail Jones (marr. diss. 1978); two *d*; *m* 1980, Mary Gimbel. *Educ:* Professional Children's Sch., NY; Columbia Univ. Served US Army, SE Asia, 1942–46. Appeared as child actor: Dead End; The Eternal Road; Sunup to Sunday; Schoolhouse on the Lot; My Heart's in the Highlands; Dir, Summer Stock, 1947–49; taught acting, High Sch. of Professional Arts; Associate Dir, CBS, 1950, Dir, 1951–57. *TV shows include:* Danger; Your Are There; Alcoa: The Sacco and Vanzetti Story; Goodyear Playhouse; Best of Broadway; Omnibus. *Films directed include:* Twelve Angry Men, 1957; Stage Struck, 1958; That Kind of Woman, 1959; The Fugitive Kind, 1960; A View from the Bridge, Long Day's Journey into Night, 1962; Fail Safe, 1964; The Pawnbroker, The Hill, 1965; The Group, 1966; The Deadly Affair, 1967; Bye Bye Braverman, Last of the Mobile Hot Shots, Child's Play, The Seagull, 1969; The Anderson Tapes, 1971; The Offence, 1973; Serpico, Murder on the Orient Express, 1974; Dog Day Afternoon, 1975; Network, 1977; Equus, 1977; The Wiz, 1979; Just Tell Me What You Want, 1979; Prince of the City, 1980; Deathtrap, 1981; The Verdict, 1982; Daniel, 1983; Garbo Talks, 1984; Power, 1985; The Morning After, 1987; Family Business, 1990; Q & A, 1991; A Stranger Among Us, 1992; Guilty as Sin, 1993; Night Falls on Manhattan, 1996; Gloria, 1999; *play:* Caligula, 1960. *Address:* c/o Jeff Berg, ICM, 8942 Wilshire Boulevard, Beverly Hills, CA 90211, USA.

LUMLEY, family name of **Earl of Scarbrough**.

LUMLEY, Viscount; Richard Osbert Lumley; *b* 18 May 1973; *s* and *heir* of 12th Earl of Scarbrough, *qv*.

LUMLEY, Joanna Lamond, OBE 1995; FRGS; actress; *b* Kashmir, India, 1 May 1946; one *s*; *m* 1st, Jeremy Lloyd (marr. diss. 1971); 2nd, 1986, Stephen Barlow. *Theatre* includes: Private Lives, tour, 1983; Hedda Gabler, Dundee, 1985; Blithe Spirit, Vaudeville, 1986; An Ideal Husband, Chichester, 1989; The Cherry Orchard, 1989; Vanilla, Brighton, transf. Lyric, 1990; The Revengers' Comedies, Strand, 1991; Who Shall I Be Tomorrow?, Greenwich, 1992; The Letter, Lyric, Hammersmith, 1995; *television* includes: General Hospital, 1973; Coronation Street, 1973; Steptoe and Son; The New Avengers, 1976–78 (BAFTA Special Award, 2000); Sapphire and Steel, 1979; The Weather in the Streets, 1983; Mistral's Daughter; Oxbridge Blues, 1984; The Glory Boys; guest presenter, Wogan; A Perfect Hero, 1989; White Rajahs of Sarawak (documentary), 1991; Lovejoy, 1992; Absolutely Fabulous, 1992–96, 2001 (2 BAFTA Awards; British Comedy Award, 1993); Class Act, 1994; Girl Friday (documentary), 1994; Joanna Lumley in the Kingdom of the Thunder Dragon (documentary), 1997; Coming Home, A Rather English Marriage, 1998; Nancherrow, Dr Willoughby, MD, 1999; Mirrorball, 2000; (co-prod) The Cazalets, 2001; *radio* includes: The Psychedelic Spy, 1990; *films* include: On Her Majesty's Secret Service; The Satanic Rites of Dracula; Trail of the Pink Panther; Curse of the Pink Panther; Shirley Valentine, 1989; Innocent Lies, 1995; James and the Giant Peach, Cold Comfort Farm, 1996; Prince Valiant, 1997; Parting Shots, Mad Cows, 1999; Maybe Baby, 2000; The Cat's Meow, 2000. Dir, Capital Radio, 1987; Gov., South Bank Centre, 2000–. Trustee, Born Free Foundn, 1987–. Hon. DLitt Kent, 1995; DUniv Oxford Brookes, 2000. *Publications:* (ed) Peacocks and Commas, 1983; Stare Back and Smile (autobiog.), 1989; Forces Sweethearts, 1993; Girl Friday, 1994; In the Kingdom of the Thunder Dragon, 1997; articles in jls. *Address:* c/o Conway Van Gelder Ltd, 18–21 Jermyn Street, SW1Y 6HP.

LUMLEY-SAVILE, family name of **Baron Savile**.

LUMSDAINE, Nicola Frances; *see* LeFanu, N. F.

LUMSDEN, Prof. Andrew Gino, PhD; FRS 1994; Professor of Developmental Neurobiology, Guy's, King's and St Thomas' Hospitals' Medical and Dental School of King's College London (formerly United Medical and Dental Schools of Guy's and St Thomas' Hospitals), London University, since 1989; *b* 22 Jan. 1947; *s* of Dr Edward Gilbert Sita-Lumsden, MD and Stella Pirie Lumsden; *m* 1970, Anne Farrington Roberg (marr. diss. 1996); two *d*. *Educ:* Kingswood Sch., Bath; St Catharine's Coll., Cambridge (BA 1968; MA 1972; Frank Smart Scholar); Yale Univ.; PhD London 1978. Fulbright Scholar, 1968–70; Lectr in Anatomy, 1973–87, Reader in Craniofacial Biology, 1987–89, Guy's Hosp. Med. Sch. Miller Foundn Vis. Prof., Univ. of California, Berkeley, 1994; Lectr, Coll. de France, Paris, 1991; Yntema Lectr, SUNY, 1993; Howard Hughes Internat. Res. Scholar, 1993–; Jenkinson Meml Lectr, Univ. of Oxford, 1994; Seymour Kreshover Lectr, NIH, 1996; Brooks Lectr, Harvard Univ., 1996. Founder FMedSci 1998. Médaille de la Ville de Paris, 1986. *Publications:* (jtly) The Developing Brain, 2001; reports in learned jls. *Recreations:* mechanical engineering, natural history, Lotus sevens. *Address:* Guy's Hospital, SE1 1UL.

LUMSDEN, Sir David (James), Kt 1985; Principal, Royal Academy of Music, 1982–93; *b* Newcastle upon Tyne, 19 March 1928; *m* 1951, Sheila Daniels; two *s* two *d*. *Educ:* Dame Allan's Sch., Newcastle upon Tyne; Selwyn Coll., Cambridge (Hon. Fellow, 1986). Organ scholar, Selwyn Coll., Cambridge, 1948–51; BA Class I, 1950; MusB (Barclay Squire Prize) 1951; MA 1955; DPhil 1957. Asst Organist, St John's Coll., Cambridge, 1951–53; Res. Student, 1951–54; Organist and Choirmaster, St Mary's, Nottingham, 1954–56; Founder and Conductor, Nottingham Bach Soc., 1954–59; Rector Chori, Southwell Minster, 1956–59; Dir of Music, Keele, 1958–59; Prof. of Harmony, Royal Academy of Music, 1959–61; Fellow and Organist, New Coll., Oxford (Hon. Fellow, 1996), and Lectr in the Faculty of Music, Oxford Univ., 1959–76; Principal, RSAMD, Glasgow, 1976–82. Conductor: Oxford Harmonic Soc., 1961–63; Oxford Sinfonia, 1967–70; BBC Scottish Singers, 1977–80; Organist, Sheldonian Theatre, 1964–76; Choragus, Oxford Univ., 1968–72. Harpsichordist to London Virtuosi, 1972–75. Member of Board: Scottish Opera, 1977–83; ENO, 1983–88. President: Inc. Assoc. of Organists, 1966–68; ISM, 1984–85; RCO, 1986–88; Chairman: NYO, 1985–94; Early Music Soc., 1985–89. Hugh Porter Lectr, Union Theological Seminary, NY, 1967; Vis. Prof., Yale Univ., 1974–75. Hon. Editor, Church Music Soc., 1970–73. Hon. FRCO 1976; Hon. RAM 1978; FRCM 1980; FRNCM 1981; FRSAMD 1982; Hon. GSM 1984; FLCM 1985; FRSA 1985; FRSCM 1987; Hon. FTCL 1988; FKC 1991. Hon. DLitt Reading, 1990. *Publications:* An Anthology of English Lute Music, 1954; Thomas Robinson's Schoole of Musicke, 1603, 1971; Articles in: The Listener; The Score; Music and Letters: Galpin Soc. Jl; La Luth et sa Musique; La Musique de la Renaissance, etc. *Recreations:* reading, theatre, photography, travel, hill-walking, etc. *Address:* Melton House, Soham, Cambs CB7 5DB.

LUMSDEN, George Innes, FRSE; CGeol, FGS, consultant in geology and scientific staff recruitment, since 1991; *b* 27 June 1926; *s* of George Lumsden and Margaret Ann Frances Lumsden (*née* Cockburn); *m* 1958, Sheila Thomson; two *s* one *d*. *Educ:* Banchory Academy; Aberdeen University (Lyon Prize in Geol.; BSc). Geological Survey of GB, 1949; District Geologist S Scotland, 1970, Asst Dir and Sen. Officer Scotland, 1980, Inst. of Geol Scis; British Geological Survey: CSO and Dep Dir, 1982–85; Dir, 1985–87; Mem., CS Commn Sci. Div's Panel of Chairmen, 1988–91; Chm. Recruitment Bds, DRA, then DERA, 1991–2001. Member: Council of Management, Macaulay Inst. for Soil Research, 1980–87; Engineering and Sci. Adv. Cttee, Derby Coll. of Higher Educn, 1983–87; Geol. Museum Adv. Panel, 1985–87; Chm., Dirs of Western European Geol Surveys' Standing Gp on Envmtl Geology, 1984–87, Hon. Pres., 1987–, Hon. Sec., 1988–95; Sec., Forum of European Geol Surveys, 1996–. *Publications:* (ed) Geology and the Environment in Western Europe, 1992, 2nd edn 1994; maps, papers and books on geol topics in official Geol Survey. *Recreations:* music, theatre, sport, gardening, word processing. *Address:* 144/9 Whitehouse Loan, Grange, Edinburgh EH9 2AN.

LUMSDEN, Iain Cobden, FFA; Group Chief Executive, Standard Life Assurance Co., since 2002; *b* 6 June 1946; *s* of John A. Lumsden and Helen H. Lumsden (*née* Foster); *m* 1970, Rosemary Hoey; one *s* one *d*. *Educ:* Exeter Coll., Oxford (BA 1967; MA). FFA 1971. Standard Life Assurance Co., 1967–: Gp Finance Dir, 1990–2001. *Address:* 30 Lothian Road, Edinburgh EH1 2DH. *T:* (0131) 225 2552.

LUMSDEN, James Alexander, MBE 1945; TD 1962; DL; Partner, Maclay, Murray & Spens, Solicitors, Glasgow and Edinburgh, 1947–82; *b* 24 Jan. 1915; *s* of late Sir James Robert Lumsden and Lady (Henrietta) Lumsden (*née* Macfarlane Reid); *m* 1947, Sheila, *d* of late Malcolm Cross and Evelyn Cross (*née* Newlands); three *s*. *Educ:* Rugby Sch.; Corpus Christi Coll., Cambridge (BA, MA 1995; LLB). Director: Bank of Scotland, 1958–85; Weir Group PLC, 1957–84; William Baird PLC, 1959–84; Murray Growth Trust PLC and other companies in Murray Johnstone Group, 1967–85 (Chm., 1971–84); Scottish Provident Instn, 1968–85 (Chm., 1977–83); Burmah Oil Co. Ltd, 1957–76 (Chm., 1971–75). Mem. Jenkins Cttee on Company Law. Mem., Queen's Body Guard for Scotland, Royal Company of Archers, 1963–. DL Dunbartonshire, 1966. *Address:* Arden-Beag, 7 Station Road, Craigendoran, Helensburgh G84 7BG. *T:* (01436) 676204. *Clubs:* Caledonian; New (Edinburgh); Western (Glasgow).

LUMSDEN, Prof. Keith Grant, FRSE; Director, Edinburgh Business School, since 1995; *b* 7 Jan. 1935; *s* of Robert Sclater Lumsden and Elizabeth Brow; *m* 1961, Jean Baillie Macdonald; one *s*. *Educ:* Univ. of Edinburgh (MA Hons Econ 1959); Stanford Univ., California (PhD 1968). FRSE 1992. Stanford University: Instructor, Dept of Econs, 1960–63; Asst Prof., Graduate Sch. of Business, 1964–67; Research Associate, Stanford Res. Inst., 1965 71; Associate Prof., Grad. Sch. of Business, 1968–75; Dir, Esmée Fairbairn Res. Centre, Heriot-Watt Univ., 1975–95. Vis. Prof., Heriot-Watt Univ., 1969–70; Affiliate Prof. of Econs, INSEAD, 1975; Acad. Dir, Sea Transport Exec. Programme, 1979; Prof. of Econs, Advanced Management Coll., Stanford Univ., 1971. Director: Economic Educn Project, 1969–74; Behavioral Res. Labs, 1970–72; Capital Preservation Fund, 1971–75; Nielsen Engineering Research, 1972–75; Hewlett-Packard Ltd, 1981–92. *Publications:* The Free Enterprise System, 1963; The Gross National Product, 1964; International Trade, 1965; (jtly) Macroeconomics, 1966, 4th edn 1981; (jtly) Macroeconomics, 1966, 4th edn 1981; (ed) New Development in the Teaching of Economics, 1967; Excess Demand and Excess Supply in World Tramp Shipping Markets, 1968; (ed) Recent Research in Economics Education, 1970; (jtly) Basic Economics: theory and cases, 1973, 2nd edn 1977; (ed) Efficiency in Universities: the La Paz papers, 1974; (jtly) Division Management Simulation, 1978; (jtly) Economics Education in the UK, 1980; (jtly) Basic Macroeconomic Models, 1981; (jtly) Running the British Economy, 1981, 6th edn 1990; (jtly) Managing the Australian Economy, 1985; (jtly) Shipping Management Model—Stratship, 1983; (jtly) Macroeconomic Database, 1984; (jtly) Strategies for Life—Stratlife, 1988; Economics, 1991; articles in professional jls. *Recreations:* tennis, deep sea game fishing. *Address:* 40 Lauder Road, Edinburgh EH9 1UE. *Clubs:* New (Edinburgh); Waverley Lawn Tennis & Squash (Edinburgh); Dalmahoy Golf and Leisure (Kirknewton); Tantallon Golf (N Berwick).

LUNCH, John, CBE 1975; VRD 1965; FCA, FCIT; Director-General of the Port of London Authority, and Board Member, 1971–76; Chairman: Comprehensive Shipping Group, 1973–75; Transcontinental Air Ltd, 1973–75; *b* 11 Nov. 1919; *s* of late Percy Valentine Lunch and Amy (*née* Somerville); *m* 1st, 1943, Joyce Barbara Clerke (*d* 1989), *d* of late Arnold Basil O'Connell Clerke and Norah Buckley (*née* Browne); two *s*; 2nd, 1995, Fiona Charis Elizabeth Fleck, *d* of late Arthur Axel Miller, MC and Charis Harrison Martin (*née* Petty), and *widow* of Peter Hugo Fleck. *Educ:* Roborough Sch., Eastbourne. FCA 1946; FCIT 1965. Served War, Lt RNVR, Medit. and Home Fleets, 1939–46 (N Atlantic convoys, Crete, N Africa, Malta convoys, Sicily D-Day landings; Torpedo specialist, 1944), subseq. Permanent RNVR, later RNR; Lt-Comdr RNR, retd list, 1969; Lt-Col RE (TA), Engr and Logistic Staff Corps (formerly Engr and Transport Staff Corps),

1971, Col, 1976, retd list, 1994. In business in City, 1946–48: Asst Man. Dir, Tokenhouse Securities Corp. Ltd, 1947, and dir several cos; British Transport Commn, 1948–61: road and rail transport and ancillary businesses; PLA, 1961; Dir of Finance, also Dir of Commerce, 1966; Asst Dir-Gen., responsible docks and harbour, 1969; Chairman: (and founder) PLA Port Users Consultative Cttee, 1966–71; Internat. Port Develt Cttee, Internat. Assoc. of Ports and Harbors, 1972–76; Pres., Inst. of Freight Forwarders, 1972–73. Chm., London Industrial Chartered Accountants, 1971–72; Member Council: Inst. of Chartered Accountants, 1970–77; Chartered Inst. of Transport, 1973–76. Mem. Cttee of Management (a Trustee), 1977–94, a Vice-Pres., 1987–94, a Life Vice-Pres., 1994, RNLI; Founder Chm., RNLI Manhood Br., 1976–78; Pres., RNLI, Hayling Island Lifeboat Station, 1978–88; Hon. Art Adviser, RNLI, 1981–99. Hon. Life Mem. Internat. Assoc. of Airport and Seaport Police, 1974. CIMgt (FBIM 1971); FCIM (FInstM 1973); FILT 1999; FRSA (Council nominee) 1976; Hon. FIFP 1986. Freeman: City of London, 1970; Watermen & Lightermen's Co. of River Thames, 1970 (Court Mem., 1976–80, Hon. Court Mem., 1980–). ADC to Governor of Louisiana, with rank Adm., 1971–. Malta GC 50th Anniv. Medal, 1992. *Publications:* The Chartered Accountant in Top Management, 1965; A Plan for Britain's Ports, 1975. *Recreations:* sailing, art, opera, horse racing. *Address:* Martins, East Ashling, Chichester, West Sussex PO18 9AX. *T:* (01243) 575252. *Clubs:* Army and Navy; Itchenor Sailing (West Sussex).

LUND, John Walter Guerrier, CBE 1975; DSc, PhD; FRS 1963; FIBiol, FCIWEM; Botanist, at Windermere Laboratory of Freshwater Biological Association, 1945–78; Deputy Chief Scientific Officer; *b* 27 Nov. 1912; *s* of George E. Lund and Kate Lund (*née* Hardwick); *m* 1949, Hilda M. Canter; one *s* one *d*. *Educ:* Sedbergh Sch.; Univ. of Manchester; London Univ. (PhD 1939; DSc 1951). Demonstrator in Botany, Univ. of Manchester, also Queen Mary Coll. and Chelsea Polytechnic, Univ. of London, 1935–38; Temp. Lectr in Botany, Univ. of Sheffield, 1936; Staff Biologist, W Midland Forensic Science Laboratory, Birmingham, 1938–45. Hon. DSc Buckingham, 1988. *Publications:* (ed with Elizabeth Howarth) Lake Sediments and Environmental History: studies in palaeolimnology and palaeoecology in honour of Winifred Tutin, 1984; (with Hilda Canter-Lund) Freshwater Algae: their microscopic world explored, 1995; papers and articles in scientific jls, symposium vols, etc. *Recreation:* gardening. *Address:* Ellerbeck, Ellerigg Road, Ambleside, Cumbria LA22 9EU. *T:* (01539) 432369.

LUND, Prof. Raymond Douglas, PhD; FRS 1992; Duke-Elder Professor of Ophthalmology, Institute of Ophthalmology, University College London, since 1995; *b* 10 Feb. 1940; *s* of Henry Douglas Lund and Rose Lund; *m* 1963, Jennifer Sylvia Hawes; two *s*. *Educ:* University College London (BSc 1st cl. Hons, PhD). LRAM. Asst Lectr, then Lectr, Anatomy Dept, UCL, 1963–66; Res. Associate, Univ. of Pennsylvania, 1966–67; Asst Prof., Anatomy Dept, Univ. of Stanford, 1967–68; Asst Prof., then Prof., Depts of Biological Structure and Neurological Surgery, Univ. of Washington, 1968–79; Prof. and Chm., Dept of Anatomy, Univ. of S Carolina, 1979–83; Prof. and Chm., Dept of Neurobiology, Anatomy and Cell Sci., Univ. of Pittsburgh, 1983–91 (Dir, Centre for Neuroscience, 1984–87); Prof. and Head of Dept of Anatomy, and Fellow of Clare College, Cambridge, 1992–95. Chm. Scientific Cttee, Internat. Spinal Res. Trust, 1994–97; Trustee, Corporate Action Trust, 1997–. Founder FMedSci 1998. NIH Merit Award, 1988. *Publications:* Development and Plasticity of the Brain, 1978; contribs to learned jls. *Recreation:* music. *Address:* Department of Pathology, Institute of Ophthalmology, Bath Street, EC1V 9EL. *T:* (020) 7608 6893.

LUND, Rodney Cookson; Director: Short Brothers, 1988–99 (Chairman, 1988–90); Hazlewood Foods, 1991–2001; *b* 16 June 1936; *s* of late Arthur and Doris Lund; *m* 1st, Lynda Brooks (marr. diss.); one *s*; 2nd, Hyacinth, (Miki), Wallace. *Educ:* Wallasey Grammar School; Liverpool University (BCom Hons). Served RAPC, 1957–59 (commissioned). Evans Medical, 1959; Carreras Rothmans, 1960–64; Partner, Urwick Orr & Partners, 1964–66 and 1969–73; Man. Dir, The Mace Voluntary Gp, 1966–69; Vice-Chm., Produce Importers Alliance, 1966–69; Exec. Director: Rank Radio International, 1973–75; British Sugar Corp., 1976–82; Woolworth Holdings, 1982–86; Chm., Nat. Bus Co., 1986–88 (Part-time Mem., 1989–92). Mem., Nationalised Industries Chairmen's Gp, 1986–88; Chm., The Enterprise Support Gp, 1991–94. CIMgt. *Recreations:* travel, opera, cooking. *Address:* 18 Billing Road, Chelsea, SW10 9UL. *T:* (020) 7352 2641.

LUNN, Rt Rev. David Ramsay; Hon. Assistant Bishop, Diocese of York, since 1998; *b* 17 July 1930. *Educ:* King's College, Cambridge (BA 1953; MA 1957); Cuddesdon College, Oxford. Deacon 1955, priest 1956, Newcastle upon Tyne; Curate of Sugley, 1955–59; N Gosforth, 1959–63; Chaplain, Lincoln Theological College, 1963–66; Sub-Warden, 1966–70; Vicar of St George, Cullercoats, 1970–75, Rector, 1975–80; Rural Dean of Tynemouth, 1975–80; Bishop of Sheffield, 1980–97. *Address:* Rivendell, 28 Southfield Road, Wetwang, Driffield, E Yorks YO25 9XX.

LUNN, Peter Northcote, CMG 1957; OBE 1951; Government Service, retired 1986; *b* 15 Nov. 1914; *e s* of late Sir Arnold Lunn; *m* 1939, Hon. (Eileen) Antoinette (*d* 1976), *d* of 15th Viscount Gormanston; two *s* two *d* (and one *s* one *d* decd). *Educ:* Eton. Joined Govt Service, 1939; Malta, 1939–44; Italy, 1944–45; W Germany, 1945–46; London, 1946–47; Vienna, 1948–50; Bern, 1950–53; Berlin, 1953–56; London, 1956–57; Bonn, 1957–62; Beirut, 1962–67; London, 1967–86. Mem., Brit. International Ski team, 1931–37, Capt. 1934–37; Capt. British Olympic Ski team, 1936; competitor, Inferno downhill ski race, 1978–86, 1988–89, 1995–2001. *Publications:* High-Speed Ski-ing, 1935; Evil in High Places, 1947; A Ski-ing Primer, 1948, rev. edn 1951; The Guinness Book of Skiing, 1983. *Club:* Ski Club of Great Britain.

LUNN-ROCKLIFFE, Victor Paul; Director, Asset Management Group, Export Credits Guarantee Department, since 1995; *b* 5 Dec. 1948; *s* of Col W. P. Lunn-Rockliffe, DSO, MC and J. Jéquier; *m* 1971, Felicity Ann O'Neill; two *d*. *Educ:* Keele Univ. (Jt Hons French History). Export Credits Guarantee Department: joined, 1973; Head, Project Underwriting Div., ME and N Africa, 1987; Head, Risk Management Div., 1989; Head, Claims Div., 1994. *Recreations:* drawing, painting, reading, walking, ballet, cinema. *Address:* Export Credits Guarantee Department, PO Box 2200, 2 Exchange Tower, Harbour Exchange Square, E14 9GS. *T:* (020) 7512 7008.

LUNNY, William Francis; Sheriff of South Strathclyde, Dumfries and Galloway, 1984–98; *b* 10 Dec. 1938; *s* of James F. Lunny and Sarah Ann Crawford or Lunny; *m* 1967, Elizabeth McDermott; two *s* one *d*. *Educ:* Our Lady's High School, Motherwell; Glasgow Univ. (MA, LLB). Solicitor, 1961–67; Depute Procurator Fiscal, 1967–74; Crown Counsel/Legal Draftsman, Antigua, 1974–76; Advocate, 1977. Barrister, Antigua, 1981. KHS 1989. *Recreations:* walking, travelling.

LUNS, Dr Joseph Marie Antoine Hubert, Officer, Order of Orange-Nassau, 1947; Knight Grand Cross, Order of the Netherlands Lion, 1971; Hon. GCMG; Hon. CH 1971; Secretary-General of NATO, 1971–84; *b* 28 Aug. 1911; *m* Baroness E. C. van Heemstra (*d* 1990); one *s* one *d*. *Educ:* sec. schs, Amsterdam and Brussels; universities of Leyden, Amsterdam, London and Berlin. Attaché of Legation, 1938; 2nd Sec., 1942; 1st Sec., 1945; Counsellor, 1949. Served in: Min. for For. Affairs, 1938–40; Berne, 1940–41; Lisbon, 1941–43; London, at Netherlands Min. for For. Affairs, 1943–44, and at Netherlands Embassy, 1944–49; Netherlands Delegn to UN, NY, 1942–52; Minister of Foreign Affairs, The Netherlands, 1952–71. MP (Second Chamber, Netherlands), July-Oct. 1956 and March-June 1959. Hon. Fellow, London Sch. of Economics, 1969. Prix Charlemagne, Aachen, 1967; Gustav Stresemann Medal, 1968. Hon. DCL: Harvard, 1970; Oxon, 1972; Exeter, 1974; Dr Humanities, Hope Coll., USA, 1974. Holds numerous foreign orders. *Publications:* The Epic of The Royal Netherlands Navy; articles on Royal Netherlands Navy in Dutch and foreign jls, and articles on international affairs in International Affairs, La Revue Politique, and others. *Recreation:* swimming. *Address:* 117 Avenue Franklin Roosevelt, 1050 Brussels, Belgium. *Clubs:* Reform (Hon. Mem.); Haagsche, De Witte (Netherlands).

LUPTON, Prof. Thomas; Professor of Organisational Behaviour, University of Manchester, 1966–86; Visiting Professor, Instituto de Estudios Superiores de la Empresa, Barcelona, 1987–94; Director of International Programmes, Escuela de Alta Dirección y Administración, Barcelona, 1990–95; *b* 4 Nov. 1918; *s* of Thomas Lupton, blacksmith, and Jane Lupton (*née* Vowell); *m* 1st, 1942, Thelma Chesney; one *d*; 2nd, 1963, Dr Constance Shirley Wilson; one *s* one *d*; 3rd, 1987, Dorothy Joyce Meredith. *Educ:* Elem. and Central Sch.; Technical Coll.; Ruskin Coll.; Oriel Coll., Oxford; Univ. of Manchester. DipEconPolSci (Oxon), MA (Oxon), PhD (Manch.). Served War, HM Forces, 1939–41 and 1944–46; Marine Engr, 1932–39, 1941–44. Research Posts: Liverpool Univ., 1951–54; Manchester Univ., 1954–57; Lectr in Sociology, Manchester Univ., 1957–59; Head of Dept of Industrial Admin, Coll. of Advanced Techn., Birmingham, 1959–64; Montague Burton Prof. of Ind. Rel., Univ. of Leeds, 1964–66; Dir, Manchester Business Sch., 1977–83. Gen. Editor, Jl of Management Studies, 1966–76; Dir, Pirelli General Cables Ltd, 1970–77; Member: Civil Service Arbitration Tribunal, 1967–70; Arbitration Panel, Dept of Employment, 1969–72; various official commns and tribunals, 1960–80. Hon. DSc Aston, 1987; Hon. DBA Manchester Metropolitan, 1997. *Publications:* On the Shop Floor, 1963; Industrial Behaviour and Personnel Management, 1964; Management and the Social Sciences, 1966, 3rd edn, 1983; Selecting a Wage Payment System (with D. Gowler), 1969; Job and Pay Comparisons (with A. M. Bowey), 1973; Wages and Salaries (with A. M. Bowey), 1974, rev. edn 1983; Achieving Change (with I. R. Tanner), 1987; articles in Jl of Management Studies, Manchester Sch., Production Engineer, etc. *Recreations:* golf, Association Football. *Address:* Foxhill, 106 Styal Road, Gatley, Cheadle, Cheshire SK8 4JR.

LUPU, Radu; pianist; *b* 30 Nov. 1945; *s* of Mayer Lupu, lawyer, and Ana Gabor, teacher of languages. *Educ:* Moscow Conservatoire. Debut at age of twelve with complete programme of own music; studied with Florica Muzicescu, Cella Delavrancea, Heinrich Neuhaus and Stanislav Neuhaus. 1st prize: Van Cliburn Competition, 1966; Enescu Internat. Competition, 1967; Leeds Internat. Pianoforte Competition, 1969. Numerous recordings include complete Mozart violin and piano sonatas, complete Beethoven Piano Concertos, 1979. *Recreations:* history, art, sport. *Address:* c/o Terry Harrison Artists Management, The Orchard, Market Street, Charlbury, Oxon OX7 3PJ. *T:* (01608) 810330.

LURIE, Prof. Alison; writer; Professor of English, Cornell University, since 1976; *b* 3 Sept. 1926; *d* of Harry Lurie and Bernice Stewart; *m* 1st, 1948, Jonathan Bishop (marr. diss. 1985); three *s*; 2nd, 1995, Edward Hower. *Educ:* Radcliffe Coll., Cambridge, Mass (AB). *Publications:* Love and Friendship, 1962; The Nowhere City, 1965; Imaginary Friends, 1967 (televised, 1987); Real People, 1969; The War Between the Tates, 1974; Only Children, 1979; Foreign Affairs, 1984 (Pulitzer Prize, 1985); The Truth About Lorin Jones, 1988; (ed) The Oxford Book of Modern Fairy Tales, 1993; Women and Ghosts (short stories), 1994; The Last Resort, 1998; *non-fiction:* The Language of Clothes, 1981; Don't Tell the Grown-ups, 1990; Familiar Spirits, 2001; *children's books:* Clever Gretchen, 1980; The Heavenly Zoo, 1980; Fabulous Beasts, 1981. *Address:* c/o English Department, Cornell University, Ithaca, NY 14853, USA.

LUSBY, John Martin; Adjudicator (panel member), Criminal Injuries Compensation Appeals Panel, since 1997; *b* 27 April 1943; *s* of late William Henry Lusby and of Florence Mary (*née* Wharam); *m* 1966, (Mary) Clare, *d* of late John Gargan and Ellen (*née* Myers); one *s* one *d*. *Educ:* Marist Coll., Hull; Ushaw Coll., Durham; Maryvale Inst., Birmingham (DipTh (with commendation) 1997); Open Univ. (MA Theol. (with distinction) 1998). DipHSM 1972; MHSM until 1996 (AHA 1972). Entered NHS, 1961; junior appointments: De la Pole Hosp., Hull, 1961–66; County Hosp., York, 1966–67; Kettering Gen. Hosp., 1967–68; Admin. Asst, United Sheffield Hosps, 1968–70; Dep. Hosp. Sec., E Birmingham Hosp, 1970–72; Hosp. Sec., Pontefract Gen. Infirmary and Headlands Hosp., Pontefract, 1972–74; Area Gen. Administrator, Kirklees AHA, 1974–76; Asst Dist Administrator (Patient Services), 1976–79, Dist Administrator, Wandsworth and E Merton Dist, 1979–81, Merton, Sutton and Wandsworth AHA(T); Area Administrator, Doncaster AHA, 1981; Dist Administrator, 1981–84, Dist Gen. Man., 1984–90, Exec. Dir, 1990, Doncaster HA; Mem., 1990–91, Gen. Manager, 1990–95, and Exec. Dir, 1991–95, Lothian Health Bd; Chm., Indep. Review Panel, NHS Complaints Procedure, Northern and Yorks Reg., NHS Exec., 1996–97. Member: Scottish Council for Postgrad. Med. and Dental Educn, 1992–95; Health Services and Public Health Res. Cttee, Chief Scientist Orgn, SHHD, 1993–95; Scottish Implementation Gp, Jun. Doctors and Dentists Hrs of Work, 1993–95; Jt Wkg Gp on Information Services, NHS in Scotland, 1993–95. Trustee: Dementia Services Develt Centre, Univ. of Stirling, 1991–95; Scottish Dementia Appeal Trust, 1994–95. Member: Catholic Theol Assoc. of GB, 1997–; Catholic Biblical Assoc. of GB, 1998–; Catholic Inst. for Internat. Relations, 1999–; Soc. for the Study of Theology, 2000–. *Recreations:* gardening, hillwalking, music, reading, travel. *Address:* Flat A, Copper Beech, 31 North Grove, N6 4SJ. *T:* (020) 8341 3426; *e-mail:* johnlusby@aol.com.

LUSCOMBE, Prof. David Edward, LittD; FSA; FRHistS; FBA 1986; Research Professor of Medieval History, University of Sheffield, since 2000; *b* 22 July 1938; *s* of Edward Dominic and Nora Luscombe; *m* 1960, Megan Phillips; three *s* one *d*. *Educ:* St Michael's Sch., North Finchley; Finchley Catholic Grammar Sch.; King's Coll., Cambridge (BA, MA, PhD, LittD). Fellow, King's Coll., Cambridge, 1962–64; Fellow and Dir of Studies in History, Churchill Coll., Cambridge, 1964–72; Sheffield University: Prof. of Medieval Hist., 1972–95; Leverhulme Personal Res. Prof. of Medieval Hist., 1995–2000; Head of Dept of History, 1973–76, 1979–84; Dep. Dean, 1983–85, Dean, 1985–87, Faculty of Arts; Pro-Vice-Chancellor, 1990–94. Vis. Prof., Univ. of Connecticut, 1993; Leverhulme European Fellow, 1973; Vis. Fellow, All Souls Coll., Oxford, 1994; British Acad./RSC Exchange Visitor to Canada, 1991; British Acad./Japan Acad. Exchange Visitor to Japan, 1996. Raleigh Lectr, British Acad., 1988. External examiner for higher degrees in Univs. of Cambridge, Oxford, London, Liverpool, Bangor, Lancaster, ANU, Toronto, Groningen, for BA degrees at Bangor, Leicester and Leeds. Dir, Historical Assoc. Summer Vacation Sch., 1976 and 1992. Member: Governing Body, later Assoc. St Edmund's House, Cambridge, 1971–84; Cttee, Ecclesiastical History Soc., 1976–79; Council, RHistS, 1981–85; Council, British Acad., 1989–97 (Publications Sec.,

1990–97; Member: Medieval Texts Cttee, 1982– (Chm., 1991–); Publications Cttee, 1987–97 (Chm., 1990–97); Postgrad. Studies Cttee, 1988–90; Humanities Res. Bd, 1994–96); Cttee on Acad. Res. Projects, 1990–97; Commonwealth Scholarships Commn in UK, 1994–2000; Auditor, HEQC, 1994–95. Mem. Council, Worksop Coll. and Ranby House, 1996–. Pres., Soc. internat. pour l'étude de la philosophie médiévale, 1997–Aug. 2002 (Vice-Pres., 1987–97); Mem. Cttee, Soc. for Study of Medieval Langs and Lit., 1991–96. Gen. Editor, Cambridge Studies in Medieval Life and Thought, 4th series, 1988– (Adv. Editor, 1983–88); Mem., Jt Supervisory Cttee, British Acad./OUP, for New DNB, 1992–99 (Associate Editor, 1993–). *Publications:* The School of Peter Abelard, 1969; Peter Abelard's Ethics, 1971 (trans. Italian, 1976); (ed jtly) Church and Government in the Middle Ages, 1976; (ed jtly) Petrus Abaelardus 1079–1142: Person, Werk und Wirkung, 1980; (jtly) David Knowles Remembered, 1991; (ed jtly) Anselm: Aosta, Bec and Canterbury, 1996; Medieval Thought, 1997 (trans. Portuguese, 2000); The Twelfth-Century Renaissance: monks, scholars and the shaping of the European mind, (in Japanese) 2000; articles in learned jls. *Recreations:* walking a spaniel, swimming, using libraries. *Address:* 4 Caxton Road, Broomhill, Sheffield S10 3DE. *T:* (0114) 268 6355.

LUSCOMBE, Rt Rev. Lawrence Edward; Bishop of Brechin, 1975–90; Primus of the Episcopal Church in Scotland, 1985–90; *b* 10 Nov. 1924; *s* of Reginald John and Winifred Luscombe; *m* 1946, Doris Carswell Morgan, BSc, MB, ChB (*d* 1992); one *d*. *Educ:* Torquay Grammar Sch.; Kelham Theological Coll.; King's Coll., London; MA, MPhil 1991, PhD 1993, Dundee. CA 1952, ASAA 1957. FSAScot 1980. Served Indian Army, 1942–47, Major. Partner, Galbraith, Dunlop & Co., Chartered Accountants, Glasgow, 1952–63. Ordained deacon, 1963; priest, 1964; Curate, St Margaret's, Glasgow, 1963–66; Rector, St Barnabas', Paisley, 1966–71; Provost of St Paul's Cathedral, Dundee, 1971–75. Hon. Canon, Trinity Cathedral, Davenport, Iowa, 1983. A Trustee, Scottish Episcopal Ch, 1985–. Hon. Res. Fellow, Dundee Univ., 1993–. Chm. of Council, Glenalmond Coll., 1987–94. FRSA 1987. Hon. DLitt Geneva Theological Coll., 1972; Hon. LLD Dundee, 1987. OStJ 1986; ChStJ 1996. *Publications:* Matthew Luscombe, Missionary Bishop, 1992; A Seminary of Learning, 1994; The Scottish Episcopal Church in the 20th Century, 1996. *Address:* Woodville, Kirkton of Tealing, by Dundee DD4 0RD. *T:* (01382) 380331.

LUSH, Christopher Duncan, CMG 1983; HM Diplomatic Service, retired; Governor, British Institute of Human Rights, since 1988; Editor, Human Rights Case Digest, since 1989; *b* 4 June 1928; *s* of late Eric Duncan Thomas Lush and Iris Leonora (*née* Greenfield); *m* 1967, Marguerite Lilian, *d* of Frederick Albert Bolden; one *s*. *Educ:* Sedbergh; Magdalen Coll., Oxford. Called to Bar, Gray's Inn, 1953. Asst Legal Adviser, FO, 1959–62; Legal Adviser, Berlin, 1962–65, Dep. Political Adviser, Berlin, 1965–66; FO (later FCO), 1966–69; Head of Chancery, Amman, 1969–71; Head of Aviation and Telecommunications Dept, FCO, 1971–73; Canadian Nat. Defence Coll., 1973–74; Counsellor, Paris, 1974–78; Counsellor, Vienna, 1978–82; Ambassador and UK Perm. Rep. to Council of Europe, Strasbourg, 1983–86. Médaille de Vermeil, Société d'Encouragement au Progrès, 1978. *Publications:* articles in Internat. and Compar. Law Qly, Connoisseur. *Club:* Travellers.

LUSH, Denzil Anton; Master of the Court of Protection, since 1996; *b* 18 July 1951; *s* of Dennis John Lush, MBE and late Hazel June Lush (*née* Fishenden). *Educ:* Devonport High Sch., Plymouth; University Coll. London (BA, MA); Corpus Christi Coll., Cambridge (LLM); Coll. of Law, Guildford. Admitted Solicitor, England and Wales, 1978; in private practice, 1978–96; admitted Solicitor and Notary Public, Scotland, 1993. Chm., Social Security Appeals Tribunals, 1994–96. Member: Law Soc. Mental Health and Disability Sub-Cttee, 1993–96; BMA Steering Gp on advance statements about medical treatment, 1994. Lay Reader, 1982–. *Publications:* Cohabitation and Co-Ownership Precedents, 1993; Elderly Clients: a precedent manual, 1996; (with Stephen Cretney) Enduring Powers of Attorney, 4th edn 1996; numerous contribs to legal publications. *Recreations:* supporting Plymouth Argyle FC and Somerset CCC, contemporary pop music. *Address:* The Court of Protection, Stewart House, 24 Kingsway, WC2B 6JX. *T:* (020) 7664 7000. *Club:* Athenæum.

LUSH, Hon. Sir George (Hermann), Kt 1979; Justice, Supreme Court of Victoria, 1966–83; *b* 5 Oct. 1912; *s* of John Fullarton Lush and Dora Louise Emma Lush; *m* 1943, Winifred Betty Wragge; three *d*. *Educ:* Carey Grammar Sch.; Ormond Coll., Melbourne Univ. (LLM). Admitted, Victorian Bar, 1935; served War, Australian Imperial Forces, 1940–45; Lecturer, Mercantile Law, Melbourne Univ., 1947–55; QC: Victoria 1957, Tasmania 1958. Chairman, Victorian Bar Council, 1964–66; President: Medico-Legal Soc., Victoria, 1962–63; Australian Bar Assoc., 1964–66; Commissioner, Overseas Telecommunications Commn, 1961–66. Chancellor, Monash Univ., 1983–92 (Mem. Council, 1969–74); Chm. Council, Ormond Coll., 1981–90. Hon. LLD Monash, 1993. *Recreations:* tennis, walking. *Address:* 37 Rochester Road, Canterbury, Vic 3126, Australia. *Clubs:* Melbourne, Melbourne Cricket (Melbourne); Lorne Country (Lorne, Vic).

LUSHINGTON, Sir John (Richard Castleman), 8th Bt *cr* 1791, of South Hill Park, Berkshire; *b* 28 Aug. 1938; *s* of Sir Henry Edmund Castleman Lushington, 7th Bt and Pamela Elizabeth Daphne, *er d* of Major Archer Richard Hunter; *S* father, 1988; *m* 1966, Bridget Gillian Margaret, *d* of late Colonel John Foster Longfield; three *s*. *Educ:* Oundle. *Heir: s* Richard Douglas Longfield Lushington, BA, Sqdn Ldr RAF [*b* 29 March 1968; *m* 2001, Christianne Jane Tipping, Flight Lieut RAF]. *Address:* Kent House, Barrington, Ilminster, Somerset TA19 0JP.

LUSK, (Ormond) Felicity (Stewart); Headmistress, Oxford High School, since 1997; *b* 25 Nov. 1955; *d* of Harold Stewart Lusk, QC (NZ), and Janet Kiwi Lusk; *m* 1976 (marr. diss. 1996); two *s*. *Educ:* Marsden Coll., Wellington, NZ; Victoria Univ (BMus); Massey Univ. (DipEd); Christchurch Teachers' Coll. (Dip Teaching); Univ. of York (Cert. Mus. Educn). Head of Music Department: Wellington E Girls' Coll., NZ, 1980–86; Aotea Coll., NZ, 1986–89; Hasmonean High School, London: Sen. Teacher and Head of Music Dept, 1990–93; Dep. Headteacher, 1993–96. Woolf Fisher Fellowship, NZ, 1985. Councillor, London Borough of Enfield, 1990–94. Member: SHA, 1993–; GSA, 1997–. Gov., GSMD, 2000–. *Recreations:* reading, conversation, travel, Oxford Harmonic Society. *Address:* Oxford High School, Belbroughton Road, Oxford OX2 6XA. *T:* (01865) 559888.

LÜST, Prof. Reimar; President, Alexander von Humboldt Foundation, Bonn, 1989–99, now Hon. President; Director General, European Space Agency, 1984–90; *b* 23 March 1923; *s* of Hero Lüst and Grete (*née* Strunck); *m* 1986, Nina Grunenberg; two *s* by a previous marriage. *Educ:* Univ. of Frankfurt; Univ. of Göttingen (Dr rer. nat.). Max-Planck-Institut of Physics: Staff Scientist, 1950–60; Head of Astrophysics Dept, 1960–63; Dir, Max-Planck-Institut of Extraterrestrial Physics, 1963–72; Pres., Max-Planck-Gesellschaft zur Förderung der Wissenschaften, 1972–84. Vis. Prof., Univs of Princeton, Chicago, New York, MIT, CIT, 1955–63; Hon. Prof., Technical Univ. of Munich, 1965; Hon. Prof., Univ. of Hamburg, 1992. Chm., German Science Council, 1969–72. Mem. and Hon. Mem. of eight academies. Dr *hc:* Sofia, 1991; Birmingham 1993. Planet No 4386 named Lüst, 1991. Adenauer-de Gaulle Prize, 1994. Grand Cross, Order of Merit (FRG), 1984; Officier, Légion d'Honneur (France), 1984; Grand Cross of Merit with Star and Shoulderblade (FRG), 1990. *Publications:* Hydrodynamik, 1955; articles in scientific jls. *Recreations:* tennis, history, ski-ing. *Address:* Max-Planck-Institute of Meteorology, Bundesstrasse 55, 20146 Hamburg, Germany. *T:* (40) 41173300.

LUSTIGER, His Eminence Cardinal Jean-Marie; Archbishop of Paris, since 1981; *b* Paris, 1926. *Educ:* Carmelite Seminary; Institut Catholique de Paris; Sorbonne (Lèsl, LenThéol). Ordained priest, 1954. Chaplain to students, Sorbonne, Paris; Dir, Centre d'étudiants Richelieu, Paris, 1959–69; Parish Pastor, Sainte Jeanne de Chantal, Paris, 1969–79; Bishop of Orléans, 1979–81. Cardinal, 1983. Mem., Académie Française, 1995–. *Publications:* Sermons d'un curé de Paris, 1978; Pain de vie, peuple de Dieu, 1981; Osez croire, 1985 (trans. Dare to Believe, 1986); Osez vivre, 1985 (trans. Dare to Live, 1989); Freude der Weihnacht, 1985, revd and enlarged edn as Petites Paroles de Nuit de Noël, 1992; Premiers pas dans la prière, 1986 (trans. First Steps in Prayer, 1988); Six sermons aux élus de la nation, 1987; The Mass, 1987 (abridged edn of La Messe, 1988); Le choix de Dieu, 1987 (trans. Choosing God, Chosen by God, 1990); The Lord's Prayer, 1988; Le Sacrement de l'onction des malades, 1990; Dieu merci, les droits de l'homme, 1990; Dare to Rejoice, 1990; Nous avons rendez-vous avec l'Europe, 1991; Devenez dignes de la condition humaine, 1995; Le Baptême de votre enfant, 1997; Soyez heureux, 1997; Pour l'Europe, un nouvel art de vivre, 1999; Les prêtres que Dieu donne, 2000; Comme Dieu vous aime, 2001. *Address:* Maison diocésaine, 7 rue Saint-Vincent, 75018 Paris, France.

LUSZTIG, Prof. George, PhD; FRS 1983; Professor of Mathematics, Massachusetts Institute of Technology, Cambridge, USA, since 1978; *b* 20 May 1946; *s* of Akos and Erzsébet Lusztig; *m* (marr. diss.); two *d*. *Educ:* Univ. of Bucharest, Rumania; Princeton Univ. (MA, PhD). Asst, Univ. of Timisoara, Rumania, 1969; Mem., Inst. for Advanced Study Princeton, 1969–71; Univ. of Warwick: Res. Fellow, 1971–72; Lectr in Maths, 1972–74; Prof. of Maths, 1974–78. Mem., US Nat. Acad. of Scis, 1992. *Publications:* The Discrete Series of GL_n over a Finite Field, 1974; and Characters of Reductive Groups over a Finite Field, 1984; Introduction to Quantum Groups, 1993. *Address:* 106 Grant Avenue, Newton, MA 02459, USA. *T:* (617) 9648579.

LUTHER, Anne Margaret, (Mrs A. N. Brearley-Smith); Director General, Action Research, 1990–2001; *b* 19 Jan. 1946; *d* of Dermot William Richard O'Leary and Eva Margaret (*née* Christie); *m* 1st, 1969, Philip John Luther (marr. diss. 1988); two *d*; 2nd, 1992, Andrew Neville Brearley-Smith. *Educ:* Ursuline Convent, Ilford; Chelsea Coll., London (BSc 1967). King's Fund Trainee, 1967–69; PA to House Governor, Westminster Hosp., 1969–71; Dir of Res., Action Research, 1982–90. Association of Medical Research Charities: Hon. Sec., 1982–87; Mem., Exec. Council, 1991–95. Mem., Prince of Wales Adv. Gp on Disability, 1990–95. Trustee, Common Investment Funds for Charities, 1991–98. Mem., Ashridge Mgt Coll. Assoc., 1984–. MInstD 1994. FRSocMed. *Recreations:* music, theatre, cookery. *Club:* Royal Society of Medicine.

LUTHER, Rt Rev. Arthur William; retired; *b* 21 March 1919; *s* of William and Monica Luther; *m* 1946, Dr Kamal Luther; one *s* two *d*. *Educ:* Nagpur University; India (MA, BT); General Theological Seminary, New York (STD 1957). Deacon, 1943; Priest, 1944; in USA and Scotland for study and parish work, 1952–54; Chaplain to Bishop of Nagpur, 1954; Head Master, Bishop Cotton School, Nagpur, 1954–57; Bishop of Nasik, 1957–70; Bishop of Bombay, 1970–73; held charge of Kolhapur Diocese concurrently with Bombay Diocese, Dec. 1970–Feb. 1972; Bishop, Church of North India, and Reg. Sec. of the Leprosy Mission, 1973–80; Promotional Sec., 1980–84. *Address:* Shripad-B, Flat 1, 60 Tulshibagwale Colony, Lane 3, Sahakar Nagar 2, Pune 411009, Maharashtra, India. *T:* 4222576.

LUTON, Jean-Marie; Chevalier de la Légion d'Honneur, 1992; Officier de l'Ordre National du Mérite, 1989; Chairman and Chief Executive Officer, Arianespace, since 1997; *b* Chamalières, 4 Aug. 1942; *m* 1967, Cécile Robine; three *s*. *Educ:* Ecole Polytechnique. Centre National de la Recherche Scientifique: researcher, 1964–71; Chargé de Recherches, 1971–74; Chargé de Mission, Service des Programmes des Organismes de Recherche, Min. for Industrial and Scientific Develt, 1971–73; Centre National d'Etudes Spatiales: Hd, Res. Progs Div., Progs and Indust. Policy Directorate, 1974–75; Hd, Planning and Projs Div., Progs and Indust. Policy Directorate, 1975–78; Dir, Progs and Planning, 1978–84; Dep. Dir. Gen., 1984–87; Dir for Space Progs, Space Systems Div., Aérospatiale, 1987–89; Director General: Centre National d' Etudes Spatiales, 1989–90; ESA, 1990–97. Mem., Internat. Acad. of Astronautics, 1986–. Astronautics Prize, French Assoc. for Aeronautics and Astronautics, 1985. *Recreations:* tennis, sailing. *Address:* c/o Arianespace, boulevard de l'Europe, 91006 Evry, France.

LUTTRELL, Col Sir (Geoffrey) Walter (Fownes), KCVO 1993; MC 1945; JP; Lord-Lieutenant of Somerset, 1978–94; *b* 2 Oct. 1919; *s* of late Geoffrey Fownes Luttrell of Dunster Castle, Somerset; *m* 1942, Hermione Hamilton, *er d* of late Capt. Cecil Gunston, MC, and Lady Doris Gunston. *Educ:* Eton; Exeter Coll., Oxford. Served War of 1939–45, with 15th/19th King's Royal Hussars, 1940–46; North Somerset Yeomanry, 1952–57; Lt-Col 1955; Hon. Col, 6th Bn LI, TAVR, 1977–87; Col 1987. Liaison Officer, Ministry of Agriculture, 1965–71. Regional Dir, Lloyds Bank, 1972–83. Member: National Parks Commn, 1962–66; Wessex Regional Cttee, Nat. Trust, 1970–85; SW Electricity Bd, 1969–78; UGC, 1973–76. Pres., Royal Bath and West and Southern Counties Soc., 1983. DL Somerset, 1958–68, Vice Lord-Lieutenant, 1968–78; High Sheriff of Somerset, 1960; JP 1961. Hon. Col Somerset ACF, 1982–89. KStJ. *Address:* Court House, East Quantoxhead, Bridgwater, Somerset TA5 1EJ. *T:* (01278) 741242. *Club:* Cavalry and Guards.

LUTZ, Marianne Christine, (Mrs C. A. Whittington-Smith); Headmistress, Sheffield High School for Girls (Girls' Public Day School Trust), 1959–83; *b* 9 Dec. 1922; *d* of Dr H. Lutz; *m* 1981, Charles Alexander Whittington-Smith, LLM, FCA (*d* 1997). *Educ:* Wimbledon High Sch., GPDST; Girton Coll., Cambridge (Schol.; MA Historical Tripos); University of London (DipEd, DipTh). Asst Mistress (History) at: Clergy Daughters' Sch., Bristol, 1946–47; South Hampstead High Sch., GPDST, 1947–59. Former Member: History Textbooks Panel for W Germany (under auspices of FO and Unesco); Professional Cttee, Univ. of Sheffield; Historical Assoc.; Secondary Heads' Assoc.; Schnauzer Club of Great Britain. *Publications:* several in connection with Unesco work and Historical Assoc. *Recreations:* crosswords, opera, art, theatre. *Address:* Evona, Hydro Close, Baslow, Bakewell, Derbyshire DE45 1SH. *T:* (01246) 582152.

LUXMOORE, Rt Rev. Christopher Charles; Bishop of Bermuda, 1984–89; Assistant Bishop of Chichester and Canon Emeritus of Chichester Cathedral, since 1991; *b* 9 April 1926; *s* of Rev. William Cyril Luxmoore and Constance Evelyn Luxmoore; *m* 1955, Judith, *d* of late Canon Verney Johnstone; four *s* one *d*. *Educ:* Sedbergh School, Yorks; Trinity Coll., Cambridge; Chichester Theol Coll. Deacon 1952, priest 1953; Asst Curate, St John the Baptist, Newcastle upon Tyne, 1952–55; Priest-in-Charge, St Bede's Ecclesiastical Dist, Newsham, 1955–57; Vicar of Newsham, 1957–58; Rector of Sangre

Grande, Trinidad, 1958–66; Vicar of Headingley, Leeds, 1967–81; Proctor in Convocation and Mem. Gen. Synod, 1975–81; Hon. Canon of Ripon Cathedral, 1980–81; Precentor and Canon Residentiary of Chichester Cathedral, 1981–84; Dean of Bermuda Cathedral, 1984–89; Archdeacon of Lewes and Hastings, 1989–91. Commissary for Bishop of Trinidad and Tobago, 1968–84. Provost, Woodard Schools Southern Div., 1989–96. *Recreations:* opera, church history. *Address:* 42 Willowbed Drive, Chichester, W Sussex PO19 2JB. *T:* (01243) 784680.

LUXON, Benjamin Matthew, CBE 1986; FGSM; baritone; *b* Camborne, Cornwall, 1937; *m* 1969, Sheila Amit; two *s* one *d. Educ:* Truro Sch.; Westminster Trng Coll.; Guildhall Sch. of Music. Teacher of Physical Education until becoming professional singer, 1963; due to severe hearing loss in 1996, eventually finished career as a professional singer. Repertoire included lieder, folk music, Victorian songs and duets, oratorio (Russian, French and English song), and operatic rôles at major opera houses at home and abroad. Major rôles included: Eugene Onegin, Don Giovanni, Wozzeck, Papageno, Julius Caesar, Posa, Gianni Schicchi, Falstaff. Numerous recordings. Appointed Bard of the Cornish Gorsedd, 1974. Third prize, Munich Internat. Festival, 1961; Gold Medal GSM, 1963. FGSM 1970; Hon. RAM, 1980; Hon. DMus: Exeter, 1980; RSAMD, 1996; Canterbury Christ Church Coll., 1997. *Recreations:* collecting English water-colours and drawings; tennis, swimming. *Address:* The Mazet, Relubbus Lane, St Hilary, Penzance, Cornwall, TR20 9DS.

LUZZATTO, Prof. Lucio, MD; FRCP, FRCPath; Scientific Director, National Institute for Cancer Research, Italy, since 2000; *b* 28 Sept. 1936; *s* of Aldo and Anna Luzzatto; *m* 1963, Paola Caboara; one *s* one *d. Educ:* Genoa Univ. (MD 1959); Pavia Univ. (Spec. Haematology 1962); Lib. Doc. Italy, 1965. FRCPath 1982; FRCP 1983. Research Fellow in Haematology, Columbia Univ., 1963–64; Lectr, then Prof. of Haematology, Univ. of Ibadan, 1964–74; Dir, Internat. Inst. of Genetics and Biophysics, Naples, 1974–81; Prof. of Haematology, RPMS, 1981–94; Hon Dir., MRC Leukaemia Res. Fund's Leukaemia Unit, 1987–93; Chm., Dept of Human Genetics, Meml Sloan-Kettering Cancer Center, NY, 1994-2000. Hon. DSc Ibadan, 1998. Pius XI Medal, 1976; Laurea ad hon., Univ. of Urbino, 1990; Chiron award, Italian Acad. of Medicine, 1995. *Publications:* numerous contribs to learned jls. *Address:* Instituto Nazionale per la Ricerca sul Cancro, Largo Rosanna Benzi 10, 16132 Genoa, Italy. *T:* (010) 352776; *e-mail:* luzzatto@hp380.ist.unige.it.

LYALL, Andrew Gardiner, CMG 1976; Under Secretary, Department of Transport, 1981–86, retired; *b* 21 Dec. 1929; *s* of late William and Helen Lyall (*née* Gardiner); *m* 1953, Olive Leslie Gennoe White; one *s* one *d. Educ:* Kirkcaldy High Sch. Joined MoT, 1951; Asst Shipping Attaché, British Embassy, Washington, DC, 1961–64; Principal, Nationalised Industry Finance and Urban Transport Planning, 1965–70; Asst Sec., Railways Div., 1970–72; seconded to FCO as Counsellor, UK Representation to European Communities, 1972–75; Assistant Secretary: Land Use Planning, DoE, 1975–76; Central Unit on Environmental Pollution, 1976–77; Under Sec., PSA, 1978–81. *Recreations:* photography, travel, walking, countryside conservation. *Address:* 5 Barrowfield, Cuckfield, Haywards Heath, West Sussex RH17 5ER. *T:* (01444) 454606. *Club:* Civil Service.

LYALL, Gavin Tudor; author; *b* 9 May 1932; *s* of J. T. and A. A. Lyall; *m* 1958, Katharine E. Whitehorn, *qv*; two *s. Educ:* King Edward VI Sch., Birmingham; Pembroke Coll., Cambridge (MA). RAF, 1951–53 (Pilot Officer, 1952). Journalist with: Picture Post, 1956–57; BBC, 1958–59; Sunday Times, 1959–63. Hon. Consultant, Air Transport Users' Cttee, CAA, 1985–94 (Mem., 1979–85); Mem., Air Travel Trust Cttee, 1986–2000. *Publications:* The Wrong Side of the Sky, 1961; The Most Dangerous Game, 1964; Midnight Plus One, 1965; Shooting Script, 1966; Venus with Pistol, 1969; Blame the Dead, 1972; Judas Country, 1975; Operation Warboard, 1976; The Secret Servant, 1980 (televised, 1984); The Conduct of Major Maxim, 1982; The Crocus List, 1985; Uncle Target, 1988; Spy's Honour, 1993; Flight From Honour, 1996; All Honourable Men, 1997; Honourable Intentions, 1999; (as Editor) Freedom's Battle: The RAF in World War II, 1968. *Recreations:* cooking, military history, model making. *Address:* 14 Provost Road, NW3 4ST. *T:* (020) 7722 2308. *Clubs:* Royal Air Force, Detection.

LYALL, Katharine Elizabeth; *see* Whitehorn, K.

LYALL, William Chalmers, MBE 1952; HM Diplomatic Service, retired; *b* 6 Aug. 1921; *s* of John Brown Lyall and Margaret Angus Leighton Stevenson Lyall; *m* 1948, Janet Lawson McKechnie; two *s* one *d. Educ:* Kelty Public and Beath Secondary schools. Min. of Labour, 1940–48; HM Forces, 1941–47; FO, 1948; Hankow, 1948–51; São Paulo, 1952–53; Manila, 1953–55; FO, 1955–57; Caracas, 1957–60; Bahrain, 1960–64; FO, 1964–65; DSAO, 1965–68; FCO, 1968–69; Consul-General, Genoa, 1969–73; FCO, 1973; Counsellor (Administration), Bonn, 1974–78. *Recreations:* music, photography.

LYALL GRANT, Maj.-Gen. Ian Hallam, MC 1944; Director General, Supply Co-ordination, Ministry of Defence, 1970–75; retired; *b* 4 June 1915; *s* of Col H. F. Lyall Grant, DSO and Lucy Ellinor (*née* Hardy); *m* 1951, Mary Jennifer Moore; one *s* two *d. Educ:* Cheltenham Coll.; RMA, Woolwich; Gonville and Caius Coll., Cambridge (MA). CEng, MICE 1968; FGA 1978. Regular Commission, RE, 1935; service in: India, Burma and Japan, 1938–46 (MC; twice mentioned in despatches); Cyprus and Egypt, 1951–52; CO 131 Para Engr Regt (TA), 1954–56; Instructor, JSSC, 1957–58; Imperial Defence Coll., 1961; Aden, 1962–63; Comdt, Royal School of Mil. Engineering, 1965–67; Maj.-Gen. 1966; Dep. QMG, 1967–70, retired 1970. Col Comdt, RE, 1972–77. President: Bengal Sappers Officers' Assoc., 1987–95; Burma Campaign Fellowship Gp, 1996– (Chm., 1991–96). *Publications:* Burma: the turning point, 1993; (with Kazuo Tamayama) Burma 1942: the Japanese Invasion, 1999. *Recreations:* travel, flyfishing, paintings, gemmology. *Address:* Friary House, 6 St Martin's Square, Chichester, W Sussex PO19 1NT. *T:* (01243) 784214. *Club:* Naval and Military.

See also M. J. Lyall Grant.

LYALL GRANT, Mark Justin; HM Diplomatic Service; Director, Africa, Foreign and Commonwealth Office, since 2000; *b* 29 May 1956; *s* of Maj.-Gen. I. H. Lyall Grant, *qv*; *m* 1986, Sheila Jean Tresise; one *s* one *d. Educ:* Eton; Trinity Coll., Cambridge (MA Law). Called to the Bar, Middle Temple, 1980; joined FCO, 1980; Second Sec., Islamabad, 1982–85; FCO, 1985–87; Private Sec. to Minister of State, FCO, 1987–89; First Sec., Paris, 1990–93; FCO 1993; seconded to European Secretariat, Cabinet Office, 1994–96; Dep. High Comr and Consul Gen., S Africa, 1996–98; Hd, EU Dept (Internal), FCO, 1998–2000. *Recreations:* golf, tennis, sailing, bridge. *Address:* c/o Foreign and Commonwealth Office, SW1A 2AH. *Club:* Royal Automobile.

LYCETT GREEN, Candida; writer; *b* 22 Sept. 1942; *d* of Sir John Betjeman, CBE and Penelope, *d* of Field Marshal Lord Chetwode, GCB, OM, GCSI; *m* 1963, Rupert Lycett Green; two *s* three *d. Educ:* St Mary's, Wantage. TV documentary films: The Front Garden, 1979; The English Woman and the Horse, 1981; A Cottage in the Country, 1983. Mem., Historic Bldgs and Monuments Commn for England (English Heritage), 1992–. Mem., PRS. *Publications:* Hadrian the Hedgehog, 1969; Hadrian in the Orient, 1971; (with Christopher Booker) Goodbye London, 1972; The Front Garden, 1974; English Cottages, 1984; Brilliant Gardens, 1989; The Perfect English Country House, 1991; John Betjeman: Letters, Vol. I, 1994, Vol. II, 1995; England: travels through an unwrecked landscape, 1996; (ed) Coming Home: an anthology of prose by John Betjeman, 1997; (ed) Betjeman's Britain, an anthology of prose and verse, 1999; Country Life's 100 Favourite Houses, 1999; (with HRH Prince of Wales) The Garden at Highgrove, 2000. *Recreation:* touring England by horse. *Address:* c/o Desmond Elliott, 403 Carrington House, Hertford Street, W1Y 7TD.

LYDDON, (William) Derek (Collier), CB 1984; Chief Planning Officer, Scottish Development Department, 1967–85; *b* 17 Nov. 1925; *s* of late A. J. Lyddon, CBE, and E. E. Lyddon; *m* 1949, Marian Louise Kaye Charlesworth, *d* of late Prof. J. K. Charlesworth, CBE; two *d. Educ:* Wrekin Coll.; University Coll., London. BA (Arch.) 1952; ARIBA 1953; DipTP 1954; AMTPI 1963; FRTPI 1973. Depute Chief Architect and Planning Officer, Cumbernauld Development Corp., 1962; Chief Architect and Planning Officer, Skelmersdale Development Corp., 1963–67. Chairman: Edinburgh Sch. of Environmental Design, 1988–96; Planning Exchange, 1991–96 (Vice-Chm., 1984–88); Vice-Chairman: Edinburgh Old Town Renewal Trust, 1991–99; Edinburgh World Heritage Trust, 1999–. Pres., Internat. Soc. of City and Regional Planners, 1981–84. Hon. Prof., Heriot-Watt Univ., 1986; Vis. Prof., Strathclyde Univ., 1986–89. FRSGS 1996. Hon. Fellow: Univ. of Edinburgh, 1986–89; Duncan Jordanstone Coll. of Art, Dundee, 1986–. Hon. DLitt Heriot-Watt, 1981. *Recreations:* walking, reading. *Address:* 31 Blackford Road, Edinburgh EH9 2DT. *T:* (0131) 667 2266.

LYELL, family name of **Baron Lyell**.

LYELL, 3rd Baron *cr* 1914, of Kinnordy; **Charles Lyell;** Bt, 1894; DL; *b* 27 March 1939; *s* of 2nd Baron, VC (killed in action, 1943), and Sophie, *d* of Major S. W. and Lady Betty Trafford; *S* father, 1943. *Educ:* Eton; Christ Church, Oxford. 2nd Lieut Scots Guards, 1957–59. CA Scotland. An Opposition Whip, 1974–79; a Lord in Waiting (Govt Whip), 1979–84; Parly Under-Sec. of State, NI Office, 1984–89; elected Mem., H of L, 1999. Mem., Queen's Body Guard for Scotland (Royal Company of Archers). DL Angus, 1988. *Heir:* none. *Address:* Kinnordy House, Kirriemuir, Angus DD8 5ER. *T:* (01575) 572848; 20 Petersham Mews, SW7 5NR. *T:* (020) 7584 9419. *Clubs:* Turf, White's.

LYELL, Rt Hon. Sir Nicholas (Walter), Kt 1987; PC 1990; QC 1980; a Recorder, since 1985; *b* 6 Dec. 1938; *s* of late Sir Maurice Legat Lyell and Veronica Mary Lyell; *m* 1967, Susanna Mary Fletcher; two *s* two *d. Educ:* Stowe Sch.; Christ Church, Oxford (MA Hons Mod. Hist.). National Service, commnd Royal Artillery, 1957–59; Walter Runciman & Co., 1962–64; called to the Bar, Inner Temple, 1965, Bencher, 1986; private practice, London (Commercial and Public Law), 1965–86, 1997–; MP (C): Hemel Hempstead, 1979–83; Mid Bedfordshire, 1983–97; NE Bedfordshire, 1997–2001. Jt Sec., Constitutional Cttee, 1979; PPS to the Attorney General, 1979–86; Parly Under-Sec. of State (Social Security), DHSS, 1986–87; Solicitor General, 1987–92; Attorney General, 1992–97. Chm., Soc. of Cons. Lawyers, 1985–86, 2001–. Vice-Chm., BFSS, 1983–86. Governor, Stowe Sch., 1990– (Chm., 2001–). *Recreations:* gardening, shooting, drawing. *Address:* Monckton Chambers, 4 Raymond Buildings, Gray's Inn, WC1R 5BP. *Clubs:* Brooks's, Pratt's, Beefsteak.

LYGO, Adm. Sir Raymond (Derek), KCB 1977; aerospace, defence and industrial consultant; Chairman, Liontrust (formerly River and Mercantile First UK Investment Trust), since 1997; *b* 15 March 1924; *s* of late Edwin T. Lygo and of Ada E. Lygo; *m* 1950, Pepper Van Osten, USA; two *s* one *d. Educ:* Valentine's Sch., Ilford; Ilford County High Sch.; Clark's Coll., Bromley. The Times, 1940; Naval Airman, RN, 1942; Naval Pilot, 1943; CO, HMS Ark Royal, 1969–71; Vice Chief of Naval Staff, 1975–78 and Chief of Naval Staff, 1978. British Aerospace: Man. Dir, Hatfield/Lostock Div., 1978–79, Group Dep. Chm., 1980; Bd Mem., 1980–89; Chm. and Chief Exec., Dynamics Gp, 1980–82; Man. Dir, 1983–86; Chief Exec., 1986–89; Chairman: BAe Inc., 1983–88; Royal Ordnance, 1987–88; BAe Enterprises Ltd, BAe (Space Systems) Ltd, BAe Hldgs Inc., 1988–89; TNT Europe Ltd and TNT Express (UK), 1992–97; Rutland Trust PLC, 1992–99; Mem., Supervisory Bd, Airbus Industrie, 1987–89. Director: James Capel Corporate Finance, 1990–92; LET, 1990–92. Dir, CBI Educn Foundn, 1985–92; Member: Council, Industrial Soc., 1985–; NEDC, 1989–91; Council, Foundn for Management Educn, 1992–. Conducted review of the management of prison service, 1991. Appeal Pres., SENSE (Nat. Deaf-Blind & Rubella Assoc.), 1983–2001; Appeal Chm., Industrial Soc., 1989–91; Dir, Southern Counties, Prince's Youth Business Trust, 1993–97; Patron, Youth Sports Trust, 1996–. Pres., FAA Officers Assoc., 1990–; Patron, Nat. FAA Assoc., 1989–. Pres., St Vincent Assoc. Freeman, City of London, 1985; Liveryman: Coachmakers' and Coach Harness Makers' Co., 1986–; Shipwrights' Co., 1988–. Life Mem., Royal Soc. of St George, 1984. FRSA; MInstD; CIMgt. Hon. FRAeS; Hon. Fellow, Univ. of Westminster (formerly Poly. of Central London), 1989. *Recreations:* flying, building, gardening, joinery. *Address:* c/o Barclays Premier Banking, 54 Lombard Street, EC3 9EX. *Clubs:* City Livery (Pres., 1996–97), Ambassadeurs; Royal Naval and Royal Albert Yacht (Portsmouth).

LYLE, Alexander Walter Barr, (Sandy), MBE 1987; professional golfer, since 1977; *b* 9 Feb. 1958; *s* of late Alex and Agnes Lyle; *m* (marr. diss.); two *s*; *m* 1989, Brigitte Jolande Huurman; one *s* one *d. Educ:* Shrewsbury local sch. Rookie of the Year, 1978; 1st in European order of merit, 1979, 1980, 1985; Open Champion, Royal St George's, 1985; won US Masters, 1988. *Publication:* Learning Golf the Lyle Way, 1986. *Recreation:* cars.

LYLE, Sir Gavin Archibald, 3rd Bt *cr* 1929; estate manager, farmer; company director; *b* 14 Oct. 1941; *s* of late Ian Archibald de Hoghton Lyle and of Hon. Lydia Yarde-Buller (who *m* 1947, as his 2nd wife, 13th Duke of Bedford; marr. diss. 1960; now Lydia Duchess of Bedford), *d* of 3rd Baron Churston; *S* grandfather, 1946; *m* 1967, Suzy Cooper (marr. diss. 1985); five *s* one *d. Heir: s* Ian Abram Lyle, *b* 25 Sept. 1968. *Address:* Glendelvine, Caputh, Perthshire PH1 4JN.

LYLE, Sandy; *see* Lyle, A. W. B.

LYLES, John, CBE 1987; JP; Lord-Lieutenant of West Yorkshire, since 1992; *b* 8 May 1929; *yr s* of Percy George Lyles and Alice Maud Mary (*née* Robinson); *m* 1953, Yvonne (*née* Johnson); two *s* two *d. Educ:* Giggleswick Sch.; Leeds Univ. (BSc Textiles 1950). Chm., S. Lyles plc, 1972–95; non-exec. Dir, Hillards plc, 1983–87. Chairman: Assoc. of Yorks and Humberside Chambers of Commerce, 1975–76; Yorks and Humberside CBI, 1983–85; Industry Year 86: Yorks and Humberside Reg.; CBI Mem., Speaker's Commn on Citizenship, 1988–90; Mem., Nat. Employers' Liaison Cttee for Volunteer and Reserve Forces, 1986–92. Mem., Yorks Cttee, NT, 1988–98. Member, Court: Leeds Univ., 1988–; Bradford Univ., 1992–. Pres., Shrievalty Assoc., 1999– (Chm., 1993–95). Patron, Royal Nat. Rose Soc., 1993–2001. Pres., Calderdale Community Foundn, 1994–; Chm., W Yorks Police Community Trust, 1996–. Hon. Colonel: 8th Bn, (Yorks) LI (Vols), 1993–96; King's Own Yorks Yeomanry (LI), 1996–99; Vice Pres., Yorks and

Humberside TAVRA, 1992– (Pres., 1997–99). JP Batley and Dewsbury, 1967; High Sheriff, W Yorks, 1985–86; DL W Yorks, 1987. DUniv Bradford, 1995. KStJ 1993. *Recreations:* gardening, photography, music, opera. *Address:* West Yorkshire Lieutenancy Office, 14 St Anne's Road, Leeds, W Yorks LS6 3NX. *T:* (0113) 224 9462. *Club:* Lansdowne.

LYMBERY, His Honour Robert Davison; QC 1967; a Circuit Judge (formerly Judge of County Courts), 1971–93; Common Serjeant in the City of London, 1990–93; *b* 14 Nov. 1920; *s* of late Robert Smith Lymbery and late Louise Lymbery; *m* 1952, (Pauline) Anne, *d* of late John Reginald and of Kathleen Tuckett; three *d. Educ:* Gresham's Sch.; Pembroke Coll., Cambridge. Served Army, 1940–46; commissioned 17/21 Lancers, 1941; Middle East, Italy, Greece (Royal Tank Regt), 1942–46, Major. Pembroke Coll., 1939–40, 1946–48 (MA, LLB 1st class hons). Foundation Exhibn. 1948; called to Bar, Middle Temple, 1949, Bencher, 1990; Harmsworth Law Scholar, 1949; practice on Midland Circuit, 1949–71. Recorder of Grantham, 1965–71; Chairman: Rutland QS, 1966–71 (Dep. Chm., 1962–66); Bedfordshire QS, 1969–71 (Dep. Chm., 1961–69); Commissioner of Assize, 1971. Freeman, City of London, 1983; Liveryman, Cutlers' Co., 1992–. *Recreations:* various. *Address:* c/o Central Criminal Court, EC4M 7EH. *Club:* Hawks (Cambridge).

LYMINGTON, Viscount; Oliver Henry Rufus Wallop; *b* 22 Dec. 1981; *s* and *heir* of Earl of Portsmouth, *qv*.

LYMPANY, Dame Moura, DBE 1992 (CBE 1979); FRAM; FRCM; concert pianist; *b* Saltash, Cornwall, 18 Aug. 1916; British; *d* of John and Beatrice Johnstone; *m* 1944, Lt-Col Colin Defries (marr. diss. 1950); *m* 1951, Bennet H. Korn, American Television Executive (marr. diss. 1961); one *s* decd. *Educ:* Belgium, Austria, England. FRAM 1948; FRCM 1995. Has made many recordings. First public performance at age of 12, 1929, at Harrogate, playing Mendelssohn G Minor Concerto. Won second prize out of 79 competitors at Ysaye International Pianoforte Competition at Brussels, 1938. Has played in USA, Canada, South America, Australia, New Zealand, India, and all principal European countries. Commander of the Order of the Crown, Belgium, 1980; Medal of Cultural Merit (Portugal), 1989; Chevalier, Ordre des Arts et des Lettres (France), 1992; Order of Prince Henry the Navigator (Portugal), 1996. *Publication:* Moura Lympany: her autobiography, 1991. *Recreations:* gardening, tapestry, reading. *Address:* c/o Transart, 8 Bristol Gardens, W9 2JG.

LYNAGH, Richard Dudley; QC 1996; a Recorder, since 2000; *b* 14 Nov. 1952; *s* of Charles Lynagh and Mary Browne; *m* 1979, Regula Wegmann; two *s* one *d. Educ:* Kettering Grammar Sch.; University Coll. London (LLB Hons). Called to the Bar, Gray's Inn, 1975; an Asst Recorder, 1999–2000. *Address:* 1 Paper Buildings, Temple, EC4Y 7EP.

LYNAM, Desmond Michael; sports broadcaster; presenter, ITV Sport, since 1999; *b* 17 Sept. 1942; *s* of Edward Lynam and Gertrude Veronica Lynam (*née* Malone); *m* 1965, Susan Eleanor Skinner (marr. diss. 1974); one *s. Educ:* Varndean Grammar Sch., Brighton; Brighton Business Coll. ACII. Business career in insurance, until 1967; also freelance journalist; reporter for local radio, 1967–69; reporter, presenter and commentator, BBC Radio, 1969–78; presenter and commentator, BBC TV Sport, 1978–99, incl. Grandstand, Sportsnight, Match of the Day, Commonwealth and Olympic Games, and World Cup; presenter: Holiday, BBC TV, 1988–89; How Do They Do That?, BBC TV, 1994–96; The Des Lynam Show, BBC Radio, 1998–99. TV Sports Presenter of the Year, TRIC, 1985, 1987, 1988, 1993, 1997; Radio Times Male TV Personality, 1989; RTS Sports Presenter of the Year, 1994, 1998; Richard Dimbleby Award, BAFTA, 1994; Variety Club of GB Media Award, 1997. *Publications:* Guide to Commonwealth Games, 1986; The 1988 Olympics, 1988; The 1992 Olympics, 1992. *Recreations:* golf, tennis, Brighton and Hove Albion, reading, theatre. *Address:* c/o Jane Morgan Management Ltd, Café Royal, 68 Regent Street, W1B 5EL.

LYNCH, David; His Honour Judge Lynch; a Circuit Judge, since 1990; *b* 23 Aug. 1939; *s* of Henry and Edith Lynch; *m* 1974, Ann Knights; two *s. Educ:* Liverpool Collegiate Grammar School. LLB London. Served RAF, 1958–61. Sharman & Sons, Solicitors, 1955–57; Bremner Sons & Corlett, Solicitors, 1961–66; Schoolmaster, 1966–68. Called to the Bar, Middle Temple, 1968; Northern Circuit; Asst Recorder, 1983–88; a Recorder, 1988–90; Liaison Judge: St Helens Justices, 1991–; Liverpool John Moores Univ., 1994–. Pres., Mental Health Review Tribunals (restricted patients), 1991–. Hon. Vice Pres., Merseyside Br., Magistrates' Assoc., 1991–. *Recreations:* classical guitar, golf, history of the Northern Circuit. *Address:* The Queen Elizabeth II Law Courts, Derby Square, Liverpool L2 1XA. *T:* (0151) 473 7373.

LYNCH, Jerome Cecil Alfonso; QC 2000; *b* 31 July 1955; *s* of late Clifford James Lynch and of Loretta Rosa Lynch; *m* 1983, Jacqueline Theresa O'Sullivan; one *s. Educ:* Lancashire Poly. (BA Hons). Called to the Bar, Lincoln's Inn, 1983; in practice at the Bar, 1983–. Co-Presenter, Nothing But the Truth, Channel 4, 1998, 1999. *Recreations:* ski-ing, golf (badly), drinking good wine. *Address:* Charter Chambers, 2 Dr Johnson's Buildings, Temple, EC4Y 7AY. *T:* (020) 7832 0300.

LYNCH, Prof. John; Director of Institute of Latin American Studies, 1974–87 and Professor of Latin American History, 1970–87, University of London, now Professor Emeritus; *b* 11 Jan. 1927; *s* of late John P. Lynch and Teresa M. Lynch, Boldon Colliery, Co. Durham; *m* 1960, Wendy Kathleen, *d* of late Frederick and Kathleen Norman; two *s* three *d. Educ:* Corby Sch. Sunderland; Univ. of Edinburgh; University College, London. MA Edinburgh 1952; PhD London 1955. FRHistS 1958. Army, 1945–48. Asst Lectr and Lectr in Modern History, Univ. of Liverpool, 1954–61; Lectr in Hispanic and Latin American History, 1961–64, Reader, 1964–70, UCL. Harrison Vis. Prof., Coll. of William and Mary, Williamsburg, 1991–92. Corresp. Member: Academia Nacional de la Historia, Argentina, 1963, Academia Nacional de la Historia, Venezuela, 1980; Academia Panameña de la Historia, 1981; Academia Chilena de la Historia, 1985; Real Academia de la Historia, Spain, 1986; Sociedad Boliviana de Historia, 1987. Dr *hc* Seville, 1990. Distinguished Service Award, Conf. on Latin American History, Amer. Histl Assoc., 1997. Comdr, Order of Isabel la Católica (Spain), 1988; Order of Andrés Bello, 1st class (Venezuela), 1995. *Publications:* Spanish Colonial Administration 1782–1810, 1958; Spain under the Habsburgs, vol. 1 1964, vol. 2 1969; (with R. A. Humphreys) The Origins of the Latin American Revolutions, 1808–1826, 1965; The Spanish American Revolutions 1808–1826, 1973; Argentine Dictator: Juan Manuel de Rosas, 1829–52, 1981; (ed) Andrés Bello: the London years, 1982; (ed) Past and Present in the Americas, 1984; Hispanoamérica 1750–1850, 1987; Bourbon Spain 1700–1808, 1989; Caudillos in Spanish America 1800–1850, 1992; Latin American Revolutions 1808–1826: old and new world origins, 1994; Massacre in the Pampas, 1872: Britain and Argentina in the age of migration, 1998; Latin America between Colony and Nation, 2001; (contrib.) Cambridge History of Latin America, vol. III 1985, vol. IV 1986. *Address:* 8 Templars Crescent, N3 3QS. *T:* (020) 8346 1089.

LYNCH, Margaret; Executive Director, War on Want, 1995–98; *b* 23 Sept. 1962; *d* of William Lynch and Rosaleen Reynolds. *Educ:* Glasgow Univ. (MA Hons). Mem., Scottish Exec., Labour Party, 1986–90; former Chair, Economic and Industry Cttee, Scottish Labour Party. Founder Mem., Scotland United, 1992. *Publications:* (ed) The Forgotten Workforce, 1991; Palestinians: the forgotten victims of the Gulf War, 1991; What Price Democracy: a referendum for Scotland, 1992. *Recreations:* painting, walking, Celtic culture.

LYNCH, Martin Patrick James; Under Secretary, Overseas Development Administration, Foreign and Commonwealth Office, 1975–83, retired; Secretary, UK Inter Professional Group, 1995–99; *b* 4 June 1924; 2nd *s* of late Frederick Lynch, DSM, and late Elizabeth Yeatman; *m* 1959, Anne, *d* of late Major Gerald McGorty, MC, RAMC; two *s* one *d* (and one *s* decd). *Educ:* London Oratory School. BA Hons London. RAF, 1942–49; Exec. Officer, HM Treasury, 1950; Asst Private Sec. to Financial Sec., 1953–54; Private Sec. to Minister Without Portfolio, 1954–55; Principal, 1958; Asst Sec., Min. of Overseas Develt, 1966 and 1971–75; Counsellor, UK Treasury and Supply Delegn, Washington, and UK Alternate Dir, World Bank, 1967–71. Asst Sec. (Admin), 1984–87, Project Manager, 1993–99, Hon. Mem., 1997, Coll. of Optometrists (formerly British Coll of Ophthalmic Opticians); Asst to Gen. Optical Council, 1989–94. Mem. Council, Assoc. for Latin Liturgy, 1973–92 (Chm., 1976–88). *Publications:* (contrib.) A Voice for All Time, 1993; The College of Optometrists: a history 1980–98, 1999. *Address:* Hillside, Combe Hill, Combe St Nicholas, Chard, Somerset TA20 3NW. *T:* (01460) 65029. *Club:* Reform.

LYNCH, Prof. Michael, PhD; FRSE; Sir William Fraser Professor of Scottish History and Palaeography, University of Edinburgh, since 1992; *b* 15 June 1946; *s* of Francis J. and Kathleen Lynch. *Educ:* Aberdeen Grammar Sch.; Univ. of Aberdeen (MA Eng. Lit. and Hist. 1st cl. hons 1969); Inst. of Historical Res., Univ. of London (PhD 1977). Lectr in History, UCNW, Bangor, 1971–79; Lectr, 1979–88; Sen. Lectr, 1988–92, Dept of Scottish History, Univ. of Edinburgh. Chm., Ancient Monuments Bd for Scotland, 1996–; Publications Sec., Scottish History Soc., 1990–93; President: Historical Assoc. of Scotland, 1992–; Soc. of Antiquaries of Scotland, 1996–99. FRHistS 1982; FRSE 1995. Editor, The Innes Review, 1984–92. *Publications:* Edinburgh and the Reformation, 1981; The Early Modern Town in Scotland, 1986; The Scottish Medieval Town, 1987; Mary Stewart: Queen in three kingdoms, 1988; Scotland: a new history, 1991, 2nd edn 1992; (ed with Julian Goodare) The Reign of James VI, 2000. *Address:* Department of Scottish History, University of Edinburgh, 17 Buccleuch Place, Edinburgh EH8 9LN. *T:* (0131) 650 4030.

LYNCH, Michael Richard, PhD; Founder and Group Chief Executive Officer, Autonomy Corporation, since 1996; *b* 16 June 1965; *s* of Michael and Dolores Lynch. *Educ:* Christ's Coll., Cambridge (BA; PhD 1991). Founder, Cambridge Neurodynamics, 1991. *Recreations:* jazz saxophone, flying helicopters. *Address:* Autonomy Corporation, Cambridge Business Park, Cowley Road, Cambridge CB4 0WZ. *T:* (01223) 421220.

LYNCH, Patrick, MA; MRIA; Professor of Political Economy (Applied Economics), University College, Dublin, 1975–80, now Emeritus; *b* 5 May 1917; *s* of Daniel and Brigid Lynch, Co. Tipperary and Dublin; *m* 1st, 1965, Mary Crotty (*née* Campbell), MA (*d* 1982); 2nd, 1991, Mary Moloney. *Educ:* Univ. Coll., Dublin. Fellow Commoner, Peterhouse, Cambridge, 1956. Entered Irish Civil Service, 1941; Asst Sec. to Govt, 1950; Univ. Lectr in Econs, UC Dublin, 1952, Associate Prof., 1966–75. Chm., Aer Lingus, 1954–75; Jt Dep. Chm., Allied Irish Banks, 1976–84. Has acted as economic consultant to OECD, Council of Europe, Dept of Finance, Dublin, Gulbenkian Inst., Lisbon. Directed surveys sponsored by Irish Govt with OECD into long-term Irish educnl needs, 1965, and into requirements of Irish economy in respect of scientific res., develt and technology, 1966; estab. Science Policy Res. Centre in Dept of Applied Econs, UC Dublin, 1969. Mem., various Irish Govt Commns and Cttees, 1952–; Member: Club of Rome, 1973; EEC Economic and Monetary Union 1980 Group, 1974; Nat. Science Council, 1968–78; Higher Educn Authority, 1968–72; Nat. Economic and Social Council, 1973–76; European Science Foundn, 1974–77; Chairman: Medico-Social Research Board, 1966–72; Public Service Adv. Council, 1973–77; Exec. Cttee, Econ. and Social Res. Inst., 1983–88; Editl Bd, Economic and Social Review; Mem. Editorial Bd, University Review. Chm., Nat. Library of Ireland Soc., 1969–72; Chm., Irish Anti-Apartheid Movement, 1972; Member: Irish Assoc. for Civil Liberty; Movement for Peace in Ireland. Chm., Inst. of Public Administration, 1973–77. Member: Governing Body UC Dublin, 1963–75; Senate NUI, 1972–77; Treasurer, RIA, 1972–80. Hon. FTCD 1995. DUniv Brunel, 1976; Hon. LLD Dublin, 1979; Hon. DEconSc: NUI, 1985; Limerick, 1994; Hon. LLD NCEA, 2000. *Publications:* Planning for Economic Development in Ireland, 1959; (with J. Vaizey) Guinness's Brewery in the Irish Economy, 1960; (jtly) Economics of Educational Costing, 1969; (with Brian Hillery) Ireland in the International Labour Organisation, 1969; (with B. Chubb) Economic Development Planning, 1969; Whither Science Policy, 1980; (ed with J. Meenan) Essays in Memory of Alexis Fitzgerald, 1987; (contrib.) Essays in memory of Dáithé Ó h-Uaithe, 1994; essays in various symposia, etc; articles in Administration, The Bell, Encycl. Britannica, Econ. History Review, Irish Hist. Studies, Irish Jl of Educn, Statist, Studies, University Review, etc. *Address:* 79 Wellington Road, Dublin 4, Ireland.

LYNCH, Roderick Robertson; Chairman and Chief Executive Officer, GSS Ltd, since 2001; *b* 22 May 1949; *s* of Nanson Lynch and Catherine (*née* Robertson); *m* 1972, Christina Williams; two *s. Educ:* Perth Acad.; Dundee Univ. (MA 1971). Served RAC, 1966–67. British Airways, 1971–89: Gen. Manager, Southern Europe, 1983–84; Man. Dir, British Airtours, 1984–86; Head, Customer Service, 1986–89; Man. Dir, Air Europe, 1989–91; Dir, Forte Hotels, 1991–93; Man. Dir, then Chief Exec., Resources, BBC, 1993–99; CEO, Olympic Airways, 1999–2000. Bd Mem., CAA, 1993–99; Dir, NATS Ltd, 1996–99. *Recreations:* Rugby football, military history, music, aviation. *Club:* Travellers.

LYNCH-BLOSSE, Sir Richard Hely, 17th Bt *cr* 1622; RAMC, 1975–85, retired; general medical practioner, since 1985 (senior partner, since 2000); *b* 26 Aug. 1953; *s* of Sir David Edward Lynch-Blosse, 16th Bt, and of Elizabeth, *er d* of Thomas Harold Payne, Welwyn Garden City; *S* father, 1971; *m* 1st, 1976, Cara (marr. diss. 1999), *o d* of George Sutherland, St Ives, Cambs; two *d*; 2nd, 2000, Jacqueline, *o d* of late Gordon Francis, Yardley Gobion, Northants. *Educ:* Royal Free Hosp. Sch. of Medicine. Commnd RAMC, July 1975; LRCP MRCS 1978; MB BS 1979; DRCOG 1983; MRCGP 1984. MO, European Sch., Culham, 1987–. Mem., Soc. of Ornamental Turners, 1992–. *Publication:* contrib. to Jl of RAMC. *Heir: cousin* David Ian Lynch-Blosse [*b* 14 Jan. 1950; *m* 1st, 1984, Mrs Barbara Susan McLaughlin (*d* 1985); 2nd, 1989, Nadine, *d* of John Baddeley; one *s* one *d*]. *Address:* The Surgery, Watery Lane, Clifton Hampden, Oxon OX14 3EL.

LYNCH-ROBINSON, Sir Dominick (Christopher), 4th Bt *cr* 1920, of Foxrock, co. Dublin; Vice Chairman and Executive Creative Director, Atlas Advertising, since 2000; *b* 30 July 1948; *o s* of Sir Niall Lynch-Robinson, 3rd Bt, DSC, and Rosemary Seaton; *S* father, 1996; *m* 1973, Victoria, *d* of Kenneth Weir; one *s* one *d*, and one step *d*. *Recreations:* reading, cinema. *Heir: s* Christopher Henry Jake Lynch-Robinson, *b* 1 Oct. 1977. *Address:* Flat 3, 34 Montagu Square, W1H 1TL.

LYNDEN-BELL, Prof. Donald, CBE 2000; FRS 1978; Professor of Astrophysics, University of Cambridge, 1972–2001; Director, Institute of Astronomy, Cambridge, 1972–77, 1982–87, and 1992–94; *b* 5 April 1935; *s* of late Lt-Col L. A. Lynden-Bell, MC and M. R. Lynden-Bell (*née* Thring); *m* 1961, Ruth Marion Truscott, MA, PhD; one *s* one *d*. *Educ:* Marlborough; Clare Coll., Cambridge (MA, PhD). Harkness Fellow of the Commonwealth Fund, NY, at the California Inst. of Technology and Hale Observatories, 1960–62; Research Fellow and then Fellow and Dir of studies in mathematics, Clare Coll., Cambridge, 1960–65; Asst Lectr in applied mathematics, Univ. of Cambridge, 1962–65; Principal Scientific officer and later SPSO, Royal Greenwich Observatory, Herstmonceux, 1965–72. Visiting Associate, Calif Inst. of Technology and Hale Observatories, 1969–70; Visiting Professorial Fellow, QUB, 1996–; H. N. Russell Lectr, AAS, 2000. Pres., RAS, 1985–87. FHMAAAS 1985. Foreign Associate: US NAS, 1990 (J. J. Carty Award, 2000); RSSAf 1994. Hon. DSc Sussex, 1987. Eddington Medal, RAS, 1984; Brouwer Prize, AAS, 1990; Gold Medal, RAS, 1993; Bruce Medal, Astronomical Soc. of the Pacific, 1998. *Publications:* contrib. to Monthly Notices of Royal Astronomical Soc. *Recreations:* hill walking, golf, squash racquets. *Address:* Institute of Astronomy, The Observatories, Madingley Road, Cambridge CB3 0HA. *T:* (01223) 337526; (028) 9027 3239.

LYNE, Prof. Andrew Geoffrey, PhD; FRS 1996; FRAS; Professor of Radio Astronomy, since 1990, and Director of Jodrell Bank Observatory, since 1998, University of Manchester at Jodrell Bank, since 1990; *b* 13 July 1942; *s* of Lionel Geoffrey Lyne and Kathleen Elizabeth Lyne; *m* 1st, Jennifer Anne Duckels; two *d*; 2nd, 1994, Diane Elizabeth Stanway; one step *s* one step *d*. *Educ:* Portsmouth GS; St John's Coll., Cambridge (MA); Manchester Univ. (PhD). Lectr in Radio Astronomy, 1969–79, Sen. Lectr, 1979–90, Manchester Univ. Vis. Scientist, CSIRO Div. of Radiophysics, Sydney, 1975–76; Leverhulme Fellow, Royal Soc., 1994. Mem., PPARC, 1997–. Herschel Medal, RAS, 1992; Sir George Thomson Gold Medal, Inst. of Measurement and Control, 1993. *Publications:* Pulsar Astronomy, 1990, 2nd edn 1998; contrib. Nature, Monthly Notes of RAS and other scientific jls. *Recreations:* tennis, golf, walking, sailing. *Address:* Jodrell Bank Observatory, Macclesfield, Cheshire SK11 9DL; Tall Trees, New Road, Moreton, Congleton, Cheshire CW12 4RX.

LYNE, Sir Roderic (Michael John), KBE 1999; CMG 1992; HM Diplomatic Service; Ambassador to Russia, since 2000; *b* 31 March 1948; *s* of Air Vice-Marshal Michael Dillon Lyne, CB, AFC and Avril Joy, *d* of Lt-Col Albert Buckley, CBE, DSO; *m* 1969, Amanda Mary, *d* of Sir Howard Frank Trayton Smith, GCMG; two *s* one *d*. *Educ:* Legbourne County Primary Sch., Lincs; Highfield Sch., Hants; Eton Coll.; Leeds Univ. (BA Hist. 1970). FCO 1970; Army Sch. of Langs, 1971; Moscow, 1972–74; Dakar, 1974–76; Eastern European and Soviet Dept, FCO, 1976–79; Rhodesia Dept, FCO, 1979; Asst Pvte Sec. to Sec. of State for Foreign and Commonwealth Affairs, 1979–82; UK Mission to UN, NY, 1982–86; Vis. Res. Fellow, RIIA, 1986–87; Counsellor and Hd of Chancery, Moscow, 1987–90; Hd of Soviet Dept, 1990–92, Hd of Eastern Dept, 1992–93, FCO; Pvte Sec. to Prime Minister, 1993–96 (on secondment); Dir for Policy Develt, CIS ME and Africa, British Gas, 1996 (on secondment); UK Perm. Rep. to Office of UN and other internat. orgns, Geneva, 1997–2000. *Recreation:* sport. *Address:* c/o Foreign and Commonwealth Office, SW1A 2AH.

LYNK, Roy, OBE 1990; consultant in human resources, since 1996; National President, Union of Democratic Mineworkers, 1987–93; General Secretary, Nottingham Section, 1985–93; *b* 9 Nov. 1932; *s* of John Thomas Lynk and Ivy Lynk; *m* 1978, Sandra Ann; three *s* three *d*. *Educ:* Station Road Higher Sch. and Healdswood Sch., Sutton-in-Ashfield; Nottingham Univ. Cert. in Industrial Relations. Miner at Teversal Colliery, Nottingham, 1947; RN 1948; Miner at various collieries, Nottingham, 1950–79. National Union of Mineworkers: Branch Sec., Sutton Colliery, 1958–79; full time Area Official, Nottingham, 1979–83; Financial Sec., Nottingham Area, 1983–85, Gen. Sec., 1985; Union of Democratic Mineworkers: formed, Dec. 1985; Nat. Gen. Sec., 1985–86. Member: European Coal and Steel Community's Consultative Cttee, 1988–93; Industrial Appeal Tribunal, Nottingham, 1993–; Board, Coal Authy, 1995–98. *Recreation:* watching football. *Address:* Columbia House, 143 Huthwaite Road, Sutton-in-Ashfield, Notts NG17 2HB.

LYNN, Bishop Suffragan of, since 1999; **Rt Rev. Anthony Charles Foottit;** *b* 28 June 1935; *s* of Percival Frederick and Mildred Foottit; *m* 1977, Rosamond Mary Alyson Buxton; one *s* two *d*. *Educ:* Lancing College; King's Coll., Cambridge (MA). Asst Curate, Wymondham, 1961–64; Vicar, Blakeney Group, 1964–71; Rector, Camelot Group, 1971–81; RD of Cary, 1979–81; St Hugh's Missioner for Lincolnshire, 1981–87; Hon. Canon of Lincoln Cathedral, 1986–87; Archdeacon of Lynn, 1987–98. *Publication:* Mission and Ministry in Rural France, 1967. *Recreations:* gardening, botany, rambling. *Address:* The Old Vicarage, Castle Acre, King's Lynn, Norfolk PE32 2AA. *T:* (01760) 755553.

LYNN, Archdeacon of; *see* Gray, Ven. M. C.

LYNN, Jonathan Adam; director, writer and actor; *b* 3 April 1943; *s* of Robin and Ruth Lynn; *m* 1967, Rita Merkelis; one *s*. *Educ:* Kingswood Sch., Bath; Pembroke Coll., Cambridge (MA). Acted in Cambridge Circus, New York, 1964; TV debut, Ed Sullivan Show, 1964; actor in repertory, Leicester, Edinburgh and Bristol Old Vic, and in London; performances include: Green Julia, 1965; Fiddler on the Roof, 1967–68; Blue Comedy, 1968; The Comedy of the Changing Years, 1969; When We Are Married, 1970; Dreyfus, 1982; actor in TV comedy programmes and plays, including: Barmitzvah Boy, 1975; The Knowledge, 1979; Outside Edge, 1982; Diana, 1984; actor in films including: Prudence and the Pill, 1967; Into the Night, 1984; Three Men and a Little Lady, 1990; Greedy (also dir.), 1994; Artistic Dir, Cambridge Theatre Co., 1977–81 (dir. 19 prodns); *director: London:* The Plotters of Cabbage Patch Corner, 1970; The Glass Menagerie, 1977; The Gingerbread Man, 1977 and 1978; The Unvarnished Truth, 1978; The Matchmaker, 1978; Songbook, 1979 (SWET Award, Best Musical, 1979); Tonight at 8.30, 1981; Arms and the Man, 1981; Pass the Butler, 1982; Loot, 1984; *National Theatre:* A Little Hotel on the Side, 1984; Jacobowski and the Colonel, 1986; Three Men on a Horse, 1987 (Olivier Award for Best Comedy); *RSC:* Anna Christie, Stratford 1979, London 1980; *Broadway:* The Moony Shapiro Songbook, 1981; *films:* Mick's People (also wrote), 1982; Clue (also wrote), 1984; Nuns on the Run (also wrote), 1990; My Cousin Vinny, 1991; The Distinguished Gentleman, 1992; Greedy (also acted), 1994; Sgt Bilko, 1996; Trial and Error, 1997; The Whole Nine Yards, 2000; *screenplay:* The Internecine Project, 1974; *TV scriptwriter:* situation comedies, including: My Brother's Keeper, 2 series, 1974 and 1975 (also co-starred); Yes, Minister (also radio scripts), 3 series, 1980, 1981 and 1982; Yes, Prime Minister, 1986, 1987; Life After Life, 1990. Writer's Award, BAFTA, 1987; Pye TV Writers Award (for Yes, Minister and Yes, Prime Minister), 1981, 1986; Broadcasting Press Guild Award, 1980, 1986; ACE Award for Amer. Cable TV Best Comedy Writing (for Yes, Prime Minister), 1988. Hon. MA Sheffield; Hon. PsyD Amer. Behavioral Studies Inst. *Publications:* A Proper Man (novel), 1976; with Antony Jay: Yes, Minister, The Diaries of a Cabinet Minister: Vol. I, 1981; Vol. II, 1982; Vol. III, 1983; The Complete Yes Minister, 1984; Yes, Prime Minister, the Diaries of the Rt Hon. James Hacker: Vol. I, 1986; Vol. II, 1987; The Complete Yes Prime Minister, 1989; Mayday (novel), 1993. *Recreation:* changing weight. *Address:* c/o Peters, Fraser & Dunlop, Ltd, Drury House, 34–43 Russell Street, WC2B 5HA.

LYNN, Maurice Kenneth, MA; Head of French, Westminster School, 1983–88 and since 1999; *b* 3 March 1951. *Educ:* Thornleigh Salesian College, Bolton; Magdalen College, Oxford (Open Scholar; BA Hons 1973; MA 1977). Asst Master, Oratory Sch., 1973–79; Asst Master, Radley Coll., 1979–83; Headmaster, The Oratory Sch., 1989–91; Westminster School: Asst Master, 1992–95; Hd, Mod. Langs, 1995–99. Dir of Europ. interests for The Oratory Sch. Assoc., 1992. *Recreations:* English Catholic poetry, twentieth century French drama, soccer, ski-ing, cricket, acting and producing, cycling, travel. *Address:* 16a Vincent Square, SW1P 2NA. *T:* (020) 7821 1959.

LYNN, Michael David; Corporate Development Director, The Stationery Office Ltd, 1996–99; *b* 18 July 1942; *s* of Martin and Dorothy Lynn; *m* 1965, Hilary Smyth; one *s* one *d*. *Educ:* Lincoln Sch. Joined HMSO 1960; Director: Publications Distribution, 1980; Finance, 1983; Print Procurement, 1984; Dir-Gen., Corporate Services, 1987; Dep. Chief Exec., 1989; Controller and Chief Exec., 1995–96. *Recreations:* swimming, chess, crosswords.

LYNN, Prof. Richard; Professor of Psychology, University of Ulster, 1972–95, now Emeritus; *b* 20 Feb. 1930; *s* of Richard and Ann Lynn; *m* 1st, 1956, Susan Maher (marr. diss. 1978); one *s* two *d*; 2nd, 1990, Susan Hampson (*d* 1998). *Educ:* Bristol Grammar Sch.; King's Coll., Cambridge (Passingham prizeman). Lectr in Psychology, Univ. of Exeter, 1956–67; Prof. of Psychology, Dublin Economic and Social Res. Inst., 1967–72. US Mensa Award for Excellence, for work on intelligence, 1985, 1988. *Publications:* Attention, Arousal and the Orientation Reaction, 1966; The Irish Braindrain, 1969; The Universities and the Business Community, 1969; Personality and National Character, 1971; An Introduction to the Study of Personality, 1972; The Entrepreneur, 1974; (ed) Dimensions of Personality, 1981; Educational Achievement in Japan, 1987; The Secret of the Miracle Economy, 1991; Dysgenics, 1996; Eugenics:a reassessment, 2001; articles on personality, intelligence and social psychology. *Recreation:* do-it-yourself house renovation. *Address:* Whitfield Court, Glewstone, Ross-on-Wye, Herefordshire HR9 6AS. *Club:* Oxford and Cambridge.

LYNN, Dame Vera, (Dame Vera Margaret Lewis), DBE 1975 (OBE 1969); singer; *b* 20 March 1917; *d* of Bertram Samuel Welch and Annie Welch; *m* 1941, Harry Lewis; one *d*. *Educ:* Brampton Rd Sch., East Ham. First public appearance as singer, 1924; joined juvenile troupe, 1928; ran own dancing school, 1932; broadcast with Joe Loss and joined Charlie Kunz, 1935; singer with Ambrose Orch., 1937–40, then went solo; voted most popular singer, Daily Express comp., 1939, and named Forces Sweetheart; own radio show, Sincerely Yours, 1941–47; starred in Applesauce, London Palladium, 1941; sang to troops in Burma, etc, 1944 (Burma Star, 1985); subseq. Big Show (radio), USA; London Laughs, Adelphi; appeared at Flamingo Hotel, Las Vegas, and many TV shows, USA and Britain, including own TV series on Rediffusion, 1955; BBC TV, 1956; BBC 2, 1970; also appearances in Holland, Denmark, Sweden, Norway, Germany, Canada, NZ and Australia; in seven Command Performances, also films and own shows on radio. 14 Gold Records; records include Auf Wiederseh'n (over 12 million copies sold), became first British artiste to top American Hit Parade. Pres., Printers' Charitable Corp., 1980. Internat. Ambassador, Variety Club Internat., 1985. Hon. Citizen: Winnipeg, 1974; Nashville, Tennessee, 1977. Freedom: City of London, 1978; City of Corner Brook, Newfoundland, 1981. FInstD. Fellow, Univ. (formerly Poly.) of E London, 1990. Hon. LLD Memorial Univ. of Newfoundland, 1977 (founded Lynn Music Scholarship, first award, 1982); Hon. MMus London, 1992. Music Publishers' Award, 1975; Show Business Personality of the Year, Grand Order of Water Rats, 1975; Ivor Novello Award, 1975; Humanitarian Award, Variety Club Internat., 1985. Comdr, Order of Orange-Nassau, Holland. *Publications:* Vocal Refrain (autobiog.), 1975; (jtly) We'll Meet Again, 1989; Unsung Heroines, 1990. *Recreations:* gardening, painting, sewing, swimming.

LYNNE, Elizabeth, (Liz); Member (Lib Dem) West Midlands Region, European Parliament, since 1999; *b* 22 Jan. 1948. *Educ:* Dorking Co. Grammar Sch. Started acting career, 1966; numerous theatre appearances in repertory and West End. Speech consultant, 1989–92 and 1997–99. Contested (L) Harwich, 1987. MP (Lib Dem) Rochdale, 1992–97; contested (Lib Dem) same seat, 1997. Lib Dem spokesperson: on health and community care, 1992–94; on social security and disability, 1994–97. *Address:* 55 Ely Street, Stratford upon Avon, Warwickshire CV37 6LN; c/o European Parliament, Rue Wiertz, 1047 Brussels, Belgium.

LYNNE, Gillian, (Mrs Peter Land), CBE 1997; director, choreographer, dancer, actress; *d* of late Leslie Pyrke and Barbara (*née* Hart); *m* 1980, Peter Land, actor. *Educ:* Baston Sch., Bromley, Kent; Arts Educnl Sch. Leading soloist, Sadler's Wells Ballet, 1944–51; star dancer, London Palladium, 1951–53; role in film, Master of Ballantrae, 1952; lead in Can-Can, Coliseum, 1954–55; Becky Sharp in Vanity Fair, Windsor, 1956; guest principal dancer: Samson and Delilah, Sadler's Wells, 1957; Aida, and Tannhauser, Covent Garden, 1957; Puck in A Midsummer Night's Dream, TV, 1958; star dancer in Chelsea at Nine (featured dance segments), TV, 1958; lead in New Cranks, Lyric, Hammersmith, 1959; roles in Wanda, Rose Marie, Cinderella, Out of My Mind, and lead in revue, 1960–61; leading lady, 5 Past Eight Show, Edinburgh, 1962; conceived, dir., chor. and starred in Collages (mod. dance revue), Edinburgh Fest., 1963, transf. Savoy; *choreographed:* The Owl and the Pussycat (1st ballet), Western Theatre Ballet, 1962; Queen of the Cats, London Palladium, 1962–63; Wonderful Life (1st film), 1963–64; Every Day's a Holiday, and Three Hats for Lisa (musical films), 1964; The Roar of the Greasepaint, and Pickwick, Broadway, 1965; The Flying Dutchman, Covent Garden, 1966; Half a Sixpence (film), 1966–67 (also staged musical nos); How Now Dow Jones, Broadway, 1967; Midsummer Marriage, Covent Garden, 1968; The Trojans, Covent Garden, 1969, 1977; Breakaway (ballet), Scottish Theatre Ballet, 1969; Phil the Fluter, Palace, 1969; Ambassador, Her Majesty's, 1971; Man of La Mancha (film), 1972; The Card, Queen's, 1973; Hans Andersen, London Palladium, 1975; The Way of the World, Aldwych, 1978; My Fair Lady, national tour and Adelphi, 1979; Parsifal, Covent Garden, 1979; (also Associate Dir) Cats, New London, 1981 (Olivier Award, 1981), Broadway 1982, nat. tour, 1983, Los Angeles, Sydney, 1985, East Berlin, 1987, Canada, Japan, Australia, Holland, Paris, 1989 (Molière Award, Best Musical); Café Soir (ballet), Houston Ballet Co., 1985; Cabaret, Strand, 1986; The Phantom of the Opera, Her Majesty's, 1986, Broadway, Japan, Vienna, 1989, Stockholm, Chicago, Hamburg, Australia, Canada, 1990; A Simple Man (ballet), Sadler's Wells, 1988; The Brontës (ballet), Northern Ballet Theatre, 1995; The Secret Garden, RSC, Stratford and Aldwych, 2000; *directed and choreographed* The Match Girls, Globe, 1966; Bluebeard, Sadler's Wells Opera, 1966, new prodn, Sadler's Wells Opera, Coliseum, 1969; Love on the Dole (musical), Nottingham Playhouse, 1970; Liberty

Ranch, Greenwich, 1972; Once Upon a Time, Duke of York's, 1972; Jasperina, Amsterdam, 1978; Cats, Vienna, 1983 (1st proscenium arch prodn; Silver Order of Merit, Austria, 1984), Paris, 1989; Valentine's Day, Chichester, 1991; Dancing in the Dark, 1991; Valentine's Day, Globe, 1992; What the World Needs, Old Globe, San Diego, 1997–98; Gigi, Vienna, 1999; Dick Whittington, Sadler's Wells, 1999; Some You Win (dance drama), Sadler's Wells, 2000; *directed:* Round Leicester Square (revue), Prince Charles, 1963; Tonight at Eight, Hampstead, 1970 and Fortune, 1971; Lillywhite Lies, Nottingham, 1971; A Midsummer Night's Dream (co-dir.), Stratford, 1977; Tomfoolery, Criterion, 1980; Jeeves Takes Charge, Fortune, 1980, off-Broadway, 1983, Los Angeles, 1985; To Those Born Later, New End, 1981; That's What Friends Are For!, May Fair, 1996; Avow, USA, 1996; (Additional Dir) La Ronde, RSC, Aldwych, 1982; (also appeared in) Alone Plus One, Newcastle, 1982; The Rehearsal, Yvonne Arnaud, Guildford and tour, 1983; Cabaret, Strand, 1986; *staged:* England Our England (revue), Princes, 1961; 200 Motels (pop-opera film), 1971; musical nos in Quilp (film), 1974; A Comedy of Errors, Stratford, 1976 (TV musical, 1977); musical As You Like It, Stratford, 1977; Songbook, Globe, 1979; Once in a Lifetime, Aldwych, 1979; new stage act for Tommy Steele, 1979; wedding sequence in Yentl (film), 1982; European Vacation II (film); Pirelli Calendar, 1988; Pickwick, Chichester and Sadler's Wells, 1993; *choreographed for television:* Peter and the Wolf (narrated and mimed all 9 parts), 1958; At the Hawk's Well (ballet), 1975; There was a Girl, 1975; The Fool on the Hill (1st Colour Special for ABC), with Australian Ballet and Sydney Symph. Orch., staged Sydney Opera House, 1975; Muppet Show series, 1976–80; (also musical staging) Alice in Wonderland, 1985; shows and specials for Val Doonican, Perry Como, Petula Clark, Nana Mouskouri, John Curry, Harry Secombe, Ray Charles, and Mike Burstein; also produced and devised Noel Coward and Cleo Laine specials; *directed for television:* Mrs F's Friends, 1981; Easy Money, 1982; Le Morte d'Arthur (also devised), 1983 (Samuel G. Engel Award); The Simple Man, 1987 (BAFTA award for direction and choreog.); The Look of Love, 1989; That's What Friends Are For!, 1996. Patron: Indep. Dancers Resettlement Trust; Liverpool Inst. for Performing Arts; Lang. of Dance Centre, Holland Pk; Doreen Bird Coll of Performing Arts; British Assoc. of Choreographers; Adventures in Motion Pictures Ltd. *Publications:* (contrib.) Cats, The Book of the Musical; articles in Dancing Times. *Address:* Lean Two Productions Ltd, 18 Rutland Street, SW7 1EF.

LYNTON, Michael Mark; President, America Online International, since 2000; Chief Executive Officer, AOL Europe, since 2001; *b* London, 1 Jan. 1960; *s* of Mark O. L. Lynton and Marion Lynton; *m* 1994, Elizabeth Jamie Alter; two *d. Educ:* Harvard Coll. (BA 1982); Harvard Business Sch. (MBA 1987). Associate, First Boston Corp., 1982–87; Pres., Hollywood Pictures, Walt Disney Co., 1987–96; Chm. and CEO, Penguin Gp, 1996–2000. *Recreations:* tennis, ski-ing. *Address:* America Online International, 22000 AOL Way, Sterling, VA 20166-9302, USA.

LYNTON, Norbert Casper; Professor of the History of Art, 1975–89, and Dean of the School of European Studies, 1985–88, University of Sussex, now Professor Emeritus; *b* 22 Sept. 1927; *s* of Paul and Amalie Christiane Lynton; *m* 1st, 1949, Janet Irving; two *s*; 2nd, 1969, Sylvia Anne Towning; two *s. Educ:* Douai Sch.; Birkbeck Coll., Univ. of London (BA Gen.); Courtauld Inst., Univ. of London (BA Hons). Lectr in History of Art and Architecture, Leeds Coll. of Art, 1950–61; Sen. Lectr, then Head of Dept of Art History and Gen. Studies, Chelsea Sch. of Art, 1961–70. London Corresp. of Art International, 1961–66; Art Critic, The Guardian, 1965–70; Dir of Exhibitions, Arts Council of GB, 1970–75; Vis. Prof. of History of Art, Open Univ., 1975; Vis. Tutor in Painting, RCA, 1989–92. Trustee, National Portrait Gallery, 1985–99; Chm., Charleston Trust, 1998–. Responsible for many exhibns and catalogues, including: Marc Vaux, NY, 1989; Victor Pasmore, NY, 1959; Ben Nicholson, Tokyo and Japanese tour, 1992–93; for British Council: Henry Moore, Delhi, 1987; Picturing People, Kuala Lumpur, Hong Kong and Singapore, 1989–90; Henry Moore: The human dimension, Leningrad, Moscow, Helsinki, 1991–92. *Publications:* (jtly) Simpson's History of Architectural Development, vol. 4 (Renaissance), 1962; Kenneth Armitage, 1962; Paul Klee, 1964; The Modern World, 1968; The Story of Modern Art, 1980, 2nd edn 1989; Looking at Art, 1981; (jtly) Looking into Paintings, 1985; Victor Pasmore, paintings and graphics 1980–92, 1992; Ben Nicholson, 1993; Jack Smith, 2000; William Tillyer: against the grain, 2000; (jtly) Yale Dictionary of Art and Artists, 2000; articles in Burlington Mag., TLS, Studio International, Architectural Design, Art in America, Smithsonian, Leonardo, Modern Painters, Prospect, etc. *Recreations:* art, people, music, travel. *Address:* 4/14 Clifton Terrace, Vine Place, Brighton BN1 3HA. *T:* (01273) 328078.

LYON; *see* Bowes Lyon.

LYON, Adrian Pirrie; His Honour Judge Lyon; a Circuit Judge, since 2000; *b* 18 Oct. 1952; *s* of Alexander Ward Lyon and Hilda Lyon; *m* 1976, Christina Margaret Harrison (*see* C. M. Lyon); one *s* one *d. Educ:* Leeds Grammar Sch.; Hampton Grammar Sch.; University Coll. London (LLB). Called to the Bar, Gray's Inn, 1975; Head of Chambers, 1997–2000. Mem., Bar Council, 1995–97. *Recreations:* travel, reading, theatre, computers. *Address:* c/o The Court Service, Northern Circuit, 15 Quay Street, Manchester M60 9FD.

LYON, Prof. Christina Margaret; Queen Victoria Professor of Law, since 1998, and Director of the Centre for the Study of the Child, the Family and the Law, since 1995, Liverpool University; a Recorder, since 2000; *b* 12 Nov. 1952; *d* of Edward Arthur Harrison and Kathleen Joan Harrison; *m* 1976, Adrian Pirrie Lyon, *qv*; one *s* one *d. Educ:* Wallasey High Sch. for Girls; University Coll. London. LLB (1st Cl. Hons) 1974; admitted Solicitor, 1977. Tutor and sometime Lectr in Law, University Coll. London, 1974–75; Trainee and Asst Solicitor, Bell & Joynson, 1975–77; Liverpool University: part-time Tutor in Law, 1976–77; Lectr in Law, 1977–80; Manchester University: Lectr in Law and Law and Social Work, 1980–86; Sub-Dean, Law Faculty, 1986; Prof. of Law, Head of Dept and of Sch. of Law, Keele Univ., 1987–93; Liverpool University: Prof. of Common Law, 1993–98; Head, Dept of Law, 1993–97; Dean, Faculty of Law, 1994–97. Asst Recorder, 1998–2000. Member: ESRC Res. Grants Bd, 1988–91; Child Policy Review Gp, Nat. Children's Bureau, 1989–; Chm., Independent Representation for Children in Need, 1991–; Member: Nat. Exec. Cttee and Fundraising Cttee, Relate, 1990–94 (Pres., N Staffs Relate, 1987–93); Merseyside Panels of Guardians *ad Litem*, 1993– (Vice-Chm., 1993–97); Child Protection and Family Justice Cttee, Nuffield Foundn, 1994–. Dr Barnardo's Research Fellow, 1987–92. Jt Editor, Jl of Social Welfare and Family Law (formerly Jl of Social Welfare Law), 1984–; Mem. Editl Bd, Representing Children, 1996–. FRSA 1991. *Publications:* Matrimonial Jurisdiction of Magistrates' Courts, 1981; Cohabitation without Marriage, 1983; (ed) Butterworth's Family Law Service Encyclopaedia, 1983, rev. edn 1998; Law of Residential Homes and Day Care Establishments, 1984; Child Abuse, 1990, 3rd edn 2000; The Law Relating to Children in Principles and Practice of Forensic Psychiatry, 1990; (ed with A. P. Lyon) Butterworth's Family Law Handbook, 1991; Atkins Court Forms on Infants, vols I and II, 1992; The Law Relating to Children, 1993; Child Abuse, 1993; Legal Issues Arising from the Care and Control of Children with Learning Disabilities who also Present Severely Challenging Behaviour, vol. I, Policy Guidance, vol. II, A Guide for Parents and Carers, 1994; Child Protection and the Civil Legal Framework in The Child Protection Handbook, 1995; Children's Rights and The Children Act 1989 in Children's Rights, 1995; Working Together: an analysis of collaborative inter-agency responses to the problem of domestic violence, 1995; Law and Body Politics, 1995; (jtly) Effective Support Services for Children, 1998; (jtly) A Trajectory of Hope, 2000; Loving Smack, Lawful Assaults: a contradiction in human rights and law, 2000. *Recreations:* riding, swimming, foreign travel, reading, theatre, opera. *Address:* Faculty of Law, University of Liverpool, Chatham Street, Liverpool L69 3BX.

LYON, Rt Hon. Clare; *see* Short, Rt Hon. C.

LYON, (Colin) Stewart (Sinclair), FIA; FSA, FRNS; General Manager (Finance), Group Actuary and Director, Legal & General Group Plc, 1980–87; *b* 22 Nov. 1926; *s* of late Col Colin Sinclair Lyon, OBE, TD and Mrs Dorothy Winstanley Lyon (*née* Thomason); *m* 1958, Elizabeth Mary Fargus Richards; four *s* one *d. Educ:* Liverpool Coll.; Trinity Coll., Cambridge (MA). FIA 1954; FSA 1972; FRNS 1955. Chief Exec., Victory Insurance Co. Ltd, 1974–76; Chief Actuary, Legal & General Assurance Soc. Ltd, 1976–85. Director: Lautro Ltd, 1987–92; Cologne Reinsurance Co. Ltd, 1987–97; City of Birmingham Touring Opera Ltd, 1987–90; Ætna Internat. (UK) Ltd, 1988–91; Pearl Gp PLC, 1991–97; UK Bd, AMP and London Life, 1991–97. Member: Occupational Pensions Bd, 1979–82; Inquiry into Provision for Retirement, 1983–85; Treasure Trove Reviewing Cttee, 1986–93. President: Inst. of Actuaries, 1982–84 (Gold Medal, 1991); British Numismatic Soc., 1966–70 (Vice-Pres., 1971–; Sanford Saltus Gold Medal, 1974). Trustee, Disablement Income Gp Charitable Trust, 1967–84; Dir, Disablement Income Gp, 1984–94 (Vice-Pres., 1995–); Trustee, Independent Living Fund, 1988–93. *Publications:* (with C. E. Blunt and B. H. I. H. Stewart) Coinage in Tenth-Century England, 1989; papers on Anglo-Saxon coinage, particularly in British Numismatic Jl; contrib. Jl of Inst. of Actuaries and Trans Internat. Congress of Actuaries. *Recreations:* numismatics, music, amateur radio (call sign GW3EIZ). *Address:* Ardraeth, Malltraeth, Bodorgan, Anglesey LL62 5AW. *T:* (01407) 840273. *Club:* Actuaries'.

LYON, George; Member (Lib Dem) Argyll and Bute, Scottish Parliament, since 1999; *b* 16 July 1956; *s* of Alister and Mary Lyon; *m* 1981, Patricia Gibson; three *d. Educ:* Rothesay Acad. Family business, farming, A. H. Lyon, 1972–74, A. K. Farms, 1994–, Isle of Bute. Mem., NFU Scotland, 1990– (Pres., 1997–99). FRAgS 2000. *Recreations:* ski-ing, football, reading, swimming. *Address:* Kildavannan Farm, Rothesay, Isle of Bute PA20 0QX. *T:* (01700) 504327. *Club:* Farmers'.

LYON, (John) David (Richard); Chief Executive, Rexam plc (formerly Bowater Industries, then Bowater plc), 1987–96; *b* 4 June 1936; *s* of John F. A. Lyon and Elizabeth Lyon (*née* Owen); *m* 1st, 1960, Nicola M. E. Bland (marr. diss. 1986); two *s* (and one *s* decd); 2nd, 1987, Lillis Lanphier. *Educ:* Wellington College; Magdalen College, Oxford (BA Modern History 1959); Harvard Business Sch. (Advanced Management Programme, 1973). 1st Bn The Rifle Brigade, Kenya and Malaya, 1954–56 (despatches). Courtaulds, 1959–70; Rank Organisation, 1970–71; Redland, 1971–87 (Dir 1976; Man. Dir, 1982); Dir, Smiths Industries, 1991–94. Chm., Stocks Austin Sice, 1997–. Mem., Adv. Cttee on Business and the Envmt, 1991–93. *Recreations:* trekking, blacksmithing. *Address:* PO Box 12, Arundel, West Sussex BN18 9ND.

LYON, John MacDonald; Director-General, Policing and Crime Reduction Group, Home Office, since 2000; *b* 12 April 1948; *m*; two *c. Educ:* Selwyn Coll., Cambridge (BA, MA). Joined Home Office, 1969; Principal, 1974; Cabinet Office, 1978–80; Asst Sec., 1982; Grade 3, 1991; Director: Sentencing and Correctional Policy, 1998–99; Police Policy, 1999. *Address:* Home Office, 50 Queen Anne's Gate, SW1H 9AT.

LYON, Mary Frances, ScD; FRS 1973; Deputy Director, Medical Research Council Radiobiology Unit, Harwell, 1982–90, retired; *b* 15 May 1925; *e d* of Clifford James Lyon and Louise Frances Lyon (*née* Kirby). *Educ:* King Edward's Sch., Birmingham; Woking Grammar Sch.; Girton Coll., Cambridge (ScD 1968; Hon. Fellow 1985). FIBiol. MRC Scientific Staff, Inst. of Animal Genetics, Edinburgh, 1950–55; MRC Radiobiology Unit, Harwell, 1955–90, Hd Genetics Div., 1962–87. Clothworkers Visiting Research Fellow, Girton Coll., Cambridge, 1970–71. Foreign Hon. Mem., Amer. Acad. Arts and Scis, 1980 (Amory Prize, 1977). Foreign Associate, US Nat. Acad. of Scis, 1979. Royal Medal, Royal Soc., 1984; Prize for Genetics, Sanremo, Italy, 1985; Gairdner Foundn Award, 1985; Allan Award, Amer. Soc. of Human Genetics, 1986; Wolf Prize for medicine, Wolf Foundn, 1996. *Publications:* papers on genetics in scientific jls. *Address:* MRC Mammalian Genetics Unit, Harwell, Oxon OX11 0RD. *T:* (01235) 834393.

LYON, Maj.-Gen. Robert, CB 1976 OBE 1964 (MBE 1960); Bursar, Loretto School, Musselburgh, 1979–91; *b* Ayr, 24 Oct. 1923; *s* of David Murray Lyon and Bridget Lyon (*née* Smith); *m* 1st, 1951, Constance Margaret Gordon (*d* 1982); one *s* one *d*; 2nd, 1992, Rosemary Jane, *d* of G. H. Allchin, Torquay. *Educ:* Ayr Academy. Commissioned, Aug. 1943, Argyll and Sutherland Highlanders. Served Italy, Germany, Palestine, Greece; transf. to Regular Commn in RA, 1947; Regtl Service, 3 RHA in Libya and 19 Field in BAOR, 1948–56; Instr, Mons Officer Cadet Sch., 1953–55; Staff Coll., 1957; DAQMG, 3 Div., 1958–60; jssc, 1960; BC F (Sphinx) Bty 7 PARA, RHA, 1961–62 (Bt Lt-Col); GSO1, ASD2, MoD, 1962–65 (Lt-Col); CO 4 Lt Regt, RA, 1965–67, Borneo (despatches), UK and BAOR (Lt-Col); as Brig.: CRA 1 Div., 1967–69, BAOR; IDC, 1970; Dir Operational Requirements, MoD, 1971–73; DRA (Maj.-Gen.), 1973–75; GOC SW District, 1975–78; retired 1979. Pres., Army Hockey Assoc., 1974–76; Chm., Army Golf Assoc., 1977–78. Chm., RA Council of Scotland, 1984–90. Col Comdt RA. Director: Braemar Civic Amenities Trust, 1986–90; Edinburgh Military Tattoo Ltd, 1988–98; Financial Forum, 1996–. Regl Dir Scotland, Manufacturing Forum, 1994–. HM Comr, Queen Victoria Sch., Dunblane, 1984–95. Pres., La Punta Urbanisation, Los Cristianos, 1995–98. FIMgt (MBIM 1978). *Publication:* Irish Roulette, 1991. *Recreations:* golf, writing, gardening. *Address:* (Apr. to Nov.) Woodside, Braemar, Aberdeenshire AB35 5YT. *T:* and *Fax:* (013397) 41667; *e-mail:* Lyonwoodside@ukonline.co.uk; (Nov. to Apr.) Appt 6 La Punta, Avenida La Habana, Los Cristianos, Tenerife, Canary Is. *T:* and *Fax:* (922) 794592; *e-mail:* Lyon@fastnetspain.net. *Clubs:* Royal Scots (Edinburgh); Hon. Company of Edinburgh Golfers; Craigendarroch Country.

LYON, Hon. Sterling Rufus Webster, PC 1982; **Hon. Mr Justice Lyon;** a Judge of the Manitoba Court of Appeal, since 1986; *b* 30 Jan. 1927; *s* of David Rufus Lyon and Ella May (*née* Cuthbert); *m* 1953, Barbara Jean Mayers; two *s* three *d. Educ:* Portage Collegiate (Governor-General's Medal); United College (BA 1948); Univ. of Manitoba Law Sch. (LLB 1953). Crown Attorney, Manitoba, 1953–57; QC (Canada) 1960. Member, Manitoba Legislative Assembly, and Executive Council, 1958–69; Attorney-General, 1958–63 and 1966–69; Minister of Municipal Affairs, 1960–61; Public Utilities, 1961–63; Mines and Natural Resources, 1963–66; Tourism and Recreation, Commissioner of Northern Affairs, 1966–68; Govt House Leader, 1966–69; Leader, Progressive Cons. Party of Manitoba, 1975–83; MLA: for Fort Garry, 1958–69; for Souris-Killarney, 1976–77; for Charleswood, 1977–86; Leader of the Opposition, Manitoba, 1976–77 and 1981–83; Premier of Manitoba and Minister of Dominion-Provincial Affairs, 1977–81.

Recreations: hunting, fishing. *Address:* Law Courts, Winnipeg, MB R3C 0P9, Canada. *T:* (204) 9452050. *Club:* Albany (Toronto).

LYON, Stewart; *see* Lyon, C. S. S.

LYON-DALBERG-ACTON, family name of **Baron Acton**.

LYONS, Maj.-Gen. Adrian William, CBE 1994; FILT; Director General, Railway Forum, since 2001; *b* 26 Dec. 1946; *s* of late Gp Capt. W. M. Lyons and M. P. Lyons (*née* Willis); *m* 1993, Rosemary Ann Farrer; one *d. Educ:* Merchant Taylors' Sch. Commnd RCT, 1966, transf. RAOC, 1972; various logistic mgt and planning appts, largely MoD based, 1977–94; psc 1980, jsdc 1986, rcds 1995; Dep. UK Mil. Rep., Brussels, 1996–98; Dir Gen. Logistic Support (Army), then Defence Logistic Support, MoD, 1998–2000. Col Comdt RLC, 2000–; Hon. Col 168 Pioneer Regt RLC(V), 2001–. Chm., Hong Kong Locally Enlisted Personnel Trust, 1998–2001. (With Sir Nicholas Jackson, Bt) composed opera, Reluctant Highwayman, first performed Broomhill Fest., 1995. Liveryman: Drapers' Co., 1997–; Carmen's Co., 1998–. *Recreations:* theatre, travel, collecting (almost) anything that makes the past come alive, esp. coins (FRNS; Mem., British Numismatic Soc.). *Address:* (office) 12 Grosvenor Place, SW1H 7XX. *T:* (020) 7259 6333.

LYONS, Alastair David, CBE 2001; Executive Chairman, Partners for Finance Ltd, since 2001; *b* 18 Oct. 1953; *o s* of late Alexander Lyons and of Elizabeth (*née* Eynon); *m* 1980, Judith Shauneen Rhodes; one *s* two *d. Educ:* Whitgift Sch.; Trinity Coll., Cambridge (Sen. Schol.; MA 2nd Cl. Hons). With Price Waterhouse & Co., 1974–79; N. M. Rothschild & Sons Ltd, 1979; H. P. Bulmer Holdings PLC, 1979–89: Gp Treas., 1979–82; Gp Financial Controller, 1983–88; Actg Gp Finance Dir, and Finance Dir, H. P. Bulmer Drinks Ltd, 1988–89; Divl Dir, Corporate Finance, Asda Gp PLC, 1989–90; Finance Dir, ASDA Stores Ltd, 1990–91; Finance Dir, 1991–94, Chief Exec., 1994–96, Nat. & Provincial Building Soc.; Man. Dir, Insurance, and Exec. Dir, Abbey National plc, 1996–97; Chief Exec., NPI, 1997–99; Dir of Corporate Projs, Nat. Westminster Gp, 1999–2000. Non-exec. Chm., Admiral Gp Ltd, 2000–; non-exec. Dir, Wishstream Ltd, 2001–. Non-executive Director: Benefits Agency, 1994–97; DSS, 1997–. Mem., Yorks Regl Cttee, NT, 1994–96. Gov., Giggleswick Sch., 1994–97. *Recreations:* cycling, running, riding, hill walking, collecting antiques. *Address:* Tolhurst Barn, Birchetts Green Lane, Ticehurst, Wadhurst, East Sussex TN5 7LJ.

LYONS, Bernard, CBE 1964; JP; DL; Chairman: UDS Group PLC, 1972–82 (Director, 1954–83; Joint Managing Director, 1966; Managing Director, 1972–79); Colmore Trust Ltd, since 1984; *b* 30 March 1913; *m* 1938, Lucy Hurst (*d* 2001); three *s* one *d. Educ:* Leeds Grammar Sch. Chairman: Yorkshire and City Properties Ltd, 1956–73; Glanfield Securities, 1958–74. Chm., Yorkshire and NE Conciliation Cttee, Race Relations Bd, 1968–70; Member: Leeds City Council, 1951–65; Community Relations Commn, 1970–72; Govt Adv. Cttee on Retail Distribution, 1970–76. Mem. Court and Council, Univ. of Leeds, 1953–58; Chm., Swarthmore Adult Educn Centre Appeal for Building Extensions, 1957–60. Chm., Leeds Judean Youth Club, 1955–70; Jt Chm., Leeds Br., CCJ, 1955–60; Life Pres., Leeds Jewish Representative Council, 1960–. JP Leeds, 1960; DL West Riding, Yorks, 1971. Hon. LLD Leeds, 1973. *Publications:* The Thread is Strong, 1981; The Narrow Edge, 1985; Tombola, 1996. *Recreations:* farming, forestry, travel, writing. *Address:* Upton Wood, Fulmer, Bucks SL3 6JJ. *T:* (01753) 662404.
See also S. R. Lyons.

LYONS, Charles Albert; General Secretary, Transport Salaried Staffs' Association, 1982–89, retired; *b* Liverpool, 13 Aug. 1929; *s* of Maurice Lyons and Catherine Jones; *m* 1958, Judith Mary Robinson; three *s. Educ:* St Mary's RC Secondary Modern Sch., Fleetwood. Wages Clerk, fishing industry, 1943–47; National Service, RAPC, 1947–49; Clerical Officer, British Rail, 1950–59; Transport Salaried Staffs' Association: Clerical Asst, 1959–64; Scottish Sec., 1965–68; London Midland Div. Officer, 1968–73; Asst Gen. Sec., 1973–77; Senior Asst Gen. Sec., 1977–82; Member: TUC Gen. Council, 1983–89 (Mem. Committees: Finance and Gen. Purposes; Equal Rights; Transport; Public Enterprise; Social Insurance and Indust. Welfare; Employment, Policy and Orgn); Hotels and Catering Industrial Training Bd, 1982–84; Railway Industry Adv. Cttee, 1982–86; Jt Council for Railways, EEC; Vice-Chm., ITF Travel Bureau Section, 1979–89; individual Mem., Labour Party, 1950–.

LYONS, Dennis John, CB 1972; CEng, FRAeS; Director General of Research, Department of the Environment, 1971–76; *b* 26 Aug. 1916; *s* of late John Sylvester Lyons and of Adela Maud Lyons; *m* 1939, Elisabeth, *d* of Arnold and Maria Friederika Müller Haefliger, Weggis, Switzerland; five *s* two *d. Educ:* Grocers' Company School; Queen Mary Coll., London Univ. (Fellow, 1969). Aerodynamics Dept, Royal Aircraft Estabt, 1937; RAFVR, 1935–41; Aerodynamics Flight Aero Dept, RAE, 1941–51; Head of Experimental Projects Div., Guided Missiles Dept, RAE, 1951; Head of Ballistic Missile Group, GW Dept, 1956; Head of Weapons Dept, RAE, 1962; Dir., Road Research Laboratory, 1965–71. Member: Adv. Board for Res. Councils, 1973–76; SRC, 1973–76; Engineering Bd, SRC, 1970–76; Natural Environment Res. Council, 1973–76. Pres. OECD Road Research Unit, 1968–72. Hon. Mem., Instn Highway Engineers. *Publications:* papers in scientific jls. *Recreations:* ski-ing, pottery-making, philately. *Address:* Summerhaven, Gough Road, Fleet, Hants GU13 8LJ. *T:* (01252) 614773.

LYONS, Edward; QC 1974; LLB; a Recorder of the Crown Court, 1972–98; *b* 17 May 1926; *s* of late A. Lyons and Mrs S. Taylor; *m* 1955, Barbara, *d* of Alfred Katz; one *s* one *d. Educ:* Roundhay High Sch.; Leeds Univ. LLB (Hons) 1951. Served Royal Artillery, 1944–48; Combined Services Russian Course, Cambridge Univ., 1946; Interpreter in Russian, Brit. CCG, 1946–48. Called to Bar, Lincoln's Inn, 1952, Bencher, 1983. MP (Lab 1966–81, SDP 1981–83) Bradford E, 1966–74, Bradford W, 1974–83; PPS at Treasury, 1969–70; SDP Parly spokesman: on home affairs, 1981–82; on legal affairs, 1982–83. Member: H of C Select Cttee on European Legislation, 1975–83; SDP Nat. Cttee, 1984–87; Chairman: PLP Legal and Judicial Gp, 1974–77; PLP Home Office Gp, 1974–79 (Dep. Chm., 1970–74). Contested: (Lab) Harrogate, 1964; (SDP) Bradford W, 1983; (SDP) Yorkshire West, European Parly Elecn, 1984. Mem., Exec. of Justice, 1974–89. *Recreations:* history, opera. *Address:* 59 Westminster Gardens, Marsham Street, SW1P 4JG. *T:* (020) 7834 1960; 4 Primley Park Lane, Leeds LS17 7JR. *T:* (0113) 268 5351.

LYONS, Sir Edward Houghton, Kt 1977; FAIM; Chairman, Totalisator Administration Board, Queensland, 1981–85. Formerly Chairman, Katies Ltd, and Gen. Manager, Industrial Acceptance Corp. Ltd; Dir, Bruck (Australia) Ltd. Trustee, National Party. *Address:* 47 Kneale Street, Holland Park Heights, Queensland 4121, Australia. *T:* (7) 33496461.

LYONS, (Isidore) Jack; Chairman: J. E. London Properties Ltd, since 1986; Natural Nutrition Company Ltd, 1989–91; Advisor, Cranbury Group, 1981–89; Director of other companies; *b* 1 Feb. 1916; *s* of Samuel H. Lyons and Sophia Niman; *m* 1943, Roslyn Marion Rosenbaum; two *s* two *d. Educ:* Leeds Grammar Sch. Dir, UDS Gp, 1955–80. Chm., Leeds Musical Festival, 1955–72, Vice-Pres., 1973; Jt Founder, 1961, and former Chm., Leeds Internat. Pianoforte Competition; Chm., London Symphony Orchestra Trust, 1970–91 (Jt Chm., 1963–70), Trustee, 1970– (Hon. Mem., LSO, 1973); Jt Chm., Southwark Rehearsal Hall Trust, 1974–95; Chm., Shakespeare Exhibn (quatercentenary celebrations Stratford-upon-Avon), 1964; Mem. Exec. Cttee, Royal Acad. of Dancing, 1964; Life Trustee, Shakespeare Birthplace Trust, 1967; Mem., Culture Adv. Cttee, UNESCO, 1973–, Dep. Chm., Fanfare for Europe, 1972–73; Chm., FCO US Bicentennial Cttee for the Arts, 1973–; Mem., Adv. Cttee of Honour, Britain's Salute to NY 1983 Bicentennial. Chairman: Sir Jack Lyons Charitable Trust; Musical Therapy Charity, 1984–85; Trustee, Heslington Foundn for Music and Associated Arts, 1987–; Dir, Wolf Trap Foundn, USA. Vice-Pres., Anglo-Italian Chamber of Commerce, 1977–. Vice-Pres., Jt Israel Appeal, 1972– (Dep. Chm. 1957); Chm., Fedn of Jewish Relief Organisations, 1958–86. Member: Canadian Veterans' Assoc., 1964; Pilgrims, 1965. Mem. Council, Internat. Triangle Res. Inst., 1983–. Patron: St Gemma's Hospice; ORT, 1997–. Dep. Chm., Governors of Carmel Coll., 1961–69; Mem. Ct, York Univ., 1965. FRSA 1973. Hon. FRAM, 1972. DUniv York, 1975. *Recreations:* music, the arts and swimming.

LYONS, Sir James (Reginald), Kt 1969; JP; Airport Manager, Cardiff Airport, 1955–75; *b* 15 March 1910; *s* of James Lyons and Hilda (*née* Driscoll); *m* 1937, Doreen Mary Fogg; one *s. Educ:* Howard Gardens High Sch.; Cardiff Technical Coll. Served War of 1939–45: Royal Tank Regt, 1940–46 (1939–45 Star, Africa Star, Italy Star, Defence Medal, War Medal of 1939–45). Civil Service, 1929–65: Post Office, Min. of Supply, Min. of Aviation. Chm., Park Lodge Property Co., till 1997. Mem., Wales Tourist Bd. Glamorgan CC, 1965–74; Cardiff City Council: Councillor, 1949–58; Alderman, 1958–74; Lord Mayor of Cardiff, 1968–69. Mem., Norfolk Cttee for investiture of Prince of Wales, 1968–69. Former Mem., BBC Broadcasting Council. Assessor under Race Relations Act, 1976. President: Welsh Games Council, 1985– (Life Vice-Pres., 1975); Cardiff Horticultural Soc., 1962–. Former Trustee, Wales and Border Counties TSB. Chairman of Governors: UC Cardiff, 1955–70; St Illtyd's Coll., 1956–86; Governor, De La Salle Prep. Sch., 1966–86. JP Cardiff, 1966–. OStJ; KCSG. *Recreations:* Rugby football, swimming, tennis. *Address:* 101 Minehead Avenue, Sully, S Glam CF6 2TL. *T:* (029) 2053 0403.

LYONS, Sir John, Kt 1987; FBA 1973; Master of Trinity Hall, Cambridge, 1984–2000; *b* 23 May 1932; *s* of Michael A. Lyons and Mary B. Lyons (*née* Sullivan); *m* 1959, Danielle J. Simonet; two *d. Educ:* St Bede's Coll., Manchester; Christ's Coll., Cambridge. MA; PhD 1961; LittD 1988. Lecturer: in Comparative Linguistics, SOAS, 1957–61; in General Linguistics, Univ. of Cambridge, 1961–64; Prof. of General Linguistics, Edinburgh Univ., 1964–76; Prof. of Linguistics, 1976–84, Pro-Vice-Chancellor, 1981–84, Sussex Univ. DèsL (*hc*) Univ. Catholique de Louvain, 1980; Hon. DLitt: Reading, 1986; Edinburgh, 1988; Sussex, 1990; Antwerp, 1992. *Publications:* Structural Semantics, 1964; Introduction to Theoretical Linguistics, 1968; New Horizons in Linguistics, 1970; Chomsky, 1970, 3rd edn 1991; Semantics, vols 1 and 2, 1977; Language and Linguistics, 1981; Language, Meaning and Context, 1981, 2nd edn 1991; Natural Language and Universal Grammar, 1991; Linguistic Semantics, 1995; articles and reviews in learned journals.

LYONS, John, CBE 1986; General Secretary, Engineers' and Managers' Association, 1977–91, and Electrical Power Engineers' Association, 1973–91; *b* 19 May 1926; *s* of Joseph and Hetty Lyons; *m* 1954, Molly McCall; two *s* two *d. Educ:* St Paul's Sch.; Polytechnic, Regent Street; Cambridge Univ. (BA Econ). RN 1944–46. Asst. to Manager of Market Research Dept, Vacuum Oil Co., 1950; Research Officer: Bureau of Current Affairs, 1951; Post Office Engineering Union, 1952–57; Asst. Sec., Instn of Professional Civil Servants 1957–66, Dep. Gen. Sec. 1966–73. Member: TUC Gen. Council, 1983–91 (Chm., Energy Cttee, 1988–91); Nat. Enterprise Bd, 1975–79; Exec. Cttee PEP, 1975–78; Council, PSI, 1978–80; Adv. Council for Applied R&D, 1978–81; Engrg Council, 1982–86; PO Bd, 1980–81, British Telecommunications Bd, 1981–83; Sec., Electricity Supply Trade Union Council (formerly Employees' Nat. Cttee for Electricity Supply Industry), 1976–91; Chm., NEDO Working Party on Industrial Trucks, 1977–80. Vice-Pres., Industrial Participation Assoc., 1976–90; British rep., Econ. and Social Cttee, EU (formerly EC), 1990–98 (Vice Pres., Energy Section, 1992–98; Pres., 1994–96, Vice Pres., 1996–98, Single Market Observatory). Governor, Kingsbury High School, 1974–86; Member: Court of Governors, LSE, 1978–84; Bd of Governors, London Business Sch., 1987–88. Hitachi Lectr, Sussex Univ., 1983; addresses to: British Assoc., 1973; IEE, 1977; Internat. Monetary Conference, 1984; Newcastle Univ., 1989. FRSA. Hon. Life Mem., EPEA, 1991; Hon. Fellow, IIEXE, 1992. *Publications:* various papers and articles. *Recreations:* several. *Address:* 305 Salmon Street, Kingsbury, NW9 8YA.

LYONS, John; MP (Lab) Strathkelvin and Bearsden, since 2001; *b* 11 July 1949; partner, Francesca Walsh; one *s* one *d. Educ:* Woodside Secondary Sch.; Stirling Univ. (MSc 2000). Mechanical engr, 1971–88; Officer UNISON, 1988–2001. Mem., Forth Valley Health Bd, 1999–2001. *Address:* c/o House of Commons, SW1A 0AA.

LYONS, Prof. Malcolm Cameron; Sir Thomas Adams's Professor of Arabic, University of Cambridge, 1985–96; Fellow, Pembroke College, Cambridge, since 1957 (President, 1989–93); *b* Indore, India, 11 Feb. 1929; *s* of Harold William Lyons and Florence Katharine (*née* Cameron); *m* 1961, Ursula Schedler. *Educ:* New Park Sch., St Andrews; Fettes Coll.; Pembroke Coll., Cambridge (Major Open Classical Schol., 1946; John Stewart of Rannoch Classical Schol. in Latin and Greek, 1948; Browne Medallist, 1948, 1949; 1st cl. hons Pts I and II, Classical Tripos, 1948, 1949; 1st cl. hons Pts I and II, Oriental Studies, Arabic and Persian, 1953; E. G. Browne Prize, 1953; MA 1954; PhD 1957; LittD 1997). RAF, 1949–51, commissioned 1950. University of Cambridge: Asst Lectr in Arabic, 1954–59; Lectr, 1959–84; Reader in Medieval Islamic Studies, 1984–85. Seconded to FO as Principal Instructor, MECAS, Lebanon, 1961–62. Founder Editor: Arabic Technical and Scientific Texts, 1966–78; Jl of Arabic Literature, 1970–. *Publications:* Galen on Anatomical Procedures (with W. Duckworth and B. Towers), 1962; In Hippocratis de Officina Medici, 1963, and De Partibus Artis Medicativae, De Causis Contentivis, De Diaeta in Morbis Acutis (in Corpus Medicorum Graecorum), 1967; An Arabic Translation of Themistius' Commentary on Aristotle's De Anima, 1973; Aristotle's Ars Rhetorica, Arabic version, 1982; (with E. Maalouf) The Poetic Vocabulary of Michel Trad, 1968; (with J. Riley-Smith and U. Lyons) Ayyubids, Mamlukes and Crusaders, 1971; (with D. Jackson) Saladin, The Politics of the Holy War, 1982; (jtly) Meredith Dewey: diaries, letters, writings, 1992; The Arabian Epic, 1995; Identification and Identity in Classical Arabic Poetry, 1999; articles and reviews in learned jls. *Recreations:* golf, ski-ing, walking. *Address:* Pembroke College, Cambridge CB1 2RF. *Club:* Royal and Ancient Golf (St Andrews).

LYONS, Sir Michael (Thomas), Kt 2000; Chief Executive, Birmingham City Council, 1994–2001; *b* West Ham, 15 Sept. 1949; *s* of Thomas Lyons and Lillian Lyons (*née* Stafford); *m* 1976, Gwendolene Jane Calvert; two *s* one *d. Educ:* Stratford Grammar Sch.; Middlesex Polytechnic (BA Soc. Scis Hons); Queen Mary Coll., London (MSc Econ). Street market trader, 1970–72; Brand Manager, Crookes-Anestan, 1971–72; Lectr and

Res. Fellow, Dept of Industrial Econs, Univ. of Nottingham, 1973–75; Sen. Res. Officer, DoE, 1975–78; W Midlands County Council: Principal Economist, 1978–82; Dep. Dir and Dir, Economic Develt, 1982–85; Chief Executive: Wolverhampton MBC, 1985–90; Notts CC, 1990–94. Sec., 1997–2001, Mem., 1999–2001, W Midlands LGA; Sec., W Midlands Regl Chamber, 1998–2001. Councillor, Birmingham City Council, 1980–83. Gov., RSC, 1999–. Hon. Prof. of Public Policy, Birmingham Univ., 1998–. FRSA. Hon. Dr Middlesex, 1997. *Publications:* (ed with A. Johnson) The Winning Bid, 1992; contribs to professional jls. *Recreations:* the demands of an energetic family, developing my kitchen skills, theatre, cinema, walking. *Address:* c/o The Council House, Victoria Square, Birmingham B1 1BB. *T.* (0121) 303 2000.

LYONS, Roger Alan; Joint General Secretary, Amicus Union, since 2002; *b* 14 Sept. 1942; *s* of late Morris and Phyllis Lyons; *m* 1971, Kitty Horvath; two *s* two *d*. *Educ:* Roe Green Junior Sch., Kingsbury; Christ's Coll., Finchley; University Coll. London (BSc Hons Econ.; Fellow, 1996). Regional Officer, ASSET, then ASTMS, 1966–70; Nat. Officer 1970–87, Asst Gen. Sec. 1987–89, ASTMS; Asst Gen. Sec., 1989–92, Gen. Sec., 1992–2001, MSF. Exec., European Metalworker Fedn, 1987–; Mem., Gen. Council, TUC, 1990–. Mem., Design Council, 1998–. Member: Council, UCL, 1997–; Bd, Univ. for Industry, 1999–. *Recreations:* family, take-aways, cinema, football (Arsenal in particular). *Address:* 22 Park Crescent, N3 2NJ. *T:* (020) 8346 6843, *Fax:* (020) 8349 9075.

LYONS, Shaun; His Honour Judge Lyons; a Circuit Judge, since 1992; Resident Judge, Wood Green Crown Court, since 1995; *b* 20 Dec. 1942; *s* of late Jeremiah Lyons and of Winifred Ruth Lyons; *m* 1970, Nicola Rosemary, *d* of late Capt. D. F. Chilton, DSO, RN; one *s* one *d*. *Educ:* Portsmouth Grammar Sch.; Inns of Court Sch. of Law. Joined RN, 1961; Lt 1966; Lt Comdr 1974; called to the Bar, Middle Temple, 1975; Comdr 1981; Captain 1988; Chief Naval Judge Advocate, 1989–92; retd RN, 1992. Asst Recorder and Recorder, 1988–92. *Clubs:* Army and Navy; Royal Yacht Squadron.

LYONS, Stuart Randolph, CBE 1993; Chairman, Colmore Trust Ltd, since 1984; *b* 24 Oct. 1943; 3rd *s* of Bernard Lyons, *qv*; *m* 1969, Ellen Harriet Zion; two *s* one *d*. *Educ:* Rugby; King's Coll., Cambridge. Man. Dir, John Collier Tailoring Ltd, 1969–74 (Chm., 1975–83); Dir, UDS Group plc, 1974–83 (Man. Dir, 1979–83); Chief Exec., Royal Doulton plc, 1985–97 (Chm., 1987–93); Director: British Ceramic Res. Ltd, 1987–94; Hogg Robinson plc, 1998–2000; Gartmore Absolute Growth & Income Trust plc, 2000–. Member: Leeds CC, 1970–74; Yorkshire and Humberside Econ. Planning Council, 1972–75; Clothing EDC, 1976–79; Ordnance Survey Review Cttee, 1978–79; Monopolies and Mergers Commn, 1981–85; Council, CBI, 1991–96; Nat. Manufacturing Council, 1992–95; Dir, Staffs TEC, 1990–93. Pres., BCMF, 1989–90; Chairman: British Ceramic Confedn, 1989–95; Staffs Develt Assoc., 1992–95; DTI Tableware Strategy Group, 1994–96; W Midlands Develt Agency, 1995–99; Vice-Chm., Industry 96 (W Midlands Fest. of Industry and Enterprise), 1994–96. Mem. Council, Keele Univ., 1989–97; Gov., Staffs Univ. (formerly Staffs Poly.), 1991–97. Contested (C) Halifax, Feb. and Oct. 1974. Hon. DLitt Keele, 1994. *Publications:* The Fleeting Years: Odes of Horace (verse trans. with introd. and notes) 1996; Can Consignia Deliver?, 2000. *Address:* 50 Seymour Walk, SW10 9NF. *T:* (020) 7352 3309, *Fax:* (020) 7376 7556; *e-mail:* gcc55@dial.pipex.com. *Clubs:* Carlton, Hurlingham.

LYONS, Prof. Terence John, DPhil; FRSE; Wallis Professor of Mathematics, University of Oxford, since 2000; Fellow, St Anne's College, Oxford, since 2000; *b* 4 May 1953; *s* of Peter Lyons and Valerie (*née* Hardie); *m* 1975, Barbara, *d* of late Joseph and Barbara Epsom; *m*; one *s* one *d*. *Educ:* St Joseph's Coll., W Norwood; Trinity Coll., Cambridge (BA Maths 1975 and 1976); Christ Church, Oxford (DPhil 1980). FRSE 1988. Jun. Res. Fellow, Jesus Coll., Oxford, 1979–81; Lectr in Maths, Imperial Coll., London, 1981–85; Colin Maclaurin Prof. of Maths, 1985–93, Hd, Dept of Maths and Stats, 1988–91, Univ. of Edinburgh; Prof. of Maths, Imperial Coll., London, 1993–2000. Hendrick Vis. Asst Prof., UCLA, 1981–82; Vis. Prof., Univ. of BC, 1990. Sen. Fellow, EPSRC, 1993–98. Vice Pres., LMS, 2000–. Mem. Editl Bd of numerous jls. Rollo Davidson Prize, 1985, Jun. Whitehead Prize, 1986, Polya Prize, 2000, LMS. *Publications:* numerous papers and articles. *Recreations:* reading, cycling, family life. *Address:* University of Oxford Mathematical Institute, 24–29 St Giles, Oxford OX1 3LB. *T:* (01865) 273544; *e-mail:* tlyons@maths.ox.ac.uk.

LYSAGHT, family name of **Baron Lisle**.

LYSCOM, David Edward; HM Diplomatic Service; Ambassador to the Slovak Republic, 1998–2001; *b* 8 Aug. 1951; *s* of late William Edward Lyscom and of Phyllis Edith May Lyscom (*née* Coyle); *m* 1973, Dr Nicole Ward; one *s* two *d*. *Educ:* Latymer Upper Sch.; Pembroke Coll., Cambridge (BA 1972). Joined HM Diplomatic Service, 1972; Vienna, 1973–76; Ottawa, 1977–79; FCO, 1979–83; First Secretary: Bonn, 1984–87; Riyadh, 1988–90; Asst Head, Aid Policy Dept, FCO, 1990–91; Counsellor, Science, Technology and Envmt, Bonn, 1991–95; Head of Envmt, Science and Energy Dept, FCO, 1995–98. *Recreations:* music, theatre, squash, tennis. *Address:* c/o Foreign and Commonwealth Office, King Charles Street, SW1A 2AH.

LYTHGO, Wilbur Reginald, OBE 1964; HM Diplomatic Service, retired; *b* 7 June 1920; *yr s* of late Alfred and Marion Lythgo, Monkton, Ayrshire; *m* 1943, Patricia Frances Sylvia Smith; two *s*. *Educ:* Palmer's Sch., Grays, Essex. Joined Home Office, 1937. Served in RASC, 1939–41 and Indian Army, 1941–46. Rejoined Home Office, 1946; British Information Services, New Delhi, 1948–54; UK High Commn, New Delhi, 1956–59; British High Commn, Ottawa, 1962–66; Head of Office Services and Supply Dept, DSAO, 1966–68; Counsellor, British Embassy, and Consul-Gen., Washington DC, 1968–71; Consul-Gen., Cleveland, Ohio, 1971–73. Hon. Kentucky Col, 1971. *Recreations:* reading, gardening. *Address:* 200 Dovercourt Avenue, Ottawa, ON K1Z 7H2, Canada. *T:* (613) 7223242.

LYTHGOE, Prof. Basil, FRS 1958; Professor of Organic Chemistry, Leeds University, 1953–78, now Emeritus; *b* 18 Aug. 1913; 2nd *s* of Peter Whitaker and Agnes Lythgoe; *m* 1946, Kathleen Cameron, *er d* of H. J. Hallum, St Andrews; two *s*. *Educ:* Leigh Grammar Sch.; Manchester Univ. Asst Lectr, Manchester Univ., 1938; Univ. Lectr, Cambridge Univ., 1946. Fellow of King's Coll., Cambridge, 1950. *Publications:* papers on chemistry of natural products, in Jl of Chem. Soc. *Recreation:* mountaineering. *Address:* 113 Cookridge Lane, Leeds LS16 7NB. *T:* (0113) 267 8837.

LYTLE, Maj.-Gen. Simon William St John, CB 1995; DL; Director, Army Sport Control Board, since 1995; *b* 1 Oct. 1940; *s* of Dr W. D. F., (Bobby), Lytle, and Anne M. E. Lytle; *m* 1966, Pamela Mary O'Ferrall; three *s*. *Educ:* Sherborne; RMA Sandhurst. Commissioned RIrF, 1960; transf. AAC, 1969; Staff College, Camberley, 1973; CO 1 Regt AAC, 1980–83; MoD, 1984–87; Comd Avn, BAOR, 1987–89; RCDS, 1989; Director: Army Recruiting, 1990–92; AAC, then Army Aviation, 1992–95. DL Hampshire, 1996. *Recreations:* sailing, bridge, tennis. *Clubs:* MCC; Leckford Golf.

LYTTELTON, family name of **Viscount Chandos** and of **Viscount Cobham**.

LYTTELTON, Humphrey Richard Adeane; musician; band-leader (specializing in Jazz); journalist; *b* Eton, Bucks, 23 May 1921; *s* of late Hon. George William Lyttelton; *m* 1st, 1948, Patricia Mary Braithwaite (marr. diss. 1952); one *d*; 2nd, 1952, Elizabeth Jill, *d* of Albert E. Richardson; two *s* one *d*. *Educ:* Sunningdale Sch.; Eton Coll.; Camberwell Sch. of Art; self-taught as regards musical educn. Served War of 1939–45: Grenadier Guards, 1941–46. Cartoonist, Daily Mail, 1949–53. Formed his own band, 1948; leader of Humphrey Lyttelton's Band, and free-lance journalist, 1953–; founded: own record label, Calligraph, 1984; own music publishers, Humph Music. Has composed over 200 original works for his band; numerous recordings and television appearances; jazz festival appearances, Nice, Bracknell, Zürich, Camden, Montreux, Newcastle, Warsaw, Edinburgh, and Glasgow. Compère, BBC radio jazz programmes: Jazz Scene, Jazz Club, The Best of Jazz, etc; Chm., I'm Sorry I Haven't a Clue, BBC R4, 1972–. Pres., Soc. for Italic Handwriting, 1990–. Hon. Prof. of Music, Keele Univ., 1993. Hon. DLitt: Warwick, 1987; Loughborough, 1988; Hon. DMus: Durham, 1989; Keele, 1992. *Publications:* I Play as I Please, 1954; Second Chorus, 1958; Take It from the Top (autobiog.), 1975; The Best of Jazz: Basin Street to Harlem, 1978, The Best of Jazz 2—Enter the Giants, 1981, both books repr. as one vol. 1997; Humphrey Lyttelton's Jazz and Big Band Quiz, 1979; Why No Beethoven? the diary of a vagrant musician, 1984; contributor: Melody Maker, 1954–2001; Reynolds News, 1955–62; Sunday Citizen, 1962–67; Harper's & Queen's, Punch, The Field, High Life. *Recreations:* birdwatching, calligraphy. *Address:* BBC, Broadcasting House, Portland Place, W1A 1AA. *T:* (020) 7580 4468; (home) Alyn Close, Barnet Road, Arkley, Herts EN5 3LJ.

LYTTLE, James Brian Chambers, OBE 1996; Secretary, Probation Board for Northern Ireland, 1987–97; *b* 22 Aug. 1932; *s* of late James Chambers Lyttle and Margaret Kirkwood Billingsley; *m* 1957, Mary Alma Davidson; four *d*. *Educ:* Bangor Grammar Sch.; Trinity Coll., Dublin (BA 1st Cl. Hons Classics). Entered NI Civil Service as Asst Principal, 1954; Private Sec. to Minister of Commerce, 1960–62; Chief Exec., Enterprise Ulster, 1972–75; Dir, Employment Service, Dept of Manpower Services, 1975–77; Dir, Industrial Develt Orgn, Dept of Commerce, 1977–81; Under Secretary, Dept of Commerce, later Dept of Economic Develt, 1977–84; Under Sec., Dept of Finance and Personnel, 1984–87. Mem., Prison Arts Foundn, 1996–. *Recreations:* reading, walking, music, poetry.

LYTTON, family name of **Earl of Lytton**.

LYTTON, 5th Earl of, *cr* 1880; **John Peter Michael Scawen Lytton;** Baron Wentworth, 1529; Bt 1838; Baron Lytton, 1866; Viscount Knebworth, 1880; Sole practitioner, John Lytton & Co., Chartered Surveyors and Valuers, since 1988; *b* 7 June 1950; *s* of 4th Earl of Lytton, OBE, and of Clarissa Mary, *d* of Brig.-Gen. C. E. Palmer, CB, CMG, DSO, RA; *S* father, 1985; *m* 1980, Ursula Alexandra (*née* Komoly); two *s* one *d*. *Educ:* Downside; Reading Univ. (BSc, Estate Management). FRICS 1987 (ARICS 1976); IRRV 1990; MCIArb (ACIArb 1991). President: Horsham Chamber of Commerce, 1995– (Chm., Horsham Chamber of Trade and Commerce, 1993–95); Sussex Assoc. of Local Councils, 1997–; Nat. Assoc. of Local Councils, 1999–; Chm., Leasehold Adv. Service (formerly Leasehold Enfranchisement Adv. Service), 1994–2000. Member: Council, CLA, 1993–99 (Exec., 1994–99); CLA Legal and Parly Cttee, 1992–; Bd, Sussex Rural Community Council. Pres., Newstead Abbey Byron Soc., 1988–. Hon. FBEng 1997. *Heir: s* Viscount Knebworth, *qv*. *Address:* (office) Estate Office, Newbuildings Place, Shipley, Horsham, West Sussex RH13 7JQ. *T:* (01403) 741650; *e-mail:* info@lytton.co.uk.

LYTTON COBBOLD, family name of **Baron Cobbold**.

LYVEDEN, 7th Baron *cr* 1859, of Lyveden, co. Northampton; **Jack Leslie Vernon;** self-employed painter and interior decorator, since 1978; *b* 10 Nov. 1938; *e s* of 6th Baron Lyveden and of Queenie Constance Vernon (*née* Ardern); *S* father, 1999; *m* 1961, Lynette June Lilley; two *s* one *d*. *Educ:* Te Aroha District High Sch. Apprentice, painting and decorating industry, 1955–60 (NZ Trade Cert.). Life Mem., Te Aroha Fire Brigade (joined Brigade, 1959; Fire Officer, 1975; Dep. Chief Fire Officer, 1981; Chief Fire Officer, 1987–94). *Heir: s* Hon. Colin Ronald Vernon, *b* 3 Feb. 1967. *Address:* 17 Carlton Street, Te Aroha, New Zealand. *Clubs:* Te Aroha, Returned Services Association.

M

MA LIN, Hon. CBE 1983; PhD; JP; Emeritus Professor of Biochemistry, and Chairman of Board of Trustees of Shaw College, since 1986, The Chinese University of Hong Kong; *b* 8 Feb. 1925; *s* of late Prof. Ma Kiam and Sing-yu Cheng; *m* 1958, Dr Meng-Hua Chen; three *d. Educ:* West China Union Univ., China (BSc); Univ. of Leeds (PhD). Post-doctorate Fellow, University College Hosp. Med. Sch., London, and St James's Hosp., Leeds, 1955–56. Assistant Lectr, 1957–59, and Lectr, 1959–64, in Clinical Chemistry, Dept of Pathology, Univ. of Hong Kong; Chinese University of Hong Kong: part-time Lectr in Chemistry, 1964; Sen. Lectr, 1965–72, Reader, 1972–73, Prof., 1973–78, in Biochemistry; Dean of Faculty of Science, 1973–75; Vice-Chancellor, 1978–87. Visiting Biochemist, Hormone Research Laboratory, Univ. of California, San Francisco, 1969. FRSA 1982. Unofficial JP, 1978. Hon. DSc Sussex, 1984; Hon. DLit East Asia, 1987; Hon. LLD: Chinese Univ. of Hong Kong, 1987; Leeds, 1996; Hon. DHL SUNY, 1989; Hon. PhD Tianjin, 1998. Order of the Rising Sun, Gold Rays, with neck ribbon (Japan), 1986; Commander's Cross, Order of Merit (FRG), 1988. *Publications:* various research papers in academic jls. *Recreations:* swimming, table-tennis. *Address:* Shaw College, The Chinese University of Hong Kong, Hong Kong.

MA, Yo-Yo; 'cellist; *b* Paris, 7 Oct. 1955 of Chinese parentage; *m* 1978, Jill A. Horner; one *s* one *d. Educ:* Harvard Univ.; Juilliard Sch. of Music, NY. First public recital at age of 5 years; winner Avery Fisher Prize, 1978; has performed under many distinguished conductors with all major world orchestras including: Berlin Philharmonic; Boston Symphony; Chicago Symphony; Israel Philharmonic; LSO; NY Philharmonic; also appears in chamber music ensembles; regular participant in festivals at Tanglewood, Edinburgh, Salzburg and other major European fests. Has made numerous recordings. Dr *hc*: Northeastern, USA, 1985; Harvard, 1991. Numerous Grammy Awards. *Address:* c/o ICM Artists Ltd, 40 W 57th Street, New York, NY 10019, USA. *T:* (212) 5565600.

MA, Yuzhen; Foreign Ministry Commissioner for People's Republic of China, Hong Kong Special Administrative Region, since 1997; *b* Sept. 1934; *s* of Ma Ziqiang and Li Jinghui; *m* 1961, Zou Jichun; one *s* one *d. Educ:* Beijing Inst. of Foreign Languages. Staff Mem., Inf. Dept, Min. of Foreign Affairs, People's Republic of China, 1954–63; Attaché and Third Sec., Burma, 1963–69; Dep. Div. Chief and Div. Chief, Inf. Dept, Min. of Foreign Affairs, 1969–80; First Sec. and Counsellor, Ghana, 1980–84; Dir, Inf. Dept, Min. of Foreign Affairs, 1984–88; Consul-Gen., Los Angeles, 1988–91; Ambassador to the UK, 1991–95; Dep. Dir, Information Office, State Council, Beijing, 1995–97. *Address:* (office) 42 Kennedy Road, Central, Hong Kong. *T:* 21066702, *Fax:* 21066298.

MA Zhengang; Ambassador of China to the Court of St James's, since 1997; *b* 9 Nov. 1940 (to a worker's family); *m* 1972, Chen Xiaodong; one *s. Educ:* Beijing Foreign Langs Univ.; post-grad. study at Ealing Tech. Coll. and LSE. Staff Mem., N American and Oceanian Affairs Dept (NAOAD), Min. of Foreign Affairs, China, 1967–70; Staff Mem., then Attaché, Yugoslavia, 1970–74; Attaché, NAOAD, 1974–81; Consul, Vancouver, 1981–85; Dep. Dir, then Dir, NAOAD, 1985–90; Counsellor, Washington, 1990–91; Dep. Dir-Gen., then Dir-Gen., NAOAD, 1991–95; Vice-Minister, Foreign Affairs Office of State Council, 1995–97. *Recreations:* table tennis, bridge, literature. *Address:* Embassy of China, 49–51 Portland Place, W1B 1JL. *T:* (020) 7299 4049.

MAAN, Bashir Ahmed, CBE 2000; JP; DL; Member, Scottish Constitutional Convention, 1988–98; Judge, City of Glasgow District Courts, 1968–97; *b* Maan, Gujranwala, Pakistan, 22 Oct. 1926; *s* of Choudhry Sardar Khan Maan and late Mrs Hayat Begum Maan; *m*; one *s* three *d. Educ:* D. B. High Sch., Qila Didar Singh; Panjab Univ.; Strathclyde Univ. (MSc 1994). Involved in struggle for creation of Pakistan, 1943–47; organised rehabilitation of refugees from India in Maan and surrounding areas, 1947–48; emigrated to UK and settled in Glasgow, 1953; Glasgow Founder Sec., Pakistan Social and Cultural Soc., 1955–65, Pres., 1966–69; Vice-Chm., Glasgow Community Relations Council, 1970–75; Pres., Standing Conf. of Pakistani Orgns in UK, 1974–77; a Dep. Chm., Commn for Racial Equality, 1977–80; Founder Chm., Scottish Pakistani Assoc., 1984–98; Pres., Nat. Assoc. of British Pakistanis, 2000–; Scottish rep., Muslim Council of Britain, 1998–; Chairman: Strathclyde CRC, 1987–93 and 1994–96; Strathclyde Interpreting Services Adv. Cttee, 1988–96. Member: Immigrants Prog. Adv. Cttee, BBC, 1972–80; Gen. Adv. Cttee, BBC, 1991–95; Scottish Selecting Panel, BBC, 1992–96. Hon. Res. Fellow, Univ. of Glasgow, 1988–91. Councillor, Glasgow Corp., 1970–75, City of Glasgow Dist, 1974–84 (Bailie, 1980–84); Mem., Glasgow City Council, 1995–, (Bailie, 1996–99); Magistrate, City of Glasgow, 1971–74; Vice-Chm. 1971–74, Chm. 1974–75, Police Cttee, Glasgow Corp.; Police Judge, City of Glasgow, 1974–75; Mem., 1995–, Convenor, 1999–, Strathclyde Jt Police Bd. Mem. Exec. Cttee, Glasgow City Labour Party, 1969–70. Contested (Lab) East Fife, Feb. 1974. Convener, Pakistan Bill Action Cttee, 1973; Member: Nat. Road Safety Cttee, 1971–75; Scottish Accident Prevention Cttee, 1971–75; Scottish Gas Consumers' Council, 1978–81; Greater Glasgow Health Bd, 1981–91; Management Bd, Scottish Council for Voluntary Orgns, 1988–95. Chm., Organising Cttee, Glasgow Internat. Sports Festival Co. Ltd, 1987–89. Mem. Bd of Governors, Jordanhill Coll. of Educn, Glasgow, 1987–91. JP 1968, DL 1982, Glasgow. Hon. LLD Strathclyde, 1999; DUniv Glasgow, 2001. *Publications:* The New Scots, 1992; articles, contrib. to press. *Recreations:* golf, reading. *Address:* 8 Riverview Gardens, Flat 6, Glasgow G5 8EL. *T:* (0141) 429 7689. *Club:* Douglas Park Golf.

MAAZEL, Lorin; symphony conductor; Music Director: Bayerischer Rundfunk Symphony Orchestra, Munich, since 1993; New York Philharmonic Orchestra, from Sept. 2002; *b* 6 March 1930; *s* of Lincoln Maazel and Marie Varencove; *m* 3rd, 1986, Dietlinde Turban; two *s* one *d*, and one *s* three *d* by previous marriages. *Educ:* Pittsburgh University. FRCM 1981. Début as a conductor at age of 9, as violinist a few years later; by 1941 had conducted foremost US Orchestras, including Toscanini's NBC; European début as conductor, 1953; active as conductor in Europe, Latin America, Australia, Japan and USA, 1954–; performances at major festivals, including Edinburgh, Bayreuth, Salzburg and Lucerne; in USA: conducted Boston Symphony, New York Philharmonic, Philadelphia Orchestra, and at Metropolitan, 1960 and 1962; Covent Garden début, 1978. Artistic Director of Deutsche Oper Berlin, 1965–71; Chief Conductor, Radio Sinfonie Orchester, Berlin, 1965–75; Associate Principal Conductor, Philharmonia (formerly New Philharmonia) Orchestra, 1970–72, Principal Guest Conductor, 1976–80; Music Director, Cleveland Orchestra, 1972–82, Conductor Emeritus, 1982; Principal Guest Conductor, 1977–88, Music Director, 1988–90, Orchestre National de France; Director, Vienna State Opera, 1982–84; Music Dir, Pittsburgh SO, 1988–96. Has made over 300 recordings. Hon. Dr of Music Pittsburgh Univ., 1968; Hon. Dr of Humanities Beaver Coll., 1973; Hon. Dr of Fine Arts, Carnegie-Mellon Univ., Pennsylvania; Hon. Dr of Music, RCM, 1984; Hon. DCL Univ. of South, Sewanee, 1988; Hon. Dr Indiana Univ., 1988. Sibelius Medal, Finland, 1969. Commander's Cross of Order of Merit, Federal Republic of Germany, 1977; Officier, Légion d'Honneur, France, 1981. *Address:* c/o Bayerischer Rundfunk, Rundfunkplatz, 80300 Munich, Germany.

MABB, David Michael; QC 2001; *b* 12 June 1956; *s* of Kenneth George Mabb and Joyce Madeleine Mabb. *Educ:* King James' Grammar Sch., Almondbury; St Nicholas Grammar Sch., Northwood; Gonville and Caius Coll., Cambridge (BA 1978; MA 1982). Called to the Bar, Lincoln's Inn, 1979. *Address:* Erskine Chambers, 30 Lincoln's Inn Fields, WC2A 3PD. *T:* (020) 7242 5532.

MABBS, Alfred Walter, CB 1982; Keeper of Public Records, 1978–82; *b* 12 April 1921; *e s* of James and Amelia Mabbs; *m* 1942, Dorothy Lowley; one *s. Educ:* Hackney Downs Sch. Served War, RAF, 1941–46. Asst Keeper, Public Record Office, 1950–66; Principal Asst Keeper, 1967–69; Records Admin. Officer, 1970–73; Dep. Keeper of Public Records, 1973–78. Pres., Internat. Council on Archives, 1980–82. Gen. Editor, Herts Record Soc., 1991–96. FRHistS 1954. FSA 1979. *Publications:* Guild Stewards Book of the Borough of Calne (vol. vii, Wilts Arch. and Record Soc.), 1953; The Records of the Cabinet Office to 1922, 1966; Guide to the Contents of the Public Record Office, vol. iii (main contributor), 1968; Exchequer of the Jews, vol. iv (jt contrib.), 1972; The Organisation of Intermediate Records Storage (with Guy Duboscq), 1974; articles and reviews in various jls. *Recreation:* retirement. *Address:* 32 The Street, Wallington, Baldock, Herts SG7 6SW.

MABEY, John Hedley; Controller of Financial Services, London Borough of Camden, since 1996; *b* 18 June 1946; *s* of Douglas Charles Mabey and Olive Ena Mabey (*née* Lipscombe); *m* 1967, Jacqueline Trudy Cassidy; two *s. Educ:* Chartered Inst. of Public Finance and Accountancy. Camden London Borough Council: Mgt Accountant, 1973–78; Asst Dir of Finance, 1978–92; Dep. Dir of Finance, 1992–96. *Recreations:* golf, squash. *Address:* Town Hall, Argyle Street, WC1H 8NG. *T:* (office) (020) 7860 5933; (home) (01494) 864618.

MABEY, Richard Thomas; writer and broadcaster; *b* 20 Feb. 1941; *s* of late Thomas Gustavus Mabey and Edna Nellie (*née* Moore). *Educ:* Berkhamsted Sch.; St Catherine's Coll., Oxford (BA Hons 1964, MA 1971). Lectr in Social Studies, Dacorum Coll. of Further Educn, 1963–65; Sen. Editor, Penguin Books, 1966–73; freelance writer, 1973–. Mem. Mgt Cttee, Soc. of Authors, 1998–. Presenter, Tomorrow's World, BBC TV, 1995. President: London Wildlife Trust, 1982–92; Richard Jefferies Soc., 1995–98; Member: Nature Conservancy Council, 1982–86; Council, Botanical Soc. of the British Isles, 1981–83; Adv. Council, Open Spaces Soc., 1992–. Dir, Common Ground, 1988–. Patron, Thomas Bewick Trust, 1986–; Mem. Adv. Council, Plantlife, 1992–. Leverhulme Trust Res. Award, 1983–84; Leverhulme Res. Fellowship, 1993–94. Hon. DSc St Andrews, 1997. *Publications:* (ed) Class, 1967; The Pop Process, 1969; Food for Free, 1972, 2nd edn 1989; Children in Primary School, 1972; The Unofficial Countryside, 1973; The Pollution Handbook, 1973; The Roadside Wildlife Book, 1974; Street Flowers, 1976 (TES Inf. Book Award); Plants with a Purpose, 1977; The Common Ground, 1980; The Flowering of Britain, 1980; (ed) Landscape with Figures, 1983; Oak and Company, 1983 (NY Acad. of Sci. Children's Book Award, 1984); In a Green Shade, 1983; Back to the Roots, 1983; (ed) Second Nature, 1984; The Frampton Flora, 1985; Gilbert White: a biography, 1986 (Whitbread Biography Award); Gen. Ed., The Journals of Gilbert White, 1986–89; (ed) The Gardener's Labyrinth, 1987; The Flowering of Kew, 1988; Home Country, 1990; (ed) The Flowers of May, 1990; A Nature Journal, 1991; Whistling in the Dark, 1993; Landlocked, 1994; (ed) The Oxford Book of Nature Writing, 1995; Flora Britannica (British Bk Awards Illustrated Book of the Year), 1996; Selected Writings 1974–1999, 1999. *Recreations:* food, woods, walking. *Address:* c/o Sheil Land Associates, 43 Doughty Street, WC1N 2LF. *Club:* Groucho.

MABEY, Roger Stanley, CMG 1997; Executive Director, Bovis Lend Lease Ltd, since 2000; *b* 11 Aug. 1944; *s* of Stanley Mabey and Edith Mabey (*née* Stride); *m* 1968, Margaret Marian Watkins; one *s* one *d. Educ:* Cleeve Sch., Cheltenham; Gloucestershire Coll. of Technology (HND 1964); Lancaster Coll. of Technology, Coventry; Eur. Centre of Continuing Educn, INSEAD. Joined Bovis, 1967; Project Manager, Bristol, 1967–73; Regl Dir, Harrow office, 1973–79; a Divl Dir, 1979–86; Dir, Bovis Construction Ltd, 1986–93; Asst Man. Dir, 1993–94, Man. Dir, 1994–97, Bovis Internat. Ltd; Exec. Dir, Bovis Construction Gp, 1998–2000. Member: DTI Adv. Gps on India, 1994, and S Africa; Market Gp, Cttee for S African Trade, 1996; BOTB, 1998. Vice Chm., Cookham Soc., 1998. FCIOB 1980; FRSA 1998. *Recreations:* travel, gardening, MGs, food, music, athletics, family. *Address:* Carrol Lodge, Sutton Road, Cookham, Maidenhead, Berks SL6 9RD.

MABON, Rt Hon. (Jesse) Dickson; PC 1977; company director and physician; Chairman, Gem and Ashtree Ltd, since 1988; *b* 1 Nov. 1925; *s* of Jesse Dickson Mabon and Isabel Simpson Montgomery; *m* 1970, Elizabeth, *o d* of Maj. William Zinn; one *s*. *Educ:* Possilpark, Cumbrae, North Kelvinside Schools. Worked in coalmining industry before Army service, 1944–48. MB, ChB (Glasgow); DHMSA; FFHom; Visiting Physician, Manor House Hospital, London, 1958–64. Political columnist, Scottish Daily Record, 1955–64; studied under Dr Kissinger, Harvard, 1963. President: Glasgow University Union, 1951–52; Scottish Union of Students, 1954–55; Chairman: Glasgow Univ. Labour Club, 1948–50; National Assoc. of Labour Students, 1949–50. Contested: (Lab) Bute and N Ayrshire, 1951; (Lab and Co-op) W Renfrewshire, 1955; Renfrew W and Inverclyde (SDP) 1983, (SDP/Alliance) 1987; (SDP) Lothians, European Parly Election, 1984. MP (Lab and Co-op 1955–81, SDP 1981–83) Greenock, Dec. 1955–1974, Greenock and Port Glasgow, 1974–83; Joint Parly Under-Sec. of State for Scotland, 1964–67; Minister of State, Scottish Office, 1967–70; Dep. Opposition Spokesman on Scotland, 1970–72 (resigned over Labour's attitude to Common Mkt); Minister of State, Dept of Energy, 1976–79. Chairman: UK Labour Cttee for Europe, 1974–76; Scottish Parly Labour Party, 1972–73, 1975–76; Member: Council of Europe, 1970–72 and 1974–76; Assembly, WEU, 1970–72 and 1974–76; North Atlantic Assembly, 1980–82; Chm., European Movement, 1975–76, Dep. Chm., 1979–83. Founder Chm., Manifesto Gp, Parly Lab. Party, 1974–76. Founder Mem., SDP, 1981; Mem., SDP Nat. Cttee, 1984–88; rejoined Labour Party, 1991. Chm., Young Volunteer Force Foundn, 1974–76. Mem., Energy Saving Trust, 1992–96; Chm., Labour Finance and Industry Gp Energy Gp, 1993–98. Fellow: Inst. of Petroleum; Inst. of Directors; Faculty of History of Medicine (Pres. 1990–94); Soc. of Apothecaries; FRSA. Freeman of City of London. *Recreations:* gardening, theatre. *Address:* 7 Kepplestone, Staveley Road, Meads, Eastbourne, E Sussex BN20 7JY. *T:* (01323) 438565, *Fax:* (01323) 438659.

MABRO, Robert Emile, CBE 1996; Fellow, St Antony's College, Oxford, since 1971; Director, Oxford Institute for Energy Studies, since 1982; *b* 26 Dec. 1934; *s* of Emile Mabro and Tatiana Mabro (*née* Bittar); *m* 1967, Judith Howey; two *d*. *Educ:* Coll. St Marc, Alexandria, Egypt; Univ. of Alexandria (BSc Engrg); SOAS, London Univ. (MSc Econs). Civil engr, Egypt, 1956–60; Leon Fellow, Univ. of London, 1966–67; Res. Officer, SOAS, 1967–69; Sen. Res. Officer in econs of ME, Univ. of Oxford, 1969–; Director: ME Centre, St Antony's Coll., Oxford, 1976–79; Oxford Energy Seminar, 1978–. Vice Chm. Bd, Econ. Res. Forum for Arab Countries, Iran and Turkey, 1994–97. Hon. Sec., Oxford Energy Policy Club, 1976–. Charles Hedlund Vis. Prof., Amer. Univ. in Cairo, 1997. Award, Internat. Assoc. for Energy Econs, 1990. Medal of the Pres. (Italy), 1985; Order of the Aztec Eagle (Mexico), 1997; Order of Francisco Miranda (Venezuela), 1999. *Publications:* The Egyptian Economy 1952–1972, 1974; (with S. Radwan) The Industrialization of Egypt 1939–73, 1976; (ed) World Energy: issues and policies, 1980; (ed) OPEC and the World Oil Market, 1986; (jtly) The Market for North Sea Crude Oil, 1986; (with P. Horsnell) Oil Markets and Prices, 1993; articles in jls. *Recreations:* cooking; collecting books, postcards, etc on Alexandria, Egypt; reading, poetry, philosophy. *Address:* (office) 57 Woodstock Road, Oxford OX2 6FA. *T:* (01865) 311377; 52 Lonsdale Road, Oxford OX2 7EP. *T:* (01865) 557623.

MAC; *see* McMurtry, S.

McADAM, Douglas Baxter; HM Diplomatic Service; Consul General, Hamburg, since 1999; *b* 25 June 1944; *s* of John Watson McAdam and Jean Cook McAdam; *m* 1965, Susan Clare Jarvis; one *s* one *d*. *Educ:* Musselburgh Burgh Sch.; Musselburgh Grammar Sch. Entered Foreign Office, 1961; served Ulan Bator, Luanda, New Delhi and FCO, 1966–78; Vice-Consul, Rio de Janeiro, 1979–82; 2nd, later 1st Sec., UK Del. MBFR, Vienna, 1983–87; FCO, 1987–90; 1st Sec., Lagos, 1990–94; FCO, 1994–95; Ambassador to Kazakhstan and Kyrgyzstan (resident in Almaty), 1996–99. Mem., RSAA, 1997. *Recreations:* trout fishing, walking, eating well. *Address:* c/o Foreign and Commonwealth Office, SW1A 2AH. *Club:* Royal Over-Seas League.

McADAM, James, CBE 1995; Chairman, Signet (formerly Ratners) Group plc, since 1992 (Chief Executive, 1992–2000); *b* 10 Dec. 1930; *s* of John Robert McAdam and Helen McAdam (*née* Cormack); *m* 1955, Maisie Una Holmes; two *d*. *Educ:* Lenzie Academy. Joined J. & P. Coats Ltd, 1945; Finance Dir, Coats Chile, 1962–66, Coats India, 1966–70, Coats Patons UK, 1972–75; Dir, 1975, Chief Exec., 1985–86, Chm., 1986–91, Coats Patons plc; Dep. Chm. and Chief Operating Officer, Coats Viyella (merged co.), 1986–91. Chm., Bisley Office Equipment Co., 1991–; Dir, Scotia Hldgs, 1991–97. Dir, London Region Post Office, 1985–87. Chairman: British Clothing Industry Assoc., 1991–; British Knitting and Clothing Confedn, 1991–; British Apparel and Textile Confedn, 1992–; Mem., Exec. Cttee, Scottish Council Develt and Industry, 1988–99. FRSA; CIMgt; FInstD. *Recreations:* theatre, gardening, travel. *Address:* Signet Group plc, 66 Grosvenor Street, W1K 3LL. *Clubs:* Royal Automobile, Farmers.

McADAM, Prof. Keith Paul William James, FRCP; Wellcome Professor of Tropical Medicine, London School of Hygiene and Tropical Medicine, London University, since 1984 (Head of Department of Clinical Sciences, 1988–94); Director, Medical Research Council Laboratories, The Gambia, since 1995 (on secondment); *b* 13 Aug. 1945; *s* of Sir Ian William James McAdam, OBE, and of Mrs L. M. Hrothgaarde Bennett (*neé* Gibson); *m* 1968, Penelope Ann (*neé* Spencer); three *d*. *Educ:* Prince of Wales School, Nairobi; Millfield School, Som.; Clare Coll., Cambridge (MA, MB BChir); Middlesex Hosp. Med. Sch. FRSTM&H; Dip. Amer. Bd of Internal Medicine, Dip. Amer. Bd of Allergy and Clinical Immunology. Medical posts at Middlesex Hosp., Royal Northern Hosp., Brompton Hosp., Nat. Hosp. for Nervous Diseases, 1969–73; Lectr in Medicine, Inst. of Med. Research, Goroka, Papua New Guinea, 1973–75; MRC Travelling Fellow, 1975–76; Vis. Scientist, Immunology Branch, Nat. Cancer Inst., NIH, Bethesda, 1976–77; Asst Prof., Tufts Univ. Sch. of Medicine, 1977–82; Associate Prof., Divs of Allergy, Exptl Medicine and Geographic Medicine, Tufts Univ., 1982–84; Consultant Physician, Hosp. for Tropical Diseases, NW1, 1984–95. *Publications:* scientific articles on immunology and tropical medicine, esp. on amyloidosis, acute phase proteins, leprosy, tuberculosis, AIDS, inflammation. *Recreations:* cricket, squash, tennis, golf, ski-ing. *Address:* Medical Research Council Laboratories, Fajara, PO Box 273, Banjul, The Gambia, West Africa. *T:* 495442/6. *Club:* MCC.

McAFEE, Raymond Noel; Commissioner, since 1996, and Director, Regional Business Services, since 2001, HM Customs and Excise; *b* 15 Dec. 1943; *s* of late James Hill and Sarah McAfee (*née* O'Kane); *m* 1966, Margot McGowan; one *s* one *d*. *Educ:* Strabane Coll.; Portadown Coll. Joined HM Customs and Excise, 1963; Officer, 1963–74; Surveyor, 1974–79; Asst Collector, 1979–85; Sen. Principal, HQ London, 1985–89; Collector, NI, 1989–93; Asst Sec., HQ London, 1993–96; Dir, Central Ops, 1996–99; Dir, Outfield, 1999–2001. FIM 1991. *Recreations:* golf, theatre, music. *Address:* (office) New King's Beam House, 22 Upper Ground, SE1 9PJ.

McAFEE, Maj.-Gen. Robert William Montgomery, CB 1999; Director of Administration, Norton Rose, since 1999; *b* 8 Nov. 1944; *s* of Andrew Montgomery McAfee and Jane Beryl McAfee; *m* 1967, Erica-May MacLennan; one *s* one *d*. *Educ:* Inverness Royal Academy; Mons Officer Cadet Sch. Commnd, RTR, 1965; served Aden, BAOR, NI (despatches), Cyprus, Gulf, Bosnia; CO 2nd RTR, 1982–84; Instructor, Staff Coll., 1985–86; Col, Higher Command and Staff Course, 1987; Comdr 6 Armd Bde, 1988–89; ACOS (Land), HQ British Forces, ME, 1990; COS HQ 1 (BR) Corps, 1991–92; RCDS 1993; DG, Army Training, 1993–95; Comdr, Multi Nat. Div. (Central), 1996–99, retired. Rep. Col Comdt, RTR, 1995–99. Chm., British Bobsleigh Assoc., 1998–2000; Dep. Pres., Army Rugby Union, 1994–99. *Recreations:* golf, ski-ing, watching Rugby and motor racing. *Address:* c/o Clydesdale Bank, 15 Academy Street, Inverness IV1 7JN. *Clubs:* Army and Navy; St Fillans Golf.

McALEESE, Kevin Stanley, CBE 1998; Head Teacher, Harrogate Grammar School, since 1992; *b* 28 Feb. 1947; *s* of late James McAleese, DFM and of Marjorie N. A. McAleese; (*née* Stromberg); *m* 1st, 1976, Dorothy Anne Nelson (*d* 1998); one *s* one *d*; 2nd, 2000, Jenny Louise Brindle (*née* Grant). *Educ:* London Nautical Sch.; Keele Univ. (BEd 1972); Univ. of Kent (MA 1985). Midshipman, subseq. Navigating Officer, Blue Funnel Line, 1964–68; Asst Teacher, West Hatch Technical High Sch., 1972–75; Head of Dept, Queen's Sch., Jt HQ Rheindahlen, 1975–78; Head of Faculty, Grange County Secondary Sch., 1978–81; Sen. Teacher, Sheppey Sch., 1981–84; Dep. Head Teacher, Geoffrey Chaucer Sch., Canterbury, 1984–87; Head Teacher, Alec Hunter High Sch., Braintree, 1987–91. FRSA 1993; FIMgt 1995. *Publications:* Managing the Margins, 1996; Balancing the Books, 2000; articles and series in TES and Managing Schools Today. *Recreations:* cinema, photography, music, walking, writing. *Address:* 11 Hazel Drive, Burn Bridge, Harrogate, N Yorks HG3 1NY.

McALEESE, Mary Patricia, (Mrs Martin McAleese); President of Ireland, since 1997; *b* 27 June 1951; *d* of Patrick Leneghan and Claire (*née* McManus); *m* 1976, Martin McAleese; one *s* two *d*. *Educ:* QUB (LLB, 1973); TCD (MA 1986); Dip. in Spanish, Inst. of Linguists, 1994; AIL. Called to the Bar: N Ireland, 1974; King's Inn, Dublin, 1978. Barrister, NI, 1974–75; Reid Prof. of Criminal Law, Criminology and Penology, TCD, 1975–79 and 1981–87; journalist and TV presenter, Radio Telefis Eireann, 1979–81 (part-time presenter, 1981–85); Queen's University, Belfast: Dir, Inst. of Professional Legal Studies, 1987–97; Pro Vice-Chancellor, 1994–97. Director: Northern Ireland Electricity, 1991–97; Channel 4 Television, 1992–97; Royal Gp of Hospitals HSS Trust, Belfast, 1996–97. *Publications:* (jtly) Reports on Irish Penal System, 1981; Children in Custody (ed Stewart and Tutt), 1987; (jtly) Sectarianism: a discussion document, 1993; Reconciled Being, 1997; contrib. legal and religious jls. *Recreations:* hill-walking, set dancing, reading, theology. *Address:* Aras an Uachtaráin, Phoenix Park, Dublin 8, Ireland.

McALISKEY, (Josephine) Bernadette, (Mrs Micheal McAliskey); Chairman, Independent Socialist Party, Ireland; *b* 23 April 1947; *d* of late John James Devlin and Elizabeth Devlin; *m* 1973, Micheal McAliskey; three *c*. *Educ:* St Patrick's Girls' Acad., Dungannon; psychology student at Queen's Univ., Belfast, 1966–69. Youngest MP in House of Commons when elected at age of 21; MP (Ind. Unity) Mid Ulster, Apr. 1969–Feb. 1974. Founder Member and Mem. Exec., Irish Republican Socialist Party, 1975–76. Contested: (Ind) N Ireland, European Parlt, 1979; (People's Democracy), Dublin N Central, Dáil Eireann, Feb. and Nov. 1982. *Publication:* The Price of my Soul (autobiog.), 1969. *Recreations:* walking, folk music, doing nothing, swimming.

McALISTER, Michael Ian, FCA; Managing Director, The Tam Programme, European Bank for Reconstruction and Development, since 1993; *b* Leeds, Yorkshire, 23 Aug. 1930; *s* of S. McAlister, CBE, and J. A. McAlister (*née* Smith); *m* 1st, 1953, Patricia (*née* Evans) (marr. diss. 1983); four *s* three *d*; 2nd, 1984, Elizabeth Anne, *o d* of Mr and Mrs Ludwig Hehn. *Educ:* Brazil; France; St John's Coll., Oxford (MA). National Service, Lieut, Intelligence Corps (MI8), 1950–51 (Acting Capt). Articled Clerk, Price Waterhouse, London, 1954–58; Private Sec. to the Duke of Windsor, 1959–61; Investment Manager, Ionian Bank Ltd, London, 1961–67; Managing Dir, Ionian Bank Trustee Co., London, 1967–68; Slater Walker Securities (Australia): Dep. Chm., 1969–70, Chm., 1970–72; Pres., Aust. Associated Stock Exchanges, 1972–74; Director: (Middle East), Lester B. Knight and Associates, USA, 1975–79; Cluff Oil Holdings, subseq. Cluff Resources, 1979–89. Chm., Woking Cons. Assoc., 1967–68. *Recreations:* carpentry, DIY. *Address:* Two Berwick Cottages, Terling Hall Road, Hatfield Peveral, Chelmsford, Essex CM3 2EY. *T:* (01245) 380158, *Fax:* (01245) 382056.

MacALISTER, Very Rev. Randal George Leslie; Dean of St Andrews, Dunkeld and Dunblane, since 1998; Rector, St Kessog's, Auchterarder and St James', Muthill, since 1998; *b* 31 Dec. 1941; *s* of James Daniel Beaton MacAlister and Doreen MacAlister (*née* Thompson); *m* 1964, Valerie Jane Letitia Nelson; three *s*. *Educ:* Royal Sch., Armagh; Trinity Coll., Dublin (BA 1963; MA 1966; Divinity Testimonium 1964). Deacon 1964, priest 1966; Curate, St Mark's, Portadown, 1964–67; Rector: St Matthew's, Keady and Armaghbreague, 1967–74, and St John's, Derrynoose, 1973–74; St Mary's, Kirriemuir, 1974–81; St John's, Greenock, 1981–87; St John's, Forfar, 1987–95; Canon, St Ninian's Cathedral, Perth, 1993–95; Chaplain, St Mark's, Sophia Antipolis, France, 1995–98. *Recreations:* gardening, hill-walking, languages, music. *Address:* St Kessog's Rectory, High Street, Auchterarder, Perthshire PH3 1AD. *T:* and *Fax:* (01764) 662525.

McALISTER, Maj.-Gen. Ronald William Lorne, CB 1977; OBE 1968 (MBE 1959); *b* 26 May 1923; 2nd *s* of late Col R. J. F. McAlister, OBE and Mrs T. M. Collins, Bath; *m* 1964, Sally Ewart Marshall; two *d*. *Educ:* Dreghorn Castle Sch., Edinburgh; Sedbergh School. Commnd 3rd QAO Gurkha Rifles, 1942; Adjt 1/3 GR Burma, 1945 (despatches); Adjt 2/10 GR Malaya, 1950–52 (despatches); Instructor, Sch. of Infantry, 1953–55; psc 1956; Bde Major 99 Gurkha Bde, Malaya, 1957–59 (MBE); jssc 1961–62; Asst Sec., Chiefs of Staff Cttee, 1962–64; 2nd in comd and CO 10th PMO Gurkha Rifles, Borneo, 1964–66 (despatches); Internal Security Duties, Hong Kong, 1967–68 (OBE); Instructor, Jt Services Staff Coll., 1968; comd Berlin Inf. Bde, 1968–71; ndc, Canada, 1971–72; Exercise Controller UK Cs-in-C Cttee, 1972–75; Dep. Commander Land Forces Hong Kong and Maj.-Gen. Brigade of Gurkhas, 1975–77; retired 1977. Col, 10th Princess Mary's Own Gurkha Rifles, 1977–85; Chm., Gurkha Brigade Assoc., 1980–90. Bursar, Wellesley House Sch., Broadstairs, 1977–88. Chm., Buckmaster Meml Home, Broadstairs, 1980–. *Publication:* (ed and contrib.) Bugle and Kukri, Vol. 2, 1986. *Recreations:* golf, gardening. *Address:* The Chalet, 41 Callis Court Road, Broadstairs, Kent CT10 3AU. *T:* (01843) 862351. *Clubs:* Army and Navy; Royal St George's Golf (Captain, 1989–90; Hon. Treas., 1991–96), Senior Golfers' Society.

McALISTER, William Harle Nelson; independent arts producer and consultant; Cultural Policy Adviser, Soros Foundations, 1992–97; *b* 30 Aug. 1940; *s* of Flying Officer William Nelson (*d* 1940) and Marjorie Isobel (*née* McIntyre); adopted by William Edwyn McAlister (whom she *m* 2nd); *m* 1968 (marr. diss. 1985); two *s* two *d*; one *s*. *Educ:* Sorbonne, Paris; Univ. of Copenhagen; University Coll. London (BA Hons Psychology, 1967). Dir, Almost Free Theatre, 1968–72; Dep. Dir, Inter-Action Trust, 1968–72; Founder Dir, Islington Bus Co., 1972–77; Director: Battersea Arts Centre, 1976–77; ICA, 1977–90; Creative Research Ltd, 1989–91; Beaconsfield Gall., 1999–; Ambient TV Ltd, 2000–. Dir, Sense of Ireland Fest., 1980; Bd Dir, London International Theatre Fest., 1983; Chm. for the Arts, IT 82 Cttee, 1982. Chm., Recreational Trust, 1972–88; Co-Founder, Fair Play for Children, 1974–75; Advr, Task Force Trust, 1972–74; Trustee: Circle 33 Housing Trust, 1972–75; Moving Picture Mime Trust, 1978–80; Shape (Arts for the Disadvantaged), 1979–81. Trustee: International House, 1989–; Africa Centre, 1990–2000; World Circuit Arts, 1996–2000. Governor: Holloway Adult Educn Inst., 1974–76; Byam Shaw Sch. of Art, 2000–. Mem. Court, RCA, 1980–90. CSCE British Deleg., Krakow, Poland, 1991. *Publications:* Community Psychology, 1975; EEC and the Arts, 1978; Art and Society, 1999; articles on arts policy. *Recreations:* mycology, angling, tennis, travel. *Address:* 151c Grosvenor Avenue, N5 2NH. *T:* (020) 7226 0205, *Fax:* (020) 7226 7971; *e-mail:* mcalister@easynet.co.uk.

MacALLAN, Andrew; *see* Leasor, T. J.

McALLION, John; Member (Lab) Dundee East, Scottish Parliament, since 1999; *b* 13 Feb. 1948; *s* of Joseph and Norah McAllion; *m* 1971, Susan Jean Godlonton; two *s*. *Educ:* St Augustine's Comprehensive School, Glasgow; St Andrews Univ. (MA Hons 2nd cl. Modern and Medieval Hist. 1972); Dundee Coll. of Education. Civil Servant, Post Office, 1967–68; History Teacher, St Saviour's High Sch., Dundee, 1973–78; Social Studies Teacher, Balgowan Sch., Dundee, 1978–82; Research Asst to Bob McTaggart, 1982–86. Regional Councillor, 1984–87, Convener, 1986–87, Tayside Regional Council. MP (Lab) Dundee East, 1987–2001. *Recreations:* sport, reading, music. *Address:* 3 Haldane Street, Dundee DD3 0HP. *T:* (01382) 826678.

McALLISTER, Ian Gerald, CBE 1996; Chairman and Chief Executive, since 1992 and Managing Director, since 1991, Ford Motor Co.; *b* 17 Aug. 1943; *s* of Ian Thomas McAllister and Margaret Mary McAllister (*née* McNally); *m* 1968, Susan Margaret Frances Mitchell; three *s* one *d*. *Educ:* Thornleigh College, Bolton; University College London (BScEcon). Ford Motor Co.: operations and marketing appts, 1964–79; Finance Director: Parts Sales, 1980; Product and Marketing Parts Ops, 1981; Car Sales Ops, 1983; Marketing Plans and Programmes, 1984; Sales, Ford Germany, 1987; Gen. Marketing Manager, Lincoln Mercury Div., USA, 1989. Vice-President: Inst. of the Motor Industry, 1992–; SMMT (Pres., 1996–98). Mem. Bd and Council, BITC. Non-exec. Dir, Scottish & Newcastle plc, 1996–. Mem. Adv. Bd, Victim Support, 1994. Member: Adv. Council, Imperial Coll., London; Bd, Anglia Univ.; Bd of Trustees, Nat. Motor Mus., Beaulieu; Adv. Cttee on Business and the Envmt, 1996–; Welfare to Work Task Force, 1997–; Bd, Qualifications and Curriculum Authority, 1997– (Dep. Chm., 2000–); Co-Chm., Cleaner Vehicles Task Force, 1997–2000. Chm., Carbon Trust, 2001–. Hon. PhD: E London, 1993; Loughborough, 1999; Hon. LLD Nottingham, 1995. *Recreations:* gardening, golf, computer studies, running. *Address:* Ford Motor Co., Eagle Way, Brentwood, Essex CM13 3BW. *T:* (01277) 253000.

McALLISTER, John Brian; Chief Executive, Sapphire House Ltd, since 1999; *b* 11 June 1941; *s* of late Thomas McAllister and of Jane (*née* McCloughan); *m* 1966, Margaret Lindsay Walker; two *d*. *Educ:* Royal Belfast Academical Instn; Queen's Univ., Belfast (BA Hons). Joined NI Civil Service as Asst Principal, Dept of Educn, 1964; Dep. Principal, Higher Educn Div., 1968; Principal: Secondary Schs Br., 1969; Re-Organisation of Local Govt Br., 1970; Principal, Dept of Finance, 1971, Dept's Central Secretariat, 1972; Asst Sec. 1973, Sen. Asst Sec. 1976, Dep. Sec., 1978–80, Dept of Educn; Dep. Sec., later Under Sec., Dept of Finance, 1980–83; Under Sec., DoE, NI, 1983–84; Dep. Chief Exec., 1984–85, Chief Exec., 1985–88, Industrial Develt Bd for NI; Chief Exec., Crestacare (formerly Cresta Hldgs Ltd), 1990–93 (Gp Man. Dir, 1988–90); consultant, 1993–94; Chief Exec., 1994–96, Chm., 1996–99, Craegmoor Healthcare. *Recreations:* watching sport of all kinds, reading. *Address:* Sapphire House Ltd, Ragnall House, 18 Peel Road, Douglas, Isle of Man IM1 4LZ.

McALPINE, family name of **Baron McAlpine of West Green**.

McALPINE OF WEST GREEN, Baron *cr* 1984 (Life Peer), of West Green in the County of Hampshire; **Robert Alistair McAlpine;** Director, Sir Robert McAlpine & Sons Ltd, 1963–95; *b* 14 May 1942; *s* of Lord McAlpine of Moffat and Ella Mary Gardner Garnett (*d* 1987); *m* 1964, Sarah Alexandra Baron (marr. diss. 1979); two *d*; *m* 1980, Romilly, *o d* of A. T. Hobbs, Cranleigh, Surrey; one *d*. *Educ:* Stowe. Joined Sir Robert McAlpine & Sons Ltd, 1958. Hon. Treasurer: Europ. Democratic Union, 1978–88; Europ. League for Econ. Co-operation, 1974–75 (Vice Pres., 1975–); Conservative and Unionist Party, 1975–90 (Dep. Chm., 1979–83). Director: George Weidenfeld Holdings Ltd, 1975–83; ICA, 1972–73. Mem., Arts Council of GB, 1981–82; Vice-President: Friends of Ashmolean Museum, 1969–; Greater London Arts Assoc., 1971–77; Vice-Chm., Contemporary Arts Soc., 1973–80. Pres., British Waterfowl Assoc., 1978–81, Patron 1981–. Member: Friends of V&A Museum, 1976–; Council, English Stage Co., 1973–75. Trustee, Royal Opera House Trust, 1974–80; Dir, Theatre Investment Fund, 1981–90 (Chm., 1985–90). Governor: Polytechnic of the South Bank, 1981–82; Stowe Sch., 1981–84; Pres., St Bartholomew's Hosp. Med. Coll., 1993–95. *Publications: as Alistair McAlpine:* The Servant, 1992; Journal of a Collector, 1994; Letters to a Young Politician, 1995; Once a Jolly Bagman (memoirs), 1997; The New Machiavelli, 1997; (jtly) Collecting and Display, 1998 Australian Memoirs, 2000; The Ruthless Leader, 2000. *Recreations:* the arts, horticulture, aviculture, agriculture. *Address:* House of Lords, SW1A 0PW. *Clubs:* Garrick, Carlton, Buck's, Pratt's, Beefsteak.
See also Hon. Sir W. H. McAlpine, Bt.

McALPINE, Alistair; *see* Baron McAlpine of West Green.

McALPINE, Christopher; *see* McAlpine, R. D. C.

McALPINE, Robert Douglas Christopher, CMG 1967; HM Diplomatic Service, retired; Director: Baring Brothers, 1969–79; H. Clarkson (Holdings) plc, 1980–87; *b* 14 June 1919; *s* of late Dr Douglas McAlpine, FRCP and late Elizabeth Meg Sidebottom; *m* 1943, Helen Margery Frances Cannan; two *s* one *d* (and one *d* decd). Educ: Winchester; New Coll., Oxford. RNVR, 1939–46. Entered Foreign Service, 1946. FO, 1946–47; Asst Private Sec. to Sec. of State, 1947–49; 2nd Sec. and later 1st Sec., UK High Commn at Bonn, 1949–52; FO, 1952–54; Lima, 1954–56; Moscow, 1956–59; FO, 1959–62; Dep. Consul-Gen. and Counsellor, New York, 1962–65; Counsellor, Mexico City, 1965–68. Town Councillor, Tetbury, 1987–91. *Recreation:* travel. *Address:* Longtree House, Cutwell, Tetbury, Glos GL8 8EB. *Club:* Oxford and Cambridge.

McALPINE, Robert James, FCIOB; Director, Alfred McAlpine plc, 1957–94 (Chairman, 1983–92); *b* 6 May 1932; *s* of late Alfred James McAlpine and of Peggy (*née* Saunders); *m* 1st, Mary Jane Anton; two *s* one *d*; 2nd, Angela Bell (*née* Langford Brooke); one *d*. *Educ:* Harrow Sch. FCIOB. Director: Chester Racecourse Co., 1976– (Chm., 1994–); Haynes Hanson & Clark, 1978– (Chm., 1993–); Hall Engrg plc, 1985–; Aintree Racecourse Co., 1988–. Chm., Export Gp for Constructional Industries, 1975–77. Mem., Jockey Club. High Sheriff, Cheshire, 1994–95. *Recreations:* racing, shooting, golf, bridge. *Address:* Tilstone Lodge, Tilstone Fearnall, Tarporley, Cheshire CW6 9HS. *Clubs:* White's, Turf, Portland, MCC.

McALPINE, Hon. Sir William (Hepburn), 6th Bt *cr* 1918, of Knott Park; FRSE; FCIT; company director; *b* 12 Jan. 1936; *s* of Lord McAlpine of Moffat (Life Peer) and Ella Mary Gardner Garnett (*d* 1987); *S* to baronetcy of father, 1990; *m* 1959, Jill Benton, *o d* of Lt-Col Sir Peter Fawcett Benton Jones, 3rd Bt, OBE, ACA; one *s* one *d*. *Educ:* Charterhouse. Life Guards, 1954–56. Dir, Sir Robert McAlpine Ltd (formerly Sir Robert McAlpine & Sons Ltd), 1956–. FRSA. High Sheriff, Bucks, 1999–2000. *Recreation:* railways. *Heir: s* Andrew William McAlpine [*b* 22 Nov. 1960; *m* 1991, Caroline Claire, *yr d* of Frederick Hodgson; four *s*]. *Address:* (office) 40 Bernard Street, WC1N 1LG. *Clubs:* Buck's, Garrick, Caledonian.
See also Baron McAlpine of West Green.

MACAN, Thomas Townley; HM Diplomatic Service; Minister and Deputy High Commissioner, New Delhi, since 1999; *b* 14 Nov. 1946; only *s* of late Dr Thomas Townley Macan and Zaida Bindloss (*née* Boddington); *m* 1976, Janet Ellen Martin, Hollidaysburg, Penn; one *s* one *d*. *Educ:* Shrewsbury Sch.; Univ. of Sussex (BA Hons Econs; Pres., Students' Union, 1967–68). MIL 1992. Joined HM Diplomatic Service, 1969; UN Dept, FCO, 1969–71; Bonn, 1971–74; Brasilia, 1974–78; Maritime, Aviation and Envmt Dept, FCO, 1978–81; Press Sec., Bonn, 1981–86; Hd, Commonwealth Co-ordination Dept, FCO, 1986–88; Hd, Trng Dept, FCO, 1988–90; Counsellor, Lisbon, 1990–94; Ambassador to Lithuania, 1995–98; on secondment to BOC Group, 1998–99. *Recreations:* steam boats, sailing, church architecture, walking. *Address:* c/o Foreign and Commonwealth Office, King Charles Street, SW1A 2AH. *Clubs:* Naval; Island Cruising (Salcombe).

McANALLY, Vice-Adm. John Henry Stuart, CB 2000; LVO 1983; Commandant, Royal College of Defence Studies, 1998–2001; *b* 9 April 1945; *s* of late Arthur Patrick McAnally and Mrs Basil Hamilton Stuart McAnally. *Educ:* Willington Prep. Sch., Putney; Westminster Sch. FNI 1999; FRIN 1999. BRNC (RN Scholarship); HM Ships Wizard, Ashanti, Walkerton, Leverton, 1963–67; USS Moale (Exchange), 1967–68; HMS Eskimo, 1968–69; HMA Ships Melbourne and Torrens, 1971–73; CO HMS Iveston, 1973–75; Adv. Navign Course, 1975; HMS Fife, 1976–77; Staff Course, 1978; HMS Birmingham and HMY Britannia, 1979–81; MoD, 1982–83; Comd HM Ships Torquay and Alacrity, 1984–86; Staff of C-in-C Fleet, 1986–87; Captain Sixth Frigate Sqdn and CO HM Ships Ariadne and Hermione, 1987–89; Asst Dir (Warfare), Dir Naval Plans, 1989–91; RCDS 1992; HCSC 1993; Dir, Naval Logistics Staff Duties and Naval Staff Duties, MoD, 1993–95; Flag Officer Trng and Recruiting, and Chief Exec., Naval Recruiting and Trng Agency, 1996–98. Younger Brother, Trinity House. MInstD. *Recreation:* golf. *Clubs:* Naval and Military, National Liberal.
See also M. B. H. McAnally.

McANALLY, Mary Basil Hamilton, (Mrs Hugh Macpherson); Managing Director, Meridian Broadcasting Ltd, since 1996; *b* 9 April 1945; *d* of late Arthur Patrick McAnally and Basil Hamilton Stuart McAnally; *m* 1979, Hugh Macpherson. *Educ:* Tiffin Girls Sch.; Wimbledon Art Sch.; London Business Sch. Internat. tennis player, 1963–67; winner, Jun. Indoor Championships of GB, 1963. Researcher, Man Alive, BBC TV, 1969; Prog. Associate, This is Your Life, Thames TV, 1969–71; Series Producer, Thames TV: Money Go Round, 1973–82; Could Do Better, What About the Workers, and The John Smith Show, 1978–80; Series Editor, For What It's Worth, Channel 4, 1982–90 (Winner, Freedom of Information Media Award, 1990); Thames TV: Editor, Daytime, 1984–87; Exec. Prod., The Time the Place, 1987–91; Head of Features, 1989–92; Meridian Broadcasting: Controller of Regl Progs and Community Affairs, 1992–94, Dir of Progs, 1994–96. Member: NCC, 1987–97; Adv. Cttee on Advertising, 1999–; Dir, Southern Screen Commn, 1997–2000; Chm., Media and Creative Industries Task Force, 1999–, and Mem. Bd, 2000–, SEEDA; Mem. Bd, SE England Cultural Consortium, 2000–. FRSA 1990; FRTS 1998. Gov., Portsmouth Univ., 1998–2000. *Publication:* (jtly) Buy Right, 1978. *Recreations:* tennis, painting, golf. *Address:* Atners Stables, Stockbridge, Hants SO20 6JF. *Clubs:* Arts, Forum UK; All England Lawn Tennis and Croquet, Cumberland Lawn Tennis, Highgate Golf, Leckford Golf.
See also J. H. S. McAnally.

MacANDREW, family name of **Baron MacAndrew**.

MacANDREW, 3rd Baron *cr* 1959, of the Firth of Clyde; **Christopher Anthony Colin MacAndrew;** farmer; *b* 16 Feb. 1945; *s* of 2nd Baron MacAndrew and Ursula Beatrice (*née* Steel) (*d* 1986); *S* father, 1989; *m* 1975, Sarah, *o d* of Lt-Col P. H. and Mrs Brazier; one *s* two *d*. *Educ:* Malvern. Comr of Income Tax, 1996–. *Recreations:* golf, tennis. *Heir: s* Hon. Oliver Charles Julian MacAndrew, *b* 3 Sept. 1983. *Address:* Hall Farm, Archdeacon Newton, Darlington, Co. Durham DL2 2YB.

McANDREW, Nicolas; Chairman, Murray Johnstone Ltd, 1992–99; *b* 9 Dec. 1934; *s* of late Robert Louis McAndrew and Anita Marian McAndrew (*née* Huband); *m* 1960, Diana Leonie Wood; two *s* one *d*. *Educ:* Winchester Coll. CA 1961. Commnd Black Watch, 1953–55. With Peat, Marwick, Mitchell & Co., 1955–61; S. G. Warburg & Co. Ltd, 1962–78: Dir, 1969–78; Chm., Warburg Investment Mgt, 1975–78; Dir, Mercury Securities Ltd, 1975–78; N. M. Rothschild & Sons Ltd, 1979–88 (Man. Dir, 1980–88); Murray Johnstone Ltd, 1988–99 (Man. Dir, 1988–92). Board Member: Highlands & Islands Enterprise, 1993–97; N of Scotland Water Authy, 1995–. Deputy Chairman: Burn Stewart Distillers PLC, 1991–99; Liverpool Victoria Friendly Soc., 1995–; Chairman: Martin Currie Enhanced Income Trust (formerly Moorgate Investment Trust) PLC, 1996–; Guinness Flight Extra Income Trust, 1995–; Derby Trust PLC, 1999–. Master, Grocers' Co., 1978–79. *Recreations:* shooting, fishing, golf, bridge. *Address:* Kilcoy Castle, Killearnan, Muir of Ord, Ross-shire IV6 7RX. *T:* (01463) 871393. *Club:* White's.

MACARA, Sir Alexander (Wiseman), Kt 1998; FRCP, FRCGP, FFPHM; Consultant Senior Lecturer in Epidemiology and Public Health Medicine, University of Bristol and Hon. Visiting Consultant, Bristol Royal Infirmary, 1976–97; Chairman of Council, British Medical Association, 1993–98; *b* 4 May 1932; *s* of late Rev. Alexander Macara, MA Hons and Marion Wiseman Macara (*née* Mackay); *m* 1964, Sylvia May Williams, BSc Hons, DipEd, *d* of late Edward Brodbeck and Ellen Florence Williams; one *s* one *d*. *Educ:* Irvine Royal Acad.; Glasgow Univ. (Carnegie Bursar; MB ChB 1958); LSHTM. DPH (Hecht Prize) 1960; FFPHM 1989 (FFCM 1973; MFCM 1972); FRIPHH 1973; FRCGP (*ad eundem gradum*) 1983; FRCP 1991; FRCPE 1997. House Physician and House Surgeon posts in Glasgow Teaching Hosps, 1958–59; General Practice experience, London and Glasgow, 1959–60; Asst MOH and Sch. MO, City and Co. of Bristol, 1960–63, then Hon. Community Physician, 1963–74; Lectr then Sen. Lectr, Univ. of Bristol, 1963–76 (Actg Head, Dept of Public Health, 1974–76). Sir Wilson Jameson Travelling Scholar, LSHTM, 1967; Vis. Prof., Univ. of Malaya, 1980; Vis. Prof. and Ext. Examnr for higher degrees, Univ. of Khartoum, 1983; Hon. Vis. Prof. in Health Studies, York Univ., 1998–; Ext. Examnr in Community Med. (Human Ecology), Univ. of Glasgow, 1979–82; Ext. Examnr, Inst. of Population Studies, Univ. of Exeter, 1993–97. Jt Chm., Jt Wkg Party of Med. Profession and DoH on Med. Services for Children, 1991–92, and Chm., Jt Wkg Party on Child Protection, 1993–94. General Medical Council: Mem., 1979–; mem. various cttees. Faculty of Community Medicine (now of Public Health Medicine): Mem. Bd, 1973–79; Treasurer, 1979–84. British Medical Association: Chm., Med. Ethics Cttee, 1982–89; Dep. Chm., 1987–89, Chm., 1989–92, Representative Body; Rep. on Standing Cttee, Doctors in the EC, 1980–; Chm. or Mem., numerous working parties, incl. Bd of Science and Educn; Fellow, 1978. Sec.-Gen., World Fedn for Educn and Res. in Public Health, 1988–96; Dir, WHO Collaborating Centre in Envmtl Health Promotion and Ecology, 1989–97; Advr and Consultant on Educn, Trng and Health Manpower Develt, WHO, 1970–; Sec., European Collaborative Health Services Studies, 1977–89; Chm., Nat. Heart Forum, 1998–. Mem. Bd of Govs, LSHTM, 1993–; Gov., Redland High Sch. for Girls, Bristol, 1998–. Lectures: Long Fox Meml, Bristol Univ., 1995; Harben, RIPH & H, 1996; Gregg Meml, AMA, 1997. Founder FMedSci 1998. FRSA 1995. Hon. Member: Hungarian Soc. Social Medicine, 1989; Italian Soc. Hygiene, Preventive Medicine and Public Health (Gold Medallist), 1991; Hon. Life Fellow, Soc. Public Health, 1991; Hon. FFOM 2000. Hon. Dr Public Health and Gerasimos Alivizatos Award, Sch. of Public Health, Athens, 1992; Hon. DSc UWE, 1998. Public Health Award, 1992, John Kershaw Award, 1994, Soc. of Public Health; James Preston Meml Award, Soc. of Public Health and BMA, 1993; Médaille d'or de l'Ordre de Médecin Français, 1998; Gold Medal, BMA, 1999. *Publications:* (jtly) Personal Data Protection in Health and Social Services, 1988; chapters in various books and articles and reports in med. jls on epidemiology, public health, envmtl health and ethics in medicine. *Recreations:* gardening, reading, music. *Address:* Elgon, 10 Cheyne Road, Stoke Bishop, Bristol BS9 2DH. *T:* (0117) 968 2838, *Fax:* (0117) 968 4602. *Club:* Athenæum.

MACARA, Sir Hugh Kenneth, 4th Bt *cr* 1911, of Ardmore, St Anne-on-the-Sea, Co. Lancaster; *b* 17 Jan. 1913; 4th *s* of Sir William Cowper Macara, 2nd Bt and Lilian Mary (*d* 1971), *d* of John Chapman; *S* brother, 1982. *Heir:* none.

McARDLE, Rear-Adm. Stanley Lawrence, CB 1975; LVO 1952; GM 1953; JP; Flag Officer, Portsmouth, and Port Admiral, Portsmouth, 1973–75; retired; *b* 1922; *s* of Theodore McArdle, Lochmaben, Dumfriesshire; *m* 1st, 1945, (Helen) Joyce, *d* of Owen Cummins, Wickham, Hants; one *d*; 2nd, 1962, Jennifer, *d* of Walter Talbot Goddard, Salisbury, Wilts; one *d*. *Educ:* Royal Hospital Sch., Holbrook, Suffolk. Joined RN, 1938; served War, 1939–45. Lieut 1945; Comdr 1956; Captain 1963. Directorate of Naval Operations and Trade, 1969; Comd HMS Glamorgan, 1970; Dir Naval Trng, Director General, Personal Services and Trng (Naval), 1971–73; Rear Admiral 1972. Dir, Endless Holdings Ltd, 1985–. JP Wilts, 1977. *Address:* The Coach House, Church Road, Farley, Salisbury, Wilts SP5 1AH.

MACARTHUR, Rev. Arthur Leitch, OBE 1981; MA, MLitt; inducted, Christ Church, Marlow-on-Thames, 1980, retired 1986; *b* 9 Dec. 1913; *s* of Edwin Macarthur and Mary Macarthur (*née* Leitch); *m* 1950, Doreen Esmé Muir; three *s* one *d*. *Educ:* Rutherford Coll.; Armstrong Coll., Durham Univ. (MA, MLitt Dunelm); Westminster Coll., Cambridge. Ordained, 1937; inducted, Clayport, Alnwick, 1937; served with YMCA in France, 1940. Inducted: St Augustine's, New Barnet, 1944; St Columba's, North Shields, 1950. Gen. Sec., Presbyterian Church of England, 1960–72; Moderator, Presbyterian Church of England, 1971–72; Jt Gen.-Sec., URC, 1972–74; Moderator, URC, 1974–75; Gen. Sec., URC, 1975–80; Moderator, Free Church Federal Council, 1980–81. Vice-Pres., BCC, 1974–77 (Chm., Admin. Cttee, 1969–74). *Publication:* Setting up Signs, 1997. *Recreations:* gardening, golf, walking. *Address:* Haywards Corner, Randalls Green, Chalford Hill, near Stroud, Glos GL6 8LH. *T:* (01453) 883700.

MacARTHUR, Brian; Associate Editor, The Times, since 1995 (Executive Editor (Features), 1991–95); *b* 5 Feb. 1940; *o s* of late S. H. MacArthur and Mrs M. MacArthur; *m* 1st, 1966, Peta Deschampsneufs (*d* 1971); 2nd, 1975, Bridget Trahair (separated; she *d* 1997); two *d*; 3rd, 2000, Maureen Waller. *Educ:* Brentwood Sch.; Helsby Grammar Sch.; Leeds Univ. (BA). Yorkshire Post, 1962–64; Daily Mail, 1964–66; The Guardian, 1966–67; The Times: Education Correspondent, 1967–70; Founder Editor, The Times Higher Educn Supplement, 1971–76; Home News Editor, 1976–78; Dep. Editor, Evening Standard, 1978–79; Chief Asst to the Editor, The Sunday Times, 1979–81; Exec. Editor (News), The Times, 1981–82; Jt Dep. Editor, The Sunday Times, 1982–84; Editor, Western Morning News, 1984–85; Editor-in-Chief, Today, 1986–87; Exec. Ed., The Sunday Times, 1987–91. Hon. MA, Open Univ., 1976. *Publications:* Eddy Shah: Today and the Newspaper Revolution, 1988; Deadline Sunday, 1991; Gulf War Despatches, 1991; (ed) The Penguin Book of Twentieth Century Speeches, 1992; (ed) The Penguin Book of Historic Speeches, 1995; (ed) The Penguin Book of Twentieth Century Protest, 1998. *Recreations:* reading, travel. *Address:* 25 Northchurch Road, N1 4ED. *T:* (020) 7275 0277; (office) (020) 7782 5801. *Club:* Garrick.

MacARTHUR, Ian, OBE 1988; Hon. Treasurer, 1991–98, and Vice-Chairman, 1992–98, Texprint Ltd, charity; *b* 17 May 1925; *yr s* of late Lt-Gen. Sir William MacArthur, KCB, DSO, OBE, MD, DSc, FRCP, KHP; *m* 1957, Judith Mary, (RGN 1976), *d* of late Francis Gavin Douglas Miller; four *s* three *d*. *Educ:* Cheltenham Coll.; The Queen's Coll., Oxford (Scholar, MA). Served War of 1939–45, with RN (Ord. Seaman) and RNVR, 1943–46 (King's Badge; Flag Lieut to C-in-C Portsmouth, 1946). Contested (U), Greenock, 1955, also by-election, Dec. 1955; MP (C) Perth and E Perthshire, 1959–Sept. 1974; an Asst Government Whip (unpaid), 1962–63; a Lord Comr of the Treasury and Govt Scottish Whip, 1963–64; Opposition Scottish Whip, 1964–65; an Opposition Spokesman on Scottish Affairs, 1965–70 (Opposition front bench, 1965–66, 1969–70). Former Member: Speaker's Conf. on Electoral Law; Select Cttees on European Legislation, on Scottish Affairs, and on Members' Interests. Chm., Scottish Cons. Mems' Cttee, 1972–73. Introduced, as Private Member's Bills: Law Reform (Damages and Solatium) (Scotland) Act, 1962; Interest on Damages (Scotland) Act, 1971; Social Work (Scotland) Act, 1972; Domicile and Matrimonial Proceedings Act, 1973. Personal Asst to the Prime Minister, Rt Hon. Sir Alec Douglas-Home, Kinross and W Perthshire By-Election, Nov. 1963. Hon. Pres., Scottish Young Unionists, 1962–65; Vice-Chm., Cons. Party in Scotland, 1972–75. Formerly Dir of Administration, J. Walter Thompson Co. Ltd. Dir, British Textile Confederation, 1977–89. FRSA 1984. Gold Cross of Merit, Polish Govt in Exile, 1971. *Address:* 15 Old Palace Lane, Richmond, Surrey TW9 1PG. *Clubs:* Naval; Puffin's (Edinburgh); Conservative (Perth).
See also R. A. G. Douglas Miller.

McARTHUR, Dr John Duncan, FRCPGlas; FRCPE; Consultant Cardiologist, Western Infirmary, Glasgow, since 1978; *b* 7 Jan. 1938; *s* of Neil McPhail McArthur and Elizabeth Duncan; *m* 1963, Elizabeth Agnew Bowie; two *s* one *d*. *Educ:* Univ. of Glasgow (BSc Hons 1960; MB ChB Hons 1963); DM Madras 1970. DObstRCOG 1965; MRCP 1966; MRCPG 1966; MRCPE 1967, FRCPE 1994; FRCPGlas 1980. Junior House Officer, Glasgow Royal Infirmary and Ayrshire Hosps, 1963–65; Senior House Officer and Registrar, Glasgow Royal Inf., 1965–67; Lectr, Sen. Lectr, Reader, Christian Med. Coll. Hosp., Vellore, India, as Missionary, Church of Scotland, 1968–73; Sen. Registrar, Medicine/Cardiology, Glasgow Teaching Hosps, 1973–78. *Publications:* articles on valvular heart disease and pacemakers. *Recreations:* DIY, gardening. *Address:* 8 Durness Avenue, Bearsden, Glasgow G61 2AQ. *T:* (0141) 563 9068, *Fax:* (0141) 586 5142; *e-mail:* jd.mcarthur@ntlworld.com.

McARTHUR, Dr Thomas Burns, (Tom); English teacher, since 1959; feature writer, since 1962; lecturer and writer on yoga and Indian philosophy, since 1962; author and language consultant, since 1970; Editor: English Today, since 1984; Oxford Companion to the English Language, since 1987; *b* 23 Aug. 1938; *s* of Archibald McArthur and Margaret Burns; *m* 1963, Fereshteh Mottahedin (*d* 1993); one *s* two *d*. *Educ:* Glasgow Univ. (MA 1958); Edinburgh Univ. (MLitt 1970; PhD 1978). Officer-Instr, RAEC, 1959–61; Asst Master, Riland Bedford Sch., Warwicks, 1961–63; Head of English, Cathedral and John Connon Sch., Bombay, India, 1965–67; Vis. Prof. in the English of the Media, Rajendra Prasad College of Mass Communication (Bharatiya Vidya Bhavan), Univ. of Bombay, 1965–67; Dir of Extra-Mural English Language Courses, Univ. of Edinburgh, 1972–79; Associate Prof. of English, Université du Québec à Trois-Rivières, Canada, 1979–83; Recognised Teacher (pt-time), 1986–, Res. Fellow, 1992–, Exeter Univ. Co-founder (with Reinhard Hartmann), Internat. Lexicography Course, Univ. of Exeter, 1987–. Consultant: Min. of Educn, Quebec, 1980–81; Société pour la promotion de l'enseignement de l'anglais (langue seconde) au Québec, 1980–83; Henson International Television (the Muppets), 1985–86; Dictionary Res. Centre, Exeter Univ., 1987–90; BBC Policy Planning Unit, 1992; also on dictionaries, encyclopedias and ELT books published by Century Hutchinson, Chambers, Collins, CUP, Longman, Macmillan, OUP and Time-Life. The Story of English (BBC radio series with D. Crystal), 1987. Member, Editorial Board: Internat. Jl of Lexicography, 1988–98; World Englishes, 1993–; Editl Advr, The Good Book Guide, 1992–; Mem., Internat. Adv. Bd, Logos, 1994–96. Hon. PhD Uppsala, 1999. *Publications:* Patterns of English series, 1972–74; English for Students of Economics, 1973; (with Beryl Atkins) Collins Dictionary of English Phrasal Verbs, 1974; (ed with A. J. Aitken) Languages of Scotland, 1979; Longman Lexicon of Contemporary English, 1981; A Foundation Course for Language Teachers, 1983; The Written Word, Books 1 and 2, 1984; Worlds of Reference, 1986; Yoga and the Bhagavad-Gita, 1986; Understanding Yoga, 1986; Unitive Thinking, 1988 (Beyond Logic and Mysticism, USA, 1990); The English Language as Used in Quebec: a survey, 1989; (ed) The Oxford Companion to the English Language, 1992, concise edn 1998; The English Languages, 1998; (ed with Alan Kernerman) Lexicography in Asia, 1998; Living Words: language, lexicography and the knowledge revolution, 1998. *Recreations:* reading, television, walking, cycling, travel. *Address:* 22–23 Ventress Farm Court, Cherry Hinton Road, Cambridge CB1 8HD. *T:* (01223) 245934, *Fax:* (01223) 241161; *e-mail:* scotsway@aol.com.

MACARTNEY, Sir John Barrington, 6th Bt *cr* 1799, of Lish, Co. Armagh; dairy farmer, retired; *b* 21 Jan. 1917; *s* of John Barrington Macartney (3rd *s* of Sir John Macartney, 3rd Bt; he *d* 1951) and Selina Koch, Hampden, Mackay, Qld, Australia; *S* uncle, Sir Alexander Miller Macartney, 5th Bt, 1960; *m* 1944, Amy Isobel Reinke (*d* 1978); one *s*. *Heir:* *s* John Ralph Macartney [*b* 24 July 1945; *m* 1966, Suzanne Marie Fowler; four *d*]. *Address:* 37 Meadow Street, North Mackay, Qld 4740, Australia.

MacASKILL, Ewen; Diplomatic Editor, The Guardian, since 2000; *b* 29 Oct. 1951; *s* of John Angus MacAskill and Catherine Euphemia MacAskill (*née* MacDonald); *m* 1976, Sarah Anne Hutchison; three *s*. *Educ:* Woodside Secondary Sch., Glasgow; Glasgow Univ. (MA Hons Modern History and Politics). Reporter, Glasgow Herald, 1973–77; VSO, working as journalist, Nat. Broadcasting Commn, Papua New Guinea, 1978–79; journalist: Reuters, 1980; Scotsman, 1981–83; China Daily, Beijing, 1984–85; Lawrence Sterne Fellow, Washington Post, 1986; Political Correspondent, 1986–90, Political Editor, 1990–96, Scotsman; Chief Pol Correspondent, Guardian, 1996–99. Mem., St Margarets Film Club. Scotland's Young Journalist of the Year, 1974. *Recreations:* mountaineering, film, books. *Address:* 11 Norman Avenue, St Margarets, Twickenham, Middx TW1 2LY. *T:* (020) 8891 0795. *Club:* Junior Mountaineering of Scotland.

MacASKILL, Kenneth Wright; solicitor; Member (SNP) Lothians, Scottish Parliament, since 1999; *b* 28 April 1958; *m*; two *s*. *Educ:* Linlithgow Acad.; Edinburgh Univ. (LLB Hons). Sen. Partner, Erskine, MacAskill & Co., solicitors. Mem., SNP, 1981– (Mem., Nat. Exec., 1984–; Treas., until 1999). Contested (SNP): Livingston, 1983, 1987; Linlithgow, 1992, 1997; Scotland Mid and Fife, EP elecns, 1989. *Address:* Scottish Parliament, Edinburgh EH99 1SP.

MACAULAY OF BRAGAR, Baron *cr* 1989 (Life Peer), of Bragar in the county of Ross and Cromarty; **Donald Macaulay.** *Educ:* Univ. of Glasgow (MA, LLB). Admitted to Faculty of Advocates, 1963; QC (Scot.) 1975. *Address:* House of Lords, SW1A 0PW.

McAVAN, Linda; Member (Lab) Yorkshire and the Humber Region, European Parliament, since 1999 (Yorkshire South, May 1998–99); *b* 2 Dec. 1962; *d* of Thomas McAvan and late Jean McAvan. *Educ:* St Joseph's RC Coll., Bradford; Heriot-Watt Univ. (BA Hons Interpreting and Translation 1984); Univ. Libre de Bruxelles (MA Internat. Relns 1991). Translator, Agence Europe Press Agency, Brussels, 1984–85; Co-ordinator and Adminr, Party of European Socialists, Brussels, 1985–88; Press Officer, European Youth Forum, Brussels, 1988–90; Head of Information Policy, EC Youth Exchange Bureau, Brussels, 1990–91; European Officer, Coalfield Communities Campaign, Barnsley, 1991–95; Sen. Strategy Officer on European Affairs, Barnsley BC, 1995–98. Dep. Leader, European Parly Lab. Party, 1999–. *Recreations:* reading, walking, swimming. *Address:* Euro Office, 79 High Street, Wath-upon-Dearne, Rotherham, S Yorks S63 7QB. *T:* (01709) 875665.

McAVEETY, Francis; Member (Lab) Glasgow Shettleston, Scottish Parliament, since 1999; *b* 27 July 1962; *s* of Philip and Anne Marie McAveety; *m* 1985, Anita Mitchell; one *s* one *d*. *Educ:* Strathclyde Univ. (BA Jt Hons English and History 1983); St Andrew's Coll. of Educn, Glasgow (post grad. teaching qualification, 1984). Teacher: Glasgow, 1984–94; Renfrewshire, 1994–99. Member (Lab): Glasgow DC, 1988–95; Glasgow City Council, 1995–99 (Convener, Arts and Culture, 1995–97; Leader, 1997–99). Dep. Minister for Local Govt, Scottish Exec., 1999–2000. DL Glasgow 1998. *Recreations:* sport, reading, record collecting. *Address:* 156 Glenbuck Avenue, Glasgow G33 1LW.

McAVOY, Prof. Brian Ramsay, MD; FRCP, FRCGP; Director, Research and Practice Support, Royal Australian College of General Practitioners, since 2000; *b* 2 Jan. 1949; *s* of Thomas Ramsay McAvoy and Christine McMillan McAvoy; *m* 1974, Dr Pauline Anne Connor (separated); one *s* one *d*. *Educ:* Eastwood Sen. Secondary Sch., Glasgow; Univ. of Glasgow (BSc; MB ChB); Leicester Univ. (MD). FRCGP 1988; FRCP 1992; FRNZCGP 1999; FRACGP 2000. Vocational Trainee in Gen. Practice, Southern Gen. Hosp. Scheme, Glasgow, 1973–76; Teaching Fellow, Dept of Family Medicine, McMaster Med. Sch., Hamilton, Ont, 1976–77; Principal in General Practice: Byfield, Northants, 1977–84; Leicester, 1984–89; Guide post, Northumberland, 1994–; Lectr, 1977–84, Sen. Lectr, 1984–89, in General Practice, Univ. of Leicester; Elaine Gurr Foundation Prof. of General Practice, Univ. of Auckland, NZ, 1989–94; William Leech Prof. of Primary Health Care, Univ. of Newcastle upon Tyne, 1994–2000. Adjunct Prof. of Gen. Practice, Univs of Melbourne and Queensland; Hon. Prof. of Gen. Practice, Monash Univ. *Publications:* (ed jtly) Asian Health Care, 1990; (contrib.) Clinical Method: a general practice approach, 1988, 2nd edn 1992; articles on med. educn, health care delivery, ethnic minority health, alcohol and health promotion. *Recreations:* running, walking, music, reading. *Address:* Royal Australian College of General Practitioners,

College House, 1 Palmerston Crescent, South Melbourne, Vic 3205, Australia. *T:* (3) 92141414, *Fax:* (3) 92141400; *e-mail:* brian.mcavoy@racgp.org.au.

McAVOY, Sir (Francis) Joseph, Kt 1976; CBE 1969; Chairman: Queensland and Australian Canegrowers Councils, 1963–82 (Member, 1952–82); Australian Canegrowers Council, 1952–82; retired; *b* 26 Feb. 1910; *s* of William Henry McAvoy and Hanorah Catherine McAvoy; *m* 1936, Mary Irene Doolan; four *s* (one *d* decd). *Educ:* Nudgee Coll., Brisbane; Sacred Heart Convent, Innisfail, Qld. Member: Goondi Mill Suppliers Cttee, 1947–82; Innisfail Canegrowers Exec., 1949–82; Metric Conversion Bd (Aust.), 1970–78; Aust. Immigration Adv. Council, 1964–72; Exec. Council of Agriculture, 1963–82; Exec., Aust. Farmers Fedn, 1969–77, Nat. Farmers Fedn, 1977–82. Vice-Pres., Internat. Fedn of Agricultural Producers, 1968–74. Paul Harris Fellow, Rotary Internat., USA, 1986. *Recreation:* lawn bowls. *Address:* PO Box 95, Innisfail, Qld 4860, Australia. *Clubs:* Rotary, IDB (Innisfail, Qld).

McAVOY, Thomas McLaughlin; MP (Lab and Co-op) Glasgow, Rutherglen, since 1987; Comptroller of HM Household, since 1997; *b* 14 Dec. 1943; *m* Eleanor Kerr; four *s*. Employee, Hoover, Cambuslang; shop steward, AEU. Mem., Strathclyde Regl Council, 1982–87; former Chm., Rutherglen Community Council. An Opposition Whip, 1990–93. *Address:* House of Commons, SW1A 0AA; 9 Douglas Avenue, Rutherglen, Lanarkshire G73 4RA.

McBAIN, (David) Malcolm, LVO 1972; HM Diplomatic Service, retired; Director (formerly Co-ordinator), British Diplomatic Oral History Programme, since 1995 (Leicester University, 1995–97, Churchill Archives Centre, Churchill College, Cambridge, since 1997); *b* 19 Jan. 1928; *s* of David Walker McBain and Lilian J. McBain; *m* 1951, Audrey Yvonne Evison; one *s* three *d*. *Educ:* Sutton County School; London School of Economics (evening student). Min. of Civil Aviation appts in Tripoli, Libya, 1949–51, New Delhi, 1953–54; Diplomatic Service: New Delhi, 1958–61; Kenya, 1963–67; Thailand, 1968–75; Brunei, 1978–81; Texas, 1981–84; Ambassador to Madagascar, 1984–87. Order of Crown of Thailand, 1972. *Recreation:* golf. *Address:* Edmeads Cottage, Teffont Magna, Salisbury, Wilts SP3 5QY.

McBAIN, Ed; *see* Hunter, Evan.

McBAIN, Malcolm; *see* McBain, D. M.

MACBEATH, Prof. Alexander Murray, PhD (Princeton, NJ); MA (Cantab); Professor of Mathematics and Statistics, University of Pittsburgh, 1979–90; *b* 30 June 1923; *s* of late Prof. Alexander Macbeath, CBE; *m* 1951, Julie Ormrod, Lytham St Anne's; two *s*. *Educ:* Royal Belfast Academical Inst.; Queen's Univ., Belfast; Clare Coll., Cambridge. Entrance Schol., Dixon Prize in Maths, Purser Studentship, 1st class hons in Maths, BA, QUB. Bletchley Park (centre for work on breaking German Enigma codes), 1943–45. Cambridge, 1945–48; Maj. Entrance Schol., Wrangler Math. Tripos, Part II, dist. Part III, BA, Owst Prize. Commonwealth Fund Fellowship, Princeton, NJ, 1948–50; Smith's Prize, 1949; PhD Princeton, 1950. Research Fellow, Clare Coll., Cambridge, 1950–51; MA Cambridge, 1951. Lectr in Maths, Univ. Coll. of North Staffordshire, 1951–53; Prof. of Maths, Queen's Coll., Dundee, 1953–62; Mason Prof. of Pure Maths, Univ. of Birmingham, 1962–79. Visiting Professor: California Inst. of Technology, 1966–67; Univ. of Pittsburgh, 1974–75; Hon. Professor: Univ. of St Andrews, 1990–94; Univ. of Warwick, 1994–. *Publications:* Elementary Vector Algebra, 1964; papers in: Jl London Mathematical Soc.; Proc. London Math. Soc.; Proc. Cambridge Philosophical Soc.; Quarterly Jl of Mathematics; Annals of Mathematics; Canadian Jl of Mathematics. *Recreation:* Scottish country dancing. *Address:* 1 Church Hill Court, Lighthorne, Warwick CV35 0AR.

McBRATNEY, George, CEng, FIMechE; Principal, College of Technology, Belfast, 1984–89; *b* 5 May 1927; *s* of George McBratney and Sarah Jane McBratney; *m* 1949, Margaret Rose Patricia, (Trissie), *d* of late John Robinson, Melbourne, Australia; one *s*. *Educ:* Coll. of Technology, Belfast (BSc(Eng) 1948); Northampton Coll. of Advanced Technol.; QUB (Dip Ed 1976). CEng, FIMechE 1971. Apprentice fitter/draughtsman, Harland and Wolff, Belfast, 1943–47; Teacher, Comber Trades Prep. Sch., 1947–54; College of Technology, Belfast: successively Asst Lectr, Lectr and Sen. Lectr, 1954–67; Asst to Principal, 1967–69; Vice-Principal, 1969–84. Council Member: IMechE, 1984–86 (Chm., NI Br., 1984–86); NI Manpower Council, 1984–; Lambeg Industrial Res. Assoc. (formerly Linen Industry Res. Assoc.), 1984–90; BTEC, 1986–89; Chm., Further Educn Adv. Cttee, Faculty of Educn, Univ. of Ulster, 1986–90. *Publications:* Mechanical Engineering Experiments, vols 1 and 2 (with W. R. Mitchell), 1962, vol. 3 (with T. G. J. Moag), 1964; (with T. G. J. Moag) Science for Mechanical Engineering Technicians, vol. 1, 1966. *Recreation:* gardening. *Address:* 16 Glencregagh Drive, Belfast BT6 0NL. *T:* (028) 9079 6123.

McBREARTY, Anthony; Senior Research Fellow, University of East London, since 1997; *b* 26 April 1946; *s* of Patrick and Mary McBrearty; *m* 1969, Heather McGowan (marr. diss. 1994), solicitor; one *s*; two *d* by former partner. Councillor (Lab) London Borough of Haringey, 1975–86 (Chm. of Personnel Cttee, 1976–79; Chm. of Housing Cttee, 1979–82); Mem. (Lab) Enfield N, 1981–86, Chm., Housing Cttee, 1982–86, GLC. Contested (Lab) W Herts, 1987. Member: Central Technical Unit, 1986–88; Hd of Policy, London Bor. of Newham, 1988–96. Mem., Mgt Cttee, Thames Reach Housing Assoc., 1987–. *Recreations:* politics, history. *Address:* 56 First Avenue, Manor Park, E12 6AN. *T:* (020) 8478 8197.

McBRIDE, Alexandra Joy; *see* Stewart, A. J.

McBRIDE, Dianne Gwenllian; *see* Nelmes, D. G.

McBRIDE, Commandant (Sara) Vonla (Adair), CB 1979; Director, City of London Region, Lloyds Bank Ltd, 1980–91; a Chairman, Civil Service Commissioners' Interview Panel, 1985–91; *b* 20 Jan. 1921; *d* of late Andrew Stewart McBride and Agnes McBride. *Educ:* Ballymena Acad., NI; TCD (Moderatorship in Mod. Lit; BA Hons). CBIM. Teacher of English and French, Ballymena Acad., 1942–45; Housemistress, Gardenhurst Sch., Burnham-on-Sea, Somerset, 1945–49. Dir, WRNS, 1976–79 (joined 1949); Hon. ADC to the Queen, 1976–79. Vice-President: Ex Services Mental Welfare Soc., 1983–; Officers' Pension Soc., 1989–96; RNLI, 1992–. Freeman, City of London, 1978. Liveryman, Shipwrights' Co., 1983–. *Publication:* Never at Sea (autobiog.), 1966. *Recreations:* golf, theatre entertaining, continental travel. *Address:* Flat 11, 8 The Paragon, Blackheath, SE3 0NY. *T:* (020) 8852 8673. *Clubs:* Army and Navy, Naval.

McBRIDE, Vonla; *see* McBride, S. V. A.

McBRIDE, William Griffith, AO 1977; CBE 1969; Medical Director, Foundation 41 (for the study of congenital abnormalities and mental retardation), 1972–2001; Consultant Obstetrician and Gynaecologist, St George Hospital, Sydney, 1957–93; *b* 25 May 1927; *s* of late John McBride, Sydney; *m* 1957, Patricia Mary, *d* of late Robert Louis Glover; two *s* two *d*. *Educ:* Canterbury High Sch., Sydney; Univ. of Sydney; Univ. of London. MB, BS Sydney 1950; MD Sydney 1962; FRCOG 1968 (MRCOG 1954); FRACOG 1979. Resident: St George Hosp., Sydney, 1950; Launceston Hosp., 1951; Med. Supt, Women's Hosp., Sydney, 1955–57; Cons. Gynaecologist, Bankstown Hosp., Sydney, 1957–66; Consultant Obstetrician and Gynaecologist: Women's Hosp., Sydney, 1966–83; Royal Hosp. for Women, 1983–88; Vis. Consultant, L.B.J. Tropical Medical Center, American Samoa, 1998–. Lectr in Obstetrics and Gynaecology, Univ. of Sydney, 1957–83; Examr in Obstetrics and Gynaecology, Univ. of Sydney, 1960–83. Vis. Prof. of Gynaecology, Univ. of Bangkok, 1968. Mem., WHO Sub-Cttee on safety of oral contraceptives, 1971. Pres. Sect. of Obstetrics and Gynæcology, AMA, 1966–73. Fellow, Senate of Univ. of Sydney, 1976–90; FRSocMed 1988; Mem., Amer. Coll. of Toxicology, 1985. Member: Soc. of Reproductive Biology; Endocrine Soc.; Teratology Soc.; Soc. for Risk Analysis; NY Acad. of Scis, 1987; AAAS, 1992. Mem. Council, Royal Agricl Soc. of NSW, 1987–; Delegate, Council meeting of Royal Agricl Socs, Calgary, 1992; breeder and judge of Hereford cattle; judged Shropshire and W Midlands Show, 1989. Member: Bd of Dirs, Australian Opera, 1979–82; Australian Opera Council, 1982–. BP Prize of Institut de la Vie, 1971 (for discovery of the teratogenic effects of the drug Thalidomide; first person to alert the world to the dangers of this drug and possibly other drugs). *Publications:* Drugs, 1960–70; Killing the Messenger, 1994; over 100 pubns in internat. med. or scientific jls including: (on teratogenic effect of the drug Thalidomide), Lancet 1961 (London); (on mutagenic effect of Thalidomide), BMJ 1994; (on Thalidomide and DNA in rats and rabbits), Teratogenesis, Carcinogenesis, Mutagenesis, 1997; (on interaction of Thalidomide with DNA or rabbit embryos), Pharmacology & Toxicology, 1999; Bitter Pills, 2001. *Recreations:* tennis, swimming, riding, music, cattle breeding. *Address:* PO Box 1327, E Sydney, NSW 2010, Australia. *Clubs:* Union, Australian Jockey, Palm Beach Surf, Royal Sydney Golf, Palm Beach Golf (Sydney).

McBURNEY, Air Vice-Marshal Ralph Edward, CBE 1945; CD; RCAF, retired; *b* Montreal, Quebec, 17 Aug. 1906; *s* of Irville Albert and Lilian McBurney, Saskatoon, Sask.; *m* 1931, Gertrude Elizabeth Bate, Saskatoon; two *s* one *d*. *Educ:* Univs of Saskatchewan and Manitoba. BSc (EE); Commenced flying training as a cadet in RCAF, 1924; Pilot Officer, 1926; employed on Forest Fire Patrols and photographic mapping; Course in RAF School of Army Co-operation and tour as Instructor in RCAF School of Army Co-operation, 1931; Course at RAF Wireless School, Cranwell, and tour as Signals Adviser at Air Force HQ, Ottawa, 1935–36; RAF Staff Coll., Andover, 1939; Dir of Signals, AFHQ, Ottawa, 1939–42; CO, RCAF Station, Trenton, Ont., 1943; CO, RCAF Station, Dishforth, Yorks, 1943; Air Cdre 1944; Base Comdr of 61 Training Base, and later, 64 Operational Base in No 6 (RCAF) Bomber Group of Bomber Comd; SASO of the Group, Dec. 1944; AOC RCAF Maintenance Comd, 1945–46; Senior Canadian Air Force Liaison Officer, London, 1946–48; AOC Air Materiel Comd, RCAF, Ottawa, 1948–52. Business Consultant, 1952–60; Chief, Technical Information Service, Nat. Research Council, Ottawa, 1960–72. Pres., Internat. Fedn for Documentation, 1968–72. *Address:* 2022 Sharon Avenue, Ottawa, ON K2A 1L8, Canada.

McBURNIE, Tony; Chairman: The Strategic Index, since 1994; The Strategic Marketing Index, since 1994; *b* 4 Aug. 1929; *s* of William McBurnie and Bessie McKenzie Harvey McBurnie; *m* 1954, René Keating; one *s* one *d*. *Educ:* Lanark Grammar Sch.; Glasgow Univ. (MA). FCIM (FInstM 1984). National Service, RAF (FO), 1951–53. Divisional Manager Mullard Ltd, 1958–65; Group Marketing Dir, United Glass Ltd, 1965–69; Chairman and Managing Director: Ravenhead Co. Ltd, 1970–79; United Glass Containers Ltd, 1979–82; Man. Dir, United Glass PT&D Gp, 1982–84; Dir, United Glass Holdings PLC, 1966–84; Dir Gen., Chartered Inst. of Marketing (formerly Inst. of Marketing), 1984–89; Managing Director: Coll. of Marketing Ltd, 1985–89; Marketing Training Ltd, 1984–89; Marketing House Publishers Ltd, 1985–89. Chairman: Reed QT Search, 1989–90; Marketing Quality Assurance, 1991–95. Director: Reed Executive plc, 1987–90; Beard Dove Ltd, 1988–97. Pres., Assoc. of Glass Container Manufacturers, 1981–83; Chm., NJIC for Glass Industry, 1982–83; Dir, European Glass Fedn, 1979–83. *Publications:* (with David Clutterbuck) The Marketing Edge, 1987; Marketing Plus, 1989. *Recreations:* golf, swimming, theatre, the arts. *Address:* Craigwood Lodge, Prince Consort Drive, Ascot, Berks SL5 8AW. *Club:* Wentworth.

McCABE, Bernice Alda; Headmistress, North London Collegiate School, since 1997; *b* 7 Oct. 1952; *d* of Alan Collis Wood and Eileen May Wood (*née* Bolton); *m* 1988, Thomas Patrick McCabe. *Educ:* Clifton High Sch. for Girls; Bristol Univ. (BA, PGCE); Leeds Metropolitan Univ. (MBA 1995). Asst English Teacher, Filton High Sch., Bristol, 1974–81; Head of English: Cotham Grammar Sch., Bristol, 1981–83; Collingwood Sch., Camberley, 1984–86; Dep. Headteacher, Heathland Sch., Hounslow, 1986–90; Headmistress, Chelmsford County High Sch. for Girls, 1990–97. Mem., GSA, 1997–. Gov., Orley Farm Sch., 1997–. FRSA 1995. *Recreations:* travel, theatre, opera, film, running, swimming. *Address:* North London Collegiate School, Canons, Edgware, Middx HA8 7RJ. *T:* (020) 8952 0912; The Old Grammar School, Cavendish, Suffolk CO10 8BB.

MACCABE, Christopher George; British Joint Secretary, British-Irish Intergovernmental Secretariat, and Associate Political Director, Northern Ireland Office, since 2000; *b* 17 Dec. 1946; *s* of late Max Maccabe, FRSA, and of Gladys Maccabe (*née* Chalmers), MBE; *m* 1974, Jenny Livingston; one *s* two *d*. *Educ:* Royal Belfast Academical Instn; Univ. of London (LLB); Queen's Univ., Belfast (LLM). Civil Servant, 1968–: Researcher, NI Cabinet Office, 1971–72, NI Office, 1972–73; Asst Private Sec. to Chief Minister, NI Power Sharing Exec., 1973–74; Private Sec. to Minister of State, NI Office, 1974–77; NI Office, 1977–80; seconded as Special Asst to Chief Constable, RUC, 1980–84; NI Office, 1984–88; Dir of Regimes, NI Prison Service, 1988–92; Hd, Political Affairs Div., NI Office, 1992–2000. Mem. Adv. Bd, Centre for Advancement of Women in Politics, QUB, 2001–. Gov., Victoria Coll., Belfast, 1989–. FRSA 2001. *Recreations:* golf, Rugby Union, reading, Anglo-Zulu War of 1879. *Address:* Windsor House, 9–15 Bedford Street, Belfast BT2 7EL. *T:* (028) 9044 3910. *Clubs:* Instonians Rugby, Dunmurry Golf (Belfast).

MacCABE, Prof. Colin Myles Joseph; Professor of English: University of Exeter, since 1998; University of Pittsburgh, since 1987; *b* 9 Feb. 1949; *s* of Myles Joseph MacCabe and Ruth Ward MacCabe; two *s* one *d*. *Educ:* Trinity College, Cambridge (BA English and Moral Scis 1971, MA 1974, PhD 1976); Ecole Normale Supérieure, 1972–73 (pensionnaire anglais). University of Cambridge: Research Fellow, Emmanuel College, 1974–76; Fellow, King's College, 1976–81; Asst Lectr, Faculty of English, 1976–81; Prof. of English Studies, 1981–85, Vis. Prof., 1985–91, Strathclyde Univ.; Head of Production, 1985–88, Head of Res., 1989–98, BFI. Chairman: John Logie Baird Centre for Research in Television and Film, 1985–91 (Dir, 1983–85); London Consortium, 1995–. Vis. Fellow, Sch. of Humanities, Griffith Univ., 1981, 1984; Mellon Vis. Prof., Univ. of Pittsburgh, 1985; Vis. Prof., Birkbeck Coll., Univ. of London, 1992–. Mem., Editl Bd, Screen, 1973–81; Editor, Critical Qly, 1990– (Critical Editor, 1987–90). *Publications:* James Joyce and the Revolution of the Word, 1979; Godard: Images, Sounds, Politics, 1980; (ed) The Talking Cure: essays in psychoanalysis and language, 1981; (ed) James

Joyce: new perspectives, 1982; Theoretical Essays: film, linguistics, literature, 1985; (ed jtly) The BBC and Public Sector Broadcasting, 1986; (ed) High Theory/Low Culture: analysing popular television and film, 1986; (ed) Futures for English, 1987; (ed jtly) The Linguistics of Writing, 1987; (with Isaac Julien) Diary of a Young Soul Rebel, 1991; (ed jtly) Who is Andy Warhol?, 1996; Performance, 1998; The Eloquence of the Vulgar, 1999. *Recreations:* eating, drinking, talking. *Address:* Department of English, University of Exeter, Exeter EX4 4QH. *T:* (01392) 264268.

McCABE, Eamonn Patrick; photographer; Picture Editor, The Guardian, 1988–2001; *b* 28 July 1948; *s* of James and Celia McCabe; *m* 1st, 1972, Ruth Calvert (marr. diss. 1993); one *s*; 2nd, 1997, Rebecca Smithers; one *d*. *Educ:* Challoner School, Finchley; San Francisco State Coll. FRPS 1990. Freelance photographer on local papers and with The Guardian for one year; staff photographer, The Observer, 1977–86 and 1987–88; official photographer for the Pope's visit to England, 1982; Picture Editor, Sportsweek, 1986–87. Dir, Newscast, 2001–. Hon. Prof., Thames Valley Univ., 1994. Fellow in Photography, Nat. Mus. of Photography and TV, Bradford, 1988. Sports photographer of the year, RPS and Sports Council, 1978, 1979, 1981, 1984; News photographer of the year, British Press Awards, 1985; Picture Editor of the Year, Nikon Press Awards, 1992, 1993, 1995, 1997, 1998. *Publications:* Sports Photographer, 1981; Eamonn McCabe, Photographer, 1987. *Recreations:* tennis, squash, cinema. *Address:* c/o The Guardian, 119 Farringdon Road, EC1R 3ER. *Club:* Chelsea Arts.

McCABE, John, CBE 1985; professional musician; composer and pianist; *b* 21 April 1939; *s* of Frank and Elisabeth McCabe; *m* 1974, Monica Christine Smith. *Educ:* Liverpool Institute High Sch. for Boys; Manchester Univ. (MusBac); Royal Manchester Coll. of Music (ARMCM); Hochschule für Musik, Munich. Pianist-in-residence, University Coll., Cardiff, 1965–68; freelance musical criticism, 1966–71. Career as composer and pianist: many broadcasts and recordings as well as concert appearances in various countries. Prizewinner in Gaudeamus Competition for Interpreters of Contemporary Music, Holland, 1969. Recordings incl. 12–CD set of complete piano music by Haydn; complete piano music of Nielsen (2 records). Awarded Special Citation by Koussevitsky Internat. Recording Foundn of USA, for recording of Symph. No 2 and Notturni ed Alba, 1974; Special Award by Composers' Guild of Gt Brit. (services to Brit. music), 1975; Ivor Novello Award (TV theme tune, Sam), 1977. Pres., ISM, 1983–84; Chm., Assoc. of Professional Composers, 1984–85. Hon. FRMCM; Hon. FLCM 1983; Hon. FRCM 1984; Hon. RAM 1985; Hon. FTCL 1989. *Compositions* include: five symphonies; two operas; five ballets, incl. Edward II, and Arthur, Pts 1 and 2; concerti; orchestral works incl. The Chagall Windows and Hartmann Variations, Notturni ed Alba, for soprano and orch., Fire at Durilgai for orch., Cloudcatcher Fells for brass band; chamber music; keyboard works; vocal compositions. *Publications:* Rachmaninov (short biog.), 1974; Bartok's Orchestral Music (BBC Music Guide), 1974; Haydn Piano Sonatas (Ariel Music Guide), 1986; Alan Rawsthorne: portrait of a composer, 1998. *Recreations:* cricket, snooker, books, films. *Address:* c/o Novello & Co. Ltd, Music Sales, 8–9 Frith Street, W1V 5TZ.

McCABE, Ven. (John) Trevor, RD 1976; Archdeacon of Cornwall, 1996–99, now Emeritus; *b* 26 Jan. 1933; *s* of John Leslie McCabe and Mary Ena McCabe; *m* 1959, Mary Thomas; three *s* one *d*. *Educ:* Falmouth Grammar Sch.; Nottingham Univ. (BA Hons); St Catherine's Coll., Oxford; Wycliffe Hall, Oxford (DipTh). Ordained, 1959; served Plymouth and Exeter; Vicar of Capel, Surrey, 1966–71; Chaplain, Isles of Scilly, 1971–81; Residentiary Canon, Bristol Cathedral, 1981–83; Vicar, Manaccan St Anthony and St Martin in Meneage, Helston, 1983–96; RD of Kerrier, 1987–90 and 1993–96; Hon. Canon of Truro, 1993–99. Chm., NHS Trust for Learning Disability, 1990–99. Served RNVR/RNR, 1955–57, 1963–83. *Recreations:* shrub gardening, local Cornish history. *Address:* Sunhill, School Lane, Budock, Falmouth TR11 5DG. *T:* (01326) 378095.

McCABE, Primrose Smith; *see* Scott, P. S.

McCABE, Stephen James; MP (Lab) Birmingham, Hall Green, since 1997; *b* 4 Aug. 1955; *s* of James and Margaret McCabe; *m* 1991, Lorraine Lea Clendon; one *s* one *d*. *Educ:* Univ. of Bradford (MA); Moray House Coll., Edinburgh (Dip. and CQSW). Social worker, Generic Team, 1977–79, Intermediate Treatment Worker, 1979–83, Wolverhampton; Manager, The Priory, Newbury, 1983–85; Lectr in Social Services, NE Worcs Coll., 1986–89; social policy researcher, BASW, and part-time child care worker, Solihull, 1989–91; Educn Advr, CCETSW, 1991–97. *Recreations:* cooking, hill-walking, reading, football. *Address:* House of Commons, SW1A 0AA. *T:* (020) 7219 3509.

McCABE, Thomas; Member (Lab) Hamilton South, Scottish Parliament, since 1999; Minister for Parliament and Chief Government Whip, since 1999; *b* 28 April 1954. *Educ:* St Martin's Secondary Sch., Hamilton; Bell Coll. of Technology, Hamilton (Dip. Public Sector Mgt). Light engrg, Hoover Factory, Cambuslang, 1974–93; Welfare Rights Officer, Strathclyde Regl Council and N Lanarks Council, 1993–98. Member (Lab): Hamilton DC, 1988–96 (Chm., Housing, 1990–92; Leader, 1992–96); S Lanarks Council, 1996–99 (Leader, 1996–99). *Recreations:* sport, reading, walking, cinema. *Address:* Hamilton South Constituency Office, 23 Beckford Street, Hamilton ML3 0BT. *T:* (01698) 454018; Scottish Parliament, George IV Bridge, Edinburgh EH99 1SP.

McCABE, Ven. Trevor; *see* McCabe, Ven. J. T.

McCAFFER, Prof. Ronald, FREng; Professor of Construction Management, since 1986, and Deputy Vice-Chancellor (formerly Senior Pro-Vice-Chancellor), since 1997, Loughborough University (formerly Loughborough University of Technology); Finance Director, European Construction Institute, since 1990; *b* 8 Dec. 1943; *s* of late John Gegg McCaffer and Catherine Turner (*née* Gourlay); *m* 1966, Margaret Elizabeth, *d* of late Cyril Warner and of Mary Huntley (*née* Mason); one *s*. *Educ:* Albert Sch., Glasgow; Univ. of Strathclyde (BSc 1965; DSc 1998); PhD Loughborough 1977. FICE 1988; FCIOB 1988; MIMgt (MBIM 1989); FREng (FEng 1991); Eur Ing 1990; MASCE 1999. Design Engr, Babtie, Shaw & Morton, 1965–67; Site Engineer: Nuclear Power Gp, 1967–69; Taylor Woodrow Construction Ltd, 1969–70; Loughborough University of Technology: Lectr, 1970–78; Sen. Lectr, 1978–83; Reader, 1983–86; Head of Civil Engrg, 1987–93; Dean of Engineering, 1992–97. Chm., Loughborough University Utilities Ltd, 1997–; Director: Loughborough Consultants Ltd, 1997–; Peterborough HE Co. Ltd, 1997–; Innovative Projects Worldwide Ltd, 1998–. Mem., Programme Cttee, 1992–95, Educn, Trng and Competence to Practice Cttee, 1995–98, Strategy Rev. Gp, 1996, Royal Acad. of Engrg. Member: Engrg Construction Industry Trng Bd, 1994–; Technical Opportunities Panel, EPSRC, 2000–; Civil Engrg Panel, 2001 RAE; Associate Parly Gp for Engrg Develt, 1995–. Visiting Professor: Univ. of Moratuwa, Sri Lanka, 1986–92; Technol Univ. of Malaysia, 1996, 2000. Moderating Examr, Engrg Council, 1988–92; past and present examr, univs in UK and overseas. Editor, Engineering, Construction and Architectural Management, 1994–. *Publications:* Modern Construction Management, 1977, 5th edn 2000; Worked Examples in Construction Management, 1978, 2nd edn 1986; Estimating and Tendering for Civil Engineering Works, 1984, 2nd edn 1991; Management of Construction Equipment, 1982, 2nd edn 1991; International Bid Preparation, 1995; International Bidding Case Study, 1995; jl articles and conf. papers. *Recreations:* bad golf, jogging, being patient with administrators. *Address:* Department of Civil Engineering, Loughborough University, Loughborough, Leics LE11 3TU. *T:* (01509) 222600, *Fax:* (01509) 223980; *e-mail:* r.mccaffer@lut.ac.uk.

McCAFFERTY, Christine; MP (Lab) Calder Valley, since 1997; *b* 14 Oct. 1945; *d* of late John and Dorothy Livesley; *m* 1st, Michael McCafferty; one *s*; 2nd, David Tarlo. *Educ:* Whalley Grange Grammar Sch. for Girls, Manchester; Footscray High Sch., Melbourne. Welfare Worker (Disabled), CHS Manchester, 1963–70; Educn Welfare Officer, Manchester Educn Cttee, 1970–72; Registrar of Marriages, Bury Registration Dist, 1978–80; Project worker, Calderdale Well Women Centre, 1989–96. Member: Calderdale MBC, 1991–97; W Yorks Police Authy, 1994–97. Chair, All Pty Gp on Population, Develt and Reproductive Health, 1999–; Mem., Council of Europe/WEU, 1999–. Chair, APG Guides. Dir, Royd Regeneration Ltd. Mem. Exec., N Reg. Assoc. for the Blind, 1993–96. Gov., Luddenden Dene Sch. *Address:* House of Commons, SW1A 0AA.

McCAFFREY, Anne Inez; writer; *b* 1 April 1926; *d* of George H. McCaffrey and Anne Dorothy McElroy-McCaffrey; *m* 1950, H. Wright Johnson (marr. diss. 1970); two *s* one *d*. *Educ:* Stuart Hall Secondary Sch., Radcliffe Coll., Harvard Univ. (BA *cum laude* 1947). Advertising copywriter and layout artist, Liberty Music Shops, NYC, 1948–50; copywriter, then Sec. to Sales Manager, Helena Rubinstein, 1950–52. Established Equine Centre, Dragonhold Stables, Co. Wicklow, 1977. Numerous awards, including: Golden Pen Award, 1982; Science Fiction Book Club Awards, 1986, 1989, 1990, 1992, 1993, 1994, 1997; Margaret A. Edwards Award for Lifetime Literary Achievement, Amer. Liby Assoc., 1999. *Publications:* Restoree, 1967; Dragonflight, 1968; Decision at Doona, 1969; (ed) Alchemy & Academe, 1970; The Ship Who Sang, 1970; Mark of Merlin, 1971; Dragonquest-2, 1971; Ring of Fear, 1971; To Ride Pegasus, 1973; Out of This World Cookbook, 1973; The White Dragon, 1975; Kilternan Legacy, 1975; Dragonsong, 1976; Dragonsinger, 1977; Get off the Unicorn, 1977; The White Dragon-3, 1978; Dinosaur Planet, 1978; Dragondrums C, 1979; Crystal Singer, 1982; The Coelura, 1983; Moreta, Dragonlady of Pern, 1983; Dinosaur Planet Survivors, 1984; Stitch in Snow, 1984; Killashandra, 1985; The Girl who Heard Dragons, 1986; The Year of the Lucy, 1986; Nerilka's Story, 1986; The Carradyne Touch, 1988 (US edn as The Lady); Dragonsdawn, 1988; Pern Portrait Gallery, 1988; Guidebook to Pern (ed. J.-L. Nye and W. Fawcett), 1989; Renegades of Pern, 1989; Pegasus in Flight, 1990; The Rowan, 1990; All the Weyrs of Pern, 1991; Damia, 1992; Crystal Line, 1992; (with M. Lackey) The Ship who Searched, 1992; Damia's Children, 1993; (with S. M. Stirling) The City who Fought, 1993; Chronicles of Pern: First Fall, 1993; Lyon's Pride, 1994; The Dolphins of Pern, 1994; The Girl who Heard Dragons (anthology) 1994; An Exchange of Gifts, 1995; Freedom's Landing, 1995; Black Horses for the King, 1996; A Diversity of Dragons, 1997; Dragonseye (UK title: Red Star Rising), 1997; Freedom's Choice, 1997; Masterharper of Pern, 1998; Freedom's Challenge, 1998; If Wishes Were Horses, 1998; Nimisha's Ship, 1999; The Tower & The Hive, 1999; Pegasus in Space-3, 2000; Skies of Pern, 2001; with J.-L. Nye: Crisis at Doona, 1992; Treaty Planet, 1994; Ship Who Won, 1994; with M. Ball: The Partner Ship, 1992; Acorna, 1997; Acorna's Quest, 1998; with E. A. Scarborough: Powers that Be, 1993; Power Lines, 1994; Power Play, 1995; books trans. into numerous foreign langs and Braille. *Recreations:* equine events, raising Maine Coon cats. *Address:* Dragonhold-Underhill, Newcastle, Co. Wicklow, Ireland. *Club:* Sloane.

McCAFFREY, Sir Thos Daniel, (Sir Tom), Kt 1979; public affairs consultant; *b* 20 Feb. 1922; *s* of William P. and B. McCaffrey; *m* 1949, Agnes Campbell Douglas; two *s* four *d*. *Educ:* Hyndland Secondary Sch. and St Aloysius Coll., Glasgow. Served War, RAF, 1940–46. Scottish Office, 1948–61; Chief Information Officer, Home Office, 1966–71; Press Secretary, 10 Downing Street, 1971–72; Dir of Information Services, Home Office, 1972–74; Head of News Dept, FCO, 1974–76; Chief Press Sec. to Prime Minister, 1976–79; Chief of Staff to Rt Hon. James Callaghan, MP, 1979–80; Chief Asst to Rt Hon. Michael Foot, MP, 1980–83; Hd, Chief Executive's Office, BPCC, 1983–84; Dir, Public Affairs, and Special Advr to the Publisher, Mirror Gp Newspapers, 1984–85. *Address:* Balmaha, 2 The Park, Great Bookham, Surrey KT23 3JL. *T:* (01372) 454171.

McCAHILL, Patrick Gerard, QC 1996; **His Honour Judge McCahill;** a Circuit Judge, since 2001; *b* 6 May 1952; *s* of John McCahill and Josephine McCahill (*née* Conaghan); *m* 1979, Liselotte Gabrielle Steiner; two *d*. *Educ:* Corby GS; St Catharine's Coll., Cambridge (1st cl. Hons; MA). FCIArb 1992. Called to the Bar, Gray's Inn, 1975 (Bacon Schol., 1973; Atkin Schol., 1975), King's Inns, Dublin, 1990; Asst Dep. Coroner for Birmingham and Solihull, 1984–99; Asst Recorder, 1993–97; a Recorder, 1997–2001. *Recreations:* humour, photography, family history. *Address:* Wolverhampton Combined Court Centre, Pipers Row, Wolverhampton WV1 3LQ.

McCALL, Sir (Charles) Patrick (Home), Kt 1971; MBE 1944; TD 1946; solicitor; Clerk of the County Council, 1960–72, Clerk of the Peace, 1960–71, and Clerk of the Lieutenancy, Lancashire, 1960–74; *b* 22 Nov. 1910; *s* of late Charles and Dorothy McCall; *m* 1934, Anne (*d* 1991), *d* of late Samuel Brown, Sedlescombe, Sussex; two *s* one *d*. *Educ:* St Edward's Sch., Oxford. Served 1939–45; Substantive Major TA. Hon. Lt-Col. Mem., Economic and Social Cttee, EEC, 1973–78. *Address:* 211–6085 Uplands Drive, Nanaimo, BC V9V IT8, Canada.

McCALL, Christopher Hugh; QC 1987; *b* 3 March 1944; *yr s* of late Robin Home McCall, CBE and Joan Elizabeth (*née* Kingdon); *m* 1981, Henrietta Francesca Sharpe. *Educ:* Winchester (Scholar); Magdalen Coll., Oxford (Demy; BA Maths, 1964; Eldon Law Scholar, 1966). Called to the Bar, Lincoln's Inn, 1966, Bencher, 1993. Second Jun. Counsel to the Inland Revenue in chancery matters, 1977–87; Jun. Counsel to Attorney Gen. in charity matters, 1981–87. Mem, Bar Council, 1973–76. Trustee, British Mus., 1999–. *Recreations:* music, travel, Egyptomania. *Address:* Maitland Chambers, 7 Stone Buildings, Lincoln's Inn, WC2A 3SZ. *T:* (020) 7406 1200; Sphinx Hill, Ferry Lane, Moulsford on Thames OX10 9JF. *T:* (01491) 652162. *Clubs:* Alpine; Leander (Henley-on-Thames).

McCALL, David Slesser, CBE 1988; DL; Chairman, Anglia Television Ltd, 1994–2001 (Director, 1970–2001; Chief Executive, 1976–94); *b* 3 Dec. 1934; *s* of Patrick McCall and Florence Kate Mary Walker; *m* 1968, Lois Patricia Elder. *Educ:* Robert Gordon's Coll., Aberdeen. Mem., Inst. of Chartered Accountants of Scotland, 1958. National Service, 1959–61. Accountant, Grampian Television Ltd, 1961–68; Company Sec., Anglia Television Ltd, 1968–76; Dir, 1970–98, Chief Exec., 1986–94, Chm., 1994–98, Anglia Television Gp. Chairman: Oxford Scientific Films Ltd, 1982–89; Greene King plc, 1995–; United Trustees Ltd, 1997–; Director: ITN, 1978–86, 1991–96; Ind. Television Publications Ltd, 1971–89; Ind. Television Assoc. Ltd, 1976–96; Sodastream Holdings Ltd, 1976–85; Norwich City Football Club, 1979–85; Channel Four Television Co., 1981–85; Radio Broadland, 1984–91; Super Channel Ltd, 1986–88; British Satellite Broadcasting, 1987–90; Regl Adv. Bd, National Westminster Bank, 1988–92; TSMS Group Ltd, 1989–96; Hodder & Stoughton Holdings Ltd, 1992–93; Cosgrove Hall Films, 1993–96; MAI plc, 1994–96; MAI Media UK Ltd, 1995–96; Meridian Broadcasting Ltd, 1994–96; Satellite Inf. Services, 1994–96; Village Roadshow Ltd, Australia, 1994–96;

Bakers Dozen Inns Ltd, 1996–; Anglia FM Ltd, 1996–99; Anglo Welsh Group PLC, 1996–2000; Bernard Matthews Gp PLC, 1996–2000; Granada Pension Trust Co. Ltd, 2000–. Chm., Norfolk and Norwich Millennium Bid, 1996–; Dep. Chm., United Broadcasting and Entertainment, 1996. Mem., ITCA, subseq. Ind. Television Assoc., 1976–95 (Chm., 1986–88); Pres., Cinema and Television Benevolent Fund, 1998– (Trustee, 1995–). Pres., Norfolk and Norwich Chamber of Commerce, 1988–90 (Dep. Pres., 1986–88); Chm., Norwich Playhouse Theatre, 1992–98. Treas., 1995–97, Chm. Council, 1997–, UEA. FRTS 1988; FRSA 1993. CIMgt (CBIM 1988). DL Norfolk, 1992. *Recreations:* sport, travel. *Address:* Woodland Hall, Redenhall, Harleston, Norfolk IP20 9QW. *T:* (01379) 854442.

McCALL, John Armstrong Grice, CMG 1964; *b* 7 Jan. 1913; 2nd *s* of Rev. Canon J. G. McCall; *m* 1951, Kathleen Mary Clarke; no *c. Educ:* Glasgow Academy; Trinity Coll., Glenalmond; St Andrews Univ.; St John's Coll., Cambridge. MA 1st class hons Hist. St Andrews, 1935. Colonial Administrative Service (HMOCS), Nigeria, 1935–67; Cadet, 1936; Class I, 1956; Staff Grade, 1958. Chm., Mid-Western Nigeria Development Corp., Benin City, 1966–67, retired 1967. Asst Chief Admin. Officer, East Kilbride Develt Corp., 1967–76. Scottish Rep., Executive Cttee, Nigerian-British Chamber of Commerce, 1977–88. Mem. 1969, Vice-Chm. 1971, S Lanarkshire Local Employment Cttee; Mem. Panel, Industrial Tribunals (Scotland), 1972–74; Gen. Sec., Scotland, Royal Over-Seas League, 1978–80. Sec., West Linton Community Council, 1980–83. *Recreations:* golf, walking. *Address:* Burnside, West Linton, Peeblesshire EH46 7EW. *T:* (01968) 660488. *Clubs:* Caledonian, Royal Over-Seas League (Hon. Life Mem.); Old Glenalmond (Chm., 1978–81); Royal and Ancient (St Andrews).

McCALL, John Donald; Director, Consolidated Gold Fields Ltd, 1959–81 (Chairman, 1969–76); *b* 1 Feb. 1911; *s* of late Gilbert Kerr McCall; *m* 1942, Vere Stewart Gardner; one *s* one *d. Educ:* Clifton Coll.; Edinburgh Univ. Gold Mining industry, S Africa, 1930–39. Served War of 1939–45: commissioned, Gordon Highlanders. Joined Consolidated Gold Fields Ltd, London, 1946 (Dir, 1959; Jt Dep. Chm., 1968). Dir, Ultramar plc, 1965–79. *Address:* 64 Pont Street, SW1X 0AE. *Club:* Caledonian.

McCALL, Sir Patrick; *see* McCall, Sir C. P. H.

McCALL, William; General Secretary, Institution of Professional Civil Servants, 1963–89; *b* 6 July 1929; *s* of Alexander McCall and Jean Corbet Cunningham; *m* 1955, Olga Helen Brunton; one *s* one *d. Educ:* Dumfries Academy; Ruskin College, Oxford. Civil Service, 1946–52; Social Insurance Dept, TUC, 1954–58; Asst Sec., Instn of Professional Civil Servants, 1958–63; Mem., Civil Service Nat. Whitley Council (Staff Side), 1963–89, Chm. 1969–71, Vice-Chm. 1983. Hon. Treasurer, Parly and Scientific Cttee, 1976–80; Part-time Mem., Eastern Electricity Board, 1977–86; Member: Cttee of Inquiry into Engrg Profession, 1977–79; PO Arbitration Tribunal, 1980–90; TUC Gen. Council, 1984–89; Pay and Employment Policy Cttee, CVCP, 1990–94; Police Complaints Authority, 1991–94. Member Council: Univ. of London, 1994–97 (Mem. Ct, 1984–94); Goldsmiths' Coll., 1989–95 (Hon. Fellow, 1996). *Address:* Foothills, Gravel Path, Berkhamsted, Herts HP4 2PF. *T:* (01442) 864974.

McCALL, Rt Rev. William David Hair; *see* Bunbury, Bishop of.

McCALLUM, Alastair Grindlay; His Honour Judge McCallum; a Circuit Judge, since 1992; *b* 28 Feb. 1947; *s* of William and Catherine McCallum; *m* 1969, Lindsay Sheila Watkins; two *d. Educ:* Gilbert Rennie, Northern Rhodesia; Leeds Univ. (LLB, LLM (Com.)). Called to the Bar, Inner Temple, 1970; Asst Recorder, 1984; Recorder, 1989; Head of Chambers, 1990. *Recreations:* golf, travel, reading. *T:* (01274) 840274. *Clubs:* Bradford Golf (Hawksworth); Applegarth.

MacCALLUM, Prof. Charles Hugh Alexander, RIBA; FRIAS; Professor of Architecture, Glasgow University, and Head, Mackintosh School of Architecture, Glasgow School of Art, 1994–2000, now Emeritus Professor; architect in private practice, since 1973; *b* Glasgow, 24 June 1935; *s* of Alister Hugh McCallum, Pitlochry, and Jessie McLean (*née* Forsyth), Perth; *m* 1963, Andrée Simone Tonnard; two *d. Educ:* Hutchesons' Grammar Sch.; Glasgow Sch. of Architecture (DA); Massachusetts Inst. of Technol. (MCP 1969). RIBA 1961; FRIAS 2001. Architect, Gillespie Kidd & Coia, Glasgow, 1957–67; Sen. Architect, Dept of Architecture and Planning, Clydebank, 1969–70; Statutory Lectr, later Exec. Dir, Sch. of Architecture, University Coll., Dublin, 1969–73; Prof. of Architectural Design, Welsh Sch. of Architecture, Univ. of Wales Coll. of Cardiff, 1986–94. Mem. Cttee, Franco-British Union of Architects, 2000–. *Recreations:* gardening, watercolours. *Publications:* (with Françoise Hamon) Louis Visconti 1791–1853, 1991; articles on architectural and engrg, in UK, France and Russia. *Address:* 11A Charlbury Road, Oxford OX2 6UT.

McCALLUM, Sir Donald (Murdo), Kt 1988; CBE 1976; FREng; FRSE; DL; General Manager, Scottish Group, 1968–85, and Director, 1970–87, Ferranti plc; Chairman, Laser Ecosse Ltd, 1990–95; *b* 6 Aug. 1922; *s* of Roderick McCallum and Lillian (*née* McPhee); *m* 1st, 1949, Barbara Black (*d* 1971); one *d*; 2nd, 1974, Mrs Margaret Illingworth (*née* Broadbent) (*d* 1997). *Educ:* George Watson's Boys' Coll.; Edinburgh Univ. (BSc). FIEE 1969; FREng (FEng 1982); FRAeS 1986; Hon. FRSGS 1993; CIMgt (CBIM 1983). Admiralty Signal Establishment, 1942–46; Standard Telecommunication Laboratories, 1946; Ferranti Ltd, 1947: Chairman: Ferranti Defence Systems Ltd, 1984–87 (Hon. Pres., 1987–90); Ferranti Industrial Electronics, 1984–87 (Hon. Pres., 1987–90). Dir, Short Bros Ltd, 1981–89; Chairman: Scottish Tertiary Education Adv. Council, 1984–87; Scottish Council Develt & Industry, 1985–91 (Pres., 1991–93; Fellow, 1993). Scottish Sub-Cttee, UGC, 1987–88; Member: UFC, 1989–91 (Chm., Scottish Cttee, 1989–91); Scottish Econ. Council, 1983–92. Member: Court, Heriot-Watt Univ., 1979–85; Governing Body, Napier Polytechnic, 1988–93; Court, Napier Univ., 1993–95; Governing Body, Edinburgh Coll. of Art, 1988–93; Bd of Trustees, Nat. Liby of Scotland, 1990–96. Hon. Life Mem., Edinburgh Univ. Students' Assoc., 1984. Liveryman, Company of Engineers, 1984; Freeman, City of London. DL City of Edinburgh, 1984. Hon. Fellow, Paisley Coll. of Technol., 1987; Fellow, SCOTVEC, 1988. DUniv Stirling, 1985; Hon. DSc: Heriot-Watt, 1986; Napier Coll. of Commerce and Technology, Edinburgh, 1986; Hon. LLD: Strathclyde, 1987; Aberdeen, 1989. British Gold Medal, RAeS, 1985. *Recreations:* photography, reading. *Address:* The Cottage, 14 Rockwood Road, Calverley, Pudsey, LS28 5AA. *T:* (0113) 256 9701. *Clubs:* Caledonian; New (Edinburgh).

McCALLUM, Googie, (Mrs John McCallum); *see* Withers, G.

McCALLUM, Helen Mary; Director of Communications, Department of Health, since 1999; *b* 23 Dec. 1952; *d* of Edward James Ward and Pauline Ward; *m* 1980, Duncan Peter Finlay McCallum; two *d. Educ:* Queen Elizabeth's Girls' Grammar Sch., Barnet; Nottingham Univ. (BA Hons English Lit.). Sabbatical Sec., Students' Union, Univ. of Nottingham, 1973–74; Admin. Asst (PR), Univ. of Sheffield, 1974–78; PRO, Univ. of Salford, 1978–81; freelance publications work, 1981–85; Alumni Officer, Univ. of Sheffield, 1985–88; Sen. PR Manager, 1989–92, Hd of Communications, 1992–94, E Anglian RHA; Hd of Communications, NHS Exec., 1994–98. Mem., Assoc. of Health Care Communicators, 1989. *Recreations:* amateur dramatics, keeping moderately fit. *Address:* 79 Gilbert Road, Cambridge CB4 3NZ.

McCALLUM, Ian Stewart; Executive Sales Manager, Save & Prosper Sales Ltd, 1989–95 (Sales Manager, 1985–87, Area Manager, 1987–89); *b* 24 Sept. 1936; *s* of late John Blair McCallum and Margaret Stewart McCallum; *m* 1st, 1957, Pamela Mary (*née* Shave) (marr. diss. 1984); one *s* two *d*; 2nd, 1984, Jean (*née* Lynch); two step *d. Educ:* Kingston Grammar Sch. Eagle Star Insurance Co. Ltd, 1953–54; National Service, Highland Light Infantry, 1954–56; Eagle Star Insce Co. Ltd, 1956–58; F. E. Wright and Co., Insurance Brokers, 1958–63; H. Clarkson (Home) Ltd, Insurance Brokers, 1963–68; Save & Prosper Group Ltd, 1968–95. Leader, Woking Borough Council, 1972–76 and 1978–81, Dep. Leader, 1981–82; Mayor of Woking, 1976–77; Chm., Assoc. of Dist Councils, 1979–84 (Leader, 1974–79); Vice-Chairman: Standing Cttee on Local Authorities and Theatre, 1977–81; UK Steering Cttee on Local Authority Superannuation, 1974–84; Member: Local Authorities Conditions of Service Adv. Bd, 1973–84; Consultative Council on Local Govt Finance, 1975–84; Council for Business in the Community, 1981–84; Audit Commn, 1983–86; Health Promotion Res. Trust, 1983–97. Vice-Chm., Sports Council, 1980–86. *Recreations:* swimming, jogging, walking, reading, bowls. *Address:* 5 Minters Orchard, Maidstone Road, St Marys Platt, near Sevenoaks, Kent TN15 8JQ. *T:* (01732) 883653.

McCALLUM, John Neil, AO 1992; CBE 1971; Chairman and Executive Producer, Fauna Films, Australia, since 1967, and John McCallum Productions, since 1976; actor and producer; *b* 14 March 1918; *s* of John Neil McCallum and Lilian Elsie (*née* Dyson); *m* 1948, Georgette Lizette Withers (*see* Googie Withers); one *s* two *d. Educ:* Oatlands Prep. Sch., Harrogate; Knox Grammar Sch., Sydney; C of E Grammar Sch., Brisbane; RADA. Served War, 2/5 Field Regt, AIF, 1941–45. Actor, English rep. theatres, 1937–39; Stratford-on-Avon Festival Theatre, 1939; Old Vic Theatre, 1940; British films and theatre, 1946–58; films include: It Always Rains On Sunday; Valley of Eagles; Miranda; London stage plays include: Roar Like a Dove; Janus; Waiting for Gillian; J. C. Williamson Theatres Ltd, Australia: Asst Man. Dir, 1958; Jt. Man. Dir, 1959–65; Man. Dir, 1966. Appeared in: (with Ingrid Bergman) The Constant Wife, London, 1973–74; (with Googie Withers) The Circle, London, 1976–77, Australia, 1982–83; (with Googie Withers) The Kingfisher, Australia, 1978–79; The Skin Game, The Cherry Orchard, and Dandy Dick, theatrical tour, England, 1981; The School for Scandal, British Council European tour, 1984; (with Googie Withers, and dir.) Stardust, tours England, 1984, Australia, 1984–85; The Chalk Garden, Chichester Fest., 1986; Hay Fever, Chichester Fest., 1988; The Royal Baccarat Scandal, Chichester Fest., 1988, Haymarket, 1989; (with Googie Withers) The Cocktail Hour, Australian and UK tour, 1989–90; (with Googie Withers) High Spirits, Australia, 1991; On Golden Pond, UK tour, 1992; The Chalk Garden, Sydney, 1995; An Ideal Husband, Old Vic, 1996, Australia, 1997–98; Lady Windermere's Fan, Chichester, 1997; A Busy Day, Bristol Old Vic and Lyric, London, 2000. Author of play, As It's Played Today, produced Melbourne, 1974. Produced television series, 1967–: Boney; Barrier Reef; Skippy; Bailey's Bird. Prod., Attack Force Z (feature film), 1980; Exec. Prod., The Highest Honor (feature film), 1982. Pres., Aust. Film Council, 1971–72. *Publication:* Life with Googie, 1979. *Recreation:* golf. *Address:* 1740 Pittwater Road, Bayview, NSW 2104, Australia. *T:* (2) 99976879. *Clubs:* Garrick, MCC; Melbourne (Melbourne); Australian, Elanora Country (Sydney).

McCALLUM, Martin; Chairman, Donmar Warehouse Theatre, since 1996; Vice Chairman, Cameron Mackintosh Ltd, since 2000; *b* 6 April 1950; *s* of Raymond and Jessie Higgins; adopted stage name of McCallum; *m* 1st, 1972, Lesley Nunnerley (marr. diss.); one *s* one *d*; 2nd, 1986, Julie Edmett (marr. diss.); one *d*; 3rd, 1989, Mary Ann Rolfe; two *s. Educ:* Barfield Sch., Surrey; Frensham Heights Sch., Surrey. Entered theatre as student asst stage manager, Castle Th., Farnham, 1967; worked throughout rep. system; Prodn Manager, NT at Old Vic, 1971–75, moved to S Bank, 1975; founded The Production Office, West End, 1978; Man. Dir, Cameron Mackintosh Ltd, 1981-2000. Pres., SOLT, 1999–. Member: Drama Panel, Arts Council of England, 1999; London's Cultural Strategy Gp, 2000–. FRSA, 1995. Mem., League of Amer. Theatres and Producers, 1988–. *Recreations:* the performing arts, music, art, gardening, running, ski-ing, travel.

MacCALLUM, Very Rev. Norman Donald; Provost of St John's Cathedral, Oban, and Priest-in-charge, St James', Ardbrecknish and Church of the Holy Spirit, Ardchattan, since 2000; *b* 26 April 1947; *s* of James MacCallum and Euphemia MacCallum (*née* Campbell); *m* 1972, Barbara MacColl Urquhart; one *s* one *d. Educ:* St John's Episcopal Sch., Ballachulish; Kinlochleven Jun. Secondary Sch.; Oban High Sch.; Edinburgh Univ. (LTh 1970); Edinburgh Theol Coll. Midlothian, E Lothian and Peebles Social Work Dept, 1970; ordained deacon, 1971, priest, 1972; Livingston Ecumenical Experiment, 1971–82; Rector, St Mary's, Grangemouth, and Priest-in-charge, St Catharine's, Bo'ness, 1982–2000; Synod Clerk, Dio. Edinburgh and Canon of St Mary's Cathedral, Edinburgh, 1996–2000. Adminr, Scottish Episcopal Clergy Appraisal Scheme, 1997–; Mem., Scottish Religious Adv. Cttee, BBC Scotland, 1997–. *Recreations:* hill-walking, photography, history. *Address:* The Rectory, Ardconnel Terrace, Oban PA34 5DJ. *T:* (01631) 562323; *e-mail:* provostoban@argyll.anglican.org.

McCALLUM, Prof. Robert Ian, CBE 1987; MD, DSc; FRCP, FRCPEd, FFOM; Hon. Consultant, Institute of Occupational Medicine, Edinburgh, since 1985; Emeritus Professor, University of Newcastle upon Tyne, since 1985; *b* 14 Sept. 1920; *s* of Charles Hunter McCallum and Janet Lyon Smith; *m* 1952, Jean Katherine Bundy Learmonth, MBE; two *s* two *d. Educ:* Dulwich Coll., London; Guy's Hosp., London Univ. (MD 1946; DSc 1971). FRCP 1970; FRCPEd 1985; FFOM 1979. Ho. phys., ho. surgeon, Guy's Hosp., 1943; ho. phys., Brompton Hosp., 1945. Rockefeller Travelling Fellowship in Medicine (MRC), USA, 1953–54. Reader in Industrial Health, 1962–81, Prof. of Occupational Health and Hygiene, 1981–85, Univ. of Newcastle upon Tyne. Hon. Physician, Industrial Medicine, Royal Victoria Infirmary, Newcastle upon Tyne, 1958–85; Hon. Consultant in Occ. Health to the Army, 1980–86. Mem., MRC Decompression Sickness Panel, 1962– (Chm., 1982–85); Chm., Health Adv. Cttee, CEGB, 1987–89. British Council: Vis. Consultant, USSR, 1977; Vis. Specialist, Istanbul, 1987; Vis. Lectr, Faculty of Medicine, Baghdad, 1987. Stanley Melville Meml Lectr, Coll. of Radiographers, 1983; Sydenham Lectr, Soc. of Apothecaries, London, 1983; Ernestine Henry Lectr, RCP, 1987. Dean, Faculty of Occ. Medicine, RCP, 1984–86; President: Sect. of Occ. Medicine, RSM, 1976–77; Soc. of Occ. Medicine, 1979–80; British Occ. Hygiene Soc., 1983–84; Mem., Adv. Cttee on Pesticides, 1975–87. Hon. Dir, North of England Industrial Health Service, 1975–84. Editor, British Jl of Industrial Medicine, 1973–79. FSAScot 1997. *Publications:* papers on pneumoconiosis, decompression sickness, dysbaric bone necrosis, and antimony toxicology. *Recreations:* gardening, swimming. *Address:* 4 Chessels Court, Canongate, Edinburgh EH8 8AD. *T:* (0131) 556 7977. *Club:* Royal Society of Medicine.

McCAMLEY, Sir Graham (Edward), KBE 1986 (MBE 1981); owner, cattle properties, since 1954; *b* 24 Aug. 1932; *s* of Edward William George and Ivy McCamley; *m* 1956, Shirley Clarice Tindale; one *s* two *d. Educ:* Rockhampton Grammar Sch. President: Aust.

Brahman Breeders, 1971–74; Central Coastal Graziers, 1974–75; Cattlemen's Union of Australia, 1976–78. Mem. Producer of Australian Meat and Livestock Co., 1982–84; Chm., Beeflands Australia Pty Ltd, 1994–97. *Recreations:* tennis, flying helicopter and fixed wing aircraft. *Clubs:* Queensland (Brisbane); Rockhampton, Rockhampton and District Masonic.

MAC CANA, Prof. Proinsias; Senior Professor, School of Celtic Studies, Dublin Institute for Advanced Studies, 1985–96, now Senior Professor Emeritus; *b* 6 July 1926; *s* of George Mc Cann and Mary Catherine Mallon; *m* 1952, Réiltín (*née* Supple); one *s* one *d*. *Educ:* St Malachy's Coll., Belfast; The Queen's Univ., Belfast (BA, MA, PhD); Ecole des Hautes Etudes, Paris. Asst Lectr, Celtic Dept, QUB, 1951–54; University College Wales, Aberystwyth: Asst Lectr in Early Irish, 1955–57; Lectr, 1957–61; Prof., Sch. of Celtic Studies, Dublin Inst. for Advanced Studies, 1961–63; Prof. of Welsh, 1963–71, Prof. of Early (incl. Medieval) Irish, 1971–85, UC Dublin. Prof. of Celtic Langs and Lits (Fall semester), Harvard Univ., 1987–92. Mem., Irish Placenames Commn, 1975–. Co-editor, Ériu (RIA Jl of Irish Studies), 1973–; General editor, Medieval and Modern Welsh Series, Dublin Inst. for Advanced Studies, 1962–; Chairman, Editorial Board: Dictionary of Medieval Latin in Celtic Countries, 1981–; Dictionary of Irish Biography, 1985–. Chm., Governing Bd, Sch. of Celtic Studies, Dublin Inst. for Advanced Studies, 1975–85. PRIA, 1979–82. Mem., Academia Europaea, 1989. Foreign Hon. Member: Amer. Acad. Arts and Scis, 1989; Royal Gustavus Adolphus Acad., Sweden, 1994. Hon. LittD Dublin, 1985; Hon. DLitt: Ulster, 1991; Wales, 1995. *Publications:* Scéalaíocht na Ríthe (collection of early Irish tales trans. into Modern Irish), 1956; Branwen Daughter of Llŷr: the second branch of the Mabinogi, 1958; Celtic Mythology, 1970; The Mabinogi, 1977; Regnum and Sacerdotium: notes on Irish Tradition (Rhŷs Meml Lecture, British Academy), 1979; The Learned Tales of Medieval Ireland, 1980; (ed jtly) Rencontres de Religions, 1986; (ed jtly) Mélusines continentales et insulaires, 1999; Collège des Irlandais Paris and Irish Studies, 2001. *Address:* 9 Silchester Road, Glenageary, Co. Dublin, Ireland. *T:* (1) 2805062. *Club:* Kildare Street and University (Dublin).

McCANDLESS, Air Vice-Marshal Brian Campbell, CB 1999; CBE 1990; FRAeS; FIEE; Air Officer Communications and Information Systems, and Air Officer Commanding Signals Units, 1996–99; *b* 14 May 1944; *s* of Norman Samuel McCandless and Rebecca Campbell; *m* 1969, Yvonne Haywood; one *s*. *Educ:* Methodist Coll., Belfast; RAF Tech. Coll., Henlow (BSc 1967); Birmingham Univ (MSc 1972); RAF Staff Coll. RAF, 1962–99: posts included: OC 26 Signals Unit, 1985–87; OC RAF Henlow, 1987–89; Dep. Chief, Architecture and Plans Div., NATO CIS Agency, Brussels, 1989–92; Dir, Comd Control and Management Inf. Systems, RAF, 1992–93; Dir, Communications and Inf. Systems, RAF, 1993–95. e-Govt Dir, Oracle Corp., 1999–2001. *Recreations:* bridge, music, sailing, hill walking. *Club:* Royal Air Force.

McCANN, Peter Toland McAree, CBE 1977; JP; DL; Lord Provost of the City of Glasgow and Lord-Lieutenant of the City of Glasgow, 1975–77; *b* 2 Aug. 1924; *s* of Peter McCann and Agnes (*née* Waddell); *m* 1958, Maura Eleanor (*née* Ferris); one *s*. *Educ:* St Mungo's Academy; Glasgow Univ. (BL). Solicitor and Notary Public. Pres., Glasgow Univ. Law Soc., 1946; Pres., St Thomas More Soc., 1959. Mem. Glasgow Corp., 1961. Chm., McCann Cttee (Secondary Educn for Physically Handicapped Children), 1971. DL Glasgow, 1978. OStJ 1977. Silver Sword, 1976, Golden Sword, 1977, City of Jeddah; Medal of King Faisal of Saudi Arabia, 1976; two Golden Swords, Royal House of Saudi Arabia, 1978. *Recreations:* music, history, model aeroplane making. *Address:* 31 Queen Mary Avenue, Glasgow G42 8DS.

McCARRAHER, His Honour David, VRD 1964; a Circuit Judge, 1984–95; *b* 6 Nov. 1922; *s* of Colin McCarraher and Vera Mabel McCarraher (*née* Hickley); *m* 1950, Betty Johnson (*née* Haywood) (*d* 1990); one *s* three *d*. *Educ:* King Edward VI Sch., Southampton; Magdalene Coll., Cambridge (MA Law). RN, 1941–45. Called to the Bar, Lincoln's Inn, 1948; practised Western Circuit until 1952, disbarred at own request to be articled; admitted solicitor, 1955; Sen. Partner in private practice, 1960–84; a Recorder, 1979–84. Mem. Panel, Dep. Circuit Judges, 1973–79. Pres., Hampshire Incorporated Law Soc., 1982–83. Founder Mem. and Past Pres., Southampton Junior Chamber of Commerce. Governor, King Edward VI Sch., Southampton, 1961–84 (Chm., 1983–84; Fellow, 1986). Sub-Lieut, RNVR, 1943–45, RNVSR, 1946–52; served to Captain RNR, 1969; CO Solent Div., RNR, 1969–72; ADC to the Queen, 1972–73; retired 1975. Hon. Sec., RNR Benevolent Fund, 1973–84. *Recreations:* family, golf. *Clubs:* Naval; Stoneham Golf (Southampton); Chipping Sodbury Golf; Royal Naval Sailing Association (Portsmouth); Southampton Police (Hon. Mem.) (Southampton).

McCARRY, Frances Jane; *see* McMenamin, F. J.

McCARTHY, family name of **Baron McCarthy**.

McCARTHY, Baron *cr* 1975 (Life Peer), of Headington; **William Edward John McCarthy,** DPhil; Emeritus Fellow of Nuffield College and Associate Fellow of Templeton College, Oxford; engaged in Industrial Arbitration and Chairman of Committees of Inquiry and Investigation, since 1968; *b* 30 July 1925; *s* of E. and H. McCarthy; *m* 1957, Margaret, *d* of Percival Godfrey. *Educ:* Holloway County; Ruskin Coll.; Merton Coll.; Nuffield Coll. MA (Oxon), DPhil (Oxon). Trade Union Scholarship to Ruskin Coll., 1953; Research Fellow of Nuffield Coll., 1959; Research Dir, Royal Commn on Trade Unions and Employers' Assocs, 1965–68; Sen. Economic Adviser, Dept of Employment, 1968–71. Chm., Railway Staff Nat. Tribunal, 1973–86; Special Advisor on Industrial Relations to Sec. of State for Social Services, 1975–77; Member: Houghton Cttee on Aid to Political Parties, 1975–76; TUC Independent Review Cttee, 1976; CS Arbitration Tribunal, 1983–; Pres., British Univ. Industrial Relations Assoc., 1975–78; Special Comr, Equal Opportunities Commn, 1977–80; Dep. Chm., Teachers' Nat. Conciliation Cttee, 1979–. Chairman: TUC Newspaper Feasibility Adv. Study Gp, 1981–83; Independent Inquiry into Rover Closure Proposals, 1989–90. Adjudicator, Nursing and Midwifery Staffs Negotiating Council, 1994–; Mem., CS Arbitration Tribunal, 1996–. Mem., H of L Select Cttee on Unemployment, 1980–82; Opposition front bench spokesman on employment, 1980–97. Mem., All Party Motor Industry Gp, 1989–; Vice Chm., All Party Friends of Music Gp, 1992–. Pres., Oxford Assoc. of Univ. Teachers, 1999–. FIPD 1995. *Publications:* The Closed Shop in Britain, 1964; The Role of Shop Stewards in British Industrial Relations, 1966; (with V. L. Munns) Employers' Associations, 1967; (with A. I. Marsh) Disputes Procedures in Britain, 1968; The Reform of Collective Bargaining at Plant and Company Level, 1971; (ed) Trade Unions, 1972, 2nd edn, 1985; (with A. I. Collier) Coming to Terms with Trade Unions, 1973; (with N. D. Ellis) Management by Agreement, 1973; (with J. F. O'Brien and V. E. Dowd) Wage Inflation and Wage Leadership, 1975; Making Whitley Work, 1977; (jtly) Change in Trade Unions, 1981; (jtly) Strikes in Post-War Britain, 1983; Freedom at Work 1985; The Future of Industrial Democracy, 1988; (with C. Jennings and R. Undy) Employee Relations Audits, 1989; (ed) Legal Intervention in Industrial Relations, 1992; New Labour at Work, 1997; Fairness at Work: past comparisons and future problems, 1999; (contrib.) Legal Regulation of the Employment Relation, 2000; articles in: Brit. Jl of Industrial Relns; Industrial Relns Jl 1995. *Recreations:* gardening, theatre, ballet, opera. *Address:* 4 William Orchard Close, Old Headington, Oxford OX3 9DR. *T:* (01865) 62016. *Club:* Reform.

McCARTHY, Arlene; Member (Lab) North West Region, European Parliament, since 1999 (Peak District, 1994–99); *b* 10 Oct. 1960; *d* of J. J. McCarthy and F. L. McCarthy; *m* 1997, Dr David Farrell. *Educ:* South Bank Poly. (BA Hons). Researcher and Press Officer to Leader of European PLP, 1990–91; Lectr in Politics, Freie Univ., Berlin, 1991–92; Head of European Affairs, Kirklees MBC, W Yorks, 1992–94. European PLP (formerly Socialist Gp and European PLP) spokesperson on regl affairs, 1994–. *Publications:* (ed jtly) Changing States: a Labour agenda for Europe, 1996; EP reports on reform of structural funds and on gen. provisions of structural funds; articles on European issues for local govt jls. *Recreations:* swimming, dancing, travel, foreign languages, music. *Address:* 3/5 St John Street, Manchester M3 4DN. *T:* (0161) 831 9848, *Fax:* (0161) 831 9849.

McCARTHY, Callum, PhD; Chairman, Gas and Electricity Markets Authority, since 2000; Chief Executive (formerly Director General), Office of Gas and Electricity Markets, since 1999 (Gas Supply, since 1998, Electricity Supply, since 1999); *b* 29 Feb. 1944; *s* of Ralph and Nan McCarthy; *m* 1966, Penelope Ann Gee; two *s* one *d*. *Educ:* Manchester Grammar Sch.; City of London Sch.; Merton Coll., Oxford (BA 1965); Stirling Univ. (PhD 1971); Grad. Sch. of Business, Stanford Univ. (Sloan Fellow; MS 1982). Operations Res., ICI, 1965–72; various posts from Economic Adv. to Under Sec., DTI, 1972–85; Dir, Kleinwort Benson, 1985–89; Man. Dir, BZW, 1989–93; CEO, Barclays Bank, Japan, 1993 96, Barclays Bank, N America, 1996–98. *Publication:* (with D. S. Davies) Introduction to Technological Economics, 1967. *Recreations:* walking, cooking, reading. *Address:* Office of Gas and Electricity Markets, 9 Millbank, SW1P 3JF.

McCARTHY, David Laurence; His Honour Judge McCarthy; a Circuit Judge, since 1995; *b* 7 April 1947; *s* of Laurence Alphonsus McCarthy and Vera May McCarthy; *m* 1981, Rosalind Marguerite Stevenson; two *s*. *Educ:* St Philip's Grammar Sch., Birmingham; Christ Church, Oxford (MA). Called to the Bar, Middle Temple, 1970; a Recorder, 1992; Midland and Oxford Circuit. *Recreations:* science fiction, playing the organ. *Address:* c/o Circuit Administrator, Midland and Oxford Circuit, The Priory Courts, Bull Street, Birmingham B4 6DW. *T:* (0121) 681 3443.

McCARTHY, Eugene Joseph; writer, since 1971; *b* 29 March 1916; *s* of Michael J. and Anna Baden McCarthy; *m* 1945, Abigail Quigley McCarthy (*d* 2001); one *s* two *d* (and one *d* decd). *Educ:* St John's Univ., Collegeville (BA); Univ. of Minnesota (MA). Teacher in public schools, 1935–40; Coll. Prof. of Econs and Sociology, and civilian techn. Asst in Mil. Intell. for War Dept, 1940–48; US Representative in Congress of 4th District, Minnesota, 1949–58; US Senator from Minnesota, 1959–70. Independent. Holds hon. degrees. *Publications:* Frontiers in American Democracy, 1960; Dictionary of American Politics, 1962; A Liberal Answer to the Conservative Challenge, 1964; The Limits of Power, 1967; The Year of the People, 1969; Other Things and the Aardvark (poetry), 1970; The Hard Years, 1975; Mr Raccoon and his Friends (children's stories), 1977; (with James Kilpatrick) A Political Bestiary, 1978; Ground Fog and Night (poetry), 1978; America Revisited: 150 years after Tocqueville, 1978; The Ultimate Tyranny: the majority over the majority, 1980; Gene McCarthy's Minnesota, 1982; Complexities and Contraries, 1982; The View from Rappahannock, 1984; Up 'Til Now, 1987; Required Reading, 1988; The View from Rappahannock II, 1989; Colony of the World, 1993; Collected Poetry, 1997; No-Fault Politics, 1997; contribs to Saturday Review, Commonweal, Harper's, New Republic, USA Today. *Address:* 271 Hawlin Road, Woodville, VA 22749, USA.

MacCARTHY, Fiona; biographer and cultural historian; *b* 23 Jan. 1940; *m* 1966, David Mellor, *qv*; one *s* one *d*. *Educ:* Wycombe Abbey Sch.; Lady Margaret Hall, Oxford (MA Hons Eng. Lang. and Lit.). FRSL 1997. Design Correspondent, Guardian, 1963–69; Women's Editor, Evening Standard, 1969–70; Literary Critic: The Times, 1980–90; Observer, 1990–98; an Associate Editor, DNB, 1998–. Sen. Fellow, RCA, 1997 (Hon. Fellow, 1990); Hon. Fellow, Centre for 19th Century Studies, Univ. of Sheffield, 1994. Hon. DLitt Sheffield, 1996. Bicentenary Medal, RSA, 1986. *Publications:* All Things Bright and Beautiful: British design 1830 to today, 1972; The Simple Life: C. R. Ashbee in the Cotswolds, 1981; The Omega Workshops: decorative arts of Bloomsbury, 1984; Eric Gill, 1989; William Morris: a life for our time, 1994 (Wolfson History Prize; Yorkshire Post Art Book Award; Writer's Guild Non-Fiction Award); Stanley Spencer: an English vision, 1997; articles in The Guardian, TLS, New York Review of Books. *Recreations:* museums, theatre, looking at new architecture. *Address:* The Round Building, Hathersage, Sheffield S32 1BA. *T:* (01433) 650220; 6 Queen Square, WC1 3AR. *T:* (020) 7278 9499.

McCARTHY, John Patrick, CBE 1992; journalist; *b* 27 Nov. 1956; *yr s* of late Pat and Sheila McCarthy; *m* 1999, Anna Ottewill. *Educ:* Haileybury; Hull Univ. (BA 1979). Joined UPITN (later WTN) as journalist, 1982. Kidnapped and held hostage in Beirut, 17 April 1986–8 Aug. 1991. BBC TV series (with Sandi Toksvig), Island Race, 1995; BBC Radio 4 series: John McCarthy's Bible Journey, 1999; A Place Called Home, 2000. Patron, Medical Foundn for the Care of Victims of Torture. Hon. DLitt Hull, 1991. *Publications:* (with Jill Morrell) Some Other Rainbow, 1993; (with Sandi Toksvig) Island Race: improbable voyage around the coast of Britain, 1995; (with Brian Keenan) Between Extremes, 1999. *Address:* c/o LAW, 14 Vernon Street, W14 0RJ.

McCARTHY, John Sidney, MBE 1984; FCIOB; Chairman, McCarthy & Stone, since 1990 (Executive Chairman, 1990–2000, non-executive, since 2001); *b* 31 Dec. 1939; *s* of John James McCarthy and Helen Caroline McCarthy; *m* 1982, Gwendoline Joan Holmes; three *s* one *d*. McCarthy & Stone: Joint Founder, 1963; Chief Exec./Chm., 1963–90. Founder, 1987, and Trustee, 1996–98, McCarthy Foundn. *Recreations:* ski-ing, shooting, sailing, subaqua diving. *Address:* Squalls Estate, Squalls Lane, Tisbury, Wilts SP3 6RX. *T:* (01202) 292480. *Club:* Royal Ocean Racing.

McCARTHY, Kieran; JP; Member (Alliance) Strangford, Northern Ireland Assembly, since 1998; *b* 9 Sept. 1942; *s* of James and Elizabeth McCarthy; *m* 1967, Kathleen Doherty; two *s* two *d*. *Educ:* Newtownards Coll. of Technol. Formerly textile worker and sales clerk; joint partner, discount drapery, 1965–87; retailer, 1987–. Councillor, 1985–, Alderman, 1997–, Ards BC. JP Ards, 1990. *Recreations:* gardening, reading, cycling. *Address:* Loughedge, 3 Main Street, Kircubbin, Co. Down BT22 2SS. *T:* (01247) 738221.

McCARTHY, Nicholas Melvyn, OBE 1983; HM Diplomatic Service, retired; High Commissioner to Cameroon, and also Ambassador (non-resident) to Gabon, Chad, Equatorial Guinea and the Central African Republic, 1995–98; *b* 4 April 1938; *s* of Daniel Alfred McCarthy and Florence Alice McCarthy; *m* 1961, Gillian Eileen Hill; three *s* one *d*. *Educ:* Queen Elizabeth's Sch., Faversham; London Univ. (BA Hons). Attaché, Saigon, 1961–64; Language Student, then Second Sec., Tokyo, 1964–69; FCO, 1969–73; First Sec., Brussels, 1973–78; FCO, 1978–80; Head of Chancery, Dakar, 1980–84; FCO, 1984–85; Consul-Gen., Osaka, 1985–90; Dep. Hd of Mission, Consul-Gen. and

Counsellor, Brussels, 1990–94. *Recreations:* golf, bridge, squash, tennis, Japanese pottery. *Address:* The Old Rectory, 34 Cross Street, Moretonhampstead, Devon TQ13 8NL.

McCARTHY, (Patrick) Peter; Regional Chairman, London North, Industrial Tribunals, 1987–90; Part-time Chairman, Industrial Tribunals, 1990–92; *b* 10 July 1919; *er s* of late William McCarthy and Mary McCarthy; *m* 1945, Isabel Mary (*d* 1994), *y d* of late Dr Joseph Unsworth, St Helens; two *s* three *d*. *Educ:* St Francis Xavier's Coll., Liverpool; Liverpool Univ. LLB 1940, LLM 1942. Admitted Solicitor, 1942; in private practice until 1974. Part-time Chm., 1972–74, full-time Chm., 1975–90, Regl Chm., Liverpool, 1977–87, Industrial Tribunals; part-time Chm., Rent Assessment Cttee, 1972–74. JP Liverpool, 1968–74. *Address:* Brook Cottage, Sham Castle Lane, Bath BA2 6JH.

McCARTHY, Richard John, FCIH; Chief Executive, Peabody Trust, since 1999; *b* 28 April 1958; *s* of John Anthony McCarthy and Anna Patricia (*née* Sheehan); *m* 1983, Judith Karen McCann; two *s* one *d*. *Educ:* Richard Challoner Sch., New Malden; Univ. of Southampton (BA Hons Geog.); Hackney Coll. FCIH 1987. Housing Officer etc, 1979–87, Ops Dir, 1987–94, Hyde Housing Assoc.; Chief Exec., S London Family Housing Assoc., 1994–99. Chm., Care and Repair, 1986–93. Mem. Council, Nat. Housing Fedn, 1998– (Chm., 2000–). *Publications:* articles in various housing jls, incl. Housing Today and Roof. *Recreations:* theatre, music, opera, tennis, football, watching Rugby. *Address:* (office) 45 Westminster Bridge Road, SE1 7JB. *T:* (020) 7928 7811.

MacCARTHY, Very Rev. Robert Brian, PhD; Dean of St Patrick's Cathedral, Dublin, since 1999 (Prebendary, 1994–99); *b* 28 March 1940; *o c* of Richard Edward MacCarthy and Dorothy MacCarthy (*née* Furney), Clonmel. *Educ:* St Columba's Coll., Rathfarnham; Trinity Coll., Dublin (BA, MA; PhD 1983); St John's Coll., Cambridge; Trinity Coll., Oxford (MA); Cuddesdon Theol Coll.; MA NUI 1965. Ordained deacon, 1979, priest, 1980; Curate, Carlow, 1979–81; Librarian, Pusey House, and Fellow, St Cross Coll., Oxford, 1981–82; Curate, 1982–83, Team Vicar, 1983–86, Bracknell; Curate, Kilkenny, 1986–88; Bp's Vicar in Kilkenny Cath., 1986–88; Domestic Chaplain to Bp of Ossory, 1986–89; Rector, Castlecomer, and RD of Carlow, 1988–95; Rector, St Nicholas' Collegiate Church, Galway and Provost of Tuam, 1995–99. *Publications:* The Estates of Trinity College, Dublin, 1992; Ancient and Modern, 1995. *Recreation:* architectural history. *Address:* The Deanery, Upper Kevin Street, Dublin 8, Ireland. *T:* (1) 4755449. *Clubs:* Kildare Street and University (Dublin); Royal Irish Yacht (Dun Laoghaire).

McCARTHY, Suzanne Joyce; Chief Executive, Financial Services Compensation Scheme, since 2001; *b* 21 Nov. 1948; *d* of Leo and Lillian Rudnick; *m* 1990, Brendan McCarthy. *Educ:* New York Univ. (BA 1970; Phi Beta Kappa); Wolfson Coll., Cambridge (Dip Social Anthropol. 1971); Lucy Cavendish Coll., Cambridge (LLM 1986). Admitted Solicitor, 1976; Solicitor in private practice, 1977–86; Lectr in Law, Univ. of Manchester, 1986–89; joined Civil Service, 1989; posts with Home Office (incl. Private Sec. to Home Sec.), Treasury, Civil Service Coll. (Dir, Policy, Govt and Europe), 1989–96; Chief Exec., HFEA, 1996–2001. Non-executive Director: Royal Brompton and Harefield NHS Trust, 1998–; Candoco Dance Co., 2000–. FRSA 2000. *Recreations:* renovating old houses, cooking and entertaining, theatre, contemporary dance. *Address:* 1 Portsoken Street, E18 8BT.

McCARTHY, Rt Hon. Sir Thaddeus (Pearcey), ONZ 1994; KBE 1974; Kt 1964; PC 1968; Justice of the Court of Appeal of New Zealand, 1963–76, President, 1973–76; Chairman, New Zealand Press Council, 1978–89; *b* 24 Aug. 1907; *s* of Walter McCarthy, Napier, merchant; *m* 1938, Joan Margaret Miller; one *s* two *d* (and one *d* decd). *Educ:* St Bede's Coll., Christchurch, New Zealand; Victoria Univ. Coll., Wellington. Master of Laws (1st Class Hons) 1931. Served War of 1939–45 in MEF with 22 Bn 2 NZEF, later as DJAG, 2 NZEF. Practised as Barrister and Solicitor until 1957 when appointed to Supreme Court. Chairman: Royal Commn on State Services, 1961–62; Winston Churchill Memorial Trust, 1966–76; Royal Commissions: on Salary and Wage Fixing Procedures in the State Services, 1968; on Social Security, 1969; on Horse Racing, Trotting and Dog Racing, 1969; on Salaries and Wages in the State Services, 1972; on Nuclear Power Generation, 1976–78; on Maori Land Courts, 1979–; Chm., Security Review Authority and Comr of Security Appeals, 1977–94. Chm. Adv. Cttee, NZ Computer Centre, 1977–86. Vice-Pres., NZ Sect., Internat. Commn of Jurists. Chm., Queen Elizabeth II Nat. Trust, 1978–84. Fellow, NZ Inst. of Public Admin, 1984. Hon. Bencher, Middle Temple, 1974. Hon. LLD Victoria Univ. of Wellington, 1978. *Recreations:* golf (Captain, Wellington Golf Club, 1952, Pres., 1973–77), sailing. *Address:* Wharenui, 274 Oriental Parade, Wellington, New Zealand. *Club:* Wellington (Wellington, NZ) (Pres., 1976–78; Trustee, 1978–).

McCARTHY, William Joseph Anthony; Director of Planning and Performance, Leeds Teaching Hospitals NHS Trust, since 2000; *b* Leeds, 14 June 1963; *s* of Shaun and Patricia McCarthy; *m* 1986, Rose Coady; four *s* one *d*. *Educ:* Prior Park, Bath; Queen Mary Coll., Univ. of London (BSc Econ.); London Sch. of Econs (MSc). Asst Economist, DoH, 1986–88; Analyst, Herts CC and ACC, 1988–91; rejoined Department of Health, 1991: Principal, 1991–94; Asst Sec., Primary Care, 1994–97; Head: of Public Expenditure Survey Br., 1997–99; of Finance and Performance Div. A, NHS Exec., 1999–2000. *Recreations:* playing with the children, eating out, weekends away, watching sport. *Address:* Leeds Teaching Hospitals NHS Trust, St James' University Hospital, Beckett Street, Leeds LS9 7TF.

McCARTIE, Rt Rev. (Patrick) Leo; Bishop of Northampton, (RC), 1990–2001; *b* 5 Sept. 1925; *s* of Patrick Leo and Hannah McCartie. *Educ:* Cotton College; Oscott College. Priest, 1949; on staff of Cotton College, 1950–55; parish work, 1955–63; Director of Religious Education, 1963–68; Administrator of St Chad's Cathedral, Birmingham, 1968–77; Aux. Bp of Birmingham, and Titular Bp of Elmham, 1977–90. Pres., Catholic Commn for Racial Justice, 1978–83; Chm., Cttee for Community Relations, Dept for Christian Responsibility and Citizenship, Bishops' Conf. on Eng. and Wales, 1983–90; Mem., Churches Main Cttee, 1996–. Church Representative: Churches Together in England, 1990; Council of Churches for Britain and Ireland, 1990. *Recreations:* music, walking. *Address:* Aston Hall, Aston by Stone, Staffordshire ST15 0BJ.

McCARTNEY, Gordon Arthur; consultant; Managing Director, Gordon McCartney Associates, since 1991; *b* 29 April 1937; *s* of Arthur and Hannah McCartney; *m* 1st, 1960, Ceris Ysobel Davies (marr. diss. 1987); two *d*; 2nd, 1988, Wendy Ann Vyvyan Titman. *Educ:* Grove Park Grammar Sch., Wrexham. Articled to Philip J. Walters, MBE (Town Clerk, Wrexham), 1954–59; admitted solicitor, 1959. Asst Solicitor, Birkenhead County Bor. Council, 1959–61; Asst Solicitor, 1961–63, Sen. Asst Solicitor, 1963–65, Bootle County Bor. Council; Dep. Clerk, Wrexham RDC, 1965–73; Clerk, Holywell RDC, 1973–74; Chief Exec., Delyn Bor. Council, 1974–81; Sec., Assoc. of Dist Councils, 1981–91; Associate, Succession Planning Associates, 1991–96. Dir, Nat. Transport Tokens Ltd, 1984–92. Secretary-General, British Section, IULA/CEMR, 1984–88; Chairman: CEMR Individual Members Gp, 1992–97; Local Govt Gp for Europe, 1997–; Co. Sec., Local Govt Internat. Bureau, 1988–91. Mem., Hansard Soc. Commn on Legislative Process, 1991–93. Director: Leisure England Ltd, 1993–; White Rock Developments Ltd, 1996–97. *Recreations:* gardening, cricket, music. *Address:* 33 Duck Street, Elton, Peterborough PE8 6RQ. *T:* (01832) 280659; 108 Frobisher House, Dolphin Square, SW1. *T:* (020) 7798 8777. *Clubs:* MCC; Northants CCC.

McCARTNEY, Hugh; Director, East Dunbartonshire Initiative for Creative Therapy and Social Care, 1997–99; *b* 3 Jan. 1920; *s* of John McCartney and Mary Wilson; *m* 1949, Margaret; one *s* two *d*. *Educ:* Royal Technical Coll., Glasgow; John Street Senior Secondary School. Apprentice in textile industry, 1934–39; entered aircraft engrg industry, Coventry, 1939; joined Rolls Royce, Glasgow, 1941; joined RAF as aero-engine fitter, 1942 and resumed employment with Rolls Royce, 1947; representative with company (later one of GKN group) specialising in manufacture of safety footware, 1951. Joined Ind. Labour Party, 1934; joined Labour Party, 1936. Town Councillor, 1955–70 and Magistrate, 1965–70, Kirkintilloch; Mem., Dunbarton CC, 1965–70. MP (Lab): Dunbartonshire E, 1970–74; Dunbartonshire Central, 1974–83; Clydebank and Milngavie, 1983–87. Scottish Regional Whip, 1979–83; Mem., Speaker's Panel of Chairmen, 1984–87. Chm., TGWU Parly Group, 1986–87. Mem., Rent Assessment Panel for Scotland, 1968–70. *Recreation:* spectating at football matches and athletic meetings (political activities permitting). *Address:* 23 Merkland Drive, Kirkintilloch G66 3PG.

See also Rt Hon. I. McCartney.

McCARTNEY, Rt Hon. Ian; PC 1999; MP (Lab) Makerfield, since 1987; Minister for Pensions, Department of Work and Pensions, since 2001; *b* 25 April 1951; *s* of Hugh McCartney, *qv*; *m* (marr. diss.); two *d* (one *s* decd); *m* 1988, Ann Parkes (*née* Kevan). *Educ:* State primary, secondary schools; Tech. Colls. Led paper boy strike, 1965; joined Labour Party, 1966; joined trade union, 1966; seaman, local govt manual worker, chef, 1966–71; unemployed, 1971–73; Labour Party Organiser, 1973–87. Councillor, Wigan Borough, 1982–87. Hon. Parly Adviser: to Greater Manchester Fire and Civil Defence Authy, 1987–92 (Mem., 1986); to Nat. Assoc. for Safety in the Home, 1989–92. Opposition spokesperson on NHS, 1992–94, on employment, 1994–96, chief spokesperson on employment, 1996–97; Minister of State: DTI, 1997–99; Cabinet Office, 1999–2001. Mem., Parly Select Cttee on Health and Social Security, 1991–92; Jt Sec., Parly Leasehold Reform Gp. Chm., T&GWU Parly Gp, 1989–91. Sponsored by TGWU. Hon. Pres., Wigan Wheelchair Fund 1987–. *Recreations:* Wigan Rugby League fanatic (supports Wigan Warriors); head of McCartney family, a family of proud working class stock. *Address:* 2 Wyatt Grove, Ashton-in-Makerfield, Wigan WN4 8SR. *T:* (01942) 712619. *Club:* Platt Bridge Labour.

McCARTNEY, Sir (James) Paul, Kt 1997; MBE 1965; musician, composer; *b* Allerton, Liverpool, 18 June 1942; *s* of James McCartney and Mary McCartney; *m* 1969, Linda Eastman (*d* 1998); one *s* two *d*, and one step *d*. *Educ:* Liverpool Inst. Mem., skiffle group, The Quarry Men, 1957–59; toured Scotland with them and Stuart Sutcliffe as the Silver Beetles, 1960; first of five extended seasons in Hamburg, Aug. 1960; made 1st important appearance as the Beatles at Litherland Town Hall, nr Liverpool, Dec. 1960; appeared as mem. of Beatles: UK, Sweden, and Royal Variety perf., London, 1963; UK, Netherlands, Sweden, France, Denmark, Hong Kong, Australia, NZ, Canada, 1964; TV appearances, USA, and later, coast-to-coast tour, 1964; UK, France, Italy, Spain, USA, Canada, 1965; West Germany, Japan, Philippines, USA, Canada, 1966; Beatles disbanded 1970; formed MPL group of cos, 1970, and own group, Wings, 1971; toured: UK, Europe, 1972–73; UK, Australia, 1975; Europe, USA, Canada, 1976; UK, 1979; Wings disbanded 1981; Europe, UK, Canada, Japan, USA, Brazil, 1989/90. Wrote (with Carl Davis) Liverpool Oratorio, 1991; *symphony:* Standing Stone, 1997. *Songs* with John Lennon include: Love Me Do; Please Please Me; From Me To You; She Loves You; Can't Buy Me Love; I Want to Hold Your Hand; I Saw Her Standing There; Eight Days a Week; All My Loving; Help!; Ticket to Ride; I Feel Fine; I'm A Loser; A Hard Day's Night; No Reply; I'll Follow The Sun; Yesterday; For No One; Here, There and Everywhere; Eleanor Rigby; Yellow Submarine; Penny Lane; All You Need Is Love; Lady Madonna; Hey Jude; We Can Work It Out; Day Tripper; Paperback Writer; When I'm Sixty-Four; A Day in the Life; Back in the USSR; Hello, Goodbye; Get Back; Let It Be; The Long and Winding Road; subseq. *songs* include: Maybe I'm Amazed; My Love; Band on the Run; Jet; Let 'Em In; Silly Love Songs; Mull of Kintyre; Coming Up; Ebony and Ivory; Tug of War; Pipes of Peace; No More Lonely Nights; My Brave Face. *Albums* with the Beatles: Please Please Me, 1963; With The Beatles, 1963; A Hard Day's Night, 1964; Beatles for Sale, 1964; Help!, 1965; Rubber Soul, 1965; Revolver, 1966; Sgt Pepper's Lonely Hearts Club Band, 1967; Magical Mystery Tour, 1967; The Beatles (White Album), 1968; Yellow Submarine, 1969; Abbey Road, 1969; Let it Be, 1970; Anthology I, II and III, 1995–96; other albums: McCartney, 1970; Ram, 1971; Wild Life, 1971; Red Rose Speedway, 1973; Band on the Run, 1973; Venus and Mars, 1975; Wings at the Speed of Sound, 1976; Wings over America, 1976; London Town, 1978; Wings Greatest, 1978; Back to the Egg, 1979; McCartney II, 1980; Tug of War, 1982; Pipes of Peace, 1983; Give My Regards to Broad Street, 1984; Press to Play, 1986; All the Best!, 1987; CHOBA B CCCP, 1988; Flowers in the Dirt, 1989; Tripping the Live Fantastic, 1990; Unplugged: The Official Bootleg, 1991; Paul McCartney's Liverpool Oratorio, 1991; Off The Ground, 1993; Paul Is Live, 1993; Flaming Pie, 1997; Standing Stone, 1999; Run Devil Run, 1999; Wingspan, 2001; Driving Rain, 2001. *Films* (with the Beatles): A Hard Day's Night, 1964; Help!, 1965; Magical Mystery Tour (TV), 1967; Yellow Submarine, 1968; Let It Be, 1970; (with Wings) Rockshow, 1981; (wrote, composed score, and acted in) Give My Regards To Broad Street, 1984; (wrote, composed score and produced) Rupert and the Frog Song, 1984 (BAFTA award, Best Animated Film); Get Back, 1991. *Film scores:* The Family Way, 1966; Live and Let Die, 1973 (title song only); Twice In A Lifetime, 1984 (title song only); Spies Like Us, 1985 (title song only); *TV scores:* Thingumybob (series), 1968; The Zoo Gang (series), 1974. Live Russian 'phone link-up, BBC Russian Service, 1989. FRCM 1995. Numerous Grammy Awards, Nat. Acad. of Recording Arts and Scis, USA, incl. Lifetime Achievement Award, 1990; Ivor Novello Awards include: for Internat. Achievement, 1980; for Internat. Hit of the Year (Ebony and Ivory), 1982; for Outstanding Contrib. to Music, 1989; PRS special award for unique achievement in popular music, 1990. Freeman, City of Liverpool, 1984. Fellow, British Acad. of Composers and Songwriters, 2000. DUniv Sussex, 1988. *Publications:* The Beatles Anthology (with George Harrison and Ringo Starr), 2000; Paintings, 2000; Blackbird Singing: poems and lyrics 1965–1999, 2001.

McCARTNEY, Robert Law; QC (NI) 1975; Member (UKU) Northern Down, Northern Ireland Assembly, since 1998; *b* 24 April 1936; *s* of William Martin McCartney and Elizabeth Jane (*née* McCartney); *m* 1960, Maureen Ann Bingham; one *s* three *d*. *Educ:* Grosvenor Grammar Sch., Belfast; Queen's Univ., Belfast (LLB Hons 1958). Admitted solicitor of Supreme Court of Judicature, NI, 1962; called to NI Bar, 1968. MP (UKU) N Down, June 1995–2001; contested (UKU) same seat, 2001. *Publications:* Liberty and Authority in Ireland, 1985; Liberty, Democracy and the Union, 2001. *Recreations:* reading (biography and military history), walking. *Address:* St Catherines, 2 Circular Road East, Cultra, Holywood, Co. Down, Northern Ireland BT18 0HA.

McCAUGHEY, (John) Davis, AC 1987; Governor of Victoria, Australia, 1986–92; *b* 12 July 1914; *s* of John and Lizzie McCaughey; *m* 1940, Jean Middlemas Henderson; three *s* two *d*. *Educ:* Pembroke Coll., Cambridge (MA; Hon. Fellow, 1988); New Coll., Edinburgh; Presbyterian Coll., Belfast. Ordained in Presbyt. Ch. in Ireland, 1942; Study Sec., SCM, 1946–52; Prof. of NT Studies, Ormond Coll., Univ. of Melbourne, 1953–64, Master of the Coll. 1959–79; Dep. Chancellor, Univ. of Melbourne, 1978–79, 1982–85. Pres., Uniting Church in Australia, 1977–79. Hon. FRACP 1988; FAHA 1990. Hon. DD Edinburgh, 1966; Hon. LLD: Melbourne, 1982; QUB, 1987; Monash, 1993; Hon. DLitt La Trobe, 1992; Hon. STD Melbourne Coll. of Divinity, 1992. *Publications:* Christian Obedience in the University, 1958; Diversity and Unity in the New Testament Picture of Christ, 1969; Piecing Together a Shared Vision (Boyer Lectures), 1988; Victoria's Colonial Governors 1839–1900, 1993; Tradition and Dissent, 1997; articles in Colloquium, Aust. Biblical Rev., etc. *Recreations:* reading, listening, golf. *Address:* 36 Chapman Street, North Melbourne, Vic 3051, Australia. *Clubs:* Melbourne, Royal Melbourne Golf.

McCAUGHREAN, Geraldine Margaret; author, since 1988; *b* 6 June 1951; *d* of Lesley Arthur Jones and Ethel Jones (*née* Thomas); *m* 1988, John McCaughrean; one *d*. *Educ:* Enfield County Grammar Sch. for Girls; Southgate Technical Coll.; Christ Church Coll. of Educn, Canterbury (BEd Hons 1977). Sec., Thames TV, 1970–73; Sec. 1977–79, and Sub-Editor, 1983–88, Marshall Cavendish; Editorial Asst, Rothmans Internat., 1980–82; Editor, Focus, 1982. Radio play, Last Call, 1991. *Publications: for children:* A Little Lower than the Angels (Whitbread Children's Book Award), 1987; A Pack of Lies (Guardian Children's Award, Carnegie Medal), 1988; Gold Dust (Beefeater Children's Novel Award), 1993; Plundering Paradise (Smarties Bronze Award), 1996; Forever X (UK Reading Assoc. Award), 1997; The Stones are Hatching, 1999; Britannia, 1999; (new version) A Pilgrim's Progress, 1999 (Blue Peter Book of the Year, 2000); The Kite Rider, 2001; Stop the Train, 2001; *for adults:* The Maypole, 1989; Fire's Astonishment, 1990; Vainglory, 1991; Lovesong, 1996; The Ideal Wife, 1997; contribs to anthologies for children and young people. *Recreation:* theatre. *Address:* c/o David Higham Associates, 5–8 Lower John Street, Golden Square, W1R 4HA.

McCAUSLAND, Benedict Maurice Perronet T.; *see* Thompson-McCausland.

McCAVE, Prof. Ian Nicholas, FGS; Woodwardian Professor of Geology, University of Cambridge, since 1985; Fellow, St John's College, Cambridge, since 1986; *b* 3 Feb. 1941; *s* of Thomas Theasby McCave and Gwendoline Marguerite McCave (*née* Langlois); *m* 1972, Susan Caroline Adams (*née* Bambridge); three *s* one *d*. *Educ:* Elizabeth Coll., Guernsey; Hertford Coll., Oxford (MA, DSc); Brown Univ., USA (PhD). FGS 1963. NATO Research Fellow, Netherlands Inst. for Sea Research, 1967–69; Lectr 1969–76, Reader 1976–84, UEA, Norwich; Hd, Dept of Earth Scis, Univ. of Cambridge, 1988–98. Visiting Professor: Oregon State Univ., 1974; MIT, 1999; Adjunct Scientist, Woods Hole Oceanographic Instn, 1978–87. Shepard Medal for Marine Geol., US Soc. for Sedimentary Geol., 1995; Huntsman Medal for Marine Scis, Canada, 1999. *Publications:* (ed) The Benthic Boundary Layer, 1976; (ed) The Deep Sea Bed, 1990; over 100 papers in jls. *Recreations:* pottering about in the garden, rowing. *Address:* Marlborough House, 23 Victoria Street, Cambridge CB1 1JP.

McCLARTY, David; Member (UU) Londonderry East, Northern Ireland Assembly, since 1998; *b* 23 Feb. 1951; *s* of Douglas and Helen McClarty; *m* 1973, (Alma) Norma (Yvonne) Walls; two *s*. *Educ:* Coleraine Academical Instn; Magee Coll., Londonderry. Sales Asst, NI Electricity, 1973; General Accident: Trainee Fire Underwriter, 1973; Dep. Manager, Fire Insurance Dept, 1978–84; Fire Underwriter, 1973–78; Insurance Consultant, D. McClarty & Co., 1984–98. Mem. (UU), Coleraine BC, 1989–; Mayor of Coleraine Borough, 1993–95. Freeman, City of London, 1995. *Recreations:* amateur dramatics, choral singing, sport in general. *Address:* 22 Slievebanna, Coleraine, Co. Londonderry BT51 3JG. *T:* (028) 7035 6734.

McCLEAN, Prof. (John) David, CBE 1994; Professor of Law, since 1973, Public Orator, 1988–91 and since 1994, University of Sheffield; *b* 4 July 1939; *s* of Major Harold McClean and Mrs Mabel McClean; *m* 1966, Pamela Ann Loader; one *s* one *d*. *Educ:* Queen Elizabeth's Grammar Sch., Blackburn; Magdalen Coll., Oxford (DCL, 1984). Called to the Bar, Gray's Inn, 1963. University of Sheffield: Asst Lectr 1961; Lectr 1963; Sen. Lectr 1968; Dean, Faculty of Law, 1978–81, 1998–2001; Pro-Vice-Chancellor, 1991–96. Vis. Lectr in Law, Monash Univ., Melbourne, 1968, Vis Prof., 1978. Chancellor: dio. of Sheffield, 1992–; dio. of Newcastle, 1998–. Vice-Chm., C of E Bd for Social Responsibility, 1978–80. Member: Gen. Synod of C of E, 1970– (Vice-Chm., House of Laity, 1979–85, Chm. 1985–95); Crown Appts Commn, 1977–87. Pres., Eur. Consortium for Church and State Res., 1995. Hon. QC 1995. *Publications:* Criminal Justice and the Treatment of Offenders (jtly), 1969; (contrib.) Halsbury's Laws of England, Vol. 8, 4th edn 1974, re-issue 1996, Vol. 2 (re-issue), 4th edn 1991; The Legal Context of Social Work, 1975, 2nd edn 1980; (jtly) Defendants in the Criminal Process, 1976; (ed jtly) Shawcross and Beaumont, Air Law, 4th edn 1977, reissue (new edn of one vol.) 1983; (jtly) Recognition and Enforcement of Judgments, etc, within the Commonwealth, 1977; (ed jtly) Dicey and Morris, Conflict of Laws, 10th edn 1980, to 13th edn 1999; Recognition of Family Judgments in the Commonwealth, 1983; International Judicial Assistance, 1992; (contrib.) Chitty, Contracts, 27th edn 1994, 28th edn 1999. *Recreation:* detective fiction. *Address:* 6 Burnt Stones Close, Sheffield S10 5TS. *T:* (0114) 230 5794. *Club:* Royal Commonwealth Society.

McCLEARY, Ann Heron, (Mrs David McCleary); *see* Gloag, A. H.

McCLELLAN, Col Sir (Herbert) Gerard (Thomas), Kt 1986; CBE 1979 (OBE 1960); TD 1955; company director; *b* 24 Sept. 1913; *s* of late George McClellan and Lilian (*née* Fitzgerald); *m* 1939, Rebecca Ann (Nancy) Desforges (*d* 1982); one *s* three *d*. Served War of 1939–45, Loyal (N Lancs) Regt, RA, London Irish Rifles, in ME and Italy (wounded; despatches). Vernons of Liverpool, 1934–82: formerly: Vice Chm. and Man. Dir, Vernons Trust Corp., Vernons Finance Corp., and Vernons Insurance Brokers; Dir, Vernons Orgn; Man. Dir, Competition Management Services. Chm., Intro-Merseyside Ltd, 1988–94; Director: JS Mortgage Corp., 1986–93; Richmond Storage & Transit Co. (UK) Ltd, 1990–93; Richmond Freight Services Ltd, 1990–93. Commanded 626 HAA (Liverpool Irish) Regt and 470 LAA (3rd West Lancs) Regt, RA TA, 1955–60; County Comdt, W Lancs ACF, 1961–66; Member: W Lancs T&AVRA, 1955–66 (Vice-Chm., 1966–68); NW England and IoM T&AVRA, 1968–70 (Vice-Chm., 1970–75; Chm., 1975–79). Former Mem. (C) for Childwall, Liverpool City Council; Member: Liverpool Cons. Assoc., 1960–95 (Vice-Chm., 1966–75; Chm., 1975–85; Vice-Pres., 1985–95); NW Area Cons. Assoc., 1971–90; Exec. Cttee, Nat. Union of Cons. and Unionist Assocs, 1982–87; Chairman: Wavertree Cons. Assoc., 1962–67 (Pres., 1967–76); Liverpool European Cons. Constituency Council, 1978–84; Merseyside W European Cons. Constit. Council, 1984–85 (Pres., 1985–88); President: Garston Cons. Assoc., 1979–90; Halewood Cons. Club, 1983–88; Vice-Pres. Woolton Ward Cons. Assoc., 1981–95; Patron, Crosby Cons. Assoc., 1994–2000 (Pres., 1986–89; Chm., 1989–91). Vice-President: Merseyside Co. SSAFA, 1975–; Incorp. Liverpool Sch. of Tropical Medicine, 1987–92. Governor: Archbp Whiteside Secondary Modern Sch. and St Brigid's High Sch., 1961–91; Mabel Fletcher Technical Coll., 1969– (Chm., 1971–86); Sandown Coll., Liverpool, 1989–91. FIAM. DL Lancs, later Merseyside, 1967–97; JP Liverpool, 1968–83; High Sheriff of Merseyside, 1980–81. *Address:* Ince Blundell Hall, Ince Blundell, Merseyside L38 6JL. *T:* (0151) 929 2269. *Clubs:* Army and Navy; Athenæum (Liverpool).

McCLELLAN, John Forrest; Under Secretary, Industry Department for Scotland (formerly Scottish Economic Planning Department), 1980–85, retired; *b* 15 Aug. 1932; *s* of John McClellan and Hester (*née* Niven); *m* 1956, Eva Maria Pressel; three *s* one *d*. *Educ:* Ferryhill Primary Sch., Aberdeen; Aberdeen Grammar Sch.; Aberdeen Univ. (MA). Served Army, 2nd Lieut, Gordon Highlanders and Nigeria Regt, RWAFF, 1954–56. Entered Civil Service, 1956; Asst Principal, Scottish Educn Dept, 1956–59; Private Sec. to Perm. Under Sec. of State, Scottish Office, 1959–60; Principal, Scottish Educn Dept, 1960–68; Civil Service Fellow, Glasgow Univ., 1968–69; Asst Sec., Scottish Educn Dept, 1969–77; Asst Under Sec. of State, Scottish Office, 1977–80. Dir, Scottish Internat. Educn Trust, 1986–2001; Mem., Management Cttee, Hanover (Scotland) Housing Assoc., 1986–. Hon. Fellow, Dundee Inst. of Technology, 1988. *Publication:* Then a Soldier, 1991. *Recreations:* gardening, walking. *Address:* 7 Cumin Place, Edinburgh EH9 2JX. *T:* (0131) 667 8446. *Club:* Royal Scots (Edinburgh).

McCLELLAND, Donovan; Member (SDLP) Antrim South, since 1998, and Deputy Speaker, since 2000, Northern Ireland Assembly; *b* 14 Jan. 1949; *s* of Dan and Virginia McClelland; *m* 1974, Noreen Patricia Young; two *s* one *d*. *Educ:* Queen's Univ., Belfast (BSc Econ). Lectr and researcher in Economics, QUB, 1973–75; Civil Servant, Dept of Agriculture, 1975–78; Lectr in Economics, Univ. of Ulster, 1978–98. Chm., Standards and Privileges Cttee, NI Assembly, 2000–. *Recreation:* reading. *Address:* 18 Roseville Crescent, Randalstown, Co. Antrim BT41 2LY.

McCLELLAND, Hon. Douglas, AC 1987; Chairman, Australian Political Exchange Council, 1993–95; *s* of Alfred McClelland and Gertrude Amy Cooksley; *m* Lorna Belva McNeill; one *s* two *d*. Mem. NSW ALP Executive, 1956–62; Hon. Dir, St George Hosp., Sydney, 1957–68. Member, Australian Senate for NSW, 1962–87; Senate appointments: Minister for the Media, 1972–75; Manager, Govt Business, 1974–75; Special Minister of State, June–Nov. 1975; Opposition spokesman on Admin. Services, 1976–77; Manager, Opposition Business, 1976–77; Dep. Leader of Opposition, May–Dec. 1977; Dep. Pres. and Chm of Cttees, 1981–82; Pres. of the Australian Senate, 1983–87; High Commissioner in UK, 1987–91; Comr-Gen., Australian Pavilion, Expo '92, Seville, Spain, 1992. Chm., Bobby Limb Foundn, 1999–; Mem. Bd of Govs, St George Bank Foundn, 1993–. *Recreations:* Patron, St George Illawarra Rugby League FC (Chm., 1998–2000); reading, making friends. *Address:* 6A Carlton Crescent, Kogarah Bay, NSW 2217, Australia. *Clubs:* City Tattersalls (Life Mem.), St George Leagues (Life Mem.) (Sydney).

McCLELLAND, George Ewart, CB 1986; Solicitor, Department of Employment, 1982–87; *b* 27 March 1927; *s* of George Ewart McClelland and Winifred (*née* Robinson); *m* 1956, Ann Penelope, *yr d* of late Judge Arthur Henry Armstrong; one *s* two *d*. *Educ:* Stonyhurst Coll.; Merton Coll., Oxford (Classical Scholar; MA). Called to the Bar, Middle Temple, 1952. Entered Solicitor's Dept, Min. of Labour, 1953; Asst Solicitor, 1969; Principal Asst Solicitor, 1978.

McCLELLAND, Prof. (William) Grigor, CBE 1994; DL; MA; MBA; former business executive and academic; *b* 2 Jan. 1922; *o c* of Arthur and Jean McClelland, Gosforth, Newcastle upon Tyne; *m* 1946, Diana Avery Close (*d* 2000); two *s* two *d*. *Educ:* Leighton Park; Balliol Coll., Oxford. First Class PPE, 1948. Friends' Ambulance Unit, 1941–46. Man. Dir, Laws Stores Ltd, 1949–65, 1978–85 (Chm., 1966–85); Sen. Res. Fellow in Management Studies, Balliol Coll., 1962–65; Dir, Manchester Business Sch., 1965–77, and Prof. of Business Administration, 1967–77, Univ. of Manchester; Dep. Chm., Nat. Computing Centre, 1966–68; Chm., Washington Develt Corp., 1977–88. Chm., EDC for the Distributive Trades, 1980–84 (Mem., 1965–70); Member: The Consumer Council, 1963–66; Economic Planning Council, Northern Region, 1965–66; IRC, 1966–71; NEDC, 1969–71; SSRC, 1971–74; North Eastern Industrial Develt Bd, 1977–86. Hon. Vis. Prof., 1977–, and Gov., 1986–98, Durham Univ. Business Sch. Chairman: Tyne Tees Telethon Trust, 1987–93; Tyne and Wear Foundn, 1988–93 (Vice-Pres., 1994–); NE Adv. Panel, Nat. Lottery Charities' Bd, 1995–97. Trustee: Joseph Rowntree Charitable Trust, 1956–94 (Chm., 1965–78); Anglo-German Foundn for the Study of Industrial Soc., 1973–79; Millfield House Foundn, 1976–; Employment Inst., 1985–92; Governor: Nat. Inst. of Econ. and Social Research; Leighton Park Sch., 1952–60 and 1962–66. CIMgt (CBIM 1966). Hon. DCL Dunelm, 1985. DL Tyne and Wear, 1988. Founding Editor, Jl of Management Studies, 1963–65. *Publications:* Quakers Visit China (ed), 1957; Studies in Retailing, 1963; Costs and Competition in Retailing, 1966; And a New Earth, 1976; Washington: over and out, 1988; Embers of War, 1997. *Recreations:* tennis, walking. *Address:* 50 Reid Park Road, Jesmond, Newcastle upon Tyne NE2 2ES; *e-mail:* grigor@mcclelland-z.freeserve.co.uk.

McCLEMENT, Rear-Adm. Timothy Pentreath, OBE 1990; Assistant Chief of Naval Staff, since 2001; *b* 16 May 1951; *s* of Capt. Reginald McClement, RN retd, and Winnifred McClement (*née* Pentreath); *m* 1980, Lynne Laura Gowans; two *s*. *Educ:* Douai Sch., Berks. Joined Royal Navy, 1971: appts in various submarines, 1975–81; passed SMCC 1981; 2nd i/c HMS Conqueror during Falklands Conflict, 1982; in command: HMS Opportune, 1983–84; Staff of Captain Submarine Sea Training as a Comand Sea Rider, 1984–87; SMCC, 1987–89 (Comdr); HMS Tireless, 1989–92 (surfaced at North Pole, 8 May 1990, and played cricket); HMS London, 1992–94 (Capt.); HMS Cornwall, 1999–2001 (led Task Gp around world, May–Nov. 2000); Rear-Adm. 2001. Freeman, City of London, 1993. *Recreations:* swimming, tennis, dog walking. *Address:* Ministry of Defence, Whitehall, SW1A 2EU. *Clubs:* Royal Navy of 1765 and 1785; Royal Thames Yacht.

MACCLESFIELD, 9th Earl of, *cr* 1721; **Richard Timothy George Mansfield Parker;** Baron Parker, 1716; Viscount Parker, 1721; *b* 31 May 1943; *s* of 8th Earl of Macclesfield and Hon. Valerie Mansfield (*d* 1994), *o d* of 4th Baron Sandhurst, OBE; *S* father, 1992; *m* 1967, Tatiana Cleone, *d* of Major Craig Wheaton-Smith; three *d* (including twins); *m* 1986, Mrs Sandra Hope Mead. *Educ:* Stowe; Worcester Coll., Oxford. *Heir: b* Hon. (Jonathan) David (Geoffrey) Parker [*b* 2 Jan. 1945; *m* 1968, Lynne Valerie Butler; one *s* two *d*]. *Address:* Shirburn Castle, Shirburn, Watlington, Oxon OX9 5DL.

MACCLESFIELD, Archdeacon of; *see* Gillings, Ven. R. J.

McCLEVERTY, Prof. Jon Armistice; Professor of Inorganic Chemistry, University of Bristol, since 1990; *b* 11 Nov. 1937; *s* of John and Nessie McCleverty; *m* 1963, Dianne Barrack; two *d*. *Educ:* Univ. of Aberdeen (BSc 1960); Imperial College, London (DIC, PhD 1963); Massachusetts Inst. of Technology. Asst Lectr, part-time, Acton Coll. of Technology, 1962–63; Asst Lectr, then Lectr, Sen. Lectr, and Reader, Univ. of Sheffield, 1964–80; Prof. of Inorganic Chem., 1980–90, and Head of Dept of Chem., 1984–90,

Univ. of Birmingham. Chairman: Cttee of Heads of Univ. Chem. Depts, 1989–91; Internat. Cttee, RSC, 1994–97; Chemistry Cttee, SERC, 1990–93; Vice-Chm., Chairman of Eur. Res. Council Chemistry Cttees, 1992–93, 1995, 1997–99 (Chm., 1996–97); Member: Science Bd, SERC, 1990–93; Technical Cttee for Chemistry, Co-operation in Sci. and Technol. in Europe, EU, 1990–96; Physical Scis and Technol. Panel, NATO Sci. Affairs Div., 1999–2002 (Chm., 2001). Pres., RSC Dalton Div., 1999–2001. Tilden Lectr, RSC, 1981. RSC Medal, for work on chem. and electrochem. of transition metals, 1985. Golden Order of Merit (Poland), 1990. *Publications:* numerous articles, principally in Jl of Chem. Soc. *Recreations:* gardening, DIY, travel, traditional jazz. *Address:* School of Chemistry, University of Bristol, Cantock's Close, Bristol BS8 1TS.

McCLINTOCK, Surg. Rear-Adm. Cyril Lawson Tait, CB 1974; OBE 1964; Medical Officer in Charge, Royal Naval Hospital, Haslar and Command Medical Adviser on staff of Commander-in-Chief Naval Home Command, 1972–75; retired 1975; *b* 2 Aug. 1916; *o* surv. *s* of late Lawson Tait McClintock, MB, ChB, Loddon, Norfolk; *m* 1966, Freda Margaret, *o d* of late Robert Jones, Caergwle, Denbighshire; two step *s*. *Educ:* St Michael's, Uckfield; Epsom; Guy's Hospital. MRCS, LRCP 1940; DLO 1955; MFCM 1975. Joined RN Medical Service, 1940; served War of 1939–45 in Western Approaches, N Africa, Eritrea, India and Singapore; Korea, 1950–51; ENT Specialist, RN Hosps, Port Edgar, Chatham, Hong Kong, Portland, Haslar, Malta and Russell Eve Building, Hamilton, Bermuda; MO i/c RN Hosp. Bighi, Malta, 1969; David Bruce RN Hosp. Mtarfa, Malta, 1970–71; Comd Med. Adviser to C-in-C Naval Forces Southern Europe, 1969–71. QHS 1971–75. FRSocMed 1948; MFCM 1974. CStJ 1973. *Recreations:* cricket, tennis, Rugby refereeing, history. *Address:* 5 Ambleside Court, Alverstoke, Hants PO12 2DJ. *Clubs:* Army and Navy, MCC.

McCLINTOCK, David, TD; writer, naturalist and plantsman; *b* 4 July 1913; *o s* of Rev. E. L. L. McClintock, Glendaragh, Crumlin, Co. Antrim, and Margaret McClintock, *d* of John Henry Buxton, Easneye, Ware, Herts; *m* Elizabeth Anne (*d* 1993), *d* of Maj. V. J. Dawson, Miserden, Glos; two *s* two *d*. *Educ:* West Downs Sch., Winchester; Harrow Sch.; Trinity Coll., Cambridge. BA 1934, MA 1940. FCA 1938; FLS 1953. 2nd Lieut, Herts Yeomanry RA TA, 1938; HQ 54 Div., Captain, 1941; Intelligence Trng Centre, 1941–43; Major, 1942; Civil Affairs Trng Centre, 1943–44; Lt-Col, 1944; BAOR, 1944–45. K-H Newsletter, 1938–46; Commercial Manager, Air Contractors Ltd, 1946–47; Chief Accountant and Admin. Officer, Coal Utilisation Council, 1951–73. Member: Wild Flower Soc., 1934– (Chm., 1981–93, Treasurer, 1978–82; Vice-Pres., 1994–97; Pres., 1997–2000); Council, Botanical Soc. of British Isles, 1954–64 (Pres., 1971–73; Hon. Mem., 1994–); Council, Kent Trust for Nature Conservation, 1958–62 (Vice-Pres., 1963–); Council, Ray Soc., 1968–72, 1976–80 (Vice-Pres., 1972–76; Pres., 1980–83; Hon. Vice-Pres., 1983–); Council, Linnean Soc., 1970–78 (Vice-Pres., 1971–74; Editl Sec., 1974–78; Editor, Biological Jl, 1976); Plant Variety Rights Adv. Panel for heathers, 1973–; Royal Horticultural Society: Scientific Cttee, 1978–94 (Vice-Chm., 1983–92; Actg Chm. 66 times), Publications Cttee, 1982–87; Council, Internat. Dendrology Soc., 1979– (Editor, 1979–83; Vice-Pres., 1990–2000); Council, Nat. Trust, 1980–84; Heather Soc., 1963– (Vice-Pres., 1980–89; Pres., 1989–2000); President: Kent Field Club, 1978–80 (Hon. Mem., 1994–); London Natural Hist. Soc., 2000–02. Internat. Registrar for heather cultivars, 1970–95; holder of national collection of Sasa bamboos, 1986–. Broadcast many times, 1962–96. Membre d'Honneur, Soc. Guernesiaise, 1968–. Veitch Meml Medal in gold, RHS, 1981; H. H. Bloomer Award, Linnean Soc., 1993; VMH 1995. *Publications:* Pocket Guide to Wild Flowers (with R. S. R. Fitter), 1956; Supplement to the Pocket Guide to Wild Flowers, 1957; (jtly) Natural History of the Garden of Buckingham Palace, 1964; Companion to Flowers, 1966; Guide to the Naming of Plants, 1969, 2nd edn 1980; Wild Flowers of Guernsey, 1975, Supplement, 1987; (with J. Bichard) Wild Flowers of the Channel Islands, 1975; Joshua Gosselin of Guernsey, 1976; (with F. Perring and R. E. Randall) Picking Wild Flowers, 1977; (ed) H. J. van de Laar, The Heather Garden, 1978; Guernsey's Earliest Flora, 1982; Heathers of the Lizard, 1998; contribs to 26 other books and over 100 periodicals, incl. more than 2,500 book reviews. *Recreations:* anything to do with wild life and gardening, music, formerly shooting, fishing, tennis etc. *Address:* Bracken Hill, Platt, Sevenoaks, Kent TN15 8JH. *T:* (01732) 884102. *Clubs:* Horticultural, Linnean Dining.

See also Baron Hazlerigg.

McCLINTOCK, Sir Eric (Paul), Kt 1981; investment banker; *b* 13 Sept. 1918; *s* of Robert and Ada McClintock; *m* 1942, Eva Lawrence; two *s* one *d*. *Educ:* De La Salle Coll., Armidale; Sydney Univ. (DPA). Supply Dept, Dept of the Navy, Australia, 1935–47; served successively in Depts of Commerce, Agriculture, and Trade, in Washington, New York, Melbourne and Canberra, 1947–61 (1st Asst Sec. on resignation); investment banking, 1962–. Chairman: McClintock Associates Ltd; Aust. Overseas Projects Corp., 1978–84; Woolworths Ltd, 1982–87; AFT Ltd, 1984–87; Plutonic Resources Ltd, 1990–96; Malaysia Mining Corp. Australia Pty Ltd, 1993–; Dep. Chm., Development Finance Corp. Ltd, 1980–87; Director: Philips Industries Holdings Ltd, 1978–85; O'Connell Street Associates Pty Ltd, 1978–; Ashton Mining Ltd, 1986–93. Chm., Trade Develt Council, 1970–74. Pres., Royal Life Saving Soc. (NSW), 1987–96. Governor, Sydney Inst., 1990–95. *Recreations:* tennis, reading, travel. *Address:* Floor 6, 2 O'Connell Street, Sydney, NSW 2000, Australia. *T:* (2) 92253244. *Clubs:* Australian (Sydney); Commonwealth (Canberra).

McCLINTOCK, Nicholas Cole, CBE 1979; Secretary-General of the Order of St John, 1968–81 (Deputy Secretary-General, 1963–68); *b* 10 Sept. 1916; *s* of late Col Robert Singleton McClintock, DSO (3rd *s* of Adm. Sir Leopold McClintock), and Mary Howard, *d* of Sir Howard Elphinstone, VC; *m* 1953, Pamela Sylvia, *d* of late Major Rhys Mansel, Smedmore, Dorset; two *s* two *d*. *Educ:* Stowe Sch.; Trinity Coll., Cambridge (MA; Capt., Univ. Fencing Team). Entered Colonial Admin. Service, N Nigeria, 1939 but went immediately on War Service with 18th and 28th Field Regts RA, Dunkirk 1940, India and Burma, 1942–45; commanded 1st Field Battery RA in final Burma campaign. Asst Principal, Appointments Dept, CO, Feb.–Oct. 1946; Asst Dist Officer, N Nigeria, 1946–49; Private Sec. to Governor (Sir John Macpherson), 1949–50; Clerk to Exec. Council and Clerk, Legislature, N Nigeria, 1951–53; Sen. Dist Officer and Actg Resident, Kano Province, 1955–59; Admin. Officer Grade 1 and Resident, Bornu Province, 1960–62. Chm., Aidis Trust, 1988–94. KStJ 1968. *Publication:* Kingdoms in the Sand and Sun, 1992. *Address:* Lower Westport, Wareham, Dorset BH20 4PR. *T:* (01929) 553252.

McCLINTOCK-BUNBURY, family name of **Baron Rathdonnell**.

McCLOY, Dr Elizabeth Carol, FRCP, FFOM; Chief Medical Officer and Medical Services Director, UNUM Ltd, 1997–98; *b* 25 April 1945; *d* of Edward Bradley and Ada Entwisle; *m* 1969, Rory McCloy (marr. diss. 1989); two *s*. *Educ:* Guildford Grammar Sch.; University Coll. and UCH, London (BSc Hons 1966; MB BS Hons 1969). MFOM 1988, FFOM 1993; FRCP 1995. Clinical Asst, Medicine, W Middlesex Univ. Hosp., 1972–83; Manchester Royal Infirmary: Sen. Clinical MO, Occupational Health, 1984–88; Consultant in Occupational Medicine, 1988–93; Dir of Occupational Health and Safety, Central Manchester Healthcare Trust, 1988–93; Chief Exec. and Dir, CS Occupnl Health Service, later CS Occupnl Health and Safety Agency, and Med. Advr to CS, 1993–96. Pres., Soc. of Occupational Medicine, 1993–94. FRSocMed. *Publications:* (ed jtly) Practical Occupational Medicine, 1994; (contrib.) Hunters Diseases of Occupations, 7th edn 1987, 8th edn 1994; (contrib.) Oxford Textbook of Medicine, 1994; articles on hepatitis. *Recreations:* theatre, gardening, antiques.

McCLUNE, Rear-Adm. (William) James, CB 1978; *b* Londonderry, 20 Nov. 1921; *s* of James McClune, MBE, Carrickmacross, Co. Monaghan, and Matilda (*née* Burns); *m* 1953, Elizabeth, *yr d* of A. E. D. Prideaux, LDS, Weymouth; one *s* one *d*. *Educ:* Model Sch. and Foyle Coll., Derry; QUB (BSc 1st Cl. Hons Elec. Eng, 1941); RN Staff Coll., Greenwich (1961); Univ. of Birmingham (Ratcliff Prizeman, MSc 1970); RN War Coll. (1971). Bronze Medal, CGLI, 1940; Belfast Assoc. of Engrs' Prize, 1940, 1941. CEng, MIEE; CIMgt. Radar Officer, RNVR, 1941–47; Eng Dept, GPO, 1947–49; RN, 1949–78; CSO (Engrg) to C-in-C Fleet, 1976–78. A Life Vice-Pres., RNLI. Patron, Monkton Combe Sch. *Recreation:* sailing. *Address:* Harlam Lodge, Lansdown, Bath; An Charraig, Port na Blagh, Co. Donegal, Ireland. *Club:* Royal Commonwealth Society.

McCLUNEY, Ian, CMG 1990; HM Diplomatic Service, retired; High Commissioner, Sierra Leone, 1993–97; *b* 27 Feb. 1937. *Educ:* Edinburgh Univ. (BSc). Served HM Forces, 1958–62. Joined FO, 1964; Addis Ababa, 1964–67; FCO, 1969–70; Baghdad, 1972–74; FCO, 1975–78; Kuwait, 1979–82; Consul-Gen., Alexandria, 1982–86; FCO, 1986–88; Ambassador to Somalia, 1989–90; Dep. High Comr, Calcutta, 1991–93. Reference Sec., Competition Commn, 2000–. *Recreation:* sailing. *Clubs:* Little Ship, Royal Over-Seas League.

McCLURE, Prof. John, MD; FRCPath; Procter Professor of Pathology, University of Manchester, since 1987; Director of Laboratory Medicine, Central Manchester Healthcare Trust, since 1996; *b* 2 May 1947; *s* of Richard Burns McClure and Isabella McClure (*née* Nelson); *m* 1970, Sheena Frances Tucker; three *d*. *Educ:* Queen's Univ. Belfast (BSc Hons, MB, BCh, BAO, MD, DMJPath). Training posts in Pathology, QUB, 1972–78; Clinical Sen. Lectr and Specialist/Sen. Specialist in Pathology, Univ. of Adelaide and Inst. of Med. and Vet. Sci., Adelaide, 1978–83; University of Manchester: Sen. Lectr and Hon. Consultant in Histopathology, 1983–87; Head of Pathological Scis, 1987–95; Associate Dean, Faculty of Medicine, 1995–98. British Red Cross: Chm., Northern Regl Council, 1998–99; Mem., Nat. Bd of Trustees, 1998– (Chm., 2001–); Pres. and Trustee, Gtr Manchester Br., 1994–99. *Publications:* papers in med. and path. jls. *Recreation:* DIY. *Address:* Directorate of Laboratory Medicine, Central Manchester Healthcare Trust, Oxford Road, Manchester M13 9WL. *T:* (0161) 276 8945.

McCLURE, Joseph Robert, MBE 2000; *b* 21 Oct. 1923; *s* of Thomas Render McClure and Catherine Bridget McClure; *m* 1943, Evelyn Joice; one *d*. *Educ:* Prior Street Sch.; Oakwellgate Sch., Gateshead. Served War, Royal Marines, 1941–46. Elected Councillor (Lab): County Borough of Gateshead, 1964–73, Dep. Mayor, 1973–74; Tyne and Wear CC, 1974–82 (Chm., 1977–78). President: Tyneside Br., Royal Marine Assoc., 1996–2001; Gateshead RBL, 1976–; Vice Pres., Northumberland/Tyne and Wear County, RBL, 1997–. JP Gateshead and Blaydon, 1979–93. *Recreation:* bowls. *Address:* 170 Rectory Road, Gateshead, Tyne and Wear NE8 4RR. *T:* (0191) 477 0709.

McCLURE, Dr Judith, FSAScot; Head of St George's School, Edinburgh, since 1994; *b* 22 Dec. 1945; *d* of James McClure and Vera (*née* Knight); *m* 1977, Roger John Howard Collins, DLitt, FRHistS, FSAScot. *Educ:* Newlands GS, Middlesbrough; Coll. of Law, London; Somerville Coll., Oxford (Shaw Lefevre Scholar; BA 1st Cl. Hons 1973; MA 1977; DPhil 1979). Canoness of St Augustine, Les Oiseaux, Westgate, Kent, 1964–70; Sir Maurice Powicke Meml Res. Fellow, LMH, Oxford, 1976–77; Lecturer: in Medieval Latin and Medieval History, Univ. of Liverpool, 1977–79; in History, Jesus, Somerville and Worcester Colls, Univ. of Oxford, 1979–81; School of St Helen and St Katherine, Abingdon: teacher of History and Politics, 1981–83; Head, History and Politics Dept, 1983–84; Asst Head, Kingswood Sch., Bath, 1984–87, Dir of Studies, 1986–87; Head, Royal Sch., Bath, 1987–93. Member: Governing Body, 1995–, Managing Cttee, 1998– (Chm., 2001–), Scottish Council of Ind. Schs; Regl Standing Cttee for Scotland, UCAS, 1997–99; Bd of Mgt, Scottish Qualifications Authy, 1999–2000; Chm., Scottish Region, and Mem. Council, GSA, 1996–99. Member: Court, Bath Univ., 1989–92; Gen. Convocation, Heriot-Watt Univ., 1994–; Member, Board of Governors: Selwyn Sch., Gloucester, 1988–90; Clifton Hall Sch., Lothian, 1995–99; Merchiston Castle Sch., 1999–. Trustee, Hopetoun House Preservation Trust, 1997–. Chm., Women of Lothian Lunch, 1998–. FRSA 1997. *Publications:* Gregory the Great: exegesis and audience, 1979; Introduction and notes to Bede's Ecclesiastical History, 1994; articles in Jl Theol Studies, Peritia, Papers of Liverpool Latin Seminar, Prep. School and in Festschriften. *Recreations:* reading, travel, thinking about the early Middle Ages. *Address:* 12A Ravelston Park, Edinburgh EH4 3DX. *Club:* University Women's.

McCLURE, Ven. Timothy Elston; Archdeacon of Bristol, since 1999; *b* 20 Oct. 1946; *s* of late Kenneth Elston McClure and of Grace Helen McClure (*née* Hoar); *m* 1969, Barbara Mary Marchant; one *s* one *d*. *Educ:* Kingston Grammar Sch.; St John's Coll., Durham (BA); Ridley Hall, Cambridge. Deacon 1970, priest 1971; Curate, Kirkheaton Parish Church, Huddersfield, 1970–73; Marketing Mgr, Agrofax Labour Intensive Products Ltd, Harrow, Middx, 1973–74; Chaplain, Manchester Poly., 1974–82; Curate, St Ambrose, Chorlton-on-Medlock, 1974–79; Team Rector, Parish of Whitworth, Manchester and Presiding Chaplain, Chaplaincies to Higher Educn in Manchester, 1979–82; Gen. Sec., SCM, 1982–92; Dir, Churches' Council for Industry and Social Responsibility, Bristol, 1992–99; Hon. Canon, Bristol Cathedral, 1992–; Lord Mayor's Chaplain, Bristol, 1996–99. Chairman: Traidcraft plc, 1990–97; Christian Conference Trust, 1998–. *Recreations:* cooking, gardening, reading. *Address:* Church House, 23 Great George Street, Bristol BS1 5QT. *T:* (0117) 906 0102.

McCLUSKEY, family name of **Baron McCluskey**.

McCLUSKEY, Baron *cr* 1976 (Life Peer), of Churchhill in the District of the City of Edinburgh; **John Herbert McCluskey;** a Senator of the College of Justice in Scotland, 1984–2000; *b* 12 June 1929; *s* of Francis John McCluskey, Solicitor, and Margaret McCluskey (*née* Doonan); *m* 1956, Ruth Friedland; two *s* one *d*. *Educ:* St Bede's Grammar Sch., Manchester; Holy Cross Acad., Edinburgh; Edinburgh Univ. Harry Dalgety Bursary, 1948; Vans Dunlop Schol., 1949; Muirhead Prize, 1949; MA 1950; LLB 1952. Sword of Honour, RAF Spitalgate, 1953. Admitted Faculty of Advocates, 1955; Standing Jun. Counsel to Min. of Power (Scotland), 1963; Advocate-Depute, 1964–71; QC (Scot.) 1967; Chm., Medical Appeal Tribunals for Scotland, 1972–74; Sheriff Principal of Dumfries and Galloway, 1973–74; Solicitor General for Scotland, 1974–79. Chm., Scottish Assoc. for Mental Health, 1985–94. Independent Chairman: Scottish Football League's Compensation Tribunal, 1988–; Scottish Football Association's Appeals Tribunal, 1990–. Reith Lectr, BBC, 1986. Editor, Butterworth's Scottish Criminal Law and Practice series, 1988–. Hon. LLD Dundee, 1989. *Publications:* Law, Justice and Democracy, 1987; Criminal Appeals, 1992, 2nd edn 2000. *Recreations:* tennis, pianoforte.

Address: c/o Parliament House, Edinburgh EH1 1RF. *T:* (0131) 225 2595. *Club:* Royal Air Force.

McCLUSKEY, Len; National Secretary, Transport and General Workers' Union, since 1990; *b* 23 July 1950; *s* of Leonard and Margaret McCluskey. *Educ:* Cardinal Godfrey High Sch., Merseyside. Dockworker, 1968–79; Transport and General Workers' Union: District Official, Merseyside, 1979–89; Political Officer, NW Region, 1985–89. Alumnus, Duke of Edinburgh's 8th Commonwealth Study Conf., 1998. *Recreations:* football, sport, reading, politics, chess. *Address:* Transport and General Workers' Union, 128 Theobalds Road, Holborn, WC1X 8TN.

McCLUSKIE, John Cameron, CB 1999; QC (Scot.) 1989; First Parliamentary Counsel, Scottish Executive (formerly First Scottish Parliamentary Counsel), since 1989; *b* 1 Feb. 1946; *s* of Thomas and Marjorie McCluskie; *m* 1970, Janis Mary Helen McArthur; one *s* one *d.* *Educ:* Hyndland Sch., Glasgow; Glasgow Univ. (LLB Hons 1967). Admitted Solicitor, Scotland, 1970; admitted Faculty of Advocates, 1974. Apprentice Solicitor, Boyds, Glasgow, 1967–69; Asst Town Clerk, Burgh of Cumbernauld, 1969–70; Legal Assistant: Macdonald, Jameson and Morris, Glasgow, 1970; SSEB, 1970–72; Asst, then Sen. Asst, Legal Sec. and Parly Draftsman, Lord Advocate's Dept, 1972–89; Legal Sec. to Lord Advocate, 1989–99. *Recreation:* growing vegetables. *Address:* Law View, Redside Farm Steadings, North Berwick, East Lothian EH39 5PE.

McCOLL, family name of **Baron McColl of Dulwich**.

McCOLL OF DULWICH, Baron *cr* 1989 (Life Peer), of Bermondsey in the London Borough of Southwark; **Ian McColl,** CBE 1997; MS, FRCS, FACS, FRCSE; Professor of Surgery, University of London at Guy's, King's and St Thomas' School of Medicine of King's College London (formerly United Medical Schools of Guy's and St Thomas' Hospitals), 1971–98; Director of Surgery, 1985–98, and Consultant Surgeon, 1971–98, Guy's Hospital; *b* 6 Jan. 1933; *s* of late Frederick George McColl and Winifred E. McColl, Dulwich; *m* 1960, Dr Jean Lennox, 2nd *d* of Arthur James McNair, FRCS, FRCOG; one *s* two *d.* *Educ:* Hutchesons' Grammar Sch., Glasgow; St Paul's Sch., London; Guy's Hosp., London. MB, BS 1957; FRCS 1962; FRCSE 1962; MS 1966; FACS 1975. Junior staff appts at St Bartholomew's, Putney, St Mark's, St Peter's, Great Ormond Street, Barnet, St Olave's and Guy's Hosps, 1957–67; Research Fellow, Harvard Med. Sch., and Moynihan Fellowship, Assoc. of Surgeons, 1967; Reader in Surgery, St Bartholomew's Hosp. Med. Coll., 1967 (Sub Dean, 1969–71). Visiting Professor: Univ. of South Carolina, 1974; Johns Hopkins Hosp., 1976. Consultant Surgeon: KCH, 1971–98 (FKC 2001); Edenbridge Dist Meml Hosp., 1978–91; Lewisham Hosp., 1983–90; Hon. Consultant in Surgery to the Army, 1982–98. External examiner in Surgery to Univs of Newcastle upon Tyne and Cardiff, QUB, TCD and NUI. Royal College of Surgeons: Examr in Pathology, 1970–76; Regl Advr, SE Reg., 1975–80; Mem. Council, 1986–94; Arris and Gale Lectr, 1964, 1965; Erasmus Wilson Lectr, 1972; Haig Gudenian Meml Lectr, 1988; Henry Cohen Meml Lectr, 1994; Lettsomian Lectr, Med. Soc. of London, 1993. Medical Advisor, BBC Television, 1976–92. PPS (Lord's) to the Prime Minister, 1994–97; a Dep. Speaker, H of L, 1994–. Member: Central Health Services Council, 1972–74; Standing Medical Adv. Cttee, 1972–82; Management Cttee, King Edward VII Hospital Fund (Chm., R&D Cttee), 1975–80; Council, Metrop. Hosp. Sunday Fund, 1986–91; Council, Imperial Cancer Res. Fund, 1986–94; Exec. Council, British Limbless Ex-Service Men's Assoc., 1991–; Chairman: King's Fund Centre Cttee, 1976–86; Govt Wkg Pty on Artificial Limb and Appliance Centres in England, 1984–86; Vice Chm., SHA for Disablement Services, 1987–91. Hon. Sec., British Soc. of Gastroenterology, 1970–74. President: Soc. of Minimally Invasive Gen. Surgery, 1991–94; Limbless Assoc. (formerly Nat. Assoc. for Limbless Disabled), 1992– (Patron and Hon. Consultant, 1989–); Internat. Wheelchair Fedn, 1991–; Assoc. of Endoscopic Surgeons of GB and Ireland, 1994–98; The Hospital Saving Assoc., 1994–2001; Leprosy Mission, 1996–; REMEDI, 1996–99; Royal Med. Foundn of Epsom Coll., 2001–; Vice-Pres., John Grooms Assoc. for Disabled People, 1990–. Governor-at-Large for England, Bd of Governors, Amer. Coll. of Surgeons, 1982–88. Pres., 1985–94, Chm. Bd of Govs, 1994–, Mildmay Mission Hosp.; Chm., Mercy Ships UK, and Dir, Mercy Ships Internat. Governor: Dulwich Coll. Prep. Sch., 1978–; James Allen's Girls' Sch., 1994– (Chm., 1998–); St Paul's Sch., 2001–. Trustee, Wolfson Foundn, Dulwich Estate, 1994–. Master, Barbers' Co., 1999–2000. Edenbridge Medal for Services to the Community, 1992; George and Thomas Hutcheson's Award, 2000. *Publications:* (ed jtly) Intestinal Absorption in Man, 1975; Talking to Patients, 1982; NHS Data Book, 1984; med. articles, mainly on gastroenterology, rehabilitation and NHS management. *Recreation:* forestry. *Address:* House of Lords, SW1A 0PW; Guy's Nuffield House, Newcomen Street, SE1 1YR. *Clubs:* Royal College of Surgeons Council, Royal Society of Medicine.

McCOLL, (Christopher) Miles; a District Judge (Magistrates' Courts) (formerly Provincial Stipendiary Magistrate), West Midlands, since 1993; *b* 18 April 1946; *s* of John Parr McColl and Lilian McColl (*née* Oddy); *m* 1971, Susan Margaret Rathbone; three *d.* *Educ:* Liverpool Coll. Admitted solicitor, 1971. Articled clerk in private practice, St Helens, 1965–69; trainee, Court Clerk, then Principal Court Clerk, Manchester City Magistrates' Court, 1969–74; Dep. Clerk to Stockport Justices, 1974–78; Clerk to Leigh Justices, 1978–93. Sec., Gtr Manchester Justices' Clerks and Courts Liaison Cttee, 1984–90; Member: Magistrates' Courts Rev. of Procedure Cttee, 1989–91; Magistrates' Courts Consultative Council, 1992–93; Children Act Procedure Adv. Gp, 1989–90; Pres. of Family Division's Cttee, 1990–92; Legal Aid Steering Cttee, 1992; Pre-trial Issues Steering Gp, 1992–93; Legal Cttee, Jt Council of HM Stipendiary Magistrates, 1997– (Chm., 2000–). Secretary: S Lancs Br., Magistrates' Assoc., 1979–85; British Juvenile and Family Courts' Soc., 1980–81; Justices' Clerks' Society: Mem. Council, 1988–93; Chm., Parly Cttee, 1989; Chm., Professional Purposes Cttee, 1989–93; Pre-trial Issues Nat. Action Manager, 1991–93; Vice-Pres., Duchy of Lancaster Br., 1993. Ed., 1979–87, Jt Ed., 1987–, Family Law. *Publications:* Court Teasers: practical situations arising in magistrates' courts, 1978; contrib. to legal jls. *Recreations:* sport, reading, music, British countryside. *Address:* Birmingham Magistrates' Court, Victoria Law Courts, Corporation Street, Birmingham B4 6QA. *T:* (0121) 212 6600.

McCOLL, Sir Colin (Hugh Verel), KCMG 1990 (CMG 1983); HM Diplomatic Service, retired; Head of MI6, 1988–94; *b* 6 Sept. 1932; *s* of Dr Robert McColl and Julie McColl; *m* 1st, 1959, Shirley Curtis (*d* 1983); two *s* two *d*; 2nd, 1985, Sally Morgan; one *s.* *Educ:* Shrewsbury School; The Queen's College, Oxford (BA; Hon. Fellow 1996). Foreign Office, 1956; Third Secretary, Bangkok, 1958, Vientiane, 1960; Second Secretary, FO, 1962; First Secretary, Warsaw, 1966; Consul and First Secretary (Disarmament), Geneva, 1973; Counsellor, FCO, 1977. Dir, Scottish American Investment Trust, 1996–; Advisory Director: Campbell Lutyens, 1995–; Mantech International, 1998–; Pegasus Security Group, 1998–. Chairman: Peers Early Educn Trust, 1996–; Pimpernel Trust, 1997–. *Recreations:* music, walks, cycling, tennis, classics. *Address:* PO Box 1105, SE1 1AG.

McCOLL, Ian, CBE 1983; Chairman, Scottish Express Newspapers Ltd, 1975–82; *b* 22 Feb. 1915; *e s* of late John and Morag McColl, Glasgow and Bunessan, Isle of Mull; *m* 1968, Brenda, *e d* of late Thomas and Mary McKean, Glasgow; one *d.* *Educ:* Hillhead High Sch., Glasgow. Served in RAF, 1940–46 (despatches, 1945): Air Crew, Coastal Comd 202 Sqdn. Joined Scottish Daily Express as cub reporter, 1933; held various editorial executive posts; Editor, Scottish Daily Express, 1961–71; Editor, Daily Express, 1971–74; Dir, Express Newspapers Ltd, 1971–82. Contested (L): Dumfriesshire, 1945; Greenock, 1950. Mem., Presbytery of Glasgow and Synod of Clydesdale, 1953–71; Mem., General Assembly Publications Cttee, until 1971; Session Clerk, Sandyford-Henderson Memorial Church of Scotland, Glasgow, 1953–71. Mem., Newlands South C of S, Glasgow, 1975–. Mem., Press Council, 1975–78; a Vice-Pres., Newspaper Press Fund, 1981–. Mem., Gen. Assembly Bd of Communication, 1983–86. Chm. Media Div., XIII Commonwealth Games, Scotland 1986, 1983–86. Mem., Saints and Sinners Club of Scotland, Chm., 1981–82. Bank of Scotland Scottish Press Life Achievement Award, 1993. *Address:* 12 Newlands Road, Newlands, Glasgow G43 2JB.

McCOLL, Isabella G.; Sheriff of Tayside, Central and Fife at Dunfermline, since 2000; *b* 7 Nov. 1952. Admitted: Solicitor, 1975; Advocate, 1993. *Address:* Sheriff Court House, 1/6 Carnegie Drive, Dunfermline KY12 7HJ.

McCOLL, Miles; *see* McColl, C. M.

McCOLLUM, Sir Liam; *see* McCollum, Sir W. P.

McCOLLUM, Rt Hon. Sir William (Paschal), (Rt Hon. Sir Liam McCollum), Kt 1988; PC 1997; **Rt Hon. Lord Justice McCollum;** a Lord Justice of Appeal, Supreme Court of Judicature, Northern Ireland, since 1997; *b* 13 Jan. 1933; *s* of Patrick McCollum and Mary Ellen McCollum (*née* Strain); *m* 1958, Anne Bernadette Fitzpatrick (CBE 1995); six *s* two *d.* *Educ:* Waterside School; St Columb's Coll., Derry; University College Dublin (BA 1953; LLB 1954). Called to the Bar of N Ireland, 1955; called to Irish Bar, 1963; QC 1971; High Court Judge, NI, 1987–97. *Address:* Royal Courts of Justice, Chichester Street, Belfast BT1 3JF.

McCOMB, Leonard William Joseph, RA 1991 (ARA 1987); RE; painter, sculptor, printmaker, potter, draughtsman; Keeper of the Royal Academy, 1995–98; *b* 3 Aug. 1930; *s* of Archibald and Delia McComb, Glasgow; *m* 1st, 1955, Elizabeth Henstock (marr. diss. 1963); 2nd, 1966, Joan Allwork (*d* 1967); 3rd, 1973, Barbara Eleonora Gittel (marr. diss. 1999). *Educ:* Manchester Art Sch.; Slade Sch. of Fine Art, Univ. of London (Dip. Fine Art, 1960). RE 1994. Teacher at art schools, Bristol, Oxford, RA schools, Slade, Goldsmiths', Sir John Cass, 1960–. Hon. Member: Royal Watercolour Soc., 1996; Royal Soc. of Printmakers, 1996. *One-man exhibitions include:* Blossoms and Flowers, Coracle Press Gall., London, 1979; Drawings, Paintings and Sculpture, Serpentine Gall., London and tour, 1983; Paintings from the South, Gillian Jason Gall., London, 1989; Drawings and Paintings, Darby Gall., London, 1993; Portraits, NY Studio Sch. Gall.; exhibits annually, Royal Acad. of Arts; *group exhibitions include:* Arts Council, 1976, 1980, 1982, 1987; RA, 1977, 1989; Venice, 1980; Whitechapel, 1981; Tate, 1984; Hirshorn Gall., Washington, 1986; Raab Gall., Berlin, 1986; Museum of Modern Art, Brussels, 1987; Gillian Jason Gall., London, 1990, 1991; Kettles Yard Gall., 1994, 1995, 1997; Walker Art Gall., Liverpool, 1995; Aspects Gall., Portsmouth, 1997; Mus. of Modern Art, Dublin, 1997; Flowers East Gall., London, 1998; *work in public collections:* Arts Council; British Council; ICA; Cambridge Univ.; Tate; V&A; BM; Ulster Mus.; Art Galls of Birmingham, Manchester, Swindon, Worcester, Eastbourne, Bedford, Belfast; *commissions* for cos and educnl bodies include paintings, plates, tapestry, plaques. Prizes include: Jubilee Prize, RA, 1986; Korn Ferry Award, 1990; Times Watercolour Comp. Prize, 1992, 1993; Nordstern Printmaking Prize, RA, 1992; RWS Prize, 1998. *Recreations:* travelling and walking in the countryside.

McCOMBE, Hon. Sir Richard (George Bramwell), Kt 2001; **Hon. Mr Justice McCombe;** a Judge of the High Court of Justice, Queen's Bench Division, since 2001; *b* 23 Sept. 1952; *s* of Barbara Bramwell McCombe, MA, FCA; *m* 1st (marr. diss.); 2nd, 1986, Carolyn Sara Birrell; one *s* one *d.* *Educ:* Sedbergh Sch.; Downing Coll., Cambridge (MA). Called to the Bar, Lincoln's Inn, 1975, Bencher, 1996; admitted (*ad hoc*) to Bars of Singapore, 1992, Cayman Is, 1993. Second Jun. Counsel to Dir-Gen. of Fair Trading, 1982–87, First Jun. Counsel, 1987–89; QC 1989; an Asst Recorder, 1993–96, Recorder, 1996–2001; Attorney Gen., Duchy of Lancaster, 1996–2001; a Dep. High Ct Judge, 1998–2001. Mem., Senate of Inns of Court and of Bar Council, 1981–86; Chm., Young Barristers' Cttee, Bar Council, 1983–84; Co-opted Mem., Bar Council Cttees, 1986–89; Mem., Gen. Council of the Bar, 1995–97 (Chm., Internat. Relns Cttee, 1997). Head of UK Delegn to Council, Bars and Law Socs of EC, 1996–98. Inspector into affairs of Norton Group PLC, 1991–92 (report, with J. K. Heywood, 1993). Mem., Singapore Acad. of Law, 1992. *Recreations:* cricket, Rugby (both as spectator), travel, flying light aircraft. *Address:* Royal Courts of Justice, Strand, WC2A 2LL. *Clubs:* Athenæum, Royal Automobile, MCC; London Scottish Football, Harlequin Football; Lancs CC.

McCOMBIE, John Alexander Fergusson, FRICS; General Manager, Glenrothes Development Corporation, 1993–96; *b* 13 Sept. 1932; *s* of Alexander William McCombie and Charlotte Mary McCombie (*née* Fergusson); *m* 1959, Seana Joy Cameron Scott; two *s* one *d.* *Educ:* Perth Acad.; Coll. of Estate Management. ARICS 1968, FRICS 1982; IRRV 1969. Nat. service, RAF, 1955–57 (MEAF). E Kilbride Develt Corp., 1959–67; Irvine Develt Corp., 1968–70; Glenrothes Develt Corp., 1970–96: Chief Estates Officer, 1970–74; Commercial Dir, 1975–93. Director: Glenrothes Enterprise Trust, 1983–94; Mid-Fife Business Trust, 1994– (Chm., 1997–); Age Concern Glenrothes Ltd, 1996–; Chm., Ecowise Fife Ltd, 1999–; Dir and Sec., 1996–, Chm., 1997–, Fife Historic Bldgs Trust; Chairman: Leven Valley Develt Trust, 1997–; Wolseley Register, Scottish Gp. Mem. Bd of Mgt, Glenrothes Coll., 1999–. *Recreations:* gardening, golf, philately, reading, veteran cars. *Address:* 13 Carnoustie Gardens, Glenrothes, Fife KY6 2QB. *T:* (01592) 755658. *Club:* Balbirnie Park Golf.

McCONNELL, Bridget Mary; Director of Cultural and Leisure Services, Glasgow City Council, since 1998; *b* 28 May 1958; *d* of Robert Rankin McLuckie and Patricia McLuckie (*née* Airlie); *m* 1990, Jack Wilson McConnell, *qv*; one *s* one *d.* *Educ:* St Patrick's Jun. Secondary Sch., Kilsyth; Our Lady's High Sch., Cumbernauld; St Andrew's Univ. (MA Hons 1982); Dundee Coll. of Commerce (DIA 1983); Stirling Univ. (MEd 1992). Curator, Doorstep Gall., Fife Regl Council, 1983–84; Arts Officer, Stirling DC, 1984–88; Principal Arts Officer, Arts in Fife, Fife Regl Council, 1988–96; Service Manager, Community Services/Arts, Libraries, Museums, Fife Council, 1996–98. Member: Bd, Workshop and Artists Studio Provision Scotland Ltd, 1985–90; Combined Arts Cttee, Scottish Arts Council, 1988–94; Chair, Scottish Youth Dance Fest., 1993–96 (Founder Mem., 1988); Co-ordinator, Fourth Internat. Conf. in Adult Educn and the Arts, 1995. *Publications:* (contrib.) Modernising Britain: creative futures, 1997; internat. conf. papers, ed conf. proceedings. *Recreations:* walking, playing the piano, swimming, reading. *Address:* (office) 20 Trongate, Glasgow G1 5ES. *T:* (0141) 287 5058.

McCONNELL, Jack Wilson; Member (Lab) Motherwell and Wishaw, Scottish Parliament, since 1999; Minister for Education, Europe and External Affairs, since 2000;

b 30 June 1960; *s* of William Wilson McConnell and Elizabeth McEwan McConnell; *m* 1990, Bridget Mary McLuckie (*see* B. M. McConnell); one *s* one *d*. *Educ:* Arran High Sch., Isle of Arran; Stirling Univ. (BSc 1983; DipEd 1983). Mathematics Teacher, Alloa, 1983–92; Gen. Sec., SLP, 1992–98. Mem. (Lab) Stirling DC, 1984–93 (Treas., 1988–92; Leader, 1990–92). Contested (Lab) Perth and Kinross, 1987. Minister for Finance, Scottish Exec., 1999–2000. Member: COSLA, 1988–92; Scottish Constitutional Convention, 1990–98. *Publications:* political articles in newspapers, jls and booklets. *Recreations:* golf, swimming, music. *Address:* 265 Main Street, Wishaw, Lanarkshire ML2 7NE. *T:* (01698) 303040.

McCONNELL, Prof. James Desmond Caldwell, FRS 1987; Professor of the Physics and Chemistry of Minerals, Department of Earth Sciences, University of Oxford, 1986–95, now Emeritus (Head of Department, 1991–95); Fellow of St Hugh's College, Oxford, 1986–95 (Hon. Fellow, 1995); *b* 3 July 1930; *s* of Samuel D. and Cathleen McConnell; *m* 1956, Jean Elspeth Ironside; one *s* two *d*. *Educ.* Queen's Univ. of Belfast (BSc, MSc 1952); Univ. of Cambridge (MA 1955; PhD 1956); MA Oxon 1986. Univ. of Cambridge: Demonstrator, 1955; Lectr, 1960; Reader, 1972–82; Churchill College: Fellow, 1962–82; Extraordinary Fellow, 1983–88; Head of Dept of Rock Physics, Schlumberger Cambridge Research, 1983–86. Alex von Humboldt Prize, Alexander von Humboldt Stiftung, Germany, 1996. *Publications:* Principles of Mineral Behaviour (with A. Putnis), 1980, Russian edn, 1983; papers in physics jls and mineralogical jls. *Recreations:* local history, hill walking, singing. *Address:* 8 The Croft, Old Headington, Oxford OX3 9BU. *T:* (01865) 769100.

McCONNELL, John, RDI 1987; FCSD; graphic designer; Director, Pentagram Design, since 1974; *b* 14 May 1939; *s* of Donald McConnell and Enid McConnell (*née* Dimberline); *m* 1963, Moira Rose Macgregor; one *s* one *d*. *Educ:* Borough Green Secondary Modern School; Maidstone College of Art (NDD). FCSD (FSIAD 1980). Employed in advertising and design, 1959–62; Lectr, Colchester College of Art, 1962–63; freelance design practice, 1963–74; co-founder, Face Photosetting, 1968. Design consultant, Boots, 1984–; non-exec. Dir, Cosalt plc, 1996–. Member: Alliance Graphique Internat., 1976; Post Office Stamp Adv. Cttee, 1984; Pres., D&AD, 1986 (President's Award, 1985); served on design competition juries, D&AD. Gold medallist at Biennale, Warsaw. *Publications:* (jtly) Living by Design, 1978; (jtly) Ideas on Design, 1986; (jtly) The Compendium, 1993; (ed jtly) Pentagram Book 5, 1999; Editor, Pentagram Papers. *Recreations:* house restoration, cooking. *Address:* 11 Needham Road, W11 2RP. *T:* (020) 7229 3477; 12 Orme Court, W2 4RL.

McCONNELL, (Sir) Robert Shean, (4th Bt *cr* 1900); *S* father, 1987, but does not use the title. *Educ:* Stowe; Queens' Coll., Cambridge (MA Urban Estate Management); Regent St Polytech. (DipTP); Univ. of BC (MSc Community and Regl Planning). FRTPI; ARICS; MIMgt. Worked as a trainee surveyor in Belfast and as a town planner in UK, Canada and USA. Lectured in town planning and principles of management at univs in UK and Australia. Mem., Bruce House Appeal Cttee. Governor: South Bank Poly., 1973–75; Tulse Hill Sch., 1976–90; Stockwell Infant Jun. Sch., 1983–88; Norwood Park Primary Sch., 1996–. Councillor (Lib Dem) Lambeth BC, 1996–. *Publications:* Theories for Planning, 1981; (contrib.) Planning Ethics, ed Hendler, 1995; (contrib.) Housing: the essential foundations, ed Balchin and Rhoden, 1998; articles in professional jls on planning matters. *Recreations:* gardening, walking, the local community, travel. *Heir:* *b* James Angus McConnell [*m* Elizabeth Jillian (*née* Harris); two *s* four *d* (incl. twins)].

McCONVILLE, Michael Anthony, MBE 1958; writer; *b* 3 Jan. 1925; *s* of late Lt-Col James McConville, MC and late Winifred (*née* Hanley); *m* 1952, Beryl Anne (*née* Jerrett); two *s* four *d*. *Educ:* Mayfield Coll.; Trinity Coll., Dublin. Royal Marines, 1943–46. Malayan Civil Service, 1950–61: served in Perak, Johore, Trengganu, Negri Sembilam, Pahang and Kedah; retd as Chm., Border War Exec. Cttee. CRO (later HM Diplomatic Service), 1961–77: Colombo, 1963–64; Kingston, Jamaica, 1966–67; Ottawa, 1967–71; Consul-Gen., Zagreb, 1974–77. Kesatria Mankgu Negara (Malaya), 1962. *Publications:* (as Anthony McCandless): Leap in the Dark, 1980; The Burke Foundation, 1985; (as Michael McConville) Ascendancy to Oblivion: the story of the Anglo-Irish, 1986; A Small War in the Balkans: the British in war time Yugoslavia, 1986; Nothing Much to Lose, 1993; (ed) Tell it to the Marines, 1994; (as Miles Noonan): Tales from the Mess, 1983; More Tales from the Mess, 1984. *Recreations:* gardening, watching Rugby. *Address:* 72 Friarn Street, Bridgwater, Som TA6 3LJ.

McCORD, Brig. Mervyn Noel Samuel, CBE 1978 (OBE 1974); MC 1951; retired; *b* 25 Dec. 1929; *s* of late Major G. McCord, MBE and Muriel (*née* King); *m* 1953, Annette Mary, *d* of C. R. W. Thomson; three *s*. *Educ:* Coleraine, NI; RMA Sandhurst. Commissioned Royal Ulster Rifles, 1949; Korea, 1950–51; School of Infantry, 1958–60; Staff Coll., Camberley, 1961–62; DAQMG, Eastern Command, Canada, 1963–65; BM, HQ 6 Infantry Brigade, 1967–69; JSSC, 1969; GSO1, HQNI, 1970–71; CO, 1st Bn The Royal Irish Rangers, 1971–74; Brig. 1975; Commander, Ulster Defence Regt, 1976–78; Dep. Comdr, Eastern Dist, 1978–81; Brig. King's Div., 1981–84. ADC to the Queen, 1981–84. Col, The Royal Irish Rangers, 1985–90 (Dep. Col, 1976–81). Chairman: SHAA, 1986–93; SHAA Retirement Homes plc, 1986–93; Dir, SHC, 1994–. *Recreations:* cricket, athletics, country sports, gardening. *Address:* c/o Drummonds, 49 Charing Cross, SW1A 2DX. *Club:* Army and Navy.

McCORKELL, George Alexander; Chief Information Officer, Department of Social Security, since 2000; *b* 6 Jan. 1944; *s* of Samuel Robert McCorkell and Sarah McCorkell; *m* 1967, Nuala McCarthy; two *s*. *Educ:* Foyle Coll., Londonderry, NI; BA Math. Open, 1978; MSc Information Systems, LSE, 1982. Computer Programmer, MoD, 1967–69; Systems Analyst: Min. of Finance, 1970–74; DHSS, 1974–76; Liaison Officer, CCTA, 1976–79; Department of Health and Social Security, later Department of Social Security: Operational Systems Team Leader, 1979–83; Principal, 1983–86; Sen. Principal, 1987–88; Director: ITSA, 1988–95; Benefits Agency, 1995–99; Chief Exec., ITSA, 1999–2000. *Recreation:* golf. *Address:* Information Technology Services Group, Department of Social Security, Peel Park Control Centre, Blackpool Industrial Estate, Brunel Way, Blackpool, Lancs FY4 5ES. *T:* (01253) 688850.

McCORKELL, Col Sir Michael (William), KCVO 1994; OBE 1964; TD 1954; JP; Lord-Lieutenant, County Londonderry, 1975–2000; *b* 3 May 1925; *s* of late Captain B. F. McCorkell, Templeard, Culmore, Co. Londonderry and of Mrs E. M. McCorkell; *m* 1950, Aileen Allen, OBE 1975, 2nd *d* of late Lt-Col E. B. Booth, DSO, Darver Castle, Dundalk, Co. Louth, Eire; three *s* one *d*. *Educ:* Aldenham. Served with 16/5 Lancers, 1943–47; Major (TA) North Irish Horse, 1951; Lt-Col 1961; comd North Irish Horse (TA); retd, 1964. T&AVR Col, NI, 1971–74; Brevet Col, 1974; Pres., T&AVR, NI, 1977–88; ADC to the Queen, 1972. Hon. Col, N Irish Horse, 1975–81. Co. Londonderry: High Sheriff 1961; DL 1962; JP 1980. *Recreations:* fishing, shooting. *Address:* Ballyarnett, 50 Beragh Hill Road, Londonderry, Northern Ireland BT48 8LY. *T:* (028) 7135 1239. *Club:* Cavalry and Guards.

MacCORMAC, Sir Richard Cornelius, Kt 2001; CBE 1994; RA 1993; PPRIBA; Partner, MacCormac, Jamieson, Prichard (formerly MacCormac, Jamieson), Architects, since 1972; President, Royal Institute of British Architects, 1991–93; *b* 3 Sept. 1938; *s* of late Henry MacCormac, CBE, MD, FRCP and Marion Maud, *d* of B. C. Broomhall, FRCS; *m* 1964, Susan Karin Landen; one *s* (and one *s* decd). *Educ:* Westminster Sch.; Trinity Coll., Cambridge (BA 1962); University College London (MA 1965). RIBA 1967. Served RN, 1957–59. Proj. Archt, London Bor. of Merton, 1967–69; estabd private practice, 1969. Major works include: Cable & Wireless Coll., Coventry (Royal Fine Art Commn/Sunday Times Bldg of the Year Award, 1994); Garden Quadrangle, St John's Coll., Oxford (Ind. on Sunday Bldg of the Year Award, 1994); Bowra Bldg, Wadham Coll., Oxford; Burrell's Fields, Trinity Coll., Cambridge; Ruskin Liby, Lancaster Univ. (Ind. on Sunday Bldg of the Year Award, 1996); Southwark Stn, Jubilee Line Extension; Wellcome Wing, Science Mus. Taught in Dept of Arch., Cambridge Univ., 1969–75 and 1979–81, Univ. Lectr, 1976–79; Studio Tutor, LSE 1998. Visiting Professor: Univ. of Edinburgh (Dept of Architecture), 1982–85; Hull Univ., 1998–99. Dir, Spitalfields Workspace, 1981–. Chm., Good Design in Housing Awards, RIBA London Region, 1977; Mem., Royal Fine Art Commn, 1983–93; Comr, English Heritage, 1995–98. Royal Academy: Member: Architecture Cttee, 1998–; Exhibns Cttee, 1998–; Council, 1998–. Advisor: British Council, 1993–; Urban Task Force, 1998. Pres., London Forum of Amenity and Civic Socs, 1997–; Trustee, Greenwich Foundn for RNC, 1998–. FRSA 1982. *Publications:* articles in Architectural Review and Archts Jl. *Recreations:* sailing, music, reading. *Address:* 9 Heneage Street, E1 5LJ. *T:* (020) 7377 9262.

McCORMACK, John P(atrick); General Motors Corporation, retired 1986; *b* New York, 23 Nov. 1923; *s* of John McCormack and Margaret (*née* Bannon); *m* 1952, Mari Martha Luhrs; two *s*. *Educ:* St John's Univ., Jamaica, NY (Bachelor of Business Admin); NY Univ., NYC (LLB). Joined General Motors, 1949; Gen. Clerk, Accounting Dept, NY, 1949, Sen. Clerk 1950, Sen. Accountant 1952; Asst to Treas., Djakarta Br., 1953; Asst Treas., Karachi Br., 1956; Asst Treas., Gen. Motors South African (Pty) Ltd, Port Elizabeth, 1958, Treas. 1961; Asst Finance Man., Overseas Div., NY, 1966; Treas., subseq. Man. Dir, Gen. Motors Continental, Antwerp, 1968; Finance Man., Adam Opel, 1970, Man. Dir and Chm. Bd, 1974; Gen. Dir, European Ops, Gen. Motors Overseas Corp., 1976; Vice Pres. i/c joint ventures and African ops, 1980; Vice Pres. i/c Latin American and S African Ops, 1983. *Recreations:* golf, photography. *Address:* c/o General Motors Corporation, General Motors Building, Detroit, Michigan 48202, USA; PO Box 1030, Pebble Beach, CA 93953-1030, USA.

McCORMACK, Mark Hume; Chairman and Chief Executive Officer, International Management Group, since 1964; *b* 6 Nov. 1930; *s* of late Ned Hume McCormack and Grace Wolfe McCormack; *m* 1st, 1954, Nancy Breckenridge McCormack (marr. diss. 1984); two *s* one *d*; 2nd, 1986, Betsy Nagelsen; one *d*. *Educ:* Princeton Univ.; William and Mary Coll. (BA); Yale Univ. (LLB). Admitted to Ohio Bar, 1957; Associate in Arter, Hadden, Wykoff & Van Duzer, 1957–63; Partner, 1964–; started Internat. Management Gp, 1962. Commentator for televised golf, BBC. *Publications:* The World of Professional Golf, annually, 1967–; Arnie: the evolution of a legend, 1967; What they don't teach you at Harvard Business School, 1984; The Terrible Truth about Lawyers, 1987; Success Secrets, 1989; What They Still Don't Teach You at Harvard Business School, 1989; The 110% Solution, 1991; Hit the Ground Running, 1993; On Negotiating, 1995; McCormack on Communications, 1996; Getting Results for Dummies, 2000; What You'll Never Learn on the Internet, 2000; monthly newsletters Success Secrets. *Recreations:* golf, tennis. *Address:* 1360 E Ninth Street #100, Cleveland, OH 44114-1782, USA. *T:* 216/522–1200. *Clubs:* Royal & Ancient Golf (St Andrews); Wentworth (Virginia Water); Sunningdale Golf (Berkshire, England); Old Prestwick (Prestwick); Royal Dornoch (Dornoch); Turnberry Hotel Golf; Deepdale (NY); Pepper Pike, Country Club of Cleveland (Ohio); Isleworth, Bay Hill (Florida); Ironwood Country (Calif).

MacCORMICK, Sir (Donald) Neil, Kt 2001; FBA 1986; Member (SNP) Scotland, European Parliament, since 1999; Regius Professor of Public Law, University of Edinburgh, since 1972 (on leave of absence, since 1999); *b* 27 May 1941; *yr s* of J. M. MacCormick, MA, LLD (Glasgow) and Margaret I. Miller, MA, BSc (Glasgow); *m* 1st, 1965, Caroline Rona Barr (marr. diss. 1992); three *d*; 2nd, 1992, Flora Margaret Britain (*née* Milne), Edinburgh. *Educ:* High School, Glasgow; Univ. of Glasgow (MA, 1st cl. Philos. and Eng. Lit.); Balliol Coll., Oxford (BA, 1st cl. Jurisprudence; MA); LLD Edinburgh, 1982. Pres., Oxford Union Soc., 1965. Called to the Bar, Inner Temple, 1971. Lecturer, St Andrew's Univ. (Queen's Coll., Dundee), 1965–67; Fellow and Tutor in Jurisprudence, Balliol Coll., Oxford, 1967–72, and CUF Lectr in Law, Oxford Univ., 1968–72; Pro-Proctor, Oxford Univ., 1971–72; University of Edinburgh: Dean of Faculty of Law, 1973–76 and 1985–88; Provost, Faculty Gp of Law and Social Scis, 1993–97; Leverhulme Personal Res. Prof., 1997–99; Vice Principal (Internat.), 1997–99. Visiting Professor: Univ. of Sydney, 1981; Univ. of Uppsala, 1991; Anne Green Vis. Prof., Univ. of Texas, 1990; Higgins Visitor, NW Sch. of Law, Oregon, 1987. Lectures: Corry, Queen's Univ., Kingston, Ont, 1981; Dewey, NY Univ., 1982; Or Emet, Osgoode Hall, 1988; Chorley, LSE, 1992; Hart, Oxford, 1993; Stevenson, Glasgow, 1994. Contested (SNP): Edinburgh North, 1979; Edinburgh, Pentlands, 1983, 1987; Argyll and Bute, 1992, 1997. President: Assoc. for Legal and Social Philosophy, 1974–76; Soc. of Public Teachers of Law, 1983–84; Vice-President: Internat. Assoc. for Phil. of Law and Social Phil., 1991–95; RSE, 1991–94. Member: Houghton Cttee on Financial Aid to Political Parties, 1975–76; Broadcasting Council for Scotland, 1985–89; ESRC, 1995–99. Hon. QC 1999. MAE, 1995; For. Mem., Finnish Acad. of Scis, 1994. FRSE 1986. Hon. LLD: Uppsala, 1986; Saarland, 1994; Queen's Univ., Kingston, Ont, 1996; Macerata, 1998; Glasgow, 1999. *Publications:* (ed) The Scottish Debate: Essays on Scottish Nationalism, 1970; (ed) Lawyers in their Social Setting, 1976; Legal Reasoning and Legal Theory, 1978; H. L. A. Hart, 1981; Legal Right and Social Democracy: essays in legal and political philosophy, 1982; (with O. Weinberger) Grundlagen des Institutionalistischen Rechtspositivismus, 1985; An Institutional Theory of Law, 1986 (trans. Italian, 1991); (ed jtly) Enlightenment, Right and Revolution, 1989; (ed jtly) Interpreting Statutes, 1991; Interpreting Precedents, 1997; Questioning Sovereignty, 1999; contribs to various symposia, jls on law, philosophy and politics. *Recreations:* hill walking, bagpiping, sailing. *Address:* 19 Pentland Terrace, Edinburgh EH10 6HA; European Parliament, 60 rue Wiertz, 1047 Brussels, Belgium.

See also I. S. MacD. MacCormick.

McCORMICK, Prof. Francis Patrick, PhD; FRS 1996; Director, Cancer Research Institute, and Wood Distinguished Professor, University of California, San Francisco, since 1997; *b* 31 July 1950; *s* of David and Jane McCormick; *m* 1979, Judith Anne Demske (marr. diss. 1995). *Educ:* Univ. of Birmingham (BSc 1972); St John's Coll., Cambridge (PhD 1975). Post-doctoral Fellow: SUNY, 1975–78; ICRF, London, 1978–81; Scientist, 1981–89, Vice-Pres., Res., 1989–91, Cetus Corp.; Vice-Pres., Res., Chiron Corp., 1991–92; Founder and Vice-Pres., Res., Onyx Pharmaceuticals, 1992–96. *Publications:* (jointly): Origins of Human Cancer, 1991; The GTPase Superfamily, 1993; The ras Superfamily of GTPases, 1993. *Recreations:* motor racing, African history. *Address:* Cancer

Research Institute, School of Medicine, University of California, San Francisco, CA 94115, USA. *T:* (415) 5021710.

MacCORMICK, Iain Somerled MacDonald; Agent, DataLocator Ltd, since 2000; *b* 28 Sept. 1939; *er s* of John MacDonald MacCormick, MA, LLB, LLD and Margaret Isobel MacCormick, MA, BSc; *m* 1st, 1964, Micky Trefusis Elsom (marr. diss.); two *s* three *d*; 2nd, 1988, Carole Burnett (*née* Story) (marr. diss.). *Educ:* Glasgow High Sch.; Glasgow Univ. (MA). Queen's Own Lowland Yeomanry, 1957–67 (Captain). Major Account Manager, 1982, Dir Liaison Manager, 1984, BT plc; Trade Consultant, Bartering Co. Ltd, 1993–95. Contested (SNP) Argyll, 1970; MP (SNP) Argyll, Feb. 1974–1979; introduced, as private member's bill, Divorce (Scotland) Act, 1976. Founder Mem., SDP, 1981. Mem., Argyll and Bute District Council, 1979–80. *Recreations:* Rugby football, sailing, local history. *Address:* 2 Dowanside Road, Glasgow G12 9DA. *T:* (0141) 334 3367. *Club:* Glasgow Art (Glasgow).

See also Sir D. N. MacCormick.

McCORMICK, Prof. James Stevenson, FRCPI, FRCGP; FFPHM; Professor of Community Health, Trinity College Dublin, 1973–91 (Dean of School of Physic, 1974–79); *b* 9 May 1926; *s* of Victor Ormsby McCormick and Margaretta Tate (*née* Stevenson); *m* 1954, Elizabeth Ann Dimond; three *s* one *d*. *Educ:* The Leys Sch., Cambridge; Clare Coll., Cambridge (BA, MB); St Mary's Hospital, W2. Served RAMC, 1960–62; St Mary's Hosp., 1963; general practice, 1964–73. Chairman: Eastern Health Board, 1970–72; Nat. Health Council, 1984–86. Pres., Irish Coll. of General Practitioners, 1986–87. Hon. MCFP 1982. *Publications:* The Doctor—Father Figure or Plumber, 1979; (with P. Skrabanek) Follies and Fallacies in Medicine, 1989; papers, espec. on General Practice and Ischaemic Heart Disease. *Recreations:* open air, patients. *Address:* The Barn, Windgates, Bray, Co. Wicklow, Ireland. *T:* (1) 2874113.

McCORMICK, John; Controller of BBC Scotland, since 1992; *b* 24 June 1944; *s* of Joseph and Roseann McCormick; *m* 1973, Jean Frances Gibbons; one *s* one *d*. *Educ:* St Michael's Acad., Irvine; Univ. of Glasgow (MA Modern History with Econ. History 1967; MEd 1970). Teacher, St Gregory's Secondary Sch., Glasgow, 1968–70; Education Officer, BBC School Broadcasting Council, 1970–75; Senior Education Officer, Scotland, 1975–82; Sec., and Head of Information, BBC Scotland, 1982–87; The Sec. of the BBC, 1987–92. Chm., Edinburgh Internat. Film Fest., 1996–; Mem. Bd, Scottish Screen, 1997–. Mem., Glasgow Sci. Centre Charitable Trust, 1999–. Mem. Court, Univ. of Strathclyde, 1996–. FRTS 1998. Hon. DLitt Robert Gordon Univ., Aberdeen, 1997; Hon. LLD Strathclyde, 1999; DUniv Glasgow, 1999. *Recreation:* newspapers. *Address:* Broadcasting House, Queen Margaret Drive, Glasgow G12 8DG. *T:* (0141) 339 8844.

McCORMICK, John Ormsby, CMG 1965; MC 1943; HM Diplomatic Service, retired; *b* Dublin, 7 Feb. 1916; *s* of Albert Victor McCormick and Sarah Beatty de Courcy; *m* 1955, Francine Guieu (*née* Pâris); one *d*; one step *s*. *Educ:* The Leys Sch., Cambridge; New Coll., Oxford. BA Hon. Mods and Greats (Oxford), 1938. Passed Competitive Exam. for Consular Service, 1939, and appointed Asst Officer, Dept of Overseas Trade. Served War of 1939–45, in Royal Corps of Signals, Africa, Sicily, Germany, 1940–45. 2nd Sec. (Commercial), British Embassy, Athens, 1945–47; FO, London, 1948–50; 1st Sec., UK High Commn, Karachi, 1950–52; Consul, New York, 1952–54; transferred to Washington, 1954–55; NATO Defence Coll., 1955; Asst Head, SE Asia Dept, FO, 1956–59; Foreign Service Officer, Grade 6, 1959; Counsellor (Commercial), British Embassy, Djakarta, 1959–62; Corps of Inspectors, FO, 1962–64; Counsellor (Commercial), British Embassy, Ankara, 1965–67; Consul-General, Lyons, 1967–72. *Publication:* The Higher Lakes of Wicklow, 1994. *Address:* Oldfort, Newcastle, Co. Wicklow, Ireland.

McCORMICK, John St Clair; FRCSE; Medical Director, Dumfries and Galloway Royal Infirmary, since 1994; *b* 20 Sept. 1939; *s* of James McCormick and Claire Anne McCormick (*née* Diskett-Heath); *m* 1964, Fiona Helen McLean; two *s*. *Educ:* St Paul's Cathedral Choir Sch.; Sedbergh Sch.; Univ. of Edinburgh (MB ChB 1964). FRCSE 1967. Consultant Surgeon: Dunfermline, 1974–79; Dumfries and Galloway Royal Infirmary, 1979-99. Royal College of Surgeons of Edinburgh: Mem. Council, 1994–; Dir of Standards, 1997–; Vice Pres., 2000–. Mem., Clinical Standards Bd, Scotland, 1999–. Freeman, Co. of Wax Chandlers, 1962. *Address:* Ivy Cottage, Kirkpatrickdurham, Castle Douglas DG7 3HG.

MacCORMICK, Sir Neil; *see* MacCormick, Sir D. N.

McCOWAN, Rt Hon. Sir Anthony (James Denys), Kt 1981; PC 1989; a Lord Justice of Appeal, 1989–97; *b* 12 Jan. 1928; *yr s* of John Haines Smith McCowan, MBE, and Marguerite McCowan, Georgetown, British Guiana; *m* 1961, Sue Hazel Anne, *d* of late Reginald Harvey and of Mrs Harvey, Braiseworth Hall, Tannington, Suffolk; two *s* one *d*. *Educ:* Queen's Coll., British Guiana; Epsom Coll.; (Open Hist. schol.) Brasenose Coll., Oxford (MA, BCL). Called to Bar, Gray's Inn, 1951, Atkin Scholar; Bencher, 1980. Dep. Chm., E Sussex QS, 1969–71; a Recorder of the Crown Court, 1972–81; QC 1972; a Judge of the High Court, QBD, 1981–89. Leader, 1978–81, Presiding Judge, 1986–89, SE Circuit; Sen. Presiding Judge, England and Wales, 1991–95. Member: Parole Bd, 1982–84; Crown Court Rule Cttee, 1982–88. Chm., Fedn of Univ. Cons. and Unionist Assocs, 1951; Founder Mem., Bow Gp, 1951 (author of its first pubn, Coloured Peoples in Britain). Pres., Old Epsomian Club, 1997–98; Vice-Pres., Queen's Coll. of Guyana Assoc. (UK), 1995–. *Recreations:* sport, history, travel.

See also J. M. Archer.

McCOWAN, Sir David William Cargill, 4th Bt *cr* 1934, of Dalwhat, Dumfries; *b* 28 Feb. 1934; *s* of Sir David James Cargill McCowan, 2nd Bt and of Muriel Emma Annie, *d* of W. C. Willmott; *S* brother, 1998; *m*; one *s* one *d*. *Heir:* *s* David McCowan; *b* 2 June 1975. *Address:* Auchendennan Farm, Alexandria, Dunbartonshire G83 8RB.

McCOWEN, Alexander Duncan, (Alec), CBE 1986 (OBE 1972); actor; *b* 26 May 1925; *s* of late Duncan McCowen and Hon. Mrs McCowen. *Educ:* Skinners' Sch., Tunbridge Wells; RADA, 1941. Repertory: York, Birmingham, etc, 1943–50; Escapade, St James's, 1952; The Matchmaker, Haymarket, 1954; The Count of Clérambard, Garrick, 1955; The Caine Mutiny Court Martial, Hippodrome, 1956; Look Back in Anger, Royal Court, 1956; The Elder Statesman, Cambridge, 1958; Old Vic Seasons, 1959–61: Touchstone, Ford, Richard II, Mercutio, Oberon, Malvolio; Dauphin in St Joan; Algy in The Importance of Being Earnest; Royal Shakespeare Company, 1962–63: Antipholus of Syracuse in The Comedy of Errors; Fool, in King Lear; Father Fontana in The Representative, Aldwych, 1963; Thark, Garrick, 1965; The Cavern, Strand, 1965; After the Rain, Duchess, 1967, Golden Theatre, NY, 1967; Hadrian VII, Birmingham, 1967, Mermaid, 1968, New York, 1969; Hamlet, Birmingham, 1970; The Philanthropist, Royal Court, 1970, NY, 1971; Butley, Criterion, 1972; The Misanthrope, NT, 1973, 1975, NY 1975; Equus, NT, 1973; Pygmalion, Albery, 1974; The Family Dance, Criterion, 1976; Antony and Cleopatra, Prospect Co., 1977; solo performance of St Mark's Gospel, Riverside Studios, Mermaid and Comedy, 1978, Globe, 1981, UK tour, 1985, Half Moon, 1990; Tishoo, Wyndham's, 1979; The Browning Version, and A Harlequinade, NT, 1980; The Portage to San Cristobal of A. H., Mermaid, 1982; Kipling (solo performance), Mermaid, 1984; The Cocktail Party, Phoenix, 1986; Fathers and Sons, Waiting for Godot, NT, 1987; Shakespeare, Cole & Co. (solo performance), UK tour, 1988; The Heiress, Chichester, 1989; Exclusive, Strand, 1989; A Single Man, Greenwich, 1990; Dancing at Lughnasa, NT, 1990, transf. Phoenix, 1991; Preserving Mr Panmure, Chichester, 1991; Caesar and Cleopatra, Greenwich, 1992; Someone Who'll Watch Over Me, Hampstead, 1992, transf. Vaudeville, NY, 1992, The Tempest, Elgar's Rondo, 1993, The Cherry Orchard, 1995, RSC, Stratford; Uncle Vanya, Chichester, 1996; Tom and Clem, Aldwych, 1997; Peter Pan, RNT, 1997; Quartet, Albery, 1999. Dir, Definitely the Bahamas, Orange Tree, Richmond, 1987. Films include: Frenzy, 1971; Travels with My Aunt, 1972; Stevie, 1978; Never Say Never Again, 1983; The Age of Innocence, 1994; Songs of New York, 2001. TV series, Mr Palfrey of Westminster, 1984. Evening Standard (later Standard) Drama Award, 1968, 1973, 1982; Stage Actor of the Year, Variety Club, 1970. *Publications:* Young Gemini (autobiog.), 1979; Double Bill (autobiog.), 1980; Personal Mark, 1984. *Recreations:* music, gardening.

McCOY, Anthony Peter; National Hunt jockey; *b* 4 May 1974. Apprentice, Jim Bolgers Stables. Champion Nat. Hunt Jockey, 1995–96, 1996–97, 1997–98, 1998–99, 1999–2000, 2000–01. Winner: Cheltenham Gold Cup on Mr Mulligan, 1997; Champion Hurdle on Make A Stand, 1997; Scottish Grand National; Grand Annual Chase on Edredon Bleu, 1998. *Publication:* (with Claude Duval) The Real McCoy: my life so far, 1998. *Recreations:* golf, football, shooting. *Address:* c/o RBI Promotions Ltd, 26 Bute Street, S Kensington SW7 3EX. *T:* (020) 7581 1111, *Fax:* (020) 7581 1826.

McCOY, Hugh O'Neill, FICS; Chairman, Baltic Exchange, 1998–2000; *b* 9 Feb. 1939; *s* of Hugh O'Neill McCoy and Nora May (*née* Bradley); *m* 1964, Margaret Daphne Corfield; two *s*. *Educ:* Dudley Grammar Sch.; Sir John Cass Coll., Univ. of London (marine qualifications). Man. Dir, Horace Clarkson plc, 1993–98; Chm., H. Clarkson & Co., 1996–98. Vice Chm., Baltic Exchange, 1993–98. Non-executive Director: Gartmore Korea Fund plc, 1993–; Hadley Shipping Co., 1998–; Dir, Benor Tankers Ltd, Hamilton, Bermuda, 1998–. Pres., Inst. Chartered Shipbrokers, 1992–94. Mem., Gen. Council, Lloyd's Register of Shipping, 1997; Council Member: Project Trust (Isle of Coll); United World Coll. of Atlantic; Mem., London Fund-raising Cttee, Missions to Seamen; Hon. Vice-Pres., Maritime Volunteer Service; Advr, CAB. Freeman, City of London; Liveryman, Co. of Shipwrights. *Recreations:* sailing, swimming, long distance walking. *Address:* The Baltic Exchange, St Mary Axe, EC3A 8BH. *T:* (020) 7369 1621. *Club:* City.

McCRACKEN, Philip Guy; Executive Director, International Retail and Information Technology, Marks & Spencer, 1999–2000; *b* 25 Nov. 1948; *m* 1972, Frances Elizabeth Addison; one *s* two *d*. *Educ:* Clee Humberston Foundn Sch., Cleethorpes; Nat. Coll. of Food Technology, Reading Univ. (BSc 1st Class Hons Food Technology). Production Manager, Mars, 1972–73; Product Development Manager, Imperial Foods, 1973–75; Marks & Spencer, 1975–2000; Man. Dir, Food Div., 1994. *Recreations:* cricket, golf, tennis.

McCREA, Rev. Dr (Robert Thomas) William; Member (DemU) Ulster Mid, Northern Ireland Assembly, since 1998; Minister, Magherafelt Free Presbyterian Church of Ulster, since 1969; *b* 6 Aug. 1948; *s* of Robert T. and Sarah J. McCrea; *m* 1971, Anne Shirley McKnight; two *s* three *d*. *Educ:* Cookstown Grammar Sch.; Theol Coll., Free Presbyterian Church of Ulster. Civil servant, 1966; Free Presbyterian Minister of the Gospel, 1967–. Dist Councillor, Magherafelt, 1973–; Mem. (DemU) Mid Ulster, NI Assembly, 1982–86. MP (DemU) Mid Ulster, 1983–97 (resigned seat Dec. 1985 in protest against Anglo-Irish Agreement; re-elected Jan. 1986); contested (DemU) same seat, 1997; MP (DemU) Antrim South, Sept. 2000–2001; contested (DemU) same seat, 2001. Dir, Daybreak Recording Co., 1981–. Gospel singer and recording artist; Silver, Gold and Platinum Discs for record sales. Hon. DD Marietta Bible Coll., Ohio, 1989. *Publication:* In His Pathway—the story of the Reverend William McCrea, 1980. *Recreations:* music, horse riding. *Address:* 11 Ballyronan Road, Magherafelt, Co. Londonderry BT45 6BP. *T:* (028) 7963 2664.

McCREADY, Prof. (Victor) Ralph, DSc; FRCR, FRCP; Hon. Consultant, Royal Marsden NHS Trust, since 1998; *b* 17 Oct. 1935; *s* of Ernest and Mabel McCready; *m* 1964, Susan Margaret Mellor; two *d*. *Educ:* Ballyclare High Sch., NI; Queen's Univ., Belfast (MB BCh, BAO, BSc, DSc); Guy's Hosp., London Univ. (MSc 1964). MRCP 1974, FRCP 1994; FRCR 1975. Mem., Scientific Staff, Inst. of Cancer Res., London, 1964–74, 1998–; Consultant, Royal Marsden Hosp., 1974–98. Civilian Consultant, RN, 1993–. Hon. FFR, RCSI, 1992. Barclay Prize, British Inst. of Radiology, 1973. *Publications:* med. articles, books and contribs to books on nuclear medicine, ultrasound and magnetic resonance. *Recreations:* aviation, music. *Address:* Royal Marsden NHS Trust, Sutton, Surrey SM2 5PT. *T:* (020) 8642 6011. *Club:* Royal Automobile.

McCREATH, Alistair William; His Honour Judge McCreath; a Circuit Judge, since 1996; *b* 6 June 1948; *s* of late James McCreath and of Ruth Mary McCreath (*née* Kellar); *m* 1976, Julia Faith Clark; one *s* one *d*. *Educ:* St Bees Sch.; Univ. of Keele (BA Hons). Called to the Bar, Inner Temple, 1972; in practice at the Bar, 1973–96; Asst Recorder, 1986–90; Recorder, 1990–96. *Recreations:* golf, walking, reading, playing on computers. *Address:* Birmingham Crown Court, Queen Elizabeth II Law Courts, Birmingham B4 7NA. *T:* (0121) 681 3300. *Clubs:* Royal Troon Golf, Blackwell Golf.

McCREESH, Paul; Founder, Director and Conductor, Gabrieli Consort & Players; *b* 24 May 1960; *s* of Patrick Michael McCreesh and Valerie McCreesh (*née* Connors); *m* 1983, Susan Hemington Jones; one *s* one *d*. *Educ:* Manchester Univ. (MusB 1981). Freelance conductor; founded Gabrieli Consort & Players, internat. ensemble specialising in renaissance and baroque music, 1982. Numerous recordings. Internat. recording awards, Australia, Denmark, France, Germany, Holland, Italy, Poland, UK, USA. *Recreations:* countryside, walking, children. *Address:* c/o Intermusica Artists' Management Ltd, 16 Duncan Terrace, N1 8BZ. *T:* (020) 7278 5455.

McCREEVY, Charlie, FCA; TD (FF) Kildare, since 1977; Minister for Finance, Republic of Ireland, since 1997; *b* 30 Sept. 1949; *s* of Charles McCreevy and Eileen Mills. *Educ:* University Coll., Dublin (BComm). FCA 1973. Partner, Tynan, Dillon and Co., Chartered Accountants, 1974–97. Mem., Kildare CC, 1979–85. Minister for: Social Welfare, 1992–93; Tourism and Trade, 1993–94; frontbench spokesperson on Finance, 1995–97. *Recreations:* golf, horse-racing, Gaelic Athletic Association. *Address:* Department of Finance, Government Buildings, Merrion Street, Dublin 2, Ireland. *T:* (1) 6767571.

McCRICKARD, Donald Cecil; Chairman, London Town plc, since 1995; Group Chief Executive, TSB Group plc, 1990–92; Chief Executive, TSB Bank plc, 1989–92; *b* 25 Dec. 1936; *s* of late Peter McCrickard and Gladys Mary McCrickard; *m* 1st, 1960, Stella May, JP (marr. diss.), *d* of Walter Edward Buttle, RN retd; two *d*; 2nd, 1991, Angela Victoria Biddulph, JP, *d* of late Robert Biddulph Mitchell and of Mary Buckley Mitchell. *Educ:*

Hove Grammar Sch.; LSE; Univ. of Malaya. Financial, marketing and gen. management appts to 1975; Chief Exec., American Express Co. UK, 1975, American Express Co. Asia, Pacific, Australia, 1980; Dir, American Express Internat. Inc., 1978–83; Man. Dir, UDT Holdings, later TSB Commercial Holdings, 1983; Chairman: Swan National, 1983; UDT Bank, 1983; Dir, and Dep. Group Man. Dir, 1987, Chief Exec., Banking, 1988, TSB Group; Chm., Hill Samuel Bank, 1991–92. Non-executive Chairman: TM Group Holdings Ltd, 1996–98; SGi Gp, 1998–; non-executive Director: Carlisle Gp, 1993–96; Nat. Counties Building Soc., 1995–; Brit Insurance Hldgs PLC (formerly Benfield & Rea Investment Trust), 1995–; Allied London Properties, 1997–2000. Chm., Barnet Enterprise Trust, 1985–88. Trustee: Crimestoppers (formerly Community Action) Trust, 1991–; Industry in Educn, 1993–. *Recreations:* golf, photography, ski-ing, theatre, writing, restaurants, the countryside. *Club:* Royal Automobile.

MacCRINDLE, Robert Alexander; QC 1963; commercial lawyer; Partner, Shearman and Sterling; *b* 27 Jan. 1928; *s* of F. R. MacCrindle; *m* 1959, Pauline Dilys, *d* of Mark S. Morgan; one *s* one *d*. *Educ:* Girvan High Sch.; King's Coll., London; Gonville and Caius Coll., Cambridge. LLB London, 1948. Served RAF, 1948–50, Flt-Lt. LLM Cantab, Chancellor's Medal, 1951. Called to Bar, Gray's Inn, 1952 (Bencher, 1969); Junior Counsel to Board of Trade (Export Credits), 1961–63; Mem., Hong Kong Bar, 1967; Avocat, Barreau de Paris, 1991. Mem., Royal Commn on Civil Liability and Compensation for Personal Injury, 1973–78. Hon. Fellow, American Coll. of Trial Lawyers, 1974. *Publication:* McNair's Law of the Air, 1953. *Recreation:* golf. *Address:* Essex Court Chambers, 24 Lincoln's Inn Fields, WC2A 3ED. *T:* (020) 7813 8000; Shearman and Sterling, 114 avenue des Champs Elysées, 75008 Paris, France. *T:* 153897000; 41 avenue Bosquet, 75007 Paris, France, *T:* 147051858. *Club:* University (New York).

McCRIRRICK, (Thomas) Bryce, CBE 1987; FREng; FIEE; Director of Engineering, BBC, 1978–87; *b* 19 July 1927; *s* of late Alexander McCrirrick and Janet McCrirrick (*née* Tweedie); *m* 1953, Margaret Phyllis Yates; two *s* (and one *s* decd). *Educ:* Galashiels Academy; Heriot Watt Coll., Edinburgh; Regent Street Polytechnic, London. BBC Radio, Studio Centres in Edinburgh, Glasgow and London, 1943–46; served RAF, 1946–49; BBC Television, 1949; Engineer-in-Charge Television Studios, 1963; Head of Engineering Television Recording, and of Studio Planning and Installation Dept, 1969; Chief Engineer, Radio Broadcasting, 1970; Asst Dir of Engrg, 1971; Dep. Dir of Engrg, 1976. Technical Assessor, Investigation into Clapham Junction Rly Accident, 1989. Pres., Soc. of Electronic and Radio Technicians, 1981–85 (Vice-Pres., 1979–80); Vice-Pres., IERE, 1985–88; Pres., IEE, 1988–89 (Dep. Pres., 1986–88, Vice-Pres., 1982–86; Hon. FIEE 1995); Mem. Council, Fellowship of Engrg, 1989–92. Gov., Imperial Coll., 1985–99; Mem. Court, Heriot-Watt Univ., 1991–94; Mem. Senate, London Univ., 1992–94. FRTS 1980; FREng (FEng 1981); FBKSTS 1982; FSMPTE 1989; Hon. FIEE 1995. Hon. DSc Heriot Watt, 1987. *Recreations:* skiing, theatre. *Address:* Surrey Place, Coach House Gardens, Fleet, Hants GU51 4QX. *T:* (01252) 623422.

McCRONE, Prof. Robert Gavin Loudon, CB 1983; FRSE 1983; Visiting Professor, Department of Business Studies, since 1994, and Hon. Fellow, Europa Institute, since 1992, University of Edinburgh; *b* 2 Feb. 1933; *s* of Robert Osborne Orr McCrone and Laura Margaret McCrone; *m* 1st, 1959, Alexandra Bruce Waddell (*d* 1998); two *s* one *d*; 2nd, 2000, Olive Pettigrew Moon (*née* McNaught); two step *d*. *Educ:* St Catharine's Coll., Cambridge (Economics Tripos; MA); University Coll. of Wales, Aberystwyth (Milk Marketing Bd Research Schol. in agricl economics; MSc 1959); Univ. of Glasgow (PhD 1964). Fisons Ltd, 1959–60; Lectr in Applied Economics, Glasgow Univ., 1960–65; Economic Consultant to UNESCO, 1964; Fellow of Brasenose Coll., Oxford, 1965–72; Mem. NEDC Working Party on Agricl Policy, 1967–68; Economic Adviser to House of Commons Select Cttee on Scottish Affairs, 1969–70; Special Economic Adviser to Sec. of State for Local Govt and Regional Planning, 1970; Head of Economics and Statistics Unit, 1970–72, Under-Sec. for Regional Develt, 1972–80, Chief Econ. Advr, 1972–92, Scottish Office; Secretary: Industry Dept for Scotland, 1980–87; Scottish Office Envmt Dept (formerly Scottish Develt Dept), 1987–92. Prof., Glasgow Univ., 1992–94. Member: Adv. Cttee, Constitution Unit (formerly Inquiry into Implementation of Constitutional Reform), 1995–97; Steering Gp for Review of Resource Allocation for NHS in Scotland (Arbuthnott Cttee), 1997–2000; Chm., Cttee of Inquiry into Professional Conditions of Service for Teachers' in Scotland, 1999–2000. Comr, Parly Boundary Commn for Scotland, 1999–. Deputy Chairman: Royal Infirmary of Edinburgh NHS Trust, 1994–99; Lothian Univs Hosps NHS Trust, 1999–2001. Member Council: Royal Economic Soc., 1977–82; Scottish Economic Soc., 1982–91; ESRC, 1986–89. Member, Board: Scottish Opera, 1992–98; Queen's Hall, Edinburgh, 1999–; Trustee: Scottish Opera Endowment Trust, 1999–; Scottish Housing Assocs Charitable Trust, 1992–98. Hon. LLD Glasgow 1986. *Publications:* The Economics of Subsidising Agriculture, 1962; Scotland's Economic Progress 1951–60, 1963; Regional Policy in Britain, 1969; Scotland's Future, 1969; (with Mark Stephens) Housing Policy in Britain and Europe, 1995; European Monetary Union and Regional Development, 1997; contribs to various economic jls. *Recreations:* music, walking. *Address:* 1 Eton Terrace, Edinburgh EH4 1QE. *T:* (0131) 343 6689. *Club:* New (Edinburgh).

McCRORIE, Linda Esther, (Mrs Peter McCrorie); *see* Gray, L. E.

McCRUDDEN, Prof. John Christopher, DPhil; Professor of Human Rights Law, University of Oxford, since 1999; Fellow, Lincoln College, Oxford, since 1980; *b* 29 Jan. 1952; *s* of Gerard and Theodora McCrudden; *m* 1990, Caroline Mary Pannell; one *s* one *d*. *Educ:* Queen's Univ., Belfast (LLB 1974); Yale Univ. (Harkness Fellow, 1974–76; LLM 1975); MA 1980, DPhil 1981, Oxon. Called to the Bar, Gray's Inn, 1996. University of Oxford: Lectr in Law, 1976–77, Jun. Res. Fellow, 1976–80, Balliol Coll.; CUF Lectr, 1980–96; Reader in Law, 1996-99. Visiting Professor: QUB, 1994–98; Univ. of Texas Sch. of Law, 1996; Univ. of Haifa, 1996; Univ. of Mich Law Sch., 1998–; Vis. Sen. Fellow, PSI, 1987–89; Vis Fellow and Lectr, Yale Law Sch., 1986. Member: Sec. of State for NI's Standing Adv. Commn on Human Rights, 1984–88; Expert Network on Application of Equality Directives, EC, 1986–; Specialist Advr, NI Affairs Select Cttee, H of C, 1999; Mem., Public Procurement Implementation Gp, NI Exec., 2001. Mem., Adv. Cttee, ESRC Res. Unit on Ethnic Relns, 1982–85. Jt Ed., Law in Context series, 1978–; Member, Editorial Board: Oxford Jl Legal Studies, 1983–; Internat. Jl Discrimination and the Law, 1996–; Jl Internat. Econ. Law, 1998–. *Publications:* (with R. Baldwin) Regulation and Public Law, 1987; (ed) Women, Employment and European Community Law, 1988; (ed) Fair Employment Handbook, 1990, 3rd edn 1995; (jtly) Racial Justice at Work: the enforcement of the Race Relations Act 1976 in employment, 1991; Equality in Law between Men and Women in the European community: United Kingdom, 1994; (ed with G. Chambers) Individual Rights and the Law in Britain, 1994; (ed) Equality between Women and Men in Social Security, 1994; (ed) Regulation and Deregulation, 1998. *Recreation:* my family. *Address:* Lincoln College, Oxford OX1 3DR. *T:* (01865) 279772.

McCRUM, (John) Robert; writer; Literary Editor, The Observer, since 1996; *b* 7 July 1953; *s* of Michael William McCrum, *qv* and Christine Mary Kathleen (*née* fforde); *m* 1st, 1979, Olivia Timbs (marr. diss. 1984); 2nd, 1995, Sarah Lyall; two *d*. *Educ:* Sherborne Sch.; Corpus Christi Coll., Cambridge (Schol.; BA 1st Cl. Hons Hı. Pennsylvania (Thouron Fellow; MA). House Reader, Chatto & Windus, and Faber Ltd: Editl Dir, 1979–89; Editor-in-Chief, 1990–96. Scriptw. producer, The Story of English, BBC TV, 1980–86. Patron, Different Str. Godwin Prize, 1979; Peabody Award, 1986; Emmy Award, 1987. *Publications*. Secret State, 1980; A Loss of Heart, 1982; The Fabulous Englishman, 1984; The St. English, 1986; The World is a Banana, 1988; Mainland, 1991; The Psycholog. Moment, 1993; Suspicion, 1996; My Year Off, 1998. *Recreation:* physiotherapy. *Address*. The Observer, 119 Farringdon Road, EC1R 3ER. *Clubs:* Royal Automobile, Groucho.

McCRUM, Michael William, CBE 1996; MA; Master of Corpus Christi College, Cambridge, 1980–94; Chairman, Cathedrals Fabric Commission for England, 1991–99; *b* 23 May 1924; 3rd *s* of Captain C. R. McCrum, RN and Ivy Hilda Constance (*née* Nicholson); *m* 1952, Christine Mary Kathleen, *d* of Sir Arthur fforde, GBE; three *s* one *d*. *Educ:* Horris Hill, Newbury; Sherborne Sch.; Corpus Christi Coll., Cambridge (Hon. Fellow, 1994). Entrance Scholar to CCC, Dec. 1942. Served RN, 1943–45 (Sub-Lt RNVR, Dec. 1943). CCC, Cambridge, 1946–48; Part I, Class. Tripos, First Class, 1947; Part II, First Class, with distinction, 1948. Asst Master, Rugby School, Sept. 1948–July 1950 (Lower Bench Master, 1949–50); Fellow CCC, Cambridge, 1949; Second Tutor, 1950–51; Tutor, 1951–62; Headmaster, Tonbridge Sch. 1962–70; Head Master of Eton, 1970–80; Vice-Chancellor, Cambridge Univ., 1987–89. Lectures: Lansdowne, Univ. of Victoria, BC, 1985; Clayesmore, Blandford Forum, 1986; Lady Margaret's Preacher, Univ. of Cambridge, 1987. Member: Council of the Senate, University of Cambridge, 1955–58, 1981–89; General Board of Faculties, 1957–62, 1987–89; Financial Bd, 1985–89; Chairman: Faculty Bd of Educn, 1981–86, 1990–93; Bd of Extra-Mural Studies, 1982–86, Cambridge. Chairman: HMC, 1974; Joint Educnl Trust, 1984–87; GBA, 1989–94 (Dep. Chm., 1982–89); Member: Oxford and Cambridge Schs Exam. Bd, 1960–62, 1966–87 (Chm., 1981–87); BBC/IBA Central Religious Affairs Cttee, 1965–69; Governing Body, Schools Council, 1969–76 (also mem., various cttees); ISJC, 1982–94 (Dep. Chm., 1989–92; Chm., 1992–94). Governor: Bradfield Coll., 1956–62; Eastbourne Coll., 1960–62; King's Sch., Canterbury, 1980–94; Sherborne Sch., 1980–94; Oakham Sch., 1981–85; United World Coll. of the Atlantic, 1981–94; Rugby Sch., 1982–94. Pres., Cambridge Soc., 1989–96. Trustee: King George VI and Queen Elizabeth Foundn of St Catharine's, Cumberland Lodge, 1983–2000; Nat. Heritage Meml Fund, 1984–90; Cambridge Foundn, 1989–99; Henry Fund, 1994–95. Hon. Freeman, Skinners' Co., 1980. Hon. DEd Victoria, BC, 1989. Comendador de la Orden de Isabel la Católica (Spain), 1988. *Publications:* Select Documents of the Principates of the Flavian Emperors AD 68–96 (with A. G. Woodhead), 1961; Thomas Arnold, Head Master, 1989; The Man Jesus, 2000; (contrib.) Dictionary of National Biography, 1971–80 and 1981–85. *Address:* 32 Clarendon Street, Cambridge CB1 1JX. *T:* (01223) 353303. *Clubs:* Athenæum, Oxford and Cambridge, East India, Devonshire, Sports and Public Schools; Hawks (Cambridge).

See also J. R. McCrum.

McCRUM, Robert; *see* McCrum, J. R.

McCUBBIN, Henry Bell; Head of European Office, Association of Greater Manchester Authorities, since 1996; *b* 15 July 1942; *s* of Henry McCubbin and Agnes (*née* Rankine); *m* 1967, Katie M. Campbell; three *d*. *Educ:* Allan Glen's Sch., Glasgow. BA Hons Open Univ. Film Cameraman: BBC TV, 1960–77; Grampian TV, 1977–89. MEP (Lab) Scotland NE, 1989–94; contested (Lab) Scotland NE, Eur. Parly elecns, 1994. *Recreations:* theatre, hill walking, politics. *Address:* European Office, Association of Greater Manchester Authorities, rue Breydel 42, Brussels 1040, Belgium.

McCULLAGH, Keith Graham, PhD; Executive Chairman, OnMedica Group plc, since 2000; Chairman, Pharmacy2U Ltd, since 2000; *b* 30 Nov. 1943; *s* of John Charles McCullagh and Kathleen Doreen McCullagh (*née* Walton); *m* 1967, Jean Elizabeth Milne; one *s* two *d*. *Educ:* Latymer Upper Sch.; Univ. of Bristol (BVSc); St John's Coll., Cambridge (PhD 1970). MRCVS 1965. Royal Soc. Leverhulme Schol., 1966; Medical Research Council: Mem., External Staff, Uganda, 1967; Mem., Scientific Staff, Dunn Nutrition Lab., Cambridge, 1967–69; Cleveland Clinic Foundation, USA: Res. Fellow, 1970; Mem., Res. Staff, 1971–73; Lectr in Veterinary Pathol., Univ. of Bristol, 1974–80; G. D. Searle & Co. Ltd: Dir of Biol., 1980–84; Dir of Res., 1984–86; Founder and Chief Exec., British Biotech plc, 1986–98. Vice Chm., European Assoc. of BioIndustries, 1996–98; Director: Medical Ventures Management Ltd, 1998–; Isis Innovation Ltd, 1998–99. Chm., HM Treasury Wkg Gp on Financing of High Technol. Businesses, 1998; Mem., DTI Adv. Gp on Competitiveness and the Single Mkt, 1997–98. Chm., BioIndustry Assoc., 1993–96. Mem., British Admiral's Cup Sailing Team, 1999. *Publications:* numerous scientific articles and reviews in learned jls. *Recreations:* squash, sailing, ski-ing, golf. *Address:* Windrush House, 30 Manor Park Avenue, Princes Risborough, Bucks HP27 9AS. *Clubs:* Royal Corinthian Yacht (Cowes and Burnham); Oxfordshire Golf, Racquets Squash (Thame).

McCULLAGH, Prof. Peter, PhD; FRS 1994; Professor, Department of Statistics, University of Chicago, since 1985 (Chairman, Department of Statistics, 1992–98); *b* N Ireland, 8 Jan. 1952; *s* of John A. McCullagh and Rita McCullagh (*née* Devlin); *m* 1977, Rosa Bogues; one *s* three *d*. *Educ:* Univ. of Birmingham (BSc 1974); Imperial Coll., London, (PhD 1977). Vis. Asst Prof., Univ. of Chicago, 1977–79; Lectr, Imperial Coll., 1979–85. FIMS, FAAAS. President's Award, Cttee of Presidents of Statistical Socs of N Amer., 1990. *Publications:* Generalized Linear Models (with J. A. Nelder), 1983, 2nd edn 1989; Tensor Methods in Statistics, 1987. *Recreation:* swimming. *Address:* Department of Statistics, University of Chicago, 5734 University Avenue, Chicago, IL 60637, USA. *T.* (312) 7028340.

McCULLIN, Donald, CBE 1993; freelance photojournalist; *b* 9 Oct. 1935; *m* 1959 (marr. diss. 1987); two *s* one *d*; one *s* by Laraine Ashton; *m* 1995, Marilyn Bridges. *Educ:* Tollington Park Secondary Sch., Morden; Hammersmith Jun. Art Sch. Started work at 15 yrs of age after death of father; National Service (RAF), 1954–56; first pictures published by The Observer, 1958; thereafter began photographic career; worked for The Sunday Times for 18 yrs, covering wars, revolutions and travel stories. Hon. FRPS 1977. DUniv: Bradford, 1993; Open, 1994. *Publications:* Destruction Business, 1971; Is Anyone Taking Any Notice, 1971; The Palestinians, 1979; Homecoming, 1979; Hearts of Darkness, 1980; Battle Beirut, a City in Crisis, 1983; Perspectives, 1987; Skulduggery, 1987; Open Skies, 1989; (with Lewis Chester) Unreasonable Behaviour (autobiog.), 1990; Sleeping with Ghosts, 1995; India, 1999. *Recreations:* protecting the English countryside, travelling the world.

McCULLOCH, Andrew Grant; Partner, Drummond Miller, WS, since 1979; President, Law Society of Scotland, 1996–97; *b* 10 Feb. 1952; *s* of late Frederick McCulloch and of Jean McCulloch (later McGregor); *m* 1988, Mave Curran; one *s* one *d*. *Educ:* Glasgow Acad.; Edinburgh Univ. (LLB, BSc SocSci). Joined Drummond & Co., Edinburgh, 1974; Solicitor-Advocate, 1994. *Recreations:* golf, opera, wine. *Address:* Westerlea, Essex Road, Edinburgh EH4 6LQ. *T:* (0131) 339 2705.

MacCULLOCH, Prof. Diarmaid Ninian John, DD; FBA 2001; FSA, FRHistS; Professor of the History of the Church, University of Oxford, since 1997; Fellow, St Cross College, Oxford, since 1995; *b* 31 Oct. 1951; *s* of Rev. Nigel MacCulloch and Jennie (*née* Chappell). *Educ:* Stowmarket Grammar Sch., Churchill Coll., Cambridge (MA, PhD 1977); Univ. of Liverpool (Dip. Archive Admin 1973); DipTh Oxon 1987; DD Oxon 2001. FSA 1978; FRHistS 1981. Jun. Res. Fellow, Churchill Coll., Cambridge, 1976–78; Tutor in Hist., Librarian and Archivist, Wesley Coll., Bristol, 1978–90; Lectr, Faculty of Theol., Oxford Univ., 1995–; Sen. Tutor, St Cross Coll., Oxford, 1996–2000. Pres., C of E Record Soc., 2001–. Co-Ed., Jl Ecclesiastical Hist., 1995–. *Publications:* Suffolk and the Tudors: politics and religion in an English county (Whitfield Prize, RHistS), 1986; Groundwork of Christian History, 1987, rev. edn 1994; The Later Reformation in England 1547–1603, 1990, rev. edn 2000; (ed) The Reign of Henry VIII: politics, policy and piety, 1995; Thomas Cranmer: a life (Whitbread Biography Prize, Duff Cooper Prize, James Tait Black Prize), 1996; Tudor Church Militant: Edward VI and the Protestant Reformation, 1999. *Recreations:* church architecture, music, drinking beer. *Address:* St Cross College, Oxford OX1 3LZ. *T:* (01865) 278458.

McCULLOCH, Prof. Ernest Armstrong, OC 1998; MD; FRSC 1974; FRS 1999; Senior Scientist Emeritus, Ontario Cancer Institute, and Princess Margaret Hospital, since 1991; University Professor, University of Toronto, 1982–91, now Emeritus; *b* 27 April 1926; *s* of Dr Albert Ernest McCulloch and Letitia Riddell McCulloch (*née* Armstrong); *m* 1953, Ona Mary Morganty; four *s* one *d*. *Educ:* Univ. of Toronto (MD Hons 1948). FRCPC 1954. Res. Fellow, Lister Inst., London, 1948–49 (Ellen Mickle Fellow); University of Toronto: Clin. Teacher, Dept of Medicine, 1954–60; Asst Prof., 1959–64, Associate Prof., 1964–66, Prof., 1966–91, Dept of Med. Biophysics; Asst Prof., 1967–68, Associate Prof., 1968–70, Prof., 1970–91, Dept of Medicine; Graduate Sec., 1969–75, Dir, 1975–79, Inst. of Med. Sci.; Asst Dean, Sch. of Graduate Studies, 1979–82; Physician, Toronto Gen. Hosp., 1960–67; Ontario Cancer Institute: Scientific Staff, 1957–91; Head, Div. of Biological Res., 1982–89; Head, Div. of Cellular and Molecular Biology, 1989–91. Vis. Prof. of Lab Medicine and Pathology, Univ. of Texas, MD Anderson Cancer Center, 1991–93; Hon. Prof., Shanxi Cancer Inst., China, 1991–. Pres., Acad. of Sci., RSC, 1987–90 (Eadie Medal, 1991). (Jtly) Annual Gairdner Award, 1969. Silver Jubilee Medal, 1977. *Publications:* more than 275 papers and reviews in med. jls. *Recreations:* sailing, gardening. *Address:* (office) 610 University Avenue, Toronto, ON M5G 2M9, Canada; (home) 480 Summerhill Avenue, Toronto, ON M4W 2E4, Canada. *Club:* Badminton and Racquet (Toronto).

McCULLOCH, Prof. Gary James, PhD; Professor of Education, University of Sheffield, since 1994; *b* 13 March 1956; *s* of Edward Joseph McCulloch and Vera Evelyn McCulloch (*née* Saunders); *m* 1984, Sarah Margaret Buyekha; one *s*. *Educ:* Caldecot Primary Sch., London; Wilson's Grammar Sch., London; Christ's Coll., Cambridge (MA, PhD History 1981). Res. Fellow, Sch. of Educn, Univ. of Leeds, 1981–83; Lectr, 1983–88, Sen. Lectr, 1988–91, in Educn, Univ. of Auckland, NZ; Prof. of Educnl Res., Lancaster Univ., 1991–94. Editor, History of Education, 1996–. FRHistS 1995. *Publications:* (jtly) Technological Revolution?, 1985; The Secondary Technical School, 1989; (jtly) Schooling in New Zealand, 1990; Philosophers and Kings, 1991; (ed) The School Curriculum in New Zealand, 1992; Educational Reconstruction, 1994; (ed jtly) Teachers and the National Curriculum, 1997; Failing the Ordinary Child?, 1998; (jtly) The Politics of Professionalism, 2000; (jtly) Historical Research in Educational Settings, 2000. *Recreations:* cinema, reading, travel, walking. *Address:* Department of Educational Studies, University of Sheffield, 388 Glossop Road, Sheffield S10 2JA; 4 Hallam Grange Croft, Sheffield S10 4BP. *T:* (0114) 222 8098.

McCULLOCH, James Rae, OBE 2001; HM Diplomatic Service, retired; Ambassador to Iceland, 1996–2000; *b* 29 Nov. 1940; *s* of William McCulloch and Catherine (*née* Rae); *m* 1965, Margaret Anderson; two *s*. *Educ:* Ardrossan Acad. Joined FO, 1958; Bamako, Mali, 1962; NY, 1964; Lusaka, 1967; FCO, 1969; Algiers, 1972; Kabul, 1973; Second Sec., FCO, 1977; Luanda, 1980; Second, subseq. First Sec. (Commercial), Bangkok, 1982; First Sec., UKMIS to UN, Geneva, 1986; FCO, 1990; Dep. Hd of Mission, Hanoi, 1992–96.

MacCULLOCH, Dr Malcolm John, MD; DPM; FRCPsych; Professor of Forensic Psychiatry, University of Wales College of Medicine, and Hon. Consultant Forensic Psychiatrist, Caswell Clinic, Bridgend & District NHS Trust, since 1997; *b* 10 July 1936; *s* of William MacCulloch and Constance Martha MacCulloch; *m* 1962, Mary Louise Beton (marr. diss. 1975); one *s* one *d*; *m* 1975, Carolyn Mary Reid; two *d*. *Educ:* King Edward VII Sch., Macclesfield, Cheshire; Manchester Univ. (MB, ChB, DPM, MD). Consultant Child Psychiatrist, Cheshire Child Guidance Service, 1966–67; Director Univ. Dept, Child Psychiatry and Subnormality, Birmingham Univ., 1967–70; Sen. Lectr, Adult Psychiatry, Univ. of Liverpool, 1970–75; PMO, DHSS, 1975–78; SPMO, Mental Health Div., DHSS, 1979–80; Dir. Special Hosps Res. Unit, London, 1979–86; Med. Dir, Park Lane Hosp., Liverpool, 1979–89; Res. Psychiatrist, Ashworth Hosp., Merseyside, 1990–93. Advr to Ontario Govt on Forensic Psychiatric Services, 1988–92. Vis. Prof., Clarke Inst. of Psychiatry, Toronto, 1987–88. *Publications:* Homosexual Behaviour: therapy and assessment, 1971; Human Sexual Behaviour, 1980; numerous med. papers on aspects of psychiatry and forensic psychiatry. *Recreations:* cars, inventing, playing music. *Address:* University of Wales College of Medicine, Division of Psychological Medicine, Heath Park, Cardiff CF4 4XN. *T:* (029) 2074 7747, *Fax:* (029) 2074 7839.

McCULLOCH, Michael Cutler; UK Executive Director, European Bank for Reconstruction and Development, 1997–2001; *b* 24 April 1943; *s* of late Ian James McCulloch and of Elsie Margaret Chadwick; *m* 1st, 1968, Melody Lawrence (marr. diss. 1975); 2nd, 1975, Robin Lee Sussman; two *d*. *Educ:* Prince of Wales Sch., Nairobi; Clare Coll., Cambridge (BA History 1964); Yale Univ. (Mellon Fellow, 1964–66; MA Internat. Relations 1967). ODM, Asst Principal, 1969; Asst Private Sec. to Minister for Overseas Develt, 1972–73, Principal, 1973, ODA; First Sec. (Aid), Dhaka, FCO, 1976–78; Resident Observer, CSSB, 1978–79; Overseas Development Administration: Rayner Scrutiny and Mgt Review Team, 1979–80; E Africa Dept, 1980–83; EC Dept, 1983–84; Principal Private Sec. to Minister for Overseas Develt, 1984–85; Asst Sec., 1985; Head: Evaluation Dept, 1985–86; British Develt Div. in E Africa, 1986–89; Finance Dept, 1990–92; Know How Fund for former Soviet Union, FCO, 1992–97. Trustee: BEARR Trust, 2001–; BBC World Service Trust, 2001–; Riders for Health, 2001–. FRSA 1995. *Recreations:* Baroque to Romantic classical music, African wildlife, photography, walking. *Address:* 12 Merchant Court, 61 Wapping Wall, E1W 3SJ. *T:* (020) 7488 0734; *e-mail:* mcculloch@btinternet.com.

McCULLOCH, Rt Rev. Nigel Simeon; *see* Wakefield, Bishop of.

McCULLOUGH, Sir (Iain) Charles (Robert), Kt 1981; a Surveillance Commissioner, since 1998; *b* 31 July 1931; *o s* of Thomas W. McCullough, CB, OBE and Lisette Hunter (*née* Gannaway); *m* 1965, Margaret Joyce, JP, LLB, BCL, AKC, *o d* of David H. Patey, Middx Hosp.; one *s* one *d*. *Educ:* Dollar Acad.; Taunton Sch. (Exhibnr); Trinity Hall, Cambridge (Dr Cooper's Law Student, 1955; BA 1955; MA 1960). National Service, 1950–52, commnd RA; RA (TA) 1952–54. Called to the Bar, Middle Temple, 1956 (Harmsworth Law Scholar, Blackstone Pupillage Prize, J. J. Powell Prize, 1956); Bencher, 1980; Treas., 2000. Practised Midland Circuit, 1957–71, Midland and Oxford Circuit, 1972–81; a Dep. Chm., Notts QS, 1969–71; QC 1971; a Recorder of the Crown Court, 1972–81; a Judge of the High Court, QBD, 1981–98. Member: Gen. Council of the Bar, 1966–70; Criminal Law Revision Cttee, 1973–; Parole Bd, 1984–86. Trustee, Uppingham Sch., 1984–94. Pres., Trinity Hall Assoc., 1986–87. *Recreations:* foreign travel, walking (particularly in hills and mountains; Mem., Lyke Wake Club), watching birds. *Address:* c/o PO Box 29105, SW1V 1ZU. *Clubs:* Garrick; Pilgrims.

McCURLEY, Anna Anderson; freelance communications consultant; Partner, Hamilton Anderson Solutions; *b* 18 Jan. 1943; *d* of George Gemmell and Mary (*née* Anderson); *m* (marr. diss.); one *d*. *Educ:* Glasgow High Sch. for Girls; Glasgow Univ. (MA); Jordanhill Coll. of Educn (Dip. in Secondary Educn); Strathclyde Univ. Secondary history teacher, 1966–72; College Methods Tutor, Jordanhill Coll. of Educn, 1972–74. Strathclyde Regional Councillor, Camphill/Pollokshaws Div., 1978–82. Sen. Exec., Dewe Rogerson, 1987–89; Head of Govt Affairs, Corporate Communications Strategy, 1990–92. Contested (C) Renfrew W and Inverclyde, 1987. MP (C) Renfrew W and Inverclyde, 1983–87. Mem., Scottish Select Cttee, 1984–87. Mem., Horserace Betting Levy Bd, 1988–97. Trustee, Nat. Galleries of Scotland, 1996–99. *Recreations:* music, cookery, cats. *Address:* Hamilton's Land, 44 High Street, Linlithgow EH49 7AE. *T:* (01506) 671880.

McCUTCHEON, Prof. John Joseph, CBE 1994; PhD, DSc; FFA; FRSE; Professor of Actuarial Studies, Heriot-Watt University, 1975–2001; *b* 10 Sept. 1940; *s* of James Thomson McCutcheon and Margaret (*née* Hutchison); *m* 1978, Jean Sylvia Constable. *Educ:* Glasgow Acad.; St John's Coll., Cambridge (MA); Univ. of Liverpool (PhD, DSc). FFA 1965. Scottish Amicable Life Assce Soc., 1962–65; Consulting Actuary, Duncan C. Fraser and Co., 1965–66; Demonstrator in Pure Maths, Univ. of Liverpool, 1966–70; Associate Prof., Univ. of Manitoba, 1970–72; Sen. Lectr, Heriot-Watt Univ., 1972–75. Pres., Faculty of Actuaries in Scotland, 1992–94. FRSE 1993. *Publications:* (with W. F. Scott) An Introduction to the Mathematics of Finance, 1986; various papers on mathematics, actuarial science, mortality studies. *Recreations:* tennis, ski-ing, opera, reading, travel. *Address:* 14 Oswald Court, Edinburgh EH9 2HY. *T:* (0131) 667 7645. *Clubs:* Woodcutters Cricket, Colinton Lawn Tennis.

McCUTCHEON, Dr William Alan, FSA, MRIA; author, lecturer and consultant; Hon. Senior Research Fellow, School of Geosciences, Queen's University, Belfast, since 1999; *b* 2 March 1934; *s* of late William John and Margaret Elizabeth McCutcheon; *m* 1956, Margaret Craig; three *s*. *Educ:* Royal Belfast Academical Instn; The Queen's University of Belfast (Hugh Wisnom Scholar, 1960; BA (Hons Geog.) 1955, MA 1958, PhD 1962). FRGS (1958–94); FSA 1970; MRIA 1983. School Teacher (Geography Specialist), Royal Belfast Academical Instn, 1956–62; Director, N Ireland Survey of Industrial Archaeology, 1962–68; Keeper of Technology and Local History, Ulster Museum, Belfast, 1968–77; Dir, Ulster Museum, 1977–82; sch. teacher (geography specialist), Ditcham Park Sch., Petersfield, 1986–93. Vis. Teacher, Glenalmond Coll., 1984, 1986. Chairman: Historic Monuments Council (NI), 1980–85; Jt Cttee on Industrial Archaeology (NI), 1981–85; Member: Malcolm Cttee on Regional Museums in Northern Ireland, 1977–78; Industrial Archaeol. Cttee, Council for British Archaeol., 1981–85. *Publications:* The Canals of the North of Ireland, 1965; Railway History in Pictures, Ireland: vol. 1 1969, vol. 2 1970; (contrib.) Travel and Transport in Ireland, 1973; (contrib.) Folk & Farm, 1976; Wheel and Spindle—Aspects of Irish Industrial History, 1977; The Industrial Archaeology of Northern Ireland, 1980 (Library Assoc. high commendation as an outstanding reference book); (contrib.) Some People and Places in Irish Science and Technology, 1985; (contrib.) An Economic and Social History of Ulster 1820–1939, 1985; numerous papers. *Recreations:* reading, classical music, photography, travel, gardening, swimming. *Address:* Ardmilne, 25 Moira Drive, Bangor, Co. Down BT20 4RW. *T:* (028) 9146 5519.

McDERMID, Ven. Norman George Lloyd Roberts; Archdeacon of Richmond, 1983–93, Emeritus since 1993; *b* 5 March 1927; *s* of Lloyd Roberts McDermid and Annie McDermid; *m* 1953, Vera Wood; one *s* three *d*. *Educ:* St Peter's School, York; St Edmund Hall, Oxford (MA); Wells Theological Coll. Deacon 1951, priest 1952; Curate of Leeds, 1951–56, in charge of St Mary, Quarry Hill, Leeds, 1953–56; Vicar of Bramley, Leeds, 1956–64; Rector of Kirkby Overblow, 1964–80; Stewardship Adviser, Ripon Diocese, 1964–76, Bradford and Wakefield, 1973–76; Vicar of Knaresborough, 1980–83. Hon. Canon of Ripon Cathedral, 1972–93, Emeritus 1993–; RD of Harrogate, 1977–83. Member: General Synod, 1970–93; Church of England Pensions Bd, 1972–78; Redundant Churches Fund, 1977–89; Central Bd of Finance of C of E, 1985–93. Church Commissioner, 1978–83. Chairman: Ripon Diocesan House of Clergy, 1981–93; Ripon Diocesan Bd of Finance, 1988–93. Mem., N Yorks County Educn Cttee, 1993–97. Chm., Bedale Probus 25 Club, 2000–. *Recreations:* investment, historic churches, pedigree cattle, gardening. *Address:* Greystones, 10 North End, Bedale, N Yorks DL8 1AB. *T:* (01677) 422210. *Club:* National Liberal.

MacDERMOT, Brian (Charles), CBE 1966; LVO 1961; HM Diplomatic Service, retired; *b* 29 Jan. 1914; *m* 1949, Mary Arden Hunter; seven *s* two *d*. Probationer Vice-Consul, Peking, China, 1936; served at: Hankow, China, 1939–40; Kobe, Japan, 1940–41; Kunming, South China, 1942; Vice-Consul, Shiraz, Persia, 1943; Paris, 1944, promoted Consul, 1945; Foreign Office, 1946; Consul, Beirut, 1948; First Secretary, Belgrade, 1950; First Secretary, Berne, 1951, acted as Charge d'Affaires, 1951, 1952, 1953; transferred to Foreign Office, 1954; transferred to Holy See, 1955, acted as Chargé d'Affaires, 1958, 1959, 1960 and 1961; HM Consul-General, Oporto, 1962–68; Ambassador and Consul-Gen., Paraguay, 1968–72. *Address:* 2 Henry's Yard, Berwick St James, Salisbury SP3 4TS.

MacDERMOT, Prof. John, MD, PhD; FRCP; Professor of Medicine and Therapeutics, Imperial College School of Medicine, since 2000; *b* 24 March 1947; *s* of Niall and Violet MacDermot; *m* 1976, Kay Krnakova; one *d*. *Educ:* Imperial Coll. of Sci. and Technol.; Charing Cross Med. Sch., Univ. of London (MD 1979); PhD Inst. of Neurology, London, 1977. FRCP 1989. Fogarty Internat. Fellow, Lab. of Biochemical Genetics, NIH, 1977–78; Wellcome Sen. Clinical Res. Fellow, RPMS, 1981–87; Professor: of Pharmacology, Univ. of Birmingham, 1987–88; of Clinical Pharmacology, RPMS, later Imperial Coll., Univ. of London, 1989–99. FMedSci 1999. *Publications:* papers on processes involved in signalling from one cell to another. *Recreations:* reading, tennis, ski-ing, cooking. *Address:* Medicine and Therapeutics (Division of Medicine), Imperial College School of Medicine, Chelsea and Westminster Hospital, 369 Fulham Road, SW10 9NH. *T:* (020) 8746 8144.

MacDERMOTT, Edmond Geoffrey; Metropolitan Stipendiary Magistrate, 1972–84. Called to Bar, Gray's Inn, 1935; Dept of Dir of Public Prosecutions, 1946–72; Asst Dir of Public Prosecutions, 1968–72.

McDERMOTT, Sir Emmet; *see* McDermott, Sir L. E.

McDERMOTT, Gerard Francis; QC 1999; a Recorder, since 1999; *b* 21 April 1956; *s* of Joseph Herbert McDermott, BSc, and Winifred Mary McDermott (*née* Limon); *m* 1992, Fiona Johnson. *Educ:* De La Salle Coll., Salford; Manchester Univ. (LLB Hons 1977). Called to the Bar, Middle Temple, 1978; Barrister, Manchester, 1979–; Attorney-at-Law, NY, 1990. General Council of the Bar: Mem., 1983–88, 1990–96 and 1998–; Chm., Internat. Relns Cttee, 1999–2000. Dir, Amer. Counsel Assoc., 1997–. *Recreations:* travel, music. *Address:* 8 King Street Chambers, Manchester M2 6AQ. *T:* (0161) 834 9560.

MacDERMOTT, Rt Hon. Sir John Clarke, Kt 1987; PC 1987; a Lord Justice of Appeal, Supreme Court of Judicature, Northern Ireland, 1987–98; *b* 1927; *s* of Baron MacDermott, PC, PC (NI), MC, and of Louise Palmer, *o d* of Rev. J. C. Johnston, DD; *m* 1953, Margaret Helen, *d* of late Hugh Dales, Belfast; four *d*. *Educ:* Campbell Coll., Belfast; Trinity Hall, Cambridge (BA); QUB. Called to Bar, Inner Temple and Northern Ireland, 1949; QC (NI) 1964. Judge, High Court of NI, 1973–87. *Address:* 6 Tarawood, Holywood, Co. Down BT18 0HS.

McDERMOTT, Sir (Lawrence) Emmet, KBE 1972; Lord Mayor of Sydney, 1969–72; Alderman, Sydney, 1962–77; Dental Surgeon; *b* 6 Sept. 1911; *s* of O. J. McDermott; *m* 1st, 1939, Arline Beatrice Olga (*d* 1987); one *s* one *d*; 2nd, 1992, Eula Macdonald, *d* of Robert Murray Ross. *Educ:* St Ignatius Coll., Sydney; Univ. of Sydney; Northwestern Univ., Chicago. MDS Sydney; DDS Northwestern; FICD, FRACDS, FACD; FAIM 1983. Hon. Consultant Dental Surgeon: Royal Prince Alfred Hosp., 1942; Eastern Suburbs Hosp., 1945; Pres., Bd of Control, United Dental Hosp., Sydney, 1967–79; Mem., NSW Dental Bd, 1967–79; Pres., Australian Dental Assoc. (NSW Br.), 1960–61; Councillor, Australian Dental Assoc., 1962–66. Mem., Liberal Party State Council, 1969; Councillor, Sydney County Council, 1973–80, Dep. Chm., 1975–77, Chm., 1977–78. Dir, City Mutual Life Assce Soc. Ltd, 1970–83, Dep. Chm., 1976–83; Member: Sydney Cove Redevelopment Authority, 1971–76; Convocation, Macquarie Univ., 1966–94; Australia-Britain Soc. (NSW Br.), Vice-Pres., 1972–77. *Recreations:* golf, swimming (Sydney Univ. Blue), bowls. *Address:* 61 Fiddens Wharf Road, Killara, NSW 2071, Australia. *T:* (2) 4984382. *Clubs:* Royal Sydney Golf, Tattersall's, Chatswood Bowling, City Bowling(all Sydney).

McDERMOTT, Patrick Anthony, MVO 1972; HM Diplomatic Service, retired; Consul General, Moscow, and to Republic of Moldova, 1998–2001 (Chargé d'Affaires, 1998, 1999); *b* 8 Sept. 1941; *e s* of Patrick McDermott and Eileen (*née* Lyons); *m* 1976, Christa, *d* of Emil and Anne-Marie Herminghaus, Krefeld, W Germany; two *s*; and two *s* by previous *m*. *Educ:* Clapham College, London. FO 1960; Mexico City, 1963; Attaché, UK Delegn to UN, NY, 1966; Vice-Consul, Belgrade, 1971; Second Sec., FCO, 1973; Second Sec., Bonn, 1973; First Sec., Paris, 1976; First Sec., FCO, 1979; Consul-Gen., and Econ. and Financial Advr to British Military Government, W Berlin, 1984; Asst Hd of Dept, FCO, 1988–89; Counsellor, Paris, 1990; Dept Head, FCO, 1995–97. Freeman, City of London, 1986. *Address:* Linkfoot House, 10 Acres Close, Helmsley, York YO62 5DS. *T:* and *Fax:* (01437) 770382; *e-mail:* patrickmcdermott@hotmail.com.

McDEVITT, Prof. Denis Gordon, MD, DSc; Professor of Clinical Pharmacology, University of Dundee, since 1984; Hon. Consultant Physician, Dundee teaching hospitals, since 1984; *b* 17 Nov. 1937; *s* of Harry and Vera McDevitt; *m* 1967, Anne McKee; two *s* one *d*. *Educ:* Queen's Univ., Belfast (MB ChB, BAO Hons 1962; MD 1968; DSc 1978). FRCPI 1977; FRCP 1978; FRCPE 1984. House Physician and Surg., 1962–63, SHO, 1963–64, Royal Victoria Hosp., Belfast; SHO, Registrar, Sen. Registrar, Dept of Therapeutics and Pharmacology, QUB and Belfast teaching hosps, 1964–68; Asst Prof. of Medicine and Cons. Physician, Christian Med. Coll., Ludhiana, India, 1968–71; Cons. Physician, Belfast teaching hosps, 1971–78; Queen's University, Belfast: Sen. Lectr, 1971–76, Reader, 1976–78, in Clin. Pharmacology and Therapeutics; Prof. of Clin. Pharmacology, 1978–83; Dean, Faculty of Medicine, Dentistry and Nursing, Univ. of Dundee, 1994–97. Merck Internat. Fellow in Clin. Pharmacology, Vanderbilt Univ., 1974–75. Civil Cons. in Exptl Medicine, RAF, 1987–. Member: British Pharmacol Soc., 1972– (SKF Medal and Lecture, 1975); Assoc. of Physicians, 1978– (Pres., 1987–88; Hon. Mem., 1988–); Medicines Commn, 1986–95 (Vice-Chm., 1992–95); GMC, 1997–; Chm., Specialist Adv. Cttee on Clin. Pharmacol. and Therapeutics, 1980–83; Vice-Chm., Ethics Cttee, Centre for Human Scis, DERA, 1994–. FFPM 1990; FRSE 1996; FRSocMed 1996; Founder FMedSci 1998. Man. Editor, European Jl of Clin. Pharmacology, 1998–. *Publications:* papers on clin. pharmacology in learned jls. *Recreations:* golf, music, opera. *Address:* Doonloughan, 1 Godfrey Street, Barnhill, Dundee DD5 2QZ. *T:* (01382) 739483. *Club:* Royal and Ancient Golf.

McDIARMID, Ian; actor, director; Joint Artistic Director, Almeida Theatre, 1989–July 2002; *b* 11 Aug. 1944; *s* of Frederick McDiarmid and late Hilda (*née* Emslie). *Educ:* Morgan Acad.; St Andrews Univ.; Royal Scottish Acad. of Music and Dramatic Art (Gold Medal, 1968). *Theatre* includes: Mephisto, Round House, 1981; Insignificance, Royal Court, 1982; Tales from Hollywood, NT, 1983; The Black Prince, Aldwych, 1989; Royal Shakespeare Company: joined, 1978; Shylock in Merchant of Venice, Henry V, The Party, 1984; Red, Black and Ignorant, War Plays, The Castle, 1985; The Danton Affair, 1986; Royal Exchange, Manchester: The Wild Duck, 1983; Edward II, 1986; Don Carlos, 1987; Associate Dir, 1986–88; Almeida: Volpone, The Rehearsal (dir), Scenes from an Execution (dir), 1990; Hippolytos, Lulu (dir), 1991; Terrible Mouth (opera), A Hard Heart (dir), 1992; School for Wives, 1993; Siren Song (opera) (dir), 1994; Tartuffe, 1996; The Cenci (opera), The Government Inspector, 1997; The Doctor's Dilemma, 1998; The Jew of Malta, 1999; The Tempest, 2000; Faith Healer, 2001; The Soldier's Tale, LSO, 1987; The King Goes Forth to France, Royal Opera House, 1987; *films* include: The Return of the Jedi, 1983; Restoration, 1996; Star Wars EPI: the phantom menace, 1999; Sleepy Hollow, 2000; *television:* Karaoke, 1996; Hillsborough, 1996; Great Expectations, 1999; All the King's Men, 1999. *Address:* Almeida Theatre, Almeida Street, N1 1TA.

MacDONAGH, Lesley Anne; Managing Partner, Lovells (formerly Lovell White Durrant), since 1995; *b* 19 April 1952; *d* of Arthur George Payne and Agnes Dowie Scott; *m* 1st, 1975, John Belton (marr. diss. 1985); one *d*; 2nd, 1987, Simon Michael Peter MacDonagh; three *s*. *Educ:* Queen Elizabeth I Sch., Wimborne; College of Law, Guildford and London. Admitted Solicitor, 1976; Partner, Lovell White Durrant, 1981–; merged with Boesebeck Droste to form Lovells, 2000. Member: Council, Law Society, 1992–2001 (Mem., Planning and Envtl Cttee, 1988–95); Lands Tribunal Consultative Cttee, 1991–95; Property Adv. Gp, 1993–. Trustee, Citizenship Foundn, 1991–. Vice-Chm., Envt Cttee, Knightsbridge Assoc., 1991–. Liveryman, Solicitors' Co., 1982– (Mem. Court, 1997–). Hon. Fellow, Soc. for Advanced Legal Studies, 1998. *Recreations:* family life, painting, drawing, dining. *Address:* Lovells, 65 Holborn Viaduct, EC1A 2DY. *T:* (020) 7296 2000.

MacDONAGH, Prof. Oliver Ormond Gerard; W. K. Hancock Professor of History, Australian National University, 1973, now Emeritus; *b* 23 Aug. 1924; *s* of Michael A. MacDonagh and Loretto (*née* Oliver); *m* 1952, Mary Carmel Hamilton; three *s* four *d*. *Educ:* Clongowes Wood Coll., Co. Kildare; University Coll. Dublin (MA); King's Inns, Dublin (BL); Univ. of Cambridge (PhD). Fellow, St Catharine's Coll., Cambridge, 1952–64, Vis. Fellow, 1986, Hon. Fellow, 1987; Foundn Prof. of History, Flinders Univ., SA, 1964–68; Prof. of Modern History, UC, Cork, 1968–73. Vis. Prof., Yale Univ., 1970; Overseas Schol., St John's Coll., Cambridge, 1981; Parnell Sen. Res. Fellow, Magdalene Coll., Cambridge, 1993–94; Res. Prof., Australian Catholic Univ., 1994–95. FASSA 1965; FAHA 1977; Corresp. FBA 1984; Hon. MRIA 1993. Hon. LittD: Flinders, 1982; Sydney, 1989; NUI, 1989. *Publications:* A Pattern of Government Growth, 1961, 2nd edn 1993; Ireland: the Union and its Aftermath, 1968, 2nd edn 1977; Early Victorian Government, 1977; The Inspector-General, 1981; States of Mind, 1983, 2nd edn 1985; The Hereditary Bondsman: Daniel O'Connell 1775–1829, 1987; The Emancipist: Daniel O'Connell 1830–1847, 1989; Jane Austen: Real and Imagined Worlds, 1991; The Life of Daniel O'Connell 1775–1847, 1991; The Sharing of the Green: a modern Irish history for Australians, 1996; (with S. R. Dennison) Guinness: 1886–1939, 1998. *Recreations:* watching Rugby, Nineteenth Century novels. *Address:* 9B Crescent Street, Fairlight, NSW 2094, Australia. *T:* (2) 99497824.

McDONAGH, Siobhain Ann; MP (Lab) Mitcham and Morden, since 1997; *b* 20 Feb. 1960; *d* of Cumin McDonagh and Breda McDonagh (*née* Doogue). *Educ:* Holy Cross Convent; Essex Univ. (BA Hons 1981). Clerical Officer, DHSS, 1981–82; Wandsworth Council: Admin. Asst, 1982–83; Receptionist, Homeless Persons Unit, 1983–86; Housing Advr, Housing Aid Centre, 1986–88; Develt Co-ordinator, Battersea Churches Housing Trust, 1988–97. Mem., South Mitcham Community Centre, 1988. *Recreations:* shopping, music, women's magazines. *Address:* 1 Crown Road, Morden SM4 5DD. *T:* (020) 8542 4835.

MACDONALD, family name of **Barons Macdonald, Macdonald of Gwaenysgor** and **Macdonald of Tradeston.**

MACDONALD, 8th Baron *cr* 1776; **Godfrey James Macdonald of Macdonald;** JP; DL; Chief of the Name and Arms of Macdonald; *b* 28 Nov. 1947; *s* of 7th Baron Macdonald, MBE, TD, and Anne (*d* 1988), *o d* of late Alfred Whitaker; *S* father, 1970; *m* 1969, Claire, *e d* of Captain T. N. Catlow, CBE, RN, Gabriel Cottage, Tunstall, Lancs; one *s* three *d*. JP Skye and Lochalsh, 1979; DL Ross and Cromarty, Skye and Lochalsh, 1986. *Heir: s* Hon. Godfrey Evan Hugo Thomas Macdonald of Macdonald, yr, *b* 24 Feb. 1982. *Address:* Kinloch Lodge, Isle of Skye. *Club:* New (Edinburgh).

McDONALD, Hon. Lord; Robert Howat McDonald, MC 1944; a Senator of the College of Justice in Scotland, 1973–89; *b* 15 May 1916; *s* of Robert Glassford McDonald, and Roberta May Howat, Paisley, Renfrewshire; *m* 1949, Barbara Mackenzie, *d* of John Mackenzie, Badcaul, Ross-shire; no *c*. *Educ:* John Neilson Institution, Paisley. MA (Glasgow) 1935; LLB (Glasgow) 1937; admitted Faculty of Advocates, 1946; QC (Scot.) 1957. Served with KOSB, 1939–46 (despatches, 1945). Sheriff Principal of Ayr and Bute, 1966–71. Mem., Criminal Injuries Compensation Board, 1964–71; Pres., Industrial Tribunals for Scotland, 1972–73; Chm., Gen. Nursing Council for Scotland, 1970–73; Chm., Mental Welfare Commn for Scotland, 1965–83; Mem., Employment Appeal Tribunal, 1976–86. Chm., Queen's Nursing Inst., Scotland, 1981–93. *Address:* 5 Doune Terrace, Edinburgh EH3 6EA. *Club:* New (Edinburgh).

MACDONALD OF GWAENYSGOR, 2nd Baron *cr* 1949, of Gwaenysgor, Flint; **Gordon Ramsay Macdonald;** business consultant; *b* 16 Oct. 1915; *er s* of 1st Baron Macdonald of Gwaenysgor, PC, KCMG; *S* father, 1966; *m* 1941, Leslie Margaret Taylor; three *d*. *Educ:* Manchester Univ. MA, Economics and Commerce. Served War, 1940–46; Army, Major, Artillery; GSO2 Operations and Intelligence (despatches, Burma). Board of Trade, 1946–53: Principal, 1946–47; UK Trade Comr, Canberra, ACT, 1947–53. With Tube Investments Ltd, and Man. Dir TI (Export) Ltd, 1953–64; Chief Exec., Telecommunications Group, Plessey Co., 1964–67; Chm., Hayek Engrg (UK) Ltd, 1967–76; Chm. and Chief Exec., Ferro Metal and Chemical Comp., and Satra Consultants (UK) Ltd, 1977. *Recreations:* golf, chess. *Heir:* none.

MACDONALD OF TRADESTON, Baron *cr* 1998 (Life Peer), of Tradeston in the City of Glasgow; **Angus John Macdonald,** CBE 1997; PC 1999; Minister for the Cabinet Office and Chancellor of the Duchy of Lancaster, since 2001; *b* 20 Aug. 1940; *s* of Colin Macdonald and Jean (*née* Livingstone); *m* 1963, Theresa McQuaid; two *d*. *Educ:* Allan Glen's Sch., Glasgow. Marine fitter, 1955–63; Circulation Manager, Tribune, 1964–65; feature writer, The Scotsman, 1965–67; Granada Television: Editor/Exec. Producer, World in Action, 1969–75; successively Head of Current Affairs, Regl Progs, Features, 1975–82; presenter, variously, Camera, Granada 500, Party conferences, Union World, Right to Reply, 1982–88; Dir of Progs, 1985–90, Man. Dir, 1990–96, Chm., 1996–98, Scottish Television, subseq. Scottish Media Gp. Chm., Taylor & Francis Group Ltd, 1997–98; Director: GMTV, 1991–97; Scottish Screen, 1997–98; Bank of Scotland, 1998; Scottish Enterprise, 1998. Parly Under-Sec. of State (Minister for Business and Industry), Scottish Office, 1998–99; Minister of State (Minister for Transport), DETR, 1999–2001. Chm., Cairngorms Partnership Bd, 1997–98. Founder Chm., Edinburgh Internat. Television Festival, 1976; Chairman: Edinburgh Film Fest., 1994–96; ITV Broadcasting Bd, 1992–94; Mem., Press and Broadcasting Adv. Cttee, MoD, 1994–95. Vice Pres., RTS, 1994–98. Vis. Prof., Film and Media Studies, Stirling Univ., 1985–98. Governor: Nat. Film and Television Sch., 1986–97; BFI, 1997–98. DUniv Stirling, 1992; Hon. DLitt: Napier, 1997; Robert Gordon, 1998. BAFTA Award, Best Factual Series (World In Action), 1973; Chairman of the Year, and Business Leader of the Year, Scottish Business Elite Awards, 1997; BAFTA Scotland Lifetime Achievement Award, 1997. *Publication:* Camera: Victorian eyewitness, 1979. *Recreations:* words, music, pictures, sports, hills. *Address:* House of Lords, SW1A 0PW. *Club:* Royal Automobile.

MACDONALD, Alastair John Peter, CB 1989; a Civil Service Commissioner, since 2001; Director General, Industry (formerly Deputy Secretary), Department of Trade and Industry, 1992–2000; *b* 11 Aug. 1940; *s* of late Ewen Macdonald and Hettie Macdonald; *m* 1969, Jane, *d* of late T. R. Morris; one *s* two *d*. *Educ:* Wimbledon Coll.; Trinity Coll., Oxford. Editorial staff of Spectator, 1962; Financial Times, 1963–68: Washington DC, 1965–66; Features Editor, 1966–68; joined Home Civil Service as Asst Principal, DEA, 1968; Principal, DTI, 1971; Sec., Lord Devlin's Commn into Industrial and Commercial Representation, 1971–72; Asst Sec., DoI, 1975; RCDS, 1980; Under Sec., DTI, 1981. Dep. Sec., DTI, 1985–90; Dep. Under Sec. of State, MoD (PE), 1990–92. Non-exec. Dir, Rank Leisure Ltd (subsid. of Rank Organisation), 1981–85. Mem., Design Council, 2001–. Pres., BCS, 2000–01. FBCS 1999. *Address:* 13 Burbage Road, SE24 9HJ.

McDONALD, Very Rev. Alexander; General Secretary, Board of Ministry, Church of Scotland, since 1988; Moderator of the General Assembly of the Church of Scotland, 1997–98; *b* 5 Nov. 1937; *s* of Alexander McDonald and Jessie Helen (*née* Low); *m* 1962, Essdale Helen (*née* McLeod); two *s* one *d*. *Educ:* Bishopriggs Higher Grade Sch.; Whitehill Senior Secondary Sch.; Stow Coll.; Scottish Coll. of Commerce; Trinity Coll., Glasgow Univ. (Dip. 1968); BA Open Univ. CMIWSc. Trainee management in timber trade, 1954–56; RAF, 1956–58; timber trade, 1958–62; Minister: St David's Church, Bathgate, 1968–74; St Mark's Church, Paisley, 1974–88. Pres., Glasgow Bn, Boys' Bde, 1998–. Broadcaster on TV and radio, 1969–. DUniv Open, 1999. *Publications:* numerous articles in jls and newspapers. *Recreations:* hill walking, swimming, reading, fishing. *Address:* (office) 121 George Street, Edinburgh EH2 4YN. *T:* (0131) 225 5722.

McDONALD, Prof. Alexander John, MA (Cantab), LLB, WS; Professor of Conveyancing, University of Dundee (formerly Queen's College), 1955–82, now Emeritus (Dean of the Faculty of Law, 1958–62, 1965); Senior Partner, Thornton, Dickie & Brand, WS, Dundee, 1978–84, Consultant to Thorntons, WS, 1984–2000; *b* 15 March 1919; *o s* of late John McDonald, and Agnes Mary Stewart McDonald; *m* 1951, Doreen Mary, *o d* of late Frank Cook, OBE; two *s* two *d*. *Educ:* Cargilfield Sch.; Fettes Coll. (open scholar); Christ's Coll., Cambridge (Classical Exhibn, BA 1942); Edinburgh Univ. (Thow Schol. and John Robertson Prize in Conveyancing; LLB with dist., 1949). Admitted as Solicitor and Writer to the Signet, 1950; Lectr in Conveyancing, Edinburgh Univ., 1952–55. *Publications:* Conveyancing Case Notes, 1981, 2nd edn 1984; Conveyancing Manual, 1982, 6th edn 1997; Registration of Title Manual, 1986. *Address:* 1 Regent Place, Broughty Ferry, Dundee DD5 1AT. *T:* (01382) 477301.

McDONALD, Alistair; Economic Development Officer, Wandsworth Borough Council, 1983–89; *b* 13 March 1925; *e s* of late John Bell McDonald and Mary McDonald; *m* 1954, Isabel Margaret Milne; two *d*. *Educ:* Fraserburgh Academy; Aberdeen Univ. (BSc 1st Cl. Hons Natural Philosophy). Served RAF and Fleet Air Arm, 1943–46. Malayan Meteorological Service, 1950–56; ICI, 1956–66; Min. of Technology, 1966–70; Dept of Trade and Industry, 1970–74; Dept of Industry, 1974–77; Director, British Shipbuilders (on secondment), 1977–79; Regional Dir, NW Region, Dept of Industry, 1979–83. *Recreation:* golf.

McDONALD, Allan Stuart; Headmaster, George Heriot's School, Edinburgh, 1970–83; *b* 20 Aug. 1922; *s* of Allan McDonald and Clementina Peebles (*née* Stuart), both of Edinburgh; *m* 1948, Margaret Wilson, *d* of late James Adams, Paisley and Stranraer, and of Margaret Wilson (*née* Ferguson); one *s* two *d*. *Educ:* Royal High Sch., Edinburgh; Giffnock and Eastwood Schs, Renfrewshire; Glasgow Univ.; Sorbonne. MA Hons 1944; DipEd 1948. Commnd, Royal Corps of Signals (21st Army Group Signals), 1943–45. Asst Master: Johnstone High Sch., 1948–50; Eastwood Sch., 1950–54; Principal Teacher: Modern Languages, Fortrose Acad., 1954–59; German, George Heriot's Sch., 1959–70; Depute Headmaster, George Heriot's Sch., 1967–70. *Recreations:* formerly Rugby, cricket; now gardening, photography. *Address:* Mearns Edge, Haulkerton Wood, Laurencekirk, Aberdeenshire AB30 1DZ.

MACDONALD, His Honour Angus Cameron; a Circuit Judge, 1979–98; *b* 26 Aug. 1931; *o s* of late Hugh Macdonald, OBE, and Margaret Cameron Macdonald (*née* Westley); *m* 1956, Deborah Anne, *d* of late John Denny Inglis, DSO, MC, JP, and Deborah Margery Meiklem Inglis (*née* Thomson); two *d* (and one *d* decd). *Educ:* Bedford Sch.; Trinity Hall, Cambridge (BA 1954; MA 1960). Nat. service, 1950–51, commissioned, TA, 1951–57. Called to Bar, Gray's Inn, 1955; Resident Magistrate, then Crown Counsel, Nyasaland Govt, 1957–65; Sen. State Counsel, Malawi Govt, 1965–67; practised, NE Circuit, 1967–79; a Recorder of the Crown Court, 1974–79. *Recreations:* singing, fishing, shooting. *Club:* Northern Counties (Newcastle upon Tyne).

McDONALD, Beverley June; *see* Hughes, B. J.

MACDONALD, Dr Calum Alasdair; MP (Lab) Western Isles, since 1987; *b* 7 May 1956; *s* of Malcolm and Donella Macdonald. *Educ:* Bayble Sch.; The Nicolson Inst.; Edinburgh Univ.; Univ. of California at Los Angeles (PhD). Parly Under-Sec. of State, Scottish Office, 1997–99. Member: TGWU; Crofters Union. *Address:* House of Commons, SW1A 0AA; 4 South Beach Street, Stornoway, Isle of Lewis HS1 2XY. *T:* (01851) 704684.

MACDONALD, Charles Adam; QC 1992; a Recorder, since 2000; *b* 31 Aug. 1949; *s* of Alasdair Cameron Macdonald, VRD, MB ChB, FRCP, FRCPGlas and Jessie Catherine Macdonald, BA; *m* 1978, Dinah Jane Manns; three *d*. *Educ:* Glasgow Academy; New Coll., Oxford (MA Hons Jurisp.). Called to the Bar, Lincoln's Inn, 1972. An Asst Recorder, 1996–99. Mem. Panel, Lloyd's Salvage Arbitrators, 1999–. Mem. Editl Bd, Internat. Maritime Law, 1994–. *Recreation:* family life. *Address:* 4 Essex Court, Temple, EC4Y 9AJ. *T:* (020) 7653 5653.

MacDONALD, Colin Cameron, CB 1999; Managing Director, Colmcille Fisheries (Iona); *b* 13 July 1943; *s* of Captain Colin D. C. MacDonald and Ann MacDonald (*née* Hough); *m* 1969, Kathryn Mary Campbell. *Educ:* Allan Glen's Sch., Glasgow; Univ. of Strathclyde (BA Hons Econ. 1967). Scottish Development Department, 1967–92: Asst Sec., Housing Div., 1988–91, Management Orgn, 1991–92; Under Sec. and Principal Estab. Officer, Scottish Office, then Scottish Exec., 1992–2000. Non-exec. Dir, TSB Bank Scotland, 1994–98. *Recreations:* tennis, fishing, music. *Address:* 4 Esdaile Bank, Edinburgh EH9 2PN. *T:* (0131) 662 8457; Caol Ithe, Iona, Argyll PA76 6SP. *T:* (01681) 700344.

McDONALD, David Arthur; Chairman, Network Housing Association, since 1996; *b* 16 Jan. 1940; *s* of late Campbell McDonald and Ethel McDonald; *m* 1st, 1963, Barbara MacCallum (marr. diss.); one *d*; 2nd, 1971, Mavis Lowe (*see* Mavis McDonald); one *s*. *Educ:* Campbell College, Belfast; Trinity College, Dublin. BA (Moderatorship) Classics. Asst Master, Classics, Methodist College, Belfast, 1963–66; Press Sec. to Minister of Education, N Ireland, 1967–68; joined Min. of Housing and Local Govt, later DoE, 1970; Asst Private Sec. to Sec. of State for the Envt, 1974–76; Asst Sec., Local Govt Finance Divs, 1977–82; Dir of Information, 1982–87; Under Sec., Construction Industry, and Sport and Recreation, Directorates, 1987–90; Dir of Information, 1990–92; Under Sec., Urban Develt and Relocation Directorate, 1992–94; Under-Sec., Cities, Countryside and Private Finance Directorate, 1994. Mem., Local Govt Area Cost Adjustment Rev. Panel, 1995–96. *Recreations:* golf, watching sport. *Clubs:* MCC; Wimbledon Park Golf.

MACDONALD, David Cameron; Chairman, National Kidney Foundation of New Zealand, since 1998; *b* 5 July 1936; *s* of James Fraser Macdonald, OBE, FRCS and Anne Sylvia Macdonald (*née* Hutcheson); *m* 1st, 1968, Melody Jane Coles (marr. diss. 1980); two *d*; 2nd, 1983, Mrs Sally Robertson; one *s* one *d*. *Educ:* St George's Sch., Harpenden; Newport Grammar Sch. Admitted a solicitor with Slaughter and May, 1962; joined Philip Hill Higginson Erlangers, later Hill Samuel & Co. Ltd, 1964. Dir, 1968; Dep. Chm., 1979–80; Dir, Hill Samuel Gp Ltd, 1979–80; Chief Exec., Antony Gibbs Holdings Ltd and Chm., Antony Gibbs & Sons, 1980–83; Chairman: Bath and Portland Gp, 1982–85; Pittards, 1985–97 (Dir, 1984); Sound Diffusion, 1987–89; Director: Coutts and Co., 1980–95; Sears, 1981–97; Merivale Moore, 1985–98; Cogent Elliott, 1986–97; Foster Yeoman Ltd, 1993–95. Sen. UK Advr, Credit Suisse First Boston, 1983–91. Dir Gen., Panel on Takeovers and Mergers, 1977–79. Adviser to Govt on Upper Clyde Shipbuilders crisis, 1971. Chm., Issuing Houses Assoc., 1975–77. Mem., BTA, 1971–82. Trustee, London City Ballet, 1983–87. *Recreations:* music, fishing. *Address:* 6 Genesis Drive, West Melton, RD1 Christchurch, New Zealand. *T:* (3) 3181688.

McDONALD, David Wylie, CMG 1978; DA, RIBA, ARIAS, FHKIA; Secretary for Lands and Works, Hong Kong, 1981–83; MLC Hong Kong, 1974–83; *b* 9 Oct. 1927; *s* of William McDonald and Rebecca (*née* Wylie); *m* 1951, Eliza Roberts Steele; two *d*. *Educ:* Harris Acad., Dundee; School of Architecture, Dundee Coll. of Art (Lorimer Meml Prize, RIAS, 1950; City Coronation Design Prize, Corporation of Dundee, 1953; DA 1953). Architect with Gauldie, Hardie, Wright and Needham, Chartered Architects, Dundee, 1953–55; Public Works Department, Hong Kong: Architect, 1955; Sen. Architect, 1964; Chief Architect, 1967; Govt Architect, 1970; Principal Govt Architect, 1972; Dir of Building Develt, 1973; Dir of Public Works, 1974. Member: Finance Cttee, Legislative Council, 1974–83; Commonwealth Parly Assoc., 1974–. Director: Mass Transit Railway Corp., Hong Kong, 1975–83; Ocean Park Ltd, Hong Kong, 1976–83; Hong Kong Industrial Estate Corp., 1981–83; Mem., Hong Kong Housing Auth., 1982–83. Mem. Exec. Cttee: Girl Guides Assoc. (Hong Kong Br.), 1977–83; Hong Kong Red Cross, 1981–83. Mem., Margaret Blackwood Hsg Assoc., 1984–; Trustee, Scottish Trust for Physically Disabled, 1984–. Mem., Mensa, 1968–. JP Hong Kong, 1972–83. Silver Jubilee Medal, 1977. *Recreations:* swimming (Coach and Manager, Hong Kong Swimming Team at Commonwealth Games, Christchurch, NZ, 1974), drawing, painting and calligraphy. *Address:* Northbank of Gray, Backmuir of Liff, Angus DD2 5QU. *T:* (01382) 580483. *Clubs:* Hong Kong (Hong Kong) (Chairman, 1977); Hong Kong Jockey (Hong Kong).

MACDONALD, Hon. Donald (Stovel); PC (Canada) 1968; CC 1994; Senior Adviser, UBS Bunting Warburg, Toronto, since 2000; *b* 1 March 1932; *s* of Donald Angus Macdonald and Marjorie Stovel Macdonald; *m* 1st, 1961, Ruth Hutchison (*d* 1987), Ottawa; four *d*; 2nd, 1988, Adrian Merchant; three step *s* three step *d* (and one step *d* decd). *Educ:* Univ. of Toronto (BA 1951); Osgoode Hall Law Sch. 1955 (LLB *ex post facto* 1991); Harvard Law Sch. (LLM 1956); Cambridge Univ. (Dip. in Internat. Law, 1957). Called to Ont Bar, 1955; Prize in Insurance Law, Law Soc. of Upper Canada, 1955; Rowell Fellow, Canadian Inst. of Internat. Affairs, 1956; McCarthy & McCarthy, law firm, Toronto, 1957–62, Partner, 1978–88; High Comr for Canada in UK, 1988–91; Counsel, McCarthy Tétrault, 1991–2000. Special Lectr, Univ. of Toronto Law Sch., 1978–83, 1986–88. MP Rosedale, 1962–78; Parly Sec. to Ministers of Justice, Finance, Ext. Affairs, Industry, 1963–68; Minister without Portfolio, 1968; Pres., Queen's Privy Council, and Govt House Leader, 1968–70; Minister of National Defence, 1970–72; Minister of Energy, Mines and Resources, 1972–75; Minister of Finance, 1975–77. Director: McDonnell Douglas Corp., 1978–88; Du Pont Canada Inc., 1978–88; Bank of Nova Scotia, 1980–88; Alberta Energy Co. Ltd, 1981–88; MacMillan-Bloedel Ltd, 1986–88; Celanese Canada, 1991–99 (Chm., 1997–99); Sun Life Assurance Co. of Canada, 1991–; TransCanada Pipelines, 1991–; Slough Estates Canada Ltd, 1991–; Siemens Canada (formerly Siemens Electric) Ltd, 1991– (Chm., 1991–); Alberta Energy Co. Ltd, 1992–; Hambros Canada Inc., 1994–98; BFC Construction Corp. (formerly Banister Foundn Inc.), 1994–99; Boise Cascade Corp., 1996–; CanEnerco Ltd, 1996–; AT&T Canada Corp., 1999; Aber Diamond Corp. (formerly Aber Resources Ltd), 1999–. Mem. Adv. Council, Mercer Management Consultants Ltd, 2000–. Chairman: Internat. Develt Res. Centre, Canada, 1981–84; Inst. for Res. on Public Policy, Montreal, 1991–97; Design Exchange, 1993–96. Chairman: Royal Commn on Econ. Union and Develt Prospects for Canada, 1982–85; Canadian Council for Public-Private Partnerships, 1993–99; Adv. Cttee on Competition in Ont's Electricity System, 1995–96; Atlantic Council of Canada, 1998–. Trustee, Clan Donald Lands Trust, Armadale, Skye, 1991–. Chm., Canadian Friends of Cambridge, 1993–97. Freeman, City of London, 1990; Liveryman, Distillers' Co. Hon. Fellow, Trinity Hall, Cambridge, 1994. LLD (*hc*): St Lawrence, 1974; New Brunswick at Saint John, 1990; Toronto, 2000; Hon. DEng Colorado Sch. of Mines, 1976. *Recreations:* cross-country skiing, tennis. *Address:* 27 Marlborough Avenue, Toronto, ON M5R 1X5, Canada. *T:* (416) 9646757. *Clubs:* York, Toronto (Toronto).

McDONALD, (Edward) Lawson, MA, MD Cantab; FRCP; FACC; Hon. Consultant Cardiologist: National Heart Hospital, since 1983 (Consultant Cardiologist, 1961–83); Canadian Red Cross Memorial Hospital, Taplow, 1960–83; Consultant Cardiologist: King Edward VII's Hospital for Officers, London, 1968–88; to King Edward VII Hospital, Midhurst, 1970–92, Emeritus, 1992; Senior Lecturer to the Institute of Cardiology, 1961–83; *b* 8 Feb. 1918; *s* of late Charles Seaver McDonald and Mabel Deborah (*née* Osborne); *m* 1953, Ellen Greig Rattray (marr. diss. 1972); one *s*. *Educ:* Felsted Sch.; Clare Coll., Cambridge; Middlesex Hospital; Harvard Univ. House appointments Middlesex Hospital, 1942–43. Temp. Surgeon-Lt, RNVR, 1943–46; served War of 1939–45, in N Atlantic and Normandy Campaigns (HMS Glasgow). RMO, Nat. Heart Hosp., 1946–47; Asst Registrar, Inst. of Cardiology, 1947–48; Med. Registrar, Middlesex Hosp., 1948–49; studied in Stockholm, 1949; Asst to Prof. of Medicine, Middlesex Hosp., 1949–52; Rockefeller Travelling Fellow in Medicine, 1952–53; Asst in Medicine, Med. Dept, Peter Bent Brigham Hosp., Boston, Mass, and Research Fellow in Medicine, Harvard Univ., 1952–53; Clinical and Research Asst, Dept of Cardiology, Middlesex Hosp., 1953–55; Asst Dir, Inst. of Cardiology and Hon. Asst Physician, Nat. Heart Hosp., 1955–61; Physician, and Physician to Cardiac Dept, London Hosp., 1960–78. Member: Cardiology Cttee, RCP, 1963–76 (Chm. Jt Adv. Cttee, RCP and British Cardiac Soc., 1973–75); Bd of Governors, National Heart and Chest Hosps, 1975–82; Council, British Heart Foundn, 1975–83. Visiting Lecturer: American Coll. of Cardiology; American Heart Assoc.; Univ. of Toronto, Queen's Univ., Kingston, Ont; Univ. of Bombay; University of Barcelona, Eliseo Migoya Inst. of Cardiology, Bilbao, Spain; Istanbul Univ., Turkey; Univs of Chicago, Cincinnati and Kansas; Harvard Univ.; Mayo Foundation, USA; Univs of Belgrade, Ljubljana and Zagreb, Yugoslavia; Nat. Univ. of Cordoba, Argentine; Univ. of Chile, and Catholic Univ., Santiago; Nat. Univ. of Colombia; Nat. Inst. of Cardiology, Mexico; Nat. Univ. of Mexico; University of San Marcos and University of Cayetano Heredia, Peru; Nat. Univ. of Venezuela; Vis. Prof., Univ. of Oregon Med. Sch.; has addressed numerous cardiac societies in Europe, Africa, Australia, Canada, NZ, USA, People's Republic of China, USSR, and South America, 1961–; St Cyres Lecturer, 1966; First Charles A. Berns Meml Lectr, Albert Einstein Coll. of Medicine, NY, 1973; Vth World Congress of Cardiology Souvenir Orator and Lectr's Gold Medallist, 1977. Advisor to the Malaysian Govt on Cardiac Services. Editorial Bd, New Istanbul Contribution to Clinical Science. Chm., 1979, and Mem., British Cardiac Soc. (Mem. Council, 1967–71); Mem., Assoc. of Physicians of Great Britain and Ireland, and other societies; FACC; Corresp. Mem. or Hon. Mem. of various socs of Cardiology or Angiology in S America. Hon. Fellow, Turkish Med. Soc.; Internat. Fellow, Council on Clinical Cardiol., Amer. Heart Assoc.; Mem., Italian Soc. of Cardiology; Hon. Member: Pakistan Cardiac Soc.; Scientific Council, Revista Portuguesa de Cardiologia. Member, Most Honourable Order of the Crown of Johore, 1980. *Publications:* (ed) Pathogenesis and Treatment of Occlusive Arterial Disease, 1960; Medical and Surgical Cardiology, 1969; (ed) Very Early Recognition of Coronary Heart Disease, 1978; numerous contribs to learned jls; also papers and addresses. *Recreations:* art, ski-ing, mountain walking, sailing. *Address:* 9 Bentinck Mansions, Bentinck Street, W1U 2ER. *T:* (020) 7935 7101, *Fax:* (020) 7467 4312.

McDONALD, Elaine Maria, OBE 1983; Director, Creative Dance Artists Trust, since 1993; *b* 2 May 1943; *d* of Wilfrid Samuel and Ellen McDonald. *Educ:* Convent of the Ladies of Mary Grammar Sch., Scarborough; Royal Ballet Sch., London. Walter Gore's London Ballet, 1962–64; Western Theatre Ballet, 1964–69; Principal Dancer, 1969–89, Artistic Controller, 1988–89, Scottish Ballet; has also danced with London Fest. Ballet, Portuguese Nat. Ballet, Galina Samsova and Andre Prokovsky's New London Ballet, Cuban Nat. Ballet; Associate Artistic Dir, Northern Ballet Th., 1990–92. Mem., Scottish Arts Council, 1986–90 (Mem., Dance and Mime Cttee, 1982–92). Patron, Dowell Trust. Hon. LittD Strathclyde, 1990. *Relevant publication:* Elaine McDonald, ed J. S. Dixon, 1983. *Recreations:* physical therapy, theatre, travel, reading.

MACDONALD, Dr Ewan Beaton, FRCP, FRCPE, FRCPGlas, FFOM, FFOMI; Senior Lecturer, Department of Public Health, University of Glasgow, since 1990; *b* 11 Jan. 1947; *s* of Dr Duncan Macdonald, MBE and Isabel Dow Macdonald; *m* 1971, Patricia Malloy; three *s* one *d. Educ:* Keil Sch.; Univ. of Glasgow (MB ChB). FFOM 1988; FRCPGlas 1992; FRCP 1994; FRCPE 1996. General medicine, Western Infirmary, Glasgow, 1971–75; National Coal Board: MO, 1975–80; PMO, Yorks, 1980–85; Hon. Consultant in Rehabilitation, Firbeck Hosp., 1980–85; IBM UK: SMO, 1986; CMO, 1987–90; Chm., IBM European Occupational Health Bd, 1988–90; Dir, SALUS (Lanarks Occupnl Health and Safety Service), 1990–. Dean, Faculty of Occupational Medicine, RCP, 1994–96; Pres., Sect. of Occupnl Medicine, Union of Eur. Med. Specialists, 2001– (Sec., 1997–2001). Founder and Chm., Kinloch Castle Friends Assoc., 1996–. *Publications:* numerous articles and chapters on occupational health. *Recreations:* mountaineering, sailing, fishing. *Address:* Department of Public Health, 2 Lilybank Gardens, University of Glasgow, Glasgow G12 8RZ. *T:* (0141) 330 4038. *Club:* Loch Lomond Sailing.

MACDONALD, Rev. Dr Finlay Angus John; Principal Clerk, since 1996, Moderator, from May 2002 (with designation Rt Rev.), General Assembly of the Church of Scotland; *b* 1 July 1945; *s* of Rev. John Macdonald, AEA, MA and Eileen Ivy Sheila (*née* O'Flynn); *m* 1968, Elizabeth Mary Stuart; two *s. Educ:* Dundee High Sch.; Univ. of St Andrews (MA 1967; BD 1970; PhD 1983). Pres. Students' Representative Council, St Andrews Univ., 1968–69. Licensed by Presbytery of Dundee, 1970; ordained by Presbytery of Stirling and Dunblane, 1971; Minister: Menstrie Parish Ch., 1971–77; Jordanhill Parish Ch., Glasgow, 1977–96. Convener, Business Cttee, Gen. Assembly, 1988–92. Gov., Jordanhill Coll., 1988–93; Lay Mem. Court, Strathclyde Univ., 1993–96. *Recreations:* music, gardening, hill-walking. *Address:* (office) 121 George Street, Edinburgh EH2 4YN. *T:* (0131) 240 2240. *Club:* New (Edinburgh).

MacDONALD, Hon. Flora Isabel, CC 1999 (OC 1993); PC (Can.) 1979; Chairperson, HelpAge International, since 1997; *b* N Sydney, Nova Scotia, 3 June 1926. *Educ:* schools in North Sydney, Nova Scotia; Empire Business Coll., Sydney, NS; Canadian Nat. Defence Coll. With Nat. HQ, Progressive Cons. Party, 1957–66 (Exec. Dir, 1961–66); Nat. Sec., Progressive Cons. Assoc. of Canada, 1966–69; Administrative Officer and Tutor, Dept of Political Studies, Queen's Univ., Kingston, 1967–73; MP (Progressive C) Kingston, Ontario, 1972–88; Sec. of State for External Affairs, Canada, 1979–80; Minister of Employment and Immigration, 1984–86; Minister for Communications, 1986–88. Vis. Scholar, Centre for Canadian Studies, Univ. of Edinburgh, 1989. Special Advr, Commonwealth of Learning, 1990–91; Chairperson, Internat. Develt Res. Centre, 1992–97. Dir, C. T. Financial Services, 1989–97. Director: Care Canada, 1993–; Partnership Africa Canada, 1997–; Future Generations, Franklin, WV, 1996–. Chairman: Canadian Co-ordinating Cttee, UN Internat. Year of Older Persons, 1999; Shastri Indo-Canada Adv. Council, 1996–. Patron, Commonwealth Human Rights Initiative. Mem., Carnegie Commn on Preventing Deadly Conflict, Washington, 1994–98. Pres., Assoc. of Canadian Clubs, 1999–. Presenter, North/South (weekly TV prog.), 1990–94. Hon. degrees from Univs in Canada, US and UK. *Publications:* papers on political subjects. *Recreations:* speedskating, mountain climbing. *Address:* #1103, 350 Queen Elizabeth Driveway, Ottawa, ON K1S 3N1, Canada.

McDONALD, F(rancis) James; Chairman, Beaumont Hospital Board of Trustees, 1992–96 (Chairman, Beaumont Hospital Foundation, 1987–92); President and Chief Operating Officer, General Motors, 1981–87; *b* Saginaw, Mich, 3 Aug. 1922; *s* of Francis and Mary McDonald; *m* 1944, Betty Ann Dettenthaler; two *s* one *d. Educ:* General Motors Inst. Served USN, 1944–46 (Lieut). Joined Saginaw Malleable Iron Plant, 1946; Transmission Div., Detroit, 1956–65; Pontiac Motor Div., 1965–68; Dir, Manufacturing Operations, Chevrolet Motor Div., 1968–69; Vice-Pres., and Mem. Admin Cttee, Gen. Motors, 1969; General Manager: Pontiac Motor Div., 1969–72; Chevrolet Motor Div., 1972–74; Exec. Vice-Pres. and a Dir, 1974; Mem. Finance Cttee, 1979; Chm., Exec. and Admin Cttees, 1981. Holds hon. degrees from univs and colls in the US, incl. Michigan State Univ. and Notre Dame Univ. *Address:* 1051 Indian Mound Trail, Vero Beach, FL 32963, USA.

MACDONALD, Howard; *see* Macdonald, J. H.

MACDONALD, Prof. (Hugh) Ian, OC 1977; Professor, Department of Economics, and Schulich School of Business (formerly Faculty of Administrative Studies), since 1974, Director, Degree Programme in Public Administration, since 1992, York University, Toronto; President Emeritus, York University, since 1984; *b* Toronto, 27 June 1929; *s* of Hugh and Winnifred Macdonald; *m* 1960, Dorothy Marion Vernon; two *s* three *d. Educ:* public schs, Toronto; Univ. of Toronto; Oxford Univ. BCom (Toronto), MA (Oxon), BPhil (Oxon). Univ. of Toronto: Lectr in Economics, 1955; Dean of Men, 1956; Asst Prof., Economics, 1962. Govt of Ontario: Chief Economist, 1965; Dep. Provincial Treas., 1967; Dep. Treas. and Dep. Minister of Economics, 1968; Dep. Treas. and Dep. Minister of Economics and Intergovernmental Affairs, 1972. Pres., York Univ., 1974–84; Dir, York Internat., 1984–94. Director: the AGF Cos, 1982–; McGraw-Hill Ryerson Ltd, 1984– (Chm., 1996–). Member, Board of Directors: World Encyclopaedia of Contemp. Theatre, 1984–; Canadian Executive Service Orgn, 1999–; Chairman: The Commonwealth of Learning, 1994; Hockey Canada, 1987; Member: Canadian Economics Assoc.; Amer. Economics Assoc.; Royal Economic Soc. (London); Canadian Assoc. for Club of Rome; Inst. of Public Admin of Canada; Lambda Alpha Fraternity (Land Economics); Amer. Soc. for Public Admin; Past President: Empire Club of Canada; Ticker Club; Couchiching Inst. Public Affairs; Canadian Rhodes Scholars Foundn; World Univ. Service of Canada; Past Chairman: Bd, Corp. to Promote Innovation Develt for Employment Advancement (Govt of Ontario); Commn on Financing of Elementary and Secondary Educn in Ontario; Ont. Municipal Trng and Educn Adv. Council; Inst. for Political Involvement; Toronto Men's Br. of CIIA; Past Member: Bd, Council for Canadian Unity, 1978–99; Admin. Bd, Internat. Assoc. of Univs; Council and Exec. Cttee, Interamerican Orgn for Higher Educn (Vice-Pres., Canada); Attorney General's Cttee on Securities Legislation; Economic Council of Canada. Chm., Annual Fund Appeal in Canada of Balliol Coll., Oxford Univ., 1994–. Hon. Councillor, Internat. Orgn for Higher Educn, 1992. Hon. Life Mem., Canadian Olympic Assoc., 1997. KLJ 1978; Citation of Merit, Court of Canadian Citizenship, 1980. Hon. LLD Toronto, 1974; DUniv Open, 1998; Hon. DLitt Sri Lanka Open, 1999. Canada Centennial Medal, 1967; Silver Jubilee Medal, 1977; Commemorative Medal, 125th Anniversary of Confedn of Canada, 1992; Award of Merit, Canadian Bureau for Internat. Educn, 1994; Vanier Medal, for distinction in public service and excellence in public admin, 2000. *Recreations:* hockey, tennis; public service in various organizations. *Address:* 7 Whitney Avenue, Toronto, ON M4W 2A7, Canada. *T:* (416) 9212908; York University, 4700 Keele Street, Toronto, ON M3J 1P3, Canada. *T:* (416) 7365632.

MACDONALD, Prof. Hugh John; Avis Blewett Professor of Music, Washington University, St Louis, since 1987 (Chair, Music Department, 1997–99); *b* 31 Jan. 1940; *s* of Stuart and Margaret Macdonald; *m* 1st, 1963, Naomi Butterworth; one *s* three *d*; 2nd, 1979, Elizabeth Babb; one *s. Educ:* Winchester College; Pembroke College, Cambridge (MA; PhD). FRCM 1987. Cambridge University: Asst Lectr, 1966–69; Lectr, 1969–71; Fellow, Pembroke Coll., 1963–71; Lectr, Oxford Univ., 1971–80, and Fellow, St John's Coll; Gardiner Prof. of Music, Glasgow Univ., 1980–87. Vis. Prof., Indiana Univ., 1979. Gen. Editor, New Berlioz Edition, 1966–. Szymanowski Medal, Poland, 1983. *Publications:* Berlioz Orchestral Music, 1969; Skryabin, 1978; Berlioz, 1981; (ed) Berlioz Selected Letters, 1995; articles in New Grove Dict. of Music and Musicians, Musical Times, Music and Letters, Revue de Musicologie. *Recreation:* bridges. *Address:* Department of Music, Washington University, One Brookings Drive, St Louis, MO 63130–4899, USA. *T:* (314) 9355519.

MACDONALD, Iain Smith, CB 1988; MD; FRCPE, FFPHM; Chief Medical Officer, Scottish Home and Health Department, 1985–88, retired; *b* 14 July 1927; *s* of Angus Macdonald, MA and Jabina Urie Smith; *m* 1958, Sheila Foster; one *s* one *d. Educ:* Univ. of Glasgow (MD, DPH). Lectr, Univ. of Glasgow, 1955; Deputy Medical Officer of Health: Bury, 1957; Bolton, 1959; joined Scottish Home and Health Dept, 1964, Dep. Chief Med. Officer, 1974–85. Mem., MRC, 1985–88. QHP 1984–87. *Address:* 4 Skythorn Way, Falkirk FK1 5NR. *T:* (01324) 625100.

MacDONALD, Ian; *see* Mayfield, Hon. Lord.

MACDONALD, Ian; *see* Macdonald, H. I.

MACDONALD, Ian Alexander; QC 1988; *b* 12 Jan. 1939; *s* of late Ian Wilson Macdonald and Helen Nicolson, MA; *m* 1st, 1968, Judith Roberts (marr. diss.); two *s*; 2nd, 1978, Jennifer Hall (marr. diss.); one *s*; 3rd, 1991, Yasmin Sharif. *Educ:* Glasgow Acad.; Cargilfield Sch., Edinburgh; Rugby Sch.; Clare Coll., Cambridge (MA, LLB). Called to the Bar, Middle Temple, 1963; Astbury Scholar, 1962–65; SE Circuit. Lectr in Law, Kingston Polytechnic, 1968–72; Senior Legal Writer and Research Consultant, Incomes Data Services Ltd, 1974–80 (monitoring develts in employment law). Mem., Cttee of Inquiry into disappearance of Gen. Humberto Delgado, 1965; Chm., Indep. Inquiry into Racial Violence in Manchester Schs, 1987–88. Special Advocate, Special Immigration Appeals Commn, 1999–. Pres., Immigration Law Practitioners' Assoc., 1984–. Mem. Editl Adv. Bd, Immigration and Nationality Law and Practice. Grand Cross, Order of Liberty (Portugal), 1995. *Publications:* Resale Price Maintenance, 1964; (with D. P. Kerrigan) The Land Commission Act 1967, 1967; Race Relations and Immigration Law, 1969; Immigration Appeals Act 1969, 1969; Race Relations: the new law, 1977; (with N. Blake) The New Nationality Law, 1982; Immigration Law and Practice, 1983, 5th edn 2001; Murder in the Playground: report of Macdonald Inquiry into Racial Violence in Manchester Schools, 1990; (contrib.) Family Guide to the Law, 1971, 1972; articles in professional jls. *Recreations:* swimming, squash, watching football, reading. *Address:* 2 Garden Court, Temple, EC4Y 9BL. *T:* (020) 7353 1633. *Club:* Cumberland Lawn Tennis.

MACDONALD OF SLEAT, Sir Ian Godfrey B.; *see* Bosville Macdonald of Sleat.

MACDONALD, Prof. Ian Grant, FRS 1979; Professor of Pure Mathematics, Queen Mary and Westfield College (formerly Queen Mary College), University of London, 1976–87, now Emeritus; *b* 11 Oct. 1928; *s* of Douglas Grant Macdonald and Irene Alice Macdonald; *m* 1954, Margaretha Maria Lodewijk Van Goethem; two *s* three *d. Educ:* Winchester Coll.; Trinity Coll., Cambridge (MA). Asst Principal and Principal, Min. of Supply, 1952–57; Asst Lectr, Univ. of Manchester, 1957–60; Lectr, Univ. of Exeter, 1960–63; Fellow, Magdalen Coll., Oxford, 1963–72; Fielden Prof. of Pure Maths, Univ. of Manchester, 1972–76. *Publications:* Introduction to Commutative Algebra (with M. F. Atiyah), 1969; Algebraic Geometry, 1969; articles in math. jls. *Address:* 56 High Street, Steventon, Abingdon, Oxon OX13 6RS.

MacDONALD, Isabel Lillias, (Mrs J. G. MacDonald); *see* Sinclair, I. L.

McDONALD, Iverach; Associate Editor, The Times, 1967–73; Director, The Times Ltd, 1968–73; *b* 23 Oct. 1908; *s* of Benjamin McDonald, Strathcool, Caithness, and Janet Seel; *m* 1935, Gwendoline (*d* 1993), *o d* of late Captain Thomas R. Brown; one *s* one *d. Educ:* Leeds Gram. Sch. Asst Editor, Yorkshire Post, 1933; sub-editor, The Times, 1935; correspondent in Berlin, 1937; diplomatic correspondent 1938; Asst Editor, 1948; Foreign Editor, 1952; Managing Editor, 1965. War of 1939–45: Capt., Gen. Staff, 1939–40; travelled extensively in Soviet Union, Far East and America; reported all allied conferences after the war, including San Francisco, 1945, Paris, 1946 and 1947, Moscow, 1947, Colombo, 1950, and Bermuda, 1953. Sen. Associate Mem., St Antony's Coll., Oxford, 1976–. *Publications:* A Man of the Times, 1976; The History of The Times, vol. V, 1939–1966, 1984; chapters in: Walter Lippmann and His Times, 1959; The Times History of our Times, 1971. *Address:* Flat 25, Emden House, Barton Lane, Headington, Oxford OX3 9JU. *T:* (01865) 744150.

McDONALD, James; *see* McDonald, F. J.

MACDONALD, Most Rev. James; *see* St John's (Newfoundland), Archbishop of, (RC).

MACDONALD, John B(arfoot), OC 1991; DDS, MS, PhD; Chairman, Addiction Research Foundation, 1981–87 (President and Chief Executive Officer, 1976–81); Executive Director, Council of Ontario Universities, 1968–76; Professor of Higher Education, University of Toronto, 1968–76; *b* 23 Feb. 1918; *s* of Arthur A. Macdonald and Gladys L. Barfoot; *m*; two *s* one *d*; *m* 1967, Liba Kucera; two *d. Educ:* Univ. of Toronto, University of Illinois, Columbia Univ. DDS (with hons) Toronto, 1942; MS (Bact) Ill, 1948; PhD (Bact) Columbia, 1953. Lectr, Prev. Dentistry, University of Toronto, and private practice, 1942–44. Canadian Dental Corps, 1944–46 (Capt.) Instr, Bacteriol, University of Toronto, and private practice, 1946–47; Res. Asst, Univ. of Illinois, 1947–48; Kellogg Fellow and Canadian Dental Assoc. Res. Student, Columbia Univ., 1948–49; University of Toronto: Asst Prof. of Bacteriol., 1949–53; Assoc. Prof. of Bacteriol., 1953–56; Chm., Div. of Dental Res., 1953–56; Prof. of Bacteriol., 1956; Cons. in Dental Educn, University of BC, 1955–56; Dir, Forsyth Dental Infirmary, 1956–62 (Cons. in Bacteriol., 1962); Prof. of Microbiol., Harvard Sch., of Dental Med., 1956–62 (Dir of Postdoctoral Studies, 1960–62); President, Univ. of British Columbia, 1962–67. Consultant: Dental Med. Section of Corporate Research Div. of Colgate-Palmolive Co., 1958–62; Donwood Foundn, Toronto, 1967 (Chm. of Bd, 1972–75); Science Council of

Canada, 1967–69; Addiction Research Foundn of Ontario, 1968–74 (Mem., 1974–76); Nat. Inst. of Health, 1968– (Mem., Dental Study Sect., 1961–65). Chm., Commn on Pharmaceutical Services of the Canadian Pharmaceutical Assoc., 1967; Mem. and Vice-Chm., Ontario Council of Health, 1981–84; Councillor-at-Large, Internat. Assoc. for Dental Research, 1963, Pres. 1968–69. Fellow, Mem. or Chm. of numerous assocs etc, both Canadian and international. FACD 1955; Hon. FICD 1965. Hon. AM, Harvard Univ., 1956; Hon. LLD: Univ. of Manitoba, 1962; Simon Fraser Univ., 1965; Hon DSc Univ. of British Columbia, 1967; Hon. LLD: Wilfred Laurier Univ., 1976; Brock Univ., 1976; Univ. of W Ontario, 1977; Hon. DSc Univ. of Windsor, 1977. *Publications:* Higher Education in British Columbia and a Plan for the Future, 1962 etc.; numerous contribs to learned jls. *Recreations:* golf, fishing. *Address:* 30 Metropolitan Crescent, Keswick, ON L4P 1L5, Canada. *Clubs:* University of BC Faculty (Vancouver); Faculty (University of Toronto).

McDONALD, Prof. John Corbett, MD; FRCP, FFCM, FFOM; Professor, Department of Occupational and Environmental Medicine, National Heart and Lung Institute (Royal Brompton Hospital), University of London, since 1990; *b* 20 April 1918; *s* of John Forbes McDonald and Sarah Mary McDonald; *m* 1942, Alison Dunstan Wells; one *s* three *d.* *Educ:* London Univ. (MD); Harvard Univ. (MS). DPH, DIH; FRCP (Canada) 1970; FRCP 1976; FFCM 1976; FFOM 1978. Served War, MO, RAMC, 1942–46. Epidemiologist, Public Health Lab. Service, 1951–64 (Dir, Epidemiol Res. Lab., 1960–64); Prof. and Head, Dept of Epidemiology and Health, McGill Univ., Montreal, 1964–76; Prof. of Occupational Health, LSHTM, London Univ., 1976–81, now Emeritus; Prof. of Epidemiol. and Hd, Sch. of Occupational Health, McGill Univ., 1981–83, Prof. Emeritus, 1988–; Chm., Dept of Clinical Epidemiology, Nat. Heart and Lung (formerly Cardiothoracic) Inst. (Royal Brompton Hosp.), Univ. of London, 1986–90. *Publications:* (ed) Recent Advances in Occupational Health, 1981; Epidemiology of Work-related Diseases, 1995, 2nd edn 2000; papers on epidemiol subjects. *Recreations:* skiing, cycling. *Address:* 4 Temple West Mews, West Square, SE11 4TJ; 232 Peabody Road, Mansonville, QC J0E 1X0, Canada. *Club:* Athenæum.

MacDONALD, Maj.-Gen. John Donald, CB 1993; CBE 1986 (OBE 1981); DL; Chief Executive (formerly General Secretary): The Earl Haig Fund, since 1994; Officers Association Scotland, since 1994; *b* 5 April 1938; *s* of Lt-Col John MacDonald, OBE; *m* 1964, Mary, *d* of Dr Graeme M. Warrack, CBE, DSO, TD; one *s* two *d.* *Educ:* George Watson's Coll., Edinburgh; RMA Sandhurst. Commnd, 1958; saw service with KOSB, RASC, RCT and Airborne Forces Berlin, UK, BAOR, N Africa, India (Defence Services Staff Coll.), 1958–71; ndc, 1976; Turkey NATO HQ Izmir, CO 4 Armoured Div., Transport Regt RCT, 1978–80; Instr Australian Comd and Staff Coll., 1980–82; Chief Instr and Comdt, RCT Officers' Sch., 1983; DCS 3 Armoured Div., 1983–86; Col Personnel Br. Sec., MoD, 1987–88; Comdr Transport, 1st BR Corps and Garrison Comdr Bielefeld, 1988–91; DG Transport and Movements, MoD, 1991–93. Col Comdt RLC, 1998–99. Gen. Sec., RBL, Scotland, 1994–2000. Chm., Sportsmatch, Scotland, 1993–98; Mem., Sports Council, Scotland, 1994–99. Queen's Councillor, Queen Victoria Sch., Dunblane, 1994–. Chm., Combined Services Rugby, 1991–93. Freeman, City of London, 1991; Hon. Mem. Ct of Assts, Carmens' Co., 1991. DL City of Edinburgh, 1996. *Recreations:* Rugby (played for Scotland, Barbarians, Combined Services and Army), ski-ing, golf, travel, music, collecting. *Address:* Ormiston Hill, Kirknewton, West Lothian EH27 8DQ. *Clubs:* Army and Navy; London Scottish, Royal & Ancient (St Andrews), Honourable Co. of Edinburgh Golfers (Muirfield), Rugby Internationalists Golfing Society.

MacDONALD, John Grant, CBE 1989 (MBE 1962); HM Diplomatic Service, retired; re-employed at Foreign and Commonwealth Office, since 1993; Representative of Secretary of State for Foreign and Commonwealth Affairs, since 1997; *b* 26 Jan. 1932; *er s* of late John Nicol MacDonald and Margaret MacDonald (*née* Vasey); *m* 1955, Jean, *o c* of late J. K. K. Harrison; one *s* two *d.* *Educ:* George Heriot's School. Entered HM Foreign (later Diplomatic) Service, 1949; FO, 1949; served HM Forces, 1950–52; FO, 1952; Berne, 1954–59; Third Sec. and Vice Consul, Havana, 1960–62; FO, 1962; DSAO, 1965; Second, later First Sec. (Comm.), Lima, 1966–71; Nat. Defence Coll., Latimer, 1971–72; Parly Clerk of FCO, 1972–75; First Sec. (Comm.), Hd of Trade Promotion Sect., Washington, 1975–79; Hd of Chancery, Dhaka, 1980–81; Hd of Chancery and HM Consul, Bogotá, 1981–84; Counsellor, FCO, 1985–86; Ambassador to: Paraguay, 1986–89; Panama, 1989–92; Head UK Delegn, and Dep. Head (Political), EC Monitor Mission, 1992; temp. duty as Charter Mark Assessor, Cabinet Office, 1994, 1995; UK Mem., OSCE Observer Gp, elections in Macedonia, 1994. Vis. Lectr, Foreign Services Inst., S Africa, 1997. *Recreations:* travel, photography, swimming. *Address:* c/o Foreign and Commonwealth Office, SW1A 2AH. *Clubs:* Naval and Military, Royal Over-Seas League.

MACDONALD, (John) Howard, CA; FCT; Director: BOC Group plc, since 1991; Weir Group plc, since 1991; *b* 5 June 1928; *s* of John and Helen Macdonald; *m* 1961, Anne Hunter; three *d.* *Educ:* Hermitage, Helensburgh. CA 1954. Thomson McLintock & Co. (served articles), 1949–55; Walter Mitchell & Sons, 1955–58; Aircraft Marine Products, 1958; Finance Manager, Keir & Cawder Arrow Drilling, 1958–60; Royal Dutch Shell Group, 1960–83, Group Treasurer, 1978–83; Chairman and Chief Executive: Dome Petroleum, 1983–88; NatWest Investment Bank, 1989–91; Director: National Westminster Bank, 1989–91; McDermott Internat. Inc., 1985–97; J. Ray McDermott Inc., 1985–97. Mem., Assoc. of Corporate Treasurers, 1979. *Recreations:* golf, theatre. *Address:* 18 Fairbourne, Cobham, Surrey KT11 2BP. *T:* (01932) 862281. *Club:* Caledonian.

MACDONALD, John Reginald; QC 1976; barrister-at-law; Commercial, Chancery and Administrative Lawyer; *b* 26 Sept. 1931; *s* of Ranald Macdonald and Marion Olive (*née* Kirkby); *m* 1958, Erica Stanton; one *s* one *d.* *Educ:* St Edward's Sch., Oxford; Queens' Coll., Cambridge. Called to Bar, Lincoln's Inn, 1955, Bencher, 1985; called to Bar of Eastern Caribbean, 1988. Represented: the people of Ocean Island, 1975; Yuri Orlov, the Soviet dissident, 1977–86; Canadian Indians, 1982; the Ilios, who were removed from Diego Garcia to make way for a US base, 1983; appeared for the people of Barbuda at the Antigua Indep. Conf. at Lancaster House in 1980; Mem., Internat. Commn of Jurists missions to investigate violence in S Africa, 1990, 1992, 1993. Drafted written constitution for the UK (We the People), proposed by Liberal Democrats, 1990, revised 1993; Mem., Jt Lib Dem Labour Cttee on Constitutional Reform, 1996–97. Contested: Wimbledon (L) 1966 and 1970; Folkestone and Hythe (L) 1983, (L/Alliance) 1987; E Kent (Lib Dem), Eur. election 1994. Chm. Council, Kent Opera, 1996–. *Recreation:* the theatre. *Address:* 12 New Square, Lincoln's Inn, WC2A 3SW. *T:* (020) 7419 8000. *Club:* MCC.

MacDONALD, John William; HM Diplomatic Service, retired; *b* 13 June 1938; *s* of John MacDonald and Anne MacDonald (*née* Richards); *m* 1960, Margaret Millam Burns. *Educ:* Boteler Grammar Sch; NDC; Manchester Businesss Sch. Foreign Office, 1955, and 1959–94; Royal Navy, 1957–59; Dipl. Service appts include Cairo, Tokyo, Dhaka, Dar es Salaam; Consul-Gen., Shanghai, 1991–94. *Recreations:* walking, golf, listening to music. *Address:* Cherry Orchard, Garden Reach, Chalfont St Giles, Bucks HP8 4BE. *Club:* Little Chalfont Golf.

MACDONALD, Sir Kenneth (Carmichael), KCB 1990 (CB 1983); Chairman: Raytheon Systems Ltd (formerly Cossor Electronics, then Raytheon Cossor, Ltd), 1991–2000; International Military Services Ltd, since 1993; Council of Voluntary Welfare Work, since 1993; *b* 25 July 1930; *s* of William Thomas and Janet Millar Macdonald; *m* 1960, Ann Elisabeth (*née* Pauer); one *s* two *d.* *Educ:* Hutchesons' Grammar Sch.; Glasgow Univ. MA (Hons Classics). RAF, 1952–54. Asst Principal, Air Ministry, 1954; Asst Private Sec. to Sec. of State, 1956–57; Private Sec. to Permanent Sec., 1958–61; HM Treasury, 1962–65; MoD, 1965; Asst Sec., 1968; Counsellor (Defence), UK Delegn to NATO, 1973–75; Asst Under-Sec. of State, 1975, Dep. Under-Sec. of State, 1980, Second Perm. Under-Sec. of State, 1988–90, MoD. Chm., Raytheon (Europe) Ltd, 1991–94. Trustee, Chatham Historic Dockyard Trust, 1992–2000. *Recreation:* golf. *Address:* c/o Barclays Bank, 27 Regent Street, SW1Y 4UB. *Club:* Royal Air Force.

MACDONALD, Kenneth Donald John; QC 1997; *b* 4 Jan. 1953; *s* of late Dr Kenneth Macdonald, scientist, and Maureen Macdonald (*née* Sheridan); *m* 1980, Linda Zuck, television producer; two *s* one *d.* *Educ:* St Edmund Hall, Oxford (BA Hons PPE 1974). Called to the Bar, Inner Temple, 1978. Mem., Treasury Counsel Selection Cttee, 2001–. Member: Cttee, Criminal Bar Assoc., 1997– (Chm., Educn Sub-Cttee, 1999–); Criminal Justice Adv. Panel, Justice, 1997–; Bar Council, 2000; Bar Public Affairs Gp, 2001–. *Recreations:* 20th century history, crime fiction, film noir, Arsenal Football Club. *Address:* Matrix Chambers, Gray's Inn, WC1R 5LN. *T:* (020) 7404 3447.

McDONALD, Rt Rev. Kevin John Patrick; *see* Northampton, Bishop of, (RC).

McDONALD, Lawson; *see* McDonald, E. L.

MACDONALD, Lewis; Member (Lab) Aberdeen Central, Scottish Parliament, since 1999; Deputy Minister for Transport and Planning, since 2001; *b* 1 Jan. 1957; *s* of late Rev. Roderick Macdonald and of Margaret Macdonald (*née* Currie); *m* 1997, Sandra Inkster; two *d.* *Educ:* Inverurie Acad.; Univ. of Aberdeen (MA, PhD). Parly Researcher, office of Frank Doran, MP, 1987–92 and 1997–99; Adviser to Tom Clarke, MP, 1993–97. Mem., Exec. Cttee, SLP, 1997–99. Convenor, Holyrood Progress Gp, 2000–01. Contested (Lab) Moray, 1997. *Recreations:* walking, football, history. *Address:* Scottish Parliament, Edinburgh EH99 1SP. *T:* (0131) 348 5000, (office) (01224) 647846.

MacDONALD, Margo, (Mrs James Sillars); Member (SNP) Lothians, Scottish Parliament, since 1999; journalist; *b* 19 April 1943; *d* of Robert and Jean Aitken; *m* 1st, 1965, Peter MacDonald (marr. diss. 1980); two *d*; 2nd, 1981, James Sillars, *qv.* *Educ:* Hamilton Academy; Dunfermline Coll. (Diploma of Physical Educn). Contested (SNP) Paisley, Gen. Elec., 1970; MP (SNP) Glasgow (Govan), Nov. 1973–Feb. 1974; contested (SNP): Glasgow (Govan), Gen. Elec., Feb. 1974 and Oct. 1974; Hamilton, by-election, May 1978. Vice-Chm., Scottish National Party, 1972–79 (Senior Vice-Chm., 1974–79); Mem., SNP Nat. Exec., 1980–81; Chm., SNP '79 Group, 1978–81. Director of Shelter (Scotland), 1978–81. *Recreations:* swimming, aquarobics, country music, Hibs FC. *Address:* Scottish Parliament, Edinburgh EH99 1SP.

McDONALD, Mavis, CB 1998; Permanent Secretary, Cabinet Office, since 2000; *b* 23 Oct. 1944; *d* of late Richard Henry and of Elizabeth Lowe; *m* 1971, David Arthur McDonald, *qv*; one *s.* *Educ:* Chadderton Grammar Sch. for Girls; London Sch. of Econs and Pol Science (BSc Econ). Min. of Housing and Local Govt, later DoE, then DETR, 1966–2000: Asst Private Sec. to Minister for Housing and Local Govt, 1969–70, to Sec. of State for the Environment, 1970–71; Private Sec. to Perm. Sec., 1973–75; Asst Sec., Central Policy Planning Unit, 1981–83; Head of Personnel Management (Envmt) Div., 1983–86; Finance, Local Authority Grants, 1986; Dep. Dir, Local Govt Finance, 1987; Under Secretary: Directorate of Admin. Resources, 1988–90; Directorate of Personnel Management, 1990–91; Directorate of Housing Resources and Management, 1990–93; Directorate of Local Govt, 1994–95; Prin. Estab. Officer, 1995; Sen. Dir, Housing, Construction, Planning and Countryside, then Dir Gen., Housing, Construction, Regeneration and Countryside Gp, 1995–2000. Non-exec. Dir, Tarmac Housing Div., 1988–91. Member: Cttee of Mgt, Broomleigh Housing Assoc., 1995–96; Bd, Ealing Family Housing Assoc., 2001. Lay Gov., Birkbeck Coll., London, 1999.

MACDONALD, Morag, (Mrs Walter Simpson), CBE 1993; Secretary of the Post Office, 1985–94; *b* 8 Feb. 1947; *d* of Murdoch Macdonald Macdonald and Isobel Macdonald (*née* Black); *m* 1st, 1970, Adam Somerville; 2nd, 1983, Walter Simpson; one *d.* *Educ:* Bellahouston Academy, Glasgow; Univ. of Glasgow (LLB Hons 1968); College of Law, London; King's Coll., London (BA 1997). Called to the Bar, Inner Temple, 1974. Joined Post Office as graduate trainee, 1968; posts in Telecommunications and Corporate HQ, 1969–79; PA to Managing Dir, Girobank, 1980; Dep. Sec., Post Office, 1983–85. Mem. Management Cttee, Industry and Parlt Trust, 1986–94. Council Mem., St George's Hosp. Med. Sch., 1994–97. FRSA 1990. *Recreations:* walking, embroidery, very indifferent piano playing. *Address:* Ardshiel, Gwydyr Road, Crieff, Perthshire PH7 4BS.

MACDONALD, Nigel Colin Lock; Partner, Ernst & Young, since 1976; *b* 15 June 1945; *s* of Trevor William and Barbara Evelyn Macdonald; *m* 1st, 1972, Elizabeth Ruth Leaney (*d* 1981); 2nd, 1983, Jennifer Margaret Webster; one *d.* *Educ:* Cranleigh Sch.; Inst. of Chartered Accountants of Scotland. Thomson McLintock & Co., 1962–68; Whinney Murray & Co., 1968–70; Whinney Murray Ernst & Ernst, Netherlands, 1970–72; Whinney Murray, later Ernst & Whinney, then Ernst & Young, 1972–. Dir, James Lock & Co., 1976– (Chm., 1986–). Mem. Council, 1989–93, Pres., 1993–94, Inst. of Chartered Accountants of Scotland. Member: Cadbury Cttee on corporate governance, 1991; Review Panel, Financial Reporting Council, 1991; Bd, BSI, 1992; Industrial Develt Adv. Bd, 1995; Additl Mem., Competition (formerly Monopolies and Mergers) Commn, 1998–. FRSA 1993. Elder, St Andrew's URC, Cheam. *Recreations:* old cars, swimming, topography. *Address:* 10 Lynwood Road, Epsom, Surrey KT17 4LD. *T:* (01372) 720853. *Clubs:* Royal Automobile, City of London.

McDONALD, Dr Oonagh, CBE 1998; research and management consultant, financial services industry; *b* Stockton-on-Tees, Co. Durham; *d* of Dr H. D. McDonald, theologian. *Educ:* Roan Sch. for Girls, Greenwich; East Barnet Grammar Sch.; Univ. of London (BD Hons 1959; MTh 1962, PhD 1974, King's Coll.). Teacher, 1959–64; Lectr in Philosophy, Bristol Univ., 1965–76. Gwilym Gibbon Res. Fellow, Nuffield Coll., Oxford, 1988–89; Sen. Res. Fellow, Univ. of Warwick, 1990. Contested (Lab): S Glos, Feb. and Oct. 1974; Thurrock, 1987. MP (Lab) Thurrock, July 1976–87. PPS to Chief Sec. to Treasury, 1977–79; Opposition front bench spokesman on defence, 1981–83, on Treasury and economic affairs, 1983–87, on Civil Service, 1983–87. Consultant, Unity Trust Bank plc, 1987–88. Non-exec. Director: Investors' Compensation Scheme, 1992–2001; Gen. Insce Standards Council, 1999–; Gibraltar Financial Services Commn, 1999–; SAGA Gp, 1995–98; Scottish Provident, 1999–; Skandia, 2001–. Director: FSA (formerly SIB), 1993–98 (Chm., Consumer Panel, 1994–95); FSA Ombudsman Scheme,

1999–. Editor, Jl of Financial Regulation and Compliance, 1998–. *Publications:* (jtly) The Economics of Prosperity, 1980; Own Your Own: social ownership examined, 1989; Parliament at Work, 1989; The Future of Whitehall, 1992. *T:* (020) 8940 5563.

MACDONALD OF CLANRANALD, Ranald Alexander; 24th Chief and Captain of Clanranald; formerly Chairman and Managing Director, Tektura Ltd; *b* 27 March 1934; *s* of late Captain Kenneth Macdonald of Inchkenneth, DSO, and late Marjory Broad Smith, Basingstoke; *S* kinsman as Chief of Clanranald, 1944; *m* 1961, Jane Campbell-Davys, *d* of late I. E. Campbell-Davys, Llandovey, Carms; two *s* one *d*. *Educ:* Christ's Hospital. Founded: Fairfix Contracts Ltd, 1963; Tektura Wallcoverings, 1970. Chm., British Contract Furnishing Assoc., 1975–76. Lieut (TA) Cameron Highlanders, 1958–68. Mem., Standing Council of Scottish Chiefs, 1957–; Pres., Highland Soc. of London, 1988–91 (Dir, 1959–80); Chief Exec., Clan Donald Lands Trust, 1978–80; Chm., Museum of the Isles, 1981–90; Founding Trustee, Lord of the Isles Galley Proj., 1989–. Vice Pres., Les Avants Bobsleigh and Toboggan Club, 1987–. Kt of Justice Constantinian Order of St George, 1982. *Recreation:* avoidance of boredom. *Heir: s* Ranald Og Angus Macdonald, younger of Clanranald, *b* 17 Sept. 1963. *Address:* Morenish House, Killin, Perthshire FK21 8TX; Boisdale, 15 Eccleston Street, SW1W 9LX. *Clubs:* Beefsteak, Pratt's; New, Puffins (Edinburgh).

MACDONALD, Richard Auld; Director General, National Farmers' Union, since 1996; *b* 31 Oct. 1954; *s* of Anthony Macdonald and Gillian Macdonald (*née* Matthews); *m* 1980, Susan Jane Reynolds; two *d*. *Educ:* Bishop's Stortford Coll.; Queen Mary Coll., London Univ. (BSc Hons Biology). National Farmers' Union: Parly Sec., 1978–85; County Sec., Devon, 1985–89; Regl Dir, SW, 1989–92; Dir, 1992–96. *Recreations:* golf, cricket, Rugby, travel. *Address:* National Farmers' Union, 164 Shaftesbury Avenue, WC2H 8HL. *T:* (020) 7331 7209; *e-mail:* richard.macdonald@nfu.org.uk; (home) Woodpeckers, Hithercroft, South Moreton, Oxon OX11 9AL. *Clubs:* Naval and Military; Moreton Cricket.

McDONALD, Robert Howat; *see* McDonald, Hon. Lord.

MACDONALD, Roderick Francis; QC (Scot.) 1988; *b* 1 Feb. 1951; *s* of late Finlay Macdonald and Catherine Maclean. *Educ:* St Mungo's Acad., Glasgow; Glasgow Univ. (LLB Hons). Admitted advocate, 1975; Advocate-Depute (Crown Counsel), 1987–93; Home Advocate-Depute (Sen. Crown Counsel), 1990–93; called to the Bar, Inner Temple, 1997. Legal Chm., Pension Appeal Tribunals for Scotland, 1995–; Member: Criminal Injuries Compensation Bd, 1995–2000; Criminal Injuries Compensation Appeals Panel, 1997–99. *Recreations:* hill walking, cycling. *Address:* 6A Lennox Street, Edinburgh EH4 1QA. *T:* (0131) 332 7240.

MACDONALD, Maj.-Gen. Ronald Clarence, CB 1965; DSO 1944 and Bar, 1945; OBE 1953; Deputy Chief of Staff, Headquarters, Allied Land Forces, Central Europe, 1962–65; *b* 1 Aug. 1911; 2nd *s* of late Col C. R. Macdonald, CMG; *m* 1st, 1939, Jessie Ross Anderson (*d* 1986); one *s* (one *d* decd); 2nd, 1986, Constance Margaret Davies. *Educ:* Rugby; RMC, Sandhurst. Royal Warwicks Regt: Commissioned, 1931; Comdr 2nd Bn, 1945–46; Comdr 1st Bn, 1953–55; Bn Comdr, France, Germany Campaign, 1944–45; Mil. Asst to CIGS, 1946–49; GSO1, HQ, West Africa Comd, 1950–53; Col Gen. Staff, SHAPE, 1955–56; Comdr 10th Inf. Bde Gp, 1956–59; DDI, War Office, 1959–60; Chief of Staff, HQ Middle East Comd, 1960–62; retired, 1965. Col Royal Warwicks Fusiliers, 1963–68; Dep. Col (Warwicks), The Royal Regt of Fusiliers, 1968–74. *Recreation:* golf. *Address:* 6 The Beeches, Shaw, Melksham, Wilts SN12 8EW.

MACDONALD, Dr Rosemary Gillespie, FRCA; Dean, Post-graduate Medical Education (Yorkshire), University of Leeds and Northern and Yorkshire NHS Executive, since 1993; *b* 25 March 1944; *d* of John Mackenzie Paterson and Mary McCauley Paterson; *m* 1968, Hamish Neil Macdonald; one *s* one *d* (twins). *Educ:* Univ. of Glasgow (MB ChB); Univ. of Bradford (PhD 1976). FRCA 1971. Lectr in Anaesthesia, Univ. of Leeds, 1973–76; Consultant Obstetric Anaesthetist, St James's Univ. Hosp., Leeds, 1976–92. *Publications:* contribs to British Jl Anaesthesia, Anaesthesia, BMJ, etc. *Recreations:* cooking, walking, opera, ballet, art, human beings. *Address:* Springbank, 11 Hall Drive, Bramhope, Leeds LS16 9JF. *T:* (0113) 203 7337.

MACDONALD, Sharman; playwright, screenwriter and novelist; *b* 8 Feb. 1951; *d* of Joseph Henry Hosgood Macdonald and Janet Rowatt Williams; *m* 1976, Kevin William Knightley; one *s* one *d*. *Educ:* Hutchesons' Girls' GS, Glasgow; George Watson's Ladies' Coll., Edinburgh; Univ. of Edinburgh (MA 1972). *Theatre:* When I Was a Girl I Used to Scream and Shout, 1984; The Brave, 1988; When We Were Women, 1988; All Things Nice, 1990; Shades, 1992; The Winter Guest, 1995; Borders of Paradise, 1995; After Juliet, 1999; *radio:* Sea Urchins, 1997 (Bronze Sony Drama Award; adapted for stage, 1998); Gladly My Cross-eyed Bear, 2000; *opera libretto:* Hey Persephone!, 1998; *films:* Wild Flowers, 1989; The Winter Guest, 1998. Most Promising Playwright Award, Evening Standard Awards, 1984. *Publications: plays:* When I Was a Girl I Used to Scream and Shout, 1984; When We Were Women, 1988; The Brave, 1988; All Things Nice, 1990; Shades, 1992; Sharman Macdonald Plays I, 1995; Sea Urchins, 1998; After Juliet, 1999; *novels:* The Beast, 1986; Night Night, 1988. *Recreation:* body boarding. *Address:* c/o Alan Brodie, 211 Piccadilly, W1V 9LD.

MacDONALD, Prof. Simon Gavin George, FRSE; Professor of Physics, University of Dundee, 1973–88, now Emeritus; *b* 5 Sept. 1923; *s* of Simon MacDonald and Jean H. Thomson; *m* 1948, Eva Leonie Austerlitz; one *s* one *d*. *Educ:* George Heriot's Sch., Edinburgh; Edinburgh Univ. (MA (1st Cl. Hons) Maths and Nat. Phil); PhD (St Andrews). FIP 1958, FRSE 1972. Jun. Scientific Officer, RAE, Farnborough, 1943–46; Lectr, Univ. of St Andrews, 1948–57; Senior Lecturer: University Coll. of the West Indies, 1957–62; Univ. of St Andrews, 1962–67; Visiting Prof., Ohio Univ., 1963; University of Dundee: Sen. Lectr, then Prof., 1967–88; Dean of Science, 1970–73; Vice-Principal, 1974–79. Convener, Scottish Univs Council on Entrance, 1977–83 (Dep. Convener, 1973–77); Chm., Stats Cttee, UCCA, 1989–93 (Mem. Exec. Cttee, 1977–93; Chm., Technical Cttee, 1979–83; Dep. Chm., 1983–89). Chm., Bd of Dirs, Dundee Rep. Th., 1975–89; Chm., Fedn of Scottish Theatres, 1978–80. *Publications:* Problems and Solutions in General Physics, 1967; Physics for Biology and Premedical Students, 1970, 2nd edn 1975; Physics for the Life and Health Sciences, 1975; articles in physics jls. *Recreations:* bridge, golf, fiction writing. *Address:* 7A Windmill Road, St Andrews KY16 9JJ. *T:* (01334) 478014. *Club:* Royal Commonwealth Society.

McDONALD, Simon Gerard; HM Diplomatic Service; Principal Private Secretary to Secretary of State for Foreign and Commonwealth Affairs, since 2001; *b* 9 March 1961; *s* of James B. McDonald and Angela (*née* McDonald); *m* 1989, Hon. Olivia Mary, *o d* of Baron Wright of Richmond, *qv*; two *s* two *d*. *Educ:* Da La Salle Coll. Grammar Sch., Salford; Pembroke Coll., Cambridge (MA). Joined FCO, 1982; Jedda, 1985; Riyadh, 1985–88; Bonn, 1988–90; FCO, 1990; Private Sec. to Perm. Under-Sec. of State, FCO, 1993–95; First Sec., Washington, 1995–98; Counsellor, Dep. Hd of Mission and Consul-Gen., Riyadh, 1998–2001. *Recreation:* talk. *Address:* c/o Foreign and Commonwealth Office, SW1A 2AH; *e-mail:* the6mcdonalds@yahoo.co.uk.

McDONALD, Sir Tom, Kt 1991; OBE 1983; Chairman: Yorkshire and Humberside and East Midlands Industrial Development Board, 1982–91; West Yorkshire Residuary Body, 1986–91; West Midlands Residuary Body, 1990–91; Education Assets Board, 1988–93; *b* 5 Aug. 1923; *s* of Robert and Edna McDonald; *m* 1951, Pamela Anne Glaisby; three *s* one *d*. *Educ:* Dewsbury Wheelwright Grammar Sch.; Leeds Univ. (BCom Hons). FCA. Armitage & Norton: Audit Manager, 1953–62; Partner, 1962–86; Chm., 1982–86. Chairman: Old Swan Hotel (Harrogate) Ltd, 1973–82; Yorkshire Chemicals, 1977–83; Yorkshire Enterprise Ltd, 1990–94; Director: Dale Electric International, 1988–93; S. Jerome & Sons (Holdings), 1988–93; Consultant, KPMG Peat Marwick, 1987–93. Dir, Opera North, 1982–95. Pres., W Yorks Soc. of Chartered Accountants, 1986–87. *Recreations:* history, travel, music. *Address:* 15 Sandmoor Green, Alwoodley, Leeds LS17 7SB. *T:* (0113) 266 4232.

McDONALD, Sir Trevor, Kt 1999; OBE 1992; newscaster, since 1990, presenter, News at Ten, ITN, 1992–99, and ITV News at Ten, since 2001; *b* Trinidad, 16 Aug. 1939; *m*; two *s* one *d*. Work on newspapers, radio and television, Trinidad, 1960–69; producer for Caribbean Service and World Service, BBC Radio, London, 1969–73; Independent Television News: reporter, 1973–78; sports corresp., 1978–80; diplomatic corresp., 1980–82; diplomatic corresp. and newscaster, 1982–87, Diplomatic Ed., 1987–89, Channel Four News; newscaster, News at 5.40, 1989–90; presenter: The ITV Evening News, 1999–2001; Tonight with Trevor McDonald, 1999–. Chancellor, South Bank Univ., 1999–. Newscaster of the Year, TRIC, 1993, 1997, 1999; Gold Medal, RTS (for outstanding contrib. to television news), 1998. *Publications:* Clive Lloyd: a biography, 1985; Vivian Richards: a biography, 1987; Queen and Commonwealth, 1989; Fortunate Circumstances (autobiog.), 1993; (ed) Trevor McDonald's Favourite Poems, 1997; Trevor McDonald's World of Poetry (anthology), 1999. *Address:* c/o ITN, 200 Gray's Inn Road, WC1 8XZ.

MACDONALD, Valerie Frances; *see* Gooding, V. F.

McDONALD, William, MBE 2000; CA; JP; Chamberlain, 1962–89, and Secretary, 1971–89, Company of Merchants of City of Edinburgh; Bursar, Carnegie Trust for the Universities of Scotland, 1990–2001; *b* 9 Nov. 1929; *yr s* of late Joseph McDonald and Margaret Pringle (*née* Gibb); *m* 1956, Anne Kidd Laird Donald; one *s* one *d*. *Educ:* Perth Acad. Served RAF, 1952–54. Sec., South Mills and Grampian Investment, Dundee, 1957–62. Clerk and Treasurer, Incorp. of Guildry in Edinburgh, 1975–89; Jt Sec., Scottish Council of Independent Schs, 1978–89. Chm., Lothian Region Valuation Appeal Cttee, 1995–2000 (Mem., 1990–95). Dep. Chief Comr of Scotland, Scout Assoc., 1977–79 (Hon. Treas., Scotland, 1989–93); Chairman: Finance Cttee, Scout Assoc., 1993–98; Audit Cttee, World Scout Bureau, 2001–; Hon. Treas., Eur. Scout Region, 1995–2000; Chm., Scottish Environmental and Outdoor Centres Assoc. (formerly Scottish Nat. Camps Assoc.), 1986–91; Mem., High Constables of Edinburgh (Colinton Ward), 1983–; Mem., Rotary Club of Edinburgh, 1989–94. *Recreations:* Scout Movement, bridge. *Address:* 1/3 Wyvern Park, Edinburgh EH9 2JY. *Club:* New (Edinburgh).

McDONALD, Very Rev. William James Gilmour; Moderator of the General Assembly of the Church of Scotland, 1989–90; Parish Minister of Mayfield, Edinburgh, 1959–92; *b* 3 June 1924; *s* of Hugh Gilmour McDonald and Grace Kennedy Hunter; *m* 1952, Margaret Patricia Watson; one *s* two *d*. *Educ:* Daniel Stewart's College, Edinburgh; Univ. of Edinburgh (MA, BD); Univ. of Göttingen. Served Royal Artillery and Indian Artillery, 1943–46. Parish Minister, Limekilns, Fife, 1953–59. Convener, Assembly Council, 1984–87. Chaplain, Edinburgh Merchant Co., 1982–. Warrack Lectr, Edinburgh and Aberdeen Univs, 1992, Glasgow and St Andrews Univs, 1995; Turnbull Trust Preacher, Scots Ch, Melbourne, 1993. Hon. DD Edinburgh, 1987. *Address:* 7 Blacket Place, Edinburgh EH9 1RN. *T:* (0131) 667 2100.

MACDONALD, Prof. William Weir, PhD, DSc; FIBiol; Selwyn Lloyd Professor of Medical Entomology, 1980–94, now Professor Emeritus, and Dean, 1983–88, Liverpool School of Tropical Medicine; *b* 5 Dec. 1927; *s* of William Sutherland Macdonald and Ina Weir; *m* 1950, Margaret Lawrie; two *d*. *Educ:* Univ. of Glasgow (BSc 1948). MSc 1964, PhD 1965, Univ. of Liverpool; DSc 1973, Univ. of Glasgow; FIBiol 1966. Strang-Steel Scholar, Glasgow Univ., 1948; Colonial Office Res. Scholar, 1949–50; Entomologist, E African Fisheries Res. Org., Uganda, 1950–52; Res. Fellow, Inst. for Med. Res., Kuala Lumpur, 1953–60; Lectr, Sen. Lectr, and Reader, Liverpool Sch. of Trop. Medicine, 1960–76; Prof. of Med. Entomology, London Sch. of Hygiene and Trop. Medicine, 1977–80. Consultant: WHO; various overseas govts. Chalmers Medal, Royal Soc. of Trop. Medicine and Hygiene, 1972. *Publications:* papers on med. entomology in scientific jls. *Recreations:* golf, gardening. *Address:* 10 Headland Close, West Kirby, Merseyside L48 3JP. *T:* (0151) 625 7857.

MACDONALD-BUCHANAN, John, MC 1945; Vice Lord-Lieutenant of Northamptonshire, 1991–2000; *b* 15 March 1925; *s* of Major Sir Reginald Macdonald-Buchanan, KCVO, MBE, MC and Hon. Lady Macdonald-Buchanan, OStJ, *o c* of 1st Baron Woolavington, GCVO; *m* 1st, 1950, Lady Rose Fane (*d* 1984), *d* of 14th Earl of Westmorland; one *s* two *d*; 2nd, 1969, Mrs Jill Rosamonde Trelawnay, *d* of Maj.-Gen. Cecil Benfield Fairbanks, CB, CBE; two *d*. *Educ:* Eton; RMC, Sandhurst; RAC, Cirencester. 2nd Lt, Scots Guards, 1943; served War, 1944–45, NW Europe; Malaya, 1948–50; retired, 1952. Mem., Horserace Betting Levy Bd, 1973–76. Steward of Jockey Club, 1969–72, Sen. Steward 1979–82. High Sheriff 1963–64, DL 1978, Northants. *Address:* Cottesbrooke Hall, Northampton NN6 8PF. *T:* (01604) 505732; 22 Cadogan Place, SW1X 9SA. *T:* (020) 7235 8615. *Clubs:* White's, Turf.

MACDONALD-DAVIES, Isobel Mary; Deputy Registrar General for England and Wales, since 1994; *b* 7 Feb. 1955; *d* of Henry Alexander Macdonald and Freda Matilda Macdonald; *m* 1977, Peter Davies; one *s* two *d*. *Educ:* Bar Convent Grammar Sch., York; St Andrews Univ. (BSc 1977). CStat 1993. Asst Statistician, OPCS, 1977–84; Statistician, Dept of Educn and OPCS, 1984–94; Registrar Gen. for England and Wales, April–June 2000. *Recreations:* family, music, reading. *Address:* Office for National Statistics, Smedley Hydro, Trafalgar Road, Southport PR8 2HH. *T:* (0151) 471 4220.

MACDONALD-SMITH, Maj.-Gen. Hugh, CB 1977; *b* 8 Jan. 1923; *s* of Alexander and Ada Macdonald-Smith; *m* 1947, Désirée Violet (*née* Williamson); one *s* one *d* (and one *d* decd). *Educ:* Llanelli Grammar Sch.; Llandovery Coll.; Birmingham Univ. BSc. CEng, FIMechE, FIEE. Commissioned REME, 1944; served: India, 1945–47; Singapore, 1956–58; BAOR, 1961–63; Technical Staff Course, 1949–51; Staff Coll., Camberley, 1953; Lt-Col, 1963; Asst Dir, Electrical and Mechanical Engineering, HQ Western Comd, 1963–65; Asst Mil. Sec., MoD, 1965–66; Comd REME, 1 (BR) Corps Troops, 1966–67; Technical Gp, REME, 1967–72; Col, 1967; Brig. 1970; Dep. Dir, Electrical and Mechanical Engineering (Eng. Pol.), (Army), 1972–75; Dir, later Dir Gen., Electrical and Mech. Engrg (Army), 1975–78; retired 1978. Col Comdt, REME, 1978–83; Rep. Col

Comdt, REME, 1979–80. Dir, TEMA, 1981–87 (Sec. to Council, 1979–80). Mem., Cttee of Inquiry into Engrg Profession, 1977–79. Mem. Council, IMechE, 1975–76. *Recreations:* golf, gardening, photography. *Address:* c/o Lloyds TSB, Bridport DT6 3QL.

McDONNELL, family name of **Earl of Antrim**.

McDONNELL, Dr Alasdair; Member (SDLP) Belfast South, Northern Ireland Assembly, since 1998; general medical practitioner, since 1979; *b* Cushendall, Co. Antrim, 1 Sept. 1949; *s* of Charles McDonnell and Margaret (*née* McIlhatton); *m* 1998, Olivia Nugent; one *s* one *d*. *Educ:* St MacNissis Coll., Garron Tower; University Coll., Dublin Med. Sch. (MB, BCh, BAO 1974). Jun. hosp. med. posts, 1975–79. Mem. (SDLP) Belfast CC, 1977–2001; Dep. Mayor, Belfast, 1995–96. Contested (SDLP) Belfast South, 2001. *Address:* 22 Derryvolgie Avenue, Belfast BT9 6FN.

McDONNELL, Christopher Thomas, CB 1991; Deputy Under-Secretary of State, Ministry of Defence, 1988–91; *b* 3 Sept. 1931; *s* of Christopher Patrick McDonnell and Jane McDonnell; *m* 1955, Patricia Anne (*née* Harvey) (*d* 1967); three *s* one *d*. *Educ:* St Francis Xavier's Coll., Liverpool; Corpus Christi Coll., Oxford (MA). WO, 1954; HM Treasury, 1966–68; RCDS, 1973; Asst Under-Sec. of State, MoD, 1976–88.

McDONNELL, David Croft; Chief Executive Worldwide, Grant Thornton, since 2001; *b* 9 July 1943; *s* of late Leslie and Catherine McDonnell; *m* 1967, Marieke (*née* Bos); three *d*. *Educ:* Quarry Bank High School, Liverpool. FCA. Qualified Chartered Accountant, 1965; Partner, Thornton Baker, later Grant Thornton, 1972; Nat. Managing Partner, Grant Thornton, 1989–2001. Chm. Bd of Trustees, Nat. Museums and Galls on Merseyside, 1995–. *Recreations:* sailing, motor racing (spectating), mountain walking. *Address:* Grant Thornton, Grant Thornton House, Melton Street, Euston Square, NW1 2EP. *T:* (020) 7383 5100.

McDONNELL, His Honour Denis Lane, OBE 1945; a Circuit Judge (formerly a County Court Judge), 1967–86; *b* 2 March 1914; *o c* of late David McDonnell, LLD and Mary Nora (*née* Lane), Riversdale, Sundays Well, Cork and Fairy Hill, Monkstown, Co. Cork and *g s* of Denny Lane, poet and Young Irelander; *m* 1940, Florence Nina (Micky), *d* of late Lt-Col Hugh T. Ryan, DSO and Clare Emily (*née* Conry), Castle View, Ballincollig, Co. Cork; three *d* (and one *s* one *d* decd). *Educ:* Christian Brothers' Coll., Cork; Ampleforth Coll.; Sidney Sussex Coll., Cambridge (MA). Served in RAFVR, Equipment and Admin. and Special Duties Branches, 1940–45 in UK and with No. 84 Gp in NW Europe (Wing Comdr). Called to Bar, Middle Temple, 1936; Bencher, 1965. Practised at Bar, 1938–40 and 1946–67. Hon. Sec., Council of HM Circuit Judges, 1979–83 (Pres., 1985). *Publications:* Kerr on Fraud and Mistake (7th edn, with J. G. Monroe), 1952; titles on carriage in Encyclopædias of Forms and Precedents and Court Forms and Precedents, and in Halsbury's Laws of England. *Recreations:* family life, listening to music, golf, gardening. *Clubs:* Piltdown Golf, Woking Golf.

McDONNELL, John Beresford William; QC 1984; *b* 26 Dec. 1940; *s* of Beresford Conrad McDonnell and Charlotte Mary McDonnell (*née* Caldwell); *m* 1968, Susan Virginia, *d* of late Wing Comdr H. M. Styles, DSO and of Audrey (*née* Jorgensen, who *m* 2nd, 1947, Gen. Sir Charles Richardson, GCB, CBE, DSO); two *s* one *d*. *Educ:* City of London School (Carpenter Scholar); Balliol College, Oxford (Domus Scholar; Hon. Mention, Craven Scholarship, 1958; 1st Cl. Hon. Mods 1960; 2nd LitHum 1962, 2nd Jurisp 1964; MA); Harvard Law Sch. (LLM 1965). Called to the Bar, Inner Temple, 1968; Bencher, Lincoln's Inn, 1993. Pres., Oxford Union Soc. and Amer. Debating Tour, 1962; Harkness Fellowship, 1964–66; Amer. Political Science Assoc. Congressional Fellowship, 1965–66 (attached Rep. Frank Thompson Jr, NJ and Senator George McGovern, SDak); Cons. Research Dept, 1966–69; HM Diplomatic Service, 1969–71, First Sec., Asst Private Sec. to Sec. of State for Foreign and Commonwealth Affairs, 1970–71; practising at Chancery Bar, 1972–. Cllr, Lambeth Borough Council, 1968–69. London Rowing Club Grand VIII, Henley, 1958. FRSA 1994. *Recreation:* sculling. *Address:* Mortham Tower, Rokeby, Barnard Castle DL12 9RZ. *T:* (01833) 626900; 17 Rutland Street, SW7 1EJ. *T:* (020) 7584 1498; New Square Chambers, Lincoln's Inn, WC2A 3SW. *T:* (020) 7419 8000. *Club:* Athenæum.

McDONNELL, John Martin; MP (Lab) Hayes and Harlington, since 1997; *b* 8 Sept. 1951; *s* of Robert and Elsie McDonnell; *m* 1st, 1971, Marilyn Jean Cooper (marr. diss. 1987); two *d*; 2nd, 1995, Cynthia Marie Pinto; one *s*. *Educ:* Great Yarmouth Grammar Sch.; Burnley Technical Coll.; Brunel Univ. (BSc); Birkbeck Coll., Univ. of London (MSc Politics and Sociology). Prodn worker, 1968–72; Research Assistant: NUM, 1976–78; TUC, 1978–82; full-time GLC Councillor, Hillingdon, Hayes and Harlington, 1982–86; Dep. Leader, GLC, 1984–85; Chm., GLC F and GP Cttee, 1982–85; Prin. Policy Advr, Camden Bor. Council, 1985–87; Secretary: Assoc. of London Authorities, 1987–95; Assoc. of London Govt, 1995–97. Editor, Labour Herald, 1985–88. Member: Gtr London Lab. Party Regl Exec. Cttee, 1982–87; for Gtr London, Lab. Party Nat. Policy Forum, 1993–; Chm., Lab. Party Irish Soc. Advr, Guildford Four Relatives Campaign, 1984–; Chair, Britain and Ireland Human Rights Centre, 1992–; Founding Mem., Friends of Ireland, 1998–. Contested (Lab): Hampstead and Highgate, 1983; Hayes and Harlington, 1992. Secretary: All Pty Britain-Kenya Gp of MPs, 1997–; All Pty Kurdish Gp, 1997–; All Pty Irish in Britain Parly Gp, 1999–; Chair: Campaign Gp of MPs, 1998–; All Party Punjabi Community in Britain Gp of MPs, 1999–. Housefather (pt-time) of family unit, children's home, 1972–87. Mem., Hayes Horticultural Show Assoc.; Hon. Vice Pres., Hayes FC. *Publications:* articles and pamphlets incl. contribs to Labour Herald, Briefing, Tribune, Campaign News. *Recreations:* gardening, reading, cycling, music, theatre, cinema, Wayfarer dinghy sailing, supporting Liverpool, Hayes and Yeading Football Clubs; generally fermenting the overthrow of capitalism. *Address:* House of Commons, SW1A 0AA; Beverley, Cedar Avenue, Hayes, Middx UB3 2NE. *Clubs:* London Irish, Blues West 14; Hillingdon Irish Society; St Claret's, Working Men's (Hayes); Hayes and Harlington Community Centre.

McDOUGALL, Hon. Barbara Jean; PC (Can.) 1984; OC; President and Chief Executive Officer, Canadian Institute of International Affairs, since 1999; *b* Toronto, 12 Nov. 1937. *Educ:* Univ. of Toronto (BA Hons Econ. and Pol Sci. 1960). Chartered Financial Analyst, 1973. Worked in financial sector in Vancouver, Edmonton and Toronto; Exec. Dir, Canadian Council Financial Analysts, 1982–84; financial columnist, national magazines and on TV. MP (PC) St Paul's, Toronto, 1984–93; Minister of State: Finance, 1984–86; Privatisation, 1986–88; Minister Responsible for Status of Women, 1986–90 and for Regulatory Affairs, 1986–88; Minister, Employment and Immigration, 1988–91; Sec. of State for External Affairs, 1991–93; Chairperson, Cabinet Cttee on Foreign Affairs and Defence Policy, 1991–93; Member Cabinet Cttees: Planning and Priorities, 1991–93; Canadian Unity and Constitutional Negotiations, 1991–93. Chairperson: Morguard Real Estate Investment Trust, 1997–99; AT&T Canada Corp., 1996–99; Director: Corel Corp., 1998–; Bank of Nova Scotia, 1999–; Stelco, Inc., 1999–; Sun Media Corp., 1999–. Director: Canadian Opera Co., 1993–; Inter-Amer. Dialogue, 1994–; Internat. Crisis Gp, 1995–; Ind. Order of Foresters, 1998–. Mem., Internat. Adv. Bd, Council on Foreign Relns, NY, 1995–. Governor, York Univ., 1995–. *Address:* Canadian Institute of International Affairs, Glendon Hall, 2nd Floor, Glendon College, 2275 Bayview Avenue, Toronto, ON M4N 3M6, Canada.

McDOUGALL, Douglas Christopher Patrick, OBE 2001; Chairman: Law Debenture Corporation plc, since 2000 (Director, 1998–2000); Independent Investment Trust plc, since 2000; *b* 18 March 1944; *s* of late Patrick McDougall and Helen (*née* Anderson); *m* 1986, Carolyn Jane Griffiths, *d* of Baron Griffiths, *qv*; two *d*. *Educ:* Edinburgh Acad.; Christ Church, Oxford (MA). Partner, 1969–89, Sen. Partner, 1989–99, Baillie Gifford & Co., Investment Managers, Edinburgh. Chairman: Foreign and Colonial Eurotrust plc, 1999–; 3i Bioscience Investment Trust plc, 2001– (Dep. Chm., 2000–01); Dep. Chm., Sand Aire Investments plc, 1999–; Director: Provincial Insce plc, 1989–94; Baillie Gifford Japan Trust plc, 1989–99; Pacific Horizon Trust plc, 1993–; Scottish Investment Trust plc, 1998–; Monks Investment Trust plc, 1999–. Chairman: Institutional Fund Managers Assoc., 1994–96; Assoc. Investment Trust Cos, 1995–97; IMRO, 1997–2000 (Dir, 1988). Mem., Investments Cttee, Cambridge Univ., 1987–. *Address:* Linplum House, Haddington, East Lothian EH41 4PE. *T:* (01620) 810242. *Clubs:* Brooks's; New (Edinburgh); Honourable Company of Edinburgh Golfers.

MacDOUGALL, Sir (George) Donald (Alastair), Kt 1953; CBE 1945 (OBE 1942); FBA 1966; economist; *b* 26 Oct. 1912; *s* of late Daniel Douglas MacDougall, Glasgow, and late Beatrice Amy Miller; *m* 1st, 1937, Bridget Christabel Bartrum (marr. diss. 1977); one *s* one *d*; 2nd, 1977, Laura Margaret Hall (*née* Linfoot) (*d* 1995). *Educ:* Kelvinside Acad., Glasgow; Shrewsbury Sch.; Balliol Coll., Oxford (Hon. Fellow, 1992). George Webb Medley Junior (1934) and Senior (1935) Scholarships in Political Economy; Asst Lecturer (later Lecturer) in Economics, University of Leeds, 1936–39; First Lord of the Admiralty's Statistical Branch, 1939–40; Prime Minister's Statistical Branch, 1940–45 (Chief Asst, 1942–45). Work on Reparations and German Industry, Moscow and Berlin, 1945; Mem. of Heavy Clothing Industry Working Party, 1946; Official Fellow of Wadham Coll., Oxford, 1945–50, Domestic Bursar, 1946–48, Hon. Fellow, 1964–; Econ. Dir, OEEC, Paris, 1948–49; Faculty Fellow, Nuffield Coll., 1947–50, Professorial Fellow, 1950–52, Official Fellow, 1952–64, First Bursar, 1958–64, Hon. Fellow, 1967–; Nuffield Reader in Internat. Economics, Oxford Univ., 1950–52; Chief Adviser, Prime Minister's Statistical Branch, 1951–53; Visiting Prof., Australian Nat. Univ., 1959; MIT Center for Internat. Studies, New Delhi, 1961; Dir, Investing in Success Equities, Ltd, 1959–62; Economic Dir, NEDO, 1962–64; Mem. Turnover Tax Cttee, 1963–64; Dir-Gen., Dept of Economic Affairs, 1964–68; Head of Govt Economic Service, and Chief Economic Adviser to the Treasury, 1969–73; Chief Economic Advr, CBI, 1973–84. Mem. Council, Royal Econ. Soc., 1950– (Hon. Sec., 1958–70; Vice-Pres., 1970–72, 1974–; Pres., 1972–74); Pres., Soc. for Strategic and Long Range Planning, 1977–85, Vice-Pres., 1968–77; Vice-Pres., Soc. of Business Economists, 1978–; Chm., Exec. Cttee NIESR, 1974–87; Mem., EEC Study Gp on Economic and Monetary Union, 1974–75; Chm., EEC Study Gp on Role of Public Finance in European Integration, 1975–77. Hon. LLD Strathclyde, 1968; Hon. LittD Leeds, 1971; Hon. DSc Aston, 1979. *Publications:* (part author) Measures for International Economic Stability, UN, 1951; The World Dollar Problem, 1957; (part author) The Fiscal System of Venezuela, 1959; The Dollar Problem: A Reappraisal, 1960; Studies in Political Economy (2 vols), 1975; Don and Mandarin: memoirs of an economist, 1987; contrib. to various economic and statistical jls. *Address:* Flat K, 19 Warwick Square, SW1V 2AB. *T:* (020) 7821 1998. *Club:* Reform.

MacDOUGALL, John William; JP; MP (Lab) Fife Central, since 2001; *b* 8 Dec. 1947; *m* Catherine; one *s* one *d*. *Educ:* Templehall Secondary Modern Sch., Kirkaldy, Fife; Rosyth Dockyard Coll.; Fife Coll.; Glenrothes Coll. Former Chm., Burntisland Initiative Recreational Trust Ltd; Chm., Community Business Fife Ltd, 1988–92. Trustee, 1996–98, Vice-Chm., 1998–, St Andrews Links Trust. Mem. (Lab) Fife Regl Council, 1982–96, Fife Council, 1995– (Leader of Admin, 1987–96; Convenor, 1996–2001). Mem. Court, St Andrews Univ. JP 1983. *Address:* (home) 60 Cromwell Road, Burntisland KY3 9EH; (office) 5 Hanover Court, Glenrothes, Fife KY7 5SB; c/o House of Commons, SW1A 0AA.

MACDOUGALL, Neil; Justice of Appeal, 1989–95, and Vice-President of the Court of Appeal, 1993–95, Supreme Court of Hong Kong; *b* 13 March 1932; *s* of Norman Macdougall and Gladys Clare Kennerly; *m* 1987, Helen Lui. *Educ:* Aquinas Coll., Perth, WA; Univ. of Western Australia (LLB 1954). Admitted Barrister and Solicitor of Supreme Court, WA, 1957, and of High Court of Australia, 1958; Solicitor of Supreme Court of England, 1976, and of Supreme Court of Hong Kong, 1977. Crown Counsel, Hong Kong, 1965; Director of Public Prosecutions, Hong Kong, 1978; a Judge of the High Court, Hong Kong, 1980; Comr, Supreme Court of Brunei, 1987; a Non-Permanent Judge, Court of Final Appeal, Hong Kong, 1997–. Chairman: Insider Dealing Tribunal, Hong Kong, 1987–88; Air Transport Licensing Authy, Hong Kong, 1992–95. *Recreations:* classical music, study of natural history, physical training. *Address:* 320 Kiln Road, Karrakup, WA 6122, Australia. *Fax:* (8) 95262869. *Club:* Hong Kong (Hong Kong).

MACDOUGALL, Patrick Lorn, FCA; Chairman: Arlington Securities plc, since 1999; West Merchant Bank Ltd (formerly Standard Chartered Merchant Bank, then Chartered WestLB), 1989–98 (Chief Executive, 1985–97); *b* 21 June 1939; *s* of late James Archibald Macdougall, WS, and of Valerie Jean Macdougall; *m* 1st, 1967, Alison Noel Offer (marr. diss. 1982); two *s*; 2nd, 1983, Bridget Margaret Young; three *d*. *Educ:* schools in Kenya; Millfield; University Coll., Oxford (MA Jurisprudence). FCA 1976. Called to the Bar, Inner Temple, 1962. Manager, N. M. Rothschild & Sons Ltd, 1967–70; Exec. Dir, Amex Bank (formerly Rothschild Intercontinental Bank Ltd), 1970–77, Chief Exec., 1977–78; Exec. Dir, Jardine Matheson Holdings Ltd, 1978–85; Gp Exec. Dir, Standard Chartered PLC, 1988–89. Member: Internat. Adv. Bd, Creditanstalt-Bankverein, Vienna, 1982–85; Mem., Sen. Adv. Council, Seagull Energy Inc., Houston, 1996–99; Director: Global Natural Resources Inc., USA, 1994–96; Nuclear Electric plc, 1994–96; Panmure Gordon & Co. Ltd, 1996–98 (Dep. Chm., 1997–98); National Provident Instn, 1997–99. Dir and Trustee, SANE, 2001–. FRSA 1988. *Recreations:* ski-ing, opera, bridge, tough crosswords. *Address:* 40 Stevenage Road, SW6 6ET. *T:* (020) 7736 3506. *Clubs:* Athenæum, Hurlingham; Hongkong, Shek O (Hong Kong).

McDOWALL, Andrew Gordon; His Honour Judge McDowall; a Circuit Judge, since 1998; *b* 2 Sept. 1948; *s* of William Crocket McDowall and Margery Haswell McDowall (*née* Wilson); *m* 1976, Cecilia Clarke; one *s* one *d*. *Educ:* Glasgow Acad.; Queen's Coll., Oxford (Open Hastings Schol.; BCL, MA). Called to the Bar, Gray's Inn, 1972; in practice at the Bar, 1972–98; a Recorder, 1993–98; South Eastern Circuit. *Recreations:* reading, music (London Orpheus Choir), squash, paronomasia. *Address:* c/o 1 King's Bench Walk, Temple, EC4Y 7DB.

MacDOWALL, Dr David William, MA, DPhil; FSA, FRAS; Chairman, Society for South Asian Studies (formerly Society for Afghan Studies), 1982–98 (Hon. Secretary, 1972–82); Hon. Research Fellow, Centre for Research in East Roman Studies, University of Warwick, since 1993; *b* 2 April 1930; *o s* of late William MacDowall and late Lilian May MacDowall (*née* Clarkson); *m* 1962, Mione Beryl, *yr d* of late Ernest Harold Lashmar and Dora Lashmar; two *d*. *Educ:* Liverpool Inst.; Corpus Christi Coll., Oxford; British Sch. at

Rome. Hugh Oldham Scholar 1947, Pelham Student in Roman History 1951; Barclay Head Prize for Ancient Numismatics, 1953 and 1956. 2nd Lieut Royal Signals, 1952. Asst Principal, Min. of Works, 1955; Asst Keeper, Dept of Coins and Medals, British Museum, 1956; Principal, Min. of Educn, 1960; Principal, Univ. Grants Cttee, 1965; Asst Sec. 1970; Master of Univ. Coll., Durham, 1973; Hon. Lectr in Classics and in Oriental Studies, Univ. of Durham, 1975; Dir, Polytechnic of N London, 1980–85. Hon. Treasurer, Royal Numismatic Soc., 1966–73; Vice-Pres., British Archaeol Assoc., 1993–95 (Hon. Treas., 1989–93); Pres., Royal Asiatic Soc., 1994–97 (Vice-Pres., 1993–94, 1997–2000). Mem. Governing Body, SOAS, 1990–97. Trustee, UK Trust, Indian Nat. Trust for Archl and Cultural Heritage, 1994–. Corresponding Member: Istituto Italiano per il Medio ed Estremo Oriente, 1987; Amer. Numismatic Soc., 1991. *Publications:* Coin Collections, their preservation, classification and presentation, 1978; The Western Coinages of Nero, 1979; (contrib.) Mithraic Studies, 1975; (contrib.) The Archaeology of Afghanistan, 1978; (ed jtly) Indian Numismatics: history, art and culture, 1992; (jtly) The Roman Coins, Republic and Empire up to Nerva, in the Provinciaal Museum G. M. Kam at Nijmegen, 1992; articles in Numismatic Chron., Jl Numismatic Soc. India, Schweizer Münzblätter, Acta Numismatica, S Asian Archaeology, Afghan Studies, S Asian Studies, Numismatic Digest, etc. *Recreations:* travel, antiquities, photography, natural history, gardening, genealogy. *Address:* Admont, Dancers End, Tring, Herts HP23 6JY. *Club:* Athenæum.

McDOWALL, Keith Desmond, CBE 1988; Chairman, Keith McDowall Associates, since 1988; *b* 3 Oct. 1929; *s* of William Charteris McDowall and Edna Florence McDowall; *m* 1st, 1957, Shirley Margaret Russell Astbury (marr. diss. 1985); two *d*; 2nd, 1988, Brenda Dean (*see* Baroness Dean of Thornton-le-Fylde). *Educ:* Heath Clark Sch., Croydon, Surrey. Served RAF, National Service, 1947–49. South London Press, 1947–55; Daily Mail, 1955–67: Indust. Corresp., 1958; Indust. Editor, 1961–67; Man. Dir, Inca Construction (UK) Co. Ltd, 1967–69; Govt Information Service: successively Chief Inf. Officer, DEA, BoT, Min. of Housing and Local Govt, DoE, and Home Office, 1969–72; Dir of Inf., NI Office, 1972–74; Dir of Inf., Dept of Employment, 1974–78; Man. Dir Public Affairs, British Shipbuilders, 1978–80. Dir, Govan Shipbuilders Ltd, 1978–80. Dir of Information, 1981–86, Dep. Dir Gen., 1986–88, CBI. Chm., Kiss FM Radio, 1990–92 (Chm., steering cttee, 1989–90). Freeman, City of London, 1997; Liveryman, Shipwrights' Co., 1998–. *Publications:* articles in newspapers and various pubns. *Recreations:* sailing, golf, mingling. *Address:* 2 Malvern Terrace, N1 1HR. *Clubs:* Reform; Medway Yacht (Rochester); Royal Cornwall Yacht (Falmouth); South Herts Golf.

McDOWALL, Stuart, CBE 1984; Chairman, Fife Healthcare NHS Trust, 1994–96; economic consultant; Senior Lecturer in Economics, University of St Andrews, 1967–91; *b* 19 April 1926; *s* of Robert McDowall and Gertrude Mary Collister; *m* 1951, Margaret Burnside Woods Gyle; three *s*. *Educ:* Liverpool Institute; St Andrews University (MA hons 1950). Personnel Manager, Michael Nairn & Co., 1955–61; Lectr in Econs, St Andrews Univ., 1961–67; Master, United Coll. of St Salvator and St Leonard, 1976–80. Dep. Chm., Central Arbitration Cttee, 1976–96; Local Govt Boundary Comr for Scotland, 1983–99; Member: Monopolies and Mergers Commn, 1985–89; Restrictive Practices Court, 1993–96. Econ. Consultant to UN in Saudi Arabia, 1985–89. Sec., Scottish Economic Soc., 1970–76. *Publications:* (with P. R. Draper) Trade Adjustment and the British Jute Industry, 1978; (with H. M. Begg) Industrial Performance and Prospects in Areas Affected by Oil Developments, 1981; articles on industrial economics and regional economics. *Recreations:* golf, hill walking. *Address:* 10 Woodburn Terrace, St Andrews, Fife KY16 8BA. *T:* (01334) 473247. *Club:* Royal and Ancient Golf (St Andrews).

MacDOWELL, Prof. Douglas Maurice, DLitt; FRSE; FBA 1993; Professor of Greek, University of Glasgow, 1971–2001; *b* 8 March 1931; *s* of Maurice Alfred MacDowell and Dorothy Jean MacDowell (*née* Allan). *Educ:* Highgate Sch.; Balliol Coll., Oxford (1st Cl. Classical Mods 1952, 1st Cl. Lit. Hum. 1954; MA, DLitt). FRSE 1991. Classics Master: Allhallows Sch., 1954–56; Merchant Taylors' Sch., 1956–58; University of Manchester: Asst Lectr, Lectr and Sen. Lectr, 1958–70; Reader in Greek and Latin, 1970–71. Vis. Fellow, Merton Coll., Oxford, 1969. Sec., Council of University Classical Depts, 1974–76; Chm. Council, Classical Assoc. of Scotland, 1976–82. *Publications:* Andokides: On the Mysteries, 1962; Athenian Homicide Law, 1963; Aristophanes: Wasps, 1971; The Law in Classical Athens, 1978; Spartan Law, 1986; Demosthenes: Against Meidias, 1990; Aristophanes and Athens, 1995; (with M. Gagarin) Antiphon and Andocides, 1998; Demosthenes: On the False Embassy, 2000. *Address:* 2 Grosvenor Court, 365 Byres Road, Glasgow G12 8AU. *T:* (0141) 334 7818. *Club:* Oxford and Cambridge.

McDOWELL, Sir Eric (Wallace), Kt 1990; CBE 1982; FCA; Partner, Wilson Hennessey & Crawford, later (following merger in 1973) Deloitte, Haskins & Sells, 1952–85 (Senior Partner, Belfast, 1980–85); *b* 7 June 1925; *s* of Martin Wallace McDowell and Edith Florence (*née* Hillock); *m* 1954, Helen Lilian (*née* Montgomery); one *s* two *d*. *Educ:* Royal Belfast Academical Instn. FCA 1957. Served War, 1943–46. Student Chartered Accountant, 1942, qualified 1948. Chm., Capita Mgt Consultants Ltd, 1992–98; Director: NI Transport Holding Co., 1971–74; Spence Bryson Ltd, 1986–89; TSB Northern Ireland, 1986–92; AIB Group Northern Ireland, 1992–97; Shepherd Ltd, 1992–. Member: Council, Inst. of Chartered Accountants in Ireland, 1968–77 (Pres., 1974–75); Industries Develt Adv. Cttee, 1971–82 (Chm., 1978–82); Adv. Cttee of NI Central Investment Fund for Charities, 1975–98 (Chm., 1980–98); NI Econ. Council, 1977–83; Industrial Develt Bd for NI, 1982–91 (Chm., 1986–91); Exec. Cttee, Relate: Marriage Guidance, NI, 1981– (Chm., 1992–96); Nat. Exec. Cttee, Relate, 1992–2000; Broadcasting Council for NI, 1983–86; Financial Reporting Review Panel, 1990–94; Senate, QUB, 1993–. Trustee, Presbyterian Church in Ireland, 1983–. Treas., Abbeyfield Belfast Soc., 1986–99. Governor, Royal Belfast Academical Instn, 1959– (Chm. of Governors, 1977–86); President: Belfast Old Instonians Assoc., 1993–94; Confedn of Ulster Socs, 1989–98. Hon. DSc(Econ) QUB, 1989. *Recreations:* music, drama, foreign travel. *Address:* Beechcroft, 19 Beechlands, Belfast BT9 5HU. *T:* (028) 9066 8771. *Clubs:* Royal Over-Seas League; Ulster Reform (Belfast).

McDOWELL, Prof. Gary Linn, PhD; FRHistS; Director, Institute of United States Studies, since 1992, and Professor of American Studies, since 1993, University of London; *b* 4 June 1949; *s* of Samuel Earl McDowell and Violet Marie McDowell (*née* Harris); *m* 1990, Brenda Jo Evans. *Educ:* Univ. of S Florida (BA 1972); Memphis State Univ. (MA 1974); Univ. of Chicago (AM 1978); Univ. of Virginia (PhD 1979). Social Studies Teacher, Dunedin Jun. High Sch., 1972–73; Asst Prof. of Political Sci., Dickinson Coll., 1979–83; Liberal Arts Fellow, Harvard Law Sch.,1981–82; Asst Prof., 1983–85, Associate Prof., 1985–86, of Political Sci., Tulane Univ.; Dir, Office of the Bicentennial of the Constitution, Nat. Endowment for the Humanities, 1984–85; Associate Dir of Public Affairs, US Dept of Justice, 1985–87; Resident Schol., Center for Judicial Studies, 1987–88; Fellow, Woodrow Wilson Internat. Center for Scholars, 1987–88; Vice Pres., Nat. Legal Center for Public Interest, 1988–89; Bradley Vis. Schol., Harvard Law Sch., 1990–92; Lectr, Harvard Univ., 1992. Mem., Fulbright Commn, 1997–. Bd, Landmark Legal Foundn, 1992–; Bd of Visitors, Pepperdine Univ. Sch. of Public Policy, 2000–. *Publications:* (ed jtly and contrib.) The American Founding, 1981; (ed jtly and contrib.) Taking the Constitution Seriously, 1981; Equity and the Constitution, 1982; Curbing the Courts, 1988; (jtly) Justice *vs* Law, 1993; (ed jtly and contrib.) Our Peculiar Security, 1993; (ed jtly and contrib.) Reason and Republicanism, 1997; (ed jtly) Juvenile Delinquency in the United States and the United Kingdom, 1999; numerous contribs to learned jls and other publications. *Recreations:* walking, reading, martinis and Cuban cigars. *Address:* Institute of United States Studies, University of London, Senate House, Malet Street, WC1E 7HU. *T:* (020) 7862 8693. *Club:* Reform.

McDOWELL, George Roy Colquhoun, CBE 1988; CEng, FIEE; Chairman, British Standards Institution, 1985–88; *b* 1 Sept. 1922; *s* of Robert Henry McDowell and Jean McDowell; *m* 1948, Joan Annie Bryan; two *s*. *Educ:* Coleraine Academical Instn; Queen's Univ., Belfast (BSc Eng). Signals Officer, RAF, 1942–46. Works Manager, Distribn Transformer Div., subseq. Works Manager, Power Transformer Div., Ferranti Ltd, 1950–69; Dir, 1969–87, Man. Dir Designate, 1969–72, Chm. and Man. Dir, 1972–87, George H. Scholes. Director: Clipsal (UK), 1983–98 (Chm., 1985–98); Clipsal Ltd, 1997–98; Elbocks Ltd, 1997–98. Chairman: Electrical Installation Equipment Manufacturers' Assoc., 1977–80; British Electrotechnical Cttee, BSI; Electrotechnical Council, BSI, 1982–85; President: British Electrical and Allied Manufacturers' Assoc., 1981–82; Internat. Electrotechnical Commn, 1987–; IEEIE; Institution of Electrical Engineers: Chm., Power Bd; Chm., Finance Cttee; Mem. Council. Hon. FIIE. Grand Decoration of Honour for Services to the Republic of Austria, 1978. *Recreations:* golf, Rugby, cricket. *Address:* 24 Oak Drive, Bramhall, Stockport, Cheshire SK7 2AD. *T:* (0161) 439 4552. *Club:* Army and Navy.

McDOWELL, Prof. John Henry, FBA 1983; FAAAS; University Professor of Philosophy, University of Pittsburgh, since 1988 (Professor of Philosophy, 1986–88); *b* 7 March 1942; *s* of Sir Henry McDowell, KBE and Norah, *d* of Walter Slade Douthwaite; *m* 1977, Andrea Lee Lehrke. *Educ:* St John's College, Johannesburg; University College of Rhodesia and Nyasaland; New College, Oxford. BA London; MA Oxon. FAAAS 1993. Fellow and Praelector in Philosophy, UC, Oxford, 1966–86, Emeritus Fellow, 1988; Univ. Lectr (CUF), Oxford Univ., 1967–86. James C. Loeb Fellow in Classical Philosophy, Harvard Univ., 1969; Visiting Professor: Univ. of Michigan, 1975; Univ. of California, Los Angeles, 1977; Univ. of Minnesota, 1982; Jadavpur Univ., Calcutta, 1983; John Locke Lectr, Oxford Univ., 1991. Sen. Fellow, Council of Humanities, Princeton Univ., 1984. *Publications:* Plato, Theaetetus (trans. with notes), 1973; (ed with Gareth Evans) Truth and Meaning, 1976; (ed) Gareth Evans, The Varieties of Reference, 1982; (ed with Philip Pettit) Subject, Thought, and Context, 1986; Mind and World, 1994; Mind, Value, and Reality (collected articles), 1998; Meaning, Knowledge, and Reality (collected articles), 1998; articles in jls and anthologies. *Recreations:* reading, music, gardening. *Address:* c/o Department of Philosophy, University of Pittsburgh, Pittsburgh, PA 15260, USA. *T:* (412) 6245792.

McDOWELL, Jonathan Bruce, RIBA; architect; Partner, McDowell+Benedetti, since 1996; Director, McDowell+Benedetti Ltd, since 1998; *b* 18 March 1957; *s* of Hamilton Blair McDowell and Pamela (*née* Howe). *Educ:* The Downs Sch.; Bootham Sch.; Downing Coll., Cambridge (MA, DipArch); Graduate Sch. of Design, Harvard Univ. RIBA 1985. Associate, Munkenbeck & Marshall, 1986–90; Principal, Jonathan McDowell Architects, 1991–96; with Renato Benedetti, formed McDowell+Benedetti, 1996; main projects include: Smithfield Regeneration, Dublin, 1992; Oliver's Wharf Penthouse, Wapping, 1996; HQ Building, Options, London, 1997; (with YRM Architects) New Univ. of the Commonwealth, Malaysia, 1998; Assoc. of Photographers, New Gall. and HQ, London, 1998; Nursing Home for Merchant Taylors' Co., Lewisham, 2000. FRSA 1999. *Recreations:* Balinese, Javanese and contemporary gamelan, travel. *Address:* (office) 62 Rosebery Avenue, EC1R 4RR. *T:* (020) 7278 8810.

McDOWELL, Kathryn Alexandra; Chief Executive, Wales Millennium Centre, since 1999; *b* 19 Dec. 1959; *d* of John McDowell and Kathleen Avril McDowell; *m* 1997, Ian Charles Stewart Ritchie, *qv*. *Educ:* Belfast High Sch.; Univ. of Edinburgh (BMus 1982); Stranmillis Coll. of Education (PGCE 1983). LTCL 1980, Hon. FTCL 1996; ARCM 1981; Hon. RCM 1999. Marketing and Educn Assistant, WNO, 1984–85; Develt Manager, Scottish Chamber Orch., 1985–89; Dep. Gen. Manager, Ulster Orch., 1989–92; Music Officer, Arts Council, 1992–94; Music Dir, Arts Council of England, 1994–99. *Recreations:* tennis, squash, travel. *Address:* Wales Millennium Centre, PO Box 2001, Cardiff CF10 5YS.

McDOWELL, Malcolm, (Malcolm Taylor); actor; *b* 13 June 1943; *m* 1992, Kelley Kuhr; one *s* one *d* by prev. marriage. *Educ:* Leeds. *Stage:* RSC Stratford, 1965–66; Entertaining Mr Sloane, Royal Court, 1975; Look Back in Anger, NY, 1980; In Celebration, NY, 1984; Holiday, Old Vic, 1987; Another Time, NY, 1993; *films:* If, 1969; Figures in a Landscape, 1970; The Raging Moon, 1971; A Clockwork Orange, 1971; O Lucky Man, 1973; Royal Flash, 1975; Aces High, 1976; Voyage of the Damned, 1977; Caligula, 1977; The Passage, 1978; Time After Time, 1979; Cat People, 1981; Blue Thunder, 1983; Get Crazy, 1983; Britannia Hospital, 1984; Gulag, 1985; Cross Creek, 1985; Sunset, 1988; Assassin of the Tsar, 1991; Milk Money, 1993; Star Trek Generations, 1994; Tank Girl, 1995; Exquisite Tenderness, 1995; Mr Magoo, 1998; Gangster No 1, 2000; *television:* Our Friends in the North, 1996. *Address:* c/o Markham and Froggatt, 4 Windmill Street, W1P 1HF.

McDOWELL, Stanley; non-executive Director, Ulster Community and Hospitals Trust, since 1998 (Chairman, Audit Committee, since 1998); Town Clerk and Chief Executive, Belfast City Council, 1989–92; *b* 14 June 1941; *s* of William McDowell and Annie Storey; *m* 1966, Charlotte Elizabeth Stockdale; three *d*. *Educ:* Royal Belfast Academical Instn; Queen's Univ. of Belfast (BSc Econ). FCIS. Belfast City and Dist Water Comrs, 1959–70; Asst Sec. (Actg), Antrim County Council, 1971–73; Roads Service Divl Finance Officer, DoE (NI), 1973–79; Belfast City Council, 1979–92; Asst Town Clerk (Admin), 1979–89. *Address:* 209 Bangor Road, Holywood, N Ireland BT18 0JG. *T:* (028) 9042 5132.

MACDUFF, Earl of; *see* Earl of Southesk.

MacDUFF, Alistair Geoffrey; QC 1993; **His Honour Judge MacDuff;** a Circuit Judge, since 1997; Designated Civil Judge, Birmingham Group, since 2000; *b* 26 May 1945; *s* of late Alexander MacDonald MacDuff and Iris Emma Jarvis (*née* Gardner); *m* 1st, 1969, Susan Christine Kitchener (*d* 1991); two *d*; 2nd 1993, Katherine Anne Buckley; one *s* one *d*. *Educ:* Ecclesfield Grammar Sch., Sheffield; LSE (LLB 1965); Sheffield Univ. (LLM 1967). Called to the Bar, Lincoln's Inn, 1969; Asst Recorder, 1983–87; a Recorder, 1987–97. *Recreations:* theatre, opera, travel, golf, Association football. *Address:* Birmingham County Court, Priory Courts, Bull Street, Birmingham B4 6DW. *Clubs:* Hendon Golf; Economicals Association Football (New Malden).

McDUFF, Prof. (Margaret) Dusa, PhD; FRS 1994; Distinguished Professor of Mathematics, State University of New York at Stony Brook, since 1998; *b* 18 Oct. 1945; *d* of Conrad Hal Waddington and Margaret Justin (*née* Blanco White); *m* 1st, 1968, David William McDuff (marr. diss. 1978); one *d*; 2nd, 1984, John Willard Milnor; one *s*. *Educ:*

Univ. of Edinburgh (BSc Hons); Girton Coll., Cambridge (PhD 1971). Lecturer: Univ. of York, 1972–76; Univ. of Warwick, 1976–78; Asst Prof., 1978–80, Associate Prof., 1980–84, Prof. of Maths, 1984–98, SUNY at Stony Brook. Asst Prof., MIT, 1974–75; Mem., Inst. for Advanced Study, Princeton, 1976 and 1977; Vis. Prof., Univ of Calif, Berkeley, 1993. Fellow, Amer. Acad. of Arts and Scis, 1995; Mem., NAS, USA, 1999. Hon. DSc: Edinburgh, 1997; York, 2000. *Publications:* (with D. Salamon): J-Holomorphic Curves and Quantum Cohomology, 1994; Introduction to Symplectic Topology, 1995. *Recreations:* chamber music, reading, walking. *Address:* Mathematics Department, State University of New York, Stony Brook, NY 11794–3651, USA. *T:* (516) 6328290.

MACE, Dr (Alan) Christopher (Hugh), CBE 1991; Deputy Director General (Operations), Immigration and Nationality Directorate, Home Office, since 1999; Chief Inspector, Immigration Service, since 2000; *b* 17 Sept. 1953; *s* of late Maurice William Mace and of Josephine Mary Mace; *m* 1979, Sian Avery; one *s* one *d*. *Educ:* Weymouth Grammar Sch.; Univ. of Exeter (BSc 1975; PhD 1981). Ministry of Defence, 1979–99: rocketry and combustion res., 1979–86; novel weapon res., 1986–88; Asst Dir, Personnel, 1988–89; Project Manager procuring Army equipt, 1990–91; Director: Res. and Internat. Collaboration, 1991–94; Finance and Secretariat, Weapons and Electronic Systems Procurement, 1994–96; on secondment as Dir, Business Develt, Avery Berkel, 1996–97; Project Dir implementing resource accounting and planning systems, MoD, 1997–99. FRSA 2000. *Publications:* res. papers on combustion. *Recreations:* music, walking. *Address:* Immigration and Nationality Directorate, Apollo House, Croydon CR9 3RR. *T:* (020) 8760 8373.

MACE, Brian Anthony; Director, Study of Personal Tax, Board of Inland Revenue, since 2000; *b* 9 Sept. 1948; *s* of late Edward Laurence Mace and of Olive (*née* Bennett); *m* 1973, Anne Margaret Cornford. *Educ:* Maidstone Grammar Sch.; Gonville and Caius Coll., Cambridge (MA Mathematics). Admin trainee, Bd of Inland Revenue, 1971–73; seconded to Secretariat, Inflation Accounting Cttee, 1974–75; Inland Revenue: Principal, 1975–82; Asst Sec., 1982–90; Under Sec., 1990–; Dir, Savings and Investment Div., 1990–98, and Capital and Valuation Div., 1995–98; Dir, Personal Tax, 1998–2000. *Recreations:* opera, chamber music and song, theatre, cricket, historic buildings. *Address:* Board of Inland Revenue, Somerset, Strand, WC2R 1LB. *T:* (020) 7438 6501.

MACE, Christopher; *see* Mace, A. C. H.

MACE, Lt-Gen. Sir John (Airth), KBE 1990 (OBE 1974; MBE 1967); CB 1986; New Zealand Chief of Defence Force, 1987–91; *b* 29 June 1932; *m* 1962, Margaret Theodocia (*née* McCallum); one *s* one *d*. *Educ:* Ashburton High Sch., NZ; Nelson Coll., NZ; RMC Duntroon, Australia. Commissioned NZ Army, 1953; NZ SAS, 1955–57; active service in Malayan Emergency (despatches, 1958); Comd SAS Sqdn, 1960–62 and 1965; Comd Co. of 1 RNZIR 1st Bn, Borneo, 1966; Vietnam, 1967; appts include: Dir of Infantry and NZ SAS; CO, 1st Bn RNZIR, Singapore; Dir, Officer Postings; Comdr, Army Logistics Support Gp; Comdr, 1st Inf. Bde Gp; Army Staff Coll., Camberley; JSSC, Canberra; Comdr, NZ Force SE Asia, 1979–80; RCDS 1981; Dep. Chief of Defence Staff, 1982–84; Chief of General Staff, 1984–87. *Recreations:* golf, walking, reading. *Clubs:* Wellington, Wellington Golf (Wellington).

MacEACHEN, Hon. Allan Joseph; PC (Canada) 1963; Senator (L) for Nova Scotia, 1984–96; *b* Inverness, Nova Scotia, 6 July 1921; *s* of Angus and Annie MacEachen. *Educ:* St Francis Xavier Univ. (BA 1944); Univ. of Toronto (MA 1946); Univ. of Chicago; MIT. Prof. of Economics, St Francis Xavier Univ., 1946–48; Head of Dept of Economics and Social Sciences; MP (L) Inverness-Richmond, NS, 1953–58, Inverness-Richmond, later Cape Breton-Highlands-Canso, NS, 1962–84. Special Asst and Consultant on Econ. Affairs to Hon. Lester Pearson, 1958; Minister: of Labour, 1963–65; of Nat. Health and Welfare, 1965–68; of Manpower and Immigration, 1968–70; of External Affairs, 1974–76; of Finance, 1980–82; Sec. of State for External Affairs, 1982–84; Pres., Privy Council and Govt Leader in House of Commons, Canada, 1970–74 and 1976–79; Dep. Prime Minister, 1977–79 and 1980–84; Dep. Leader of the Opposition and Opposition House Leader, 1979–80; called to Senate, 1984, Leader of Govt in Senate, 1984, Leader of Opposition in Senate, 1984–91. Co-Chm., Canada-Germany Conf., 1984–. Mem. Bd Trustees, Internat. Crisis Gp, NY, 1995–. Member, Bd of Governors: St Francis Xavier Univ.; Gaelic Coll. of Celtic Arts and Crafts, NS. Mem., Royal Celtic Soc., Edinburgh. Hon. degrees: universities: St Francis Xavier; Acadia; St Mary's; Dalhousie; Wilfrid Laurier; Loyola Coll.; Canadian Coast Guard Coll.; UC of Cape Breton. Grand Cross, Order of Merit (Germany), 1993. *Address:* RR1, Whycocomagh, NS B0E 3M0, Canada. *Clubs:* Rideau, Le Cercle Universitaire (Ottawa); Halifax (Halifax, NS); Princeton (New York).

McEACHERN, Allan; Hon. Chief Justice McEachern; Chief Justice of British Columbia, since 1988; *b* 20 May 1926; *s* of John A. and L. B. McEachern; *m* 1953, Gloria L. (*d* 1997); two *d*. *Educ:* Univ. of British Columbia (BA 1949; LLB 1950). Called to the Bar of British Columbia, 1951. Partner, Russell and DuMoulin, Barristers, 1950–79; Chief Justice, Supreme Court of BC, 1979–88. Hon. LLM Univ. of BC, 1990. *Recreations:* walking, sailing, gardening. *Address:* The Law Courts, 800 Smithe Street, Vancouver, BC V6Z 2E1, Canada. *T:* (604) 6602710.

McEACHRAN, Colin Neil; QC (Scot.) 1982; *b* 14 Jan. 1940; *s* of Eric Robins McEachran and Nora Helen Bushe; *m* 1967, Katherine Charlotte Henderson; two *d*. *Educ:* Trinity Coll., Glenalmond; Merton Coll., Oxford (BA 1961); Univ. of Glasgow (LLB 1963); Univ. of Chicago (Commonwealth Fellow; JD 1965). Admitted Solicitor, 1966; admitted to Faculty of Advocates, 1968. Advocate Depute, 1975–78. Mem., Scottish Legal Aid Bd, 1990–98; Pres., Pension Appeal Tribunals for Scotland, 1995–. Chm., Commonwealth Games Council for Scotland, 1995–99. *Recreations:* target rifle shooting (Silver Medal, Commonwealth Games, NZ, 1974), hill walking. *Address:* 13 Saxe-Coburg Place, Edinburgh EH3 5BR. *T:* (0131) 332 6820.

MACEDO, Prof. Helder Malta, PhD; Camoens Professor of Portuguese, University of London at King's College, since 1982; *b* 30 Nov. 1935; *s* of Adelino José de Macedo and Aida Malta de Macedo; *m* 1960, Suzette Armanda (*née* de Aguiar). *Educ:* Faculty of Law, Univ. of Lisbon; King's Coll., Univ. of London (BA, PhD); FKC 1991. Lectr in Portuguese and Brazilian Studies, KCL, 1971–82; Sec. of State for Culture, Portuguese Govt, 1979. Visiting Professor: Harvard Univ., 1981; Ecole des Hautes Etudes et Sciences Sociales, Paris, 1992, 1995. Pres., Internat. Assoc. of Lusitanists, 1994–99. Fellow, Academia das Ciências de Lisboa, 1987. Editor, Portuguese Studies Jl, 1985–. Comendador, Ordem de Santiago da Espada (Portugal), 1993. *Publications:* Nós, Uma Leitura de Cesário Verde, 1975, 4th edn 1999; Do Significado Oculto da 'Menina a Moça', 1977, 2nd edn 1999; Poesia 1957–77, 1978; Camões e a Viagem Iniciática, 1980; The Purpose of Praise: Past and Future in The Lusiads of Luís de Camões, 1983; Cesário Verde: O Romântico e o Feroz, 1988; Partes de Africa, 1991; Viagem de Inverno, 1994; Pedro e Paula, 1998, 2nd edn 1998 (Brazilian edn, 1999); Viagens do Olhar, 1998; Vicios e Virtudes, 2000. *Address:* Department of Portuguese and Brazilian Studies, King's College London, Strand, WC2R 2LS. *T:* (020) 7873 2507.

McELHERAN, John; Principal Assistant Solicitor (Under Secretary), Ministry of Agriculture, Fisheries and Food, 1983–89; *b* 18 Aug. 1929; *s* of late Joseph Samuel McElheran and Hilda McElheran (*née* Veale); *m* 1956, Jean Patricia Durham; one *s* two *d*. *Educ:* Archbishop Holgate's Grammar Sch., York; St Edmund Hall, Oxford (MA English, DipEd). Solicitor. Short period of teaching; articled clerk, Thomson & Hetherton, York, 1954; Asst Solicitor 1959, Partner 1962, Leathes Prior & Son, Norwich; Senior Legal Asst, Land Commn, Newcastle upon Tyne, 1967; Sen. Legal Asst 1971, Asst Solicitor 1974, Dept of Trade and Industry and successor Depts. *Recreation:* photography. *Address:* 12 Bedern, York YO1 7LP. *T:* (01904) 628987. *Club:* Civil Service.

McENERY, John Hartnett; author, consultant and conceptual analyst, since 1981; *b* 5 Sept. 1925; *y s* of late Maurice Joseph and Elizabeth Margaret McEnery (*née* Maccabe); *m* 1977, Lilian Wendy, *yr d* of late Reginald Gibbons and Lilian Gibbons (*née* Cox). *Educ:* St Augustine's Sch., Coatbridge; St Aloysius Coll., Glasgow; Glasgow Univ. (MA(Hons)). Served War of 1939–45: RA, 1943–47; Staff Captain, Burma Command, 1946–47. Glasgow Univ., 1947–49. Asst Principal, Scottish Educn Dept, 1949; Principal, 1954; Cabinet Office, 1957; HM Treasury, 1959; Min. of Aviation, 1962; UK Delegn to NATO, 1964; Counsellor (Defence Supply), British Embassy, Bonn, 1966; Asst Sec., Min. of Technology, 1970; Dept of Trade and Industry, 1970–72; Under-Sec. and Regional Dir for Yorks and Humberside, DTI, 1972, Dept of Industry, 1974–76; Under Sec., Concorde and Nationalisation Compensation Div., Dept of Industry, 1977–81. *Publications:* Manufacturing Two Nations—the sociological trap created by the bias of British regional policy against service industry, 1981; Towards a New Concept of Conflict Evaluation, 1985; Epilogue in Burma 1945–48: the military dimension of British withdrawal, 1990; articles in Jl of Economic Affairs. *Recreations:* various games and sports, chess, travel. *Address:* 37 Leinster Avenue, East Sheen, SW14 7JW. *Club:* Hurlingham.

McENERY, Judith Mary; *see* Chessells, J. M.

McENERY, Peter; actor; Associate Artist, Royal Shakespeare Co.; *b* 21 Feb. 1940; *s* of Charles and Mary McEnery; *m* 1978; one *d*. *Educ:* various state and private schs. First stage appearance, Brighton, 1956; first London appearance in Flowering Cherry, Haymarket, 1957; *stage:* rôles with RSC include, 1961–: Laertes, Tybalt, Johnny Hobnails in Afore Night Come, Bassanio, Lorenzaccio, Orlando, Sachs in The Jail Diary of Albie Sachs, Pericles, Brutus, Antipholus of Ephesus, Godber in A Dream of People; other rôles include: Rudge in Next Time I'll Sing to You, Criterion, 1963; Konstantin in The Seagull, Queen's, 1964; Harry Winter in The Collaborators, Duchess, 1973; Trigorin in The Seagull, Lyric, 1975; Edward Gover in Made in Bangkok, Aldwych, 1986; Fredrik in A Little Night Music, Chichester, transf. Piccadilly, 1989; Torvald in The Doll's House, Robert in Dangerous Corner, Chichester, 1994; Menelaus in Women of Troy, NT, 1995; Hector Hushabye in Heartbreak House, Almeida, 1997; Claudius in Hamlet, RNT, 2000; directed: Richard III, Nottingham, 1971; The Wound, Young Vic, 1972. *Films* include: Tunes of Glory, 1961; Victim, 1961; The Moonspinners, 1963; Entertaining Mr Sloane, 1970; *television:* Clayhanger, 1976; The Jail Diary of Albie Sachs, 1980; Pictures, 1983; The Collectors, 1986; The Mistress, 1986; Witchcraft, 1992. *Recreations:* steam railway preservation, ski-ing, American football. *Address:* c/o ICM, 76 Oxford Street, W1M 0DD.

McENTEE, Peter Donovan, CMG 1978; OBE 1963; HM Diplomatic Service, retired; Governor and Commander-in-Chief of Belize, 1976–80; *b* 27 June 1920; *s* of Ewen Brooke McEntee and Caroline Laura Clare (*née* Bayley); *m* 1945, Mary Elisabeth Sherwood; two *d*. *Educ:* Haileybury Coll., Herts. Served War, HM Forces, 1939–45, KAR (Major). HM Overseas Civil Service, 1946–63: Dist Commissioner; retired as Principal of Kenya Inst. of Administration; First Secretary: Commonwealth Relations Office, 1963; Lagos, 1964–67; Commonwealth Office (later Foreign and Commonwealth Office), 1967–72; Consul-Gen., Karachi, 1972–75. *Recreations:* music, natural history. *Address:* Flat 2, Glebe House, The Street, Ickham, Canterbury, Kent CT3 1QN. *Club:* Royal Over-Seas League (Chm., 1992–95; Vice Pres., 1995).

MACER, Dr Richard Charles Franklin, MA, PhD; consultant on biotechnology and genetics, 1985–95; *b* 21 Oct. 1928; *s* of Lionel William Macer and Adie Elizabeth Macer; *m* 1952, Vera Gwendoline Jeapes; three *d*. *Educ:* Worthing High Sch.; St John's Coll., Cambridge. Research, St John's Coll., Cambridge, 1949–55, Hutchinson Res. Student, 1952–53; Hd of Plant Pathology Section, Plant Breeding Inst., Cambridge, 1955–66; Dir and Dir of Res., Rothwell Plant Breeders Ltd, Lincs, 1966–72; Prof. of Crop Production, Univ. of Edinburgh, 1972–76; Dir, Scottish Plant Breeding Station, 1976–81; Gen. Manager, Plant Royalty Bureau Ltd, 1981–85. *Publications:* papers on fungal diseases of cereals. *Recreations:* hill walking, archaeology, reading. *Club:* Farmers'.

McEVOY, David Dand; QC 1983; **His Honour Judge McEvoy;** a Circuit Judge, since 1996; *b* 25 June 1938; *s* of David Dand McEvoy and Ann Elizabeth McEvoy (*née* Breslin); *m* 1974, Belinda Anne Robertson; three *d*. *Educ:* Mount St Mary's Coll.; Lincoln Coll., Oxford. BA (PPE). 2nd Lieut The Black Watch, RHR, 1958–59. Called to the Bar, Inner Temple, 1964; a Recorder, 1979–96. *Recreations:* golf, fishing. *Address:* c/o Worcester Combined Court Centre, Shirehall, Worcester WR1 1TR. *T:* (01905) 730800. *Clubs:* Garrick; Blackwell Golf; Seniors Golfing Society; Highland Brigade.

McEWAN, Hon. Lord; Robin Gilmour McEwan; a Senator of the College of Justice in Scotland, since 2000; *b* 12 Dec. 1943; *s* of late Ian G. McEwan and of Mary McEwan, Paisley, Renfrewshire; *m* 1973, Sheena, *d* of late Stewart F. McIntyre and of Lilian McIntyre, Aberdour; two *d*. *Educ:* Paisley Grammar Sch.; Glasgow Univ. (1st Cl. Hons LLB; PhD). Faulds Fellow in Law, Glasgow Univ., 1965–68; admitted to Faculty of Advocates, 1967; QC (Scot.) 1981. Standing Jun. Counsel to Dept of Energy, 1974–76; Advocate Depute, 1976–79; Sheriff of S Strathclyde, Dumfries and Galloway, at Lanark, 1982–88, at Ayr, 1988–2000; Temp. Judge, Court of Session and High Court of Justiciary, 1991–99. Chm., Industrial Tribunals, 1981–82; Mem., Scottish Legal Aid Bd, 1989–96. *Publications:* Pleading in Court, 1980, 2nd edn 1995; (with Ann Paton) A Casebook on Damages in Scotland, 1983; contrib. Stair Memorial Encyclopaedia of the Laws of Scotland, 1987. *Recreation:* golf. *Address:* Court of Session, Parliament House, Parliament Square, Edinburgh EH1 1RQ. *T:* (0131) 225 2595. *Clubs:* New (Edinburgh); Honourable Company of Edinburgh Golfers, Prestwick Golf.

McEWAN, Geraldine, (Mrs Hugh Cruttwell); actress; *b* 9 May 1932; *d* of Donald and Norah McKeown; *m* 1953, Hugh Cruttwell, *qv*; one *s* one *d*. *Educ:* Windsor County Girls' School. Acted with Theatre Royal, Windsor, 1949–51; Who Goes There, 1951; Sweet Madness, 1952; For Better For Worse, 1953; Summertime, 1955; Love's Labour's Lost, Stratford-on-Avon, 1956; The Member of the Wedding, Royal Court Theatre, 1957; The Entertainer, Palace, 1957–58; Stratford-on-Avon, 1958: Pericles; Twelfth Night; Much Ado About Nothing; 1961: Much Ado About Nothing; Hamlet; Everything in the Garden, Arts and Duke of York's, 1962; School for Scandal, Haymarket, and USA, 1962; The Private Ear, and The Public Eye, USA, 1963; Loot, 1965; National Theatre, 1965–71: Armstrong's Last Goodnight; Love For Love; A Flea in Her Ear; The Dance of Death; Edward II; Home and Beauty; Rites; The Way of the World; The White Devil; Amphitryon 38; Dear Love, Comedy, 1973; Chez Nous, Globe, 1974; The Little Hut,

Duke of York's, 1974; Oh Coward!, Criterion, 1975; On Approval, Haymarket, 1975; Look After Lulu, Chichester, and Haymarket, 1978; A Lie of the Mind, Royal Court, 1987; Lettice and Lovage, Globe, 1988; Hamlet, Riverside Studio, 1992; The Bird Sanctuary, Abbey, Dublin, 1994; Grace Note, Old Vic, 1997; The Chairs, Royal Court Downstairs, 1997, USA 1998; Hay Fever, Savoy, 1999; National Theatre: The Browning Version and Harlequinade, 1980; The Provok'd Wife, 1980; The Rivals, 1983; Two Inches of Ivory, 1983; You Can't Take It With You, 1983; The Way of the World, 1995. Directed: As You Like It, Birmingham Rep., transf. Phoenix, 1988; Treats, Hampstead, 1989; Waiting for Sir Larry, Edinburgh, 1990; Four Door Saloon, Hampstead, 1991; Keyboard Skills, Bush, 1993. *Television series:* The Prime of Miss Jean Brodie, 1978; The Barchester Chronicles, 1982; Mapp and Lucia, 1985, 1986; Oranges are not the only Fruit, 1990; Mulberry, 1992, 1993; The Red Dwarf, 1999. *Films:* The Adventures of Tom Jones, 1975; Escape from the Dark, 1978; Foreign Body, 1986; Henry V, 1989; Robin Hood, Prince of Thieves, 1991; Moses, 1996; The Love Letter, 1999; Titus, 2000; Love's Labour's Lost, 2000. *Address:* c/o Marmont Management Ltd, Langham House, 302–308 Regent Street, W1R 5AL.

McEWAN, Ian Russell, CBE 2000; FRSL; author; *b* 21 June 1948; *s* of late Major (retd) David McEwan and of Rose Lilian Violet Moore; *m* 1982, Penny Allen (marr. diss. 1995); two *s* two *d*; *m* 1997, Annalena McAfee. *Educ:* Woolverstone Hall Sch.; Univ. of Sussex (BA Hons Eng. Lit.); Univ. of East Anglia (MA Eng. Lit.). Began writing, 1970. FRSL 1982; FRSA; Fellow, Amer. Acad. of Arts and Scis, 1995. Hon. DLitt Sussex, 1989; Hon. DLit London, 1998; Hon. LittD E Anglia, 1993. Shakespeare Prize, FVS Foundn, Hamburg, 1999. *Films:* The Ploughman's Lunch, 1983; Last Day of Summer, 1984; Soursweet, 1988; The Innocent, 1993; The Good Son, 1994. *Publications:* First Love, Last Rites, 1975 (filmed, 1997); In Between the Sheets, 1978; The Cement Garden, 1978 (filmed, 1993); The Imitation Game, 1981; The Comfort of Strangers, 1981 (filmed, 1991); Or Shall we Die? (oratorio; score by Michael Berkeley), 1982; The Ploughman's Lunch (film script), 1985; The Child in Time, 1987 (Whitbread Award; Prix Fémina, 1993); Soursweet (film script), 1989; The Innocent, 1990; Black Dogs, 1992; The Daydreamer, 1994; The Short Stories, 1995; Enduring Love, 1997; Amsterdam (novel), 1998 (Booker Prize, 1998); Atonement, 2001. *Recreations:* hiking, tennis. *Address:* c/o Jonathan Cape, Random Century House, 20 Vauxhall Bridge Road, SW1V 2SA.

McEWAN, Leslie James; JP; Director of Social Work, City of Edinburgh Council, since 1996; *b* 26 Feb. 1946; *s* of Charles and Ann McEwan; *m* 1966, Catherine Anne Currie; two *s*. *Educ:* St Andrews Univ. (MA); Dundee Univ. (Dip Social Admin); Univ. of Edinburgh (Dip Social Work). Midlothian, East Lothian and Peebles: Child Care Officer, Children's Dept, 1967–69; Social Worker, 1969–71; Sen. Social Worker, 1971–74; Social Work Advr, 1974–75; Divisional Director of Social Work: Midlothian-Lothian Reg., 1975–80; West Lothian, 1980–85; Lothian Region: Depute Dir of Social Work, 1985–90; Sen. Depute Dir, 1990–95; Director, 1995–96. JP Midlothian, 1973. *Recreations:* fly-fishing, golf, woodturning. *Address:* (office) Shrubhill House, Leith Walk, Edinburgh EH7 4PD; 1 Eskglades, Dalkeith, Midlothian EH22 1UZ.

McEWAN, Robin Gilmour; *see* McEwan, Hon. Lord.

MacEWEN, Ann Maitland, RIBA (DisTP), MRTPI; Planning Consultant; *b* 15 Aug. 1918; *d* of Dr Maitland Radford, MD, DPH, MOH St Pancras, and Dr Muriel Radford; *m* 1st, 1940, John Wheeler, ARIBA, AADip (Hons), Flt-Lt, RAF (killed on active service, 1945); two *d*; 2nd, 1947, Malcolm MacEwen (*d* 1996); one *d*. *Educ:* Howell's Sch., Denbigh, N Wales; Architectural Assoc. Sch. of Architecture (AA Dip., RIBA); Assoc. for Planning and Regional Reconstruction Sch. of Planning (SP Dip., MRTPI). Architectural Asst, 1945–46; Planning Asst, Hemel Hempstead New Town Master Plan, 1946–47; Architect-Planner with LCC, 1949–61; Mem., Colin Buchanan's Gp, Min. of Transport, which produced official report, Traffic in Towns, 1961–63; res. work, Transport Section, Civil Engineering Dept, Imperial Coll., 1963–64; Partner, Colin Buchanan and Partners, 1964–73. Senior Lectr, Bristol Univ. Sch. of Advanced Urban Studies, 1974–77; Hon. Res. Fellow, UCL, 1977–87. Mem., Noise Adv. Council, 1971–73. RIBA Distinction in Town Planning, 1967. *Publications:* National Parks—Cosmetics or Conservation? (with M. MacEwen), 1982; (with Joan Davidson) The Livable City, 1983; (with M. MacEwen) Greenprints for the Countryside? the story of Britain's National Parks, 1987. *Address:* Manor House, Wootton Courtenay, Minehead, Somerset TA24 8RD. *T:* (01643) 841325.

McEWEN, Hilary Mary; *see* Mantel, H. M.

McEWEN, Prof. James, FRCP, FFPHM, FFOM, FMedSci; Professor of Public Health, University of Glasgow, since 2000 (Henry Mechan Professor of Public Health, 1989–2000); President, Faculty of Public Health Medicine, Royal Colleges of Physicians of the United Kingdom, 1998–2001; *b* 6 Feb. 1940; *s* of Daniel McEwen and Elizabeth Wells (*née* Dishington); *m* 1964, Elizabeth May Archibald; one *s* one *d*. *Educ:* Dollar Acad.; Univ. of St Andrews (MB ChB 1963). FFPHM 1981; FFOM 1990; FRCPGlas 1991; FRCP 1999; FRCPE 1999. Asst MO of Health, City of Dundee, 1965–66; Lectr, Univ. of Dundee, 1966–74; Sen. Lectr, Univ. of Nottingham, 1975–81; CMO, Health Educn Council, 1981–82; Prof. of Community Medicine, King's Coll. Sch. of Medicine and Dentistry, Univ. of London, 1983–89. Hon. Consultant in Public Health Medicine, Gtr Glasgow Health Bd, 1989–; non-exec. Dir, Glasgow Royal Infirmary and Univ. NHS Trust, 1994–99. Mem., NRPP, 1996. Distinguished Visitor, Univ. of Tucuman, Argentina, 1993. FCPS (Pak), 1996; Founder FMedSci 1998. Hon. FFPHMI 1997. *Publications:* (with A. Finlayson) Coronary Heart Disease and Patterns of Living, 1977; (jtly) Measuring Health Status, 1986; (ed jtly) Oxford Textbook of Public Health, 3rd edn 1997; contrib. articles on public health, health services and quality of life. *Recreations:* Church, gardening, architectural heritage. *Address:* Department of Public Health, University of Glasgow, 1 Lilybank Gardens, Glasgow G12 8RZ. *T:* (0141) 330 5013; Auchanachie, Ruthven, Huntly AB54 4SS. *Club:* Royal Society of Medicine.

McEWEN, Sir John (Roderick Hugh), 5th Bt *cr* 1953; journalist; *b* 4 Nov. 1965; *s* of Sir Robert Lindley McEwen, 3rd Bt, of Marchmont and Bardrochat, and of Brigid Cecilia, *d* of late James Laver, CBE, and Veronica Turleigh; *S* brother, 1983; *m* 2000, Rachel, *er d* of Gerald Soane, Wallington, Surrey. *Educ:* Ampleforth; University Coll. London. *Heir: cousin* Adam Hugo McEwen, *b* 9 Feb. 1965. *Address:* 32/5 Montgomery Street, Edinburgh EH7 5JS.

MACEY, Rear-Adm. David Edward, CB 1984; Registrar and Secretary, Order of the Bath, 1990–2001; *b* 15 June 1929; *s* of Frederick William Charles Macey and Florence May Macey; *m* 1st, 1958, Lorna Therese Verner (decd), *o d* of His Honour Judge Oliver William Verner; one *s* one *d*, and one step *s* two step *d*; 2nd, 1982, Fiona (marr. diss. 1994), *o d* of Vice-Adm. Sir William Beloe, KBE, CB, DSC; 3rd, 1996, Rosemary Bothway, *o d* of Percy Crotch. *Educ:* Sir Joseph Williamson's Mathematical Sch., Rochester; Royal Naval Coll., Dartmouth. Midshipman, 1948; Cruisers, Carriers, Destroyers, 1950–63; Comdr, 1963; Amer. Staff Coll., 1964; Comdr, RNC Dartmouth, 1970; Captain, 1972; Directorate Naval Plans, 1972–74; RCDS, 1975; Dir, RN Staff Coll., 1976–78; Dir, Naval Manpower, 1979–81; Rear-Adm., 1981; Dep. Asst Chief of Staff (Ops), SACEUR, 1981–84. ADC to HM the Queen, 1981. Gentleman Usher of the Scarlet Rod, Order of the Bath, 1985–90. Receiver-Gen., Canterbury Cathedral, 1984–98; Mem., Archbps' Commn on Cathedrals, 1992–94. *Recreations:* walking, cricket, cooking. *Address:* Bell Tower House, Painter's Forstal, Faversham, Kent ME13 0EL. *Clubs:* Anglo-Belgian, MCC; Band of Brothers (Kent).

MACEY, Air Vice-Marshal Eric Harold, OBE, 1975; Director General of Training (Royal Air Force), 1989–91, retired; *b* 9 April 1936; *s* of Harold Fred and Katrina Emma Mary Macey; *m* 1957, Brenda Ann Bracher; one *s* one *d*. *Educ:* Shaftesbury Grammar School; Southampton Tech. Coll. Asst Sci. Officer, Min. of Supply, 1953–54; RAF, 1954; commissioned, 1955; Pilot's Wings, 1956; RAF Staff Coll., 1966; RCDS 1983; AOC and Comdt, RAF Coll., Cranwell, 1985–87; ACDS (Policy and Nuclear), 1987–89. President: RAF Chilmark Assoc., 1994–; Bournemouth Red Arrows Assoc., 1995–; Vice-President: 214 Sqdn Assoc., 1990–; 101 Sqdn Assoc., 1999–; Salisbury RFC, 1990–; Bomber Comd Assoc., 1998–. *Recreations:* music, walking, DIY. *Address:* Ebblemead, Homington, Salisbury, Wilts SP5 4NL.

McFADDEN, Jean Alexandra, CBE 1992; JP; DL; MA, LLB; Lecturer in Law, University of Strathclyde, since 1992; Chair, Scottish Charity Law Commission, since 2000; Vice Lord Lieutenant of City of Glasgow, 1980–92; *b* 26 Nov. 1941; *d* of John and Elma Hogg; *m* 1966, John McFadden (*d* 1991). *Educ:* Univ. of Glasgow (MA 1st Cl. Hons Classics); Univ. of Strathclyde (LLB 1st Cl. Hons). Principal Teacher of Classics, Strathclyde Schools, 1967–86; part-time Lectr in Law, Univ. of Glasgow, 1991–92. Entered Local Govt as Mem. of Glasgow Corp. for Cowcaddens Ward, 1971 then (following boundary changes) Mem., Glasgow DC for Scotstoun Ward, 1984–96; Mem., City of Glasgow Council, 1995– (Convener, 1995–96; Chair: Labour Gp, 1995–; Social Strategy Cttee, 1996–99); Chm., Manpower Cttee, 1974–77; Leader, Labour Gp, 1977–86, 1992–94; Leader, 1980–86, 1992–94, Treas., 1986–92, Glasgow DC. Convener, Scottish Local Govt Information Unit, 1984–; Pres., Convention of Scottish Local Auths, 1990–92; Member Board: SDA, 1989–91; Glasgow Develt Agency, 1992–2000. Member: Health Appts Adv. Cttee, Scottish Exec. (formerly Scottish Office), 1995–2000; Ancient Monuments Bd for Scotland, 2000–. Chm., Mayfest (Glasgow Internat. Arts Fest.), 1983–92. JP Glasgow, 1972; DL 1980. *Recreations:* cycling, theatre, walking, golf, West Highland terriers. *Address:* 16 Lansdowne Crescent, Glasgow G20 6NQ. *T:* (0141) 334 3522.

McFADYEAN, Colin William; Deputy Headteacher, Ilminster Avenue Primary School, Bristol Education Authority, since 1999; *b* 11 March 1943; *s* of Captain Angus John McFadyean, MC, 1st Bn London Scottish Regt (killed in action, 1944) and late Joan Mary McFadyean (*née* Irish); *m* 1970, Jeanette Carol Payne; one *s*. *Educ:* Plymouth Coll.; Bristol Grammar Sch.; Loughborough Coll. of Education; Keele Univ. (DLC hons, Adv. DipEd). Phys. Educn teacher, Birmingham, 1965–67; Phys. Educn Lectr, 1967–72, Sen. Lectr, 1972–74, Cheshire; Dep. Dir, Nat. Sports Centre, Lilleshall, 1974–78; Chief Coach, Jubilee Sports Centre, Hong Kong, 1979–82; Sports Master and House Master, Dulwich Coll., 1983–85; Dir Gen., NPFA, 1985–87; with Croydon Educn Authy, 1988–90; teacher, Avon, then Bristol Educn Authy, 1991–98; Dep. Headteacher, Oldbury Court Primary Sch., 1998–99. Dir Coaching, Bristol FC (Rugby Union), 1990–91; Coach, Moseley FC, 1991–93; Coach, 1992–99, Dir of Rugby, 1998–99, Cleve RFC. Internat. Rugby career includes: 11 England caps, 1966–68; 4 Tests British Lions *v* NZ, 1966; (captain) *v* Ireland, 1968; (captain) *v* Wales, 1968; scored 5 tries, 1 dropped goal (in 15 Tests); other sport: coach to Hong Kong disabled team to Olympics, Arnhem, 1980; Adviser, Hong Kong table tennis team to World Championships, Yugoslavia, 1981. Broadcaster with Hong Kong TV and commercial radio. *Recreations:* tennis, golf, music. *Address:* The Barn, Parkfield Road, Pucklechurch, South Glos BS16 9PN. *Clubs:* British Sportsman's; England Rugby International's; Rugby Internationals Golf, Saltford Golf; Moseley Football (Vice-Pres.); Penguins Rugby Football (Vice-Pres), Cleve Rugby Football (Vice-Pres.).

MACFADYEN, Hon. Lord; Donald James Dobbie Macfadyen; a Senator of the College of Justice in Scotland, since 1995; *b* 8 Sept. 1945; *er s* of late Donald James Thomson Macfadyen and Christina Dick Macfadyen; *m* 1971, Christine Balfour Gourlay Hunter; one *s* one *d*. *Educ:* Hutchesons' Boys' Grammar Sch., Glasgow; Glasgow Univ. (LLB 1967). Admitted to Faculty of Advocates, 1969, Vice-Dean 1992–95. Advocate Depute, 1979–82; Standing Jun. Counsel to Dept of Agric. and Fisheries for Scotland, 1977–79, to SHHD, 1982–83; QC (Scot.) 1983. Part-time Chm., Med. Appeal Tribunals and Vaccine Damage Tribunals, 1989–95; Temp. Judge, Court of Session, 1994–95. Vice Chm., Judges' Forum, Internat. Bar Assoc., 2000–. Chm. Council, Cockburn Assoc. (Edinburgh Civic Trust), 2001–. FCIArb 1993. *Address:* 66 Northumberland Street, Edinburgh EH3 6JE. *T:* (0131) 556 6043, *Fax:* (0131) 556 9149. *Club:* New (Edinburgh).

MACFADYEN, Donald James Dobbie; *see* Macfadyen, Hon. Lord.

MACFADYEN, Air Marshal Ian David, CB 1991; OBE 1984; FRAeS; Lieutenant Governor, Isle of Man, since 2000; *b* 19 Feb. 1942; *s* of Air Marshal Sir Douglas Macfadyen, KCB, CBE and of Lady Macfadyen (*née* Dafforn, now Mrs P. A. Rowan); *m* 1967, Sally Harvey; one *s* one *d*. *Educ:* Marlborough; RAF Coll., Cranwell. Joined RAF, 1960; Cranwell cadet, 1960–63 (Sword of Honour); 19 Sqdn, 1965–68; HQ, RAF Strike Command, 1969; Flying Instructor, RAF Coll., Cranwell, 1970–73; RAF Staff Coll., 1973; 111 Sqdn, 1974–75; Flt Comdr, 43 Sqdn, 1975–76; HQ 2 ATAF, RAF Germany, 1976–79; comd 29 Sqdn, 1980–84; comd 23 Sqdn, 1984; MoD, 1984–85; comd RAF Leuchars, Fife, 1985–87; RCDS, 1988; MoD, 1989–90; COS, then Comdr, HQ British Forces ME, Riyadh, 1990–91; ACDS, Op. Requirements (Air Systems), 1991–94; Dir Gen., Saudi Arabia Armed Forces Project, 1994–98; retd, 1999. Trustee, RAF Mus. (Chm. Trustees, 1999–2001). Liveryman, GAPAN, 1999–. QCVSA 1974. *Recreations:* shooting, photography, gliding, golf, aviation history, painting. *Address:* Government House, Onchan, Isle of Man IM3 1RR. *Clubs:* Royal Air Force; Royal & Ancient (St Andrews).

McFALL, John; MP (Lab and Co-op) Dumbarton, since 1987. An Opposition Whip, 1989–91; Opposition front bench spokesman: for education and home affairs, 1992; on Scottish Affairs, 1992–97; a Lord Comr of HM Treasury (Govt Whip), 1997–98; Parly Under-Sec. of State, NI Office, 1998–99. Member, Select Committee: on Defence, 1988; on Sittings of the House, 1991; on Information, 1990–97; Chm., HM Treasury Select Cttee, 2001–; Mem. Exec. Cttee, Parly Gp for Energy Studies, 1988–97; Secretary: Retail Industry Gp, 1992–97; Roads Study Gp, 1989–; Hon. Sec., Parly and Scientific Cttee, 1989–92. Vis. Prof., Strathclyde Business Sch., Univ. of Strathclyde. *Recreations:* running, golf, reading. *Address:* 14 Oxhill Road, Dumbarton G82 4DG. *T:* (01389) 31437.

McFALL, Richard Graham; Chairman, 1980–86, Director, 1976–86, Fleming Enterprise Investment Trust plc (formerly Crossfriars Trust plc); *b* 31 Jan. 1920; 3rd *s* of Henry Joseph Marshall and Sarah Gertrude McFall; *m* 1945, Clara Louise Debonnaire Mitford; one *s* one *d*. *Educ:* Holmwood Prep. Sch., Lancs; Clifton Coll., Bristol. Joined Pacol Ltd, 1938; Mil.

Service, HAC, 1939–40; Colonial Office, 1941–45 (Asst Sec., then Sec., W African Produce Control Bd); Motor & Air Products Ltd, 1946–48; re-joined Pacol Ltd, 1949, Dir 1951; Chm., London Cocoa Terminal Market Assoc., 1954–55; Chm., Cocoa Assoc. of London, 1958–59; Dir 1962–82, Man. Dir 1965–74, Chm., 1970–76, Vice-Chm., 1976–78, Gill & Duffus Group PLC. *Recreation:* golf. *Address:* Springfold Cottage, Green Dene, East Horsley, Surrey KT24 5RG. *T:* (01483) 283282. *Clubs:* Farmers'; Effingham Golf.

McFARLAND, Alan; *see* McFarland, R. A.

McFARLAND, Prof. David John, DPhil; Professor of Biological Robotics, University of the West of England, since 2000; Fellow, Balliol College, Oxford, 1966–2000, now Emeritus; *b* 31 Dec. 1938; *s* of John Cyril and Joan Elizabeth McFarland; *m* 1962, Frances Jill Tomlin; one *s* one *d*. *Educ:* Leighton Park Sch., Reading; Liverpool Univ. (BSc 1st Cl. Hons Zoology, 1961); Oxford Univ. (DPhil Psychology, 1965). Lectr in Psychology, Durham Univ., 1964; Oxford University: Lectr in Psychology, 1966–74; Reader in Animal Behaviour, 1974–2000; Tutor in Psychology, Balliol Coll., 1966–2000. Hofmeyer Fellow, Univ. of the Witwatersrand, 1974; Visiting Professor: Dalhousie Univ., 1968; Rutgers Univ., 1971; Univ. of Penn, 1977; SUNY, Stonybrook, 1978; Univ. of Oregon, 1978; Univ. of Münster, Germany, 1989. Pres., Internat. Ethological Conf., 1981. Editor, Animal Behaviour, 1969–74. *Publications:* (with J. McFarland) An Introduction to the Study of Behaviour, 1969; Feedback Mechanisms in Animal Behaviour, 1971; (ed) Motivational Control Systems Analysis, 1974; (ed) The Oxford Companion to Animal Behaviour, 1981; (with A. Houston) Quantitative Ethology: the state space approach, 1981; (ed) Functional Ontogeny, 1982; Animal Behaviour, 1985, 3rd edn 1999; Problems of Animal Behaviour, 1989; Biologie des Verhaltens, (Germany) 1989, 2nd edn 1999; (with T. Bosser) Intelligent Behavior in Animals and Robots, (USA) 1993; articles in scientific learned jls. *Recreations:* keeping animals, pottery. *Address:* Balliol College, Oxford OX1 3BJ. *T:* (01865) 277760.

McFARLAND, Sir John (Talbot), 3rd Bt *cr* 1914, of Aberfoyle, Londonderry; TD 1967; Chairman: Malvay Ltd (formerly Lanes (Business Equipment)), since 1977; J. T. McFarland Holdings, since 1984; McFarland Farms Ltd, since 1980; Information and Imaging Systems Ltd, since 1994; *b* 3 Oct. 1927; *s* of Sir Basil Alexander Talbot McFarland, 2nd Bt, CBE, ERD, and Anne Kathleen (*d* 1952), *d* of late Andrew Henderson; *S* father, 1986; *m* 1957, Mary Scott, *d* of late Dr W. Scott Watson, Londonderry; two *s* two *d*. *Educ:* Marlborough College; Trinity Coll., Oxford. Captain RA (TA), retired 1967. Chm., R. C. Malseed & Co. Ltd, 1957–90; Chairman, 1977–84: Lanes (Derry) Ltd; Lanes (Fuel) Oils Ltd; Lanes Patent Fuels Ltd; Holmes Coal Ltd; Alexander Thompson & Co. Ltd; Nicholl Ballintyne Ltd; J. W. Corbett Ltd; Wattersons Ltd. Chm., Londonderry Lough Swilly Railway Co., 1978–81; Director: Londonderry Gaslight Co., 1958–89; Donegal Holdings Ltd, 1963–85; G. Kinnaird & Son Ltd, 1981–95; Windy Hills Ltd, 1994–95; Wallcoatings Dublin Ltd, 1996–. Member: Londonderry County Borough Council, 1955–69; NW HMC, 1960–73; Londonderry Port and Harbour Commrs, 1965–73. Jt Chm., Londonderry and Foyle Coll., 1971–76. High Sheriff, Co. Londonderry 1958, City of County of Londonderry 1965–67; DL Londonderry 1962, resigned 1982. *Recreations:* golf, shooting. *Heir: er s* Anthony Basil Scott McFarland [*b* 29 Nov. 1959; *m* 1988, Anne Margaret, BA, ACA, *d* of T. K. Laidlaw, Gernonstown, Slane, Co. Meath. *Educ:* Marlborough Coll.; Trinity College, Dublin (BA). ACA]. *Address:* Dunmore House, Carrigans, Lifford, Co. Donegal. *T:* (74) 40120, *Fax:* (74) 40336. *Clubs:* Kildare Street and University (Dublin); Northern Counties (Londonderry).

McFARLAND, (Robert) Alan; Member (UU) North Down, Northern Ireland Assembly, since 1998; *b* 9 Aug. 1949; *s* of Dr Albert John Black McFarland and Mary Elizabeth Florence McFarland (*née* Campbell); *m* 1979, Celia Mary Sharp; one *s* two *d*. *Educ:* Rockport Sch., Craigavad, Co. Down; Campbell Coll., Belfast; RMA, Sandhurst. Commnd RTR, 1975; various regtl appts, 1975–81 (despatches, 1981); SO, Orgn and Deployment, HQ 4th Armd Div., 1981–83; Sqn Ldr, Challenger Tank Sqn and HQ Sqn 2nd RTR, 1983–86; SO, Public Relns, HQ SW Dist and UK Mobile Force, 1987–89; Mgt Consultant, MoD, 1989–92; retd in rank of Major, 1992. Parly Asst to Rev. Martin Smyth, MP and Rt Hon. James Molyneaux, MP, H of C, 1992–95; Dir, Somme Heritage Centre, Newtownards, 1996–98. *Recreations:* military history, folk music. *Address:* c/o Parliament Buildings, Stormont, Belfast BT4 3XX.

MACFARLANE, family name of **Baron Macfarlane of Bearsden**.

MACFARLANE OF BEARSDEN, Baron *cr* 1991 (Life Peer), of Bearsden in the district of Bearsden and Milngavie; **Norman Somerville Macfarlane,** KT 1996; Kt 1983; DL; FRSE; Hon. Life President: Macfarlane Group PLC (Chairman, 1973–98, Managing Director, 1973–90, Hon. Life President, 1999, Macfarlane Group (Clansman) PLC); United Distillers PLC, 1996 (Chairman, 1987–96); Lord High Commissioner, General Assembly, Church of Scotland, 1992, 1993 and 1997; *b* 5 March 1926; *s* of Daniel Robertson Macfarlane and Jessie Lindsay Somerville; *m* 1953, Marguerite Mary Campbell; one *s* four *d*. *Educ:* High Sch. of Glasgow. FRSE 1991. Commnd RA, 1945; served Palestine, 1945–47. Founded N. S. Macfarlane & Co. Ltd, 1949; became Macfarlane Group (Clansman) PLC, 1973. Underwriting Mem. of Lloyd's, 1978–97; Chairman: The Fine Art Society PLC, 1976–98 (Hon. Life Pres., 1998); American Trust PLC, 1984–97 (Dir, 1980–); Guinness PLC, 1987–89 (Jt Dep. Chm., 1989–92); Director: Clydesdale Bank PLC, 1980–96 (Dep. Chm., 1993–96); General Accident Fire & Life Assce Corp. plc, 1984–96; Edinburgh Fund Managers plc, 1980–98. Dir, Glasgow Chamber of Commerce, 1976–79; Member: Council, CBI Scotland, 1975–81; Bd, Scottish Develt Agency, 1979–87. Chm., Glasgow Develt Agency (formerly Glasgow Action), 1985–92. Vice Chm., Scottish Ballet, 1983–87 (Dir, 1975–); Dir, Scottish National Orch., 1977–82; Pres., Royal Glasgow Inst. of the Fine Arts, 1976–87; Mem., Royal Fine Art Commn for Scotland, 1980–82; Scottish Patron, National Art Collection Fund, 1978–; Governor, Glasgow Sch. of Art, 1976–87; Trustee: Nat. Heritage Meml Fund, 1984–97; Nat. Galls of Scotland, 1986–97. Dir, Third Eye Centre, 1978–81. Hon. Pres., Charles Rennie Mackintosh Soc., 1988–. Hon. Pres., High Sch. of Glasgow, 1992– (Chm. Govs, 1979–92); Mem. Court, Univ. of Glasgow, 1979–87; Regent, RCSE, 1997–. President: Stationers' Assoc. of GB and Ireland, 1965; Co. of Stationers of Glasgow, 1968–70; Glasgow High Sch. Club, 1970–72. Patron, Scottish Licensed Trade Assoc., 1992–. DL Dunbartonshire, 1993. CIMgt 1996. HRSA 1987; HRGI 1987; Hon. FRIAS 1984; Hon. FScotvec 1991; Hon. FRCPSGlas 1992; Hon. Fellow, Glasgow Sch. of Art, 1993. Hon. LLD: Strathclyde, 1986; Glasgow, 1988; Glasgow Caledonian, 1993; Aberdeen, 1995; DUniv Stirling, 1992; Dr (*hc*) Edinburgh, 1992. *Recreations:* golf, cricket, theatre, art. *Address:* Macfarlane Group PLC, Clansman House, 21 Newton Place, Glasgow G3 7PY; 50 Manse Road, Bearsden, Glasgow G61 3PN. *Clubs:* Glasgow Art, Royal Scottish Automobile (Glasgow); New (Edinburgh); Hon. Co. of Edinburgh Golfers, Glasgow Golf.

McFARLANE OF LLANDAFF, Baroness *cr* 1979 (Life Peer), of Llandaff in the County of South Glamorgan; **Jean Kennedy McFarlane;** Professor and Head of Department of Nursing, University of Manchester, 1974–88, now Professor Emeritus; *b* 1 April 1926; *d* of late James and Elvina Alice McFarlane. *Educ:* Howell's Sch., Llandaff; Bedford Coll., London (BScSoc); Birkbeck Coll., London (MA; Fellow, 1997). SRN, SCM, HV Tutor's Cert.; FRCN 1976; FCNA 1984. Staff Nurse, St Bartholomew's Hosp., 1950–51; Health Visitor, Cardiff CC, 1953–59; Royal Coll. of Nursing: Organising Tutor, Integrated Course, Educn Div., London, 1960–62; Educn Officer, Birmingham, 1962–66; Res. Project Ldr (DHSS sponsored), London, 1967–69; Dir of Educn, Inst. of Advanced Nursing Educn, London, 1969–71; Univ. of Manchester: Sen. Lectr in Nursing, Dept of Social and Preventive Medicine, 1971–73; Sen. Lectr and Head of Dept of Nursing, 1973–74. Member: Royal Commn on NHS, 1976–79; Commonwealth War Graves Commn, 1983–88. Chm., English Bd for Nursing, Midwifery and Health Visiting, 1980–83. Mem., Gen. Synod of C of E, 1990–95. Hon. FRCP 1990. Hon. MSc Manchester, 1979; Hon. DSc Ulster, 1981; Hon. DEd CNAA, 1983; Hon. MD Liverpool, 1990; Hon. DLit Glamorgan, 1995; Hon. LLD Manchester, 1998. *Publications:* The Problems of Developing Criteria of Quality for Nursing Care (thesis), 1969; The Proper Study of the Nurse, 1970; (with G. Castledine) The Practice of Nursing using the Nursing Process, 1982. *Recreations:* music, walking, travelling, photography. *Address:* 5 Dovercourt Avenue, Heaton Mersey, Stockport SK4 3QB. *T:* (0161) 432 8367.

MACFARLANE, Prof. Alan Donald James, FRAI; FRHistS; FBA 1986; Professor of Anthropological Science, University of Cambridge, since 1991; *b* 20 Dec. 1941; *s* of Donald Kennedy Macfarlane and Iris Stirling Macfarlane; *m* 1st, 1966, Gillian Ions; one *d*; 2nd, 1981, Sarah Harrison. *Educ:* Sedbergh School; Worcester College, Oxford (MA, DPhil); LSE (MPhil); SOAS (PhD). University of Cambridge: Senior Research Fellow in History, King's College, 1971–74; Univ. Lectr in Social Anthropology, 1975–81; Reader in Historical Anthropology, 1981–91. Lectures: Frazer Meml, Liverpool Univ., 1974; Malinowski Meml, LSE, 1978; Radcliffe-Brown Meml, Univ. of Lancaster, 1992; Marett Meml, Univ. of Oxford, 1995; F. W. Maitland Meml, Univ. of Cambridge, 2000. Rivers Meml Medal, RAI, 1984; William J. Goode Award, Amer. Sociol Assoc., 1987. Principal consultant and presenter, The Day the World Took Off (millennium series), C4, 2000. *Publications:* Witchcraft in Tudor and Stuart England, 1970; The Family Life of Ralph Josselin, 1970; Resources and Population, 1976; (ed) The Diary of Ralph Josselin, 1976; Reconstructing Historical Communities, 1977; Origins of English Individualism, 1978; The Justice and the Mare's Ale, 1981; A Guide to English Historical Records, 1983; Marriage and Love in England, 1986; The Culture of Capitalism, 1987; The Cambridge Database System User Manual, 1990; (jtly) The Nagas: hill peoples of North-east India, 1990; (ed and trans. with S. Harrison) Bernard Pignède, The Gurungs of Nepal, 1993; The Savage Wars of Peace, 1997; The Riddle of the Modern World, 2000; The Making of the Modern World, 2001. *Recreations:* walking, gardening, second-hand book hunting. *Address:* 25 Lode Road, Lode, near Cambridge CB5 9ER. *T:* (01223) 811976.

MacFARLANE, Prof. Alistair George James, CBE 1987; FRS 1984; FREng; FRSE; Principal and Vice-Chancellor of Heriot-Watt University, 1989–96; *b* 9 May 1931; *s* of George R. MacFarlane; *m* 1954, Nora Williams; one *s*. *Educ:* Hamilton Academy; Univ. of Glasgow. BSc 1953, DSc 1969, Glasgow; PhD London 1964; MSc Manchester 1973; MA 1974, ScD 1979, Cantab. FIEE; FREng (FEng 1981); FRSE 1990. Metropolitan-Vickers, Manchester, 1953–58; Lectr, Queen Mary Coll., Univ. of London, 1959–65, Reader 1965–66; Reader in Control Engrg, Univ. of Manchester Inst. of Sci. and Technology, 1966–69, Prof. 1969–74; Prof. of Engrg and Hd of Information Engrg Div., Univ. of Cambridge, 1974–88; Fellow, 1974–88, Vice-Master, 1980–88, Hon. Fellow, 1989–, Selwyn Coll., Cambridge. Chm., Cambridge Control Ltd, 1985–90; Non-Executive Director: Lothian and Edinburgh Enterprise Ltd, 1990–96; British Nuclear Fuels plc, 1995–2000. Member: Council, SERC, 1981–85; Computer Board, 1983–88; Adv. Cttee for Safety of Nuclear Installations, 1987–90; Engrg Tech. Adv. Cttee, DTI, 1991–93; BT Adv. Forum, 1997–98. Chm., Res. Councils' High Performance Computing Strategy Gp, 1995–98. Comr, Nat. Commn on Educn, 1991–93; Academic Advr, 1997–2000, CEO and Dir, 2000–01, Univ. of Highlands and Islands project; Chairman: Scottish Univs Wkg Party on Teaching and Learning in an Expanding Higher Educn System, 1991–92 (MacFarlane Report, 1992); Scottish Council for Res. in Educn, 1992–98; Scottish Library and Information Council, 1994–98. Royal Society: Vice-Pres., 1997–99; Mem. Council, 1997–99; Chm., Educn Cttee, 2000–. Trustee, Scottish Internat. Educn Trust, 1994–. Hon. DEng: UMIST, 1995; Glasgow, 1995; DUniv: Heriot-Watt, 1997; Paisley, 1997; Hon. DSc Abertay Dundee, 1998; Hon. DLitt Lincolnshire and Humberside, 1999. Medals: Centennial, ASME, 1980; Sir Harold Hartley, Inst. of Measurement and Control, 1982; Achievement, IEE, 1992; Faraday, IEE, 1993. *Publications:* Engineering Systems Analysis, 1964; Dynamical System Models, 1970; (with I. Postlethwaite) A Complex Variable Approach to the Analysis of Linear Multivariable Feedback Systems, 1979; (ed) Frequency-Response Methods in Control Systems, 1979; (ed) Complex Variable Methods for Linear Multivariable Feedback Systems, 1980; (with S. Hung) Multivariable Feedback: a quasi-classical approach, 1982; (with G. K. H. Pang) An Expert Systems Approach to Computer-Aided Design of Multivariable Systems, 1987. *Address:* Dalnacroich, Strathconon, by Muir of Ord, Ross-shire IV6 7QQ. *T:* and *Fax:* (01997) 477281. *Club:* New (Edinburgh).

MACFARLANE, Rev. Alwyn James Cecil; Parish Minister of Newlands (South), Church of Scotland, 1968–85; Extra Chaplain to the Queen in Scotland, since 1992 (Chaplain, 1977–92); *b* 14 June 1922; *s* of James Waddell Macfarlane and Ada Cecilia Rankin; *m* 1953, Joan Cowell Harris; one *s* one *d*. *Educ:* Cargilfield Sch.; Rugby Sch.; Oxford Univ. (MA); Edinburgh Univ. Served War: N Africa, Italy, Greece; Liaison Officer in Black Watch with 12th Bde, 1942–46. Ordained, 1951; served in parishes in Ross-shire, Edinburgh, Glasgow, Australia. *Recreations:* photography, walking. *Address:* Flat 12, Homeburn House, 177 Fenwick Road, Giffnock, Glasgow G46 6JD.

McFARLANE, Andrew Ewart; QC 1998; a Recorder, since 1999; a Deputy High Court Judge, since 2000; *b* 20 June 1954; *s* of Gordon McFarlane and Olive McFarlane (*née* Davies); *m* 1981, Susanna Jane Randolph; four *d*. *Educ:* Shrewsbury Sch.; Durham Univ. (BA Hons Law 1975); Univ. of Wales (LLM Canon Law 1998). Called to the Bar, Gray's Inn, 1972; an Asst Recorder, 1995–99; Midland and Oxford Circuit. *Publications:* (with David Hershman) Children: law and practice, 1991; (contrib.) Family Court Practice, 2001. *Recreations:* family life, the countryside, theatre. *Address:* 1 King's Bench Walk, Temple, EC4Y 7DB. *T:* (020) 7936 1500.

MACFARLANE, Anne Bridget; Master of the Court of Protection, 1982–95; *b* 26 Jan. 1930; *d* of late Dr David Griffith and Dr Grace Griffith; *m* 1957, James Douglas Macfarlane (*d* 1999); two *d*. *Educ:* nine schools; Bristol Univ. (LLB). Admitted Solicitor, 1954. HM Land Registry, 1966–75; Registrar, Bromley County Court, 1975–82. *Publications:* (contrib.) Atkin's Court Forms, 2nd edn 1983; Older Adults' Decision-Making and the Law, 1996. *Recreation:* collecting Victorian tiles. *Club:* Law Society (Hon. Life Mem., 1996).

MACFARLANE, Sir (David) Neil, Kt 1988; Chairman: Associated Nursing Services, since 1994; Securicor plc, since 1995 (Director, since 1992); *b* 7 May 1936; *yr s* of late

Robert and of Dulcie Macfarlane; *m* 1961, June Osmond King, Somerset; two *s* one *d*. *Educ:* St Aubyn's Prep. Sch.; Bancroft's, Woodford Green. Short Service Commission, Essex Regt, 1955–58; served TA, 265 LAA, RA, 1961–66. Joined Shell Mex and BP, 1959; contested (C): East Ham (North), 1970; Sutton and Cheam, by-election, 1972. Parly Under-Sec. of State (Dep. Minister for the Arts), DES, 1979–81; Parly Under-Sec. of State, DoE, 1981–85 (with spec. responsibility for Sport, 1981–85, for Children's Play, 1983–85). Mem., All Party Select Cttee on Science and Technology, 1974–79; MP (C) Sutton and Cheam, Feb. 1974–1992. Chm., Rushman Lloyd PLC, 1994–97; Director: RMC, 1987–; Bradford and Bingley Bldg Soc., 1987–2000. Chairman: Sports Aid Foundn, 1986–87; Golf Fund PLC; Vice-Pres. PGA, 1985–. Trustee, England and Wales Cricket Foundn, 1997–. Mem., National Trust, 1976–. *Publication:* Sport and Politics: a world divided, 1986. *Recreations:* golf, cricket-watching. *Clubs:* MCC, Lord's Taverners; Essex County Cricket; Leander (Henley); Royal & Ancient Golf; Huntercombe Golf; Sunningdale Golf; Wentworth Golf.

MACFARLANE, Sir George (Gray), Kt 1971; CB 1965; BSc; Dr Ing (Dresden); FREng; retired; Member of the Board, British Telecommunications Corporation, 1981–84; Corporate Director, British Telecom plc, 1984–87; *b* 8 Jan. 1916; *s* of late John Macfarlane, Airdrie, Lanarks; *m* 1941, Barbara Grant, *d* of Thomas Thomson, Airdrie, Lanarks; one *s* one *d*. *Educ:* Airdrie Academy; Glasgow Univ.; Technische Hochschule, Dresden, Germany. FREng (FEng 1976); FIMA; FPhysS. On scientific staff, Air Ministry Research Establishment, Dundee and Swanage, 1939–41; Telecommunications Research Establishment (TRE), Malvern, 1941–60; Deputy Chief Scientific Officer (Individual Merit Post), 1954–60; Deputy Director, National Physical Laboratory, 1960–62; Director, Royal Radar Establishment, 1962–67; Controller (Research), Min. of Technology and Min. of Aviation Supply, 1967–71; Controller, Research and Develt Establishments and Research, MoD, 1971–75. Member: PO Review Cttee, 1976–77; PO Bd, 1977–81; NEB, 1980–85 and NRDC, 1981–85 (subseq. British Technology Gp). Mem., Bd of Trustees, Imperial War Museum, 1978–86. Deputy-Pres., IEE, 1976–78 (Vice-Pres., 1972–74), Hon. FIEE, 1988; Hunter Meml Lecturer, IEE, 1966; Council Mem., Fellowship of Engrg, 1982–87 (Vice-Pres. 1983–86). Hon. LLD Glasgow. Glazebrook Medal and Prize, Inst. of Physics, 1978. *Publications:* papers in IEE, Proc. Phys. Society, Phys. Review. *Recreations:* walking, gardening. *Address:* Red Tiles, 17 Orchard Way, Esher, Surrey KT10 9DY. *T:* (01372) 463778. *Club:* Athenæum.

McFARLANE, Sir Ian, Kt 1984; Chairman and Managing Director: Southern Pacific Petroleum NL, since 1968; Central Pacific Minerals NL, since 1968; Chairman, Trans Pacific Consolidated Ltd, since 1964; *b* 25 Dec. 1923; *s* of Stuart Gordon McFarlane, CMG, MBE and Mary Grace McFarlane; *m* 1956, Ann, *d* of M. A. Shaw, Salt Lake City, USA; one *s* two *d*. *Educ:* Melbourne Grammar School; Harrow; Sydney Univ. (BSc, BE); MIT (MS). Served War of 1939–45, RANVR. Morgan Stanley & Co., 1949–59; Mem., Sydney Stock Exchange, 1959–64; Partner, Ord, Minnett, T. J. Thompson & Partners, 1959–64; Dep. Chm., Magellan Petroleum, 1964–70; Director: Trans City Discount Ltd, 1960–64; Consolidated Rutile Ltd, 1964–68; International Pacific Corp., 1967–73; Aust. Gen. Insurance Co., 1968–74; Mercantile Mutual Insurance Co., 1969–74; Concrete Construction, 1972–74; International Pacific Aust. Investments, 1972–73; Morgan Stanley Internat., NYC, 1976–80. Mem. Council, Imperial Soc. of Knights Bachelor, 1985–. Founder, Sir Ian McFarlane Travelling Professorship in Urology, 1980. Chm., Royal Brisbane Hosp. Res. (formerly Hosp.) Foundn, 1985–93; Member: Appeal Bd, Pain and Mgt Res. Centre, Royal North Shore Hosp., 1994–; Nat. Trust St John's Cathedral Completion Fund, Brisbane, 1997–. Life Governor, Royal Prince Alfred Hosp., Sydney, 1982; Founding Governor, St Luke's Hosp. Foundn, Sydney, 1982–. Fellow Commoner, Christ's Coll., Cambridge, 1987. Fellow, Aust. Inst. of Mining and Metallurgy, 1993; FAICD (FIDA 1983). Hon. Col Kentucky, 1984–. KCGSJ 1999. *Address:* 40 Wentworth Road, Vaucluse, NSW 2030, Australia. *Clubs:* Australian (Sydney); Queensland (Brisbane); Commonwealth (Canberra); University (NY); Royal Sydney Golf; Brisbane Polo; Cruising Yacht of Australia, Royal Motor Yacht of NSW, Rose Bay Surf (Sydney).

McFARLANE, Prof. Ian Dalrymple, MBE 1946; FBA 1978; Professor of French Literature, University of Oxford, 1971–83, now Emeritus; Professorial Fellow, Wadham College, Oxford, 1971–83, now Emeritus Fellow; *b* 7 Nov. 1915; *s* of James Blair McFarlane and Valérie Edith Liston Dalrymple; *m* 1939, Marjory Nan Hamilton; one *s* one *d*. *Educ:* Lycée St-Charles, Marseilles; Tormore Sch., Upper Deal, Kent; Westminster Sch.; St Andrews Univ. MA 1st class Hons, 1938; Carnegie Research Scholar, 1938–39. Served 1st Bn Black Watch, RHR, 1940–45. Apptd Lectr in French, Cambridge Univ., 1945; Gonville and Caius College: elected Fellow, 1947 (Hon. Fellow, 1990); appointed Senior Tutor, 1956; Prof. of French Language and Literature, St Andrews, 1961–70. Zaharoff Lectr, Oxford, 1984; Hon. Faculty Prof., University Coll., Cardiff, 1984. Hon. Sen. Res. Fellow, Inst. of Romance Studies, Univ. of London, 1990. Member, Scottish Cert. of Educn Examination Board, 1964; Member Academic Planning Board, University of Stirling, 1964–67; Mem. Cttee on Research and Develt in Modern Languages, 1966. Pres., MHRA, 1986. Doctor of Univ. of Paris, 1950; Dr *hc*, Univ. of Tours, 1982; Hon. DLitt St Andrews, 1982. Officier des Palmes Académiques, 1971. *Publications:* critical edn of M. Scève's Délie, 1966; Renaissance France 1470–1589, 1974; Buchanan, 1981; The Entry of Henri II into Paris, 1549, 1982; various, in learned periodicals. *Recreations:* cricket, music. *Address:* Wadham College, Oxford OX1 3PN.

MACFARLANE, Ian John; Governor, Reserve Bank of Australia, since 1996; *b* 22 June 1946; *s* of Gordon H. and Lilias E. M. Macfarlane; *m* 1970; one *s* one *d*. *Educ:* Monash Univ. Inst. of Econs and Stats, Oxford Univ., 1971–72; OECD, Paris, 1973–78; Reserve Bank of Australia, 1979–: various posts, 1979–88; Head, Res. Dept, 1988–90; Asst Gov. (Economic), 1990–92; Dep. Gov., 1992–96. *Address:* Reserve Bank of Australia, 65 Martin Place, Sydney, NSW 2000, Australia. *T:* (2) 95519507, *Fax:* (2) 95518030; GPO Box 3947, Sydney, NSW 2001, Australia; *e-mail:* rbainfo@rba.gov.au.

McFARLANE, James Sinclair, CBE 1986; CEng, FIM; CIMgt; Director General, Engineering Employers' Federation, 1982–89; *b* 8 Nov. 1925; *s* of John Mills McFarlane and Hannah McFarlane; *m* 1951, Ruth May Harden; three *d*. *Educ:* Manchester Grammar Sch.; Emmanuel Coll., Cambridge (MA, PhD). CEng, FIM 1961. ICI Ltd, 1949–53; Henry Wiggin & Co. Ltd, 1953–69; Chm. and Man. Dir, Smith-Clayton Forge Ltd (GKN Ltd), 1969–76; Man. Dir, Garringtons Ltd (GKN Ltd), 1976–77; Guest Keen & Nettlefolds Ltd: Gen. Man., Personnel, 1977–79; Exec. Dir, 1979–82. Mem., NEDC, 1982–89; a Civil Service Comr (pt-time), 1983–88. *Publications:* contrib. scientific and technical jls. *Recreation:* music. *Address:* 24 Broad Street, Ludlow, Shropshire SY8 1NJ. *T:* (01584) 872495. *Club:* Caledonian.

MACFARLANE, Sir Neil; *see* Macfarlane, Sir D. N.

MacFARLANE, Neil; *see* MacFarlane, S. N.

MacFARLANE, Maj.-Gen. Robert Goudie, MBE 1952; FRCP; FRCPE; Deputy Secretary, Scottish Council for Postgraduate Medical Education, 1975–84; *b* 1 March 1917; *s* of late Archibald Forsyth MacFarlane and Jessie Robertson Goudie; *m* 1945, Mary Campbell Martin; three *s*. *Educ:* Hillhead High Sch., Glasgow; Glasgow Univ. MB, ChB, 1940; MD 1955; FRCPE 1964; MRCP 1970; FRCP 1979. Served War: commissioned RAMC, 1941; in Madagascar, India, Burma, 1941–45. Specialist in Medicine and Consultant Physician, 1948–; CO, British Mil. Hosp., Iserlohn, 1968–70; Prof. of Mil. Med., Royal Army Medical Coll., 1970–71; Consulting Physician, BAOR, 1971–73. Dir. of Army Medicine and Consulting Physician to the Army, 1973–74. QHP 1973. *Address:* 6 Redholm, Greenheads Road, North Berwick, East Lothian EH39 4RA.

MacFARLANE, Prof. (Stephen) Neil, DPhil; Lester B. Pearson Professor of International Relations, and Fellow of St Anne's College, University of Oxford, since 1996; Director, Centre for International Studies, Oxford, since 1997; *b* 7 March 1954; *s* of David Livingstone MacFarlane and Gertrude Cecile (*née* Straight); *m* 1981, Anne Church Bigelow; three *s* one *d*. *Educ:* Dartmouth Coll., NH (AB); Balliol Coll., Oxford (MA, MPhil, DPhil 1982). University of Virginia, USA: Asst Prof., 1984–87; Associate Prof., 1987–91; Dir, Center for Russian and E European Studies, 1990–91; Queen's University, Kingston, Ontario: Prof. of Political Studies, 1991–96; Dir, Centre for Internat. Relns, 1995–96. *Publications:* Intervention and Regional Security, 1985; The Idea of National Liberation, 1985; Western Engagement in the Caucasus and Central Asia, 1999; Politics and Humanitarian Action, 2000; articles in Internat. Affairs, Internat. Jl, Survival, Post-Soviet Affairs, World Politics, Security Studies, Third World Qly. *Recreations:* cross-country ski-ing, walking, skating. *Address:* St Anne's College, Oxford OX2 6HS. *T:* (01865) 274800.

MACFARLANE, Maj.-Gen. William Thomson, CB 1981; Consultant/Administrator, Sion College, 1984–93; *b* Bath, 2 Dec. 1925; *s* of late James and Agnes Macfarlane; *m* 1955, Dr Helen D. Meredith; one *d*. Commissioned Royal Signals, 1947. Served Europe, Near East, ME, and Far East. Commanded 16th Parachute Bde Signal Squadron, 1961–63; Military Asst, Commander FARELF, 1964–66; Comd 1st Div. HQ and Signal Regt, BAOR, 1967–70; Services Mem., Cabinet Office Secretariat, 1970–72; Comd, Corps Royal Signals, 1972–73; Dir of Public Relations (Army), MoD, 1973–75; C of S, UKLF, 1976–78; Chief, Jt Services Liaison Organisation, Bonn, 1978–80. Exec. Dir, Hong Kong Resort Co. Ltd, 1981–84; Dir, Compton Manor Estates (formerly Farms) Ltd, 1990–. Col Comdt, 1980–85, Rep. Col Comdt, 1985, Royal Corps of Signals. *Club:* Naval and Military.

MacFARQUHAR, Prof. Roderick Lemonde; Professor of Government, since 1984, Leroy B. Williams Professor of History and Political Science, since 1990, and Chairman, Department of Government, since 1998, Harvard University; *b* 2 Dec. 1930; *s* of Sir Alexander MacFarquhar, KBE, CIE, and of Berenice Whitburn; *m* 1964, Emily Jane Cohen (*d* 2001); one *s* one *d*. *Educ:* Fettes Coll.; Oxford Univ. (BA); Harvard Univ. (AM); LSE (PhD). Specialist on China, Daily Telegraph (and later Sunday Telegraph), 1955–61; Founding Editor, China Quarterly, 1959–68; Rockefeller Grantee, 1962; Reporter, BBC TV programme Panorama, 1963–64. Associate Fellow, St Antony's Coll., Oxford, 1965–68. Mem., Editorial Bd, New Statesman, 1965–69; Ford Foundation Grant, 1968; Senior Research Fellow, Columbia Univ., 1969; Senior Research Fellow, RIIA, 1971–74 (Mem. Council, 1978–83); Co-presenter, BBC Gen. Overseas Services 24 Hours prog., 1972–74, 1979–80. Governor, SOAS, 1978–83; Dir, Fairbank Center for E Asian Res., Harvard Univ., 1986–92. Contested: (Lab) Ealing South, 1966; (Lab) Meriden, March 1968; (SDP) Derbys S, 1983. MP (Lab) Belper, Feb. 1974–1979; PPS to Minister of State, FCO, March 1974; resignation accepted, April 1975; reappointed June 1975; PPS to Sec. of State, DHSS, 1976–78. Member: N Atlantic Assembly, 1974–79; Select Cttee for Sci. and Technology, 1976–79; Trilateral Commn, 1976–98 (Mem. Exec. Cttee, 1976–84); Exec. Cttee, Fabian Soc., 1976–80. Leverhulme Res. Fellow, 1980–83; Fellow: Woodrow Wilson Center, Smithsonian Instn, 1980–81; Amer. Acad. of Arts and Scis, 1986–. Vis. Prof. of Govt, Harvard, 1982; Vis. Fellow, St Antony's Coll., Oxford, 1983; inaugurated: Inchon Meml Lectureship, Korea Univ., 1987; Merle Goldman History Lectureship, Boston Univ., 1997. *Publications:* The Hundred Flowers, 1960; The Sino-Soviet Dispute, 1961; Chinese Ambitions and British Policy (Fabian Pamphlet), 1966; (ed) China under Mao, 1966; Sino-American Relations, 1949–71, 1972; The Forbidden City, 1972; The Origins of the Cultural Revolution: Vol. 1, Contradictions among the People 1956–1957, 1974; Vol. 2, The Great Leap Forward 1958–1960, 1983; Vol. 3, The Coming of the Cataclysm 1961–1966, 1997 (Levenson 20th Century China Prize, Assoc. for Asian Studies, 1999); (ed jtly) Cambridge History of China, Vol. 14, 1987, Vol. 15, 1991; (ed jtly) The Secret Speeches of Chairman Mao, 1989; (ed) The Politics of China 1949–1989, 1993, 2nd edn, as The Politics of China, the Eras of Mao and Deng, 1997; (ed jtly) The Paradox of China's Post-Mao Reforms, 1999; articles in Foreign Affairs, The World Today, Atlantic Monthly, Pacific Affairs, Commentary, Newsweek, NY Review of Books, etc. *Recreations:* reading, listening to music, travel. *Address:* Fairbank Center, 1737 Cambridge Street, Cambridge, MA 02138, USA.

McFEELY, Elizabeth Sarah Anne C.; *see* Craig McFeely.

McFETRICH, (Charles) Alan; Deputy Chairman, Tenon Group PLC, since 2000; Managing Partner, External Affairs, Coopers & Lybrand, 1994–96; *b* 15 Dec. 1940; *s* of late Cecil McFetrich, OBE, FCA and Kathleen M. McFetrich (*née* Proom); *m* 1990, Janet Elizabeth Henkel (*née* Munro); two *s* one *d* from previous *m*. *Educ:* Oundle Sch.; Magdalene Coll., Cambridge. FCA. Trainee Accountant, Graham Proom & Smith, 1959–61 and 1964–66; Deloitte Haskins & Sells: Accountant, 1966–68; Consultant, 1968–73; Consultancy Partner, 1973–80; seconded to Dept of Industry, 1981–82; Nat. Operations Partner, 1983–85; Nat. Managing Partner, 1985–90; Coopers & Lybrand Deloitte, later Coopers & Lybrand: Man. Partner, 1990–92; Exec. Partner, 1992–94. FRSA 1989. *Recreations:* gardening, theatre.

McGAHERN, John, FRSL; author; *b* 12 Nov. 1934; *s* of Francis McGahern and Susan McManus; *m* 1973, Madeline Green. Research Fellow, Univ. of Reading, 1968–71; O'Connor Prof., Colgate Univ., 1969, 1972, 1977, 1979 and 1983. Member: Aosdana Irish Acad of Letters. British Northern Arts Fellow, 1974–76. McCauley Fellowship, 1964; British Arts Council Award, 1967; Soc. of Authors Award, 1975; Amer. Irish Foundn Literary Award, 1985; Irish Times/Aer Lingus Award, 1990; GPA Award, 1992. Hon. LitD TCD, 1991. Chevalier de l'Ordre des Arts et des Lettres (France), 1989. *Publications:* The Barracks, 1962 (AE Meml Award, 1962); The Dark, 1965; Nightlines, 1970; The Leavetaking, 1975; Getting Through, 1978; The Pornographer, 1979; High Ground, 1985; The Rockingham Shoot, 1987; Amongst Women, 1990; The Power of Darkness, 1991; The Collected Stories, 1992. *Address:* c/o Faber & Faber, 3 Queen Square, WC1N 3AU.

McGANN, Prof. Jerome John, PhD; John Stewart Bryan University Professor, University of Virginia, since 1997 (John Stewart Bryan Professor of English, 1987–97); *b* 22 July 1937; *s* of John J. McGann and Marie V. McGann (*née* Lecouffe); *m* 1960, Anne Lanni; two *s* one *d*. *Educ:* Le Moyne Coll. (BS); Syracuse Univ. (MA); Yale Univ. (PhD 1966). Asst Prof., then Prof., Univ. of Chicago, 1966–75; Professor: Johns Hopkins Univ., 1975–81; CIT, 1981–87. Fulbright Fellow, 1965–66; Guggenheim Fellow, 1970–71 and 1976–81; NEH Fellow, 1975–76 and 1987–89. Lectures: Clark, Trinity Coll., Cambridge,

1988; Carpenter, Univ. of Chicago, 1988; Alexander, Univ. of Toronto, 1986; Beckman, Univ. of Calif (Berkeley), 1992; Lansdowne, Univ. of Victoria, 1994; Patten, Indiana Univ., 1995; Byron, Univ. of Nottingham, 1998; Hulme, Univ, of London, 1998. Fellow, Amer. Acad. of Arts and Scis, 1994. Hon. DHL Chicago, 1997. Melville Kane Award, Amer. Poetry Soc., 1973; Distinguished Schol. Award, Byron Soc., 1989; Wilbur Cross Medal, Yale Univ., 1994. *Publications:* Fiery Dust: Byron's poetic development, 1969; (ed) Pelham, or The Adventures of a Gentleman, by Edward Bulwer-Lytton, 1972; Swinburne: an experiment in criticism, 1972; Don Juan in Context, 1976; Air Heart Sermons (poems), 1976; (with J. Kauffman) Writing Home (poems), 1978; (with J. Kahn) Nerves in Patterns (poems), 1979; (ed) Byron: the complete poetical works, Vol. I 1980, Vols II and III 1981, Vols IV and V 1986, Vol. VI 1991, Vol. VII 1993; The Romantic Ideology: a critical investigation, 1983; A Critique of Modern Textual Criticism, 1983, 2nd edn 1992; The Beauty of Inflections: literary investigations in historical method and theory, 1985; (ed) Textual Studies and Literary Interpretation, 1985; (ed jtly) The Manuscripts of the Younger Romantics: Byron, Vol. I 1985, Vol. II 1986, Vols III and IV 1988; (ed) Historical Studies and Literary Criticism, 1985; (ed) The Oxford Authors Byron, 1986; Social Values and Poetic Acts, 1987; Towards a Literature of Knowledge, 1989; (ed) Victorian Connections, 1989; (ed) Postmodern Poetries, 1990; The Textual Condition, 1991; (ed) The New Oxford Book of Romantic Period Verse, 1993; Black Riders: the visible language of modernism, 1993; (ed) A Symposium on Russian Postmodernism, 1993; (ed) Byron: the Oxford poetry library, 1994; Four Last Poems (poems), 1996; Poetics of Sensibility: a revolution in literary style, 1997; Complete Writings and Pictures of Dante Gabriel Rossetti: a hypermedia research archive, 1999; D. G. Rossetti and The Game that Must be Lost, 2000. *Recreation:* squash. *Address:* 555 Spring Lane, Charlottesville, VA 22903, USA. *T:* (804) 9795127.

McGARRITY, J(ames) Forsyth, CB 1981; MA, MEd, BSc; HM Senior Chief Inspector of Schools (Scotland), 1973–81; *b* 16 April 1921; *s* of late James McGarrity and Margaret Davidson; *m* 1951, Violet S. G. Philp, MA; one *s* one *d*. *Educ:* Bathgate Academy; Glasgow Univ. Schoolmaster, 1949–57; HM Inspector of Schools, 1957–68; HM Chief Inspector of Schools, 1968–73. *Recreations:* golf, gardening. *Address:* 30 Oatlands Park, Linlithgow, Scotland EH49 6AS. *T:* (01506) 843258.

McGARRY, Ian; General Secretary, British Actors' Equity Association, since 1991; *b* 27 Feb. 1941; *s* of John and Jean McGarry; *m* 1964, Christine Smith (marr. diss. 1989); one *s*. *Educ:* Chichester High Sch.; Lewes County Grammar Sch. Labour Party Constituency Agent, Putney, 1964–76; Asst General Sec., Equity, 1976–91. *Recreations:* golf, football (spectator), horse racing. *Address:* Guild House, Upper St Martin's Lane, WC2H 9EG. *T:* (020) 7379 6000.

McGARVEY, Alan; independent specialist in economic and industrial development, since 1996; *b* 22 June 1942; *s* of William Johnson McGarvey and Rosina McGarvey; *m* 1st, 1967, Eileen Cook (*d* 1992); 2nd, 1997, Shirlee Ann Gleeson. *Educ:* Wallsend Grammar Sch.; Coll. of Further Educn; Newcastle Univ. (BSc); Cranfield Sch. of Management (MBA). C. A. Parsons, 1958–64 (apprentice); RTZ, 1968–71; Decca Gp, 1972–76; MK Electric, 1976–78; Director, Small Company Div., NEB, 1978–82; Chief Exec., Greater London Enterprise Bd, 1982–86; management consultant, 1986–88; Man. Dir, Greater Manchester Econ. Develt Ltd, 1987–90; regl develt specialist, 1990–93; specialist, Regl and Small and Medium Enterprises Develt, EU Commn, 1993–96 Labour Party, 1974–, Mem., Wandsworth Borough Council, 1981–86 (Dep. Opposition Leader, 1982–83); Chm., Battersea Constituency Labour Parties, 1978–82. Exec. Mem., Wandsworth CRC, 1973–82; Board Member: Battersea Arts Centre Trust, 1982–88; Northern Chamber Orch., 1988–93; Member: Jt Governing Board, Centre for Development of Industry (EEC-ACP Lomé), 1981–90; Adv. Council, Cttee for Industrial Co-operation (EEC-ACP), 1990–96. Governor, Polytech. of South Bank, 1985–87; Chm. Govs, Medlock Sch., Manchester, 1989–91. *Recreations:* home and garden, science fiction; amateur sculptor. *Address:* Willowbank, 9 Anglesey Drive, Poynton SK12 1BT. *T:* (01625) 873869, *Fax:* (01625) 873698; *e-mail:* mcgarvey01@aol.com.

McGARVIE, Hon. Richard Elgin, AC 1994; Governor of Victoria, 1992–97; *b* 21 May 1926; *s* of Richard Fleming McGarvie and Mabel Catherine McGarvie; *m* 1953, Lesley, *d* of K. G. and G. D. Kerr; two *s* two *d*. *Educ:* Camperdown High Sch.; Univ. of Melbourne (LLB Hons, BCom). AB, RAustNR, 1944–46. Admitted Victorian Bar, 1952; QC 1963; Judge, Supreme Court of Victoria, 1976–92. Mem., Law Faculty, Melbourne Univ., 1957–88. Chm., Nat. Cttee on Discrimination in Employment and Occupation, 1973–76; Member: Adv. Cttee on Aust. Judicial System, Constitutional Commn, 1985–87; Constitutional Convention on Republic, 1998. Chm., Victorian Bar Council, 1973–75; Treas., Exec. Law Council of Aust., 1974–76; Dep. Chm., then Chm., Aust. Inst. of Judicial Admin, 1980–86 (Mem., 1976–). Mem. Council, Monash Univ., 1980; Chancellor, La Trobe Univ., 1981–92. Hon. LLD Melbourne, 1990; Monash, 1997; DUniv La Trobe, 1995. *Publications:* (jtly) Cases and Materials on Contract, 1962, 4 edns; Democracy: choosing Australia's republic, 1999; papers on law, judiciary, governorship, and head of state/republican issue; author of McGarvie model for head of state in Australia. *Recreations:* reading, sailing, golf. *Address:* 1/62 Grange Road, Sandringham, Vic 3191, Australia. *T:* (3) 95216802. *Clubs:* Royal Automobile, West Brighton (Victoria); Melbourne Cricket.

McGEE, Prof. James O'Donnell, FMedSci; Professor of Morbid Anatomy, University of Oxford, 1975–99, now Emeritus; Fellow of Linacre College, Oxford, since 1975; *b* 27 July 1939; *s* of Michael and Bridget McGee; *m* 1961, Anne Lee; one *s* two *d*. *Educ:* Univ. of Glasgow. MB, ChB, PhD, MD; MA (Oxon). FRCPath 1986; FRCPGlas 1989. Various appts in Univ. Dept of Pathology, Royal Infirmary, Glasgow, 1962–69; Roche Inst. of Molecular Biology, Nutley, NJ: MRC Fellow 1969–70; Vis. Scientist 1970–71; Distinguished Vis. Scientist, 1981 and 1989; Dept of Pathology, Royal Infirmary, Glasgow: Lectr 1971–74; Sen. Lectr, 1974–75. Member: Scientific Cttee, 1978–88, Grants Cttee, 1988–92, Cancer Res. Campaign; Cttee on Safety of Medicines, 1987–89 (Safety and Efficacy Sub Cttee, 1984–87); Kettle Meml Lectr, RCPath, 1980; Annual Guest Lecturer: Royal Coll. of Physicians, Ireland, 1986; Royal Acad. of Medicine (Ireland), 1985. Founder FMedSci 1998. Bellahouston Gold Medal, Glasgow Univ., 1973. *Publications:* Biopsy Pathology of Liver, 1980, 2nd edn 1988; In Situ Hybridisation: principles and practice, 1990; Oxford Textbook of Pathology, 1992: vol. 1, Principles of Pathology, vols 2a, 2b, Pathology of Systems; The Natural Immune System: The Macrophage, 1992; The Natural Killer Cell, 1992; Diagnostic Molecular Pathology, vols 1 and 2, 1992; papers in scientific jls on liver disease, breast and cervical cancers, telematics/telepathology in health care. *Recreations:* talking with my family, swimming. *Address:* Linacre College, Oxford OX1 3JA.

McGEGAN, (James) Nicholas; Music Director: Philharmonia Baroque Orchestra, San Franciso, since 1985; Irish Chamber Orchestra, 2001; Artistic Director, Göttingen Handel Festival, Germany, since 1991; *b* 14 Jan. 1950; *s* of late (James Edward) Peter McGegan and Christine Mary McGegan (*née* Collier). *Educ:* Corpus Christi, Cambridge (BA, MA); Magdalen Coll., Oxford. LTCL 1969. Royal College of Music: Prof., 1973–79; Dir, Early Music, 1976–80; Artist-in-Residence, Washington Univ., St Louis, Mo, 1979–85; Principal Conductor, Drottningholm Court Th., Sweden, 1993–96 (Vänners Hederstecken, 1996); Principal Guest Conductor, Scottish Opera, 1993–98. Baroque series Dir, St Paul Chamber Orch., 1999. Hon. RCM 1978. Has made numerous recordings, incl. opera and oratorios. Handel Prize, Halle, Germany, 1993. *Publication:* (ed) Philidor, Tom Jones, 1978. *Recreations:* history, cooking, good wine. *Address:* 722 Wildcat Canyon Road, Berkeley, CA 94708, USA. *T:* (510) 5280862; 1 Kew Terrace, Glasgow G12 0TD. *T:* (0141) 339 0786. *Clubs:* East India, Savile.

McGEOCH, Prof. Duncan James, PhD; FRSE; Director, Medical Research Council Virology Unit, Glasgow, since 1995; *b* 13 Sept. 1944; *s* of Peter and Christine McGeoch; *m* 1971, Jennifer A. Wylie; two *s*. *Educ:* Hutchesons' Grammar Sch., Glasgow; Univ. of Glasgow (BSc 1967; PhD 1971). FRSE 1987. Jane Coffin Childs Postdoctoral Fellow, Dept of Microbiology and Molecular Genetics, Harvard Med. Sch., 1971–73; Researcher, Virology Div., Dept of Pathology, Univ. of Cambridge, 1973–76; Mem. of Scientific Staff, MRC Virology Unit, Glasgow, 1976–95. Hon. Prof., Univ. of Glasgow, 1996–. Editor-in-Chief, Jl of General Virology, 1988–92. Fleming Award, Soc. for Gen. Microbiology, 1980. *Publications:* scientific papers. *Recreations:* reading, mountains and sea, ski-ing, walking, sailing.

McGEOCH, Vice-Adm. Sir Ian (Lachlan Mackay), KCB 1969 (CB 1966); DSO 1943; DSC 1943; Director, Midar Systems Ltd, since 1986; *b* 26 March 1914; 3rd *s* of L. A. McGeoch; *m* 1937, Eleanor Somers, *d* of Rev. Canon Hugh Farrie; two *s* two *d*. *Educ:* Pangbourne Coll. Joined RN, 1931. Comd HM Submarine Splendid, 1942–43; Staff Officer (Ops) 4th Cruiser Sqdn, 1944–45; Comd: HMS Fernie, 1946–47; 4th Submarine Squadron, 1949–51; 3rd Submarine Squadron, 1956–57; Dir of Undersurface Warfare, Admiralty, 1959; IDC 1961; Comd HMS Lion 1962–64; Admiral Pres., RNC, Greenwich, 1964–65; Flag Officer Submarines, 1965–67; Flag Officer, Scotland and Northern Ireland, 1968–70. Trustee, Imperial War Mus., 1977–87. Member: The Queen's Body Guard for Scotland, Royal Co. of Archers, 1969–; Hon. Co. of Master Mariners, 1999–. MPhil Edinburgh, 1975. FNI 1986. Editor, The Naval Review, 1972–80. *Publications:* (jtly) The Third World War: a future history, 1978; (jtly) The Third World War: the untold story, 1982; An Affair of Chances, 1991; The Princely Sailor, 1996. *Recreations:* sailing, the arts. *Address:* Hill House, High Street, Ixworth, Bury St Edmunds, Suffolk IP31 2HN. *Clubs:* Army and Navy, Special Forces; Royal Yacht Squadron, Royal Naval Sailing Association (Cdre 1968–70), Royal Cruising, Royal Harwich Yacht.

McGEOUGH, Prof. Joseph Anthony, CEng, FIMechE, FIEE; Regius Professor of Engineering, University of Edinburgh, since 1983 (Head, Department of Mechanical Engineering, 1983–91); *b* 29 May 1940; *s* of late Patrick Joseph McGeough and Gertrude (*née* Darroch); *m* 1972, Brenda Nicholson; two *s* one *d*. *Educ:* St Michael's Coll., Irvine; Glasgow Univ. (BSc, PhD); Aberdeen Univ. (DSc). Vacation-apprentice, Malcolm & Allan Ltd, 1957–61; Research Demonstrator, Leicester Univ., 1966; Sen. Res. Fellow, Queensland Univ., 1967; Res. Metallurgist, International Research & Development Co. Ltd, Newcastle upon Tyne, 1968–69; Sen. Res. Fellow, Strathclyde Univ., 1969–72; Lectr 1972–77, Sen. Lectr 1977–80, Reader 1980–83, Dept of Engineering, Aberdeen Univ. Royal Society/SERC Industrial Fellow, 1987–89; Hon. Prof., Nanjing Univ. of Aeronautics and Astronautics, 1992–; Visiting Professor: Univ. degli Studi di Napoli Federico II, 1994; Glasgow Caledonian Univ., 1997–. Chm., Scottish Br., IMechE, 1993–95 (Chm., Edinburgh and SE Scotland Panel, 1988–92); Mem. Council, IMechE, 2000–. Chm., CIRP UK Bd, 2000–. Hon. Vice-Pres., Aberdeen Univ. Athletic Assoc., 1981–. Editor, Processing of Advanced Materials, 1991–94; CIRP Ed., Jl of Materials Processing Technol., 1995–. FRSE 1990. *Publications:* Principles of Electrochemical Machining, 1974; Advanced Methods of Machining, 1988; (ed) Micromachining of Engineering Materials, 2001; papers mainly in Journal of Mech. Engrg Science; contrib. Encyclopaedia Britannica, Encyclopaedia of Electrochemistry. *Recreations:* golf, hill-walking. *Address:* 39 Dreghorn Loan, Colinton, Edinburgh EH13 0DF. *T:* (0131) 441 1302.

McGEOWN, Prof. Mary Graham, (Mrs J. M. Freeland), CBE 1985; FRCP, FRCPE, FRCPI; Professorial Fellow, Queen's University of Belfast, since 1988; *b* 19 July 1923; *d* of James Edward McGeown and Sarah Graham Quinn; *m* 1949, Joseph Maxwell Freeland (*d* 1982); three *s*. *Educ:* Lurgan College; Queen's University of Belfast (MB, BCh, BAO, with hons, 1946; MD, PhD). House Physician and Surgeon, Royal Victoria Hosp., Belfast, 1947–48; Sen. House Physician, Royal Belfast Hosp. for Sick Children, 1948; Asst Lectr in Pathology, 1948–50, in Biochemistry, 1950–53, QUB; res. grant, MRC, 1953–56; Res. Fellow, Royal Victoria Hosp., 1956–58; Belfast City Hospital: Sen. Hosp. MO, 1958–62; Consultant Nephrologist, 1962–88; Physician in Admin. Charge, Renal Unit, 1968–88. Hon. Reader in Nephrology, QUB, 1972–87. Chm., UK Transplant Management Cttee, 1983–90; Hon. Treas., Renal Assoc., 1986–89 (Pres., 1983–86); Pres., Ulster Med. Soc., 1985–86. Chm., Corrigan Club, 1987. Mem., Unrelated Living Transplant Regulatory Authority, 1990–96; Hon. Member: British Transplantation Soc.; Eur. Dialysis Transplant Assoc.; Eur. Renal Assoc. Lectures: Graves, Royal Acad. of Medicine, Ireland, 1963; Corrigan, 1987, J. Creery Ferguson, 1997, RCPI. Hon. DSc New Univ. of Ulster, 1983; Hon. DMSc QUB, 1991. *Publications:* Clinical Management of Electrolyte Disorders, 1983; Clinical Management of Renal Transplantation, 1992; numerous papers and chapters in books on calcium metabolism, renal stones, phosphate metabolism, parathyroid function and disease, renal transplantation, kidney diseases. *Recreations:* gardening, antique collecting, genealogy. *Address:* 14 Osborne Gardens, Belfast BT9 6LE. *T:* (028) 9080 2934.

McGHEE, George Crews; Legion of Merit; businessman; former diplomat; Director: Mobil Oil Co., 1969–82; Procter and Gamble Co., 1969–82; American Security & Trust Co., 1969–82; Trans World Airlines, 1976–82; *b* Waco, Texas, 10 March 1912; *s* of George Summers McGhee and Magnolia (*née* Spruce); *m* 1938, Cecilia Jeanne DeGolyer; two *s* four *d*. *Educ:* Southern Methodist Univ., Dallas; Univ. of Oklahoma; Oxford Univ. (Rhodes Schol.); Univ. of London. BS (Oklahoma) 1933; DPhil (Oxon) 1937. Served with US Navy, 1943–45 (Asiatic ribbon with three battle stars). Geologist and geophysicist, 1930–40; Oil producer, sole owner, McGhee Production Co., 1940–. Special Asst to Under-Sec of State for Economic Affairs, 1946; Coordinator for Aid to Greece and Turkey, 1947; Asst Sec. of State for Near Eastern, South Asian and African Affairs, 1949; US Ambassador to Turkey, 1951–53; Consultant, Nat. Security Council, 1958; Mem. President's Cttee to Study Mil. Asst Program, 1958; Counselor of Dept of State and Chm. of State Dept Policy Planning Council, 1961; Under-Sec. of State for Political Affairs, 1961; Bd, Panama Canal Co., 1962; Actg Sec., Cuban Missile Crisis, Oct. 1963; US Ambassador to the Federal Republic of Germany, 1963–68; Ambassador-at-Large, 1968–69. Chairman: English Speaking Union of US, 1969–74; Business Council for Internat. Understanding, 1969–73; Vice-Chm., Inst. for Study of Diplomacy, 1978–; Member Board: Geo. C. Marshall Res. Foundn, 1972–85; German–American Cultural Fund, 1992–; Amer. Council on Germany, 1969–86; Resources for Future, 1977–82; Asia Foundn, 1974–84; Atlantic Council, 1975–; Atlantic Inst. for Internat. Affairs, 1977–88;

Smithsonian Nat. Associates, 1971– (Chm., 1975–76); Population Crisis Cttee, 1969–82; Council of Amer. Ambassadors, 1983–; Amer. Inst. for Contemp. German Studies, 1983–; Nat. Tree Trust, 1992–; President's Circle, Nat. Acad. of Scis, 1989–; Circle, Nat. Gall. of Art, 1991–; Carnegie Council, 1990–; Council for Econ. Develt Sub-cttee on Global Econ. Strategy for US, 1991–. Member: Inst. of Turkish Studies, 1983–86; Sackler Gall. Vis. Cttee, Smithsonian Instn. Trustee: Duke Univ.; Cttee for Economic Develt, 1957–72; Aspen Inst. for Humanistic Studies, 1958–; Salzburg Seminar, 1969–71; Nat. Civil Service League, 1969–71; Folger Library Council, 1983–85. Chm., Saturday Review World, 1974–77. Mem., Amer. Philos. Soc., 1993–. Hon. Fellow, Queen's Coll., Oxford, 1969. Distinguished Service Citation, Univ. of Oklahoma, 1952; Hon. DCL, Southern Methodist Univ., 1953; Hon. LLD: Tulane Univ., 1957; Univ. of Maryland, 1965; Hon. DSc, Univ. of Tampa, 1969. Ouissam Alaouite Cherifien, Govt Morocco, 1950; Hon. Citizen, Ankara, Turkey, 1954; Outstanding Citizen Award, Amer. Friends of Turkey, 1983. *Publications:* Envoy to the Middle World, 1983; (ed) Diplomacy for the Future, 1987; At the Creation of a New Germany, 1989; (ed) National Interest and Global Goals, 1989; The US-Turkish-NATO Middle East Connection, 1990; Dance of the Billions, 1990; International Community: a goal for a New World Order, 1992; Life in Alanya: Turkish delight, 1992; On the Frontline in the Cold War—an Ambassador Reports, 1997; I Did It This Way, 2001; The Ambassador, 2001; contribs to Foreign Affairs, Gewerkschaftliche Rundschau, Werk und Wir, Europa Archiv, Universitas, Ruperto-Carola Weltraumfahrt-Raketentechnik, Europa, Washington Post, New York Times, etc. *Recreations:* hunting, tennis, photography. *Address:* Farmer's Delight, 36276 Mountville Road, Middleburg, VA 20117–3308, USA. *Clubs:* Bohemian (California); Metropolitan, Cosmos (Washington, DC); Century Association (New York).

McGHIE, Hon. Lord; James Marshall McGhie; Chairman, Scottish Land Court, since 1996; President, Lands Tribunal for Scotland, since 1996; *b* 15 Oct. 1944; *s* of James Drummond McGhie and Jessie Eadie Bennie; *m* 1968, Ann Manuel Cockburn; one *s* one *d*. *Educ:* Perth Acad.; Edinburgh Univ. (LLB Hons). Called to the Scottish Bar, 1969; QC (Scot.) 1983; Advocate-depute, 1983–86. Pt-time Chm., Medical Appeal Tribunal, 1987–92; Mem., Criminal Injuries Compensation Bd, 1992–96. *Recreations:* various. *Address:* 3 Lauder Road, Edinburgh EH9 2EW. *T:* (0131) 667 8325.

McGHIE, James Marshall; *see* McGhie, Hon. Lord.

MacGIBBON, Dr Barbara Haig, (Mrs John Roberts), CB 1988; FRCPath; Chairman, Commission on Environmental Health, 1996–97; Assistant Director (Medical), National Radiological Protection Board, 1988–93; *b* 7 Feb. 1928; *d* of Ronald Ross MacGibbon and Margaret Fraser; *m* 1954, John Roberts; one *s* one *d*. *Educ:* Lady Margaret Hall, Oxford; University College Hosp. Registrar, then Res. Assistant, Dept of Haematology, Royal Postgraduate Med. Sch., 1957–64; Sen. Registrar, Sen. Lectr/Hon. Consultant, then Sen. Res. Fellow, Dept of Haematology, St Thomas' Hosp. Med. Sch., 1969–79; SMO, then PMO, Toxicology and Environmental Health, DHSS, 1979; SPMO, DHSS, 1983–88. Chm., Panel on Energy, WHO Commn on Health and Envmt, 1990–92; Consultant, MRC Inst. for Envmt and Health, 1994–97. *Publications:* (ed) Concern for Europe's Tomorrow: health and environment in the WHO European region, 1995; articles in various med. jls.

McGILL, Angus, MBE 1990; journalist; *b* 26 Nov. 1927; *s* of Kenneth and Janet McGill. *Educ:* Warehousemen, Clerks' and Drapers' Schools, Addington, Surrey. Reporter, Shields Gazette, 1944; Army service; feature writer, Evening Chronicle, Newcastle, 1948; Londoner's Diary, Evening Standard, 1957; columnist, Evening Standard, 1961–92. Chm., Knobs & Knockers, 1964–77. British Press Award, descriptive writer of the Year, 1968. *Publications:* Augusta, comic strip (drawn by Dominic Poelsma), 1968–; Yea Yea Yea (novel), 1969; (with Kenneth Thomson) Live Wires, 1982; London Pub Guide, annually 1995–97. *Address:* 83 Winchester Court, Vicarage Gate, W8 4AF. *T:* (020) 7937 2166.

MACGILL, Kerry Michael Peter; His Honour Judge Macgill; a Circuit Judge, since 2000; *b* 30 April 1950; *s* of Alan and Betty Macgill; *m* 1973, Janet Hazeldine; one *s* one *d*. *Educ:* Holborn Coll. of Law (LLB Hons London, 1971). Asst Solicitor, T. I. Clough & Co., 1975–77; Partner, Lumb & Kenningham, which later became Lumb & Macgill, criminal law practice, 1977–2000. *Recreations:* walking, golf, sailing. *Address:* Leeds Combined Court Centre, 1 Oxford Row, Leeds LS1 3BG.

McGILL, Maj.-Gen. Nigel Harry Duncan, CB 1966; Chief of Staff to Commandant-General, Royal Marines, 1967–68, retired, 1968; *b* 15 Oct. 1916; *s* of Lt-Col H. R. McGill; *m* 1944, Margaret Constance Killen; two *s* one *d*. *Educ:* Victoria Coll., Jersey. Commissioned 2nd Lt RM 1934; Maj.-Gen. 1964; Comdr, Portsmouth Group, RM, 1964–67. Representative Col Comdt RM, 1977–78. Exec., Rolls Royce Ltd, 1968–78. *Recreation:* golf. *Address:* Alderwood, Manor Farm Road, Fordingbridge, Hants SP6 1DY.

McGILL, Rt Rev. Stephen; Bishop of Paisley, (RC), 1968–88, now Bishop Emeritus; *b* Glasgow, 4 Jan. 1912; *s* of Peter McGill and Charlotte Connolly. *Educ:* St Aloysius', Glasgow; Blairs College, Aberdeen; Coutances, France; Institut Catholique, Paris (STL). Ordained Priest of St Sulpice, 1936. St Mary's College, Blairs, Aberdeen: Spiritual Director, 1940–51; Rector, 1951–60; Bishop of Argyll and the Isles, 1960–68. *Address:* 13 Newark Street, Greenock PA16 7UH.

MacGILLIVRAY, Barron Bruce, FRCP; Consultant in Clinical Neurophysiology and Neurology, Royal Free Hospital, 1964–93 (Dean, School of Medicine, 1975–89); Consultant in Clinical Neurophysiology, National Hospital for Nervous Diseases, 1971–93; *b* 21 Aug. 1927; *s* of late John MacGillivray and of Doreene (*née* Eastwood), S Africa; *m* 1955, Ruth Valentine; two *s* one *d*. *Educ:* King Edward VII Sch., Johannesburg; Univ. of Witwatersrand (BSc Hons 1949); Univ. of Manchester; Univ. of London (MB, BS 1962). FRCP 1973. House Surg., House Phys., Manchester Royal Infirm., 1955–56; RMO, Stockport and Stepping Hill Hosp., 1957–59; Registrar, subseq. Sen. Registrar, Nat. Hosp. for Nervous Diseases, Queen Sq., London, 1959–64; Res. Fellow, UCLA, 1964–65. Pro-Vice Chancellor, Medicine, Univ. of London, 1985–87. Member: Camden and Islington AHA(T), 1975–78; NE Thames RHA, 1979–84; CVCP, 1983–87; Senate, Collegiate Council, Univ. of London; Univ. rep., Council, Sch. of Pharmacy, St George's Hosp. Med. Sch. (Treasurer, 1996–2000), and British Postgraduate Med. Fedn; Examr and Teacher, Univ. of London. Mem., Complaints Review Cttee, DHSS, 1993–94. Pres., Electrophys. Technicians Assoc., 1976–82. MRI 1975; FRSocMed; FRSA. *Publications:* papers in sci. jls on cerebral electrophysiol., epilepsy, computing and cerebral death. *Recreations:* sailing, photography. *Address:* 21 The Avenue, Wraysbury, Staines TW19 5EY. *T:* (01784) 482304.

MacGILLIVRAY, Prof. Ian, MD, FRCP; FRCOG; Regius Professor of Obstetrics and Gynæcology, University of Aberdeen, 1965–84 (Dean of Medical Faculty, 1976–79), now Emeritus Professor; *b* 25 Oct. 1920; *yr s* of W. and A. MacGillivray; *m* 1950, Edith Mary Margaret Cook; one *s* twin *d*. *Educ:* Vale of Leven Academy, Alexandria; University of Glasgow (MB, ChB 1944; MD 1953); MRCOG 1949, FRCOG 1959; FRCPGlas 1973. Gardiner Research Schol., 1949–51, Lectr in Midwifery, 1951–53, Univ. of Glasgow; Senior Lecturer: in Obstetrics and Gynæcology, Univ. of Bristol, 1953–55; in Midwifery and Gynæcology, Univ. of Aberdeen, 1955–61; Prof. of Obstetrics and Gynæcology, University of London, at St Mary's Hospital Medical Sch., 1961–65. Mem., GMC, 1979–84. Founder Pres., Internat. Soc. for Study of Hypertension in Pregnancy, 1976–80; Pres., Internat. Soc. for Twin Studies, 1980–83; Mem. Council, RCOG, 1974–80. *Publications:* Outline of Human Reproduction, 1963; Combined Textbook of Obstetrics and Gynaecology, 1976; Human Multiple Reproduction, 1976; Pre-eclampsia: the hypertensive disease of pregnancy, 1983; contrib. to: British Medical Journal, Lancet, Journal of Obstetrics and Gynæcology of the British Empire; Clinical Science. *Address:* Errogie, 35A Coombe Lane, Stoke Bishop, Bristol BS9 2BL. *T:* (0117) 940 0478.

McGILLIVRAY, Robert, CEng, FICE, FCIWEM; Chairman, Fisheries Committee for Hydro-Electric Schemes, Scotland, 1992–March 2002; Chief Engineer and Under Secretary, Scottish Development Department, 1987–91; *b* 11 May 1931; *o s* of late William Gilchrist McGillivray and of Janet Love Jamieson; *m* 1955, Pauline, *e d* of late Alexander Davie; one *s*. *Educ:* Boroughmuir Sch., Edinburgh; Univ. of Edinburgh (BSc CivEng.). National Service, 1949–51. Training with J. & A. Leslie & Reid, CE, 1955–57; Asst Engr, Midlothian CC, 1957–60; CE, Dept of Agric. & Fisheries for Scotland, 1960–72; Scottish Development Department: Prin. CE, 1972–75; Engrg Inspector, 1976–80; Asst Chief Engr, 1980–85; Dep. Chief Engr, 1985–87. *Publication:* A History of the Clan MacGillivray (with George B. Macgillivray), 1973. *Recreations:* music, genealogy, Highland history. *Address:* Fairview, 88/3 Barnton Park View, Edinburgh EH4 6HJ. *T:* (0131) 339 1667.

McGIMPSEY, Michael; Member (UU) Belfast South, since 1998, and Minister of Culture, Arts and Leisure, since 1999, Northern Ireland Assembly; *b* 1 July 1948; *s* of Henry and Isabel McGimpsey; *m* 1970, Maureen Elisabeth Speers; one *s* one *d*. *Educ:* Regent House Grammar Sch.; Trinity Coll., Dublin (BA 1970). Mem. (UU), Belfast CC, 1993–2001. *Recreations:* reading, gardening, walking. *T:* (028) 9181 3948.

McGINLEY, Aideen, OBE 2000; Permanent Secretary, Department of Culture, Arts and Leisure, Northern Ireland Assembly, since 1999; *b* 31 May 1954; *d* of Joseph Slevin and Terry Slevin (*née* O'Brien); *m* 1975, James McGinley; two *s* one *d*. *Educ:* Salford Univ. (BSc Hons Envmtl Sci. 1975); Univ. of Ulster (MSc Social Policy, Admin and Planning 1983). Community Services Officer: Fermanagh DC, 1976; Strabane DC, 1976–89; Fermanagh District Council: Principal Officer, Policy and Planning, 1989–92; Dir of Develt, 1992–95; Chief Exec., 1995–2000. DUniv Ulster, 1998. *Recreation:* family. *Address:* Department of Culture, Arts and Leisure, Interpoint, 20–24 York Street, Belfast BT15 1AQ. *T:* (028) 9025 8820.

McGINTY, Lawrence Stanley; Health and Science Editor, ITN, since 1989 (Science Editor, 1987–89); *b* 2 July 1948; *s* of Lawrence McGinty and Hilda (*née* Hardman); *m* 1969, Joan Allen. *Educ:* Stand Grammar Sch., Whitefield, Bury; Liverpool Univ. (BSc Zoology). Asst Editor, Chemistry in Britain, 1971–72; Technology Editor, then Health and Safety Editor, later News Editor, New Scientist, 1972–82; Science Correspondent, Channel 4 News, 1982–87. Guest Lectr, Ecole Polytechnique, 1984. Special Advisor: WHO, 2000; IAEA, 2001. Silver Jubilee Medal, 1977. *Recreations:* fine wine, books, walking. *Address:* ITN, 200 Gray's Inn Road, WC1X 8XZ. *T:* (020) 74304290.

McGIRR, Prof. Edward McCombie, CBE 1978; BSc, MD Glasgow; FRCP, FRCPE, FRCPGlas; FACP (Hon.); FFCM; FRSE; Dean, 1974–81, Administrative Dean, 1978–81, and Professor of Administrative Medicine, 1978–81 now Professor Emeritus, Faculty of Medicine, University of Glasgow; Dean of Faculties, University of Glasgow, 1992–94; Physician, Glasgow Royal Infirmary, 1952–81; Honorary Consultant Physician to the Army in Scotland, 1975–81; *b* 15 June 1916; *yr s* of William and Ann McGirr, Hamilton, Lanarkshire; *m* 1949, Diane Curzon (*d* 1996), *y c* of Alexander Woods, MBE, TD, DL, and Edith E. C. Woods, Birmingham and London; one *s* three *d*. *Educ:* Hamilton Academy; Glasgow Univ. BSc 1937; MB, ChB (Hons) Glasgow, 1940; MD (Hons) and Bellahouston Medal, 1960. Served RAMC, 1941–46, in UK, India, Burma, Siam, Indo-China; Medical Specialist; demobilized with hon. rank of Major. Glasgow University: various appointments incl. Lectr and Sen. Lectr in Medicine, at Royal Infirmary, Glasgow, 1947–61; Muirhead Prof. of Medicine, 1961–78. Visitor, Royal Coll. of Physicians and Surgeons of Glasgow, 1968–70, President 1970–72. Member: Medical Appeals Tribunals, 1961–88; Nat. Radiological Protection Bd, 1976–83; Scottish Health Service Planning Council, 1977–84 (Chm., 1978–84); Nat. Med. Consultative Cttee, 1977–81; Med. Sub-Cttee, UGC, 1977–81; GNC for Scotland, 1978–83; Greater Glasgow Health Bd, 1979–85; Nat. Bd for Nursing, Midwifery and Health Visiting for Scotland, 1980–83; Cttee of ten, Tenovus-Scotland, 1981–89; BBC/IBA Scottish Appeals Adv. Cttee, 1982–86; Chairman: Scottish Council for Postgrad. Med. Educn, 1979–85; Scottish Council for Opportunities for Play Experience, 1985–87; Professional Adv. Panel, Prince and Princess of Wales Hospice, 1985–87; Working Party on Play in Scotland, 1986–87; Clyde Estuary Amenity Council, 1986–90. Member: Assoc. of Physicians of Gt Britain and Ireland, 1955– (mem. of editorial panel, Quarterly Journal of Medicine, 1968–76; Mem. Council, 1972–76; Hon. Mem., 1990–); Scottish Soc. of Physicians; Scottish Soc. for Experimental Med. (Treas., 1960–66); Pres., Harveian Soc. of Edin., 1979; Corresp. Member: Amer. Thyroid Assoc.; Medical Research Soc. (mem. of council, 1967–69); Royal Medico-Chirurgical Soc. of Glasgow (Pres., 1965–66). Hon. DSc Glasgow, 1994. *Publications:* chiefly in relation to thyroid gland dysfunction, nuclear medicine, medical education, policy planning in the NHS, and 18th century medical history. *Recreations:* family life, curling. *Address:* Anchorage House, Bothwell, by Glasgow G71 8NF. *T:* (01698) 852194. *Club:* Royal Scottish Automobile.

McGIVERN, Eugene, CB 1997; Member, Civil Service Appeal Board, since 1998; Under Secretary, Board of Inland Revenue, 1986–98; *b* 15 Sept. 1938; *s* of late James and Eileen McGivern; *m* 1960, Teresa Doran; two *s* one *d*. *Educ:* St Mary's Grammar School, Belfast. Joined Inland Revenue, 1955; seconded to Welsh Office as Private Sec. to Minister of State, 1967–69; Inland Revenue, 1969–98.

McGLADE, Prof. Jacqueline Myriam, PhD; NERC Professor, Department of Mathematics, University College London, since 2000; *b* 30 May 1955; *d* of Bryan Maurice Cox and Maria Alphonsonia (*née* LeClair); *m* 1977, James McGlade (marr. diss. 1994); two *d*. *Educ:* UCNW (BSc; Hon. Fellow, Univ. of Wales, 1999); Univ. of Guelph, Canada (PhD 1981). FRICS 1989. Sen. Res. Scientist, Federal Govt of Canada, 1981–87; Adrian Fellow, Darwin Coll., Cambridge, 1987–90; Associate Prof., Cranfield Inst. of Technology, 1987–88; Schol., Internat. Fedn of Insts of Advanced Studies, Maastricht, 1988–93; Dir, and Prof. of Theoretical Ecology, Forschungszentrum Jülich, 1988–92; Prof. of Biol Scis, Univ. of Warwick, 1992–98 (Hon. Prof., 1998–); Dir, Centre for Coastal and Marine Scis, NERC, 1998–2000. Trustee, Earth Centre, 1990–; Member: Bd, Envmt Agency, 1998–; Marine Foresight Panel, 1999–; Envmt Panel, UK-China Forum, 1999–. Hon. Mem., Internat. Inst. for Dynamical Systems, 1991. FRSA 1997; FLS 1998. Jubileum Award, Chalmers Univ., Sweden, 1991; Minerva Prize, FZ Jülich, Germany, 1992. *Publications:* Advanced Ecological Theory, 1999; papers on math. biology, fisheries, marine sci. and governance. *Recreations:* sailing, diving, ski-ing, climbing. *Address:* 10 The Coach House, Compton Verney, Warwick CV35 9HJ.

McGLASHAN, John Reid Curtis, CBE 1974; HM Diplomatic Service, retired 1979; *b* 12 Dec. 1921; *s* of late John Adamson McGlashan and Emma Rose May McGlashan; *m* 1947, Dilys Bagnall (*née* Buxton Knight); one *s* two *d*. *Educ:* Fettes; Christ Church, Oxford (Rugger Blue, 1945). RAF (Bomber Command), 1940–45 (POW, 1941–45). Entered Foreign Service, 1953; Baghdad, 1955; Tripoli, 1963; Madrid, 1968; Counsellor, FCO, 1970–79. *Recreations:* gardening, reading. *Address:* Allendale, Selsey Bill, West Sussex PO20 9DB. *Club:* Vincent's (Oxford).

MacGLASHAN, Maureen Elizabeth, CMG 1997; HM Diplomatic Service, retired; Ambassador to the Holy See, 1995–98; *b* 7 Jan. 1938; *d* of Kenneth and Elizabeth MacGlashan. *Educ:* Luton High Sch.; Girton Coll., Cambridge (MA, LLM). Joined FO, 1961; 2nd Sec., Tel Aviv, 1964–67; FCO, 1967–72; Head of Chancery, East Berlin, 1973–75; UK Representation to EEC, 1975–77; seconded to Home Civil Service, 1977–82; Counsellor, Bucharest, 1982–86; Asst Dir, Res. Centre for Internat. Law, and bye-Fellow, Girton Coll., Cambridge Univ., 1986–90; Counsellor, Consul-Gen. and Dep. Head of Mission, Belgrade, 1990; Head, Western European Dept, FCO, 1991–92; on secondment to CSSB, 1992–95. Ed., Iran–US Claims Tribunal Reports, vols 8–22. *Publications:* (trans.) Weil, Maritime Delimitation, 1989; Consolidated Index to the International Law Reports, vols 36–80, 1990, vols 81–100, 1996, vols 1–120, 2001. *Address:* 16G Main Street, Largs, Ayrshire KA30 8AB. *Club:* University Women's.

McGONAGLE, Stephen; Senator, Seanad Éireann, Dublin, 1983–87; *b* 17 Nov. 1914; *m*; five *s* one *d*. *Educ:* Christian Brothers', Derry. Chairman, NI Cttee, Irish Congress of Trade Unions, 1959; Vice-Chm., Derry Develt Commn, 1969–71; Pres., Irish Congress of Trade Unions, 1972–73; Mem., NI Economic Council, Indust. Tribunal, Indust. Ct, until 1973; Dist Sec., Irish Transport and General Workers' Union, Dec. 1973; NI Parly Comr For Admin, and Comr for Complaints, 1974–79; Chm., NI Police Complaints Bd, 1977–83. *Recreations:* fishing, boating, reading.

McGONIGAL, Christopher Ian; His Honour Judge McGonigal; North Eastern Circuit Mercantile Judge, since 1997; *b* 10 Nov. 1937; *s* of Harold Alfred Kelly McGonigal and Cora McGonigal (*née* Bentley); *m* 1961, Sara Ann Sander; three *s* one *d*. *Educ:* Ampleforth Coll., York; Corpus Christi Coll., Oxford (MA). Coward Chance: articled clerk, 1963–65; Asst Solicitor, 1965–68; Sen. Litigation Partner, 1969–79, 1983–87; Sen. Resident Partner, Dubai, Sharjah, Bahrain and Jeddah offices, 1979–83; Clifford Chance: Jt Sen. Litigation Partner, 1987–95; Sen. Partner, Contentious Business Area, 1995–97. Asst Recorder, 1990–95; Recorder, 1995–97. *Recreations:* gardening, opera, local history. *Address:* c/o Leeds Mercantile Court, Leeds LS1 3BE. *T:* (0113) 283 0040.

McGOUGAN, Donald; Director of Finance, City of Edinburgh Council, since 1995; *b* 26 Dec. 1950; *s* of Louis and Sidney McGougan; *m* 1991, Mandy Dodgson; one *s* one *d*. *Educ:* Hermitage Acad., Helensburgh. CPFA 1976. Trainee Accountant, Midlothian CC, 1971–75; Professional Asst, City of Edinburgh DC, 1975–77; Falkirk District Council: Sen. Accountant, 1977–79; Principal Asst, 1979–81; Depute Dir of Finance, 1981–87; City of Edinburgh District Council: Depute Dir of Finance, 1987–95; acting Dir of Finance, 1995–96. *Recreations:* family, golf, football. *Address:* (office) Wellington Court, 10 Waterloo Place, Edinburgh EH1 3EG. *T:* (0131) 469 3005.

McGOUGH, Roger, OBE 1997; poet; *b* 9 Nov. 1937; *s* of Roger Francis and Mary Agnes McGough; *m* 1st, 1970 (marr. diss. 1980); two *s*; 2nd, 1986, Hilary Clough; one *s* one *d*. *Educ:* St Mary's Coll., Crosby, Liverpool; Hull Univ. (BA, Grad. Cert. Ed.). Fellow of Poetry, Univ. of Loughborough, 1973–75. Mem. Exec. Council, Poetry Soc., 1989–. Hon. Prof., Thames Valley Univ., 1993; Hon. Fellow, John Moores Univ., 1999. Hon. MA Nene Coll., 1998. *Television:* Kurt, Mungo, BP and Me (BAFTA Award), 1984. Lyrics for Wind in the Willows, Broadway, 1985–86; The Elements (RTS Award), 1993. *Publications:* Watchwords, 1969; After The Merrymaking, 1971; Out of Sequence, 1972; Gig, 1972; Sporting Relations, 1974; In The Glassroom, 1976; Summer with Monika, 1978; Holiday on Death Row, 1979; Unlucky For Some, 1981; Waving at Trains, 1982; Melting into the Foreground, 1986; Selected Poems 1967–1987, 1989; You at the Back, 1991; Defying Gravity, 1992; The Spotted Unicorn, 1998; The Way Things Are, 1999; *children's books:* Mr Noselighter, 1977; The Great Smile Robbery, 1982; Sky in the Pie, 1983; The Stowaways, 1986; Noah's Ark, 1986; Nailing the Shadow, 1987; An Imaginary Menagerie, 1988; Helen Highwater, 1989; Counting by Numbers, 1989; Pillow Talk, 1990; The Lighthouse That Ran Away, 1991; My Dad's a Fire-eater, 1992; Another Custard Pie, 1993; Lucky, 1993; Stinkers Ahoy!, 1995; The Magic Fountain, 1995; The Kite and Caitlin, 1996; Bad, Bad Cats, 1997; Until I Met Dudley, 1997; contributed to: Penguin Modern Poets, No 10, Mersey Sound, 1967, rev. edn 1983; Oxford Book of 20th Century Verse, 1973; The Norton Anthology of Modern Poetry, 1973; Penguin Modern Poets, No 4 (new series), 1995; edited: Strictly Private, 1981; Kingfisher Book of Comic Verse, 1986; The Kingfisher Book of Poems about Love, 1997; The Ring of Words (anthology), 1998. *Address:* c/o Peters Fraser and Dunlop, Drury House, 34–43 Russell Street, WC2B 5HA. *T:* (020) 7376 7676. *Club:* Chelsea Arts (Chm., 1984–86; Trustee, 1992–).

McGOVERN, George Stanley; United States Senator, 1963–81; US Permanent Representative to United Nations Food and Agriculture Organisation, 1998–2001; *b* Avon, S Dakota, 19 July 1922; *s* of Rev. Joseph C. McGovern and Francis (*née* McLean); *m* 1943, Eleanor Faye Stegeberg; one *s* three *d* (and one *d* decd). *Educ:* Dakota Wesleyan Univ. (BA); Northwestern Univ. (MA, PhD). Served World War II, USAAF (DFC). Prof. of History and Govt, Dakota Wesleyan Univ., 1950–53. Exec. Sec., S Dakota Democratic Party, 1953–56; Mem., 1st Dist, S Dakota, US House of Reps, 1957–61; Dir, Food for Peace Programme, 1961–62; Senator from South Dakota, 1963–81. Democratic nominee for US President, 1972. Visiting Professor: Columbia Univ., 1977; Univ. of Pa, 1978; Northwestern Univ., 1981; Univ. of New Orleans, 1982; University Coll., Dublin, 1982; Duke Univ., 1985; Univ. of Munich, 1987. Mem., Amer. Hist. Assoc. *Publications:* The Colorado Coal Strike, 1913–14, 1953; War Against Want, 1964; Agricultural Thought in the Twentieth Century, 1967; A Time of War, A Time of Peace, 1968; (with Leonard F. Guttridge) The Great Coalfield War, 1972; An American Journey, 1974; Grassroots, an Autobiography, 1978; Terry: my daughter's life-and-death struggle with alcoholism, 1996; The Third Freedom: ending hunger in our time, 2001.

McGOWAN, family name of **Baron McGowan**.

McGOWAN, 3rd Baron *cr* 1937; **Harry Duncan Cory McGowan;** Managing Director, WestLB Panmure Ltd, since 1999 (Chairman, 1995–99); Partner, Panmure, Gordon & Co., 1971–86; *b* 20 July 1938; *e s* of Harry Wilson McGowan, 2nd Baron McGowan, and Carmen (*d* 1996), *d* of Sir (James) Herbert Cory, 1st Bt; *S* father, 1966; *m* 1962, Lady Gillian Angela Pepys, *d* of 7th Earl of Cottenham; one *s* two *d*. *Educ:* Eton. Non-executive Director: BNB Resources plc; Halma plc; Wassall plc. Mem., Jockey Club. *Heir:* *s* Hon. Harry John Charles McGowan [*b* 23 June 1971; *m* 2001, Emma, *d* of Duncan Hattersley Smith]. *Address:* Highway House, Lower Froyle, Alton, Hants GU34 4NB. *T:* (01420) 22104; 12 Stanhope Mews East, SW7 5QU. *T:* (020) 7370 2346. *Clubs:* Boodle's, Cavalry and Guards.

McGOWAN, Alan Patrick, PhD; Archivist, Royal Naval College, Greenwich, 1989–98; Curator Emeritus, National Maritime Museum, since 1989 (Chief Curator, 1986–88; Callender Curator, 1989–91); *b* 16 Nov. 1928; *s* of Hugh McGowan and Alice Chilton; *m* 1958, Betty Eileen, *e d* of Mr and Mrs F. L. MacDougall, Ontario; three *s*. *Educ:* Spring Grove Grammar Sch.; Borough Road Coll.; Univ. of Western Ontario (BA, MA); Univ. of London (PhD). Served RASC (Air Freight), 1947–49. Asst Master (History), 1953–63; Lectr, Univ. of Western Ont Summer Sch., 1964; Canada Council Fellow, 1964–66; Asst Keeper, 1967–71, Keeper, 1980, Head, 1971–86, Dept of Ships, National Maritime Museum. Associate Prof. of History, Univ. of Western Ont Summer Sch., 1977. Member: Council, Navy Records Soc., 1968–; Adv. Council on Export of Works of Art, 1972–88; Victory Adv. Technical Cttee, 1974– (Chm., 1983–); Mary Rose Adv. Cttee, 1974–78; Ships Cttee, Maritime Trust, 1977–88; Council, Soc. for Nautical Res., 1981–; Cttee, Falkland Islands Foundn, 1981–83. Associate RINA, 1980–88. Liveryman, Co. of Shipwrights, 1984–. *Publications:* (ed) Jacobean Commissions of Enquiry, 1608 and 1618, vol. 113 of Navy Records Society, 1971; Royal Yachts, 1975; (with J. Fabb) The Victorian and Edwardian Navy in Photographs, 1976; (ed and prefaced) Steel's Naval Architecture, 1976; Sailor, 1977; (ed and prefaced) Steel's Rigging and Seamanship, 1978; The Century before Steam, 1980; Tiller and Whipstaff, 1981; HMS Victory 1758–1998: the career and restoration of an icon, 1999; articles in jls of history and in encyclopaedia. *Recreations:* golf, reading, music. *Address:* c/o National Maritime Museum, Greenwich, SE10 9NF.

McGOWAN, Bruce Henry, MA; FRSA; Headmaster, Haberdashers' Aske's School, Elstree, 1973–87; *b* 27 June 1924; *er s* of late Rt Rev. Henry McGowan, sometime Bishop of Wakefield, and Nora Heath McGowan (*née* Godwin); *m* 1947, Beryl McKenzie (*née* Liggitt); one *s* three *d*. *Educ:* King Edward's Sch., Birmingham; Jesus Coll., Cambridge. War service, Royal Artillery, 1943–46 (India and Burma). Asst Master, King's Sch., Rochester, 1949–53; Senior History Master, Wallasey Gram. Sch., 1953–57; Headmaster: De Aston Sch., Market Rasen, Lincs, 1957–64; Solihull Sch., 1964–73. Page Scholar of the English-Speaking Union, 1961. Member: Church Assembly, 1963–70; Public Schools Commn, 1968–70; Council, Church Schools Co., 1986–92 (Chm., 1987–92); Cttee, GBGSA, 1989–93; GBA, 1992–95; Chairman: Boarding Schools Assoc., 1967–69; Headmasters' Conference, 1985 (Chairman: London Div. 1977; Community Service Cttee, 1976–80; Political and Public Relations Cttee, 1981–84). Comr, Duke of York's Royal Mil. Sch., Dover, 1986–96; Governor: Bristol Grammar Sch., 1983–95; St George's Sch., Harpenden, 1977–81, 1984–97; Greycotes Sch., Oxford, 1987–96; Ellesmere Coll., 1992–94; Adv. Gov., St Benedict's Sch., Ealing, 1989–2001. Church Warden, St Mary's, N Leigh, Oxford, 1993–96. Fellow Woodard Corp., 1990–94. *Recreations:* foreign travel, walking, music, the theatre. *Address:* The Bell House, 29 Union Street, Woodstock, Oxon OX20 1JF. *Club:* East India.

MACGOWAN, Christopher John; Chief Executive, Society of Motor Manufacturers and Traders, since 1999; *b* 26 April 1947; *s* of Rev. John Macgowan and Dorothy Macgowan; *m* 1st, 1968, Victoria Lindey (*d* 1989); two *d*; 2nd, 1995, Amanda Fuller. *Educ:* Orwell Park, Marlborough Coll. Export Rep. (Canada), British Leyland, 1965–73; PR Manager, Massey-Ferguson, 1973–90; Sales Dir, Ransomes, 1990–94; Chief Exec., Retail Motor Ind. Fedn, 1994–99. Freeman, City of London, 1997. *Recreations:* information technology, National Hunt racing. *Address:* (office) Forbes House, Halkin Street, SW1X 7DS. *T:* (020) 7235 7000. *Club:* Royal Automobile.

McGOWAN, Prof. David Alexander, PhD; Professor of Oral Surgery, University of Glasgow, 1977–99, now Emeritus; Hon. Consultant in Oral Surgery, Greater Glasgow Health Board, 1977–99; *b* 18 June 1939; *s* of George McGowan, MBE, and Annie, (Nan), Hall McGowan (*née* Macormac); *m* 1968, Margaret Vera Macauley; one *s* two *d*. *Educ:* Portadown Coll.; QUB (BDS 1961; MDS 1970); London Hosp. Med. Coll., London Univ. (PhD). FDSRCS 1964; FFDRCSI 1966; FDSRCPSGlas 1978; FDSRCSE 1999. Oral Surgery trng, Royal Victoria Hosp., Belfast and Aberdeen Royal Infirmary, 1961–67; Lectr in Dental Surgery, QUB, 1968; Department of Oral and Maxillo-Facial Surgery, London Hospital Medical College: Lectr, 1968–70; Sen. Lectr, 1970–77; Sen. Tutor, 1970–73; Consultant, 1971–77; Dep. Head, 1973–77. Chm., Nat. Dental Adv. Cttee, Scotland, 1995–99. Post-grad. Advr in Dentistry for W Scotland, 1977–90; Dean: Dental Faculty, RCPSG, 1989–92; Glasgow Univ. Dental Sch., 1990–95; Senate Assessor, Court, Univ. of Glasgow, 1995–99; Mem., GDC, 1989–99 (Dep. Chm., Exec., 1995–99). Univ. Fellow, Univ. of Western Australia, 1986; Caldwell Lectr, Univ. of Glasgow, 1993. Gold Medal, Bulgarian Acad. of Medicine, 1992; University Medal: Malta, 1999; Helsinki, 2000. *Publications:* (jtly) Outline of Oral Surgery, part 1, 1985; An Atlas of Minor Oral Surgery, 1989 (trans. Italian 1991, trans. French 1993), 2nd edn 1999; (jtly) The Maxillary Sinus and its Dental Implications, 1993;(jtly) Outline of Oral Surgery, parts 1 and 2, 1998; numerous articles in jls. *Recreations:* sailing, dog-walking, reading novels, listening to music. *Address:* Rhu Lodge, Rhu, Helensburgh G84 8NF. *T:* (home) (01436) 821315, (office) (0141) 211 9650, *Fax:* (01436) 820261. *Clubs:* Royal Society of Medicine; Royal Northern and Clyde Yacht.

McGOWAN, Ian Duncan; Librarian, National Library of Scotland, since 1990; *b* 19 Sept. 1945; *s* of Alexander McGowan and Dora (*née* Sharp); *m* 1971, Elizabeth Ann Weir; two *d*. *Educ:* Liverpool Inst.; Exeter Coll., Oxford (BA 1st Cl. Hons Russian Lang. and Lit., 1967); Sch. of Slavonic and E European Studies, Univ. of London. National Library of Scotland: Asst Keeper, 1971–78; Keeper (Catalogues and Automation), 1978–88; Sec. of the Library, 1988–90. Chm., Nat. Preservation Adv. Cttee, 1994–96; Pres., Scottish Library Assoc., 1998 (Vice-Pres., 1996–97); Chm., Britain-Russia Centre, Scotland, 1999–. Founding Fellow, Inst. of Contemporary Scotland, 2000. FRSA 1999. *Recreations:* books, gardens. *Address:* 23 Blackford Road, Edinburgh EH9 2DT. *T:* (0131) 667 2432. *Club:* New (Edinburgh).

McGOWAN, John; Sheriff in Ayr, since 2000; *b* 15 Jan. 1944; *s* of Arthur McGowan and Bridget McCluskey; *m* 1966, Elise Smith; two *s*. *Educ:* St Joseph's Acad., Kilmarnock; Glasgow Univ. (LLB). Admitted Solicitor, 1967; Temp. Sheriff, 1986–93; Sheriff in Glasgow, 1993–2000. Chm., DHSS Appeal Tribunal, 1980–86. Mem. Council, Law Soc. of Scotland, 1982–85. *Recreations:* golf, tennis, curling, theatre. *Address:* 19 Auchentrae Crescent, Ayr KA7 4BD. *T:* (01292) 260139.

McGOWAN, Prof. Margaret Mary, (Mrs Sydney Anglo), CBE 1998; PhD; FBA 1993; Professor of French, 1974–97, Senior Pro-Vice-Chancellor, 1992–97, Research Professor, since 1997, University of Sussex; *b* 21 Dec. 1931; *d* of George McGowan and Elizabeth (*née* McGrail); *m* 1964, Prof. Sydney Anglo. *Educ:* Stamford High Sch.; Univ. of Reading (BA, PhD). Lecturer: Univ. of Strasbourg, 1955–57; Univ. of Glasgow, 1957–64; University of Sussex: Lectr, 1964–68; Reader, 1968–74; Dean, Sch. of European Studies, 1977–80; Pro-Vice-Chancellor (Arts and Social Studies), 1981–86. Mem. Bd, European Strategic Mgt Unit, 1995–. Vice-Pres., British Acad., 1996–98. Vice-Chm. Bd, British

Inst. in Paris, 1978–99; Gov., Ardingly Coll., 1994–. Freeman, City of Tours, 1986. Hon. DLitt Sussex, 1999. *Publications:* L'Art du Ballet de Cour, 1963; Montaigne's Deceits, 1974; Ideal Forms in the Age of Ronsard, 1985; Louis XIII's Court Ballets, 1989; Moy qui me voy: studies of the self, 1990; The Vision of Rome in Late Renaissance France, 2000. *Recreations:* music, cooking, tennis. *Address:* 59 Green Ridge, Withdean, Brighton BN1 5LU.

McGOWAN, Maura Patricia; QC 2001; a Recorder, since 1996; *b* 27 Jan. 1957; *d* of Matthew Vincent McGowan and Bridget McGowan (*née* Helebert). *Educ:* Virgo Fidelis Convent, London; St Mary's Coll., Leeds; Manchester Univ. (LLB Hons). Called to the Bar, Middle Temple, 1980; in practice, specialising in criminal law. *Recreations:* cricket, fishing, opera, theatre, reading, gossip. *Address:* 2 Bedford Row, WC1R 4BU. *T:* (020) 7440 8888. *Club:* Irish.

McGOWAN, Michael; *b* 19 May 1940; *m*; two *s* one *d*. *Educ:* Leicester University. Formerly: lecturer; BBC journalist; co-operative employment development officer, Kirklees Council, to 1984. MEP (Lab) Leeds, 1984–99. *Address:* 9 Clarence Road, Horsforth, Leeds LS18 4LB.

McGRADY, Edward Kevin; MP (SDLP) Down South, since 1987; Member (SDLP) Down South, Northern Ireland Assembly, since 1998; *b* 3 June 1935; *y s* of late Michael McGrady and late Lilian Leatham; *m* 1959, Patricia, *d* of Wm Swail and Margaret Breen; two *s* one *d*. *Educ:* St Patrick's High Sch., Downpatrick. ACA 1957, FCA 1962. Former Partner, M. B. McGrady & Co., chartered accountants and insurance brokers. Councillor, Downpatrick UDC, 1961–89; Chm. of UDC, 1964–73; Vice-Chm., Down District Council, 1973, 1975–76, 1977, Chm. 1974, 1976, 1978, 1981, 1982. 1st Chm. of SDLP, 1971–73; 1st Chm. of SDLP Assembly Party; Chief Whip, SDLP, 1979–; SDLP Parly Chief Whip, 1987–; SDLP Party Assembly Chief Whip, 1998–. Mem. (SDLP) S Down: NI Assembly, 1973–75; NI Constitutional Convention, 1975–76; NI Assembly, 1982–86; Head of Office of Executive Planning and Co-ordination (Minister for Co-ordination, Jan.-May 1974); contested (SDLP) Down S, gen. elections, 1979, 1983 and 1986. Mem., NI Affairs Cttee, H of C. *Recreations:* golf, badminton, choral work. *Address:* Cois Na Cille, Saul Brae, Downpatrick, Co. Down BT30 6NL. *T:* (028) 4461 2882, *Fax:* (028) 4461 9574; *e-mail:* e.mcgrady@sdlp.ie; House of Commons, SW1A 0AA. *T:* (020) 7219 4481.

McGRAIL, Prof. Seán Francis, FSA; Visiting Professor of Maritime Archaeology, University of Southampton, since 1991; Chief Archaeologist, National Maritime Museum, 1976–86; *b* 5 May 1928; *m* 1955, Ursula Anne Yates, BA; one *s* three *d*. *Educ:* Royal Navy (Master Mariner); Univ. of Bristol (BA); Univ. of London (PhD); Campion Hall, Oxford (MA 1987); DSc Oxon 1989. FSA 1981; MIFA 1983. Served RN, 1946–68: Seaman Officer; awarded Wings (pilot), 1952; qualified as Air Warfare Instr, 1954, as Instrument Rating Examnr, 1958; comd 849 Sqdn, FAA, 1962–63. Undergrad., Univ. of Bristol, 1968–71 (Harry Crook Scholar, 1969–71); Postgrad. Student, Inst. of Archaeology, London, 1972–73; Postgrad. Student (pt-time), UCL, 1973–78; National Maritime Museum, 1972–86, Hd of Archaeol Res. Centre, 1976–86. Leverhulme Res. Fellow, 1991–94; Visiting Professor: of Maritime Archæology, Oxford Univ., 1986–93; Danish Nat. Museum's Centre for Maritime Archaeology, Roskilde, 1994; Univ. of Haifa, 1995. Mem., Adv. Cttee on Historic Wrecks, Dept. of Nat. Heritage (formerly DoE), 1974–98. Mem., Wardour Catholic Cemetery Trust, 1976–; Vice-Chm., Trust for Preservation of Oxford Coll. Barges, 1987–95. Prehistoric and medieval excavations, Norway, Denmark, Orkney, Ireland and Britain, 1974–93; maritime ethnographic fieldwork, Bangladesh and east coast of India, 1994–. *Publications:* Building and Trials of a Replica of an Ancient Boat, 1974; Logboats of England and Wales, 1978; Rafts, Boats and Ships, 1981; Ancient Boats, 1983; Ancient Boats of North West Europe, 1987, 2nd edn 1998; Medieval Boat and Ship Timbers from Dublin, 1993; Studies in Maritime Archaeology, 1997; Boats of the World, 2001; *edited:* Sources and Techniques in Boat Archaeology, 1977; Medieval Ships and Harbours, 1979; Paul Johnstone, Seacraft of Prehistory, 1980, 2nd edn 1988; Brigg 'raft' and her Prehistoric Environment, 1981; Woodworking Techniques before 1500, 1982; Aspects of Maritime Archaeology and Ethnography, 1984; (with J. Coates) Greek Trireme of 5th Century BC, 1984; (with E. Kentley) Sewn Plank Boats, 1985; Maritime Celts, Saxons and Frisians, 1990; articles in archaeological and maritime jls. *Recreations:* strategic gardening, real ale specialist. *Address:* Institute of Archaeology, 36 Beaumont Street, Oxford OX1 2PG. *T:* (01865) 278240.

McGRATH, Prof. Alister Edgar, DPhil; Principal, Wycliffe Hall, Oxford, since 1995; Titular Professor of Historical Theology, University of Oxford, since 1999; *b* 23 Jan. 1953; *s* of Edgar P. McGrath and Annie J. M. McGrath (*née* McBride); *m* 1980, Joanna Ruth Collicutt; one *s* one *d*. *Educ:* Wadham Coll., Oxford (BA 1975); Linacre Coll., Oxford; Merton Coll., Oxford (MA, DPhil 1978; BD 1983); St John's Coll., Cambridge. Ordained deacon, 1980, priest, 1981; Curate, St Leonard's Ch, Wollaton, Nottingham, 1980–83; Lectr, Wycliffe Hall, Oxford, 1983–95. Hon. DD Virginia Theol Seminary, 1996. *Publications:* Explaining Your Faith. . . Without Losing Your Friends, 1988; Justification by Faith, 1988; Justitia Dei: history of the Christian doctrine of justification, Vol. I 1989, Vol. II 1993; Doubt: handling it honestly, 1990; Luther's Theology of the Cross: Martin Luther's theological breakthrough, 1990; Cloud of Witnesses: ten great Christian thinkers, 1990; Genesis of Doctrine, 1990; Life of John Calvin: a study in the shaping of Western culture, 1990; Affirming Your Faith: exploring the Apostles' Creed, 1991; Bridge Building: creative Christian apologetics, 1992; Intellectual Origins of the European Reformation, 1992; Making Sense of the Cross, 1992; Reformation Thought: an introduction, 1992; Roots that Refresh, 1992; Suffering, 1992; (with J. McGrath) Dilemma of Self Esteem: the Cross and Christian confidence, 1992; (ed) Blackwell Encyclopedia of Modern Christian Thought, 1993; Christian Theology: an introduction, 1993; Making of Modern German Christology: from the Enlightenment to Pannenberg, 1993; Renewal of Anglicanism, 1993; Jesus: who He is and why He matters, 1994; Evangelicalism and the Future of Christianity, 1994; A Passion for Truth, 1996; (ed jtly) Doing Theology for the People of God, 1996; J. I. Packer: a biography, 1997; The Foundations of Dialogue in Science and Religion, 1998; Historical Theology: an introduction to the history of Christian thought, 1998; T. F. Torrance: an intellectual biography, 1999; Theology for Amateurs, 2000; The Unknown God: searching for spiritual fulfilment, 2000; The Journey: a pilgrim in the lands of the spirit, 2000; (ed) Christian Literature: an anthology, 2000; In the Beginning: the story of the King James Bible, 2001; contrib. articles to learned jls. *Recreations:* walking, Australian wines. *Address:* Wycliffe Hall, Oxford OX2 6PW. *T:* (01865) 274200.

McGRATH, Sir Brian (Henry), GCVO 2001 (KCVO 1993; CVO 1988); an Extra Equerry to the Duke of Edinburgh, since 1996 (Assistant Private Secretary, 1982; Private Secretary, 1982–92; Treasurer, 1984–2000); *b* 27 Oct. 1925; *s* of William Henry and Hermione Gioja McGrath; *m* 1959, Elizabeth Joan Bruce (*née* Gregson-Ellis) (*d* 1977); two *s*, and one step *d*. *Educ:* Eton College. Served War of 1939–45, Irish Guards, 1943–46, Lieut. Cannon Brewery Co., 1946–48; Victoria Wine Co.: joined, 1948; Dir, 1949; Chm., 1960–82; Dir, 1960, Chm., 1975–82, Grants of St James's Ltd; Dir, Allied Breweries Ltd (subseq. Allied-Lyons plc), 1970–82; Chm., Broad Street Securities, 1983–92. Younger Brother of Trinity House, 1993. Master of Wine. *Recreations:* golf, gardening, shooting. *Address:* Flat 3, 9 Cheyne Gardens, SW3 5QU. *Clubs:* Boodle's, White's.

McGRATH, Dr Elizabeth, FBA 1998; Curator, Photographic Collection, Warburg Institute, University of London, since 1991; *b* 20 March 1945; *d* of Thomas McGrath and Emilie McGrath (*née* Melvin). *Educ:* St Joseph's High Sch., Kilmarnock; Glasgow Univ. (MA 1967); PhD London 1971. Photographic Collection, Warburg Inst., London Univ., 1970–; Jt Ed., Jl of Warburg and Courtauld Insts, 1977–. Durning Lawrence Lectr, UCL, 1989; Slade Prof. of Fine Art, Oxford Univ., 1990. Hans Reimer Prize, Hamburg Univ., 1996; Mitchell Prize for the History of Art, 1998; Eugène Baie Prize for Flemish Cultural History, Province of Antwerp. *Publications:* Rubens: Subjects from History, vol. XIII in *Corpus Rubenianum*, 1997; contrib. to Jl of Warburg and Courtauld Insts, Burlington Mag., etc. *Address:* Warburg Institute, University of London, Woburn Square, WC1H 0AB. *T:* (020) 7862 8949.

McGRATH, Ian; *see* McGrath, J. C.

McGRATH, James Aloysius; Hotspur, Racing Correspondent of the Daily Telegraph, since 1991; BBC television commentator; *b* 13 June 1952; *s* of Brian James McGrath and Kathleen May McGrath; *m* 1977, Anita Lee; two *s* two *d*. *Educ:* Xavier Coll., Melbourne. Cadet racing writer, The Australian, 1972–73; Racing Corresp., China Mail (Hong Kong), 1973–74; Chief Racing Writer, South China Morning Post (Hong Kong), 1975–86; writer, Racing Post, 1986–90; Racing Corresp., Sunday Telegraph, 1988–95. Racing Commentator: BBC, 1992–; (Sen. Racing Commentator, 1997); Satellite Information Services, 1993–97. *Recreations:* golf, ski-ing, watching cricket. *Address:* The Travers, Chobham, Woking, Surrey GU24 8SZ. *T:* (01276) 857155. *Clubs:* Hong Kong Jockey, Hong Kong Golf, Hong Kong Football (Hong Kong).

McGRATH, John Brian; Chairman, The Boots Co. plc, since 2000 (non-executive Director, since 1998); *b* 20 June 1938; *m* 1964, Sandy Watson; one *s* one *d*. *Educ:* Brunel Univ. (BSc 1st Cl. Hons Applied Physics). UKAEA, 1962–65; NCB, 1965–67; Ford Motor Co., 1967–71; Jaguar Cars, 1971–75; Stone-Platt, 1976–82; Man. Dir, Construction and Mining Div. and Chief Exec., Compair, 1982–85; joined Grand Metropolitan PLC, 1985: Gp Dir, Watney Mann & Truman Brewers Ltd, 1985; Chm. and Man. Dir, Grand Metropolitan Brewing, 1986–88; Jt Man. Dir, Internat. Distillers & Vintners, 1988–91; IDV Ltd: Man. Dir and Chief Operating Officer, 1991–92; Chief Exec., 1992–93; Chm. and Chief Exec., 1993–96; Group Chief Executive: Grand Metropolitan PLC, 1996–97; Diageo, 1997–2000. Chm., Scotch Whisky Assoc., 1995–2000. *Address:* The Boots Co. plc, Nightingale House, 65 Curzon Street, W1Y 7PE.

McGRATH, Prof. John Christie, (Ian); pharmacologist and physiologist; Regius Professor of Physiology, since 1991, and Head, Division of Neuroscience and Biomedical Systems, since 1997, University of Glasgow; *b* 8 March 1949; *s* of John Christie McGrath and Margaret Gilmore Cochrane McGrath (*née* Murray); *m* 1970, Wilma Nicol; one *s* one *d*. *Educ:* Cross Arthurlie Primary Sch.; John Neilson Instn; Univ. of Glasgow (BSc 1st class Hons 1970; PhD 1974). Wellcome Interdisciplinary Research Fellowship, Dept of Pharmacology and Univ. Dept of Anaesthesia, Glasgow Royal Infirmary, Univ. of Glasgow, 1973–75; Institute of Biomedical and Life Sciences (formerly Institute of Physiology), University of Glasgow: Lectr, 1975; Wellcome Trust Research Leave Fellowship, 1982; Sen. Lectr, Reader, Titular Prof., 1983–91; Co-Dir, Clinical Res. Initiative, 1994–99. Chm. Standing Cttee, Heads of UK Physiology Depts, 2000–. Member: British Pharmacol Soc. 1975 (Sandoz Prize, 1980); Cttee, Physiolog. Soc., 1988– (Mem., 1978); Internat. Soc. for Heart Research, 1989; Amer. Soc. for Pharmacology and Experimental Therapeutics, 1991; Amer. Physiol Soc., 1994. Mem., Labour Party. Member Editorial Board: British Jl of Pharmacology, 1985–91, 2001–; Jl of Cardiovascular Pharmacology, 1988–; Pharmacological Reviews, 1990–98; Jl of Vascular Res., 1991–. 1st Pfizer Award for Biology, 1983. *Publications:* contribs to learned jls in fields of pharmacology and physiology. *Recreations:* running, politics, travel. *Address:* Institute of Biomedical and Life Sciences, University of Glasgow, Glasgow G12 8QQ. *T:* (0141) 330 4483, *Fax:* (0141) 330 2923; *e-mail:* i.mcgrath@bio.gla.ac.uk.

McGRATH, John Peter; writer and director, theatre, film and television; Director, Freeway Films, since 1983; *b* 1 June 1935; *s* of John Francis McGrath and Margaret McGrath; *m* 1962, Elizabeth Maclennan; two *s* one *d*. *Educ:* Alun Grammar Sch., Mold; St John's Coll., Oxford. Theatre (playwright), 1958–61; BBC Television, 1960–65; film (screenwriting) and theatre (writing and directing), 1965–70; theatre, with regular forays into television and film, as writer and director, 1970–; founded 7:84 Theatre Co., 1971, Artistic Dir, 1971–88; Dir, C4 Television, 1989–94. Judith E. Wilson Vis. Fellow, Cambridge, 1979, 1988; Vis. Prof. in Media Studies, RHBNC, 1996–. Has produced or directed over 75 plays in the theatre, and written over 40 plays, including: Why the Chicken, 1959; The Tent, 1960; Comrade Jacob, 1968; Soft or a Girl, 1971; Trees in the Wind, 1971; Sergeant Musgrave Dances On (adaptation), 1972; Boom, 1974; Lay Off, 1975; Out of Our Heads, 1976; Trembling Giant, 1977; Bitter Apples, 1979; Nightclass, 1981; Rejoice!, 1982; The Catch, 1982; Women in Power, 1983; Women of the Dunes, 1983; Six Men of Dorset (adaptation), 1984; The Albannach (adaptation), 1984; The Baby and the Bathwater, 1984; All the Fun of the Fair, 1985; There is a Happy Land, 1986; Mairi Mhor, 1987; Border Warfare, 1989; John Brown's Body, 1990; Watching for Dolphins, 1991; The Wicked Old Man, 1992; The Silver Darlings (adaptation), 1994; Reading Rigoberta, 1995; The Four Estaites, 1996; The Last of the MacEachans, 1996; many TV plays performed on BBC and ITV; prod. film Carrington, 1995; co-prod. film Ma Vie En Rose, 1997; screenplays: The Bofors Gun, 1967; Billion Dollar Brain, 1967; The Virgin Soldiers (adaptation), 1968; The Reckoning, 1968; Blood Red Roses, 1986 (dir); The Dressmaker, 1988 (exec. producer); The Long Roads, 1993; wrote libretto for Alexander Goehr's opera, Behold the Sun; writes songs and poems. Writer's Award, BAFTA, 1994; Lifetime Achievement Award, Writers Guild of GB, 1997. DUniv Stirling, 1992. *Publications: plays:* Events While Guarding the Bofors Gun, 1966; Random Happenings in the Hebrides, 1972; Bakke's Night of Fame, 1973; The Cheviot, The Stag and The Black Black Oil, 1974, 2nd edn 1981; The Game's A Bogey, 1974; Fish in the Sea, 1977; Little Red Hen, 1977; Yobbo Nowt, 1978; Joe's Drum, 1979; Blood Red Roses (filmed for TV, 1986), and Swings and Roundabouts, 1981; Six Pack: six plays for Scotland, 1996; *general:* A Good Night Out, 1981; The Bone Won't Break, 1990. *Address:* c/o Freeway Films, 33A Pembroke Square, W8 6PD.

McGRATH, William Joseph; Founder and Chief Executive Officer, Greenfield Services Ltd, since 1996; Managing Director, British Gas Energy Centres, since 1999; *b* 30 Sept. 1940; *s* of William George McGrath and Wallis (*née* Reinwold); *m* 1963, Mary Teresa Bridget Galvin; two *d*. *Educ:* St John's RC Sch., Tamworth, Staffs; Open Univ. (BA Hons). With Cunard Steamship Co. Ltd, 1956–68; G. J. Keddie & Sons Ltd, 1968–75; Director: Asda Stores Ltd, 1975–81; Comet PLC, 1981–84; Founder and Chief Exec. Officer, Builders Mate, 1984–87; Dir, Wickes PLC, 1990–93 (Dep. Chm., 1993); Chief Exec. Officer, Pentos Gp, 1994–95; Chm. and CEO, British Home Doors, 2000– (non-exec. Dir, 1995; non-exec. Chm., 1997). Non-executive Chairman: Gasflair Ltd, 1999–;

Hiatt Ltd, 2000–; non-executive Director: Cashbuild, South Africa, 1995–; Gainsborough Building Soc., 2000–. MInstD 1984; MCIM 1989. FRSA 1994. Wine and Spirit Educn Trust (Cert., Higher Cert. Dist. and Dip.). Compagnon de Beaujolais, 1976. KSC 1962. *Recreations:* chess, walking, gardening. *Address:* Manor House, Gringley on the Hill, Notts DN10 4RG. *T:* (01777) 817716. *Club:* East India.

MacGREGOR, family name of **Baron MacGregor of Pulham Market**.

MacGREGOR OF PULHAM MARKET, Baron *cr* 2001 (Life Peer), of Pulham Market in the County of Norfolk; **John Roddick Russell MacGregor,** OBE 1971; PC 1985; *b* 14 Feb. 1937; *s* of late Dr. N. S. R. MacGregor; *m* 1962, Jean Mary Elizabeth Dungey; one *s* two *d. Educ:* Merchiston Castle Sch., Edinburgh; St Andrews Univ. (MA, 1st cl. Hons); King's Coll., London (LLB; FKC 1988). Univ. Administrator, 1961–62; Editorial Staff, New Society, 1962–63; Special Asst to Prime Minister, Sir Alec Douglas-Home, 1963–64; Conservative Research Dept, 1964–65; Head of Private Office of Rt Hon. Edward Heath, Leader of Opposition, 1965–68. MP (C) S Norfolk, Feb. 1974–2001. An Opposition Whip, 1977–79; a Lord Comr of HM Treasury, 1979–81; Parly Under-Sec. of State, DoI, 1981–83; Minister of State, MAFF, 1983–85; Chief Sec. to HM Treasury, 1985–87; Minister of Agriculture, Fisheries and Food, 1987–89; Sec. of State for Educn and Sci., 1989–90; Lord Pres. of the Council and Leader of H of C, 1990–92; Sec. of State for Transport, 1992–94. Hill Samuel & Co. Ltd, 1968–79 (Dir, 1973–79), Dep. Chm., 1994–96; Director: Associated British Foods, 1994–; Slough Estates, 1995–; Uniq (formerly Unigate), 1996–; London & Manchester Gp, 1997–98; Friends Provident, 1998–; Supervisory Bd, DAFS Netherlands NV, 2000–. Chairman: Fedn of University Cons. and Unionist Assocs, 1959; Bow Group, 1963–64; 1st Pres., Conservative and Christian Democratic Youth Community, 1963–65; Vice-President: ACC, 1995–97; LGA, 1997–99. Mem., Cttee on Standards in Public Life, 1998–. Member: Council, KCL, 1996–; Council, IOD, 1996–. Formerly Treasurer, Federal Trust for Educn and Research; formerly Trustee, European Educnl Research Trust. Hon. LLB Westminster, 1996. *Publications:* contrib. The Conservative Opportunity; also pamphlets. *Recreations:* music, reading, travelling, gardening, conjuring (Member: Magic Circle, 1989; Inner Magic Circle, 2000). *Address:* House of Lords, SW1A 0PW.

McGREGOR, Prof. Alan Michael, MD; FRCP; Professor of Medicine, Head of Division of Medicine and Dean of Research, Guy's, King's and St Thomas' School of Medicine of King's College London (formerly King's College School of Medicine and Dentistry), since 1986; *b* 3 Aug. 1948. *Educ:* Selwyn Coll., Cambridge (BA 1971; MB, BChir 1974; MA 1982; MD 1982). MRCP 1977, FRCP 1985. MRC Trng Fellow, Royal Victoria Infirmary, Newcastle upon Tyne, 1977–80; Lectr, 1980, Wellcome Sen. Res. Fellow, 1981–86, Dept of Medicine, Univ. of Wales Coll. of Medicine. Hon. Consultant Physician, KCH NHS Trust. Mem., MRC, 1995–2000 (Chm., Physiological Medicine and Infections Bd). FKC 1997; Founder FMedSci, 1998. *Publications:* (ed) Immunology of Endocrine Diseases, 1986; contrib. learned jls. *Address:* Division of Medicine, Guy's, King's and St Thomas' School of Medicine of King's College London, Bessemer Road, SE5 9PJ.

MacGREGOR, Alastair Rankin; QC 1994; *b* 23 Dec. 1951; *s* of Alexander MacGregor and Anna MacGregor (*née* Neil); *m* 1982, Rosemary Kerslake; one *s* one *d. Educ:* Glasgow Acad.; Edinburgh Univ.; New Coll., Oxford Univ. (MA). Called to the Bar, Lincoln's Inn, 1974. *Address:* One Essex Court, Temple, EC4Y 9AR. *T:* (020) 7583 2000.

See also R. N. MacGregor.

McGREGOR, Rev. Alistair Gerald Crichton; QC (Scot.) 1982; WS; Minister, North Leith Parish Church, Edinburgh, since 1987; *b* 15 Oct. 1937; *s* of late James Reid McGregor, CB, CBE, MC, and Dorothy McGregor; *m* 1965, Margaret Lees or McGregor; two *s* one *d. Educ:* Charterhouse; Pembroke Coll., Oxford (BA (Hons) Jurisprudence); Edinburgh Univ. (LLB; BD). Intelligence Corps, 1956–58. Solicitor and WS, 1965–66; Advocate, 1967–82. Clerk to Court of Session Rules Council, 1972–75; Standing Junior Counsel to: SHHD, 1977–79; Scottish Develt Dept, 1979–82. Chm., Family Care (Scotland), 1983–88; Director: Apex (Scotland), 1988–98; Kirk Care Housing Assoc., 1994–97. Governor: Dean Orphanage Trust, 1998–; Loretto Sch., 2000–. Licensed, Church of Scotland, 1986. *Recreations:* squash, tennis. *Address:* 22 Primrose Bank Road, Edinburgh EH5 3JG. *T:* (0131) 551 2802.

McGREGOR, Hon. Alistair John; QC 1997; *b* 11 March 1950; *s* of Baron McGregor of Durris; *m* 1985, Charlotte Ann East; one *s* one *d. Educ:* Haberdashers' Aske's Sch., Elstree; Queen Mary Coll., London Univ. (LLB Hons). Called to the Bar, Middle Temple, 1974. *Recreations:* music, sport. *Address:* 11 King's Bench Walk, Temple, EC4Y 7EQ. *T:* (020) 7583 0610. *Club:* Garrick.

McGREGOR, Dr Angus; Regional Medical Officer, West Midlands Regional Health Authority, 1979–88; Visiting Professor, University of Keele, 1988–94; *b* 26 Dec. 1926; *s* of Dr William Hector Scott McGregor and Dr Olwen May Richards; *m* 1951, May Burke, BA; one *d. Educ:* Solihull Sch.; St John's Coll., Cambridge. MA, MD; FRCP; FFCM; DPH. Junior hospital posts, 1950; Army service, RAMC, 1951–52; general practice, 1953; Asst MOH, Chester, 1954–56; Deputy Medical Officer of Health: Swindon, 1957–58; Hull, 1958–65; MOH and Port MO, Southampton, 1965–74; District Community Physician, East Dorset, 1974–79. Mem. Bd, FCM, RCP, 1982–88. FRSA 1986. *Publications:* (with T. Bunbury) Disciplining and Dismissing Doctors in the NHS, 1988; contrib. papers to medical journals. *Recreation:* piano. *Address:* (home) Withyholt, 26 Lyttelton Road, Droitwich Spa, Worcestershire WR9 7AA. *T:* (01905) 776077. *Club:* Royal Over-Seas League.

MACGREGOR, Sir Edwin (Robert), 7th Bt *cr* 1828; Mayor, District of Sooke, since 1999; Deputy Minister, Ministry of Lands and Parks, Province of British Columbia, Victoria, BC, 1991–92, retired; *b* 4 Dec. 1931; *e s* of Sir Robert McConnell Macgregor, 6th Bt, and of Annie Mary Lane; *S* father, 1963; *m* 1st, 1952, (Margaret Alice) Jean Peake (marr. diss. 1981); one *s* two *d* (and one *s* decd); 2nd, 1982, Helen Linda Herriott; two step *d. Educ:* University of British Columbia. BASc 1955, MASc 1957, Metallurgical Engineering. Plant Manager, 1965–72, Marketing Manager, Metals, 1972–74, Union Carbide Canada Ltd. Dep. Minister, Min. of Crown Lands, BC, 1989–91. Life Mem., Assoc. of Professional Engrs and Geoscientists, Province of British Columbia. *Publications:* contribs to Trans Amer. Inst. of Mining, Metallurgical and Petroleum Engrg, Jl Amer. Chem. Soc. *Recreations:* reading; participation in several outdoor sports such as golf, swimming, fishing, etc.; music. *Heir: s* Ian Grant Macgregor, *b* 22 Feb. 1959. *Address:* Scarlet Oak, 6136 Kirby Road, Sooke, BC V0S 1N0, Canada.

McGREGOR, Ewan Gordon; actor; *b* 31 March 1971; *s* of James and Carol McGregor; *m* 1995, Eve Mavrakis. *Theatre:* What the Butler Saw, 1992; Little Malcolm, Comedy, 1998–99; *films:* Family Style, Being Human, 1993; Shallow Grave, 1994; Trainspotting, Swimming with the Fishes, Emma, The Pillow Book, Brassed Off, 1996; The Serpent's Kiss, Blue Juice, A Life Less Ordinary, 1997; Nightwatch, Velvet Goldmine, Little Voice, Desserts, Anno Domini, 1998; The Phantom Menace, Rogue Trader, Eye of the Beholder, Tube Tales (also dir.), 1999; Nora (co-producer, 2000); Moulin Rouge, 2001; *television* includes: Lipstick on Your Collar, Scarlet and Black, 1993; Doggin' Around, 1994; Karaoke, 1996. Hon. DLitt Ulster, 2001. *Recreation:* motor bikes. *Address:* c/o Lindy King, PFD, Drury House, 34 Russell Street, WC2B 5HA. *T:* (020) 7344 1010.

McGREGOR, Prof. Gordon Peter, DPhil; Professor of Education, University of Leeds, 1991–95, now Emeritus; *b* Aldershot, Hants, 13 June 1932; 2nd *s* of William A. K. McGregor and Mary A. McGregor (*née* O'Brien); *m* 1957, Jean Olga Lewis; three *d. Educ:* Bishop Road Jun. Sch., Bristol; St Brendan's Coll., Bristol; Univ. of Bristol (Open Schol.; BA Hons); Univ. of East Africa (MEd); Univ. of Sussex (DPhil); Dip. Coll. of Teachers of the Blind. Educn Officer, RAF, 1953–56; Asst Master, Worcester Coll. for the Blind, 1956–59; Asst Master, King's Coll., Budo, Uganda, 1959–62; Lecturer in English Language, Makerere Univ. Coll., Uganda 1963–66; Univ. of Zambia: Sen Lecturer in Educn, 1966–68; Reader and Head of Dept of Education, 1968–70; Prof. of Educn, 1970; Principal, Bishop Otter Coll., Chichester, 1970–80; Principal, Coll., then UC, of Ripon and York St John, Leeds Univ., 1980–95. Danforth Fellow, Colorado Coll., USA, 1972; Commonwealth Educn Consultant, Sri Lanka, 1973; British Council ELT Consultant, Iraq, 1975; CUAC Consultant, univ. colls, India and Australia, 1996; Visiting Professor: Univ. of Fort Hare, 1997; Makerere Univ., 1998–; Westminster Inst., Oxford Brookes Univ., 2001–. Chairman: York Diocesan Educn Council, 1980–95; Council of Church and Associated Colls, 1990–95; Member: UK Commn for UNESCO, 1984–86; Voluntary Sector Consultative Council, 1985–89. Vice-Chm. Govs, York Theatre Royal, 1992–95. Hon. Fellow, Coll. of Ripon and York St John, 2001. Hon. DLitt: Ripon Coll., Wisconsin, 1986; York Coll., Penn, 1993; Southampton, 1999; Hon. DHumLitt Union Coll., NY, 1996. *Publications:* King's College, Budo, The First Sixty Years, 1967; Educating the Handicapped, 1967; English for Education?, 1968; Teaching English as a Second Language (with J. A. Bright), 1970; English in Africa, (UNESCO), 1971; Bishop Otter College and Policy for Teacher Education 1839–1980, 1981; A Church College for the 21st Century?: the first 150 years of Ripon and York St John, 1991; Towards True Education, 1994; English for Life?, 2001; numerous articles. *Recreations:* music, literature, theatre, film, travel, walking, swimming, armchair Rugby and cricket, watching my wife bird-watching. *Address:* Hollyhocks, High Street, Selsey, W Sussex PO20 0RD. *T:* (01243) 602680.

MACGREGOR, Rt Rev. Gregor; Bishop of Moray, Ross and Caithness, 1994–98; *b* 17 Nov. 1933; *m* 1956, Elizabeth Jean Harris; one *s* three *d. Educ:* St Andrews Univ. (MA 1964; BD 1967). Ordained deacon, 1976, priest, 1977; NSM, Elie and Earlsferry, and Pittenweem, 1977–81; Rector, Glenrothes, 1981–86; Vice-Provost, Cumbrae, 1986; Rector, Dollar, 1987–90; Mission Priest, St Luke, Wester Hailes, 1991–94. *Address:* Flat 11, John Ker Court, 42 Polwarth Gardens, Edinburgh EH11 1LM. *T:* (0131) 229 6938.

MacGREGOR OF MacGREGOR, Brig. Sir Gregor, 6th Bt *cr* 1795; ADC 1979; 23rd Chief of Clan Gregor; *b* 22 Dec. 1925; *o s* of Capt. Sir Malcolm MacGregor of MacGregor, 5th Bt, CB, CMG, and Hon. Gylla Lady MacGregor of MacGregor, OBE (*d* 1980); *S* father, 1958; *m* 1958, Fanny, *o d* of C. H. A. Butler, Shortgrove, Newport, Essex; two *s. Educ:* Eton. Commissioned Scots Guards, 1944; served War of 1939–45. Served in Palestine, 1947–48; Malaya, 1950–51; Borneo, 1965. Staff Coll. Course, 1960; Brigade Major, 16th Parachute Bde Gp, 1961–63; Joint Services Staff Coll., 1965; commanding 1st Bn Scots Guards, 1966–69; GSO1 (BLO) Fort Benning, USA, 1969–71; Col Recruiting, HQ Scotland, 1971; Lt-Col commanding Scots Guards, 1971–74; Defence and Mil. Attaché, British Embassy, Athens, 1975–78; Comdr, Lowlands, 1978–80. Grand Master Mason of Scotland, 1988–93. Mem. of the Royal Company of Archers (Queen's Body Guard for Scotland), 1949–. *Heir: s* Major Malcolm Gregor Charles MacGregor of MacGregor, Scots Guards [*b* 23 March 1959; *m* 1988, Cecilia, *er d* of Sir Ilay Campbell of Succoth, Bt, *qv*]. *Address:* Bannatyne, Newtyle, Blairgowrie, Perthshire PH12 8TR. *T:* (01828) 650314. *Club:* New (Edinburgh).

McGREGOR, Harvey; QC 1978; DCL; Warden, New College, Oxford, 1985–96 (Fellow, 1972–85; Hon. Fellow, 1996); *b* 25 Feb. 1926; *s* of late William Guthrie Robertson McGregor and Agnes (*née* Reid). *Educ:* Inverurie Acad.; Scarborough Boys' High Sch.; Queen's Coll., Oxford (Hastings Scholar; BA 1951, BCL 1952, MA 1955, DCL 1983). Dr of Juridical Science, Harvard, 1962. Called to the Bar, Inner Temple, 1955, Bencher, 1985. Flying Officer, RAF, 1946–48. Bigelow Teaching Fellow, Univ. of Chicago, 1950–51; Vis. Prof., New York Univ. and Rutgers Univ., 1963–69 (various times). Consultant to Law Commn 1966–73. Pres., Harvard Law Sch. Assoc. of UK, 1981–2001; Mem., Acad. of European Private Lawyers, 1994–. Ind. Chm., London Theatre Council and The Theatre Council (formerly Provincial Theatre Council), 1992– (Dep. Ind. Chm., 1971–92); Pres., Oxford Stage Co., 1992–; Trustee, Oxford Union Soc., 1977– (Chm. Trustees, 1994–). Fellow, Winchester Coll., 1985–96. Trustee, Migraine Trust, 1999–. Mem. Editorial Cttee, 1967–86, Mem., Editorial Bd, 1986–, Modern Law Review. Privilegiate, St Hilda's Coll., Oxford, 2001. *Publications:* McGregor on Damages, 12th edn 1961–, 16th edn 1997; Contract Code, 1993; (contrib.) International Encyclopedia of Comparative Law, 1972; articles in legal jls. *Recreations:* music, theatre, travel. *Address:* (chambers) 4 Paper Buildings, Temple, EC4Y 7EX. *T:* (020) 7353 3366; (residence) Gray's Inn Chambers, Gray's Inn, WC1R 5JA. *T:* (020) 7242 4942; 29 Howard Place, Edinburgh EH3 5JY. *T:* (0131) 556 8680. *Clubs:* Garrick; New (Edinburgh).

McGREGOR, Sir Ian (Alexander), Kt 1982; CBE 1968 (OBE 1959); FRS 1981; FRSE; Visiting Professor (formerly Professorial Fellow), Department of Tropical Medicine, Liverpool School of Tropical Medicine, 1981–94; *b* 26 Aug. 1922; *s* of John McGregor and Isabella (*née* Taylor), Cambuslang, Lanarks; *m* 1954, Nancy Joan, *d* of Frederick Small, Mapledurham, Oxon; one *s* one *d. Educ:* Rutherglen Academy; St Mungo Coll., Glasgow. LRCPE, LRCSE, LRFPS(G) 1945; DTM&H 1949; MRCP 1962; FRCP 1967; FFCM 1972; Hon. FRCPGlas 1984. Mil. Service, 1946–48 (despatches). Mem. Scientific Staff, Human Nutrition Research Unit, MRC, 1949–53; Dir, MRC Laboratories, The Gambia, 1954–74, 1978–80; Head of Laboratory of Trop. Community Studies, Nat. Inst. for Med. Research, Mill Hill, 1974–77; Mem., External Staff, MRC, 1981–84. Chm., WHO Expert Cttee on Malaria, 1985–89; Member: WHO Adv. Panel on Malaria, 1961–99; Malaria Cttee, MRC, 1962–71; Cttee on Nutrition Surveys, Internat. Union of Nutrition Sciences, 1971–75; Tropical Medicine Res. Bd, MRC, 1974–77, 1981–83; Steering Cttee on Immunology of Malaria, WHO, 1978–89; Council, Liverpool Sch. of Trop. Medicine, 1982–95; Steering Cttee on Applied Field Res. in Malaria, WHO, 1984–90; Council, Royal Soc., 1985–87. Lectures: Heath Clark, London Sch. of Hygiene and Tropical Medicine, 1983–84; Fred Soper, Amer. Soc. of Trop. Medicine and Hygiene, 1983; Lord Cohen History of Medicine, Liverpool Univ., 1989; Albert Norman Meml, Inst. of Med. Lab. Scis, 1992; Manson Orator, RSTM&H, 1994. Pres., Royal Soc. of Trop. Medicine and Hygiene, 1983–85 (Vice-Pres., 1981–83; Hon. Fellow, 1995). FRSE 1987. Hon. Fellow: Liverpool Sch. of Trop. Medicine, 1980; RSTM&H, 1995; Hon. Member: Amer. Soc. of Trop. Medicine and Hygiene, 1983; British Soc. for Parasitology, 1988. Hon. LLD Univ. of Aberdeen, 1983; Hon. DSc Glasgow, 1984. Chalmers Medal, Royal Soc. Trop. Med. and Hygiene, 1963; Stewart Prize, BMA, 1970; Darling Foundn Medal,

WHO, 1974; Laveran Medal, Société de Pathologie Exotique de Paris, 1983; Glaxo Prize for Medical Writing, 1989; Mary Kingsley Medal, Liverpool Sch. of Trop. Medicine, 1994. *Publications:* (ed with W. Wernsdorfer) Malaria: the principles and practice of malariology, 1988; scientific papers on infections, nutrition, immunity, child health and community medicine in tropical environments. *Recreations:* ornithology, golf, fishing. *Address:* Greenlooms House, Homington, Salisbury, Wilts SP5 4NL.

McGREGOR, Sir James David, Kt 1997; OBE 1976; ISO 1973; Member, Executive Council, Hong Kong, 1995–97; retired; *b* 30 Jan. 1924; *s* of David Nelson McGregor and Ann Horsburgh McGregor; *m* 1st, 1947, Doreen Davis (marr. diss.); one *d*; 2nd, 1963, Christine K. C. Hung; one *s* one *d*. *Educ:* Morgan Acad., Dundee; No 1 Sch. of Tech. Trng, Halton (RAF). RAF service, 1940–54 (armament specialist and aeronautical inspector). Hong Kong Government: Exec. Officer, 1954; Dep. Dir, Commerce and Industry Dept and Dep. Comr of Customs, 1972–75; Dir, Hong Kong General Chamber of Commerce, 1975–88; elected MLC, Hong Kong, 1988–95. JP Hong Kong, 1967–97. Hon. LLD Napier, 1995. *Publications:* Life and Death (short stories), 1995; numerous articles on politics, economics, Hong Kong and Asian affairs. *Recreations:* golf, snooker, writing, embroidery. *Address:* 1233 Pacific Drive, Tsawwassen, Delta, BC V4M 2K2, Canada. *T:* (604) 9433299. *Clubs:* Hong Kong, Hong Kong Jockey.

McGREGOR, James Stalker; Chairman, Honeywell Ltd, 1981–89; *b* 30 Oct. 1927; *s* of John McGregor and Jean McCabe; *m* 1953, Iris Millar Clark; one *s*. *Educ:* Dumfries Acad.; Royal Tech. Coll., Glasgow (ARTC); Glasgow Univ. BSc (Hons); CEng, MIMechE; CBIM. Production Engr, Rolls Royce Ltd, 1952–56; Sales Engr, Sandvik Swedish Steels, 1956–57; Honeywell Control Systems: Assembly Manager, later Production Control Manager and Admin Manager, 1957–65; Divl Dir, Temperature Controls Gp, 1965–71; Man. Dir, 1971–86. Hon. LLD Strathclyde, 1984. *Recreation:* golf. *Address:* 10 Seeleys Road, Beaconsfield, Bucks HP9 1BY.

MacGREGOR, Joanna Clare, FTCL, FRAM; concert pianist; *b* 16 July 1959; *d* of Alfred MacGregor and Angela (*née* Hughes); *m* 1986, Richard Williams; (one *d* decd). *Educ:* S Hampstead Sch. for Girls; New Hall, Cambridge (BA Hons); Royal Acad. of Music (FRAM 1991). FTCL 1995. Gresham Prof. of Music (jtly), 1997–2000. Has appeared as a soloist with leading orchestras, including: RPO, LSO, English Chamber Orch., BBC SO, City of London Sinfonia, NYO, London Mozart Players; has toured worldwide, incl. Netherlands, Scandinavia, Africa, Australia, NZ, USA and Far East. Classical repertoire, also jazz and new music (has commissioned and premiered over 50 new works); jtly organised Platform Fest. of New Music, ICA, 1991–93; Artistic Dir, SoundCircus, Bridgewater Hall, Manchester, 1996 and creator, SoundCircus recording label, 1998; has made numerous recordings. Mem., Arts Council of England, 1998–. Trustee, Young Concert Artists Trust, 1985–88. Presenter: BBC Radio 3; Strings, Bow and Bellows (series), BBC TV, 1995. European Encouragement Prize for Music, 1995; South Bank Show Award for Classical Music, 2000. *Publication:* Joanna MacGregor's Piano World (3 vols), 1999. *Address:* c/o Ingpen and Williams, 26 Wadham Road, SW15 2LR. *T:* (020) 8874 3222.

MACGREGOR, John Malcolm, CVO 1992; HM Diplomatic Service; Director, Wider Europe, Foreign and Commonwealth Office, since 2000; *b* 3 Oct. 1946; *s* of late Dr D. F. Macgregor and of K. A. Macgregor (*née* Adams); *m* 1982, Judith Anne Brown; three *s* one *d*. *Educ:* Kibworth Beauchamp Grammar Sch., Leics; Balliol Coll., Oxford (BA 1967). ARCO 1965. Taught at Cranleigh Sch., Surrey, 1969–73; joined HM Diplomatic Service, 1973; 1st Sec. (political), New Delhi, 1975; FCO, 1979; Pvte Sec. to Minister of State, FCO, 1981; Assistant, Soviet Dept, FCO, 1983; Dep. Head of Mission, Prague, 1986; Head of Chancery, Paris, 1990–93; Head of EU Dept (Ext.), 1993–95; Dir Gen. for Trade Promotion in Germany and Consul-Gen., Düsseldorf, 1995–98; Ambassador to Poland, 1998–2000. *Recreations:* music, languages, bricolage, travel. *Address:* c/o Foreign and Commonwealth Office, King Charles Street, SW1A 2AH. *T:* (020) 7270 3000.

MacGREGOR, Neil; *see* MacGregor, R. N.

McGREGOR, Peter, CEng, FIEE; writer and consultant; Director General, Export Group for the Constructional Industries, 1984–91 (Consultant, 1991–94); *b* 20 May 1926; *s* of Peter McGregor and Margaret Thomson McGregor (*née* McAuslan); *m* 1954, Marion, *d* of H. T. Downer; one *s* one *d*. *Educ:* Cardiff High Sch.; Univ. of Birmingham; London Sch. of Economics (BSc (Econs)). National Service, RE, 1946–48. Various appointments, Ferranti Ltd, 1950–74, incl. Works Manager, Distribution Transformer Dept, Sales Manager, Transformer Div., Gen. Manager, Power Div.; Dir, Industrie Elettriche di Legnano (Italy), 1970–74; Associate Dir, Corporate Renewal Associates Ltd, 1988–93. Dir, Oxford Univ. Business Summer Sch., 1972; first Sec. Gen., Anglo-German Foundn for Study of Industrial Soc., 1974–81; Industrial Dir (Dep. Sec.), NEDO, 1981–84. Chm., Textile Machinery EDC, 1982–86; Dir, Templeton Technol. Seminar, 1985. Member: N American Adv. Gp, BOTB, 1968–74; Europ. Trade Cttee, BOTB, 1981–83; Adv. Bd, Public Policy Centre, 1984–88; Cttee on Exchange Rate, Public Policy Centre, 1984–87. Industrial Advr to Liberal Party, 1960–73; an Industrial Advr to Social and Liberal Democrats, 1988–90; Chm., Hazel Grove Liberal Assoc., 1971–74; contested (L) Ilford South, 1964. Mem., Königswinter Conf. steering cttee, 1976–90. Hon. Treasurer, Anglo-German Assoc., 1983–91. Elder and Hon. Treas., St Columba's Ch, Oxford, 1992–97. MCIM; FIMgt; FRSA 1981–97. *Publications:* The Retreat or The Cybernetic Infraction (novel), 1997; various articles and pamphlets especially on industrial relations, company structure, market economy. *Recreations:* walking, reading, listening to music, writing, conversation, gardening, drawing attention to the Emperor's lack of clothes. *Address:* Dacre Cottage, Longworth, Oxon OX13 5HH. *T:* (01865) 821463. *Club:* Caledonian.

MacGREGOR, (Robert) Neil; Director, National Gallery, since 1987; *b* 16 June 1946; *s* of Alexander Rankin MacGregor and Anna MacGregor (*née* Neil). *Educ:* Glasgow Acad.; New Coll., Oxford (Hon. Fellow); Ecole Normale Supérieure, Paris; Univ. of Edinburgh; Courtauld Inst. of Art. Mem., Faculty of Advocates, Edinburgh, 1972. Lectr in History of Art and Architecture, Univ. of Reading, 1976; Editor, The Burlington Magazine, 1981–86. Trustee, Pilgrim Trust, 1990–. Kuratorium, Zentralinstitut für Kunstgeschichte, Munich, 1992–; Mem., Supervisory Bd, Rijksmuseum, Amsterdam, 1995–. Hon. Mem., Royal Scottish Acad., 1995; Hon. FBA 2000. DUniv York, 1992; Dr *hc*: Edinburgh, 1994; Reading, 1997; Leicester, 1997; Exeter, 1998; Strathclyde, 1998; Hon. DLitt: Oxford, 1998, London, 1999. *Publications:* A Victim of Anonymity: the master of the St Bartholomew Altarpiece, 1994; (jtly) Seeing Salvation: images of Christian art, 2000; contribs to Apollo, The Burlington Magazine, etc. *Address:* National Gallery, Trafalgar Square, WC2N 5DN.

See also A. R. MacGregor.

MacGREGOR, Susan Katriona, (Sue), OBE 1992; Presenter, Today, BBC Radio Four, since 1984; *b* 30 Aug. 1941; *d* of late Dr James MacGregor and Margaret MacGregor. *Educ:* Herschel School, Cape, South Africa. Announcer/producer, South African Broadcasting Corp., 1962–67; BBC Radio reporter, World at One, World This Weekend, PM, 1967–72; Presenter: Woman's Hour, BBC Radio 4, 1972–87; Tuesday Call, 1973–86; Conversation Piece, 1978–94; Around Westminster, BBC TV, 1990–92. Vis. Prof. of Journalism, Nottingham Trent Univ., 1995–. Mem. Bd, RNT, 1998–. Member: RCP Cttee on Ethical Issues in Medicine, 1985–2001; Marshall Aid Commemoration Commn, 1989–98. FRSA 1983; Hon. MRCP 1995. Hon. DLitt: Nottingham, 1996; Nottingham Trent, 2000; Staffordshire, 2001; Hon. LLD Dundee, 1997. *Recreations:* theatre, cinema, ski-ing. *Address:* c/o BBC News Centre, W12 8QT.

McGREGOR-JOHNSON, Richard John; His Honour Judge McGregor-Johnson; a Circuit Judge, since 1998; *b* 11 July 1950; *s* of Maxwell and Pamela McGregor-Johnson; *m* 1974, Elizabeth Weston; one *s* one *d*. *Educ:* Dean Close Sch., Cheltenham; Bristol Univ. (LLB 1972). Called to the Bar, Inner Temple, 1973, Bencher, 2001; an Asst Recorder, 1990–94; a Recorder, 1994–98. *Recreations:* choral singing, dinghy sailing. *Address:* Crown Court, 6–8 Penrhyn Road, Kingston upon Thames, Surrey KT1 2BB.

McGRIGOR, Captain Sir Charles Edward, 5th Bt *cr* 1831; DL; Rifle Brigade, retired; Member Royal Company of Archers (HM Body Guard for Scotland); *b* 5 Oct. 1922; *s* of Lieut-Colonel Sir Charles McGrigor, 4th Bt, OBE, and Lady McGrigor, *d* of Edward Lygon Somers Cocks, Bake, St Germans, Cornwall; *S* father, 1946; *m* 1948, Mary Bettine, *e d* of Sir Archibald Charles Edmonstone, 6th Bt; two *s* two *d*. *Educ:* Eton. War of 1939–45 (despatches); joined Army, 1941, from Eton; served with Rifle Bde, N. Africa, Italy, Austria. ADC to Duke of Gloucester, 1945–47, in Australia and England. Exon, Queen's Bodyguard, Yeoman of the Guard, 1970–85. Mem. Cttee of Management, and a Vice-Pres., RNLI. DL Argyll and Bute, 1987. *Recreations:* fishing, gardening. *Heir:* *s* James Angus Rhoderick Neil McGrigor, *qv*. *Address:* Upper Sonachan, Dalmally, Argyll PA33 1BJ.

McGRIGOR, James Angus Rhoderick Neil; Member (C) Highlands and Islands, Scottish Parliament, since 1999; *b* 19 Oct. 1949; *er s* and *heir* of Sir Charles Edward McGrigor, Bt, *qv*; *m* 1st, 1987, Caroline Roboh (marr. diss. 1993); two *d*; 2nd, 1997, Emma Mary Louise Fellowes; one *s*. *Educ:* Cladich Sch., Argyll; Sunningdale Sch., Berks; Eton College. Shipping, 1969–71; stockbroking, 1971–74; farmer, 1975–. Mem., Queen's Body Guard for Scotland, Royal Co. of Archers, 1990. *Recreations:* fishing, music, literature. *Address:* Ardchonnel, by Dalmally, Argyll PA33 1BW. *Clubs:* White's, New, Chelsea Arts.

McGROUTHER, Prof. (Duncan) Angus, MD; FRCS, FRCSGlas, FRCSE; Professor of Plastic and Reconstructive Surgery, University of Manchester, since 2001; *b* 3 March 1946; *s* of Dr John Ingram McGrouther and Margot Christina Cooke Gray; *m* 1967, Sandra Elizabeth Jackson; one *s* one *d*. *Educ:* Glasgow High Sch.; Univ. of Glasgow (MB ChB 1969; MD Hons 1988); Univ. of Strathclyde (MSc Bioengineering 1975). Glasgow Royal Infirmary, 1969–74; Cruden Med. Res. Fellow, Bioengrg Unit, Univ. of Strathclyde, 1972–73; Registrar and Sen. Registrar in Plastic Surgery, Canniesburn Hosp., Glasgow, 1975–78; Assistentarzt, Klinikum Rechts der Isar, Munich, 1978; Consultant Plastic Surgeon: Shotley Bridge Gen. Hosp. and Sunderland Dist Gen. Hosp., 1979–80; Canniesburn Hosp., 1981–89; Prof. of Plastic and Reconstructive Surgery (first estabd British chair), UCL, 1989–2001. Christine Kleinert Vis. Prof., Univ. of Louisville, 1988. Kay-Kilner Prize, British Assoc. of Plastic Surgeons, 1979; Pulvertaft Prize, British Soc. for Surgery of the Hand, 1981. *Publications:* papers on anatomy, biomechanics, plastic surgery, hand surgery, microsurgery, and wound healing. *Recreations:* mountains, sea, books. *Address:* Department of Plastic Surgery, Wythenshawe Hospital, Southmoor Road, Manchester M23 9LT.

McGUCKIAN, John Brendan; Chairman, Ulster Television, since 1990; *b* 13 Nov. 1939; *s* of late Brian McGuckian and of Pauline (*née* McKenna); *m* 1970, Carmel, *d* of Daniel McGowan; two *s* two *d*. *Educ:* St McNissis Coll., Garrontower; Queen's Univ. of Belfast (BSc). Chairman: Cloughmills Mfg Co., 1967–; Tedcastle Hldgs, 1999–; Director: Munster & Leinster Bank, 1972–; Allied Irish Bank plc, 1976–; Harbour Group Ltd, 1978–; Aer Lingus plc, 1979–84; Unidare plc, 1987–; Irish Ferries plc, 1988–; Derry Development Commn, 1968–71; Dep. Chm., Laganside Corp., 1988–92; and other directorships. Chairman: Internat. Fund for Ireland, 1990–93; IDB for NI, 1991–98. Sen. Pro-Chancellor and Chm. of Senate, QUB. *Address:* Ardverna, Cloughmills, Ballymena, Co. Antrim, Northern Ireland BT44 9NL. *T:* (028) 2763 8121; Lisgoole Abbey, Culkey, Enniskillen BT92 2FP.

McGUFFIN, Prof. Peter, PhD; FRCP, FRCPsych, FMedSci; Professor of Psychiatric Genetics and Director, Social, Genetic and Developmental Psychiatry Research Centre, Institute of Psychiatry, London, since 1998; *b* 4 Feb. 1949; *s* of Captain W. B. McGuffin, RD, RNR and M. M. McGuffin; *m* 1972, Prof. Anne E. Farmer; one *s* two *d*. *Educ:* Univ. of Leeds (MB ChB); Univ. of London (PhD). MRCP 1976, FRCP 1988; MRCPsych 1978, FRCPsych 1990. St James Univ. Hosp., Leeds, 1972–77; Registrar, Sen. Registrar, Maudsley Hosp., 1977–79; MRC Fellow, MRC Sen. Clinical Fellow, Inst. of Psychiatry, 1979–86; Hon. Consultant, Maudsley and King's Coll. Hosps, 1983–86; Prof. of Psychological Medicine, Univ. of Wales Coll. of Medicine, 1987–98. Vis. Fellow, Washington Univ., St Louis, 1981–82. Founder FMedSci 1998. Pres., Internat. Soc. of Psychiatric Genetics, 1996–. *Publications:* Scientific Principles of Psychopathology, 1984; A Psychiatric Catechism, 1987; Schizophrenia, the Major Issues, 1988; The New Genetics of Mental Illness, 1991; Seminars in Psychiatric Genetics, 1994; Essentials of Postgraduate Psychiatry, 1997; articles, research papers on psychiatry and genetics. *Recreations:* classical guitar, music, tennis, running, horse riding. *Address:* Institute of Psychiatry, de Crespigny Park, Denmark Hill, SE5 8AF; 68 Heol-y-Delyn, Lisvane, Cardiff CF4 5SR.

McGUGAN, Irene Margaret; Member (SNP) North East Scotland, Scottish Parliament, since 1999; *b* 29 Aug. 1952; *d* of late James Millar Duncan and of Phyllis Margaret Duncan (*née* Smith, now Mrs John Nicoll); *m* 1971, James McGugan; one *s* one *d*. *Educ:* Robert Gordon's Inst. of Technol. (CQSW 1982; Dip. Social Work 1982); Dundee Univ. (Advanced Cert. in Child Protection Studies 1991). VSO, India, 1970–71; full-time mother and voluntary worker, 1971–80; Social Work Dept, Tayside Regl Council, 1985–96, Angus Council, 1996–99 (Manager, Community Support, 1998–99). Elder, Church of Scotland, 1985. *Recreations:* Gaelic, malt whisky, cycling, music, theatre. *Address:* (constituency office) 70 Rosemount Place, Aberdeen AB25 2XJ. *T:* (01224) 623150.

McGUIGAN, Rupert Iain Sutherland; HM Diplomatic Service, retired; Managing Director, Private Trust Corporation (East Africa) Ltd, since 1999; *b* 25 June 1941; *s* of Hugh and Sue McGuigan; *m* 1968, Rosemary Rashleigh Chaytor; two *d*. *Educ:* Marlborough Coll.; Magdalene Coll., Cambridge (MA Law). With BP Ltd, 1964–72; HM Diplomatic Service, 1972–97: First Secretary: New Delhi, 1974–77; Kingston, Jamaica, 1978–81; Permanent Under-Secretaries Dept, FCO, 1981–85; Bridgetown, 1985–88; Counsellor: Lagos, 1989–93; Kingston, Jamaica, 1994–96. Private Sec. to the Princess Royal, 1997–99. *Recreations:* most ball games, amateur dramatics, philately, singing in the bath. *Address:* Goodhope, Halls Lane, Waltham St Lawrence, Berks RG10 0JB. *T:* (0118) 934 0989; PO Box 288, Village Market, Nairobi, Kenya. *Clubs:* Hawks (Cambridge); Worplesdon Golf.

McGUIGAN BURNS, Simon Hugh; *see* Burns.

McGUINESS, Robert Clayton, PhD; Managing Director, NPL Management Ltd, since 2000; *b* 31 Dec. 1951; *s* of Robert McGuiness and Agnes McGuiness; *m* 1982, Beate Winkelmann; two *d. Educ:* Univ. of Glasgow (BSc (Hons) 1973; PhD 1976). ICI plc, 1976–2000: ICI Paints, 1976–93; Gen. Manager Marketing and Planning, ICI Autocolor, 1993–96; Vice Pres., Refinish, Glidden Co., N. America, 1996–98; Chief Exec., ICI Autocolor, 1999. *Recreations:* golf, ski-ing. *Address:* Oak Lodge, Bray Road, Maidenhead, Berks SL6 1UF. *T:* (01628) 621699; National Physical Laboratory, Queen's Road, Teddington, Middlesex TW11 0LW. *Club:* Aspect Park Golf (Remenham Hill).

McGUINNESS, Maj.-Gen. Brendan Peter, CB 1986; consultant in education and training, now retired; Adviser on Engineering to Schools and Colleges, University of Birmingham, 1994–96; Director of Education and Training Liaison, Engineering Employers' Federation, West Midlands, 1988–94 (Head of Educational Liaison, 1987–88); *b* 26 June 1931; *s* of Bernard and May McGuinness; *m* 1968, Ethne Patricia (*née* Kelly); one *s* one *d. Educ:* Mount St Mary's College. psc, rcds. Commissioned Royal Artillery, 1950; regimental duty, 1950–60; Staff, 1960–62; sc 1963; Adjutant, 1964–65; Staff, 1965–68 (despatches, Borneo, 1966); Battery Comdr, 1968–70; Staff Coll. Directing Staff, 1970–72; CO 45 Medium Regt, 1972–75; CRA 1st Armd Div., 1975–77; RCDS 1978; MoD Staff, 1979–81; Dep. Comdr, NE District, 1981–83; GOC W Dist, 1983–86. Hon. Col, Birmingham Univ. OTC, 1987–97; Hon. Regtl Col, 45 Field Regt, 1985–91. Mem. Cttee, Hereford and Worcester Br., STA, 1991–96. Project Dir, 1987–88, Gov., 1988–, The City Technol. Coll., Kingshurst; Mem. Court, Birmingham Univ., 1992–94; Governor: King's Coll. for the Arts and Technol., Guildford, 1999–; King's Internat. Coll. for Business and the Arts, Camberley, 2000–; Guest Gov., Cirencester Coll., 1998–. Dir, Acafess Community Trust, 1992–94 (Chm., 1992). *Recreations:* tennis, hill walking, beagling. *Address:* 107 Gloucester Street, Cirencester, Glos GL7 2DW. *T:* (01285) 657861. *Club:* Army and Navy.

McGUINNESS, Frank; playwright; Writer in Residence, Department of English, University College, Dublin, since 1987; *b* 29 July 1953; *s* of Patrick McGuinness and Celine O'Donnell-McGuinness. *Educ:* University College, Dublin (BA 1974; MPhil 1976). *Plays:* The Factory Girls, 1982, Observe the Sons of Ulster Marching Towards the Somme, Baglady, 1985, Abbey Th.; Innocence, Gate Th., 1986; Carthaginians, Abbey, 1988; Peer Gynt (version), Gate, 1988; Mary and Lizzie, RSC, 1989; Three Sisters (version), Gate, 1990; Someone Who'll Watch Over Me, Vaudeville, transf. NY, 1992; The Bird Sanctuary, Abbey, 1994; A Doll's House (version), Playhouse, transf. NY, 1996; Mutabilitie, Caucasian Chalk Circle (version), 1997, RNT; Electra (version), Donmar, transf. NY, 1997; The Storm (version), Almeida, 1998; Dolly West's Kitchen, Abbey, transf. Old Vic, 1999; Miss Julie (version), Haymarket, 2000; *television:* The Hen House, 1989. Hon. DLitt Ulster, 2000. Evening Standard Award, 1986; Ewart-Biggs Prize, 1987; NY Critics Circle Award, 1992; Writers' Guild Award, 1992; Ireland Fund Literary Award, 1992; Tony Award, 1997. Officier de la République française, 1996. *Publications:* The Factory Girls, 1982; Observe the Sons of Ulster Marching Towards the Somme, 1986; Innocence, 1987; Carthaginians, and Baglady, 1988; Mary and Lizzie, 1989; Someone Who'll Watch Over Me, 1992; Booterstown (poems), 1994; Plays, vol. 1, 1996; Mutabilitie, 1997; Dolly West's Kitchen, 1999; The Sea With No Ships (poems), 1999; Plays, vol. 2, 2002; *versions:* Peer Gynt, 1990; Three Sisters, 1990; A Doll's House, 1996; Electra, 1997; The Storm, 1998; Miss Julie, 2000. *Recreations:* walking, horse-racing, Irish art. *Address:* Department of Anglo-Irish Literature, University College, Dublin, Belfield, Dublin 4, Ireland.

McGUINNESS, Rt Rev. James Joseph; Bishop of Nottingham, (RC), 1974–2000, now Emeritus; *b* 2 Oct. 1925; *s* of Michael and Margaret McGuinness. *Educ:* St Columb's College, Derry; St Patrick's College, Carlow; Oscott College, Birmingham. Ordained, 1950; Curate of St Mary's, Derby, 1950–53; Secretary to Bishop Ellis, 1953–56; Parish Priest, Corpus Christi Parish, Clifton, Nottingham, 1956–72; Vicar General of Nottingham Diocese, 1969; Coadjutor Bishop of Nottingham and Titular Bishop of St Germans, 1972–74. *Recreation:* gardening. *Address:* Nazareth House, Priory Street, Old Lenton, Nottingham NG7 2NX.

McGUINNESS, Martin; MP (SF) Ulster Mid, since 1997; Member (SF) Ulster Mid, since 1998, and Minister of Education, since 1999, Northern Ireland Assembly; *b* 23 May 1950. *Educ:* Christian Brothers' Tech. Coll. Mem., NI Assembly, 1982–86. Chief Negotiator, Sinn Féin. Contested (SF) Foyle, 1983, 1987, 1992. *Address:* Sinn Féin, 55 Falls Road, Belfast BT12 4PD.

McGUIRE, Anne Catherine; MP (Lab) Stirling, since 1997; a Lord Commissioner of HM Treasury (Government Whip), since 2001; *b* 26 May 1949; *d* of Albert Long, CBE and Agnes Long (*née* Coney); *m* 1972, Leonard F. McGuire; one *s* one *d. Educ:* Our Lady and St Francis Sch., Glasgow; Univ. of Glasgow (MA Hons 1971); Notre Dame Coll. of Educn. Registrar and Sec., Court's Dept, Univ. of Glasgow, 1971–74; teacher, 1983–85; fieldworker, 1985–89, Nat. Officer, Scotland, 1989–93, CSV; Dep. Dir, Scottish Council for Voluntary Orgns, 1993–97. PPS to Sec. of State for Scotland, 1997–98; an Asst Govt Whip, 1998–2001. *Recreations:* walking, Scottish traditional music, reading. *Address:* House of Commons, SW1A 0AA. *T:* (020) 7219 5014.

McGUIRE, Gerald, OBE 1974; Vice-President, Council for National Parks, 1983–90 and since 1995 (President, 1990–92; Vice-Chairman, 1981–83); *b* 12 July 1918; *s* of John Charles McGuire and Adelaide Maud McGuire (*née* Davies); *m* 1942, Eveline Mary Jenkins; one *s* one *d. Educ:* Trinity County Sch., Wood Green. Youth Hostels Association: Reg. Sec., N Yorks, 1944–64; National Countryside and Educn Officer, 1964–74; Dep. Nat. Sec., 1974–82; Pres., N England Region, 1989–95. President: Ramblers Assoc., 1975–78 (Vice Pres., 1978–; Pres., Lake Dist Area, 1983–86; Pres., E Yorks and Derwent Area, 1987–90); Assoc. of National Park and Countryside Voluntary Wardens, 1978–80; Chm., Countryside Link Gp, 1982–86. Member: N York Moors Nat. Park Cttee, 1953–72, 1985–91; Exec. Cttee, CPRE, 1966–76, 1981–84; Gosling Cttee on Footpaths, 1967–68; Countryside Commn, 1976–79; Commn on Energy and the Environment, 1978–81; Recreation and Conservation Cttee, Yorks Water Authority, 1984–89; Yorks Regional Cttee, Nat. Trust, 1985–93; Jt Adv. Cttee, Howardian Hills Area of Outstanding Natural Beauty, 1992–97. Vice Pres., Open Spaces Soc., 1982–98 (Vice Chm. 1971–76); Vice Chairman: Standing Cttee on Nat. Parks, 1970–76; Council for Environmental Conservation, 1981–82; Trustee, Gatliff Trust, 1983–94. Hon. Mem., Cyclists Touring Club, 1978–. Cert. of Merit, Internat. Youth Hostel Fedn, 1983; Richard Schirrmann (Founder's) Medal, German Youth Hostels Assoc., 1983; Nat. Blood Transfusion Service Award for 100 donations, 1983; CPRE Medal, 1998. *Recreations:* reading, music, walking in the countryside. *Address:* 24 Castle Howard Drive, Malton, North Yorks YO17 7BA. *T:* (01653) 692521.

McGUIRE, Michael Thomas Francis; *b* 3 May 1926; *m* 1954, Marie T. Murphy; three *s* two *d. Educ:* Elementary Schools. Coal miner. Whole-time NUM Branch Secretary, 1957–64. Joined Lab. Party, 1951. MP (Lab): Ince, 1964–83; Makerfield, 1983–87. PPS to Minister of Sport, 1974–77. Member: Council of Europe, 1977–87; WEU, 1977–87. *Recreations:* most out-door sports, especially Rugby League football; traditional music, especially Irish traditional music. *Address:* 11A Daresbury Road, Eccleston, St Helens, Lancs WA10 5DR.

McGURK, John Callender; Editorial Director, The Scotsman Publications Ltd, since 2001; *b* 12 Dec. 1952; *s* of John B. McGurk and Janet McGurk; *m* 1984, Karen Patricia Anne Ramsay; one *s* one *d. Educ:* Tynecastle Sen. Secondary Sch., Edinburgh. Trainee Journalist, Scottish County Press, 1970–73; Reporter: Evening Post, Nottingham, 1973–75; Scottish Daily News, 1975; Reporter and Broadcaster, Radio Clyde, 1975–78; Sunday Mail: Reporter, 1978–84; News Editor, 1984–88; Dep. Editor, 1988–89; Editor, Sunday Sun, Newcastle, 1989–91; Dep. Editor, Daily Record, 1991–94; broadcaster and media consultant, 1994–95; Editor: Evening News, Edinburgh, 1995–97; Scotland on Sunday, 1997–2001. Chm., Editors' Cttee, Scottish Daily Newspaper Soc., 2001–. Mem., Press Complaints Commn, 1999–. *Recreations:* newspapers, dining out, playing and paying for my children, therefore given up golf. *Address:* (office) 108 Holyrood Road, Edinburgh EH8 8AS. *T:* (0131) 620 8246.

MACH, David Stefan, RA 1998; sculptor; *b* 18 March 1956; *s* of Joseph Mach and Martha (*née* Cassidy); *m* 1979, Lesley June White. *Educ:* Buckhaven High Sch.; Duncan of Jordanstone Coll. of Art (Dip. and Post Dip. in Art); Royal Coll. of Art (MA). Full-time sculptor and occasional vis. lectr, 1982–; Associate Prof., Sculpture Dept, Edinburgh Coll. of Art, 1999–; Prof. of Sculpture, Royal Acad., 2000–. Work includes Train, Darlington, largest contemp. sculpture in the UK, 1998; sculptures exhibited at galleries in England, Scotland, NY, São Paolo Biennale, Venice Biennale. City of Glasgow Lord Provost Prize, 1992. *Recreations:* gardening, tennis, travelling, driving, film, television. *Address:* 64 Canonbie Road, Forest Hill, SE23 3AG. *T:* (020) 8699 1668; *e-mail:* davidmach@davidmach.com. *Club:* Chelsea Arts.

McHALE, His Honour Keith Michael; a Circuit Judge, 1980–2000; *b* 26 March 1928; *s* of late Cyril Michael McHale and Gladys McHale; *m* 1966, Rosemary Margaret Arthur; one *s* one *d.* Called to the Bar, Gray's Inn, 1951. *Address:* Oak Lodge, Albemarle Road, Beckenham, Kent BR3 5HS.

McHENRY, Brian Edward; Senior Civil Service Lawyer, since 1996; Member, Crown Appointments Commission, since 1997; *b* 12 Dec. 1950; *s* of Alexander Edward McHenry and Winifred Alice McHenry (*née* Wainford); *m* 1979, Elizabeth Anne Lipsey; two *s. Educ:* Dulwich Coll.; New Coll., Oxford (MA). Called to the Bar, Middle Temple, 1976. Treasury Solicitor's Dept, 1978–92, 2000; on secondment as: legal advr, Monopolies and Mergers Commn, 1992–96; Solicitor: N Wales Tribunal of Inquiry into Child Abuse, 1996–97; BSE Inquiry, 1998–2000; Chief Legal Advr, Competition Commn, 2000–. General Synod of Church of England: Mem., 1980–85 and 1987–; Vice-Chm., House of Laity, 2000–; Chm., Standing Orders Cttee, 1991–99; Member: Standing Cttee, 1990–95; Legislative Cttee, 1981–85 and 1991–95 (Dep. Chm., 2001–); Business Cttee, 1999–; elected Mem., Archbishops' Council, 1999–2000; Lay Vice-Pres., Southwark Diocesan Synod, 1988–96 and 1997–99. A Reader, C of E, 1976–. *Recreations:* jogging, swimming, walking, travel, history, Arsenal FC. *Address:* 21 Maude Road, SE5 8NY.

McHENRY, Donald F.; University Research Professor of Diplomacy and International Affairs, Georgetown University, since 1981; *b* 13 Oct. 1936; *s* of Limas McHenry and Dora Lee Brooks; *m* Mary Williamson (marr. diss.); one *s* two *d. Educ:* Lincoln Senior High Sch., East St Louis, Ill; Illinois State Univ. (BS); Southern Illinois Univ. (MSc); Georgetown Univ. Taught at Howard Univ., Washington, 1959–62; joined Dept of State, 1963; Head of Dependent Areas Section, Office of UN Polit. Affairs, 1965–68; Asst to Sec. of State, US, 1969; Special Asst to Counsellor, Dept of State, 1969–71; Lectr, Sch. of Foreign Service, Georgetown Univ.; Guest Scholar, Brookings Inst., and Internat. Affairs Fellow, Council on Foreign Relations (on leave from State Dept), 1971–73; resigned from State Dept, 1973; Project Dir, Humanitarian Policy Studies, Carnegie Endowment for Internat. Peace, Washington, 1973–76; served in transition team of President Carter, 1976–77; Ambassador and Deputy Rep. of US to UN Security Council, 1977–79, Permanent Rep., 1979; US Ambassador to UN, 1979–81. Director: Internat. Paper Co., 1981–; Fleet Boston Financial Co.; Bank of Boston Corp., 1981–; SmithKline Beecham plc, 1982–; Coca-Cola, 1982–; American Telephone and Telegraph, 1987–; Inst. for Internat. Economics; American Ditchley Foundn. Chm., Bd of Dirs, Africare; Mem. Bd of Govs, UNA of USA. Mem., American Acad. of Arts and Scis, 1992. Hon. degrees: Dennison, Duke, Eastern Illinois, Georgetown, Harvard, Illinois State, Michigan, Princeton, Southern Illinois, Tufts, and Washington Univs; Amherst, Bates, Boston and Williams Colleges. Superior Honor Award, Dept of State, 1966. Mem. Council on Foreign Relations and Editorial Bd, Foreign Policy Magazine. *Publication:* Micronesia: Trust Betrayed, 1975. *Address:* Georgetown University, 37th and O Streets, NW, Washington, DC 20057, USA.

MACHIN, Anthony; *see* Machin, E. A.

MACHIN, David; Under Treasurer, Gray's Inn, 1989–2000; *b* 25 April 1934; *s* of late Noel and Joan Machin; *m* 1963, Sarah Mary, *yr d* of late Col W. A. Chester-Master, DL; two *d. Educ:* Eton (Oppidan Scholar); Trinity Coll., Cambridge. National Service, 1952–54 (2nd Lieut Welsh Guards). Editor, William Heinemann Ltd, 1957–66; Literary Agent, Gregson & Wigan Ltd and London International, 1966–68; Partner, A. P. Watt & Son, 1968–70; Director: Jonathan Cape Ltd, 1970–78; Chatto, Bodley Head and Jonathan Cape Ltd, 1977–78, 1981–87; Jt Man. Dir, 1981, Man. Dir, 1982–87, The Bodley Head Ltd; Dir, Triad Paperbacks Ltd, 1983–86; Gen. Sec., The Society of Authors, 1978–81. Chm. of Trustees, Inns of Court Gainsford Trust, 1992–2000. Vice-Chm., Hammersmith Democrats, 1988–89. Hon. Bencher, Gray's Inn, 2000. *Publications:* (contrib.) Outlook, 1963; articles in The Author, The Bookseller, Graya. *Address:* 20 Lansdown Crescent, Bath BA1 5EX. *Club:* Garrick.

MACHIN, (Edward) Anthony; QC 1973; a Recorder of the Crown Court, 1976–90; a Judge of the Courts of Appeal of Jersey and Guernsey, 1988–95; *b* 28 June 1925; *s* of Edward Arthur Machin and Olive Muriel Smith; *m* 1953, Jean Margaret McKanna; two *s* one *d. Educ:* Christ's Coll., Finchley; New Coll., Oxford. MA 1950; BCL 1950; Vinerian Law Scholar, 1950; Tancred Student, 1950; Cassel Scholar, 1951. Called to Bar, Lincoln's Inn, 1951, Bencher, 1980; retired from practice, 1996. Chm., Exeter Flying Club, 1999. *Publications:* Redgrave's Factories Acts, 1962, 1966, 1972; Redgrave's Offices and Shops, 1965 and 1973; Redgrave's Health and Safety in Factories, 1976, 1982; Health and Safety at Work, 1980; Health and Safety, 1990; (contrib.) Medical Negligence, 1990 and 1994. *Recreations:* music, learning the organ, flying, web-surfing, languages. *Address:* Strand End, Strand, Topsham, Exeter EX3 0BB. *T:* (01392) 877992.

MACHIN, John Vessey; His Honour Judge Machin; a Circuit Judge since 1997; *b* 4 May 1941; *s* of late William Vessey Machin and Dona Machin (*née* Pryce), Worksop; *m* 1967, Susan Helen, *d* of Edgar Frank Emery; one *s* one *d. Educ:* Dragon Sch., Oxford; Westminster Sch. Called to the Bar, Middle Temple, 1965; Midland and Oxford Circuit;

Asst Recorder, 1990–94; Recorder, 1994–97. Chm., Agricl Land Tribunal (Eastern Area), 1999– (Dep. Chm., 1986–99). Member, Council: Ranby House Sch., 1986–; Worksop Coll., Notts, 1986–; Fellow, Woodard Corp., 1988–. *Recreations:* rural and aquatic pursuits. *Address:* c/o Lincoln Combined Court Centre, 360 High Street, Lincoln LN5 7RL. *Clubs:* Farmers', United Services (Nottingham); Newark Rowing.

MACHIN, Kenneth Arthur, QC 1977; **His Honour Judge Machin;** a Circuit Judge, since 1984 (sitting at Central Criminal Court, 1986–90) (Deputy Circuit Judge, 1976–79); *b* 13 July 1936; *o s* of Thomas Arthur Machin and Edith May Machin; *m* 1983, Amaryllis Francesca (Member of Court of Common Council, Cripplegate Ward, City of London), *o d* of Dr Donald and Lucille Bigley. *Educ:* St Albans School. Called to the Bar, 1960; South Eastern Circuit and Central Criminal Court; a Recorder of the Crown Court, 1979–84; Chief Social Security Comr, 1990–2001; Chief Child Support Comr, 1993–2001. Mem., Judicial Studies Bd, 1992– (Chm., Tribunals Cttee). Freeman, City of London. *Recreations:* painting, martello towers. *Address:* Central Criminal Court, Old Bailey, EC4M 7EH.

MACHIN, Thomas Paul Edwin; Director, MacGregor Associates, since 2000; *b* 14 Sept. 1944; *s* of late Thomas Edwin Machin and Elizabeth Pamela Machin (*née* Collett); *m* 1970, Elizabeth-Ann Suttle. *Educ:* St Joseph's Coll., Stoke-on-Trent; London Sch. of Economics (BSc Econs). Plessey Co., 1966–69; Massey Ferguson, 1969–74; joined British Leyland, 1974; Dir, Engrg Services, 1980–82; Personnel Dir, Cowley, 1983–87; Eur. Employee Relns and Mgt Develt Dir, Lawson Mardon Gp (Europe), 1987–91; Human Resources Dir, James Neill Hldgs Ltd, 1991–92; CEO, States of Jersey Estabt Cttee, 1992–95; Chief Executive, BPIF, 1995–2000. Chairman: Indust. Relns Cttee, BPIF, 1989–91; Trade Assoc. Council, CBI, 2000; Pres., Yorks Publicity Assoc., 1998. FIPD 1986; FRSA 1996. Freeman, City of London, 1998; Liveryman, Co. of Stationers and Newspaper Makers, 1998–. *Recreations:* golf, retired Association Football referee, walking, spectator sports (especially horse racing and Association Football). *Address:* 271 Kenilworth Road, Balsall Common, Coventry CV7 7EL. *T:* (01676) 532546. *Clubs:* National Liberal; Leamington and County Golf.

MACHRAY, Alastair Hulbert; Editor, Daily Post, since 1995; *b* 19 June 1961; *s* of Douglas Basil Machray and June Hulbert; *m* 1987, Lynne Elizabeth Ward; one *s*. *Educ:* Glasgow Acad.; Greencroft Comprehensive. Reporter, Sunderland Echo, 1979–82; sports journalist, Journal, Newcastle, 1982–85; editor, Football Pink, Newcastle, 1985–86; sports journalist, Today, 1986–88; Evening Chronicle, Newcastle: Sub Editor, 1988; Asst Chief Sub Editor, 1988–89; Dep. Chief Sub Editor, 1989–90; Design Editor, 1990–93; Asst Editor, Liverpool Echo, 1994–95. *Recreations:* golf, cricket, family, cinema, travel. *Address:* PO Box 48, Old Hall Street, Liverpool L69 3EB. *T:* (0151) 227 2000.

McHUGH, James, CBE 1989; FREng; Chairman, British Pipe Coaters Ltd, 1991–96; *b* 4 May 1930; *s* of late Edward McHugh and Martha (*née* Smith); *m* 1953, Sheila (*née* Cape); two *d*. *Educ:* Carlisle Grammar Sch.; various colls. FREng (FEng 1986); FIMechE, FIGasE, FInstPet; FIQA; CIMgt. FRSA. Served Army, National Service. Entered Gas Industry, 1947; technical and managerial appts in Northern and E Midlands Gas Bds; Prodn Engr 1967, Dir of Engrg 1971, W Midlands Gas Bd; British Gas Corporation, subseq. British Gas plc: Dir of Ops, 1975; Mem., 1979; Man. Dir, Prodn and Supply, 1982; Man. Dir, 1986; Gp Exec. Mem., 1986–91. Director: Lloyd's Register Quality Assurance Ltd, 1985–; UK Accreditation Service, 1995–2000. Member: Meteorological Cttee, MoD, 1981–85; Engrg Council, 1989–92; President: IGasE, 1986–87; Inst. of Quality Assurance, 1992–97; World Quality Council, 1997–. Freeman, City of London, 1984; Liveryman, Engineers' Co., 1984–. *Recreations:* mountaineering, dinghy sailing. *Clubs:* Royal Automobile, Anglo-Belgian.

McILWAIN, Alexander Edward, CBE 1985; WS; President, Law Society of Scotland, 1983–84; Consultant, Leonards, Solicitors, Hamilton, 1995–97 (Partner, 1963–95, Senior Partner, 1984–95); *b* 4 July 1933; *s* of Edward Walker McIlwain and Gladys Edith Horne or McIlwain; *m* 1961, Moira Margaret Kinnaird; three *d*. *Educ:* Aberdeen Grammar Sch.; Aberdeen Univ. MA 1954; LLB 1956. Pres., Students Representative Council, Univ. of Aberdeen, 1956–57. Commnd RCS, 1957–59, Lieut. Admitted Solicitor in Scotland, 1957; SSC, 1966. Burgh Prosecutor, Hamilton, 1966–75; District Prosecutor, Hamilton, 1975–76; Dean, Soc. of Solicitors of Hamilton, 1981–83; Vice Pres., Law Soc. of Scotland, 1982–83; Hon. Sheriff, Sheriffdom of South Strathclyde, Dumfries and Galloway at Hamilton, 1982; Temp. Sheriff, 1984. WS 1985. Chairman: Legal Aid Central Cttee, 1985–87; Hamilton Sheriff Court Project, 1991–94 and 1996–99; Member: Lanarkshire Health Bd, 1981–91; Central Adv. Cttee on Justices of the Peace, 1987–96; Supreme Court (formerly Review) Cttee, Scottish Legal Aid Bd, 1987–93; Cameron Cttee on Shrieval Trng, 1994–96; Criminal Injuries Compensation Appeal Panel, 1997–; Judicial Studies Cttee, 1997–2000; Criminal Injuries Compensation Bd, 1998–2000. Pres., Temporary Sheriffs' Assoc., 1995–98 (Vice Pres., 1993–95). Chm., Lanarkshire Scout Area, 1981–91; Mem. Council, Scout Assoc., 1987–97. Founder Fellow, Inst. of Contemp. Scotland, 2000. Hon. Mem., Amer. Bar Assoc., 1983. *Recreations:* gardening, listening to music. *Address:* Craigievar, Bothwell Road, Uddingston, Glasgow G71 7EY. *T:* (01698) 813368.

McINDOE, Very Rev. John Hedley; Minister of St Columba's Church, Pont Street, London, 1988–2000; Moderator of the General Assembly of The Church of Scotland, 1996–97; *b* 31 Aug. 1934; *s* of William McIndoe and May (*née* Hedley); *m* 1960, Evelyn Kennedy Johnstone; three *d*. *Educ:* Greenock Acad.; Glasgow Univ. (MA Hons (Classics), 1956; BD (with distinction), 1959); Hartford Seminary, Conn, USA (STM, 1960). Ordained, 1960; Asst Minister, Paisley Abbey, 1960–63; Minister: Park Church, Dundee, 1963–72; St Nicholas Parish Church, Lanark, 1972–88. Hon. DD Glasgow, 2000. *Recreations:* theatre, films. *Address:* 5 Dunlin, Westerlands Park, Glasgow G12 0FE. *T:* (0141) 579 1366. *Club:* Caledonian.

McINDOE, William Ian, CB 1978; Deputy Secretary, Department of the Environment, 1979–86; *b* 11 March 1929; *s* of John McIndoe, Leven, Fife and Agnes Scott; *m* 1st, 1954, Irene Armour Mudie (*d* 1966); one *s* two *d*; 2nd, 1971, Jamesanna Smart (*née* MacGregor). *Educ:* Sedbergh; Corpus Christi Coll., Oxford. 2nd Lieut 2 RHA, 1951–53; CRO, 1953–63, served in Canberra and Salisbury, 1956–62, Private Sec. to Sec. of State, 1962–63; Private Sec. to Sec. of Cabinet, later Asst Sec., Cabinet Office, 1963–66; Scottish Office, 1966–76, Under-Sec., 1971; Dep. Sec., Cabinet Office, 1976–79. Dep. Chm., Housing Corp., 1986–90. *Address:* Gifford Cottage, Main Street, Gifford, E Lothian EH41 4QH. *T:* (01620) 810363.

McINERNEY, Prof. John Peter, OBE 1995; Glanely Professor of Agricultural Policy and Director of Agricultural Economics Unit, University of Exeter, since 1984; *b* 10 Jan. 1939; *s* of Peter McInerney and Eva McInerney; *m* 1961, Audrey M. Perry; one *s* one *d*. *Educ:* Colyton Grammar Sch., Colyford, Devon; Univ. of London (BScAgric Hons); Univ. of Oxford (DipAgricEcons); Iowa State Univ. (PhD). Lectr in Agricl Econs, Wye Coll., Univ. of London, 1964–66; Lectr and Sen. Lectr in Agricl Econs, Univ. of Manchester, 1967–78; Prof. of Agricl Econs and Management, Univ. of Reading, 1978–84. Research Economist and Cons., World Bank, Washington, 1972–97. President: Agricl Econs Soc., 1996–97; Rural Educn and Develt Assoc., 1996–97; Member: Mgt Cttee, MAFF/DTI LINK Sustainable Livestock Prog., 1996–; Farm Animal Welfare Council, MAFF, 1996–; Bd, UK Register of Organic Food Standards, 1997–; MAFF Independent Scientific Gp on Cattle TB, 1998–. Governor, Silsoe Res. Inst., 1996–. Phi Kappa Phi 1964, Gamma Sigma Delta 1964. FRSA 1995. Hon. FRASE 1999. Massey Ferguson Nat. Agricl Award, 1998. *Publications:* The Food Industry: economics and policy (jtly), 1983; Badgers and Bovine Tuberculosis (jtly), 1986; Disease in Farm Livestock: economics and policy (jtly), 1987; Diversification in the Use of Farm Resources, 1989; Economic Analysis of Milk Quotas, 1992; Agriculture at the Crossroads, 1998; Who Cares?: a study of farmers' involvement in countryside management, 2000; chapters in: Current Issues in Economic Policy, 1975, 2nd edn 1980; Resources Policy, 1982; Grassland Production, 1999, etc; articles in Jl of Agricl Econs, Amer. Jl of Agricl Econs, Canadian Jl of Agricl Econs, Outlook on Agric., Jl of RASE, Farm Mgt, Preventive Vet. Medicine, Agricl Progress. *Recreations:* doing it myself, tentative farming, introspection. *Address:* c/o Agricultural Economics Unit, University of Exeter, Exeter EX4 6TL. *T:* (01392) 263837; *e-mail:* J.P.McInerney@exeter.ac.uk. *Club:* Templeton Social.

MacINNES, Archibald, CVO 1977; Under Secretary, Property Services Agency, Department of the Environment, 1973–79; retired 1989; *b* 10 April 1919; *s* of Duncan and Catherine MacInnes; *m* 1950, Nancey Elisabeth Blyth (*d* 1976); one *s* two *d*. *Educ:* Kirkcudbright Academy; Royal Technical Coll., Glasgow. FIMechE. Scott's Shipbuilding and Engineering Co., Greenock, 1937–44; Colonial Service, Nigeria, 1945–59; War Office Works Organisation: Gibraltar, 1959–63; Southern Comd, Salisbury, Wilts, 1963–64; MPBW, Bristol, 1964–68; DoE, Germany, 1968–72; Dir, London Region, PSA, DoE, 1972–79; part-time Planning Inspector, DoE, 1980–89. FIMgt. Coronation Medal. *Recreations:* golf, shooting, fishing. *Address:* Lower Road, Homington, Salisbury, Wilts SP5 4NG. *T:* (01722) 718336.

MacINNES, Barbara Mary; *see* Stocking, B. M.

MacINNES, Hamish, OBE 1979; BEM; Founder and Leader, Glencoe Mountain Rescue Team, 1960–94; author and film consultant, major movies; Director, Glencoe Productions Ltd, since 1989; *b* 7 July 1930. Dep. Leader, British Everest Expedition, 1975. Hon. Dir, Leishman Meml Res. Centre, Glencoe, 1975–92; Mountain Rescue Cttee for Scotland (Past Sec.). Founder and Hon. Pres., Search and Rescue Dog Assoc.; Past Pres., Alpine Climbing Group; Pres., Guide Dogs for the Blind Adventure Gp, 1986–. Designer of climbing equipment, incl. the first all metal ice axe, terrodactyl ice tools, the MacInnes stretchers, etc. Hon. LLD Glasgow, 1983; Hon. DSc: Aberdeen, 1988; Heriot-Watt, 1992; DU Stirling, 1997. *Publications:* Climbing, 1964; Scottish Climbs, 2 vols, 1971, 2nd edn (1 vol.) 1981; International Mountain Rescue Handbook, 1972, 4th edn 1998; Call-Out: mountain rescue, 1973, 4th edn 1986; Climb to the Lost World, 1974; Death Reel (novel), 1976; West Highland Walks, vols 1 and 2, 1979, Vol. 3, 1983, Vol. 4, 1988; Look Behind the Ranges, 1979; Scottish Winter Climbs, 1980; High Drama (stories), 1980; Beyond the Ranges, 1984; Sweep Search, 1985; The Price of Adventure, 1987; My Scotland, 1988; The Way Through the Glens, 1989; Land of Mountain and Mist, 1989; books have been translated into Russian, Japanese and German. *Address:* Tigh A'Voulin, Glencoe, Argyll PA49 4HX.

McINNES, John Colin; DL; QC (Scot.) 1990; Sheriff Principal of South Strathclyde, Dumfries and Galloway, since 2000; *b* 21 Nov. 1938; *s* of late Mr I. W. McInnes, WS, and of Mrs Lucy McInnes, Cupar, Fife; *m* 1966, Elisabeth Mabel Neilson; one *s* one *d*. *Educ:* Cargilfield Sch., Edinburgh; Merchiston Castle Sch., Edinburgh; Brasenose Coll., Oxford (BA); Edinburgh Univ. (LLB). 2nd Lieut 8th Royal Tank Regt, 1957–58; Lieut Fife and Forfar Yeomanry/Scottish Horse (TA), 1958–64. Advocate, 1963. In practice at Scottish Bar, 1963–73; Tutor, Faculty of Law, Edinburgh Univ., 1965–73; Sheriff of the Lothians and Peebles, 1973–74, of Tayside Central and Fife, 1974–2000. Member and Vice-President: Security Service Tribunal, 1989–; Intelligence Services Tribunal, 1994–; Mem., Investigatory Powers Tribunal, 2000–. Member: Cameron Gp on Shrieval Trng, 1995–96; Scottish Criminal Justice Forum, 1996–2000; Judicial Studies Cttee (Scotland), 1996–2000. Comr of Northern Lighthouses, 2000–. Pres., Sheriffs' Assoc., 1995–97. Director: R. Mackness & Co. Ltd, 1963–70; Fios Group Ltd, 1970–72 (Chm., 1970–72). Chm., Fife Family Conciliation Service, 1988–90. Mem. Court, St Andrews Univ., 1983–91. DL Fife, 1997. Hon. LLD St Andrews, 1994. Contested (C) Aberdeen North, 1964. *Publication:* Divorce Law and Practice in Scotland, 1990. *Recreations:* shooting, fishing, ski-ing, photography. *Address:* Sheriff Court House, Graham Street, Airdrie ML6 6EE. *T:* (01236) 751121.

MacINNES, Keith Gordon, CMG 1984; HM Diplomatic Service, retired; Ambassador and UK Permanent Representative to OECD, Paris, 1992–95; *b* 17 July 1935; *s* of late Kenneth MacInnes and of Helen MacInnes (*née* Gordon); *m* 1st, 1966, Jennifer Anne Fennell (marr. diss. 1980); one *s* one *d*; 2nd, 1985, Hermione Pattinson. *Educ:* Rugby; Trinity Coll., Cambridge (MA); Pres., Cambridge Union Soc., 1957. HM Forces, 1953–55. FO, 1960; Third, later Second Secretary, Buenos Aires, 1961–64; FO, 1964 (First Sec., 1965); Private Sec. to Permanent Under-Sec., Commonwealth Office, 1965–68; First Sec. (Information), Madrid, 1968–70; FCO, 1970–74; Counsellor and Head of Chancery: Prague, 1974–77; Dep. Perm. Rep., UK Mission, Geneva, 1977–80; Head of Information Dept, FCO, 1980–83; Asst Under-Sec. of State and Principal Finance Officer, FCO, 1983–87; Ambassador to the Philippines, 1987–92. *Recreations:* golf, bridge. *Address:* c/o Child & Co., 1 Fleet Street, EC4Y 1BD.

McINTOSH, family name of **Baron McIntosh of Haringey** and **Baroness McIntosh of Hudnall**.

McINTOSH OF HARINGEY, Baron *cr* 1982 (Life Peer), of Haringey in Greater London; **Andrew Robert McIntosh;** Captain of the Yeomen of the Guard (Deputy Government Chief Whip), since 1997; *b* 30 April 1933; *s* of late Prof. A. W. McIntosh and Jenny (*née* Britton); *m* 1962, Naomi Ellen Sargant; two *s*. *Educ:* Haberdashers' Aske's Hampstead Sch.; Royal Grammar Sch., High Wycombe; Jesus Coll., Oxford (MA); Ohio State Univ. (Fellow in Econs, 1956–57). Gallup Poll, 1957–61; Hoover Ltd, 1961–63; Market Res. Manager, Osram (GEC) Ltd, 1963–65; IFF Research Ltd: Man. Dir, 1965–81; Chm., 1981–88; Dep. Chm., 1988–97. Chm., SVP United Kingdom Ltd, 1983–92. Member: Hornsey Bor. Council, 1963–65; Haringey Bor. Council, 1964–68 (Chm., Develt Control); Greater London Council: Member for Tottenham, 1973–83; Chm., NE Area Bd, 1973–74, W Area Bd, 1974–76, and Central Area Bd, 1976; Opposition Leader on Planning and Communications, 1977–80; Leader of the Opposition, 1980–81. House of Lords: Opposition spokesman on educn and science, 1985–87, on industry matters, 1983–87, on the environment, 1987–92, on home affairs, 1992–97; Dep. Leader of the Opposition, 1992–97; Chm., Computer Sub-Cttee, H of L Offices Cttee, 1984–92. Mem., Metrop. Water Bd, 1967–68. Market Research Society: Ed. of Jl, 1963–67; Chm., 1972–73; Pres., 1995–98. Chairman: Assoc. of Neighbourhood Councils, 1974–80; Fabian Soc., 1985–86 (Mem., NEC, 1981–87). Principal, Working Men's Coll., NW1, 1988–97; Governor, Drayton Sch., Tottenham, 1967–83. *Publications:*

Industry and Employment in the Inner City, 1979; (ed) Employment Policy in the UK and United States, 1980; Women and Work, 1981; jl articles on theory, practice and findings of survey research. *Recreations:* cooking, reading, music. *Address:* 27 Hurst Avenue, N6 5TX. *T:* (020) 8340 1496, *Fax:* (020) 8348 4641.
See also N. E. Sargant.

McINTOSH OF HUDNALL, Baroness *cr* 1999 (Life Peer), of Hampstead in the London Borough of Camden; **Genista Mary McIntosh;** Executive Director, Royal National Theatre, 1990–96 and since 1997; *b* 23 Sept. 1946; *d* of late Geoffrey Tandy and Maire Tandy; *m* 1971, Neil Scott Wishart McIntosh, *qv* (marr. diss.); one *s* one *d. Educ:* Univ. of York (BA Philosophy and Sociology). Press Sec., York Festival of Arts, 1968–69; Royal Shakespeare Co.: Casting Dir, 1972–77; Planning Controller, 1977–84; Sen. Administrator, 1986–90; Associate Producer, 1990; Chief Exec., Royal Opera House, Covent Gdn, 1997. Dir, Marmont Management Ltd, 1984–86. Board Member: Roundhouse Trust, 1999–; WNO, 2000–. Trustee, Nat. Endowment for Sci., Technol. and the Arts, 1998–. DUniv York, 1998. *Address:* Royal National Theatre, Upper Ground, SE1 9PX. *T:* (020) 7452 3333.

McINTOSH, Prof. Angus, FRSE 1978; FBA 1989; consultant on linguistics problems; hon. consultant, Institute for Historical Dialectology (formerly Gayre Institute for Medieval English and Scottish Dialectology), University of Edinburgh, since 1986; *b* 10 Jan. 1914; *s* of late Kenneth and Mary McIntosh (*née* Thompson), Cleadon, Sunderland, Co. Durham; *m* 1st, 1939, Barbara (*d* 1988), *d* of late Dr William Seaman and Mrs Bainbridge (*née* June Wheeler), New York City; two *s* one *d*; 2nd, 1988, Karina Williamson (*née* Side), *widow* of Colin Williamson, Fellow of Jesus Coll., Oxford; two step *s* one step *d. Educ:* Ryhope Grammar Sch., Co. Durham; Oriel Coll., Oxford (BA, 1st Class Hons, English Lang., and Lit., 1934); Merton Coll., Oxford (Harmsworth Scholar); (Dip. of Comparative Philology, University of Oxford, 1936); Harvard Univ. (Commonwealth Fund Fellow, 1936–38; AM 1937). MA (Oxford) 1938. Lecturer, Dept of English, University College, Swansea, 1938–46. Served War of 1939–45, beginning as trooper in Tank Corps, finishing as Major in Intelligence Corps. University Lecturer in Mediæval English, Oxford, 1946–48; Lecturer in English, Christ Church, Oxford, 1946–47; Student of Christ Church, 1947–48; University of Edinburgh: Forbes Prof. of English Language and General Linguistics, 1948–64, later Forbes Prof. of Eng. Lang., 1964–79; Dir, Middle English Dialect Atlas Project, 1979–86; Hon. Sen. Res. Fellow, Dept of English Language, Glasgow Univ., 1993–. Co-Chm., Hon. Adv. Bd, Pergamon Encyclopedia of Lang. and Linguistics, 1988–94. Rockefeller Foundation Fellowship, US, June-Sept. 1949; Leverhulme Emeritus Res. Fellow, 1984–86. Hon. Pres., Scottish Text Soc., 1989– (Pres., 1977–89). For. Mem., Finnish Acad. of Science and Letters, 1976. Hon. DPhil Poznan Univ., 1972; Hon. DLitt: Durham, 1980; Glasgow, 1994. Sir Israel Gollancz Prize, British Acad., 1989. *Publications:* books, articles and reviews on English language and related topics. *Recreations:* gardening, painting, music. *Address:* 32 Blacket Place, Edinburgh EH9 1RL. *T:* (0131) 667 5791.
See also T. Williamson.

McINTOSH, Anne Caroline Ballingall; MP (C) Vale of York, since 1997; *b* 20 Sept. 1954; *d* of Dr Alastair Ballingall McIntosh and Grethe-Lise McIntosh (*née* Thomsen); *m* 1992, John Harvey. *Educ:* Harrogate Coll., Harrogate, Yorks; Univ. of Edinburgh (LLB Hons); Univ. of Aarhus, Denmark. Admitted to Faculty of Advocates, 1982. Stagiaire, EEC, Brussels, 1978; unqualified legal advr in private EEC practice, Brussels, 1979–80; Bar apprentice with Simpson and Marwick, WS, and devilling at Scottish Bar, 1980–82; private legal practice, Brussels, specialising in EEC law, 1982–83; Secretariat Mem., responsible for transport, youth, culture, educn and tourism, and relations with Scandinavia, Austria, Switzerland and Yugoslavia, EDG, Europ. Parlt, 1983–89. European Parliament: Mem. (C), NE Essex, 1989–94, Essex N and Suffolk S, 1994–99; a Jun. Whip, EDG, 1989–92; Mem., Transport and Legal Affairs Cttees; EDG Spokesman on Rules Cttee, 1989–95, Transport and Tourism Cttee, 1992–99; Mem., Norway Parly Delegn, 1989–95, Polish Parly Delegn, 1995–97, Czech Parly Delegn, 1997–99. Member: Select Cttee on Envmt, Transport and the Regions, 1999–2001; Select Cttee on Transport, Local Govt and the Regions, 2001–; Exec., 1922 Cttee, 2000–; European Scrutiny Cttee; European Standing Cttee. President: Anglia Enterprise in Europe, 1989–; Yorkshire First, Enterprise in Yorks, 1995–. Member: Governing Council, Anglia Poly. Univ.; Senate, Univ. of Essex; Gov., Writtle Coll. Hon. LLD Anglia Poly. Univ., 1997. *Recreations:* swimming, cinema, walking. *Address:* House of Commons, SW1A 0AA; Conservative Office, Westgate, Thirsk, N Yorks, YO7 1QS. *T:* (01845) 527240.

McINTOSH, David Angus; Senior Partner, Davies Arnold Cooper, Solicitors, since 1978; President, Law Society, 2001–July 2002; *b* 10 March 1944; *s* of late Robert Angus McIntosh and of Monica Joan (*née* Hillier, now Sherring); *m* 1968, Jennifer Mary Dixon; two *d. Educ:* Selwood Co. Sch., Frome; Coll. of Law, London. Admitted solicitor, 1969. Joined Davies Arnold Cooper, 1963. Law Society of England and Wales: Mem. Council, 1996–; Vice-Pres., 2000–01; Chm., Exec. Cttee, 2000–; Member: Court of Appeal Users' Cttee, 1998–2000; Interim Exec. Cttee, 1999; Vice-Chm., 1997–98, Chm., 1999–2000, Civil Litigation Cttee. Chm., Cttee on Consumer Affairs, Advertising, Unfair Competition and Product Liability, Internat. Bar Assoc., 1995–99; Mem., Exec. Cttee (US), Internat. Assoc. Defense Counsel, 1995–98. *Publications:* Personal Injury Awards in EC Countries, 1990; Civil Procedures in EC Countries, 1993; Personal Injury Awards in EU and EFTA Countries, 1994; numerous contribs on compensation, insurance and products liability to learned jls. *Recreations:* golf, trying to keep fit, choosing ties! *Address:* c/o Davies Arnold Cooper, 6–8 Bouverie Street, EC4Y 8DD. *T:* (020) 7936 2222. *Clubs:* Caledonian; Chigwell Golf; Real Sotogrande Golf (Spain).

MACINTOSH, Dr Farquhar, CBE 1982; Rector (Headmaster), The Royal High School, Edinburgh, 1972–89; *b* 27 Oct. 1923; *s* of John Macintosh and Kate Ann Macintosh (*née* MacKinnon); *m* 1959, Margaret Mary Inglis, Peebles; two *s* two *d. Educ:* Portree High Sch., Skye; Edinburgh Univ. (MA); Glasgow Univ. (DipEd). Served RN, 1943–46; commnd RNVR, 1944. Headmaster, Portree High Sch., 1962–66; Rector, Oban High Sch., 1967–72. Member: Highlands and Islands Develt Consultative Council, 1965–82; Broadcasting Council for Scotland, 1975–79; Chairman: BBC Secondary Programme Cttee, 1972–80; School Broadcasting Council for Scotland, 1981–85; Scottish Examination Bd, 1977–90; Scottish Assoc. for Educnl Management and Admin, 1979–82; Highlands and Is Educn Trust, 1988–97 (Chm., Educn Cttee, 1973–97); Gaelic Educn Action Gp, 1994–; European Movt (Scotland), 1996– (Chm., Educn Cttee, 1993–96). Chm. of Governors, Jordanhill Coll. of Educn, 1970–72; Mem. Court, Edinburgh Univ., 1975–91; Chm., Sabhal Mor Ostaig (Gaelic Coll.), Skye, 1991–; Mem., Foundn and Bd of Govs (formerly Bd of Dirs), Univ. of Highlands and Islands, 1996– (Chm., Forum, 1999–). Governor: St Margaret's Sch., Edinburgh, 1989–98 (Vice-Chm., Bd of Govs, 1996–98); Royal Blind Sch., 1990– (Chm. Educn Exec. Cttee, 1994–). Elder, Church of Scotland. FEIS 1970; FScotvec 1990. Hon. DLitt Heriot-Watt, 1980; Dr *hc* Edinburgh, 1992. *Publications:* (contrib.) Celtic Connections, vol. I, 1999; regular contribs to TES Scotland; contrib. to European Jl of Educn. *Recreations:* hill-walking, occasional fishing, Gaelic, travel. *Address:* 12 Rothesay Place, Edinburgh EH3 7SQ. *T:* (0131) 225 4404. *Clubs:* East India; Rotary of Murrayfield and Cramond (Edinburgh).
See also K. Macintosh.

McINTOSH, Rev. Canon Hugh; Honorary Canon, St Mary's Cathedral, Glasgow, since 1983; *b* 5 June 1914; *s* of Hugh Burns McIntosh and Mary (*née* Winter); *m* 1951, Ruth Georgina, *er d* of late Rev. William Skinner Wilson and Enid (*née* Sanders); two *s* one *d. Educ:* Hatfield Coll., Durham (Exhibr); Edinburgh Theological Coll. (Luscombe Schol.). LTh, 1941; BA (dist.), 1942; MA 1945. Deacon and Priest, 1942. Precentor and Senior Chaplain, St Paul's Cathedral, Dundee, 1942–46; Senior Chaplain, St Mary's Cathedral, Edinburgh, 1946–49; Curate, St Salvador's, Edinburgh, 1949–51; Rector, St Adrian's, Gullane, 1951–54; Rector, St John's, Dumfries, 1954–66; Canon of St Mary's Cathedral, Glasgow, and Synod Clerk of Glasgow and Galloway, 1959; Provost of St Mary's Cathedral, Glasgow, 1966–70; Rector, Christ Church, Lanark, 1970–83. *Recreations:* reading, writing, and (a little) arithmetic. *Address:* 2 Ridgepark Drive, Lanark ML11 7PG. *T:* (01555) 663458.

McINTOSH, Vice-Admiral Sir Ian (Stewart), KBE 1973 (MBE 1941); CB 1970; DSO 1944; DSC 1942; Management Selection Consultant, 1973–78; *b* 11 Oct. 1919; *s* of late A. J. McIntosh, Melbourne, Australia; *m* 1943, Elizabeth Rosemary Rasmussen (*d* 1995); three *s* (one *d* decd). *Educ:* Geelong Grammar Sch. Entered RN, 1938; comd HM Submarine: H44, 1942; Sceptre, 1943–44; Alderney, 1946–48; Aeneas, 1950–51; Exec. Officer, HMS Ark Royal, 1956–58; comd 2nd Submarine Sqn, 1961–63; comd HMS Victorious, 1966–68; Dir-Gen., Weapons (Naval), 1968–70; Dep. Chief of Defence Staff (Op. Req.), 1971–73, retd 1973. Captain, 1959; Rear-Adm., 1968; Vice-Adm., 1971. Chairman: Sea Cadet Assoc., 1973–83; HMS Cavalier Trust, 1974–88. *Recreations:* friends, reading, music. *Address:* 19 The Crescent, Alverstoke, Hants PO12 2DH. *T:* (023) 9258 0510. *Club:* Royal Over-Seas League.

MACINTOSH, Joan, CBE 1978; *b* 23 Nov. 1919; *née* Burbidge; *m* 1952, Ian Gillies Macintosh (*d* 1992); one *s* two *d* (and one *s* decd). *Educ:* Amer. and English schs; Oxford Univ. (MA Modern History). BBC, 1941–42; Amer. Div., Min. of Inf., 1942–45; HM Foreign Service, 1945–52; retd on marriage. Voluntary work in India, 1953–69; CAB Organiser, Glasgow, 1972–75. Chm. Council, Insurance Ombudsman Bureau, 1981–85; Lay Observer for Scotland (Solicitors (Scotland) Act), 1981–89; Chm., Scottish Child Law Centre, 1989–92; Mem., Royal Commn on Legal Services in Scotland, 1975–80; Mem., Scottish Constitutional Commn, 1994. Chm., Scottish Consumer Council, 1975–80; Vice-Chm., National Consumer Council, 1976–84; Vice-Pres., Nat. Fedn of Consumer Gps, 1982–97; Member: Council, Victim Support Scotland, 1992–96; Auchterarder Community Council, 1995–98. Hon. Pres., Scottish Legal Action Group, 1990. Hon. LLD: Dundee, 1982; Strathclyde, 1991; DUniv Stirling, 1988. *Recreations:* tapestry, local history. *Address:* Wynd End, Auchterarder, Perthshire PH3 1AD. *T:* (01764) 662499.

McINTOSH, John Charles, OBE 1996; Headmaster, The London Oratory School, since 1977; *b* 6 Feb. 1946; *s* of Arthur and Betty McIntosh. *Educ:* Ebury Sch.; Shoreditch Coll.; Sussex Univ. (MA). The London Oratory School: Asst Master, 1967–71; Dep. Headmaster, 1971–77. Member: Nat. Curriculum Council, 1990–93; Centre for Policy Studies Educn Gp, 1982–; Inst. of Econ. Affairs Educn Adv. Council, 1988–91; Health Educn Council, 1985–88. Mem., Catholic Union of GB, 1978–. FRSA 1981. Hon. FCP 1998. *Recreations:* playing the organ, opera, ballet, theatre. *Address:* The London Oratory School, Seagrave Road, SW6 1RX; *e-mail:* headmaster@London-oratory.org; 75 Alder Lodge, River Gardens, Stevenage Road, SW6 6NR. *T:* (020) 7385 4576, *Fax:* (020) 7610 0834; *e-mail:* cantemus@aol.com. *Clubs:* Athenæum, East India.

MACINTOSH, Kenneth; Member (Lab) Eastwood, Scottish Parliament, since 1999; *b* 15 Jan. 1962; *s* of Dr Farquhar Macintosh, *qv*; *m* 1998, Claire, *d* of Douglas and Deirdre Kinloch Anderson; one *s. Educ:* Royal High Sch., Edinburgh; Edinburgh Univ. (MA Hons History). Joined BBC, 1987; worked in News Information, Breakfast News, Breakfast with Frost, BBC Westminster, Newsgathering and Nine O'Clock News; Sen. Broadcast Journalist, News and Current Affairs, 1995–99. *Recreations:* sport (including football, tennis and golf), music, reading. *Address:* Millworks, 28 Field Road, Busby G76 8SE. *T:* (0141) 644 3330.

McINTOSH, Lyndsay June; Member (C) Central Scotland, Scottish Parliament, since 1999; *b* 12 June 1955; *d* of Lawrence and Mary Clark; *m* 1981, Gordon McIntosh; one *s* one *d. Educ:* Duncanrig Sen. Secondary Sch.; Dundee Coll. of Technology (Dip. Mgt Studies). Legal Secretary, 1973–75; Civil Servant, Inland Revenue, 1975–84; business consultant, 1996–99. Lay Inspector of Schools, 1994–99. Scottish Parliament: former Dep. Convenor, Justice 2 Cttee; Cons. spokesman on social justice, equal opportunities and women's issues. JP N Lanarks, 1993–99. *Recreations:* reading, gardening, swimming, sport of kings, F1, stadium concerts. *Address:* Scottish Parliament, George IV Bridge, Edinburgh EH99 1SP. *T:* (0131) 348 5639.

McINTOSH, Melinda Jane Frances; *see* Letts, M. J. F.

McINTOSH, Prof. Naomi Ellen Sargant, (Lady McIntosh of Haringey); *see* Sargant, N. E.

McINTOSH, Dr Neil; Edward Clarke Professor of Child Life and Health, University of Edinburgh, since 1987; *b* 21 May 1942; *s* of William and Dorothy McIntosh; *m* 1967, Sheila Ann Clarke; two *s* one *d. Educ:* University College Hosp., London (MB BS; DSc Med 1995); Univ. of Southampton (BSc). Sen. Registrar in Paediatrics, UCH, 1973–78; Res. Fellow in Paediatric Endocrinology, Univ. of Calif, San Francisco, 1975–76; Sen. Lectr and Consultant Paediatrician, St George's Hosp. and Med. Sch., 1978–87; Hon. Consultant Paediatrician, Royal Hosp. for Sick Children, Edinburgh, 1987–; Hon. Neonatologist, Royal Infirmary, Edinburgh, 1987–. Consultant Advr in Neonatology to British Army, 1984–. Pres., European Soc. for Pediatric Res., 1993–94. Editor, Current Topics in Neonatology, 1996–. *Publication:* (ed with A. G. M. Campbell) Forfar and Arneil's Textbook of Paediatrics, 4th edn 1993, 5th edn 1998. *Recreations:* music, family. *Address:* 32 Queens Crescent, Edinburgh EH9 2BA. *T:* (0131) 536 0801.

McINTOSH, Neil Scott Wishart; Chief Executive, Centre for British Teachers, since 1990; *b* 24 July 1947; *s* of William Henderson McIntosh and Mary Catherine McIntosh; *m* 1st, 1971, Genista Mary Tandy (*see* Baroness McIntosh of Hudnall) (marr. diss. 1990); one *s* one *d*; 2nd, 1991, Melinda Jane Frances Letts, *qv*; one *s* one *d. Educ:* Merchiston Castle Sch., Edinburgh; Univ. of York (BA Politics); London Sch. of Econs (MSc Industrial Relations). Res. Associate, PEP, 1969–73; Res. Dir, Southwark Community Develt Proj., 1973–76; Dir, Shelter, 1976–84; Dir, VSO, 1985–90. Councillor, London Bor. of Camden, 1971–77; Chm., Housing Cttee, 1974–76. Dir, Stonham Housing Assoc., 1982–98. Vice Pres., BSA, 1985–91. Founder and Chm., Homeless Internat., 1988–91; Treasurer, Campaign for Freedom of Information, 1984– (Co-Chm., 1997–); Mem., Independent Broadcasting Telethon Trust, 1987–94. *Publication:* The Right to Manage?, 1971 (2nd edn 1976). *Recreations:* golf, sailing, theatre. *Clubs:* Reform; The Springs Golf; Plockton Sailing.

McINTOSH, Sir Neil William David, Kt 2000; CBE 1990; JP; DL; Convener, Scottish Council for Voluntary Organisations, since 1996; *b* 30 Jan. 1940; *s* of Neil and Beatrice McIntosh; *m* 1965, Marie Elizabeth Lindsay; one *s* two *d*. *Educ:* King's Park Sen. Secondary Sch., Glasgow. ACIS 1967; FIPM 1987. J. & P. Coats, 1957–59; Honeywell Controls, 1959–62; Berks, Oxford and Reading Jt O&M Unit, 1962–64; Stewarts & Lloyds, 1964–66; Sen. O&M Officer, Lanark CC, 1966–69; Estabt/O&M Officer, Inverness CC, 1969–75; Personnel Officer, 1975–81, Dir of Manpower Services, 1981–85, Highland Regl Council; Chief Executive: Dumfries and Galloway Regl Council, 1985–92; Strathclyde Regl Council, 1992–96. Chm., Commn on Local Govt and Scottish Parlt, 1998–99. Mem. Bd, British Telecom, Scotland, 1998–. Chm., Nat. Cos Contact Gp, 1996–98; Hd, COSLA Consultancy, 1996–99. Director: Training 2000 (Scotland) Ltd, 1993; Quality Scotland Foundn, 1993; Sportability Strathclyde, 1994. Scottish Advr, Joseph Rowntree Foundn, 2000–. Chief Counting Officer, Scottish Parlt Referendum, 1997; Mem., UK Electoral Commn, 2001–. Trustee: Nat. Museums of Scotland, 1999–; Dumfries Theatre Royal Trust, 2000–. Mem., Comunn na Gaidhlig Wkg Gp on Status of Gaelic Lang. DL Dumfries, 1998; JP 1999. FRSA 1989. Hon. DHL Syracuse Univ., USA, 1993; Hon. LLD Glasgow Caledonian, 1999. *Recreations:* antique bottle collecting, bowling, local history, hill walking. *Address:* Birnock Lodge, Well Road, Moffat DG10 9JT.

McINTOSH, Dr Robert; Chief Executive, Forest Enterprise, since 1997 (Director, Operations, 1994–97); *b* 6 Oct. 1951; *s* of Robert Hamilton McIntosh and Kathleen McIntosh; *m* 1985, Elizabeth Anne Boon. *Educ:* Linlithgow Acad.; Edinburgh Univ. (BSc Hons 1973; PhD 1985); MICFor 1974. Dist Officer, 1973–78, Res. Project Leader, 1979–84, Forestry Commn; Forest Dist Manager, Kielder Forest, 1984–94. *Publications:* papers and articles in forestry jls. *Recreations:* shooting, stalking, farming. *Address:* Forest Enterprise, 231 Corstorphine Road, Edinburgh EH12 7AT; East Brackley Grange, by Kinross KY13 9LU. *T:* (01577) 862057. *Club:* Farmers'.

McINTOSH, Sir Ronald (Robert Duncan), KCB 1975 (CB 1968); Chairman, APV plc, 1982–89; Director: S. G. Warburg & Co. Ltd, 1978–90; Foseco plc, 1978–90; London & Manchester Group plc, 1978–90; *b* 26 Sept. 1919; *s* of Thomas Steven McIntosh, MD, FRCPE and Christina Jane McIntosh; *m* 1951, Doreen Frances, *o d* of Commander Andrew MacGinnity, RNR and Margaret MacGinnity, Frinton-on-Sea. *Educ:* Charterhouse (Scholar); Balliol Coll., Oxford. Served in Merchant Navy, 1939–45; Second Mate, 1943–45. Assistant Principal, Board of Trade, 1947; General Manager, Dollar Exports Board, 1949–51; Commercial Counsellor, UK High Commn, New Delhi, 1957–61; Under-Secretary: BoT, 1961–64; DEA, 1964–66; Dep. Under-Sec. of State, Dept of Economic Affairs, 1966–68; Dep. Secretary, Cabinet Office, 1968–70; Dep. Under-Sec. of State, Dept of Employment, 1970–72; Dep. Sec., HM Treasury, 1972–73; Dir-Gen. Nat. Economic Development Office, and Mem. NEDC, 1973–77. Chairman: Danish–UK Chamber of Commerce, 1990–92; British Health Care Consortium (for the former Soviet Union), 1992–97. Mem., Council, CBI, 1980–90; Co-Chm., British-Hungarian Round Table, 1980–84. Chm., Centre for Eur. Agricl Studies, Wye Coll., 1979–83. CIMgt. Hon. DSc Aston, 1977. *Recreations:* sailing, travel. *Address:* 24 Ponsonby Terrace, SW1P 4QA. *Club:* Royal Thames Yacht.

MacINTYRE, Prof. Alasdair Chalmers; Research Professor of Philosophy, University of Notre Dame, since 2000; *b* 12 Jan. 1929; *o s* of Eneas John MacIntyre, MD (Glasgow), and Margaret Emily Chalmers, MB, ChB (Glasgow); *m* 1977, Lynn Sumida Joy; one *s* three *d* by previous marriages. *Educ:* Epsom Coll. and privately; Queen Mary Coll., Univ. of London (Fellow, 1984); Manchester Univ. BA (London); MA (Manchester); MA (Oxon). Lectr in Philosophy of Religion, Manchester Univ., 1951–57; Lectr in Philosophy, Leeds Univ., 1957–61; Research Fellow, Nuffield Coll., Oxford, 1961–62; Sen. Fellow, Council of Humanities, Princeton Univ., 1962–63; Fellow and Preceptor in Philosophy, University Coll., Oxford, 1963–66; Prof. of Sociology, Univ. of Essex, 1966–70; Prof. of History of Ideas, Brandeis Univ., 1970–72; Univ. Prof. in Philos. and Political Sci., Boston Univ., 1972–80; Luce Prof., Wellesley Coll., 1980–82; W. Alton Jones Prof. of Philosophy, Vanderbilt Univ., 1982–88; McMahon/Hank Prof. of Philosophy, Univ. of Notre Dame, Indiana, 1988–94; Arts and Scis Prof. of Phil., Duke Univ., 1995–2000. Pres., Eastern Div., Amer. Phil Assoc., 1984. Fellow, Amer. Acad. of Arts and Scis, 1985; Corresp. FBA, 1994. Hon. Mem., Phi Beta Kappa, 1973. Hon. DHL Swarthmore, 1983; Hon. DLit: QUB, 1988; Williams Coll., Mass, 1993; DU Essex, 1990. *Publications:* Marxism and Christianity, 1954 (revised, 1968); New Essays in Philosophical Theology (ed, with A. G. N. Flew), 1955; Metaphysical Beliefs (ed), 1956; The Unconscious: a conceptual analysis, 1958; A Short History of Ethics, 1965; Secularisation and Moral Change, 1967; Marcuse: an exposition and a polemic, 1970; Sociological Theory and Philosophical Analysis (ed with D. M. Emmet), 1971; Against the Self-Images of the Age, 1971; After Virtue, 1981; Whose Justice? Which Rationality?, 1988; Three Rival Versions of Moral Enquiry, 1990. *Address:* Philosophy Department, University of Notre Dame, Notre Dame, IN 46556, USA.

McINTYRE, Prof. Alasdair Duncan, CBE 1994; FRSE 1975; Emeritus Professor of Fisheries and Oceanography, Aberdeen University, since 1986; *b* 17 Nov. 1926; *s* of Alexander Walker McIntyre and Martha Jack McIntyre; *m* 1967, Catherine; one *d*. *Educ:* Hermitage Sch., Helensburgh; Glasgow Univ. BSc (1st class Hons Zoology) 1948; DSc 1973. Scottish Home Department (since 1960, DAFS) Marine Laboratory, Aberdeen: Develt Commn Grant-aided Student, 1948–49; Scientific Officer, 1950; Head, Lab. Environmental Gp, 1973; Dep. Dir, 1977; Dir, 1983. Dir of Fisheries Res. Services for Scotland, Dept of Agric. and Fisheries for Scotland, 1983–86. UK Co-ordinator, Fisheries Res. and Develt, 1986. President: Scottish Marine Biological Assoc., later Scottish Assoc. for Marine Sci., 1988–93; Estuarine and Coastal Scis Assoc., 1992–96; Sir Alister Hardy Foundn for Ocean Sci., 1992–99; Chairman: UN Gp of Experts on Scientific Aspects of Marine Pollution (GESAMP), 1981–84; Adv. Cttee on Marine Pollution, Internat. Council for the Exploration of the Sea, 1982–84; Marine Forum for Envmtl Issues, 1988–98; Atlantic Frontier Envmtl Forum, 1996–; Falkland Is Exploration and Production Envmtl Forum, 1997–; Assessor: Donaldson Inquiry into protection of UK coastline from pollution by merchant shipping, 1993–94; Donaldson Review of Salvage and Intervention Command and Control, 1997–99. Member: NCC for Scotland, 1991; Res. Bd, Scottish Natural Heritage, 1992–96. Hon. Res. Prof., Aberdeen Univ., 1983–86. Chm., Trustees of Buckland Foundn, 1994–99 (Vice Chm., 1988–94). Ed., Fisheries Research, 1988–. Hon. Dr Stirling, 1997. *Publications:* over 100 articles in scientific jls on marine ecology and pollution. *Recreations:* cooking, wine, walking. *Address:* 63 Hamilton Place, Aberdeen AB15 5BW. *T:* (01224) 645633.

McINTYRE, Sir Alister; *see* McIntyre, Sir M. A.

McINTYRE, Sir Donald (Conroy), Kt 1992; CBE 1985 (OBE 1977); opera singer, free-lance; *b* 22 Oct. 1934; *s* of George Douglas McIntyre and Mrs Hermyn McIntyre; *m*; three *d*. *Educ:* Mount Albert Grammar Sch.; Auckland Teachers' Trng Coll.; Guildhall Sch. of Music. Debut in Britain, Welsh National Opera, 1959; Sadler's Wells Opera, many roles, 1960–67; Royal Opera, Covent Garden, from 1967; also Vienna, Bayreuth, La Scala, Milan and Metropolitan, NY. *Principal roles:* Barak, in Die Frau Ohne Schatten, Strauss; Wotan and Wanderer, in The Ring, Wagner; Hollander, Wagner; Hans Sachs, in Die Meistersinger von Nurnberg, Wagner; Heyst, in Victory, Richard Rodney Bennett; Macbeth, Verdi; Scarpia, in Tosca, Puccini; Count, in Figaro, Mozart; Dr Schön, in Wozzeck, Berg; title role in Cardillac, Hindemith; Siegfried, Metropolitan, NY; Rocco, in Fidelio; Prospero, in Un Re in Ascolto, Berio; Balstrode, in Peter Grimes, Britten; Bayreuth: Wotan, Wanderer, Hollander; Telramund, in Lohengrin; Klingsor, Amfortas and Gurnemanz in Parsifal; Bayreuth Centenary Ring, 1976–81. *Video and films include:* Der Fliegende Holländer, 1975; Electra, 1976; Die Meistersinger, 1984; Bayreuth Centenary Ring, 1976–81; recordings include Pelléas et Mélisande, Il Trovatore, The Messiah, Oedipus Rex, The Ring, Beethoven's 9th Symphony, Damnation of Faust, Bayreuth Centenary Ring. Fidelio Award, 1989. *Recreations:* gardening, swimming, tennis, farming. *Address:* Foxhill Farm, Jackass Lane, Keston, Bromley, Kent BR2 6AN. *T:* (01689) 855368; c/o Ingpen & Williams, 26 Wadham Road, SW15 2LR.

McINTYRE, Prof. Donald Ian; Professor of Education, since 1996, and Head of School of Education, since 1997, University of Cambridge; Fellow of Hughes Hall, Cambridge, since 1996; *b* 3 Jan. 1937; *s* of George McIntyre and Mary Gladys McIntyre (*née* Bell); *m* 1964, Anne Roberta Brown; two *s* one *d*. *Educ:* George Watson's Coll., Edinburgh; Edinburgh Univ. (MA; MEd). Math. Teacher, Dunfermline High Sch., 1960–61; Lectr in Educn, Moray House Coll., Edinburgh, 1961–65, 1967–69; Res. Tutor in Math. Educn, Univ. of Hull, 1965–67; Sen. Res. Fellow, subseq. Lectr, and Sen. Lectr, Reader in Educn, Univ. of Stirling, 1969–85; Reader in Educnl Studies, Univ. of Oxford, 1986–95. *Publications:* jointly: Teachers and Teaching, 1969; Schools and Socialization, 1971; Investigations of Microteaching, 1977; Making Sense of Teaching, 1993; The School Mentor Handbook, 1993; Effective Teaching and Learning, 1996. *Recreations:* writing, golf, walking, visiting Scotland and France. *Address:* School of Education, University of Cambridge, 17 Trumpington Street, Cambridge CB2 1QA. *T:* (01223) 332888; School of Education, University of Cambridge, Shaftesbury Road, Cambridge CB2 2BX. *T:* (01223) 369631. *Address:* Hughes Hall, Cambridge CB1 2EW.

MACINTYRE, Donald John; Chief Political Commentator, Independent, since 1996; *b* 27 Jan. 1947; *s* of Kenneth Mackenzie Campbell Macintyre and Margaret Macintyre (*née* Freeman); partner, Sarah Spankie; one *s*. *Educ:* Bradfield Coll.; Christ Church, Oxford (BA Lit.Hum.); UC, Cardiff (Dip. Journalism Studies). Reporter, Sunday Mercury, 1971–75; Industrial Reporter, Daily Express, 1975–77; Labour Corresp., The Times, 1977–83; Labour Editor: Sunday Times, 1983–85; The Times, 1985–86; Independent, 1986–87; Political Editor: Sunday Telegraph, 1987–89; Sunday Correspondent, 1989–90; Independent on Sunday, 1990–93; Independent, 1993–96. *Publications:* Talking about Trade Unions, 1979; (jtly) Strike!, 1985; Mandelson and the Making of New Labour, 1999. *Recreations:* cinema, walking, bad chess. *Address:* Press Gallery, House of Commons, SW1A 0AA. *T:* (020) 7219 6580. *Clubs:* Beefsteak, Soho House.

MacINTYRE, Prof. Iain, FMedSci; FRS 1996; Professor and Research Director, William Harvey Research Institute, St Bartholomew's and the Royal London School of Medicine and Dentistry (Queen Mary and Westfield College), since 1995; *b* 30 Aug. 1924; *s* of John MacIntyre, Tobermory, Mull, and Margaret Fraser Shaw, Stratherick, Inverness-shire; *m* 1947, Mabel Wilson Jamieson, MA, *y d* of George Jamieson and J. C. K. K. Bell, Largs, Ayrshire; one *d*. *Educ:* Jordanhill Coll. Sch., Glasgow; Univ. of Glasgow (MB, ChB 1947); PhD 1960, DSc 1970, London. MRCPath 1963 (Founder Mem.), FRCPath 1971; FRCP 1977 (MRCP 1969). Asst Clinical Pathologist, United Sheffield Hosps, and Hon. Demonstrator in Biochem., Sheffield Univ., 1948–52; Royal Postgraduate Medical School: Registrar in Chemical Pathology, 1952–54; first Sir Jack Drummond Meml Fellow, 1954–56; Asst Lectr in Chem. Path., 1956–59; Reader in Chem. Path., 1963–67; Dir, Endocrine Unit, 1967–89; Chm., Academic Bd, 1985–89; Sen. Res. Fellow, Dept of Medicine, 1989–91; Prof., Chem. Path., London Univ., 1967–89, now Emeritus; Res. Dir, William Harvey Res. Inst., St Bartholomew's Hosp. Med. Coll., 1991–94. Director: Dept of Chem. Path., Hammersmith Hosp., 1982–89; Chelsea Hosp. for Women, Queen Charlotte's Hosp. for Women, 1986–89. Vis. Scientist, Nat. Insts of Health, Bethesda, 1960–61; Commonwealth Fund Schol., Australia, 1968; Visiting Professor: San Francisco Medical Center, 1964; Melbourne Univ., 1979–80; St George's Hosp. Med. Sch., 1989–; Vis. Lectr, Insts of Molecular Biol. and Cytol., USSR Acad. of Scis, 1978. Lectures: A. J. S. McFadzean, Univ. of Hong Kong, 1981; Transatlantic, Amer. Endocrine Soc., 1987; Per Edman Meml, St Vincent's Inst. of Medical Res., Australia, 1990. Mem., Hammersmith and Queen Charlotte's SHA, 1982–89. Chm. Organizing Cttee, Hammersmith Internat. Symposium on Molecular Endocrinology, 1967–81; Member: Org Cttee, Hormone and Cell Regulation Symposia, 1976–79; Adv. Council, Workshop on Vitamin D, 1977–79. Pres., Bone and Tooth Soc., 1984–87; Member: Cttee, Soc. for Endocrinology, 1978–80; Biochem. Soc.; NIH Alumni Assoc; Assoc. of Amer. Physicians, 1998; Amer. Endocrine Soc.; Amer. Soc. for Bone and Mineral Res.; European Calcified Tissue Soc.; Assoc. of Clin. Biochemists. Vice-Pres., English Chess Assoc., 1989–. Member Editorial Board: Clinical Endocrinology, 1975–79; Molecular and Cellular Endocrinology, 1975–80; Jl of Endocrinological Investigation; Jl of Mineral and Electrolyte Metabolism; Jl of Investigative and Cell Pathol.; Jl of Metabolic Bone Disease and Related Res. Hon. Mem., Assoc. of American Physicians, 1998. Founder FMedSci 1998. Hon. MD: Turin, 1985; Sheffield, 2001. Gairdner Internat. Award, Toronto, 1967; Elsevier Award, Internat. Confs on Calcium Regulating Hormones, Inc., 1992; John B. Johnson Award, Paget Foundn, 1995. *Publications:* articles in endocrinology. *Recreations:* tennis, chess, music. *Address:* Great Broadhurst Farm, Broad Oak, Heathfield, East Sussex TN21 8UX. *T:* (01435) 883515. *Clubs:* Athenæum; Queen's, Hurlingham.

MACINTYRE, Iain Melfort Campbell, MD; FRCSE, FRCPE; FSAScot; Consultant Surgeon, Western General Hospital, Edinburgh, since 1979; Surgeon to the Queen in Scotland, since 1997; *b* 23 June 1944; *s* of John Macintyre, MA, BD, FSAScot and Mary (*née* Campbell); *m* 1969, Tessa Lorna Mary Millar; three *d*. *Educ:* Daniel Stewart's Coll., Edinburgh; Edinburgh Univ. (MB ChB, MD 1992). FRCSE 1974; FRCPE 1997. FSAScot 1997. Lectr in Surgery, Edinburgh Univ., 1974–78; Vis. Prof., Univ. of Natal, 1978–79. Royal College of Surgeons of Edinburgh: Mem. Council, 1991–2000; Dir of Educn and Wade Prof., 1997–2000. Mem., Nat. Med. Adv. Cttee, 1992–95. *Recreations:* sailing, golf, reading. *Address:* 20 Lygon Road, Edinburgh EH16 5QB. *Club:* Bruntsfield Links Golfing Society.

McINTYRE, Air Vice Marshal Ian Graeme; Chief Executive, Defence Dental Agency, since 1997; *b* 9 July 1943; *s* of Arthur McIntyre and Eileen McIntyre (*née* Patmore); *m* 1966, Joan; two *s*. *Educ:* Royal Masonic Inst. for Boys; Durham Univ. (BDS); BPMF, Inst. of Dental Surgery, London Univ. (MSc). MGDS RCS, DDPH RCS; FDSRCSE *ad hominem* 1998. Commnd RAF, 1961; Triservice Advr in Gen. Dental Practice, 1989; Asst Dir, Dental Service, RAF, 1991; CO, RAF Inst. of Dental Health and Trng, 1994; Dir, Clinical Services, Defence Dental Agency and Dir, RAF Dental Branch, 1995; QHDS, 1995–2001. *Recreations:* hill walking, gardening, watching Rugby. *Address:* HQ Defence Dental Agency, RAF Halton, Aylesbury, Bucks HP22 5RG. *T:* (01296) 623535. *Club:* Royal Air Force.

McINTYRE, Ian James; writer and broadcaster; *b* Banchory, Kincardineshire, 9 Dec. 1931; *y s* of late Hector Harold McIntyre, Inverness, and late Annie Mary Michie, Ballater; *m* 1954, Leik Sommerfelt, 2nd *d* of late Benjamin Vogt, Kragerø, Norway; two *s* two *d*. *Educ:* Prescot Grammar Sch.; St John's Coll., Cambridge (Scholar; Med. and Mod. Langs Tripos, Pts I and II; BA 1953; MA); Coll. of Europe, Bruges. Pres., Cambridge Union, 1953. Commnd, Intelligence Corps, 1955–57. Current affairs talks producer, BBC, 1957; Editor, At Home and Abroad, 1959; Man. Trng Organiser, BBC Staff Trng Dept, 1960; Programme Services Officer, ITA, 1961; staff of Chm., Cons. Party in Scotland, 1962; Dir of Inf. and Res., Scottish Cons. Central Office, 1965; contested (C) Roxburgh, Selkirk and Peebles, 1966; long-term contract, writer and broadcaster, BBC, 1970–76; presenter and interviewer, Analysis, and other programmes on politics, for. affairs and the arts; travelled widely in Europe, N America, Africa, Asia and ME; Controller: BBC Radio 4, 1976–78; BBC Radio 3, 1978–87. Associate Ed., The Times, 1989–90. *Publications:* The Proud Doers: Israel after twenty years, 1968; (ed and contrib.) Words: reflections on the uses of language, 1975; Dogfight: the transatlantic battle over Airbus, 1992; The Expense of Glory: a life of John Reith, 1993; Dirt and Deity: a life of Robert Burns, 1995; Garrick, 1999 (Annual Book Prize, Soc. for Theatre Res., 2000); articles and book reviews in The Listener, The Times, The Independent. *Recreation:* family life. *Address:* Spylaw House, Newlands Avenue, Radlett, Herts WD7 8EL. *T:* (01923) 853532. *Clubs:* Beefsteak; Union (Cambridge).

McINTYRE, Very Rev. Prof. John, CVO 1985; DD, DLitt; FRSE; Professor of Divinity, University of Edinburgh, 1956–86, now Emeritus; Dean of the Order of the Thistle, 1974–89; Chaplain to the Queen in Scotland, 1975–86; an Extra Chaplain to the Queen in Scotland, 1974–75 and since 1986; Moderator of the General Assembly of the Church of Scotland, 1982; *b* 20 May 1916; *s* of late John C. McIntyre, Bathgate, Scotland, and Annie McIntyre; *m* 1945, Jessie B., *d* of late William Buick, Coupar Angus; two *s* one *d*. *Educ:* Bathgate Academy; University of Edinburgh; MA 1938; BD 1941; DLitt 1953. Ordained, 1941; Locum Tenens, Parish of Glenorchy and Inishail, 1941–43; Minister of Parish of Fenwick, Ayrshire, 1943–45; Hunter Baillie Prof. of Theology, St Andrew's Coll., University of Sydney, 1946–56; Principal of St Andrew's Coll., 1950–56 (Hon. Fellow, 1990); Principal Warden, Pollock Halls of Residence, Univ. of Edinburgh, 1960–71; actg Principal and Vice-Chancellor, Edinburgh Univ., 1973–74, 1979; Principal, New Coll., and Dean of Faculty of Divinity, 1968–74. FRSE 1977 (Vice-Pres., 1983–86). DD *hc* Glasgow, 1961; DHL *hc*, Coll. of Wooster, Ohio, 1983; Dr *hc* Edinburgh, 1987. *Publications:* St Anselm and His Critics, 1954; The Christian Doctrine of History, 1957; On the Love of God, 1962; The Shape of Christology, 1966, 2nd edn 1998; Faith, Theology and Imagination, 1987; The Shape of Soteriology, 1992; The Shape of Pneumatology, 1997; Theology after the Storm, 1997; articles and reviews in various learned jls of Theology. *Address:* 317 Mayfield Court, 27 West Savile Terrace, Edinburgh EH9 3DT. *T:* (0131) 667 1203.

McINTYRE, (John) Paul; Deputy Director General, Enterprise and Innovation, Department of Trade and Industry, since 2000; *b* 4 Dec. 1951; *s* of John McIntyre and Julia McIntyre; *m* 1984, Jennifer Eastabrook; two *d*. *Educ:* Austin Friars, Carlisle; Churchill Coll., Cambridge (BA Econs). Joined HM Treasury, 1974: on secondment to: UK Delegn to IMF/IBRD, Washington, 1977–78; Hambros Bank, City of London, 1983–85; Assistant Secretary: Social Security Policy, 1987–90; Monetary and Debt Mgt Policy, 1990–94; Dep. Dir, Internat. Finance, 1995–99. *Recreations:* family, cricket, reading, music. *Address:* Department of Trade and Industry, 1 Victoria Street, SW1H 0ET. *Clubs:* MCC; Mandarins Cricket.

McINTYRE, Sir (Meredith) Alister, Kt 1992; Chief Technical Advisor, Caribbean Regional Negotiating Machinery, Kingston, Jamaica, since 1998; *b* Grenada, 29 March 1932; *s* of Meredith McIntyre and Cynthia Eileen McIntyre; *m* Marjorie Hope; three *s* one *d*. *Educ:* LSE (BSc (Econ) 1st Cl. Hons 1957); Nuffield Coll., Oxford (BLitt 1963). Fulbright-Hays Fellow, Columbia Univ., 1963–64; Asst Prof., Woodrow Wilson Sch. of Public Affairs, Princeton Univ., 1962; University of the West Indies: Lectr in Economics, 1960–64; Sen. Lectr and Chm. of Social Scis, 1964–67; Dir, Inst. of Social and Econ. Res., 1964–74; Sec.-Gen., Caribbean Community Secretariat, 1974–77; Dir, Commodities Div., UNCTAD, 1977–82; Dep. Sec.-Gen., UNCTAD, 1982–87; Asst Sec.-Gen., UN, 1987–88. Vice-Chancellor, Univ. of West Indies, 1988–98. Hon. LLD: West Indies, 1980; Sheffield, 1995; Toronto, 1996. Comdr, Order of Distinction (Jamaica), 1975; Cacique's Crown of Honour (Guyana), 1978; Order of Merit (Jamaica), 1992; Order of the Caribbean Community, 1994. *Recreations:* swimming, sailing, reading. *Address:* 14 Jacks Hill Road, Kingston 6, Jamaica.

McINTYRE, Michael; *see* McIntyre, T. M.

McINTYRE, Prof. Michael Edgeworth, PhD; FRS 1990; Professor of Atmospheric Dynamics, Cambridge University, since 1993; Co-director, Cambridge Centre for Atmospheric Science, since 1992; *b* 28 July 1941; *s* of Archibald Keverall McIntyre and Anne Hartwell McIntyre; *m* 1968, Ruth Hecht; one step *d* two step *s*. *Educ:* King's High School, Dunedin, NZ; Univ. of Otago, NZ; Trinity Coll., Cambridge. PhD Cantab 1967 (geophysical fluid dynamics); postdoctoral Fellow, Woods Hole Oceanographic Inst., 1967. Research Associate, Dept of Meteorology, MIT, 1967; Cambridge University: Asst Dir of Research, 1969; Res. Fellow, St John's Coll., 1968–71; Univ. Lectr, 1972; Reader in Atmospheric Dynamics, 1987; SERC, then EPSRC, Sen. Res. Fellow, 1992–97. Member: Atmospheric Sci. Cttee, NERC, 1989–94; Sci. Steering Gp, UK Univs Global Atmos. Modelling Project, NERC, 1990–; Workshop on Tropical Cyclone Disasters, IUTAM/IUGG/ICSU, 1990–91; Scientific Steering Cttee, STRATEOLE experiment, 1992–; Scientific Adv. Cttee and Organizing Cttee, Prog. on Maths of Atmosphere and Ocean Dynamics, Isaac Newton Inst., 1995–96. Member: Academia Europaea, 1989; Euro. Geophys. Soc. (Julius Bartels Medal, 1999), Amer. Geophys. Union, Catgut Acoust. Soc.; FRMetS; Fellow, Amer. Met. Soc., 1991 (Carl-Gustaf Rossby Res. Medal, 1987); FAAAS 1999. *Publications:* numerous papers in professional jls, incl. papers on lucidity principles. *Recreations:* music, gliding. *Address:* 98 Windsor Road, Cambridge CB4 3JN.

McINTYRE, Prof. Neil, FRCP; Professor of Medicine, Royal Free Hospital School of Medicine, 1978–99; Hon. Consultant Physician, Royal Free Hospital, 1968–99; *b* 1 May 1934; *s* of John William McIntyre and Catherine (*née* Watkins); *m* 1966, Wendy Ann Kelsey; one *s* one *d*. *Educ:* Porth County School for Boys; King's Coll. London (BSc 1st Cl. Hons Physiol); King's Coll. Hosp. (MB BS (Hons), MD). House Officer: KCH, 1959; Hammersmith Hosp., 1960; RAF Med. Br. (Flt Lieut), 1960–63; MRC Res. Fellow, Registrar, Lectr in Medicine, Royal Free Hosp., 1963–66; MRC Travelling Fellowship, Harvard Med. Sch., 1966–68; Royal Free Hospital School of Medicine: Sen. Lectr 1968–73, Reader in Medicine 1973–78; Chm., Dept of Medicine, 1983–94; Vice Dean, 1993–96; Dir of Med. Educn, UCL Med. Sch. and Royal Free Hosp. Sch. of Med., 1993–95. Non-exec. Dir, N Middlesex Hosp. NHS Trust, 1991–96. MRSocMed 1968. Liveryman, Soc. of Apothecaries, 1971–. Sam E. Roberts Medal, Univ. of Kansas Med. Sch., 1980. *Publications:* Therapeutic Agents and the Liver, 1965; The Problem Orientated Medical Record, 1979; Lipids and Lipoproteins, 1990; Clinical Hepatology, 1991; papers on liver disease, lipoprotein metabolism, med. educn. *Recreations:* reading, photographing medical statues, golf. *Address:* 20 Queens Court, Wembley, Middx HA9 7QU. *Clubs:* Athenæum; Highgate Golf.

McINTYRE, Paul; *see* McIntyre, J. P.

MACINTYRE, Prof. Sarah Jane, (Sally), OBE 1998; PhD; FRSE; Director, MRC Social and Public Health Sciences (formerly Medical Sociology) Unit, Glasgow, since 1984; *b* 27 Feb. 1949; *d* of late Rev. Angus Macintyre and Evelyn Macintyre; *m* 1980, Dr Guy Paul Muhlemann. *Educ:* Univ. of Durham (BA 1970); Bedford Coll., London (MSc 1971); Univ. of Aberdeen (PhD 1976). FRSE 1998. Res. Fellow, Aberdeen Univ., 1971–75; non-clinical scientist, MRC Med. Sociology Unit, 1975–84. Hon. Prof., Univ. of Glasgow, 1991–. Founder FMedSci 1998. Hon. MFPHM 1993. *Publications:* Single and Pregnant, 1977; (jtly) Antenatal Care Assessed, 1985; contrib. jl articles on sociological and public health topics. *Recreations:* mountaineering, rock-climbing, ski-ing, running, yoga. *Address:* MRC Social and Public Health Sciences Unit, 4 Lilybank Gardens, Glasgow G12 8RZ. *T:* (0141) 357 3949. *Club:* Pinnacle.

McINTYRE, (Theodore) Michael; Senior Executive, HSBC Private Banking, since 1996; *b* 9 Dec. 1941; *s* of James Penton McIntyre and Susan E. M. McIntyre; *m* 1969, Jill Yvonne Mander; one *s* one *d*. *Educ:* Marlborough Coll. Hongkong and Shanghai Banking Corporation Ltd: E Malaysia, Kowloon, Japan, Hong Kong and Brazil, 1959–91; Dep. CEO, 1991–92; CEO, 1992–96, UK. SBStJ 1989. *Recreations:* reading, golf, tennis, sailing. *Address:* Flat 3, 69 Alderney Street, SW1V 4HH. *T:* (020) 7834 9719.

MACINTYRE, William Ian, CB 1992; Head, Communications and Information Industries Directorate, Department of Trade and Industry, since 1996; *b* 20 July 1943; *s* of late Robert Miller Macintyre, CBE and of Florence Mary Macintyre; *m* 1967, Jennifer Mary Pitblado; one *s* two *d*. *Educ:* Merchiston Castle School, Edinburgh; St Andrews University. MA. British Petroleum Co. Ltd, 1965–72; ECGD, 1972–73; DTI, later Dept of Energy, 1973–77; seconded to ICFC, 1977–79; Asst Sec., Dept of Energy, Gas Div., 1979–83; Under-Sec. 1983, Dir-Gen., Energy Efficiency Office, 1983–87; Under Sec., Electricity Div., 1987–88, Electricity Div. B, 1988–91, Dept of Energy; Under Sec., Coal Div., Dept of Energy, then DTI, 1991–94; Head, Telecoms Div., DTI, 1994–95. Mem., Froebel Inst., 1999–. Mem. Council, Univ. of Surrey Roehampton, 2000–; Gov., Froebel Coll., 2001–. *Address:* Department of Trade and Industry, 151 Buckingham Palace Road, SW1W 9SS.

McINTYRE, William Ian Mackay, CBE 1990; PhD; FRCVS; Professor Emeritus of Veterinary Medicine, University of Glasgow, since 1991 (Senior Lecturer, 1951–61, Professor, 1961–83); *b* 7 July 1919; *s* of George John and Jane McIntyre; *m* 1948, Ruth Dick Galbraith; three *s*. *Educ:* Altnaharra Primary and Golspie Secondary Sch., Sutherland; Royal (Dick) Veterinary Coll. (MRCVS); University of Edinburgh (PhD). FRCVS 1983. Clinical Asst, Royal (Dick) Veterinary Coll., 1944–48; Lectr, Vet. Med., Royal (Dick) Vet. Coll., 1948–51. Seconded to University of East Africa, University Coll., Nairobi, as Dean, Faculty of Veterinary Science, and Prof., Clinical Studies, 1963–67. Dir, International Trypanotolerance Centre, The Gambia, 1984–89. Hon. DVM Justus Liebig Univ., Giessen, 1987. *Publications:* various, on canine nephritis, parasitic diseases and vaccines, clinical communications, and African Trypanosomiasis. *Address:* Stuckenduff, Shandon, Helensburgh G84 8NW. *T:* (01436) 820571.

McISAAC, Shona; MP (Lab) Cleethorpes, since 1997; *b* 3 April 1960; *d* of Angus and Isa McIsaac; *m* 1994, Peter Keith. *Educ:* St Aidan's Coll., Durham (BSc Geography). Formerly: Lifeguard, Tooting Pool; Sub-Editor: Chat; Bella; Woman; food writer, Slimmer. Mem. (Lab) Wandsworth BC, 1990–97. Mem., Select Cttee on Standards and Privileges, 1997–2001. *Recreations:* food, football, cycling, archaeology. *Address:* House of Commons, SW1A 0AA. *T:* (020) 7219 3000.

McIVOR, Rt Hon. Basil; *see* McIvor, Rt Hon. W. B.

McIVOR, Donald Kenneth; Executive-in-residence, Queen's University Business School; Director and Senior Vice-President, Exxon Corporation, Irving, Texas (formerly New York), 1985–92; *b* 12 April 1928; *s* of Kenneth MacIver McIvor and Nellie Beatrice McIvor (*née* Rutherford); *m* 1953, Avonia Isabel Forbes; four *s* one *d*. *Educ:* Univ. of Manitoba (BSc Hons in Geol.). Joined Imperial Oil, 1950; operational and res. assignments, Exploration Dept, 1950–58; gen. planning and res. management positions, 1958–68; Asst Manager and Manager, Corporate Planning, 1968–70; Exploration Manager, 1970–72; Nat. Defence Coll., 1972–73; Sen. Vice-Pres., 1973–75; Exec. Vice-Pres., 1975–77; Vice-Pres., oil and gas exploration and prodn, Exxon Corp., NY, 1977–81; Dep. Chm., Imperial Oil, 1981; Chm. and Chief Exec. Officer, Imperial Oil, 1982–85. Member: Canadian Soc. of Petroleum Geologists; American Petroleum Inst.

McIVOR, (Frances) Jane; District Judge (Magistrates' Courts), South East London, since 2001; *b* NI, 22 Oct. 1959; *d* of Rt Hon. (William) Basil McIvor, *qv* and (Frances) Jill McIvor, *qv*; *m* 1988, Girish Thanki; one *s* one *d*. *Educ:* sch. in Belfast; Univ. of E Anglia (LLB 1982). Called to the Bar, Inner Temple, 1983; in practice on S Eastern Circuit; Actg Metropolitan Stipendiary Magistrate, 1998–2001. *Recreations:* entertaining, family life. *Address:* Croydon Magistrates' Court, Altyre Road, Croydon CR9 3NG.

McIVOR, (Frances) Jill, CBE 1994; Northern Ireland Parliamentary Commissioner for Administration and for Complaints, 1991–96; *b* 10 Aug. 1930; *d* of Cecil Reginald Johnston Anderson and Frances Ellen (*née* Henderson); *m* 1953, William Basil McIvor, *qv*; two *s* one *d*. *Educ:* Methodist Coll.; Lurgan Coll.; Queen's Univ. of Belfast (LLB Hons). Called to Bar of Northern Ireland, 1980. Asst Librarian (Law), QUB, 1954–55; Tutor in Legal Res., Law Faculty, QUB, 1965–74; editorial staff, NI Legal Qtly, 1966–76; Librarian, Dept of Dir of Public Prosecutions, 1977–79. NI Mem., IBA, 1980–86; Dep. Chm., Radio Authy, 1990–94. Chm., Lagan Valley Regional Park Cttee, 1984–89 (Mem., 1975); Member: Ulster Countryside Cttee, 1984–89; Fair Employment Agency, 1984–89; Fair Employment Commn, 1990–91; Lay Panel, Juvenile Court, 1976–77; GDC, 1979–91; Exec., Belfast Voluntary Welfare Soc., 1981–88; Adv. Council, 1985–90, Bd, 1987–90, Co-operation North; Adv. Panel on Community Radio, 1985–86; NI Adv. Cttee, British Council, 1986–98. Chairman: Ulster–NZ Trust, 1987–; Educnl Guidance Service for Adults, 1988–90. NZ Hon. Consul for NI, 1996–. Mem. Bd of Visitors, QUB, 1988–. FRSA 1988–2001. DUniv Ulster, 1997. QSM 1993. *Publications:* Irish Consultant (and contrib.), Manual of Law Librarianship, 1976; (ed) Elegantia Juris: selected writings of F. H. Newark, 1973; Chart of the English Reports (new edn), 1982. *Recreations:* New Zealand, gardening. *Address:* 98 Spa Road, Ballynahinch, Co. Down BT24 8PP. *T:* (028) 9756 3534. *Club:* Royal Over-Seas League.
See also F. J. McIvor.

McIVOR, Rt Hon. (William) Basil, OBE 1991; PC (NI) 1971; *b* 17 June 1928; 2nd *s* of Rev. Frederick McIvor, Methodist clergyman and Lilly McIvor; *m* 1953, Frances Jill Anderson (*see* F. Jill McIvor); two *s* one *d*. *Educ:* Methodist Coll., Belfast; Queen's Univ., Belfast. LLB 1948. Called to NI Bar, 1950; Jun. Crown Counsel, Co. Down, Sept. 1974,

Resident Magistrate, Dec. 1974. MP (UU) Larkfield, NI Parlt, 1969; Minister of Community Relations, NI, 1971–72; Member (UU) for S Belfast, NI Assembly, 1973–75; Minister of Education, NI, 1974. Founder Mem., 1976–, Chm., 1988–, Fold Housing Assoc. Chm., All Children Together (the pioneering movement for integrated educn by consent), 1990–92 (Mem., 1974–). Governor, Campbell Coll., 1975– (Chm., 1983–85); Chm. Bd of Governors, Lagan Coll., Belfast, 1981– (the first integrated RC and Protestant school in NI). *Publication:* Hope Deferred: experiences of an Irish Unionist, 1998. *Recreations:* golf, music, gardening. *Address:* Larkhill, 98 Spa Road, Ballynahinch, Co. Down BT24 8PP. *T:* (028) 9756 3534. *Club:* Royal Over-Seas League.
See also F. Jane McIvor.

MACK, (Brian) John, DPhil; FSA; Senior Keeper, British Museum; *b* 10 July 1949; *s* of Brian Mack and Joan Alexandra Mack (*née* Kelly); *m* 1975, Caroline Jenkins, *d* of Rev. Dr D. T. Jenkins, *qv*; one *s* one *d*. *Educ:* Campbell Coll., Belfast; Univ. of Sussex (MA); Merton Coll., Oxford (DPhil 1975). FSA 1994. Res. Asst, 1976, Asst Keeper, 1977, Keeper, 1991–99, Dept of Ethnography, BM. Vis. Prof., UCL, 1996–. Member: Council, British Inst. in Eastern Africa, 1981–; Council, RAI, 1983–86; Council, African Studies Assoc., 1986–88; British Acad. Bd for Academy-sponsored Insts and Schs, 1996–; Conseil d'orientation de l'établissement publique de Musée du Quai Branly, Paris, 1999–2000; Pitt-Rivers Cttee, Univ. of Oxford, 2000–. Trustee, Horniman Mus. and Public Park, 1998–. Mem. Editl Bd, Art History, 1982–91. Nat. Art Collections Fund Award for Images of Africa, BM, 1991. *Publications:* (with J. Picton) African Textiles (Craft Adv. Council Book of the Year), 1979, 2nd edn 1989; Zulus, 1980; (with P. T. Robertshaw) Culture History in the Southern Sudan, 1982; (with M. D. McLeod) Ethnic Sculpture, 1984; Madagascar, Island of the Ancestors, 1986; Ethnic Jewellery, 1988; Malagasy Textiles, 1989; Emil Torday and the Art of the Congo 1900–1909, 1990; (with C. Spring) African Textile Design, 1991; Masks, the Art of Expression, 1994; (with K. Yoshida) Images of Other Cultures, 1997; Africa, Arts and Cultures, 2000; articles and revs in learned jls. *Address:* British Museum, Great Russell Street, WC1B 3DG. *T:* (020) 7636 1555.

MACK SMITH, Denis, CBE 1990; FBA 1976; FRSL; Extraordinary Fellow, Wolfson College, Oxford, 1987–2000 (Hon. Fellow, 2000); Emeritus Fellow, All Souls Coll., Oxford, 1987; *b* 3 March 1920; *s* of Wilfrid Mack Smith and Altiora Gauntlett; *m* 1963, Catharine Stevenson; two *d*. *Educ:* St Paul's Cathedral Choir Sch.; Haileybury Coll.; Peterhouse, Cambridge Univ. (organ and history schols). MA Cantab, MA Oxon. Asst Master, Clifton Coll., 1941–42; Cabinet Offices, 1942–46; Fellow of Peterhouse, Cambridge, 1947–62 (Hon. Fellow, 1986); Tutor of Peterhouse, 1948–58; Univ. Lectr, Cambridge, 1952–62; Sen. Res. Fellow, 1962–87, Sub-Warden, 1984–86, All Souls Coll., Oxford. Chm., Assoc. for Study of Modern Italy, 1987–. For. Hon. Mem., Amer. Acad. of Arts and Sciences, 1972. Public Orator of the Repubblica di San Marino, 1982; Hon. Citizen, Santa Margherita Ligure, 1999. Awards: Thirlwall, 1949; Serena, 1960; Elba, 1972, 1994; Villa di Chiesa, 1973; Mondello, 1975; Nove Muse, 1976; Duff Cooper Meml., 1977; Wolfson Literary, 1977; Rhegium Julii, 1983; Presidential Medal, Italy, 1984; Polifemo d'Argento, 1988; Fregene, 1990; Sileno d'Oro, 1996. Grande Ufficiale dell'Ordine al Merito della Repubblica Italiana, 1996 (Commendatore, 1978). *Publications:* Cavour and Garibaldi 1860, 1954, enlarged 2nd edn 1985; Garibaldi, 1957; (jtly) British Interests in the Mediterranean and Middle East, 1958; Italy, a Modern History, 1959; Medieval Sicily, 1968; Modern Sicily, 1968; Da Cavour a Mussolini, 1968; (ed) The Making of Italy 1796–1870, 1968, 2nd edn 1988; (ed) Garibaldi, 1969; (ed) E. Quinet, Le Rivoluzioni d'Italia, 1970; Victor Emanuel, Cavour and the Risorgimento, 1971; (ed) G. La Farina, Scritti Politici, 1972; Vittorio Emanuele II, 1972, 2nd edn 1994; Mussolini's Roman Empire, 1976; (jtly) Un Monumento al Duce, 1976; Cento Anni di Vita Italiana attraverso il Corriere della Sera, 1978; L'Italia del Ventesimo Secolo, 1978; (ed) G. Bandi, I mille: da Genova a Capua, 1981; Mussolini, 1981; (ed) F. De Sanctis, Un Viaggio Elettorale, 1983; Cavour, 1985; (jtly) A History of Sicily, 1986; Italy and its Monarchy, 1989; Mazzini, 1993; Modern Italy: a political history, 1997; La Storia Manipolata, 1998; Jt Editor, Nelson History of England, 1962–. *Address:* White Lodge, Osler Road, Headington, Oxford OX3 9BJ. *T:* (01865) 762878.

McKANE, Prof. William, FRSE 1984; FBA 1980; Professor of Hebrew and Oriental Languages, University of St Andrews, 1968–90, now Emeritus; Principal of St Mary's College, St Andrews, 1982–86; *b* 18 Feb. 1921; *s* of Thomas McKane and Jemima Smith McKane; *m* 1952, Agnes Mathie Howie; three *s* two *d*. *Educ:* Univ. of St Andrews (MA 1949); Univ. of Glasgow (MA 1952, PhD 1956, DLitt 1980). RAF, 1941–45. University of Glasgow: Asst in Hebrew, 1953–56; Lectr in Hebrew, 1956–65; Sen. Lectr, 1965–68; Dean, Faculty of Divinity, St Andrews, 1973–77. Fellow, Nat. Humanities Center, NC, USA, 1987–88. Foreign Sec., Soc. for Old Testament Study, 1981–86 (Pres., 1978); Chm., Peshitta project (Old Testament in Syriac), Internat. Org. for Study of Old Testament. Corresponding Mem., Göttingen Akad. der Wissenschaften. DD (*hc*) Edinburgh, 1984. Burkitt Medal, British Acad., 1985. *Publications:* Prophets and Wise Men, 1965; Proverbs: a new approach, 1970; Studies in the Patriarchal Narratives, 1979; Jeremiah 1–25 (International Critical Commentary series), 1986; Selected Christian Hebraists, 1989; A Late Harvest, 1995; Jeremiah 26-52 (International Critical Commentary Series), 1996; Micah: introduction and commentary, 1998; articles and reviews in British and European learned jls. *Recreations:* St Andrews association football blue (1949), walking. *Address:* 51 Irvine Crescent, St Andrews, Fife KY16 8LG. *T:* (01334) 73797. *Club:* Royal and Ancient Golf (St Andrews).

MACKANESS, George Bellamy, MB, BS, DPhil; FRS 1976; President, Squibb Institute for Medical Research and Development, 1976–87, retired; *b* Sydney, Australia, 20 Aug. 1922; *s* of James V. Mackaness and Eleanor F. Mackaness; *m* 1945, Gwynneth Patterson; one *s*. *Educ:* Sydney Univ. (MB, BS Hons 1945); London Univ. (DCP 1948); Univ. of Oxford (Hon. MA 1949, DPhil 1953). Resident MO, Sydney Hosp., 1945–46; Resident Pathologist, Kanematsu Inst. of Pathology, Sydney Hosp., 1946–47; Dept of Path., Brit. Postgrad. Med. Sch., London Univ., 1947–48 (DCP); ANU Trav. Scholarship, Univ. of Oxford, 1948–51; Demonstrator and Tutor in Path., Sir William Dunn Sch. of Path., Oxford, 1949–53; Dept of Experimental Pathology, Australian National University: Sen. Fellow, 1954–58; Associate Prof. of Exp. Path., 1958–60; Professorial Fellow, 1960–63; Vis. Investigator, Rockefeller Univ., NY, 1959–60; Prof. of Microbiology, Univ. of Adelaide, 1963–65; Dir, Trudeau Inst. for Med. Res., NY, 1965–76; Adjunct Prof. of Path., NY Univ. Med. Center, 1969–. Director: Josiah Macy Jr Foundn, 1982–86; Squibb Corp., 1984–87. Member: Allergy and Immunol. Study Sect., Nat. Insts of Health, 1967–71; Bd of Sci. Counsellors, Nat. Inst. of Allergy and Infect. Diseases, 1971–75; Armed Forces Epidemicol Bd, 1967–73; Bd of Governors, W. Alton Jones Cell Science Center, 1970–72; Council, Tissue Culture Assoc., 1973–; Bd of Sci. Consultants, Sloan-Kettering Inst. Member: Amer. Assoc. of Immunologists; Amer. Assoc. for Advancement of Science; Reticuloendothelial Soc.; Lung Assoc.; Internat. Union Against Tuberculosis; Amer. Soc. of Microbiologists. Fellow, Amer. Acad. of Arts and Scis, 1978. Paul Ehrlich-Ludwig Darmstaedter Prize, 1975; Novartis Prize, 1998. *Address:* 677 Lake Frances Drive, St Michael's Place, James Island, SC 29412, USA. *T:* (843) 7623951.

MACKAY, family name of **Earl of Inchcape, Lord Reay** and **Barons Mackay of Clashfern, Mackay of Drumadoon** and **Tanlaw**.

MACKAY OF CLASHFERN, Baron *cr* 1979 (Life Peer), of Eddrachillis in the District of Sutherland; **James Peter Hymers Mackay,** KT 1997; PC 1979; FRSE 1984; Editor-in-Chief, Halsbury's Laws of England, since 1998; Lord High Chancellor of Great Britain, 1987–97; *b* 2 July 1927; *s* of James Mackay and Janet Hymers; *m* 1958, Elizabeth Gunn Hymers; one *s* two *d*. *Educ:* George Heriot's Sch., Edinburgh. MA Hons Maths and Nat. Philosophy, Edinburgh Univ., 1948; Lectr in Mathematics, Univ. of St Andrews, 1948–50; Major Schol., Trinity Coll., Cambridge, in Mathematics, 1947, taken up 1950; Senior Schol. 1951; BA (Cantab) 1952; LLB Edinburgh (with Distinction) 1955. Admitted to Faculty of Advocates, 1955; QC (Scot.) 1965; Standing Junior Counsel to: Queen's and Lord Treasurer's Remembrancer; Scottish Home and Health Dept; Commissioners of Inland Revenue in Scotland; Sheriff Principal, Renfrew and Argyll, 1972–74; Vice-Dean, Faculty of Advocates, 1973–76; Dean, 1976–79; Lord Advocate of Scotland, 1979–84; a Senator of Coll. of Justice in Scotland, 1984–85; a Lord of Appeal in Ordinary, 1985–87. Chancellor, Heriot-Watt Univ., 1991–. Part-time Mem., Scottish Law Commn, 1976–79. Hon. Master of the Bench, Inner Temple, 1979. Fellow: Internat. Acad. of Trial Lawyers, 1979; Inst. of Taxation, 1981; Amer. Coll. of Trial Lawyers, 1990. Dir, Stenhouse Holdings Ltd, 1976–77. Mem., Insurance Brokers' Registration Council, 1977–79. A Comr of Northern Lighthouses, 1975–84; Elder Brother of Trinity House, 1990. Hon. Mem., SPTL, 1986. Hon. Fellow: Trinity Coll., Cambridge, 1989; Girton Coll., Cambridge, 1990; Hon. FRCSE 1989; Hon. FRCP 1990; Hon. FRCOG 1996; Hon. FICE 1988. Hon. LLD: Edinburgh, 1983; Dundee, 1983; Strathclyde, 1985; Aberdeen, 1987; St Andrews, 1989; Cambridge, 1989; Coll. of William and Mary, Va, 1989; Birmingham, 1990; Nat. Law Sch. of India, 1994; Bath, 1994; Glasgow, 1994; De Montfort, 1999; Hon. DCL: Newcastle, 1990; Oxford, 1998; Hon. Dr jur Robert Gordon, 2000. *Publication:* Armour on Valuation for Rating, 5th edn (Consultant Editor), 1985. *Recreations:* walking, travel. *Address:* House of Lords, SW1A 0PW. *Clubs:* Athenæum, Caledonian; New (Edinburgh).

MACKAY OF DRUMADOON, Baron *cr* 1995 (Life Peer), of Blackwaterfoot in the district of Cunninghame; **Donald Sage Mackay;** PC 1996; a Senator of the College of Justice in Scotland, since 2000; *b* 30 Jan. 1946; *s* of Rev. Donald George Mackintosh Mackay and Jean Margaret Mackay; *m* 1979, Lesley Ann Waugh; one *s* two *d*. *Educ:* George Watson's Boys' Coll., Edinburgh; Univ. of Edinburgh (LLB 1966; LLM 1968); Univ. of Virginia (LLM 1969). Law apprentice, 1969–71; Solicitor with Allan McDougall & Co., SSC, Edinburgh, 1971–76; called to the Scottish Bar, 1976; Advocate Depute, 1982–85; QC (Scot.) 1987; Solicitor-General for Scotland, 1995; Lord Advocate, 1995–97. Mem., Criminal Injuries Compensation Bd, 1989–95. Opposition spokesman on constitutional and legal affairs, H of L, 1997–2000. *Recreations:* golf, gardening, Isle of Arran. *Address:* 39 Hermitage Gardens, Edinburgh EH10 6AZ. *T:* (0131) 447 1412, *Fax:* (0131) 447 9863; Seafield, Lamlash, Isle of Arran KA27 8JT, *T:* (01770) 600646; Parliament House, Edinburgh EH1 1RQ. *T:* (0131) 225 2595, *Fax:* (0131) 225 8213. *Club:* Western (Glasgow).

MACKAY, Prof. Alan Lindsay, FRS 1988; Professor of Crystallography, Birkbeck College, University of London, 1986–91, now Emeritus; *b* 6 Sept. 1926; *s* of Robert Lindsay Mackay, OBE, MC, BSc, MD and Margaret Brown Mackay, OBE, MB ChB, JP; *m* 1951, Sheila Thorne Hague, MA; two *s* one *d*. *Educ:* Wolverhampton Grammar Sch.; Oundle Sch.; Trinity Coll., Cambridge (BA, MA); BSc, PhD, DSc London. Lectr, Reader, Prof., Dept of Crystallography, Birkbeck Coll., 1951–91. Visiting Professor: Univ. of Tokyo, 1969; Univ. of Tsukuba, 1980; Korean Advanced Inst. of Sci. and Tech., 1987; Hon. Professor: Central China Univ; Sichuan Inst. of Sci. Studies; China Inst. for Sci. Studies; Univ. de Paris-Sud, 1989. Zaheer Lectr, New Delhi, 1977. Foreign Member: Academia Mexicana de Ciencias, 1998; Korean Acad. of Sci. and Technol., 1999. *Publications:* The Harvest of a Quiet Eye, 1977; (with A. N. Barrett) Spatial Structure and the Microcomputer, 1987; (ed) A Dictionary of Scientific Quotations, 1991; papers in learned jls. *Recreation:* Asian studies. *Address:* 22 Lanchester Road, N6 4TA. *T:* (020) 8883 4810.

McKAY, Prof. Alexander Gordon, OC 1988; FRSC 1965; Professor of Classics, McMaster University, 1957–90, now Emeritus; Adjunct Professor of Humanities, 1990–96, and Fellow, Vanier College, since 1992, York University; President, Royal Society of Canada, 1984–87; *b* 24 Dec. 1924; *s* of Alexander Lynn McKay and Marjory Maude Redfern Nicoll McKay; *m* 1964, Helen Jean Zulauf; two step *d*. *Educ:* Trinity Coll., Toronto (Hons BA Classics 1946); Yale Univ. (MA 1947); Princeton Univ. (AM 1948; PhD 1950). Classics faculty: Wells Coll., NY, 1949–50; Univ. of Pennsylvania, 1950–51; Univ. of Manitoba, 1951–52; Mount Allison Univ., 1952–53; Waterloo Coll., Ont., 1953–55; Univ. of Manitoba, 1955–57; McMaster Univ., 1957–90: Chm. of Dept, 1962–68, 1976–79; Founding Dean of Humanities, 1968–73; Senator, 1968–73, 1985–87. Dist. Vis. Prof., Univ. of Colorado, 1973; Prof. i/c, Intercollegiate Center for Classical Studies in Rome (Stanford Univ.), 1975; Mem. Inst. for Advanced Study, Princeton, 1979, 1981; Vis. Schol., Univ. of Texas, Austin, 1987; Vis. Fellow Commoner, Trinity Coll., Cambridge, 1988; Distinguished Vis. Lectr, Concordia Univ., Montreal, 1992–93. Dir, Internat. Union of Academies, 1980–83, 1986–90 (Vice-Pres., 1983–86). Vice-Pres., Bristol Inst. of Hellenic and Roman Studies, 1998–. Hon. LLD: Manitoba, 1986; Brock Univ., Ont, 1990; Queen's Univ., Kingston, 1991; Hon. DLitt: McMaster, 1992; Waterloo, 1993. KStJ 1986. Silver Jubilee Medal, 1977; 125th Anniversary of the Confederation of Canada Medal, 1992. *Publications:* Naples and Campania: texts and illustrations, 1962; Roman Lyric Poetry: Catullus and Horace, 1962; Vergil's Italy, 1970; Cumae and the Phlegraean Fields, 1972; Naples and Coastal Campania, 1972; Houses, Villas and Palaces in the Roman World, 1975, German edn 1980; Roman Satire, 1976; Vitruvius, Architect and Engineer, 1978; Roma Antiqua: Latium and Etruria, 1986; Selections from Vergil's Aeneid Books I, IV, VI: Dido and Aeneas, 1988; Tragedy, Love and Change, 1994; Arma Virumque: heroes at war, 1998. *Recreations:* pianoforte, travel. *Address:* 1 Turner Avenue, Hamilton, ON L8P 3K4, Canada. *T:* (905) 5261331, *Fax:* (905) 5269245; *e-mail:* ag.mckay@sympatico.ca. *Clubs:* Yale (NY); University (Pittsburgh); Tamahaac (Ancaster, Hamilton); Arts and Letters, X (Toronto); President's (McMaster Univ.).

McKAY, Allan George; Director of Information Services, British Gas, 1994–95; *b* 5 Sept. 1935; *s* of George Allan McKay and Wilhelmina McKay; *m* 1962, Margaret Currie Baxter; one *s* two *d*. *Educ:* Royal High School, Edinburgh. FCCA, ACIS, CIGasE. Accountant, Scottish Gas Board, 1961; Dir of Finance, Scottish Gas, 1975; Deputy Chairman: British Gas East Midlands, 1982; British Gas North Thames, 1987; Chairman: British Gas North Eastern, 1989; British Gas North Western, 1993. *Recreations:* golf, gardening. *Address:* Avonmead, Tiddington Road, Stratford-upon-Avon, Warks CV37 7AF.

McKAY, Allen; JP; *b* 5 Feb. 1927; *s* of Fred and Martha Anne McKay; *m* 1949, June Simpson (*d* 1997); one *s*. *Educ:* Hoyland Kirk Balk Secondary Modern School; extramural studies, Univ. of Sheffield. Clerical work, Steel Works, 1941–45; general mineworker,

1945–47; Mining Electrical Engineer, 1947–65; NCB Industrial Relations Trainee, 1965–66; Asst Manpower Officer, Barnsley Area, NCB, 1966–78. MP (Lab) Pensistone, July 1978–1983; Barnsley West and Penistone, 1983–92. Opposition Whip, 1981. JP Barnsley, 1971. *Recreation:* reading. *Address:* 24 Springwood Road, Hoyland, Barnsley, South Yorks S74 0AZ. *T:* (01226) 743418.

MacKAY, Rt Hon. Andrew (James); PC 1998; MP (C) Bracknell, since 1997 (Berkshire East, 1983–97); *b* 27 Aug. 1949; *s* of Robert James MacKay and Olive Margaret MacKay; *m* 1st 1975, Diana Joy (*née* Kinchin) (marr. diss. 1996); one *s* one *d*; 2nd, 1997, Julie Kirkbride, *qv*; one *s*. *Educ:* Solihull. MP (C) Birmingham, Stechford, March 1977–1979; PPS to Sec. of State for NI, 1986–89, to Sec. of State for Defence, 1989–92; an Asst Govt Whip, 1992–93; a Lord Comr of HM Treasury (Govt Whip), 1993–95; Vice Chamberlain of HM Household, 1995–96; Treasurer of HM Household (Dep. Govt Chief Whip), 1996–97; Opposition front bench spokesman on NI, 1997–2001. Mem., Environment Select Cttee, 1985–86; Sec., Cons. Parly For. Affairs Cttee, 1985–86. Mem., Conservative Party Nat. Exec., 1979–82. *Recreations:* golf, squash, good food. *Address:* House of Commons, SW1A 0AA. *T:* (020) 7219 4109. *Clubs:* Berkshire Golf; Aberdovey Golf; Royal & Ancient Golf (St Andrews).

MacKAY, Angus; Member (Lab) Edinburgh South, Scottish Parliament, since 1999; Minister for Finance and Local Government, since 2000; *b* 10 Sept. 1964. *Educ:* St Augustine's High Sch., Edinburgh; Edinburgh Univ. (MA Hons Politics and History, 1986). Formerly Campaign Officer, Shelter (Scotland); Parly Asst to Dr Mo Mowlam, 1990–92. Mem. (Lab) City of Edinburgh Council, 1995–99 (Convener, Finance Cttee, 1997–99). Dep. Minister for Justice, Scottish Parlt, 1999–2000. *Address:* Scottish Parliament, Edinburgh EH99 1SP.

MACKAY, Prof. Angus Iain Kenneth, PhD; FBA 1991; Professor of History, University of Edinburgh, 1985–97; *b* 1939; *m* 1962; one *s* one *d*. *Educ:* Edinburgh Univ. (MA 1962; PhD 1969). Lectr, Reading Univ., 1965–69; Lectr, then Sen. Lectr, 1969–82, Reader, 1982–85, Edinburgh Univ. *Publications:* Spain in the Middle Ages, 1977; Money, Prices and Politics in Fifteenth-century Castile, 1981; Society, Economy and Religion in late Mediaeval Castile, 1987; (with R. Bartlett) Mediaeval Frontier Societies, 1989; (with D. Ditchburn) Atlas of Medieval Europe, 1997; contribs to learned jls. *Address:* 43 Liberton Drive, Edinburgh EH16 6NL.

MACKAY, Charles, CB 1986; FIBiol; Chief Agricultural Officer, Department of Agriculture and Fisheries for Scotland, 1975–87; *b* 12 Jan. 1927; *s* of Hugh and Eliza Mackay; *m* 1956, Marie A. K. Mackay (*née* Mitchell); one *s* one *d*. *Educ:* Strathmore Sch., Sutherland; Lairg Higher Grade Sch., Sutherland; Univ. of Aberdeen (BScAgric); Univ. of Kentucky (MSc). Department of Agriculture and Fisheries for Scotland: Temporary Inspector, 1947–48; Asst Inspector, 1948–54; Inspector, 1954–64; Sen. Inspector, 1964–70; Technical Develt Officer, 1970–73; Dep. Chief Agricl Officer, 1973–75. Hon. Order of Kentucky Colonels, 1960. *Recreations:* fishing, golf. *Address:* The Cottage, 3 West Shinness, Lairg, Sutherland IV27 4DW. *T:* (01549) 402114.

MACKAY, Charles Dorsey; Chairman: Eurotunnel Group, since 2001 (non-executive Director, since 1997; Deputy Chairman, 1999–2001); Eurotunnel PLC, since 1999; The Channel Tunnel Group Ltd, since 1999; *b* 14 April 1940; *s* of late Brig. Kenneth Mackay, CBE, DSO and Evelyn Maud (*née* Ingram); *m* 1964, Annmarie Joder-Pfeiffer; one *s* one *d* (and one *s* decd). *Educ:* Cheltenham Coll.; Queens' Coll., Cambridge (MA); INSEAD (MBA). British Petroleum Co., 1957–69; commercial apprentice, 1957–59; univ. apprentice, Cambridge, 1959–62; marketing assistant, London, 1962–63; Regl Sales Manager, Algeria, 1963–65; Commercial Dir, Burundi/Rwanda/Congo, 1965–68; sponsored at INSEAD, France, 1968–69; McKinsey & Co. Inc., 1969–76: Consultant; Sen. Engagement Manager, 1972–76; worked in London, Paris, Amsterdam, Dar es Salaam; Pakhoed Holding NV, Rotterdam, 1976–81: Dir, 1976–77, Chm., 1977–81, Paktrans Div.; Chloride Group plc, 1981–86: Dir, 1981–86; Chm., Overseas Div., 1981–85; Chm., Power Electronics Div., 1985–86; Inchcape plc, 1986–96: Dir, 1986–96; Chief Exec., 1991–96; Dep. Chm., 1995–96; Chm., Inchcape (Hong Kong) Ltd and Dodwell and Co. Ltd, 1986–87; Chm. and Chief Exec., Inchcape Pacific Ltd, 1987–91. Chairman: DSL Gp Ltd, 1996–97; TDG plc, 2000–; Dep. Chm., Thistle Hotels Plc, 1996–; non-executive Director: Union Insurance Soc. of Canton Ltd, 1986–91; Hongkong and Shanghai Banking Corp. Ltd, 1986–92; Midland Bank plc, 1992–93; HSBC Holdings plc, 1992–98; British Airways plc, 1993–96; Johnson Matthey PLC, 1999–; Mem. Supervisory Bd, Gucci Gp NV, 1997–. Mem. Bd, INSEAD, 2000–. *Recreations:* travel, tennis, ski-ing, classical music, opera, chess. *Address:* Eurotunnel Group, 1 Northumberland Avenue, Trafalgar Square, WC2N 5BW. *T:* (020) 8938 6823. *Club:* Hong Kong (Hong Kong).

MacKAY, Colin, CBE 2001; FRCS, FRCSE, FRCSGlas, FRCP, FRCPI, FFPHM, FRCPE; President, Royal College of Physicians and Surgeons of Glasgow, 1997–2000; *b* 8 Nov. 1936; *s* of Kenneth MacKay and Margaret Blair Dawson MacKay; *m* 1966, Dr Helen Paul Miskimmin; one *s* two *d*. *Educ:* Univ. of Glasgow (BSc Hons; MB ChB (Commendation)). FRCS 1966; FRCSE 1966; FRCSGlas 1966; FRCP 1999; FRCPI 1999; FFPHM 1999; FRCPE 2000. Surgical trng, Western Infirmary, Glasgow, 1961–69; MRC Travelling Fellow, Boston Univ., 1969–70; Sen. Lectr in Surgery, Univ. of Glasgow, 1970–82; Consultant Surgeon, Western Infirmary/Gartnavel Gen. Hosp., Glasgow, 1982–96. Royal College of Physicians and Surgeons of Glasgow: Mem. Council, 1972–; Hon. Treas., 1976–86; Vice Pres., Surgical, 1992–94; Visitor, 1996–97. FACP 1998; FCMSA 1998; Fellow, Acad. of Medicine, Singapore 1998. *Publications:* (with I. McA. Ledingham) Textbook of Surgical Physiology, 1978, 2nd edn 1988; contribs to med. jls in field of surgical gastroenterology, in general, and peptic ulcer and gallstone disease, in particular. *Recreations:* travel, walking in the distinguished company of a golden retriever. *Address:* 73 Buchanan Drive, Bearsden, Glasgow G61 2EP. *T:* (0141) 942 8759. *Club:* Royal Scottish Automobile (Glasgow).

MACKAY, Hon. Sir Colin (Crichton), KT 2001; **Hon. Mr Justice Mackay;** a Judge of the High Court, Queen's Bench Division, since 2001; *b* 26 Sept. 1943; *s* of Sir James Mackerron Mackay, KBE, CB, and Katherine Millar Crichton Mackay (*née* Hamilton); *m* 1969, Rosamond Diana Elizabeth Collins; one *d* two *s*. *Educ:* Radley Coll.; Corpus Christi Coll., Oxford (Open Classical Schol; MA). Harmsworth Entrance Exhibnr, 1965, and Astbury Schol., 1967; called to the Bar, Middle Temple, 1967, Bencher, 1995; QC 1989, a Recorder, 1992–2001. *Recreations:* opera, sport, Scotland. *Address:* Royal Courts of Justice, Strand, WC2A 2LL. *Club:* Vincent's (Oxford).

McKAY, Sheriff Colin Graham; Sheriff of North Strathclyde at Kilmarnock, since 2001; *b* 20 Jan. 1942; *s* of Patrick Joseph McKay and Mary Kieran; *m* 1966, Sandra Anne Coli; one *d* one *s*. *Educ:* St Aloysius' Coll., Glasgow; Clongowes Wood Coll., by Dublin; Univ. of Glasgow (MA, LLB). Admitted Solicitor, 1966; in private practice, 1966–90; Temporary Sheriff, 1985–90; Sheriff of N Strathclyde: (floater), 1990–95; at Oban and Fort William, 1995–2001. *Recreations:* sailing, hillwalking, watching Rugby. *Address:* Sheriff Court House, St Marnock Street, Kilmarnock KA1 1ED.

MACKAY, David Ian; His Honour Judge Mackay; a Circuit Judge, since 1992; *b* 11 Nov. 1945; *s* of David and Jessie Mackay, Higher Tranmere, Birkenhead; *m* 1974, Mary Elizabeth Smith; one *s* two *d*. *Educ:* Birkenhead Sch.; Brasenose Coll., Oxford (Schol.; BA Jurisprudence 1968; MA 1992). Called to the Bar, Inner Temple, 1969; practised on Northern Circuit, 1970–92; Asst Recorder, 1986–89; Recorder, 1989–92. Official Referee's business, 1993–98; Provincial Judge, Technology and Construction Court, 1998–. Gov., Birkenhead Sch., 1979– (Chm., 1991–); Chm., Birkenhead Sch. Foundn Trust, 1998–. *Recreations:* history, transport, France. *Address:* Queen Elizabeth II Law Courts, Derby Square, Liverpool L2 1XA. *Club:* Athenæum (Liverpool).

MACKAY, David James, FCIT; Chief Executive, John Menzies plc, since 1997; *b* 20 May 1943; *s* of David Mackay and Lena Mackay (*née* Westwater); *m* 1966, Jane Brown Hunter; one *s* one *d*. *Educ:* Kirkcaldy High Sch.; post experience programmes at Edinburgh and Bradford Univs. FCIT 1993. Various exec. posts in John Menzies plc, 1964–97, including: Transport Manager, NI, 1965; Asst Regl Dir, Southern & London, 1973; Ops Dir, Edinburgh, 1978; Man. Dir, Wholesale, 1984. CIMgt 1998. *Recreations:* golf, walking. *Address:* John Menzies plc, 108 Princes Street, Edinburgh EH2 3AA. *T:* (0131) 225 8555. *Clubs:* Press (Edinburgh); Bruntsfield Golf (Edinburgh); Aberdour Golf (Fife).

MACKAY, Donald George; Hon. Research Fellow, Aberdeen University, since 1990; *b* 25 Nov. 1929; *s* of William Morton Mackay and Annie Tainsh Higgs; *m* 1965, Elizabeth Ailsa Barr (*d* 1999); two *s* one *d*. *Educ:* Morgan Academy, Dundee; St Andrews Univ. (MA); Aberdeen Univ. (PhD). Assistant Principal, Scottish Home Dept, 1953; Asst Private Sec. to Sec. of State for Scotland, 1959–60; Asst Sec., Royal Commn on the Police, 1960–62; Principal, SHHD, 1962–66; Sec., Royal Commission on Local Govt in Scotland, 1966–69; Asst Sec., Scottish Develt Dept, 1969–79; Asst Sec., 1980–83, Under Sec., 1983–85, Dept of Agric. and Fisheries for Scotland; Under Sec., Scottish Develt Dept., 1985–88. Mem., Scottish Agricl Wages Bd, 1991–97. *Publication:* Scotland's Rural Land Use Agencies, 1995. *Recreations:* hill walking, photography, music. *Address:* 38 Cluny Drive, Edinburgh EH10 6DX. *T:* (0131) 447 1851.

MacKAY, Sir Donald (Iain), Kt 1996; FRSE; FRSGS; Chairman, Grampian Holdings, since 1998 (Director, since 1987); *b* 27 Feb. 1937; *s* of William and Rhona MacKay; *m* 1961, Diana Marjory (*née* Raffan); one *s* two *d*. *Educ:* Dollar Academy; Univ. of Aberdeen (MA). FRSE 1988. English Electric Co., 1959–62; Lectr in Political Economy, Univ. of Aberdeen, 1962–65; Lectr in Applied Economics, Univ. of Glasgow, 1965–68, Sen. Lectr, 1968–71; Prof. of Political Economy, Univ. of Aberdeen, 1971–76; Prof. of Economics, Heriot-Watt Univ., Edinburgh, 1976–82, Professorial Fellow 1982–90; Hon. Prof., 1990–. Chairman: Pieda plc, 1974–97; Scottish Enterprise, 1993–97; Director: Scottish Mortgage Trust; Edinburgh Income and Value Trust, 1999–; DTZ Hldgs, 1999–. Mem., Scottish Econ. Council, 1985–99. Consultant to Sec. of State for Scotland, 1971–99. Chairman: Scottish Sci. Trust, 1997–; Edinburgh Business Sch., 1997–. Gov., NIESR, 1981–. FRSGS 1996. Hon. LLD Aberdeen, 1994; DUniv Stirling, 1994. *Publications:* Geographical Mobility and the Brain Drain, 1969; Local Labour Markets and Wage Structures, 1970; Labour Markets under Different Employment Conditions, 1971; The Political Economy of North Sea Oil, 1975; (ed) Scotland 1980: the economics of self-government, 1977; articles in Econ. Jl, Oxford Econ. Papers, Manch. Sch., Scottish Jl Polit. Econ., Jl Royal Stat. Soc. *Recreations:* tennis, golf, bridge. *Address:* Newfield, 14 Gamekeeper's Road, Edinburgh EH4 6LU.

MACKAY, Douglas Ian; QC (Scot) 1993; *b* 10 Aug. 1948; *s* of Walter Douglas Mackay and Karla Marie Anna Fröhlich; *m* 1970, Susan Anne Nicholson; two *s* one *d*. *Educ:* Inverness High Sch.; Aberdeen Univ. (LLB). Admitted advocate, 1980. *Recreations:* Scottish art, travel, mountaineering, shooting, gundogs. *Address:* St Ann's House, Lasswade, Midlothian EH18 1ND. *T:* (0131) 660 2634; Mount Pleasant Farm, Fortrose, Ross-shire IV10 8SH.

MACKAY, Eileen Alison, (Lady Russell), CB 1996; non-executive Director, Royal Bank of Scotland Group plc, since 1996; *b* 7 July 1943; *d* of Alexander William Mackay and Alison Jack Ross; *m* 1983, (Alastair) Muir Russell (*see* Sir A. M. Russell). *Educ:* Dingwall Acad.; Edinburgh Univ. (MA Hons Geography). Dept of Employment, Scottish HQ, 1965–72; Scottish Office, 1972–78; HM Treasury, 1978–80; CPRS, Cabinet Office, 1980–83; Scottish Office, 1983–96: Under Sec., Housing, Envmt Dept, 1988–92; Principal Finance Officer, 1992–96. Chm., Castlemilk Partnership, 1988–92; Director: Moray Firth Maltings, 1988–99; Edinburgh Investment Trust plc, 1996–; Scottish TV (Regional) Ltd, 1998–99; Scottish Enterprise Edinburgh and Lothian, 1998–; Scottish Financial Enterprise Ltd, 2000–. Chm., Standing Adv. Cttee on Trunk Road Assessment, 1996–99. Mem., Commn on Local Govt and the Scottish Parlt, 1998–99. Member: Bd, Scottish Screen, 1997–99; ESRC, 1999–; Scottish Business and Biodiversity Gp, 1999–; Accountancy Review Bd, 2000–. Mem. Bd, Margaret Blackwood Housing Assoc., 1996–. Trustee, David Hume Inst., 1996–; Mem. Court, Univ. of Edinburgh, 1997–. *Address:* c/o Royal Bank of Scotland, 42 St Andrew Square, Edinburgh EH2 2YE. *Club:* New (Edinburgh).

MACKAY, Eric Beattie; Editor of The Scotsman, 1972–85; *b* 31 Dec. 1922; *s* of Lewis Mackay and Agnes Johnstone; *m* 1954, Moya Margaret Myles Connolly (*d* 1981); three *s* one *d*. *Educ:* Aberdeen Grammar Sch.; Aberdeen Univ. (MA). Aberdeen Bon-Accord, 1948; Elgin Courant, 1949; The Scotsman, 1950; Daily Telegraph, 1952; The Scotsman, 1953: London Editor, 1957; Dep. Editor, 1961. *Recreations:* travel, reading, theatre. *Address:* 5 Strathearn Place, Edinburgh EH9 2AL. *T:* (0131) 466 0143.

MACKAY, Francis Henry, FCCA; Chairman: Compass Group plc, since 1999; Kingfisher plc, since 2001; *b* 24 Oct. 1944; *m* 1963, Christine Leach; one *s* two *d*. FCCA 1967. Finance Dir, 1986–91, Chief Exec. and Dep. Chm., 1991–99, Compass Gp plc; Jt Dep. Chm., Granada Compass, 2000–01. Non-exec. Dir, Centrica plc, 1997–2001. *Address:* Compass Group plc, Cowley House, Guildford Street, Chertsey, Surrey KT16 9BA. *T:* (01932) 573000.

MACKAY, Air Vice-Marshal (Hector) Gavin, OBE 1987; AFC 1982; FRAeS; Air Officer Commanding, and Commandant, Royal Air Force College, Cranwell, since 2000; *b* 3 Oct. 1947; *s* of John MacLean Mackay and Isobel Margaret Mackay (*née* Mackay); *m* 1971, Elizabeth Stark Bolton; one *s* one *d*. *Educ:* Dingwall Acad.; Glasgow Univ. (BSc Civil Engrg 1970); RAF Coll., Cranwell. FRAeS 1997. Qualified Flying Instructor, RAF Linton-on-Ouse, 1973–75; Harrier Pilot: No 20 Sqdn, RAF Wildenrath, 1976–77; No 3 (F) Sqdn, RAF Gutersloh, 1977–79; Flight Comdr, No 1 (F) Sqdn, RAF Wittering, 1979–82; RNSC, 1982; Central Tactics and Trials Orgn, 1983–84; OC Examng Wing, CFS, 1984–87; Concept Studies and Operational Requirements, MoD, 1987–90; Station Comdr, RAF Gutersloh, 1991–93; Dep. Dir Air Offensive, MoD, 1993; rcds 1994; ACOS Ops, HQ AIRCENT, 1995–96; Comdt, CFS, 1996–99; Hd, Jt Force 2000 Implementation Team, 1999–2000. Upper Freeman, GAPAN 1997. *Recreations:* flying, golf, walking. *Address:* The Lodge, Cranwell, Sleaford, Lincs NG34 8HD. *T:* (01400) 261354. *Club:* Royal Air Force.

McKAY, Rt Hon. Sir Ian (Lloyd), KNZM 1998; PC 1992; Chartered Arbitrator; Judge of the Court of Appeal of New Zealand, 1991–97; *b* 7 March 1929; *s* of Neville James McKay and Kathleen Mary (*née* McGrath); *m* 1958, Ruth Constance Younger; four *s* two *d*. *Educ:* Victoria Coll., Univ. of NZ (BA, LLB). FCIArb; FAMINZ(Arb). Barrister and Solicitor, High Court of NZ, 1952; in practice as barrister and solicitor with Swan Davies & McKay, Wellington, later Swan Davies McKay & Co., then Young Swan McKay & Co., subseq. Young Swan Morison McKay, and Kensington Swan, 1953–91; Sen. Partner, 1967–91. Chm., various govt law reform cttees, 1971–87. Dir, public and private cos, 1970–91. Fellow, Internat. Acad. Trial Lawyers, USA, 1982–. Hon. Mem., Amer. Bar Assoc., 1981. *Publications:* Laws NZ—Defamation; The Act of Piobaireachd; papers to nat. confs and jls of various professional bodies. *Recreations:* Highland bagpipe music, tennis. *Address:* PO Box 17028, Wellington, New Zealand. *T:* (4) 4768950, *Fax:* (4) 4767950. *Club:* Wellington (Wellington, NZ).

MACKAY, Ian Stuart, FRCS; Consultant Otorhinolaryngologist, Royal Brompton Hospital and Charing Cross Hospital, London, since 1977; *b* 16 June 1943; *s* of Rev. Gordon Mackay and Sylvia Mackay (*née* Spencer); *m* 1st, 1968, Angela Gascoigne-Pees (marr. diss. 1981); one *s* one *d*; 2nd, 1981, Madeleine Hargreaves (*née* Tull); one *d*. *Educ:* Kearsney Coll., Natal, South Africa; Royal Free Hosp. Sch. of Medicine, London (MB BS 1968). FRCS 1974. Cons. Otorhinolaryngologist, Metropolitan ENT Hosp., 1977–86. Hon. Senior Lecturer: Nat. Heart and Lung Inst., 1985–; Inst. of Laryngology and Otology, Univ. of London, 1985–; Hon. Consultant, King Edward VII Hosp. for Officers, 1995–. Vis. Prof., Mayo Clinic, 1996. Hon. Treasurer: European Acad. of Facial Surgery, 1978–93; British Academic Conf. in Otolaryngology, 1992–; Mem. Council, Laryngology and Rhinology Section, RSocMed, 1996– (Pres., Nov. 2002–); Founder Mem., British Allergy Foundn, 1995; Pres., British Assoc. of Otolaryngologists, 1999–Nov. 2002; (Pres.-elect, 1996–99); Chm., Fedn of Surgical Specialty Assocs, 2001–. Mem. Editl Bd, Amer. Jl of Rhinology, 1995–. *Publications:* (ed) Scott-Brown's Otolaryngology, Rhinology Vols, 5th edn 1987, 6th edn 1997; (contrib.) Facial Plastic Surgery, 1986; Otolaryngology, 1987, 2nd edn 1997; (ed) Rhinitis: mechanisms and management, 1989; chapters in books and papers, mainly on rhinoplasty and endoscopic sinus surgery. *Recreation:* sailing. *Address:* 55 Harley Street, W1G 8QR. *T:* (020) 7580 5070. *Club:* Royal Society of Medicine.

McKAY, Sir John (Andrew), Kt 1972; CBE 1966; QPM 1968; HM Chief Inspector of Constabulary for England and Wales, 1970–72; *b* 28 Nov. 1912; *s* of late Denis McKay, Blantyre, Lanarkshire; *m* 1st, 1947, Gertrude Gillespie Deighan (*d* 1971); two *d*; 2nd, 1976, Mildred Grace Kilday, *d* of late Dr Emil Stern and Grace Mildred Pleasants, San Francisco. *Educ:* Glasgow Univ. MA Glasgow, 1934. Joined Metropolitan Police, 1935; Metropolitan Police Coll., 1937–38; seconded to Army for service with Military Govt in Italy and Austria, 1943–47 (Lt-Col); Asst Chief Constable, then Deputy Chief Constable, Birmingham, 1953–58; Chief Constable of Manchester, 1959–66; HM Inspector of Constabulary, 1966–70. Freeman of City of London, 1972. OStJ 1963. Hon. MA, Manchester, 1966; Hon. Fellow, Manchester Polytechnic, subseq. Manchester Metropolitan Univ., 1971. *Address:* 212 Mocking Bird Circle, Santa Rosa, CA 95409, USA. *T:* (707) 5388285.

McKAY, Dr John Henderson, CBE 1987; JP; DL; Tutor and Associate Lecturer, Open University, since 1993; Hon. Vice President, Royal Caledonian Horticultural Society, since 1997 (Vice President, 1993–97); *b* 12 May 1929; *s* of Thomas Johnstone McKay and Patricia Madeleine Henderson; *m* 1964, Catherine Watson Taylor; one *s* one *d*. *Educ:* West Calder High School. BA Hons, PhD, Open University. Labourer, clerk, Pumpherston Oil Co. Ltd, 1948–50; National Service, Royal Artillery, 1950–52; Officer and Surveyor, Customs and Excise, 1952–85. Mem., 1974–77 and 1978–88, Lord Provost and Lord Lieutenant, 1984–88, City of Edinburgh DC; Chm., Edinburgh Internat. Fest. Soc., 1984–88; Jt Chm., Edinburgh Mil. Tattoo Policy Cttee, 1984–88; Councillor, Royal Caledonian Horticultural Soc., 1974–78, 1980–81, 1984–88 (Sec. and Treas., 1988–93). Convener, Business Cttee, 1992–96, Assessor on Univ. Court, 1996–99, Gen. Council of Edinburgh Univ. Chm., Scottish Wkg People's History Trust, 1992–2000; Trustee: Inst. of Occupl Medicine Res. Trust, 1992–; Almond Valley Collections Trust, 1994–; Edinburgh Quartet Trust, 1994– (Chm., 1995–2000); Hon. Pres., Scottish Craftsmanship Assoc., 1987–2000; Hon. Vice-Pres., St Andrew Soc., 1989–; Patron, Scotland Yard Adventure Centre, 1988–. JP 1984, DL 1988, Edinburgh. Dr *hc* Edinburgh, 1989. *Publication:* (jtly) The Pumpherston Story, 2001. *Recreations:* gardening, listening to music. *Address:* 2 Buckstone Way, Edinburgh EH10 6PN. *T:* (0131) 445 2865. *Club:* Lothianburn Golf (Edinburgh).

MacKAY, Julie; *see* Kirkbride, J.

MACKAY, Maj.-Gen. Kenneth, CB 1969; MBE 1943; idc, psc; GOC, Field Force Command Australia, Nov. 1973–Feb. 1974, retired; *b* 17 Feb. 1917; *m* 1943, Judith, *d* of F. Littler; two *s* one *d*. *Educ:* University High Sch., Melbourne; RMC Duntroon. Served War of 1939–45: Artillery, and Liaison Officer HQ 9th Australian Division, Middle East, 1940–41; ME Staff Sch., 1942; Bde Maj. 26 Bde, 1942–44; MO 12, War Office, 1944–45; Joint Sec., JCOSA, 1945–48; CO, 67 Inf. Bn, 1948; CO, 3 Bn Royal Aust. Regt, 1949; AHQ, 1949–52; Chief Instructor, Sch. of Tactics and Admin. 1952–55; Asst Aust. Defence Rep. UK, 1955–57; successively Dir of Maintenance, Personnel Admin., Quartering and Military Training, 1957–61; IDC, 1962; Dir Military Operations and Plans, Army HQ, Canberra, 1962–66; Comdr Aust. Force Vietnam, 1966; Commander 1st Division Australian Army, 1967–68; QMG AHQ, 1968–71; GOC Eastern Comd, 1971–73. *Recreations:* fishing, golf. *Address:* Unit 31, Glenaeon, Glenaeon Avenue, Belrose, NSW 2085, Australia. *Clubs:* Australian (Sydney); Gordon Golf, New South Wales Golf.

McKAY, Neil Stuart, CB 2001; Chief Operating Officer, Department of Health, since 2000; *b* 19 Feb. 1952; *s* of late Roy McKay and of Alison Maude McKay (*née* Dent); *m* 1978, Deirdre Mary McGinn; two *s*. *Educ:* Dame Allan's Boys' Sch., Newcastle upon Tyne. Trainee Adminr, Newcastle upon Tyne Univ. HMC, 1970–72; Asst Hosp. Sec., Dunston Hill Hosp., Gateshead HMC, 1972–74; Admin Asst, Gateshead AHA, 1974–75; Unit Adminr, Dryburn Hosp., Durham AHA, 1975–76; Commng Officer, St George's Hosp., Merton, Sutton and Wandsworth AHA, 1976–80; Dist Planning Adminr, 1980–82, Hosp. Adminr, Springfield Hosp., 1982–85, Wandsworth HA; Gen. Manager, Doncaster Royal Infirmary, 1985–88; Gen. Manager, 1988–91, Chief Exec., 1991–96, Northern Gen. Hosp. NHS Trust, Sheffield; Regl Dir, Trent Regl Office, 1996–2000, Dep. Chief Exec., 2000, NHS Exec., DoH. *Recreations:* sport of all kinds (especially following Sunderland AFC), reading, gardening. *Address:* Department of Health, Quarry House, Quarry Hill, Leeds LS2 7UE.

MACKAY, Neville Patrick; Chief Executive, Resource: Council for Museums, Archives and Libraries, since 2000; *b* 22 June 1958; *s* of Edward William Charles Mackay and Constance Evelyn Mackay; *m* 1996, Gillian Anne Prole; two *d*. *Educ:* Brentwood Sch.; Lancaster Univ. (BA Hons Geog. 1979); University Coll. London. Researcher, DoE, 1983–90; DFE, 1990–92; Department for National Heritage, later Department for Culture, Media and Sport: 1992–99; Dep. Hd, Heritage Div., 1995–97; Hd, Libraries and Inf. Div., 1997–99. *Recreations:* motor sports, walking, camping, being with my family. *Address:* c/o Resource: Council for Museums, Archives and Libraries, 16 Queen Anne's Gate, SW1H 9AA. *T:* (020) 7273 1444.

MacKAY, Prof. Norman, CBE 1997; MD; FRCPGlas, FRCPE, FRCSE, FRCGP, FRCP; Dean of Postgraduate Medicine and Professor of Postgraduate Medical Education, University of Glasgow, since 1989; *b* 15 Sept. 1936; *s* of Donald MacKay and Catherine MacLeod; *m* 1961, Grace Violet McCaffer; two *s* two *d*. *Educ:* Glasgow Univ. (MB ChB, MD). FRCPGlas 1973; FRCPE 1975; FRCSE 1993; FRCGP 1993. Junior posts, Glasgow hosps, 1959–66; Lectr in Medicine, Nairobi, 1966–67; Sen. Registrar, Victoria Infirmary, Glasgow, 1967–68; Acting Sen. Lectr, Materia Medica, Univ. of Glasgow, 1968–72; Acting Consultant Physician, Falkirk, 1972–73; Consultant Physician, Victoria Infirmary, 1973–89, Hon. Consultant, 1989–94. Pres., RCPSG, 1994–97 (Hon. Sec., 1973–83; Visitor, 1992–94). Vice-Chm., Copmed. FCPS(Pak) 1993; FRACP; FAMS; FRCPI; FAMM; Hon. FACP 1995; Hon. FCPS Bangladesh; Hon. FRCS. *Publications:* articles in med. jls. *Recreations:* gardening, golf, soccer. *Address:* 5 Edenhall Grove, Newton Mearns, Glasgow G77 5TS. *T:* (0141) 616 2831.

MACKAY, Peter, CB 1993; director and consultant; Secretary, Scottish Office Industry Department, 1990–95; *b* Arbroath, 6 July 1940; *s* of John S. Mackay, FRCS, and Patricia M. Atkinson; *m* 1964, Sarah Holdich; one *s* two *d*. *Educ:* Glasgow High Sch.; St Andrews Univ. (MA Political Economy). Teacher, Kyogle High Sch., NSW, 1962–63; joined Scottish Office as Asst Principal, 1963; various posts, incl. Private Sec. to successive Ministers of State, 1966–68 and Secs of State, 1973–75; Nuffield Travelling Fellow, Canada, Australia and NZ, 1978–79; seconded: as Dir for Scotland, MSC, 1983–85; as Under Sec., Manpower Policy, Dept of Employment, London, 1985–86; Under Sec., Further and Higher Educn, Scottish Educn Dept, 1987–89; Principal Establishment Officer, Scottish Office, 1989–90. Director: British Linen Bank, 1996–2000; Business Banking Div., Bank of Scotland, 1999–; Pacific Horizon Investment Trust plc, 2001–. Member: Competition (formerly Monopolies and Mergers) Commn, 1996–; Bd, Scottish Natural Heritage, 1996–. Vis. Prof., Strathclyde Grad. Business Sch., 1996–2000. Comr, Northern Lighthouse Bd, 1999–. Mem. Court, Napier Univ., 1996. Hon. LLD Robert Gordon's, 1996. *Recreations:* high altitudes and latitudes, dinghy sailing, sea canoeing. *Address:* 6 Henderland Road, Edinburgh EH12 6BB. *T:* and *Fax:* (0131) 337 2830. *Clubs:* Clyde Canoe, Scottish Arctic.

MacKAY, Prof. Robert Sinclair, PhD; FRS 2000; FInstP; Professor of Mathematics, University of Warwick, since 2000; *b* 4 July 1956; *s* of Donald Maccrimmon MacKay and Valerie MacKay (*née* Wood); *m* 1992, Claude Noëlle Baesens. *Educ:* Trinity Coll., Cambridge (BA Math.; MA); Princeton (PhD Astrophys. Scis). FInstP 2000. Res. Asst, QMC, 1982–83; Vis. Researcher, Institut des Hautes Etudes Scientifiques, Bures-sur-Yvette, France, 1983–84; Lectr, 1984–90, Reader, 1990–93, Prof., 1993–95, Mathematics, Univ. of Warwick; Prof. of Nonlinear Dynamics, and Fellow of Trinity Coll., Univ. of Cambridge, 1995–2000. Nuffield Foundn Sci. Res. Fellow, 1992–93; Res. Associate, 1994–95, Vis. Prof., 1995, CNRS, Université de Bourgogne, France. (First) Stephanos Pnevmatikos Internat. Award for Res. in Nonlinear Phenomena, 1993; Jun. Whitehead Prize, London Math. Soc., 1994. *Publications:* Hamiltonian Dynamical Systems, 1987; Renormalisation in area-preserving maps, 1993; papers in learned jls. *Address:* Mathematics Institute, University of Warwick, Coventry CV4 7AL.

MACKAY, Ronald David; *see* Eassie, Hon. Lord.

McKAY, Sir William (Robert), KCB 2001 (CB 1996); Clerk of the House of Commons, since 1998; *b* 18 April 1939; *s* of late William Wallace McKay and of Margaret H. A. Foster; *m* 1962, Rev. Margaret M., *d* of late E. M. Fillmore, OBE; twin *d*. *Educ:* Trinity Academy, Leith; Edinburgh Univ. (MA Hons). Clerk in the House of Commons, 1961; Clerk of Financial Cttees, H of C, 1985–87; Clerk of the Journals, H of C, 1987–91; Clerk of Public Bills, H of C, 1991–94; Clerk Asst, H of C, 1994–97. Secretary: to the House of Commons Commn, 1981–84; to the Public Accounts Commn, 1985–87. *Publications:* (ed) Erskine May's Private Journal 1883–86, 1984; Secretaries to Mr Speaker, 1986; Clerks in the House of Commons 1363–1989: a biographical list, 1989; (ed) Observations, Rules and Orders of the House of Commons: an early procedural collection, 1989; (ed jtly) Erskine May's Parliamentary Practice, 22nd edn 1997; (contrib.) Halsbury's Laws of England, 4th edn; contrib. historical jls. *Recreation:* reading Scottish history. *Address:* House of Commons, SW1A 0AA; Knowes of Elrick Smithy, Aberchirder, Huntly, Aberdeenshire AB54 7PN.

MACKAY-DICK, Maj.-Gen. Sir Iain (Charles), KCVO 1997; MBE 1981; Clerk to the Trustees and Chief Executive, Morden College, since 1997; *b* 24 Aug. 1945; *s* of John Mackay-Dick and Margaret Edith Mackay-Dick (*née* Forty); *m* 1971, Carolynn Hilary Holmes; three *d*. *Educ:* St Edmund's Sch., Hindhead; Sherborne Sch.; RMAS; Staff Coll., Camberley (psc, hcsc). Commnd, Scots Guards, 1965; served Malaysia, Borneo, Germany, Falkland Is, Cyprus and UK to 1986; Comdt, Jun. Div. Staff Coll., Warminster, 1986–88; Comdr, 11 Armoured Bde, 1989–91; Dep. Mil. Sec. (A), 1991–92; GOC 1st Armoured Div., Verden, 1992–93; GOC Lower Saxony Dist, Verden, 1993; Comdr British Forces Falkland Is, 1993–94; GOC London Dist and Maj. Gen. commanding Household Div., 1994–97. Mem., RUSI, 1979–. Hon. Col, 256 (City of London) Field Hosp., RAMC(V), 2000–. Member: Public Schools Old Boys Soc.; LTA; South Atlantic Medal Assoc. Freeman, City of London, 2000. FIMgt 1996. *Publication:* (contrib.) Central Region versus Out of Area (essays), 1990. *Recreations:* most sports (represented Army in lawn tennis and squash (Army Squash Champion, 1971)), walking, gardening, military history. *Address:* Morden College, 19 St Germans Place, Blackheath SE3 0PW. *T:* (020) 8858 3365. *Clubs:* Edinburgh Angus (Edinburgh); Jesters; Guards' Golfing Society, Army Golfing Society.

McKEAN, Prof. Charles Alexander, FRSE; FSAScot; Professor of Scottish Architectural History, Dundee University, since 1998 (Professor of Architecture, 1995–98); *b* 16 July 1946; *s* of John Laurie McKean and Nancy Burns Lendrum; *m* 1975, Margaret Elizabeth Yeo; two *s*. *Educ:* Fettes Coll., Edinburgh; Univ. of Bristol (BA Hons). Regional Secretary, RIBA, 1968–79; Sec. and Treas., RIAS, 1979–94; Architectural Correspondent: The Times, 1977–83; Scotland on Sunday, 1988–89; Trustee, Thirlestane Castle Trust, 1983–; Director, Workshops and Artists Studios Scotland (WASPS), 1980–85; Member: Scottish Arts Council Exhibitions Panel, 1980–83; Adv. Council for the Arts in Scotland, 1984–87; Edinburgh Common Purpose Adv. Cttee, 1990–94; Mem. Council, and Chm. Buildings Cttee, Nat. Trust for Scotland, 1995–. Lectures: Bossom, RSA, 1986; RCS Prestigious, 1992. Hon. Mem., Saltire Soc. FRSE 1999; FRSA. Hon. FRIBA 1989; Hon. FRIAS 1994. Hon. DLitt Robert Gordon, 1993. General Editor, RIAS/Landmark Trust series to Scotland, 1982–. Architectural Journalist of the Year, 1979 and 1983; Building Journalist of the Year, 1983. *Publications:* (with David Atwell) Battle of Styles, 1974; Guide to Modern Buildings in London 1965–75, 1976; Fight Blight, 1977; Architectural Guide to Cambridge and East Anglia 1920–80, 1980; Edinburgh—an illustrated architectural guide, 1982, 3rd edn 1983; (with David Walker) Dundee—an illustrated introduction through its buildings, 1984, 2nd edn 1986; Stirling and the Trossachs, 1984; The Scottish Thirties, 1987; The District of Moray—an illustrated introduction, 1987; (jtly) Central Glasgow—an illustrated architectural guide, 1989; Banff and Buchan—an illustrated architectural guide, 1990; For a Wee Country, 1990; Edinburgh: portrait of a city, 1991; Edinburgh—an illustrated architectural guide, 1992; (with David Walker) Dundee—an illustrated architectural guide, 1993; Value or Cost, 1994; Claim, 1998; The Making of the Museum of Scotland, 2001. *Recreations:* gardening, topography, books and glass collecting. *Address:* 10 Hill Park Road, Edinburgh EH4 7AW. *T:* (0131) 336 2753. *Club:* Scottish Arts.

MacKEAN, Thomas Neill; His Honour Judge MacKean; a Circuit Judge, since 1993; *b* 4 March 1934; *s* of late Andrew Neill MacKean and Mary Dale MacKean (*née* Nichol); *m* 1962, Muriel Hodder; four *d*. *Educ:* Sherborne; Trinity Hall, Cambridge (BA). 2nd Lt, Royal Hampshire Regt, 1952–54. Partner, Hepherd Winstanley & Pugh, solicitors, Southampton, 1960–93; HM Coroner, Southampton and New Forest, 1990–93; a Recorder, 1991–93. *Recreations:* sailing, walking, working. *Address:* Portsmouth Combined Court, Winston Churchill Avenue, Portsmouth PO1 2EB. *Clubs:* Royal Cruising; Royal Southern Yacht (Hamble).

McKEARNEY, Philip, CMG 1983; HM Diplomatic Service, retired; *b* 15 Nov. 1926; *s* of Philip McKearney, OBE; *m* 1950, Jean Pamela Walker; two *s*. *Educ:* City of London Sch.; Hertford Coll., Oxford. 4/7th Dragoon Guards, 1946–53; joined HM Diplomatic Service, 1953; 3rd Sec., British Embassy, Damascus, 1955–56; 1st Sec., British Legation, Bucharest, 1959–62; British Political Agent, Qatar, 1962–65; Counsellor and Consul-Gen., Baghdad, 1968–70; Counsellor, Belgrade, 1970–74; Inspector, FCO, 1975–77; Consul-General: Zagreb, 1977–80; Boston, Mass, 1980–83; Amb. to Romania, 1983–86; Dir, Foreign Service Prog., Oxford Univ., 1987–88.

McKECHIN, Ann; MP (Lab) Glasgow, Maryhill, since 2001; *b* 22 April 1961; *d* of William Joseph McKechin and Anne McKechin (*née* Coyle). *Educ:* Strathclyde Univ. (LLB, DLP). Solicitor, 1983–; Partner, Pacitti Jones, Glasgow, 1990–2000. *Recreations:* films, dancing, art history. *Address:* House of Commons, SW1A 0AA. *T:* (020) 7219 8239.

MACKECHNIE, Sir Alistair (John), Kt 1993; financial consultant, since 1992; *b* 15 Nov. 1934; *s* of Frank Harper McIvor Mackechnie and Ellen Annie (*née* Brophy); *m* 1961, Countess Alexandra Kinsky, *er d* of Count Frederick-Carl Kinsky; three *d*. *Educ:* St Patrick's Coll., Wellington, NZ; Victoria Univ. of Wellington, NZ. ACA 1957. Nat. Service: commnd NZ Scottish Regt, 1955. Director: Henderson Admin, 1976–88; BSI-Thornhill Investment Mgt, 1989–. Twickenham Conservative Association: Chm., 1985–88; Pres., 1989–; Greater London Area Conservatives: Dep. Chm., 1988–90; Chm., 1990–93; Vice-Pres., 1993–; Mem., Exec. Cttee, Nat. Union of Cons. and Unionist Assocs, 1988–. Mem. Council, Back Care (formerly Nat. Back Pain Assoc.), 1994–. Governor: St Mary's UC, 1997–; St Catherine's Sch., Twickenham, 1997–. *Recreations:* theatre, travel, bird-watching, hill-walking. *Club:* Carlton.

McKECHNIE, George; Director of Participation and Communications, Education and Learning Wales, since 2001; *b* 28 July 1946; *m* 1971, Janequin (*née* Morris); two *s*. *Educ:* Portobello Sen. Secondary Sch., Edinburgh. Reporter: Paisley and Renfrewshire Gazette, 1964–66; Edinburgh Evening News, 1966; Scottish Daily Mail, 1966–68; Daily Record, 1968–73; Dep. News Editor and News Editor, Sunday Mail, 1974–76; Asst Editor, 1976–81, Editor, 1981–94, Evening Times, Glasgow; Editor, The Herald, Glasgow, 1994–97; Dir of Public Affairs, Beattie Media, 1998–99; Dir of Communications, Council of Welsh TECs, 1999–2001. Director: George Outram & Co., 1986–92; Caledonian Newspaper Publishing, 1992–97. Member: Press Complaints Commn, 1992–94; Adv. Bd, Assoc. of British Editors; Chairman: Editor's Cttee, Scottish Daily News Soc., 1989–91; Scottish Foundn, 1985–97. *Recreations:* reading, walking, cinema, Hearts FC, Swansea RFC. *Address:* Mumbles Hill House, 1 Mumbles Hill, Mumbles, Swansea SA3 4HZ.

McKECHNIE, Dame Sheila (Marshall), DBE 2001 (OBE 1995); Director, Consumers' Association, since 1995; a Director, Bank of England, since 1998; *b* Falkirk, 3 May 1948. *Educ:* Falkirk High School; Edinburgh Univ. (MA Politics and History); Warwick Univ. (MA Industrial Relations). Research Asst, Oxford Univ., 1971–72; Asst Gen. Sec., Wall Paper Workers Union Staff Section, 1972–74; WEA Tutor, Manchester, 1974–76; Health and Safety Officer, ASTMS, 1976–85; Dir, Shelter, 1985–94. DUniv Open, 1994; Hon. DSc(SocSci) Edinburgh, 1994. *Address:* Consumers' Association, 2 Marylebone Road, NW1 4DF; *e-mail:* mckechnies@which.co.uk.

McKEE, Major Sir Cecil; *see* McKee, Major Sir William Cecil.

McKEE, (Charles Dean) Grant; television executive producer; Director of Programmes, Yorkshire Television, 1993–95; *b* 18 Aug. 1951; *s* of Cdr Eric McKee, RN, OBE and Betty (*née* Dean); *m* 1991, Jill Turton; one *d*. *Educ:* Clifton Coll.; Exeter Coll., Oxford (LLB). Journalist: Goole Times, 1974–76; Yorkshire Post, 1976–78; Yorkshire Television, 1979–95: journalist and documentary producer, 1979–88; Editor, First Tuesday, 1988–93; Controller, Documentaries and Current Affairs, 1988–93. *Publication:* (with R. Franey) Time Bomb: Irish bombers, English justice and the Guildford Four, 1988. *Recreations:* travel, cricket, countryside. *Address:* 10 Woodbine Terrace, Leeds LS6 4AF.

McKEE, David John; writer, illustrator, painter and film maker; *b* 2 Jan. 1935; *m* Barbara Ennuss (decd); two *s* one *d*. *Educ:* Tavistock Grammar Sch.; Plympton Grammar Sch.; Plymouth Coll. of Art; Hornsey Coll. of Art. Freelance cartoonist, 1955–; films incl. Mr Benn (13 films), 1970; Founder, and Director, King Rollo Films Ltd, 1979–. *Publications:* include: Bronto's Wings, 1964; Two Can Toucan, 1964; Mr Benn series, 1967–; Elmer, 1968; Melric the Magician, 1970; Two Admirals, 1977; Tusk Tusk, 1978; King Rollo, 1979; Adventures of King Rollo, 1982; Not Now Bernard, 1980; I Hate My Teddy Bear, 1982; Further Adventures of King Rollo, 1983; Two Monsters, 1985; King Rollo's Letter and Other Stories, 1986; Sad Story of Veronica Who Played the Violin, 1988; Snow Woman, 1989; Elmer Again, 1991; Zebra's Hiccups, 1991; Elmer on Stilts, 1993; Isabel's Noisy Tummy, 1994; Elmer and Wilbur, 1994; Elfed, 1995; Charlotte's Piggy Bank, 1996; Monster and the Teddy Bear, 1997; Prince Peter and the Teddy Bear, 1999; Elmer and the Teddy Bear, 1999; Mary's Secret, 1999. *Address:* c/o Andersen Press, 20 Vauxhall Bridge Road, SW1V 2SA.

McKEE, Grant; *see* McKee, C. D. G.

McKEE, Dr Robert Andrew; Chief Executive, Library Association, since 1999; *b* 16 Aug. 1950; *s* of Rev. Harry McKee and Nancy McKee; *m* 1976, Victoria Alexandra Lippman; one *s* one *d*. *Educ:* Bury Grammar Sch.; St Catherine's Coll., Oxford (BA 1971); Shakespeare Inst., Univ. of Birmingham (MA 1972; PhD 1976); Birmingham Poly. (DipLib 1977). ALA 1979. Trainee and Resources Librarian, Birmingham Liby Service, 1974–79; Tutor Librarian, Solihull Coll. of Technol., 1979–84; Principal Lectr, Dept of Liby and Inf. Studies, Birmingham Poly., 1984–88; Dir, Libraries and Arts, 1988–96, Asst Chief Exec., 1996–99, Solihull MBC. MIInfSc 1986. FRSA 1991. *Publications:* The Information Age, 1985; Public Libraries into the 1990s, 1987; Planning Library Service, 1989; contribs to jl literature of liby and inf. studies. *Recreations:* walking, music, watching football (Bury FC) and cricket, enjoying the company of family and friends. *Address:* Library Association, 7 Ridgmount Street, WC1E 7AE. *T:* (020) 7255 0691; *e-mail:* Bob.McKee@la-hq.org.uk.

McKEE, Major Sir (William) Cecil, Kt 1959; ERD; JP; Estate Agent; *b* 13 April 1905; *s* of late W. B. McKee and M. G. B. Bulloch; *m* 1932, Florence Ethel Irene Gill; one *d*. *Educ:* Methodist Coll., Belfast; Queen's Univ., Belfast. Alderman, Belfast Corporation, 1934; High Sheriff, Belfast, 1946; Deputy Lord Mayor, 1947, Lord Mayor of Belfast, 1957–59. JP Belfast, 1957. Pres., NI Br., Inst. of Dirs, 1957–59. Served with Royal Artillery in War of 1939–45. KStJ. 1982. Hon. LLD Queen's Univ., Belfast, 1960. *Recreation:* golf. *Address:* 8 Ailsa Road, Holywood, Co. Down BT18 0AS. *Clubs:* Ulster Reform (Belfast); Royal County Down Golf.

McKEE, Dr William James Ernest, MD; Regional Medical Officer and Advisor, Wessex Regional Health Authority, 1976–89; *b* 20 Feb. 1929; *s* of John Sloan McKee, MA, and Mrs Annie Emily McKee (*née* McKinley); *m* Josée Tucker; three *d*. *Educ:* Queen Elizabeth's, Wakefield; Trinity Coll., Cambridge; Queen's Coll., Oxford. MA, MD, BChir (Cantab); LRCP, MRCS, FFCM. Clinical trng and postgrad. clinical posts at Radcliffe Infirmary, Oxford, 1952–57; med. res., financed by Nuffield Provincial Hosps Trust, 1958–61; successive posts in community medicine with Metrop. Regional Hosp. Bds, 1961–69; Sen. Admin. Med. Officer, Liverpool Regional Hosp. Bd, 1970–74; Regional Med. Officer, Mersey RHA, 1974–76. Chairman: Regional Med. Officers' Gp, 1984–86; Wessex Regl Working Party to review policy for Mental Handicap Services, 1979; UK Head of Delegation, EEC Hosp. Cttee, 1986–89; Member: Council for Postgrad. Med. Educn in England and Wales, 1975–85; Hunter Working Party on Med. Admin, 1972–83; DHSS Adv. Cttee on Med. Manpower Planning, 1982–85; DHSS Jt Planning Adv. Cttee on Med. Manpower, 1985–89; Bd of Faculty of Medicine, Univ. of Southampton, 1976–89. QHP 1987–90. *Publications:* papers on tonsillectomy and adenoidectomy in learned jls. *Recreations:* fly-fishing, golf. *Address:* 22a Bereweeke Avenue, Winchester SO22 6BH. *T:* (01962) 861369.

MacKEITH, Prof. Margaret Anne, CBE 1997; PhD; FRTPI; FRGS; Consultant, MacKeith Dickinson & Partners Ltd, since 2000; Pro Vice-Chancellor, University of Central Lancashire (formerly Lancashire Polytechnic), 1995–99; *b* 26 June 1939; *d* of James and Gertrude Crane; *m* 1962, Charles Gordon MacKeith; two *s*. *Educ:* Shirebrook Grammar Sch., Derbyshire; Univ. of Manchester (DipTP, MA); Heriot Watt Univ. (PhD). FRTPI 1980; FRGS 1976; MIEnvSc 1977. Planning Officer, Lancs CC, 1961–63; Consultant to MacKeith Dickinson and Partners, 1963–74; Prin. Planning Officer, Blackpool BC, 1967–69 and 1974–75; Lancashire Polytechnic: Sen., then Prin. Lectr, 1975–87; Hd, Sch. of Construction and Surveying, 1987–90; Dean, Faculty of Technol., 1987–90, Faculty of Design and Technol., 1990–95. Consultant, TradePoint Systems USA, 1999. Mem., Royal Fine Art Commn, 1993–99. Member: BTEC Cttees, 1988–93; NW Cttee, OFFER, 1990–93; Landscape Adv. Cttee, Dept of Transport, 1991–93; NRA NW Cttee, 1994–97. Trustee, Nat. Museums and Galls on Merseyside, 2000–. Hon. Prof., Transylvania Univ., Romania, 1998. FRSA 1990. Dr *hc* Cluj, Romania, 1994. *Publications:* Shopping Arcades 1817–1939, 1985; History and Conservation of Shopping Arcades, 1986; articles and conf. papers on conservation, engrg educn and women in engrg and technol. *Recreations:* travel, architectural history, music, opera. *Address:* 104 Breck Road, Poulton-le-Fylde, Lancs FY6 7HT. *T:* (01253) 884774; 4 Breton House, Barbican, EC2Y 8DG.

McKELLEN, Sir Ian (Murray), Kt 1991; CBE 1979; actor and director since 1961; *b* 25 May 1939; *s* of late Denis Murray McKellen and Margery (*née* Sutcliffe). *Educ:* Wigan Grammar Sch.; Bolton Sch.; St Catharine's Coll., Cambridge (BA; Hon. Fellow, 1982). Cameron Mackintosh Prof. of Contemporary Theatre, Univ. of Oxford, 1991–92. Pres., Marlowe Soc., 1960–61. Elected to Council of Equity, 1971–72. Hon. DLitt Nottingham, 1989. 1st appearance (stage): Belgrade Theatre, Coventry, in a Man for all Seasons, Sept. 1961. Arts Theatre, Ipswich, 1962–63; Nottingham Playhouse, 1963–64; 1st London stage appearance, Duke of York's in A Scent of Flowers, 1964 (Clarence Derwent Award); Recruiting Officer, Chips with Everything, Cambridge Theatre Co., 1971; Founder Mem., Actors Company: Ruling the Roost, 'Tis Pity She's a Whore, Edin. Fest., 1972; Knots, Wood-Demon, Edin. Fest., 1973, and with King Lear, Brooklyn Acad. of Music, Wimbledon Theatre season, 1974; *London stage appearances:* A Lily in Little India, St Martin's; Man of Destiny/O'Flaherty VC, Mermaid Theatre; Their Very Own and Golden City, Royal Court, 1966; The Promise, Fortune, 1967 (also Broadway); White Lies/Black Comedy, Lyric; Richard II, Prospect Theatre Co., 1968 (revived with Edward II, Edin. Fest., British and European tours); Hamlet, Cambridge, 1971 (British and European tours); Ashes, Young Vic, 1975; Bent, Royal Court, Criterion, 1979 (SWET Award, 1979); Short List, Hampstead, 1983; Cowardice, Ambassadors, 1983; Henceforward, Vaudeville, 1988; *with Royal National Theatre:* Much Ado About Nothing, Old Vic, 1965; Armstrong's Last Goodnight, Trelawney of the Wells, Chichester Fest., 1965; Venice Preserv'd, Wild Honey (Laurence Olivier Award, Plays and Players Award; Los Angeles and NY, 1986–87), Coriolanus (London Standard Award), South Bank, 1984–85; as Assoc. Dir, produced and acted in The Duchess of Malfi, The Real Inspector Hound with The Critic, The Cherry Orchard (Paris and Chicago), 1984–85; Bent, 1990 (also Garrick); Kent in King Lear, and title role, Richard III, 1990 (Laurence Olivier Award; Assoc. Prod. for world tour, 1990–91); Napoli Milionaria, 1991; Uncle Vanya, 1992; Richard III, US tour, 1992; An Enemy of the People, Peter Pan, 1997–98; *with Royal Shakespeare Co.:* Dr Faustus, Edin. Fest. and Aldwych, 1974; Marquis of Keith, Aldwych, 1974–75; King John, Aldwych, 1975; Too Good to be True, Aldwych and Globe, 1975; Romeo and Juliet, The Winter's Tale, Macbeth (Plays and Players Award, 1976), Stratford, 1976–77; Every Good Boy Deserves Favour, RFH, 1977, Barbican, 1982; Romeo and Juliet, Macbeth, Pillars of the Community (SWET Award, 1977), Days of the Commune, The Alchemist (SWET Award, 1978), Aldwych and RSC Warehouse, 1977–78; Prod. RSC Tour, 1978: Three Sisters, Twelfth Night, Is There Honey Still for Tea; Iago in Othello, The Other Place, Stratford and Young Vic, 1989, BBC TV (Evening Standard and London Critics' Award); *with W Yorks Playhouse, Leeds:* The Seagull, Present Laughter, 1998; The Tempest, 1999; *Directed:* Liverpool Playhouse, 1969; Watford and Leicester, 1972; A Private Matter, Vaudeville, 1973; The Clandestine Marriage, Savoy, 1975; *other performances include:* Words, Words, Words (solo recital), Edin. Fest. and Belfast Fest., 1976 (with Acting Shakespeare, Edin. and Belfast, 1977); Amadeus, Broadhurst, NY, 1980–81 (Drama Desk, NY Drama League, Outer Critics' Circle and Tony Awards); A Knight Out, NY, S Africa, UK, 1994–95; Dance of Death, NY, 2001; *Acting Shakespeare tours:* Israel, Norway, Denmark, Sweden, 1980; Spain, France, Cyprus, Israel, Poland, Romania, 1982; Los Angeles and Ritz, NYC (Drama Desk Award), 1983; San Francisco, Washington DC, Los Angeles, Olney, Cleveland, San Diego, Boston (Elliot Norton Award), 1987 Playhouse, London, 1987–88. *Films,* 1968–: A Touch of Love, The Promise, Alfred the Great, Priest of Love, Scarlet Pimpernel, Plenty, Zina, Scandal, The Ballad of Little Jo, Six Degrees of Separation, The Shadow, Jack and Sarah, Restoration; Richard III (European Actor of the Year, Berlin Film Fest.), 1996; Swept from the Sea, 1996; Apt Pupil, 1997; Bent, 1997; Gods and Monsters, 1998; X-Men, 2000; The Fellowship of the Ring, 2001. Has appeared on television, 1966–, incl. Walter, 1982 (RTS Performance Award for 1982); Walter and June, 1983; Mister Shaw's Missing Millions,

1993; Tales of the City, 1993; Cold Comfort Farm, 1995; Rasputin, 1996 (Golden Globe Award). *Address:* c/o ICM, Oxford House, 76 Oxford Street, W1N 0AX. *T:* (020) 7636 6565, *Fax:* (020) 7323 0101.

McKELVEY, Very Rev. Houston; *see* McKelvey, Very Rev. R. S. J. H.

McKELVEY, Rev. Dr Robert John; Principal, Northern College, Manchester, 1979–93; Moderator, General Assembly of the United Reformed Church, 1994–95; *b* 12 Oct. 1929; *s* of Robert John McKelvey and Eleanor McMaster McKelvey (*née* Earls); *m* 1957, Martha Esther Skelly; two *s* one *d. Educ:* Paton Congregational Coll.; Nottingham Univ. (BA 1955); Pittsburgh Theol Seminary (MTh 1956); Mansfield Coll., Oxford (DPhil 1959). Tutor, 1959–67, Principal, 1968–74, Adams United Coll., S Africa; Pres., Federal Theol Seminary of S Africa, 1970–71; Dir, Internship Trng, United Congregational Church of S Africa, 1975–78; Pres., Northern Fedn for Trng in Ministry, 1984–86. *Publications:* The New Temple: the Church in the New Testament, 1969; The Millennium and the Book of Revelation, 1999; contributor to: New Bible Dictionary, 1962; The Illustrated Bible Dictionary, 1980; New 20th Century Encyclopedia of Religious Knowledge, 2nd edn 1991; New Dictionary of Biblical Theology, 2000; learned jls incl. NT Studies, Jl of Theol Studies. *Recreations:* gardening, walking, travel, oddjobbery. *Address:* 64 Brooklawn Drive, Withington, Manchester M20 3GZ. *T:* (0161) 434 4936.

McKELVEY, Very Rev. Dr (Robert Samuel James) Houston, TD; Dean of Belfast, since 2001; *b* 3 Sept. 1942; *s* of Robert and Annie McKelvey; *m* 1969, Eileen Roberta; one *s. Educ:* Queen's Univ., Belfast (BA 1965; MA (Ed) 1988); TCD; Garrett-Evangl Theol Seminary, Evanston, Ill. (DMin 1993). Ordained deacon, 1967, priest, 1968; Curate, Dunmurry, 1967–70; Rector, Kilmakee, 1970–82; Sec., Gen. Synod Bd of Educn (NI), 1982–2001. Ed., Ch of Ire. Gazette, 1975–82. CF (TAVR), 1970–99. QVRM 2000. *Publications:* Forty Days with Jesus, 1991; The Apostles' Creed, 1992; Children at the Table, 1993; In Touch with God, 1997; God, our Children, and Us, 1999. *Recreations:* sailing, photography, travel. *Address:* Belfast Cathedral, Donegall Street, Belfast BT1 2HB. *T:* (028) 9032 8332, *Fax:* (028) 9023 8855. *Club:* Ulster (Belfast).

McKELVEY, William; *b* Dundee, 8 July 1934; *m*; two *s. Educ:* Morgan Acad.; Dundee Coll. of Technology. Joined Labour Party, 1961; formerly Sec. Organiser, Lab. Party, and full-time union official. Mem., Dundee City Council. MP (Lab) Kilmarnock, 1979–83, Kilmarnock and Loudoun, 1983–97. Chm., Select Cttee on Scottish Affairs, 1992–97. *Address:* 41 Main Street, Kilmaurs, Ayrshire KA3 2SY.

McKELVIE, Peter, FRCS, FRCSE; Consultant Ear, Nose and Throat Surgeon: London Hospital, 1971–98 (Hon. Consulting Surgeon, Bart's and the London (formerly Royal Hospitals) NHS Trust, since 1998); Royal National Throat, Nose and Ear Hospital, London, 1972–95 (Hon. Consulting Surgeon, since 1995); *b* 21 Dec. 1932; *s* of William Bryce McKelvie, MD, ChM, FRCSE, DLO, and Agnes E. McKelvie (*née* Winstanley), Headmistress; *m* Myra Chadwick, FRCP, Cons. Dermatologist; one *d. Educ:* Manchester Grammar Sch.; Rugby Sch.; Univ. of Manchester (MB ChB, MD, ChM). FRCS 1962, FRCSE 1989. House Surgeon: Manchester Royal Inf., 1957; Royal Nat. Throat, Nose and Ear Hosp., London, 1958; Lectr in Anatomy, KCL, 1959; Casualty Surg., St Mary's Hosp., London, 1960; Reader in Laryngology, UCL, 1968–70; Dean, Inst. of Laryngology and Otology, London, 1984–89. Examiner: London Univ.; Royal Colls of Surgeons of England, Edinburgh and Glasgow. MRSM 1966 (Pres., Laryngology Sect., 1992–93). *Publications:* numerous, on head and neck cancer. *Recreations:* mirth, watching young surgeons develop, Mediterranean Basin. *Address:* Elmcroft, 9 Farm Way, Northwood, Middx HA6 3EG. *T:* (01923) 823544.

McKENDRICK, Emma Elizabeth Ann; Headmistress, Downe House, since 1997; *b* 24 June 1963; *d* of Ian and Ann Black; *m* 1987, Iain Alastair McKendrick. *Educ:* Bedford High Sch.; Univ. of Liverpool (BA Hons German with Dutch); Univ. of Birmingham (PGCE). Royal School, Bath: Teacher of German, 1986–88; Head of Sixth Form and Careers, 1988–90; Housemistress for Sixth Form, 1989–90; Dep. Head, 1990–93; Headmistress, 1994–97. Governor: Hatherop Castle Prep. Sch., 1997–; Study Sch., Wimbledon, 1998–; Manor Prep. Sch., Oxford, 1998–; Godstone Prep. Sch., 2000–. *Recreations:* travel, theatre. *Address:* St Peter's House, Downe House, Cold Ash, Thatcham, Berks RG18 9JJ. *T:* (01635) 200286. *Club:* Lansdowne.

McKENDRICK, Prof. Ewan Gordon; Professor of English Private Law, University of Oxford, since 2000; Fellow, Lady Margaret Hall, Oxford, since 2000; *b* 23 Sept. 1960; *s* of Norman and Muriel McKendrick; *m* 1983, Rosemary Grace Burton-Smith; four *d. Educ:* Univ. of Edinburgh (LLB Hons); Pembroke Coll., Oxford (BCL). Lecturer in Law: Central Lancashire Poly., 1984–85; Univ. of Essex, 1985–88; LSE, 1988–91; Fellow, St Anne's Coll., Oxford and Linnells Lectr in Law, Univ. of Oxford, 1991–95; Prof. of English Law, UCL, 1995–2000; called to the Bar, Gray's Inn, 1998; in practice as barrister, 1998–. *Publications:* Contract Law, 1990, 4th edn 2000; (with A. Burrows) Cases and Materials on the Law of Restitution, 1997; (with N. E. Palmer) Interests in Goods, 1993, 2nd edn 1997; (ed) Chitty on Contracts, 27th and 28th edns 1999; Sale of Goods, 2000. *Recreation:* reading. *Address:* Lady Margaret Hall, Oxford OX2 6QA. *T:* (01865) 274300; 3 Verulam Buildings, Gray's Inn, WC1R 5NT. *T:* (020) 7831 8441.

McKENDRICK, Prof. Melveena Christine, PhD; FBA 1999; Professor of Spanish Golden Age Literature, Culture and Society, University of Cambridge, since 1999; Fellow of Girton College, Cambridge, since 1970; *b* 23 March 1941; *d* of James Powell Jones and Catherine Letitia Jones (*née* Richards); *m* 1967, Neil McKendrick, *qv*; two *d. Educ:* Neath Girls' Grammar Sch.; Dyffryn Grammar Sch., Port Talbot; King's Coll., London (BA 1st cl. Hons Spanish); Girton Coll., Cambridge (PhD 1967). Girton College, Cambridge: Jex-Blake Res. Fellow, 1967–70; Tutor, 1970–83; Sen. Tutor, 1974–81; Dir of Studies in Modern Langs, 1984–95; Lectr in Spanish, 1980–92, Reader in Spanish Lit. and Soc., 1992–99, Univ. of Cambridge; British Acad. Reader, 1992–94. Vis. Prof., Univ. of Victoria, 1997. Member: Gen. Bd, Cambridge Univ., 1993–97 (Chair, Educn Cttee, 1995–97); Humanities Res. Bd, British Acad., 1996–98; Arts and Humanities Res. Bd, 1998–99. Consultant Hispanic Ed., Everyman, 1993–99; Member, Editorial Board: Donaire, 1994–; Revista Canadiense de Estudios Hispánicos, 1995–; Bulletin of Hispanic Studies (Glasgow), 1998–. *Publications:* Ferdinand and Isabella, 1968; A Concise History of Spain, 1972; Woman and Society in the Spanish Drama of the Golden Age, 1974; Cervantes, 1980 (trans. Spanish 1986); (ed) Golden-Age Studies in Honour of A. A. Parker, 1984; Theatre in Spain 1490–1700, 1989 (trans. Spanish 1994); (jtly) El Mágico Prodigioso, 1992; The Revealing Image: stage portraits in the theatre of the Golden Age, 1996; Playing the King: Lope de Vega and the limits of conformity, 2000; contributed to: Critical Studies of Calderón's Comedias, 1973; Women in Hispanic Literature, 1983; El mundo del teatro en el siglo de oro, 1989; Teatro y prácticas escénicas en los siglos XVI y XVII, 1991; Feminist Readings on Spanish and Spanish-American Literature, 1991; Hacia Calderón, 1991; The Comedia in the Age of Calderón, 1993; Teatro y Poder, 1994; Heavenly Bodies, 1996; Texto e Imagen en Calderón, 1996; Calderón 1600–1681, 2000; Calderón: protagonista eminente del barro europeo, 2000; Spanish Theatre: studies in honour of Victor F. Dixon, 2001; articles on Early Modern Spanish theatre in many jls. *Recreations:* cooking, being abroad, reading, films, my husband and daughters. *Address:* The Master's Lodge, Gonville and Caius College, Cambridge CB2 1TA. *T:* (01223) 332417.

McKENDRICK, Neil, FRHistS; historian; Master of Gonville and Caius College, Cambridge, since 1996; Reader in Social and Economic History, University of Cambridge, since 1995; *b* 28 July 1935; *s* of late Robert Alexander McKendrick and Sarah Elizabeth Irvine; *m* 1967, Melveena Jones (*see* M. McKendrick); two *d. Educ:* Alderman Newton's Sch., Leicester; Christ's Coll., Cambridge (Entrance Schol.; BA 1st cl. Hons (with distinction) History, 1956; MA 1960; Hon. Fellow, 1996). FRHistS 1971. Cambridge University: Res. Fellow, Christ's Coll., 1958; Asst Lectr in History, 1961–64; Lectr, 1964–95; Sec. to Faculty Bd of History, 1975–77; Chm., History Faculty, 1985–87; Gonville and Caius College: Fellow, 1958–96; Lectr in History, 1958–96; Dir of Studies in History, 1959–96; Tutor, 1961–69. Lectures: Earl, Univ. of Keele, 1963; Inaugural, Wallace Gall., Colonial Williamsburg, 1985; Chettyar Meml, Univ. of Madras, 1990. Member: Tancred's Charities, 1996; Sir John Plumb Charitable Trust, 1999–; Properties Cttee, Nat. Trust, 1999–; Vice-Pres., Cains Foundn in America, 1998–. *Publications:* (ed) Historical Perspectives: studies in English thought and society, 1974; (jtly) The Birth of a Consumer Society: the commercialization of eighteenth century England, 1982, 2nd edn 1983; (ed jtly) Business Life and Public Policy, 1986; L'Impressa Industria Commercio Banca XIII–XVIII, 1991; The Birth of Foreign & Colonial: the world's first investment trust, 1993; Il Tempo Libero Economia e Societa Secc XIII–XVIII, 1995; (jtly) 'F & C': a history of Foreign & Colonial Investment Trust, 1999; contributed to: Essays in Economic History, ed E. M. Carus Wilson, 1962; Rise of Capitalism, ed D. S. Landes, 1966; Changing Perspectives in the History of Science, ed M. Teich and R. M. Young, 1971; The Historical Development of Accounting, ed B. S. Yamey, 1978; Science and Culture in the Western Tradition, ed J. Burke, 1987; Industry and Modernization, ed Wang Jue-fei, 1989; The Social History of Western Civilization, ed R. Golden, 1992; The Other Side of Western Civilization, ed P. Stearns, 1992; The History of Enterprise, ed S. Jones and J. Inggs, 1993; The Industrial Revolution in Britain, ed J. Hoppit and E. A. Wrigley, 1994; Europäische Konsumgeschichte, ed H. Siegrist, H. Kaelble and J. Kocka, 1997; articles in learned jls, mainly on Josiah Wedgwood and the Industrial Revolution. *Recreations:* gardening, antiques, claret, photography, my wife and daughters. *Address:* The Master's Lodge, Gonville and Caius College, Cambridge CB2 1TA. *T:* (01223) 332404, *Fax:* (01223) 332336; Howe House, Huntingdon Road, Cambridge CB3 0LX. *T:* (01223) 276856. *Club:* Athenæum.

McKENNA, David, CBE 1967 (OBE 1946; MBE 1943); FCIT; Member, British Railways Board, 1968–76 (part-time Member, 1976–78); *b* 16 Feb. 1911; *s* of late Rt Hon. Reginald McKenna and Pamela Margaret McKenna (*née* Jekyll); *m* 1934, Lady Cecilia Elizabeth Keppel, *d* of 9th Earl of Albemarle, MC; three *d. Educ:* Eton; Trinity Coll., Cambridge. London Passenger Transport Board, 1934–39, and 1946–55; Asst General Manager, Southern Region of BR, 1955–61; Chief Commercial Officer, HQ, BR, 1962; General Manager, Southern Region of BR, and Chairman Southern Railway Board, 1963–68; Chairman, British Transport Advertising, 1968–81. Mem., Dover Harbour Bd, 1969–80. Dir, Isles of Scilly Steamship Co., 1976–92. War Service with Transportation Service of Royal Engineers, 1939–45; Iraq, Turkey, India and Burma; Lieut-Colonel. Pres., Chartered Inst. of Transport, 1972. Chairman of Governors, Sadler's Wells, 1962–76. Vice-Pres., Royal College of Music; Chairman of Bach Choir, 1964–76. FRCM. Commandeur de l'Ordre National du Mérite, 1974. *Publications:* various papers on transport subjects. *Recreations:* music, sailing. *Address:* Rosteague, Portscatho, Truro, Cornwall TR2 5EF. *Clubs:* Brooks's; Royal Cornwall Yacht (Falmouth).

McKENNA, Hon. Francis Joseph, (Frank); PC (Can.) 1987; Counsel, McInnes Cooper, since 1998; *b* 19 Jan. 1948; *s* of Durward and Olive McKenna; *m* Julie Friel; two *s* one *d. Educ:* Apohaqui Elementary Sch.; Sussex High Sch.; St Francis Xavier Univ. (BA); Queen's Univ.; Univ. of New Brunswick (LLB). Lawyer; Mem., NB and Canadian Bar Assocs. MLA (L) Chatham, NB, 1982–97; Leader, NB Liberal Party, 1985–97; Premier of NB, 1987–97. Dir of various provincial nat. and internat. corps, incl. Bank of Montreal, Noranda Inc. Hon. DSP Moncton, 1988; Hon. LLD New Brunswick, 1988. Vanier Award, 1988. *Address:* McInnes Cooper, PO Box 1368, Moncton, NB E1C 8T6, Canada.

McKENNA, Martin Nicholas; His Honour Judge McKenna; a Circuit Judge, since 2000; *b* 19 Nov. 1955; *s* of Bernard Malcolm McKenna and Anne Rose McKenna; *m* 1st, 1979, Deborah Jane Scott (marr. diss. 1995); two *d*; 2nd, 1996, Sarah Louise Malden; two step *d. Educ:* Birmingham Univ. (LLB 1st Cl. Hons); Lincoln Coll., Oxford. Admitted Solicitor, 1980. Joined Evershed & Tomkinson, Solicitors, 1978: Associate, 1984–87; Partner, 1987–2000; Head of Litigation Dept, 1994–99. Midland and Oxford Circuit. *Recreations:* Rugby, cricket, sailing, ski-ing. *Address:* Priory Courts, 33 Bull Street, Birmingham B4 6DW. *Club:* East India.

McKENNA, Prof. Patrick Gerald, (Gerry), PhD; Vice-Chancellor and President, University of Ulster, since 1999; *b* 10 Dec. 1953; *s* of late Gerald Joseph and Mary Teresa McKenna; *m* 1976, Philomena Winifred McArdle; two *s. Educ:* Univ. of Ulster (BSc 1st Cl. Hons 1976); PhD Genetics, QUB, 1979. FIBMS 1982; FIBiol 1988. Lectr, Human Biology, NUU, 1979–84; University of Ulster: Sen. Lectr, Biology, 1984–88; Dir, Biomedical Scis Res. Centre, 1985–88; Prof. and Head of Dept of Biol and Biomed. Scis, 1988–94; Dean, Faculty of Science, 1994–97; Pro-Vice-Chancellor (Res.), 1997–99. Chairman: NI Foresight, Life and Health Technologies Panel, 1995–99; UU-Online.com; non-executive Director: NI Med. Physics Agency, 1995–; NI Sci. Park Foundn, 1999–; E-University Hldg Co.; UUTECH Ltd; Univ. of Ulster Sci. Res. Parks Ltd. Vice Chm., Ulster Cancer Foundn, 1999–. Mem. Council, Inst. of Biomed. Sci., 1996–. Mem., Shadow Bd for E-nursing educn. Freedom, Borough of Coleraine, 2001. FRSA 1999. Hon. DSc NUI, 2001. *Publications:* numerous scientific papers. *Recreations:* reading, the turf. *Address:* University of Ulster, Coleraine, Northern Ireland BT52 1SA. *T:* (028) 7032 4329. *Club:* Reform.

MacKENNA, Robert Ogilvie, MA, ALA; University Librarian and Keeper of the Hunterian Books and MSS, Glasgow, 1951–78; *b* 21 March 1913; *s* of late Dr John G. MacKenna and Katherine Ogilvie; *m* 1942, Ray, *o d* of late Samuel Mullin, Glasgow. *Educ:* Paisley Grammar Sch.; Glasgow Univ. Assistant Librarian, Glasgow Univ., 1936; Sub-Librarian, Leeds Univ., 1946; Librarian, King's Coll., Newcastle upon Tyne (University of Durham), 1948–51. Served War as officer, RNVR, 1939–45. Trustee, National Library of Scotland, 1953–79. President, Scottish Library Association, 1966; Chairman, Standing Conference of National and University Libraries, 1967–69. President Scottish Cricket Union, 1968. Editor: The Philosophical Journal, 1976–77; Glasgow Cathedral Lecture Series, 1986–. *Publication:* Glasgow University Athletic Club: the story of the first hundred years, 1981. *Recreations:* watching and talking cricket, reading. *Address:* 40 Kelvin Court, Glasgow G12 0AE. *Club:* College (Glasgow).

McKENNA, Rosemary, CBE 1995; MP (Lab) Cumbernauld and Kilsyth, since 1997; *b* 8 May 1941; *d* of Cornelius Harvey and Mary (*née* Crossan); *m* 1963, James S. McKenna; three *s* one *d. Educ:* St Augustine's, Glasgow; Notre Dame Coll. (Dip. Primary Educn).

Private sec., 1958–64; teacher, various primary schs, 1974–94. Member (Lab): Cumbernauld and Kilsyth DC, 1984–96 (Leader, 1984–88 and 1992–94; Provost, 1988–92); N Lanarks Council, 1995–97. Pres., COSLA, 1994–96. PPS to Minister of State for Foreign and Commonwealth Affairs, 1998–2001. Mem., Select Cttee on culture, media and sport, and procedure. Mem., Cttee of Regions of EU, 1994–98; Chm., UK and European Standing Cttees, CEMR, 1996–98. Chm., Scottish Libraries and Inf. Council, 1998–. *Recreations:* reading, travelling, family gatherings. *Address:* House of Commons, SW1A 0AA. *T:* (020) 7219 4003.

MACKENZIE, family name of **Earl of Cromartie** and **Barons MacKenzie of Culkein** and **Mackenzie of Framwellgate**.

MACKENZIE of Gairloch; *see* Inglis of Glencorse.

MacKENZIE OF CULKEIN, Baron *cr* 1999 (Life Peer), of Assynt in Highland; **Hector Uisdean MacKenzie;** Associate General Secretary, UNISON, 1993–2000; *b* 25 Feb. 1940; *s* of George MacKenzie and Williamina Budge Sutherland; *m* 1961, Anna Morrison (marr. diss.); one *s* three *d. Educ:* Nicholson Inst., Stornoway, Isle of Lewis; Portree High Sch., Skye; Leverndale School of Nursing, Glasgow; West Cumberland School of Nursing, Whitehaven. RGN, RMN. Student Nurse, Leverndale Hosp., 1958–61; Asst Lighthouse Keeper, Clyde Lighthouses Trust, 1961–64; Student Nurse, 1964–66, Staff Nurse 1966–69, West Cumberland Hosp.; Confederation of Health Service Employees: Asst Regl Sec., 1969; Regl Sec., Yorks and E Midlands, 1970–74; Nat. Officer, 1974–83; Asst Gen. Sec., 1983–87; Gen. Sec., 1987–93. Co. Sec., UIA Insurance Ltd, 1996–2000. Pres., TUC, 1998–99. *Recreations:* work, reading, aviation. *Address:* House of Lords, SW1A 0PW. *T:* (020) 7219 8515, *Fax:* (020) 7219 5979.

MACKENZIE OF FRAMWELLGATE, Baron *cr* 1998 (Life Peer), of Durham in the co. of Durham; **Brian Mackenzie,** OBE 1998; *b* 21 March 1943; *s* of Frederick George Mackenzie and Lucy Mackenzie (*née* Ward); *m* 1965, Jean Seed; two *s. Educ:* Eastbourne Sch., Darlington; London Univ. (LLB Hons 1974); FBI Nat. Acad. (graduate 1985). Durham Constabulary, 1963–98: Constable, 1963; Sgt (Trng), 1970; Det. Insp., Hd of Drug Squad, 1976; Chief Insp., Hd of Crime Computer Unit, 1979; Supt (Det.), attached to Home Office, 1980; Territorial Comdr Supt, 1983; Divl Comdr, Chief Supt, 1989–98. Nat. Pres., Police Superintendents' Assoc. of England and Wales, 1995–98 (Vice Pres., 1993–95). Studied and lectured extensively on police methods, visiting Europe, USA and Canada. Regular broadcasts on TV and radio on law and policing issues. *Publications:* articles in legal and policing jls. *Recreations:* after-dinner speaking, swimming, music, travel. *Address:* House of Lords, SW1A 0PW. *Club:* Dunelm (Durham).

MACKENZIE, Sir Alexander Alwyne Henry Charles Brinton M.; *see* Muir Mackenzie.

MACKENZIE, Archibald Robert Kerr, CBE 1967; HM Diplomatic Service, retired; *b* 22 Oct. 1915; *s* of James and Alexandrina Mackenzie; *m* 1963, Virginia Ruth Hutchison. *Educ:* Glasgow, Oxford, Chicago and Harvard Universities. Diplomatic Service, with duty at Washington, 1943–45; United Nations, 1946–49; Foreign Office, 1949–51; Bangkok, 1951–54; Cyprus, 1954; Foreign Office, 1955–57; OEEC, Paris, 1957–61; Commercial Counsellor, HM Embassy, Rangoon, 1961–65; Consul-General, Zagreb 1965–69; Ambassador, Tunisia, 1970–73; Minister (Econ. and Social Affairs), UK Mission to UN, 1973–75. Brandt Commission, 1978–80. *Recreation:* golf. *Address:* Strathcashel Cottage, Rowardennan, near Glasgow G63 0AW. *T:* (01360) 870262. *Club:* Royal Scottish Automobile (Glasgow).

MACKENZIE, Colin Scott; DL; Sheriff of Grampian, Highland and Islands at Lerwick and Kirkwall, since 1992; Vice Lord-Lieutenant, Western Isles, 1984–92; *b* 7 July 1938; *s* of late Major Colin Scott Mackenzie, BL and Mrs Margaret S. Mackenzie, MA; *m* 1966, Christeen Elizabeth Drysdale McLauchlan. *Educ:* Nicolson Inst., Stornoway; Fettes Coll., Edinburgh; Edinburgh Univ. (BL 1959). Admitted Solicitor and Notary Public, 1960; Procurator Fiscal, Stornoway, 1969–92. Clerk to the Lieutenancy, Stornoway, 1975–92. Dir, Harris Tweed Assoc. Ltd, 1979–95; Trustee, Western Isles Kidney Machine Trust, 1977–. Council Mem for Western Isles, Orkney, Shetland etc, Law Soc. of Scotland, 1985–92. General Assembly, Church of Scotland: Comr, Presbytery of Lewis, 1991–92; Mem., Bd of Social Responsibility, 1991–95; Convenor, Study Gp into Young People and the Media, 1991–93. DL Islands Area of Western Isles, 1975. *Publications:* The Last Warrior Band, 2001; contrib. Stair Memorial Encyclopaedia of Laws of Scotland, 1987. *Recreations:* amateur radio, boating, fishing, local history, shooting, trying to grow trees. *Address:* Middlebank, 3 Bells Road, Lerwick, Shetland ZE1 0QB. *T:* (01595) 695808; Park House, 8 Matheson Road, Stornoway, Western Isles HS1 2NQ. *T:* (01851) 702008. *Clubs:* New (Edinburgh); Royal Northern and University (Aberdeen); Royal Scottish Automobile (Glasgow).

McKENZIE, Dan Peter, PhD; FRS 1976; Royal Society Research Professor, Department of Earth Sciences, Cambridge University, since 1996; Fellow of King's College, Cambridge, 1965–73 and since 1977; *b* 21 Feb. 1942; *s* of William Stewart McKenzie and Nancy Mary McKenzie; *m* 1971, Indira Margaret Misra; one *s. Educ:* Westminster Sch.; King's Coll., Cambridge (BA 1963, PhD 1966). Cambridge University: Sen. Asst in Res., 1969–75; Asst Dir of Res., 1975–79; Reader in Tectonics, 1979–84; Prof. of Earth Scis, 1984–96. Hon. MA Cambridge, 1966. (Jtly) Geology and Geophysics Prize, Internat. Balzan Foundn of Italy and Switzerland, 1981; (jtly) Japan Prize, Science and Technology Foundn of Japan, 1990; Royal Medal, Royal Soc., 1991; Gold Medal, RAS, 1992. *Publications:* papers in learned jls. *Recreation:* gardening. *Address:* Bullard Laboratories, Madingley Road, Cambridge CB3 0EZ. *T:* (01223) 337177.

MACKENZIE, Rear-Adm. David John, CB 1983; FNI; Royal Navy, retired 1983; Director, Atlantic Salmon Trust, 1985–97 (Life Vice-President, 1998); *b* 3 Oct. 1929; *s* of late David Mackenzie and of Alison Walker Lawrie; *m* 1965, Ursula Sybil Balfour; two *s* one *d. Educ:* Cargilfield Sch., Barnton, Edinburgh; Royal Naval Coll., Eaton Hall, Cheshire. Cadet to Comdr, 1943–72: served in East Indies, Germany, Far East, Home and Mediterranean Fleets, and commanded: HMML 6011, HM Ships: Brinkley, Barrington, Hardy, Lincoln, Hermione; Captain 1972; Senior Officers War Course, 1972; commanded HMS Phoenix (NBCD School), 1972–74; Captain F8 in HMS Ajax, 1974–76; Director of Naval Equipment, 1976–78; Captain: HMS Blake, 1979; HMS Hermes, 1980; Rear Admiral 1981; Flag Officer and Port Admiral, Gibraltar, Comdr Gibraltar Mediterranean, 1981–83. Younger Brother of Trinity House, 1971–. Member, Queen's Body Guard for Scotland (Royal Company of Archers), 1976–. Vice Pres., Nautical Inst., 1985–93. Pres., King George's Fund for Sailors (Scotland), 1996–. *Recreations:* shooting and fishing. *Address:* Easter Meikle Fardle, Meikleour, Perthshire PH2 6EF. *Club:* New (Edinburgh).

MacKENZIE, Prof. David Neil, PhD; FBA 1996; Professor of Iranian Studies, University of Göttingen, 1975–94, Professor Emeritus since 1994; *b* 8 April 1926; *s* of David MacKenzie and Ada MacKenzie (*née* Hopkins); *m* 1951, Gina Schaefer (marr. diss. 1981); three *s* one *d. Educ:* Sch. of Oriental and African Studies, Univ. of London (BA 1951; MA 1953; PhD 1958). School of Oriental and African Studies, University of London: Lectr in Kurdish, 1955–61; Lectr in Iranian Langs, 1961–65; Univ. Reader in Iranian Langs, 1965–75. *Publications:* Kurdish Dialect Studies, I & II, 1961–62; Poems from the Divan of Khushâl Khân Khattak, 1965; The Dialect of Awroman (Hawrāmān-i Luhōn), 1966; The 'Sūtra of the Causes and Effects of Actions' in Sogdian, 1970; A Concise Pahlavi Dictionary, 1971, 2nd edn 1986; The Buddhist Sogdian Texts of the British Library, 1976; The Khwarezmian Element in the Qunyat al-munya, 1990; Iranica Diversa, I and II, 1999; contrib. Festschriften; numerous articles in learned jls, esp. Bull. SOAS. *Recreation:* music. *Address:* 5 Column Grounds, Llanfairpwll, Anglesey LL61 5NJ. *T:* (01248) 715270.

MacKENZIE, Gillian Rachel, (Mrs N. I. MacKenzie); *see* Ford, G. R.

MACKENZIE, Sir Guy; *see* Mackenzie, Sir J. W. G.

MACKENZIE, Ian Clayton, CBE 1962; HM Diplomatic Service, retired; Ambassador to Korea, 1967–69; *b* 13 Jan. 1909; *m* 1948, Anne Helena Tylor; one *s* one *d. Educ:* Bedford Sch.; King's Coll., Cambridge. China Consular Service, 1932–41; Consul, Brazzaville, 1942–45, Foreign Office, 1945; 1st Sec., Commercial, Shanghai, 1946–49; Santiago, Chile, 1949–53; Commercial Counsellor: Oslo, 1953–58; Caracas, 1958–63; Stockholm, 1963–66. *Address:* Koryo, Armstrong Road, Brockenhurst, Hants SO42 7TA. *T:* (01590) 623453.

MACKENZIE, James, BSc; CEng, FIM; a Managing Director, British Steel Corporation, 1976–85; *b* 2 Nov. 1924; *s* of James Mackenzie and Isobel Mary Chalmers; *m* 1950, Elizabeth Mary Ruttle; one *s* one *d. Educ:* Queen's Park Sch., Glasgow; Royal Technical Coll., Glasgow (BSc). The United Steel Companies Ltd, Research and Develt Dept, 1944–67; British Steel Corporation, 1967–85. Chm., Wade Building Services Ltd, 1987–99; former Dir, Geo. Cohen Sons & Co. Ltd; Dir, Lloyds Register Quality Assce Ltd, 1985–98. President: Inst. of Ceramics, 1965–67; Metals Soc., 1983–85. *Address:* Westhaven, Beech Waye, Gerrards Cross, Bucks SL9 8BL. *T:* (01753) 886461.

MacKENZIE, James Alexander Mackintosh, CB 1988; FREng; Chief Road Engineer, Scottish Development Department, 1976–88, retired; *b* Inverness, 6 May 1928; *m* 1970, Pamela Dorothy Nixon; one *s* one *d. Educ:* Inverness Royal Acad. FICE, FIHT; FREng (FEng 1982). Miscellaneous local govt appts, 1950–63; Chief Resident Engr, Durham County Council, 1963–67; Dep. Dir, 1967–71, Dir, 1971–76, North Eastern Road Construction Unit, MoT, later DoE. *Recreations:* golf, fishing. *Address:* Pendor, 2 Dean Park, Longniddry, East Lothian EH32 0QR. *T:* (01875) 852643.

MACKENZIE, Sir James William Guy, 5th Bt *cr* 1890, of Glen Muick, Aberdeenshire; Chairman, Kerrier Direct Services Board, 1995–98 (Vice-Chairman, 1994–95); *b* 6 Oct. 1946; *s* of Lt-Col Eric Dighton Mackenzie, CMG, CVO, DSO (*d* 1972), 4th *s* of Sir Allan Russell Mackenzie, 2nd Bt, and Elizabeth Kathrine Mary, *d* of Captain James William Guy Innes, CBE; *S* cousin, 1993; *m* 1st, 1972, Paulene Patricia Simpson (marr. diss. 1980); two *d*; 2nd, 1996, Sally Ann (*née* Howard). *Educ:* Stowe. Vice-Pres., Crown Royale Internat., USA, 1979–81. Mem. (Ind) Kerrier DC, 1993–. *Recreations:* watching cricket, music, unusual architecture. *Heir: b* Allan Walter Mackenzie, 6 Nov. 1952. *Address:* Tresowes Hill Farm, Helston, Cornwall TR13 9SY.

MACKENZIE, Gen. Sir Jeremy (John George), GCB 1998 (KCB 1992); OBE 1982; Governor, Royal Hospital, Chelsea, since 1999; *b* 11 Feb. 1941; *s* of late Lt-Col John William Elliot Mackenzie, DSO, QPM and of Valerie (*née* Dawes); *m* 1969, Elizabeth Lyon (*née* Wertenbaker); one *s* one *d. Educ:* Duke of York Sch., Nairobi, Kenya. psc, HCSC. Commnd Queen's Own Highlanders, 1961; Canadian Forces Staff Coll., 1974; Bde Major, 24 Airportable Bde, 1975–76; CO 1 Queen's Own Highlanders, NI and Hong Kong, 1979–82; Instructor, Staff Coll., 1982–83; Col Army Staff Duties 2, 1983–84; Comdr 12th Armoured Bde, 1984–86; Service Fellowship, King's Coll., Univ. of London, 1987; Dep. Comdt, 1987–89, Comdt, 1989, Staff Coll; GOC 4th Armoured Div., BAOR, 1989–91; Comdr 1st (British) Corps, 1991–92; Comdr, Ace Rapid Reaction Corps, 1992–94; Dep. SACEUR, 1994–98; ADC Gen. to the Queen, 1997–98. Colonel Commandant: WRAC, 1990–92; AGC, 1992–98; Colonel: Highlanders Regt, 1994–2001; APTC, 1999–. Brig., Queen's Body Guard for Scotland, Royal Company of Archers, 1986–. Pres., Services Br., British Deer Soc., 1993–; Life Vice-Pres., Combined Services Winter Sports Assoc., 1994. Comdr, US Legion of Merit, 1997 and 1999; Cross of Merit 1st Class (Czech Republic), 1998; Officers' Cross, Order of Merit (Hungary), 1998; Order of Madara Horseman, 1st Cl. (Bulgaria), 1999. *Publication:* The British Army and the Operational Level of War, 1989. *Recreations:* shooting, fishing, painting. *Address:* Royal Hospital, Chelsea, SW3 4SR. *Club:* Caledonian.

McKENZIE, John Cormack, FREng; FICE; Hon. Secretary, Overseas Affairs, Fellowship of Engineering, 1988–92; Vice-Chairman, Thomas Telford Ltd, 1982–90; Director, H. R. Wallingford plc, 1990–95; *b* 21 June 1927; *s* of William Joseph McKenzie and Elizabeth Frances Robinson; *m* 1954, Olga Caroline Cleland; three *s* one *d. Educ:* St Andrews Coll.; Trinity Coll., Dublin (MA, MAI); Queen's Univ., Belfast (MSc). FREng (FEng 1984); FIPM, FIEI, FIE(Aust). McLaughlin & Harvey, and Sir Alexander Gibb & Partners, 1946–48; Asst Lectr, QUB, 1948–50; Edmund Nuttall Ltd, 1950–82, Dir, 1967–82; Chm., Nuttall Geotechnical Services Ltd, 1967–82; Dir, British Wastewater Ltd, 1978–82. Secretary: ICE, 1982–90; Commonwealth Engineers' Council, 1983–90; Sec. Gen., World Fedn of Engrg Orgs, 1987–97 (Treas., 1997–); Vice-Pres., Register of Engrs for Disaster Relief. Pres., Beaconsfield Adv. Centre, 1978–. Hon. DSc: Tajikistan, 1993; Nottingham, 1997. *Publications:* papers: Research into some Aspects of Soil Cement, 1952; Engineers: Administrators or Technologists?, 1971; (contrib.) Civil Engineering Procedure, 3rd edn 1979; Comparison of the Market and Command Economics, 1990; Wealth Creation, 1992; Sustainable Development and the Maintenance of Economic Viability, 1994; The Contribution of Engineers to the UN International Decade for Natural Disaster Reduction, 1994; International Application of Ethics for Engineers, 1996; Beyond the Bottom Line, 1996; Quo Vadis, 1997; The Complete Engineer, 1997. *Recreations:* philately, collecting ancient pottery, climbing. *Address:* 20 Ledborough Lane, Beaconsfield, Bucks HP9 2PZ. *Club:* Athenæum.

McKENZIE, Prof. John Crawford; Governor and Director of International Development, The London Institute, since 1996 (Rector, 1986–96); *b* 12 Nov. 1937; *s* of late Donald Walter McKenzie and Emily Beatrice McKenzie; *m* 1960, Ann McKenzie (*née* Roberts); two *s. Educ:* London School of Economics and Political Science (BScEcon); Bedford Coll., London (MPhil). Lecturer, Queen Elizabeth Coll., Univ. of London, 1961; Dep. Director, Office of Health Econs, 1966; Market Inf. Manager, Allied Breweries Ltd, 1968; various posts, Kimpher Ltd, 1969, finally Chief Exec., Kimpher Marketing Services, 1973; Head of Dept, London Coll. of Printing, 1975; Principal: Ilkley Coll., 1978; Bolton Inst. of Higher Educn, 1982; Rector, Liverpool Poly., 1984. Visiting Professor: Queen Elizabeth Coll., 1976–80; Univ. of Newcastle, 1981–87. Director: Antiquarian Pastimes Ltd, 1984–; Developments at The London Inst. Ltd, 1989–; The Cochrane Theatre Co.

Ltd, 1990–; New Frontiers in Educn Ltd, 1993–. Mem., Adv. Council, Univ. of Sarawak, Malaysia, 1994–; Advr, Japan Coll. of Foreign Langs, Tokyo, 1997–. Chevalier de l'Ordre des Arts et des Lettres (France), 1992. *Publications:* (ed jtly) Changing Food Habits, 1964; (ed jtly) Our Changing Fare, 1966; (ed jtly) The Food Consumer, 1987; many articles in Proc. Nutrition Soc., British Jl Nutrition, Nutrition Bull., etc. *Recreation:* collecting antiquarian books and works of art. *Address:* The London Institute, 65 Davies Street, W1K 5DA. *T:* (020) 7514 6000. *Clubs:* Athenæum, Chelsea Arts.

McKENZIE, Rear-Adm. John Foster, CB 1977; CBE 1974 (OBE 1962); *b* Waiuku, 24 June 1923; *s* of Dr J. C. McKenzie; *m* 1st, 1945, Doreen Elizabeth (*d* 1996), *d* of Dr E. T. and Dr G. M. McElligot; one *s* one *d*; 2nd, 1996, Jocelyn Elva McIntosh. *Educ:* Timaru Boys' High Sch.; St Andrews Coll., Christchurch, NZ. Served War of 1939–45: Royal Navy; transferred to Royal New Zealand Navy, 1947; Head, Defence Liaison Staff, London, 1966–68; Imperial Defence Coll., 1969; Asst Chief of Defence Staff (Policy), Defence HQ, NZ, 1970–71; Deputy Chief of Naval Staff, 1972; Commodore, Auckland, 1973–75; Chief of Naval Staff, and Mem. Defence Council, 1975–77, retired 1977. ADC 1972–75. *Recreations:* gardening, fishing. *Address:* 1/38 Seaview Road, Remuera, Auckland 1005, New Zealand.

McKENZIE, Julia Kathleen, (Mrs Jerry Harte); actress, singer and director; *b* 17 Feb. 1941; *d* of Albion McKenzie and Kathleen Rowe; *m* 1972, Jerry Harte. *Educ:* Guildhall School of Music and Drama. Hon. FGSM, 1988. *Stage:* Maggie May, 1965; Mame, 1969; Promises, Promises, 1970; Company, 1972; Cowardy Custard, 1973; Cole, 1974; Side by Side by Sondheim, 1977 (London and Broadway); Norman Conquests, 1978; Ten Times Table, 1979; On the 20th Century, 1981; Guys and Dolls, NT, 1982; Schweyk in 2nd World War, NT, 1982; Woman in Mind, Vaudeville, 1986; Follies, Shaftesbury, 1987; Into the Woods, Phoenix, 1990; Sweeney Todd, NT, 1993; Communicating Doors, Gielgud, 1995; Kafka's Dick, Piccadilly, 1998; directed: Stepping Out, Duke of York's, 1984; Steel Magnolias, Lyric, 1989; Just So, Watermill, Bagnor, Berks, 1989; Putting it Together, Old Fire Station, Oxford, 1992, NY, 1993; A Little Night Music, Tokyo, 1999; Honk! The Ugly Duckling, NT, 1999; The Royal Family, Th. Royal, Haymarket, 2001; *films:* Shirley Valentine, 1989; The Old Curiosity Shop, 1994; *television films:* Those Glory Glory Days, 1980; Hotel Du Lac, 1986; Adam Bede, 1992; Jack and the Beanstalk—the Real Story, 2001; *series:* Fame is the Spur, 1982; Blott on the Landscape, 1985; Fresh Fields, 1984–86; French Fields, 1989–91; *television plays:* Dear Box No, 1983; Sharing Time, 1984; Absent Friends, 1985; Julia and Company (TV special), 1986; The Shadowy Third, 1995; numerous TV musicals. *Recreations:* cooking, gardening. *Address:* c/o April Young Ltd, 11 Woodlands Road, Barnes, SW13 0JZ. *T:* (020) 8876 7030.

MacKENZIE, Kelvin Calder; Chairman and Chief Executive, The Wireless Group plc; *b* 22 Oct. 1946; *m* 1969, Jacqueline Mary Holland; two *s* one *d*. Editor, The Sun, 1981–94; Man. Dir, British Sky Broadcasting, 1994; Dir, 1994–98, Gp Man. Dir, 1998, Mirror Group plc. *Address:* The Wireless Group plc, 18 Hatfields, SE1 8DJ.

MacKENZIE, Kenneth John, CB 1996; Secretary, Scottish Executive (formerly Scottish Office) Development Department, 1998–2001; *b* 1 May 1943; *s* of John Donald MacKenzie and Elizabeth Pennant Johnston Sutherland; *m* 1975, Irene Mary Hogarth; one *s* one *d*. *Educ:* Woodchurch Road Primary School, Birkenhead; Birkenhead School; Pembroke College, Oxford (Exbnr; MA Mod. Hist.); Stanford Univ., Calif (AM Hist.). Scottish Home and Health Dept, 1965; Private Sec. to Jt Parly Under Sec. of State, Scottish Office, 1969–70; Scottish Office Regional Develt Div., 1970–73; Scottish Educn Dept, 1973–76; Civil Service Fellow, Glasgow Univ., 1974–75; Principal Private Sec. to Sec. of State for Scotland, 1977–79; Asst Sec., Scottish Economic Planning Dept, 1979–83; Scottish Office: Finance Div., 1983–85; Principal Finance Officer, 1985–88; Under Sec., Home and Health Dept, 1988–91; Under Sec., 1991–92, Sec., 1992–95, Agric. and Fisheries Dept; Cabinet Office (on secondment): Dep. Sec. (Hd of Economic and Domestic Affairs Secretariat), 1995–97; Hd, Constitution Secretariat, 1997–98. Mem., BBSRC (formerly AFRC), 1992–95. Mem., Edinburgh CS Dramatic Soc. Elder, St Cuthbert's Parish Church. *Address:* 30 Regent Terrace, Edinburgh EH7 5BS.

MACKENZIE, Lorimer David Maurice; Director, Development Strategy for Enterprises, European Commission, since 1996; *b* 4 Aug. 1940; *s* of William David Beveridge Mackenzie and Elizabeth Reid (*née* Peters); *m* 1959, Penelope Marsh Happer; two *s* two *d*. *Educ:* Hermitage Park Sch., Leith; Royal High Sch., Edinburgh; Edinburgh Univ. (MA Hons Mental Philosophy). Department of Agriculture and Fisheries, Scottish Office: Asst Principal, 1964–68; Principal, 1968–73; Commission of the European Communities: Head of Division: Agricl Res., 1973–77; Food Aid, 1978–82; Develt of Trade, 1982–92; Dir, Budget and Gen. Affairs, Directorate Gen. of Fisheries, 1992–96. *Recreations:* Scottish history and literature. *Address:* Hoogvorstweg 4, 3080 Tervuren, Belgium; 41 Great King Street, Edinburgh EH3 6QR. *Clubs:* Royal Commonwealth Society; New (Edinburgh).

McKENZIE, Michael, CB 1999; QC 1991; Master of the Crown Office and Queen's Coroner and Attorney, Registrar of Criminal Appeals and of the Courts Martial Appeal Court, and Master of the Queen's Bench Division, High Court of Justice, since 1988; *b* Hove, Sussex, 25 May 1943; *s* of Robert John McKenzie and Kitty Elizabeth McKenzie; *m* 1964, Peggy Dorothy, *d* of Thomas Edward William Russell and Dorothy Mabel Russell; three *s*. *Educ:* Varndean Grammar Sch., Brighton. Town Clerk's Dept, Brighton, 1961–63; Asst to Clerk of the Peace, Brighton Quarter Sessions, 1963–67; Sen. Clerk of the Court, 1967–70, Dep. Clerk of the Peace, 1970–71, Middlesex Quarter Sessions; called to the Bar, Middle Temple, 1970, Bencher, 1993; Deputy to Courts Administrator, Middlesex Crown Court, 1972–73; Courts Administrator (Newcastle), NE Circuit, 1974–79; Courts Administrator, Central Criminal Court, and Coordinator for Taxation of Crown Court Costs, S Eastern Circuit, 1979–84; Dep. Circuit Administrator, SE Circuit, 1984–86; Asst Registrar, Ct of Appeal Criminal Div., 1986–88. Mem., Criminal Cttee, Judicial Studies Bd, 1988–. Hon. Mem., Litigation Section, State Bar, California, 1995. Freeman, City of London, 1979. FRSA 1990. Hon. Fellow, Kent Sch. of Law, Canterbury Univ., 1991. *Publication:* (ed) Rules of Court: criminal procedure, annually 1994–97. *Recreations:* Northumbrian stick dressing, fell walking. *Address:* Royal Courts of Justice, Strand, WC2A 2LL.

MACKENZIE, Michael Philip; Director-General, Food and Drink Federation, 1986–2001; *b* 26 June 1937; *s* of Brig. Maurice Mackenzie, DSO, and Mrs Vivienne Mackenzie; *m* 1966, Jill (*née* Beckley); one *s* one *d*. *Educ:* Downside Sch.; Lincoln Coll., Oxford (BA); Harvard Business Sch., USA. United Biscuits plc, 1966–86: Prodn Dir, various businesses within United Biscuits, 1974–83; Man. Dir, D. S. Crawford Bakeries, 1983–86. FRSA. *Recreations:* walking, gardening, opera, theatre. *Address:* Ebony Cottage, Reading Street, near Tenterden, Kent TN30 7HT. *Club:* Travellers.

MACKENZIE, Sir Peter Douglas, 13th Bt *cr* 1673 (NS), of Coul, Ross-shire; *b* 23 April 1949; *s* of Henry Douglas Mackenzie (*d* 1965) and Irene Carter Freeman; *S* kinsman, 1990; *m* 1982, Jennifer, *d* of Ridley Boyce; two *d*. *Heir: kinsman* Miles Roderick Turing Mackenzie [*b* 18 April 1952; *m* 1983, Hiroko Sato].

MACKENZIE, Sir Roderick McQuhae, 12th Bt *cr* 1703, of Scatwell; FRCP(C); medical practitioner, pediatrician; *b* 17 April 1942; *s* of Captain Sir Roderick Edward François McQuhae Mackenzie, 11th Bt, CBE, DSC, RN and Marie Evelyn Campbell (*d* 1993), *o c* of late William Ernest Parkinson; *S* father, 1986; *m* 1970, Nadezhda, (Nadine), Baroness von Rorbas, *d* of Georges Frederic Schlatter, Baron von Rorbas; one *s* one *d*. *Educ:* Sedbergh; King's College London. MB, BS; MRCP; DCH. *Heir: s* Gregory Roderick McQuhae Mackenzie, *b* 8 May 1971. *Recreations:* classical music (violin, viola), horseback riding (3-Day eventing), windsurfing. *Address:* 2431 Udell Road NW, Calgary, AB T2N 4H4, Canada; *e-mail:* rmmacken@cadvision.com.

McKENZIE, Sir Roy (Allan), ONZ 1995; KBE 1989; Director, Rangatira Ltd, 1946–93; *b* 7 Nov. 1922; *s* of John Robert McKenzie and Ann May McKenzie (*née* Wrigley); *m* 1949, Shirley Elizabeth Howard; two *s* one *d*. *Educ:* Timaru Boys' High Sch. ACA 1948. Executive, 1949–70, Exec. Dir, 1955, McKenzie NZ Ltd; Chairman: Rangatira Investment Co. Ltd, 1968–85; J. R. McKenzie Trust, 1970–87. Chairman and Founder: McKenzie Educn Foundation; Roy McKenzie Foundn; Chm., Te Omanga Hospice, 1979–. Patron, Outward Bound Trust NZ, 1977– (Chm., 1968). Hon. DLitt Massey, 1992. Rotary Internat. Service Above Self Award, 1995; Rotary Paul Harris Five Jewel Award, 1997. *Publications:* The Roydon Heritage, 1978; Footprints: harnessing an inheritance into a legacy, 1998. *Recreations:* tennis, ski-ing, tramping, breeding standardbreds (horses). *Address:* 21 Marine Drive, Lowry Bay, Eastbourne, New Zealand. *T:* (4)684492.

MACKENZIE, Ruth, OBE 1995; Special Adviser to Secretary of State for Culture, Media and Sport, since 1999; *b* 24 July 1957; *d* of Kenneth Mackenzie and Myrna Blumberg. *Educ:* South Hampstead High Sch.; Sorbonne, Paris; Newnham Coll., Cambridge (MA English 1982). Editor's Asst, Time Out magazine, 1980–81; Co-founder, Dir and writer, Moving Parts Theatre Co., 1980–82; Fellow in Theatre, and Dir, Theatre in the Mill, Bradford Univ., 1982–84; Drama Officer, Arts Council of GB, 1984–86; Head of Strategic Planning, South Bank Centre, 1986–90; Exec. Dir, Nottingham Playhouse, 1990–97; Gen. Dir, Scottish Opera, 1997–99. Artistic Dir, Bradford Multicultural Fest., 1983–84; Artistic Programmer, Theatr Clwyd, 1995–96; Theatre Programmer, Barbican Centre, 1995–97. Member: Bd, Women in Entertainment, 1987–89; Bd, Paines Plough Theatre Co., 1990–96; Touring Panel, 1992–, Lottery Panel, 1994–97, Arts Council of England (formerly of GB); Dance and Drama Panel, British Council, 1992–97; Bd, London Internat. Fest. of Theatre, 1993–97; Nat. Develt Forum, ABSA, 1994–96; Bd, New Millennium Experience Co., 1997–99; Panel 2000, 1998–99. FRSA. Hon. Fellow, Univ. of Nottingham, 1994. Hon. DLitt: Nottingham Trent, 1994; Nottingham, 1997. *Address:* c/o Department for Culture, Media and Sport, 2–4 Cockspur Street, SW1Y 5DH.

MACKENZIE, Wallace John, OBE 1974; Director, Slough Estates plc, 1972–91 (Group Managing Director, 1975–86); *b* 2 July 1921; *s* of Wallace D. Mackenzie and Ethel F. Williamson; *m* 1951, Barbara D. Hopson; two *s* one *d*. *Educ:* Harrow Weald County Grammar Sch. Gen. Manager, Slough Estates Canada Ltd, 1952–72; Dep. Man. Dir, Slough Estates Ltd, 1972–75. Dir, Investors in Industry plc, 1982–86; Chm., Trust Parts Ltd, 1986–94 (Dir, 1985). Member: Commn for New Towns, 1978–94; London Residuary Body, 1985–95. Trustee, Lankelly Foundn, 1985–. *Recreations:* golf, bridge. *Address:* 1 Brampton Mews, Pound Lane, Marlow, Bucks SL7 2SY. *T:* (01628) 478310.

McKENZIE JOHNSTON, Henry Butler, CB 1981; Vice-Chairman, Commission for Local Administration in England, 1982–84 (Commissioner, 1981–84); *b* 10 July 1921; *er s* of late Colin McKenzie Johnston and late Bernardine (*née* Fawcett Butler); *m* 1949, Marian Allardyce Middleton, *e d* of late Brig. A. A. Middleton and late Winifred (*née* Salvesen); one *s* two *d*. *Educ:* Rugby. Served with Black Watch (RHR), 1940–46; Adjt 6th Bn, 1944–45; Temp. Major 1945. Staff of HM Embassy, Athens, 1946–47; entered Foreign (subseq. Diplomatic) Service, 1947; Paris, 1948–51; British High Commn, Germany, 1951–54; FO, 1954–56; 1st Sec. (Commercial), Montevideo, 1956–60; FO, 1960–63; Counsellor (Information), Mexico City, 1963–66; Dep. High Comr, Port of Spain, 1966–67; seconded to Min. of Overseas Develt, 1968–70; Consul-Gen., Munich, 1971–73; seconded to Office of Parly Comr, 1973–79, transferred permanently, 1979–81; Dep. Parly Comr for Admin, 1974–81. Mem., Broadcasting Complaints Commn, 1986–90. Mem., Social Security Appeal Tribunal, Kensington, subseq. Central London, 1985–88. Chm., British-Mexican Soc., 1977–80. *Publication:* Missions to Mexico: a tale of British diplomacy in the 1820s, 1992; Ottoman and Persian Odysseys: James Morier, creator of Hajji Baba of Ispahan, and his brothers, 1998. *Address:* 6 Pembroke Gardens, W8 6HS. *Clubs:* Athenæum, Hurlingham.

McKENZIE-PRICE, Isobel Clare; Editorial Director, IPC Home Interest Magazines (Ideal Home, Living etc, Homes and Ideas, 25 Beautiful Homes, Homes & Gardens, Country Homes & Interiors), since 1998; *b* 11 Jan. 1956; *d* of Edward Charles Price and Patricia Price (*née* Edgeley); *m* 1st, 1977, Andrew James Alistair McKenzie (marr. diss. 1981); 2nd, 1983, William Woods; one *s* three *d*. *Educ:* Horsham Girls High Sch.; Univ. of Leeds (BA Hons). Homes Editor, Over 21, 1979–80; Dep. Editor, Wedding and Home, 1983–85; Mem., Launch Team, Country Living, 1985–86; Dep. Editor, Essentials, 1986–90; Editor: Mother and Baby, 1990–91; Parents, 1991–92; Period Living, 1993–94; Editor in Chief, Elle Decoration, and Period Living, 1994–96; Publishing Consultant, Inspirations, 1997; Exec. Editor, Prima, and Launch Editor, Your Home, 1997–98. *Recreations:* family, new media, country walking. *Address:* Southbank Publishing Ltd, IPC Magazines, King's Reach Tower, SE1 9LS. *T:* (020) 7261 5000.

McKENZIE SMITH, Ian, OBE 1992; PRSA (ARSA 1973, RSA 1987); PPRSW (RSW 1981); artist (painter); President, Royal Scottish Academy, since 1998 (Deputy President and Treasurer, 1990–91; Secretary, 1991–98); City Arts and Recreation Officer, City of Aberdeen, 1989–96; *b* 3 Aug. 1935; *y s* of James McKenzie Smith and Mary Benzie; *m* 1963, Mary Rodger Fotheringham; two *s* one *d*. *Educ:* Robert Gordon's Coll., Aberdeen; Gray's Sch. of Art, Aberdeen; Hospitalfield Coll. of Art, Arbroath; Aberdeen Coll. of Educn. SSA 1960; AAS 1963; FSAScot 1970; ASIAD 1975; FMA 1987. Teacher of art, 1960–63; Educn Officer, Council of Industrial Design, Scottish Cttee, 1963–68; Dir, Aberdeen Art Gall. and Museums, 1968–89 (Hon. Mem. 2000). Work in permanent collections: Scottish Nat. Gall. of Modern Art; Scottish Arts Council; Arts Council of NI; Contemp. Art Soc.; Aberdeen Art Gall. and Museums; Glasgow Art Gall. and Museums; City Art Centre, Edinburgh; Perth Art Gall.; McManus Gall., Dundee; Abbot Hall Art Gall., Kendal; Hunterian Mus., Glasgow; Nuffield Foundn; Carnegie Trust; Strathclyde Educn Authority; Lothian Educn Authority; RSA; DoE; Robert Fleming Holdings; IBM; Deutsche Morgan Grenfell; Grampian Hosps Art Trust; Lord Chancellor. Mem., Cttee of Enquiry into Econ. Situation of Visual Artists, Gulbenkian Foundn, 1978. Trustee, Nat. Galls of Scotland, 1999–. Member: Scottish Arts Council, 1970–77 (Chm., Art Cttee, 1975–77); Scottish Museums Fedn, 1970–86; Scottish Museums Council, 1980–87 (Chm., Industrial Cttee, 1985–87); Aberdeen Univ. Museums Cttee and Music Cttee, 1970–96; ICOM Internat. Exhibns Cttee, 1986–96; Museums and Galls Commn, 1997–2000; Nat. Heritage, Scottish Gp, 1977–99; Bd of Mgt, Grampian Hosps Art Project, 1987–2000; Adv. Council on Export of Works of Art, 1991–; Curatorial Cttee,

1991–, Council, 1996–99, Bldgs Cttee, 1998–, Art Advr, 2000–, NT for Scotland. Arts Advr, COSLA, 1976–85. Pres., RSW, 1988–98. Governor: Edinburgh Coll. of Art, 1976–88; The Robert Gordon Univ. (formerly Robert Gordon Inst. of Technology), 1989–95. External Assessor: Glasgow Sch. of Art, 1982–86; Duncan of Jordanstone Coll. of Art, 1982–86; Scottish Arts Council Gifting Scheme, 1997. Board Member: RSA Enterprises, and Friends of RSA, 1972–; Scottish Sculpture Workshop, 1979–2000; Aberdeen Maritime Mus. Appeal, 1981–98. Vice Pres., NADFAS, 2000–. Trustee: Painters Workshop (Scotland), 1975–89; John Kinross Fund, 1990–; Alexander Naysmith Fund, 1990–; Spalding Fund, 1990–; Sir William Gillies Fund, 1990–; Hospitalfield Trust, 1991–; McBey Trust, 2000–. FSS 1981; FRSA 1973. Hon. RA 1999; Hon. RHA 1999; Hon. RUA 1999; Hon. RWA 2000. Hon. Mem., Peacock Printmakers, 1993. Hon. LLD Aberdeen, 1991; Hon. DArt Robert Gordon, 2000. Inst. of Contemp. Prints Award, 1969; Guthrie Award, 1971, Gillies Award, 1980, RSA; ESU Thyne Scholarship, 1980. *Address:* 70 Hamilton Place, Aberdeen AB15 5BA. *T:* (01224) 644531, *Fax:* (01224) 626253. *Clubs:* Caledonian, Royal Over-Seas League, Scottish Arts (Edinburgh); Royal Northern (Aberdeen).

MACKENZIE SMITH, Peter; Director of Education, Marconi (formerly General Electric Co.) plc, since 1997; *b* 12 Jan. 1946; *s* of Antony and Isobel Mackenzie Smith; *m* 1973, Sandra Gay-French; three *d*. *Educ:* Downside; Jesus Coll., Cambridge (BA Classical Tripos). Teacher: British Inst., Oporto, 1967–68; Internat. House, London, 1969; British Council, 1969–97: Asst Rep., Lagos, 1969–72; Asst Cultural Attaché, Cairo, 1972–77; Regl Dir, Southampton, 1977–80; Educnl Contracts Dept, 1980–83; Dep. Rep., Cairo, 1983–87; Director: Educnl Contracts, 1987–89; Projects Div., 1989–92; Nigeria and W Africa, 1992–94; Export Promotion, 1994–96; Africa and S Asia, 1996–97. *Address:* 30 Prothero Road, SW6 7LZ.

McKEON, Andrew John; Head of Medicines, Pharmacy and Industry Division, Department of Health, since 2000; *b* 22 Sept. 1955; *s* of Kenneth and Maurine McKeon; *m* 1989, Hilary Neville; one *s* one *d*. *Educ:* William Hulme's Grammar Sch., Manchester; St Catharine's Coll., Cambridge. Joined DHSS, 1976. *Address:* 8 Poplar Road, SW19 3JR.

McKEOWN, Dr John; Chief Executive Officer, United Kingdom Atomic Energy Authority, since 1997; *b* 10 March 1945; *s* of Edward McKeown and Anne McGladrigan; *m* 1967, Maureen Susan Doherty; one *s* one *d*. *Educ:* Univ. of Glasgow (BSc 1966; PhD 1971); Harvard Business Sch. CEGB Res. Fellow, 1971–73; Asst, Forward Planning, 1973–76; South of England Electricity Board: Sen. Engr, 1976–79, Principal Engr, 1979–83, Control and Instrumentation Div.; Manager: Electrical Dept, 1983–88; Nuclear Safety, 1988–90; Scottish Nuclear: Director: Safety, 1990–92; Projects, 1992–95; Safety & Envmt, 1995–96; Principal, John McKeown and Associates, 1996–97. Director: UK Nirex, 1997–; British Nuclear Industry Forum, 1998–. *Recreations:* golf, music. *Address:* (office) Marshall Building, 521 Harwell, Didcot, Oxon OX11 0RA. *T:* (01235) 436880. *Club:* Frilford Heath Golf.

McKEOWN, Prof. Patrick Arthur, OBE 1991; MSc; FREng, FIEE, FIMechE; FIQA; Professor of Precision Engineering, 1974–96, now Emeritus, Director of Cranfield Unit for Precision Engineering, 1969–96, Cranfield University (formerly Institute of Technology); Director, Pat McKeown and Associates, since 1995; *b* 16 Aug. 1930; *s* of Robert Matthew McKeown and Augusta (*née* White); *m* 1954, Mary Patricia Heath; three *s*. *Educ:* Cambridge County High Sch. for Boys; Bristol Grammar Sch.; Cranfield Inst. of Technol. (MSc). CEng, MIMechE 1969; FIEE (FIProdE 1971); FIQA 1973; FREng (FEng 1986). National Service, RE, 1949–51; Suez Campaign, 1956: Captain RE; port maintenance. Student apprentice, Bristol Aircraft Co. Ltd, Bristol, 1951–54 (HNC National State Scholarship); Cranfield Inst. of Technol., 1954–56; Société Genevoise, Newport Pagnell and Geneva, 1956–68 (Technical and Works Dir, 1965); Hd of Dept for Design of Machine Systems. Cranfield Inst. of Technol., 1975–85. Chairman: Cranfield Precision Systems Ltd, 1984–87; Cranfield Moulded Structures Ltd, 1984–91; Cranfield Precision Engrg Ltd, 1987–95 (Chief Exec., 1987–92); non-executive Director: Control Techniques plc, 1990–95; AMTRI, 1990–92; Cranfield Aerospace Ltd, 2001–. Vice-Pres., Inst. of Qual. Assurance, 1976; Pres., CIRP (Internat. Instn for Prodn Engrg Research), 1988–89. Member: Evaluation Panel, National Bureau of Standards, Washington, USA; Metrology and Standards Requirements Bd, DTI, 1983–86; Advanced Manufg Technol. Cttee, DTI, 1983–87; Vis. Cttee, RCA, 1984–87; ACARD working gp, 1987–88. Internat. Advr, Gintic Inst. of Manufg Technology, Singapore, 1991–97. Vis. Prof., Univ. of Calif, Berkeley, 1994. Clayton Meml Lectr, IMechE, 1986. Pres., Eur. Soc. for Precision Engrg and Nametechnol., 1998–2000. Charter Fellow, Soc. of Manufacturing Engineers, 1985. Hon. DSc: Connecticut, 1996; Cranfield, 1996. Fulbright Award (Vis. Prof. of Mechanical Engrg, Univ. of Wisconsin-Madison), 1982; F. W. Taylor Award, Soc. of Manufacturing Engrs, 1983; Thomas Hawksley Gold Medal, IMechE, 1987; Mensforth Gold Medal, IProdE, 1988; Life Achievement Award, Amer. Soc. for Precision Engrg, 1998; Faraday Medal, IEE, 1999. *Publications:* papers in CIRP Annals; project reports and lectures for Royal Acad. of Engrg. *Recreations:* walking, travel, enjoyment of wine, good food, music, theatre. *Address:* 37 Church End, Biddenham, Bedford MK40 4AR. *T:* (01234) 267678, *Fax:* (01234) 262560; *e-mail:* patmckeown@kbnet.co.uk.

McKERN, Leo, (Reginald McKern), AO 1983; actor; *b* 16 March 1920; *s* of Norman Walton McKern and Vera (*née* Martin); *m* 1946, Joan Alice Southa (Jane Holland); two *d*. *Educ:* Sydney Techn. High Sch. Engrg apprentice, 1935–37; artist, 1937–40; AIF (Corp., Engrs), 1940–42; actor, 1944; arrived England, 1946; CSEU tour, Germany; Arts Council tours, 1947; Old Vic, 1949–52; Shakespeare Meml Theatre, 1952–54; Old Vic last season, 1962–63; New Nottingham Playhouse, 1963–64; *stage:* Toad of Toad Hall, Princes, 1954; Queen of the Rebels, Haymarket, 1955; Cat on a Hot Tin Roof, Aldwych, 1958; Brouhaha, Aldwych, 1958; Rollo, Strand, 1959; A Man for all Seasons, Globe, 1960; The Thwarting of Baron Bolligrew, RSC, Aldwych, 1965; Volpone, Garrick, 1967; The Wolf, Apollo, 1973; The Housekeeper, Apollo, 1982; Number One, Queen's, 1984; Boswell for the Defence, Australia, later Playhouse, 1989, tour 1991; Hobson's Choice, Chichester, tour, then Lyric, 1995; When We Are Married, Chichester, then Savoy, 1996; She Stoops to Conquer, Sydney Opera House, 1999; *films:* The French Lieutenant's Woman, 1983; Ladyhawke, 1984; The Chain, 1985; Travelling North, 1986; On Our Selection, 1996; Molokai, 1998; *television:* Rumpole of the Bailey (series), 1977–; Reilly—Ace of Spies, 1983; King Lear, 1983; Monsignor Quixote; Murder With Mirrors (film), 1985; The Master Builder, 1988; The Last Romantics (film), 1992; A Foreign Field, 1993; Circles of Deceit (film), 1996. *Publication:* Just Resting (biographical memoir), 1983. *Recreations:* sailing, swimming, photography, painting, environment preservation. *Address:* c/o Richard Hatton Ltd, 29 Roehampton Gate, SW15 5JR.

MACKERRAS, Sir (Alan) Charles (MacLaurin), AC 1997; Kt 1979; CBE 1974; Hon. RAM 1969; FRCM; FRNCM; Principal Guest Conductor: Scottish Chamber Orchestra, 1992–95, now Conductor Laureate; Czech Philharmonic Orchestra, since 1997; Music Director, Orchestra of St Luke's, New York, since 1998; Guest Conductor: Vienna State Opera; Paris Opera; Munich Opera; Opera Australia; Royal Opera House Covent Garden; Metropolitan Opera; *b* Schenectady, USA, 17 Nov. 1925; *s* of late Alan Patrick and Catherine Mackerras, Sydney, Australia; *m* 1947, Helena Judith (*née* Wilkins); two *d*. *Educ:* Sydney Grammar Sch.; Sydney Conservatorium of Music; student with Vaclav Talich, Prague Acad. of Music. FRCM 1987; FRNCM 1999. Principal Oboist, Sydney Symphony Orchestra, 1943–46; Staff Conductor, Sadler's Wells Opera, 1948–54; Principal Conductor BBC Concert Orchestra, 1954–56; freelance conductor with most British and many continental orchestras; concert tours in USSR, S Africa, USA, 1957–66; First Conductor, Hamburg State Opera, 1966–69; Musical Dir, Sadler's Wells Opera, later ENO, 1970–77; Chief Guest Conductor, BBC SO, 1976–79; Chief Conductor, Sydney Symphony Orch., ABC, 1982–85; Principal Guest Conductor, Royal Liverpool Philharmonic Orch., 1986–88; Mus. Dir, WNO, 1987–92 (Conductor Emeritus, 1992–); Principal Guest Conductor: San Francisco Opera, 1993–96 (now Conductor Emeritus); RPO, 1993–96; frequent radio and TV broadcasts; many commercial recordings, notably Handel, Janáček, Mozart operas and symphonies, Brahms and Beethoven symphonies; appearances at many internat. festivals and opera houses. Hon. FTCL 1999. Hon. DMus: Hull, 1990; Nottingham, 1991; York, Brno, Brisbane, 1994; Oxford, 1997; Prague Acad. of Music, 1999; Napier Univ., 2000. Evening Standard Award for Opera, 1977; Janáček Medal, 1978; Gramophone Record of the Year, 1977, 1980, 1999; Gramophone Operatic Record of the Year Award, 1983, 1984, 1994, 1999; Gramophone Best Choral Record, 1986; Grammy Award for best opera recording, 1981; Chocs de l'Année Award, Le Monde de la Musique, 1998; Edison Award, 1999; Lifetime Achievement Award and Chopin Prize, Cannes, 2000. Medal of Merit (Czech Republic), 1996. *Publications:* ballet arrangements of Sullivan's Pineapple Poll and of Verdi's Lady and the Fool; Arthur Sullivan's lost Cello Concerto, 1986; contrib. 4 appendices to Charles Mackerras: a musicians' musician, by Nancy Phelan 1987; articles in Opera Magazine, Music and Musicians and other musical jls. *Recreations:* languages, yachting. *Address:* 10 Hamilton Terrace, NW8 9UG. *T:* (020) 7286 4047, *Fax:* (020) 7289 5893.

McKERROW, June; charity advisor; Director, Mental Health Foundation, 1992–2000; *b* 17 June 1950; *d* of Alexander Donald and Lorna McKerrow. *Educ:* Brunel Univ. (MPhil 1977). Housing management in local govt and housing assocs, 1967–80; Dir, Stonham Housing Assoc., 1980–92. Mem. Cttee, English Rural Housing Assoc., 1997–99. Trustee and Vice-Chm., Shelter, 1985–93; Trustee: Homeless Internat., 1988–93; Cherwell Housing Trust, 1992–97; Charity Projects, 1993–97; Patron, Revolving Doors Agency, 1993–99; Chm., Housing Assocs Charitable Trust, 1998–. Mem., British Council, UN Internat. Year of Shelter for the Homeless, 1987. Non-exec. Dir, Oxfordshire Mental Healthcare NHS Trust, 2000–. Mem. Court, Oxford Brookes Univ., 1999–. *Address:* 22 Buckingham Street, Oxford OX1 4LH.

McKERROW, Neil Alexander Herdman; Bursar and Clerk to the Governors, Sedbergh School, since 1997; *b* 17 May 1945; *s* of Anderson Herdman McKerrow, TD, MB ChB and Joan Ysobel Cuthbertson (*née* Clark); *m* 1971, Penelope Mackinlay (*née* Chiene); one *s* two *d*. *Educ:* Sedbergh Sch.; Emmanuel Coll., Cambridge (MA). Reckitt & Colman (Overseas) Ltd, 1968–69; commnd 1st Bn Queen's Own Highlanders (Seaforth and Camerons), service in Trucial-Oman States, BAOR, 1969–73 (Capt.); Marketing Manager, Distillers Co., 1973–75; Macdonald Martin Distilleries, later Glenmorangie plc: Export Dir, 1975–81; Sales Marketing Dir, 1981–87; Man. Dir, 1987–94; Chief Exec., Forest Enterprise, Forestry Commn, 1995–96. Member: Royal Scottish Pipers Soc., 1971–; High Constabulary, Port of Leith, 1976–; Incorp. of Malt Men, 1990–. Gov., Belhaven Hill Sch., Dunbar, 1997–. *Recreations:* fishing, outdoor pursuits, most sports, malt whisky, local history, traditional jazz. *Address:* (office) Malim Lodge, Sedbergh LA10 5RY. *T:* (01539) 620303. *Clubs:* London Scottish; New (Edinburgh); Hawks (Cambridge); Royal & Ancient Golf (St Andrews).

MACKESON, Sir Rupert (Henry), 2nd Bt *cr* 1954; *b* 16 Nov. 1941; *s* of Brig. Sir Harry Ripley Mackeson, 1st Bt, and Alethea, Lady Mackeson (*d* 1979), *d* of late Comdr R. Talbot, RN; *S* father, 1964; *m* 1968, Hon. Camilla Keith (marr. diss. 1973), *d* of Baron Keith of Castleacre, *qv*. *Educ:* Harrow; Trinity Coll., Dublin (MA). Captain, Royal Horse Guards, 1967, retd 1968. *Publications:* (as Rupert Collens): (jtly) 'Snaffles' on Racing and Point-to-Pointing, 1988; (jtly) 'Snaffles' on Hunting, 1989; Look at Cecil Aldin's Dogs and Hounds, 1990; 25 Legal Luminaries from Vanity Fair, 1990; Cecil Aldin's Dog Models, 1994. *Recreations:* art, racing. *Heir:* none.

MACKESY, Dr Piers Gerald, FRHistS; FBA 1988; Fellow of Pembroke College, Oxford, 1954–87, now Emeritus; *b* 15 Sept. 1924; *s* of Maj.-Gen. Pierse Joseph Mackesy, CB, DSO, MC and Dorothy (*née* Cook), (novelist as Leonora Starr); *m* 1st, 1957, Sarah Davies; one *s* two *d*; 2nd, 1978, Patricia Timlin (*née* Gore). *Educ:* Wellington Coll.; Christ Church, Oxford (1st cl. Hons Modern Hist., 1950; DPhil 1953; DLitt 1978). FRHistS 1965. Lieut, The Royal Scots Greys (NW Europe, 1944–47); Captain, TA, 1950–57. Robinson Schol., Oriel Coll., Oxford, 1951–53; Harkness Fellow, Harvard Univ., 1953–54; Vis. Fellow, Inst. for Advanced Study, Princeton, 1962–63; Vis. Prof., CIT, 1966; Huntingdon Lby, San Marino, Calif, 1967. Lectures: Lees-Knowles, Cambridge, 1972; American Bicentennial, at Williamsburg, Va, Clark Univ., Naval War Coll., US Mil. Acad., Nat. War Coll., Peabody Mus., N Eastern Univ., Capitol Historical Soc. Member, Council: Inst. for Early Amer. Hist. and Culture, 1970–73; Nat. Army Mus., 1983–92; Soc. for Army Historical Res., 1985–94. *Publications:* The War in the Mediterranean 1803–10, 1957; The War for America 1775–83, 1964, 2nd edn 1993; Statesmen at War: the Strategy of Overthrow 1798–99, 1974; The Coward of Minden: the affair of Lord George Sackville, 1979; War without Victory: the downfall of Pitt 1799–1802, 1984; British Victory in Egypt, 1801: the end of Napoleon's conquest, 1995 (Templer Medal, Soc. for Army Histl Res., 1995); contribs to various books and jls. *Recreation:* not gardening. *Address:* Westerton Farmhouse, Dess, by Aboyne, Aberdeenshire AB34 5AY. *T:* (013398) 84415. *Club:* Army and Navy.

MACKEY, Prof. James Patrick; Thomas Chalmers Professor of Theology, 1979–99, now Emeritus, and Director of Graduate School and Associate Dean, 1995–99, University of Edinburgh (Hon. Fellow, Faculty of Divinity, 1999); *b* 9 Feb. 1934; *e s* of Peter Mackey and Esther Mackey (*née* Morrissey); *m* 1973, Hanorah Noelle Quinlan; one *s* one *d*. *Educ:* Mount St Joseph Coll., Roscrea; Nat. Univ. of Ireland (BA); Pontifical Univ., Maynooth (LPh, BD, STL, DD); Queen's Univ. Belfast (PhD); postgraduate study at Univs of Oxford, London, Strasbourg. Lectr in Philosophy, QUB, 1960–66; Lectr in Theology, St John's Coll., Waterford, 1966–69; Associate Prof. and Prof. of Systematic and Philosophical Theol., Univ. of San Francisco, 1969–79; Dean, Faculty of Divinity, Edinburgh Univ., 1984–88. Visiting Professor: Univ. of California, Berkeley, 1974; Dartmouth Coll., NH, 1989; TCD, 1999–; Curricular Consultant, UC Cork, 1999–. Mem., Centre for Hermeneutical Studies, Univ. of California, Berkeley, 1974–79. Organiser, Internat. Conf. on the Cultures of Europe, Derry, 1992. *Television series:* The Hall of Mirrors, 1984; The Gods of War, 1986; Perspectives, 1986–87; radio programmes. Associate Editor: Herder Correspondence, 1966–69; Concilium (church history section), 1965–70; Horizons, 1973–79; Editor, Studies in World Christianity, 1995–. *Publications:* The Modern Theology of Tradition, 1962; Life and Grace, 1966; Tradition and Change in the Church, 1968; Contemporary Philosophy of Religion, 1968; (ed) Morals, Law and

Authority, 1969; The Church: its credibility today, 1970; The Problems of Religious Faith, 1972; Jesus: the man and the myth, 1979; The Christian Experience of God as Trinity, 1983; (ed) Religious Imagination, 1986; Modern Theology: a sense of direction, 1987; (with Prof. J. D. G. Dunn) New Testament Theology in Dialogue, 1987; (ed) Introduction to Celtic Christianity, 1989; Power and Christian Ethics, 1993; (ed) The Cultures of Europe, 1994; The Critique of Theological Reason, 2000; contribs to theol. and philosoph. jls. *Recreations:* yachting; rediscovery of original Celtic culture of these islands. *Address:* 15 Glenville Park, Dunmore Road, Waterford, Eire. *Clubs:* Edinburgh University; Port Edgar Yacht (W Lothian).

MACKEY, Air Vice-Marshal Jefferson; Chief Executive, Defence Dental Agency, 1996–97; *b* 24 Oct. 1936; *s* of late James Mackey and of Cicely (*née* Hitchman); *m* 1959, Sheila Mary Taylor; one *s* two *d*. *Educ:* Latymer Upper Sch.; Guy's Hosp. (BDS, LDS RCS). Asst Dir, Defence Dental Services, 1982–86; Officer Comdg RAF Inst. of Dental Health and Trng, 1986–87; Principal Dental Officer, RAF Support Command, 1987–90; Dir, RAF Dental Services, 1990–94; Dir, Defence Dental Services, 1992–96. QHDS 1987–97. FISM; FIMgt; FRGS. *Address:* Takali, Oxford Road, Stone, Bucks HP17 8PB. *T:* (01296) 748823. *Clubs:* Royal Air Force; Mentmore Golf and Country.

MACKEY, Most Rev. John, CBE 1983; Bishop of Auckland, NZ, (RC), 1974–83; *b* Bray, Co. Wicklow, 11 Jan. 1918; *s* of Malachy Mackey and Kathleen (*née* Byrne). *Educ:* Auckland Univ. (MA, DipEd); Notre Dame Univ., USA (PhD). Emigrated to NZ, 1924. Ordained priest, 1941; Adminr for Auckland Diocesan Schs, 1951–71; Lectr, Holy Cross Seminary, 1972–74; formerly Professor in Theological Faculty, National Seminary of Mosgiel, Dunedin. *Publications:* The Making of a State Education System, 1967; Reflections on Church History, 1975; Looking at Ourselves, 1994. *Address:* 3 Karaka Street, Takapuna, Auckland, New Zealand.

MACKEY, William Gawen; Partner, 1952, Managing Partner UK Operations, 1981–86, Ernst & Whinney; retired 1986; *b* 22 Sept. 1924; *s* of William Gawen Mackey and Jane Mackey; *m* 1948, Margaret Reeves Vinycomb; two *s*. *Educ:* Dame Allan's Sch., Newcastle upon Tyne. Qualified Chartered Accountant, 1949. Served RN, 1942–45 (Sub-Lt). Joined Ernst & Whinney, 1952, Newcastle; transf. London, 1973, with responsibility for corporate restructuring and insolvency services in UK. Receiver: Airfix; British Tanners; Laker; Stone-Platt. Chm., Insolvency Sub Cttee, CCAB, 1978–82; Dir, Inst. Corporate Insolvency Courses, 1974–80. *Publications:* articles and lectures on corporate management, restructuring and insolvency. *Recreations:* opera, gardening, France. *Address:* Eynesse, Ste Foy La Grande 33220, France. *T:* 557410042, *Fax:* 557410070.

McKIBBIN, Dr Ross Ian, FBA 1999; Fellow, and Tutor in Modern History, St John's College, Oxford, since 1972; *b* 25 Jan. 1942; *s* of Arnold Walter McKibbin and Nance Lilian (*née* Spence). *Educ:* Univ. of Sydney (BA, MA); St Antony's Coll., Oxford (DPhil 1970). Lectr in Hist., Univ. of Sydney, 1968–70; Jun. Res. Fellow, Christ Church, Oxford, 1970–72. *Publications:* The Evolution of the Labour Party 1910–1924, 1974, 2nd edn 1991; The Ideologies of Class, 1990; Classes and Cultures: England 1918–1951, 1998. *Recreations:* gardening, squash, tennis. *Address:* St John's College, Oxford OX1 3JP. *T:* (01865) 277344.

MACKIE, family name of **Baron Mackie of Benshie**.

MACKIE OF BENSHIE, Baron *cr* 1974 (Life Peer), of Kirriemuir; **George Yull Mackie,** CBE 1971; DSO 1944; DFC 1944; Chairman: Caithness Glass Ltd, 1966–84; Caithness Pottery Co. Ltd, 1975–84; The Benshie Cattle Co. Ltd; Land and Timber Services Ltd, since 1986; *b* 10 July 1919; *s* of late Maitland Mackie, OBE, Hon. LLD; *m* 1st, 1944, Lindsay Lyall Sharp (*d* 1985), *y d* of late Alexander and Isabella Sharp, OBE, Aberdeen; three *d* (one *s* decd); 2nd, 1988, Jacqueline, *widow* of Andrew Lane, and *d* of late Col. Marcel Rauch. *Educ:* Aberdeen Grammar Sch.; Aberdeen Univ. Served War of 1939–45, RAF; Bomber Command, (DSO, DFC); Air Staff, 1944. Farming at Ballinshoe, Kirriemuir, 1945–89. Contested (L) South Angus, 1959; MP (L) Caithness and Sutherland, 1964–66; contested (L) Scotland NE, European Parliamentary election, 1979. Pres., Scottish Liberal Party, 1983–88 (Chm., 1965–70); Member: EEC Scrutiny Cttee (D), House of Lords; Liberal Shadow Admin; Exec., IPU; Council of Europe, 1986–97 (Mem. and Rapporteur, Cttee on Agricl and Rural Develt, 1990–97); WEU, 1986–; Liberal, then Lib Dem, Spokesman, House of Lords, until 2000: Devolution, Agriculture, Scotland, Industry. Chm., Cotswold Wine Co. (UK) Ltd, 1983–85. Dir, Scottish Ballet, 1986–88. Rector, Dundee Univ., 1980–83. Hon. LLD Dundee, 1982. *Publication:* Policy for Scottish Agriculture, 1963. *Address:* Benshie Cottage, Oathlaw, by Forfar, Angus DD8 3PQ. *T:* (01307) 850376. *Clubs:* Garrick, Farmers', Royal Air Force.
See also I. L. Aitken, A. G. Sharp, Sir R. L. Sharp.

MACKIE, Air Cdre (Retd) Alastair Cavendish Lindsay, CBE 1966; DFC 1943 and Bar 1944; Director General, Health Education Council, 1972–82; Director, Ansador Ltd, since 1983; *b* 3 Aug. 1922; *s* of George Mackie, DSO, OBE, MD, Malvern, Worcs and May (*née* Cavendish); *m* 1944, Rachel Goodson; two *s*. *Educ:* Charterhouse. Royal Air Force, 1940–68; Under Treas., Middle Temple, 1968; Registrar, Architects' Registration Council, 1970; Sec., British Dental Assoc., 1971; Pres., Internat. Union for Health Educn, 1979–82. Vice-Pres., CND, 1990–. *Recreation:* allotmenteering. *Address:* 4 Warwick Drive, SW15 6LB. *T:* (020) 8789 4544. *Club:* Royal Air Force.
See also D. L. Mackie.

MACKIE, Prof. Andrew George; Professor of Applied Mathematics, 1968–88, Vice-Principal 1975–80, University of Edinburgh; *b* 7 March 1927; *s* of late Andrew Mackie and Isobel Sigsworth Mackie (*née* Storey); *m* 1959, Elizabeth Maud Mackie (*née* Hebblethwaite); one *s* one *d*. *Educ:* Tain Royal Acad.; Univ. of Edinburgh (MA); Univ. of Cambridge (BA); Univ. of St Andrews (PhD). Lecturer, Univ. of Dundee, 1948–50; Bateman Res. Fellow and Instructor, CIT, 1953–55; Lecturer: Univ. of Strathclyde, 1955–56; Univ. of St Andrews, 1956–62; Prof. of Applied Maths, Victoria Univ. of Wellington, NZ, 1962–65; Res. Prof., Univ. of Maryland, 1966–68. Visiting Professor: CIT, 1984; Univ. of NSW, 1985. FRSE 1962. *Publications:* Boundary Value Problems, 1965, 2nd edn 1989; numerous contribs to mathematical and scientific jls. *Recreation:* golf. *Address:* 31/7 Hermitage Drive, Edinburgh EH10 6BY. *T:* (0131) 447 2164.

MACKIE, Clive David Andrew, FCA, FSS; Consultant, Institute of Actuaries, 1992–94; *b* 29 April 1929; *s* of David and Lilian Mackie; *m* 1953, Averil Ratcliff; one *s* three *d*. *Educ:* Tiffin Sch., Kingston-on-Thames. FCA 1956; FSS 1982. Director: cos in Grundy (Teddington) Group, 1959–67; D. Sebel & Co. Ltd, 1967–70; post in admin of higher educn, 1970–73; Institute of Actuaries: Dep. Sec., 1973–77; Sec., 1977–83; Sec.-Gen., 1983–92. Mem., Catenian Assoc., 1972–. *Recreations:* music (post 1780), cricket, carpentry, amateur dramatics, working with the Nat. Service of Talking Newspaper Assoc. of UK. *Address:* Withermere, Burwash, East Sussex TN19 7HN. *T:* (01435) 882427. *Clubs:* Gallio; Actuaries; Sussex CC.

MACKIE, David Lindsay; QC 1998; Head of Litigation, Allen & Overy, since 1988; a Recorder, since 1992; a Deputy High Court Judge, since 1998; *b* 15 Feb. 1946; *s* of Air Cdre Alastair Cavendish Lindsay Mackie, *qv*; *m* 1st, 1971 (marr. diss.); two *s* one *d*; 2nd, 1989, Phyllis Marilyn Gershon. *Educ:* St Edmund Hall, Oxford (BA Modern History 1967). FCIArb 1990. Admitted Solicitor, 1971. Joined Allen & Overy, 1968, Partner, 1975–. Asst Recorder, 1988–92. Mem., Civil and Family Cttee, Judicial Studies Bd, 1991–96; Dep. Chair, Royal Courts of Justice Advice Bureau, 1998–. Trustee, Solicitors Pro Bono Gp, 1997–. *Recreation:* climbing. *Address:* Allen & Overy, One New Change, EC4M 9QQ. *T:* (020) 7330 3000.

MACKIE, Eric Dermott, OBE 1987; Executive Chairman, Swansea Dry Docks Ltd, 1995–2000; *b* 4 Dec. 1924; *s* of James Girvan and Ellen Dorothy Mackie; *m* 1950, Mary Victoria Christie; one *s* one *d*. *Educ:* Coll. of Technology, Belfast. CEng; MIMechE, FIMarE, FRINA. 1st Class MoT Cert. (Steam and Diesel). Trained with James Mackie & Son (Textile Engrs), 1939–44; Design draughtsman, Harland & Wolff, Belfast, 1944–48; 2nd Engineer (sea-going) in both steam and diesel ships for Union Castle Mail Steamship Co., 1948–53; Harland & Wolff, Belfast, 1953–75: Test Engr; Manager, Shiprepair Dept; Gen. Manager i/c of Southampton branch; Gen. Manager i/c of ship prodn and shiprepair, Belfast; Man. Dir, James Brown Hamer, S Africa, 1975–79; Chief Exec. and Man. Dir of Shiprepair in UK, British Shipbuilders, 1979–81; Chm. and Man. Dir, Govan Shipbuilders, later Govan Kvaerner Ltd, 1979–90. Mem., Governing Bd, British Marine Technology. Denny Gold Medal, IMarE, 1987. *Publications:* articles for marine engrg instns on various subjects pertaining to marine engrg and gen. engrg. *Recreations:* golf, swimming, reading. *Address:* Middle Barton, Whittingham, near Alnwick, Northumberland NE66 4SU. *T:* (01665) 574648. *Clubs:* Caledonian; Durban, Rand (Johannesburg, SA).

MACKIE, George, DFC 1944; RSW 1968; RDI 1973; freelance graphic artist and painter; Head of Design, Gray's School of Art, Aberdeen, 1958–80 (retd); *b* 17 July 1920; *s* of late David Mackie and late Kathleen Grantham; *m* 1952, Barbara Balmer, ARSA, RSW, RGI; two *d*. Served Royal Air Force, 1940–46. Consultant in book design to Edinburgh University Press, 1960–87. Paintings in various private and public collections incl. HRH the Duke of Edinburgh's and Scottish Nat. Gall. of Modern Art. Major retrospective exhibitions: Books, mostly scholarly, and some Ephemera, Nat. Library of Scotland, 1991; Dartmouth Coll., NH, USA, 1991. *Publication:* Lynton Lamb: Illustrator, 1979. *Address:* 32 Broad Street, Stamford, Lincs. PE9 1PJ. *T:* (01780) 753296. *Club:* Double Crown.

MACKIE, Prof. George Owen, FRS 1991; DPhil; Professor of Biology, University of Victoria, 1968–94, Professor Emeritus since 1995; *b* 20 Oct. 1929; *s* of late Col (Frederick) Percival Mackie, CSI, OBE, IMS and Mary E. H. Mackie (*née* Owen); *m* 1956, Gillian V. Faulkner; three *s* two *d*. *Educ:* Oxford (BA 1954; MA 1956; DPhil 1956). FRSC 1982. Univ. of Alberta, 1957–68; Univ. of Victoria, 1968–; Chm., Biol. Dept, 1970–73. Editor, Canadian Jl of Zoology, 1980–89. Fry Medal, Canadian Soc. of Zoologists, 1989. *Publications:* (ed) Coelenterate Ecology and Behavior, 1976; numerous research articles in books and jls. *Recreations:* chamber music ('cello), earthenware pottery. *Address:* University of Victoria, Department of Biology, PO Box 3020, Victoria, BC V8W 3N5, Canada. *T:* (250) 7217146.

MACKIE, Dr Karl Joseph; Chief Executive, Centre for Effective Dispute Resolution, since 1990; *b* 31 March 1947; *s* of John Mackie and Ethel Mackie (*née* Freeman); *m* 1st, 1968, Ann Douglas (marr. diss.); one *s* one *d*; 2nd, 2001, Eileen Carroll. *Educ:* Buckhaven High Sch.; Univ. of Edinburgh (MA Hons), DipEd; Univ. of London (LLB ext.); Univ. of Nottingham (PhD 1987); Open Univ. (MBA Psychol 1990). FCIArb 1992. Accredited Mediator, CEDR. Called to the Bar, Gray's Inn, 1982; Res. Associate, Univ. of Edinburgh, 1971–72; various posts, 1972–73; Lectr, then Sen. Lectr, Law and Social Psychology, Univ. of Nottingham, 1973–90; Partner, Network Associates Strategy Consultants, 1985–90. Hon. Prof. in Alternative Dispute Resolution, Univ. of Birmingham, 1994–2001. Mem., Panel of Independent Mediators and Arbitrators, ACAS, 1980–. Member: Educn. Cttee, Bar Assoc. for Commerce, Finance and Industry, 1987–90; Law Soc., Specialisation Cttee, 1989–92. FRSA 1993. Mem. editl cttee, various jls. *Publications:* (ed jtly) Learning Lawyers' Skills, 1989; Lawyers in Business and the Law Business, 1989; (ed) A Handbook of Dispute Resolution, 1991; (jtly) Commercial Dispute Resolution, 1995, 2nd edn as The ADR Practice Guide, 2000; (with E. Carroll) International Mediation: the art of business diplomacy, 2000. *Recreation:* film, swimming, ski-ing, writing. *Address:* Centre for Effective Dispute Resolution, 95 Gresham Street, EC2V 7NA. *T:* (020) 7600 0500.

MACKIE, Lily Edna Minerva, (Mrs John Betts), OBE 1986; Head Mistress, City of London School for Girls, 1972–86; *b* 14 April 1926; *d* of late Robert Wood Mackie and late Lilian Amelia Mackie (*née* Dennis); *m* 1985, John Betts (*d* 1992). *Educ:* Plaistow Grammar Sch.; University Coll., London (BA); Lycée de Jeunes Filles, Limoges; Université de Poitiers. Asst Mistress: Ilford County High Sch. for Girls, 1950–59; City of London Sch. for Girls, 1960–64; Head Mistress: Wimbledon County Sch., 1964–69; Ricards Lodge High Sch., Wimbledon, 1969–72. *Recreations:* theatre, music, gardening, travel. *Address:* Cotswold, 59–61 Upper Tooting Park, SW17 7SU.

MACKIE, Neil, CBE 1996; FRSE; international concert tenor; Professor of Singing, since 1985, and Head of Vocal Studies, since 1994, Royal College of Music; *b* 11 Dec. 1946; *yr s* of late William Fraser Mackie and Sheila Roberta (*née* Taylor); *m* 1973, Kathleen Mary Livingstone, soprano; two *d*. *Educ:* Aberdeen Grammar Sch.; Royal Scottish Acad. of Music and Drama (DipMusEd, DipRSAMD; FRSAMD 1992); Royal Coll. of Music (Foundn Scholar 1970; ARCM Hons; FRCM 1996). London recital début, Wigmore Hall, 1972; London concert début with English Chamber Orch., 1973; world premières include works by Peter Maxwell Davies, Britten, Henze and Kenneth Leighton; numerous recordings. FRSA. Hon DMus Univ. of Aberdeen, 1993. CStJ 1996. *Recreations:* reading, charity work, occasional gardening. *Address:* Royal College of Music, Prince Consort Road, SW7 2BS. *T:* (020) 7591 4343, *Fax:* (020) 7589 7740; 70 Broadwood Avenue, Ruislip, Middx HA4 7XR. *T:* (01895) 632115, *Fax:* (01895) 625765; *e-mail:* neil@mackies.freeserve.co.uk. *Club:* Athenæum.

McKIE, Peter Halliday, CBE 1995; CChem, FRSC, FIQA; Chairman: PHM Associates, since 1996; QUBIS Ltd, since 1998; *b* 20 March 1935; *s* of Harold and Winifred McKie; *m* 1959, Jennifer Anne Parkes; three *s* one *d*. *Educ:* Bangor Grammar Sch.; Queen's Univ., Belfast (BSc Chem.; Hon. DSc 1993). CChem, FRSC 1988; FIQA 1987. Shift Supervisor, Courtaulds Ltd, 1956–59; Supervisor, Du Pont Mfg, Londonderry, 1959–77; Manager, Du Pont Waynesbro Orlon Plant, USA, 1977–79; Asst Works Dir, Du Pont, Londonderry, 1979–81; Man. Dir, Du Pont Scandinavia and Du Pont Finland, 1981–84; Prodn Manager, Du Pont Europe, 1984–87; Chm., Du Pont (UK) Ltd, 1987–96; Manager, Du Pont Belle Plant, W Virginia, USA, 1995–96. Chm., Industrial Res. & Technol. Unit, Dept. of Econ. Develt, NI, 1994–2001. Vis. Prof., Dept of Engrg, QUB, 1991–. FInstD 1987. *Recreations:* photography, sport, classic cars and motor cycles. *Address:* 3 The Rookery, Killinchy, Co. Down BT23 6SY.

MacKIE, Prof. Rona McLeod, (Lady Black), CBE 1999; MD; FRCP, FRCPath; FRSE; Professor of Dermatology, University of Glasgow, since 1978; *b* Dundee, 22 May 1940; *d* of late Prof. (James) Norman Davidson, CBE, FRS and Morag McLeod, PhD; *m* 1st, 1962, Euan Wallace MacKie (marr. diss. 1992); one *s* one *d*; 2nd, 1994, Sir James Whyte Black, *qv*. *Educ:* Channing Sch., London; Laurel Bank Sch., Glasgow; Univ. of Glasgow (MB ChB 1963; MD with commendation 1970; DSc 1994). FRCPath 1984; FRCP 1985. Junior hosp. posts, Glasgow, 1964–70; Lectr in Dermatology, Glasgow Univ., 1971–72; Consultant Dermatologist, Greater Glasgow Health Bd, 1972–78. Pres., British Assoc. of Dermatologists, 1994–95 (Sir Archibald Gray Medallion, 1999); FRSE 1983 (Meeting Sec., 1994–97). *Publications:* textbooks and contribs to learned jls in field of skin cancer, particularly malignant melanoma. *Recreations:* family, opera, golf, gardening. *Address:* Department of Dermatology, Robertson Building, The University, Glasgow G12 8QQ. *Club:* Glasgow Art.

McKIERNAN, Most Rev. Francis J., DD; Bishop of Kilmore, (RC), 1972–98; *b* 3 Feb. 1926; *s* of Joseph McKiernan and Ellen McTague. *Educ:* Aughawillan National School; St Patrick's Coll., Cavan; University College, Dublin; St Patrick's Coll., Maynooth. BA, BD, HDE. St Malachy's Coll., Belfast, 1951–52; St Patrick's Coll., Cavan, 1952–53; University Coll., Dublin, 1953–54; St Patrick's Coll., Cavan, 1954–62; Pres., St Felim's Coll., Ballinamore, Co. Leitrim, 1962–72. Editor of Breifne (Journal of Breifne Historical Society), 1958–72. *Address:* 5 Brookside, Cavan, Ireland. *T:* (49) 4361804.

MACKILLIGIN, David Patrick Robert, CMG 1994; HM Diplomatic Service, retired; Governor, British Virgin Islands, 1995–98; *b* 29 June 1939; *s* of R. S. Mackilligin, CMG, OBE, MC and Patricia (*née* Waldegrave); *m* 1976, Gillian Margaret Zuill Walker; two *d*. *Educ:* St Mary's Coll., Winchester; Pembroke Coll., Oxford (2nd Cl. Hons PPE). Asst Principal, CRO, 1961–62; Third, later Second Sec., Pakistan, 1962–66; Asst Private Sec. to Sec. of State for Commonwealth Relations, 1966–68; Private Sec. to Minister Without Portfolio, 1968–69; Dep. Comr, Anguilla, 1969–71 (Actg Comr, July-Aug. 1970); First Sec., Ghana, 1971–73; First Sec., Head of Chancery and Consul, Cambodia, 1973–75 (Chargé d'Affaires at various times); FCO, 1975–80 (Asst Head of W African Dept, 1978–80); Counsellor (Commercial and Aid), Indonesia, 1980–85; NATO Defence Coll., Rome, 1985–86; Counsellor (Economic and Commercial), and Dir of Trade Promotion, Canberra, 1986–90; High Comr, Belize, 1991–95. *Recreations:* walking and swimming in remote places, ruins, second-hand bookshops, theatre, literature. *Address:* c/o Foreign and Commonwealth Office, King Charles Street, SW1A 2AH. *Clubs:* Oxford and Cambridge, Reform, Royal Commonwealth Society.

McKILLOP, Prof. James Hugh, FRCP, FRCR, FMedSci; Muirhead Professor of Medicine, since 1989, and Associate Dean for Medical Education, since 2000, University of Glasgow; *b* 20 June 1948; *s* of Patrick McKillop and Helen Theresa McKillop; *m* 1972, Caroline Annis Oakley; two *d*. *Educ:* St Aloysius' Coll.; Univ. of Glasgow (BSc, MB ChB; PhD 1979. FRCPGlas 1986; FRCPE 1990; FRCP 1992; FRCR 1994. University of Glasgow: Lectr in Medicine, 1975–82; Sen. Lectr in Medicine, 1982–89; Harkness Fellow, Stanford Univ., California, 1979–80. Chairman: Intercollegiate Standing Cttee on Nuclear Medicine, 1995–99; Admin of Radioactive Substances Adv. Cttee, DoH, 1996–. Pres., British Nuclear Medicine Soc., 1990–92; Congress Pres., Eur. Assoc. of Nuclear Medicine, 1997; Mem., Exec. Cttee, Assoc. of Physicians of UK and Ire., 2000–. *Publications:* (with D. L. Citrin) Atlas of Technetium Bone Scans, 1978; (with A. G. Chalmers and P. J. Robinson) Imaging in Clinical Practice, 1988; (with I. Fogelman) Clinicians' Guide to Nuclear Medicine: benign and malignant bone disease, 1991; 250 papers mainly on nuclear medicine and cardiology. *Recreations:* opera (esp. Verdi), reading fiction, soccer. *Address:* University Department of Medicine, Royal Infirmary, Glasgow G31 2ER. *T:* (0141) 211 4675. *Club:* Royal Society of Medicine.

McKILLOP, Murdoch Lang, CA; a Senior Partner, Global Corporate Finance, Arthur Andersen; *b* 30 Oct. 1947; *s* of Graham Lang McKillop and Margaret Morris (*née* Stark); *m* 1972, Elizabeth Leith; two *d*. *Educ:* Kelvinside Acad., Glasgow; Univ. of Strathclyde (BA Hons 1971). CA 1975; FSPI 1996. Joined Arthur Andersen, Glasgow, as grad. trainee, 1971; Partner, 1984–; Jt Administrator, Maxwell Private Gp, 1991–; Joint Administrative Receiver: Leyland Daf Ltd, 1993; Ferranti Internat. plc, 1994, and others; Worldwide Head, Corporate Recovery and Turnaround, Arthur Andersen, 1996–98. Pres., Soc. of Practitioners of Insolvency, 1998–99; Jun. Vice-Pres., ICAS, 2001–Apr. 2002. *Recreation:* sailing. *Address:* 415 Spice Quay, Butlers Wharf, 32 Shad Thames, SE1 2YL. *Club:* Royal Highland Yacht (Oban).

McKILLOP, Dr Thomas Fulton Wilson; Director, since 1996, Chief Executive, since 1999, AstraZeneca (formerly Zeneca Group) PLC; *b* 19 March 1943; *s* of Hugh McKillop and Annie (*née* Wilson); *m* 1966, Elizabeth Kettle; one *s* two *d*. *Educ:* Irvine Royal Acad.; Univ. of Glasgow (BSc 1st Cl. Hons; PhD Chem. 1968); Centre de Mécanique Ondulatoire Appliquée, Paris. Res. scientist, ICI Corporate Lab., 1969–75; ICI Pharmaceuticals: Hd, Natural Products Res., 1975–78; Res. Dir, France, 1978–80; Chemistry Manager, 1980–84; Gen. Manager, Res., 1984–85, Develt, 1985–89; Technical Dir, 1989–94; CEO, Zeneca Pharmaceuticals, 1994–99. Non-executive Director: Amersham Internat. PLC, 1992–97; Nycomed Amersham PLC, 1997–2000; Lloyds TSB Gp PLC, 1999–. Pro-Chancellor and Mem. Gen. Council, Univ. of Leicester, 1998–. MRI; MRSC; MACS; Mem., Soc. for Drug Res. Trustee, Darwin Trust of Edinburgh, 1995–. Hon. LLD Manchester, 1999; Hon. DSc: Glasgow, 2000; Leicester, 2000; Huddersfield, 2000. *Recreations:* music, sport, reading, walking, carpentry. *Address:* c/o AstraZeneca PLC, 15 Stanhope Gate, W1K 1LN. *T:* (020) 7304 5000. *Club:* Wilmslow Golf.

MACKINLAY, Andrew Stuart; MP (Lab) Thurrock, since 1992; *b* 24 April 1949; *s* of Danny Mackinlay and Monica (*née* Beanes); *m* 1972, Ruth Segar; two *s* one *d*. *Educ:* Salesian Coll., Chertsey. ACIS; DMA. A clerk, Surrey CC, 1965–75; Nalgo official, 1975–92. An Opposition Whip, 1992–93; Member: Transport Select Cttee, 1992–97; Foreign Affairs Select Cttee, 1997–; Chm., All-Party Poland Gp, 1997– (Sec., 1992–97). A Vice Pres., Assoc. of Dist Councils. *Recreations:* studying battlefields of World War I in France and Belgium, Non-league football. *Address:* House of Commons, SW1A 0AA. *T:* (020) 7219 3000. *Club:* Chadwell Working Men's.

MACKINLAY, Jack Lindsay; Chairman, Bradford & Bingley plc (formerly Bradford & Bingley Building Society), since 1995 (Director, since 1990); *b* 24 Jan. 1936; *m* 1961, Catherine Elizabeth Houston; one *s* one *d*. FCA, FCMA. Rowntree plc, 1964–89 (Dir, 1973–89); Dir, Argos, 1990–97; Chm., RPC Gp, 1992–2000. *Recreations:* golf, music. *Address:* Bradford & Bingley plc, PO Box 88, Crossflatts, Bingley, W Yorks BD16 2UA. *T:* (01274) 555555.

McKINLAY, Peter, CBE 1998; Chairman, Wise Group, since 1998; *b* 29 Dec. 1939; *s* of late Peter McKinlay and of Mary Clegg (*née* Hamill); *m* 1963, Anne Rogerson Aitken Thomson; two *s* one *d*. *Educ:* Univ. of Glasgow (MA Hons). GPO HQ, Edinburgh, 1963–67; Scottish Office, 1967–91: Private Sec. to Minister of State, 1974–75; Director, Scottish Prison Service, 1988–91; Chief Executive, Scottish Homes, 1991–99. Nat. Exec., First Div. Assoc., 1977–80. Non-exec. Dir, D. S. Crawford Ltd, 1984–86; Chm., Bute Beyond 2000 (formerly Bute Partnership), 1993–98; Mem. Bd, Cairngorms Partnership, 1998–99. Dir, Common Purpose, 1993–97. FRSA 1998. Hon. DBA Napier, 1999. *Recreations:* family, friends, garden, TV, reading, food, drink. *Address:* Wise Group, 72 Charlotte Street, Glasgow G1 5DW. *Club:* Machrihanish Golf.

McKINLAY, Robert Murray, CBE 1993; FREng, FRAeS; President, Bristol Chamber of Commerce and Industry, 1994–97; *b* 12 Jan. 1934; *s* of Robert Graham McKinlay and Mary Murray; *m* 1957, Ellen Aikman Stewart; two *s*. *Educ:* Vale of Leven Acad.; Royal Tech. Coll., Glasgow (BSc Hons, ARTC). Flight testing and project engineering, Bristol Helicopters and Westlands, 1956–66; British Aircraft Corporation, 1966–79: Systems Develt Manager; Designer in charge; Asst Chief Engr; Asst Dir, Flight Test; Concorde Design Dir; British Aerospace, 1979–94: Dir, Airbus; Gp Dir, Man. Dir, Airbus Div.; Man. Dir, Commercial Aircraft; Chm., Airbus, 1991–94. Non-executive Director: Prematec, 2000–; B. F. Goodrich, Aerospace, Europe, 1998–. Vis. Prof., Dept Aerospace Engrg, Glasgow Univ., 1994–. Chm. of Govs, Colston's Girls' Sch., 1996–. FREng (FEng 1992). Hon. DTech Bristol, 1991; Hon. DEng Glasgow, 2001. British Gold Medal, RAeS, 1995. *Recreations:* sailing, golf, piano, woodworking. *Address:* 43 Glenavon Park, Bristol BS9 1RW. *T:* (0117) 968 6253. *Club:* Society of Merchant Venturers (Bristol).

McKINLEY, Air Vice-Marshal David Cecil, CB 1966; CBE 1957; DFC 1940; AFC 1944, Bar 1945; RAF; *b* 18 Sept. 1913; *s* of David McKinley, Civil Engineer, and May McKinley (*née* Ward); *m* 1940, Brenda Alice (*née* Ridgway); three *s*. *Educ:* Bishop Foy Sch., Waterford; Trinity Coll., Dublin. Radio Engineering, Ferranti Ltd, 1935. Entered (regular) Royal Air Force, 1935; served continuously since that date; AOC Malta and Dep. C-in-C (Air), Allied Forces, Mediterranean, 1963–65; SASO, Transport Command, 1966, Air Support Command, 1967–68; retired 1968. Freeman, The Guild of Air Pilots and Air Navigators, 1959. FIN 1949. *Recreations:* sailing, fishing, water ski-ing, gardening. *Address:* 4 Courtil Lubin, Alderney, Channel Islands. *T:* (01481) 822497; HSBC, Alderney, CI. *Club:* Royal Air Force.

McKINLEY, John Key; Chairman and Chief Executive Officer, Texaco Inc., 1980–86 (President, 1971–83), retired; *b* Tuscaloosa, Ala, 24 March 1920; *s* of Virgil Parks McKinley and Mary Emma (*née* Key); *m* 1946, Helen Grace Heare; two *s*. *Educ:* Univ. of Alabama (BS Chem. Engrg, 1940; MS Organic Chemistry, 1941); Harvard Univ. (Graduate, Advanced Management Program, 1962). Served War, AUS, Eur. Theatre of Ops, 1941–45 (Major; Bronze Star). Texaco Inc., 1941–86: Asst Dir of Res., Beacon, NY, 1957–59; Asst to the Vice-Pres., 1959–60; Manager of Commercial Develt Processes, 1960; Gen. Man., Worldwide Petrochemicals, NYC, 1960–67, Vice-Pres., Petrochem. Dept, 1967–71 (also Vice-Pres. i/c Supply and Distribution); Sen. Vice-Pres., Worldwide Refining, Petrochems, Supply and Distbn, 1971, Pres. and Dir, 1971–83; Director: Texaco Inc., 1971–92; Merck & Co., Inc., 1982–90; Manufacturers Hanover Corp., 1980–90; Hanover Trust Co., 1980–90; Martin Marietta, 1985–90; Apollo Computer, 1987–89; Burlington Industries Inc., 1977–87; Federated Dept Stores, Inc., 1990–. Hon. Dir, Amer. Petroleum Inst. Man. Dir, Met. Opera Assoc., 1980–; National Chm., Met. Opera Centennial Fund, 1980. Dir, Americas Soc. Member: Bd of Overseers, Meml Sloan-Kettering Cancer Center, 1981–91; Brookings Council, 1986; Business Council. Fellow, Amer. Inst. of Chem. Engrs; Sesquicentennial Hon. Prof., Univ. of Alabama; Hon. LLD: Univ. of Alabama, 1972; Troy State Univ., 1974. *Address:* Tuscaloosa, AL, USA; Darien, CT 06820; Buffalo, Wyoming. *Clubs:* Links, Brook (NYC); Wee Burn Country (Darien); Augusta National Golf (Georgia); Blind Brook (Purchase, NY); North River Yacht (Tuscaloosa).

McKINNEY, Her Honour (Sheila Mary) Deirdre; a Circuit Judge, 1981–2001; *b* 20 Oct. 1928; *d* of Patrick Peter McKinney and Mary Edith (*née* Conoley). *Educ:* Convent of the Cross, Boscombe, Bournemouth. Called to the Bar, Lincoln's Inn, 1951; a Recorder of the Crown Court, 1978–81.

McKINNON, Rt Hon. Donald Charles; PC 1992; Secretary-General of the Commonwealth, since 2000; *b* 27 Feb. 1939; *s* of Maj.-Gen. Walter Sneddon McKinnon, CB, CBE; *m* 1st, 1964, Patricia Maude Moore (marr. diss. 1995); three *s* one *d*; 2nd, 1995, Clare de Lore; one *s*. *Educ:* Lincoln Univ., New Zealand. AREINZ. Farm Manager, 1964–72; Farm Management Consultant, 1973–78; Real Estate Agent, 1974–78. MP (Nat. Party) NZ, 1978–99, for Albany, 1978–96; Dep. Leader of the Opposition, 1987–90; Dep. Prime Minister, 1990–96; Leader of the House, 1993–96; Minister: of External Relations, then Foreign Affairs, and Trade, 1990–99; of Pacific Island Affairs, 1991–98; for Disarmament and Arms Control, 1996–99; i/c War Pensions, 1998–99. *Recreations:* enthusiastic jogger and tennis player. *Address:* Commonwealth Secretariat, Marlborough House, Pall Mall, SW1Y 5HX. *T:* (020) 7747 6103.

McKINNON, Sir James, Kt 1992; CA, FCMA; Director General, Office of Gas Supply, 1986–93; *b* 1929. *Educ:* Camphill School. CA 1952, FCMA 1956. Company Secretary, Macfarlane Lang & Co. Ltd, Glasgow, 1955–65; Business Consultant, McLintock, Moores & Murray, Glasgow, 1965–67; Finance Director, Imperial Group plc, London, 1967–86. Chm., Ionica, 1993–98. Pres., Inst. of Chartered Accountants of Scotland, 1985–86. *Publications:* papers to learned jls and articles in Accountants' magazine. *Recreation:* ski-ing.

McKINNON, Prof. Kenneth Richard, AO 1995; FACE; Chairman: McKinnon Walker Pty Ltd, since 1995; IMB Pty Ltd, since 2000; Chairman, Australian Press Council, since 2000; *b* 23 Feb. 1931; *s* of Charles and Grace McKinnon; *m* 1st, 1956 (marr. diss.); one *s*; 2nd, 1981, Suzanne H., *d* of W. Milligan. *Educ:* Univ. of Adelaide; Univ. of Queensland (BA; BEd); Harvard Univ. (EdD). FACE 1972. Teacher, headmaster and administrator, 1957–65; Dir of Educn, Papua New Guinea, 1966–73; Chm., Australian Schs Commn, 1973–81; Vice-Chancellor, 1981–95, and Prof. Emeritus, Univ. of Wollongong; Vice-Chancellor, James Cook Univ. of N Qld, 1997. Chairman: Bd of Educn, Vic, 1982–85; Australian Nat. Commn for UNESCO, 1984–88; Illawara Technology Corp., 1983–; Marine Sci. and Technol. Review, 1988; Nuclear Res. Reactor Review, 1993; Reviewer, Marine Scis Orgns, 1993. Pres., AVCC, 1991–92. Member: Australia Council, 1974–77 (Dep. Chm., 1976–77); Primary Industries and Energy Res. Council, 1991–92; Prime Minister's Science Council, 1991–92. Consultant in the Arts, Aust. Govt, 1981. Dir, Coll. of Law, 1993–. Hon. DLitt: Wollongong, 1994; Deakin, 1994; NSW, 1995; DUniv James Cook, 1998. *Publications:* Realistic Educational Planning, 1973; Oceans of Wealth, 1988; Benchmarking in Universities, 2000; articles in jls and papers. *Recreations:* swimming, theatre, music, reading. *Address:* 14 Norfolk House, 1 Sutherland Crescent, Darling Point, NSW 2027, Australia. *T:* (2) 93623427, *Fax:* (2) 93632551. *Club:* Commonwealth (Canberra, Australia).

MACKINNON, Neil Joseph; Floating Sheriff, at Edinburgh, since 2000; *b* 24 Jan. 1956; *s* of late Donald Patrick Mackinnon and Catriona Traese Mackinnon (*née* Sinclair); *m* 1990, Anne Helen Gavagan; one *d*. *Educ:* St Aloysius' Coll., Glasgow; Univ. of Glasgow (LLB Hons 1978). Admitted solicitor, Scotland, 1980; Advocate, Scots Bar, 1984. Mem., Rules Council, Court of Session, 1997–99. *Recreations:* Scottish Gaelic literature, travel, hill-walking, classical archaeology. *Address:* 7 Middleby Street, Edinburgh EH9 1TD. *T:* (0131) 662 4905. *Club:* Broomieknowe Golf.

MACKINNON, Dame Patricia; *see* Mackinnon, Dame U. P.

McKINNON, Hon. Sir Stuart (Neil), Kt 1988; **Hon. Mr Justice McKinnon;** a Judge of the High Court of Justice, Queen's Bench Division, since 1988; *b* 14 Aug. 1938; *s* of His Honour Neil Nairn McKinnon, QC; *m* 1966, Rev. Helena Jacoba Sara (*née* van Hoorn) (marr. diss. 1999); two *d. Educ:* King's Coll. Sch., Wimbledon; Council of Legal Educn; Trinity Hall, Cambridge (BA, LLB 1963; MA 1967). Called to the Bar, Lincoln's Inn, 1960, Bencher, 1987; Junior at the Common Law Bar, 1964–80; QC 1980; a Recorder, 1985–88. Chm., Lord Chancellor's Mddx Adv. Cttee on JPs, 1990–97. Pres., Cambridge Univ. Law Soc., 1962–63. *Recreation:* golf. *Address:* Royal Courts of Justice, Strand, WC2A 2LL. *Club:* Addington Golf.
See also W. N. McKinnon.

MACKINNON, Dame (Una) Patricia, DBE 1977 (CBE 1972); *b* Brisbane, 24 July 1911; *d* of Ernest T. and Pauline Bell; *m* 1936, Alistair Scobie Mackinnon; one *s* one *d. Educ:* Glennie School and St Margaret's School, Queensland. Member Cttee of Management, Royal Children's Hospital, Melbourne, 1948–79; Vice-President, 1958; President, 1965–79; Chm., Research Bd, 1967–85. *Recreations:* gardening, reading history and biographies. *Address:* 5 Ross Street, Toorak, Vic 3142, Australia. *Club:* Alexandra (Melbourne).

McKINNON, Warwick Nairn; His Honour Judge Warwick McKinnon; a Circuit Judge, since 1998; *b* 11 Nov. 1947; *s* of His Honour Neil McKinnon, QC; *m* 1978, Nichola Juliet Lloyd; one *s* one *d. Educ:* King's Coll. Sch., Wimbledon; Christ's Coll., Cambridge (MA). Called to the Bar, Lincoln's Inn, 1970; in practice on SE Circuit; Asst Recorder, 1991–95; Recorder, 1995–98. Chm., Essex Criminal Justice Strategy Cttee, 1999–2001. *Recreations:* music, opera, travel, gardening, cricket. *Address:* Queen Elizabeth Building, Temple, EC4Y 9BS. *T:* (020) 7583 5766.
See also Hon. Sir S. N. McKinnon.

MACKINTOSH, family name of **Viscount Mackintosh of Halifax**.

MACKINTOSH OF HALIFAX, 3rd Viscount *cr* 1957; **John Clive Mackintosh;** Bt 1935; Baron 1948; FCA; Partner, PricewaterhouseCoopers (formerly Price Waterhouse), since 1992; *b* 9 Sept. 1958; *s* of 2nd Viscount Mackintosh of Halifax, OBE, BEM; *S* father, 1980; *m* 1st, 1982, Elizabeth Lakin (marr. diss. 1993); two *s*; 2nd, 1995, Claire Jane, *y d* of Stanislaw Nowak; one *d. Educ:* The Leys School, Cambridge; Oriel College, Oxford (MA in PPE). FCA 1995. President, Oxford Univ. Conservative Assoc., 1979. Chartered accountant. *Recreations:* cricket, bridge, golf. *Heir:* *s* Hon. Thomas Harold George Mackintosh, *b* 8 Feb. 1985. *Address:* (office) No 1 London Bridge, SE1 9QL. *Clubs:* MCC, Royal Automobile, Coningsby.

MACKINTOSH, Sir Cameron (Anthony), Kt 1996; producer of musicals; Chairman, Cameron Mackintosh Ltd, since 1981; Director, Delfont/Mackintosh, since 1991; *b* 17 Oct. 1946; *s* of late Ian Mackintosh and of Diana Mackintosh. *Educ:* Prior Park Coll., Bath. Hon. Fellow, St Catherine's Coll., Oxford, 1990. Decided to be producer of musical stage shows at age 8, after seeing Slade's Salad Days; spent brief period at Central Sch. of Speech and Drama; stage hand at Theatre Royal, Drury Lane; later Asst Stage Manager; worked with Emile Littler, 1966, with Robin Alexander, 1967; produced first musical, 1969. Co-owner, with First Leisure, of Prince Edward, Prince of Wales and Strand Theatres, 1991. *London productions:* Little Women, 1967; Anything Goes, 1969; Trelawney, 1972; The Card, 1973; Winnie the Pooh, 1974; Owl and Pussycat Went to See, 1975; Godspell, 1975; Side by Side by Sondheim, 1976; Oliver!, 1977, new prodn 1994; Diary of a Madam, 1977; After Shave, 1977; Gingerbread Man, 1978; Out on a Limb, 1978; My Fair Lady, 1979; Oklahoma!, 1980; Tomfoolery, 1980; Jeeves Takes Charge, 1981; Cats, 1981; Song and Dance, 1982; Blondel, 1983; Little Shop of Horrors, 1983; Abbacadabra, 1983; The Boyfriend, 1984; Les Misérables, 1985; Café Puccini, 1985; Phantom of the Opera, 1986; Follies, 1987; Miss Saigon, 1989; Just So, 1990; Five Guys Named Moe, 1991; Moby Dick, 1992; Putting It Together, 1992; Carousel, 1993; Oliver!, 1994; Martin Guerre, 1996; The Fix, 1997; The Witches of Eastwick, 2000; My Fair Lady, 2001. Observer Award for Outstanding Achievement in Memory of Kenneth Tynan, Olivier Awards, 1991. *Recreations:* taking holidays, cooking. *Address:* Cameron Mackintosh Ltd, 1 Bedford Square, WC1B 3RA. *T:* (020) 7637 8866. *Club:* Groucho.

MACKINTOSH, Catherine Anne, (Mrs C. D. Peel), FRCM, FRSAMD; violinist; *b* 6 May 1947; *d* of late Duncan Robert Mackintosh and Mary Isa Mackintosh; *m* 1973, Charles David Peel; one *s* one *d. Educ:* Cranborne Chase Sch.; Dartington Coll. of Arts; Royal Coll. of Music (ARCM; FRCM 1994). FRSAMD 1998. Prof. of Baroque and Classical Violin and Viola, Royal Coll. of Music, 1977–. Vis. Prof., Early Music, RSAMD, 1989–. Leader, Acad. of Ancient Music, 1973–87; Mem., Julian Bream Consort, 1978–88; Founding Mem., Purcell Quartet, 1984–; Co-Leader, Orch. of Age of Enlightenment, 1987–. *Recreations:* trombone playing, crosswords, eating. *Address:* 15 Ranelagh Road, W5 5RJ.

McKINTOSH, Ian Stanley; His Honour Judge McKintosh; a Circuit Judge, since 1988; *b* 23 April 1938; *s* of late (Herbert) Stanley and of Gertrude McKintosh; *m* 1967, (Alison) Rosemary, *e d* of Kenneth Blayney Large and Margaret Wharton Large; two *s* one *d. Educ:* Leeds Grammar Sch.; Exeter Coll., Oxford (MA). Admitted Solicitor of the Supreme Court, 1966. Served RAF, 1957–59. Articled to Town Clerk, Chester and to Laces & Co., Liverpool, 1962–66; Dept of Solicitor to Metropolitan Police, New Scotland Yard, 1966–69; Partner, Lemon & Co., Swindon, 1969–88; a Dep. Circuit Judge, 1976–81; a Recorder, 1981–88. Mem., Local Gen. and Area Appeals Cttees, SW Legal Aid Area, 1970–89. Mem., Stonham Housing Assoc. (Chm., Swindon Br.). *Recreations:* family, cricket, sailing, rowing, talking. *Address:* The Castle, Exeter EX4 3TH. *Clubs:* MCC, XL.

MACKINTOSH, (John) Malcolm, CMG 1975; HM Diplomatic Service, retired; *b* 25 Dec. 1921; *s* of late James Mackintosh, MD, LLD, FRCP, and Marjorie Mackintosh; *m* 1946, Elena Grafova; one *s* one *d* (and one *s* decd). *Educ:* Mill Hill; Edinburgh Academy; Glasgow Univ. MA (Hons) 1948. Served War, Middle East, Italy and Balkans, 1942–46; Allied Control Commn, Bulgaria, 1945–46. Glasgow Univ., 1946–48. Programme Organiser, BBC Overseas Service, 1948–60; Foreign Office, engaged on research, 1960–68; Asst Sec., Cabinet Office, 1968–87. Sen Fellow in Soviet Studies, IISS, 1989–91; Hon. Sen. Res. Fellow, KCL, 1987–91; Hon. Lectr in Internat. Relns, St Andrews Univ., 1991–97; Hon. Vis. Fellow, SSEES, 1994–. *Publications:* Strategy and Tactics of Soviet Foreign Policy, 1962, 2nd edn 1963; Juggernaut: a history of the Soviet armed forces, 1967. *Recreations:* walking, climbing. *Address:* 21 Ravensdale Avenue, N12 9HP. *T:* (020) 8445 9714. *Clubs:* Garrick, Royal Over-Seas League.

MACKINTOSH, Malcolm; *see* Mackintosh, J. M.

MACKINTOSH, Prof. Nicholas John, DPhil; FRS 1987; Professor of Experimental Psychology, and Professorial Fellow of King's College, University of Cambridge, 1981–Oct. 2002; *b* 9 July 1935; *s* of Dr Ian and Daphne Mackintosh; *m* 1st, 1960, Janet Ann Scott (marr. diss. 1978); one *s* one *d*; 2nd, 1978, Bundy Wilson (marr. diss. 1989); two *s*; 3rd, 1992, Leonora Caroline Brosan, *d* of Dr G. S. Brosan, *qv*; one *s. Educ:* Winchester; Magdalen Coll., Oxford. BA 1960, MA, DPhil 1963. Univ. Lectr, Univ. of Oxford, 1964–67; Res. Fellow, Lincoln Coll., Oxford, 1966–67; Res. Prof., Dalhousie Univ., 1967–73; Prof., Univ. of Sussex, 1973–81. Visiting Professor: Univ. of Pennsylvania, 1965–66; Univ. of Hawaii, 1972–73; Bryn Mawr Coll., 1977. Editor, Qly Jl of Experimental Psychology, 1977–84. *Publications:* (ed with W. K. Honig) Fundamental Issues in Associative Learning, 1969; (with N. S. Sutherland) Mechanisms of Animal Discrimination Learning, 1971; The Psychology of Animal Learning, 1974; Conditioning and Associative Learning, 1983; Animal Learning and Cognition, 1994; Cyril Burt: fraud or framed?, 1995; IQ and Human Intelligence, 1998; papers in psychological journals. *Address:* King's College, Cambridge CB2 1ST. *T:* (01223) 351386.

McKITTERICK, Dr David John, FSA, FRHistS; FBA 1995; Fellow and Librarian, Trinity College, Cambridge, since 1986; *b* 9 Jan. 1948; *s* of Rev. Canon J. H. B. McKitterick and Marjory McKitterick (*née* Quarterman); *m* 1976, Rosamond Deborah Pierce (*see* R. D. McKitterick); one *d. Educ:* King's Coll. Sch., Wimbledon; St John's Coll., Cambridge (Scholar; BA 1969; MA 1973; LittD 1994); University College London (DipLib 1971). Staff, Cambridge Univ. Library, 1969–70, 1971–86; Fellow, Darwin Coll., Cambridge, 1978–86. Lyell Reader in Bibliography, Univ. of Oxford, 2000; Sandars Reader in Bibliography, University of Cambridge, 2001–02. Hon. Curator, Early Printed Books, Fitzwilliam Mus. Chm., Adv. Cttee on Books, Council for Care of Churches; Vice-Pres., 1990–98, Pres., 1998–2000, Bibliog. Soc.; Pres., Cambridge Bibliog. Soc., 1991–. Trustee, Wordsworth Trust. *Publications:* The Library of Sir Thomas Knyvett of Ashwellthorpe 1539–1618, 1978; (ed) Stanley Morison and D. B. Updike: Selected Correspondence, 1979; (ed) Stanley Morison: selected essays on the history of letter forms in manuscript and print, 1981; (with John Dreyfus) A History of the Nonesuch Press, 1981; Four Hundred Years of University Printing and Publishing at Cambridge 1584–1984, 1984; Cambridge University Library: a history: the eighteenth and nineteenth centuries, 1986; A New Specimen Book of Curwen Pattern Papers, 1987; (ed jtly) T. F. Dibdin: *Horae Bibliographicae Cantabrigiensis*, 1988; Wallpapers by Edward Bawden, 1989; (ed) Andrew Perne: quatercentenary studies, 1991; Catalogue of the Pepys Library at Magdalene College, Cambridge, VII: facsimile of Pepys's catalogue, 1991; A History of Cambridge University Press, vol. 1: printing and the book trade in Cambridge 1534–1698, 1992, vol 2: scholarship and commerce 1698–1872, 1998; (ed) The Making of the Wren Library, 1995; contribs to learned jls. *Address:* Trinity College, Cambridge CB2 1TQ. *T:* (01223) 338513. *Clubs:* Roxburghe, Double Crown (President, 1994–95).
See also W. H. McKitterick.

McKITTERICK, Prof. Rosamond Deborah, FRHistS; Professor of Mediaeval History, University of Cambridge, since 1999; Fellow of Newnham College, Cambridge, since 1974; *b* Chesterfield, Derbys, 31 May 1949; *d* of Rev. Canon C. A. Pierce, OBE, MA, BD and Melissa (*née* Heaney); *m* 1976, David John McKitterick, *qv*; one *d. Educ:* Univ. of WA (BA 1st cl. Hons 1970); Univ. of Cambridge (MA 1977; PhD 1976; LittD 1991); Univ. of Munich (Graduate Student). FRHistS 1980; Fellow, European Medieval Acad., 1993. University of Cambridge: Asst Lectr, 1979–85; Lectr, 1985–91; Reader, 1991–97; Prof. of Early Mediaeval European Hist., 1997–99; Newnham College: Dir of Studies in Anglo-Saxon, Norse and Celtic, 1979–93; Vice-Principal, 1996–98. Hugh Balsdon Fellow, British Sch. at Rome, 2001–June 2002. Guest Lectr in univs in Germany, Austria, USA, Australia, Denmark, Eire, France, Netherlands and Norway, 1978–; lecture tours: USA, 1982, 1990, 1994; Germany, 1987; UK; speaker, internat. confs on early medieval studies, Belgium, France, Netherlands, Germany, Italy, USA, UK, Eire and Austria. Corresp. Fellow, Monumenta Germaniae Historica, Germany, 1999. Vice-Pres., RHistS, 1994–98, 2000–. Editor: Cambridge Studies in Medieval Life and Thought; Cambridge Studies in Palaeography and Codicology, 1989–; Corresp. Ed., Early Medieval Europe, 1999– (Editor, 1992–99). *Publications:* The Frankish Church and the Carolingian Reforms 789–895, 1977; The Frankish Kingdoms under the Carolingians 751–987, 1983; The Carolingians and the Written Word, 1989; The Uses of Literacy in early medieval Europe, 1990; (with Lida Lopes Cardozo) Lasting Letters, 1992; Carolingian Culture: emulation and innovation, 1993; Books, Scribes and Learning in the Frankish Kingdoms, Sixth to Ninth Centuries, 1994; (ed and contrib.) The New Cambridge Medieval History II, 700–900, 1995; Frankish Kings and Culture in the Early Middle Ages, 1995; (ed jtly and contrib.) Edward Gibbon and Empire, 1996; (ed and contrib.) The Short Oxford History of Europe: the early middle ages 400–1000, 2001; The Migration of Ideas in the Early Middle Ages, 2002; (ed and contrib.) The Times Atlas of the Medieval World, 2002; articles in many collections of essays and conf. proc. and jls, incl. English Hist. Rev., Library, Studies in Church History, Trans of RHistS, Early Medieval Europe, Francia, Scriptorium; reviews for TLS and English and continental learned jls. *Recreations:* music, fresh air. *Address:* Newnham College, Cambridge CB3 9DF. *T:* (01223) 335700.

McKITTERICK, William Henry; Director of Social Services, City and County of Bristol, since 1995; *b* 21 Sept. 1949; *s* of Rev. Canon J. H. B. McKitterick and M. G. McKitterick (*née* Quarterman); *m* 1972, Jennifer M. Fisher; one *s* one *d. Educ:* King's College Sch.; Hatfield Poly. (BA, CQSW); Bradford Univ. (MA 1982). Social Worker: Leics, 1973–75; Oldham, 1975–78; Social Services Manager: Manchester, 1978–84; Oldham, 1984–89; Wakefield, 1989–93; Head of Service, and Dep. Dir of Social Services, Wakefield, 1993–95. *Recreations:* family, walking, choral singing, books. *Address:* Holly Bank, Grove Orchard, Blagdon, Bristol BS40 7DR. *T:* (home) (01761) 463407; (office) (0117) 903 7860.
See also D. J. McKitterick.

McKITTRICK, Neil Alastair; His Honour Judge McKittrick; a Circuit Judge, since 2001; *b* 1 Jan. 1948; *s* of late Ian James Arthur McKittrick and of Mary Patricia McKittrick (*née* Hobbs); *m* 1975, Jean Armstrong; one *s* one *d. Educ:* King's Sch., Ely; College of Law, Guildford. LLB London. Solicitor, 1972. Articled Clerk and Asst Solicitor, Cecil Godfrey & Son, Nottingham, 1967–73; Prosecuting Solicitor, Notts, 1973–77; Clerk to the Justices, 1977–89 (Darlington 1977, E Herts 1981, N Cambs 1986–89); Stipendiary Magistrate, subseq. Dist Judge (Magistrates' Courts), Middx, 1989–2001; a Recorder, 1996–2001. Member: Council, Justices' Clerks' Soc., 1985–89 (Chm., Professional Purposes Cttee, 1987–89); President's Family Cttee, 1985–89; Justice Cttee on Witnesses, 1986; Domestic Courts Cttee, Magistrates' Assoc., 1988–91; Adv. Gp, Magistrates' Training Courses, 1989–96; Middlesex Probation Cttee, 1990–2001. Editor, Justice of the Peace, 1985–89; Licensing Editor, Justice of the Peace Reports, 1983–; Editor, Jl of Criminal Law, 1990–2000 (Mem., Editl Bd, 1985–2000). *Publications:* (ed jtly) Wilkinson's Road Traffic Offences, 14th edn to 18th edn, 1997; (with Pauline Callow) Blackstone's Handbook for Magistrates, 1997, 2nd edn 2000; papers and articles in learned jls. *Recreations:* visiting churches, racecourses. *Address:* Peterborough Combined Courts Centre, Crown Building, Rivergate, Peterborough PE1 1EJ. *T:* (01733) 349161.

MACKLEY, Ian Warren, CMG 1989; CVO 1999; HM Diplomatic Service, retired; High Commissioner to Ghana, and Ambassador (non-resident) to Togo, 1996–2000; *b* 31 March 1942; *s* of late Harold William Mackley and of Marjorie Rosa Sprawson (*née* Warren); *m* 1st, 1968, Jill Marion (*née* Saunders) (marr. diss. 1988); three *s*; 2nd, 1989, Sarah Anne Churchley; one *s* one *d*. *Educ:* Ardingly College. FO, 1960; Saigon, 1963; Asst Private Sec. to Ministers of State, FCO, 1967; Wellington, 1969; First Sec., 1972; FCO 1973; Head of Inf. Services, New Delhi, 1976; Asst Head, UN Dept, FCO, 1979; seconded to ICI, 1982; Counsellor, Dep. Hd of UK Delegn to Conf. on Confidence- and Security-Building Measures and Disarmament in Europe, Stockholm, 1984–86; Chargé d'Affaires, Kabul, 1987–89; Dep. High Comr, Canberra, 1989–93; Head of Training, FCO, 1993–96. Pres., Kabul Golf and Country Club, Afghanistan, 1987–89. *Recreations:* golf, armchair sport. *Address:* Ridgecoombe, Penton Grafton, Andover, Hants SP11 0RR.

MACKLIN, David Drury, CBE 1989; DL; *b* 1 Sept. 1928; *s* of Laurence Hilary Macklin and Alice Dumergue (*née* Tait); *m* 1955, Janet Smallwood; four *s*. *Educ:* Felsted Sch., Essex; St John's Coll., Cambridge. MA. Articled to Baileys Shaw & Gillett, Solicitors, 1951–54; Assistant Solicitor: Coward Chance & Co., 1954–56; Warwickshire CC, 1956–61; Devon CC, 1961–69; Dep. Clerk, Derbyshire CC, 1969–73; Chief Executive: Lincolnshire CC, 1973–79; Devon CC, 1979–88. Mem., Boundary Commn for England, 1989–99. Chm., Community Council of Devon, 1992–96; Mem., Devon and Cornwall Housing Assoc., 1989–98. Founder Mem., ViRSA Educnl Trust (Chm., 1994–98). DL Devon, 1991. *Recreations:* sailing, music, golf, theatre, walking. *Address:* The Garden Cottage, Station Road, Topsham, Exeter EX3 0DT. *T:* and *Fax:* (01392) 873160.

MACKLIN, Prof. John Joseph, PhD; Principal and Vice-Chancellor, University of Paisley, since 2001; *b* 9 Oct. 1947; *s* of James and Mary Macklin; *m* 1969, Pauline Ruben; one *s* two *d*. *Educ:* Queen's Univ., Belfast (BA 1st cl. French, 1st cl. Spanish; PhD 1976). University of Hull: Lectr in Hispanic Studies, 1973–85; Sen. Lectr, 1985–87; Hd of Dept, 1986–87; University of Leeds: Cowdray Prof. of Spanish, 1988–2001; Dean, Faculty of Arts, 1992–94; Dean for Res. in Humanities, 1994–99; Pro-Vice-Chancellor, 1999–2001. Comdr, Orden de Isabel la Católica (Spain), 1994. *Publications:* Tigre Juan and El curandero de sa honra, 1980; The Modernist Fictions of Ramón Pérez de Ayala, 1988; The Scripted Self, 1995; contrib. to Bull. Hispanic Studies, MLR, Hispanic Rev., Cuadernos Hispanoamericanos, Neophilologus, Anales de la literatura española contemporánea. *Recreations:* walking, cinema, current affairs, art history. *Address:* Office of Principal and Vice-Chancellor, University of Paisley, Paisley PA1 2BE. *T:* (0141) 848 3670.

MACKNEY, Paul Leon John; General Secretary, National Association of Teachers in Further and Higher Education, since 1997; *b* 25 March 1950; *s* of Rev. L. E. Mackney and Margaret Mackney; *m* 1982, Cherry M. Sewell; one *s* one *d*. *Educ:* Exeter Univ. (BA Hons); Birmingham Poly. (RSA DipTEFL); Wolverhampton Poly. (FE CertEd); Warwick Univ. (MA Industrial Relns 1986). Trainee probation officer, 1971–73; General Studies Lectr, Poole Tech. Coll., 1974–75; Hall Green Technical College: ESOL Organiser, 1975–79; Trade Union Studies Tutor, 1980–85; Head, Birmingham Trade Union Studies Centre, S Birmingham Coll., 1986–92; W Midlands Regl Official, NATFHE, 1992–97. Pres., Birmingham TUC, 1980–84 (Life Mem.). *Publication:* Birmingham and the Miners Strike, 1986. *Recreations:* music, guitar, singing. *Address:* National Association of Teachers in Further and Higher Education, 27 Britannia Street, WC1X 9JP. *T:* (020) 7837 3636. *Club:* Union (Birmingham).

MACKRELL, Judith Rosalind; Dance Critic, The Guardian, since 1994; *b* 26 Oct. 1954; *d* of Alec Mackrell and Margaret (*née* Atkinson, later Halsey); *m* 1977, Simon Henson; two *s*. *Educ:* York Univ. (BA 1st Cl. Hons Eng. and Philosophy); Oxford Univ. Part-time Lectr in English and Dance at various estabts incl. Oxford Univ., Oxford Poly. and Roehampton Inst., 1981–86; Dance Critic, Independent, 1986–94. Free-lance dance writer and arts broadcaster, 1986–. Hon. Fellow, Laban Centre for Dance, 1996. *Publications:* Out of Line, 1994; Reading Dance, 1997; (with Darcey Bussell) Life in Dance, 1998; (ed with Debra Craine) The Oxford Dictionary of Dance, 2000. *Recreations:* travel, food, music, reading, my family. *Address:* 73 Greenwood Road, E8 1NT. *T:* (020) 7249 5553.

MACKRELL, Keith Ashley Victor; Deputy Chairman, BG plc, since 2000; Chairman, Enterprise LSE, since 1992; *b* 20 Oct. 1932; *s* of late Henry George Mackrell and Emily Winifred Mackrell (*née* Elcock); *m* 1960, June Yvonne Mendoza, *qv*; one *s* three *d*. *Educ:* Peter Symonds Sch.; London School of Economics (Harold Laski Schol.; BSc Econs 1953; Hon. Fellow, 1999). Dir, Shell International, 1976–91, Regl Co-ordinator, East and Australasia, 1979–91. Non-executive Director: Standard Chartered Bank, 1991–; Regalian Properties, 1991–; Rexam (formerly Bowater) plc, 1991–98; Fairey Gp plc, 1993–99; BG plc, 1994–2000; Dresdner Emerging Markets Investment Trust, 1998–; Govett Asian Recovery Trust, 1998–; Net Profit Publications, 1998–. Gov., LSE, 1991–. FInstD 1976; CIMgt (CBIM 1978). Hon. LLD Nat. Univ. of Singapore, 1991. *Recreations:* tennis, squash, theatre, reading. *Address:* c/o BG plc, Eagle House, 108–110 Jermyn Street, SW1Y 6RH. *T:* (020) 7707 4858. *Clubs:* Hurlingham, Wimbledon.

MACKSEY, Kenneth John, MC 1944; freelance author, since 1968, and publisher, since 1982; *b* 1 July 1923; *s* of Henry George Macksey and Alice Lilian (*née* Nightingall); *m* 1946, Catherine Angela Joan Little; one *s* one *d*. *Educ:* Goudhurst Sch.; Sandhurst; Army Staff Coll., Camberley. Served War, RAC: trooper, 1941–44; commnd 141st Regt RAC (The Buffs), 1944; Western Europe, 1944–45; Royal Tank Regt, 1946; served: India, 1947; Korea, 1950; Germany, 1957 and 1960–62; Singapore, 1958–60; retd, 1968. Dep. Editor, Purnell's History of the Second World War, and History of the First World War, 1968–70. Consultant to Canadian Armed Forces, 1981–91; Mil. Consultant, Discovery Channel, 1993. Town Councillor, 1972–83. *Publications:* To the Green Fields Beyond, 1965 (2nd edn 1977); The Shadow of Vimy Ridge, 1965; Armoured Crusader: the biography of Major-General Sir Percy Hobart, 1967; Afrika Korps, 1968 (4th edn 1976); Panzer Division, 1968 (4th edn 1976); Crucible of Power, 1969; Tank, 1970 (3rd edn 1975); Tank Force, 1970; Beda Fomm, 1971; Tank Warfare, 1971; Vimy Ridge, 1972; Guinness Book of Tank Facts and Feats, 1972 (3rd edn 1980); The Guinness History of Land Warfare, 1973 (2nd edn 1976); Battle, 1974; The Partisans of Europe, 1975; (jtly) The Guinness History of Sea Warfare, 1975; Guderian, Panzer General, 1975 (3rd edn 1992); (with Joan Macksey) The Guinness Guide to Feminine Achievements, 1975; (jtly) The Guinness History of Air Warfare, 1976; The Guinness Book of 1952, 1977; The Guinness Book of 1953, 1978; The Guinness Book of 1954, 1978; Kesselring: the making of the Luftwaffe, 1978, 2nd edn 1996; Rommel: battles and campaigns, 1979 (2nd edn 1997); The Tanks, vol. 3, 1979; Invasion: the German invasion of England July 1940, 1980 (2nd edn 1990); The Tank Pioneers, 1981; A History of the Royal Armoured Corps, 1914–1975, 1983; Commando Strike, 1985; First Clash, 1985; Technology in War, 1986; Godwin's Saga, 1987; Military Errors of World War II, 1987; Tank versus Tank, 1988 (2nd edn 1991); For Want of a Nail, 1989; (jtly) The Penguin Encyclopedia of Modern Warfare, 1991, 2nd edn 1993; Penguin Encyclopedia of Weapons and Military Technology, 1994; (ed) The Hitler Options, 1995; From Triumph to Disaster, 1996, new edn as Why the Germans Lose at War, 1999; Turning Points (memoirs), 1997; Without Enigma, 2000; contributor to DNB; articles and reviews in RUSI Jl, Army Qly, Brit. Army Rev., and The Tank. *Recreations:* umpiring ladies hockey, listening to music, living in Beaminster. *Address:* Whatley Mill, Beaminster, Dorset DT8 3EN. *T:* (01308) 862321.

McKUEN, Rod; poet, composer, author, performer, columnist, classical composer; *b* Oakland, Calif, 29 April 1933. Has appeared in numerous films, TV, concerts, nightclubs, and with symphony orchestras. Composer: modern classical music; scores for motion pictures and TV. President: Stanyan Records; Discus Records; New Gramophone Soc.; Mr Kelly Prodns; Montcalm Prodns; Stanyan Books; Cheval Books; Biplane Books; Rod McKuen Enterprises; Vice-Pres., Tamarack Books; Dir, Animal Concern; Member, Advisory Board: Fund for Animals; Internat. Educn; Market Theatre, Johannesburg; Member, Board of Directors: National Ballet Theatre; Amer. Dance Ensemble; Amer. Guild of Authors and Composers; Exec. Pres., Amer. Guild of Variety Artists; Member: Amer. Soc. of Composers, Authors and Publishers; Writers' Guild; Amer. Fedn of TV and Radio Artists; Screen Actors' Guild; Equity; Modern Poetry Assoc.; Amer. Guild of Variety Artists; AGAC; Internat. Platform Assoc. Mem., Bd of Governors, National Acad. of Recording Arts and Sciences; Trustee: Univ. of Nebraska; Freedoms Foundn. Nat. spokesperson for Amer. Energy Awareness; Internat. spokesperson for Cttee for Prevention of Child Abuse (also Nat. Bd Mem.). Numerous awards, including: Grand Prix du Disc, Paris, 1966, 1974, 1975 and 1982; Golden Globe Award, 1969; Grammy for best spoken word album, Lonesome Cities, 1969; Entertainer of the Year, 1975; Man of the Year Award, Univ. of Detroit, 1978; awards from San Francisco, LA, Chattanooga, Topeka, Lincoln and Nebraska; Freedoms Foundn Patriot Medal, 1981; Salvation Army Man of the Year, 1982. Over 200 record albums; 41 Gold and Platinum records internationally; nominated Pulitzer Prize in classical music for The City, 1973. *Publications: poetry:* And Autumn Came, 1954; Stanyan Street and Other Sorrows, 1966; Listen to the Warm, 1967; Lonesome Cities, 1968; Twelve Years of Christmas, 1968; In Someone's Shadow, 1969; A Man Alone, 1969; With Love, 1970; Caught in the Quiet, 1970; New Ballads, 1970; Fields of Wonder, 1971; The Carols of Christmas, 1971; And to Each Season, 1972; Pastorale, 1972; Grand Tour, 1972; Come to Me in Silence, 1973; America: an Affirmation, 1974; Seasons in the Sun, 1974; Moment to Moment, 1974; Beyond the Boardwalk, 1975; The Rod McKuen Omnibus, 1975; Alone, 1975; Celebrations of the Heart, 1975; Finding my Father: one man's search for identity (prose), 1976; The Sea Around Me, 1977; Hand in Hand, 1977; Coming Close to the Earth, 1978; We Touch the Sky, 1979; Love's Been Good to Me, 1979; Looking for a Friend, 1980; An Outstretched Hand (prose), 1980; The Power Bright and Shining, 1980; Too Many Midnights, 1981; Rod McKuen's Book of Days, 1981; The Beautiful Strangers, 1981; The Works of Rod McKuen: Vol. 1, Poetry, 1950–82, 1982; Watch for the Wind . . ., 1982; Rod McKuen—1984 Book of Days, 1983; The Sound of Solitude, 1983; Suspension Bridge, 1984; Another Beautiful Day, 1984, vol. 2, 1985; Valentines, 1986; Intervals, 1987; *major classical works:* Symphony No One; Concerto for Guitar and Orchestra; Concerto for Four Harpsichords; Concerto for Cello and Orch.; Concerto for Bassoon and Orch.; Seascapes; Concerto for Piano and Orchestra; Adagio for Harp and Strings; Piano Variations; The Black Eagle (opera); Birch Trees (Concerto for Orch.); various other classical commns; numerous lyrics; *film and television scores:* Joanna, 1968; Travels with Charley, 1968; The Prime of Miss Jean Brodie (Academy Award Nomination), 1969; Me, Natalie, 1969; The Loner, 1969; A Boy Named Charlie Brown (Academy Award Nomination), 1970; Come to your Senses, 1971; Scandalous John, 1971; Wildflowers, 1971; The Borrowers, 1973; Lisa Bright and Dark, 1973; Hello Again, 1974; Emily, 1975; The Unknown War, 1979; Man to Himself, 1980; Portrait of Rod McKuen, 1982; The Beach, 1984. *Address:* PO Box 2783, Los Angeles, CA 90078–2790, USA.

MACKWORTH, Sir Digby (John), 10th Bt *cr* 1776, of The Gnoll, Glamorganshire; pilot, easyJet, since 2000; *b* 2 Nov. 1945; *s* of Sir David Arthur Geoffrey Mackworth, 9th Bt and his 1st wife, Mary Alice, (Molly), (*née* Grylles); *S* father, 1998; *m* 1971, Antoinette Francesca McKenna; one *d*. *Educ:* Wellington Coll. Lieut, Australian Army Aviation Corps, 1966; basic flying trng, 63 course, RAAF, Point Cook; helicopter pilot, 28 Commonwealth Bde, Malaysia; 161 (Indep.) Reconnaissance Flt, Australian Task Force, Viet-Nam. Pilot: Bristow Helicopters, Trinidad, Iran, 1972–77; British Airways Helicopters, Shetland, Aberdeen, China, India, 1977–89; British Airways, Heathrow, 1989–2000. *Recreation:* amateur workshop practice. *Heir: kinsman* Norman Humphrey Mackworth [*b* 1917; *m* 1941, Jane Felicity Thring; two *s* one *d*]. *Address:* Blagrove Cottage, Fox Lane, Boars Hill, Oxford OX1 5DS. *T:* (01865) 735543.

MACKWORTH, Rosalind Jean, CBE 1994; Social Fund Commissioner for Great Britain, 1987–96, and for Northern Ireland, 1987–96; Senior Partner, Mackworth Rowland, Solicitors; *b* 10 Aug. 1928; *d* of Rev. Albert Walters, FRMetS and Alma Walters, sometime Comptroller to Archbishop of Canterbury; *m* 1960, Richard Charles Audley Mackworth, MA, MSc, DIC, CEng; two *d*. *Educ:* twelve small schools, following father's postings; Queen's Univ. Belfast (BA); Girton Coll., Cambridge (MA); Law Soc. professional exams. Joined Gregory Rowcliffe, Solicitors, 1956; set up own practice, 1967; amalgamated practice, Mackworth Rowland, 1982. Mem., VAT Tribunals, 1976–. Chm., Judicial Commn, Euro. Union of Women, 1984–87 (Vice-Chm., British Section, 1986–87). *Recreations:* everything except golf. *Address:* Mackworth Rowland, 3 Zenobia Mansions, Queen's Club Gardens, W14 9TD. *T:* (020) 7385 4996.

McLACHLAN, Dr Andrew David, FRS 1989; Scientific Staff, Medical Research Council Laboratory of Molecular Biology, Cambridge, 1967–2000; Fellow of Trinity College, Cambridge, since 1959; *b* 25 Jan. 1935; *s* of late Donald Harvey McLachlan and Katherine (*née* Harman); *m* 1959, Jennifer Margaret Lief Kerr; three *s*. *Educ:* Winchester Coll. (Schol.); Trinity Coll., Cambridge (BA, MA, PhD, ScD). Res. Fellow, Trinity Coll., 1958; Harkness Fellow, USA, 1959–61; Lectr in Physics, Trinity Coll., 1961–87; Lectr in Chemistry, Cambridge Univ., 1965–67. Visiting Professor: CIT, 1964; Brandeis Univ., 1975; UCLA, 1989. *Publications:* (with A. Carrington) Introduction to Magnetic Resonance, 1967; papers in various jls, including Jl of Molecular Biology, Nature, and Proceedings of the Royal Soc. *Recreations:* walking, music, camping. *Address:* Trinity College, Cambridge CB2 1TQ. *T:* (home) (01223) 361318; *e-mail:* admcl@mrc-lmb.cam.ac.uk.

McLACHLAN, Gordon, CBE 1967; BCom; FCA; Secretary, Nuffield Provincial Hospitals Trust, 1956–86; *b* 12 June 1918; *s* of late Gordon McLachlan and Mary McLachlan (*née* Baird); *m* 1951, Monica Mary Griffin; two *d*. *Educ:* Leith Academy; Edinburgh Univ. Served with RNVR, 1938–46; Gunnery Specialist, 1943–46. Accountant, Edinburgh Corp., 1946–48; Dep. Treas., NW Met. Regional Hosps Bd, 1948–53; Accountant Nuffield Foundn, Nuffield Provincial Hosps Trust, Nat. Corp. for Care of Old People, 1953–56. Asst Dir, Nuffield Foundn, 1955–56. Henry Cohen Lectr, Univ. of Jerusalem, 1969; Parker B. Francis Foundn Distinguished Lectr, Amer. Coll. of Hosp. Admin, 1976; Sir David Bruce Lectr, RAMC, 1982; Rock Carling Fellow, 1989–90. Consultant, American Hospitals Assoc. and American Hospitals Research and Educational Trust, 1964–65; Member Council, American Hospitals Research and Educational Trust, 1965–74 (citation for meritorious service, AHA, 1976); Mem., Inst. of

Medicine, Nat. Acad. of Sciences, Washington DC, 1974–. General Editor, Nuffield Provincial Hospitals Trust publications, 1956–86; Consulting Editor, Health Services Research Journal (US), 1966–74. Hon. FRCGP 1978. Hon. LLD Birmingham, 1977. *Publications:* What Price Quality?, 1990; A History of the Nuffield Provincial Hospitals Trust 1940–90, 1992; editor of many publications on Nuffield Provincial Hospitals Trust list; contrib. to Lancet, Practitioner, Times, Twentieth Century, etc. *Recreations:* reading, watching ballet, theatre, Rugby football. *Address:* 95 Ravenscourt Road, W6 0UJ. *T:* (020) 8748 8211. *Club:* Caledonian.

McLACHLAN, Hon. Ian (Murray), AO 1989; MP (L) Barker, South Australia, 1990–98; Minister for Defence, Australia, 1996–98; *b* 2 Oct. 1936; *s* of I. McLachlan; *m* 1964, Janet Lee; two *s* one *d. Educ:* Collegiate Sch. of St Peter, SA; Jesus Coll., Cambridge. Played cricket for SA, 1961–64. Director: SA Brewing, 1978–90 (Dep. Chm., 1983–90); Elders IXL, 1980–90. Shadow Minister: for Industry and Commerce, 1990–93; for Infrastructure and Nat. Develt, 1993–94; for Envmt and Heritage, 1994–95. Pres., Nat. Farmers' Fedn, 1984–88. *Address:* 5 Fuller Court, Walkerville, Adelaide, SA 5081, Australia.

McLACHLIN, Rt Hon. Beverley; PC 2000; Chief Justice, Supreme Court of Canada, since 2000; *b* Pincher Creek, Alberta, 7 Sept. 1943; *m* 1st, 1967, Roderick McLachlin (*d* 1988); one *s*; 2nd, 1992, Frank E. McArdle. *Educ:* Univ. of Alberta (MA 1968, LLB 1968). Called to the Bar: Alberta, 1969; BC, 1971; practised law: with Wood, Moir, Hyde and Ross, Edmonton, 1969–71; with Thomas, Herdy, Mitchell & Co., Fort St John, BC, 1971–72; with Bull, Housser and Tupper, Vancouver, 1972–75; Lectr, 1974–75, Associate Prof., 1975–78, Prof., 1981, Univ. of BC, 1974–81; Judge: County Court of Vancouver, 1981; Supreme Court of BC, 1981–85; Court of Appeal, BC, 1985–88; Chief Justice, Supreme Court of BC, 1988–89; Judge, Supreme Court of Canada, 1989–2000. Hon. LLD: BC, 1990; Alberta, 1991; Toronto, 1995; York, 1999; Law Soc. of Upper Canada, 2000. *Publications:* contrib. to learned jls. *Address:* Supreme Court of Canada, 301 Wellington Street, Ottawa, ON K1A 0J1, Canada.

MACLAGAN, Michael, CVO 1988; FSA; FRHistS; Richmond Herald of Arms, 1980–89; *b* 14 April 1914; *s* of Sir Eric Robert Dalrymple Maclagan, KCVO, CBE, and Helen Elizabeth (*née* Lascelles); *m* 1st, 1939, Brenda Alexander (marr. diss. 1946); one *s*; 2nd, 1949, Jean Elizabeth Brooksbank Garnett, *d* of late Lt-Col W. B. Garnett, DSO; two *d* (one *s* decd). *Educ:* Winchester Coll.; Christ Church, Oxford (BA 1st Cl. Hons Modern History, MA). FSA 1948; FRHistS 1961; FSG 1970; FHS 1972. Lectr, Christ Church, Oxford, 1937–39; Fellow of Trinity Coll., 1939–81, Emeritus Fellow 1981, Sen. Proctor, 1954–55. 2/Lieut TA, 1938; served war, 1939–46: 16/5 Lancers; sc; Major, GSOII War Office. Slains Pursuivant, 1948–70; Portcullis Pursuivant, 1970–80. Vis. Professor, Univ. of S Carolina, 1974; Fellow of Winchester Coll., 1975–89; Sen. Librarian, Oxford Union, 1960–70; Trustee, Oxford Union, 1970–99. Councillor, Oxford CBC, 1946–74; Sheriff, 1964–65; Lord Mayor of Oxford, 1970–71. Chm., Oxford Dio. Adv. Cttee, 1961–85. Master of Scriveners' Co., 1988–89. OStJ 1952. *Publications:* (ed) Bede: Ecclesiastical History I and II, 1949; Trinity College, 1955, rev. edn 1963; (jtly) The Colour of Heraldry, 1958; (ed) Richard de Bury: Philobiblon, 1960; 'Clemency' Canning, 1962 (Wheatley Gold Medal); City of Constantinople, 1968; (with J. Louda) Lines of Succession, 1981 (trans. French, 1984; 3rd edn 1992); articles in DNB, VCH, etc. *Recreations:* real tennis, wine, walking, travel. *Address:* 20 Northmoor Road, Oxford OX2 6UR. *T:* (01865) 558536; Trinity College, Oxford OX1 3BH. *Clubs:* Cavalry and Guards, Pratt's; Oxford Union (Oxford).

McLAGGAN, Murray Adams; JP; Lord Lieutenant of Mid Glamorgan, since 1990; *b* 29 Sept. 1929; *s* of Sir John Douglas McLaggan, KCVO, FRCS, FRCSE and Elsa Violet Lady McLaggan (*née* Adams), MD, DPH; *m* 1959, Jennifer Ann Nicholl; two *s* one *d. Educ:* Winchester College; New College, Oxford (MA 1st Cl. Hons). Called to the Bar, Lincoln's Inn, 1955; Student and Tutor in Law, Christ Church, Oxford, 1957–66. Member: Parly Boundary Commn for Wales, 1980–97; Regl Adv. Bd, Wales, NRA, 1990–96 (Chm., Regl Flood Defence Cttee, 1990–97); Adv. Cttee for Wales, Environment Agency, 1996–98; former Chm., Forestry Commn Regional Adv. Cttee (Wales). Chm., Nat. Trust Cttee for Wales, 1991–93 (Dep. Chm., 1984–91). High Sheriff Mid Glamorgan, 1978–79, DL 1982; JP Glamorgan, 1968. *Recreations:* bibliophily, dendrology, amateur operatics. *Address:* Merthyr Mawr House, Bridgend CF32 0LR. *T:* (01656) 652038.

McLAREN, family name of **Baron Aberconway.**

McLAREN, (Dame) Anne Laura, (Dr Anne McLaren), DBE 1993; DPhil; FRCOG, FMedSci; FRS 1975; Principal Research Associate, Wellcome/Cancer Research Campaign Institute, since 1992, and Hon. Fellow, King's College, Cambridge, since 1996; *b* 26 April 1927; *d* of 2nd Baron Aberconway; *m* 1952, Donald Michie (marr. diss.); one *s* two *d. Educ:* Univ. of Oxford (MA, DPhil). FRCOG *ad eund* 1986. Post-doctoral research, UCL, 1952–55 and Royal Vet. Coll., London, 1955–59; joined staff of ARC Unit of Animal Genetics at Edinburgh Univ., 1959; Dir, MRC Mammalian Develt Unit, 1974–92; Res. Fellow, King's Coll., Cambridge, 1992–96. Fullerian Prof. of Physiology, Royal Instn, 1990–; Professorial Fellow, Univ. of Melbourne, 1998–. Mem., ARC, 1978–83; Mem., HFEA, 1990–. Vice-Pres., Royal Soc., 1992–96 (Mem. Council, 1985–87; Foreign Sec., 1991–96); Pres., BAAS, 1993–94. Mem., Cttee of Managers, Royal Instn, 1976–81; Chm., Governing Body, Lister Inst. of Preventive Medicine, 1994–; Trustee, Natural Hist. Mus., 1994–. Founder MAE 1988; Founder FMedSci 1998. Hon. Fellow, UCL, 1993. Scientific Medal, Zool Soc. London, 1967; Royal Medal, Royal Soc., 1990. *Publications:* Mammalian Chimaeras, 1976; Germ Cells and Soma, 1980; papers on reproductive biology, embryology, genetics and immunology in sci. jls. *Address:* Wellcome/CRC Institute, Tennis Court Road, Cambridge CB2 1QR; 40 Ainger Road, NW3 3AT.

McLAREN, Clare, (Mrs Andrew McLaren); *see* Tritton, E. C.

McLAREN, Prof. Digby Johns, OC 1987; FRS 1979; FRSC 1968; President, Royal Society of Canada, 1987–90; *b* 11 Dec. 1919; *s* of James McLaren and Louie Kinsey; *m* 1942, Phyllis Matkin; two *s* one *d. Educ:* Sedbergh Sch.; Queens' Coll., Cambridge (BA, MA); Univ. of Michigan (PhD). Served RA (Gunner to Captain), ME and Italy, 1940–46. Field Geologist, Geological Survey of Canada, in Alberta and British Columbia Rocky Mountains, District of Mackenzie, Yukon Territory, Arctic Islands, 1948–80; first Dir, Inst. of Sedimentary and Petroleum Geology, Calgary, Alberta, 1967–73; Dir Gen., Geological Survey of Canada, 1973–80; Prof., Dept of Geology, Univ. of Ottawa, 1981–89; Sen. Science Adviser, Dept of Energy, Mines and Resources, Ottawa, 1981–84. Pres., Commn on Stratigraphy, IUGS, 1972–76; Chm. of Bd, Internat. Geol Correlation Programme, UNESCO-IUGS, 1976–80; IUGS Deleg. to People's Republic of China to advise on participation in international science, 1977. President: Paleontol Soc., 1969; Canadian Soc. Petroleum Geologists, 1971; Geol Soc. of America, 1981; Hon. Mem. and Leopold von Buch Medallist, Geol Soc. of Germany, 1982; Corresp. Mem., Geol Soc. of France, 1975; Foreign Associate, Nat. Acad. of Scis, USA, 1979. For. Mem., Amer. Philosophical Soc., 1994; For. Hon. Fellow, European Union of Geoscis, 1983; Hon. FGS 1989. Hon. DSc: Ottawa, 1980; Carleton, 1993; Waterloo, 1996. Gold Medal (for Pure and Applied Science), Professional Inst. of Public Service of Canada, 1979; Edward Coke Medal, Geol Soc. of London, 1985; Logan Medal, Geol Assoc. of Canada, 1987; Hollis D. Hedberg Award in Energy, Inst. for Study of Earth and Man, 1994. *Publications:* (ed) Resources and World Development (proceedings of 2 Dahlem Workshops), 1987; memoirs, bulletins, papers, geological maps, and scientific contribs to journals on regional geology, paleontology, geological time, correlation, extinctions and global change and resource depletion. *Recreations:* ski-ing, swimming, gardening, music. *Address:* 607–420 Mackay Street, Ottawa, ON K1M 2C4, Canada. *T:* (613) 7423067.

McLAREN, Ian Alban Bryant; QC 1993; a Recorder, since 1996 (an Assistant Recorder, 1992–96); *b* 3 July 1940; *yr s* of Alban McLaren and Doris (*née* Hurst); *m* 1964, Margaret Middleton, BA; two *s* one *d. Educ:* Sandbach Sch., Blackpool Grammar Sch.; Univ. of Nottingham (LLB 1961). Called to the Bar, Gray's Inn, 1962 (Macaskie Schol.); in practice at the Bar, 1962–; Law Tutor, Univ. of Nottingham, 1962–64; Hd of Ropewalk Chambers, 2000–. Pres., Notts Medico-Legal Soc., 1997–98. Fellow, Soc. for Advanced Legal Studies. *Recreations:* gardening, photography. *Address:* 24 The Ropewalk, Nottingham NG1 5EF. *T:* (0115) 947 2581.

McLAREN, Sir Robin (John Taylor), KCMG 1991 (CMG 1982); HM Diplomatic Service, retired; Director: Invesco Asia Trust, since 1995; Fidelity Asian Values, since 1997; Govett Asian Recovery Trust, since 1998; *b* 14 Aug. 1934; *s* of late Robert Taylor McLaren and of Marie Rose McLaren (*née* Simond); *m* 1964, Susan Ellen Hatherly; one *s* two *d. Educ:* Richmond and East Sheen County Grammar Sch. for Boys; Ardingly Coll.; St John's Coll., Cambridge (Schol.; MA). Royal Navy, 1953–55. Entered Foreign Service, 1958; language student, Hong Kong, 1959–60; Third Sec., Peking, 1960–61; FO, 1961–64; Asst Private Sec. to Lord Privy Seal (Mr Edward Heath), 1963–64; Second, later First Sec., Rome, 1964–68; seconded to Hong Kong Govt as Asst Political Adviser, 1968–69; First Sec., FCO, 1970–73; Dep. Head of Western Organisations Dept, 1974–75; Counsellor and Head of Chancery, Copenhagen, 1975–78; Head of Hong Kong and Gen. Dept, 1978–79, of Far Eastern Dept, 1979–81, FCO; Political Advr, Hong Kong, 1981–85; Ambassador to Philippines, 1985–87; Asst Under Sec. of State, FCO, 1987–90; Sen. British Rep., Sino-British Jt Liaison Gp, 1987–89; Dep. Under Sec. of State, FCO, 1990–91; Ambassador to People's Republic of China, 1991–94. Member Council: Ardingly Coll., 1996– (Chm., 1999–); RHBNC, 1997– (Chm., 1999–). *Recreations:* music, China, reading. *Address:* 11 Hillside, Wimbledon, SW19 4NH. *Clubs:* Oxford and Cambridge; Hong Kong (Hong Kong).

MacLAREN, Hon. Roy; PC (Can.) 1983; High Commissioner for Canada in the United Kingdom, 1996–2000; *b* 26 Oct. 1934; *s* of Wilbur MacLaren and Anne (*née* Graham); *m* 1959, Alethea Mitchell MacLaren; two *s* one *d. Educ:* schs in Vancouver, Canada; Univ. of BC (BA); Univ. of Cambridge (MA); Univ. of Harvard; Univ. of Toronto (MDiv). With Canadian Diplomatic Service, in Saigon, Hanoi, Prague, Geneva, NY (UN) and Ottawa, 1957–69; Dir, Public Affairs, Massey Ferguson Ltd, 1969–73; President: Ogilvy & Mather (Canada) Ltd, 1974–76; Canadian Business Media Ltd, 1977–93; Director: Deutsche Bank (Canada), 1984–93; London Life Assurance, 1984–93; Royal LePage Ltd, 1985–93. MP (L) Etobicoke N, 1979–96; Parly Sec., Energy, 1980–82; Minister of: State Finance, 1983; Nat. Revue, 1984; Internat. Trade, 1993–96. Non-executive Director: Standard Life; Brascan; Canadian Tire; Patheon; Slough Estates (Canada). Comr, Commonwealth War Graves Commn, 1996–2000; Trustee, Imperial War Mus., 1996–2000; Dir, Bletchley Park Trust; Mem. Adv. Cttee, Scott Polar Res. Inst., 1998–2000. Mem. Council, IISS; Chairman: Canadian Inst. of Internat. Affairs; Canada-Europe Round Table. Hon. Col, 7th Toronto Regt, Royal Canadian Artillery, 1995–. Hon. DSL Toronto, 1996. *Publications:* Canadians in Russia 1918–1919, 1976; Canadians on the Nile 1882–1898, 1978; Canadians Behind Enemy Lines 1939–1945, 1981; Honourable Mentions, 1986; African Exploits: the diaries of William Stairs 1887–1892, 1997. *Recreations:* cross country walking, ski-ing. *Address:* (office) 425 Russell Hill Road, Toronto, ON M5P 2S4, Canada. *Clubs:* Athenæum, White's, Pratt's; Rideau (Ottawa); Toronto; Royal Canadian Yacht.

McLAREN-THROCKMORTON, Clare; *see* Tritton, E. C.

McLATCHIE, Cameron, CBE 1996 (OBE 1988); Chairman and Chief Executive, British Polythene Industries plc (formerly Scott & Robertson), since 1988; *b* 18 Feb. 1947; *s* of Cameron McLatchie and Maggie McLatchie (*née* Maxwell Taylor); *m* 1973, Leslie Mackie; two *s* one *d. Educ:* Univ. of Glasgow (LLB). Apprentice CA, Whinney, Murray & Co., 1968–70; Admin. Asst, subseq. Prodn Manager, then Prodn Dir, Thos Boag & Co. Ltd, 1971–74; Managing Director: Anaplast Ltd, 1975–83; Scott & Robertson plc, 1983–88. Non-executive Director: Motherwell Bridge Hldgs Ltd, 1993–97; Hiscox Select plc, 1993–98 (Chm.); Royal Bank of Scotland Gp, 1998–. Dep. Chm., Scottish Enterprise, 1997–2000 (Mem. Bd, 1990–95). Member: Adv. Cttee on Business and the Envmt, 1991–93; Sec. of State for Scotland's Adv. Gp on Sustainable Develt, 1994–95; Bd, Scottish Envmtl Protection Agency, 1995–97. DUniv. Paisley 2000. *Recreations:* golf, bridge, gardening. *Address:* British Polythene Industries plc, 96 Port Glasgow Road, Greenock PA15 2RP. *T:* (01475) 501000.

McLAUCHLAN, Derek John Alexander, CBE 1998; CEng, FIEE; FRAeS; FInstP; Secretary-General, Civil Air Navigation Services Organisation, Geneva, since 1997; *b* 5 May 1933; *s* of Frederick William McLauchlan and Nellie (*née* Summers); *m* 1960, Dr Sylvia June Smith (*see* S. J. McLauchlan); two *d. Educ:* Queen Elizabeth's Hospital, Bristol; Bristol Univ. (BSc). CEng, FIEE 1988; FRAeS 1993; FInstP 1997. BAC, 1954–66; European Space Technol. Centre, 1966–70; Marconi Space and Defence Systems, 1970–76; ICL, 1976–88; Renishaw Research, 1988–89; Dir Gen., Projects and Engrg, CAA, 1989–91; Chief Exec., NATS, 1991–97; Mem. Bd, CAA, 1991–97. Non-exec. Chm., Architecture Projects Management Ltd, 1994–96. Chm., Jt Air Navigation Services Council, 1996–97; Mem. Council, Air League, 1994–. *Recreations:* music, theatre, walking. *Address:* 7 Holmwood Close, East Horsley, Leatherhead, Surrey KT24 6SS. *T:* (01483) 285144.

McLAUCHLAN, Prof. Keith Alan, PhD; FRS 1992; Professor of Chemistry, Oxford University, since 1996; Fellow of Hertford College, Oxford, since 1965; *b* 8 Jan. 1936; *s* of Frederick William McLauchlan and Nellie (*née* Summers); *m* 1958, Joan Sheila Dickenson; one *s* one *d. Educ:* Queen Elizabeth's Hosp., Bristol; Univ. of Bristol (BSc, PhD); Univ. of Oxford (MA). Post-doctoral Fellow, NRCC, Ottawa, 1959–60; Post-doctoral Fellow, then Sen. Scientific Officer, NPL, Teddington, 1960–65. Oxford University: Lectr, 1965–94; Reader in Physical Chemistry, 1994–96; Chairman: Inter-deptl Cttee for Chemistry, 1990–93; Cttee of Heads of Sci. Depts, 1991–93; Member: Gen. Bd, 1993–97; Hebdomadal Council, 1998–2000. Erskine Fellow, Univ. of Christchurch, NZ, 1997; Eminent Scientist, RIKEN, Tokyo, 2000–. Visiting Professor: Tata Inst., Bombay, 1986; Univ. of Konstanz, Germany, 1990; Univ. of Padua, 1998; Ecole Normale Supérieure, Paris, 1998; George Willard Wheland Vis. Prof., Univ. of Chicago, 1998. Chm., Electron Spin Resonance Discussion Gp, RSC, 1989–92. Pres.,

Internat. Soc. for Electron Paramagnetic Resonance, 1993–96. Mem., Scientific Adv. Bd, Electro Magnetic Field Biol Res. Trust, 1995–. Silver Award for Chemistry, IES, 1993; Bruker Prize, RSC, 1997. Radio and television appearances. *Publications:* Magnetic Resonance, 1972; contrib. chaps in books; papers and review articles in Molecular Physics, Chemical Physics Letters, etc. *Recreations:* gardening, walking, ski-ing, reading. *Address:* Physical and Theoretical Chemistry Laboratory, South Parks Road, Oxford OX1 3QZ. *T:* (01865) 275424; *e-mail:* keith.mclauchlan@chem.ox.ac.uk; 29 Cumnor Hill, Oxford OX2 9EY. *T:* (01865) 862528.

McLAUCHLAN, Madeline Margaret Nicholls; Head Mistress, North London Collegiate School, 1965–85; *b* 4 June 1922; *o c* of late Robert and Gertrude McLauchlan, Birmingham. *Educ:* King Edward VI Grammar Sch. for Girls, Camp Hill, Birmingham; Royal Holloway College, University of London. Asst Mistress: Shrewsbury High Sch., GPDST, 1944; Manchester High Sch., 1952. Senior Walter Hines Page Scholar, E-SU, 1955. Head Mistress, Henrietta Barnett Sch., 1958. Chm., Schoolboy and Schoolgirl Exchange Cttee, E-SU (Mem., Educn Cttee, 1966); Member: Exec. Cttee, Assoc. of Head Mistresses, 1966–76, Chm., 1974–76; Exec. Cttee, UCCA, 1968–85; Direct Grant Cttee, GBGSA, 1972–; Assisted Places Cttee, ISJC, 1980–85; Council, Westfield Coll., Univ. of London, 1975–78; Council, The Francis Holland Schools Trust, 1985– (Chm., 1993–99); Vice-Pres., Church Schs Co., 1996– (Mem. Council, 1985–96); Chm., Brecknock DFAS, 1999. Governor: Imperial Coll., 1968–85; Bedford Coll., 1981–85; St Christopher's Sch., NW3, 1985–98; Rougemont Sch., Newport, Gwent, 1988–92; Llanbedr Village Sch., 1989–; NYO, 1985–93 (Mem. Council, 1975, Vice-Chm. Council, 1981). Freeman, Goldsmiths' Co., 1986. *Recreations:* music, mountain walking, housekeeping. *Address:* The Coach House, Moor Park, Llanbedr, Crickhowell, Powys NP8 1SS. *Clubs:* English-Speaking Union, University Women's.

McLAUCHLAN, Dr Sylvia June, FFPHM; Director General, The Stroke Association, 1993–97; *b* 8 June 1935; *d* of Sydney George Smith and Muriel May (*née* Treweek); *m* 1960, Derek John Alexander McLauchlan, *qv*; two *d*. *Educ:* High Sch. for Girls, Chichester; Univ. of Bristol (MB ChB 1959); Univ. of Manchester (MSc 1981). FFPHM 1989. GP, Bristol, 1960–66; MO, Dept of Public Health, Portsmouth, 1970–76; Clinical MO, Macclesfield, 1976–77; Community Medicine Dept, NW RHA, 1977–86; Public Health Dept, SW Thames RHA, 1986–91; Dir of Public Health, Ealing HA, 1991–93. Chm., Primary Care Facilitation Trust, 1997–; Trustee, East Thames Care. Gov., Treloar Sch. *Recreations:* theatre, gardening, cooking. *Address:* 7 Holmwood Close, East Horsley, Surrey KT24 6SS.

McLAUCHLAN, Thomas Joseph; Stipendiary Magistrate, 1966–82; *b* 15 May 1917; *s* of Alexander and Helen McLauchlan; *m* 1945, Rose Catherine Gray, MA. *Educ:* St Aloysius Coll., Glasgow; Univ. of Glasgow (BL). War service, Merchant Navy and RAF Y Section, Signals Intell., Wireless Officer, 1940–46. Legal Asst to Manager of large industrial insurance co., 1947–49; Clerk to Glasgow Police Courts, 1949–66. JP Scotland. *Address:* 1B Lennox Court, 14 Sutherland Avenue, Bearsden, Glasgow G61 3JW. *T:* (0141) 942 9446.

McLAUGHLIN, Eleanor Thomson; JP; DL; Lord Provost and Lord Lieutenant of Edinburgh, 1988–92; *b* 3 March 1938; *d* of Alexander Craig and Helen Thomson; *m* 1959, Hugh McLaughlin; one *s* two *d*. *Educ:* Broughton School. Mem. (Lab), Edinburgh District Council, 1974–96. Chairman: Edinburgh Festival Soc., 1988–; Edinburgh Military Tattoo Ltd, 1988–. JP Edinburgh, 1975; DL Edinburgh, 1993. *Recreations:* Shetland lace knitting, gardening (Alpine plants). *Address:* 28 Oxgangs Green, Edinburgh EH13 9JS. *T:* (0131) 445 4052.

McLAUGHLIN, Prof. Martin Leonard, DPhil; Fiat Serena Professor of Italian Studies, University of Oxford, and Fellow, Magdalen College, Oxford, since 2001; *b* 4 Dec. 1950; *s* of George Vincent McLaughlin and Ann Josephine McLaughlin; *m* 1974, Catherine Ann Gallagher; one *d*. *Educ:* St Aloysius' Coll., Glasgow; Glasgow Univ. (MA); Balliol Coll., Oxford (MA; DPhil 1984). Lectr, Italian Dept, Edinburgh Univ., 1977–90; Lectr in Italian, and Student, Christ Church, Oxford, 1990–2001. Reviews Ed., Italian Studies, 1989–94; Italian Ed., 1994–2001, Gen. Ed., 2001–, Modern Lang. Rev. Member, Executive Committee: Soc. for Italian Studies, 1987–94; MHRA, 1994–. John Florio Prize for Translation, 2000. *Publications:* (ed jtly) Leopardi: a Scottis Quair, 1987; Literary Imitation in the Italian Renaissance, 1995; Italo Calvino, 1998; (trans.) Italo Calvino, Why Read the Classics?, 1999; (ed) Britain and Italy from Romanticism to Modernism, 2000. *Recreations:* football, travel, cinema, walking. *Address:* Magdalen College, Oxford OX1 4AU.

McLAUGHLIN, Mitchel; Member (SF) Foyle, Northern Ireland Assembly, since 1998; National Chairperson, Sinn Féin, since 1994; *b* 29 Oct. 1945; *m* 1975, Mary-Lou Fleming; three *s*. Mem. (SF) Derry CC, 1985–99. Sinn Féin: Mem., Nat. Exec., 1981–; peace negotiator, 1997–. Member: Civil Rights Assoc., 1968–; Nat. H-Blocks/Armagh Cttee, 1980–81. *Address:* Sinn Féin Foyle Constituency Office, 15 Cable Street, Derry City BT48 9HY. *T:* (028) 7130 9264, *Fax:* (028) 7130 8781.

MacLAURIN, family name of **Baron MacLaurin of Knebworth**.

MacLAURIN OF KNEBWORTH, Baron *cr* 1996 (Life Peer), of Knebworth in the county of Hertfordshire; **Ian Charter MacLaurin,** Kt 1989; DL; Chairman, Tesco PLC, 1985–97 (Managing Director, 1973–85; Deputy Chairman, 1983–85; Director, 1970); Chairman, England and Wales Cricket Board (formerly Test and County Cricket Board), since 1996; *b* Blackheath, 30 March 1937; *s* of Arthur George and Evelina Florence MacLaurin; *m* 1961, Ann Margaret (*née* Collar) (*d* 1999); one *s* two *d*. *Educ:* Malvern Coll., Worcs. Served in RAF, 1956–58. Joined Tesco, 1959. Non-executive Director: Enterprise Oil, 1984–90; Guinness PLC, 1986–95; National Westminster Bank plc, 1990–97; Gleneagles Hotels plc, 1992–97; Whitbread plc, 1997–2001 (Dep. Chm., 1999–); Vodafone AirTouch (formerly Vodafone), 1997– (Chm., Vodafone, 1998–99; Dep. Chm., 1999–2000, Chm., 2000–, Vodafone AirTouch). Chm., Food Policy Gp, Retail Consortium, 1980–84; Pres., Inst. of Grocery Distribution, 1989–92. Trustee, Royal Opera House Trust, 1992. Governor and Mem. Council, Malvern Coll.; Chancellor, Univ. of Hertfordshire, 1996–. Mem. Cttee, MCC, 1986–96. FRSA 1986; FIM 1987; Hon. FCGI 1992. Liveryman, Carmen's Co., 1982–. DL Herts, 1992. DUniv Stirling, 1987; Hon. LLD Hertfordshire, 1995. *Publication:* Tiger by the Tail (memoirs), 1999. *Recreation:* golf. *Address:* (office) 14 Great College Street, SW1P 3RX. *Clubs:* MCC, Lord's Taverners, XL, Band of Brothers; Royal & Ancient Golf (St Andrews).

MACLAY, family name of **Baron Maclay**.

MACLAY, 3rd Baron *cr* 1922, of Glasgow; **Joseph Paton Maclay;** DL; Bt 1914; Group Marketing Executive, Acomarit Group, since 1993; *b* 11 April 1942; *s* of 2nd Baron Maclay, KBE, and of Nancy Margaret, *d* of R. C. Greig, Hall of Caldwell, Uplawmoor, Renfrewshire; *S* father, 1969; *m* 1976, Elizabeth Anne, *o d* of G. M. Buchanan, Delamere, Pokataroo, NSW; two *s* one *d*. *Educ:* Winchester; Sorbonne Univ. Managing Director: Denholm Maclay Co. Ltd, 1970–83; Denholm Maclay (Offshore) Ltd, 1975–83; Triport Ferries (Management) Ltd, 1975–83; Dep. Man. Dir, Denholm Ship Management Ltd, 1982–83; Man. Dir, Milton Timber Services Ltd, 1984–90; Dir, Denholm Ship Management (Holdings) Ltd, 1991–93. Director: Milton Shipping Co. Ltd, 1970–83; Marine Shipping Mutual Insce Co., 1982–83; Altnamara Shipping PLC, 1994–; Pres., Hanover Shipping Inc., 1982–83. Director: British Steamship Short Trades Assoc, 1978–83; N of England Protection and Indemnity Assoc., 1976–83. A Comr of Northern Lighthouses, 1996– (Vice Chm. 2001_01, Chm., 2001–, Bd). Chm., Scottish Br., British Sailors Soc., 1979–81; Vice-Chm., Glasgow Shipowners & Shipbrokers Benevolent Assoc., 1982–83 and 1996–97 (Pres., 1998–99). Chm., Scottish Maritime Mus., 1998–. Trustee, Cattanach Charitable Trust, 1991–. DL Renfrewshire, 1986. *Heir: s* Hon. Joseph Paton Maclay, *b* 6 March 1977. *Address:* Duchal, Kilmacolm, Renfrewshire PA13 4RS.

McLAY, Hon. James Kenneth, (Jim); Managing Director and Principal, J. K. McLay Ltd (international business consultants), since 1987; *s* of late Robert McLay and Joyce McLay; *m* 1983, Marcy Farden. *Educ:* St Helier's Sch.; King's Sch.; King's Coll.; Auckland Univ. (LLB 1967); Pennsylvania State Univ. (EMP 1987). Solicitor in practice on own account, 1971; barrister 1974. MP (National Party) for Birkenhead, NZ, 1975–87; Attorney-Gen. and Minister of Justice, 1978–84; Government Spokesperson for Women, 1979–84; Dep. Prime Minister, 1984; Leader, National Party and Leader of the Opposition, 1984–86. Mem., Ministerial Wkg Party on Accident Compensation and Incapacity, 1990–91; NZ Comr, Internat. Whaling Commn, 1993–. Chairman: Wholesale Electricity Market Study, 1991–92; Wholesale Electricity Market Develt Gp, 1993–94. Chairman: OMNIPORT Napier Ltd, 1988–; Roading Adv. Gp, 1997; Project Manukau Audit Gp, 1998–; Director: Evergreen Forests Ltd, 1995–; Motor Sport New Zealand Ltd, 1996–99; Mem. Adv. Bd, Westfield NZ Ltd, 1998–. Advr, UK Cons. Party Commn on Bank of England, 1999–2000. *Recreation:* trout fishing. *Address:* PO Box 8885, Symonds Street Post Office, Auckland 1, New Zealand.

MacLEAN, Rt Hon. Lord; Ranald Norman Munro MacLean; PC 2001; a Senator of the College of Justice in Scotland, since 1990; *b* 18 Dec. 1938; *s* of late John Alexander MacLean, CBE; *m* 1963, Pamela Ross (marr. diss. 1993); two *s* one *d* (and one *s* decd). *Educ:* Inverness Royal Acad.; Fettes Coll.; Clare Coll., Cambridge Univ. (BA); Edinburgh Univ. (LLB); Yale Univ., USA (LLM). Called to the Scottish Bar, 1964; QC (Scot.) 1977; Advocate Depute, 1972–75, Home Advocate Depute, 1979–82; Standing Jun. Counsel, Health and Safety Exec. (Scotland), 1975–77; Member: Council on Tribunals, 1985–90 (Chm., Scottish Cttee, 1985–90); Scottish Legal Aid Bd, 1986–90. Member: Stewart Cttee on Alternatives to Prosecution, 1977–82; Parole Bd for Scotland, 1998–2000; Chm., Cttee on Serious Violent and Sexual Offenders, 1999–2000. Mem., Ind. Rev. Commn on Scottish Football, Scottish Football Assoc., 1995–97. Trustee, Nat. Liby of Scotland, 1967–90. Chm. of Council, Cockburn Assoc., 1988–96. Chm. Govs, Fettes Coll., 1996–. FSAScot 1994; FRSE 2000. *Publication:* (ed jtly) Gloag and Henderson, Introduction to the Law of Scotland, 7th edn 1968, 8th edn 1980. *Recreations:* hill walking, Munro collecting, swimming. *Address:* 38 Royal Terrace, Edinburgh EH7 5AH. *Clubs:* New (Edinburgh); Royal Scottish Automobile (Glasgow).

MACLEAN of Dochgarroch, Very Rev. Canon Allan Murray; historian; Provost of St John's Cathedral, Oban, 1986–99; *b* 22 Oct. 1950; *o s* of late Rev. Donald Maclean of Dochgarroch and Loraine Maclean of Dochgarroch (*née* Calvert); *m* 1990, Anne (*née* Cavin), *widow* of David Lindsay; two *s* one *d*. *Educ:* Dragon School, Oxford; Trinity College, Glenalmond; Univ. of Edinburgh (MA 1st cl. Hons Scottish History); Cuddesdon Coll. and Pusey House, Oxford. Deacon 1976, Priest 1977; Chaplain of St Mary's Cathedral, Edinburgh, 1976–81; Rector of Holy Trinity, Dunoon, 1981–86; Exam. Chaplain to Bishop of Argyll and the Isles, 1983–93. Hon. Canon, St John's Cathedral, Oban, 1999–. Pres., Clan Maclean Assoc., 1994–98 (Vice-Pres., 1982–94). Editor: Clan Maclean, 1975–85; Argyll and the Isles, 1984–93. *Publication:* Telford's Highland Churches, 1989. *Recreations:* topography, history, genealogy, architecture. *Address:* 5 North Charlotte Street, Edinburgh EH2 4HR. *T:* (0131) 225 8609; Hazelbrae House, Glen Urquhart, Inverness IV63 6TJ. *T:* (01456) 476267. *Clubs:* New, Puffin's (Edinburgh).

MACLEAN of Dunconnel, Sir Charles (Edward), 2nd Bt *cr* 1957, of Dunconnel, co. Argyll; *b* 31 Oct. 1946; *s* of Sir Fitzroy Hew Maclean of Dunconnel, 1st Bt, KT, CBE and of Hon. Veronica Fraser, *d* of 16th Lord Lovat, KT, GCVO, KCMG, CB, DSO and *widow* of Lt Alan Phipps, RN; *S* father, 1996; *m* 1986, Deborah, *d* of Lawrence Young; four *d*. *Educ:* Eton; New Coll., Oxford. *Publications:* The Wolf Children, 1979; The Watcher, 1983; Island on the Edge of the World: story of St Kilda, 1992; (with C; S. Sykes) Scottish Country, 1993; Romantic Scotland, 1995; The Silence, 1996. *Heir: b* Alexander James Simon Aeneas Maclean [*b* 9 June 1949; *m* 1st, 1983, Sarah (marr. diss. 1989), *d* of Hugh Janson; 2nd, 1993, Sarah, *d* of Nicolas Thompson]. *Address:* Strachur House, Strachur, Cairndow, Argyll PA27 8BX.

See also Maj.-Gen. J. J. J. Phipps.

McLEAN, Colin, CMG 1977; MBE 1964; HM Diplomatic Service, retired; UK Permanent Representative to the Council of Europe (with the personal rank of Ambassador), 1986–90; *b* 10 Aug. 1930; *s* of late Dr L. G. McLean and H. I. McLean; *m* 1953, Huguette Marie Suzette Leclerc; one *s* one *d*. *Educ:* Fettes; St Catharine's Coll., Cambridge (MA). 2RHA, 1953–54. District Officer, Kenya, 1955–63; Vice-Principal, Kenya Inst. of Administration, 1963–64; HM Diplomatic Service, 1964; served Wellington, Bogotá and FCO, 1964–77; Counsellor, Oslo, 1977–81; Head of Trade Relations and Export Dept, FCO, 1981–83; High Comr in Uganda, 1983–86. *Recreation:* sailing. *Address:* 28 The Heights, Foxgrove Road, Beckenham, Kent BR3 5BY. *T:* (020) 8650 9565.

MACLEAN, Colin William, OBE 2000; FRCVS; Chairman, Royal Berkshire and Battle Hospitals NHS Trust, since 2000; *b* 19 June 1938; *s* of late Kenneth Percy Maclean and Elsie Violet (*née* Middleton); *m* 1959, Jacqueline Diana Brindley; two *d*. *Educ:* William Hulme's Grammar Sch., Manchester; Liverpool Univ. Sch. of Vet. Sci. (BVSc; MVSc 1971). MRCVS 1961, FRCVS 1969. Veterinary Surgeon and Partner, veterinary practice, Thornley, Glos, and Wickham, Hants, 1961–66; Unilever Ltd: Chief Vet. Advr, 1966–72; Manager, Pig Breeding, 1972–74; Man. Dir, Farm Mark Ltd and Masterbreeders Ltd, 1974–76; Area Gen. Manager (S), BOCM Silcock Ltd, 1980–83; Glaxo Group: Dep. Man. Dir, 1983–88; Product Develt Dir, Glaxo Animal Health Ltd, 1983–88; Technical Dir, 1988–92, Dir-Gen., 1992–99, MLC. *Publications:* contrib. to Veterinary Record, Res. Vet. Sci., Jl Comparative Pathology. *Recreations:* squash, Rugby, theatre, travel. *Address:* Crackwillow, Cocklane, Bradfield, Reading RG7 6HW. *Club:* Farmers'.

MACLEAN, Rt Hon. David (John); PC 1995; MP (C) Penrith and the Border, since July 1983; *b* 16 May 1953. Asst Govt Whip, 1987–88; a Lord Comr of HM Treasury (Govt Whip), 1988–89; Parly Sec., MAFF, 1989–92; Minister of State: DoE, 1992–93; Home Office, 1993–97; Opposition Chief Whip, 2001–. *Address:* House of Commons, SW1A 0AA.

McLEAN, Denis Bazeley Gordon, CMG 1989; writer; Member, New Zealand Press Council, since 1999; *b* Napier, NZ, 18 Aug. 1930; *s* of John Gordon McLean and Renée Maitland Smith; *m* 1958, Anne Davidson, Venado Tuerto, Argentina; two *s* one *d. Educ:* Nelson Coll., NZ; Victoria Univ. Coll., NZ (MSc); Rhodes Schol. 1954; University Coll., Oxford (MA). Jun. Lectr in Geology, Victoria UC, 1953–54; joined Dept of External Affairs of NZ Govt, London, 1957; served in: Wellington, 1958–60; Washington, 1960–63; Paris, 1963–66; Kuala Lumpur, 1966–68; Asst Sec. (Policy), MoD, Wellington, 1969–72; RCDS, 1972; Dep. High Comr, London, 1973–77; Dep. Sec. of Defence, NZ, 1977, Sec. of Defence, 1979–88; Ambassador to US, 1991–94; Warburg Prof. in Internat. Relns, Simmons Coll., Boston, Mass, 1995–98. Visiting Fellow: Strategic and Defence Studies Centre, ANU, Canberra, 1989; Guest Scholar, Woodrow Wilson Center, and Sen. Associate, Carnegie Endowment for Internat. Peace, Washington, 1990–91; Distinguished Fellow, US Inst. of Peace, 1994–95. *Publications:* The Long Pathway: Te Ara Roa, 1986; Peace Operations and Commonsense, 1996. *Recreations:* walking, looking at art, writing, geology. *Address:* 11 Dekka Street, Khandallah, Wellington, New Zealand. *Club:* Wellington (NZ).

MACLEAN, Sir Donald (Og Grant), Kt 1985; optometrist, practising in Ayr, since 1965; *b* 13 Aug. 1930; *s* of Donald Og Maclean and Margaret Maclean (*née* Smith); *m* 1958, Muriel Giles (*d* 1984); one *s* one *d. Educ:* Morrison's Academy, Crieff; Heriot Watt Univ. FBOA; FCOptom. RAMC, 1952–54. Optical practice: Newcastle upon Tyne, 1954–57; Perth, 1957–65. Chm., Ayr Constituency Cons. Assoc., 1971–75; Scottish Conservative and Unionist Association: Vice-Pres., 1979–83; Pres., 1983–85; Chm., W of Scotland Area, 1977–79; Exec. Mem., Nat. Union, 1979–89; Scottish Conservative Party: Dep. Chm., 1985–89; Vice-Chm., 1989–91; Chm., Carrick, Cumnock and Doon Valley Cons. Assoc., 1998–2000. Chm., Ayrshire and Arran Local Optical Cttee, 1986–88. Chm., Ayrshire Medical Support Ltd, 1995–. Chm., Bell Hollingworth Ltd, 1996–99. Freeman: Spectacle Makers' Co., 1986 (Liveryman, 1989–); City of London, 1987. Dean of Guildry, Royal Burgh of Ayr, 1993–95. *Recreations:* coastal shipping, reading, photography, philately. *Address:* Dun Beag II, 22 Woodend Road, Alloway, Ayr KA7 4QR.

MACLEAN, Rear-Adm. Euan, CB 1986; FRINA, FIMechE; Director General Fleet Support Policy and Services, 1983–86; *b* 7 July 1929; *s* of John Fraser Maclean and Dorothy Mary Maclean; *m* 1954, Renée Shaw; two *d. Educ:* BRNC Dartmouth; RNEC Keyham/Manadon. FRINA 1980; FIMechE 1980. Joined Exec. Br., RN, 1943; transf. to Engr Br., 1947; sea service in HMS Sirius, Illustrious, Gambia, Ocean, Indefatigable, Defender, Hermes, Eagle and Ark Royal, 1950–72; on loan to Royal Malaysian Navy, 1965–68; Prodn Dept, Portsmouth Dockyard, 1968–71; HMS Ark Royal, 1971–72; Exec. Officer, HMS Sultan, 1973; Dep. Prodn Man., Devonport Dockyard, 1974–77; Fleet Marine Engr Officer, 1977–79; student, RCDS, 1980; Prodn Man., Portsmouth Dockyard, 1981–83. ADC to the Queen, 1982. Comdr 1965, Captain 1974, Rear-Adm. 1983. *Recreations:* cycling, writing limericks (sometimes coincident).

McLEAN, Geoffrey Daniel, CBE 1988; QPM 1981; Assistant Commissioner (Territorial Operations), Metropolitan Police, 1984–91; *b* 4 March 1931; *s* of late William James McLean and Matilda Gladys (*née* Davies); *m* 1959, Patricia Edna Pope; two *s* two *d.* Following service in RA, joined Metropolitan Police, 1951; Chief Supt, 1969; Staff Officer to HMCIC, Home Office, 1970–72; Comdr, 1975; Graduate, RCDS, 1978; Dep. Asst Comr, 1979; Dep. Comdt, Police Staff Coll., 1981–83. *Recreations:* Met. Police Athletics Assoc. (Chm., 1984); Met. Police Football Club (Chm., 1984); Met. Police Race-Walking Club (Chm., 1978); riding.

MacLEAN, Vice-Adm. Sir Hector Charles Donald, KBE 1962; CB 1960; DSC 1941; JP; DL; *b* 7 Aug. 1908; *s* of late Captain D. C. H. Maclean, DSO, The Royal Scots; *m* 1933, Opre, *d* of late Captain Geoffrey Vyvyan, Royal Welch Fusiliers; one *s* two *d. Educ:* Wellington. Special Entry into Navy, 1926; Captain 1948; idc 1951; Comd HMS Saintes and 3rd Destroyer Sqdn, 1952–53; Dir of Plans, Admiralty, 1953–56; Comd HMS Eagle, 1956–57; Chief of Staff, Home Fleet, 1958–59; Chief of Allied Staff, Mediterranean, 1959–62; Vice-Adm. 1960; retired 1962. JP Norfolk, 1963; DL Norfolk, 1977. *Address:* Deepdale Old Rectory, Brancaster Staithe, King's Lynn, Norfolk PE31 8DD. *T:* (01485) 210281.

McLEAN, Hector John Finlayson, CBE 1995; Secretary, Crown Appointments Commission, and Archbishops' Appointments Secretary, 1987–95; a Civil Service Commissioner, 1996–2001; *b* 10 Feb. 1934; *s* of late Dr Murdoch McLean, MB ChB and Dr Edith Muriel Finlayson McLean (*née* McGill), MB ChB, DPH, DOMS; *m* 1959, Caroline Elizabeth Lithgow; one *s* two *d. Educ:* Dulwich Coll.; Pembroke Coll., Cambridge (BA Hons 1958; MA 1997); Harvard Business Sch., Switzerland (SMP6 1976). FCIPD (FIPM 1965); 2nd Lieut, KOSB, 1954–55. Imperial Chemical Industries, 1958–87: Central Staff Dept, 1958; various personnel and admin. posts in Dyestuffs and Organics Divs, 1959–72; Personnel Manager, Organics Div., 1972–74; Polyurethanes Business Area Manager, 1974–75; Dir, Agricl Div., 1975–86. Non-exec. Chairman: People & Potential Ltd, 1987–97; Positive People Develt (formerly Teesside Positive People), 1987–94. Mem. Exec. Cttee, N of England Develt Council, 1978–83; Teesside Industrial Mission: Mem., Management Cttee, 1978–85; Chm., 1982–85; Dir, Cleveland Enterprise Agency, 1982–87. Mem., Northern Regl Council, CBI, 1981–85; Trustee: NE Civic Trust, 1976–88; Northern Heritage Trust, 1984–87; Swindon Family Mediation Service, 2000–. Mem., Chemical and Allied Products ITB, 1979–82. Gov. Teesside Polytechnic, 1978–84; Mem. Council, Newcastle Univ., 1985–87. FRSA 1991. Pres., Alleyn Club, 1997–98 (Vice Pres., 1996–97). *Recreations:* family, music (especially choral music), travel, gardening, walking. *Address:* College Farm House, Purton, near Swindon, Wilts SN5 4AE. *T:* (01793) 770525. *Club:* Oxford and Cambridge.

MACLEAN, Hector Ronald; Sheriff of Lothian and Borders, at Linlithgow, since 1988; *b* 6 Dec. 1931; *s* of Donald Beaton Maclean and Lucy McAlister; *m* 1967, Hilary Elizabeth Jenkins; three *d. Educ:* High Sch. of Glasgow; Glasgow Univ. Admitted to Faculty of Advocates, 1959. Sheriff of N Strathclyde (formerly Renfrew and Argyll), 1968–88. *Recreation:* golf. *Address:* Barrfield, Houston, Johnstone, Renfrewshire. *T:* (01505) 612449.

McLEAN, His Honour Ian Graeme; a Circuit Judge, 1980–97; *b* Edinburgh, 7 Sept. 1928; *s* of Lt-Gen. Sir Kenneth McLean, KCB, KBE; *m* 1957, Eleonore Maria Gmeiner, Bregenz, Austria; two *d. Educ:* Aldenham Sch.; Christ's Coll., Cambridge. BA Hons Law 1950; MA 1955. Intell. Corps, 1946–48. Called to English Bar, Middle Temple, Nov. 1951; admitted Faculty of Advocates, Edinburgh, 1985; practised London and on Western Circuit, 1951–55; Crown Counsel, Northern Nigeria, 1955–59; Sen. Lectr and Head of Legal Dept of Inst. of Administration, Northern Nigeria, 1959–62; Native Courts Adviser, 1959–62; returned to English Bar, 1962; practised London and South Eastern Circuit, 1962–70; Adjudicator under Immigration Acts, 1969–70; Metropolitan Stipendiary Magistrate, 1970–80. *Publications:* Cumulative Index West African Court of Appeal Reports, 1958; (with Abubakar Sadiq) The Maliki Law of Homicide, 1959; (with Sir Lionel Brett) Criminal Law Procedure and Evidence of Lagos, Eastern and Western Nigeria, 1963; (with Cyprian Okonkwo) Cases on the Criminal Law, Procedure and Evidence of Nigeria, 1966; (with Peter Morrish) A Practical Guide to Appeals in Criminal Courts, 1970; (with Peter Morrish) The Crown Court, an index of common penalties, etc, 1972–2000; (ed, with Peter Morrish) Harris's Criminal Law, 22nd edn, 1972; (with Peter Morrish) The Magistrates' Court, an index of common penalties, annually 1973–92; (with Peter Morrish) The Trial of Breathalyser Offences, 1975, 3rd edn 1990; A Practical Guide to Criminal Appeals, 1980; A Pattern of Sentencing, 1981; (with John Mulhern) The Industrial Tribunal: a practical guide to employment law and tribunal procedure, 1982; (with Sheriff Stone) Fact-Finding for Magistrates, 1990; contrib. Archbold's Criminal Pleadings, 38th edn, and Halsbury's Laws of England, 4th edn, title Criminal Law. *Recreations:* gardening, writing, languages. *Address:* c/o First Direct, 40 Wakefield Road, Leeds LS98 1FD.

MACLEAN, Prof. Ian Walter Fitzroy, DPhil; FRHistS; FBA 1994; Titular Professor of Renaissance Studies, Oxford University, and Senior Research Fellow, All Souls College, Oxford, since 1996; *b* 9 Feb. 1945; *s* of James Walter Maclean and Elsie May Maclean (*née* Davis); *m* 1971, Pauline Jennifer Henderson; one *s* two *d. Educ:* Christ's Hosp.; Wadham Coll., Oxford (BA 1st Cl. Hons Mod. Lang. 1966; MA, DPhil 1971). FRHistS 1989. Sen. Scholar, Wadham Coll., Oxford, 1967–69; Lectr in French, Univ. of Leeds, 1969–72; Oxford University: CUF Lectr in French, 1972–93; Reader in French, 1994–96; Fellow, 1972–96, Supernumerary Fellow, 1996–, Queen's Coll.; Dir, European Humanities Res. Centre, 1994–99. Vis. Fellow, Humanities Res. Centre, Canberra, 1983; Vis. Scholar, Herzog August Bibliothek, Wolfenbüttel, 1986, 1995; Vis. Prof., Catholic Univ. of Nijmegen, 1993; Dist. Vis. Schol., Centre for Renaissance and Reformation Studies, Victoria Univ., Univ. of Toronto, 1994. MAE 1998. Chevalier, Ordre des Arts et des Lettres (France), 1997. *Publications:* Woman Triumphant: feminism in French literature, 1977; The Renaissance Notion of Woman, 1980; (ed and contrib.) Montaigne, 1982; (ed and contrib.) The Political Responsibility of Intellectuals, 1990; Meaning and Interpretation in the Renaissance: the case of law, 1992; (trans.) Potocki, The Manuscript Found in Saragossa, 1995; Montaigne philosophe, 1996; articles and essays in learned jls, collective vols, etc. *Recreations:* music, fishing, wine. *Address:* All Souls College, Oxford OX1 4AL. *T:* (01865) 279379.

McLEAN, (John David) Ruari (McDowall Hardie), CBE 1973; DSC 1943; freelance typographer and author; *b* 10 June 1917; *s* of late John Thomson McLean and late Isabel Mary McLean (*née* Ireland); *m* 1945, Antonia Maxwell Carlisle (*d* 1995); two *s* one *d. Educ:* Dragon Sch., Oxford; Eastbourne Coll. First studied printing under B. H. Newdigate at Shakespeare Head Press, Oxford, 1936. Industrial printing experience in Germany and England, 1936–38; with The Studio, 1938; Percy Lund Humphries, Bradford, 1939. Served Royal Navy, 1940–45. Penguin Books, 1945–46; Book Designer (freelance), 1946–53; Tutor in Typography, Royal College of Art, 1948–51; Typographic Adviser to Hulton Press, 1953; Founder Partner, Rainbird, McLean Ltd, 1951–58; Founder Editor, and Designer, Motif, 1958–67. Typographic Consultant to The Observer, 1960–64; Hon. Typographic Adviser to HM Stationery Office, 1966–80. Sandars Reader in Bibliography, Univ. of Cambridge, 1982–83; Alexander Stone Lectr in Bibliophily, Univ. of Glasgow, 1984. Member: Nat. Council for Diplomas in Art and Design, 1971; Vis. Cttee of RCA, 1977–83; Academic Adv. Cttee, Heriot-Watt Univ. for Edinburgh Coll. of Art, 1978–96. Crown Trustee, Nat. Library of Scotland, 1981–2001. American Printing History Assoc. Individual Award, 1993. Croix de Guerre (French), 1942. *Publications:* George Cruikshank, 1948; Modern Book Design, 1958; Wood Engravings of Joan Hassall, 1960; Victorian Book Design, 1963, rev. edn 1972; Tschichold's Typographische Gestaltung (trans.), 1967; (ed) The Reminiscences of Edmund Evans, 1967; Magazine Design, 1969; Victorian Publishers' Book-bindings in Cloth and Leather, 1973; Jan Tschichold, Typographer, 1975; Joseph Cundall, 1976; (ed) Edward Bawden: A Book of Cuts, 1979; Thames and Hudson Manual of Typography, 1980; Victorian Publishers' Book-Bindings in Paper, 1983; The Last Cream Bun (drawings by Roger Pettiward), 1984; Benjamin Fawcett, Engraver and Colour Printer, 1988; (ed) Edward Bawden, War Artist, 1989; Nicolas Bentley drew the Pictures, 1990; Tschichold's Die neue Typographie (trans.), 1994; (ed) Typographers on Type, 1995; Jan Tschichold: a life in typography, 1997; True to Type, 2000; How Typography Happens, 2000; Half Seas Under, 2001. *Recreations:* reading, acquiring books. *Address:* The Studio, Sanquhar House, Sanquhar, Dumfriesshire DG4 6JL. *T:* and *Fax:* (01659) 58021. *Clubs:* Double Crown; New (Edinburgh).

MACLEAN, Kate; Member (Lab) Dundee West, Scottish Parliament, since 1999; *b* 16 Feb. 1958; *d* of late Alexander Robertson and Sarah Robertson; *m* 1978 (marr. diss.); one *s* one *d. Educ:* Craigie High Sch., Dundee. Mem. (Lab) Dundee City Council, 1988–99 (Leader, 1992–99). Convener, Equal Opportunities Cttee, Scottish Parliament, 1999–. Vice-Pres., COSLA, 1996–99. *Address:* Scottish Parliament, Edinburgh EH99 1SP.

McLEAN, Keith Richard, FCCA; Partner, Key Health Consulting, since 1998; Director: Harrogate Management Centre Ltd, since 1996; Key Health Marketing Ltd, since 1998; *b* 27 Oct. 1947; *s* of Bertie and Elsie McLean; *m* 1973, Patricia Ann Morrell; one *d. Educ:* J. Rowntree Sch., York. FCCA 1975; IPFA 1989; MHSM 1992. Hospital Management Committees: Clerical Officer, York B, 1964–67; Higher Clerical Officer, Leicester No 4, 1967–68; Internal Auditor, Nottingham No 4, 1968–70; Sen. Accountant, Huddersfield, 1970–74; Dep. Area Treas., Calderdale HA, 1974–79; Dist Finance Officer, Derbys AHA, 1979–82; North Derbyshire Health Authority: Dist Treas., 1982–85; Dist Treas. and Dep. Dist Gen. Manager, 1985–87; Dir of Finance and Corporate Strategist, Leics HA, 1987–89; Yorkshire Regional Health Authority: Regl Dir of Finance, 1990–91; Regl Gen. Manager, 1991–94; Regl Gen. Manager, Trent RHA and Regl Dir, NHS Exec., Trent, 1994–96. Principal Res. Fellow, Sheffield Univ., 1996–2000. Nat. Chm., Healthcare Financial Mgt Assoc., 1992–93. FRSA 1994. *Recreations:* golf, snooker. *Address:* University of Sheffield, Regent Court, 30 Regent Street, Sheffield S1 4DA. *T:* (0114) 282 5454. *Club:* Oakdale Golf (Harrogate).

MacLEAN, Kenneth Smedley, MD, FRCP; Consultant Physician to Guy's Hospital, 1950–79, now Emeritus; *b* 22 Nov. 1914; *s* of Hugh MacLean and Ida Smedley; *m* 1939, Joan Hardaker; one *s* one *d* (and one *s* decd). *Educ:* Westminster; Clare Coll., Cambridge. MRCS, LRCP, 1939; House appts at Guy's, 1939; MB, BChir 1939. RNVR, 1939–46, Surg.-Lt and Surg.-Lt-Comdr. MRCP 1946; House Officer and Medical Registrar, Guy's Hosp., 1946–48; MD Cantab 1948; FRCP 1954; elected to Assoc. of Physicians of Great Britain and Ireland, 1956. Assistant Director, Dept of Medicine, Guy's Hospital Medical Sch., 1949, Director, 1961–63. Chm., University Hosps Assoc., 1975–78. Pres., Assurance Medical Soc., 1985–87. *Publication:* Medical Treatment, 1957. *Recreation:* golf. *Address:* 7 Icehouse Wood, Oxted, Surrey RH8 9DN. *T:* (01883) 716652.

MACLEAN, Hon. Sir Lachlan Hector Charles, 12th Bt *cr* 1631 (NS), of Duart and Morvern; CVO 2000; DL; Major, Scots Guards, retired; 28th Chief of Clan Maclean; *b* 25 Aug. 1942; *s* of Baron Maclean, KT, GCVO, KBE, PC and of Elizabeth, *er d* of late Frank Mann; *S* to baronetcy of father, 1990; *m* 1966, Mary Helen, *e d* of W. G. Gordon; two *s* two *d* (and one *d* decd). *Educ:* Eton. DL Argyll and Bute, 1993. *Heir:* *s* Malcolm Lachlan Charles Maclean [*b* 20 Oct. 1972; *m* 1998, Anna, *e d* of Giles Sturdy]. *Address:* Arngask House, Glenfarg, Perthshire PH2 9QA.

McLEAN, Prof. Malcolm, PhD; CEng, FIM; Professor of Materials, Imperial College of Science, Technology and Medicine, University of London, since 1990 (Head, Department of Materials, 1990–2000); *b* 19 Dec. 1939; *s* of Andrew Bell McLean and Jane Pattison McLean (*née* Kilmartin); *m* 1967, Malinda Ruth Conner; two *s*. *Educ:* Ayr Acad.; Univ. of Glasgow (BSc Natural Phil. 1962; PhD 1965). CEng 1991; FIM 1984. Ohio State Univ., 1965–67; NPL, 1969–90 (Grade 6, Sect. Leader in mech. behaviour of materials at high temps). Fellow, Amer. Soc. Metals, 1992. Rosenhain Medallist, Inst. Metals, 1986. *Publications:* Directionally solidified materials for high temperature service, 1983; (Series Editor) Characterisation of high temperature materials, Vols 1–7, 1988–89; articles on materials sci. and engrg in learned jls. *Recreations:* travel, music, politics. *Address:* Department of Materials, Imperial College of Science, Technology and Medicine, Prince Consort Road, SW7 2BP; 20 Strawberry Hill Road, Twickenham, Middx TW1 4PT. *T:* (020) 8892 0617.

MACLEAN, Sir Murdo, Kt 2000; Chief Executive, Tridos Solutions Ltd, since 2000; Chairman, SiScape Technology Ltd, since 2001; *b* 21 Oct. 1943; *s* of late Murdo Maclean and of Johanna (*née* Martin). *Educ:* Glasgow. Temp. Clerk, Min. of Labour Employment Exchange, Govan, Glasgow, 1963–64; BoT, 1964–67; Prime Minister's Office, 1967–72; Dept of Industry, 1972–78; Private Sec. to Govt Chief Whip, 1979–2000. Freeman, City of London, 1994. FRSA 1990. *Address:* SiScape Technology Ltd, 77A High Street, Brentwood, Essex CM14 4RR. *Club:* Garrick.

MACLEAN, Prof. Norman; JP; PhD; FIBiol, FLS; Professor of Genetics, since 1992, and Head of Department of Biology, since 1993; University of Southampton; *b* 23 Sept. 1932; *s* of late Alexander Maclean and Christine Walker; *m* 1962, Dr Jane Kay Smith; one *s* one *d*. *Educ:* George Heriot's Sch., Edinburgh; Edinburgh Sch. of Agriculture; Edinburgh Univ. (SDA, BSc 1st cl. Hons, PhD 1962). FIBiol 1990; FLS 1992. Asst Lectr in Zoology, Edinburgh Univ., 1961–64; Sir Henry Wellcome Travelling Fellow, 1964–65; Res. Associate, Rockefeller Inst., NY, 1964; Lectr in Biology, Sen. Lectr and Reader, Southampton Univ., 1965–92. Mem., Scientific Adv. Cttee, Aquagene Inc., Fla, 1999–. Trustee, Marwell Preservation Trust, 1995–. Edinburgh University: MacGillivray Prize in Zoology, 1956; Moira Lindsay Stuart Prize in Zoology, 1957; Gunning Victoria Jubilee Prize, 1960. JP Southampton, 1976. *Publications:* Control of Gene Expression, 1976; The Differentiation of Cells, 1977; Haemoglobin, 1978; Trout and Grayling: an angler's natural history, 1980; (jtly) DNA, Chromatin and Chromosomes, 1981; (ed jtly) Eukaryotic Genes: structure, activity and regulation, 1983; (ed) Oxford Surveys on Eukaryotic Genes, vols 1–7, 1984–90; (jtly) Cell Commitment and Differentiation, 1987; Macmillan Dictionary of Genetic and Cell Biology, 1987; Genes and Gene Regulation, 1989, 3rd edn 1992; Animals with Novel Genes, 1994; articles in learned jls. *Recreations:* gardening, fly fishing, tennis, reading. *Address:* 10 Russell Place, Southampton SO17 1NU. *T:* (023) 8055 7649. *Club:* Abbotts Barton Angling.

McLEAN, Peter Standley, CMG 1985; OBE 1965; Head of East Asia Department, Overseas Development Administration, 1985–87; *b* 18 Jan. 1927; *s* of late William and Alice McLean; *m* 1954, Margaret Ann Minns; two *s* two *d*. *Educ:* King Edward's Sch., Birmingham; Wadham Coll., Oxford (MA). Served Army, 1944–48; Lieut, 15/19th King's Royal Hussars. Colonial Service, Uganda, 1951–65, retired from HMOCS as Permanent Sec., Min. of Planning and Economic Develt; Ministry of Overseas Development: Principal, 1965; Private Sec. to Minister for Overseas Develt, 1973; Head of Eastern and Southern Africa Dept, 1975; Head of Bilateral Aid and Rural Develt Dept, 1979; Minister and UK Perm. Rep to FAO, 1980. Chm., Africa Grants Cttee, Comic Relief, 1989–92. Chm., Internat. Health Solutions Trust, 1997–. *Recreations:* watching sport, DIY, painting. *Address:* 17 Woodfield Lane, Ashtead, Surrey KT21 2BQ. *T:* (01372) 278146.

McLEAN, Philip Alexander, CMG 1994; HM Diplomatic Service, retired; Director-General, Canning House (Hispanic and Luso-Brazilian Council), since 1999; *b* 24 Oct. 1938; *s* of late Wm Alexander McLean and Doris McLean (*née* Campbell); *m* 1960, Dorothy Helen Kirkby; two *s* one *d*. *Educ:* King George V Sch., Southport; Keble Coll., Oxford (MA Hons). National Service, RAF, 1956–58. Industry, 1961–68; entered HM Diplomatic Service by Open Supplementary Competition, 1968; Second, later (1969) First, Secretary, FCO; La Paz, 1970–74: Head of Chancery, 1973; FCO, 1974–76; Dep. Director of British Trade Development Office and Head of Industrial Marketing, New York, 1976–80; Counsellor and Consul-Gen., Algiers, 1981–83; Diplomatic Service Inspector, 1983–85; Hd, S America Dept, FCO, 1985–87; Consul-Gen., Boston, 1988–91; Minister and Dep. Head of Mission, Peking, 1991–94; Ambassador to Cuba, 1994–98. Robin Humphreys Vis. Res. Fellow, Inst. of Latin American Studies, London Univ., 1999–2000. Hon. LLD American Internat. Coll., 1991. *Recreations:* hill walking, food and drink, friends. *Address:* Hill Cottage, Reading Road, Goring-on-Thames RG8 0LH. *Club:* Oxford and Cambridge.

MacLEAN, Ranald Norman Munro; *see* MacLean, Rt Hon. Lord.

McLEAN, Ruari; *see* McLean, J. D. R. McD. H.

McLEAN, Prof. Sheila Ann Manson, PhD; FRSE; FRCPE; International Bar Association Professor of Law and Ethics in Medicine, since 1990, and Director, Institute of Law and Ethics in Medicine, since 1985, Glasgow University; *b* 20 June 1951; *d* of William Black and Bethia Black (*née* Manson); *m* 1976, Alan McLean (marr. diss. 1987). *Educ:* Glasgow High Sch. for Girls; Glasgow Univ. (LLB 1972; MLitt 1978; PhD 1987). FRSE 1996; FRCPE 1997. Area Reporter, Children's Panel, 1972–75; Lectr, 1975–85, Sen. Lectr, 1985–90, Sch. of Law, Glasgow Univ. Chm., Scottish Criminal Cases Review Commn, 1999–. Chairman: Review of consent provisions of Human Fertilisation and Embryology Act, DoH, 1997–98; Ind. Review Gp on Organ Retention at Post Mortem, 2000–01; Member: UKCC, 1993–98; UK Xenotransplantation Interim Regulatory Authy, 1997–; Vice Chair, Multi-Centre Res. Ethics Cttee for Scotland, 1997–98; Mem., SHEFC, 1996–; Mem., Broadcasting Council for Scotland, 1991–96. FRSA 1996. *Publications:* (jtly) Medicine, Morals and the Law, 1983; A Patient's Right to Know: information disclosure, the doctor and the law, 1989; (jtly) The Case for Physician Assisted Suicide, 1997; Old Law, New Medicine, 1999; *edited:* Legal Issues in Medicine, 1981; (jtly) Human Rights: from rhetoric to reality, 1986; (jtly) The Legal Relevance of Gender, 1988; Legal Issues in Human Reproduction, 1989; Law Reform and Human Reproduction, 1992; Compensation for Personal Injury: an international perspective, 1993; Law Reform and Medical Injury Litigation, 1995; Law and Ethics in Intensive Care, 1996; Death, Dying and the Law, 1996; Contemporary Issues in Law, Medicine and Ethics, 1996. *Recreations:* playing guitar, singing, reading. *Address:* School of Law, The University, Glasgow G12 8QQ. *T:* (0141) 330 5577. *Club:* Lansdowne.

McLEAN, Dr Thomas Pearson, CB 1990; FRSE; CPhys, FInstP; Professor of Electrical Engineering and Science, Royal Military College of Science, Shrivenham, 1992–95; *b* Paisley, 21 Aug. 1930; *s* of Norman Stewart McLean and Margaret Pearson McLean (*née* Ferguson); *m* 1957, Grace Campbell Nokes; two *d*. *Educ:* John Neilson Instn, Paisley; Glasgow Univ. (BSc, PhD); Birmingham Univ. Royal Radar Estabt (becoming Royal Signals and Radar Estabt, 1976), 1955–80: Head of Physics Gp, 1973–77; Dep. Dir, 1977–80; Ministry of Defence: Under Sec., Dir Gen. Air Weapons and Electronic Systems, 1980–83; Dir, RARDE, 1984–86; Dep. Controller, Aircraft, 1987; Dir, Atomic Weapons Estabt, 1987–90. Member: Physics Cttee, SRC, 1968–73; Optoelectronics Cttee, Rank Prize Funds, 1972–81; Council, Inst. of Physics, 1980–84. Hon. Prof. of Physics, Birmingham Univ., 1977–80. Dep. Editor, Jl of Physics C, 1976–77. *Publications:* papers in Physical Rev., Jl of Physics, etc. *Recreations:* music, mathematics, computing.

MACLEAN, Prof. William James, RSA 1991; RSW 1997; Professor of Fine Art, University of Dundee, since 1995; *b* 12 Oct. 1941; *s* of Capt. John Maclean and Mary Isabella (*née* Reid); *m* 1968, Marian Leven; two *s* one *d*. *Educ:* Inverness Royal Acad.; HMS Conway MN Cadet Trng Sch., N Wales; Gray's Sch. of Art, Aberdeen (DA 1966; Post-Grad. Dip. 1967). Midshipman, Blue Funnel Line, 1957–59; school teacher, 1971–81; Lectr in Drawing and Painting, Dundee Coll. of Art, 1981–94. Solo exhibns in GB and abroad; *work in Collections of:* Arts Council of GB; British Mus.; Nat. Art Collection; Fitzwilliam Mus. and Art Gall., Cambridge; Yale Centre for British Art; Scottish Nat. Gall. of Modern Art, etc. Mem., RGI, 1996. Hon. DLitt St Andrews. *Publication:* Will Maclean: sculptures and box constructions, 1987; *relevant publication:* Symbols of Survival: the art of Will Maclean, by Prof. Duncan Macmillan, 1992. *Recreations:* reading, walking. *Address:* 18 Dougall Street, Tayport, Fife DD6 9JD. *T:* (01382) 552219.

MacLEARY, Alistair Ronald; Member, Lands Tribunal for Scotland, since 1989; *b* 12 Jan. 1940; *s* of Donald Herbert MacLeary and Jean Spiers (*née* Leslie); *m* 1967, Mary-Claire Cecilia (*née* Leonard); one *s* one *d*. *Educ:* Inverness Royal Acad.; Coll. of Estate Management, London; Edinburgh Coll. of Art, Heriot-Watt Univ.; Strathclyde Univ. MSc, DipTP; FRICS, FRTPI. Gerald Eve & Co., 1963–65; Murrayfield Real Estate Co., 1965–67; Dept of Environment (on secondment), 1971–73; Wright, Partners, 1967–76; MacRobert Prof. of Land Economy, 1976–89, Dean, Faculty of Law, 1982–85, Aberdeen Univ. Univ. of Auckland Foundn Visitor and Fletcher Challenge Vis. Fellow, 1985; Memorialist, MacAuley Inst. for Soil Science, 1986–87. Mem., Cttee of Inquiry into Acquisition and Occupancy of Agricl Land, 1977–79; Chm., Watt Cttee, Energy Working Gp on Land Resources, 1977–79; Mem., Exec. Cttee, Commonwealth Assoc. of Surveying and Land Economy, 1980–85 (Chm., Bd of Surveying Educn, 1981–90); Member: Home Grown Timber Adv. Cttee, Forestry Commn, 1981–87; NERC, 1988–91 (Chm., Terrestrial and Freshwater Sci. Cttee, 1990–91). Mem., Gen. Council, RICS, 1983–87 (Pres., Planning and Develt Divl Council, 1984–85). Mem., MacTaggart Chair Adv. Bd, Glasgow Univ., 1992–2000. FRSA, FIMgt. Hon. Fellow, Commonwealth Assoc. of Surveying and Land Economy, 1992. Founder and Editor, Land Development Studies (subseq. Jl of Property Research), 1983–90. *Publications:* (ed with N. Nanthakumeran) Property Investment Theory, 1988; National Taxation for Property Management and Valuation, 1990. *Recreations:* hill walking, field sports, golf. *Address:* St Helen's, Ceres, Fife KY15 5NQ. *T:* (01334) 828862. *Club:* Royal Northern and University (Aberdeen).

See also D. W. MacLeary.

MacLEARY, Donald Whyte; Principal Répétiteur to the Principal Artists, Royal Ballet, since 1999 (Répétiteur, 1981–94; Senior Répétiteur, 1994–99); *b* Glasgow, 22 Aug. 1937; *s* of Donald Herbert MacLeary, MPS, and Jean Spiers (*née* Leslie). *Educ:* Inverness Royal Academy; The Royal Ballet School. Principal male dancer, 1959–78, Ballet Master, 1978–81, Royal Ballet. *Classical Ballets:* (full length) Swan Lake, Giselle, 1958; Sleeping Beauty, Cinderella, Sylvia, 1959; Ondine, La Fille Mal Gardée, 1960; (centre male rôle) in Ashton's Symphonic Variations, 1962; Sonnet Pas de Trois, 1964; Romeo and Juliet, 1965; Eugene Onegin, Stuttgart, 1966; Apollo, 1966; Nutcracker, 1968; Swan Lake with N. Makarova, 1972. *Creations:* (1954–74): Solitaire, The Burrow, Danse Concertante, Antigone, Diversions, Le Baiser de la Fée, Jabez and the Devil, Raymonda Pas de Deux (for Frederick Ashton), two episodes in Images of Love; Song of the Earth; Lilac Garden (revival); Jazz Calendar; Raymonda (for Nureyeff); The Man in Kenneth MacMillan's Checkpoint; leading role in Concerto no 2 (Balanchine's Ballet Imperial, renamed); Elite Syncopations, 1974; Kenneth MacMillan's Four Seasons Symphony; the Prince in Cinderella. Toured Brazil with Royal Ballet, Spring 1973. Guest dancer, Scottish Ballet, 1979. *Recreations:* reading, theatre, records (all types); riding, swimming. *Club:* Queen's.

See also A. R. MacLeary.

MACLEAY, Rev. Canon John Henry James; Dean of Argyll and The Isles, 1987–99; Rector of St Andrew's, Fort William, 1978–99; retired; *b* 7 Dec. 1931; *s* of James and Isabella Macleay; *m* 1970, Jane Speirs Cuthbert; one *s* one *d*. *Educ:* St Edmund Hall, Oxford (MA); College of the Resurrection, Mirfield. Deacon 1957, priest 1958, Southwark; Curate: St John's, East Dulwich, 1957–60; St Michael's, Inverness, 1960–62, Rector 1962–70; Priest-in-charge, St Columba's, Grantown-on-Spey with St John the Baptist's, Rothiemurchus, 1970–78; Canon of St Andrew's Cathedral, Inverness, 1977–78; Canon of St John's Cathedral, Oban and Synod Clerk, Diocese of Argyll and the Isles, 1980–87. Hon. Canon, Oban Cathedral, 1999–. *Recreations:* fishing, reading, visiting cathedrals and churches. *Address:* 47 Riverside Park, Lochyside, Fort William PH33 7RB. *T:* (01397) 700117.

McLEAY, Hon. Leo Boyce; MP (Lab) Watson, New South Wales, since 1993 (Grayndler, 1979–93); Chief Opposition Whip and Deputy Manager of Opposition business, House of Representatives, Australia, since 1996; *b* 5 Oct. 1945; *s* of Ron and Joan McLeay; *m* 1969, Janice Delaney; three *s*. *Educ:* De La Salle Sch., Marrickville; North Sydney Technical Coll. Telephone technician, 1962–76; Asst Gen. Sec., ALP (NSW), 1976–79; Dep. Speaker, 1986–89, Speaker, 1989–93, Chief Govt Whip, 1993–96, House of Representatives, Australia. *Recreations:* fishing, reading. *Address:* Parliament House, Canberra, ACT 2600, Australia. *T:* (2) 62774083. *Club:* Canterbury Rugby League (NSW).

McLEISH, Rt Hon. Henry (Baird); PC 2000; Member (Lab) Fife Central, Scottish Parliament, since 1999; *b* 15 June 1948; *s* of Harry McLeish and late Mary McLeish; *m* 1968, Margaret Thomson Drysdale (*d* 1995); one *s* one *d*; *m* 1998, Julie Fulton. *Educ:* Heriot-Watt Univ. (BA Hons planning). Research Officer, Social Work Dept, Edinburgh, 1973–74; Planning Officer, Fife County Council, 1974–75; Planning Officer, Dunfermline DC, 1975–87; part time Lectr/Tutor, Heriot-Watt Univ., 1973–87; part-time employment consultant, 1984–87. Member: Kirkcaldy DC (Chm., Planning Cttee, 1974–77); Fife Regl Council (Chm., Further Educn Cttee, 1978–82; Leader, Council, 1982–87). MP (Lab) Central Fife, 1987–2001. Minister of State, Scottish Office, 1997–99; Scottish Executive: Minister for Enterprise and Lifelong Learning, 1999–2000; First Minister, 2000–01. *Recreations:* reading, malt whisky (history and development of), history, life and works of Robert Burns, Highlands and Islands of Scotland. *Address:* Scottish Parliament, George IV Bridge, Edinburgh EH99 1SP; 12 Little Carron Gardens, St Andrews, Fife KY16 8QL. *Clubs:* Denbeath Miners' Welfare; Glenrothes Football Recreation.

MacLELLAN, Maj.-Gen. (Andrew) Patrick (Withy), CB 1981; CVO 1989; MBE 1964; Resident Governor and Keeper of the Jewel House, HM Tower of London, 1984–89; *b* 29 Nov. 1925; *y s* of late Kenneth MacLellan and Rachel Madeline MacLellan (*née* Withy); *m* 1954, Kathleen Mary Bagnell; one *s* twin *d*. *Educ:* Uppingham. Commnd Coldstream Guards, 1944; served Palestine 1945–48, N Africa 1950–51, Egypt 1952–53, Germany 1955–56; psc 1957; DAA&QMG 4th Guards Brigade Group, 1958–59; Mil. Asst to Chief of Defence Staff, 1961–64; Instructor, Staff Coll., Camberley, 1964–66; GSO1 (Plans) Far East Comd, 1966–67; CO 1st Bn Coldstream Guards, 1968–70; Col GS Near East Land Forces, 1970–71; Comdr 8th Inf. Brigade, 1971–72; RCDS 1973; Dep. Comdr and COS, London District, 1974–77; Pres., Regular Commns Bd, 1978–80. Vice-Pres., Officers' Assoc. Mem. Cttee, Royal Humane Soc.; Chm., Adv. Council, First Aid Nursing Yeomanry (The Princess Royal's Volunteer Corps). FIMgt (FBIM 1970). Mem. (Walbrook Ward), Court of Common Council, City of London, 1989– (Chm., Police Cttee, 1995–97). Freeman: City of London, 1984; Co. of Watermen and Lightermen; Liveryman, Fletchers' Co., 1986– (Master, 1997–98). Chevalier de la Légion d'Honneur, 1960; Order of the Sacred Treasure (Japan), 1998. *Address:* c/o Bank of Scotland, London Chief Office, 38 Threadneedle Street, EC2P 2EH. *Clubs:* White's, Pratt's.

McLELLAN, Very Rev. Andrew Rankin Cowie; Minister, Parish Church of St Andrew and St George, Edinburgh, since 1986; Moderator of the General Assembly of the Church of Scotland, 2000–01; *b* 16 June 1944; *s* of Andrew Barclay McLellan and Catherine Hilda McLellan (*née* Cowie); *m* 1975, Irene Lamont Meek; twin *s*. *Educ:* Kilmarnock Acad.; Madras Coll., St Andrews; St Andrews Univ. (MA 1965); Glasgow Univ. (BD 1968); Union Theol Seminary, NY (STM 1969). Asst Minister, St George's West, Edinburgh, 1969–71; Minister: Cartsburn Augustine, Greenock, 1971–80; Viewfield, Stirling, 1980–86. Tutor, Glasgow Univ., 1978–82; Chaplain, HM Prison, Stirling, 1982–85. Chairman: George St Assoc. of Edinburgh, 1990–93; Scottish Religious Adv. Cttee, BBC, 1996–; Convener, Church and Nation Cttee, Gen. Assembly of the Church of Scotland, 1992–96. Warrack Lectr on Preaching, Divinity Faculties of Scotland, 2000. Mem., Inverclyde DC, 1977–80. *Publications:* Preaching for these People, 1997; Gentle and Passionate, 2001. *Recreations:* sport, travel, books. *Address:* 25 Comely Bank, Edinburgh EH4 1AJ. *T:* (0131) 332 5324.

McLELLAN, Prof. David, DPhil; Professor of Political Theory, University of Kent, 1975–99; *b* 10 Feb. 1940; *s* of Robert Douglas McLellan and Olive May Bush; *m* 1967, Annie Brassart; two *d*. *Educ:* Merchant Taylors' Sch.; St John's Coll., Oxford (MA, DPhil). University of Kent: Lectr in Politics, 1966–71; Sen. Lectr in Politics, 1972–73; Reader in Political Theory, 1973–75. Visiting Professor: State Univ. of New York, 1969; Goldsmiths Coll., Univ. of London, 1999–; Guest Fellow in Politics, Indian Inst. of Advanced Studies, Simla, 1970. *Publications:* The Young Hegelians and Karl Marx, 1969 (French, German, Italian, Spanish and Japanese edns); Marx before Marxism, 1970, 2nd edn 1972; Karl Marx: The Early Texts, 1971; Marx's Grundrisse, 1971, 2nd edn 1973; The Thought of Karl Marx, 1971 (Portuguese and Italian edns); Karl Marx: His Life and Thought, 1973, 22nd edn 1976 (German, Italian, Spanish, Japanese, Swedish and Dutch edns); Marx (Fontana Modern Masters), 1975; Engels, 1977; Marxism after Marx, 1979; (ed) Marx: the first hundred years, 1983; Karl Marx: the legacy, 1983; Ideology, 1986; Marxism and Religion, 1987; Simone Weil: Utopian pessimist, 1989; Christianity and Politics, 1990; Religion and Public Life, 1992; Unto Caesar: the political relevance of Christianity, 1993; Case Law and Political Theory, 1996; (ed) Political Christianity, 1997. *Recreations:* chess, Raymond Chandler, hill walking. *Address:* c/o Rutherford College, University of Kent, Canterbury, Kent CT2 7NX.

MacLELLAN, Maj.-Gen. Patrick; *see* MacLellan, A. P. W.

McLELLAND, Charles James; Director General, Association of British Travel Agents, 1987; *b* 19 Nov. 1930; *s* of Charles John McLelland and Jessie Steele Barbour; *m* 1961, Philippa Mary Murphy; one *s* three *d*. *Educ:* Kilmarnock Acad.; Glasgow Acad.; Glasgow Univ. (MA). Commissioned Royal Artillery, 1952–54. Sub-Editor, Leader Writer, Glasgow Herald, 1954–58; Scriptwriter, European Productions, BBC, 1958–61; Head of Programmes, Radio Sarawak, 1962–64; Indian Programme Organiser, BBC, 1964–67; Asst Head, Arabic Service, BBC, 1967–71; Head of Arabic Service, 1971–75; Controller, BBC Radio 2, 1976–80 (also Radio 1, 1976–78); Dep. Man. Dir and Dir of Progs, BBC Radio, 1980–86. Chm., EBU Radio Prog. Cttee, 1985–86; Pres., Overseas Broadcasters' Club, 1985–89, Hon. Vice-Pres., 1990–. Mem. Council, Officers' Assoc., 1989–. Trustee, Bourke Trust, 1991–92. *Address:* 14 High Street, Tisbury, Wilts SP3 6HG.

MACLENNAN, family name of **Baron Maclennan of Rogart**.

MACLENNAN OF ROGART, Baron *cr* 2001 (Life Peer), of Rogart in Sutherland; **Robert Adam Ross Maclennan;** PC 1997; President, Liberal Democrats, 1994–98; Barrister-at-Law; *b* 26 June 1936; *e s* of late Sir Hector MacLennan and Isabel Margaret Adam; *m* 1968, Mrs Helen Noyes, *d* of late Judge Ammi Cutter, Cambridge, Mass, and *widow* of Paul H. Noyes; one *s* one *d*, and one step *s*. *Educ:* Glasgow Academy; Balliol Coll., Oxford; Trinity Coll., Cambridge; Columbia Univ., New York City. Called to the Bar, Gray's Inn, 1962. MP Caithness and Sutherland, 1966–97 (Lab, 1966–81, SDP, 1981–88, Lib Dem, 1988–97), (Lib Dem) Caithness, Sutherland and Easter Ross, 1997–2001. Parliamentary Private Secretary: to Secretary of State for Commonwealth Affairs, 1967–69; to Minister without Portfolio, 1969–70; an Opposition Spokesman: on Scottish Affairs, 1970–71; on Defence, 1971–72; Parly Under-Sec. of State, Dept of Prices and Consumer Protection, 1974–79; opposition spokesman on foreign affairs, 1980–81; SDP spokesman on agriculture, fisheries and food, 1981–87; Leader, SDP, 1987–88; Jt Leader, SLD, 1988; Lib Dem spokesman on home affairs and the arts, 1988–94, on constitutional affairs and culture, 1994–2001. Member: House of Commons Estimates Cttee, 1967–69; House of Commons Select Cttee on Scottish Affairs, 1969–70; Public Accounts Cttee, 1979–99. Mem., Latey Cttee on Age of Majority, 1968. *Publications:* libretti: The Lie, 1992; Friend of the People, 1999. *Recreations:* theatre, music, visual arts. *Address:* House of Lords, SW1A 0PW.

MacLENNAN, Dr David Herman, FRS 1994; FRSC 1985; University Professor, University of Toronto, since 1993; *b* 3 July 1937; *s* of Douglas Henry MacLennan and Sigridur MacLennan (*née* Sigurdson; *m* 1965, Linda Carol Vass; two *s* (one *d* decd). *Educ:* Swan River Collegiate Inst., Canada; Univ. of Manitoba (BSA 1959); Purdue Univ. (MS 1961; PhD 1963). Postdoctoral Fellow, 1963–64, Asst Prof., 1964–68, Inst. for Enzyme Res., Univ. of Wisconsin; Banting and Best Department of Medical Research, University of Toronto: Associate Prof., 1969–74; Prof., 1974–93; Acting Chm., 1978–80; Chm., 1980–90; J. W. Billes Prof. of Med. Res., 1987–. Principal Investigator, Canadian Genetic Diseases Network, 1991–; Consultant, Merck, Sharp & Dohme, PA, 1992–98. Member: Med. Adv. Bd, Muscular Dystrophy Assoc., Canada, 1976–87; Scientists' Review Panel, MRC Canada, 1988–90; Univ. of Ottawa Heart Inst. Res. Review Panel, 1991–94; Chm., Molecular Biol. and Pathol. Cttee, Heart and Stroke Foundn of Canada, 1995–99; Gairdner Foundn Review Panel, 1999–2001; Med. Adv Bd, 2001–. Fellow, Internat. Soc. Heart Res., 2001; For. Associate, NAS, USA, 2001. Hon. DSc Manitoba, 2001. Awards include: Ayerst Award, Canadian Biochem. Soc., 1974; Internat. Lectr Award, Biophys. Soc., 1990; Gairdner Foundn Internat. Award, 1991; Izaak Walton Killam Meml Prize for Health Scis, Canada Council, 1997; Jonas Salk Award, Ontario March of Dimes, 1998; Royal Soc. Glaxo Wellcome Prize, Medal and Lecture, 2000. *Publications:* ed and contribs to numerous learned jls. *Recreations:* collecting and restoring Canadian antique furniture, reading fiction, listening to classical music, gardening, ski-ing. *Address:* Banting and Best Department of Medical Research, University of Toronto, C. H. Best Institute, 112 College Street, Toronto, ON M5G 1L6, Canada. *T:* (416) 9785008; 293 Lytton Boulevard, Toronto, ON M5N 1R7, Canada. *T:* (416) 4879729.

MacLENNAN, David Ross; HM Diplomatic Service; *b* 12 Feb. 1945; *s* of David Ross MacLennan and Agnes McConnell; *m* 1964, Margaret Lytollis; two *d*. *Educ:* West Calder High Sch. FO, 1963; ME Centre for Arab Studies, 1966–69; Third, later Second Sec., Aden, 1969–71; Second, later First Sec., FCO, 1972–75; First Sec., UK Delegn to OECD, Paris, 1975–79; First Sec., Hd of Chancery, Abu Dhabi, 1979–82; Asst Hd, N America Dept, FCO, 1982–84; EEC, Brussels, 1984–85; Counsellor, Kuwait, 1985–88; Dep. High Comr, Nicosia, 1989–90; Consul Gen., Jerusalem, 1990–93; Counsellor, Head of Africa Dept (Equatorial), FCO, and Comr, British Indian Ocean Territory, 1994–96; Ambassador to Lebanese Republic, 1996–2000. *Recreations:* archaeology, natural history. *Address:* c/o Foreign and Commonwealth Office, SW1A 2AH.

MACLENNAN, Prof. Duncan, CBE 1997; FRSE; Mactaggart Professor of Land Economics and Finance, University of Glasgow, since 1990; Special Adviser to the First Minister of Scotland, since 1999; *b* 12 March 1949; *s* of James Dempster Maclennan and Mary Mackechnie (*née* Campbell); *m* (separated); one *s* one *d*. *Educ:* Allan Glen's Sch., Glasgow; Univ. of Glasgow (MA, MPhil). FRSE 1999. Lectr in Pol Econ., Aberdeen Univ., 1976–79; Glasgow University: Lectr in Applied Econs, 1979–81; Sen. Lectr, 1981–84; Titular Prof., 1984–88; Prof. of Urban Studies, 1988–90; Director: Centre for Housing Res. and Urban Studies, 1983–96; Cities Programme, ESRC, 1996–99. Susman Prof. of Real Estate Finance, Wharton Bus. Sch., 1988; Regent's Prof., Univ. of Calif at Berkeley, 1996. Chairman: Care and Repair (Scotland), 1987–94; Shelter (Scotland) Adv. Council, 1989–; Dir, Joseph Rowntree Res. Programme, 1988–94; Chm., Joseph Rowntree Area Regeneration Steering Gp, 1996–2000; Mem. Bd, Scottish Homes, 1989–99. Mem., HM Treasury Panel of Advisers, 1995–. FRSA 1993. *Publications:* Regional Policy in Britain, 1979; Housing Economics, 1982; Paying for Britain's Housing, 1990; The Housing Authority of the Future, 1991; Fairer Subsidies, Faster Growth, 1992; Fixed Commitments, Uncertain Incomes, 1997; Changing Places, Engaging People, 2000; contribs to Urban Studies, Housing Studies, Economic Jl, Applied Econs. *Recreations:* gardening, cooking, Rugby, watching Glasgow get better. *Address:* 3 Glenburn Road, Bearsden, Glasgow G61 4PT. *T:* (0141) 942 1394.

McLENNAN, Gordon; General Secretary, Communist Party of Great Britain, 1975–89; *b* Glasgow, 12 May 1924; *s* of a shipyard worker; *m*; four *c*. *Educ:* Hamilton Crescent Sch., Partick, Glasgow. Engineering apprentice, Albion Motors Ltd, Scotstoun, 1939, later engineering draughtsman. Elected Glasgow Organiser, Communist Party, 1949; Sec., Communist Party in Scotland, 1957; Nat. Organiser, Communist Party of GB, 1966. *Recreations:* golf and other sports; cultural interests. *Address:* c/o Democratic Left, 6 Cynthia Street, N1 9JF.

MacLENNAN, Graeme Andrew Yule, CA; Director, Phillips & Drew Fund Management, 1990–93; Chairman, Noble Asset Management, since 2000 (Director, since 1998); *b* 24 Aug. 1942; *s* of Finlay and Helen MacLennan; *m* 1st, 1973, Diane Marion Gibbon (*née* Fyfe) (marr. diss. 1989); two *s* two *d*; 2nd, 1989, Diana Rosemary Steven (*née* Urie). *Educ:* Kelvinside Academy, Glasgow. Asst Investment Manager, Leopold Joseph & Sons Ltd, London, 1964–68; Investment Man., Murray Johnstone & Co., Glasgow, 1969–70; Edinburgh Fund Managers: Investment Man., 1970; Dir, 1980, Jt Man. Dir, 1983–88; Investment Dir, Ivory & Sime plc, 1988–90; Hd, Investment Trust Business, LGT Asset Management, 1995–98; non-executive Director: HTR Japanese Smaller Cos Trust, 1993–96; Premium Trust, 1993–; TriVen VCT, 1999–; Financial Services Compensation Scheme, 2000–; TriVest VCT, 2000–. MSI; FRSA. *Recreations:* hill walking, fishing. *Address:* The Old School House, 5 Main Street, Killearn, Glasgow G63 9RJ. *T:* (01360) 550127.

MacLENNAN, Prof. Ian Calman Muir, PhD; FRCP, FRCPath; Professor of Immunology, since 1979 and Director, MRC Centre for Immune Regulation, since 1999, University of Birmingham; *b* Inverness, 30 Dec. 1939; *s* of late Calman MacLennan and Mary Helen MacLennan (*née* Muir, subseq. Roxburgh) and step *s* of William Alexander Roxburgh; *m* 1965, Pamela Bennett; two *s*. *Educ:* Guy's Hosp. Med. Sch., Univ. of London (BSc Anatomy 1962; MB BS 1965; PhD 1970). FRCPath 1985; FRCP 1995. SHO, MRC Rheumatism Res. Unit, Taplow, 1966–69 (ARC Res. Fellow); Lectr, Nuffield Dept of Clin. Medicine, Oxford Univ., 1969–79; Hd, Dept of Immunology, 1979–1998, Hd, Div. of Immunity and Infection, 1998–2000, Univ. of Birmingham. Medical Research Council: Co-ordinator, trials in Multiple Myeloma, 1980–98; Chm., Wkg Party on Leukaemia in Adults, 1982–92; Dep. Chm., Cell Biol. and Disorders Bd, 1983–87 (Chm., Grants Cttee A, 1982–84); Mem. Council, and Chm., Molecular and Cellular Medicine Bd, 2000–. Sec., British Soc. for Immunol., 1973–79. Founding Fellow FMedSci, 1998. Mem., Birmingham Med. Res. Expeditionary Soc., 1986–. Hon. Life Mem., Scandinavian Soc. Immunol., 1995. *Publications:* numerous contribs to learned jls, incl. Immunological Reviews, Nature, Annual Rev. of Immunol., Jl Exptl Medicine. *Recreations:* climbing, ski-ing, observing the natural world, listening to and supporting the City of Birmingham SO. *Address:* MRC Centre for Immune Regulation, University of Birmingham, Birmingham B15 2TT.

McLENNAN, William Patrick, CBE 1997; AM 1992; Australian Statistician, Australian Bureau of Statistics, 1995–2000; *b* 26 Jan. 1942; *s* of William Freeman McLennan and Linda Maude Shannon; *m* 1968, Christine Elizabeth Alexander; one *s* one *d*. *Educ:* Australian National University (BEcon Hons). Statistician, Aust. Bureau of Statistics, 1960–92; Dep. Aust. Statistician, 1986–92; Dir, CSO, and Head of Govt Statistical Service, UK, 1992–95. Vis. Fellow, Nuffield Coll., Oxford, 1992–95. *Recreations:* sport, Rugby, squash, golf. *Address:* 47 MacKellar Crescent, Cook, ACT 2614, Australia.

MacLEOD, Dr Calum Alexander, CBE 1991; Chairman: Aberdeen Development Capital plc, since 1986; Grampian Television, since 1993 (Deputy Chairman, 1982–93); *b* 25 July 1935; *s* of Rev. Lachlan Macleod and Jessie Mary Morrison; *m* 1962, Elizabeth Margaret Davidson; two *s* one *d*. *Educ:* Nicolson Inst., Stornoway; Glenurquhart High Sch.; Aberdeen Univ. Partner, Paull & Williamsons Advocates, Aberdeen, 1964–80; Chairman: Aberdeen Petroleum, 1982–92; Harris Tweed Assoc. Authority, 1984–93 (Vice-Chm., 1993–95); Deputy Chairman: Scottish Eastern Investment Trust, 1988–99; Britannia Life, 1992–94 (Chm., 1990–92); Britannia Building Society, 1993–94 and 1999–2000 (Chm., 1994–99); SMG plc (formerly Scottish Media Group), 1997– (acting Chm., 1998–99); Martin Currie Portfolio Investment Trust plc, 1999–; Director: North Bd, Bank of Scotland, 1980–2000; Bradstock Gp, 1994–98; Macdonald Hotels, 1995–. Member: White Fish Authy, 1973–80; N of Scotland Hydro-Electric Bd, 1976–84; Highlands and Islands Develt Bd, 1984–91; Chm., Grampian Health Bd, 1993–2000.

Chairman: Chancellor's Assessor, Aberdeen Univ., 1979–90; Robert Gordon's Coll., 1981–94; SATRO North Scotland, 1986–90; Scottish Council of Indep. Schs, 1992–97; Trustee, Carnegie Trust for the Univs of Scotland, 1997–; Gov., Caledonian Res. Foundn, 1990–94. Hon LLD Aberdeen, 1986. *Recreations:* golf, motoring, Hebridean coastal walking, reading, music. *Address:* 6 Westfield Terrace, Aberdeen AB25 2RU. *T:* (01224) 846600. *Clubs:* Royal Northern and University (Aberdeen); Royal Aberdeen Golf; Nairn Golf.

McLEOD, Sir Charles Henry, 3rd Bt *cr* 1925; *b* 7 Nov. 1924; *o surv. s* of Sir Murdoch Campbell McLeod, 2nd Bt, and Annette Susan Mary (*d* 1964), *d* of Henry Whitehead, JP, 26 Pelham Crescent, SW7; *S* father, 1950; *m* 1957, Gillian (*d* 1978), *d* of Henry Bowlby, London; one *s* two *d*. *Educ:* Winchester. Diploma Master Brewer, 1950. Member, London Stock Exchange, 1955–. Part-time in-house proof-reader and freelancer, 1998–. Represented India, Squash Rackets Internat., 1956–58. *Heir: s* James Roderick Charles McLeod [*b* 26 Sept. 1960; *m* 1990, Helen M. Cooper, *d* of Captain George Cooper, OBE, RN]. *Clubs:* MCC; I Zingari, Free Foresters, Jesters.

McLEOD, Prof. David, FRCS, FRCOphth; Professor, and Head of Department of Ophthalmology, University of Manchester, since 1988; Hon. Consultant Ophthalmologist, Manchester Royal Eye Hospital, since 1988; *b* 16 Jan. 1946; *s* of Norman McLeod and Anne McLeod (*née* Heyworth); *m* 1967, Jeanette Allison Cross; one *s* one *d*. *Educ:* Univ. of Edinburgh (BSc 1st cl. Hons Physiology 1966; MB ChB Hons 1969). FRCS 1974; FRCOphth 1989. House Physician and Surg., Edinburgh Royal Infirmary, 1969–70; Sen. House Officer and Res. Fellow, Princess Alexandra Eye Pavilion, Edinburgh, 1970–72; Moorfields Eye Hospital: RSO, 1972–75; Fellow in Vitreoretinal Surgery and Ultrasound, 1975–78; Consultant Ophthalmic Surg., 1978–88. Civilian Consultant Ophthalmologist, RAF, 1984–. Vis. Prof., UMIST, 1996–. Vice-Pres., Royal Coll. of Ophthalmologists, 1997–2001. Mem., Club Jules Gonin, Lausanne. *Publications:* over 120 publications on retinal vascular disease, diabetic retinopathy, vitreoretinal surgery, vitreous pathology. *Recreations:* golf, ballroom dancing. *Address:* Royal Eye Hospital, Oxford Road, Manchester M13 9WH. *T:* (0161) 276 5620; Langdale, 370 Chester Road, Woodford, Stockport, Cheshire SK7 1QG. *Clubs:* Royal Air Force; Bramall Park Golf.

MacLEOD, Donald Alexander; HM Diplomatic Service, retired; study course organiser, since 1990; *b* 23 Jan. 1938; *er s* of late Col Colin S. MacLeod of Glendale, OBE, TD, and of Margaret Drysdale Robertson MacLeod; *m* 1963, Rosemary Lilian Abel (*née* Randle); two *s* two *d*. *Educ:* Edinburgh Academy; Pembroke Coll., Cambridge, 1958–61 (BA). National Service, Queen's Own Cameron Highlanders, 1956–58. HM Foreign Service, 1961; School of Oriental and African Studies, London, 1961–62; British Embassy, Rangoon, 1962–66; Private Sec. to Minister of State, Commonwealth Office, 1966–69; First Secretary, Ottawa, 1969–73; FCO, 1973–78; First Sec./Head of Chancery, Bucharest, 1978–80; Counsellor (Econ. and Commercial), Singapore, 1981–84. Dep. High Comr, Bridgetown, 1984–87; Hd of Protocol Dept, FCO, 1987–89. *Address:* Kinlochfollart, by Dunvegan, Isle of Skye IV55 8WQ.

McLEOD, Fiona Grace; Member (SNP) West of Scotland, Scottish Parliament, since 1999; *b* 3 Dec. 1957; *d* of John McLeod and Irene McLeod (*née* Robertson); *m* 1979, Dr Andrew David Rankine; one *s*. *Educ:* Glasgow Univ. (MA Hons Medieval and Modern Hist.); Strathclyde Univ. (Postgrad. DipLib). ALA. Librarian: Balfron High Sch., 1983–87; Glasgow North Coll. of Nursing, 1987–90; Marie Curie Centre Huntershill Liby, 1995–98. *Recreations:* Scottish castles, walking. *Address:* Scottish Parliament, Edinburgh EH99 1SP. *T:* (0131) 348 5669.

MACLEOD, Sir Hamish; *see* Macleod, Sir N. W. H.

MacLEOD, Prof. Iain Alasdair, PhD; CEng, FICE, FIStructE; Professor of Structural Engineering, University of Strathclyde, since 1981; *b* 4 May 1939; *s* of Donald MacLeod and Barbara (*née* MacKenzie); *m* 1967, Barbara Jean Booth; one *s* one *d*. *Educ:* Lenzie Acad.; Univ. of Glasgow (BSc 1960, PhD 1966). CEng 1968; FIStructE 1982; FICE 1984. Asst Engr, Crouch & Hogg, Glasgow, 1960–62; Asst Lectr in Civil Engrg, Univ. of Glasgow, 1962–66; Structural Engineer: H. A. Simons Internat., Vancouver, Canada, 1966–67; Portland Cement Assoc., Skokie, USA, 1968–69; Lectr in Civil Engrg, Univ. of Glasgow, 1969–73; Prof. and Head of Dept of Civil Engrg, Paisley Coll. of Technol., 1973–81. Vice-Pres., IStructE, 1989–90; Mem., Standing Cttee on Structural Safety, IStructE and ICE, 1990–97. FRSA. Lewis Kent Award, IStructE, 1998. *Publications:* Analytical Modelling of Structural Systems, 1990; over 80 published papers. *Recreations:* sailing, hill walking. *Address:* Department of Civil Engineering, University of Strathclyde, Glasgow G4 0NG. *T:* (0141) 548 3275.

McLEOD, Brig. Ian, CMG 1999; OBE 1983; MC 1965; Division for Relations with Armed and Security Forces, International Committee of the Red Cross, since 1999; *b* 19 June 1941; *s* of David Drummond McLeod and Eleanor McLeod (*née* Williams); *m* 1966, Janet Edith Prosser Angus; one *s* two *d*. *Educ:* Rhondda Co. Grammar Sch.; RMA Sandhurst; sc 1973; ndc 1991; BA Open Univ. 1990. Commnd Parachute Regt, 1961; service in 3 Para, UK, Gulf and Aden, 1961–67; Jungle Warfare Sch., Malaya, 1967–69; 2 Para, 1969–71; SC, 1971–73; HQ 44 Para Bde (V), 1974–75; 82 AB Div., US Army, 1976–77; Co. Comd, 3 Para, BAOR, 1977–79; GSO2, Defence Ops Analysis Estabt, 1979–81; CO 1 Para, 1981–84; SO1, SC, 1984–86; Col Operational Requirements, MoD, 1986–87; UK Liaison Officer, US Army, 1987–89; Comd, 42 Inf. Bde, 1989–91; Defence Advr, British High Commn, Islamabad, 1992–94; retd 1995; Mem., EC Monitor Mission to former Yugoslavia, 1995–97; Dep. Hd, Regl Office in Brcko of High Rep. for Bosnia, 1997–98; Mem., Kosovo Verification Mission, OSCE, 1998–99. Freeman, City of London, 1992. *Recreations:* travel, ski-ing, military history. *Address:* c/o HSBC, 33 The Borough, Farnham, Surrey GU9 7NJ.

MACLEOD, Ian Buchanan, FRCSE; Hon. Secretary, Royal College of Surgeons of Edinburgh, 1993–96; Consultant Surgeon, Royal Infirmary, Edinburgh, and Hon. Senior Lecturer, Department of Clinical Surgery, University of Edinburgh, 1969–93; Surgeon to the Queen in Scotland, 1987–93; *b* 20 May 1933; *s* of Donald Macleod, MB, ChB, and Katie Ann Buchanan; *m* 1961, Kathleen Gillean Large; one *s* one *d*. *Educ:* Wigan Grammar Sch.; Univ. of Edinburgh (BSc Hons; MB ChB Hons). FRCSE 1962. Resident appts, Royal Inf., Edinburgh, 1957–59. National Service, MO RAMC, 1959–61. Res. Fellow, Lectr and Sen. Lectr, Univ. of Edinburgh, 1962–93; Hon. and Cons. Surg., Royal Inf., Edinburgh, 1969–93. Editor, Journal of Royal College of Surgeons of Edinburgh, 1982–87. *Publications:* Principles and Practice of Surgery (with A. P. M. Forrest and D. C. Carter), 1985; (contrib.) A Companion to Medical Studies, 1968, 3rd edn 1985; (contrib.) Farquharson's Textbook of Operative Surgery, 1986; papers in surgical jls. *Recreations:* golf, photography. *Address:* Derwent House, 32 Cramond Road North, Edinburgh EH4 6JE. *T:* (0131) 336 1541. *Clubs:* Bruntsfield Links Golfing Society (Edinburgh); Honourable Company of Edinburgh Golfers (Muirfield).
See also N. R. B. Macleod.

MACLEOD, Jean Grant; *see* Scott, J. G.

McLEOD, Rev. John; Minister of Resolis and Urquhart, 1986–93; Chaplain to the Queen in Scotland, 1978–96, an Extra Chaplain, since 1996; *b* 8 April 1926; *s* of Angus McLeod and Catherine McDougall; *m* 1958, Sheila McLeod; three *s* two *d*. *Educ:* Inverness Royal Academy; Edinburgh Univ. (MA); New Coll., Edinburgh. Farming until 1952; at university, 1952–58; ordained, Inverness, 1958. Missionary in India: Jalna, 1959–68; Poona, 1969–74; involved in rural development with special emphasis on development and conservation of water resource; also responsible for pastoral work in Church of N India, St Mary's, Poona, 1970–74; Church of Scotland Minister, Livingston Ecumenical Team Ministry, 1974–86. *Recreations:* hill walking, gardening. *Address:* Benview, 19 Balvaird, Muir of Ord, Ross-shire IV7 6RQ. *T:* (01463) 871286.

MacLEOD, John; Chairman, British Beet Research Organisation, since 2000; Professor of Horticulture, Royal Horticultural Society, since 2001; *b* 16 Aug. 1939; *s* of James Rae MacLeod and Mollie McKee MacLeod (*née* Shaw); *m* 1966, Janet Patricia Beavan, sculptor; one *s* (and one *s* decd). *Educ:* Nicolson Inst., Stornoway; Univ. of Glasgow (BSc Hons Agr. 1962); Michigan State Univ. (MS 1964). ARAgS 1998. NAAS, later ADAS, MAFF, 1964–90. Director: Arthur Rickwood Exptl Farm, 1982–85; ADAS Exptl Farms, MAFF, 1985–90; NIAB, Cambridge, 1990–99. Pres., Groupe Consultatif Internat. de Recherche sur le Colza, Paris, 1993–97; Vice-Chm., BCPC, 2000–. *Recreations:* long term restoration of a 16th century farmhouse and garden, sculpture, early music, walking. *Address:* British Beet Research Organisation, The Research Station, Great North Road, Thornhaugh, Peterborough PE8 6HJ; Church Farm House, Over, Cambs CB4 5NX.

MacLEOD OF MacLEOD, John; 29th Chief of MacLeod; *b* 10 Aug. 1935; second *s* of late Captain Robert Wolrige-Gordon, MC, and Joan, *d* of Hubert Walter and Dame Flora MacLeod of MacLeod, DBE; officially recognised in name of MacLeod of MacLeod by decree of Lyon Court, 1951; *S* grandmother, 1976; *m* 1973, Melita Kolin; one *s* one *d*. *Educ:* Eton. *Heir: s* Hugh Magnus MacLeod, younger of MacLeod. *Address:* Dunvegan Castle, Isle of Skye. *T:* (01470) 521206.
See also P. Wolrige-Gordon.

McLEOD, Prof. John Bryce, DPhil; FRS 1992; Professor of Mathematics, University of Pittsburgh, since 1988; *b* 23 Dec. 1929; *s* of John McLeod and Adeline Annie (*née* Bryce); *m* 1956, Eunice Martin Third; three *s* one *d*. *Educ:* Aberdeen Grammar Sch.; Univ. of Aberdeen (MA 1950); Oxford Univ. (BA 1952, MA, DPhil 1958). Rotary Foundn Fellow, Univ. of BC, 1952–53; Educn Officer, RAF, 1953–55; Harmsworth Sen. Scholar, Merton Coll., Oxford, 1955–56; Jun. Lectr in Maths, Oxford Univ., 1956–58; Lectr, Univ. of Edinburgh, 1958–60; University of Oxford: Fellow, Wadham Coll., 1960–91; Lectr in Maths, 1960–88; Jun. Proctor, 1963–64; Sen. Fellow, SERC, 1986–91. *Publications:* numerous papers in mathematical jls. *Recreations:* travel, music, gardening. *Address:* Department of Mathematics, University of Pittsburgh, Pittsburgh, PA 15260, USA. *T:* (412) 6241273.

MacLEOD, Hon. Sir (John) Maxwell (Norman), 5th Bt *cr* 1924, of Fuinary, Morven, Co. Argyll; *b* 23 Feb. 1952; *s* of Baron MacLeod of Fuinary (Life Peer), MC and Lorna Helen Janet (*d* 1984), *er d* of late Rev. Donald Macleod; *S* to baronetcy of father, 1991. *Educ:* Gordonstoun. *Heir: b* Hon. Neil David MacLeod, *b* 25 Dec. 1959. *Address:* Fuinary Manse, Loch Aline, Morven, Argyll PA34 5XU.

McLEOD, Keith Morrison, CBE 1975; Financial Controller, British Airports Authority, 1971–75; *b* 26 May 1920; *yr s* of John and Mary McLeod; *m* 1943, Patricia Carter; two *s* one *d*. *Educ:* Bancroft's School. Asst Auditor, Exchequer and Audit Dept, 1939; served RAF, 1941–46; Asst Principal, Min. of Supply, 1948; Principal, 1950; BJSM, Washington, 1955–57; Asst Sec., Min. of Supply, 1957; Cabinet Office, 1962; Finance Dir, British Airports Authority, 1966. *Address:* 161 Banstead Road, Banstead, Surrey SM7 1QH. *T:* (020) 8393 9005.

McLEOD, Kirsty, (Mrs Christopher Hudson); author and journalist, since 1976; *b* 23 Dec. 1947; *d* of late Alexander McLeod and Elizabeth Davidson McLeod; *m* 1978, Christopher Hudson; one *s*. *Educ:* St Leonard's Sch., St Andrews; St Anne's Coll., Oxford (MA). Editorial staff, IPC Magazines, 1970–73; Editor, Fontana Books, 1974–76; Columnist, Daily Telegraph, 1991–93. English Heritage: Comr, 1995–2001; Chm., Historic Parks and Gardens Adv. Cttee, 1998–2001 (Mem., 1995–2001). *Publications:* The Wives of Downing Street, 1976; Drums and Trumpets: the House of Stuart, 1977; The Last Summer: May to September 1914, 1983; A Passion for Friendship: Sibyl Colefax and her circle, 1991; Battle Royal: Edward VIII and George VI, 1999; numerous newspaper articles. *Recreation:* gardening. *Address:* Little Dane, Biddenden, Kent TN27 8JT. *T:* (01580) 291214.

McLEOD, Prof. Malcolm Donald, FRSE; Professor, since 1993, and Vice-Principal, External Relations and Marketing, since 1999, Hunterian Museum and Art Gallery, Glasgow (Director, 1990–99); Chairman, Scottish Museums Council, since 1996; *b* 19 May 1941; *s* of Donald McLeod and Ellen (*née* Fairclough); *m* 1st, 1965, Jacqueline Wynborne (marr. diss. 1980); two *s* one *d*; 2nd, 1980, Iris Barry. *Educ:* Birkenhead Sch.; Hertford and Exeter Colls, Oxford (MA, BLitt). FRSE 1995. Lectr, Dept of Sociology, Univ. of Ghana, 1967–69; Asst Curator, Museum of Archaeology and Ethnology, Cambridge, 1969–74; Lectr, Girton Coll., Cambridge, 1969–74; Fellow, Magdalene Coll., Cambridge, 1972–74; Keeper of Ethnography, British Museum, 1974–90. Member: Hist. and Current Affairs Selection Cttee, Nat. Film Archive, 1978–84; Council, Museums Assoc., 1983–86; UK Unesco Cultural Adv. Cttee, 1980–85. Consultant, Manhyia Palace Mus., Kumasi, Ghana, 1994–99; Curator, RSE, 1999–. Hon. Lecturer: Anthropology Dept, UCL, 1976–81; Archæology Dept, Glasgow Univ., 1991–. Lectures: Marett, Exeter Coll., Oxford, 1982; Sydney Jones, Liverpool Univ., 1984; Arthur Batchelor, UEA, 1987; Rivers, Cambridge, 1993. Trustee: Sainsbury Unit, UEA, 1991–2000; Oriental Mus., Univ. of Durham, 1994–2000; Hunterian Collection, London, 1998–; Scottish Mus. of the Year Awards, 1999–. *Publications:* The Asante, 1980; Treasures of African Art, 1980; (with J. Mack) Ethnic Art, 1984; (with E. Bassani) Jacob Epstein: collector, 1987; An English-Kriolu, Kriolu-English Dictionary, 1990; Collecting for the British Museum, 1994; articles and reviews in learned jls. *Address:* Tweediemill, Sandford, Strathaven ML10 6PL. *Club:* Athenæum.

McLEOD, (Margaret) Kirsty; *see* McLeod, K.

MacLEOD, Hon. Sir Maxwell; *see* MacLeod, Hon. Sir J. M. N.

MACLEOD, Sir (Nathaniel William) Hamish, KBE 1994 (CBE 1992); Financial Secretary, Hong Kong, 1991–95; *b* 6 Jan. 1940; *s* of George Henry Torquil Macleod and Ruth Natalie Wade; *m* 1970, Fionna Mary Campbell; one *s* one *d*. *Educ:* Univ. of St Andrews (MA Soc. Sci. Hons); Univ. of Bristol (Dip. Soc. Sci. Sociology); Birmingham Coll. of Commerce. FCIS 1995. Commercial trainee, Stewarts & Lloyds, Birmingham, 1958–62; Hong Kong Government: Admin. Officer, 1966; Dir of Trade and Chief Trade Negotiator, 1983–87; Secretary for Trade and Industry, 1987–89; Sec. for the Treasury,

1989–91. Director: Scottish Community (formerly Caledonian) Foundation, 1995–; Highland Distilleries, 1995–99; Scottish Oriental Smaller Cos Trust, 1995–; Chm., Fleming Asian Investment Trust, 1997–. *Recreations:* golf, walking. *Address:* 20 York Road, Trinity, Edinburgh EH5 3EH. *T:* (0131) 552 5058, *Fax:* (0131) 551 4996. *Clubs:* Hong Kong, Royal Hong Kong Yacht; Kilspindie Golf.

MACLEOD, Nigel Ronald Buchanan; QC 1979; a Recorder of the Crown Court, since 1981; a Deputy High Court Judge, since 1992; *b* 7 Feb. 1936; *s* of Donald Macleod, MB, ChB, and Katherine Ann Macleod; *m* 1966, Susan Margaret (*née* Buckley); one *s* one *d*. *Educ:* Wigan Grammar Sch. (school captain); Christ Church, Oxford (MA, BCL). Served RAF, 1954–56. Called to the Bar, Gray's Inn, 1961 (Bencher, 1993), Inner Temple *ad eundem* 1984. Asst Comr, Boundary Commn for England, 1981–85; a Pres., Mental Health Review Tribunals, 1999–. Chm., Planning and Environment Bar Assoc., 1998–2000 (Vice Chm., 1994–98); Mem., Gen. Council of the Bar, 1998–2000. Fellow, Soc. for Advanced Legal Studies, 1998; Observer to Governing Body, St Alban's Primary Sch., Camden, 1998–. *Publications:* contribs to legal jls. *Recreations:* boats, gardening. *Address:* Russet House, 27 Warwick Road, Upper Boddington, Northants NN11 6DH. *T:* (01327) 264256; 4 Verulam Buildings, Gray's Inn, WC1R 5LQ. *T:* (020) 7404 7752. *Club:* Garrick.

See also I. B. Macleod.

MacLEOD, Norman Donald; QC (Scot.) 1986; MA, LLB; Advocate; Sheriff Principal of Glasgow and Strathkelvin, 1986–97; *b* 6 March 1932; *s* of late Rev. John MacLeod, Edinburgh and Catherine MacRitchie; *m* 1957, Ursula Jane, *y d* of late George H. Bromley, Inveresk; two *s* two *d*. *Educ:* Mill Hill Sch.; George Watson's Boys' Coll., Edinburgh; Edinburgh Univ.; Hertford Coll., Oxford. Passed Advocate, 1956. Colonial Administrative Service, Tanganyika: Dist. Officer, 1957–59; Crown Counsel, 1959–64; practised at Scots Bar, 1964–67; Sheriff of Glasgow and Strathkelvin (formerly Lanarkshire at Glasgow), 1967–86; Hon. Sheriff N Strathclyde. Vis. Prof., Law Sch., Univ. of Strathclyde, 1988–98. Comr, Northern Lighthouse Bd, 1986–97 (Chm., 1990–91). *Recreations:* sailing, gardening. *Address:* Calderbank, Lochwinnoch, Renfrewshire PA12 4DJ. *T:* (01505) 843340.

MACLEOD CLARK, Prof. Dame Jill, DBE 2000; PhD; Professor of Nursing, Head of School of Nursing and Midwifery and Deputy Dean of Faculty of Medicine and Health, University of Southampton, since 1999; *b* 11 June 1944; *d* of George William Charles Tearle Gibbs and late Edith Vera Macleod Gibbs; *m* 1st, 1967, Andrew William Clark (marr. diss. 1983); two *s*; 2nd, 1989, William Arthur Bridge. *Educ:* UCH (RGN 1965); LSE (BSc Hons 1972); KCL (PhD 1982). FRCN 1997. Various clin. posts, London, Birmingham and Bedford, 1965–76; Nursing Officer, DoH, 1976–78; Res. Fellow, 1978–81, Lectr in Nursing, 1981–86, Chelsea Coll., London Univ.; King's College London: Sen. Lectr in Nursing, 1986–90; Prof. of Nursing, 1990–93; Dir, Nightingale Inst., 1993–99. *Publications:* Research for Nursing, 1979; Communication in Nursing Care, 1981; Further Research of Nursing, 1989; numerous res. based papers in learned jls on health promotion, smoking cessation, health prof. educn and communication in health care. *Recreations:* sailing, singing. *Address:* 80 Walpole House, 126 Westminster Bridge Road, SE1 7UN. *Club:* Royal Southampton Yacht.

McLERNAN, Kieran Anthony; Sheriff of Grampian, Highlands and Islands at Banff and Peterhead, since 1991 and at Aberdeen, since 2000; *b* 29 April 1941; *s* of James John McLernan and Delia (*née* McEvaddy); *m* 1979, Joan Doherty Larkins; one *s* three *d*. *Educ:* St Aloysius' Coll., Glasgow; Glasgow Univ. (MA 1961; LLB 1965). Admitted solicitor, 1965; Tutor, Glasgow Univ., 1985–91. Temp. Sheriff, 1986–91. KCHS 1998 (KHS 1990). *Recreations:* golf, hockey, ski-ing, etc. *Address:* Sheriff Courthouse, Low Street, Banff AB4 1AU; Peockstone Farm, Lochwinnoch, Strathclyde PA12 4LE. *T:* (01505) 842128.

McLETCHIE, David William; Member (C) Lothians, Scottish Parliament, since 1999; Leader, Conservative Group, Scottish Parliament, since 1999; *b* 6 Aug. 1952; *s* of James Watson McLetchie and Catherine Alexander McLetchie (*née* Gray); *m* 1st, 1977, Barbara Gemmell Baillie (*d* 1995); one *s*; 2nd, 1998, Sheila Elizabeth Foster. *Educ:* Leith Acad.; George Heriot's Sch., Edinburgh; Edinburgh Univ. (LLB Hons). Admitted solicitor, 1976; joined Tods Murray, WS, Edinburgh, 1976, Partner, 1980–; specialises in trusts, estates and tax. *Recreations:* golf, watching football, music, reading crime fiction and political biographies. *Address:* Scottish Parliament, Edinburgh EH99 1SP. *T:* (0131) 348 5659. *Clubs:* New (Edinburgh), Bruntsfield Links Golfing Society, North Berwick Golf.

McLINTOCK, Sir (Charles) Alan, Kt 1999; CA; President, Woolwich Building Society, 1995–97 (Director, 1970–95; Deputy Chairman, 1980–84; Chairman, 1984–95); Chairman: Allchurches Trust, since 1986 (Director, since 1975); Central Board of Finance of the Church of England, 1992–98; Director, Royal Artillery Museums Ltd, since 1996; *b* 28 May 1925; *s* of late Charles Henry McLintock, OBE, and Alison McLintock; *m* 1955, Sylvia Mary Foster Taylor; one *s* three *d*. *Educ:* Rugby School. Served Royal Artillery, 1943–47; commnd 1945; Captain RHA 1946. With Thomson McLintock & Co., Chartered Accountants, 1948–87; qualified, 1952; Partner, 1954; Sen. Partner, KMG Thomson McLintock, 1982–87; Partner, Klynveld Main Goerdeler (KMG), 1979–87. Chairman: Grange Trust, 1973–81 (Dir, 1958–81); Border and Southern Stockholders Investment Trust, subseq. Govett Strategic Investment Trust, 1975–94; Stockholders Investment Trust, subseq. Govett Atlantic Investment Trust, 1978–92; Ecclesiastical Insce Office, subseq. Ecclesiastical Insce Gp, 1981–93 (Dir, 1972–93); Director: Trust Houses Ltd, 1967–71; Lake View Investment Trust, later Govett Oriental Investment Trust, 1971–90 (Chm., 1975–90); National Westminster Bank, 1979–90 (Adv. Bd, 1990–91); M & G Gp, 1982–94; AJ's Family Restaurants, 1987–96; Acxiom UK (formerly Southwark Computer Services), 1988–90; Cheltenham & Gloucester Coll. Develt Trust, 1996–. Mem., Archbishops' Commn on organisation of C of E, 1994–96. Vice-Pres., Metropolitan Assoc. of Building Socs, 1985–90. Trustee, Church Urban Fund, 1990–98. Chairman of Governors: Rugby Sch., 1988–95 (Gov., 1973–95); Westonbirt Sch., 1991–2000 (Gov., 1977–2000); Vice-Pres., Clergy Orphan Corp., 1984–97 (Mem., Cttee of Management, 1963–84); Member: Royal Alexandra and Albert Sch. Bd of Management, 1965–88; Council, London Univ., 1987–99. Hon. DBA Greenwich, 1994. *Recreations:* music, family pursuits. *Address:* Manor House, Westhall Hill, Burford, Oxon OX18 4BJ. *T:* (01993) 822276. *Club:* Army and Navy.

See also M. G. A. McLintock.

McLINTOCK, Michael George Alexander; Chief Executive, M&G Group Limited (formerly Prudential M&G Asset Management), since 1999; *b* 24 March 1961; *s* of Sir (Charles) Alan McLintock, *qv*; *m* 1996, Nicola Fairles Ogilvy Watson; two *d*. *Educ:* Malvern Coll.; St John's Coll., Oxford (scholar; BA 1st cl. hons Mod. History and Econs). Morgan Grenfell & Co. Ltd, 1983; Baring Brothers & Co. Ltd, 1987; M&G Group plc, 1992, Chief Exec., 1997–99. Dir, Prudential plc, 2000–. *Recreations:* family, friends, good wine. *Address:* (office) Laurence Pountney Hill, EC4R 0HH. *T:* (020) 7626 4588. *Club:* MCC.

McLINTOCK, Sir Michael (William), 4th Bt *cr* 1934, of Sanquhar, Co. Dumfries; *b* 13 Aug. 1958; *s* of Sir William Traven McLintock, 3rd Bt and Andrée, *d* of Richard Lonsdale-Hands; *S* father, 1987. *Heir: b* Andrew Thomson McLintock, *b* 2 Dec. 1960.

McLOUGHLIN, Catherine Mary Anne, CBE 1998; Chair, St George's Healthcare NHS Trust, since 1999; *b* 26 July 1943; *d* of Peter Patrick McLoughlin and Catherine (*née* McHugh). *Educ:* Ravenswell Convent, Bray, Co. Wicklow. Gen. nurse trng, N Middx Hosp., 1961–64; post-registration psychiatric trng, 1965–66, then specialist posts, 1966–73, Bethlem Royal and Maudsley Hosp.; Principal Nursing Officer, Paddington and N Kensington HA, 1979–85; Dist Gen. Manager, Haringey HA, 1985–89; Dir of Nursing and Dep. Chief Nursing Officer, DoH, 1989–90, retd. Chair: Bromley FHSA, 1992–94; Bromley HA, 1994–99; NHS Confedn, 1997–2000. Chair, Nat. Network Art in Health, 2000–. Dr *hc* Middx 1995. *Recreations:* reading, art, walking, driving. *Address:* 96 Croydon Road, Anerley, SE20 7AB.

McLOUGHLIN, Elizabeth Mary, CBE 1997; Command Secretary, Adjutant General, Ministry of Defence, since 1997; *b* 10 April 1947; *d* of Donald Norwood Menzies and late Doreen Mary Menzies (*née* Collinson); *m* 1976, John McLoughlin; three *s*. *Educ:* South Hampstead High Sch.; University College London (BA Hons History). Res., 1969–72; joined MoD, 1972; various posts, 1972–88; Sen. Civil Service, 1988. *Recreations:* gardening, reading – and not working! *Address:* Trenchard Lines, Upavon, Pewsey, Wilts SN9 6BE.

McLOUGHLIN, George Leeke, CB 1988; Deputy Director of Public Prosecutions for Northern Ireland, 1982–87; *b* 2 July 1921; *e s* of Charles M. and Rose W. McLoughlin; *m* 1953, Maureen Theresa McKaigney (*d* 1998); two *s* six *d*. *Educ:* St Columb's College, Londonderry; Queen's Univ. Belfast (BA). Barrister, N Ireland, practised 1945–58; joined HMOCS 1958; Resident Magistrate, 1958, Crown Counsel, 1958–63, Northern Rhodesia; Parly Draftsman, Zambia, 1965; Solicitor General, Zambia, 1968–70, retired; Office of Law Reform, N Ireland, 1971–72; Sen. Asst Dir of Public Prosecutions, NI (Under Secretary, NI Civil Service), 1973–82. *Recreations:* photography, armchair sports following. *Address:* 27 Tullymacnous Road, near Killyleagh, Toye, Downpatrick, Co. Down, Northern Ireland BT30 9PW.

McLOUGHLIN, Most Rev. James; *see* Galway and Kilmacduagh, Bishop of, (RC).

McLOUGHLIN, Patrick Allen; MP (C) West Derbyshire, since May 1986; *b* 30 Nov. 1957; *s* of Patrick and Gladys Victoria McLoughlin; *m* 1984, Lynne Newman; one *s* one *d*. *Educ:* Cardinal Griffin Roman Catholic Sch., Cannock. Mineworker, Littleton Colliery, 1979–85; Marketing Official, NCB, 1985–86. PPS to Sec. of State for Trade and Industry, 1988–89; Parly Under-Sec. of State, Dept of Transport, 1989–92, Dept of Employment, 1992–93, DTI, 1993–94; an Asst Govt Whip, 1995–96; a Lord Comr of HM Treasury (Govt Whip), 1996–97; Opposition Pairing Whip, 1997–98; Dep. Opposition Chief Whip, 1998–. *Address:* House of Commons, SW1A 0AA.

MACLURE, Sir John (Robert Spencer), 4th Bt *cr* 1898; Headmaster, Croftinloan School, Pitlochry, Perthshire, 1978–92 and 1997–98; *b* 25 March 1934; *s* of Sir John William Spencer Maclure, 3rd Bt, OBE, and Elspeth (*d* 1991), *er d* of late Alexander King Clark; *S* father, 1980; *m* 1964, Jane Monica, *d* of late Rt Rev. T. J. Savage, Bishop of Zululand and Swaziland; four *s*. *Educ:* Winchester College. DipEd. 2nd Lt, 2nd Bn KRRC, 1953–55, BAOR; Lt, Royal Hampshire Airborne Regt, TA. Assistant Master: Horris Hill, 1955–66 and 1974–78; St George's, Wanganui, NZ, 1967–68; Sacred Heart Coll., Auckland, NZ, 1969–70; St Edmund's, Hindhead, Surrey, 1971–74. *Heir: s* John Mark Maclure [*b* 27 Aug. 1965; *m* 1996, Emily, *d* of Peter Frean; one *s* one *d*]. *Address:* Trerice, Chevithorne, Tiverton, Devon EX16 7PY; *e-mail:* maclurej@aol.com; 24 Heron Circle, Kommetjie, Cape Town, 7975, SA. *Clubs:* MCC; Royal Green Jackets; Royal and Ancient (St Andrews); Royal North Devon Golf; Tiverton Golf.

MACLURE, (John) Stuart, CBE 1982; Editor, Times Educational Supplement, 1969–89; *b* 8 Aug. 1926; *s* of Hugh and Bertha Maclure, Highgate, N6; *m* 1951, Constance Mary Butler; one *s* two *d*. *Educ:* Highgate Sch.; Christ's Coll., Cambridge. MA. Joined The Times, 1950; The Times Educational Supplement, 1951; Editor, Education, 1954–69. Hon. Prof. of Educn, Keele Univ., 1981–84; Dist. Vis. Fellow, PSI, 1989–90; Associate Fellow, Centre for Educn and Industry, Warwick Univ., 1991–94. President: Br. Sect., Comparative Educn Soc. in Europe, 1979; Educnl Sect., BAAS, 1983; Member: Educnl Adv. Council, IBA, 1979–84; Consultative Cttee, Assessment of Performance Unit, 1974–82. Regents' Lecturer, Univ. of California, Berkeley, 1980. Gov., Commonwealth Inst., 1991–97. Hon. Fellow, City of Sheffield Polytechnic, 1976; Hon. FCP 1985; Hon. Fellow, Westminster Coll., 1990. DUniv Open, 1991. *Publications:* Joint Editor (with T. E. Utley) Documents on Modern Political Thought, 1956; Editor, Educational Documents, 1816–1963, 1965; A Hundred Years of London Education, 1970; (with Tony Becher) The Politics of Curriculum Change, 1978; (ed with Tony Becher) Accountability in Education, 1979; Education and Youth Employment in Great Britain, 1979; Educational Development and School Building, 1945–1973, 1984; Education Re-formed, a guide to the Education Reform Act, 1988; A History of Education in London 1870–1990, 1990; Missing Links—The Challenge to Further Education, 1991; (ed with Peter Davies) Learning to Think—Thinking to Learn, 1992; The Inspectors' Calling—HMI and the Shaping of Educational Policy, 2001. *Address:* 109 College Road, Dulwich, SE21 7HN. *Club:* MCC.

McLUSKEY, Very Rev. J(ames) Fraser, MC; MA, BD, DD; Minister at St Columba's Church of Scotland, Pont Street, London, 1960–86; Moderator of the General Assembly of the Church of Scotland, 1983–84; *b* 19 Sept. 1914; *s* of James Fraser McLuskey and Margaret Keltie; *m* 1st, 1939, Irene (*d* 1959), *d* of Pastor Calaminus, Wuppertal; two *s*; 2nd, 1966, Ruth Quartermaine (*née* Hunter), *widow* of Lt-Col Keith Briant. *Educ:* Aberdeen Grammar Sch.; Edinburgh Univ. Ordained Minister of Church of Scotland, 1938; Chaplain to Univ. of Glasgow, 1939–47. Service as Army Chaplain, 1943–46 (1st Special Air Service Regt, 1944–46); Sub Warden Royal Army Chaplains' Training Centre, 1947–50; Minister at Broughty Ferry East, 1950–55; Minister at New Kilpatrick, Bearsden, 1955–60. *Publications:* Parachute Padre, 1951; The Cloud and the Fire, 1994. *Recreations:* walking, music, reading. *Address:* 54/5 Eildon Terrace, Edinburgh EH3 5LU. *Clubs:* Caledonian, Special Forces; New (Edinburgh).

McMAHON, Andrew, (Andy); *b* 18 March 1920; *s* of Andrew and Margaret McMahon; *m* 1944; one *s* one *d*. *Educ:* District School, Govan. Boilermaker, Govan shipyards, 1936; unemployed, 1971–79. MP (Lab) Glasgow, Govan, 1979–83; first and only Boilermaker to enter House of Commons. Member, Glasgow Dist Council, 1973–79. Chm., Scottish Arab Friendship Assoc., 1972–85; Sec. Gen., British-Iraqi Friendship Assoc., 1989 (Pres., 1986–89). *Recreations:* youth work, care and comfort for elderly. *Address:* 21 Morefield Road, Govan, Glasgow G51 4NG.

McMAHON, Sir Brian (Patrick), 8th Bt *cr* 1817; engineer; *b* 9 June 1942; *s* of Sir (William) Patrick McMahon, 7th Bt, and Ruth Stella (*d* 1982), *yr d* of late Percy Robert

Kenyon-Slaney; *S* father, 1977; *m* 1981, Kathleen Joan (marr. diss. 1991), *d* of late William Hopwood. *Educ:* Wellington. BSc, AIM. Assoc. Mem., Inst of Welding. *Heir: brother* Shaun Desmond McMahon [*b* 29 Oct. 1945; *m* 1971, Antonia Noel Adie; *m* 1985, Jill Rosamund, *yr d* of Dr Jack Cherry; two *s*]. *Address:* Oak Ridge, School Road, Thorney Hill, Bransgore, Christchurch, Dorset BH23 8DS.

McMAHON, Sir Christopher William, (Sir Kit), Kt 1986; Director, Angela Flowers, since 1992; *b* Melbourne, 10 July 1927; *s* of late Dr John Joseph McMahon and late Margaret Kate (*née* Brown); *m* 1st, 1956, Marion Kelso; two *s*; 2nd, 1982, Alison Barbara Braimbridge, *d* of late Dr J. G. Cormie and late Mrs B. E. Cormie. *Educ:* Melbourne Grammar Sch.; Univ. of Melbourne (BA Hons Hist. and English, 1949); Magdalen Coll., Oxford. 1st cl. hons PPE, 1953. Tutor in English Lit., Univ. of Melbourne, 1950; Econ. Asst, HM Treasury, 1953–57; Econ. Adviser, British Embassy, Washington, 1957–60; Fellow and Tutor in Econs, Magdalen Coll., Oxford, 1960–64 (Hon. Fellow, 1986); Tutor in Econs, Treasury Centre for Admin. Studies, 1963–64; Mem., Plowden Cttee on Aircraft Industry, 1964–65; entered Bank of England as Adviser, 1964; Adviser to the Governors, 1966–70; Exec. Dir, 1970–80; Dep. Governor, 1980–85; Chief Exec. and Dep. Chm., 1986–87, Chm., 1987–91, Midland Bank. Director: Eurotunnel, 1987–91; Hongkong and Shanghai Banking Corp., 1987–91; Royal Opera House, 1989–97; Taylor Woodrow, 1991–2000 (Dep. Chm., 1997–2000); Newspaper Publishing, 1993–94; Aegis, 1993–99; FI Gp, 1994–2001; History World, 2001–; Chairman: Coutts Consulting Gp, 1992–96; Pentos, 1993–95. Mem., Gp of Thirty, 1978–84; Chairman: Working Party 3, OECD, 1980–85; Young Enterprise, 1989–92; Centre for Study of Financial Innovation, 1993–95. Mem. Court, Univ. of London, 1984–86; Gov., Birkbeck Coll., 1991–. Trustee: Whitechapel Art Gall., 1984–92; Royal Opera House Trust, 1984–86. Hon. Fellow, UCNW, 1988. Chevalier, Légion d'Honneur (France), 1990. *Publications:* Sterling in the Sixties, 1964; (ed) Techniques of Economic Forecasting, 1965. *Recreations:* looking at pictures, buying books, going to the movies, helping in the garden. *Address:* The Old House, Burleigh, Stroud GL5 2PQ. *Club:* Garrick.

McMAHON, Hugh Robertson; UK Political Editor, World Parliamentarian magazine, since 1999; *b* 17 June 1938; *s* of Hugh McMahon and Margaret Fulton Robertson; *m* 1986, Helen Grant; one *s* one *d*. *Educ:* Glasgow University (MA Hons); Jordanhill College. Assistant Teacher: Largs High School, 1962–63; Stevenston High School, 1963–64; Irvine Royal Academy, 1964–68; Principal Teacher of History, Mainholm Academy, Ayr, 1968–71; Principal Teacher of History and Modern Studies, 1971–72, Asst Head Teacher, 1972–84, Ravenspark Academy, Irvine. MEP (Lab) Strathclyde W, 1984–99; contested (Lab) Scotland, 1999. European Parliament: Mem., Budgetary Control Cttee, 1987–92; Social Affairs, Employment and Working Envmt Cttee, 1984–99 (Vice Chm., 1992–94); Fisheries Cttee, 1994–99; Mem., Interparly Delegn with Czech Republic, 1997–99. Formerly Rep. of Scottish MEPs, Scottish Exec. Cttee, Labour Party. *Recreations:* golf, reading, walking, languages. *Address:* 9 Low Road, Castlehead, Paisley PA2 6AQ. *T:* (0141) 889 0885, *Fax:* (0141) 889 4790. *Clubs:* Saltcoats & Kilbirnie Labour; Ravenspark Golf; Irvine Bogside Golf.

McMAHON, Sir Kit; *see* McMahon, Sir C. W.

McMAHON, Rt Rev. Malcolm Patrick; *see* Nottingham, Bishop of, (RC).

McMAHON, Michael Joseph; Member (Lab) Hamilton North and Bellshill, Scottish Parliament, since 1999; *b* 18 Sept. 1961; *s* of Patrick McMahon and Bridget Clarke; *m* 1983, Margaret Mary McKeown; one *s* two *d*. *Educ:* Glasgow Caledonian Univ. (BA Hons Social Scis (Politics and Sociology) 1996). Welder, Terex Equipment Ltd, 1977–92; freelance socio-political researcher, 1996–99. *Recreations:* swimming, hill walking, supporting Celtic FC. *Address:* 7 Forres Crescent, Bellshill, Lanarkshire ML4 1HL. *T:* (01698) 747997.

McMAHON, Rt Rev. Thomas; *see* Brentwood, Bishop of, (RC).

McMANNERS, Rev. Prof. John, CBE 2000; DLitt; FBA 1978; Fellow and Chaplain, All Souls College, Oxford, 1984–2001 (Hon. Fellow, 2001); *b* 25 Dec. 1916; *s* of Rev. Canon Joseph McManners and Mrs Ann McManners; *m* 1951, Sarah Carruthers Errington; two *s* two *d*. *Educ:* St Edmund Hall, Oxford (BA 1st cl. hons Mod. History, 1939; Hon. Fellow, 1983); Durham Univ. (DipTheol 1947; Hon. Fellow, St Chad's Coll., 1992); DLitt Oxon, 1980. Military Service, 1939–45 in Royal Northumberland Fusiliers (Major). Priest, 1948; St Edmund Hall, Oxford: Chaplain, 1948; Fellow, 1949–56; Dean, 1951; Prof., Univ. of Tasmania, 1956–59; Prof., Sydney Univ., 1959–66; Professorial Fellow, All Souls Coll., Oxford, 1965–66; Prof. of History, Univ. of Leicester, 1967–72; Canon of Christ Church and Regius Prof. of Ecclesiastical History, Oxford Univ., 1972–84. Lectures: Birkbeck, 1976, Trevelyan, 1989, Cambridge; John Coffin Meml, London Univ., 1982; Sir Owen Evans, Univ. of Wales, 1984; F. D. Maurice, King's Coll., London, 1985; Zaharoff, 1985, Hensley Henson, 1986, A.B. Emden Meml, 1992, Oxford. Dir d'études associé, Ecole Pratique des Hautes Etudes, sect. IV, Paris, 1980–81. Mem., Doctrinal Commn of C of E, 1978–82. Trustee, Nat. Portrait Gallery, 1970–78; Mem. Council, RHistS, 1971; Pres., Ecclesiastical Hist. Soc., 1977–78. FAHA 1970. Hon. DLitt Durham, 1984. Officer, Order of King George I of the Hellenes, 1945; Comdr, Ordre des Palmes académiques (France), 1991. *Publications:* French Ecclesiastical Society under the Ancien Régime: a study of Angers in the 18th Century, 1960; (ed) France, Government and Society, 1965, 2nd edn 1971; Lectures on European History 1789–1914: Men, Machines and Freedom, 1966; The French Revolution and the Church, 1969; Church and State in France 1870–1914, 1972; Death and the Enlightenment, 1981 (Wolfson Literary Award, 1982); (ed) The Oxford Illustrated History of Christianity, 1990; Church and Society in 18th Century France, 2 vols, 1998; contrib.: New Cambridge Modern History vols VI and VIII; Studies in Church History, vols XII, XV and XXII. *Recreation:* tennis. *Address:* All Souls College, Oxford OX1 4AL. *T:* (01865) 279368.

MacMANUS, Dr Bernard Ronald; Vice-Chancellor, Bournemouth University, 1992–94; *b* 25 April 1936; *s* of Ronald MacManus and Doris Evelyn MacManus (*née* Sherriff); *m* 1959, Patricia Mary Greet; one *s* one *d*. *Educ:* St Boniface's Coll., Devon; Plymouth Poly.; Univ. of Birmingham (BScEng, PhD). Head, Dept of Mech. Production and Aeronautical Engrg, Manchester Poly., 1972–73; Dean, Faculty of Engrg, Sunderland Poly., 1973–78; Dep. Dir, Glasgow Coll. of Technology, 1978–83; Director: Dorset Inst. of Higher Educn, 1983–91; Bournemouth Poly., 1991–92. *Publications:* contribs to learned jls on manufacturing systems. *Recreations:* swimming, classic cars, music. *Address:* Thurlstone, Chapel Lane, Osmington, Dorset DT3 6ET.

McMANUS, Declan Patrick Aloysius, (Elvis Costello); musician and composer; *b* 25 Aug. 1954; *s* of Ross McManus and Lillian McManus (*née* Costello); *m* 1974, Mary; one *s*; *m* 1986, Cait O'Riordan. Formed Elvis Costello and the Attractions, 1977; has collaborated with, amongst others, Brodsky Quartet, Swedish Radio Symphony Orchestra and Burt Bacharach. Dir, S Bank Centre Meltdown, 1995. Recordings include: *albums:* My Aim is True, 1977; This Year's Model, 1978; Armed Forces, 1979; Trust, 1981; Almost Blue, 1981; Imperial Bedroom, 1982; Punch the Clock, 1983; Blood and Chocolate, 1986; Spike, 1989; Mightly Like the Rose, 1991; (with Brodsky Quartet) The Juliet Letters, 1993; Brutal Youth, 1994; Extreme Honey, 1997; Painted from Memory, 1998; (with Anne Sofie von Otter) For the Stars, 2001; *singles:* Alison, 1977; Watching the Detectives, 1977; (I Don't Want to Go to) Chelsea, 1978; Oliver's Army, 1979; Accidents Will Happen, 1979; Good Year for the Roses, 1981; Everyday I Write the Book, 1983; Pills and Soap, 1983; The People's Limousine, 1985; Little Atoms, 1996; She, 1999.

McMANUS, Francis Joseph; solicitor; *b* 16 Aug. 1942; *s* of Patrick and Celia McManus; *m* 1971, Carmel V. Doherty, Lisnaskea, Co. Fermanagh; two *s* one *d*. *Educ:* St Michael's, Enniskillen; Queen's University, Belfast. BA 1965; Diploma in Education, 1966. Subsequently a Teacher. MP (Unity) Fermanagh and S Tyrone, 1970–Feb. 1974. Founder Mem. and Co-Chm., Irish Independence Party, 1977–. *Address:* Lissadell, Drumlin Heights, Enniskillen, Co. Fermanagh, N Ireland. *T:* Enniskillen (028) 6632 3401.

McMANUS, Dr James John; Chairman, Parole Board for Scotland, since 2000; Senior Lecturer in Law, University of Dundee, since 1976; *b* 23 June 1950; *s* of David McManus and Alice McManus (*née* Vallelly); *m* 1974, Catherine MacKellaig; one *s* four *d*. *Educ:* Our Lady's High Sch., Motherwell; Univ. of Edinburgh (LLB); Univ. of Dundee (PhD 1985). Lectr, UC, Cardiff, 1972–74; Lectr, Univ. of Dundee, 1974–76. Comr, Scottish Prisons Complaints Commn, 1994–99. Expert Advr, Cttee for Prevention of Torture, Council of Europe, 1992–. *Publications:* Lay Justice, 1992; Prisons, Prisoners and the Law, 1994. *Recreations:* golf, ski-ing. *Address:* Department of Law, The University, Dundee DD1 4HN. *T:* (01382) 344634; Parole Board, Saughton House, Broomhouse Drive, Edinburgh EH11 3XA. *T:* (0131) 244 8755.

McMANUS, Jonathan Richard; QC 1999; *b* 15 Sept. 1958; *s* of Frank Rostron McManus and Benita Ann McManus. *Educ:* Neale Wade Comprehensive, March; Downing Coll., Cambridge (MA). Called to the Bar, Middle Temple, 1982. *Publications:* Education and the Courts, 1998; contrib. Economic, Social and Cultural Rights: their implementation, in United Kingdom Law, ed Burchill, Harris and Owers, 1999. *Recreations:* music, travel, photography. *Address:* 4–5 Gray's Inn Square, Gray's Inn, WC1R 5JP. *T:* (020) 7404 5252.

McMASTER, Brian John, CBE 1987; Director, Edinburgh International Festival, since 1991. International Artists' Dept, EMI Ltd, 1968–73; Controller of Opera Planning, ENO, 1973–76; Gen Administrator, subseq. Man. Dir, WNO, 1976–91; Artistic Dir, Vancouver Opera, 1984–89. *Address:* Edinburgh International Festival, The Hub, Castlehill, Edinburgh EH1 2NE. *T:* (0131) 473 2032.

McMASTER, Hughan James Michael; Chief Architect and Director of Works, Home Office, 1980–87, retired; *b* 27 July 1927; *s* of William James Michael and Emly McMaster; *m* 1950; one *s* two *d*. *Educ:* Christ's Coll., Finchley; Regent Street Polytechnic (DipArch). ARIBA 1951. Served RAF, India and Far East, 1946–48. Joined Civil Service, 1961; Navy Works, 1961–69; Whitehall Development Gp, Directorate of Home Estate Management and Directorate of Civil Accommodation, 1969–76; Defence Works (PE and Overseas), 1976–80. *Recreations:* gardening, cycling, theatre, music.

McMASTER, Prof. Paul; Professor of Hepatobiliary Surgery and Transplantation, and Consultant Surgeon, Queen Elizabeth Hospital, University of Birmingham, since 1980; *b* 4 Jan. 1943; *s* of Dr James McMaster and Sarah Jane McMaster (*née* Lynn); *m* 1969, Helen Ruth Bryce; two *s* one *d*. *Educ:* Liverpool Coll.; Univ. of Liverpool (MB ChB 1966; ChM 1979); MA Cantab 1978. FRCS 1971. House Surgeon, subseq. House Physician, Liverpool Royal Infirmary, Univ. of Liverpool, 1966–67; SHO in Urology and Transplantation, RPMS, Hammersmith Hosp., 1967–68; Registrar in Surgery, Addenbrooke's Hosp., 1969–72; Sen. Registrar and Res. Fellow, 1972–76, Sen. Lectr in Surgery, 1976–80, Univ. Dept of Surgery, Addenbrooke's Hosp., Cambridge Univ. Visiting Professor: Univs of Rome, Genoa, Cairo, Concepción; RACS Foundn, 1998. FICS. *Publications:* numerous articles on immuno suppression, liver transplantation, devolt of laparoscopic and hepatobiliary surgery, advances in major hepatic and biliary surgery. *Recreations:* gardening, sailing, reading. *Address:* Liver Unit, Queen Elizabeth Hospital, Edgbaston, Birmingham B15 2TH. *T:* (0121) 627 2413.

McMASTER, Peter, CB 1991; FRICS; Member, Lord Chancellor's Panel of Independent Inspectors, 1991–2001; *b* 22 Nov. 1931; *s* of Peter McMaster and Ada Nellie (*née* Williams); *m* 1955, Catherine Ann Rosborough; one *s* one *d*. *Educ:* Kelvinside Academy, Glasgow; RMA Sandhurst; RMCS Shrivenham. BScEng London. Called to the Bar, Middle Temple, 1969. Commissioned into Royal Engineers, 1952; served Middle and Far East; retired (major), 1970; joined Civil Service, 1970; W Midland Region, Ordnance Survey, 1970–72; Caribbean Region, Directorate of Overseas Survey, 1972–74; Headquarters, 1974–91, Dir Gen., 1985–91, Ordnance Survey. Vis. Prof., Kingston Polytechnic, subseq. Kingston Univ., 1991–93. Member Council: BCS, 1983–92; RGS, 1990–93. FIIM 1990. *Recreations:* travel, walking, chess. *Address:* Hillhead, Stratton Road, Winchester, Hampshire SO23 0JQ. *T:* (01962) 862684.

McMENAMIN, Frances Jane, (Mrs Ian McCarry); QC (Scot.) 1998; *b* 21 May 1951; *d* of Francis and Agnes McMenamin; *m* 1991, Ian McCarry. *Educ:* Our Lady of Lourdes Primary Sch., Glasgow; Notre Dame High Sch., Glasgow; Strathclyde Univ. (BA, LLB 1974). Admitted Solicitor, 1976; admitted to Faculty of Advocates, 1985. Legal Apprentice, Hughes, Dowdall & Co., Solicitors, 1974–76; Procurator Fiscal Depute, 1976–84; advocate specialising in criminal law, 1985–; Temp. Sheriff, 1991–97; Advocate Depute, 1997–2000. Vis. Lectr, Scottish Police Coll., Tulliallan Castle, 1991–. *Recreations:* spending time with husband, family and friends, golf, exercise classes, reading, travelling. *Address:* (home) 59 Hamilton Drive, Glasgow G12 8DP. *T:* (0141) 339 0519; Advocates' Library, Parliament House, Parliament Square, Edinburgh EH1 1RF. *T:* (0131) 226 5071. *Clubs:* Hole in the Head (Edinburgh); Milngavie Golf.

McMICHAEL, Prof. Andrew James, FRS 1992; Director, Medical Research Council Human Immunology Unit, John Radcliffe Hospital, Oxford, 1998, now Hon. Director; Professor of Molecular Medicine and Director, Weatherall Institute of Molecular Medicine, Oxford University, since 2000; Fellow of Corpus Christi College, Oxford, since 2000; *b* 8 Nov. 1943; *s* of Sir John McMichael, FRS and late Sybil McMichael; *m* 1968, Kathryn Elizabeth Cross; two *s* one *d*. *Educ:* St Paul's Sch., London; Gonville and Caius Coll., Cambridge (MA; BChir 1968; MB 1969); St Mary's Hosp. Med. Sch., London. PhD 1974; MRCP 1971; FRCP 1985. House Physician, St Mary's Hosp., Royal Northern Hosp., Hammersmith Hosp. and Brompton Hosp., 1968–71; MRC Jun. Res. Fellow, National Inst. for Med. Res., 1971–74; MRC Travelling Fellow, Stanford Univ. Med. Sch., 1974–76; Oxford University: Wellcome Sen. Clin. Fellow, Nuffield Depts of Medicine and Surgery, 1977–79; University Lectr in Medicine and Hon. Consultant Physician, 1979–82; MRC Clinical Res. Prof. of Immunology, 1982–98; Prof. of Immunology, 1999–2000; Fellow, Trinity Coll., 1983–2000. Member: Adv. Bd, Beit Meml Trust, 1984–; MRC AIDS Steering Cttee, 1988–94; Res. Grants Council, Hong Kong, 1990–99; Council, Royal Soc., 1998–99. Founder FMedSci 1998. *Publications:* (ed with J. W. Fabre) Monoclonal Antibodies in Clinical Medicine, 1982; articles on genetic control of human immune response, antiviral immunity and AIDS. *Recreations:* working in the garden and getting wet.

MACMILLAN, family name of **Earl of Stockton**.

MACMILLAN OF OVENDEN, Viscount; Daniel Maurice Alan Macmillan; *b* 9 Oct. 1974; *s* and *heir* of Earl of Stockton, *qv*.

McMILLAN, Alan Austen, CB 1986; Solicitor to the Secretary of State for Scotland, 1984–87; *b* 19 Jan. 1926; *s* of Allan McMillan and Mabel (*née* Austin); *m* 1949, Margaret Moncur; two *s* two *d.* *Educ:* Ayr Acad.; Glasgow Univ. Served in Army, 1944–47. Qualified Solicitor in Scotland, 1949; Legal Assistant, Ayr Town Council, 1949–55; Scottish Office: Legal Assistant, 1955–62; Sen. Legal Assistant, 1962–68; Asst Solicitor, 1968–82, seconded to Cabinet Office Constitution Unit, 1977–78; Dep. Solicitor, 1982–84. *Recreations:* reading, music, theatre.

MACMILLAN, Sir (Alexander McGregor) Graham, Kt 1983; Director, Scottish Conservative Party, 1975–84; *b* 14 Sept. 1920; *s* of James Orr Macmillan and Sarah Dunsmore (*née* Graham); *m* 1947, Christina Brash Beveridge (*d* 1998); two *s* two *d.* *Educ:* Hillhead High Sch., Glasgow. Served War, RA, 1939–46. Conservative Agent: W Lothian, 1947–50; Haltemprice, 1950–53; Bury St Edmunds, 1953–60; Dep. Central Office Agent, NW Area, 1960–61; Central Office Agent, Yorks Area, 1961–75. Chairman: M & P Financial Services Ltd, 1986–87 (Dir, 1984–87); Mid-Anglian Enterprise Agency Ltd, 1988–92 (Gov., 1987–97); Exec. Sec., YorCan Communications Ltd, 1989–94. Chairman: Bury St Edmunds Round Table, 1959–60 (Pres., 1997–); Bury St Edmunds Br., Multiple Sclerosis Soc., 1987–95. Mem., Transport Users' Consultative Cttee for E England, 1987–95. Hon. Sec., Suffolk Assoc. of Boys' Clubs, 1986–88. Governor, Leeds Grammar Sch., 1968–75. *Recreations:* fishing, watching cricket and rugby. *Address:* 46 Crown Street, Bury St Edmunds, Suffolk IP33 1QX. *T:* (01284) 704443.

MACMILLAN, Alexander Ross, FCIBS, CIMgt; Director, 1974–87, Chief General Manager, 1971–82, Clydesdale Bank PLC; *b* 25 March 1922; *s* of Donald and Johanna Macmillan; *m* 1961, Ursula Miriam Grayson; two *s* one *d.* *Educ:* Tain Royal Acad. FCIBS (FIBScot 1942); CIMgt (CBIM 1980). Served War, RAF, 1942–46 (despatches, King's Birthday Honours, 1945). Entered service of N of Scotland Bank Ltd, Tain, 1938; after War, returned to Tain, 1946; transf. to Supt's Dept, Aberdeen, and thereafter to Chief Accountant's Dept, Clydesdale Bank, Glasgow, 1950, on amalgamation with N of Scotland Bank; Chief London Office, 1952; Gen. Manager's Confidential Clerk, 1955; Manager, Piccadilly Circus Br., 1958; Supt of Branches, 1965; Gen. Manager's Asst, 1967; Asst Gen. Man., 1968. Director: The High Sch. of Glasgow Ltd, 1979–92; Caledonian Applied Technology Ltd, 1982–87; Highland-North Sea Ltd, 1982–2000 (Chm., 1982–); John Laing plc, 1982–86; Martin-Black PLC, 1982–85; Radio Clyde Ltd, 1982–93; Scottish Develt Finance Ltd, 1982–92; Kelvin Technology Develts Ltd, 1982–96; Compugraphics Internat. Ltd, 1982–87; Highland Deephaven Ltd, 1983–2000; TEG Products Ltd, 1986–87; New Generation Housing Soc. Ltd, 1986–95; Castle Wynd Housing Soc. Ltd, 1987–89; Wilsons Garage (Argyll) Ltd, 1987–94; Wilsons Fuels Ltd, 1987–94; EFT Gp (formerly Edinburgh Financial Trust) plc, 1987–93; Balmoral Gp Ltd, 1988–93; North of Scotland Radio Ltd, 1989–93; Radio Clyde Holdings plc, 1991–93; Gilmorhill Power Management Ltd, 1994–96; Nemoquest Ltd, 1994–96; Dumwilco Ltd, 1995–96; Chm., First Northern Corporate Finance Ltd, 1983–87. Chm., Nat. House Bldg Council (Scotland), 1982–88. Mem. Court, Univ. of Glasgow, 1981–96. Freeman, Royal Burgh of Tain, 1975. DUniv Glasgow, 1989. *Recreation:* golf. *Address:* 4 Cochrane Court, Fairways, Milngavie, Glasgow G62 6QT.

MacMILLAN, Prof. Andrew, OBE 1992; RSA 1990; RIBA; FRIAS; Professor of Architecture, Glasgow University, and Head, Mackintosh School of Architecture, 1973–94, now Emeritus Professor; *b* 11 Dec. 1928; *s* of Andrew Harkness MacMillan of Murlaggan and Mary Jane McKelvie; *m* 1955, Angela Lillian McDowell; one *s* three *d.* *Educ:* Maryhill Public Sch.; North Kelvinside Sen. Secondary Sch., Glasgow; Glasgow Sch. of Architecture (MA 1973). FRIAS 1973. Apprenticeship, Glasgow Corp. Housing Dept, 1945–52; Architectural Asst, East Kilbride New Town Develt Corp., 1952–54; Asst Architect, 1954–63, Partner, 1966–88, Gillespie Kidd & Coia; consultant architect in private practice, 1988–. Davenport Vis. Prof., Yale Univ., 1986. Mem., Scottish Arts Council, 1978–82; Vice-Pres. for Educn, RIBA, 1981–85; Vice President: Prince and Princess of Wales Hospice, 1981–; Charles Rennie Mackintosh Soc., 1984–; Patron, Arts Educn Trust, 1988–. Royal Scottish Acad. Gold Medal, 1975; RIBA Bronze Medal, 1985; RIBA Award for Arch., 1966, 1967, 1968 and 1982; Saltire awards and Civic Trust awards at various times. *Publications:* books, papers and articles mainly dealing with urban design, urban building, architectural educn, Glasgow arch. of 20th century, and Charles Rennie Mackintosh. *Recreations:* travel, sailing, watercolours. *Address:* The Penthouse, 28 Wilson Street, Glasgow G1 1SS. *T:* (0141) 552 2481.

MACMILLAN, Deborah Millicent, (Lady Macmillan); artist; *b* Boonah, Qld, 1 July 1944; *d* of Dr Dudley Williams and Nina Deborah (*née* Darvall); *m* 1st, 1966, Denis Allard (marr. diss. 1973); 2nd, 1974, Sir Kenneth Macmillan; one *d.* *Educ:* Wenona, N Sydney; Nat. Art Sch., E Sydney (Painting and Sculpture Dip.). Member: Bd, Royal Opera House, 1993–96; Exec. Cttee, Royal Acad. Dancing, 1994–; Council, Arts Council of England, 1996–98 (Chm., Dance Panel, 1996–98); Chm., Friends of Covent Gdn, 1995–96. Hon. Member: Bd, American Ballet Theatre, 1993–; Nat. Cttee, Houston Ballet, 1993–. Gov., Nat. Youth Dance Trust, 1999–; Trustee, Wimbledon Sch. of Art, 2000–. Custodian, Sir Kenneth Macmillan's choreography, 1992–. *Exhibitions:* solo show, Charlotte Lampard Gall., 1984; mixed show, Camden Arts Centre, 1990; Royal Acad. Summer Exhibn, 1990; Accrochage, Fischer Fine Art, 1990; Contemporary Art Soc. Mkt, 1990; Drawing Show, Thumb Gall., 1990; Art for Equality, ICA, 1991; Leicestershire Collection, 1992; solo show, Turtle Key Arts Centre, 1995; Gillian Jason Contemporary Portraits Real and Imagined, 1993; Jason Rhodes Gp Show, 1995; mixed show, Glyndebourne Fest. Opera, 1997–; solo Show, Chelsea Arts Club, 1999. *Recreations:* gardening, any displacement activity. *Address:* c/o Simpson Fox, 52 Shaftesbury Avenue, W1V 7DE. *Club:* Chelsea Arts.

MACMILLAN, Duncan; *see* Macmillan, J. D.

MACMILLAN, Very Rev. Gilleasbuig Iain, CVO 1999; Minister of St Giles', The High Kirk of Edinburgh, since 1973; Chaplain to the Queen in Scotland, since 1979; Dean of the Order of the Thistle, since 1989; *b* 21 Dec. 1942; *s* of Rev. Kenneth M. Macmillan and Mrs Mary Macmillan; *m* 1965, Maureen Stewart Thomson; one *d.* *Educ:* Oban High School; Univ. of Edinburgh. MA, BD. Asst Minister, St Michael's Parish, Linlithgow, 1967–69; Minister of Portree Parish, Isle of Skye, 1969–73. Extra Chaplain to the Queen in Scotland, 1978–79. Hon. Chaplain: Royal Scottish Academy; Royal Coll. of Surgeons of Edinburgh; Soc. of High Constables of City of Edinburgh. Hon. FRCSE 1998. Hon. DD Alma Coll., 1997; Dr *hc* Edinburgh, 1998. *Publication:* A Workable Belief, 1993. *Address:* St Giles' Cathedral, Edinburgh EH1 1RE. *T:* (0131) 225 4363. *Club:* New (Edinburgh).

MACMILLAN, Sir Graham; *see* Macmillan, Sir A. M. G.

McMILLAN, Hamilton; *see* McMillan, N. H.

MACMILLAN, Iain Alexander, CBE 1978; LLD; Sheriff of South Strathclyde, Dumfries and Galloway at Hamilton, 1981–92; Temporary Sheriff, 1992–94; *b* 14 Nov. 1923; *s* of John and Eva Macmillan; *m* 1954, Edith Janet (*née* MacAulay); two *s* one *d.* *Educ:* Oban High Sch.; Glasgow Univ. (BL). Served war, RAF, France, Germany, India, 1944–47. Glasgow Univ., 1947–50. Subseq. law practice; Sen. Partner, J. & J. Sturrock & Co., Kilmarnock, 1952–81. Law Society of Scotland: Mem. Council, 1964–79; Pres., 1976–77. Pres., Temp. Sheriffs' Assoc., 1993–94. Chairman: Lanarkshire Br., Scottish Assoc. for Study of Delinquency, 1986–92; Victim Support, E Ayrshire, 1998–. Hon. LLD Aberdeen, 1975. *Recreation:* golf. *Address:* 2 Castle Drive, Kilmarnock KA3 1TN. *T:* (01563) 525864.

MacMILLAN, Jake; *see* MacMillan, John.

MacMILLAN, Dr James Loy; composer and conductor: part-time teacher, Royal Scottish Academy of Music and Drama, since 1989; composer/conductor, BBC Philharmonic, since 2000; *b* 16 July 1959; *s* of James MacMillan and Ellen MacMillan (*née* Loy); *m* 1983, Lynne Frew; one *s* two *d.* *Educ:* Edinburgh Univ. (BMus); Durham Univ. (PhD 1987). Lectr, Univ. of Manchester, 1986–88; Composer in Residence, St Magnus Fest., Orkney, 1989; Featured Composer: Musica Nova, Glasgow, 1990; Huddersfield Contemp. Music Fest., 1991; Edinburgh Fest., 1993; Raising Sparks Fest., S Bank and Barbican, 1997; Affiliate Composer, Scottish Chamber Orch., 1990–; Vis. Composer, Philharmonia, 1991–; Vis. Prof., Univ. of Strathclyde, 1997–. FRSAMD 1996. Hon. FRIAS 1997. DUniv Paisley, 1995; Hon. DLitt Strathclyde, 1996; Hon. DMus St Andrews, 2001. Gramophone Award, 1993; Classic CD Award, 1994; Royal Philharmonic Soc. Award, 1995. *Compositions* include: Busquéda (music theatre), 1988; Visions of a November Spring (string quartet no 1), 1988; Tryst (for orch.), 1989; Tuireadh (clarinet quintet), 1991; Confession of Isobel Gowdie (for orch.), 1990; Veni, Veni Emmanuel (percussion concerto), 1992; Visitatio Sepulchri (one-act opera), 1993; Seven Last Words (chorus and strings), 1994; Britannia (overture), 1995; Ines de Castro (opera), 1996; The World's Ransoming (concerto for cor anglais), 1996; 'Cello Concerto, 1996; I–a Meditation on Iona (for chamber orch.), 1997; Ninian (clarinet concerto), 1997; 14 Little Pictures (for piano trio), 1997; Vigil (symphony), 1997; Raising Sparks (for mezzo-sop. and ensemble), 1997; Why is this night different? (string quartet no 2), 1998; Quickening (for chorus, orch., boys' choir and four soloists), 1999; Symphony no 2, 1999; The Birds of Rhiannon, 2001. *Recreations:* fatherhood, Glasgow Celtic FC. *Address:* c/o Boosey & Hawkes Music Publishers Ltd, 295 Regent Street, W1R 8JH. *T:* (020) 7580 2060.

MacMILLAN, Prof. John, (Jake), PhD Glasgow; DSc Bristol; FRS 1978; CChem, ARIC; Alfred Capper Pass Professor of Organic Chemistry, 1985–90, and Head of Department of Organic Chemistry, 1983–90, University of Bristol, now Professor Emeritus and Senior Research Fellow; *b* 13 Sept. 1924; *s* of John MacMillan and Barbara Lindsay; *m* 1952, Anne Levy; one *s* two *d.* *Educ:* Lanark Grammar Sch.; Glasgow Univ. Res. Chemist, Akers Res. Labs, ICI Ltd, 1949; Associate Res. Manager, Pharmaceuticals Div., ICI Ltd, 1962; Lectr in Org. Chemistry, Bristol Univ., 1963, Reader 1968, Prof. 1978. Pres., Internat. Plant Growth Substance Assoc., 1973–76. For. Associate, Nat. Acad. of Scis, USA, 1991. *Publications:* (ed) Encyclopedia of Plant Physiology, New Series vol. 9, 1980; (ed jtly) Gibberellins, 1991; (jtly) GC-MS of Gibberellins and Related Compounds: methodology and a library of reference spectra, 1991; research papers in learned jls on natural organic products, esp. plant growth hormones. *Recreations:* golf, gardening, theatre, music. *Address:* 1 Rylestone Grove, Bristol BS9 3UT. *T:* (0117) 962 0535.

MACMILLAN, Prof. (John) Duncan, PhD; Curator, Talbot Rice Gallery, since 1979, and Professor of History of Scottish Art, since 1994, University of Edinburgh; *b* 7 March 1939; *s* of William Miller Macmillan and Mona Constance Mary Tweedie; *m* 1971, Vivien Rosemary Hinkley; two *d.* *Educ:* Gordonstoun Sch.; St Andrews Univ. (MA Hons 1961); Courtald Inst., London (Dip. Hist. of Art 1964); Edinburgh Univ. (PhD 1974). Lectr, 1964–81, Curator of Univ. Collections, 1987–, Edinburgh Univ. Art critic: The Scotsman, 1994–2000; Business am, 2000–. Visting Fellow: Yale Centre for British Art, 1991; Japan Soc. for Promotion of Science, 1995. Convener, Scottish Univ. Museums Gp, 1992–99; Chm., Edinburgh Galls Assoc., 1995–98; Vice-Chm., European Union Cultural Forum; Chm., Torvean Project Steering Gp, 1997–; Member: Council, Edinburgh Fest. Soc., 1991–97; Cttee, Univ. Museums Gp, 1992–99; Heritage Unit Adv. Bd, Robert Gordon Univ.; comité consultatif, French Inst., Edinburgh, 1997–. Member Editorial Board: Scotlands, 1994–; British Art Jl, 1999–. Hon. Keeper of Portraits, RCSE. Hon. RSA; FRSA. *Publications:* (jtly) Miró in America, 1983; Painting in Scotland: the Golden Age 1707–1843, 1986; Scottish Art 1460–1990, 1990 (Scottish Book of the Year, Saltire Soc., 1992), 2nd edn, Scottish Art 1460–2000, 2000; Symbols of Survival: the art of Will Maclean, 1992 (Scottish Arts Council Book Award, 1993); The Paintings of Steven Campbell: the story so far, 1993; Scottish Art in the Twentieth Century, 1994 (Scottish Arts Council Book Award, 1995); (jtly) Peter Brandes: stained glass, 1994; (jtly) Eugenio Carmi, 1996; Elizabeth Blackadder, 1999; numerous exhibn catalogues, articles, etc. *Recreations:* walking, landscape photography. *Address:* 20 Nelson Street, Edinburgh EH3 6LJ. *T:* (0131) 556 7100; Wester Balnagrantach, Glen Urquhart, Inverness-shire. *T:* (01456) 450727.

MACMILLAN, John Kenneth; Regional Chairman, Employment (formerly Industrial) Tribunals, Nottingham, since 1997; *b* 8 July 1946; *s* of Kenneth Lionel Macmillan, OBE and late Marjorie Ethel Macmillan; *m* 1st, 1972, Mary Lister (marr. diss.); 2nd, 1977, Dawn Nelson (marr. diss.); one *d*; 3rd, 1995, Pauline Anne Swain; two step *d.* *Educ:* Carlton-le-Willows Grammar Sch., Nottingham. Admitted Solicitor, 1970; Asst Solicitor, 1970, Litigation Partner, 1971–81, Haden and Stretton, Solicitors. Pt-time Chm., 1981–87, full-time Chm., 1987–97, Industrial Tribunals, Birmingham; Mem., President's Trng Panel, 1992–. Ed., Employment Tribunals Members Handbook, 1999–. Hon. Sec., RSNC, 1992–. *Recreations:* nature conservation, theatre, gardening, fly fishing. *Address:* (office) 3rd Floor, Byron House, Maid Marian Way, Nottingham NG1 6HS.

MacMILLAN, Lt-Gen. Sir John Richard Alexander, KCB 1988; CBE 1978 (OBE 1973); DL; fruit farmer; GOC Scotland and Governor of Edinburgh Castle, 1988–91; *b* 8 Feb. 1932; *m* 1964, Belinda Lumley Webb; one *s* two *d.* *Educ:* Trinity Coll., Cambridge (BA 1953; MA 1958); rcds, psc. Commnd Argyll and Sutherland Highlanders, 2nd Lieut, 1952; GSO2 (Ops Int. Trng), Trucial Oman Scouts, 1963–64; BM, HQ 24 Inf. Bde, 1967–69; Chief Recruiting and Liaison Staff, Scotland, 1970; CO, 1st Bn The Gordon Highlanders, 1971–73; GSO1 (DS), Staff Coll., 1973–75; Col GS, Mil. Ops 4, 1975–76; Brig., 1976; Bde Comd, 39 Inf. Bde, 1977–78; RCDS 1979; COS, 1 (Br.) Corps,

1980–82; Maj.-Gen., 1982; GOC Eastern Dist, 1982–84; ACGS, MoD, 1984–87; Lt-Gen., 1988. Col, The Gordon Highlanders, 1978–86; Col Comdt, Scottish Div., 1986–91; Hon. Col, Aberdeen Univ. OTC, 1987–97. Chm. Exec Cttee, Scottish Conservation Projects Trust, 1992–98; Chm., Erskine Hosp. (formerly Princess Louise Scottish Hosp.), 1995–. DL Stirling and Falkirk, 1998. *Address:* c/o Northern Bank, 9 Donegall Square North, Belfast BT1 5GJ.

MACMILLAN, Matthew, CBE 1983 (OBE 1977); Controller, English Language and Literature Division, British Council, 1978–83; *b* 14 July 1926; *s* of late David Craig Macmillan and Barbara Cruikshank Macmillan (*née* Gow); *m* 1949, Winifred (*née* Sagar); one *s* two *d. Educ:* Robert Gordon's Coll., Aberdeen; Aberdeen Univ. (MA Hons); Manchester Univ. (Teacher's Dip.). Served Royal Air Force, 1944–47. Schoolmaster, Chatham House Grammar Sch., Ramsgate, 1951–57; Sen. Lectr, Univ. of Science and Technology, Kumasi, Ghana, 1958–62; Associate Prof., University Coll. of Cape Coast, Ghana, 1962–64; Prof. of English, Univ. of Khartoum, The Sudan, 1965–70; British Council, London: Director, English-Teaching Information Centre, 1970–72; Dep. Controller, English Teaching Div., 1972–74; Asst Educn Adviser (English Studies), British Council, India, 1974–78; Prof. of English, 1983–89, Principal, 1986–89, University Coll., Univ. of E Asia, Macau; Prof., English Programmes, E Asia Open Inst., Hong Kong, 1989–90. English examiner, Trinity Coll. London, 1992–99. Mem., ESU, 1993–. *Publications:* articles on the teaching of English as a second/foreign language. *Recreations:* travel, antiques. *Address:* Yeoman's Cottage, 49 North Lane, Canterbury, Kent CT2 7EF. *T:* (01227) 766429. *Club:* Royal Commonwealth Society.

MACMILLAN, Maureen; Member (Lab) Highlands and Islands, Scottish Parliament, since 1999; *b* 9 Feb. 1943; *m* 1965, Michael Muirdon Macmillan, LLB; two *s* two *d. Educ:* Oban High Sch.; Edinburgh Univ. (MA Hons); Moray House. English Teacher, 1983–99. Co-founder, Ross-shire Women's Aid, 1980–. Mem., EIS, 1980–. *Address:* Scottish Parliament, Edinburgh EH99 1SP.

McMILLAN, Neil Macleod, CMG 1997; Deputy Permanent Representative, UK Mission to the United Nations, Geneva, since 2001; *b* 21 Oct. 1953; *s* of John Howard McMillan, CBE and Ruby Hassell McMillan (*née* Meggs); *m* 1st, 1978, Karin Lauritzen (marr. diss. 1985); 2nd, 1994, Lena Madvig Madsen; one *s. Educ:* Westminster City Sch.; Univ. of Regensburg; Univ. of Kiel, Germany; Exeter Univ. (BA Hons Mod. Langs 1977). Admin. Trainee, Dept of Prices and Consumer Protection, 1978–79; Dept of Industry, 1980–81; HEO (Develt), Dept of Trade, 1981–82; Private Sec. to Minister for Industry and IT, 1982–84; seconded to Govt Commn on Telecommunications Reform, Federal Min. of Research, Bonn, 1985; Principal, DTI, 1986–87; First Sec., UK Representation to EU, Brussels, 1987–91; Department of Trade and Industry: Dir, Internat. Communications Policy, 1991–98; Dir, EU Internal Trade Policy, 1998–2000. Chairman: European Telecommunications Regulatory Cttee, 1992–96; WTO Negotiating Gp on Basic Telecommunications Services, 1994–97; World Telecommunications Policy Forum, 1998. *Recreations:* reading, church architecture. *Address:* c/o Foreign and Commonwealth Office, King Charles Street, SW1A 2AH. *Club:* Athenæum.

McMILLAN, (Norman) Hamilton, CMG 1997; OBE 1984; Director of Operations, CIEX Ltd, since 1997; *b* 28 Oct. 1946; *s* of Neil McMillan and Alma McMillan (*née* Hall); *m* 1969, Carolyn Vivienne Barltrop; one *s* one *d. Educ:* Brentwood Sch.; Balliol Coll., Oxford. Joined HM Diplomatic Service, 1968; Third Sec., FCO, 1968–70; Third, later Second Sec., Vienna, 1970–72; Second, later First Sec., FCO, 1972–77; First Secretary: Rome, 1977–81; Dhaka, 1981–84; Cairo, 1984–86; Counsellor: (Chancery), Vienna, 1989–93; FCO, 1993–97. *Recreations:* board games, music with bite, cosmology. *Address:* CIEX Ltd, 6 Buckingham Gate, SW1E 6JP. *Club:* Oriental.

MACMILLAN, Dr Robert Hugh; Professor of Vehicle Design and Head of School of Automotive Studies, 1977–82, Dean of Engineering, 1980–82, Cranfield Institute of Technology; *b* Mussoorie, India, 27 June 1921; *s* of H. R. M. Macmillan and E. G. Macmillan (*née* Webb); *m* 1950, Anna Christina Roding, Amsterdam; one *s* two *d. Educ:* Felsted Sch.; Emmanuel Coll., Cambridge. Technical Branch, RAFVR, 1941; Dept of Engrg, Cambridge Univ., 1947; Asst Prof., MIT, 1950–51; Prof. of Mech. Engrg, Swansea, 1956; Dir, Motor Industry Res. Assoc., 1964–77; Associate Prof., Warwick Univ., 1965–77. 20th Leonardo Da Vinci Lectr, 1973. Mem. Council, Loughborough Univ., 1966–81, 1988–91; Chm. Council, Automobile Div., IMechE, 1976–77; Member: Noise Adv. Council, 1970–77; Internat. Technical Commn, FIA, 1975–88; FISITA: Mem. Council, 1970–80; Chm., London Congress, 1972. Approved Lectr for NADFAS, 1985–98; official guide, Winslow Hall, 1985–97, Ascott, 1988–93; Steward, Bath Abbey, 2000–. Editor, The Netherlands Philatelist, 1984–88. MIEE; FIMechE; FRPSL. Hon. DTech Loughborough, 1992. Gold Medal, FISITA, 1970. *Publications:* Theory of Control, 1951; Automation, 1956; Geometric Symmetry, 1978; Dynamics of Vehicle Collisions, 1983; Netherlands Stamps 1852–1939, 1996. *Recreations:* music, philately, national heritage. *Address:* 1 The Empire, Grand Parade, Bath BA2 4DF. *T:* (01225) 329687. *Clubs:* Royal Air Force, Royal Over-Seas League.

MACMILLAN, Very Rev. William Boyd Robertson; Moderator of the General Assembly of the Church of Scotland, 1991–92; an Extra Chaplain to the Queen in Scotland, since 1997 (Chaplain, 1988–97); *b* 3 July 1927; *s* of Robert and Annie Simpson Macmillan; *m* 1962, Mary Adams Bisset Murray. *Educ:* Royal High Sch., Edinburgh; Univ. of Aberdeen (MA, BD). Served RN, 1946–48. Minister: St Andrew's, Bo'ness, 1955–60; Fyvie, 1960–67; Bearsden, South, 1967–78; Dundee Parish Church (St Mary's), 1978–93; Chaplain, City of Dundee DC, 1978–93. Convener, General Assembly, Church of Scotland: Bd of Practice and Procedure, 1985–88; Business Cttee, 1985–88. Mem. Cttee, Chaplains to HM Forces, 1995–99. Chm. Bd of Dirs, High Sch. of Dundee, 1993–96. Chm., Murray Home, 1994–96; Trustee, Scottish Nat. War Meml, 1994–; Mem., Cttee of Mgt, Royal Soc. for Relief of Indigent Gentlewomen, Scotland, 1994–. Pres., Scottish Church Soc., 1994–97. Freeman of Dundee, 1991. Hon. LLD Dundee, 1990; Hon. DD Aberdeen, 1991. ChStJ 1993 (Prelate, 1993–96). *Recreations:* reading, golf, exploring towns. *Address:* 3/5 Craigend Park, Edinburgh EH16 5XY. *Club:* New (Edinburgh).

McMILLAN-SCOTT, Edward; Member (C) Yorkshire and the Humber Region, European Parliament, since 1999 (York, 1984–94; North Yorkshire, 1994–99); *b* 15 Aug. 1949; *s* of late Walter Theodore Robin McMillan-Scott, ARIBA and of Elizabeth Maud Derrington Hudson; *m* 1972, Henrietta Elizabeth Rumney Hudson, solicitor; two *d. Educ:* Blackfriars School, Llanarth; Blackfriars School, Laxton; Exeter Technical College. Tour director in Europe, Scandinavia, Africa and USSR, 1968–75; PR exec., then parly consultant, 1976–84; political adviser to Falkland Islands Govt, London office 1983–84. European Parliament: Member: For. Affairs and Security Cttee, 1989–; Transport Cttee, 1989–92; Chairman: 1979 Cttee (Cons. back-bench cttee), 1994–95; Conservatives in EP, 1997– (Treas., 1995). Mem. Bd, Cons. Party, 1998–. Mem. Court, Univ. of York. Trustee, BBC World Service Trng Trust, 1999–. *Recreations:* music, reading. *Address:* European Parliament, 2 Queen Anne's Gate, SW1H 9AA.

McMINN, Prof. Robert Matthew Hay; Emeritus Professor of Anatomy, Royal College of Surgeons and University of London; *b* 20 Sept. 1923; *o s* of Robert Martin McMinn, MB, ChB, Auchinleck and Brighton, and Elsie Selene Kent; *m* 1948, Margaret Grieve Kirkwood, MB, ChB, DA; one *s* one *d. Educ:* Brighton Coll. (Schol.); Univ. of Glasgow (Scottish Univ. Champion, 440 yds hurdles, 1944). MB, ChB 1947, MD (commendation) 1958, Glasgow; PhD Sheffield 1956; FRCS 1978. Hosp. posts and RAF Med. Service, 1947–50; Demonstrator in Anatomy, Glasgow Univ., 1950–52; Lectr in Anatomy, Sheffield Univ., 1952–60; Reader 1960–66, Prof. of Anatomy 1966–70, King's Coll., London Univ.; Sir William Collins Prof. of Human and Comparative Anatomy, RCS, Conservator, Hunterian Museum, RCS, and Prof. of Anatomy, Inst. of Basic Med. Scis, London Univ., 1970–82, prematurely retd. Late Examnr to RCS, RCPSG and Univs of London, Cambridge, Edinburgh, Belfast, Singapore, Malaya and Makerere. Arris and Gale Lectr, RCS, 1960; Arnott Demonstrator, RCS, 1970. Former Treas., Anatomical Soc. of Gt Britain and Ireland; Foundn Sec., British Assoc. of Clinical Anatomists (Special Presentation Award, 2000); FRSocMed; Member: Amer. Assoc. of Anatomists; Amer. Assoc. of Clinical Anatomists; BMA; Trustee, Skin Res. Foundn. *Publications:* Tissue Repair, 1969; The Digestive System, 1974; The Human Gut, 1974; (jtly) Colour Atlas of Human Anatomy, 1977, 4th edn 1998; (jtly) Colour Atlas of Head and Neck Anatomy, 1981, 2nd edn 1994; (jtly) Colour Atlas of Foot and Ankle Anatomy, 1982, 2nd edn 1995; (jtly) Colour Atlas of Applied Anatomy, 1984; (jtly) Picture Tests in Human Anatomy, 1986; (jtly) The Human Skeleton, 1987; (ed) Last's Anatomy, 8th edn 1990, 9th edn 1994; (jtly) McMinn's Functional and Clinical Anatomy, 1995; (jtly) Concise Handbook of Human Anatomy, 1998; articles in various med. and sci. jls. *Recreations:* motoring, photography, archaeology, short-wave radio, deputy organist, Craignish Parish Church. *Address:* Achnafuaran, Ardfern, Lochgilphead, Argyll PA31 8QN. *T:* (01852) 500274.

McMULLAN, Rt Rev. Gordon; Bishop of Down and Dromore, 1986–97; *b* 1934; *m* 1957, Kathleen Davidson; two *s. Educ:* Queen's Univ., Belfast (BSc Econ 1961, PhD 1971); Ridley Hall, Cambridge. Dipl. of Religious Studies (Cantab) 1978; ThD Geneva Theol Coll., 1988; MPhil TCD, 1990; DMin Univ. of the South, USA, 1995. Deacon 1962, priest 1963, dio. Down; Curate of Ballymacarrett, 1962–67; Central Adviser on Christian Stewardship to Church of Ireland, 1967–70; Curate of St Columba, Knock, Belfast, 1970–71; Rector of St Brendan's, East Belfast, 1971–76; Rector of St Columba, Knock, Belfast, 1976–80; Archdeacon of Down, 1979–80; Bishop of Clogher, 1980–86. Merrill Fellow/Resident Fellow, Harvard Divinity Sch., 1997–98. *Publications:* A Cross and Beyond, 1976; We are called …, 1977; Everyday Discipleship, 1979; Reflections on St Mark's Gospel, 1984; Growing Together in Prayer, 1990; Reflections on St Luke's Gospel, 1994; Opposing Violence/Building Bridges, 1996. *Address:* 26 Wellington Park, Bangor, Co. Down, N Ireland BT20 4PJ.

McMULLAN, His Honour Michael Brian; a Circuit Judge, 1980–95; *b* 15 Nov. 1926; *s* of late Joseph Patrick McMullan and Frances McMullan (*née* Burton); *m* 1960, Rosemary Jane Margaret, *d* of late Stanley Halse deL. de Ville; one *s* two *d. Educ:* Manor Farm Road Sch.; Taunton's Sch., Southampton; The Queen's College, Oxford (MA). Called to the Bar, Gray's Inn, 1960. National Service, Army, 1946–48. Colonial Administrative Service: Gold Coast and Ghana, Political Administration, Ashanti, Min. of Finance, Accra, Agricl Development Corp., 1949–60. In practice as Barrister, SE Circuit, 1961–80; a Recorder of the Crown Court, 1979. *Club:* Oxford and Cambridge.

McMULLEN, Prof. David Lawrence, FBA 1994; Professor of Chinese, University of Cambridge, since 1989; Fellow of St John's College, Cambridge, since 1967; *b* 10 Aug. 1939; *m* 1983, Sarah Jane Clarice Croft; two *d. Educ:* Monkton Combe Sch., Bath; St John's Coll., Cambridge (BA, MA, PhD). National Service, RAF, 1957–59. Taiwan Min. of Educn Schol., 1963–64; Harkness Commonwealth Fellowship, 1965–67; Asst Lectr 1967, Lectr 1972, in Chinese Studies, Cambridge Univ. Pres., British Assoc. for Chinese Studies, 1985–87. *Publications:* Concordances and Indexes to Chinese Texts, 1975; State and Scholars in T'ang China, 1988; contribs to jls of E Asian studies. *Recreation:* gardening. *Address:* Grove Cottage, 35 High Street, Grantchester, Cambridge CB3 9NF. *T:* (01223) 840206.

McMULLEN, Dr Ian James, FBA 2001; Lecturer in Japanese, University of Oxford, since 1972; Fellow, Pembroke College, Oxford, since 1989; *b* 10 Aug. 1939; *s* of late Alexander Lawrence McMullen and Muriel Felicity McMullen (*née* Sikes); *m* 1970, Bonnie Shannon; one *s. Educ:* Monkton Combe Sch., Bath; St John's Coll., Cambridge (BA, MA; PhD 1969). Nat. Service, RAF, 1957–59. Schol., Min. of Educn, Japan, 1963–64; Lectr, 1965, Asst Prof., 1966–70, Associate Prof., 1970–72, Univ. of Toronto; Fellow, St Antony's Coll., Oxford, 1972–89. Pres., British Assoc. Japanese Studies, 1997–98. *Publications:* Genji Garden: the origins of Kumazawa Banzan's commentary on the Tale of Genji, 1991; Idealism, Protest and the Tale of Genji, 1999; contribs to jls of E Asian studies. *Recreation:* gardening. *Address:* Wilton Lodge, 44 Osberton Road, Oxford OX2 7NU. *T:* (01865) 559859.

McMULLEN, Jeremy John; QC 1994; QC (NI) 1996; a Recorder, since 2000; *b* 14 Sept. 1948; *s* of John Ezra McMullen and Irene McMullen; *m* 1973, Deborah Cristman; one *s* one *d. Educ:* William Hulme's Grammar Sch., Manchester; Brasenose Coll., Oxford (MA); LSE (MSc). Called to the Bar, Middle Temple, 1971, NI, 1994; Associate Attorney, New York, 1971–73; General, Municipal, Boilermakers' Union: Legal Officer, 1973–77; Regl Officer, London, 1977–84; in practice at the Bar, 1984–; an Asst Recorder, 1998–2000; Sports Arbitrator, 2000–. Chm. (part-time), Employment (formerly Industrial) Tribunals, 1993–. Chair: Industrial Law Soc., 1989–93; Employment Law Bar Assoc., 1994–95. *Publications:* Rights at Work, 1978, 2nd edn 1983; (contrib.) Penguin Guide to Civil Liberties, 1989; Employment Tribunal Procedure, 1996; Employment Precedents, 1996. *Recreations:* squash, cycling, under-gardener, family allotment. *Address:* Old Square Chambers, 1 Verulam Buildings, Gray's Inn, WC1R 5LQ. *Clubs:* Reform, West London Trade Union.

McMULLIN, Rt Hon. Sir Duncan (Wallace), Kt 1987; PC 1980; Judge of Court of Appeal, New Zealand, 1979–89; commercial arbitrator, since 1990; *b* 1 May 1927; *s* of Charles James McMullin and Kathleen Annie Shout; *m* 1955, Isobel Margaret, *d* of Robert Ronald Atkinson, ED; two *s* two *d. Educ:* Auckland Grammar Sch.; Univ. of Auckland (LLB). Judge of Supreme Court, 1970–79. Chm., Royal Commn on Contraception, Sterilisation and Abortion in NZ, 1975–77. Chairman: Wanganui Computer Centre Policy Cttee, 1989–93; Market Surveillance Panel, Electricity Marketing Corp., 1994–. Chm., NZ Conservation Authority, 1996–2000. FIArb of NZ, 1990. *Recreations:* forestry, farming, conservation. *Address:* 4/456 Remuera Road, Auckland, New Zealand. *T:* (9) 5246583.

McMURRAY, Prof. Cecil Hugh, FRSC, FIFST; Chief Scientific Officer, Department of Agriculture and Rural Development for Northern Ireland, since 1988; *b* 19 Feb. 1942; *s* of late Edwin McMurray and of Margaret (*née* Smyth); *m* 1967, Ann Stuart; two *s* one *d. Educ:* Royal Belfast Academical Instn; Queen's University, Belfast (BSc 1965; BAgr 1966); PhD Bristol, 1970. FRSC 1981; FIFST 1987. Res. Fellow, Dept of Chem., Harvard Univ., 1970–72; Head of Biochem. Dept, Vet. Res. Lab., Dept of Agric. for NI, 1972–84;

Prof. of Food and Agricl Chem., QUB, and concurrently DCSO, Dept of Agric. for NI, 1984–88 (Hon. Prof., QUB, 1998–). Expert Advr, WHO, 1983, 1986; Assessor to: AFRC, 1988–94; Priorities Bd for R&D in Agric. and Food, 1988–93; Technology Bd for NI, 1988–92; NERC, 1992–93; Adv. Cttee on microbiol safety of food, 1992–; Dir, NI Public Sector Overseas, 1994–. Mem., Steering Gp on chem. aspects of food surveillance, 1992–95. Pres., Agricl Gp, BAAS, 1986–87. Mem. Cttee, Coronary Prevention Gp, 1985–89. Trustee, Agricl Inst. for NI, 1985–; Mem. Governing Body, Rowett Res. Inst., Aberdeen, 1986–89, 1993–. Mem. Editl Bd, Fertiliser Res., 1985–92. *Publications:* (ed jtly) Detection Methods for Irradiated Foods: current status, 1996; over 100 scientific publications in various jls incl. Biochemical Jl, Jl of Amer. Chemical Soc., Clin. Chem., CIBA Foundn Symposia, Jl of Chromatography, British Vet. Jl, Vet. Record, Jl Assoc. of Analytical Chem., Trace Metals in Man and Domestic Animals, Biology of Total Envmt. *Recreations:* reading, photography, walking. *Address:* Department of Agriculture and Rural Development for Northern Ireland, Dundonald House, Upper Newtownards Road, Belfast BT4 3SB. *T:* (028) 9052 4635.

McMURRAY, David Bruce, MA; Headmaster, Oundle School, 1984–99; *b* 15 Dec. 1937; *s* of late James McMurray, CBE, and of Kathleen McMurray (*née* Goodwin); *m* 1962, Antonia Murray; three *d. Educ:* Loretto Sch.; Pembroke Coll., Cambridge (BA, MA). National service, Royal Scots, 1956–58, 2nd Lieut. Pembroke Coll., Cambridge, 1958–61; Asst Master, Stowe Sch., 1961–64; Fettes College: Asst Master, 1964–72; Head of English, 1967–72; Housemaster, 1972–76; Headmaster, Loretto Sch., 1976–84. HM Comr, Queen Victoria Sch., Dunblane, 1977–87; Mem., Edinburgh Fest. Council, 1980–84. FRSA 1989. CCF Medal, 1976, and Bar, 1984. *Recreations:* cricket, golf, sub-aqua diving, poetry. *Address:* 7 Amisfield Park, Haddington, East Lothian EH41 4QE. *T:* (01620) 825474. *Clubs:* MCC, Free Foresters; New (Edinburgh).

MacMURRAY, Her Honour Mary Bell McMillan, (Mrs Ian Mills); QC 1979; a Circuit Judge, 1988–96; *d* of Samuel Bell MacMurray and Constance Mary MacMurray (*née* Goodman); *m* 1971, Ian Donald Mills. *Educ:* Queen Margaret's School, Escrick, York. Called to the Bar, Lincoln's Inn, 1954, Bencher, 1986. Barrister-at-Law, 1954–88; a Recorder of the Crown Court, 1978–88. Coronation Medal, 1953. *Recreation:* golf. *Address:* c/o Courts Administrator, Westgate House, Westgate Road, Newcastle upon Tyne NE1 1RR. *Clubs:* Durham County; Whitburn Golf; Lady Taverners.

McMURTRY, Hon. (Roland) Roy; Chief Justice of Ontario, since 1996 (Associate Chief Justice, 1991–94, Chief Justice, 1994–96, Ontario Court of Justice (General Division)); *b* 31 May 1932; *s* of Roland Roy McMurtry and Doris Elizabeth Belcher; *m* 1957, Ria Jean Macrae; three *s* three *d. Educ:* St Andrew's Coll., Aurora, Ont; Trinity Coll., Univ. of Toronto (BA Hons); Osgoode Hall Law Sch., Toronto (LLB). Called to the Bar of Ontario, 1958; QC 1970. Partner: Benson, McMurtry, Percival & Brown, Toronto, 1958–75; Blaney, McMurtry, Stapells, 1988–91. Elected to Ontario Legislature, 1975; re-elected, 1977 and 1981; Attorney General for Ontario, 1975–85; Solicitor General for Ontario, 1978–82. High Comr in UK, 1985–88. Freeman, City of London, 1986. Hon. LLD: Ottawa, 1983; Law Soc. of Upper Canada, 1984; Leeds, 1988; York, 1991; Toronto, 1998. *Recreations:* painting, ski-ing, tennis. *Address:* 130 Queen Street West, Toronto, ON M5H 2N5, Canada. *T:* (416) 3275000. *Clubs:* Albany, York (Toronto).

McMURTRY, Stanley, (Mac); social and political cartoonist, Daily Mail, since 1970; *b* 4 May 1936; *s* of Stanley Harrison McMurtry and Janet Lind McMurtry; *m* 1st, 1958, Maureen Flaye (marr. diss. 1980); one *s* one *d*; 2nd, 1981, Janet Elizabeth Rattle. *Educ:* Sharmans Cross Secondary Sch., Birmingham; Birmingham Coll. of Art. Cartoon film animator, 1956–65; social and political cartoonist, Daily Sketch, 1968–70; freelance cartoonist, for Punch and other magazines, 1960–; TV scriptwriter with Bernard Cookson, for Tommy Cooper and Dave Allen, 1973–76. Social and Political Cartoonist of the Year, 1983, Master Cartoonist, 2000, Cartoonist Club of GB; Cartoonist of Year Award, 1982, 1984 and 1999, UK Press Gazette. *Publications:* The Bunjee Venture (for children), 1977 (cartoon film, 1979); Mac's Year Books, annually, 1980–; contrib. short story to Knights of Madness, ed Peter Haining, 1998. *Recreations:* motorcycling, golf, tennis, writing. *Address:* 10 Groveside Court, Lombard Road, SW11 3RQ. *T:* (020) 7585 1893. *Clubs:* Chelsea Arts, Saints and Sinners.

MACNAB OF MACNAB, James Charles; The Macnab; 23rd Chief of Clan Macnab; *b* 14 April 1926; *e s* of late Lt-Col James Alexander Macnabb, OBE, TD (*de jure* 21st of Macnab), London, SW3, and Mrs Ursula Walford (*née* Barnett), Wokingham, Berks; *S* gt uncle Archibald Corrie Macnab of Macnab, (*de facto*) 22nd Chief, 1970; *m* 1959, Hon. Diana Mary, DL, *er d* of Baron Kilmany, MC, PC, and of Monica Helen, (Lady Kilmany), OBE, JP, *o c* of late Geoffrey Lambton, 2nd *s* of 4th Earl of Durham; two *s* two *d. Educ:* Cothill House; Radley Coll.; Ashbury Coll., Ottawa. Served in RAF and Scots Guards, 1944–45; Lieut, Seaforth Highldrs, 1945–48. Asst Supt, then Acting Dep. Supt, Fedn of Malaya Police Force, 1948; retd, 1957. Mem., Western DC of Perthshire, 1961–64; CC, Perth and Kinross Jt County Council, 1964–75; Mem., Central Regional Council, 1978–82. Exec., subseq. Sen., Consultant, Hill Samuel Investment Services, 1982–92. Member, Royal Company of Archers, Queen's Body Guard in Scotland. Capt., Seaforth Highldrs, TA, 1960–64. JP Perthshire, 1968–75, Stirling, 1975–86. *Recreations:* shooting, travel. *Heir: s* James William Archibald Macnab, younger of Macnab [*b* 22 March 1963; *m* 1994, Dr Jane Mackintosh, *d* of late Dr David Mackintosh; one *s* one *d*]. *Address:* Leuchars Castle Farmhouse, Leuchars, St Andrews, Fife KY16 0EY. *T:* (01334) 838777. *Club:* New (Edinburgh).

McNAB, John Stanley; Chief Executive, Port of Tilbury London Ltd (formerly Port of Tilbury (Port of London Authority)), 1987–96; *b* 23 Sept. 1937; *s* of Robert Stanley McNab and Alice Mary McNab; *m* 1st, 1961, Carol Field (marr. diss. 1978); two *d*; 2nd, 1980, Jacqueline Scammell (marr. diss. 1997). *Educ:* Gravesend Grammar Sch. FCCA 1976; FCIT 1992. Nat. Service, Royal Engineers, Libya, 1956–58. Port of London Authority: joined 1954; Accountant, India and Millwall Docks, 1965, Upper Docks, 1970; Man. Dir, PLA (Thames) Stevedoring, 1973; Dir, Upper Docks, 1974; Exec. Dir (Manpower) and Group Board Mem., 1978; Dir, Tilbury, 1983. Dir, Internat. Transport Ltd, 1992–96. FRSA 1991; MIMgt (MBIM 1970). Freeman: City of London, 1988; Co. of Watermen and Lightermen of River Thames, 1988. *Recreations:* golf, swimming, tennis, DIY, learning Spanish and Portuguese. *Address:* 1 The Heythrop, Chelmsford, Essex CM2 6BX. *T:* (01245) 491997.

McNAB JONES, Robin Francis, FRCS; Consultant Otolaryngologist, 1959–99; Surgeon: ENT Department, St Bartholomew's Hospital, 1961–87; Royal National Throat, Nose and Ear Hospital, 1962–83; *b* 22 Oct. 1922; *s* of late E. C. H. Jones, CBE, and M. E. Jones, MBE; *m* 1950, Mary Garrett; one *s* three *d. Educ:* Manchester Grammar Sch.; Dulwich Coll.; Med. Coll., St Bartholomew's Hosp. (MB BS 1945); FRCS 1952. Ho. Surg., St Bart's, 1946–47; MO, RAF, 1947–50; Demonstrator of Anatomy, St Bart's, 1950–52; Registrar, Royal Nat. Throat, Nose and Ear Hosp., 1952–54; Sen. Registrar, ENT Dept, St Bart's, 1954–59; Lectr, Dept of Otolaryngology, Univ. of Manchester, 1959–61; Dean, Inst. of Laryngology and Otology, Univ. of London, 1971–76; Vice-Pres., St Bart's Hosp. Med. Coll., 1984–87. Mem., Court of Examiners, 1972–78, and Mem. Council (for Otolaryngology), 1982–87, RCS; External Examiner, RCSI, 1980–83, 1988–91. Hon. Sec., Sect. of Otology, 1965–68, Pres., Sect. of Laryngology, 1981–82, RSocMed. *Publications:* various chapters in standard med. textbooks; contribs to med. jls. *Recreations:* tennis, ski-ing, golf, fishing, gardening. *Address:* 91 Barnfield Wood Road, Beckenham, Kent BR3 2ST. *T:* (020) 8650 0217.

MACNAGHTEN, Sir Patrick (Alexander), 11th Bt *cr* 1836; farmer; *b* 24 Jan. 1927; *s* of Sir Antony Macnaghten, 10th Bt, and of Magdalene, *e d* of late Edmund Fisher; *S* father, 1972; *m* 1955, Marianne, *yr d* of Dr Erich Schaefer and Alice Schaefer, Cambridge; three *s. Educ:* Eton; Trinity Coll., Cambridge (BA Mechanical Sciences). Army (RE), 1945–48. Project Engineer, Cadbury Bros (later Cadbury Schweppes), 1950–69; in General Management, Cadbury-Schweppes Ltd, 1969–84. *Recreations:* fishing, shooting. *Heir: s* Malcolm Francis Macnaghten, *b* 21 Sept. 1956. *Address:* Dundarave, Bushmills, Co. Antrim, Northern Ireland BT57 8ST. *T:* (028) 2073 1215.

McNAIR, family name of **Baron McNair**.

McNAIR, 3rd Baron *cr* 1955, of Gleniffer; **Duncan James McNair;** *b* 26 June 1947; *s* of 2nd Baron McNair and Vera, *d* of Theodore James Faithfull; *S* father, 1989. *Educ:* Bryanston. Former Mem., Parly Gps on Drug Misuse, Alcohol Misuse, Population Develt and Reproductive Health; Vice Chm., Parly Waterways Gp, 1995–99. Mem., Sub-Cttee E (Enmvt), EC Select Cttee, 1990–92. Member: Resource Use Institute Ltd, 1994–; Adv. Bd, Effective Educn Assoc., 1996–; Council for Human Rights and Religious Freedom, 1996–; Chairman: Unitax Assoc., 1994–; Emission Control Systems International Ltd, 1996–. *Heir: b* Hon. William Samuel Angus McNair, *b* 19 May 1958.

McNAIR, Archibald Alister Jourdan, (Archie); Co-founder, 1955, and Chairman, 1955–88, Mary Quant Group of Companies; Founder, 1971, and Chairman, 1971–88, Thomas Jourdan plc; *b* 16 Dec. 1919; *s* of late Donald McNair and Janie (*née* Jourdan); *m* 1954, Catherine Alice Jane, *d* of late John and Margaret Fleming; one *s* one *d. Educ:* Blundell's. Served War, 1939–45: River Thames Formation. Photographer, 1950–57. *Recreations:* sculpting, gardening, chess. *Address:* c/o Coutts & Co., 440 Strand, WC2R 0QS. *Club:* Hurlingham.

See also D. B. Vernon.

MACNAIR, His Honour (Maurice John) Peter; a Circuit Judge, 1972–91; *b* 27 Feb. 1919; *s* of late Brig. J. L. P. Macnair and Hon. Mrs Macnair (*née* Atkin); *m* 1952, Vickie Reynolds, *d* of Hugh Reynolds; one *s* two *d. Educ:* Bembridge Sch.; St Paul's Sch.; St Edmund Hall, Oxford. BA 1947. Served War of 1939–45, Western Desert, Sicily, Italy; wounded 1944; Captain, RA. Called to Bar, Gray's Inn, 1948. Dep. Chm., W Sussex QS, 1968–72. *Recreations:* reading, painting. *Address:* 28 Rawlings Street, SW3 2LS.

See also K. S. Gavron.

McNAIR-WILSON, Sir Patrick (Michael Ernest David), Kt 1989; company director and consultant; *b* 28 May 1929; *s* of Dr Robert McNair-Wilson; *m* 1953, Diana Evelyn Kitty Campbell Methuen-Campbell, *d* of Hon. Laurence Methuen-Campbell; one *s* four *d. Educ:* Eton. Exec. in French Shipping Co., 1951–53; various appointments at Conservative Central Office, 1954–58; Staff of Conservative Political Centre, 1958–61; Director, London Municipal Society, 1961–63; Executive with The British Iron and Steel Federation, 1963–64. Partner, Ferret PR and Public Affairs, 1995–. Dir, Photo-Me International Plc, 1996–. MP (C): Lewisham W, 1964–66; New Forest, Nov. 1968–1997. Opposition Front Bench Spokesman on fuel and power, 1965–66; Vice-Chm., Conservative Parly Power Cttee, 1969–70; PPS to Minister for Transport Industries, DoE, 1970–74; Opposition Front Bench Spokesman on Energy, 1974–76; Chm., Jt Lords and Commons Select Cttee on Private Bill Procedure, 1987–88; Mem., Select Cttee on Members Interests, 1985–86. Editor of The Londoner, 1961–63. *Recreations:* sailing, pottery, flying. *Address:* Godfrey's Farm, Beaulieu, Hants SO42 7YP.

McNALLY, family name of **Baron McNally**.

McNALLY, Baron *cr* 1995 (Life Peer), of Blackpool in the county of Lancashire; **Tom McNally;** Consultant, Weber Shandwick Worldwide, since 2001; *b* 20 Feb. 1943; *s* of John P. McNally and Elizabeth May (*née* McCarthy); *m* 1st, 1970, Eileen Powell (marr. diss. 1990); 2nd, 1990, Juliet Lamy Hutchinson; two *s* one *d. Educ:* College of St Joseph, Blackpool; University Coll., London (BScEcon; Fellow 1995). President of Students' Union, UCL, 1965–66; Vice-Pres., Nat. Union of Students, 1966–67; Asst Gen. Sec. of Fabian Society, 1966–67; Labour Party researcher, 1967–68; Internat. Sec. of Labour Party, 1969–74; Political Adviser to: Foreign and Commonwealth Sec., 1974–76; Prime Minister, 1976–79. MP (Lab 1979–81, SDP 1981–83) Stockport S; SDP Parly spokesman on educn and sport, 1981–83. Mem., Select Cttee on Industry and Trade, 1979–83. Contested (SDP) Stockport, 1983. Public Affairs Adviser, GEC, 1983–84; Dir-Gen., Retail Consortium, and Dir, British Retailers Association, 1985–87; Head of Public Affairs, Hill & Knowlton, 1987–93; Hd of Public Affairs, 1993–96, Vice-Chm., 1996–2001, Shandwick Consultants. FRSA; FIPR. Pres., St Albans Lib Dems. *Recreations:* playing and watching sport, reading political biographies. *Address:* House of Lords, SW1A 0PW.

McNALLY, Eryl Margaret; Member (Lab) Eastern Region, England, European Parliament, since 1999 (Bedfordshire and Milton Keynes, 1994–99); *b* 11 April 1942; *d* of late Llywelyn Williams, MP and Elsie Williams; *m* 1964, James Frederick McNally; one *s* one *d. Educ:* Newbridge Grammar Sch.; Bristol Univ. (BA Langs); University Coll., Swansea (PGCE). Modern langs teacher, 1964–84; advisory work, Bucks CC, 1985–93; freelance schools inspector, OFSTED, 1993–94. Councillor: Abbots Langley Parish Council, 1970–73; Watford RDC, 1972–74; Three Rivers DC, 1973–77; Herts CC, 1986–95. *Publications:* articles on language teaching and teacher training in professional jls. *Recreations:* learning languages, reading, world music, films. *Address:* 30 Follet Drive, Abbots Langley, Herts WD5 0LP. *T:* (01923) 662711.

McNALLY, Joseph, (Joe); Chief Executive, 1984–2001, Vice President, 1989–2001, Compaq Computer Ltd; *b* 17 July 1942; *s* of Joseph McNally and Emily McNally; *m* 1968, Anne Buglass; one *s* one *d. Educ:* Gateshead GS; King's Coll., Newcastle. Programmer, ICL, 1966–68; sales manager, Honeywell, 1968–79; Chief Exec. Designate, FMC/Harris, 1979–83; Founder Man. Dir, Compaq Computer UK, 1984. MInstD 1984. *Recreations:* shooting, fishing, gardening. *Address:* Compaq Computer Ltd, Hotham House, 1 Heron Square, Richmond, Surrey TW9 1EJ. *Clubs:* Farmers', St James's, Royal Automobile.

McNAMARA, (Joseph) Kevin; MP (Lab) Kingston-upon-Hull North, Jan. 1966–1974 and since 1997 (Kingston-upon-Hull Central, 1974–83; Hull North, 1983–97); *b* 5 Sept. 1934; *s* of late Patrick and Agnes McNamara; *m* 1960, Nora (*née* Jones), Warrington; four *s* one *d. Educ:* various primary schools; St Mary's Coll., Crosby; Hull Univ. (LLB). Head of Dept of History, St Mary's Grammar Sch., Hull, 1958–64; Lecturer in Law, Hull Coll. of Commerce, 1964–66. Opposition spokesman on defence, 1982–83, on defence and disarmament, 1983–85, dep. opposition spokesman on defence, 1985–87, opposition spokesman on Northern Ireland, 1987–94, on Civil Service, 1994–95. Member: Select Cttee on For. Affairs, 1977–82 (former Chm., Overseas Devlt Sub-Cttee); Parly Assembly, NATO, 1984–88; Vice-Chm., Economic Cttee, NATO, 1985–87; former Chairman: Select Cttee on Overseas Devlt; PLP NI Gp; Sec., Parly Gp, TGWU. Chm., All Party Irish In Britain Gp; Vice-Chm., British-Irish Inter-Parly Body; Founder Mem., Friends of the Good Friday Agreement. Former Mem., UK Delegn to Council of Europe. Commendatore, Order Al Merito della Repubblica Italiana, 1977. *Recreations:* family and outdoor activities. *Address:* House of Commons, SW1A 0AA; 145 Newland Park, Hull HU5 2DX.

McNAMARA, Air Chief Marshal Sir Neville (Patrick), KBE 1981 (CBE 1972); AO 1976; AFC 1961; Royal Australian Air Force, retired 1984; *b* Toogoolawah, Qld, 17 April 1923; *s* of late P. F. McNamara; *m* 1950, Dorothy Joan Miller; two *d*. *Educ:* Christian Brothers Coll., Nudgee, Qld. Enlisted RAAF, 1941; commnd 1944; Fighter Pilot WWII with No 75 Sqdn, Halmaheras and Borneo; served with No 77 Sqdn in Japan on cessation of hostilities; Air Traffic Control duties, HQ NE Area, 1949; Flying Instructor, Central Flying Sch., 1951–53; operational tour with No 77 Sqdn in Korean War; Pilot Trng Officer, HQ Trng Comd, 1954–55; Staff Officer, Fighter Operations Dept Air, 1955–57; CO No 25 Sqdn W Australia, 1957–59; CO No 2 Operational Conversion Unit, 1959–61; CO and Sen. Air Staff Officer, RAAF Staff, London, 1961–63; Director of Personnel (Officers), Dept Air, 1964–66; OC RAAF Contingent, Thailand, 1966–67; Air Staff Officer, RAAF Richmond, 1967–69; Dir-Gen., Organisation Dept Air, 1969–71; Comdr RAAF Forces Vietnam, 1971–72; Aust. Air Attaché, Washington, 1972–75; Dep. Chief of Air Staff, 1975–79; Chief of Air Staff, 1979–82; Chief of Defence Force Staff, 1982–84. RAAF psc, pfc, jssc. *Recreations:* golf, fishing. *Club:* Commonwealth (Canberra).

McNAMARA, Robert Strange; Medal of Freedom with Distinction; *b* San Francisco, 9 June 1916; *s* of Robert James McNamara and Clara Nell (*née* Strange); *m* 1940, Margaret McKinstry Craig (decd); one *s* two *d*. *Educ:* University of California (AB); Harvard Univ. (Master of Business Administration). Asst Professor of Business Administration, Harvard, 1940–43. Served in USAAF, England, India, China, Pacific, 1943–46 (Legion of Merit); released as Lieut-Colonel. Joined Ford Motor Co., 1946; Executive, 1946–61; Controller, 1949–53; Asst General Manager, Ford Div., 1953–55; Vice-President, and General Manager, Ford Div., 1955–57; Director, and Group Vice-President of Car Divisions, 1957–61, President, 1960–61; Secretary of Defense, United States of America, 1961–68; Pres., The World Bank, 1968–81; Director: Royal Dutch Petroleum, 1981–87; Bank of America, 1981–87; Corning, 1981–90; The Washington Post, 1981–89. Trustee: Urban Inst.; Trilateral Commn. Hon. degrees from: Harvard, Calif, Mich, Columbia, Ohio, Princeton, NY, Notre Dame, George Washington, Aberdeen, St Andrews, Fordham and Oxford Univs; Williams, Chatham and Amherst Colls. Phi Beta Kappa. Albert Pick Jr Award, Univ. of Chicago (first recipient), 1979; Albert Einstein Peace Prize, 1983; Franklin D. Roosevelt Freedom from Want Medal, 1983; Amer. Assembly Service to Democracy Award; Dag Hammarskjöld Hon. Medal; Extrepreneurial Excellence Medal, Yale Sch. of Organization and Management; Olive Branch Award for Outstanding Book on subject of World Peace, 1987; Sidney Hillman Foundn Award, 1987; Onassis Athinai Prize, 1988. *Publications:* The Essence of Security, 1968; One Hundred Countries, Two Billion People: the dimensions of development, 1975; The McNamara Years at the World Bank, 1981; Blundering into Disaster, 1987; Out of the Cold, 1990; In Retrospect: the tragedy and lessons of Vietnam, 1995; Argument Without End, 2000; Wilson's Ghost, 2001. *Address:* 1350 I Street NW, Suite 500, Washington, DC 20005–3305, USA.

McNAUGHT, John Graeme; His Honour Judge McNaught; a Circuit Judge, since 1987; *b* 21 Feb. 1941; *s* of Charles William McNaught and Isabella Mary McNaught; *m* 1966, Barbara Mary Smith; two *s* one *d*. *Educ:* King Edward VII Sch., Sheffield; The Queen's Coll., Oxford (BA Jurisprudence, 1962). Bacon Scholar, Gray's Inn, 1962; called to the Bar, Gray's Inn, 1963; a Recorder, 1981–87; Hon. Recorder, Devizes, 1996–. Mem., Parole Bd for England and Wales, 1998–. Chm., Wilts Criminal Justice Strategy Cttee, 2000–. UK Council Mem., Commonwealth Magistrates' and Judges' Assoc., 1997–. *Address:* The Swindon Combined Court Centre, Islington Street, Swindon SN1 2HG.

McNAUGHTON, Lt-Col Ian Kenneth Arnold; Chief Inspecting Officer of Railways, Department of Transport, 1974–82; *b* 30 June 1920; *er s* of late Brig. F. L. McNaughton, CBE, DSO and Betty, *d* of late Rev. Arnold Pinchard, OBE; *m* 1946, Arthea, *d* of late Carel Begeer, Voorschoten, Holland; two *d*. *Educ:* Loretto Sch.; RMA Woolwich; RMCS Shrivenham. BScEng, CEng, FIMechE, FIRSE. 2nd Lieut RE, 1939; served War of 1939–45, NW Europe (Captain) (despatches); GHQ MELF, 1949 (Major); Cyprus, 1955; OC 8 Rly Sqdn, 1958; Port Comdt Southampton, 1959 (Lt-Col); SOI Transportation HQ BAOR, 1960; retd 1963. Inspecting Officer of Rlys, Min. of Transport, 1963. Chm., Rlys Industry Adv. Cttee, Health and Safety Commn, 1978–82. *Recreations:* gardening, foreign travel. *Address:* Chawton Glebe, Alton, Hants GU34 1SH. *T:* (01420) 83395.

MacNAUGHTON, Joan; Director General, Policy, Lord Chancellor's Department, since 1999; *b* 12 Sept. 1950; *d* of Duncan McNaughton and Marion McNaughton (*née* Caldwell); *m* 1979, William Alexander Jeffrey, *qv*. *Educ:* Notre Dame Coll. Sch., Liverpool; Warwick Univ. (BSc Hons Physics). Home Office: Admin. Trainee, 1972–74; HEO (Develt), 1974–76; Asst Sec. to Royal Commn on Criminal Procedure, 1976–80; Criminal Policy Dept, 1981–85; Prin. Private Sec. to Dep. Prime Minister and Lord Pres. of the Council, 1985–87; Head, Women and Young Offenders Div., Prison Service, 1987–89; Dir, Prison Service Industries and Farms, 1989–91; Head, Criminal Policy Div., 1991–92; Prin. Private Sec. to Home Secretary, 1992–95; Chief Exec., Police IT Orgn, 1996–99. *Recreations:* reading, music, hill walking, watching soccer, films. *Address:* Lord Chancellor's Department, Selborne House, Victoria Street, SW1E 6QW. *Club:* Reform.

MACNAUGHTON, Prof. Sir Malcolm (Campbell), Kt 1986; MD; FRCPG; FRCOG; FFFP; FRSE; Muirhead Professor of Obstetrics and Gynaecology, University of Glasgow, 1970–90, now Emeritus; *b* 4 April 1925; *s* of James Hay and Mary Robieson Macnaughton; *m* 1955, Margaret-Ann Galt; two *s* three *d*. *Educ:* Glasgow Academy; Glasgow Univ. (MD). Lectr, Univ. of Aberdeen, 1957–61; Sen. Lectr, Univ. of St Andrews, 1961–66; Hon. Sen. Lectr, Univ. of Dundee, 1966–70. Pres., RCOG, 1984–87; Vice-Pres., Royal Coll. of Midwives, 1992–. Pres., British Fertility Soc., 1992–95. Hon. FACOG; Hon. FSLCOG; Hon. FRCAnaes; Hon. FRACOG. Hon. LLD Dundee, 1988. *Publications:* Combined Textbook of Obstetrics and Gynaecology (ed jtly), 9th edn 1976; (ed and contrib.) Handbook of Medical Gynaecology, 1985; numerous papers in obstetric, gynaecological, endocrine and general medical jls. *Recreations:* fishing, walking, curling. *Address:* Beechwood, 15 Boclair Road, Bearsden, Glasgow G61 2AF. *T:* (0141) 942 1909. *Club:* Glasgow Academical (Glasgow).

McNAUGHTON, Prof. Peter Anthony, DPhil; Sheild Professor of Pharmacology, University of Cambridge, since 1999; Fellow of Christ's College, Cambridge, 1983–91 and since 1999; *b* 17 Aug. 1949; *s* of Anthony Henry McNaughton and Dulcie Helen McNaughton; *m* 1985, Linda Ariza; one *s* two *d*. *Educ:* Univ. of Auckland, NZ (BSc 1970); Balliol Coll., Oxford (DPhil 1974); MA Cantab 1976. University of Cambridge: Res. Fellow, Clare Coll., 1974–78; Physiological Laboratory: Elmore Med. Res. Student, 1977–78; Univ. Demonstrator, 1978–83; Univ. Lectr, 1983–91; Nuffield Sci. Res. Fellow, 1988–89; King's College London: Halliburton Prof. of Physiology, and Head of Physiology, 1991–99; Dean of Basic Med. Scis, 1993–96. Hon. Prof., Dept of Optometry and Vision Scis, Univ. of Wales, Cardiff, 1998–. Member: Biochemistry and Cell Biology Panel, BBSRC, 1996–2000; Neurosci. Panel, Wellcome Trust, 1999–2001; Chm., Bio-imaging Initiative Panel, BBSRC, 1998–2002. Member: Physiological Soc., 1979– (Mem. Cttee, 1988–92); British Pharmacological Soc., 1999–. *Publications:* articles in fields of physiology, pharmacology and neuroscience in learned jls. *Address:* Department of Pharmacology, University of Cambridge, Tennis Court Road, Cambridge CB2 1QJ.

McNEE, Sir David (Blackstock), Kt 1978; QPM 1975; Commissioner, Metropolitan Police, 1977–82; non-executive director and adviser to a number of public limited companies; *b* 23 March 1925; *s* of John McNee, Glasgow, Lanarkshire; *m* 1952, Isabella Clayton Hopkins (*d* 1997); one *d*. *Educ:* Woodside Senior Secondary Sch., Glasgow. Joined City of Glasgow Police, 1946. Apptd Dep. Chief Constable, Dunbartonshire Constabulary, 1968; Chief Constable: City of Glasgow Police, 1971–75; Strathclyde Police, 1975–77. Lectures: Basil Henriques, Bristol Univ., 1978; London, in Contemporary Christianity, 1979; Dallas, Glasgow, 1980; Peter le Neve Foster Meml, RSA, 1981. President: Royal Life Saving Soc., 1982–90; National Bible Soc. of Scotland, 1983–96; Glasgow City Cttee, Cancer Relief, 1987–93; Glasgow Battalion, Boys' Brigade, 1984–87; Hon. Vice-Pres., Boys' Bde, 1980–; Vice-Pres., London Fedn of Boys Clubs, 1982–. Patron, Scottish Motor Neurone Assoc., 1982–97. Hon. Col, 32 (Scottish) Signal Regt (V), TA, 1988–92. Freeman of the City of London, 1977. FIMgt (FBIM 1977); FRSA 1981. KStJ 1991. *Publication:* McNee's Law, 1983. *Recreations:* fishing, golf, music. *Clubs:* Caledonian, Naval (Life Mem.).

McNEIL, (David) John, CBE 1988; WS; NP; Partner, Morton Fraser (formerly Morton Fraser Milligan), since 1968; President, Law Society of Scotland, 1986–87; *b* 24 March 1937; *s* of Donald S. McNeil and Elizabeth (*née* Campbell); *m* 1962, Georgina Avril Sargent; one *s* two *d*. *Educ:* Daniel Stewart's Coll., Edinburgh; Edinburgh Univ. (MA Hons, LLB). Apprenticed to Davidson & Syme, WS, Edinburgh, 1959–62; admitted Solicitor in Scotland, 1962; WS 1964; Partner, Fraser, Stodart and Ballingall, 1964–68. Mem. Council, Law Soc. of Scotland, 1972–92. Mem., Warnock Inquiry into Aspects of Human Infertility and Embryology, 1982–84. *Recreations:* golf, snooker, music and opera, theatre. *Address:* St Catherine's Royal Terrace, Linlithgow, West Lothian EH49 6HQ. *T:* (01506) 843100. *Clubs:* New, Bruntsfield Golf (Edinburgh).

McNEIL, Duncan; Member (Lab) Greenock and Inverclyde, Scottish Parliament, since 1999; *b* 7 Sept. 1950; *m* Margaret; one *s* one *d*. Apprentice, Cartsdyke Shipyard; shipbuilder; Officer, GMB. Mem., Labour Party Scottish Exec.; Chm., Local Govt Cttee. Mem., Enterprise and Lifelong Learning Cttee, Scottish Parlt, 1999–. *Address:* Scottish Parliament, Edinburgh EH99 1SP.

McNEIL, Ian Robert; JP; FCA; Partner, Moores Rowland, Chartered Accountants, 1958–98; *b* 14 Dec. 1932; *s* of Robert and Doris Mary McNeil; *m* 1963, Ann Harries-Rees; two *d*. *Educ:* Brighton Coll. ACA 1955. Partner, Nevill Hovey Gardner (later amalgamated into Moores Rowland), 1958. Dep. Chm., Financial Reporting Council, 1991–92; Mem., Takeover Panel, 1991–92. Member: Lord Chancellor's Adv. Cttee on Legal Educn and Conduct, 1994–99; Legal Services Consultative Panel, 2000–. Institute of Chartered Accountants in England and Wales: Vice-Pres., 1989–90; Dep. Pres., 1990–91; Pres., 1991–92. Governor, Hurstpierpoint Coll., 1999–. Trustee and Hon. Treas., Action Research, 1999–2000. Liveryman: Curriers' Co., 1959 (Master, 1994–95); Chartered Accountants' Co., 1989. JP Hove 1967 (Chm., Hove Bench, 1988–89); Mem. Council, Magistrates' Assoc., 1983–89. *Address:* Lancasters, West End Lane, Henfield, West Sussex BN5 9RB. *T:* (01273) 492606. *Club:* Athenæum.

MACNEIL OF BARRA, Prof. Ian Roderick; The Macneil of Barra; Chief of Clan Macneil and of that Ilk; Baron of Barra; Wigmore Professor of Law, Northwestern University, 1980–99, now Emeritus; *b* 20 June 1929; *s* of Robert Lister Macneil of Barra and Kathleen, *d* of Orlando Paul Metcalf, NYC, USA; *m* 1952, Nancy, *e d* of James Tilton Wilson, Ottawa, Canada; two *s* one *d* (and one *s* decd). *Educ:* Univ. of Vermont (BA 1950); Harvard Univ. (LLB 1955). Lieut, Infty, Army of US, 1951–53 (US Army Reserve, 1950–69, discharged honorably, rank of Major). Clerk, US Court of Appeals, 1955–56; law practice, Concord, NH, USA, 1956–59. Cornell Univ., USA: Asst Prof. of Law, 1959–62; Associate Prof., 1962–63; Prof. of Law, 1962–72 and 1974–76; Ingersoll Prof. of Law, 1976–80; Prof. of Law, Univ. of Virginia, 1972–74. Visiting Professor of Law: Univ. of East Africa, Dar es Salaam, Tanzania, 1965–67; Harvard Univ., 1988–89; Guggenheim Fellow, 1978–79; Vis. Fellow, Wolfson Coll., Oxford, 1979. Hon. Vis. Fellow, Faculty of Law, Edinburgh Univ., 1979 and 1987. Member: American Law Inst.; Standing Council of Scottish Chiefs. FSAScot. *Publications:* Bankruptcy Law in East Africa, 1966; (with R. B. Schlesinger, *et al*) Formation of Contracts: A Study of the Common Core of Legal Systems, 1968; Contracts: Instruments of Social Co-operation-East Africa, 1968; (with R. S. Morison) Students and Decision Making, 1970; Contracts: Exchange Transactions and Relations, 1971, 2nd edn 1978; The New Social Contract, 1980; American Arbitration Law, 1992; (jtly) Federal Arbitration Law, 1994. *Heir: s* Roderick Wilson Macneil, Younger of Barra [*b* 22 Oct. 1954; *m* 1988, Sau Ming, *d* of Chun Kwan, Hong Kong]. *Address:* Carlton Grange, 95/6 Grange Loan, Edinburgh EH9 2ED. *T:* (0131) 667 6068; Taigh A'Mhonaidh, Garrygall, Castlebay, Isle of Barra, Scotland HS9 5UH. *T:* (01871) 810300; (seat) Kisimul Castle, Isle of Barra.

McNEIL, John; *see* McNeil, D. J.

MacNEIL, Most Rev. Joseph Neil; Archbishop of Edmonton (Alberta), (RC), 1973–99; *b* 15 April 1924; *s* of John Martin MacNeil and Kate MacNeil (*née* MacLean). *Educ:* St Francis Xavier Univ., Antigonish, NS (BA 1944); Holy Heart Seminary, Halifax, NS; Univs of Perugia, Chicago and St Thomas Aquinas, Rome (JCD 1958). Priest, 1948; pastor, parishes in NS, 1948–55; Chancery Office, Antigonish, 1958–59; admin, dio. Antigonish, 1959–60; Rector, Antigonish Cathedral, 1961; Dir of Extension Dept, St Francis Xavier Univ., Antigonish, 1961–69; Vice-Pres., 1962–69; Bishop of St John, NB, 1969–73. Pres., Canadian Conf. of Catholic Bishops, 1979–81 (Vice-Pres., 1977–79); Member: Commn on Ecumenism, 1985–91; Perm. Council, 1993–95; Commn on Mission, 1991–96); Chm., Alberta Bishops' Conf., 1973–99. Chancellor, Univ. of St Thomas, Fredericton, NB, 1969. Founding Mem., Inst. for Res. on Public Policy, 1968–80; Mem., Bd of Directors: The Futures Secretariat, 1981–; Centre for Human Develt, Toronto, 1985–. Chairman: Bd, Newman Theol Coll., Edmonton, 1973–99; Bd, St Joseph's Coll., Alberta Univ., 1973–99. Member, Bd of Management: Edmonton Gen. Hosp., 1983–92; Edmonton Caritas Health Gp, 1992–99. *Address:* (office) 8421–101 Avenue, Edmonton, Alberta T6A 0L1, Canada.

McNEILL, James Walker; QC (Scot.) 1991; *b* 16 Feb. 1952; *s* of late James McNeill and Edith Anna Howie Wardlaw; *m* 1986, Katherine Lawrence McDowall; two *s* one *d*. *Educ:*

Dunoon Grammar Sch.; Cambridge Univ. (MA); Edinburgh Univ. (LLB). Advocate 1978; Standing Junior Counsel: to Dept of Transport in Scotland, 1984–88; to Inland Revenue in Scotland, 1988–91. *Recreations:* music, hill-walking, golf, sailing, travel. *Address:* 28 Kingsburgh Road, Edinburgh EH12 6DZ. *Clubs:* New (Edinburgh); Hon. Company of Edinburgh Golfers; Isle of Colonsay Golf.

McNEILL, Prof. John, PhD; Director Emeritus, Royal Ontario Museum, Toronto, since 1997 (Director, 1991–97; President, 1995–97); Hon. Associate, Royal Botanic Garden, Edinburgh, since 1998 (Regius Keeper, 1987–89); *b* 15 Sept. 1933; *s* of Thomas McNeill and Helen Lawrie Eagle; *m* 1st, 1961, Bridget Mariel Winterton (marr. diss. 1990); two *s*; 2nd, 1990, Marilyn Lois James. *Educ:* George Heriot's, Edinburgh; Univ. of Edinburgh (BSc Hons, PhD 1960). Asst Lectr and Lectr, Dept of Agricl Botany, Univ. of Reading, 1957–61; Lectr, Dept of Botany, Univ. of Liverpool, 1961–69; Plant (later Biosystematics) Research Institute, Agriculture Canada, Ottawa: Res. Scientist, 1969–77, Chief, Vascular Plant Taxonomy Sect., 1969–72; Sen. Res. Scientist, 1977–81; Prof. and Chm., Dept of Biology, Univ. of Ottawa, 1981–87; Associate Dir Curatorial, Royal Ontario Mus., Toronto, 1989–90, Acting Dir, 1990–91; Dir, George R. Gardiner Mus. of Ceramic Art, Toronto, 1991–96. Hon. Prof., Univ. of Edinburgh, 1989; Prof., Dept of Botany, Univ. of Toronto, 1990–; Adjunct Prof., Univ. of Ottawa, 1987–91. Mem. Editl Cttee, 1985–, Chm. Mgt Cttee, 1998–, Flora North America; Ed., Nomenclature section, Taxon (jl of Internat. Assoc. for Plant Taxonomy), 2000–. *Publications* include: Phenetic and phylogenetic classification (jt ed), 1964; (jtly) Grasses of Ontario, 1977; (jt ed) International Code of Botanical Nomenclature, 1983, 1988, 1994, 2000; (jtly) Preliminary Inventory of Canadian Weeds, 1988; (jt ed) Flora of North America north of Mexico, vols 1 and 2, 1993, vol. 3, 1997, vol. 22, 2000; (jt ed) International Code of Nomenclature for Cultivated Plants, 1995; over 20 chapters or sections of sci. books and over 90 contribs to sci. res. jls. *Recreation:* botanical nomenclature. *Address:* Royal Botanic Garden, 20A Inverleith Row, Edinburgh EH3 5LR; *e-mail:* jmcneill@rbge.org.uk.

McNEILL, Johnston David John; Chief Executive, Rural Payments Agency, since 2001; *b* 15 Aug. 1956; *s* of David McNeill and Mary McNeill (*née* Kane); *m* 1983, Jennifer Fowler (marr. diss. 1997); one *s* two *d*. *Educ:* Lurgan Coll.; Southampton Coll. of Technology (HND Mech. Engrg); Univ. of Ulster (BA); Univ. of Central Lancashire (MBA); Portsmouth Univ. (PGDipPM, MA); PGDipM. Marine engr, 1974–79; mgt posts, private sector cos, 1979–88; Dep. Gen. Manager, Lancs CC, 1988–90; Asst Dir, Southampton CC, 1990–92; Dir of Contract Services, Belfast CC, 1992–94; Chief Executive: Meat Hygiene Service, MAFF, 1994–2000; Food Standards Agency, 2000–01. FIPD. Freeman, City of London; Liveryman, Butchers' Co. *Recreations:* ski-ing, rowing, yacht sailing, guitar, PhD studies at University of Portsmouth, socialising with friends and family. *Address:* 3 de Grey Court, Clifton, York YO3 6AZ. *T:* (01904) 455500. *Club:* Farmers.

McNEILL, Pauline Mary; Member (Lab) Glasgow Kelvin, Scottish Parliament, since 1999; *b* 12 Sept. 1962; *d* of John Patrick McNeill and Teresa Ward or McNeill; *m* 1999, William Joseph Cahill; two step *s*. *Educ:* Glasgow Coll. of Building and Printing (Dip. 1986); Strathclyde Univ. (LLB 1999). Pres., NUS, 1986–88; Regl Orgnr, GMB Scotland, 1988–99. *Recreations:* guitar, singing, rock music, keep fit. *Address:* Woodside House, 20–23 Woodside Place, Glasgow G3 7QF. *T:* (0141) 304 4534.

McNEILL, Peter Grant Brass, PhD; QC (Scot.) 1988; Sheriff of Lothian and Borders at Edinburgh, 1982–96, temporary Sheriff, 1996–98; *b* Glasgow, 3 March 1929; *s* of late William Arnot McNeill and late Lillias Philips Scrimgeour; *m* 1959, Matilda Farquhar Rose, *d* of late Mrs Christina Rose; one *s* three *d*. *Educ:* Hillhead High Sch., Glasgow; Morrison's Academy, Crieff; Glasgow Univ. MA (Hons Hist.) 1951; LLB 1954; Law apprentice, Biggart Lumsden & Co., Glasgow, 1952–55; Carnegie Fellowship, 1955; Faulds Fellowship, 1956–59; Scottish Bar, 1956; PhD, 1961. Hon. Sheriff Substitute of Lanarkshire, and of Stirling, Clackmannan and Dumbarton, 1962; Standing Junior Counsel to Scottish Development Dept (Highways), 1964; Advocate Depute, 1964–65; Sheriff of Lanarks, subseq. redesignated Glasgow and Strathkelvin, at Glasgow, 1965–82. Pres., Sheriffs' Assoc., 1982–85. Chm., Review Bd, Chinook Helicopter Accident, 1988. Mem., Scottish Records Adv. Council, 1989–95. Mem. Council, Scottish Nat. Dictionary Assoc. Ltd, 1987– (Chm., 1997–2001); Chm. Council, Stair Soc., 1990–98. *Publications:* (ed) Balfour's Practicks (Stair Society), 1962–63; (ed jtly) An Historical Atlas of Scotland *c*400–*c*1600, 1975; Adoption of Children in Scotland, 1982, 3rd edn 1998; (ed jtly) Atlas of Scottish History to 1707, 1996; legal and historical articles in Encyclopaedia Britannica, Juridical Review, Scots Law Times, Glasgow Herald, DNB, New DNB, etc. *Recreations:* legal history, gardening, bookbinding. *Address:* 31 Queensferry Road, Edinburgh EH4 3HB. *T:* (0131) 332 3195.

McNEISH, Prof. Alexander Stewart, FRCP; Warden, St Bartholomew's and Royal London School of Medicine and Dentistry, 1997–2001, and Deputy Principal, Queen Mary and Westfield College, 1999–2001 (Vice Principal, 1997–99), London University; *b* 13 April 1938; *s* of Angus Stewart McNeish and Minnie Howieson (*née* Dickson); *m* 1963, Joan Ralston (*née* Hamilton); two *s* one *d*. *Educ:* Glasgow Acad.; Univ. of Glasgow (MB); Univ. of Birmingham (MSc). FRCP 1977; FRCPGlas 1985; FRCPCH 1996. Sen. Lectr in Paediatrics and Child Health, Univ. of Birmingham, 1970–76; Foundn Prof. of Child Health, Univ. of Leicester, 1976–80; University of Birmingham: Leonard Parsons Prof. of Paediatrics and Child Health, 1980–95; Dir, Inst. of Child Health, 1980–93; Dean, Faculty of Medicine and Dentistry, 1987–92; Dir of R&D, W Midlands RHA, 1992–95; Dir, MRC Clinical Scis Centre, Hammersmith Hosp., 1995–97. Mem., GMC, 1984–95. Founder FMedSci 1998. *Publications:* papers on paediatric gastroenterology in Lancet, BMJ and in Archives of Disease in Childhood. *Recreations:* golf, music. *Address:* St Bartholomew's and Royal London School of Medicine and Dentistry, West Smithfield, EC1A 7BE; 128 Westfield Road, Edgbaston, Birmingham B15 3JQ. *T:* (0121) 454 6081. *Clubs:* Athenæum; Blackwell Golf.

McNICOL, David Williamson, CBE 1966; Australian Diplomatic Service, retired; *b* 20 June 1913; *s* of late Donald McNicol, Adelaide; *m* 1947, Elsa Margaret, *d* of N. J. Hargrave, Adelaide; one *s*. *Educ:* Carey Grammar Sch., Melbourne; Kings Coll., Adelaide; Adelaide Univ. (BA). RAAF, 1940–45, Pilot, 201 and 230 Sqdns RAF, Atlantic, Madagascar, Italy and Dodecanese. Australian Minister to Cambodia, Laos and Vietnam, 1955–56; idc 1957; Australian Comr to Singapore, 1958–60; Asst Sec., Dept of External Affairs, Australia, 1960–62; Australian High Comr to Pakistan, 1962–65 and to New Zealand, 1965–68; Australian Ambassador to Thailand, 1968–69; Australian High Comr to Canada, 1969–73; Dep. High Comr for Australia in London, 1973–75; Ambassador to S Africa, and High Comr to Botswana, Lesotho and Swaziland, 1975–77. *Recreations:* golf, gardening. *Address:* Unit 7/23, Burkitt Street, Page, ACT 2614, Australia. *Clubs:* Naval and Military (Melbourne); Royal Canberra Golf.

McNICOL, Prof. Donald; Vice-Chancellor, University of Tasmania, since 1996; *b* 18 April 1939; *s* of Ian Robertson McNicol and Sadie Isabelle Williams; *m* 1963, Kathleen Margaret Wells; one *s* two *d*. *Educ:* Unley High Sch.; Univ. of Adelaide (BA 1964); St John's Coll., Cambridge (PhD 1967). Fellow, Aust. Psych. Soc. Lectr in Psychology, Univ. of Adelaide, 1967–71; Research Fellow, St John's Coll., Cambridge, 1968–69; Sen. Lectr in Psych., Univ. of NSW, 1971–74; Associate Prof. in Psych., Univ. of NSW, 1975–81; Prof. of Psych., Univ. of Tasmania, 1981–86, now Emeritus Prof.; Comr for Univs and Chm., Univs Adv. Council, Commonwealth Tertiary Educn, 1986–88; Vice-Chancellor, Univ. of New England, NSW, 1988–90; Vice-Chancellor and Principal, Univ. of Sydney, 1990–96. President: AVCC, 1994–95; Assoc. of Univs of Asia Pacific, 1998–99; AHEIA, 2000–. FRSA. *Publication:* A Primer of Signal Detection Theory, 1972. *Recreations:* walking, jazz, reading. *Address:* University of Tasmania, GPO Box 252–51, Hobart, Tas 7001, Australia. *T:* (3) 62262003.

McNICOL, Prof. George Paul, CBE 1992; FRSE 1984; Principal and Vice-Chancellor, University of Aberdeen, 1981–91; *b* 24 Sept. 1929; *s* of Martin and Elizabeth McNicol; *m* 1959, Susan Ritchie; one *s* two *d*. *Educ:* Hillhead High Sch., Glasgow; Univ. of Glasgow. MD, PhD, FRCP, FRCPG, FRCPE, FRCPath. House Surg., Western Infirmary, Glasgow, 1952; House Phys., Stobhill Gen. Hosp., Glasgow, 1953; Regimental MO, RAMC, 1953–55; Glasgow Medical Sch., 1955–71: various posts in clinical acad. med., 1955–65; Hon. Cons. Phys., 1966–71; Reader in Medicine, 1970–71; Prof. of Medicine and Hon. Cons. Phys., Leeds Gen. Infirmary, 1971–81; Chm., Bd of Faculty of Medicine, Leeds Univ., 1978–81. Harkness Fellow, Commonwealth Fund, Dept of Internal Medicine, Washington Univ., 1959–61; Hon. Clinical Lectr and Hon. Cons. Phys., Makerere UC Med. Sch. Extension, Kenyatta Nat. Hosp., Nairobi (on secondment from Glasgow Univ.), 1965–66. Chm. Med. Adv. Cttee, Cttee of Vice-Chancellors and Principals, 1985–90; Member: British Council Cttee on Internat. Co-op. in Higher Educn, 1985–91; Council, ACU, 1988–91; former Mem., Adv. Council on Misuse of Drugs. Chm., Part I Examining Bd, Royal Colls of Physicians (UK). Vice-Chm., Raigmore Hosp. NHS Trust, 1993–95. Chm., Bd of Governors, Rowett Res. Inst., 1981–89; Mem., Bd of Governors, N of Scotland Coll. of Agriculture, 1981–91; Co-Pres., EU Standing Cttee for Med. Trng, 1990–93. Mem., Exec. Cttee, Scottish Council (Develt and Industry), 1989–91. Mem. Aberdeen Local Bd, Bank of Scotland, 1983–92. FRSA 1985. Hon. FACP. Foreign Corresp. Mem., Belgian Royal Acad. of Medicine, 1985. Hon. DSc Wabash Coll., Indiana, 1989; Hon. LLD Aberdeen, 1992. *Publications:* papers in sci. and med. jls on thrombosis and bleeding disorders. *Recreations:* water-colour painting, learning Spanish, bonsai cultivation. *Address:* 17 Barton Farm, Cerne Abbas, Dorset DT2 7LF. *T:* (01300) 341758; *e-mail:* george.mcnicol@btinternet.com.

See also A. H. Smallwood.

MacNISH, Alastair Jesse Head, FCCA; Chief Executive, South Lanarkshire Council, 1995–99; Chairman, Leadership Advisory Panel, Scottish Executive, 1999–2000; *b* 4 Feb. 1947; *m* 1970, Jean Ferguson Bell; one *s* two *d*. *Educ:* Gourock High Sch. FCCA 1972. Chief Auditor, Renfrew CC, 1973–75; Strathclyde Regional Council: Principal Accountant, 1975–77; Asst Dir of Educn, 1977–87; Depute Dir of Social Work, 1987–95. Clerk: Strathclyde Jt Fire Bd, 1995–99; Lanarkshire Jt Valuation Bd, 1995–99. Mem., Scotland Adv. Cttee, EOC, 1996–2000. MIPD 1994. *Recreations:* golf, curling, bridge. *Address:* c/o Scottish Executive, Victoria Quay, Edinburgh EH6 6QQ. *Club:* Gourock Golf (Capt. 1998–99).

McNISH, Althea Marjorie, (Althea McNish Weiss), CMT 1976; freelance textile designer, since 1957; *b* Trinidad; *d* of late J. Claude McNish, educnl reformer, and late Margaret (*née* Bourne); *m* 1969, John Weiss. *Educ:* Port-of-Spain, by her father and others; London Coll. of Printing; Central School of Art and Crafts; Royal Coll. of Art. NDD, DesRCA; FCSD (FSIA 1968, MSIA 1960). Painted throughout childhood; after design educn in London, freelance practice in textile and other design; commns from Ascher and Liberty's, 1957; new techniques for laminate murals, for SS Oriana and hosp. and coll. in Trinidad; Govt of Trinidad and Tobago travelling schol., 1962; interior design (for Govt of Trinidad and Tobago) in NY, Washington and London, 1962; Cotton Bd trav. schol. to report on export potential for British printed cotton goods in Europe, 1963; collection of dress fabric designs for ICI and Tootal Thomson for promotion of Terylene Toile, 1966; special features for Daily Mail Ideal Home Exhibn, 1966–78; (with John Weiss) etched silver dishes, 1973–; interior design for Sec.-Gen. of Commonwealth, 1975; bedlinen collection for Courtaulds, 1978; (with John Weiss) textile design develt for BRB, 1978–81; textile hangings for BRB Euston offices, 1979; banners for Design Centre, 1981; (with John Weiss) improvements to London office of High Comr for Trinidad and Tobago, 1981; advr on exhibn design for Govt of Trinidad and Tobago, Commonwealth Inst., 1982–84; fashion textile designs for Slovene textile printers, 1985–91; furnishing textile designs for Fede Cheti, Milan, 1986–91; murals and hangings for Royal Caribbean Cruise Line: MS Nordic Empress, 1990; MS Monarch of the Seas, 1991. Paintings and various work in exhibitions include: individual and gp exhibns, London, 1954–; paintings, Jamaica, 1975; hangings, Kilkenny, 1981; hangings, individual exhibn, Peoples Gall., 1982; hangings, Magazine Workspace, Leicester, 1983; textile designs in exhibitions: Inprint, Manchester and London, 1964–71; Design Council/BoT, USA and Sweden, 1969, London, 1970, London and USA, 1972; Design-In, Amsterdam, 1972–74; Design Council, 1975–80; The Way We Live Now, V&A Mus., 1978; Indigo, Lille, 1981–82; Commonwealth Fest. Art Exhibn, Brisbane, 1982; Designs for British Dress and Furnishing Fabrics, V&A Mus., 1986; Make or Break, Henry Moore Gall., 1986; Surtex, New York, 1987; Ascher, V&A Mus., 1987; Transforming the Crown: African, Asian and Caribbean Artists in Britain 1966–96, NY, 1996; work represented in permanent collection of V&A Mus. Vis. Lecturer: Central Sch. of Art and Crafts and other colls and polytechnics, 1960–; USA, 1972; Italy, W Germany and Slovenia, 1985–; Advisory Tutor in Furnishing and Surface Design, London Coll. of Furniture, 1972–90. External assessor for educnl and professional bodies, incl. CSD and NCDAD/CNAA, 1966–; Mem. jury for Leverhulme schols, 1968; Judge: Portuguese textile design comp., Lisbon, 1973; 'Living' Design Awards, 1974; Carnival selection panels, Arts Council, 1982 and 1983. Vice-Pres., SIAD, 1977–78; Design Council: Mem., selection panels for Design Awards and Design Index, 1968–80; Mem. Bd, 1974–81; Mem., Jubilee Souvenir Selection Panel, 1976; Mem., Royal Wedding Souvenir Selection Panel, 1981. Member: Fashion and Textiles Design Bd, CNAA, 1975–78; London Local Adv. Cttee, IBA, 1981–; Formation Cttee, London Inst., ILEA, 1985. Mem. Governing Body, Portsmouth Coll. of Art, 1972–81. *BBC-TV:* studio setting for Caribbean edn of Full House, 1973. Has appeared, with work, in films for COI and Gas Council. Chaconia Medal (Gold) (Trinidad and Tobago), 1976, for service to art and design; Scarlet Ibis Award (Trinidad and Tobago), 1993. *Publications:* textile designs produced in many countries, 1957–; designs illustrated in: V. D. Mendes and F. M. Hinchcliffe, Ascher, 1987; Did Britain Make It?, ed P. Sparke, 1986; M. Schoeser, Fabrics and Wallpapers, 1986; M. Schoeser and C. Rufey, English and American Textiles from 1790 to the Present, 1989; B. Philips, Fabrics and Wallpapers, 1991; S. Calloway, The House of Liberty, 1992; A. Walmsley, The Caribbean Artists Movement 1966–1972, 1992; published in Decorative Art, Designers in Britain and design jls. *Recreations:* ski-ing, travelling, music, gardening. *Address:* 142 West Green Road, N15 5AD. *T:* (020) 8800 1686. *Club:* Soroptimist.

MACNIVEN, Duncan, TD 1985; Commissioner and Head of Corporate Services, Forestry Commission, since 1999; *b* 1 Dec. 1950; *s* of John and Jenny Macniven; *m* 1976, Valerie Margaret Clark; two *d*. *Educ:* Melville Coll., Edinburgh; Aberdeen Univ. (MA

1973; MLitt 1978). Joined Scottish Office, 1973; Principal, 1978–85; Asst Sec., 1986–90; Dep. Dir, Historic Scotland, 1990–95; Head of Police Div., 1995–97; Head of Police, Fire and Emergencies Gp, 1997–99. RE, TA, 1969–85 (Major, 1983–85). *Recreations:* active church membership, being outdoors, walking, cycling, ski-ing, exploring, Scottish history. *Address:* Forestry Commission, 231 Corstorphine Road, Edinburgh EH12 7AT. *T:* (0131) 314 6252.

McNULTY, Anthony James; MP (Lab) Harrow East, since 1997; a Lord Commissioner of HM Treasury (Government Whip), since 2001; *b* 3 Nov. 1958; *s* of James Anthony McNulty and Eileen Anne McNulty. *Educ:* Univ. of Liverpool (BA Hons); Virginia Poly. Inst. and State Univ. (MA). Business School, Polytechnic of North London: Research Asst, 1983–85; Res. Fellow and part-time Lectr, 1985–86; part-time Lectr, PCL and Kingston Poly., 1984–86; Sen. Lectr, then Principal Lectr, Business Sch., Poly. of N London, later Univ. of N London, 1986–97. Mem. (Lab), Harrow LBC, 1986–97 (Dep. Leader, 1990–96, Leader, 1996–97, Labour Gp). Mem., Regl Exec., Gtr London Labour Party, 1985–87. Mem., NI Grand Cttee. PPS to Min. of State, DfEE, 1997–99; an Asst Govt Whip, 1999–2001. *Publications:* various academic works on local govt, public sector mgt, trng and small firms. *Recreations:* eating out, theatre, films, Rugby, current affairs. *Address:* House of Commons, SW1A 0AA. *T:* (020) 7219 4108, *Fax:* (020) 7219 2417; Harrow East Labour Party, Labour Centre, 18 Byron Road, Harrow, Middx HA3 7ST. *T:* (020) 8427 2100; *e-mail:* McNulty@parliament.uk.

McNULTY, Des(mond); Member (Lab) Clydebank and Milngavie, Scottish Parliament, since 1999; *b* Stockport, 28 July 1952; *m;* two *s. Educ:* St Bede's Grammar Sch., Manchester; York Univ.; Glasgow Univ. Subject Leader in Sociology, 1990–97, Head of Strategic Planning, 1997–99, Glasgow Caledonian Univ. Non-exec. Dir, Gtr Glasgow Health Bd, 1998–99. Member (Lab): Strathclyde Regl Council, 1990–96; Glasgow City Council, 1995–99. Scottish Parliament: Member: Transport and Envmt Cttee, 1999–; Corporate Body, 1999–; Enterprise and Lifelong Learning Cttee, 2000–. Chairman: Glasgow Healthy City Partnership, 1996–99; Glasgow 1999 Fest. of Architecture and Design. Dep. Chm., Wise Gp, 1997–. Mem., Kemp Commn on Future of Vol. Sector in Scotland, 1995–97. Mem. Ct, Glasgow Univ., 1994–99. *Address:* Scottish Parliament, Edinburgh EH99 1SP. *T:* (0131) 348 5918; (constituency office) Clydebank Central Library, Dumbarton Road, Clydebank G81 1XH. *T:* (0141) 952 7711.

McNULTY, Sir (Robert William) Roy, Kt 1998; CBE 1992; Chairman, Civil Aviation Authority, since 2001 (Member of Board, 1999–2000); *b* 7 Nov. 1937; *s* of Jack and Nancy McNulty; *m* 1963, Ismay Ratcliffe Rome; one *s* two *d. Educ:* Portora Royal School, Enniskillen; Trinity College, Dublin (BA, BComm). Audit Manager, Peat Marwick Mitchell & Co., Glasgow, 1963–66; Accounting Methods Manager, Chrysler UK, Linwood, 1966–68; Harland & Wolff, Belfast: Management Accountant, 1968–72; Computer Services Manager, 1972–74; Management Services Manager, 1975–76; Sen. Management Consultant, Peat Marwick Mitchell & Co., Belfast, 1977–78; Short Brothers plc: Exec. Dir, Finance and Admin, 1978–85; Dep. Managing Dir, 1986–88; Man. Dir and Chief Exec., 1988–92; Pres., Shorts Gp, Bombadier Aerospace, 1992–96; Chm., 1996–99. Chm., NATS Ltd, 1999–2001. Chm., The Odyssey Trust Co. Ltd, 1997–99; non-executive Director: Norbrook Laboratories Ltd, 1990–; Ulster Bank Ltd, 1996–2000. Mem., Council, SBAC, 1988–99 (Pres., 1993–94; Treas., 1995–99). Member: IDB for NI, 1992–98; Steering Gp for UK Foresight Programme, 1997–2000; Chairman: NI Growth Challenge, 1993–98; Technology Foresight Defence and Aerospace Panel, 1994–95; DTI Aviation Cttee, 1995–98. Industrial Prof., Dept of Engineering, Univ. of Warwick. Vice Pres., EEF, 1997–. Hon. FRAeS 1995; CIMgt. Hon. DSc QUB, 1999. *Recreations:* walking, golf, reading. *Address:* Civil Aviation Authority, CAA House, 45–59 Kingsway, WC2B 6TE. *Club:* Naval and Military.

McPARTLIN, Noel; Advocate, since 1976; Sheriff of Grampian, Highland and Islands at Elgin, since 1985; *b* 25 Dec. 1939; *s* of Michael Joseph McPartlin and Ann Dunn or McPartlin; *m* 1965, June Anderson Whitehead; three *s* three *d. Educ:* Galashiels Acad.; Edinburgh Univ. (MA, LLB). Solicitor in Glasgow, Linlithgow and Stirling, 1964–76. Sheriff of Grampian, Highland and Islands at Peterhead and Banff, 1983–85. *Recreation:* country life. *Club:* Elgin.

McPHAIL, Angus William, MA; Warden, Radley College, since 2000; *b* 25 May 1956; *s* of Peter Bigham McPhail and Sylvia Bridget McPhail (*née* Campbell); *m* 1980, Elizabeth Hirsch; two *s* one *d. Educ:* Abingdon Sch.; University Coll., Oxford (BA Hons 1978; MA 1982). Overseas Dept, Bank of England, 1978–82; Asst Master, Glenalmond Coll., 1982–85; Head of Econs and Housemaster, Sedbergh Sch., 1985–93; Headmaster, Strathallan Sch., 1993–2000. *Recreations:* cricket, golf, music, walking. *Address:* Radley College, Abingdon, Oxon OX14 2HR. *Clubs:* East India; West Sussex Golf; Cryptics Cricket.

MacPHAIL, Sir Bruce (Dugald), Kt 1992; FCA; Managing Director, Peninsular and Oriental Steam Navigation Co., since 1985; *b* 1 May 1939; *s* of late Dugald Ronald MacPhail and Winifred Marjorie MacPhail; *m* 1st, 1963, Susan Mary Gregory (*d* 1975); three *s*; 2nd, 1983, Caroline Ruth Grimston Curtis-Bennett (*née* Hubbard). *Educ:* Haileybury Coll.; Balliol Coll., Oxford (MA); Harvard Business Sch., Mass, USA (MBA 1967). FCA 1976. Articled, Price Waterhouse, 1961–65; Hill Samuel & Co. Ltd, 1967–69; Finance Director: Sterling Guarantee Trust Ltd, 1969–74; Town & City Properties Ltd, 1974–76; Man. Dir, Sterling Guarantee Trust, 1976–85. Non-exec. Dir, Chelsfield Plc, 1999–. Gov., Royal Ballet Sch., 1982–99; Life Gov. and Mem. Council, Haileybury Coll., 1992–; Chairman: Council, Templeton Coll., Oxford, 1993–95; Council for Sch. of Management Studies, Univ. of Oxford, 1995–. Barclay Fellow, Templeton Coll., Oxford, 1995–. Trustee, Sir Jules Thorn Charitable Trust, 1994–. *Recreations:* reading, wine, scuba diving. *Address:* Thorpe Lubenham Hall, Lubenham, Market Harborough, Leics LE16 9TR.

MACPHAIL, Iain Duncan; QC (Scot.) 1989; Sheriff of Lothian and Borders, since 1995; *b* 24 Jan. 1938; *o s* of late Malcolm John Macphail and Mary Corbett Duncan; *m* 1970, Rosslyn Graham Lillias, *o d* of E. J. C. Hewitt, MD, TD, Edinburgh; one *s* one *d. Educ:* George Watson's Coll.; Edinburgh and Glasgow Univs. MA Hons History Edinburgh 1959, LLB Glasgow 1962. Admitted to Faculty of Advocates, 1963; in practice at Scottish Bar, 1963–73; Faulds Fellow in Law, Glasgow Univ., 1963–65; Lectr in Evidence and Procedure, Strathclyde Univ., 1968–69 and Edinburgh Univ., 1969–72; Standing Jun. Counsel to Scottish Home and Health Dept and to Dept of Health and Social Security, 1971–73; Extra Advocate-Depute, 1973; Sheriff: of Lanarks, later Glasgow and Strathkelvin, 1973–81; of Tayside, Central and Fife, 1981–82; of Lothian and Borders, 1982–89; Mem., Scottish Law Commn, 1990–94. Chm., Scottish Assoc. for Study of Delinquency, 1978–81. Arthur Goodhart Prof. of Legal Sci., Cambridge Univ., 2001–02. Hon. LLD Edinburgh, 1992. *Publications:* Law of Evidence in Scotland (Scottish Law Commn), 1979; Evidence, 1987; Sheriff Court Practice, 1988; articles and reviews in legal jls. *Address:* Sheriff Court House, 27 Chambers Street, Edinburgh EH1 1LB. *T:* (0131) 225 2525. *Club:* New (Edinburgh).

MACPHERSON, family name of **Barons Macpherson of Drumochter** and **Strathcarron.**

MACPHERSON OF DRUMOCHTER, 2nd Baron *cr* 1951; **(James) Gordon Macpherson;** Chairman and Managing Director of Macpherson, Train & Co. Ltd, and Subsidiary and Associated Companies, since 1964; Chairman, A. J. Macpherson & Co. Ltd (Bankers), since 1973; founder Chairman, Castle Dairies (Caerphilly) Ltd; *b* 22 Jan. 1924; *s* of 1st Baron Macpherson of Drumochter and Lucy Lady Macpherson of Drumochter (*d* 1984); *S* father, 1965; *m* 1st, 1947, Dorothy Ruth Coulter (*d* 1974); two *d* (one *s* decd); 2nd, 1975, Catherine, *d* of Dr C. D. MacCarthy; one *s* two *d. Educ:* Loretto; Wells House, Malvern. Served War of 1939–45, with RAF; 1939–45 Campaign medal, Burma Star, Pacific Star, Defence Medal, Victory Medal. Founder Chm. and Patron, British Importers Confedn, 1968–72. Member: Council, London Chamber of Commerce, 1958–73 (Gen. Purposes Cttee, 1959–72); East European Trade Council, 1969–71; PLA, 1973–76; Exec. Cttee, W India Cttee, 1959–83 (Dep. Chm. and Treasurer, 1971, Chm. 1973–75); Highland Soc.of London, 1975–. Freeman of City of London, 1969; Mem., Butchers' Co., 1969–. Governor, Brentwood Sch. JP Essex, 1961–76; Dep. Chm., Brentwood Bench, 1972–76; Mem. Essex Magistrates Court Cttee, 1974–76. Hon. Game Warden for Sudan, 1974; Chief of Scottish Clans Assoc. of London, 1972–74; Member: Macpherson Clan Assoc. (Chm., 1963–64); Sen. Golfers' Soc., 1981–91. Life Managing Governor, Royal Scottish Corp., 1975–. Founder Mem., WWF, 1961. FRSA 1971; FRES 1940; FZS 1965. *Recreations:* shooting, fishing, golf, bridge. *Heir:* *s* Hon. James Anthony Macpherson, *b* 27 Feb. 1979. *Address:* Kyllachy, Tomatin, Inverness-shire IV13 7YA. *T:* (01808) 511212. *Clubs:* Boodle's, Shikar; Royal and Ancient (St Andrews); Thorndon Park Golf (capt. 1962–63); Hartswood Golf (Founder Pres., 1970–74).

McPHERSON, Prof. Andrew Francis, FBA 1993; Professor of Sociology, 1989–96, now Emeritus, and Co-Director, Centre for Educational Sociology, 1972–96, University of Edinburgh; *b* 6 July 1942; *m* 1st, 1965, Eldwyth Mary Boyle (*d* 2000); one *s* one *d*; 2nd, 1989, Alison Jean Elphinstone Edward or Arnott. *Educ:* Ripon Grammar Sch.; The Queen's Coll., Oxford (BA Hist.). DPSA; FEIS; FSCRE; FRSE. Lectr in Sociology, Univ. of Glasgow, 1965; University of Edinburgh: Res. Fellow in Education, 1968; Lectr in Sociology, 1973; Sen. Lectr, 1978; Reader, 1983. *Publications:* (with G. Neave) The Scottish Sixth, 1976; (with L. Gow) Tell Them from Me, 1980; (jtly) Reconstructions of Secondary Education, 1983; (with C. Raab) Governing Education, 1988; academic articles on history and sociology of education. *Recreations:* family, music, sport. *Address:* c/o Centre for Educational Sociology, Department of Education and Society, University of Edinburgh, St John's Land, Holyrood Road, Edinburgh EH8 8AQ.

McPHERSON, Ann, CBE 2000; FRCP, FRCGP; Principal in General Practice, Oxford, since 1979; Fellow, Green College, Oxford, since 2000; *b* 22 June 1945; *d* of late Max Egelnick and of Sadie Egelnick; *m* 1968, Prof. Klim McPherson; one *s* two *d. Educ:* Copthall Co. Grammar Sch.; St George's Hosp. Med. Sch., London (MB BS 1968); DCH 1972; MRCGP (with dist.) 1978, FRCGP 1993; FRCP 2001. Pt-time trng posts in paediatrics and gen. practice, London, Harvard and Oxford, 1968–76; pt-time Lectr, Dept of Primary Care, Oxford Univ., 2001–. Active in res. in women's health and teenage health. *Publications:* (*edited:* with A. Anderson) Women's Problems in General Practice, 1983; (jtly) Miscarriage, 1984, 2nd edn 1990; Cervical Screening: a practical guide, 1985, 2nd edn (jtly) 1992; Fresher Pressure: how to survive as a student, 1994; (with D. Waller) Women's Health in General Practice, 4th edn 1997; (with N. Durham) Women's Health: by women, for women, about women, 1998; with A. Macfarlane: Mum I Feel Funny, 1982; Diary of a Teenage Health Freak, 1987, 2nd edn as The New Diary of the Teenage Health Freak, 1996; I'm a Health Freak Too, 1989, 2nd edn as The Diary of the Other Health Freak, 1996; Me and My Mates, 1991; The Virgin Now Boarding, 1992; Adolescents: the Agony, the Ecstacy, the Answers: a book for parents, 1999. *Recreations:* swimming, playing tennis, reading, walking, chatting. *Address:* 25 Norham Road, Oxford OX2 6SF. *T:* (01865) 558743; (office) (01865) 240501.

MACPHERSON, Ewen Cameron Stewart; Chief Executive, 3i Group plc, 1992–97 (Director, 1989–97); *b* 19 Jan. 1942; *s* of G. P. S. Macpherson and Elizabeth Margaret Cameron (*née* Smail); *m* 1982, Hon. Laura Anne Baring, *d* of 5th Baron Northbrook; two *s. Educ:* Fettes Coll., Edinburgh; Queens' Coll., Cambridge (MA; Hon. Fellow, 1996); London Business Sch. (MSc; Alumni Achievement Award, 1997). Rep., Massey-Ferguson (Export) Ltd, 1964–68; various appointments, ICFC, 1970–82; 3i Group plc and subsidiaries: Dir, City Office, 1982–90; Mem., Exec. Cttee, 1985–97; Man. Dir, Finance & Planning, 1990–92. Non-executive Director: M&G Group, 1996–99; Scottish Power, 1996–; Foreign & Colonial Investment Trust, 1997–; Booker, 1998–2000; Law Debenture Corp., 1998–2001; Glynwed Internat., 1998–2000 (Chm., 1998–2000); Pantheon Internat. Participations, 1998–; Sussex Place Investment Mgt, 1999–; Chm., Merrill Lynch New Energy Technology plc, 2000–. Indep. Trustee, Glaxo-Wellcome Pension Fund, 1997– (Chm., 2000–). Governor, NIESR, 1993–. Trustee, Develt Trust, Nat. Hist. Mus., 1998–2000. *Recreations:* gardening, sailing, classic cars. *Address:* Aston Sandford, Bucks HP17 8LP. *T:* (01844) 291335. *Clubs:* Caledonian, City of London; Royal Lymington Yacht.

McPHERSON, James Alexander Strachan, CBE 1982; JP; FSA (Scot.); Lord-Lieutenant of Grampian Region (Banffshire), since 1987; Solicitor, since 1954; *b* 20 Nov. 1927; *s* of Peter John McPherson and Jean Geddie Strachan; *m* 1960, Helen Marjorie Perks, MA; one *s* one *d. Educ:* Banff Academy; Aberdeen Univ. MA, BL, LLB. National Service, 1952–54; commissioned RA. Solicitor; Partner, Alexander George & Co., Macduff, 1954–95 (Senior Partner, 1986–95; Consultant, 1995–2000). Macduff Town Council: Mem., 1958–75; Treasurer, 1965–72; (last) Provost, 1972–75; Banff County Council: Mem., 1958–75; Chm., Educn Cttee, 1967–70; Chm., Management and Finance Cttee, 1970–75; (last) Convener, County Council, 1970–75; Member: Assoc. of County Councils for Scotland, 1965–75; COSLA, 1974–86; Grampian Regional Council, 1974–90 (Chm., Public Protection Cttee, 1974–86); Police Adv. Bd for Scotland, 1974–86. Mem., Scottish Solicitors Discipline Tribunal, 1990–95; Pres., Banffshire Soc. of Solicitors, 1976–79. Former mem., numerous Scottish Cttees and Boards. Governor, Scottish Police Coll., 1974–86. Mem. Court, Aberdeen Univ., 1993–97. Chairman: Banff and Buchan JP Adv. Cttee, 1987–98; Aberdeenshire JP Adv. Cttee, 1998–; Hon. Sheriff, Grampian Highland and Islands at Banff, 1972–. JP Banff and Buchan, 1974. *Recreations:* sailing, swimming, reading, local history. *Address:* Dun Alastair, Macduff, Banffshire AB44 1XD. *T:* (home) (01261) 832377; (office) (01261) 832201. *Clubs:* Royal Northern and University (Aberdeen); Banff Town and County; Duff House Royal Golf.

MACPHERSON, Mary Basil Hamilton; *see* McAnally, M. B. H.

MACPHERSON, Nicholas Ian; Managing Director, Public Services, HM Treasury, since 2001; *b* 14 July 1959; *s* of Ewen Macpherson and Nicolette Macpherson (*née* Van der Bijl); *m* 1983, Suky Jane Appleby; two *s. Educ:* Eton Coll.; Balliol Coll., Oxford; University Coll. London. Economist: CBI, 1982–83; Peat Marwick and Mitchell, 1983–85; joined HM Treasury, 1985; Principal Private Sec. to Chancellor of the Exchequer, 1993–97; Head of Work Incentives Policy, 1997–98; Dep. Dir, then Dir,

(Welfare Reform), Budget and Public Finances, 1998–2001. *Address:* HM Treasury, 1 Parliament Street, SW1P 3AG. *T:* (020) 7270 5939.

M'PHERSON, Prof. Philip Keith, CEng, FIEE; Managing Director, Systems and Value Ltd, since 2001; *b* 10 March 1927; *s* of Ven. Kenneth M'Pherson and Dulce M'Pherson; *m* 1975, Rosalie Margaret, *d* of Richard and Mary Fowler. *Educ:* Marlborough Coll.; Royal Naval Engineering Coll.; Royal Naval Coll., Greenwich; Massachusetts Inst. of Technology (SM); MA Oxon. Engineer Officer, Royal Navy, 1948–59; research in Admiralty Gunnery Estabt, 1955–59, retired as Lt-Comdr, 1959. Head, Dynamics Gp, Atomic Energy Estabt, UKAEA, 1959–65, SPSO, 1963; Fellow of St John's Coll., Oxford, 1965–67; Prof. of Systems Sci., later Systems Engrg and Management, 1967–87, and Pro-Vice-Chancellor, 1982–87, City Univ. Vis. Scholar, Internat. Inst. of Applied Systems Analysis, Austria, 1976–77; Adjunct Prof., Xian Jiaotong Univ., China, 1980–84; Visiting Professor: City Univ., 1987; RCMS, 1990. Man. Dir, MacPherson Systems Ltd, 1984. Member: Executive Cttee, UK Automation Council, 1964–68; SRC Control Engrg Cttee, 1970–75; Chairman: IMechE Automatic Control Gp, 1967–69; IEE Systems Engrg Gp Cttee, 1966–69; IEE Control and Automation Div., 1967–69; IEE Systems Engrg Cttee, 1984–90; Soc. for General Systems Research (UK), 1973–76. Archbishops' Commn on Rural Areas, 1988–89. Freeman, City of London, 1985; Liveryman, Engineers' Co., 1986. *Publications:* many papers in the scientific literature. *Recreations:* walking, singing, making things. *Clubs:* City Livery, Royal Over-Seas League.

MACPHERSON of Biallid, Sir (Ronald) Thomas (Stewart), (Tommy), Kt 1992; CBE (mil.) 1968; MC 1943, Bars 1944 and 1945; TD 1960; DL; Chairman: Boustead plc, since 1986; Annington Holdings PLC, since 1996; *b* 4 Oct. 1920; 5th *s* of Sir Thomas Stewart Macpherson, CIE, LLD, and Lady (Helen) Macpherson (*née* Cameron); *m* 1953, Jean Henrietta, *d* of late David Butler Wilson; two *s* one *d*. *Educ:* Cargilfield; Fettes Coll. (scholar); Trinity Coll., Oxford (1st open classical scholar; MA 1st Cl. Hons PPE). Athletics Blue and Scottish International; British Team World Student Games, Paris, 1947; represented Oxford in Rugby football and hockey, 1946–47; played Rugby for London Scottish, 1945–55; played hockey for Mid Surrey and Anglo Scots, 1956–59. Reader Middle Temple. 2nd Lieut. Queen's Own Cameron Highlanders TA, 1939; Scottish Commando, parachutist, 1940; POW, 1941–43, escaped 1943; Major 1943 (despatches). Consultant, Italo-Yugoslav Border Commn, 1946. CO 1st Bn London Scottish TA, 1961–64; Col TA London Dist, 1964–67. Mem., Queen's Body Guard for Scotland (Royal Co. of Archers). Chairman: Mallinson-Denny Gp, 1981–82 (Dir, 1948–82; Man. Dir, 1967–81); Birmid Qualcast, 1982–88; Cosmopolitan Textile Co., 1983–91; Allstate Reinsurance Ltd, 1983–96; Employment Conditions Abroad Ltd, 1983–93; Webb-Bowen Internat. Ltd, 1984–94; SNTC (France), 1985–95; Owl Creek Investments plc, 1989–91; Wineworld (London) PLC, 1996–2000; Internet Network Services Ltd, 1995–99; Entuity Ltd, 2000–; Nexus Investments Ltd, 2001–; XchangePoint Ltd, 2001–; Dep. Chm., Keller Group plc, 1991–99. Exec. Dir, Brooke Bond Gp plc, 1981–82; Director: Transglobe Expedition Ltd, 1976–83; Scottish Mutual Assurance Soc., 1982–91; C. H. Industrials PLC, 1983–91; NCB, 1983–86; English Architectural Glazing Ltd, 1985–99; TSB Scotland, 1986–91; Independent Insurance plc, 1987–93; Fitzwilton (UK) plc, 1990–; Soc. Générale Merchant Bank, 1991–93; Architectural Glazing (Scotland) Ltd, 1998–99; UK Consultant, Sears Roebuck & Co., Chicago, 1984–98; Consultant: Bain & Co., 1987–99; Candover Investment plc, 1989–95. Founder Chm., Nat. Employment Liaison Cttee for TA and Reserves, 1986–94; Chm., ABCC, 1986–88; Pres., Eurochambres (Assoc. of European Chambers of Commerce), 1992–94; Vice-Pres., London Chamber of Commerce, 1985– (Chm., Council, 1980–82). Member: Council, CBI (Chm., London and SE Reg., CBI, 1975–77); Scottish Council Develt and Industry, London; Prices and Incomes Bd, 1968–69; Council, GBA, 1979–83; Council, Strathclyde Univ. Business Sch., 1982–86. Foundn Trustee, Acad. of European Law, Germany, 1994–. Chm., 1961–79, Pres., 1979–, Achilles Club; Vice-Pres., Newtonmore Camanachd Club; President: Commando Assoc., 2000–; Highland Soc. of London, 2001–. Governor, Fettes Coll., 1984–92. Prime Warden, Co. of Dyers, 1985–86; Mem., Carpenters' Co. FRSA, FIMgt. DL 1977, High Sheriff, 1983–84, Greater London. Chevalier, Légion d'Honneur, and Croix de Guerre with 2 palms and star, France; Medaglia d'Argento and Resistance Medal, Italy; Kt of St Mary of Bethlehem. *Recreations:* fishing, squash, shooting, outdoor sport. *Address:* 27 Archery Close, W2 2BE. *T:* (020) 7262 8487; Craigdhu, Newtonmore, Inverness-shire PH20 1BS. *T:* (01528) 544200, *Fax:* (01528) 544274. *Clubs:* Hurlingham, MCC; New (Edinburgh).

MACPHERSON, Sir Thomas; *see* Macpherson, Sir R. T. S.

MACPHERSON OF CLUNY (and Blairgowrie), Sir William (Alan), Kt 1983; TD 1966; Cluny Macpherson; 27th Chief of Clan Macpherson; Judge of the High Court of Justice, Queen's Bench Division, 1983–96; *b* 1 April 1926; *s* of Brig. Alan David Macpherson, DSO, MC, RA (*d* 1969) and late Catharine Richardson Macpherson; *m* 1962, Sheila McDonald Brodie; two *s* one *d*. *Educ:* Wellington Coll., Berkshire; Trinity Coll., Oxford (MA; Hon. Fellow, 1991). Called to Bar, Inner Temple, 1952; Bencher, 1978; QC 1971; a Recorder of the Crown Court, 1972–83; Presiding Judge, Northern Circuit, 1985–88; Pres., Interception of Communications Tribunal, 1990–2000. Mem., Bar Council and Senate, 1981–83; Hon. Mem., Northern Circuit, 1987. Served, 1944–47, in Scots Guards (Capt.). Commanded (Lt-Col) 21st Special Air Service Regt (TA), 1962–65, Hon. Col, 1983–91; Mem., Queen's Body Guard for Scotland, Royal Co. of Archers, 1977–, Brigadier 1989. Gov., Royal Scottish Corporation, 1972–96 (Vice-Pres., 1989–). Mem., Tay Dist Salmon Fisheries Bd, 1996–99. *Recreations:* golf, fishing, archery; Past Pres., London Scottish FC. *Heir:* *s* Alan Thomas Macpherson yr of Cluny and Blairgowrie. *Address:* Newton Castle, Blairgowrie, Perthshire PH10 6SU. *Clubs:* Caledonian, Highland Society of London (Pres., 1991–94); New (Edinburgh); Blairgowrie Golf; Denham Golf.

MACPHIE, Maj.-Gen. Duncan Love; Executive Director, St John Ambulance, 1994–95 (Medical Director, 1993–94); *b* 15 Dec. 1930; *s* of Donald Macphie and Elizabeth Adam (*née* Gibson); *m* 1957, Isobel Mary Jenkins; one *s* two *d*. *Educ:* Hutchesons' Grammar Sch.; Glasgow Univ. MB ChB. Stonehouse and Hairmyres Hosps, 1957–58; commnd RAMC, 1958; RMO, 1st Bn The Royal Scots, 1958–61; GP, Glasgow, 1961–63; RMO, 3 RHA, 1963–67; CO, BMH Dharan, Nepal, 1970–72; CO, 24 Field Ambulance, 1972–75; CO, BMH Munster, 1976–78; ADMS, 4 Armd Div., 1978–80; Asst DGAMS, MoD, 1980–83; CO, Queen Elizabeth Mil. Hosp., Woolwich, 1983–85; Chief, Med. Plans Branch, SHAPE, 1985–87; Comdr Med., BAOR, 1987–90, retd. QHS 1985–90. Col Comdt, RAMC, 1990–95. Warden, St John Ophthalmic Hosp., Jerusalem, 1999. *Recreations:* gardening, Rugby, cricket, classical music, reading.

McQUAID, James, CB 1997; PhD; FREng, FIMinE; Director, Science and Technology, and Chief Scientist, Health and Safety Executive, 1996–99; *b* 5 Nov. 1939; *s* of late James and Brigid McQuaid; *m* 1968, Catherine Anne, *d* of late Dr James John Hargan and of Dr Mary Helen Hargan; two *s* one *d*. *Educ:* Christian Brothers' Sch., Dundalk; University Coll., Dublin (BEng); Jesus Coll., Cambridge (PhD); DSc NUI 1978. MIMechE 1972; FIMinE 1986; FREng (FEng 1991). Graduate engrg apprentice, British Nylon Spinners, 1961–63; Sen. Res. Fellow 1966–68, Sen. Scientific Officer 1968–72, PSO 1972–78, Safety in Mines Res. Estabt; seconded as Safety Advr, Petrochemicals Div., ICI, 1976–77; Health and Safety Executive: Dep. Dir, Safety Engrg Lab., 1978–80, Dir, 1980–85; Res. Dir, 1985–92; Dir, Strategy and Gen. Div. and Chief Scientist, 1992–96. Chm., Electrical Equipment Certification Management Bd, 1985–92; Member: Safety in Mines Res. Adv. Bd, 1985–92; Council, Midland Inst. of Mining Engrs, 1987– (Vice-Pres., 1991–93, Pres., 1993–94); Council, IMinE, 1991–95; Council, Royal Acad. Engrg, 1995–98; Adv. Bd for Mech. Engrg, Univ. of Liverpool, 1987–92; Exec. Cttee, RoSPA, 1992–94. Mem. Court, 1985–, Mem. Council, 1993–, Vis. Prof. of Mechanical Engrg, 1996–, Univ. of Sheffield; Vis. Prof. of Sustainable Develt, Ulster Univ., 1999–. Pres., Sheffield Trades Hist. Soc., 1989–91. Mem., Council, S Yorks Trades Hist. Trust, 1989– (Chm., 1999–). FRSA 2000. Hon. DEng Sheffield, 2000. *Publications:* numerous papers in technical jls. *Recreations:* ornamental turning, model engineering, industrial archaeology. *Address:* 61 Pingle Road, Sheffield S7 2LL. *T:* (0114) 236 5349. *Club:* Athenæum.

McQUAIL, Paul Christopher; Visiting Senior Research Fellow, Constitution Unit, University College London; Consultant, various public bodies, since 1994; *b* 22 April 1934; *s* of Christopher McQuail and Anne (*née* Mullan); *m* 1964, Susan Adler; one *s* one *d*. *Educ:* St Anselm's, Birkenhead; Sidney Sussex Coll., Cambridge. Min. of Housing and Local Govt, 1957; Principal, 1962; Asst Sec., 1969; DoE, 1970; Special Asst to Permanent Sec. and Sec. of State, 1972–73; Sec., Royal Commn on the Press, 1974–77; Under Sec., DoE, 1977–88; Chief Exec., Hounslow Bor. Council, 1983–85 (on secondment); Dep. Sec., DoE, 1988–94. Member: Environment and Planning Cttee, ESRC, 1983–87; Policy Cttee, CPRE, 1995–2001; Chairman: Nat. Urban Forestry Unit, 1995–; Nat. Retail Planning Forum, 1995–; Alcohol Concern, 1996–. *Publications:* Origins of DoE, 1994; Cycling to Santiago, 1995; A View from the Bridge, 1995; (with Katy Donnelly) English Regional Government, 1996; Soviet Children's Books of the Twenties and Thirties: the Adler Collection, 2000; Unexplored Territory: elected regional assemblies in England, 2001. *Recreations:* trees, books, alpinism and other harmless pleasures. *Address:* 158 Peckham Rye, SE22 9QH.

MACQUAKER, Donald Francis, CBE 1991; solicitor, retired; Partner, T. C. Young & Son, Glasgow, 1957–93, Consultant, 1993–96; *b* 21 Sept. 1932; *s* of Thomas Mason Macquaker, MC, MA, BL and Caroline Bertha Floris Macquaker; *m* 1964, Susan Elizabeth, *d* of Mr and Mrs W. A. K. Finlayson, High Coodham, Symington, Ayrshire; one *s* one *d*. *Educ:* Winchester Coll.; Trinity Coll., Oxford (MA); Univ. of Glasgow (LLB). Admitted Solicitor, 1957. Mem. Bd of Management, Glasgow Royal Maternity Hosp. and associated hosps, 1965–74 (Vice-Chm., 1972–74); Greater Glasgow Health Board: Mem., 1973–87; Chm., 1983–87; Convener, F and GP Cttee, 1974–83; Chm., Common Services Agency for Scottish Health Service, 1987–91. Dir, Lithgows Ltd, 1987–98. Dir, Prince and Princess of Wales Hospice, Glasgow, 1991–94. Chm., Western Meeting Club, Ayr Racecourse, 1996–. *Recreations:* shooting, fishing, gardening. *Address:* Blackbyres, by Ayr KA7 4TS. *T:* (01292) 441088. *Club:* Leander (Henley-on-Thames).

McQUARRIE, Sir Albert, Kt 1987; Chairman: A. McQuarrie & Son (Great Britain) Ltd, 1946–88; Sir Albert McQuarrie & Associates Ltd, since 1988; *b* 1 Jan. 1918; *s* of Algernon Stewart McQuarrie and Alice Maud Sharman; *m* 1st, 1945, Roseleen McCaffery (*d* 1986); one *s*; 2nd, 1989, Rhoda Annie Gall. *Educ:* Highlanders Acad., Greenock; Greenock High Sch.; Royal Coll. of Science and Technology, Univ. of Strathclyde. MSE, PEng 1945. Served in HM Forces, 1939–45 (Officer in RE). Dir, Hunterston Develt Co., 1989–. Former Dean of Guild, Gourock Town Council; Chm., Fyvie/Rothienorman/Monquhitter Community Council, 1975–79. Contested (C): Kilmarnock, 1966; Caithness and Sutherland, Oct. 1974; Banff and Buchan, 1987; Highlands and Islands, European Parly elecn, 1989. MP (C): Aberdeenshire E, 1979–83; Banff and Buchan, 1983–87. Chm., British/Gibraltar All Party Gp, 1979–87; Vice Chm., Conservative Fisheries Sub Cttee, 1979–87; Secretary: Scotch Whisky All Party Gp, 1979–87; Scottish Cons. Backbench Cttee, 1985–87; Member: Select Cttees on Scottish Affairs, 1979–83, on Agriculture, 1983–85, on Private Bill Procedure, 1987; Speaker's Panel of Chairmen, 1986–87. Mem. Council, Soc. of Engineers, 1978–87. Dep. Chm., Ayr Cons. Assoc., 1992–; Hon. Pres., Banff and Buchan Cons. and Unionist Assoc., 1989–. Vice Chm., Mintlaw Community Council, 1999–. Pres., Gourock Horticultural Soc., 1993– (Hon. Vice-Pres., 1954–93). FRSH 1952. Freeman, City of Gibraltar, 1982. KSJ 1991; GCSJ 1999 (Grand Prior of UK and Eire, 1999–). Granted armorial bearings, 1991. *Recreations:* golf, bridge, music, soccer, swimming, horticulture. *Address:* Kintara House, Newton Road, Mintlaw AB42 5EF. *T:* (01771) 623955, *Fax:* (01771) 623956. *Clubs:* Lansdowne; Royal Scottish Automobile (Glasgow).

MACQUARRIE, Rev. Prof. John, TD 1962; FBA 1984; Lady Margaret Professor of Divinity, University of Oxford, and Canon of Christ Church, 1970–86; *b* 27 June 1919; *s* of John Macquarrie and Robina Macquarrie (*née* McInnes); *m* 1949, Jenny Fallow (*née* Welsh); two *s* one *d*. *Educ:* Paisley Grammar Sch.; Univ. of Glasgow. MA 1940; BD 1943; PhD 1954; DLitt 1964; DD Oxon 1981. Royal Army Chaplains Dept, 1945–48; St Ninian's Church, Brechin, 1948–53; Lecturer, Univ. of Glasgow, 1953–62; Prof. of Systematic Theology, Union Theological Seminary, NY, 1962–70. Consultant, Lambeth Conf., 1968 and 1978. Hon. degrees: STD: Univ. of the South, USA, 1967; General Theological Seminary, NY, 1968; DD: Glasgow, 1969; Episcopal Seminary of SW, Austin, Texas, 1981; Virginia Theol Seminary, 1981; Univ. of Dayton, 1994; DCnL, Nashotah House, Wisconsin, 1986. *Publications:* An Existentialist Theology, 1955; The Scope of Demythologising, 1960; Twentieth Century Religious Thought, 1963, 5th edn 2001; Studies in Christian Existentialism, 1965; Principles of Christian Theology, 1966; God-Talk, 1967; God and Secularity, 1967; Martin Heidegger, 1968; Three Issues in Ethics, 1970; Existentialism, 1972; Paths in Spirituality, 1972; The Faith of the People of God, 1972; The Concept of Peace, 1973; Thinking about God, 1975; Christian Unity and Christian Diversity, 1975; The Humility of God, 1978; Christian Hope, 1978; In Search of Humanity, 1982; In Search of Deity (Gifford Lectures), 1984; Theology, Church and Ministry, 1986; Jesus Christ in Modern Thought, 1990 (HarperCollins Religious Book Prize, 1991); Mary for All Christians, 1991, new edn 2001; Heidegger and Christianity, 1994; Invitation to Faith, 1995; The Mediators, 1995; A Guide to the Sacraments, 1997; Christology Revisited, 1998; On Being a Theologian, 1999. *Address:* 206 Headley Way, Headington, Oxford OX3 7TA. *T:* (01865) 761889.

MacQUEEN, Prof. John; Professor of Scottish Literature and Oral Tradition, University of Edinburgh, 1972–88, now Professor Emeritus, and Hon. Fellow, Faculty of Arts, 1993; *b* 13 Feb. 1929; *s* of William L. and Grace P. MacQueen; *m* 1953, Winifred W. McWalter; three *s*. *Educ:* Hutchesons' Boys' Grammar Sch.; Glasgow Univ.; Cambridge Univ. MA English Lang. and Lit., Greek, Glasgow; BA, MA Archaeology and Anthropology, Section B, Cambridge. RAF, 1954–56 (Flying Officer). Asst Prof. of English, Washington Univ., Missouri, 1956–59; University of Edinburgh: Lectr in Medieval English and Scottish Literature, 1959–63; Masson Prof. of Medieval and Renaissance Literature, 1963–72; Dir, Sch. of Scottish Studies, 1969–88; Endowment Fellow, 1988–92. Barclay Acheson Vis. Prof. of Internat. Relations, Macalester Coll., Minnesota, 1967; Vis. Prof. in Medieval Studies, Australian Nat. Univ., 1971; Winegard Vis. Prof., Univ. of Guelph, Ont, 1981.

Chairman: British Branch, Internat. Assoc. of Sound Archives, 1978–80; Exec. Cttee, Scottish Nat. Dictionary Assoc., 1978–87; Scottish Dictionary Jt Council, 1988–92; Pres., Scottish Text Soc., 1989–92; Mem., Scottish Film Council, 1981–92 (Chm., Archive Cttee, 1980–92). FRSE 1992. Hon. DLitt NUI, 1985. Fletcher of Saltoun Award, 1990. *Publications:* St Nynia, 1961, 2nd edn 1991; (with T. Scott) The Oxford Book of Scottish Verse, 1966; Robert Henryson, 1967; Ballattis of Luve, 1970; Allegory, 1970; (ed with Winifred MacQueen) A Choice of Scottish Verse, 1470–1570, 1972; Progress and Poetry, 1982; Numerology, 1985; The Rise of the Historical Novel, 1989; (ed with Winifred MacQueen) Scotichronicon, Bks III and IV, 1989, Bks I and II, 1993, Bk V, 1995; (ed) Humanism in Renaissance Scotland, 1990; articles and reviews in learned jls. *Recreations:* music, walking, archaeology. *Address:* Slewdonan, Damnaglaur, Drummore, Stranraer DG9 9QN. *T:* (01776) 840637.

McQUIGGAN, John, MBE 1955; Executive Director, United Kingdom-South Africa Trade Association Ltd, 1978–86; retired at own request from HM Diplomatic Service, 1977; *b* 24 Nov. 1922; *s* of John and Sarah Elizabeth McQuiggan; *m* 1950, Doris Elsie Hadler; three *s* one *d. Educ:* St Edwards Coll., Liverpool. Served War, in RAF, 1942–47 (W Africa, Europe and Malta). Joined Dominions Office, 1940; Administration Officer, British High Commission, Canberra, Australia, 1950–54; Second Sec., Pakistan, Lahore and Dacca, 1954–57; First Sec. (Inf.), Lahore, 1957–58; Dep. Dir, UK Inf. Services, Australia (Canberra and Sydney), 1958–61; Dir, Brit. Inf. Services, Eastern Nigeria (Enugu), 1961–64; Dir, Brit. Inf. Services in Uganda, and concurrently First Sec., HM Embassy, Kigali, Rwanda, 1964–69; W African Dept, FCO, 1969–73; HM Consul, Chad, 1970–73 (London based); Dep. High Comr and Counsellor (Econ. and Commercial), Lusaka, Zambia, and sometime Actg High Comr, 1973–76. Dir-Gen., Brit. Industry Cttee on South Africa, 1986. Mem., Royal African Soc.; MIPR 1964; Mem., Internat. Public Relations Assoc., 1975. Fellow, Inst. of Dirs. *Publications:* A Time to Heal, 2001; pamphlets and contribs to trade and economic, technical woodworking, and religious jls. *Recreations:* tennis, carpentry, craftwork. *Address:* 7 Meadowcroft, Bickley, Kent BR1 2JD. *T:* (020) 8467 0075. *Club:* Royal Over-Seas League.

McQUILLAN, William Rodger; HM Diplomatic Service, retired; *b* 18 March 1930; *s* of late Albert McQuillan and Isabella Glen McQuillan; *m* 1970, Sheriell May Fawcett; one *s* two *d. Educ:* Royal High Sch., Edinburgh; Edinburgh Univ.; Yale Univ. Served RAF, 1954–57. Asst Sec., Manchester Univ. Appointments Board, 1957–65; HM Diplomatic Service, 1965–83: First Sec., CRO, 1965; Lusaka, 1968, Head of Chancery, 1969; First Sec. (Commercial), Santiago, Chile, 1970; Counsellor and HM Consul, Guatemala City, 1974; Head of Inf. Policy Dept, FCO, 1978–81; Ambassador to Iceland, 1981–83. *Address:* Lidston House, Edderton, Ross-shire IV19 1LF.

MacQUITTY, (Joanna) Jane; freelance wine writer and broadcaster, since 1982; Wine and Drink Correspondent, The Times, since 1982; *b* 14 Oct. 1953; *d* of William Baird MacQuitty and Betty (*née* Bastin); *m* 1988, Philip Killingworth Hedges; one *s* two *d. Educ:* Benenden Sch. Wine and food writer, House & Garden, 1975–82; Editor, Which Wine Guide, and Which Wine Monthly, 1982–84; Wine Editor, Good Housekeeping, 1984–2000. Wine Lectr and Judge, 1982–. Member: Circle of Wine Writers, 1977–; Soc. of Authors, 1982–. Glenfiddich Awards: Wine Writer of the Year, 1981; Whisky Writer of the Year, 1981; Special Award (for Which Wine Guide), 1983. *Publications:* Which Wine Guide, 1983, rev. edn 1984; Jane MacQuitty's Guide to Champagne and Sparkling Wines, 1986, 3rd edn 1993; Jane MacQuitty's Guide to Australian and New Zealand Wines, 1988. *Recreations:* my family, eating, drinking, talking, sleep. *Address:* c/o The Times Week-End, 1 Pennington Street, E98 1TT. *Club:* Riverside.

MacRAE, Sir (Alastair) Christopher (Donald Summerhayes), KCMG 1993 (CMG 1987); HM Diplomatic Service, retired; Secretary General, Order of St John, 1997–2000; *b* 3 May 1937; *s* of Dr Alexander Murray MacRae and Dr Grace Maria Lynton Summerhayes MacRae; *m* 1963, Mette Willert; two *d. Educ:* Rugby; Lincoln Coll., Oxford (BA Hons English); Harvard (Henry Fellow in Internat. Relations). RN, 1956–58. CRO, 1962; 3rd, later 2nd Sec., Dar es Salaam, 1963–65; ME Centre for Arab Studies, Lebanon, 1965–67; 2nd Sec., Beirut, 1967–68; FCO, 1968–70; 1st Sec. and Head of Chancery: Baghdad, 1970–71; Brussels, 1972–76; attached Directorate-Gen. VIII, European Commn, Brussels, on secondment from FCO, 1976–78; Ambassador to Gabon, 1978–80, and to Sao Tomé and Principé (non-resident), 1979–80; Head of W Africa Dept, FCO, 1980–83, and Ambassador (non-resident) to Chad, 1982–83; Political Counsellor and Head of Chancery, Paris, 1983–87; Minister and Head of British Interests Section, Tehran, 1987; Vis. Fellow, IISS, 1987–88; Support Services Scrutiny, FCO, 1988; Under Sec. (on secondment), Cabinet Office, 1988–91; High Comr to Nigeria, and concurrently Ambassador (non-resident) to Benin, 1991–94; High Comr to Pakistan, 1994–97. KStJ 1997.

McRAE, Frances Anne, (Mrs Hamish McRae); *see* Cairncross, F. A.

McRAE, Hamish Malcolm Donald; Associate Editor, The Independent, since 1991; *b* 20 Oct. 1943; *s* of Donald and Barbara McRae (*née* Budd); *m* 1971, Frances Anne Cairncross, *qv*; two *d. Educ:* Fettes College; Trinity College, Dublin (BA Hons Economics and Political Science). Liverpool Post, 1966–67; The Banker, 1967–72 (Asst Editor, 1969, Dep. Editor, 1971); Editor, Euromoney, 1972–74; Financial Editor, The Guardian, 1975–89; Business and City Editor, The Independent, 1989–91. Vis. Prof., UMIST, 1999–. Wincott Foundn financial journalist of the year, 1979. *Publications:* (with Frances Cairncross) Capital City: London as a financial centre, 1973, 5th edn 1991; (with Frances Cairncross) The Second Great Crash, 1975; Japan's role in the emerging global securities market, 1985; The World in 2020, 1994; (with Tadashi Nakamae) Wake-up, Japan, 1999. *Recreations:* walking, ski-ing, cooking. *Address:* 6 Canonbury Lane, N1 2AP.

MACRAE, John Esmond Campbell, CMG 1986; DPhil; HM Diplomatic Service, retired; *b* 8 Dec. 1932; *s* of Col Archibald Campbell Macrae, IMS, and Euretta Margaret Skelton; *m* 1962, Anne Catherine Sarah Strain; four *s. Educ:* Sheikh Bagh Sch., Kashmir; Fettes Coll., Edinburgh; Christ Church Oxford (Open Scholar); Princeton, USA. DPhil, MA. Atomic Energy and Disarmament Dept, Foreign Office, 1959–60; 2nd Sec., British Embassy, Tel Aviv, 1961–64; 1st Secretary: Djakarta, 1964; Vientiane, 1964–66; FO, NE African Dept, 1966; Central Dept, 1967–69; Southern African Dept, 1970–72; UK Mission to the UN, New York (dealing with social affairs, population and outer space), 1972–75; Counsellor, Science and Technology, Paris, 1975–80; Head of Cultural Relns Dept, FCO, 1980–85; RCDS, 1985; Ambassador: to Senegal, and (non-resident) to Mali, Cape Verde, Guinea and Guinea-Bissau, 1985–90; to Mauritania (non-resident), 1986–92 and to Morocco, 1990–92. *Recreations:* music, travel, picnics in unusual places. *Address:* Les Aires, 26110 Mirabel aux Baronnies, France.

MacRAE, Kenneth Charles; His Honour Judge MacRae; a Circuit Judge, since 1990; *b* 14 March 1944; *s* of William and Ann MacRae; *m* 1981, Hilary Vivien Williams; one *d. Educ:* Redruth County Grammar School; Cornwall Tech. Coll.; Fitzwilliam Coll., Cambridge (BA Hons). Called to the Bar, Lincoln's Inn, 1969; a Recorder of the Crown Court, 1985. *Recreations:* gardening, walking, music. *Address:* The Crown Court, 6–8 Penrhyn Road, Kingston-upon-Thames KT1 2BB. *T:* (020) 8240 2500.

McRAE, Lindsay; *see* Duncan, L.

MACREADIE, John Lindsay; a National Officer, Civil and Public Services Association, since 1970 (Deputy General Secretary, 1987–92); *b* 19 Sept. 1946; *s* of John and Mary Macreadie; *m* 1967, Roisin Ann Boden; one *s* one *d. Educ:* Primary and Secondary State Schools, Glasgow. Civil Servant, 1964–70. Mem., TUC General Council, 1987–88. *Recreations:* politics, football, cinema. *Address:* 1 The Green, Morden, Surrey SM4 4HJ. *T:* (020) 8542 5880. *Club:* William Morris Labour (Wimbledon).

MACREADY, Sir Nevil (John Wilfrid), 3rd Bt *cr* 1923; CBE 1983; Chairman, Mental Health Foundation, 1993–97; *b* 7 Sept. 1921; *s* of Lt-Gen. Sir Gordon (Nevil) Macready, 2nd Bt, KBE, CB, CMG, DSO, MC, and Elisabeth (*d* 1969), *d* of Duc de Noailles; *S* father, 1956; *m* 1949, Mary, *d* of late Sir Donald Fergusson, GCB; one *s* three *d. Educ:* Cheltenham; St John's Coll., Oxford. Served in RA (Field), 1942–47 (despatches); Staff Captain, 1945. BBC European Service, 1947–50. Vice-Pres. and Gen. Manager, Mobil Oil Française, 1972–75; Man. Dir, Mobil Oil Co. Ltd, 1975–85. Pres., Inst. of Petroleum, 1980–82. Chairman: Crafts Council, 1984–91; Horseracing Adv. Council, 1986–93; Dep. Chm., British Horseracing Bd, 1993–95. Pres., Royal Warrant Holders' Assoc., 1979–80; Trustee V&A Museum, 1985–95. *Recreations:* racing, fishing, theatre, music. *Heir: s* Charles Nevil Macready [*b* 19 May 1955; *m* 1st, 1981, Lorraine McAdam (marr. diss. 1994); one *s* one *d*; 2nd, 2001, Gillian Simms]. *Address:* The White House, Odiham, Hants RG29 1LG. *T:* (01256) 702976. *Clubs:* Boodle's; Jockey (Paris).

MacROBBIE, Prof. Enid Anne Campbell, FRS 1991; FRSE; Professor of Plant Biophysics, University of Cambridge, 1987–99, now Emeritus professor; Fellow of Girton College, since 1958; *b* 5 Dec. 1931; *d* of late George MacRobbie and Agnes Kerr MacRobbie (*née* Campbell). *Educ:* Mary Erskine Sch., Edinburgh; Univ. of Edinburgh (BSc, PhD); MA, ScD Cantab. FRSE 1998. Res. Fellow, Univ. of Copenhagen, 1957–58; Cambridge University: Res. Fellow, Botany Sch., 1958–62; Demonstrator in Botany, 1962–66; Lectr in Botany, 1966–73; Reader in Plant Biophysics, 1973–87. Mem., BBSRC, 1996–99. Foreign Associate, Nat. Acad. of Scis, USA, 1999. *Publications:* papers in sci jls. *Address:* Girton College, Cambridge CB3 0JG. *T:* (01223) 338999.

McROBERT, Rosemary Dawn Teresa, OBE 1985; Deputy Director, Consumers' Association, 1980–88; *b* Maymyo, Burma, 29 Aug. 1927; *e d* of late Lt-Col Ronald McRobert, MB, ChB, FRCOG, IMS, and Julie Rees. *Educ:* privately and at Gloucestershire College of Educn. Journalist and broadcaster on consumer subjects, 1957–63; Founder editor, Home Economics, 1954–63; Chief Information Officer, Consumer Council, 1965–70; Consumer Representation Officer, Consumers' Assoc., 1971–73; Adviser on consumer affairs in DTI and Dept of Prices and Consumer Protection, 1973–74; Dir, Retail Trading Standards Assoc., 1974–80. Member Council: Inst. of Consumer Ergonomics, 1974–81; Consumers' Assoc., 1974–79; Advertising Standards Authority, 1974–80; Member: Adv. Council on Energy Conservation, 1974–82; Design Council, 1975–84; Post Office Review Cttee, 1976; Policyholders' Protection Bd, 1976–92; Nuffield Enquiry into Pharmacy Services, 1984–86; Council for Licensed Conveyancers, 1989–94; British Hallmarking Council, 1989–97. Chm., Management Cttee, Camden Consumer Aid Centres, 1977–80. Vice-Pres., Patients Assoc., 1988–95. Director: Investors Compensation Scheme, 1988–96; CSM Parliamentary Consultants, 1988–. Liveryman, Glovers' Co., 1979. *Address:* Well House, Bolton Street, Lavenham, Suffolk CO10 9RG. *Club:* Reform.

MacRORY, Avril; Head of Millennium Event Programmes, BBC Television, 1998–2000; *b* 5 April 1956; *d* of Patrick Simon MacRory and Elizabeth (*née* Flynn); *m* 1983, Val Griffin; one *s. Educ:* University College, Dublin (BA Hons 1978). Producer and Director, RTE, 1979; Head of Variety, RTE, 1986; Commissioning Editor, Music, Channel 4, 1988; Head of Music Progs, BBC TV, 1993–98. Pres., Internat. Music Zentrum, Vienna, 1992–. *Recreations:* sailing, music, reading.

MACRORY, Prof. Richard Brabazon, CBE 2000; Professor of Environmental Law, University College, London, since 1999; Barrister-at-law; *b* 30 March 1950; *s* of Sir Patrick Macrory and late Lady Marjorie Elizabeth Macrory; *m* 1979, Sarah Margaret Briant; two *s. Educ:* Westminster Sch.; Christ Church, Oxford (BA 1972; MA 1976). Called to the Bar, Gray's Inn, 1974; Legal Advr, Friends of the Earth Ltd, 1975–78; Imperial College, London: Lectr, 1980–89; Associate Dir, 1990–94, Centre for Envmtl Technol.; Reader in Envmtl Law, 1989–91; Denton Hall Prof. of Envmtl Law, 1991–94; Dir, Envmtl Change Unit, Univ. of Oxford, 1994–95; Prof. of Envmtl Law, Imperial Coll., London, 1995–99; Supernumerary Fellow, Linacre Coll., Oxford, 1996–. Chairman: UK Envmtl Law Assoc., 1986–88; Hon. Standing Council, CPRE, 1981–92; Steering Cttee, European Envmtl Adv. Councils, 2001–; Member: Envmtl Adv. Bd, Shanks and McKewan plc, 1989–91; UK Nat. Adv. Cttee on Eco-labelling, 1990–91; Royal Commn on Envmtl Pollution, 1991–; Expert Strategy Panel, Inter-Agency Cttee for Global Envmtl Change, 1995–96; Bd, Envmt Agency, 1999–. Specialist Adviser: H of L Select Cttee on EC, 1991–92, and 1996–97; H of C Select Cttee on Envmt, 1989–92, 1993–. Mem. Bd, Durham Univ. European Law Inst., 1991–. Hon. Chm., Merchant Ivory Prodns Ltd, 1992–. Hon. Vice-Pres., Nat. Soc. for Clean Air, 1997–. Rapporteur, UK Nat. Biotechnology Conf., 1996; UK nominated expert arbitrator, Law of the Sea Convention, 1998–. Editor, Jl of Envmtl Law, 1988–; Legal Corresp., Ends Report, 1982–. *Publications:* Nuisance, 1982; Water Law: principles and practice, 1985; Water Act 1989, 1989; (with D. Gilbert) Pesticide Related Law, 1989; (with S. Hollins) Bibliography of Community Environmental Law, 1995; articles and reviews in legal and tech. jls. *Recreations:* cinema, board-games, reading, cycling. *Address:* Crossing Farmhouse, Tackley, Oxford OX5 3AT. *T:* (01869) 331151; Brick Court Chambers, 15–19 Devereux Court, WC2R 3JJ. *T:* (020) 7583 0777, *Fax:* (020) 7583 9401; Faculty of Laws, University College, Bentham House, Endsleigh Gardens, WC1H 0EG, *T:* (020) 7679 1543, *Fax:* (020) 7387 9597; *e-mail:* r.macrory@ucl.ac.uk.

MACROSSAN, Hon. John Murtagh, AC 1993; Chancellor, Griffith University, since 1998; *b* 12 Mar. 1930; *m* 1961, Margery Newton; one *s. Educ:* St Columban's Coll., Brisbane; Univ. of Queensland; Univ. of Oxford. Admitted Qld Bar, 1951; QC 1967; Judge, 1980–89, Chief Justice, 1989–98, of Supreme Court, Qld. *Address:* Griffith University, Nathan Campus, Brisbane, Qld 4111, Australia.

MacSHANE, Denis, PhD; MP (Lab) Rotherham, since May 1994; Parliamentary Under-Secretary of State, Foreign and Commonwealth Office, since 2001; *b* 21 May 1948; *e s* of late Jan Matyjaszek and of Isobel MacShane; *m* 1987, Nathalie Pham; one *s* four *d. Educ:* Merton Coll., Oxford (MA); Birkbeck Coll., London. (PhD). BBC reporter, 1969–77; Pres., NUJ, 1978–79; Policy Dir, Internat. Metalworkers Fedn, 1980–92; Dir, European Policy Inst., 1992–94. PPS, FCO, 1997–2001. Vis. Parly Fellow, St Antony's Coll., Oxford, 1998–99. Mem. Council, RIIA, 1999–. *Publications:* Solidarity: Poland's Independent Trade Union, 1981; François Mitterand: a political Odyssey, 1982; Black

Workers, Unions and the Struggle for Democracy in South Africa, 1984; International Labour and the Origins of the Cold War, 1992; Britain's Steel Industry in the 21st Century, 1996. *Recreations:* walking, family, novels, poetry. *Address:* House of Commons, SW1A 0AA. *Club:* East Dene Working Men's.

McSHARRY, Deirdre; Editor-in-Chief, Country Living, 1986–89; *b* 4 April 1932; *d* of late Dr John McSharry and Mrs Mary McSharry. *Educ:* Dominican Convent, Wicklow; Trinity Coll., Dublin. Woman's Editor, Daily Express, 1962–66; Fashion Editor, The Sun, 1966–72; Editor, Cosmopolitan, 1973–85; Consultant, Nat. Magazine Co., and Magazine Div., The Hearst Corp., 1990–95; Ed., Countryside mag., NY, 1991–92. Curator, exhibn, Inspirations: the textile tradition, Amer. Mus. in Britain, 2001. Mem. Council and Chm. Bath Friends, Amer. Mus. in Britain, Bath, 1995–. Magazine Editor of the Year, PPA, 1981, 1987; Mark Boxer Award, British Soc. of Magazine Editors, 1992. *Recreation:* the arts. *Address:* Southfield House, 16 High Street, Rode, Somerset BA11 6NZ.

MacSHARRY, Raymond; Chairman: London City Airport, since 1996; Telecom Éireann, since 1999; Irish Forestry Board, since 1999; Director: Bank of Ireland, since 1993; Jefferson Smurfit Group, since 1993; Ryanair, since 1993 (Chairman, 1993–96); *b* Sligo, April 1938; *m* Elaine Neilan; three *s* three *d*. *Educ:* St Vincent's Nat. Sch., Sligo; Ballincutranta Nat. Sch., Beltra, Co. Sligo; Marist Brothers Nat. Sch., Sligo; Summerhill Coll., Sligo. TD (FF) for Sligo Leitrim, 1969–89; opposition front bench spokesman on Office of Public Works, 1973–75; Mem., Cttee of Public Accts, 1969–77; Minister of State, Dept of Finance and the Public Service, 1977–79; Minister of Agriculture, 1979–81; opposition spokesman on Agric., 1981–82; Tánaiste and Minister for Finance, 1982; Minister for Finance and the Public Service, 1987–88. Mem., Commn of EC, 1989–92. Formerly Member: New Ireland Forum; Nat. Exec., Fianna Fáil Party (later, also an Hon Treas.). Mem. for Connaught/Ulster, Europ. Parlt, 1984–87; Mem., Council of Ministers, 1984–87. Governor, Europ. Investment Bank, 1982. Dir, Hannon's Poultry, Roscommon, 1993–. Councillor, Sligo CC, 1967–78; Chairman: Bd of Management, Sligo Reg. Tech. Coll., 1970–78; Sligo Hosp. Exec. Cttee, 1972–78; NW Health Bd, 1974–75 (Mem., 1971–78); Member: Sligo Corp., 1967–78 (Alderman, 1974–78); Town of Sligo Vocational Educn Cttee, 1967–78; Bd of Management, Sligo-Leitrim Reg. Develt Org., 1973–78; Sligo Jun. Chamber, 1965– (PP). Freeman, Borough of Sligo, 1993. Hon. Dr NUI, 1994; Hon. DEconSc Limerick, 1994. Grand Cross, Order of Leopold II (Belgium), 1993. *Address:* 46 Upper Mount Street, Dublin 2, Eire. *T:* (1) 6762459, *Fax:* 6762489; Alcantara, Pearse Road, Sligo, Eire.

MacSWEEN, Sir Roderick (Norman McIver), Kt 2000; MD; FRCS, FRCPE, FRCPGlas, FRCPath, FMedSci; FIBiol; FRSE; Professor of Pathology, University of Glasgow, 1984–99, now Emeritus; President, Royal College of Pathologists, 1996–99; *b* 2 Feb. 1935; *s* of Murdo MacLeod MacSween and Christina (*née* McIver); *m* 1961, Dr Marjory Pentland Brown; one *s* one *d*. *Educ:* Inverness Royal Acad.; Glasgow Univ. (BSc Hons 1956; MD 1973). FRCPGlas 1972; FRCPE 1974; FRCPath 1976; FIBiol 1987; FRSE 1985; FRCS 2000. University of Glasgow: Lectr, then Sen. Lectr in Pathology, 1965–78; Titular Prof. in Pathology, 1978–84. Instructor in Pathology, Univ. of Colo, Denver, 1968–69; Otago Savings Bank Vis. Prof., Univ. of Otago, NZ, 1983. President: Royal Medico-Chirurgical Soc. of Glasgow, 1978–79; British Div., Internat. Acad. of Pathology, 1989–91; Chm., Acad. of Med. Royal Colls, 1998–2000. Hon. Librarian, RCPSG, 1985–95. Founder FMedSci 1998. Hon. Fellow, Coll. of Pathologists of S Africa, 1998; Hon. FRCP 1999; Hon. FRCSE 2000. Ed., Histopathology, 1984–95. *Publications:* (ed jtly) Pathology of the Liver, 1979, 4th edn 2001; (ed with P. P. Anthony) Recent Advances in Histopathology Nos 11–16, 1992–94; (ed with K. Whaley) Muir's Textbook of Pathology, 13th edn 1992. *Recreations:* golf, gardening, hill-walking . . . and more golf! *Address:* 32 Calderwood Road, Newlands, Glasgow G43 2RU. *Clubs:* Athenæum; Glasgow Golf, Dunaverty Golf (Past Capt.), Machrihanish Golf (Past Capt.).

MACTAGGART, Fiona; MP (Lab) Slough, since 1997; *b* 12 Sept. 1953; *d* of Ian Auld Mactaggart and Rosemary Belhaven. *Educ:* Cheltenham Ladies' Coll.; King's Coll., London (BA Hons); Inst. of Educn, London (MA). Gen. Sec., London Students' Organisation, 1977–78; Vice-Pres., 1978–80, Nat. Sec., 1980–81, NUS; Gen. Sec., Jt Council for Welfare of Immigrants, 1982–86. Mem. (Lab) Wandsworth BC, 1986–90 (Leader of the Opposition, 1988–90). Teacher, Lyndhurst Sch., Camberwell, 1988–92; Lectr, Inst. of Educn, 1992–97. PPS to Sec. of State for Culture, Media and Sport, 1997–2001. Chm., PLP Women's Exec., 2001–. Chm., Liberty (NCCL), 1994–96. *Address:* House of Commons, SW1A 0AA.

MACTAGGART, Sir John (Auld), 4th Bt *cr* 1938, of King's Park, City of Glasgow; FRICS; *b* 21 Jan. 1951; *s* of Sir Ian Auld Mactaggart, 3rd Bt and of Rosemary, *d* of Sir Herbert Williams, 1st Bt, MP; *S* father, 1987; *m* 1st, 1977, Patricia (marr. diss. 1990), *y d* of late Major Harry Alastair Gordon, MC; 2nd, 1991, Caroline, *y d* of Eric Williams; two *s* two *d*. *Educ:* Shrewsbury; Trinity Coll., Cambridge (MA). Chairman: Central and City Ltd, 1981–; Western Heritable Investment Co. Ltd, 1987–. Dir, The Scottish Ballet, 1988–97. *Heir: s* Jack Auld Mactaggart, *b* 11 Sept. 1993. *Address:* 63A South Audley Street, W1Y 5FB.

MACTAGGART, William Alexander, CBE 1964; Chairman, 1960–70, and Managing Director, 1945–68, Pringle of Scotland Ltd, Knitwear Manufacturers, Hawick; *b* 17 Aug. 1906; *o s* of late William Alexander and Margaret Mactaggart, Woodgate, Hawick; *m* 1932, Marjorie Laing Innes; two *s* one *d*. *Educ:* Sedbergh Sch., Yorks. Joined Robert Pringle & Son Ltd (later Pringle of Scotland Ltd), 1925; Dir, 1932; Joint Managing Dir, 1933. Served War of 1939–45: Captain, RASC, Holland, Belgium, France, 1942–45. *Address:* Bewlie House, Lilliesleaf, Melrose, Roxburghshire TD6 9ER. *T:* (01835) 870267.

MacTAGGART, Air Vice-Marshal William Keith, CBE 1976 (MBE 1956); CEng, FIMechE; FRAeS; Consultant: MPE Ltd, 1989–91 (Managing Director, 1984–89); Adwest plc, 1989–91; *b* 15 Jan. 1929; *s* of Duncan MacTaggart and Marion (*née* Keith); *m* 1st, 1949 Christina Carnegie Geddes (marr. diss. 1977); one *s* two *d*; 2nd, 1977, Barbara Smith Brown (marr. diss. 1994), *d* of Adm. Stirling P. Smith, late USN, and Mrs Smith; one step *d*; 3rd, 1995, Kathleen Mary Wilkie, *d* of William and Beatrice Booth. *Educ:* Aberdeen Grammar Sch.; Aberdeen Univ. (BScEng 1948). FIMechE 1973; FRAeS 1974; FIMgt (FBIM 1978). Commnd RAF, 1949; 1949–67: Engr Officer; Pilot; AWRE, Aldermaston (Montebello and Maralinga atomic trials); attended RAF Staff Coll., and Jt Services Staff Coll.; Def. Intell.; Systems Analyst, DOAE, West Byfleet, and MoD (Air); Head of Systems MDC, RAF Swanton Morley, 1968; OC RAF Newton, 1971 (Gp Captain); Dep. Comd Mech. Engr, HQ Strike Comd, 1973; Dir of Air Armament, MoD (PE), 1973 (Air Cdre); RCDS, 1977; Vice-Pres. (Air), Ordnance Bd, 1978 (Air Vice-Marshal), Pres., 1978–80. Dep. Chm., Tomash Holdings Ltd, 1980–84. *Recreations:* music, travel. *Address:* Croft Stones, Lothmore, Helmsdale, Sutherland KW8 6HP. *T:* (01431) 821439. *Club:* Royal Air Force.

MacTHOMAS OF FINEGAND, Andrew Patrick Clayhills; 19th Chief of Clan MacThomas (Mac Thomaidh Mhor); Public Affairs Director, Barclays PLC, since 1997; *b* 28 Aug. 1942; *o s* of late Captain Patrick Watt MacThomas of Finegand and Elizabeth Cadogan Fenwick MacThomas (*née* Clayhills-Henderson); *S* father, 1970; *m* 1985, Anneke Cornelia Susanna, *o d* of A. and S. Kruyning-Van Hout, Netherlands; one *s* one *d*. *Educ:* St Edward's, Oxford. FSA (Scot.) 1973. Pres., Clan MacThomas Soc., 1970–; Hon. Vice-Pres., Clan Chattan Assoc., 1970–. *Recreations:* tennis, family. *Heir: s* Thomas David Alexander MacThomas, Yr of Finegand, *b* 1 Jan. 1987. *Address:* c/o Barclays PLC, 54 Lombard Street, EC3P 3AH.

MACUR, Julia; QC 1998; a Recorder, since 1999; *b* 17 April 1957; *d* of Boleslaw Macur and Betsy Macur; *m* 1981; two *s*. *Educ:* Sheffield Univ. (LLB 1978). Called to the Bar, Lincoln's Inn, 1979; Midland and Oxford Circuit. *Address:* St Ive's Chambers, Whittall Street, Birmingham B4 6DH. *T:* (0121) 236 0863.

McVEIGH, Charles Senff, III; Co-Chairman (formerly Chairman), Salomon Smith Barney (formerly Salomon Brothers International Ltd), since 1987; *b* New York, 4 July 1942; *s* of Charles S. McVeigh, Jr and Evelyn B. McVeigh; *m* 1993, Jennifer Champneys; one *s* four *d*. *Educ:* Univ. of Virginia (BA); Long Island Univ. (MBA). Officer, Morgan Guaranty Trust Co., 1965–1971; joined Salomon Brothers, 1971: Vice-Pres. and Manager, NY Internat. Dept, 1974–75; Hd, Salomon Bros Internat., London, 1975–87; General Partner, 1977–81; Mem., European Mgt Cttee, 1981–. Non-exec. Dir, Savilles plc, 2000–. Mem. Supervisory Bd, Zagreb Achka Banca. Mem., Fulbright Commn, 1993–. Pres., Amer. Chamber of Commerce, 1998–; Member Board: LIFFE, 1983–89; London Stock Exchange, 1986–92; CEDEL, 1994–; Member: City Capital Mkts Cttee, 1989–94; Legal Risk Rev. Cttee, 1990–92. *Recreations:* field sports, gardening. *Address:* Salomon Smith Barney, Citi Group Centre, 33 Canada Square, Canary Wharf, E14 5LB. *Clubs:* White's; Brook, Anglers' (NYC).

McVEIGH, (Robert) Desmond; Managing Director, Longdown Financial Services Ltd, since 1995; *b* 10 Jan. 1939; *s* of Rev. Robert Walker McVeigh and of late Evelyn Mary (*née* McCoubrey); *m* 1966, Gillian Ann Nash; two *s* one *d*. *Educ:* Methodist Coll., Belfast; QUB (LLB Hons); Univ. of Michigan (LLM). Citibank, London, 1967–71; GATX, London, 1971–72; Citibank, 1972–74; First Nat. Bank, Dallas, 1974–77; Saudi Internat. Bank, London, 1977–85; Lloyds Merchant Bank, 1985–87; independent consultant, 1987–92; Chief Exec., IDB for NI, 1993–95. Vis. Prof. of Finance and Industrial Relations, Warsaw Univ., 1994–. CIMgt 1994. *Recreations:* golf, tennis, music. *Address:* Moor Villa, 31 Compton Way, Moor Park, Farnham, Surrey GU10 1QT. *T:* and *Fax:* (01252) 781688. *Club:* Royal Over-Seas League.

MacVICAR, Rev. Kenneth, MBE (mil.) 1968; DFC 1944; Extra Chaplain to the Queen in Scotland, since 1991 (Chaplain in Ordinary, 1974–91); Minister of Kenmore and Lawers, Perthshire, 1950–90; *b* 25 Aug. 1921; *s* of Rev. Angus John MacVicar, Southend, Kintyre; *m* 1946, Isobel Guild McKay; three *s* one *d*. *Educ:* Campbeltown Grammar Sch.; Edinburgh Univ.; St Andrews Univ. (MA); St Mary's Coll., St Andrews. Mem., Edinburgh Univ. Air Squadron, 1941; joined RAF, 1941: Pilot, 28 Sqdn, RAF, 1942–45, Flt Comdr, 1944–45 (despatches, 1945). Chaplain, Scottish Horse and Fife and Forfar Yeomanry/Scottish Horse, TA, 1953–65. Convener, Church of Scotland Cttee on Chaplains to HM Forces, 1968–73. Clerk to Presbytery of Dunkeld, 1955. District Councillor, 1951–74. *Recreation:* golf. *Address:* Illeray, Kenmore, Aberfeldy, Perthshire PH15 2HE. *T:* (01887) 830514.

MACVICAR, Neil; QC (Scot.) 1960; MA, LLB; Sheriff of Lothian and Borders (formerly the Lothians and Peebles), at Edinburgh, 1968–85; *b* 16 May 1920; *s* of late Neil Macvicar, WS; *m* 1949, Maria, *d* of Count Spiridon Bulgari, Corfu; one *s* two *d*. *Educ:* Loretto Sch.; Oriel Coll., Oxford; Edinburgh Univ. Served RA, 1940–45. Called to Scottish Bar, 1948. Chm., Med. Appeal Tribunals, 1961–67 and 1987–94. Chancellor, Dio. of Edinburgh, 1961–74. Chm. of Govs, Dean Orphanage and Cauvin's Trust, 1967–85. *Publications:* A Heart's Odyssey (memoirs), 1991; Grace Notes: variations on a Greek theme, 1995. *Address:* 25 Blackford Road, Edinburgh EH9 2DT. *T:* (0131) 667 2362; Kapoutsi, Gastouri, Corfu, Greece. *T:* (661) 56110. *Clubs:* New (Edinburgh); Anagnostiki Etairia (Corfu).

McVIE, Prof. (John) Gordon, MD; Director General, Cancer Research Campaign, since 1996 (Scientific Director, 1989–96); *b* 13 Jan. 1945; *s* of John McVie and Lindsaye Woodburn McVie (*née* Mair); *m* 1998, Claudia Joan Burke; three *s* by previous marriage. *Educ:* Royal High Sch., Edinburgh; Univ. of Edinburgh (BSc Hons; MB, ChB; MD 1978) MRCP 1971. Edinburgh University: MRC Fellow, 1970–71; Lectr in Therapeutics, 1971–76; CRC Sen. Lectr in Oncology, Glasgow Univ., 1976–80; Netherlands Cancer Institute, Amsterdam: Hd, Clinical Res. Unit, 1980–84; Clinical Res. Dir, 1984–89. Vis. Prof., BPMF, London Univ., 1990–. Member: Council, Scottish Action for Smoking and Health, 1975–80; Royal College of Physicians: Collegiate Mems Cttee, 1975–80; Standing Cttee on Smoking, 1976–80; MRC Cancer Therapy Cttee UK, 1984–92; Bd of Dirs, Netherlands Cancer Inst., 1984–89; Permanent Cttee on Oncology, Min. of Health, Netherlands, 1986–89; European Organisation for Research and Treatment of Cancer: Chairman: Lung Cancer Co-operation Gp, 1981–88; Pharmacokinetics and Metabolism Gp, 1984–87 (Mem., 1981–87); Protocol Rev. Cttee, 1984–91; Pres., 1994. Examiner: RCPE, 1976–94; RCPSG, 1978–84. Chm., UICC Fellowships Prog., 1990–98. Member: Nat. Review of Resource Allocation, Scottish Office, 1998–99; Internat. Scientific Cttee, Italian Govt, 1998; Steering Cttee, Alliance of World Cancer Res. Orgns. Mem., editl bds of numerous jls related to cancer; Editor-in-Chief, European Cancer News, 1987–97; European Ed., Jl Nat. Cancer Inst., 1994–. FRCPE 1981; FRCPSGlas 1987; FRCP 1997; FMedSci 1999. Hon. DSc: Abertay Dundee 1996; Nottingham 1997; Portsmouth 1999. *Publications:* Cancer Assessment and Monitoring, 1979; Autologous Bone Marrow Transplantation and Solid Tumours, 1984; Microspheres and Drug Therapy, 1984; Clinical and Experimental Pathology and Biology of Lung Cancer, 1985; contrib. chapters in books and jls. *Recreations:* opera, theatre, cooking, Italian wine. *Address:* (office) 10 Cambridge Terrace, NW1 4JL. *T:* (020) 7224 1333. *Club:* New (Edinburgh).

McWALTER, Tony; MP (Lab and Co-op) Hemel Hempstead, since 1997; *b* 20 March 1945; *s* of late Joe McWalter and Anne Murray; *m* 1991, Karry Omer; one *s* two *d*. *Educ:* UC Wales, Aberystwyth (BSc 1968); McMaster Univ., Canada (MA 1969); University Coll., Oxford (BPhil 1971; MLitt 1983). School teacher, Cardinal Wiseman Sch., Greenford, 1963–64; lorry driver, E. H. Patterson Transport, 1964; Lecturer in Philosophy: Thames Poly., 1972–74; Hatfield Poly., then Univ. of Hertfordshire, 1974–97 (Dir of Computing, 1989–92). Member, Select Committee: NI, 1997–2000; Sci. & Technol., 2001–. Mem., Nat. Cttee for Philosophy, 1984– (Treas., 1984–97). Mem., External Adv. Bd, Faculty of Lit. Hum., Oxford Univ., 2000–. Hon. Vice-Pres., Herts Conservation Soc., 1997–. *Publication:* (ed jtly) Kant and His Influence, 1990. *Recreations:* playing with my children, tennis, bridge, croquet, theatre. *Address:* House of Commons, SW1A 0AA. *T:* (020) 7219 4547; (constituency) (01442) 251251. *Fax:* (01442) 241268.

McWATTERS, George Edward; Director of Corporate Affairs, HTV Group plc, 1989–91; Chairman: TVMM, 1988–91; HTV West, 1969–88; *b* India, 17 March 1922; *s* of Lt-Col George Alfred McWatters and Ellen Mary Christina McWatters (*née* Harvey); *m* 1st, 1946, Margery Robertson (*d* 1959); 2nd, 1960, Joy Anne Matthews; one *s*. *Educ:* Clifton Coll., Bristol. Vintners' Scholar, 1947. Served War of 1939–45: enlisted ranks Royal Scots, 1940; commissioned 14th Punjab Regt, Indian Army, 1941–46. John Harvey & Sons (family wine co.): joined, 1947; Dir, 1951; Chm., 1956–66; estab. a holding co. (Harveys of Bristol Ltd), 1962, but Showerings took over, 1966, and he remained Chm. until resignation, Aug. 1966; Chm., John White Footwear Holdings Ltd, later Ward White Gp Ltd, 1967–82; Actg Chm., HTV Group plc, 1985–86; Chm., HTV Ltd, 1986–88 (Vice-Chm., 1969–86). Chm., Bristol Avon Phoenix, 1987–90; Director: Bristol and West Bldg Soc., 1985–92 (Vice-Chm., 1988–92); Martins Bank, 1960–70; Local Adv. Dir (Peterborough), Barclays Bank, 1970–82; Local Dir (Northampton), Commercial Union Assce Co., 1969–82; Dir, Bain Clarkson Ltd, 1982–95. Mem., CBI Grand Council, 1970–82. Mem. Cttee, Automobile Assoc., 1962–89. Chairman: Council, Order of St John, Avon, 1983–93; Bishop of Bristol's Urban Fund, 1989–95; Millennium Appeal, RWEA, 1996–; Vice-Pres., Avon Wildlife Trust, 1989– (Chm., Appeal Cttee, 1982). Pres., Avon and Bristol Fedn of Boys Clubs, 1985–94. Governor: Clifton Coll., 1958–; Kimbolton Sch., 1970–82. Master, Soc. of Merchant Venturers, 1986. City Councillor, Bristol, 1950–53. JP, Bristol, 1960–67; JP, Marylebone, 1969–71; High Sheriff, Cambridgeshire, 1979. *Recreations:* swimming, walking. *Address:* 4 Rivers Street, Bath, Avon BA1 2PZ. *T:* (01225) 337725. *Club:* MCC.

McWATTERS, Stephen John; Headmaster, The Pilgrims' School, 1976–83, retired; *b* 24 April 1921; *er s* of late Sir Arthur Cecil McWatters, CIE and Mary McWatters (*née* Finney); *m* 1957, Mary Gillian, *o d* of late D. C. Wilkinson and Mrs G. A. Wilkinson; one *s* two *d*. *Educ:* Eton (Scholar); Trinity Coll., Oxford (Scholar, MA). 1st Cl. Class. Mods, 1941. Served in The King's Royal Rifle Corps, 1941–45. Distinction in Philosophy section of Litterae Humaniores, Oxford, 1946. Asst Master, Eton Coll., 1947–63 (Master in Coll., 1949–57, Housemaster, 1961–63); Headmaster, Clifton Coll., 1963–75. Governor: Clifton Coll., 1977–; Milton Abbey Sch., 1978–94. *Recreations:* music, bird-watching. *Address:* 26 Edgar Road, Winchester SO23 9TN. *T:* (01962) 867523.

McWEENY, Prof. Roy; Professor of Theoretical Chemistry, University of Pisa, 1982–97, Professor Emeritus, since 1998; *b* 19 May 1924; *o s* of late Maurice and Vera McWeeny; *m* 1947, Patricia M. Healey (marr. diss. 1979); one *s* one *d*; *m* 1982, Virginia Del Re. *Educ:* Univ. of Leeds; University Coll., Oxford. BSc (Physics) Leeds 1945; DPhil Oxon 1949. Lectr in Physical Chemistry, King's Coll., Univ. of Durham, 1948–57; Vis. Scientist, Physics Dept, MIT, USA, 1953–54; Lectr in Theoretical Chemistry, Univ. Coll. of N Staffs, 1957–62; Associate Dir, Quantum Chemistry Gp, Uppsala Univ., Sweden, 1960–61; Reader in Quantum Theory, 1962–64, Prof. of Theoretical Chemistry, 1964–66, Univ. of Keele; Prof. of Theoretical Chem., 1966–82, and Hd of Chemistry Dept, 1976–79, Sheffield Univ. Vis. Prof., America, Japan, Europe. Mem., Acad. Européenne des Scis, des Arts et des Lettres, 1988. *Publications:* Symmetry, an Introduction to Group Theory and its Applications, 1963; (with B. T. Sutcliffe) Methods of Molecular Quantum Mechanics, 1969, 2nd edn as sole author, 1989; Spins in Chemistry, 1970; Quantum Mechanics: principles and formalism, 1972; Quantum Mechanics: methods and basic applications, 1973; Coulson's Valence, 3rd rev. edn 1979; contrib. sections in other books and encyclopædias; many research papers on quantum theory of atomic and molecular structure in Proc. Royal Soc., Proc. Phys. Soc., Phys. Rev., Revs. Mod. Phys., Jl Chem. Phys., etc. *Recreations:* drawing, sculpture, travel. *Address:* Via Consoli del Mare 3, 56126 Pisa, Italy.

McWHA, Prof. James Alexander, PhD; Vice-Chancellor and President, Massey University, New Zealand, since 1996; *b* 28 May 1947; *s* of David McWha and Sarah Isabel McWha (*née* Caughey); *m* 1970, Jean Lindsay Farries; one *s* two *d*. *Educ:* Queen's Univ., Belfast (BSc, BAgr Hons); Glasgow Univ. (PhD Plant Physiol. 1973). Lectr in Plant Physiol., 1973–79, Hd, Dept of Plant and Microbial Scis, 1980–85, Univ. of Canterbury; Prof. of Agricl Botany, QUB and Dep. CSO, Dept of Agriculture for NI, 1985–89; Dir, DSIR Fruit and Trees (NZ), 1989–92; CEO, Horticulture and Food Res. Inst., NZ, 1992–95; Dir, Dairy Res. Inst., NZ, 1996–97. Member: Council, NIAB, Cambridge, 1986–89; Bd, NZ Foundn for Res. Sci. and Technol., 1992–95. Dir, Industrial Res. Ltd, 1996–. *Publications:* numerous scientific and educnl articles. *Address:* Tiritea, Private Bag 11-222, Massey University, Palmerston North, New Zealand. *T:* (office) (6) 3505087.

McWHINNEY, Jeffrey Harold; Chief Executive, British Deaf Association, since 1995; *b* 9 May 1960; *s* of late Harold George McWhinney and of Mabel Joan McWhinney (*née* Carlisle); *m* 1989, Brigitte François; three *s* one *d*. *Educ:* Jordanstown Schs, Belfast; Mary Hare Grammar Sch., Newbury; Kingston Univ. (Cert. Mgt 1992; Dip. Mgt 1993). Develt Officer, Breakthrough Trust, 1984–87; Head of Community Services, Disability Resources Team, 1987–91; Sen. Economic Develt Officer, Economic Develt Office, Wandsworth BC, 1991–94; Dir, Greenwich Assoc. of Disabled People, 1994–95. Dir, Sign Campaign, 1993–; Chief Exec., Big D Trading Co., 1996–. Mem., Assoc. of Chief Execs of Nat. Voluntary Orgns, 1995–. MInstD 1996. Deaf Acad. Award, 1996. *Publications:* Deaf Consciousness, 1992; numerous articles in various professional and specialist jls. *Recreations:* golf, reading, politics, family activities, travel. *Address:* (office) 1 Worship Street, EC2A 2AB.

MACWHINNIE, Sir Gordon (Menzies), Kt 1992; CBE 1984 (OBE 1977); JP; FCA; Chairman: Allied Group Ltd, since 1998; Allied Properties Ltd, since 1998; Director, Bermuda Trust (Hong Kong) Ltd, since 1996; *b* 13 Nov. 1922; *s* of Arthur William Philip Macwhinnie and Nellie Evelyn (*née* Rand); *m* 1948, Marjorie Grace Benwell; two *s*. *Educ:* Westminster Sch. FCA 1958 (ACA 1948). War Service, 1941–46: Capt., No 1 Commando, Burma and FE. Joined Peat Marwick Mitchell & Co., 1948, Sen. Partner, Hong Kong, 1968–78; chm. and dir of cos, 1978–; consultant in private practice, 1978–. Chm. and Mem., Govt cttees, 1978–. Council Mem., Hong Kong Univ. of Science and Technol., 1988–98. Hon. DLitt Hong Kong Poly., 1991; Hon. DBA Hong Kong Univ. of Sci. and Technol., 1995. *Recreations:* golf, horse-racing, watching cricket, football, athletics, etc. *Address:* Apt 703, de Ricou, The Repulse Bay, 109 Repulse Bay Road, Hong Kong. *T:* 28031302, *Fax:* 28129874. *Clubs:* Oriental; Royal & Ancient Golf (St Andrews); Piltdown Golf; Hong Kong Golf (Pres.), Hong Kong, Hong Kong Jockey (Chm., 1989–91).

McWHIRTER, Prof. John Graham, PhD; FRS 1999; FREng; Senior Fellow, Signal Processing Group, Defence Evaluation and Research Agency, since 1996; *b* 28 March 1949; *s* of late Francis David McWhirter and Elizabeth McWhirter (*née* Martin); *m* 1973, Avesia Vivianne Wolfe; one *s* one *d*. *Educ:* Newry High Sch.; Queen's Univ., Belfast (BSc 1st Cl. Hons Maths 1970; PhD 1973). CMath, FIMA 1988; FIEE 1994; FREng (FEng 1996); FInstP 1999. Defence Evaluation and Research Agency: Higher Scientific Officer, 1973–77; SSO, 1977–80; PSO, 1980–86; SPSO, 1986–96. Visiting Professor: Electrical Engrg Dept, Queen's Univ., Belfast, 1986–; Sch. of Engrg, UC, Cardiff, 1997–. Vice Pres., IMA, 1998–99 (Chm. and Proceedings Ed., IMA Internat. Conf. on Maths in Signal Processing, 1988, 1992, 1996 and 2000). Hon. DSc QUB, 2000. J. J. Thomson Medal, IEE, 1994. *Publications:* over 120 res. papers; inventor or jt inventor of 28 UK, European, US and Canadian patents. *Recreations:* swimming for exercise, building and flying radio-controlled model gliders. *Address:* Defence Evaluation Research Agency, St Andrew's Road, Malvern, Worcs WR14 3PS. *T:* (01684) 895384. *Club:* Malvern Soaring Association.

McWHIRTER, Norris Dewar, CBE 1980; author, publisher, broadcaster; Director, Guinness Publications Ltd (formerly Guinness Superlatives Ltd), 1954–96 (Managing Director, 1954–76); *b* Winchmore Hill, N London, 12 Aug. 1925; *er (twin) s* of William Allan McWhirter, Managing Director of Associated Newspapers and Northcliffe Newspapers Group, and Margaret Williamson; *m* 1st, 1957, Carole (*d* 1987), *d* of late George H. Eckert; one *s* one *d*; 2nd, 1991, Tessa Mary, *d* of late Joseph Dunsdon Pocock and Dorothy Pocock (*née* von Weichardt). *Educ:* Marlborough; Trinity Coll., Oxford. BA (Internat. Rel. and Econs), MA (Contract Law). Served RN, 1943–46: Sub-Lt RNVR, 2nd Escort Gp, Atlantic; minesweeping Pacific. Dir, McWhirter Twins Ltd, 1950–; Chm., Wm McWhirter & Sons, 1955–86; co-founder, Redwood Press (Chm., 1966–72); Dir, Gieves Group plc, 1972–95. Founder Editor (with late Ross McWhirter till 1975) and compiler, Guinness Book of Records, 1954–86 (1st edn 1955), Adv. Editor, 1986–96; by 1999, in 37 languages; over 83 million sales. Athletics Correspondent: Observer, 1951–67; Star, 1951–60; BBC TV Commentator, Olympic Games, 1960–72; What's In the Picture, 1957; The Record Breakers, 1972–94; Guinness Hall of Fame, 1986. Mem., Sports Council, 1970–73. Pres., Freedom Assoc. (Chm., 1983–2000). Pres., Marlburian Club, 1983–84. Contested (C) Orpington, 1964, 1966. Trustee: Ross McWhirter Foundn (Chm., 1994–); Police Convalescent and Rehabilitation Trust. *Publications:* Get To Your Marks, 1951; (ed) Athletics World, 1952–56; Dunlop Book of Facts, 5 edns, 1964–73; Guinness Book of Answers, 1976, 10th edn 1995; Ross: story of a shared life, 1976; Guinness Book of Essential Facts, 1979 (US); (jtly) Treason at Maastricht, 1994; Time and Space, 1998; Book of Extremes, 1998; Book of Millennium Records, 1999; Book of Historical Records, 2000. *Recreations:* family tennis, watching athletics (Oxford 100 yds, Scotland 1950–52, GB in Norway 1951) and Rugby football (Saracens and Mddx XV, 1950). *Address:* c/o Room 222, South Bank House, Black Prince Road, SE1 7SJ. *Clubs:* Carlton; Vincent's (Oxford); Achilles.

McWIGGAN, Thomas Johnstone, CBE 1976; aviation electronics consultant; Secretary General, European Organisation for Civil Aviation Electronics, 1979–87; *b* 26 May 1918; *s* of late Thomas and Esther McWiggan; *m* 1947, Eileen Joyce Moughton; two *d*. *Educ:* UC Nottingham. Pharmaceutical Chemist. FIEE, FRAeS, SMIEEE. Signals Officer (Radar), RAFVR, 1941–46. Civil Air Attaché (Telecommunications) Washington, 1962–65; Dir of Telecommunications (Plans), Min. of Aviation, 1965; Dir of Telecommunications (Air Traffic Services), BoT, 1967; Dir Gen. Telecommunications, Nat. Air Traffic Services, 1969–79 (CAA, 1972–79). *Publications:* various technical papers. *Recreations:* photography, cabinet-making, gardening. *Address:* The Squirrels, Liberty Rise, Addlestone, Weybridge, Surrey KT15 1NU. *T:* (01932) 843068.

MacWILLIAM, Very Rev. Alexander Gordon; Dean of St Davids Cathedral, 1984–90; *b* 22 Aug. 1923; *s* of Andrew George and Margaret MacWilliam; *m* 1951, Catherine Teresa (*née* Bogue); one *s*. *Educ:* Univ. of Wales (BA Hons Classics, 1943); Univ. of London (BD 2nd Cl. Hons, 1946, PhD 1952, DipEd 1962). Deacon 1946, priest 1947; Curate of Penygroes, Gwynedd, 1946–49; Minor Canon, Bangor Cathedral, 1949–55; Rector of Llanfaethlu, Gwynedd, 1955–58; Head of Dept of Theology, Trinity Coll., Carmarthen, Dyfed, 1958–74; Head of School of Society Studies, Trinity Coll. (Inst. of Higher Education, Univ. of Wales), 1974–84; Canon of St Davids Cathedral and Prebendary of Trefloden, 1978. Examining Chaplain to Bishop of St Davids, 1969. Vis. Prof. of Philosophy and Theology, Central Univ. of Iowa, USA, 1983. Prov. Grand Master, S Wales Western Div., United Grand Lodge of England, 1992–. *Publications:* contribs to Learning for Living (Brit. Jl of Religious Education), UCW Jl of Educn. *Recreations:* travel to archaeological sites and art centres, classical music, food and wine. *Address:* Pen Parc, Smyrna Road, Llangain, Carmarthen, Carmarthenshire SA33 5AD.

McWILLIAM, John David; MP (Lab) Blaydon, since 1979; *b* 16 May 1941; *s* of Alexander and Josephine McWilliam; *m* 1st, 1965, Lesley Mary Catling; two *d*; 2nd, 1994, Mary McLoughlin (marr. diss. 1997); 3rd, 1998, Helena Lovegreen. *Educ:* Leith Academy; Heriot Watt Coll.; Napier College of Science and Technology. Post Office Engineer, 1957–79. Councillor, Edinburgh CC, 1970–75 (last Treasurer of City of Edinburgh and only Labour one, 1974–75); Commissioner for Local Authority Accounts in Scotland, 1974–78. Member: Scottish Council for Technical Educn, 1973–85; Select Cttee on Educn, Science and the Arts, 1980–83; Select Cttee on Procedure, 1984–87; Services Cttee (Chm., Computer sub-cttee, 1983–87); Select Cttee on Defence, 1987–99; Speaker's Panel of Chairmen, 1988–97. Dep. to the Shadow Leader of the House of Commons, 1983; Opposition Whip, 1984–87. Mem., Gen. Adv. Council, BBC, 1984–89. *Recreations:* reading, listening to music, angling. *Clubs:* Chopwell Social, Chopwell RAOB (Chopwell); Ryton Social (Ryton); Blackhall Mill Social (Blackhall Mill); Greenside and District Social (Greenside); Winlaton Hallgarth, Winlaton West End (Winlaton). *Address:* House of Commons, SW1A 0AA.

McWILLIAM, Sir Michael (Douglas), KCMG 1996; Chairman, Royal Commonwealth Society, since 1996 (Deputy Chairman, 1982–91); *b* 21 June 1933; *s* of Douglas and Margaret McWilliam; *m* 1960, Ruth Arnstein; two *s*. *Educ:* Cheltenham Coll.; Oriel Coll., Oxford (MA); Nuffield Coll., Oxford (BLitt). Kenya Treasury, 1958; Samuel Montagu & Co., 1962; joined Standard Bank, subseq. Standard Chartered Bank, 1966; Gen. Manager, 1973; Gp Man. Dir, 1983–88; Dir, SOAS, Univ. of London, 1989–96 (Hon. Fellow, 1997). Member: Bd, Commonwealth Development Corp., 1990–96; Council, ODI, 1991–. Chm., Superannuation Fund, London Univ., 1990–97; Director: Shanghai Fund, 1992–99, Bangladesh Fund, 1993–99, Indo-Cam Gp; Simba Fund, ING Baring, 1995–2000; Indo-Cam Mosais, 1998–. Chairman: Royal African Soc., 1996– (Mem. Council, 1979–91); Centre for the Study of African Economies, Oxford, 1998–. Pres. Council, Cheltenham Coll., 1988–92 (Mem., 1977–92). *Publication:* The Development Business: a history of the Commonwealth Development Corporation. *Address:* 18 Northumberland Avenue, WC2N 5BJ. *Club:* Royal Commonwealth Society.

McWILLIAMS, Sir Francis, GBE 1992; FREng; conciliator and arbitrator, since 1978; Chairman, Centre for Economics and Business Research, since 1992; Lord Mayor of London, 1992–93; *b* 8 Feb. 1926; *s* of John J. and Mary Anne McWilliams; *m* 1950, Winifred (*née* Segger); two *s*. *Educ:* Holy Cross Acad., Edinburgh; Edinburgh Univ. (BSc Eng 1945); Inns of Court Sch. of Law. FICE. Engineer in local govt, 1945–54; Town Engineer, Petaling Jaya New Town, Malaysia, 1954–64; Consulting Civil and Struct. Engineer, Kuala Lumpur, 1964–76. Bar student, 1976–78; called to the Bar, Lincoln's Inn, 1978, Bencher, 1993. Dir, Hong Kong & Shanghai Bank (Malaysia), 1993–99. Chm., British/Malaysian Soc., 1994–2001. Mem., Common Council, City of London, 1978–80; Alderman, Ward of Aldersgate, 1980–96; Sheriff, City of London, 1988–89. Master: Arbitrators' Co., 1985–86; Engineers' Co., 1990–91; Loriners' Co., 1995–96; Pres., Aldersgate Ward Club, 1980–96. Chm., St John's Ambulance City Br., 1992–96. Pres., Instn of Incorp. Exec. Engrs, 1994–97. Vice Chm. Trustees, Foundn for Manufg and

Industry, 1994–2000. FCGI; FREng (FEng 1991). Hon. DCL City; Hon. DEng Kingston, 1994; Dr *hc* Edinburgh, 1994. KStJ 1992; KSG 1993. PJK, Selangor, Malaysia, 1963; Dato Seri Selera, Selangor, 1973. Order of Merit (Senegal), 1989; Order of Independence (Cl. III) (UAE), 1989. *Recreations:* golf, ski-ing. *Address:* 85 North Road, Hythe, Kent CT21 5ET. *T:* (01303) 261800. *Clubs:* Hon. Company of Edinburgh Golfers, Muirfield; Hythe Imperial Golf; Royal Selangor Golf (Kuala Lumpur).

MADARIAGA, Prof. Isabel Margaret de, FRHistS; FBA 1990; Professor of Russian Studies, University of London at School of Slavonic and East European Studies, 1981–85, now Professor Emerita; *b* 27 Aug. 1919; *d* of late Salvador de Madariaga and Constance Archibald, MA; *m* 1943, Leonard Bertram Schapiro, CBE, FBA (marr. diss 1976; he *d* 1983). *Educ:* Ecole Internationale, Geneva; Instituto Escuela, Madrid and fifteen other schools; Univ. of London (BA, PhD). FRHistS 1967. BBC Monitoring Service, 1940–43; Min. of Information (later COI), 1943–47; Economic Information Unit, HM Treasury, 1947–48; Editl Asst, Slavonic and East European Review, 1951–64; Asst Lectr and Lectr, LSE, intermittently, 1951–66; Lectr in Modern History, Univ. of Sussex, 1966–68; Sen. Lectr in Russian Hist., Univ. of Lancaster, 1968–71; Reader in Russian Studies, SSEES, Univ. of London, 1971–81. Corresp. Mem., Royal Spanish Acad. of History, 1991. Member, Editorial Boards: Government and Opposition, 1965–; Slavonic and E European Review, 1971–86; European History Qly, 1971–. *Publications:* Britain, Russia and the Armed Neutrality, 1963; (with G. Ionescu) Opposition, 1968; Russia in the Age of Catherine the Great, 1981; Catherine the Great: a short history, 1990 (trans. German, 1993; Spanish, 1994; Portuguese, 1996; Turkish, 1997); Politics and Culture in Eighteenth-Century Russia, 1998; articles in learned jls. *Recreation:* music. *Address:* 25 Southwood Lawn Road, Highgate, N6 5SD. *T:* (020) 8341 0862. *Club:* Oxford and Cambridge.

MADDEN, (Albert) Frederick (McCulloch), DPhil; Reader in Commonwealth Government, Oxford, 1957–84; Professorial (Charter) Fellow of Nuffield College, 1958–84, Emeritus Fellow since 1984, Pro-Proctor, 1988–89; *b* 27 Feb. 1917; *e s* of A. E. and G. McC. Madden; *m* 1941, Margaret, *d* of Dr R. D. Gifford; one *s* one *d*. *Educ:* privately, by mother; Bishop Vesey's Grammar Sch.; Christ Church, Oxford. Boulter and Gladstone exhibns; BA 1938, BLitt 1939, DPhil 1950. Dep. Sup., Rhodes House Library, 1946–48; Beit Lectr, 1947–57; Sen. Tutor to Overseas Service Courses, 1950–; Co-Dir, Foreign Service Course, 1959–72; Dir, Inst. of Commonwealth Studies, 1961–68; Vice-Chm., History Bd, 1968–73. Co-founder, Oxford Samaritans, 1961. Canadian Vis. Fellow, 1970; Vis. Prof., Cape Town, 1973; Vis. Fellow, Res. Sch., ANU, 1974. Dir, Hong Kong admin. course, 1975–86. Dir, Prospect Theatre, 1963–66. FRHistS 1952. *Publications:* (with V. Harlow) British Colonial Developments, 1774–1834, 1953; (with K. Robinson) Essays in Imperial Government, 1963; chapter in Cambridge History of British Empire III, 1959; Imperial Constitutional Documents, 1765–1965, 1966; (with W. Morris-Jones) Australia and Britain, 1980; (with D. K. Fieldhouse) Oxford and the Idea of Commonwealth, 1982; Perspectives on Imperialism and Decolonisation (Festschrift), 1984; Select Documents on the Constitutional History of the British Empire: Vol. I, The Empire of the Bretaignes 1165–1688, 1985; Vol. II, The Classical Period of the First British Empire 1689–1783, 1986; Vol. III, Imperial Reconstruction 1763–1840, 1987; Vol. IV, Settler Self-government 1840–1900, 1989; Vol. V, The Dependent Empire and Ireland 1840–1900, 1991; Vol. VI, The Dominions and India since 1900, 1993; Vol. VII, The Dependent Empire 1900–48, 1994; Vol. VIII, The End of Empire 1948–97, 2000; reviews in English Historical Review, etc. *Recreations:* acting (Cranmer in Quatercentenary, St Mary's, Oxford, and 186 other parts); photographing islands and highlands, hill towns, country houses, churches; Renaissance art; writing music and listening; taking services. *Address:* 1 Penstones Court, Marlborough Lane, Stanford-in-the-Vale, Oxfordshire SN7 8SW. *T:* (01367) 718068.

See also D. C. A. McC. Madden.

MADDEN, David Christopher Andrew McCulloch, CMG 1996; HM Diplomatic Service; Ambassador to Greece, since 1999; *b* 25 July 1946; *s* of Dr A. F. McC. Madden, *qv* and (Alice) Margaret Madden; *m* 1970, Penelope Anthea Johnston; one *s* two *d*. *Educ:* Magdalen Coll. Sch., Oxford; Merton Coll., Oxford (Postmaster; MA); Courtauld Inst. of Art, London Univ. (MA). FCO, 1970–72; British Mil. Govt, Berlin, 1972–75; Cabinet Office, 1975–77; Moscow, 1978–81; Athens, 1981–84; FCO, 1984–87; Counsellor, 1987; Dep. Hd of Mission, Belgrade, 1987–90; Head, Southern European Dept, FCO, 1990–94; High Comr, Republic of Cyprus, 1994–99. *Recreations:* cricket, rowing, tennis, reading, pets, animal welfare. *Address:* Foreign and Commonwealth Office, King Charles Street, SW1A 2AH.

MADDEN, Frederick; *see* Madden, A. F. McC.

MADDEN, Dr (John) Lionel, CBE 1999; Librarian, National Library of Wales, 1994–98; *b* 8 Aug. 1938; *s* of late Cyril Madden and of Edith (*née* Mottram); *m* 1965, Georgina Mary Hardwick; one *s* one *d*. *Educ:* King Edward VII Grammar Sch., Sheffield; Lincoln Coll., Oxford (MA 1964); University Coll. London (DipLib 1963); Univ. of Leicester (PhD 1970). ALA 1964. Asst Librarian, Univ. of Hull, 1963–67; Bibliographer, Univ. of Leicester Victorian Studies Centre, 1967–72; Sen. Lectr, Coll. of Librarianship, Wales, 1973–87; Keeper of Printed Books, Nat. Liby of Wales, 1987–94. Mem., Pubns Bd, Leicester Univ. Press, 1968–72; Chm., Pubns Bd, Tennyson Soc., 1973–77. Pres., Welsh Liby Assoc., 1994–98; Chairman: Welsh Books Council, 1996– (Vice-Chm., 1994–96); Liby and Inf. Services Council, Wales, 1998–2001; Capel (Welsh Chapels Heritage Soc.), 1999–. Trustee, St Deiniol's Liby, Hawarden, 1994–. Hon. Fellow, Dept of Inf. and Liby Studies, Univ. of Wales, Aberystwyth, 1989–93, Hon. Prof., 1993–; Hon. Fellow, Univ. of Wales, Lampeter, 1998–. Hon. FLA 1998. Hon. Mem., Gorsedd Beirdd Ynys Prydain, 1995–. *Publications:* Thomas Love Peacock, 1967; How to Find Out about the Victorian Period, 1970; Robert Southey: the critical heritage, 1972; Sir Charles Tennyson: an annotated bibliography, 1973; The Nineteenth Century Periodical Press in Britain, 1976; Primary Sources for Victorian Studies, 1977; (ed jtly) Investigating Victorian Journalism, 1990; articles in learned jls. *Recreation:* walking. *Address:* Hafren, Cae'r Gôg, Aberystwyth SY23 1ET. *T:* (01970) 617771.

MADDEN, Max; *b* 29 Oct. 1941; *s* of late George Francis Leonard Madden and Rene Frances Madden; *m* 1972, Sheelagh Teresa Catherine Howard. *Educ:* Lascelles Secondary Modern Sch.; Pinner Grammar Sch. Journalist: East Essex Gazette; Tribune (political weekly); Sun, London; Scotsman, London; subseq. Press and Information Officer, British Gas Corp., London; Dir of Publicity, Labour Party, 1979–82. MP (Lab): Sowerby, Feb. 1974–1979; Bradford West, 1983–97.

MADDEN, Michael; Under Secretary, Ministry of Agriculture, Fisheries and Food, 1985–96, retired; *b* 12 Feb. 1936; *s* of late Harold Madden and Alice Elizabeth (*née* Grenville); *m* 1st, 1960, Marion Will (marr. diss. 1977); two *s* one *d*; 2nd, 1994, Angela Grace Abell. *Educ:* King Edward VII Sch., Sheffield. Exec. Officer, Min. of Transport and Civil Aviation, 1955; Ministry of Agriculture, Fisheries and Food: Asst Principal, 1963–67; Asst Private Sec. to Minister, 1966–67; Principal, 1967; Asst Sec. (as Head, Tropical Foods Div.), 1973; Under Sec., 1985; Head, Management Services Gp, 1985; Flood Defence, Plant Protection and Agricl Resources, 1990; Envmt Policy Gp, 1991–96. *Recreations:* walking, eating and drinking with friends, music, planning expeditions. *Address:* 2A Brampton Road, St Albans, Herts AL1 4PW. *Club:* Farmers.

MADDEN, Sir Peter John, 3rd Bt *cr* 1919, of Kells, co. Kilkenny; *b* 10 Sept. 1942; *s* of Lt-Col John Wilmot Madden, MC, RA, *yr s* of 1st Bt, and Beatrice Catherine (*née* Sievwright); *S* uncle, 2001; *m* 1993, Mrs Vellie Laput Co; three step *d*. *Educ:* Blundell's; RMA Sandhurst. Late Captain, RA. *Heir:* *b* Charles Jonathan Madden [*b* 11 Aug. 1949; *m* 1980, Kirsteen Victoria Noble; one *s* one *d*].

MADDICOTT, Dr John Robert Lewendon, FBA 1996; FSA; Fellow and Lecturer in Modern History, Exeter College, Oxford, since 1969; *b* Exeter, 22 July 1943; *e s* of late Robert Maddicott, Ipplepen, Devon, and Barbara (*née* Lewendon); *m* 1965, Hilary, *d* of late Thomas and Violet Owen; two *d*. *Educ:* Cheltenham Grammar Sch.; King Edward's Sch., Bath; Worcester Coll., Oxford (BA 1st cl. 1964; DPhil 1968). FSA 1980. Jun. Lectr, Magdalen Coll., Oxford, 1966–67; Asst Lectr, Univ. of Manchester, 1967–69; Sub-Rector, Exeter Coll., Oxford, 1988–90. Vis. Prof., Univ. of S Carolina, 1983. Raleigh Lectr, British Acad., 2001. Jt Editor, English Hist. Review, 1990–2000. *Publications:* Thomas of Lancaster 1307–22, 1970; The English Peasantry and the Demands of the Crown, 1294–1341, 1975; Law and Lordship: Royal Justices as Retainers in Thirteenth- and Fourteenth-Century England, 1978; Simon de Montfort, 1994; contribs to learned jls. *Recreations:* hill walking, poetry, book collecting. *Address:* Exeter College, Oxford OX1 3DP. *T:* (01865) 279621.

MADDISON, Prof. Angus; Professor of Economics, University of Groningen, Netherlands, 1978–96, now Emeritus; *b* 6 Dec. 1926; *s* of Thomas Maddison and Jane (*née* Walker); *m* 1st, Carol Hopkins; two *s*; 2nd, Penelope Pearce; one *d*. *Educ:* Darlington Grammar Sch.; Selwyn Coll., Cambridge (BA, MA; Hon. Fellow 1999); McGill Univ., Montreal; Johns Hopkins Univ.; Univ. Aix-en-Provence (docteur d'état). Pilot Officer, RAF, 1948–49. Lectr in Econ. Hist., Univ. of St Andrews, 1951–52; Head of Econs Div., later Dir, Develt Assistance, then Fellow, Develt Centre, OEEC and OECD, Paris, 1953–66; Dir, Res. Project on Econ. Growth, Twentieth Century Fund, NY, 1966–69; Res. Fellow and Econ. Advr, Harvard Univ. Centre for Internat. Affairs, 1969–71; Head, Central Analysis Div., OECD, Paris, 1971–78. Visiting Lecturer or Professor: Univ. of Calif, Berkeley, 1968; Nuffield Coll., Oxford, 1975; Université Paris Dauphine, 1981; ANU, 1982; St Antony's Coll., Oxford, 1988; Internat. Develt Centre, Japan, 1989; Universitá Ca' Foscari, Venice, 1990; Univ. of Turin, 1993; NY Univ., 1993; SOAS, London Univ., 1996–99; ASERI, Univ. del Sacro Cuore, Milan, 1997; Keio Univ., Fujisawa, 1998; Kuznets Meml Lecture, Yale Univ., 1998. Consultant: EU, ECAFE, ECE, ECLAC, FAO, GATT, IADB, UNESCO, UN, UNIDO; World Bank; govts of Brazil, Ghana, Greece, Mexico and Pakistan. Corresp. FBA 1994. Foreign Hon. Member: Amer. Econ. Assoc., 1989; Amer. Acad. of Arts and Scis, 1996; Foreign Mem., Russian Acad. of Scis in Econs and Business, 1992. Medal, Univ. of Helsinki, 1986. *Publications:* Economic Growth in the West, 1964; Foreign Skills and Technical Assistance in Economic Development, 1965; Economic Growth in Japan and the USSR, 1969; Economic Progress and Policy in Developing Countries, 1970; Class Structure and Economic Growth: India and Pakistan since the Moghuls, 1971; Phases of Capitalist Development, 1982; Two Crises: Latin America and Asia 1929–38 and 1973–83, 1985; The World Economy in the Twentieth Century, 1989; Dynamic Forces in Capitalist Development, 1991; The Political Economy of Poverty, Equity and Growth: Brazil and Mexico, 1992; Explaining the Economic Performance of Nations: essays in time and space, 1995; Monitoring the World Economy, 1995; Chinese Economic Performance in the Long Run, 1998; numerous articles in econ. and financial jls. *Recreations:* collecting furniture, books and hats. *Address:* Chevincourt, 60150, France. *T:* 344760532, *Fax:* 344766514.

MADDISON, David George; His Honour Judge Maddison; a Circuit Judge, since 1992; *b* 22 Jan. 1947; *s* of Claude and Clarice Maddison; *m* 1976, Indira Mary Antoinette Saverymuttu; three *s*. *Educ:* King's Sch., Chester; Grey Coll., Univ. of Durham (BA 1968). Called to the Bar, Inner Temple, 1970; practised on Northern Circuit, 1972–92; a Recorder, 1990–92. Mem., Parole Bd, 1996–. *Publication:* (ed) Bingham's Negligence Cases, 4th edn 1996. *Recreations:* classical music, playing the piano, singing, tennis, golf, watching football. *Address:* c/o Queen Elizabeth II Law Courts, Derby Square, Liverpool L2 1XA. *Clubs:* East India; Athenæum (Liverpool); Liverpool Cricket.

MADDOCK, family name of **Baroness Maddock.**

MADDOCK, Baroness *cr* 1997 (Life Peer), of Christchurch in the co. of Dorset; **Diana Margaret Maddock;** President, Liberal Democrats, 1998–99; *b* 19 May 1945; *d* of Reginald Derbyshire and Margaret Evans; *m* 1966, Robert Frank Maddock; two *d*; *m* 2001, Rt Hon. Alan Beith, *qv*. *Educ:* Brockenhurst GS; Shenstone Training Coll.; Portsmouth Polytechnic. Teacher: Weston Park Girls' Sch., Southampton, 1966–69; Extra-Mural Dept, Stockholm Univ., 1969–72; Sholling Girls' Sch., Southampton, 1972–73; Anglo-Continental Sch. of English, Bournemouth, 1973–76; Greylands Sch. of English, Southampton, 1990–91. Councillor (L, subseq. Lib Dem), Southampton CC, 1984–93. Contested (Lib Dem) Southampton Test, 1992. MP (Lib Dem) Christchurch, July 1993–1997; contested (Lib Dem) same seat, 1997. Sec., All-Party Parly Gp on Homelessness and Housing Need; Vice Chm., All-Party Parly Gp on Electoral Reform. Lib Dem spokesman on housing, H of L, 1997–. Pres., Nat. Housing Forum; a Vice Pres., Nat. Housing Fedn. Trustee, Nat. Energy Foundn. *Recreations:* theatre, music, reading, travel. *Address:* House of Lords, SW1A 0PW.

MADDOCKS, Arthur Frederick, CMG 1974; HM Diplomatic Service, retired; Ambassador and UK Permanent Representative to OECD, Paris, 1977–82; *b* 20 May 1922; *s* of late Frederick William Maddocks and Celia Elizabeth Maddocks (*née* Beardwell); *m* 1945, Margaret Jean Crawford Holt; two *s* one *d*. *Educ:* Manchester Grammar Sch.; Corpus Christi Coll., Oxford. Army, 1942–46; Foreign (later Diplomatic) Service, 1946–82: Washington, 1946–48; FO, 1949–51; Bonn, 1951–55; Bangkok, 1955–58; UK Delegn to OEEC, 1958–60; FO, 1960–64; UK Delegn to European Communities, Brussels, 1964–68; Political Adviser, Hong Kong, 1968–72; Dep. High Comr and Minister (Commercial), Ottawa, 1972–76. Mem., OECD Appeals Tribunal, 1984–89. *Address:* Lynton House, 83 High Street, Wheatley, Oxford OX33 1XP. *Club:* Hong Kong (Hong Kong).

MADDOCKS, Bertram Catterall; His Honour Judge Maddocks; a Circuit Judge, since 1990; *b* 7 July 1932; *s* of His Honour George Maddocks and of Mary Maddocks (*née* Day); *m* 1964, Angela Vergette Forster; two *s* one *d*. *Educ:* Malsis Hall, near Keighley; Rugby; Trinity Hall, Cambridge (schol.; MA; Law Tripos Part 2 1st Cl. 1955). Nat. Service, 2nd Lieut, RA, 1951; Duke of Lancaster's Own Yeomanry (TA), 1958–67. Called to the Bar, Middle Temple, 1956; Harmsworth Schol.; Mem., Lincoln's Inn; a Recorder, 1983–90. Pt-time Chm., VAT Tribunals, 1977–92. *Recreations:* real tennis, lawn tennis, ski-ing, bridge. *Address:* Moor Hall Farm, Prescot Road, Aughton, Lancashire

L39 6RT. *T:* (01695) 421601. *Clubs:* Queen's; Northern Counties (Newcastle); Manchester Tennis and Racquet.

MADDOCKS, Fiona Hamilton; Chief Music Critic, The Observer, since 1997; *m* 1st, R. Cooper (marr. diss.); two *d*; 2nd, 1995, Tom Phillips, *qv*. *Educ:* Blackheath High Sch. (GPDST), London; Royal Coll. of Music; Newnham Coll., Cambridge (MA; Associate, 1985–97). Taught English Literature, Istituto Orsoline, Cortina d'Ampezzo, Italy, 1977–78; Medici Soc., London, 1978–79; News trainee, Producer and Sen. Producer, LBC, 1979–82; Founder Producer/Editor, Comment, 1982–85, Asst Commng Editor, Music, 1985–86, Channel 4; The Independent: Dep. Arts Editor, 1986–88, and writer; Music Editor and Associate Arts Editor, 1988–91; feature writer, Observer, Independent, Spectator and other pubns, 1991–; Founding Editor, 1992–97, Adv. Editor, 1997–98, BBC Music Magazine; Editor, BBC Proms Guide, 1998–99; Exec. Editor, LSO Living Music Magazine, 1998–. Board Mem., Opera magazine, 1998–. Mem. Exec. Cttee, SPNM, 1990–91; Mem., Critics' Circle, 1995 (Mem. Council, 1997–99). Trustee, Masterprize, 1997–2001. Gov., Sherborne Sch., 2001–. BP Arts Journalism Press Award, 1991. *Publication:* Hildegard of Bingen, 2001. *Recreations:* playing chamber music, Italy. *Address:* c/o The Observer, 119 Farringdon Road, EC1R 3ER.

MADDOCKS, Rt Rev. Morris Henry St John; Adviser on the Ministry of Health and Healing to Archbishops of Canterbury and York, 1983–95; Hon. Assistant Bishop, Diocese of Chichester, since 1987; Prebendary of Chichester Cathedral, since 1992; *b* 28 April 1928; *s* of late Rev. Canon Morris Arthur Maddocks and Gladys Mabel Sharpe; *m* 1955, Anne Miles; no *c*. *Educ:* St John's Sch., Leatherhead; Trinity Coll., Cambridge (BA 1952; MA 1956); Chichester Theological Coll. Ordained in St Paul's Cathedral, London, 1954; Curate: St Peter's, Ealing, 1954–55; St Andrews, Uxbridge, 1955–58; Vicar of: Weaverthorpe, Helperthorpe and Luttons Ambo, 1958–61; S Martin's on the Hill, Scarborough, 1961–71; Bishop Suffragan of Selby, 1972–83. Chm., Churches' Council for Health and Healing, 1982–85 (Co-Chm., 1975–82); Co-Founder, with wife, of Acorn Christian Healing Trust, 1983. *Publications:* The Christian Healing Ministry, 1981; The Christian Adventure, 1983; Journey to Wholeness, 1986; A Healing House of Prayer, 1987; Twenty Questions about Healing, 1988; The Vision of Dorothy Kerin, 1991. *Recreations:* music, walking, gardening. *Address:* 3 The Chantry, Cathedral Close, Chichester, W Sussex PO19 1PZ. *T:* (01243) 788888.

MADDOX, Sir John (Royden), Kt 1995; writer and broadcaster; Editor, Nature, 1966–73 and 1980–95; *b* 27 Nov. 1925; *s* of A. J. and M. E. Maddox, Swansea; *m* 1st, 1949, Nancy Fanning (*d* 1960); one *s* one *d*; 2nd, 1960, Brenda Power Murphy; one *s* one *d*. *Educ:* Gowerton Boys' County Sch.; Christ Church, Oxford; King's Coll., London. Asst Lecturer, then Lecturer, Theoretical Physics, Manchester Univ., 1949–55; Science Correspondent, Guardian, 1955–64; Affiliate, Rockefeller Institute, New York, 1962–63; Asst Director, Nuffield Foundation, and Co-ordinator, Nuffield Foundation Science Teaching Project, 1964–66; Man. Dir, Macmillan Journals Ltd, 1970–72; Dir, Macmillan & Co. Ltd, 1968–73; Chm., Maddox Editorial Ltd, 1972–74; Dir, Nuffield Foundn, 1975–80. Member: Royal Commn on Environmental Pollution, 1976–81; Genetic Manipulation Adv. Gp, 1976–80; British Library Adv. Council, 1976–81; Council on Internat. Devélt, 1977–79; Chm. Council, Queen Elizabeth Coll., 1980–85; Mem. Council, King's Coll. London, 1985–89. Mem., Crickadarn and Gwendwr Community Council, 1981–. Hon. FRS 2000. Hon. DTech Surrey, 1982; Hon. DSc: UEA, 1992; Liverpool, 1994; Glamorgan, 1997; Hon. DLitt Nottingham Trent, 1996. *Publications:* (with Leonard Beaton) The Spread of Nuclear Weapons, 1962; Revolution in Biology, 1964; The Doomsday Syndrome, 1972; Beyond the Energy Crisis, 1975; What Remains to be Discovered, 1998. *Address:* 9 Pitt Street, W8 4NX. *T:* (020) 7937 9750. *Club:* Athenæum.

MADDOX, Ronald, PRI 1989 (RI 1959); artist, illustrator and designer; *b* 5 Oct. 1930; *s* of Harold George and Winifred Maddox; *m* 1st, 1958, Camilla Farrin (*d* 1995); two *s*; 2nd, 1997, Diana Goodwin. *Educ:* Hertfordshire College of Art and Design, St Albans; London College of Printing and Graphic Art. FCSD, FSAI; Hon. RWS 1990. Nat. Service, RAF, 1949–51, Air Min. Design Unit. Designer, illustrator, art director, London advertising agencies, 1951–61; private practice, 1962–; commissioned by nat. and multinat. cos and corps, govt depts, public authorities, TV; designer British postage stamps and philatelic material, 1972– (winner Prix de l'art Philatelique, 1987); exhibns, RA, RI, London and provincial galls; paintings in royal, govt and public bodies' collections. Council, AGBI. Trustee, Royal Acad./British Institution Fund, 1996–2000. Vice-Pres., RI, 1979; Governor, Fedn of British Artists, 1989– (Chm., 1997); Hon. Member: Soc. of Architect Artists; Fedn of Canadian Artists; United Soc. of Artists; Campine Assoc. of Watercolours, Belgium; PS; Soc. of Graphic Artists. FRSA. Freeman, City of London; Hon. Freeman, Co. of Painter-Stainers, 2000. Winsor & Newton/RI Award, 1981, 1991; Rowland Hilder landscape painting Award, RI, 1996, 2000. *Recreations:* compulsive drawing, walking, cycling, gardening. *Address:* Herons, 21 New Road, Digswell, Herts AL6 0AQ. *T:* (01438) 714884.

MADDOX, Stephen; Chief Executive, Metropolitan Borough of Wirral, since 1997; *b* Merseyside. *Educ:* Univ. of Kent (BA 1974). Joined Wirral MBC as articled clerk, 1974; admitted as solicitor, 1977; Dep. Borough Solicitor and Sec., Wirral MBC, 1991–98. *Address:* Metropolitan Borough of Wirral, Town Hall, Brighton Street, Wallasey, Wirral CH44 8ED.

MADDRELL, Geoffrey Keggen; Chairman: Westbury plc, since 1992; Unite Group plc, since 1999; Glenmorangie plc (formerly Macdonald Martin Distilleries), since 1994; LDV Ltd, since 1995; ProShare, since 1994 (Chief Executive, 1991–94); Ivory and Sime ISIS Trust plc, since 1993; *b* 18 July 1936; *s* of Captain Geoffrey Douglas Maddrell and Barbara Marie Kennaugh; *m* 1964, Winifred Mary Daniel Jones; two *s* one *d*. *Educ:* King William's Coll., Isle of Man; Corpus Christi Coll., Cambridge (MA Law and Econs); Columbia Univ., New York (MBA). Lieut, Parachute Regt, 1955–57. Shell Internat. Petroleum Co. Ltd, 1961–69; Boston Consulting Gp, Boston, USA, 1971–72; Bowater Corp., 1972–86, apptd to main bd, 1979; joined Tootal Gp as Man. Dir, 1986, Chief Exec., 1987–91. Chm., Manchester TEC, 1988–91; Civil Service Comr, 1992–96, 2000–. Chm., Friends of Airborne Forces, 1996–. Gov., UMIST, 1987–. *Recreations:* club running, golf, travel. *Address:* 28 Sussex Street, SW1V 4RL. *T:* (020) 7834 3874.

MADDRELL, Dr Simon Hugh Piper, FRS 1981; Fellow of Gonville and Caius College, Cambridge, since 1964; Hon. Reader, Cambridge University, since 1991; *b* 11 Dec. 1937; *s* of late Hugh Edmund Fisher Maddrell and Barbara Agnes Mary Maddrell; *m* 1st, 1961, Anna Myers (marr. diss. 1985, she *d* 1997); three *s* one *d*; 2nd, 1990, Katherine Mona Mapes. *Educ:* Peter Symonds' Sch., Winchester; St Catharine's Coll., Cambridge. BA, MA, PhD 1964, ScD 1978. Res. Fellow, Dalhousie Univ., Canada, 1962–64; SPSO, AFRC Unit of Invertebrate Chem. and Physiology, subseq. Unit of Insect Neurophysiology and Pharmacology, Cambridge Univ., 1968–90; College Fellow and Lectr, Gonville and Caius Coll., Cambridge, 1968–. Financial Sec. and Investments Manager, Co. of Biologists Ltd, 1965–. Scientific Medal, Zool Soc. of London, 1976. *Publication:* Neurosecretion, 1979. *Recreations:* golf, gardening, wine-tasting, cinema. *Address:* Gonville and Caius College, Cambridge CB2 1TA; Ballamaddrell, Ballabeg, Arbory, Isle of Man IM9 4HD. *T:* (01624) 822787.

MADEL, Sir (William) David, Kt 1994; *b* 6 Aug. 1938; *s* of late William R. Madel and Eileen Madel (*née* Nicholls); *m* 1971, Susan Catherine, *d* late Lt-Comdr Hon. Peter Carew; one *s* one *d*. *Educ:* Uppingham Sch.; Keble Coll., Oxford. MA Oxon 1965. Graduate Management Trainee, 1963–64; Advertising Exec., Thomson Organisation, 1964–70. Contested (C) Erith and Crayford Nov. 1965, 1966. MP (C): S Bedfordshire, 1970–83; Bedfordshire SW, 1983–2001. PPS to Parly Under-Sec. of State for Defence, 1973–74, to Minister of State for Defence, 1974, to Rt Hon. Sir Edward Heath, KG, MBE, MP, 1991–97; an Opposition Whip, 1997–99. Chm., Cons. Backbench Educn Cttee, 1983–85; Vice-Chm., Cons. Backbench Employment Cttee, 1974–81; Member: Select Cttee on Educn, Sci. and Arts, 1979–83, on Transport, 1995–97, on Foreign Affairs, 1999–2001; H of C European Legislation Cttee, 1983–97. *Recreations:* cricket, tennis, reading, walking. *Address:* 120 Pickford Road, Markyate, Herts AL3 8RL. *Clubs:* Carlton, Coningsby; Mid-Cheshire Pitt (Chester).

MADELUNG, Prof. Wilferd Willy Ferdinand, FBA 1999; Laudian Professor of Arabic, University of Oxford, 1978–98; *b* 26 Dec. 1930; *s* of Georg Madelung and Elisabeth (*née* Messerschmitt); *m* 1963, A. Margaret (*née* Arent); one *s*. *Educ:* Eberhard Ludwig Gymnasium, Stuttgart; Univs of Georgetown, Cairo, Hamburg. PhD (Hamburg). Cultural Attaché, W German Embassy, Baghdad, 1958–60. Vis. Professor, Univ. of Texas, Austin, 1963; Privatdozent, Univ. of Hamburg, 1963–64; University of Chicago: Asst Prof., 1964; Associate Prof., 1966; Prof. of Islamic History, 1969. Guggenheim Fellowship, 1972–73. Decoration of Republic of Sudan (4th cl.), 1962. *Publications:* Der Imam al-Qāsim ibn Ibrāhīm und die Glaubenslehre der Zaiditen, 1965; Religious Schools and Sects in Medieval Islam, 1985; Religious Trends in Early Islamic Iran, 1988; Religious and Ethnic Movements in Medieval Islam, 1992; The Succession to Muhammad, 1996; articles in learned jls and Encyc. of Islam. *Recreation:* travel. *Address:* 21 Belsyre Court, Oxford OX2 6HU.

MADEN, Prof. Margaret; Professor of Education, Keele University, since 1995; *b* 16 April 1940; *d* of Clifford and Frances Maden. *Educ:* Arnold High Sch. for Girls, Blackpool; Leeds Univ. (BA Hons); Univ. of London Inst of Educn (PGCE). Asst Teacher of Geography, Stockwell Manor Comprehensive Sch., SW9, 1962–66; Lectr, Sidney Webb Coll. of Educn, 1966–71; Dep. Head, Bicester Comprehensive Sch., Oxon, 1971–75; Headmistress, Islington Green Comprehensive Sch., 1975–82; Dir, Islington Sixth Form Centre, 1983–86; Principal Advr, Tertiary Develt, ILEA, 1986–87; Dep. County Educn Officer, 1987–88, County Educn Officer, 1989–95, Warwickshire CC. Mem., Nat. Commn on Educn, 1991–93. Member: Council, PSI, 1994–; Basic Skills Agency, 1998–; Prince's Trust Adv. Gp, 2001–. Hon. Pres., BEMAS, 1995–99. Hon. FCP 1994. *Publications:* contributions to: Dear Lord James, 1971; Teachers for Tomorrow (ed Calthrop and Owens), 1971; Education 2000 (ed Wilby and Pluckrose), 1979; The School and the University, an International Perspective (ed Burton R. Clark), 1984; School Co-operation: new forms of Governance (ed Ransom and Tomlinson), 1994; (ed jtly) Success Against the Odds, 1995; Shifting Gear: changing patterns of educational governance in Europe, 2000; (ed) Success Against the Odds—5 Years On, 2001. *Recreations:* European painting, writing and films; politics, opera. *Address:* 12 Dale Close, Oxford OX1 1TU. *T:* and *Fax:* (01865) 721372.

MADGE, James Richard, CB 1976; Deputy Secretary, Department of the Environment, on secondment as Chief Executive, Housing Corporation, 1973–84; *b* 18 June 1924; *s* of James Henry Madge and Elisabeth May Madge; *m* 1955, Alice June Annette (*d* 1975), *d* of late Major Horace Reid, Jamaica; two *d*. *Educ:* Bexhill Co. Sch.; New Coll., Oxford. Pilot in RAFVR, 1942–46. Joined Min. of Civil Aviation, 1947; Principal Private Secretary: to Paymaster-General, 1950–51; to Minister of Transport, 1960–61; Asst Secretary, Min. of Transport, 1961–66; Under-Sec., Road Safety Gp, 1966–69; Head of Policy Planning, 1969–70; Under-Sec., Housing Directorate, DoE, 1971–73. Churchwarden, St Mary Abbots, Kensington, 1987–. *Recreations:* lawn tennis, swimming, furniture-making. *Address:* 56 Gordon Place, Kensington, W8 4JF. *T:* (020) 7937 1927.

MADONNA; *see* Ciccone, M. L. V.

MAEHLER, Prof. Herwig Gustav Theodor, FBA 1986; Professor of Papyrology, University College London, 1981–2000, now Emeritus; *b* 29 April 1935; *s* of Ludwig and Lisa Maehler; *m* 1963, Margaret Anderson; two *d*. *Educ:* Katharineum Lübeck (Grammar Sch.); Univs of Hamburg (PhD Classics and Classical Archaeol.), Tübingen and Basel. British Council Schol., Oxford, 1961–62; Res. Assistant, Hamburg Univ., 1962–63, Hamburg Univ. Liby, 1963–64; Keeper of Greek Papyri, Egyptian Mus., W Berlin, 1964–79; Habilitation for Classics, 1975, Lectr in Classics, 1975–79, Free Univ. of W Berlin; Reader in Papyrology, UCL, 1979–81. Corresp. Mem., German Archaeol Inst., 1979. *Publications:* Die Auffassung des Dichterberufs im frühen Griechentum bis zur Zeit Pindars, 1963; Die Handschriften des S Jacobi-Kirche Hamburg, 1967; Urkunden römischer Zeit, (BGU XI), 1968; Papyri aus Hermupolis (BGU XII), 1974; Die Lieder des Bakchylides, Part 1, 2 vols, 1982, Part 2, 1997; (with G. Cavallo) Greek Bookhands of the Early Byzantine Period, 1987; editions of Bacchylides and Pindar, 1970, 1987, 1989, 1992; articles in learned jls. *Address:* Birkenhöhe 17, 22949 Ammersbek, Germany.

MAFFEY, family name of **Baron Rugby**.

MAGEE, Bryan; writer; Visiting Professor, King's College, London, 1994–2000 (Hon. Senior Research Fellow in History of Ideas, 1984–94); *b* 12 April 1930; *s* of Frederick Magee and Sheila (*née* Lynch); *m* 1954, Ingrid Söderlund (marr. diss.); one *d*. *Educ:* Christ's Hospital; Lycée Hôche, Versailles; Keble Coll., Oxford (Open Scholar; MA 1956; Hon. Fellow, 1994). Pres., Oxford Union, 1953. Henry Fellow in Philosophy, Yale, 1955–56. Music criticism for many publications, 1959–; Theatre Critic, The Listener, 1966–67; regular columnist, The Times, 1974–76. Mem., Arts Council, 1993–94 (Chm., Music Panel, 1993–94). Current Affairs Reporter on TV; Critic of the Arts on BBC Radio 3; own broadcast series include: Conversations with Philosophers, BBC Radio 3, 1970–71; Men of Ideas, BBC TV 2, 1978; The Great Philosophers, BBC TV 2, 1987; What's the Big Idea?, BBC Radio 3, 1991–92. Silver Medal, RTS, 1978. Contested (Lab): Mid-Bedfordshire, Gen. Elec., 1959; By-Elec., 1960; MP (Lab 1974–82, SDP 1982–83) Leyton, Feb. 1974–1983; contested (SDP) Leyton, 1983. Elected to Critics' Circle, 1970, Pres., 1983–84. Judge: for Evening Standard annual Opera Award, 1973–84; for Laurence Olivier Annual Opera Awards, 1990–91, 1993–95; Chm. of Judges, Royal Philharmonic Soc. opera awards, 1991–2000. Lectr in Philosophy, Balliol Coll., Oxford, 1970–71; Visiting Fellow: All Souls Coll., Oxford, 1973–74; New Coll., Oxford, 1995; Merton Coll., Oxford, 1998; St Catherine's Coll., Oxford, 2000; Peterhouse, Cambridge, 2001; Vis. Schol., 1991–93, Vis. Fellow, 1993–94, Wolfson Coll., Oxford; Vis. Schol. in Philos., Harvard, 1979, Sydney Univ., 1982, Univ. of California, Santa Barbara, 1989 (Girvetz Meml Lectr); German Marshall Fund Fellow to USA, 1989; Vis. Prof., Trinity Univ., San Antonio, Texas, 1997. Charles Carter Lectr, Univ. of Lancaster, 1985; Bithell Meml Lectr, Univ. of London, 1989. Lecturer: Seattle Opera, 1989, 1991, 1995; Royal Opera House,

1990; San Francisco Opera, 1990; Belgian Nat. Opera, 1991; Bayreuth Festspielhaus, 1994; Los Angeles Opera, 1995 and 1997; Hawaii Opera, 2000; Royal Inst. of Philosophy, 1992, 1994. Hon. Pres., Edinburgh Univ. Philosophy Soc., 1987–88. Governor, 1979–, Mem. Council, 1982–, Ditchley Foundn; Acad. Visitor, LSE, 1994–96. Hon. Fellow, QMC, 1988; Fellow: QMW, 1989; Royal Philharmonic Soc., 1990. *Publications:* Crucifixion and Other Poems, 1951; Go West Young Man, 1958; To Live in Danger, 1960; The New Radicalism, 1962; The Democratic Revolution, 1964; Towards 2000, 1965; One in Twenty, 1966; The Television Interviewer, 1966; Aspects of Wagner, 1968, rev. edn 1988; Modern British Philosophy, 1971; Popper, 1973; Facing Death, 1977; Men of Ideas, 1978, 2nd edn as Talking Philosophy, 2001; The Philosophy of Schopenhauer, 1983, rev. edn 1997; The Great Philosophers, 1987; Misunderstanding Schopenhauer, 1990; (with M. Milligan) On Blindness, 1995, 2nd edn, as Sight Unseen, 1998; Confessions of a Philosopher, 1997; The Story of Philosophy, 1998; Wagner and Philosophy, 2000. *Recreations:* music, theatre. *Address:* Wolfson College, Oxford OX2 6UD. *Clubs:* Garrick, Savile.

MAGEE, Ian; Chief Executive, Court Service, Lord Chancellor's Department, since 1998; *b* 9 July 1946. *Educ:* Leeds Univ. (BA Hist.). Joined DHSS, 1969; Private Sec. to Minister for Social Security, 1976–78; Asst Controller, Management Services, London N, 1983–84; seconded to Cabinet Office Enterprise Unit, 1984–86; Department of Social Security, 1986–98: Dep. to Dir of Personnel, 1986–89; Territorial Dir, Benefits Agency, 1990–93; Chief Exec., IT Services Agency, 1993–98. Non-exec. Dir, Laing Management Contracting, 1989–91. Member Advisory Board: Lancaster Univ. Sch. of Management, 1994–98; KPMG Impact, 1994–99. *Recreations:* sport, slow horses, Leeds United. *Address:* (office) Court Service, Southside, 105 Victoria Street, SW1E 6QT. *Club:* MCC.

MAGGS, Air Vice-Marshal William Jack, CB 1967; OBE 1943; MA; Fellow and Domestic Bursar, Keble College, Oxford, 1969–77, Emeritus Fellow since 1981; *b* 2 Feb. 1914; *s* of late Frederick Wilfrid Maggs, Bristol; *m* 1940, Margaret Grace, *d* of late Thomas Liddell Hetherington, West Hartlepool; one *s* one *d*. *Educ:* Bristol Grammar Sch.; St John's Coll., Oxford (MA). Management Trainee, 1936–38. Joined RAF, 1939; Unit and Training duties, 1939–42; Student, Staff Coll., 1942; Planning Staffs, and participated in, Algerian, Sicilian and Italian landings, 1942–44; SESO Desert Air Force, 1944; Jt Admin. Plans Staff, Cabinet Offices, Whitehall, 1945–48; Instructor, RAF Coll., Cranwell, 1948–50; comd No 9 Maintenance Unit, 1950–52; exchange officer at HQ, USAF Washington, 1952–54; Student Jt Services Staff Coll., 1954–55; No 3 Maintenance Unit, 1955–57; Dep. Director of Equipment, Air Ministry, 1958–59; SESO, HQ, NEAF, Cyprus, 1959–61; Student, Imperial Defence Coll., 1962; Director of Mech. Transport and Marine Craft, Air Ministry, 1963–64; Director of Equipment, Ministry of Defence (Air), 1964–67; SASO, RAF Maintenance Comd, 1967–69. Group Captain, 1958; Air Commodore, 1963; Air Vice-Marshal, 1967. Governor, Bristol Grammar Sch., 1980–89. *Recreations:* golf, gardening. *Club:* Royal Air Force.

MAGINNESS, Alban Alphonsus; barrister; Member (SDLP) Belfast North, Northern Ireland Assembly, since 1998; *b* 9 July 1950; *s* of Alphonsus and Patricia Maginness; *m* 1978, Carmel McWilliams; three *s* five *d*. *Educ:* St Malachy's Coll., Belfast; Univ. of Ulster (BA Hons Mod. Hist. 1973); Queen's Univ., Belfast. Called to the Bar: NI, 1976; Ireland, 1984; in practice at NI Bar, specialising in civil litigation. Chm., SDLP, 1985–91. Mem. (SDLP) Belfast CC, 1985–; Lord Mayor of Belfast, 1997–98 (first SDLP Mayor). Contested (SDLP) Belfast North, 1997, 2001. Chm., Regl Develt Cttee, NI Assembly, 1999–. Member: NI Forum, 1996–98; Forum for Peace and Reconciliation, Dublin, 1994–96. Trustee, Ormeau Baths Gall., 1994–; Mem. Bd, Ulster Orch., 1997–. *Recreations:* theatre, history, reading, walking, music. *Address:* 96 Somerton Road, Belfast BT15 4DE. *T:* (028) 9077 0558; (office) 228 Antrim Road, Belfast BT15 2AN. *T:* (028) 9022 0520.

MAGINNIS, family name of **Baron Maginnis of Drumglass**.

MAGINNIS OF DRUMGLASS, Baron *cr* 2001 (Life Peer), of Carnteel in the County of Tyrone; **Kenneth Wiggins Maginnis;** *b* 21 Jan. 1938; *m* 1961, Joy Stewart; two *s* two *d*. *Educ:* Royal Sch., Dungannon; Stranmillis Coll., Belfast, Served UDR, 1970–81, commissioned 1972, Major. Party spokesman on internal security and defence. Mem., Dungannon District Council, 1981–93; Mem. (UU) Fermanagh and S Tyrone, NI Assembly, 1982–86. Contested (UU) Fermanagh and S Tyrone, Aug. 1981. MP (UU) Fermanagh and S Tyrone, 1983–2001 (resigned seat Dec. 1985 in protest against Anglo-Irish Agreement; re-elected Jan. 1986). Mem., H of C Select Cttee on Defence, 1984–86, on NI, 1994–97. Vice Pres., UU Council, 1990–. Chm., Moygashel Community Develt Assoc. *Address:* House of Lords, SW1A 0PW; 1 Park Lane, Dungannon, Co. Tyrone.

MAGINNIS, John Edward; JP; *b* 7 March 1919; *s* of late Edward Maginnis and Mary E. Maginnis, Mandeville Hall, Mullahead, Tanderagee; *m* 1944, Dorothy, *d* of late R. J. Rusk, JP, of Cavanaleck, Fivemiletown, Co. Tyrone; one *s* four *d*. *Educ:* Moyallon Sch., Co. Down; Portadown Technical Coll. Served War of 1939–45, Royal Ulster Constabulary. MP (UU) Armagh, Oct. 1959–Feb. 1974. JP, Co. Armagh, 1956. Group Secretary, North Armagh Group, Ulster Farmers' Union, 1956–59. Hon. LLD, 1990. *Recreations:* football, hunting, shooting. *Address:* Mandeville Hall, 68 Mullahead Road, Tandragee, Craigavon, Co. Armagh, N Ireland BT62 2LB. *T:* (028) 3884 0260.

MAGNUS, Sir Laurence (Henry Philip), 3rd Bt *cr* 1917, of Tangley Hill, Wonersh; Vice Chairman, Lexicon Partners Ltd, since 2001; non-executive Chairman: Ins-Sure Services Ltd, since 2001; Red Box Systems Ltd, since 2001; *b* 24 Sept. 1955; *s* of Hilary Barrow Magnus, QC (*d* 1987), and of Rosemary Vera Anne Magnus (*née* Masefield); *S* uncle, Sir Philip Magnus-Allcroft, 2nd Bt, CBE, 1988; *m* 1983, Jocelyn Mary, *d* of R. H. F. Stanton; two *s* one *d*. *Educ:* Eton College; Christ Church, Oxford (MA). Corporate Finance Executive, 1977–84, Head of Corporate Finance, Singapore Branch, 1984–87, Samuel Montagu & Co. Ltd; Group Country Manager, Singapore Region, Midland Bank plc (Singapore), 1987–88; Exec. Dir, 1988–95 and Dep. Head, UK Corporate Finance Div., 1994–95, Samuel Montagu & Co. Ltd; Dir, Phoenix Securities Ltd, 1995–97 (acquired by Donaldson, Lufkin & Jenrette, 1997); Managing Director: Donaldson, Lufkin & Jenrette Internat., 1997–2000 (acquired by Credit Suisse First Boston, 2000); Credit Suisse First Boston, 2000–01. Mem., Finance Cttee, Nat. Trust, 1997–. *Recreations:* reading, fishing, walking. *Heir: s* Thomas Henry Philip Magnus, *b* 30 Sept. 1985. *Address:* c/o Lexicon Partners Ltd, No 1 Cornhill, EC3V 3ND. *T:* (020) 7743 6337, *Fax:* (020) 7743 6331; *e-mail:* lmagnus@lexiconpartners.com. *Clubs:* Brooks's, City of London; Millennium.

MAGNUS, Prof. Philip Douglas, FRS 1985; R. P. Doherty, Jr–Welch Regents Professor of Chemistry, University of Texas at Austin, since 1989; *b* 15 April 1943; *s* of Arthur Edwin and Lillian Edith Magnus; *m* 1963, Andrea Claire (*née* Parkinson); two *s*. *Educ:* Imperial College, Univ. of London (BSc, ARCS, PhD, DSc). Asst Lectr, 1967–70, Lectr, 1970–75, Imperial College; Associate Prof., Ohio State Univ., 1975–81; Prof. of Chemistry, 1981–87, Distinguished Prof., 1987–88, Indiana Univ. Corday Morgan Medal, RSC, 1978; Janssen Prize, Belgian Chemical Soc. and Janssen Foundn, 1992; Robert Robinson Medal, RSC, 1996. *Publications:* papers in leading chemistry jls. *Recreations:* golf, chess. *Address:* 3111D Windsor Road, Austin, TX 78703, USA. *T:* (512) 4713966.

MAGNUSSON, Magnus, Hon. KBE 1989; MA (Oxon); FRSE; writer and broadcaster; *b* 12 Oct. 1929; *s* of late Sigursteinn Magnusson, Icelandic Consul-Gen. for Scotland, and Ingibjorg Sigurdardottir; *m* 1954, Mamie Baird; one *s* three *d* (and one *s* decd). *Educ:* Edinburgh Academy; Jesus Coll., Oxford (MA; Hon. Fellow, 1990). Subseq. Asst Editor, Scottish Daily Express and Asst Editor, The Scotsman. Presenter, various television and radio programmes including: Chronicle, 1966–80; Mastermind, 1972–97; Pebble Mill at One; BC, The Archaeology of the Bible Lands; Tonight; Cause for Concern; All Things Considered; Living Legends; Vikings!; Birds For All Seasons. Editor: The Bodley Head Archaeologies; Popular Archaeology, 1979–80. Chairman: Ancient Monuments Bd for Scotland, 1981–89; Cairngorms Working Party, 1991–93; NCC for Scotland, 1991–92; Scottish Natural Heritage, 1992–99. Stewards, York Archaeol Trust; Scottish Churches Architectural Heritage Trust, 1978–85; Scottish Youth Theatre, 1976–78; Member: Bd of Trustees, Nat. Museums of Scotland, 1985–89; UK Cttee for European Year of the Environment, 1987; Pres., RSPB, 1985–90; Hon. Vice-President: Age Concern Scotland; RSSPCC. Rector, Edinburgh Univ., 1975–78. FSAScot 1974; FRSE 1980; FRSA 1983; Hon. FRIAS 1987; FSA 1991; FRSGS 1991. Dr *hc* Edinburgh, 1978; DUniv: York, 1981; Paisley, 1993; Hon. DLitt: Strathclyde, 1993; Napier Univ., 1994; Glasgow, 2001; Glasgow Caledonian, 2001. Scottish Television Personality of the Year, 1974; Iceland Media Award, 1985; Medlicott Medal, HA, 1989. Knight of the Order of the Falcon (Iceland), 1975, Knight Commander, 1986; Silver Jubilee Medal, 1977. *Publications:* Introducing Archaeology, 1972; Viking Expansion Westwards, 1973; The Clacken and the Slate (Edinburgh Academy, 1824–1974), 1974; Hammer of the North (Norse mythology), 1976, 2nd edn, Viking Hammer of the North, 1980; BC, The Archaeology of the Bible Lands, 1977; Landlord or Tenant? a view of Irish history, 1978; Iceland, 1979; Vikings!, 1980; Magnus on the Move, 1980; Treasures of Scotland, 1981; Lindisfarne: The Cradle Island, 1984; Iceland Saga, 1987; I've Started, So I'll Finish, 1997; Rum: nature's island, 1997; Magnus Magnusson's Quiz Book, 2000; Scotland: the story of a nation, 2000; *translations:* The Icelandic Sagas, Vol. I, 1999, Vol. II, 2002; (all with Hermann Pálsson): Njal's Saga, 1960; The Vinland Sagas, 1965; King Harald's Saga, 1966; Laxdaela Saga, 1969; (all by Halldor Laxness): The Atom Station, 1961; Paradise Reclaimed, 1962; The Fish Can Sing, 1966; World Light, 1969; Christianity Under Glacier, 1973; (by Samivel) Golden Iceland, 1967; *contributor:* The Glorious Privilege, 1967; The Future of the Highlands, 1968; Strange Stories, Amazing Facts, 1975; Pass the Port, 1976; Book of Bricks, 1978; Chronicle, 1978; Discovery of Lost Worlds, 1979; Pass the Port Again, 1981; Second Book of Bricks, 1981; *introduced:* Ancient China, 1974; The National Trust for Scotland Guide, 1976; Karluk, 1976; More Lives Than One?, 1976; Atlas of World Geography, 1977; Face to Face with the Turin Shroud, 1978; Modern Bible Atlas, 1979; Living Legends, 1980; The Hammer and the Cross, 1980; Household Ghosts, 1981; Great Books for Today, 1981; The Voyage of Odin's Raven, 1982; Robert Burns: Bawdy Verse & Folksongs, 1982; Mastermind 4, 1982; Northern Voices, 1984; The Village, 1985; Secrets of the Bible Seas, 1985; Beowulf, 1987; Complete Book of British Birds, 1988; Trustlands, 1989; The Wealth of a Nation, 1989; The Return of Cultural Treasures, 1990; William Morris: Icelandic Journals, 1996; *edited:* Echoes in Stone, 1983; Readers Digest Book of Facts, 1985; Chambers Biographical Dictionary, 5th edn 1990; The Nature of Scotland, 1991, 2nd edn 1997. *Recreations:* digging and delving. *Address:* Blairskaith House, Balmore-Torrance, Glasgow G64 4AX. *T:* (01360) 620226.

MAGONET, Rabbi Prof. Jonathan David; Principal, since 1985, Professor, since 1996, Leo Baeck College; *b* 2 Aug. 1942; *s* of Alexander Philip and Esther Magonet; *m* 1974, Dorothea (*née* Foth); one *s* one *d*. *Educ:* Westminster Sch.; Middlesex Hosp. Med. Sch. (MB BS). Leo Baeck Coll.; Univ. of Heidelberg (PhD). Junior hosp. doctor, 1966–67; Leo Baeck College: Rabbinic studies, 1967–71; Head of Dept of Bible Studies, 1974–85. Vis. Fellow, Tel Aviv Univ., 1990–91; Guest Professor: Kirchliche Hochschule, Wuppertal, Germany, 1992–93, 1995; Carl van Ossietzky Univ., Oldenburg, 1999. Vice-Pres., World Union for Progressive Judaism, 1988–. Co-Editor, European Judaism, 1992– (Mem. Editl Bd, 1978–); Member, Editorial Board: Christian-Jewish Relations, 1987–; Jl of Progressive Judaism, 1993–. FRSA. Verdienstkreuz (Germany), 1999. *Publications:* Form and Meaning: studies in literary techniques in the Book of Jonah, 1976; (ed jtly) Forms of Prayer, vol. I, Daily and Sabbath Prayerbook, 1977, vol. III, Days of Awe Prayerbook, 1985, vol. II, Pilgrim Festival Prayerbook, 1995; (ed jtly) The Guide to the Here and Hereafter, 1988; A Rabbi's Bible, 1991; Bible Lives, 1992; (jtly) How to Get Up When Life Gets You Down, 1992; (ed jtly) The Little Blue Book of Prayer, 1993; A Rabbi Reads the Psalms, 1994; (jtly) Kindred Spirits, 1995; (ed) Jewish Explorations of Sexuality, 1995; The Subversive Bible, 1997; (ed) Das Jüdische Gebetbuch, 2 vols, 1997; Mit der Bibel durch das Jüdische Jahr, 1998; The Explorer's Guide to Judaism, 1998; (jtly) Sun, Sand and Soul, 1999; Abraham-Jesus-Mohammed: interreligiöser dialog aus Jüdischer perspektive, 2000; From Autumn to Summer: a Biblical journey through the Jewish year, 2000. *Address:* 18 Wellfield Avenue, N10 2EA. *T:* (020) 8444 3025.

MAGOS, Adam László, MD; Consultant Obstetrician and Gynaecologist, and Hon. Senior Lecturer, Royal Free Hospital, London, since 1991; Consultant Gynaecologist, King Edward VII Hospital for Officers, London, since 1992; *b* 26 Sept. 1953; *s* of László Pál Aurel Magos and Eva Mária Magos (*née* Benjamin); *m* 1991, Anne Cyprienne Coburn; three *s*. *Educ:* Whitgift Sch., Croydon; KCL (BSc 1975); King's Coll. Hosp. Sch. of Medicine (MB BS 1978; MD 1986). MRCOG 1986, FRCOG 1998. House Officer, KCH, 1980–82; Res. Fellow in Obstetrics and Gynaecol., Dulwich Hosp., 1982–84; Registrar, KCH and Dulwich Hosp., 1984–86; Lectr, Nuffield Dept of Obstetrics and Gynaecology, John Radcliffe Hosp., Univ. of Oxford, 1986–90; Sen. Lectr and Hon. Consultant, Academic Dept of Obstetrics and Gynaecology, Royal Free Hosp., Univ. of London, 1990–91. Treas., British Soc. for Gynaecol Endoscopy, 1989–92; Member: Wkg Gp on New Technol. in Endoscopic Gynaecol Surgery, RCOG, 1993–94; MAS Trng Sub-Cttee, RCOG, 1998–. Hon. Member: Aust. Gynaecol Endoscopy Soc., 1994; Egyptian Soc. for Gynaecol Endoscopy, 1996. Ed., Gynaecological Endoscopy, 1990–93. Syntex Award, Internat. Soc. of Reproductive Medicine, 1988. *Publications:* (ed jtly) Endometrial Ablation, 1993; contribs to books on premenstrual syndrome, hysteroscopic surgery and laparoscopic surgery and to professional jls. *Recreations:* music, cooking, saxophone. *Address:* King Edward VII Hospital for Officers, Beaumont Street, W1N 2AA. *T:* (020) 7486 4411; Royal Free Hospital, Pond Street, NW3 2QG. *T:* (020) 7431 1321.

MAGOWAN, Ven. Alistair James; Archdeacon of Dorset, since 2000; *b* 10 Feb. 1955; *s* of Samuel and Marjorie Magowan; *m* 1979, (Margaret) Louise Magowan (*née* Atkin); one *s* two *d*. *Educ:* King's Sch., Worcester; Leeds Univ. (BSc Hons Animal Physiol. and Nutrition); Trinity Coll., Bristol (DipHE). Ordained deacon, 1981, priest, 1982; Curate: St John the Baptist, Owlerton, Sheffield, 1981–84; St Nicholas, Durham, 1984–89; Chaplain, St Aidan's Coll., Durham Univ., 1984–89; Vicar, St John the Baptist, Egham, 1989–2000; RD, Runnymede, 1993–98. Canon, Salisbury Cathedral, 2000–. Chm., Guildford Diocesan Bd of Educn, 1995–2000. *Recreations:* walking, fly fishing, oil painting, stamp collecting. *Address:* Bowmoor House, Anvil Road, Pimperne, Blandford, Dorset DT11 8UQ.

MAGUIRE, Adrian Edward; National Hunt jockey; *b* 29 April 1971; *s* of Joseph Maguire and of late Phyllis Maguire; *m* 1995, Sabrina; one *d. Educ:* Kilmessan Nat. Sch.; Trim Vocational Sch. Winner: Irish Grand National, on Omerta, 1991; Hennessy Gold Cup, on Sibton Abbey, 1992; Cheltenham Gold Cup, on Cool Ground, 1992; King George VI Chase, on Barton Bank, 1993; Queen Mother Champion Chase, on Viking Flagship, 1994; Scottish National, on Baronet, 1998; Whitbread Gold Cup, on Call It A Day, 1998. *Address:* 17 Willes Close, Faringdon, Oxon SN7 7DU.

MAGUIRE, (Albert) Michael, MC 1945; MM 1943; QC 1967; *b* 30 Dec. 1922; *s* of late Richard Maguire and Ruth Maguire. *Educ:* Hutton Grammar Sch.; Trinity Hall, Cambridge (BA 1948). Served War of 1939–45, North Irish Horse (Captain), in Africa (MM) and Italy (MC). Inns of Court Regt, 1946. War Crimes Investigation Unit, 1946. Called to the Bar, Middle Temple, 1949 (Harmsworth Scholar); Bencher, 1973; Leader, Northern Circuit, 1980–84. Last Recorder of Carlisle (1970–71). *Address:* Goldsmith Building, Temple, EC4Y 7BL; Chestnuts, 89 Lower Bank Road, Fulwood, Preston PR2 4NU. *T:* (01772) 719291.

MAGUIRE, (Benjamin) Waldo, OBE 1973; *b* 31 May 1920; *s* of Benjamin Maguire and Elizabeth Ann Eldon; *m* 1944, Lilian Joan Martin (*d* 1998); four *s. Educ:* Portadown Coll.; Trinity Coll., Dublin. BA 1st cl. hons Philosophy. Intell. Service, WO and FO, 1942–45; BBC Latin American Service, 1945; BBC Radio News, 1946–55; BBC TV News, 1955; Editor, BBC TV News, 1962–64; Controller, News and Public Affairs, NZ Broadcasting Corp., 1965–66; BBC Controller, NI, 1966–72; Head of Information Programmes, NZ TV2, 1975–76. *Recreations:* gardening, conversation, angling. *Address:* c/o The Sloane Nursing Home, Beckenham, Kent.

MAGUIRE, Hugh, FRAM; violinist and conductor; Director of Strings, Britten-Pears School for Advanced Music Studies, since 1978; Professor of Violin, Royal Academy of Music, since 1957; *b* 2 Aug. 1926; *m* 1st, 1953, Suzanne Lewis (marr. diss. 1987), of International Ballet; two *s* three *d*; 2nd, 1988, Tricia Catchpole. *Educ:* Belvedere Coll., SJ, Dublin; Royal Academy of Music, London (David Martin); Paris (Georges Enesco). Leader: Bournemouth Symphony Orchestra, 1952–56; London Symphony Orchestra, 1956–62; BBC Symphony Orchestra, 1962–67; Cremona String Quartet, 1966–68; Allegri String Quartet, 1968–76; Melos Ensemble, 1972–85; Orch. of Royal Opera House, Covent Garden, 1983–91. Artistic Dir, Irish Youth Orch. String coach, European Commn Youth Orch. Mem., Irish Arts Council. Hon. MMus Hull, 1975; Hon. DLitt Univ. of Ulster, 1986; Hon. DMus NUI, 1992. Harriet Cohen Internat. Award; Councils Gold Medal (Ireland), 1963; Cobbett Medal, Musicians' Co., 1982. *Address:* Manor Farm, Benhall, Suffolk IP17 1HN. *T:* (01728) 603245.

MAGUIRE, John Joseph; QC (Scot) 1990; Sheriff Principal of Tayside, Central and Fife, 1990–98; *b* 30 Nov. 1934; *y s* of Robert Maguire, Solicitor, Glasgow, and Julia Maguire; *m* 1962, Eva O'Hara, Tralee, Co. Kerry; two *s* two *d. Educ:* St Mary's Coll., Blairs; Pontifical Gregorian Univ., Rome (PhL 1955); Edinburgh Univ. (LLB 1958). Mem., Faculty of Advocates, 1958; Standing Junior to MPBW, 1963–68; Sheriff Substitute: Airdrie, 1968; Glasgow, 1973. Member: Deptl Cttee on Alternatives to Prosecution, 1977–82; Parole Bd for Scotland, 2000–. Pres., Sheriffs' Assoc., 1989–90 (Sec., 1982–87). *Recreations:* reading, pottering in the garden. *Address:* Spring Lodge, Hatton Way, Perth PH2 7DP. *T:* (01738) 636260. *Club:* Royal Perth Country and City.

MAGUIRE, Mairead C.; *see* Corrigan-Maguire.

MAGUIRE, Michael; *see* Maguire, A. M.

MAGUIRE, Waldo; *see* Maguire, B. W.

MAHATHIR bin MOHAMAD, Dato Seri Dr; MHR for Kubang Pasu, since 1974; Prime Minister of Malaysia, since 1981; *b* 20 Dec. 1925. *Educ:* Sultan Abdul Hamid Coll.; College of Medicine, Singapore (MB BS). Medical Officer, Kedah and Perlis, 1953–57; in private practice, 1957–64. MHR for Kota Star Selatan, 1964–69; Mem., Senate, 1972–74; Minister of: Education, 1974–77; Trade and Industry, 1977–81; Home Affairs, 1986–99; Dep. Prime Minister, 1976–81. President, United Malays Nat. Organisation, 1981– (Mem., Supreme Council, 1972–). *Publication:* The Malay Dilemma, 1969; The Way Forward (essays), 1998. *Address:* Office of the Prime Minister, 50502 Kuala Lumpur, Malaysia.

MAHER, Christina Rose, OBE 1994; Founder and Director, Plain English Campaign, since 1979; *b* 21 April 1938; *d* of late Fred Lewington and Maureen (*née* Collen); *m* 1959, George Bernard Maher; three *s* one *d. Educ:* St Cecilia's Sch., Liverpool. Community worker, 1969–98. Founder: Tuebrook Bugle (first community newspaper), 1971; Liverpool News (first newspaper for people with learning difficulties), 1974. Chm., Impact Printers Foundn, 1974–98; Founder, Salford Form Market (for NCC), 1975. Hon. MA Manchester, 1995; DUniv Open, 1997. *Publications:* Plain English Story, 1980; How to Write Letters/Reports in Plain English, 1995; Decade of Drivel, 1996; Language on Trial, 1996; A to Z for Lawyers, 1996. *Recreations:* swimming, dance, theatre, driving, keep fit. *Address:* Thorny Lee Farm, Combs, Derbys SK23 9UJ. *T:* (01298) 813109.

MAHER, Terence; His Honour Judge Maher; a Circuit Judge, since 1995; *b* 20 Dec. 1941; *s* of late John Maher and of Bessie Maher; *m* 1965 (marr. diss. 1983); two *d. Educ:* Burnley Grammar Sch.; Univ. of Manchester. LLB (hons). Admitted Solicitor, 1966; articled to Town Clerk, Burnley; Asst Sol., City of Bradford, 1966–68; Prosecuting Sol., Birmingham Corp., 1968–70; Dep. Pros. Sol., Thames Valley Police, 1970–73; Asst Sol. and partner, Cole & Cole, Oxford, 1973–83; Metropolitan Stipendiary Magistrate, 1983–95; a Chm., Inner London Juvenile, subseq. Youth, Courts and Family Proceedings Court, 1985–95; a Recorder, 1989–95. Gen. Sec., Univ. of Manchester Students' Union, 1962–63; Chm., Chipping Norton Round Table, 1975–76; Treasurer/Vice-Chm. and Chm., Oxford and District Solicitors' Assoc., 1980–83; Mem., Law Society Standing Cttee on Criminal Law, 1980–85. Mem. Editl Bd, Jl of Criminal Law, 1982–95. *Recreations:* walking, reading, anything to do with France and the French. *Address:* c/o Luton Crown Court, 7 George Street, Luton LU1 2AA. *Club:* Frewen (Oxford).

MAHER, Terence Anthony, FCCA; Chairman: Maher Booksellers Ltd, since 1995; Race Dynamics Ltd, since 1998; *b* 5 Dec. 1935; *s* of late Herbert and Lillian Maher; *m* 1960, Barbara (*née* Grunbaum); three *s. Educ:* Xaverian Coll., Manchester. ACCA 1960, FCCA 1970. Carborundum Co. Ltd, 1961–69; First National Finance Corp., 1969–72; Founder, Chm. and Chief Exec., Pentos plc, 1972–93; Chairman: Dillons Bookstores, 1977–93; Athena Internat., 1980–93; Ryman, 1987–93; Tempus Publishing (formerly Chalford Publishing) Co. Ltd, 1994–98. Mem., Adv. Council on Libraries, 1997–98. Contested (L): Accrington, 1964; Runcorn, 1966. Founder Trustee, Lib Dem, 1988–. Trustee, Photographers' Gall., 1994–97. FRSA 1988. Led successful campaign to abolish price control on books. *Publications:* (jtly) Counterblast, 1965; (jtly) Effective Politics, 1966; Against My Better Judgement (memoir), 1994. *Recreations:* reading, ski-ing, tennis, walking, music, bridge. *Address:* 33 Clarence Terrace, Regent's Park, NW1 4RD. *T:* (020) 7723 4254; The Old House, Whichford, near Shipston-on-Stour, Warwickshire CV36 5PG. *T:* (01608) 684614. *Club:* Savile.

MAHER, Very Rev. William Francis, SJ; Provincial Superior of the English Province of the Society of Jesus, 1976–81; *b* 20 June 1916. *Educ:* St Ignatius' College, Stamford Hill; Heythrop College, Oxon. STL. Entered the Society of Jesus, 1935; ordained priest, 1948; Principal, Heythrop College, 1974–76. *Address:* Our Lady of the Rosary, 40 Margaret Street, Ammanford, Dyfed SA18 2NP. *T:* (01269) 592533.

MAHFOUZ, Naguib; Egyptian novelist; *b* Gamallya, Cairo, 11 Dec. 1911; *s* of Abdel Aziz Ibrahim and Fatma Mostapha Mahfouz; *m* 1954, Attiyah-Allah; two *d. Educ:* King Fuad I Univ. (now Cairo Univ.). Civil servant, 1934; Sec., King Fuad I Univ., 1936–38; Min. of Religious Affairs, 1939–54; Dept Arts and Censorship Bd, 1954–59; Dir, Foundn for Cinema, State Cinema Orgn, Cairo, 1959–69; cons. cinema affairs, Min. of Culture, 1969–71. Staff mem., Ar-Risala; contribs to Al-Hilal, Al-Ahram. Hon. Mem., Amer. Acad. and Inst. of Arts and Letters. Nat. Prize for Letters, Egypt, 1970. Collar of the Republic, 1972; Nobel Prize for Literature, 1988. *Publications fiction:* Hams al-junun, 1938; 'Abath al-aqdar (Games of Fate), 1939; Radubis (Radobis), 1943; Kifah Tibah (The Struggle of Thebes), 1944; Al-Qahira al-jadida (New Cairo), 1945; Khan al-Khalili, 1946; Zuqaq al-middaq (Midaq Alley), 1947; Al-Sarab (The Mirage), 1948; Bidaya wa nihaya (The Beginning and the End), 1949; trilogy, Al-thulathiya: vol. 1, Bayn al-qasrayn (Palace Walk), 1956 (Egyptian State Prize); vol. 2, Qasr al-shawq (Palace of Desire), 1957; vol. 3, Al-Sukkariyya (Sugar Street), 1957; Awlad haritna (Children of Our Alley), 1959; Al-Liss wa'l-kilab (The Thief and the Dogs), 1961; Al-Samman wa'l-kharif (Autumn Quail), 1962; Dunya Allah (God's World), 1962; Al-Tariq (The Search), 1964; Al-Shahhaz (The Beggar), 1965; Bayt sayyi'al-sum'a, 1965; Tharthara fawq al-nil (Adrift on the Nile), 1966; Miramar, 1967; Khammarat al-qitt al-aswad, 1969; Taht al-midhalla, 1969; Hikaya a bi-la bidaya wa-la nihaya, 1971; Shahr al-'asal, 1971; Al-Maraya (Mirrors), 1972; Al-Hubb taht al-matar, 1973; Al-jarima, 1973; Al-Karnak, 1974; Hikayat haratina (Fountain and Tomb), 1975; Qalb al-layl, 1975; Hadrat al-muhtaram (Respected Sir), 1975; Malhamat al-harafish (The Harafish), 1977; Al-hubb fawqa Hadabat al-Haram, 1979; Al-shaytan ya'iz, 1979; Asr al Hubb, 1980; Afrah al-qubba (Wedding Song), 1981; Layali alf layla (Arabian Nights and Days), 1982; Ra'aytu fima yara al-na'im, 1982; Al-Baqi min al-zaman saa, 1982; Amama al'arsh, 1982; Rihlat Ibn Fattuma (The Journey of Ibn Fattouma), 1983; Al-tandhim al-sirri, 1984; Yawm qutila al-zaim (The Day the Leader was Killed), 1985; Al-Aish fi-l-haqiqa (Akhenaton: Dweller in Truth), 1985; Hadith al sabah wa-al-masa, 1987; Sabah al-ward, 1987; Qushtumor, 1988; Al-Fajr al-Kadhib, 1988; Asda al-sira al dhatiyya (Echoes of an Autobiography), 1996. *Address:* (agent) c/o The American University in Cairo Press, 113 Kasr al-Aini Street, Cairo 11511, Egypt. *Fax:* (2) 7941440.

MAHLER, Dr Halfdan Theodor; Director-General, World Health Organization, 1973–88, now Emeritus; Secretary-General, International Planned Parenthood Federation, 1989–95; consultant, international health, since 1996; *b* 21 April 1923; *m* 1957, Dr Ebba Fischer-Simonsen; two *s. Educ:* Univ. of Copenhagen (MD, EOPH). Planning Officer, Internat. Tuberculosis Campaign, Ecuador, 1950–51; Sen. WHO Med. Officer, Nat. TB Programme, India, 1951–61; Chief MO, Tuberculosis Unit, WHO/HQ, Geneva, 1961–69; Dir, Project Systems Analysis, WHO/HQ, Geneva, 1969–70; Asst Dir-Gen., WHO, 1970–73. Hon. FFPHM 1975; Hon. FRSocMed 1976; Hon. FRCGP 1986; Hon. FRSTM&H, 1993; Hon. Fellow: Indian Soc. for Malaria and other Communicable Diseases, Delhi; Faculty of Community Med., RCP, 1975; Hon. Professor: Univ. Nacional Mayor de San Marcos, Lima, Peru, 1980; Fac. of Medicine, Univ. of Chile, 1982; Beijing Med. Coll., China, 1983; Shanghai Med. Univ., 1986; Bartel World Affairs Fellow, Cornell, 1988; Peking Univ., 1994; Hon. Advr, China FPA, 1994. Hon. Fellow: LSHTM, 1979; Coll. of Physicians and Surgeons, Dacca, Bangladesh, 1980; Hon. Member: Soc. médicale de Genève; Union internat. contre la Tuberculose; Société Française d'Hygiène, de Médecine Sociale et Génie Sanitaire, 1977; Med. Assoc. of Argentina, 1985; Latin American Med. Assoc., 1985; Italian Soc. of Tropical Medicine, 1986; APHA, 1988; Swedish Soc. of Medicine, 1988; Hon. Foreign Corresp. Mem., BMA, 1990; Hon. Life Mem., Uganda Medical Assoc., 1976; Assoc. Mem., Belgian Soc. of Trop. Medicine; Mem., Inst. of Medicine, USA, 1989; List of Honour, Internat. Dental Fedn, 1984; Hon. Academician: Nat. Acad. of Medicine, Mexico, 1988; Nat. Acad. of Medicine, Buenos Aires, 1988. FRCP 1981. Hon. LLD: Nottingham, 1975; McMaster, 1989; Exeter, 1990; Toronto, 1990; Hon. MD: Karolinska Inst., 1977; Charles Univ., Prague, and Mahidol Univ., Bangkok, 1982; Aarhus, 1988; Copenhagen, 1988; Aga Khan, Pakistan, 1989; Newcastle upon Tyne, 1990; Hon. Dr de l'Univ. Toulouse (Sciences Sociales), 1977; Hon. Dr Public Health, Seoul Nat. Univ., 1979; Hon DSc: Lagos, 1979; Emory, Atlanta, 1989; SUNY, 1990; Hon. Dr Med. Warsaw Med. Acad., 1980; Hon. Dr Faculty of Medicine, Univ. of Ghent, Belgium, and Universidad Nacional Autonoma de Nicaragua, Managua, 1983; Hon. DHL CUNY, 1989; Dr *hc*: Universidad Nacional 'Federico Villarreal', Lima, Peru, 1980; Semmelweis Univ. of Medicine, Budapest, 1987. Jane Evangelisty Purkyne Medal, Prague, 1974; Comenius Univ. Gold Medal, Bratislava, 1974; Carlo Forlanini Gold Medal, 1975; Ernst Carlsens Foundn Prize, Copenhagen, 1980; Georg Barfred-Pedersen Prize, Copenhagen, 1982; Hagedorn Medal and Prize, Denmark, 1986; Freedom from Want Medal, Roosevelt Inst., 1988; Bourgeoisie d'Honneur, Geneva, 1989; UK–US Hewitt Award, RSM, 1992; Dr Ved Vias Puri Meml Award, FPA of India, 1994; UN Population Award, 1995; Andrija Stampar Award, Assoc. of Schs of Public Health in European Region, 1995. Grand Officier: l'Ordre Nat. du Bénin, 1975; l'Ordre Nat. Voltaïque, 1978; l'Ordre du Mérite, République du Sénégal, 1982; Ordre National Malgache (Madagascar), 1987; Comdr (1st cl.), White Rose Order of Finland, 1983; Commandeur, l'Ordre National du Mali, 1982; Grand Cordon, Order of the Sacred Treasure (Japan), 1988; Storkors Af Dannebrogsordenen (Denmark), 1988; Grand Cross: Order of the Falcon (Iceland), 1988; Order of Merit (Luxembourg), 1990. *Publications:* papers etc on the epidemiology and control of tuberculosis, the political, social, economic and technological priority setting in the health sector, and the application of systems analysis to health care problems. *Recreations:* sailing, ski-ing. *Address:* 12 chemin du Pont-Ceard, 1290 Versoix, Switzerland; *e-mail:* halfdan.mahler@bluewin.ch.

MAHLER, Prof. Robert Frederick, FRCP, FRCPE; Editor, Journal of Royal College of Physicians, 1987–94, Editor Emeritus, since 1994; Consultant Physician, Clinical Research Centre, Northwick Park Hospital, Harrow, 1979–90, retired; *b* 31 Oct. 1924; *s* of Felix Mahler and Olga Lowy; *m* 1951, Maureen Calvert; two *s. Educ:* Edinburgh Academy; Edinburgh Univ. BSc; MB, ChB. Research fellowships and univ. posts in medicine, biochemistry and clinical pharmacology at various med. schs and univs: in Gt Britain: Royal Postgrad. Med. Sch., Guy's Hosp., Manchester, Dundee, Cardiff; in USA: Harvard Univ., Univ. of Indiana; in Sweden: Karolinska Inst., Stockholm; Prof. of Med., Univ. of Wales, 1970–79. Royal College of Physicians: Mem. Council, 1974–76; Censor, 1976–78; Bradshaw Lectr, 1977. Member: MRC, 1977–81; Commonwealth Scholarship Commn, 1980–93; Council, Imperial Cancer Res. Fund, 1984–94; Res. Cttee, British Diabetic Assoc., 1984–87; Scientific Co-ord. Cttee, Arthritis and Rheumatism Council,

1986–91. *Publications:* contribs to British and Amer. med. and scientific jls. *Recreations:* opera, music, theatre. *Address:* 14 Manley Street, NW1 8LT. *Club:* Royal Society of Medicine.

MAHMOOD, Khalid; MP (Lab) Birmingham Perry Barr, since 2001; *b* 1962. Formerly: engr, advr, Danish Internat. Trade Union. Mem., Birmingham CC, 1990–93. *Address:* (office) 1 George Street, West Bromwich, West Midlands B70 6NT; c/o House of Commons, SW1A 0AA.

MAHON, Alice; MP (Lab) Halifax, since 1987; *b* 28 Sept. 1937; *m*; two *s*. *Educ:* Bradford Univ. (BA Hons). Lectr, Bradford and Ilkley Community Coll. Member: Calderdale Bor. Council, 1982–87; Calderdale DHA. PPS to Sec. of State for Culture, Media and Sport, 1997. Mem., Select Cttee on Health, 1991–97. Mem., Nato Parly (formerly N Atlantic) Assembly, 1992–. *Address:* House of Commons, SW1A 0AA.

MAHON, Charles Joseph; His Honour Judge Mahon; a Circuit Judge, since 1989; *b* 16 Aug. 1939; *s* of late Frank and Amy Agnes Mahon; *m* 1974, Lavinia Gough (*née* Breaks); one *d* and one step *s* two step *d*. *Educ:* Chetham's Hosp.; Gonville and Caius Coll., Cambridge (BA, LLB). Called to the Bar, Gray's Inn, 1962. Parachute Regt, TA, 1966–72. *Recreations:* music, books, walking.

MAHON, Sir Denis; *see* Mahon, Sir J. D.

MAHON, Sir (John) Denis, Kt 1986; CBE 1967; MA Oxon; FBA 1964; art historian; Trustee of the National Gallery, 1957–64 and 1966–73; Member, Advisory Panel, National Art-Collections Fund, since 1975; *b* 8 Nov. 1910; *s* of late John FitzGerald Mahon (4th *s* of Sir W. Mahon, 4th Bt) and Lady Alice Evelyn Browne (*d* 1970), *d* of 5th Marquess of Sligo. *Educ:* Eton; Christ Church, Oxford (Hon. Student, 1996). Has specialised in the study of 17th-Century painting in Italy and has formed a collection of pictures of the period (exhibited Nat. Gall., 1997); is a member of the Cttee of the Biennial Exhibitions at Bologna, Italy; has long campaigned for fiscal measures to encourage support from private individs for art galls and museums. Awarded Medal for Benemeriti della Cultura by Pres. of Italy for services to criticism and history of Italian art, 1957; Archiginnasio d'Oro, City of Bologna, 1968; Serena Medal for Italian Studies, British Acad., 1972. Elected Accademico d'Onore, Clementine Acad., Bologna, 1964; Sen. Fellow, RCA, 1988; Corresp. Fellow: Accad. Raffaello, Urbino, 1968; Deputazione di Storia Patria per le provincie di Romagna, 1969. Ateneo Veneto, 1987. Hon. Citizen, Cento, 1982. Hon. DLitt: Newcastle, 1969; Oxford, 1994; Rome (La Sapienza), 1998. *Publications:* Studies in Seicento Art and Theory, 1947; Mostra dei Carracci, Catalogo critico dei Disegni, 1956 (1963); Poussiniana, 1962; Catalogues of the Mostra del Guercino (Dipinti, 1968; Disegni, 1969); (with Nicholas Turner) The Drawings of Guercino in the Collection of Her Majesty the Queen at Windsor Castle, 1989; catalogues of exhibitions for 4th centenary of Guercino's birth, 1991–92; contributed to: Actes of Colloque Poussin, 1960; Friedlaender Festschrift, 1965; Problemi Guardeschi, 1967; (consultant) Luigi Salerno, I Dipinti del Guercino, 1988; articles, including a number on Caravaggio and Poussin, in art-historical periodicals, *eg*, The Burlington Magazine, Apollo, The Art Bulletin, Journal of the Warburg and Courtauld Institutes, Bulletin of the Metropolitan Museum of New York, Gazette des Beaux-Arts, Art de France, Paragone, Commentari, Zeitschrift für Kunstwissenschaft; has collaborated in the compilation of catalogues raisonnés of exhibitions, *eg*, Artists in 17th Century Rome (London, 1955), Italian Art and Britain (Royal Academy, 1960), L'Ideale Classico del Seicento in Italia (Bologna, 1962), Omaggio al Guercino (Cento, 1967). *Address:* 33 Cadogan Square, SW1X 0HU. *T:* (020) 7235 7311, (020) 7235 2530.

MAHON, Colonel Sir William (Walter), 7th Bt *cr* 1819 (UK), of Castlegar, Co. Galway; *b* 4 Dec. 1940; *s* of Sir George Edward John Mahon, 6th Bt and Audrey Evelyn (*née* Jagger) (*d* 1957); *S* father, 1987; *m* 1968, Rosemary Jane, *yr d* of late Lt-Col M. E. Melvill, OBE, Symington, Lanarks; one *s* two *d*. *Educ:* Eton. Commnd Irish Guards, 1960; served UK, Germany, Malaysia, Aden, Hong Kong, Pakistan, Spain. Mem., HM Body Guard, Hon. Corps of Gentlemen at Arms, 1993. Fundraising, Macmillan Cancer Relief, 1993–. *Recreations:* shooting, collecting, military history. *Heir:* *s* James William Mahon, *b* 29 Oct. 1976. *Club:* Army and Navy.

MAHONEY, Dennis Leonard; Chairman and Chief Executive Officer, Aon Ltd (formerly Aon Group Ltd), since 1997; *b* 20 Sept. 1950; *s* of late Frederick Mahoney; *m* 1st, Julia McLaughlin (marr. diss.); one *s* one *d*; 2nd, 1988, Jacqueline Fox; one *s* two *d*. *Educ:* West Hatch Technical High School; Harvard Business Sch. (PMD 1983). *Address:* 8 Devonshire Square, EC2M 4PL.

MAHONEY, Rev. Prof. John Aloysius, (Jack), SJ; Founding Director, Lauriston Centre for Contemporary Belief and Action, Edinburgh, and Hon. Fellow, Faculty of Divinity, Edinburgh University, since 1998; Emeritus Professor of Moral and Social Theology, University of London, since 1999; *b* Coatbridge, 14 Jan. 1931; *s* of Patrick Mahoney and Margaret Cecilia Mahoney (*née* Doris). *Educ:* Our Lady's High Sch., Motherwell; St Aloysius' Coll., Glasgow; Univ. of Glasgow (MA 1951). LicPhil 1956; LicTheol 1963; DTheol *summa cum laude*, Pontifical Gregorian Univ., Rome, 1967. Entered Society of Jesus, 1951; ordained priest, 1962; Jesuit Tertianship, NY, 1963–64. Lectr in Moral and Pastoral Theology, Heythrop Coll., Oxon, 1967–70, and Heythrop Coll., London, 1970–86; Principal, Heythrop Coll., London, 1976–81 (Fellow, 2000); F. D. Maurice Prof. of Moral and Social Theology, KCL, 1986–93; Founding Dir, KCL Business Ethics Res. Centre, 1987–93; Dean, Faculty of Theol., London Univ., and Faculty of Theol. and Religious Studies, KCL, 1990–92; Dixons Prof. of Business Ethics and Social Responsibility, London Business Sch., 1993–98. Mercers' Sch. Meml Prof. of Commerce, Gresham Coll., London, 1987–93; Martin D'Arcy Meml Lectr, Campion Hall, Oxford, 1981–82. Mem., Internat. Theol. Commn, Rome, 1974–80; Sector Pres., Nat. Pastoral Congress, 1980; Mem., Internat. Study Gp on Bioethics, Internat. Fedn of Catholic Univs, 1984–93. Pres., Catholic Theolog. Assoc., 1984–86. Chaplain to Tablet Table, 1983–98; Domestic Chaplain to Lord Mayor of London, 1989–90. CIMgt 1993. Hon. Fellow: Gresham Coll., City of London, 1999–; St Mary's UC, Strawberry Hill, 1999–. Governor, St Aloysius' Coll., Glasgow, 1999–, Chm., 2000. Founding Editor, Business Ethics, A European Review, 1992–98. *Publications:* Seeking the Spirit, 1981; Bioethics and Belief, 1984; The Making of Moral Theology, 1987; The Ways of Wisdom, 1987; Teaching Business Ethics in the UK, Europe and USA, 1990; (ed) Business Ethics in a New Europe, 1992. *Recreations:* bridge, unrequited golf. *Address:* 28 Lauriston Street, Edinburgh EH3 9DJ. *T:* (0131) 228 6621; *e-mail:* jmlaur@aol.com.

MAHY, Brian Wilfred John, PhD, ScD; Senior Scientist, National Center for Infectious Diseases, Centers for Disease Control and Prevention, Atlanta, since 2000; Adjunct Professor, Emory University, since 1993; *b* 7 May 1937; *s* of Wilfred Mahy and Norah Dillingham; *m* 1st, 1959, Valerie Pouteaux (marr. diss. 1986); two *s* one *d*; 2nd, 1988, Penny Scott (*née* Cunningham). *Educ:* Elizabeth Coll., Guernsey; Univ. of Southampton (BSc, PhD); Univ. of Cambridge (MA, ScD). Res. Biologist, Dept of Cancer Res., London Hosp. Med. Coll., Univ. of London, 1962–65; Asst Dir, Res. Virology, Dept of Pathology, Cambridge Univ., 1965–79; Fellow and Tutor, University (Wolfson) Coll., 1967–84; Librarian, Wolfson Coll., 1975–80; Huddersfield Lectr in Special Path. (Virology), 1979–84; Head, Div. of Virology, Cambridge, 1979–84; Head, Pirbright Lab., AFRC Inst. for Animal Health (formerly Animal Virus Res. Inst. and AFRC Inst. for Animal Disease Res.), 1984–89; Dir, Div. of Viral and Rickettsial Diseases, Centers for Disease Control and Prevention, Atlanta, GA, 1989–2000. Vis. Prof., Univ. of Minnesota, 1968; Eleanor Roosevelt Internat. Cancer Fellow, Dept of Microbiol., Univ. of California, San Francisco, 1973–74; Vis. Prof., Inst. für Virologie, Univ. of Würzburg, 1980–81. Convener, Virus Group, 1980–84, Mem. Council, 1983–87, Soc. for General Microbiology; Vice-Chm., 1987–90, Chm., 1990–93, Past Chm., 1994–96, Virology Div., Vice Pres., 1995–99, Pres., 1999–Aug. 2002, Internat. Union of Microbiol Socs. FRSocMed 1985; Fellow: Infectious Diseases Soc. of America, 1992; Amer. Acad. of Microbiol., 1998–. Editor-in-Chief, Virus Research, 1983–; US Editor: Jl of Med. Virology, 1994–; Reviews in Med. Virology, 2000–. *Publications:* (jtly) The Biology of Large RNA Viruses, 1970; Negative Strand Viruses, 1975; Negative Strand Virus and the Host Cell, 1978; Lactic Dehydrogenase Virus, 1975. A Dictionary of Virology, 1981; Virus Persistence, 1982; The Microbe 1984: pt 1, Viruses, 1984; Virology: a practical approach, 1985; The Biology of Negative Strand Viruses, 1987; Genetics and Pathogenicity of Negative Strand Viruses, 1989; Concepts in Virology: from Ivanovsky to the present, 1993; Virology Methods Manual, 1996; Immunobiology and Pathogenesis of Persistent Virus Infections, 1996; A Dictionary of Virology, 1996, 3rd edn 2001; (ed jtly) Topley & Wilson's Microbiology and Microbial Infections, 9th edn, Vol. 1, 1998; numerous articles on animal virology in learned jls. *Recreations:* playing the violin in chamber and orchestral groups, gardening. *Address:* National Center for Infectious Diseases (C12), Centers for Disease Control and Prevention, 1600 Clifton Road, NE, Atlanta, GA 30333, USA.

MAHY, Margaret May, ONZ 1993; writer; *b* 21 March 1936; *d* of Francis George Mahy and Helen May Penlington; two *d*. *Educ:* Whakatane Primary and High Schs; Univ. of NZ (BA). Asst Librarian, Petone Public Library, 1959; Asst Children's Librarian, Christchurch Public Library, 1960; Librarian i/c of school requests, Sch. Library Service (Christchurch Br.), 1967; Children's Librarian, Christchurch Public Library, 1977; full time writer, 1980–. Hon. DLitt Canterbury, 1993. Carnegie Medal, 1982, 1984; Esther Glen Medal. *Publications: picture books:* The Dragon of an Ordinary Family, 1969; A Lion in the Meadow, 1969; Mrs Discombobulous, 1969; Pillycock's Shop, 1969; The Procession, 1970; The Little Witch, 1970; Sailor Jack and the Twenty Orphans, 1970; The Princess and the Clown, 1971; The Boy with Two Shadows, 1971; The Man whose Mother was a Pirate, 1972; The Railway Engine and the Hairy Brigands, 1973; Rooms for Rent/Rooms to Let, 1974; The Witch in the Cherry Tree, 1974; The Rare Spotted Birthday Party, 1974; Stepmother, 1974; The Ultra-Violet Catastrophe, 1975; The Great Millionaire Kidnap, 1975; The Wind Between the Stars, 1976; David's Witch Doctor, 1976; Leaf Magic, 1976; The Boy who was Followed Home, 1977; Jam, 1985; The Great White Man-Eating Shark, 1989; The Tin Can Band and Other Poems, 1989; Making Friends, 1990; The Pumpkin Man and the Crafty Creeper, 1990; The Seven Chinese Brothers, 1990; The Dentist's Promise, 1991; Keeping House, 1991; The Queen's Goat, 1991; The Horrendous Hullabaloo, 1992; The Three-Legged Cat, 1993; A Busy Day for a Good Grandmother, 1993; The Christmas Tree Tangle, 1994; The Rattlebang Picnic, 1994; The Big Black Bulging Bump, 1995; Boom, Baby, Boom, Boom!, 1996; Beaten by a Balloon, 1997; Summery Saturday Morning, 1998; Simply Delicious!, 1999; *collections of stories:* three Margaret Mahy Story Books, 1972, 1973, 1975; A Lion in the Meadow, 1976; Nonstop Nonsense, 1977; The Great Piratical Rumbustification and The Librarian and the Robbers, 1978; The Chewing-Gum Rescue, 1982; The Birthday Burglar and a Very Wicked Headmistress, 1984; The Downhill Crocodile Whizz, 1986; Mahy Magic, 1986; The Three Wishes, 1986; The Door in the Air, 1988; Bubble Trouble, 1991; Tick Tock Tales, 1993; *junior novels:* Clancy's Cabin, 1974; The Bus Under the Leaves, 1975; The Pirate Uncle, 1977; Raging Robots and Unruly Uncles, 1981; The Pirates' Mixed-Up Voyage, 1983; The Blood and Thunder Adventure on Hurricane Peak, 1989; The Cousins Quartet, books 1–4, 1994; The Greatest Show off Earth, 1994; Tingleberries, Tuckertubs and Telephones: a tale of love and ice-cream, 1995; The Five Sisters, 1996; The Horribly Haunted School, 1997; Dinsmore Down in the Dump, 1999; A Villain's Night Out, 1999; *novels for older readers:* The Haunting, 1982; The Changeover, 1984; The Catalogue of the Universe, 1985; Aliens in the Family, 1986; The Tricksters, 1986; Memory, 1987; Dangerous Spaces, 1991; Underrunners, 1992; The Other Side of Silence, 1995; Operation Terror, 1997; *for schools:* The Crocodile's Christmas Jandals, 1982; The Bubbling Crocodile, 1983; Mrs Bubble's Baby, 1983; Shopping with a Crocodile, 1983; Going to the Beach, 1984; The Great Grumbler and the Wonder Tree, 1984; Fantail Fantail, 1984; A Crocodile in the Garden, 1985; The Crocodile's Christmas Thongs, 1985; Horrakapotchkin, 1985; *for emergent readers:* Ups and Downs, 1984; Wibble Wobble, 1984; The Dragon's Birthday, 1984; The Spider in the Shower, 1984; The Adventures of a Kite, 1985; Sophie's Singing Mother, 1985; The Earthquake, 1985; The Cake, 1985; The Catten, 1985; Out in the Big Wide World, 1985; A Vary Happy Bathday, 1985; Clever Hamburger, 1985; Muppy's Ball, 1986; Baby's Breakfast, 1986; The Tree Doctor, 1986; The Garden Party, 1986; The Man who Enjoyed Grumbling, 1986; The Trouble with Heathrow, 1986; The Pop Group, 1986; Feeling Funny, 1986; A Pet to the Vet, 1986; The New House Villain, 1986; Tai Taylor is Born, 1986; The Terrible Topsy-Turvy Tissy-Tossy Tangle, 1986; Trouble on the Bus, 1986; Mr Rumfitt, 1986; My Wonderful Aunt, 1986; The Funny, Funny Clown Face, 1986; The Haunting of Miss Cardamon, 1987; The Girl Who Washed by Moonlight, 1987; The King's Jokes, 1987; The Mad Puppet, 1987; *verse:* Seventeen Kings and Forty-Two Elephants, 1972; *non-fiction:* Look Under 'V', 1977. *Recreations:* reading, gardening. *Address:* No 1 RD, Lyttelton, New Zealand. *T:* (3) 299703.

MAIANI, Prof. Luciano; Director General, Organisation Européenne pour la Recherche Nucléaire (CERN), since 1999 (President of Council, since 1997); President, Istituto Nazionale di Fisica Nucleare, Italy, since 1993; Professor of Theoretical Physics, University of Rome, since 1984; *b* 16 July 1941. *Educ:* Univ. of Rome (degree in Physics 1964). Research Associate: Istituto Superior di Sanità, 1964; Univ. of Florence, 1964; Fellow, Lyman Lab. of Physics, Univ. of Harvard, 1969; Prof., Inst. of Theoretical Physics, Univ. of Rome, 1976; Vis. Prof., Ecole Normale Supérieure, Paris, 1977; Vis. Prof., 1979–80, 1985–86, Mem. Council, 1993–, CERN. Fellow, APS, 1991 (J. Sakurai Prize, 1987). *Address:* CERN, 1211 Geneva 23, Switzerland.

MAIBAUM, Prof. Thomas Stephen Edward, PhD; CEng, FIEE; Professor, Foundations of Software Engineering, King's College London, since 1999; *b* 18 Aug. 1947; *s* of Leslie Maibaum and Olga Maibaum (*née* Klein); *m* 1971, Janet Hilless; one *s* one *d*. *Educ:* Toronto Univ. (BSc); PhD London Univ. Postdoctoral Fellow, 1973, Asst Prof., 1974–81, Univ. of Waterloo; Imperial College, University of London: Lectr, Dept of Computing, 1981–86; Reader in Computing Science, 1986–90; Hd, Dept of Computing, 1989–97; Prof., Foundns of Software Engrg, 1990–99. Vis. Prof., Pontifícia Universidade Católica de Rio de Janeiro, 1977, 1981 (Hon. Prof., 1992); Royal Soc./SERC Industrial Fellow, 1984; Marie Curie Fellowship (EU), Univ. of Lisbon, 1997–98. FRSA. Engrg

Foresight Award, Royal Acad. Engrg, 1998. *Publications:* (jtly) The Specification of Computer Programs, 1987; (ed jtly) Handbook of Logic in Computer Science, vol. I, 1992, vol. II, 1992, vol. III, 1995, vol. IV, 1995, vol. V, 2000. *Recreations:* memorising the films of Mel Brooks, music, opera, travel, literature. *Address:* Department of Computer Science, King's College London, Strand, WC2R 2LS; 39 Inchmery Road, SE6 2NA. *T:* (020) 7848 2895.

MAIDEN, Sir Colin (James), Kt 1992; ME, DPhil; Chairman: Fisher & Paykel Industries Ltd, since 1989; Tower Insurance Ltd (formerly National Insurance Company of New Zealand Ltd), since 1988; Director, Independent Newspapers Ltd (Chairman, 1994–2001); Vice-Chancellor, University of Auckland, New Zealand, 1971–94; *b* 5 May 1933; *s* of Henry A. Maiden; *m* 1957, Jenefor Mary Rowe; one *s* three *d*. *Educ:* Auckland Grammar Sch.; Univ. of Auckland, NZ (ME); Exeter Coll., Oxford (DPhil; Hon. Fellow, 1994). Post-doctorate research, Oxford Univ. (supported by AERE, Harwell), 1957–58; Head of Hypersonic Physics Section, Canadian Armament Research and Develt Estabt, Quebec City, Canada, 1958–60; Sen. Lectr in Mechanical Engrg, Univ. of Auckland, 1960–61; Head of Material Sciences Laboratory, Gen. Motors Corp., Defense Research Laboratories, Santa Barbara, Calif, USA, 1961–66; Manager of Process Engineering, Gen. Motors Corp., Technl Centre, Warren, Michigan, USA, 1966–70. Chairman: NZ Synthetic Fuels Corp. Ltd, 1980–90; Sedgwick Gp (NZ) Ltd, 1996–98 (Dir, 1994–98); Transpower NZ Ltd, 1997– (Dir, 1994–); Director: Mason Industries Ltd, 1971–78; Farmers Trading Co. Ltd, 1973–86; Wilkins & Davies Co. Ltd, 1986–89; Winstone Ltd, 1978–88; NZ Steel Ltd, 1988–92; ANZ Banking Gp (NZ) Ltd, 1990–93; NZ Refining Co. Ltd, 1991–; Progressive Enterprises Ltd, 1992–2000; DB Group Ltd, 1994–; Tower Ltd, 1995–; Foodland Associated Ltd (WA), 2000–. Chairman: NZ Energy R&D Cttee, 1974–81; Liquid Fuels Trust Bd, 1978–86. Chm., NZ Vice-Chancellors' Cttee, 1977–78, and 1991; Hon. Treasurer, ACU, 1988–98. Member: Spirit of Adventure Trust Bd, 1972–80; NZ Metric Adv. Bd, 1973–77. NZ Agent for Joint NZ/US Sci. and Technol Agreement, 1974–81. Hon. FIPENZ 1999. Hon. LLD Auckland, 1994. Thomson Medal, Royal Soc. NZ, 1986; Medal, Univ. of Bonn, 1983; Symons Award, ACU, 1999. Silver Jubilee Medal, 1977. *Publications:* numerous scientific and technical papers. *Recreation:* tennis. *Address:* 7 Chatfield Place, Remuera, Auckland, New Zealand. *T:* (9) 5290380. *Clubs:* Vincent's (Oxford); Northern (Auckland); Remuera Racquets, International Lawn Tennis of NZ, Auckland Golf.

MAIDEN, (James) Dennis, CEng; FFB; Director General, Federation of Master Builders, 1991–97; *b* 28 June 1932; *s* of James William Maiden and Elsie (*née* Brotherton); *m* 1953, Irene Harris; one *s* one *d*. *Educ:* Wath-upon-Dearne Grammar Sch. CEng 1966; MIMechE 1966; FFB 1987. Engrg Consultant, Husband & Co., 1958–63; Chief Engr, British Shoe Corp., 1963–67; Construction Industry Training Board: Develt Manager, 1967–73; Gen. Manager, 1973–76; Dir of Trng, 1976–85; Chief Exec., 1985–90; Dir-Gen. designate, Fedn of Master Builders, 1990–91. Chief Exec., Construction Ind. Services Ltd, 1991–97; Managing Director: Nat. Register of Warranted Builders Ltd, 1991–97; Trade Debt Recovery Service Ltd, 1991–97. Pres., Kings Lynn Inst. of Mgt, 1988. Chm., Park House Hotel for Disabled People, 1983–88 and 1995–99. Trustee, Leonard Cheshire Foundn, 1987–92; Pres., Norfolk Outward Bound Assoc., 1988. Hon. Mem., C & G, 1981; CIMgt 1986; MIPM 1971. FRSA 1987. Freeman, City of London, 1988; Liveryman, Co of: Constructors, 1988; Plumbers, 1989. *Recreations:* golf, gardening, theatre. *Address:* Micklebring, Church Lane, Bircham, Kings Lynn, Norfolk PE31 6QW. *T:* (01485) 578336. *Club:* Hunstanton Golf.

MAIDEN, Prof. Martin David, PhD; Professor of the Romance Languages, University of Oxford, since 1996; Fellow of Trinity College, Oxford, since 1996; *b* 20 May 1957; *s* of Kenneth Henry Maiden and Betty Maiden (*née* Liddiard). *Educ:* King Edward VI Sch., Southampton; Trinity Hall, Cambridge (MA, MPhil, PhD). Lectr in Italian, Univ. of Bath, 1982–89; Univ. Lectr in Romance Philology, and Fellow of Downing Coll., Cambridge, 1989–96. Pres., Società Internazionale di Linguistica e Filologia Italiana, 1989–91; Mem. Council, Philological Soc., 1996–2000. Consultant Ed., Etudes romanes, 2001–. *Publications:* Interactive Morphonology: metaphony in Italy, 1991; (ed with J. C. Smith) Linguistic Theory and the Romance Languages, 1995; A Linguistic History of Italian, 1995; (ed with M. Parry) The Dialects of Italy, 1997; Storia linguistica dell' italiano, 1998; (with C. Robusielli) A Reference Grammar of Modern Italian, 2000; articles in various jls, incl. Romance Philology, Zeitschrift für romanische Philologie, Jl of Linguistics. *Recreation:* travel. *Address:* 62 Cunliffe Close, Oxford OX2 7BL. *T:* (01865) 511753.

MAIDEN, Robert Mitchell, FCIBS; Managing Director, Royal Bank of Scotland plc, and Executive Director, Royal Bank of Scotland Group plc, 1986–91; *b* 15 Sept. 1933; *s* of Harry and Georgina Maiden; *m* 1958, Margaret Mercer (*née* Nicolson). *Educ:* Montrose Acad., Tayside, Scotland. Royal Bank of Scotland: various appts, 1950–74; Supt of branches, 1974–76; Treasurer, 1976–77; Chief Accountant, 1977–81; Gen. Man. (Finance), 1981–82; Exec. Dir, 1982–86. Vice-Chm., CC-Bank AG, Germany, 1991–93; Chm., Lothian and Edinburgh Enterprise, 1994–96. Member: Accounts Commn for Scotland, 1992–99; Scottish Panel of Adjudicators, Investors in People, Scotland, 1996–2001. Gov., Napier Univ. (formerly Napier Poly.), 1988–98. Trustee, C of S Pension Scheme, 1991–96. FIMgt; FRSA. *Recreations:* music, golf, reading. *Address:* Trinafour, 202 Braid Road, Edinburgh EH10 6HS. *Club:* New (Edinburgh).

MAIDMENT, Francis Edward, (Ted); Headmaster, Shrewsbury School, 1988–2001; *b* 23 Aug. 1942; *s* of Charles Edward and late Olive Mary Maidment. *Educ:* Pocklington Sch., York; Jesus Coll., Cambridge (Scholar). Asst Master, Lancing Coll., 1965–81 (Housemaster, 1975–81); Headmaster, Ellesmere Coll., Shropshire, 1982–88. Governor: Cheltenham Ladies' Coll.; Abberley Hall Sch.; Malsis Sch.; Packwood Haugh Sch.; Prestfelde Sch. *Recreations:* singing, medieval history, modest tennis. *Address:* The Coach House, Glansevern Hall, Berriew, Welshpool, Powys SY21 8AH. *Clubs:* East India, Devonshire, Sports and Public Schools; Gilgil (Kenya).

MAIDMENT, Neil, CMG 1996; Director (non-executive), Hong Kong Institute of Biotechnology Ltd, since 1996; *b* Oxford, 18 Aug. 1938; *s* of late Kenneth John Maidment, Founding Vice-Chancellor, Univ. of Auckland and Isobel Felicity Maidment (*née* Leitch); *m* 1983, Sandie Shuk-Ling Yuen. *Educ:* Magdalen Coll. Sch., Oxford; King's Sch., Auckland; King's Coll., Auckland; Univ. of Auckland (Life Mem., Students' Assoc.). South British Insurance Co. Ltd, Auckland, Singapore, Calcutta, Bombay, 1958–65; Glaxo Group: Far Eastern Surgical Rep., Singapore, Kuala Lumpur, 1965–68; Manager: Hong Kong, 1968–70; Manila, 1971; Director and General Manager: Glaxo Hong Kong Ltd, 1971–93; Glaxo China Ltd, 1988–93; Area Dir, North Asia, 1990–93; Exec. Dir, Glaxo Wellcome plc (formerly Glaxo Hldgs plc), responsible for Asia Pacific, 1993–95, and for Africa, Middle East and Turkey, 1994–95. Member: Pharmacy and Poisons Appeal Tribunal, Hong Kong, 1979–88; Sub-Cttee on Biotechnology, Hong Kong, 1988–89; UK/Hong Kong Scholarships Cttee, 1988–94. Pres., Hong Kong Assoc. of Pharmaceutical Industry, 1977–78; Chm., British Chamber of Commerce, Hong Kong, 1989–90. *Publication:* (with H. Scrimgeour and H. Williams) Arthur Scrimgeour—a life, 1990. *Recreations:* reading, travelling in China. *Address:* PO Box 23022, Wanchai, Hong Kong; Les Jumelles, 20658 Lakeshore, Baie d'Urfé, QC H9X 1R4, Canada. *Clubs:* Hong Kong, Hong Kong Jockey (Hong Kong); Saturday (Calcutta).

MAIDMENT, Ted; *see* Maidment, F. E.

MAIDSTONE, Viscount; Tobias Joshua Stormont Finch Hatton; *b* 21 June 1998; *s* and *heir* of Earl of Winchilsea and Nottingham, *qv*.

MAIDSTONE, Bishop Suffragan of, since 2001; **Rt Rev. Graham Alan Gray;** *b* 21 April 1947; *s* of late Alan Cray and Doris Mary Kathleen Cray; *m* 1973, Jacqueline Webster; two *d*. *Educ:* Leeds Univ. (BA 1968); St John's Coll., Nottingham. Ordained deacon, 1971, priest, 1972; Asst Curate, St Mark, Gillingham, 1971–75; N Area Co-ordinator, Youth Dept, CPAS, 1975–78; Asst Curate, 1978–82, Vicar, 1982–92, St Michael-le-Belfrey, York; Principal, Ridley Hall Theol Coll., 1992–2001. Six Preacher, Canterbury Cathedral, 1997. *Recreations:* listening to rock music, following sport, reading theology. *Address:* Bishop's House, Pett Lane, Charing, Ashford, Kent TN27 0DL.

MAIDSTONE, Archdeacon of; *see* Evans, Ven. P. A. S.

MAIER, Prof. John Paul, DPhil; FRS 1999; Professor of Physical Chemistry, University of Basel, since 1991; *b* 15 Nov. 1947; *s* of Dr H. E. Maier and S. Maier; three *d* (one *s* decd). *Educ:* Univ. of Nottingham (BSc Hons Chemistry 1966); Balliol Coll., Oxford (DPhil Physical Chemistry 1972). University of Basel: Royal Soc. Fellow, 1973–74; Res. Associate, 1975–78; Lectr in Chemistry, 1978–81; Associate Prof. in Physical Chemistry, 1982–90. Werner Prize, Swiss Chem. Soc., 1979; Marlow Medal, RSC, 1980; Chemistry Prize, Göttingen Sci. Acad., 1986; Nat. Latsis Prize, Swiss Nat. Sci Foundn, 1987. *Recreations:* bridge, golf. *Address:* Institute for Physical Chemistry, Klingelbergstrasse 80, 4056 Basel, Switzerland. *T:* (61) 2673826, *Fax:* (61) 2673855; *e-mail:* j.p.maier@unibas.ch.

MAILER, Joanna Mary; *see* Shapland, J. M.

MAILER, Norman; *b* 31 Jan. 1923; *s* of Isaac Barnett Mailer and Fanny Schneider; *m* 1st, 1944, Beatrice Silverman (marr. diss., 1951); one *d*; 2nd, 1954, Adèle Morales (marr. diss., 1962); two *d*; 3rd, 1962, Lady Jeanne Campbell (marr. diss., 1963); one *d*; 4th, 1963, Beverly Bentley; two *s*; 5th, Carol Stevens; one *d*; 6th, Norris Church; one *s*. *Educ:* Harvard. Infantryman, US Army, 1944–46. Co-founder of Village Voice, 1955; an Editor of Dissent, 1953–63. Democratic Candidate, Mayoral Primaries, New York City, 1969. Directed films: Wild 90, 1967; Beyond the Law, 1967; Maidstone, 1968; Tough Guys Don't Dance, 1988. Pulitzer Prize for Fiction, 1980. *Publications:* The Naked and the Dead, 1948; Barbary Shore, 1951; The Deer Park, 1955 (dramatized, 1967); Advertisements for Myself, 1959; Deaths For The Ladies, 1962; The Presidential Papers, 1963; An American Dream, 1964; Cannibals and Christians, 1966; Why Are We In Vietnam?, 1967 (a novel); The Armies of the Night, 1968 (Pulitzer Prize, 1969); Miami and the Siege of Chicago, 1968 (National Book Award, 1969); Of a Fire on the Moon, 1970; The Prisoner of Sex, 1971; Existential Errands, 1972; St George and the Godfather, 1972; Marilyn, 1973; The Faith of Graffiti, 1974; The Fight, 1975; Some Honorable Men, 1975; Genius and Lust, 1976; A Transit to Narcissus, 1978; The Executioner's Song, 1979; Of a Small and Modest Malignancy, Wicked and Bristling with Dots, 1980; Of Women and Their Elegance, 1980; The Essential Mailer, 1982; Ancient Evenings, 1983; Tough Guys Don't Dance, 1984; Harlot's Ghost, 1991; Oswald's Tale: an American mystery, 1995; Picasso: portrait of Picasso as a young man, 1996; The Gospel According to the Son, 1997; The Time of Our Time, 1998. *Address:* c/o Random House Inc., 201 E 50th Street, New York, NY 10022, USA.

MAIN, Very Rev. Prof. Alan, TD 1982; PhD; Professor of Practical Theology, since 1980 and Master, since 1992, Christ's College, Aberdeen; Moderator of the General Assembly of the Church of Scotland, 1998–99; *b* 31 March 1936; *s* of James E. W. Main and Mary A. R. Black; *m* 1960, Anne Louise Swanson; two *d*. *Educ:* Robert Gordon's Coll., Aberdeen; Aberdeen Univ. (MA 1957; BD 1960; PhD 1963); Union Theol Seminary, NY (STM 1961). Minister, Chapel of Garioch Parish, Aberdeenshire, 1963–70; Chaplain to Univ. of Aberdeen, 1970–80. *Publications:* Worship Now, 1989; (ed) But Where Shall Wisdom Be Found?, 1995; (ed) Northern Accents, 2001; articles in jls on pastoral care and counselling, military ethics, medical ethics. *Recreations:* music (piano and organ), golf, bee-keeping. *Address:* Faculty of Divinity, King's College, University of Aberdeen, Old Aberdeen AB24 2UB; Kirkfield, Barthol Chapel, Inverurie AB51 8TD. *Club:* Royal Northern and University (Aberdeen).

MAIN, Air Vice-Marshal John Bartram, CB 1996; OBE 1979 (MBE 1977); FREng; Military Adviser, Matra Marconi Space UK Ltd, since 1996; *b* 28 Jan. 1941; *s* of late Wing Comdr James Taylor Main, OBE and Nellie Ethel Toleman; *m* 1965, Helen Joyce Lambert; two *d*. *Educ:* Portsmouth Grammar Sch.; Birmingham Univ. (BSc Elect. Eng.); RAF Tech. Coll., Henlow. CEng, FIEE, FIIE. Commissioned Engr Branch, RAF, 1960; served Benson, Hiswa (Aden), Thorney Island; Dir of Sci. and Tech. Intell., MoD, 1970–74; OC No 33 Signals Unit, Cyprus, 1974–77; CO RAF Digby, 1977–79; RAF Staff Coll., 1979–80; RAF Signals Engrg Estabt, 1980–83; Head, Tech. Intell. (Air), 1983–87; RCDS 1986; Dep. Comd Aerosystems Engr, HQ Strike Comd, 1987–88; Comdt, RAF Sigs Engrg Estabt and Air Cdre Sigs, HQ RAF Support Comd, 1988–89; Dir, Command, Control, Communication and Inf. Systems (Policy and Op. Requirements), 1989–93; DG Support Services (RAF), 1993–94; AO Communications and Inf. Systems, and AOC Signals Units, HQ Logistics Comd, 1994–96. Military Advr, Astrium, 1996–2001. FREng 2001; FRAeS. *Recreations:* gardening, cycling, tennis, sailing, reading. *Address:* Robin's Mead, 120 Manor Way, Aldwick Bay, West Sussex PO21 4HN. *Club:* Royal Air Force.

MAIN, His Honour John Roy; QC 1974; a Circuit Judge, 1976–95; *b* 21 June 1930; *yr s* of late A. C. Main, MIMechE; *m* 1955, Angela de la Condamine Davies, *er d* of late R. W. H. Davies, ICS; two *s* one *d*. *Educ:* Portsmouth Grammar Sch.; Hotchkiss Sch., USA; Brasenose Coll., Oxford (MA). Called to Bar, Inner Temple, 1954; a Recorder of Crown Court, 1972–76. Mem. Special Panel, Transport Tribunal, 1970–76; Dep. Chm., IoW QS, 1971. Pres., Transport Tribunal, 1996–97 (Chm., 1997–2000). Gov., Portsmouth Grammar Sch., 1988–2000. *Recreations:* walking, gardening, music. *Address:* 4 Queen Anne Drive, Claygate, Surrey KT10 0PP. *T:* (01372) 466380.

MAIN, Sir Peter (Tester), Kt 1985; ERD 1964; Chairman, The Boots Company PLC, 1982–85; *b* 21 March 1925; *s* of late Peter Tester Main and Esther Paterson (*née* Lawson); *m* 1st, 1952, Dr Margaret Fimister, MB, ChB (*née* Tweddle) (*d* 1984); two *s* one *d*; 2nd, 1986, May Hetherington Anderson (*née* McMillan). *Educ:* Robert Gordon's Coll., Aberdeen; Univ. of Aberdeen (MB, ChB 1948, MD 1963; Hon. LLD 1986). MRCPE 1981, FRCPE 1982. Captain, RAMC, 1949–51; MO with Field Ambulance attached to Commando Bde, Suez, 1956; Lt-Col RAMC (AER), retd 1964. House Surg., Aberdeen Royal Infirmary, 1948; House Physician, Woodend Hosp., Aberdeen, 1949; Demonstrator, Univ. of Durham, 1952; gen. practice, 1953–57; joined Res. Dept, Boots,

1957; Dir of Res., 1968; Man. Dir, Industrial Div., 1979–80; Dir, 1973–85, Vice-Chm., 1980–81, The Boots Company PLC. Chm., Inveresk Res. Internat., 1986–89; Dir, 1985–91, Vice-Chm., 1990–91, W. A. Baxter and Sons Ltd; Dir, John Fleming and Co., 1985–89. Chm., Cttee of Inquiry into Teachers' Pay and Conditions, Scotland, 1986; Member: NEDC, 1984–85; Scottish Health Service Policy Board, 1985–88; SDA, 1986–91. Governor, Henley Management Coll., 1983–86; Chm., Grantown Heritage Trust, 1987–91; Trustee, Univ. of Aberdeen Develt Trust, 1988–97. CIMgt (FBIM 1978). *Recreations:* fly fishing, Scottish music. *Address:* Ninewells House, Chirnside, Duns, Berwickshire TD11 3XF.

MAINES, James Dennis, CB 1998; CEng, FIEE; Consultant; Director General, Command Information Systems, Ministry of Defence, 1995–97; *b* 26 July 1937; *s* of Arthur Burtonwood Maines and Lilian Maines (*née* Carter); *m* 1st, 1960, Janet Enid Kemp (marr. diss. 1997); three *s*; 2nd, 1997, Janet Elizabeth Bussey (*née* Franks); two step *d. Educ:* Leigh Grammar School; City University (BSc). Joined RSRE (then RRE), Malvern, 1956 (Sandwich course in applied physics, 1956–60); Head of Guided Weapons Optics and Electronics Group, 1981; Head, Microwave and Electro-optics Group, 1983; Head, Sensors, Electronic Warfare and Guided Weapons, ARE, Portsdown, 1984–86; Dep. Dir (Mission Systems), RAE, 1986–88; Dir Gen., Guided Weapons and Electronics Systems, MoD, 1988–95. Wolfe Award for outstanding MoD research (jtly), 1973. *Publications:* (jtly) Surface Wave Filters (ed Matthews), 1977; papers in learned jls. *Recreations:* sailing, cricket, golf, music, painting, non-labour intensive gardening. *Address:* Hollybush Cottage, Folly Hill, Farnham, Surrey GU9 0DR.

MAINGARD de la VILLE ès OFFRANS, Sir (Louis Pierre) René, (Sir René Maingard), Kt 1982; CBE 1961; company chairman and director, Mauritius; *b* 9 July 1917; *s* of Joseph René Maingard de la Ville ès Offrans and Véronique Hugnin; *m* 1946, Marie Hélène Françoise Raffray; three *d. Educ:* St Joseph's Coll.; Royal Coll. of Mauritius; Business Training Corp., London. Clerk, Rogers & Co. Ltd, 1936, Man. Dir, 1948. Chairman: Rogers & Co. Ltd, 1956–82; Mauritius Steam Navigation Co. Ltd, 1964–; Mauritius Portland Cement Co. Ltd, 1960–; De Chazal du Mée Associates Ltd, 1982–. Director: Mauritius Commercial Bank Ltd, 1956–; New Mauritius Dock Co. Ltd, 1948–. Formerly, Consul for Finland in Mauritius. Chevalier 1st Cl., Order of the White Rose, Finland, 1973. *Recreations:* golf, fishing, boating. *Address:* Rogers & Co. Ltd, PO Box 60, Port Louis, Mauritius. *T:* 086801. *Clubs:* Royal Air Force; Dodo, Mauritius Naval & Military Gymkhana (Mauritius).

MAINI, Prof. Ravinder Nath, FRCP; Professor of Rheumatology, since 1989 and Head, Kennedy Institute of Rheumatology Division, since 2000, Imperial College School of Medicine at Charing Cross Hospital Campus (formerly Charing Cross and Westminster Medical School), University of London; *b* 17 Nov. 1937; *s* of Sir Amar (Nath) Maini, CBE and Saheli (*née* Mehra); *m* 1st, 1963, Marianne Gorm (marr. diss. 1986); one *s* one *d* (and one *s* decd); 2nd, 1987, Geraldine Room; two *s. Educ:* Cambridge Univ. (BA; MB, BChir 1962). MRCP 1966, FRCP 1977; FRCPE 1994. Jun. med. appts, Guy's, Brompton and Charing Cross Hosps, 1962–70; Consultant Physician: St Stephen's Hosp., London, 1970–76; Rheumatology Dept, Charing Cross Hosp., 1970; Hon. Consultant, Charing Cross Hosp., Hammersmith Hosps NHS Trust; Prof. of Immunology of Rheumatic Diseases, Charing Cross and Westminster Med. Sch., 1981–89; Dir, Kennedy Inst. of Rheumatology, 1990–2000 (Head, Clinical Immunology Div., 1979). President: Brit. Soc. Rheumatology, 1989–90 (Heberden Orator, 1988); Brit. League Against Rheumatism, 1985–89; Chm., Res. Subcttee, 1980–85, and Mem., Scientific Co-ordinating Cttee, 1980–95, Arthritis and Rheumatism Council; Chm., Standing Cttee for Investigative Rheumatology, European League Against Rheumatism, 1990–97; Mem., Exec. Cttee, Assoc. Physicians of GB and Ire., 1989–91; Chm., Rheumatology Cttee, RCP, 1992–96 (Croonian Lectr, 1995; Lumleian Lectr, 1999); Mem., European Union of Medical Specialists, 1994– (Pres., Sect. of Rheumatology, 1996–99; Chm., Eur. Bd of Rheumatology, 1996–99). Samuel Hyde Lectr, RSocMed, 1998. FMedSci 1999. Hon. Member: Australian Rheumatism Assoc., 1977; Norwegian Soc. for Rheumatology, 1988; Amer. Coll. of Rheumatology, 1988; Hellenic Rheumatology Soc., 1989; Hungarian Rheumatology Soc., 1990; Scandinavian Soc. for Immunology, 1996; Mexican Soc. for Rheumatology, 1996. Dr *hc* Univ. René Descartes, Paris, 1994. Carol Nachman Prize for rheumatology (with Prof. M. Feldmann), city of Wiesbaden, 1999; Dist. Investigator Award, Amer. Coll. of Rheumatology, 1999; Crafoord Prize (with Prof. M. Feldmann), Royal Swedish Acad. of Scis, 2000; Courtin-Clarins Prize (with Prof. M. Feldmann and Prof. J.-M. Dayer), Assoc. de Recherche sur la Polyarthrite, 2000. *Publications:* Immunology of Rheumatic Diseases, 1977; (ed) Modulation of Autoimmune Disease, 1981; (contrib.) Textbook of the Rheumatic Diseases, 6th edn 1986; (ed) T cell activation in health and disease, 1989; (ed) Rheumatoid Arthritis, 1992; (contrib.) Oxford Textbook of Rheumatology, 1993; (section ed.) Rheumatology, 1993; (ed jtly) Manual of Biological Markers of Disease, Sect. A, Methods of Autoantibody Detection, 1993, Sect. B, Autoantigens, 1994, Sect. C, Clinical Significance of Autoantibodies, 1996; (contrib.) Oxford Textbook of Medicine, 2001; articles in learned jls. *Recreations:* music appreciation, walking. *Address:* Kennedy Institute of Rheumatology, 1 Aspenlea Road, W6 8LH. *T:* (020) 8383 4444. *Club:* Reform.

MAINWARING, Captain Maurice Kildare C.; *see* Cavenagh-Mainwaring.

MAIR, Alexander, MBE 1967; Chief Executive and Director, Grampian Television Ltd, 1970–87, retired; *b* 5 Nov. 1922; *s* of Charles Mair and Helen Dickie; *m* 1953, Margaret Isobel Gowans Rennie. *Educ:* Skene, Aberdeenshire; Webster's Business Coll., Aberdeen; Sch. of Accountancy, Glasgow. Fellow, CIMA, 1992 (Associate, 1953). Chief Accountant, Bydand Holdings Ltd, 1957–60; Company Sec., Grampian Television, 1961–70; apptd Dir, 1967; Director: ITN, 1980–87; Cablevision (Scotland) Ltd, 1983–88; TV Publication Ltd, 1970–87. Chairman: British Regional Television Assoc., 1973–75; ITCA Management Cttee, 1980–87; RGIT Ltd, 1989–98. Pres., Aberdeen Junior Chamber of Commerce, 1960–61; Mem. Council, Aberdeen Chamber of Commerce, 1973–96 (Vice-Pres., 1987–89; Pres., 1989–91). Gov., Robert Gordon's Coll., Aberdeen, 1987–. FRSA 1973. FRTS 1987. *Recreations:* golf, ski-ing, gardening. *Address:* Ravenswood, 66 Rubislaw Den South, Aberdeen AB15 4AY. *T:* (01224) 317619. *Club:* Royal Northern (Aberdeen).

MAIR, Alexander Stirling Fraser, (Alistair), MBE 1987; DL; Chairman, 1991–98, and Managing Director, 1977–98, Caithness Glass Ltd; *b* 20 July 1935; *s* of Alexander W. R. Mair and Agnes W. (*née* Stirling); *m* 1st, 1961, Alice Anne Garrow (*d* 1975); four *s*; 2nd, 1977, Mary Crawford Bolton; one *d. Educ:* Robert Gordon's Coll., Aberdeen; Aberdeen Univ. (BSc (Eng)); BA Hist. Open Univ. 2001. SSC, RAF, 1960–62. Rolls-Royce, Glasgow: grad. apprentice, 1957–59; various appts, until Product Centre Manager, 1963–71; Man. Dir, Caithness Glass, Wick, 1971–75; Marketing Dir, Worcester Royal Porcelain Co., 1975–77. Director: Grampian Television, 1986–; Crieff Hydro Ltd, 1994– (Chm., 1996–); Murray VCT 3 PLC, 1998–. Vice Chm., Scottish Cons. and Unionist Party, 1992–93; Chm., Perth Cons. and Unionist Assoc., 1999–. Mem. Council, CBI, 1985–97 (Chm., Scotland, 1989–91). Pres., British Glass Manufacturers' Confedn, 1997–98; Chm., Crieff and Dist Aux. Assoc. (Richmond House), 1993–99. Hon. Pres., Perth and Kinross Assoc., Duke of Edinburgh's Award Scheme, 1993–. Mem. Court, Aberdeen Univ., 1993– (Convener, Jt Planning, Finance and Estates Cttee, 1998–; Chancellor's Assessor and Vice Chm., 2000–); Gov., Morrison's Acad., Crieff, 1985– (Chm., 1996–); Comr, Queen Victoria Sch., Dunblane, 1992–97. FIMgt; FRSA 1986. DL Perth and Kinross 1993. *Recreations:* walking, gardening, swimming, current affairs, history. *Address:* Woodend, Madderty, by Crieff, Perthshire PH7 3PA. *T:* and *Fax:* (01764) 683210. *Club:* Royal Scottish Automobile (Glasgow).

MAIR, John Magnus; Director of Social Work, Edinburgh, 1969–75; Lecturer in Social Medicine, University of Edinburgh, 1959–75; *b* 29 Dec. 1912; *s* of Joseph Alexander Mair and Jane Anderson; *m* 1940, Isobelle Margaret Williamson (*d* 1969); three *s. Educ:* Anderson Inst., Lerwick; Univs of Aberdeen (MB, ChB) and Edinburgh (DPH). MFCM. Asst GP, Highlands and Islands Medical Service, 1937–40; RAMC, 1940–45; Edinburgh Public Health Dept (latterly Sen. Depute Medical Officer of Health), 1945–69. *Recreation:* golf. *Address:* 67 Elliot Road, Hendon, NW4 3EB. *Club:* Grampian (Corby).

MAIR, Prof. Robert James, PhD; FREng, FICE; Professor of Geotechnical Engineering, University of Cambridge, since 1998; Master of Jesus College, Cambridge, since 2001; Founding Director, Geotechnical Consulting Group, London, since 1983; *b* 20 April 1950; *s* of William Austyn Mair, *qv*; *m* 1981, Margaret Mary Plowden O'Connor; one *s* one *d. Educ:* Leys Sch.; Clare Coll., Cambridge (MA 1975; PhD 1979). FICE 1990; FREng (FEng 1992). Scott Wilson Kirkpatrick and Partners, Consulting Engineers: Engr, London and Hong Kong, 1971–76; Sen. Engr, London, 1980–83; Res. Asst, Dept of Engrg, Univ. of Cambridge, 1976–79; Fellow, St John's Coll., Cambridge, 1998–2001. Special Prof., Dept of Civil Engrg, Univ. of Nottingham, 1994–97; Royal Acad. of Engrg Vis. Prof., Univ. of Cambridge, 1997–98. Mem., Commn of Enquiry into Collapse of Toulon Tunnel, French Govt, 1997. Mem. Council, and various cttees, ICE, 1993–95. *Publications:* (with D. M. Wood) Pressuremeter Testing: methods and interpretation, 1987; technical papers, mainly in jls of soil mechanics and geotechnical engrg; conf. proceedings, principally on underground construction and tunnelling. *Recreations:* supporting QPR, sailing, tennis, golf, long walks. *Address:* Master's Lodge, Jesus College, Cambridge CB5 8BL. *T:* (01223) 339442, *Fax:* (01223) 339304; *e-mail:* master@jesus.cam.ac.uk; rjm50@eng.cam.ac.uk. *Clubs:* Hurlingham; Royal Solent Yacht.

MAIR, Prof. William Austyn, CBE 1969; MA; FREng; Francis Mond Professor of Aeronautical Engineering, University of Cambridge, 1952–83; Head of Engineering Department, 1973–83; Fellow of Downing College, Cambridge, 1953–83, Hon. Fellow, 1983; *b* 24 Feb. 1917; *s* of William Mair, MD; *m* 1944, Mary Woodhouse Crofts; two *s. Educ:* Highgate Sch.; Clare Coll., Cambridge. Aerodynamics Dept, Royal Aircraft Establishment, Farnborough, 1940–46; Dir, Fluid Motion Laboratory, Univ. of Manchester, 1946–52. Mem. various cttees, Aeronautical Research Council, 1946–80. Dir, Hovercraft Development Ltd, 1962–81. John Orr Meml Lectr, S Africa, 1983. Chm., Editorial Bd, Aeronautical Qly, 1975–81. FRAeS (Silver Medal 1975); FREng (FEng 1984). Hon. DSc Cranfield, 1990. *Publications:* (with D. L. Birdsall) Aircraft Performance, 1992; papers on aerodynamics. *Address:* 7 The Oast House, Pinehurst, Grange Road, Cambridge CB3 9AP. *T:* (01223) 350137.

See also R. J. Mair.

MAIS, Francis Thomas; Secretary, Royal Northern College of Music, 1982–90; *b* 27 June 1927; *s* of Charles Edward Mais and Emma (*née* McLoughlin); *m* 1st, Margaret Edythe Evans (*d* 1984); one *d*; 2nd, 1987, Joan Frost-Smith. *Educ:* Barnsley Grammar Sch.; Christ's Coll., Cambridge (MA). Northern Ireland Civil Service, 1951–82: Permanent Secretary: Dept of Commerce, 1979–81; Dept of Manpower Services, 1981–82. Governor, Associated Bd, Royal Schs of Music, 1985–92. Hon. RNCM 1987. *Address:* No 2 Applegarth, Fairybead Lane, Stainton, Penrith, Cumbria CA11 0DD. *T:* (01768) 210531.

MAISEY, Prof. Michael Norman, BSc, MD; FRCP; FRCR; Professor and Chairman of Radiological Sciences, Guy's, King's and St Thomas' Hospitals' School of Medicine, King's College London (formerly United Medical and Dental Schools of Guy's and St Thomas's Hospitals), since 1984; *b* 10 June 1939; *s* of Harold Lionel Maisey and Kathleen Christine Maisey; *m* 1965, Irene Charlotte (*née* Askay); two *s. Educ:* Caterham Sch.; Guy's Hosp. Med. Sch. (BSc, MD). ABNM 1972; FRCP 1980; FRCR 1989. House appts, 1964–66; Registrar, Guy's Hosp., 1966–69; Fellow, Johns Hopkins Med. Instns, 1970–72; Guy's Hospital: Sen. Registrar, 1972–73; Consultant Physician, Endocrinology and Nuclear Medicine, 1973–; Med. Dir and Chm. of Mgt Bd, 1991–93; Med. Dir, Guy's and St Thomas's Hosp. NHS Trust, 1993–96. Hon. Consultant to the Army in Nuclear Medicine, 1978–. Pres., BIR, 2000–01. *Publications:* Nuclear Medicine, 1980; (ed jtly) Clinical Nuclear Medicine, 1983, 3rd edn 1998; (jtly) An Atlas of Normal Skeletal Scintigraphy, 1985; (jtly) An Atlas of Clinical Nuclear Medicine, 1988, 2nd edn 1994; (jtly) New Developments in Myocardial Imaging, 1993; Clinical Positron Emission Tomography, 1999; books and papers on thyroid diseases, nuclear medicine and medical imaging. *Address:* Guy's Hospital, St Thomas Street, SE1 9RT. *T:* (020) 7955 4531.

MAISNER, Air Vice-Marshal Aleksander, CB 1977; CBE 1969; AFC 1955; *b* 26 July 1921; *s* of Henryk Maisner and Helene Anne (*née* Brosin); *m* 1946, Mary (*née* Coverley) (*d* 1997); one *s* one *d. Educ:* High Sch. and Lyceum, Czestochowa, Poland; Warsaw Univ. Labour Camps, USSR, 1940–41; Polish Artillery, 1941–42; Polish Air Force, 1943–46; joined RAF, 1946; Flying Trng Comd, 1946–49; No 70 Sqdn Suez Canal Zone, 1950–52; No 50 Sqdn RAF Binbrook, 1953–55; No 230 (Vulcan) OCU, RAF Waddington, 1955–59; psa 1960; OC Flying Wing, RNZAF Ohakea, 1961–62; Dirg Staff, RAF Staff Coll., Andover, 1963–65; DD Air Plans, MoD, 1965–68; CO, RAF Seletar, Singapore, 1969–71; Asst Comdt, RAF Coll., Cranwell, 1971–73; Dir, Personnel (Policy and Plans), MoD, 1973–75; Asst Air Sec., 1975; Dir-Gen. of Personnel Management, RAF, 1976. Personnel Exec., Reed Internat. Ltd, 1977–82; Dir, Industry and Parlt Trust, 1984–87. Governor, Shiplake Coll., 1978–96. Pres., Polish Air Force Assoc., 1982–. Comdr's Cross with Star, Order of Polonia Restituta (Poland), 1990; Comdr's Cross, OM (Poland), 1992; OM with Star (Poland), 1998. *Recreations:* gardening, reading. *Club:* Royal Air Force.

MAISONROUGE, Jacques Gaston; management consultant; *b* Cachan, Seine, 20 Sept. 1924; *s* of Paul Maisonrouge and Suzanne (*née* Cazas); *m* 1948, Françoise Andrée Féron; one *s* four *d. Educ:* Lycée Voltaire and Saint Louis, Paris. Studied engineering; gained dip. of Ecole Centrale des Arts et Manufactures. Engineer, 1948; various subseq. appts in IBM Corp., France; Chm. and Chief Exec. Officer, IBM World Trade Europe/ME/Africa Corp., 1974–81; Pres., IBM Europe, 1974–81; Sen. Vice-Pres., 1972–84, and Mem. Bd of Dirs, 1983–84, IBM Corp.; Chm., IBM World Trade Corp., 1976–84; Vice Chm., Liquid Air Corp., 1984–86; Dir-Gen. of Industry, France, 1986–87; Chm. of Bd, French Centre for Foreign Trade, 1987–89. Director: L'Air Liquide, 1964–94; IBM Europe/ME/Africa, 1987–94. Chm., Bd of Trustees, Ecole Centrale des Arts et Manufactures, 1976–87; Chancellor, Internat. Acad. of Management, 1987–93. Gov., American Hosp. of Paris, 1988–. Nat. Pres., France–US Assoc., 1994–. Grand Officier, Ordre de la Légion d'Honneur; Commander: Ordre National du Mérite; des Palmes Académiques; Order of

Merit of the Italian Republic; Order of Saint Sylvester; Order of Star of North (Sweden); Grand Officer, Order of Malta. *Publication:* Inside IBM: a European's story, 1985. *Recreations:* interested in sport (tennis). *Address:* 3 boulevard Flandrin, 75116 Paris, France. *Club:* Automobile of France, Cercle Interallié.

MAITLAND, family name of **Earl of Lauderdale**.

MAITLAND, Viscount, Master of Lauderdale; **Ian Maitland;** Marketing Adviser, London School of Economics and Political Science, 1995–2001; *b* 4 Nov. 1937; *s* and *heir* of Earl of Lauderdale, *qv*; *m* 1963, Ann Paule, *d* of Geoffrey Clark; one *s* one *d*. *Educ:* Radley Coll., Abingdon; Brasenose Coll., Oxford (MA Modern History). Various appointments since 1960; with Hedderwick Borthwick & Co., 1970–74; National Westminster Bank, 1974–95: Regl Manager, Maghreb, 1986, ME and N Africa, 1989–91; Sen. Regl Manager, Africa and ME, 1991–95. Director: Maitland Consultancy Services Ltd, 1995–; Tradefinanceguru.com Ltd, 2000–. Lecturer: NY Inst. of Finance, 1997–2000; Euromoney Instnl Investor (formerly Euromoney Publications) PLC, 1998–2000; LSE Gurukul Scholarship Course, 1999. Royal Naval Reserve (Lieutenant), 1963–73; Mem., Queen's Body Guard for Scotland, Royal Co. of Archers, 1986–. Freeman, City of London, 1998; Liveryman, Fanmakers' Co., 1998–. *Recreations:* photography, sailing. *Heir: s* Master of Maitland, *qv*. *Address:* 150 Tachbrook Street, SW1V 2NE; *e-mail:* maitland@lauderdale.u-net.com. *Clubs:* Royal Ocean Racing; New (Edinburgh).

MAITLAND, Master of; Hon. John Douglas Maitland; *b* 29 May 1965; *s* and *heir* of Viscount Maitland, *qv*; *m* 2001, Rosamund, *yr d* of Nigel Bennett. *Educ:* Emanuel School; Radley College; Van Mildert College, Durham (BSc). *Recreations:* cycling, camping, sailing. *Address:* 150 Tachbrook Street, SW1V 2NE.

MAITLAND, Alastair George, CBE 1966; Consul-General, Boston, 1971–75, retired; *b* 30 Jan. 1916; *s* of late Thomas Douglas Maitland, MBE, and Wilhelmina Sarah Dundas; *m* 1st, 1943, Betty Hamilton (*d* 1981); two *s* one *d*; 2nd, 1986, Hazel Margaret Porter. *Educ:* George Watson's Coll., Edinburgh; Universities of Edinburgh (MA First Class Hons), Grenoble and Paris, Ecole des Sciences Politiques. Vice-Consul: New York, 1938; Chicago, 1939; New York, 1939; Los Angeles, 1940; apptd to staff of UK High Commissioner at Ottawa, 1942; apptd to Foreign Office, 1945; Brit. Middle East Office, Cairo, 1948; Foreign Office, 1952; UK Delegation to OEEC, Paris, 1954; Consul-General: at New Orleans, 1958–62; at Jerusalem, 1962–64; at Cleveland, 1964–68; Dir-Gen., British Trade Develt Office, NY, 1968–71. Hon. LLD Lake Erie Coll., Ohio, 1971. CStJ. *Recreations:* music, golf, gardening, reading. *Address:* Box 31, Heath, MA 01346, USA.

MAITLAND, Charles Alexander, (10th Bt *cr* 1918, of Clifton, Midlothian); *b* 3 June 1986; *s* of Sir Richard John Maitland, 9th Bt (*d* 1994). Has not yet established his claim to the title.

MAITLAND, David Henry, CVO 1988; Chief Executive, 1966–81, and Chairman, 1979–81, Save & Prosper Group; *b* 9 May 1922; *s* of George and Mary Annie Maitland; *m* 1955, Judeth Mary Gold; three *d*. *Educ:* Eton; King's College, Cambridge. FCA. Army, 1941–46, Captain, Oxf. & Bucks Light Inf. Articled Whinney Smith & Whinney, 1946; qualified ACA 1950; Mobil Oil Co., 1952–60; Save & Prosper Group: Comptroller, 1960; Managing Dir, 1966; non-exec. Dir, 1981; retired 1987. Dir, HFC Bank, 1989–95. Chm., Unit Trust Assoc., 1973–75; Member: City Capital Markets Cttee, 1975–84; Inflation Accounting Steering Group, 1976–80; Council, Duchy of Lancaster, 1977–87; Bethlem Royal Hosp. and Maudsley Hosp. SHA, 1982–90; Royal Commn for 1851 Exhibn, 1984–97; Treloar Trust (formerly Lord Mayor Treloar Trust), 1984–. Vice-Chm., Crafts Council, 1989–90 (Mem., 1984–90). Mem., Cttee of Management, Inst. of Psychiatry, 1984–96 (Chm., 1987–90). *Address:* Angel House, 4 High Street, Odiham, Hants RG29 1LG. *Club:* City of London (Chm., 1985–88).

MAITLAND, Sir Donald (James Dundas), GCMG 1977 (CMG 1967); Kt 1973; OBE 1960; Visiting Professor, Bath University; *b* 16 Aug. 1922; *s* of Thomas Douglas Maitland and Wilhelmina Sarah Dundas; *m* 1950, Jean Marie Young, *d* of Gordon Young; one *s* one *d*. *Educ:* George Watson's Coll.; Edinburgh Univ (MA). Served India, Middle East, and Burma, 1941–47 (Royal Scots; Rajputana Rifles). Joined Foreign Service, 1947; Consul, Amara, 1950; British Embassy, Baghdad, 1950–53; Private Sec. to Minister of State, Foreign Office, 1954–56; Director, Middle East Centre for Arab Studies, Lebanon, 1956–60; Foreign Office, 1960–63; Counsellor, British Embassy, Cairo, 1963–65; Head of News Dept, Foreign Office, 1965–67; Principal Private Sec. to Foreign and Commonwealth Secretary, 1967–69; Ambassador to Libya, 1969–70; Chief Press Sec., 10 Downing St, 1970–73; UK Permanent Rep. to UN, 1973–74; Dep. Under-Sec. of State, FCO, 1974–75; UK Mem., Commonwealth Group on Trade, Aid and Develt, 1975; Ambassador and UK Perm. Rep. to EEC, 1975–79; Dep. to Perm. Under-Sec. of State, FCO, Dec. 1979–June 1980; Perm. Under-Sec. of State, Dept of Energy, 1980–82. Chairman: Independent Commn for World-Wide Telecommunications Develt, 1983–85; UK Nat. Cttee for World Communications Year, 1983; HEA, 1989–94. Govt Dir, Britoil, 1983–85; Director: Slough Estates, 1983–92; Northern Engrg Industries, 1986–89. Dep. Chm., IBA, 1986–89. Chm., Charlemagne Inst. (formerly Christians for Europe), 1984–97. Mem., Commonwealth War Graves Commn, 1983–87. President: Bath Inst. for Rheumatic Diseases, 1986–95 and 1997–; Federal Trust for Educn and Res., 1987–; Vice-Pres., Centre Européen de Prospective et de Synthèse, Paris, 1990–95; Governor, Westminster Coll., Oxford, 1990–97 (Chm., 1994–97). Hon. Fellow, Bath Spa UC, 2000. Hon. LLD Bath, 1995; Hon. DLitt UWE, 2000. *Publications:* Diverse Times, Sundry Places (autobiog.), 1996; The Boot and Other Stories, 1999; The Running Tide, 2000; articles on internat. affairs, sovereignty, world telecommunications, public health. *Recreations:* hill-walking, music. *Address:* Murhill Farm House, Limpley Stoke, Bath BA2 7FH. *T:* (01225) 723157.

MAITLAND, Lady (Helen) Olga, (Lady Olga Hay); journalist; *b* 23 May 1944; *er d* of Earl of Lauderdale, *qv*; *m* 1969, Robin Hay, *qv*; two *s* one *d*. *Educ:* Sch. of St Mary and St Anne, Abbots Bromley; Lycée Français de Londres. Reporter, Fleet St News Agency, Blackheath and Dist Reporter, 1965–67; journalist, Sunday Express, 1967–91, Daily Mail, 1998–. ILEA Candidate, Holborn and St Pancras, 1986; contested (C) Bethnal Green and Stepney, 1987. MP (C) Sutton and Cheam, 1992–97; contested (C) same seat, 1997, 2001. PPS to Minister of State, NI Office, 1996. Member, Select Committee: on Procedure, 1992–95; on Educn, 1992–96; on Social Security, 1995–96; on Health, 1996–97. Formerly Sec., Cons. back bench Defence Cttee; Sec., Cons. back bench NI Cttee, 1992–97. Founder and Chm., Families for Defence, 1983–; Pres., Defence and Security Forum, 1992–. *Publications:* Margaret Thatcher: the first ten years, 1989; Faith in the Family, 1997; (contrib.) Peace Studies in our Schools, 1984; (contrib.) Political Indoctrination in Schools, 1985. *Recreations:* family, the arts, travel. *Address:* 21 Cloudesley Street, N1 0HX. *T:* (020) 7837 9212.

MAITLAND DAVIES, Keith Laurence; a District Judge (Magistrates' Courts) (formerly Metropolitan Stipendiary Magistrate), since 1984; *b* 3 Feb. 1938; *s* of Wyndham Matabele Davies, QC and Enid Maud Davies; *m* 1964, Angela Mary (*née* Jenkins); two *d* one *s*. *Educ:* Winchester; Christ Church, Oxford (MA). Called to the Bar, Inner Temple, 1962; private practice, 1962–84. *Address:* c/o West London Magistrates' Court, 181 Talgarth Road, W6 8DN.

MAITLAND-MAKGILL-CRICHTON, Maj.-Gen. Edward; *see* Crichton.

MAITLAND SMITH, Geoffrey; Chairman, Fiske plc, since 2000; chartered accountant; *b* 27 Feb. 1933; *s* of late Philip John Maitland Smith and Kathleen (*née* Goff); *m* 1986, Lucinda Enid, *d* of late Lt-Col Gerald Owen Whyte. *Educ:* University Coll. Sch., London. Partner, Thornton Baker & Co., Chartered Accountants, 1960–70; Sears plc: Dir, 1971–95; Dep. Chm., 1978–84; Jt Chm., 1984; Chief Exec., 1978–88; Chm., 1985–95; Chairman: Selfridges Ltd, 1985–93; Mallett plc, 1986–89; Hammerson plc, 1993–99 (Dir, 1990–99); W. and F. C. Bonham and Sons Ltd, 1996–2000; Dep. Chm., Midland Bank plc, 1992–96 (Dir, 1986–96); Director: Asprey plc, 1980–93; Central Independent Television plc, 1983–85; Courtaulds plc, 1983–90; Imperial Group plc, 1984–86; HSBC Holdings plc, 1992–96. Mem. Bd, Financial Reporting Council, 1990–98. Chm., 1996 British Olympic Games Appeal, 1994–97. Hon. Vice Pres., Inst. of Marketing, 1987–94. Chm. Council, University Coll. Sch., 1987–96. *Recreation:* opera. *Address:* Manor Barn, Fifield, Oxon OX7 6HF. *Club:* Boodle's.

MAITLIS, Prof. Peter Michael, FRS 1984; Professor of Chemistry, 1972–97, Research Professor, since 1997, Sheffield University; *b* 15 Jan. 1933; *s* of Jacob Maitlis and Judith Maitlis; *m* 1959, Marion (*née* Basco); three *d*. *Educ:* Univ. of Birmingham (BSc 1953); Univ. of London (PhD 1956, DSc 1971). Asst Lectr, London Univ., 1956–60; Fulbright Fellow and Res. Associate, Cornell Univ., 1960–61, Harvard Univ., 1961–62; Asst Prof, 1962–64, Associate Prof., 1964–67, Prof., 1967–72, McMaster Univ., Hamilton, Ont, Canada; Prof. of Inorganic Chemistry, Univ. of Sheffield, 1972–. Chm., Chemistry Cttee, SERC, 1985–88. Fellow, Alfred P. Sloan Foundn, USA, 1968–70; Tilden Lectr, RSC, 1979–80; Sir Edward Frankland Prize Lectr, RSC, 1985; Ludwig Mond Lectr, RSC, 1996–97. Member: Royal Soc. of Chemistry (formerly Chem. Soc.), 1952– (Pres., Dalton Div., 1985–87); Amer. Chemical Soc., 1963–; Council, Royal Soc., 1991–93; BBC Sci. Consultative Gp, 1989–93. Foreign Mem., Accademia Nazionale dei Lincei, Italy, 1999. E. W. R. Steacie Prize (Canada), 1971; Medallist, RSC (Noble Metals and their Compounds), 1981; Kurnakov Medal, Russian Acad. of Scis, 1998. *Publications:* The Organic Chemistry of Palladium, vols 1 and 2, 1971; many research papers in learned jls. *Recreations:* travel, music, reading, walking. *Address:* Department of Chemistry, The University, Sheffield S3 7HF. *T:* (0114) 222 9320.

MAJOR; *see* Henniker-Major, family name of Baron Henniker.

MAJOR, Rt Hon. John, CH 1999; PC 1987; *b* 29 March 1943; *s* of late Thomas Major and Gwendolyn Minny Coates; *m* 1970, Norma Christina Elizabeth Johnson (*see* Dame N. C. E. Major); one *s* one *d*. *Educ:* Rutlish. AIB. Banker, Standard Chartered Bank: various executive posts in UK and overseas, 1965–79. Member, Lambeth Borough Council, 1968–71 (Chm. Housing Cttee, 1970–71). Contested (C) St Pancras North (Camden), Feb. 1974 and Oct. 1974. MP (C) Huntingdonshire, 1979–83, Huntingdon, 1983–2001. PPS to Ministers of State at the Home Office, 1981–83; an Asst Govt Whip, 1983–84; a Lord Comr of HM Treasury (a Govt Whip), 1984–85; Parly Under-Sec. of State for Social Security, DHSS, 1985–86; Minister of State for Social Security, DHSS, 1986–87; Chief Sec. to HM Treasury, 1987–89; Sec. of State for Foreign and Commonwealth Affairs, 1989; Chancellor of the Exchequer, 1989–90; Prime Minister and First Lord of the Treasury, 1990–97. Jt Sec., Cons. Parly Party Environment Cttee, 1979–81. Mem., European Adv. Bd, 1998–, Chm., European Bd, 2001–, Carlyle Gp; Chm., European Adv. Council, Emerson Electric Co., 1999–; Member: Bd, Mayflower Corporation, 2000–; European Bd of Dirs, Siebel Systems, Inc., 2001–; Sen. Advr, Credit Suisse First Boston, 2001–. Chm., Ditchley Council; Mem., InterAction Council, Tokyo, 1998–. Chm., Westminster Woodland, 1998–. Pres., Nat. Asthma Campaign, 1998–; Patron: Child of Achievement Awards; Mercy Ships; Prostate Cancer Charity; Support for Africa; Atlantic Partnership, 2001–; FCO Assoc., 2001–; Professional Cricketers' Assoc. Mem. Bd, Warden Housing Assoc., 1975–83. Member: Bd of Advrs, Baker Inst., Houston, 1998–; Internat. Bd of Govs, Peres Center for Peace, Israel, 1997–. Pres., Surrey CCC, 2000–02, now Hon. Life Vice-Pres. *Publication:* The Autobiography, 1999. *Recreations:* music, theatre, opera, reading, travel, cricket and other sports. *Clubs:* Buck's, Carlton, Farmers', Pratt's, MCC (Mem. Cttee, 2001–).

MAJOR, John, LVO 1998; FRICS; Chairman, Clegg Kennedy Drew, Land Agents and Chartered Surveyors, since 1998; *b* 16 June 1945; *s* of John Robert Major and Vera Major; *m* 1967, (Mary) Ruth Oddy; one *s* one *d*. *Educ:* Wellingborough Sch.; RAC, Cirencester. FRICS 1980. Partner, Osmond Tricks, Bristol, 1980–85; Land Agent, Castle Howard, N Yorks, 1986–91; Land Agent to HM the Queen, Sandringham Estate, 1991–98. Dir, F.P.D. Savills, 2000–. *Recreation:* sailing. *Address:* Tysdale Manor, Tydd St Mary, Wisbech, Cambridgeshire PE13 5QY. *Club:* Farmers.

MAJOR, Dame Malvina (Lorraine), DBE 1991 (OBE 1985); opera singer; *b* 28 Jan. 1943; *d* of Vincent William Major and Eva Gwendolen (*née* McCaw); *m* 1965, Winston William Richard Fleming (*d* 1990); one *s* two *d*. *Educ:* Hamilton Technical Coll.; London Opera Centre. Studied with Dame Sister Mary Leo, Auckland; winner: NZ Mobil Song Quest, 1963; Melbourne Sun Aria Contest, Australia, 1964; Kathleen Ferrier Award, London, 1966. Camden Fest., London; Salzburg Fest., 1968 (internat. début as Rosina in Barber of Seville), 1969, 1991; returned to NZ, 1970; La Finta Giardiniera, Th. de la Monnaie, Brussels, 1985; Vienna, Amsterdam, New York, Antwerp, Salt Lake City, 1986; Don Giovanni, Drottningholme, Brighton Fest., 1987; Covent Garden début as Rosalinde in Die Fledermaus, 1990; with Australian Opera, and in E Berlin, 30 rôles, including: La Bohème; Madame Butterfly; Faust; Il Seraglio; Rigoletto; Don Pasquale; Lucia di Lammermoor; Magic Flute; Tosca; Merry Widow; La Traviata; Eugene Onegin; Elisabetta Regina d'Inghilterra; Marriage of Figaro; also extensive concert repertoire, TV and recordings. Established Dame Malvina Major Foundn for educn in performing arts, 1992. Entertainer and Internat. Performer of the Year, NZ, 1992; NZ Classical Disc Award, 1993 and 1994. *Recreations:* golf, sewing, family. *Address:* PO Box 11–175, Wellington, New Zealand.

MAJOR, Dame Norma (Christina Elizabeth), DBE 1999; *b* 12 Feb. 1942; *d* of late Norman Wagstaff and Edith Johnson; *m* 1970, Rt Hon. John Major, *qv*; one *s* one *d*. *Educ:* Peckham Sch. for Girls; Battersea Coll. of Domestic Science (Teachers' Cert.). Teacher, Sydenham Sch. and St Michael and All Angels Sch., Camberwell, 1963–70. Campaigned with husband, 7 Gen. Elecns, 1974–97. Dir, WNO, 1999–. A Nat. Vice Pres., Mencap, 1995– (President: Mencap Challenge Fund; Mencap, Huntingdon); a Vice Pres., John Grooms Assoc.; Patron: Crossroads Care, 1991–; Spinal Res. Trust; Rowan Foundn. *Publications:* Joan Sutherland, 1987; Chequers: the Prime Minister's country house and its history, 1996. *Recreations:* opera, theatre, reading.

MAK, Prof. Tak Wah, FRS 1994; Professor, since 1984, and Head, Division of Cellular and Molecular Biology, Ontario Cancer Research Institute, University of Toronto; *b* Canton, China, 4 Oct. 1946; *s* of Kent and Linda Mak; *m* 1969, Shirley Lau; two *d. Educ:* Univ. of Wisconsin (BSc 1967; MSc 1969); Univ. of Alberta (PhD 1972). Research Assistant: Univ. of Wisconsin, Madison, 1967–69; Univ. of Alberta, 1969–72; University of Toronto: Postdoctoral Fellow, 1972–74; Asst Prof., 1974–78; Associate Prof., 1978–84. Dir and Res. Vice Pres., Amgen Inst. *Publications:* (ed) Molecular and Cellular Biology of Hemopolitic Stem Cell Differentiation, 1981; (ed) Molecular and Cellular Biology of Neiplasia, 1983; (ed) Cancer: perspective for control, 1986; (ed) The T Receptor, 1987; (ed) AIDS: ten years later, 1991; articles in jls. *Address:* (home) 130 Glen Road, Toronto, ON M4W 2W3, Canada; (office) Ontario Cancer Research Institute, 610 University Avenue, Room 8–712, Toronto, ON M5G 2M9, Canada.

MAKAROVA, Natalia; dancer and choreographer; *b* Leningrad, 21 Nov. 1940; *m* 1976, Edward Karkar; one *s. Educ:* Vaganova Ballet Sch.; Leningrad Choreographic Sch. Mem., Kirov Ballet, 1959–70; London début, as Giselle, Covent Garden, 1961; joined American Ballet Theatre, 1970; formed dance co., Makarova & Co., 1980; Guest Artist: Royal Ballet, Covent Garden, 1972; London Festival Ballet, 1984. Has danced many classical and contemporary rôles in UK, Europe and USA, 1970–92; appearances include: La Bayadère (which she also staged, and choreographed in part), NY Met, 1980, Manchester, 1985; On Your Toes, London and NY, 1984–86; choreographed new prodn of Swan Lake for London Fest. Ballet, London and tour, 1988. Honoured Artist of RSFSR, 1970. *Publications:* A Dance Autobiography, 1979; On Your Toes, 1984. *Address:* 323 Marina Boulevard, San Francisco, CA 94123, USA.

MAKEHAM, Peter Derek James; Director General, Finance and Analytical Services, Department for Education and Skills (formerly Department for Education and Employment), since 2000; *b* 15 March 1948; *s* of Derrick James Stark Makeham and Margaret Helene Makeham; *m* 1972, Carolyne Rosemary Dawe; one *s* three *d. Educ:* Chichester High Sch. for Boys; Nottingham Univ. (BA); Leeds Univ. (MA Lab Econs). Economist, Dept of Employment, 1971–82; on secondment to Unilever, 1982–83; HM Treasury, 1983–84; Enterprise Unit, Cabinet Office, 1984–85; Dept of Employment, 1985–87; DTI, 1987–90; Dept of Employment, subseq. Dept for Educn and Employment, now Dept for Educn and Skills, 1990–; Head of Strategy and Employment Policy Div., 1992–95; Director: Employment and Adult Trng, 1995–97; School Orgn and Funding, 1997–99; Teachers Gp, 1999–2000. *Recreation:* sailing. *Address:* Department for Education and Skills, Sanctuary Buildings, Great Smith Street, SW1P 3BT. *T:* (020) 7925 5573.

MAKEPEACE, John, OBE 1988; FCSD; FIMgt, FRSA; designer and furniture maker, since 1961; Founder and Director, The Parnham Trust and Parnham College (formerly School for Craftsmen in Wood), 1977; *b* 6 July 1939; *m* 1st, 1964, Ann Sutton (marr. diss. 1979); 2nd, 1983, Jennie Moores (*née* Brinsden). *Educ:* Denstone Coll., Staffs. Study tours: Scandinavia 1957; N America, 1961; Italy, 1968; W Africa, 1972; USA, 1974; Japan, 1994. Furniture in private and corporate collections in Europe, USA, Asia and S Africa. *Public Collections:* Cardiff Museum; Fitzwilliam Museum, Cambridge; Leeds Museum; Court Room, Worshipful Co. of Innholders; Board Room, Grosvenor Estate Holdings; Art Inst., Chicago; Museum für Kunsthandwerk, Frankfurt; Royal Museum of Scotland; V & A Museum; Lewis Collection, Richmond, USA; Banque Générale du Luxembourg. *Exhibitions:* Herbert Art Gall., Coventry, 1963; New Art Centre, London, 1971; Fine Art Soc., London, 1977; Interior, Kortrijk, Belgium, 1978, 1992, 1994; Royal Show, Stoneleigh, 1981–87; Crafts Council Open, 1984; National Theatre, 1980, 1986; Parnham at Smiths Gall., 1988–91; Sotheby's, 1988, 1992, 1993, 1997; New Art Forms, Chicago, 1989–92; Tokyo, 1990; ARCO, Madrid, 1993; Chicago Contemporary Art Fair, 1993–96; Art '93, London; Conservation by Design, Providence, USA, 1993; Creation, Claridge's, 1994; Banque de Luxembourg, 1995; British Embassy, Brussels, 1995; Smithsonian Instn, 1996; Rotunda, Hong Kong, 1996; Chicago Design Show, 1997; Mayor Gall., 1997; Great British Design, Cologne, 1997; Crafts Council, 1999; Maastricht Fair, 1999–2001; Sotheby's Contemporary Decorative Arts, 2000. *Consultancies/Lectures:* Crafts Council (and Mem.), 1972–77; India Handicrafts Bd, 1975; Jammu and Kashmir Govt, 1977; Belgrade Univ., 1978; Artist in Context, V&A Mus., 1979; Chm., Wood Programme, World Crafts Conf., Kyoto, Japan, 1979; Australian Crafts Council, 1980; Oxford Farming Conf., 1990; Furniture Technols Conf., Oxford, 2000; Furniture Soc., USA, 2000; Design Fest., Barcelona, 2001. Trustee, V & A Mus., 1987–91. *Television films:* Made by Makepeace, 1975; History of English Furniture, 1978; Heritage in Danger, 1979; First Edition, 1980; Touch Wood, 1982; Tomorrow's World, 1986. Winner, Observer Kitchen Design, 1971; Hooke Park Winner, UK Conservation Award, 1987; British Construction Industry Award, 1990; Amer. Inst. of Archts Award, 1993. *Relevant publication:* John Makepeace: a spirit of adventure in craft and design, by Jeremy Myerson, 1995. *Recreations:* friends, travel, contemporary art. *Address:* Parnham House, Beaminster, Dorset DT8 3NA. *T:* (01308) 862204. *Club:* Athenæum.

MAKEPEACE, Richard Edward; HM Diplomatic Service; Ambassador to Sudan, since 1999; *b* 24 June 1953; *s* of late Edward Dugard Makepeace and of Patricia Muriel Makepeace; *m* 1980, Rupmani Catherine Pradhan; two *s. Educ:* St Paul's Sch.; Keble Coll., Oxford. Joined FCO, 1976; MECAS, 1977–78; Muscat, 1979–81; Prague, 1981–85; FCO, 1985–86; Private Sec. to Parly Under-Sec. of State, FCO, 1987–88; UK Perm. Repn to EC, 1989–93; Dep. Head, Personnel Mgt Dept, FCO, 1993–95; Counsellor and Dep. Hd of Mission, Cairo, 1995–98. *Recreations:* travel, reading, music. *Address:* c/o Foreign and Commonwealth Office, SW1A 2AH.

MAKEPEACE-WARNE, Maj.-Gen. Antony, CB 1992; MBE 1972; Director, Army Museums Ogilby Trust, since 1996; Commandant, Joint Service Defence College, 1990–92; *b* 3 Sept 1937; *e s* of late Keith Makepeace-Warne and Nora (*née* Kelstrup); *m* 1966, Jill Estelle Seath; two *d. Educ:* Taunton School; Open Univ. (BA Hons 1990). Commissioned KOYLI, 1960; served BAOR, Malaya, Aden, Berlin, MoD, to 1969; Staff College, 1970; 2nd Bn LI, 1971–72; 24 Airportable Bde, 1972–74; Instructor, Staff Coll., 1975–77; CO 1st Bn LI, 1977–80; Col ASD2, MoD, 1980–82; Comdr, Berlin Inf. Bde, 1982–84; RCDS 1985; ACOS HQ UKLF, 1986–88; GS Study of Indiv. Trg Orgn, 1988–89. Dep. Col, LI (Somerset and Cornwall), 1987–89; Colonel, The Light Infantry, 1990–92. Member: Council, Assoc. of Independent Museums, 1996–; Council, Museums Assoc., 1997–. *Publications:* Exceedingly Lucky: a history of the Light Infantry 1968–1993, 1993; The British Army Today and Tomorrow 1993/94, 1993; Brassey's Companion to the British Army, 1995. *Address:* c/o Lloyds TSB, Cox's & King's, 7 Pall Mall, SW1Y 5NA. *Club:* Army and Navy.

MAKGILL, family name of **Viscount of Oxfuird**.

MAKGILL CRICHTON MAITLAND, Major John David; Lord-Lieutenant of Renfrewshire, 1980–94; *b* 10 Sept. 1925; *e s* of late Col Mark Edward Makgill Crichton Maitland, CVO, DSO, DL, JP, The Island House, Wilton, Salisbury, Wilts, and late Patience Irene Fleetwood Makgill Crichton Maitland (*née* Fuller); *m* 1st, 1954, Jean Patricia (*d* 1985), *d* of late Maj.-Gen. Sir Michael Creagh, KBE, MC, Pigeon Hill, Homington, Salisbury; one *s* one *d*; 2nd, 1987, Mary Ann Vere, *o d* of late Major Charles Herbert Harberton Eales, MC, and *widow* of Capt. James Quintin Penn Curzon. *Educ:* Eton. Served War, 1944–45, Grenadier Guards. Continued serving until 1957 (temp. Major, 1952; retd 1957), rank Captain (Hon. Major). Renfrew CC, 1961–75. DL Renfrewshire 1962, Vice-Lieutenant 1972–80. *Address:* Daluaine, Rhynie, Huntly, Aberdeenshire AB54 4WA. *T:* (01464) 861638.

MAKHLOUF, Gabriel; Director, International, Board of Inland Revenue, since 1998; *b* 3 Feb. 1960; *s* of Antoine Makhlouf and Aïda Makhlouf (*née* Lazian); *m* 1984, Sandy Cope; one *s. Educ:* Prior Park Coll., Bath; Univ. of Exeter (BA Hons Econs); Univ. of Bath (MSc Industrial Relns). Board of Inland Revenue: HM Inspector of Taxes, 1984–89; Policy Advr, 1989–92; Head of Secretariat, Change Mgt Gp, 1992–93; Head of Direct Tax Br., Fiscal Policy, HM Treasury, 1993–95; Asst Dir, Personal Tax Div., Bd of Inland Revenue, 1995–97; HM Treasury: Principal Private Sec. to Chancellor of Exchequer, 1997–98; Head, Work Incentives and Poverty Analysis, 1998. Chm., Cttee on Fiscal Affairs, OECD, 2000–. *Address:* Revenue Policy International, Board of Inland Revenue, Victory House, 30–34 Kingsway, WC2B 6ES. *T:* (020) 7438 6762.

MAKHULU, Most Rev. Walter Paul Khotso, CMG 2000; Archbishop of Central Africa, 1980–2000, now Emeritus; Bishop of Botswana, 1979–2000; *b* Johannesburg, 1935; *m* 1966, Rosemary Sansom; one *s* one *d. Educ:* St Peter's Theological Coll., Rosettenville; Selly Oak Colls, Birmingham. Deacon 1957, priest 1958, Johannesburg; Curate: Johannesburg, 1957–60; Botswana, 1961–63; St Carantoc's Mission, Francistown, Botswana, 1961–63; St Andrew's Coll., Selly Oak, Birmingham, 1963–64; Curate: All Saints, Poplar, 1964–66; St Silas, Pentonville, with St Clement's, Barnsbury, 1966–68; Vicar of St Philip's, Battersea, 1968–75; Secretary for E Africa, WCC, 1975–79. A President: WCC, 1983–91; All Africa Conf. of Churches, 1981–86. Hon. DD: Kent, 1988; Gen. Theol Seminary, NY, 1990. Officier, Ordre des Palmes Académiques (France), 1981; PH 2000. *Address:* Cheyne House, 10 Crondace Road, Fulham, SW6 4BB. *T:* (020) 7371 9419; *e-mail:* bishmak@makhulu.fsnet.co.uk.

MAKIN, Claire Margaret, FRICS; Chambers Director, 13 King's Bench Walk, since 1998; *b* 21 March 1951; *d* of late James Ernest Makin, CBE and Mary Makin (*née* Morris); *m* 1978, David Anthony Bowman. *Educ:* City Univ. (MBA). FRICS 1988; ACIArb 1985. Partner, Richard Ellis, 1978–90; Consultant, Price Waterhouse, 1990–91; Partner, Bernard Thorpe, 1991–93; Dir, DTZ Debenham Thorpe, 1993–95; Chief Exec., RICS, 1995–97. FRSA 1991. *Recreations:* travelling, food and wine, restoring old houses. *Address:* 62 Queens Gate, SW7 5JP.

MAKINS, family name of **Baron Sherfield**.

MAKINSON, John Crowther, CBE 2001; Finance Director, Pearson plc, since 1996; *b* 10 Oct. 1954; *s* of Kenneth Crowther Makinson and Phyllis Georgina Makinson (*née* Miller); *m* 1985, Virginia Clare Macbeth; two *d. Educ:* Repton Sch.; Christ's Coll., Cambridge (BA Hons). Journalist: Reuters, 1976–79; Financial Times, 1979–86; Vice Chm., Saatchi & Saatchi (US), 1986–89; Partner, Makinson Cowell, 1989–94; Man. Dir, Financial Times, 1994–96. *Recreations:* music, cooking. *Address:* 25 Richmond Crescent, N1 0LY. *Club:* Groucho.

MAKINSON, William, CBE 1977; engineering management consultant, now retired; *b* 11 May 1915; *s* of Joshua Makinson and Martha (*née* Cunliffe); *m* 1952, Helen Elizabeth Parker; one *s* three *d. Educ:* Ashton-in-Makerfield Grammar Sch.; Manchester Univ. Asst Lecturer, Electronics, Manchester Univ., 1935–36; Education Officer, RAF Cranwell, 1936–39; RAE Farnborough, 1939–52; Hon. Squadron-Ldr, RAF, 1943–45; Superintendent, Blind Landing Experimental Unit, 1952–55; Defence Research Policy Staff, 1955–56; Managing Director, General Precision Systems Ltd, 1956–64; Group Jt Managing Director, Pullin, 1964–65; Mem., NRDC, 1967–80 (Man. Dir, 1974–80, Chief Exec., Engrg Dept, 1965–74). *Publications:* papers to Royal Aeronautical Society. *Recreation:* golf. *Address:* 2 Miller Place, West Common, Gerrards Cross, Bucks SL9 7QQ. *T:* (01753) 893219.

MAKKAWI, Dr Khalil; Chevalier, Order of Cedar, Lebanon; Ambassador and Permanent Representative of Lebanon to the United Nations, New York, 1990–94; *b* 15 Jan. 1930; *s* of Abdel Basset Makkawi and Rosa Makkawi; *m* 1958, Zahira Sibaei; one *s* one *d. Educ:* Amer. Univ. of Beirut (BA Polit. Science); Cairo Univ. (MA Polit. Science); Colombia Univ., NY, USA (PhD Internat. Relations). Joined Lebanese Min. of Foreign Affairs, 1957; UN Section at Min., 1957–59; Attaché to Perm. Mission of Lebanon to UN, New York, 1959, Dep. Perm. Rep., 1961–64; First Sec., Washington, 1964–66; Chief of Internat. Relations Dept, Min. of For. Affairs, Beirut, 1967–70; Counsellor, London, 1970–71; Minister Plenipotentiary, London, 1971–73; Ambassador to: German Democratic Republic, 1973–78; Court of St James's, and Republic of Ireland, 1979–83; Dir of Political Dept, Min. of Foreign Affairs, Beirut, 1983–85; Amb. to Italy, and Permanent Rep. to UNFAO, 1985–90. Mem., Lebanese Delegn to UN Gen. Assembly Meetings, 14th-39th Session; Chairman of Lebanese Delegations to: Confs and Councils, FAO, 1985–89; Governing Councils, IFAD, 1985–89; 16th Ministerial Meeting, Islamic conf. in Fès, 1986; 8th Summit Conf. of Non-Aligned Countries, Harare, 1986; Ministerial Meeting, Mediterranean Mems, Non-Aligned Countries, Brioni, Yugoslavia, 1987; IMO Conf., Rome, 1988; Vice-Pres., Lebanese delegn to ME peace negotiations, Washington, 1993–94. A Vice-Chm., Exec. Bd, UNICEF, 1993–95, Pres., 1995–. Grand Cross of Merit (Italian Republic). *Recreations:* sports, music. *Address:* c/o Ministry of Foreign Affairs, Beirut, Lebanon.

MAKLOUF, Raphael David; sculptor; painter; Chairman, Tower Mint, since 1975; *b* Jerusalem, 10 Dec. 1937; *m* 1968, Marillyn Christian Lewis, *d* of Gwilym Hugh Lewis, DFC; two *s* one *d. Educ:* studied art at Camberwell School of Art, under Karel Vogel, 1953–58. Official commissions: Tower of London, Carnegie Hall, NY, etc. Portrait effigy of the Queen on all UK and Commonwealth coinage minted 1985–97, on Britannia gold coins minted 1989–97. Bronze portraits of the Queen, 1988, at Royal Nat. Theatre, Richmond Riverside Develt and Westminster Sch. Science Building, unveiled by the Queen. 15 Stations of Cross for new Brentwood Cathedral, 1992. Sitters have included: HM Queen; HRH Prince Philip; Rt Hon Margaret Thatcher. Designs for National Trust and English Heritage. FRSA 1985. *Address:* 3 St Helena Terrace, Richmond, Surrey TW9 1NR. *Clubs:* City Livery, Garrick, Chelsea Arts; Riverside Raquet Centre.

MAKSYMIUK, Jerzy; conductor; Chief Conductor, 1983–93, Conductor Laureate, since 1993, BBC Scottish Symphony Orchestra; *b* Grodno, Poland, 9 April 1936. *Educ:* Warsaw Conservatory. First Prize, Paderewski Piano Comp., 1964; worked at Warsaw Grand Theatre, 1970–72; founded Polish Chamber Orchestra, 1972; UK début, 1977; toured all over world incl. European festivals of Aix-en-Provence and Vienna and BBC Promenade concerts; Principal Conductor, Polish Nat. Radio Orch., 1975–77; toured extensively in E Europe and USA; has conducted orchestras in Europe, USA and Japan including: Orch. Nat. de France, Tokyo Metropolitan Symphony, Ensemble Orchestral de Paris, Israel Chamber Orch., Rotterdam Philharmonic and Hong Kong Philharmonic; in UK has conducted BBC Welsh and BBC Philharmonic Orchs, CBSO, LSO, London

Philharmonic, ENO, Bournemouth Sinfonietta and Royal Liverpool Phil. Orch.; début for ENO with Don Giovanni, London Coliseum, 1990. Has made numerous recordings. Hon. DLitt Strathclyde, 1990. *Address:* c/o IMG Artists (Europe), 616 Chiswick High Road, W4 5RX.

MAKUTA, Hon. Friday Lewis; Chief Justice of Malaŵi, 1985–93; *b* 25 Oct. 1936; *s* of late Lewis and Anne Makuta; *m* 1962; four *s* one *d*. *Educ:* Malamulo Mission; Dedza Secondary Sch. Called to the Bar, Middle Temple, 1967. Joined Civil Service, Malaŵi, 1967; State Advocate, 1967; Chief Legal Aid Advocate, 1970; Dir of Public Prosecutions, 1972; Judge of the High Court, 1975; Attorney Gen. and Sec. for Justice, 1976; SC 1979; Dep. Sec. to the Pres. and Cabinet, 1984. *Address:* PO Box 320, Mulanje, Malaŵi. *T:* 465384. *Club:* Civil Service (Lilongwe, Malaŵi).

MALAHIDE, Patrick; *see* Duggan, P. G.

MALAM, Colin Albert; Football Correspondent, Sunday Telegraph, since 1973; *b* 16 Oct. 1938; *s* of Albert and Irene Malam; *m* 1971, Jacqueline Cope; four *s*. *Educ:* Liverpool Inst. High Sch. for Boys; Sidney Sussex Coll., Cambridge (BA Hons History). Trainee, Liverpool Daily Post and Echo, 1961–64; News Reporter, Birmingham Post, 1964–65; Press Officer: Westward TV, 1965–66; GEC (Telecommunications) Ltd, Coventry, 1966; Football Writer, later Football Correspondent, Birmingham Post, 1966–70; Football Writer, The Sun, 1970–73. *Publications:* World Cup Argentina, 1978; Gary Lineker: strikingly different, 1993; (with Terry Venables) The Best Game in the World, 1996; The Magnificent Obsession: Keegan, Sir John Hall, Newcastle and sixty million pounds, 1997. *Recreations:* listening to music, especially jazz, reading anything, watching cricket. *Address:* (office) 1 Canada Square, Canary Wharf, E14 5DT. *T:* (020) 7538 5000.

MALAND, David; barrister; *b* 6 Oct. 1929; *s* of Rev. Gordon Albert Maland and Florence Maud Maland (*née* Bosence); *m* 1953, Edna Foulsham; two *s*. *Educ:* Kingswood Sch.; Wadham Coll., Oxford (BA Hons Mod. Hist., 1951; MA 1957; Robert Herbert Meml Prize Essay, 1959). Nat. service commn RAF, 1951–53. Asst Master, Brighton Grammar Sch., 1953–56; Senior History Master, Stamford Sch., 1957–66; Headmaster: Cardiff High Sch., 1966–68; Denstone Coll., 1969–78; High Master, Manchester Grammar Sch., 1978–85. Schoolmaster Commoner, Merton Coll., Oxford, 1975. Chm., Assisted Places Sub-Cttee of Headmasters' Conf., 1982–83. Called to the Bar, Gray's Inn, 1986; in practice, 1987–95. Gen. Gov., British Nutrition Foundn, 1987–95. Governor: Stonyhurst Coll., 1973–80; Abingdon Sch., 1979–91; GPDST, 1984–88. *Publications:* Europe in the Seventeenth Century, 1966; Culture and Society in Seventeenth Century France, 1970; Europe in the Sixteenth Century, 1973; Europe at War, 1600–1650, 1980; (trans.) La Guerre de Trente Ans, by Pagès, 1971; articles and reviews in History. *Address:* Windrush, Underhill Lane, Westmeston, Hassocks, East Sussex BN6 8XG. *Clubs:* Athenæum; Austrian Alpine.

MALBON, Vice-Adm. Sir Fabian (Michael), KBE 2001; Director, TOPMAST, since 2001; *b* 1 Oct. 1946; *s* of Rupert Charles Malbon and June Marion Downie; *m* 1969, Susan Thomas; three *s*. *Educ:* Brighton, Hove and Sussex Grammar Sch. Joined RN, Dartmouth, 1965; jun. postings, 1969–82; CO, HMS Torquay, 1982–84; MoD, 1984; Comdr Sea Training, 1985–87; CO, HMS Brave, 1987–88; Dir, Naval Service Conditions, MoD, 1988–90; RCDS 1991; CO, HMS Invincible, 1992–93; Naval Sec. and CE Naval Manning Agency, MoD, 1996–98; Dep. C-in-C, Fleet, 1990–2001. Mem., RNSA. *Recreation:* sailing. *Club:* Cruising Association.

MALCANGI, Evelyn Elizabeth Ann; *see* Glennie, E. E. A.

MALCOLM, Prof. Alan David Blair, DPhil; Chief Executive, Institute of Biology, since 1998; *b* 5 Nov. 1944; *s* of late David Malcolm and Helena Malcolm (*née* Blair); *m* 1972, Susan Waller; two *d*. *Educ:* King's Coll. Sch., Wimbledon; Merton Coll., Oxford (MA, DPhil 1970). Demonstrator, Oxford Univ., 1969–72; EMBO Fellow, Max-Planck-Institute, 1971; Lectr, Univ. of Glasgow, 1972–76; St Mary's Hospital Medical School: Lectr, 1976–79; Sen. Lectr, 1979–81; Reader, 1981–84; Prof. of Biochem., Charing Cross and Westminster Med. Sch., 1984–92; Dir Gen., Flour, Milling and Baking Res. Assoc., 1992–94; Dir, BBSRC Inst. of Food Res., 1994–98. Vis. Fellow, Yale Univ., 1982; Hon. Res. Fellow, UCL, 1984–89. Vice-Chm., Technol. Foresight Food and Drink Panel, 1995–99; Member: MAFF Food Adv. Cttee, 1995–; EU Standing Cttee on Fruit and Vegetables, 1998–; UK Deleg. to Eur. Cttee of Biol Assocs, 1998–; Council, Parly Scientific Cttee, 2000–; Expert Advr, H of C Select Cttee on Genetically Modified Organisms, 1999. Chm., Res. and Scientific Cttee, Arthritis and Rheumatism Council, 1990–92; Mem., Royal Soc. Cttee on Genetically Modified Organisms, 1998; Scientific Gov., 1995–, Vice-Chm. Council, 1996–98, Chm., 1998–, British Nutrition Foundn. Chm., Biochemical Soc., 1992–95. Mem. Court, ICSTM, Univ. of London, 1998–. Member Editorial Board: Internat. Jl Food Science Nutrition, 1997–; Pesticide Outlook, 1998–; Outlook on Agriculture, 1999–. *Publications:* Enzymes, 1971; Molecular Medicine, vol. 1, 1984, vol. 2, 1987; numerous articles, symposia, etc. *Address:* Institute of Biology, 20 Queensberry Place, SW7 2DZ. *T:* (020) 7581 8333.

MALCOLM, Hon. David Kingsley, AC 1992; **Hon. Justice Malcolm;** Chief Justice of Western Australia, since 1988, and Lieutenant-Governor, since 1990; *b* 6 May 1938; *s* of Colin Kingsley Malcolm and Jeanne (*née* Cowan); *m* 1st, 1965, Jennifer Birney (marr. diss. 1997); (one *s* decd); 2nd, 1997, Kaaren Brizland; one *d*. *Educ:* Guildford Grammar Sch.; Univ. of Western Australia (LLB 1st Cl. Hons); Oxford Univ. (Rhodes Schol.; BCL 1st Cl. Hons). Partner, Muir Williams Nicholson, 1964–67; Counsel, Asst Gen. Counsel, Dep. Gen. Counsel, Asian Development Bank, Manila, 1967–70; Partner, Muir Williams Nicholson & Co., 1970–79; Independent Bar, 1980–88. QC: WA, 1980; NSW, 1983. Member: Law Reform Commn of WA, 1966–67 and 1975–82 (Chm., 1976, 1979–82); Copyright Tribunal, 1978–86; Chm., Town Planning Appeal Tribunal, 1979–86. Mem., Council of Law Soc. of WA, 1966–67, 1985–88 (Vice-Pres., 1986–88); Pres., WA Bar Assoc., 1982–84; Vice Pres., Aust. Bar Assoc., 1984; Dep. Chm., 1990–95, Chm., 1995–, Judicial Sect., Law Assoc. for Asia and Pacific; Chm. WA Br., Internat. Commn of Jurists, 1994–; Chm., Conf. of Chief Justices of Asia and Pacific, Beijing, 1995, Manila, 1997, Seoul, 1999. Mem. Council, Internat. Soc. for the Reform of Criminal Law, 1992–. Chairman, Advisory Board: Neuromuscular Res. Inst. of Aust., 1989–95; Crime Res. Centre, Univ. of WA, 1991–; Chm., Bd of Trustees, Francis Burt Legal Educn Centre and Law Mus., 1995–; Member: Council, Guildford Grammar Sch., 1971–98 (Dep. Chm., 1974–80; Chm., 1980–83); Senate, Univ. of WA, 1988–94; Constitutional Centenary Foundn Council, 1991–2000. Chm., Bd of Trustees, Special Airborne Resources Trust, 1996–. Patron, various community and sporting orgns. Hon. FRAPI 1984. Hon. Bencher, Lincoln's Inn, 1999. Paul Harris Fellow, Rotary Internat., 1997. Citizen of the Year, WA, 2000. *Publications:* articles in various learned jls, incl. Aust. Law Jl, Aust. Bar Rev., Aust. Business Law Rev., Univ. of WA Law Rev., LAWASIA Jl. *Recreations:* Rugby Union, windsurfing. *Address:* Chief Justice's Chambers, Supreme Court, Perth, WA 6000, Australia. *T:* (chambers) (8) 94215337. *Club:* Weld (Perth, WA).

MALCOLM, Derek Elliston Michael; Film Critic, The Guardian, 1971–97; President: International Film Critics, since 1990 (Chairman, UK Section, since 1982); British Federation of Film Societies, since 1993; *b* 12 May 1932; *s* of J. Douglas Malcolm and Dorothy Taylor; *m* 1st, 1962, Barbara Ibbott (marr. diss. 1966); one *d*; 2nd, 1994, Sarah Gristwood. *Educ:* Eton; Merton College, Oxford (BA Hons Hist.). Actor, amateur rider (National Hunt), 1953–56; Drama Critic, Gloucestershire Echo, 1956–62; Sub-Editor, The Guardian, 1962–69; Racing correspondent, The Guardian, 1969–71. Dir, London Internat. Film Fest., 1982–84. Gov., BFI, 1989–92. Pres., Critics' Circle of UK, 1980 (Chm., Film Section, 1978–81). Internat. Publishing Cos Critic of the Year, 1972. *Publication:* Robert Mitchum, 1984. *Recreations:* cricket, tennis, squash, music. *Address:* 28 Avenue Road, Highgate, N6 5DW. *T:* and *Fax:* (020) 8348 2013; The Dower House, Hull Place, Sholden, Kent CT14 0AQ. *T:* and *Fax:* (01304) 364614.

MALCOLM, Ellen; RSA 1976 (ARSA 1968); *b* 28 Sept. 1923; *d* of John and Ellen Malcolm; *m* 1962, Gordon Stewart Cameron, RSA (*d* 1994). *Educ:* Aberdeen Acad.; Gray's Sch. of Art, Aberdeen. DA (Aberdeen) 1944. Teacher of Art, Aberdeen Grammar Sch. and Aberdeen Acad., 1945–62. Paintings in public galleries in Southend, Aberdeen, Perth, Milngavie, Edinburgh, and in private collections in Scotland, England, Wales, America, Switzerland, Sweden and Australia. Chalmers-Jervise Prize, 1946; Guthrie Award, Royal Scottish Acad., 1952; David Cargill Award, Royal Glasgow Inst., 1973. *Recreation:* reading. *Address:* c/o Dr I. Malcolm, 4 Deemount Gardens, Aberdeen AB11 7UE.

MALCOLM, James Ian, OBE 1995; HM Diplomatic Service; Deputy High Commissioner, Jamaica, since 1997; *b* 29 March 1946; *e s* of William Kenneth Malcolm and late Jennie Malcolm (*née* Cooper); *m* 1967, Sheila Nicholson Moore; one *s* one *d*. *Educ:* Royal High Sch., Edinburgh. Joined Foreign Office, 1966; UKDEL NATO, Brussels, 1969–72; Burma, 1972–74; FCO, 1974–77; Commercial Attaché, Kenya, 1977–80; Consul, Syria, 1980–83; Second Sec. (Commercial), Angola, 1983–85; Second, later First, Sec., FCO, 1985–87; First Secretary: (Political/Econ.), Indonesia, 1987–94; FCO, 1994–97. *Recreations:* reading and research in British history in Sumatra and Jamaica, golf, riding motorcycles. *Address:* c/o Foreign and Commonwealth Office, King Charles Street, SW1A 2AH. *Club:* Royal Over-Seas League.

MALCOLM, Sir James (William Thomas Alexander), 12th Bt *cr* 1665 (NS), of Balbedie and Innertiel, Co. Fife; DL; *b* 15 May 1930; *s* of Lt-Col A. W. A. Malcolm, CVO (*d* 1989) and Hester Mary Malcolm (*née* Mann) (*d* 1992); *S* cousin, 1995; *m* 1955, Gillian Heather (*née* Humpherus); two *s* two *d*. *Educ:* Eton Coll.; RMA Sandhurst; Staff Coll., Camberley (psc). CO 1st Bn Welsh Guards, 1970–72; Regimental Col, Welsh Guards, 1972–76. Appeals Dir, British Heart Foundn, 1976–89. High Sheriff, 1991–92, DL 1991, Surrey. *Recreations:* golf, cricket. *Heir:* *s* Col Alexander James Elton Malcolm, OBE [*b* 30 Aug. 1956; *m* 1982, Virginia (*née* Coxon); two *s* one *d*]. *Address:* Highgrove, Wrecclesham Hill, Wrecclesham, Farnham, Surrey GU10 4JN. *T:* (01252) 712167. *Clubs:* MCC; Royal St George's Golf (Sandwich); Berkshire Golf (Ascot).

MALCOLM of Poltalloch, Robin Neill Lochnell; Chief of Clan Malcolm; Vice Lord-Lieutenant of Argyll and Bute, 1996–2001; *b* 11 Feb. 1934; *s* of Lt-Col George Ian Malcolm of Poltalloch, A&SH and Enid Gaskell; *m* 1962, Susan Freeman; two *s* two *d*. *Educ:* Eton; North of Scotland Coll. of Agriculture. National Service, 1 Argyll and Sutherland Highlanders, 1952–54; TA service, 8 A&SH, 1954–64. Shipping, and British Iron & Steel Co., 1955–62; farming at Poltalloch, 1963–. Convenor, Highlands and Islands Cttee, NFU, 1972–74; Member: HIDB Consultative Council, 1973–77, 1988–91; Bd, Argyll and Isles Enterprise, 1991–98; Bd, SW Region, Scottish Natural Heritage, 1993–99. Pres., Scottish Agricl Orgn Soc. Ltd, 1983–86. Mem., Argyll and Bute DC, 1976–92; Argyll and Bute: DL, 1974; JP 1976. *Recreations:* shooting, swimming. *Address:* Duntrune Castle, Kilmartin, Argyll PA31 8QQ. *T:* (01546) 510283.

MALCOLM, Dr Wilfred Gordon, CBE 1994; Vice-Chancellor, University of Waikato, New Zealand, 1985–94; Chairman, Academic Audit Unit, New Zealand Universities; *b* 29 Nov. 1933; *s* of Norman and Doris Malcolm; *m* 1959, Edmée Ruth Prebensen; two *s* four *d*. *Educ:* Victoria Univ. of Wellington (MA, PhD); Emmanuel Coll., Cambridge (BA). Victoria University of Wellington: Lectr in Mathematics, 1960–62; Gen. Sec., Inter Varsity Fellowship of Evangelical Unions, 1963–66; Lectr/Reader in Mathematics, 1967–74; Prof. of Pure Mathematics, 1975–84. Vis. Prof., Univ. of Brunei Darussalam, 1997–99. Chm., Ministerial Adv. Cttee on Employment Relations Educn. *Address:* 76 Hamurana Road, Omokoroa, Bay of Plenty, New Zealand.

MALCOMSON, Prof. James Martin, PhD; FBA 2000; Professor of Economics, and Fellow, All Souls College, University of Oxford, since 1999; *b* 23 June 1946; *s* of E. Watlock Malcomson and Madeline Malcomson (*née* Stuart); *m* 1979, Sally Claire Richards; (one *d* decd). *Educ:* Gonville and Caius Coll., Cambridge (BA, MA); Harvard Univ. (MA, PhD 1973). Res. Fellow in Econs, 1971–72, Lectr, 1972–83, Sen. Lectr, 1983–85, Univ. of York; Prof. of Econs, Univ. of Southampton, 1985–98. Vis. Fellow, Université Catholique de Louvain, Belgium, 1983–84. *Publications:* (contrib.) Efficiency Wage Models of the Labor Market, 1986; (contrib.) Handbook of Labor Economics, 1999; (contrib.) Handbook of Health Economics, 2000; numerous articles in learned jls. *Recreations:* walking, music, film, theatre. *Address:* All Souls College, Oxford OX1 4AL. *T:* (01865) 279379.

MALCOMSON, Thomas Herbert; HM Diplomatic Service, retired; Ambassador to Panama, 1992–96; *b* 9 Oct. 1937; *m* 1st, 1960, Barbara Hetherington (marr. diss. 1985); one *s* two *d*; 2nd, 1986, Blanca Ruiz de Castilla; twin *d*. *Educ:* Univ. of Glasgow. Joined FO, subseq. FCO, 1961; Bangkok, 1963; São Paulo, 1967; FCO, 1971; Colombo, 1972; Consul, Chiang Mai, 1975; FCO, 1978; Dep. High Comr, Brunei, 1981; Acting High Comr, Solomon Is, 1984; Lima, 1985; FCO, 1989. *Address:* c/o Foreign and Commonwealth Office, SW1A 2AH.

MALDEN, Viscount; Frederick Paul de Vere Capell; Deputy Head Teacher, Skerton County Primary School, Lancaster, 1990–95 (Acting Head, 1992–93); *b* 29 May 1944; *s* and *heir* of 10th Earl of Essex, *qv*. *Educ:* Skerton Boys' School; Lancaster Royal Grammar School; Didsbury College of Education, Manchester; Northern School of Music. ACP, LLCM(TD), ALCM. Assistant teacher, Marsh County Junior School, 1966–72; Deputy Head, 1972–75; Acting Head, 1975–77; Deputy Head Teacher, Marsh County Primary School, 1977–78; Head Teacher, Cockerham Parochial CE School, Cockerham, Lancaster, 1979–80; in charge of Pastoral Care, Curriculum Develt and Music, Skerton County Primary School, Lancaster, 1981–90. Patron: Morecambe Philharmonic Choir, 1990–; Friends of Cassiobury Park, Watford, 1998–. FRSA. *Recreation:* music. *Address:* 35 Pinewood Avenue, Brookhouse, Lancaster LA2 9NU.

MALDEN, Charles Peter S.; *see* Scott-Malden.

MALE, Anthony Hubert, (Tony), CMG 1997; FIL; National Executive Adviser for Languages, Department for Education and Skills (formerly Department for Education and

Employment), since 2001; Director, Central Bureau for Educational Visits and Exchanges, 1986–99, and Secretary, UK Centre for European Education, 1989–99, British Council; *b* 16 March 1939; *s* of Hubert Edward Male and Louise Irene Lavinia (*née* Thomas); *m* 1960, Françoise Andrée Germaine Pinot, LèsL; one *s* one *d*. *Educ:* Yeovil Sch.; Exeter Univ. (BA, PGCE); Sorbonne. FIL 1990. Housemaster, 1962–74, Head, Comparative Internat. Studies, 1970–74, Tiverton GS; Central Bureau for Educational Visits and Exchanges: Head, Teacher and Sch. Exchange, Europe, 1974–76; Asst Dir, 1976–78; Dep. Dir, 1978–84; Sec., 1984–86. Expert, Eur. Commn, 1977–99; Consultant, Council of Europe, 1982–99. Chm., Langs Nat. Working Gp, 2001–. Pres., Fédn Internat. des Organisations de Correspondances et d'Exchanges Scolaires (FIOCES), 1986–94. Member: Adv. Panel, Langs Lead Body, 1991–98; Council, Inst. Linguists, 1997–99. Member: Bd of Dirs, Nat. Youth Jazz Orch., 1975–; Jury, Concours Internat. de Guitare, Radio France, 1993–. Trustee, Amer. Field Service, 1981–86; Internat. House, 1989–98; Lefèvre Trust, 1991–93; Technol. Colls Trust, 1996–99. Gov., Richmond Coll., 1990–99. FRSA 1985. Hon. FCP 1993; Hon. Fellow, Westminster Coll., Oxford, 1999. Hon. Mem., British Council, 1999. Chevalier, 1977, Comdr, 1992, Ordre des Palmes Académiques (France); Chevalier, Ordre National du Mérite (France), 1984; Chevalier, Ordre de Leopold II (Belgium), 1981; Comdr, Orden del Mérito Civil (Spain), 1999. *Publications:* contrib. articles on inter-cultural exchange, modern langs and internat. dimension in education. *Recreations:* music, flamenco and jazz guitar, travel, photography. *e-mail:* 100564.346@compuserve.com. *Club:* Travellers.

MALE, David Ronald, CBE 1991; FRICS; Consultant, Gardiner & Theobald, Chartered Quantity Surveyors, since 1992 (Senior Partner, 1979–91); a Church Commissioner, 1989–93; *b* 12 Dec. 1929; *s* of Ronald Male and Gertrude Simpson; *m* 1959, Mary Louise Evans; one *s* two *d*. *Educ:* Aldenham Sch., Herts. Served RA, 2nd Lieut, 1948–49. With Gardiner & Theobald, 1950–. Mem., Gen. Council, RICS, 1976–93 (Pres., 1989–90); Pres., Quantity Surveyors Divl Council, 1977–78. Member: Bd of Dirs, Building Centre, 1970–80; Govt Construction Panel, 1973–74; EDC for Building, 1982–86; Chm., NEDC Commercial Bldg Steering Gp, 1984–88; Dir, London and Bristol Developments, 1985–91. Member: Bd of Management, Macmillan Cancer Relief (formerly Cancer Relief Macmillan Fund), 1992–2000; Court of Benefactors, RSocMed, 1986–. Mem. Bd of Govs, Wilson Centre, Cambridge, 1993–97; Governor: Aldenham Sch., 1974–93; Downe House, 2000–; Pres., Old Aldenhamian Soc., 1986–89. Master, Chartered Surveyors' Co., 1984–85; Liveryman, Painter-Stainers' Co., 1961–93. *Recreations:* opera and ballet, golf. *Address:* 6 Bowland Yard, Kinnerton Street, SW1X 8EE. *Clubs:* Boodle's, Garrick, MCC (Mem. Cttee, 1984–96 and 1997–99; Mem., Estates Sub-Cttee, 1984–2000).

MALE, Peter Royston, (Roy); Chief Executive, Addenbrooke's NHS Trust, since 1998; *b* 16 March 1948; *s* of Royston Stanley Male and Patricia Male (*née* Kennedy); *m* 1975, Susan Bootle; one *s*. *Educ:* Nottingham High Sch.; King's Coll. Sch., Wimbledon; St John's Coll., Cambridge (BA 2nd Cl. Hons 1970; MA 1974). MHSM 1974; DipHSM 1974; MIPD 1987. Grad. trainee, NHS, Sheffield Reg., 1970–72; Doncaster Royal Infirmary, 1972–73; Fazakerley Hosp., 1973–75; Dist Personnel Officer, S Sefton, 1975–77; Area Personnel Officer, Norfolk HA, 1977–87; Director: of Personnel and Admin, Liverpool HA, 1987–90; of Personnel, Cambridge HA, 1990–92; Dep. Chief Exec., Addenbrooke's NHS Trust, 1992–98. *Publications:* papers and contribs to jls. *Recreations:* cricket, keyboard, gardening.

MALECELA, Cigwiyemisi John Samwel; MP (Chama cha Mapinduzi Party) Mtera, Tanzania, since 1995; *b* 20 April 1934; *m*; four *c*. *Educ:* Alliance Secondary Sch., Dodoma; St Andrews Coll., Minaki, Dar es Salaam; Univ. of Bombay (BCom); post-grad. studies, Cambridge Univ. Dist Officer, Mbeya Region, 1960–61; appts for Tanganyikan Govt, 1962–64: Consul to USA and Sec. of Mission to UN, New York, 1962–63; Regl Comr, Lake Reg., 1963–64; for Tanzania: Ambassador to UN, 1964–68, to Ethiopia, 1968; Minister: for East African Community Affairs, 1969–71; for Foreign Affairs, 1972–75; for Agriculture, 1975–80; for Minerals, 1980–82; for Communications and Transport, 1982–85; Administrator, Tanzania's Public Debt, 1985; Regional Comr, Iringa, 1987; High Comr for Tanzania in UK, and non-resident Ambassador to Ireland, 1989–90; Prime Minister and First Vice Pres., Tanzania, 1990–95; Vice Chm., Chama cha Mapinduzi, ruling party, 1992–95. Member: Internat. Ind. Commn for Worldwide Telecommunication Develt, 1983; Commonwealth Eminent Persons Group on S Africa, 1985; Gp of 34 World Eminent Persons on Disarmament and Internat. Security, Stockholm, 1988. *Address:* Box number 2324, Dodoma, Tanzania.

MALEK, Ali; QC 1996; a Recorder, since 2000; *b* 19 Jan. 1956; *s* of Ali Akbar Malek and late Irene Elizabeth (*née* Johnson); *m* 1989, Francesca Shoucair; two *d*. *Educ:* Bedford Sch.; Keble Coll., Oxford (MA, BCL). Called to the Bar, Gray's Inn, 1980; in practice at the Bar, 1980–; Asst Recorder, 1998–2000. *Publications:* various articles on banking law. *Recreations:* running, ski-ing, golf, music. *Address:* 3 Verulam Buildings, Gray's Inn, WC1R 5NT. *T:* (020) 7831 8441. *Club:* Vincent's (Oxford).
See also H. M. Malek.

MALEK, Hodge Mehdi; QC 1999; *b* 11 July 1959; *s* of Ali Akbar Malek and late Irene Elizabeth Malek (*née* Johnson); *m* 1986, Inez Dies Louise Vegelin van Claerbergen; two *s* one *d*. *Educ:* Bedford Sch.; Sorbonne, Univ. of Paris; Keble Coll., Oxford (MA 1981; BCL 1982). Called to the Bar, Gray's Inn, 1983 (Birkenhead Schol.; Atkin Schol.; Band Schol.); in practice at the Bar, 1983–. Mem., Supplementary Treasury Panel (Common Law), 1995–99. *Publications:* (with P. B. Matthews) Discovery, 1992; Disclosure, 2001; articles on law and history. *Recreations:* swimming, ski-ing, history. *Address:* 4/5 Gray's Inn Square, Gray's Inn, WC1R 5AY. *T:* (020) 7404 5252.
See also A. Malek.

MALES, Stephen Martin; QC 1998; a Recorder, since 2000; *b* 24 Nov. 1955; *s* of Dennis Albert Males and Mary Winifred Males (*née* Bates); *m* 1982, Daphne Clytie Baker; three *s*. *Educ:* Skinners' Sch.; St John's Coll., Cambridge (MA). Called to the Bar, Middle Temple, 1978; Asst Recorder, 1999–2000. *Recreation:* sailing. *Address:* 20 Essex Street, WC2R 3AL. *T:* (020) 7583 9294. *Club:* Bewl Valley Sailing.

MALET, Sir Harry (Douglas St Lo), 9th Bt *cr* 1791, of Wilbury, Wiltshire; JP; farmer, Australia and England; *b* 26 Oct. 1936; *o s* of Col Sir Edward William St Lo Malet, 8th Bt, OBE and Baroness Benedicta von Maasburg (*d* 1979); *S* father, 1990; *m* 1967, Julia Gresley, *d* of Charles Harper, Perth, WA; one *s*. *Educ:* Downside; Trinity Coll., Oxford (BA Eng. Lit.). Commnd QRIH, 1958–61. JP W Somerset, 1982. *Recreation:* equestrian sports. *Heir: s* Charles Edward St Lo Malet [*b* 30 Aug. 1970; *m* 1997, Rachel, *d* of T. P. S. Cane; one *d*]. *Address:* Wrestwood, RMB 184, Boyup Brook, WA 6244, Australia. *Club:* Weld (Perth).

MALIK, Rt Rev. Ghais Abdel; President Bishop of the Central Synod of the Episcopal Church in Jerusalem and the Middle East, 1996–2000; Bishop in Egypt, 1984–2000; *b* 21 May 1930; *m* 1956, Fawzia Emsak Gouany; two *s* one *d*. *Educ:* Cairo Univ. (DipEd 1960); St George's Coll., Jerusalem. Ordained deacon 1962, priest 1963, Cairo; Curate, 1963–66, Rector, 1966–84, Jesus Light of the World Ch., Old Cairo; cons. Bishop of Egypt, with N Africa, Ethiopia, Somalia, Eritrea and Djibouti, 1984. Vice-Chm., Council of Anglican Provinces of Africa, 1992–99; Chm., Fellowship of Middle East Evangelical Churches, 1997–2001. *Recreations:* walking, reading, maintenance of harmoniums, fishing. *Address:* c/o Diocesan Office, PO Box 87, Zamalek, Cairo, Egypt.

MALIM, Rear-Adm. Nigel Hugh, CB 1971; LVO 1960; DL; FIMechE; *b* 5 April 1919; *s* of late John Malim, Pebmarsh, and Brenda Malim; *m* 1944, Moonyeen, *d* of late William and Winefride Maynard; two *s* one *d*. *Educ:* Weymouth Coll.; RNEC Keyham. Cadet, RN, 1936; HMS Manchester, 1940–41; HMS Norfolk, 1942; RNC Greenwich, 1943–45; HMS Jamaica, 1945–47; Staff of RNEC, 1948–50; Admty, 1951–54; HMS Triumph, 1954–56; Admty, 1956–58; HM Yacht Britannia, 1958–60; District Overseer, Scotland, 1960–62; Asst, and later Dep., Dir Marine Engrg, 1962–65; idc 1966; Captain, RNEC Manadon, 1967–69; Chief Staff Officer Technical to C-in-C, W Fleet, 1969–71, retd. Man. Dir, Humber Graving Dock & Engrg Co. Ltd, 1972–82. Chm., Fabric Council, Lincoln Cathedral, 1985–91. DL Lincoln, 1987. *Recreations:* offshore racing and cruising. *Address:* The Old Vicarage, Caistor, Lincoln LN7 6UG. *Clubs:* Royal Ocean Racing; Royal Naval Sailing Association.

MALIN, Prof. Stuart Robert Charles; Professor of Geophysics, Bosphorus University, Istanbul, 1994–2001; Visiting Professor: Department of Physics and Astronomy, University College London, since 1983; University of Cairo, since 1996; *b* 28 Sept. 1936; *s* of late Cecil Henry Malin and Eleanor Mary Malin (*née* Howe); *m* 1963, Irene Saunders (*d* 1997); two *d*; *m* 2001, Lindsey Jean MacFarlane. *Educ:* Royal Grammar Sch., High Wycombe; King's College, London. BSc 1958, PhD 1972, DSc 1981; FInstP 1971; CPhys 1985; FRAS 1961 (Mem. Council, 1975–78). Royal Greenwich Observatory, Herstmonceux: Asst Exptl Officer, 1958; Scientific Officer, 1961; Sen. Scientific Officer, 1965; Institute of Geological Sciences, Herstmonceux and Edinburgh: PSO, 1970; SPSO (individual merit), 1976, and Hd of Geomagnetism Unit, 1981; Hd of Astronomy and Navigation, Nat. Maritime Museum, 1982; Maths teacher: Dulwich Coll., 1988–91, 1992–94; Haberdashers' Aske's Hatcham Coll., 1991–92. Cape Observer, Radcliffe Observatory, Pretoria, 1963–65; Vis. Scientist, Nat. Center for Atmospheric Res., Boulder, Colorado, 1969; Green Schol., Scripps Instn of Oceanography, La Jolla, 1981. Consultant, Rahmi M. Koç Müzesi, Istanbul, 1995–2001. Pres., Jun. Astronomical Soc., 1989–91. Associate Editor, Qly Jl, RAS, 1987–92; Editor, Geophysical Jl Internat., 1996–. *Publications:* (with Carole Stott) The Greenwich Meridian, 1984; Spaceworks, 1985; The Greenwich Guide to the Planets, 1987; The Greenwich Guide to Stars, Galaxies and Nebulae, 1989; The Story of the Earth, 1991; (with Rahmi M. Koç) Rahmi M. Koç Müzesi Tanıtımı, 1997; contribs to scientific jls. *Recreations:* croquet, clocks. *Address:* 30 Wemyss Road, Blackheath, SE3 0TG. *T:* (020) 8318 3712.

MALINS, Humfrey Jonathan, CBE 1997; MP (C) Woking, since 1997; lawyer and consultant; a Recorder, since 1996; *b* 31 July 1945; *s* of Rev. Peter Malins and late Lilian Joan Malins; *m* 1979, Lynda Ann; one *s* one *d*. *Educ:* St John's Sch., Leatherhead; Brasenose Coll., Oxford (MA Hons Law). College of Law, Guildford, 1967; joined Tuck and Mann, Solicitors, Dorking, 1967, qual. as solicitor, 1971; Partner, Tuck and Mann, 1973; an Asst Recorder, 1991–96; Actg Dist Judge (formerly Actg Met. Stipendiary Magistrate), 1992–. Councillor, Mole Valley DC, Surrey, 1973–83 (Chm., Housing Cttee, 1980–81). Contested (C): Toxteth Division of Liverpool, Feb. and Oct. 1974; E Lewisham, 1979. MP (C) Croydon NW, 1983–92; contested (C) same seat, 1992. PPS to Minister of State, Home Office, 1987–89, to Minister of State, DoH, 1989–92. Chm. of Trustees, Immigration Adv. Service, 1993–96. *Recreations:* Rugby football, golf, gardening, soup making. *Address:* House of Commons, SW1A 0AA. *Clubs:* Vincent's (Oxford); Richmond Rugby Football; Walton Heath Golf.
See also J. H. Malins.

MALINS, Julian Henry; QC 1991; a Recorder, since 2000; *b* 1 May 1950; *s* of Rev. Peter Malins and late (Lilian) Joan Malins (*née* Dingley); *m* 1972, Joanna Pearce; three *d*. *Educ:* St John's School, Leatherhead; Brasenose College, Oxford (MA). Called to the Bar, Middle Temple, 1972, Bencher, 1996. Mem., General Council of the Bar, 1986–. Mem., Court of Common Council, City of London, 1981–. Governor: Mus. of London, 1998–; GSMD, 1999–. *Recreations:* fishing, chess, conversation. *Address:* Littleton Chambers, 3 King's Bench Walk North, Temple, EC4Y 7HR. *T:* (020) 7583 5275.
See also H. J. Malins.

MALINS, Penelope, (Mrs John Malins); *see* Hobhouse, P.

MALJERS, Floris Anton, Hon. KBE 1992; Chairman, Unilever NV, and Vice Chairman, Unilever PLC, 1984–94; *b* 12 Aug. 1933; *s* of A. C. J. Maljers and L. M. Maljers-Kole; *m* 1958, J. H. Maljers-de Jongh; two *s* (one *d* decd). *Educ:* Univ. of Amsterdam. Joined Unilever, 1959; various jobs in the Netherlands until 1965; Man. Dir, Unilever-Colombia, 1965–67; Man. Dir, Unilever-Turkey, 1967–70; Chairman, Van den Bergh & Jurgens, Netherlands, 1970–74; Co-ordinator of Man. Group, edible fats and dairy, and Dir of Unilever NV and Unilever PLC, 1974–94. Member: Unilever's Special Committee, 1982–94; Supervisory Bd, KLM Royal Dutch Airlines, 1991– (Vice Chm., 1994; Chm., 2000); Supervisory Bd, Philips Electronics NV, 1993–99 (Chm., 1994); Supervisory Bd, Vendex NV, subseq. Vendex-KBB NV, 1996– (Vice Chm., 1998); Bd, Rand Europe, 1999–; Director: Guinness plc, 1994–98; Amoco Petroleum, Chicago, 1994–98; BP (formerly BP Amoco), 1998–; Diageo plc, 1998. Gov., Europ. Policy Forum, 1993–. Chm., Concertgebouw, 1987–; Mem. Bd, Nat. Mus. of Archaeology, 1993–. Chairman: Bd of Trustees, Utrecht Univ. Hosp., 1994–; Rotterdam Sch. of Mgt, Erasmus Univ., 1999–. *Address:* PO Box 11550, 2502 AN The Hague, Netherlands.

MÄLK, Raul; Ambassador of the Republic of Estonia to the Republic of Ireland, since 1996, and to Portugal, since 2000; *b* 14 May 1952; *s* of Linda and August Mälk. *Educ:* Tartu State Univ. Jun. Res. Fellow, Inst. of Economy, Acad. of Scis, 1975–77; freelance editor, subseq. Editor in Chief, Estonian Radio, 1977–90; Dep. Head and Counsellor, Office of President of Supreme Council, 1990–92; Ministry of Foreign Affairs, Tallinn: Counsellor, 1992–93; Chief of Minister's Office, 1993–94; Dep. Permanent Under Sec. (political affairs, press and inf.), 1994–96; Ambassador to UK, 1996–2001; Minister of Foreign Affairs, Estonia, 1998–99. *Publications:* numerous articles in Estonian and Finnish newspapers; material for Estonian radio and television broadcasts, incl. comment on internat. and home news, and parly reports. *Recreations:* theatre, music, attending sports events (football, basketball, track and field). *Address:* c/o Ministry of Foreign Affairs, Rävala 9, Tallinn 0100, Estonia. *Club:* Farmers'.

MALLABER, (Clare) Judith; MP (Lab) Amber Valley, since 1997; *b* 10 July 1951; *d* of late Kenneth Mallaber and Margaret Joyce Mallaber. *Educ:* N London Collegiate Sch.; St Anne's Coll., Oxford (BA Hons). Res. Officer, NUPE, 1975–85; Local Govt Information Unit, 1985–96 (Dir, 1987–95). Mem., Select Cttee on Educn and Employment, 1997–. Mem. Adv. Council, Northern Coll., Barnsley, 1995–. *Address:* House of Commons, SW1A 0AA.

MALLABY, Sir Christopher (Leslie George), GCMG 1996 (KCMG 1988; CMG 1982); GCVO 1992; HM Diplomatic Service, retired; Managing Director, UBS Warburg (formerly Warburg Dillon Read), since 2000; *b* 7 July 1936; *s* of late Brig. A. W. S. Mallaby, CIE, OBE, and Margaret Catherine Mallaby (*née* Jones); *m* 1961, Pascale Françoise Thierry-Mieg; one *s* three *d*. *Educ:* Eton; King's Coll., Cambridge. British Delegn to UN Gen. Assembly, 1960; 3rd Sec., British Embassy, Moscow, 1961–63; 2nd Sec., FO, 1963–66; 1st Sec., Berlin, 1966–69; 1st Sec., FCO, 1969–71; Harvard Business Sch., 1971; Dep. Dir, British Trade Develt Office, NY, 1971–74; Counsellor and Head of Chancery, Moscow, 1975–77; Head of Arms Control and Disarmament Dept, FCO, 1977–79, Head of East European and Soviet Dept, 1979–80, Head of Planning Staff, 1980–82, FCO; Minister, Bonn, 1982–85; Dep. Sec., Cabinet Office, 1985–88; Ambassador to Germany, 1988–92; Ambassador to France, 1993–96. Adviser to: UBS, 1996–2000; RMC, 1996–2000; Herbert Smith, 1997–2001; Louis Dreyfus Group, 1998–; Mem. Supervisory Bd, Mannesmann AG, 2000–; non-executive Director: Sun Life and Provincial Hldgs plc, 1996–2000; Charter European Investment Trust, 1996–. Founder, 1995 and Trustee, 1996–, Entente Cordiale Scholarships. Trustee: Tate Gall., 1996–99; Reuters, 1998–. Chairman: Primary Immunodeficiency Assoc., 1996–; Adv. Bd, GB Centre, Humboldt Univ., Berlin, 1997–; Adv. Bd, German Studies Inst., Birmingham Univ., 1998–. Grand Cross, Order of Merit (Germany), 1992; Grand Officier, Légion d'Honneur (France), 1996. *Recreation:* grandchildren. *Address:* c/o UBS Warburg, 1 Finsbury Avenue, EC2M 2PG. *Clubs:* Brooks's, Beefsteak, Grillions.

MALLALIEU, Baroness *cr* 1991 (Life Peer), of Studdridge in the County of Buckinghamshire; **Ann Mallalieu;** QC 1988; *b* 27 Nov. 1945; *d* of Sir (Joseph Percival) William Mallalieu and of Lady Mallalieu; *m* 1979, Timothy Felix Harold Cassel (*see* Sir T. F. H. Cassel); two *d*. *Educ:* Holton Park Girls' Grammar Sch., Wheatley, Oxon; Newnham Coll., Cambridge (MA, LLM; Hon. Fellow, 1992). (First woman) Pres., Cambridge Union Soc., 1967. Called to the Bar, Inner Temple, 1970, Bencher, 1992; a Recorder, 1985–93. Mem., Gen. Council of the Bar, 1973–75. Opposition spokesman on home affairs and on legal affairs, H of L, 1992–97. Chm., Indep. Council of the Ombudsman for Corporate Estate Agents, 1993–2000. Pres., Countryside Alliance, 1998–. Chm., Suzy Lamplugh Trust, 1997–2000. *Recreations:* sheep, hunting, poetry, horseracing. *Address:* House of Lords, SW1A 0PW. *T:* (020) 7219 3000.

MALLET, John Valentine Granville, FSA; FRSA; Keeper, Department of Ceramics, Victoria and Albert Museum, 1976–89; *b* 15 Sept. 1930; *s* of late Sir Victor Mallet, GCMG, CVO, and Lady Mallet (*née* Andreae); *m* 1958, Felicity Ann Basset; one *s*. *Educ:* Winchester Coll.; Balliol Coll., Oxford (BA Modern History; Hon. Fellow, 1992). Mil. service in Army: commnd; held temp. rank of full Lieut in Intell. Corps, 1949–50. Messrs Sotheby & Co., London, 1955–62; Victoria and Albert Museum: Asst Keeper, Dept of Ceramics, 1962; Sec. to Adv. Council, 1967–73. Indep. Mem., Design Selection Cttee, Design Council, 1981–89; Member: Exec. Cttee, Nat. Art Collections Fund, 1989–; Art Adv. Cttee, Nat. Mus. of Wales, Cardiff, 1991–94; Wissenschaftlicher Beirat, Ceramica-Stiftung, Basel, 1990–; Arts Adv. Panel, Nat. Trust, 1996–; Pres., English Ceramic Circle, 1999–. Mem., Court of Assistants, Fishmongers' Co., 1970– (Prime Warden, 1983–84). *Publications:* (with F. Dreier) The Hockemeyer Collection: maiolica and glass, 1998; articles on ceramics in Burlington Magazine, Apollo, Trans English Ceramic Circle, and Faenza. *Recreation:* tennis. *Address:* 11 Pembroke Square, W8 6PA.
See also P. L. V. Mallet.

MALLET, Philip Louis Victor, CMG 1980; HM Diplomatic Service, retired; *b* 3 Feb. 1926; *e s* of late Sir Victor Mallet, GCMG, CVO and Christiana Jean, *d* of Herman A. Andreae; *m* 1953, Mary Moyle Grenfell Borlase; three *s*. *Educ:* Winchester; Balliol Coll., Oxford. Army Service, 1944–47. Entered HM Foreign (subseq. Diplomatic) Service, 1949; served in: FO, 1949; Baghdad, 1950–53; FO, 1953–56; Cyprus, 1956–58; Aden, 1958; Bonn, 1958–62; FO, 1962–64; Tunis, 1964–66; FCO, 1967–69; Khartoum, 1969–73; Stockholm, 1973–76; Head of Republic of Ireland Dept, FCO, 1977–78; High Comr in Guyana and non-resident Ambassador to Suriname, 1978–82. *Address:* Wittersham House, Wittersham, Kent TN30 7ED. *Club:* Brooks's.
See also J. V. G. Mallet.

MALLET, Sir (William) George, GCSL; GCMG 1997; CBE; Governor-General of St Lucia, 1996–97; *b* 24 July 1923; *m* Beryl Bernadine Leonce. *Educ:* RC Boys' Sch.; Castries Intermediate Sch. Mem., Castries City Council, 1952–64; MLC, 1958–79, MHA, 1979–96, St Lucia; Minister for Trade, Industry, Agric. and Tourism, 1964–79; Minister for Trade, Industry and Tourism, 1982–92; Dep. Prime Minister, Minister for For. Affairs, and Minister for Caribbean Community Affairs, 1992–96. *Address:* The Morne, Castries, St Lucia.

MALLETT, Conrad Richard, FRICS; Member, Lands Tribunal, 1980–92; *b* 11 May 1919; *s* of Captain Raymond Mallett, OBE, MN and Joyce Mallett (*née* Humble); *m* 1942, Elisabeth (Paulina) Williams; one *s* two *d*. *Educ:* Wellingborough Sch. Ordinary Airman to Lieut Comdr (A), RNVR, 1939–46 (despatches 1941). Partner, Montagu Evans and Son, Chartered Surveyors, London and Edinburgh, 1950–80. *Recreation:* cruising under sail. *Address:* 2 Hadley Hurst Cottages, Hadley Common, Barnet, Herts EN5 5QF. *T:* (020) 8449 5933.

MALLETT, Edmund Stansfield; Director of Applications Programmes, European Space Agency, Paris, 1981–85, retired; *b* 21 April 1923; *s* of Cecil Finer Mallett and Elsie Stansfield; *m* 1st, 1953, Nancy Campbell (*d* 1983); three *s*; 2nd, 1985, Jocelyn Maynard Ghent, BA, MA, PhD. *Educ:* Bradford Grammar Sch.; Leeds Univ. (BSc). CEng, MIEE; FBIS. Gramophone Co., 1944; Fairey Aviation Co., 1948; Royal Aircraft Establishment: joined 1950; Head, Data Transmission and Processing Div., 1961; Supt, Central Unit for Scientific Photography, 1966; Head, Instrumentation Div., 1968; Head of Instruments Br., Min. of Technol., 1969; Head of Instrumentation and Ranges Dept, RAE, 1971; Director Space, DoI, 1976; Under Sec., and Head of Res. and Technol. Requirements and Space Div., DoI, 1978; Dir, Nat. Maritime Inst., 1979. *Publications:* papers and articles on instrumentation and measurement. *Recreations:* music, art, genealogy, solving problems. *Address:* 580 Prospect Avenue, Rockcliffe Park, Ottawa, ON K1M 0X7, Canada. *T:* (613) 7487219.

MALLETT, Francis Anthony, CBE 1984; Chief Executive, South Yorkshire County Council, 1973–84; Clerk of the Lieutenancy, South Yorkshire, 1974–84; solicitor; *b* 13 March 1924; *s* of Francis Sidney and Marion Mallett; *m* 1956, Alison Shirley Melville, MA; two *s* one *d*. *Educ:* Mill Hill; London Univ. (LLB). Army, 1943–47: commissioned, Royal Hampshire Regt, 1944; served in Middle East, Italy and Germany. Second Dep. Clerk, Herts CC, 1966–69; Dep. Clerk, West Riding CC, 1969–74. Chairman: Assoc. of Local Authority Chief Execs, 1979–84; Crown Prosecution Service Staff Commn, 1985–87; Mem., W Yorks Residuary Body, 1985–91. *Recreations:* gardening, fishing. *Address:* Lurley Manor, Tiverton, Devon EX16 9QS. *T:* (01884) 255363. *Club:* Lansdowne.

MALLICK, Sir Netar (Prakash), Kt 1998; DL; FRCP, FRCPE, FRCPI; Professor of Renal Medicine, University of Manchester, since 1994; Hon. Consultant in Renal Medicine, Manchester Royal Infirmary, since 1970; *b* 3 Aug. 1935; *s* of Bhawani Das Mallick and Shanti Devi Mallick; *m* 1960, Mary Wilcockson; three *d*. *Educ:* Queen Elizabeth's Grammar Sch., Blackburn; Manchester Univ. (BSc Hons 1956; MB ChB 1959; Pres., Students' Union, 1958–59). FRCP 1976; FRCPE 1992; FRCPI 1999. Surgical Res. Fellow, Harvard Univ., 1960; Dept of Medicine, Welsh Nat. Sch. of Medicine, 1963–67; Manchester University: Lectr, 1967–72; Sen. Lectr, 1972–92; Hon. Prof. in Renal Medicine, 1992–; Physician in Charge, Dept of Renal Medicine, Manchester Royal Infirmary, 1973–. Medical Director: Central Manchester Healthcare NHS Trust, 1997–2000; Advisory Distinction Awards, 1999–. Vice Chm., Blackburn, Hyndburn and Ribble Valley HA, 1985–90. Pres., Renal Assoc., 1988–91; Chairman: European Dialysis and Transplantation Assoc. Registry, 1991–94; Union Européenne des Médecins Specialistes, 1993–98 (Pres., Bd of Nephrology, 1993–97). Pres., Manchester Lit. and Phil. Soc., 1986–88. DL Greater Manchester, 1999. *Publications:* (ed) Glucose Polymers in Health and Disease, 1977; Renal Disease in General Practice, 1979; (ed) Williams, Colour Atlas of Renal Diseases, 2nd edn 1993; Atlas of Nephrology, 1994; papers on renal disease and health provision in learned jls. *Recreations:* theatre, literature, cricket and other sports. *Address:* Department of Renal Medicine, Central Manchester Healthcare NHS Trust, Manchester Royal Infirmary, Oxford Road, Manchester M13 9WL. *T:* (0161) 276 4411.

MALLINCKRODT, Georg Wilhelm von; *see* von Mallinckrodt.

MALLINSON, Anthony William; Senior Partner, Slaughter and May, 1984–86; *b* 1 Dec. 1923; *s* of Stanley Tucker Mallinson and Dora Selina Mallinson (*née* Burridge); *m* 1955, Heather Mary Gardiner (*d* 1999). *Educ:* Cheam School; Marlborough College; Gonville and Caius College, Cambridge (Exbnr 1948, Tapp Post-Graduate Scholar, 1949, BA, LLM). Served RA, 1943–47, Major. Admitted solicitor, England and Wales, 1952, Hong Kong, 1978; Partner, Slaughter and May, 1957–86; Solicitor to Fishmongers' Co., 1964–86. Mem. London Bd, Bank of Scotland, 1985–93; Director: Baring Stratton (formerly Stratton) Investment Trust, 1986–94; Morgan Grenfell Asset Management Ltd, 1986–91. Mem., BoT Cttee examining British Patent System (Banks Cttee), 1967–70; Chm., Cinematograph Films Council, 1973–76. Hon. Legal Adviser to Accounting Standards Cttee, 1982–86; Member: Council, Section on Business Law, Internat. Bar Assoc., 1984–90; (co-opted) Law Soc. Co. Law Cttee, 1986–92; Financial Services Tribunal, 1988–97; Financial Reporting Review Panel, 1991–95; Registration Cttee, TCCB, 1986–96; Trustee, Essex CCC, 1990– (Mem. Exec. Cttee, 1986–92). *Recreations:* watching sport, particularly cricket, reading. *Address:* 21 Cottesmore Court, Stanford Road, W8 5QN. *T:* (020) 7937 2739. *Clubs:* Royal Commonwealth Society, MCC, Cricketers'.

MALLINSON, Sir James; *see* Mallinson, Sir W. J.

MALLINSON, John Russell; Speaker's Assistant Counsel, House of Commons, since 1996; *b* 29 June 1943; *s* of Wilfred and Joyce Helen Mallinson; *m* 1968, Susan Rebecca Jane Godfree; one *s* one *d*. *Educ:* Giggleswick Sch.; Balliol Coll., Oxford (Keasbey Schol. 1963; BA). Solicitor (Hons.), 1972. Asst Solicitor, Coward Chance, 1972–74; Sen. Legal Assistant, DTI, 1974–79; Assistant Solicitor: Law Officers' Dept, AG's Chambers, 1979–81; DTI, 1982–84; Under Sec. (Legal), DTI, 1985–89; Corporation of Lloyd's: Gen. Manager, 1989–92; Solicitor, 1992–95; Mem., Lloyd's Regulatory Bd, 1993–95. *Recreations:* reading, conversation, music, looking at paintings. *Address:* 4 Nunappleton Way, Hurst Green, Surrey RH8 9AW. *T:* (01883) 714775.

MALLINSON, William Arthur, CBE 1978; FREng; Vice Chairman, Smiths Industries PLC, 1978–85; *b* 12 June 1922; *s* of Arthur Mallinson and Nellie Jane Mallinson; *m* 1948, Muriel Ella Parker; two *d*. *Educ:* William Hulme's Grammar Sch., Manchester; Faculty of Technol., Manchester Univ. (BScTech 1st Cl. Hons). MIEE, MIMechE, MRAeS; FREng (FEng 1985). Electrical Officer, Tech. Br., RAFVR, 1943–47; Elec. Designer, Electro-Hydraulics Ltd, 1947–51; Ferranti Ltd: Proj. Engr, GW Dept, 1951–55; Chief Engr, Aircraft Equipment Dept, 1955–68; Smiths Industries Ltd, 1968–85: Technical Dir, then Gen. Man., Aviation Div.; Divl Man. Dir; Main Bd Dir; Corporate Man. Dir. Member: Airworthiness Requirements Bd, CAA, 1981–85; Electronics and Avionics Requirements Bd, DTI, 1983–85 (Chm., Aviation Cttee, 1984–85). FIMgt (FBIM 1976). *Recreations:* music, horticulture. *Address:* Chestnut Cottage, Dukes Covert, Bagshot, Surrey GU19 5HU. *T:* (01276) 472479.

MALLINSON, Sir (William) James, 5th Bt *cr* 1935, of Walthamstow; indologist; researching for DPhil at Balliol College, Oxford, since 1995; *b* 22 April 1970; *s* of Sir William John Mallinson, 4th Bt and of Rosalind Angela Mallinson (*née* Hoare); *S* father, 1995. *Educ:* Eton Coll.; St Peter's Coll., Oxford (BA Sanskrit); SOAS, London Univ. (MA). *Recreations:* juggling, yoga, paragliding. *Heir: cousin* Anthony William Mallinson [*b* 1 Dec. 1923; *m* 1955, Heather Mary (*née* Gardiner) (*d* 1999)]. *Club:* Bembridge Sailing (Isle of Wight).

MALLON, Rt Rev. Mgr Joseph Laurence; Parish Priest, St Brendan, Harwood, Bolton, since 1995; *b* 8 Aug. 1942; *s* of John Mallon and Mary (*née* O'Neill). *Educ:* St Nathy's Coll., Ballaghadereen; St Kiernan's Coll., Kilkenny. Ordained priest, Dio. of Salford, 1966; Curate: St Joseph's, Bury, 1966–67; St Anne's, Stretford, 1967–73; commnd into RAChD, 1973; service in England, NI, Germany and Cyprus; Sen. RC Chaplain, BAOR, 1988; Prin. RC Chaplain and VG (Army), 1989–93, retired; Parish Priest, St Anne's, Ancoats, Manchester, 1993–95. Prelate of Honour, 1989. *Recreations:* bridge, golf, recreational mathematics, The Times crossword. *Address:* St Brendan's Presbytery, 171 Longsight, Harwood, Bolton, Lancs BL2 3JF.

MALLON, Most Rev. Peter J.; *see* Regina, Archbishop of, (RC).

MALLON, Seamus; MP (SDLP) Newry and Armagh, since Jan. 1986; Member (SDLP) Newry and Armagh, Northern Ireland Assembly, since 1998; *b* 17 Aug. 1936; *s* of Francis P. Mallon and Jane O'Flaherty; *m* 1966, Gertrude Cush; one *d*. *Educ:* St Joseph's Coll. of Educn. Member: NI Assembly, 1973–74 and 1982; NI Convention, 1975–76; Irish Senate, 1981–82; New Ireland Forum, 1983–84; Armagh Dist Council, 1973–86. Dep. First Minister (designate), 1998–99, Dep. First Minister, 1999–2001, NI Assembly. Dep. Leader, SDLP, 1978–2001. Member: Select Cttee on Agric., 1987–97; Anglo-Irish Inter-Parly Body, 1990–. Author of play, Adam's Children, prod. radio, 1968, and stage, 1969. *Recreations:* angling, gardening. *Address:* 5 Castleview, Markethill, Armagh BT60 1QP. *T:* (028) 3755 1411; House of Commons, SW1A 0AA; (office) 15 Cornmarket, Newry, Co. Down BT35 8BG; (office) 6 Seven Houses, Armagh, Co. Armagh BT61 7LJ.

MALLOWS, Surg. Rear-Adm. (Harry) Russell; Senior Medical Officer, Shell Centre, 1977–85; *b* 1 July 1920; *s* of Harry Mallows and Amy Mallows (*née* Law); *m* 1st, 1942, Rhona Frances Wyndham-Smith (*d* 1997); one *s* two *d*; 2nd, 1999, Jean Richardson. *Educ:* Wrekin Coll.; Christ's Coll., Cambridge (MA, MD); UCH, London. FFPHM, FFOM, DPH, DIH. SMO, HM Dockyards at Hong Kong, Sheerness, Gibraltar and Singapore, 1951–67; Naval MO of Health, Scotland and NI Comd, and Far East Stn, 1964–68; Dir of Environmental Medicine, Inst. of Naval Medicine, 1970–73; Comd MO, Naval Home Comd, 1973–75; QHP, 1974–77; Surgeon Rear-Adm. (Ships and Estabts), 1975–77; retd 1977. CStJ 1976. *Publications:* articles in BMJ, Royal Naval Med. Service Jl, Proc. RSM. *Recreations:* music, travel. *Address:* 1 Shear Hill, Petersfield, Hants GU31 4BB. *T:* (01730) 263116.

MALMESBURY, 7th Earl of, *cr* 1800; **James Carleton Harris;** Baron 1788; Viscount FitzHarris 1800; DL; *b* 19 June 1946; *o s* of 6th Earl of Malmesbury, TD; *S* father, 2000; *m* 1969, Sally Ann, *yr d* of Sir Richard Newton Rycroft, 7th Bt; three *s* two *d*. *Educ:* Eton; Queen's Coll., St Andrews (MA). DL Hampshire, 1997. *Heir: s* Viscount FitzHarris, *qv*. *Address:* Greywell Hill, Greywell, Hook, Hants RG29 1DG. *T:* (01256) 703565.

MALMESBURY, Archdeacon of; *see* Hawker, Ven. A. F.

MALONE, Dr Caroline Ann Tuke, (Mrs S. K. F. Stoddart), FSA; Keeper, Department of Prehistory and Early Europe, British Museum, since 2000; *b* 10 Oct. 1957; *d* of Lt Col Henry Charles Malone and Margaret Hope (*née* Kayll); *m* 1983, Dr Simon Kenneth Fladgate Stoddart, *qv*; two *d*. *Educ:* St Mary's Sch., St Leonards on Sea; New Hall, Cambridge (MA Hons Archaeol. and Anthropol. 1984); Trinity Hall, Cambridge (PhD Archaeol. 1986). FSA 1993. Italian Govt Scholarship, Rome Univ., 1980–81; Rome Scholarship in Archaeol., Brit. Sch. in Rome, 1981–82; Curator, Alexander Keiller Mus., Avebury, 1985–87; Inspector of Ancient Monuments, English Heritage, 1987–90; Lectr, then Sen. Lectr, Univ. of Bristol, 1990–97; Cambridge University: Tutor in Archaeol., Continuing Educn, 1997–2000; Affiliated Lectr, Dept of Archaeology, 1998–2000; Pro Proctor, 1998–99, Sen. Proctor, 1999–2000, Dep. Proctor, 2000–01; Fellow, New Hall, 1997–2000. Co Director: Gubbio Archaeol. Project, 1983–88; Gozo Project, Malta, 1987–98; Troina Project, Sicily, 1997–. Ed., Antiquity, 1998–2000. Mem., Inst. of Field Archaeologists, 1986–. Fellow, McDonald Inst. for Archaeol Res., 1996. *Publications:* (ed with S. Stoddart) Papers in Italian Archaeology, Vols 1–4, 1985; Avebury, 1989; (ed with S. Stoddart) Territory, Time and State: the archaeological development of the Gubbio basin, 1994; contrib. numerous academic papers, articles and reviews. *Recreations:* gardening, pottery, good books, ancient monuments. *Address:* British Museum, Great Russell Street, WC1B 3DG. *T:* (020) 7323 8454.

MALONE, (Peter) Gerald; Editor, The Sunday Times Scotland, 1989–90, Editorial Consultant, 1990; *b* 21 July 1950; *s* of P. A. and J. Malone; *m* 1981, Dr Anne S. Blyth; two *s* one *d*. *Educ:* St Aloysius Coll., Glasgow; Glasgow Univ. (MA, LLB). Admitted solicitor, 1972. MP (C): Aberdeen S, 1983–87; Winchester, 1992–97; contested (C) Winchester, 1997. PPS to Parly Under Secs of State, Dept of Energy, 1985, and to Sec. of State, DTI, 1985–86; an Asst Government Whip, 1986–87; Dep. Chm., Cons. Party, 1992–94; Minister of State, DoH, 1994–97. Dir of European Affairs, Energy and Envmtl Policy Center, Harvard Univ., 1987–90; Presenter, Talk In Sunday, Radio Clyde, 1988–90. Chm., CGA, 1991. *Recreations:* opera, motoring. *Club:* Conservative (Winchester).

MALONE, Rt Rev. Vincent; Auxiliary Bishop of Liverpool, (RC), and Titular Bishop of Abora, since 1989; *b* 11 Sept. 1931; *s* of Louis Malone and Elizabeth Malone (*née* McGrath). *Educ:* St Francis Xavier's Coll, Liverpool; St Joseph's Coll., Upholland; Liverpool Univ. (BSc 1959); Cambridge Univ. (CertEd 1960; DipEd 1964). FCP 1967. Chaplain to Notre Dame Training Coll., Liverpool, 1955–59; Curate, St Anne's, Liverpool, 1960–61; Asst Master, Cardinal Allen Grammar School, Liverpool, 1961–71; RC Chaplain to Liverpool Univ., 1971–79; Administrator, Liverpool Metropolitan Cathedral, 1979–89. *Address:* 17 West Oakhill Park, Liverpool L13 4BN. *T:* (0151) 228 7637, *Fax:* (0151) 475 0841; *e-mail:* vmalone@onetel.net.uk.

MALONE-LEE, Michael Charles, CB 1995; Vice Chancellor, Anglia Polytechnic University, since 1995; *b* 4 March 1941; *s* of Dr Gerard Brendan and Theresa Malone-Lee; *m* 1971, Claire Frances Cockin; two *s*. *Educ:* Stonyhurst College; Campion Hall, Oxford (MA). Ministry of Health, 1968; Principal Private Sec. to Sec. of State for Social Services, 1976–79; Asst Sec., 1977; Area Administrator, City and East London AHA, 1979–81; District Administrator, Bloomsbury Health Authy, 1982–84; Under Secretary, 1984, Dir, Personnel Management, 1984–87, DHSS; Prin. Fin. Officer, Home Office, 1987–90; Dep. Sec. (Dir of Corporate Affairs, NHS Management Exec.), DoH, 1990–93; Dep. Sec. (Head of Policy Gp), Lord Chancellor's Dept, 1993–95. Non-exec Dir, ICI (Agrochemicals), 1986–89. Dir, Essex TEC, 1996–; Chairman: BBC E Regl Adv. Council, 1997–99; Essex Learning and Skills Council, 2000–. Mem., Review Body for Nursing Staff, Midwives, Health Visitors and Professions allied to Medicine, 1998–2001. Chm. Governors, New Hall Sch., 1999–. CIMgt. *Recreations:* natural history, marathon running. *Address:* Anglia Polytechnic University, Victoria Road South, Chelmsford, Essex CM1 1LL.

MALONEY, Michael John; JP; MA; Principal, Moreton Hall, 1990–92; *b* 26 July 1932; *s* of John William Maloney and Olive Lois Maloney; *m* 1960, Jancis Ann (*née* Ewing); one *s* one *d*. *Educ:* St Alban's Sch.; Trinity Coll., Oxford (MA). Nat. Service, 2nd Lieut RA, served with RWAFF, 1955–57. May & Baker Ltd, 1957–58; Asst Master, Shrewsbury Sch., 1958–66; Sen. Science Master, Housemaster, Dep. Headmaster, Eastbourne Coll., 1966–72; Headmaster: Welbeck Coll., 1972–85; Kamazu Acad., Malaŵi, 1986–89. JP Worksop, 1975–86, Shrewsbury, 1991. *Publication:* (with D. E. P. Hughes) Advanced Theoretical Chemistry, 1964. *Recreations:* ornithology, cryptography, very hard crosswords. *Address:* Lower Lane Cottage, Chirbury, Montgomery, Powys SY15 6UD. *T:* (01938) 561303.

MALOUF, David George Joseph, AO 1987; writer; *b* 20 March 1934; *s* of George and Welcolme Malouf. *Educ:* Brisbane Grammar Sch.; Univ. of Queensland (BA Hons Eng Lang. and Lit.). Teacher, St Anselm's Coll., Birkenhead, 1962–68; Lectr, Dept of English, Univ. of Sydney, 1968–78. Boyer Lectr, ABC, 1998. Hon. DLitt: Macquarie, 1990; Queensland, 1991; Sydney, 1998. *Publications:* Johnno: a novel, 1975; An Imaginary Life, 1978; Child's Play, 1981; Fly Away Peter, 1981; Harland's Half Acre, 1984; Antipodes (stories), 1985; 12 Edmondstone Street, 1986; The Great World, 1990; Remembering Babylon, 1993; The Conversations at Curlow Creek, 1996; A Spirit of Play (Boyer Lectures), 1998; Untold Tales, 1999; Dream Stuff (stories), 2000; *poetry:* Bicycle and Other Poems, 1970; Neighbours in a Thicket, 1974; First Things Last, 1981; Selected Poems, 1993; *libretti:* Baa Baa Black Sheep, 1993; Jane Eyre, 2000. *Address:* c/o Rogers, Coleridge & White, 20 Powis Mews, W11 1JN.

MALPAS, Prof. James Spencer, DPhil; FRCR, FRCP, FRCPCH; Master, London Charterhouse, 1996–2001; Consultant Physician, St Bartholomew's Hospital, since 1973; Professor of Medical Oncology, 1979–95, now Professor Emeritus, and Director, Imperial Cancer Research Fund Medical Oncology Unit, 1976–95, St Bartholomew's Hospital; *b* 15 Sept. 1931; *s* of Tom Spencer Malpas, BSc, MICE and Hilda Chalstrey; *m* 1957, Joyce May Cathcart; two *s*. *Educ:* Sutton County Grammar Sch.; St Bartholomew's Hosp., London Univ. Schol. in Sci., 1951; BSc Hons, 1952; MB BS, 1955; DPhil, 1965; FRCP 1971; FRCR 1983; FFPM 1989; FRCPCH 1997. Junior appts in medicine, St Bartholomew's Hosp. and Royal Post-Grad. Med. Sch.; Nat. Service in RAF, 1957–60; Aylwen Bursar, St Bartholomew's Hosp., 1961; Lectr in Medicine, Oxford Univ., 1962–65; St Bartholomew's Hospital: Sen. Registrar in Medicine, 1966–68; Sen. Lectr in Medicine, 1968–72; Dean, 1969–72, Gov., 1972–74, Treasurer, 1986–87, and Vice Pres., 1987–93, of Med. Coll.; Dep. Dir (Clinical), ICRF, 1986–90. Cooper Res. Schol. in Med., 1966, 1967, 1968. Examiner in Medicine: Univ. of Oxford, 1974; Univ. of London, 1985, 1986. Asst Registrar, RCP, 1975–80; Treasurer, Postgrad. Med. Fellowship, 1984–87. Pres., Assoc. of Cancer Physicians, 1994–99. Trustee: Special Trustees, St Bart's Hosp., 1997–; Med. Coll. of St Bart's Hosp. Trust, 1999–. Lockyer Lectr, RCP, 1978; Skinner Lectr, RCR, 1986; Subodh Mitra Meml Orator, New Delhi, 1991; Louise Buchanan Lectr, Assoc. of Cancer Physicians, 1993. Editor, British Jl of Cancer, 1992–. *Publications:* (ed jtly) Multiple Myeloma, 1994, 2nd edn 1997; contrib. many medical textbooks; papers in BMJ, Brit. Jl Haematology, Jl Clinical Oncology, etc. *Recreations:* travel, history, painting, sailing, amateur molecular biologist, avoiding gardening. *Address:* 253 Lauderdale Tower, Barbican, EC2Y 8BY. *T:* (020) 7920 9337. *Club:* Little Ship.

MALPAS, Sir Robert, Kt 1998; CBE 1975; FREng, FIMechE, FIChemE; Chairman, Cookson Group, 1991–98; *b* 9 Aug. 1927; *s* of late Cheshyre Malpas and of Louise Marie Marcelle Malpas; *m* 1956, Josephine Dickenson. *Educ:* Taunton Sch.; St George's Coll., Buenos Aires; Durham Univ. (BScMechEng (1st Cl. Hons)). Joined ICI Ltd, 1948; moved to Alcudia SA (48.5 per cent ICI), Spain, 1963; ICI Europa Ltd, Brussels, 1965; Chm., ICI Europa Ltd, 1973; ICI Main Board Dir, 1975–78; Pres., Halcon International Inc., 1978–82; a Man. Dir, BP, 1983–89; Chm., PowerGen, 1990; Director: BOC Group, 1981–96; Eurotunnel, 1987–99 (Co-Chm., 1996–98); Repsol, SA, 1989–. Member: Engineering Council, 1983–88 (Vice-Chm., 1984–88); ACARD, 1983–86; Chairman: LINK Steering Gp, 1987–93; NERC, 1993–96. FREng (FEng 1978; Sen. Vice Pres., 1988–92). Hon. FRSC 1988; Hon. FIMechE 1999. FRSA. Hon. Fellow, Univ. of Westminster, 1992. Hon. DTech Loughborough, 1983; DUniv Surrey, 1984; Hon. DEng Newcastle, 1991; Hon. DSc: Bath, 1991; Durham, 1997. Order of Civil Merit, Spain, 1967. *Recreations:* sport, music, theatre. *Address:* 2 Spencer Park, SW18 2SX. *Clubs:* Royal Automobile; Mill Reef (Antigua).

MALPASS, Brian William, PhD; CChem; writer; Chief Executive, De La Rue Co. plc, 1987–89; *b* 12 Sept. 1937; *s* of William and Florence Malpass; *m* 1960, Hazel Anne; two *d*. *Educ:* Univ. of Birmingham (Open Schol.; Frankland Prize 1960; BScChem 1st Cl. Hons, PhD). MRSC. Passfield Res. Laboratories, 1963–68; De La Rue Co., 1968–89; Finance Dir, 1980–84; Man. Dir, Thomas De La Rue Currency Div., 1984–87. *Publications:* Bluff Your Way in Science, 1993; Bluff Your Way in Chess, 1993; numerous papers in scientific jls. *Recreations:* golf, cinema. *Address:* 13 Spinfield Mount, Marlow, Bucks SL7 2JU. *Club:* Maidenhead Golf.

MALTA, Archbishop of, (RC), since 1976; **Most Rev. Joseph Mercieca;** STD, JUD; *b* Victoria, Gozo, 11 Nov. 1928. *Educ:* Gozo Seminary; Univ. of London (BA); Gregorian Univ., Rome (STD); Lateran Univ., Rome (JUD). Priest, 1952; Rector of Gozo Seminary in late 1960s; Permanent Judge at Sacred Roman Rota and Commissioner to Congregation for the Sacraments and Congregation for the Doctrine of the Faith, 1969; Auxiliary Bishop of Malta, and Vicar-General, 1974–76. Consultor, Supreme Tribunal of Apostolic Segnatura suis, 1992–. *Address:* Archbishop's Curia, PO Box 29, Valletta, Malta. *T:* 234317.

MALTBY, Antony John; JP; MA; Headmaster of Trent College, 1968–88; *b* 15 May 1928; *s* of late G. C. Maltby and Mrs Maltby (*née* Kingsnorth); *m* 1959, Jillian Winifred (*née* Burt) (*d* 2000); four *d*. *Educ:* Clayesmore Sch., Dorset; St John's Coll., Cambridge. BA Hons (History) 1950; MA. Schoolmaster: Dover Coll., 1951–58; Pocklington Sch., 1958–68. Mem. (Indep. C), Ashford BC, 1991. JP: Ilkeston, 1980; Ashford, 1992; DL Derbyshire, 1984–91. *Recreations:* community matters, travel. *Address:* Little Singleton Farm, Great Chart, Ashford, Kent TN26 1JS. *T:* (01233) 629397. *Club:* Hawks (Cambridge).

MALTBY, Colin Charles; Chief Executive, BP Investment Management Ltd, since 2000; *b* 8 Feb. 1951; *s* of George Frederick Maltby and Dorothy Maltby; *m* 1983, Victoria Angela Valerie Elton; one *s* two *d*. *Educ:* George Heriot's Sch., Edinburgh; King Edward's Sch., Birmingham; Christ Church, Oxford (MA, MSc); Stanford Business Sch. Pres., Oxford Union, 1973; Chm., Fedn of Cons. Students, 1974–75. With N. M. Rothschild & Sons, 1975–80; Director: Kleinwort Benson Investment Mgt Ltd, 1984–95 (Chief Exec., 1988–95); Banque Kleinwort Benson SA, Geneva, 1985–88; Kleinwort Benson Gp plc, 1989–95; CCLA Investment Mgt Ltd, 1997– (Chm., 1999–); Chm., Kleinwort Overseas Investment Trust plc, 1992–96; Chief Investment Officer, Equitas, 1996–2000. Director: RM plc, 1997–99; H. Young Hldgs plc, 1997–. Mem., Finance Cttee, Funding Agency for Schs, 1996–99. FRSA 1993; MRI; Mem., ICA. *Recreations:* music, ski-ing. *Address:* 51 Addison Avenue, W11 4QU.

MALTRAVERS, Lord; Henry Miles Fitzalan-Howard; *b* 3 Dec. 1987; *s* and *heir* of Earl of Arundel and Surrey, *qv*. A Page of Honour to the Queen, 1999–.

MALVERN, 3rd Viscount *cr* 1955, of Rhodesia and of Bexley, Kent; **Ashley Kevin Godfrey Huggins;** *b* 26 Oct. 1949; *s* of 2nd Viscount Malvern, and of Patricia Marjorie, *d* of Frank Renwick-Bower, Durban, S Africa; *S* father, 1978. *Heir: uncle* Hon. (Martin) James Huggins, *b* 13 Jan. 1928.

MALVERN, John, FRCSE, FRCOG; Consultant Obstetrician and Gynaecologist, Queen Charlotte's and Chelsea Hospital for Women (formerly Queen Charlotte's Hospital and Chelsea Hospital), since 1973; Hon. Consultant Gynaecologist, King Edward VII Hospital for Officers, since 1997; *b* 3 Oct. 1937; *s* of late Harry Ladyman Malvern, CBE, and Doreen Malvern (*née* Peters); *m* 1965, Katharine Mary Monica, *d* of late Hugh Guillebaud; one *s* two *d*. *Educ:* Fettes Coll., Edinburgh; Royal London Hosp. Med. Sch., Univ. of London (BSc 1st Cl. Hons 1959; MB BS 1963). FRCSE 1968; FRCOG 1984. Various jun. posts in surgery and obstetrics and gynaecology at Royal London Hosp., Plymouth Gen. Hosp., Hosp. for Women, Soho Sq., Middx Hosp., Queen Charlotte's and Chelsea Hosp. Hon. Sen. Lectr, RPMS, then ICSTM, 1973–99. Ninian M. Falkiner Lectr, Rotunda Hosp., Dublin, 1980. Chm., Acad. Gp, Inst. Obstetrics and Gynaecol., 1986–88. Royal College of Obstetricians and Gynaecologists: Officer and Hon. Treas., 1991–98; Mem. Council, 1977–83 and 1987–90; Pres., Obstetric and Gynaecol Section, RSocMed, 1989. Former Examiner for RCOG: Central Midwives Bd; Univs of London, Liverpool, Edinburgh, Manchester, Benghazi, Colombo, Khartoum and Hong Kong. Member: Central Manpower Cttee, 1981–84; PPP Healthcare Trust Ltd, 1998–. Member: Blair Bell Res. Soc., 1970–; Internat. Continence Soc., 1971–; Fothergill Club, 1977–; Gynaecol Vis. Soc., 1979–; Hon. Mem., New England Obstetrical and Gynecol Soc., 2000. Liveryman, Soc. of Apothecaries, 1978–. *Publications:* (ed jtly) The Unstable Bladder, 1989; (ed jtly) Lecture Notes on Gynaecology, 1996; contributor to: Turnbull's Obstetrics, 1985, 2nd edn 1995; Basic Sciences in Obstetrics and Gynaecology, 1992; Gynaecology by Ten Teachers, 1995; various contribs on urogynaecology and obstetrics.

Recreations: wine tasting, history of art, travel. *Address:* 82 Harley Street, W1G 7HW. *T:* (020) 7636 2766; 30 Roedean Crescent, Roehampton, SW15 5JU. *T:* (020) 8876 4943. *Clubs:* Royal Society of Medicine, Hurlingham.

See also Sir H. R. Wilmot.

MALYAN, Hugh David; Member (Lab), since 1994, Leader, since 2000, Croydon Borough Council; *b* 7 June 1959; *s* of Cyril and Brenda Malyan; *m* 1983, Ruth Margaret; one *s* one *d. Educ:* Strand Grammar Sch., Brixton. Trustee Savings Bank, 1975–78; fireman, London Fire Bde, 1978–92. Chm., Educn Cttee, Croydon BC. *Recreations:* amateur dramatics (Mem., Downsview Players), singing, football (Crystal Palace supporter!). *Address:* Town Hall, Katharine Street, Croydon, Surrey CR0 1NX. T: (020) 8686 4433.

MAMALONI, Solomon Sunaone; MP (People's Alliance Party), Solomon Islands; Prime Minister of Solomon Islands, 1981–85, 1989–93 and 1994–97; *b* 21 June 1943. *Educ:* King George VI School; Te-Aute College, NZ. Exec. Officer, Civil Service, later Clerk to Legislative Council; MP Makira, 1970–76, West Makira, 1976–77 and 1980–; Chief Minister, British Solomon Islands, 1974–76; founder and leader, People's Progress Party (merged with Rural Alliance Party to form People's Alliance Party, 1979). Man. Dir, Patosha Co., 1977. *Address:* National Parliament Building, Honiara, Guadalcanal, Solomon Islands.

MAMATSASHVILI, Teimuraz; Ambassador of Georgia to the Court of St James's, since 1995, and to the Republic of Ireland, since 1998; *b* 10 Nov. 1942; *s* of David Mamatsashvili and Maria Robakidze; *m* 1967, Irina Arkhangelskaya; two *d. Educ:* Georgian Polytechnical Inst. (Engineer); Acad. of Foreign Trade of USSR (Economist). Senior Engineer: Sci. Inst. of Metrology, 1965–70; USSR Trade Rep. in Australia, 1974–77; Dir, foreign trade orgn Licensintorg, Moscow, 1977–89; USSR Trade Rep., Tokyo, 1989–92; Minister of Foreign Economic Relations, Georgia, 1992–93. Rep. to IMO, 1995–; Gov., EBRD, 1996–. Orders of the Soviet Union, 1971, 1988. *Recreations:* hunting, gardening. *Address:* 3 Hornton Place, W8 4LZ. *T:* (020) 7937 8233. *Club:* Arts.

MAMBA, George Mbikwakhe, Hon. GCVO 1987; Minister of Foreign Affairs, Swaziland, 1988–94; *b* 5 July 1932; *s* of Ndabazebelungu Mamba and Getrude Mthwalose Mamba, and *g s* of late Chief Bokweni Mamba; *m* 1960, Sophie Sidzandza Sibande; three *s* two *d. Educ:* Franson Christian High Sch.; Swazi National High Sch.; Morija Teacher Trng Coll.; Cambridge Inst. of Educn; Nairobi Univ. Head Teacher, Makhonza Mission Sch., 1956–60; Teacher, Kwaluseni Central Sch., 1961–65; Head Teacher, Enkamheni Central Sch., 1966–67; Inspector of Schs, Manzini Dist, 1969–70; Welfare/Aftercare Officer, Prison Dept, 1971–72; Counsellor, Swaziland High Commn, Nairobi, 1972–77; High Comr to UK and concurrently High Comr to Malta, Ambassador to Denmark, Sweden and Norway, and Perm. Deleg. to UNESCO, 1978–88, Sen. High Comr, 1984 and Doyen of Diplomatic Corps, 1985–88. Vice-Pres., Swaziland NUT, 1966–67. Field Comr, Swaziland Boy Scouts Assoc., 1967–68, Chief Comr, 1971–72. *Publication:* Children's Play, 1966. *Recreations:* scouting, reading. *Address:* c/o Ministry of Foreign Affairs, PO Box 518, Mbabane, Swaziland.

MAMET, David Alan; writer; stage and film director; *b* 30 Nov. 1947; *s* of Bernard Morris Mamet and Lenore June Mamet (*née* Silver); *m* 1st, 1977, Lindsay Crouse (marr. diss.); 2nd, 1991, Rebecca Pidgeon. *Educ:* Goddard College, Plainfield, Vt (BA Eng. Lit. 1969); Neighbourhood Playhouse Sch., NY. Founding Mem. and first Artistic Dir, St Nicholas Theater Co., Chicago, 1974. *Plays written and produced include:* American Buffalo, 1976; A Life in the Theatre, 1976; The Water Engine, 1977; The Woods, 1977; Lakeboat, 1980; Glen Garry Glen Ross, 1984 (film, 1992); Speed the Plow, 1987; Bobby Gould in Hell, 1989; The Old Neighborhood (trilogy), 1990, UK 1998; Oleanna, 1992; The Cryptogram, 1994; *written and directed:* Boston Marriage, 1999, UK, 2001; *written for films:* The Verdict, 1980; The Untouchables, 1986; House of Games, 1986; (with Shel Silverstein) Things Change, 1987; Hoffa, 1990; Homicide, 1991; Uncle Vanya on 42nd Street, 1994; The Edge, 1998; Wag the Dog, 1998; (jtly) Hannibal, 2001; State and Main (also dir.), 2001; *films directed:* House of Games, 1986; Things Change, 1988; Homicide, 1991; The Winslow Boy, 1999. Pulitzer Prize for Drama, 1984. *Publications:* Writing in Restaurants, 1986; Some Freaks, 1989; The Hero Pony, 1990; On Directing Film, 1991; The Cabin, 1992; The Village, 1994; Passover, 1996; True or False—Heresy and Common Sense for the Actor, 1998; The Old Religion, 1998; Wilson: a consideration of the sources, 2000. *Address:* c/o Howard Rosenstone, Rosenstone/Wender Agency, 3 East 48th Street, New York, NY 10017, USA.

MAMO, Sir Anthony (Joseph), Kt 1960; OBE 1955; Companion of Honour, National Order of Merit (Malta), 1990; *b* 8 Jan. 1909; *s* of late Joseph Mamo and late Carla (*née* Brincat); *m* 1939, Margaret Agius; one *s* two *d. Educ:* Royal Univ. of Malta. BA 1931; LLD 1934. Mem. Statute Law Revision Commn, 1936–42; Crown Counsel, 1942–51; Prof., Criminal Law, Malta Univ., 1943–57; Dep. Attorney-Gen., 1952–54, Attorney-Gen., 1955, Malta; Chief Justice and President, Court of Appeal, Malta, 1957–71; President, Constitutional Court, Malta, 1964–71; Governor-General, Malta, 1971–74; President, Republic of Malta, 1974–76. QC (Malta) 1957. Hon. DLitt Malta, 1969; Hon. LLD Libya, 1971. KStJ 1969. Gieh ir-Repubblika (Malta), 1992; Gieh Birkirkara (Malta), 1996. *Address:* Casa Arkati, Constitution Street, Mosta, Malta. *T:* 434342. *Clubs:* Casino, Maltese.

MAN, Archdeacon of; *see* Partington, Ven. B. H.

MANASSEH, Leonard Sulla, OBE 1982; RA 1979 (ARA 1976); RWA; FRIBA; Partner, Leonard Manasseh Partnership (formerly Leonard Manasseh & Partners), since 1950; *b* 21 May 1916; *s* of late Alan Manasseh and Esther (*née* Elias); *m* 1st, 1947 (marr diss. 1956); one *s* (and one *s* decd); 2nd, 1957, Sarah Delaforce; two *s* (one *d* decd). *Educ:* Cheltenham College; The Architectural Assoc. Sch. of Architecture (AA Dip.). ARIBA 1941, FRIBA 1964; FCSD (FSIAD 1965); RWA 1972 (Pres., 1989–94, PPRWA 1995). Asst Architect, CRE N London and Guy Morgan & Partners; teaching staff, AA and Kingston Sch. of Art, 1941–43; Fleet Air Arm, 1943–46; Asst Architect, Herts CC, 1946–48; Senior Architect, Stevenage New Town Develt Corp., 1948–50; won Festival of Britain restaurant competition, 1950; started private practice, 1950; teaching staff, AA Sch. of Architecture, 1951–59; opened office in Singapore and Malaysia with James Cubitt & Partners (Cubitt Manasseh & Partners), 1953–54. Member: Council, Architectural Assoc., 1959–66 (Pres., 1964–65); Council of Industrial Design, 1965–68; Council, RIBA 1968–70, 1976–82 (Hon. Sec., 1979–81); Council, National Trust, 1977–91; Ancient Monuments Bd, 1978–84; Bd, Chatham Historic Dockyard Trust, 1984–. Pres., Franco-British Union of Architects, 1978–79. Governor: Alleyn's Sch., Dulwich, 1987–95; Dulwich Coll., 1987–95; Dulwich Picture Gallery, 1987–94 (Chm., 1988–93). FRSA 1967. *Work includes:* houses, housing and schools; industrial work; power stations; conservation plan for Beaulieu Estate; Nat. Motor Museum, Beaulieu; Wellington Country Park, Stratfield Saye; Pumping Station, Weymouth; British Museum refurbishment; (jtly) New Research Centre, Loughborough, British Gas. *Publications:* Office Buildings (with 3rd Baron Cunliffe), 1962, Japanese edn 1964; (jtly) Snowdon Summit Report (Countryside Commission), 1974; Eastbourne Harbour Study (Trustees, Chatsworth Settlement), 1976; New Service Yard, Hampstead Heath (Corp. of London), 1993; (jtly) planning reports and studies. *Recreations:* photography, painting, being optimistic. *Address:* 6 Bacon's Lane, Highgate, N6 6BL. *T:* (020) 8340 5528, *Fax:* (020) 8347 6313. *Clubs:* Athenæum, Arts, Royal Automobile.

MANCE, Rt Hon. Sir Jonathan (Hugh), Kt 1993; PC 1999; **Rt Hon. Lord Justice Mance;** a Lord Justice of Appeal, since 1999; *b* 6 June 1943; *e s* of late Sir Henry Stenhouse Mance and of Lady (Joan Erica Robertson) Mance; *m* 1973, Mary Howarth Arden (*see* Rt Hon. Dame M. H. Arden); one *s* two *d. Educ:* Charterhouse; University Coll., Oxford (MA). Called to the Bar, Middle Temple, 1965, Bencher, 1989. QC 1982; a Recorder, 1990–93; a Judge of the High Court, QBD, Commercial List, 1993–99. Worked in Germany, 1965. Chm., Banking Appeal Tribunals, 1992–93. Dir, Bar Mutual Indemnity Fund Ltd, 1987–94. Chm., Consultative Council of European Judges, 2000–. Chm., Hampstead Counselling Service, 2000. Pres., British Insurance Law Assoc., 2000– (Dep. Pres., 1998–2000). Chm., Bar Lawn Tennis Soc., 2000–. *Publications:* (asst editor) Chalmer's Sale of Goods, 1981; (ed jtly) Sale of Goods, Halsbury's Laws of England, 4th edn 1983; lectures and articles on insurance and other legal subjects. *Recreations:* tennis, languages, music. *Address:* Royal Courts of Justice, Strand, WC2A 2LL. *Club:* Cumberland Lawn Tennis.

MANCE, Rt Hon. Dame Mary Howarth; *see* Arden, Rt Hon. Dame M. H.

MANCHAM, Sir James Richard Marie, KBE 1976; international trade consultant, since 1981; Chairman, Mahé Publications Ltd, since 1984; Founding President, Republic of the Seychelles, 1976–77; Founder and Chairman, Crusade for the Restoration of Democracy in Seychelles, since 1990; Leader of revived Seychelles Democratic Party, since 1992; *b* 11 Aug. 1939; adopted British nationality, 1984; *e s* of late Richard Mancham and Evelyne Mancham, MBE (*née* Tirant); *m* 1963, Heather Jean Evans (marr. diss. 1974); one *s* one *d*; *m* 1985, Catherine Olsen; one *s. Educ:* Seychelles Coll.; Wilson Coll., London. Called to Bar, Middle Temple, 1961. Auditeur Libre à la Faculté de Droit ès Sciences Economiques, Univ. of Paris, 1962; Internat. Inst. of Labour Studies Study Course, Geneva, Spring 1968. Legal practice, Supreme Court of Seychelles. Seychelles Democratic Party (SDP), Pres. 1964; Mem. Seychelles Governing Council, 1967; Leader of Majority Party (SDP), 1967; Mem., Seychelles Legislative Assembly, 1970–76; Chief Minister, 1970–75; Prime Minister, 1975–76; Leader of Opposition, 1993–98; led SDP to Seychelles Constitutional Conf., London, 1970 and 1976. Founder, Seychelles Weekly, 1962. Lecturer, 1981, on struggle for power in Indian Ocean, to US and Eur. univs and civic gps; Lectr on geo-politics of Indian Ocean, Internat. Univ. of Japan, 1996. Promoter, Internat. Inst. of Nat. Reconciliation Between Nations, 1997. Delegate: to Conf. on Challenges of Demilitarisation of Africa in Arusha, Tanzania, 1998; to Convocation of Family Fedn for World Peace and Unification Internat., Seoul, 1999; to internat. confs on world peace. Hon. Patron, Indo-Seychelles Chamber of Commerce, 1995. Mem., Internat. Palm Soc., 1994. Hon. Trustee, Cary Ann Lindblad Intrepid Foundn, 1986–. Hon. Mem., Internat. Consultative Bd, Inst. for Strategic Studies and Develt, Bracakaric Univ., Belgrade, 1998. Hon. Citizen: Dade County, Florida, 1963; New Orleans, 1965. FRSA 1968. Cert. of Merit for Distinguished Contribn to Poetry, Internat. Who's Who in Poetry, 1974. Chevalier, Chaîne des Rôtisseurs, 1993. Officier de la Légion d'Honneur, 1976; Grande Médaille de la Francophonie, 1976, Grande médaille vermeille, Paris, 1976; Quaid-i-Azam Medallion (Pakistan), 1976; Gold Medal, City of Pusan, Repub. of Korea, 1976; Gold Medal for Tourism, Mexico, 1977; Gold Medal of Chamber of Commerce and Industries of France, 1977; Gold Medal des Excellences Européennes, 1977; Plaque of Appreciation, Rotary Club of Manila, Philippines, 1987; Gold Medal, Municipality of Dubai, 1995; Gold Medal, City of Bombay, 1996. *Publications:* Reflections and Echoes from Seychelles, 1972 (poetry); L'Air des Seychelles, 1974; Island Splendour, 1980; Paradise Raped, 1983; Galloo—The undiscovered paradise, 1984; New York's Robin Island, 1985; Peace of Mind, 1989; Adages of an Exile, 1991; Oh, Mighty America, 1998. *Recreations:* travel, fishing, birdfeeding, journalism, writing. *Address:* PO Box 29, Mahé, Seychelles. *Clubs:* Royal Automobile, Annabel's, Les Ambassadeurs, Wig and Pen; Intrepids (NY); Cercle Saint Germain des Prés (Paris).

MANCHESTER, 12th Duke of, *cr* 1719; **Angus Charles Drogo Montagu;** Baron Montagu, Viscount Mandeville, 1620; Earl of Manchester, 1626; *b* 9 Oct. 1938; *yr s* of 10th Duke of Manchester, OBE, and Nell Vere (*d* 1966); *S* brother, 1985; *m* 1st, 1961, Mary Eveleen McClure (marr. diss. 1970); two *s* one *d*; 2nd, 1971, Diane Pauline Plimsaul (marr. diss. 1985); 3rd, 1989, Mrs Ann-Louise Bird, *d* of Dr Alfred Butler Taylor, Cawthorne, S Yorks; 4th, 2000, Biba Hiller. *Educ:* Gordonstoun.

MANCHESTER, Bishop of, since 1993; **Rt Rev. Christopher John Mayfield;** *b* 18 Dec. 1935; *s* of Dr Roger Bolton Mayfield and Muriel Eileen Mayfield; *m* 1962, Caroline Ann Roberts; two *s* one *d. Educ:* Sedbergh School; Gonville and Caius Coll., Cambridge (MA 1961); Linacre House, Oxford (Dip. Theology); MSc Cranfield Univ. 1984. Deacon 1963, priest 1964, Birmingham; Curate of St Martin-in-the-Bull Ring, Birmingham, 1963–67; Lecturer at St Martin's, Birmingham, 1967–71; Chaplain at Children's Hospital, Birmingham, 1967–71; Vicar of Luton, 1971–80 (with East Hyde, 1971–76); RD of Luton, 1974–79; Archdeacon of Bedford, 1979–85; Bishop Suffragan of Wolverhampton, 1985–93. Mem., H of L, 1998–. *Recreations:* family, gardening, walking. *Address:* Bishopscourt, Bury New Road, Manchester M7 4LE. *T:* (0161) 792 2096.

MANCHESTER, Dean of; *see* Riley, Very Rev. K. J.

MANCHESTER, Archdeacon of; *see* Wolstencroft, Ven. A.

MANCHESTER, William; Purple Heart (US) 1945; author; Fellow, East College, 1968–86, writer in residence since 1974, and Adjunct Professor of History, 1979–92, now Professor Emeritus, Wesleyan University; Fellow, Pierson College, Yale University, since 1991; *b* 1 April 1922; *s* of William Raymond Manchester and Sallie E. R. (*née* Thompson); *m* 1948, Julia Brown Marshall (*d* 1998); one *s* two *d. Educ:* Springfield Classical High School; Univ. of Massachusetts; Dartmouth Coll., NH; Univ. of Missouri. Served US Marine Corps, 1942–45. Reporter, Daily Oklahoman, 1945–46; Reporter, foreign corresp., war corresp., Baltimore Sun, 1947–55; Man. editor, Wesleyan Univ. Publications, 1955–64; Fellow, Center for Advanced Studies, 1959–60, Lectr in English, 1968–69, Wesleyan Univ. Trustee: Friends of Univ. of Massachusetts Library, 1970–76 (Pres., 1970–72); Winston Churchill Travelling Fellowships, 1992–96; Mem., Soc. of Amer. Historians. Guggenheim Fellow, 1959; Hon. Dr of Humane Letters: Univ. of Mass, 1965; Univ. of New Haven, 1979; Hon. LittD: Skidmore Coll., 1987; Univ. of Richmond, 1988; Hon. LHD Russell Sage Coll., NY, 1990. Dag Hammarskjold Internat. Prize in Literature, 1967; Overseas Press Club (New York) Award for Best Book of the Year on Foreign Affairs, 1968; Univ. of Missouri Medal, 1969; Connecticut Book Award, 1974; President's Cabinet Award, Detroit Univ., 1981; Frederick S. Troy Medal, 1981; McConaughy Award, 1981; Lincoln Literary Award, 1983; Distinguished Public Service Award, Conn Bar Assoc., 1985; Washington Irving Lit. Award, 1991; Sarah Josepha Hale Award, 1993. *Publications:* Disturber of the Peace, 1951 (publ. UK as The Sage of

Baltimore, 1952); The City of Anger, 1953; Shadow of the Monsoon, 1956; Beard the Lion, 1958; A Rockefeller Family Portrait, 1959; The Long Gainer, 1961; Portrait of a President, 1962; The Death of a President, 1967; The Arms of Krupp, 1968; The Glory and the Dream, 1974; Controversy and other Essays in Journalism, 1976; American Caesar, 1978; Goodbye, Darkness, 1980; One Brief Shining Moment, 1983; The Last Lion: vol. 1, Visions of Glory, 1932–1940, 1983; vol. 2, Alone, 1987 (publ. UK as The Caged Lion, Winston Spencer Churchill 1932–1940, 1988); This is Our Time, 1989; A World Lit Only By Fire, 1992; contrib. to Encyclopedia Britannica and to periodicals. *Recreation:* photography. *Address:* Wesleyan University, Middletown, CT 06459, USA. *T:* (860) 6853884. *Club:* Century (New York).

MANCHESTER, Sir William (Maxwell), KBE 1987 (CBE 1973); FRCS, FRACS, FACS; retired; *b* 31 Oct. 1913; *s* of James Manchester and Martha Browne; *m* 1945, Lois Yardley Cameron (*d* 1990). *Educ:* Waimate Primary Sch.; Timaru Boys' High Sch.; Otago Univ. Med. Sch. MB ChB 1938. FRCS 1949; FRACS 1957; FACS 1973. NZ Medical Corps: joined as RMO, Feb. 1940; 2nd NZ Exped. Force, May 1940; seconded for training as plastic surgeon, Nov. 1940; served in UK, Egypt and NZ (mostly in plastic surgery) until 1947. Head of plastic surgical services, Auckland Hosp Bd, 1950–79; Prof. of Plastic and Reconstructive Surgery, Univ. of Auckland, 1977–79; private plastic surgery practice, 1979–89; Mem., Auckland Hosp. Bd, 1980–89. Mem., James IV Assoc. of Surgeons, 1969. *Publications:* chapters in: Operative Surgery, 1956, 3rd edn 1976; Long-term Results in Plastic and Reconstructive Surgery, 1980; The Artistry of Reconstructive Surgery, 1987; Management of Cleft Lip and Palate, ed J. Bardach and H. L. Morris, 1990; contribs to British and US med. jls. *Recreations:* classical music, gardening, cooking. *Address:* Watch Hill, Jeffs Road, RD1, Papatoetoe, Auckland, New Zealand. *T:* (9) 2746702. *Club:* Northern (Auckland).

MANCROFT, family name of **Baron Mancroft.**

MANCROFT, 3rd Baron *cr* 1937, of Mancroft in the City of Norwich; **Benjamin Lloyd Stormont Mancroft;** Bt 1932; *b* 16 May 1957; *s* of 2nd Baron Mancroft, KBE, TD and Diana Elizabeth (*d* 1999), *d* of late Lt-Col Horace Lloyd, DSO; *S* father, 1987; *m* 1990, Emma Louisa, *e d* of Thomas Peart; two *s* one *d. Educ:* Eton. MFH, Vale of White Horse Hunt, 1987–89. Chm., Inter Lotto (UK) Ltd, 1995–. Chairman: Addiction Recovery Foundn, 1989–; Drug and Alcohol Foundn, 1993–; Deputy Chairman: British Field Sports Soc., 1993–98; Phoenix House Housing Assoc., 1993–96. Dir, Countryside Alliance, 1998–. Member Executive: Nat. Union of Cons. and Unionist Assocs, 1989–95; Assoc. of Cons. Peers, 1989–95. Elected Mem., H of L, 1999. Pres., Alliance of Ind. Retailers, 1996–. Patron: Sick Dentists' Trust, 1991–; Patsy Hardy Trust, 1991–; Osteopathic Centre for Children, 1996–. *Heir: s* Hon. Arthur Louis Stormont Mancroft, *b* 3 May 1995. *Address:* House of Lords, SW1A 0PW. *Club:* Pratt's.

MANDELA, Nelson Rolihlahla, Hon. OM 1995; President of South Africa, 1994–99; President, African National Congress, 1991–97 (Deputy President, 1990–91); *b* 1918; *s* of Chief of Tembu tribe; *m* Winnie Mandela (marr. diss. 1996); two *d*; *m* 1998, Graca, *widow* of Samora Machel. *Educ:* Univ. Coll., Fort Hare; Univ. of Witwatersrand. Legal practice, Johannesburg, 1952. On trial for treason, 1956–61 (acquitted); sentenced to five years' imprisonment, 1962; tried for further charges, 1963–64, and sentenced to life imprisonment; released, 1990. Holds hon. degrees from Oxford, Cambridge and other UK univs. Hon. QC 2000. Jawaharlal Nehru Award, India, 1979; Simon Bolivar Prize, UNESCO, 1983; Sakharov Prize, 1988; (with F. W. De Klerk) Nobel Peace Prize, 1993. *Publications:* No Easy Walk to Freedom, 1965; Long Walk to Freedom, 1994. *Address:* c/o President's Office, Private Bag X 1000, Cape Town 8000, South Africa.

MANDELSON, Rt Hon. Peter (Benjamin); PC 1998; MP (Lab) Hartlepool, since 1992; *b* 21 Oct. 1953; *s* of late George Mandelson and of Hon. Mary, *o c* of Baron Morrison of Lambeth, CH, PC. *Educ:* Hendon County Grammar Sch.; St Catherine's Coll., Oxford (Hons degree, PPE). Econ. Dept, TUC, 1977–78; Chm., British Youth Council, 1978–80; producer, LWT, 1982–85; Dir of Campaigns and Communications, Labour Party, 1985–90. An Opposition Whip, 1994–95; Opposition spokesman on Civil Service, 1995–97; Minister without Portfolio, Cabinet Office, 1997–98; Sec. of State for Trade and Industry, 1998, for N Ireland, 1999–2001. Mem. Council, London Bor. of Lambeth, 1979–82. Industrial Consultant, SRU Gp, 1990–92. Chm., UK- Japan 21st Century Gp, 2001–. *Publications:* Youth Unemployment: causes and cures, 1977; Broadcasting and Youth, 1980; (jtly) The Blair Revolution, 1996. *Recreations:* swimming, country walking. *Address:* c/o House of Commons, SW1A 0AA; 30 Hutton Avenue, Hartlepool TS26 9PN. *T:* (01429) 866173.

MANDELSTAM, Prof. Joel, FRS 1971; Emeritus Professor, University of Oxford, and Emeritus Fellow, Linacre College, since 1987; *b* S Africa, 13 Nov. 1919; *s* of Leo and Fanny Mandelstam; *m* 1954, Dorothy Hillier (*d* 1996); one *s* one *d*; *m* 1975, Mary Maureen Dale. *Educ:* Jeppe High Sch., Johannesburg; University of Witwatersrand. Lecturer, Medical Sch., Johannesburg, 1942–47; Queen Elizabeth Coll., London, 1947–51; Scientific Staff, Nat. Institute for Med. Research, London, 1952–66; Iveagh Prof. of Microbiology, and Fellow of Linacre College, Univ. of Oxford, 1966–87; Deptl Demonstrator, Sir William Dunn Sch. of Pathology, Univ. of Oxford, 1987–90. Fulbright Fellow, US, 1958–59; Vis. Prof., Univ. of Adelaide, 1971. Mem., ARC, 1973–83. Leewenhoek Lectr, Royal Soc., 1975. Editorial Board, Biochemical Journal, 1960–66. *Publications:* Biochemistry of Bacterial Growth (with K. McQuillen and I. Dawes), 1968; articles in journals and books on microbial biochemistry. *Address:* 13 Cherwell Lodge, Water Eaton Road, Oxford OX2 7QH.

MANDELSTAM, Prof. Stanley, FRS 1962; Professor Emeritus of Physics, University of California. *Educ:* University of the Witwatersrand, Johannesburg, Transvaal, South Africa (BSc); Trinity Coll., Cambridge (BA). PhD, Birmingham. Formerly Professor of Math. Physics, University of Birmingham; Prof. Associé, Univ. de Paris Sud, 1979–80 and 1984–85. Fellow, Amer. Acad. of Arts and Scis., 1992. Dirac Medal and Prize, Internat. Centre for Theoretical Physics, 1991; Dannie Heinemann Prize for Mathematical Physics, APS, 1992. *Publications:* (with W. Yourgrau) Variational Principles in Dynamics and Quantum Theory, 1955 (revised edn, 1956); papers in learned journals. *Address:* Department of Physics, University of California, Berkeley, CA 94720, USA.

MANDER, Sir Charles (Marcus), 3rd Bt *cr* 1911; Underwriting Member of Lloyd's, 1957–92; Director: Manders (Holdings) Ltd, 1951–58; Mander Brothers Ltd, 1948–58; Headstaple Ltd, since 1977; *b* 22 Sept. 1921; *o s* of Sir Charles Arthur Mander, 2nd Bt, and late Monica Claire Cotterill, *d* of G. H. Neame; *S* father, 1951; *m* 1945, Maria Dolores Beatrice, *d* of late Alfred Brodermann, Hamburg; two *s* one *d. Educ:* Eton Coll., Windsor; Trinity Coll., Cambridge. Commissioned Coldstream Guards, 1942; served War of 1939–45, Canal Zone, 1943; Italy, 1943, Germany, 1944; War Office (ADC to Lieut-General R. G. Stone, CB), 1945 Chairman: Arlington Securities Ltd, 1977–83; London & Cambridge Investments Ltd, 1984–91. High Sheriff of Staffordshire, 1962–63. *Recreations:* shooting, music. *Heir: s* Charles Nicholas Mander [*b* 23 March 1950; *m* 1972, Karin Margareta, *d* of Arne Norin; four *s* one *d*]. *Address:* Little Barrow Farm, Moreton-in-Marsh, Glos GL56 0XU. *T:* (01451) 830265.

MANDER, Prof. Lewis Norman, FRS 1990; Professor of Chemistry, Australian National University, since 1980; *b* 8 Sept. 1939; *s* of John Eric and Anne Frances Mander; *m* 1965, Stephanie Vautin; one *s* two *d. Educ:* Mount Albert Grammar Sch.; Univ. of Sydney (PhD 1965). FRACI 1980; FAA 1983. Postdoctoral Fellow, Univ. of Michigan, 1964–65; Postdoctoral Associate, Caltech, 1965–66; Lectr and Sen. Lectr in Organic Chem., Univ. of Adelaide, 1966–75; Sen. Fellow, 1975–80, Dean, 1981–86 and 1992–95, Res. Sch. of Chem., ANU. Nuffield Commonwealth Fellow, Cambridge, 1972; Fulbright Sen. Schol., Caltech, 1977, Harvard, 1986. H. G. Smith Medal, RACI, 1981; Flintoff Medal and Prize, RSocChem, 1990. *Publications:* numerous articles in learned jls, mainly on synthesis of organic molecules. *Recreations:* bushwalking, speleology. *Address:* Research School of Chemistry, Australian National University, Canberra, ACT 0200, Australia. *T:* (2) 61253761, *Fax:* (2) 61258114.

MANDER, Michael Harold; His Honour Judge Mander; DL; a Circuit Judge, since 1985 (Resident Judge, Shrewsbury Crown Court); *b* 27 Oct. 1936; *e s* of late Harold and Ann Mander; *m* 1960, Jancis Mary Dodd, *er d* of late Revd Charles and Edna Dodd. *Educ:* Workington Grammar School; Queen's College, Oxford (MA, 2nd cl. hons Jurisp.; Rigg Exbnr). Nat. Service, RA (2nd Lieut) to 1957. Articled clerk; solicitor, 2nd cl. hons, 1963; called to the Bar, Inner Temple, 1972. Asst Recorder, 1982–85. Dep. Chm., Agricultural Lands Tribunal, 1983–85. Freeman: Information Technologists' Co., 1994; City of London, 1995. DL Shropshire, 2000. Mem., The Magic Circle. *Recreation:* life under the Wrekin. *Address:* Garmston, Eaton Constantine, Shrewsbury SY5 6RL. *T:* (01952) 510288. *Club:* Wrekin Rotary (Hon. Mem.).

MANDER, Noel Percy, MBE 1979; FSA; Managing Director, N. P. Mander Ltd, since 1946; *b* 19 May 1912; *s* of late Percy Mander and Emily Pike, Hoxne, Suffolk; *m* 1948, Enid Watson; three *s* two *d. Educ:* Haberdashers Aske's Sch., Hatcham. Organ building from 1930, interrupted by war service with RA (Hampshire Bde) in N Africa, Italy and Syria, 1940–46. FSA 1974. Mem., Nat. Council of Christians and Jews (former Chm., N London Council). Former Governor, Sir John Cass Foundn. Liveryman, Musicians' Co.; Past Master, Parish Clerks' Co. of City of London; Mem., Art Workers' Guild. Churchill Life Fellow, Westminster Coll., Fulton, 1982; Hon. DFA Westminster Coll., 1984. Builder of Winston Churchill Meml Organ, Fulton, Missouri, and organs in many parts of world; organ builder to St Paul's Cathedral London and Canterbury Cathedral, and to HM Sultan of Oman. *Publications:* St Lawrence Jewry, A History of the Organs from the Earliest Times to the Present Day, 1956; St Vedast, Foster Lane, A History of the Organs from Earliest Times to the Present Day, 1961; St Vedast Foster Lane, in the City of London: a history of the 13 United Parishes, 1973; (with C. M. Houghton) St Botolph Aldgate: a history of the organs from the Restoration to the Twentieth Century, 1973. *Recreations:* archaeology, horology, reading. *Address:* The Street, Earl Soham, Woodbridge, Suffolk IP13 7SM. *T:* (01728) 685312; The Lodge, St Peter's Organ Works, St Peter's Close, E2 7AF. *T:* (020) 7739 4746. *Club:* Savage.

MANDEVILLE, Viscount; Alexander Charles David Drogo Montagu; *b* 11 Dec. 1962; *s* and *heir* of 12th Duke of Manchester, *qv*; *m* 1992, Wendy Dawn, *d* of Michael Buford; one *s* one *d. Educ:* Geelong Grammar Sch., Vic; Kimbolton Sch., Cambridgeshire. *Heir: s* Alexander Montagu, Lord Kimbolton, *b* 13 May 1993. *Address:* c/o British Consulate-General, 11766 Wilshire Boulevard, Los Angeles, CA 90025–6538, USA.

MANDUCA, John Alfred; High Commissioner for Malta in London, 1987–90; (concurrently) Ambassador to Norway, Sweden and Denmark, 1988–90, and to Ireland, 1990; *b* 14 Aug. 1927; *s* of Captain Philip dei Conti Manduca and Emma (*née* Pullicino); *m* 1954, Sylvia Parnis; two *s* two *d. Educ:* St Edward's Coll., Malta. Served 11 HAA Regt, Royal Malta Artillery (T), 1952–55 (commnd 1953). Joined Allied Malta Newspapers Ltd, 1945, Dep. Editor, 1953–62; Malta Correspondent, The Daily Telegraph and The Sunday Telegraph, 1946–62; joined Broadcasting Authority, Malta, 1962; BBC attachment, 1963; Chief Exec., Broadcasting Authority, Malta, 1963–68; Dir and Manager, Malta Television Service Ltd, 1968–71; Man. Dir, Rediffusion Gp of Cos in Malta, 1971–76; Chm., Tourist Projects Ltd, 1976–83; Dir Gen., Confedn of Private Enterprises, 1983–87; Dir, RTK Radio, 1991–93. Chairman: Malta Br., Inst. of Journalists, 1957, 1959 and 1961; Hotels and Catering Establishments Bd, 1970–71; Hon. Treas., Malta Br., Inst. of Dirs, 1975; Member: Tourist Bd, 1969–70; Broadcasting Authority, 1979–81. Trustee: Lady Strickland Trust for Malta, 1991–; Lady Strickland Trust for St Edward's Coll., 1997–. Chm. Bd of Governors, St Edward's Coll., 1995–98 (Mem., 1966–75, 1991–94). Editor, Treasures of Malta, 1994–. *Publications:* Tourist Guide to Malta and Gozo, 1967, 7th edn 1980; Tourist Guide to Harbour Cruises, 1974, 3rd edn 1981; Connoisseur's Guide to City of Mdina, 1975, 3rd edn 1985; Gen. Ed., Malta Who's Who, 1987; (ed) Antique Maltese Clocks, 1992. *Recreations:* collecting Melitensia, current affairs, gardening. *Address:* Beaulieu, Bastion Square, Citta Vecchia (Mdina) RBT 12, Malta. *T:* 454009, *Fax:* 452608. *Clubs:* Royal Over-Seas League; Casino Maltese (Malta).

MANDUCA, Paul Victor Sant; Chief Executive, Rothschild Asset Management, since 1999; *b* 15 Nov. 1951; *s* of Victor Manduca and Elizabeth Manduca (*née* Johnson); *m* 1982, Ursula Vogt; two *s. Educ:* Harrow Sch.; Hertford Coll., Oxford (Hons Mod. Langs). Colegrave & Co., 1973–75; Rowe & Pitman, 1976–79; Hill Samuel Inv. Management, 1979–83; Touche Remnant, 1983–92: Dir 1986; Vice-Chm. 1987; Chm., 1989–92; Dir, Henderson (formerly TR) Smaller Cos Investment Trust (formerly Trustees Corp.), 1986–; Man. Dir, TR Industrial & General, 1986–88; Chm., TR High Income, 1989–94; Gp Dep. Man. Dir, Henderson Administration PLC, 1992–94; Chief Exec., Threadneedle Asset Mgt, 1994–99. Chm., FTSE Trains, 1997–. Director: Clydesdale IT, 1987–88; Eagle Star Hldgs, 1994–99; Allied Dunbar Assurance, 1994–99; Gresham Trust, 1994–99 (Chm., 1996–99); MEPC PLC, 1999–2000. Chm., Assoc. of Investment Trust Cos, 1991–93 (Dep. Chm., 1989–91); Mem., Takeover Panel, 1991–93. Liveryman, Bakers' Co., 1988–. *Recreations:* golf, squash, shooting. *Address:* (office) 1 King William Street, EC4N 7AR. *Clubs:* White's, Lansdowne; Wentworth Golf; St George's Hill Golf.

MANDUELL, Sir John, Kt 1989; CBE 1982; FRAM, FRCM, FRNCM, FRSAMD; composer; Principal, Royal Northern College of Music, 1971–96; *b* 1928; *s* of Matthewman Donald Manduell, MC, MA, and Theodora (*née* Tharp); *m* 1955, Renna Kellaway; three *s* one *d. Educ:* Haileybury Coll.; Jesus Coll., Cambridge; Univ. of Strasbourg; Royal Acad. of Music. FRAM 1964; FRNCM 1974, CRNCM 1996; FRCM 1980; FRSAMD 1982; FWCMD 1991; Hon. FTCL 1973; Hon. GSM 1986. BBC: music producer, 1956–61; Head of Music, Midlands and E Anglia, 1961–64; Chief Planner, The Music Programme, 1964–68; University of Lancaster: Dir of Music, 1968–71; Mem. Court and Council, 1972–77, 1979–83. University of Manchester: Hon. Lectr in Music, 1976–96; Mem. Court, 1990–. Prog. Dir, Cheltenham Festival, 1969–94. Arts Council: Mem. Council, 1976–78, 1980–84; Mem. Music Panel, 1971–76, Dep. Chm., 1976–78, Chm., 1980–84; Mem. Touring Cttee, 1975–80, Chm., 1976–78; Mem. Trng Cttee, 1973–77. Mem. Music Adv. Cttee, British Council, 1963–72, Chm., 1973–80; Chm. Music Panel, North West Arts, 1973–79; Man., NW Arts Bd, 1991–97. President: British

Arts Fests Assoc., 1988– (Vice-Chm., 1977–81, Chm., 1981–88); European Assoc. of Music Academies (now Assoc. of European Conservatoires), 1988–96 (Hon. Pres., 1996); Manchester Olympic Fest., 1990; ISM, 1991–92; European Music Year (1985): Dep. Chm. UK Cttee, 1982–85; Member: Eur. Organising Cttee, 1982–86; Eur. Exec. Bureau, 1982–86; Internat. Prog. Cttee, 1982–84; Mem. Exec. Cttee, Composers' Guild of GB, 1984–87 (Vice Chm., 1987–89, Chm., 1989–92); Gulbenkian Foundn Enquiry into Trng Musicians, 1978; Mem. Opera Bd, 1988–95, Mem. Bd, 1989–95, Royal Opera House; Chairman: Cttee of Heads of Music Colls, 1986–90; Nat. Curriculum Music Working Gp, 1990–91; European Opera Centre, 1995–; Nat. Assoc. of Youth Orchestras, 1996–; Governor: Chetham's Sch., 1971–; National Youth Orch., 1964–73, 1978–96; President: Lakeland Sinfonia, 1972–89; Jubilate Choir, 1979–91; Director: London Opera Centre, 1971–79; Associated Bd of Royal Schools of Music, 1973–96; Northern Ballet Theatre, 1973–86 (Chm., 1986–89); Manchester Palace Theatre Trust, 1978–84; London Orchestral Concert Bd, 1980–85; Young Concert Artists' Trust, 1983–93; Lake Dist Summer Music Fest., 1984– (Chm., 1996–); Mem. Bd, Hallé Concerts Soc. (Dep. Chm., 1997–99). Hon. Member: Roy. Soc. of Musicians, 1972; Chopin Soc. of Warsaw, 1973. Engagements and tours as composer and lectr in Canada, Europe, Hong Kong, S Africa and USA. Chairman: BBC TV Young Musicians of the Year, 1978, 1980, 1984; Munich Internat. Music Comp., 1979, 1982, 1984, 1985, 1995, 1997, 1998, 1999, 2001; Geneva Internat. Music Comp., 1986, 1990, 1991, 1996; Chm. or mem., national and internat. music competition juries. FRSA 1981; Fellow, Manchester Polytechnic, 1983. Hon. DMus: Lancaster, 1990; Manchester, 1992; RSAMD 1996. First Leslie Boosey Award, Royal Phil. Soc. and PRS, 1980. Chevalier de l'Ordre des Arts et des Lettres (France), 1990. *Publications:* (contrib.) The Symphony, ed Simpson, 1966; *compositions:* Chansons de la Renaissance, 1956; Gradi, 1963; Diversions for Orchestra, 1970; String Quartet, 1976; Prayers from the Ark, 1981; Double Concerto, 1985; Vistas, 1997; Into the Ark, 1997; Flute Concerto, 2001. *Recreations:* cricket, travel, French culture. *Address:* European Opera Centre, 68 Grosvenor Street, Manchester M1 7EW. *T:* (0161) 273 8111. *Club:* MCC.

MANGHAM, Maj.-Gen. William Desmond, CB 1978; Director, The Brewers' Society, 1980–90; *b* 29 Aug. 1924; *s* of late Lt-Col William Patrick Mangham and Margaret Mary Mangham (*née* Donnachie); *m* 1960, Susan, *d* of late Col Henry Brabazon Humfrey; two *s* two *d*. *Educ:* Ampleforth College. 2nd Lieut RA, 1943; served India, Malaya, 1945–48; BMRA 1st Div. Egypt, 1955; Staff, HQ Middle East, Cyprus, 1956–58; Instructor, Staff Coll., Camberley and Canada, 1962–65; OC 3rd Regt Royal Horse Artillery, 1966–68; Comdr RA 2nd Div., 1969–70; Royal Coll. of Defence Studies, 1971; Chief of Staff, 1st British Corps, 1972–74; GOC 2nd Div., 1974–75; VQMG, MoD, 1976–79. Colonel Commandant: RA, 1979–88; RHA, 1983–88. Advisory Governor, Ampleforth Coll., 1990–98. Mem., Gordon Foundn, 1980–. *Recreations:* shooting, golf. *Address:* Redwood House, Woolton Hill, Newbury, Berks RG20 9UZ. *Club:* Army and Navy.

MANGO, Prof. Cyril Alexander, FBA 1976; Bywater and Sotheby Professor of Byzantine and Modern Greek, 1973–95, and Emeritus Fellow of Exeter College, Oxford University; *b* 14 April 1928; *s* of Alexander A. Mango and Adelaide Damonov; *m* 1st, 1953, Mabel Grover; one *d*; 2nd, 1964, Susan A. Gerstel; one *d*; 3rd, 1976, Maria C. Mundell. *Educ:* Univ. of St Andrews (MA); Univ. of Paris (Dr Univ Paris). From Jun. Fellow to Lectr in Byzantine Archaeology, Dumbarton Oaks Byzantine Center, Harvard Univ., 1951–63; Lectr in Fine Arts, Harvard Univ., 1957–58; Visiting Associate Prof. of Byzantine History, Univ. of California, Berkeley, 1960–61; Koraës Prof. of Modern Greek and of Byzantine History, Language and Literature, King's Coll., Univ. of London, 1963–68; Prof. of Byzantine Archaeology, Dumbarton Oaks Byzantine Center, 1968–73. FSA. *Publications:* The Homilies of Photius, 1958; The Brazen House, 1959; The Mosaics of St Sophia at Istanbul, 1962; The Art of the Byzantine Empire, Sources and Documents, 1972; Architettura bizantina, 1974; Byzantium, 1980; Byzantium and its Image, 1984; Le Développement Urbain de Constantinople, 1985. *Address:* 12 High Street, Brill, Aylesbury, Bucks HP18 9ST.

MANGOLD, Thomas Cornelius; Reporter, BBC TV Panorama, since 1976; *b* 20 Aug. 1934; *s* of Fritz Mangold and Dorothea Mangold; *m* 1st, 1972, Valerie Ann Hare (*née* Dean) (marr. diss. 1991); three *d*; 2nd, 2000, Kathryn Mary Colleton Parkinson-Smith. *Educ:* Dorking Grammar Sch. Reporter, Croydon Advertiser, 1952. Served RA, 1952–54. Reporter: Croydon Advertiser, 1955–59; Sunday Pictorial, 1959–62; Daily Express, 1962–64; BBC TV News, 1964–70; BBC TV 24 Hours, later Midweek, 1970–76. *Publications:* (jtly) The File on the Tsar, 1976; (jtly) The Tunnels of Cu Chi, 1985; Cold Warrior, 1991; Plague Wars, 1999. *Recreations:* writing, playing Blues harp. *Address:* c/o BBC TV, White City, W12 7TS. *T:* (020) 8752 7100.

MANKTELOW, Rt Rev. Michael Richard John; Hon. Assistant Bishop: of Chichester, since 1994; of Gibraltar in Europe, since 1994; Bursalis Prebendary, Chichester Cathedral, since 1997; *b* 23 Sept. 1927; *s* of late Sir Richard Manktelow, KBE, CB, and late Helen Manktelow; *m* 1966, Rosamund Mann; three *d*. *Educ:* Whitgift School, Croydon; Christ's Coll., Cambridge (MA 1952); Chichester Theological Coll. Deacon 1953, priest 1954, Lincoln; Asst Curate of Boston, Lincs, 1953–57; Chaplain of Christ's Coll., Cambridge, 1957–61; Chaplain of Lincoln Theological Coll., 1961–64, Sub-Warden, 1964–66; Vicar of Knaresborough, 1966–73; Rural Dean of Harrogate, 1972–77; Vicar of St Wilfrid's, Harrogate, 1973–77; Hon. Canon of Ripon Cathedral, 1975–77; Bishop Suffragan of Basingstoke, 1977–93; Canon Residentiary, 1977–91, Vice-Dean, 1987–91, Hon. Canon, 1991–93, Canon Emeritus, 1993, Winchester Cathedral. President: Anglican and Eastern Churches Assoc., 1980–97; Assoc. for Promoting Retreats, 1982–87. *Publication:* Forbes Robinson: disciple of love, 1961; John Moorman: Anglican, Franciscan, Independent, 1999. *Recreations:* music, walking. *Address:* 2 The Chantry, Canon Lane, Chichester, West Sussex PO19 1PZ. *T:* (01243) 531096.

MANLEY, Brian William, CBE 1994; FREng, FIEE, FInstP; FCGI; Managing Partner, Manley Moon Associates, 1988–2001; President, Institute of Physics, 1996–98; *b* 30 June 1929; *s* of late Gerald William Manley and Ellen Mary Manley (*née* Scudder); *m* 1954, Doris Winifred Dane; one *s* one *d*. *Educ:* Shooters Hill Sch.; Woolwich Poly.; Imperial Coll. of Science and Technology (BSc, DIC). FInstP 1967; FIEE 1974; FREng (FEng 1984); FCGI 1990. Served RAF, 1947–49. Mullard Research Labs, 1954–68; Commercial Gen. Manager, Mullard Ltd, 1969–75; Managing Director: Pye Business Communications, 1975–77; TMC Ltd, 1977–82; Philips Data Systems, 1979–82, Gp Man. Dir, Philips Business Systems, 1980–83; Chm. and Man. Dir, MEL Defence Systems, 1983–86; Dir, Philips Electronic & Associated Industries Ltd, 1983–87; Chairman: AT&T Network Systems (UK) Ltd, 1986–89; Moondisks Ltd, 1994–2001. Mem. Bd, Teaching Co. Scheme, 1996–98. Pres., IEE, 1991–92; Sen. Vice Pres., Royal Acad. of Engrg, 1993–96. Centenary Fellow, Univ. of Greenwich, 1991. Sen. Pro-Chancellor and Chm. Council, Univ. of Sussex, 1995–2001. Trustee: RC dio. Arundel and Brighton, 1999–; Daphne Jackson Trust, 1999–. Hon. FIEE 1999. Hon. DSc: Loughborough, 1995; City, 1998; Sussex, 2002. *Publications:* many papers on electronics, communications and engrg educn. *Recreations:* walking, gardening, second-hand bookshops, searching for my Irish roots. *Address:* Hopkins Crank, Ditchling Common, Sussex BN6 8TP. *T:* (01444) 233734. *Club:* Athenæum.

MANLEY, Ivor Thomas, CB 1984; consultant in government/industry relations; Deputy Secretary, Department of Employment, 1987–91; *b* 4 March 1931; *s* of Frederick Stone and Louisa Manley; *m* 1952, Joan Waite; one *s* one *d*. *Educ:* Sutton High Sch., Plymouth. Entered Civil Service, 1951; Principal: Min. of Aviation, 1964–66; Min. of Technology, 1966–68; Private Secretary: to Rt Hon. Anthony Wedgwood Benn, 1968–70; to Rt Hon. Geoffrey Rippon, 1970; Principal Private Sec. to Rt Hon. John Davies, 1970–71; Asst Sec., DTI, 1971–74; Department of Energy: Under-Sec., Principal Estabt Officer, 1974–78, Under Sec., Atomic Energy Div., 1978–81; Dep. Sec., 1981–87. UK Governor, IAEA, 1978–81; Mem., UKAEA, 1981–86. Chm., Task Force on Tourism and the Envmt, 1990–91; Board Member: Business in the Community, 1988–89; BTA, 1991–95 (Chm., Marketing Cttee, 1991–95); Volunteer Centre, UK, 1992–2000; Consortium on Opportunities for Volunteering, 1996–2000; Third Age Trust, 1999–. *Recreations:* walking, reading, Univ. of the Third Age. *Address:* 28 Highfield Avenue, Aldershot, Hants GU11 3BZ. *T:* (01252) 322707.

MANN, Anthony; *see* Mann, G. A.

MANN, Prof. Anthony Howard, MD; FRCP, FRCPsych; Professor of Epidemiological Psychiatry, Institute of Psychiatry, King's College London, since 1989; *b* 11 Dec. 1940; *s* of Alfred Haward Mann and Marjory Ethel (*née* Weatherly). *Educ:* Rugby Sch.; Jesus Coll., Cambridge (MD 1982); St Bartholomew's Hosp. FRCPsych 1984; FRCP 1986. Res. worker, and Sen. Lectr, Inst. of Psychiatry, 1972–80; Sen. Lectr, then Prof. of Psychiatry, Royal Free Hosp., 1980–89. *Publications:* numerous contribs to scientific jls on psychiatry of old age, general practice and epidemiology. *Recreations:* friends, travel. *Address:* 75 Chesil Court, Chelsea Manor Street, SW3 5QS; Quartier Le Clos, Menerbes 84560, France.

MANN, Prof. (Colin) Nicholas (Jocelyn), CBE 1999; PhD; FBA 1992; Dean, School of Advanced Study, University of London, since 2002; *b* 24 Oct. 1942; *s* of Colin Henry Mann and Marie Elise Mann (*née* Gosling); *m* 1964, Joëlle Bourcart; one *s* one *d*. *Educ:* Eton; King's Coll., Cambridge (MA, PhD). Res. Fellow, Clare Coll., Cambridge, 1965–67; Lectr, Univ. of Warwick, 1967–72; Vis. Fellow, All Souls Coll., Oxford, 1972; Fellow and Tutor, Pembroke Coll., Oxford, 1973–90, Emeritus Fellow, 1991–; Dir, Warburg Inst., and Prof. of Hist. of Classical Tradition, Univ. of London, 1990–2001. Visiting Professor: Univ. of Toronto, 1996; Coll. de France, 1998. Member Council: Mus. of Modern Art, Oxford, 1984–92 (Chm., 1988–90); Contemporary Applied Arts, 1994– (Chm., 1996–99); British Acad., 1995–98, 1999– (For. Sec., 1999–); RHBNC, 1996–98; Mem., British Library Adv. Council, 1997–. Trustee, Cubitt Artists, 1996–99. Fellow, European Medieval Acad., 1993. Romance Editor, Medium Ævum, 1982–90. *Publications:* Petrarch Manuscripts in the British Isles, 1975; Petrarch, 1984; A Concordance to Petrarch's Bucolicum Carmen, 1984; (ed jtly) Lorenzo the Magnificent: culture and politics, 1996; (ed jtly) Medieval and Renaissance Scholarship, 1996; (ed jtly) Giordano Bruno 1583–1585: the English experience, 1997; (ed jtly) The Image of the Individual: portraits in the Renaissance, 1998; (ed jtly) Photographs at the Frontier: Aby Warburg in America 1895–1896, 1998; articles in learned jls. *Recreations:* yoga, poetry, sculpture. *Address:* School of Advanced Study, Senate House, Malet Street, WC1E 7HU. *T:* (020) 7862 8659.

MANN, David William; Chairman, Charteris plc, since 1996; *b* 14 June 1944; *s* of William and Mary Mann; *m* 1968, Gillian Mary Edwards; two *s*. *Educ:* Felixstowe Grammar Sch.; Jesus Coll., Cambridge (MA). CEng; FBCS. CEIR, 1966–69; Logica: joined 1969; Dir, 1976; Man. Dir, UK Ops, 1979; Dep. Gp Man. Dir, 1982; Gp Man. Dir and Chief Exec., 1987; Dep. Chm., 1993–94. Chairman: Cambridge Display Technol., 1995–97; Flomerics Gp, 1995–; Director: Industrial Control Services Gp, 1994–2000; Druid Gp, 1996–2000; Room Underwriting Systems, 1996–; Cadcentre Group, 1999–; Eurolink Managed Services, 1999–2000; Ansbacher Hldgs, 2000–. Mem., Engineering Council, 1993–95. Pres., British Computer Soc., 1994–95. Master, Information Technologists' Co., 1997–98. CIMgt 1994; FInstD 1994. *Recreations:* gardening, walking, ski-ing, golf. *Address:* Theydon Copt, Forest Side, Epping, Essex CM16 4ED. *T:* (01992) 575842. *Club:* Athenæum.

MANN, Eric John; Controller, Capital Taxes Office, 1978–81; *b* 18 Dec. 1921; *s* of Percival John Mann and Marguerite Mann; *m* 1960, Gwendolen Margaret Salter; one *d* (one *s* decd). *Educ:* University Coll. Sch., Hampstead; Univ. of London (LLB). Entered Inland Revenue, 1946; Dep. Controller, Capital Taxes Office, 1974. *Publications:* (ed jtly) Green's Death Duties, 5th-7th edns, 1962–71. *Address:* Lawn Gate Cottage, Moccas, Herefordshire HR2 9LF.

MANN, Dr Felix Bernard; medical practitioner; *b* 10 April 1931; *s* of Leo and Caroline Mann; *m* 1986, Ruth Csorba von Borsai. *Educ:* Shrewsbury House; Malvern Coll.; Christ's Coll., Cambridge; Westminster Hosp. MB, BChir, LMCC. Practised medicine or studied acupuncture in England, Canada, Switzerland, France, Germany, Austria and China. Founder, Medical Acupuncture Soc., 1959. *Publications:* Acupuncture; the ancient Chinese art of healing, 1962, 2nd edn 1971; The Treatment of Disease by Acupuncture, 1963; The Meridians of Acupuncture, 1964; Atlas of Acupuncture, 1966; Acupuncture: cure of many diseases, 1971; Scientific Aspects of Acupuncture, 1977; Textbook of Acupuncture, 1987; Reinventing Acupuncture, 1992, 2nd edn 2000; also edns in Italian, Spanish, Dutch, Finnish, Portuguese, German, Japanese and Swedish; contrib. various jls on acupuncture. *Recreations:* walking in the country and mountains. *Address:* 15 Devonshire Place, W1G 6HF. *T:* (020) 7935 7575. *Club:* Royal Society of Medicine.

MANN, George Anthony; QC 1992; *b* 21 May 1951; *s* of George Edgar and Ilse Beate Mann; *m* 1979, Margaret Ann Sherret; two *d*. *Educ:* Chesterfield Grammar Sch.; Perse Sch., Cambridge; St Peter's Coll., Oxford (BA 1973; MA 1977). Called to the Bar, Lincoln's Inn, 1974. *Recreations:* French horn playing, music, computers. *Address:* Enterprise Chambers, 9 Old Square, Lincoln's Inn, WC2A 3SR.

MANN, Prof. Gillian Lesley, (Jill), FBA 1990; Endowed Professor, Department of English, University of Notre Dame, Indiana, since 1999; *b* 7 April 1943; *d* of late Edward William Ditchburn and Kathleen Ditchburn (*née* Bellamy); *m* 1964, Michael Mann (marr. diss. 1976). *Educ:* Bede Grammar Sch., Sunderland; St Anne's Coll., Oxford (BA 1964; Hon. Fellow, 1990); Clare Hall, Cambridge (MA; PhD 1971). Research Fellow, Clare Hall, 1968–71; Lectr, Univ. of Kent at Canterbury, 1971–72; Official Fellow, 1972–88, Professorial Fellow, 1988–98, Life Fellow, 1999, Girton Coll., Cambridge; Asst Lectr, 1974–78, Lectr, 1978–88, Prof. of Medieval and Renaissance English, 1988–98, Cambridge Univ. British Academy Research Reader, 1985–87. *Publications:* Chaucer and Medieval Estates Satire, 1973; Ysengrimus, 1987; (ed with Piero Boitani) The Cambridge Chaucer Companion, 1986; Geoffrey Chaucer, 1991; articles on Middle English and Medieval Latin. *Recreations:* walking, travel. *Address:* Girton College, Cambridge CB3 0JG; Department of English, University of Notre Dame, Notre Dame, IN 46556, USA.

MANN, Jillian Rose, FRCP, FRCPCH; Consultant Paediatric Oncologist, Birmingham Children's Hospital, since 1979; *b* 29 April 1939; *d* of William Farmcote Mann and Vera Maud Mann. *Educ:* Pate's Grammar Sch. for Girls, Cheltenham; St Thomas' Hosp. Med. Sch., London (MB BS 1962). LRCP 1962, MRCP 1966, FRCP 1980; MRCS 1962; DCH 1964; FRCPCH 1997. Postgrad. trng, St Thomas' and Great Ormond St Children's Hosps, 1963–67, and Birmingham Children's Hosp., 1967–71; Consultant Paediatrician, S Birmingham, and Consultant Associate in Haematological Diseases, Birmingham Children's Hosp., 1972–79. Hon. Prof. of Paediatric Oncology, Univ. of Birmingham, 1997–. Member: Cttee on Med. Aspects of Radiation in the Envmt, DoH, 1985–89; Standing Med. Adv. Cttee, DoH, 1986–90. Member: Leukaemia in Childhood Wkg party, MRC, 1975–2000; Med. and Scientific Adv. Panel, Leukaemia Res. Fund, 1985–88. Mem. Council, RCP, 1988–91; RCP and RCPCH: Regl Advr, 1994–99; Examr for MRCP/MRCPCH, 1994–. Founder Mem., 1977, Sec., 1977–81, Chm., 1983-86, UK Children's Cancer Study Gp. Chm., Educn and Trng Cttee, Soc. Internat. d'Oncologie Pédiatrique Europe and Eur. Soc. of Paediatric Haematol. and Immunol., 2000–. Mem., Lunar Soc., Birmingham, 1994–. Eur. Women of Achievement Award, Humanitarian Section, EUW, 1996; Nye Bevan Lifetime Achievement Award, 2000. *Publications:* numerous book chapters and contribs to learned jls mostly on childhood leukaemia, cancer and blood diseases; numerous abstracts of contribs to nat. and internat. scientific meetings. *Recreations:* music, country pursuits. *Address:* Oncology Department, Birmingham Children's Hospital, Steelhouse Lane, Birmingham B4 6NH. *T:* (0121) 333 8238.

MANN, John; MP (Lab) Bassetlaw, since 2001; *b* 10 Jan. 1960; *s* of James Mann and Brenda Cleavin; *m* 1985, Joanna White; one *s* two *d*. *Educ:* Manchester Univ. (BA Econ). MIPD. Hd of Res. and Educn, AEU, 1988–90; Nat. Trng Officer, TUC, 1990–95; Liaison Officer, Nat. Trade Union and Lab Party, 1995–2000. Dir, Abraxas Communications Ltd, 1998–. Mem. (Lab), Lambeth BC, 1986–90. *Publication:* (with Phil Woolas) Labour and Youth: the missing generation, 1985. *Recreations:* football, cricket, hill walking. *Address:* House of Commons, SW1A 0AA. *Clubs:* Manton Miners'; Worksop Town.

MANN, John Frederick; educational consultant; *b* 4 June 1930; *e s* of Frederick Mann and Hilda G. (*née* Johnson); *m* 1966, Margaret (*née* Moore); one *s* one *d*. *Educ:* Poole and Tavistock Grammar Schs; Trinity Coll., Oxford (MA); Birmingham Univ. Asst Master, Colchester Royal Grammar Sch., 1954–61; Admin. Asst, Leeds County Bor., 1962–65; Asst Educn Officer, Essex CC, 1965–67; Dep. Educn Officer, Sheffield County Bor., 1967–78; Sec., Schools Council for the Curriculum and Exams, 1978–83; Dir of Educn, London Bor. of Harrow, 1983–88. Member: Iron and Steel Industry Trng Bd, 1975–78; Exec., Soc. of Educn Officers, 1976–78; Sch. Broadcasting Council, 1979–83; Council, British Educn Management and Admin Soc., 1979–84; Cttee, Soc. of Educn Consultants, 1990–95 (Sec., 1990–94; Vice Chm., 1994–95). Governor: Welbeck Coll., 1975–84; Hall Sch., 1985–88. Chm., Brent Samaritans, 1995–99. Hon. Fellow, Sheffield Polytechnic, 1980; Hon. FCP, 1986. FRSA. JP Sheffield, 1976–79. *Publications:* Education, 1979; Highbury Fields School, 1994; contrib. to Victoria County History of Essex, Local Govt Studies, and Educn. *Recreations:* travel, books, theatre, gardening. *Address:* 109 Chatsworth Road, NW2 4BH. *T:* (020) 8459 5419.

MANN, Martin Edward; QC 1983; a Recorder, since 1990; a Deputy High Court Judge, Chancery Division, since 1992; *b* 12 Sept. 1943; *s* of late S. E. Mann and M. L. F. Mann; *m* 1966, Jacqueline Harriette (*née* Le Maître); two *d*. *Educ:* Cranleigh Sch. Called to the Bar, Gray's Inn, 1968 (Lord Justice Holker Sen. Exhibn), Lincoln's Inn, 1973 (*ad eund*); Bencher, Lincoln's Inn, 1991. Mem., Senate of the Inns of Court and the Bar, 1979–82; Chm., Bar Council Fees Collection Cttee, 1993–95. *Publication:* (jtly) What Kind of Common Agricultural Policy for Europe, 1975. *Recreations:* farming, the arts. *Address:* 24 Old Buildings, Lincoln's Inn, WC2A 3UJ. *T:* (020) 7404 0946; Kingston St Mary, Somerset. *Club:* Garrick.

MANN, Rt Rev. Michael Ashley, KCVO 1989; Assistant Bishop, diocese of Gloucester, since 1989; Dean of Windsor, 1976–89; Chairman, St George's House, 1976–89; Register, Order of the Garter, 1976–89; Domestic Chaplain to the Queen, 1976–89; Prelate, Order of St John, 1990–99; *b* 25 May 1924; *s* of late H. G. Mann and F. M. Mann, Harrow; *m* 1st, 1949, Jill Joan Jacques (*d* 1990); one *d* (one *s* decd); 2nd, 1991, Elizabeth Pepys. *Educ:* Harrow Sch.; RMC Sandhurst; Wells Theological Coll.; Graduate School of Business Admin., Harvard Univ. Served War of 1939–45: RMC, Sandhurst, 1942–43; 1st King's Dragoon Guards, 1943–46 (Middle East, Italy, Palestine). Colonial Admin. Service, Nigeria, 1946–55. Wells Theological Coll., 1955–57; Asst Curate, Wolborough, Newton Abbot, 1957–59; Vicar: Sparkwell, Plymouth, 1959–62; Christ Church, Port Harcourt, Nigeria, 1962–67; Dean, Port Harcourt Social and Industrial Mission; Home Secretary, The Missions to Seamen, 1967–69; Residentiary Canon, 1969–74, Vice-Dean, 1972–74, Norwich Cathedral; Adviser to Bp of Norwich on Industry, 1969–74; Bishop Suffragan of Dudley, 1974–76. Church Comr, 1977–85; Comr, Royal Hospital Chelsea, 1985–91. Dep. Chm., Imperial War Museum, 1990–96 (Trustee, 1980–96); Trustee: Army Museums Ogilby Trust, 1984–96; British Library, 1990–93; Military Records Soc., 1992–. Pres., Soc. of Friends of Nat. Army Mus., 1989– (Chm., 1989–97). Governor: Harrow Sch., 1976–91 (Chm., 1980–88); Atlantic Coll., 1987–91. Nat. Chaplain, Royal British Legion, 1992–. CIMgt. KStJ 1990. *Publications:* A Windsor Correspondence, 1984; And They Rode On, 1984; A Particular Duty, 1986; China 1860, 1989; Some Windsor Sermons, 1989; Survival or Extinction, 1989; Regimental History of 1st Queen's Dragoon Guards, 1993; The Trucial Oman Scouts, 1994; The Veterans, 1997; Sermons for Soldiers, 1998. *Recreations:* military history, philately, ornithology. *Address:* The Cottage, Lower End Farm, Eastington, Northleach, Glos GL54 3PN. *T:* and *Fax:* (01451) 860767; *e-mail:* michael.mann@virgin.net. *Club:* Cavalry and Guards.

MANN, Murray G.; *see* Gell-Mann.

MANN, Nicholas; *see* Mann, C. N. J.

MANN, Patricia Kathleen Randall, (Mrs Pierre Walker), OBE 1996; Consultant, J. Walter Thompson Co. Ltd, and Director, JWT Trustees; *b* 26 Sept. 1937; *d* of late Charles Mann and of Marjorie Mann (*née* Heath); *m* 1962, Pierre George Armand Walker (*d* 1997); one *d*. *Educ:* Clifton High School, Bristol. FCAM, FIPA; CIMgt. Joined J. Walter Thompson Co., 1959, Copywriter, 1959–77, Head of Public Affairs, 1978; Dir of External Affairs, J. Walter Thompson Gp, and Vice Pres. Internat., JWT, 1981–97. Director: Yale and Valor plc, 1985–91; Woolwich (formerly Woolwich Equitable) Building Soc., 1983–96; British Gas plc, 1995–97; Centrica, 1997–; Hill & Knowlton Internat. (Brussels), 1998–. Mem., Monopolies and Mergers Commn, 1984–93. Member: Council, Inst. of Practitioners in Advertising, 1965–97 (Hon. Sec., 1979–83); Advertising Creative Circle, 1965–; Council, Nat. Advertising Benevolent Soc., 1973–77; Council, Advertising Standards Authy, 1973–86; Board, European Advertising Tripartite, 1981–97; Board, European Assoc. of Advertising Agencies, 1984–97; Gas Consumers Council, 1981–90; Board, UK CEED, 1984–; Food Adv. Cttee, MAFF, 1986–95; Kingman Cttee on English, DES, 1987; EC Commerce and Distribution Commn, 1989–2001; Sen. Salaries Rev. Body, 1994–2000; CBI Europe Cttee, 1996–; Mgt Council, Canada-UK Colloquia, 2001–. Vice President: History of Advertising Trust, 1997–; Eur. Food Law Assoc. UK, 1998–. Chm., Debating Soc., 2000–. Governor: CAM Educn Foundn, 1971–77; Admin. Staff Coll., Henley, 1976–92; ESU, 1999–; Mem. Ct, Brunel Univ., 1976– (Council, 1976–86). Editor, Consumer Affairs, 1978–98. Mem., Awards Nomination Panel, RTS, 1974–78. Mackintosh Medal, Advertising Assoc., 1977. FRSA. DUniv Brunel, 1996. *Publications:* 150 Careers in Advertising, 1971; Advertising, 1979; (ed) Advertising and Marketing to Children, 1980; various articles. *Recreation:* word games. *Address:* 269 Lonsdale Road, Barnes, SW13 9QL. *T:* (020) 8748 8345, *Fax:* (020) 8255 4313. *Clubs:* Reform, Women's Advertising, London Cornish Association.

MANN, Pauline, (Mrs R. D. Mann); *see* Vogelpoel, P.

MANN, Sir Rupert (Edward), 3rd Bt *cr* 1905; *b* 11 Nov. 1946; *s* of Major Edward Charles Mann, DSO, MC (*g s* of 1st Bt) (*d* 1959), and of Pamela Margaret, *o d* of late Major Frank Haultain Hornsby; *S* great uncle, 1971; *m* 1974, Mary Rose, *d* of Geoffrey Butler, Stetchworth, Newmarket; two *s*. *Educ:* Malvern. *Heir: s* Alexander Rupert Mann, *b* 6 April 1978. *Address:* Billingford Hall, Diss, Norfolk IP21 4HN. *Clubs:* MCC; Norfolk.

MANNERS, family name of **Baron Manners,** and **Duke of Rutland.**

MANNERS, 5th Baron *cr* 1807; **John Robert Cecil Manners;** DL; Consultant, Osborne, Clarke & Co., Solicitors, Bristol (Partner, 1952–84); *b* 13 Feb. 1923; *s* of 4th Baron Manners, MC, and of Mary Edith, *d* of late Rt Rev. Lord William Cecil; *S* father, 1972; *m* 1949, Jennifer Selena (*d* 1996), *d* of Ian Fairbairn; one *s* two *d*. *Educ:* Eton; Trinity College, Oxford. Served as Flt-Lieut, RAFVR, 1941–46. Solicitor to the Supreme Court, 1949. Official Verderer of the New Forest, 1983–. DL Hampshire, 1987. *Recreations:* hunting and shooting. *Heir:* s Hon. John Hugh Robert Manners [*b* 5 May 1956; *m* 1983, Lanya Mary Jackson, *d* of late Dr H. E. Heitz and of Mrs Ian Jackson; two *d*]. *Address:* Sabines, Avon, Christchurch, Dorset BH23 7BQ. *Club:* Brooks's.

MANNERS, Elizabeth Maude, TD 1962; MA; Headmistress of Felixstowe College, Suffolk, 1967–79; Member, East Anglia Regional Health Authority, 1982–85; *b* 20 July 1917; *d* of William George Manners and Anne Mary Manners (*née* Sced). *Educ:* Stockton-on-Tees Sec. Sch.; St Hild's Coll., Durham Univ. BA (Dunelm) 1938; MA 1941. Teacher of French at: Marton Grove Sch., Middlesbrough, 1939–40; Ramsey Gram. Sch., IOM, 1940–42; Consett Sec. Sch., Durham, 1942–44; Yarm Gram. Sch., Yorks, 1944–54; Deputy Head, Mexborough Gram. Sch., Yorks, 1954–59; Head Mistress, Central Gram. Sch. for Girls, Manchester, 1959–67. Vice-President: Girl Guides Assoc., Co. Manchester, 1959–67; Suffolk Agric. Assoc., 1967–82. Member: Educn Cttee, Brit. Fedn of Univ. Women, 1966–68; Council, Bible Reading Fellowship, 1973–81; Cttee, E Br., RSA, 1974–90; Cttee, ISIS East, 1974–79. Mem. (C), Suffolk CC, 1977–85 (Member: Educn Cttee, 1977–85; Staff Joint and Personnel Cttees, 1981–85; Vice-Chm., Secondary Educn Cttee, 1981–85); Mem. (C), Felixstowe Town Council, 1991–95; Mem., Suffolk War Pensions Cttee, 1980–90. Sponsor, the Responsible Society, 1982–90. Chm. Governors, Felixstowe Deben High Sch., 1985–88. Enlisted ATS (TA), 1947; commissioned, 1949. FRSA 1972. Coronation Medal, 1953. *Publications:* The Vulnerable Generation, 1971; The Story of Felixstowe College, 1980. *Recreations:* narrow boating, choral singing, theatre, motoring, good food and wine. *Address:* 6 Graham Court, Hamilton Gardens, Felixstowe, Suffolk IP11 7ES.

MANNERS, Prof. Gerald; Professor of Geography, University College London, 1980–97, now Emeritus; Chairman, City Parochial Foundation and Trust for London, since 1996 (Trustee, since 1977); *b* 7 Aug. 1932; *s* of George William Manners and Louisa Hannah Manners; *m* 1st, 1959, Anne (*née* Sawyer) (marr. diss. 1982); one *s* two *d*; 2nd, 1982, Joy Edith Roberta (*née* Turner); one *s*. *Educ:* Wallington County Grammar School; St Catharine's College, Cambridge (MA). Lectr in Geography, University Coll. Swansea, 1957–67; Reader in Geography, UCL, 1967–80. Vis. Schol., Resources for the Future, Inc., Washington DC, 1964–65; Vis. Associate, Jt Center for Urban Studies, Harvard and MIT, 1972–73; Vis. Fellow, ANU, 1990. Dir, Economic Associates Ltd, 1964–74. Member: Council, Inst. of British Geographers, 1967–70; LOB 1970–80; SE Economic Planning Council, 1971–79; Council, TCPA, 1980–89; Subscriber, Centre for Environmental Studies Ltd, 1981–99. Specialist Advisor to: H of C Select Cttee on Energy, 1980–92; H of L Select Cttee on Sustainable Develt, 1994–95; H of C Envmtl Audit Cttee, 1999–; Advr to Assoc. for Conservation of Energy, 1981–; Chairman: Regl Studies Assoc., 1981–84; RSA Panel of Inquiry into regl problem in UK, 1982–83. Mem., Central Governing Body, City Parochial Foundn, 1977– (Chm., Estate Cttee, 1987–2001). Trustee: Chelsea Physic Garden, 1980–83; EAGA Charitable Trust, 1993–. Sadler's Wells Foundn (formerly Sadler's Wells Foundn and Trust): Gov., 1978–95; Vice-Chm., 1982–86; Chm. Theatre Bd, 1986–93; Chm., 1986–95; Vice-Pres., 1995–99; Mem. Council, ENO Works, 1996–99. Mem. Court, City Univ., 1985–. *Publications:* Geography of Energy, 1964, 2nd edn 1971; South Wales in the Sixties, 1964; Changing World Market for Iron Ore 1950–1980, 1971; (ed) Spatial Policy Problems of the British Economy, 1971; Minerals and Man, 1974; Regional Development in Britain, 1974, 2nd edn 1980; Coal in Britain, 1981; Office Policy in Britain, 1986; contribs to edited volumes and learned jls. *Recreations:* music, dance, theatre, walking, undergardening. *Address:* 338 Liverpool Road, Islington, N7 8PZ. *T:* (020) 7607 7920, *Fax:* (020) 7609 2306.

MANNERS, Hon. Thomas (Jasper); Director, Lazard Brothers, 1965–89 (Deputy Chairman, 1986–89); *b* 12 Dec. 1929; *y s* of 4th Baron Manners, MC, and of Mary Edith, *d* of late Rt Rev. Lord William Cecil; *m* 1955, Sarah, *d* of Brig. Roger Peake, DSO; three *s*. *Educ:* Eton. Lazard Brothers & Co. Ltd, 1955–89; Director: Legal & General Gp, 1972–93; Scapa Gp, 1970–96; Davy Corp., 1985–91. *Recreations:* shooting, fishing. *Address:* The Old Malt House, Ashford Hill, Thatcham, Berks RG19 8BN. *T:* (0118) 981 4865. *Clubs:* Pratt's, White's.

MANNING, Prof. Aubrey William George, OBE 1998; DPhil, FRSE, FIBiol; Professor of Natural History, University of Edinburgh, 1973–97, now Emeritus; *b* 24 April 1930; *s* of William James Manning and Hilda Winifred (*née* Noble); *m* 1st, 1959, Margaret Bastock, DPhil (*d* 1982); two *s*; 2nd, 1985, Joan Herrmann, PhD; one *s*. *Educ:* Strode's School, Egham, Surrey; University Coll., London (BSc); Merton Coll., Oxford (DPhil). FRSE 1975; FIBiol 1980; FRZSScot 1997. Commnd RA, 1954–56. University of Edinburgh: Asst Lectr, 1956–59; Lectr, 1959–68; Reader, 1968–73. Mem., Bd of Trustees, Nat. Museums of Scotland, 1997–. Sec. Gen., Internat. Ethological Cttee, 1971–79; Pres., Assoc. Study Animal Behaviour, 1983–86; Member: Scottish Cttee, NCC, 1982–88; NCC Adv. Cttee on Science, 1984–88; Pop. Studies Panel, Wellcome Trust, 1995–99; Pres., Biology Sect., BAAS, 1993; Chm. Council, Scottish Wildlife Trust, 1990–96. Chm., Edinburgh Brook Adv. Centre, 1975–82. Presenter, TV series: Earth Story, 1998; Talking Landscapes, 2001. Dr *hc* Univ. Paul Sabatier, Toulouse, 1981. Dobzhansky Meml Award, Behavior Genetics Assoc., 1994; Assoc. Study Animal Behaviour Medal, 1998. *Publications:* An Introduction to Animal Behaviour, 1967, 5th edn (with M. Dawkins) 1998; papers on animal behaviour in learned jls. *Recreations:* woodland regeneration, hill-walking, architecture, 19th century novels. *Address:* The Old Hall, Ormiston, East Lothian EH35 5NJ. *T:* (01875) 340536.

MANNING, Sir David Geoffrey, KCMG 2001 (CMG 1992); HM Diplomatic Service; Head of Defence and Overseas Secretariat, Cabinet Office, and Foreign Policy Adviser to the Prime Minister, since 2001; *b* 5 Dec. 1949; *s* of John Robert Manning and Joan Barbara Manning; *m* 1973, Catherine Marjory Parkinson. *Educ:* Ardingly Coll.; Oriel Coll., Oxford; Johns Hopkins Sch. of Advanced Internat. Studies, Bologna (Postgrad. Diploma in Internat. Relations, 1972). FCO, 1972; Warsaw, 1974–76; New Delhi, 1977–80; FCO, 1980–84; First Sec., Paris, 1984–88; Counsellor, seconded to Cabinet Office, 1988–90; Political Counsellor and Head of Political Sect., Moscow, 1990–93; Hd of Eastern Dept, FCO, 1993–94; Hd of Policy Planning Staff, FCO, 1994–95; Ambassador to Israel, 1995–98; Dep. Under-Sec. of State, FCO, 1998–2000; Perm. Rep., UK Delegn to NATO, 2000–01. British Mem., Contact Gp on Bosnia, Internat. Conf. on Former Yugoslavia, April–Nov. 1994. *Address:* c/o 10 Downing Street, SW1A 2AA.

MANNING, Dr Geoffrey, CBE 1986; FInstP; Visiting Professor, Department of Physics and Astronomy, University College London, since 1987; *b* 31 Aug. 1929; *s* of Jack Manning and Ruby Frances Lambe; *m* 1951, Anita Jacqueline Davis; two *s* one *d. Educ:* Tottenham Grammar Sch.; Imperial Coll., London Univ. BSc, PhD; ARCS. Asst Lectr in Physics, Imperial Coll., 1953–55; Research worker: English Electric Co., 1955–56; Canadian Atomic Energy Co., 1956–58; Calif Inst. of Technol., 1958–59; AERE, 1960–65; Rutherford Laboratory, Science Research Council: Gp Leader, 1965–69; Dep. Dir, 1969–79; Head of High Energy Physics Div., 1969–75; Head of Atlas Div., 1975–79; Dir, Rutherford (Rutherford & Appleton Labs), 1979–81; Dir, Rutherford Appleton Lab., SERC, 1981–86 (Hon. Scientist, 1994–); Chm., Active Memory Technology Ltd, 1986–92; non-exec. Dir, Recogniton Res., 1991–94; Consultant: to UFC on formation of UKERNA, 1991–93; Cambridge Parallel Processing, 1992–94. Mem., Visiting Cttee, Physics Dept, Imperial Coll., 1988–92. Vis. Scientist, Fermi Nat. Accelerator Lab., 1994–95. Chairman: Parallel and Novel Architectures Sub Cttee, DTI, 1988–91; Systems Architecture Cttee, DTI/SERC, 1991–92 (Mem., 1988–91); Mem., IT Adv. Bd, DTI/SERC, 1991–92. Glazebrook Medal and Prize, Inst. of Physics, 1986. *Recreations:* golf, squash, ski-ing. *Address:* 38 Sunningwell Village, Abingdon, Oxon OX13 6RB. *T:* (01865) 736123.

MANNING, Dr Geoffrey Lewis, FRCSE; FDSRCS; Chairman, North Staffordshire Hospital NHS Trust, since 1993; *b* 21 Sept. 1931; *s* of late Isaac Harold Manning and Florence Hilda Manning (*née* Tomlin); *m* 1978, Patricia Margaret Wilson; one *d. Educ:* Rossall Sch., Fleetwood, Lancs; Univ. of Birmingham (LDS, BDS 1953; MB, ChB 1961). FDSRCS 1964; FRCSE 1986. Nat. service, Capt., RADC, 1954–56. Senior Registrar: Central Middx Hosp., 1964–66; Mt Vernon Hosp., 1966–68; Parkland Meml Hosp., Dallas, 1967; Consultant Oral Surgeon, N Staffs Hosp., 1968–93. Mem., N Staffs DHA, 1986–92. Leader, Health Task Force, Prince of Wales Business Leaders Forum, 1993–. Mem., British Fedn of Pottery Manufacturers. Hon. DSc Keele, 2000. *Recreations:* gardening, brick-laying, classic cars. *Address:* The Old Hall, Haughton, Stafford ST18 9HB. *T:* (01785) 780273. *Club:* Trentham Golf.

MANNING, Jane Marian, OBE 1990; freelance concert and opera singer (soprano), since 1965; *b* 20 Sept. 1938; *d* of Gerald Manville Manning and Lily Manning (*née* Thompson); *m* 1966, Anthony Edward Payne, *qv. Educ:* Norwich High Sch.; Royal Academy of Music (LRAM 1958); Scuola di Canto, Cureglia, Switzerland. GRSM 1960, ARCM 1962. London début (Park Lane Group), 1964; first BBC broadcast, 1965; début Henry Wood Promenade Concerts, 1972; founded own ensemble, Jane's Minstrels, 1988; regular appearances in leading concert halls and festivals in UK and Europe, with leading orchestras and conductors; many broadcasts and gramophone recordings, lectures and master classes. Specialist in contemporary music (over 300 world premières given); Warsaw Autumn Fest., 1975–78, 1987, 1992; Wexford Opera Fest., 1976; Scottish Opera, 1978; Brussels Opera, 1980. Canadian début, 1977; tours: of Australia and New Zealand, 1978, 1980, 1982, 1984, 1986, 1990, 1996; of USA, 1981, 1983, 1985, 1986, 1987, 1988, 1989, 1991, 1993, 1996, 1997. Milhaud Vis. Prof., Mills Coll. Oakland, 1983; Lucie Stern Vis. Prof., Mills Coll., Oakland, 1981 and 1986; Vis. Artist, Univ. of Manitoba, Canada, 1992; Vis. Prof., RCM, 1995–; Hon. Prof., Keele Univ., 1996–July 2002. Vice Pres., SPNM, 1984–. Chm., Nettlefold Fest. Trust, 1990–; Member: Exec. Cttee, Musicians Benevolent Fund, 1989–; Arts Council Music Panel, 1990–95; Internat. Jury, Gaudeamus Young Interpreters Competition, Holland, 1976, 1979, 1987; Jury, Eur. Youth Competition for Composers, Eur. Cultural Foundn, 1985. Hon. ARAM 1972, Hon. FRAM 1984; FRCM 1998. DUniv York, 1988. Special award, Composers Guild of Gt Britain, 1973. *Publications:* (chapter in) How Music Works, 1981; New Vocal Repertory, vol. I, 1986, vol. II, 1998; (chapter in) A Messiaen Companion, 1996; articles in Composer, and Music and Musicians. *Recreations:* reading, cinema, ornithology. *Address:* 2 Wilton Square, N1 3DL. *T:* (020) 7359 1593, *Fax:* (020) 7226 4369.

MANNING, Jeremy James C.; *see* Carter-Manning.

MANNING, Mary Elizabeth; Executive Director, Academy of Medical Sciences, since 2000; *b* 1 Nov. 1947; *d* of late Charles Frederick Kent and Marie Lucia Kent (*née* Hall); *m* 1972, Keith Quentin Frederick Manning; two *d. Educ:* Stoodley Knowle Sch. for Girls, Torquay; Bedford Coll., Univ. of London (BA Hons Hist. 1968). Royal Insce Co., 1968–69; Desk Officer, 1969–72, Attaché, British High Commn, Singapore, 1972–73, MoD; English lang. teacher, La Petite Ecole Française, Sofia, 1975–78; Royal Society: Meetings Officer, 1987–95; Manager, Scientific Prog., 1995–97; Hd, Sci. Promotion, 1997–2000. Mem., Steering Gp for Public Understanding of Sci., Engrg and Technol. EPSRC, 1999–. Mem., BAAS, 1995–. *Recreations:* music, walking, family and friends, France. *Address:* Academy of Medical Sciences, 10 Carlton House Terrace, SW1Y 5AH. *T:* (020) 7969 5285.

MANNING, Hon. Patrick Augustus Mervyn; MP (People's National Movement) San Fernando East, since 1971; Leader of the Opposition, Trinidad and Tobago, 1986–90 and since 1996; *b* 17 Aug. 1946; *s* of late Arnold and Elaine Manning; *m* 1972, Hazel Kinsale; two *s. Educ:* Rose Bank Private Sch.; San Fernando Govt Sch.; Presentation Coll.; Univ. of West Indies, Jamaica (BSc Special Hons Geology 1969). Texaco Trinidad Inc.: Refinery Operator, 1965–66; Geologist, 1969–71. Parliamentary Secretary: Min. of Petroleum and Mines, 1971–73; Office of the Prime Minister, 1973–74; Min. of Planning and Develt, 1974–75; Min. of Industry and Commerce, 1975–76; Min. of Works, Transport and Communications, 1976–78; Minister: Min. of Finance (Maintenance and Public Service), 1978–81; Prime Minister's Office (Information), 1979–81; Minister of: Inf. and of Industry and Commerce, 1981; Energy and Natural Resources, 1981–86; Prime Minister of Trinidad and Tobago, 1991–95. Leader, People's National Movement, 1987–. *Recreations:* table tennis, chess, reading. *Address:* Port of Spain, Trinidad and Tobago.

MANNING, Paul Andrew, QPM 1996; Assistant Commissioner, Metropolitan Police, 1994–2000; *b* 29 May 1947; *s* of Owen Manning and Joyce Cynthia Manning (*née* Murgatroyd); *m* 1967, Margaret Anne Bucknall; two *s. Educ:* Forest of Needwood High Sch., Rolleston-on-Dove; Cranfield Inst. of Technology (MSc). Metropolitan Police Cadet, 1964; Constable, 1966, Chief Supt, 1985, Staffordshire Police; Asst Chief Constable, Avon and Somerset Constabulary, 1988; Dep. Chief Constable, Herts Constabulary, 1992. Chm., ACPO Traffic Cttee, 1997–2000 (Sec., 1996–97). Director: Educnl Broadcasting Services Trust, 1997–; London Police Educn Ltd, 1997–. Mem., Amwell Rotary Club. FCIT; FILT. *Recreations:* hill walking, Rotary. *Address:* 6 The Chestnuts, Hertford SG13 8AQ. *T:* (01992) 422106, *Fax:* (01992) 413080.

MANNINGHAM-BULLER, family name of **Viscount Dilhorne**.

MANNION, Rosa; soprano; *b* 29 Jan. 1962; *d* of Patrick Anthony Mannion and Maria (*née* MacGregor); *m* 1985, Gerard McQuade; two *s. Educ:* Seafield Grammar Sch., Crosby; Royal Scottish Acad. of Music and Drama (BA). Débuts: Scottish Opera, 1984; Edinburgh Fest., 1985; ENO, 1987; Glyndebourne Fest. Opera, 1988; principal soprano: Scottish Opera, 1984–86; ENO, 1989–92; major rôles include: Gilda in Rigoletto; Violetta in La Traviata; Manon (title rôle); Magnolia in Show Book; Pamina in Die Zauberflöte; Minka in Le Roi malgré lui; Sophie in Werther; Oscar in A Masked Ball; Atalanta in Xerxes; Constanze in Die Entführung aus dem Serail; Countess in Figaro's Wedding; Sophie in Der Rosenkavalier. Has given many concerts and recitals. Winner, Internat. Singing Competition, Scottish Opera, 1988. *Address:* c/o IMG Artists, 616 Chiswick High Road, W4 5RX.

MANOR, Prof. James Gilmore, DPhil; Professorial Fellow, Institute of Development Studies, University of Sussex, since 1987 (Head of Research, 1988–91); *b* 21 April 1945; *s* of James Manor and Ann (*née* Jones); *m* 1974, Brenda Cohen; one *s. Educ:* Yale Univ. (BA 1967); Univ. of Sussex (DPhil 1975). Asst Lectr in History, Chinese Univ. of Hong Kong, 1967–69; Tutor, SOAS, 1973–75; Asst Prof. of History, Yale, 1975–76; Lectr in Politics, Univ. of Leicester, 1976–85; Prof. of Govt, Harvard, 1985–87; Dir, and Prof. of Commonwealth Politics, Inst. of Commonwealth Studies, Univ. of London, 1994–97. Sen. Res. Fellow, US Nat. Endowment for the Humanities, 1980–81; Vis Fellow, MIT, 1982. Consultant to: Dutch Govt, 1989–90; World Bank, 1994–97; Swedish Govt, 1995. Editor, Jl of Commonwealth and Comparative Politics, 1980–88. *Publications:* Political Change in an Indian State, 1977; (ed with P. Lyon) Transfer and Transformation, 1983; (ed) Sri Lanka in Change and Crisis, 1984; The Expedient Utopian, 1989; (ed) Rethinking Third World Politics, 1991; (ed with C. Colclough) States or Markets?, 1991; Power, Poverty and Poison, 1993; Nehru to the Nineties, 1994. *Recreations:* reading, theatre. *Address:* Institute of Development Studies, University of Sussex, Falmer, Brighton BN1 9RE. *T:* (01273) 606261.

MANS, Keith Douglas Rowland; Public Affairs Adviser, Society of British Aerospace Companies, since 1997; Director, Royal Aeronautical Society, since 1998; *b* 10 Feb. 1946; *s* of Maj.-Gen. R. S. N. Mans, *qv; m* 1972, Rosalie Mary McCann; one *s* two *d. Educ:* Berkhamsted School; RAF College Cranwell; Open Univ. (BA). FRAeS. Pilot, RAF, 1964–77 (Flight Lieut); Pilot, RAF Reserve, 1977–. Retail Manager, John Lewis Partnership, 1978–87. MP (C) Wyre, 1987–97; contested (C) Lancaster and Wyre, 1997. PPS to Minister of State, Dept of Health, 1990–92, to Sec. of State for Health, 1992–95. Member: H of C Environment Select Cttee, 1987–91; Select Cttee on Defence, 1995–97; Chairman: Parly Envmt Gp, 1993–97; Parly Aerospace Gp, 1994–97; Vice-Chm., Back bench Fisheries Cttee, 1987–96; Secretary: Back bench Aviation Cttee, 1987–90; Back bench Envmt Cttee, 1990–91; All Party Aviation Gp, 1991–94. Vice Chm., Air League, 1997–. *Recreation:* flying. *Address:* 3 Dell Way, Ealing, W13 8JH. *Clubs:* Royal Air Force, Carlton.

MANS, Maj.-Gen. Rowland Spencer Noel, CBE 1971 (OBE 1966, MBE 1956); Director, Military Assistance Office, 1973–76, retired; *b* 16 Jan. 1921; *s* of Thomas Frederick Mans and May Seigenberg; *m* 1945, Veeo Ellen Sutton; three *s. Educ:* Surbiton Grammar Sch.; RMC, Sandhurst; jssc, psc. Served War, Queen's Royal Regt and King's African Rifles, 1940–45. Regtl and Staff Duty, 1945–59; Instr, Staff Colleges, Camberley and Canada, 1959–63; Comd, 1st Tanganyika Rifles, 1963–64; Staff Duty, Far East and UK, 1964–68; Comd, Aldershot, 1969–72; DDPS (Army), 1972–73. Col, Queen's Regt, 1978–83 (Dep. Col (Surrey), 1973–77). Defence consultant and writer on defence and political affairs. Mem., Hampshire CC, 1984–89. Pres., KAR & EAF Assoc., 1997–. *Publications:* Kenyatta's Middle Road in a Changing Africa, 1977; Canada's Constitutional Crisis, 1978. *Recreations:* writing, reading, gardening. *Address:* Ivy Bank Cottage, Vinegar Hill, Milford-on-Sea, Hants SO41 0RZ. *T:* (01590) 643982. *Clubs:* Army and Navy; Royal Lymington Yacht.

See also K. D. R. Mans.

MANSAGER, Felix Norman, Hon. KBE 1976 (Hon. CBE 1973); Honorary Director, Hoover Co. USA (President-Chairman, Hoover Co. and Hoover World-wide Corporation, 1966–75); Director, Hoover Ltd UK (Chairman, 1966–75); *b* 30 Jan. 1911; *s* of Hoff Mansager and Alice (*née* Qualseth); *m* Geraldine (*née* Larson); one *s* two *d. Educ:* South Dakota High Sch., Colton. Joined Hoover Co. as Salesman, 1929; Vice-Pres., Sales, 1959; Exec. Vice-Pres. and Dir, 1961. Dir, Belden and Blake Energy Co. Member: Council on Foreign Relations; Newcomen Soc. in N America; Trustee, Graduate Theological Union (Calif); The Pilgrims of the US; Assoc. of Ohio Commodores; Masonic Shrine (32nd degree Mason); Mem. and Governor, Ditchley Foundn; Member Board of Trustees: Ohio Foundn of Indep. Colls; Indep. Coll. Funds of America. Hon. Mem., World League of Norsemen. Marketing Award, British Inst. of Marketing, 1971. Executive Prof. of Business (Goodyear Chair), Univ. of Akron (Mem. Delta Sigma Pi; Hon. Mem., Beta Sigma Gamma). Hon. Fellow, UC Cardiff, 1973. Hon. Dr of Laws Capital Univ., 1967; Hon. LLD Strathclyde, 1970; Hon. DHL Malone Coll., Canton, Ohio, 1972; Hon. PhD Walsh Coll., Canton, 1974; Hon. Dr Humanities Wartburg Coll., Waverly, Iowa, 1976; Medal of Honor, Vassa Univ., Finland, 1973; Person of Year, Capital Univ. Chapter of Tau Pi Phi, 1981. Grand Officer, Dukes of Burgundy, 1968; Chevalier: Order of Leopold, 1969; Order of St Olav, Norway, 1971; Legion of Honour, France, 1973; Grande Officiale, Order Al Merito della Republica Italiana, 1975. *Recreation:* golf. *Address:* 3421 Lindel Court NW, Canton, OH 44718, USA. *Clubs:* Metropolitan (NYC); Congress Lake Country (Hartville, Ohio); Torske (Hon.) (Minneapolis).

MANSEL, Sir Philip, 15th Bt *cr* 1621; Chairman and Managing Director of Eden-Vale Engineering Co. Ltd, 1962–98, retired; *b* 3 March 1943; *s* of Sir John Mansel, 14th Bt and Hannah, *d* of Ben Rees; *S* father, 1947; *m* 1968, Margaret, *o d* of Arthur Docker; two *s* one *d. Heir: s* John Philip Mansel, *b* 19 April 1982. *Address:* 2 Deyncourt Close, Darras Hall, Ponteland, Northumberland NE20 9JY.

MANSEL, Prof. Robert Edward, FRCS; Professor of Surgery, since 1992, and Chairman, Hospital-Based Division, University of Wales College of Medicine; *b* 1 Feb. 1948; *s* of Regnier Ranulf Dabridgecourt Mansel and Mary Germaine Mansel (*née* Littlewood); *m* 1987, Elizabeth Clare, *d* of John Francis Skone and Daphne Viola (*née* Rees); two *s* four *d. Educ:* Llandovery Coll.; Charing Cross Hosp. Med. Sch., Univ. of London (MB BS, MS). LRCP 1971; FRCS 1975. Res. Fellow, 1976–78, Lectr and Sen. Lectr, 1979–89, Univ. of Wales Coll. of Medicine; Prof. of Surgery, Univ. of Manchester, 1989–92. Chm., Breast Speciality Gp, British Assoc. of Surgical Oncology, 1997–2002.

UICC Fellow, Univ. of Texas at San Antonio, 1982–83; Churchill Meml Fellowship, 1982; James IV Fellowship, James IV Assoc., 1989. Hunterian Prof., RCS, 1989. *Publications:* Fibrocystic Breast Disease, 1986; (with L. E. Hughes and D. J. T. Webster) Benign Breast Disease, 1989, 2nd edn 2000; Atlas of Breast Disease, 1994; contribs to surgical jls. *Recreations:* fishing, Rugby, travel, chess. *Address:* University Department of Surgery, University of Wales College of Medicine, Heath Park, Cardiff CF14 4XN. *T:* (029) 2074 2749, *Fax:* (029) 2076 1623.

MANSEL-JONES, David; Chairman, Huntingdon Research Centre plc, 1978–86 (Vice-Chairman, 1974–78); *b* 8 Sept. 1926; *o s* of Rees Thomas Jones and Ceinwen Jones; *m* 1952, Mair Aeronwen Davies; one *s*. *Educ:* St Michael's Sch., Bryn; London Hospital. MB, BS 1950; MRCP 1973; FFPM 1992. Jun. Surgical Specialist, RAMC; Dep. Med. Dir, Wm R. Warner & Co. Ltd, 1957–59; Med. Dir, Richardson-Merrell Ltd, 1959–65; formerly PMO, SMO and MO, Cttee on Safety of Drugs; formerly Med. Assessor, Cttee on Safety of Medicines; Consultant to WHO, 1970–86; Senior PMO, Medicines Div., DHSS, 1971–74. Vis. Prof., Gulbenkian Science Inst., Portugal, 1981; Examiner, Dip. Pharm. Med., Royal Colls of Physicians, UK, 1980–87. *Publications:* papers related to safety of medicines. *Recreations:* music, painting. *Address:* 39 St John's Court, Princes Road, Felixstowe, Suffolk IP11 7SG. *T:* (01394) 275984.

MANSEL LEWIS, Sir David (Courtenay), KCVO 1995; Lord-Lieutenant of Dyfed, since 1979 (Lieutenant, 1974–79; HM Lieutenant for Carmarthenshire, 1973–74); JP; *b* 25 Oct. 1927; *s* of late Charlie Ronald Mansel Lewis and Lillian Georgina Warner, *d* of Col Sir Courtenay Warner, 1st Bt, CB; *m* 1953, Lady Mary Rosemary Marie-Gabrielle Montagu-Stuart-Wortley, OBE, JP, 4th *d* of 3rd Earl of Wharncliffe; one *s* two *d*. *Educ:* Eton; Keble Coll., Oxford (BA). Served in Welsh Guards, 1946–49; Lieut 1946, RARO. Chairman: SW Div., Royal Forestry Soc., 1963–93; S Wales Woodlands, 1969–85; Founder Chm., Carmarthen-Cardigan Cttee, 1968–, Regl Chm., S Wales, 1985–, STA. Member, Court: Nat. Mus. of Wales, 1974–91 (Mem. Council, 1987–91); UCW Aberystwyth, 1974–. President: Llanelli Art Soc., 1956–; Carmarthen–Cardigan Br., 1977–91, Dyfed Br., 1991–, CLA; Dyfed Wildlife Trust, 1978–; Gŵyl Llanelli Fest., 1979–; Dyfed Br., Magistrates' Assoc., 1979–; Burry Port RNLI, 1982–; Welsh Assoc. of Male Voice Choirs, 1997–; Chm., Llanelli Millennium Coastal Park Trustees, 1999–. Patron: Carmarthen RBL, 1974–; Tall Ships Council of Wales, 1991–; Commonwealth Games Council for Wales, 1996–; Wales Gurkha Villages Aid Trust, 1999–. Chm. of Trustees, Llandovery Coll., 2001– (Trustee, 1985–2001). President: W Wales, 1979–90, Wales, 1995–99, TAVRA; Dyfed SSAFA, 1986–. FRSA; Hon. Fellow, Trinity Coll., Carmarthen, 1997. High Sheriff, Carmarthenshire, 1965; JP 1969; DL 1971. KStJ (Sub Prior for Wales, 1998–). *Recreations:* music, sailing. *Address:* Stradey Castle, Llanelli, Dyfed SA15 4PL. *T:* (01554) 774626. *Clubs:* Lansdowne; Royal Yacht Squadron (Cowes); Burry Port Yacht (Founder Cdre, 1966; Pres., 1975–).

MANSELL, Gerard Evelyn Herbert, CBE 1977; Managing Director, External Broadcasting, BBC, 1972–81; Deputy Director-General, BBC, 1977–81; retired; *b* 16 Feb. 1921; 2nd *s* of late Herbert and Anne Mansell, Paris; *m* 1956, Diana Marion Sherar; two *s*. *Educ:* Lycée Hoche, Versailles; Lycée Buffon, Paris; Ecole des Sciences Politiques, Paris; Chelsea Sch. of Art. Joined HM Forces, 1940; served in Western Desert, Sicily and NW Europe, 1942–45 (despatches). Joined BBC European Service, 1951; Head, Overseas Talks and Features Dept, 1961; Controller, BBC Radio 4 (formerly Home Service), and Music Programme, 1965–69; Dir of Programmes, BBC, Radio, 1970. Chairman: British Cttee, Journalists in Europe, 1978–95; Jt Adv. Cttee on Radio Journalism Trng, 1981–87; Sony Radio Awards Organising Cttee, 1983–87; Communications Adv. Cttee, UK Nat. Commn for UNESCO, 1983–85; Friends of UNESCO, 1986–88; Member: Communication and Cultural Studies Bd, CNAA, 1982–87; Exec. Cttee, GB–China Centre, 1986–96 (Vice-Chm., 1988–96); Franco-British Council, 1990–; Sandford St Martin Trust, 1991–. Governor, Falmouth Sch. of Art and Design, 1988–97; Chairman: New Hampstead Garden Suburb Trust, 1984–90, 1992–93; Burgh House Trust, Hampstead, 1995–98, 1999–. Hon. Vis. Fellow, Grad. Centre for Journalism, City Univ., 1992–. FRSA 1979. Sony Gold Award for Services to Radio, 1988. French Croix de Guerre, 1945. *Publications:* Tragedy in Algeria, 1961; Let Truth be Told, 1982. *Address:* 15 Hampstead Hill Gardens, NW3 2PH.

MANSELL, Nigel Ernest James, OBE 1991; racing driver; *b* 8 Aug. 1953; *s* of Eric and Joyce Marshall; *m* Rosanne Elizabeth Perry; two *s* one *d*. *Educ:* Wellsbourne and Hall Green Bilateral Schools; Matthew Bolton Polytechnic; Solihull Tech. Coll.; N Birmingham Polytechnic (HND). Engineering apprenticeship with Lucas; lab. technician, Lucas Aerospace, later product manager; senior sales engineer, tractor div., Girling. Began racing in karts; won 11 regional championships, 1969–76; Formula Ford and Formula Three, 1976–79; Formula Two, later Formula One, 1980; Lotus team, 1981–84; Williams-Honda team, 1985–87; Williams-Judd team, 1988; Ferrari team, 1989–90; Williams-Renault team, 1991–92 and 1994 (part time); McLaren team, 1995; first competed in a Grand Prix, Austria, 1980; won 31 Grands Prix, 1980–94 (record); Formula One World Drivers Champion, 1992; American Newman-Haas IndyCar Team, 1993; IndyCar Champion, 1993. Ed.-in-Chief, Formula 1 Mag., 2001–. Grand Fellow, MIRCE Akad. for System Operational Sci., 2000. *Publications:* (with Derick Allsop) Driven to Win, 1988; (with Derick Allsop) Mansell and Williams, The Challenge for the Championship 1992; (with Jeremy Shaw) Nigel Mansell's IndyCar Racing, 1993; (with James Allen) Nigel Mansell, My Autobiography, 1995. *Recreation:* golf.

MANSELL-JONES, Richard Mansell; Chairman, Brown, Shipley & Co., since 1992; *b* 4 April 1940; *s* of late Arnaud Milward Jones and Winifred Mabel (*née* Foot); *m* 1971, Penelope Marion, *y d* of Major Sir David Henry Hawley, 7th Bt. *Educ:* Queen Elizabeth's, Carmarthen; Worcester College, Oxford (MA). FCA. Articled to Price, Waterhouse & Co., 1963–68; with N. M. Rothschild & Sons, 1968–72; with Brown, Shipley & Co., 1972–88 (Dir, 1974–84; Dep. Chm., 1984–88); non-exec. Dir, 1982–88, Chm., 1988–2000, Barlow International PLC (formerly J. Bibby & Sons). Director: Brown, Shipley Holdings, 1985–92; Barr & Wallace Arnold Trust, 1984–93; Barlow Ltd (formerly Barlow Rand Ltd), 1988–2001; Rand Mines Ltd, 1988–93; Barloworld Hldgs, 1990–; Standard Bank London, 1992–; Standard Internat. Holdings, 2000–; Chm., Millfield Gp, 2001–. Mem. Council, CBI, 1999–2000. Patron, Shaw Trust, 1996– (Trustee, 1990–96). MSI 1992. CIMgt. *Address:* (office) Founders Court, Lothbury, EC2R 7HE. *T:* (020) 7606 9833. *Clubs:* Beefsteak, Boodle's, City of London.

MANSER, John; *see* Manser, P. J.

MANSER, Michael John, CBE 1993; RA 1995; architect in private practice, The Manser Practice (formerly Michael Manser Associates, then Manser Associates), since 1961; President, Royal Institute of British Architects, 1983–85; *b* 23 March 1929; *s* of late Edmund George Manser and Augusta Madge Manser; *m* 1953, Dolores Josephine Bernini; one *s* one *d*. *Educ:* Sch. of Architecture, Polytechnic of Central London (DipArch). RIBA 1954; RWA 1994. Intermittent architectural journalist and lectr; News Editor, Architectural Design, 1961–64; Architectural Correspondent, The Observer, 1961–64. TV and radio, 1963–. Councillor: RIBA, 1977–80 and 1982; RSA, 1987–93 (Founder and Chm., Art for Architecture Award Scheme, 1990–93); Assessor, Art in the Workplace Awards, 1988–; Chairman: Art and Work Awards, 1996–; Nat. Home Builder Design Awards, 1998–; Nat. House Builders Award, 1999–; Stirling Prize Award, RIBA, 2000; RIBA Rep., Council, Nat. Trust, 1991–93; Member: London Transport Design Policy Cttee, 1991–95; Westminster CC Public Art Adv. Panel, 1999–; Ext. Examiner, Faculty of Architecture, Kingston Univ., 1995–98. Royal Academy: Member: Council, 1998; Architectural Cttee, 1998–; Audit Cttee, 1999–; Works Cttee, 1999–; Remuneration Cttee, 2000–. Hon. Fellow, Royal Architectural Inst. of Canada, 1985. Civic Trust Awards, 1967, 1973 and 1991; Award for Good Design in Housing, DoE, 1975; Europ. Architectural Heritage Year Award, 1975; RIBA Award and Regional Award, 1991, 1995; ICE Merit Award, 1995; Structural Steel Design Award, 1995. *Publications:* (with José Manser) Planning Your Kitchen, 1976; (contrib.) Psychiatry in the Elderly, 1991; (contrib.) Companion to Contemporary Architectural Thought, 1993. *Recreations:* going home, architecture, music, books, boats, sketching, gardening (under supervision). *Address:* Morton House, Chiswick Mall, W4 2PS. *Club:* Brooks's.

MANSER, (Peter) John, CBE 1992; DL; FCA; Chairman, Robert Fleming Holdings Ltd, 1997–2000 (Director, since 1972; Group Chief Executive, 1990–97); *b* 7 Dec. 1939; *s* of late Peter Robert Courtney Manser and Florence Delaplaine Manser; *m* 1969, Sarah Theresa Stuart (*née* Todd); two *d*. *Educ:* Marlborough Coll. Man. Dir, Jardine Fleming & Co. Ltd, 1975–79; Chief Exec., Save & Prosper Gp Ltd, 1983–88; Chm., Robert Fleming & Co. Ltd, 1990–97. Chairman: Delancey Estates, 1998–; Intermediate Capital Gp, 2001–; Director: Capital Shopping Centres, 1994–2000; Shaftesbury, 1997–; Keppel Tatlee Bank, 2000–. Dep. Chm., FIMBRA, 1984–85; Dir, SIB, 1986–93; Chm., London Investment Banking Assoc., 1994–98; Vice-Pres., BBA, 1994–98. Dir, Cancer Research Campaign, 1985–2000. Chm., Wilts Community Foundn, 1997–. Pres., Marlburian Club, 1999–2000. DL Wilts, 1999. *Recreations:* gardening, walking, shooting, saving pubs. *Address:* Chisenbury Priory, East Chisenbury, Pewsey, Wilts SN9 6AQ. *Clubs:* Boodle's, MCC.

MANSFIELD, family name of **Baron Sandhurst**.

MANSFIELD AND MANSFIELD, 8th Earl of, *cr* 1776 and 1792 (GB); **William David Mungo James Murray;** JP, DL; Baron Scone, 1605; Viscount Stormont, 1621; Baron Balvaird, 1641; (Earl of Dunbar, Viscount Drumcairn, and Baron Halldykes in the Jacobite Peerage); Hereditary Keeper of Bruce's Castle of Lochmaben; First Crown Estate Commissioner, 1985–95; *b* 7 July 1930; *o s* of 7th Earl of Mansfield and Mansfield, and of Dorothea Helena (*d* 1985), *y d* of late Rt Hon. Sir Lancelot Carnegie, GCVO, KCMG; *S* father, 1971; *m* 1955, Pamela Joan, *o d* of W. N. Foster, CBE; two *s* one *d*. *Educ:* Eton; Christ Church, Oxford. Served as Lieut with Scots Guards, Malayan campaign, 1949–50. Called to Bar, Inner Temple, 1958; Barrister, 1958–71. Mem., British Delegn to European Parlt, 1973–75; an opposition spokesman in the House of Lords, 1975–79; Minister of State: Scottish Office, 1979–83; NI Office, 1983–84. Mem., Tay Salmon Fisheries Bd, 1971–79. Director: General Accident, Fire and Life Assurance Corp. Ltd, 1972–79, 1985–98; American Trust, 1985–; Pinneys of Scotland, 1985–89; Ross Breeders Ltd, 1989–90. Ordinary Dir, Royal Highland and Agricl Soc., 1976–79. President: Fédn des Assocs de Chasse de l'Europe, 1977–79; Scottish Assoc. for Care and Resettlement of Offenders, 1974–79; Scottish Assoc. of Boys Clubs, 1976–79; Royal Scottish Country Dance Soc., 1977–; Chm., Scottish Branch, Historic Houses Assoc., 1976–79. Mem., Perth CC, 1971–75; Hon. Sheriff for Perthshire, 1974–; JP 1975, DL 1980, Perth and Kinross. Hon. Mem., RICS, 1994. *Publications:* articles on agriculture, land management and wine. *Heir: s* Viscount Stormont, *qv*. *Address:* Scone Palace, Perthshire PH2 6BE; 16 Thorburn House, Kinnerton Street, SW1X 8EX. *Clubs:* White's, Pratt's, Turf, Beefsteak.

MANSFIELD, Prof. Averil (Olive), (Mrs J. W. P. Bradley), CBE 1999; FRCS; Professor of Vascular Surgery, Academic Surgical Unit, St Mary's Hospital and Imperial College School of Medicine (formerly St Mary's Hospital Medical School), since 1993 (Director, Academic Surgical Unit, 1993–99); Consultant Surgeon, St Mary's Hospital, since 1982; *b* 21 June 1937; *m* 1987, John William Paulton Bradley. *Educ:* Liverpool Univ. (MB 1960; ChM 1972). FRCS 1966. Consultant Surgeon: Royal Liverpool Hosp., 1972–80; Hillingdon Hosp., 1980–82; RPMS, subseq. ICSM, 1980–. Royal College of Surgeons: Chm., Court of Examrs, 1990–92; Mem. Council, 1990–; Vice-Pres., 1998–2000; President: Assoc. of Surgeons of GB and Ireland, 1992–93; Vascular Surgical Soc. of GB and Ireland, 1996–97; Sect. of Surgery, RSocMed, 1997–98. Hon. FRACS 1996; Hon. FACS 1998. Hon. MD Liverpool, 1994. *Publications:* Clinical Surgery in General, 1993; articles on vascular surgery. *Recreations:* playing the piano, walking in the Lake District, restoring old wrecks. *Address:* 31 Radnor Mews, W2 2SA.

MANSFIELD, David James; Group Chief Executive, Capital Radio, since 1997; *b* 12 Jan. 1954; *m* 1979, Alison Patricia Pullin; two *s* one *d*. Gen. Sales Manager, Scottish TV, 1977–85; Sales and Marketing Dir, Thames TV, 1985–93; Capital Radio: Gp Commercial Dir, 1993–97; Gp Man. Dir, May–July 1997. *Address:* Capital Radio, 30 Leicester Square, WC2H 7LA.

MANSFIELD, Rear-Adm. David Parks, CB 1964; *b* 26 July 1912; *s* of Comdr D. Mansfield, RD, RNR; *m* 1939, Jean Craig Alexander (*d* 1984); one *s* one *d*. *Educ:* RN Coll., Dartmouth; RN Engineering Coll., Keyham. Lt (E) 1934; HMS Nelson, 1934–36; Staff of C-in-C Med., 1936–39; HMS Mauritius, 1939–42; Lt-Comdr (E) 1942; HMS Kelvin, 1942–43; Chatham Dockyard, 1943–46; Comdr (E) 1945; Admty (Aircraft Maintenance Dept), 1946–49; Staff of FO Air (Home), 1949–51; HMS Kenya, 1951–53; RN Engrg Coll., 1953–55; Captain 1954; RNAS Anthorn (in command), 1955–57; RN Aircraft Yard, Fleetlands (Supt.), 1957–60; Admty Dir of Fleet Maintenance, 1960–62; Rear-Adm. 1963; Rear-Adm. Aircraft, on Staff of Flag Officer Naval Air Command, 1963–65. *Recreation:* family affairs. *Address:* The Lawn, Holybourne, Alton, Hants GU34 4ER.

MANSFIELD, Vice-Adm. Sir (Edward) Gerard (Napier), KBE 1974; CVO 1981; retired 1975; *b* 13 July 1921; *s* of late Vice-Adm. Sir John Mansfield, KCB, DSO, DSC, and Alice Talbot Mansfield; *m* 1943, Joan Worship Byron, *d* of late Comdr John Byron, DSC and Bar, and late Frances Byron; two *d*. *Educ:* RNC, Dartmouth. Entered Royal Navy, 1935. Served War of 1939–45 in destroyers and Combined Ops (despatches), taking part in landings in N Africa and Sicily. Comdr, 1953; comd HMS Mounts Bay, 1956–58; Captain 1959; SHAPE, 1960–62; Captain (F) 20th Frigate Sqdn, 1963–64; Dir of Defence Plans (Navy), 1965–67; Cdre Amphibious Forces, 1967–68; Senior Naval Member, Directing Staff, IDC, 1969–70; Flag Officer Sea Training, 1971–72; Dep. Supreme Allied Comdr, Atlantic, 1973–75. Chm., Assoc. of RN Officers, 1975–86; Chm. Council, Operation Raleigh, 1984–89. Chm., Crondall Parish Council, 1977–81. Mem. Admin. Council, Royal Jubilee Trusts, 1978–81. *Recreations:* golf, gardening. *Address:* White Gate House, Heath Lane, Ewshot, Farnham, Surrey GU10 5AH. *T:* (01252) 850325. *Club:* Army and Navy.

MANSFIELD, Dr Eric Harold, FRS 1971; FREng, FRAeS, FIMA; Chief Scientific Officer (Individual Merit), Royal Aircraft Establishment, 1980–83; *b* 24 May 1923; *s* of

Harold Goldsmith Mansfield and Grace Phundt; *m* 1947; two *s* one *d*; *m* 1974, Eunice Lily Kathleen Shuttleworth-Parker. *Educ:* St Lawrence Coll., Ramsgate; Trinity Hall, Cambridge (MA, ScD). Research in Structures Department, Royal Aircraft Establishment, Farnborough, Hants, 1943–83. Vis. Prof., Dept of Mechanical Engrg, Univ. of Surrey, 1984–90. Member: British Nat. Cttee for Theoretical and Applied Mechanics, 1973–79; Gen. Assembly of IUTAM, 1976–80; Council, Royal Soc., 1977–78. FREng (FEng 1976). James Alfred Ewing Gold Medal for Engrg Res., ICE, 1991; Royal Medal, Royal Soc., 1994. UK winner (with I. T. Minhinnick), World Par Bridge Olympiad, 1951. Member, Editorial Advisory Boards: Internat. Jl of Non-linear Mechanics, 1965–95; Internat Jl of Mechanical Scis, 1977–84. *Publications:* The Bending and Stretching of Plates, 1964, 2nd edn 1989; Bridge: The Ultimate Limits, 1986; contribs to: Proc. Roy. Soc., Phil. Trans., Quarterly Jl Mech. Applied Math., Aero Quarterly, Aero Research Coun. reports and memos, and to technical press. *Recreations:* duplicate bridge, palaeontology, snorkling. *Address:* Manatoba, Dene Close, Lower Bourne, Farnham, Surrey GU10 3PP. *T:* (01252) 713558.

MANSFIELD, Sir Gerard; *see* Mansfield, Sir E. G. N.

MANSFIELD, Hon. Guy (Rhys John); QC 1994; a Recorder, since 1993; *b* 3 March 1949; *o s* and *heir* of 5th Baron Sandhurst, *qv*; *m* 1976, Philippa St Clair Verdon-Roe; one *s* one *d*. *Educ:* Harrow Sch.; Oriel Coll., Oxford (MA). Called to the Bar, Middle Temple, 1972; Bencher, 2000. Mem., Gen. Council of the Bar, 1998– (Chm., Remuneration and Terms of Work (formerly Legal Aid and Fees) Cttee, 1998–99; Mem., Gen. Mgt Cttee, 1998–; Chm., Legal Services Cttee, 2000–). *Recreations:* cricket, opera. *Address:* 1 Crown Office Row, Temple, EC4Y 7HH. *T:* (020) 7797 7500. *Clubs:* MCC; Leander (Henley-on-Thames); United (Jersey).

MANSFIELD, Michael; QC 1989; *b* 12 Oct. 1941; *s* of Frank Le Voir Mansfield and Marjorie Mansfield; *m* 1965, Melian Mansfield (*née* Bordes) (marr. diss. 1992); three *s* two *d*; 2nd, 1992, Yvette Vanson; one *s*. *Educ:* Highgate Sch.; Keele Univ. (BA Hons). Called to the Bar, Gray's Inn, 1967. Estabd set of chambers of which head, 1984. Vis. Prof. of Law, Westminster Univ., 1997–. Hon. Fellow, Kent Univ., 1994. Hon. LLD: South Bank, 1995; Keele, 1995; Hertfordshire, 1995; Middx, 1999. *Publication:* Presumed Guilty, 1994. *Recreations:* my children's interests. *Address:* 14 Tooks Court, Cursitor Street, EC4Y 1JY. *T:* (020) 7405 8828.

MANSFIELD, Sir Peter, Kt 1993; FRS 1987; Professor of Physics, University of Nottingham, 1979–94, now Professor Emeritus; *b* 9 Oct. 1933; *s* of late Rose Lilian Mansfield (*née* Turner) and late Sidney George Mansfield; *m* 1962, Jean Margaret Kibble; two *d*. *Educ:* William Penn Sch., Peckham; Queen Mary Coll., London (BSc 1959, PhD 1962; Fellow, 1985). Research Associate, Dept of Physics, Univ. of Illinois, 1962–64; Lectr, Univ. of Nottingham, 1964, Sen. Lectr, 1968, Reader, 1970–79; Sen. Visitor, Max Planck Inst. für Medizinische Forschung, Heidelberg, 1972–73. Society of Magnetic Resonance in Medicine: Gold Medal, 1983; President, 1987–88. Founder FMedSci 1998. Hon. Member: Soc. of Magnetic Resonance Imaging, 1994; British Inst. of Radiology, 1993; Hon. FRCR 1992; Hon. FInstP 1996. Hon. MD Strasbourg, 1995; Hon. DSc Kent, 1996; Hon. Dr Jagellonian Univ., Krakow, 2000. Sylvanus Thompson Lectr and Medal, 1988, Barclay Medal, 1993, British Inst. of Radiology; Gold Medal, Royal Soc. Wellcome Foundn, 1984; Duddell Medal and Prize, Inst. of Physics, 1988; Antoine Béclère Medal, Internat. Radiol Soc. and Antoine Béclère Inst., 1989; Mullard Medal and Award, Royal Soc., 1990; ISMAR Prize, 1992; Gold Medal, Eur. Assoc. of Radiol., 1995; Garmisch-Partenkirchen Prize for Magnetic Resonance Imaging, 1995; Rank Prize, 1997. *Publications:* NMR Imaging in Biomedicine (with P. G. Morris), 1982; (ed with E. L. Hahn) NMR Imaging, 1991; (ed) MRI in Medicine, 1995; papers in learned jls on nuclear magnetic resonance. *Recreations:* languages, reading, travel, flying (Private Pilot's Licence, Private Pilot's Licence for Helicopters). *Address:* Magnetic Resonance Centre, Department of Physics, University of Nottingham, Nottingham NG7 2RD. *T:* (0115) 951 4740, *Fax:* (0115) 951 5166.

MANSFIELD, Sir Philip (Robert Aked), KCMG 1984 (CMG 1973); HM Diplomatic Service, retired; Ambassador to the Netherlands, 1981–84; *b* 9 May 1926; *s* of Philip Theodore Mansfield, CSI, CIE and Helen Rosamond Aked; *m* 1953, Elinor Russell MacHatton; two *s*. *Educ:* Winchester; Pembroke Coll., Cambridge. Grenadier Guards, 1944–47. Sudan Political Service, 1950–55. Entered HM Diplomatic Service, 1955; served in: Addis Ababa, Singapore, Paris, Buenos Aires; Counsellor and Head of Rhodesia Dept, FCO, 1969–72; RCDS, 1973; Counsellor and Head of Chancery, 1974–75, Dep. High Comr, 1976, Nairobi; Asst Under Sec. of State, FCO, 1976–79; Ambassador and Dep. Perm. Representative to UN, 1979–81. Consultant to: Rank Xerox, 1987–95; BPB Industries, 1987–95. *Recreations:* reading, walking, cooking. *Address:* Palmers Farm, St Breward, Bodmin, Cornwall PL30 4NT. *T:* (01208) 850460. *Club:* Royal Commonwealth Society.

MANSFIELD, Prof. Terence Arthur, FRS 1987; FIBiol; Professor of Plant Physiology, University of Lancaster, since 1977; *b* 18 Jan. 1937; *s* of Sydney Walter Mansfield and Rose (*née* Sinfield); *m* 1963, Margaret Mary James; two *s*. *Educ:* Univ. of Nottingham (BSc); Univ. of Reading (PhD). FIBiol 1984. University of Lancaster: Lectr, then Reader, 1965–77; Dir, Inst. of Envmtl and Biol Scis, 1988–94; Provost of Sci. and Engrg, 1993–96. Member: AFRC, 1989–93; Eur. Envmtl Res. Orgn, 1994–. *Publications:* Physiology of Stomata, 1968; Effects of Air Pollutants on Plants, 1976; Stomatal Physiology, 1981; Plant Adaption to Environmental Stress, 1993; many contribs to books and jls in plant physiology. *Recreations:* cricket, hill walking, classical music. *Address:* 25 Wallace Lane, Forton, Lancs PR3 0BA. *T:* (01524) 791338. *Club:* Shireshead and Forton Cricket (Pres., 1993–).

MANSFIELD, Terence Gordon; Managing Director, National Magazine Co., since 1982; Chairman, COMAG, since 1984; Director, since 1993, and a Vice President, since 2000, Hearst Corporation USA; *b* 3 Nov. 1938; *s* of Archer James Mansfield and Elizabeth Mansfield; *m* 1965, Helen Leonora Russell; two *d*. *Educ:* Maynard Road Jun. Sch., Essex; SW Essex Technical Sch. MInstM 1969; MInstD 1976. D. H. Brocklesby, Advertising Agents, 1954; S. H. Benson, Advertising Agents, 1956; served RAF, Christmas Island, 1957–59; Conde Nast Publications, 1960–66; Queen Magazine, 1966; National Magazine Co.: Advertisement Man., Harpers and Queen, 1969; Publisher, Harpers and Queen, 1975; Dep. Man. Dir, National Magazine Co., 1980; Dir, PPA, 1982–. Chm., Trng Bd, Periodicals Trng Council, 2000–. Member: Advertising Assoc.; Marketing Soc. 1975–; British Fashion Council, 1988–; Action Research (formerly Action Res. for Crippled Child), 1989–; Adv. Bd for Victim Support, 1990–. Trustee: United World Coll., 1977–; St Bride's Church, 2001–. Friend of Epping Forest. Freeman, City of London, 1989; Liveryman, Stationers' & Newspaper Makers' Co., 1997–. *Recreations:* family, running, walking dogs. *Address:* 5 Grosvenor Gardens Mews North, SW1W 0JP. *T:* (020) 7730 7740. *Clubs:* Mark's, Harry's Bar, Solus; Hanbury Manor.

MANSINGH, Lalit; Foreign Secretary, Ministry for External Affairs, India; *b* 29 April 1941; *s* of late Dr Mayadhar Mansingh and of Hemalata Mansingh; *m* 1976, Indira Singh; one *s* one *d*. *Educ:* Utkal Univ. (MA). Res. Fellow, Sch. of Internat. Studies, New Delhi, 1960–61; Lectr in Political Science, Utkal Univ., 1961–63; Indian Foreign Service: Probationer, 1963–64; Third, then Second Sec., Geneva, 1964–67; Under Secretary: Min. of External Affairs, 1967–69; Min. of Finance, 1969–71; Dep. Chief of Mission, Kabul, 1971–74; Dep. Sec., Min. of Finance, 1975–76; Dep. Chief of Mission, Brussels, 1976–80; Ambassador to UAE, 1980–83; Joint Secretary: Min. of External Affairs, 1983–84; Min. of Finance, 1984–85; Dir Gen., Indian Council for Cultural Relations, 1985–89; Dep. Chief of Mission, with rank of Ambassador, Washington, 1989–92; High Comr, Lagos, 1993–94; Dean, Foreign Service Inst., New Delhi, 1995–96; Sec. (West), Min. of External Affairs, 1997–98; High Comr in UK, 1998–99. *Publication:* (ed.-in-chief) Indian Foreign Policy: agenda for the 21st century, 2 vols, 1998. *Recreations:* art, culture. *Address:* Ministry for External Affairs, South Block, New Delhi 110 011, India. *Clubs:* Travellers; India International Centre, India Habitat Centre, Gymkhana (New Delhi); Bhubaneswar (Bhubaneswar); International Centre (Goa).

MANSON, Ian Stuart; Chief Crown Prosecutor, West Midlands Area, Crown Prosecution Service, 1986–89; *b* 15 March 1929; *s* of late David Alexander Manson and Elsie May (*née* Newton); *m* 1957, Pamela Horrocks-Taylor; three *s*. *Educ:* Heath Grammar Sch., Halifax; Clare Coll., Cambridge (Open Exhibnr; BA Hons). Admitted Solicitor, 1956. Asst Prosecuting Solicitor, Bradford, 1956–57; Prosecuting Solicitor: Southampton, 1957–58; Portsmouth, 1958–60; Asst Prosecuting Solicitor, Birmingham, 1960–66; Prosecuting Solicitor, W Midlands Police Authority, 1966–74; Chief Prosecuting Solicitor, W Midlands CC, 1974–86. *Recreations:* reading, music, gardening.

MANT, Prof. David Clive Anthony, FRCP, FRCGP; Professor of General Practice and Fellow of Kellogg College, University of Oxford, since 1998. *Educ:* Churchill Coll., Cambridge (BA 1972; MA 1976); Birmingham Univ. (MB ChB 1977); London Sch. of Hygiene and Tropical Medicine (MSc (Community Medicine) 1983). MRCGP 1982, FRCGP 1999; MFPHM 1984; FRCP 1999. Trainee in gen. practice, E Oxford Health Centre, 1981–82; Registrar in Community Medicine, Oxford RHA, 1982–84; Clin. Lectr, 1984–93, and Sen. Scientist, Gen. Practice Res. Gp, 1987–93, Oxford Univ.; Prof. of Primary Care Epidemiology, Southampton University, 1993–98; Dir of R&D, S and W Reg., NHS Exec., DoH, 1996–98 (on secondment). Hon. Prof., Bristol Univ., 1996–98. FMedSci 1998.

MANTEL, Hilary Mary, (Mrs G. McEwen); author; *b* 6 July 1952; *d* of Henry Thompson and Margaret Mary Thompson (*née* Foster, later Mrs Jack Mantel); *m* 1973, Gerald McEwen. *Educ:* London Sch. of Econs; Sheffield Univ. (BJur). FRSL 1990. Shiva Naipaul Meml Prize, 1987; Winifred Holtby Award, RSL, 1990; Southern Arts Literature Prize, 1990; Cheltenham Fest. Prize, 1990; Book of Year Award, Sunday Express, 1992. *Publications:* Every Day is Mother's Day, 1985; Vacant Possession, 1986; Eight Months on Ghazzah Street, 1988; Fludd, 1990; A Place of Greater Safety, 1992; A Change of Climate, 1994; An Experiment in Love, 1995 (Hawthornden Prize for Literature, 1996); The Giant, O'Brien, 1998. *Recreation:* sleeping. *Address:* A. M. Heath & Co., 79 St Martin's Lane, WC2N 4AA.

MANTELL, Rt Hon. Sir Charles (Barrie Knight), Kt 1990; PC 1997; **Rt Hon. Lord Justice Mantell;** a Lord Justice of Appeal, since 1997; *b* 30 Jan. 1937; *s* of Francis Christopher Knight Mantell and Elsie Mantell; *m* 1960, Anne Shirley Mantell; two *d*. *Educ:* Manchester Grammar Sch.; Manchester Univ. (LLM). Called to the Bar, Gray's Inn, 1960, Bencher, 1990. Flying Officer, RAF, 1958–61. In practice at Bar, London and Manchester, 1961–82; a Recorder of the Crown Court, 1978–82; QC 1979; Judge of Supreme Court, Hong Kong, 1982–85; a Circuit Judge, 1985–90; Judge, High Court of Justice, QBD, 1990–97; Presiding Judge, Western Circuit, 1993–96. *Recreations:* reading, watching cricket. *Address:* Royal Courts of Justice, Strand, WC2A 2LL. *Club:* Hong Kong (Hong Kong).

MANTHORPE, John Jeremy, CB 1994; Chief Executive, 1985–96, and Chief Land Registrar, 1990–96, HM Land Registry; *b* 16 June 1936; *s* of William Broderick and Margaret Dora Manthorpe; *m* 1967, Kathleen Mary Ryan; three *s* one *d*. *Educ:* Beckenham and Penge Grammar School. HM Land Registry: Plans Branch, 1952; Principal Survey and Plans Officer, 1974; Controller (Registration), 1981–85. CIMgt 1994; Hon. RICS (Hon. ARICS 1992). *Recreations:* walking and watching the Ashdown Forest. *Address:* Beurles, Fairwarp, Uckfield, East Sussex TN22 3BG. *T:* (01825) 712795.

MANTLE, Richard John; General Director, Opera North, since 1994; *b* 21 Jan. 1947; *s* of late George William Mantle, OBE and Doris Griffiths; *m* 1970, Carol June Mountain. *Educ:* Tiffin Sch.; Ealing Coll. of Advanced Technology. Personnel Officer, Beecham Group, 1969–72; Associate Dir, J. Walter Thompson Co., 1973–79; Personnel Dir, then Dep. Man. Dir, ENO, 1980–85; Man. Dir, Scottish Opera, 1985–91; Gen. Dir, Edmonton Opera, Canada, 1991–94. Mem. Adv. Council, RSCM, 2000–. Chm., St Mary and St Anne Abbotts Bromley Foundn, 1999–. A Guardian, Shrine of Our Lady of Walsingham, 1998–. *Recreations:* music, reading, the country, English churches. *Address:* Cleveland House, Barrowby Lane, Kirkby Overblow, Harrogate, N Yorks HG3 1HQ. *T:* (01423) 815924, *Fax:* (01423) 815926; *e-mail:* richardmantle@aol.com. *Club:* Athenæum.

MANTON, 3rd Baron *cr* 1922, of Compton Verney; **Joseph Rupert Eric Robert Watson;** DL; Landowner and Farmer; *b* 22 Jan. 1924; *s* of 2nd Baron Manton and Alethea (*d* 1979), 2nd *d* of late Colonel Philip Langdale, OBE; *S* father, 1968; *m* 1951, Mary Elizabeth, twin *d* of Major T. D. Hallinan, Ashbourne, Glounthaune, Co. Cork; two *s* three *d* (of whom two *s* one *d* are triplets). *Educ:* Eton. Joined Army, 1942; commissioned Life Guards, 1943; Captain, 1946; retired, 1947; rejoined 7th (QO) Hussars, 1951–56. DL Humberside, 1980. *Recreations:* hunting, shooting, racing. *Heir: s* Major the Hon. Miles Ronald Marcus Watson, Life Guards [*b* 7 May 1958; *m* 1984, Elizabeth, *e d* of J. R. Story; two *s*]. *Address:* Houghton Hall, Sancton, York YO4 3RE. *T:* (01430) 873234. *Clubs:* White's, Jockey.

See also Baron Hesketh.

MANTON, Sir Edwin (Alfred Grenville), Kt 1994; Senior Adviser, American International Group Inc., since 1982; *b* 22 Jan. 1909; *s* of John H. Manton and Emily C. Manton (*née* Denton); *m* 1936, Florence V. Brewer; one *d*. *Educ:* Shaftesbury GS; Coll. of Insurance, NY. AIIA. With B. W. Noble, Paris, 1927–33; American International Underwriters Corp.: Casualty Underwriter, 1933–37; Sec., 1937–38; Vice-Pres., 1938–42; Pres., 1942–69; Chm., 1969–75. Hon. DHL Coll. of Insurance, NY. *Publications:* various papers in insurance press. *Recreations:* walking, art, formerly cricket and hockey. *Address:* American International Group, 70 Pine Street, 59th Floor, New York, NY 10270–0002, USA.

MANTON, Prof. Nicholas Stephen, PhD; FRS 1996; FInstP; Professor of Mathematical Physics, University of Cambridge, since 1998; Fellow, St John's College, Cambridge, since 1997; *b* 2 Oct. 1952; *s* of Franz Eduard Sigmund Manton and Lily Manton (*née* Goldsmith); *m* 1989, Terttu Anneli Aitta; one *s*. *Educ:* Dulwich Coll.; St John's Coll., Cambridge (BA, MA, PhD 1978). FInstP 1996. Joliot-Curie Fellow, Ecole

Normale Supérieure, Paris, 1978–79; Res. Fellow, MIT, 1979–81; Asst Res. Physicist, Inst. for Theoretical Physics, Univ. of Calif, Santa Barbara, 1981–84; Cambridge University: Sen. Res. Student, St John's Coll., 1985–87; Lectr, 1987–94; Reader in Mathematical Physics, 1994–98; Dir of Studies in Applied Maths, St John's Coll., 1997–98. Vis. Prof., Inst. for Theoretical Physics, SUNY, Stony Brook, 1988; Scientific Associate, CERN, Geneva, 2001. Mem., British Team, Internat. Mathematical Olympiad, 1971. Jun. Whitehead Prize, London Mathematical Soc., 1991. *Publications:* papers in mathematical and theoretical physics in various jls incl. Nuclear Physics, Physics Letters, Physical Rev., Communications in Mathematical Physics, and conf. proceedings. *Recreations:* music, Finland and its culture. *Address:* Department of Applied Mathematics and Theoretical Physics, Centre for Mathematical Sciences, University of Cambridge, Wilberforce Road, Cambridge CB3 0WA. *T:* (01223) 337900; St John's College, Cambridge CB2 1TP.

MANUELLA, Sir Tulaga, GCMG 1996; MBE 1981; Governor General, Tuvalu, since 1994; Chancellor, University of the South Pacific, 1997–2000; *b* 26 Aug. 1936; *s* of Teuhu Manuella and Malesa Moevasa; *m* 1957, Milikini Uinifaleti; two *s* three *d*. *Educ:* primary sch., Ocean Is. Gilbert and Ellice Islands Colony: sub-accountant and ledger keeper, 1953–55; clerical officer, 1955–57; Sen. Asst, then Asst Accountant, Treasury, 1957–75; Tuvalu Government: Asst Accountant, Accountant, then Actg Financial Sec., Min. of Finance, 1976–84; Financial Secretary, Financial Division: Church of Tuvalu, 1984–86; Pacific Conf. of Churches, Suva, Fiji, 1987–91; Co-ordinator of Finance and Admin, Ekalesia Kelisiano, Tuvalu, 1992–94. Patron, Pacific Islands Soc. in Britain and Ireland, 1995. *Address:* PO Box 50, Vaiaku, Funafuti, Tuvalu.

MANWARING, Randle (Gilbert), MA; FSS, FPMI; poet and author; retired company director; *b* 3 May 1912; *s* of late George Ernest and Lilian Manwaring; *m* 1941, Betty Violet (*d* 2001), *d* of H. P. Rout, Norwich; three *s* one *d*. *Educ:* private schools. MA Keele, 1982. Joined Clerical, Medical and Gen. Life Assce Soc., 1929. War service, RAF, 1940–46, W/Cdr; comd RAF Regt in Burma, 1945. Clerical, Medical & Gen. Pensions Rep., 1950; joined C. E. Heath & Co. Ltd, 1956: Asst Dir, 1960, Dir, 1964, Man. Dir. 1969; Founder Dir (Man.), C. E. Heath Urquhart (Life and Pensions), 1966–71, and a Founder Dir, Excess Life Assce Co., 1967–75; Dir, Excess Insurance Group, 1975–78; Insurance Adviser, Midland Bank, 1971; first Man. Dir, Midland Bank Ins. Services, 1972–74, Vice-Chm., 1974–77, Dir, 1977–78. Chm., Life Soc., Corp. of Insce Brokers, 1965–66; Dep. Chm., Corp. of Insce Brokers, 1970–71; Pres., Soc. of Pensions Consultants, 1968–70. Chairman of Governors: Luckley-Oakfield Sch., 1972–83; Northease Manor Sch., 1972–84. Diocesan Reader (Chichester), 1968–; Mem., C of E Evangelical Council, 1980–82; Lay Pres., Chichester Diocesan Evangelical Union, 1989–91; Mem., Diocesan Synod, 1985–98; Lay Chm., Uckfield Deanery Synod, 1993–99; Churchwarden, St Peter-upon-Cornhill, London, 1985–90. Chm., Vine Books Ltd; Dir, Crusaders Union Ltd, 1960–91 (Vice-Pres., 1983–). Vice-Pres., RAFA, 1990–. Chm. of Trustees, Careforce, 1980–87. Chm., Probus Club, Uckfield, 1989–90. *Publications:* The Heart of this People, 1954; A Christian Guide to Daily Work, 1963; Thornhill Guide to Insurance, 1976; The Run of the Downs, 1984; From Controversy to Co-existence, 1985; The Good Fight, 1990; A Study of Hymnwriting and Hymnsinging in the Christian Church, 1991; (for children) The Swallows, the Fox and the Cuckoo, 1998; *poems:* Posies Once Mine, 1951; Satires and Salvation, 1960; Under the Magnolia Tree, 1965; Slave to No Sect, 1966; Crossroads of the Year, 1975; From the Four Winds, 1976; In a Time of Unbelief, 1977; Poem Prayers for Growing People, 1980; The Swifts of Maggiore, 1981; In a Time of Change, 1983; Collected Poems, 1986; Some Late Lark Singing, 1992; Love So Amazing, 1995; Trade Winds, 2001; contrib. poems and articles to learned jls in GB and Canada; contrib. hymns to several hymn books. *Recreations:* music, reading, following cricket. *Address:* Marbles Barn, Newick, Lewes, East Sussex BN8 4LG. *T:* (01825) 723845. *Clubs:* Royal Air Force, MCC; Sussex County Cricket.

MANZIE, Sir (Andrew) Gordon, KCB 1987 (CB 1983); Director, Altnamara Shipping plc, since 1994; *b* 3 April 1930; *s* of late John Mair and Catherine Manzie; *m* 1955, Rosalind Clay; one *s* one *d*. *Educ:* Royal High Sch. of Edinburgh; London Sch. of Economics and Political Science (BScEcon). Joined Civil Service as Clerical Officer, Scottish Home Dept, 1947. National Service, RAF, 1949. Min. of Supply: Exec. Officer (Higher Exec. Officer, 1957). Private Sec. to Perm. Sec., Min. of Aviation, 1962; Sen. Exec. Officer, 1963; Principal, 1964; Sec. to Cttee of Inquiry into Civil Air Transport (Edwards Cttee), 1967; Asst Sec., Dept of Trade and Industry, on loan to Min. of Posts and Telecommunications, 1971; Dept of Industry, 1974; Under-Sec., Dir, Office for Scotland, Depts of Trade and Industry, 1975; Under Sec., Scottish Economic Planning Dept, 1975–79; Dir, Industrial Develt Unit, 1980–81, Dep. Sec., 1980–84, Dept of Industry (Dept of Trade and Industry, 1983–84); Second Perm. Sec. and Chief Exec., PSA, DoE, 1984–90, retd. Chairman: Anglo Japanese Construction Ltd, 1990–95; Forthspan Ltd, 1993–97; Thistle Water, 1995–97; Yorkshire Link Ltd, 1996–97; Director: Altnacraig Shipping, 1990–96; Motherwell Bridge Hldgs, 1990–97; Trafalgar House Construction Hldgs Ltd, later Kvaerner Construction, 1991–97; Trafalgar House, later Kvaerner, Corporate Develt Ltd, 1991–97; Mem., Adv. Bd, LEK Partnership, 1992–2000. Gov., LSE, 1994–. Trustee, Stort Trust, 1990–; Pres., Bishop's Stortford Caledonian Soc., 1987–93. CIMgt (CBIM 1987); Hon. FCIOB 1990. *Recreations:* golf, reading, watching Rugby football. *Address:* 28 Manor Links, Bishop's Stortford, Herts CM23 5RA. *T:* (01279) 651960. *Club:* Caledonian.

MANZINI, Raimondo; Italian Ambassador to the Court of St James's, 1968–75; *b* Bologna, 25 Nov. 1913. *Educ:* Univ. of California (Berkeley); Clark Univ., Mass. (MA); Dr of Law, Bologna Univ. Entered Diplomatic Service, 1940; served San Francisco, 1940–41; Lisbon, 1941–43; Min. of Foreign Affairs in Brindisi, Salerno, Rome, 1943–44; London, 1944–47; Consul General for Congo, Nigeria and Gold Coast, 1947–50; Consul General, Baden Baden, 1951–52; Head of Information Service, CED, Paris, 1952–53; Ministry of Foreign Affairs, 1953–55; Adviser to the Minister of Foreign Trade, 1955–58; Chef de Cabinet of Minister for Foreign Affairs, 1958; Diplomatic Adviser to the Prime Minister, 1958–59; Advr to Minister of Industry, 1960–64; Perm. Rep. to OECD, Paris, 1965–68; Sec.-Gen., Min. of Foreign Affairs, 1975–78. Gran Croce, Ordine Merito Repubblica, 1968; Hon. GCVO 1969; Commandeur, Légion d'Honneur (France), 1976. *Address:* Villa Bellochio, 83 Boulevard de Garavan, Menton, France.

MANZOOR, Zahida Parveen, CBE 1998; Regional Chair, Northern and Yorkshire Regional Office of NHS, Department of Health, since 1997; Co-founder and Director, Intellisys Ltd, since 1996; *b* 25 May 1958; *d* of Nazir Ahmed and Mahroof Ahmed; *m* 1984, Dr Madassar Manzoor; two *d*. *Educ:* Leeds Univ. (HVCert 1983); Bradford Univ. (MA Applied Social Studies 1989). Student nurse to Staff Nurse, W Suffolk AHA, 1977–80 (SRN 1980); Staff Nurse, then Staff Midwife, Birmingham AHA, 1980–82 (SCM 1981); Health Visitor, Durham AHA, 1983–84; Lectr, Thomas Danby Coll., 1984–86 and 1987–88; NE Regl Prog. Dir, Common Purpose Charitable Trust, 1990–92; Chm., Bradford HA, 1992–97. Comr and Dep. Chm., CRE, 1993–98. Ind. Assessor, FCO, 1998–. Mem., Bradford Congress, 1992–96; Dir, Bradford City Challenge, 1993–96. Trustee: W Yorks Police Community Trust, 1996–98; Uniting Britain Trust, 1996–; NSPCC, 1997–. Mem. Ct, Univ. of Bradford, 1992–98; Governor: Sheffield Hallam Univ., 1991–93; Bradford and Airedale Coll. of Health, 1992–93; Keighley Coll., 1994–95. Vice-Patron, Regl Crime Stoppers, 1998. Hon. DSc Bradford, 1999. *Recreations:* antiques, gardening, painting, historic buildings. *Address:* The Nunnery, Harewood Road, Arthington, W Yorks LS21 1PR.

MAPLE, Graham John; District Judge, Principal Registry of Family Division, High Court of Justice, since 1991; *b* 18 Dec. 1947; *s* of Sydney George and Thelma Olive Maple; *m* 1974, Heather Anderson; two *s*. *Educ:* Shirley Secondary Modern Sch.; John Ruskin Grammar Sch., Croydon; Bedford Coll., London (LLB 1973). Lord Chancellor's Dept, 1968; Sec., Principal Registry of Family Div., 1989. Member: Outer London, Court Service Cttee, 1991–96; Family Courts Forum, 1996–. Church Warden, St Mildred Parish Church, Tenterden, 1992–98. Consulting Editor, Rayden and Jackson on Divorce and Family Matters, 1998–. *Publications:* (Co-Editor) Rayden and Jackson on Divorce, 12th edn 1974, to 17th edn 1998; (Co-Editor) The Practitioner's Probate Manual, 21st edn 1979; (ed) Holloway's Probate Handbook, 8th edn 1987. *Recreations:* archaeology, Roman Britain, steam and model railways. *Address:* Principal Registry, Family Division, High Court of Justice, First Avenue House, 42–48 High Holborn, WC1V 2NP.

MAPLES, John Cradock; MP (C) Stratford-on-Avon, since 1997; *b* 22 April 1943; *s* of late Thomas Cradock Maples and Hazel Mary Maples; *m* 1986, Jane Corbin; one *s* one *d*. *Educ:* Marlborough Coll., Wiltshire; Downing Coll., Cambridge; Harvard Business Sch., USA. Called to the Bar, Inner Temple, 1965. Chm. and Chief Exec., Saatchi & Saatchi Govt Communications Worldwide, 1992–96; Chm., Rowland Sallingbury Casey, 1994–96. MP (C) W Lewisham, 1983–92; contested (C) W Lewisham, 1992. PPS to Financial Sec. to HM Treasury, 1987–90; Econ. Sec. to HM Treasury, 1990–92; Opposition front bench spokesman on health, 1997–98, on defence, 1998–99, on foreign affairs, 1999–2000. Jt Dep. Chm., Cons. Party, 1994–95. *Recreations:* sailing, ski-ing. *Address:* House of Commons, SW1A 0AA.

MAR, Countess of (*suo jure*, 31st in line from Ruadri, 1st Earl of Mar, 1115); Premier Earldom of Scotland by descent; Lady Garioch, *c* 1320; **Margaret of Mar;** *b* 19 Sept. 1940; *er d* of 30th Earl of Mar, and Millicent Mary Salton; *S* father, 1975; recognised in surname "of Mar" by warrant of Court of Lord Lyon, 1967, when she abandoned her second forename; *m* 1st, 1959, Edwin Noel Artiss (marr. diss. 1976); one *d*; 2nd, 1976, (cousin) John Salton (marr. diss. 1981); 3rd, 1982, J. H. Jenkin, MA (Cantab), FRCO, LRAM, ARCM. Lay Mem., Immigration Appeal Tribunal, 1985–. Mem., EU Sub-Cttee on environment, health and consumer affairs, H of L, 1995–; Dep. Speaker, H of L, 1997–; elected Mem., H of L, 1999. Chm., Honest Food, 2000–. Chm., Environmental Medicine Foundn, 1997–. Patron: Dispensing Doctors' Assoc., 1985–96; Gulf Veterans Assoc., 1995–; Worcs Mobile Disabled Gp, 1991–; Pres., Elderly Accommodation Counsel, 1994–. Governor, King's Sch., Gloucester, 1984–87. *Heir: d* Mistress of Mar, *qv*. *Address:* St Michael's Farm, Great Witley, Worcester WR6 6JB. *T:* (01299) 896608.

MAR, Mistress of; Lady Susan Helen of Mar; interior designer; *b* 31 May 1963; *d* and *heiress* of Countess of Mar, *qv*; *m* 1989, Bruce Alexander Wyllie; two *d*. *Educ:* King Charles I School, Kidderminster; Christie College, Cheltenham. *Address:* Firethorn Farm Cottage, Plough Lane, Ewhurst Green, Cranleigh, Surrey GU6 7SG.

MAR, 14th Earl of, *cr* 1565, **and KELLIE**. 16th Earl of, *cr* 1619; **James Thorne Erskine;** Baron Erskine 1429; Viscount Fentoun 1606; Baron Dirleton 1603; Baron Erskine of Alloa Tower (Life Peer) 2000; Premier Viscount of Scotland; Hereditary Keeper of Stirling Castle; DL; *b* 10 March 1949; *s* of 13th Earl of Mar and 15th Earl of Kellie, and Pansy Constance Erskine, OBE (*d* 1996); *S* father, 1993; *m* 1974, Mrs Mary Mooney, *yr d* of Dougal McD. Kirk. *Educ:* Eton; Moray Coll. of Education, 1968–71; Inverness Coll. (building course, 1987–88). Page of Honour to the Queen, 1962, 1963. Community Service Volunteer, York, 1967–68; Community Worker, Richmond-Craigmillar Parish Church, Edinburgh, 1971–73; Sen. Social Worker, Family and Community Services, Sheffield District Council, 1973–76; Social Worker: Grampian Regional Council, Elgin, 1976–77, Forres, 1977–78; Highland Regional Council, Aviemore, 1979; HM Prison, Inverness, 1979–81; Inverness W, Aug.-Dec. 1981; Community Worker, Merkinch Centre, Inverness, Jan.-July 1982; Community Service Supervisor, Inverness, 1983–87; building technician, 1989–91; project worker, SACRO Intensive Probation Project, Falkirk, 1991–93; boatbuilder, 1993. Sits in H of L as Lib Dem. Contested (Lib Dem) Ochil, Scottish Parly elecn, 1999. Chm., Strathclyde Tram Inquiry, 1996; Parly Comr, Burrell Collection (lending) Inquiry, 1997. Pilot Officer, RAuxAF, 1979, attached to 2622 Highland Sqdn, RAuxAF Regt; Flying Officer, RAuxAF, 1982–86; RNXS, 1985–89. DL Clackmannan, 1991. *Heir: b* Hon. Alexander David Erskine [*b* 26 Oct. 1952; *m* 1977, Katherine Shawford, *e d* of Thomas Clark Capel; one *s* one *d*]. *Recreations:* canoeing, hill walking, railways, gardening, restoration of Alloa Tower. *Address:* Hilton Farm, Alloa, Scotland FK10 3PS. *Club:* Farmers'.

MARA, Rt Hon. Ratu Sir Kamisese Kapaiwai Tuimacilai, GCMG 1983; KBE 1969 (OBE 1961); CF 1996; MSD 1996; PC 1973; Tui Nayau; Tui Lau; President of the Republic of Fiji, 1994–2000; Hereditary High Chief of the Lau Islands; *b* 13 May 1920; *s* of late Ratu Tevita Uluilakeba, Tui Nayau; *m* 1951, Adi Lady Lala Mara (Roko Tui Dreketi); two *s* five *d* (and one *s* decd). *Educ:* Fiji; Sacred Heart Coll., NZ; Otago Univ., NZ; Wadham Coll., Oxford (MA; Hon. Fellow, 1971); London Sch. of Economics (Dip. Econ. & Social Admin.), Hon. Fellow, 1985. Administrative Officer, Colonial Service, Fiji, Oct. 1950; Fijian MLC, 1953–89, and MEC, 1959–61 (elected MLC and MEC, 1959). Member for Natural Resources and Leader of Govt Business; Alliance Party, 1964–66 (Founder of Party); Chief Minister and Mem., Council of Ministers, Fiji, 1967; Prime Minister, Fiji, 1970–87, Republic of Fiji, 1987–92; Minister for Foreign Affairs and Civil Aviation, 1986–87. Mem. Bd, Internat. Raoul Wallenberg Foundns, 2001–. Hon. Dr of Laws: Univ. of Guam, 1969; Univ. of Papua New Guinea, 1982; Hon. LLD: Univ. of Otago, 1973; New Delhi, 1975; Hon. DPolSc Korea, 1978; Hon. Dr Tokai Univ., 1980; DU Univ. of South Pacific, 1980. Man of the Pacific Award, 1984. KStJ. Grand Cross, Order of Lion, Senegal, 1975; Order of Diplomatic Service Merit, Korea, 1978. *Publication:* The Pacific Way: a memoir, 1997. *Recreations:* athletics, cricket, Rugby football, golf, fishing. *Clubs:* Oxford and Cambridge, Achilles (London); Defence (Suva, Fiji).

See also Ratu E. Nailatikau.

MARAN, Prof. Arnold George Dominic, MD; FRCS, FRCSE, FRCPE, FACS; Professor of Otolaryngology, University of Edinburgh, 1988–2000; *b* 16 June 1936; *s* of John and Hilda Maran; *m* 1962, Anna De Marco; one *s* one *d*. *Educ:* Daniel Stewart's Coll., Edinburgh; Univ. of Edinburgh (MB, ChB 1959; MD 1963); Univ. of Iowa. FRCSE 1962; FACS 1974; FRCPE 1989; FRCS 1991. Basic trng in surgery, Edinburgh, followed by specialty head and neck trng, Univ. of Iowa; consultant otolaryngologist, Dundee Royal Infirmary, 1967–73; Prof. of Otolaryngology, W Virginia Univ., 1974–75; consultant otolaryngologist, Royal Infirmary of Edinburgh, 1975–88. Chm., Intercollegiate Bd in Otolaryngology, 1988–91; Sec., Conf. of Royal Colls, Scotland, 1992. Royal College of Surgeons of Edinburgh: Hon. Treasurer, 1976–81; Mem.

Council, 1981–86; Hon. Sec., 1988–92; a Vice-Pres., 1995–97; Pres., 1997–2000. President: Scottish Otolaryngol Soc., 1991–92; Laryngology Section, RSM, 1990. Sixteen visiting professorships; fifteen eponymous lectures. Hon. FDSRCS 1995; Hon. FCS(SoAf) 1997; Hon. FCSHK 1997; Hon Fellow, Acad. of Medicine, Singapore, 1998. Hon. Member: S African Otolaryngol Soc., 1986; S African Head and Neck Soc., 1986; Irish Otolaryngol Soc., 1990 (Wilde Medal, 1990); Assoc. of Surgeons of India, 1991. Yearsley Medal, 1985, Semon Medal, 1990, London Univ.; Jobson Horne Prize, BMA, 1985; W. J. Harrison Prize, 1989, Howells Prize, 1991, RSM; Leon Goldman Medal, Univ. of Cape Town, 1994. Order of Gorka Dakshina Bahu (Nepal), 1998. *Publications:* Head and Neck Surgery, 1972, 4th edn 2000; Clinical Otolaryngology, 1979; Clinical Rhinology, 1990; Head and Neck Surgery for the General Surgeon, 1991; (ed) Logan Turner's Diseases of Nose, Throat and Ear, 11th edn, 1992; contribs to 14 textbooks; 150 articles. *Recreations:* golf, classical music, playing jazz piano. *Address:* 27 Learmonth Terrace, Edinburgh EH4 1NZ. *T:* (0131) 332 0055; 2 Double Dykes Road, St Andrews KY16 9DX. *T:* (01334) 472939. *Clubs:* New (Edinburgh); Royal and Ancient Golf (St Andrews); Bruntsfield Golfing Society (Edinburgh).

MARBER, Patrick; writer and director; *b* 19 Sept. 1964; *s* of Brian Marber and Angela (*née* Benjamin). *Educ:* Wadham Coll., Oxford. *Plays:* Dealer's Choice, RNT and Vaudeville, 1995 (Writers' Guild and Evening Standard Awards, 1995); After Miss Julie, BBC, 1995; Closer, RNT, 1997, transf. Lyric, 1998, NY, 1999 (Evening Standard, Time Out, Critic's Circle and Olivier Best Play Awards, 1998); Howard Katz, RNT, 2001. *Publications:* Dealer's Choice, 1995; After Miss Julie, 1995; Closer, 1997; Howard Katz, 2001.

MARCEAU, Marcel; Officier de la Légion d'Honneur; Grand Officier de l'Ordre National du Mérite; Commandeur des Arts et des Lettres de la République Française; mime; Founder, Compagnie de Mime Marcel Marceau, 1949 (Director, 1949–64); Director: International School of Mime of Paris Marcel Marceau, since 1978; New Mimodrama Co., since 1993; *b* Strasbourg, 22 March 1923; *s* of Charles and Anne Mangel; two *s* two *d*. *Educ:* Ecole des Beaux Arts; Arts Décoratifs, Limoges; Ecole Etienne Decroux; Ecole Charles Dullin. First stage appearance, in Paris, 1946; with Barrault/ Renaud Co., 1946–49; founded his company, 1949; since then has toured constantly, playing in 65 countries. Created about 100 pantomimes (most famous are The Creation of the World, The Cage, The Maskmaker, The Tree, Bip Liontamer, Bip hunts Butterfly, Bip plays David and Goliath, Bip at a Society Party, Bip in the Modern and Future Life, Bip Soldier, etc), and 26 mimodrames, and in particular the character 'Bip' (1947); *Mimodrames:* Bip et la fille des rues, 1947; Bip et L'Oiseau, 1948; Death Before Dawn, 1948; The Fair, 1949; The Flute Player, 1949; The Overcoat, 1951; Moriana and Galvan, Pierrot of Montmartre, 1952; Les Trois Perruques, 1953; Un Soir aux Funambules, 1953; La Parade en bleu et noir, 1956; le 14 juillet, 1956; Le Mont de Piété, 1956; Le Loup de Tsu Ku Mi, 1956; Le Petit Cirque, 1958; Les Matadors, 1959; Paris qui rit, Paris qui pleure, 1959; Don Juan, 1964; Candide, 1970, with Ballet de l'Opéra de Hambourg; Le Chapeau Melon, 1997; *films:* The Overcoat, 1951; Barbarella, 1967; Scrooge (BBC London), 1973; Shanks, US, 1973; Silent Movie, 1976. Has made frequent TV appearances and many short films for TV, incl. Pantomimes, 1954, A Public Garden, 1955, Le mime Marcel Marceau, 1965, The World of Marcel Marceau, 1966, 12 short films with Enc. Brit., NY, 1974. Member: Acad. of Arts and Letters (DDR); Akad. der schönen Künste, Munich; Acad. des Beaux Arts, Paris. Emmy Awards (US), 1955, 1968. Hon. Dr, Univ. of Oregon; Dr *hc* Univ. of Princeton, 1981. Gold Medal of Czechoslovak Republic (for contribution to cultural relations). *Publications:* Les 7 Péchés Capitaux (lithographs); Les Rêveries de Bip (lithographs); La Ballade de Paris et du Monde (text, lithographs, water-colours, drawings in ink and pencil); Alphabet Book; Counting Book; L'Histoire de Bip (text and lithographs); The Third Eye (lithoprint); Pimporello. *Recreations:* painting, poetry, fencing. *Address:* Compagnie de Mime Marcel Marceau, 32 rue de Londres, 75009 Paris, France. *T:* 142804832, *Fax:* 148749187.

MARCH AND KINRARA, Earl of; Charles Henry Gordon Lennox; *b* 8 Jan. 1955; *s* and *heir* of Duke of Richmond, Lennox and Gordon, *qv*; *m* 1st, 1976, Sally (marr. diss. 1989), *d* of late Maurice Clayton and of Mrs Denis Irwin; one *d*; 2nd, 1991, Hon. Janet Elizabeth, *d* of 3rd Viscount Astor and of Bronwen, *d* of His Honour Sir (John) Alan Pugh; three *s* one *d* (of whom one *s* one *d* are twins). *Educ:* Eton. *Heir: s* Lord Settrington, *qv*. *Address:* Goodwood House, Chichester, West Sussex PO18 0PY.

MARCH, Lionel John, ScD; Professor of Design and Computation, School of the Arts and Architecture, University of California, Los Angeles, since 1994; *b* 26 Jan. 1934; *o s* of Leonard James March and Rose (*née* Edwards); *m* 1st, 1960, Lindsey Miller (marr. diss. 1984); one *s* two *d*; 2nd, 1984, Maureen Vidler; one step *s* two step *d*. *Educ:* Hove Grammar Sch. for Boys; Magdalene Coll., Cambridge (MA, ScD). FIMA, FRSA. Nat. Service: Sub-Lt, RNVR, 1953–55. Harkness Fellow, Commonwealth Fund, Harvard Univ. and MIT, 1962–64; Asst to Sir Leslie Martin, 1964–66; Lectr in Architecture, Univ. of Cambridge, 1966–69; Dir, Centre for Land Use and Built Form Studies, Univ. of Cambridge, 1969–73; Prof., Dept of Systems Design, Univ. of Waterloo, Ontario, 1974–76; Prof. of Design, Faculty of Technology, Open Univ., 1976–81; Rector and Vice-Provost, RCA, 1981–84; Prof., Grad. Sch. of Architecture and Urban Planning, 1984–94, Hd of Architecture/Urban Design Prog. 1984–91, UCLA. Chm., Applied Res. of Cambridge Ltd, 1969–73. Mem., Governing Body, Imperial Coll. of Science and Technology, 1981–84. General Editor (with Leslie Martin), Cambridge Urban and Architectural Studies, 1970–; Founding Editor, Environment and Planning B, Planning and Design, 1974–. *Publications:* (with Philip Steadman) The Geometry of Environment, 1971; (ed with Leslie Martin) Urban Space and Structures, 1972; (ed) The Architecture of Form, 1976; (ed with Judith Sheine) R. M. Schindler: composition and construction, 1993; Architectonics of Humanism, 1998. *Address:* The How House, 2422 Silver Ridge Avenue, Silver Lake, Los Angeles, CA 90039, USA. *T:* (213) 6647760.

MARCH, Prof. Norman Henry; Coulson Professor of Theoretical Chemistry, University of Oxford, 1977–94; Fellow of University College, Oxford, 1977–94, Emeritus since 1994; *b* 9 July 1927; *s* of William and Elsie March; *m* 1949, Margaret Joan Hoyle (*d* 1994); two *s*. *Educ:* King's Coll., London Univ. University of Sheffield: Lecturer in Physics, 1953–57; Reader in Theoretical Physics, 1957–61; Prof. of Physics, 1961–72; Prof. of Theoretical Solid State Physics, Imperial Coll., Univ. of London, 1973–77. Hon. DTech Chalmers, Gothenburg, 1980. *Publications:* The Many-Body Problem in Quantum Mechanics (with W. H. Young and S. Sampanthar), 1967; Liquid Metals, 1968; (with W. Jones) Theoretical Solid State Physics, 1973; Self-Consistent Fields in Atoms, 1974; Orbital Theories of Molecules and Solids, 1974; (with M. P. Tosi) Atomic Dynamics in Liquids, 1976; (with M. Parrinello) Collective Effects in Solids and Liquids, 1983; (with S. Lundqvist) The Theory of the Inhomogeneous Electron Gas, 1983; (with M. P. Tosi) Coulomb Liquids, 1984; (with M. P. Tosi) Polymers, Liquid Crystals and Low-Dimensional Solids, 1984; (with R. A. Street and M. P. Tosi) Amorphous Solids and the Liquid State, 1985; Chemical Bonds outside Metal Surfaces, 1986; (with P. N. Butcher and M. P. Tosi) Crystalline Semiconducting Materials and Devices, 1986; (with B. M. Deb) The Single Particle Density in Physics and Chemistry, 1987; (with S. Lundqvist and M. P. Tosi) Order and Chaos in Nonlinear Physical Systems, 1988; (with J. A. Alonso) Electrons in Metals and Alloys, 1989; Liquid Metals, 1990; Chemical Physics of Liquids, 1990; Electron Density Theory of Atoms and Molecules, 1992; (with J. F. Mucci) Chemical Physics of Free Molecules, 1993; Electron Correlation in Molecules and Condensed Phases, 1996; (with L. S. Cederbaum and K. C. Kulander) Atoms and Molecules in Intense External Fields, 1997; Electron Correlation in the Solid State, 1999; (with C. W. Lung) Mechanical Properties of Metals, 1999; many scientific papers on quantum mechanics and statistical mechanics in Proceedings Royal Society, Phil. Magazine, Phys. Rev., Jl of Chem. Phys, etc. *Recreations:* music, chess, cricket. *Address:* Elmstead, 6 Northcroft Road, Englefield Green, Egham, Surrey TW20 0DU. *T:* (01784) 433078.

MARCH, Valerie, (Mrs Andrew March); *see* Masterson, V.

MARCHAMLEY, 4th Baron *cr* 1908; **William Francis Whiteley;** *b* 27 July 1968; *o s* of 3rd Baron Marchamley and of Sonia Kathleen Pedrick; *S* father, 1994. *Heir:* none.

MARCHANT, Clare Wynne; Director of Social Services and Housing, London Borough of Bromley, 1993–2000; *b* 13 June 1941; *d* of Glyn and Elma Morgan; *m* 1980, Harold Marchant. *Educ:* Horley Endowed Sch.; Banbury Grammar Sch.; UC Wales, Aberystwyth (BA Hons Philosophy 1963); UC Wales, Cardiff (DipSocSc 1964); Birmingham Univ. (Dip. Applied Social Sci. 1965). London Borough of Lewisham: Child Care Officer, 1965–67; Team Leader, 1967–71; Social Services Dist Officer, 1971–74; Principal Social Worker, 1974–87; Asst Dir (Social Services), RBK&C, 1987–93. *Recreations:* writing, sleeping, genealogy, local history, photography, enjoying myself. *Address:* Shaftesbury House, 15 Royal Circus Street, Greenwich, SE10 8SN.

MARCHANT, Ven. George John Charles; Archdeacon Emeritus and Canon Emeritus of Durham, since 1983; *b* 3 Jan. 1916; *s* of late T. Marchant, Little Stanmore, Mddx; *m* 1944, Eileen Lillian Kathleen, *d* of late F. J. Smith, FCIS; one *s* three *d*. *Educ:* St John's Coll., Durham (MA, BD); Tyndale Hall, Bristol. Deacon 1939, priest 1940, London; Curate of St Andrew's, Whitehall Park, N19, 1939–41; Licence to officiate, London dio., 1941–44 (in charge of Young Churchmen's Movement); Curate of St Andrew-the-Less, Cambridge (in charge of St Stephen's), 1944–48; Vicar of Holy Trinity, Skirbeck, Boston, 1948–54; Vicar of St Nicholas, Durham, 1954–74; Rural Dean of Durham, 1964–74; Hon. Canon of Durham Cathedral, 1972–74; Archdeacon of Auckland and Canon Residentiary, Durham Cathedral, 1974–83. Pre-Retirement Advr, Dio. Norwich Clergy, 1990–2000. Member of General Synod, 1970–80 (Proctor in Convocation for Dio. Durham). Chm. Editorial Bd, Anvil, 1983–91. *Publications:* (ed) Moving Forward to Retirement, 1996; contributed to: Baker's Dictionary of Theology, 1960; Bishops in the Church, 1966; articles in Evangelical Qly, Churchman, and Anvil; book reviews. *Recreations:* reading, music, bird watching, gardening. *Address:* 28 Greenways, Eaton, Norwich NR4 6PE. *T:* (01603) 458295.

MARCHANT, Graham Leslie; arts management consultant, since 1989; General Manager, Contemporary Dance Trust, 1994–98; *b* 2 Feb. 1945; *s* of late Leslie and Dorothy Marchant. *Educ:* King's School, Worcester; Selwyn College, Cambridge (MA). Administrator, Actors' Company, 1973–75; General Manager, English Music Theatre, 1975–78; Gen. Administrator, Opera North, 1978–82; Administrator, Tricycle Theatre, 1983–84; Chief Exec., Riverside Studios, 1984; Managing Dir, Playhouse Theatre Co., 1985–86; Dir, Arts Co-ordination, Arts Council, 1986–89; Head of Site Improvement, South Bank Centre, 1989–92. Director: Ballet Rambert Ltd, 1991–93; Lyric Theatre (Hammersmith) Trust, 1993–97; Chairman: London Dance Network, 1998–99; Nat. Dance Co-ordinating Cttee, 2000–; Director: Shobana Jeyasingh Dance Co., 1999–. FRSA 1999. *Recreations:* reading, gardening. *Address:* 43 Canonbury Square, N1 2AW.

MARCHWOOD, 3rd Viscount *cr* 1945, of Penang and of Marchwood, Southampton; **David George Staveley Penny;** Bt 1933; Baron 1937; Managing Director, since 1987, Chairman, since 1997, Moët Hennessy UK Ltd (formerly Moët & Chandon (London) Ltd); *b* 22 May 1936; *s* of 2nd Viscount Marchwood, MBE and Pamela (*d* 1979), *o d* of John Staveley Colton-Fox; *S* father, 1979; *m* 1964, Tessa Jane (*d* 1997), *d* of W. F. Norris; three *s*. *Educ:* Winchester College. 2nd Lt, Royal Horse Guards (The Blues), 1955–57. Joined Schweppes Ltd, 1958, and held various positions in the Cadbury Schweppes group before joining his present company. *Recreations:* Real tennis, golf, shooting, racing. *Heir: s* Hon. Peter George Worsley Penny [*b* 8 Oct. 1965; *m* 1995, Annabel, *d* of Rex Cooper; one *s* one *d*]. *Address:* Filberts, Aston Tirrold, near Didcot, Oxon OX11 9DG. *T:* (01235) 850386. *Clubs:* White's, MCC.

MARCKUS, Melvyn; Consultant, Cardew & Co., since 1998; *b* 1 Jan. 1944; *s* of late Norman Myer Marckus and of Violet Frances Mary Marckus (*née* Hughes); *m* 1st, 1970, Rosemary Virden (marr. diss. 1985); one *s* one *d*; 2nd, 1987, Rachel Mary Frances, *d* of Lord King of Wartnaby, *qv*. *Educ:* Worthing Grammar Sch. Journalist: Scotsman, 1962–66; Daily Mail, 1966–67; Guardian, 1967; Daily Mail, 1967–70; Daily Express, 1970–72; Sunday Telegraph, 1972–82 (Jt Dep. City Editor, 1979–82); Observer, 1982–93: City Editor, 1982–93; Editor, Observer Business, 1984–93; an Asst Editor, 1987; Exec. Dir, 1987; City Editor, The Times, 1993–96; Columnist, The Express, 1996–99. Consultant, Luther Pendragon, 1996–98. *Recreations:* fishing, films, literature. *Address:* Cardew & Co., 12 Suffolk Street, SW1Y 4HQ.

MARCUS, Prof. Rudolph Arthur; Arthur Amos Noyes Professor of Chemistry, California Institute of Technology, since 1978; *b* Montreal, 21 July 1923; *s* of Meyer Marcus and Esther Marcus (*née* Cohen); *m* 1949, Laura Hearne; three *s*. *Educ:* McGill Univ. (BSc Chemistry 1943; PhD 1946; Hon. DSc 1988). Postdoctoral research: NRCC, Ottawa, 1946–49; Univ. of N Carolina, 1949–51; Polytechnic Institute, Brooklyn: Asst Prof., 1951–54; Associate Prof., 1954–58; Prof., 1958–64; Acting Head, Div. of Phys. Chem., 1961–62; Prof., 1964–78, Head, Div. of Phys. Chem., 1967–68, Univ. of Illinois. Vis. Prof. of Theoretical Chem., Univ. of Oxford, 1975–76; Linnett Vis. Prof. of Chem., Univ. of Cambridge, 1996; Hon. Professor: Fudan Univ., Shanghai, 1994–; Inst. of Chem., Chinese Acad. of Scis, Beijing, 1995–. Mem., Sci. Cttees and Nat. Adv. Cttees, incl. External Adv. Bd, Nat. Sci. Foundn Center for Photoinduced Charge Transfer, 1990–; Internat. Advr in Chem., World Scientific Publishing, 1987; mem., numerous editl bds; Lectr, USA, Asia, Australia, Canada, Europe, Israel, USSR. Mem., Nat. Acad. of Sciences and other learned bodies; Foreign Member: Royal Soc., 1987; RSCan, 1993; Chinese Acad. of Scis, 1998. Hon. MRSC; Hon. Member: Internat. Soc. of Electrochemistry; Korean Chemical Soc., 1996. Hon. Fellow, UC, Oxford, 1995. Hon. DSc Oxford, 1995. Prizes incl. Wolf Prize in Chem., 1985; Nat. Medal of Science, 1989; Nobel Prize in Chem., 1992. *Publications:* contribs to sci jls, incl. articles on electrochemistry, electron transfer, unimolecular reactions. *Recreations:* tennis, ski-ing, music. *Address:* Noyes Laboratory of Chemical Physics, Caltech 127–72, Pasadena, CA 91125, USA. *T:* (626) 3956566; 331 S Hill Avenue, Pasadena, CA 91106–3405, USA.

MARDELL, Mark Ian; Political Correspondent, BBC News at Six, since 2000; *b* 10 Sept. 1957; *s* of Donald and Maureen Mardell; *m* 1990, Joanne Veale; one *s* one *d*. *Educ:* Priory

Sch., Banstead; Epsom Coll.; Univ. of Kent at Canterbury (BA Hons Politics 1979). Journalist: Radio Tees, 1980–82; Radio Aire, 1982; Indep. Radio News, 1983–87; Industrial Ed. and Reporter, Sharp End (C4), 1987–89; Political Corresp., BBC, 1989–93; Political Ed., Newsnight, 1993–2000. *Recreations:* reading, music, swimming. *Address:* 8 Heights Close, Banstead, Surrey SM7 1DR. *T:* (01737) 356526.

MARDELL, Peggy Joyce, CBE 1982; Regional Nursing Officer, North West Thames Regional Health Authority, 1974–82; *b* 8 July 1927; *d* of Alfred Edward and Edith Mary Mardell. *Educ:* George Spicer Sch., Enfield; Highlands Hosp., London (RFN); E Suffolk Hosp., Ipswich (Medallist, SRN); Queen Charlotte's Hosp. Battersea Coll. of Further Educn (Hons Dip., RNT). Queens Inst. of District Nursing, Guildford, 1951–52 (SCM); Ward Sister, Night Sister, Bethnal Green Hosp., 1953–55; Sister Tutor, Royal Surrey County Hosp., 1957–64; Asst Regional Nursing Officer, NE Metrop. Regional Hosp. Bd, 1964–70; Chief Regional Nursing Officer, NW Metrop. Regional Hosp. Bd, 1970–74. Lectr, British Red Cross, 1958–60; Examr, Gen. Nursing Council, 1962–70; Nurse Mem., Surrey AHA, 1977–82; Member: Royal Coll. of Nursing; Regional Nurse Trng Cttee, 1970–82; Assessor for Nat. Nursing Staff Cttee, 1970–82. *Recreations:* renovating old furniture, gardening, reading. *Address:* 3 Corvill Court, Shelley Road, Worthing, W Sussex BN11 4DF. *T:* (01903) 211876.

MARDER, His Honour Bernard Arthur; QC 1977; a Circuit Judge, 1983–98; President of the Lands Tribunal, 1993–98 (Member, 1989–98); *b* 25 Sept. 1928; *er s* of late Samuel and Marie Marder; *m* 1953, Sylvia Levy (MBE 1988); one *s* one *d*. *Educ:* Bury Grammar Sch.; Manchester Univ. (LLB 1951). Called to the Bar, Gray's Inn, 1952. A Recorder of the Crown Court, 1979–83. Formerly Asst Comr, Local Govt and Parly Boundary Commns; Chairman: Panel of Inquiry into W Yorks Structure Plan, 1979; Mental Health Review Tribunals, 1987–89. Pres., Land Inst., 1997–99. Mem. Bd, Orange Tree Theatre, 1986–2000; Trustee: Richmond Parish Lands Charity, 1987–96 (Chm., 1993–96); Richmond Museum, 1996–; Petersham Meadows Trust, 1999–. Hon. FSVA 1994; Hon. RICS 1999. *Recreations:* music, theatre, wine, walking.

MAREK, John, PhD; Member (Lab) Wrexham, National Assembly for Wales, since 1999; Deputy Presiding Officer, since 2000; *b* 24 Dec. 1940; *m* 1964, Anne. *Educ:* Univ. of London (BSc (Hons), PhD). Lecturer in Applied Mathematics, University College of Wales, Aberystwyth, 1966–83. MP (Lab) Wrexham, 1983–2001. Opposition frontbench spokesman: on health, 1985–87; on treasury and economic affairs, and on the Civil Service, 1987–92. *Publications:* various research papers. *Address:* National Assembly for Wales, Cardiff Bay, Cardiff CF99 1NA. *T:* (constituency office) (01978) 364334.

MARGADALE, 2nd Baron *cr* 1964, of Islay, Co. Argyll; **James Ian Morrison,** TD, DL; director of companies; farmer; *b* 17 July 1930; *e s* of 1st Baron Margadale, TD and Hon. Margaret Esther Lucie Smith (*d* 1980), 2nd *d* of Viscount Hambleden; *S* father, 1996; *m* 1952, Clare Barclay; two *s* one *d*. *Educ:* Eton Coll.; Royal Agricultural Coll., Cirencester. 2nd Lieut, Life Guards, 1949–50; Major, Royal Wilts Yeo., 1960–68; Hon. Colonel: A (RWY) Sqn Royal Yeomanry RAC TA, and B (RWY) Sqn Royal Wessex Yeomanry, 1982–89; Royal Wessex Yeomanry RAC TA, 1984–89. Member, Queen's Body Guard for Scotland, 1960–. County Councillor, Wilts, 1955 and 1973–77, County Alderman, 1969; Chairman, W Wilts Conservative Assoc., 1967–71, Pres., 1972–84; Chm., Wilts CLA, 1978–81. Chm., Tattersalls Cttee, 1969–80. DL 1977, High Sheriff 1971, Wiltshire. *Recreations:* racing, shooting, hunting. *Heir:* *s* Hon. Alastair John Morrison [*b* 4 April 1958; *m* 1988, Lady Sophia Louise Sydney Murphy (marr. diss. 1999), *yr d* of Duke and Duchess of Devonshire, *qqv*; one *s* one *d*; *m* 1999, Mrs Amanda Wace, *d* of late Michael Fuller]. *Address:* Fonthill House, Tisbury, Salisbury, Wilts SP3 5SA; Islay Estate Office, Bridgend, Islay, Argyll PA44 7PA. *Clubs:* White's, Jockey.

See also Hon. Sir C. A. Morrison, Hon. M. A. Morrison, Viscount Trenchard.

MARGÁIN, Hugo B., Hon. GCVO 1975; Ambassador of Mexico to the United States, 1965–70 and 1977–82; *b* 13 Feb. 1913; *s* of Cesar R. Margáin and Maria Teresa Gleason de Margáin; *m* 1941, Margarita Charles de Margáin; two *s* three *d* (and one *s* decd). *Educ:* National Univ. of Mexico (UNAM); National Sch. of Jurisprudence (LLB). Prof. of Constitutional Law, 1947, of Constitutional Writs, 1951–56, and of Fiscal Law, 1952–56, Univ. of Mexico. Govt posts include: Dir-Gen., Mercantile Transactions Tax, 1951–52, and Dir-Gen., Income Tax, 1952–59, Min. for Finance. Official Mayor, Min. for Industry and Commerce, 1959–61; Dep. Minister of Finance, Sept. 1961–Dec. 1964; Sec. of Finance, Aug. 1970–May 1973; Ambassador to the UK, 1973–77. Chm., Nat. Commn on Corporate Profit-Sharing (ie labour participation), 1963–64; Govt Rep. on Bd of Nat. Inst. for Scientific Res., 1962–63 (Chm. of Bd, 1963–64). Holds hon. degrees from univs in USA. *Publications:* Avoidance of Double Taxation Based on the Theory of the Source of Taxable Income, 1956; Preliminary Study on Tax Codification, 1957; (with H. L. Gumpel) Taxation in Mexico, 1957; Civil Rights and the Writ of Amparo in Administrative Law, 1958; The Role of Fiscal Law in Economic Development, 1960; Profit Sharing Plan, 1964; Housing Projects for Workers (Infonavit), 1971. *Recreations:* riding, swimming. *Address:* Fujiyama No 745, Col. Las Aguilas, Del. Alvaro Obregón, México 01710 DF, México.

MARGASON, Geoffrey, CEng, FICE; Director, Transport and Road Research Laboratory, Crowthorne, 1984–88, retired (Deputy Director, 1980–84); *b* 19 Sept. 1933; *s* of Henry and Edna Margason; *m* 1958, Bernice Thompson; one *s* two *d*. *Educ:* Humberston Foundation Sch., Cleethorpes; Loughborough College of Advanced Technology (DLCEng). With British Transport Commission and Mouchel Associates, Consulting Engineers, until 1960; Transport and Road Research Laboratory: Researcher in Geotechnics, 1960–69; Research Manager in Construction Planning, Scottish Br. and Transport Planning, 1969–75; Sen. Research Manager in Transport Operations, 1975–78; Head of Research and Science Policy Unit, Depts of Environment and Transport, 1978–80. *Publications:* papers in jls of various professional instns and to nat. and internat. confs on range of topics in highway transportation; reports of TRRL. *Recreations:* pétanque, golf. *Address:* Franche Cottage, Pankridge Street, Crondall, Farnham, Surrey GU10 5QZ. *T:* (01252) 850399. *Club:* Crondall Pétanque.

MARGERISON, Thomas Alan; author, journalist and broadcaster on scientific subjects; Consultant, British Nuclear Forum, since 1989; *b* 13 Nov. 1923; *s* of late Ernest Alan Margerison and Isabel McKenzie; *m* 1950, Pamela Alice Tilbrook; two *s*. *Educ:* Huntingdon Grammar Sch.; Hymers Coll., Hull; King's Sch., Macclesfield; Sheffield University. Research Physicist, 1949; film script writer, Film Producers Guild, 1950; Scientific Editor, Butterworths sci. pubns, Ed. Research, 1951–56; Man. Editor, Heywood Pubns and National Trade Press, 1956. First Scientific Editor, The New Scientist, 1956–61; Science Corresp., Sunday Times, 1961; Dep. Editor, Sunday Times Magazine, 1962; Man. Dir, Thomson Technical Developments Ltd, 1964; Dep. Man. Dir, 1967–69, Chief Exec., 1969–71, London Weekend Television; Dir, 1966, Chm., 1971–75, Computer Technology Ltd. Formerly Dir, Nuclear Electricity Information Gp. Chm., Communications Cttee, UK Nat. Commn for UNESCO. Worked for many years with Tonight team on BBC. Responsible for applying computers to evening newspapers in Reading and Hemel Hempstead. *Publications:* articles and television scripts, indifferent scientific papers; (ed) popular science books. *Recreation:* sailing. *Club:* Savile.

MARGESSON, family name of **Viscount Margesson.**

MARGESSON, 2nd Viscount *cr* 1942, of Rugby; **Francis Vere Hampden Margesson;** *b* 17 April 1922; *o s* of 1st Viscount Margesson, PC, MC, and Frances H. Leggett (*d* 1977), New York; *S* father, 1965; *m* 1958, Helena, *d* of late Heikki Backstrom, Finland; one *s* three *d*. *Educ:* Eton; Trinity Coll., Oxford. Served War of 1939–45, as Sub-Lt, RNVR. A Director of Thames & Hudson Publications, Inc., New York, 1949–53. ADC to Governor of the Bahamas, 1956; Information Officer, British Consulate-General, NY, 1964–70. *Heir:* *s* Major the Hon. Richard Francis David Margesson, Coldstream Guards [*b* 25 Dec. 1960; *m* 1990, Wendy Maree, *d* of James Hazelton]. *Address:* 63 The Hills, Port Ewen, New York, NY 12466, USA.

MARGETSON, Sir John (William Denys), KCMG 1986 (CMG 1979); HM Diplomatic Service, retired; Gentleman Usher of the Blue Rod, since 1992; *b* 9 Oct. 1927; *yr s* of Very Rev. W. J. Margetson and Marion Jenoure; *m* 1963, Miranda, *d* of Sir William Menzies Coldstream, CBE and Mrs Nancy Spender; one *s* one *d*. *Educ:* Blundell's; St John's Coll., Cambridge (choral scholar; MA). Lieut, Life Guards, 1947–49. Colonial Service, District Officer, Tanganyika, 1951–60 (Private Sec. to Governor, Sir Edward Twining, subseq. Lord Twining, 1956–57); entered Foreign (subseq. Diplomatic) Service, 1960; The Hague, 1962–64; speech writer to Foreign Sec., Rt Hon. George Brown, MP, 1966–68; Head of Chancery, Saigon, 1968–70; Counsellor 1971, seconded to Cabinet Secretariat, 1971–74; Head of Chancery, UK Delegn to NATO, 1974–78; Ambassador to Vietnam, 1978–80; seconded to MoD as Senior Civilian Instructor, RCDS, 1981–82; Ambassador and Dep. Perm. Rep. to UN, NY, and Pres., UN Trusteeship Council, 1983–84; Ambassador to the Netherlands, 1984–87; Special Rep. of the Sec. of State for For. and Commonwealth Affairs, 1994–98. Dir, John S. Cohen Foundn, 1988–93. Chm., Foster Parents Plan (UK), 1988–90. Patron, Suffolk Internat. Trade Gp, 1988–90; Jt Pres., Suffolk and SE Cambridgeshire 1992 Club, 1988–90. Chairman: RSCM, 1988–94; Jt Cttee, London Royal Schs of Music, 1991–94; Yehudi Menuhin Sch., 1990–94; Trustee: Fitzwilliam Museum Trust, 1990–98; Ouseley Trust, 1991–97; Music in Country Churches, 1993–2000. Hon. RCM 1992; FRSCM 1994. *Recreation:* music. *Club:* Brooks's.

MARGETTS, Robert John, CBE 1996; FREng; FIChemE; Chairman: Legal & General Group PLC, since 2000 (Vice Chairman, 1998–2000); BOC Group, since 2002; Chairman, Natural Environment Research Council, since 2001; *b* 10 Nov. 1946; *s* of John William and Ellen Mary Margetts; *m* 1969, Joan Sandra Laws; three *s* one *d*. *Educ:* Highgate Sch.; Trinity Hall, Cambridge (BA Natural Scis and Chem. Engrg). FIChemE 1985; FREng (FEng 1988). Joined ICI, 1969: Process Design Engr, Agricl Div., Billingham, 1969; subseq. various managerial posts, including: Director: Agricl Div., 1982–85; Petrochemicals and Plastics Div., 1985; Res. and Ops, ICI Chemicals and Polymers Gp, 1987; ICI PLC: Dir, ICI Engrg, 1987–89; Gen. Manager, Personnel, 1989–90; Chm. and Chief Exec., Tioxide Gp PLC, 1991–92; Exec. Dir, 1992–97; Vice Chm., 1998–2000; Chm., ICI Pension Fund Trustee Ltd, 1994–2000. Non-exec. Dir, 1996–, Chm., Audit Cttee, 1998–2000, Legal & Gen. Gp PLC; non-executive Director: English China Clays PLC, 1992–99; Anglo American PLC, 1999–; Chm. Europe, Huntsman Corp. (USA), 2000–. Gov., Mem. Finance Cttee, and Chm., IRC in Process Systems, ICSTM, 1991–; Member: Council for Ind. and Higher Educn, 1992–; Bd, CEFIC, 1993–95 and 1998–2000; Council, CIA, 1993–96 and 2001–; Council for Sci. and Technol., 1998–; Adv. Cttee on Business and the Envmt, 1999–; Chm., Action for Engrg, 1995–97. Vice-Pres., Royal Acad. of Engrg, 1994–97. Hon. FIC 1999. Hon. DEng Sheffield, 1997. *Recreations:* sailing, ski-ing, tennis, watersports. *Address:* Legal & General Group PLC, Temple Court, 11 Queen Victoria Street, EC4N 4TP.

MARGOLYES, Miriam; actress; *b* 18 May 1941; *d* of late Dr Joseph Margolyes and Ruth (*née* Walters). *Educ:* Oxford High Sch.; Newnham Coll., Cambridge; Guildhall Sch. of Music and Drama (LGSM 1959). *Films* include: Rime of the Ancient Mariner, 1976; Stand Up, Virgin Soldiers, 1977; Little Shop of Horrors, 1986; The Good Father, 1987; Body Contact, 1987; Little Dorrit, 1988; Pacific Heights, 1990; I Love You to Death, 1990; The Butcher's Wife, 1991; As You Like It, 1992; Ed and His Dead Mother, 1993; The Age of Innocence, 1993; Immortal Beloved, 1994; Babe, 1995; Balto, 1995; James and the Giant Peach, 1996; Romeo and Juliet, 1996; Different for Girls, 1996; The IMAX Nutcracker, 1997; The First Snow of Winter, 1998; Left Luggage, 1998; Sunshine, 1999; Dreaming of Joseph Lees, 1999; End of Days, 1999; House!, 2000; Cats and Dogs, 2001; *theatre* includes: Dickens' Women (one-woman show), Duke of York's, 1991; She Stoops to Conquer, Queen's, 1993; The Killing of Sister George, Ambassador's, 1995; *television* includes: Take a Letter Mr Jones, A Kick Up the Eighties, The History Man, 1981; Blackadder, 1983, 1986, 1988; Oliver Twist, 1985; Poor Little Rich Girl, 1987; The Life and Loves of a She Devil, 1990; Frannie's Turn, 1992; Cold Comfort Farm, 1995; The Phoenix and the Carpet, 1997; Supply & Demand, 1998; Vanity Fair, 1998; *radio performances* include The Queen and I, 1993. Best Supporting Actress, LA Critics Circle, 1989; Best Supporting Actress, BAFTA, 1993. *Recreations:* reading, talking, eating, Italy. *Address:* c/o Peters, Fraser & Dunlop, Drury House, 34–43 Russell Street, WC2B 5HA. *Fax:* (020) 7836 9539.

MARGRIE, Victor Robert, CBE 1984; FCSD; studio potter; *b* 29 Dec. 1929; *s* of Robert and Emily Miriam Margrie; *m* 1955, Janet Smithers (separated); three *d*. *Educ:* Southgate County Grammar Sch.; Hornsey Sch. of Art (NDD, ATD 1952). FSIAD 1975. Part-time teaching at various London art colls, 1952–56; own workshop, making stoneware and latterly porcelain, 1954–71; Head of Ceramics Dept, Harrow Sch. of Art, 1956–71 (founded Studio Pottery Course, 1963); Sec., Crafts Adv. Cttee, 1971–77; Dir, Crafts Council, 1977–84; Professorial appt, RCA, 1984–85; own studio, Bristol, 1985. One-man exhibns, British Craft Centre (formerly Crafts Centre of GB), 1964, 1966 and 1968; represented in V&A Museum and other collections. Vice-Chm., Crafts Centre of GB, 1965; Member: Cttee for Art and Design, DATEC, 1979–84; Cttee for Art and Design, CNAA, 1981–84; Design Bursaries Bd, RSA, 1980–84; Working Party, Gulbenkian Craft Initiative, 1985–88; Fine Art Adv. Cttee, British Council, 1983–86; UK National Commn for UNESCO, 1984–85 (also Mem., Culture Adv. Cttee); Adv. Council, V&A Mus., 1979–84; Craftsmen Potters Assoc., 1960–89; Internat. Acad. of Ceramics, 1972–; Cttee, Nat. Video and Electronic Archive of the Crafts, 1993–. Ext. Examiner, Royal Coll. of Art: Dept of Ceramics and Glass, 1977; Dept of Silversmithing and Jewellery, 1978–80; Ext. Advisor, Dept of Ceramics, UWE (formerly Bristol Polytechnic), 1987–; Mem., Bd of Studies in Fine Art, Univ. of London, 1989–94; Advr, Faculty of Fine Art, Cardiff Inst. of Higher Educn, 1992–94; Vis. Prof., Univ. of Westminster (formerly Poly. of Central London), 1992–96. Governor: Herts Coll. of Art and Design, 1977–79; Camberwell Sch. of Art and Crafts, 1975–84; W Surrey Coll. of Art and Design, 1978–87; Loughborough Coll. of Art and Design, 1984–89, 1990–93. Associate Editor: Studio Pottery, 1993–2000; Ceramics in Society, 2000–. *Publications:* contributed to: Oxford Dictionary of Decorative Arts, 1975; Europaische Keramik Seit

1950, 1979; Lucie Rie, 1981; contrib. specialist pubns and museum catalogues. *Address:* Bowlders, Doccombe, Moretonhampstead, Devon TQ13 8SS. *T:* (01647) 440264.

MARÍN-GONZALEZ, Manuel; Grand Cross of Isabel la Católica; Visiting Professor, University of Carlos III, Madrid, 1999; *b* 21 Oct. 1949; *m* 1983; two *d. Educ:* Univ. of Madrid; Centre d'études européennes, Univ. of Nancy; Collège d'Europe, Bruges. MP for Ciudad Real, La Mancha, 1977–82; Sec. of State for relations with EEC, 1982–85; a Vice Pres., CEC, later EC, 1986–99. Mem., Spanish Socialist Party, 1974–.

MARINCOWITZ, Dr John; Headmaster, Queen Elizabeth's School, Barnet, since 1998; *b* 19 Dec. 1950; *s* of Nicholas and Diana Marincowitz; *m* 1979, Miriam Salie; one *s* one *d. Educ:* St John's Coll., Johannesburg; Witwatersrand Univ. (BA); UCW, Aberystwyth (BA Hons); SOAS, London Univ. (PhD 1985); Inst. of Educn, London Univ. (NPQH). History teacher, Trafalgar High Sch., Cape Town, 1979–82; Queen Elizabeth's School, Barnet: history teacher, 1985–86; Hd of Year, 1986–88; Hd of Sixth Form, Senior Master, 1988–98. Chm. Govs, Little Heath Sch., Herts, 1994–98. FRSA 1998. Mem., RYA, 1999. *Recreations:* sailing, non-fiction, classical music and jazz, Rugby Union (particular interest in English and African sides). *Address:* c/o Queen Elizabeth's School, Queen's Road, Barnet, Herts EN5 4DQ. T: (020) 8441 4646.

MARINKER, Prof. Marshall, OBE 1991; FRCGP; Visiting Professor in General Practice, Guy's, King's and St Thomas' School of Medicine of King's College London (formerly United Medical and Dental Schools of Guy's and St Thomas' Hospitals), since 1991; *b* 2 March 1930; *s* of Isidor and Sarah Marinker; *m* 1st, 1955; two *s* one *d*; 2nd, 1978, Jeanette Miller. *Educ:* Haberdashers' Aske's Sch., Hampstead; Middlesex Hosp. Med. Sch., Univ. of London (MB, BS 1956). FRCGP 1972. Principal in Gen. Practice, Grays, 1959–73; Sen. Lectr, St Mary's Hosp. Med. Sch., 1971–73; Foundation Prof. of Gen. Practice and Head, Dept of Community Health, Univ. of Leicester, 1974–82; Dir, MSD Foundn, 1982–92; Dir of Medical Educn, MSD Ltd, 1992–95. Visiting Professor: Univ. of Iowa, 1973; Univ. of Tampere, 1976; Roche Vis. Prof., NZ Coll. of GPs, 1977; Dozar Prof., Ben Gurion Univ., 1981; Sir James Wattie Meml Vis. Prof., NZ, 1982. Chm., R&D Cttee, High Security Psychiatric Services Bd, NHS, 1996–. Royal College of General Practitioners: Res. Registrar, 1967–70; William Pickles Lectr, 1974; Mem. Council, 1974–89; Chm., Educn Div., 1981–84; Chair, Cttee on Med. Ethics, 1987–89; George Abercrombie Prize, 1991. Chm., Council of Europe Wkg Party on the Future of Gen. Practice, 1975–77. Freeman, City of London, 1995. Hon. DM Tampere, 1982. *Publications:* (jtly) Treatment or Diagnosis?, 1970, 2nd edn 1984; (jtly) The Future General Practitioner, 1972; (ed jtly) Practice: a handbook of primary medical care, annually 1978–; (ed jtly) Teaching General Practice, 1981; (ed jtly) Towards Quality in General Practice, 1986; (ed) Medical Audit and General Practice, 1990, 2nd edn 1995; (ed) Controversies in Health Care Policy, 1995; (ed) Sense and Sensibility in Health Care, 1996; (jtly) Clinical Futures, 1998; pamphlets, lectures and papers on theory of gen. practice, med. educn, health service policy and med. ethics. *Recreations:* conversation, poetry, theatre, classical music, reading good thrillers, communing with my dog. *Address:* 8 St Peter's Church, 124 Dartmouth Park Hill, N19 5HL. *T:* (020) 7263 1586, *Fax:* (020) 7263 6759; *e-mail:* marshall@marinker.com.

MARIO, Dr Ernest; Chief Executive, since 1993, and Chairman, since 1997, Alza Corporation, Mountain View (Co-Chairman, 1993–97); *b* 12 June 1938; *s* of Jerry and Edith Mario; *m* 1961, Mildred Martha Daume; three *s. Educ:* Rutgers College of Pharmacy, New Brunswick, NJ (BSc Pharmacy); Univ. of Rhode Island (MS; PhD). Vice Pres., Manufacturing Operation, Smith Kline, 1974; E. R. Squibb & Sons: Vice Pres., Manufacturing for US Pharmaceutical Div., 1977; Vice Pres. and Gen. Man., Chemical Div., 1979; Pres., Chemical Engrg Div. and Sen. Vice Pres. of company, 1981; Pres. and Chief Exec. Officer, Squibb Medical Product, 1983; elected to Bd, 1984; joined Glaxo Inc. as Pres. and Chief Exec. Officer, 1986; apptd to Bd of Glaxo Holdings, 1988; Chief Exec., 1989–93; Dep. Chm., 1991–93. Chairman: Nat. Foundn for Infectious Diseases, Washington, 1989; American Foundn for Pharmaceutical Educn, NY, 1991–. *Recreations:* golf, swimming. *Address:* Alza, 1900 Charleston Road, Mountain View, CA 94043, USA.

MARJORIBANKS, Sir James Alexander Milne, KCMG 1965 (CMG 1954); Chairman, Scotland in Europe, 1979–90; *b* 29 May 1911; *y s* of Rev. Thomas Marjoribanks of that Ilk, DD, and Mary Ord, *d* of William Logan, Madras CS; *m* 1936, Sonya Patricia (*d* 1981), *d* of David Stanley-Alder, Alderford Grange, Sible Hedingham, Essex, and Sylvia Marie Stanley; one *d. Educ:* Merchiston; Edinburgh Academy; Edinburgh Univ. (MA, 1st class hons). Entered Foreign Service, Nov. 1934; HM Embassy, Peking, 1935–38; Consulate-General, Hankow, 1938; Marseilles, 1939–40; Consul, Jacksonville, 1940–42; Vice-Consul, New York, 1942–44; Asst to UK Political Rep., Bucharest, 1944–45; Foreign Office, 1945–49; Dep. to Secretary of State for Foreign Affairs in Austrian Treaty negotiations, 1947–49; Official Secretary, UK High Commn, Canberra, 1950–52; Dep. Head of UK Delegation to High Authority of European Coal and Steel Community, 1952–55; Cabinet Office, 1955–57; HM Minister (Economic), Bonn, 1957–62; Asst Under-Secretary of State, Foreign Office, 1962–65; Ambassador and Head of UK Delegn to European Economic Community, European Atomic Energy Community and ECSC, 1965–71. Director: Scottish Council (Develt and Industry), 1971–81 (Vice-Pres., 1981–83); The Distillers Co. Ltd, 1971–76; Governing Mem., Inveresk Research International, 1978–90. Gen. Council Assessor, Edinburgh Univ. Ct, 1975–79. *Recreation:* hill walking. *Club:* New (Edinburgh).

MARJORIBANKS, Prof. Kevin McLeod, PhD; FSS; FASSA; FACE; Professor of Education, University of Adelaide, 1975–86, and since 1994 (Vice-Chancellor, 1987–93); *b* 25 July 1940; *s* of Hugh and Irene Marjoribanks; *m* 1962, Janice Humphreys; one *s* one *d. Educ:* Universities of: New South Wales (BSc); New England (BA); Harvard (MA); Toronto (PhD). FSS 1977; FASSA 1982; FACE 1983. Asst Prof., Univ. of Toronto, 1969; Lectr, Univ. of Oxford, 1970–74; Pro Vice-Chancellor, Univ. of Adelaide, 1986. Visiting Professor: Stanford Univ., 1979; Haifa Univ., 1983; (in Educn) Oxford Univ., 1994–95; Harvard Univ., 1994–95. *Publications:* Environments for Learning, 1974; Families and their Learning Environments, 1979; Ethnic Families and Children's Achievements, 1980; The Foundations of Children's Learning, 1989; Families, Schools and Learning: a study of children's learning environments, 1993; Australian Education: a review of research, 1999–. *Recreations:* writing, music listening, walking. *Address:* 81 Molesworth Street, North Adelaide, SA 5006, Australia. *Club:* Adelaide.

MARK, Dr Alan Francis, DCNZM 2001; CBE 1989; FRSNZ 1978; Professor of Botany, University of Otago, 1975-98, now Professor Emeritus; *b* 19 June 1932; *s* of Cyril Lionel Mark and Frances Evelyn Mark (*née* Marshall); *m* 1958, Patricia Kaye Davie; two *s* two *d. Educ:* Univ. of New Zealand (BSc 1953; MSc 1955); Duke Univ., N Carolina (James B. Duke Fellow, 1957; Phi Beta Kappa, 1958; PhD 1958). Sen. Res. Fellow, 1960–64, Res. Advr, 1965–2000, Hellaby Indigenous Grasslands Res. Trust; University of Otago: Lectr in Botany, 1960–65; Sen. Lectr, 1966–69; Associate Prof., 1969–75. Chm., Guardians of Lakes Manapouri, Monowai and Te Anau, 1973–99. Mem., Royal NZ Forest and Bird Protection Soc. *Publications:* (with Nancy M. Adams) New Zealand Alpine Plants, 1973, 3rd edn 1995; contrib. numerous scientific papers. *Recreations:* enjoying the outdoors, nature conservation. *Address:* 205 Wakari Road, Helensburgh, Dunedin, New Zealand. *T:* (3) 4763229, (office) (3) 4797573; *e-mail:* amark@otago.ac.nz.

MARK, Janet Marjorie; freelance writer, since 1976; *b* 22 June 1943; *d* of Colin Denis Brisland and Marjorie Léa Brisland (*née* Harrow); *m* 1969, Neil Mark (marr. diss. 1989); one *s* one *d. Educ:* Ashford (Kent) Grammar Sch.; Canterbury Coll. of Art. (NDD 1965). Secondary Sch. teacher, 1965–71. *Publications* include: Thunder and Lightnings, 1976 (Penguin/Guardian Award, Carnegie Medal); The Ennead, 1978; Divide and Rule, 1979; Nothing to be Afraid of, 1980; Aquarius, 1982; Feet, 1983 (Angel Award); Handles, 1983 (Carnegie Medal); Zeno was Here, 1987 (Angel Award); A Can of Worms, 1990; The Hillingdon Fox, 1991; Great Frog and Mighty Moose, 1992; They Do Things Differently There, 1994; A Fine Summer Knight, 1995; The Tale of Tobias, 1995; God's Story, 1997; The Sighting, 1997; The Eclipse of the Century, 1999; Heathrow Nights, 2000; reviews and articles for Signal Magazine and TES. *Recreation:* gardening. *Address:* 98 Howard Street, Oxford OX4 3BG. *T:* (01865) 727702.

MARK, Sir Robert, GBE 1977; Kt 1973; QPM 1965; Commissioner, Metropolitan Police, 1972–77 (Deputy Commissioner, 1968–72); *b* Manchester, 13 March 1917; *y s* of late John Mark and Louisa Mark (*née* Hobson); *m* 1941, Kathleen Mary Leahy (*d* 1997); one *s* one *d. Educ:* William Hulme's Grammar Sch., Manchester. Constable to Chief Superintendent, Manchester City Police, 1937–42, 1947–56; Chief Constable of Leicester, 1957–67; Assistant Commissioner, Metropolitan Police, 1967–68. Vis. Fellow, Nuffield Coll., Oxford, 1970–78 (MA Oxon 1971). Member: Standing Advisory Council of Penal System, 1966; Adv. Cttee on Police in Northern Ireland, 1969; Assessor to Lord Mountbatten during his Inquiry into Prison Security, 1966. Royal Armoured Corps, 1942–47: Lieut, Phantom (GHQ Liaison Regt), North-West Europe, 1944–45; Major, Control Commission for Germany, 1945–47. Lecture tour of N America for World Affairs Council and FCO, Oct. 1971; Edwin Stevens Lecture to the Laity, RCM, 1972; Dimbleby Meml Lecture (BBC TV), 1973. Director: Phoenix Assurance Co. Ltd, 1977–85; Control Risks Ltd, 1982–87. Mem. Cttee, AA, 1977–87; Governor and Mem. Admin. Bd, Corps of Commissionaires, 1977–86; Hon. Freeman, City of Westminster, 1977. Hon. LLM Leicester Univ., 1967; Hon. DLitt Loughborough, 1976; Hon. LLD: Manchester, 1978; Liverpool, 1978. KStJ 1977. *Publications:* Policing a Perplexed Society, 1977; In the Office of Constable, 1978. *Address:* Esher, Surrey KT10 8LU.

MARKESINIS, Prof. Basil Spyridonos, PhD, LLD, DCL; FBA 1997; Professor of Common Law and Civil Law, and Chairman of Institute of Global Law, University College London, since 2001; Senior Adviser on European Affairs, Clifford Chance, since 1999; *b* 10 July 1944; *s* of Spyros B. Markesinis (former Prime Minister of Greece) and Ieta Markesinis; *m* 1970, Eugenie (*née* Trypanis); one *s* one *d. Educ:* Univ. of Athens (LLB, DIur); MA, PhD, LLD Cambridge; DCL Oxford. Asst Prof., Law Faculty, Univ. of Athens, 1965–68; Gulbenkian Res. Fellow, Churchill Coll., Cambridge, 1970–74; called to the Bar, Gray's Inn, 1973, Bencher, 1991; Fellow of Trinity Coll., Cambridge, and Univ. Lectr in Law, 1975–86; Denning Prof. of Comparative Law, Univ. of London, at QMC, subseq. QMW, 1986–93; Dep. Dir, Centre for Commercial Law Studies, Univ. of London, 1986–93; Prof. of Eur. Private Law, UCL, 1993–95; University of Oxford: Fellow: LMH, 1995–99; Brasenose Coll., 1999–2000; Clifford Chance Prof. of European Law, 1995–99, of Comparative Law, 1999–2000; Founder Dir, Centre, then Inst., of Eur. and Comparative Law, 1995–2000; Prof. of Anglo-Amer. Private Law, Leiden Univ., 1986–2000, and Founder and Dir, Leiden Inst. of Anglo-American Law, 1987–2000. Advocate to Greek Supreme Court, 1976–86. Visiting Professor: Univs of Paris I and II; Siena; Rome; Cornell; Michigan (Ann Arbor); Texas (Austin); Francqui Vis. Prof., Univ. of Gent, 1989–90; Jamail Regents' Prof. of Law, Univ. of Texas, Austin, 1998–. Lectures: Atkin, Reform Club, 1989; Shimizu, LSE, 1989; Lionel Cohen Meml, Hebrew Univ. of Jerusalem, 1993; Wilberforce, 1998. Mem., Council of Management, British Inst. of Internat. and Comparative Law, 1993–2000. Associate Fellow, Internat. Acad. of Comp. Law, 1987–98; Mem., Amer. Law Inst., 1989; Corresponding Fellow: Royal Belgian Acad., 1990; Acad. of Athens, 1994; Foreign Fellow, Royal Netherlands Acad. of Arts and Scis, 1995; Corresp. Collaborator, UNIDROIT, 1992. Hon. QC 1998. DIur (*hc*): Ghent, 1992; Paris I (Panthéon-Sorbonne), 1998; Munich, 1999. Humboldt Forschungspreise, 1996; Univ. Prize, Leiden, 1996. Officer's Cross, Order of Merit (Germany), 1992; Officier, Ordre des Palmes Académiques (France), 1992; Officier, Légion d'Honneur (France), 2000 (Chevalier, 1995); Comdr, Order of Merit (Germany), 1998; Kt Comdr, Order of Merit (Italy), 1999 (Officer, 1995); Comdr, Order of Honour (Greece), 2000. *Publications:* The Mother's right to Guardianship according to the Greek Civil Code, 1968; The Theory and Practice of Dissolution of Parliament, 1972 (Yorke Prize); The English Law of Torts, 1976; (jtly) An Outline of the Law of Agency, 1979, 4th edn 1998; (jtly) Richterliche Rechtspolitik im Haftungsrecht, 1981; (jtly) Tortious Liability for unintentional harm in the Common Law and the Civil Law, 2 vols, 1982; (jtly) Tort Law, 1984, 4th edn 1999; The German Law of Torts: a comparative introduction, 1986, 4th edn 2002; (gen. ed. and contrib.) The Gradual Convergence: foreign ideas, foreign influences and English law on the eve of the 21st century, 1994; (ed and contrib.) Bridging the Channel, 1996; Foreign Law and Comparative Methodology: a subject and a thesis, 1997; (jtly) The German Law of Contract and Restitution, 1998; (gen. ed. and contrib.) Protecting Privacy, 1998; The Impact of the Human Rights Bill on English Law, 1998; (jtly) Tortious Liability of Statutory Bodies, 1999; Always on the Same Path: essays on foreign law and comparative methodology, 2001; ed. and contrib. many articles in learned jls in Belgium, Canada, England, France, Germany, Greece, Israel, Italy and USA. *Recreations:* painting, music, archaeological digging, chess. *Address:* University College London Institute of Global Law, Bentham House, Endsleigh Gardens, WC1H 0EG. *T:* (020) 7679 1478; Middleton Stoney House, Middleton Stoney, Bicester, Oxfordshire OX6 8SA. *T:* (01869) 343560.

MARKEY, Air Vice-Marshal Peter Desmond, OBE 1986; General Manager, NATO Maintenance and Supply Agency, Luxembourg, since 1999; *b* 28 March 1943; *s* of Althorpe Hazel Christopher Markey and Marjorie Joyce Markey (*née* Thomas); *m* 1966, Judith Mary Widdowson; one *s* one *d. Educ:* RAF Coll. Cranwell; Open Univ. (BA 1980); Cranfield Univ. (MSc 1994). RAF Supply Officer: commissioned 1964; served Singapore, France and UK to 1981; NDC, 1981–82; HQ Strike Comd, 1982–83; HQ AFCENT, Netherlands, 1983–85; MoD Carlisle, 1986–88; Station Comdr, Carlisle, 1988 89; RCDS 1990; MoD Central Staff, 1991; Dept of AMSO, 1991; HQ Logistics Comd, 1994; Dir Gen., Support Mgt, RAF, 1995–97; Dir of Resources, NATO, Luxembourg, 1997–99. *Publications:* papers and contribs to learned jls. *Recreations:* running, mountain walking, travelling. *Address:* NAMSA, 8302 Capellen, Luxembourg. *T:* 30636501. *Club:* Royal Air Force.

MARKHAM, Sir Charles (John), 3rd Bt *cr* 1911; *b* 2 July 1924; *s* of Sir Charles Markham, 2nd Bt, and Gwladys, *e d* of late Hon. Rupert Beckett; *S* father 1952; *m* 1949, Valerie (*d* 1998), *o d* of Lt-Col E. Barry-Johnston, Makuyu, Kenya; two *s* one *d. Educ:* Eton. Served War of 1939–45, Lieut in 11th Hussars (despatches). Vice-Chm., Nairobi Co. Council, 1953–55; MLC Kenya, 1955–60. Pres., Royal Agricultural Soc., Kenya, 1958. KStJ 1973. *Heir:* *s* Arthur David Markham [*b* 6 Dec. 1950; *m* 1977, Carolyn, *yr d* of Captain Mungo

Park; two *d*]. *Address:* PO Box 42263, Nairobi, Kenya, East Africa. *Club:* Cavalry and Guards.

MARKIDES, Vanias; High Commissioner for the Republic of Cyprus in the United Kingdom, 1995–97; *b* 26 July 1937; *s* of Vias and Andromachi Markides; *m* 1962, Ioulia Michaeloudes; one *s*. *Educ:* Athens Univ. (LLB). Ministry of Foreign Affairs: Second Sec., Nicosia, 1961; Head of Consular and Cultural Affairs, Cyprus High Commn, London, 1966–68; Counsellor, 1971; Dir, First Political Div., 1975–88; Minister, Plenipotentiary, 1979; Ambassador, 1985; Permt Rep. to UN, Geneva, 1988–92; Rep. of Cyprus to UN Commn on Human Rights, 1990–92; Permt Sec., 1994–95. Dir, Office of Studies on the Cyprus Problem, 1992–95. Merito Civil Gran Cruz (Spain), 1987. *Recreations:* classical philosophy, music.

MARKING, Sir Henry (Ernest), KCVO 1978; CBE 1969; MC 1944; CompRAeS 1953; FCIT; Deputy Chairman and Managing Director, British Airways, 1972–77; *b* 11 March 1920; *s* of late Isaac and Hilda Jane Marking. *Educ:* Saffron Walden Gram. Sch.; University Coll., London. Served War of 1939–45: 2nd Bn The Sherwood Foresters, 1941–45; North Africa, Italy and Middle East; Adjutant, 1944–45. Middle East Centre of Arab Studies, Jerusalem, 1945–46. Admitted solicitor, 1948. Asst Solicitor, Cripps, Harries, Hall & Co., Tunbridge Wells, 1948–49; Asst Solicitor, 1949, Sec., 1950, Chief Exec., 1964–72, Chm., 1971–72, BEA; Mem. Bd, BOAC, 1971–72; Mem., British Airways Board, 1971–80. Chm., Rothmans UK, 1979–86; Director: Rothmans International, 1979–86; Barclays International, 1977–86. Mem., 1969–77, Chm., 1977–84, British Tourist Authority. Trustee, 1962–95, Chm. Internat. Cttee, 1970–91, Leonard Cheshire Foundn. FIMgt (FBIM 1971). *Club:* Reform.

MARKL, Prof. Hubert, Dr rer. nat.; President, Max-Planck-Gesellschaft, since 1996; *b* 17 Aug. 1938; *m* Eva Markl; one *s*. *Educ:* Univ. of Munich (Dr rer. nat. 1962). Scientific Assistant: Zoological Inst., Univ. of Munich, 1962–63; Zoological Inst., Univ. of Frankfurt, 1963–67; Res. Associate, Biological Labs, Harvard Univ. and Rockefeller Univ., 1965–66; Associate Prof., Zoological Inst., Univ. of Frankfurt, 1967–68; Prof. of Zoology and Dir, Zoological Inst., Technical Univ. of Darmstadt, 1968–74; Prof. of Biology, Univ. of Konstanz, 1974– (on leave of absence). Heinrich-Hertz Vis. Prof., Univ. of Karlsruhe, 1994–95. Vice Pres., Alexander von Humboldt Foundn, 1986–91; President: Deutsche Forschungsgemeinschaft, 1986–91 (Mem. Senate, 1974–77; Vice Pres., 1977–83); Ges. Deutscher Naturforscher und Ärtze, 1993–94; Berlin-Brandenburg Acad. of Scis, 1993–95; Chm., DFG-Commn for Primate Res., 1974–77; Member: Supervisory Bd, German Primate Centre, 1978–83; Adv. Bd, Max-Planck Inst. for Biological Cybernetics, 1976–85, 1992–; Adv. Bd, Max-Planck Inst. for Behavioural Physiology, 1982–85. Member: Deutsche Akad. der Naturforscher Leopoldina, 1985; Berlin-Brandenburg Acad. of Scis, 1993; MAE 1988; FAAAS 1981. Hon. Dr rer. nat.: Saarland, 1992; Dublin, 1997; Potsdam, 1999; Hon. DHL Jewish Theol Seminary, NY, 2000; Hon. DPhil: Tel Aviv, 2001; Hebrew Univ. of Jerusalem, 2001. *Publications:* Biophysik, 1977 (trans. English 1983); Evolution of Social Behaviour, 1980; Natur und Geschichte, 1983; Neuroethology and Behavioral Physiology, 1983; Evolution, Genetik und menschliches Verhalten, 1986; Natur als Kulturaufgabe, 1986; Wissenschaft: zur Rede gestellt, 1989; Wissenschaft im Widerstreit, 1990; Die Fortschrittsdroge, 1992; Wissenschaft gegen Zukunftsangst, 1998. *Address:* Max-Planck-Gesellschaft zur Förderung der Wissenschaften, Postfach 101062, 80084 Munich, Germany. *T:* (89) 21081211.

MARKLAND, John Anthony, CBE 1999; PhD; Chairman, Scottish Natural Heritage, since 1999; *b* 17 May 1948; *s* of late Thomas Henry Markland and of Rita Markland (*née* Shippen); *m* 1970, Muriel Harris; four *d*. *Educ:* Bolton Sch., Lancs; Dundee Univ. (MA Geog. 1970; PhD 1975). CDipAF 1979; ACIS 1982. Demographer, Somerset CC, 1974–76; Sen. Professional Asst (Planning Res.), Tayside Regl Council, 1976–79; Fife Regional Council: PA to Chief Exec., 1979–83; Asst Chief Exec., 1983–86; Chief Exec., 1986–95; Chief Exec., Fife Council, 1995–99. Chm., Scottish Br., SOLACE, 1993–95. Chairman: Forward Scotland Ltd, 1996–2000; Scottish Leadership Foundn, 2001–; non-executive Director: Going for Green, 1997–; Environmental Campaigns, 1999–; Environmental Campaigns (Scotland), 2000–; Perth Rep. Theatre Ltd, 2000–. Member: Jt Nature Conservation Cttee, 1999–; Cairngorm Partnership Panel, 1999–. *Recreation:* finding the easiest way up Scotland's Munros. *Address:* Moreland House, Cleish, Kinross KY13 0LP. *T:* (01577) 850278.

MARKOVA, Dame Alicia, DBE 1963 (CBE 1958); **(Dame Lilian Alicia Marks);** Prima Ballerina Assoluta; Professor of Ballet and Performing Arts, College-Conservatory of Music, University of Cincinnati, since 1970; President, English National (formerly London Festival) Ballet, since 1986; *b* London, 1 Dec. 1910; *d* of Arthur Tristman Marks and Eileen Barry. With Diaghilev's Russian Ballet Co., 1925–29; Rambert Ballet Club, 1931–33; Vic-Wells Ballet Co., 1933–35; Markova-Dolin Ballet Co., 1935–37; Ballet Russe de Monte Carlo, 1938–41; Ballet Theatre, USA, 1941–46. Appeared with Anton Dolin, guest and concert performances, 1948–50. Co-Founder and Prima Ballerina, Festival Ballet, 1950–51; Guest Prima Ballerina: Buenos Aires, 1952; Royal Ballet, 1953 and 1957; Royal Danish Ballet, 1955; Scala, Milan, 1956; Teatro Municipal, Rio de Janeiro, 1956; Festival Ballet, 1958 and 1959; Guest appearances at Metropolitan Opera House, New York, 1952, 1953–54, 1955, 1957, 1958; partnered Ram Gopal, Prince's Th., London and Edin. Fest., 1960; Dir, Metropolitan Opera Ballet, 1963–69; produced Les Sylphides for Festival Ballet and Aust. Ballet, 1976, for Royal Ballet School and Northern Ballet Theatre, 1978, for Royal Winnipeg Ballet, Canada, 1979. Guest Professor: Royal Ballet Sch., 1973–; Paris Opera Ballet, 1975; Australian Ballet Sch., 1976; Yorkshire Ballet Seminars, 1975–; Pres., All England Dance Competition, 1983–. Vice-Pres., Royal Acad. of Dancing, 1958–; Governor, Royal Ballet, 1973–; President: Pavlova Meml Mus., 1978; London Ballet Circle, 1981–; Trust of the Arts Educational Schs, 1984–;. Concert, television and guest appearances (general), 1952–61. BBC series, Markova's Ballet Call, 1960; Masterclass, BBC2, 1980. Queen Elizabeth II Coronation Award, Royal Acad. of Dancing, 1963; Special Ballet Award, Evening Standard, 1994. Hon. DMus: Leicester, 1966; East Anglia, 1982. *Publications:* Giselle and I, 1960; Markova Remembers, 1986; *relevant publication:* Markova: the legend, by Maurice Leonard, 1995. *Address:* c/o Royal Ballet School, Talgarth Road, W14 9DE.

MARKOWITZ, Prof. Harry M., PhD; Professor of Finance and Economics, Baruch College, City University of New York, 1982–93; *b* 24 Aug. 1927; *s* of Morris Markowitz and Mildred (*née* Gruber); *m* Barbara Gay. *Educ:* Univ. of Chicago (PhB Liberal Arts 1947; MA 1950, PhD 1954 Econs). Res. Associate, Rand Corp., 1952–60 and 1961–63; Consultant, Gen. Electric Corp., 1960–61; Chm., Bd and Technical Dir, Consolidated Analysis Centres Inc., 1963–68; Prof. of Finance, UCLA, 1968–69; Pres., Arbitrage Management Co., 1969–72, Consultant, 1972–74; Vis. Prof. of Finance, Wharton Bus. Sch., 1972–74; Res. Staff Mem., T. J. Watson Res. Center, IBM, 1974–83; Adj. Prof. of Finance, Rutgers Univ., 1980–82; Consultant, Daiwa Securities, 1990–2000. Director: Amer. Finance Assoc.; TIMS. Fellow: Econometric Soc.; Amer. Acad. Arts and Sciences, 1987. Von Neumann Theory Prize, ORSA/TIMS, 1989; Nobel Prize for Economics, 1990. *Publications:* Portfolio Selection: efficient diversification of investments, 1959, 2nd edn 1991; Simscript: a simulation programming language, 1963; (jtly) Studies in Process Analysis: economy-wide production capabilities, 1963 (trans. Russian 1967); (jtly) The Simscript II Programming Language, 1969; (jtly) The EAS-E Programming Language, 1981; (jtly) Adverse Deviation, 1981; Mean-Variance Analysis in Portfolio Choice and Capital Markets, 1987; contrib. chapters to numerous books and papers in professional jls, incl. Jl of Finance, Management Science, Jl of Portfolio Management. *Recreations:* music, canoeing, snorkeling.

MARKS, family name of **Baron Marks of Broughton**.

MARKS OF BROUGHTON, 3rd Baron *cr* 1961, of Sunningdale in the Royal Co. of Berks; **Simon Richard Marks;** *b* 3 May 1950; *s* of 2nd Baron Marks of Broughton and his 1st wife, Ann Catherine (*née* Pinto); *S* father, 1998; *m* 1982, Marion, *o d* of Peter F. Norton; one *s* three *d*. *Educ:* Eton; Balliol Coll., Oxford (BA 1968). *Heir: s* Hon. Michael Marks, *b* 13 May 1989.

MARKS, Bernard Montague, OBE 1984; Life President, Alfred Marks Bureau Group of Companies, 1985 (Managing Director and Chairman, 1946–84); *b* 11 Oct. 1923; *s* of Alfred and Elizabeth Marks; *m* 1956, Norma Renton (*d* 1990); one *s* (and one *s* decd). *Educ:* Highgate Public Sch.; Royal Coll. of Science. Served Somerset LI, seconded to RWAFF (Staff Capt.), 1944–46. Chm. or Vice-Chm., Fedn of Personnel Services of GB, 1965–79, 1983–84. Mem., Equal Opportunities Commn, 1984–86. *Publication:* Once Upon A Typewriter, 1974. *Recreations:* bridge, golf, theatre. *Address:* 29G Eaton Square, SW1W 9DF. *Club:* St George's Hill Golf.

MARKS, Prof. David Francis, PhD; CPsychol, FBPsS; Professor of Psychology, City University, London, since 2000; *b* 12 Feb. 1945; *s* of Victor William Francis Marks and Mary Dorothy Marks; *m* 1991, Yoriko Taniguchi. *Educ:* Southern Grammar Sch. for Boys, Portsmouth; Reading Univ. (BSc); Sheffield Univ. (PhD 1970). FBPsS 1984; CPsychol 1988; Chartered Health Psychologist, 1998. Sen. Demonstrator, Sheffield Univ., 1966–69; Lectr, 1970–74, Sen. Lectr, 1978–86, Univ. of Otago, NZ; Middlesex Polytechnic, subseq. University: Prof. of Psychology, 1986–2000; Head, Sch. of Psychology, 1986–91; Head, Health Research Centre, 1989–2000. Visiting Professor: Oregon, 1976; Washington, 1977; Hamamatsu Univ. Sch. of Medicine, Fukuoka Univ., Japan, 1984; Rome, 1997; Hon. Res. Fellow, UCL, 1977. Mem., DoH Scientific Cttee on Tobacco and Health, 1994–98; Convenor, Task Force on Health Psychol., Eur. Fedn of Professional Psychologists' Assocs, 1993–97. Sen. Asst Ed., Jl of Mental Imagery, 1987–96; Asst Ed., British Jl of Psychology, 1990–95; Ed., Jl Health Psychol., 1996–. Developer of first smoking cessation prog. on the internet. Gold Disk for Music Therapy, NZ Min. of Health, 1979. *Publications:* The Psychology of the Psychic, 1980, 2nd edn 2000; Theories of Image Formation, 1986; Imagery: current developments, 1990; The Quit for Life Programme, 1993; Improving the Health of the Nation, 1996; Health Psychology: theory, research and practice, 2000; Dealing with Dementia, 2000; The Health Psychology Reader, 2002; Methods in Health Psychology, 2002; numerous book chapters and contribs to Nature, Science, Brit. Jl of Psych., Jl of Mental Imagery, and many other jls. *Recreations:* travel, photography, films, art. *Address:* City University, Northampton Square, EC1V 0HB; *e-mail:* d.marks@city.ac.uk.

MARKS, Dennis Michael; broadcaster, writer and film-maker, since 1997; General Director, English National Opera, 1993–97; *b* 2 July 1948; *s* of Samuel Marks and Kitty Ostrovsky; *m*; one *s* one *d*. *Educ:* Haberdashers' Aske's Sch., Elstree; Trinity Coll., Cambridge (1st Cl. Hons English Tripos). British Broadcasting Corporation, 1969–81: TV researcher, 1969–71; Dir, TV music and arts, 1972–78; Dir/Producer, Bristol Arts Unit, 1978–81; Dir/Producer, 3rd Eye Prodns, 1981–85; BBC TV: Editor, music progs, 1985–88; Asst Head of Music and Arts Dept, 1988–91; Hd of Music Progs, 1991–93. Pres., Internat. Music Centre, Vienna, 1989–92. *Publications:* Great Railway Journeys, 1981; Repercussions, 1985. *Recreations:* cooking, travel. *Address:* 7 Molines Wharf, Narrow Street, Limehouse, E14 8BP.

MARKS, Frederick Charles, OBE 1983; Commissioner for Local Administration in Scotland, 1994–2000; *b* 3 Dec. 1934; *s* of James Marks and Elizabeth (*née* McInnes); *m* 1959, Agnes Miller Bruce; two *s* one *d* (and one *s* decd). *Educ:* Wishaw High Sch.; Univ. of Glasgow (MA Hons; LLB). Admitted solicitor, 1960. Legal Asst, Burgh of Motherwell and Wishaw, 1957–61; Solicitor, Burgh of Kirkcaldy, 1961–63; Depute Town Clerk, City and Royal Burgh of Dunfermline, 1963–68; Town Clerk, Burgh of Hamilton, 1968–75; Chief Exec., Motherwell Dist, 1974–83; Gen. Manager, Scottish Special Housing Assoc., 1983–89; Dep. Chm., Local Govt Boundary Commn for Scotland, 1989–94. Vice-Chairman: Queen Margaret Hosp. NHS Trust, Dunfermline, 1994–99; Fife Acute Hosps NHS Trust, 1999–. *Address:* Dunkeld, 33 Townhill Road, Dunfermline, Fife KY12 0JD.

MARKS, Prof. Isaac Meyer, MD; Professor of Experimental Psychopathology, Institute of Psychiatry, University of London, 1978–2000, now Emeritus; Senior Research Investigator, Imperial College, London University, at Charing Cross Hospital Campus; *b* 16 Feb. 1935; *s* of Morris Norman and Anna Marks; *m* 1957, Shula Eta Winokur (*see* S. E. Marks); one *s* one *d*. *Educ:* Univ. of Cape Town (MB ChB 1956; MD 1963); Univ. of London (DPM 1963). Consultant Psychiatrist and research worker, Bethlem-Maudsley Hosp. and Inst. of Psychiatry, 1978–2000. Salmon Medallist, NY Acad. of Medicine, 1978; IT Effectiveness Award, Health Care '98, 1998. *Publications:* Patterns of Meaning in Psychiatric Patients, 1965; Fears & Phobias, 1969; (jtly) Clinical Anxiety, 1971; (jtly) Psychotherapy, 1971; (jtly) Nursing in Behavioural Psychotherapy, 1977; Living with Fear, 1978, 2nd edn 2001; Cure and Care of Neuroses, 1981; Psychiatric Nurse Therapists in Primary Care, 1985; Behavioural Psychotherapy, 1986; (jtly) Anxiety and its Treatment, 1986; Fears, Phobias and Rituals, 1987; (ed jtly) Mental Health Care Delivery, 1990; (jtly) Problem-centred care planning, 1995; (jtly) BT Steps—Behavioural self-assessment and self care for OCD, 1996; 380 scientific papers. *Recreations:* hiking, gardening, theatre, cinema. *Address:* 303 North End Road, W14 9NS. *T:* (020) 7610 2594.

MARKS, John Emile, CBE 1970; Chairman, Peckerbond Ltd; *m* 1975, Averil May Hannah (*née* Davies); two *s* two *d* by former marriage. *Educ:* Eton College. Served War of 1939–45 (despatches 1944). *Recreations:* snooker, bowls. *Address:* Teignmouth, Devon.

MARKS, John Henry, MD; FRCGP; General Practitioner, Boreham Wood, 1954–90; Chairman of Council, British Medical Association, 1984–90; Medical Director, National Medical Examination Network (Definitech) Ltd, since 1992; *b* 30 May 1925; *s* of Lewis and Rose Marks; *m* 1954, Shirley Evelyn, *d* of Alic Nathan, OBE; one *s* two *d*. *Educ:* Tottenham County Sch.; Edinburgh Univ. MD; FRCGP; D(Obst)RCOG. Served RAMC, 1949–51. Chairman: Herts LMC, 1966–71; Herts Exec. Council, 1971–74; Member: NHS Management Study Steering Cttee, 1971–72; Standing Med. Adv. Cttee, 1984–90; Council for Postgrad. Med. Educn, 1984–90. British Medical Association: Fellow, 1976; Member: Gen. Med. Services Cttee, 1968–90 (Dep. Chm., 1974–79); Council, 1973–98; GMC, 1979–84, 1990–94; Chairman: Representative Body, 1981–84; Foundn for AIDS, 1987–99. Member, Council: ASH, 1991–99; Assurance Medical Soc., 1999–. *Publications:* The Conference of Local Medical Committees and its Executive: an historical view, 1979; papers on the NHS and general medical practice. *Recreations:* philately, walking, gardening. *Address:* Brown Gables, Barnet Lane, Elstree, Herts WD6 3RQ. *T:* (020) 8953 7687.

MARKS, Jonathan Clive; QC 1995; *b* 19 Oct. 1952; *s* of late Geoffrey Jack Marks, LDS RCS and Patricia Pauline Marks, LLB; *m* 1st, 1982, Sarah Ann Russell (marr. diss. 1991); one *s* one *d*; 2nd, 1993, (Clementine) Medina Cafopoulos; two *s* two *d*. *Educ:* Harrow; University Coll., Oxford (BA Hons Jurisp.); Inns of Court Sch. of Law. Called to the Bar, Inner Temple, 1975; in practice, Common Law and Commercial Law, Western Circuit. Vis. Lecturer in Advocacy: Univs of Malaya and Mauritius; Sri Lanka Law Coll. Contested (SDP): Weston-Super-Mare, 1983; Falmouth and Camborne, 1987; EP elecn, Cornwall and Plymouth, 1984. Mem., Lib Dem Cttee for England, 1988–89; Chm., Lib Dem Lawyers Assoc., 2001–. Freeman, City of London, 1975; Liveryman, Patternmakers' Co., 1975– (Mem. Ct Assts, 1998–). *Recreations:* tennis, ski-ing, theatre, opera, food, wine, travel. *Address:* 4 Pump Court, Temple, EC4Y 7AN. *T:* (020) 7353 2656. *Club:* Royal Automobile.

MARKS, Dr Louis Frank; film and television producer; *b* 23 March 1928; *s* of Michael Marks and Sarah Abrahams; *m* 1957, Sonia Herbstman; two *d*. *Educ:* Christ's Coll., London; Balliol Coll., Oxford (MA, BLitt, DPhil 1957). Sen. History teacher, Beltane Sch., 1951–53; founder and editor, Books and Bookmen, 1956; freelance scriptwriter, TV series, 1958–69; joined BBC, 1970; Script Editor, Series Dept, 1970; Plays Dept, 1972; Drama Producer, 1974; producer, film and TV Drama, 1976–; productions include: The Lost Boys (RTS Award, 1979); Play of the Month, later Festival, 1979–86, incl. Lady Windermere's Fan and Ghosts (ACE Awards, 1988, 1992); Loving, 1996; Plotlands (serial), 1997. films include: Silas Marner (Banff Film Fest. Award, 1986); Memento Mori (Writers' Guild Award, 1992); The Trial, 1993; TV adaptation: Middlemarch (serial), 1994 (Writers' Guild Award, BPG TV Award for best serial, Voice of the Listener and Viewer Award for excellence in broadcasting and best TV prog., 1994). *Publications:* (ed and trans.) Antonio Gramsci: the modern prince, 1957; articles in Archivio Storico Italiano and Italian Renaissance Studies. *Address:* Paddock Lodge, The Green, Hampton Court, East Molesey, Surrey KT8 9BW. *T:* (020) 8979 5254.

MARKS, Michael John Paul, CBE 1999; Executive Vice President, Merrill Lynch & Co. Inc., since 2001; Executive Chairman: Merrill Lynch Europe, Middle East and Africa, since 1998 (Chief Operating Officer, 1997–98); Merrill Lynch Investment Managers and International Private Client Group, since 2001; *b* 28 Dec. 1941; *m* 1967, Rosemary Ann Brody; one *s* two *d*. *Educ:* St Paul's Sch. Joined Smith Brothers, subseq. Smith New Court, 1960; Partner, 1969–84; Dir, 1975; Man. Dir, Smith New Court International, 1984–87; Chief Exec., 1987–94, Chm., 1995, Smith New Court PLC; Dep. Chm., Jt Hd of Global Equities, and Mem. Exec. Mgt Cttee, Merrill Lynch Internat., 1995–97. Non-exec. Dir, Rothschilds Continuation, 1990–95; Mem., Internat. Markets Adv. Bd, Nasdaq Stock Market, 1991–. Director: Securities Inst., 1992–93; London Stock Exchange, 1994–; Trustee, Stock Exchange Benevolent Fund, 1994–97. *Address:* (office) 25 Ropemaker Place, EC2Y 9LY.

MARKS, Prof. Richard Charles, PhD; FSA; Professor in Medieval Stained Glass, University of York, since 1992; *b* 2 July 1945; *s* of William Henry Marks and Jeannie Eileen Marks (*née* Pigott); *m* 1970, Rita Spratley. *Educ:* Berkhamsted Sch.; Queen Mary Coll., Univ. of London (BA (Hons) History); Courtauld Inst. of Art, Univ. of London (MA, PhD, History of European Art). Research Asst for British Acad. *Corpus Vitrearum Medii Aevi* Cttee, 1970–73; Asst Keeper, Dept of Medieval and Later Antiquities, British Mus., 1973–79; Keeper of Burrell Collection and Asst Dir, Glasgow Museums and Art Galls, 1979–85; Dir, Royal Pavilion, Art Gall. and Museums in Brighton, 1985–92. Chm., Group of Directors of Museums, 1989–92; Mem. Cttee, 1985–, Pres. Internat. Bd, 1995–, *Corpus Vitrearum Medii Aevi*, British Academy. Liveryman, Glaziers' Co., 1990. FSA 1977 (Mem. Council, 1990–94; Vice-Pres., 1991–94). *Publications:* (jtly) British Heraldry from its origins to *c* 1800, 1978; (jtly) The Golden Age of English Manuscript Painting, 1980; Burrell Portrait of a Collector, 1983, 2nd edn 1988; The Glazing of the Collegiate Church of the Holy Trinity, Tattershall, Lincs, 1984; (jtly) Sussex Churches and Chapels, 1989; Stained Glass in England during the Middle Ages, 1993; The Medieval Stained Glass of Northamptonshire, 1998; articles and reviews in learned jls. *Recreations:* opera, cricket, rowing, parish churches, travelling in the Levant. *Address:* c/o Centre for Medieval Studies, University of York, The King's Manor, York Y01 2EP; Hillcroft, 11 Stewkley Road, Soulbury, Bucks LU7 0DH. *Clubs:* MCC; Clydesdale Amateur Rowing (Glasgow); North British Rowing (the Borders).

MARKS, Richard Leon; QC 1999; a Recorder, since 1994; *b* 20 Nov. 1953; *s* of Harry and Denise Marks; *m* 1987, Jane Elizabeth Tordoff; one *s* one *d*. *Educ:* Clifton Coll.; Univ. of Manchester (LLB Hons). Called to the Bar, Gray's Inn, 1975; Northern Circuit; an Asst Recorder, 1991–94. Pres., Restricted Patients Panel, Mental Health Review Tribunal, 2000–. *Recreations:* travel, cinema, Clarice Cliff, MUFC. *Address:* Peel Court Chambers, 45 Hardman Street, Manchester M3 3PL.

MARKS, Prof. Shula Eta, OBE 1996; PhD; FBA 1995; Professor of Southern African History, School of Oriental and African Studies, University of London, 1993–2001, now Emeritus; *b* Cape Town, S Africa, 14 Oct. 1936; *d* of Chaim and Frieda Winokur; *m* 1957, Isaac M. Marks, *qv*; one *s* one *d*. *Educ:* Univ. of Cape Town (Argus Scholar, 1958–59; BA 1959). PhD London, 1967. Came to London, 1960; Lectr in the History of Southern Africa, SOAS and Inst. of Commonwealth Studies, 1963–76, Reader, 1976–83; Dir, 1983–93, Prof. of Commonwealth Hist., 1984–93, Inst. of Commonwealth Studies, London Univ.; Vice-Chancellor's Visitor to NZ, 1978. Dir, Ford Foundn Grant to Univ. of London on S African History, 1975–78; Mem., Commonwealth Scholarships Commn, 1993–. Member: Adv. Council on Public Records, 1989–94; Humanities Res. Bd, British Acad., 1997–98; AHRB, 1998–2000. Pres., African Studies Assoc. of UK, 1978; Chairman: Internat. Records Mgt Trust, 1989–; Council for Assisting Refugee Academics (formerly Soc. for Protection of Sci. and Learning), 1993–. Editor, Jl of African History, 1971–77; Mem. Council, Jl of Southern African Studies, 1974– (Founding Mem., 1974; Chm. Bd, 1998–). Hon. DLitt Cape Town, 1994; Hon. DSocSc Natal, 1996. *Publications:* Reluctant Rebellion: an assessment of the 1906–8 disturbances in Natal, 1970; (ed with A. Atmore) Economy and Society in Pre-industrial South Africa, 1980; (ed with R. Rathbone) Industrialization and Social Change in South Africa, 1870–1930, 1982; (ed with P. Richardson) International Labour Migration: historical perspectives, 1983; The Ambiguities of Dependence in Southern Africa: class, nationalism and the state in twentieth-century Natal, 1986; (ed) Not either an experimental doll: the separate worlds of three South African women, 1987; (ed with Stanley Trapido) The Politics of Race, Class & Nationalism in Twentieth Century South Africa, 1987; Divided Sisterhood: race, class and gender in the South African nursing profession, 1994; chapters in Cambridge Hist. of Africa, vols 3, 4 and 6; contrib. Jl of African Hist. and Jl of Southern African Studies.

MARKS, Victor James; Cricket Correspondent, The Observer, since 1990; *b* 25 June 1955; *s* of late Harold George Marks and Phyllis Joan Marks; *m* 1978, Anna Stewart; two *d*. *Educ:* Blundell's Sch.; St John's Coll., Oxford (BA). Professional cricketer, 1975–89: played for: Oxford Univ., 1975–78 (Capt., 1976 and 1977); Somerset, 1975–89; WA, 1986–87; played in 6 Test Matches and 34 One-Day Internationals for England. Summariser, Test Match Special, BBC, 1989–. Cricket Chm., Somerset CCC, 1999–. Mem., Editl Bd, The Cricketer, 1990–. *Publications:* Somerset Cricket Scrapbook, 1984; Marks out of XI, 1985; TCCB Guide to Better Cricket, 1987; (with R. Drake) Ultimate One-Day Cricket Match, 1988; Wisden Illustrated History of Cricket, 1989; (with R. Holmes) My Greatest Game, 1994. *Recreation:* golf. *Address:* c/o The Observer, 119 Farringdon Road, EC1B 1AH.

MARKUS, Prof. Robert Austin, OBE 2000; FBA 1985; Professor of Medieval History, Nottingham University, 1974–82, now Emeritus; *b* 8 Oct. 1924; *s* of Victor Markus and Lily Markus (*née* Elek); *m* 1955, Margaret Catherine Bullen; two *s* one *d*. *Educ:* Univ. of Manchester (BSc 1944; MA 1948; PhD 1950). Mem., Dominican Order, 1950–54; Asst Librarian, Univ. of Birmingham, 1954–55; Liverpool University: Sub-Librarian, 1955–59; Lectr, Sen. Lectr, Reader in Medieval Hist., 1959–74. Mem., Inst. for Advanced Study, Princeton, 1986–87; Distinguished Professor of Early Christian Studies: Catholic Univ. of America, Washington, 1988–89; Univ. of Notre Dame, 1993. Pres., Assoc. Internationale d'Etudes Patristiques, 1991–95. *Publications:* Christian Faith and Greek Philosophy (with A. H. Armstrong), 1964; Saeculum: history and society in the theology of St Augustine, 1970; Christianity in the Roman world, 1974; From Augustine to Gregory the Great, 1983; The End of Ancient Christianity, 1990; Gregory the Great and his World, 1997; contribs to Jl of Ecclesiastical Hist., Jl of Theol Studies, Byzantion, Studies in Church Hist., etc. *Recreation:* music. *Address:* 100 Park Road, Chilwell, Beeston, Nottingham NG9 4DE. *T:* (0115) 925 5965.

MARLAND, Michael, CBE 1977; FCP; General Editor, Heinemann School Management Series, since 1971; *b* 28 Dec. 1934; *m* 1st, 1955, Eileen (*d* 1968); four *s* one *d*; 2nd, 1971, Rose (marr. diss. 1977); 3rd, 1989, Linda; one *s*. *Educ:* Christ's Hospital Sch.; Sidney Sussex Coll., Cambridge (MA). Head of English, Abbey Wood Sch., 1961–64; Head of English and subseq. Dir of Studies, Crown Woods Sch., 1964–71; Headmaster, Woodberry Down Sch., 1971–79; founder Headteacher, N Westminster Community Sch., 1980–99. Hon. Prof., Dept of Educn, Univ. of Warwick, 1980–92. Member: many educn cttees, incl. Bullock Cttee, 1972–75; Commonwealth Inst. Educn Cttee, 1982–; Arts Council of GB Educn Cttee, 1988–92; Educn and Human Develt Cttee, ESRC (formerly SSRC), 1983–88; Nat. Assoc. for Educn in the Arts, 1986–; Nat. Book League Council, 1984; Finniston Cttee on Technol. in Educn, 1985–88; Video Adv. Cttee, British Bd of Film Classification, 1989–; Educn Cttee, ESU; Careers Cttee, ICE; Bd, Young Persons' Concert Foundn; Nat. Adv. Forum, DIVERT. Chairman: Schools Council English Cttee, 1978–81; Books in Curriculum Res. Project, 1982–; Royal Ballet Educn Adv. Council, 1983–; Nat. Assoc. for Pastoral Care in Educn, 1982–86; Royal Opera House Educnl Adv. Council, 1984–95; Nat. Textbook Ref. Library Steering Cttee, 1984–; Exec., City of Westminster Arts Council; Mentoring Cttee, City of Westminster Race Equality Council. Mem., Paddington and N Kensington DHA, 1982–84. Patron, Tagore Foundn. FCP 1999. Hon. DEd Kingston, 2000; DUniv Surrey Roehampton, 2001. *Publications:* Towards The New Fifth, 1969; The Practice of English Teaching, 1970; Peter Grimes, 1971; Head of Department, 1971; Pastoral Care, 1974; The Craft of the Classroom, 1975, rev. edn 1993; Language Across the Curriculum, 1977; Education for the Inner City, 1980; Departmental Management, 1981; Sex Differentiation and Schooling, 1983; Short Stories for Today, 1984; Meetings and Partings, 1984; School Management Skills, 1985; The Tutor and the Tutor Group, 1990; Marketing the School, 1991; (with Peter Ribbins) Leadership in the Secondary School: portraits of headship, 1994; Scenes from Plays, 1996; (with Rick Rogers) The Art of the Tutor, 1997; Managing the Arts in the Curriculum, 2001; General Editor of: The Student Drama Series; Longman Imprint Books; The Times Authors; Heinemann Organisation in Schools Series; Longman Tutorial Resources; English Poetry Plus; contrib. Times Educnl Supplement. *Recreations:* music, literature. *Address:* 22 Compton Terrace, N1 2UN. *T:* (020) 7226 0648; The Green Farmhouse, Cranmer Green, Walsham-le-Willows, Bury St Edmunds, Suffolk IP31 3BJ. *T:* (01359) 259483.

MARLAND, Paul; farmer, since 1967; *b* 19 March 1940; *s* of Alexander G. Marland and Elsa May Lindsey Marland; *m* 1st, 1965, Penelope Anne Barlow (marr. diss. 1982); one *s* two *d*; 2nd, 1984, Caroline Ann Rushton. *Educ:* Gordonstoun Sch., Elgin; Trinity Coll., Dublin (BA, BComm). Hopes Metal Windows, 1964; London Press Exchange, 1965–66. MP (C) Gloucester West, 1979–97; contested (C) Forest of Dean, 1997; contested (C) South West Region, EP elecns, 1999. Jt PPS to Financial Sec. to the Treasury and Economic Sec., 1981–83, to Minister of Agriculture, Fisheries and Food, 1983–86. Chm., back bench Agric. Cttee, 1989–97. *Recreations:* ski-ing, shooting, riding, fishing. *Address:* Ford Hill Farm, Temple Guiting, Cheltenham, Glos GL54 5XU.

MARLAR, Robin Geoffrey; management consultant, since 1968; with Sunday Times, since 1954 (Cricket Correspondent, 1970–96); *b* 2 Jan. 1931; *o s* of late E. A. G. Marlar and Winifred Marlar (*née* Stevens); *m* 1st, 1955, Wendy Ann Dumeresque (*d* 2000); two *s* four *d*; 2nd, 1980, Hon. Gill Taylor, 2nd *d* of Baron Taylor of Hadfield. *Educ:* King Edward's Sch., Lichfield; Harrow; Magdalene Coll., Cambridge (BA). Asst Master, Eton Coll., 1953–54; Librarian, Arundel Castle, 1954–59; Captain, Sussex CCC, 1955–59; sportswriter, Daily Telegraph, 1954–60; De La Rue Co., 1960–68; Consultant and Partner, Spencer-Stuart and Associates, 1968–71; Founder, Marlar Group of Consultancies, 1971. Contested (C): Bolsover, 1959; Leicester NE, July 1962; contested (Referendum) Newbury, May 1993. *Publications:* The Story of Cricket, 1978; (ed) The English Cricketers Trip to USA and Canada 1859, 1979; Decision Against England, 1983. *Recreations:* gardening, sport. *Clubs:* Garrick, MCC (Mem. Cttee, 1999); Sussex CCC (Chm., 1997–98).

MARLBOROUGH, 11th Duke of, *cr* 1702; **John George Vanderbilt Henry Spencer-Churchill;** DL; Baron Spencer, 1603; Earl of Sunderland, 1643; Baron Churchill, 1685; Earl of Marlborough, 1689; Marquis of Blandford, 1702; Prince of the Holy Roman Empire; Prince of Mindelheim in Suabia; late Captain Life Guards; *b* 13 April 1926; *s* of 10th Duke of Marlborough and Hon. Alexandra Mary Hilda Cadogan, CBE (*d* 1961), *d* of late Henry Arthur, Viscount Chelsea; *S* father, 1972; *m* 1st, 1951, Susan Mary (marr. diss., 1960; she; *m* 1962, Alan Cyril Heber-Percy), *d* of Michael Hornby; one *s* one *d* (and one *s* decd); 2nd, 1961, Mrs Athina Livanos (marr. diss. 1971; she *d* 1974), *d* of late Stavros G. Livanos, Paris; 3rd, 1972, Rosita Douglas; one *s* one *d* (and one *s* decd). *Educ:* Eton. Lieut Life Guards, 1946; Captain, 1953; resigned commission, 1953. Chairman: Martini & Rossi, 1979–96; London Paperweights Ltd, 1974–. Mem., Trusthouse Charitable Trust (formerly Forte Council), 1994–. President: Thames and Chilterns Tourist Board, 1974–; Oxfordshire Branch, CLA, 1978–; Oxfordshire Assoc. for Young People, 1972–; Oxford Br., SSAFA, 1977–; Sports Aid Foundn (Southern), 1981–; Oxford United Football Club, 1964–; Dep. Pres., Nat. Assoc. of Boys' Clubs, 1987–; Chm., Badminton Conservation Trust, 1997–; Mem. Council, Winston Churchill Meml Trust, 1966–; Patron, Oxfordshire Br., BRCS. CC 1961–64, Oxfordshire; JP 1962; DL 1974. *Heir: s* Marquis of Blandford, *qv*. *Address:* Blenheim Palace, Woodstock, Oxon OX20 1PX. *Clubs:* Portland, White's.

MARLER, David Steele, OBE 1984; Director, Egypt, British Council, 1997–2001; *b* 19 March 1941; *s* of Steele Edward and Dorothy Marler; *m* 1963, Belinda Mary Handisyde; two *s*. *Educ:* Brighton, Hove and Sussex Grammar Sch.; Merton Coll., Oxford (Postmaster; BA, MA). British Council, 1962–2001: seconded SOAS, 1962–63; Asst Rep., Bombay, 1963; Regional Officer, India, 1967; Dep. Rep., Ethiopia, 1970; Rep., Ibadan, Nigeria, 1974; Dir, Policy Res., 1977; Rep., Cyprus, 1980; seconded SOAS, 1984; National Univ., Singapore, 1985; Rep., China, 1987–90; Director: Asia, Pacific and Americas Div., 1990–92; Turkey, Azerbaijan and Uzbekistan, 1993–97. *Recreations:* sailing, travel, reading, walking. *Address:* c/o British Council, 10 Spring Gardens, SW1A 2BN. *T:* (020) 7930 8466. *Club:* Changi Sailing (Singapore).

MARLER, Dennis Ralph Greville, FRICS; Chairman, Falcon Property Trust, 1988–95; *b* 15 June 1927; *s* of late Greville Sidney Marler, JP, FRICS and Ivy Victoria (*née* Boyle); *m* 1952, Angela (*née* Boundy); one *s* one *d*. *Educ:* Marlborough. Served Royal Lincolnshire Regt, Palestine, 1946–48; articled pupil, Knight, Frank & Rutley, 1948–50; Partner, Marler & Marler, 1950–83; Jt Man. Dir, 1966–76, Man. Dir, 1976–85, Chm., 1985–90, Capital & Counties plc; Chairman: Knightsbridge Green Hotel Ltd, 1966–; Pension Fund Property Unit Trust, 1987–89. Member: NEDO Working Party for Wood Report (Public Client and Construction Industry), 1974–75; Adv. Bd, Dept of Construction Management, Univ. of Reading, 1981–88; DHSS Nat. Property Adv. Gp, 1984–91; FCO *ad hoc* Adv. Panel on Diplomatic Estate, 1985–90; RSA Art for Architecture Panel, 1990–93. A Vice-Pres., TCPA, 1983–97; Pres., British Property Fedn, 1983–84. A Vice-Pres., RNIB, 1994–99. Mem. Ct of Assistants, Merchant Taylors' Co., 1984–. CIMgt; FRSA. *Recreations:* reading, golf, gardening. *Address:* Park Farm, St Minver, Cornwall PL27 6QS. *T:* (01208) 862141. *Clubs:* Royal Thames Yacht, Roehampton; St Enodoc Golf.

MARLESFORD, Baron *cr* 1991 (Life Peer), of Marlesford in the County of Suffolk; **Mark Shuldham Schreiber;** DL; political consultant, farmer and journalist; *b* 11 Sept. 1931; *s* of late John Shuldham Schreiber, AE, DL, Marlesford Hall, Suffolk and Maureen Schreiber (*née* Dent); *m* 1969, Gabriella Federica, *d* of Conte Teodoro Veglio di Castelletto d'Uzzone; two *d*. *Educ:* Eton; Trinity Coll., Cambridge. Nat. Service in Coldstream Guards, 1950–51. Fisons Ltd, 1957–63; Conservative Research Dept, 1963–67; Dir, Conservative Party Public Sector Research Unit, 1967–70; Special Advr to the Govt, 1970–74; Special Adviser to Leader of the Opposition, 1974–75; Editorial Consultant, 1974–91, lobby correspondent, 1976–91, The Economist. Ind. Nat. Dir, Times Newspaper Holdings, 1991–; Director: Royal Ordnance Factories, 1972–74; British Railways (Anglia), 1988–92; Eastern Electricity plc, 1990–95. Adviser: Mitsubishi Corp. Internat. NV, 1990–; John Swire & Sons Ltd, 1992–. Member: Govt Computer Agency Council, 1973–74; Countryside Commn, 1980–92; Rural Development Commn, 1985–93; Chm., CPRE, 1993–98. Pres., Suffolk Preservation Soc., 1997–. Mem., East Suffolk CC, 1968–70. DL Suffolk, 1991. *Recreation:* gadfly on bureaucracy. *Address:* Marlesford Hall, Woodbridge, Suffolk IP13 0AU; 5 Kersley Street, SW11 4PR. *Club:* Pratt's.

MARLING, Sir Charles (William Somerset), 5th Bt *cr* 1882; *b* 2 June 1951; *s* of Sir John Stanley Vincent Marling, 4th Bt, OBE, and Georgina Brenda (Betty) (*d* 1961), *o d* of late Henry Edward FitzRoy Somerset; *S* father, 1977; *m* 1979, Judi P. Futrille; three *d*. *Address:* The Barn, The Street, Eversley, Hants RG27 0PJ.

MARLOW, Antony Rivers; *b* 17 June 1940; *s* of late Major Thomas Keith Rivers Marlow, MBE, RE retd, and Beatrice Nora (*née* Hall); *m* 1962, Catherine Louise Howel (*née* Jones) (*d* 1994); three *s* two *d*. *Educ:* Wellington Coll.; RMA Sandhurst; St Catharine's Coll., Cambridge (2nd Cl. Hons (1) Mech. Sciences, MA). Served Army, 1958–69; retd, Captain RE; management consultant and industrial/commercial manager, 1969–79. MP (C) Northampton North, 1979–97; contested (C) same seat, 1997. *Recreations:* farming, Rugby spectator, opera, ballet.

MARLOW, David Ellis; Chief Executive, 3i Group, 1988–92; *b* 29 March 1935; *m* 1959, Margaret Anne Smith; one *d* (one *s* decd). Chartered Accountant. Investors in Industry, subseq. 3i, 1960–92. Director: Brixton Estate plc, 1993–; Trinity Mirror plc, 1992–. *Recreations:* playing tennis, the piano, the organ and the 'cello; ski-ing and scrambling in the Alps. *Address:* The Platt, Elsted, Midhurst, Sussex GU29 0LA. *T:* (01730) 825261. *Clubs:* Athenæum; Cercle de l'Union Interalliée (Paris).

MARLOWE, Hugh; *see* Patterson, Harry.

MARMION, Prof. Barrie P., AO 1994; Visiting Professor, Department of Pathology, University of Adelaide (Adelaide Medical School), since 1985; *b* 19 May 1920; *s* of J. P. and M. H. Marmion, Alverstoke, Hants; *m* 1953, Diana Ray Newling, *d* of Dr P. Ray Newling, Adelaide, SA; one *d*. *Educ:* University Coll. and University Coll. Hosp., London. MD London 1947, DSc London 1963; FRCPath 1962, FRCPA 1964, FRCPE 1970, FRACP 1984; FRSE 1976. House Surg., UCH, 1942; Bacteriologist, Public Health Laboratory Service, 1943–62; Rockefeller Trav. Fellow, at Walter and Eliza Hall Inst., Melbourne, 1951–52; Foundation Prof., Microbiology, Monash Univ., Melbourne, Australia, 1962–68; Prof. of Bacteriology, Univ. of Edinburgh, 1968–78; Dir, Div. of Virology, Inst. of Med. and Vet. Science, Adelaide, 1978–85, retd. DUniv Adelaide, 1990. Distinguished Fellow Award (Gold Medal), RCPath Australia, 1986. *Publications:* (ed) Mackie and McCartney's Medical Microbiology, 12th edn 1975 to 14th edn 1996; numerous papers on bacteriology and virology. *Recreations:* swimming, music. *Address:* Department of Pathology, University of Adelaide, North Terrace, Adelaide, SA 5000, Australia.

MARMOT, Prof. Sir Michael (Gideon), Kt 2000; PhD; FRCP, FFPHM, FMedSci; Professor of Epidemiology and Public Health, University College London, since 1985 (MRC Professor, since 1995), and London School of Hygiene and Tropical Medicine at University College London, since 1990; Director, International Centre for Health and Society, University College London, since 1994; *b* 26 Jan. 1945; *s* of Nathan Marmot and Alice Marmot (*née* Weiner); *m* 1971, Alexandra Naomi Ferster; two *s* one *d*. *Educ:* Univ. of Sydney (BSc Hons, MB BS Hons); Univ. of California, Berkeley (PhD Epidemiology). FFPHM (FFCM 1989); FRCP 1996. RMO, Royal Prince Alfred Hosp., 1969–70, Fellowship in Thoracic Medicine, 1970–71, Univ. of Sydney; Res. Fellow and Lectr, Dept of Biomedical and Envmtl Health Scis, Univ. of California, Berkeley, 1971–76 (Fellowships from Berkeley and Amer. Heart Assoc., 1972–76); Lectr and Sen. Lectr in Epidemiology, LSH&TM, 1976–85; Hon. Consultant, Public Health Medicine, Camden (formerly Bloomsbury) and Islington DHA, 1990–. Vis. Prof., RSocMed, 1987. Chm., Cardiovascular Review Gp, Cttee on Med. Aspects of Food Policy, 1990–; Member: Royal Commn on Envmtl Pollution, 1995–; CMO's Working Gp on Health of the Nation, 1993–. Chm., Behavioural Scis Section, Academia Europaea, 1996–. Founder FMedSci 1998. *Publications:* (ed jtly and contrib.) Coronary Heart Disease Epidemiology, 1992; (ed jtly) Social Determinants of Health, 1999; contribs to OPCS Medical and Population Studies; numerous papers in learned jls. *Recreations:* tennis, viola. *Address:* Department of Epidemiology and Public Health, University College London, 1–19 Torrington Place, WC1E 6BT; Wildwood Cottage, 17 North End, NW3 7HR. *T:* (020) 8458 2125.

MARNOCH, Rt Hon. Lord; Michael Stewart Rae Bruce; PC 2001; Senator of the College of Justice in Scotland, since 1990; *b* 26 July 1938; *s* of late Alexander Eric Bruce, Advocate in Aberdeen, and late Mary Gordon Bruce (*née* Walker); *m* 1963, Alison Mary Monfries Stewart; two *d*. *Educ:* Loretto Sch.; Aberdeen Univ. (MA, LLB). Admitted Faculty of Advocates, 1963; QC Scot. 1975; Standing Counsel: to Dept of Agriculture and Fisheries for Scotland, 1973; to Highlands and Islands Develt Bd, 1973; Advocate Depute, 1983–86. Mem., Criminal Injuries Compensation Bd, 1986–90. Hon. Vice Pres., Salmon and Trout Assoc., 1994– (Chm., Scotland, 1989–94). Hon. LLD Aberdeen, 1999. *Recreations:* fishing, golf. *Clubs:* New (Edinburgh); Honourable Company of Edinburgh Golfers; Rosehall Golf (Turriff), Duff House Royal Golf (Banff).

MAROWITZ, Charles; Artistic Director: Malibu Stage Company, since 1990; Texas Stage Company, since 1994; Director and Dramaturge, California Repertory Theatre, Long Beach, since 1996; *b* 26 Jan. 1934; Austrian mother, Russian father; *m* 1982, Jane Elizabeth Allsop. *Educ:* Seward Park High Sch.; University Coll. London. Dir, In-Stage Experimental Theatre, 1958; Asst Dir, Royal Shakespeare Co., 1963–65; Artistic Director: Traverse Theatre, 1963–64; Open Space Theatre London, 1968–81; Open Space Theatre of Los Angeles, 1982; Associate Dir, LA Theater Center, 1984–89. Drama Critic: Encore Magazine, 1956–63; Plays and Players, 1958–74; The Village Voice, 1955–; The NY Times, 1966–; West Coast critic: Theatre Week magazine, 1990–97; In-Theater magazine, 1997–; Official Drama critic, Jewish Jl, 1998–; columnist, LA View, 1994–. *West End* Director: Loot, Criterion, 1967; The Bellow Plays, Fortune, 1966; Fortune and Men's Eyes, Comedy, 1969; productions *abroad:* Woyzeck, 1965, The Shrew, 1979, Nat. Theatre, Bergen; Hedda, 1978, Enemy of the People, 1979, Nat. Theatre, Oslo; Measure for Measure, Oslo New Theatre, 1981; The Father, Trondheim, 1981; Ah Sweet Mystery of Life, Seattle, 1981; A Midsummer Night's Dream, Odense, Denmark, 1983; Tartuffe, Molde, Norway, 1985; Marat/Sade, Rutgers, 1993; Merry Wives of Windsor, Dallas Shakespeare Fest., 1993; Bashville in Love, Texas, 1995; productions in *Los Angeles:* Artaud at Rodez, 1982; Sherlock's Last Case, 1984; The Petrified Forest, 1985; The Fair Penitent, 1986; The Shrew, 1986; Importance of Being Earnest, 1987; What the Butler Saw, 1988; Wilde West, 1989; Variations on Measure for Measure, 1990; A MacBeth, 1991. Order of the Purple Sash, 1969. *Publications:* The Method as Means, 1960; The Marowitz Hamlet, 1967; A Macbeth, 1970; Confessions of a Counterfeit Critic, 1973; Open Space Plays, 1974; Measure for Measure, 1975; The Shrew, 1975; Artaud at Rodez, 1976; Variations on The Merchant of Venice; The Act of Being, 1977; The Marowitz Shakespeare, 1978; New Theatre Voices of the 50s and 60s, 1981; Sex Wars, 1982; Prospero's Staff, 1986; Potboilers (collection of plays), 1986; Recycling Shakespeare, 1991; Burnt Bridges, 1991; Directing The Action, 1992; (trans.) Cyrano de Bergerac, 1995; Alarums and Excursions, 1996; The Other Way, 1997; Boulevard Comedies, 1999; Stage Fright, 2000; Stagedust (collection of reviews), 2001; Roar of the Canon (collection of Shakespeare criticism), 2001. *Recreation:* balling. *Address:* 3058 Sequit Drive, Malibu, CA 90265, USA.

MARQUAND, Prof. David (Ian), FBA 1998; FRHistS; Principal, Mansfield College, Oxford, 1996–Sept. 2002; *b* 20 Sept. 1934; *s* of Rt Hon. Hilary Marquand, PC; *m* 1959, Judith Mary (*née* Reed); one *s* one *d*. *Educ:* Emanuel Sch.; Magdalen Coll., Oxford; St Antony's Coll., Oxford (Sen. Schol.). 1st cl. hons Mod. Hist., 1957. FRHistS 1986. Teaching Asst, Univ. of Calif., 1958–59; Leader Writer, The Guardian, 1959–62; Research Fellow, St Antony's Coll., Oxford, 1962–64; Lectr in Politics, Univ. of Sussex, 1964–66. Contested: (Lab) Barry, 1964; (SDP) High Peak, 1983; MP (Lab) Ashfield, 1966–77; PPS to Minister of Overseas Develt, 1967–69; Jun. Opposition Front-Bench Spokesman on econ. affairs, 1971–72; Member: Select Cttee on Estimates, 1966–68; Select Cttee on Procedure, 1968–73; Select Cttee on Corp. Tax, 1971; British Deleg. to Council of Europe, 1970–73. Chief Advr, Secretariat-Gen., European Commission, 1977–78; Prof. of Contemporary History and Politics, Salford Univ., 1978–91; Prof. of Politics, 1991–96 (Hon. Prof., 1997–), and Dir, Political Economy Research Centre, 1993–96, Sheffield Univ. Vis. Scholar, Hoover Instn, Stanford, USA, 1985–86. Jt Ed., Political Qly, 1987–97. Member: Nat. Steering Cttee, SDP, 1981–88; Policy Cttee, Soc & Lib Dem, 1988–90. Trustee, Aspen Inst., Berlin, 1982–; Member: Adv. Council, Inst. of Contemporary British History, 1987–; Bd of Trustees, IPPR, 1992–; Adv. Council, Demos, 1993–; Social Justice Commn, 1993–94; Commn on Wealth Creation and Social Cohesion, 1994–95. Thomas Jefferson Meml Lectr, Univ. of Calif at Berkeley, 1981. FRSA. Hon. DLitt Salford, 1996. George Orwell Meml Prize (jtly), 1980; Sir Isaiah Berlin Prize, Pol Studies Assoc., 2001. *Publications:* Ramsay MacDonald, 1977; Parliament for Europe, 1979; (with David Butler) European Elections and British Politics, 1981; (ed) John Mackintosh on Politics, 1982; The Unprincipled Society, 1988; The Progressive Dilemma, 1991, 2nd edn 1999; (ed with Anthony Seldon) The Ideas That Shaped Post-War Britain, 1996; The New Reckoning, 1997; (ed with R. Nettler) Religion and Democracy, 2000; contrib. to: The Age of Austerity, 1964; A Radical Future, 1967; Coalitions in British Politics, 1978; Britain in Europe, 1980; The Political Economy of Tolerable Survival, 1980; The Rebirth of Britain, 1982; European Monetary Union Progress and Prospects, 1982; Social Theory and Political Practice, 1982; The Changing Constitution, 1985; Thatcherism, 1987; The Radical Challenge, 1987; The Ruling Performance, 1987; The Alternative, 1990; Debating the Constitution, 1993; Re-inventing the Left, 1994; articles and reviews in The Guardian, The Times, The Sunday Times, New Statesman, Encounter, Commentary, and in academic jls. *Recreation:* walking. *Address:* Mansfield College, Mansfield Road, Oxford OX1 3TF.

MÁRQUEZ, Gabriel García; Colombian novelist; *b* 1928; *m* Mercedes García Márquez; two *s*. *Educ:* Univ. of Bogotá; Univ. of Cartagena. Corresp., El Espectador, Rome and Paris; formed Cuban Press Agency, Bogotá; worked for Prensa Latina, Cuba, later as Dep. Head, NY office, 1961; lived in Venezuela, Cuba, USA, Spain, Mexico; returned to Colombia, 1982; divides time between Mexico and Colombia. Rómulo Gallegos Prize, 1972; Nobel Prize for Literature, 1982. *Publications:* La hojarasca, 1955 (Leaf Storm, 1973); El coronel no tiene quien la escriba, 1961 (No One Writes to the Colonel, 1971); La mala hora, 1962 (In Evil Hour, 1980); Los funerales de la Mamá Grande, 1962; Cien años de soledad, 1967 (One Hundred Years of Solitude, 1970); La increíble y triste historia de la cándida Eréndira, 1972 (Innocent Erendira and other stories, 1979); El otoño del patriarca, 1975 (The Autumn of the Patriarch, 1977); Crónica de una muerte anunciada, 1981 (Chronicle of a Death Foretold, 1982; filmed, 1987); (with P. Mendoza) El olor de la Guayaba, 1982 (Fragrance of Guava, ed T. Nairn, 1983); El amor en los tiempos del cólera, 1984 (Love in the Time of Cholera, 1988); Relato de un naufrago (The Story of a Shipwrecked Sailor, 1986); Clandestine in Chile: adventures of Miguel Littín, 1986; Amores Difíciles, 1989 (Of Love and Other Demons, 1995); El General en su Laberinto, 1989 (The General in his Labyrinth, 1991); Collected Stories, 1991; Doce cuentos peregrinos, 1992 (Strange Pilgrims, 1993); News of a Kidnapping (non-fiction), 1997. *Address:* c/o Agencia Literaria Carmen Balcelos, Diagonal 580, Barcelona, Spain.

MARQUIS, family name of **Earl of Woolton**.

MARQUIS, James Douglas, DFC 1945; Managing Director, Irvine Development Corporation, 1972–81; *b* 16 Oct. 1921; *s* of James Charles Marquis and Jessica Amy (*née* Huggett); *m* 1945, Brenda Eleanor, *d* of Robert Reyner Davey; two *s*. *Educ:* Shooters Hill Sch., Woolwich. Local Govt, 1938–41. Served War: RAF: 1941–46 (RAF 1st cl. Air Navigation Warrant, 1945), Navigation Officer, 177 Sqdn, 224 Gp, and AHQ Malaya (Sqdn Ldr 1945). Local Govt, 1946–56; Harlow Develt Corp., 1957–68; Irvine Develt Corp.: Chief Finance Officer, 1968–72; Dir of Finance and Admin., 1972. Pres., Ayrshire Chamber of Industries, 1979–80. Mem., Scottish Bonsai Assoc. FRMetS 1945; CPFA (IPFA 1950); FCIS 1953. *Publication:* An Ayrshire Sketchbook, 1979. *Recreations:* sketching and painting (five one-man exhibns, incl. one in Sweden; works in collections: Japan, Sweden, Norway, Denmark, Australia, USA, Canada); gardening, bonsai, suiseki. *Address:* 3 Knoll Park, Ayr KA7 4RH. *T:* (01292) 442212.

MARR, Andrew William Stevenson; Political Editor, BBC, since 2000; *b* 31 July 1959; *s* of Donald and Valerie Marr; *m* 1987, Jacqueline Ashley, *qv*; one *s* two *d*. *Educ:* Dundee High Sch.; Craigflower, Fife; Loretto School, Musselburgh; Trinity Hall, Cambridge (BA). Trainee and gen. reporter, 1982–85, Parly Corresp., 1985–86, The Scotsman; Political Corresp., The Independent, 1986–88; Political Editor: The Scotsman, 1988; The Economist, 1989–92; political columnist and Associate Editor, 1992–96, Editor, 1996–98, Editor-in-Chief, 1998, The Independent; columnist, The Observer, and The Express, 1998–2000. Columnist of the Year, 1994; Creative Media Journalist of Year, 2000; Pol Journalist of Year, C4/House Mag., 2001. *Publications:* The Battle for Scotland, 1992; Ruling Britannia, 1995; The Day Britain Died, 2000. *Recreations:* reading, painting, talking. *Address:* c/o BBC Westminster, 4 Millbank, SW1P 3JA.

MARR, (Sir) Leslie Lynn, (2nd Bt *cr* 1919, but does not use the title); MA Cambridge; painter and draughtsman; late Flight Lieutenant RAF; *b* 14 Aug. 1922; *o s* of late Col John Lynn Marr, OBE, TD, (and *g s* of 1st Bt,) and Amelia Rachel, *d* of late Robert Thompson, Overdinsdale Hall, Darlington; *S* grandfather, 1932; *m* 1st, 1948, Dinora Delores Mendelson (marr. diss. 1956); one *d*; 2nd, 1962, Lynn Heneage; two *d*. *Educ:* Shrewsbury; Pembroke Coll., Cambridge. Has exhibited at Ben Uri, Drian, Woodstock, Wildenstein, Whitechapel, Campbell and Franks Galls, London; also in Norwich, Belfast, Birmingham, Newcastle upon Tyne, Bristol and Paris. *Publication:* From My Point of View: personal record of some Norfolk churches, 1979. *Heir: cousin* James Allan Marr [*b* 17 May 1939; *m* 1965, Jennifer, *yr d* of late J. W. E. Gill; two *s* one *d*].

MARR-JOHNSON, Frederick James Maugham; His Honour Judge Marr-Johnson; a Circuit Judge, since 1991; *b* 17 Sept. 1936; *s* of late Kenneth Marr-Johnson and Hon. Diana Marr-Johnson; *m* 1966, Susan Eyre; one *s* one *d*. *Educ:* Winchester Coll.; Trinity Hall, Cambridge (MA). Called to the Bar, Lincoln's Inn, 1962, Bencher, 1999; practised on SE Circuit, 1963–91. Judge of Mayor's and City of London Court, 1999–. *Recreation:* sailing. *Address:* 33 Hestercombe Avenue, SW6 5LL. *T:* (020) 7731 0412. *Clubs:* Royal Yacht Squadron (Cowes); Bar Yacht (Rear Cdre, 1999–2000).

MARRACK, Rear-Adm. Philip Reginald, CB 1979; CEng, FIMechE, FIMarE; *b* 16 Nov. 1922; *s* of Captain Philip Marrack, RN and Annie Kathleen Marrack (*née* Proud); *m* 1954, Pauline Mary (*née* Haag); two *d*. *Educ:* Eltham Coll.; Plymouth Coll.; RNC Dartmouth; RN Engineering Coll., Manadon. War service at sea, HM Ships Orion and Argus, 1944–45; Advanced Engineering Course, RNC Greenwich, 1945–47; HM Submarines Templar and Token, 1947–50; served in Frigate Torquay, Aircraft Carriers Glory and Hermes, and MoD; Captain 1965; Commanded Admiralty Reactor Test Estab., Dounreay, 1967–70; CSO (Mat.) on Staff of Flag Officer Submarines, and Asst Dir (Nuclear), Dockyard Dept, 1970–74; Rear-Adm. 1974; Dir, Naval Ship Production, 1974–77; Dir, Dockyard Production and Support, 1977–81, retd. *Recreations:* fly fishing, gardening, viticulture, wine making.

MARRE, Romola Mary, (Lady Marre), CBE 1979; Vice Chairman, City Parochial Foundation, 1989–93 (Trustee, 1975–89); *b* 25 April 1920; *d* of late Aubrey John Gilling and Romola Marjorie Angier; *m* 1943, Sir Alan Samuel Marre, KCB (*d* 1990); one *s* one *d*. *Educ:* Chelmsford County High Sch. for Girls; Bedford Coll., Univ. of London. BA Hons Philosophy. Asst Principal (Temp.), Min. of Health, 1941–42; Sgt, subseq. Jun. Comdr, ATS Officer Selection Bd, 1942–45. Organiser, West Hampstead Citizen's Advice Bureau, 1962–65; Dep. Gen. Sec., Camden Council of Social Service, 1965–73; Adviser on Community Health Councils to DHSS, 1974–75; Chairman: London Voluntary Service Council (formerly London Council of Social Service), 1974–84; Cttee on the Future of the Legal Profession, 1986–88; Panel of Four Commn of Enquiry into Human Aids to Communication, 1990–92; Camden and Islington (formerly Bloomsbury, Camden and Islington) HA Dist Ethics Cttee, 1993–2000; Member: Lord Chancellor's Adv. Cttee on Legal Aid, 1975–80; Milk Marketing Bd, 1973–82; BBC and IBA Central Appeals Adv. Cttee, 1980–87 (Chm., 1984–87); Council of Management, Charity Projects, 1987–90; Dep. Chm., Royal Jubilee Trusts, 1981–88; Chairman: Volunteer Centre, 1973–78; Adv. Gp on Hospital Services for children with cancer in North Western Region, Jan.–June 1979; Prince of Wales' Adv. Gp on Disability, 1982–84; Child Mental Health Res. Trust, 1996–; Founder Pres., Barnet Voluntary Service Council, 1979–. *Recreations:* cooking, gardening, painting, talking. *Address:* 27 Edmunds Walk, N2 0HU. *T:* (020) 8883 4420.

MARRIN, John Wheeler; QC 1990; a Recorder, since 1997; *b* 24 Aug. 1951; *s* of late Dr Charles Ainsworth Marrin and of Cecilia Margaret Marrin (*née* Staveley); *m* 1984, Paquita Carmen Bulan de Zulueta; one s three *d*. *Educ:* Sherborne Sch.; Magdalene Coll., Cambridge (MA). Called to the Bar, Inner Temple, 1974. *Recreations:* music, ski-ing, horse-racing, travel. *Address:* Keating Chambers, 10 Essex Street, WC2R 3AA. *T:* (020) 7544 2600. *Club:* Royal Automobile.

MARRINER, Sir Neville, Kt 1985; CBE 1979; conductor; Founder and Director, Academy of St Martin in the Fields, since 1956; *b* 15 April 1924; *s* of Herbert Henry Marriner and Ethel May Roberts; *m* 1955, Elizabeth Mary Sims; one *s* one *d*. *Educ:* Lincoln Sch.; Royal College of Music (ARCM). Taught music at Eton Coll., 1948; Prof., Royal Coll. of Music, 1950. Martin String Quartet, 1949; Jacobean Ensemble, 1951; London Symphony Orchestra, 1954; Music Director: Los Angeles Chamber Orchestra, 1968–77; Minnesota Orchestra, 1979–86; Stuttgart Radio Symphony Orch., 1984–89. Artistic Director: South Bank Summer Music, 1975–77; Meadow Brook Festival, Detroit Symphony Orchestra, 1979–83; Barbican Summer Festival, 1985–87. Hon. ARAM; Hon. FRCM 1983; Fellow, Hong Kong Acad. Music, 1998. Hon. MusD: RSAMD; Univ. of Hull. Kt, Order of the Star of the North (Sweden), 1984; Officer, Ordre des Arts et des Lettres (France), 1995. *Club:* Garrick.

MARRIOTT, Arthur Leslie; QC 1997; Solicitor, Debevoise & Plimpton, since 1997; a Deputy High Court Judge, since 1997; a Recorder, since 1998; *b* 30 March 1943; *s* of Arthur Leonard Marriott and Helen Gracie Marriott (*née* Patterson). *Educ:* Selhurst Grammar Sch. for Boys, Croydon; Gymnasium Christian Ernestinum, Bayreuth, Germany; Coll. of Law. FCIArb 1990. Admitted Solicitor, England and Wales, 1966, Hong Kong, 1976; with Wilmer, Cuter & Pickering, 1988–97. *Publication:* (with Henry Brown) Alternative Dispute Resolution: principles and practice, 1993, 2nd edn 1999. *Recreations:* fishing, music. *Address:* (office) Tower 42, 25 Old Broad Street, EC2N 1HQ. *T:* (020) 7786 9000. *Clubs:* Athenæum, Royal Automobile.

MARRIOTT, Bryant Hayes; Director of Broadcasting, Seychelles Broadcasting Corporation (formerly Radio Television Seychelles), 1991–93; *b* 9 Sept. 1936; *s* of Rev. Horace Marriott and Barbara Marriott; *m* 1963, Alison Mary Eyles; one *s* two *d*. *Educ:* Tormore Sch., Upper Deal, Kent; Marlborough Coll., Wilts; New Coll., Oxford (MA). Joined BBC, 1961; Studio Manager, 1961; Producer, 1963; Staff Training Attachments Officer, 1973; Chief Asst to Controller Radio 1 and 2, 1976; Head of Recording Services, 1979; Controller, Radio Two, 1983; Controller, Special Duties, Radio BBC, 1990–91. *Recreations:* gardening, sailing, drumming. *Address:* 4 School Pasture, Burnham Deepdale, King's Lynn, Norfolk PE31 8DF. *Club:* Brancaster Staithe Sailing.

MARRIOTT, Sir Hugh Cavendish S.; *see* Smith-Marriott.

MARRIOTT, Martin Marriott; Headmaster, Canford School, 1976–92; *b* 28 Feb. 1932; *s* of late Rt Rev. Philip Selwyn Abraham, Bishop of Newfoundland, and Elizabeth Dorothy Cicely, *d* of late Sir John Marriott; *m* 1956, Judith Caroline Guerney Lubbock; one *s* two *d*. *Educ:* Lancing College; New College, Oxford. MA, DipEd. RAF Educn Branch, 1956–59. Asst Master, Heversham Grammar Sch., 1959–66; Asst Master, Housemaster, Second Master, Acting Master, Haileybury College, 1966–76. Chm., HMC, 1989. *Recreations:* grandchildren, golf, gardening. *Address:* Morris' Farm House, Baverstock, near Dinton, Salisbury, Wilts SP3 5EL. *T:* (01722) 716874. *Club:* East India.

MARRIOTT, Richard, TD 1965; Lord-Lieutenant of East Riding of Yorkshire, since 1996; *b* 17 Dec. 1930; *s* of late Rowland Arthur Marriott and Evelyn (*née* Caillard), Cotesbach Hall, Leics; *m* 1959, Janet (Sally) Coles; two *s*. *Educ:* Eton Coll.; Brasenose Coll., Oxford (Schol.). 2nd Lieut, Rifle Bde, 1950–51; Lt-Col comdg 21st SAS Regt (Artists) TA, 1966–69. With Brown Shipley & Co. Ltd, 1954–63; Partner, Mullens & Co. (Govt Brokers), 1964–86; Dir, Mercury Asset Mgt, 1986–96. Mem., Rural Develt Commn, Humberside, 1986–95. Vice-President: Officers' Assoc. (Chm., 1977–86); RUSI, 1993–98; Financial Adviser: Army Benevolent Fund, 1969–97 (Treas., 1997–2000); Airborne Forces Security Fund, 1972–; Trustee, Special Air Service Assoc., 1994–. Pres., Yorks Agricl Soc., 1995–96. Member Council: Nat. Army Mus., 1991–; Hull Univ., 1994–2000; Vice-Pres., Brynmor Jones Lby, Hull, 1988–. Trustee: Burtle Trust, 1985–98 (Dep. Chm., 1990–96); York Minster Fund, 1987–2000; Chm., Burton Constable Foundn, 1992–. Mem., Adv. Panel, Greenwich Hosp., 1981–. High Sheriff, Humberside, 1991–92. *Recreations:* books, the arts, travel, field sports. *Address:* Boynton Hall, Bridlington, E Yorks YO16 4XJ. *Clubs:* Beefsteak, Special Forces, White's.

MARRIS, James Hugh Spencer; Director, Newcastle Race Course, since 1994; Regional Chairman, British Gas, Northern, 1988–93; *b* 30 July 1937; *s* of Harry V. Marris and Agnes E. Hutchinson; *m* 1963, Susan Mary Husband; one *s* one *d*. *Educ:* King William's College, Isle of Man; Royal Technical College, Salford. ARTCS, CEng, FIGasE. Dir of Engineering, E Midlands Gas, 1978–82; Regional Dep. Chm., Eastern Gas, 1982–83; HQ Dir (Ops), British Gas, 1983–87. *Publications:* contribs to IGasE Jl. *Recreations:* golf, gardening. *Address:* 3 Apple Tree Rise, Corbridge, Northumberland NE45 5HD. *T:* (01434) 633509.

MARRIS, Robert; MP (Lab) Wolverhampton South West, since 2001; *b* 8 April 1955; *s* of Dr Charles Marris and Margaret Chetwode Marris, JP; partner, Julia Pursehouse. *Educ:* St Edward's Sch., Oxford; Univ. of British Columbia (BA Sociology and Hist. (double 1st) 1976; MA Hist. 1979); Birmingham Poly. Trucker, 1977–79; trolley bus driver, 1979–82; law student, 1982–84; articled clerk, 1985–87; solicitor, 1987–. *Recreations:* Wolves, Canadiana, bicycling. *Address:* House of Commons, SW1A 0AA. *T:* (020) 7219 3000.

MARRIS, Prof. Robin Lapthorn; Professor of Economics, 1981–86, and Head of Department of Economics, 1983–86, Birkbeck College, University of London, now Professor Emeritus; *b* 31 March 1924; *s* of Eric Denyer Marris, CB, and late Phyllis, *d* of T. H. F. Lapthorn, JP; *m* 1st, 1949, Marion Ellinger; 2nd, 1954, Jane Evelina Burney Ayres; one *s* two *d*; 3rd, 1972, Anne Fairclough Mansfield; one *d*. *Educ:* Bedales Sch.; King's Coll., Cambridge. BA 1946, ScD 1968, Cantab. Asst Principal, HM Treasury, 1947–50; UN, Geneva, 1950–52; Fellow of King's Coll., Cambridge, 1951–76; Lectr, 1951–72, Reader, 1972–76, in Econs, Univ. of Cambridge; Prof. 1976–81 and Chm., 1976–79, Dept of Economics, Univ. of Maryland. Visiting Professor: Univ. of California, Berkeley, 1961; Harvard, 1967; Trento Univ., Italy, 1989–91. Dir, World Economy Div., Min. of Overseas Develt, 1964–66. Mem., Vis. Cttee, Open Univ., 1982–. *Publications:* Economic Arithmetic, 1958; The Economic Theory of Managerial Capitalism, 1964; The Economics of Capital Utilisation, 1964; (with Adrian Wood) The Corporate Economy, 1971; The Corporate Society, 1974; The Theory and Future of the Corporate Economy and Society, 1979; The Higher Education Crisis, 1987; Reconstructing Keynsian Economics with Imperfect Competition, 1991; Economics, Bounded Rationality and the Cognitive Revolution, 1992; How to Save the Underclass, 1996; Managerial Capitalism in Retrospect, 1998; Ending Poverty, 1999; contrib. Econ. Jl, Rev. Econ. Studies, Economica, Jl Manchester Stat. Soc., Jl Royal Stat. Soc., Amer. Econ. Rev., Qly Jl of Econs, Jl of Economic Literature, etc. *Recreations:* cooking, ski-ing, sailing. *Address:* Lingard House, Chiswick Mall, W4 2PJ.

See also S. N. Marris.

MARRIS, Stephen Nicholson; economic consultant; *b* 7 Jan. 1930; *s* of Eric Denyer Marris, CB, and Phyllis May Marris (*née* Lapthorn); *m* 1955, Margaret Swindells; two *s* one *d*. *Educ:* Bryanston School; King's College, Cambridge. MA, PhD. Nat. Inst. of Economic and Social Research, 1953–54; economist and international civil servant; with Org. for European Economic Co-operation, later Org. for Economic Co-operation and Development (OECD), 1956–83: Dir, Economics Branch, 1970; Economic Advr to Sec.-Gen., 1975; Sen. Fellow, Inst. for Internat. Econs, Washington, 1983–88. Vis. Res. Prof. of Internat. Economics, Brookings Instn, Washington DC, 1969–70; Vis. Prof., Institut d'Etudes Politiques, Paris, 1986. Hon. Dr Stockholm Univ., 1978. *Publication:* Deficits and the Dollar: the World Economy at Risk, 1985. *Recreation:* sailing. *Address:* 8 Sentier des Pierres Blanches, 92190 Meudon, France. *T:* 146269812.

See also R. L. Marris.

MARRISON, Rev. Dr Geoffrey Edward; Hon. Fellow, South East Asian Studies, since 1992, Senior Fellow, since 1998, University of Hull (Associate, Centre for South-East Asian Studies, 1989–91); *b* 11 Jan. 1923; *s* of John and Rose Marrison; *m* 1958, Margaret Marian Millburn; one *s* three *d*. *Educ:* SOAS, Univ. of London (BA Malay 1948, PhD

Linguistics 1967); Bishops' Coll. Cheshunt; Kirchliche Hochschule, Berlin. Indian Army, 1942–46. SOAS, 1941–42 and 1946–49; ordained Priest, Singapore, 1952; in Malaya with USPG, 1952–56; Vicar of St Timothy, Crookes, Sheffield, 1958–61; Linguistics Adviser British and Foreign Bible Soc., 1962–67, incl. service in Assam, 1962–64; Asst Keeper, British Museum, 1967–71, Dep. Keeper 1971–74; Dir and Keeper, Dept of Oriental Manuscripts and Printed Books, British Library, 1974–83; permission to officiate, dio. of Carlisle, 1983–; Tutor, Carlisle Diocesan Training Inst., 1984–. Res. studies on Indonesian literatures, Leiden and Indonesia, 1990–91. Hon. Canon of All Saints Pro-Cathedral, Shillong, 1963. FRAS. *Publications:* The Christian Approach to the Muslim, 1958; A Catalogue of the South-East Asian Collections of Professor M. A. Jaspan (1926–1975), 1989; A Catalogue of the South-East Asian History Collections of Dr D. K. Bassett (1931–1989), 1992; A Catalogue of the Collections of Rev. Dr Harry Parkin on Asian Religions and Batak Studies (1926–1990), 1993; A Catalogue of the Collections of Dr Roy Bruton on Sarawak, and on the Sociology of Education, 1994; Sasak and Javanese Literature of Lombok, 1999; Catalogue of Javanese and Subak Texts, 1999; articles in Jl Malayan Branch Royal Asiatic Soc., Bible Translator. *Recreations:* ethno-linguistics of South and South East Asia, Christian and oriental art. *Address:* Emmaus, 1 Ainsworth Street, Ulverston, Cumbria LA12 7EU. *T:* (01229) 586874.

MARS-JONES, Adam; writer; Film Critic, The Times, 1999–2001; *b* 26 Oct. 1954; *s* of Hon. Sir William Mars-Jones, MBE. *Educ:* Westminster School; Trinity Hall, Cambridge (BA 1976). Film Critic, The Independent, 1986–99. *Publications:* Lantern Lecture (stories), 1981 (Somerset Maugham Award 1982); (with Edmund White) The Darker Proof (stories), 1987, 2nd edn 1988; Venus Envy (essay), 1990; Monopolies of Loss (stories), 1992; The Waters of Thirst (novel), 1993; Blind Bitter Happiness (essays), 1997. *Recreations:* organ-playing, baby-sitting. *Address:* 42B Calabria Road, Highbury, N5 1HU. *T:* (020) 7226 2890. *Club:* London Apprentice.

MARSALIS, Wynton; trumpeter; *b* New Orleans, 18 Oct. 1961; *s* of Ellis and Dolores Marsalis. *Educ:* New Orleans Center for the Creative Arts; Berkshire Music Center (Harvey Shapiro Award); Juilliard Sch., NY (Schol.). Mem., Art Blakey's Jazz Messengers, 1980–81; formed own jazz quintet, 1981; has played with major orchestras worldwide, incl. New Orleans Philharmonic, LSO, English Chamber Orch. *Compositions* include: In This House, On This Morning; Blood on the Fields, 1997 (Pulitzer Prize for Music, 1997); Knozz-Moe-King; Jazz (ballet score). Numerous recordings (Grammy Awards for jazz and classical performances). *Publications:* Sweet Swing Blues on the Road, 1994; Marsalis on Music, 1995. *Address:* c/o Agency for the Performing Arts, 9200 West Sunset Boulevard, Suite 1200, West 12 Hollywood, CA 90069–5812, USA.

MARSDEN, Edmund Murray; Director (formerly Minister (Cultural Affairs)), India, and Regional Director, South Asia, British Council, since 2000; *b* 22 Sept. 1946; *s* of Christopher Marsden and Ruth Marsden (*née* Kershaw); *m* 1975, Christine Vanner (*d* 1980); *m* 1981, Megan McIntyre; one *s*. *Educ:* Winchester College; Trinity College, Cambridge. Partner, Compton Press, Salisbury, 1968–70; Nuffield Foundn Publications Unit, 1970–71; British Council: Ghana, 1971; Belgium, 1973; Algeria, 1975; Management Accountant, 1977; Syria, 1980; Dir, Educn Contracts, 1982; Turkey, 1987; Dir, Corporate Affairs, 1990–93; Asst Dir-Gen., 1993–99; Chm., Intermediate Technol. Develt Gp, 1995–97 and 1998–2000. *Address:* c/o Foreign and Commonwealth Office, King Charles Street, SW1A 2AH; 17 Kasturba Gandhi Marg, New Delhi 110 001, India. *T:* (11) 3353906, *Fax:* (11) 3357710; *e-mail:* edmund.marsden@in.britishcouncil.org.

MARSDEN, Frank; JP; *b* Everton, Liverpool, 15 Oct. 1923; *s* of Sidney Marsden and Harriet Marsden (*née* Needham); *m* 1943, Muriel Lightfoot; three *s*. *Educ:* Abbotsford Road Sec. Mod. Sch., Liverpool. Served War, with RAF Bomber Command, 115 Sqdn (Warrant Officer), 1941–46. Joined Lab. Party and Co-op. Movement, 1948. MP (Lab) Liverpool, Scotland, Apr. 1971–Feb. 1974. Local Councillor: Liverpool St Domingo Ward, May 1964–67; Liverpool Vauxhall Ward, 1969–71; Knowsley DC, 1976–. Chm. Liverpool Markets, 1965–67; Past Mem. Exec. Cttee: Liverpool Trades Council; Liverpool Lab. Party. JP (City of Liverpool), 1969. *Recreations:* jazz music, gardening. *Address:* 2 Thunderbolt Cottage, 6 Alder Lane, Knowsley, Prescot, Merseyside L34 9EQ. *T:* (0151) 546 8666.

MARSDEN, Gordon; MP (Lab) Blackpool South, since 1997; *b* 28 Nov. 1953; *s* of late George Henry Marsden and of Joyce Marsden. *Educ:* Stockport Grammar Sch.; New Coll., Oxford (BA 1st cl. Hons History; MA); Warburg Inst., London Univ. (postgrad. res.); Harvard Univ. (Kennedy Schol. in Internat. Relations). Tutor and Associate Lectr, Arts Faculty, Open Univ., 1977–97; PR Consultant, 1980–85; Chief Public Affairs Advr, English Heritage, 1984–85; Editor, History Today, 1985–97; Consultant Ed., New Socialist, 1989–90. Chm., Fabian Soc., 2000–. Contested (Lab) Blackpool S, 1992. PPS, Lord Chancellor's Dept, 2001–. Mem., Select Cttee on Educn and Employment, 1998–2001. Vice-President: All Party Arts and Heritage Gp; PLP Educn and Employment Cttee, 1997–. Pres., British Resorts Asssoc., 1998–. Mem. Bd, Inst. of Historical Res., 1995–. Mem. Editl Bd, The House Mag., 1997–. *Publications:* (ed) Victorian Values: personalities and perspectives in Nineteenth Century society, 1990, 2nd edn 1998; (contrib.) The English Question, 2000; contrib. Political Qly, History Today, New Statesman. *Recreations:* world music, travel, medieval culture. *Address:* House of Commons, SW1A 0AA. *T:* (020) 7219 1262.

MARSDEN, Dr John Christopher; Executive Secretary, Linnean Society, since 1989; *b* 4 March 1937; *s* of Ewart and May Marsden; *m* 1962, Jessany Margaret Hazel Macdonald; two *s*. *Educ:* Bristol Grammar Sch.; Keble Coll., Oxford (MA, DPhil). FRSC; FIBiol. Lectr in Biology, Univ. of York, 1965–71; Sen. Res. Fellow, Inst. of Child Health, 1971–72; Reader in Cell Physiology, City of London Polytechnic, 1972–74; Polytechnic of Central London: Head of Life Scis, 1974–86; Dean, Faculty of Engrg and Sci., 1986–88, retired. *Publications:* Enzymes and Equilibria (with C. F. Stoneman), 1974; numerous contribs to biol. jls. *Recreations:* book collecting, cookery. *Address:* 7 Surrey Close, Tunbridge Wells, Kent TN2 5RF. *T:* (01892) 533784; *e-mail:* taxon@pavilion.co.uk.

MARSDEN, Jonathan Mark; Deputy Surveyor of the Queen's Works of Art, since 1996; *b* 15 Feb. 1960; *s* of Rear-Adm. Peter Nicholas Marsden, *qv*. *Educ:* Sherborne Sch.; Univ. of York (BA Hons Hist.). Asst Curator, The Treasure Houses of Britain exhibn, Nat. Gall. of Art, Washington, 1983–85; Historic Buildings Rep., Nat. Trust N Wales Reg., 1986–92, Thames and Chilterns Reg., 1992–96. *Publications:* several National Trust guidebooks; contribs to learned jls. *Recreations:* gardening, shooting, music, beach cricket. *Address:* 43 Cleaver Square, SE11 4EA. *Club:* Travellers.

MARSDEN, Paul William Barry; MP (Lab) Shrewsbury and Atcham, since 1997; *b* 18 March 1968; *s* of Thomas Darlington Marsden and Audrey Marsden; *m* 1994, Michelle Sarah Bayley (*née* Somerville); two *s*. *Educ:* Open Univ. (Dip. Mgt 1995); Newcastle Coll. (Dip. Business Excellence 2000). Quality Manager: Taylor Woodrow, 1990–94; NatWest Bank, 1994–96; Mitel Telecom, 1996–97. Mem., Select Cttee on Agric., 1997–2001; Chm., All Party Gp on Mgt, 1998. Vice President: Offa's Dyke Assoc., 1997–; Heart of Wales Travellers' Assoc., 1997–. Member: Shropshire Chamber of Commerce, Trng & Enterprise, 1997–; Agric. & Rural Economy Cttee, CLA, 1997–2001. MIMgt 1996; MInstD 2001. *Recreations:* marathon running, gardening, American political history, family, rural affairs. *Address:* (office) 3rd Floor, Talbot House, Market Street, Shrewsbury SY1 1LG. *T:* (01743) 341422, *Fax:* (01743) 341261; *e-mail:* marsdenp@parliament.uk.

MARSDEN, Rear-Adm. Peter Nicholas; *b* 29 June 1932; *s* of Dr James Pickford Marsden and Evelyn (*née* Holman); *m* 1956, Jean Elizabeth Mather; two *s* one *d*. *Educ:* Felsted Sch., Essex. Joined RN, 1950; Commander, 1968; Captain, 1976; Commodore, Admiralty Interview Bd, 1983–84; Sen. Naval Mem., DS, RCDS, 1985–88. Exec. Dir, 21st Century Trust, 1989–92. *Recreations:* golf, beagling, gardening. *Address:* c/o National Westminster Bank, Standishgate, Wigan, Lancs WN1 1UJ.

See also J. M. Marsden.

MARSDEN, Dr Rosalind Mary; HM Diplomatic Service; Director, Asia-Pacific, Foreign and Commonwealth Office, since 1999; *b* 1950; *d* of late Major Walter Stancliffe Marsden and Winifred Howells. *Educ:* Woking County Grammar Sch. for Girls; Somerville Coll., Oxford (BA 1st Cl. Hons Mod. Hist.); St Antony's Coll., Oxford (DPhil). Joined FCO, 1974; Tokyo, 1976–80; Policy Planning Staff, 1980–82; EC Dept (Internal), 1983–84; Bonn, 1985–88; Hong Kong Dept, 1989–91; on secondment to National Westminster Bank Gp, 1991–93; Political Counsellor, Tokyo, 1993–96; Hd, UN Dept, FCO, 1996–99. *Recreations:* mountain walking, reading, travel. *Address:* c/o Foreign and Commonwealth Office, King Charles Street, SW1A 2AH.

MARSDEN, Sir Simon (Neville Llewelyn), 4th Bt *cr* 1924, of Grimsby, co. Lincoln; fine art photographer; author; *b* 1 Dec. 1948; *s* of Sir John Denton Marsden, 2nd Bt and of Hope (now Dowager Lady Marsden), *yr d* of late G. E. Llewelyn; *S* brother, 1997; *m* 1st, 1970, Catherine Thérèsa Windsor-Lewis (marr. diss. 1978); 2nd, 1984, Caroline Stanton; one *s* one *d*. *Educ:* Ampleforth Coll., Yorks; Sorbonne Univ., Paris. Photographer, 1969–; group exhibns, 1972–, include: London, NY, Paris, European and USA tour; one-man exhibns, 1975–, include: London, NY, Dublin, Paris, Brussels, Tokyo; work in collections including: Arts Council of GB, V & A Mus., Saatchi Collection, London; Bibliothèque Nationale, Paris; J. Paul Getty Mus., Malibu, Cleveland Mus. of Art, USA. Radio and TV appearances, 1986–, incl. Ghosthunter (docu-drama), Granada TV, 1992. Arts Council of GB Awards, 1975 and 1976. *Publications:* In Ruins: the once great houses of Ireland, 1980; The Haunted Realm: ghosts, witches and other strange tales, 1986; Visions of Poe, 1988; Phantoms of the Isles: further tales from the haunted realm, 1990; The Journal of a Ghosthunter: in search of the undead from Ireland to Transylvania, 1994; Beyond the Wall: the lost world of East Germany, 1999; Venice, City of Haunting Dreams, 2001. *Recreations:* sport, walking, historic buildings, reading. *Heir: s* Tadgh Orlando Denton Marsden, *b* 25 Dec. 1990. *Address:* The Presbytery, Hainton, Market Rasen, Lincs LN8 6LR. *T:* (01507) 313646. *Club:* Chelsea Arts.

MARSDEN, Susan; Part-time Chairman: Social Security Appeal Tribunals (Leeds), 1987–97; Disability Appeal Tribunals, 1992–97; *b* 6 Dec. 1931; *d* of late John Marsden-Smedley and Agatha (*née* Bethell). *Educ:* Downe House Sch.; Girton Coll., Cambridge (MA). Called to the Bar, Middle Temple, 1957. Worked in consumer organisations in Britain and US, 1957–65; Senior Research Officer, Consumer Council, 1966–70; Legal Officer, Nuffield Foundation Legal Advice Research Unit; 1970–72; Exec. Dir, 1972–78, and Course Dir, 1978–81, Legal Action Gp (Editor, LAG Bulletin, 1972–78); Sec., Public Sector Liaison, RIBA, 1981–84; Asst Dir, Nat. Assoc. of CAB, 1985–86. Chair, Greater London CAB Service, 1979–85; Member: Council, National Assoc. of CAB, 1980–84; Royal Commn on Legal Services, 1976–79; Yorks Regional Rivers Adv. Cttee, Nat. Rivers Authority, 1989–96; Council, Leeds Civic Trust, 1989–92. Chair, EYE on the Aire, 1988–93. Sec., Access Cttee, and Local Access Officer, WR Ramblers' Assoc., 2001–. *Publication:* Justice Out of Reach, a case for Small Claims Courts, 1969. *Recreations:* conservation along the River Aire, tree planting and preservation, gardening, walking, looking at modern buildings. *Address:* Flat 5, 28 Newlay Lane, Horsforth, Leeds LS18 4LE. *T:* (0113) 258 0936.

MARSDEN, William, CMG 1991; HM Diplomatic Service, retired; Director: Las Delicias SA; Turismo Pacifico, Costa Rica; *b* 15 Sept. 1940; *s* of Christopher Marsden and Ruth (*née* Kershaw); *m* 1964, Kaia Collingham; one *s* one *d*. *Educ:* Winchester Coll.; Lawrenceville Sch., USA; Trinity Coll., Cambridge (MA); London Univ. (BSc Econs). FO, 1962–64; UK Delegn to NATO, 1964–66; Rome, 1966–69; seconded as Asst to Gen. Manager, Joseph Lucas Ltd, 1970; First Sec., FCO, 1971–76; First Sec. and Cultural Attaché, Moscow, 1976–79; Asst Head, European Community Dept, FCO, 1979–81; Counsellor, UK Representation to EEC, 1981–85; Head, E Africa Dept, FCO, and Comr, British Indian Ocean Territory, 1985–88; Ambassador to Costa Rica, and concurrently Ambassador to Nicaragua, 1989–92; Minister (Trade), Washington, 1992–94; Asst Under-Sec. of State, later Dir, (Americas), FCO, 1994–97; Ambassador to Argentina, 1997–2000. Chairman: Diplomatic Service Assoc., 1987–88; Twickenham Town Cttee, 1981–88. MIMgt. *Address:* Townend, Chelmorton, Derbyshire SK17 9SH. *T:* (020) 7834 3275.

MARSH, family name of **Baron Marsh**.

MARSH, Baron *cr* 1981 (Life Peer), of Mannington in the County of Wiltshire; **Richard William Marsh;** PC 1966; Kt 1976; FZS; FCIT; Chairman: Mannington Management Services, since 1989; Laurentian Financial Group plc, since 1986; *b* 14 March 1928; *s* of William Marsh, Belvedere, Kent; *m* 1st, 1950, Evelyn Mary (marr. diss. 1973), *d* of Frederick Andrews, Southampton; two *s*; 2nd, 1973, Caroline Dutton (*d* 1975); 3rd, 1979, Felicity, *d* of Baron McFadzean of Kelvinside. *Educ:* Jennings Sch., Swindon; Woolwich Polytechnic; Ruskin Coll., Oxford. Health Services Officer, National Union of Public Employees, 1951–59; Mem., Clerical and Administrative Whitley Council for Health Service, 1953–59; MP (Lab) Greenwich, Oct. 1959–April 1971; promoted Offices Act 1961; Member: Select Cttee Estimates, 1961; Chm. Interdepartmental Cttee to Co-ordinate Govt Policy on Industrial Training, 1964; Parly Sec., Min. of Labour, 1964–65; Joint Parly Sec., Min. of Technology, 1965–66; Minister of Power, 1966–68; Minister of Transport, 1968–69. Chairman: British Railways Bd, 1971–76; Newspaper Publishers' Assoc., 1976–90; British Iron and Steel Consumers' Council, 1977–82; Allied Investments Ltd, 1977–81; Member: NEDC, 1971–; Freight Integration Council, 1971–; Council, CBI, 1970–. Chairman: Allied Medical Group, 1977–81; Vivat Hldgs PLC, 1982–88; TV-am, 1983–84 (Dep. Chm., 1980–83); Lopex PLC, 1986–97 (Dir, 1985–97); China & Eastern Investments Trust, Hong Kong, 1990–98 (Dir, 1987–98); Gartmore British Income & Growth Trust, 1994–; Dep. Chm., United Medical Enterprises Ltd, 1978–81; Director: Imperial Life of Canada UK, 1983–; Imperial Life Assurance Co. of Canada, 1983–; Charles Church Developments, 1987–97; Laurentian Group Corp. (Montreal), 1990–94; Advisor: Nissan Motor Co., 1981–; Fujitec, 1982–. Pres., Council ECSC, 1968. Governor: British Transport Staff Coll. (Chm.); London Business Sch. FIMgt; FInstD; FInstM. *Publication:* Off the Rails (autobiog.), 1978. *Address:* House of Lords, SW1A 0PW.

MARSH, Barrie; *see* Marsh, G. B.

MARSH, Derek Richard, CVO 1999; Deputy Head of Mission and Consul-General, Republic of Korea, since 1997 (on secondment); *b* 17 Sept. 1946; *s* of Reginald and Minnie Marsh; *m* 1969, Frances Anne Roberts; one *s* one *d*. *Educ:* Queen's Coll., Oxford (Schol.; MA 1973). Ministry of Defence: Asst Principal, 1968–72; Asst Private Sec. to Minister of State for Defence, 1973–74; Principal, 1974–78; ndc, 1975; Admin. Sec., Sovereign Base Areas, Cyprus, 1978–81; Asst Sec., 1982–86; rcds 1987; Department of Trade and Industry: Head of Air 1 and 2, 1988–91; Director: Companies House, 1991–93; Projects Export Promotion, 1994–97. Non-executive Director: Felixstowe Dock and Railway Co., 1990–91; Bovis Homes Ltd, 1992–93. *Recreations:* travel, reading, running. *Address:* c/o Foreign and Commonwealth Office, King Charles Street, SW1A 2AH.

MARSH, Rt Rev. Edward Frank; Bishop of Central Newfoundland, 1990–2000; *b* 25 Oct. 1935; *m* 1962, Emma Marsh; one *s* two *d*. *Educ:* Dalhousie Univ., NS (BCom 1956); Univ. of Newfoundland (BA 1960); Queen's Coll., Newfoundland (LTh 1961; BD 1969). Deacon 1959, priest 1960; Curate, Corner Brook, 1959–63; Incumbent, Harbour Breton, 1963–69; Curate, Wickford, 1969–71; Incumbent, Indian Bay, 1971–73; Curate, St John the Baptist Cathedral, St John's, 1973–77; Rector of Cartwright, dio. East Newfoundland, 1977–81; Rector, Holy Trinity, Grand Falls, 1981–90.

MARSH, Ven. (Francis) John, DPhil; Archdeacon of Blackburn, 1996–2001; *b* 3 July 1947; *s* of William Frederick and Helena Mary Marsh; *m* 1974, Gillian Popely; two *d*. *Educ:* York Univ. (BA 1969; DPhil 1976); Cert Theol Cambridge, 1975. ATCL 1965; ARCM 1966; ARCO 1971. Ordained deacon, 1975, priest, 1976; Assistant Curate: St Matthew's, Cambridge, 1975–78; Christ Church, Pitsmoor, Sheffield, 1979–81; Dir of Pastoral Trng, St Thomas', Crookes, Sheffield, 1981–85; Vicar, Christ Church, South Ossett, Wakefield, 1985–96. Rural Dean of Dewsbury, 1993–96. Mem., Gen. Synod of C of E, 1990–96, 1997–. Chm. Trustees, Anglican Renewal Ministries, 1989–. Mem., Adv. Bd, RSCM, 2000–.

MARSH, Rear-Adm. Geoffrey Gordon Ward, CB 1985; OBE 1969; jssc; Project Manager, NATO Frigate 90, Hamburg, 1988–90, retired; *m*; one *s* one *d*. *Educ:* St Albans Sch.; Queens' Coll., Cambridge. Britannia Royal Naval Coll., 1947; served on HM Ships: Indefatigable; Victorious; Carron; Norfolk; Girdle Ness; Bristol; involved in develt of Sea Dart missile; Hd of Propulsion Machinery Control, Ship Dept; Asst Dir (Surface Warfare), Naval Op. Req.; Dir, Weapons Co-ordination and Acceptance (Naval), MoD, 1978–80; i/c HMS Thunderer, 1980–82; ACNS (Op. Req.), 1982–84; Dep. Controller, Warships Equipment, MoD (Navy), 1984–87; Chief Naval Engr Officer, 1985–87. *Address:* c/o The Naval Secretary, Ministry of Defence, Old Admiralty Building, Whitehall, SW1A 2BE.

MARSH, Gordon Victor, MA; FHSM; Member, Police Complaints Authority, 1989–94 and 1995–96; *b* 14 May 1929; *s* of late Ven. Wilfred Carter Marsh, Devil's Lake, North Dakota, USA and Rosalie (*née* Holliday); *m* Millicent, *e d* of late Christopher Thomas and Edith Rowsell; one *s* one *d*. *Educ:* Grammar Schs, Swindon; Keble Coll., Oxford (MA); Inst. of Health Service Administrators (FHA 1964); Sloan Business Sch., Cornell Univ., USA. NHS admin. posts, England and Wales, 1952–72; Administrator and Sec., Bd of Governors, UCH, 1972–74; Area Administrator, Lambeth, Southwark and Lewisham AHA(T), 1974–82; Dep. Health Service Comr, 1982–89, retd. Vice-Chm., Assoc. of Chief Administrators of Health Authorities, 1980–82; Member: Council, National Assoc. of Health Authorities, 1979–82; Adv. Bd, Coll. of Occupational Therapists, 1974–95. Chm., Trelawn Cttee of Richmond Fellowship, 1970–83; Hon. Sec. to Congregational Meeting and Wandsman, St Paul's Cathedral, 1980–. *Publications:* articles in professional jls. *Recreations:* music, gardening. *Address:* Springwater, St Lucian's Lane, Wallingford, Oxon OX10 9ER. *T:* (01491) 836660; *e-mail:* gmarsh@supanet.com. *Clubs:* Oxford and Cambridge, Nikaean.

See also Rev. Canon R. St J. J. Marsh.

MARSH, (Graham) Barrie; FCIArb; solicitor; Partner, Mace & Jones, Solicitors, Liverpool and Manchester, 1959–99 (Senior Partner, 1980–97); *b* 18 July 1935; *s* of Ernest Heaps Marsh and Laura Greenhalgh Marsh; *m* 1961, Nancy Smith; one *s* two *d*. *Educ:* Bury Grammar Sch.; Loughborough Grammar Sch.; Liverpool Univ. (LLB Hons). FCIArb 1982. Admitted as Solicitor, 1957. Nat. Chm., Young Solicitors Gp, Law Soc., 1975; President: Liverpool Law Soc., 1978–79; Solicitors' Disciplinary Tribunal, 1988–2001; Liverpool Publicity Assoc., 1980. Chairman: Merseyside Chamber of Commerce and Industry, 1984–86; Radio City PLC, 1988–91. Non-exec. Dir, Liverpool HA, 1996–2000. Trustee, Nat. Museums and Galls on Merseyside, 1998–. Hon. Belgian Consul, Liverpool, and for NW, 1987–96. *Publications:* Employer and Employee: a complete and practical guide to the modern law of employment, 1977, 3rd edn 1990; contribs to legal and personnel jls on all aspects of employment law and industrial relations. *Recreations:* golf, Liverpool Football Club, bird-watching, hill-walking. *Address:* Calmer Hey, Benty Heath Lane, Willaston, South Wirral CH64 1SA. *T:* (0151) 327 4863; *e-mail:* barriemarsh@hotmail.com. *Clubs:* Army and Navy; Heswall Golf (Cheshire).

MARSH, Jean Lyndsey Torren; actress, writer; Artistic Director, Adelphi University Theatre, Long Island, New York, 1981–83; *b* 1 July 1934; *d* of late Henry Charles and of Emmeline Susannah Marsh; *m* 1955, Jon Devon Roland Pertwee (marr. diss. 1960; he *d* 1996). Began as child actress and dancer; *films:* Return to Oz; Willow; danced in Tales of Hoffmann, Where's Charley?, etc; Fatherland, 1995 (Cable Ace Award for Best Supporting Actress, 1996); acted in repertory companies: Huddersfield, Nottingham, etc; Broadway debut in Much Ado About Nothing, 1959; West End debut, Bird of Time, 1961; *stage:* Habeas Corpus, The Importance of Being Earnest, Too True to be Good, Twelfth Night, Blithe Spirit, Whose Life is it Anyway?, Uncle Vanya, On the Rocks, Pygmalion, Hamlet, The Chalk Garden; *television:* series, Nine to Five; co-created and co-starred (Rose) in series Upstairs Downstairs (Emmy, 1975); co-created series, The House of Eliott; Alexei Sayle Show; The Ghost Hunter; *radio* incl. Bleak House. Hon. DH Maryland Coll., NY, 1980. *Publications:* The Illuminated Language of Flowers, 1978; The House of Eliott, 1993; Fiennders Keepers, 1996; Iris, 1999; articles for Sunday Times, Washington Post, New York Times, Los Angeles Times, Daily Telegraph. *Recreations:* walking, reading, cooking, eating, drinking, listening to music. *Address:* c/o Michael Whitehall Associates, 125 Gloucester Road, SW7 4TE.

MARSH, Ven. John; *see* Marsh, Ven. F. J.

MARSH, Sir John (Stanley), Kt 1999; CBE 1993; Professor of Agricultural Economics and Management, later of Agricultural and Food Economics, Reading University, 1984–97, now Emeritus; *b* 5 Oct. 1931; *s* of Stanley Albert Marsh and Elsie Gertrude Marsh (*née* Powell); *m* 1958, Kathleen Edith Casey; one *s* one *d*. *Educ:* St John's Coll., Oxford (BA PPE 1955; MA 1958); Reading Univ. (Dip. Agricl Econs 1956). CIBiol, FIBiol 1997. Res. Economist, 1956–63, Lectr, 1963–71, Reader in Agricl Econs, 1971–77, Reading Univ.; Prof. of Agricl Econs, Aberdeen Univ., and Chm. of Econs Gp, N of Scotland Coll. of Agriculture, Aberdeen, 1977–84; Reading University: Dean, Faculty of Agriculture and Food, 1986–89; Dir, Centre for Agricl Strategy, 1990–97. Chairman: Agricl Wages Bd for England and Wales, 1991–99; RURAL, 1997–; Pres., British Inst. of Agricl Consultants, 1998–. FRASE 1991; FRAgS 1992. *Publications:* contribs to books; numerous articles in learned jls. *Recreations:* photography, caravanning, Methodist local preacher. *Address:* 15 Adams Way, Earley, Reading, Berks RG6 5UT. *T:* (0118) 986 8434. *Clubs:* Farmers'; Caravan (East Grinstead).

MARSH, Prof. Leonard George, OBE 1992; MEd; DPhil; Principal, Bishop Grosseteste College, 1974–96; *b* 23 Oct. 1930; third *c* of late Ernest Arthur Marsh and Anne Eliza (*née* Bean); *m* 1953, Ann Margaret Gilbert; one *s* one *d*. *Educ:* Ashford (Kent) Grammar Sch.; Borough Road Coll., London Inst. of Educn (London Univ. Teachers' Certif. and Academic Dip.); Leicester Univ. (MEd); DPhil York, 1988. Lectr in Educn and Mathematics, St Paul's Coll., Cheltenham, 1959–61; Lectr, 1961–63, Sen. Lectr, 1963–65, Principal Lectr and Head of Postgraduate Primary Educn Dept, 1965–74, Goldsmiths' Coll., London. Hon. Prof., Hull Univ., 1987–. Visiting Lectr, Bank Street Coll., New York, and Virginia Commonwealth Univ.; former Consultant, OECD, Portugal; Educnl Consultant, Teacher Trng Proj., Botswana, 1981; Dir, Sindh Pakistan Primary Educn Develt Prog., 1992–96; Specialist tour to India for British Council; Mem., SCAA, 1993–97. Dir (non-exec.), A & C Black plc, 1994–2000. Member: Gen. Adv. Council, IBA, 1977–82; N Lincolnshire AHA, 1984–90; Chm., Nat. Assoc. for Primary Educn, 1981–83. Gov., Canterbury Christ Church Coll., 1997–. FRSA. Hon. FCP (FCP 1989). Hon. DLitt Hull, 1996. *Publications:* Let's Explore Mathematics, Books 1–4, 1964–67; Children Explore Mathematics, 1967, 3rd edn 1969; Exploring Shapes and Numbers, 1968, 2nd edn 1970; Exploring the Metric System, 1969, 2nd edn 1969; Exploring the Metric World, 1970; Approach to Mathematics, 1970; Alongside the Child in the Primary School, 1970; Let's Discover Mathematics, Books 1–5, 1971–72; Being A Teacher, 1973; Helping your Child with Maths—a parents' guide, 1980; The Guinness Mathematics Book, 1980; The Guinness Book for Young Scientists, 1982. *Recreations:* photography, theatre, walking, films. *Address:* Broomfields, 16 The Meadow, Chislehurst, Kent BR7 6AA. *T:* (020) 8467 6311. *Club:* Athenæum.

MARSH, Mary Elizabeth; Director and Chief Executive, National Society for the Prevention of Cruelty to Children, since 2000; *b* 17 Aug. 1946; *d* of George Donald Falconer and Lesley Mary (*née* Wilson); *m* 1968, Juan Enrique Marsh (*d* 1999); four *s*. *Educ:* Birkenhead High Sch., GPDST; Univ. of Nottingham (BSc); London Business Sch. (MBA). Teacher, Icknield High Sch., 1968; St Christopher School, Letchworth: teacher, 1969–72; Dep. Hd, 1980–90; Head: Queens' Sch., Watford, 1990–95; Holland Park Sch., 1995–2000. *Recreations:* swimming, reading, music, good company, walking in mountains and by the sea. *Address:* NSPCC, 42 Curtain Road, EC2A 3NH. *T:* (020) 7825 2586. *Club:* Reform.

MARSH, Nevill Francis, CBE 1969; Director-General, St John Ambulance, 1972–76; *b* 13 Aug. 1907; *m* 1st, 1935, Betty Hide (decd); one *s* one *d*; 2nd, 1989, Gillian Hodnett. *Educ:* Oundle Sch., Northants; Clare Coll., Cambridge (MA). Traction Motor Design Staff, Metropolitan-Vickers Electrical Co. Ltd, 1930–32; Mid-Lincolnshire Electric Supply Co. Ltd: Dist Engineer, 1932–38; Engineer and Manager, 1938–48; Chief Commercial Officer, E Midlands Electricity Board, 1948–55; Dep.-Chm., N Eastern Electricity Board, 1955–57; Dep.-Chm., E Midlands Electricity Board, 1957–59; Chm., East Midlands Electricity Board, 1959–61; a Dep. Chm., Electricity Council, 1962–71; Chm., British Electrotechnical Cttee, 1970–72. Dir for Gtr London, St John Ambulance Assoc., 1971–72. Also formerly: Dir, Altrincham Electric Supply Ltd, and Public Utilities (Elec.) Ltd, and Supervising Engineer, Campbeltown & Mid-Argyll Elec. Supply Co. Ltd, and Thurso & District Elec. Supply Co. Ltd. FIEE; Pres. of Assoc. of Supervising Electrical Engineers, 1966–68. KStJ 1973. *Publications:* jt contrib. Jl Inst. Electrical Engineers, 1955. *Address:* Gill's Cottage, 23 High Street, Morton, near Bourne, Lincs PE10 0NR. *T:* (01778) 570601. *Club:* Royal Air Force.

MARSH, Norman Stayner, CBE 1977; QC 1967; Law Commissioner, 1965–78; Member, Royal Commission on Civil Liability and Compensation for Personal Injury, 1973–78; *b* 26 July 1913; 2nd *s* of Horace Henry and Lucy Ann Marsh, Bath, Som; *m* 1939, Christiane Christinnecke (*d* 2000), 2nd *d* of Professor Johannes and Käthe Christinnecke, Magdeburg, Germany; two *s* two *d*. *Educ:* Monkton Combe Sch.; Pembroke Coll., Oxford (2nd Class Hons, Final Honour Sch. of Jurisprudence, 1935; 1st Cl. Hons BCL; Hon. Fellow, 1978). Vinerian Scholar of Oxford Univ., Harmsworth Scholar of Middle Temple, called to Bar, 1937; practice in London and on Western Circuit, 1937–39; Lieut-Col Intelligence Corps and Control Commission for Germany, 1939–46. Stowell Civil Law Fellow, University Coll., Oxford, 1946–60; University Lecturer in Law, 1947–60; Estates Bursar, University Coll., 1948–56; Secretary-General, International Commission of Jurists, The Hague, Netherlands, 1956–58. Member: Bureau of Conference of Non-Governmental Organisations with Consultative Status with the United Nations, 1957–58; Internat. Cttee of Legal Science (Unesco), 1960–63. Dir of British Institute of International and Comparative Law, 1960–65. Mem., Younger Cttee on Privacy, 1970–72. Hon. Vis. Prof. in Law, KCL, 1972–77. Vice-Chm., Age Concern, England, 1979–86. General editor, International and Comparative Law Quarterly, 1961–65, Mem., Editorial Board, 1965–93. *Publications:* The Rule of Law as a supra-national concept, in Oxford Essays in Jurisprudence, 1960; The Rule of Law in a Free Society, 1960; Interpretation in a National and International Context, 1974; (editor and part-author) Public Access to Government-held Information, 1987; articles on common law and comparative law in English, American, French and German law jls. *Address:* 10 Trinity Close, The Pavement, Clapham, SW4 0JD. *T:* (020) 7622 2865.

See also B. K. Cherry.

MARSH, Prof. Paul Rodney; Esmée Fairbairn Professor of Finance, London Business School, since 1998 (Professor of Management and Finance, 1985–98); *b* 19 Aug. 1947; *s* of Harold Marsh and Constance (*née* Miller); *m* 1971, Stephanie Beatrice (*née* Simonow). *Educ:* Poole Grammar Sch.; London School of Economics (BScEcon, 1st Cl. Hons); London Business Sch. (PhD). Systems Analyst, Esso Petroleum, 1968–69; Scicon, 1970–71; London Business School, 1974–: Bank of England Res. Fellow, 1974–85; Dir, Sloan Fellowship Prog., 1980–83; Non-exec. Dir, Centre for Management Develt, 1984–; Mem. Gov. Body, 1986–90; Faculty Dean, 1987–90; Dep. Principal, 1989–90; Dir, Masters in Finance Prog., 1993–. Member: CBI Task Force on City-Industry Relationships, 1986–88; Exec. Cttee, British Acad. of Management, 1986–88. Non-executive Director: M&G Investment Management Ltd, 1989–97; M&G Gp, 1998–99; Majedie Investments, 1999–; Dir, Hoare Govett Indices Ltd, 1991–. Gov. Examg Bd, Securities Inst., 1994–. *Publications:* Cases in Corporate Finance, 1988; Managing Strategic Investment Decisions, 1988; Accounting for Brands, 1989; Short-termism on Trial, 1990; The HGSC Smaller Companies Index, 2000; The Millennium Book: a century of investment returns, 2000; Millennium Book II: 101 years of investment returns, 2001; numerous articles in Jl of Financial Econs, Jl of Finance, Jl of Business, Harvard Business Review, Jl of Inst. of Actuaries, Managerial Finance, Res. in Marketing, Mergers and Acquisitions, Investment Analyst, Long Range Planning, etc. *Recreations:* gardening, investment. *Address:* London Business School, Sussex Place, Regent's Park, NW1 4SA. *T:* (020) 7262 5050; *e-mail:* pmarsh@london.edu.

MARSH, Rev. Canon Richard St John Jeremy, PhD; Canon Residentiary and Director, Education Centre, Canterbury Cathedral, since 2001; *b* 23 April 1960; *s* of Gordon Victor Marsh, *qv*; *m* 1984, Elizabeth Mary Mullins; one *s* one *d*. *Educ:* Trinity Sch. of John Whitgift; Keble Coll., Oxford (BA 1982; MA 1986); Coll. of the Resurrection, Mirfield; Durham Univ. (PhD 1991). Deacon 1985, priest 1986; Curate, Grange St Andrew, Runcorn, 1985–87; Chaplain and Solway Fellow, UC, Durham, 1987–92; Asst Sec. for Ecum. Affairs to Abp of Canterbury, 1992–95, Sec., 1995–2000. Licensed to officiate, Dio. London, 1993–; Canon, Dio. Gibraltar in Europe, 1995–; Non-Res. Canon, Canterbury Cathedral, 1998–2001. *Publication:* Black Angels, 1998. *Recreations:* music, cooking. *Address:* 22 The Precincts, Canterbury, Kent CT1 2EP. *T:* (01227) 865229. *Club:* Athenæum.

MARSHALL, family name of **Baron Marshall of Knightsbridge**.

MARSHALL OF KNIGHTSBRIDGE, Baron *cr* 1998 (Life Peer), of Knightsbridge in the City of Westminster; **Colin Marsh Marshall,** Kt 1987; Chairman: British Airways, since 1993; Invensys (formerly Siebe, then BTR Siebe) plc, since 1999; *b* 16 Nov. 1933; *s* of Marsh Edward Leslie and Florence Mary Marshall; *m* 1958, Janet Winifred (*née* Cracknell); one *d*. *Educ:* University College Sch., Hampstead. Progressively, cadet purser to Dep. Purser, OSNC, 1951–58; Hertz Corp., 1958–64: management trainee, Chicago and Toronto, 1958–59; Gen. Man., Mexico, Mexico City, 1959–60; Asst to Pres., New York, 1960; Gen. Manager: UK London, 1961–62; UK Netherlands and Belgium, London, 1962–64; Avis Inc., 1964–79: Reg. Man./Vice-Pres., Europe, London, 1964–66; Vice-Pres. and Gen. Man., Europe and ME, London, 1966–69; Vice-Pres. and Gen. Man., International, London, 1969–71; Exec. Vice-Pres. and Chief Operating Officer, New York, 1971–75; Pres. and Chief Operating Officer, New York, 1975–76; Pres. and Chief Exec. Officer, New York, 1976–79; Co-Chm., 1979; Exec. Vice-Pres., Norton Simon Inc., New York, 1979–81; Dir and Dep. Chief Exec., Sears Holdings plc, 1981–83; British Airways, 1983–: Chief Exec., 1983–95; Dep. Chm., 1989–93. Chm., Inchcape plc, 1996–2000; Dep. Chm., British Telecommunications plc, 1996–2001. Board Member: HSBC Holdings, 1992–; US Air, 1993–96; Qantas, 1993–96 and 2000–01; NY Stock Exchange, 1994–2000; Royal Automobile Club Ltd, 1998–99. Dep. Chm., Financial Reporting Council, 1996–99. Chm. Trustees, Conference Bd, NY, 2000–. Member: Council, Inst. of Dirs, 1982–; Chartered Inst. of Marketing, 1989–96 (Pres., 1989–94); Marketing Council, 1995– (Chm., 1995–96); Vice Pres., Advertising Assoc., 1988–; Pres., 1996–98, Dep. Pres., 1998–99, CBI. Vice Chm., World Travel & Tourism Council, 1990–99; Pres., Commonwealth Youth Exchange Council, 1998–. Chm., London Development Partnership, 1998–2000. Mem., Hong Kong Assoc., 1996–2000. Trustee, RAF Museum, 1991–2000. Hon. DHL Suffolk, Boston, USA, 1984; Hon. LLD: Bath, 1989; American Univ. in London, Richmond Coll., 1993; Lancaster, 1997; Hon. DSc: Buckingham, 1990; Cranfield, 1997; Hon. DCL Durham, 1997; Hon. LittD Westminster, 1999; Hon. Dr Business London Guildhall, 2000. *Recreations:* tennis, ski-ing. *Address:* c/o British Airways, Berkeley Square House, Berkeley Square, W1J 6BA. *T:* (020) 7930 4915. *Clubs:* Royal Automobile, All England Lawn Tennis and Croquet, Queen's.

MARSHALL, Mrs Alan R.; *see* Marshall, V. M.

MARSHALL, Alan Ralph; Managing Director, ARM Educational Consultants Ltd, 1991–94; *s* of Ralph Marshall and Mabel Mills; *m* 1958, Caterina Gattico; one *s* one *d*. *Educ:* Shoreditch College (Teacher's Cert. 1953); London Univ. (Dip Ed 1959; MPhil 1965); Eastern Washington State Univ. (MEd 1964); Stanford Univ. (MA 1969). Teacher, schools in UK and USA, 1954–62; Lectr, Shoreditch Coll., 1962–68; Vis. Prof., Eastern Washington State Univ., 1964–65; Field Dir, Project Technology, Schools Council, 1970–72; Editor, Nat. Centre for School Technology, 1972–73; Course Team Chm., Open Univ., 1973–76; HM Inspector, DES, 1976–91, HM Chief Inspector of Schools, 1985–91. Hon. DEd CNAA, 1990. *Publications:* (ed) School Technology in Action, 1974; (with G. T. Page and J. B. Thomas) International Dictionary of Education, 1977; Giving Substance to a Vision, 1990; articles in jls. *Recreations:* travel, reading. *Address:* 98 Wheathampstead Road, Harpenden, Herts AL5 1JB.

MARSHALL, Alexander Badenoch, (Sandy); Director, Maersk Co. Ltd, 1979–95 (Vice-Chairman, 1983–87; Chairman, 1987–93); *b* 31 Dec. 1924; *m* 1961, Mona Kurina Douglas Kirk, South Africa; two *s* one *d*. *Educ:* Trinity Coll., Glenalmond; Worcester Coll., Oxford (MA). Served War, Sub-Lieut RNVR, 1943–46. P&O Group of Companies: Mackinnon Mackenzie & Co., Calcutta, 1947–59; Gen. Manager, British India Steam Navigation Co., 1959–62; Man. Dir, Trident Tankers Ltd, 1962–68; Dir, 1968–79, Man. Dir, 1972–79, Peninsular and Oriental Steam Navigation Co.; Chairman: Bestobell Plc, 1979–85; Commercial Union Assurance Co. plc, 1983–90 (Dir, 1970–90); Royal Bank of Canada Hldgs UK Ltd, 1988–95; Vice-Chm., The Boots Co. Plc, 1985–91 (Dir, 1981–91); Director: Royal Bank of Canada, 1985–95; Seascope Shipping Hldgs Plc, 1997–99. Pres., Chamber of Shipping of UK, 1994–95. Co-Chm., British-N American Cttee, 1984–90. *Publication:* Taking the Adventure, 2000. *Recreations:* travel, hill walking, golf. *Address:* Crest House, Woldingham, Surrey CR3 7DH. *Clubs:* Oriental; Tollygunge (Calcutta).

MARSHALL, Sir Arthur Gregory George, Kt 1974; OBE 1948; DL; Life President, Marshall of Cambridge (Holdings), 1990; *b* 4 Dec. 1903; *s* of David Gregory Marshall, MBE, and Maude Edmunds Wing; *m* 1931, Rosemary Wynford Dimsdale (*d* 1988), *d* of Marcus Southwell Dimsdale; two *s* one *d*. *Educ:* Tonbridge Sch.; Jesus Coll., Cambridge (Hon. Fellow, 1990). Engrg, MA. Joined Garage Company of Marshall (Cambridge) Ltd, 1926, which resulted in estabt of Aircraft Company, now Marshall of Cambridge (Aerospace) Ltd, 1929, Chm. and Jt Man. Dir, 1942–89. Chm., Aerodrome Owners Assoc., 1964–65; Member: Air Cadet Council, 1951–59 and 1965–76; Adv. Council on Technology, 1967–70. Liveryman, GAPAN, 1997– (Guild Award of Honour, 2000). Hon. Old Cranwellian, 1979; CRAeS 1980; Companion, Air League, 1996. JP Linton, 1951–61; DL 1968, High Sheriff of Cambridgeshire and Isle of Ely, 1969–70. Hon. DSc Cranfield, 1992; Hon. LLD Cantab, 1996. Masefield Gold Medal, British Assoc. of Aviation Consultants, 1998. Order of Istiqlal, First Class (Jordan), 1990. *Publications:* The Marshall Story: a century of wheels and wings, 1994; No 104 (City of Cambridge) Squadron Air Training Corps 1939–1994, 1995. *Recreations:* Cambridge Athletics Blue, Olympic Team Reserve, 1924; flying. *Address:* Horseheath Lodge, Linton, Cambridge CB1 6PT. *T:* (01223) 891318. *Clubs:* Royal Air Force (Hon. Mem., 1969); Hawks (Cambridge).

See also M. J. Marshall.

MARSHALL, Arthur Stirling-Maxwell, CBE 1986 (OBE 1979); HM Diplomatic Service, retired; *b* 29 Jan. 1929; *s* of Victor Stirling-Maxwell Marshall and Jeannie Theodora Hunter; *m* 1st, 1955, Eleni Kapralou, Athens (*d* 1969); one *s* two *d*; 2nd, 1985, Cheryl Mary Hookens, Madras; one *d*. *Educ:* Daniel Stewart's Coll., Edinburgh. Served Royal Navy, 1947–59. Foreign Office, 1959; Middle East Centre for Arab Studies, Lebanon, 1959–61; Political Officer, British Political Agency, Bahrain and Registrar of HBM Court for Bahrain, 1961–64; Attaché, Athens, 1964–67; Information Officer, Rabat, Morocco, 1967–69; Commercial Secretary: Nicosia, Cyprus, 1970–75; Kuwait, 1975–79; Deputy High Commissioner, Madras, 1980–83; Counsellor, Kuwait, 1983–85; Ambassador to People's Democratic Republic of Yemen, 1986–89. *Recreations:* music, nature. *Address:* 147 Highbury Grove, N5 1HP.

MARSHALL, Prof. Barry James, FRS 1999; FRACP; Professor of Microbiology, University of Western Australia, since 2000; *b* 30 Sept. 1951; *s* of Robert and Marjorie Marshall; *m* 1972, Adrienne Joyce Feldman; one *s* three *d*. *Educ:* Univ. of Western Australia (MB BS). FRACP 1983. Clinical asst (res.), Gastroenterology Dept, Royal Perth Hosp., 1985–86; University of Virginia: Res. Fellow in Medicine, Div. of Gastroenterology, 1986–87; Asst Prof. of Medicine, 1988–92, Associate Prof., 1992, Prof., 1993; Clinical Prof., 1993–96; Prof. of Res. in Internal Medicine, 1996–2000; Clinical Prof. of Medicine, 1997–2000, NH&MRC Burnet Fellow and Prof. of Medicine, 1998–2000, Univ. of WA. Hon. Res. Fellow in Gastroenterology, Sir Charles Gairdner Hosp., 1997. (Jtly) Warren Alpert Prize, Harvard Med. Sch., 1995; Albert Lasker Award, NYC, 1995; (jtly) Paul Ehrlich Prize, Frankfurt, 1997; Kilby Prize, Dallas, 1997; Dr A. H. Heineken Prize for Medicine, Amsterdam, 1998; Florey Medal, Aust. Inst. for Pol Sci., Canberra, 1998; Buchanan Medal, Royal Soc., 1998; Benjamin Franklin Medal for Life Sci., Philadelphia, 1999. *Publications:* Campylobacter pylori, 1988; Helicobacter pylori in peptic ulceration and gastritis, 1991; Helicobacter Pylori, 1990 (Proc. 2nd Internat. Symposium), 1991; Gastroenterology Clinics of North America, 2000; contribs to jls incl. The Lancet, Amer. Jl Gastroenterol., Jl Infectious Diseases, Jl Nuclear Medicine, Jl Clinical Pathol., Digestive Diseases and Scis, Gastroenterol., Scandinavian Jl Gastroenterol., Jl Clinical Microbiol., Alimentary Pharmacol. and Therapeutics. *Recreations:* computers, photography, electronics. *Address:* Helicobacter Pylori Research Laboratory, Department of Microbiology, University of Western Australia, QE2 Medical Centre, Nedlands, WA 6009, Australia. *T:* (8) 93464815.

MARSHALL, Hon. (Cedric) Russell, CNZM 2001; High Commissioner for New Zealand in the United Kingdom, from March 2002; *b* 15 Feb. 1936; *s* of Cedric Thomas Marshall and Gladys Margaret Marshall; *m* 1961, Barbara May Watson; two *s* one *d*. *Educ:* Nelson Coll.; Christchurch Teachers Coll.; Auckland Univ. (DipTeaching, 1966); BA Victoria Univ., 1992. Primary teacher, Nelson, 1955–56; Trinity Methodist Theol Coll., 1958–60; Methodist Minister: Christchurch, Spreydon, 1960–66; Masterton, 1967–71; teacher, Wanganui High Sch., 1972. MP (Lab) Wanganui, 1972–90; Opposition education spokesman, 1976–84; Chief Opposition Whip, 1978–79; Minister of Education, 1984–87, for the Environment, 1984–86, of Conservation, 1986–87, of Disarmament and Arms Control, 1987–89, of Foreign Affairs, 1987–90, for Pacific Island Affairs, 1988–90. Chairman: Commonwealth Observer Mission to Seychelles election, 1993; Commonwealth Observer Mission to South Africa, 1994; Mem., Commonwealth Observer Mission to Lesotho elections, 1993. Chairman: NZ Commn for UNESCO, 1990–99; Polytechnics Internat. New Zealand, 1994–; Education New Zealand, 1998–2002; Tertiary Educn Adv. Commn, 2000–02; Member: UNESCO Exec. Bd, 1995–99 (Chm., Finance and Admin Commn, 1997–99); Public Adv. Cttee for Disarmament and Arms Control, 1997–; Mem. Council, 1994–, Pro-Chancellor, 1999, Chancellor, 2000–02, Victoria Univ. of Wellington. Chairman: Cambodia Trust (Aotearoa–NZ), 1994–; Cambodia Trust (UK), 2001– (Trustee, 2000–); Trustee: Africa Information Centre, 1978–95 (Chm., 1991–95); Nelson Mandela Trust (NZ), 1995–. Patron, Genealogical Res. Inst. of NZ, 1987–. Hon. PhD Univ. of Khon Kaen, Thailand, 1989. *Recreations:* reading, listening to music, genealogy. *Address:* New Zealand High Commission, New Zealand House, Haymarket SW1Y 4TQ; 249 Tinakori Road, Thorndon, Wellington 7001, New Zealand. *T:* (4) 4711935, *Fax:* (4) 4711939.

MARSHALL, Charles Michael John; Senior NHS Specialist, District Audit, since 2001; *b* 25 Sept. 1954; *s* of George William Marshall and Lucy Cameron Marshall (*née* MacInnes); *m* 1985, Margaret Hutchinson (marr. diss. 1990). *Educ:* Royal Grammar Sch., Newcastle upon Tyne; King's Coll. London. Civil Servant, Lord Chancellor's Dept, MoD and Privy Council Office, 1976–86 (Private Sec. to Lord Privy Seal and Leader of H of C, 1983–85); General Manager: Dulwich Hosp., 1986–88; King's Coll. and Dulwich Hosps, 1988–89; Dist Gen. Manager, Newcastle HA, 1989–92; Chief Exec., UCL Hosps NHS Trust, 1992–98; Dir, Charles Marshall Consulting Ltd, 1998. Vis. Prof. in Health Service Mgt, UCL, 1995–; Vis. Fellow, King's Fund Coll., 1994–96. Member: Council, Nat. Assoc. for Educn of Sick Children, 1995–97; Trusts Council, NAHAT, 1996–97; Council, St Oswald's Hospice, 1998–; Hon. Sec., Middx Hosp. Special Trustees, 1994–98. Mem. Ct of Govs, LSHTM, 1999–.

MARSHALL, Prof. Christopher John, DPhil; FRS 1995; Director, Cancer Research Campaign Centre for Cell and Molecular Biology, Institute of Cancer Research, since 1994; *b* 19 Jan. 1949; *s* of Lillian and James Marshall; *m* 1973, Vivien Roma Morrall (marr. diss. 1997); two *s* one *d*. *Educ:* King Henry VIII Sch., Coventry; Churchill Coll., Cambridge (MA); Lincoln Coll., Oxford (DPhil). Postdoctoral Fellow: ICRF, 1973–78; Sidney Farber Cancer Inst., Boston, USA, 1978–80; Research Scientist, Inst. of Cancer Research, 1980–. Gibb Life Fellow, CRC, 1992. Mem., EMBO, 1993; Founder FMedSci 1998. Novartis Prize and Medal, Biochemical Soc., 1999. *Publications:* contribs to learned jls. *Recreation:* cycling. *Address:* Chester Beatty Laboratories, Institute of Cancer Research, 237 Fulham Road, SW3 6JB. *T:* (020) 7352 9772. *Club:* Norwood Paragon Cycling.

MARSHALL, David; MP (Lab) Glasgow, Shettleston, since 1979 (sponsored by TGWU); former transport worker; *b* 7 May 1941; *m*; two *s* one *d*. *Educ:* Larbert, Denny and Falkirk High Schs; Woodside Sen. Secondary Sch., Glasgow. Joined Labour Party, 1962; former Lab. Party Organiser for Glasgow; Mem., TGWU, 1960–. Chm., Select Cttee, Scottish Affairs, 1997– (Mem., 1981–83, 1994–). Hon. Sec. and Hon Treas., Scottish Gp of Labour MPs, 1981–. Private Member's Bill, The Solvent Abuse (Scotland) Act, May 1983. Member: Glasgow Corp., 1972–75; Strathclyde Reg. Council, 1974–79 (Chm., Manpower Cttee); formerly: Chm., Manpower Cttee, Convention of Scottish Local Authorities; Mem., Local Authorities Conditions of Service Adv. Bd. *Recreations:* gardening, music. *Address:* House of Commons, SW1A 0AA; 32 Enterkin Street, Glasgow G32 7BA.

MARSHALL, David Arthur Ambler; FRAeS; Director General, Society of British Aerospace Companies, since 1997; *b* 4 April 1943; *s* of Henry R. Marshall and Joan E. Marshall; *m* 1968, Karen Elizabeth Marker; two *d*. *Educ:* Brighton Coll.; Churchill Coll., Cambridge (MA). FRAeS 1994. Joined Rolls Royce Ltd as Apprentice, 1961; Develt Engr, 1970–73; Co. Rep., Airbus, 1973–75; Manager, Eur. Sales, 1975–78; Commercial Manager, 1978–83; Head of Business Planning, 1983–87; Gen. Manager, Mktg, 1987–89; Dir, Business Planning, 1989–90; Commercial Dir, 1990–93; Dir, Business Develt, 1993–96. FRSA 1998. Freeman, City of London, 1999; Liveryman, Fan Makers' Co. *Recreations:* garden railways, music. *Address:* (office) 60 Petty France, SW1H 9EU. *T:* (020) 7227 1002.

MARSHALL, Sir Denis (Alfred), Kt 1982; solicitor; with Barlow Lyde & Gilbert, 1937–83, now a consultant; *b* 1 June 1916; *s* of Frederick Herbert Marshall and Winifred Mary Marshall; *m* 1st, 1949, Joan Edith Straker (*d* 1974); one *s*; 2nd, 1975, Jane Lygo.

Educ: Dulwich Coll. Served War: HAC, 1939; XX Lancs Fusiliers (Temp. Major), 1940–46. Articled to Barlow Lyde & Gilbert, Solicitors, 1932–37; admitted Solicitor, 1937. Mem. Council, Law Soc., 1966–86, Vice-Pres., 1980–81, Pres., 1981–82. Member: Insurance Brokers Registration Council, 1979–91; Criminal Injuries Compensation Bd, 1982–90; Council, FIMBRA, 1986–90. *Recreations:* sailing, gardening. *Address:* 15 Coombe Road, Dartmouth, Devon TQ6 9PQ.

MARSHALL, Dr Edmund Ian; Lecturer in Management Science, University of Bradford, 1984–2000; *b* 31 May 1940; *s* of Harry and Koorali Marshall; *m* 1969, Margaret Pamela, *d* of John and Maud Antill, New Southgate, N11; one *d.* *Educ:* Magdalen Coll., Oxford (Mackinnon Schol.; Double 1st cl. hons Maths, and Junior Mathematical Prize, 1961); PhD Liverpool, 1965. *Educ:* Various univ. appts in Pure Maths, 1962–66; mathematician in industry, 1967–71. Mem., Wallasey County Borough Council, 1963–65. Contested (L) Louth Div. of Lincs, 1964 and 1966; joined Labour Party, 1967. MP (Lab) Goole, May 1971–1983; PPS to Sec. of State for NI, 1974–76, to Home Sec., 1976–79; Chm., Trade and Industry sub-cttee of House of Commons Expenditure Cttee, 1976–79; Mem., Chairmen's Panel in House of Commons, 1981–82; Opposition Whip, 1982–83; joined SDP, 1985. Contested (SDP/Alliance) Bridlington, 1987. Non-Exec. Dir, Wakefield FHSA, 1990–96; Dir, Wakefield Healthcare Commn, 1994–96. Member: British Methodist Conf., 1969–72, 1980 and 1985–97 (Vice-Pres., 1992); World Methodist Conf., 1971; British Council of Churches, 1972–78; Sec., Associate (formerly All-Party) Parly Gp related to Council of Church Colls, 1994–; Bishop of Wakefield's Advr for Ecumenical Affairs, 1998–. Methodist Local Preacher, 1959–; Reader in C of E, 1994–. Mem., Gen. Synod of C of E, 2000–. Governor: Woodhouse Grove Sch., Bradford, 1986–94; Wakefield Grammar School Foundn, 1989–97. *Publications:* (jtly) Europe: What Next? (Fabian pamphlet), 1969; Parliament and the Public, 1982; Business and Society, 1993; (jtly) The Times Book of Best Sermons, 1995; various papers in mathematical and other jls. *Recreations:* word games, music. *Address:* 14 Belgravia Road, Wakefield, West Yorks WF1 3JP. *Clubs:* Royal Over-Seas League; Yorkshire County Cricket.

MARSHALL, Dr Frank Graham, FIEE; technology consultant, since 1998; Group Research and Development Director, Colt Group Ltd, 1990–98; *b* 28 March 1942; *s* of Frank and Vera Marshall; *m* 1965, Patricia Anne (*née* Bestwick); two *s* one *d.* *Educ:* Birmingham Univ. (BSc Physics); Nottingham Univ. (PhD Physics). FIEE 1984. Joined Royal Signals and Radar Estabt (MoD) (Physics and Electronic Device Res.), 1966; Sen. Principal Scientific Officer, 1975–80; seconded to HM Diplomatic Service as Science and Technology Counsellor, Tokyo, 1980–82. Man. Dir, Plessey Electronic Systems Res., later Plessey Res. Roke Manor, 1983–87; Technical Dir, Plessey Naval Systems, 1987–90. (Jtly) IEEE Best Paper award, 1973; (jtly) Wolfe Award, 1973. *Publications:* numerous papers on electronic signal processing devices in various jls. *Recreations:* country life, electronics; *e-mail:* fgm@sunspot.co.uk.

MARSHALL, Geoffrey, MA, PhD; FBA 1971; Provost, The Queen's College, Oxford, 1993–99 (Fellow and Tutor in Politics, 1957–93; Hon. Fellow, 1999); *b* 22 April 1929; *s* of Leonard William and Kate Marshall; *m* 1957, Patricia Ann Christine Woodcock; two *s.* *Educ:* Arnold Sch., Blackpool, Lancs; Manchester Univ. (MA); MA Oxon; PhD Glasgow. Research Fellow, Nuffield Coll., 1955–57. Andrew Dixon White Vis. Prof., Cornell Univ., Ithaca, NY, 1985–91. Pres., Study of Parliament Gp, 1994–2000. Mem. Oxford City Council, 1965–74; Sheriff of Oxford, 1970–71. *Publications:* Parliamentary Sovereignty and the Commonwealth, 1957; Some Problems of the Constitution (with G. C. Moodie), 1959; Police and Government, 1965; Constitutional Theory, 1971; Constitutional Conventions, 1984; Ministerial Responsibility, 1989. *Recreation:* Blackpool FC. *Address:* 33 The Villas, Rutherway, Oxford OX2 6QY. *T:* (01865) 516114.

MARSHALL, Gordon, DPhil; FBA 2000; AcSS; Chief Executive, and Deputy Chairman, Economic and Social Research Council, since 2000; *b* 20 June 1952; *s* of Robert Marshall and Ina Marshall (*née* McPhie); *m* 1975, Heather Alexander (marr. diss. 1999); one *s*; partner, Marion Headicar. *Educ:* Falkirk High Sch.; Univ. of Stirling (BA 1st Cl. Hons Sociol. 1974); Nuffield Coll., Oxford (DPhil 1978). Postdoctoral Res. Fellow, Nuffield Coll., Oxford, 1977–78; Lectr and Sen. Lectr, Dept of Sociol., Univ. of Essex, 1978–90; Prof. of Sociol., Univ. of Bath, 1990–93; Official Fellow in Sociol., Nuffield Coll., Oxford, 1993–99. British Acad./Leverhulme Trust Sen. Res. Fellow, 1992–93. AcSS 2000. *Publications:* Presbyteries and Profits, 1980; In Search of the Spirit of Capitalism, 1982; (jtly) Social Class in Modern Britain, 1987; In Praise of Sociology, 1990; (jtly) Oxford Dictionary of Sociology, 1994, 2nd edn 1998; (jtly) Against the Odds?, 1997; (jtly) Repositioning Class, 1997; contrib. numerous articles to jls and symposia. *Recreations:* sailing, fretting about Ipswich Town FC. *Address:* Courtyard House, 49 High Street, Sutton Courtenay, Oxon OX14 4AT. *T:* (01235) 848386.

MARSHALL, Hazel Eleanor, (Mrs H. C. J. Marshall); *see* Williamson, H. E.

MARSHALL, Howard Wright; retired; Under Secretary, Department of Transport, 1978–82; *b* 11 June 1923; *s* of Philip Marshall, MBE, and Mary Marshall; *m* 1st (marr. diss.); two *s*; 2nd, 1963, Carol Yvonne (*née* Oddy); one *d.* *Educ:* Prudhoe West Elementary, Northumberland; Queen Elizabeth Grammar Sch., Hexham. Served War, RAF, 1941–46; POW, 1943–45. Min. of Health, Newcastle upon Tyne, 1940; Regional Offices, Ministries of Health, Local Govt and Planning, Housing and Local Govt, 1948–55; HQ, Min. of Housing and Local Govt, 1955–59; National Parks Commn, 1959–62; Min. of Housing and Local Govt, later DoE, 1962; Asst Sec., 1968; Under Sec., 1976; Regional Dir, Eastern Region, Depts of Environment and Transport, 1976–78; Chm., East Anglia Regional Economic Planning Bd, 1976–78. *Recreations:* gardening, sport. *Address:* Brackenwood, Farthing Green Lane, Stoke Poges, Bucks SL2 4JH. *T:* (01753) 662974. *Clubs:* Caterpillar; Wexham Park Golf and Leisure.

MARSHALL, Rev. Canon Hugh Phillips; Vicar of Wendover, 1996–2001; *b* 13 July 1934; *s* of Dr Leslie Phillips Marshall and Dr (Catherine) Mary Marshall; *m* 1962, Diana Elizabeth Gosling; one *s* three *d.* *Educ:* Marlborough Coll.; Sidney Sussex Coll., Cambridge (BA, MA); Bishop's Hostel, Lincoln. RN, 1952–54. Ordained deacon 1959, priest 1960, Dio. London; Curate, St Stephen with St John, Westminster, 1959–65; Vicar of St Paul, Tupsley, Hereford, 1965–74; Vicar and Team Rector of Wimbledon, 1974–87; Rural Dean of Merton, 1979–85; Vicar of Mitcham, Surrey, 1987–90; Chief Sec., ABM, 1990–96. Hon. Canon: Southwark Cathedral, 1989, Hon. Canon Emeritus, 1990; St John's Cathedral, Bulawayo, 1996. Commissary to Bishop of Matabeleland, 1989–. Mem., SE Reg. Awards Cttee, Nat. Lottery Charities Bd, 1998–. *Recreations:* DIY, cooking, gardening, travel. *Address:* 7 The Daedings, Deddington, Oxon OX15 0RT. *T:* (01869) 337761.

MARSHALL, James; MP (Lab) Leicester South, Oct. 1974–1983, and since 1987; *b* 13 March 1941; *m* 1962, Shirley (marr. diss.), *d* of W. Ellis, Sheffield; one *s* one *d*; *m* 1986, Susan, *d* of G. Carter, Leicester. *Educ:* City Grammar Sch., Sheffield; Leeds Univ. BSc, PhD. Joined Lab Party, 1960. Mem., Leeds City Council, 1965–68; Leicester City Council: Mem., 1971–76; Chm., Finance Cttee, 1972–74; Leader, 1974. Contested (Lab): Harborough, 1970; Leicester South, Feb. 1974, 1983. An Asst Govt Whip, 1977–79. *Address:* House of Commons, SW1A 0AA.

MARSHALL, James; Assistant Auditor General, National Audit Office, since 1993; *b* 16 March 1944; *s* of James Marshall and late Winifred Marshall (*née* Hopkins); *m* 1980, Patricia Anne Smallbone; one *s.* *Educ:* Sacred Heart Coll., Droitwich; King Charles I Grammar Sch., Kidderminster; Jesus Coll., Cambridge (MA). Joined Inland Revenue, 1966: Asst Principal, 1966–69; Private Sec. to Chm. of Bd, 1969–70; Principal, 1970–74; First Sec., Budget and Fiscal, UK Repn to EC, Brussels, 1974–77; First Asst, UK Mem. of Court, European Court of Auditors, 1977–80; Asst Sec., Inland Revenue, 1980–88; Consultant, CJA Mgt Recruitment, 1988–89; Dir, Nat. Audit Office, 1989–93. *Recreations:* reading, walking, entertaining, music. *Address:* National Audit Office, Buckingham Palace Road, SW1W 9SP; 56 Melody Road, SW18 2QF. *T:* (020) 8870 3308.

MARSHALL, Jeremy; *see* Marshall, John J. S.

MARSHALL, John, MA; Headmaster, Robert Gordon's College, Aberdeen, 1960–77; *b* 1 July 1915; *s* of Alexander Marshall and Margaret Nimmo Carmichael; *m* 1940, May Robinson Williamson; two *d.* *Educ:* Airdrie Acad.; Glasgow Univ. MA (1st cl. hons Classics), 1935; Medley Memorial Prizeman, History 1934; John Clark Schol., Classics, 1935. Asst Master: Bluevale Sch., 1937–39; Coatbridge Sec. Sch., 1939–41; Principal Teacher of Classics, North Berwick High Sch., 1941–50; Rector, North Berwick High Sch., 1950–60. Mem., Adv. Coun. on Educn for Scotland, 1955–57; Trustee, Scottish Sec. Schools Travel Trust, 1960–78 (Chm., 1971–78; Sec., 1978–80); Pres., Headmasters' Assoc. of Scotland, 1962–64; Member: HMC, 1960–77; Gen. Teaching Coun. for Scotland, 1966–70; Exec. Cttee, UCCA, 1970–78; Co-ordinator, Scottish Scheme of Oxford Colls' Admissions, 1978–84. Trustee, Gordon Cook Foundn, 1974– (Chm., 1992–93). JP City of Aberdeen, 1967–95. *Publications:* Off the Beaten Track in Switzerland, 1989; The Visitor's Guide to Switzerland, 1990, 2nd edn 1995; The Visitor's Guide to The Rhine and Mosel, 1992; numerous articles on educational and travel subjects. *Recreations:* photography, writing, language studies, travel. *Address:* 11 Hazledene Road, Aberdeen AB15 8LB. *T:* (01224) 318003. *Club:* Royal Northern and University (Aberdeen).

MARSHALL, Prof. John, CBE 1990; FRCP, FRCPE; Professor of Clinical Neurology in the University of London, 1971–87, now Emeritus; *b* 16 April 1922; *s* of James Herbert and Bertha Marshall; *m* 1946, Margaret Eileen Hughes; two *s* three *d.* *Educ:* Univ. of Manchester (MB ChB 1946, MD 1951, DSc 1981). FRCPE 1957, FRCP 1966; DPM 1952. Sen. Registrar, Manchester Royal Infirmary, 1947–49; Lt-Col RAMC, 1949–51; MRC research worker, 1951–53; Sen. Lectr in Neurology, Univ. of Edinburgh, 1954–56; Reader in Clinical Neurology, Univ. of London, 1956–71. Chm., Disability Living (formerly Attendance) Allowance Bd, 1982–93. Knight of the Order of St Sylvester (Holy See), 1962, KCSG 1986 (KSG 1964). Auenbrugger Medal, Univ. of Graz, 1983. *Publications:* The Management of Cerebrovascular Disease, 1965, 3rd edn 1976; The Infertile Period, Principles and Practice, 1963, 2nd rev. edn 1969; Love One Another, 1995. *Recreations:* gardening, walking. *Address:* 203 Robin Hood Way, SW20 0AA. *T:* (020) 8942 5509.

MARSHALL, Prof. John, PhD; Frost Professor of Ophthalmology and Chairman, Department of Ophthalmology, Guy's, King's and St Thomas' School of Medicine of King's College London (formerly United Medical and Dental Schools of Guy's and St Thomas' Hospitals), since 1991; *b* 21 Dec. 1943; *s* of Henry Thomas George Marshall and Ellen Emily Martha Marshall; *m* 1972, Judith Anne Meadows. *Educ:* Inst. of Ophthalmology, Univ. of London (BSc; PhD 1968). Institute of Ophthalmology: Lectr in Anatomy, 1968–73; Sen. Lectr in Visual Sci., 1973–80; Reader in Exptl Pathology, 1981–83; Sembal Prof. of Exptl Ophthalmology, 1983–91; Hon. Consultant in Ophthalmology, St Thomas' Hosp., 1992–. Ed., numerous scientific jls, 1985–. Advr on lasers to WHO, 1974–80, to Internat. Red Cross, 1989–95. Dir, DIOMED, 1991–97. Trustee, Brit. Retinitis Pigmentosa Soc., 1978–. Gov., Moorfields Eye Hosp., 1988–90. Numerous patents on applications of lasers to eye surgery, 1968–. FRSA 1989. Hon. Fellow, Coll. of Optometrists, 1997. Nettleship Medal, 1980, Ashton Medal, 1993, RCOphth; Mackenzie Medal, Tennant Inst. of Ophthalmol., Glasgow, 1985; Raynor Medal, Intraocular Implant Soc., UK, 1988; Ridley Medal, Internat. Soc. for Cataract and Refractive Surg., 1990; Wilkening Award, Laser Inst. of Amer., 1999; Ida Mann Medal Oxford, 2000; Lord Crook Gold Medal, Spectacle Makers' Co., 2001; Doyne Medal, Oxford Congress of Ophthalmol., 2001; Barraquer Medal, Internat. Soc. of Refractive Surg., 2001. *Publications:* Hazards of Light, 1986; Laser Technology in Ophthalmology, 1988; Vision and Visual Systems, 1991; Annual of Ophthalmic Laser Surgery, 1992; numerous papers in scientific jls, concerning effect of lasers, light and aging on ocular tissues. *Recreations:* work!, reading. *Address:* Wildacre, 27 Cedar Road, Farnborough, Hants GU14 7AU. *T:* (01252) 543473. *Clubs:* Athenæum, Royal Automobile.

MARSHALL, John Alexander, CB 1982; General Secretary, Distressed Gentlefolk's Aid Association, 1982–89; *b* 2 Sept. 1922; *s* of James Alexander Marshall and Mena Dorothy Marshall; *m* 1947, Pauline Mary (*née* Taylor); six *s.* *Educ:* LCC elem. sch.; Hackney Downs School. Paymaster General's Office, 1939; FO, 1943; HM Treasury, 1947: Principal, 1953; Asst Sec., 1963; Under-Sec., 1972; Cabinet Office, 1974–77; Northern Ireland Office, 1977–82, Dep. Sec., 1979–82. *Recreations:* literature, music. *Address:* 48 Long Lane, Ickenham, Mddx UB10 8TA. *T:* (01895) 672020.

MARSHALL, John Gibb, (John Sessions); actor, writer; *b* 11 Jan. 1953; *s* of John Marshall and Esmé Richardson. *Educ:* Univ. of Wales (MA). Plays and one-man shows, 1982–85; *television:* Spitting Image, 1986; Porterhouse Blue, 1987; A Day in Summer, 1988; Whose Line is it Anyway?, 1988; Single Voices, 1990; Ackroyd's Dickens, 1990; Jute City, 1991; Life with Eliza, 1992; The Soldier's Tale, 1993; A Tour of the Western Isles, 1993; Citizen Locke, 1994; The Treasure Seekers, 1996; Tom Jones, 1997; My Night with Reg, 1997; Stella Street (3 series), 1997, 1998, 2000; In the Red, 1998; The Man, 1999; Gormenghast, 2000; Randall & Hopkirk Deceased, 2000; Murder Rooms; one-man shows: New Year Show, 1988; On the Spot, 1989; Tall Tales, 1991; Likely Stories, 1994; *theatre:* The Life of Napoleon, Albery, 1987; The Common Pursuit, Phoenix, 1988; The American Napoleon, Phoenix, 1989; Die Fledermaus, Royal Opera House, 1990; Travelling Tales, Haymarket, 1991; Tartuffe, Playhouse, 1991; My Night with Reg, Royal Court, 1994; Paint, said Fred!, Royal Acad., 1996; *films:* The Bounty, 1984; Whoops Apocalypse, 1986; Castaway, 1987; Henry V, 1989; Sweet Revenge, 1990; The Pope Must Die, 1991; Princess Caraboo, 1994; In the Bleak Midwinter, 1995; The Scarlet Tunic, 1998; Cousin Bette, 1998; A Midsummer Night's Dream, 1999; One of the Hollywood Ten, 2000; Gangs of New York, 2001; *radio:* Whose Line is it Anyway?, 1988; Beachcomber, 1989; Mightier than the Sword, 1992; Figaro gets Divorced, 1993; Poonsh, 1993; The Good Doctor, 1994; Private Passions, 1997–99; The Reith Affair, 1998; Saturday Night Fry, 1998; The Destiny of Nathalie X, 1998; Season's Greetings, 1999; The Man who came to Dinner; Reconstructing Louis; Dante's Inferno. *Recreation:* dinner parties. *Address:* c/o Markham & Froggatt, 4 Windmill Street, W1P 1HF. *T:* (020) 7636 4412. *Club:* Groucho.

MARSHALL, (John) Jeremy (Seymour); Chief Executive, De La Rue Co. plc, 1989–98; *b* 18 April 1938; *s* of late Edward Pope Marshall and Nita Helen Marshall (*née* Seymour); *m* 1962, Juliette Butterley; one *s* two *d*. *Educ:* Sherborne Sch.; New Coll., Oxford (MA Chem.). Nat. Service, Royal Signals, 1956–58. Wiggins Teape, 1962–64; Riker Labs, 1964–67; CIBA Agrochemicals, 1967–71; Hanson Trust: Managing Director: Dufaylite Developments, 1971–76; SLD Olding, 1976–79; Chief Executive: Lindustries, 1979–86; Imperial Foods, 1986–87; BAA plc, 1987–89. Director: John Mowlem & Co., 1991–97; Camelot Gp, 1993–98; BTR plc, 1995–98; Hillsdown Holdings, 1998–2000. Hon. Treas., Design Museum (Trustee, 1996). Mem. Council, Sch. of Mgt Studies, Oxford Univ., 1995–. CIMgt (CBIM 1991); FCIT 1989. *Recreations:* squash, lawn tennis, shooting, music. *Address:* Willow House, Bourn, Cambridge CB3 7SQ. *T:* (01954) 719435. *Club:* Royal Automobile.

MARSHALL, John Leslie; Chairman, Beta Global Emerging Markets Investment Trust plc, 2000–01 (Director, 1999–2001); *b* 19 Aug. 1940; *s* of late Prof. William Marshall and Margaret Marshall; *m* 1978, Susan Elizabeth (marr. diss. 2000), *d* of David Mount, Petham, Kent; two *s*. *Educ:* Glasgow Academy; St Andrews Univ. (MA). ACIS. Asst Lecturer in Economics, Glasgow Univ., 1962–66; Lectr in Economics, Aberdeen Univ., 1966–70; Mem., Internat. Stock Exchange; Carr Sebag & Co., 1979–82; Partner, 1983–86, Dir, 1986–90, Analyst, 1990–93, Kitcat & Aitken; Analyst: London Wall Equities, subseq. Mees Pierson Securities (UK) Ltd, 1993–97; New Japan Securities, 1998–99. Sen. Financial Journalist, Shares mag., 1999–. Member (C): Aberdeen Town Council, 1968–70; Ealing Borough Council, 1971–86 (Chm., Finance Bd, 1978–82; Chm., Local Services Cttee, 1982–84); Barnet LBC, 1998– (Chm., Cons. Gp, 1998–2000). Contested (C): Dundee East, 1964 and 1966; Lewisham East, Feb. 1974. MEP (C) London N, 1979–89; Asst Whip, EDG, Eur. Parlt, 1986–89. MP (C) Hendon South, 1987–97; contested (C) Finchley and Golders Green, 1997, 2001. PPS to Minister for the Disabled, Dept of Social Security, 1989–90, to Sec. of State for Social Security, 1990–92, to Leader of H of C, 1992–95. Mem., Select Cttee on health, 1995–97; Vice Chm., All Pty Mental Health Gp, 1996–97. Chm., British Israel Parly Gp, 1991–97; Vice Pres., Anglo-Israel Assoc., 2001– (Chm., 1994–2000). Consultant, Bus and Coach Council, 1991–97. Chm., Friends of the Northern Line, 1994–97. Chm., Dermatrust Appeal, 1998–. *Publications:* articles on economics in several professional jls; pamphlets on economic questions for Aims. *Recreations:* watching cricket, football and Rugby; gardening, bridge, theatre. *Clubs:* Carlton, East Finchley Constitutional, MCC; Middlesex County Cricket.

MARSHALL, John Roger; Chairman: Supply Chain Partnering, since 1996; Building Software Ltd, since 1997; *b* 20 April 1944; *s* of John Henry Marshall and Betty Alaine Rosetta Marshall; *m* (marr. diss.); one *s* two *d*. *Educ:* Rendcomb College; Bristol Univ. (BSc Hons Civil Eng.). MICE, CEng, FIHT. Balfour Beatty Consultants, W. C. French and R. McGregor & Sons, 1966–70; Mears Construction, 1970–78; Henry Boot, 1978–83; Man. Dir, Mowlem Management, 1983–87; Dir, 1987–95, Man. Dir, 1989–94, Chief Exec., 1994–95, John Mowlem and Co. PLC. Non-executive Director: St Aldwyns Enterprises Ltd, 1996–; BRE Ltd, 1998–. *Recreation:* arts (visual, dramatic and operatic). *Address:* Copplestone House, Manley Lane, Tiverton, Devon EX16 4NH.

MARSHALL, Laurence Arthur; His Honour Judge Marshall; a Circuit Judge, since 1991; *b* 1 June 1931; *s* of Reginald Herbert Marshall and Nora Marshall; *m* 1st, 1959, Marian Charlotte Mowlem Burt (marr. diss. 1979); two *s* two *d*; 2nd, 1980, Gloria Elizabeth Kindersley. *Educ:* Ardingly Coll.; King's Coll., London (LLB). Called to the Bar, Gray's Inn, 1956. *Recreation:* building. *Address:* The Old Post Office, Stourton, Shipston on Stour, Warwicks CV36 5HG. *T:* (01608) 686363. *Club:* Royal London Yacht.

MARSHALL, Margaret Anne, OBE 1999; concert and opera singer; soprano; *b* 4 Jan. 1949; *d* of Robert and Margaret Marshall; *m* 1970, Dr Graeme Griffiths King Davidson; two *d*. *Educ:* High School, Stirling; Royal Scottish Academy of Music and Drama (DRSAMD). Recital début, Wigmore Hall, 1975; performs regularly with all major British orchs, also with ENO and Scottish Opera; opera début as Euridice, in Orfeo, Florence; major rôles include: Countess Almaviva in The Marriage of Figaro; Fiordiligi in Così fan Tutte; Elvira and Donna Anna in Don Giovanni; Violetta in La Traviata; Marschallin in Der Rosenkavalier; Constanze in The Seraglio; many concert and opera performances in Europe and N America; numerous recordings. First Prize, Munich International Competition, 1974. *Recreations:* squash, golf. *Address:* Woodside, Main Street, Gargunnock, Stirling FK8 3BP. *Club:* Gleneagles Country.

MARSHALL, Mark Anthony, CMG 1991; HM Diplomatic Service, retired; Ambassador to the Republic of Yemen (formerly Yemen Arab Republic) and the Republic of Djibouti, 1987–93; *b* 8 Oct. 1937; *s* of late Thomas Humphrey Marshall, CMG and of Nadine, *d* of late Mark Hambourg; *m* 1970, Penelope Lesley Seymour; two *d*. *Educ:* Westminster Sch.; Trinity Coll., Cambridge (BA). MECAS, 1958; Third Sec., Amman, 1960; FO, 1962; Commercial Officer, Dubai, 1964; FO, 1965; Aden, 1967; First Sec., 1968; Asst Dir of Treasury Centre for Admin. Studies, 1968; UK Delegn to Brussels Conf., 1970; First Sec./Head of Chancery, Rabat, 1972; First Sec., FCO, 1976; Counsellor: Tripoli, 1979–80; Damascus, 1980–83; Head of Finance Dept, FCO, 1984–87. *Recreations:* swimming, golf, fell walking.

MARSHALL, Prof. Mary Tara, OBE 1997; Director, Dementia Services Development Centre, University of Stirling, since 1989; *b* 13 June 1945; *d* of Percy Edwin Alan and Phyllis April Trix Johnson-Marshall. *Educ:* Edinburgh Univ. (MA); London School of Economics (DSA); Liverpool Univ. (Dip. in Applied Social Studies). Child Care Officer, Lambeth, 1967–69; Social Worker, Liverpool Personal Service Soc. Project, 1970–74; Organiser, res. project, Age Concern, Liverpool, 1974–75; Lectr in Applied Social Studies, Liverpool Univ. 1975–83; Dir, Age Concern, Scotland, 1983–89. Mem., Royal Commn on Long Term Care for the Elderly, 1998–99. Member: Liverpool Housing Trust, 1976–; Edinvar Housing Assoc. Bd, 1988–; Gov., PPP Healthcare Med. Trust Ltd, 1998–. Member: Centre for Policy on Ageing, 1986– (Gov., 1994–2000); BASW, 1970–; British Soc. of Gerentology, 1977–. Member: Adv. Bd, Jl of Dementia Care; Editl Adv. Bd, Health & Social Care in the Community; Editl Bd, Alzheimer's Care Qly. Hon. DEd Queen Margaret Coll., 1998. *Publications:* Social Work with Old People, 1983, 3rd edn (with M. Dixon), 1996; "I Can't Place This Place At All": working with people with dementia and their carers, 1996; book reviews, papers, reports and articles. *Recreations:* birdwatching, photography. *Address:* Dementia Services Development Centre, University of Stirling, Stirling FK9 4LA. *T:* (01786) 467740.

MARSHALL, Sir Michael; *see* Marshall, Sir R. M.

MARSHALL, Rt Rev. Michael Eric, MA; Bishop in Residence, Holy Trinity, Sloane Street, since 1997; an Assistant Bishop: Diocese of London, since 1984; Diocese of Chichester, since 1992; *b* Lincoln, 14 April 1936. *Educ:* Lincoln Sch.; Christ's Coll., Cambridge (Tancred Scholar, Upper II: Hist. Pt 1 and Theol Pt 1a, MA); Cuddesdon Theological Coll. Deacon, 1960; Curate, St Peter's, Spring Hill, Birmingham, 1960–62; Tutor, Ely Theological Coll. and Minor Canon of Ely Cath., 1962–64; Chaplain in London Univ., 1964–69; Vicar of All Saints', Margaret Street, W1, 1969–75; Bishop Suffragan of Woolwich, 1975–84. Preb. of Wightring in Chichester Cathedral and Wightring Theol Lectr, 1990–. Dir of Evangelism, Chichester Theol Coll., 1991–97; Archbishops' Advr on Evangelism, 1992–97; Leader, Springboard, 1992–97. Founder and Director: Inst. of Christian Studies, 1970; Internat. Inst. for Anglican Studies, 1982; Founding Episcopal Dir, Anglican Inst., St Louis, Missouri, 1984–92; Member: Gen. Synod, 1970, also Diocesan and Deanery Synods; Liturgical Commn; Anglican/Methodist Liaison Commn until 1974; SPCK Governing Body; USPG Governing Body; Exam. Chap. to Bp of London, 1974. Has frequently broadcast on BBC and commercial radio; also lectured, preached and broadcast in Canada and USA. *Publications:* A Pattern of Faith, 1966 (co-author); Glory under Your Feet, 1978; Pilgrimage and Promise, 1981; Renewal in Worship, 1982; The Anglican Church, Today and Tomorrow, 1984; Christian Orthodoxy Revisited, 1985; The Gospel Conspiracy in the Episcopal Church, 1986; The Restless Heart, 1987; The Gospel Connection, 1991; The Freedom of Holiness, 1992; Free to Worship, 1996; Founder and co-editor, Christian Quarterly. *Recreations:* music, cooking. *Address:* 97a Cadogan Lane, SW1X 9DU.

MARSHALL, Michael John, CBE 1999; DL; Chairman and Chief Executive, Marshall of Cambridge (Holdings) Ltd, since 1990; Vice Lord-Lieutenant of Cambridgeshire, since 1992; *b* 27 Jan. 1932; *s* of Sir Arthur Gregory George Marshall, *qv*; *m* 1st, 1960, Bridget Wykham Pollock (marr. diss. 1977); two *s* two *d*; 2nd, 1979, Sibyl Mary Walkinshaw (*née* Hutton); two step *s*. *Educ:* Eton Coll.; Jesus Coll., Cambridge (MA Hist.; rowing Blue, 1954, rep. GB in Eur. championships, 1955). IEng; FRAeS; FIMI. Nat. Service, Flying Officer, RAF, 1950–52. Joined Marshall of Cambridge (Eng) Ltd, 1955: Dep. Chm. and Man. Dir, Marshall (Cambridge) Ltd, 1964–90. Dir, Eastern Electricity Bd, 1971–77; Chm., BL Cars Distributor Council, 1977, 1983 (Mem., 1975–84); Vice-President: Inst. Motor Ind., 1980–; EEF, 1993–; Chm., Cambs Manpower Cttee, 1980–83. Vice-Chm., Cambs Youth Involvement Cttee, Silver Jubilee Fund, 1977–78; Chm., Cambridge Olympic Appeal, 1984; Mem., Ely Cathedral Restoration Appeal Co. Cttee, 1987–; Pres., Cambridge Soc. for Blind, 1989–92; Chm., Prince's Trusts' Cambs Appeal Cttee, 1991–92; Pres., Cambridge '99 Rowing Club, 1996–. Chairman: Civilian Cttee, 104 (City of Cambridge) Sqdn, ATC, 1975–; Beds and Cambs Wing, ATC, 1987–93; Member: Air Cadet Council, 1994–; Council, Air League, 1995– (Chm., 1998–); Air Squadron, 1998–. CIMgt 1997; FRSA. Freeman, City of London, 1988; Liveryman, GAPAN, 1989–. Cambridgeshire: High Sheriff, 1988–89; DL 1989. DUniv Anglia Poly., 2001. *Recreations:* flying, watching others take exercise! *Address:* (office) c/o Marshall of Cambridge (Holdings) Ltd, The Airport, Newmarket Road, Cambridge CB5 8RX. *T:* (01223) 373245, *Fax:* (01223) 324224; *e-mail:* mjm@marcamb.co.uk. *Clubs:* Royal Air Force, Air Squadron; Hawks, Cambridge County (Cambridge); Leander (Henley-on-Thames); Eton Vikings.

MARSHALL, Noël Hedley, CMG 1986; HM Diplomatic Service, retired; *b* 26 Nov. 1934; *s* of late Arthur Hedley Marshall, CBE, and Margaret Louise Marshall (*née* Longhurst). *Educ:* Leighton Park Sch.; Lawrenceville Sch., NJ (E-SU Exchange Scholar, 1953–54); St John's Coll., Cambridge (BA 1957, MA 1992; Sir Joseph Larmor Award, 1957). Pres., Cambridge Union Soc., 1957. Entered Foreign (later Diplomatic) Service; FO, 1957–59; Third Sec., Prague, 1959–61; FO, 1961–63; Second (later First) Sec., Moscow, 1963–65; CRO, 1965–66; First Sec. (Economic): Karachi, 1966–67; Rawalpindi, 1967–70; Chargé d'affaires *ai*, Ulan Bator, 1967; FCO, 1970–74; First Sec. (later Counsellor) Press, Office of UK Permanent Rep. to European Communities, Brussels, 1974–77; NATO Defence Coll., Rome, 1977–78; Counsellor, UK Delegn to Cttee on Disarmament, Geneva, 1978–81; Head of N America Dept, FCO, 1982–85; Overseas Inspector, 1985–86; Minister, Moscow, 1986–89; Co-ordinator, British Days in the USSR, Kiev, 1990; UK Perm. Rep. to Council of Europe (with personal rank of Ambassador), 1990–93. Skippered own yacht Sadko on circumnavigation of world, 1994–97 (Challenge Cup, Royal Cruising Club; Rose Medal, Ocean Cruising Club; Lacey Trophy, Cruising Assoc.). FRGS 1998. *Publications:* contrib. to sailing jls. *Recreations:* sailing, the theatre. *Clubs:* Royal Ocean Racing, Royal Cruising.

MARSHALL, Prof. Sir (Oshley) Roy, Kt 1974; CBE 1968; High Commissioner for Barbados in the United Kingdom, 1989–91; Vice-Chancellor, Hull University, 1979–85, Emeritus Professor since 1985; *b* 21 Oct. 1920; *s* of Fitz Roy and Corene Carmelita Marshall; *m* 1st, 1945, Eirwen Lloyd (*d* 1998); one *s* three *d*; 2nd, 2000, Hon. Marie Elizabeth Bourne Hollands, CHB. *Educ:* Harrison Coll., Barbados, WI; Pembroke Coll., Cambridge; University Coll., London (Fellow, 1985). Barbados Scholar, 1938; BA 1945, MA 1948 Cantab; PhD London 1948. Barrister-at-Law, Inner Temple, 1947. University Coll., London: Asst Lecturer, 1946–48; Lecturer, 1948–56; Sub-Dean, Faculty of Law, 1949–56; Prof. of Law and Head of Dept of Law, Univ. of Sheffield, 1956–69, Vis. Prof. in Faculty of Law, 1969–80; on secondment to University of Ife, Ibadan, Nigeria, as Prof. of Law and Dean of the Faculty of Law, 1963–65; Vice-Chancellor, Univ. of West Indies, 1969–74; Sec.-Gen., Cttee of Vice-Chancellors and Principals, 1974–79. Chairman: Commonwealth Educn Liaison Cttee, 1974–81; Cttee on Commonwealth Legal Co-operation, 1975; Commonwealth Standing Cttee on Student Mobility, 1982–94; Council for Educn in the Commonwealth, 1985–91; Review Cttee on Cave Hill Campus, Univ. of WI, 1986; Constitutional Commn on the Turks and Caicos Islands, 1986; Member: Police Complaints Bd, 1977–81; Council, RPMS, 1976–83; Council, ACU, 1979–85; Management Cttee, Universities Superannuation Scheme Ltd, 1980–85; UGC for Univ. of S Pacific, 1987; Chm., Bd of Governors, Hymers Coll., Hull, 1985–89; Vice-Chm., Governing Body of Commonwealth Inst., 1980–81; Mem., Bd of Governors, Commonwealth of Learning, 1988–91; Trustee, Commonwealth Foundn, 1981. Hon. LLD: Sheffield, 1972; West Indies, 1976; Hull, 1986; Hon. DLitt CNAA, 1992. *Publications:* The Assignment of Choses in Action, 1950; A Casebook on Trusts (with J. A. Nathan), 1967; Theobald on Wills, 12th edn, 1963. *Recreations:* racing and cricket. *Address:* Evanston, Nelson Road, Navy Gardens, Christ Church C 27, Barbados, West Indies. *T:* 426 2474. *Club:* Royal Commonwealth Society.

MARSHALL, Peter, QPM 1979; Commissioner of Police for the City of London, 1978–85; *b* 21 June 1930; *s* of late Christopher George Marshall and Sylvia Marshall; *m* 1954, Bridget Frances Humphreys; three *s* one *d*. *Educ:* St Clement Danes Holborn Estate Grammar Sch. Trooper, 8th Royal Tank Regt, 1948–50. Police Officer, Metropolitan Police, 1950–78. *Recreations:* reading, gardening. *Address:* The Cottage, Cock Lane, Elham, Canterbury, Kent CT4 6TL.

MARSHALL, Sir Peter (Harold Reginald), KCMG 1983 (CMG 1974); Chairman, Joint Commonwealth Societies Council, since 1993; *b* 30 July 1924; 3rd *s* of late R. H. Marshall; *m* 1st, 1957, Patricia Rendell Stoddart (*d* 1981); one *s* one *d*; 2nd, 1989, Judith, *widow* of E. W. F. Tomlin. *Educ:* Tonbridge; Corpus Christi Coll., Cambridge (Hon. Fellow 1989). RAFVR, 1943–46. HM Foreign (later Diplomatic) Service, 1949–83: FO, 1949–52; 2nd Sec. and Private Sec. to Ambassador, Washington, 1952–56; FO, 1956–60; on staff of Civil Service Selection Board, 1960; 1st Sec. and Head of Chancery, Baghdad,

1961, and Bangkok, 1962–64; Asst Dir of Treasury Centre for Administrative Studies, 1965–66; Counsellor, UK Mission, Geneva, 1966–69, Counsellor and Head of Chancery, Paris, 1969–71; Head of Financial Policy and Aid Dept, FCO, 1971–73; Asst Under-Sec. of State, FCO, 1973–75; UK Rep. on Econ. and Social Council of UN, 1975–79; Ambassador and UK Perm. Rep. to Office of UN and Other Internat. Organisations at Geneva, 1979–83; Commonwealth Dep. Sec. Gen. (Econ.), 1983–88. Chm., Commonwealth Trust and Royal Commonwealth Soc., 1988–92; Pres., Queen Elizabeth House, Oxford, 1990–94; Vice Pres., Council for Educn in World Citizenship, 1985–98; Member: Exec. Cttee, Pilgrims, 1986–; Council, VSO, 1989–95; ODI, 1989–99; Governor, E-SU of the Commonwealth, 1984–90; Trustee: King George VI and Queen Elizabeth Foundn of St Catharine's, 1987–; Magna Carta Trust, 1993–. Vis. Lectr, Diplomatic Acad. of London, 1989–. Hon. Fellow, Univ. of Westminster, 1992. *Publications:* The Dynamics of Diplomacy, 1990; (contrib.) The United Kingdom—The United Nations (ed Jensen and Fisher), 1990; (ed) Diplomacy Beyond 2000, 1996; Positive Diplomacy, 1997; (ed) Are Diplomats Really Necessary?, 1998; (ed) The Information Explosion: a challenge for diplomacy, 1998. *Recreations:* music, golf. *Address:* 26 Queensdale Road, W11 4QB. *Clubs:* Travellers, Royal Commonwealth Society.

MARSHALL, Peter Izod; Chairman, Ocean Group (formerly Ocean Transport and Trading), 1987–97; *b* 16 April 1927; *s* of Charles and Gwendoline Marshall; *m* 1955, Davina Mary (*née* Hart); one *s* one *d*. *Educ:* Buxton College. FCA; LRAM. Commercial Dir, EMI Electronics, 1962–67; Dir of Finance, Norcros, 1967–77; Dep. Chief Exec., Plessey Co., 1977–87; Dir, Hogg Robinson plc, 1987–96; Dep. Chm., Astec (BSR) plc, 1989–99; Chm., Plessey Pension Trust Ltd, 1990–97. *Recreations:* music, swimming, golf. *Address:* Moyns, Christchurch Road, Virginia Water, Surrey GU25 4PJ. *T:* (01344) 842118. *Clubs:* Les Ambassadeurs; Wentworth.

MARSHALL, Prof. Peter James, FBA 1992; DPhil; Rhodes Professor of Imperial History, King's College, London, 1980–93, now Emeritus; *b* 28 Oct. 1933; *s* of Edward Hannaford Marshall and Madeleine (*née* Shuttleworth). *Educ:* Wellington College; Wadham Coll., Oxford (BA 1957; MA, DPhil 1962; Hon. Fellow, 1997). Military service, King's African Rifles, Kenya, 1953–54. Assistant Lecturer, Lecturer, Reader, Professor, History Dept, King's Coll., London, 1959–80 (FKC 1991). Mem., History Wkg Gp, National Curriculum, 1989–90. Pres., RHistS, 1996–2000 (Vice-Pres., 1987–91; Hon. Vice-Pres., 2000–). Editor, Journal of Imperial and Commonwealth History, 1975–81; Associate Editor, Writings and Speeches of Edmund Burke, 1976–. *Publications:* Impeachment of Warren Hastings, 1965; Problems of Empire: Britain and India 1757–1813, 1968; (ed, with J. A. Woods) Correspondence of Edmund Burke, vol. VII, 1968; The British Discovery of Hinduism, 1972; East India Fortunes, 1976; (ed) Writings and Speeches of Edmund Burke, vol. V, 1981, vol. VI, 1991, vol. VII, 2000; (with Glyndwr Williams) The Great Map of Mankind, 1982; Bengal: the British bridgehead (New Cambridge History of India, Vol. II, 2), 1988; Trade and Conquest: studies on the rise of British dominance in India, 1993; (ed) Cambridge Illustrated History of the British Empire, 1996; (ed) Oxford History of the British Empire, Vol. II, The Eighteenth Century, 1998; articles in Economic History Rev., History, Modern Asian Studies, etc. *Address:* 7 Malting Lane, Braughing, Ware, Herts SG11 2QZ. *T:* (01920) 822232.

MARSHALL, Peter James, CMG 1996; HM Diplomatic Service, retired; Consul General, Atlanta, USA, 1997–2001; *b* 25 June 1944; *s* of George Aubrey Marshall and Joan Marshall; *m* 1966, Roberta Barlow; one *s* three *d*. *Educ:* Ripon Grammar Sch. Min. of Aviation, 1963–64; CRO, 1964–65; seconded to Commonwealth Secretariat, 1965–67; served Malta, 1967–70; Vice Consul (Commercial), Johannesburg, March–Dec. 1970; 2nd Sec. (Commercial/Information), Kaduna, 1970–74; Vice Consul (Commercial), San Francisco, 1974–79; First Sec., FCO, 1979–83; Dep. High Comr, Malta, 1983–88; First Sec., FCO, 1988–90; Dep. Head, News Dept, FCO, 1990–94; Counsellor, Consul Gen. and Dep. Head of Mission, later Chargé d'Affaires, Algiers, 1994–95; Ambassador to Algeria, 1995–96. *Recreations:* gardening, travel, sailing, flying, grandchildren. *Address:* 37 Steeple Heights Drive, Biggin Hill, Kent TN16 3UN.

MARSHALL, Very Rev. Peter Jerome; Dean of Worcester, since 1997; *b* 10 May 1940; *s* of Guy and Dorothy Marshall; *m* 1965, Nancy Jane Elliott; one *s* two *d*. *Educ:* St John's, Leatherhead; Upper Canada Coll., Toronto; McGill Univ. (BSc); Westcott House, Cambridge. Ordained deacon, 1963, priest, 1964; Curate, St Mary, E Ham, 1963–66; Curate, St Mary, Woodford, and Curate i/c, St Philip and St James, S Woodford, 1966–71; Vicar, St Peter, Walthamstow, 1971–81; Dep. Dir of Training, dio. of Chelmsford, 1981–84; Canon Residentiary, Chelmsford Cathedral, 1981–85; Dio. Dir of Training, Ripon, and Canon Residentiary, Ripon Cathedral, 1985–97. Chm. Pastoral Cttee, dio. of Worcester, 1997–. Chm., Barking and Havering AHA, 1976–82. *Recreations:* swimming, walking, sailing, films. *Address:* The Deanery, 10 College Green, Worcester WR1 2LH. *T:* (01905) 27821.

MARSHALL, Air Cdre Philippa Frances, CB 1971; OBE 1956; Director of the Women's Royal Air Force, 1969–73; *b* 4 Nov. 1920; *d* of late Horace Plant Marshall, Stoke-on-Trent. *Educ:* St Dominic's High Sch., Stoke-on-Trent. Joined WAAF, 1941; Comd WRAF Admin. Officer, Strike Comd, 1968–69, Air Cdre 1969; ADC, 1969–73. *Recreations:* music, cookery. *Club:* Royal Air Force.

MARSHALL, Robert Leckie, OBE 1945; Principal, Co-operative College, and Chief Education Officer, Co-operative Union Ltd, 1946–77; *b* 27 Aug. 1913; *s* of Robert Marshall and Mary Marshall; *m* 1944, Beryl Broad; one *s*. *Educ:* Univ. of St Andrews (MA Mediaeval and Modern History; MA 1st Cl. Hons English Lit.); Commonwealth Fellow, Yale Univ. (MA Polit. Theory and Govt). Scottish Office, 1937–39. Served War, 1939–46: RASC and AEC; finally Comdt, Army Sch. of Educn. Pres., Co-op. Congress, 1976. Missions on Co-op. develt to Tanganyika, Nigeria, India, Kenya, S Yemen and Thailand. Member: Gen. Adv. Council, and Complaints Rev. Bd, IBA, 1973–77; Monopolies and Mergers Commn, 1976–82; Distributive Studies Bd, Business Educn Council, 1976–79; Treas., Council for Educnl Advance, 1974–77; Chm., Quest House, Loughborough, 1980–86; Vice-Chm., Charnwood Community Council, 1980–90. Mem. Court, Loughborough Univ. of Technol., 1981–91. Hon. MA Open Univ., 1977; Hon. DLitt Loughborough Univ. of Technol., 1977. Jt Editor, Jl of Soc. for Co-operative Studies, 1967–95. *Publications:* Lippen on Angus—a celebration of North Angus Co-operative Society, 1983; contribs to educnl and co-op jls. *Recreations:* walking, reading, golf. *Address:* Holly Cottage, 15 Beacon Road, Woodhouse Eaves, Leics LE12 8RN. *T:* (01509) 890612.

MARSHALL, Sir (Robert) Michael, Kt 1990; DL; company director, author, and retired politician; *b* 21 June 1930; *s* of late Robert Ernest and Margaret Mary Marshall, Hathersage; *m* 1972, Caroline Victoria Oliphant, *d* of late Alexander Hutchison, Strathairly, Scotland; two step *d*. *Educ:* Bradfield Coll.; Harvard Univ. (MBA 1960); Stanford Univ. Joined United Steel Cos Ltd, 1951; Branch Man., Calcutta, 1954–58; Man. Dir, Bombay, 1960–64; Commercial Dir, Workington, 1964–66; Man. Dir, Head Wrightson Export Co. Ltd, 1967–69; Management Consultant, Urwick Orr & Partners Ltd, 1969–74. MP (C) Arundel, Feb. 1974–1997; Parly Under-Sec. of State, DoI, 1979–81. Chairman: Parly Space Cttee, 1982–97; IPU, 1987–90 (Vice Chm., 1985–87); Parly IT Cttee, 1986–97 (Vice-Chm., 1982–86); Vice-Chairman: Cons. Party Parly Industry Cttee, 1976–79; All Party Parly Cttee on Management, 1974–79; Member: Select Cttee on Defence, 1982–87; Procedure Cttee, 1994–95. Adviser: British Aerospace, 1982–97; Cable and Wireless, 1982–98; SWET, 1984–97; Williams Hldgs, 1988–97; Matra Marconi Space Ltd, then Astrium, 1997–2001; Chairman, Advisory Board: Lava Systems Inc. (Canada), 1992–98; MCI/SHL Systemhouse (Europe) Ltd, 1992–98. Non-executive Director: General Offshore (UK) Ltd, 1992–98; Pathlore Software Corp. (USA), 1995–; Impatica com (Canada), 1998–. Visiting Lecturer: Judge Inst. of Mgt Studies, Cambridge, 1997; Chief Execs Orgn, USA, Toronto, Hong Kong, 1998; Bristol Univ., 2001. Member Council: British Assoc. for Central and Eastern Europe, 1994–97; Assoc. of MBAs, 1995–98; RIIA, 1997–99; Foundn for Mgt Educn; Mem. Adv. Panel, Data Protection Registrar, 1995–98. Life Member: Equity; BAFTA; RSL. Trustee, Theatres Trust, 1987–99; Chm., Chichester Fest. Theatre Trust Co., 1997–. Trustee, UC, Chichester. Hon. DL New England Coll., 1982. Liveryman, Information Technologists' Co. DL W Sussex, 1990. FRSA. *Publications:* Top Hat and Tails: the story of Jack Buchanan, 1978; (ed) The Stanley Holloway Monologues, 1979; More Monologues and Songs, 1980; The Book of Comic and Dramatic Monologues, 1981; The Timetable of Technology, 1982; No End of Jobs, 1984; Gentlemen and Players, 1987; (contrib.) A Celebration of Lords and Commons Cricket, 1989; (contrib.) My Lord's, 1990; Cricket at the Castle, 1995; (contrib.) The Planetary Interest, 1998; More Sussex Seans, 1999. *Recreations:* writing, travel, cricket, commentating, golf. *Address:* Old Inn House, Slindon, Arundel, W Sussex BN18 0RB. *Clubs:* Garrick, MCC, Lord's Taverners, Cricket Writers'; Sussex (Worthing); Royal & Ancient Golf (St Andrews); Goodwood Golf; Arundel Castle Cricket.

MARSHALL, Prof. Robin, PhD; FRS 1995; Professor of Experimental Physics, Manchester University, since 1992; *b* 5 Jan. 1940; *s* of Robert Marshall and Grace Eileen Marshall (*née* Ryder); *m* 1963; two *s* one *d*. *Educ:* Ermysted's Grammar Sch., Skipton; Univ. of Manchester (BSc 1962; PhD 1965). DSIR Research Fellow, 1965–67; Vis. Scientist, Deutsches Elektronen Synchrotron, Hamburg, 1967–68; Res. Scientist, MIT, 1968–70; Scientist, Daresbury Lab., 1970–78; PSO, 1978–86, Sen. Principal (IM), 1986–92, Rutherford Appleton Lab. Dir and Co. Sec., Frontiers Science and Television Ltd., 1999–. Max Born Medal and Prize, German Physical Soc., 1997. *Publications:* High Energy Electron-Positron Physics, 1988; Electron-Positron Annihilation Physics, 1990; numerous scientific papers. *Recreation:* nurturing ducks on Manchester's inner city canals. *Address:* Department of Physics and Astronomy, University of Manchester, Manchester M13 9PL. *T:* (0161) 275 4170.

MARSHALL, Sir Roy; *see* Marshall, Sir O. R.

MARSHALL, Hon. Russell; *see* Marshall, Hon. C. R.

MARSHALL, Steven, FCMA; Group Chief Executive, Railtrack Group PLC, 2000–April 2002 (Group Finance Director, 1999–2000); *b* 11 Feb. 1957; *s* of late Victor Marshall and of Kathleen Marshall. *Educ:* Isleworth Grammar Sch. Mgt accountant, BOC Gp, 1977–81; Marketing Analyst, then Systems Accountant, Black & Decker, 1981–84; Treasury Controller, then Sector Financial Controller, Burton Gp, 1984–87; Dep. Gp Finance Dir, and Co. Sec., Parkdale Hldgs plc, 1987–89; Gp Investor Relns Dir, then Eur. Finance Dir, IDV, Grand Metropolitan plc, 1990–95; Gp Finance Dir, 1995–98, Gp Chief Exec., 1998–99, Thorn plc. FCMA 1987. *Recreations:* international travel, natural history, soccer. *Address:* c/o Railtrack House, Euston Square, NW1 2EE. *T:* (020) 7557 8000.

MARSHALL, Thomas Daniel; DL; Member (Lab), Newcastle City Council, since 1986; Lord Mayor of Newcastle, 1998–99; *b* 6 Nov. 1929; *s* of James William and Leonora Mary Marshall; *m* 1953, Eileen James (*d* 1995); one *s*; *m* 2000, Catherine Fix, San Diego. *Educ:* St George's RC Elementary Sch., Bell's Close, Newcastle upon Tyne; Ruskin Coll.; Open Univ. Post Office, then Nat. Assistance Board, 1960; DHSS, 1966. Councillor, Newburn UDC, 1967; Mem., Tyne and Wear CC, 1974–86 (Chm., 1978–79). Chairman: Nat. Resource for Innovative Trng, Res. and Employment Ltd; Tyne and Wear PTA; Tyne and Wear Enterprise Trust; Throckley Community Hall Ltd; Newburn Riverside Recreation Assoc. Ltd; Grange Day Centre Ltd; Director: NE Innovation Centre and Development Co.; Bowes Railway Co.; Tyneside Stables Project Ltd; Owners Ltd; Newburn Sports Services Ltd; Gateshead Enterprise Agency; Vice Chm. and Exec. Mem., Northern Reg. Assembly Develt Cttee. Trustee: Building Preservation Trust Ltd; Grange Welfare Assoc. DL Tyne and Wear, 1999. *Recreation:* reading. *Address:* 7 Hallow Drive, Throckley, Newcastle upon Tyne NE15 9AQ. *T:* (0191) 267 0956. *Clubs:* Grange Welfare; Newburn Memorial (Newcastle).

MARSHALL, Valerie Margaret, (Mrs A. R. Marshall); Director, Greig, Middleton & Co. Ltd, since 1990; *b* 30 March 1945; *d* of Ernest Knagg and Marion Knagg; *m* 1972, Alan Roger Marshall; two *s* one *d*. *Educ:* Brighton and Hove High Sch.; Girton Coll., Cambridge (MA); London Graduate Sch. of Business Studies (MSc). LRAM. Financial Controller, ICFC, 1969–80; Scottish Development Agency: Investment Exec., 1980–84; Investment Man., 1984–88; Head of Business Enterprise, 1988–90. Director: Renfrew Development Co. Ltd, 1988–90; Scottish Food Fund, 1988–90. Member: Scottish Cttee, Design Council, 1975–77; Monopolies and Mergers Commn, 1976–81. Chm., Scottish Music Inf Centre, 1986–90. Governor: Glasgow Sch. of Art, 1989–90; Tonbridge GS for Girls, 1993–. *Recreations:* music, ballet, collecting antiquarian books, walking, entertaining. *Address:* 2 Farnaby Drive, Sevenoaks, Kent TN13 2LQ.

MARSHALL, Wayne; organ recitalist and solo pianist, conductor and composer; *b* 13 Jan. 1961; *s* of Wigley Marshall and Costella (*née* Daniel). *Educ:* Chetham's Sch., Manchester; Royal Coll. of Music; Vienna Hochschule. Organ Schol., Manchester Cathedral and St George's Chapel, Windsor. Dir, W11 Opera Gp, 1991; Associate Music Dir and Conductor, Carmen Jones, Old Vic, 1991; Guest Chorus Dir, Royal Opera Hse, 1992; Organist-in-Residence, Bridgewater Hall, Manchester, 1996–. Organ, solo piano, and duo recitals throughout UK, and overseas incl. US, European and Far East concert series and fests; conductor and soloist with leading orchestras in UK and overseas, incl. CBSO, RPO, London Philharmonic, BBCSO, Berlin Philharmonic and LA Philharmonic. Has made numerous recordings incl. organ music, and works by Hindemith and Gershwin. Artist of Year Award, BBC Music Mag., 1998; ECHO Award, 1998. *Address:* c/o Askonas Holt Ltd, Lonsdale Chambers, 27 Chancery Lane, WC2A 1PF. *T:* (020) 7400 1706, *Fax:* (020) 7400 1799.

MARSHALL-ANDREWS, Robert Graham; QC 1987; MP (Lab) Medway, since 1997; a Recorder of the Crown Court, since 1982; *b* 10 April 1944; *s* of late Robin and Eileen Nora Marshall; *m* 1968, Gillian Diana Elliott; one *s* one *d*. *Educ:* Mill Hill Sch.; Univ. of Bristol (LLB; winner, Observer Mace Nat. Debating Competition, 1965). Called to the Bar, Gray's Inn, 1967, Bencher, 1996; Oxford and Midland Circuit. Contested (Lab) Medway, 1992. Founder Mem., Old Testament Prophets, 1996. Dep. Chm., Theatre Council, 1997–. Trustee: George Adamson Trust, 1988–; Geffrye Museum, 1990–. Chm. of Govs, Grey Court Sch., 1988–94. *Publications:* The Palace of Wisdom (novel), 1989; contrib. political articles to nat. periodicals. *Recreations:* theatre, reading, Rugby (watching), travelling about. *Address:* House of Commons, SW1A 0AA; 4 Paper Buildings, Temple, EC4Y 7EX. *T:* (020) 7353 3366. *Club:* Druidston (Broadhaven, Pembrokeshire).

MARSHALL EVANS, David; *see* Evans.

MARSHAM, family name of **Earl of Romney**.

MARSLEN-WILSON, Lorraine Komisarjevsky; *see* Tyler, L. K.

MARSLEN-WILSON, Prof. William David, PhD; FBA 1996; Director, MRC Cognition and Brain Sciences Unit (formerly MRC Applied Psychology Unit), Cambridge, since 1997; Fellow, Wolfson College, Cambridge, since 2000; *b* Salisbury, Wilts, 5 June 1945; *s* of David William Marslen-Wilson and Pera (*née* Funk); *m* 1982, Lorraine Komisarjevsky Tyler, *qv*; one *s* one *d*; one *d*. *Educ:* St John's Coll., Oxford (BA 1st cl. Philosophy and Psychology 1967); PhD MIT 1973. Asst Prof., Cttee on Cognition and Communication, Dept of Behavioral Scis, Chicago Univ., 1973–78; Scientific Associate, Max Planck Inst. for Psycholinguistics, Nijmegen, 1977–82; Lectr, Dept of Exptl Psychol., Cambridge Univ., 1982–84; Co-Dir, Max Planck Inst. for Psycholinguistics, 1985–87; Sen. Scientist, MRC Applied Psychol. Unit, Cambridge, 1987–90; Prof. of Psychology, 1990–97, College Fellow, 2000–, Birkbeck Coll., London Univ. MAE 1996. *Publications:* (ed) Lexical Representation and Process, 1989; over 100 contribs to learned jls incl. Science, Nature, Psychological Rev., Jl of Exptl Psychol., Cognition, Lang. and Cognitive Processes. *Recreations:* photography, cooking, gardening. *Address:* MRC Cognition and Brain Sciences Unit, 15 Chaucer Road, Cambridge CB2 2EF. *T:* (01223) 355294, *Fax:* (01223) 500250.

MARSON, Anthony; Finance Director, C. B. Marketing and Investments Ltd, 1997, retired; *b* 12 Jan. 1938; *m* 1963, Margaret Salmond; three *s*. *Educ:* Bristol Univ. (BA). Finance Dir, Pharmaceutical Div., Beecham Gp, 1968–90; Gp Finance Dir, PSA Services, DoE, 1990–93. *Address:* Bullbeggars House, Church Hill, Woking, Surrey GU21 4QE.

MARSON, Geoffrey Charles; QC 1997; a Recorder, since 1995; *b* 30 March 1952; *s* of Charles Marson and Muriel Annie Marson; *m* 1992, Denise Lynn Gresty; two *s*. *Educ:* Malton Grammar Sch.; King's Coll. London (LLB Hons). Called to the Bar, Gray's Inn, 1975; Asst Recorder, 1991–95; Head of Chambers. Pt-time Pres., Mental Health Review Tribunals (Restricted Panel). *Recreations:* family, wine, cooking, travel. *Address:* 25 Park Square (West), Leeds LS1 2PW. *T:* (0113) 245 1841.

MARTEN, Francis William, CMG 1967; MC 1943; formerly Counsellor, Foreign and Commonwealth Office; *b* 8 Nov. 1916; *er s* of late Vice-Adm. Sir Francis Arthur Marten and late Lady Marten (*née* Phyllis Raby Morgan); *m* 1940, Hon. Avice Irene Vernon (*d* 1964); one *s* one *d*; 2nd, 1967, Miss Anne Tan; one *s*. *Educ:* Winchester Coll.; Christ Church, Oxford. Served HM Forces, 1939–46. Entered HM Foreign Service, 1946; served FO, 1946–48; Washington, 1948–52; FO, 1952–54; Teheran, 1954–57; NATO Defence Coll., Paris, 1957–58; Bonn, 1958–62; Leopoldville, 1962–64; Imperial Defence Coll., 1964–65; Dep. High Comr, Eastern Malaysia, 1965–67; ODM, 1967–69. *Recreation:* gardening. *Address:* 113 Pepys Road, SE14 5SE. *T:* (020) 7639 1060.

MARTIN, Archer John Porter, CBE 1960; FRS 1950; MA, PhD; *b* 1 March 1910; *s* of Dr W. A. P. and Mrs L. K. Martin; *m* 1943, Judith Bagenal; two *s* three *d*. *Educ:* Bedford Sch.; Peterhouse, Cambridge, Hon. Fellow, 1974. Nutritional Lab., Cambridge, 1933–38; Chemist, Wool Industries Research Assoc., Leeds, 1938–46; Research Dept, Boots Pure Drug Co., Nottingham, 1946–48; staff, Medical Research Council, 1948–52; Head of Phys. Chem. Div., National Inst. of Medical Research, 1952–56; Chemical Consultant, 1956–59; Director, Abbotsbury Laboratories Ltd, 1959–70; Consultant to Wellcome Research Laboratories, 1970–73. Extraordinary Prof., Technological Univ. of Eindhoven, 1965–73; Professorial Fellow, Univ. of Sussex, 1973–78; Robert A. Welch Prof. of Chemistry, Univ. of Houston, Texas, 1974–79; Invited Prof. of Chemistry, Ecole Polytechnique Fédérale de Lausanne, 1980–84. Berzelius Gold Medal, Swedish Medical Soc., 1951; (jointly with R. L. M. Synge) Nobel Prize for Chemistry, 1952; John Scott Award, 1958; John Price Wetherill Medal, 1959; Franklin Institute Medal, 1959; Leverhulme Medal, Royal Society, 1963; Koltoff Medal, Acad. of Pharmaceutical Science, 1969; Callendar Medal, Inst. of Measurement and Control, 1971; Fritz-Pregl Medal, Austrian Soc. of Microchem. and Analytical Chem., 1985. Hon. DSc Leeds, 1968; Hon. LLD Glasgow, 1973.

MARTIN, (Arthur) Bryan, CB 1987; Member of Health and Safety Executive, 1985–88, and Director, Resources and Planning Division, 1977–88; Head of UK Delegation, and Alternate Chairman, Channel Tunnel Safety Authority, 1989–92; *b* 16 July 1928; *s* of Frederick Arthur Martin and Edith Maud Martin; *m* 1953, Dyllis Naomi Eirne Johnstone-Hogg; two *s*. *Educ:* Bristol Grammar Sch.; Royal Mil. Coll. of Science (BSc). Joined Army, REME, 1948; commnd, 1948; Lt-Col, 1967–69; served in UK, Germany, Malaya (despatches, 1959), Cyprus and Aden; joined Civil Service (Dept of Employment), 1969, as direct entrant principal; Asst Sec., Factory Inspectorate, 1973; Under Sec., HSE, 1977. Director: Docklands Light Railway, 1993–98; Angel Train Contracts, 1996–99.

MARTIN, Barry Robert; Headmaster, Hampton School, since 1997; *b* 18 July 1950; *s* of late Robert Martin and Peggy Martin; *m* 1983, Fiona MacLeod; one *s* one *d*. *Educ:* Kingston Grammar Sch.; St Catharine's Coll., Cambridge (MA; Hockey Blue 1973); Inst. of Education, London Univ. (PGCE); Loughborough Univ. (MBA). Asst Master, Kingston GS, 1973–75; Bank of England Overseas Dept, 1975–77; Hd of Econs and Business Studies and Housemaster, Caterham Sch., 1978–83; Hd of Econs, Repton Sch., 1983–85; Housemaster and Dir of Studies, Mill Hill Sch., 1985–92; Principal, Liverpool Coll., 1992–97. Chief Examr, Cambridge A Level Business Studies, 1988–. FRSA 1994; FIMgt 1997. *Publications:* jointly: The Complete A–Z Business Studies Handbook, 1994, 2nd edn 1996; The Complete A–Z Economics and Business Studies Handbook, 1996; Business Studies, 1999; articles in Business Rev. *Recreation:* Cornwall. *Address:* Hampton School, Hanworth Road, Hampton, Middx TW12 3HD. *T:* (020) 8979 5526. *Clubs:* East India; Hawks (Cambridge).

MARTIN, Sir Bruce; *see* Martin, Sir R. B.

MARTIN, Bryan; *see* Martin, A. B.

MARTIN, Charles Edmund, MA; Headmaster, Bristol Grammar School, 1986–99; *b* 19 Sept. 1939; *s* of late Flight Lieut Charles Stuart Martin and of Sheila Martin; *m* 1966, Emily Mary Bozman; one *s* (one *d* decd). *Educ:* Lancing College; Selwyn College, Cambridge (Hons English; MA); Bristol University (PGCE). VSO, Sarawak, 1958–59; Asst Master, Leighton Park School, Reading, 1964–68; Day Housemaster and Sixth Form Master, Sevenoaks School, 1968–71; Head of English Dept and Dep. Headmaster, Pocklington School, 1971–80; Headmaster, King Edward VI Camp Hill Boys' School, Birmingham, 1980–86. Sec., 1992–93, Chm., 1993–94, HMC SW Div.; Divl Rep., HMC Cttee, 1992–94; Member: ISC Assisted Places Cttee, 1997–99; HMC Bridges and Partnership Cttee, 1998–99. Chief Examr, A-level English, UCLES, 1978–83. VSO selector, 1999–. Gov., John Cabot City Technol. Coll., 2000–. *Recreations:* travel, hill walking, theatre, ornithology. *Address:* 47 Hampton Park, Redland, Bristol BS6 6LQ.

MARTIN, Christopher; *see* Martin, K.

MARTIN, Christopher George; management consultant; Director of Personnel, British Broadcasting Corporation, 1981–89, retired; *b* 29 May 1938; *s* of George and Lizbette Martin; *m* 1st, 1960, Moira Hughes (marr. diss. 1975); one *s* one *d*; 2nd, 1981, Elizabeth Buchanan Keith; one *s* decd. *Educ:* Beckenham Sch., Kent. Royal Marines, 1956–62. Group Personnel Manager: Viyella Internat., 1964–70; Great Universal Stores, 1970–74; Personnel Dir, Reed Paper & Board, 1974–76; UK Personnel Dir, Air Products Ltd, 1976–78; Gp Personnel Controller, Rank Organisation Ltd, 1978–81. CIMgt (CBIM 1984); FIPM 1984. *Publication:* contrib. Jl of Textile Inst. *Recreations:* music, sailing. *Address:* Cailhavel, 31540 St Felix-Lauragais, France.

MARTIN, Christopher Sanford; Headmaster, Millfield School, 1990–98; *b* 23 Aug. 1938; *s* of late Geoffrey Richard Rex Martin and Hazel Matthews; *m* 1968, Mary Julia Parry-Evans; one *s* one *d*. *Educ:* St Andrews Univ. (MA Mod. Langs; PGCE). Commissioned 2/10 Gurkha Rifles, 1957. Taught at Westminster Sch., 1963–78, at Philips, Exeter Acad., USA, 1966; Head Master, Bristol Cathedral Sch., 1979–90. Member: Privy Council Educnl Panel, 1986–96; Engrg Council Educn Cttee, 1988–96; Adv. Gp on teaching as a profession, Teacher Trng Agencies, 1995–98. Chairman: SW Div., HMC, 1987; Choir Schools' Assoc., 1987–89; HMC/SHA Working Party on teacher shortage, 1987–90; Students Partnership Worldwide, 1998–; Nat. Rep., HMC Cttee, 1987–89. Founded Textbooks for Africa scheme (ODA), 1988. Chairman: Mental Health Foundn, 2000–; Hanover Foundn, 2001–. *Recreations:* walking, sailing, ski-ing, rebuilding a farmhouse in SW France. *Address:* 51 Portland Road, Holland Park, W11 4LJ.

MARTIN, Sir Clive (Haydn), Kt 2001; OBE 1981; TD; DL; Chairman, MPG Ltd (formerly Staples Printers Ltd), since 1978; Lord Mayor of London, 1999–2000; *b* 20 March 1935; *s* of Thomas Stanley Martin and Dorothy Gladys Martin; *m* 1959, Linda Constance Basil Penn; one *s* three *d*. *Educ:* St Albans Sch.; Haileybury and Imperial Service Coll.; London Sch. of Printing and Graphic Arts. FCIS 1966; FCMA 1971; FIOP 1985. Nat. Service, Germany, commnd RE (Survey), 1956–58. Man. Dir, Staples Printers Ltd, 1972–85. ADC to The Queen, 1982–86. City of London: Alderman, Aldgate Ward, 1985–; Sheriff, 1996–97. Master, Stationers' and Newspaper Makers' Co., 1997–98. Hon. Artillery Company: CO, 1978–80; Regtl Col, 1981–83; Master Gunner, Tower of London, 1981–83. Hon. DCL City, 1999. *Recreations:* ocean racing, cycling, walking. *Address:* MPG Ltd, The Gresham Press, Old Woking, Surrey GU22 9LH. *Clubs:* Oriental, Royal Ocean Racing.

MARTIN, Rev. Prof. David Alfred, PhD; International Fellow (formerly Senior Professorial Fellow), Institute for the Study of Economic Culture, Boston University, since 1990; Professor of Sociology, London School of Economics and Political Science, London University, 1971–89, now Emeritus; Hon. Professor, Lancaster University, since 1993; *b* 30 June 1929; *s* of late Frederick Martin and late Rhoda Miriam Martin; *m* 1st, 1953, Daphne Sylvia Treherne (*d* 1975); one *s*; 2nd, 1962, Bernice Thompson; two *s* one *d*. *Educ:* Richmond and East Sheen Grammar Sch.; Westminster Coll. (DipEd 1952); Westcott House, Cambridge. BSc (Ext.) 1st Cl. Hons, London Univ., 1959; PhD 1964. School teaching, 1952–59; postgrad. scholar, LSE, 1959–61; Asst Lectr, Sheffield Univ., 1961–62; Lectr, LSE, 1962–67, Reader, 1967–71. JSPS Scholar, Japan, 1978–79; Scurlock Prof. of Human Values, Southern Methodist Univ., Dallas, Texas, 1986–90. Lectures: Cadbury, Birmingham Univ., 1973; Ferguson, Manchester Univ., 1977; Gore, Westminster Abbey, 1977; Firth, Nottingham Univ., 1980; Forwood, Liverpool Univ., 1982; Prideaux, Exeter Univ., 1984; F. D. Maurice, KCL, 1991; Sarum, Oxford Univ., 1994–95; Gunning, Edinburgh Univ., 1997; Select Preacher, Cambridge Univ., 1979. Pres., Internat. Conf. of Sociology of Religion, 1975–83. Ordained Deacon, 1983, Priest 1984; Hon. Asst Priest, Guildford Cathedral, 1983–98. Hon. DTheol Helsinki, 2000. *Publications:* Pacifism, 1965; A Sociology of English Religion, 1967; The Religious and the Secular, 1969; Tracts against the Times, 1973; A General Theory of Secularisation, 1978; Dilemmas of Contemporary Religion, 1978; (ed) Crisis for Cranmer and King James, 1979; The Breaking of the Image, 1980; (ed jtly) Theology and Sociology, 1980; (ed jtly) No Alternative, 1981; (ed jtly) Unholy Warfare, 1983; Divinity in a Grain of Bread, 1989; Tongues of Fire, 1990; The Forbidden Revolutions, 1996; Reflections on Sociology and Theology, 1997; Does Christianity Cause Wars?, 1997; Pentecostalism—The World Their Parish, 2001; contrib. Encounter, TLS, THES, Daedalus, TES. *Recreation:* piano accompaniment. *Address:* Cripplegate Cottage, 174 St John's Road, Woking, Surrey GU21 1PQ. *T:* (01483) 762134.

MARTIN, David John Pattison; barrister; Partner, A., D., P. & E. Farmers, since 1968; *b* 5 Feb. 1945; *s* of late John Besley Martin, CBE and Muriel Martin; *m* 1977, Basia Dowmunt; one *s* three *d* (and one *d* decd). *Educ:* Norwood Sch., Exeter; Kelly College; Fitzwilliam College, Cambridge (BA Hons 1967). Governor, Dummer Academy, USA, 1963–64; called to the Bar, Inner Temple, 1969; practised until 1976; returned to the Bar, 1998; formerly Dir, family caravan and holiday business. Teignbridge District Councillor (C), 1979–83. Contested Yeovil, 1983. MP (C) Portsmouth South, 1987–97; contested (C) same seat, 1997; PPS to Minister of State, Defence Procurement, 1990, to Sec. of State, Foreign and Commonwealth Affairs, 1990–94. Contested (C): South West Region, EP elecns, 1999; Rugby and Kenilworth, 2001. *Recreations:* music, golf. *Address:* Queen Square Chambers, 56 Queen Square, Bristol BS1 4PR. *Club:* Hawks (Cambridge).

MARTIN, David Weir; Member (Lab) Scotland, European Parliament, since 1999 (Lothians, 1984–99); a Vice President of the European Parliament, since 1989; *b* 26 Aug. 1954; *s* of William Martin and Marion Weir; *m* 1979, Margaret Mary Cook; one *s* one *d*. *Educ:* Liberton High School; Heriot-Watt University (BA Hons Econs); Leicester Univ. (MA 1997). Stockbroker's clerk, 1970–74; animal rights campaigner, 1975–78. Lothian Regional Councillor, 1982–84. Leader, British Lab Gp, European Parliament, 1987–88. Vice-Pres., Internat. Inst. for Democracy; Vice-President: Nat. Playbus Assoc., 1985–; Advocates for Animals (formerly Scottish Soc. for Prevention of Vivisection), 1993–. Dir, St Andrew Animal Fund, 1986–. *Publications:* Europe: an ever closer union, 1991; Fabian pamphlets on the Common Market and on EC enlargement; Wheatley pamphlet on European Union. *Recreations:* soccer, reading. *Address:* (office) PO Box 27030, Edinburgh EH10 7YP. *T:* (0131) 654 1606.

MARTIN, Prof. Derek H.; Professor of Physics, Queen Mary and Westfield College (formerly Queen Mary College), University of London, 1967–94, Emeritus Professor since 1995 (Hon. Fellow, 1996); *b* 18 May 1929; *s* of Alec Gooch Martin and Winifred Martin; *m* 1951, Joyce Sheila Leaper; one *s* one *d*. *Educ:* Hitchin Boys' Grammar Sch.; Eastbourne Grammar Sch.; Univ. of Nottingham. BSc; PhD. Queen Mary College, London: Lectr, 1954–58, 1962–63; Reader in Experimental Physics, 1963–67; Dean, Faculty of Science, 1968–70; Head of Dept of Physics, 1970–75. DSIR Res. Fellow,

1959–62; Visiting Professor: Univ. of Calif, Berkeley, 1965–66; Univ. of Essex, 1995–97. Member: Astronomy, Space and Radio Bd, SRC, 1975–78; Bd, Athlone Press, 1973–79; Royal Greenwich Observatory Cttee, 1977–80; Senate, Univ. of London, 1981–86; Court, Univ. of Essex, 1986–. Fellow, Inst. of Physics (Hon. Sec., 1984–94); Mem., Internat. Astronomical Union. NPL Metrology Award, 1983. Editor, Advances in Physics, 1974–84. *Publications:* Magnetism in Solids, 1967; Spectroscopic Techniques, 1967; numerous articles and papers in Proc. Royal Soc., Jl of Physics, etc. *Address:* Hermanus, Hillwood Grove, Brentwood, Essex CM13 2PD. *T:* (01277) 210546. *Club:* Athenæum.

MARTIN, Evelyn Fairfax, OBE 1994; Company Secretary, National Council of Women of GB, since 1992 (National President, 1986–88); Co-Chair, Women's National Commission, 1991–93; *b* 12 Aug. 1926; *d* of late Kenneth Gordon Robinson and Beatrice Robinson (*née* Munro); *m* 1949, Dennis William Martin; three *d* (and one *d* decd). *Educ:* Belvedere Girls' Sch., Liverpool; Huyton Coll. for Girls, Liverpool; Mrs Hoster's Secretarial Coll. Foster parent, 1960–71. Chairman: Battered Wives Hostel, Calderdale, 1980–82; Calderdale Well Woman Centre, 1982–86; Calderdale CHC, 1982–84; Women's Health and Screening Delegn, 1985–91. FRSA 1991. *Recreations:* gardening, foreign travel, animals. *Address:* 32 Clifton Road, Halifax HX3 0BT. *T:* (01422) 360438; *e-mail:* evelyn.martin@btinternet.com. *Club:* University Women's.

MARTIN, (Francis) Troy K.; *see* Kennedy Martin.

MARTIN, Frank; Principal Establishment and Finance Officer, Teacher Training Agency, since 1999 (on secondment); *b* 1 April 1946; *s* of Frank and Sylvia Martin; *m* 1975, Jean Richardson; one *s* one *d. Educ:* Alsop High Sch. for Boys, Liverpool; Sidney Sussex Coll., Cambridge (BA Hist.); LSE (MSc Internat. Relns). COI, 1969–73; DTI, 1973–76; HM Treasury, 1976–: Dep. Dir, Central Unit on Purchasing, 1987–89; Principal Establishment and Finance Officer, CSO, 1989–93, on secondment; Second Treasury Officer of Accounts, 1994–98. *Recreations:* reading, gardening, listening to music. *Address:* Teacher Training Agency, Portland House, Stag Place, SW1E 5TT.

MARTIN, Frank Vernon, MA (Oxon); graphic artist; printmaker; engraver; illustrator; *b* Dulwich; 14 Jan. 1921; *er s* of late Thomas Martin; *m* 1942, Mary Irene Goodwin; three *d. Educ:* Uppingham Sch.; Hertford Coll., Oxford (History Schol.); St Martin's Sch. of Art. Army, 1941–46. Studied wood engraving with Gertrude Hermes and etching with John Buckland Wright. In free-lance professional practice as wood engraver and book illustrator, 1948–. Teacher of etching and engraving, Camberwell Sch. of Art, 1953–80 (Hd of Dept of Graphic Arts, 1976–80). Printmaker, 1966–; etchings, drypoints, woodcuts in colour. Twenty-four one-man exhibitions in UK, Europe and USA, 1956–; works in various public and private collections in UK and abroad. RE 1955–74; MSIA 1955–71; Mem., Soc. of Wood Engravers; Hon. Academician, Accademia delle Arti del Disegno, Florence, 1962. *Publications:* (also illus.) Newhaven-Dieppe, 1996; Twenty-eight Wood Engravings, 1999; *relevant publication:* The Wood Engravings of Frank Martin, by Hal Bishop, 1998. *Address:* 55 St Mary's Grove, W4 3LW.

MARTIN, Geoffrey; *see* Martin, T. G.

MARTIN, Prof. Geoffrey Haward, CBE 1986; DPhil; FSA, FRHistS; Research Professor of History, University of Essex, since 1990; *b* 27 Sept. 1928; *s* of late Ernest Leslie Martin and Mary H. Martin (*née* Haward); *m* 1953, Janet, *d* of late Douglas Hamer, MC and Enid Hamer; three *s* one *d. Educ:* Colchester Royal Grammar Sch.; Merton Coll., Oxford (MA, DPhil); Univ. of Manchester. FSA 1975; FRHistS 1958. University of Leicester (formerly University Coll. of Leicester): Lectr in Econ. History, 1952–65; Reader in History, 1966–73; Prof. of History, 1973–82; Public Orator, 1971–74; Pro-Vice-Chancellor, 1979–82; Hon. Archivist, 1989–. Keeper of Public Records, 1982–88. Vis. Prof. of Medieval History, Carleton Univ., Ottawa, 1958–59 and 1967–68; Vis. Res. Fellow, 1971, Sen. Res. Fellow, 1990–93, Merton Coll., Oxford; Sen. Res. Fellow, Loughborough Univ. of Technol., 1987–95; Hon. Res. Fellow, Dept of Library and Archive Studies, UCL, 1987–; Dist. Vis. Prof. of History, Univ. of Toronto, 1989; Emeritus Fellow, Leverhulme Trust, 1989–91. Evelyn Wrench Lectr, ESU, 1992. Chairman: Board of Leicester University Press, 1975–82; Selection Cttee, Miners' Welfare National Educn Fund, 1978–84; British Records Assoc., 1982–91 (Vice-Pres., 1992–); Commonwealth Archivists' Assoc., 1984–88; Arts and Humanities Res. Degrees Sub-Cttee, CNAA, 1986–92; Mem., RCHM, 1987–94. Vice-Pres., RHistS, 1984–88; Mem. Council, Soc. of Antiquaries, 1989–91; Pres., Cumberland and Westmorland Antiquarian and Archaeological Soc., 1999–. Gov., Museum of London, 1989–95. Hon. Gen. Editor, Suffolk Record Soc., 1956–94. Res. Associate, New DNB, 1997–. Dist. Mem., Sistema Nacional de Archivos, Mexico, 1988. DUniv Essex, 1989. Besterman Medal, Library Assoc., 1972. *Publications:* The Town: a visual history, 1961; Royal Charters of Grantham, 1963; (with Sylvia McIntyre) Bibliography of British and Irish Municipal History, vol. 1, 1972; Ipswich Recognizance Rolls: a calendar, 1973; (with Philomena Connolly) The Dublin Guild Merchant Roll *c* 1190–1265, 1992; Portsmouth Royal Charters 1194–1974, 1995; Knighton's Chronicle 1337–96, 1995; (with J. R. L. Highfield) History of Merton College, Oxford, 1997; contribs to learned jls, etc. *Recreations:* fell-walking, reflecting, gardening. *Address:* Flat 27, Woodside House, Woodside, Wimbledon, SW19 7QN. *T:* (020) 8946 2570. *Club:* Oxford and Cambridge.

MARTIN, Prof. Geoffrey Thorndike, PhD, LittD; FSA; Edwards Professor of Egyptology and Head of Department of Egyptology, University College London, 1988–93, now Emeritus; *b* 28 May 1934; *s* of late Albert Thorndike Martin and Lily Martin (*née* Jackson). *Educ:* Palmer's Sch., Grays Thurrock; University Coll. London (BA 1963); Corpus Christi Coll., Cambridge; Christ's Coll., Cambridge (MA 1966; PhD 1969; LittD 1994). Chartered Librarian (ALA, 1958–60); FSA 1975. Cataloguer, Brit. Nat. Bibliography, 1957–60; Lady Wallis Budge Res. Fellow in Egyptology, Christ's Coll., Cambridge, 1966–70; University College London: Lectr in Egyptology, 1970–78; Reader in Egyptian Archaeology, 1978–87; Prof. (*ad hominem*) of Egyptology, 1987–88. Wilbour Fellow, Brooklyn Museum, 1969; Rundle Fellow, Aust. Centre for Egyptology, Macquarie Univ., 1985, 1995, 2000; Jane and Morgan Whitney Art Hist. Fellow, Met. Mus. of Art, 1999–2001. Vis. Prof., Collège de France, 1986. Glanville Lectr, Cambridge, 1990. Assisted at excavations of Egypt Exploration Society at: Buhen, Sudan, 1963; Saqqara, Egypt, 1964–68, 1970–71 (Site Dir, 1971–74; Field Dir, 1975–98); Field Director: Epigraphic Mission, Amarna, Egypt, 1969, 1980; Leiden Excavations, Saqqara, 1999–2000 (Hon. Dir, 2001–); Jt Field Dir, Amarna Royal Tombs Project, Valley of the Kings, Thebes, 1998–. Mem. Cttee, Egypt Exploration Soc., 1969–97; Rep. for GB, Council of Internat. Assoc. Egyptologists, 1976–82; Mem. Cttee, Bd of Management, Gerald Averay Wainwright Near Eastern Archaeol Fund, Oxford Univ., 1985–89; Hon. Keeper of Muniment Room, 1997–, Hon. Keeper of the Plate, 2000–; Fellow Commoner, 1998–, Christ's Coll., Cambridge. Patron, Thurrock Local History Soc., 1996–. Corresp. Mem., German Archaeol Inst., 1982. *Publications:* Egyptian Administrative and Private-Name Seals, 1971; The Royal Tomb at El-Amarna, vol. 1, 1974, vol. 2, 1989; The Tomb of Hetepka, 1979; The Sacred Animal Necropolis at North Saqqara, 1981; (with V. Raisman) Canopic Equipment in the Petrie Collection, 1984; Scarabs, Cylinders and other Ancient Egyptian Seals, 1985; The Tomb Chapels of Paser and Raia, 1985; Corpus of Reliefs of the New Kingdom, vol. 1, 1987; (with A. El-Khouly) Excavations in the Royal Necropolis at El-Amarna, 1987; The Memphite Tomb of Horemheb, 1989; The Hidden Tombs of Memphis, 1991 (German edn 1994); Bibliography of the Amarna Period and its aftermath, 1991; The Tomb of Tia and Tia, 1997; The Tombs of Three Memphite Officials, 2001; contribs to learned and other jls. *Recreations:* travel, English history, book collecting, bibliography. *Address:* c/o Christ's College, Cambridge CB2 3BU.

MARTIN, Sir George (Henry), Kt 1996; CBE 1988; Chairman: AIR Group of companies, since 1965; Heart of London Radio, since 1994; Director, Chrysalis Group, since 1978; *b* 3 Jan. 1926; *s* of Henry and Bertha Beatrice Martin; *m* 1st, 1948, Sheena Rose Chisholm; one *s* one *d*; 2nd, 1966, Judy Lockhart Smith; one *s* one *d. Educ:* St Ignatius Coll., Stamford Hill, London; Bromley County Sch., Kent; Guildhall Sch. of Music and Drama (Hon. FGSM 1998). Sub-Lieut, FAA, RNVR, 1944–47. BBC, July 1950; EMI Records Ltd, Nov. 1950–1965; formed AIR Gp of cos (originally Associated Independent Recordings Ltd), 1965; built AIR Studios, 1969; built AIR Studios, Montserrat, 1979; completed new AIR Studios, Lyndhurst Hall, 1992; company merged with Chrysalis Gp, 1974; produced innumerable records, including all those featuring The Beatles; scored the music for fifteen films; nominated for Oscar for A Hard Day's Night, 1964; Grammy Awards, USA, 1964, 1967 (two), 1973, 1993, 1996; Ivor Novello Awards, 1963, 1979; Music Industry Trusts' Award, 1998. Hon. RAM 1999. Hon. DMus Berklee Coll. of Music, Boston, Mass, 1989; Hon. MA Salford, 1992. *Publications:* All You Need Is Ears, 1979; Making Music, 1983; Summer of Love, 1994. *Recreations:* boats, sculpture, tennis, snooker. *Address:* c/o AIR Studios, Lyndhurst Hall, Hampstead, NW3 5NG. *Clubs:* Oriental; Alderney Sailing.

MARTIN, Prof. (George) Steven, PhD; FRS 1998; Professor, Department of Molecular and Cell Biology, since 1989, and Research Virologist, Cancer Research Laboratory, since 1983, University of California at Berkeley; *b* 19 Sept. 1943; *s* of Kurt and Hanna Martin; *m* 1969, Gail Zuckman; one *s. Educ:* Queens' Coll., Cambridge (MA 1966; PhD 1968). Postdoctoral Fellow, Virus Lab., Univ. of Calif, Berkeley, 1968–71; staff mem., ICRF, London, 1971–75; University of California, Berkeley: Asst Prof., 1975–79, Associate Prof., 1979–83, Prof., 1983–89, Dept of Zool.; Asst Res. Virologist, 1975–79, Associate Res. Virologist, 1979–83, Cancer Res. Lab. Jane Coffin Childs Meml Fund Fellow, 1968–70; Amer. Cancer Soc. Dernham Fellow, 1970–71; John Simon Guggenheim Meml Foundn Fellow, 1991–92. Scholar Award in Cancer Res., Amer. Cancer Soc., 1991–92. *Publications:* contribs to Nature, Science, Cell and other scientific jls. *Recreations:* hiking, bicycling, reading. *Address:* University of California at Berkeley, Department of Molecular and Cell Biology, 401 Barker Hall #3204, Berkeley, CA 94720–3204, USA. *T:* (510) 6421508.

MARTIN, Gerard James; QC 2000; a Recorder, since 2000; *b* 27 May 1955; *m* 1980, Deirdre Martin; three *s. Educ:* St Joseph's Coll., Blackpool; Trinity Hall, Cambridge (BA Law). Called to the Bar, Middle Temple, 1978; Asst Recorder, 1997–2000. *Recreations:* most sports, good food and wine. *Address:* Exchange Chambers, Pearl Assurance House, Derby Square, Liverpool L2 9XX.

MARTIN, Lt-Gen. Henry James, CBE 1943; DFC; Chief of Defence Staff, South African Defence Force, retired; *b* 10 June 1910; *s* of Stanley Charles Martin and Susan C. Fourie; *m* 1940, Renée Viljoen; one *s* two *d. Educ:* Grey Coll. Sch., Bloemfontein; Grey Univ. Coll., Bloemfontein. Joined S African Air Force, 1935, and played important rôle in British Empire Training Scheme in South Africa; commanded No 12 Sqdn in Western Desert (DFC, Croix Militaire de première classe Belgique); commanded No 3 Wing (a unit of Desert Air Force) and campaigned from El Alamein to Tunis; returned to Union, 1943. *Recreation:* rugger (represented Orange Free State, 1931–34, Transvaal, 1935–37, South Africa, 1937). *Address:* 42 Newlands Park, PO Box 370, Newlands Plaza, 0049, S Africa.

MARTIN, Ian; Deputy Special Representative of UN Secretary-General, UN Mission in Ethiopia and Eritrea, since 2000; *b* 10 Aug. 1946; *s* of Collin and Betty Martin. *Educ:* Brentwood Sch.; Emmanuel Coll., Cambridge; Harvard Univ. Ford Foundn Representative's Staff, India, 1969–70, Pakistan, 1970–71, Bangladesh, 1972; Community Relations Officer, Redbridge Community Relations Council, 1973–75; Gen. Sec., Jt Council for the Welfare of Immigrants, 1977–82 (Dep. Gen. Sec., 1976–77; Exec. Cttee Mem., 1982–86); Gen. Sec., The Fabian Soc., 1982–85; Sec. Gen., Amnesty Internat., 1986–92 (Hd, Asia Res. Dept, 1985–86). Dir for Human Rights, UN/OAS Internat. Civilian Mission in Haiti, 1993, 1994–95; Chief, UN Human Rights Field Op., Rwanda, 1995–96; Special Advr, UN High Comr for Human Rights, 1998; Dep. High Rep. for Human Rights, Bosnia and Herzegovina, 1998–99; Special Rep. of UN Sec.-Gen., East Timor Popular Consultation, 1999. Sen. Associate, Carnegie Endowment for Internat. Peace, 1993, 1994; Visiting Fellow: Human Rights Centre, Univ. of Essex, 1996–97; Internat. Peace Acad., NY, 2000. Member: Exec. Cttee, NCCL, 1983–85; Redbridge and Waltham Forest AHA, 1977–82; Redbridge HA, 1982–83. Councillor, London Borough of Redbridge, 1978–82. *Publications:* Immigration Law and Practice (with Larry Grant), 1982; Self-Determination in East Timor, 2001; *contributed to:* Labour and Equality, Fabian Essays, 1980; Civil Liberties, Cobden Trust Essays, 1984; Public Interest Law (ed J. Cooper and R. Dhavan), 1986; Hard Choices (ed J. Moore), 1998. *Address:* 346 Ben Jonson House, Barbican, EC2Y 8NQ.

MARTIN, Ian Alexander; Chairman, Heath Lambert Fenchurch Holdings (formerly Erycinus), since 1997; *b* 28 Feb. 1935; *s* of Alexander Martin and Eva (*née* Gillman); *m* 1963, Phyllis Mitchell-Bey; one *s* two *d. Educ:* Univ. of St Andrews (MA). Mem., Inst. of Chartered Accountants, Scotland. Dir, Mine Safety Appliances Co. Ltd, 1969–72; Div. Dir, ITT Europe, 1977–79; Grand Metropolitan: Dir, 1985–94; Gp Man. Dir, 1991–93; Dep. Chm., 1993–94; Chairman: Intercontinental Hotels, 1986–88; Burger King Corp., 1989–93; Pillsbury Co., 1989–93; Internat. Distillers and Vintners, 1992–93; Chm. and Chief Exec., Glenisla Gp Ltd, 1994–97; Chm., 1995–2001, Chief Exec., 2001, Unigate, then Uniq; Chairman: Baxi Gp (formerly Newmond), 1997–; William Hill, 1999–; 365 Corporation PLC, 1999–; SSL International, 2001–; Director: St Paul Companies Inc., 1989–96; Grocery Manufacturers of America, 1989–93; Granada Group, 1992–; House of Fraser, 1994–2000; Nat. Commn on Children, USA, 1990–93. Chm., Europe Cttee, CBI, 1993–94; Mem. Adv. Cttee, Ian Jones & Partners, 1998–. Trustee, Duke of Edinburgh's Award Scheme, 1991–98; Dir, Friends of the Youth Award Inc., 1991–98; Patron, Cities in Schools, 1994–. Freeman, City of London, 1982. CIMgt (CBIM 1986). *Recreations:* angling, golf, music. *Address:* HLF Insurance Holdings Ltd, Friary Court, 65 Crutched Friars, EC3N 2NP. *T:* (020) 7560 3573. *Clubs:* Buck's; Wentworth Golf.

MARTIN, James Brown; General Secretary, Educational Institute of Scotland, 1988–95; *b* 6 Dec. 1953; *s* of James and Annie Martin; *m* 1975, Anne McNaughton; one *s* one *d. Educ:* Larbert Village and High Schs; Heriot-Watt Univ. (BAEcon); Moray House College of Educn. Teacher, Falkirk High Sch., 1975–79; Field Officer 1979–83, Asst Sec. 1983–88, EIS. Member: Gen. Council, Scottish TUC, 1987; Exec., ETUCE, 1988; Exec., Education International, 1993. Mem., Forth Valley Enterprise Bd, 1989.

Recreations: Hibernian FC, watching football. *Address:* 1 Orchard Grove, Polmont, Stirlingshire FK2 0XE.

MARTIN, Janet, (Mrs K. P. Martin); Relief Warden (Assisted Independence), Test Valley Housing, 1988–91; *b* Dorchester, Dorset, 8 Sept. 1927; *d* of James Wilkinson and Florence Steer; *m* 1951, Peter Martin (retired Southampton HA, Senior Consultant AT&T (ISTEL) Ltd); one *s* one *d*. *Educ:* Dorchester Grammar Sch., Dorset; Weymouth Tech. Coll.; occupational training courses. PA to Group Sec., Herrison HMC, 1949; admin./clerical work, NHS and other, 1956; social research fieldwork, mainly NHS (Wessex mental health care evaluation team), and Social Services (Hants CC and Nat. Inst. for Social Work), 1967–76; residential social worker (children with special needs), Southampton, 1976–78; Social Services Officer, Test Valley, 1978–86; Senior Residential Care Officer (Elderly), Test Valley Social Services, 1986–87. Interviewer, MRC 'National' Survey, 1970–85; Psychosexual Counsellor, Aldermoor Clinic, 1981–84. Mem., Press Council, 1973–78. Vice Chm., Dorchester Labour Party. *Recreations:* buildings, books. *Address:* The Old Stables, Linden Avenue, Dorchester, Dorset DT1 1EJ. *T:* (01305) 269839.

MARTIN, John; *see* Martin, L. J.

MARTIN, Vice-Adm. Sir John (Edward Ludgate), KCB 1972 (CB 1968); DSC 1943; FNI; retired; Lieutenant-Governor and Commander-in-Chief of Guernsey, 1974–80; *b* 10 May 1918; *s* of late Surgeon Rear-Admiral W. L. Martin, OBE, FRCS and Elsie Mary Martin (*née* Catford); *m* 1942, Rosemary Ann Deck; two *s* two *d*. *Educ:* RNC, Dartmouth. Sub Lt and Lt, HMS Pelican, 1938–41; 1st Lt, HMS Antelope, 1942; navigation course, 1942; Navigation Officer, 13th Minesweeping Flotilla, Mediterranean, 1943–44, including invasions N Africa, Sicily, Pantelleria, Salerno; RNAS Yeovilton, 1944; Navigation Officer: HMS Manxman and HMS Bermuda, 1944–46; HMS Nelson, 1947; HMS Victorious, 1948; Staff Coll., 1949; Navigation Officer, HMS Devonshire, 1950–51; Dirg Staff, Staff Coll., 1952–54; Jt Services Planning Staff, Far East, 1954–55; Exec. Off., HMS Superb, 1956–57; Jt Services Staff Coll., 1958; Dep. Dir Manpower Planning and Complementing Div., Admty, 1959–61; Sen. Naval Off., W Indies, 1961–62; Comdr Brit. Forces Caribbean Area, 1962–63; Capt. Britannia Royal Naval Coll., Dartmouth, 1963–66; Flag Officer, Middle East, 1966–67; Comdr, British Forces Gulf, 1967–68 (despatches); Dir-Gen., Naval Personal Services and Training, 1968–70; Dep. Supreme Allied Comdr, Atlantic, 1970–72. Comdr 1951; Captain 1957; Rear-Adm. 1966; Vice-Adm. 1970. Pres., Nautical Inst., 1975–78. *Recreations:* fishing, shooting, beagling (Jt Master Britannia Beagles, 1963–66), sailing. *Clubs:* Army and Navy; Royal Naval Sailing Association; Royal Yacht Squadron.

MARTIN, Prof. John Francis, MD; FRCP; British Heart Foundation Professor of Cardiovascular Medicine, University College London, since 1996; Hon. Consultant Physician, University College Hospitals NHS Trust, since 1996; *b* 8 July 1943; *s* of Francis Martin and Marie-Antoinette Martin (née Bessler); *m* 1979, Íde Leddy (marr. diss. 1987); *m* 1991, Elisabeth Gaillochet (marr. diss. 1995). *Educ:* English Coll., Valladolid, Spain; Univ. of Sheffield (MB ChB 1973; MD 1981). FRCP 1989. Lectr in Medicine, Sheffield Univ., 1975–79; Sen. Lectr, Univ. of Melbourne, 1979–81; Hon. Consultant Physician, St Vincent's Hosp., Melbourne, 1979–81; Sen. Lectr, Sheffield Univ., 1981–86; Hon. Consultant Physician, Hallamshire Hosp., 1981–86; Hd, Cardiovascular Res., Wellcome Foundn Res. Labs, 1986–96; Sen. Lectr, 1986–90, BHF Prof. of Cardiovascular Sci., 1990–96, KCL; Hon. Consultant Physician, KCH, 1986–96. Founder, Eurogene (biotech. co.), 1997. Mem., Animal Procedures Cttee, Home Office, 1998–. Pres., Eur. Soc. for Clinical Investigation, 1992–95; Vice Pres., Eur. Soc. Cardiology, 2001– (FESC 1995; Mem. Bd, 1998–2000). Captain, RAMC(V), 1977–83, Major, 1983–86; now RARO. FMedSci 2000. *Publications:* Platelet Heterogeneity, Biology and Pathology, 1990; contrib. articles to learned jls on cardiovascular biol. and medicine, particularly arteriosclerosis, thrombosis and acute coronary syndromes and gene therapy. *Recreations:* poetry, Mediaeval philosophy. *Address:* Department of Medicine, University College London, 5 University Street, WC1E 6JJ. *T:* (020) 7209 6532; 21 West Square, SE11 4SN. *T:* (020) 7735 2212. *Club:* Athenæum.

MARTIN, John Howard Sherwell, FRICS; Senior Partner, Knight Frank, since 1996; *b* 7 Aug. 1945; *s* of John Robert Henry Martin and Lilian Vera Sherwell; *m* 1971, Linda Susan Johnson; one *s* two *d*. *Educ:* Emanuel Sch. FRICS 1971. Trainee Surveyor, GLC, 1965–71; joined Knight Frank & Rutley, 1971: Partner, 1978–96. Non-exec. Dir, Baltic Exchange, 1993–98. Trustee, St Clement Danes Holborn Estate Charity, 1987–2000. *Recreations:* travel, antiques, gardening. *Address:* (office) 20 Hanover Square, W1S 1HZ. *T:* (020) 7629 8171. *Clubs:* Oriental, Home House.

MARTIN, John Neville, FREng, FICE, FIStructE; Chairman, Ove Arup Partnership, 1992–95; *b* 9 April 1932; *s* of Reginald Martin and Dorothy Sylvia Martin (*née* Bray); *m* 1964, Julia Mary Galpin; three *s* one *d*. *Educ:* Royal Grammar Sch., Guildford. FICE 1957; FIStructE 1957; FREng (FEng 1988). Articled pupil with Engr and Surveyor, Woking UDC, 1949–52; Nat. Service, RE, 1952–54; Asst Engr, Sir William Halcrow & Partners, Consulting Engrs, 1954–57; with Ove Arup Partnership, Consulting Engrs, 1957–95. Chm., Ove Arup Foundn, 1996–2000. Chm., Haslemere Dist Scout Council, 1995–. *Publications:* various papers for engrg jls (IStructE). *Recreations:* Scouting, mountain-walking, music, country dancing. *Address:* Broadheath, Nutcombe Lane, Hindhead, Surrey GU26 6BP. *T:* (01428) 604616.

MARTIN, John Sharp Buchanan; Head of Transport (formerly Transport and Planning) Group, Scottish Executive (formerly Scottish Office) Development Department, since 1998; *b* 7 July 1946; *s* of David Buchanan Martin and Agnes Miller (*née* Craig); *m* 1971, Catriona Susan Stewart Meldrum; one *s* one *d*. *Educ:* Bell-Baxter High Sch., Cupar, Fife; Univ. of St Andrews (BSc). Asst Principal, Scottish Educn Dept, 1968–71; Private Sec. to Parly Under-Sec. of State for Scotland, 1971–73; Scottish Office: Principal, 1973–80, seconded to Rayner Scrutinies, 1979–80; Asst Sec., 1980–92; Under-Sec., Sch. Educn and Sport, Educn, subseq. Educn and Industry Dept, 1992–98. *Recreations:* tennis, golf, cricket, philately. *Address:* c/o Scottish Executive Development Department, Victoria Quay, Edinburgh EH6 6QQ. *T:* (0131) 244 0629. *Clubs:* Colinton Lawn Tennis, Merchants of Edinburgh Golf, Woodcutters Cricket (Edinburgh).

MARTIN, John Sinclair, CBE 1977; farmer; Chairman, Anglian Flood Defence Committee, Environment Agency (formerly National Rivers Authority), 1989–97; *b* 18 Sept. 1931; *s* of Joseph and Claire Martin, Littleport, Ely; *m* 1960, Katharine Elisabeth Barclay, MB, BS; three *s* one *d*. *Educ:* The Leys Sch., Cambridge; St John's Coll., Cambridge (MA, Dip. in Agriculture). Chairman: Littleport and Downham IDB, 1971–88; JCO Arable Crops and Forage Bd, 1973–76; Eastern Regional Panel, MAFF, 1981–86 (Mem., 1972–78); Great Ouse Local Land Drainage Cttee, AWA, 1983–88; Anglian Drainage Cttee, 1988–89; Member: Eastern Counties Farmers' Management Cttee, 1960–70; ARC, 1968–78; Great Ouse River Authority, 1970–74; Lawes Agricl Trust Cttee, 1982–84; MAFF Priorities Bd, 1984–88; Anglian Water Authority, 1988–89; Vice-Pres., Assoc. of Drainage Authorities, 1986–. Chairman: Ely Br., NFU, 1963; Cambs NFU, 1979. High Sheriff, Cambs, 1985–86. *Address:* Denny Abbey, Waterbeach, Cambridge CB5 9PQ. *T:* (01223) 860282. *Club:* Farmers'.

MARTIN, John Vandeleur; QC 1991; *b* 17 Jan. 1948; *s* of Col Graham Vandeleur Martin, MC and Margaret Helen (*née* Sherwood); *m* 1974, Stephanie Johnstone Smith; two *s* one *d*. *Educ:* Malvern Coll.; Pembroke Coll., Cambridge (MA). Called to the Bar, Lincoln's Inn, 1972, Bencher, 1999. Dep. High Court Judge, Chancery Div., 1993. Liveryman, Drapers' Co., 1973. *Recreations:* almost any opera, swimming in warm water. *Address:* Wilberforce Chambers, 8 New Square, Lincoln's Inn, WC2A 3QP. *T:* (020) 7306 0102.

MARTIN, John William Prior; HM Diplomatic Service, retired; Counsellor, Foreign and Commonwealth Office, 1985–89; *b* 23 July 1934; *er s* of late Stanley Gordon Martin and Frances Heather (*née* Moore); *m* 1960, Jean Fleming; three *s* one *d*. *Educ:* CIM Sch., Chefoo and Kuling; Bristol Grammar Sch.; St John's Coll., Oxford (MA). National Service, 1953–55 (2nd Lieut Royal Signals). Joined FO, 1959; Beirut, 1960; Saigon, 1963; Language Student, Hong Kong, 1965–67; Dar es Salaam, 1968; FCO, 1971; Singapore, 1974; FCO, 1978; Kuala Lumpur, 1982. *Recreations:* conservation, travel, ornithology.

MARTIN, Jonathan Arthur, OBE 1995; sports broadcasting consultant; Controller, Television Sport, BBC Broadcast, 1996–98; *b* 18 June 1942; *s* of Arthur Martin and Mabel Gladys Martin (*née* Bishop); *m* 1967, Joy Elizabeth Fulker; two *s*. *Educ:* Gravesend Grammar School; St Edmund Hall, Oxford (BA 1964, English; MA 1992). Joined BBC as general trainee, 1964; producer, Sportsnight, 1969; producer, Match of the Day, 1970; editor, Sportsnight and Match of the Day, 1974; exec. producer, BBC TV Wimbledon tennis coverage, 1979–81; producer, Ski Sunday and Grand Prix, 1978–80; managing editor, Sport, 1980; Head of Sport, 1981–87, Head of Sport and Events, 1987–96, BBC TV. Vice-Pres., EBU Sports Gp, 1984–98. *Recreations:* ski-ing, golf, watching sport, especially Watford FC. *Address:* Arkle, Valentine Way, Chalfont St Giles, Bucks HP8 4JB. *Club:* Harewood Downs Golf.

MARTIN, Kit; Director, Phoenix Trust (UK Historic Building Preservation Trust), 1997–2001; *b* 6 May 1947; *s* of Sir (John) Leslie Martin, RA, and Sadie Speight, architect; *m* 1st, 1970, Julia Margaret Mitchell (marr. diss. 1978); 2nd, 1980, Sally Martha, *d* of late Sqdn Ldr Edwin Brookes; one *d*. *Educ:* Eton; Jesus Coll., Cambridge (BA 1969; DipArch 1972; MA 1973). Started Martin & Weighton, architectural practice, 1969–76; partner involved in numerous projects to restore and save listed bldgs in UK, France and Italy; Dir, Kit Martin (Historic Houses Rescue) Ltd, 1974–; initiated rescue and conversion of listed bldgs of outstanding architectural interest, including: Dingley Hall, Northants, 1976–79; Gunton Park, Norfolk, 1980–84; Cullen House, Banffshire, 1982–85; Tyninghame House, E Lothian, 1988–92; Burley on the Hill, Rutland, 1993–97; Formakin, Renfrewshire, 1994–99; Maristow, Devon, 1995–99 (several schemes have won local, nat. or European awards); Dir, Historic Bldgs Rescue Ltd, 1993–; initiated rescue and conversion of several listed bldgs, including Royal Naval Hosp., Norfolk to housing, and a chapel. Mem., Historic Bldgs Council for Scotland, 1987–99. Trustee, Save Europe Heritage, 1994–. Hon. FRIBA 2000. *Publications:* The Country House: to be or not to be, 1982; Save Jamaica's Heritage (UNESCO Award), 1990. *Recreations:* ski-ing, squash, private flying with wife, landscape gardening, including restoration of Gunton Park according to historic principles. *Address:* (office) Park Farm, Gunton Park, Hanworth, Norfolk NR11 7HL.

MARTIN, Sir Laurence (Woodward), Kt 1994; DL; Senior Adviser, Center for Strategic and International Studies, Washington (Arleigh Burke Professor of Strategy, 1998–2000); *b* 30 July 1928; *s* of Leonard and Florence Mary Martin; *m* 1951, Betty Parnall; one *s* one *d*. *Educ:* St Austell Grammar Sch.; Christ's Coll., Cambridge (MA); Yale Univ. (MA, PhD). Flying Officer, RAF, 1948–50; Instr, Yale Univ., 1955–56; Asst Prof., MIT, 1956–61; Rockefeller Fellow for Advanced Study, 1958–59; Associate Prof., Sch. of Advanced Internat. Studies, The Johns Hopkins Univ., 1961–64; Wilson Prof. of Internat. Politics, Univ. of Wales, 1964–68; Prof. of War Studies, King's Coll., Univ. of London, 1968–77, Fellow 1983–; Vice-Chancellor, Univ. of Newcastle upon Tyne, 1978–90, Emeritus Prof., 1991; Dir, RIIA, 1991–96. Research Associate, Washington Center of Foreign Policy Research, 1964–76, 1979–. Lees-Knowles Lectr, Cambridge, 1981; BBC Reith Lectr, 1981. Member: SSRC, 1969–76 (Chm. Res. Grants Bd); Internat. Res. Council, Center for Internat. and Strategic Studies (formerly Georgetown Center of Strategic Studies), 1969–77, 1979– (Co-Chm., 1998–); Council, IISS, 1975–83. Consultant, Sandia Labs. DL Tyne and Wear, 1986. Hon. DCL Newcastle, 1991. *Publications:* The Anglo-American Tradition in Foreign Affairs (with Arnold Wolfers), 1956; Peace without Victory, 1958; Neutralism and Non-Alignment, 1962; The Sea in Modern Strategy, 1967; (jtly) America in World Affairs, 1970; Arms and Strategy, 1973; (jtly) Retreat from Empire?, 1973; (jtly) Strategic Thought in the Nuclear Age, 1979; The Two-Edged Sword, 1982; Before the Day After, 1985; The Changing Face of Nuclear Warfare, 1987; (jtly) British Foreign Policy, 1997. *Address:* 35 Witley Court, Coram Street, WC1N 1HD.

MARTIN, (Leonard) John, CBE 1995; Consulting Actuary, Watson Wyatt (formerly R. Watson & Sons), since 1954; *b* 20 April 1929; *s* of Leonard A. Martin and Anne Elisabeth Martin (*née* Scudamore); *m* 1956, Elisabeth Veronica Hall Jones; one *s* one *d*. *Educ:* Ardingly Coll. FIA, FSS, FPMI. Joined R. Watson & Sons, 1952, Partner 1954, Sen. Partner 1984–94. Dir, NPI Insurance Co., 1993–. Pres., Inst. of Actuaries, 1992–94; Chm., Consultative Group of Actuaries in Europe, 1988–91; Rapporteur, Cttee of Actuaries, UN, 1988–. Liveryman, GAPAN. *Recreations:* flying, sailing, singing. *Address:* Pitt House, Ducie Avenue, Bembridge, Isle of Wight PO35 5NF. *Club:* Naval.

MARTIN, Leslie Vaughan; Directing Actuary (Superannuation and Research), Government Actuary's Department, 1974–79; *b* 20 March 1919; *s* of late Hubert Charles Martin and late Rose Martin (*née* Skelton); *m* 1949, Winifred Dorothy Hopkins; one *s* one *d*. *Educ:* Price's Sch., Fareham. FIA 1947. Served with RAMC and REME, 1940–46. Deptl Clerical Officer, Customs and Excise, 1936–38; joined Govt Actuary's Dept, 1938; Asst Actuary, 1949; Actuary, 1954; Principal Actuary, 1962. Mem. Council, Inst. of Actuaries, 1971–76; Vice-Chm., CS Medical Aid Assoc., 1976–79. Churchwarden, St Barnabas, Dulwich, 1965–70, 1977–79, Vice-Chm. of PCC, 1970–79; Treasurer: Morchard Bishop Parochial Church Council, 1980–83; Cadbury Deanery Synod, 1981–88; Chulmleigh Deanery Synod, 1989–97; Lapford PCC, 1991–93. *Recreations:* crosswords, chess, scrabble. *Address:* Pickwick House, Down St Mary, Crediton, Devon EX17 6EQ. *T:* (01363) 84581.

MARTIN, Lewis Vine; Executive Director, 1995–2002, Chief Executive, Priory of England and Islands, 1999–2002, St John Ambulance; *b* 14 Nov. 1939; *s* of Lewis and Else Martin; *m* 1964, Patricia Mary Thorne; two *d*. *Educ:* Clarks Coll., Cardiff. Exec. posts in marketing, investment, admin, major projects and gen. management, UK and Europe, Mobil Oil Co. Ltd, 1955–95. *Recreations:* keep fit, swimming, gardening, Rugby (spectator now). *Address:* c/o St John Ambulance, National Headquarters, 27 St John's Lane, EC1M 4BU. *T:* (020) 7324 4000.

MARTIN, Michael C.; *see* Craig-Martin.

MARTIN, Rt Hon. Michael John; PC 2000; MP Glasgow, Springburn, since 2000; Speaker of the House of Commons, since 2000; *b* 3 July 1945; *s* of Michael and Mary Martin; *m* 1966, Mary McLay; one *s* one *d*. *Educ:* St Patrick's Boys' Sch., Glasgow. Sheet metal worker; AUEW Shop Steward, Rolls Royce, Hillington, 1970–74; Trade Union Organiser, 1976–79; Mem., and sponsored by, AEEU. MP (Lab) Glasgow, Springburn, 1979–2000 (when elected Speaker). PPS to Rt Hon. Denis Healey, MP, 1981–83; Member: Select Cttee for Trade and Industry, 1983–86; Speaker's Panel of Chairmen, 1987–2000; First Dep. Chm. of Ways and Means, and a Dep. Speaker, H of C, 1997–2000. Chm., Scottish Grand Cttee, 1987–97. Councillor: for Fairfield Ward, Glasgow Corp., 1973–74; for Balornock Ward, Glasgow DC, 1974–79. Mem., Coll. of Piping, 1989–. *Recreations:* hill walking, local history, piping. *Address:* Speaker's House, Westminster, SW1A 0AA.
See also P. *Martin*.

MARTIN, His Honour Oliver Samuel; QC 1970; a Circuit Judge, 1975–93; *b* 26 Nov. 1919; *s* of Sidney Edward Martin and Nita Martin; *m* 1st, 1954, Marion Eve (marr. diss. 1982); two *s*; 2nd, 1982, Gloria Audrey. *Educ:* King's College Sch., Wimbledon; London University. Served RNVR, 1939–46. Called to Bar, Gray's Inn, 1951. Dep. Chm. E Sussex QS, 1970–71; a Recorder of the Crown Court, 1972–75. *Recreations:* golf, music, reading, writing, holidays.

MARTIN, Hon. Paul; PC (Canada) 1993; MP (L) for Lasalle-Emard, Quebec, since 1988; Minister for Finance, Canada, since 1993; *b* Windsor, Ont, 28 Aug. 1938; *s* of Paul Joseph James Martin and Eleanor Alice Martin; *m* 1965, Sheila Ann Cowan; three *s*. *Educ:* Univ. of Ottawa; Univ. of Toronto (BA Philos. and Hist. 1962); Univ. of Toronto Law Sch. (LLB 1965). Merchant seaman on salvage ops in Arctic; worked in Legal Dept, ECSC, Luxembourg; with Osler, Hoskin & Harcourt, Toronto; called to the Bar, Ontario, 1966; with Power Corp. of Canada; Chm. and Chief Exec. Officer, Canada Steamship Lines; Corporate Dir for several major cos. Critic for: Treasury Bd and Urban Develt, until 1991; Envmt and Associate Finance Critic, 1991–93; Minister responsible for Federal Office of Regl Develt, 1993–97. First Chm., G-20, 1999–. Co-Chm., Nat. Platform Cttee, Liberal Party of Canada, 1993. *Address:* House of Commons, Room 515 S, Center Block, Ottawa, ON K1A 0A6, Canada. *T:* (613) 9924284, *Fax:* (613) 9924291.

MARTIN, Paul; Member (Lab) Glasgow Springburn, Scottish Parliament, since 1999; *b* 17 March 1967; *s* of Rt Hon. Michael John Martin, *qv*; *m* 1997, Fiona Allen. *Educ:* All Saints Secondary Sch.; Barmulloch Coll., Glasgow. Mem. (Lab) City of Glasgow Council, 1995–99. *Address:* Scottish Parliament, Edinburgh EH99 1SP; 15 Strathkelvin Avenue, Glasgow G64 1RR.

MARTIN, Paul, PhD; Fellow, Wolfson College, Cambridge, 1985–86 and since 2001; writer and consultant, since 2001; *b* 11 May 1958; *s* of Joseph Martin and Pamela Vague. *Educ:* Christ's Coll., Cambridge (MA, PhD). Harkness Fellow and Postdoctoral Schol., Stanford Univ., 1982–83; Asst Lectr, Cambridge Univ., 1984–86; MoD, 1986–2000; Dir of Communication, Cabinet Office, 2000–01. *Publications:* (with Patrick Bateson) Measuring Behaviour, 1986, 2nd edn 1993; The Sickening Mind, 1997; (with Patrick Bateson) Design for a Life, 1999.

MARTIN, Paul James, (Paul Merton); comedian, actor, writer; *b* 9 July 1957; *s* of Albert and Mary Martin; *m* 1991, Caroline Quentin (marr. diss. 1999); *m* 2000, Sarah Parkinson. *Educ:* Wimbledon Coll. Civil Servant, Dept of Employment; *stage:* stand-up comic: London Comedy Store, 1981–; London cabaret circuit, 1982–88; toured England, Scotland and Ireland, 1993; London Palladium, 1994; Live Bed Show, Garrick, 1994; *television* includes: series: Comedy Wavelength, 1987; Whose Line is it Anyway?, 1989–93; Have I Got News For You, 1990–; Paul Merton—the series, 1991, 1993; Paul Merton's Life of Comedy, 1995; Paul Merton's Palladium Story (2 programmes), 1995; Paul Merton in Galton & Simpson, 1996, 1997; The Paul Merton Show, 1996; Room 101, 1999–; *films:* An Evening with Gary Lineker, 1994; The Suicidal Dog, 2000 (writer and dir); *radio* series include: Just a Minute, 1988–; I'm Sorry I Haven't a Clue, 1993–; The Masterson Inheritance, 1993–96; Two Priests and a Nun go into a Pub, 2000; Late, 2001. *Publications:* (with Julian Clary) My Life with Fanny the Wonderdog, 1988; Paul Merton's History of the 20th Century, 1993; Have I Got News For You, 1994; My Struggle, 1995. *Recreations:* tropical fish, walking, film comedy. *Address:* c/o International Artistes Ltd, Mezzanine Floor, 235 Regent Street, W1R 8AX. *T:* (020) 7439 8401, *Fax:* (020) 7409 2070.

MARTIN, Peter; *see* Martin, R. P.

MARTIN, Peter Anthony; Treasurer, Metropolitan Police Authority, since 2000; *b* 8 Dec. 1946; *s* of Frank and Renie Martin; *m* 1970, Jennifer Margaret (*née* Shaw); one *s* four *d*. *Educ:* Nottingham High Sch.; St John's Coll., Oxford (BA Hons); Univ. of Kent at Canterbury (MA Management). CIPFA 1973. Accountant, Derbyshire CC, 1969–76; Asst County Treasurer, W Sussex CC, 1976–81; Kent County Council: Dep. County Treas., 1981–86; County Treas., later Finance Dir, 1986–97; Dir, Peter Martin Consultancy Ltd, 1997–2001. Treas., Kent Police Authy, 1995–2000. Local Authy Assocs' Revenue Support Grant Principal Negotiator, 1991–94. Pres., Soc. of Co. Treasurers, 1996–97. *Recreations:* cricket, reading, family. *Address:* Woodside, Hadlow Park, Hadlow, Tonbridge, Kent TN11 0HZ.

MARTIN, Maj.-Gen. Peter Lawrence de Carteret, CBE 1968 (OBE 1964); President, Lady Grover's Hospital Fund for Officers' Families, since 1989 (Chairman, 1975–85; Vice President, 1985–89); President, Normandy Veterans' Association, since 1995 (Vice President, 1989–95); *b* 15 Feb. 1920; *s* of late Col Charles de Carteret Martin, MD, ChD, IMS and of Helen Margaret Hardinge Grover; *m* 1st, 1949, Elizabeth Felicia (marr. diss. 1967), *d* of late Col C. M. Keble; one *s* one *d*; 2nd, 1973, Mrs Valerie Singer (marr. diss. 1997). *Educ:* Wellington Coll.; RMC Sandhurst. FBIM 1979 (MBIM 1970). Commnd Cheshire Regt, 1939; BEF (Dunkirk), 1940; Middle East, 1941; N Africa 8th Army, 1942–43 (despatches); invasion of Sicily, 1943; Normandy landings and NW Europe, 1944 (despatches); Palestine, 1945–47; GSO2 (Int.), HQ British Troops Egypt, 1947; Instructor, RMA Sandhurst, 1948–50; psc 1951; Bde Major 126 Inf. Bde (TA), 1952–53; Chief Instructor MMG Div. Support Weapons Wing, Sch. of Infantry, 1954–56; Malayan Ops, 1957–58 (despatches); DAAG GHQ FARELF, 1958–60; CO 1 Cheshire, N Ireland and BAOR, 1961–63; AA&QMG Cyprus District, 1963–65; comd 48 Gurkha Inf. Bde, Hong Kong, 1966–68; Brig. AQ HQ Army Strategic Comd, 1968–71; Dir, Personal Services (Army), 1971–74. Col The 22nd (Cheshire) Regt, 1971–78; Col Comdt, Mil. Provost Staff Corps, 1972–74. Services Advr, Variety Club of GB, 1976–86. Member: Ex-Services Mental Welfare Soc., 1977–91; Nat. Exec. Cttee, Forces Help Soc., 1975–97. *Recreations:* golf, ski-ing, ex-Services associations. *Address:* 17 Station Street, Lymington, Hants SO41 3BA. *T:* and *Fax:* (01590) 672620. *Club:* Army and Navy.

MARTIN, Prof. Raymond Leslie, AO 1987; MSc, PhD, ScD, DSc; FRACI, FRSC, FTSE, FAA; Professor of Chemistry, Monash University, Melbourne, 1987–92, now Emeritus (Vice-Chancellor, 1977–87); Chairman, Australian Science and Technology Council, 1988–92; *b* 3 Feb. 1926; *s* of Sir Leslie Harold Martin, CBE, FRS, FAA and late Gladys Maude Elaine, *d* of H. J. Bull; *m* 1954, Rena Lillian Laman; three *s* one *d*. *Educ:* Scotch Coll., Melbourne; Univ. of Melb. (BSc, MSc); Sidney Sussex Coll., Cambridge (PhD, ScD). FRACI 1956; FRSC (FRIC 1974); FTSE (FTS 1989); FAA 1971. Resident Tutor in Chemistry, Queen's Coll., Melb., 1947–49 (Fellow, 1979–); Sidney Sussex Coll., Cambridge: 1851 Exhibn Overseas Scholar, 1949–51; Sen. Scholar, 1952–54; Res. Fellow, 1951–54; Sen. Lectr, Univ. of NSW, 1954–59; Section Leader, 1959–60, and Associate Res. Manager, 1960–62, ICIANZ; Prof. of Inorganic Chem., 1962–72, and Dean of Faculty of Science, 1971, Univ. of Melb.; Australian National University, Canberra: Prof. of Inorganic Chem., Inst. of Advanced Studies, 1972–77, Prof. Emeritus 1977; Dean, Res. Sch. of Chem., 1976–77; DSc. Vis. Scientist: Technische Hochschule, Stuttgart, 1953–54; Bell Telephone Labs, NJ, 1967; Vis. Prof., Columbia Univ., NY, 1972. Royal Aust. Chemical Institute: Smith Medal, 1968; Olle Prize, 1974; Inorganic Medal, 1978; Leighton Medal, 1989; Fed. Pres., 1968–69. Chm., Internat. Commn on Atomic Weights and Isotopic Abundances, 1983–87; Mem., Prime Minister's Science Council, 1989–92. Director: Circadian Technologies Ltd, 1986–; Heide Park and Art Gall., 1988–92; Winston Churchill Meml Trust, 1983– (Nat. Chm., 1995–2000); Chairman: Syngene Ltd, 1996–; Optiscan Pty Ltd, 1997–; Trustee, Selby Scientific Foundn, 1990–. Council Mem., Victorian Coll. of the Arts, 1984–98 (Dep. Pres., 1991; Pres., 1992–95). Hon. LLD Monash, 1992; Hon. DSc Melbourne, 1996. Silver Jubilee Medal, 1977. *Publications:* papers and revs on physical and inorganic chem. mainly in jls of London, Amer. and Aust. Chem. Socs. *Recreations:* ski-ing, golf, lawn tennis (Cambridge Univ. team *v* Oxford, Full Blue; Cambs County Colours). *Address:* PO Box 98, Mount Eliza, Vic 3930, Australia. *Clubs:* Melbourne (Melbourne); Hawks (Cambridge); Frankston Golf (Victoria); Royal South Yarra Lawn Tennis.

MARTIN, Richard Graham; Vice-Chairman, Allied-Lyons, 1988–92 (Director, 1981–92; Chief Executive, 1989–91); *b* 4 Oct. 1932; *s* of Horace Frederick Martin, MC and Phyllis Jeanette Martin; *m* 1958, Elizabeth Savage; two *s* one *d*. *Educ:* Sherborne School; St Thomas's Hosp. Med. Sch., 1953–54. 2nd Lt, RA, 1951–52. Joined Friary Holroyd & Healy's Brewery, 1955, Dir, 1959; Dir, Friary Meux, 1963–66; Managing Dir, Ind Coope (East Anglia), 1966–69; Director: Joshua Tetley & Son, 1969–72; Allied Breweries, 1972–92; Chief Exec., Joshua Tetley & Son, 1972–78; Vice-Chm., Joshua Tetley & Son and Tetley Walker, 1978–79; Chm., Ind Coope, 1979–85; Man. Dir, 1985–86, Chm. and Chief Exec., 1986–88, Allied Breweries; Chairman: J. Lyons & Co. Ltd, 1989–91; Hiram Walker, 1991 (Dir, 1989–91); Allied-Lyons, later Allied-Domecq, Pensions and Trustee Services, 1992–95; non-exec. Dir, Gibbs Mew plc, 1995–98. Chm., Brewers' Soc., 1991–92 (Vice-Chm., 1989–91). Pres., Shire Horse Soc., 1981–82. *Recreations:* travel, music, food.

MARTIN, Sir (Robert) Bruce, Kt 1992; QC 1977; Chairman, The Bob Martin Co., since 1980; *b* 2 Nov. 1938; *s* of late Robert Martin and Fay Martin; *m* 1967, Elizabeth Georgina (*née* Kiddie) (marr. diss. 1995); one *s* one *d*. *Educ:* Shrewsbury Sch.; Liverpool Univ. (LLB Hons 1959). Called to the Bar, Middle Temple, 1960; a Recorder of the Crown Court, 1978–86. Vice-Chm., Mersey RHA, 1986–88 (Mem. 1983–88); Chairman, N Western RHA, 1988–94; NHS Litigation Authy, 1996–99. *Recreations:* music, golf, ski-ing. *Address:* 4 Montpelier Terrace, SW7 1JP. *Clubs:* Reform; Royal Birkdale Golf; Inanda (Johannesburg).

MARTIN, Robert George H.; *see* Holland-Martin.

MARTIN, Robert Logan, (Roy); QC (Scot.) 1988; *b* 31 July 1950; *s* of Robert Martin and Dr Janet Johnstone Logan or Martin; *m* 1984, Fiona Frances Neil; one *s* two *d*. *Educ:* Paisley Grammar Sch.; Univ. of Glasgow (LLB). Solicitor, 1973–76; admitted to Faculty of Advocates, 1976; Mem., Sheriff Court Rules Council, 1981–84; Standing Junior Counsel to Dept of Employment in Scotland, 1983–84; Advocate-Depute, 1984–87; called to the Bar, Lincoln's Inn, 1990. Admitted to Bar of NSW, 1987. Chairman: Industrial Tribunals, 1991–96; Police Appeals Tribunal, 1997–. Chm., Scottish Planning, Local Govt and Envmtl Bar Gp, 1991–96. Affiliate, RIAS, 1995. Hon. Sec., Wagering Club, 1982–91. *Recreations:* shooting, ski-ing, modern architecture, vintage motor cars. *Address:* Kilduff House, Athelstaneford, North Berwick, East Lothian EH39 5BD. *Club:* New (Edinburgh).

MARTIN, Robin Geoffrey; Director, Hewetson plc, 1980–98 (Chairman, 1980–88); *b* 9 March 1921; *s* of Cecil Martin and Isabel Katherine Martin (*née* Hickman); *m* 1946, Margery Chester Yates; two *s* one *d*. *Educ:* Cheltenham Coll.; Jesus Coll., Cambridge (MA). FIQ. Tarmac Ltd: Dir 1955; Gp Man. Dir 1963; Dep. Chm. 1967; Chm. and Chief Exec., 1971–79; Dir, Serck Ltd, 1971, Dep. Chm., 1974, Chm., 1976–81; Director: Burmah Oil Co,. 1975–85; Ductile Steels Ltd, 1977–82. Mem., Midlands Adv. Bd, Legal and General Assurance Soc. Ltd, 1977–84. Chm., Ironbridge Gorge Develt Trust, 1976–78. Life Governor, Birmingham Univ., 1970–85. *Recreations:* gardening, bridge.

MARTIN, Robin Rupert; Director, Cross-Cutting Policy, Board of Inland Revenue, since 2000; *b* 28 Feb. 1946; *s* of late Rupert Claude Martin and Ellen Martin (*née* Wood); *m* 1972, Jane Elizabeth Mackenzie Smith; three *s*. *Educ:* Harrow Sch.; Worcester Coll., Oxford (MA Hons). VSO: Thailand, 1964–65; India, 1969–70; joined Home Civil Service, 1970: Private Sec. to Chm., Bd of Inland Revenue, 1973–74; Office of Chancellor of Duchy of Lancaster, Cabinet Office, 1976–79; Asst Sec., 1981; Under Sec., 1993; Principal Finance Officer, Bd of Inland Revenue, 1993–2000. *Recreations:* infrequent leisurely hill-walking, cricket, second-hand books. *Address:* Board of Inland Revenue, Somerset House, WC2R 1LB. *Club:* MCC.

MARTIN, Roger John Adam; formerly HM Diplomatic Service; Vice-President, Somerset Wildlife Trust, since 2001; *b* 21 Jan. 1941; *s* of late Geoffrey (Richard Rex) Martin and of Hazel (*née* Matthews); *m* 1972, Ann Cornwell (*née* Sharp); one *s*. *Educ:* Westminster School; Brasenose College, Oxford (BA). VSO, Northern Rhodesia, 1959–60; Commonwealth Office, 1964–66; Second Sec., Djakarta, 1967, Saigon, 1968–70; First Sec., FCO, 1971–74, Geneva, 1975–79; seconded to Dept of Trade, as Head of Middle East/North Africa Br., 1981–83; Dep. High Comr, Harare, 1983–86; resigned. Vis. Fellow, Univ. of Bath. Mem., Nat. Exec., VSO, 1988–96; Dir, Som Trust for Nature Conservation, subseq. Som Wildlife Trust, 1988–2001. Member: Regional Committees: Envmt Agency, 1990–; MAFF, 1993–97; Planning Conf., 1996–2000; Heritage Lottery Fund, 2001–. Founder Mem., SW Regl Chamber, 1998. Exmoor Nat. Park Authy, 1998–; Chm., SW Reg., CPRE, 2001–; Pres., Mendip Soc., 2001–. Hon. Dr UWE, 2001. *Publication:* Southern Africa: the price of apartheid, 1988. *Recreations:* environmental issues, walking, archaeology. *Address:* Coxley House, Coxley, near Wells, Somerset BA5 1QS. *T:* (01749) 672180.

MARTIN, Ronald, MBE 1945; *b* 7 Nov. 1919; *o s* of late Albert and Clara Martin; *m* 1943, Bettina, *o d* of late H. E. M. Billing; one *d*. *Educ:* St Olave's Grammar Sch. Asst

Traffic Superintendent, GPO, 1939. Served War of 1939–45, Royal Signals, NW Europe. GPO: Asst Princ., 1948; Princ., 1950; Treasury, 1954; Princ. Private Sec. to PMG, 1955; Staff Controller, GPO, London, 1956; Asst Sec., 1957; Dir Establishments and Organisation, GPO, 1966; Dir Telecommunications Personnel, 1967; Dir of Marketing, Telecommunications HQ, 1968–75; Sen. Dir, Customer Services, 1975–79. *Recreations:* music, motoring, horology. *Address:* 23 Birch Close, Send, Woking, Surrey GU23 7BZ.

MARTIN, Ronald Noel, CB 1998; FRCVS; Chief Veterinary Officer, Department of Agriculture for Northern Ireland, 1990–98; *b* 15 Dec. 1938; *s* of Robert John and Margretta Martin; *m* 1962, Alexandrina Margaret McLeod; two *s*. *Educ:* Royal (Dick) Sch. of Veterinary Studies, Univ. of Edinburgh (BVMS). FRCVS 1995 (MRCVS 1961). Private veterinary practice, 1960–64; Ministry of Agriculture, later Department of Agriculture, for Northern Ireland: Vet. Officer, 1964–69; Divl Vet. Officer, 1969–73; Sen. Principal Vet. Officer, 1973–78; Dep. Chief Vet. Officer, 1978–90. *Recreations:* gardening, walking, cycling. *Address:* 8 Whiteside, Mountain Road, Newtownards, Co. Down BT23 4UP. *T:* (028) 9181 3962.

MARTIN, Roy; *see* Martin, Robert L.

MARTIN, (Roy) Peter, MBE 1970; author and critic; *b* 5 Jan. 1931; *s* of Walter Martin and Annie Mabel Martin; *m* 1st, 1951, Marjorie Peacock (marr. diss. 1960); 2nd, Joan Drumwright (marr. diss. 1977); two *s*; 3rd, 1978, Catherine Sydee. *Educ:* Highbury Grammar Sch.; Univ. of London (BA 1953, MA 1956); Univ. of Tübingen. Nat. Service (RAF Educn Branch), 1949–51. Worked as local govt officer, schoolteacher and tutor in adult educn; then as British Council officer, 1960–83; service in Indonesia, Hungary (Cultural Attaché) and Japan (Cultural Counsellor). *Publications:* (with Joan Martin) Japanese Cooking, 1970; The Chrysanthemum Throne, 1997; (as James Melville): The Wages of Zen, 1979; The Chrysanthemum Chain, 1980; A Sort of Samurai, 1981; The Ninth Netsuke, 1982; Sayonara, Sweet Amaryllis, 1983; Death of a Daimyo, 1984; The Death Ceremony, 1985; Go Gently Gaijin, 1986; The Imperial Way, 1986; Kimono For A Corpse, 1987; The Reluctant Ronin, 1988; A Haiku for Hanae, 1989; A Tarnished Phoenix, 1990; The Bogus Buddha, 1990; The Body Wore Brocade, 1992; Diplomatic Baggage, 1994; The Reluctant Spy, 1995; (as Hampton Charles): Miss Seeton At The Helm, 1990; Miss Seeton, By Appointment, 1990; Advantage Miss Seeton, 1990. *Recreations:* music, books. *Address:* c/o Curtis Brown, 28/29 Haymarket, SW1Y 4SP. *Clubs:* Travellers, Detection.

MARTIN, Stanley William Frederick, CVO 1992 (LVO 1981); JP; HM Diplomatic Service, retired; Extra Gentleman Usher to the Queen, since 1993; Protocol Consultant, Foreign and Commonwealth Office, since 1993; Diplomatic Consultant, Grosvenor House, since 1999; *b* 9 Dec. 1934; *s* of Stanley and Winifred Martin; *m* 1960, Hanni Aud Hansen, Copenhagen; one *s* one *d*. *Educ:* Bromley Grammar Sch.; University Coll., Oxford (MA Jurisprudence; Pres., OU Law Soc., 1957); Inner Temple (student Scholar). Nat. Service, 2nd Lieut RASC, 1953–55. Entered CRO, 1958; Asst Private Sec. to Sec. of State, 1959–62; First Secretary: Canberra, 1962–64; Kuala Lumpur, 1964–67; FCO (Planning Staff and Personnel Dept), 1967–70; seconded to CSD (CSSB), 1970–71; HM Asst Marshal of the Diplomatic Corps, 1972–81; First Asst Marshal, 1981–92; Associate Head of Protocol Dept, FCO, 1986–92. Vis. Prof., Diplomatic Acad., Poly. of Central London, subseq. Univ. of Westminster, 1987– (Hon. Fellow, 1998). Diplomatic Consultant, Hyde Park Hotel, then Mandarin Oriental Hyde Park, 1993–99. Member: Cttee, London Diplomatic Assoc., 1972–; Central Council, Royal Over-Seas League, 1982– (Exec. Cttee, 1993–); Council, Oxford Univ. Soc., 1993–; Adv. Council, Spanish Inst. of Protocol Studies, 1997–. Trustee: Attlee Foundn, 1993–99; Toynbee Hall, 1996–99; Vice-Patron, Apex Trust, 1995–; Advr, Consular Corps of London, 1993–. Mem., Commonwealth Observer Gp, Guyana elecns, 1997. Freelance lectr, 1993–. FRSA 1985. JP Inner London, 1993–2000. Freeman of the City of London, 1988. Companion, Order of Distinguished Service (Brunei), 1992. *Publications:* (jtly) Royal Service: history of the Royal Victorian Order, Medal and Chain, vol. I 1996, vol. II 2001; (contrib.) Diplomatic Handbook, 2nd edn 1977 to 7th edn 1998; contribs to Jl of Orders and Medals Res. Soc., Jl of Royal Over-Seas League, Diplomat mag. *Recreations:* collecting books, manuscripts and obituaries, historical research and writing, walking, siestas, watching old films in the afternoon. *Address:* 14 Great Spilmans, Dulwich, SE22 8SZ. *T:* (020) 8693 8181. *Clubs:* Travellers, Royal Over-Seas League.

MARTIN, Stephen Harcourt; Chief Executive, Education and Learning Wales, since 2001; *b* 4 Sept. 1952; *s* of Robert Harcourt Martin and Joan Winifred Martin (*née* Carpenter); *m* 1988, Amanda Suna Hodges; one *s* one *d*. *Educ:* Watford GS for Boys; Haywards Heath GS; Hull Univ. (Pol Studies). Nursing Assistant, De La Pole Psych. Hosp., Willerby, 1973–74; Welsh Office: Exec. Officer, Town and Country Planning Div., 1974–77; Admin Trainee, Health and Industry Depts, 1977–79; Pvte Sec. to successive Perm. Secs, 1979–81; Principal: Health Dept, 1981–85; Housing Div., 1985–87; Asst Sec., Health and Social Services Divs, 1987–92; Under Sec., later Dir, Educn Dept, 1992–97; Prin. Establishments Officer, 1997–99; Sec. and Dir of Policy, Welsh Fourth Channel Authy, 1999–2000; Chief Exec., HEFCW, 2000–01. *Recreations:* music, literature. *Address:* Education and Learning Wales, Linden Court, The Orchards, Ilex Close, Llanishen, Cardiff CF14 5DZ. *T:* (029) 2076 1861.

MARTIN, Hon. Stephen Paul; MP (Lab) for Cunningham, NSW, since 1984; *b* 24 June 1948; *s* of Harold and Vera Martin; *m* 1971, Carol O'Keeffe; one *s* three *d*. *Educ:* ANU (BA); Univ. of Alberta (MA); Sydney Univ. (MTCP); Univ. of NSW (Dip. Ed). High School teacher, 1970–74; Univ. Lectr, 1975–77; Town Planner, NSW Dept of Planning and Environment, 1977–84. Chm., Banking, Finance and Public Administration Cttee, 1987–91; Parly Sec. to Minister for Foreign Affairs and Trade, 1991–93; Speaker, House of Reps, Aust., 1993–96; Shadow Minister: for Sport and Tourism, and for Veterans' Affairs, 1996–97; for Small Business, Customs, Sport and Tourism, 1997–98; for Defence, 1998–. *Recreations:* swimming, Rugby League, movies. *Address:* House of Representatives, Parliament House, Canberra, ACT 2600, Australia. *T:* (2) 62774363. *Club:* Illawarra Steelers (Wollongong).

MARTIN, Steven; *see* Martin, G. S.

MARTIN, (Thomas) Geoffrey; Head of Representation of European Commission in the United Kingdom, since 1994; *b* 26 July 1940; *s* of Thomas Martin and Saidee Adelaide (*née* Day); *m* 1968, Gay (Madeleine Annesley) Brownrigg; one *s* three *d*. *Educ:* Queen's Univ., Belfast (BSc Hons). President, National Union of Students of England, Wales and Northern Ireland, 1966–68; City of London: Banking, Shipping, 1968–73; Director, Shelter, 1973–74; Diplomatic Staff, Commonwealth Secretariat, 1974–79; Head of EC Office, NI, 1979–85; Head of EC Press and Inf. Services, SE Asia, 1985–87; Hd of External Relations, EC Office, London, 1987–93. *Address:* European Commission, Jean Monnet House, 8 Storey's Gate, SW1P 3AT. *Club:* Travellers.

MARTIN, Prof. Thomas John, AO 1996; MD, DSc; FRACP, FRCPA; FRS 2000; FAA; Director, St Vincent's Institute of Medical Research, University of Melbourne, since 1988; *b* 24 Jan. 1937; *s* of Thomas Michael and Ellen Agnes Martin; *m* 1964, Christine Mayo Conroy (*d* 1995); two *s* four *d*. *Educ:* Xavier Coll.; Univ. of Melbourne (MB BS 1960; MD 1969; DSc 1979). FRACP 1969; FRCPA 1985; FAA 1996. Registrar and Res. Fellow, RPMS, London, 1965–66; Sen. Res. Fellow, 1967–68, Sen. Lectr, 1968–73, Dept of Medicine, Univ. of Melbourne; Prof. of Chemical Pathology, Univ. of Sheffield, 1974–77; Prof. of Medicine, Univ. of Melbourne, 1977–98, now Emeritus (Chm., Dept of Medicine, 1985–98). Vis. Prof., RPMS, 1973. Hon. MD Sheffield, 1992. *Publications:* more than 400 scientific papers, reviews and book chapters on endocrinology, bone cell biology, cancer and clinical medicine. *Recreations:* music, golf, fly-fishing, travel. *Address:* 1/6 Findon Crescent, Kew, Vic 3101, Australia. *T:* (3) 98528424. *Club:* Melbourne.

MARTIN, Timothy Randall; Founder, 1979, and Chairman, since 1983, J. D. Wetherspoon plc; *b* 28 April 1955; *s* of Ray and Olive Martin; *m* Felicity Owen; one *s* three *d*. *Educ:* Nottingham Univ. (LLB). Called to the Bar, 1980. *Address:* J. D. Wetherspoon plc, Wetherspoon House, Central Park, Reeds Crescent, Watford, Herts WD1 1QH. *T:* (01923) 477777. *Club:* Exeter Squash.

MARTIN-BATES, James Patrick, MA; JP; FCIS; CIMgt; Director: Atkins Holdings Ltd, 1986–90 (Chairman, 1987–89); W. S. Atkins Ltd, 1986–94; W. S. Atkins Group Ltd, 1970–86; *b* 17 April 1912; *er s* of late R. Martin-Bates, JP, Perth, Scotland; *m* 1939, Clare, *d* of late Prof. James Miller, MD, DSc; one *s* two *d*. *Educ:* Perth Academy; Glenalmond; Worcester Coll., Oxford. BA 1933; MA 1944. Lamson Industries, 1933–36; Dorman Long & Co. Ltd, 1936–38; PE Group, 1938–61: Man. Dir, Production Engineering Ltd, 1953–59; Vice-Chm., PE Holdings, 1959–61; Director: Hutchinson Ltd, 1958–78; Avery's Ltd, 1970–77; Charringtons Industrial Holdings Ltd, 1972–77. Principal, Administrative Staff Coll., Henley-on-Thames, 1961–72. Chm., Management Consultants Association, 1960; Member: Council, British Institute of Management, 1961–66; UK Advisory Council on Education for Management, 1961–66; Council, Glenalmond, 1963–82; Bd of Visitors, HM Borstal, Huntercombe, 1964–67; The Council for Technical Education and Training for Overseas Countries, 1962–73; Council, University Coll., Nairobi, 1965–68; Council, Chartered Institute of Secretaries, 1965–74; EDC for Rubber Industry, 1965–69; Council, Univ. of Buckingham (formerly University Coll. at Buckingham), 1977–87. Governor, Aylesbury Grammar Sch., 1983–89. UN Consultant in Iran, 1972–78. High Sheriff of Buckinghamshire, 1974; Chm., Marlow Bench, 1978–82. FCIS 1961; CIMgt (FBIM 1960); Fellow Internat. Acad. of Management, 1964. DUniv Buckingham, 1986. Burnham Medal, BIM, 1974. *Publications:* The History of the Maurice Lubbock Memorial Fund, 1993; various articles in Management Journals. *Recreations:* golf, fishing. *Address:* Ivy Cottage, Fingest, near Henley-on-Thames, Oxon RG9 6QD. *T:* (01491) 638202. *Clubs:* Caledonian; Royal and Ancient (St Andrews); Huntercombe Golf.

MARTIN-JENKINS, Christopher Dennis Alexander; Chief Cricket Correspondent, The Times, since 1999; BBC cricket commentator, since 1973; *b* 20 Jan. 1945; *s* of late Dennis Frederick Martin-Jenkins, TD and Dr Rosemary Clare Martin-Jenkins (*née* Walker); *m* 1971, Judith Oswald Hayman; two *s* one *d*. *Educ:* Marlborough; Fitzwilliam Coll., Cambridge (BA (Modern Hist.); MA). Dep. Editor, The Cricketer, 1967–70; sports broadcaster, 1970–73, Cricket Correspondent, 1973–80, 1984–91, BBC; Editor, 1981–88, Editl Dir, 1988–91, The Cricketer International; Cricket Correspondent, Daily Telegraph, 1991–99. President: Rugby Fives Assoc., 1993–95; W Sussex Assoc. of Umpires and Scorers, 1995–; Cricket Soc., 1998–. Trustee, Brian Johnston Meml Trust, 1995–2000 (Chm., 1998–2000). *Publications:* Testing Time, 1974; Assault on the Ashes, 1975; MCC in India, 1977; The Jubilee Tests and the Packer Revolution, 1977; In Defence of the Ashes, 1979; Cricket Contest, 1980; The Complete Who's Who of Test Cricketers, 1980; The Wisden Book of County Cricket, 1981; Bedside Cricket, 1981; Twenty Years On: Cricket's years of change, 1984; Cricket: a way of life, 1984; (ed) Cricketer Book of Cricket Eccentrics, 1985; (ed) Seasons Past, 1986; (ed jtly) Quick Singles, 1986; Grand Slam, 1987; Cricket Characters, 1987; Sketches of a Season, 1989; Ball by Ball, 1990; (jtly) Summers Will Never Be the Same, 1994; The Spirit of Cricket (anthology), 1994; World Cricketers, 1996; An Australian Summer, 1999. *Recreations:* cricket, golf, music, theatre, walking. *Address:* The Times, 1 Pennington Street, E1 9XN. *Clubs:* MCC; I Zingari, Free Foresters, Arabs, Marlborough Blues, Cranleigh Cricket, Albury Cricket, Rudgwick Cricket, Horsham Cricket; West Sussex Golf.

MARTINDALE, Air Vice-Marshal Alan Rawes, CB 1984; Royal Air Force, retired; *b* 20 Jan. 1930; *s* of late Norman Martindale and Edith (*née* Rawes); *m* 1952, Eileen Alma Wrenn; three *d*. *Educ:* Kendal Grammar Sch.; University Coll., Leicester (BA History, London Univ., 1950). Commissioned RAF, 1951; served, 1951–71: RAF Driffield, Oakington, Eindhoven, Stafford, Wickenby, Faldingworth and Marham; Instructor, RAF Coll., Cranwell; Staff AHQ Malta; RAF Staff Coll., Bracknell, MoD, Jt Services Staff Coll. (student and Directing Staff), and HQ Maintenance Comd; Dep. Dir of Supply Management, MoD, Harrogate, 1971–72; Comd Supply Officer, RAF Germany, 1972–74; Dir of Supply Management, MoD, Harrogate, 1974–75; RCDS, 1976; Air Cdre Supply and Movements, RAF Support Comd, 1977; Dep. Gen. Man., NAMMA, 1978–81; Dir of Supply Policy (RAF), MoD, 1981–82; Dir Gen. of Supply (RAF), 1982–84; retd 1985. Dist Gen. Manager, Hastings HA, 1985–90; Census Area Manager, S Kent and Hastings, 1990–91. Chm., Battle Festival, 1991–96. *Recreations:* golf, gardening. *Address:* Stores Barn, The Old Stable Yard, Radway, Warwicks CV35 0UQ. *Club:* Royal Air Force.

MARTINEAU, Charles Herman; Chairman, Electricity Consultative Council for South of Scotland, 1972–76; *b* 3 Sept. 1908; *s* of Prof. Charles E. Martineau, Birmingham; *m* 1939, Margaret Shirley Dolphin; two *s* one *d*. *Educ:* King Edward's Sch., Birmingham. Jas Williamson & Son Ltd, Lancaster and Nairn-Williamson Ltd, Kirkcaldy: Man. Dir, 1952–66. Part-time Mem., S of Scotland Electricity Bd, 1971–76. Mem., Fife CC, 1967 (Vice-Convener, 1970–73); Mem., Fife Regional Council, 1978–82. *Recreations:* chess, golf. *Address:* Gladsmuir, Hepburn Gardens, St Andrews, Fife. *T:* (01334) 473069. *Club:* Royal & Ancient (St Andrews).

MARTINEAU, David Nicholas Nettlefold; His Honour Judge Martineau; a Circuit Judge, since 1994; *b* 27 March 1941; *s* of Frederick Alan Martineau and Vera Ruth Martineau (*née* Naylor); *m* 1968, Elizabeth Mary Allom; one *s* one *d*. *Educ:* Eton; Trinity Coll., Cambridge (MA, LLM). Called to the Bar, Inner Temple, 1964; Asst Recorder, 1982–86; Recorder 1986–94. Mem., Exec. Cttee, Cystic Fibrosis Trust, 1990–. *Recreations:* ski-ing, water ski-ing, wind-surfing, music, wine and food. *Address:* Blackfriars Crown Court, Pocock Street, SE1 0BJ. *T:* (020) 7922 5800. *Clubs:* MCC; Hawks (Cambridge).

MARTINEAU, Malcolm John; pianist, accompanist; Professor, Royal Academy of Music, since 1987; *b* 3 Feb. 1960; *s* of George Martineau and Hester Dickson. *Educ:* George Watson's Coll., Edinburgh; St Catharine's Coll., Cambridge (BA 1981); Royal Coll. of Music. Début, Wigmore Hall, 1984; has accompanied many leading singers, incl. Thomas Allen, Dame Janet Baker, Barbara Bonney, Della Jones, Dame Felicity Lott, Ann Murray, Bryn Terfel, Anne Sofie von Otter, Frederica von Stade, and instrumentalists, incl. Emma Johnson; has accompanied master classes, Britten-Pears Sch. Presented song recital series: Debussy and Poulenc, St John's, Smith Square; Britten, Wigmore Hall; Jt Artistic Dir, Liederreise, St John's, Smith Sq., 1998. Recordings incl. complete folk song settings of Beethoven and Britten, instrumental and vocal music incl. Arnold, Brahms, Fauré, Schubert, Schumann, Strauss and song recitals, with various artists. Hon. RAM 1998. Accompanist's Prize, Walther Grüner Internat. Lieder Competition, 1983. *Recreations:* theatre-going, cooking. *Address:* c/o Askonas Holt, Lonsdale Chambers, 27 Chancery Lane, WC2A 1PF. *T:* (020) 7400 1700.

MARTINEAU-WALKER, Roger Antony; *see* Walker.

MARTINEZ, Arthur C.; Chairman and Chief Executive Officer, Sears, Roebuck and Co., since 1995; *b* 25 Sept. 1939; *s* of Arthur F. Martinez and Agnes M. Martinez (*née* Caulfield); *m* 1966, Elizabeth Rusch; one *s* one *d*. *Educ:* Polytechnic Univ. (BSME); Harvard Univ. (MBA 1965). Exxon Chemical Co., 1960; Dir of Planning, Internat. Paper Co., 1967–69; Asst to Pres., Talley Industries, 1969–70; Dir of Finance, 1970–73, Vice-Pres., 1973–80, RCA Corp.; Sen. Vice-Pres. and Chief Financial Officer, 1980–84, Exec. Vice-Pres., 1984–87, Vice-Chm., 1990–92, Saks Fifth Avenue; Gp Chief Exec., Retail Div., and Sen. Vice Pres., Batus Inc., 1987–90; Chm. and Chief Exec. Officer, Sears Merchandise Gp, 1992–95. Bd Mem., Ameritech Corp.; Vice-Chm., Federal Reserve Bank of Chicago. Chm., Nat. Minority Supplier Develt Council, 1994–97. Chm., Bd of Trustees, Polytechnic Univ., 1990–; Trustee: Northwestern Univ.; Art Inst. of Chicago; Chicago Symphony Orch.; Northwestern Univ. Hosp. *Address:* Sears, Roebuck & Co., 3333 Beverly Road, Hoffman Estates, IL 60179, USA.

MARTINI, His Eminence Cardinal Carlo Maria, SJ; Archbishop of Milan, since 1980; *b* 15 Feb. 1927; *s* of Leonardo and Olga Maggia. *Educ:* Pontifical Gregorian Univ. (DTheol); Pontifical Biblical Inst. (Doctorate in holy scripture). Ordained priest, 1952; Rector, Pontifical Biblical Inst., 1969–78; Rector, Gregorian Univ., 1978–79. Cardinal 1983. Pres., Consilium Conferentiarum Episcopalium Europae, 1987–93. *Address:* Piazza Fontana 2, 20122 Milano, Italy. *T:* (2) 85561.

MARTLEW, Eric Anthony; MP (Lab) Carlisle, since 1987; *b* 3 Jan. 1949; *m* 1970, Elsie Barbara Duggan. *Educ:* Harraby Secondary School, Carlisle; Carlisle Tech. Coll. Nestlé Co. Ltd, 1966–87: joined as lab. technician; later Personnel Manager, Dalston Factory, Carlisle. Member: Carlisle County Borough Council, 1972–74; Cumbria CC, 1973–88 (Chm., 1983–85). Mem., Cumbria Health Authy, later E Cumbria HA, 1977–87 (Chm., 1977–79). Opposition spokesman on defence, 1992–95; an Opposition Whip, 1995–97; PPS to Chancellor of Duchy of Lancaster, 1997–98, to Leader of H of L, 1998–2001. *Recreations:* photography, fell walking, horse racing. *Address:* 3 Chatsworth Square, Carlisle, Cumbria CA1 1HB. *T:* (01228) 511395.

MARTONMERE, 2nd Baron *cr* 1964; **John Stephen Robinson;** *b* 10 July 1963; *s* of Hon. Richard Anthony Gasque Robinson (*d* 1979) and of Wendy Patricia (who *m* subseq. Ronald De Mara), *d* of late James Cecil Blagden; *S* grandfather, 1989. *Educ:* Lakefield College School; Senaca College. *Heir:* *b* David Alan Robinson, *b* 15 Sept. 1965. *Address:* 390 Russell Hill Road, Toronto, ON M4V 2V2, Canada.

MARTYN, Charles Roger Nicholas; Master of the Supreme Court, 1973–95; part-time Adjudicator, Immigration Appellate Authority, 1991–95; *b* 10 Dec. 1925; *s* of Rev. Charles Martyn; *m* 1960, Helen, *d* of Frank Everson; two *s* one *d*. *Educ:* Charterhouse, 1939–44; Merton Coll., Oxford, 1947–49. MA (Hons) Mod. Hist. Joined Regular Army, 1944; commissioned 60th Rifles (KRRC), 1945; CMF, 1946–47; special release, 1947. Articles, 1950–52, and admitted as solicitor, 1952. Sherwood & Co., Parly Agents (Partner), 1952–59; Lee, Bolton & Lee, Westminster (Partner), 1961–73; Notary Public, 1969. Mem. and Dep. Chm., No 14 Legal Aid Area Cttee, 1967–73; Hon. Legal Adviser to The Samaritans (Inc), 1955–73. Chairman: Family Welfare Assoc., 1973–78 (Chief Trustee of 129 public charities and 6 almshouses); NHS Complaints Panel for Gtr London, 1999–; Member: Gtr London Citizens' Advice Bureaux Management Cttee, 1974–79; Council, St Gabriel's Coll. (Further Education), Camberwell, 1973–77 (Vice-Chm.); Council, Goldsmiths' Coll., Univ. of London, 1988–94 (Mem., Delegacy, 1977–88). *Recreations:* walking, sailing (Vice-Cdre, Thames Barge Sailing Club, 1962–65), observing people, do-it-yourself, nigrology. *Address:* 29 St Albans Road, NW5 1RG. *T:* (020) 7267 1076.

MARTYN-HEMPHILL, family name of **Baron Hemphill**.

MARWICK, Prof. Arthur John Brereton, FRHistS; Professor of History, The Open University, since 1969; *b* 29 Feb. 1936; *s* of William Hutton Marwick and Maeve Cluna Brereton; unmarried; one *d*. *Educ:* George Heriot's School, Edinburgh; Edinburgh Univ. (MA, DLitt); Balliol Coll., Oxford (BLitt). Asst Lectr in History, Univ. of Aberdeen, 1959–60; Lectr in History, Univ. of Edinburgh, 1960–69; Dean and Dir of Studies in Arts, Open Univ., 1978–84. Vis. Prof. in History, State Univ. of NY at Buffalo, 1966–67; Vis. Scholar, Hoover Instn and Vis. Prof., Stanford Univ., 1984–85; Directeur d'études invité, l'Ecole des Hautes Etudes en Sciences Sociales, Paris, 1985; Visiting Professor: Rhodes Coll., Memphis, 1991; Univ. of Perugia, 1991. FRSA 1999. *Publications:* The Explosion of British Society, 1963; Clifford Allen, 1964; The Deluge, 1965, new edn 1991; Britain in the Century of Total War, 1968; The Nature of History, 1970, 3rd edn 1989; War and Social Change in the Twentieth Century, 1974; The Home Front, 1976; Women at War 1914–1918, 1977; Class: image and reality in Britain, France and USA since 1930, 1980, rev. edn 1990; (ed) Illustrated Dictionary of British History, 1980; British Society since 1945, 1982, 3rd edn 1996; Britain in Our Century, 1984; (ed) Class in the Twentieth Century, 1986; Beauty in History: society, politics and personal appearance c 1500 to the present, 1988; (ed) Total War and Social Change, 1988; (ed) The Arts, Literature and Society, 1990; Culture in Britain since 1945, 1991; The Sixties: cultural revolution in Britain, France, Italy and the United States *c.* 1958–*c.* 1974, 1998; (ed) Windows on the Sixties: exploring key texts of media and culture, 2000; A History of the Modern British Isles 1914–1999: circumstances, events and outcomes, 2000; The Nature of History: knowledge, evidence, language, 2001; The Arts in the West since 1945, 2001; contribs to English Hist. Review, Amer. Hist. Review, Jl of Contemporary Hist. *Recreations:* wine, women, tennis. *Address:* 67 Fitzjohns Avenue, Hampstead, NW3 6PE. *T:* (020) 7794 4534. *Clubs:* Open University Football, Open University Tennis.

MARWICK, George Robert; JP; farmer and company director; Lord-Lieutenant of Orkney, since 1997 (Vice Lord-Lieutenant, 1995–97); *b* 27 Feb. 1932; *s* of late Robert William Marwick, BSc Hons, MICE, Civil Engr, and Agnes Kemp Marwick (*née* Robson); *m* 1st, 1958, Hanne Jensen (marr. diss. 1989); three *d*; 2nd, 1990, Norma Gerrard (*née* Helm). *Educ:* Port Regis, Dorset; Bryanston Sch., Dorset; Edinburgh Sch. of Agriculture (SDA 1953). Chm. and Man. Dir, Swannay Farms Ltd, 1972–; Chairman: Campbeltown Creamery Ltd, 1974–90; Campbeltown Creamery (Hldgs) Ltd, 1974–90; Director: North Eastern Farmers Ltd, 1968–98; Orkney Islands Shipping Co., 1972–87. Chm., N of Scotland Water Bd, 1970–73; Member: Scottish Agricl Cons. Panel (formerly Winter Keep Panel), 1964–98; Countryside Commn for Scotland, 1978–86; Council, NT for Scotland, 1979–84. Ind. Mem., Orkney CC, then Orkney Is Council, 1968–78 (Vice-Convenor, 1970–74; Convenor, 1974–78). JP, 1970, DL, 1976, Orkney. Hon. Sheriff of Grampian, Highlands and Is, 2000. *Recreations:* shooting, motor sport. *Address:* Swannay House, by Evie, Orkney KW17 2NP. *T:* (01856) 721365, *Fax:* (01856) 721227. *Clubs:* Farmers'; New (Edinburgh).

MARWICK, Patricia, (Tricia); Member (SNP) Mid Scotland and Fife, Scottish Parliament, since 1999; *b* 5 Nov. 1953; *m* 1975, Frank Marwick; one *s* one *d*. *Educ:* Fife. Former public affairs officer, Shelter. Mem., SNP, 1985– (Mem. NEC, 1997–). Contested (SNP) Fife Central, 1992, 1997. *Address:* Scottish Parliament, Edinburgh EH99 1SP.

MARYCHURCH, Sir Peter (Harvey), KCMG 1985; Chairman, Associated Board of the Royal Schools of Music, 1994–2000; Director, Government Communications Headquarters, 1983–89; *b* 13 June 1927; *s* of Eric William Alfred and Dorothy Margaret Marychurch; *m* 1965, June Daphne Ottaway (*née* Pareezer). *Educ:* Lower School of John Lyon, Harrow. Served RAF, 1945–48. Joined GCHQ, 1948; Asst Sec. 1975; Under Sec. 1979; Dep. Sec. 1983. Chairman: Cheltenham Arts Festivals Co., 1994–2000; Cheltenham Internat. Fest. of Music, 1993–97; Cheltenham and Cotswold Relate, 1990–97; Pres., Cheltenham Arts Council, 1998–. FRSAMD 1998. Hon. RNCM 2000. Medal for Distinguished Public Service, US Dept of Defense, 1989. *Recreations:* theatre, music (especially opera), gardening. *Address:* HSBC, 2 The Promenade, Cheltenham, Glos GL50 1LS. *Club:* Naval and Military.

MARYON DAVIS, Dr Alan Roger, FFPHM; Consultant in Public Health Medicine, Lambeth, Southwark and Lewisham Health Authority (formerly West Lambeth, then South East London, Health Authority), since 1988; Senior Lecturer in Public Health, King's College London (formerly United Medical and Dental Schools), since 1988; *b* 21 Jan. 1943; *s* of Cyril Edward Maryon Davis and Hilda May Maryon Davis; one *s*; *m* 1981, Glynis Anne Davies; two *d*. *Educ:* St Paul's Sch.; St John's Coll., Cambridge (MA 1968; MB BChir 1970); St Thomas's Hosp. Med. Sch.; London Sch. of Hygiene and Tropical Medicine. MSc (Social Med.) London 1978; MRCP 1972; MFCM 1978, FFPHM (FFCM 1986); FRIPHH 1989. Early med. career in gen. medicine and rheumatology, later in community medicine; MO, 1977–84, CMO, 1984–87, Health Educn Council; Sen. Med. Adviser, Health Educn Authority, 1987–88; Hon. Consultant, Paddington and N Kensington HA, 1985–88; Hon. Sen. Lectr in Community Medicine, St Mary's Hosp. Med. Sch., 1985–88. Mem. Council, RIPH&H, 1989–. Writer and broadcaster on health matters, 1975–; BBC radio series include Action Makes the Heart Grow Stronger (Med. Journalist's Assoc. Radio Award), 1983; BBC television series include: Body Matters, 1985–89; Health UK, 1990–91. Editor-in-Chief, Health Education Jl, 1984–88; Med. Advice Columnist, Woman magazine, 1988–. *Publications:* Family Health and Fitness, 1981; Body Facts, 1984; (with J. Thomas) Diet 2000, 1984; (with J. Rogers) How to Save a Life, 1987; PSSST—a Really Useful Guide to Alcohol, 1989; Cholesterol Check, 1991; The Good Health Guide, 1994; Ruby's Health Quest, 1995; The Body-clock Diet, 1996. *Recreations:* eating well, drinking well, singing (not so well) with the humorous group Instant Sunshine. *Address:* 4 Sibella Road, Clapham, SW4 6HX. *T:* (020) 7720 5659.

MASCHLER, Fay; restaurant critic, Evening Standard, since 1972; *b* 15 July 1945; *d* of Mary and Arthur Frederick Coventry; *m* 1970, Thomas Michael Maschler, *qv* (marr. diss. 1987); one *s* two *d*; *m* 1992, Reginald Bernard John Gadney. *Educ:* Convent of the Sacred Heart, Greenwich, Conn. Copywriter, J. Walter Thompson, 1964; journalist, Radio Times, 1969. *Publications:* Cooking is a Game You Can Eat, 1975; A Child's Book of Manners, 1979; Miserable Aunt Bertha, 1980; Fay Maschler's Guide to Eating Out in London, 1986; Eating In, 1987; Howard & Maschler on Food, 1987; Teach Your Child to Cook, 1988; Evening Standard Restaurant Guides, annually, 1993–. *Address:* 12 Fitzroy Square, W1P 5HQ. *Clubs:* Groucho, Car Clamp.

MASCHLER, Thomas Michael; Publisher, Jonathan Cape Children's Books, since 1991; Director, Jonathan Cape Ltd, since 1960 (Chairman, 1970–91); *b* 16 Aug. 1933; *s* of Kurt Leo Maschler and of Rita Masseron (*née* Lechner); *m* 1970, Fay Coventry (*see* Fay Maschler) (marr. diss. 1987); one *s* two *d*; *m* 1988, Regina Kulinicz. *Educ:* Leighton Park School. Production Asst, Andre Deutsch, 1955; Editor, MacGibbon & Kee, 1956–58; Fiction Editor, Penguin Books, 1958–60; Jonathan Cape: Editorial Dir, 1960; Man. Dir, 1966. Associate Producer, The French Lieutenant's Woman (film), 1981. *Publications:* (ed) Declarations, 1957; (ed) New English Dramatists Series, 1959–63. *Address:* 20 Vauxhall Bridge Road, SW1V 2SA.

MASCORD, Dr David John; Headmaster, Bristol Grammar School, since 1999; *b* 18 Oct. 1950; *s* of George and Evelyn Mascord; *m* 1974, Veronica Mary Chalton Peers; two *s*. *Educ:* York Univ. (BA 1st Cl. Hons Chemistry 1972); St John's Coll., Cambridge (PhD 1976; PGCE with Dist.). Head of Chemistry, Wellington Coll., 1981–86; Sen. Teacher, Aylesbury GS, 1986–89; Asst Hd, 1989–98, Dep. Hd, 1998–99, Bristol GS. *Publications:* contrib. articles in Faraday Discussions of Chem. Soc., Molecular Physics, Jl Chem. Industry. *Recreations:* walking, swimming, personal computing, cooking, reading, particularly Charles Dickens, sketching, painting. *Address:* Bristol Grammar School, University Road, Bristol BS8 1SR. *T:* (0117) 973 6006, *Fax:* (0117) 946 7485.

MASEFIELD, Sir Charles (Beech Gordon), Kt 1997; CEng, FRAeS, FIMechE; Group Marketing Director, BAE SYSTEMS, since 1999; *b* 7 Jan. 1940; *s* of Sir Peter (Gordon) Masefield, *qv*; *m* 1970, Fiona Anne Kessler; two *s*. *Educ:* Eastbourne Coll.; Jesus Coll., Cambridge (MA). CEng 1984; FRAeS 1980; FIMechE 1984. Sales Exec., Beagle Aircraft, 1964–70; Hawker Siddeley Aviation: Test Pilot, 1970–76; Dep. Chief Test Pilot, Manchester, 1976–78; British Aerospace, Manchester: Chief Test Pilot, 1978–80; Project Dir, 1980–81; Prodn Dir, 1981–84; Gen. Manager, 1984–86; Man. Dir, BAe Hatfield, Manchester, Prestwick, 1986–92; President: BAe Commercial Aircraft, 1992–93; Avro Internat. Aerospace, 1993–94; Sen. Vice-Pres. and Commercial Dir, Airbus Industrie, Toulouse, 1993–94; Hd, Defence Export Services Orgn, 1994–98; Vice-Chm, GEC, 1998–99. Pres., RAeS, 1994–95. FRSA 1999. *Recreation:* occasional golf. *Address:* BAE SYSTEMS, Warwick House, PO Box 87, Farnborough Aerospace Centre, Farnborough, Hants GU14 6YU; Ashlea, Kinsbourne Green, Harpenden, Herts AL5 3PJ. *T:* (01582) 763901.

MASEFIELD, (John) Thorold, CMG 1986; HM Diplomatic Service, retired; Governor and Commander-in-Chief of Bermuda, 1997–2001; *b* 1 Oct. 1939; *e s* of late Dr Geoffrey Bussell Masefield, DSc and of Mildred Joy Thorold Masefield (*née* Rogers); *m* 1962, Jennifer Mary, *d* of late Rev. Dr H. C. Trowell, OBE and late K. M. Trowell, MBE; two *s* one *d* (and one *d* decd). *Educ:* Dragon Sch., Oxford; Repton Sch.; St John's Coll., Cambridge (Scholar) (MA). Joined CRO, 1962; Private Sec. to Permanent Under Sec., 1963–64; Second Secretary: Kuala Lumpur, 1964–65; Warsaw, 1966–67; FCO, 1967–69; First Sec., UK Delegn to Disarmament Conf., 1970–74; Dep. Head, Planning Staff, FCO, 1974–77; Far Eastern Dept, FCO, 1977–79; Counsellor, Head of Chancery and Consul Gen., Islamabad, 1979–82; Head of Personnel Services Dept, FCO, 1982–85; Head, Far Eastern Dept, FCO, 1985–87; Fellow, Center for Internat. Affairs, Harvard Univ., 1987–88; seconded to CSSB, 1988–89; High Comr, Tanzania, 1989–92; Asst Under-Sec.

of State, FCO, 1992–94; High Comr, Nigeria, also concurrently Ambassador (non-resident) to the Republics of Benin and of Chad, 1994–97. KStJ 1997. *Publication:* article in International Affairs. *Recreations:* fruit and vegetables. *Address:* c/o Foreign and Commonwealth Office, SW1A 2AH. *Clubs:* Royal Commonwealth Society; Mid Ocean Golf.

MASEFIELD, Sir Peter (Gordon), Kt 1972; MA Cantab; CEng; Hon. FRAeS; FCIT; President: Brooklands Museum Trust, since 1993 (Chairman, 1987–93); Croydon Airport Society, since 1962; aviation historian; *b* Trentham, Staffs, 19 March 1914; *e s* of late Dr W. Gordon Masefield, CBE, MRCS, and Marian A. Masefield (*née* Lloyd-Owen); *m* 1936, Patricia Doreen, 3rd *d* of late Percy H. Rooney, Wallington, Surrey; three *s* one *d*. *Educ:* Westminster Sch.; Chillon Coll., Switzerland; Jesus Coll., Cambridge (BA (Eng) 1935). On Design Staff, The Fairey Aviation Co. Ltd, 1935–37; Pilot's licence, 1937–77; joined The Aeroplane newspaper, 1937, Technical Editor, 1939–43; Air Correspondent Sunday Times, 1940–43; War Corresp. with RAF and US Army Eighth Air Force on active service, 1939–43; Editor, The Aeroplane Spotter, 1941–43; Chm. Editorial Cttee, The Inter-Services Journal on Aircraft Recognition, MAP, 1942–45; Personal Adviser to the Lord Privy Seal (Lord Beaverbrook) and Sec. of War Cabinet Cttee on Post War Civil Air Transport, 1943–45; first British Civil Air Attaché, British Embassy, Washington, DC, 1945–46 (Signator to Anglo-American Bermuda Air Agreement, 1946); Dir-Gen. of Long Term Planning and Projects, Ministry of Civil Aviation, 1946–48; Chief Executive and Mem. of Board of BEA, 1949–55; Managing Dir, Bristol Aircraft Ltd, 1956–60; Man. Dir, Beagle Aircraft Ltd, 1960–67, Chm., 1968–70; Dir, Beagle Aviation Finance Ltd, 1962–71. Chm., British Airports Authority, 1965–71. Chm., Nat. Jt Council for Civil Air Transport, 1950–51; Member: Cairns Cttee on Aircraft Accident Investigation, 1960; Min. of Aviation Advisory Cttees on Civil Aircraft Control and on Private and Club Flying and Gliding; Aeronautical Research Council, 1958–61; Board, LTE, 1973–82 (Chm. and Chief Exec., London Transport, 1980–82); CAA Flight Time Limitations Bd, 1986–91. Mem., Cambridge Univ. Appointments Bd, 1956–69. Director: Pressed Steel Co. Ltd, 1960–68; Worldwide Estates Ltd, 1972–88; Nationwide Building Soc., 1973–86; British Caledonian Aviation Gp Plc, 1975–88 (Dep. Chm., 1978–87); LRT Internat., 1982–91; Chm., Project Management Ltd, 1972–88. President: RAeS, 1959–60 (Mem. Council, 1945–65); Inst. of Travel Managers, 1967–71; Duxford Aviation Soc., 1970–; British Assoc. of Aviation Consultants, 1972–84 (Patron, 1984–); IRTE, 1979–81; Internat. Fedn of Airworthiness, 1980–83 (Patron, 1983–88); Bd Mem., Imperial War Mus. and HMS Belfast, 1942–44; Chm., Bd of Trustees, Imperial War Museum, 1977–78; Mem. Council, Royal Aero Club (Chm., Aviation Cttee, 1960–65; Chm., 1968–70). Chm., Bd of Governors, Reigate Grammar Sch., 1979–91; Governor, Ashridge Management Coll., 1981–91. FRSA (Chm. Council, 1977–79; Vice-Pres., 1979, now Vice-Pres. Emeritus); CIMgt. Hon. FAIAA; Hon. FCASI; Hon. DSc Cranfield, 1977; Hon. DTech Loughborough, 1977. Liveryman, GAPAN; Freeman, City of London. *Publications:* To Ride the Storm, 1982; articles on aviation, transport, management, and First World War. *Recreations:* reading, writing, gardening. *Address:* Rosehill, Doods Way, Reigate, Surrey RH2 0JT. *T:* (01737) 242396. *Clubs:* Athenæum, Royal Aero; National Aviation (Washington).

See also Sir C. B. G. Masefield.

MASEFIELD, Thorold; *see* Masefield, J. T.

MASERI, Attilio, MD; FRCP; FACC; Professor of Cardiology, and Director of Institute of Cardiology, Catholic University of Rome, Italy, since 1991; *b* 12 Nov. 1935; *s* of Adriano and Antonietta Albini, Italian nobles; *m* 1960, Countess Francesca Maseri Florio di Santo Stefano; one *s*. *Educ:* Classic Lycée Cividale, Italy; Padua Univ. Med. Sch. Special bds in Cardiology, 1963, in Nuclear Medicine, 1965, Italy. Research fellow: Univ. of Pisa, 1960–65; Columbia Univ., NY, 1965–66; Johns Hopkins Univ., Baltimore, 1966–67; University of Pisa: Asst Prof., 1967–70; Prof. of Internal Medicine, 1970; Prof. of Cardiovascular Pathophysiology, 1972–79; Prof. of Medicine (Locum), 1977–79; Sir John McMichael Prof. of Cardiovascular Medicine, RPMS, Univ. of London, 1979–91. King Faisal Prize for Medicine, 1992; Dist. Scientist Award, Amer. Coll. of Cardiology, 1997. Chevalier d'honneur et devotion, SMO Malta. *Publications:* Myocardial Blood Flow in Man, 1972; Primary and Secondary Angina, 1977; Perspectives on Coronary Care, 1979; Ischemic Heart Disease: a rational basis for clinical practise and clinical research, 1995; articles in major internat. cardiological and med. jls. *Recreations:* skiing, tennis, sailing. *Address:* Via Zandonai 9–11, 00194 Rome, Italy. *Club:* Queen's.

MASHAM OF ILTON, Baroness *cr* 1970 (Life Peer); **Susan Lilian Primrose Cunliffe-Lister, (Countess of Swinton);** DL; *b* 14 April 1935; *d* of Sir Ronald Sinclair, 8th Bt and Reba Blair (who *m* 2nd, 1957, Lt-Col H. R. Hildreth, MBE; she *d* 1985), *d* of Anthony Inglis, MD; *m* 1959, Lord Masham (now Earl of Swinton, *qv*); one *s* one *d* (both adopted). *Educ:* Heathfield School, Ascot; London Polytechnic. Has made career in voluntary social work. Mem., Peterlee and Newton Aycliffe New Town Corp., 1973–85. Mem., Select Cttee on Sci. and Technol., 1997–. All-Party Parliamentary Committees: Vice-Chairman: Drug Misuse, 1984–; AIDS, 1988–; Member: Disablement, 1970–; Penal Affairs, 1975–; Member, All-Party Parliamentary Groups on: Children, 1982–; Breast Cancer, 1993–; Skin, 1994–; Epilepsy, 1994–; Primary Care and Public Health, 1998–; British Council Associate Parly Gp, 1999–. President: N Yorks Red Cross, 1963–88 (Patron, 1989–); Yorks Assoc. for the Disabled, 1963–98; Spinal Injuries Assoc., 1982–; Chartered Soc. of Physiotherapy, 1975–82; Papworth and Enham Village Settlements, 1973–85; Registration Council of Scientists in Health Care, 1991–; Countrywide Workshops Charitable Trust, 1993–97; Vice-President: British Sports Assoc. for the Disabled; Disabled Drivers Assoc.; Assoc. of Occupnl Therapists; Action for Dysphasic Adults; Hosp. Saving Assoc.; Chairman: Bd of Dirs, Phoenix House (Drug Rehabilitation), 1986–92 (Patron, 1992–); Home Office Working Gp on Young People and Alcohol, 1987; Member: Yorks RHA, 1982–90; N Yorks FHSA, 1990–95; Bd of Visitors, Wetherby Young Offenders Instn (formerly Wetherby Youth Custody Centre), 1963–94; Winston Churchill Meml Trust, 1980–; Council, London Lighthouse, 1991–98; Trustee, Spinal Res. Trust; Patron: Disablement Income Gp; Yorks Faculty of GPs; Mem. and Governor, Ditchley Foundn, 1980–; former Mem., Volunteer Centre. Freedom, Borough of Harrogate, 1989. DL North Yorks, 1991. Hon. FRCGP 1981; Hon. FCSP 1996; Hon. Fellow, Bradford and Ilkley Community Coll., 1988. Hon. MA Open, 1981; DUniv York, 1985; Hon. LLD: Leeds, 1988; Teesside, 1993; Hon. DSc Ulster, 1990; Hon. DLitt Keele, 1993. *Publication:* The World Walks By, 1986. *Recreations:* breeding highland ponies, swimming, table tennis, fishing, flower decoration, gardening. *Address:* Dykes Hill House, Masham, near Ripon, N Yorks HG4 4NS. *T:* (01765) 689241; 46 Westminster Gardens, Marsham Street, SW1P 4JG. *T:* (020) 7834 0700.

MASHELKAR, Raghunath Anant, PhD; FRS 1998; Director General, Council of Scientific & Industrial Research, and Secretary, Department of Scientific and Industrial Research, India, since 1995; *b* 1 Jan. 1943; *s* of late Anant Tukaram Mashelkar and Anjani Anant Mashelkar; *m* 1970, Vaishali R. Mashelkar; one *s* two *d*. *Educ:* Univ. of Bombay (BChemEngrg 1966; PhD 1969). Sen. Scientist, 1976–86, Dir, 1989–95, Nat. Chemical Lab., Pune. Pres., Indian Sci. Congress, 1999–2000. Fellow: Indian Acad. of Scis, 1983 (Vice Pres., 1995–97); Indian Nat. Sci. Acad., 1984 (Viswakarma Medal, 1988); Maharashtra Acad. of Scis, 1985 (Pres., 1991–94); Third World Acad. of Scis, 1994. Hon. DSc: Salford, 1993; Kanpur, 1995; Delhi, 1998; Gukrahati, Anna (Chennai), Pretoria, 2000; London, 2001. Herdillia Award, Indian Inst. of Chem. Engrs, 1982; K. G. Naik Gold Medal, 1985; Republic Day Award, NRDC, 1995; Atur Sangtani Award, Atur Foundn, 1998. Padmashri, 1991; Padmabhushan, 2000. *Publications:* (ed jtly) Advances in Transport Processes, vol. 1, 1980, vol. 2, 1982, vol. 3, 1983, vol. 4, 1986, vol. 8, 1992, vol. 9, 1993; (ed jtly and contrib.) Frontiers in Chemical Reaction Engineering, vols 1 and 2, 1984; (ed jtly) Transport Phenomena in Polymeric Systems, vol. 1, 1987, vol. 2, 1989; (ed jtly) Advances in Transport Phenomena in Fluidizing Systems, 1987; (ed jtly) Recent Trends in Chemical Reaction Engineering, vols 1 and 2, 1987; (ed jtly) Reactions and Reaction Engineering, 1987; (ed jtly and contrib.) Heat Transfer Equipment Design, 1988; (ed jtly) Readings in Solid State Chemistry, 1994; (ed jtly and contrib.) Dynamics of Complex Fluids, 1998; (ed jtly and contrib.) Structure and Dynamics in the Mesoscopic Domain, 1999; numerous articles in jls and contribs to books. *Address:* Council of Scientific and Industrial Research, 2 Rafi Marg, New Delhi 110001, India. *T:* (office) 3717053, 3710472; (home) 4648851, 4649359.

MASIRE, Quett Ketumile Joni, Hon. GCMG 1991; Naledi Ya Botswana; President of Botswana, 1980–98; *b* 23 July 1925; *m* 1957, Gladys Olebile; three *s* three *d*. *Educ:* Kanye; Tiger Kloof. Founded Seepapitso Secondary School, 1950; reporter, later Dir, African Echo, 1958; Mem., Bangwaketse Tribal Council, Legislative Council (former Mem., Exec. Council); founder Mem., Botswana Democratic Party (Editor, Therisanyo, 1962–67); Member, Legislative Assembly (later National Assembly): Kanye S, 1966–69; Ngwaketse-Kgalagadi, 1974–79; Dep. Prime Minister, 1965–66; Vice-Pres. and Minister of Finance and Development Planning, 1966–80. *Address:* PO Box 70, Gaborone, Botswana. *T:* 353391.

MASKELL, Prof. Duncan John, PhD; Marks and Spencer Professor of Farm Animal Health, Food Science and Food Safety, Cambridge University, since 1996; Fellow, Wolfson College, Cambridge, since 1998; *b* 30 May 1961; *s* of Leslie George Maskell and Mary Sheila Horsburgh Maskell; *m* 1992, Dr Sarah Elizabeth Peters; one *s* one *d*. *Educ:* Gonville and Caius Coll., Cambridge (MA, PhD). Res. Scientist, Wellcome Biotech, 1985–88; Res. Fellow, Inst. of Molecular Medicine, John Radcliffe Hosp., Univ. of Oxford, 1988–92; Lectr, Dept of Biochemistry, Imperial Coll., London Univ., 1992–96. Member: Res. Review Gp, Food Standards Agency, 2000–; Agri-Food Cttee, 1997– (Chm., 2000–), Strategy Bd, 2000–, BBSRC. *Publications:* numerous papers in learned jls. *Recreations:* watching cricket, Manchester United, cooking, fine wine, music. *Address:* Centre for Veterinary Science, Department of Clinical Veterinary Medicine, Madingley Road, Cambridge CB3 0ES. *T:* (01223) 339868.

MASKEY, Alexander; Member (SF) Belfast West, Northern Ireland Assembly, since 1998; *b* 8 Jan. 1952; *s* of Alexander and Teresa Maskey; *m* 1976, Elizabeth McKee; two *s*. *Educ:* Christian Brothers' Primary Sch.; Donegall Street, Belfast; St Malaghy's Coll., Belfast. Mem. (SF), Belfast CC, 1983–. Member: Nat. Cttee, Ard Chomairle, 1994–; N Ireland Forum, 1996–98. Contested (SF) Belfast S, 2001. *Recreations:* photography, reading. *Address:* James Connolly House, 147 Andersonstown Road, Belfast BT11 9BW.

MASLIN, David Michael E.; *see* Eckersley-Maslin.

MASON, family name of **Baron Mason of Barnsley**.

MASON OF BARNSLEY, Baron *cr* 1987 (Life Peer), of Barnsley in South Yorkshire; **Roy Mason;** PC 1968; DL; *b* 18 April 1924; *s* of Joseph and Mary Mason; *m* 1945, Marjorie, *d* of Ernest Sowden; two *d*. *Educ:* Carlton Junior Sch.; Royston Senior Sch.; London Sch. of Economics (TUC Scholarship). Went underground at 14 years of age, 1938–53; NUM branch official, 1947–53; mem. Yorks Miners' Council, 1949. MP (Lab): Barnsley, March 1953–1983; Barnsley Central, 1983–87. Labour party spokesman on Defence and Post Office affairs, 1960–64; Minister of State (Shipping), Bd of Trade, 1964–67; Minister of Defence (Equipment), 1967–April 1968; Postmaster-Gen., April–June 1968; Minister of Power, 1968–69; President, Bd of Trade, 1969–70; Labour party spokesman on Civil Aviation, Shipping, Tourism, Films and Trade matters, 1970–74; Secretary of State for: Defence, 1974–76; Northern Ireland, 1976–79; opposition spokesman on agriculture, fisheries and food, 1979–81. Mem., Council of Europe and WEU, 1973. Chm., Yorkshire Gp of Labour MPs, 1972–74; Chm., Miners Gp of MPs, 1974, Vice-Chm., 1980. Chairman: Prince's Trust, S Yorks, 1985–; Barnsley Business and Innovation Centre, 1990. DL South Yorks, 1992. DUniv Sheffield Hallam, 1993. *Recreations:* work, provided one stays on top of it, fly-fishing, cravatology (tie-designing). *Address:* 12 Victoria Avenue, Barnsley, S Yorks S70 2BH. *Club:* Lords and Commons Fly-Fishing (founder, and Pres., 1983–).

MASON, Alastair Michael Stuart, FRCP; Partner, Partners in Care, since 1994; *b* 4 March 1944; *s* of Adair Stuart and Rosemary Mason; *m* 1967; two *s* two *d*. *Educ:* Downside Sch.; London Hosp., London Univ. MB BS. MRCP, FRCP 1993; MRCS; FFPHM 1991. Hosp. junior appts, 1967–73; Sen. Medical Officer, Dept of Health, 1974–84; Sen. Manager, Arthur Andersen & Co., 1984–88; RMO, S Western RHA, 1988–94. *Publications:* (ed) Walk don't run, 1985; Information for Action, 1988. *Recreations:* walking, reading, theatre. *Address:* 5 The Cobblers Close, Gotherington, Glos GL52 9HF.

MASON, Hon. Sir Anthony (Frank), AC 1988; KBE 1972 (CBE 1969); Chancellor, University of New South Wales, 1994–99; Chief Justice, High Court of Australia, 1987–95; *b* Sydney, 21 April 1925; *s* of F. M. Mason; *m* 1950, Patricia Mary, *d* of Dr E. N. McQueen; two *s*. *Educ:* Sydney Grammar Sch.; Univ. of Sydney. BA, LLB. RAAF Flying Officer, 1944–45. Admitted to NSW Bar, 1951; QC 1964. Commonwealth Solicitor-General, 1964–69; Judge, Court of Appeal, Supreme Court of NSW, 1969–72; Justice, High Court of Australia, 1972–87; Judge, Supreme Court of Fiji, 1995–; Non-permanent Judge, HK Court of Final Appeal, 1997–; Pres., Solomon Islands Court of Appeal, 1997–99. Mem., Permanent Court of Arbitration, 1987–99. Mem., Panel of Arbitrators and Advrs, INTELSAT, 1965–69; Presiding Arbitrator, Internat. Centre for Settlement of Investment Disputes (dispute under N Amer. Free Trade Agreement), Washington, 1999–2000. Nat. Fellow, Res. Sch. of Social Scis, ANU, 1995–99; Arthur Goodhart Prof. in Legal Sci., and Vis. Fellow, Gonville and Caius Coll., Cambridge, 1996–97. Vice-Chm., UN Commn on Internat. Trade Law, 1968. Chairman: Nat. Liby of Australia, 1995–98; Adv. Bd, Nat. Inst. for Law, Ethics and Public Affairs, Griffith Univ., 1995–99; Member: Council of Management, British Inst. of Internat. and Comparative Law, 1987–; Council, ANU, 1969–72; Pro-Chancellor, ANU, 1972–75. Mem., Amer. Law Inst., 1995. FASSA 1989. Hon. Bencher, Lincoln's Inn, 1987. Hon. LLD: ANU, 1980; Sydney, 1988; Melbourne, 1992; Monash, 1995; Griffith, 1995; Deakin, 1995; NSW, 2000. Hon. DCL Oxford, 1993. *Recreations:* gardening, tennis, swimming. *Address:* 1 Castlereagh Street, Sydney, NSW 2000, Australia.

MASON, Sir (Basil) John, Kt 1979; CB 1973; FRS 1965; DSc (London); Director-General of the Meteorological Office, 1965–83; Chancellor, University of Manchester

Institute of Science and Technology, 1994–96 (President, 1986–94); *b* 18 Aug. 1923; *s* of late John Robert and Olive Mason, Docking, Norfolk; *m* 1948, Doreen Sheila Jones; two *s*. *Educ:* Fakenham Grammar Sch.; University Coll., Nottingham. Commissioned, Radar Branch RAF, 1944–46. BSc 1st Cl. Hons Physics (London), 1947, MSc 1948; DSc (London) 1956. Shirley Res. Fellow, Univ. of Nottingham, 1947; Asst Lectr in Meteorology, 1948, Lectr, 1949, Imperial Coll.; Warren Res. Fellow, Royal Society, 1957; Vis. Prof. of Meteorology, Univ. of Calif, 1959–60; Prof. of Cloud Physics, Imperial Coll. of Science and Technology (Univ. of London), 1961–65. Dir, Royal Soc. prog. on Acidification of Surface Waters, 1983–90; Sen. Advr, Centre for Envmtl Technol. (formerly Global Envt Res. Centre), Imperial Coll., 1990–; Chairman: WMO/ICSU Scientific Cttee, World Climate Res. Prog., 1984–88; Co-ordinating Cttee, Marine Science and Technol., 1988–91. Hon. Gen. Sec. British Assoc., 1965–70; President: Physics Section, British Assoc., 1965; Inst. of Physics, 1976–78; BAAS, 1982–83; Nat. Soc. for Clean Air, 1989–91; Assoc. for Science Educn, 1992; Pres., 1968–70, Hon. Mem., 1985, Royal Meteorol. Soc.; Sen. Vice-Pres., 1976–86, and Treasurer, 1976–86, Royal Soc.; Pres., Soc. of Envmtl Engrs, 1999–. UK Perm. Rep., World Meteorological Orgn, 1965–83 (Mem. Exec. Cttee, 1966–75 and 1977–83). Member: ABRC, 1983–87; Astronomy, Space Radio Bd, SERC, 1981–85. Chm. Council, 1970–75, Pro-Chancellor, 1979–85, Surrey Univ. Lectures: James Forrest, ICE, 1967 and 1993; Kelvin, IEE, 1968; Dalton, RIC, 1968; Bakerian, Royal Soc., 1971; Hugh MacMillan, IES, 1975; Symons, Royal Meteorol. Soc., 1976; Halley, Oxford, 1977; Rutherford, Royal Soc., Larmor, Cambridge, Linacre, Oxford, and H. L. Welch, Toronto, 1990; Loretto, Edinburgh, 1993; Sir Henry Tizard, Westminster Sch., 1999. Mem., Academia Europaea, 1989; Hon. Mem., Amer. Meteorol Soc., 1988; Foreign Mem., Norwegian Acad. of Sci. and Letters, 1993. Hon. Fellow: Imperial Coll. of Science and Technology, 1974; UMIST, 1979. Hon. DSc: Nottingham, 1966; Durham, 1970; Strathclyde, 1975; City, 1980; Sussex, 1983; Plymouth Polytechnic, 1990; Heriot-Watt Univ., 1991; UMIST, 1994; Reading, 1998; Hon. ScD East Anglia, 1988. Hugh Robert Mill Medal, Royal Meteorol. Soc., 1959; Charles Chree Medal and Prize, Inst. Physics and Phys. Soc., 1965; Rumford Medal, Royal Soc., 1972; Glazebrook Medal, Inst. Physics, 1974; Symons Meml Gold Medal, Royal Meteorol. Soc., 1975; Royal Medal, Royal Soc., 1991. *Publications:* The Physics of Clouds, 1957, 2nd edn 1971; Clouds, Rain and Rain-Making, 1962, 2nd edn 1975; The Surface Waters Acidification Programme, 1990; Acid Rain, 1992; papers in physics and meteorological journals. *Recreations:* foreign travel, music. *Address:* 64 Christchurch Road, East Sheen, SW14 7AW.

MASON, Benedict; composer, sound artist and film maker. *Educ:* King's Coll., Cambridge (schol.; MA); Royal Coll. of Art (MA). Guido d'Arezzo, 1988; John Clementi Collard Fellowship, 1989; Fulbright Fellow, 1990; Deutsche Akademischer Austauschdienst Künstlerprogramm, Berlin, 1994. *Compositions* include: Hinterstoisser Traverse, 1986; 1st String Quartet, 1987; Lighthouses of England and Wales, 1987 (Britten Prize, 1988); Oil and Petrol Marks on a Wet Road are sometimes held to be Spots where a Rainbow Stood, 1987; Horn Trio, 1987; Six Piano Etudes, 1988; Chaplin Operas, 1989; Sapere Aude for Eighteenth Century Period Instrument Orchestra, 1989; Dreams that do what they're told, 1990; Concerto for the Viola Section accompanied by the Rest of the Orchestra, 1990; Nodding Trilliums and Curve-lined Angles, 1990; Self Referential Songs and Realistic Virelais, 1990; Rilke Songs, 1991; Animals and the Origins of the Dance, 1992; Quantized Quantz, 1992; !, 1992; Colour and Information, 1993; 2nd String Quartet, 1993; Playing Away: an opera about Germany, Opera, Pop Music and Football, 1994. *Sound/theatre installations:* Ohne Missbrauch der Aufmerksamkeit, 1993; Second Music for a European Concert Hall: Ensemble Modern/Freiburg Barockorchester/Benoît Régent/Mozartsaal, 1994; third music for a european concert hall (espro: eic: i love my life), 1994; Clarinet Concerto, 1995; ASKO/PARADISO: the Fifth Music. Résumé with C. P. E. Bach, 1995; Schumann-Auftrag: Live Hörspiel ohne Worte, 1996; SEVENTH. (for David Alberman and Rolf Hind) PIANO.WITH.VIOLIN.TO.TOUR.ALL. HALLS.MUSIC, 1996; Carré, Nederlands Kamerkoor, Schoenberg Ensemble, Eighth Music for a European Concert Hall (First Music for a Theatre), 1996; Steep Ascent within and away from a Non European Concert Hall: Six Horns, Three Trombones and a Decorated Shed, 1996; Trumpet Concerto, 1997; The Four Slopes of Twice among Gliders of her Gravity (two Steinway model D pianos, two Ampico player pianos and one human being), 1997; Szene für Jean Nouvel (drei Frauenstimmen, drei Spiegelstimmen, Orch., Sampler und Film), 1998. Solo exhibn, gastronomic amorous gymnastic etc music, Berlin, 1997. *Films:* Horn, 1980; Doppler Between, 1983; Resonating Toner, 1985; all stages, 1987; Leading Articles, 1990; Reassurance, 1991; Disclaimer, 1995. Ernst von Siemens Prize, 1992; Paul Fromm Award, 1995; Britten Award, 1996. *Recreation:* litigation. *Address:* The Music Inc., 12A, 30 Fifth Avenue, New York, NY 10011, USA.

MASON, David Arthur; Director of Social Services, Warwickshire County Council, 1991–97; *b* 13 May 1946; *s* of Arthur J. Mason and Vera M. Mason. *Educ:* Birmingham Polytechnic (Cert. Social Work, 1970); Univ. of Aston in Birmingham (MSc Public Sector Management, 1981). Social worker, 1966–70; Sen. Social worker, Hounslow, 1970–72; Unit Organiser, Birmingham Family Service Unit, 1972–75; Area Man., Birmingham, 1975–81; Divl Dir of Social Services, Warwickshire, 1981–84; Director of Social Services: Knowsley, 1985–87; Liverpool CC, 1987–91.

MASON, Sir David (Kean), Kt 1992; CBE 1987; BDS, MD; FRCSGlas, FDSRCPS Glas, FDSRCSE, FRCPath; FRSE; Professor of Oral Medicine and Head of the Department of Oral Medicine and Pathology, University of Glasgow Dental School, 1967–92, now Professor Emeritus; Dean of Dental Education, University of Glasgow, 1980–90; *b* 5 Nov. 1928; *s* of George Hunter Mason and Margaret Kean; *m* 1967, Judith Anne Armstrong; two *s* one *d*. *Educ:* Paisley Grammar Sch.; Glasgow Acad.; St Andrews Univ. (LDS 1951, BDS 1952); Glasgow Univ. (MB, ChB 1962, MD (Commendation) 1967). FDSRCSE 1957; FDSRCPS Glas 1967 (Hon. FDSRCPS Glas 1990); FRCSGlas 1973; FRCPath 1976 (MRCPath 1967); FRSE 1999. Served RAF, Dental Br., 1952–54. Registrar in Oral Surgery, Dundee, 1954–56; gen. dental practice, 1956–62; Vis. Dental Surgeon, Glasgow Dental Hosp., 1956–62, Sen. Registrar 1962–64; Sen. Lectr in Dental Surgery and Pathology, Univ. of Glasgow, 1964–67; Hon. Consultant Dental Surgeon, Glasgow, 1964–67. Chm., National Dental Consultative Cttee, 1976–80 and 1983–87; Member: Medicines Commn, 1976–80; Dental Cttee, MRC, 1973–80; Physiol Systems Bd, MRC, 1976–80; Jt MRC/Health Depts/SERC Dental Cttee, 1984–87; GDC, 1976–94 (Mem., Disciplinary Cttee, 1980–85; Health Cttee, 1985–89; Pres., 1989–94); Dental Cttee, UGC, 1977–87 (Chm., 1983–87); Supervised Trng Gp, UGC, 1984–86; Dental Rev. Wkg Party, UGC, 1986–87; Jt Cttee for Higher Trng in Dentistry, 1977–84; Dental Strategy Rev. Gp, 1980–81; Scientific Prog. Cttee, FDI, 1980–87; Consultant to Commn on Dental Res., FDI, 1973–80. President: W of Scotland Br., BDA, 1983–84; British Soc. for Dental Res., 1984–86; British Soc. for Oral Medicine, 1984–86; GDC, 1989–94; Convener, Dental Council, RCPGlas, 1977–80. Lectures: Charles Tomes, RCS, 1975; Holme, UCH, London, 1977; Caldwell Meml, Univ. of Glasgow, 1983; Evelyn Sprawson, London Hosp. Med. Coll., 1984. Hon. FFDRCSI 1988; Hon. FRCSE 1995. Hon. DDS Wales, 1991; Hon. LLD Dundee, 1993; Hon. DSc Western Ontario, 1997; DUniv Glasgow, 1998. John Tomes Prize, RCS, 1979; Colyer Medal, RCS, 1992. *Publications:* (jtly) Salivary Glands in Health and Disease, 1975; (jtly) Introduction to Oral Medicine, 1978; (jtly) Self Assessment: Manual I, Oral Surgery, 1978; Manual II, Oral Medicine, 1978; (ed jtly) Oral Manifestations of Systemic Disease, 1980, 2nd edn 1990; (jtly) World Workshop on Oral Medicine, 3 vols, 1988, 1993, 1999. *Recreations:* golf, tennis, gardening, enjoying the pleasures of the countryside. *Address:* Greystones, Houston Road, Kilmacolm, Renfrewshire PA13 4NY. *Clubs:* Royal Scottish Automobile (Glasgow); Royal & Ancient Golf, Elie Golf House, Kilmacolm Golf.

MASON, Frances Jane G.; *see* Gumley-Mason.

MASON, Sir Frederick (Cecil), KCVO 1968; CMG 1960; HM Diplomatic Service, retired; *b* 15 May 1913; *s* of late Ernest Mason and Sophia Charlotte Mason (*née* Dodson); *m* 1941, Karen Rørholm; two *s* one *d* (and two *d* decd). *Educ:* City of London Sch.; St Catharine's Coll., Cambridge. Vice-Consul: Antwerp, 1935–36; Paris, 1936–37; Leopoldville, 1937–39; Elisabethville, 1939–40; Consul at Thorshavn during British occupation of Faroes, 1940–42; Consul, Colon, Panama, 1943–45; First Sec., British Embassy, Santiago, Chile, 1946–48; First Sec. (Information), Oslo, 1948–50; Asst Labour Adviser, FO, 1950–53; First Sec. (Commercial), UK Control Commission, Bonn, 1954–55; Counsellor (Commercial), HM Embassy, Athens, 1955–56; Counsellor (Economic), HM Embassy, Tehran, 1957–60; Head of Economic Relations Dept, Foreign Office, 1960–64; Under-Sec., Ministry of Overseas Development, 1965, and CRO, 1966; Ambassador to Chile, 1966–70; Under-Sec. of State, FCO, Oct. 1970–Apr. 1971; Ambassador and Perm. UK Rep. to UN and other Internat. Orgns, Geneva, 1971–73. Dir, New Court Natural Resources, 1973–83. British Mem., Internat. Narcotics Control Bd, Geneva, 1974–77. Chm., Anglo-Chilean Soc., 1978–82. Grand Cross, Chilean Order of Merit, 1968. *Publication:* Ropley Past and Present, 1989. *Recreations:* walking, painting. *Address:* The Forge, Ropley, Hants SO24 0DS. *T:* (01962) 772285. *Club:* Canning.

MASON, His Honour (George Frederick) Peter; QC 1963; FCIArb 1986; a Circuit Judge, 1970–87; *b* 11 Dec. 1921; *s* of George Samuel and Florence May Mason, Keighley, Yorks; *m* 1st, 1950 (marr. diss. 1977); two *s* two *d* (and one *d* decd); 2nd, 1981, Sara, *er d* of Sir Robert Ricketts, Bt, *qv*. *Educ:* Lancaster Royal Grammar Sch.; St Catharine's Coll., Cambridge. Open Exhibnr St Catharine's Coll., 1940. Served with 78th Medium Regt RA (Duke of Lancaster's Own Yeo.) in Middle East and Italy, 1941–45, latterly as Staff Capt. RA, HQ 13 Corps. History Tripos Pt 1, 1st cl. hons with distinction, 1946; called to Bar, Lincoln's Inn, 1947; MA 1948; Cholmeley Schol., 1949. Asst Recorder of Huddersfield, 1961; Dep. Chairman: Agricultural Land Tribunal, W Yorks and Lancs, 1962; West Riding of Yorks Quarter Sessions, 1965–67; Recorder of York, 1965–67; Dep. Chm., Inner London QS, 1970; Dep. Chm., NE London QS, 1970–71; Senior Judge: Snaresbrook Crown Ct, 1974–81; CCC, 1982; Inner London Crown Court, 1983–87. Member: Council, Assoc. of Futures Brokers and Dealers, 1987–91; London Court of Internat. Arbitration, 1990–2000; Bd, Securities and Futures Authy, 1991–93; Amer. Arbitration Assoc., 1992–; Bd, Internat. Petroleum Exchange, 1993–98; Special Cttee, London Metal Exchange, 1995–. Freeman, City of London, 1977. Liveryman, Wax Chandlers' Co., 1980–. *Recreations:* music, cycling, carpentry. *Address:* 11 King's Bench Walk, Temple, EC4Y 7EQ. *T:* (020) 7353 3337/8; Lane Cottage, Amberley, Glos GL5 5AB. *T:* (01453) 872412, *Fax:* (01453) 878557; *e-mail:* masonamberley@compuserve.com. *Clubs:* Athenæum; Hawks.

MASON, Sir Gordon (Charles), Kt 1993; OBE 1982; JP; *b* 8 Nov. 1921; *s* of Joseph Henry Mason and May Louisa Mason; *m* 1944, Tui Audrey King; two *s* one *d*. *Educ:* Kaipara Flats. In local government, New Zealand, 1960–92: Dep. Chm., 1965–72, Co. Chm., 1972–89; Mayor, Rodney DC, 1989–92. Chm., Local Govt Trng Bd, 1981–89; Pres., NZ Counties Assoc., 1984–87. Past Master: Rodney Masonic Lodge; Rotary; Lions. JP NZ, 1968. *Recreations:* travel, gardening. *Address:* Kaipara Flats RD4, Warkworth, New Zealand. *T:* (9) 4225718. *Clubs:* Bowling (NZ); RSA (Warkworth, NZ).

MASON, (James) Stephen, CB 1988; Counsel to the Speaker, House of Commons, 1994–2000; *b* 6 Feb. 1935; *s* of Albert Wesley Mason and Mabel (*née* Topham); *m* 1961, Tania Jane Moeran (*see* T. J. Mason); one *s* two *d*. *Educ:* Windsor County Grammar Sch.; Univ. of Oxford (MA, BCL). Called to the Bar, Middle Temple, 1958; in practice, 1961–67; Office of Parly Counsel, 1967–94: Parly Counsel, 1980–94. *Recreations:* being an indulgent father, reading, playing the piano. *Address:* Cannon Cottage, Well Road, NW3 1LH.

MASON, Jane; *see* Mason, T. J.

MASON, Sir John; *see* Mason, Sir B. J.

MASON, Sir John (Charles Moir), KCMG 1980 (CMG 1976); Chairman, Pirelli Cables Australia Ltd, 1993–99 (Director, 1987–99); *b* 13 May 1927; *o s* of late Charles Moir Mason, CBE and late Madeline Mason; *m* 1954, Margaret Newton; one *s* one *d*. *Educ:* Manchester Grammar Sch.; Peterhouse, Cambridge. Lieut, XX Lancs Fusiliers, 1946–48; BA 1950, MA 1955, Cantab; Captain, Royal Ulster Rifles, 1950–51 (Korea); HM Foreign Service, 1952; 3rd Sec., FO, 1952–54; 2nd Sec. and Private Sec. to Ambassador, British Embassy, Rome, 1954–56; 2nd Sec., Warsaw, 1956–59; 1st Sec., FO, 1959–61; 1st Sec. (Commercial), Damascus, 1961–65; 1st Sec. and Asst Head of Dept, FO, 1965–68; Dir of Trade Develt and Dep. Consul-Gen., NY, 1968–71; Head of European Integration Dept, FCO, 1971–72; seconded as Under-Sec., ECGD, 1972–75; Asst Under-Sec. of State (Economic), FCO, 1975–76; Ambassador to Israel, 1976–80; High Commissioner to Australia, 1980–84. Chairman: Thorn-EMI (Australia), 1985–94; Lloyd's Bank (NZA), Sydney, 1985–90; Lloyds International Ltd, 1985–90; Vickers Shipbuilders (Australia), 1985–92; Bd of Advice, Spencer Stuart and Associates, Sydney, 1985–96; Multicon, 1987–92; Prudential (Australia and NZ), later Prudential Corp. Australia, 1987–92; Prudential Assets Management, 1987–92; Prudential Funds Management, 1987–92; Director: Nat. Bank of NZ, 1984–90; Wellcome (Australia) Ltd, 1985–90; Fluor Daniel (Australia) Ltd, 1985–93; Sen. Internat. Advr, Fluor Corp., USA, 1989–93. Public Mem., Australia Press Council, 1992–99; Member: Professional Conduct Cttees, NSW Bar Assoc., 1992–99; NSW Law Soc., 1994–99. Chairman: North Shore Heart Foundn, Sydney, 1986–92; Bequests Cttee, RACP, 1992–95; Mem., Finance Cttee, State Cancer Council, NSW, 1993–95. Nat. Dep. Chm., Churchill Meml Trust, Aust., 1995–2001. *Publication:* Diplomatic Despatches From a Son to his Mother, 1998. *Address:* 147 Dover Road, Dover Heights, NSW 2030, Australia; c/o Lloyds TSB, 7 Pall Mall, SW1Y 5NA. *Club:* Union (Sydney).

MASON, Prof. John Kenyon French, CBE 1973; MD; FRSE; Regius Professor of Forensic Medicine, University of Edinburgh, 1973–85, now Emeritus; *b* 19 Dec. 1919; *s* of late Air Cdre J. M. Mason, CBE, DSC, DFC and late Alma French; *m* 1943, Elizabeth Latham (decd); two *s*. *Educ:* Downside Sch.; Cambridge Univ.; St Bartholomew's Hosp. MD, FRCPath, DMJ, DTM&H; LLD Edinburgh 1987. FRSE 1995. Joined RAF, 1943; Dir of RAF Dept of Aviation and Forensic Pathology, 1956; retd as Group Captain, Consultant in Pathology, 1973. Pres., British Assoc. in Forensic Medicine, 1981–83. L. G. Groves Prize for Aircraft Safety, 1957; R. F. Linton Meml Prize, 1958; James Martin

Award for Flight Safety, 1972; Douglas Weightman Safety Award, 1973; Swiney Prize for Jurisprudence, 1978; Lederer Award for Aircraft Safety, 1985. *Publications:* Aviation Accident Pathology, 1962; (ed) Aerospace Pathology, 1973; Forensic Medicine for Lawyers, 1978, 4th edn 2001; (ed) The Pathology of Violent Injury, 1978, 3rd edn as The Pathology of Trauma, 2000; Law and Medical Ethics, 1983, 5th edn 1999; Butterworth's Medico-Legal Encyclopaedia, 1987; Human Life and Medical Practice, 1989; Medico-legal Aspects of Reproduction, 1990, 2nd edn 1998; The Courts and the Doctor, 1990; (ed) Forensic Medicine: an illustrated text, 1993; papers in medical and legal jls. *Address:* 66 Craiglea Drive, Edinburgh EH10 5PF. *Club:* Royal Air Force.

MASON, Sir John (Peter), Kt 1994; CBE 1989; solicitor; Chairman, North Lincolnshire Primary Care Trust, since 2001; Chairman, National Union of Conservative and Unionist Associations, 1992–93 (Vice Chairman, 1989–92); *b* 25 Dec. 1940; *m* Margaret; one *s* two *d. Educ:* Scunthorpe GS. Admitted solicitor, 1964; Sen. Partner, Mason Baggott & Garton, solicitors, Scunthorpe, 1976–. Chairman: Scunthorpe HA, 1981–93; Scunthorpe and Goole Hosps NHS Trust, 1993–2001. Conservative Party: Chm., E Midlands Area, 1985–89; Dep. Chm., Bd of Finance, 1994–; Mem., Nat. Union Exec. Cttee, 1977–98 (Chm., European Cttee, 1989–92). *Address:* Mason, Baggott & Garton, 13/19 Wells Street, Scunthorpe, N Lincs DN15 6HN.

MASON, Prof. (John) Stanley, PhD; CEng; Principal and Vice-Chancellor, Glasgow Caledonian University, 1993–97 (Principal, Glasgow College of Technology, then Glasgow Polytechnic, 1988–93); *b* 30 Jan. 1934; *s* of George and Grace Mason; *m* Florence; two *s. Educ:* Wigan Grammar Sch.; Nottingham Univ. (BSc 1st cl. Hons Mining Engrg 1958); Liverpool Poly. (PhD 1972). With NCB, 1950–54 and 1958–59; Maths Master, Leeds Grammar Sch., 1959–62; Lt, RN, 1963–66 (ME and RNEC, Manadon); Prin. Lectr in Mechanical Engrg, Liverpool Poly., 1966–68; Sen. Res. Fellow, Nottingham Univ., 1968–69; Hd, Fluid Mechanics and Thermodynamics Div., Liverpool Poly., 1969–73; Hd, Sch. of Mechanical Engrg and Dean, Faculties of Engrg and Technol., Thames Poly., 1973–87; Depute Dir, Glasgow Coll., 1987–88. Mem., SERC, 1990–94. Silver Plate, USA Powder and Bulk Solids Conf., 1985. *Publications:* (jtly) Bulk Solids Handling Technology, 1987; numerous papers. *Recreations:* travel, sport.

MASON, Rt Rev. Kenneth Bruce, AM 1984; retired; Chairman, Australian Board of Missions, General Synod of the Anglican Church of Australia, 1983–93; *b* 4 Sept. 1928; *s* of Eric Leslie Mason and Gertrude Irene (*née* Pearce); unmarried. *Educ:* Bathurst High Sch.; Sydney Teachers' Coll.; St John's Theological Coll., Morpeth (ThL 1953); Univ. of Queensland (BA, DipDiv 1964). Primary Teacher, 1948–51; deacon, 1953; priest, 1954; Member, Brotherhood of the Good Shepherd, 1954; Parish of: Gilgandra, NSW, 1954–58; Darwin, NT, 1959–61; Alice Springs, NT, 1962; resigned from Brotherhood, 1965; Trinity Coll., Melbourne Univ.: Asst Chaplain, 1965; Dean, 1966–67; Bishop of the Northern Territory, 1968–83. Member, Oratory of the Good Shepherd, 1962, Superior, 1981–87. *Recreations:* attending opera, listening to music, walking, railways. *Address:* PO Box 544, Glebe, NSW 2037, Australia.

MASON, Rev. Canon Kenneth Staveley; Canon Theologian, Scottish Episcopal Church, 1995–96; Canon of St Mary's Cathedral, Edinburgh, 1989–96, now Canon Emeritus; *b* 1 Nov. 1931; *s* of Rev. William Peter Mason and Anna Hester (*née* Pildrem); *m* 1958, Barbara Thomson; one *s* one *d. Educ:* Imperial College of Science, London (BSc, ARCS); BD (ext.) London; Wells Theological Coll. Assistant Curate: St Martin, Kingston upon Hull, 1958; Pocklington, 1961; Vicar of Thornton with Allerthorpe and Melbourne, 1963; Sub-Warden and Librarian, KCL, at St Augustine's Coll., Canterbury, 1969; Dir, Canterbury Sch. of Ministry, 1977, Principal, 1981. Examining Chaplain to Archbp of Canterbury, 1979–91; Six Preacher in Canterbury Cath., 1979–84; Hon. Canon of Canterbury, 1984–89; Principal, Edinburgh Theol Coll., later Dir, Theol Inst., Scottish Episcopal Church, 1989–95. *Publications:* George Herbert, Priest and Poet, 1980; Anglicanism, a Canterbury essay, 1987; Priesthood and Society, 1992; Catholic Tradition and the Ordination of Women, 1993. *Recreation:* bird-watching. *Address:* 2 Williamson Close, Ripon HG4 1AZ. *T:* (01765) 607041.

MASON, Monica; Principal Répétiteur, since 1984, Assistant Director, since 1991, Royal Ballet; *b* 6 Sept. 1941; *d* of Richard Mason and Mrs E. Fabian; *m* 1968, Austin Bennett. *Educ:* Johannesburg, SA; Royal Ballet Sch., London. Joined Royal Ballet in Corps de Ballet, 1958; Sen. Principal until 1989; created role of Chosen Maiden in Rite of Spring, 1962; also created roles in: Diversions, Elite Syncopations, Electra, Manon, Romeo and Juliet, Rituals, Adieu, Isadora, The Four Seasons, The Ropes of Time. Assistant to the Principal Choreographer, Royal Ballet, 1980–84. DUniv Surrey, 1996. *Address:* Royal Opera House, Covent Garden, WC2E 9DD.

MASON, Dr Pamela Georgina Walsh; FRCPsych; Vice-Chairman, Taunton and Somerset NHS Trust, 1991–97; Senior Principal Medical Officer (Under Secretary), Department of Health and Social Security, 1979–86, retired; re-employed as Senior Medical Officer, Department of Health, 1986–90; *d* of late Captain George Mason and Marie Louise Walsh; god-daughter and ward of late Captain William Gregory, Hon. Co. of Master Mariners; *m* 1st, 1949, David Paltenghi (*d* 1961); two *s*; 2nd, 1965, Jan Darnley-Smith (*d* 1996). *Educ:* Christ's Hosp. Sch.; Univ. of London, Royal Free Hosp. Sch. of Medicine (MRCS, LRCP, 1949; MB, BS 1950). DPM 1957; MRCPsych 1971. Various appointments at: Royal Free Hosp., 1951–53; Maudsley Hosp. and Bethlem Royal Hosp., 1954–58; Guy's Hosp., 1958–60; Home Office, 1961–71; DHSS, later DoH, 1971–90. Vis. Psychiatrist, Holloway Prison, 1962–67; Adviser: C of E Children's Soc., 1962–; Royal Philanthropic Soc., 1962–; WRAF Health Educn Scheme, 1962–67. Consultant to: Law Commn, 1991–93; Carnegie Inquiry into the Third Age, 1991–92; Nat. Audit Office, 1992–94. Chairman: WHO Working Gp on Youth Advisory Services, 1976; WHO Meeting of Nat. Mental Health Advrs, 1979. Member: Council of Europe Select Cttee of Experts on Alcoholism, 1976–77; Cttee of Experts on Legal Problems in the Medical Field, 1979–80; UK Delegn to UN Commn on Narcotic Drugs, 1980–86; Organising Cttee, World Summit of Ministers of Health on Progs for AIDS Prevention, 1988; Review of Prison Med. Services, 1990. Chm. Appeals Cttee, Somerset Red Cross, 1999–. FRSocMed. QHP 1984–87. *Publications:* contribs to various professional jls and Govt pubns. *Recreations:* antiquities, humanities, ballet, films, tennis, seafaring and expeditions. *Address:* Flat 54, Berkeley Plaza, 39 Hill Street, Mayfair, W1J 5LZ. *T:* (020) 7491 4028.

MASON, Dr Paul James, FRS 1995; Chief Scientist, Meteorological Office, since 1991; *b* 16 March 1946; *s* of Charles Ernest Edward Mason and Phyllis Mary Mason (*née* Swan); *m* 1968, Elizabeth Mary Slaney; one *s* one *d. Educ:* Univ. of Nottingham (BSc Physics 1967); Univ. of Reading (PhD Geophysics 1972). Meteorological Office: SO, 1967–71; SSO, 1971–74; PSO, 1974–79; Head, Meteorological Res. Unit, Cardington, 1979–85; Asst Dir, Boundary Layer Br., 1985–89; Dep. Dir, Physical Res., 1989–91. Vis. Prof., Univ. of Surrey, 1995–. Member: Editing Cttee, Qly Jl Meteorology, 1983–88; Editl Bd, Boundary Layer Meteorology, 1988–. Royal Meteorological Society: Mem. Council, 1989–90; Vice Pres., 1990–92 and 1994–95; Pres., 1992–94. L. G. Groves Prize for Meteorology, MoD, 1980; Buchan Prize, RMetS, 1986. *Publications:* scientific papers in meteorology and fluid dynamics jls. *Recreations:* walking, exploring the countryside. *Address:* Meteorological Office, Room 321a, London Road, Bracknell, Berks RG12 2SZ. *T:* (01344) 854604.

MASON, Peter; *see* Mason, G. F. P.

MASON, Peter Geoffrey, MBE 1946; High Master, Manchester Grammar School, 1962–78; *b* 22 Feb. 1914; *o s* of Harry Mason, Handsworth, Birmingham; *m* 1st, 1939, Mary Evelyn Davison (marr. diss.); three *d*; 2nd, 1978, Elizabeth June Bissell (*d* 1983); 3rd, 1985, Marjorie Payne. *Educ:* King Edward's Sch., Birmingham; Christ's Coll., Cambridge (Scholar). Goldsmith Exhibitioner, 1935; Porson Scholar, 1936; 1st Class, Classical Tripos, Pts 1 and 2, 1935, 1936. Sixth Form Classical Master, Cheltenham Coll., 1936–40, Rugby Sch., 1946–49; Headmaster, Aldenham Sch., 1949–61. War Service, 1940–46: commissioned into Intelligence Corps, 1940; various staff appointments including HQ 21 Army Group; later attached to a dept of the Foreign Office. Member: Advisory Cttee on Education in the Colonies, 1956; ITA Educnl Adv. Council, 1964–69; Council, University of Salford, 1969–87; Council, British Volunteer Programme (Chm., 1966–74); Chairman: Council of Educn for World Citizenship, 1966–83; Reg. Conf. on IVS, 1972–82; (first), Eur. Council of Nat. Assocs of Indep. Schs, 1988–94, Hon. Life Pres., 1994; Hon. Dir of Research, ISIS, 1981–. *Publications:* Private Education in the EEC, 1983; Private Education in the USA and Canada, 1985; Private Education in Australia and New Zealand, 1987; Independent Education in Southern Africa, 1990; Independent Education in Western Europe, 1992, 2nd edn 1997; articles and reviews in classical and educational journals. *Recreations:* travel, fly-fishing, walking. *Address:* Leeward, Longborough, Moreton-in-Marsh, Glos GL56 0QR. *T:* and *Fax:* (01451) 830147; *e-mail:* xbf15@dial.pipex.com. *Club:* East India.

MASON, Peter James; Chief Executive Officer, AMEC plc, since 1996; *b* 9 Sept. 1946; *s* of Harvey John Mason and Jenny Mason (*née* Wilson); *m* 1st, 1969, Elizabeth Ann McLaren (marr. diss. 1992); two *s*; 2nd, 1997, Beverly Ann Hunter. *Educ:* Marr Coll., Troon; Univ. of Glasgow (BSc Hons Engrg 1968). Norwest Holst Group Ltd, 1980–92; Man. Dir, Civil Engrg Div., 1980–86; CEO, 1986–92; Chm., 1990–92; BICC plc, 1992–96: Dir, 1993–96; CEO, 1992–96, Chm., 1994–96, Balfour Beatty Ltd. Board Mem., British Trade Internat., 2000–. *Recreations:* opera, sailing, gardening. *Address:* c/o 65 Carter Lane, EC4V 5HF. *T:* (020) 7634 0009.

MASON, Rt Rev. Peter Ralph; *see* Ontario, Bishop of.

MASON, Rachel Anne, (Mrs A. L. Mason); *see* Squire, R. A.

MASON, Air Vice-Marshal Richard Anthony, CB 1988; CBE 1981; Professor, Birmingham University, since 1996 (Director, Centre for Studies in Security and Diplomacy, 1988–2001); *b* 22 Oct. 1932; *s* of William and Maud Mason; *m* 1956, Margaret Stewart; one *d. Educ:* Bradford Grammar Sch.; St Andrews Univ. (MA); London Univ. (MA); DSc Birmingham 1997. Commissioned RAF, 1956; Director of Defence Studies, 1977; Director of Personnel (Ground), 1982; Deputy Air Secretary, 1984; Air Sec., 1985–89. Leverhulme Airpower Res. Dir, Foundn for Internat. Security, 1989–94. Hon. Freeman, Bor. of Cheltenham, 2001. *Publications:* Air Power in the Next Generation (ed), 1978; Readings in Air Power, 1979; (with M. J. Armitage) Air Power in the Nuclear Age, 1981; The RAF Today and Tomorrow, 1982; British Air Power in the 1980s, 1984; The Soviet Air Forces, 1986; War in the Third Dimension, 1986; Air Power and Technology, 1986; To Inherit the Skies, 1990; Air Power: a centennial appraisal, 1994; Air and Space Power: revised roles and technology, 1998; articles in internat. jls on defence policy and strategy. *Recreations:* Rugby, writing, gardening. *Address:* c/o Lloyds TSB, Montpelier Walk, Cheltenham GL50 1SH. *Club:* Royal Air Force.

MASON, Prof. Sir Ronald, KCB 1980; FRS 1975; Professor of Chemistry, University of Sussex, 1971–88 (Pro-Vice-Chancellor, 1977); Chairman: British Ceramic Research Ltd, 1990–96; University College Hospitals NHS Trust, 1992–2001; *b* 22 July 1930; *o s* of David John Mason and Olwen Mason (*née* James); *m* 1952, E. Pauline Pattinson; three *d*; *m* 1979, Elizabeth Rosemary Grey-Edwards. *Educ:* Univ. of Wales (Fellow, University College Cardiff, 1981); London Univ. (Fellow, UCL, 1996). CChem, FRSC; FIM 1993. Research Assoc., British Empire Cancer Campaign, 1953–61; Lectr, Imperial Coll., 1961–63; Prof. of Inorganic Chemistry, Univ. of Sheffield, 1963–71; Chief Scientific Advr, MoD, 1977–83. Vis. Prof., Univs in Australia, Canada, France, Israel, NZ and US, inc. A. D. Little Prof., MIT, 1970; Univ. of California, Berkeley, 1975; Ohio State Univ., 1976; North Western Univ., 1977; Prof. associé, Univ. de Strasbourg, 1976; Erskine Vis. Prof., Christchurch, NZ, 1977; Prof., Texas, 1982; Vis. Prof. of Internat. Relns, UCW, 1985–95. Schmidt Meml Lectr, Israel, 1977. SRC: Mem., 1971–75; Chm. Chemistry Cttee, 1969–72; Chm. Science Bd, 1972–75; Consultant and Council Mem., RUSI, 1984–88; UK Mem., UN Commn of Disarmament Studies, 1984–92; Chairman: Council for Arms Control, 1986–90; Engrg Technol. Cttee, DTI, 1991–93. Pres., BHRA, 1986–94 (Chm., BHR Gp, 1990–95); Member: ABRC, 1977–83; BBC Adv. Group, 1975–79. Chairman: Hunting Engineering Ltd, 1987 (Dep. Chm., 1985–87); Science Applications Internat. Corp. (UK) Ltd, 1993–96; Xtreamis plc, 1998–2000. Pres., Inst. of Materials, 1995–96. Foundation Chm., Stoke Mandeville Burns and Reconstructive Surgery Res. Trust, 1990–94. Hon. FIMechE 1997. Hon. DSc: Wales, 1986; Keele, 1992. Corday-Morgan Medallist, 1965, and Tilden Lectr, 1970, Chemical Society; Medal and Prize for Structural Chem., Chem. Soc., 1973. *Publications:* (ed) Advances in Radiation Biology, 1964 (3rd edn 1969); (ed) Advances in Structure Analysis by Diffraction Methods, 1968 (6th edn 1978); (ed) Physical Processes in Radiation Biology, 1964; many papers in Jl Chem. Soc., Proc. Royal Soc., etc, and on defence issues. *Address:* Chestnuts Farm, Weedon, Bucks HP22 4NH.

MASON, Stanley; *see* Mason, J. S.

MASON, Stephen; *see* Mason, J. S.

MASON, Prof. Stephen Finney, FRS 1982; FRSC; Emeritus Professor of Chemistry, University of London; *b* 6 July 1923; *s* of Leonard Stephen Mason and Christine Harriet Mason; *m* 1955, Joan Banus; three *s. Educ:* Wyggeston Sch., Leicester; Wadham Coll., Oxford. MA, DPhil, DSc. Demonstrator, Mus. of Hist. of Sci., Oxford Univ., 1947–53; Research Fellow in Med. Chemistry, ANU, 1953–56; Reader in Chemical Spectroscopy, Univ. of Exeter, 1956–64; Professor of Chemistry: Univ. of East Anglia, 1964–70; KCL, 1970–87. Fellow, Wolfson Coll., Cambridge, 1988–90; FKC 1997. *Publications:* A History of the Sciences: main currents of scientific thought, 1953; Molecular Optical Activity and the Chiral Discriminations, 1982; Chemical Evolution: origin of the elements, molecules and living systems, 1991; articles in Jl Chem. Soc., 1945–. *Recreations:* history and philosophy of science. *Address:* 12 Hills Avenue, Cambridge CB1 7XA. *T:* (01223) 247827.

MASON, (Tania) Jane; Regional Chairman of Employment Tribunals, London Central Region, since 2000; *b* 25 Sept. 1936; *d* of late Edward Warner Moeran, sometime MP, and of Pymonie (*née* Fincham); *m* 1961, James Stephen Mason, *qv*; one *s* two *d. Educ:*

Frensham Heights Sch. Called to the Bar, Inner Temple, 1961. Law Reporter, Judicial Cttee of Privy Council, 1976–83; Asst Legal Advr, British Council, 1983–86; full-time Chm. of Industrial Tribunals, 1986–92; Regional Chairman: Industrial Tribunals, London S Reg., 1992–97; Industrial, later Employment, Tribunals, London N Reg., 1997–2000. *Recreations:* country life, English novels, culinary arts. *Address:* Cannon Cottage, Well Road, Hampstead, NW3 1LH. *T:* (020) 7435 2917. *Club:* Reform.

MASON, Timothy Ian Godson; arts and heritage consultant; Director, Museums & Galleries Commission, 1995–2000; *b* 11 March 1945; *s* of late Ian Godson Mason and Muriel (*née* Vaile); *m* 1975, Marilyn Ailsa Williams; one *d* one *s*. *Educ:* St Alban's Sch., Washington, DC; Bradfield Coll., Berkshire; Christ Church, Oxford (MA). Assistant Manager, Oxford Playhouse, 1966–67; Assistant to Peter Daubeny, World Theatre Season, London, 1967–69; Administrator: Ballet Rambert, 1970–75; Royal Exchange Theatre, Manchester, 1975–77; Director: Western Australian Arts Council, 1977–80; Scottish Arts Council, 1980–90; Consultant on implementation of changes in structure of arts funding, Arts Council of GB, 1990–91; Chief Exec., London Arts Bd, 1991–95. Mem., Gen. Adv. Council, BBC, 1990–96. *Recreations:* family, travelling, the arts. *Address:* 30 Chatsworth Way, SE27 9HN. *T:* (020) 8761 1414.

MASON, William Ernest, CB 1983; Deputy Secretary (Fisheries and Food), Ministry of Agriculture, Fisheries and Food, 1982–89, retired; *b* 12 Jan. 1929; *s* of Ernest George and Agnes Margaret Mason; *m* 1959, Jean (*née* Bossley); one *s* one *d*. *Educ:* Brockley Grammar Sch.; London Sch. of Economics (BScEcon). RAF, 1947–49; Min. of Food, 1949–54; MAFF, 1954; Principal 1963; Asst Sec. 1970; Under Sec., 1975; Fisheries Sec., 1980. Dir, Allied-Lyons, then Allied Domecq, PLC, 1989–98; consultant on food and drink industry, 1989–98. Member: Econ. Develt Cttee for Distrib. Trades, 1975–80; Econ. Develt Cttee for Food and Drink Manufg Inds, 1976–80; Adv. Bd, Inst. of Food Res., 1993–98. FRSA 1989; FIGD 1989; Hon. FIFST 1989. Hon. Keeper of the Quaiche, 1989–. *Recreations:* music, reading, modern British painting. *Address:* 82 Beckenham Place Park, Beckenham, Kent BR3 5BT. *T:* (020) 8650 8241. *Club:* Reform.

MASRI, Taher Nashat, Order of the Renaissance (Jewelled), Jordan, 1991; Order of Al-Kawkab, Jordan, 1974; Hon. GBE 1988; Member of Senate, Jordan, since 1998; *b* 5 March 1942; *s* of Nashat Masri and Hadiyah Solh; *m* 1968, Samar Bitar; one *s* one *d*. *Educ:* North Texas State Univ. (BBA 1965). Central Bank of Jordan, 1965–73; MP Nablus District, Jordan, 1973–74, 1984–88, 1989–97; Minister of State for Occupied Territories Affairs, 1973–74; Ambassador to: Spain, 1975–78; France, 1978–83; Belgium (non-resident), 1978–80; Britain, 1983–84; Perm. Delegate to UNESCO, 1978–83; Foreign Minister, 1984–89 and 1991; Dep. Prime Minister and Minister of State for Economic Affairs, April–Aug. 1989; Chm., Foreign Relations Cttee, 1989–91; Prime Minister of Jordan and Minister of Defence, June–Nov. 1991; Speaker of Lower House of Parlt, 1993–94. Rapporteur, Royal Commn for Drafting of Nat. Charter, 1989. Chm., Bd of Trustees, Jordan Univ. of Sci. and Technol., 1999–. Grand Cross, Order of Civil Merit, Spain, 1977; Order of Isabel the Catholic, Spain, 1978; Commander, Legion of Honour, France, 1981. *Address:* PO Box 5550, Amman 11183, Jordan. *T:* (6) 592600, (office) 4642227, *Fax:* (6) 4642226.

MASSE, Hon. Marcel, OQ; PC (Can.); Président, Commission franco-québécoise sur les lieux de mémoire communs, since 1997; *b* 27 May 1936; *s* of Rosaire Masse and Angeline Masse (*née* Clermont); *m* 1960, Cécile, *d* of René and Clementine Martin; one *s* one *d*. *Educ:* Ecole Normale Jacques-Cartier, Montréal; Univ. de Montréal; Inst. of Pol Sci., Paris; Sorbonne, Paris; City of London Coll.; Inst. Européen d'Admin. des Affaires, Fontainebleau. History teacher, Joliette, Québec, 1962–66; Mem., Québec Nat. Assembly, 1966–73 (Minister, 1966–70); Dir, Lavalin Inc., Montréal, 1974–84; MP (Progressive C) Frontenac, Québec, 1984–93; Minister of Communications, Canada, 1984–86, 1989–91; Minister of Energy, Mines and Resources, 1986–89; Minister of National Defence, 1991–93; Quebec Deleg. Gen. in Paris, 1996–97. Pres., Commn des biens culturels du Québec, 1997–2000. Officer, Legion of Honour (France). *Recreations:* reading, music, fishing, ski-ing. *Address:* 165 chemin Côte St Catherine, Apt 1109, Outremont, QC H2V 2A7, Canada. *Club:* Garrison (Quebec).

MASSER, Prof. (Francis) Ian, PhD; Professor of Urban Planning, International Institute for Aerospace Survey and Earth Sciences, Netherlands, since 1998; *b* 14 Sept. 1937; *s* of late Francis Masser and Isabel Masser (*née* Haddaway); *m* 1st, 1962, Alexandra Arnold (*d* 1988); two *d*; 2nd, 1996, Susan Parkin. *Educ:* Malton Grammar Sch.; Univ. of Liverpool (BA, MCD, PhD 1975; LittD 1993). MRTPI 1964. Leverhulme Res. Fellow, UC of Rhodesia and Nyasaland, 1960–61; Associate Planner, Shankland Cox Associates, 1962–64; Lectr, then Sen. Lectr, Univ. of Liverpool, 1964–75; Prof. and Hd of Inst. of Urban and Regional Planning, Univ. of Utrecht, 1975–79; University of Sheffield: Prof. of Town and Regl Planning, 1979–98; Hd, Dept of Town and Regional Planning, 1979–86; Dean, Faculty of Architectural Studies, 1981–84 and 1992–95; Chm., Sheffield Centre for Envmtl Res., 1979–92. Visiting Professor: Hitotsubashi Univ., Tokyo, 1986; Poly. of Turin, 1993–94. Ed., Papers of Regl Sci. Assoc., 1975–80. Nat. Co-ordinator, ESRC Regl Res. Lab. Initiative, 1986–91; Co-Dir, ESF GISDATA scientific prog., 1991–97. Councillor: Regl Sci. Assoc., 1975–78 (Vice-Pres., 1980–81); Assoc. for Geographic Information, 1991–94, 1999–; Chm., Res. Assessment Evaluation Cttee on Geographical and Envmtl Sci., Assoc. of Univs in Netherlands, 1995–96; Pres., European Umbrella Orgn for Geographic Information, 1999–. FRSA 1983. *Publications:* Analytical Models for Urban and Regional Planning, 1972; Inter-regional Migration in Tropical Africa, 1975; (ed) Spatial Representation and Spatial Interaction, 1978; (ed) Evaluating Urban Planning Efforts, 1983; (ed) Learning from Other Countries, 1985; (ed) Handling Geographic Information, 1991; Geography of Europe's Futures, 1992; (ed) Diffusion and Use of Geographic Information Technologies, 1993; (ed) Planning for Cities and Regions in Japan, 1994; Geographical Information Systems and Organisations, 1995; (ed) GIS Diffusion, 1996; Governments and Geographic Information, 1998. *Recreations:* walking, travel. *Address:* White Cottage, Priestcliffe, near Buxton, Derbys SK17 9TN. *T:* (01298) 85232.

MASSEREENE, 14th Viscount *cr* 1660, **AND FERRARD,** 7th Viscount *cr* 1797; **John David Clotworthy Whyte-Melville Foster Skeffington;** Baron Loughneugh (Ire.), 1660; Baron Oriel (Ire.), 1790; Baron Oriel (UK), 1821; stockbroker with M.D. Barnard & Co.; *b* 3 June 1940; *s* of 13th Viscount and Annabelle Kathleen, *er d* of H. D. Lewis; *S* father, 1992; *m* 1970, Ann Denise, *er d* of late Norman Rowlandson; two *s* one *d*. *Educ:* St Peter's Court, Millfield; Institute Monte Rosa. Grenadier Guards, 1958–61. Stock Exchange, 1961–64; motor trade, 1964–70; Stock Exchange, 1970–; various dirships; landowner. *Recreations:* vintage cars, stalking, shooting. *Heir:* *s* Hon. Charles John Clotworthy Whyte-Melville Foster Skeffington, *b* 7 Feb. 1973. *Clubs:* Turf, Pratt's.

MASSEVITCH, Prof. Alla Genrikhovna; Chief Scientist of the Astronomical Institute of the Russian Academy of Sciences, since 1988 (Vice-President, 1952–88); Professor of Astrophysics, Moscow University, since 1946; *b* Tbilisi, Georgia, USSR, 9 Oct. 1918; *d* of Genrick Massevitch and Natalie Zhgenti; *m* 1942, Joseph Friedlander; one *d*. *Educ:* Moscow Univ. Lectured at the Royal Festival Hall, London, and at the Free Trade Hall, Manchester, etc., on The Conquest of Space, 1960; in charge of network of stations for tracking Sputniks, in Russia, 1957–93. Pres. Working Group 1 (Tracking and Telemetring) of COSPAR (Internat. Cttee for Space Research) 1961–66. Pres., Commission 35 (Internal Structure of Stars) of the Internat. Astronom. Union, 1967–70; Dep. Sec. Gen., UNISPACE 82 (UN Conf. on Exploration and Peaceful Uses of Outer Space), Vienna, 1981–83. Chm., Space Science Studies Cttee, Internat. Acad. of Astronautics, 1983–86; Associate Editor, Astrophysics and Space Science, 1987–94; Mem. Editorial Bd, Astrophysics (Russian), 1985–; Editor of series: Vital Problems of Astrophysics, 1987–; Vital Problems of Space Research, 1987–. Foreign Member: Royal Astronomical Soc., 1963; Indian Nat. Acad. of Sciences, 1979; Austrian Acad. Scis, 1985; Internat. Acad. Astronautics, 1964. Vice-President: Inst. for Russian-American Relations (formerly Soviet-American Relations), 1967–; USSR Peace Cttee, 1977–92 (Mem. Bd, 1965–92); Mem. Bd, Internat. Peace Cttee, 1965–92. Hon. Mem., Russian Acad. of Cosmonautics, 1996. Internat. Award for Astronautics (Prix Galabert), 1963; Govtl decorations, USSR, Sign of Honour, 1963, Red Banner, 1975; USSR State Prize, 1975. Hon. Scientist Emeritus, 1978. *Publications:* Use of Satellite Tracking Data for Geodesy (monograph), 1980; Physics and Evolution of Stars (monograph), 1988; 159 scientific papers on the internal structure of the stars, stellar evolution, and optical tracking of artificial satellites, in Russian and foreign astronomical and geophysical journals. *Address:* 48 Pjatnitskaja Street, Moscow 109017, Russia. *T:* (095) 2313980, *Fax:* (095) 2302081; Pushkarev per 6, Apt 4, Moscow 103045; *e-mail:* vmyakutin@inasan.zssi.zu. *Club:* Club for Scientists (Moscow).

MASSEY, family name of **Baroness Massey of Darwen.**

MASSEY OF DARWEN, Baroness *cr* 1999 (Life Peer), of Darwen in the county of Lancashire; **Doreen Elizabeth Massey;** independent consultant in health education, sex education and sexual health; *b* 5 Sept. 1938; *d* of Mary Ann Hall (*née* Sharrock) and Jack Hall; *m* 1966, Dr Leslie Massey; two *s* one *d*. *Educ:* Darwen Grammar Sch., Lancs; Birmingham Univ. (BA Hons French 1961); DipEd 1962; Inst. of Educn, London Univ. (MA 1985). Graduate service overseas, Gabon, 1962–63; teacher: S Hackney Sch., 1964–67; Springside Sch., Philadelphia, 1967–69; Pre-School Play Group Association, 1973–77; teacher, Walsingham Sch., London, 1977–83 (co-ordinator Health Educn, Head of Year, senior teacher); advisory teacher for personal, social and health educn, ILEA, 1983–85; Manager, Young People's Programme, Health Educn Council, 1985–87; Dir of Educn, 1987–89, Dir, 1989–94, FPA. Member: Brook Adv. Centres; Nat. Trust; Dir, Adv. Council on Alcohol and Drug Educn; Trustee, Trust for Study of Adolescence; school governor. FRSA 1992. *Publications:* Sex Education: Why, What and How?, 1988; Sex Education Factpack, 1988; (jtly) Sex Education Training Manual, 1991; (ed) Sex Education Resource Book, 1994; (ed) The Lover's Guide Encyclopedia, 1996; articles on sex educn, family planning, health educn. *Recreations:* reading, cinema, theatre, opera, art and design, yoga, pilates, sports, vegetarian cookery, travel. *Address:* 66 Lessar Avenue, SW4 9HQ.

MASSEY, Anna (Raymond); actress; *b* 11 Aug. 1937; *d* of late Raymond Massey and Adrianne Allen; *m* 1st, 1958, Jeremy Huggins (marr. diss., 1963; he *d* 1995); one *s*; 2nd, 1988, Uri Andres. *Educ:* London; New York; Switzerland; Paris; Rome. *Plays:* The Reluctant Debutante, 1955; Dear Delinquent, 1957; The Elder Statesman, 1958; Double Yolk, 1959; The Last Joke, 1960; The Miracle Worker, 1961; The School for Scandal, 1962; The Doctor's Dilemma, 1963; The Right Honourable Gentleman, 1964; The Glass Menagerie, 1965; The Prime of Miss Jean Brodie, 1966; The Flip Side, 1967; First Day of a New Season, 1967; This Space is Mine, 1969; Hamlet, 1970; Spoiled, 1971; Slag, 1971; Jingo, 1975; Play, 1976; The Seagull, 1981; Broadway Bound, 1991; A Hard Heart, 1992; Grace, 1992; Moonlight, 1993; *at National Theatre:* Heartbreak House, 1975; Close of Play, 1979; Summer; The Importance of Being Earnest; A Kind of Alaska, and Family Voices, in Harold Pinter trio Other Places, 1982; King Lear, 1986; Mary Stuart, 1996. *Films:* Gideon's Day, 1957; Peeping Tom, 1960; Bunny Lake is Missing, 1965; The Looking Glass War, 1969; David Copperfield, 1969; De Sade, 1971; Frenzy, 1972; A Doll's House, 1973; Sweet William, 1979; The Corn is Green, 1979; Five Days One Summer, 1982; Another Country, 1984; The Chain, 1985; Le Couleur du Vent, 1988; The Tall Guy, 1989; Haunted, 1995; The Grotesque, 1995; The Slab Boys, 1997; Déjà Vu, 1997; Captain Jack, 1999; Mad Cows, 1999; Dark Blue World, 2000; Room to Rent, 2001. *Films for television:* Journey into the Shadows, Sakharov, 1984; Sacred Hearts, 1985; Hotel du Lac, 1986; The Christmas Tree, 1987; Sunchild, 1988; A Tale of Two Cities, 1989; Man From the Pru, 1990; The Sleeper, 2000; The Importance of Being Earnest, 2001; numerous appearances in TV plays, including Shalom, Joan Collins, 1990; A Respectable Trade (series), 1998. *Address:* c/o Markham and Froggatt Ltd, 4 Windmill Street, W1P 1HF.

MASSEY, (Robert) Graham; Managing Director, The Science Archive Ltd, since 1996; *b* 28 Sept. 1943; *s* of Robert Albert Massey and Violet Edith Massey (*née* Smith); *m* 1965, Allison Ruth Duerden; one *s* one *d*. *Educ:* Manchester Grammar Sch.; Balliol Coll., Oxford (BA 1st Cl. Hons History). Joined BBC 1965 as general trainee; Producer, Science and Features Dept, 1970; Producer, 1972, Editor, 1981–85, Horizon; Series Producer, Making of Mankind (with Richard Leakey), 1979–81; Head, Special Features Unit, BBC Drama, 1985–89; Head, Science and Features Dept, BBC, 1989–91; Dir, Co-productions, 1991–92, Dir, Internat., 1992–94, BBC Enterprises. *Recreations:* theatre, cinema, cooking. *Address:* 2 Gregory Place, Holland Street, W8 4NG.

MASSEY, Roy Cyril, MBE 1997; Organist and Master of the Choristers, Hereford Cathedral, 1974–2001; *b* 9 May 1934; *s* of late Cyril Charles Massey and Beatrice May Massey; *m* 1975, Ruth Carol Craddock Grove. *Educ:* Univ. of Birmingham (BMus); privately with David Willcocks. FRCO (CHM); ADCM; ARCM; FRSCM (for distinguished services to church music) 1972. Organist: St Alban's, Conybere Street, Birmingham, 1953–60; St Augustine's, Edgbaston, 1960–65; Croydon Parish Church, 1965–68; Warden, RSCM, 1965–68; Conductor, Croydon Bach Soc., 1966–68; Special Comr of RSCM, 1964–; Organist to City of Birmingham Choir, 1954–; Organist and Master of Choristers, Birmingham Cath., 1968–74; Dir of Music, King Edward's Sch., Birmingham, 1968–74. Conductor, Hereford Choral Soc., 1974–2001; Conductor-in-Chief, alternate years Associate Conductor, Three Choirs Festival, 1975–2001; Advisor on organs to dioceses of Birmingham and Hereford, 1974–. Mem. Council and Examiner, RCO, 1970 94 and 1997–; Mem., Adv. Council, 1976–78, Council, 1984–98, RSCM; Mem. Council, Friends of Cathedral Music, 1999–. President: Birmingham Organists' Assoc., 1970–75; Cathedral Organists' Assoc., 1982–84; IAO, 1991–93. Fellow, St Michael's Coll., Tenbury, 1976–85. DMus Lambeth, 1990. *Recreations:* motoring, old buildings, climbing the Malvern Hills. *Address:* 2 King John's Court, Tewkesbury, Glos GL20 6EG.

MASSEY, Prof. Vincent, PhD; FRS 1977; J. Lawrence Oncley Distinguished University Professor of Biological Chemistry, University of Michigan, since 1995; *b* 28 Nov. 1926; *s* of Walter Massey and Mary Ann Massey; *m* 1950, Margot Eva Ruth Grünewald; one *s* two *d*. *Educ:* Univ. of Sydney (BSc Hons 1947); Univ. of Cambridge (PhD 1952).

Scientific Officer, CSIRO, Australia, 1947–50; Ian McMaster Scholar, Cambridge, 1950–53, ICI Fellow, 1953–55; Researcher, Henry Ford Hosp., Detroit, 1955–57; Lectr, then Sen. Lectr, Univ. of Sheffield, 1957–63; Prof. of Biol Chemistry, Univ. of Michigan, 1963–95. Visiting Professor: Univ. of Ill, 1960; Univ. of Konstanz, Germany, 1973–74 (Permanent Guest Prof., 1975–); Inst. of Applied Biochem., Mitake, Japan, 1985; Guest Prof., Yokohama City Univ., Japan, 1988. Mem., NAS, USA, 1995–. Hon. DSc Tokushima Univ. Med. Sch., 1994. *Publications:* (ed jtly) Flavins and Flavoproteins, 1982, Flavins and Flavoproteins 1996, 1997 (proc. of internat. symposia); over 400 articles in scholarly jls and books. *Recreations:* walking, sailing, gardening. *Address:* Department of Biological Chemistry, University of Michigan, Ann Arbor, MI 48109, USA. *T:* (734) 7647196, *Fax:* (734) 7634581; *e-mail:* massey@umich.edu.

MASSEY, William Greville Sale; QC 1996; barrister; *b* 31 Aug. 1953; *s* of Lt Col Patrick Massey, MC and Bessie Lee Massey (*née* Byrne); *m* 1978, Cecilia D'Oyly Awdry; three *s*. *Educ:* Harrow; Hertford Coll., Oxford (Entrance Schol.; MA). Called to the Bar, Middle Temple, 1977 (Harmsworth Exhibnr). Member: Revenue Bar Assoc., 1978–; Chancery Bar Assoc., 1980–; London Commercial and Common Law Bar Assoc., 1980–. *Recreations:* chess, cricket, opera, gardening, ski-ing. *Address:* Pump Court Tax Chambers, 16 Bedford Row, WC1R 4EB. *T:* (020) 7414 8080.

MASSIE, Allan Johnstone, FRSL; author and journalist; *b* 19 Oct. 1938; *s* of late Alexander Johnstone Massie and Evelyn Jane Wilson Massie (*née* Forbes); *m* 1973, Alison Agnes Graham Langlands; two *s* one *d*. *Educ:* Drumtochty Castle Sch.; Trinity College, Glenalmond; Trinity College, Cambridge (BA). Schoolmaster, Drumtochty Castle Sch., 1960–71; TEFL, Rome, 1972–75; fiction reviewer, The Scotsman, 1976–; Creative Writing Fellow: Edinburgh Univ., 1982–84; Glasgow and Strathclyde Univs, 1985–86; columnist: Glasgow Herald, 1985–88; Sunday Times Scotland, 1987–91; Daily Telegraph, 1991–; The Scotsman, 1992–; Daily Mail, 1994–; Sunday Times Scotland, 1996–. Mem., Scottish Arts Council, 1989–91. Trustee, Nat. Museums of Scotland, 1995–98. FRSL 1982; Hon. FRIAS 1997. *Publications: fiction:* Change and Decay In All Around I See, 1978; The Last Peacock, 1980; The Death of Men, 1981; One Night in Winter, 1984; Augustus, 1986; A Question of Loyalties, 1989; The Hanging Tree, 1990; Tiberius, 1991; The Sins of the Fathers, 1991; Caesar, 1993; These Enchanted Woods, 1993; The Ragged Lion, 1994; King David: a novel, 1995; Shadows of Empire, 1997; Antony, 1997; Nero's Heirs, 1999; The Evening of the World, 2001; *non-fiction:* Muriel Spark, 1979; Ill-Met by Gaslight, 1980; The Caesars, 1983; A Portrait of Scottish Rugby, 1984; Colette, 1986; 101 Great Scots, 1987; Byron's Travels, 1988; Glasgow, 1989; The Novel Today, 1990; Edinburgh, 1994; *plays:* Quintet in October; The Minstrel and the Shirra; First-Class Passengers. *Recreations:* reading, lunching, watching cricket, Rugby, horse-racing, smoking, walking the dogs. *Address:* Thirladean House, Selkirk TD7 5LU. *T:* (01750) 20393. *Clubs:* Academy; Selkirk RFC.

MASSIE, Herbert William, CBE 2000 (OBE 1984); Chairman, Disability Rights Commission, since 2000; *b* 31 March 1949; *s* of Herbert Douglas and Lucy Joan Massie. *Educ:* Portland Trng Coll. for Disabled, Mansfield; Hereward Coll., Coventry; Liverpool Poly. (BA Hons 1977); Manchester Poly. (CQSW). Wm Rainford Ltd, 1967–68; W Cheshire Newspapers Ltd, 1968–70; Liverpool Assoc. for Disabled, 1970–72; Disabled Living Foundn, 1977; RADAR, 1978–99 (Dir, 1990–99). Member: Management Cttee, Disabled Drivers Assoc., 1968–71; Exec. Cttee, Assoc. of Disabled Professionals, 1979 (Vice Chm., 1986–94; former Trustee); Careers Service Adv, Council for England, 1979–83; Voluntary Council for Handicapped Children (later Council for Disabled Children), 1980–93 (Vice-Chm., 1985–93); Exec. Cttee, OUTSET, 1983–91; MSC Wkg Party to Review Quota Scheme for Employment of Disabled People, 1984–85; Access Cttee for England, 1984–93; Disabled Persons Tspt Adv. Cttee, 1986–; BR Adv. Gp on Disabled People, 1986–94; Tripscope, 1986– (Vice-Chm., 1989); Nat. Adv. Council on Employment of People with Disabilities, 1991–98; Independent Commn on Social Justice, 1993–94; DSS Panel of Experts on Incapacity Benefit, 1993–94; Cabinet Office Adv. Panel on Equal Opportunities in Sen. CS, 1994–; Nat. Disability Council, 1996–2000 (Dep. Chm., 1997–2000); Bd, Eur. Disability Forum, 1996–2000; Adv. Cttee, New Deal Task Force, 1997–2000; Disability Rights Task Force, 1997–99. 1990 BEAMA Foundation for Disabled People: Sec., 1986–90; Trustee, 1990–2000. Vice Pres., Foundn for Assistive Technol., 2000–; Mem., Honour Council, Rehabilitation Internat., 2000– (UK Nat. Sec., 1993–2000, Dep. Vice-Pres., Europe, 1996–2000). Patron, Disabled Living Services (Manchester), 1990–; Trustee: Independent Living Fund, 1990–93; Habinteg Housing Assoc., 1991–; Mobility Choice, 1998–; Inst. for Employment Studies, 2000–; CSV, 2001–. FRSA 1988. Snowdon Award, 1995. *Publications:* (with M. Greaves) Work and Disability, 1977, 1979; Aspects of the Employment of Disabled People in the Federal Republic of Germany, 1982; (with M. Kettle) Employer's Guide to Disabilities, 1982, 2nd edn 1986; (jtly) Day Centres for Young Disabled People, 1984; Travelling with British Rail, 1985; (with J. Weyers) Wheelchairs and their Use, 1986; (with J. Male) Choosing a Wheelchair, 1990; (with J. Isaacs) Seat Belts and Disabled People, 1990; Social Justice and Disabled People, 1994; Getting Disabled People to Work, 2000; reports and numerous articles. *Recreations:* photography, reading. *Address:* 7th Floor, 222 Gray's Inn Road, WC1X 8HL. *T:* (020) 7211 4547; *e-mail:* bert.massie@drc-gb.org; (home) 4 Moira Close, N17 6HZ. *T:* (020) 8808 0185; *e-mail:* bert@massie.com.

MASSINGHAM, John Dudley, CMG 1986; HM Diplomatic Service, retired; Consul General and Director of Trade Promotion, Johannesburg, 1987–90; *b* 1 Feb. 1930; *yr s* of Percy Massingham and Amy (*née* Sanders); *m* 1952, Jean Elizabeth Beech (*d* 1995); two *s* two *d*. *Educ:* Dulwich Coll.; Magdalene Coll., Cambridge (MA); Magdalen Coll., Oxford. HM Overseas Civil Service, N Nigeria, 1954–59; BBC, 1959–64; HM Diplomatic Service, 1964–: First Secretary, CRO, 1964–66; Dep. High Comr and Head of Chancery, Freetown, 1966–70; FCO, 1970–71; seconded to Pearce Commn, Jan.–May 1972; First Sec. (Information), later Aid (Kuala Lumpur), 1972–75; First Sec. and Head of Chancery, Kinshasa, 1976–77; Chief Sec., Falkland Islands Govt, 1977–79; Consul-General, Durban, June–Dec. 1979; Counsellor (Economic and Commercial), Nairobi, 1980–81; Governor and C-in-C, St Helena, 1981–84; High Comr to Guyana and non-resident Ambassador to Suriname, 1985–87. *Recreations:* bird watching, nature conservation work. *Address:* 24 Cherry Orchard, Pershore, Worcs WR10 1EL.

MASSY, family name of **Baron Massy**.

MASSY, 9th Baron *cr* 1776 (Ire.); **Hugh Hamon John Somerset Massy;** *b* 11 June 1921; *o s* of 8th Baron, and Margaret, 2nd *d* of late Richard Leonard, Meadsbrook, Ashbourne, Co. Limerick, and *widow* of Dr Moran, Tara, Co. Meath; *S* father 1958; *m* 1943, Margaret, *d* of late John Flower, Barry, Co. Meath; four *s* one *d*. *Educ:* Clongowes Wood Coll.; Clayesmore Sch. Served War, 1940–45, Private, RAOC. *Heir:* *s* Hon. David Hamon Somerset Massy, *b* 4 March 1947.

MASSY-GREENE, Sir (John) Brian, AC 1989; Kt 1972; Chairman, Hazelton Air Lines (formerly Hazelton Air Services Investments) Ltd, 1984–97; *b* Tenterfield, NSW, 20 April 1916; *s* of late Sir Walter Massy-Greene, KCMG, and Lula May Lomax; *m* 1942, Margaret Elizabeth Ritchie Sharp, *d* of late Dr Walter Alexander Ramsay Sharp, OBE; two *s* two *d*. *Educ:* Sydney C of E Grammar Sch.; Geelong Grammar Sch.; Clare Coll., Cambridge (MA). Served War 1939–45: New Guinea, AIF, as Lieut, 1942–45. Joined Metal Manufacturers Ltd, as Staff Cadet, 1939; later transferred to their wholly-owned subsid. Austral Bronze Co. Pty Ltd; Gen. Manager, 1953–62. Managing Dir, 1962–76, and Chm., 1966–77, Consolidated Gold Fields Australia Ltd; Chairman: The Bellambi Coal Co. Ltd, 1964–72; Goldsworthy Mining Ltd, 1965–76; The Mount Lyell Mining & Railway Co. Ltd, 1964–76; Lawrenson Alumasc Holdings Ltd, 1964–73 (Dir, 1962–73); Pacific Dunlop (formerly Dunlop Olympic) Ltd, 1979–86 (Dir, 1968–86; Vice-Chm., 1977–79); Santos Ltd, 1984–88 (Dir, 1984); Commonwealth Banking Corp., 1985–88 (Dep. Chm., 1975–85; Dir, 1968–88); Director: Associated Minerals Consolidated Ltd, 1962–76; Commonwealth Mining Investments (Australia) Ltd, 1962–72 and 1978–85; Consolidated Gold Fields Ltd, London, 1963–76; Dalgety Australia Ltd, 1967–78 (Dep. Chm., 1975–78); Zip Holdings Ltd, 1964–73; Australian European Finance Corp., 1975–89 (Chm., 1987–88); Nat. Mutual Life Assoc. Ltd, 1977–85. Member: Exec. Cttee, Australian Mining Industry Council, 1967–78 (Pres. 1971); Manuf. Industries Adv. Council, 1968–77; NSW Adv. Cttee, CSIRO, 1968–75. Mem., Aust. Inst. Mining and Metallurgy. FAIM; FIEAust. *Recreations:* farming, fishing, flying. *Address:* c/o Level 9, 1 York Street, Sydney, NSW 2000, Australia. *T:* (2) 92500077. *Club:* Australian.

MASTER, Simon Harcourt; Group Deputy Chairman, since 1989, and Chairman, General Books Division, since 1992, Random House (formerly Random Century) Group, (Group Managing Director, 1989–90); *b* 10 April 1944; *s* of Humphrey Ronald Master and Rachel Blanche Forshaw (*née* Plumbly); *m* 1969, Georgina Mary Cook Batsford, *d* of Sir Brian Batsford; two *s*. *Educ:* Ardingly Coll.; Univ. de La Rochelle. Hatchards Booksellers, 1963; Pan Books Ltd, 1964, Sen. Editor, 1967; Sen. Editor, B. T. Batsford Ltd, 1969; Pan Books Ltd: Editorial Dir, 1971; Publishing Dir, 1973; Man. Dir, 1980–87; Chief Exec., Random House UK Ltd, 1987–89; Vice Pres., Internat. Random House Inc., 1987–90; Chm. and Chief Exec., Arrow, 1990–92; Vice Pres., Random House (Delaware) Ltd, 1997–99. Non-exec. Dir, HMSO, 1990–95. Publishers Association: Mem. Council, 1989–95, Mem. Bd, 1997–98; Vice Pres., 1995–96 and 2000–01; Pres., 1996–97 and 2001– April 2002). *Recreations:* gardening, golf, old cars. *Address:* Flat 1, St George's Mansions, Causton Street, SW1P 4RZ. *T:* (020) 7630 7121. *Clubs:* Groucho; Sherborne Golf.

MASTERMAN, Crispin Grant, FCIArb; **His Honour Judge Masterman;** a Circuit Judge, since 1995; *b* 1 June 1944; *s* of late Osmond Janson Masterman and Anne Masterman (*née* Bouwens); *m* 1976, Clare Fletcher; one *s* two *d*. *Educ:* St Edward's Sch., Oxford; Univ. of Southampton (BA). FCIArb 1991. Called to the Bar, Middle Temple, 1971; a Recorder, 1988–95. Mem., Council, Cardiff Univ., 1995–. *Recreations:* family and friends, walking, golf. *Address:* 28 South Rise, Llanishen, Cardiff CF14 0RH. *T:* (029) 2075 4072.

MASTERS, Brian Geoffrey John; author; *b* 25 May 1939; *s* of Geoffrey Howard Masters and Mabel Sophia Charlotte (*née* Ingledew). *Educ:* Wilson's Grammar Sch., London; University Coll., Cardiff (BA 1st cl. Hons 1961); Université de Montpellier. FRSA 1989. *Publications:* Molière, 1969; Sartre, 1969; Saint-Exupéry, 1970; Rabelais, 1971; Camus: a study, 1973; Wynyard Hall and the Londonderry Family, 1974; Dreams about HM The Queen, 1974; The Dukes, 1975; Now Barabbas Was A Rotter: the extraordinary life of Marie Corelli, 1978; The Mistresses of Charles II, 1980; Georgiana, Duchess of Devonshire, 1981; Great Hostesses, 1982; Killing for Company: the case of Dennis Nilsen, 1985 (Gold Dagger Award, CWA); The Swinging Sixties, 1985; The Passion of John Aspinall, 1988; Maharana: the Udaipur Dynasty, 1990; Gary, 1990; The Life of E. F. Benson, 1991; The Shrine of Jeffrey Dahmer, 1993; (ed and trans.) Voltaire's Treatise on Tolerance, 1994; Masters on Murder, 1994; The Evil That Men Do, 1996; She Must Have Known: the trial of Rosemary West, 1996; Thunder in the Air: great actors in great roles, 2000. *Recreations:* etymology, stroking cats. *Address:* 47 Caithness Road, W14 0JD. *T:* (020) 7603 6838; 6 Place E. Granier, 34160 Castries, France. *T:* (4) 67875834. *Clubs:* Garrick, Beefsteak, Pratt's, Aspinall's.

MASTERS, Dr Christopher; Chairman, Aggreko plc, since 1997; *b* 2 May 1947; *s* of Wilfred and Mary Ann Masters; *m* 1971, Gillian Mary (*née* Hodson); two *d*. *Educ:* Richmond Sch.; King's Coll. London (BSc, AKC); Leeds Univ. (PhD). Research Chemist, Shell Research, Amsterdam, 1971–77; Corporate Planner, Shell Chemicals UK, 1977–79; Business Develt Manager, Christian Salvesen, 1979–81; Dir of Planning, Merchants Refrigerating Co., NY, 1981–82; Managing Director: Christian Salvesen Seafoods, 1983–86; Christian Salvesen Industrial Services, 1984–89; Chief Exec., Christian Salvesen PLC, 1989–97. Director: British Assets Trust plc, 1990–; Scottish Widows' Fund or Life Assurance Soc, 1992–2000. Chm., Young Enterprise Scotland, 1993–96; Mem., SHEFC, 1995– (Chm., 1998–). Director: Scottish Opera, 1994–99 (Vice Chm., 1996–99); Scottish Chamber Orch., 1995–. FRSE 1996. *Publications:* Homogeneous Transition—Metal Catalysis, 1981, Russian edn 1983; numerous research papers and patents. *Recreations:* music, wine. *Address:* Aggreko plc, Ailsa Court, 121 West Regent Street, Glasgow G2 2SD. *T:* (0141) 225 5900.

MASTERS, Sheila Valerie; *see* Baroness Noakes.

MASTERSON, Valerie, (Mrs Andrew March), CBE 1988; opera and concert singer; *d* of Edward Masterson and Rita McGrath; *m* 1965, Andrew March; one *s* one *d*. *Educ:* Holt Hill Convent; studied in London and Milan on scholarship, and with Edwardo Asquez. Début, Landestheater Salzburg; appearances with: D'Oyly Carte Opera, Glyndebourne Festival Opera, ENO, Royal Opera, Covent Garden, etc; appears in principal opera houses in Paris, Aix-en-Provence, Toulouse, Munich, Geneva, Barcelona, Milan, San Francisco, Chile, etc; leading roles in: La Traviata, Le Nozze di Figaro, Manon, Faust, Alcina, Die Entführung aus dem Serail, Così fan tutte, La Bohème, Semele (SWET award, 1983), Die Zauberflöte, Julius Caesar, Rigoletto, Romeo and Juliet, Carmen, Count Ory, Mireille, Louise, Idomeneo, Les Dialogues des Carmélites, The Merry Widow, Xerxes, Orlando, Lucia di Lammermoor. Recordings include: La Traviata; Elisabetta, Regina d'Inghilterra; Der Ring des Nibelungen; The Merry Widow; Julius Caesar; Scipione; several Gilbert and Sullivan operas. Broadcasts regularly on radio and TV. Vice-Pres., British Youth Opera, 1995–. FRCM; Hon. RAM 1994. Hon. DLitt South Bank, 1999. *Recreations:* tennis, swimming. *Address:* c/o Music International, 13 Ardilaun Road, Highbury, N5 2QR.

MASTERTON-SMITH, Cdre Anthony Philip, RN; CEng; Chief Executive, Royal College of Physicians, since 1998; *b* 2 Aug. 1944; *s* of late Edward Masterton-Smith and Pauline Masterton-Smith (*née* Pilgrim); *m* 1975, Jennifer Sue Sprigings; one *s* one *d*. *Educ:* UCS, Hampstead; BRNC Dartmouth; RNEC Manadon. CEng, MIEE 1973. Royal Navy, 1962–98: HM Ships Fiskerton, Victorious, Llandaff, Bacchante, Scylla, Southampton; Staff of FO Sea Training, 1978–80; CO, HMS Royal Arthur, 1982–84; JSDC, 1986; Dep. Dir, Naval Recruiting, 1988–91; Defence and Naval Attaché, Tokyo, 1992–95; Cdre, BRNC Dartmouth, 1995–98. *Recreations:* opera, gardening, walking, sport. *Address:* Royal College of Physicians, 11 St Andrew's Place, Regent's Park, NW1 4LE.

MASUI, Prof. Yoshio, PhD; FRS 1998; Professor, University of Toronto, 1978–97, now Emeritus; *b* Kyoto, 6 Oct. 1931; adopted Canadian nationality, 1983; *s* of Fusa-jiro Masui and Toyoko Masui; *m* 1959, Yuriko Suda; one *s* one *d*. *Educ:* Kyoto Univ. (BSc 1953; MSc 1955; PhD 1961). Lectr, 1958–65, Asst Prof., 1965–68, Prof. Emeritus, 1999, Konan Univ., Japan; Staff Biologist, 1966–68, Lectr, 1969, Yale Univ.; Associate Prof. of Zoology, Univ. of Toronto, 1969–78. Hon. DSc Toronto, 1999. Albert Lasker Basic Medical Res. Award, 1998. *Address:* Department of Zoology, University of Toronto, 25 Harbord Street, Toronto, ON M5S 3G5, Canada. *T:* (416) 9783493.

MASUR, Kurt; German conductor; Music Director, New York Philharmonic Orchestra, 1992–Sept. 2002 (Guest Conductor, 1981–92); Principal Conductor, London Philharmonic Orchestra, since 2000; *b* 18 July 1927; *m* 3rd, Tomoko Sakurai, soprano; one *s*; four *c* by previous marriages. *Educ:* Nat. Music Sch., Breslau; Leipzig Conservatory. Orch. Coach, Nat. Theatre of Halle, Saxony, 1948–51; Conductor: Erfurt City Theatre, 1951–53; Leipzig City Theatre, 1953–55; Dresden Philharmonic Orch., 1955–58; Music Director: Mecklenburg State Theatre, Schwerin, 1958–60; Komische Oper, E Berlin, 1960–64; Chief Conductor, Dresden Philharmonic Orch., 1967–72; Artistic Dir, Gewandhaus Orch. of Leipzig, 1970–96 (Hon. Mem., 1981; Conductor Laureate, 1996); Guest Conductor: Cleveland Orch, 1974; Philadelphia Orch.; Boston SO; Berlin Philharmonic Orch.; Leningrad Philharmonic Orch.; l'Orchestre de Paris; RPO. Prof., Leipzig Acad. of Music, 1975–. *Address:* New York Philharmonic Orchestra, Avery Fisher Hall, New York, NY 10023, USA; c/o London Philharmonic Orchestra, County Hall, Riverside Building, Westminster Bridge Road, SE1 7PB.

MATACA, Most Rev. Petero; *see* Suva, Archbishop of, (RC).

MATANE, Sir Paulias (Nguna), Kt 1986; CMG 1980; OBE 1975; writer; *b* 21 Sept. 1931; *s* of Ilias Maila Matane and Elsa Toto; *m* 1957, Kaludia Peril Matane; two *s* two *d*. *Educ:* Teacher's College (Dip. Teaching and Education). Asst Teacher, Tauran Sch., PNG, 1957, Headmaster, 1958–61; School Inspector, 1962–66; Dist Sch. Inspector and Dist Educn Officer, 1967–68; Supt, Teacher Educn, 1969; Foundn Mem., Public Service Bd, 1969–70; Sec., Dept of Business Develt, 1971–74; Ambassador to USA, Mexico and UN, and High Comr to Canada, 1975–80; Sec., Foreign Affairs, PNG, 1980–85. Chairman: Treid Pacific (PNG) Pty Ltd, 1986–90; Newton Pacific (PNG) Pty Ltd, 1995–. Chairman: Review Cttee on Philosophy of Educn, 1986; Cocoa Industry Investigating Cttee, 1987; Foundn for Peoples of South Pacific, PNG, 1989–94; PNG Censorship Bd, 1990–97; Children, Women and Families in PNG: a situation analysis, 1996. Producer of regular progs for TV, 1990–, and radio, 1998. Hon. DTech Univ. of Technol., Lae, 1985; Hon. PhD Univ. of PNG, 1986. UN 40th Anniv. Medal, 1985. *Publications:* Kum Tumun of Minj, 1966; A New Guinean Travels through Africa, 1971; My Childhood in New Guinea, 1972; What Good is Business?, 1972; Two New Guineans Travel through SE Asia, 1974; Aimbe the Challenger, 1974; Aimbe the School Dropout, 1974; Aimbe the Magician, 1976; Aimbe the Pastor, 1979; Two Papua New Guineans Discover the Bible Lands, 1987; To Serve with Love, 1989; Chit Chat, vol. 1, 1991, vol. 2, Let's Do It PNG, 1994, vol. 3, 2000; East to West—the longest train trip in the world, 1991; Trekking Through the New Worlds, 1995; Voyage to Antarctica, 1996; Laughter Made in PNG, 1996; Amazing Discoveries in 40 Years of Marriage, 1997; The Other Side of Port Moresby—in pictures, 1998; A Trip of a Lifetime, 1998; The Word Power, 1998; Waliling United Church: then and now, 1998; Coach Adventures Down Under, 1999; Management Problems in Papua New Guinea: some solutions, 2000; Further Management Problems in Papua New Guinea: their solutions, 2000; Management for Excellence, 2001; Exploring the Holy Lands, 2001; Exploring South East Asia, 2 vols, 2001. *Recreations:* reading, gardening, squash, fishing, writing. *Address:* PO Box 680, Rabaul, ENBP, Papua New Guinea. *Clubs:* Tamukavar, Tauran Ex Student and Citizens' (Papua New Guinea).

MATE, Rt Rev. Martin; Bishop of Eastern Newfoundland and Labrador, 1980–92; *b* 12 Nov. 1929; *s* of John Mate and Hilda Mate (*née* Toope); *m* 1962, Florence Hooper, Registered Nurse; two *s* three *d*. *Educ:* Meml Univ. of Newfoundland; Queen's Coll., St John's, Newfoundland (LTh); Bishop's Univ., Lennoxville, PQ. BA (1st Cl. Hons), MA. Deacon 1952, priest 1953; Curate, Cathedral of St John the Baptist, St John's, Newfoundland, 1952–53; Deacon-in-charge and Rector, Parish of Pushthrough, 1953–58; Incumbent, Mission of St Anthony, 1958–64; Rural Dean, St Barbe, 1958–64; Rector of Cookshire, Quebec, 1964–67; Rector of Catalina, Newfoundland, 1967–72; RD of Bonavista Bay, 1970–72; Rector of Pouch Cove/Torbay, 1972–76; Treasurer, Diocesan Synod of E Newfoundland and Labrador, 1976–80. *Publication:* Pentateuchal Criticism, 1967. *Recreations:* carpentry, hunting, fishing, camping. *Address:* 57 Penney Crescent, St John's, NF A1A 5J5, Canada.

MATES, James Michael; Washington Correspondent, ITN, since 1997; *b* 11 Aug. 1961; *s* of Michael John Mates, *qv*; *m* 1991, Fiona Margaret Bennett; two *s* one *d*. *Educ:* Marlborough Coll.; Farnham Coll.; Leeds Univ. (BA Hons). Joined Independent Television News, 1983: Tokyo corresp., 1989–91; North of England corresp., 1991–92; Moscow corresp., 1992–94; Diplomatic Ed., 1994–97. *Recreations:* bridge, tennis, composting. *Address:* c/o Independent TV News, 200 Gray's Inn Road, WC1X 8XZ.

MATES, Lt-Col Michael John; MP (C) East Hampshire, since 1983 (Petersfield, Oct. 1974–1983); *b* 9 June 1934; *s* of Claude John Mates; *m* 1959, Mary Rosamund Paton (marr. diss. 1980); two *s* two *d*; *m* 1982, Rosellen (marr. diss. 1995), *d* of Mr and Mrs W. T. Bett; one *d*. *Educ:* Salisbury Cathedral Sch.; Blundell's Sch.; King's Coll., Cambridge (choral schol.). Joined Army, 1954; 2nd Lieut, RUR, 1955; Queen's Dragoon Guards, RAC, 1961; Major, 1967; Lt-Col, 1973; resigned commn 1974. Minister of State, NI Office, 1992–93. Vice-Chm., Cons. NI Cttee, 1979–81 (Sec., 1974–79); Chairman: Select Cttee on Defence, 1987–92 (Mem., 1979–92); Select Cttee on NI, 2001–; Cons. Home Affairs Cttee, 1987–88 (Vice-Chm., 1979–87); All-Party Anglo-Irish Gp, 1979–92; Sec., 1922 Cttee, 1987–88, 1997–; Mem., Intell. and Security Cttee, 1994–; introduced: Farriers Registration Act, 1975; Rent Amendment Act, 1985. Farriers' Co.: Liveryman, 1975–; Asst, 1981; Master, 1986–87. *Address:* House of Commons, SW1A 0AA.
See also J. M. Mates.

MATHER, Lt-Col Anthony Charles McClure, CVO 1998; OBE 1990 (MBE 1965); Secretary, Central Chancery of the Orders of Knighthood and Assistant Comptroller, Lord Chamberlain's Office, 1991–99; *b* 21 April 1942; *s* of late Eric James Mather and Stella Mather (*née* McClure); *m* 1966, Gaye, *d* of late Dr Eric Lindsay Dickson and Mrs Louise Tillett; one *s* two *d*. *Educ:* Eton College. Commissioned, Grenadier Guards, 1962; served UK, British Guyana, Germany and Hong Kong; retired 1991. An Extra Equerry to the Queen, 1992–. Freeman, City of London, 1998. *Recreations:* gardening, fishing, music. *Address:* The Horseshoes, Chirton, near Devizes, Wilts SN10 3QR. *T:* (01380) 840261. *Club:* Army and Navy.

MATHER, Sir Carol; *see* Mather, Sir D. C. MacD.

MATHER, Sir (David) Carol (Macdonell), Kt 1987; MC 1944; *b* 3 Jan. 1919; *s* of late Loris Emerson Mather, CBE; *m* 1951, Hon. Philippa Selina Bewicke-Copley, *o d* of 5th Baron Cromwell, DSO; one *s* three *d*. *Educ:* Harrow; Trinity Coll., Cambridge. War of 1939–45: commissioned Welsh Guards, 1940; served in Western Desert Campaigns, Commandos, SAS, 1941–42; PoW, 1942; escaped, 1943; NW Europe, 1944–45 (despatches); wounded, 1945; Palestine Campaign, 1946–48. Asst Mil. Attaché, British Embassy, Athens, 1953–56; GSO 1, MI Directorate, War Office, 1957–61; Mil. Sec. to GOC-in-C, Eastern Command, 1961–62; retd as Lt-Col, 1962. Conservative Research Dept, 1962–70; contested (C) Leicester (NW), 1966. MP (C) Esher, 1970–87. An Opposition Whip, 1975–79; a Lord Comr of HM Treasury, 1979–81; Vice-Chamberlain of HM Household, 1981–83; Comptroller of HM Household, 1983–86. FRGS. *Publications:* Aftermath of War: everyone must go home, 1992; When the Grass Stops Growing, 1997. *Club:* Brooks's.

MATHER, Graham Christopher Spencer; solicitor; President: European Policy Forum, since 1992; European Media Forum, since 1997; European Financial Forum, since 1999; *b* 23 Oct. 1954; *er s* of Thomas and Doreen Mather; *m* 1st, 1981, Fiona Marion McMillan (marr. diss. 1995), *e d* of Sir Ronald McMillan Bell, QC, MP and of Lady Bell; two *s*; 2nd, 1997, Geneviève, *widow* of James Seton Fairhurst. *Educ:* Hutton Grammar School; New College, Oxford (Burnet Law Scholar); MA Jurisp. Institute of Directors: Asst to Dir Gen., 1980; Head of Policy Unit, 1983; Institute of Economic Affairs: Dep. Dir, 1987; Gen. Dir, 1987–92. MEP (C) Hampshire N and Oxford, 1994–99. Mem., HM Treasury Working Party on Freeports, 1982. Member: Monopolies and Mergers Commission, 1989–94; Appeal Tribunal, Competition Commn, 2000–. Vis. Fellow, Nuffield Coll., Oxford, 1992–2000. Mem., Westminster City Council, 1982–86; contested (C) Blackburn, 1983. Radio and television broadcaster. Consultant, Tudor Investment Corp., 1992–; Advr, BIFU, 1997–99. Vice-President: Strategic Planning Soc., 1993–; Assoc. of Dist Councils, 1994–97. Past Asst Grand Registrar, United Grand Lodge of England, 1997. *Publications:* lectures, papers and contribs to jls; contribs to The Times. *Address:* European Policy Forum, 125 Pall Mall, SW1Y 5EA. *T:* (020) 7839 7565, *Fax:* (020) 7839 7339; *e-mail:* graham.mather@epfltd.org. *Clubs:* Oxford and Cambridge, Carlton.

MATHER, John Douglas, FCIT, FILDM; CIMgt; Chief Executive, National Freight Consortium plc, 1984–93; *b* 27 Jan. 1936; *s* of John Dollandson and Emma May Mather; *m* 1958, Hilda Patricia (*née* Kirkwood); one *s* (one *d* decd). *Educ:* Manchester Univ. (BACom, MAEcon). MIPM. Personnel Management: Philips Electrical, 1959–66; Convoys Ltd, 1966–67; Personnel Management, Transport Management, National Freight Company, 1967–93. Non-executive Director: Charles Sidney plc (formerly Bletchley Motor Gp), 1993–98; Computer Management Gp, 1993–98; Miller Gp, 1993–; CIT Hldgs, 1994–; CIT Ventures, 1996–; St Mary's (Paddington) NHS Trust, 1995–97. Chairman: Bedfordshire TEC, 1991–93; Camden Business Partnership, 1991–; London Regeneration Consortium plc, 1993–95. Member: Adv. Bd, Cranfield Sch. of Management, 1992–97; Council, Cranfield Univ., 1993–. Trustee, Help The Aged, 1993– (Chm., 1995–). Mem., Co. of Carmen. *Recreations:* golf, gardening, travel. *Address:* Roundhale, Love Lane, Kings Langley, Hertfordshire WD4 9HW. *T:* (01923) 263063. *Clubs:* Royal Automobile; Woburn Golf and Country; La Sella Golf and Country.

MATHER, Richard Martin; Principal, Rick Mather Architects, since 1973; *b* 30 May 1937; *s* of late Richard John Mather and Opal Mather (*née* Martin). *Educ:* Sch. of Architecture and Allied Arts, Univ. of Oregon (BArch); Dept of Urban Design, Architectural Assoc. Teacher, UCL, Univ. of Westminster, and Harvard Grad. Sch. of Design, 1967–88; RIBA External Examiner to univs and colls in England and Scotland, 1986– (Mem. Council, RIBA, 1998–2000). Consultant Architect: Architectural Assoc., 1978–92 (Mem. Council, 1992–96); UEA, 1988–92; Univ. of Southampton, 1996–. Trustee, V & A Mus., 2000–. Projects include: Schs of Educn and of Inf. Systems, and Climatic Res. Unit, UEA (Archtl Design Award, 1986; RIBA Award, 1988); Times Newspaper HQ, London (RIBA Award, 1992); Zen Restaurants, London, Montreal and Hong Kong; further UEA buildings (RIBA Award, 1994; Civic Trust Award, 1995); All Glass Extension and Structure, London (RIBA Nat. Award, 1994); ARCO Building, Keble Coll., Oxford, 1995 (RIBA Award, 1996; Civic Trust Award, 1997); new private house, Hampstead, 1997 (RIBA Nat. Award, 1998; AIA Award, 1997; Civil Trust Award, 1998); ISMA Centre, Univ. of Reading, 1998 (RIBA Award, Civic Trust Award, 1999); Neptune Court, Nat. Maritime Mus., 1999 (Civic Trust Award, 2000); Wallace Collection, 2000; Dulwich Picture Gall., 2000; London South Bank Centre Masterplan, 2000; Masterplans for Ashmolean Mus., Oxford and Stowe Sch., 2001. *Recreations:* gardens, food, ski-ing. *Address:* Rick Mather Architects, 123 Camden High Street, NW1 7JR. *T:* (020) 7284 1727.

MATHERS, Peter James, LVO 1995; HM Diplomatic Service; Counsellor, Commercial and Economic, Stockholm, since 1998; *b* 2 April 1946; *s* of Dr James Mathers and Margaret Mathers (*née* Kendrick); *m* 1983, Elisabeth Hoeller; one *s* one *d*. *Educ:* Bradfield Coll., Berks. Army SSC, 1968–71. Joined HM Diplomatic Service, 1971: SOAS (Persian), 1972–73; Tehran, 1973–75; Bonn, 1976–78; FCO, 1978–81; Copenhagen, 1981–85; Tehran, 1986–87; FCO, 1987–88; on secondment to UN Office, Vienna, 1988–91; FCO, 1991–95; Dep. High Comr, Barbados and Eastern Caribbean, 1995–98. *Address:* c/o Foreign and Commonwealth Office, King Charles Street, SW1A 2AH.

MATHERS, Sir Robert (William), Kt 1981; *b* 2 Aug. 1928; *s* of William Mathers and Olive Ida (*née* Wohlsen); *m* 1957, Betty Estelle Greasley; three *d*. *Educ:* Church of England Grammar Sch., E Brisbane. FAIM; FRMIA 1982. Chm. and Man. Dir, Mathers Enterprises Ltd, 1973–88; Chm., Kinney Shoes (Australia) Ltd, 1988–90; Dep. Chm., Bligh Coal Ltd, 1981–88; Director: Finlayson Timber & Hardware Pty Ltd, 1986–98; Nat. Mutual Life Assoc. of Australasia, 1988–96; Kidston Gold Mines, 1988–96; Buderim Ginger, 1989–95; Coles Myer, 1992–96; Leutenegger, 1992–95; Touraust Funds Management, 1994–96; Australian Tourism Co., 1994–96. Mem., Aust. Adv. Bd, Kmart Corp., USA, 1991–94. Life Mem., Retailers Assoc. of Qld, 1990 (Mem. Council, 1952–90); Pres., Footwear Retailers Assoc., 1960–63. Member: Council, Australian Bicentennial Authority, 1980–89; Finance Adv. Cttee for XII Commonwealth Games, 1979; Australiana Fund, 1980–94; Brisbane Adv. Bd, Salvation Army, 1990–96; Adv. Bd, Bond Univ. Sch. of Business, 1991–96; Councillor: Griffith Univ., 1978–88; Enterprise Australia, 1983–92; Deputy Chairman: Nat. Finance Cttee, Australian Stockman's Hall of Fame and Outback Heritage Centre, 1984–89; Organising Cttee, Brisbane Bid for 1992 Olympics, 1985–88. Trustee: WWF, Australia, 1981–87; Queensland Art Gall., 1983–87 (Founding Cttee Mem., Qld Art Gall. Foundn, 1979). Hon. FAMI 1984; FRSA 1989. DUniv Griffith, 1992. Cavaliere, Order of Merit (Italy), 1983. *Recreations:* golf, tennis, swimming. *Address:* 2/88 Macquarie Street, St Lucia, Qld 4067, Australia. *T:* (7) 38703339. *Clubs:* Rotary, Royal Queensland Yacht Squadron, Tattersalls, Brisbane Polo, Queensland Rugby Union, Indooroopilly Golf (Brisbane).

MATHESON, Alexander, OBE 1990; JP; FRPharmS; Lord-Lieutenant of the Western Isles, since 2001 (Vice Lord-Lieutenant, 1994–2001); Chairman, Highlands and Islands

Airports Ltd, since 2001; *b* 16 Nov. 1941; *s* of Alex Matheson, MB ChB and Catherine Agnes Matheson (*née* Smith), MA; *m* 1965, Irene Mary Davidson, BSc Hons, MSc; two *s* two *d*. *Educ:* Nicolson Inst., Stornoway; Robert Gordon Inst. of Technol., Aberdeen. MRPharmS 1965, FRPharmS 1993. Pharmacist. Man. Dir, 1966–82 and Chm., 1967–, Roderick Smith Ltd. Member: Stornoway Town Council, 1967–75 (Provost, 1971–75); Ross and Cromarty CC, 1967–75. Member: Stornoway Trust Estate, 1967– (Chm., 1971–81); Stornoway Pier and Harbour Commn, 1968– (Chm., 1971–72 and 1993–); Western Isles Island Council, 1974–94 (Convener, 1982–90); Western Isles Health Bd, 1974–2001 (Chm., 1993–2001). Pres., Islands Commn of Peripheral Maritime Regions of Europe, 1988–93. JP Western Is, 1971; Hon. Sheriff, Stornoway, 1972. *Recreations:* genealogy, research and lecturing on local history. *Address:* 33 Newton Street, Stornoway, Isle of Lewis HS1 2RW. *T:* (01851) 702082, *Fax:* (01851) 700415.

MATHESON, Catherine; Executive Director, War on Want, since 1998 (Projects Director, 1996–98); *b* 24 Jan. 1958; *d* of Donald and Alice Matheson; *m* 1988, Duncan Green; two *s*. *Educ:* Lady Margaret Hall, Oxford (BA Hons Hist.); Open Univ. (Postgrad. Dip. Develt Mgt). News trainee, 1981–83, Sub-editor, World Service, 1983–85, BBC; El Salvador corresp., Guardian, 1985–87; Central America corresp., BBC, 1985–87; journalist, for Asia, 1987–92, for Latin America/Caribbean, 1993–96, Christian Aid. Mem., TGWU. *Recreations:* cycling, swimming, touch Rugby, salsa dancing. *Address:* War on Want, Fenner Brockway House, 37–39 Great Guildford Street, SE1 0ES. *T:* (020) 7620 1111.

MATHESON, Duncan, MA, LLM; QC 1989; **His Honour Judge Matheson;** a Circuit Judge, since 2000. Bencher, Inner Temple, 1994. Jun. Counsel in Legal Aid Matters, Law Soc., 1981–89; a Recorder, 1985–2000. Chairman, Legal Aid Area Committee: London S, 1989–92; London, 1992–95. *Address:* Middlesex Guildhall, Broad Sanctuary, SW1P 3BB.

MATHESON of Matheson, Major Sir Fergus (John), 7th Bt *cr* 1882, of Lochalsh, Co. Ross; Chief of Clan Matheson; *b* 22 Feb. 1927; *yr s* of Gen. Sir Torquhil George Matheson, 5th Bt, KCB, CMG and Lady Elizabeth Matheson, ARRC (*d* 1986), *o d* of 8th Earl of Albemarle; *S* brother, 1993; *m* 1952, Hon. Jean Elizabeth Mary Willoughby, *yr d* of 11th Baron Middleton, KG, MC; one *s* two *d*. *Educ:* Eton. Major, Coldstream Guards, 1945–64. One of HM Body Guard of the Hon. Corps of Gentlemen-at-Arms, 1979–97 (Standard Bearer, 1993–97). Pres., St John Ambulance, Norfolk, 1993–96. *Heir:* (to baronetcy and chiefship): *s* Lt-Col Alexander Fergus Matheson, yr of Matheson, Coldstream Guards [*b* 26 Aug. 1954; *m* 1983, Katharine Davina Mary, *o d* of Sir W. R. M. Oswald, *qv*; two *s* one *d*]. *Address:* The Old Rectory, Hedenham, Norfolk NR35 2LD.

MATHESON, Sir (James Adam) Louis, KBE 1976 (MBE 1944); CMG 1972; FTSE; FREng; Vice-Chancellor, Monash University, Melbourne, 1959–76; Chancellor, Papua New Guinea University of Technology, 1973–75; Chairman, Australian Science and Technology Council, 1975–76; *b* 11 Feb. 1912; *s* of William and Lily Edith Matheson; *m* 1937, Audrey Elizabeth Wood; three *s*. *Educ:* Bootham Sch., York; Manchester Univ. (MSc 1933). Lectr, Birmingham Univ., 1938–46 (PhD 1946); Prof. of Civil Engineering, Univ. of Melbourne, Australia, 1946–50; Beyer Prof. of Engineering, Univ. of Manchester, 1951–59. Hon. FICE (Mem. Council, 1965); Hon. FIEAust (Mem. Council, 1961–81, Vice-Pres., 1970–74, Pres., 1975–76); FTSE (FTS 1976); FREng (FEng 1980). Member: Mission on Technical Educn in W Indies, 1957; Royal Commn into failure of King's Bridge, 1963; Ramsay Cttee on Tertiary Educn in Victoria, 1961–63; CSIRO Adv. Council, 1962–67; Exec., Aust. Council for Educational Research, 1964–69; Interim Council, Univ. of Papua New Guinea, 1965–68; Enquiry into Post-Secondary Educn in Victoria, 1976–78; Chairman: Council, Papua New Guinea Inst. of Technology, 1966–73; Aust. Vice-Chancellors' Cttee, 1967–68; Assoc. of Commonwealth Univs, 1967–69; Newport Power Stn Review Panel, 1977; Schools Commn Buildings Cttee, 1977–81; Victorian Planning and Finance Cttee, Commonwealth Schools Commn, 1979–83; Sorrento Harbour Inquiries, 1984 and 1987; St Kilda Harbour Inquiry, 1986. Trustee, Inst. of Applied Science (later Science Mus. of Victoria), 1963–83 (Pres., 1969–73). Dir, Nauru Phosphate Corp., 1977–79. Hon. DSc Hong Kong, 1969; Hon. LLD: Manchester, 1972; Monash, 1975; Melbourne, 1975. Kernot Meml Medal, 1972; Peter Nicol Russell Medal, 1976. *Publications:* Hyperstatic Structures: Vol. 1, 1959; Vol. 2, 1960; Still Learning, 1980; various articles on engineering and education. *Recreations:* music, woodcraft. *Address:* 26/166 West Toorak Road, South Yarra, Victoria 3141, Australia.

MATHESON, Very Rev. James Gunn; Moderator of General Assembly of Church of Scotland, 1975–76; *b* 1 March 1912; *s* of Norman Matheson and Henrietta Gunn; *m* 1937, Janet Elizabeth Clarkson (*d* 1997); three *s* one *d* (and one *d* decd). *Educ:* Inverness Royal Academy; Edinburgh Univ. (MA, BD). Free Church of Olrig, Caithness, 1936–39; Chaplain to HM Forces, 1939–45 (POW Italy, 1941–43); St Columba's Church, Blackhall, Edinburgh, 1946–51; Knox Church, Dunedin, NZ, 1951–61; Sec. of Stewardship and Budget Cttee of Church of Scotland, 1961–73; Parish Minister, Portree, Isle of Skye, 1973–79; retired 1979. Hon. DD Edinburgh, 1975. *Publications:* Do You Believe This?, 1960; Saints and Sinners, 1975; contrib. theol jls. *Recreations:* gardening, fishing. *Address:* 17 Cumberland Street, Edinburgh EH3 6RT.

MATHESON, Maj.-Gen. John Mackenzie, OBE 1950; TD 1969; retired; *b* Gibraltar, 6 Aug. 1912; *s* of late John Matheson and late Nina Short, Cape Town; *m* 1942, Agnes (*d* 1995), *d* of Henderson Purves, Dunfermline; one *d*. *Educ:* George Watson's Coll., Edinburgh; Edinburgh Univ. (Vans Dunlop Schol.). MB, ChB 1936; MRCP 1939; MD 1945; FRCSEd 1946; FRCS 1962; FRCP 1972. Royal Victoria Hosp. Tuberculosis Trust Research Fellow, 1936–37; Lieut, RAMC (TA), 1936. Served War of 1939–45: Middle East, N Africa and Italy; Regular RAMC Commn, 1944 (despatches). Clinical Tutor, Surgical Professorial Unit, Edinburgh Univ., 1947–48; Med. Liaison Officer to Surgeon-Gen. US Army, Washington, DC, 1948–50; Asst Chief, Section Gen. Surgery, Walter Reed Army Hosp., Washington, DC, 1950–51; Cons. Surgeon: MELF, 1963–64; BAOR, 1967; Far East, 1967–69; Jt Prof. Mil. Surg., RAM Coll. and RCS of Eng., 1964–67; Brig. 1967; Comdt and Dir of Studies, Royal Army Med. Coll., 1969–71; Postgrad. Dean, Faculty of Medicine, Univ. of Edinburgh, 1971–80. QHS 1969–71. Hon. Col, 205 (Scottish) Gen. Hosp., T&AVR, 1978–80. Alexander Medal, 1961; Simpson-Smith Memorial Lectr, 1967; Gordon-Watson Lectr, RCS of Eng., 1967; Mitchiner Meml Lectr, RAM Coll., Millbank, 1988. Senior Fellow, Assoc. of Surgeons of GB and Ireland; British Medical Association: Mem., Armed Forces Cttee, 1983–88; Mem., Bd of Educn and Science, 1985–88; Pres., Lothian Div., 1978–80. President: Scottish Br., Royal Soc. of Tropical Medicine and Hygiene, 1978–80; Military Surgical Soc., 1984–86; Edinburgh Univ. Graduates Assoc., 1987–89 (Vice-Pres., 1985–86); Chm. Council, Edinburgh Royal Infirmary Samaritan Soc., 1983–. *Publications:* (contrib.) Military Medicine, in Dictionary of Medical Ethics, 1977; papers (on gun-shot wounds, gas-gangrene and sterilisation) to medical jls. *Recreation:* travel. *Address:* 2 Orchard Brae, Edinburgh EH4 1NY.

MATHESON, Sir Louis; *see* Matheson, Sir J. A. L.

MATHESON, Michael; Member (SNP) Central Scotland, Scottish Parliament, since 1999; *b* 8 Sept. 1970; *s* of Edward and Elizabeth Matheson. *Educ:* Queen Margaret Coll., Edinburgh (BSc Occupational Therapy); Open Univ. (BA; Dip. Applied Social Scis). CPSM State Registered Occupational Therapist. Community Occupational Therapist: Social Work Dept, Highland Regl Council, 1991–93; Central Regl Council, 1993–97; Social Work Services, Stirling Council, 1997–99. SNP Dep. spokesperson on health and social policy, 1997–98; Dep. Opposition spokesman for justice and equality, Scottish Parlt, 1999–. Member: Ochils Mountain Rescue Team; BSES. *Recreations:* mountaineering, travel, supporting Partick Thistle FC. *Address:* Scottish Parliament, Edinburgh EH99 1SP. *T:* (0131) 348 5671, *Fax:* (0131) 348 5895; (constituency office) *T:* (01324) 849670, *Fax:* (01324) 849671.

MATHESON, Stephen Charles Taylor, CB 1993; Deputy Secretary, 1989–2000, and Deputy Chairman, Inland Revenue, 1993–2000; *b* 27 June 1939; *s* of Robert Matheson and Olive Lovick; *m* 1960, Marna Rutherford Burnett; two *s*. *Educ:* Aberdeen Grammar Sch.; Aberdeen Univ. (MA hons English Lang. and Lit., 1961). HM Inspector of Taxes, 1961–70; Principal, Bd of Inland Revenue, 1970–75; Private Sec. to Paymaster General, 1975–76, to Chancellor of the Exchequer, 1976–77; Board of Inland Revenue, 1977–2000; Project Manager, Computerisation of Pay As You Earn Project; Under Sec., 1984; Dir of IT, 1984; Comr, 1989; Dir Gen. (Management), 1989–94, (Policy and Technical), 1994–2000. FBCS (Pres., 1991–92); FBIPM 1996. Hon. DBA De Montfort Univ., 1994. *Publications:* Maurice Walsh, Storyteller, 1985; (contrib.) The Listowel Literary Phenomenon, 1994. *Recreations:* Scottish and Irish literature, book collecting, cooking, music.

MATHEW, Brian Frederick; Editor, Curtis's Botanical Magazine, since 1993; *b* 30 Aug. 1936; *s* of Frederick Mathew and Ethel Mathew (*née* Baines); *m* 1966, Helen Margaret Briggs; one *s*. *Educ:* Oxted County Grammar Sch.; RHS Sch. of Horticulture (RHS Dip. in Horticulture (Hons) 1962). Botanist, Royal Botanic Gardens, Kew, 1967–92, Hon. Res. Fellow, 1999. VMH 1992. *Publications:* Dwarf Bulbs, 1973; The Genus Daphne, 1976; The Larger Bulbs, 1978; A Field Guide to Bulbs of Europe, 1981; The Iris, 1981, 2nd edn 1989; The Crocus, 1982; A Field Guide to the Bulbous Plants of Turkey, 1984; Hellebores, 1989; The Genus Lewisia, 1989; Allium Section Allium, 1996; Growing Bulbs, 1997; Bulbs: the four seasons, 1998. *Recreations:* gardening, photography.

MATHEW, John Charles; QC 1977; *b* 3 May 1927; *s* of late Sir Theobald Mathew, KBE, MC, and Lady Mathew; *m* 1952, Jennifer Jane Mathew (*née* Lagden); two *d*. *Educ:* Beaumont Coll. Served, Royal Navy, 1945–47. Called to Bar, Lincoln's Inn, 1949; apptd Junior Prosecuting Counsel to the Crown, 1959; First Sen. Prosecuting Counsel to the Crown, 1974–77. Elected a Bencher of Lincoln's Inn, 1970. *Recreations:* golf, shooting, cinema. *Address:* 47 Abingdon Villas, W8 6XA. *T:* (020) 7937 7535. *Club:* Garrick.

MATHEW, Robert Knox, (Robin); QC 1992; *b* 22 Jan. 1945; *s* of late Robert Mathew, TD, MP and Joan Leslie (*née* Bruce); *m* 1968, Anne Rosella Elliott; one *d*. *Educ:* Eton Coll.; Trinity Coll., Dublin (BA 1967). City and financial journalist, 1968–76. Called to the Bar, Lincoln's Inn, 1974. Asst Parly Boundary Comr, 1992–98. *Recreations:* country pursuits, racing, ski-ing. *Address:* 12 New Square, Lincoln's Inn, WC2A 3SW; Church Farm, Little Barrington, Burford, Oxon OX18 5TE. *T:* (01451) 844311, *Fax:* (01451) 844768. *Club:* Boodle's.

MATHEWS, Hon. Jeremy Fell, CMG 1989; Attorney General of Hong Kong, 1988–97; *b* 14 Dec. 1941; *s* of George James and Ivy Priscilla Mathews; *m* 1st, 1968, Sophie Lee (marr. diss. 1992); two *d*; 2nd, 1992, Halima Guterres. *Educ:* Palmer's Grammar Sch., England. Qualified as solicitor, London, 1963; private practice, London, 1963–65; Dep. Dist Registrar in the High Court of Australia, Sydney, 1966–67; Hong Kong Government: Crown Counsel, 1968; Dep. Law Draftsman, 1978; Dep. Crown Solicitor, 1981; Crown Solicitor, 1982. *Recreations:* reading, trekking, music. *Clubs:* Hong Kong; Hong Kong Football.

MATHEWS, Marina Sarah Dewe, (Mrs John Dewe Mathews); *see* Warner, M. S.

MATHEWS, Michael Robert; Partner, Clifford Chance, 1971–2000; President, Law Society of England and Wales, 1998–99; *b* 3 Nov. 1941; *s* of George Walter Mathews and Betty Mathews (*née* Willcox); *m* 1966, Ann Gieve; two *s* one *d*. *Educ:* Uppingham Sch.; King's Coll., Cambridge (MA). Admitted solicitor, 1966; joined Coward Chance (later Clifford Chance), 1963. Vice Pres. and Chm., City of London Law Soc., 1992–95; Law Society of England and Wales: Mem. Council, 1995–; Dep. Vice Pres. and Treas., 1996–97; Vice Pres., 1997–98. Master, City of London Solicitors' Co., 1999–2000. Hon. LLD City, 1999. *Recreations:* walking, watching good cricket. *Address:* 12 Clare Lawn Avenue, East Sheen, SW14 8BL.

MATHEWS, Terence Francis, CBE 1995; Consultant, Financial Services Authority, since 1999; *b* 1 May 1935; *s* of Frank Mathews and Alice Elizabeth (*née* Lever); *m* 1st, 1958, Anna Dawson (marr. diss. 1973); one *s* one *d*; 2nd, 1976, Barbara Scott. *Educ:* Balham Central Sch. Nat. Service, RAF, 1953–55. HM Treasury, 1952–86; Building Socs Commn, 1986–96, Comr, 1988–96, retd. Mem., Gibraltar Financial Services Commn, 1995–. *Recreation:* amateur theatre. *Address:* Financial Services Authority, 25 The North Colonnade, Canary Wharf, E14 5HS.

MATHEWSON, Sir George (Ross), Kt 1999; CBE 1985; BSc, PhD, MBA; FRSE; CEng, MIEE; Chairman: Royal Bank of Scotland Group, since 2001 (Director, since 1987; Deputy Chairman, 2000–01); Royal Bank of Scotland, since 2001 (Director, since 1987); National Westminster Bank, since 2001; *b* 14 May 1940; *s* of George Mathewson and Charlotte Gordon (*née* Ross); *m* 1966, Sheila Alexandra Graham (*née* Bennett); two *s*. *Educ:* Perth Academy; St Andrews Univ. (BSc, PhD); Canisius Coll., Buffalo, NY (MBA). Assistant Lecturer, St Andrews Univ., 1964–67; various posts in Research & Development, Avionics Engineering, Bell Aerospace, Buffalo, NY, 1967–72; joined Industrial & Commercial Finance Corp., Edinburgh, 1972; Area Manager, Aberdeen, 1974, and Asst General Manager and Director, 1979; Chief Exec. and Mem., Scottish Develt Agency, 1981–87; Royal Bank of Scotland Group: Dir of Strategic Planning and Develt, 1987–90; Dep. Gp Chief Exec., 1990–92; Gp Chief Exec., 1992–2000. Director: Scottish Investment Trust Ltd, 1981–; Citizens Financial Gp, Inc., 1989–; Direct Line Gp Ltd (formerly Direct Line Insurance plc), 1990–2001. FCIBS 1994; CIMgt (CBIM 1985); FRSE 1988. Hon. LLD: Dundee, 1983; St Andrews, 2000. *Publications:* various articles on engineering/finance. *Recreations:* Rugby, tennis, business. *Address:* 29 Saxe Coburg Place, Edinburgh EH3 5BP; Royal Bank of Scotland, 42 St Andrew Square, Edinburgh EH2 2YE. *Club:* New (Edinburgh).

MATHIAS, Prof. Christopher Joseph, DPhil, DSc; FRCP, FMedSci; Professor of Neurovascular Medicine, University of London, since 1991, at Imperial College School of Medicine (St Mary's Hospital), Imperial College of Science, Technology and Medicine, and Institute of Neurology, University College London; Consultant Physician, since 1982: St Mary's Hospital; National Hospital for Neurology and Neurosurgery; *b* 16 March 1949;

s of late Lt Elias Mathias, IN and Hilda Mathias (*née* Lobo); *m* 1977, Rosalind (Lindy) Margaret, *d* of late Ambrose Jolleys, Cons. Paediatric Surgeon and of Betty Jolleys; two *s* one *d*. *Educ:* St Aloysius Sch., Visakhapatnam; St Joseph's E. H. Sch., Bangalore; St John's Med. Coll., Bangalore Univ. (MB BS 1972); Worcester Coll., Oxford; Wolfson Coll., Oxford (DPhil 1976); Univ. of London (DSc 1995). LRCSE, LRCPSGlas 1974; MRCP 1978, FRCP 1987. Rhodes Schol., 1972–75; Res. Officer and Hon. Registrar, Dept of Neurology, Churchill Hosp., Oxford, 1972–76; Clinical Asst and Res. Fellow, Nat. Spinal Injuries Centre, Stoke Mandeville Hosp., 1973–76; Sen. Hse Officer, Dept of Medicine, RPMS/Hammersmith Hosp., 1976–77; Registrar in Medicine, St Mary's Hosp., Portsmouth and Dept of Renal Medicine, Univ. of Southampton, 1977–79; Wellcome Trust Sen. Res. Fellow in Clinical Sci. at St Mary's Hosp. Med. Sch., 1979–84; Wellcome Trust Sen. Lectr in Med. Sci., St Mary's Hosp. Med. Sch. and Inst. of Neurol., 1984–92. Prof. Ruitinga Foundn Award and Vis. Prof., Acad. Med. Centre, Univ. of Amsterdam, 1988; Nimmo Vis. Prof., Univ. of Adelaide, 1996; Vis. Prof., Univ. of Hawaii, 1999. Dr J. Thomas Meml Oration, St John's Med. Coll., Bangalore Univ., 1988; Lectures: Lord Florey Meml, and Dorothy Mortlock, Royal Adelaide Hosp., Univ. of Adelaide, 1991; BP Regl, RCP, 1992; Thailand Neurological Soc., 1995; Sir Hugh Cairns Meml, Adelaide, 1996; Allan Birch Meml, London, 1997; Abbie Meml, Univ. of Adelaide, 1999; Coll., RCP, 2001; Sir Robert Menzies Meml Foundn, Sydney, 2001. Chairman: Clinical Autonomic Res. Soc., 1987–90 (first Sec., 1982–86); Res. Cttee, World Fedn of Neurol., 1993–97 (Mem., 1989–93); Scientific Panel, European Fedn of Neurol Socs, 1994–99; Pres., Eur. Fedn of Autonomic Socs, 1998–; Member: Scientific Cttee, Internat. Spinal Res. Trust, 1996–; Bd of Dirs, Amer. Autonomic Soc., 1996–. Consultant, ESA, 1997–2000; Mem., Jt ESA/NASA Neuroscience Rev. Panel, 1997. Mem., NW Thames Regl Adv. Cttee for Distinction Awards, 1999–; Chm., Dr P. M. Shankland (Pushpa Chopra) Charitable Trust Prize Fund, 1998–. Patron, Autonomic Disorders Assoc. Sarah Matheson Trust, 1997–. FMedSci 2001. Founder Editor-in-Chief, Clinical Autonomic Res., 1991–; Member, Editorial Board: Hypertension, 1990–93; Jl of Pharmaceutical Medicine, 1991–95; Functional Neurol., 1990–; High Blood Pressure and Cardiovascular Prevention, 1992–; Jl of Hypertension, 1994–97; Parkinsonism and Related Disorders, 1995–. *Publications:* (ed jtly) Mild Hypertension: current controversies and new approaches, 1984; (ed jtly) Concepts in Hypertension, 1989; (ed with Sir Roger Bannister) Autonomic Failure: a textbook of clinical disorders of the autonomic nervous system, 3rd edn 1992, 4th edn 1999; chaps in neurol. and cardiovascular textbooks; papers on nervous system and hormonal control of circulation in neurological, cardiovascular and other medical disorders. *Recreations:* gardening, badminton, watching cricket and football, observing human (and canine) behaviour. *Address:* Meadowcroft, West End Lane, Stoke Poges, Bucks SL2 4NE. *Clubs:* Athenæum; Vincent's (Oxford).

MATHIAS, Surg. Rear-Adm. (D) Frank Russell Bentley; retired 1985; Director, Naval Dental Services, 1983–85, and Deputy Director of Defence Dental Services (Organisation), Ministry of Defence, 1985; *b* 27 Dec. 1927; *s* of Thomas Bentley Mathias and Phebe Ann Mathias; *m* 1954, Margaret Joyce (*née* Daniels); one *s* one *d*. *Educ:* Narberth Grammar Sch.; Guy's Hosp., London. LDSRCS Eng. 1952. House Surgeon, Sussex County Hosp., Brighton, 1952–53; joined RN, 1953; principal appointments: Staff Dental Surgeon, Flag Officer Malta, 1972; Flotilla Dental Surgeon, Flag Officer Submarines, 1972–74; Comd Dental Surgeon, Flag Officer Naval Air Comd, 1974–76; Dep. Dir, Naval Dental Services, 1976–80; Comd Dental Surgeon to C-in-C Naval Home Comd, 1980–83. QHDS 1982–85. OStJ 1981.

MATHIAS, Pauline Mary; Headmistress, More House School, 1974–89; *b* 4 Oct. 1928; *d* of Francis and Hilda Donovan; *m* 1954, Prof. Anthony Peter Mathias; two *s*. *Educ:* La Retraite High School; Bedford College, London (BA Hons; DipEd). Head of English Dept, London Oratory Sch., 1954–64; Sen. Lectr in English and Admissions Tutor, Coloma Coll. of Education, 1964–74. Mem., ITC, 1991–96. Pres., GSA, 1982–83; Vice-Pres., Women's Careers Foundn, 1985–89; Chairman: ISIS, 1984–86; GBGSA, 1994–98 (Dep. Chm., 1992–94). Governor: Westminster Cathedral Choir Sch., 1978–; ESU, 1986–92; St Felix Sch., Southwold, 1986–95 (Chm., 1990–95); London Oratory Sch., 1987– (Dep. Chm., 1994–); St Mary's Sch., Ascot, 1995–; Godolphin and Latymer Sch., 1995–98. *Address:* 18 Lee Road, Aldeburgh, Suffolk IP15 5HG.

MATHIAS, Dr Peter, CBE 1984; MA, DLitt; FBA 1977; Master of Downing College, Cambridge, 1987–95 (Hon. Fellow, 1995); *b* 10 Jan. 1928; *o c* of John Samuel and late Marian Helen Mathias; *m* 1958, Elizabeth Ann, *d* of Robert Blackmore, JP, Bath; two *s* one *d*. *Educ:* Colston's Sch., Bristol; Jesus Coll., Cambridge (Schol.; Hon. Fellow, 1987). 1st cl. (dist) Hist. Tripos, 1950, 1951; DLitt: Oxon, 1985; Cantab, 1987. Research Fellow, Jesus Coll., Cambridge, 1952–55; Asst Lectr and Lectr, Faculty of History, Cambridge, 1955–68; Dir of Studies in History and Fellow, Queens' Coll., Cambridge, 1955–68 (Hon. Fellow, 1987); Tutor, 1957–68; Senior Proctor, Cambridge Univ., 1965–66; Chichele Prof. of Economic History, Oxford Univ., and Fellow of All Souls Coll., Oxford, 1969–87. Mem., Council of the Senate, Cambridge Univ., 1991–94. Visiting Professor: Univ. of Toronto, 1961; School of Economics, Delhi, 1967; Univ. of California, Berkeley, 1967; Univ. of Pa, 1972; Virginia Gildersleeve, Barnard Coll., Columbia Univ., 1972; Johns Hopkins Univ., 1979; ANU, Canberra, 1981; Geneva, 1986; Leuven, 1990; San Marino, 1990; Waseda, 1996; Osaka Gakuin, 1998; Free Univ., Bolzano, 1999. Chairman: Business Archives Council, 1968–72 (Vice-Pres., 1980–84 and 1995–; Pres., 1984–95); Econ. and Social History Cttee, SSRC, 1975–77 (Mem., 1970–77); Acad. Adv. Council, University Coll., Buckingham, 1979–84 (Mem., 1984–98); Wellcome Trust Adv. Panel for History of Medicine, 1981–88; Friends of Kettle's Yard, 1989–95; Fitzwilliam Mus. Enterprises Ltd, 1990–; Syndic of Fitzwilliam Mus., 1987–98; Bd of Continuing Educn, 1991–95; Nat. Adv. Council, British Library, 1994–2000 (Mem., Adv. Cttee (Humanities and Social Scis), 1990–94); Central European Univ. Press, 2000–; Member: ABRC, 1983–89; Round Table, Council of Industry and Higher Educn, 1989–94; Beirat Wissenschaftskolleg, Berlin, 1992–98; Bd of Patrons, Eur. Banking Hist. Assoc., 1995–. Treasurer, Econ. Hist. Soc., 1968–88 (Pres., 1989–92; Vice Pres., 1992–); Hon. Treasurer, British Acad., 1980–89; International Economic History Association: Sec., 1959–62; Pres., 1974–78; Hon. Pres., 1978–; Vice Pres., Internat. Inst. of Economic History Francesco Datini, Prato, 1987–99 (Mem. Exec. Cttee, 1972–99); Jerusalem Cttee, 1978–93; Mem., Academia Europaea, 1989; Trustee and Mem. Council, GB Sasakawa Foundn, 1994– (Chm., 1997–); Foreign Member: Royal Danish Acad., 1982; Royal Belgian Acad., 1988. Curator, Bodleian Library, 1972–87. FRHistS 1972 (Vice-Pres., 1976–80). Hon. DLitt: Buckingham, 1985; Birmingham, 1988; Hull, 1992; Warwick, 1995; De Montfort, 1995; East Anglia, 1999. Asst Editor, Econ. Hist. Rev., 1955–57; Gen. Editor, Debates in Economic History, 1967–86. *Publications:* The Brewing Industry in England 1700–1830, 1959, repr. 1993; English Trade Tokens, 1962; Retailing Revolution, 1967; The First Industrial Nation, 1969, rev. edn 1983); (ed) Science and Society 1600–1900, 1972; The Transformation of England, 1979; L'Economia Britannica dal 1815 al 1914, 1994; General Editor, Cambridge Economic History of Europe, 1968–93. *Recreation:* travel. *Address:* Bassingbourn Mill, Mill Lane, Bassingbourn, near Royston, Herts SG8 5PP. *T:* (01763) 248708.

MATHIAS, Sean Gerard; writer and director; *b* 14 March 1956; *s* of John Frederick Mathias and Anne Josephine Patricia Mathias (*née* Harding). *Educ:* Bishop Vaughan Comprehensive Sch., Swansea. *Writer: plays:* Cowardice, Ambassadors, 1983; A Prayer for Wings, and Infidelities, Edinburgh Fest., 1985; Poor Nanny, King's Head, Islington, 1989; Swansea Boys, RNT Studio, 1991; *screenplay:* The Lost Language of Cranes, 1991. *Director: film:* Bent, 1996 (Prix de la Jeunesse, Cannes, 1997); *plays:* Exceptions, New End, 1989; Bent, RNT, transf. Garrick, 1990; Uncle Vanya, RNT, 1992; Ghosts, Sherman Th., Cardiff, 1993; Les Parents Terribles, RNT, 1994; Design for Living, Donmar, transf. Gielgud, 1994; Indiscretions, NY, 1995; A Little Night Music, RNT, 1995; Marlene, Oldham, transf. Lyric, 1996, NY, 1999; Antony and Cleopatra, RNT, 1998; Suddenly Last Summer, Comedy, 1999; Servicemen, Dance of Death, NY, 2001. Dir of the Year, Evening Standard Awards, and Critics' Circle Awards, 1994. *Publications: plays:* A Prayer for Wings, 1985; Infidelities, 1985; *novella:* Manhattan Mourning, 1989. *Address:* c/o Judy Daish Associates, 2 St Charles Place, W10 6EG. *T:* (020) 8964 8811.

MATHIES, Monika W.; *see* Wulf-Mathies.

MATHIESON, Hon. Dame Janet Hilary; *see* Smith, Hon. Dame J. H.

MATHISON, Peter Yorke; Chief Executive, Benefits Agency, Department of Social Security, 1995–2000; *b* 29 March 1945; *m* 1966, Betty McCarthy. *Educ:* Lancashire Poly. (BA Business Studies 1983). FCMA 1981. Rover Group: Financial Controller, 1982–84, Systems Manager, 1984–86, Leyland Trucks; Ops Dir, Engines and Foundry Plants, 1986–88; Gen. Manager, Power Systems Div., Lucas Aerospace, 1989; Man. Dir, Guns and Vehicles Div., Royal Ordnance, 1990–91; Chief Exec., War Pensions Agency, DSS, 1992–95. *Recreations:* theatre, good restaurants, travelling, meeting people.

MATLHABAPHIRI, Hon. Gaotlhaetse Utlwang Sankoloba; MP, Botswana, 1979–80, and since 1989; *b* 6 Nov. 1949; *s* of late Sankoloba and Khumo Matlhabaphiri; four *d*. *Educ:* Diamond Corporation Training Sch.; London; Friederick Ebert Foundn, Gaborone (Labour Economics). Clerk, Standard Chartered Bank, 1971–72; teacher, also part-time Dep. Head Master, Capital Continuation Classes, Gaborone, 1971–72; diamond sorter valuator, 1973–79; Gen. Sec., Botswana Democratic Party Youth Wing, 1978–85, 1992–96 and 1996–98; Asst Minister of Agriculture, 1979–85; Mem., Central Cttee, Botswana Democratic Party, 1982–85, 1991–95 and 1995–99 (Chm., Labour Cttee, 1991); Ambassador of Botswana to Nordic countries, 1985–86; High Comr for Botswana in UK, 1986–88 (concurrently Ambassador (non-resident) to Romania and Yugoslavia). Asst Gen. Sec., Bank Employees Union, 1972; Gen. Sec., Botswana Diamond Sorters Valuators Union, 1976–79; Chairman: Botswana Fedn of Trade Unions, 1979; Parly Public Accounts Cttee, 1993–94; Law Reform Cttee, 1993–94; Citizen Cttee of Botswana, 1998–. Mem. Bd, Botswana Develt Corp., 1998–. Member: CPA; Botswana Br., IPU Cttee, 1993; UEESA. Conductor/Dir, Botswana Democratic Party Internat. Choir. Governor, IFAD, 1980–84. *Recreations:* footballer, athlete; choral music. *Address:* c/o PO Box 2475, Gaborone, Botswana. *Clubs:* Royal Over-Seas League, Royal Commonwealth Society; Gaborone Township Rollers.

MATLOCK, Prof. Jack Foust; American career diplomat; George F. Kennan Professor, Institute for Advanced Study, Princeton, 1996–2001; *b* 1 Oct. 1929; *s* of late Jack F. Matlock and of Nellie Matlock (*née* McSwain); *m* 1949, Rebecca Burrum; four *s* one *d*. *Educ:* Duke Univ. (BA 1950); Columbia Univ. (MA 1952). Editor and translator on Current Digest of the Soviet Press, 1952–53; Russian language and literature Instructor, Dartmouth Coll., 1953–56; joined US Foreign Service, 1956; served in Moscow, Austria, Ghana, Zanzibar, Tanzania; Vis. Prof. of Political Science, Vanderbilt Univ., 1978–79; Dep. Dir, Foreign Service Inst., 1979–80; Chargé d'Affaires, Moscow, 1981; Ambassador to Czechoslovakia, 1981; Special Asst to President for Nat. Security Affairs and Sen. Dir, European and Soviet Affairs on Nat. Security Council Staff, 1983–86; Ambassador to Soviet Union, 1987–91. Kathryn and Shelby Cullom Davis Prof., Columbia Univ., 1993–96. Masaryk Award, 1983; Superior Honor Award, Dept of State, 1981; Presidential Meritorious Service Award, 1984, 1987. *Publications:* Handbook to Russian edn of Stalin's Works, 1972; Autopsy on an Empire: the American Ambassador's account of the collapse of the Soviet Union, 1995; articles on US-Soviet relations. *Address:* 940 Princeton-Kingston Road, Princeton, NJ 08540, USA. *Club:* Century Association (NY).

MATOKA, Dr Peter Wilfred; Senior Lecturer, University of Zambia, since 1995; *b* 8 April 1930; *m* 1957, Grace Joyce; two *s* one *d*. *Educ:* Mwinilunga Sch.; Munali Secondary Sch.; University Coll. of Fort Hare (BA Rhodes); American Univ., Washington (Dipl. Internat. Relations); Univ. of Zambia (MA); Univ. of Warwick (PhD 1994). MP Mwinilunga, Parlt of Zambia, 1964–78; Minister: of Information and Postal Services, 1964–65; of Health, 1965–66; of Works, 1967; of Power, Transport and Works, 1968; of Luapula Province, 1969; High Comr for Zambia in UK and Ambassador to the Holy See, 1970–71; Minister of Health, 1971–72; Minister of Local Govt and Housing, 1972–77; Minister of Economic and Technical Co-operation and Pres., Africa, Caribbean and Pacific Gp of States, 1977; retd from active politics, 1992; Sen. Regl Advr, Econ. Commn for Africa, UN, Addis Ababa, 1979–83; High Comr in Zimbabwe, 1984–89. Mem. Central Cttee, United National Independence Party, 1971–78 and 1984–91 (Chairman: Social and Cultural Cttee, 1989–90; Sci. and Technol. Cttee, 1990–91). Life Mem., CPA, 1974. Pres., AA of Zambia, 1969–70. Kt of St Gregory the Great, 1964; Mem., Knightly Assoc. of St George the Martyr, 1986–. *Publication:* Child Labour in Zambia, 1999. *Recreations:* reading, walking, watching television. *Address:* PO Box 50101, Lusaka, Zambia; (home) 26D Ibex Hill Township, Lusaka, Zambia.

MATOLENGWE, Rt Rev. Patrick Monwabisi; a Bishop Suffragan of Cape Town, 1976–88, retired; Dean and Assisting Bishop, All Saints' Cathedral, Diocese of Milwaukee, since 1990; *b* 12 May 1937; *s* of David and Emma Matolengwe; *m* 1967, Crecencia Nompumelelo (*née* Nxele); three *s* two *d*. *Educ:* Healdtown Institution, Fort Beaufort (matric.); Lovedale Teacher Training Coll., Alice; Bishop Gray Coll., Cape Town; Federal Theol Sem., Alice (Cert. Theol.). MTh and DD, Nashotah House Seminary, 1992; DMin, United Theol Seminary, 1996. Teaching, 1959–60; Court Interpreter, 1960–61; theological studies, 1962–65; Curacy at Herschel, Dio. Grahamstown, 1965–68; Rector of Nyanga, Dio. Cape Town, 1968–76, of St Luke's Church, Whitewater, Dio. of Milwaukee, 1988–89. *Recreations:* scouting, singing, music, reading, tennis. *Address:* 818 E Juneau Avenue, Milwaukee, WI 53202, USA.

MATRENZA, Richard Anthony; High Commissioner for Malta in London, 1997–99; *b* 17 Oct. 1936; *s* of Domenic and Esther Sultana; *m* 1957, Doris Mercieca; one *s* one *d*. *Educ:* St Michael's Teacher Training Coll., Malta; Univ. of Oxford (Dip. Politics and Econs 1965). Teacher, 1954–60; Trade Union Negotiator, 1960–69; Management Consultant and Industrial Relations Specialist, 1970–96. MInstD. *Publications:* Libraries in Malta, 1956; L-Istorja ta' Louis Pasteur, 1959; professional papers. *Recreations:* industrial archaeology, collecting comics (late 1940s and early 1950s). *Address:* 41 Triq Kristofru, Valletta, Malta VLTO3. *T:* 356 240584.

MATSUURA, Koïchiro; Director-General of UNESCO, since 1999; *b* 29 Sept. 1937; *s* of Seichi and Kiyoko Matsuura; *m* 1967, Takako Kirikae; two *s*. *Educ:* Univ. of Tokyo; Havenford Coll., USA (MBA). Counsellor, Embassy of Japan, USA, 1977–80; Consul Gen., Hong Kong, 1985–88; Dir-Gen., Econ. Co-operation Bureau, 1988–90, N American Affairs Bureau, 1990–92, Min. of Foreign Affairs; Dep. Minister for Foreign Affairs (Sherpa for Japan at G-7 Summit), 1992–94; Ambassador of Japan to: Djibouti, 1994–99; France, 1994–99; Andorra, 1996–99. Chm., World Heritage Cttee, UNESCO, 1998–99. Bintang Jasa Utama (Indonesia), 1993; Grand Officer, Nat. Order of Merit (France), 1994; Comdr, Nat. Order of 27 June (Djibouti), 1997. *Publications:* In the Forefront of Economic Co-operation Diplomacy, 1990; History of Japan-United States Relations, 1992; Focusing on the Future: Japan's global role in a changing world, 1993; The G-7 Summit: its history and perspectives, 1994; Development and Perspectives of the Relations between Japan and France, 1995; Japanese Diplomacy at the Dawn of the 21st Century, 1998. *Recreations:* Go, tennis, golf, mountain climbing. *Address:* UNESCO, 7 Place de Fontenoy, 75007 Paris, France. *T:* (1) 45681310.

MATT; *see* Pritchett, Matthew.

MATTAJ, Iain William, PhD; FRS 1999; FRSE; Scientific Co-ordinator, European Molecular Biology Laboratory, since 1999; *b* 5 Oct. 1952; *s* of George Eugeniusz Mattaj and Jane Margaret Mattaj; *m* 1974, Ailsa McCrindle. *Educ:* Edinburgh Univ. (BSc); Leeds Univ. (PhD 1980). Postdoctoral research: Friedrich Miescher Inst., Basel, 1979–82; Biocentre, Basel Univ., 1982–85; Gp Leader, 1985–90, Programme Co-ordinator, 1990–99, EMBL, Heidelberg. Exec. Ed., EMBO Jl, 1990–. Mem., EMBO, 1989. Pres., Ribonucleic Acid Soc., 1998–2000. FRSE 2000. *Publications:* numerous contribs to scientific jls. *Recreations:* squash, music, literature. *Address:* European Molecular Biology Laboratory, Meyerhofstrasse 1, 69117 Heidelberg, Germany. *T:* (6221) 387393.

MATTHEW, Chessor Lillie, FRIBA, FRIAS; Principal, Duncan of Jordanstone College of Art, Dundee, 1964–78, retired; *b* 22 Jan. 1913; *s* of William Matthew and Helen Chessor Matthew (*née* Milne); *m* 1939, Margarita Ellis; one *s*. *Educ:* Gray's School of Art; Robert Gordon's Coll., Aberdeen. Diploma in Architecture; AMRTPI 1948; FRIBA 1958; FRIAS 1958. Lectr, Welsh Sch. of Architecture, Cardiff, 1936–40. Served RAF, 1940–46, Flt-Lt. Sen. Lectr, Welsh Sch. of Architecture, Cardiff, 1946–57; Head of Sch. of Architecture, Duncan of Jordanstone Coll. of Art, Dundee, 1958–64. Mem., Royal Fine Art Commn for Scotland, 1966–78. JP 1974. *Recreations:* hill walking, foreign travel. *Address:* Craigmhor, 36 Albany Road, West Ferry, Dundee DD5 1NW. *T:* (01382) 778364.

MATTHEWMAN, His Honour Keith; QC 1979; a Circuit Judge, 1983–2001; *b* 8 Jan. 1936; *e s* of late Lieut Frank Matthewman and Elizabeth Matthewman; *m* 1962, Jane (*née* Maxwell); one *s*. *Educ:* Long Eaton Grammar Sch.; University College London (LLB). Called to the Bar, Middle Temple, 1960. School teacher, Barking, Essex, 1958–59, and Heanor, Derbys, 1960–61; Commercial Assistant, Internat. Div., Rolls-Royce Ltd, 1961–62; practice at the Bar, 1962–83, Midland Circuit, later Midland and Oxford Circuit; a Recorder of the Crown Court, 1979–83. Mem. Cttee, Council of HM's Circuit Judges, 1984–89. Member: Notts Probation Cttee, 1986–2001; Parole Bd, 1996–. A Pres., Mental Health Review Tribunals, 1993–99. Ext. Examr, Bar vocational course, Nottingham Trent Univ., 2000–. Inaugural Pres., Friends of the Galleries of Justice (Nottingham), 1998–. Mem. (Lab), Heanor UDC, 1960–63. TV appearances include Crimestalker, Central TV, 1993. *Recreations:* gardening, reading. *Address:* c/o Crown Court, Nottingham NG1 7EJ. *Club:* Beeston Fields Golf (Bramcote).

MATTHEWS, Rt Rev. Anthony Francis Berners H.; *see* Hall-Matthews.

MATTHEWS, Colin, DPhil; composer; Prince Consort Professor of Composition, Royal College of Music, since 2001; *b* 13 Feb. 1946; *s* of Herbert and Elsie Matthews; *m* 1977, Belinda Lloyd; one *s* two *d*. *Educ:* Univ. of Nottingham (BA Classics, MPhil Composition); Univ. of Sussex (DPhil). Studied composition with Arnold Whittall and Nicholas Maw, 1967–70; collaborated with Deryck Cooke on performing version of Mahler's Tenth Symphony, 1964–74; asst to Benjamin Britten, 1971–76; worked with Imogen Holst, 1972–84; taught at Univ. of Sussex, 1971–72, 1976–77. Associate Composer: LSO, 1990–99; Hallé Orch., 2001–. Dir, Holst Estate and Holst Foundn, 1973–; Trustee, Britten-Pears Foundn, and Dir, Britten Estate, 1983– (Chm., 2000–); Mem. Council and Exec. Cttee, SPNM, 1981–93, 1994–; Exec. Mem. Council, Aldeburgh Foundn, 1984–93; Dir, PRS, 1992–95. Founder, NMC Recordings Ltd, 1988. Gov., RNCM, 2000–. Patron, Musicians against Nuclear Arms, 1985–. Hon. DMus Nottingham, 1998. Scottish National Orch. Ian Whyte Award, 1975; Park Lane Group Composer Award, 1983; Royal Philharmonic Soc. Award, 1996. *Principal works:* Fourth Sonata, 1974; Night Music, 1976; Sonata no 5 'Landscape', 1977–81; String Quartet no 1, 1979; Oboe Quartet, 1981; The Great Journey, 1981–88; Divertimento for Double String Quartet, 1982; Toccata Meccanica, 1984; Night's Mask, 1984; Cello Concerto, 1984; Suns Dance, 1985; Five Duos, 1985; Three Enigmas, 1985; String Quartet no 2, 1985; Pursuit (ballet), 1986; Monody, 1986–87; Eleven Studies in Velocity, 1987; Two Part Invention, 1987; Cortège, 1988; Hidden Variables, 1989; Quatrain, 1989; Second Oboe Quartet, 1990; Five Concertinos, 1990; Chiaroscuro, 1990; Machines and Dreams, 1990; Broken Symmetry, 1990–91; Renewal, 1990–96; Contraflow, 1992; Memorial, 1992; String Quartet no 3, 1994; … through the glass, 1994; 23 Frames, 1995; Cello Concerto no 2, 1996; Renewal, 1996; My Life So Far (film score), 1998; Two Tributes, 1999; Aftertones, 2000; Pluto, 2000; Continuum, 2000; Horn Concerto, 2001. *Publications:* contribs to Musical Times, Tempo, TLS, etc. *Recreations:* wine, very amateur astrophysics. *Address:* c/o Faber Music Ltd, 3 Queen Square, WC1N 3AU. *T:* (020) 7278 6881, *Fax:* (020) 7278 3817. *Club:* Leyton Orient Supporters'.

See also D. J. Matthews.

MATTHEWS, Brother Daniel (Fairbairn), SSF; Minister General, Society of Saint Francis, since 1997; *b* 7 Sept. 1936; *s* of Maxwell and Mary Matthews. *Educ:* S Shields Marine Coll. (1st Cl. Marine Engrg); Bishop Patteson Theological Coll., Kohimarama, Solomon Is (DipTh). Chief Engr (Marine), 1957–63; Society of St Francis: Guardian, Solomon Is, 1975–81; Provincial Minister, Australia and NZ, 1981–97. *Recreations:* walking, reading. *Address:* Society of Saint Francis, The Friary, Hilfield, Dorchester, Dorset DT2 7BE.

MATTHEWS, David; *see* Matthews, William D.

MATTHEWS, David John; composer; *b* 9 March 1943; *s* of Herbert and Elsie Matthews; *m* 1995, Jean Hasse. *Educ:* Bancroft's Sch., Woodford; Univ. of Nottingham (BA Classics). Studied composition with Anthony Milner, 1967–69; Asst to Benjamin Britten, 1966–70. Musical Dir, Deal Fest., 1989–; Composer in Association, Britten Sinfonia, 1997–. Collaborated with Deryck Cooke on performing version of Mahler's Tenth Symphony, 1964–74. Hon. DMus Nottingham, 1997. *Compositions include:* 3 songs for soprano and orchestra, 1968; String Quartet No 1, 1970; Symphony No 1, 1975; String Quartet No 2, 1976; Symphony No 2, 1977; String Quartet No 3, 1977; September Music, for small orch., 1979; Ehmals und Jetzt, 6 songs for soprano and piano, 1979; The Company of Lovers, 5 choral songs, 1980; String Quartet No 4, 1981; Serenade, for chamber orch., 1982; Violin Concerto No 1, 1982; The Golden Kingdom, 9 songs for high voice and piano, 1983; Piano Trio No 1, 1983; Clarinet Quartet, 1984; Symphony No 3, 1985; In the Dark Time, for orch., 1985; Variations for strings, 1986; The Flaying of Marsyas, for oboe and string quartet, 1987; Chaconne, for orch., 1987; Cantiga, for soprano and chamber orch., 1988; The Ship of Death, for chorus, 1989; Piano Sonata, 1989; String Trio, 1989; Romanza, for 'cello and small orch., 1990; The Music of Dawn, for orch., 1990; Symphony No 4, 1990; Capriccio, for 2 horns and strings, 1991; String Quartet No 6, 1991; Oboe Concerto, 1992; The Sleeping Lord, for sop. and ensemble, 1992; A Vision and a Journey, for orch., 1993; Piano Trio No 2, 1993; A Congress of Passions, for voice, oboe and piano, 1994; Vespers, for soli, chorus and orch., 1994; Skies now are Skies, for tenor and string quartet, 1994; A Song and Dance Sketchbook, for piano quartet, 1995; Sinfonia, for orch., 1995; Moments of Vision, for chorus, 1995; Two Pieces for Strings: Little Chaconne, 1996, Fall Dances, 1999; Hurrahing in Harvest, for chorus, 1997; Variations, for piano, 1997; Burnham Wick, for small orch., 1997; Violin Concerto No 2, 1998; String Quartet No 8, 1998; Symphony No 5, 1999; String Quartet No 9, 2000; Aubade, for chamber orch., 2001; String Quartet No 10, 2001. *Publications:* Michael Tippett, 1980; Landscape into Sound, 1992; contribs to Musical Times, Tempo, TLS. *Recreations:* walking, sketching. *Address:* c/o Faber Music Ltd, 3 Queen Square, WC1N 3AU.

See also Colin Matthews.

MATTHEWS, Douglas, FRSL; FLA; Librarian, The London Library, 1980–93; *b* 23 Aug. 1927; *s* of Benjamin Matthews and Mary (*née* Pearson); *m* 1968, Sarah Maria Williams (marr. diss. 1991); two *d*. *Educ:* Acklam Hall Sch., Middlesbrough; Durham Univ. (BA). FRSL 1999. Assistant: India Office Library, 1952–62; Kungl. Biblioteket, Stockholm, 1956–57; Librarian, Home Office, 1962–64; Dep. Librarian, London Library, 1965–80. Mem. Cttee, Royal Literary Fund, 1993–. Mem. Court, Univ. of Sussex, 1983–94. *Address:* 1 Priory Terrace, Mountfield Road, Lewes, Sussex BN7 2UT. *T:* (01273) 475635. *Club:* Garrick.

MATTHEWS, Edwin James Thomas, TD 1946; Chief Taxing Master of the Supreme Court, 1979–83 (Master, 1965–78); *b* 2 May 1915; *s* of Edwin Martin Matthews (killed in action, 1916); *m* 1939, Katherine Mary Hirst, BA (Oxon.), Dip. Soc. Sc. (Leeds); two *d*. *Educ:* Sedbergh Sch., Yorks. Admitted as Solicitor of Supreme Court, 1938; practice on own account in Middlesbrough, 1938–39. Served in Royal Artillery, 1939–46, UK, France and Belgium (Dunkirk 1940); released with rank of Major. Partner, Chadwick Son & Nicholson, Solicitors, Dewsbury, Yorks, 1946–50; Area Sec., No. 6 (W Midland) Legal Aid Area Cttee of Law Soc., 1950–56; Sec. of Law Soc. for Contentious Business (including responsibility for administration of Legal Aid and Advice Schemes), 1956–65. Toured Legal Aid Offices in USA for Ford Foundation and visited Toronto to advise Govt of Ontario, 1963. Mem., Council, British Academy of Forensic Sciences, 1965–68. Special Consultant to NBPI on Solicitors' Costs, 1967–68; General Consultant, Law Soc., 1983–84. Member: Lord Chancellor's Adv. Cttee on Legal Aid, 1972–77; Working Party on Legal Aid Legislation, 1974–76; Working Party on the Criminal Trial, 1980–83; Supreme Ct Procedure Cttee, 1982–83. Lectr, mainly on costs and remuneration for solicitors and counsel, for Coll. of Law, Legal Studies and Services Ltd and to various provincial Law Socs, 1983–89. *Publications:* contrib. Halsbury's Laws of England, 1961 and Atkins Encyclopaedia of Forms and Precedents, 1962; (with Master Graham-Green) Costs in Criminal Cases and Legal Aid, 1965; (jointly) Legal Aid and Advice Under the Legal Aid and Advice Acts, 1949 to 1964, 1971; (ed jtly) Supreme Court Practice; contribs to legal journals. *Recreations:* trout fishing, theatre, gardening, French wines. *Address:* 11 Old Parsonage Court, Otterbourne, Winchester, Hants SO21 2EP. *T:* (01962) 862478.

MATTHEWS, Prof. Geoffrey, MA, PhD; CMath, FIMA; Shell Professor of Mathematics Education, Centre for Science and Mathematics Education, Chelsea College, University of London, 1968–77, now Emeritus; *b* 1 Feb. 1917; *s* of Humphrey and Gladys Matthews; *m* 1st, 1941, Patricia Mary Jackson; one *s* one *d*; 2nd, 1972, Julia Comber. *Educ:* Marlborough; Jesus Coll., Cambridge (MA); PhD (London). CMath 1991; FIMA 1964. Wiltshire Regt, Intelligence Officer 43rd (Wessex) Div., 1939–45, Captain (dispatches, 1945; US Bronze Star, 1945). Teacher: Haberdashers' Aske's Sch., 1945–50; St Dunstan's Coll., 1950–64, Dep. Head and head of mathematics dept; Organiser, Nuffield Mathematics Teaching Project, 1964–72; Co-director (with Julia Matthews), Schools Council Early Mathematical Experiences project, 1974–79; Co-dir (with Prof. K. W. Keohane) SSRC funded prog. Concepts in Secondary Sch. Maths and Sci., 1974–79. Hon. Res. Associate, Greenwich Univ., 1996. Presenter of BBC TV programmes in series Tuesday Term, Middle School Mathematics, and Children and Mathematics; consultant to BBC series Maths in a Box and You and Me, and to ATV series Towards Mathematics. Consultant to maths teaching projects in Italy, Greece, Portugal, Sri Lanka and Thailand; has lectured extensively abroad. Pres., Mathematical Assoc., 1977–78 (Hon. Mem., 1990); Founder Mem., Commonwealth Assoc. of Sci. and Maths Educators, 1964; Member: Internat. Cttee, 3rd Congress, ICME, 1976; Council, Inst. of Maths and its Applications, 1978–81; Cttee, Soc. of Free Painters and Sculptors, 1978–89. One man shows, Loggia Gall., 1986, 1989; St Martin's-in-the-Fields Gall., 1993, 1996. *Publications:* Calculus, 1964; Matrices I & II, 1964; Mathematics through School, 1972; Mainly on the Bright Side, 1989, 2nd edn 2001; papers in Proc. Kon. Akad. Wetensch. (Amsterdam); numerous articles in Math. Gaz., etc. *Recreations:* painting, travel. *Address:* 50 Sydney Road, Bexleyheath, Kent DA6 8HG. *T:* (020) 8303 4301.

MATTHEWS, Geoffrey Vernon Townsend, OBE 1986; Director of Research and Conservation, 1955–88, and Deputy Director, 1973–88, Wildfowl Trust, Slimbridge; *b* 16 June 1923; *s* of Geoffrey Tom Matthews and Muriel Ivy Townsend; *m* 1st, 1946, Josephine (marr. diss. 1961), *d* of Col Alured Charles Lowther O'Shea Bilderdeck; one *s* one *d*; 2nd, 1964, Janet Kear, *qv* (marr. diss. 1978); 3rd, 1980, Mary Elizabeth, *d* of William Evans; one *s* one *d*. *Educ:* Bedford Sch.; Christ's Coll., Cambridge (MA, PhD). RAF Operational Res., Bomber and SE Asia Comds (Sci. Officer/Flt Lieut), 1943–46. Post-doctoral res., Cambridge Univ., 1950–55; Special Lectr, Bristol Univ., 1965–88; Hon. Lectr 1966–69, Professorial Fellow 1970–90, UC, Cardiff. Dir, Internat. Waterfowl Res. Bureau, 1969–88, Counsellor of Honour, 1989–. Served on numerous non-govtl and govtl cttees; travelled widely. Pres., Assoc. for the Study of Animal Behaviour, 1971–74; Vice-Pres., British Ornithologists' Union, 1972–75, Union Medal, 1980. FIBiol, 1974; Corresp. Fellow, Amer. Ornithologists Union, 1969–. RSPB Medal, 1990. Officer, Dutch Order of Golden Ark, 1987. *Publications:* Bird Navigation, 1955, 2nd edn 1968; The Ramsar Convention on Wetlands, 1993 (trans. German and Japanese); chapters contributed to 44 multi-authored books; more than 100 papers in sci. and conservation jls. *Recreations:* fossil hunting, collecting zoological stamps, reading, household maintenance. *Address:* 32 Tetbury Street, Minchinhampton, Glos GL6 9JH. *T:* (01453) 884769. *Club:* Victory.

MATTHEWS, George Lloyd; Archivist, Democratic Left (formerly Communist Party of Great Britain); *b* 24 Jan. 1917; *s* of James and Ethel Matthews, Sandy, Beds; *m* 1940,

Elisabeth Lynette Summers; no *c. Educ:* Bedford Modern Sch.; Reading Univ. Pres., Reading Univ. Students Union, 1938–39; Vice-Pres., Nat. Union of Students, 1939–40; Vice-Pres., University Labour Fedn, 1938–39. County Chm., Nat. Union of Agricultural Workers, 1945–49; Mem. Exec. Cttee, Communist Party, 1943–79; Asst Gen. Sec., Communist Party, 1949–57; Asst Editor, 1957–59, Editor, 1959–74, Daily Worker, later Morning Star; Head of Press and Publicity Dept, Communist Party of GB, 1974–79. *Publication:* (ed with F. King) About Turn, 1990. *Recreation:* music. *Address:* c/o Democratic Left, 6 Cynthia Street, N1 9JF. *T:* (020) 7278 4443.

MATTHEWS, Henry Melvin; Managing Director, Texaco Ltd, 1982–88; *b* 26 Feb. 1926; *s* of Phillip Lawrence and Agnes K. Matthews; *m* 1947, Margaret Goodridge; one *s* two *d. Educ:* Columbia University; Tufts Univ. (BSNS, BSME). Commnd Ensign, 1945, USNR; retired 1986. General Manager, Texaco Europe, USA, 1976; Vice Pres. Manufacture and Marketing, Texaco Europe, USA, 1980. Mem., US Navy League, London. *Recreations:* tennis, golf, swimming, gardening, music (choir), YMCA, Congregational Church. *Address:* (winter) 6280 Winged Foot Drive, Stuart, FL 34997, USA; (summer) Three Winds, 338 West Beach Road, Charlestown, RI 02813, USA. *Club:* Mariner Sands CC (Stuart, Fla).

MATTHEWS, Hugh; QC (Scot) 1992; Sheriff of Glasgow and Strathkelvin since 1997; *b* 4 Dec. 1953; *s* of Hugh Matthews and Maureen Matthews (*née* Rea). *Educ:* St Columba's Primary Sch., Kilmarnock; St Joseph's Acad., Kilmarnock; Glasgow Univ. (LLB Hons). Admitted to Faculty of Advocates, 1979; Standing Jun. Counsel, Dept of Employment, Office in Scotland, 1984–88; Advocate-depute, 1988–93; temp. Sheriff, 1993–97. *Recreations:* Star Trekking, ancient history, golf, Celtic Football Club, pub quizzes, having fun. *Address:* Glasgow Sheriff Court, 1 Carlton Place, Glasgow G5 9DA. *Club:* Pollok Golf (Glasgow).

MATTHEWS, Jeffery Edward, FCSD; freelance graphic designer and consultant, since 1952; *b* 3 April 1928; *s* of Henry Edward Matthews and Sybil Frances (*née* Cooke); *m* 1953, (Sylvia Lilian) Christine (*née* Hoar) (*d* 1994); one *s* one *d. Educ:* Alleyn's; Brixton Sch. of Building (Interior Design; NDD). AIBD 1951; FCSD (FSIAD 1978). Graphic designer with J. Edward Sander, 1949–52; part-time tutor, 1952–55. Lettering and calligraphy assessor for SIAD, 1970–. Designs for Post Office: decimal to pay labels, 1971; fount of numerals for definitive stamps, 1981; stamps: United Nations, 1965; British bridges, 1968; definitives for Scotland, Wales, NI and IOM, 1971; Royal Silver Wedding, 1972; 25th Anniversary of the Coronation, 1978; London, 1980; 80th birthday of the Queen Mother, 1980; Christmas, 1980; Wedding of Prince Charles and Lady Diana Spencer, 1981; Quincentenary of College of Arms, 1984; 60th birthday of the Queen, 1986; Wedding of Prince Andrew and Sarah Ferguson, 1986; Order of the Thistle Tercentenary of Revival, 1987; 150th Anniversary of the Penny Black, 1990; self-adhesive definitives, 1993; The Queen's Beasts, 1998; Jeffery Matthews miniature sheet, 2000; also first-day covers, postmarks, presentation packs, souvenir books and posters; one of three stamp designers featured in PO film, Picture to Post, 1969. Other design work includes: title banner lettering and coat of arms, Sunday Times, 1968; cover design and lettering for official prog., Royal Wedding, 1981; The Royal Mint, commemorative medal, Order of the Thistle, 1987; Millennium commemorative crown piece, 1999; official heraldry and symbols, HMSO; hand-drawn lettering, COI; stamp designs, first-day covers, calligraphy, packaging, promotion and bookbinding designs, logotypes, brand images and hand-drawn lettering, for various firms including Unicover Corp., USA, Harrison & Sons Ltd, Metal Box Co., John Dickinson, Reader's Digest Assoc. Ltd, Encyc. Britannica Internat. Ltd, ICI and H. R. Higgins (Coffee-man) Ltd. Work exhibited in A History of Bookplates in Britain, V&A Mus., 1979. Citizen and Goldsmith of London (Freedom by Patrimony), 1949. FRSA 1987. *Publications:* (contrib.) Designers in Britain, 1964, 1971; (contrib.) 45 Wood-engravers, 1982; (contrib.) Royal Mail Year Book, 1984, 1986, 1987, 1998. *Recreations:* furniture restoration, playing the guitar, gardening, DIY.

MATTHEWS, John, CBE 1990; FRAgS; Director, Institute of Engineering Research, Agricultural and Food Research Council (formerly National Institute of Agricultural Engineering), 1984–90; *b* 4 July 1930; *s* of John Frederick Matthews and Catherine Edith Matthews (*née* Terry); *m* 1982 (marr. diss. 1993); two *d*; *m* 2000, June Robinson. *Educ:* Royal Latin School, Buckingham. BSc (Physics) London. CPhys, FInstP; CEng; FIAgrE 1970 (Hon. FIAgrE 1994). Scientist, GEC Res. Labs, 1951–59; National Institute of Agricultural Engineering: joined 1959; Head of Tractor Performance Dept, 1967–73; Head of Tractor and Cultivation Div., 1973–83; Asst Dir, 1983–84; Dir, 1984–90. Vis. Prof., Cranfield Inst. of Technology, 1987. Vice Chm., Ceredigion and Mid-Wales NHS Trust (Dir, 1992–). Mem., Bd of Management, AFRC, 1986–90. Formerly Chm., Technical Cttees, Internat. Standards Orgn and OECD; Pres., Inst. of Agricl Engineers, 1986–88. Pro-Chancellor, Univ. of Luton, 1993–98 (Chm. of Govs, Luton Coll. of Higher Educn, 1989–93). Fellow: Ergonomics Soc.; Academie Georgofili, Italy, 1991. Research Medal, RASE, 1983. Max Eyth Medallion (Germany), 1990; Chevalier de Merite Agricole (France), 1992. *Publications:* (contrib.) Fream's Elements of Agriculture, 1984; (ed) Progress in Agricultural Physics and Engineering, 1991; contribs to other books and jls on agricultural engineering and ergonomics. *Recreations:* farming, gardening, Lions International club, travel. *Address:* Carron, Aberporth, Cardigan, Ceredigion SA43 2DA.

MATTHEWS, Prof. John Burr Lumley, (Jack), FRSE; Director, 1988–96 and Secretary, 1988–99, Scottish Association for Marine Science (formerly Scottish Marine Biological Association) (Hon. Fellow 1999); *b* 23 April 1935; *s* of Dr John Lumley Matthews and Susan Agnes Matthews; *m* 1962, Jane Rosemary Goldsmith; one *s* two *d. Educ:* Warwick Sch.; St John's Coll., Oxford (MA, DPhil). FRSE 1988. Res. Scientist, Oceanographic Lab., Edinburgh, 1961–67; University of Bergen: Lectr, Sen. Lectr, Marine Biology, 1967–78; Prof., Marine Biology, 1978–84; Dep. Dir, Scottish Marine Biol Assoc., 1984–88; Dir, Dunstaffnage Marine Lab., NERC, 1988–94. Vis. Prof., Oceanography, Univ. of British Columbia, 1977–78; Hon. Prof., Biology, Univ. of Stirling, 1984–. Member: Cttee for Scotland, Nature Conservancy Council, 1989–91; SW Regl Bd, Scottish Natural Heritage, 1992–97 (Dep. Chm., 1994–97). Sec., Internat. Assoc. of Biol Oceanography, 1994–. Mem., Bd and Acad. Council, Univ. of the Highlands and Islands Ltd, 1993–96. Trustee, Hebridean Whale & Dolphin Trust, 2000–. FRSA 1989. *Publications:* (ed jtly) Freshwater on the Sea, 1976; contribs to marine sci. jls. *Recreations:* hill-walking, cross-country ski-ing, pethau cymreig. *Address:* Grianaig, Rockfield Road, Oban, Argyll PA34 5DH. *T:* (01631) 562734.

MATTHEWS, Dr John Duncan, CVO 1989; FRCPE; retired; Consultant Physician, Royal Infirmary, Edinburgh, 1955–86; Hon. Senior Lecturer, University of Edinburgh, 1976–86; *b* 19 Sept. 1921; *s* of Joseph Keith Matthews and Ethel Chambers; *m* 1945, Constance Margaret Moffat; two *s. Educ:* Shrewsbury; Univ. of Cambridge (BA); Univ. of Edinburgh (MB, ChB). FRCPE 1958. Surgeon, High Constables and Guard of Honour, Holyroodhouse, 1961–87, Moderator, 1987–89. Hon. Consultant in Medicine to the Army in Scotland, 1974–86; Examr in Medicine, Edinburgh and Cambridge Univs and Royal Colleges of Physicians. Vice-Pres., RCPE, 1982–85; Mem./Chm., various local and national NHS and coll. cttees. Sec., Edinburgh Medical Angling Club, 1963–86. *Publications:* occasional articles in med. jls on diabetes and heart disease. *Recreations:* cricket (Free Foresters, Grange, and Scotland), fishing, golf, gardening. *Address:* 3 Succoth Gardens, Edinburgh EH12 6BR.

MATTHEWS, Prof. John Frederick, DPhil; FRHistS; FSA; FBA 1990; Professor of Roman History, Departments of Classics and History, Yale University, since 1996 (Chair of Classics, since 1998); *b* 15 Feb. 1940; *s* of Jack and Mary Matthews; *m* 1st, 1965, Elaine Jackson (marr. diss. 1995); two *d*; 2nd, 1995, Veronika Grimm. *Educ:* Wyggeston Boys' Sch., Leicester; Queen's Coll., Oxford (MA 1965; DPhil 1970). FRHistS 1986; FSA 1993. Oxford University: Dyson Jun. Res. Fellow in Greek Culture, Balliol Coll., 1965–69; Conington Prize, 1971; Univ. Lectr in Middle and Late Roman Empire, 1969–90; Reader, 1990–92; Prof. of Middle and Later Roman History, 1992–96; Official Fellow, Corpus Christi Coll., 1969–76; Fellow, and Praelector in Ancient History, Queen's College, Oxford, 1976–96. Inst. for Advanced Study, Princeton, 1980–81; British Acad. Reader in Humanities, 1988–90; Fellow, Nat. Humanities Center, N Carolina, 1995–96. Chm. of Govs, Cheney Sch., Oxford, 1986–91. *Publications:* Western Aristocracies and Imperial Court AD 364–425, 1975; (with T. J. Cornell) Atlas of the Roman World, 1982; Political Life and Culture in late Roman Society, 1985; The Roman Empire of Ammianus, 1989; (with Peter Heather) The Goths in the Fourth Century, 1991; Laying Down the Law: a study of the Theodosian Code, 2000. *Recreations:* playing the piano, listening to music. *Address:* 160 McKinley Avenue, New Haven, CT 06515, USA. *T:* (203) 3898137.

MATTHEWS, Michael Gough; pianist, teacher, adjudicator and consultant; Director, Royal College of Music, 1985–93; *b* 12 July 1931; *s* of late Cecil Gough Matthews and Amelia Eleanor Mary Matthews. *Educ:* Chigwell School; Royal College of Music (Open Scholarship, 1947; Hopkinson Gold Medal, 1953; ARCM, FRCM 1972); ARCO; Diploma del Corso di Perfezionamento St Cecilia, Rome. Diploma of Honour and Prize, Chopin Internat. Piano Competition, 1955; Italian Govt Scholarship, 1956; Chopin Fellowship, Warsaw, 1959. Pianist; recitals, broadcasts, concerts, UK, Europe and Far East. Supervisor Junior Studies, RSAMD, 1964–71; Royal College of Music: Dir, Junior Dept, and Prof. of Piano, 1972–75; Registrar, 1975; Vice-Dir, 1978–84. Teacher and adjudicator of internat. competitions. Hon. Dir, Royal Music Foundn, Inc., USA, 1985–. Member: NYO GB; Royal Philharmonic Soc., 1985–; Music Study Gp, EEC, 1989–; Comité d'Honneur, Presence de l'Art, Paris, 1990–; Council, Purcell Tercentenary Trust, 1992. Vice-President: RCO, 1985–; Nat. Youth Choir, 1986–; Herbert Howells Soc., 1987–; Hon. Vice-Pres., Royal Choral Soc., 1992–. Chm., Parkhouse Award, 1997–99. Consultant to HM the Sultan of Oman, 1993–, to Jaguar Cars, 1993–. Hon. FLCM 1976; Hon. RAM 1979; FRSAMD 1986; FRNCM 1991; FRSA; Hon. GSM 1987. Recordings of piano music by Fauré, 1995 and 1997, and Brahms, 1999. *Publications:* various musical entertainments; arranger of educational music. *Recreation:* gardening. *Address:* Laurel Cottages, South Street, Mayfield, E Sussex TN20 6DD. *T:* and *Fax:* (01435) 873065. *Club:* Athenæum.

MATTHEWS, Percy; *b* 24 July 1921; *s* of Samuel and Minnie Matthews; *m* 1946, Audrey Rosenthal; one *s* two *d. Educ:* Parmiters Sch., London. Overseas Associate, J. O. Hambro & Co. Hon. Fellow, St Peter's Coll., Oxford. Freeman, City of London. *Recreations:* painting, golf. *Address:* 20 Pavilion Court, Frognal Rise, NW3 6PZ.

MATTHEWS, Sir Peter (Alec), Kt 1975; AO 1980; Chairman, Pegler-Hattersley plc, 1979–87 (Director, 1977–87); Director: Lloyds Bank, 1974–91 (Chairman, Central London Regional Board, 1978–91); Cookson Group (formerly Lead Industries Group), 1980–91; Hamilton Oil Great Britain, 1981–91; *b* 21 Sept. 1922; *s* of Major Alec Bryan Matthews and Elsie Lazarus Barlow; *m* 1946, Sheila Dorothy Bunting; four *s* one *d. Educ:* Shawnigan Lake Sch., Vancouver Island; Oundle Sch. Served Royal Engineers (retired as Major), 1940–46. Joined Stewarts and Lloyds Ltd, 1946; Director of Research and Technical Development, 1962; Member for R&D, BSC, 1968–70, Dep. Chm., 1973–76; Vickers PLC: Man. Dir, 1970–79; Chm., 1980–84; Director: British Electric Traction Plc, 1976–87; Sun Alliance and London Insurance, 1979–89; Lloyds & Scottish, 1983–86. Chm., Armed Forces Pay Review Body, 1984–89; Mem., Top Salaries Review Body, 1984–89. Member: BOTB, 1973–77; Export Guarantees Adv. Council, 1973–78; Status Review Cttee, ECGD, 1983–84; Pres., Sino-British Trade Council, 1983–85. Member: NRDC, 1974–80; Engineering Industries Council, 1976–84 (Chm., 1980–84); Adv. Council for Applied R&D, 1976–80. Pres., Engineering Employers Fedn, 1982–84; Chm., Council, University Coll., London, 1980–89 (Hon. Fellow, 1982). CBIM, FRSA. *Recreations:* sailing, gardening. *Address:* Chalkwell, Nether Wallop, Stockbridge, Hants SO20 8HE. *T:* (01264) 782136. *Club:* Royal Yacht Squadron (Cowes).

MATTHEWS, Prof. Peter Bryan Conrad, FRS 1973; MD, DSc; Professor of Sensorimotor Physiology, 1987–96, now Emeritus and Student of Christ Church, 1958–96, now Emeritus, University of Oxford; *b* 23 Dec. 1928; *s* of Prof. Sir Bryan Matthews, CBE, FRS; *m* 1956, Margaret Rosemary Blears; one *s* one *d. Educ:* Marlborough Coll.; King's Coll., Cambridge; Oxford Univ. Clinical School. Oxford University: Univ. Lectr in Physiology, 1961–77; Reader, 1978–86; Tutor, Christ Church, 1958–86. Sir Lionel Whitby Medal, Cambridge Univ., 1959; Robert Bing Prize, Swiss Acad. of Med. Science, 1971. *Publications:* Mammalian Muscle Receptors and their Central Actions, 1972; papers on neurophysiology in various scientific jls. *Address:* University Laboratory of Physiology, Parks Road, Oxford OX1 3PT. *T:* (01865) 272500.

MATTHEWS, Prof. Peter Hugoe, LittD; FBA 1985; Professor of Linguistics, University of Cambridge, 1980–2001, now Emeritus (Head of Department of Linguistics, 1980–96); Fellow, since 1980, Praelector, since 1987, St John's College, Cambridge; *b* 10 March 1934; *s* of John Hugo and Cecily Eileen Emsley Matthews; *m* 1984, Lucienne Marie Jeanne Schleich; one step *s* one step *d. Educ:* Montpellier Sch., Paignton; Clifton Coll.; St John's Coll., Cambridge (MA 1960; LittD 1988). Lectr in Linguistics, UCNW, 1961–65 (on leave Indiana Univ., Bloomington, 1963–64); University of Reading: Lectr in Linguistic Science, 1965–69; Reader, 1969–75; Prof., 1975–80 (on leave as Fellow, King's Coll., Cambridge, 1970–71, and as Fellow, Netherlands Inst. of Advanced Study, Wassenaar, 1977–78). Pres., Philological Soc., 1992–96 (Vice-Pres., 1996–). Hon. Mem., Linguistic Soc. of America, 1994–. An Editor, Jl of Linguistics, 1970–79. *Publications:* Inflectional Morphology, 1972; Morphology, 1974, 2nd edn 1991; Generative Grammar and Linguistic Competence, 1979; Syntax, 1981; Grammatical Theory in the United States from Bloomfield to Chomsky, 1993; The Concise Oxford Dictionary of Linguistics, 1997; A Short History of Structural Linguistics, 2001; articles and book chapters. *Recreations:* cycling, gardening. *Address:* 10 Fendon Close, Cambridge CB1 7RU. *T:* (01223) 247553; 22 Rue Nina et Julien Lefevre, 1952 Luxembourg. *T:* 224146.

MATTHEWS, Sir Peter (Jack), Kt 1981; CVO 1978; OBE 1974; QPM 1970; DL; Chief Constable of Surrey, 1968–82; *b* 25 Dec. 1917; *s* of Thomas Francis Matthews and Agnes Jack; *m* 1944, Margaret, *er d* of Cecil Levett, London; one *s. Educ:* Blackridge Public Sch., West Lothian. Joined Metropolitan Police, 1937; Flt-Lt (pilot) RAF, 1942–46; Metropolitan Police, 1946–65; seconded Cyprus, 1955; Chief Supt P Div. 1963–65; Chief Constable: of East Suffolk, 1965–67; of Suffolk, 1967–68. President: British Section,

Internat. Police Assoc., 1964–70 (Internat. Pres. 1966–70); Assoc. of Chief Police Officers of England, Wales and NI, 1976–77 (Chm., Sub-Cttee on Terrorism and Allied Matters, 1976–82; Rep. at Interpol, 1977–80); Chief Constables' Club, 1980–81; Vice-Chm., Home Office Standing Adv. Cttee on Police Dogs, 1982– (Chm., 1978–82; Chm., Training Sub-Cttee, 1972–82); led British Police Study Team to advise Singapore Police, 1982; specialist advr to Parly Select Cttee on Defence, 1984; Mem., MoD Police Review Cttee, 1985. Pres., Woking Br., Aircrew Assoc., 1990–2000. Lecture tour of Canada and USA, 1979; Lecturer: Airline Training Associates Ltd, 1984–91; International Military Services Ltd, 1987–91. Final Reader, HM The Queen's Police Gold Medal Essay Competition, 1983–92. FIMgt (CBIM 1978). DL Surrey, 1981. Special Cert. for Extraordinary Service, Office of Special Investigation, USAF, 1968. *Club:* Royal Air Force.

MATTHEWS, Philip Rodway B.; *see* Bushill-Matthews.

MATTHEWS, Prof. Robert Charles Oliver, (Robin), CBE 1975; FBA 1968; Master, 1975–93, and Fellow, since 1993, Clare College, Cambridge; Professor of Political Economy, Cambridge University, 1980–91, now Emeritus; *b* 16 June 1927; *s* of Oliver Harwood Matthews, WS, and Ida Finlay; *m* 1948, Joyce Hilda Lloyds; one *d. Educ:* Edinburgh Academy; Corpus Christi Coll., Oxford (Hon. Fellow, 1976). Student, Nuffield Coll., Oxford, 1947–48; Lectr, Merton Coll., Oxford, 1948–49; University Asst Lectr in Economics, Cambridge, 1949–51, and Univ. Lectr, 1951–65; Fellow of St John's Coll., Cambridge, 1950–65; Drummond Prof. of Political Economy, Oxford, and Fellow of All Souls Coll., 1965–75. Vis. Prof., Univ. of California, Berkeley, 1961–62. Chm., SSRC, 1972–75. A Managing Trustee, Nuffield Foundn, 1975–96; Trustee, Urwick Orr and Partners Ltd, 1978–86. Pres., Royal Econ. Soc., 1984–86; Mem., OECD Expert Group on Non-inflationary Growth, 1975–77. Chm., Bank of England Panel of Academic Consultants, 1977–93. FIDE Internat. Master of chess composition, 1965. For. Hon. Mem., Amer. Acad. of Arts and Scis, 1985; Hon. Mem., Amer. Econ. Assoc., 1993. Hon. DLitt: Warwick, 1980; Abertay Dundee, 1996. *Publications:* A Study in Trade Cycle History, 1954; The Trade Cycle, 1958; (with M. Lipton and J. M. Rice) Chess Problems: introduction to an art, 1963; (with F. H. Hahn) Théorie de la Croissance Economique, 1972; (ed) Economic Growth: trends and factors, 1981; (with C. H. Feinstein and J. C. Odling-Smee) British Economic Growth 1856–1973, 1982; (ed with G. B. Stafford) The Grants Economy and Collective Consumption, 1982; (ed) Slower Growth in the Western World, 1982; (ed with J. R. Sargent) Contemporary Problems of Economic Policy: essays from the CLARE Group, 1983; (ed) Economy and Democracy, 1985; Mostly Three-Movers: collected chess problems, 1995; articles in learned journals. *Address:* Clare College, Cambridge CB2 1TL. *Club:* Reform.

MATTHEWS, Suzan Patricia, (Mrs A. R. Matthews); QC 1993; a Recorder, since 1995; *b* 5 Dec. 1947; *y c* of late Sidney Herbert Clark and Susan Hadnett Clark (*née* Mathews); *m* 1970, Anthony Robert Matthews; one *s. Educ:* Univ. of Bradford (BSc Hons Business Admin 1972). Called to the Bar, Middle Temple, 1974. Asst Recorder, 1991–95. Asst Boundary Comr, 1992–. Councillor, SE Region, Gas Consumers' Council, 1987–96. Member: Criminal Injuries Compensation Appeals Panel, 1996–; Adv. Bd on Family Law, 1997–; Criminal Injuries Compensation Bd, 1999–2000; Mental Health Rev. Tribunal (Restricted Patients) Panel, 1999–. Pres., The Valley Trust. *Recreations:* historical research, music, gardening. *Address:* Guildford Chambers, Stoke House, Leapale Lane, Guildford, Surrey GU1 4LY. *T:* (01483) 539131; *e-mail:* suzanmatthewsqc@cs.com.

MATTHEWS, Timothy John; Chief Executive, Highways Agency, since 2000; *b* 24 June 1951; *s* of Kenneth James Matthews and Vera Joan Matthews (*née* Fittall); *m* 1984, Sally Vivien Davies; two *s. Educ:* Peterhouse, Cambridge (BA Hons History). Admin. Trainee, DHSS, 1974; Private Sec. to Perm. Sec., DHSS, 1978–79; Dist Gen. Administrator, Bloomsbury HA, 1984; Gen. Manager, Middlesex Hosp., 1985; Dist Gen. Manager, Maidstone HA, 1988; Chief Executive: St Thomas' Hosp., 1991; Guy's and St Thomas' Hosp. Trust, 1993–2000. Director: S Bank Careers, 1996–2000; Focus Central London TEC, 1997–2001; S Bank Employers' Gp, 1998–2000. Trustee, Kent Community Housing Trust, 1991–94. *Recreations:* allotment gardening, opera. *Address:* 70 Rosendale Road, West Dulwich, SE21 8DP. *Club:* Surrey CC.

MATTHEWS, Rt Rev. Victoria; *see* Edmonton (Alberta), Bishop of.

MATTHEWS, Rev. Canon William Andrew; Vicar of Bradford-on-Avon, since 1981; Chaplain to the Queen, since 2001; *b* 8 Jan. 1944; *s* of Charles and Olive Matthews; *m* 1969, Jean Elizabeth McNicholas; one *s. Educ:* Malmesbury Grammar Sch.; Univ. of Reading (BA 1965; MA 1994); St Stephen's House, Oxford. Ordained deacon, 1967, priest, 1968; Curate: St Alban's, Westbury Park, Bristol, 1967–70; Marlborough, 1970–73; Priest i/c, 1973–75, Vicar, 1975–81, Winsley. RD, Bradford-on-Avon, 1984–94; Canon and Preb., Salisbury Cath., 1988–. *Recreation:* palaeography. *Address:* Holy Trinity Vicarage, 18A Woolley Street, Bradford-on-Avon, Wilts BA15 1AF. *T:* (01225) 864444; *e-mail:* w.a.matthews@btinternet.com.

MATTHEWS, (William) David; His Honour Judge Matthews; a Circuit Judge, since 1992; *b* 19 Nov. 1940; *s* of Edwin Kenneth William Matthews and Bessie Matthews; *m* 1965, Pauline Georgina May Lewis; two *s. Educ:* Wycliffe Coll. Admitted Solicitor, 1964; Partner, T. A. Matthews & Co., 1965–92; a Recorder, 1990–92. Chm., W Mercia Criminal Justice Strategy Cttee. Pres., Herefordshire, Breconshire and Radnorshire Incorp. Law Soc., 1988–89. Mem. Council, Three Counties Agricl Soc., 1978–2001. Gov., Wycliffe Coll., 1985–90. *Recreations:* cricket, boats. *Address:* Birmingham Crown Court, Queen Elizabeth II Law Courts, Newton Street, Birmingham. *T:* (0121) 681 3300.

MATTHÖFER, Hans; Member of the Bundestag (Social Democrat), 1961–87; *b* Bochum, 25 Sept. 1925; *m* Traute Matthöfer (*née* Mecklenburg). *Educ:* primary sch.; studied economics and social sciences in Frankfurt/Main and Madison, Wis, USA, 1948–53 (grad. Economics). Employed as manual and clerical worker, 1940–42; Reich Labour Service, 1942; conscripted into German Army, 1943 (Armoured Inf.), final rank NCO. Joined SPD (Social Democratic Party of Germany), 1950; employed in Economics Dept, Bd of Management, IG Metall (Metalworkers' Union) and specialized in problems arising in connection with automation and mechanization, 1953 (Head of Educn Dept, 1961). Member, OEEC Mission in Washington and Paris, 1957–61; Vice-Pres., Gp of Parliamentarians on Latin American Affairs (Editor of periodical Esprés Español until end of 1972); Mem., Patronage Cttee of German Section of Amnesty Internat.; Pres., Bd of Trustees, German Foundn for Developing Countries, 1971–73; Parly State Sec. in Federal Min. for Economic Co-operation, 1972; Federal Minister for Research and Technology, 1974, of Finance, 1978–82, for Posts and Telecommunications, 1982. Mem. of Presidency and Treasurer, SPD, 1985–87. Chm., Exec. Bd, Beteiligungsges. der Gewerkschaften (formerly für Gemeinwirtschaft) AG, trade union holding, 1987–97. Counsellor to Govt of Bulgaria, 1997–. Publisher, Vorwärts, 1985–88. *Publications:* Der Unterschied zwischen den Tariflöhnen und den Effektivverdiensten in der Metallindustrie der Bundesrepublik, 1956; Technological Change in the Metal Industries (in two parts), 1961–62; Der Beitrag politischer Bildung zur Emanzipation der Arbeitnehmer—Materialien zur Frage des Bildungsurlaubs, 1970; Streiks und streikähnliche Formen des Kampfes der Arbeitnehmer im Kapitalismus, 1971; Für eine menschliche Zukunft—Sozialdemokratische Forschungs—und Technologiepolitik, 1976; Humanisierung der Arbeit und Produktivität in der Industriegesellschaft, 1977, 1978, 1980; Agenda 2000: Vorschläge zur Wirtschafts- und Gesellschaftspolitik, 1993; numerous articles on questions of trade union, development, research and finance policies. *Address:* Schreyerstrasse 38, 61476 Kronberg im Taunus, Germany.

MATTILA, Karita Marjatta; opera singer, soprano; *b* 5 Sept. 1960; *d* of Erkki and Arja Mattila; *m* 1992, Tapio Kuneinen. *Educ:* Sibelius Acad., Helsinki; private studies in London. Début: Finnish Nat. Opera, 1983; Royal Opera House, Covent Garden, 1986; Metropolitan Opera, NY, 1990; has performed in opera houses worldwide; has performed with conductors incl. Abbado, Haitink, Mehta and Solti; has worked with theatre directors incl. Luc Bondy and Lev Dodin; concert and recital performances. Has made numerous recordings. Outstanding Perf. Award, Evening Standard, 1997; François Reichenbech Prize, Académie du Disque Lyrique, 1997. *Address:* c/o IMG Artists Europe, 616 Chiswick High Road, W4 5RX. *T:* (020) 8233 5800.

MATTINGLEY, Brig. Colin Grierson, CBE 1985 (OBE 1980); Clerk to the Grocers' Company, 1988–98; *b* 12 Oct. 1938; *s* of Lt-Col Wallace Grierson Mattingley, KOSB and Jeanette McLaren Mattingley (*née* Service); *m* 1964, Margaretta Eli Kühle; two *d. Educ:* Wellington Coll; RMA Sandhurst. rcds, ndc, psc. Commnd KOSB, 1958; sc 1971; comd 1st Bn KOSB, 1979–81; Jun. Directing Staff, RCDS, 1981–82; Comdr, 8 Inf. Bde, 1982–84; Dir, Army Service Conditions, 1985–87; retd 1988. Col, KOSB, 1990–95. *Recreations:* sketching, walking, landscape gardening. *Address:* Stockers House, Broad Street, Somerton, Som TA11 7NH. *Clubs:* Army and Navy, St James's.

MATTINGLY, Dr Stephen, TD 1964, FRCP; Consultant Physician, Middlesex Hospital, 1958–81, now Emeritus; Consultant Physician, 1956–82 and Medical Director, 1972–82, Garston Manor Rehabilitation Centre; Hon. Consultant in Rheumatology and Rehabilitation to the Army, 1976–81; *b* 1 March 1922; *s* of Harold Mattingly, CBE and Marion Grahame Meikleham; *m* 1945, Brenda Mary Pike; one *s. Educ:* Leighton Park Sch.; UCH (MB, BS); Dip. in Physical Med., 1953. FRCP 1970. House-surg., UCH, 1947; Regtl MO, 2/10 Gurkha Rifles, RAMC Far East, 1947–49; House-surg. and Registrar, UCH, 1950–55; Sen. Registrar, Mddx Hosp., 1955–56. Reg. Med. Consultant for London, S-Eastern, Eastern and Southern Regions, Dept of Employment, 1960–74. Mem., Attendance Allowance Bd, 1978–83. Lt-Col RAMC TA, 1952–67. *Publications:* (contrib.) Progress in Clinical Rheumatology, 1965; (contrib.) Textbook of Rheumatic Diseases, ed Copeman, 1969; (contrib.) Fractures and Joint Injuries, ed Watson Jones, 5th edn 1976, 6th edn 1982; (ed) Rehabilitation Today, 1977, 2nd edn 1981; Aspects of Brington: a Northamptonshire Country Parish, 1997, 2nd edn 1998. *Recreation:* gardening. *Address:* Highfield House, Steeple Lane, Little Brington, Northants NN7 4HN. *T:* (01604) 770271.

MATUTES JUAN, Abel; Minister for Foreign Affairs, Spain, 1996–2000; *b* 31 Oct. 1941; *s* of Antonio Matutes and Carmen Juan; *m* Nieves Prats Prats; one *s* three *d. Educ:* University of Barcelona (Law and Economic Sciences). Prof., Barcelona Univ., 1963; Vice-Pres., Employers Organization for Tourism, Ibiza-Formentera, 1964–79; Mayor of Ibiza, 1970–71; Senator, Ibiza and Formentera in Alianza Popular (opposition party), 1977–79; Vice-Pres., Partido Popular (formerly Alianza Popular), 1979– (Pres., Economy Cttee); Mem., EEC, 1986–94; MEP for Spain, 1994–96. Pres., Nat. Electoral Cttee; Spokesman for Economy and Finance, Grupo Popular in Congress (Parlt). *Recreation:* tennis. *Address:* POB 416, Ibiza. *Clubs:* Golf Rocalliza (Ibiza); de Campo Tennis (Ibiza).

MAUCERI, John Francis; Principal Conductor, Hollywood Bowl Orchestra, since 1997 (Conductor, 1991–96); Music Director, Pittsburgh Opera, since 2001; *b* 12 Sept. 1945; *s* of Gene B. Mauceri and Mary Elizabeth (*née* Marino); *m* 1968, Betty Ann Weiss; one *s. Educ:* Yale Univ. (BA, MPhil). Music Dir, Yale Symphony Orch., 1968–74; Associate Prof., Yale Univ., 1974–84; Music Director: Washington Opera, 1979–82; Orchestras, Kennedy Center, 1979–91; Amer. Symphony Orch., NYC, 1985–87; Scottish Opera, 1987–93; Teatro Regio, Torino, 1994–98; Leonard Bernstein Fest., LSO, 1986; Conductor, Amer. Nat. Tour, Boston Pops Orch., 1987; co-Producer, musical play, On Your Toes, 1983; Musical Supervisor, Song and Dance, Broadway, 1985. Vis. Prof., Yale Univ., 2001. Dir, Charles Ives Soc., 1986–91 (Mem., 1986–); Mem., Adv. Bd, Amer. Inst. for Verdi Studies, 1986–; Consultant for Music Theater, Kennedy Center for Performing Arts, Washington, 1982–91; Trustee, Nat. Inst. for Music Theater, 1986–91. Mem. Adv. Bd, Kurt Weill Edn, 1993–. Fellow, Amer. Acad. Berlin, 1999. Television appearances; numerous recordings (Grammy award for Candide recording, 1987; Edison Klassiek Award, 1991; Deutsche Schallplatten Prize, 1991, 1994); soundtrack to film Evita, 1996. Antoinette Perry Award, League of NY Theatres and Producers, 1983; Drama Desk Award, 1983; Outer Critics Circle Award, 1983; Arts award, Yale Univ., 1985; Olivier award for Best Musical for Candide, adaptation for Scottish Opera/Old Vic prodn, 1988; Wavenden All Music Award for Conductor of the Year, 1989; Emmy Award, 1994, 1998; Soc. for Preservation of Film Music Award, 1995; Diapason d'Or, 1997. *Publications:* (contrib.) Sennets and Tuckets: a Bernstein celebration (ed Ledbetter), 1988; various articles for Scottish Opera programmes, newspapers, magazines and jls. *Address:* c/o David Foster, ICM Artists, 40 West 57th Street, New York, NY 10019, USA.

MAUCHLINE, Lord; Michael Edward Abney-Hastings; ranger with New South Wales Pastures Protection Board; *b* 22 July 1942; *s* and *heir* of Countess of Loudoun (13th in line), *qv* and *s* of Captain Walter Strickland Lord (whose marriage to the Countess of Loudoun was dissolved, 1945; his son assumed, by deed poll, 1946, the surname of Abney-Hastings in lieu of his patronymic); *m* 1969, Noelene Margaret McCormick, 2nd *d* of Mr and Mrs W. J. McCormick, Barham, NSW; two *s* three *d* (of whom one *s* one *d* are twins). *Educ:* Ampleforth. *Address:* 74 Coreen Street, Jerilderie, NSW 2716, Australia.

MAUD, Hon. Sir Humphrey (John Hamilton), KCMG 1993 (CMG 1982); HM Diplomatic Service, retired; Deputy Secretary General (Economic and Social Affairs) of the Commonwealth, 1993–99; *b* 17 April 1934; *s* of Baron Redcliffe-Maud, GCB, CBE and Jean, *yr d* of late J. B. Hamilton, Melrose; *m* 1963, Maria Eugenia Gazitua; three *s. Educ:* Eton (Oppidan Scholar); King's Coll., Cambridge (Scholar; Classics and History); MA. Mem., NYO, 1949–52. Instructor in Classics, Univ. of Minnesota, 1958–59; entered Foreign Service, 1959; FO, 1960–61; Madrid, 1961–63; Havana, 1963–65; FO, 1966–67; Cabinet Office, 1968–69; Paris, 1970–74; Nuffield Coll., Oxford (Econs), 1974–75; Head of Financial Relations Dept, FCO, 1975–79; Minister, Madrid, 1979–82; Ambassador, Luxembourg, 1982–85; Asst Under Sec. of State, FCO, 1985–88; High Comr, Cyprus, 1988–90; Ambassador to Argentina, 1990–93. Chairman: Commonwealth Disaster Mgt Agency Ltd, 1999–; Emerging Markets Partnership—Financial Advisors, 1999–. Member, Council: British Diabetic Assoc., 1986–90; RCM, 1987–. Dir, Orchestra of St John's, 1997–. Trustee, Parkhouse Award, 1994–. *Recreations:* golf, music ('cellist), bird-watching. *Address:* 31 Queen Anne's Grove, W4 1HW. *Clubs:* Oxford and Cambridge, Garrick; Royal Mid-Surrey Golf.

MAUDE, family name of **Viscount Hawarden.**

MAUDE, Rt Hon. Francis (Anthony Aylmer); PC 1992; MP (C) Horsham, since 1997; *b* 4 July 1953; *s* of Baron Maude of Stratford-upon-Avon, TD, PC; *m* 1984, Christina Jane, *yr d* of late Peter Hadfield, Shrewsbury; two *s* three *d. Educ:* Abingdon Sch.; Corpus Christi Coll., Cambridge (MA (Hons) History; Avory Studentship; Halse Prize). Called to Bar, Inner Temple, 1977 (scholar; Forster Boulton Prize). Councillor, Westminster CC, 1978–84. MP (C) Warwicks N, 1983–92; contested (C) Warwicks N, 1992. PPS to Minister of State for Employment, 1984–85; an Asst Government Whip, 1985–87; Parly Under Sec. of State, DTI, 1987–89; Minister of State, FCO, 1989–90; Financial Sec. to HM Treasury, 1990–92; Shadow Chancellor, 1998–2000; Shadow Foreign Sec., 2000–01. Chm., Govt's Deregulation Task Force, 1994–97. Director: Salomon Brothers, 1992–93; Asda Gp, 1992–99; Man. Dir, 1993–97, Adv. Dir, 1997–98, Morgan Stanley & Co. *Recreations:* ski-ing, cricket, reading, music. *Address:* House of Commons, SW1A 0AA.

MAUGHAN, Air Vice-Marshal Charles Gilbert, CB 1976; CBE 1970; AFC; Independent Panel Inspector, Department of the Environment, 1983–94; *b* 3 March 1923. *Educ:* Sir George Monoux Grammar Sch.; Harrow County Sch. Served War, Fleet Air Arm (flying Swordfishes and Seafires), 1942–46. Joined RAF, 1949, serving with Meteor, Vampire and Venom sqdns in Britain and Germany; comd No 65 (Hunter) Sqdn, Duxford, Cambridgeshire (won Daily Mail Arch-to-Arc race, 1959). Subseq. comd: No 9 (Vulcan) Sqdn; flying bases of Honington (Suffolk) and Waddington (Lincs); held a staff post at former Bomber Comd, Air Staff (Ops), Strike Command, 1968–70; Air Attaché, Bonn, 1970–73; AOA Strike Command, 1974–75; SASO RAF Strike Command, 1975–77. Gen. Sec., Royal British Legion, 1978–83. *Address:* Whitestones, Tresham, Wotton-under-Edge, Glos GL12 7RW.

MAULEVERER, (Peter) Bruce; QC 1985; FCIArb; a Recorder, since 1985; *b* 22 Nov. 1946; *s* of late Algernon Arthur Mauleverer and Hazel Mary Mauleverer; *m* 1971, Sara (*née* Hudson-Evans); two *s* two *d. Educ:* Sherborne School; University College, Univ. of Durham (BA 1968). Called to the Bar, Inner Temple, 1969, Bencher 1993. Vice-Chm., Internat. Law Assoc., 1993– (Hon. Sec.-Gen., 1986–93). Vice-Pres., Internat. Social Sci. Council, UNESCO, 1998–2000. *Recreations:* sailing, ski-ing, travel. *Address:* Eliot Vale House, Eliot Vale, Blackheath, SE3 0UW. *T:* (020) 8852 2070.

MAUNDER, Prof. Leonard, OBE 1977; BSc; PhD; ScD; FREng; FIMechE; Professor of Mechanical Engineering, 1967–92, now Emeritus (Professor of Applied Mechanics, 1961), Dean of the Faculty of Applied Science, 1973–78, University of Newcastle upon Tyne; *b* 10 May 1927; *s* of Thomas G. and Elizabeth A. Maunder; *m* 1958, Moira Anne Hudson; one *s* one *d. Educ:* Bishop Gore Grammar Sch., Swansea; University Coll. of Swansea (BSc; Hon. Fellow, 1989); Edinburgh Univ. (PhD); Massachusetts Institute of Technology (ScD). Instructor, 1950–53, and Asst Prof., 1953–54, in Dept of Mech. Engrg, MIT; Aeronautical Research Lab., Wright Air Development Center, US Air Force, 1954–56; Lecturer in Post-Graduate Sch. of Applied Dynamics, Edinburgh Univ., 1956–61. Christmas Lectr, Royal Instn, 1983. Member: NRDC, 1976–81; SRC Engrg Bd, 1976–80; Adv. Council on R&D for Fuel and Power, Dept of Energy, 1981–92; British Technology Gp, 1981–92; ACOST, 1987–93; Dep. Chm., Newcastle Hospitals Management Cttee, 1971–73. President: Internat. Fedn Theory of Machines and Mechanisms, 1976–79; Engrg, BAAS, 1980; Vice-Pres., IMechE, 1975–80; Chm., Engrg Educn (formerly Continuum) Exec. Bd, Royal Acad. of Engrg, 1997–. Hon. Foreign Mem., Polish Soc. Theoretical and Applied Mechanics, 1984. Hon. Fellow, UC, Swansea, 1989. *Publications:* (with R. N. Arnold) Gyrodynamics and Its Engineering Applications, 1961; Machines in Motion, 1986; numerous papers in the field of applied mechanics. *Address:* The Old Forge Building, University of Newcastle, Newcastle upon Tyne NE1 7RU. *Fax:* (0191) 222 7153; *e-mail:* leonard.maunder@ncl.ac.uk.

MAUNDRELL, Rev. Canon Wolseley David; Canon and Prebendary of Chichester Cathedral, 1981–89; Priest-in-charge (NSM), Stonegate, 1989–94; *b* 2 Sept. 1920; *s* of late Rev. William Herbert Maundrell, RN, and Evelyn Helen Maundrell; *m* 1950, Barbara Katharine Simmons (*d* 1985); one *s* one *d. Educ:* Radley Coll.; New Coll., Oxford. Deacon, 1943; Priest, 1944; Curate of Haslemere, 1943; Resident Chaplain to Bishop of Chichester, 1949; Vicar of Sparsholt and Lainston, Winchester, 1950; Rector of Weeke, Winchester, 1956; Residentiary Canon of Winchester Cathedral, 1961–70 (Treasurer, 1961–70; Vice-Dean, 1966–70); Examining Chaplain to Bishop of Winchester, 1962–70; Asst Chaplain of Holy Trinity Church, Brussels, 1970–71; Vicar of Icklesham, E Sussex, 1972–82; Rural Dean of Rye, 1978–84; Rector of Rye, 1982–89. Chm., Chichester DAC for Care of Churches, 1977–90. *Address:* 13 North Walls, Chichester, West Sussex PO19 1DA. *T:* (01243) 537359.

MAUNG, U Hla; Ambassador of the Union of Myanmar to the Court of St James's, 1992–96, concurrently accredited to Denmark, Norway and Sweden; *b* 8 Nov. 1932; *s* of U Pya and Daw Amar; *m* 1955, Daw Khin Myint; four *s* two *d. Educ:* Univ. of Yangon (BA Econs); Vanderbilt Univ., USA (MA Econs; Dip. in Econ. Devclt). Ministry of Planning and Finance, Yangon: Asst Dir, 1966–72; Dir-Gen., 1972–78; Asian Development Bank, Manila: Alternate Exec. Dir, 1978–80; Exec. Dir, 1981–83; Dir-Gen., Min. of Planning and Finance, Yangon, 1983–84; Ambassador to: Philippines, 1984–87; Yugoslavia, 1987–92. Kyein Wut Pi Pya Ye/Taya U Pade So Mo Ye Tazeik, 1989; Pyi Thu Wun Htan Taziek, 1989; Naingngandaw Ayechan Thayarye Tazeik, 1989; Pyi Thu Wun Htan Kaung Taziek, 1992. *Publications:* articles on econs to Myanmar monthly jls. *Recreations:* reading, swimming. *Address:* c/o Ministry of Foreign Affairs, Prome Court, Prome Road, Yangon, Myanmar.

MAUNSELL, (Caroline) Harriet, OBE 1994; Chairman, Occupational Pensions Regulatory Authority, since 2001 (Member, since 1997); *b* 22 Aug. 1943; *d* of Dr Geoffrey Sharman Dawes and Margaret Joan Monk; *m* 1986, Michael Brooke Maunsell, *qv. Educ:* Somerville Coll., Oxford (MA 1965). Barrister, 1973; Solicitor, 1978. Courtaulds Ltd, 1965–77; Lovell White & King, subseq. Lovells, 1977–97, Partner, 1980–97. Mem., Occupational Pensions Bd, 1987–97 (Dep. Chm., 1992–97; Chm., 1993); Mem. Council, Occupational Pensions Adv. Service, 1990–93. Co-founder and first Chm., Assoc. of Pension Lawyers, 1984–85 (Mem. cttees, 1984–97). Dir, Ambache Chamber Orchestra, 1996–; Council Mem., Cheltenham Ladies' Coll., 1998–. *Publication:* (with Jane Samsworth) Guide to the Pensions Act 1995, 1995. *Recreations:* reading, gardening, opera, travel, playing the piano, singing in a choral society. *Address:* Occupational Pensions Regulatory Authority, Invicta House, Trafalgar Place, Brighton BN1 4DW. *T:* (01273) 627609; 41 Colebrooke Row, N1 8AF.

MAUNSELL, Michael Brooke; Senior Fellow, British Institute of International and Comparative Law, 1998–2000; *b* 29 Jan. 1942; *s* of Captain Terence Augustus Ker Maunsell, RN and Elizabeth (*née* Brooke); *m* 1st, 1965, Susan Pamela Smith (*see* S. P. Maunsell) (marr. diss. 1986); 2nd, 1986, (Caroline) Harriet Dawes (*see* C. H. Maunsell). *Educ:* Monkton Combe Sch.; Gonville and Caius Coll., Cambridge (MA, LLB). Admitted Solicitor, 1967; with Lovell White & King (Solicitors), 1967–88: Partner, 1971–88; Admin Partner, 1978–83; Partner, 1988–97, Managing Partner, 1993–97, Lovell White Durrant. Dir, J. M. Jones & Sons (Holdings) Ltd, 1981–91. Chm., Educn and Trng Cttee, City of London Law Soc., 1978–91; Mem., London (No 13) Local, then Area, Legal Aid Cttee, 1971–89. Trustee: Highgate Cemetery Charity, 1988–95; Kings Corner Project (Islington), 1997–. Gov., Grey Coat Hosp., Westminster, 1997–. Liveryman, City of London Solicitors' Co., 1973–. *Recreations:* opera, theatre, travel, good living. *Address:* 41 Colebrooke Row, N1 8AF. *T:* (020) 7226 7128.

MAUNSELL, Susan Pamela; a Director, Office of the Parliamentary Commissioner for Administration, 1993–2001; *b* 30 Jan. 1942; *d* of George Cruickshank Smith and Alice Monica Smith (*née* Davies); *m* 1965, Michael Brooke Maunsell, *qv* (marr. diss. 1986). *Educ:* Nottingham High Sch. for Girls (GPDST); Girton Coll., Cambridge (schol.; BA classics; MA). Ministry of Health: Asst Principal, 1964; Private Sec. to Perm. Sec., 1967, to Parly Sec., 1968; Department of Health and Social Security: Principal, 1969; Asst Sec., 1976; Regl Controller, London S Social Security Reg., 1981–85; various HQ policy posts, 1985–89; Under Sec., Policy Div. A, DSS, 1989–92. Mem., CSAB, 1993–99. Chair, Age Concern Bromley, 1997–2001. FRSA 1995. *Recreations:* travel, books, theatre, cinema, riding, food, wine. *Address:* 27 Longton Avenue, SE26 6RE. *T:* (020) 8778 5605; *e-mail:* SusanMaunsell@compuserve.com.

MAURICE, Dr Rita Joy; Director of Statistics, Home Office, 1977–89; *b* 10 May 1929; *d* of A. N. Maurice and F. A. Maurice (*née* Dean). *Educ:* East Grinstead County Sch.; University Coll., London. BSc (Econ) 1951; PhD 1958. Asst Lectr, subseq. Lectr in Economic Statistics, University Coll., London, 1951–58; Statistician, Min. of Health, 1959–62; Statistician, subseq. Chief Statistician, Central Statistical Office, 1962–72; Head of Economics and Statistics Div. 6, Depts of Industry, Trade and Prices and Consumer Protection, 1972–77. Member: Council, Royal Statistical Soc., 1978–82; Parole Bd, 1991–94; Retail Prices Index Adv. Cttee, 1992–94. *Publications:* (ed) National Accounts Statistics: sources and methods, 1968; articles in statistical jls. *Address:* 10 Fairfax Place, Swiss Cottage, NW6 4EH.

MAUROY, Pierre; Senator, Nord, since 1992; *b* 5 July 1928; *s* of Henri Mauroy and Adrienne Mauroy (*née* Bronne); *m* 1951, Gilberte Deboudt; one *s. Educ:* Lycée de Cambrai; Ecole normale nationale d'apprentissage de Cachan. Joined Young Socialists at age of 16 (Nat. Sec., 1950–58); teacher of technical educn, Colombes, 1952; Sec.-Gen., Syndicat des collèges d'enseignement technique de la Fédération de l'Education nationale, 1955–59; Sec., Fedn of Socialist Parties of Nord, 1961; Mem., Political Bureau, 1963, Dep. Gen. Sec., 1966, Socialist Party; Mem. Exec. Cttee, Fédération de la gauche démocratique et socialiste, 1965–68; First Sec., Fedn of Socialist Parties of Nord and Nat. Co-ordination Sec., Socialist Party, 1971–79; First Sec., Socialist Party, 1988–92. Member, from Le Cateau, and Vice-Pres., Conseil Gen. du Nord, 1967–73; Town Councillor and Deputy Mayor of Lille, 1971, Mayor, 1973–2001, Vice-Pres., Town Corp., 1971–81; Deputy, Nord, 1973–81, 1986–92; Prime Minister of France, 1981–84. Pres., Regional Council, Nord-Pas-de-Calais, 1974–81; Socialist Rep. and Vice-Pres., Political Commn, EEC, 1979–81. Political Dir, Action Socialiste Hebdo, 1979–; President: Communauté Urbaine de Lille, 1989–; Fédération nationale Léo Lagrange; Fédération Nationale des Elus Socialistes et Républicains, 1987–90; Socialist International, 1992–99; Fondation Jean Jaurès, 1992–. *Publications:* Héritiers de l'avenir, 1977; C'est ici le chemin, 1982; A gauche, 1985; Parole de Lillois, 1994; Léo Lagrange, 1996. *Address:* Sénat, 75291 Paris Cedex 06, France; 17–19 rue Voltaire, 59800 Lille, France.

MAVOR, Prof. John, FREng; FRSE; Principal and Vice-Chancellor, Napier University, since 1994; *b* 18 July 1942; *s* of Gordon Hattersley Mavor and Wilhelmina Baillie McAllister; *m* 1968, Susan Christina Colton; two *d. Educ:* City Univ., London; London Univ. (BSc, PhD, DSc(Eng)). FInstP; FIEEE; FIEE. AEI Res. Labs, London, 1964–65; Texas Instruments Ltd, Bedford, 1968–70; Emihus Microcomponents, Glenrothes, 1970–71; University of Edinburgh: Lectr, 1971; Reader, 1979; Lothian Chair of Microelectronics, 1980; Head of Dept of Electrical Engrg, 1984–89; Prof. of Electrical Engrg, 1986–94; Dean, 1989–94, and Provost, 1992–94, Faculty of Sci. and Engrg. Hon. DSc: Greenwich, 1998; City, 1998. *Publications:* MOST Integrated Circuit Engineering, 1973; Introduction to MOS LSI Design, 1983; over 150 technical papers in professional electronics jls. *Recreations:* gardening, walking, steam railways. *Address:* Napier University, 219 Colinton Road, Edinburgh EH14 1DJ.

MAVOR, Michael Barclay, CVO 1983; MA; Head Master, Loretto School, since 2001; *b* 29 Jan. 1947; *s* of late William Ferrier Mavor and Sheena Watson Mavor (*née* Barclay); *m* 1970, Jane Elizabeth Sucksmith; one *s* one *d. Educ:* Loretto School; St John's Coll., Cambridge (Exhibn and Trevelyan Schol.; Pres., Johnian Soc., 2000). MA (English); CertEd. Woodrow Wilson Teaching Fellow, Northwestern Univ., Evanston, Ill, 1969–72; Asst Master, Tonbridge Sch., 1972–78; Course Tutor (Drama), Open Univ., 1977–78; Headmaster, Gordonstoun Sch., 1979–90; Head Master, Rugby Sch., 1990–2001. Chm., HMC, 1997. Mem., Queen's Body Guard for Scotland, Royal Co. of Archers, 1997–. *Recreations:* theatre, writing, golf, fishing, cricket. *Address:* Loretto School, Musselburgh, Midlothian EH21 7RE. *Club:* Hawks (Cambridge).

MAVOR, Ronald Henry Moray, CBE 1972; author; *b* 13 May 1925; *s* of late Dr O. H. Mavor, CBE (James Bridie) and Rona Bremner; *m* 1959, Sigrid Bruhn (marr. diss. 1989); one *s* one *d* (and one *d* decd). *Educ:* Merchiston Castle Sch.; Glasgow Univ. MB, ChB 1948; MRCPGlas 1955, FRCPGlas 1989. In medical practice until 1957, incl. periods in RAMC, at American Hosp., Paris, and Deeside Sanatoria. Drama Critic, The Scotsman, 1957–65; Dir, Scottish Arts Council, 1965–71. Prof., 1981–90, and Head, 1983–90, Dept of Drama, Univ. of Saskatchewan (Vis. Prof., 1977–78, 1979–81), Prof. Emeritus. Vice-Chm., Edinburgh Festival Council, 1975–81 (Mem., 1965–81); Mem. Gen. Adv. Council, BBC, 1971–76; Mem. Drama Panel, British Council, 1973–79. Vis. Lectr on Drama, Guelph, Ontario, and Minneapolis, 1976. FRSA 1991. *Plays:* The Keys of Paradise, 1959; Aurelie, 1960; Muir of Huntershill, 1962; The Partridge Dance, 1963; A Private Matter (originally A Life of the General), 1973; The Quartet, 1980; A House on Temperance, 1981; The Grand Inquisitor, 1990. *Publications:* Art the Hard Way, in, Scotland, 1972; A Private Matter (play), 1974; Dr Mavor and Mr Bridie, 1988. *Address:* 19 Falkland Street, Glasgow G12 9PY. *T:* (0141) 339 3149; 250 rue Nationale, 46000 Cahors, France. *T:* 565238531.

MAW, (John) Nicholas; composer; *b* 5 Nov. 1935; *s* of Clarence Frederick Maw and Hilda Ellen (*née* Chambers); *m* 1960, Karen Graham; one *s* one *d. Educ:* Wennington Sch., Wetherby, Yorks; Royal Academy of Music. Studied in Paris with Nadia Boulanger and Max Deutsch, 1958–59. Fellow Commoner in Creative Arts, Trinity Coll., Cambridge, 1966–70; Visiting Professor of Composition: Yale Music Sch., 1984–85, 1989; Boston Univ., 1986; Prof. of Music, Milton Avery Grad. Sch. of Arts, Bard Coll., NY, 1990–99; Prof. of Composition, Peabody Conservatory of Music, Baltimore, 1999–. Midsummer Prize, Corp. of London, 1980; Konssevitsky Foundn Award, 1990; Sudler Internat. Wind Band Prize, John Philip Sousa Soc., 1992; Stoeger Prize for Chamber Music, Chamber Music Soc., Lincoln Center, 1993. *Compositions include: operas:* One-Man Show, 1964; The Rising of The Moon, 1970; *for orchestra:* Sinfonia, 1966; Sonata for Strings and Two

Horns, 1967; Serenade, for small orchestra, 1973, 1977; Life Studies, for 15 solo strings, 1973; Odyssey, 1974–86; Summer Dances, 1981; Spring Music, 1983; The World in the Evening, 1988; Shahnama, 1992; Dance Scenes, 1995; Variations in Old Style, 1995, subseq. retitled Romantic Variations; *for instrumental soloist and orchestra:* Sonata Notturna, for cello and string orchestra, 1985; Little Concert, for oboe and chamber orchestra, 1987; Violin Concerto, 1993; *for voice and orchestra:* Nocturne, 1958; Scenes and Arias, 1962; *for wind band:* American Games, 1991; *chamber music:* String Quartet, no 1, 1965, no 2, 1983, no 3, 1994; Chamber Music for wind and piano quintet, 1962; Flute Quartet, 1981; Ghost Dances, for chamber ensemble, 1988; Piano Trio, 1991; *instrumental music:* Sonatina for flute and piano, 1957; Essay for organ, 1961; Personae for piano, nos I-III, 1973, IV–VI, 1985; Music of Memory, for solo guitar, 1989; Sonata for solo violin, 1997; Narration for solo cello, 2001; *vocal music:* The Voice of Love, for mezzo soprano and piano, 1966; Six Interiors, for high voice and guitar, 1966; La Vita Nuova, for soprano and chamber ensemble, 1979; Five American Folksongs, for high voice and piano, 1988; Roman Canticle, for mezzo soprano, flute, viola and harp, 1989; *choral music:* Five Epigrams, for chorus, 1960; Round, for chorus and piano, 1963; Five Irish Songs, for mixed chorus, 1973; Reverdie, five songs for male voices, 1975; Te Deum, for treble and tenor soli, chorus, congregation and organ, 1975; Nonsense Rhymes; songs and rounds for children, 1975–76; The Ruin, for double choir and solo horn, 1980; Three Hymns, for mixed choir and organ, 1989; One Foot in Eden Still, I Stand (motet for choir and soloists), 1990; Hymnus, for chorus and orch., 1996. *Address:* c/o Faber Music Ltd, 3 Queen Square, WC1N 3AU.

MAWBY, Colin (John Beverley); Conductor, National Irish Chamber Choir, 1996–2001; *b* 9 May 1936; *e s* of Bernard Mawby and Enid Mawby (*née* Vaux); *m* 1987, Beverley Courtney; two *s*. *Educ:* St Swithun's Primary Sch., Portsmouth; Westminster Cathedral Choir Sch.; Royal Coll. of Music. Organist and Choirmaster of Our Lady's Church, Warwick St, W1, 1953; Choirmaster of Plymouth Cath., 1955; Organist and Choirmaster of St Anne's, Vauxhall, 1957; Asst Master of Music, Westminster Cath., 1959; Master of Music, 1961–75; Dir of Music, Sacred Heart, Wimbledon, 1978–81; Choral Dir, Radio Telefis Eireann, 1981–95. Conductor: Westminster Chamber Choir, 1971–78; Westminster Cathedral String Orchestra, 1971–78; New Westminster Chorus, 1972–80; Horniman Singers, 1979–80. Prof. of Harmony, Trinity Coll. of Music, 1975–81. Director (Catholic) Publisher, L. J. Cary & Co., 1963; Vice-Pres., Brit. Fedn of *Pueri Cantores*; 1966; Member: Council, Latin Liturgical Assoc., 1969; Adv. Panel, Royal Sch. of Church Music, 1974; Music Sub-Cttee, Westminster Arts Council, 1974. Hon. FGCM 1988. Broadcaster and recording artist; free lance journalism. *Publications:* Church music including twenty-three Masses, anthems, motets, two children's operas and Holy Week music. *Recreations:* gardening, wine drinking. *Address:* Gerrardstown, Garlow Cross, Navan, Co. Meath, Ireland. *T:* (46) 29394; *e-mail:* colinmawby@oceanfree.net.

MAWBY, Peter John; Headmaster, Lancaster Royal Grammar School, 1983–2001; *b* 17 Aug. 1941; *s* of Norman James Mawby and May Mawby (*née* Huse); *m* 1968, Gillian Fay Moore; one *s* one *d*. *Educ:* Sedbergh Sch.; Queens' Coll., Cambridge (MA 1966). Assistant Teacher: Shrewsbury Sch., 1964–65; St John's Sch., Leatherhead, 1965–68; Head of Biology, Edinburgh Acad., 1968–79; Head of Science, Cheltenham Coll., 1979–83. Member: Council, Brathay Exploration Gp, 1989–95; Court, Lancaster Univ., 1989–2001; Headteacher Mentoring Exec. Cttee, Grant-Maintained Schs' Centre, 1992–99. *Publications:* (with M. B. V. Roberts) Biology 11–13, 1983; Biology Questions, 1985; Longman Science 11–14: Biology, 1991, 3rd edn 1996. *Recreations:* sport, music, ornithology. *Address:* Low Hill, Haverbreaks, Lancaster LA1 5BJ. *Club:* East India.

MAWER, Philip John Courtney; Secretary-General: Archbishops' Council, since 1999; General Synod of the Church of England, since 1990; *b* 30 July 1947; *s* of Eric Douglas and Thora Constance Mawer; *m* 1972, Mary Ann Moxon; one *s* two *d*. *Educ:* Hull Grammar Sch.; Edinburgh Univ. (MA Hons Politics 1971); DPA (London Univ. External) 1973. Senior Pres., Student Representative Council, 1969–70. Home Office, 1971; Private Sec. to Minister of State, 1974–76; Nuffield and Leverhulme Travelling Fellowship, 1978–79; Sec., Lord Scarman's Inquiry into Brixton disturbances, 1981; Asst Sec., Head of Industrial Relations, Prison Dept, 1984–87; Principal Private Sec. to Home Sec. (Rt Hon. Douglas Hurd), 1987–89; Under-Secretary, Cabinet Office, 1989–90. Non-exec. Dir, Ecclesiastical Insce Gp, 1996–. Trustee, All Churches Trust, 1992–; Mem. Governing Body, SPCK, 1994–. Patron, Church Housing Trust, 1996–. FRSA 1991. *Recreations:* family and friends. *Address:* Church House, Great Smith Street, SW1P 3NZ. *T:* (020) 7898 1000.

MAWER, Ronald K.; *see* Knox-Mawer.

MAWHINNEY, Rt Hon. Sir Brian (Stanley), Kt 1997; PC 1994; MP (C) Cambridgeshire North West, since 1997 (Peterborough, 1979–97); *b* 26 July 1940; *s* of Frederick Stanley Arnot Mawhinney and Coralie Jean Mawhinney; *m* 1965, Betty Louise Oja; two *s* one *d*. *Educ:* Royal Belfast Academical Instn; Queen's Univ., Belfast (BSc); Univ. of Michigan, USA (MSc); Univ. of London (PhD). Asst Prof. of Radiation Research, Univ. of Iowa, USA, 1968–70; Lectr, subsequently Sen. Lectr, Royal Free Hospital School of Medicine, 1970–84. Mem., MRC, 1980–83. Mem., Gen. Synod of C of E, 1985–90. PPS to Ministers in HM Treasury, Employment and NI, 1982–86; Under Sec. of State for NI, 1986–90; Minister of State: NI Office, 1990–92; DoH, 1992–94; Sec. of State for Transport, 1994–95; Minister without Portfolio, 1995–97; Opposition front bench spokesman on home affairs, 1997–98. Pres., Cons. Trade Unionists, 1987–90 (Vice-Pres., 1984–87); Chm. of Cons. Party, 1995–97. Mem., AUT. Contested (C) Stockton on Tees, Oct. 1974. Non-exec. dir of cos in USA, England and NI. *Publications:* (jtly) Conflict and Christianity in Northern Ireland, 1976; In the Firing Line, 1999. *Recreations:* sport, reading. *Address:* House of Commons, SW1A 0AA.

MAWHOOD, Caroline Gillian, (Mrs J. P. Nettel); Assistant Auditor General, National Audit Office, since 1996; *b* 17 July 1953; *d* of John Lennox Mawhood and Joan Constance Dick; *m* 1980, Julian Philip Nettel; two *s*. *Educ:* Queen Anne's Sch., Caversham; Bristol Univ. (BScSoc Geography). CIPFA. Joined Exchequer and Audit Dept, 1976, Dep. Dir, 1989–92; Office of the Auditor General, Canada, 1992–93; Dir of Corporate Policy, Nat. Audit Office, 1993–95. *Publication:* (contrib.) State Audit in the European Union, 1996. *Recreations:* golf, tennis, swimming, bridge. *Address:* National Audit Office, 157–197 Buckingham Palace Road, SW1W 9SP. *T:* (020) 7798 7533. *Clubs:* Roehampton, Wimbledon Park Golf.

MAWREY, Richard Brooks; QC 1986; a Recorder of the Crown Court, since 1986; *b* 20 Aug. 1942; *s* of Philip Stephen Mawrey and Alice Brooks Mawrey; *m* 1965, Gillian Margaret Butt, *d* of Francis Butt and Alice Margaret Butt; one *d*. *Educ:* Rossall School; Magdalen College, Oxford (BA, 1st class Hons Law, 1963; Eldon Law Scholar, 1964; MA 1967). Albion Richardson Scholar, Gray's Inn, 1964; called to the Bar, Gray's Inn, 1964; Lectr in Law, Magdalen College, Oxford, 1964–65, Trinity College, Oxford, 1965–69. Co-Founder and Trustee, Historic Gardens Foundn, 1995–. *Publications:* Computers and the Law, 1988; specialist editor: Consumer Credit Legislation, 1983; Butterworths County Court Precedents, 1985; Bullen & Leake & Jacob's Precedents of Pleadings, 1990, 2001; Butterworths Civil Court Pleadings, 1999. *Recreations:* history, opera, cooking. *Address:* 2 Harcourt Buildings, Temple, EC4Y 9DB. *T:* (020) 7583 9020.

MAWSON, David, OBE 1990; JP; DL; FSA; Partner, Feilden and Mawson, Architects, Norwich, 1957–90, Consultant, since 1990; *b* 30 May 1924; *s* of John William Mawson and Evelyn Mary Mawson (*née* Bond); *m* 1951, Margaret Kathlyn Norton; one *s* one *d*. *Educ:* Merchant Taylors' Sch., Sandy Lodge; Wellington Coll., NZ; Auckland Univ., NZ; Kingston-upon-Thames Coll. of Art. Royal Navy, 1945–47. Architect, 1952–. Architect, Norwich Cathedral, 1977–90. Chairman: Norfolk Soc. (CPRE), 1971–76 (Vice Pres. 1976–96; Pres., 1996–2000); 54 Gp, 1982–; Norfolk Professional Firms Gp, 1994–; Friends of Norwich Museums, 1985–2000; Founder and Chm., British Assoc. of Friends of Museums, 1973–89 (Vice-Pres., 1989–); Founder Pres., World Fedn of Friends of Museums, 1975–81, Past Pres., 1981–; Pres., Costume and Textile Assoc. for Norfolk Museums, 1989–. Mem., Cttee of Nat. Heritage, 1973–89; Trustee: Norfolk Historic Bldgs Trust, 1975–90 (Dir, 1990–); Theatre Royal, Norwich, 1991–99; Vice-Pres., Norfolk Gardens Trust, 1991– (Founder, and Chm., 1988–91); Council Mem., Assoc. of Gardens Trusts, 1994–98. Mem., Norfolk Assoc. of Architects, 1952–94 (Pres., 1979–81); Hon. Treas., Heritage Co-ordination Gp, 1981–87. Trustee, Wymondham Bridewell Preservation Trust, 1994–. First Gov., Wymondham Coll., 1991–99. Pres., Norwich Venta Probus Club, 2001–02. JP Norwich, 1972; DL Norfolk, 1986. FSA 1983. Hon. MA UEA, 1995. *Publication:* paper on British Museum Friends Socs in Proc. of First Internat. Congress of Friends of Museums, Barcelona, 1972; contrib. Jl of Royal Soc. of Arts. *Recreations:* gardening, yachting. *Club:* Norfolk (Norwich) (Pres., 1986–87).

MAWSON, Stuart Radcliffe; Consultant Surgeon, Ear Nose and Throat Department, King's College Hospital, London, 1951–79, Head of Department, 1973–79, Hon. Consultant, 1979; *b* 4 March 1918; *s* of late Alec Robert Mawson, Chief Officer, Parks Dept, LCC, and Ena (*née* Grossmith), *d* of George Grossmith Jr, Actor Manager; *m* 1948, June Irene, *d* of George Percival; two *s* two *d*. *Educ:* Canford Sch.; Trinity Coll., Cambridge; St Thomas's Hosp., London. BA Cantab 1940, MA 1976; MRCS, LRCP 1943; MB, BChir Cantab 1946; FRCS 1947; DLO 1948. House Surg., St Thomas's Hosp., 1943; RMO XIth Para. Bn, 1st Airborne Div., Arnhem, POW, 1944–45; Chief Asst, ENT Dept, St Thomas's Hosp., 1950; Consultant ENT Surgeon: King's Coll. Hosp., 1951; Belgrave Hosp. for Children, 1951; Recog. Teacher of Oto-Rhino-Laryngology, Univ. of London, 1958. Chm., KCH Med. Cttee and Dist Management Team, 1977–79. FRSocMed (Pres. Section of Otology, 1974–75); Liveryman, Apothecaries' Soc.; former Mem. Council, Brit. Assoc. of Otolaryngologists. *Publications:* Diseases of the Ear, 1963, 6th edn 1998; (jtly) Essentials of Otolaryngology, 1967; (contrib.) Scott-Brown's Diseases of the Ear, Nose and Throat, 4th edn 1979; (contrib.) Modern Trends in Diseases of the Ear, Nose and Throat, 1972; Arnhem Doctor, 1981, repr. 2000; numerous papers in sci. jls. *Address:* Whinbeck, Knodishall, Saxmundham, Suffolk IP17 1UF. *Clubs:* Aldeburgh Golf, Aldeburgh Yacht.

MAXEY, Peter Malcolm, CMG 1982; HM Diplomatic Service, retired 1986; *b* 26 Dec. 1930; *m* 1st, 1955, Joyce Diane Marshall; two *s* two *d*; 2nd, Christine Irene Spooner. *Educ:* Bedford Sch.; Corpus Christi Coll., Cambridge. Served HM Forces, 1949–50. Entered Foreign Office, 1953; Third Sec., Moscow, 1955; Second Sec., 1956; First Sec., Helsinki, 1962; Moscow, 1965; First Sec. and Head of Chancery, Colombo, 1968; seconded to Lazard Bros, 1971; Inspector, 1972; Deputy Head UK Delegation to CSCE, Geneva, 1973; Head of UN Dept, FCO, 1974; NATO Defence Coll., Rome, 1977; Dublin, 1977; on secondment as Under Sec., Cabinet Office, 1978–81; Ambassador, GDR, 1981–84; Ambassador and Dep. Perm. Rep. to UN, NY, 1984–86. Editorial Dir, Global Analysis Systems, 1986–88.

MAXTON, John Alston; *b* Oxford, 5 May 1936; *s* of late John Maxton, agr. economist, and Jenny Maxton; *m* 1970, Christine Maxton; three *s*. *Educ:* Lord Williams' Grammar Sch., Thame; Oxford Univ. Lectr in Social Studies, Hamilton Coll. Chm., Assoc. of Lectrs in Colls of Educn, Scotland; Member: Educnl Inst. of Scotland; Socialist Educnl Assoc.; MSF. Joined Lab. Party, 1970. MP (Lab) Glasgow, Cathcart, 1979–2001. Opposition spokesman on health, local govt, and housing in Scotland, 1985–87, on Scotland, 1987–92; Scottish and Treasury Whip, 1984–85. Member: Scottish Select Cttee, 1981–83; Public Accounts Cttee, 1983–84; Culture, Media and Sport (formerly Nat. Heritage) Select Cttee, 1992–2001; Speaker's Panel of Chairmen, 1994–97. *Recreations:* family, listening to jazz, running.

MAXWELL, family name of **Barons de Ros** and **Farnham**.

MAXWELL, David Campbell F.; *see* Finlay-Maxwell.

MAXWELL, Ian Robert Charles; Publisher, Maximov Publications Ltd, since 1995; *b* 15 June 1956; *s* of late (Ian) Robert Maxwell, MC; *m* 1st, 1991, Laura Plumb (marr. diss. 1998); 2nd, 1999, Tara Dudley Smith. *Educ:* Marlborough; Balliol Coll., Oxford (MA). Pergamon Press, 1978–83; Prince's Charitable Trust, 1983–84; British Printing & Communication Corporation, later Maxwell Communication Corporation, 1985–91 (Jt Man. Dir, 1988–91); Chm., Agence Centrale de Presse, 1986–89; Chairman and Publisher: Mirror Gp Newspapers, 1991 (Dir, 1987–91); The European Newspaper, 1991 (Dir, 1990–91). Mem., Nat. Theatre Develt Council, 1986–91; Pres., Club d'Investissement Media, 1988–91. Vice Chm., Derby County Football Club, 1987–91 (Chm., 1984–87). *Recreations:* music, ski-ing, water-skiing, football.

See also K. F. H. Maxwell.

MAXWELL, Prof. James Rankin, PhD, DSc; FRS 1997; Senior Research Fellow, University of Bristol, since 1999; *b* 20 April 1941; *s* of John J. and Helen M. T. Maxwell; *m* 1964, Joy Millar Hunter; one *d* (one *s* decd). *Educ:* Univ. of Glasgow (BSc; PhD 1967); DSc Bristol 1982. Research Asst, Univ. of Glasgow, 1967; Postdoctoral Res. Chemist, Univ. of Calif, Berkeley, 1967–68; University of Bristol: Postdoctoral Fellow, 1968–69; Res. Associate, 1969–72; Lectr, 1972–78; Reader, 1978–90; Prof. of Organic Geochemistry, 1990–99; Hd, Envmtl and Analytical Chem. Section, 1991–99. Geochemistry Fellow, Geochem. Soc., USA and European Assoc. Geochem., 1996. J. Clarence Karcher Medal, Univ. of Oklahoma, 1979; Treibs Medal, Geochem. Soc., USA, 1989. *Publications:* numerous papers in learned jls. *Recreations:* walking, gardening, cooking. *Address:* School of Chemistry, University of Bristol, Cantock's Close, Bristol BS8 1TS. *T:* (0117) 928 7669.

MAXWELL, John Hunter, CA; Chairman: Wellington Underwriting plc, since 2000; Ceedemo Ltd; Deputy Chairman, Atlantic Telecom Group; Director General, Automobile Association, 1996–2000; *b* 25 Sept. 1944; *s* of John Hunter Maxwell, OBE and Susan Elizabeth Una Smith; *m* 1967, Janet Margaret Frew; three *s*. *Educ:* Melville Coll., Edinburgh; Dumfries Acad.; Edinburgh Univ. CA 1967. T. Hunter Thompson & Co., CA, Edinburgh, 1962–67; Regl Dir, Far East, Rank Xerox Ltd, 1967–83; Gp Financial Controller, Grand Metropolitan plc, 1983–86; Chief Executive: Provincial Gp, 1986–92; BPB Industries plc, 1992–93; non-exec. Dir, Alliance & Leicester, 1993–94; Corporate Develt Dir, Prudential Corp. plc, 1994–96; non-exec. Dir, Provident Financial,

2000–. Mem. Council, IAM, 1997–. CIMgt 1992; FIMI 1997; FRSA 1997. Trustee, Friends of UCL, 1995–; Gov., Royal Ballet Sch., 2000–. Hon. Treas., Cruising Assoc., 1973–74. Freeman, City of London, 1998; Liveryman, Coachmakers' and Coach Harness Makers' Co., 1998–. *Recreations:* sailing, classic cars, travel, arts. *Address:* Blackwell Hall, Blackwell Hall Lane, Latimer, Bucks HP5 1TN. *Fax:* (01494) 762122. *Clubs:* Royal Thames Yacht; Itchenor Sailing (Chichester); Stoke Poges Golf.

MAXWELL, Kevin Francis Herbert; Chairman, Telemonde Inc., since 1999; *b* 20 Feb. 1959; *s* of late (Ian) Robert Maxwell, MC; *m* 1984, Pandora Deborah Karen Warnford-Davis; two *s* four *d*. *Educ:* Marlborough Coll.; Balliol Coll., Oxford (MA Hons). Chairman: Maxwell Communication Corporation, 1991 (Dir, 1986–91); Macmillan Inc., 1991 (Dir, 1988–91); Dir, Guinness Mahon Hldgs, 1989–92. Chm., Oxford United FC, 1987–92. Trustee, New Sch. for Social Research, NYC, 1989–92. *Recreations:* water colour painting, football. *Address:* Moulsford Manor, Moulsford, Oxon OX10 9HU.
See also I. R. C. Maxwell.

MAXWELL, Sir Michael (Eustace George), 9th Bt *cr* 1681 (NS), of Monreith, Wigtownshire; ARICS; *b* 28 Aug. 1943; *s* of Major Eustace Maxwell (*d* 1971) and of Dorothy Vivien, *d* of Captain George Bellville; *S* uncle, 1987. *Educ:* Eton; College of Estate Management. *Recreations:* microlights, curling, tennis, ski-ing. *Address:* Laundry House, Farming Woods, Brigstock, Northants NN14 3JA; 56 Queensmill Road, SW6 6JS. *Clubs:* Stranraer Rugby; Port William Tennis.

MAXWELL, Sir Nigel Mellor H.; *see* Heron-Maxwell.

MAXWELL, Richard; QC 1988; a Recorder, since 1992; a Deputy High Court Judge, since 1998; *b* 21 Dec. 1943; *s* of Thomas and Kathleen Marjorie Maxwell; *m* 1966, Judith Ann Maxwell; two *s* two *d*. *Educ:* Nottingham High Sch.; Hertford College, Oxford (MA). Lectr in Law, 1966–68; called to the Bar, Inner Temple, 1968. An Asst Recorder, 1989–92. *Recreations:* squash (daily), running (weekly), half marathon (annually), fly fishing (in season), ski-ing, mountain-biking, roller-blading, golf, wine, single malt whisky. *Clubs:* Nottingham and Notts United Services; Nottingham Squash Rackets; Darley Dale Flyfishers'; Beeston Fields Golf.

MAXWELL, Robert James, CVO 1998; CBE 1993; JP; FRCPE; Secretary and Chief Executive, The King's Fund, 1980–97; *b* 26 June 1934; *s* of Dr George B. Maxwell, MC and Cathleen Maxwell; *m* 1960, Jane FitzGibbon; three *s* two *d*. *Educ:* Leighton Park Sch.; New Coll., Oxford (BA 1st Cl. Hons, MA; Newdigate Prize for Poetry); Univ. of Pennsylvania (MA); LSE (PhD); Univ. of Tromsø (Dip. in Health Econs). FCMA; FRCPE 1997; 2nd Lieut, Cameronians (Scottish Rifles), 1952–54. Union Corp., 1958–66; McKinsey & Co., 1966–75; Administrator to Special Trustees, St Thomas' Hosp., 1975–80. Pres., European Healthcare Management Assoc., 1985–87; Pres., Open Section, RSocMed, 1986–88; Chm. Council, Foundn for Integrated Medicine, 1998–. Chm., Court, LSHTM, 1985–95; Governor: NISW, 1981–98; UMDS, 1989–98; Director: Guy's and Lewisham Trust, 1990–93; Lewisham NHS Trust, 1993–98; Severn NHS Trust, 1998–; Mem., Bd of Management, Med. Defence Union, 1990–98 (Hon. Fellow, 1998). Chm., Leighton Park Sch., 1981–. FRSA 1995. Hon. FRCGP 1994; Hon. MRCP 1987; Hon. Mem., Assoc. of Anaesthetists, 1990. Trustee: Joseph Rowntree Foundn, 1994–; Thrive (formerly Horticultural Therapy), 1998–; Pharmacy Res. Trust, 1999–. JP Inner London Youth and Family Courts (Chm.), 1971–98; JP S Glos, 1999. DUniv Brunel, 1993; Hon. DLitt West of England, 1993. *Publications:* Health Care: the growing dilemma, 1974; Health and Wealth, 1981; Reshaping the National Health Service, 1988; Spotlight on the Cities, 1989; An Unplayable Hand?: BSE, CJD and British Government, 1997. *Recreations:* poetry, walking, stained glass, not quite catching up with correspondence. *Address:* Pitt Court Manor, North Nibley, Dursley, Glos GL11 6EL. *Clubs:* Brooks's, Royal Society of Medicine.

MAXWELL, Simon Jeffrey; Director, Overseas Development Institute, since 1997; *b* 1 May 1948; *s* of Frederick Norman Maxwell and Ruth Maxwell (*née* Salinsky); *m* 1973, Catherine Elizabeth Pelly; three *s*. *Educ:* Lycée d'Anvers; Solihull Sch.; St Edmund Hall, Oxford (BA PPE 1970); Univ. of Sussex (MA Devtl Econs 1973). United Nations Development Programme: Jun. Professional Officer, Nairobi, 1970–72; Asst Res. Rep., New Delhi, 1973–77; Agricl Economist, ODA, Santa Cruz, Bolivia, 1978–81; Fellow, Inst. of Develt Studies, Univ. of Sussex, 1981–97. Member: Oxfam Field Cttee for Latin America, 1981–84; Ind. Gp on British Aid, 1982–; UN Adv. Gp on Nutrition, 1990–96; Program Adv. Panel, Foundn for Develt Co-operation, 1997–. External Examiner, Wye Coll., Univ. of London, 1995–98; Gov., Inst. of Develt Studies, 1996–97. Mem. Council, Develt Studies Assoc., 1998–. Trustee, Action for Conservation through Tourism, 1998–; Patron, One World Broadcasting Trust, 1998–. *Publications:* numerous pubns on poverty, food security, aid and agricl develt. *Recreations:* the five essentials: sailing, cycling, singing, swimming, shape. *Address:* Overseas Development Institute, 111 Westminster Bridge Road, SE1 7HR. *T:* (020) 7922 0300; 20 West Drive, Brighton, E Sussex BN2 2GD.

MAXWELL DAVIES, Sir Peter, Kt 1987; CBE 1981; composer and conductor; *b* 8 Sept. 1934; *s* of Thomas and Hilda Davies. *Educ:* Leigh Grammar Sch.; Manchester Univ. (MusB (Hons) 1956); Royal Manchester Coll. of Music. FRNCM 1978. Studied with Goffredo Petrassi in Rome (schol. 1957); Harkness Fellow, Grad. Music Sch., Princetown Univ., NJ, 1962. Dir of Music, Cirencester Grammar Sch., 1959–62; lecture tours in Europe, Australia, NZ, USA, Canada and Brazil; Visiting Composer, Adelaide Univ., 1966; Founder and Co-Dir, with Harrison Birtwistle, of Pierrot Players, 1967–71; Prof. of Composition, Royal Northern Coll. of Music, 1975–80; Founder and Artistic Director: The Fires of London, 1971–87; St Magnus Fest., Orkney Is, 1977–86 (Pres., 1986–); Artistic Dir, Dartington Hall Summer Sch. of Music, 1979–84; Associate Conductor/Composer: Scottish Chamber Orch., 1985–94 (Composer Laureate, 1994–); BBC Philharmonic Orch., 1992–2001; RPO, 1992–2000. Retrospective Festival, South Bank Centre, 1990. President: Schs Music Assoc., 1983–; Composers' Guild of GB, 1986–; Nat. Fedn of Music Socs, 1989–; Cheltenham Arts Fests, 1994–96; SPNM, 1995–. Series for Schools Broadcasts, BBC Television. FRCM 1994; FRSAMD 1994. Hon. Member: RAM, 1979; Guildhall Sch. of Music and Drama, 1981; Royal Philharmonic Soc., 1987; RSA, 2001. Hon. DMus: Edinburgh, 1979; Manchester, 1981; Bristol, 1984; Open Univ., 1986; Glasgow, 1993; Durham, 1994; Hull, 2001; Hon. DL Aberdeen, 1981; Hon. DLitt: Warwick, 1986; Salford, 1999. Cobbett Medal, for services to chamber music, 1989; (first) Award, Assoc. of British Orchs, 1991; Gulliver Award, 1991. Officier de l'Ordre des Arts et des Lettres (France), 1988. *Major compositions include: orchestral:* First Fantasia on an In Nomine of John Taverner, 1962, Second Fantasia, 1964; St Thomas Wake, 1968; Worldes Blis, 1969; Symphony No 1, 1976; Symphony No 2, 1980; Sinfonia Concertante, 1982; Symphony No 3, 1985; An Orkney Wedding, with Sunrise, 1985; Violin Concerto, 1985; Concerto for trumpet and orch., 1988; Symphony No 4, 1989; Ojai Festival Overture, 1991; A Spell for Green Corn: The MacDonald Dances, 1993; Symphony No 5, 1994; Cross Lane Fair, 1994; The Beltane Fire, 1995; Symphony No 6, 1996; Mavis in Las Vegas, 1997; Sails in St Magnus, retitled Orkney Saga, I and II, 1997, III, 1999, V, 2000; Strathclyde Concertos: No 1, 1986; No 2, 1988; No 3, for horn, trumpet and orch., 1989; No 4, for clarinet and orch., 1990; No 5 for violin, viola and string orch., 1991; No 6, for flute and orch., 1991; No 7, for double bass and orch., 1992; No 8, for bassoon and orch., 1993; No 9, for woodwind and strings, 1994; No 10, for orch., 1996; Symphony No 7, and No 8 (Antarctic), 2000; *instrumental:* Sonata for trumpet and piano, 1955; Piano Sonata, 1981; Brass Quintet, 1981; Concerto for piccolo, 1996; Concerto for piano, 1997; Trumpet Quintet, 1999; Horn Concerto, 1999; *for ensemble:* Alma redemptoris mater, 1957; Antechrist, 1967; Missa super L'Homme Armé, 1968; Ave Maris Stella, 1975; A Mirror of Whitening Light, 1977; Image, Reflection, Shadow, 1982; *opera:* Taverner, 1970; The Martyrdom of Saint Magnus, 1976; The Two Fiddlers, 1978; The Lighthouse, 1979; Cinderella, 1979; Resurrection, 1987; The Doctor of Myddfai, 1995; *music theatre:* Eight Songs for a Mad King, 1969; Vesalii Icones, 1969; Miss Donnithorne's Maggot, 1974; Le Jongleur de Notre Dame, 1978; The No 11 Bus, 1984; The Great Bank Robbery, 1989; Mr Emmet Takes a Walk, 1999; *ballet:* Salome, 1978; Caroline Mathilde, 1990; *for accompanied voices:* Five Motets, 1959; O Magnum Mysterim, 1960; Revelation and Fall, 1966; From Stone to Thorn, 1971; Stone Litany, 1973; Black Pentecost, 1979; Solstice of Light, 1979; Into the Labyrinth, 1983; The Turn of the Tide, 1992; The Three Kings, 1995; Job, 1997; The Jacobite Rising, 1997; Sea Elegy, 1998. *Address:* c/o Mrs Judy Arnold, 50 Hogarth Road, SW5 0PU.

MAXWELL-HYSLOP, Kathleen Rachel, FSA; FBA 1991; archaeologist, retired; *b* 27 March 1914; *d* of Sir Charles Clay, CB, FBA and Hon. Lady Clay; *m* 1938, Aymer Robert Maxwell-Hyslop (*d* 1993); one *s* two *d*. *Educ:* Downe House Sch.; Sorbonne; London Univ. (Acad. Postgrad. Dip. in Archaeology of Western Asia). FSA 1950. Institute of Archaeology, University of London: Asst Lectr, 1947–52; Lectr in W Asiatic Archaeology, 1952–66. Archaeol research and travel in Turkey, Cyprus, Iraq, Jordan, Israel, 1950–89; lectured in Philadelphia, MIT, Teheran, Amman; excavations in British Isles, Turkey, Cyprus, Iraq and Iran, 1936–90. *Publications:* Western Asiatic Jewellery *c.* 3000–612 BC, 1971; articles in Iraq, Levant, Jl of Archaeol Science, Anatolian Studies and jls in USA and Turkey. *Recreations:* gardening, painting, piano. *Address:* Water Lane House, Little Tew, Chipping Norton, Oxon OX7 4JG. *T:* (01608) 683226.

MAXWELL-HYSLOP, Sir Robert John, (Sir Robin), Kt 1992; *b* 6 June 1931; 2nd *s* of late Capt. A. H. Maxwell-Hyslop, GC, RN, and late Mrs Maxwell-Hyslop; *m* 1968, Joanna Margaret, *er d* of Thomas McCosh; two *d*. *Educ:* Stowe; Christ Church, Oxford (MA). Hons Degree in PPE Oxon, 1954. Joined Rolls-Royce Ltd Aero Engine Div., as graduate apprentice, Sept. 1954; served 2 years as such, then joined Export Sales Dept; PA to Sir David Huddie, Dir and GM (Sales and Service), 1958; left Rolls-Royce, 1960. Contested (C) Derby (North), 1959; MP(C) Tiverton Div. of Devon, Nov. 1960–1992. Member: Trade and Industry Select Cttee, 1971–92; Standing Orders Cttee, 1977–92; Procedure Select Cttee, 1978–92. Former Chm., Anglo-Brazilian Parly Gp. Politician of the Year Award (first recipient), Nat. Fedn of Self-employed and Small Businesses, 1989. *Publication:* (ed) Secretary to the Speaker: Ralph Verney's correspondence, 1999. *Recreation:* naval and South American history. *Address:* 4 Tiverton Road, Silverton, Exeter, Devon EX5 4JQ.

MAXWELL SCOTT, Sir Dominic James, 14th Bt *cr* 1642, of Haggerston, Northumberland; *b* 22 July 1968; *s* of Sir Michael Fergus Maxwell Scott, 13th Bt and of Deirdre Moira, *d* of late Alexander McKechnie; *S* father, 1989. *Educ:* Eton; Sussex Univ. *Heir: b* Matthew Joseph Maxwell Scott, *b* 27 Aug. 1976. *Address:* c/o 130 Ritherdon Road, SW17 8QQ.

MAXWELL-SCOTT, Dame Jean (Mary Monica), DCVO 1984 (CVO 1969); Lady in Waiting to HRH Princess Alice, Duchess of Gloucester, since 1959; *b* 8 June 1923; *d* of Maj.-Gen. Sir Walter Maxwell-Scott of Abbotsford, 1st Bt, CB, DSO, DL and Mairi MacDougall of Lunga. *Educ:* Couvent des Oiseaux, Westgate-on-Sea. VAD Red Cross Nurse, 1941–46. *Recreations:* gardening, reading, horses. *Address:* Abbotsford, Melrose, Roxburghshire TD6 9BQ. *T:* (01896) 752043. *Club:* New Cavendish.

MAY, family name of **Barons May** and **May of Oxford**.

MAY, 3rd Baron *cr* 1935, of Weybridge; **Michael St John May;** Bt 1931; late Lieut, Royal Corps of Signals; *b* 26 Sept. 1931; *o s* of 2nd Baron May and of Roberta, *d* of George Ricardo Thoms; *S* father, 1950; *m* 1st, 1958, Dorothea Catherine Ann (marr. diss. 1963), *d* of Charles McCarthy, Boston, USA; 2nd, 1963, Jillian Mary, *d* of Albert Edward Shipton, Beggars Barn, Shutford, Oxon; one *s* one *d*. *Educ:* Wycliffe Coll., Stonehouse, Glos; Magdalene Coll., Cambridge. 2nd Lieut, Royal Signals, 1950. *Recreations:* sailing, travel. *Heir: s* Hon. Jasper Bertram St John May, *b* 24 Oct. 1965. *Address:* Gautherns Barn, Sibford Gower, Oxon OX15 5RY; 10 Rabbit Row, W8 4DX.

MAY OF OXFORD, Baron *cr* 2001 (Life Peer), of Oxford in the County of Oxfordshire; **Robert McCredie May,** AC 1998; Kt 1996; FRS 1979; Royal Society Research Professor, Department of Zoology, Oxford University, and Imperial College, London, since 1988; Fellow of Merton College, Oxford, since 1988; President, Royal Society, since 2000; *b* 8 Jan. 1936; *s* of Henry W. May and Kathleen M. May; *m* 1962, Judith (*née* Feiner); one *d*. *Educ:* Sydney Boys' High Sch.; Sydney Univ. BSc 1956, PhD (Theoretical Physics) 1959, Gordon Mackay Lectr in Applied Maths, Harvard Univ., 1959–61; Sydney Univ.: Sen. Lectr in Theoretical Physics, 1962–64; Reader, 1964–69; Personal Chair, 1969–73; Princeton University: Prof. of Biology, 1973–88; Class of 1877 Prof. of Zoology, 1975–88; Chm., Univ. Res. Bd, 1977–88; Chief Scientific Advr to the Govt and Hd of the OST, 1995–2000. Vis. Prof., Imperial Coll., 1975–88; visiting appointments at: Harvard, 1966; California Inst. of Technology, 1967; UKAEA Culham Lab., 1971; Magdalen Coll., Oxford, 1971; Inst. for Advanced Study, Princeton, 1972; King's Coll., Cambridge, 1976. Pres., British Ecol Soc., 1992–93; Chm., Natural History Mus., 1994–98 (Trustee, 1991–93); Trustee: WWF (UK), 1990–94; Royal Botanic Gardens, Kew, 1991–96; Nuffield Foundn, 1993–. Member: Smithsonian Council, USA, 1988–; Jt Nature Conservation Council, 1989–95. Founder FMedSci 1998. Overseas Mem., Australian Acad. of Sci., 1991; For. Associate, US Nat. Acad. of Scis, 1992. Linnean Medal, 1991; Crafoord Prize, Royal Swedish Acad. of Scis, 1996. *Publications:* Stability and Complexity in Model Ecosystems, 1973, 2nd edn 1974; Theoretical Ecology: Principles and Applications, 1976, 2nd edn 1981; Population Biology of Infectious Diseases, 1982; Exploitation of Marine Communities, 1984; Perspectives in Ecological Theory, 1989; Infectious Diseases of Humans: dynamics and control, 1991; Extinction Rates, 1994; articles in mathematical, biol and physics jls. *Recreations:* tennis, running, bridge. *Address:* Royal Society, 6 Carlton House Terrace, SW1Y 5AG.

MAY, Rt Hon. Sir Anthony (Tristram Kenneth), Kt 1991; PC 1998; **Rt Hon. Lord Justice May;** a Lord Justice of Appeal, since 1997; Deputy Head of Civil Justice, since 2000; *b* 9 Sept. 1940; *s* of late Kenneth Sibley May and Joan Marguérite (*née* Oldaker); *m* 1968, Stella Gay Pattisson; one *s* two *d*. *Educ:* Bradfield Coll.; Worcester Coll., Oxford (Trevelyan Scholar 1960, Hon. Scholar 1962; MA; Hon. Fellow, 1999). Inner Temple Scholar, 1965; called to the Bar, 1967, Bencher, 1985; QC 1979; a Recorder, 1985–91; a Judge of the High Court of Justice, QBD, 1991–97. Jun. Counsel to DoE for Land Commn Act Matters, 1972–75; Chm., Commn of Inquiry, Savings and Investment Bank Ltd, IoM, 1990. A Judge, Employment Appeal Tribunal, 1993–97; Judge in Charge, Non-

Jury List, 1995–97. Chm., Security Vetting Appeals Panel, 1997–2000. Vice-Chm., Official Referees Bar Assoc., 1987–91. Mem., Civil Procedure Rule Cttee, 1997–. Vice-Pres., Guildford Choral Soc., 1991– (Chm., 1980–91). Mem. Council, Wycombe Abbey Sch., 1997–. *Publication:* (ed) Keating on Building Contracts, 5th edn 1991, 6th edn 1995. *Recreations:* gardening, music, books, bonfires. *Address:* Royal Courts of Justice, Strand, WC2A 2LL. *Club:* Garrick.

MAY, Prof. Brian Albert, FREng; independent development adviser; Professor of Agricultural Engineering, 1982–91, and Head, Cranfield Rural Institute, 1989–91, Cranfield Institute of Technology; Emeritus Professor, 1992; *b* 2 June 1936; *s* of Albert Robert and Eileen May; *m* 1961, Brenda Ann Smith; three *s*. *Educ:* Faversham Grammar Sch.; Aston Univ., Birmingham. Design Engineer, Massey Ferguson, 1958–63; National College of Agricultural Engineering: Lectr, 1963–68; Sen. Lectr, 1968–72; Principal Lectr, 1972–75; Head of Environmental Control and Processing Dept, 1972–75; Cranfield Institute of Technology: Prof. of Environmental Control and Processing, 1975–82; Head, Nat. Coll. of Agricl Engrg, later Silsoe Coll., 1976–89; Dean, Faculty of Agricl Engrg, Food Prodn and Rural Land Use, 1977–86. Dir, British Agricl Export Council, 1985–88. Member: Res. Requirements Bd on Plants and Soils, AFRC, 1980–86; Engrg Adv. Cttee, AFRC, 1984–88; Standing Cttee on University Entrance Requirements, 1984–91; Agric. and Vet. Cttee, 1985–91, Engrg and Technol. Adv. Cttee, 1991–95, British Council. Pres., IAgrE, 1984–86; FRAgS (Mem. Council, 1984–91); FREng (FEng 1990; Member: Overseas Affairs Cttee, 1991–95; Undergrad. Adv. Gp, 1993–). Governor, British Soc. for Res. in Agricl Engrg, 1979–90. Chm., Ramsgate Soc., 1995–; Vice Chm., Kent History Fedn, 1999–. Chm. of Govs, Thanet Coll., 1997–. *Publications:* Power on the Land, 1974; The Ramsgate Millennium Book, 2001; papers in agricl and engrg jls. *Recreations:* cricket, gardening, reading. *Address:* 23 Spencer Square, Ramsgate, Kent CT11 9LA. *T:* (01843) 580746; *e-mail:* BAMay@compuserve.com. *Club:* Farmers'.

MAY, Charles Alan Maynard, FREng, FIEE; lately Senior Director, Development and Technology, British Telecom; retired 1984; *b* 14 April 1924; *s* of late Cyril P. May and Katharine M. May; *m* 1947, Daphne, *o d* of late Bertram Carpenter; one *s* two *d*. *Educ:* The Grammar Sch., Ulverston, Cumbria; Christ's Coll., Cambridge (Mech. Sciences tripos 1944, MA). FIEE 1967; FREng (FEng 1982). Served REME and Indian Army, 1944–47. Entered Post Office Engrg Dept, 1948; Head of Electronic Switching Gp, 1956; Staff Engr, Computer Engrg Br., 1966; Dep. Dir (Engrg), 1970; Dir of Research, Post Office, later British Telecom, 1975–83. Dir, SIRA Ltd, 1982–89. Chm., IEE Electronics Divl Bd, 1977–78; Member: Council, IEE, 1970–72 and 1976–80; BBC Engrg Adv. Cttee, 1978–84; Adv. Cttee on Calibration and Measurement, 1978–83; Adv. Cttee, Dept of Electronic and Electrical Engrg, Sheffield Univ., 1979–82; Communications Systems Adv. Panel, Council of Educnl Technology, 1980–83; Ind. Adv. Bd, Sch. of Eng. and Applied Scis, Sussex Univ., 1981–84; Council, ERA Technology, 1983–88. Graham Young Lectr, Glasgow Univ., 1979. Vis. Examr, Imperial Coll., Univ. of London, 1980–82; External Examnr, NE London Polytechnic, 1982–86. Governor, Suffolk Coll. of Higher and Further Educn, 1980–83. *Publications:* contribs on telecommunications to learned jls. *Recreations:* gardening, snooker, bridge. *Address:* Corner Cottage, High Park Avenue, East Horsley, Leatherhead, Surrey KT24 5DD. *T:* (01483) 282521.

MAY, David; *see* May, M. D.

MAY, Douglas James; QC (Scot) 1989; a Social Security Commissioner and a Child Support Commissioner, since 1993; *b* 7 May 1946; *s* of Thomas May and Violet Mary Brough Boyd or May. *Educ:* George Heriot's Sch., Edinburgh; Edinburgh Univ. Advocate 1971. Temporary Sheriff, 1990–99. Contested (C): Edinburgh E, Feb. 1974; Glasgow Cathcart, 1983. Pres., Edinburgh Photographic Soc., 1996–99. *Recreations:* golf, photography (ARPS), travel, concert going. *Address:* Office of the Social Security Commissioners, 23 Melville Street, Edinburgh EH3 7PW. *T:* (0131) 225 2201. *Clubs:* Scottish Arts (Edinburgh); Merchants of Edinburgh Golf (Captain, 1997–99), Bruntsfield Links Golfing Society, Luffness New Golf.

MAY, Gordon Leslie, OBE 1982; retired solicitor; *b* 19 Nov. 1921; *s* of A. Carveth May and Isobella May; *m* 1945, Nina Cheek; one *s* two *d*. *Educ:* Worcester College for the Blind; Manchester Univ. War service, 1939–45. Admitted Solicitor, 1947; South Eastern Gas Board: Solicitor, 1956; Secretary, 1961; Executive Board Member, 1968; British Gas Corporation: Dep. Chairman, SW Region, 1974; Corp. Sec., 1977–84; Mem. Executive, 1982–84. Consultant, Keene Marsland, solicitors, 1984–87. Mem. Exec. Council, RNIB, 1975–89. Chm. Bd of Governors, Worcester Coll. for the Blind, 1980–87. Liveryman, Solicitors' Co., 1963. *Recreation:* sailing. *Address:* Walsall House, High Street, Upnor, Rochester, Kent ME2 4XG. *T:* (01634) 297197. *Club:* Medway Yacht (Upnor).

MAY, Graham; retired from Civil Service, 1981; *b* 15 Dec. 1923; *s* of Augustus May; *m* 1952, Marguerite Lucy Griffin; four *s*. *Educ:* Gravesend County Sch. for Boys; Balliol Coll., Oxford (BA). War Service, Royal Artillery, 1942–46. Asst Principal, Min. of Works, 1948, Principal 1952; seconded to Treasury, 1961–63; Asst Sec., MPBW, 1963; Under Sec., DoE, 1972–81. *Address:* 14 Wells Close, Tenterden, Kent TN30 6QJ.

MAY, James Nicholas Welby; Director-General, UK Offshore Operators Association, since 1997; *b* 21 Feb. 1949; *s* of Richard Percy May and Caroline Rosemary Welby May (*née* Jack); *m* 1979, Diana Mary Tamplin; two *s*. *Educ:* Sherborne Sch., Dorset; Southampton Univ. (BSc 1970); College of Law. Called to the Bar, Lincoln's Inn, 1974. Programme Officer, UNEP, 1976–77; Project Officer, IUCN, 1977–78; Legal Officer, Friends of the Earth, 1978–79; Legal Adviser, NFU, 1980–89; Dir-Gen., British Retail Consortium, 1989–97. Sec., Footwear Distributors' Fedn, 1989–97; Member: Countryside Commn Common Land Forum, 1984–86; Nat. Retail Trng Council, 1989–97; Distributive Occupational Standards Council, 1993–97; Council, 1996–, Trade Assoc. Council, 1998–, CBI; Meteorological Cttee, 1997–99. Non-exec. Dir, Meteorological Office, 2000–. Non-exec. Chm., Common Data Access Ltd, 2000–. Trustee, Sherborne Sch. Foundn, 1999–. FRSA; MInstD; AIMgt; MInstPet. *Recreations:* travel, tennis, ski-ing. *Address:* UK Offshore Operators Association, 232–242 Vauxhall Bridge Road, SW1V 1AU; *e-mail:* info@ukooa.co.uk. *Clubs:* Roehampton; Royal Northern and University (Aberdeen).

MAY, Air Vice-Marshal John Anthony Gerard, CB 1995; CBE 1993; FRAeS; Air Officer Training and Air Officer Commanding Training Group, Headquarters Personnel and Training Command, and Chief Executive, Training Group Defence Agency, 1994–97; *b* 12 Nov. 1941; *s* of late Anthony Frederick May and Beatrice Mary (*née* Niblett); *m* 1964, Margaret Anne Chester; two *s*. *Educ:* City of London Sch. FRAeS 1997. Joined RAF 1961; flying trng, then Qualified Flying Instr, Linton-on-Ouse; Lightning aircraft, 1966; served with Nos 56, 5 and 19 Sqns; Staff Coll., Camberley, 1977; Chief Flying Instr, RAF Cranwell, 1979; Stn Comdr, Binbrook, 1985; Dep. Dir of Air Defence, MoD, 1987; Air Cdre Policy and Plans, RAF Support Comd, 1989; AOC No 38 Gp, and SASO, HQ Strike Comd, 1993–94. QCVSA 1971. *Recreations:* alpine ski-ing, classic cars, RAFVR(T) air experience flying for cadets. *Address:* 157 Sapley Road, Hartford, Huntingdon, Cambs PE29 1YT. *Club:* Royal Air Force.

MAY, John Otto, CBE 1962 (OBE 1949); HM Diplomatic Service; retired; *b* 21 April 1913; *s* of late Otto May, FRCP, MD; *m* 1939, Maureen McNally; one *d*. *Educ:* Sherborne; St John's Coll., Cambridge. Apptd to Dept of Overseas Trade, 1937. Private Sec. to Comptroller-General, 1939; Asst Commercial Secretary: Copenhagen, 1939; Helsinki, 1940; Ministry of Economic Warfare (Representative in Caracas), 1942–44; First Sec. (Commercial): Rome, 1945, Bucharest, 1948; Foreign Office, 1950–53; First Sec., Helsinki, 1954. Acted as Chargé d'Affaires in 1954, 1955, and 1956; Counsellor (Commercial) and Consul-General, HM Embassy, Athens, 1957–60; Consul-General: Genoa, 1960–65; Rotterdam, 1965–68; Gothenburg, 1968–72. Coronation Medal, 1953. *Recreations:* travel, photography, walking, philately. *Address:* 6 Millhedge Close, Cobham, Surrey KT11 3BE. *T:* (01932) 864645. *Club:* Oxford and Cambridge.

MAY, Prof. (Michael) David, DSc; FRS 1991; Professor and Head of Department of Computer Science, Bristol University; *b* Holmfirth, 24 Feb. 1951; *s* of Douglas May. *Educ:* Queen Elizabeth's GS, Wakefield; King's Coll., Cambridge (BA 1972; MA 1976); DSc Southampton. Lectr, Dept of Computer Sci., Warwick Univ.; Technology Manager (Computer Architecture), Inmos Ltd, Bristol. Vis. Prof. of Engrg Design, Oxford Univ., 1991. *Publication:* (ed jtly) Networks, Routers and Transputers: function, performance and application, 1993. *Address:* Department of Computer Science, University of Bristol, Merchant Venturers' Building, Woodland Road, Bristol BS8 1UB. *T:* (0117) 954 5134; 9 Eaton Crescent, Clifton, Bristol BS8 2EJ. *T:* (0117) 974 2586.

MAY, Richard George; His Excellency Judge May; a Judge of the International Criminal Tribunal for the Former Yugoslavia, since 1997; *b* 12 Nov. 1938; *s* of late George William May, MB, and Phyllis May; *m* 1974, Radmila Monica, *er d* of late J. D. A. Barnicot, OBE, and Elizabeth Barnicot; one *s* two *d*. *Educ:* Haileybury; Selwyn Coll., Cambridge. National Service, 2nd Lieut, DLI, 1958–60. Called to the Bar, Inner Temple, 1965; Midland and Oxford Circuit; a Recorder, 1985–87; a Circuit Judge, 1987–97. Vis. Fellow, US Federal Judicial Center, Washington, 1997. Contested (Lab): Dorset South, 1970; Finchley, 1979. Councillor, Westminster CC, 1971–78 (Leader of the Opposition, 1974–77). *Publications:* (ed jtly) Phipson on Evidence, 12th edn 1976, 13th edn 1982; Criminal Evidence, 1986, 4th edn 1999; (ed jtly) Essays on ICTY Procedure and Evidence, 2001; articles on criminal procedure and evidence. *Address:* International Criminal Tribunal for the Former Yugoslavia, Churchillplein 1, PO Box 13888, 2501 EW The Hague, Netherlands. *Club:* Savile.

MAY, Stuart; *see* May, W. H. S.

MAY, Theresa Mary; MP (C) Maidenhead, since 1997; *b* 1 Oct. 1956; *d* of Rev. Hubert Brasier and Zaidee Brasier (*née* Barnes); *m* 1980, Philip John May. *Educ:* St Hugh's Coll., Oxford (MA). Bank of England, 1977–83; Inter-Bank Res. Orgn, 1983–85; Assoc. for Payment Clearing Services, 1985–97 (Hd of European Affairs Unit, 1989–96). Mem. (C), Merton LBC, 1986–94. Contested (C): Durham NW, 1992; Barking, June 1994. Opposition frontbench spokesman on educn and employment, 1998–99; Shadow Sec. of State for Educn and Employment, 1999–2001; Shadow Sec. for Transport, Local Govt and the Regions, 2001–. *Recreations:* walking, cooking. *Address:* House of Commons, SW1A 0AA. *Clubs:* Carlton (Associate Mem.); Maidenhead Conservative.

MAY, Valentine Gilbert Delabere, CBE 1969; *b* 1 July 1927; *s* of Claude Jocelyn Delabere May and Olive Gilbert; *m* 1st, 1955, Penelope Sutton; one *d*; 2nd, 1980, Petra Schroeder; one *d*. *Educ:* Cranleigh Sch.; Peterhouse Coll., Cambridge. Trained at Old Vic Theatre Sch. Director: Ipswich Theatre, 1953–57; Nottingham Playhouse, 1957–61; Bristol Old Vic Company, 1961–75; plays directed at Bristol which transf. to London incl.: War and Peace, 1962; A Severed Head, 1963; Love's Labour's Lost, 1964 (also British Council European tour); Portrait of a Queen, 1965; The Killing of Sister George, 1965; The Italian Girl, 1968; Mrs Mouse, Are You Within, 1968; Conduct Unbecoming, 1969; It's a Two-Foot-Six Inches Above the Ground World, 1970; Poor Horace, 1970; Trelawny, 1972; The Card, 1973. Directed at Old Vic: Richard II, 1959; Mourning Becomes Electra, 1961; Tribute to the Lady, 1974–75. Dir, Yvonne Arnaud Theatre, Guildford, 1975–92; plays directed which transferred to London: Baggage, 1976; Banana Ridge, 1976; The Dark Horse, 1978; House Guest, 1981. Directed: Little Me, Prince of Wales, 1984; Royal Baccarat Scandal, Chichester Fest., 1988, London, 1989; Henry IV (by Pirandello), London, 1990; The Accused, Haymarket Theatre Royal, 2000. Dir, Ludlow Festival, 1993–96: The Taming of the Shrew, Richard III, King Lear. Overseas prodns include: Romeo and Juliet, and Hamlet (NY and USA tour); The Taming of the Shrew (Hong Kong Fest. and Latin America tour); Broadway prodns: A Severed Head; Portrait of a Queen; The Killing of Sister George; Conduct Unbecoming; Murder Among Friends; Pygmalion. Hon. MA Bristol, 1975. *Recreations:* reading, architecture, music, astronomy. *Address:* Manor House Farm, Peasmarsh, Guildford, Surrey GU3 1LY. *T:* (01483) 563547.

MAY, (William Herbert) Stuart; Senior Partner, Theodore Goddard, Solicitors, 1989–97; *b* 5 April 1937; *s* of Arthur Douglas May and Jean Reid; *m* 1966, Sarah Margaret (*née* Maples); four *s*. *Educ:* Taunton School; Wadham College, Oxford (MA). Qualified Solicitor, 1965, with Theodore Goddard, Partner 1970. *Recreations:* gardening, walking, reading, golf. *Address:* Lower Farm, Hadstock, Cambridge CB1 6PF.

MAYALL, Prof. James Bardsley Lawson, FBA 2001; Sir Patrick Sheehy Professor of International Relations, University of Cambridge, and Fellow, Sidney Sussex College, Cambridge, since 1998; *b* 14 April 1937; *s* of Robert Cecil Mayall and Rhoda Anne (*née* Stote); *m* 1st, 1964, Margaret Berry (marr. diss. 1990); one *d*; 2nd, 1991, Avril Doris Whalley. *Educ:* Shrewsbury Sch.; Sidney Sussex Coll., Cambridge (BA Hist. Tripos 1960; MA 1998). Sir John Dill Fellow, Princeton Univ., NJ, 1960–61; BoT, 1961–64; British High Commn, New Delhi, 1964–65; London School of Economics: Dept of Internat. Relns, 1966–98; Prof. of Internat. Relns, 1991–98, Prof. Emeritus, 1998–; Chm., Steering Cttee, Centre for Internat. Studies, 1991–98. Mem. Council, RIIA, 1992–98 (Associate Editor, Survey and Documents of Internat. Affairs, 1967–71). *Publications:* Africa and the Cold War, 1971; (Associate Ed.) Survey of International Affairs 1963, 1977; (ed jtly) A New International Commodity Regime, 1979; (ed jtly) The End of the Post-War Era: documents on Great Power relns 1968–75, 1980; (ed) The Community of States: a study in international political theory, 1982; Nationalism and International Society, 1990; (ed jtly) The Fallacies of Hope: the post Colonial record of the Commonwealth Third World, 1991; (ed) The New Interventionism 1991–94: United Nations experience in Cambodia, Former Yugoslavia and Somalia, 1996; World Politics: progress and its limits, 2000. *Recreations:* cooking, gardening, watching cricket, walking the dog. *Address:* Centre of International Studies, Fitzwilliam House, 32 Trumpington Street, Cambridge CB2 1QY. *T:* (01223) 335333. *Club:* MCC.

MAYER, Anthony; *see* Mayer, R. A. J.

MAYER, Prof. Colin Peter; Peter Moores Professor of Management Studies, Saïd Business School (formerly School of Management Studies), since 1994, and Director, Oxford Financial Research Centre, since 1998, University of Oxford; Fellow of Wadham

College, Oxford, since 1994; *b* 12 May 1953; *s* of late Harold Charles Mayer and Anne Louise Mayer; *m* 1979, Annette Patricia Haynes; two *d*. *Educ:* St Paul's Sch.; Oriel College, Oxford; Wolfson College, Oxford (MA, MPhil, DPhil); Harvard Univ. HM Treasury, 1976–78; Harkness Fellow, Harvard, 1979–80; Fellow in Economics, St Anne's College, Oxford, 1980–86; Price Waterhouse Prof. of Corporate Finance, City Univ. Business Sch., 1987–92; Prof. of Econs and Finance, Univ. of Warwick, 1992–94. Chm., ESF Network in Financial Markets, 1989–94; Dir, Oxford Economic Research Associates Ltd, 1987–. Delegate, OUP, 1996–. Hon. Fellow, St Anne's Coll., Oxford, 1993. Mem. Council, REconS, 1998–. Associate Editor: Jl of Internat. Financial Management; Jl of Corporate Finance; European Financial Management Jl; Fiscal Studies; Oxford Review of Economic Policy. *Publications:* (with J. Kay and J. Edwards) Economic Analysis of Accounting Profitability, 1986; (with J. Franks) Risk, Regulation and Investor Protection, 1989; (with A. Giovannini) European Financial Integration, 1991; (with X. Vives) Capital Markets and Financial Intermediation, 1993; (with T. Jenkinson) Hostile Takeovers, 1994; articles in economic and finance jls. *Recreations:* piano, jogging, reading philosophy and science. *Address:* Wadham College, Oxford OX1 3PN. *T:* (01865) 228476.

MAYER, John; *see* Mayer, R. J.

MAYER, (Ralph) Anthony (Jeffrey), CBE 2000; Chief Executive, Greater London Authority, since 2000; *b* 24 Feb. 1946; *s* of George Mayer and Margaret (*née* Jones); *m* 1971, Ann Gowen; one *s* one *d*. *Educ:* City of Bath Boys' Sch.; Lycée Michelet, Paris; St Edmund Hall, Oxford (BA Hons PPE). Ministry of Housing and Local Government, subseq. Department of the Environment, 1967–85: Asst Principal, 1967–72; seconded as Pvte Sec. to Parly Sec., CSD, 1971–72; Principal, 1972–81; seconded as Mem., CPRS, 1974–76, and as Prin. Pvte Sec. to Sec. of State for Transport, 1980–82; Asst Sec., 1981–85; Asst Dir, N. M. Rothschild and Sons, 1985–87; Man. Dir (Finance and Admin), Rothschild Asset Management, 1987–91; Chief Exec., Housing Corp., 1991–2000; Actg Chief Exec., Transport for London, 2000. *Recreations:* hill walking, bridge, golf, yachting. *Address:* Greater London Authority, Romney House, Marsham Street, SW1P 3PY. *T:* (020) 7983 4000.

MAYER, Prof. Roland George, PhD; Professor of Classics, King's College London, since 1996; *b* Annapolis, Md, 24 July 1947; *s* of Roland George Mayer, Jr and Mary Clare Devine. *Educ:* Univ. of Calif at Berkeley (BA 1967); Peterhouse, Cambridge (BA 1972; PhD 1977). Res. Fellow, Bedford Coll., Univ. of London, 1976–79; Lectr, 1979–88, Sen. Lectr, 1988–98, Birkbeck Coll., Univ. of London; Sen. Lectr, KCL, 1989–96. Editor, Classical Review, 1994–. *Publications: edited:* Lucan, Civil War 8, 1982; Horace, Epistles 1, 1994; Tacitus, Dialogus, 2001; (with M. Coffey) Seneca, Phaedra, 1990. *Recreations:* opera, South German Baroque churches. *Address:* Department of Classics, King's College London, Strand, WC2R 2LS. *T:* (020) 7848 2058; *e-mail:* roland.mayer@kcl.ac.uk.

MAYER, Prof. (Roland) John; FRCPath; Professor of Molecular Cell Biology, since 1986 and Head of Molecular Cell Biology, School of Biomedical Sciences, since 1997, University of Nottingham; *b* 30 April 1943; *s* of George and Ethel Mayer; *m* 1967, Elaine Ing; two *s*. *Educ:* Univ. of Birmingham (BSc 1st Cl., 1965; PhD 1968); DSc Nottingham 1980. Lectr, Sen. Lectr and Reader, Univ. of Nottingham, 1970–86. *Publications:* (with J. H. Walker) Immunochemical Methods in the Biological Sciences: enzymes and proteins, 1980; (with J. H. Walker) Immunochemical Methods in Cell and Molecular Biology, 1987; (with F. J. Doherty) Intracellular Protein Degradation, 1992; contribs to learned jls. *Recreation:* golf. *Address:* School of Biomedical Sciences, University of Nottingham Medical School, Queen's Medical Centre, Nottingham NG7 2UH. *T:* (0115) 970 9369.

MAYER, Thomas, CBE 1985; FREng; Chairman, Eldonray Ltd, since 1990; *b* 17 Dec. 1928; *s* of Hans and Jeanette Mayer; *m* 1st, 1956 (marr. diss. 1975); one *s* one *d*; 2nd, 1975, Jean Patricia Burrows. *Educ:* King's Sch., Harrow; Regent Street Polytechnic (BScEng). FIEE 1964; FRTS 1968; FREng (FEng 1987); CRAeS 1990. Broadcasting Div., Marconi Co. Ltd, 1948–68; Man. Dir, Marconi Elliott Micro-Electronics Ltd, 1968–69; Man. Dir, Marconi Communication Systems Ltd, 1969–81; Man. Dir, 1981–86, Chm., 1981–90, THORN EMI Electronics Ltd; Chief Exec., THORN EMI Technology Gp, 1986–88; Exec. Dir, THORN EMI plc, 1987–90. Chairman: THORN EMI Varian Ltd, 1981–89; Holmes Protection Gp, 1990–91; ITT Defence Ltd, 1993–97; Director: Thorn Ericsson, 1981–88; Systron Donner Corp., 1983–90; Inmos Corp., 1985–88; Babcock Thorn Ltd, 1985–90; THORN EMI Australia, 1987–88; non-executive Director: Devonport Management Ltd, 1990–97; Eurodis Electron (formerly Electron House) plc, 1991–. Chm., UK Nat. Widescreen Television Forum, DTI, 1991–97. Member: Council, IEE, 1971–74; Council, Electronic Engrg Assoc., 1974–75, 1981–87 (Pres., 1982–83); Nat. Electronics Council, 1983–98; SBAC, 1984–90 (Pres., 1987–88). Liveryman, Worshipful Co. of Engineers, 1984–. *Recreations:* golf, swimming, theatre. *Address:* 1590 A.D., Burton Lane, Monks Risborough, Bucks HP27 9JF. *T:* (01844) 274549. *Club:* Ellesborough Golf.

MAYES, Maj.-Gen. Frederick Brian, CB 1995; FRCS; Director General, Army Medical Services, 1993–96; *b* 24 Aug. 1934; *s* of late Harry Frederick and Constance Enid Mayes; *m* 1962, Mary Anna Georgina Roche; one *s* two *d* (and one *s* decd). *Educ:* Wyggeston Grammar Sch., Leicester; St Mary's Hosp. Med. Sch. (MB BS London 1958). Commissioned Lieut RAMC, 1960; served Aden, E Africa, BAOR, UK; Consultant in Surgery, 1972; CO, BMH Hannover, 1984–87; CO, Cambridge Mil. Hosp., Aldershot, 1987–88; Consultant Surgeon, HQ BAOR, 1988–90; Comdr Med., HQ BAOR, 1990–93. QHS, 1991–96. Pres., St John's Ambulance, Germany, 1990. CStJ 1993. *Recreations:* off-shore sailing, bridge, mountaineering. *Address:* Mornington, 9 Searle Road, Farnham, Surrey GU9 8LJ. *T:* (01252) 715453.

MAYES, Ian; QC 1993; a Recorder, since 2000; *b* 11 Sept. 1951; *yr s* of late Harold Mayes, MBE, journalist, and of Beatrice Mayes; *m* 1986, Shirley A. Bothroyd, *qv*; two *s*. *Educ:* Highgate Sch. (Foundation Schol.); Trinity Coll., Cambridge. Called to the Bar, Middle Temple, 1974 (Harmsworth Schol.; Bencher, 2001). Dept of Trade Inspection, London Capital Group Ltd, 1975–77; Standing Counsel to Inland Revenue, 1983–93. Chm., Disciplinary Tribunal, Lloyd's of London. Mem., Justice Cttee on Fraud Trials. *Recreation:* photography. *Address:* 3 (North) King's Bench Walk, Temple, EC4Y 7HR. *T:* (020) 7797 8600.

MAYES, Rt Rev. Michael Hugh Gunton; *see* Limerick and Killaloe, Bishop of.

MAYES, Shirley Ann, (Mrs Ian Mayes); *see* Bothroyd, S. A.

MAYFIELD, Hon. Lord; Ian MacDonald, MC 1945; a Senator of the College of Justice in Scotland, 1981–95; *b* 26 May 1921; *s* of H. J. and J. M. MacDonald; *m* 1946, Elizabeth de Vessey Lawson; one *s* one *d*. *Educ:* Colston's Sch., Bristol; Edinburgh Univ. (MA, LLB). Served 1939–46: Royal Tank Regt (Capt.). TA Lothians and Border Horse, later Queen's Own Lowland Yeomanry, 1948–62. Called to Bar, 1952; QC (Scot.) 1964. Mem., Criminal Injuries Compensation Board, 1972–74. Sheriff Principal of Dumfries and Galloway, Feb.-Dec. 1973; Pres., Industrial Tribunals for Scotland, 1973–81; Scottish Chm., Employment Appeal Tribunal, 1986–92. *Recreation:* sport. *Address:* Shiskine, Duncur Road, Muirfield, Gullane, E Lothian, EH31 2EF. *T:* (01620) 842084. *Clubs:* Royal Scottish Automobile (Glasgow); Hon. Company of Edinburgh Golfers.

MAYFIELD, Rt Rev. Christopher John; *see* Manchester, Bishop of.

MAYFIELD, Lt-Col Richard, DSO 1972; LVO 2000; Lieutenant, HM Body Guard of the Honourable Corps of Gentlemen-at-Arms, 1998–2000; *b* 2 Nov. 1930; *s* of Col Bryan Mayfield (formerly Scots Guards) and Rowena Lucy (*née* Hordern); *m* 1964, Rosemary Elisabeth Carlton, *d* of Col and Mrs Donald Matheson; one *s* two *d*. *Educ:* Radley Coll. Commnd Scots Guards, 1949; served FE, ME and Europe; Lt-Col 1971; in comd 1st Bn, Scots Guards, 1971–74; retd 1974. Mem., HM Body Guard of Hon. Corps of Gentlemen-at-Arms, 1981–2000 (Clerk of the Cheque and Adjutant, 1994–98). *Recreations:* shooting, ski-ing, collecting watercolours. *Address:* Ewhurst Park, Ramsdell, Tadley, Hants RG26 5RG. *T:* (01256) 850051. *Club:* Army and Navy.

MAYHEW, family name of **Baron Mayhew of Twysden**.

MAYHEW OF TWYSDEN, Baron *cr* 1997 (Life Peer), of Kilndown in the co. of Kent; **Patrick Barnabas Burke Mayhew,** Kt 1983; PC 1986; QC 1972; DL; *b* 11 Sept. 1929; *o surv. s* of late A. G. H. Mayhew, MC; *m* 1963, Jean Elizabeth Gurney, OBE 1997, MA (Cantab), BD, FKC, *d* of John Gurney; four *s*. *Educ:* Tonbridge; Balliol Coll., Oxford (MA). President, Oxford Union Society, 1952. Commnd 4th/7th Royal Dragoon Guards, national service and AER, captain. Called to Bar, Middle Temple, 1955, Bencher 1980. Non-exec. Dir, Western Provident Assoc., 1997– (Vice-Chm., 2000). Contested (C) Camberwell and Dulwich, 1970. MP (C): Royal Tunbridge Wells, Feb. 1974–1983; Tunbridge Wells, 1983–97. Parly Under Sec. of State, Dept of Employment, 1979–81; Minister of State, Home Office, 1981–83; Solicitor General, 1983–87; Attorney General, 1987–92; Sec. of State for NI, 1992–97. Mem. Exec., 1922 Cttee, 1976–79; Vice Chm., Cons. Home Affairs Cttee, 1976–79. Chm., Prime Minister's Adv. Cttee on Business Appts, 2000–. DL Kent, 2001. *Address:* House of Lords, SW1A 0PW. *Clubs:* Garrick, Pratt's, Beefsteak; Tunbridge Wells Constitutional.

MAYHEW, David Lionel; Chairman, Cazenove Group plc, since 2001; *b* 20 May 1940; *s* of Lionel Geoffrey Mayhew and Biddy Vowe Mayhew; *m* 1966, Virginia Ann Wonnacott; two *s* one *d*. *Educ:* Eton Coll. With Panmure Gordon, 1961–69; Cazenove & Co., 1969–, Partner, 1971–. *Recreations:* farming, country pursuits. *Address:* (office) 12 Tokenhouse Yard, EC2R 7AN. *T:* (020) 7588 2828. *Clubs:* Boodles, City of London; Swinley Golf; New Zealand Golf.

MAYHEW, Judith; Chairman, Policy and Resources Committee, Corporation of London, since 1997; Special Adviser to the Chairman, Clifford Chance, since 2000; City and Business Adviser to the Mayor of London, since 2000; *b* 18 Oct. 1948; *m* 1976 (marr. diss. 1986). *Educ:* Univ. of Otago, NZ (LLM 1973). Barrister and Solicitor, NZ, 1973; admitted Solicitor, England and Wales, 1993. Lectr in Law, Univ. of Otago, 1970–73; Lecturer in Law and Sub Dean: Univ. of Southampton, 1973–76; King's Coll., London, 1976–89; Dir, Anglo Franch law degree, Sorbonne, Paris, 1976–89; Dir of Training and Employment Law, Titmuss Sainer Dechert, 1989–94; Dir of Educn and Trng, Wilde Sapte, 1994–99. Mem., Court of Common Council, 1986; Chm., Educn Cttee, Corp. of London, 1989–95. Director: Gresham Coll., 1990–; ESU, 1993–99; Geffrye Mus., 1995–99; Internat. Financial Services London (formerly British Invisibles), 1996–; City Disputes Panel, 1996–99; London First Centre, 1996–; London First, 1997–; 4Ps, 1997–; London Development Partnership, 1998–2000; London Develt Agency, 2000–; Tower Hamlets Educn Business Partnership, 2001–. Trustee, Natural History Mus., 1998–; Mem. Council, BM Develt Trust, 2001–. Governor: London Guildhall Univ., 1992–99, 2000–; Birkbeck Coll., London Univ., 1993–; Imperial Coll., London Univ., 2001–. *Recreations:* opera, theatre, old English roses, tennis. *Address:* Corporation of London, Guildhall, EC2P 2EJ. *Club:* Guildhall.

MAYHEW, Kenneth; Reader in Economics, University of Oxford, since 1996; Fellow and Tutor in Economics, since 1976, and Vicegerent, since 2000, Pembroke College, Oxford; Director, ESRC Research Centre on Skills, Knowledge and Organisational Performance, since 1998; *b* 1 Sept. 1947; *s* of late Albert Chadwick Mayhew and of Alice Mayhew (*née* Leigh). *Educ:* Manchester Grammar Sch.; Worcester Coll., Oxford (MA); London School of Economics (MScEcon). Economic Asst, HM Treasury, 1970–72; Res. Officer, Queen Elizabeth House, Oxford, 1972; Asst Res. Officer, then Res. Officer, Inst. of Economics and Statistics, Oxford, 1972–81; Economic Dir, NEDO, 1989–91. Vis. Associate Prof., Cornell Univ., 1981. Advr, CBI, 1983. Editor, Oxford Bull. of Econs and Stats, 1976–88; Associate Editor: Oxford Review of Economic Policy, 1984–; Oxford Economic Papers, 1997–. *Publications:* Trade Unions and the Labour Market, 1983; (ed with D. Robinson) Pay Policies for the Future, 1983; (ed with A. Bowen) Improving Incentives for the Low Paid, 1990; (ed with A. Bowen) Reducing Regional Inequalities, 1991; (ed jtly) Providing Health Care, 1991; (ed jtly) Britain's Training Deficit, 1994; reports and numerous articles on labour econs and industrial relns in learned jls. *Recreations:* travel, literature. *Address:* Pembroke College, Oxford OX1 1DW. *T:* (01865) 276434. *Club:* Reform.

MAYHEW, Prof. Leslie Dennis, PhD; Department of Geography, Birkbeck College, University of London, since 1998; *b* 7 Nov. 1947; *s* of Charles and Violet Mayhew; *m* 1984, Karin Sigmund; two *s* one *d*. *Educ:* Birkbeck Coll., London (BSc Hons (1st class); PhD 1979). Dir of OR, later Business Develt Manager, Benefits Agency, and sen. post in Finance/Planning, DHSS, then DSS, 1979–93; Dir of Central Services and Prin. Estabts and Finance Officer, CSO, 1993–96; Gp Dir for Admin. Services and Registration, ONS, 1996–98. Res. Schol., Internat. Inst. for Applied Systems Analysis, Vienna, 1980–82 and 1999–; Vis. Prof., Birkbeck Coll., London Univ., 1995–98. *Publications:* Urban Hospital Location, 1986; contrib. learned jls and periodicals in health, transport, geography and operational res. (current research: ageing, disability, congestion and road charging). *Recreations:* tennis, music, travelling. *Address:* Department of Geography, Birkbeck College, University of London, 7–15 Gresse Street, W1P 2LL. *T:* (020) 7631 6494; *e-mail:* l.mayhew@geog.bbk.ac.uk, lesmayhew@hotmail.com.

MAYHEW-SANDERS, Sir John (Reynolds), Kt 1982; MA; FCA; Chief Executive, 1975–83, and Chairman, 1978–83, John Brown PLC (Director, 1972–83); *b* 25 Oct. 1931; *e s* of Jack Mayhew-Sanders, FCA; *m* 1958, Sylvia Mary (*d* 1995), *d* of George S. Colling; three *s* one *d*. *Educ:* Epsom Coll.; RNC, Dartmouth; Jesus Coll., Cambridge (MA Engrg). FCA 1958. RN, 1949–55. Mayhew-Sanders & Co., Chartered Accountants, 1955–58; P-E Consulting Gp Ltd, 1958–72 (Dir, 1968–72). Director: Dowty Gp, 1982–85; Rover Gp (formerly BL plc), 1980–89; Chm., Heidrick and Struggles UK, 1985–87; Chief Exec., Samuelson Gp, 1987. Member: Management Bd, Engineering Employers' Fedn, 1977–81; BOTB, 1980–83; BBC Consultative Gp on Industrial and Business Affairs, 1981–83; Chm., Overseas Projects Bd, 1980–83; Pres., British-Soviet Chamber of Commerce, 1982–88; Vice-Pres., Inst. of Export, 1982. Governor, Sadler's Wells Foundn, 1983–89. CIMgt (CBIM 1980); FRSA 1983. *Recreations:* fishing, shooting, astronomy, music. *Address:* Great Deptford House, High Bickington, Umberleigh, N Devon EX37 9BP.

MAYLAND, Rev. Canon Ralph; VRD 1962 and bar 1972; non-stipendiary Priest-in-Charge, Brancepeth, 1994–96; *b* 31 March 1927; *s* of James Henry and Lucy Mayland; *m* 1959, Rev. Jean Mary Goldstraw; one *d* and one adopted *d*. *Educ:* Cockburn High Sch., Leeds; Leeds City Training Coll.; Westminster Coll., London Univ.; Ripon Hall, Oxford. Schoolteacher, 1945–46; RN, 1946–51; perm. commn, RNR, 1952, Chaplain, 1961–82; 3rd yr student, 1951–52; schoolteacher, 1952–57; theol student, 1957–59. Curate of Lambeth, 1959–62; Priest-in-charge, St Paul's, Manton, Worksop, 1962–67; Vicar, St Margaret's, Brightside, 1968–72; Chaplain, Sheffield Industrial Mission, 1968–75; Vicar, St Mary's, Ecclesfield, 1972–82; Chaplain to Master Cutler, 1979–80; Canon and Treasurer, York Minster, 1982–94, Canon Emeritus, 1994–. Hon. Chaplain, HMS York, 1989–; Chaplain, 8th Destroyer Assoc., 2000–. Life Mem., Royal Naval Assoc. *Recreation:* collecting Victorian children's literature. *Address:* Minster Cottage, 51 Sands Lane, Barmston, Driffield, East Yorkshire YO25 8PQ. *T:* (01262) 468709. *Club:* Nikaean.

MAYNARD, Prof. Alan Keith; Professor of Health Economics, since 1997, Director, York Health Policy Group, since 1998, University of York; *b* 15 Dec. 1944; *s* of Edward Maynard and Hilda (*née* McCausland); *m* 1968, Elizabeth Shanahan; two *s* two *d*. *Educ:* Univ. of Newcastle upon Tyne (BA Hons 1st cl. 1967); Univ. of York (BPhil 1968). Asst Lectr and Lectr, Univ. of Exeter, 1968–71; University of York: Lectr in Econs, 1971–77; Sen. Lectr, then Reader in Econs and Dir, Grad. Programme in Health Econs, 1977–83; Prof. of Econs and Founding Dir, Centre for Health Econs, 1983–95; Sec., Nuffield Provincial Hosps Trust, 1995–96. Vis. Prof., LSE, 1995–; Hon. Prof., Univ. of Aberdeen, 2000–. Mem., York HA, 1982–91; non-exec. Mem., York Hosp. NHS Trust, 1991–97; Chm., York NHS Trust, 1997–. Member: ESRC, 1986–88; Health Services Res. Cttee, MRC, 1986–92; Police Foundn Inquiry into 1971 Misuse of Drugs Act, 1997–2000; Chm., Evaluation Panel, Fourth Health and Med. Res. Programme, EC, 1990–91. Hon. MFPHM. Founding Ed., Health Economics, 1992–. *Publications:* Health Care in the European Community, 1976; (ed jtly) The Public Private Mix for Health, 1982; (with A. B. Atkinson and C. Trinder) Parents and Children, 1983; (ed jtly) Preventing Alcohol and Tobacco Problems, 1989; (ed jtly) Controlling Legal Addictions, 1990; (ed jtly) Competition in Health Care, 1991; (ed jtly) Purchasing and Providing Cost Effective Health Care, 1993; (ed with Ian Chalmers) Non Random Reflections on Health Services Research, 1997; contrib. numerous articles to various jls. *Recreations:* walking, reading, watching cricket, football. *Address:* York Health Policy Group, Department of Health Studies, University of York, Heslington, York YO10 5DD. *Clubs:* Royal Society of Medicine, Royal Commonwealth Society.

MAYNARD, Edwin Francis George; Overseas Business Consultant; Member, Export Council Advisory Panel; HM Diplomatic Service, retired; Deputy High Commissioner, Calcutta, 1976–80; *b* 23 Feb. 1921; *s* of late Edwin Maynard, MD, FRCS, DPH, and late Nancy Frances Tully; *m* 1945, Patricia Baker; one *s* one *d*; *m* 1963, Anna McGettrick; two *s*. *Educ:* Westminster. Served with Indian Army (4/8th (PWO) Punjab Regt and General Staff) (Major, GSO II), Middle East and Burma, 1939–46. BBC French Service, 1947; Foreign Office, 1949; Consul and Oriental Sec., Jedda, 1950; Second, later First, Sec., Benghazi, 1952; FO 1954; Bogota, 1956; Khartoum, 1959; FO, 1960; Baghdad, 1962; Founder Dir, Diplomatic Service Language Centre, 1966; Counsellor, Aden, 1967; Counsellor, New Delhi, 1968–72; Minister (Commercial), 1972–76, Chargé d'Affaires, 1974–75, Buenos Aires. *Recreations:* shooting, fishing, languages, gardening. *Address:* Littlebourne Court, Littlebourne, Canterbury, Kent CT3 1TU. *Club:* Brooks's.

MAYNARD, Prof. Geoffrey Walter; Economic Adviser, Investcorp International Ltd, since 1986; Director of Economics, Europe and Middle East, Chase Manhattan Bank, 1977–86 (Economic consultant, 1974); Director, Chase Manhattan Ltd, 1977–86; *b* 27 Oct. 1921; *s* of Walter F. Maynard and Maisie Maynard (*née* Bristow); *m* 1949, Marie Lilian Wright; two *d*. *Educ:* London School of Economics. BSc(Econ); PhD. Served War, 1941–45, RAF. Lectr and Sen. Lectr, UC of S Wales, Cardiff, 1951–62; Economic Consultant, HM Treasury 1962–64; Economic Advr, Harvard Univ. Develt Adv. Gp in Argentina, 1964–65; University of Reading: Reader, 1966–68; Prof. of Economics, 1968–76; Vis. Prof. of Economics, 1976–. Editor, Bankers' Magazine, 1968–72; Under-Sec. (Econs), HM Treasury, 1972–74 (on leave of absence); Dep. Chief Economic Advr, HM Treasury, 1976–77; occasional consultant, IBRD, Overseas Develt Administration of FCO. Mem., Econ. Affairs Cttee, ESRC, 1982–85. Mem. Governing Body, Inst. of Develt Studies, Sussex, 1984–91; Mem. Council, Inst. of Fiscal Studies, 1988–2000. *Publications:* Economic Development and the Price Level, 1962; (jtly) International Monetary Reform and Latin America, 1966; (jtly) A World of Inflation, 1976; The Economy under Mrs Thatcher, 1988; chapters in: Development Policy: theory and practice, ed G. Papanek, 1968; Commonwealth Policy in a Global Context, ed Streeten and Corbet, 1971; Economic Analysis and the Multinational Enterprise, ed J. Dunning, 1974; Special Drawing Rights and Development Aid (paper), 1972; articles in Economic Jl, Oxford Economic Papers, Jl of Development Studies, World Development, etc. *Address:* 219 Queens Quay, 58 Upper Thames Street, EC4V 3EH. *Club:* Reform.

MAYNARD, Roger Paul; Director of Investment and Joint Ventures, British Airways, since 1996; Director: Qantas, since 1993; Iberia, since 2000; *b* 10 Feb. 1943; *s* of Leonard John Maynard and May Gertrude Blake; *m* 1966, Ruth Elizabeth Wakeling; three *s* (including twin *s*). *Educ:* Purley Grammar Sch., Surrey; Queens' Coll., Cambridge (MA Hons Economics). Asst Principal, Bd of Trade, 1965; Second Secretary, UK Mission to UN and Internat. Organisations, Geneva, 1968; Principal: Dept of Industry, Shipbuilding Division, 1972; Dept of Trade, Airports Policy, 1975; Asst Sec., Dept of Industry, Air Division, 1978; Counsellor, Aviation and Shipping, British Embassy, Washington, 1982; British Airways: Vice Pres., Commercial Affairs, N America, 1987–89; Exec. Vice Pres., N America, 1989; Dir, Investor Relations and Marketplace Performance, 1989–91; Dir, Corporate Strategy, 1991–96. Dir, US Air, 1993–96. *Recreations:* cricket, golf, music. *Address:* 43 Rosebank, Holyport Road, Fulham, SW6 6LO. *T:* (office) (020) 8738 6013.

MAYNARD SMITH, Prof. John, FRS 1977; Professor of Biology, University of Sussex, 1965–85, now Emeritus; *b* 6 Jan. 1920; *s* of Sidney Maynard Smith and Isobel Mary (*née* Pitman); *m* 1941; two *s* one *d*. *Educ:* Eton Coll.; Trinity Coll., Cambridge (BA Engrg, 1941); UCL (BSc Zool., 1951; Fellow, 1979). Aircraft stressman, 1942–47; Lectr in Zool., UCL, 1952–65; first Dean of Biol Sciences, Univ. of Sussex, 1965–72. For. Associate, US Nat. Acad. of Scis, 1982; Mem., Hungarian Acad. of Scis, 1993. Hon. DSc: Kent, 1983; Oxon, 1987; Sussex, 1988; Chicago, 1988; Edinburgh, 1995. Balzan Prize, Fondazione Internazionale Premio E. Balzan, 1991; Crafoord Prize, Royal Swedish Acad. of Sci., 1999; Darwin Medal, 1986, Royal Medal, 1997, Copley Medal, 1999, Royal Soc. *Publications:* The Theory of Evolution, 1958, 3rd edn 1975; Mathematical Ideas in Biology, 1968; On Evolution, 1972; Models in Ecology, 1974; The Evolution of Sex, 1978; Evolution and the Theory of Games, 1982; The Problems of Biology, 1985; Evolutionary Genetics, 1989; (with E. Szathmáry) The Major Transitions in Evolution, 1995; (with E. Szathmáry) The Origins of Life, 1999. *Recreations:* gardening, talking. *Address:* The White House, Kingston Ridge, Lewes, East Sussex BN7 3JX. *T:* (01273) 474659.

MAYNE, Ann, (Mrs Roger Mayne); *see* Jellicoe, P. A.

MAYNE, Prof. David Quinn, FRS 1985; FREng; Professor of Electrical and Computer Engineering, University of California, Davis, 1989–96, now Professor Emeritus; Senior Research Fellow, Department of Electrical and Electronic Engineering, Imperial College, London University, since 1996; *b* 23 April 1930; *s* of Leslie Harper Mayne and Jane Quin; *m* 1954, Josephine Mary Hess; three *d*. *Educ:* Univ. of the Witwatersrand, Johannesburg (BSc (Eng), MSc); DIC, PhD, DSc London. FIEE, FIEEE; FREng (FEng 1987). Lectr, Univ. of Witwatersrand, 1950–54, 1956–59; R&D Engineer, British Thomson Houston Co., Rugby, 1955–56; Imperial College: Lectr, 1959–67, Reader, 1967–71; Prof. of Control Theory, 1971–89, now Prof. Emeritus; Sen. Sci. Res. Fellow, 1979–80; Hd of Dept of Electrical Engrg, 1984–88. Research Consultant, 1974–, at Univs of California (Berkeley, and Santa Barbara), Lund, Newcastle NSW, and Wisconsin. Res. Fellow, Harvard Univ., 1970; Vis. Prof., Academia Sinica, Beijing, Shanghai and Guanzhou, 1981. Corresp. Mem., Nacional Acad. de Ingenieria, Mexico, 1983. Hon. DEng Lund Univ., 1995. *Publications:* Differential Dynamic Programming, vol. 24 in Modern Analytic and Computational Methods in Science and Mathematics (with D. H. Jacobson, ed R. Bellman), 1970; Geometric Methods in System Theory, proc. NATO Advanced Study Inst., (ed. with R. W. Brockett), 1973; contribs to learned jls. *Recreations:* walking, cross-country ski-ing. *Address:* 123 Elgin Crescent, W11 2JH.

MAYNE, Eric; Under Secretary, General Functions Group, Department of Economic Development, Northern Ireland, 1986–87, retired; *b* 2 Sept. 1928; *s* of Robert P. Mayne and Margaret Mayne; *m* 1954, Sarah Boyd (*née* Gray); three *s* two *d*. *Educ:* Bangor Grammar Sch. Univ. of Reading (BSc); Michigan State Univ. (MS). Horticultural Advisor, Min. of Agriculture, NI, 1949–56; Kellogg Foundation Fellow, 1956–57; Horticultural Advisor, HQ Min. of Agriculture, NI, 1957–64; Principal Officer, 1964–67; Gen. Manager, NI Agric. Trust, 1967–74; Sen. Asst Secretary, Dept of Agriculture, NI, 1974–79; Dep. Sec., Dept of Manpower Services, NI, 1979–82; Under Sec., Dept of Econ. Develt, NI, 1982–87. *Recreations:* gardening, winemaking.

MAYNE, John Fraser, CB 1986; Principal Establishment and Finance Officer, Department of Health and Social Security, then Department of Health, 1986–90; *b* 14 Sept. 1932; *s* of late John Leonard Mayne and Martha Laura (*née* Griffiths); *m* 1958, Gillian Mary (*née* Key); one *s* one *d*. *Educ:* Dulwich Coll.; Worcester Coll., Oxford. National Service, Royal Tank Regt, 1951–53. Air Min., 1956–64; HM Treasury, 1964–67; MoD, 1967–70; Asst Private Sec. to Sec. of State for Defence, 1968–70; Cabinet Office and Central Policy Rev. Staff, 1970–73; MoD, 1973–78; Private Sec. to Sec. of State for Def., 1975–76; Asst Under-Sec. of State (Air Staff), 1976–78; Principal Establishments and Finance Officer, NI Office, 1979–81; Dir Gen. of Management Audit, MoD, 1981–83; Dep. Sec., Cabinet Office (MPO), 1984–86. Non-exec. Mem., Hampstead HA, 1991–93. Associate, PA Consulting Group, 1990–95; Dir, Carnegie Young People Initiative, 1996–98. Member: Council, RUSI, 1986–89; Public Policy Unit, 1992–97. Trustee, Nat. AIDS Trust, 1992–. Freeman, City of London, 1983. *Recreations:* music, walking, restoring furniture, cooking, gardening. *Address:* Hazlefield House, Auchencairn, Castle Douglas DG7 1RF; 2 Ashley Gardens, Ambrosden Avenue, SW1P 1QD. *Club:* New (Edinburgh).

MAYNE, Very Rev. Michael Clement Otway, KCVO 1996; Dean of Westminster, 1986–96, now Dean Emeritus; Dean of the Order of the Bath, 1986–96; *b* 10 Sept. 1929; *s* of late Rev. Michael Ashton Otway Mayne and Sylvia Clementina Lumley Ellis; *m* 1965, Alison Geraldine McKie; one *s* one *d*. *Educ:* King's Sch., Canterbury; Corpus Christi Coll., Cambridge (MA); Cuddesdon Coll., Oxford. Curate, St John the Baptist, Harpenden, 1957–59; Domestic Chaplain to the Bishop of Southwark, 1959–65; Vicar of Norton, Letchworth, 1965–72; Head of Religious Progs, BBC Radio, 1972–79; Vicar of Great St Mary's, Cambridge (the University Church), 1979–86. Select Preacher: Univ. of Cambridge, 1988; Univ. of Oxford, 1989, 1993. Mem. Council, St Christopher's Hospice, 1988–. Chairman: London Ecumenical AIDS Forum, 1992–96; Sandford St Martin Trust, 1993–99. Trustee: Royal Foundn of Grey Coat Hosp., 1986–96; King George VI and Queen Elizabeth Foundn of St Catherine's, Cumberland Lodge, 1992–. Chm. Governors, Westminster Sch., 1986–96. *Publications:* Prayers for Pastoral Occasions, 1982; (ed) Encounters, 1985; A Year Lost and Found, 1987; This Sunrise of Wonder, 1995; Pray, love, remember, 1998; Learning to Dance, 2001. *Recreations:* theatre, bird-watching, books, silence. *Address:* 37 St Mark's Road, Salisbury, Wilts SP1 3AY. *T:* (01722) 331069.

MAYNE, Richard (John); writer; broadcaster; *b* 2 April 1926; *s* of John William Mayne and Kate Hilda (*née* Angus); *m* 1st, Margot Ellingworth Lyon; 2nd, Jocelyn Mudie Ferguson; two *d*. *Educ:* St Paul's Sch., London; Trinity Coll., Cambridge (1st Cl. Hons Pts I and II, Hist. Tripos; MA and PhD). War service, Royal Signals, 1944–47. Styring, Sen., and Res. Scholar, and Earl of Derby Student, Trinity Coll., Cambridge, 1947–53; Leverhulme European Scholar, Rome, and Rome Corresp., New Statesman, 1953–54; Asst Tutor, Cambridge Inst. of Educn, 1954–56; Official: ECSC, Luxembourg, 1956–58; EEC, Brussels, 1958–63; Dir of Documentation Centre, Action Cttee for United States of Europe, and Personal Asst to Jean Monnet, Paris, 1963–66; Paris Corresp., Encounter, 1966–71, Co-Editor, 1985–90, Contributing Editor, 1990–91. Vis. Prof., Univ. of Chicago, 1971; Dir of Federal Trust for Educn and Res., 1971–73; Head of UK Offices, 1973–79, Special Advr, 1979–80, EEC. Hon. Professorial Fellow, UCW, Aberystwyth, 1986–89. Film critic: Sunday Telegraph, 1987–89; The European, 1990–98. *Publications:* The Community of Europe, 1962; The Institutions of the European Community, 1968; The Recovery of Europe, 1970 (rev. edn 1973); The Europeans, 1972; (ed) Europe Tomorrow, 1972; (ed) The New Atlantic Challenge, 1975; (trans.) The Memoirs of Jean Monnet, 1978 (Scott-Moncrieff Prize, 1979); Postwar: the dawn of today's Europe, 1983; (ed) Western Europe: a handbook, 1986; Federal Union: the pioneers, 1990; (trans.) Europe: a history of its peoples, 1990; (trans.) A History of Civilisations, 1993; (trans.) Illustrated History of Europe, 1993; The Language of Sailing, 2000. *Recreations:* travel, sailing, fell-walking. *Address:* Albany Cottage, 24 Park Village East, Regent's Park, NW1 7PZ. *T:* (020) 7387 6654. *Clubs:* Groucho; Les Misérables (Paris).

MAYNE, William; writer; *b* 16 March 1928; *s* of William and Dorothy Mayne. *Educ:* Cathedral Choir Sch., Canterbury, 1937–42 (then irregularly). Has pursued a career as novelist and has had published a large number of stories for children and young people—about 120 altogether, beginning in 1953 and going on into the foreseeable future. Lectr in Creative Writing, Deakin Univ., Geelong, Vic, Aust., academic years, 1976 and 1977; Fellow in Creative Writing, Rolle Coll., Exmouth, 1979–80. Library Assoc's Carnegie Medal for best children's book of the year (1956), 1957; Guardian Award for Children's Fiction, 1993; (jtly) Kurt Maschler Award, 1997. *Address:* c/o David Higham Associates, 5–8 Lower John Street, Golden Square, W1R 4HA.

MAYO, 10th Earl of, *cr* 1785; **Terence Patrick Bourke;** Baron Naas, 1766; Viscount Mayo, 1781; Lieut RN (retired); Managing Director, Irish Marble Ltd, Galway, 1965–82;

b 26 Aug. 1929; *s* of Hon. Bryan Longley Bourke (*d* 1961) and Violet Wilmot Heathcote Bourke (*d* 1950); *S* uncle, 1962; *m* 1st, 1952, Margaret Jane Robinson Harrison (marr. diss. 1987; she *d* 1992); three *s*; 2nd, 1987, Sally Anne, *o d* of F. G. Matthews; one *s*. *Educ:* St Aubyns, Rottingdean; RNC Dartmouth. Lieut, RN, 1952; Fleet Air Arm, 1952; Suez, 1956; Solo Aerobatic Displays, Farnborough, 1957; invalided, 1959. Mem., Gosport Borough Council, 1961–64; Pres., Gosport Chamber of Trade, 1962; Gov., Gosport Secondary Schs, 1963–64. Mem., Liberal Party, 1963–65; contested (L) Dorset South, 1964. *Heir: s* Lord Naas, *qv*.

MAYO, Col (Edward) John, OBE 1976; Director General, Help the Aged, 1983–96; *b* 24 May 1931; *s* of late Rev. Thomas Edward Mayo, JP, and Constance Muriel Mayo; *m* 1st, 1961, Jacqueline Margaret Anne Armstrong, MBE 1985, Lieut WRAC (*d* 1993), *d* of late Brig. C. D. Armstrong, CBE, DSO, MC; one *s*; 2nd, 1998, Pamela Joyce Shimwell. *Educ:* King's Coll., Taunton. Commissioned into Royal Regt of Artillery, 1951; served Malta and N Africa 36 HAA Regt, 1951–55; ADC to Governor of Malta, 1953–54; 2nd Regt RHA, BAOR, 1955–58; ADC to C-in-C BAOR/Comdr Northern Army Gp, 1958–60; 20 Field Regt, RA UK, 1960–61; Adjt 20 Field Regt, RA Malaya, 1961–63; Adjt 254 (City of London) Regt RA(TA), 1963–64; Instr RMA, Sandhurst, 1964–66; GS03 Mil. Operations, MoD, 1966–68; Second in Comd 20 Heavy Regt, RA BAOR, 1968–70; GS02 Instr Staff Coll., 1970–72; commanded 17 Trng Regt and Depot RA, 1972–74, and The Depot Regt RA, 1974–75; GS01 Public Relations MoD, 1976–79; Col GS; Public Information BAOR, 1979–83; retired 1983. Dir, Executive Communication Consultants (IOM) Ltd, 1999–. Mem. Bd, HelpAge Sri Lanka; Trustee: HelpAge India, 1985–99; HelpAge Kenya; Global Cancer; Combat Stress. Patron, The Homeless Fund. *Publications:* miscellaneous articles on military matters. MIPR 1981. FRSA 1987. *Recreations:* fishing, gardening, sailing, riding, travelling, collecting and restoring antiques. *Address:* Ballamoar Castle, Sandygate, Isle of Man IM7 3AJ. *T:* (01624) 897504, *Fax:* (01624) 898144. *Clubs:* Army and Navy, Special Forces, MCC.

MAYO, Col John; *see* Mayo, Col E. J.

MAYO, Rear-Adm. Robert William, CB 1965; CBE 1962; *b* 9 Feb. 1909; *s* of late Frank Mayo, Charminster; *m* 1st, 1942, Sheila (*d* 1974), *d* of late John Colvill, JP, of Campbeltown; one *s*; 2nd, 1980, Mrs Betty Washbrook. *Educ:* Weymouth Coll.; HMS Conway. RNR and officer with Royal Mail Steam Packet Co., 1926–37; Master's Certificate; transferred to Royal Navy, 1937; qualified Anti-Submarine Specialist, 1938; served Hong Kong and Malayan Area, 1939–41; Fleet Destroyers Atlantic and N Russian Convoys, 1942–44; commanded: HMS Aberdeen and Escort Gp 56, Atlantic, 1944–45; HMS Chevron, Mediterranean, 1947–48; HMS Theseus, 1951–52; served Korean War; Capt., HMS Osprey, 1956–58; Capt. i/c Clyde (US submarines), 1959–61; Capt., HMS St Angelo (Malta Naval Base), 1961–63; Rear-Adm. and Naval Dep. to C-in-C AFNORTH, 1964–66; retired, 1966.

MAYO, Simon Herbert; Hon. Mr Justice Mayo; Vice President, Court of Appeal of the High Court, Hong Kong, since 2000; *b* 15 Nov. 1937; *s* of late Herbert and Marjorie Mayo; *m* 1966, Catherine Yin Ying Young; one *s* one *d*. *Educ:* Harrow Sch. Admitted a solicitor, England and Wales, 1961, Hong Kong, 1963; called as barrister and solicitor, W Australia, 1967. Asst Legal Advr, GEC, 1961; Asst Solicitor, Deacons, Solicitors, Hong Kong, 1963; in private practice, WA, 1967. Asst Registrar, 1968, Registrar, 1976, Supreme Court of Hong Kong; a Judge of the High Court, Hong Kong, 1980–95; Justice of Appeal, Court of Appeal of Supreme, then High, Court, Hong Kong, 1995–2000. *Recreations:* golf, music, literature, walking. *Address:* High Court, Hong Kong. *T:* 28254603. *Clubs:* Hong Kong, Sheko Country (Hong Kong).

MAYOR, Hugh Robert, QC 1986; **His Honour Judge Mayor;** a Circuit Judge, since 1992; *b* 12 Oct. 1941; *s* of George and Grace Mayor; *m* 1970, Carolyn Ann Stubbs; one *s* one *d*. *Educ:* Kirkham Grammar Sch.; St John's Coll., Oxford (MA). Lectr, Univ. of Leicester, 1964 (MA). Called to the Bar, Gray's Inn, 1968; a Recorder, 1982–92. *Address:* Crown and County Court, Rivergate, Peterborough PE1 1EJ.

MAYOR ZARAGOZA, Federico; Director-General of UNESCO, 1987–99; *b* Barcelona, 27 Jan. 1934; *s* of Federico Mayor and Juana Zaragoza; *m* 1956, Maria Angeles Menéndez; two *s* one *d*. *Educ:* Madrid Complutense Univ. Granada University: Prof. of Biochemistry, 1963–73; Rector, 1968–72; Prof. of Biochemistry, Univ. Autónoma, Madrid, 1973. Dir, 1974–78, Scientific Chm., 1983–87, Molecular Biology Centre, Higher Council for Scientific Research. Under-Sec., Min. for Educn and Science, 1974–75; Pres., Commn for Study of Special Set of Rules for the four Catalan Provinces, 1976; Mem., Cortes (Parliament) for Granada, 1977–78; Dep. Dir-Gen., UNESCO, 1978–81; Minister for Educn and Science, Spain, 1981–82; Special Advr to Dir-Gen., UNESCO, 1982; Dir, Inst. of Sciences of Man, Madrid, 1983–87. Mem., European Parlt, 1987. Pres., Foundn for Culture of Peace, Madrid, 1999–. *Address:* Mar Caribe, 15 Interland, Majadahonda, 28220 Madrid, Spain.

MAYR-HARTING, Prof. Henry Maria Robert Egmont, DPhil; FBA 1992; Regius Professor of Ecclesiastical History, University of Oxford, and Lay Canon of Christ Church, Oxford, since 1997; *b* 6 April 1936; *s* of Herbert Mayr-Harting and Anna Mayr-Harting (*née* Münzer), Prague; *m* 1968, Caroline Henry; one *s* one *d*. *Educ:* Douai School; Merton Coll., Oxford (BA Mod. Hist. 1957; MA; DPhil 1961). Asst Lectr and Lectr in Medieval History, Univ. of Liverpool, 1960–68; Fellow, and Tutor in Medieval History, St Peter's Coll., Oxford, 1968–97; Reader in Medieval History, Oxford Univ., 1993–97. Vis. Fellow, Peterhouse, Cambridge, 1983; Slade Prof. of Fine Art, Oxford Univ., 1987–88; Brown Foundn Fellow, Univ. of the South, Tennessee, 1992. Corresp. Mem., Austrian Acad. of Scis, 2001. Hon. DLitt: Lawrence Univ., Wisconsin, 1998; Univ. of the South, Tennessee, 1999. *Publications:* The Acta of the Bishops of Chichester 1075–1207, 1965; The Coming of Christianity to Anglo-Saxon England, 1972, 3rd edn 1991; What to do in the Penwith Peninsula, Cornwall, in less than perfect weather, 1987, 2nd edn 1988; Ottonian Book Illumination: an historical study, 2 vols, 1991, 2nd edn 1999; Two Conversions to Christianity: the Bulgarians and the Anglo-Saxons, 1994; (ed with Richard Harries) Christianity: two thousand years, 2001; articles in learned jls. *Recreations:* music, especially playing keyboard instruments; watching cricket. *Address:* Christ Church, Oxford OX1 1DP. *T:* (01865) 286334. *Club:* Athenæum.

MAYS, Colin Garth, CMG 1988; HM Diplomatic Service, retired; Bursar, Yehudi Menuhin School, 1991–97; *b* 16 June 1931; *s* of William Albert Mays and Sophia May Mays (*née* Pattinson); *m* 1956, Margaret Patricia, *d* of Philemon Robert Lloyd and Gladys Irene (*née* Myers); one *s*. *Educ:* Acklam Hall Sch.; St John's Coll., Oxford (Heath Harrison Scholar). Served in Army, 1949–51; entered HM Foreign (subseq. Diplomatic) Service, 1955; FO, 1955–56; Sofia, 1956–58; Baghdad, 1958–60; FO, 1960; UK Delegn to Conf. of 18 Nation Cttee on Disarmament, Geneva, 1960; Bonn, 1960–65; FO, 1965–69; Prague, 1969–72; FCO, 1972–77; Head of Information Administration Dept, 1974–77; Counsellor (Commercial), Bucharest, 1977–80; seconded to PA Management Consultants, 1980–81; Diplomatic Service Overseas Inspector, 1981–83; High Commissioner: Seychelles, 1983–86; Bahamas, 1986–91. Liveryman, Painter-Stainers' Co., 1981. *Recreations:* sailing, swimming, travel. *Club:* Travellers.

MAYSTADT, Dr Philippe; President, and Chairman, Board of Directors, European Investment Bank, since 2000; *b* 14 March 1948; *s* of Auguste Maystadt and Marie-Thérèse Deblon; *m* 1970, Suzanne Franquin; two *s* one *d*. *Educ:* Catholic Univ. of Louvain, Belgium (PhD Law 1970); Claremont Grad. Sch., LA (MA Public Admin). Asst Prof., Catholic Univ. of Louvain, 1970–77; MHR, Charleroi, Belgium, 1977–91, 1995–98; Mem., Senate, 1991–95, 1999; Sec. of State for Walloon Reg., 1979–80; Minister: for CS and Scientific Policy, 1980–81; of Budget, Scientific Policy and Planning, 1981–85; of Econ. Affairs, 1985–86; Dep. Prime Minister and Minister of Econ. Affairs, 1986–88; Minister of Finance, 1988–98; Minister of Finance and Foreign Trade, June–Sept. 1995; Dep. Prime Minister and Minister of Finance and Foreign Trade, 1995–98. Pres., Parti Social Chrétien, 1998–99. Chairman: G-10 Ministers of Finance, 1990–91; Council of Ministers of Economy and Finance of EC, 1993; Interim Cttee, IMF, 1993–98; Council of Governors, EBRD, 1997–98. Part-time Prof., Faculty of Law, Catholic Univ. of Louvain, 1989–. *Publications:* (with A. Jacquemin) Les aspects juridiques de l'intervention de l'Etat dans la vie économique, 1975 (Prix spécial de l'Association des juristes d'entreprises); Ecouter et puis Décider, 1988; (with F. Dermine-Minet) Comprendre l'économie: le marché et l'Etat à l'heure de la mondialisation, 1998. *Address:* European Investment Bank, 100 Boulevard Konrad Adenauer, 2950 Luxembourg. *T:* 43794464.

MAZANKOWSKI, Rt Hon. Donald (Frank); PC (Can.) 1979; OC 2000; Deputy Prime Minister of Canada, 1986–93; Minister of Finance, 1991–93; *b* 27 July 1935; *s* of late Frank Mazankowski and Dora (*née* Lonowski); *m* 1958, Lorraine Poleschuk; three *s*. *Educ:* High Sch., Viking, Alberta. MP (Progressive Conservative), Vegreville, 1968–93; Minister for Transport and Minister responsible for Canadian Wheat Bd, 1979–80; Minister of Transport, 1984–86; Pres. of Queen's Privy Council for Canada, 1986–91; Minister of Agriculture, 1988–91; Minister responsible for Privatization, 1988; Govt House Leader and Pres. of Privy Council, 1986–91. Director: Gulf Canada Resources Ltd, 1993–; Shaw Communications Inc., 1993–; Investors Group, 1994–; Great West Life Co., 1994–; Power Corp. of Canada, 1996–; Gulf Indonesia Resources, 1997–; Weyerhaeusel Co., 1997–; IMC Global Inc., 1997–; ATCO Gp, 1999–. Chairman: Canadian Genetics Diseases Network, 1998–; Premier's Adv. Council on Health, Alberta, 2000–. Hon. DEng Technical Univ. of Nova Scotia, 1987; Hon. LLD Alberta, 1993. *Address:* PO Box 1350, Vegreville, AB T9C 1S5, Canada; *e-mail:* maz1@agt.net.

MAZRUI, Prof. Ali A., DPhil; Albert Schweitzer Professor in the Humanities, State University of New York, Binghamton, since 1989; *b* Kenya, 24 Feb. 1933; *s* of Al'Amin Ali Mazrui, Judge of Islamic Law, and Safia Suleiman Mazrui; marr. diss.; three *s*; two *s* by Pauline Uti. *Educ:* Univ. of Manchester (BA with distinction 1960); Columbia Univ. (MA 1961); Oxford Univ. (DPhil 1966). Makerere University, Kampala, Uganda: Lectr, 1963–65; Prof. and Head of Dept of Political Science, 1965–73; Dean, Faculty of Social Sciences, 1967–69; Res. Prof., Univ. of Jos, Nigeria, 1981–86; Prof. of Pol Science and of Afroamerican and African Studies, Univ. of Michigan, 1974–91; Andrew D. White Prof.-at-Large, Cornell Univ., 1986–92, Emeritus and Sen. Scholar, 1992–; Ibn Khaldun Prof.-at-Large, Sch. of Islamic and Social Scis, Leesburg, 1997–. Vis. Prof., Univs of London, Manchester, Sussex, Leeds, Harvard, Calif (LA), Northwestern, Stanford, Colgate, Ohio State, Bridgewater State Coll., Mass, Denver, Pennsylvania State, McGill, Canada, Nairobi, Cairo, Baghdad, Singapore and Australian National, 1965–; Walter Rodney Vis. Prof., Univ. of Guyana, 1997–98. Expert Adviser: World Bank, 1988–91; UN Commn on Transnational Corps, 1987–92. Member: Adv. Cttee, Trans-Africa Run for Wildlife Foundn, Inc., 1987–; Adv. Bd of Dirs, Detroit Chapter, AFRICARE, 1987–; Pan-African Adv. Council to UNICEF, 1988–. Pres., African Studies Assoc. of USA, 1978–79; Vice-President: Internat. Congress of African Studies, 1978–; Internat. African Inst., 1987–; World Congress of Black Intellectuals, 1988–. BBC Reith Lectr, 1979; Presenter, The Africans (BBC TV series), 1986. *Publications:* Towards a Pax Africana, 1967; The Anglo-African Commonwealth, 1967; On Heroes and Uhuru-Worship, 1967; Violence and Thought, 1969; (with R. I. Rotberg) Protest and Power in Black Africa, 1970; The Trial of Christopher Okigbo (novel), 1971; Cultural Engineering and Nation-Building in East Africa, 1972; (with Hasu Patel) Africa in World Affairs: the next thirty years, 1973; World Culture and the Black Experience, 1974; Soldiers and Kinsmen in Uganda, 1975; The Political Sociology of the English Language: an African perspective, 1975; A World Federation of Cultures: an African perspective, 1976; Africa's International Relations, 1977; The Warrior Tradition in Modern Africa, 1978; Political Values and the Educated Class in Africa, 1978; The African Condition (The Reith Lectures), 1980; (with Michael Tidy) Nationalism and New States of Africa, 1984; The Africans: a triple heritage, 1986; Cultural Forces in World Politics, 1990; Africa since 1935 (Vol. VIII, UNESCO General History of Africa), 1993; (with A. M. Mazrui) The Power of Babel: language and governance in Africa's experience, 1998. *Address:* 313 Murray Hill Road, Vestal, NY 13850, USA. *T:* (607) 7774494.

MBEKEANI, Nyemba W.; Chief Executive, Mkulumadzi Farm Bakeries Ltd, since 1981; Chairman, Spearhead Holdings Ltd, since 1987; *b* 15 June 1929; Malawi parentage; *m* 1950, Lois Moses (*née* Chikankheni); two *s* three *d*. *Educ:* Henry Henderson Institute, Blantyre; London Sch. of Economics (Economic and Social Administration, 1963). Local Government Officer, 1945–58; political detention in Malawi and Southern Rhodesia, 1959–60; Business Executive, 1960–61; Local Govt Officer, 1963–64; Foreign Service, 1964; High Commissioner for Malawi in London, 1964–67; Ambassador to USA and Permanent Rep. at the UN, 1967–72; Ambassador to Ethiopia, 1972–73; Gen. Manager, Malaŵi Housing Corp., 1973–81. Farmer, company director, tea broker, baker, confectioner. Chm., Petroleum Control Commn, 1987–93; Comr, Malaŵi Electoral Commn, 1998. Board Member: Lingadzi Farming Co., 1987–; Sable Farming Co., 1987–. Trustee, Small Farmers Fertilizer Revolving Fund, 1988–. Counsellor, Malaŵi Univ. Council, 1984–93; Chm., Malaŵi Polytechnic Bd of Govs, 1988–93. *Recreation:* flower gardening. *Address:* PO Box 2095, Blantyre, Malaŵi. *T:* 641418; *Telex:* 44847 Lumadzi MI.

MBEKI, Thabo Mvuyelwa, Hon. GCMG 2000, President of South Africa, since 1999 (Deputy President, 1994–99); President, African National Congress, since 1997 (Deputy President, 1994–97); *b* 18 June 1942; *s* of late Govan and of Epainette Mbeki; *m* 1974, Zanele Dlamini. *Educ:* St John's High Sch., Umtata; Lovedale Inst.; Sussex Univ. (MA Econs; Hon. LLD 1995). Youth organiser, ANC, Johannesburg, 1961–62; left S Africa, 1962; worked in ANC Offices, London, 1967–70; mil. training, USSR, 1970; African National Congress: Asst Sec., Revolutionary Council, 1971–72; Mem., NEC, 1975–; Acting Rep., Swaziland, 1975–76; Rep. Nigeria, 1976–78; Political Sec., President's Office, 1978; Dir, Information and Publicity, 1984–89; Hd, Dept of Internat. Affairs, 1989–94 (Hd, delegn talks with S African Govt which led to unbanning of ANC and release of political prisoners, 1989; Mem., delegn concerning talks with S African Govt, 1990); Chm., 1993. *Address:* Private Bag X9146, Cape Town 8000, South Africa.

M'BOW, Amadou-Mahtar; Director-General of Unesco, 1974–87; *b* 20 March 1921; *s* of Fara-N'Diaye M'Bow and N'Goné Casset, Senegal; *m* 1951, Raymonde Sylvain; one *s* two *d*. *Educ:* Univ. of Paris. Teacher, Rosso Coll., Mauritania, 1951–53; Dir, Service of Fundamental and Community Educn, Senegal, 1953–57; Min. of Education and Culture, 1957–58; Teacher at Lycée Faidherbe, St-Louis, Senegal, 1958–64; Prof., Ecole Normale Supérieure, Dakar, 1964–66; Minister of Educn, 1966–68; Mem. Nat. Assembly, Senegal, 1968–70; Minister of Culture, Youth and Sports 1968–70; Asst Dir-Gen. for Educn, UNESCO, 1970–74. Member: Acad. des Sciences d'Outre-Mer, 1977; Acad. of Kingdom of Morocco, 1981; Hon. Mem., Royal Acad. Fine Arts, San Temo, Spain, 1977; For. Mem., Acad. of Athens, 1983. Hon. Professor: Ecole normale supérieure, Dakar, 1979; Indep. Univ. of Santo Domingo, 1978; Nat. Indep. Univ. of Mexico, 1979. Hon. Dr: Buenos Aires, 1974; Granada (Lit. and Phil.), Sherbrooke (Educn), West Indies (Laws), 1975; Open, Kliment Okhridski, Sofia, Nairobi (Lit.), 1976; Malaya (Lit.), Philippines (Laws); Venice (Geog.), Uppsala (Soc. Scis), Moscow (Soc. Scis), Paris I, 1977; Andes (Philos.), Peru (Educn Scis), Haiti, Tribhunvan Univ., Nepal (Lit.), State Univ., Mongolia, Khartoum (Law), Sri Lanka, 1978; Charles Univ., Prague (Phil.), Tashkent, Québec, 1979; Nat. Univ. of Zaïre, Madras, Belgrade, Ivory Coast, Sierra Leone, 1980; Univ. Gama Filho, Brazil, 1981; Nat. Univ. of Lesotho, 1981; Univ. of Benin, 1981; Technical Univ. of Middle East, Ankara, 1981; Univ. of Ankara, 1981, Univ. of Gand, Belgium, 1982; Nat. Univ. of Seoul, 1982; State Univ. of Kiev, 1982; Laval Univ., Quebec, 1982; Quaid-i-Azam Univ., Islamabad, 1983; Jawaharlal Nehru Univ., New Delhi, 1983; Aix-Marseilles Univ., 1983; Beijing Univ., China, 1983; Kim Il Sung Univ., PDR of Korea (Pedagogy), 1983; Lucknow Univ., India (Lit.), 1983; Chulalongkorn Univ., Thailand (Pedagogy), 1983; Sokoto Univ., Nigeria (Lit.), 1984; Malta Univ., 1986; Polytechnic Univ. of Catalonia, Cauca Univ. Popayan (Colombia), Univ. of Mayor, Real y Pontificia de San Francisco Xavier de Chuquisara, Sucre (Bolivia), 1987; Grand Tribute, Univ. Candido Mendes, Brazil, 1981. Order of Merit, Senegal; Grand Cross: Order of the Liberator, Order of Andres Bello and Order of Francisco de Miranda, Venezuela; Order of Merit and Juan Montalvo National Order of Merit (Educn), Ecuador; Order of Miguel Antonio Caro y Rufino José Cuervo, Colombia; Order of Stara Planina, Bulgaria; Order of the Sun, Peru; Order of Merit of Duarte, Sanchez and Mella, Dominican Republic; National Order of the Lion, Senegal; Order of Alphonso X the Sabio, Spain; Order of the Southern Cross and Order of Merit of Guararapes, Brazil; Order of Distinguished Diplomatic Service Merit, Republic of Korea; Order of Sikatuna, Philippines; Order of Merit, Indonesia; Order of Merit, Syrian Arab Republic; Order of Merit, Jordan; Order of the Arab Republic of Egypt; Order of Felix Varela, Cuba; Grand Cross: Order of Nat. Flag (PDR of Korea); Order of Meritorious Action (Libya); Nat. Order of Andean Condor (Bolivia); Grand Order of Education (Bolivia); Grand Officer: National Order of Ivory Coast; National Order of Guinea; Order of Merit, Cameroon; National Order of Merit, Mauritania; Order of Independence, Tunisia; Commander: Order of Academic Palms; National Order of Upper Volta; Order of the Gabonese Merit; Order of Arts and Letters, France; Grand Medal, Order of the Inconfidência, State of Minas Gerais, Brazil; Medal: Order of Merit of Caetés, Olinda, Brazil; Order of Manual José Hurtado, Panama; Superior Decoration for Education, Jordan. Man and his World Peace Prize, Canada, 1978; Gold Medal of Olympic Order, 1981; Gold Medal of ALECSO (Arab Educnl, Cultural and Scientific Orgn), 1981; Internat. Dimitrov Prize, 1982; Gold Medal: Champion of Africa, 1986, of Andalucia, 1987. *Publications:* Le temps des peuples, ed R. Laffont, 1982; Where the Future Begins, 1982; Hope for the Future, 1984; Unesco: universality and international intellectual co-operation, 1985; numerous monographs, articles in educnl jls, textbooks, etc. *Address:* Fondation Paix et Développement, BP 3473, Bd Djily Mbaye & Macadou Ndiaye, Imm Fahd 14ème étage, Dakar, Senegal.

MEACHER, Rt Hon. Michael (Hugh); PC 1997; MP (Lab) Oldham West and Royton, since 1997 (Oldham West, 1970–97); Minister of State (Minister for the Environment), Department for Environment, Food and Rural Affairs, since 2001(Department of the Environment, Transport and the Regions, 1997–2001); *b* 4 Nov. 1939; *s* of late George Hubert and Doris May Meacher; *m* 1st, 1962, Molly Christine (*née* Reid) (marr. diss. 1987); two *s* two *d*; 2nd, 1988, Mrs Lucianne Sawyer. *Educ:* Berkhamsted Sch., Herts; New College, Oxford. Greats, Class 1. Sec. to Danilo Dolci Trust, 1964; Research Fellow in Social Gerontology, Univ. of Essex, 1965–66; Lecturer in Social Administration: Univ. of York, 1967–69; London Sch. of Economics, 1970. Parly Under-Secretary of State: DoI, 1974–75; DHSS, 1975–76; Dept of Trade, 1976–79; Mem., Shadow Cabinet, 1983–97; chief opposition spokesman on health and social security, 1983–87, on employment, 1987–89, on social security, 1989–92, on development and co-operation, 1992–93, on Citizen's Charter, 1993–94, on transport, 1994–95, on employment, 1995–96, on envmtl protection, 1996–97. Mem., Treasury Select Cttee, 1980–83 (a Chm. of its sub-cttee). Chm., Labour Co-ordinating Cttee, 1978–83; Member: Nat. Exec.'s Campaign for Press Freedom; Labour Party NEC, 1983–88. Vis. Prof., Univ. of Surrey, Dept of Sociology, 1980–87. *Publications:* Taken for a Ride: Special Residential Homes for the Elderly Mentally Infirm, a study of separatism in social policy, 1972; Fabian pamphlets incl. The Care of the Old, 1969; Wealth: Labour's Achilles Heel, in Labour and Equality, ed P. Townsend and N. Bosanquet, 1972; Socialism with a Human Face, 1981; Diffusing Power: the key to Socialist revival, 1992; numerous articles. *Recreations:* music, sport, reading. *Address:* House of Commons, SW1A 0AA; 34 Kingscliffe Gardens, SW19 6NR.

MEAD, Deryk; Chief Executive, NCH (formerly NCH Action for Children), since 1996; *b* 3 July 1945; *s* of Joe and Ruth Mead; *m* 1967, Susan Margaret Kay; two *s*. *Educ:* Univ. of Manchester (BSc, MSc); Univ. of Leeds (DipPSW); CQSW. Approved Sch. Officer, Burnley, 1969–74; Principal Officer, Social Services, Lancs, 1974–79; Deputy Director of Social Services: Rochdale, 1979–88; Cumbria, 1987–91; Dir of Social Services, Gloucestershire, 1991–96. Mem., FRSA 1992; MInstD. *Publications:* contrib. to numerous publications. *Recreations:* fell running, rock and ice climbing. *Address:* (office) 85 Highbury Park, N5 1UD. *Club:* Worcestershire County Cricket.

MEAD, Dr Keith Owen, CB 2000; CEng, FIEE; CMath, FIMA; Director of Technology and Engineering, Government Communications Headquarters, 1994–2000; *b* 14 Oct. 1945; *s* of Kenneth Stanley Mead and Constance Louise Mead; *m* 1971, Fiona McDonald McCall; one *s* one *d*. *Educ:* Southend High Sch. for Boys; Sussex Univ. (BSc); Liverpool Univ. (PhD 1971). CEng 1996, FIEE 1996; CMath 1996, FIMA 1996. Joined GCHQ, 1970; PSO, 1975; Asst Sec., 1987; RCDS 1990; Under Sec., 1994. Mem. Council, IMA, 1999–. *Publications:* maths res. papers in learned jls. *Recreations:* playing the piano, teaching and arranging music, walking; *e-mail:* keith@meadkr.demon.co.uk.

MEAD, Dr Timothy John; Registrary, University of Cambridge, and Fellow, Wolfson College, Cambridge, since 1997; *b* 31 May 1947; *s* of Ernest Arthur Mead and Catherine Beryl Louisa Mead (*née* Midlane); *m* 1971, Anne Frances Glasson; one *s* one *d*. *Educ:* Queen Mary Coll., Univ. of London (BSc Hons 1969); Churchill Coll., Cambridge (PhD 1972). Admin. Asst, Univ. of Sheffield, 1972–75; University of Southampton: Asst Registrar, 1976–79; Asst Sec., 1979–82; Sen. Asst Registrar, 1982–86; Dep. Registrar and Academic Sec., Univ. of Nottingham, 1986–91; Registrar, 1991–97, and Sec., 1996–97, Univ. of Kent at Canterbury. Dir, Univs and Colls Staff Develt Agency, 1996–. *Publications:* articles in Jl of Chemical Soc. *Recreations:* music, natural history, running. *Address:* The Old Schools, Trinity Lane, Cambridge CB2 1TN. *T:* (01223) 332293.

MEAD, Prof. William Richard, FBA 1994; Professor and Head of Department of Geography, University College, London, 1966–81, now Emeritus Professor; *b* 29 July 1915; *s* of William Mead and Catharine Sarah Stevens; unmarried. *Educ:* Aylesbury Gram. Sch. (Foundation Governor, 1981–); London Sch. of Economics (Hon. Fellow 1979). PhD 1946, DSc(Econ) 1968, London. Served RAF, 1940–46. Asst Lectr and Lectr, University of Liverpool, 1947–49; Rockefeller Fellowship, held in Finland, 1949–50; Lectr, 1950, Reader, 1953, University Coll., London. Chm. Council, Sch. of Slavonic and E European Studies, 1978–80. Chm., Anglo-Finnish Soc., 1966–95; President: Inst. of British Geographers, 1971 (Hon. Mem., 1989); Geog. Assoc., 1981–82 (Hon. Mem., 1991); Hon. Sec., Royal Geographical Society, 1967–77 (Vice Pres., 1977–81, Hon. Vice-Pres., 1981–). Pres., Crabtree Foundn, 1997–98. Brown Meml Lectr, Univ. of Minnesota, 1983. Hon. Member: Finnish Geog. Soc.; Fenno-Ugrian Soc.; Porthan Soc.; Sydsvenska geografiska sällskapet; Det norske Videnskaps. Akademi, 1976; Det Norske Geografiske Selskab; Foreign Mem., Finnish Acad. of Science and Letters. Gill Memorial Award, 1951, Founder's Medal, 1980, RGS; Wahlberg Gold Medal, Swedish Geographical Soc., 1983; Fennia Medal, Finnish Geographical Soc., 1988; Res. Medal, RSGS, 1988. Dr *hc* University of Uppsala, 1966; DPhil *hc* Univ. of Helsinki, 1969; PhD *hc* Lund, 1987. Chevalier, Swedish Order of Vasa, 1962; Comdr, Orders of: Lion of Finland, 1963 (Chevalier, 1953); White Rose of Finland, 1976; Polar Star of Sweden, 1977. *Publications:* Farming in Finland, 1953; Economic Geography of Scandinavian States and Finland, 1958; (with Helmer Smeds) Winter in Finland, 1967; Finland (Modern Nations of the World Series), 1968; (with Wendy Hall) Scandinavia, 1972; The Scandinavian Northlands, 1973; (with Stig Jaatinen) The Åland Islands, 1974; An Historical Geography of Scandinavia, 1981; An Experience of Finland, 1993; Aylesbury: a personal memoir from the 1920s, 1996; Aylesbury Grammar School 1598–1998, 1997; other books on Norway, Sweden, Canada and USA. *Recreations:* riding, music. *Address:* 6 Lower Icknield Way, Aston Clinton, near Aylesbury, Bucks HP22 5JS.

MEADE, family name of **Earl of Clanwilliam**.

MEADE, Eric Cubitt, FCA; Senior Partner, Deloitte Haskins & Sells, Chartered Accountants, 1982–85; *b* 12 April 1923; *s* of William Charles Abbott Meade and Vera Alicia Maria Meade; *m* 1960, Margaret Arnott McCallum; two *s* one *d*. *Educ:* Ratcliffe College. FCA 1947. Served War, Hampshire Regt, 1942–46; N Africa, Italy, prisoner of war, 1944–45; Captain. Chartered Accountant, 1947. Mem. Council, Inst. of Chartered Accountants in England and Wales, 1969–79 (Chm., Parly and Law Cttee, 1974–76; Chm., Investigation Cttee, 1976–77); Chm., Consultative Cttee., Accountancy Bodies Ethics Cttee, 1977–83; Mem. Council, FIMBRA, 1986–87; Lay Mem., Solicitors Complaints Bureau, 1986–89; Mem., Audit Commn, 1986–89. *Recreations:* tennis, bowls. *Address:* 56 Hurlingham Court, Ranelagh Gardens, Fulham, SW6 3UP. *T:* (020) 7736 5382. *Club:* Hurlingham.

MEADE, Patrick John, OBE 1944; consultant in meteorology to various international organisations, 1974–88; Director of Services, and Deputy Director-General, Meteorological Office, 1966–73; *b* 23 Feb. 1913; *s* of late John Meade, Caterham, Surrey; *m* 1937, Winifred Jessie, *d* of Bertram Kent, Fawley, Hants; one *s* one *d* (and one *s* decd). *Educ:* Sir Joseph Williamson's Math. Sch., Rochester; Imperial Coll. of Science and Technology (Royal College of Science). ARCSc, BSc; Lubbock Mem. Prize in Maths, London Univ., 1933. Entered Met. Office, 1936; Southampton, 1937; Flt Lt RAFVR, Fr., 1939–40; Sqdn Leader, Sen. Met. Off., GHQ Home Forces, 1940–42; Wing Comdr (Gp Capt. 1944), Chief Met. Off., MAAF, 1943–45; Chief Met. Off., ACSEA, 1945–46; Head of Met. Office Trng Sch., 1948–52; London Airport, 1952–55; Research, 1955–60; idc 1958; Dep. Dir for Outstations Services, 1960–65. Hon. Sec., Royal Meteorological Society, 1956–61, Vice-Pres., 1961–63. *Publications:* papers in jls on aviation meteorology and on meteorological aspects of air pollution, atmospheric radioactivity and hydrology. *Recreations:* music, gardening. *Address:* Luccombe, Coronation Road, South Ascot, Berks SL5 9LP. *T:* (01344) 623206.

MEADE, Richard John Hannay, OBE 1974; Bureau Member, and Chairman of Northern European Group of Nations, International Equestrian Federation, 1990–98; *b* 4 Dec. 1938; *s* of John Graham O'Mahony Meade and late Phyllis Brenda Meade; *m* 1977, Angela Dorothy Farquhar; two *s* one *d* (and one *s* decd). *Educ:* Lancing College; Magdalene College, Cambridge (Engineering Degree). Competed for GB in 3-day equestrian events, 1963–82; won 3 Olympic gold medals: team gold, 1968; team and individual gold, Munich, 1972; World Championships individual medals include: silver, Burghley, 1996; silver, Punchestown, 1970; World Championships team medals include: gold, Punchestown, 1970; gold, Luhmûhlen, 1982; European Championships team medals include: gold, Punchestown, 1967; gold, Burghley, 1971; gold, Horsens, 1981; won Burghley 1964 and Badminton 1970 and 1982. Mem., 3-day Event Cttee, Internat. Equestrian Fedn, 1977–80; Pres., British Equestrian Fedn, 1989–92; Chm., British Horse Foundn, 1991–. *Publication:* Fit for Riding, 1984. *Address:* Church Farm, West Littleton, Chippenham, Wilts SN14 8JB. *T:* (01225) 891226.

MEADE, Prof. Thomas Wilson, CBE 1994; DM; FRCP, FMedSci; FRS 1996; Department of Epidemiology and Population Health, London School of Hygiene and Tropical Medicine, since 2001; Director, Medical Research Council Epidemiology and Medical Care Unit, Wolfson Institute of Preventive Medicine (formerly at Northwick Park Hospital), and Professor of Epidemiology, St Bartholomew's and the Royal London Hospital School of Medicine and Dentistry, Queen Mary and Westfield College (formerly Medical College of St Bartholomew's Hospital), London University, 1970–2001; *b* 21 Jan. 1936; *s* of James Edward Meade, CB, FBA, and of Elizabeth Margaret (*née* Wilson); *m* 1962, Helen Elizabeth Perks; one *s* two *d*. *Educ:* Westminster Sch.; Christ Church, Oxford; St Bartholomew's Hosp. Sen. Lectr, Dept of Public Health, London Sch. of Hygiene and Tropical Medicine, 1968–70 (on secondment to Schieffelin Leprosy Research Sanatorium, S India, 1969–70). Chm., MRC/Wellcome Trust/DoH Expert Working Gp on UK Population Sample Collections, 1999–; Member: MRC Physiological Systems and Disorders Bd, 1974–78; MRC Health Services Res. Panel and Cttee, 1981–90; Wellcome Trust Physiology and Pharmacology Panel, 1990–95; Council, Royal Soc., 1998–99. Founder FMedSci 1998. Internat. Balzan Prize, Fondazione Internazionale Premio E. Balzan, 1997; MRC Millennium Medal, 2002. *Publications:* papers on thrombosis and arterial disease. *Recreations:* oboe, growing vegetables. *Address:* 28 Cholmeley Crescent, N6 5HA. *T:* (020) 8340 6260. *Club:* Leander (Henley-on-Thames).

MEADE-KING, Charles Martin, MA; Headmaster, Plymouth College, 1955–73, retired; *b* 17 Aug. 1913; *s* of late G. C. Meade-King, solicitor, Bristol; *m* 1948, Mary (*née* Frazer); one *s* one *d*. *Educ:* Clifton Coll.; Exeter Coll., Oxford (Stapeldon Scholar). Asst Master, King's Sch., Worcester, 1935–38; Asst Master, Mill Hill Sch., 1938–40. Intelligence Corps, 1940–45. Housemaster, Mill Hill Sch., 1945–55. *Recreations:* history, arts, games. *Address:* Mistledown, Iron Mine Lane, Dousland, Yelverton, Devon PL20 6NA. *T:* (01822) 852237.

MEADES, Jonathan Turner; journalist, writer and television performer; *b* 21 Jan. 1947; *s* of late John William Meades and Margery Agnes Meades (*née* Hogg); *m* 1st, 1980, Sally Dorothy Renée, *d* of Raymond Brown; twin *d*; 2nd, 1988, Frances Anne (marr. diss. 1997), *d* of Sir William Bentley, KCMG; two *d*. *Educ:* King's Coll., Taunton; RADA; Bordeaux Univ. Editor, Event, 1981–82; Features Editor, Tatler, 1982–85; Restaurant Critic, The Times, 1986–2001. Contributor to magazines and newspapers, 1971–, including: Books and Bookmen, Time Out, Observer, Architects Jl, Sunday Times, Harpers and Queen, Vogue, Literary Review, Tatler, A La Carte, Independent, Sunday Correspondent, Mail on Sunday, Evening Standard. *Television: series:* The Victorian House, 1987; Abroad in Britain, 1991; Further Abroad, 1994; Even Further Abroad, 1997; *films:* Jerry Building, 1994; Heart Bypass, 1998; Travels with Pevsner: Worcestershire, 1998; Victoria Died in 1901 and is Still Alive Today, 2001; tvssfbmjtn, 2001; *film script:* L'Atlantide, 1991. *Publications:* This is Their Life, 1979; An Illustrated Atlas of the World's Great Buildings, 1980; Filthy English, 1984; Peter Knows what Dick Likes, 1989; Pompey, 1993; Fowler Family Blood, 2001. *Recreations:* buildings, mushrooms, sloth. *Address:* c/o David Godwin Associates, 55 Monmouth Street, WC2H 9DG. *T:* (020) 7240 9992. *Clubs:* Groucho, Academy.

MEADOW, Sir (Samuel) Roy, Kt 1997; FRCP, FRCPE, FRCPCH; Head of Department of Paediatrics and Child Health, St James's University Hospital, Leeds, 1980–98, now Emeritus Professor; *b* 9 June 1933; *m* 1st, 1962, Gillian Margaret Maclennan; one *s* one *d*; 2nd, 1978, Marianne Jane Harvey. *Educ:* Wigan Grammar Sch.; Bromsgrove Sch.; Worcester Coll., Oxford (BA Hons Physiol. 1957; MA, BM BCh 1960). DRCOG 1962; DCH 1963; MRCP 1964, FRCP 1974; FRCPE 1996; FRCPCH 1997. Partner GP, Banbury, 1962–64; junior appts at Guy's Hosp., Evelina Children's Hosp., Hosp. for Sick Children, London and Royal Alexandra Hosp., Brighton, 1964–67; MRC Sen. Res. Fellow, Birmingham Univ., 1967–68; Sen. Lectr and Consultant Paediatrician, Leeds Univ., 1970–80. Consultant Advr to CMO, DoH, 1997–2000. Blackwell Vis. Prof., NZ Paediatric Assoc., 1989; Kildorrory Lectr, Irish Paed. Assoc., 1987; Charles West Lectr, RCP, 1993. Chm., Assoc. for Child Psychology and Psychiatry, 1983–84; President: BPA, 1994–96 (Chm., Acad. Bd, 1990–94); RCPCH, 1996–97. Enuresis Resource and Inf. Centre, 1996–. Editor, Archives of Diseases in Childhood, 1979–87. Dawson Williams Prize, BMA, 1994; James Spence Medal, RCPCH, 1999. *Publications:* Lecture Notes on Paediatrics, 1973, 7th edn 2001; Bladder Control and Enuresis, 1973; The Child and His Symptoms, 1978; ABC of Child Abuse, 1989, 3rd edn 1997; Paediatric Kidney Disease, 1992; reports and papers on teratogenicity of anticonvulsant drugs, Munchausen Syndrome by proxy child abuse, childhood urinary tract disorders and child abuse. *Recreation:* gardening. *Address:* Weeton Grange, Weeton, Leeds LS17 0AP. *T:* (01423) 734234, *Fax:* (01423) 734726.

MEADOWCROFT, Michael James; politician, writer and public affairs consultant; *b* 6 March 1942; marr. diss.; one *s* one *d*; *m* 2nd, 1987, Elizabeth Bee. *Educ:* King George V Sch., Southport; Bradford Univ. (MPhil 1978). Chm., Merseyside Regl Young Liberal Orgn, 1961; Liberal Party Local Govt Officer, 1962–67; Sec., Yorks Liberal Fedn, 1967–70; Asst Sec., Joseph Rowntree Social Service Trust, 1970–78; Gen. Sec., Bradford Metropolitan Council for Voluntary Service, 1978–83. Senior Vis. Fellow, PSI, 1989. Dir, Electoral Reform Consultancy Services, 1992–94. Member: Leeds City Council, 1968–83; W Yorks MCC, 1973–76, 1981–83. Dir, Leeds Grand Theatre and Opera House, 1971–83. Chm., Liberal Party Assembly Cttee, 1977–81; Pres. Elect, 1987–88, Pres., 1993–, Liberal Party. Contested (L) Leeds W, Feb. and Oct. 1974, 1987, 1992. MP (L) Leeds W, 1983–87. Chm., Electoral Reform Soc., 1989–93. Has undertaken 39 missions to 25 new and emerging democracies; Co-ordinator: UN Electoral Assistance Secretariat, Malawi, 1994; OSCE Internat. Observer Mission, Russian Presidential elecn, 1996, Bulgaria, 1996, Bosnia Refugee Vote, 1996; EU Observation Unit, Suriname Nat. Assembly elecns, 2000; Advr on Jerusalem, EU Electoral Unit, Palestinian Assembly elecns, 1995–96; Consultant, Cttee for Free and Fair Elections, Cambodia, 1997; European Co-Dir, EC Support to Democratic Electoral Process in Cambodia, 1998; Post-Electoral Advr, Indonesian Assembly elecns, 1999. *Publications:* Liberal Party Local Government Handbook (with Pratap Chitnis), 1963; Success in Local Government, 1971; Liberals and a Popular Front, 1974; Local Government Finance, 1975; A Manifesto for Local Government, 1975; The Bluffer's Guide to Politics, 1976; Liberal Values for a New Decade, 1980; Social Democracy—Barrier or Bridge?, 1981; Liberalism and the Left, 1982; Liberalism and the Right, 1983; Liberalism Today and Tomorrow, 1989; The Politics of Electoral Reform, 1991; Diversity in Danger, 1992; The Case for the Liberal Party, 1992; (with E. Bee) Faugères: a guide to the Appellation, 1996; Focus on Freedom, 1997, new edn 2001. *Recreations:* music (including jazz), French philately. *Address:* Waterloo Lodge, 72 Waterloo Lane, Bramley, Leeds LS13 2JF. *T:* (0113) 257 6232, *Fax:* (0113) 257 9009; *e-mail:* meadowcroft@bramley.demon.co.uk. *Clubs:* National Liberal; Leeds, Armley Liberal, Bramley Liberal, Burley Liberal, Kirkstall Liberal, Upper and Lower Wortley Liberal (Leeds).

MEADOWS, Prof. Arthur Jack, FInstP; FLA; FIInfSc; Professor of Library and Information Studies, Loughborough University, since 1986; *b* 24 Jan. 1934; *s* of Arthur Harold Meadows and Alice Elson; *m* 1958, Isobel Jane Tanner Bryant; one *s* two *d*. *Educ:* New Coll., Oxford (MA Physics; DPhil Astronomy); University Coll. London (MSc History and Philosophy of Science). Fulbright Schol., Vis. Fellow, Mt Wilson and Palomar Observatories, Asst Prof., Univ. of Illinois, 1959–61; Lectr, Univ. of St Andrews, 1961–63; Asst Keeper, British Mus., 1963–65; University of Leicester: Hd of Dept and Prof., Astronomy and History of Science Depts, 1965–86; Hd of Primary Communications Res. Centre, 1975–86; Hd of Office for Humanities Communication, 1982–86; Loughborough University: Hd, Library and Inf. Stats Unit, 1986–97; Hd, Computers in Teaching Initiative Centre for Liby and Inf. Studies, 1989–97; Pro-Vice-Chancellor, 1995–96. Hon. Life Vice-Pres., LA, 1995. Hon. DSc City, 1995. *Publications:* Stellar Evolution, 1967; The High Firmament: a survey of astronomy in English literature, 1969; Early Solar Physics, 1970; Science and Controversy, 1972; Communication in Science, 1974; Greenwich Observatory: recent history (1836–1975), 1975; The Scientific Journal, 1979; (jtly) Dictionary of New Information Technology, 1982; (jtly) The Lamp of Learning: Taylor & Francis and the development of science publishing, 1984; (jtly) Maxwell's Equations and their Applications, 1985; Space Garbage, 1985; (jtly) Dictionary of Computing and Information Technology, 1987; The Origins of Information Science, 1987; (jtly) The History of Scientific Discovery, 1987; (jtly) Principles and Practice of Journal Publishing, 1987, rev. edn as Journal Publishing, 1997; Infotechnology, 1989; Innovation in Information, 1994; (jtly) Front Page Physics, 1994; (jtly) Project ELVYN, 1995; Communicating Research, 1998; about 250 articles. *Recreation:* sleeping in church services. *Address:* 47 Swan Street, Seagrave, Leics LE12 7NL. *T:* (01509) 812557.

MEADOWS, Bernard William; sculptor; Professor of Sculpture, Royal College of Art, 1960–80; *b* Norwich, 19 Feb. 1915; *s* of W. A. F. and E. M. Meadows; *m* 1939, Marjorie Winifred Payne; two *d*. *Educ:* City of Norwich Sch. Studied at Norwich Sch. of Art, 1934–36; worked as Asst to Henry Moore, 1936–40; studied at Royal College of Art, 1938–40 and 1946–48. Served with RAF, 1941–46. Commissioned by Arts Council to produce a work for Festival of Britain, 1951. Rep. (Brit. Pavilion) in Exhib. of Recent Sculpture, Venice Biennale, 1952; in Exhib., Kassel, Germany, 1959, etc. Exhibited in International Exhibitions of Sculpture (Open Air): Battersea Park, 1951, 1960; Musée Rodin, Paris, 1956; Holland Park, 1957; in 4th International Biennial, São Paulo, Brazil, 1957; also in Exhibns (Open Air) in Belgium and Holland, 1953–. *One man exhibitions:* Gimpel Fils, London, 1957, 1959, 1963, 1965, 1967; Paul Rosenberg, New York, 1959, 1962, 1967; Taranman, London, 1979. *Works in Collections:* Tate Gallery; Victoria and Albert Museum; Arts Council; British Council; Museum of Modern Art, New York; also in public collections in N and S America, Israel, Australia, and in Europe. Mem., Royal Fine Art Commn, 1971–76. Awarded Italian State Scholarship, 1956. *Publication:* 34 etchings and box (for Molloy by Samuel Beckett), 1967. *Address:* 34 Belsize Grove, NW3 4TR. *T:* (020) 7722 0772.

MEADOWS, Graham David; Director, Regional Policy, Commission of European Communities, since 1989; *b* 17 Dec. 1941; *s* of late Albert Edward Meadows and Jessica Maude Titmus; two *d*. *Educ:* Edinburgh Univ. MA Hons Political Economy. Journalist, 1958–69, specialising latterly in agric. affairs; European corresp., Farmers' Weekly (based in Brussels), 1973–75; EC 1975–; Mem., agric. policy unit; adviser on agricl, fisheries and envt policy, Office of Pres. of EEC (Gaston E. Thorn), 1981–84; Chef de Cabinet of Stanley Clinton Davis, Mem. of EEC responsible for transport, envmt and nuclear safety, 1985–89. *Recreations:* mountain walking, reading in the history of economic thought. *Address:* Commission of the European Communities, 200 rue de la Loi, 1049 Brussels, Belgium. *T:* (2) 2956181.

MEADOWS, Pamela Catherine, (Mrs P. A. Ormerod); Senior Research Fellow, National Institute of Economic and Social Research, since 1998; *b* 9 Jan. 1949; *d* of Sidney James Meadows and Hilda Catherine (*née* Farley); *m* 1975, Paul Andrew Ormerod; one *s*. *Educ:* Kenya High Sch., Nairobi; Penrhos Coll., Colwyn Bay; Univ. of Durham (BA Econs 1970); Birkbeck Coll., Univ. of London (MSc Econs 1978). Research Officer, NIESR, 1970–74; Sen. Econ. Asst, then Econ. Advr, Home Office, 1974–78; Department of Employment: Econ. Advr, 1978–88; Grade 5, 1988–92; Chief Economic Advr, and Hd of Econs, Res. and Evaluation Div., 1992–93; Dir, PSI, 1993–98. Vis. Prof., Arbetslivsinstitutet, Stockholm, 1998–. Mem., Better Regulation Task Force, 1997–. Trustee, Employment Policy Inst., 1995–; Mem. Exec. Cttee, Public Mgt and Policy Assoc., 1998–. Gov., Birkbeck Coll., 1997–. *Address:* 35 The Avenue, Kew, Richmond, Surrey TW9 2AL.

MEADWAY, (Richard) John, PhD; Under Secretary, Department of Trade and Industry, 1989–96; *b* 30 Dec. 1944; *s* of late Norman Pardey Meadway and of Constance Meadway (now Kellaway); *m* 1968, Rev. Dr Jeanette Valerie (*née* Partis); two *d*. *Educ:* Collyer's Sch., Horsham; Peterhouse, Cambridge (MA NatScis); Edinburgh Univ. (PhD); Oxford Univ. (MA). Asst Principal, Min. of Technology, 1970; Private Secretary: to Minister for Trade and Consumer Affairs, 1973; to Sec. of State for Prices and Consumer Protection, 1974; to the Prime Minister, 1976–78; Asst Sec., Dept of Trade, later DTI, 1979–89; Hd of Overseas Trade Div. 2, 1989–94, Hd of Export Control and Non-Proliferation Div., 1994–96, DTI. UK Gov., IAEA, 1994–96. Dir of Fitness to Practise, GMC, 1997–98. Trustee, Refugee Legal Centre, 1999–. FRSA 1995. *Publications:* papers on the amino-acid sequences of proteins. *Recreations:* reading, travel. *Address:* 4 Glebe Avenue, Woodford Green, Essex IG8 9HB. *T:* (020) 8491 6040. *Club:* Reform.

MEAGER, Michael Anthony, ARIBA; Director of Estates, Department of Health, 1989–91; *b* 15 Feb. 1931; *s* of late Arthur Pattison Meager and Dora Edith Meager (*née* Greeves); *m* 1954, Val Cranmer Benson, *d* of late H. C. Benson; two *s* one *d*. *Educ:* Royal Naval Coll., Dartmouth; Clacton County High Sch.; Architectural Assoc. Sch. of Architecture. ARIBA 1955; AADip 1956. National Service, RE, 1955–57: commnd 1956, served Cyprus, 1956–57. HMOCS, Kenya, 1958–63; architect in private practice, 1964–66; Department of Health (formerly MoH and DHSS), 1966–91: Chief Arch., 1986–88; Dir of Health Building, 1988–89.

MEAKIN, Wilfred, CB 1982; CEng, FIMechE; defence systems consultant (W. M. Associates); Executive Director, Royal Ordnance plc, 1986; Chairman, Royal Ordnance Inc., 1986; *b* 3 Oct. 1925. *Educ:* engineering apprenticeship in industry. Served War of 1939–45, RN. Technical Asst, ROF, Maltby, 1951; posts in ROF and former Inspectorate of Armaments; Asst Dir, ROF, Blackburn, 1966–72; Dir, ROF, Birtley, 1972–75; Dir, ROF Leeds, during 1975; Dir-Gen., Ordnance Factories (Weapons and Fighting Vehicles), 1975–79; Chief Exec. and Dep. Chm., Bd of ROF, later Royal Ordnance plc, 1979–86. Hon. FCGI.

MEALE, (Joseph) Alan; MP (Lab) Mansfield, since 1987; *b* 31 July 1949; *s* of late Albert Henry and Elizabeth Meale; *m* 1983, Diana Gilhespy; one *s* one *d*. *Educ:* St Joseph's RC School; Ruskin College, Oxford; Sheffield Hallam Univ. (MA 1997). Seaman, British Merchant Navy, 1964–68; engineering worker, 1968–75; Nat. Employment Develt Officer, NACRO, 1977–80; Asst to Gen. Sec., ASLEF, 1980–83; Parly and Political Advisor to Michael Meacher, MP, 1983–87. An Opposition Whip, 1992–94; PPS to Dep. Leader of Lab. Party, 1994–97, to Dep. Prime Minister, 1997–98; Parly Under-Sec. of State, DETR, 1998–99. Mem., Select Cttee on Home Affairs, 1989–92; Treas., Parly All Party Football Gp, 1989; Chm., British Cyprus Cttee, 1992–; Treas., British Section, CPA Cyprus Gp. Member: Parly Court of Referees; MSF Parly Cttee, 1997–. *Recreations:* reading, writing. *Address:* 5 Clumber Street, Mansfield, Notts NG18 1NT. *T:* (01623) 660531; House of Commons, SW1A 0AA. *Clubs:* Woodhouse Working Men's, Bellamy Road Working Men's, Mansfield Town Association Football (Mansfield).

MEANTI, Dr Luigi; Chairman, ENI SpA, Rome, 1993–96; *b* Milan, 14 Aug. 1928; *m*; two *s*. *Educ:* Poly. of Milan (Dr Ing). Asst Prof., Poly. of Milan, 1954–57; SNAM SpA, Milan: mem. staff, R&D dept, 1958–65; with gas planning dept, 1966–69; Dep. Gen. Manager, 1970–72; Gen. Manager, 1973–80; Vice-Pres. and Man. Dir, 1981–91; Hon. Pres., 1991–. Pres., Internat. Gas Union, Zürich, 1991–94; Vice Pres., EUROGAS, 1991–93. Hon. Member: IGasE, 1992; Assoc. Tecnique de l'Industrie du Gaz, Paris, 1993. *Address:* c/o ENI SpA, Piazzale E. Mattei, 00144 Rome, Italy. *T:* (6) 5982326.

MEARA, Rev. Canon David Gwynne; Rector, St Bride's Church, Fleet Street, since 2000; *b* 30 June 1947; *s* of Gwynne and Winifred Meara; *m* 1973, Rosemary Anne, *d* of John and Audrey Alexander; two *s* two *d*. *Educ:* Merchant Taylors' Sch., Northwood; Oriel Coll., Oxford (BA Lit. Hum. 1970; BA Theol. 1972; MA 1973); Cuddesdon Theol Coll., Oxford. Lambeth Dip. 1975. Ordained deacon, 1973, priest, 1974; Curate, Christchurch, Reading, 1973–77; Chaplain, Univ. of Reading, 1977–82; Vicar, Basildon, Aldworth and Ashampstead, 1982–94; RD, Bradfield, 1990–94; Rector, 1994–2000, Area Dean, 1996–2000, Buckingham. Sec., 1980–2000, Chm., 1990–2000, Oxford Diocesan Adv. Gp on Mission; Mem., Oxford DAC, 1998–2000. Hon. Canon, Christ Church Cathedral, Oxford, 1997–; Chaplain: Co. of Stationers and Newspaper Makers, 2000–; Co. of Marketors, 2000–. FSA 1994. *Publications:* The Foundation of St Augustine at

Reading, 1982; Victorian Memorial Brasses, 1983; A. W. N. Pugin and the Revival of Memorial Brasses, 1991; *contributions to:* Blue Guide to English Parish Churches, (Berkshire), 1985; Catalogue of Pugin Exhibition, V & A Mus., 1994; Catalogue of Pugin Exhibition, NY, 1995; Monumental Brasses as Art and History, 1996. *Recreations:* church-crawling, opera, theatre, art galleries, amateur dramatics, malt whisky. *Address:* St Bride's Rectory, Fleet Street, EC4Y 8AU. *T:* (020) 7427 0133. *Club:* Athenæum.

MEARS, Dr Adrian Leonard; CPhys, FInstP; Technical Director, Defence Evaluation and Research Agency, since 1995 (Chief Knowledge Officer, 1998–2000); *b* 27 May 1944; *s* of Leonard Mears and Marjorie (*née* Isaac); *m* 1969, Barbara Bayne; two *s*. *Educ:* Highgate Sch.; Christ Church, Oxford (DPhil, MA). Res. Associate, Univ. of Md, USA, 1969–71; joined RRE (later Royal Signals and Radar Establishment), 1971: worked on display technology, optoelectronics and lasers, 1971–81; Hd, Signal Processing, 1981–86; Dir of Science (Comd, Control, Communications and Inf. Systems), MoD, 1987–89; Dep. Dir and Commercial Dir, RSRE, 1990–91; Tech. and Quality Dir, DRA, 1991–95. *Recreations:* walking, theatre, music. *Address:* Defence Evaluation and Research Agency, Farnborough, Hants GU14 0LX. *T:* (01252) 394555.

MEARS, Rt Rev. John Cledan; Bishop of Bangor, 1983–92; *b* 8 Sept. 1922; *s* of Joseph and Anna Lloyd Mears; *m* 1949, Enid Margaret; one *s* one *d*. *Educ:* Univ. of Wales, Aberystwyth (BA Philosophy 1943); Wycliffe Hall, Oxford; St Deiniol's Library, Hawarden. MA Wales 1948 (research, Blaise Pascal). Deacon 1947, priest 1948, St Asaph; Curate: Mostyn, 1947–49; Rhosllannerchrugog, 1949–55; Vicar of Cwm, 1955–58; Lecturer, St Michael's Coll., Llandaff and Univ. of Wales, Cardiff, 1959–73; Chaplain, 1959–67; Sub-warden, 1967–73; Vicar of St Mark's, Gabalfa, Cardiff, 1973–82. Examining Chaplain, 1960–73; Hon. Canon of Llandaff Cathedral, 1981–82; Sec. of Governing Body, Church in Wales, 1977–82. *Publications:* reviews in Theology, articles in Efrydiau Athronyddol, Diwynyddiaeth, and Barn. *Recreations:* hiking, mountaineering. *Address:* 25 Avon Ridge, Thornhill, Cardiff CF14 9AU. *T:* (029) 2061 5505.

MEARS, Martin John Patrick; solicitor in private practice; President of the Law Society, 1995–96; *b* 12 Feb. 1940; *s* of J. F. Mears and E. Mears; seven *c*. *Educ:* St Illtyd's College, Cardiff; Wadham Coll., Oxford (MA, BCL). Solicitor, 1966. Editor, legal satirical jl, Caterpillar. *Publications:* numerous articles in national, regional and legal press. *Recreations:* Law Society, journalism, travel, reading. *Address:* Old Rectory, Haddiscoe, Norwich NR14 6PS. *Clubs:* Oxford and Cambridge; Norfolk (Norwich).

MEATH, 15th Earl of, *cr* 1627; **John Anthony Brabazon;** Baron Ardee (Ire.) 1616; Baron Chaworth (UK) 1831; *b* 11 May 1941; *er s* of 14th Earl of Meath, and of Elizabeth Mary (*née* Bowlby); *S* father, 1998; *m* 1973, Xenia Goudime; one *s* two *d*. *Educ:* Harrow. Page of Honour to the Queen, 1956–57. Served Grenadier Guards, 1959–62. *Heir:* *s* Lord Ardee, *qv*. *Address:* Killruddery, Bray, Co. Wicklow, Ireland.

MEATH, Bishop of, (RC), since 1990; **Most Rev. Michael Smith;** *b* 6 June 1940; *s* of John Smith and Bridget Fagan. *Educ:* Gilson Endowed Sch., Oldcastle; St Finian's Coll., Mullingar; Lateran Univ., Rome (DCL 1966). Ordained priest, 1963; Curate, Clonmellon, 1967–68; Chaplain: St Loman's Hosp., 1968–74; Sacred Heart Hosp., 1975–84; Auxiliary Bp of Meath, 1984–88; Coadjutor Bp of Meath, 1988–90. Diocesan Sec., dio. of Meath, 1968–84; Sec., Irish Bishops' Conf., 1984– (Asst Sec., 1970–84). *Recreations:* golf, walking. *Address:* Bishop's House, Dublin Road, Mullingar, Co. Westmeath, Ireland. *T:* (44) 48841, 42038, *Fax:* (44) 43020.

MEATH AND KILDARE, Bishop of, since 1996; **Most Rev. Richard Lionel Clarke,** PhD; *b* 25 June 1949; *s* of Dudley Hall Clarke and Norah Constance (*née* Quine); *m* 1975, Linda Margaret Thompson; one *s* one *d*. *Educ:* Trinity Coll., Dublin (MA 1979; PhD 1990); King's Coll., London (BD 1975). Ordained deacon, 1975, priest, 1976; Assistant Curate: Holywood, Down, 1975–77; St Bartholomew with Christ Church, Leeson Park, Dublin, 1977–79; Dean of Residence, Trinity Coll., Dublin, 1979–84; Rector, Bandon Union of Parishes, dio. of Cork, 1984–93; Dean of Cork and Incumbent of St Fin Barre's Union of Parishes, Cork, 1993–96. *Publication:* And Is It True?, 2000. *Recreation:* music. *Address:* Bishop's House, Moyglare, Maynooth, Co. Kildare, Ireland. *T:* (1) 6289354.

MEDAWAR, Nicholas Antoine Macbeth, QC 1984; **His Honour Judge Medawar;** a Circuit Judge, since 1987; *b* 25 April 1933; *e s* of Antoine Medawar and Innes (*née* Macbeth); *m* 1st, 1962, Joyce Catherine (*née* Crosland-Boyle) (marr. diss.); one *s* (one *d* decd); 2nd, 1977, Caroline Mary, *d* of Harry Samuel Collins, of Nottingham and Buckley. *Educ:* Keswick School; Trinity College, Dublin. BA Mod., LLB. Called to the Bar, Gray's Inn, 1957. Nat. Service, RASC, 1957–59, 2nd Lieut. A Recorder of the Crown Court, 1985–87. A Legal Assessor, Gen. Optical Council, 1984–87. Mem. Ethnic Minorities Adv. Cttee, Judicial Studies Bd, 1993–96. *Recreations:* divers. *Address:* 4 Paper Buildings, Temple, EC4Y 7EX.

MEDD, David Leslie, OBE 1964; Consultant Architect, Department for Education (formerly Department of Education and Science), since 1978; *b* 5 Nov. 1917; *s* of Robert Tate Medd and Dorothy (*née* Rogers); *m* 1949, Mary Beaumont Crowley (*see* M. B. Medd). *Educ:* Oundle; Architectural Assoc. (AA Dip. Hons). ARIBA 1941. Architects' Dept, Herts CC, 1946–49. Develt Gp, Architects and Building Br., Min. of Educn, later DES, 1949–78; private architectural work, 1978–. Commonwealth Fund Fellowship, 1958–59. Hon. DSc: Edinburgh, 1974; Hull, 1993. SADG Medal (France), 1941; Distinguished Service Certificate, BSI, 1992. *Publications:* School Furniture, 1981; contrib. to numerous learned jls, incl. HMSO building bulletins. *Recreations:* art, music, furniture making, gardening. *Address:* 5 Pennyfathers Lane, Harmer Green, Welwyn, Herts AL6 0EN. *T:* (01438) 714654. *Club:* Royal Over-Seas League.

MEDD, Mary Beaumont, (Mrs D. L. Medd), OBE 1964; retired; *b* 4 Aug. 1907; *d* of Ralph Henry Crowley and Muriel Crowley (*née* Priestman); *m* 1949, David Leslie Medd, *qv*. *Educ:* Bedales Sch.; Architectural Assoc. Pre-war work connected with housing and Building Centre, London; Hertfordshire County Council: Educn Dept, 1941–46; Architects' Dept, 1946–49; Develt Gp, Architects and Building Br., Min. of Educn, later DES, 1949–72; consultancy work, educnl and architectural, in England and abroad, 1972–93. Hon. DSc Hull, 1993. SADG Medal (France), 1932. *Publications:* contribs to jls and books, educnl and architectural, incl. HMSO building bulletins. *Recreations:* art, music, architecture, travel. *Address:* 5 Pennyfathers Lane, Harmer Green, Welwyn, Herts AL6 0EN. *T:* (01438) 714654.

MEDHURST, Brian; Managing Director (International Division), Prudential Corporation plc, 1985–94; *b* 18 March 1935; *s* of late Eric Gilbert Medhurst and Bertha May (*née* Kinggett); *m* 1960, Patricia Anne Beer; two *s* one *d*. *Educ:* Godalming Grammar Sch.; Trinity Coll., Cambridge (MA). FIA 1962 (Mem. Council, 1982–87). Joined Prudential Assurance Co. Ltd, 1958; Deputy Investment Manager, 1972; Investment Manager, 1975; Jt Chief Investment Manager, 1981; Gen. Manager, 1982. *Recreations:* chess, golf, piano duets, tree felling. *Address:* Woodcroft, Yelverton, Devon PL20 6HY. *T:* (01822) 853337. *Clubs:* North Hants Golf, Yelverton Golf.

MEDINA, Earl of; Henry David Louis Mountbatten; *b* 19 Oct. 1991; *s* and *heir* of Marquess of Milford Haven, *qv*.

MEDLEY, George Julius, OBE 1989; Director, WWF-UK (World Wide Fund for Nature) (formerly World Wildlife Fund (UK)), 1978–93; *b* 2 Aug. 1930; *s* of late Brig. Edgar Julius Medley, DSO, OBE, MC and Norah Medley (*née* Templer); *m* 1952, Vera Frances Brand; one *s* one *d*. *Educ:* Winchester College; Wye College, Univ. of London. BSc (Hort.). Fruit farmer, 1952–56; Manager, Chemical Dept, Harrisons & Crosfield, Colombo, 1957–63; Dir, Fisons (Ceylon), 1960–63; Tech. Develt Manager, Tata Fison, Bangalore, 1963–64; Gen. Manager Pesticides Div., Tata Fison Industries, Bombay, 1964–68; Sales Manager, Western Hemisphere, Agrochemicals, Fisons Internat. Div., 1968–69; Overseas Manager, Fisons Agrochemical Div., 1970–71; Dep. Managing Dir, Glaxo Labs, India, 1972–73, Managing Dir, 1973–77. Chm., Alexis Productions Ltd, 1994–; Dir, Edward Jewson Services to Charities Ltd, 1993–. Member: Radioactive Waste Management Adv. Cttee, 1991–98; UK Ecolabelling Bd, 1995–99. Vice-Pres., Organisation of Pharmaceutical Producers of India, 1974–77; Founder Mem. and Vice-Chm., Inst. of Charity Fundraising Managers, 1983 (Chm., 1984–85); Treasurer: Wilts WI Market Soc., 1993–99; Wilts Wildlife Trust, 1994–99 (Pres., 1999–); Trustee: Farming and Wildlife Adv. Gp, 1984–93; Internat. Inst. for Envmt and Develt, 1989–93; Falkland Islands Foundn, 1985–92. FIMgt; FICFM 1988. Officer, Order of Golden Ark (Netherlands), 1993. *Publications:* contrib. to Strategic Planning Soc. Jl. *Recreations:* gardening, DIY. *Address:* Hoddinotts House, Tisbury, Wilts SP3 6QQ. *T:* (01747) 870677.

MEDLICOTT, Michael Geoffrey; Chief Executive (formerly Managing Director), Servus (formerly Opus) Holdings plc, since 1997; *b* 2 June 1943; *s* of Geoffrey Henry Medlicott and Beryl Ann Medlicott (*née* Burchell); *m* 1st, 1973, Diana Grace Fallaw (marr. diss. 1998); one *s* three *d*; 2nd, 1999, Susan Caroline Whittall. *Educ:* Downside School; Lincoln College, Oxford (Scholar; MA). Management Trainee, P&O-Orient Lines, 1965–66; Shipping Asst, Mackinnon, Mackenzie & Co., Bombay, 1966–68, Tokyo, 1968–69; Asst to Management, P&O-Orient Lines, 1969–71; P&O Cruises: Develt Analyst, 1971–73; Asst Fleet Manager, 1973–75; Gen. Manager, Fleet, 1975–80; Gen. Manager, Europe, 1980–83; Dir, Europe, 1983–86; Man. Dir, Swan Hellenic, 1983–86; Man. Dir, P&O Air Holidays, 1980–86; Dir, P&O Travel, 1980–84; Chief Exec., BTA, 1986–93; Vice Pres., Europe, 1993–96, Europe and Asia, 1996–97, Delta Airlines Inc. Chairman: Delta Aeroflot Travel Enterprises (Moscow), 1996–97; Servus Facilities Mgt Ltd, 1998–; Servus bzb Ltd, 2000–; Transaction Dir, Nomura Internat. Principal Finance Gp, 1997–2000; Director: Deltair UK Investments, 1995–96; Lesteris Ltd, 1995–96; Gatwick Handling Internat. Ltd, 1995–96; Grand Facilities Mgt Holdings Ltd, 1998–2000. Chm., European Travel Commn, 1992–93 (Chm., Planning Cttee, 1990–92). Member: Council of Management: Passenger Shipping Assoc., 1983–86; Heritage of London Trust, 1987–; London Tourist Bd, 1992–93; Council, Tidy Britain Gp, 1988–; Bd, British–Amer. Chamber of Commerce, 1996–97. Member: Adv. Panel, Languages Lead Body, Dept of Employment, 1990–93; Adv. Council, Univ. of Surrey Tourism Dept, 1991–; Hon. Bd, Univ. Center of Hellenic and European Studies, Piraeus, 1994–. Trustee, British Travel & Educnl Trust, 1986–93. LEA Gov., Ecchinswell and Sydmonton C of E Primary Sch., 1999–. Mem., Royal Philatelic Soc. FRSA 1986. Queen Mother's Birthday Award for Envmtl Improvement, 1993, 1995. *Publications:* contribs to British West Indies Study Circle Bulletin, 1970–. *Recreations:* philately, theatre, travelling in perfect company. *Address:* Servus Holdings Ltd, Ireland House, 150 New Bond Street, W1S 2TU. *Club:* Oxford and Cambridge.

MEDLYCOTT, Sir Mervyn (Tregonwell), 9th Bt *cr* 1808, of Ven House, Somerset; *b* 20 Feb. 1947; *s* of Thomas Anthony Hutchings Medlycott (*d* 1970) (2nd *s* of 7th Bt) and of Mrs Cecilia Mary Medlycott, Cowleaze, Edmondsham, Dorset, *d* of late Major Cecil Harold Eden; *S* uncle, 1986. Genealogist; FSG 1990; Pres., Somerset and Dorset Family History Soc., 1986– (Founder and Hon. Sec., 1975–77; Chm., 1977–84; Vice-Pres., 1984–86). *Heir:* none. *Address:* The Manor House, Sandford Orcas, Sherborne, Dorset DT9 4SB. *T:* (01963) 220206.

MEDWAY, Lord; John Jason Gathorne-Hardy; *b* 26 Oct. 1968; *s* and *heir* of 5th Earl of Cranbrook, *qv*.

MEEK, Brian Alexander, OBE 1982; JP; Director, Capital Publicity Ltd, since 1987; *b* 8 Feb. 1939; *s* of Walter Harold Meek and Elsbeth Dearden Meek; *m* 1st, 1962, Glenda (*née* Smith) (marr. diss. 1983); one *s* one *d*; 2nd, 1983, Frances (*née* Horsburgh). *Educ:* Royal High Sch. of Edinburgh; Edinburgh Commercial Coll. Sub-editor, The Scotsman and Edinburgh Evening Dispatch, 1958–63; Features and Leader Writer, Scottish Daily Express, 1963–74; Rugby Football Correspondent, Scottish Daily Express and Sunday Express, 1974–86; Political Columnist, Glasgow Herald, 1986–. Dep. Chm., Livingston Develt Corp., 1986–97. Councillor: Edinburgh Corp., 1969–74; Edinburgh Dist Council, 1974–82 (Chm., Recreation Cttee, 1974–77); Lothian Regional Council, 1974–92 (Leader, Conservative Opposition, 1974–82, 1986–90; Convener and Leader of the Admin, 1982–86); Edinburgh DC, 1992–96; City of Edinburgh Council, 1995– (Chm., Cons. Gp, 1995–). Vice-Pres., Scottish Cons. and Unionist Assoc., 1989–92. Magistrate, Edinburgh, 1971, JP 1974. *Recreations:* golf, theatre, cinema, travel. *Address:* City Chambers, High Street, Edinburgh EH1 1YJ. *T:* (0131) 200 2000.

MEEK, Prof. John Millar, CBE 1975; DEng; FREng, FInstP, FIEE; David Jardine Professor of Electrical Engineering, University of Liverpool, 1946–78; Public Orator, 1973–76, and Pro-Vice-Chancellor, 1974–77, University of Liverpool; *b* Wallasey, 21 Dec. 1912; *s* of Alexander Meek and Edith Montgomery; *m* 1942, Marjorie, *d* of Bernard Ingleby; two *d*. *Educ:* Monkton Combe Sch.; University of Liverpool. College Apprentice, Metropolitan-Vickers Electrical Co. Ltd, 1934–36; Research Engineer, Metropolitan-Vickers Electrical Co. Ltd, 1936–38, 1940–46. Commonwealth Fund Research Fellow, Physics Dept, University of California, Berkeley, 1938–40. Mem. of Council, IEE, 1945–48, 1960–73 (Vice-Pres. 1964–68, Pres., 1968–69), Faraday Medal, 1975. Mem., IBA (formerly ITA), 1969–74. FREng (FEng 1976). Hon. DSc Salford, 1971. *Publications:* The Mechanism of the Electric Spark (with L. B. Loeb), 1941; Electrical Breakdown of Gases (with J. D. Craggs), 1953, new edn 1978; High Voltage Laboratory Technique (with J. D. Craggs), 1954; papers in various scientific journals concerning research on electrical discharges in gases. *Recreations:* golf, gardening, theatre. *Address:* 4 The Kirklands, West Kirby, Wirral CH48 7HW. *T:* (0151) 625 5850.

MEEK, Marshall, CBE 1989; RDI 1986; FREng, FRINA, FIMarE; Chairman, Argonautics Maritime Technologies Ltd, since 1995; Director: North of England (formerly European) Microelectronics Institute, since 1996; President, Royal Institution of Naval Architects, 1990–93 (Vice President, 1979–90); *b* 22 April 1925; *s* of Marshall Meek and Grace R. Smith; *m* 1957, Elfrida M. Cox; three *d*. *Educ:* Bell Baxter School, Cupar; Glasgow University (BSc Naval Arch. 1946). FIES 1963; FREng (FEng 1990).

Caledon Shipbuilding Co., 1942–49; Asst Naval Architect, BSRA, 1949–53; Naval Architect, Ocean Fleets, 1953–79 (Dir, 1964–79); Head of Ship Technology, British Shipbuilders, 1979–84; Managing Dir, National Maritime Inst., 1984–85; Dep. Chm., British Maritime Technology, 1985–86. Visiting Professor in Naval Architecture: Strathclyde Univ., 1972–83; UCL, 1983–86. Mem., Lloyds Register of Shipping Technical Cttee, 1979–2001. Chm., Marine Technology Bd, 1984–88; Member: Defence Scientific Adv. Council, 1989–94; Marine Safety Agency (formerly Surveyor General's) Res. Cttee, Dept of Transport, 1992–98; Cadland (Royal Yacht replacement) Cttee, 1996–. Pres., NECInst., 1984–86. Chm., NE Coast Engrg Trust, 1994–96. Master, RDI, 1997–99. Mem.,Northumberland Br., Gideons International in UK, 1986– (Chm., 2000–); Trustee, Northumberland and Newcastle upon Tyne Police Court Mission Fund, 1990–. JP City of Liverpool, 1977–79. FRSA 1968 (Mem. Council, 1995; Vice Pres., 1997–99; Mem., Design Adv. Gp, 1997–99; Chm., Student Engrg Design Award Panel, 1997–2000; Chm., NE Reg., 1992–97). *Publications:* numerous papers to RINA and other marine jls. *Recreations:* gardening, reading, church activities. *Address:* Coppers, Hillside Road, Rothbury, Northumberland NE65 7PT. *T:* (01669) 621403. *Club:* Caledonian.

MEEKE, (Robert) Martin (James); QC 2000; a Recorder, since 1999; *b* 25 Dec. 1950; *s* of James Alexander Meeke and Mildred Alverta Meeke; *m* 1973, Beverley Ann Evans; one *s* one *d*. *Educ:* Allhallows Sch., Devon; Bristol Univ. (LLB Hons). Called to the Bar, Gray's Inn, 1973. *Address:* Colleton Chambers, Colleton Crescent, Exeter EX2 4DG. *T:* (01392) 274898.

MEERES, Norman Victor, CB 1963; Under-Secretary, Ministry of Defence, 1971–73, retired; *b* 1 Feb. 1913; *m* 1938, Elizabeth Powys Fowler; two *s* one *d*. *Educ:* Sloane Sch., Chelsea; Magdalene Coll., Cambridge. Asst Principal, Air Ministry, 1935; Principal, 1940, Asst Sec., 1944, Ministry of Aircraft Prod.; Asst Sec., Min. of Supply, 1946; Under Secretary: Min. of Supply, 1956; Min. of Aviation, 1959–67; seconded to Dipl. Service in Australia, with title Minister (Defence Research and Civil Aviation), 1965–68; Under-Sec., Min. of Technology, 1969–70. ARCM (piano teaching), 1974. *Recreations:* music, lawn tennis. *Address:* 89 Grove Way, Esher, Surrey KT10 8HF. *T:* (020) 8398 1639.

MEESE, Edwin, III; lawyer; Distinguished Fellow, Heritage Foundation, Washington, since 1988; Distinguished Visiting Fellow, Hoover Institution, Stanford University, Calif, since 1988; *b* Oakland, Calif, 1931; *s* of Edwin Meese Jr and Leone Meese; *m* 1958, Ursula Herrick; one *s* one *d* (and one *s* decd). *Educ:* Oakland High Sch.; Yale Univ. (BA 1953); Univ. of Calif at Berkeley (JD 1958). Dep. Dist Attorney, Alameda County, 1959–67; Sec. of Legal Affairs to Gov. of Calif, Ronald Reagan, 1967–69; Exec. Assistant and C of S to Gov. of Calif, 1969–75; Vice-Pres., Rohr Industries, 1975–76; Attorney at Law, 1976–80; Dir, Center for Criminal Justice Policy and Management, Univ. of San Diego, 1977–81; Prof. of Law, Univ. of San Diego Law Sch., 1978–81; Counsellor to Pres. of USA, 1981–85; Attorney Gen. of USA, 1985–88. Hon. LLD: Delaware Law Sch.; Widener Univ.; Univ. of San Diego; Valparaiso Univ.; California Lutheran Coll.; Universidad Francisco Marroquin, Guatemala. *Publications:* With Reagan: the inside story, 1992; contribs to professional jls. *Address:* The Heritage Foundation, 214 Massachusetts Avenue, NE, Washington, DC 20002, USA.

MEGAHEY, Leslie; writer and director, film, television and theatre; *b* 22 Dec. 1944; *s* of Rev. Thomas and Beatrice Megahey. *Educ:* King Edward VI Grammar Sch., Lichfield; Pembroke Coll., Oxford. BBC general trainee, 1965; radio drama, script editor, producer, 1967; director, producer, TV arts series, 1968–; Exec. Producer, Arena, 1978–79; Editor, Omnibus, 1979–81, Co-Editor, 1985–87; Head of Music and Arts, BBC TV, 1988–91; other *television:* The RKO Story; Artists and Models; The Orson Welles Story; numerous drama-documentaries; *films:* Schalcken the Painter, 1979; Cariani and the Courtesans, 1987; Duke Bluebeard's Castle (filmed opera), 1988; The Hour of the Pig, 1993; *theatre:* (dir and co-author) Jack—a night on the town, Criterion, 1994, NY, 1996. Mem., Arts Council Adv. Panel, Film and TV, 1985–89. Awards: BAFTA, 1980; Prague, 1975; Asolo, 1985; NY, 1987; Banff, 1987; Royal Philharmonic, 1989; Prix Italia, 1989. *Address:* c/o Peters Fraser & Dunlop, Drury House, 34–43 Russell Street, WC2B 5HA.

MEGAHY, Thomas; *b* 16 July 1929; *s* of Samuel and Mary Megahy; *m* 1954, Jean (*née* Renshaw); three *s*. *Educ:* Wishaw High Sch.; Ruskin Coll., Oxford, 1953–55; College of Educn (Technical), Huddersfield, 1955–56 and 1968–69; London Univ. (external student), 1959–63. BScEcon London; DipEcon and PolSci Oxon; DipFE Leeds. Left school at 14 to work on railway; National Service, RN, 1947–49; railway signalman, 1950–53. Lecturer: Rotherham Coll. of Technology, 1956–59; Huddersfield Technical Coll., 1960–65; Park Lane Coll., Leeds, 1965–79. MEP (Lab) SW Yorks, 1979–99. European Parliament: Vice Pres., 1987–89; Dep. Leader, British Labour Group of MEPs, 1985–87; Member: Social Affairs Cttee, 1984–99; Transport and Tourism Cttee, 1989–99; Hungarian Jt Cttee, 1992–99; Substitute Mem., Social Affairs Cttee, 1984. Active member of Labour Party, 1950–; Chm., Scottish Labour League of Youth; Executive Mem., Dewsbury CLP, 1962–. Councillor, Mirfield UDC, 1963–74; Leader, Kirklees Metropolitan Borough Council, 1973–76; Opposition Leader, 1976–78. Member, Yorks and Humberside REPC, 1974–77; Vice-President: AMA, 1979–97; Yorks and Humberside Develt Assoc., 1981–. *Address:* 6 Lady Heton Grove, Mirfield, West Yorks WF14 9DY. *T:* (01924) 492680.

MEGARRY, Rt Hon. Sir Robert (Edgar), Kt 1967; PC 1978; FBA 1970; a Judge of the Chancery Division of the High Court of Justice, 1967–76; the Vice-Chancellor: of that Division, 1976–81; of the Supreme Court, 1982–85; *b* 1 June 1910; *e s* of late Robert Lindsay Megarry, OBE, MA, LLB, Belfast, and of late Irene, *d* of Maj.-Gen. E. G. Clark; *m* 1936, Iris, *e d* of late Elias Davies, Neath, Glam; three *d*. *Educ:* Lancing Coll.; Trinity Hall, Cambridge (MA, LLD; Hon. Fellow, 1973). Music Critic, Varsity, 1930–32. Solicitor, 1935–41; taught for Bar and Solicitors' exams, 1935–39; Mem., Faculty of Law, Cambridge Univ., 1939–40; Certificate of Honour, and called to Bar, Lincoln's Inn, 1944, in practice, 1946–67; QC 1956–67; Bencher, Lincoln's Inn, 1962, Treasurer 1981. Principal, 1940–44, and Asst Sec., 1944–46, Min. of Supply; Book Review Editor and Asst Ed., Law Quarterly Review, 1944–67; Dir of Law Society's Refresher Courses, 1944–47; Sub-Lector, Trinity Coll., Cambridge, 1945–46; Asst Reader, 1946–51, Reader, 1951–67, Hon. Reader, 1967–71 in Equity in the Inns of Court (Council of Legal Educn); Member: Gen. Council of the Bar, 1948–52; Lord Chancellor's Law Reform Cttee, 1952–73; Senate of Inns of Court and Bar, 1966–70, 1980–82; Adv. Council on Public Records, 1980–85; Consultant to BBC for Law in Action series, 1953–66; Chairman: Notting Hill Housing Trust, 1967–68; Bd of Studies, and Vice-Chm., Council of Legal Educn, 1969–71; Friends of Lancing Chapel, 1969–93; Incorporated Council of Law Reporting, 1972–87; Comparative Law Sect., British Inst. of Internat. and Comp. Law, 1977–89; President: Soc. of Public Teachers of Law, 1965–66; Lancing Club, 1974–98; Selden Soc., 1976–79. Visiting Professor: New York Univ. Sch. of Law, 1960–61; Osgoode Hall Law Sch., Toronto, 1964; Regents' Prof., UCLA, 1983; Lectures: John F. Sonnett, Fordham Univ., 1982; Tyrrell Williams, Washington Univ., St Louis, 1983; Leon Ladner, Univ. of British Columbia, 1984. Visitor: Essex Univ., 1983–90; Clare Hall, Cambridge, 1984–89. Hon. LLD: Hull, 1963; Nottingham, 1979; Law Soc. of Upper Canada (Osgoode Hall), 1982; London, 1988; DU Essex, 1991. Hon. Life Member: Canadian Bar Assoc., 1971; Amer. Law Inst., 1985. *Publications:* The Rent Acts, 1939, 11th edn: Vols 1 and 2, 1988; Vol. 3, 1989, 2nd edn as Megarry's Assured Tenancies by T. M. Fancourt, 1999; A Manual of the Law of Real Property, 1946, 7th edn (ed with Prof. M. P. Thompson), 1993; Lectures on the Town and Country Planning Act, 1947, 1949; Miscellany-at-Law, 1955; (with Prof. Sir William Wade QC) The Law of Real Property, 1957, 6th edn (ed C. Harpum) 2000; Lawyer and Litigant in England (Hamlyn Lectures, 1962); Arabinesque-at-Law, 1969; Inns Ancient and Modern, 1972; A Second Miscellany-at-Law, 1973; Editor, Snell's Equity, 23rd edn 1947, 27th edn (with P. V. Baker, QC), 1973; contrib. to legal periodicals. *Recreations:* heterogeneous. *Address:* The Institute of Advanced Legal Studies, 17 Russell Square, WC1B 5DR. *T:* (020) 7682 5800; 5 Stone Buildings, Lincoln's Inn, WC2A 3XT. *T:* (020) 7242 8607.

MEGAW, Arthur Hubert Stanley, CBE 1951; MA Cantab; FSA; *b* Dublin, 1910; *s* of late Arthur Stanley Megaw; *m* 1937, Elene Elektra (decd), *d* of late Helias Mangoletsi, Koritsa, Albania; no *c*. *Educ:* Campbell Coll., Belfast; Peterhouse, Cambridge (Walston Student, 1931). Macmillan Student, British School of Archæology at Athens, 1932–33, Asst Dir, 1935–36; Dir of Antiquities, Cyprus, 1936–60; Field Dir, Byzantine Institute, Istanbul, 1961–62; Dir, British Sch. of Archæology, Athens, 1962–68. CStJ 1967. *Publications:* (with A. J. B. Wace) Hermopolis Magna-Ashmunein, Alexandria, 1959; (with E. J. W. Hawkins) The Church of the Panagia Kanakariá in Cyprus, its Mosaics and Frescoes, 1977; various papers in archæological journals. *Recreation:* travel. *Address:* 27 Perrin's Walk, NW3 6TH.

MEGGESON, Michael; Solicitor and Notary Public; Senior Partner, Warner, Goodman & Streat, 1986–94; a Recorder of the Crown Court, 1981–92; *b* 6 Aug. 1930; *s* of Richard Ronald Hornsey Meggeson and Marjorie Meggeson; *m* 1975, Alison Margaret (*née* Wood). *Educ:* Sherborne; Gonville and Caius Coll., Cambridge. BA 1953; MA 1963. Nat. Service, RA, 1949–50; 5th Bn Royal Hampshire Regt, TA, 1950–63. Admitted a Solicitor, 1957; Asst Solicitor, 1957–59, Partner, 1959–94, Warner & Sons, subseq. Warner Goodman & Co., and Warner, Goodman & Streat; Dep. Circuit Judge, 1978–81. Mem. Cttee, Solicitors Staff Pension Fund, 1980– (Chm., Cttee of Management, 1988–92); Pres., Hampshire Incorp. Law Soc., 1981–82. *Recreations:* sailing, golf, gardening, music. *Address:* Church Farm, Langrish, near Petersfield, Hants GU32 1RQ. *T:* (01730) 264470. *Clubs:* Royal Southern Yacht (Hamble); Hayling Island Golf, Liphook Golf.

MEHAFFEY, Rt Rev. James; *see* Derry and Raphoe, Bishop of.

MEHEW, Peter; Assistant Under Secretary of State (Civilian Management) (C), Ministry of Defence, 1983–86, retired; *b* 22 Jan. 1931; *er s* of Oliver Mehew and Elsie (*née* Cox); *m* 1st, 1956, Gwyneth Sellors (*d* 1982); one *s* one *d*; 2nd, 1992, Margaret McComish; one step *s*. *Educ:* Bishop Wordsworth's Sch.; St Catharine's Coll., Cambridge (BA 1954). Asst Principal, Admiralty, 1954, Principal 1959; Assistant Secretary: CSD, 1970–73; MoD, 1973–80; Dep. Head, UK Delegn to Negotiations on Mutual and Balanced Force Reductions, 1975–77; Asst Under Sec. of State (Sales Admin), MoD, 1981–83. Fellow Commoner, CCC Cambridge, 1980. *Address:* 6 Anderson Road, Salisbury SP1 3DX. *T:* (01722) 326364.

MEHROTRA, Prof. Ram Charan, MSc, DPhil, PhD, DSc; Vice-Chancellor, University of Allahabad, since 1991; Professor of Chemistry, University of Rajasthan, Jaipur, 1962–82, now Emeritus; *b* 16 Feb. 1922; *s* of late R. B. Mehrotra; *m* 1944, Suman; one *s* two *d*. *Educ:* Allahabad Univ. (MSc 1943, DPhil 1948); London Univ. (PhD 1952, DSc 1964). Research Chemist, Vigyan Kala Bhawan, Meerut, 1943–44; Lectr, Allahabad Univ., 1944–54; Reader, Lucknow Univ., 1954–58; Prof., 1958–62, Dean, Faculty of Science, 1959–62, Gorakhpur Univ.; Prof., 1962–74, Dean, Faculty of Science, 1962–65, Chief Rector, 1965–67, Vice-Chancellor, 1968–69 and 1972–73, Rajasthan Univ., Jaipur; Vice-Chancellor, Univ. of Delhi, 1974–79. Mem., UGC, 1982–85. President: Chemistry Section, Indian Sci. Congress, 1967; Indian Chemical Soc., 1976–77; Indian Science Congress, 1978–79; Vice-Pres., Indian Nat. Science Acad., 1977–78; Member: Inorganic Chem. Div., IUPAC, 1977–81; Inorganic Nomenclature Commn, 1981–; Convener, Internat. Symposium, Nanjing, 1987. Fedn of Asian Chem. Socs Lecture, Seoul, 1987. Sir S. S. Bhatnagar award, 1965; Fedn of Indian Chambers of Commerce and Industry award, 1975; Prof. T. R. Seshadri's Birthday Commem. Medal, 1976; P. C. Ray Meml Medal, 1981; Golden Jubilee Medal, Inst. of Science, Bombay, 1983; Popularization of Science Award (by the Prime Minister), 1985; J. C. Ghosh Medal, Indian Chem. Soc., 1986; Achievement Award, Inst. of Oriental Phil., 1987; Platinum Jubilee Distinguished Service Award, Indian Science Congress, 1988; Atma Ram Award, for popularization of science, 1989; Dhar Meml Award, Diamond Jubilee Nat. Acad. of Science, 1991; Chatterjee Award, Indian Science Congress Assoc., 1991. Hon. DSc Meerut, 1976. *Publications:* (contrib.) Sol-Gel Science and Technology, 1989; Organometallic Chemistry, 1991; (contrib.) Chemistry, Spectroscopy and Applications of Sol-Gel Glasses, 1991; (contrib.) Chemistry of Silicon and Tin, 1991; treatises on: Metal Alkoxides and Metal β-Diketonates and Allied Derivatives, 1978; Metal Carboxylates, 1983; numerous research papers in nat. and internat. jls of chemistry; continuous references in the chemistry progress reports of Chem. Soc. London. *Recreation:* photography. *Address:* P4, University Campus, Jaipur 302004, India. *T:* (office) 510306; (home) 511476; Allahabad University, Allahabad–211002, India.

MEHTA, Bharat, OBE 2000; Clerk to the Trustees, City Parochial Foundation, since 1998; *b* 5 March 1956; *s* of Maganlal Jinabhai Mehta and Rattanben Mehta; *m* 1990, Sally Anne Chambers; two *d*. *Educ:* Plymouth Poly. (BA Hons Psychology 1979); UCL (MSc Ergonomics 1981). Researcher, MRC, 1979–80; Community Develt Worker, Pensioners Link, 1981–84; Policy Officer, NCVO, 1984–86; Principal Officer, Waltham Forest LBC, 1987–89; Dir of Develt, 1989–93, CEO, 1993–98, Nat. Schizophrenia Fellowship. Patron, Revolving Doors Agency, 1998–. Mem. Bd, London Community Foundn, 2001–. Chm., Governing Body, Bowes Primary Sch., 2000–. Fellow, British American Proj., 1996; Graduate, Common Purpose, 1996. *Publication:* contrib. British Jl of Psychology. *Recreations:* field hockey, swimming, history. *Address:* 18 Kelvin Avenue, Palmers Green, N13 4TG. *T:* (020) 8888 9873. *Clubs:* Southgate Adelaide Hockey, Griffins Hockey.

MEHTA, Ved (Parkash); writer; *b* Lahore, 21 March 1934; 2nd *s* of late Dr Amolak Ram Mehta (former Dep. Director General of Health Services, Govt of India), and Shanti Devi Mehta (*née* Mehra); naturalized citizen of USA, 1975; *m* 1983, Linn Fenimore Cooper, *d* of late William L. Cary and Katherine Cary; two *d*. *Educ:* Arkansas Sch. for the Blind; Pomona Coll. (BA 1956); Balliol Coll., Oxford (Hazen Fellow, 1956–59; BA Hons Mod. Hist. Oxon, 1959; MA 1962; Hon. Fellow, 1999); Harvard Univ. (MA 1961). Phi Beta Kappa, 1955. Harvard Prize Fellow, 1959–60; Residential Fellow, Eliot House, Harvard Univ., 1959–61; Guggenheim Fellow, 1971–72, 1977–78; Ford Foundn Travel and Study Grantee, 1971–76, Public Policy Grantee, 1979–82; MacArthur Prize Fellow, 1982–87. Staff writer, The New Yorker, 1961–94. Yale University: Rosenkranz Chair in Writing, 1990–93; Lectr in History, 1990, 1991, 1992; Lectr in English, 1991–93; Associate Fellow,

1988–; Residential Fellow, 1990–93, Berkeley Coll. Vis. Schol., Case Western Reserve Univ., 1974; Beatty Lectr, McGill Univ., 1979; Vis. Prof. of Literature, Bard Coll., 1985, 1986; Noble Foundn Vis. Prof. of Art and Cultural History, Sarah Lawrence Coll., 1988; Vis. Fellow (Literature), Balliol Coll., 1988–89; Vis. Prof. of English, NY Univ., 1989–90; Arnold Bernhard Vis. Prof. of English and History, Williams Coll., 1994; Randolph Distinguished Vis. Prof. of English and History, Vassar Coll., 1994–96; Sen. Fellow, Freedom Forum, Media Studies Center, 1996–97; Fellow, Center for Advanced Study in Behavioral Scis, 1997–98. Mem. Council on Foreign Relations, 1979–. Mem. Usage Panel, Amer. Heritage Dictionary, 1982. Fellow, NY Inst. for Humanities, 1988–92. Hon. DLitt: Pomona, 1972; Bard, 1982; Williams, 1986; Bowdoin Coll., 1995; DUniv Stirling, 1988. Assoc. of Indians in America Award, 1978; Silver Medal, Signet Soc., Harvard, 1983; Distinguished Service Award, Asian/Pacific Americans Liby Assoc., 1986; NYC Mayor's Liberty Medal, 1986; Centenary Barrows Award, Pomona Coll., 1987; Literary Lion Medal, 1990, Literary Lion Centennial Award, 1996, NY Public Liby; NY State Asian-American Heritage Month Award, 1991. *Publications:* Face to Face, 1957 (Secondary Educn Annual Book Award, 1958; serial reading on BBC Light prog., 1958, dramatization on Home prog., 1959; reissued 1967, 1978); Walking the Indian Streets, 1960 (rev. edn 1971); Fly and the Fly-Bottle, 1963, 2nd edn 1983 introd. Jasper Griffin; The New Theologian, 1966; Delinquent Chacha (fiction), 1967; Portrait of India, 1970, 2nd edn 1993; John Is Easy to Please, 1971; Mahatma Gandhi and His Apostles, 1977, reissued 1993; The New India, 1978; Photographs of Chachaji, 1980; A Family Affair: India under three Prime Ministers, 1982; Three Stories of the Raj (fiction), 1986; Rajiv Gandhi and Rama's Kingdom, 1995; A Ved Mehta Reader: the craft of the essay, 1998; Continents of Exile (autobiography): Daddyji, 1972; Mamaji, 1979; Vedi, 1982; The Ledge Between the Streams, 1984; Sound-Shadows of the New World, 1986; The Stolen Light, 1989; Up at Oxford, 1993; Remembering Mr Shawn's New Yorker: the invisible art of editing, 1998; All For Love: a personal history of desire and disappointment (memoirs), 2001; numerous translations; articles and stories in Amer., British and Indian newspapers and magazines, 1957–. Writer and commentator of TV documentary film Chachaji: My Poor Relation, PBS, 1978, BBC, 1980 (DuPont Columbia Award for Excellence in Broadcast Journalism, 1977–78). *Recreation:* listening to Indian and Western music. *Address:* 139 East 79th Street, New York, NY 10021, USA. *T:* (212) 7377487, *Fax:* (212) 4727220. *Club:* Century Association (NY) (Trustee, 1973–75; Wine Cttee, 2000–).

MEHTA, Zubin; Music Director for life, Israel Philharmonic Orchestra (Musical Adviser, 1962–78); Artistic Director, Maggio Musicale Fiorentino, since 1986; General Music Director, Bavarian State Opera, since 1998; *b* 29 April 1936; *s* of Mehli Mehta; *m* 1st, 1958, Carmen Lasky (marr. diss. 1964); one *s* one *d*; 2nd, 1969, Nancy Kovack. *Educ:* St Xavier's Coll., Bombay; Musikakademie, Vienna. First Concert, Vienna, 1958; first prize internat. comp., Liverpool, 1958; US debut, Philadelphia Orch., 1960; debut with Israel and Vienna Philharmonic Orchs, 1961; apptd Music Director, Montreal Symphony Orch., 1961; European tour with this orch., 1962; guest conducting, major European Orchs, 1962; Music Director: Los Angeles Philharmonic Orch., 1962–78; New York Philharmonic, 1978–91. Opera debut, Montreal, Tosca, 1964; debut Metropolitan Opera, Aida, 1965; operas at Metropolitan incl.: Tosca, Turandot, Otello, Carmen, Mourning becomes Elektra (world première), Trovatore, etc. Tours regularly with Israel Philharmonic Orchs and occasionally with Vienna Phil. Orch.; regular guest conducting with Vienna Phil., Berlin Phil., Orch. de Paris. Hon. Doctorates: Colgate Univ.; Brooklyn Coll.; Westminster Coll.; Occidental Coll.; Sir George Williams Univ., Canada; Weizmann Inst. of Science, Israel; Tel-Aviv Univ. Holds numerous awards; Israel Wolf Foundn Prize, 1996; Padma Bhushan (India), 1967; Commendatore of Italy; Médaille d'Or Verneil, City of Paris, 1984. *Address:* 27 Oakmont Drive, Los Angeles, CA 90049–1901, USA. *T:* (310) 4443111.

MEIER, Maj.-Gen. Anthony Leslie, CB 1995; OBE 1981; Director (non-executive), Eastbourne Hospitals NHS Trust, since 1994; *b* 3 Sept. 1937; *s* of late Eric Leslie Francis Meier and Vera Madge Meier (*née* Terry); *m* 1973, Susanne Jennifer Manley; two *s* one *d*. *Educ:* Latymer Upper Sch.; RMA Sandhurst. Commissioned RASC, 1957, later RCT; regtl appts, Germany and on secondment to Brigade of Gurkhas, Far East, 1958–68; Staff Coll., 1969; MoD, 31 Sqn GTR, NDC, HQ BAOR, CO 8 Regt RCT, to 1981; Col GS Coord (COS), Staff Coll., 1981–84; NATO Defence Coll., Rome, 1984–85; HQ AFCENT, 1985–87; Dir of Intell. (Warsaw Pact), MoD, 1988–90; Dir-Gen., Management and Support of Intell., MoD, 1991–94. Dir, Macmillan Appeal for Brighton and Hove Hospice, 1994–96. Adjudicator, Criminal Injuries Compensation Appeals Panel, 1997–. Chm., Bd of Govs, St Bede's Prep. Sch., Eastbourne, 1994–99; Dep. Chm., Bd of Govs, St Bede's Sch., Sussex, 1999–; Special Comr, Duke of York's Royal Mil. Sch., 1998–. *Publications:* Notes on the Warsaw Pact Ground Forces, 1972; articles in Internat. Defense Review. *Recreation:* sport. *Address:* c/o National Westminster Bank, 5 Meads Street, Eastbourne, E Sussex BN20 7QT.

MEIER, David Benjamin; His Honour Judge Meier; a Circuit Judge, since 1993; Designated Care Judge for Buckinghamshire; *b* 8 Oct. 1938; *s* of Arnold Meier, PhD and Irma Meier; *m* 1964, Kathleen Lesly Wilton; one *d*. *Educ:* Bury Grammar Sch.; King's College London (LLB). Admitted Law Society, 1964; Solicitor. Metropolitan Stipendiary Magistrate, 1985–93; a Recorder, 1991–93. Pres., Mental Health Tribunals, 1988–2000; Chairman: Juvenile Court, 1988–93; Family Panel, 1991–93. Pres., N Middx Law Soc., 1984–85. *Recreations:* riding, cricket, golf. *Address:* c/o Milton Keynes County Court, 351 Silbury Boulevard, Witan Gate East, Milton Keynes MK9 2DT.

MEIER, Richard Alan; principal architect, Richard Meier & Partners (formerly Richard Meier & Associates, New York), since 1963; *b* Newark, NJ, 12 Oct. 1934; *s* of Jerome Meier and Carolyn Meier (*née* Kalenbacher); *m* 1978, Katherine Gormley (marr. diss. 1987); one *s* one *d*. *Educ:* Cornell Univ. (BAArch 1957). FAIA. Architect with: Frank Grad & Sons, NJ, 1957; Davis Brody & Wisniewski, NY, 1958–59; Skidmore, Owings & Merrill, 1959–60; Marcel Breuer & Associates, 1960–63. Adjunct Prof. of Architecture, Cooper Union, 1963–73; Visiting Professor: Yale Univ., 1975, 1977; Harvard Univ., 1977; UCLA, 1987, 1988. *Major works* include: Smith House, Darien, Conn, 1967, and houses in Harbor Springs, E Hampton, Malibu, Dallas, New York, Florida, Pittsburgh and Naples; Bronx Developmental Center, NY, 1977; Atheneum, New Harmony; High Mus. of Art, Atlanta, 1983; Mus. für Kunsthandwerk, Frankfurt, 1984; City Hall and Central Liby, The Hague; Canal Plus HQ, Paris; Mus. of Contemp. Art, Barcelona; Getty Center, LA, 1997. *Exhibitions* include: XV Triennale, Milan, 1973; Mus. of Modern Art, NY, 1975, 1981; Princeton Univ., 1976; Cooper-Hewitt Mus., NY, 1976–77; Athens, 1982–83; Tokyo, 1988; Naples, 1991; Rome, 1993; Nagoya, 1996; Paris, 1999. 5 Architectural Record awards, 1964–77; 15 AIA Awards, 1968–99; Pritzker Prize for Architecture, 1984; RIBA Gold Medal, 1988; 5 Progressive Architecture awards, 1979–95; AIA Gold Medal, 1997; Praemium Imperiale, Japan, 1997. Comdr, Ordre des Arts et Lettres (France), 1992 (Officier, 1984). *Publications:* On Architecture, 1982; Richard Meier, Architect, vol. 1 1984, vol. 2 1991, vol. 3 1999; contribs to professional jls. *Address:* 475 10th Avenue, New York, NY 10018–1120, USA.

MEINERTZHAGEN, Peter Richard; Chairman, Hoare Govett, since 1991; *b* 16 April 1946; *s* of late Daniel Meinertzhagen and of Marguerite Meinertzhagen (*née* Leonard); *m* 1967, Nikki Phillips; five *d*. *Educ:* Eton College; Sorbonne. Hoare & Co.: joined 1965; Partner, 1973; Dir, Institutional Sales, 1973–90; Chm., Hoare Govett Corporate Finance, 1990–. *Recreations:* golf, tennis, horse-racing, music. *Address:* 20 Tite Street, SW3 4HZ. *T:* (020) 7352 6806. *Club:* White's.

MEIRION-JONES, Prof. Gwyn Idris, FSA 1981; author and consultant on historic buildings; *b* 24 Dec. 1933; *e s* of late Maelgwyn Meirion-Jones and Enid Roberts, Manchester; *m* 1961, Monica, *e d* of late George and Marion Havard, Winchester. *Educ:* North Manchester Grammar School; King's College London (BSc, MPhil, PhD). National Service, RAF, 1954–56. Schoolmaster, 1959–68; Lectr in Geography, Kingston Coll. of Technology, 1968; Sir John Cass Coll., later City of London Polytechnic, now London Guildhall University: Sen. Lectr i/c Geography, 1969; Principal Lectr i/c, 1970; Head of Geography, 1970–89; Personal Chair, 1983–89, now Prof. Emeritus; Hon. Research Fellow, 1989–98. Leverhulme Research Fellow, 1985–87; Vis. Prof. of Archaeol., Univ. of Reading, 1995–. Dir, Soc. of Antiquaries, 2001–. British Assoc. for the Advancement of Science: Sec., 1973–78, Recorder, 1978–83, Pres., 1992–93, Section H (Anthropology and Archaeology); Mem. Council, 1977–80; Mem. Gen. Cttee, 1977–83; Ancient Monuments Society: Mem. Council, 1974–79 and 1983–94; Hon. Sec., 1976–79; Vice-Pres., 1979–; Editor, 1985–94. Member: Comité Scientifique des Musées du Finistère, 1984–; Royal Commn on Historical Monuments of England, 1985–97; Adv. Cttee on Bldgs and Domestic Life, Welsh Folk Mus., 1991–95. Hon. Pres., Domestic Buildings Res. Gp (Surrey), 1991– (Pres., 1986–91). Editor, Medieval Village Res. Gp, 1978–86. Hon. Corresp. Mem., Soc. Jersiaise, 1980–90 and 1990–; Corresp. Mem., Compagnie des Architectes en Chef des Monuments Historiques, 1989–. Exhibitions: vernacular architecture of Brittany, on tour 1982–89; Architecture vernaculaire en Bretagne (15e–20e siècles), Rennes and tour, 1984–89. *Publications:* La Maison traditionnelle (bibliog.), 1978; The Vernacular Architecture of Brittany, 1982; (with Michael Jones) Aimer les Châteaux de Bretagne, 1991 (trans. English and German); (with Michael Jones) Les Châteaux de Bretagne, 1992; (jtly) Manorial Domestic Buildings in England and Northern France, 1993; Historic Buildings and Dating by Dendrochronology, 1997; (jtly) La Ville de Cluny et ses Maisons XIe–XVe siècles, 1997; (jtly) The Seigneurial Residence in Europe, 2001; papers in sci., archaeol and ethnol jls. *Recreations:* food, wine, music, walking, fly-fishing. *Address:* Department of Archaeology, University of Reading, Reading RG6 6AA. *T:* (0118) 931 8132; 11 Avondale Road, Fleet, Hants GU13 9BH. *T:* and *Fax:* (01252) 614300; *e-mail:* gmj@dircon.co.uk. *Club:* Athenæum.

MEISEL, Prof. John, CC 1999 (OC 1989); PhD; FRSC; President, Royal Society of Canada, 1992–95; Sir Edward Peacock Professor of Political Science, Queen's University, Canada, 1983–94, now Emeritus; Co-Editor (formerly Editor), International Political Science Review, 1979–95; *b* 23 Oct. 1923; *s* of Fryda S. Meisel and Anne Meisel (*née* Heller); *m* 1949, Murie A. Kelly (decd). *Educ:* Pickering Coll.; Univ. of Toronto (BA, MA); LSE (PhD). FRSC 1974. Political scientist; Queen's University, Canada: Instructor to Prof., 1949–79; Hardy Prof. of Political Science, 1963–79. Vis. Prof., Yale, 1976–77; Commonwealth Dist. Vis. Prof., UK, 1978. Chm., Canadian Radio-TV and Telecommunications Commn, 1980–83. President: Canadian Pol. Sci. Assoc., 1973–74; Social Sci. Fedn of Canada, 1975–76. Hon. LLD: Brock; Calgary; Carleton; Queen's; Guelph; Toronto; Regina; DU Ottawa; Hon. DLitt Waterloo; Hon. DSS Laval. Canada Medals: Confedn Centennial, 1967; 125th Anniv. Confedn, 1992; Silver Jubilee Medal, 1977. *Publications:* The Canadian General Election of 1957, 1962; Papers on the 1962 Election, 1964; Working Papers on Canadian Politics, 1972; (with Vincent Lemieux) Ethnic Relations in Canadian Voluntary Associations, 1972; Cleavages, Parties and Values in Canada, 1974; (with Jean Laponce) Debating the Constitution, 1994; numerous articles in acad. jls. *Recreations:* visual and performing arts, swimming, cross-country ski-ing, hiking, bird watching, flower admiring, indoor gardening, printed word. *Address:* Colimaison, Tichborne, ON K0H 2V0, Canada. *T:* (613) 2792380, *Fax:* (613) 2793391; Queen's University, Kingston, ON K7L 3N6, Canada. *T:* (613) 5336227, *Fax:* (613) 5336848; *e-mail:* meiselj@qsilver.queensu.ca. *Clubs:* Rideau (Ottawa); University (Toronto).

MEIXNER, Helen Ann Elizabeth, (Mrs Helen Thornton), CMG 2001; Regional Director, South-East Europe, 2000–01, and Director, Romania, 1997–2001, British Council; *b* 26 May 1941; *d* of Henry Gerard and Valerie Meixner; *m* Jack Edward Clive Thornton, CB, OBE (*d* 1996). *Educ:* Sydney C of E Grammar Sch. for Girls, Darlinghurst; Univ. of Queensland (BA 1961). Teacher, Abbotsleigh Girls' Sch., Wahroonga, 1962; Educn Asst, ABC, 1963–64; joined British Council, 1966; Recruitment Unit, Zagreb Office, Exchanges, Courses, Staff Recruitment, Dir-Gen's and Personnel Depts; Head, Design, Production and Publishing Dept, 1984–86; Dep. Dir, Personnel and Head, Personnel Dept, 1986–91; Dir of Libraries, Books and Information Div., 1991–94; Dep. Dir, Professional Services and Head, Consultancy Gp, 1994–96; Dir, 1996–97, Regl Dir, 1997–2000, Central Europe. Member: Council, Ranfurly Liby Service, 1991–94; Exec. Cttee, VSO, 1995–97; Council, Book Aid Internat., 2001–. Dir, Cornerhouse, Manchester, 1993–95. JP Inner London, 1988–98. *Recreations:* music, reading, walking, travel. *Address:* 131 Dalling Road, W6 0ET. *T:* (020) 8748 7692.

MELANESIA, Archbishop of, since 1994; **Most Rev. Ellison Leslie Pogo,** KBE 2000; Bishop of Central Melanesia, since 1994; *b* 9 Dec. 1947; *s* of Stephen Zaku and Sarah Duri; *m* 1978, Roslyn (*née* Kairopo); one *s* two *d*. *Educ:* Bishop Patteson Theol Coll., Kohimarama, Solomon Is; St John's Theol Coll., Auckland, NZ (LTh). Asst Priest, Anderson's Bay, Dunedin, 1979–81; Bishop of Ysabel, Solomon Is, 1981–94. Mem., Exec. Cttee, Pacific Conf. of Churches, 1984–; Comr for Pacific Region, Unit IV (Sharing and Service), WCC, 1989–; Ex Officio Mem., Pacific Ecumenical Regl Gp, 1989–. Chm., Bd of Govs, Pacific Theol Coll., Suva, Fiji, 1994–. *Recreations:* reading, gardening. *Address:* Archbishop's House, PO Box 19, Honiara, Solomon Islands. *T:* (office) 21892, 21137, (home) 22339.

MELANESIA, CENTRAL, Bishop of; *see* Melanesia, Archbishop of.

MELBOURNE, Archbishop of, and Metropolitan of the Province of Victoria, since 2000; **Most Rev. Peter Robert Watson;** *b* 1 Jan. 1936; *s* of Noel Frederick and Helen Elizabeth Watson; *m* 1962, Margo Eleanor Deans; three *d*. *Educ:* Canterbury Boys' High Sch., Sydney; Sydney Univ. (BEc); Moore Theological Coll., Sydney (ThL). Asst Priest, St Paul's, Chatswood, 1961–63; Curate-in-Charge, Lalor Park and Seven Hills, 1963–73; Rector, Lalor Park and Seven Hills, 1973–74; RD of Prospect, 1968–74; Canon, Prov. Cathedral of St John, Parramatta, 1969–74; Rector: St Luke's, Miranda, 1974–84; St Thomas, North Sydney, 1984–89; Area Dean, North Sydney, 1986–89; Bishop of Parramatta, 1989–93, of South Sydney, 1993–2000; an Asst Bp of Sydney, 1989–2000. *Recreations:* caravanning, squash, swimming. *Address:* Bishopscourt, 120 Clarendon Street, East Melbourne, Vic 3002, Australia; The Anglican Centre, 209 Flinders Lane,

Melbourne, Vic 3000, Australia. *T:* (3) 9653 4220, *Fax:* (3) 9650 2184; *e-mail:* Archbishop@melbourne.anglican.com.au.

MELBOURNE, Archbishop of, (RC), since 2001; **Most Rev. Denis James Hart;** *b* Melbourne, 13 May 1941; *s* of Kevin James Hart and Annie Eileen Larkan. *Educ:* Xavier Coll., Kew; Corpus Christi Coll., Werribee; Corpus Christi Coll., Glen Waverley. Ordained priest, 1967; Chaplain, Repatriation Hosp., Heidelberg, 1967–68; Asst Priest, N Balwyn, 1968; Asst Priest and Master of Ceremonies, St Patrick's Cathedral, Melbourne, 1969–74; Prefect of Ceremonies, Archdio. Melbourne, 1970–96; Advocate and Notary, Regional Matrimonial Tribunal, 1975–85; Exec. Sec., Nat. Liturgical Commn, Aust. Catholic Bps' Conf., 1975–90; Parish Priest, St Joseph's, W Brunswick, 1987–96; Vicar Gen. and Moderator of the Curia, 1996–2001; Aux. Bp, Archdio. Melbourne, 1997–2001; Titular Bp of Vagada, 1997. Mem., Cttee for Laity, 1998, Cttee for Liturgy, 2000, Aust. Catholic Bps' Conf. *Address:* St Patrick's Cathedral, Melbourne, Vic 3002, Australia.

MELBOURNE, Assistant Bishops of; *see* Curnow, Rt Rev. A. W.; St John, Rt Rev. A. R.; Wilson, Rt Rev. J. W.

MELCHETT, 4th Baron *cr* 1928; **Peter Robert Henry Mond;** Bt 1910; Executive Director, Greenpeace UK, 1989–2000 (Chairman, 1986–89); *b* 24 Feb. 1948; *s* of 3rd Baron Melchett and of Sonia Elizabeth Sinclair, *qv; S* father, 1973. *Educ:* Eton; Pembroke Coll., Cambridge (BA); Keele Univ. (MA). Res. Worker, LSE and Addiction Res. Unit, 1973–74. A Lord in Waiting (Govt Whip), 1974–75; Parly Under-Sec. of State, DoI, 1975–76; Minister of State, NI Office, 1976–79. Chm., working party on pop festivals, 1975–76; Chm., Community Industry, 1979–85. Chairman: Wildlife Link, 1979–87; Greenpeace Japan, 1994–2001; Mem. Bd, Greenpeace Internat., 2001–. Vice-Pres., Ramblers' Assoc., 1984– (Pres., 1981–84). *Address:* Courtyard Farm, Ringstead, Hunstanton, Norfolk PE36 5LQ.

MELDING, David Robert Michael; Member (C) South Wales Central, National Assembly for Wales, since 1999; *b* 28 Aug. 1962; *s* of David Graham Melding and Edwina Margaret Melding (*née* King). *Educ:* Dwr-y-felin Comprehensive Sch., Neath; UC Cardiff (BScEcon); Coll. of William and Mary, Virginia (MA). Cons. Res. Dept, 1986–89; Dep. Dir, Welsh Centre for Internat. Affairs, 1989–96; Manager, Carers Nat. Assoc. in Wales, 1996–99. *Recreations:* swimming, golf, reading, collecting popes and parrots (usually stamps). *Address:* National Assembly for Wales, Cardiff Bay, Cardiff CF99 1NA. *T:* (029) 2089 8328.

MELDRUM, Maj.-Gen. Bruce, CB 1991; OBE 1986; Chief of New Zealand General Staff, 1989–92; *b* 15 March 1938; *s* of late Ian Maitland Meldrum and of Vivienne Meldrum; *m* 1960, Janet Louise Boyling; one *s* one *d. Educ:* Feilding Agricl High Sch., NZ; RMC Duntroon. Lieut, RNZAC, 1959; Troop Comdr, Queen Alexandra's Regt, 1960–62; RAC Sch. of Tank Technol., UK, 1962–63; Sen. Instructor, then Chief Instructor, Sch. of Armour, Waiouru, 1963–66; OC 1 Armoured Sqdn, 1966–68; with US 11th Armoured Cavalry Regt, S Vietnam, Nov.–Dec. 1966; Staff Officer: Trng Directorate, Army HQ, 1968–69; HQ NZ Force Far East, Singapore, 1969–71; HQ NZ V Force, Saigon, 1971–72; Australian Comd and Staff Coll., 1972; Bde Maj., HQ 1 Inf. Bde, 1972–74; Lt-Col 1974; Staff Officer, HQ Field Force Comd, 1974–76; Dir, Ops and Plans, Army Gen. Staff, 1976–78; Australian JSSC, 1978; Special Projects Officer, 1978–80; Col 1980; Defence Advr, NZ High Commn, Kuala Lumpur, 1980–83; Comdr, Army Trng Gp, 1983–85; rcds, 1985–86; DCGS, 1986–89; Brig. 1987; Maj.-Gen. 1989. *Recreations:* golf, walking, reading. *Clubs:* Wellington, Wellesley (Wellington, NZ).

MELDRUM, Graham, CBE 1994; QFSM 1989; FIFireE; HM Chief Inspector of Fire Services, since 1998; *b* 23 Oct. 1945; *s* of George Meldrum and Agnes (*née* Gordon); *m* 1964, Catherine Meier; one *s* one *d. Educ:* Inverurie Acad., Aberdeenshire. FIFireE 1995. Fireman to Station Officer, London Fire Bde, 1963–73; Instructor, in the rank of Asst Divl Officer, Fire Service Coll., 1973–74; Divl Officer III, Hants Fire Service, 1974–76; Tyne and Wear: Divl Officer II, 1976–79; Divl Officer I, 1979–80; Sen. Divl Officer, 1980–83; West Midlands: Asst Chief Officer, 1983–84; Dep. Chief Fire Officer, 1984–90; Chief Fire Officer, 1990–97. Pres., Chief and Asst Chief Fire Officers' Assoc., 1994–95; Chairman: Fire Services Nat. Benevolent Fund, 1994; CACFOA (Research) Ltd, 1988–; CACFOA (Services) Ltd, 1988–. DUniv 1997. OStJ 1998. *Publications:* papers on fire engrg in jls. *Recreations:* computers, motor-cycling, railways, industrial archaeology, community work. *Address:* HM Inspectorate of Fire Services, Horseferry House, Dean Ryle Street, SW1P 2AW. *T:* (020) 7217 8599, *Fax:* (020) 7217 8959; *e-mail:* graham.meldrum@homeoffice.gsi.gov.uk.

MELDRUM, James; Director, Administrative Services, Scottish Executive, since 1999; *b* 9 Aug. 1952; *s* of late George and Marion Meldrum. *Educ:* Lenzie Academy; Glasgow Univ. (MA Hons). Joined Scottish Office 1973; Principal, 1979–86; Dep. Dir, Scottish Courts Admin, 1986–91; Head, Investment Assistance Div., Scottish Office Industry Dept, 1991–94; Registrar General for Scotland, 1994–99. *Recreations:* reading, music. *Address:* (office) Saughton House, Broomhouse Drive, Edinburgh EH11 3XD. *T:* (0131) 244 4311, *Fax:* (0131) 244 4313. *Club:* Royal Commonwealth Society.

MELDRUM, Keith Cameron, CB 1995; Chief Veterinary Officer, Ministry of Agriculture, Fisheries and Food, 1988–97; *b* 19 April 1937; *s* of Dr Walter James Meldrum and Mrs Eileen Lydia Meldrum; *m* 1st, 1962, Rosemary Ann (*née* Crawford) (marr. diss. 1980); two *s* one *d*; 2nd, 1982, Vivien Mary (*née* Fisher). *Educ:* Uppingham; Edinburgh Univ. Qualified as veterinary surgeon, 1961; general practice, Scunthorpe, 1961–63; joined MAFF, Oxford, 1963; Divl Vet. Officer, Tolworth, 1972, Leamington Spa, 1975; Dep. Regional Vet. Officer, Nottingham, 1978; Regional Vet. Officer, Tolworth, 1980; Asst Chief Vet. Officer, Tolworth, 1983; Dir of Vet. Field Service, 1986. UK Deleg., Office Internat. des Epizooties, 1988–97. Mem. Council, RCVS, 1988–97. Gov., Inst. of Animal Health, 1988–97. Hon. FRSH. Bledisloe Vet. Award, RASE, 1995. *Recreations:* outdoor activities. *Address:* The Orchard, Swaynes Lane, Merrow, Guildford, Surrey GU1 2XX. *Clubs:* Farmers'; North London Rifle (Bisley).

MELGUND, Viscount; Gilbert Timothy George Lariston Elliot-Murray-Kynynmound; *b* 1 Dec. 1953; *s* and *heir* of 6th Earl of Minto, *qv; m* 1983, Diana, *yr d* of Brian Trafford; two *s* one *d* (and one *s* decd). *Educ:* Eton; North East London Polytechnic (BSc Hons 1983). ARICS. Lieut, Scots Guards, 1972–76. Mem., Royal Co. of Archers, Queen's Body Guard for Scotland, 1983–. *Heir: s* Hon. Gilbert Francis Elliot-Murray-Kynynmound, *b* 15 Aug. 1984. *Club:* White's.

MELHUISH, Sir (Michael) Ramsay, KBE 1993; CMG 1982; HM Diplomatic Service, retired; *b* 17 March 1932; *s* of late Henry Whitfield Melhuish and Jeanette Ramsay Pender Melhuish; *m* 1961, Stella Phillips; two *s* two *d. Educ:* Royal Masonic Sch., Bushey; St John's Coll., Oxford (BA). FO, 1955; MECAS, 1956; Third Sec., Bahrain, 1957; FO, 1959; Second Sec., Singapore, 1961; First Sec. (Commercial) and Consul, Prague, 1963; First Sec. and Head of Chancery, Bahrain, 1966; DSAO (later FCO), 1968; First Sec., Washington, 1970; Counsellor, Amman, 1973; Head of N America Dept, FCO, 1976; Counsellor (Commercial), Warsaw, 1979–82; Ambassador, Kuwait, 1982–85; High Comr, Zimbabwe, 1985–89; Ambassador, Thailand, 1989–92. Head, EC Monitor Mission, Zagreb, July–Dec. 1992. *Recreations:* tennis, golf. *Address:* 9 Greycoat Gardens, Greycoat Place, SW1P 2QA. *Club:* Oxford and Cambridge.

MELIA, Dr Terence Patrick, CBE 1993; Chairman, Learning and Skills Development Agency, since 2000; *b* 17 Dec. 1934; *s* of John and Kathleen Melia (*née* Traynor); *m* 1976, Madeline (*née* Carney); one *d. Educ:* Sir John Deane's Grammar Sch., Northwich; Leeds Univ. (PhD). CChem, FRSC. Technical Officer, ICI, 1961–64; Lectr, then Sen. Lectr, Salford Univ., 1964–70; Principal, North Lindsey Coll. of Technology, 1970–74; HM Inspector of Schools, 1974–92: Regional Staff Inspector, 1982–84; Chief Inspector, Further and Higher Educn, 1985–86; Chief Inspector, Higher Educn, 1985–91; Sen. Chief Inspector, HM Inspectorate of Schs, 1991–92; Chief Inspector, FEFC, 1993–96. Vis. Prof., Leeds Metropolitan Univ., 1993–. Chairman: Further Educn Staff Develt Forum, 1996–99; Further Educn Develt Agency, 1997–2000; Further Educn NTO, 1999–2001; Educn Policy Cttee, RSA Exams Bd, 1996–99. Hon. DSc Salford, 1998. *Publications:* Masers and Lasers, 1967; papers on thermodynamics of polymerisation, thermal properties of polymers, effects of ionizing radiation, chemical thermodynamics, nucleation kinetics, thermal properties of transition metal compounds and gas kinetics. *Recreations:* golf, gardening.

MELINSKY, Rev. Canon (Michael Arthur) Hugh; Principal, Northern Ordination Course, 1978–88; *b* 25 Jan. 1924; *s* of late M. M. Melinsky and Mrs D. M. Melinsky; *m* 1949, Renate (*née* Ruhemann); three *d. Educ:* Whitgift Sch., Croydon; Christ's Coll., Cambridge (BA 1947, MA 1949); London Univ. Inst. of Education (TDip 1949); Ripon Hall, Oxford. Asst Master: Normanton Grammar Sch., 1949–52; Lancaster Royal Grammar Sch., 1952–57. Curate: Wimborne Minster, 1957–59; Wareham, 1959–61; Vicar of St Stephen's, Norwich, 1961–68; Chaplain of Norfolk and Norwich Hosp., 1961–68; Hon. Canon and Canon Missioner of Norwich, 1968–73; Chief Sec., ACCM, 1973–77. Chairman: C of E Commn on Euthanasia, 1972–75; Inst. of Religion and Medicine, 1973–77; Mem., Social Policy Cttee, C of E Bd for Social Responsibility, 1982–92; Mem. Cttee for Theological Educn, ACCM, 1985–88. Hon. Res. Fellow, Dept of Theol Studies, Manchester Univ., 1984. *Publications:* The Modern Reader's Guide to Matthew, 1963; the Modern Reader's Guide to Luke, 1963; Healing Miracles, 1967; (ed) Religion and Medicine, 1970; (ed) Religion and Medicine 2, 1973; Patterns of Ministry, 1974; (ed) On Dying Well, 1975, 2nd edn 2000; Foreword to Marriage, 1984; (contrib.) The Weight of Glory, 1991; The Shape of the Ministry, 1992; (contrib.) Tentmaking: perspectives on self-supporting ministry, 1998; A Code-breaker's Tale, 1998. *Address:* 15 Parson's Mead, Norwich, Norfolk NR4 6PG. *T:* (01603) 455042.

MELLAART, James, FBA 1980; Lecturer in Anatolian Archaeology, Institute of Archaeology, University of London, 1964–91; *b* 14 Nov. 1925; *s* of J. H. J. Mellaart and A. D. Van Der Beek; *m* 1954, Arlette Meryem Cenani; one *s. Educ:* University College, London. BA Hons (Ancient Hist. and Egyptology) 1951. Archaeol field surveys in Anatolia as Scholar and Fellow of British Inst. of Archaeol. at Ankara, 1951–56; excavations at Hacilar, 1957–60; Asst Dir, British Inst. of Archaeol. at Ankara, 1959–61; excavations at Çatal Huyük, Turkey, 1961–63 and 1965; Foreign Specialist, Lectr at Istanbul Univ., 1961–63. Corresp. Mem., German Archaeol Inst., 1961. *Publications:* Earliest Civilisations of the Near East, 1965; The Chalcolithic and Early Bronze Ages in the Near East and Anatolia, 1966; Çatal Hüyük, a Neolithic Town in Anatolia, 1967; Excavations at Hacilar, 1970; The Neolithic of the Near East, 1975; The Archaeology of Ancient Turkey, 1978; Çatal Hüyük and Anatolian Kilims, 1989; (with Ann Murray) Beycesultan, vol. III 2, 1995; chapters in Cambridge Ancient History; numerous articles in Anatolian Studies, etc. *Recreations:* geology, Turkish ceramics, clan history, Gaelic and classical music, Seljuk art. *Address:* 13 Lichen Court, 79 Queen's Drive, N4 2BH. *T:* (020) 8802 6984.

MELLARS, Prof. Paul Anthony, ScD; FBA 1990; Fellow, since 1981, President, since 1992, Corpus Christi College, Cambridge; Professor of Prehistory and Human Evolution, Cambridge University, since 1997; *b* 29 Oct. 1939; *s* of Herbert and Elaine Mellars; *m* 1969, Anny Chanut. *Educ:* Woodhouse Grammar Sch., Sheffield; Fitzwilliam Coll., Cambridge (Exhibnr; BA 1st Cl. Hons Archaeol. and Anthropol. 1962; MA 1965; PhD 1967; ScD 1988). FSA 1977. Sir James Knott Res. Fellow, Univ. of Newcastle upon Tyne, 1968–70; University of Sheffield: Lectr in Prehistory and Archaeol., 1970–75; Sen. Lectr, 1975–80; Reader, 1980–81; University of Cambridge: Lect, 1981–91; Reader in Archaeology, 1991–97. British Academy: Res. Reader, 1989–91; Reckitt Archaeol. Lectr, 1991; Vis. Prof., SUNY (Binghamton), 1974; Vis. Fellow, ANU, 1981; Danish Res. Council Vis. Lectr, Copenhagen and Aarhus Univs, 1985. President: Hunter Archaeol. Soc., 1975–80; Prehistoric Soc., 1998– (Vice Pres., 1992–95); Chm., Archaeol. Sci. Cttee, Council for British Archaeol., 1980–87; Mem. Council, British Acad., 1994–97 (Chm., Archaeol. Sect., 1995–). MAE 1999. Hon. Mem., Italian Inst. of Prehistoric & Protohistoric Sciences, 1997. *Publications:* (ed) The Early Postglacial Settlement of Northern Europe, 1976; Excavations of Oronsay, 1987; (ed) Research Priorities of Archaeological Science, 1987; (ed) The Human Revolution, 1989; (ed) The Emergence of Modern Humans, 1990; The Middle Palaeolithic: adaptation, behaviour & variability, 1991; (ed) The Origin of Modern Humans and the Impact of Science-based Dating, 1992; The Neanderthal Legacy, 1996; (ed) Modelling the Early Human Mind, 1996; Star Carr in Context, 1998; articles in archaeol. jls. *Recreations:* music, foreign travel. *Address:* Long Gable, Elsworth, Cambs CB3 8HX. *T:* (01954) 267275; Department of Archaeology, Downing Street, Cambridge CB2 3DZ. *T:* (01223) 333520.

MELLENEY, Clare Patricia; *see* Montgomery, C. P.

MELLERS, Prof. Wilfrid Howard, OBE 1982; DMus; Composer; Professor of Music, University of York, 1964–81, now Emeritus; *b* 26 April 1914; *s* of Percy Wilfrid Mellers and Hilda Maria (*née* Lawrence); *m* 1st, 1940, Vera Muriel (*née* Hobbs) (marr. diss.); 2nd, 1950, Peggy Pauline (*née* Lewis) (marr. diss. 1975); two *d*; 3rd, 1987, Robin Hildyard. *Educ:* Leamington Coll.; Downing Coll., Cambridge (Hon. Fellow 2001); BA Cantab 1939; MA Cantab 1945; DMus Birmingham 1962. FGSM 1982. Supervisor in English and College Lecturer in Music, Downing Coll., Cambridge, 1945–48; Staff Tutor in Music, Extra Mural Dept, University of Birmingham, 1949–60; Visiting Mellon Prof. of Music, University of Pittsburgh, USA, 1960–62; Vis. Prof., City Univ., 1984–. Hon. DPhil City, 1981. *Publications:* Music and Society, 1946; Studies in Contemporary Music, 1948; François Couperin and the French Classical Tradition, 1950, 2nd edn 1987; Music in the Making, 1951; Man and his Music, 1957; Harmonious Meeting, 1964; Music in a New Found Land, 1964, 2nd edn 1987; Caliban Reborn: renewal in 20th-century music, 1967 (US), 1968 (GB); Twilight of the Gods: the Beatles in retrospect, 1973; Bach and the Dance of God, 1981; Beethoven and the Voice of God, 1983; A Darker Shade of Pale: a backdrop to Bob Dylan, 1984; Angels of the Night: popular female singers of our time, 1986; The Masks of Orpheus, 1987; Vaughan Williams and the Vision of Albion, 1989, 2nd edn 1997; Le Jardin Parfumé: homage to Federico Mompou, 1990; The Music of

Percy Grainger, 1992; The Music of Francis Poulenc, 1993; New Worlds and Old (selected music journalism), 1997; Singing in the Wilderness, 2001; Celestial Music: some masterpieces of European religious music, 2001; *compositions* include: Requiem Canticle; Cloud Canticle; Canticum Incarnationi, 1960; Chants and Litanies of Carl Sandburg, 1960; Missa Brevis, 1961; Aubade, 1961–2001; Alba in 9 Metamorphoses, 1962; Rose of May, 1964; Life-Cycle, 1967; Yeibichai, 1968; Canticum Resurrectionis, 1968; Natalis Invicti Solis, 1969; The Word Unborn, 1970; The Ancient Wound, 1970; De Vegetabilis et Animalibus, 1971; Venery for Six Plus, 1971; Sun-flower: the Quaternity of William Blake, 1972–73; Opus Alchymicum, 1972–95; The Key of the Kingdom, 1976; Rosae Hermeticae, 1977; A Blue Epiphany, 1977; Shaman Songs, 1980; The Wellspring of Loves, 1981; Hortus Rosarium, 1986; The Echoing Green, 1995. *Address:* Oliver Sheldon House, 17 Aldwark, York YO1 7BX. *T:* (01904) 638686.

MELLING, Dr Jack; Director, Karl Landsteiner Institute, Vienna, since 2001; *b* 8 Feb. 1940; *s* of John Melling and Mary (*née* Marsden); *m* 1967, Susan Ewart. *Educ:* Rivington and Blackrod Grammar Sch.; Manchester Univ. (BSc, MSc); Bath Univ. (PhD). FRPharmS 1977; FIBiol 1979; FRCPath 1996. Res. Asst, Bath Univ., 1965–68; Lectr, Heriot-Watt Univ., 1968–69; SSO, then PSO, MoD, 1969–79; Dir, Vaccine Res. and Prodn Lab., PHLS, 1979–87; Dep. Dir, 1987–93, Dir, 1993–96, Centre for Applied Microbiology and Res., Porton Down; Dir, Biological Develt Center, Salk Inst. for Biol Studies, USA, 1996–2001. Visiting Professor: Rutgers Univ., 1979–84; Aston Univ., 1981–96; Westminster Univ., 1995–; Gastprofesseur, Inst. for Social and Preventive Medicine, Univ. of Zürich, 1999–. Society of Chemical Industry: Mem. Council, 1983–86, 1998–; Sec., 1975–81, Chm., 1981–83, Biotechnology Gp; Chm. Pubns Cttee, 1999–. Member: British Nat. Cttee for Microbiol., 1978–84; MRC Cttee on Develt of Vaccines and Immunol Products, 1979–96; Cttee on Safety of Medicines Biologicals Subcttee, 1982–99; Ind. Register Defence Scientific Adv. Council, 1994–98. Sec., British Co-ordinating Cttee for Biotechnol., 1981–85; Sen. Scientific Advr, Internat. AIDS Vaccine Initiative, 1999–. Editor, Jl of Chem. Technol. and Biotechnol., 1985–; Mem. Editl Bd, Vaccine, 1983–. Lampitt Medal, SCI, 1993. *Publications:* Continuous Culture Applications and New Fields, 1977; Adhesion of Micro-organisms to Surfaces, 1979; The Microbial Cell Surface and Adhesion, 1981; Biosafety in Industrial Technology, 1994; papers in scientific jls. *Recreations:* ski-ing, shooting, walking. *Address:* Karl Landsteiner Institute, Rennweg 95B, 1030 Vienna, Austria. *T:* (676) 7236834, *Fax:* (1) 20620800; *e-mail:* jmelling@ptdprolog.net. *Clubs:* Athenæum, Royal Society of Medicine; Parkstone Yacht (Poole).

MELLITT, Prof. Brian, FREng; Chairman, Building Research Establishment, since 1998; *b* 29 May 1940; *s* of John and Nellie Mellitt; *m* 1961, Lyn Waring; one *s* one *d*. *Educ:* Loughborough Univ.; Imperial College, London Univ. (BTechEng, DIC). FIEE, FIMechE, FIRSE; FREng (FEng 1990). Student apprentice, 1956, Junior Engineer, 1962, R&D Engineer, 1964, English Electric Co.; Lectr and Sen. Lectr, Huddersfield Polytechnic, 1966–67; Research Dept, British Rlys Bd, 1968–70; University of Birmingham: Lectr, 1971; Sen. Lectr, 1979; Prof., 1982; Head of Dept of Electronic and Electrical Engrg, 1986; Dean, Faculty of Engrng, 1987–88; Hon. Prof. of Electronic Engrg, 1989; Dir Engrg, London Underground Ltd, 1989–95; Dir, Metro Power, 1990–95; Dir of Engrg and Prodn, Railtrack PLC, 1995–99; Engrg Advr, Railtrack (UK), 1999–2000. Consultant Engineer, railway related organisations, 1972–88. Chairman: BMCONSULT Ltd, 1999–; Metro-Consulting Ltd, 2000–; SIRA Ltd, 2001–; Dir, Railway College Ltd, then Catalis Rail Trng, 1998–2000; Rail Advr, NM Rothschild, 1999–. President: Welding Inst., 2000–01; IEE, 2001–Oct. 2002 (Vice Pres., 1996–99; Dep. Pres., 1999–2001). Editor, IEE Procs (B), 1978–. Hon. Fellow, Assoc. of Project Managers, 1998. Hon. DTech Loughborough, 1991; Hon. DSc Huddersfield, 1998; Hon. DEng Birmingham, 1999. Leonardo da Vinci Award, Italian Assoc. for Industrial Design, 1989. *Publications:* contribs on electric railway topics to learned jls. *Recreation:* bridge. *Address:* The Priory, 36 Church Street, Stilton, Cambs PE7 3RF. *T:* (01733) 240573. *Club:* Athenæum.

MELLON, Sir James, KCMG 1988 (CMG 1979); HM Diplomatic Service, retired; Chairman: Regent Europe Asset Management, since 2000; BFS Asian Assets Trust, since 2000; *b* 25 Jan. 1929; *m* 1st, 1956, Frances Murray (*d* 1976); one *s* three *d*; 2nd, 1979, Mrs Philippa Shuttleworth (*née* Hartley). *Educ:* Glasgow Univ (MA). Dept of Agriculture for Scotland, 1953–60; Agricultural Attaché, Copenhagen and The Hague, 1960–63; FO, 1963–64; Head of Chancery, Dakar, 1964–66; UK Delegn to European Communities, 1967–72; Counsellor, 1970; Hd of Sci. and Technol. Dept, FCO, 1973–75; Commercial Counsellor, East Berlin, 1975–76; Head of Trade Relations and Export Dept, FCO, 1976–78; High Comr in Ghana and Ambassador to Togo, 1978–83; Ambassador to Denmark, 1983–86; Dir-Gen. for Trade and Investment, USA, and Consul-Gen., New York, 1986–88. Chairman: Scottish Homes, 1989–96; Thamesmead Town, 1993–96. *Publications:* A Danish Gospel, 1986; Og Gamle Danmark, 1992. *Address:* Regent Europe, 39 St James's Street, SW1A 1JQ. *Club:* New (Edinburgh).

MELLOR, Christopher John; Chief Executive, awg plc (formerly Anglian Water PLC), since 2000; *b* 3 March 1949; *s* of late John Whitaker Mellor and Mary Mellor (*née* Thompson); *m*; four *d*. Chartered Accountant, 1972. Various posts in local govt finance, 1967–79; joined Anglian Water Authy, subseq. Anglian Water PLC, then awg plc, 1979: Sen. Accountant, 1979–85; Principal Accountant, 1985–87; Hd, Privatisation Unit, 1987–88; Hd, Finance and Planning, 1988–90; Principal Accountant, then Head, Financial Planning, 1988–90; Gp Finance Dir, 1990–98; Gp Man. Dir, 1998–2000. *Recreations:* music, painting, golf. *Address:* awg plc, Anglian House, Ambury Road, Huntingdon, Cambs PE29 3NZ. *T:* (01480) 323257.

MELLOR, David, CBE 2001 (OBE 1981); DesRCA; RDI 1962; FCSD; designer, manufacturer and retailer; Chairman, Crafts Council, 1982–84; *b* 5 Oct. 1930; *s* of Colin Mellor; *m* 1966, Fiona MacCarthy, *qv*; one *s* one *d*. *Educ:* Sheffield College of Art; Royal College of Art (DesRCA and Silver Medal, 1953, Hon. Fellow 1966); British School at Rome. Set up silver-smithing workshop, Sheffield, 1954; designer and maker of silver for Worshipful Co. of Goldsmiths, Cutlers' Co., Southwell Minster, Essex Univ., Darwin Coll., Cambridge, among others, and range of silver tableware for use in British embassies; designer of fountain in bronze for Botanic Gdns, Cambridge, 1970; concurrently opened industrial design office. Consultancies, 1954–, include: Walker & Hall, Abacus Municipal, Glacier Metal, ITT, Post Office, British Rail, James Neill Tools; Magis Furniture; Cons. to DoE on design of traffic signals, 1965–70. Trustee: V & A Museum, 1984–88; Peak Park Trust, 1992–96. Work in collections: Goldsmiths' Co., V&A, Millennium Galls, Sheffield, Mus. of Modern Art, NY; retrospective exhibn, Design Mus., 1998. Awards: Design Centre: 1957, 1959, 1962, 1965, 1966; Design Council: 1974, 1977; RSA Presidential Award for Design Management, 1981. Liveryman, Goldsmiths' Co., 1980; Freeman, Cutlers' Co. of Hallamshire, 1981. FCSD (FSIAD 1964; CSD Medal 1988). Hon. Fellow, Sheffield City Polytechnic, 1979; Hon. DLitt Sheffield Univ., 1986; Hon. DDes De Montfort, 1997; Hon. Dr RCA, 1999. *Address:* The Round Building, Hathersage, Sheffield S32 1BA. *T:* (01433) 650220.

MELLOR, Prof. David Hugh, FBA 1983; Pro-Vice-Chancellor, University of Cambridge, 2000–01; Professor of Philosophy, University of Cambridge, 1986–89; Fellow, Darwin College, Cambridge, since 1971 (Vice-Master, 1983–87); *b* 10 July 1938; *s* of Sydney David Mellor and Ethel Naomi Mellor (*née* Hughes). *Educ:* Manchester Grammar School; Pembroke College, Cambridge (BA Nat. Scis and Chem. Eng, 1960; MA; PhD 1968; ScD 1990; MEng 1992); Univ. of Minnesota (Harkness Fellowship; MSc Chem. Eng, 1962). Technical Officer, ICI Central Instruments Lab., 1962–63; Cambridge University: Research Student in Philosophy, Pembroke Coll., 1963–68; Fellow, Pembroke Coll., 1965–70; Univ. Asst Lectr in Philosophy, 1965–70; Univ. Lectr in Philosophy, 1970–83; Univ. Reader in Metaphysics, 1983–85. Vis. Fellow in Philosophy, ANU, 1975; Radcliffe Trust Fellow in Philosophy, 1978–80. Hon. Prof. of Philosophy, Univ. of Keele, 1989–92. President: British Soc. for the Philos. of Science, 1985–87; Aristotelian Soc., 1992–93. Editor: British Journal for the Philosophy of Science, 1968–70; Cambridge Studies in Philosophy, 1978–82. Hon. PhD Lund, 1997. *Publications:* The Matter of Chance, 1971; Real Time, 1981; Matters of Metaphysics, 1991; The Facts of Causation, 1995; Real Time II, 1998; articles in Mind, Analysis, Philosophy of Science, Philosophy, Philosophical Review, Ratio, Isis, British Jl for Philosophy of Science, Jl of Philosophy. *Recreation:* theatre. *Address:* 25 Orchard Street, Cambridge CB1 1JS. *T:* (01223) 740017.

MELLOR, Rt Hon. David John; PC 1990; QC 1987; broadcaster, journalist and international business adviser; *b* 12 March 1949; *s* of Mr and late Mrs Douglas H. Mellor; *m* 1974, Judith Mary Hall (marr. diss. 1995); two *s*. *Educ:* Swanage Grammar Sch.; Christ's Coll., Cambridge (BA Hons 1970). FZS 1981. Called to the Bar, Inner Temple, 1972; in practice thereafter. Chm., Cambridge Univ. Conservative Assoc., 1970; contested West Bromwich E, Oct. 1974; MP (C) Putney, 1979–97; contested (C) same seat, 1997. PPS to Leader of Commons and Chancellor of the Duchy of Lancaster, 1981; Parly Under-Sec. of State, Dept of Energy, 1981–83, Home Office, 1983–86; Minister of State: Home Office, 1986–87; Foreign and Commonwealth Office, 1987–88; Dept of Health, 1988–89; Home Office, 1989–90; Privy Council Office (Minister for the Arts), 1990; Chief Sec. to the Treasury, 1990–92; Sec. of State for Nat. Heritage, 1992. Sec., Cons. Parly Legal Cttee, 1979–81; Vice-Chm., Greater London Cons. Members Cttee, 1980–81. Chairman: Sports Aid Foundn, 1993–97; Football Task Force, 1997–99. Special Trustee, Westminster Hosp., 1980–87; Mem. Council, NYO, 1981–; Mem. Bd, ENO, 1993–95. Pres., Bournemouth SO, 2000–. Presenter: 6.06, 1993–99, Mellor, 1999–, BBC Radio 5; Vintage Years (series), BBC Radio 3, 1993–2000; The Midnight Hour, BBC2, 1997–99; Across the Threshold (series), Classic FM, 1998–. Music Critic, Mail on Sunday, 2000–; columnist: The Guardian, 1992–94; The People, 1998–; sports columnist, Evening Standard, 1997–. BBC Radio Personality of the Year, Variety Club of GB, 1995. Hon. Associate, BVA, 1986. *Recreations:* classical music, reading, football.

MELLOR, David John; His Honour Judge David Mellor; a Circuit Judge, since 1989; *b* 12 Oct. 1940; *s* of John Robert Mellor and Muriel Mary (*née* Field); *m* 1966, Carol Mary Clement, LLB, BA, AKC, Barrister, *o d* of David Morris Clement, *qv*; two *d*. *Educ:* Plumtree Sch., S Rhodesia; King's Coll., London (LLB). Called to the Bar, Inner Temple, 1964; a Recorder, 1986–89; Principal Judge in Civil Matters for counties of Cambridge, Norfolk and Suffolk, 1991–98; Resident Judge, Norwich, 1998–. *Address:* Norwich Combined Court, Bishopgate, Norwich NR3 1UR. *T:* (01603) 761776. *Club:* Norfolk (Norwich).

MELLOR, Derrick, CBE 1984; HM Diplomatic Service, retired; re-employed at Foreign and Commonwealth Office, since 1984; Occasional Lecturer, School of Oriental and African Studies, since 1987; *b* 11 Jan. 1926; *s* of William Mellor and Alice (*née* Hurst); *m* 1954, Kathleen (*née* Hodgson); two *s* one *d*. Served Army, 1945–49. Board of Trade, 1950–57; Trade Commission Service, 1958–64: served Kuala Lumpur and Sydney; HM Diplomatic Service, 1964–: served Copenhagen, Caracas, Asuncion (Ambassador, 1979–84) and London; Trng Consultant, FCO, 1987–. Project Dir for S Amer., GAP Activity Projects (GAP) Ltd, 1993–. *Recreations:* tennis, golf, skiing. *Address:* Summerford Farmhouse, Withyham, E Sussex TN7 4DA. *T:* (01892) 770826. *Club:* Army and Navy.

MELLOR, Fiona; *see* MacCarthy, F.

MELLOR, Hugh Wright; Secretary and Director, National Corporation for Care of Old People (now Centre for Policy on Ageing), 1973–80; *b* 11 Aug. 1920; *s* of late William Algernon and Katherine Mildred Mellor; *m* 1944, Winifred Joyce Yates. *Educ:* Leys Sch., Cambridge; London Univ. (BScEcon). Friends Relief Service, 1940–45; Sec., St Albans Council of Social Service, 1945–48; Community Develt Officer, Hemel Hempstead Develt Corp., 1948–50; Asst Sec., Nat. Corp. for Care of Old People, 1951–73. Pres., Hanover Housing Assoc., 1994–99 (Chm., 1980–85). *Publication:* The Role of Voluntary Organisations in Social Welfare, 1985. *Recreations:* walking, reading, music. *Address:* Lark Rise, Risborough Road, Great Kimble, Aylesbury, Bucks HP17 0XS. *Club:* Royal Commonwealth Society.

MELLOR, Ian, MA; Headmaster, Stockport Grammar School, since 1996; *b* 30 June 1946; *s* of William Crompton Mellor and Annie Mellor; *m* 1969, Margery Ainsworth; three *s*. *Educ:* Manchester Grammar Sch.; Sidney Sussex Coll., Cambridge (MA, DipEd). Asst Modern Langs teacher, King's Sch., Chester, 1968–73; Head of Modern Languages: Kirkham Grammar Sch., Lancs, 1974–76; Bristol Grammar Sch., 1976–84; Dep. Head, Sale Boys' Grammar Sch., 1984–90; Head, Sir Roger Manwood's Sch., Sandwich, 1991–96. *Recreations:* Association football, cricket, reading, music of the 1960s, philatelic flaws and watermark varieties, bridge. *Address:* Shaa House, Stockport Grammar School, Buxton Road, Stockport, Cheshire SK2 7AF.

MELLOR, Julie Thérèse; Chair, Equal Opportunities Commission, since 1999; *b* 29 Jan. 1957; *d* of Gp Capt. Edward Vernon Mellor and late Patricia Ann Mellor; *m* 1990, Nick Reed; one *s* one *d*. *Educ:* Winchester Co. High Sch. for Girls; Brasenose Coll., Oxford (BA Hons Exptl Psychol.). Eleanor Emerson Fellow in Labour Educn, Cornell Univ., NY and teacher, Inst. for Educn Res. on Women and Work, 1979–81; Employee Relns Advr, Shell UK, 1981–83; Econ. Develt Officer, London Borough of Islington, 1983–84; Sen. Employment Policy Advr and Dep. Hd, Contract Compliance, Equal Opportunities Unit, ILEA, 1984–89; Equal Opportunities Manager, TSB Gp, 1989–91; Dir of Equal Opportunities and Corporate Human Resources Dir, British Gas, 1992–96; owner and principal consultant, Julie Mellor Consultants, 1996–99. Mem., CRE, 1995–. Member: Equal Opportunities Panel, CBI, 1993–96; Minister's Nat. Adv. Council on Employment of Disabled People, 1993–95; Minister's Co-ordinating Gp, Eur. Year Against Racism, 1997. *Recreations:* theatre, travel, food, family. *Address:* Equal Opportunities Commission, 36 Broadway, SW1H 0XH. *T:* (020) 7222 1110.

MELLOR, His Honour Kenneth Wilson; QC 1975; a Circuit Judge, 1984–97; *b* 4 March 1927; *s* of Samuel Herbert Mellor; *m* 1957, Sheila Gale; one *s* three *d*. *Educ:* King's College Cambridge (BA 1949; LLB 1950; MA 1951). RNVR, 1944–47 (Sub Lieut). Called to the Bar, Lincoln's Inn, 1950. Dep. Chm., Hereford QS, 1969–71; a Recorder, 1972–84. Chm., Agricultural Land Tribunal (West Midlands).

MELLOR, Ronald William, CBE 1984; FREng, FIMechE; Secretary, Institution of Mechanical Engineers, 1987–93; *b* 8 Dec. 1930; *s* of William and Helen Edna Mellor; *m* 1956, Jean Sephton; one *s* one *d*. *Educ:* Highgate School; King's College London (BSc Eng). FIMechE 1980; FREng (FEng 1983). Ford Motor Co.: Manager Cortina Product Planning, 1964; Manager Truck Product Planning, 1965; Chief Research Engineer, 1969; Chief Engine Engineer, 1970; Chief Body Engineer, Ford Werke AG, W Germany, 1974; Vice Pres. Car Engineering, Ford of Europe Inc., 1975–87; Dir, Ford Motor Co. Ltd, 1983–87. Mem., Bd of Govs, Anglia Polytechnic Univ., 1993–. Liveryman, Co. of Carmen, 1990–. Thomas Hawksley Lectr, IMechE, 1983. *Recreation:* yachting.

MELLOWS, Prof. Anthony Roger, TD 1969; PhD, LLD; Solicitor of the Supreme Court, since 1960; Professor of the Law of Property in the University of London, 1974–90, now Emeritus; Deputy Lord Prior, Order of St John, since 1999; *b* 30 July 1936; *s* of L. B. and M. P. Mellows; *m* 1973, Elizabeth, DStJ, *d* of Ven. B. G. B. Fox, MC, TD, and of Hon. Margaret Joan Fox, *d* of 1st Viscount Davidson, PC, GCVO, CH, CB. *Educ:* King's Coll., London (AKC 1957; LLB 1957; LLM 1959; PhD 1962; BD 1968; LLD 1973; Fellow 1980). Commissioned Intelligence Corps (TA), 1959, Captain 1964; served Intell. Corps (TA) and (T&AVR) and on the Staff, 1959–71; RARO, 1971–91. Admitted a solicitor, 1960; private practice, 1960–; Sen. Partner, Messrs Alexanders Easton Kinch, 1962–96, now Consultant, Messrs Hunters. Asst Lectr in Law, King's Coll., London, 1962, Lectr, 1964, Reader, 1971; Dir of Conveyancing Studies, 1969; Dean, Fac. of Laws, Univ. of London, 1981–84, and of Fac. of Laws, KCL, 1981–85; Hd of Dept of Laws, KCL, 1984–87; Mem. Council, KCL, 1972–80. Mem., Archbishops' Millennium Adv. Gp, 1995–2000; Chm., Archbishops' Rev. of Bishops' Needs and Resources, 1999–. Trustee: Kincardine Foundn, 1972–84; Nineveh Trust, 1985–90; London Law Trust, 1968– (Chm. Trustees); Lambeth Fund, 1995–; Marit and Hans Rausing Charitable Foundn, 1996–; Order of St John and British Red Cross Soc. Jt Cttee, 1987–. FRSA 1959. Freeman of the City of London, 1963. GCStJ 1991 (KStJ 1988; CStJ 1985; OStJ 1981; Mem. Council, 1981–88; Registrar, 1988–91; Chancellor, 1991–99); Comdr, Ordine Pro Merito Melitensi, SMO Malta, 1999. *Publications:* Local Searches and Enquiries, 1964, 2nd edn 1967; Conveyancing Searches, 1964, 2nd edn 1975; Land Charges, 1966; The Preservation and Felling of Trees, 1964; The Trustee's Handbook, 1965, 3rd edn 1975; Taxation for Executors and Trustees, 1967, 6th edn 1984; (jtly) The Modern Law of Trusts, 1966, 5th edn 1983; The Law of Succession, 1970, 4th edn 1983; Taxation of Land Transactions, 1973, 3rd edn 1982. *Address:* 22 Devereux Court, Temple Bar, WC2R 3JJ. *Club:* Athenæum.

MELLOWS, Heather Jean, (Mrs A. Johnson), FRCOG; Consultant Obstetrician and Gynaecologist, Doncaster and Bassetlaw Hospitals NHS Trust, since 1988; *b* 13 March 1951; *d* of late A. Paul Mellows, DFC, MA, LLB and of Jean Mellows (*née* Wells); *m* 1982, Anthony Johnson; two step *s*. *Educ:* Parsons Mead Sch., Ashtead, Surrey; Rosebery Co. Sch. for Girls, Epsom; Royal Free Hosp. Sch. of Medicine (MB BS 1974). FRCOG 1993; MFFP 1993. Pre-registration house officer posts: Royal Free Hosp., 1974; St Andrew's Hosp., Bow, 1975; house officer posts: Croydon Gen. Hosp., 1975; Royal Free Hosp., 1976; SHO posts: Queen Charlotte's Hosp., 1976; Chelsea Hosp. for Women, 1977; Res. Asst, Queen Charlotte's Hosp., 1978–79; Registrar, Univ. Dept Obstetrics and Gynaecol., Cape Town, SA, 1980–81; Senior Registrar: Queen Charlotte's Hosp., 1982; Jessop Hosp. for Women, Sheffield, 1983–85; Sen. Clin. MO, Family Planning and Related Services, Sheffield, 1986–87; Associate Postgrad. Dean, Faculty of Medicine, Nottingham Univ., 1999–2001; Postgrad. Clin. Tutor, Bassetlaw Hosp., 1997–. Regl Assessor in Obstetrics, Confidential Enquiry into Maternal Deaths, 1993–; Mem., Regl Panel for Confidential Enquiry into Stillbirths and Deaths in Infancy, 1993–; Advr, Confidential Enquiry into Perioperative Deaths, 2000–01; Mem. Panel, Sec. of State's Inquiry into Quality and Practice within the NHS, arising from the actions of Rodney Ledward, 1999–2000 (reported, 2000). Royal College of Obstetricians and Gynaecologists: Member of Council: 1986–92, 1994–96 and 1999–; Faculty of Family Planning, 2000–; Chm., Hosp. Recognition Cttee, 1994–96; Jun. Vice Pres., 2001–. *Address:* Brookhouse Hall, Laughton, Sheffield S25 1YA. *T:* (01909) 562399.

MELLY, (Alan) George (Heywood); professional jazz singer; with John Chilton's Feetwarmers, since 1974; *b* 17 Aug. 1926; *s* of Francis Heywood and Edith Maud Melly; *m* 1955, Victoria Vaughan (marr. diss. 1962); one *d*; *m* 1963, Diana Margaret Campion Dawson; one *s* and one step *d*. *Educ:* Stowe School. Able Seaman, RN, 1944–47. Art Gallery Asst, London Gallery, 1948–50; sang with Mick Mulligan's Jazz Band, 1949–61. Wrote Flook strip cartoon balloons (drawn by Trog (Wally Fawkes)), 1956–71. Critic, The Observer: pop music, 1965–67; TV, 1967–71; films, 1971–73. Film scriptwriter: Smashing Time, 1968; Take a Girl Like You, 1970. Pres., British Humanist Assoc., 1972–74. Critic of the Year, IPC Nat. Press Awards, 1970. *Publications:* I Flook, 1962; Owning Up, 1965; Revolt into Style, 1970; Flook by Trog, 1970; Rum Bum and Concertina, 1977; (with Barry Fantoni) The Media Mob, 1980; Tribe of One: Great Naive and Primitive Painters of the British Isles, 1981; (with Walter Dorin) Great Lovers, 1981; Mellymobile, 1982; (ed) Edward James, Swans Reflecting Elephants: my early years, 1982; Scouse Mouse, 1984; It's All Writ Out for You: the life and work of Scottie Wilson, 1986; (with Michael Woods) Paris and the Surrealists, 1991; Don't tell Sybil: an intimate memoir of E. L. T. Mesens, 1997. *Recreations:* trout fishing, singing and listening to blues of 1920s, collecting modern paintings. *Address:* 81 Frithville Gardens, Shepherds Bush, W12 7JQ. *Clubs:* Colony Room, Chelsea Arts.

MELMOTH, Christopher George Frederick Frampton, CMG 1959; South Asia Department, International Bank for Reconstruction and Development, 1962–75, retired; *b* 25 Sept. 1912; *s* of late George Melmoth and Florence Melmoth; *m* 1946, Maureen Joan (*née* Brennan); three *d*. *Educ:* Sandringham Sch., Forest Gate. Accountant Officer, Co-ordination of Supplies Fund, Malta, 1942–45; Administrative Officer, Hong Kong, 1946–55; Minister of Finance, Uganda, 1956–62. *Recreation:* walking. *Address:* Hoptons Cottage, Kemerton, Tewkesbury, Glos GL20 7JE.

MELMOTH, Graham John; Chief Executive, Co-operative Group (CWS) Ltd (formerly Co-operative Wholesale Society), since 1996; *b* 18 March 1938; *s* of Harry James Melmoth and Marjorie Doris Melmoth (*née* Isitt); *m* 1967, Jennifer Mary Banning; two *s*. *Educ:* City of London Sch. FCIS 1972. National Service, 1957–59 (Lieut), RA. Asst Sec., Chartered Inst. of Patent Agents, 1961–65; Sec., BOC-AIRCO, 1965–69; Dep. Sec., Fisons, 1969–72; Sec., Letraset, 1972–75; CWS, then Co-operative Group (CWS) Ltd, 1975–: Director: Co-operative Bank plc, 1992–; Co-operative Press Ltd, 1994–98; Co-operative Insurance Soc. Ltd, 1996–. Chm., Ringway Developments plc, 1995– (Dir, 1988–); Dir, Unity Trust Bank plc, 1992–98. Chairman: Manchester TEC Ltd, 1999–2001 (Dir, 1997–2001); Manchester Enterprises Ltd, 2001– (Dir, 1997–2000, Chm., 1999–2000, Manchester TEC Ltd). Mem. Council, NACRO, 1998–. Trustee: New Lanark Conservation Trust, 1987–; Nat. Mus. of Labour History, 1995–2001. Pres., Internat. Co-operative Alliance, Geneva, 1995–97. FIGD 1996; FRSA 1996; CIMgt 1997. *Recreations:* opera, theatre, Co-operative history. *Address:* Co-operative Group (CWS) Ltd, New Century House, Manchester M60 4ES. *T:* (0161) 834 1212. *Club:* Reform.

MELROSE, Prof. Denis Graham; Professor of Surgical Science, Royal Postgraduate Medical School, 1968–83, Emeritus since 1983; *b* 20 June 1921; *s* of late Thomas Robert Gray Melrose, FRCS and Floray Collings; *m* 1945, Ann, *d* of late Kathleen Tatham Warter; two *s*. *Educ:* Sedbergh Sch.; University Coll., Oxford; UCH London. MA, BM, BCh, MRCP, FRCS. Junior appts at Hammersmith Hosp. and Redhill County Hosp., Edgware, 1945; RNVR, 1946–48; subseq. Lectr, later Reader, Royal Postgrad. Med. Sch.; Nuffield Travelling Fellow, USA, 1956; Fulbright Fellow, 1957; Associate in Surgery, Stanford Univ. Med. Sch., 1958. Fellow: RPMS, 1993; ICSM, 1999. *Publications:* numerous papers in learned jls and chapters in books, particularly on heart surgery, heart lung machine and med. engrg. *Recreations:* sailing, ski-ing. *Address:* Ca'n Rosa, Apartado 499, 07820 Sant Antoni de Portmany, Ibiza, Baleares, Spain. *Club:* Royal Naval Sailing Association.

MELVILL JONES, Prof. Geoffrey, FRS 1979; FRSC 1979; FCASI; FRAeS; Emeritus Professor, McGill University, since 1992; Adjunct Professor, since 1992, Research Professor, since 2001, University of Calgary; *b* 14 Jan. 1923; *s* of Sir Bennett Melvill Jones, CBE, AFC, FRS and Dorothy Laxton Jotham; *m* 1953, Jenny Marigold Burnaby; two *s* two *d*. *Educ:* King's Choir Sch.; Dauntsey's Sch.; Cambridge Univ. (BA, MA, MB, BCh). Appointments in UK, 1950–61: House Surgeon, Middlesex Hosp., 1950; Sen. Ho. Surg., Otolaryngology, Addenbrooke's Hosp., Cambridge, 1950–51; MO, RAF, 1951; Scientific MO, RAF Inst. of Aviation Medicine, Farnborough, Hants, 1951–55; Scientific Officer (external staff), Medical Research Council of Gt Britain, 1955–61; McGill University: Dir, Aviation, later Aerospace Med. Res. Unit, 1961–88; Associate Prof., 1961–68; Full Prof., 1968–91; Hosmer Res. Prof. of Physiol., 1978–91. Fellow, Aerospace Medical Assoc., 1969; FCASI 1965; FRAeS 1981. First recipient, Dohlman Medal for research in the field of orientation and postural control, 1986; Robert Bárány Jubilee Gold Medal for most significant research on vestibular function during past 5 years; Ashton Graybiel Lectureship Award, US Navy, 1989; Stewart Meml Lectureship Award, RAeS, 1989; Buchanan-Barbour Award, RAeS, 1990; McLaughlan Medal, RSCan, 1991. *Publications:* Mammalian Vestibular Physiology, 1979 (NY); Adaptive Mechanisms in Gaze Control, 1985; research papers in physiological jls. *Recreations:* outdoor activities, music. *Address:* Department of Clinical Neurosciences, Faculty of Medicine, University of Calgary, 3330 Hospital Drive NW, Calgary, AB T2N 4N1, Canada. *T:* (403) 220 8764/4307, *Fax:* (403) 283 8731.

MELVILLE; *see* Leslie Melville, family name of Earl of Leven and Melville.

MELVILLE, 9th Viscount *cr* 1802; **Robert David Ross Dundas;** Baron Duneira 1802; *b* 28 May 1937; *s* of Hon. Robert Maldred St John Melville Dundas (2nd *s* of 7th Viscount) (killed in action, 1940), and of Margaret Connell (who; *m* 2nd, 1946, Gerald Bristowe Sanderson), *d* of late Percy Cruden Ross; *S* uncle, 1971; *m* 1982, Fiona Margaret Stilgoe, *d* of late Roger and of Mrs Stilgoe, Stogumber, Som; two *s*. *Educ:* Wellington College. District Councillor, Lasswade, Midlothian; Mem., Midlothian CC, 1964–67. Pres., Lasswade Civic Soc. Lieutenant, Ayrshire Yeomanry; Captain (Reserve), Scots Guards. *Recreations:* fishing, shooting, golf, chess. *Heir:* *s* Hon. Robert Henry Kirkpatrick Dundas, *b* 23 April 1984. *Address:* Wey House, Norton Fitzwarren, Taunton, Som TA4 1BT. *Clubs:* Cavalry and Guards; House of Lords Motor; Midlothian County; Bonnyrigg and Lasswade District Ex-Servicemen's.

MELVILLE, Anthony Edwin; Headmaster, The Perse School, Cambridge, 1969–87; *b* 28 April 1929; *yr s* of Sir Leslie Melville, *qv*; *m* 1964, Pauline Marianne Surtees Simpson, *d* of Major A. F. Simpson, Indian Army; two *d*. *Educ:* Sydney Church of England Grammar Sch.; Univ. of Sydney (BA); King's Coll., Cambridge (MA). Sydney Univ. Medal in English, 1950; Pt II History Tripos, 1st cl. with dist., 1952; Lightfoot Schol. in Eccles. History, 1954. Asst Master, Haileybury Coll., 1953. *Recreations:* reading, gardening, music. *Address:* 4 Field Way, Cambridge CB1 8RW. *Club:* East India.

MELVILLE, Prof. David, CBE 2001; PhD; CPhys, FInstP; Vice-Chancellor, University of Kent at Canterbury, since 2001; *b* 4 April 1944; *s* of late Frederick George Melville and Mary Melville; *m*; one *s* two *d*. *Educ:* Clitheroe Royal Grammar Sch.; Sheffield Univ. (BSc 1st Cl. Hons 1965; PhD 1969); Columbia Univ. CPhys, FInstP 1978. Southampton University: Lectr in Physics, 1968–78; Sen. Lectr, 1978–84; Lancashire Polytechnic: Prof. of Physics and Head, Sch. of Physics and Astronomy, 1985–86; Asst Dir, 1986–89; Vice-Rector, 1989–91; Dir, Middlesex Polytechnic, 1991–92; Vice-Chancellor, Middlesex Univ., 1992–96; Chief Exec., FEFC, 1996–2001. ICI Res. Fellow, 1968; Visiting Professor: Univ. of Parma, Italy, 1974–80; Oporto Univ., Portugal, 1983; Univ. of Warwick, 1997–; Visiting Scientist: ICI Corporate Lab., Runcorn, 1975; Consiglio Nazionale delle Ricerche, Italy, 1976–80. Vice-Chm., CVCP, 1995–96. Member: Council, BNF Metals Technol. Centre, 1986–92; SERC Materials Commn, 1988–92; SERC Condensed Matter Sub-Cttee, 1986–88; SERC Physics Cttee, 1988–92; SERC Metals and Magnetic Materials Cttee, 1988–92; Council for Industry and Higher Educn, 1994–96; Council, Inst. of Employment Studies, 1998–; Jt DfEE/DCMS Educn and Libraries Task Gp, 1999–2000; Chairman: SERC Magnetism and Magnetic Materials Initiative, 1989–91; UK and Republic of Ireland Chapter, Magnetics Soc., IEEE, 1988–93; Internat. Congress on Magnetism, Edinburgh, 1991. Hon. Pres., Co. of Middx Trust, 1992–. DUniv: Middlesex, 1997; Derby, 2000; Hon. DSc: Sheffield, 1997; Southampton, 2001. *Publications:* articles on magnetism, magnetic materials and biophysics in scientific and engrg jls. *Recreations:* sailing, walking, ski-ing. *Address:* The Registry, The University, Canterbury, Kent CT2 7NZ. *T:* (01227) 823201.

MELVILLE, James; *see* Martin, R. P.

MELVILLE, Sir Leslie Galfreid, KBE 1957 (CBE 1953); Member of the Board of the Reserve Bank, Australia, 1959–63, and 1965–74; Member, Commonwealth Grants Commission, 1979–82 (Chairman, 1966–74); *b* 26 March 1902; *s* of Richard Ernest Melville and Lilian Evelyn Thatcher; *m* 1925, Mary Maud Scales; two *s*. *Educ:* Sydney Church of England Grammar Sch. Bachelor of Economics, University of Sydney, 1925; Public Actuary of South Australia, 1924–28; Prof. of Economics, University of Adelaide, 1929–31; Economic Adviser to Commonwealth Bank of Australia, 1931–49; Asst Gov. (Central Banking) Commonwealth Bank of Australia, 1949–53; Mem. of Commonwealth Bank Bd, 1951–53; Exec. Dir of International Monetary Fund and International Bank for Reconstruction and Development, 1950–53. Mem. of Cttees on Australian Finances and Unemployment, 1931 and 1932, Financial Adviser to Australian Delegates at Imperial Economic Conference, 1932; Financial Adviser to Australian Delegate at World Economic Conference, 1933; Mem. of Financial and Economic Advisory Cttee, 1939; Chm. of Australian Delegation to United Nations Monetary Conf. at Bretton Woods, 1944; Mem. of Advisory Council of Commonwealth Bank, 1945–51; Chm. UN Sub-Commn on Employment and Economic Stability, 1947–50; Member: Immigration Planning Council, 1956–61; Develt Adv. Service of Internat. Bank, 1963–65; Chm. of Tariff Bd, Australia, 1960–62; Chm., Tariff Adv. Cttee of Papua and New Guinea, 1969–71. Vice-Chancellor Australian National Univ., Canberra, ACT, 1953–60. Hon. LLD: Toronto, 1958; ANU, 1978; Hon. DSc Econ Sydney, 1980. *Address:* Unit 61 The Grange, 67 MacGregor Street, Deakin, Canberra, ACT 2600, Australia. *Club:*

Commonwealth.
See also A. E. Melville.

MELVILLE-ROSS, Timothy David; Chairman: Investors in People UK, since 1999; NewsCast, since 2000; *b* 3 Oct. 1944; *s* of late Antony Stuart Melville-Ross and of Anne Barclay Fane; *m* 1967, Camilla Mary Harlackenden; two *s* one *d*. *Educ:* Uppingham School; Portsmouth College of Technology (Dip Business Studies, 2nd cl. hons). FCIS. British Petroleum, 1963–73; Rowe, Swann & Co., stockbrokers, 1973–74; joined Nationwide Building Soc., 1974: Dir and Chief Gen. Man., 1985–87; Dir and Chief Exec., 1987–94; Dir Gen., Inst. of Dirs, 1994–99. Dep. Chm., Monument Oil and Gas plc, 1997–99 (Dir, 1992–99); Chairman: DTZ Holdings plc, 2000–; Bank Insinger de Beaufort NV, 2000–; Director: Bovis Homes plc, 1998–; Royal London Mutual Insce Ltd, 1999–; Manganese Bronze plc, 2000–. Member Council: Industrial Soc., 1986–95; Inst. of Business Ethics, 1994–; Essex Univ., 1995–. Pro-Chancellor, Univ. of Sussex, 2000–. Trustee, Uppingham Sch., 1988–2000. FRSA; CIMgt; FCIS; FCIB. *Recreations:* music, reading, bridge, tennis, the countryside.

MELVYN HOWE, Prof. George; *see* Howe.

MENCHÚ, Rigoberta; human rights activist; Goodwill Ambassador, UNESCO, since 1996; *b* 1959; *d* of late Vicente Menchú, Mayan resistance leader and founder, Cttee of Peasant Unity (CUC), Guatemala, and Juana Menchú; *m* 1995, Angel Canil. Works for indigenous peoples' rights; founded Rigoberta Menchú Tum Foundn, Guatemala City; Member: CUC; United Representation of Guatemalan Opposition; Five Hundred Years of Resistance Campaign; UN Working Group on Indigenous Populations; UN Internat. Indian Treaty Council. Nobel Peace Prize, 1992. Pres., Indigenous Initiative for Peace, UN, 1999. *Publications:* (with Elisabeth Burgos-Debray) I, Rigoberta Menchú, 1983 (trans. English 1984; in 12 other langs); (with Gianni Minà y Dante Liano) Rigoberta: grandson of the Mayas, 1998 (trans. Italian and English).

MENDEL, Paul David, MBE 2000; Consultant, Council of Christians and Jews, since 1999 (Director, 1992–98); broadcaster and speaker; *b* 14 Oct. 1930; *s* of late Eric Lazarus Mendel and Esther (*née* Graber); *m*; one *s* one *d*; *m* 1989, Rosalind Alder. *Educ:* St Christopher's Sch., Letchworth. Nat. Service, 1949–51, Capt. RMP. Former Member: Middx CC; Barnet BC. Dep. Dir, Defence and Gp Relns, Bd of Deputies of British Jews, 1982–84; Council of Christians and Jews: Asst Dir, 1985–87; Dep. Dir, 1987–92. Mem., Interfaith Network Exec., 1987–. JP Juvenile and W Central PSD, 1955–83 (sometime Chm.). *Recreations:* travel, reading, people. *Address:* 100 Lyncroft Mansions, Lyncroft Gardens, NW6 1JY. *T:* (020) 7794 6989.

MENDELSOHN, Robert Victor, JD; Group Chief Executive and Director, Royal & Sun Alliance Insurance Group plc, since 1997; *b* NYC, 18 July 1946; *s* of Harold Victor Mendelsohn and Mary Ellen (*née* Muldoon); *m* 1968, Patricia Fielding; one *s* one *d*. *Educ:* Georgetown Univ. (AB 1968); Harvard Univ. (JD 1971). Called to the Bar, NY, 1971; Attorney, Willkie Farr & Gallagher, NYC, 1971–74; Pres. and Dir, W. R. Berkley Corp., Greenwich, Conn, 1974–93; Chief Exec., 1994–97, Chm., 1997–, Royal & Sun Alliance USA, Inc., Charlotte, NC. Director: Amer. Insce Assoc., 1994– (Chm., 1999–2000); Internat. Insce Soc., 1999–; Chm. Council, Insce Co. Execs, 1998–2000. Mem., UK-China Forum, 1999–. Mem., Bd of Regents, Georgetown Univ., Washington, 1999–. Trustee, Jose Limon Dance Foundn, 1979–. *Recreations:* golf, walking, ski-ing, sailing. *Address:* (office) 30 Berkeley Square, W1J 6EW. *T:* (020) 7569 6120; PO Box 1000, 9300 Arrowpoint Boulevard, Charlotte, NC 28201–1000, USA. *T:* (704) 5222000.

MENDELSON, Prof. Maurice Harvey; QC 1992; DPhil; Professor of International Law, University of London at University College London, since 1987; *b* 27 Aug. 1943; *s* of William Maizel Mendelson and Anne (*née* Aaronson); *m* 1968, Katharine Julia Olga Kertesz; two *d*. *Educ:* St Marylebone Grammar Sch.; New Coll., Oxford (BA 1st Cl. Hons Jurisprudence 1964; MA; DPhil 1971). Called to the Bar, Lincoln's Inn, 1965 (Bencher, 2000); Internat. Law Fund Schol., 1966; Leverhulme European Res. Schol., 1966–67; Lectr in Laws, KCL, 1968–74; Kennedy Law Schol., Lincoln's Inn, 1970–73; Official Fellow and Tutor in Law, St John's Coll., Oxford, and Univ. Lectr in Law, Oxford, 1975–86. Fulbright Vis. Schol., Harvard Law Sch., 1977; Visiting Professor: Univ. of N Carolina, 1982; Univ. of Pennsylvania, 1986; Univ. of Paris II, 1993; Univ. of NSW, 1999. Mem., Bd of Editors, British Yearbook of Internat. Law, 1995–, and other specialist jls. *Publications:* articles in internat. law jls, etc; reports to Internat. Law Assoc. *Recreations:* the arts, painting, swimming, tennis, riding. *Address:* Faculty of Laws, University College London, Bentham House, 4 Endsleigh Gardens, WC1H 0EG. *T:* (020) 7679 1428; Blackstone Chambers, Blackstone House, Temple, EC4Y 9BW. *T:* (020) 7583 1770. *Club:* Athenæum.

MENDES, Samuel Alexander, CBE 2000; Artistic Director, Donmar Warehouse Theatre, since 1992; *b* 1 Aug. 1965; *s* of Valerie Hélène Mendes (*née* Barnett) and James Peter Mendes. *Educ:* Magdalen Coll. Sch., Oxford; Peterhouse, Cambridge (BA English, 1st Cl. Hons). Asst Dir, Chichester Festival, 1987–88, Artistic Director, Minerva Studio Theatre, 1989: productions included: Heartlands, 1988; Summerfolk, 1989; Love's Labour's Lost, 1989; productions at *Donmar Warehouse*, 1992–, include: Assassins, 1992; Translations, 1993; Cabaret, 1993, NY (Tony Award for Best Revival of Musical), 1998; Glengarry Glen Ross, 1994; The Glass Menagerie, 1995; Company, 1995; Habeas Corpus, 1996; The Fix, 1997; The Front Page, 1997; The Blue Room, 1998, NY, 1999; To the Green Fields and Beyond, 2000; productions as freelance director: *Royal Shakespeare Co.:* Troilus and Cressida, 1990; The Alchemist, 1991; Richard III, 1992; The Tempest, 1993; *Royal National Theatre:* The Sea, 1991; The Rise and Fall of Little Voice, 1992; The Birthday Party, 1994; Othello, 1997; Kean, Old Vic, 1990; The Plough and the Stars, Young Vic, 1991; Oliver!, Palladium, 1994. *Film:* American Beauty (Academy Award for Best Dir and Best Picture), 1999. Numerous other awards. *Address:* c/o Donmar Films, 26–28 Neal Street, WC2H 9QQ.

MENDL, His Honour James Henry Embleton; a Circuit Judge at Knightsbridge Crown Court, 1974–93; *b* 23 Oct. 1927; *s* of late R. W. S. Mendl, barrister and author, and Dorothy Williams Mendl (*née* Burnett), and *g s* of late Sir S. F. Mendl, KBE; *m* 1971, Helena Augusta Maria Schrama, *d* of late J. H. and H. H. Schrama-Jekat, The Netherlands. *Educ:* Harrow; University Coll., Oxford (MA). Called to Bar, Inner Temple, 1953; South Eastern Circuit. Commissioned, Worcestershire Regt, 1947; served: Egypt, with 2nd N Staffs, 1947–48; with Royal Signals (TA), 1952–54, and Queen's Royal Regt (TA) (Captain, 1955), 1954–56. Councillor, Royal Borough of Kensington and Chelsea, 1964–74 (Vice-Chm., Town Planning Cttee, 1969; Chm. (Vice-Chm. 1970), Libraries Cttee, 1971). Contested (C) Gateshead East, 1966. Liveryman, Musicians' Co., 1997–. *Recreations:* music, reading, theatre. *Clubs:* Garrick, Lansdowne.

MENDOZA, June Yvonne, AO 1989; RP; ROI; artist; *d* of John Morton and Dot (*née* Mendoza), musicians; *m* 1960, Keith Ashley Victor Mackrell, *qv*; one *s* three *d*. *Educ:* Lauriston Girls' Sch., Melbourne; St Martin's Sch. of Art. Member: RP 1970; ROI 1968. Portraits for govt, regts, industry and commerce, academia, medicine, theatre, sport (*eg* Chris Evert for Wimbledon Mus.), and in public and private collections internationally. These include: Queen Elizabeth II; Queen Elizabeth the Queen Mother; Prince and Princess of Wales; Margaret Thatcher; John Major; Prime Minister of Australia, Sir John Gorton; Prime Minister of Fiji, Ratu Sir Kamisese Mara; Prime Minister of Singapore, Goh Chok Tong; former Prime Minister of Singapore, Lee Kuan Yew; Pres. of Iceland, Vigdis Finnbogadottir; Pres. of Philippines, Corazón Aquino; Donald Coggan, Robert Runcie, and George Carey, severally, while Archbishop of Canterbury; large group paintings include: The House of Commons in Session, 1986; House of Representatives, for new Parliament building in Canberra; private series of musicians include: Sir Yehudi Menuhin; Sir Georg Solti; Dame Joan Sutherland; Paul Tortelier; Sir Michael Tippett. Lectures internationally; appearances on art programmes, TV and radio. Hon. Mem., Soc. of Women Artists, 1986. Hon. DLitt: Bath, 1986; Loughborough, 1994. *Address:* 34 Inner Park Road, SW19 6DD.

MENDOZA, Vivian P.; *see* Pereira-Mendoza.

MENEM, Carlos Saúl; President of Argentina, 1989–99; *b* 2 July 1935; *s* of Saúl Menem and Mohibe Akil; *m* 1966, Zulema Fátima Yoma (marr. diss.); one *d* (one *s* decd); *m* 2001, Cecilia Bolloco. *Educ:* Córdoba Univ. Legal Advr, Confederacíon General del Trabajo, La Rioja, 1955–70; lawyer, La Rioja, 1958; Gov., La Rioja, 1973–76, 1983–89; imprisoned, 1976–81. Pres., Partido Justicialista, La Rioja, 1963–. Vice Pres., Confedn of Latin American Popular Parties, 1990–. Founder, Juventud Peronista (Peronist youth gp), 1955. *Publications:* Argentina, Now or Never; Argentina Year 2000; (jtly) The Productive Revolution.

MENEVIA, Bishop of, (RC), since 1987; **Rt Rev. Daniel Joseph Mullins;** *b* 10 July 1929; *s* of Timothy Mullins. *Educ:* Mount Melleray; St Mary's, Aberystwyth; Oscott Coll.; UC of S Wales and Mon, Cardiff (Fellow, University Coll., Cardiff). Priest, 1953; Curate at: Barry, 1953–56; Newbridge, 1956; Bargoed, 1956–57; Maesteg, 1957–60; Asst Chaplain to UC Cardiff, 1960–64; Sec. to Archbp of Cardiff, 1964–68; Vicar General of Archdiocese of Cardiff, 1968; Titular Bishop of Stowe and Auxiliary Bishop in Swansea, 1970–87. Pres., Catholic Record Soc. Member of Court, UC, Swansea. Hon. Fellow, St David's University Coll., Lampeter, 1987. *Recreations:* golf, walking. *Address:* Bryn Rhos, 79 Walter Road, Swansea SA1 4PS.

MENEVIA, Bishop Coadjutor of, (RC); *see* Jabalé Rt Rev. J. M.

MENHENNET, Dr David, CB 1991; Librarian of the House of Commons, 1976–91; Visiting Research Fellow, Goldsmiths College, London University, since 1990; *b* 4 Dec. 1928; *s* of William and Everill Menhennet, Redruth, Cornwall; *m* 1954, Audrey, *o d* of William and Alice Holmes, Accrington, Lancs; two *s*. *Educ:* Truro Sch., Cornwall; Oriel Coll., Oxford (BA 1st Cl. Hons 1952); Queen's Coll., Oxford. Open Scholarship in Mod. Langs, Oriel Coll., Oxford, 1946; Heath Harrison Trav. Scholarship, 1951; Bishop Fraser Res. Scholar, Oriel Coll., 1952–53; Laming Fellow, Queen's Coll., Oxford, 1953–54; Zaharoff Trav. Scholarship, 1953–54. MA 1956, DPhil 1960, Oxon. Library Clerk, House of Commons Library, 1954; Asst Librarian i/c Res. Div., 1964–67; Dep. Librarian, 1967–76. Mem., Study of Parliament Gp, 1964–90; Chm. Adv. Cttee, Bibliographic Services, British Library, 1986–92 (Mem., 1975–86); Mem. Exec. Cttee, Friends of Nat. Libraries, 1991–96. FRSA 1966 (Life Fellow 2001). Freeman, City of London, 1990; Liveryman, Stationers' Co., 1990. Gen. Editor, House of Commons Library Documents series, 1972–90. *Publications:* (with J. Palmer) Parliament in Perspective, 1967; The Journal of the House of Commons: a bibliographical and historical guide, 1971; (ed with D. C. L. Holland) Erskine May's Private Journal, 1857–1882, 1972; (contrib.) The House of Commons in the Twentieth Century, ed S. A. Walkland, 1979; (contrib.) The House of Commons: Services and Facilities 1972–1982, ed M. Rush, 1983; The House of Commons Library: a history, 1991, 2nd edn 2000; Essays and Articles on Bernardin de Saint-Pierre 1737–1814, 1998; articles in Lib. Assoc. Record, Parliamentarian, Parly Affairs, Polit. Qly, New Scientist, Contemp. Rev., Jl of Librarianship, Jl of Documentation, Book Collector. *Recreations:* National Trust activities, visiting Cornwall, French literature. *Address:* 50 Kelsey Lane, Beckenham, Kent BR3 3NE. *T:* (020) 8650 7787. *Club:* Athenæum.

MENIN, Rt Rev. Malcolm James; Bishop Suffragan of Knaresborough, 1986–97; *b* 26 Sept. 1932; *s* of Rev. James Nicholas Menin and Doreen Menin; *m* 1958, Jennifer Mary Cullen; one *s* three *d*. *Educ:* Dragon School; St Edward's School; University Coll., Oxford (MA); Cuddesdon Coll. Curate: Holy Spirit, Southsea, 1957–59; St Peter and St Paul, Fareham, 1959–62; Vicar of St James, Norwich, later St Mary Magdalene with St James, Norwich, 1962–86; RD Norwich East, 1981–86; Hon. Canon, Norwich Cathedral, 1982–86. *Recreations:* walking, photography, carpentry. *Address:* 32c Bracondale, Norwich NR1 2AN. *T:* (01603) 627987.

MENKES, Suzy Peta, (Mrs S. P. Menkes-Spanier); Fashion Editor, International Herald Tribune, since 1988; *b* 24 Dec. 1943; *d* of Edouard Gerald Lionel Menkès and Betty Curtis Lightfoot; *m* 1969, David Graham Spanier (*d* 2000); three *s* (one *d* decd). *Educ:* Univ. of Cambridge (MA). Editor, Varsity newspaper, Cambridge, 1966; Jun. Reporter, The Times, 1966–69; Fashion Editor, Evening Standard, 1969–77; Women's Editor, Daily Express, 1977–80; Fashion Editor: The Times, 1980–87; The Independent, 1987–88. Freeman: City of Milan, 1986; City of London, 1987. British Press Awards Commendations, 1983 and 1984; Eugenia Sheppard Award for Fashion Journalism, Council of Fashion Designers of America, 1995. *Publications:* The Knitwear Revolution, 1983; The Royal Jewels, 1985, 3rd edn 1988; The Windsor Style, 1987; Queen and Country, 1992. *Recreations:* family life, reading, opera, Royal history. *Address:* c/o International Herald Tribune, 6 bis rue des Graviers, 92521 Neuilly Cedex, France. *T:* (1) 41439428.

MENNELL, Stuart Leslie; Director, Strategic Developments, National Maritime Museum, since 2001; *b* 17 Oct. 1948; *s* of Albert Edward Mennell and Iris Mennell (*née* Jackson); *m* 1970, Margaret Hirst (*d* 2000); three *d*. *Educ:* Barlby High Sch., E Yorks. Ministry of Social Security, 1968–72; HM Customs & Excise: Preventive Duties, 1972–75; VAT, 1975–78; Regl Personnel Officer, 1978–82; Statistical Office, 1982–84; HQ Personnel Manager, 1984–86; Estate Manager, 1986–88; National Maritime Museum: Estabt Officer, 1988–89; Personnel & Corporate Planning Manager, 1989–93; Dir, Collections and Mus. Services Div., 1993–2001. MIPD 1989; MIMgt 1992. *Recreations:* badminton, classic motor cycles, walking. *Address:* National Maritime Museum, Romney Road, Greenwich, SE10 9NF. *T:* (020) 8312 6612. *Club:* Ferrers Badminton (SE Essex).

MENON, Prof. David Krishna, MD; PhD; FRCP, FRCA, FMedSci; Professor of Anaesthesia, University of Cambridge, since 2000; *b* 21 Aug. 1956; *s* of Parakat Govindan Kutty Menon and Violet Rebecca Menon; *m* 1988, Wendy Humphreys; one *s*. *Educ:* Univ. of Madras (MB BS, MD 1992); RPMS, Univ. of London (PhD 1995). FRCA 1988; FRCP 1999. Residency in Internal Medicine, Jawaharlal Inst., Pondicherry, India, 1978–83; Registrar: in Medicine, Professorial Med. Unit, Leeds Gen. Infirmary, 1984–86;

in Anaesthetics, Royal Free Hosp., London, 1987–88; MRC Res. Fellow, Robert Steiner Magnetic Resonance Unit, Hammersmith Hosp., 1989–91; Clinical Lectr, 1992–93, Lectr in Anaesthesia, 1993–2000, Univ. of Cambridge; Lead Consultant and Dir, Neurocritical Care, Addenbrooke's Hosp., 1997–2001. Founder FMedSci 1998. *Publications:* Textbook of Neuroanaesthesia and Critical Care, 1998; contrib. to several textbooks, incl. Oxford Textbook of Critical Care, 1999, and Oxford Textbook of Medicine, 2001; contribs to various jls on topics of critical care and neuroscis. *Recreations:* basketball, science fiction, cooking. *Address:* University Department of Anaesthesia, Box 93, Addenbrooke's Hospital, Hills Road, Cambridge CB2 2QQ. *T:* (01223) 217889. *Club:* Royal Society of Medicine.

MENON, Prof. Mambillikalathil Govind Kumar, MSc, PhD; FRS 1970; Dr Vikram Sarabhai Distinguished Professor, Department of Space, Government of India, since 1999; President, International Council of Scientific Unions, 1988–93; *b* 28 Aug. 1928; *s* of Kizhekepat Sankara Menon and Mambillikalathil Narayaniamma; *m* 1955, Indumati Patel; one *s* one *d*. *Educ:* Jaswant Coll., Jodhpur; Royal Inst. of Science, Bombay (MSc); Univ. of Bristol (PhD). Tata Inst. of Fundamental Research: Reader, 1955–58; Associate Prof., 1958–60; Prof. of Physics and Dean of Physics Faculty, 1960–64; Senior Prof. and Dep. Dir (Physics), 1964–66, Dir, 1966–75. Chm., Electronics Commn, and Sec., Dept of Electronics, Govt of India, 1971–78; Scientific Advr to Minister of Defence, Dir-Gen. of Defence Res. and Develt Orgn, and Sec. in the Ministry of Defence for Defence Res., 1974–78; Dir-Gen., Council of Scientific and Industrial Res., 1978–81; Sec. to Govt of India, Dept of Science and Technology, 1978–82, Dept of the Envmt, 1980–81; Chm., Commn for Addtnl Sources of Energy, 1981–82; Mem., Planning Commn, 1982–89; Chm., Science Adv. Cttee to the Cabinet, 1982–85; Scientific Advr to the Prime Minister, 1986–89; Minister of State for Sci. and Technology, India, 1989–90; MP (Janata Dal) Rajasthan, Rajya Sabha, 1990–96. M. N. Saha Dist. Fellow, Nat. Acad. of Scis, India, 1994–99. Pres., India Internat. Centre, 1983–88; Member: UN Sec.-Gen.'s Adv. Cttee on Application of Sci. and Technol. to Develt, 1972–79 (Chm. for 2 yrs); Bd of Dirs, Internat. Fedn of Insts for Advanced Study, Stockholm, 1992–99. President: Indian Sci. Congress Assoc., 1981–82; Indian Statistical Inst., 1990–. Fellow: Indian Acad. of Sciences (Pres., 1974–76); Indian Nat. Science Acad. (Pres., 1981–82); Founding Fellow, Third World Acad. of Sciences; Hon. Fellow: Nat. Acad. of Sciences, India (Pres., 1987–88); Indian Inst. of Sciences, Bangalore; Hon. FInstP 1998; For. Hon. Member: Amer. Acad. of Arts and Scis; Russian Acad. of Scis; Mem., Pontifical Acad. of Scis, Vatican; Hon. Pres., Asia Electronics Union; Hon. Mem., Instn of Electrical & Electronics Engrs Inc., USA. Mem. Governing Council, UN Univ., 1986–92; Chm. Bd, Inst. for Advanced Studies, UN Univ., Tokyo, 1996–2001. Hon. DSc: Jodhpur Univ., 1970; Delhi Univ., 1973; Sardar Patel Univ., 1973; Allahabad Univ., 1977; Roorkee Univ., 1979; Banaras Hindu Univ., 1981; Jadavpur Univ., 1981; Sri Venkateswara Univ., 1982; Indian Inst. of Tech. Madras, 1982; Andhra Univ., 1984; Utkal Univ., 1984; Aligarh Muslim Univ., 1986; Bristol Univ., 1990; N Bengal Univ., 1989; Indian Inst. of Technology, Kharagpur, 1990; Guru Nanak Dev Univ., 1996; Hon. Dr Engrg Stevens Inst. of Tech., USA, 1984. Royal Commn for Exhibn of 1851 Senior Award, 1953–55; Shanti Swarup Bhatnagar Award for Physical Sciences, Council of Scientific and Industrial Research, 1960; Khaitan Medal, RAS, 1973; Pandit Jawaharlal Nehru Award for Sciences, Madhya Pradesh Govt, 1983; G. P. Chatterjee Award, 1984; Om Prakash Bhasin Award for Science and Technol., 1985; C. V. Raman Medal, INSA, 1985; J. C. Bose Triennial Gold Medal, Bose Inst., 1983; (first) Ashutosh Mukherjee Gold Medal, Indian Science Congress Assoc., 1988; Gujar Mal Modi Award, Gujar Mal Modi Sci. Foundn, 1994; Abdus Salam Award, Third World Acad. of Scis, 1997. National Awards: Padma Shri, 1961; Padma Bhushan, 1968; Padma Vibhushan, 1985. *Publications:* 135, on cosmic rays and elementary particle physics. *Recreations:* photography, bird-watching. *Address:* C–63 Tarang Apts, 19 IP Ext., Mother Dairy Road, Patparganj, Delhi 110092, India; *e-mail:* mgkmenon@ren02.nic.in. *Clubs:* National Liberal; India International Centre (New Delhi).

MENOTTI, Gian Carlo; composer; Founder, Spoleto Festivals, Italy and Charleston, USA; *b* Cadegliano, Italy, 7 July 1911. *Educ:* The Curtis Institute of Music, Philadelphia, Pa. Has been resident in the United States since 1928. Teacher of Composition at Curtis Inst. of Music, 1948–55. First performances of works include: Amelia Goes to the Ball (opera), 1936; The Old Maid and the Thief (radio opera), 1939 (later staged); The Island God, 1942; Sebastian (Ballet), 1943; Piano Concerto in F, 1945; The Medium (opera), 1946 (later filmed); The Telephone (opera), 1947; Errand into the Maze (ballet), 1947; The Consul (opera), 1950 (Pulitzer Prize); Apocalypse (orchestral), 1951; Amahl and the Night Visitors (television opera), 1951; Violin Concerto in A Minor, 1952; The Saint of Bleeker Street (opera), 1954 (Pulitzer Prize); The Unicorn, The Gorgon, and the Manticore, 1956; Maria Golovin (television opera), 1958; The Last Savage (opera), 1963; The Death of the Bishop of Brindisi (oratorio), 1963; Martin's Lie (opera), 1964; Canti della Lontananza (song cycle), 1967; Help, Help, the Globolinks (opera), 1968; The Leper (drama), 1970; Triplo Concerto a Tre (symphonic piece), 1970; The Most Important Man (opera), 1971; Fantasia for 'cello and orch., 1971; Tamu-Tamu (opera), 1973; The Egg (opera), 1976; The Trial of the Gypsy (opera), 1976; Landscapes & Remembrances, for chorus and orch., 1976; Symphony no 1, 1976; Chip & his Dog (opera), 1978; Juana la Loca (opera), 1979; Mass, O Pulchritudo, 1979; Song of Hope (cantata), 1980; A Bride from Pluto (opera), 1982; St Teresa (cantata), 1982; The Boy Who Grew Too Fast (opera), 1982; Goya (opera), 1986; Giorno di Nozze (opera), 1988; wrote libretto for Vanessa (opera, by Samuel Barber), 1958. Internationally recognised as a producer; has worked at the greatest opera houses, including La Scala, Metropolitan, Paris Opéra, Vienna Staatsoper. Guggenheim Award, 1946, 1947; Kennedy Centre Award, 1984; NYC Mayor's Liberty Award; Hon. Association, Nat. Inst. of Arts and Letters. *Publications:* his major works have been published, also some minor ones; he is the author of all his libretti, most of which have been written in English. *Address:* c/o Thea Dispeker, 59 East 54th Street, New York, NY 10022, USA; Yester House, Gifford, Haddington, East Lothian EH41 4JF.

MENTER, Sir James (Woodham), Kt 1973; MA, PhD, ScD Cantab; FRS 1966; CPhys; FInstP; Principal, 1976–86, Fellow, 1986, Queen Mary College, London University; *b* 22 Aug. 1921; *s* of late Horace Menter and late Jane Anne Lackenby; *m* 1947, Marjorie Jean, *d* of late Thomas Stodart Whyte-Smith, WS; two *s* one *d*. *Educ:* Dover Grammar Sch.; Peterhouse, Cambridge. PhD 1949, ScD 1960. Experimental Officer, Admty, 1942–45; Research, Cambridge Univ., 1946–54 (ICI Fellow, 1951–54; Sir George Beilby Mem. Award, 1954); Tube Investments Research Laboratories, Hinxton Hall, 1954–68; Dir of Research and Develt, Tube Investments Ltd, 1965–76. Director: Tube Investments Res. Labs, 1961–68; Tube Investments Ltd, 1965–86; Round Oak Steelworks Ltd, 1967–76; British Petroleum Co., 1976–87; Steetley Co., 1981–85. Member: SRC, 1967–72; Cttee of Inquiry into Engrg Profession, 1977–79; a Vice-Pres., Royal Society, 1971–76, Treasurer, 1972–76; Royal Institution: a Manager, 1982–84; a Vice-Pres., 1983–85; Chm. Council, 1984–85. Fellow, Churchill Coll., Cambridge, 1966–88. President: Inst. of Physics, 1970–72; Metals Soc., 1976; Dep. Chm., Adv. Council Applied R&D, 1976–79. Mem. (part-time), BSC, 1976–79. Member: Bd of Govs, London Hosp. Med. Coll., 1976–86; Ct of Governors, City of London Polytechnic, 1982–85; Court, Stirling Univ., 1988–94. Hon. FRMS 1974; Hon. FRSE 1992. Hon. DTech Brunel, 1974; DUniv Stirling, 1995. Bessemer Medal, Iron and Steel Inst., 1973; Glazebrook Medal and Prize, Inst. of Physics, 1977. *Publications:* scientific papers in Proc. Royal Society, Advances in Physics, Jl Iron and Steel Inst., etc. *Recreation:* fishing. *Address:* Carie, Kinloch Rannoch, by Pitlochry, Perthshire PH17 2QJ. *T:* (01882) 632341.

MENTETH, Sir James (Wallace) Stuart-, 6th Bt, *cr* 1838; *b* 13 Nov. 1922; *e s* of 5th Bt and Winifred Melville (*d* 1968), *d* of Daniel Francis and *widow* of Capt. Rupert G. Raw, DSO; *S* father, 1952; *m* 1949, Dorothy Patricia, *d* of late Frank Greaves Warburton; two *s*. *Educ:* Fettes; St Andrews Univ.; Trinity Coll., Oxford (MA). Served War of 1939–45, with Scots Guards, 1942–44; on active service in North Africa and Italy (Anzio) (severely wounded). *Recreations:* gardening, ornithology. *Heir:* *s* Charles Greaves Stuart-Menteth [*b* 25 Nov. 1950; *m* 1976, Nicola St Lawrence; four *d*].

MENTZ, Donald, AM 1994; Executive Director, Crawford Fund for International Agricultural Research, Australia, since 1999; *b* 20 Oct. 1933; *s* of Stanley Mentz and Marie Agnes (*née* Bryant); *m* 1959, Mary Josephine (*née* Goldsworthy); one *s* two *d*. *Educ:* Hampton High School, Victoria; Dookie Agricultural College, Victoria (DDA); Melbourne Univ. (BAgSci); Australian Nat. Univ. (BEcon). Dept of External Territories, Australia, 1969–73; Aust. Develt Assistance Bureau, Dept of Foreign Affairs, 1973–77; Dept of Business and Consumer Affairs, 1977–78; Dir of Operations, Asian Develt Bank, Philippines, 1979–81; Dep. Sec., Dept of Business and Consumer Affairs, Aust., 1981–82; Dep. Sec., Dept of Territories and Local Govt, 1983–84; Dir Gen., Commonwealth Agricl Bureaux, later CAB Internat., 1985–92; Man. Dir, Mentz Internat. Trading, 1993–99. *Recreations:* ski-ing, gardening. *Address:* Flat 1, 25 Longridge Road, Earls Court, SW5 9SB. *T:* (020) 7835 1208. *Clubs:* Athenæum; Commonwealth (Canberra).

MENZIES, Duncan Adam Young; QC (Scot.) 1991; *b* 28 Aug. 1953; *s* of late Douglas William Livingstone Menzies and Margaret Adam (*née* Young); *m* 1979, Hilary Elizabeth McLauchlan Weston; two *s*. *Educ:* Cargilfield; Glenalmond (schol.); Wadham Coll., Oxford (schol.; MA); Edinburgh Univ. (LLB). Admitted Advocate, 1978; Standing Junior Counsel to Admiralty, 1984–91; Temp. Sheriff, 1996–97; Home Advocate Depute, 1998–. Chm., Scottish Planning, Local Govt and Envmtl Bar Gp, 1997–. Contested (C): Midlothian, 1983; Edinburgh Leith, 1987. Founder, Scottish Wine Soc., 1976. *Recreations:* shooting, golf, wine. *Address:* Leaston House, Humbie, East Lothian EH36 5PD. *T:* (01875) 833219. *Clubs:* New (Edinburgh); Honourable Company of Edinburgh Golfers.

MENZIES, John Maxwell; Life President, John Menzies, since 1997 (Chairman, 1952–97); *b* 13 Oct. 1926; *s* of late John Francis Menzies, and of Cynthia Mary Graham; *m* 1953, Patricia Eleanor, *d* of late Comdr Sir Hugh Dawson, Bt, CBE and Lady Dawson; four *d*. *Educ:* Eton. Lieut Grenadier Guards. Berwickshire CC, 1954–57. Director: Scottish American Mortgage Co., 1959–63; Standard Life Assurance Co., 1960–63; Vidal Sassoon Inc., 1969–80; Gordon & Gotch plc, 1970–85; Atlantic Assets Trust, 1973–88 (Chm., 1983–88); Ivory & Sime Enterprise Capital plc (formerly Independent Investment Co. plc), 1973–96 (Chm., 1983–96); Ivory & Sime plc, 1980–83; Fairhaven International (formerly Nimslo International), 1980–88; Rocky Mountains Oil & Gas, 1980–85; Personal Assets Trust PLC, 1981–92; Bank of Scotland, 1984–94; Guardian Royal Exchange, 1985–96; Malcolm Innes Galls (formerly Malcolm Innes & Partners), 1989–2000; Kames Dairies Ltd, 1995– . Trustee, Newsvendors' Benevolent Instn, 1974–95 (Pres., 1968–74; Life Vice Pres., 1996). Mem. Bd of Trustees, Nat. Library of Scotland, 1991–99. Mem., Royal Co. of Archers, HM's Body Guard for Scotland. Landowner. *Recreations:* shooting, reading, travel. *Address:* Kames, Duns, Berwickshire. *T:* (01890) 840202. *Clubs:* Boodle's, Beefsteak; New (Edinburgh).

MENZIES, Lt-Gen. Robert Clark, OBE 1989; QHS 1996; FRCPE, FRCPath, FFPHM; Surgeon General to the Armed Forces, since 2000; *b* 1 June 1944; *s* of late Flt Lieut Robert Clark Menzies and Jane, (Jean), Reid Menzies; *m* 1967, Joanna, (Joan), Letitia Lindsay Dunning; one *s* one *d*. *Educ:* Kilmarnock Acad.; Glasgow Univ. (MB ChB 1967); DMJ (Pathology) 1976. MRCPath 1980, FRCPath 1992; FFPHM 1999; FRCPE 2000. OC, Med. Reception Stn, Warminster, 1969; Trainee Pathologist, Leishman Lab., Cambridge Mil. Hosp., 1971–72; Pathologist, BMH, Rinteln, 1973–75; Registrar in Pathology, Queen Alexandra Mil. Hosp., 1975–76; British Army Exchange Pathologist, Armed Forces Inst. of Pathology, Washington, 1976–78 (Chief, Missile Trauma Pathology Br. and Hon. Professional Lectr, George Washington Univ.); Sen. Registrar in Pathology, Leishman Lab., Cambridge Mil. Hosp., 1978–81; Lectr in Forensic Medicine, Charing Cross Hosp. Med. Sch., 1981–83; Consultant Pathologist, Leishman Lab., 1983–85; Prof. of Mil. Pathology, Royal Army Med. Coll. and RCPath, 1985–89; CO, BMH Rinteln, 1989–92; Dir of Army Pathology, 1992–94; CO, 217 (London) Gen. Hosp. RAMC(V), 1994–95; Commander Medical: HQ London Dist, 1995–96; HQ Land Comd, 1996–99; Dir Gen., AMS, 1999–2000. Freeman, City of London, 1995. FRSocMed 1985. *Publications:* articles on pathology, particularly forensic pathology, in jls. *Recreations:* walking, travelling, photography, reading, music. *Address:* Ministry of Defence, Main Building, Whitehall, SW1A 2HB. *Club:* Army and Navy.

MENZIES-WILSON, William Napier, CBE 1985; Chairman, Ocean Transport & Trading plc, Liverpool, 1980–86 (Director, 1973–88); *b* 4 Dec. 1926; *s* of James Robert Menzies-Wilson and Jacobine Napier Williamson-Napier; *m* 1953, Mary Elizabeth Darnell Juckes; two *s* one *d*. *Educ:* Winchester; New Coll., Oxford (MA); North Western Univ., Chicago. Joined Stewarts & Lloyds Ltd, 1950; Managing Director, Stewarts & Lloyds of South Africa Ltd, 1954–61, Chairman, 1961; Director, Stewarts & Lloyds Ltd, 1964; Dir, Supplies & Transport, British Steel Corporation, 1967–73; Chairman: Wm Cory & Son Ltd, 1973–77; Viking Resources Trust, 1986–89; Director: Overseas Containers Holdings, 1979–86; Dunlop Holdings, 1982–84; NFC, 1986–95. Pres., Gen. Council of British Shipping, 1984–85; Mem. Exec. Bd, Lloyd's Register of Shipping, 1984–87. Chm., Bd of Trustees, Help the Aged, 1988–95. *Recreations:* shooting, golf, gardening. *Address:* Last House, Old, Northampton NN6 9YA. *T:* (01604) 781346. *Club:* Hon. Co. of Edinburgh Golfers.

MEON, Archdeacon of The; *see* Hancock, Ven. P.

MERCER, Prof. Alan; Professor of Operational Research, University of Lancaster, 1968–98, now Emeritus; *b* 22 Aug. 1931; *s* of Harold Mercer and Alice Ellen (*née* Catterall); *m* 1954, Lillian Iris (*née* Pigott); two *s*. *Educ:* Penistone Grammar Sch.; Cambridge Univ. (MA; DipMathStat); London Univ. (PhD). NCB, 1954–56; UKAEA, 1956–62; Armour & Co. Ltd, 1962–64; Univ. of Lancaster, 1964–: Chm., Sch. of Management and Organisational Scis, 1982–85. Mem., Central Lancashire Develt Corp., 1971–85; Mem., 1985–89, Chm., 1986–89, Warrington and Runcorn Develt Corp. Chm., Employers' Side of Whitley Council for New Towns Staff, 1979–89 (Mem., 1971–89); Mem., Management and Industrial Relns Cttee, SSRC, 1972–76, 1980–82; Chm., Industry and Employment Cttee, ESRC, 1984–87 (Vice Chm., 1982–84); Mem., NW Econ. Planning Council, 1973–79. Jt Editor, European Journal of Operational Research, 1977–98. *Publications:* Operational Distribution Research (jtly), 1978; Innovative Marketing Research, 1991; numerous papers in learned jls. *Recreations:* travel, sport. *Address:* South Cottage, Calton, Airton, Skipton, North Yorks BD23 4AD. *T:* (01729) 830542.

MERCER, Rt Rev. Eric Arthur John; *b* 6 Dec. 1917; *s* of Ambrose John Mercer, Kent; *m* 1951, Rosemary Wilma, *d* of John William Denby, Lincs; one *s* one *d*. *Educ:* Dover Gram. Sch.; Kelham Theol. Coll. Enlisted Sherwood Foresters, 1940; Capt. and Adjt, 14th Foresters, 1943; served Italy (despatches), 1944; Staff Coll., Haifa, 1944; DAA&QMG, 66 Inf. Bde, Palestine, 1945; GSO2 (SD), HQ, MEF, 1945. Returned Kelham Theol. Coll., 1946–47. Ordained, Chester; Curate, Coppenhall, Crewe, 1947–51; Priest in charge, Heald Green, 1951–53; Rector, St Thomas', Stockport, 1953–59; Chester Diocesan Missioner, 1959–65; Rector, Chester St Bridget, 1959–65; Hon. Canon of Chester Cathedral, 1964; Bishop Suffragan of Birkenhead, 1965–73; Bishop of Exeter, 1973–85. Church Commissioners: Dep. Chm., Pastoral Cttee, 1976–85; Mem., Bd of Governors, 1980–85. Nat. Chm., CEMS, 1974–78. *Publication:* (contrib.) Worship in a Changing Church, 1965. *Address:* Frickers House, Chilmark, Salisbury SP3 5AJ. *T:* (01722) 761400.
See also P. J. Mercer.

MERCER, Geoffrey Dallas; His Honour Judge Mercer; a Circuit Judge, South Eastern Circuit, since 1991; *b* 17 Dec. 1935; *s* of Leon Dallas Mercer, FRCS and Veronica Kathleen Mary Lillian Mercer (*née* Pitt-Lancaster). *Educ:* Clifton Coll., Bristol; St John's Coll., Cambridge (MA, LLM). Called to the Bar, Gray's Inn, 1960; practised at the Bar, 1961–91; Hd of Chambers, 1985–91. Former English Youth International and Cheshire County golfer. *Recreations:* golf, music.

MERCER, Prof. Ian Dews, CBE 1996; Secretary General, Association of National Park Authorities, 1996–2001; Hon. Professor of Rural Conservation Practice, University of Wales, since 1991; *b* 25 Jan. 1933; *s* of Eric Baden Royds Mercer and Nellie Irene Mercer; *m* 1st, 1957, Valerie Jean Hodgson; four *s*; 2nd, 1976, Pamela Margaret Gillies (*née* Clarkson). *Educ:* King Edward VI Sch., Stourbridge; Univ. of Birmingham (BA Hons). Sub-Lieut RNR, 1954–56. Field Centre appts, Preston Montford, 1956–57, Juniper Hall, 1957–59; Warden, Slapton Ley, 1959–68; Lectr, St Luke's Coll., Exeter, 1968–70; Warden, Malham Tarn Field Centre, 1970–71; County Conservation Officer, Devon CC; 1971–73; National Park Officer, Dartmoor, 1973–90; Chief Exec., Countryside Council for Wales, 1990–95. Chm., Envmtl Trng Orgn, 1996–98; Mem., Inland Waterways, Amenity Adv. Council, 1995–2001. President: Field Studies Council, 1986–; Devon Wildlife Trust, 1986–. Governor: Univ. of Plymouth, 1996–; Stover Sch., 1996–. FRAgS 1999; Hon. FLI 1997. Hon. LLD Exeter, 1994; Hon. DSc Plymouth, 1995. *Publications:* Nature Guide to the West Country, 1981; chapters in books on conservation matters. *Recreations:* painting, golf, gardening in France, teaching adults birds and landscape. *Address:* Ponsford House, Moretonhampstead, Devon TQ13 8NL. *T:* (01647) 440612. *Club:* Farmers'.

MERCER, Patrick John, OBE 1997 (MBE 1992); MP (C) Newark and Retford, since 2001; *b* 26 June 1956; *s* of Rt Rev. Eric Arthur John Mercer, *qv*; *m* 1990, Catriona Jane Beaton; one *s*. *Educ:* King's Sch., Chester; Exeter Coll., Oxford (MA Mod. Hist. 1980). Commnd 1st Worcs and Sherwood Foresters, 1975: served NI, 1975–77; Captain: BAOR and W Belfast, 1980–83 (despatches); Instructor, Brecon, 1984–86; Major: Chief Instructor, Ugandan Sch. of Inf., 1986; Jun. Inf. Bn, Shorncliffe, 1986–88; sc, Camberley, 1988; Co. Comdr, Omagh, NI, 1989–90 (GOC's Commendation); SO2 (Ops), HQ NI, 1991–92; Chief Instructor, Platoon Comdr's Course, 1993; Lieut Col, SO1 Instructor, Staff Coll., Camberley, 1994–95; CO, Tidworth, Bosnia, Canada, 1995–97; Col, Hd of Strategy, Army Trng and Recruitment Agency, 1997–99; Defence Corresp., Today prog., BBC Radio, 1999. Mem., KCL team tasked with writing defence policy for E Timor, 2000. *Publications:* Inkermann: the soldiers' battle, 1997; Give Them a Volley and Charge, 1997; contrib. jls and newspapers. *Recreations:* water-colour painting, history, bird watching, country sports. *Address:* House of Commons, SW1A 0AA; Newark and Retford Conservative Association, London Road, Newark, Notts NG24 1TN. *T:* (01636) 703269. *Club:* Army and Navy.

MERCER, Dr Robert Giles Graham; Headmaster, Prior Park College, since 1996; *b* 30 May 1949; *s* of late Leonard and Florence Elizabeth Mercer; *m* 1974, Caroline Mary Brougham; one *s*. *Educ:* Austin Friars School, Carlisle; Churchill College, Cambridge (Scholar; 1st cl. Hist. Tripos, Pts I and II; MA); St John's College, Oxford (Sen. Schol., DPhil). Head of History, Charterhouse, 1974–76; Asst Principal, MoD, 1976–78; Dir of Studies and Head of History, Sherborne School, 1979–85; Headmaster, Stonyhurst Coll., 1985–96. Chm., Catholic Ind. Schs Conf., 2000–. Gov., All Hallows Prep. Sch., Shepton Mallett, 1999–. *Publication:* The Teaching of Gasparino Barzizza, 1979. *Recreations:* art, music, travel, swimming. *Address:* Prior Park College, Bath, Avon BA2 5AH. *T:* (01225) 835353. *Club:* East India.

MERCER, Rt Rev. Robert William Stanley, CR; Diocesan Bishop, Anglican Catholic Church of Canada, since 1989 (Assistant Bishop, 1988–89); *b* 10 Jan. 1935; *s* of Harold Windrum Mercer and Kathleen Frampton. *Educ:* Grey School, Port Elizabeth, S Africa; St Paul's Theological Coll., Grahamstown, SA (LTh). Deacon 1959, priest 1960, Matabeleland; Asst Curate, Hillside, Bulawayo, 1959–63; Novice, CR, 1963; professed, 1965; at Mirfield, 1963–66; at St Teilo's Priory, Cardiff, 1966–68; Prior and Rector of Stellenbosch, S Africa, 1968–70; deported from SA, 1970; Chaplain, St Augustine's School, Penhalonga, Rhodesia, 1971–72; Rector of Borrowdale, Salisbury, Rhodesia, 1972–77; Bishop of Matabeleland, 1977–87. Sub-Prelate, Order of St John of Jerusalem, 1981. *Address:* 225 First Avenue, Ottawa, ON K1S 2G5, Canada.

MERCER, Roger James, FSA, FSAScot; FRSE; Secretary, Royal Commission on the Ancient and Historical Monuments of Scotland, since 1990; *b* 12 Sept. 1944; *o s* of Alan Mercer and Patricia (*née* Hicks); *m* 1970, Susan Jane Fowlie; one *s* one *d*. *Educ:* Harrow County Grammar Sch.; Edinburgh Univ. (MA). MIFA. Inspector of Ancient Monuments, DoE, 1969–74; Lectr and Reader, Dept of Archaeology, Univ. of Edinburgh, 1974–89. Mem., Ancient Monuments Bd for Scotland, 1988–; Vice President: Soc. of Antiquaries of Scotland, 1988–91; Council for British Archaeology, 1990–94; Prehistoric Soc., 1989–92. British Acad. Readership, 1989; Hon. Professor of Archaeology: Univ. of Durham, 1996–; Univ. of Edinburgh, 1999–. FSAScot 1971; FSA 1976; FRSE 1995. *Publications:* Beaker Studies in Europe (ed), 1979; Hambledon Hill—a Neolithic Landscape, 1980; Grimes Graves—Excavations 1971–72, 1981; Carn Brea—a Neolithic Defensive Complex, 1981; (ed) Farming Practice in British Prehistory, 1981; Causewayed Enclosures, 1990; articles and reviews in learned jls. *Recreations:* music, books, good food. *Address:* Home House, 4 Old Church Lane, Duddingston, Edinburgh EH15 3PX. *T:* (0131) 661 2931. *Club:* New (Edinburgh).

MERCHANT, Ismail Noormohamed; film producer, since 1960; Partner, Merchant Ivory Productions, since formation, 1961; *b* 25 Dec. 1936; *s* of Noormohamed Haji Abdul Rehman and Hazra Memon. *Educ:* St Xavier's Coll., Bombay (BA); New York Univ. (MBA). Collaborator with Ruth Prawer Jhabvala and James Ivory on most of the following: *feature films:* The Householder, 1963; Shakespeare Wallah, 1965 (won Best Actress award, Berlin Film Fest., 1965); The Guru, 1969; Bombay Talkie, 1970; Savages, 1972; The Wild Party, 1976; Roseland, 1977; The Europeans, 1979 (official Brit. entry, Cannes Film Fest.); Quartet, 1981; Heat and Dust, 1983 (Brit. entry, Cannes Film Fest.); The Bostonians, 1984 (feature, Cannes Film Fest.); A Room with a View, 1986; Maurice, 1987 (Silver Lions for Best Picture, Best Actor and Best Composer); The Deceivers, 1988; The Perfect Murder, 1988; Slaves of New York, 1989; Mr and Mrs Bridge, 1990; The Ballad of the Sad Cafe, 1991; Howards End, 1992; The Remains of the Day, 1993; (directed) In Custody, 1994; Jefferson in Paris, 1995; Feast of July, 1995; Surviving Picasso, 1996; (directed) The Proprietor, 1996; Gaach, 1997; A Soldier's Daughter Never Cries, 1998; Side Streets, 1998; (directed) Cotton Mary, 1999; The Golden Bowl, 2000; *shorts:* The Creation of Woman, 1960 (Academy award nomination); Helen, Queen of the Nautch Girls, 1973; (directed) Mahatma and the Mad Boy, 1974; Sweet Sounds, 1976; *television:* Adventures of a Brown Man in Search of Civilization, 1972 (BBC); Autobiography of a Princess, 1975 (TV special, NY); Hullabaloo over Georgie and Bonnie's Pictures, 1978 (feature, LWT); Jane Austen in Manhattan, 1980 (feature, LWT and Polytel); (directed for Channel 4) The Courtesans of Bombay, 1983; The Curry Connection, 1990 (series, Channel 4); Street Musicians of Bombay, 1995 (Channel 4). *Publications:* Ismail Merchant's Indian Cuisine, 1986; Hullabaloo In Old Jaypoore, 1988; Ismail Merchant's Florence, 1994; Ismail Merchant's Passionate Meals, 1994; Once Upon a Time—The Proprietor, 1996; Ismail Merchant's Paris: filming and feasting in France, 1999. *Recreations:* squash, bicycling, cooking. *Address:* 400 East 52nd Street, New York, NY 10022, USA. *T:* (212) 5828049; Garden View, Sutter Street, Bombay, India. *T:* 2020083.

MERCHANT, John Richard; Director of Resources, Voluntary Service Overseas, since 1995; *b* 4 June 1945; *s* of William Henry Merchant and Eileen Merchant; *m* 1966, Eileen McGill; two *s*. *Educ:* Gravesend Grammar Sch.; Sheffield Univ. (BSc); Cranfield Inst. of Technol. (MSc). FIS. Lyons Bakery Ltd, 1966–69; Lectr, Cranfield Inst. of Technol., 1969–75; Statistician, MoD, 1975–79; Chief Statistician, CS Coll., 1979–82; Asst Sec., Cabinet Office (MPO), 1982–84; Principal Finance and Estabt Officer, DPP, 1984–86, Crown Prosecution Service, 1986–88; Under Sec., 1985; Sec. and Dir, Council Policy and Admin, SERC, 1988–94; Grade 3, Office of Public Service and Science, 1994. *Recreations:* Nigerian postal history, fishing. *Address:* (office) 317 Putney Bridge Road, SW15 2PN. *T:* (020) 8780 7283.

MERCHANT, Piers Rolf Garfield; Director of Campaigns, London Chamber of Commerce and Industry, since 2001; Executive Director, Made in London, since 2000; *b* 2 Jan. 1951; *s* of Garfield Frederick Merchant and Audrey Mary Rolfe-Martin; *m* 1977, Helen Joan Burrluck; one *s* one *d*. *Educ:* Nottingham High School; Univ. of Durham. BA (Hons) Law and Politics, MA Political Philosophy. Reporter, Municipal Correspondent, Chief Reporter, Dep. News Editor, The Journal, 1973–80; News Editor, The Journal, 1980–82; Editor, Conservative Newsline, 1982–84. Dir of Corporate Publicity, NEI plc, 1987–90; Dir of Public Affairs, The Advertising Assoc., 1990–92; Man. Dir, Cavendish Gp plc, 1998–2000 (non-exec. Dir, 2000–). Contested (C) Newcastle upon Tyne Central, 1979. MP (C): Newcastle upon Tyne Central, 1983–87; Beckenham, 1992–Oct. 1997. PPS to Sec. of State for Social Security, 1992–97. Co-Chm., Freeflow of Information Cttee, Internat. Parly Gp, 1986–91; Vice-Chm., All-Party Parly Cttee on AIDS, 1987. Non-executive Director: Eur. Public Health Foundn, 1993–; Tyne and Wear Waste Saver Ltd, 1996–98; London Asset Mgt Ltd, 2000–. Mem., Senior Common Room, University Coll., Durham. *Publications:* newspaper articles and features. *Recreations:* swimming, walking, genealogy, electronics, computers. *T:* (020) 7630 9294.

MERCIECA, Most Rev. Joseph; *see* Malta, Archbishop of, (RC).

MEREDITH, Most Rev. Bevan; Archbishop of Papua New Guinea, Primate of the Province of Papua New Guinea, 1990–95; Bishop of New Guinea Islands, 1977–95; licensed to officiate, diocese of Brisbane; *b* Alstonville, NSW, 14 Aug. 1927; 3rd *c* of Stanley Meredith and Edith Meredith (*née* Witchard). *Educ:* Univ. of Queensland; St Francis Theol Coll., Brisbane. Teacher, Slade Sch., Warwick, Qld and Housemaster, Highfields House, 1948–53; Staff, Martyrs' Meml Sch., PNG, 1954–58; deacon 1961, priest 1962, St Thomas, Toowong; Priest-in-charge, Managalas, PNG, 1963–67; Asst Bp of New Guinea, 1967–77. *Recreations:* music, photography, philately. *Address:* 23 Coronet Drive, Bray Park, Qld 4500, Australia. *T:* and *Fax:* (7) 38896993.

MEREDITH, David Michael; District Judge (Magistrates' Courts) (formerly Stipendiary Magistrate), Leicestershire, since 1995; *b* 2 May 1945; *s* of George and Phyllis Maude Meredith; *m* 1977, Lynn Graham; one *s*. *Educ:* King Edward VII Sch., Sheffield; St Edmund Hall, Oxford (BA, DipEd). Asst Teacher, Chorlton High Sch., 1969–70, and King Edward VII Sch., Sheffield, 1970–74; admitted solicitor, 1977; Articled Clerk and Asst Solicitor, 1975–81, Partner, 1981–95, Graysons, Sheffield. *Recreations:* football, bad golf, theatre, travel. *Address:* Leicester Magistrates' Court, Pocklington's Walk, Leicester LE1 9BE. *T:* (0116) 255 3666. *Club:* Vincent's (Oxford).

MEREDITH, John Michael; barrister-at-law; Magistrate, Deputy District Judge and Coroner, Hong Kong, 1988–94, retired; *b* 23 Oct. 1934; *s* of late John Stanley Meredith and Lily Meredith; *m*; one *s* three *d*; *m* 1988, Linda (*née* Crossland). *Educ:* Crossley and Porter Schs, Halifax, Yorks; Leeds Univ. (LLB Hons 1956). Called to the Bar, Gray's Inn, 1958; Junior, NE Circuit, 1964; a Recorder, 1976–88. Dir, 1955–64, Chm. Dirs, 1964–88, J. T. Meredith (Carboniser) Ltd. *Recreations:* shooting, sailing. *Address:* China Rose, c/o Puerto Galera Yacht Club, Puerto Galera, Mindoro Island, Philippines. *Clubs:* Royal Hong Kong Yacht (Life Mem.); Puerto Galera Yacht.

MEREDITH, Richard Alban Creed, MA; Head Master, Monkton Combe School, 1978–90; *b* 1 Feb. 1935; *s* of late Canon R. Creed Meredith; *m* 1968, Hazel Eveline Mercia Parry; one *s* one *d*. *Educ:* Stowe Sch.; Jesus Coll., Cambridge. Asst Master (Modern Langs), 1957–70, Housemaster, 1962–70, King's Sch., Canterbury; Headmaster, Giggleswick Sch., 1970–78. CMS Area Sec., dios of Derby, Leicester and Southwell, 1990–98. *Recreations:* walking, foreign travel, music, gardening. *Address:* Beacon Knoll, 334 Beacon Road, Loughborough LE11 2RD. *T:* (01509) 212008.

MEREDITH DAVIES, (James) Brian; *see* Davies.

MERI, Lennart; President, Republic of Estonia, since 1992; *b* Tallinn, 29 March 1929; *s* of Georg-Peeter Meri and Alice-Brigitta Meri (*née* Engmann); *m* Helle Pihlak; two *s* one *d*. *Educ:* schs in Berlin, Paris, Yaransk and Tallinn; Tartu Univ., Siberia (grad *cum laude* in hist. 1953). Family deported to Siberia, 1941–46. Hd, MS Section, and dramatist, Vanemuine Theatre, 1953–55; producer, Estonian Radio, 1955–61; scriptwriter, 1963–68, and producer, 1968–71, 1986–88, Tallinnfilm (*films* depicting the history of Finno-Ugric people include: Veelinnurahvas, 1970; Linnutee tuuled, 1977; Kaleva hääled, 1986; Toorumi pojad, 1989; Šamaan, 1997); For. Relns Sec., Estonian Writers Union, 1985–87; Founder and Dir, Estonian Inst., 1988–90; Minister of Foreign Affairs, 1990–92; Ambassador to Finland, April–Oct. 1992. Active in Estonian Popular Front and Nat. Heritage Preservation Assoc., during 1980s. Member: Internat. Council, Meml Foundn for Victims of Communism, 1995–; Inter-Parly Council against Antisemitism, 1997–.

Member: Estonian Writers Union, 1963; Estonian Cinematographers Union, 1966; Eur. Acad. of Arts, Scis and Humanities (Co-Pres., Cttee of Honour, 1993–). For. Mem., Kalevala Soc., Finland, 1975; Corresp. Mem., Finnish Literary Soc., 1976; Hon. Mem., Writers' Union, Finland, 1982. Hon. DLitt: Helsinki, 1986; Lapland (Finland), 1999. East-West Liberty Award, Inst. for East-West Studies, New York, 1996; Coudenhove-Kalergi European Award, Coudenhove-Kalergi Foundn, 1996; Crans Montana Universal Forum Foundn Award, 1997. Holds foreign decorations. *Publications:* Kobrade ja karakurtide jälgedes (Following the trails of cobras and black widows), 1959; Laevapoisid rohelisel ookeanil (Shipmates on the Green Ocean), 1961; Tulemägede maale (To the land of fiery mountains), 1964; Virmaliste väraval (At the gate of Northern Lights), 1974; Hõbevalge (Silverwhite), 1976; Lähenevad rannad (Approaching coasts), 1977; Hõbevalgem (Silverwhiter), 1984; (jtly) 1940 Eestis (1940 in Estonia: documents and materials), 1989; Tulen maasta, jonka nimi on Viro (Coming from the country called Estonia), 1995; Presidential Speeches, 1996 (trans. German); translations of works by Remarque, Vercors, Greene, Boulle and Solzhenitsyn. *Recreations:* history, literature, maps. *Address:* Kadriong Palace, 15050 Tallinn, Estonia. *T:* (2) 6316202.

MERIFIELD, Sir Anthony (James), KCVO 2000; CB 1994; The Ceremonial Officer, Cabinet Office, 1994–2000; *b* 5 March 1934; *s* of late Francis Bertram Merifield and Richardina (*née* Parker); *m* 1980, Pamela Pratt. *Educ:* Chesterfield Sch.; Shrewsbury Sch.; Wadham Coll., Oxford (MA). National Service, 1952–54, Royal Tank Regt. HM Overseas Civil Service, Kenya, 1958–65; Department of Health and Social Security: Principal, 1965–71; Asst Sec., 1971–77; Under Secretary, 1978–82; Under Sec., NI Office, 1982–85; Dir of Regl Liaison, NHS Management Bd, DHSS, subseq. NHS Management Exec., DoH, 1986–91; Head of Sen. and Public Appts Gp, Cabinet Office, 1991–94. *Address:* c/o Lloyds TSB, High Street, Oxford OX1 4AA. *T:* (home) (020) 8670 1546. *Clubs:* Athenæum, Royal Commonwealth Society; Achilles; Dulwich and Sydenham Hill Golf.

MERLE, Robert Jean Georges; Croix du Combattant, 1945; Officier de l'Instruction publique, 1953; Professor of English Literature, University of Paris X, Nanterre, since 1965; Titular Professor: University of Rennes, Brittany, since 1944 (on leave, 1950–51); University of Toulouse, since 1957; University of Caen-Rouen, since 1960; University of Algiers, since 1963; *b* 29 Aug. 1908; father an officer; *m* 1st; one *d*; *m* 2nd, 1949; three *s* one *d*; 3rd, 1965; one *s*. *Educ:* Lycée Michelet, Paris; Sorbonne, Paris. Professor, 1944. Mobilised, 1939; Liaison agent with BEF (prisoner, 1940–43). *Publications:* Oscar Wilde, 1948, 3rd edn 1996; Week-end à Zuydcoote, 1949 (awarded Prix Goncourt); La Mort est mon métier, 1953; L'Ile, 1962 (awarded Prix de la Fraternité) (translated, as The Island, 1964); Un Animal doué de raison, 1967 (translated, as The Day of the Dolphin, 1969); Derrière la vitre, 1970; Malevil, 1972 (Campbell Award, USA); Les hommes protégés, 1974 (translated, as The Virility Factor, 1977); Madrapour, 1976; Fortune de France, 1978; En nos vertes années, 1979; Paris ma bonne ville, 1980; Le Prince que voilà, 1982; La violente amour, 1983; La Pique du jour, 1985; Le Jour ne se lève pas pour nous, 1986; L'Idole, 1987 (translated, as The Idol, 1989); Le Propre de l'Homme, 1989; La Volte des Vestugadins, 1991; L'Enfant-roi, 1993; Les Roses de la Vie, 1995; Le Lys et la Pourpre, 1997; La gloire et le périls, 1999; *plays:* Nouveau Sisyphe, 1950; Flamineo (inspired by Webster's White Devil), 1953; Pièces pies et impies, 1995; *historical essays:* Moncada, 1965; Ben Bella, 1965; translations, articles. *Recreation:* swimming. *Address:* La Malmaison, Grosrouvre, 78490 Montfort L'Amaury, France.

MERLO, David, CEng; Director of Research, British Telecommunications plc, 1983–89; *b* 16 June 1931; *s* of Carlo G. Merlo and Catherine E. Merlo (*née* Stringer); *m* 1952, Patricia Victoria Jackson; two *s*. *Educ:* Kilburn Grammar Sch., London; London Univ. (BScEng 1st Cl. Hons 1954); W. B. Esson schol. of IEE, 1953, and IEE Electronics Premium, 1966. CEng 1967, FIEE 1973. Post Office Research Br., 1948; Executive Engineer, 1955; Sen. Scientific Officer, 1959; Principal Sci. Officer, 1967; Head of Division, 1974; Dep. Director of Research, 1977. Visiting Lecturer: Northampton Polytechnic, 1955–61; Regent Street Polytechnic, 1960–69; Governor, Suffolk College of Higher and Further Education, 1984–89. Served on numerous technical committees in telecommunications field. FRSA 1988. Patent award, 1970. *Publications:* miscellaneous contribs to learned jls. *Recreations:* reading, photography, wine. *Address:* Heather Lodge, Levington, Ipswich IP10 0NA. *T:* (01473) 659508.

MERLYN-REES, family name of **Baron Merlyn-Rees**.

MERLYN-REES, Baron *cr* 1992 (Life Peer), of Morley and South Leeds in the County of West Yorkshire and of Cilfynydd in the County of Mid Glamorgan; **Merlyn Merlyn-Rees;** PC 1974; *b* Cilfynydd, South Wales, 18 Dec. 1920; *s* of late L. D. and E. M. Rees; name changed to Merlyn-Rees by deed poll, 1992; *m* 1949, Colleen Faith (*née* Cleveley); three *s*. *Educ:* Elementary Schools, S Wales and Wembley, Middx; Harrow Weald Grammar School; London School of Economics; London Univ. Institute of Education. Nottingham Univ. Air Sqdn; Served RAF, 1941–46; demobilised as Sqdn Ldr. Teacher in Economics and History, Harrow Weald Grammar School, 1949–60. Organised Festival of Labour, 1960–62. Lecturer in Economics, Luton Coll. of Technology, 1962–63; contested (Lab) Harrow East, Gen. Elections 1955 and 1959 and by-election, 1959. MP (Lab) South Leeds, June 1963–83, Morley and Leeds South, 1983–92. PPS to Chancellor of the Exchequer, 1964; Parly Under-Sec. of State, MoD (Army), 1965–66; MoD (RAF), 1966–68; Home Office, 1968–70; Mem., Shadow Cabinet, 1972–74; Opposition spokesman on NI affairs, 1972–74; Sec. of State for NI, 1974–76; Home Sec., 1976–79; Shadow Home Sec., 1979–80; Opposition spokesman on Energy, 1980–83. Member: Cttee to examine operation of Section 2 of Official Secrets Act, 1971; Falklands Is Inquiry Cttee, 1982. Pres., Video Standards Council, 1990–. Pres., South Leeds Groundwork Trust (Chm., 1987–97). Chancellor, Univ. of Glamorgan, 1994–2001. Hon. Fellow, Goldsmiths' Coll., London Univ., 1984. Hon. LLD: Wales, 1987; Leeds, 1992. *Publications:* The Public Sector in the Mixed Economy, 1973; Northern Ireland: a personal perspective, 1985. *Recreation:* reading. *Address:* c/o House of Lords, SW1A 0PW.

MERRICKS, Walter Hugh; Chief Ombudsman, Financial Ombudsman Service, since 1999; *b* 4 June 1945; 2nd *s* of late Dick and Phoebe Merricks, Icklesham, Sussex; *m* 1982, Olivia Montuschi; one *s* one *d*, and one step *s*. *Educ:* Bradfield College, Berks; Trinity College, Oxford. MA Hons (Jurisp). Articled Clerk with Batt, Holden, 1968–70; admitted Solicitor, 1970; Hubbard Travelling Scholar, Montreal, 1971; Dir, Camden Community Law Centre, 1972–76; Lectr in Law, Brunel Univ., 1976–81; legal affairs writer, New Law Journal, 1982–85; Law Society: Sec., Professional and Public Relations, 1985–87; Asst Sec.-Gen. (Communications), 1987–95; Dir, Professional and Legal Policy, 1995–96; Insurance Ombudsman, 1996–99. Member: Royal Commn on Criminal Procedure, 1978–81; Fraud Trials (Roskill) Cttee, 1984–86. Mem., Victim Support Wkg Party on Financial Compensation, 1992–93. Chairman: British and Irish Ombudsman Assoc., 2001–; Nat. Gamete Donation Trust, 2000–; Membership Sec., Donor Conception Network. Mem. Council, King Alfred Sch., 1991–99. *Address:* c/o Financial Ombudsman Service, South Quay Plaza, 183 Marsh Wall, E14 9SR. *T:* (020) 7964 1000; *e-mail:* enquiries@financial-ombudsman.gov.uk.

MERRIFIELD, Prof. Robert Bruce; Professor, since 1966, John D. Rockefeller Jr Professor, since 1984, Rockefeller University; *b* 15 July 1921; *s* of George and Lorene Merrifield; *m* 1949, Elizabeth L. Furlong; one *s* five *d*. *Educ:* Univ. of California, Los Angeles (BA 1943, Chemistry; PhD 1949, Biochemistry). Chemist, Philip R. Park Research Foundn, 1943–44; Research Asst, UCLA Med. Sch., 1948–49; Asst to Associate Prof., Rockefeller Inst. for Med. Research, 1949–66. Nobel Guest Prof., Uppsala, 1968. Member: Amer. Chem. Soc.; Amer. Soc. of Biological Chemists; Amer. Inst. of Chemists; Nat. Acad. of Sciences. Associate Editor, Internat. Jl of Peptide and Protein Research; Mem. Editl Bd of Analytical Biochemistry. Numerous hon. degrees from Amer. univs and colls. Lasker Award for Basic Med. Research, 1969; Gairdner Award, 1970; Intra-Science Award, 1970; Amer. Chem. Soc. Award for Creative Work in Synthetic Organic Chemistry, 1972; Nichols Medal, 1973; Instrument Specialties Co. Award, Univ. of Nebraska, 1977; Alan E. Pierce Award, 1979; Nobel Prize in Chemistry, 1984; Hirschmann Award in Peptide Chem., ACS, 1990; Josef Rudinger Award, Eur. Peptide Soc., 1990. Order of San Carlos (Columbia), 1984. *Publications:* numerous papers in sci. jls, esp. on peptide chemistry, solid phase peptide synthesis. *Address:* The Rockefeller University, 1230 York Avenue, New York, NY 10021, USA. *T:* (212) 3278244.

MERRILL, Fiona Claire, (Mrs R. W. T. Merrill); *see* Reynolds, F. C.

MERRIMAN, Air Vice-Marshal Alan; *see* Merriman, H. A.

MERRIMAN, Air Vice-Marshal (Henry) Alan, CB 1985; CBE 1973; AFC 1957, and Bar 1961; DL; defence and aerospace consultant; *b* 17 May 1929; *s* of Henry Victor Merriman and Winifred Ellen Merriman; *m* 1965, Mary Brenda Stephenson; three *d*. *Educ:* Hertford Grammar Sch.; RAF Coll., Cranwell. Graduate, Empire Test Pilots Sch. FRAeS 1977. Commnd, 1951; Qual. Flying Instr, 263 F Sqdn, Empire Test Pilots Sch., Fighter Test Sqdn, A&AEE, Central Fighter Estabt, and RAF Staff Coll., 1952–63; Personal Air Sec. to Minister of Defence for RAF, 1964–66; Jt Services Staff Coll., 1966; OC Fighter Test Sqdn, A&AEE, 1966–69; HQ 38 Gp, 1969–70; Stn Comdr, RAF Wittering, 1970–72; RCDS, 1973; CO Empire Test Pilots Sch., 1974–75; Comdt, A&AEE, 1975–77; Dir, Operational Requirements (1), 1977–81; Mil. Dep. to Head of Defence Sales, 1981–84. Pres., NW Essex Aircrew Assoc., 1990–; Vice-Pres., N Herts Aircrew Assoc., 1992–; Herts County Rep., RAF Benevolent Fund, 1995. Queen's Commendation for Valuable Services in the Air, 1956. DL Herts, 1995. *Recreations:* classic cars and aircraft, gardening. *Address:* Kingswood, Millfield Lane, Hitchin, Herts SG4 7NH. *Club:* Royal Air Force.

MERRITT, Prof. John Edward; Emeritus Professor, The Open University, since 1987; educational research in association with Charlotte Mason College, Ambleside, 1985–91; *b* 13 June 1926; *s* of Leonard Merritt and Janet (*née* Hartford); *m* 1948, Denise Edmondson; two *s*. *Educ:* Univ. of Durham (BA); Univ. of London (DipEdPsychol). ABPsS; FRSA. Sandhurst, 1945–46; Trng Officer, Border Regt, 1946–48. Educnl Psychologist, Lancs LEA, 1957–59; Sen. Educnl Psychologist, Hull LEA, 1959–63; Lectr, Inst. of Educn, Univ. of Durham, 1964–71; Prof. of Teacher Educn, Open Univ., 1971–85, retd. Emeritus Fellow, Leverhulme Trust, 1986–88. Pres., UK Reading Assoc., 1969–70; Chm., 5th World Congress on Reading, Vienna, 1974; Mem., Nat. Cttee of Inquiry into Reading and Use of English (Bullock Cttee), 1972–75. Hon. FCP 1994. *Publications:* Reading and the Curriculum (ed), 1971; A Framework for Curriculum Design, 1972; (ed jtly) Reading Today and Tomorrow, 1972; (ed jtly) The Reading Curriculum, 1972; Perspectives on Reading, 1973; What Shall We Teach, 1974; numerous papers in educnl jls. *Recreations:* fell walking, orienteering, climbing, ski-ing, theatre. *Address:* Wetherlam, 20 Fisherbeck Park, Ambleside, Cumbria LA22 0AJ. *T:* (01539) 432259.

MERRITT, Lindsay; *see* Nicholson, L.

MERRITT, Prof. Neil; Vice-Chancellor, University of Portsmouth, 1992–94 (President, Portsmouth Polytechnic, 1991–92); *b* 3 March 1939; *s* of the late Leslie Alfred Merritt and Gladys Irene (*née* Green); *m* 1961, Jean Fisher (former Headmistress, Heathfield Sch., GPDST, Pinner); one *s* one *d*. *Educ:* Ilford County High Sch.; Univ. of Hull (LLB). Asst Lectr, City of London Coll., 1962–63; Lectr, Slough Coll., 1963–65; Staff Tutor, Further Educn Staff Coll., 1965–68; Head, Faculty of Management and Arts, Norfolk Coll. of Arts and Technology, 1968–73; Vice-Principal, Mid-Essex Technical Coll., 1973–74; Pro-Dir, Chelmer Inst. of Higher Educn, 1975–76; Vis. Prof. of Law, Indiana Univ., 1974 and 1976; Dir, Ealing Tech. Coll., later Ealing Coll. of Higher Educn, then Polytechnic of W London, 1977–91 (Prof. *ad hominem*, 1989). Secretary, then Chairman: Assoc. of Law Teachers, 1965–71; Standing Conf. of Principals, 1977–91; Member: Adv. Cttee on Legal Educn, 1972–76; CNAA Legal Studies Bd, 1978–84; Nat. Adv. Body for Public Sector Higher Educn Bd, 1982–88 (Mem., Chm.'s Study Gp, 1983–88); Trustee, then Vice-Chm., Central Bureau for Educnl Visits and Exchanges, 1980–88; Chairman: Cttee for Business and Finance, BTEC, 1982–85; Polytechnic and Colls Employers Forum, 1990–92; Pres., European Assoc. of Higher Educn, 1990–92; Co-Chm., Cttee for Higher Educn in EC, 1991–92. Chm., Hillingdon Hosp. Trust, 1991–94. FRSA. *Publications:* (with E. G. H. Clayton) Business Law, 1966; articles in professional jls on law, and higher educn policy. *Recreations:* opera, writing, sailing, tempera.

MERRIVALE, 3rd Baron *cr* 1925, of Walkhampton, Co. Devon; **Jack Henry Edmond Duke;** *b* 27 Jan. 1917; *o s* of 2nd Baron Merrivale, OBE, and Odette, *d* of Edmond Roger, Paris; *S* father, 1951; *m* 1st, 1939, Colette (marr. diss. 1974), *d* of John Douglas Wise, Bordeaux, France; one *s* one *d*; 2nd, 1975, Betty, *widow* of Paul Baron. *Educ:* Dulwich; private tuition, SW France; Ecole des Sciences Politiques, Paris. Served War of 1939–45, RAF, 1940; Flight-Lieut, 1944 (despatches). Formerly Chm., Scotia Investments Plc; Chm., Grecian Investments (Gibraltar) Ltd (formerly Leisure Investments (Gibraltar) Ltd), 1990–; Pres., Inst. of Traffic Administration, 1953–70; Chm., 1961–86, Pres., 1986–96, Anglo-Malagasy Soc.; Chairman: British Cttee for Furthering of Relations with French-speaking Africa, 1973; GB–Senegal Friendship Assoc., 1990. Founder Mem., Club de Dakar, 1974. Freeman, City of London, 1979; Hon. Freedom, City of Gibraltar, 2001. FRSA 1964. Chevalier, Nat. Order of Malagasy, 1968; Commander, Nat. Order of the Lion (Senegal), 1992. *Recreations:* sailing, photography. *Heir:* *s* Hon. Derek John Philip Duke, *b* 16 March 1948. *Address:* 16 Brompton Lodge, SW7 2JA. *T:* (020) 7581 5678.

MERRON, Gillian Joanna; MP (Lab) Lincoln, since 1997; *b* 12 April 1959. *Educ:* Wanstead High Sch.; Univ. of Lancaster (BSc Hons (Mgt Scis)). Formerly: Business Develt Advr; Local Govt Officer; Sen. Officer, UNISON, Lincolnshire. Mem., Lab. Pty, 1982–. PPS to Minister of State for the Armed Forces, 1998–99, to Minister of State for Defence Procurement, 1999–2001, MoD. Mem., Select Cttee on Trade and Industry, 1997–98. Vice-Chm., PLP Back bench Cttee on Foreign and Commonwealth Affairs, 1997–98; Chm., E Midlands Gp of Lab. MPs, 1999–. Mem. Bd, Westminster Foundn for Democracy, 1998–. Grad., Armed Forces Parly Scheme (RAF), 1997–98. *Recreations:* walking, films, Lincoln City FC. *Address:* House of Commons, SW1A 0AA.

MERRY, David Byron, CMG 2000; HM Diplomatic Service; High Commissioner, Gaborone, since 2001; *b* 16 Sept. 1945; *s* of late Colin Merry and of Audrey Merry (*née*

Handley); *m* 1967, Patricia Ann Ellis; one *s* two *d*. *Educ:* King Edward VII Sch., Sheffield; Ecclesfield Grammar Sch. Min. of Aviation, 1961–65; entered HM Diplomatic Service, 1965; Bangkok, 1969–73; Budapest, 1974–77; FCO, 1977–81; First Sec. (Econ.) and Civil Air Attaché, Bonn, 1981–85; Head of Chancery, E Berlin, 1985–88; FCO, 1989–93; Counsellor and Dep. Head of Mission, Manila, 1993–97; Dep. High Comr, Karachi, 1997–2000; FCO, 2000–01. *Recreations:* swimming, walking. *Address:* c/o Foreign and Commonwealth Office, King Charles Street, SW1A 2AH.

MERRYLEES, Prof. Andrew, RSA 1991; RIBA; FRIAS, FCSD; consultant in private architectural practice, Merrylees & Robertson; *b* 13 Oct. 1933; *s* of Andrew Merrylees and Mary McGowan Craig; *m* 1959, Maie Crawford; two *s* one *d*. *Educ:* Glasgow Sch. of Architecture (BArch 1956; DipTP 1957). RIBA 1958; FRIAS 1977; FCSD 1978. Joined Sir Basil Spence, Glover & Ferguson, 1952: student, 1952–57; architect, 1957–68; Associate, 1968; Partner, 1972–85; Principal, Andrew Merrylees Associates, then Andrew Merrylees Grierson & Robertson, subseq. Merrylees & Robertson, 1985–2000, merged with Hypostyle, 2001. Consultant Architect: SCONUL, 1964–79; UC Dublin, 1973–91. Hon. Prof. of Architecture, Univ. of Dundee, 1998–. Member: Adv. Council for Arts in Scotland, 1989–97; Council, RIAS, 1991–94. Mem., Edinburgh Fest. Soc., 1979–. *Major projects* include: university buildings at Edinburgh (Civic Trust Award, for Univ. Liby, 1969), Heriot-Watt, Dublin, Liverpool, Newcastle and Aston in Birmingham; Scottish HQ for AA; Sorting Office for PO, Edinburgh (Art in Architecture Award, Saltire Soc., 1983); Nat. Liby of Scotland (SCONUL Award, 1996); British Golf Mus., St Andrews; Motherwell Heritage Centre. FRSA 1993. Winner, numerous design competitions, including: UC Dublin Liby; Liverpool Univ. Arts Liby; Conf. Centre, Heriot-Watt Univ.; John Logie Baird Visions Centre, Glasgow; Dundee Sci. Centre. Numerous awards, including: Bronze Medal, RIBA, 1968; Gold Medal, Royal Scottish Acad., 1984. *Recreations:* architecture, painting, cooking. *Address:* 204 Bonkle Road, Newmains, Lanarkshire ML2 9AA. *T:* (01698) 384914. *Club:* Scottish Arts (Edinburgh).

MERSEY, 4th Viscount *cr* 1916, of Toxteth; **Richard Maurice Clive Bigham;** Lord Nairne 1681; Baron Mersey 1910; film director; *b* 8 July 1934; *e s* of 3rd Viscount Mersey, and 12th Lady Nairne (*d* 1995); *S* father, 1979; *m* 1961, Joanna, *d* of late John A. R. G. Murray, CBE; one *s*. *Educ:* Eton and Balliol. Irish Guards, 1952–54 (final rank Lt). Films incl. documentaries for Shell, LEPRA and Government (various awards, London and Venice). President: SIESO, 1987–91; Combined Heat and Power Assoc., 1989–92. FRGS. Hon. FRAM 1995. *Publications:* The Hills of Cork and Kerry, 1987; Pole Power: changing the face of Poland's energy for the European Union, 2001. *Heir: s* Hon. Edward John Hallam Bigham, Master of Nairne, *b* 23 May 1966. *Address:* Bignor Park, Pulborough, West Sussex RH20 1HG. *T:* (01798) 869214.

MERTENS DE WILMARS, Baron Josse (Marie Honoré Charles); Grand Croix de l'Ordre de la Couronne; Chevalier de l'Ordre de Léopold; Judge, 1967–80, and President, 1980–84, Court of Justice of the European Communities; Emeritus Professor, Faculty of Law, Catholic University of Leuven, since 1971; Member of the University Curatorium, 1972–90; *b* 12 June 1912; *s* of (Marie Antoine Joseph) Albert Mertens and Jeanne Eugénie Marie Anne Meert; *m* 1939, Elisabeth Simonne M. Hubertine van Ormelingen; three *s* five *d*. *Educ:* Abdijschool, Zevenkerke, Bruges; Catholic Univ. of Leuven (Dr in Law, Dr in Pol. and Diplomatic Science). Hon. Assessor, Legislative Dept of Council of State (Conseil d'Etat) (Assessor, 1950–52). Mem., Chambre des Représentants de Belgique (Lower House of Parlt), 1952–62; former Mem., Bar Council. Hon. Mem., Bar of Antwerp. Chief Editor, Revue Internationale Droit Economique, 1989–93. CStJ. Groot kruis van de Orde van Orange Nassau (Neth.); Grand Croix de l'Ordre de la Couronne de Chêne (Lux.); Grosskreuz des Verdienstordens der Bundesrepublik Deutschland. *Publications:* several works on Belgian and European Law. *Address:* 192 Jan Van Rijswijcklaan, 2020 Antwerpen, Belgium. *T:* (3) 2380768, *Fax:* (3) 2486504.

MERTHYR, Barony of (*cr* 1911); title disclaimed by 4th Baron; *see under* Lewis, Trevor Oswin.

MERTON, Viscount; Simon John Horatio Nelson; *b* 21 Sept. 1971; *s* and *heir* of 9th Earl Nelson, *qv*.

MERTON, John Ralph, MBE (mil.) 1942; painter; *b* 7 May 1913; *s* of late Sir Thomas Merton, KBE, FRS; *m* 1939, Viola Penelope von Bernd; two *d* (and one *d* decd). *Educ:* Eton; Balliol Coll., Oxford. Served War of 1939–45 (MBE); Air Photo reconnaissance research, Lieut-Col 1944. Works include: Mrs Daphne Wall, 1948; The Artist's daughter, Sarah, 1949; Altar piece, 1952; The Countess of Dalkeith, at Drumlanrig, 1958; A myth of Delos, 1959; Clarissa, 1960; Mrs Julian Sheffield, 1970; Sir Charles Evans, 1973; Iona Colquhoun Duchess of Argyll, 1982; Triple Portrait of Sir David Piper, 1984 (in Nat. Portrait Gall.); James Meade, 1987; Triple Portrait of HRH The Princess of Wales (for Cardiff City Hall), 1987; HM The Queen (at Windsor Castle), 1989; Paul H. Nitze (in Johns Hopkins Univ.), 1991; Triple Portrait of Duke of Grafton (for Nat. Portrait Gall.), 1992; Lord and Lady Romsey with a mirror reflecting Broadlands, 1997; double portrait drawing of two children, 1999 (exhibited RA, 2000); two paintings, from own photos, of coral trees under S China Sea off Tioman Is, N Malaysia: vertical tree (a mile off shore), 2000; horizontal tree (in shallower water), 2001. Legion of Merit (USA), 1945. *Publication:* A Journey Through an Artist's Life, 1994. *Recreations:* music, making things, underwater photography. *Address:* Pound House, Oare, near Marlborough, Wilts SN8 4JA. *T:* (01672) 563539.

See also Hon. Sir R. A. Morritt.

MERTON, Paul; *see* Martin, P. J.

MERTON, Prof. Robert C., PhD; John and Natty McArthur University Professor, Graduate School of Business, Harvard University, since 1998; *b* 31 July 1944; *s* of Robert K. Merton and Suzanne C. Merton; *m* 1966, June Rose (separated 1996); two *s* one *d*. *Educ:* Columbia Univ. (BS Engrg Math. 1966); California Inst. of Technology (MS Applied Math. 1967); MIT (PhD Econs 1970). Massachusetts Institute of Technology: Asst Prof., 1970–73, Associate Prof., 1973–74, Prof., 1974–80, of Finance; J. C. Penney Prof. of Management, 1980–88; George Fisher Baker Prof. of Business Admin, Graduate Sch. of Business, Harvard Univ., 1988–98. Mem., NAS, 1993; Fellow: Amer. Acad. of Arts and Scis; Econometric Soc.; Internat. Assoc. of Financial Engrs. Hon. Prof., Hautes Etudes Commerciales, France, 1995; Hon. LLD Chicago, 1991; Hon. DEconSc Lausanne, 1996; Dr *hc* Paris Dauphine, 1997; Hon. Dr Mgt Sci, Nat. Sun Yat-sen Univ., China, 1998. Internat. Prize, Accademia Nazionale dei Lincei, 1993; Nobel Prize for Economics, 1997; Michael I. Pupin Medal for Service to the Nation, Columbia Univ., 1998. *Publications:* Continuous-Time Finance, 1990, 2nd edn 1992; (jtly) Casebook in Financial Engineering: applied studies of financial innovation, 1995; (jtly) The Global Financial System: a functional perspective, 1995; (jtly) Finance, 2000; contribs to scientific jls. *Address:* Morgan Hall 397, Harvard Business School, Soldiers Field, Boston, MA 02163, USA. *T:* (617) 495 6678, *Fax:* (617) 495 8863.

MERVYN DAVIES, David Herbert; *see* Davies.

MERZ, (Joachim) Friedrich; Member (CDU/CSU) Bundestag, since 1994; *b* 11 Nov. 1955; *m* 1981, Charlotte Gass; one *s* two *d*. *Educ:* Univ. of Bonn. Mil. service, 1975–76. Practical trng in judicial and other legal work, Saarbrücken and Johannesburg, SA, 1982–85; magistrate, Saarbrücken, 1985–86; lawyer, Bonn, 1986–89; Partner, Leinen & Derichs, Cologne, Berlin, Brussels, 1990–. MEP (CDU/CSU) S Westfalia, 1989–94. Mem., Finance Cttee and Cttee for Eur. Affairs, Bundestag, 1994–. CDU/CSU Parliamentary Group: co-ordinator, on Finance Cttee, 1996–; Dep. Chm., 1998–2000; Chm., 2000–; Member: Bd, CDU Nordrhein-Westfalen, 1997–; Fed. Bd, CDU party, 1998–. *Address:* Bundeshaus, Platz der Republik, 11011 Berlin, Germany.

MESHER, John; Social Security Commissioner and Child Support Commissioner, since 1993; *b* 25 June 1947; *s* of Percy Charles Mesher and Dorothy Mesher; *m* 1973, Hilary Anne Wilkens; one *s* and *d* (and one *d* decd). *Educ:* Bancroft's Sch.; University Coll., Oxford (BA Jurisp, BCL); Yale Law Sch. (LLM). Called to the Bar, Gray's Inn, 1970; Lectr in Laws, QMC, 1969–76; University of Sheffield: Lectr in Law, Sen. Lectr and Reader, 1976–93; Simmons & Simmons Res. Fellow in Pensions Law, 1988–93; Prof. Associate, 1993–. Part-time Chm. of Social Security, Medical, and Disability Appeals Tribunals, 1981–93, Pensions Appeal Tribunals, 1995–; Dep. Social Security Comr, 1991–93. Editor, Occupational Pensions Law Reports, 1992–; Section Editor, Encyclopedia of Employment Law, 1991–. *Publications:* Compensation for Unemployment, 1976; (ed) CPAG's Supplementary Benefit Legislation Annotated, 1983, 10th edn, as Income-Related Benefits: the Legislation, 1993; contribs to learned jls. *Address:* Office of the Social Security and Child Support Commissioners, Harp House, 83 Farringdon Street, EC4A 4DH. *T:* (020) 7353 5145.

MESIĆ, Stjepan; President, Republic of Croatia, since 2000; *b* 24 Dec. 1934; *s* of Josip and Mandica Mesić; *m* 1961, Milka; two *d*. *Educ:* Univ. of Zagreb (LLB). Mayor, Orahovica, Croatia, 1967–71; former MP Socialist Republic of Croatia; involved in Croatian Spring movt and served one-year jail sentence; Sec., 1990, Hd, Exec. Cttee, 1992, Croatian Democratic Union; Prime Minister, Socialist Republic of Croatia, May–Aug. 1990; last Pres., Yugoslavia, May–Dec. 1991; Speaker, Parlt of Republic of Croatia, 1992–94; Founder, Croatian Indep. Democrats Party (HND), 1994; Mem., Croatian Nat. Party (HNS), 1997–2000 (Exec. Vice-Pres. and Pres., Zagreb Br.). Charles Univ. Medal, 2001. Homeland War Meml Medal (Croatia), 1993; State Order of Star of Romania, 2000; Grand Star, Decoration of Honour for Merit (Austria), 2001; Golden Order, Gjergj Kastrioti Skënderbeu (Albania), 2001; Grand Cross, Order of Saviour (Greece), 2001. *Publication:* The Break-up of Yugoslavia: political memoirs, 1992, 2nd edn 1994. *Recreations:* Nanbudo, swimming. *Address:* Office of the President of the Republic of Croatia, Pantovčak 241, 10 000 Zagreb, Croatia. *T:* (1) 4565191, *Fax:* (1) 4565299.

MESSEL, Prof. Harry, CBE 1979; BA, BSc, BMilSci; PhD (NUI) 1951; Professor and Head of the School of Physics, and Director of Science Foundation for Physics, University of Sydney, Australia, 1952–87, now Emeritus Professor; Chancellor, Bond University, 1992–97 (Executive Chancellor, 1993–96); *b* 3 March 1922. *Educ:* Rivers Public High Sch., Rivers, Manitoba. Entered RMC of Canada, 1940, grad. with Governor-General's Silver Medal, 1942. Served War of 1939–45: Canadian Armed Forces, Lieut, Canada and overseas, 1942–45. Queen's Univ., Kingston, Ont., 1945–48 (BA 1st Cl. Hons in Mathematics, 1948; BSc Hons in Engineering Physics, 1948); St Andrews Univ., Scotland, 1948–49; Institute for Advanced Studies, Dublin, Eire, 1949–51; Sen. Lectr in Mathematical Physics, University of Adelaide, Australia, 1951–52. Mem., Aust. Atomic Energy Commn, 1974–81; Sen. Vice-Chm., Species Survival Commn, IUCN, 1978– (Chm., Crocodile Specialist Gp, 1989–). Hon. DSc Sydney; Hon. DHL Schiller Internat., 1994. *Publications:* Chap. 4, Progress in Cosmic Ray Physics, vol. 2, (North Holland Publishing Company), 1953; co-author and editor of: A Modern Introduction to Physics (Horwitz-Grahame, Vols I, II, III, 1959, 1960, 1962); Selected Lectures in Modern Physics, 1958; Space and the Atom, 1961; A Journey through Space and the Atom, 1962; The Universe of Time and Space, 1963; Light and Life in the Universe, 1964; Science for High School Students, 1964; Time, 1965; Senior Science for High School Students, 1966; (jt) Electron-Photon Shower Distribution Function, 1970; (jt) Multistrand Senior Science for High School Students, 1975; Australian Animals and their Environment, 1977; Time and Man, 1978; Tidal Rivers in Northern Australia and their Crocodile Populations (20 monographs), 1979–87; The Study of Populations, 1985; editor of: From Nucleus to Universe, 1960; Atoms to Andromeda, 1966; Apollo and the Universe, 1967; Man in Inner and Outer Space, 1968; Nuclear Energy Today and Tomorrow, 1969; Pioneering in Outer Space, 1970; Molecules to Man, 1971; Brain Mechanisms and the Control of Behaviour, 1972; Focus on the Stars, 1973; Solar Energy, 1974; Our Earth, 1975; Energy for Survival, 1979; The Biological Manipulation of Life, 1981; Science Update, 1983; The Study of Population, 1985; Highlights in Science, 1987; numerous papers published in: Proc. Physical Soc., London; Philosophical Magazine, London; Physical Review of America. *Recreations:* conservation, water ski-ing, hunting, fishing and photography. *Address:* 74 Montevideo Drive, Clear Island Waters, Qld 4226, Australia. *T:* (7) 55755873, *Fax:* (7) 55755874.

MESSER, Cholmeley Joseph; Chairman, Hamilton Insurance, 1995–2000; Director, HFC Bank plc, 1993–99; *b* 20 March 1929; *s* of late Col Arthur Albert Messer, DSO. CBE, FRIBA, and Lilian Hope Messer (*née* Dowling); *m* 1956, Ann Mary Power; two *d*. *Educ:* Wellington Coll. Solicitor. Served KRRC, 2nd Lieut, 1948–49. Articled Lawrance Messer & Co., Solicitors, London 1949–54; Partner, 1957–66; Save & Prosper Group: Exec. Dir, 1967–72; Dep. Man. Dir, 1973–80; Man. Dir, 1980–84; Chm., 1981–89. Chm., Code of Advertising Practice Cttee, Advertising Standards Authority, 1977–78; Vice-Chm., Internat. Bar Assoc. Cttee on Investment Cos Funds and Trusts, 1978–81; Chm., Unit Trust Assoc., 1981–83; Mem., 1989–92, Chm., 1992–98, London Pension Funds Authy. Chm., British Bobsleigh Assoc., 1989–92. *Recreations:* armchair sport, gardening, golf, railways. *Address:* The Manor House, Normandy, Guildford, Surrey GU3 2AP. *T:* (01483) 810910. *Clubs:* City of London, MCC.

MESSITER, Malcolm; oboist; Founder and Managing Director: Messiter Software, since 1985; Trans-Send International Ltd, since 1992; *b* 1 April 1949; *s* of late Ian and of Enid Messiter; *m* 1972, Christine (marr. diss. 1990); one *d*. *Educ:* Bryanston Sch.; Paris Conservatoire; Royal Coll. of Music (ARCM Hons 1971). First Oboe: BBC Concert Orchestra, 1971–77; London Mozart Players, 1977–83; London Festival Orchestra, 1985–; many solo concerts. Several recordings. Founder, Virtual Orchestra Co. Ltd, 1999. *Publications:* personal computer software and manuals. *Recreations:* wine, music, opera, model aeroplanes. *Address:* 47 Sutton Crescent, Barnet, Herts EN5 2SW.

MESSMER, Pierre Auguste Joseph; Grand Croix de la Légion d'Honneur; Compagnon de la Libération; Croix de Guerre, 1939–45; Médaille de la Résistance; Member, Académie Française, 1999; Député (RPR) from Moselle, 1968–88; *b* Vincennes (Seine), 20 March 1916; *s* of Joseph Messmer, industrialist, and of Marthe (*née* Farcy); *m* 1947, Gilberte Duprez. *Educ:* Lycées Charlemagne and Louis-le Grand; Faculty of Law, Paris; Ecole Nationale de la France d'Outre-Mer. Pupil Administrator of Colonies, 1938. Served War of 1939–45: Free French Forces, 1940; African Campaigns (Bir-Hakeim), France,

Germany; parachuted Tonkin; PoW of Vietminh, 1945. Sec.-Gen., Interministerial Cttee of Indochina, 1946; Dir of Cabinet of E. Bollaert (High Commissioner, Indochina), 1947–48; Administrator-in-Chief of France Overseas, 1950; Governor: of Mauritania, 1952, of Ivory Coast, 1954–56; Dir of Cabinet of G. Defferre (Minister, France Overseas), Jan.-April 1956; High Commissioner: Republic of Cameroon, 1956–58; French Equatorial Africa, 1958; French West Africa, July 1958–Dec. 1959; Minister of Armed Forces: (Cabinets: M. Debré, 5 Feb. 1958–14 April 1962; G. Pompidou, April-Nov. 1962, 6 Dec. 1962–7 Jan. 1966, 8 Jan. 1966–1 April 1967, 7 April 1967–10 July 1968; M. Couve de Murville, 12 July 1968–20 June 1969); Minister of State in charge of Depts and Territories Overseas, Feb. 1971–72; Prime Minister, 1972–74; Mem. European Parliament, 1979–80. Pres., RPR Federal Cttee, Moselle, 1968–88. Mayor of Sarrebourg, 1971–89. Mem., l'Institut (Académie des Sciences Morales et Politiques), 1988; Secrétaire perpétuel, Acad. des Sciences Morales et Politiques, 1995–98. Officer, American Legion. *Publications:* (jtly) Les écrits militaires de Charles de Gaulle: essai d'analyse thématique, 1986; Après tant de batailles, 1992. *Recreations:* tennis, sailing. *Address:* 23 quai de Conti, 75006 Paris, France.

MESTEL, Prof. Leon, PhD; FRS 1977; Professor of Astronomy, University of Sussex, 1973–92, now Emeritus; *b* 5 Aug. 1927; *s* of late Rabbi Solomon Mestel and Rachel (*née* Brodetsky); *m* 1951, Sylvia Louise Cole; two *s* two *d. Educ:* West Ham Secondary Sch., London; Trinity Coll., Cambridge (BA 1948, PhD 1952). ICI Res. Fellow, Dept of Maths, Univ. of Leeds, 1951–54; Commonwealth Fund Fellow, Princeton Univ. Observatory, 1954–55; University of Cambridge: Univ. Asst Lectr in Maths, 1955–58; Univ. Lectr in Maths, 1958–66; Fellow of St John's Coll., 1957–66; Vis. Mem., Inst. for Advanced Study, Princeton, 1961–62; J. F. Kennedy Fellow, Weizmann Inst. of Science, Israel, 1966–67; Prof. of Applied Maths, Manchester Univ., 1967–73. Eddington Medal, RAS, 1993. *Publications:* Magnetohydrodynamics (with N. O. Weiss), 1974 (Geneva Observatory); Stellar Magnetism, 1999; papers, revs and conf. reports on different branches of theoretical astrophysics. *Recreations:* reading, music. *Address:* 13 Prince Edward's Road, Lewes, E Sussex BN7 1BJ. *T:* (01273) 472731.

MESTON, family name of **Baron Meston**.

MESTON, 3rd Baron *cr* 1919, of Agra and Dunottar; **James Meston,** QC 1996; **His Honour Judge Meston;** a Circuit Judge, since 1999; *b* 10 Feb. 1950; *s* of 2nd Baron Meston and Diana Mary Came, *d* of Capt. O. S. Doll; *S* father, 1984; *m* 1974, Jean Rebecca Anne, *d* of John Carder; one *s* two *d. Educ:* Wellington College; St Catharine's Coll., Cambridge (MA); Leicester Univ. (LLM). Barrister, Middle Temple, 1973; Jun. Counsel to Queen's Proctor, 1992–96; a Recorder, 1997–99. Legal Assessor, 1991–99, Sen. Legal Assessor, 1999, UKCC. Appeal Steward, BBB of C, 1993–. Pres., British Soc. of Commerce, 1984–92. *Heir: s* Hon. Thomas James Dougall Meston, *b* 21 Oct. 1977. *Address:* Queen Elizabeth Building, Temple, EC4Y 9BS. *Club:* Hawks (Cambridge).

METCALF, Christopher Sherwood John; His Honour Judge Metcalf; a Circuit Judge, since 2001; *b* 18 May 1945; *s* of Bernard Metcalf and Margaret Metcalf; *m* 1977, Pamela Falconer; two *s* two *d. Educ:* The Leys Sch., Cambridge; W Georgia Coll., USA (Rotary Internat. Schol. 1963). Called to the Bar, Middle Temple, 1972; in practice on Midland and Oxford Circuit, 1972–2001; Asst Recorder, 1991–95; Recorder, 1995–2001. *Recreations:* foreign travel, church architecture, private enterprise, games, choral music. *Address:* Leicester Combined Court Centre, 90 Wellington Street, Leicester LE1 6HG.

METCALF, Prof. David Harry, PhD; Professor of Industrial Relations, London School of Economics, since 1985; Ombudsman, European Bank for Reconstruction and Development, since 1997; *b* 15 May 1942; *s* of Geoffrey and Dorothy Metcalf; *m* 1968, Helen Pitt (*see* Dame Helen Metcalf); one *s. Educ:* Manchester Univ. (BA Econ 1964; MA 1966); London Univ. (PhD 1971). Apprentice welder, English Electric, 1959–61; Lectr in Econs, LSE, 1967–75; Special Advr to Minister for Social Security, 1976–79; Prof. of Econs, Kent Univ., 1978–85. Comr, Low Pay Commn, 1997–. Editor, British Jl Industrial Relns, 1990–95. Jockey Club Steward, Lingfield Park, Plumpton and Folkestone. *Publications:* Low Pay, Occupational Mobility and Minimum Wage Policy in Britain, 1983; New Perspectives on Industrial Disputes, 1993; articles in Econ. Jl, Industrial and Labor Relns Rev., etc. *Recreations:* horse-racing (owner and investor), watching Tottenham Hotspur FC. *Address:* 18 St Georges Avenue, N7 0HD. *T:* (020) 7607 5902; *e-mail:* d.metcalf@lse.ac.uk. *Club:* MCC.

METCALF, Prof. David Michael, DPhil, DLitt; Professor of Numismatics, University of Oxford, 1996–98; Keeper of Heberden Coin Room, Ashmolean Museum, Oxford, 1982–98; Fellow of Wolfson College, Oxford, 1982–98, now Emeritus; *b* 8 May 1933; *s* of Rev. Thomas Metcalf and Gladys Metcalf; *m* 1958, Dorothy Evelyn (*née* Uren); two *s* one *d. Educ:* St John's College, Cambridge. MA, DPhil, DLitt; FSA. Asst Keeper, Ashmolean Museum, 1963. President: Royal Numismatic Soc., 1994–99 (Sec., and Editor, Numismatic Chronicle, 1974–84); UK Numismatic Trust, 1994–99. *Publications:* Coinage in South-eastern Europe 820–1396, 1979; Coinage of the Crusades and the Latin East, 1983, 2nd edn 1995; (ed with D. H. Hill) Sceattas in England and on the Continent, 1984; Coinage in Ninth-century Northumbria, 1987; Thrymsas and Sceattas in the Ashmolean Museum, Oxford: vol. 1, 1993, vol. 2, 1993, vol. 3, 1994; Corpus of Lusignan Coinage, vol. 2, 1996, vol. 1, 1998, vol. 3, 2000; Suevic Coinage, 1997; An Atlas of Anglo-Saxon Coin Finds, 1998; articles on numismatics in various jls. *Address:* 40 St Margaret's Road, Oxford OX2 6LD.

METCALF, Prof. Donald, AC 1993 (AO 1976); FRS 1983, FRACP, FRCPA, FAA; Assistant Director and Head of Cancer Research Unit, Walter and Eliza Hall Institute of Medical Research, Melbourne, 1965–96; Research Professor of Cancer Biology, University of Melbourne, 1986–96, now Professor Emeritus; *b* 26 Feb. 1929; *s* of Donald Davidson Metcalf and Enid Victoria Metcalf (*née* Thomas); *m* 1954, Josephine Emily Lentaigne; four *d. Educ:* Sydney University. MD, BSc (med). Resident MO, Royal Prince Alfred Hosp., Sydney, 1953–54; Surgeon-Lieut, RANR, 1953–58; Carden Fellow in Cancer Res., Walter and Eliza Hall Inst. of Med. Res., 1954–65. Vis. Fellow, Harvard Med. Sch., 1956–58; Visiting Scientist: Roswell Park Meml Inst., Buffalo, 1966–67; Swiss Inst. for Experimental Cancer Res., Lausanne, 1974–75; Radiobiological Res. Inst., Rijswijk, 1980–81; Royal Soc. Guest Res. Fellow, Cambridge Univ., 1981. *Publications:* The Thymus, 1966; (with M. A. S. Moore) Haemopoietic Cells, 1971; Hemopoietic Colonies, 1977; Hemopoietic Colony Stimulating Factors, 1984; The Molecular Control of Blood Cells, 1988; (with N. A. Nicola) The Hemopoietic Colony Stimulating Factors, 1995; numerous scientific papers on cancer and leukaemia. *Recreations:* music, tennis. *Address:* 268 Union Road, Balwyn, Victoria 3103, Australia. *T:* (3) 98361343.

METCALF, Dame Helen, DBE 1998; Headteacher, Chiswick Community School, since 1988; *b* 7 Oct. 1946; *d* of Thomas Pitt and Winifred Pitt (*née* Nicholas); *m* 1968, Prof. David Harry Metcalf, *qv*; one *s. Educ:* Manchester Univ. (BA); London Sch. of Econs (MSc). Head of 6th Form and history teacher, Islington Green Comprehensive, 1974–82; Dep. Head, Acland Burghley Comprehensive, 1982–88. Mem. (Lab), Islington LBC, 1971–78. FRSA 1996. *Recreations:* gardening, travel, politics, detective stories. *Address:* Chiswick Community School, Burlington Lane, W4 3UN. *T:* (020) 8747 0031.

METCALF, Malcolm, MC 1944; DL; Chairman, Surrey County Council, 1978–81; *b* 1 Dec. 1917; *s* of Charles Almond Metcalf and Martha Fatherly Atkins Metcalf; *m* 1945, Charis Thomas; two *s. Educ:* Merchant Taylors' Sch., Crosby. ACIS. Army service, 1939–46. Contested (C) Barrow-in-Furness, 1959; Mem., Surrey CC, 1965–89 (Leader, 1973–77; Vice-Chm., 1977–78); Member: Metrop. Water Board, 1965–74 (Vice-Chm. 1971–72); Thames Conservancy, 1970–74; Thames Water Authority, 1973–78, 1981–87. Mem., Assoc. of County Councils, 1975–88. DL Surrey, 1979. *Address:* 1 The Lodge, Watts Road, Thames Ditton KT7 0DE. *T:* (020) 8398 3057. *Clubs:* MCC, Burhill Golf (Walton-on-Thames).

METCALF, Ven. Robert Laurence; Archdeacon of Liverpool, since 1994; *b* 18 Nov. 1935; *s* of late Victor Noel Metcalf and Phyllis Maud Metcalf (*née* Dunwell); *m* 1964, Rachel Margaret Herring; two *s* three *d. Educ:* St John's Coll., Durham Univ. (BA 1960; rowing colours, 1960); Cranmer Hall, Durham (DipTheol 1962). Nat. Service, REME, 1955–57. Ordained deacon, 1962, priest, 1963; Curate: Christ Church, Bootle, 1962–65; i/c St John's, Widnes, 1965–67; Vicar, St Catharine, Wigan, 1967–75; Dir, Wigan Br., Samaritans, 1970–75; Rector, Holy Trinity, Wavertree, 1974–94; Chaplain: Liverpool Royal Sch. for the Blind, 1975–94; Blue Coat Sch., Liverpool, 1975–94; Diocesan Dir of Ordinands, Liverpool, 1982–94; Hon. Canon, Liverpool Cathedral, 1988. Chm., Pre-theol Educn Panel, Ministry Div., Archbps' Council, 1999–. Mem., Toxteth Rotary Club (Pres., 1995–96). Occasional broadcaster, BBC Radio Merseyside. *Publications:* contrib.: Prayers for Today's Church, 1972; For All the Family, 1984; Prayers for Today's World, 1993; Reconciliation. *Recreations:* walking, rowing, reading novels (political intrigue!), holidaying. *Address:* 38 Menlove Avenue, Allerton, Liverpool L18 2EF. *T:* (0151) 724 3956, *Fax:* (0151) 729 0587; *e-mail:* BobMetcalf@ukgateway.net.

METCALFE, Adrian Peter, OBE 2001; international sport and media consultant; *b* 2 March 1942; *s* of Hylton and Cora Metcalfe; *m* Catherine, Baroness von Delvig; one *s* one *d* by former marriage. *Educ:* Roundhay Sch., Leeds; Magdalen Coll., Oxford. Reporter, Sunday Express, 1964; Dep. Editor, World of Sport, ABC TV, 1965; Producer, Sports Arena, LWT, 1968; Presenter, CBS Sports Spectacular, 1972–76; Man. Dir, AMO Productions, 1976; Sen. Commissioning Editor, Sport and Features, Channel 4 TV, 1981; Commentator, ITV, 1966–87; Director of Programmes: Eurosport, 1989–91; Tyne Tees Television Ltd, 1991–92; Dir, Venue Production, Atlantic Olympic Games, 1994–96; Chm., API Television, 1996–98; Exec. Publr, worldsport.com, 1998–99. GB Record, 400m, 45·7, ranked No 1 in the world at 400m, 1961; Gold Medal, 400m and 4×400m, World Student Games, 1963; Silver Medal, 4×400m, Tokyo Olympics, 1964; 7 British Records, 4 European Records, 1961–64. Pres., OUAC, 1962–63. Mem., UK Sports Council, 1998– (Chm., Major Events Steering Gp, 1999–); Life Vice-Pres. and Trustee, Sports Aid Foundn, 1990–. *Recreations:* still running, Russian culture. *Address:* 45 Tunis Road, W12 7EZ. *T:* (020) 8749 9233.

METCALFE, Prof. David Henry Harold, OBE 1989; Professor of General Practice, University of Manchester School of Medicine, 1978–92, now Professor Emeritus; *b* 3 Jan. 1930; *s* of Henry R. Metcalfe and Mary Metcalfe (*née* Evans); *m* 1957, Anne (*née* Page); three *s. Educ:* Leys School, Cambridge; Cambridge Univ. (clinical course at Liverpool) (MA, MB, BChir); MSc Manchester. FRCGP; FFPHM. United Liverpool Hosps, 1956–58; Principal in gen. practice, Hessle, E Yorks, 1960–70; Asst Prof. in Family Medicine, Univ. of Rochester, NY, 1970–72; Sen. Lectr (GP), Dept of Community Health, Nottingham Univ. Med. Sch., 1972–78. Dir, DHSS Urban Primary Care Res. Unit, 1978–92. Vice-Chm., RCGP, 1983–84. *Publications:* papers on medical information handling, doctor-patient communication, patterns of general practice, and medical educn. *Recreations:* photography, sailing, hill walking. *Address:* Westgate Barn, Milburn, Penrith, Cumbria CA10 1TW. *T:* (01768) 361947.

METCALFE, Hugh, OBE 1969; FREng, FRAeS; Director, Redcliffe Holdings, since 1996; *b* 26 June 1928; *s* of late Clifford Metcalfe, CBE and Florence Ellen Metcalfe; *m* 1952, Pearl Allison Carter (*d* 1998); three *s*; *m* 1999, Jennifer Mary Reid. *Educ:* Harrow County Grammar School; Imperial College, Univ. of London. BSc, ARCS. FREng (FEng 1983). RAF, 1946–48; joined Bristol Aeroplane Co., 1951; Divisional Dir, 1974; British Aerospace Dynamics Group: Group Dir, Naval Weapons, 1978; Man. Dir, Bristol Div., 1980; Man. Dir, Hatfield Div., 1981; Chief Exec., 1982; Dir, 1982–88, and Dep. Chief Exec. (Ops), 1986–88, BAe; Dir, SAC Internat., then Ricardo Internat., later Ricardo Gp, 1989–95. Pres., RAeS, 1989–90. Hon. DSc Hatfield Polytechnic, 1988; Hon. DEng Bristol Univ., 1992. RAeS gold medal, 1984. *Recreation:* choral music. *Address:* 46 Frogwell Park, Chippenham SN14 0RB. *Clubs:* Athenæum; Leander; Savage's (Bristol).

METCALFE, Prof. James Charles, PhD; Professor of Mammalian Cell Biochemistry, University of Cambridge, since 1996; Fellow, Darwin College, Cambridge, since 1975; *b* 20 July 1939; *s* of Cyril Tom Metcalfe and Olive Kate (*née* Ayling); *m* 1st, 1969, Susan Milner (marr. diss.); one *s* one *d*; 2nd, 1983, Aviva Miriam Tolkovsky. *Educ:* St Paul's Sch.; Sidney Sussex Coll., Cambridge (MA; PhD 1965). Research Fellow, Dept of Pharmacology, Cambridge Univ. and Dept of Pharmacology, Harvard Med. Sch., 1965–67; Mem. Scientific Staff, MRC Molecular Pharmacology Unit, Dept of Pharmacology, Cambridge, 1967–72; Res. Fellow, Dept of Chemistry, Stanford Univ., 1968; Perm. MRC appt, 1970; Div. of Molecular Pharmacology, NIMR, 1972–73; Univ. Lectr, Dept of Pharmacology, Cambridge, 1974; Sir William Dunn Reader, Dept of Biochem., Cambridge, 1974–96. Chm., Scientific Cttee, CRC, 1995–2000. Mem., EMBO, 1981. Fogarty Internat. Schol., NIH, 1979. Colworth Medal, Biochem. Soc., 1973. *Publications:* papers in scientific jls. *Recreations:* walking in France, reading, ski-ing. *Address:* Department of Biochemistry, University of Cambridge, Tennis Court Road, Downing Site, Cambridge CB2 1QW. *T:* (01223) 333633.

METCALFE, Julian Edward; Founder and Chairman, Pret a Manger, since 1986; *b* 14 Dec. 1959; *s* of David Metcalfe and Alexa (*née* Boycun); *m* 1993, Melanie Willson; two *s. Educ:* Harrow; Central London Poly. (BSc). *Recreation:* eating. *Address:* (office) 16 Palace Street, SW1E 5PT. *T:* (020) 7827 8000. *Club:* White's.

METCALFE, Stanley Gordon; Chairman: Queens Moat Houses plc, 1993–2001; Ranks Hovis McDougall PLC, 1989–93, retired (Managing Director, 1981–89, Chief Executive, 1984–89, and Deputy Chairman, 1987–89); *b* 20 June 1932; *s* of Stanley Hudson Metcalfe and Jane Metcalfe; *m* 1968, Sarah Harter; two *d. Educ:* Leeds Grammar Sch.; Pembroke Coll., Oxford (MA). Commnd Duke of Wellington's Regt, 1952. Trainee, Ranks, Hovis McDougall, 1956–59; Director, Stokes & Dalton, Leeds, 1963–66; Managing Director, McDougalls, 1966–69; Director, Cerebos Ltd, 1969–70; Managing Director: RHM Overseas Ltd, 1970–73; RHM Cereals Ltd, 1973–79; Director, Ranks Hovis McDougall Ltd, 1979. Member: Exec. Cttee, FDF, 1987–93 (Pres., 1990–92); Priorities Bd for R&D in Agriculture and Food, 1987–92; CBI President's Cttee, 1990–93; Council, Business in the Community, 1990–93. Chm., Adv. Bd, Inst. of Food Research, 1988–. President,

Nat. Assoc. of British and Irish Millers, 1978. *Recreations:* cricket, golf, theatre. *Address:* The Oast House, Lower Froyle, Alton, Hants GU34 4LX. *T:* (01420) 22310. *Clubs:* Boodle's, MCC; IZ, Arabs.

METFORD, Prof. John Callan James; Professor of Spanish, 1960–81, now Emeritus Professor, Head of Department of Hispanic and Latin American Studies, 1973–81, University of Bristol; *b* 29 Jan. 1916; *s* of Oliver Metford and Florence Stowe Thomas; *m* 1944, Edith Donald; one *d. Educ:* Porth Grammar Sch.; Universities of Liverpool, Yale and California. Commonwealth Fund Fellow, 1939–41; British Council Lecturer in Brazil, 1942–44; Regional Officer, Latin American Department of the British Council, 1944–46; Lectr in Latin American Studies, Univ. of Glasgow, 1946–55; Bristol University: Head of Dept of Spanish and Portuguese, 1955–73; Prof., 1960–81; Dean of Faculty of Arts, 1973–76; Chm., Sch. of Modern Langs, 1976–79. Vis. Prof., Lehigh Univ., USA, 1968–69. Chm., Council of Westonbirt Sch., 1976–83; Mem., Central Cttee of Allied Schs, 1970–83; Governor, Coll. of St Matthias, Bristol, 1960–79; Mem., St Matthias Trust, 1979–96; Professorial Mem., Council of Univ. of Bristol, 1972–74; Founder Trustee, The Octagon, Univ. of West England (formerly Bristol Poly.), 1993–96. Mem., Diocesan Adv. Cttee, Bristol, 1984–93. *Publications:* British Contributions to Spanish and Spanish American Studies, 1950; San Martín the Liberator, 1950, 2nd edn 1970; Modern Latin America, 1964; Falklands or Malvinas?, rev. edn of J. Goebel: The Struggle for the Falkland Islands, 1982; Dictionary of Christian Lore and Legend, 1983; The Christian Year, 1991; articles in Bull. of Spanish Studies, Bull. of Hispanic Studies, Liverpool Studies in Spanish, International Affairs, Contemporary Review, etc. *Recreations:* opera, iconography. *Address:* 58 Westfield House, Cote Lane, Westbury-on-Trym, Bristol BS9 3UN. *T:* (0117) 949 4858.

METGE, Dame (Alice) Joan, DBE 1987; research anthropologist and writer; *b* 21 Feb. 1930; *d* of Cedric Leslie Metge and Alice Mary (*née* Rigg). *Educ:* Auckland Univ. (MA); London School of Economics (PhD). Jun. Lectr, Geography Dept, Auckland Univ., 1952; research and doctoral study, 1953–61; Lectr, Univ. Extension, Auckland Univ., 1961–64; University of Wellington: Sen. Lectr, Anthropology Dept, 1965–67, Associate Prof., 1968–88. Fifth Captain James Cook Res. Fellow, 1981–83. Hutchinson Medal, LSE, 1958; Elsdon Best Meml Medal, Polynesian Soc., 1987; Te Rangi Hiroa Medal, Royal Soc. of NZ, 1997. *Publications:* A New Maori Migration, 1964; The Maoris of New Zealand, 1967, rev. edn 1976; (with Patricia Kinloch) Talking Past Each Other, 1978; In and Out of Touch, 1986; Te Kohao o Te Ngira, 1990; New Growth From Old, 1995; Korero Tahi–Talking Together, 2001. *Recreations:* theatre, music, reading, gardening. *Address:* 3 Mariri Road, Onehunga, Auckland 1006, New Zealand. *T:* (9) 6345757.

METHAM, Patricia; Head, Roedean School, since 1997; *b* Cairo, 1 March 1945; *d* of John (Jack) Andrews and Jane Starrett Andrews; *m* 1st, 1966, Nicholas Hern (marr. diss.); two *d*; 2nd, 1986, Dr Tim Metham. *Educ:* Upper Chine Sch., Isle of Wight; Bristol Univ. (BA English and Drama). English and Drama Teacher: Dartford Girls' Grammar Sch., 1966–67; Sir Leo Schultz High Sch., Hull, 1967; Newland High Sch., Hull, 1967–72; Wimbledon High Sch., 1975–82 (School-Teacher Fellow, Merton Coll., Oxford, 1981); Head of English and Sixth Form, Francis Holland Sch., London, 1982–87; Head: Farlington Sch., Horsham, 1987–92; Ashford, Sch., 1992–97. Vice Chm., Ind. Schs Exams Bd, 1999. JP, Horsham, then Ashford, 1991–97. *Publications:* editor of seven critical play texts. *Recreations:* theatre, choral singing, travel to centres of archaeological and cultural interest (in Europe, particularly), good food and good wine. *Address:* Roedean House, Roedean School, Brighton, Sussex BN2 5RQ.

METHUEN, family name of **Baron Methuen**.

METHUEN, 7th Baron *cr* 1838; **Robert Alexander Holt Methuen;** electrical engineer, retired from Roll-Royce plc, 1994; *b* 22 July 1931; *y s* of 5th Baron Methuen and Grace (*d* 1972), *d* of Sir Richard Durning Holt, 1st Bt; *S* brother, 1994; *m* 1st, 1958, Mary Catharine Jane (marr. diss. 1993), *o d* of late Ven. C. G. Hooper; two *d*; 2nd, 1994, Margrit Andrea, *o d* of Friedrich Hadwiger. *Educ:* Shrewsbury; Trinity Coll., Cambridge. Elected Mem., H of L, 1999. *Heir: cousin* James Paul Archibald Methuen-Campbell, *b* 25 Oct. 1952.

METHUEN, Very Rev. John Alan Robert; Dean of Ripon, since 1995; *b* 14 Aug. 1947; *s* of late Rev. Alan Robert Methuen and Ruth Josephine Tyrrell Methuen; *m* 1970, Bridget Mary (*née* Andrews); two *d. Educ:* Upton Prep. Sch., Windsor; Eton Coll. Choir Sch.; St John's Sch., Leatherhead; Brasenose Coll., Oxford (Colquitt Exhibnr 1966; BA 1969; MA 1972); Cuddesdon Coll., Oxford. Asst Curate, Fenny Stratford and Water Eaton Team Ministry, Milton Keynes, 1971–74; Asst Chaplain, Eton Coll., 1974–77; Priest-in-Charge, St James, Dorney and Warden of Dorney Parish-Eton Coll. Conf. Centre, 1974–77; Vicar, St Mark, Reading, 1977–83; Rector, The Ascension, Hulme, Manchester, 1983–95. Church Comr, 1998–. Master, Ripon Hosps of St John the Baptist and St Mary Magdalen, 1995–. Member: Egypt Exploration Soc., 1991–; N Yorks Ancient Egyptian Soc., 1996–. Lectr, Swan Hellenic Cruises, 1996–. Gerald Avery Near Eastern Archaeolog. Prize, Oxford Univ., 1965. Writer and Dir, The Christian Life (series of 8 educnl videos), 1990–93. *Publications:* various lectures and papers. *Recreations:* drama and theatre, concerts and music-making; film-making, writing and broadcasting; history and archaeology; pilgrimage and travel (especially as leader and lecturer). *Address:* The Minster House, Ripon, North Yorkshire HG4 1PE. *T:* (01765) 603615. *Clubs:* Leeds City (Leeds); Ripon City (Ripon).

METHUEN, Richard St Barbe; QC 1997; *b* 22 Aug. 1950; *s* of late John Methuen and of Rosemary Methuen; *m* 1974, Mary Catherine Griffiths, LLB, MA, *d* of David Howard Griffiths, *qv*; one *s* two *d. Educ:* Marlborough College. Called to the Bar, Lincoln's Inn, 1972. Mem., Professional Conduct Cttee, Bar Council, 1993–98. Head of Chambers, 2000–. *Address:* 12 King's Bench Walk, Temple, EC4Y 7EL. *T:* (020) 7583 0811; *e-mail:* methuen@12kbw.co.uk.

METTERS, Dr Jeremy Stanley, CB 1994; FRCOG, FFPHM; Deputy Chief Medical Officer, Department of Health, 1989–99; *b* 6 June 1939; *s* of late Thomas Lee Metters and Henrietta Currey; *m* 1962, Margaret Howell; two *s* one *d. Educ:* Eton; Magdalene College, Cambridge; St Thomas' Hosp. (MB BChir 1963, MA 1965). MRCOG 1970, FRCOG 1982; FFPHM 1997. House officer posts, St Thomas' Hosp. and Reading, 1963–66; Lectr in Obst. and Gyn., St Thomas' Hosp., 1968–70; Registrar in Radiotherapy, 1970–72; DHSS 1972; SPMO (Under Sec.), 1984; Dep. Chief Scientist, DHSS, later Dept of Health, 1986–89. Member: Council of Europe Cttee on Bioethics (formerly Ethical and Legal Problems relating to Human Genetics), 1983–89; ESRC, 1986–88. *Publications:* papers in med. and sci. jls. *Recreations:* DIY, steam preservation.

METTYEAR, Michael King; His Honour Judge Mettyear; a Circuit Judge, since 1992; *b* 22 Sept. 1946; *s* of Charles Frank Henry King and Vera May (*née* Moore); *m* 1984, Gail Stafford; one *s* one *d. Educ:* LLB London (external). Called to the Bar, Middle Temple, 1973; a Recorder, 1990–92. Mem., Sentencing Adv. Panel, 1999–. *Recreations:* tennis, travel. *Address:* Hull Combined Court Centre, Lowgate, Hull HU1 2EZ. *T:* (01482) 586161.

METZ, David Henry, PhD; Visiting Professor, Centre for Ageing and Public Health, London School of Hygiene and Tropical Medicine, since 2000; Partner, Population Ageing Associates, since 2001; *b* 11 March 1941; *s* of Lewis and Esther Metz; *m* 1st, 1966, Marilyn Ann Yeatman (marr. diss. 1980); one *s*; 2nd, 1994, Monica Mary Threlfall. *Educ:* City of London Sch.; University Coll. London (BSc Chem, MSc Biochem); King's Coll. London (PhD Biophysics). Virology Division, National Institute for Medical Research, 1967–76: Fellow, Helen Hay Whitney Foundn, 1967–69; Mem., MRC Scientific Staff, 1969–76; Res. Fellow, Dept of Microbiol., Harvard Med. Sch., and Children's Hosp. Med. Center, Boston, 1972–73; Dept of Energy, 1976–86; Dep. Dir-Gen., Office of Gas Supply, 1986–89; Dept of Energy, 1989–92; Chief Scientist, Dept of Transport, 1992–97; Dir, AgeNet, Wolfson Inst. of Preventive Medicine, 1997–2000. Member: Mgt Bd, TRRL, 1993–96; Res. and Technol. Cttee, BR, 1994–96; Res. Adv. Council, NATS, 1997–99. Mem. Mgt Bd, Oxford Dementia Centre, 1999–. *Publications:* papers in sci. jls. *Recreations:* cooking, riding. *Address:* 14 Montpelier Grove, NW5 2XD. *T:* (020) 7681 8040.

METZGER, Rev. Prof. Bruce Manning; George L. Collord Professor of New Testament Language and Literature, Princeton Theological Seminary, 1964–84, now Emeritus; *b* Middletown, Pa, 9 Feb. 1914; *o s* of late Maurice R. Metzger and Anna Manning Metzger; *m* 1944, Isobel Elizabeth, *e d* of late Rev. John Alexander Mackay, DD; two *s. Educ:* Lebanon Valley Coll. (BA 1935); Princeton Theol Seminary (ThB 1938, ThM 1939); Princeton Univ. (MA 1940, PhD 1942, Classics). Ordained, United Presbyterian Church, USA, 1939; Princeton Theological Seminary: Teaching Fellow in NT Greek, 1938–40; Instr. in NT, 1940–44; Asst Prof., 1944–48; Associate Prof., 1948–54; Prof., 1954–64. Dist. Vis. Prof., Fuller Theol Sem., 1970; Visiting Professor: Gordon–Conwell Theol Sem., 1978; Caribbean Grad. Sch. of Theol., Jamaica, 1990; Seminario Internacional Teológico Bautista, Buenos Aires, 1991; Schol. in Residence, Tyndale Hse, Cambridge, 1969; Visiting Fellow: Clare Hall, Cambridge, 1974; Wolfson Coll., Oxford, 1979; Vis. Lectr, Sem. Theol. Presbyt. do Sul, Campinas, Brazil, 1952; Lectr, New Coll. for Advanced Christian Studies, Berkeley, 1978; many lectures to some 100 other academic instns on 5 continents. Chairman, Amer. Cttee on Versions, Internat. Greek NT Project, 1950–; Secretary: Panel of Translators, Rev. Standard Version of Apocrypha, 1952–57; Amer. Textual Criticism Seminar, 1954–56; Member: Kurat. of Vetus Latina Inst., Beuron, 1959–; Adv. Cttee, Inst. of NT Textual Res., Münster, Germany, 1961–; Inst. for Advanced Study, Princeton, 1964 and 1974; Chairman: Cttee on Trans., Amer. Bible Soc., 1964–70; Amer. Exec. Cttee, Internat. Greek NT Project, 1970–88; Cttee of Translators, New RSV of the Bible, 1977–90. President: Soc. of Biblical Lit., 1971; Stud. Novi Test. Soc., 1971–72; N Amer. Patristic Soc., 1972; Soc. for Textual Scholarship, 1995; Corresp. Fellow Brit. Acad., 1978; Hon. Fellow and Corresp. Mem., Higher Inst. of Coptic Studies, Cairo, 1955; Mem., Amer. Philosophical Soc., 1986–. Hon. DD: Lebanon Valley Coll., 1951 (also Dist. Alumnus award of Alumni Assoc. 1961); St Andrews, 1964; Hon. DTheol Münster, 1971; Hon. LHD Findlay Coll., 1962; Hon. DLitt Potchefstroom, 1985. *Publications:* The Saturday and Sunday Lessons from Luke in the Greek Gospel Lectionary, 1944; Lexical Aids for Students of New Testament Greek, 1946, enlarged edn 1955 (trans. Malagasy, Portuguese, Korean); A Guide to the Preparation of a Thesis, 1950, 2nd edn 1961; Index of Articles on the New Testament and the Early Church Published in Festschriften, 1951, Supplement 1955; Annotated Bibliography of the Textual Criticism of the New Testament, 1955; (jtly) The Text, Canon, and Principal Versions of the Bible, 1956; An Introduction to the Apocrypha, 1957 (trans. Korean); Index to Periodical Literature on the Apostle Paul, 1960, 2nd edn 1970; Lists of Words Occurring Frequently in the Coptic New Testament (Sahidic Dialect), 1961; (jtly) The Oxford Concise Concordance to the Revised Standard Version of the Holy Bible, 1962; (jtly) The Oxford Annotated Bible, 1962; Chapters in the History of New Testament Textual Criticism, 1963; The Text of the New Testament, its Transmission, Corruption, and Restoration, 1964 (trans. German, Japanese, Korean, Chinese, Italian, Russian), 3rd enlarged edn 1992; The Oxford Annotated Apocrypha, 1965; The New Testament, its Background, Growth, and Content, 1965 (trans. Chinese, Korean); Index to Periodical Literature on Christ and the Gospels, 1966; (ed jtly) The Greek New Testament, 1966, 4th edn 1993; Historical and Literary Studies, Pagan, Jewish, and Christian, 1968; A Textual Commentary on the Greek New Testament, 1971, 2nd edn 1994; The New Oxford Annotated Bible with the Apocrypha, expanded edn 1977; The Early Versions of the New Testament, their Origin, Transmission, and Limitations, 1977; New Testament Studies, Philological, Versional, and Patristic, 1980; Manuscripts of the Greek Bible, an Introduction to Greek Palaeography, 1981 (trans. Japanese); (general editor) Reader's Digest Condensed Bible, 1982 (trans. Italian, French, Korean); The Canon of the New Testament, its Origin, Development, and Significance, 1987 (trans. Italian, Russian, Korean, German); (jtly) The Making of the New Revised Standard Version of the Bible, 1991; Breaking the Code, Understanding the Book of Revelation, 1993 (trans. Chinese, Korean); (ed) The Oxford Companion to the Bible, 1993; Reminiscences of an Octogenarian, 1997; (ed) The Oxford Guide to People and Places of the Bible, 2001; (ed) New Testament Tools and Studies, thirty vols, 1960–2000; numerous articles in learned jls and encycs. *Recreations:* reading, woodworking. *Address:* 20 Cleveland Lane, Princeton, New Jersey 08540, USA. *T:* (609) 9244060. *Club:* Nassau (Princeton, New Jersey).

MEXBOROUGH, 8th Earl of, *cr* 1766; **John Christopher George Savile;** Baron Pollington, 1753; Viscount Pollington, 1766; *b* 16 May 1931; *s* of 7th Earl of Mexborough, and Josephine Bertha Emily (*d* 1992), *d* of late Captain Andrew Mansel Talbot Fletcher; *S* father, 1980; *m* 1st, 1958, Lady Elizabeth Hariot (marr. diss. 1972; she *d* 1987), *d* of 6th Earl of Verulam; one *s* (one *d* decd); 2nd, 1972, Mrs Catherine Joyce Vivian, *d* of late J. K. Hope, CBE; one *s* one *d*. MIMI. *Heir: s* Viscount Pollington, *qv*. *Address:* Arden Hall, Hawnby, York YO6 5LS. *T:* (01439) 798348; 13 Ovington Mews, SW3 1LT. *T:* (020) 7589 3669. *Clubs:* White's; All England Lawn Tennis and Croquet; Air Squadron; Mill Reef (Antigua).

MEYER, Sir Anthony John Charles, 3rd Bt *cr* 1910; lecturer on European affairs; *b* 27 Oct. 1920; *o s* of Sir Frank Meyer, MP, 2nd Bt, Ayot House, Ayot St Lawrence, Herts; *S* father, 1935; *m* 1941, Barbadee Violet, *o c* of late A. Charles Knight, JP, FSA, and of Mrs Charles Knight, Herne Place, Sunningdale; one *s* three *d. Educ:* Eton (Capt. of Oppidans); New Coll., Oxford. Served Scots Guards, 1941–45 (wounded). Entered HM Foreign Service, 1946; HM Embassy, Paris, 1951; 1st Sec., 1953; transferred to HM Embassy, Moscow, 1956; London, 1958. MP (C): Eton and Slough, 1964–66; W Flint, 1970–83, Clwyd NW, 1983–92. PPS to Sec. of State for Employment, 1972–74. Chm., Franco-British Parly Relations Cttee, 1979–92; Vice-Chm., Cons. European Affairs Cttee, 1979–89. Vice-Chm., Franco-British Council, 1986–; Mem. Bd British Council of European Movement, 1990–99, then Mem. Mgt Bd, British European Movement, 1999–2001; Chm., Federal Union, 2000–. Trustee of Shakespeare National Memorial Theatre. Officier, Légion d'Honneur, France, 1983. *Publications:* A European Technological Community, 1966; Stand Up and Be Counted, 1990. *Recreations:* music, travel, skiing, cooking. *Heir: s* Anthony Ashley Frank Meyer [*b* 23 Aug. 1944; *m* 1966, Susan Mathilda (marr. diss. 1980), *d* of John Freestone; one *d*]. *Address:* 9 Cottage Place, Brompton Square, SW3 2BE. *T:* (020) 7589 7416. *Club:* Beefsteak.

MEYER, Sir Christopher (John Rome), KCMG 1998 (CMG 1988); HM Diplomatic Service; Ambassador to the United States of America, since 1997; *b* 22 Feb. 1944; *s* of Flight Lieut R. H. R. Meyer (killed in action 1944) and Mrs E. P. L. Meyer (now Mrs S. Landells); *m* 1976, Françoise Elizabeth Hedges (marr. diss.), *d* of Air Cdre Sir Archibald Winskill, *qv*; two *s*, and one step *s*; *m* 1997, Catherine Laylle; two step *s*. *Educ:* Lancing College; Peterhouse, Cambridge (MA History); Johns Hopkins Sch. of Advanced Internat. Studies, Bologna. Third Sec., FO, 1966–67; Army Sch. of Education, 1967–68; Third, later Second, Sec., Moscow, 1968–70; Second Sec., Madrid, 1970–73; First Sec., FCO, 1973–78; First Sec., UK Perm. Rep. to European Communities, 1978–82; Counsellor and Hd of Chancery, Moscow, 1982–84; Head of News Dept, FCO, 1984–88; Fellow, Center for Internat. Affairs, Harvard, 1988–89; Minister (Commercial), 1989–92, Minister and Dep. Hd of Mission, 1992–93, Washington; Press Sec. to Prime Minister (on secondment to Cabinet Office), 1994–96; Ambassador to Germany, 1997. *Address:* c/o Foreign and Commonwealth Office, King Charles Street, SW1A 2AH.

MEYER, Rev. Conrad John Eustace; *b* 2 July 1922; *s* of William Eustace and Marcia Meyer; *m* 1960, Mary Wiltshire; no *c*. *Educ:* Clifton Coll.; Pembroke Coll., Cambridge; Westcott House. BA 1946, MA 1948. Served War of 1939–45: Royal Navy (commissioned from lower deck), 1942–46. Lieut (S) RNVR, post war, until apptd Chaplain, RNVR, 1950–54. Deacon, 1948; Priest, 1949; Asst Curate: St Francis, Ashton Gate, Bristol, 1948–51; Kenwyn, Truro, 1951; Falmouth Parish Church, 1954; Vicar of Devoran, Truro, 1956–65; Diocesan Youth Chaplain, 1956; Asst Dir of Religious Educn, 1958; Diocesan Sec. for Educn, 1960–69; Archdeacon of Bodmin, 1969–79; Hon. Canon of Truro, 1966–79; Examining Chaplain to Bishop of Truro, 1973–79; Bishop Suffragan of Dorchester, 1979–87 (Area Bishop, 1985–87); Hon. Asst Bishop, dio. of Truro, 1990–94. Received into RC Ch, 1994; ordained priest, 1995; Hon. Canon, Plymouth RC Cathedral, 2001. Hon. Diocesan Sec., Nat. Soc., 1960–69. Society for Promoting Christian Knowledge: Mem. Governing Body, 1972–90; Chairman: Projects Cttee, 1973–87; Appeals Cttee, 1987–90; Vice Chm., 1988–90; Vice-Pres., 1990–. Chairman: Federation of Catholic Priests, 1976–79; Church Union Exec. Cttee, 1979–84; The Churches' Group on Funerals at Cemeteries and Crematoria, 1980–89. Fellow, Woodard Corp. of Schools, 1967–92; Provost, Western Div., Woodard Corp., 1970–92 (Hon. Fellow, 1993–94). Hon. FICDDS. *Recreations:* swimming, walking, military history, civil defence, archaeology. *Address:* Hawk's Cliff, 38 Praze Road, Newquay, Cornwall TR7 3AF. *Club:* Royal Commonwealth Society.

MEYER, Julie; Founder and Chief Executive Officer, Ariadne Capital, since 2000; *b* 28 Aug. 1966. *Educ:* Valparaiso Univ. (BA Dist. 1988); INSEAD (MBA 1997). Consultant: AC3, Paris, 1989–91; Meyer Gp, Paris, 1992–93; Account Manager, Cunningham Communication, 1994–97; Associate, Roland Berger & Partner, Paris, 1997; independent consultant, London and Paris, 1997–98; Jt Founder, 1998 and Chief Marketing Officer, 1998–2000, First Tuesday; Asst Dir, NewMedia Investors, 1998–99. *Recreations:* Pastis and Amaretto, any kind of sport, taking weekend trips and sleeping late, genealogy, carrying on family traditions, finding John Galt. *Address:* Ariadne Capital, 28 Queen Street, EC4R 1BB.

MEYER, Michael Siegfried; Chairman and Chief Executive, EMESS plc, 1983–2000; *b* 2 May 1950; *s* of late Ernest Meyer and of Gretta Gillis; *m* 1st, 1984, Jill Benedict (marr. diss. 1990); one *d*; 2nd, 1994, Livia Hannah, *o d* of Maj.-Gen. Monty Green. *Educ:* South African College School, Cape Town. FCIS. Company Secretary, Heenan Beddow International, 1973–75; Director, 1976–79, Chief Exec., 1980–82, EMESS; Director: Royal Sovereign Group, 1986–90; Henderson Smaller Cos Investment Trust, 1990–; Walker Greenbank, 1991–97; Design Trust, 1994–. *Recreations:* watching and playing cricket, watching Rugby, theatre. *Address:* 53 Chelsea Crescent, Chelsea Harbour, SW10 0XB. *T:* (020) 7352 8706. *Clubs:* Naval and Military, MCC, Lansdowne; Western Province Cricket (Cape Town).

MEYER, Roelof Petrus, (Roelf Meyer); Chairman, Civil Society Initiative, since 2000; *b* 16 July 1947; *m* 1971, Carené Lubbe; two *s* two *d*. *Educ:* Ficksburg High Sch.; Univ. of OFS (BComm, LLB). Practised as attorney, Pretoria and Johannesburg, until 1980; MP (Nat. Party) S Africa, 1979–97 (for Johannesburg West, 1979–94); MP (UDM), 1999–2000; Deputy Minister, S Africa, 1986–91; Minister of: Defence, 1991–92; Constitutional Develt, 1992–96; Provincial Affairs, 1994–96. Co-Founder, 1997, Dep. Pres., 1998–2000, United Democratic Movt. *Recreations:* reading, jogging, cycling. *Address:* PO Box 2271, Brooklyn Square, Pretoria, 0075, South Africa. *T:* (12) 4204437, *Fax:* (12) 4203886; *e-mail:* rmeyer@lantic.net.

MEYER, Dr Rolf Arthur; Chairman of the Board, and Chief Executive Officer, Ciba Specialty Chemicals Inc., 1997–2000; *b* Switzerland, 31 Oct. 1943; *m* 1969, Elisabeth Lehmann; one *s*. *Educ:* Univ. of St Gallen, Switzerland (MBA 1967; PhD Political Sci. 1973). Various mkting and financial posts in Swiss textile ind., 1967–73; joined Ciba, 1973: financial analyst, HQ, Basle, 1973–76; Controller, Gp Co., SA, 1976–79; Manager, strategic planning and control and mkting and prodn depts, Basle, 1979–85; Corporate Vice-Pres., Ciba-Geigy Corp., USA, 1985–92 (Dir, US Corp., 1991–92); Chief Financial Officer and Mem., Exec. Cttee, 1992–97. Director: Swiss Stock Exchange, 1992–99; UBS, 1992–; Siber Hegner, 1996–.

MEYER, Rear Adm. Stephen Richard; Chief of Staff, Permanent Joint Headquarters, since 2001; *b* 28 Aug. 1950; *s* of Ernest Frederick Meyer and Rita Agnes Meyer (*née* Humphrey); *m* 1977, Erica Michelle Diana, *d* of Captain N. Hall, Jersey; two *d*. *Educ:* Merchant Taylors' Sch., Crosby; BRNC, Dartmouth. Joined RN, 1968; served HMS Tenby, Charybdis, Beachampton, Apollo, and USS Raleigh, 1969–74; loaned Sultan of Oman's Navy, i/c Sultan's Naval Vessel Al Mansur, 1975; comd HMS Bildeston, 1975–77; Flag Lieut to Adm. Sir Henry Leach, 1977–79; qualified principal warfare officer, 1980; served HM ships Coventry and Broadsword, 1980–83; commanded: HMS Galatea, 1985–86; HMS Liverpool, 1986–88; HMS Fearless, 1990–91; Head of Maritime Intelligence, 1992–93; Dir of Navy Plans, 1994–97; comd, HMS Illustrious, 1997–98; Head of Jt Force 2000 Study Team, 1998; Military Advr to High Representative, Sarajevo, 1999–2000; Comdr UK Task Gp UKMarFor, and Comdr Anti Submarine Warfare Striking Force, 2000–01. *Recreations:* family, home, friends. *Address:* c/o Naval Secretary, Victory Building, HM Naval Base, Portsmouth PO1 3LS.

MEYJES, Sir Richard (Anthony), Kt 1972; DL; President, Association of Optometrists, 1995–2000; *b* 30 June 1918; *s* of late Anthony Charles Dorian Meyjes and Norah Isobel Meyjes; *m* 1939, Margaret Doreen Morris; three *s*. *Educ:* University College School, Hampstead. War Service, RASC, Sept. 1939–Jan. 1946 (temp. Captain). Qualified as Solicitor, June 1946; Legal Dept, Anglo-Saxon Petroleum Co., 1946–56; Manager, Thailand and Vietnam Division, Shell International Petroleum Co., 1956–58; Marketing Manager, Shell Co. of Philippines, Ltd, Manila, 1958–61; President, 1961–64; Head of Regional Marketing Div., Shell International Petroleum Co., London, 1964–66; Marketing Coordinator, 1966–70; seconded to HM Govt (Mr Heath's Admin) as Head of Business Team, 1970–72; Dir and Group Personnel Co-ordinator, Shell International Petroleum Co. Ltd, 1972–76. Director: Foseco Minsep, later Foseco plc, 1976–89 (Dep. Chm., 1986–89); Coates Bros plc, 1976–83 (Chm., 1978–83); Portals Hldgs, 1976–88. Vice-Pres., Assoc. of Optometrists, 1988–95. Chm. Council, Univ. of Surrey, 1980–85. DL, 1983, High Sheriff, 1984, Surrey. Master, Worshipful Co. of Spectacle Makers, 1985–87. CIMgt; FInstD; Hon. FCOptom; FRSA. DUniv Surrey, 1988. Officer of Philippine Legion of Honour, 1964. *Recreations:* gardening, walking. *Address:* 31 Mayfield, Rowledge, Farnham, Surrey GU10 4DZ. *T:* (01252) 794726. *Clubs:* Royal Over-Seas League, Institute of Directors.

MEYLER, John William F.; *see* Forbes-Meyler.

MEYNELL, Benedict William; Hon. Director-General, Commission of the European Communities, since 1981; *b* 17 Feb. 1930; *s* of late Sir Francis Meynell, RDI, and of Lady (Vera) Meynell, MA; *m* 1st, 1950, Hildamarie (*née* Hendricks) (marr. diss. 1965); two *d*; 2nd, 1967, Diana (*née* Himbury) (marr. diss. 1971). *Educ:* Beltane Sch.; Geneva Univ. (Licencié-ès-sciences politiques); Magdalen Coll., Oxford (Doncaster schol.; MA). Asst Principal, Bd of Inland Revenue, 1954–56; Asst Principal, BoT, 1957–59, Principal, 1959–68; Principal British Trade Commissioner, Kenya, 1962–64; Board of Trade: Principal Private Sec. to Pres., 1967–68; Asst Sec., 1968–70; Commercial Counsellor, Brit. Embassy, Washington, DC, 1970–73; a Dir, EEC, responsible for relations with Far East, and for commercial safeguards and textiles negotiations, 1973–77, for relations with N America, Japan and Australasia, 1977–81. *Publications:* (paper) International Regulation of Aircraft Noise, 1971; contribs: Japan and Western Europe, ed Tsoukalis and White, 1982; A Survey of External Relations, in Yearbook of European Law 1982; Servir l'Etat, 1987 (Cahiers de l'Homme series). *Address:* New Cottage, Greatham Lane, Pulborough, West Sussex RH20 2ES. *T:* (01798) 872688. *Club:* Savile.

MEYRIC HUGHES, Henry Andrew Carne; independent curator and consultant; Director of Exhibitions, South Bank Centre (Hayward Gallery, National Touring Exhibitions, Arts Council Collection), 1992–96; *b* 1 April 1942; *s* of late Reginald Richard Meyric Hughes and of Jean Mary Carne Meyric Hughes (*née* Pratt); *m* 1968, Alison Hamilton Faulds; one *s* one *d*. *Educ:* Shrewsbury Sch.; Univs of Rennes and Munich; University Coll., Oxford (BA Hons); Univ. of Sussex (MA). British Council, 1968–92: Berlin, Lima, Paris, Milan, London; Dir, Fine Arts Dept, later Visual Arts Dept, 1986–92. British Comr, Venice Biennale and São Paulo Bienal, 1986–92. Dir, Riverside Trust, 1986–95; Mem. Court, RCA, 1986–92; Mem., Faculty of Fine Arts, British Sch. at Rome, 1988–94. Board Member: Manifesta (formerly Eur. Visual Arts Manifestation), 1993– (Chm., 1995–97, 1998; Hon. Pres.); Internat. Assoc. of Curators of Contemp. Art Exhibs, 1992–97; Inst. of Internat. Visual Arts, 1995–; Konsthallen, Göteborg, 1995–2000. Member, Scientific Committee: Museum Moderner Kunst Stiftung Ludwig Wein, Vienna, 2001–; Galleria d'Arte Moderna, Bologna, 2001–. Silver Medal, Czech Soc. for Internat. Cultural Relations, 1986. Officier, l'Ordre Nat. des Arts et des Lettres (France), 1997. *Publications:* articles on visual arts and cultural relations, UK and overseas, 1966–. *Recreations:* music, reading, Europe. *Address:* 13 Ashchurch Grove, W12 9BT. *T:* and *Fax:* (020) 8749 4098.

MEYRICK, Sir David (John Charlton), 4th Bt *cr* 1880; *b* 2 Dec. 1926; *s* of Colonel Sir Thomas Frederick Meyrick, 3rd Bt, TD, DL, JP, and Ivy Frances (*d* 1947), *d* of Lt-Col F. C. Pilkington, DSO; *S* father, 1983; *m* 1962, Penelope Anne, *d* of late Comdr John Bertram Aubrey Marsden-Smedley, RN; three *s*. *Educ:* Eton; Trinity Hall, Cambridge (MA). FRICS. *Heir: s* Timothy Thomas Charlton Meyrick, [*b* 5 Nov. 1963. *Educ:* Eton; Bristol Univ.]. *Address:* Bush House, Gumfreston, Tenby, Pembrokeshire SA70 8RA.

MEYRICK, Sir George (Christopher Cadafael Tapps Gervis), 7th Bt *cr* 1791, of Hinton Admiral; *b* 10 March 1941; *s* of Sir George David Eliott Tapps Gervis Meyrick, 6th Bt, MC and of Ann, *d* of late Clive Miller; *S* father, 1988; *m* 1968, Jean Louise, *d* of late Lord William Montagu Douglas Scott and of Lady William Montagu Douglas Scott; two *s* one *d*. *Educ:* Eton; Trinity College, Cambridge (MA). FRICS. *Heir: s* George William Owen Tapps Gervis Meyrick, *b* 3 April 1970. *Address:* Hinton Admiral, Christchurch, Dorset BH23 7DU; Bodorgan, Isle of Anglesey LL62 5LW. *Club:* White's.

MEYSEY-THOMPSON, Sir (Humphrey) Simon, 4th Bt *cr* 1874; *b* 31 March 1935; *s* of Guy Herbert Meysey-Thompson (*d* 1961), and Miriam Beryl Meysey-Thompson (*d* 1985); *S* kinsman, Sir Algar de Clifford Charles Meysey-Thompson, 1967. *Address:* 10 Church Street, Woodbridge, Suffolk IP12 1DH.

MIAKWE, Hon. Sir Akepa, KBE 1989 (OBE 1982); Chairman, Eastern Highlands Development Corporation, Papua New Guinea, since 1982; *b* 1934; *s* of Umakue Miakwe and Obio Opae; *m* Kora Maho; seven *s* five *d*. *Educ:* Grade 3, Kabiufa Primary Sch. Local Govt Councillor, 1960–77 (Pres., 1962–64, Sen. Vice-Pres., 1965–72); MP Goroka, 1972–76, Unggai/Bena, 1977–82; Minister for Correctional Services and Liquor Licensing under Nat. Party. Mem. Bd Dirs, Eastern Highlands Capital Authority, 1989–; Dir, New Guinea Highlands Coffee Exports Pty Ltd, 1992–. Mem. Council, Univ. of Papua New Guinea, 1991–94. *Address:* Eastern Highlands Development Corporation Pty Ltd, PO Box 971, Goroka, Eastern Highlands Province, Papua New Guinea. *T:* 7322057, *Fax:* 7321961.

MIALL, (Rowland) Leonard, OBE 1961; research historian; *b* 6 Nov. 1914; *e s* of late Rowland Miall and S. Grace Miall; *m* 1st, 1941, Lorna (*d* 1974), *o d* of late G. John Rackham; three *s* one *d*; 2nd, 1975, Sally Bicknell, *e d* of late Gordon Leith. *Educ:* Bootham Sch., York (Scholar); Freiburg Univ.; St John's Coll., Cambridge (Sizar), MA. Pres. Cambridge Union, 1936; Ed. Cambridge Review, 1936. Lectured in US, 1937; Sec. British-American Associates, 1937–39; joined BBC; inaugurated talks broadcast to Europe, 1939; BBC German Talks and Features Editor, 1940–42. Mem. British Political Warfare Mission to US, 1942–44 (Dir of News, San Francisco, 1943; Head of New York Office, 1944); Personal Asst to Dep. Dir-Gen., Political Warfare Exec., London, 1944; attached to Psychological Warfare Division of SHAEF, Luxembourg, 1945. Rejoined BBC: Special Correspondent, Czechoslovakia, 1945; Actg Diplomatic Corresp., 1945; Chief Corresp. in US, 1945–53; Head of Television Talks, 1954; Asst Controller, Current Affairs and Talks, Television, 1961; Special Asst to Dir of Television, planning start of BBC-2, 1962; Asst Controller, Programme Services, Television, BBC, 1963–66; BBC Rep. in US, 1966–70; Controller, Overseas and Foreign Relations, BBC, 1971–74; Research Historian, BBC, 1975–84. Inaugurated BBC Lunchtime Lectures, 1962; Advisor, Cttee on Broadcasting, New Delhi, 1965; Delegate to Commonwealth Broadcasting Confs, Jamaica, 1970, Kenya, 1972, Malta, 1974. Dir, Visnews Ltd (Dep. Chm., 1984–85); Overseas Dir, BAFTA, 1974–; Mem. Council, RTS, 1984–91. FRTS 1986; FRSA. Cert. of Appreciation, NY City, 1970. *Publications:* Richard Dimbleby, Broadcaster, 1966; Inside the BBC, 1994; contribs to DNB and various jls. *Recreation:* writing. *Address:* Maryfield Cottage, High Street, Taplow, Maidenhead, Berks SL6 0EX. *T:* (01628) 604195. *Clubs:* Garrick; Union (Cambridge).

MICHAEL, Rt Hon. Alun (Edward); PC 1998; JP; MP (Lab and Co-op) Cardiff South and Penarth, since 1987; Minister of State (Minister for Rural Affairs), Department for Environment, Food and Rural Affairs, since 2001; *b* 22 Aug. 1943; *m* 1966, Mary Crawley; two *s* three *d*. *Educ:* Colwyn Bay GS; Keele Univ. (BA Hons English and Phil.). Journalist, South Wales Echo, 1966–71; Youth and Community Worker, Cardiff, 1972–84; Area Community Education Officer, Grangetown and Butetown, 1984–87. Mem., Cardiff City Council, 1973– 89 (sometime Chm., Finance, Planning, Performance Review, and Econ. Develt, and Chief Whip, Labour Gp). Dir, Cardiff and Vale Enterprise. An Opposition Whip, 1987–88; Opposition frontbench spokesman: on Welsh Affairs, 1988–92; on Home Affairs and the voluntary sector, 1992–97; Minister of State, Home Office, 1997–98; Sec. of State for Wales, 1998–99; Mem. (Lab and Co-op) Wales Mid and West, and First Sec. for Wales, Nat. Assembly for Wales, 1999–2000. Chairman: Co-operative Parly Gp, 1988–92; Parly Friends of Co-operative Ideal, 1988–92; Member: Nat. Exec., Co-op. Party, 1988–92; Parly Cttee, Co-op. Union, 1988–94. Chairman: All-Party Gp on Alcohol Misuse, 1991–93; All-Party, Penal Affairs Gp; Parly Friends of WNO, 1991–; Jt Chm., All-Party Gp on Somalia, 1989–; Vice-Chm., All-Party Penal Affairs Gp, 1991–; Jt Sec., All-Party Gp for Further and Tertiary Educn, 1990–; Sec., All-Party Panel for Personal Social Services, 1990–93. Mem. Bd, Crime Concern. Vice-Pres., YHA; formerly Mem. Exec., Nat. Youth Bureau. Formerly Vice-Pres., Bldg Socs Assoc. Dep. Chm., Cardiff Bay Opera House Trust, 1994–96; Mem. Bd, Cardiff and Vale Enterprise, 1982–93; plays leading role locally in community develt projects. JP Cardiff, 1972 (Chm., Cardiff Juvenile Bench, 1986–87; formerly Mem., S Glam Probation Cttee). *Recreations:* long-distance running, mountain walking, opera, listening to classical music, reading. *Address:* House of Commons, SW1A 0AA. *T:* (020) 7219 3441. *Clubs:* Penarth Labour; Grange Stars; Earlswood.

MICHAEL, Sir Duncan, Kt 2001; PhD; FREng; Chairman of Trustees, Ove Arup Partnership, since 1995 (Director, since 1977); *b* 26 May 1937; *s* of Donald Michael and Lydia Cameron MacKenzie; *m* 1960, Joan Clay; two *s* one *d*. *Educ:* Beauly Public School; Inverness Royal Academy. BSc Edinburgh; PhD Leeds. FICE 1975; FIStructE 1975; FREng (FEng 1984); FHKIE 1981. Lectr, Leeds Univ., 1961; Ove Arup Partnership: Engr, 1962; Chm., 1995–2000. Member: Council, IStructE, 1977–80, 1983–89; Jt Bd of Moderators of Engrg Instns, 1985–92; SE Asia Trade Adv. Group, BOTB, 1982–85; Civil Engineering Cttee, SERC, 1980–83; Council, Royal Acad. Engrg, 1994– (Chm., Awards Cttee, 1995–99; Vice Pres., 1999–); Vice-Chm., Council of Tall Buildings & Urban Habitat, 1980–96; Member: Educn and Trng Affairs Cttee, CBI, 1997–; State of the Nation Assessment Panel, ICE, 2000–. Chairman: Engrg Adv. Bd, Aberdeen Univ., 1998–; Adv. Bd, Master of Research, Univ. of Dundee, 2000–; Steering Gp on Design for Sustainable Engrg, Univ. of Cambridge, 2000–; Member: Industrial Adv. Cttee, Churchill Coll., Cambridge, 2000–; Academic Adv. Bd, Univ. of Highlands and Islands proj. Fellowship of Engrg Vis. Prof., Aberdeen Univ., 1989–94; Vis. Prof., Leeds Univ., 1990–94. Fellow, Inst. of Scottish Shipbldrs and Engrs, 2000; Mem., Smeatonian Soc. of Civil Engrs. Hon. DEng: Abertay Dundee, 1997; UMIST, 1999; Hon. DSc Aberdeen, 2001. Gold Medal, IStructE, 2000. *Publications:* Skyscrapers, 1987; lectures and engineering papers in technical jls. *Recreations:* garden, Scottish archaeology, opera. *Address:* 21 Marryat Road, SW19 5BB. *Club:* Caledonian.

MICHAEL, Prof. Ian David Lewis; King Alfonso XIII Professor of Spanish Studies, University of Oxford, since 1982; Fellow, Exeter College, Oxford, since 1982; *b* 26 May 1936; *o s* of late Cyril George Michael and Glenys Morwen (*née* Lewis). *Educ:* Neath Grammar Sch.; King's Coll., London (BA First Class Hons Spanish 1957); PhD Manchester 1967. University of Manchester: Asst Lectr in Spanish, 1957–60; Lectr in Spanish, 1960–69; Sen. Lectr in Spanish, 1969–70; University of Southampton: Prof. of Spanish and Hd of Spanish Dept, 1971–82; Dep. Dean, Faculty of Arts, 1975–77, 1980–82; Sen. Curator and Chm., Univ. Library Cttee, 1980–82; Oxford University: Curator, Taylor Instn, 1994–2000; Chm., Faculty Bd of Mod. Langs, 1999–2000. Leverhulme Faculty Fellow in European Studies (at Madrid), 1977–78; first British-Spanish Foundn Vis. Prof., Complutensian Univ., Madrid, 1993–94. Member: Gp of Three for Spain (Humanities research review), Eur. Science Foundn, 1987; Welsh Acad. (Eng. Lang. Section), 1995–. Pres., Assoc. of Hispanists of GB and Ire., 1990–92. Comdr, Order of Isabel la Católica (Spain), 1986. *Publications:* The Treatment of Classical Material in the Libro de Alexandre, 1970; Spanish Literature and Learning to 1474, in, Spain: a Companion to Spanish studies, 1973, 3rd edn 1977; The Poem of the Cid, 1975, new edn 1984; Poema de Mio Cid, 1976, 2nd edn 1979; Gwyn Thomas, 1977; chapter on Poem of My Cid in New Pelican Guide to English Literature. I ii, 1983; (ed) Sound on Vision: studies on Spanish cinema, 1999; (ed) Context, Meaning and Reception of Celestina, 2000; articles in various learned jls and Festschriften; *as David Serafín:* Saturday of Glory, 1979 (John Creasey Meml Award, CWA, 1980); Madrid Underground, 1982; Christmas Rising, 1982; The Body in Cadiz Bay, 1985; Port of Light, 1987; The Angel of Torremolinos, 1988. *Recreations:* horticulture; collecting Art Nouveau and Art Déco, particularly ceramics; writing pseudonymous fiction; opera. *Address:* Exeter College, Oxford OX1 3DP. *T:* (01865) 270484, *Fax:* (01865) 270757. *Club:* Organon.

MICHAEL, Ian (Lockie), CBE 1972; Deputy Director, Institute of Education, University of London, 1973–78; *b* 30 Nov. 1915; 4th *c* of late Reginald Warburton Michael and Margaret Campbell Kerr; *m* 1942, Mary Harborne Bayley, *e c* of late Rev. William Henry Bayley; one *s* one *d*. *Educ:* St Bees Sch.; private study. BA (London) 1938; PhD (Bristol) 1963. Schoolmaster: St Faith's Sch., Cambridge, 1935–40; Junior Sch., Leighton Park, 1941–45, Headmaster, 1946–49; Lectr in Educn, Bristol Univ., 1950–63; Prof. of Educn, Khartoum Univ., 1963–64; Vice-Chancellor, Univ. of Malaŵi, 1964–73. Leverhulme Emeritus Fellowship, 1978–79, 1979–80; Vis. Prof. of Educn, Univ. of Cape Town, 1981. Hon. DLitt Malaŵi, 1974. *Publications:* English Grammatical Categories and the Tradition to 1800, 1970; The Teaching of English from the Sixteenth Century to 1870, 1987; Early Textbooks of English, 1993; Literature in School 1700–1830, 1999. *Address:* 9 Cornwallis House, Cornwallis Grove, Bristol BS8 4PG. *T:* (0117) 973 5977.

MICHAEL, Sir Peter (Colin), Kt 1989; CBE 1983; CIMgt; Chairman: Classic FM, since 1993 (Director, since 1991); Pilot Investment Trust, 1993–97; *b* 17 June 1938; *s* of Albert and Enid Michael; *m* 1962, Margaret Baldwin; two *s*. *Educ:* Whitgift Sch., Croydon; Queen Mary Coll., Univ. of London (BSc Elec. Engrg; Fellow, 1983). Chairman: Micro Consultants Group, 1969–85; Quantel Ltd, 1974–89; Databasix Ltd, 1986–88; UEI plc, 1986–89 (Dep. Chm., 1981–85); Cray Electronics, 1989–93. Dir, Rutherford Asset Management, 1995–97; non-executive Director: GWR Gp plc, 1996–; Altodigital plc, 1999–. Chairman: Peter Michael Winery, Calif, 1982–; Donnington Valley Hotel, 1991–; The Vineyard at Stockcross, 1997–; Pelican Cancer Centre, 1999–; Virtual Music Store Ltd, 2000–. Member: Adv. Council for Applied R&D, 1982–85; NCB, 1983–86; ACARD Sub-Gp on Annual Review of Govt Funded R&D, 1985–86; Technol. Requirements Bd, DTI, 1986–88; Adv. Cttee, Royal Mint, 1999–. Paper on City financing of electronics companies to PITCOM, 1988. Chairman: Royal Soc. of British Sculptors Appeal, 1992; Chelsea Harbour '93 Internat. Sculpture Exhibn Appeal; The Sculpture Company, 1995–99. Chm., Greenham Common Community Trust, 1996–. Lectures: Humphrey Davies, QMC, 1984; IEE Electronics, 1984. Freeman, Goldsmiths' Co., 1984. Freeman, City of London, 1984; Liveryman, Goldsmiths' Co., 1988. CIMgt (CBIM 1982). FRSA 1984. Hon. FBKSTS 1981. The Guardian Young Businessman of the Year, 1982. *Recreations:* tennis, opera, classical music, wine, sculpture, writing rhyme. *Address:* (office) 3 The Pentangle, Park Street, Newbury, Berks RG14 1EA. *T:* (01635) 552502.

MICHAELS, Prof. Leslie, MD; FRCPath, FRCP(C); Professor of Pathology, Institute of Laryngology and Otology, London University, 1973–90 (Dean, 1976–81); Emeritus Professor, Department of Histopathology, University College London Medical School (formerly University College and Middlesex School of Medicine), since 1990; *b* 24 July 1925; *s* of Henry and Minnie Michaels; *m* Edith (*née* Waldstein); two *d*. *Educ:* Parmiter's Sch., London; King's Coll., London; Westminster Med. Sch., London (MB, BS; MD). FRCPath 1963, FRCP(C) 1962. Asst Lectr in Pathology, Univ. of Manchester, 1955–57; Lectr in Path., St Mary's Hosp. Med. Sch., London, 1957–59; Asst Prof. of Path., Albert Einstein Coll. of Medicine, New York, 1959–61; Hosp. Pathologist, Northern Ont, Canada, 1961–70; Sen. Lectr, Inst. of Laryn. and Otol., 1970–73. *Publications:* Pathology of the Larynx, 1984; Ear, Nose and Throat Histopathology, 1987, 2nd edn 2001; scientific articles in jls of medicine, pathology and otolaryngology. *Recreations:* reading, music, walking. *Address:* Romany Ridge, Hillbrow Road, Bromley, Kent BR1 4JL.

MICHAELS-MOORE, Anthony; *see* Moore.

MICHEL, Prof. (Christopher) Charles, DPhil; Professor of Physiology, Imperial College School of Medicine (formerly St Mary's Hospital Medical School), 1984–2000; *b* 23 March 1938; *s* of late Maurice and May Michel; *m* 1965, Rosalind McCrink; one *s* one *d*. *Educ:* Leeds Grammar Sch.; Queen's Coll., Oxford (BA 1959, 1st cl. Physiol.; MA, DPhil 1962; BM BCh 1965). MRCP 1986, FRCP 1996. US Public Health Postdoctoral Res. Fellow, 1962; Oxford University: Deptl Demonstrator in Physiol., 1964–67; Univ. Lectr in Physiol., 1967–84; Fellow and Praelector in Physiol., Queen's Coll., 1966–84. Lectures: Oliver-Sharpey, RCP, 1985; Annual Prize Review, Physiol. Soc., 1987; Starling Centenary, World Congress for Microcirculation, 1996. Sec., Physiol Soc., 1980–83; Chm., RN Personnel Res. Cttee, 1991–96, Army Personnel Res. Cttee, 1993–94, MRC. Hon. Mem., Amer. Physiol. Soc., 1993. Malpighi Prize, Eur. Soc. for Micro-circulation, 1984. *Publications:* (ed with E. M. Renkin) American Handbook of Physiology: the microcirculation, 1984; articles in learned jls. *Recreations:* running, walking, reading. *Address:* Sundial House, High Street, Alderney, Channel Islands GY9 3UG.

MICHEL, Prof. Dr Hartmut; Director, Max-Planck-Institut of Biophysics, Frankfurt am Main, since 1987; *b* Ludwigsburg, W Germany, 18 July 1948; *s* of Karl Michel and Frieda Michel; *m* 1979, Ilona Leger-Michel; one *s* one *d*. *Educ:* Universities of: Tübingen (Dip. in biochem.); Würzburg (PhD); Munich (habilitation for biochemistry, 1986). Res. associate with D. Oesterhelt, Univ. of Würzburg, 1977–79; group leader in D. Oesterhelt's dept, Max-Planck-Inst. of Biochemistry, Martinsried, until 1987. Various prizes, including: Biophysics Prize of Amer. Phys. Soc., 1986; Otto Klung Prize for Chemistry, 1986; (jtly) Otto Bayer Prize, 1988; (jtly) Nobel Prize for Chemistry, 1988. *Publication:* (ed) Crystallization of Membrane Proteins, 1990. *Recreations:* nature, wild life, physical exercise, readings on history and travel. *Address:* Max-Planck-Institut für Biophysik, Heinrich-Hoffmann-Strasse 7, 60528 Frankfurt am Main, Germany. *T:* (69) 96769401, *Fax:* (69) 96769423.

MICHEL, Louis; Deputy Prime Minister and Minister of Foreign Affairs, since 1999, and Senator, Belgium; *b* 2 Sept. 1947; *m*; two *c*. German lang. teacher, 1968; Lectr, Inst. Supérieur de Commerce, St Louis; Prof. of Dutch, English and German Lit., Ecole Normale Provinciale, Jodoigne, 1968–78. MHR (PRL), 1978–99; Mem., parly commns on Finance, Budget, Instnl Reforms, and Commn on supervising electoral expenditures. Mem., Benelux Interparly Consultative Council. Dep. Pres., Liberal Internat. Mem. Bd, ELDR. Liberal Reform Party (PRL): Sec.-Gen., 1980–82; Pres., 1982–90 and 1995–; Pres., Parly Gp in Council of Walloon Reg., 1991–92; Parly Gp in House of Reps, 1992–95. Alderman, 1977–83, Mayor, 1983–, Jodoigne. Comdr, Order of Leopold (Belgium); Grand-Croix, Order of: Royal Suédois de l'Etoile Polaire (Sweden), 2001; Infante Dom Henrique (Portugal), 2000; Orange-Nassau (Netherlands), 2000; Isabel la Católica (Spain). *Publications:* (with D. Ducarme) Le defi vert, 1980; (with P. Monfils) L'enfant, 1984; Libres et forts-project éducatif pour réussir le futur, 1986; Wallons et optimistes, 1997; De echte Walen, 1997; Rendre Confiance, 1998; Objectif 100 La Wallonnie j'y crois!, 1998. *Address:* Ministry of Foreign Affairs, Rue des Petits Carmes 15, 1000 Brussels, Belgium. *T:* (2) 5018211.

MICHELL, John; *see* Michell, M. J.

MICHELL, Keith; actor since 1948; *b* Adelaide; *s* of Joseph Michell and Alice Maud (*née* Aslat); *m* 1957, Jeannette Sterke; one *s* one *d*. *Educ:* Port Pirie High Sch.; Adelaide Teachers' Coll.; Sch. of Arts and Crafts; Adelaide Univ.; Old Vic Theatre School. Formerly taught art. *Stage:* First appearance, Playbox, Adelaide, 1947; Young Vic Theatre Co., 1950–51; first London appearance, And So To Bed, 1951; Shakespeare Meml. Theatre Co., 1952–56, inc. Australian tour, 1952–53 (Henry IV Part 1, As You Like It, Midsummer Night's Dream, Troilus and Cressida, Romeo and Juliet, Taming of the Shrew, All's Well That Ends Well, Macbeth, Merry Wives of Windsor); Don Juan, Royal Court, 1956; Old Vic Co., 1956 (Antony and Cleopatra, Much Ado about Nothing, Two Gentlemen of Verona, Titus Andronicus); Irma La Douce, Lyric, 1958, Washington, DC, 1960 and Broadway, 1960–61; The Chances, Chichester Festival, 1962; The Rehearsal, NY, 1963; The First Four Hundred Years, Australia and NZ, 1964; Robert and Elizabeth, Lyric, 1964; The King's Mare, 1966; Man of La Mancha, 1968–69, NY, 1970; Abelard and Heloise, 1970, Los Angeles and NY, 1971; Hamlet, Globe, 1972; Dear Love, Comedy, 1973; The Crucifer of Blood, Haymarket, 1979; On the Twentieth Century (musical), Her Majesty's, 1980; Pete McGynty and the Dreamtime (own adap. of Peer Gynt), Melbourne Theatre Co., 1981; Captain Beaky Christmas Show, Lyric, Shaftesbury Ave., 1981–82; The Tempest, Brisbane, 1982; opened Keith Michell Theatre, Port Pirie, with one-man show, 1982; Amadeus (UK tour), 1983; La Cage Aux Folles, San Francisco and NY, 1984, Sydney and Melbourne, 1985; Portraits, Malvern Fest., 1987; Aspects of Love, Edmonton and Toronto, 1991–92, Chicago, 1992; Scrooge, Melbourne, 1993; Caesar and Cleopatra, Edmonton, 1994; Brazilian Blue, Brisbane, 1995; Family Matters (tour), 1998; *Chichester Festival Theatre:* Artistic Director, 1974–77; Tonight We Improvise, Oedipus Tyrannus, 1974; Cyrano de Bergerac, Othello, 1975; (dir and designed) Twelfth Night, 1976; Monsieur Perrichon's Travel, 1976; The Apple Cart, 1977; (dir and designed) In Order of Appearance, 1977; Murder in the Cathedral (Chichester Cathedral), 1977; Henry VIII, 1991; toured Australia with Chichester Co., 1978 (Othello, The Apple Cart); acted in: On the Rocks, 1982; Jane Eyre, 1986; The Royal Baccarat Scandal, 1988, transf. Theatre Royal Haymarket, 1989; Henry VIII, 1991; Monsieur Amilcar (Minerva), 1995. *Films include:* Dangerous Exile; The Hell Fire Club; Seven Seas to Calais; The Executioner; House of Cards; Prudence and the Pill; Henry VIII and his Six Wives; Moments, The Deceivers. *Television includes:* Henry VIII in the Six Wives of Henry VIII (series), 1972; Keith Michell at Chichester, 1974; My Brother Tom, 1986; Captain James Cook, 1987; Murder She Wrote (series), 1990. Many recordings.

First exhibn of paintings, 1959; subseq. one-man exhibns at John Whibley Gall., London, Wright Hepburn and Webster Gall., NY, Century Gall., Henley-on-Thames, Wylma Wayne Gall., London, Vincent Gall., Adelaide. Many awards. *Publications:* (ed and illus.) Twelve Shakespeare Sonnets (series of lithographs produced 1974), 1981; illus. and recorded Captain Beaky series, 1975; (also illus.) Practically Macrobiotic, 1987. *Recreations:* painting, photography, swimming, cooking. *Address:* c/o Chatto & Linnit, 123a Kings Road, SW3 4PL.

MICHELL, Michael John; Director: Prestbury Enterprises Ltd; Agip UK Ltd; *b* 12 Dec. 1942; *s* of late John Martin Michell and of Pamela Mary Michell; *m* 1st, 1965, Pamela Marianne Tombs (marr. diss. 1978); two *s* (one *d* decd); 2nd, 1978, Alison Mary Macfarlane; two *s*. *Educ:* Marlborough College; Corpus Christi College, Cambridge (BA 1964). Min. of Aviation, 1964; Private Sec. to Sir Ronald Melville, 1968–69; Concorde Div., 1969–73; Sec. to Sandilands Cttee on inflation accounting, 1973–75; Private Sec. to Sec. of State for Industry, 1975–77; HM Treasury, 1977–80; Industrial Policy Div., Dept of Industry, 1980–82; RCDS 1983; Department of Trade and Industry: Head, Air Div., 1884–88; Chief Exec., Radio Div., subseq. Radiocommunications Agency, 1988–93; Head, Oil and Gas Div., 1993–98. *Address:* 10 Ebury Bridge Road, SW1W 8PZ. *Club:* Brooks's.

MICHELL, Prof. Robert Hall, FRS 1986; Royal Society Research Professor at the University of Birmingham, since 1987; *b* 16 April 1941; *s* of Rowland Charles Michell and Elsie Lorna Michell; two *s* one *d*. *Educ:* Crewkerne School, Somerset; Univ. of Birmingham (BSc Med. Biochem. and Pharmacol. 1962; PhD Med. Biochem. 1965; DSc 1978). Research Fellow, Birmingham, 1965–66, 1968–70, Harvard Med. Sch., 1966–68; Birmingham University: Lectr in Biochemistry, 1970–81; Sen. Lectr, 1981–84; Reader, 1984–86; Prof. of Biochemistry, 1986–87. Mem., Physiol. Systems and Disorders Bd, 1985–90, Chm., Grants Cttee B, 1988–90, MRC; Member: Fellowships Cttee, BHF, 1992–97; Fellowships Selection Panel, Lister Inst. of Preventive Medicine, 1999–; Vice-Chm., Fellowship Review Panel, Human Frontiers Sci. Prog. Mem., Biochem. Panel, 1996 RAE, Biol Scis Panel, 2001 RAE, HEFCE. Member: Adv. Bd, Beit Meml Trust, 1993–; Council, Royal Soc., 1996–97; Pres., Med. Scis Sect., BAAS, 1993–94. Mem., EMBO, 1991. Member, Editorial Boards: Jl Neurochem., 1974–80; Cell Calcium, 1979–89; Biochem. Jl, 1983–88; Current Opinion in Cell Biology, 1988–; Procs Royal Soc. B, 1989–97; Jl of Molecular Endocrinology, 1992–99; Molecular Membrane Biology, 1993–. CIBA Medal, Biochemical Soc., 1988. *Publications:* (with J. B. Finean and R. Coleman) Membranes and their Cellular Functions, 1974, 3rd edn 1984; (ed with J. B. Finean) Membrane Structure, vol. 1 of New Comprehensive Biochemistry, 1981; (ed with J. W. Putney, Jr) Inositol Lipids in Cellular Signalling, 1987; (ed with M. J. Berridge) Inositol Lipids and Transmembrane Signalling, 1988; (ed jtly) Inositol Lipids and Cellular Signalling, 1989; contribs to Nature, Biochem. Jl and sci. jls. *Recreations:* birdwatching, wilderness, pottery. *Address:* 59 Weoley Park Road, Birmingham B29 6QZ. *T:* (0121) 472 1356.

MICHELL, Roger Harry; director; *b* 5 June 1956; *s* of H. D. Michell, DSO, DFC, and Jillian Green; *m* 1992, Kate Buffery; one *s* one *d*. *Educ:* Clifton Coll., Bristol; Queens' Coll., Cambridge (BA Hons). With Royal Court Th., 1978–80, Royal Shakespeare Th., 1985–91. Judith E. Wilson Sen. Fellow, Cambridge Univ., 1990. *Plays* include: Private Dick, Edinburgh and Whitehall, 1980; The Catch, Royal Court, 1981; White Glove, Lyric, Hammersmith, 1982; Marya, Old Vic., 1990; My Night with Reg, Royal Court and Criterion, 1995; Some Sunny Day, Hampstead, 1996; Royal Shakespeare Company: Merchant of Venice, 1986; Dead Monkey, 1986; Hamlet, 1987; Temptation, 1987; Conversation, 1987; Constant Couple, 1988; Restoration, 1988; Some Americans Abroad, 1989; Redevelopment, 1989; Two Shakespearian Actors, 1990; Royal National Theatre: The Coup, 1991; Under Milk Wood, 1995; The Homecoming, 1997; Blue/Orange, 2000; *television* includes: Buddha of Suburbia, 1994; Ready When You Are, Mr Patel, 1995; My Night with Reg, 1997; Michael Redgrave, My Father, 1998; *films:* Persuasion, 1995; Titanic Town, 1999; Notting Hill, 1999; Changing Lanes, 2001. *Recreations:* children, cooking, wines of Southern Rhône. *Address:* c/o ICM, 79 Oxford Street, W1N 9FD.

MICHELMORE, Clifford Arthur, CBE 1969; Television Broadcaster and Producer; Managing Director: Michelmore Enterprises Ltd, since 1969; Communications Consultants Ltd, since 1969; Director, CP Video, since 1988; *b* 11 Dec. 1919; *s* of late Albert, (Herbert), Michelmore and Ellen Alford; *m* 1950, Jean Metcalfe (Broadcaster) (*d* 2000); one *s* one *d*. *Educ:* Cowes Senior Sch., Isle of Wight. Entered RAF, 1935; commnd 1940; left RAF 1947. Head, Outside Broadcasts and Variety, BFN, 1948; Dep. Station Dir, BFN, also returned to freelance as Commentator and Producer, 1949. Entered Television, 1950. Man. Dir, RM/EMI Visual Programmes, 1971–81. Has taken part in numerous radio and television programmes in Britain, Europe and the USA. Introduced: "Tonight" series, 1957–65; 24 Hours series, 1965–68; General Election Results programmes, 1964, 1966, 1970; So You Think . . . ., 1966–; Our World, 1967; With Michelmore (interviews); Talkback; Apollo Space Programmes, 1960–70; Holiday, 1969–86; Chance to Meet, 1970–73; Wheelbase, 1972; Getaway, 1975; Globetrotter, 1975; Opinions Unlimited, 1977–79; Presenter: Day by Day (Southern TV), 1980; Sudden Change (HTV), 1982; Cliff Michelmore Show (BBC Radio), 1982–83; Home on Sunday (BBC TV), 1983–90; Waterlines (BBC Radio Four), 1984–94; Lifeline (BBC TV), 1986–96; Coastline (BBC Radio Four), 1991–94; Cliff's Country, 1992 (BBC Radio Four); Scrapbook, 1996; A Year to Remember, 1996– (BBC Radio Two). Made films: Shaping of a Writer, 1977; Hong Kong: the challenge, 1978. FRSA 1975. Television Society Silver Medal, 1957; Guild of TV Producers Award, Personality of the Year, 1958; TV Review Critics Award, 1959; Variety Club Award, 1961. *Publications:* (ed) The Businessman's Book of Golf, 1981; Cliff Michelmore's Holidays By Rail, 1986; (with Jean Metcalfe) Two-Way Story (autobiog.), 1986; Some of These Days, 1987; contribs to Highlife, Financial Weekly; various articles on television, broadcasting and travel. *Recreations:* golf, doing nothing. *Address:* Northend Barn, South Harting, Petersfield, Hants GU31 5NR. *T:* (01730) 825665. *Clubs:* Royal Air Force, MCC.

MICHELS, David Michael Charles; Chief Executive, Hilton Group plc, since 2000; *b* 8 Dec. 1946; *s* of Klaus Peter and Thelma Sadie Michels; *m* 1973, Michele Ann Arnold; one *s* one *d*. *Educ:* Hendon Coll. FHCIMA. Grand Metropolitan, 1966–81; Ladbrokes: Sales and Marketing Dir, Hotels, 1981–83; Man. Dir, Leisure Div., 1983–85; Man. Dir, Ladbroke Hotels, 1985–87; Hilton International: Sen. Vice-Pres., Sales and Marketing, 1987–89; Dep. Chm., Hilton UK and Exec. Vice-Pres., Hilton Worldwide, 1989–91; Chief Exec., Stakis plc, 1991–99; Chief Exec., Hilton Internat. Hotels, 1999–2000. Hon. DLitt Glasgow Caledonian, 1993. *Recreations:* tennis, poker, reading. *Address:* Hilton Group plc, Maple Court, Central Park, Reeds Crescent, Watford WD1 1HZ. *T:* (020) 7856 8000. *Club:* Vanderbilt.

MICHIE, family name of **Baroness Michie of Gallanach**.

MICHIE OF GALLANACH, Baroness *cr* 2001 (Life Peer), of Oban in Argyll and Bute; **Janet Ray Michie;** *b* 4 Feb. 1934; *d* of Baron Bannerman of Kildonan, OBE and Lady Bannerman of Kildonan; *m* 1957, Dr Iain Michie, MB, FRCP, *s* of Malcolm and Margaret Michie; three *d*. *Educ:* Aberdeen High Sch. for Girls; Lansdowne House Sch., Edinburgh; Edinburgh Coll. of Speech Therapy. LCST, MCST. Area Speech Therapist, Argyll and Clyde Health Board, 1977–87. Chm., Argyll Lib. Assoc., 1973–76; Vice-Chm., Scottish Lib. Party, 1977–79; Chair, Scottish Lib. Democrats, 1992–93. Contested (L): Argyll, 1979; Argyll and Bute, 1983. MP Argyll and Bute, 1987–2001 (L 1987–88, Lib Dem 1988–2001). Lib Dem spokesman on transport and rural devélt, 1987–88, on Scotland, 1988–97, on women's issues, 1988–94. Member: Select Cttee on Scottish Affairs, 1992–97; Chairmen's Panel, 1997–2001. Jt Vice Chm., All Party Parly Gp on Whisky Industry, 1990–2001. Member: Scottish NFU; Scottish Crofters' Union. Vice-Pres., Royal Coll. of Speech and Language Therapists, 1996–2001. Hon. Pres., Clyde Fishermen's Assoc. Hon. Associate, Nat. Council of Women of GB. *Recreations:* golf, swimming, gardening, watching Rugby. *Address:* House of Lords, SW1A 0PW. *Club:* National Liberal.

MICHIE, Prof. David Alan Redpath, OBE 1997; RSA 1972 (ARSA 1964); RGI 1984; Head, School of Drawing and Painting, Edinburgh College of Art, 1982–90; Professor Emeritus, Heriot-Watt University, 1991; *b* 30 Nov. 1928; *s* of late James Michie and late Anne Redpath, OBE, ARA, RSA; *m* 1951, Eileen Anderson Michie; two *d*. *Educ:* Edinburgh Coll. of Art (DA). National Service, 1947–49; Edinburgh Coll. of Art, 1949–53 (studied painting); travelling scholarship, Italy, 1953–54; Lectr in Painting, Gray's Sch. of Art, Aberdeen, 1958–62; Lectr in Painting, Edinburgh Coll. of Art, 1962–82, Vice-Principal, 1974–77. Visiting Professor of Painting: Acad. of Fine Art, Belgrade, 1979; Univ. of Calif, Santa Barbara, 1992. Member: Gen. Teaching Council for Scotland, 1976–80; Edinburgh Festival Soc., 1976–; Museums and Galls Commn, 1991–96. Mem. Court, Heriot-Watt Univ., 1979–82. Pres., Soc. of Scottish Artists, 1961–63. One Man Exhibitions: Mercury Gallery, London, 1967, 1969, 1971, 1974, 1980, 1983, 1992, 1996, 1999; Mercury Gall., Edinburgh, 1986; Lothian Region Chambers, 1977; Scottish Gall., Edinburgh, 1980, 1994, 1998; Kasteel de Hooge Vuursche, Baarn, Netherlands, 1991. RWA 1991–2000. FRSA 1990. *Recreation:* music. *Address:* 17 Gilmour Road, Edinburgh EH16 5NS. *T:* (0131) 667 2684.

MICHIE, Prof. Donald, DPhil (Oxon), DSc (Oxon); Professor of Machine Intelligence, Edinburgh University, 1967–84, Professor Emeritus, since 1984; *b* 11 Nov. 1923; *s* of late James Kilgour Michie and Marjorie Crain Michie; *m* 1st, 1949, Zena Margaret Davies (marr. diss.); one *s*; 2nd, 1952, Anne McLaren (marr. diss.); one *s* two *d*; 3rd, 1971, Jean Elizabeth Hayes (*née* Crouch). *Educ:* Rugby Sch.; Balliol Coll., Oxford (Schol., MA). Fellow Royal Soc. Edinburgh 1969; Fellow Brit. Computer Soc., 1971. War Service in FO, Bletchley, 1942–45; Res. Associate, Univ. of London, 1952–58; University of Edinburgh: Sen. Lectr, Surg. Science, 1958; Reader in Surg. Science, 1962; Dir of Expermtl Programming Unit, 1965; Chm. of Dept of Machine Intelligence and Perception, 1966; Dir, Machine Intelligence Res. Unit, 1974–84; Prof., Computer Sci., Univ. of Strathclyde, 1984–92; Turing Institute, Glasgow: Dir of Res., 1984–86; Chief Scientist, 1986–92; Sen. Fellow, 1992–94. Technical Dir, Intelligent Terminals Ltd (Knowledgelink), 1984–92. Royal Soc. Lectr in USSR, 1965; Wm Withering Lectr, Univ. of Birmingham, 1972; Vis. Lectr, USSR Acad. Sci., 1973, 1985; Geo. A. Miller Lectr, Univ. of Illinois, 1974, 1984; Herbert Spencer Lectr, Univ. of Oxford, 1976; Samuel Wilks Meml Lectr, Princeton Univ., 1978; S. L. A. Marshall Lectr, US Army Res. Inst. for the Behavioural and Soc. Scis, 1990; C. C. Garvin Lectr, Virginia Polytech. Inst. and State Univ., 1992. Chief Editor, Machine Intelligence series, 1967–. Chm., A. M. Turing Trust, 1975–97. Treas., Human-Computer Learning Foundn, 1995–. Fellow, Amer. Assoc. Artificial Intell., 1990. Hon. DSc: CNAA, 1991; Salford, 1992; Aberdeen, 1999; DUniv: Stirling, 1996; York, 2000. (With A. McLaren) Pioneer Award, Internat. Embryo Transfer Soc., 1988; Achievement Award, IEE, 1995; Feigenbaum Medal, World Congress on Expert Systems, 1996; Res. Excellence Award, Internat. Jt Conf. on Artificial Intelligence, 2001. *Publications:* (jtly) An Introduction to Molecular Biology, 1964; On Machine Intelligence, 1974, 2nd edn 1986; Machine Intelligence and Related Topics, 1982; (jtly) The Creative Computer, 1984; papers in tech. and sci. jls. *Recreation:* writing. *Address:* 6 Inveralmond Grove, Edinburgh EH4 6RA. *Club:* New (Edinburgh).

MICHIE, William; *b* 24 Nov. 1935; *m*; two *s*. *Educ:* Abbeydale Secondary Sch., Sheffield; Sheffield Polytechnic. Nat. Service, RAF, 1957–59. Formerly: apprentice electrician; maintenance electrician; Lab. Technician, Computer Applications; unemployed, 1981–83. Joined Labour Party, 1965; Co-op. Party, 1966. Mem., AEEU (formerly AUEW, then AEU), 1952– (former Br. Trustee; former Standing Orders Cttee Deleg., Lab. Party Yorks Regl Conf.). Member: Sheffield City Council, 1970–84 (Chairman: Planning, 1974–81; Employment, 1981–83; Gp Sec./Chief Whip, 1974–83); South Yorks CC, 1974–86 (Area Planning Chm., 1974–81). MP (Lab) Sheffield, Heeley, 1983–2001. Member: Privileges Select Cttee, 1994–96; Members' Interests Select Cttee, 1993–96; Jt Cttee on Parly Privilege, 1997–2001. Chm., AEEU Parly Gp, 1997–2001 (Mem., 1983–2001). *Recreations:* pub darts, gardening, Sheffield Wednesday.

MICKLEWHITE, Sir Michael; *see* Caine, Sir Michael.

MIDDLEBURGH, Rabbi Dr Charles Hadley; Executive Director, Union of Liberal and Progressive Synagogues, since 1997; *b* 2 Oct. 1956; *s* of late Hyman Middleburgh and of Elizabeth Middleburgh; *m* 1984, Gilly Blyth. *Educ:* Brighton Coll.; University Coll. London (BA Hons, PhD 1982); Leo Baeck Coll. Lay reader, Brighton and Hove Progressive Synagogue, 1975–77; Minister, Kingston Liberal Synagogue, 1977–83; ordained 1986; Rabbi, Harrow and Wembley Progressive Synagogue, 1983–97. Lectr in Bible, Aramaic, Rabbinic Practice, Leo Baeck Coll., 1985–. Occasional broadcaster, BBC Radio 4 and World Service, 1997–. FZS 1997; FRSA 1998. *Publications:* (Associate Ed.) Union of Liberal and Progressive Synagogues Daily, Sabbath and Festival Prayer Book, 1995; (ed jtly) Union of Liberal and Progressive Synagogues High Holy Days Prayerbook, 2002. *Recreations:* animal photography, running, cycling, needlepoint, horse-riding, playing with tigers. *Address:* Union of Liberal and Progressive Synagogues, Montagu Centre, 21 Maple Street, W1T 4BE. *T:* (020) 7580 1663; *e-mail:* charles@ulps.org.

MIDDLEHURST, Tom; Member (Lab) Alyn and Deeside, National Assembly for Wales, since 1999; *b* 25 June 1936; *s* of late James Middlehurst and Agnes Middlehurst; *m* 1986, Patricia Mary; one *s* one *d* from a previous marriage. *Educ:* Ormskirk Grammar Sch.; Wigan Tech. Coll.; Liverpool Poly. Engrg apprentice, 1952–57; Underground Engr, NCB, 1957–63; engr, 1963–71; Local Govt Officer, Flintshire, later Clwyd, CC, 1971–93. Mem. (Lab), Alyn and Deeside DC, 1986–95; Mem. (Lab), Clwyd CC, 1993–95 (Chm., Housing Cttee; Chm., Personnel Cttee); Leader (Lab), Flintshire CC, 1995–99. Chm., Welsh Local Govt Assoc., 1997–99. National Assembly for Wales: Sec. for Post-16 Educn and Training, 1999–2000; Mem., N Wales Cttee, 1999–. Mem., Labour Party, 1961–. *Address:* National Assembly for Wales, Cardiff Bay, Cardiff CF99 1NA.

MIDDLEMAS, Prof. Robert Keith; Professor of History, University of Sussex, 1986–98, now Emeritus; *b* 26 May 1935; *s* of late Robert James Middlemas, Solicitor and of Eleanor Mary (*née* Crane), Howick, Northumberland; *m* 1958, Susan Mary, *d* of

Laurence Edward Paul Tremlett and Marjorie Isobel Derrington Bell; one *s* three *d. Educ:* Stowe Sch.; Pembroke Coll., Cambridge (Exhibnr, scholar, BA 1st cl. History 1958); DPhil 1972, DLitt 1982, Sussex. 2nd Lieut, Northumberland Fusiliers, 1954–55 (served in Kenya); Clerk, House of Commons, 1958–66; Lectr in History, Univ. of Sussex, 1966–76, Reader, 1976–86. Visiting Professor: Stanford Univ. and Hoover Instn, Stanford, 1984; Univ. of Beijing, 1989. Member: UK Nat. Cttee, Unesco, 1980–86; Council, Inst. of Contemporary British History; Council and Res. Cttee, Foundn for Manufg and Industry, 1993–. FRSA. Co-Founder and Editor, Catalyst: a jl of public debate, 1985–87. *Publications:* The Master Builders, 1963; The Clydesiders, 1965; (with John Barnes) Baldwin, 1969; Diplomacy of Illusion, 1972; (ed) Thomas Jones: Whitehall Diary, vols I and II, 1969–70, vol. III, 1972; Politics in Industrial Society, 1979; Cabora Bassa, 1975; Power and the Party, 1980; Industry, Unions and Government, 1984; Power, Competition and the State, vol. I, Britain in Search of Balance 1940–61, 1986, vol. 2, Threats to the Post-War Settlement: Britain 1961–74, 1990; vol. 3, The End of the Post-War Era: Britain since 1974, 1991; Orchestrating Europe: informal politics of the European Community since 1973, 1995; articles and reviews in learned jls. *Recreations:* sports, sailing, fishing, landscape gardening; Member, UK Nat. Rifle Team, Canadian tour, 1958. *Address:* West Burton House, West Burton, Pulborough, West Sussex RH20 1HD. *T:* (01798) 831516. *Clubs:* Flyfishers'; North London Rifle (Bisley).

MIDDLESBROUGH, Bishop of, (RC), since 1993; **Rt Rev. John Crowley;** *b* Newbury, 23 June 1941. Ordained priest, 1965; Holy Trinity Parish, Brook Green, W6, 1965–68; Catholic Missionary Soc., 1968–74; Private Sec. to Cardinal Hume, 1974–82; Vicar Gen. for Westminster dio., 1982–86; Auxiliary Bishop of Westminster (Bishop in Central London), and Titular Bishop of Tala, 1986–92. Chairman, Catholic Fund for Overseas Development, 1988–2000. *Address:* Bishop's House, 16 Cambridge Road, Middlesbrough, Cleveland TS5 5NN. *T:* (01642) 818253.

MIDDLESEX, Archdeacon of; *see* Colmer, Ven. M. J.

MIDDLETON, 12th Baron *cr* 1711; **Digby Michael Godfrey John Willoughby,** MC 1945; DL; Bt 1677; *b* 1 May 1921; *er s* of 11th Baron Middleton, KG, MC, TD, and Angela Florence Alfreda (*d* 1978), *er d* of Charles Hall, Eddlethorpe Hall, Malton, Yorks; *S* father, 1970; *m* 1947, Janet, *o d* of General Sir James Marshall-Cornwall, KCB, CBE, DSO, MC; three *s. Educ:* Eton; Trinity Coll., Cambridge. BA 1950; MA 1958. Served War of 1939–45: Coldstream Guards, 1940–46; NW Europe, 1944–45 (despatches, MC, Croix de Guerre); Hon. Col, 2nd Bn Yorkshire Volunteers, TAVR, 1976–88. Mem., H of L Select Cttee on Europ. Communities, 1985–97; Chm., H of L Sub-Cttee D, Agriculture and Food, 1989–92, 1994–97. Pres., CLA, 1981–83; Member: Yorks and Humberside Econ. Planning Council, 1968–79; Nature Conservancy Council, 1986–89. DL 1963, JP 1958, CC 1964–74, ER of Yorks; CC N Yorks, 1974–77. *Heir: s* Hon. Michael Charles James Willoughby [*b* 14 July 1948; *m* 1974, Hon. Lucy Sidney, *y d* of 1st Viscount De L'Isle, VC, KG, GCMG, GCVO, PC; two *s* three *d*]. *Address:* Birdsall House, Malton, N Yorks YO17 9NR. *Club:* Boodle's.

MIDDLETON, Bishop Suffragan of, since 1999; **Rt Rev. Michael Augustine Owen Lewis;** *b* 1953; *m* 1979, Julia Donneky (*née* Lennox); two *s* one *d. Educ:* Merton Coll., Oxford (BA 1975; MA 1979); Cuddesdon Coll. (BA Oxon 1977). Ordained deacon, 1978, priest, 1979; Curate, Salfords, 1978–80; Chaplain, Thames Poly., 1980–84; Vicar, Welling, 1984–91; Team Rector, Worcester SE Team Ministry, 1991–99; Rural Dean, Worcester E, 1993–99; Canon, Worcester Cathedral, 1998–99. Chm., Manchester Diocesan Bd of Educn, 2000–; Warden of Readers and Lay Assts, dio. of Manchester, 2001–. *Address:* The Hollies, Manchester Road, Rochdale, Lancs OL11 3QY.

MIDDLETON, (David) Miles, CBE 1992; Chairman, Tees Valley Learning and Skills Council, since 2000; Partner, Middleton Associates, since 1993; *b* 15 June 1938; *s* of late Harry Middleton and of Dorothy Hannah Middleton (*née* Nisbet); *m* 1st, 1962, Mary Gale (marr. diss. 1979); one *s* one *d*; 2nd, 1980, Elizabeth, (Bobbie), Lancaster; two step *s* two step *d. Educ:* Sedbergh Sch. ACA 1962, FCA 1972. Articled Clerk, Strachan & Co., 1956–61; Audit Sen., Coopers Brothers & Co., 1962–64; Coopers & Lybrand: Manager, Zürich, 1964–68; Newcastle upon Tyne office, 1968–71, 1986–90; Middlesbrough office, 1971–86; Partner, 1974; Sen. Partner, NE Practice, 1990–93. Chairman: Northern Enterprise Ltd, 1988–; Rural Develt Commn, 1997–99. Mem. Bd, NE Regl Develt Agency, 1999–. Pres., British Chamber of Commerce, 1990–92. *Address:* Ingleboro, St Helen's Lane, Corbridge, Northumberland NE45 5JD. *T:* (01434) 633545; (office) 19 Dacre Street, SW1H 0DH. *T:* (020) 7340 2900. *Clubs:* Royal Over-Seas League; Northern Counties (Newcastle upon Tyne); Hexham Golf; Bassenthwaite Sailing.

MIDDLETON, Donald King, CBE 1981; HM Diplomatic Service, retired; Chairman, Leominster Abbeyfield Society, 1993–97; *b* 24 Feb. 1922; *s* of late Harold Ernest Middleton and Ellen Middleton; *m* 1st, 1945, Marion Elizabeth Ryder (*d* 1988); one *d*; 2nd, 1996, Mary Elaine Aston. *Educ:* King Edward's Sch., Birmingham; Saltley College. Min. of Health, 1958–61; joined Commonwealth Relations Office, 1961; First Sec., British High Commn, Lagos, 1961–65; Head of Chancery, British Embassy, Saigon, 1970–72; British Dep. High Commissioner, Ibadan, 1973–75; HM Chargé d'Affaires, Phnom Penh, 1975; seconded to NI Office, Belfast, 1975–77; High Comr, Papua New Guinea, 1977–82. *Address:* Stone House, Ledgemoor, near Weobley, Herefordshire HR4 8RN.

MIDDLETON, Edward Bernard; Partner, PKF, Chartered Accountants; *b* 5 July 1948; *s* of Bernard and Bettie Middleton; *m* 1971, Rosemary Spence Brown; three *s. Educ:* Aldenham Sch., Elstree; Chartered Accountant, 1970. Joined London office of Pannell Kerr Forster, 1971; Nairobi office, 1973; Audit Manager, London office, 1975; Partner, 1979; seconded to DTI as Dir, Industrial Develt Unit, 1984–86. Dir, PKF Hotel Consultancy Services. Mem. sub-cttee, Consultative Cttee of Accountancy Bodies, 1980–84. Hon. Treas., Hospitality Action; Mem. Council, British Assoc. of Hospitality Accountants, 1997–. *Recreations:* sailing, photography. *Address:* Barrans, Bury Green, Little Hadham, Ware, Herts SG11 2ES. *T:* (01279) 658684. *Club:* Reform.

MIDDLETON, Dame Elaine (Madoline), DCMG 1998; MBE 1976; Executive Director, National Committee for Families and Children, Belize, 1994–98; *d* of Elstan Kerr and Leolyn Kerr Gillett; *m* 1961, Winston Middleton; one *s* two *d. Educ:* Belize Teachers' Trng Coll. (Teacher's Cert 1957); UC, Swansea (Dip. Social Welfare and Admin 1961; Dip. Applied Social Studies 1966); Univ. of the Union Inst., Ohio (BA in Social Work 1990). Primary Sch. Teacher, Salvation Army Sch. and Methodist Schs, Belize City, Dangriga and Gales Point, Manatee, 1947–57; Social Development Department, Belize: Probation Officer, 1957–62; Dep. Head, 1963–68; Head of Dept, 1969–81; Dir-Gen., Belize Red Cross Soc., 1981–83; lived and worked in USA, 1983–94. Member: Consortium for Belizean Develt, 1985–; Women's Commn of Belize, 1997–. Sec., Bd of Mgt, Wesley Coll.; Pres., YWCA of Belize. *Recreations:* reading, community work. *Address:* 16 4th Street, King's Park, Belize City, Belize. *T:* (2) 34760.

MIDDLETON, Francis; Advocate; Sheriff of Glasgow and Strathkelvin (formerly of Lanarkshire) at Glasgow, 1956–78, retired; Temporary Sheriff, 1979; *b* 21 Nov. 1913; Scottish; *m* 1942, Edith Muir; two *s* one *d. Educ:* Rutherglen Academy; Glasgow Univ. MA, LLB 1937. Practising as Solicitor, 1937–39; volunteered Sept. 1939; Cameronian Scottish Rifles; commissioned to 6th Battn 11th Sikh Regt, Indian Army, 1940; Captain 1940; Major 1942, injured; Interpreter 1st Class in Hindustani, 1943; posted to Judge Advocate's Branch, 1944; released Dec. 1945. Admitted Faculty of Advocates in Scotland, 1946. Sheriff Substitute of Inverness, Moray, Nairn and Ross and Cromarty, 1949–52, Fife and Kinross, 1952–56. Mem., Rotary Club. *Recreations:* reading, gardening. *Address:* 20 Queens Court, Helensburgh G84 7AH. *T:* (01436) 678965.

MIDDLETON, Rear-Adm. (John) Patrick (Windsor), CB 1992; Secretary, Royal Commission for the Exhibition of 1851, since 1995; *b* 15 March 1938; *s* of late Comdr John Henry Dudley Middleton, RN and Norna Mary Tessimond (*née* Hitchings); *m* 1962, Jane Rodwell Gibbs; one *s* one *d. Educ:* Cheltenham College; BRNC Dartmouth; RNEC Manadon. CEng, MIMechE, MIMarE. Entered Royal Navy 1954; CSO(E) to Flag Officer Submarines, 1981; CSO(E) Falkland Islands, 1983; Captain Naval Drafting, 1984; Dir, In Service Submarines, 1987; CSO (Engrg), later (Support), to C-in-C Fleet, 1989–92, retd. Gov., CARE for People with Learning Disabilities, 1993– (Chm. Govs, 1998–); Trustee, Mariners, 1995–97. Liveryman: Armourers and Brasiers' Co., 1971– (Mem. Ct of Assts, 1995–; Master, 2001–June 2002). *Recreations:* sailing, walking. *Address:* Manora, Chilmark, Wilts SP3 5AH. *T:* (01722) 716231. *Clubs:* Army and Navy; Royal Naval Sailing Association (Portsmouth).

MIDDLETON, Lawrence John, CMG 1985; PhD; HM Diplomatic Service; Ambassador to the Republic of Korea, 1986–90, retired; *b* 27 March 1930; *s* of John James Middleton and Mary (*née* Horgan); *m* 1963, Sheila Elizabeth Hoey; two *s* one *d. Educ:* Finchley Catholic Grammar Sch.; King's Coll., London (BSc 1951, PhD 1954). Scientific Officer, ARC, 1954–60 and 1962–63; Cons. to FAO and to UN Cttee on Effects of Atomic Radiation, 1960–62; CENTO Inst. of Nuclear Science, 1963–65; Principal, Min. of Agriculture, 1966–68; First Sec., FO, 1968; Washington, 1969–71; Kuala Lumpur, 1971–74; Counsellor (Commercial), Belgrade, 1974–78; Dir of Research, FCO, 1978–80; Cabinet Office, 1980–82; Counsellor, UK Delegn to Conf. on Disarmament, Geneva, 1982–84; Sen. DS, RCDS, 1984–86. Mem. Council, 1994–2001, Vice-Pres., 1998–2001, Royal Asiatic Soc. (FRAS 1992); Chm., Anglo-Korean Soc., 1995–. Chm., N Oxford Defence Assoc., 1995–2000. *Publications:* articles on plant physiology and nuclear science in biology, 1954–63. *Address:* 12 Polstead Road, Oxford OX2 6TN. *Club:* Frilford Heath Golf.

MIDDLETON, Rear Adm. Linley Eric, CB 1986; DSO; FRAeS; *m* 1965, Pamela Mannerings (*née* Lewis); three *s. Educ:* Dale Coll., Kingwilliamstown. Qualified as FAA pilot, 1952; served HMS Indefatigable, HMS Centaur, HMS Bulwark, HMS Eagle, HMS Mounts Bay, HMS Victorious and HMS Ark Royal, 1952–63; BRNC Dartmouth, 1964–65; CO, 809 Naval Air Squadron in HMS Hermes, 1966–67; Naval Staff, MoD, 1968–69; CO, HMS Whitby, 1970–71; Staff of Flag Officer, Naval Air Comd, 1971–73; Capt. 2nd Frigate Sqn and CO, HMS Undaunted, 1973–74, and CO, HMS Apollo, 1974–75; Chief Staff Officer to Flag Officer Carriers & Amphibious Ships, 1975–77; Dir, Naval Air Warfare, 1978–79; CO, HMS Hermes, 1980–82; Asst Chief of Naval Staff (Ops), 1983–84; Flag Officer, Naval Air Comd, 1984–87, retired. Man. Dir, British Internat. Helicopters, 1987–92. Liveryman: Coach Makers' and Coach Harness Makers' Co., 1983; GAPAN, 1993 (Upper Freeman, 1987).

MIDDLETON, Michael Humfrey, CBE 1975; Director, Civic Trust, 1969–86; *b* 1 Dec. 1917; *s* of Humfrey Middleton and Lilian Irene (*née* Tillard); *m* 1954, Julie Margaret Harrison; one *s* two *d. Educ:* King's Sch., Canterbury. Art Critic, The Spectator, 1946–56; Art Editor and Asst Editor, Picture Post, 1949–53; Exec. Editor, Lilliput, 1953–54; Editor, House and Garden, 1955–57; Sec. and Dep. Dir, Civic Trust, 1957–69; Mem. Council, Soc. of Industrial Artists and Designers, 1953–55, 1968–70; UK Sec.-Gen., European Architectural Heritage Year, 1972–75. Member: Adv. Cttee on Trunk Road Assessment, 1977–80; UK Commn for UNESCO, 1976–80. Hon. Fellow: RIBA, 1974; Landscape Inst., 1986. Film scripts include A Future for the Past, 1972. Council of Europe Pro Merito Medal, 1976. *Publications:* Soldiers of Lead, 1948; Group Practice in Design, 1967; Man Made the Town, 1987; Cities in Transition, 1991; contributor to many conferences and jls, at home and abroad, on art, design and environmental matters. *Recreation:* looking. *Address:* 84 Sirdar Road, W11 4EG. *T:* (020) 7727 9136.

MIDDLETON, Rev. Canon Michael John; Canon of Westminster, since 1997; Treasurer, since 1997, and Almoner, since 2000, Westminster Abbey; *b* 21 July 1940; *s* of Bernard and Gladys Middleton; *m* 1965, Anne Elisabeth Parker; two *s* one *d. Educ:* Weymouth Grammar Sch.; St Cuthbert's Soc., Durham (BSc); Fitzwilliam Coll., Cambridge (MA); Westcott House, Cambridge. Ordained: deacon, 1966; priest, 1967; Curate, St George's Jesmond, Newcastle, 1966–69; Chaplain: St George's Grammar Sch., Cape Town, 1969–72; King's School, Tynemouth, 1972–77; Vicar, St George's, Jesmond, Newcastle, 1977–85; Rector of Hexham, 1985–92; Archdeacon of Swindon, 1992–97. Hon. Canon of Newcastle, 1990. Proctor in Convocation, 1980–92. *Recreations:* walking, Westerns. *Address:* 1 Little Cloister, Westminster Abbey, SW1P 3PL. *T:* (020) 7654 4804, *Fax:* (020) 7654 4811; *e-mail:* michael.middleton@westminster-abbey.org.

MIDDLETON, Miles; *see* Middleton, D. M.

MIDDLETON, Rear-Adm. Patrick; *see* Middleton, Rear-Adm. J. P. W.

MIDDLETON, Sir Peter (Edward), GCB 1989 (KCB 1984); Director, since 1991 and Chairman, since 1999, Barclays Bank (Deputy Chairman, 1991–98; Chairman, BZW Banking Division, 1991–98); *b* 2 April 1934; *m* 1st, 1964, Valerie Ann Lindup (*d* 1987); one *d* (one *s* decd); 2nd, 1990, Constance Owen. *Educ:* Sheffield City Grammar Sch.; Sheffield Univ. (BA; Hon. DLitt 1984); Bristol Univ. Served RAPC, 1958–60. HM Treasury: Senior Information Officer, 1962; Principal, 1964; Asst Director, Centre for Administrative Studies, 1967–69; Private Sec. to Chancellor of the Exchequer, 1969–72; Treasury Press Secretary, 1972–75; Head of Monetary Policy Div., 1975; Under Secretary, 1976; Dep. Sec., 1980–83; Permanent Sec., 1983–91. Director: Bass PLC, 1992–2001; General Accident Fire & Life Assurance Corp. plc, later CGU plc, 1992–98; United Utilities PLC (formerly NW Water Gp), 1994– (Vice-Chm., 1998–99; Chm., 1999–2000; Dep. Chm., 2000–01). Chm., Sheffield Urban Regeneration Co. Ltd (Sheffield 1), 2000–. Dir, Internat. Monetary Conf., 2001–. Member: Adv. Bd, Nat. Econ. Res. Associates 1991; Exec. Cttee, Centre for Econ. Policy Res. Vis. Fellow, Nuffield Coll., Oxford, 1981–89. Dir, Inst. of Contemporary British History, 2001– (Chm., 1992–2001). Mem. Council, 1991–, Chancellor, 1999–, Univ. of Sheffield (Pro-Chancellor, 1997–99); Mem. Council, Manchester Business Sch., 1985–92; Governor: London Business Sch., 1984–90; Ditchley Foundn, 1985–; NIESR, 1991–. Dir, English Chamber Orch. and Music Soc., 1992–. Cdre, Civil Service Sailing Assoc., 1984–92. *Recreations:* hill walking, music, outdoor sports. *Address:* Barclays Bank plc, 54 Lombard Street, EC3P 3AH. *Club:* Reform.

MIDDLETON, Peter James; Transaction Director, Nomura International plc, since 2000; *b* 10 Feb. 1940; *s* of Roy and Freda Middleton; *m* 1st, 1968, Yvonne Summerson (marr. diss. 1996); two *s* one *d*; 2nd, 1996, Anita Mehra; one *s*. *Educ:* Univ. of Paris; Univ. of Hull (BA Hons). HM Diplomatic Service, 1969–85: Second Sec., Jakarta, 1969–71; First Sec., Dar-es-Salaam, 1973–74; Paris, 1978–82; Midland Bank, 1985–87, Head of Banking Ops, 1986–87; Gp Chief Exec., Thomas Cook Gp, 1987–92; Chief Executive: Lloyd's of London, 1992–95; Salomon Brothers Internat., later Salomon Smith Barney, 1995–98; Chm., Football League, 1998–2000; Chief Exec., World Snooker Assoc., 1999–2000. Chm., London Luton Airport, 1999–2000; Dir, GTL Resources, 2000–. *Recreations:* soccer, horse-racing, music. *Address:* Nomura International plc, Nomura House, 1 St Martin's-le-Grand, EC1A 4NP.

MIDDLETON, Stanley; novelist; *b* Bulwell, Nottingham, 1 Aug. 1919; *y s* of Thomas and Elizabeth Ann Middleton; *m* 1951, Margaret Shirley, *y d* of Herbert and Winifred Vera Welch; two *d*. *Educ:* High Pavement Sch.; University Coll., Nottingham (later Univ. of Nottingham). Served Army (RA and AEC), 1940–46. Head of English Dept, High Pavement Coll., Nottingham, 1958–81. Judith E. Wilson Vis. Fellow, Emmanuel Coll., Cambridge, 1982–83. FRSL 1998. Hon. MA Nottingham, 1975; MUniv Open, 1995; Hon. DLitt: De Montfort, 1998; Nottingham Trent, 2000. *Publications:* novels: A Short Answer, 1958; Harris's Requiem, 1960; A Serious Woman, 1961; The Just Exchange, 1962; Two's Company, 1963; Him They Compelled, 1964; Terms of Reference, 1966; The Golden Evening, 1968; Wages of Virtue, 1969; Apple of the Eye, 1970; Brazen Prison, 1971; Cold Gradations, 1972; A Man Made of Smoke, 1973; Holiday (jtly, Booker Prize), 1974; Distractions, 1975; Still Waters, 1976; Ends and Means, 1977; Two Brothers, 1978; In A Strange Land, 1979; The Other Side, 1980; Blind Understanding, 1982; Entry into Jerusalem, 1983; The Daysman, 1984; Valley of Decision, 1985; An After Dinner's Sleep, 1986; After a Fashion, 1987; Recovery, 1988; Vacant Places, 1989; Changes and Chances, 1990; Beginning to End, 1991; A Place to Stand, 1992; Married Past Redemption, 1993; Catalysts, 1994; Toward the Sea, 1995; Live and Learn, 1996; Brief Hours, 1997; Against the Dark, 1998; Necessary Ends, 1999; Small Change, 2000. *Recreations:* music, walking, listening, argument, water-colour painting. *Address:* 42 Caledon Road, Sherwood, Nottingham NG5 2NG. *T:* (0115) 962 3085. *Club:* PEN.

MIDDLETON, Timothy John; Deputy Legal Adviser, Home Office, since 1997; *b* 15 Sept. 1953; *s* of William Smith Middleton and Brenda Mary Middleton; *m* 1983, Janet Kathleen Elliott; one *s* two *d*. *Educ:* King Edward VII Grammar Sch., Coalville, Leics; Balliol Coll., Oxford (MA Jurisprudence); Coll. of Law. Called to the Bar, Gray's Inn, 1977; Legal Asst, 1979–83, Sen. Legal Asst, 1983–85, MAFF; on secondment to Directorate Gen. VI (Agriculture), CEC, 1985–87; Lawyer: MAFF, 1987–89; Legal Secretariat to Law Officers, 1989–92; Legal Dir, Intervention Bd, 1992–94; Hd of a Legal Div., MAFF, 1994–97. Gov., Broadwater Sch., Godalming, 1999–. Churchwarden, St John the Evangelist, Farncombe, 2000–. *Recreations:* modern literature, theatre, cooking. *Address:* Home Office, 50 Queen Anne's Gate, SW1H 9AT. *T:* (020) 7273 3098.

MIDLETON, 12th Viscount *cr* 1717 (Ire.); **Alan Henry Brodrick;** Baron Brodrick of Midleton, Co. Cork 1715; Baron Brodrick of Peper Harow 1796; Keeper of Horology, John Gershom Parkington Collection of Time Measurement Instruments, Bury St Edmunds, since 1986; Museum Manager, British Horological Institute, since 2001 (Chairman, 1999–2000); *b* 4 Aug. 1949; *s* of Alan Rupert Brodrick (*d* 1972) (*g g s* of 7th Viscount) and of Alice Elizabeth, *d* of G. R. Roberts; *S* uncle, 1989; *m* 1978, Julia Helen, *d* of Michael Pitt; two *s* one *d*. *Educ:* St Edmund's School, Canterbury. British Horological Institute: FBHI; Mem. Council, 1993; Chm. Museum and Liby Cttee, 1994; Chm., Mus. Trust, 1995. *Recreation:* bicycling. *Heir:* *s* Hon. Ashley Rupert Brodrick, *b* 25 Nov. 1980. *Address:* c/o British Horological Institute, Upton Hall, Upton, Newark, Notts NG23 5TE. *Club:* Athenæum.

MIDORI; *see* Goto, Mi Dori.

MIDWINTER, Eric Clare, OBE 1992; MA, DPhil; Chairman, Community Education Development Centre, 1995–2001; *b* 11 Feb. 1932; *m*; two *s* one *d*. *Educ:* St Catharine's Coll., Cambridge (BA Hons History); Univs of Liverpool (MA Educn) and York (DPhil). Educational posts, incl. Dir of Liverpool Educn Priority Area Project, 1955–75; Head, Public Affairs Unit, Nat. Consumer Council, 1975–80; Dir, Centre for Policy on Ageing, 1980–91. Chairman: Council, Adv. Centre for Educn, 1976–84; London Transport Users Consultative Cttee, 1977–84; London Regl Passengers' Cttee, 1984–96. Mem., POW Adv. Cttee on Disability, 1990–95. Pres., Assoc. of Cricket Statisticians and Historians, 1997–. Vis. Prof. of Educn, Univ. of Exeter, 1993–. DUniv Open, 1989. *Publications:* Victorian Social Reform, 1968; Law and Order in Victorian Lancashire, 1968; Social Administration in Lancashire, 1969; Nineteenth Century Education, 1970; Old Liverpool, 1971; Projections: an education priority project at work, 1972; Social Environment and the Urban School, 1972; Priority Education, 1972; Patterns of Community Education, 1973; (ed) Teaching in the Urban Community School, 1973; (ed) Pre-School Priorities, 1974; Education and the Community, 1975; Education for Sale, 1977; Make 'Em Laugh: famous comedians and their world, 1978; Schools and Society, 1980; W. G. Grace: his life and times, 1981; Age is Opportunity: education and older people, 1982; (ed) Mutual Aid Universities, 1984; The Wage of Retirement: the case for a new pensions policy, 1985; Fair Game: myth and reality in sport, 1986; Caring for Cash: the issue of private domiciliary care, 1986; Redefining Old Age, 1987; The Lost Seasons: wartime cricket 1939–1945, 1987; (ed) Retired Leisure, 1987; Polls Apart? Older Voters and the 1987 General Election, 1987; New Design for Old, Function, Style and Older People, 1988; Red Roses Crest the Caps: a history of Lancashire cricket, 1989; Creating Chances: arts by older people, 1990; Old Order: crime and older people, 1990; Out of Focus: old age, the press and broadcasting, 1991; Brylcreem summer: the 1947 cricket season, 1991; An Illustrated History of County Cricket, 1992; Lifelines, 1994; The Development of Social Welfare in Britain, 1994; First Knock: cricket's opening pairs, 1994; European Year '93, 1995; 150 Years: a celebration: Surrey CCC, 1995; Thriving People: the growth and prospects of the U3A in the UK, 1995; Darling Old Oval: history of Surrey County Cricket Club, 1995; State Educator: the life and enduring influence of W. E. Forster, 1996; Pensioned Off: retirement and income examined, 1997; Yesterdays: the way we were, 1998; The Billy Bunter Syndrome: or why Britain failed to create a relevant secondary school system, 1998; (ed) MCC Yearbook, 1998, 1999, MCC Annual, 2000–; From Meadowland to Multinational: a review of cricket's social history, 2000; Yesterdays: our finest hours, 2001; Literary Lords: cricket in literature, 2001; Mellow Fruitfulness: Midwinter on the autumn of life, 2001. *Recreations:* sport, comedy. *Clubs:* Savage, Players, MCC; Lancashire CCC.

MIDWINTER, Prof. John Edwin, OBE 1984; PhD; FRS 1985; FREng; Pender Professor of Electronic Engineering, University College London, since 1991; President, Institution of Electrical Engineers, 2000–01; *b* 8 March 1938; *s* of Henry C. and Vera J. Midwinter; *m* 1961, Maureen Anne Holt; two *s* two *d*. *Educ:* St Bartholomew's Grammar Sch., Newbury, Berks; King's Coll., Univ. of London (BSc Physics, 1961; AKC 1961). PhD Physics, London (ext.), 1968. MInstP 1973; FIEE 1980; FIEEE 1983; FREng (FEng 1984). Joined RRE, Malvern, as Scientific Officer, 1961 (research on lasers and non-linear optics); Sen. Scientific Officer, 1964–68; Perkin Elmer Corp., Norwalk, Conn, USA, 1968–70; Res. Center, Materials Research Center, Allied Chemical Corp., Morristown, NJ, USA, 1970–71; Head of Optical Fibre Develt, PO Res. Centre, Martlesham, 1971–77; Head, Optical Communications Technol., British Telecom Res. Labs, 1977–84; University College London: BT Prof. of Optoelectronics, 1984–91; Head, Dept of Electronic Engrg, later of Electronic and Electrical Engrg, 1988–98; Vice Provost, 1994–99. Dep. Pres., IEE, 1998–2000 (Vice Pres., 1994; Chm., Electronics Div., 1991–92). Lectures: Bruce Preller, RSE, 1983; Clifford Patterson, Royal Soc.,1983; Cantor, RSA, 1984. Hon. DSc: Nottingham, 2000; Loughborough, 2001. Electronics Div. Premium, 1976, J. J. Thompson Medal, 1987, Faraday Medal, 1997, IEE. *Publications:* Applied Non-Linear Optics, 1972; Optical Fibers for Transmission, 1979 (Best Book in Technol. Award, Amer. Publishers' Assoc., 1980); over 200 papers on lasers, non-linear optics and optical communications. *Recreations:* country and mountain walking, ski-ing. *Address:* Department of Electronic and Electrical Engineering, University College London, Torrington Place, WC1E 7JE. *T:* (020) 7388 0427, (020) 7387 7050.

MIDWINTER, Stanley Walter, CB 1982; Chief Planning Inspector (Director of Planning Inspectorate), Departments of the Environment and Transport, 1978–84; *b* 8 Dec. 1922; *s* of late Lewis Midwinter and Beatrice (*née* Webb); *m* 1954, Audrey Mary Pepper (*d* 1988); one *d*. *Educ:* Regent Street Polytechnic Sch.; Sch. of Architecture (DipArch, ARIBA 1948); Sch. of Planning and Res. for Regional Develt (AMTPI 1952, FRTPI 1965); Dip. in Sociol., Univ. of London, 1976. Served War, RE, 1942–46: N Africa, Italy, Greece. Planning Officer, LCC, 1949–54; Bor. Architect and Planning Officer, Larne, NI, 1955–60; joined Housing and Planning Inspectorate, 1960; Dep. Chief Inspector, 1976. Assessor at Belvoir Coalfield Inquiry, 1979. Town Planning Institute: Exam. Prize, 1952; Thomas Adams Prize, 1955; President's Prize, 1958. *Publications:* articles in TPI Jl.

MIERS, Sir (Henry) David (Alastair Capel), KBE 1985; CMG 1979; HM Diplomatic Service, retired; Chairman, Society of Pension Consultants, since 1998; *b* 10 Jan. 1937; *s* of late Col R. D. M. C. Miers, DSO, QO Cameron Highlanders, and Honor (*née* Bucknill); *m* 1966, Imelda Maria Emilia, *d* of Jean-Baptiste Wouters, Huizingen, Belgium; two *s* one *d*. *Educ:* Winchester; University Coll., Oxford. Tokyo, 1963; Vientiane, 1966; Private Sec. to Minister of State, FO, 1968; Paris, 1972; Counsellor, Tehran, 1977–79; Hd, Middle Eastern Dept, FCO, 1980–83; Ambassador to Lebanon, 1983–85; Asst Under-Sec. of State, FCO, 1986–89; Ambassador: to Greece, 1989–93; to Netherlands, 1993–96. Chairman: British-Lebanese Assoc., 1998–; Anglo-Hellenic League, 1999–.

MIFLIN, Dr Benjamin John, PhD; Chairman, Crop Evaluation Ltd, since 2000; Director, Institute of Arable Crops Research and IACR-Rothamsted, 1994–99, Lawes Trust Fellow, since 1999; *b* 7 Jan. 1939; *s* of late Stanley Miflin and Kathleen (*née* Davies); *m* 1964, Hilary Newman; three *d*. *Educ:* Univ. of Nottingham (BSc); Univ. of Illinois (MS); QMC and Imperial Coll., London (PhD 1965). FIBiol 1997; FRASE 1996. Lectr in Plant Scis (Plant Biochem.), Sch. of Agric., Univ. of Newcastle upon Tyne, 1965–73; Hd, Biochem. Dept, 1973–85, and Div. of Molecular Scis, 1983–85, Rothamsted Exptl Stn, Harpenden; Hd, Internat. R & D, Ciba-Geigy Seeds, Basle, 1986–93. Vis. Prof., Univ. of Nottingham, 1981–85 and 1994–2000. Mem., Adv. Cttee on Novel Foods and Processes, 1995–98. Corresp. Mem., Amer. Soc. of Plant Physiologists, 1986. *Publications:* (ed) The Biochemistry of Plants, Vol. 5, 1980, (ed with P. J. Lea) Vol. 16, 1990; (ed) Oxford Surveys of Plant Cell and Molecular Biology, Vols 1–7, 1984–91; numerous papers in field of plant biochem. and related subjects. *Recreations:* ski-ing, gardening, photography. *Address:* IACR-Rothamsted, Harpenden, Herts AL5 2JQ. *T:* (01582) 763133.

MIFSUD BONNICI, Dr Carmelo, BA, LLD; Prime Minister of Malta, 1984–87; *b* 17 July 1933; *s* of Dr Lorenzo Mifsud Bonnici, and Catherine (*née* Buttigieg). *Educ:* Govt sch. and Lyceum, Malta; Univ. of Malta (BA, LLD); Univ. Coll. London. Lectr in Industrial and Fiscal Law, Univ. of Malta, 1969–86. Legal Consultant, General Workers' Union, 1969–83; Dep. Leader, Labour Party, responsible for Party affairs, 1980–82; Designate Leader of the Labour Movement, 1982; co-opted to Parlt, 1983, Minister of Labour and Social Services, 1983; Sen. Dep. Prime Minister, 1983–84; Leader, Labour Party, 1984–92; MP First District, 1987–96. *Recreation:* reading. *Address:* Hamrun, Malta.

MIFSUD BONNICI, Dr Ugo; President of Malta, 1994–99; *b* 8 Nov. 1932; *m* 1959, Gemma Bianco; two *s* one *d*. *Educ:* Lyceum, Malta; Univ. of Malta (BA 1952; LLD 1955). Elected MP, 2nd Electoral Div., 1966–94; Shadow Minister of Educn, 1971; President: General Council, 1976; Admin. Council, 1976; Minister of: Educn, 1987; Educn and the Interior, 1987–92; Educn and Human Resources, 1992. Campanion of Honour, Nat. Order of Merit (Malta). *Publications:* Biex il-Futur Jerga' Jibda, 1976; Il-Linja t-Tajba, 1980; Biex il-Futur Rega' Beda, 1992; Il-Manwal tal-President, 1997; Kif Sirna Republika, 1999. *Recreations:* reading, writing, listening to music. *Address:* 18 Triq Erin Serracino Inglott, Bormla, Malta. *Club:* Casino Maltese.

MILAN, Archbishop of; *see* Martini, His Eminence Cardinal C. M.

MILBANK, Sir Anthony (Frederick), 5th Bt *cr* 1882; DL; farmer and landowner since 1977; *b* 16 Aug. 1939; *s* of Sir Mark Vane Milbank, 4th Bt, KCVO, MC, and Hon. Verena Aileen, Lady Milbank (*d* 1995), *yr d* of 11th Baron Farnham, DSO; *S* father, 1984; *m* 1970, Belinda Beatrice, *yr d* of Brig. Adrian Gore, DSO; two *s* one *d*. *Educ:* Eton College. Brown, Shipley & Co. Ltd, 1961–66; M&G Securities Ltd, 1966–77. Chairman: Moorland Assoc., 1987–2001; Northern Uplands Moorland Regeneration Project, 1999–2001; Member: NCC Cttee for England, 1989–91; CLA Exec. Cttee, 1989–94; Council, RSPB, 1993–98. Pres., Yorks Wildlife Trust, 1990. High Sheriff of Durham, 1991–92; DL N Yorks, 1998. *Recreations:* various. *Heir:* *s* Edward Mark Somerset Milbank, *b* 9 April 1973. *Address:* Barningham Park, Richmond, N Yorks DL11 7DW.

MILBERG, Dr Joachim; Chairman, Board of Management, BMW AG, since 1999; *b* Verl, Westfalia, 10 April 1943. *Educ:* Bielefeld State Engrg Coll.; Berlin Tech. Univ. (Dr ing 1972). Apprentice machine fitter, 1959–62; scientific asst, Inst. Machine Tool and Prodn Technol., Berlin Tech. Univ., 1970–72; Exec. Manager, 1972–78, Hd, Automatic Lathe Div., 1978–81, Werkzeugmaschinenfabrik Gildemeister AG; Prof. of Machine Tools and Ops Res., Munich Tech. Univ., 1981–93; Mem., Bd of Mgt, Prodn, 1993–98, Engrg and Prodn, 1998–99, BMW AG. *Address:* BMW Haus, Petuelring 130, 80788 Munich, Germnay.

MILBORNE-SWINNERTON-PILKINGTON, Sir Thomas Henry; *see* Pilkington.

MILBOURN, Dr Graham Maurice; Director, National Institute of Agricultural Botany, 1981–90, retired; *b* 4 Sept. 1930; *s* of late Frank McLaren Milbourn, BSc and Winifred May Milbourn; *m* 1956, Louise Lawson, BSc Hons; three *s*. *Educ:* Reading Univ. (BSc, MSc, PhD). Served RN, 1948–50. Asst Lectr, Reading Univ., 1953–56; Radiobiological Lab., ARC, 1956–61; Sen. Lectr, Crop Production, Wye Coll., London Univ., 1961–77;

Prof. of Crop Production, Sch. of Agric., Edinburgh Univ., 1977–81. Vis. Prof., Silsoe Coll., Cranfield Univ. (formerly Inst. of Technology), 1991–. Pres., Assoc. Applied Biologists, 1991. *Publications:* papers on physiology of cereals and vegetables, uptake of radio-nucleides by crops. *Recreation:* sailing.

MILBURN, Rt Hon. Alan; PC 1998; MP (Lab) Darlington, since 1992; Secretary of State for Health, since 1999; *b* 27 Jan. 1958; partner, Dr Ruth Briel; two *s*. *Educ:* Stokesley Comprehensive Sch.; Lancaster Univ. (BA). Co-ordinator, Trade Union Studies Information Unit, Newcastle, 1984–90; Sen. Business Development Officer, N Tyneside MBC, 1990–92. Opposition front bench spokesman on health, 1995–96, on Treasury and econ. affairs, 1996–97; Minister of State, DoH, 1997–98; Chief Sec. to HM Treasury, 1998–99. Mem., Public Accounts Cttee, 1994–95; Chair, PLP Treasury Cttee, 1992–95. *Address:* House of Commons, SW1A 0AA.

MILBURN, Sir Anthony (Rupert), 5th Bt *cr* 1905; landowner; *b* 17 April 1947; *s* of Major Rupert Leonard Eversley Milburn (*yr s* of 3rd Bt) (*d* 1974) and of Anne Mary, *d* of late Major Austin Scott Murray, MC; *S* uncle, 1985; *m* 1977, Olivia Shirley, *y d* of Captain Thomas Noel Catlow, CBE, DL, RN; two *s* one *d*. *Educ:* Hawtreys, Savernake Forest; Eton College; Cirencester Agricultural Coll. ARICS. *Recreations:* sporting and rural pursuits. *Heir: s* Patrick Thomas Milburn, *b* 4 Dec. 1980. *Address:* Guyzance Hall, Acklington, Morpeth, Northumberland NE65 9AG. *T:* (01665) 513047. *Club:* New (Edinburgh).

MILBURN, Donald B.; *see* Booker-Milburn.

MILDMAY, Sir Walter John Hugh St J.; *see* St John-Mildmay.

MILDON, His Honour Arthur Leonard; QC 1971; a Circuit Judge, 1986–96; *b* 3 June 1923; *er s* of late Rev. Dr W. H. Mildon, Barnstaple; *m* 1950, Iva, *er d* of late G. H. C. Wallis, Plymouth; one *s* one *d*. *Educ:* Kingswood Sch., Bath; Wadham Coll., Oxford (MA). Pres., Oxford Univ. Liberal Club, 1948. Army Service, 1942–46: Lieut, 138th (City of London) Field Regt, RA; Captain, 1st Army Group, RA. Called to Bar, Middle Temple, 1950, Bencher, 1979, Lent Reader, 1999; Member of Western Circuit; Dep. Chm., Isle of Wight QS, 1967–71; a Recorder, 1972–85. Mem., Bar Council, 1973–74. Pres., Medico-Legal Soc., 1994–96. *Recreation:* sailing. *Address:* c/o 4 New Square, Lincoln's Inn, WC2A 3RJ. *T:* (020) 7822 2000. *Club:* Royal Solent Yacht.
See also D. W. Mildon.

MILDON, David Wallis; QC 2000; *b* 19 Sept. 1955; *s* of His Honour Arthur Leonard Mildon, *qv*; *m* 1983, Lesley Mary Richardson; one *s* one *d*. *Educ:* Emmanuel Coll., Cambridge (LLB; MA). Called to the Bar, Middle Temple, 1980; in practice at the Bar, 1980–. *Recreations:* music, sailing. *Address:* Essex Court Chambers, 24 Lincoln's Inn Fields, WC2A 3ED. *T:* (020) 7813 8000.

MILDON, Russell; Director, Audit of Agricultural Expenditure, Personnel and Administration, European Commission, since 2001; *b* 22 Aug. 1949; *s* of R. F. Mildon and J. Mildon (*née* Kröpfl); *m* 1973, Micheline Williams; two *s* one *d*. *Educ:* Royal Holloway Coll., London Univ. (Open Schol.; BSc Hons); Brunel Univ. (MTech). With Commission of the European Communities, 1974–: Statistics, studies and reports (Agricl), 1974–81; Gen. Affairs Gp, 1981–83; Private Sec. to Dep. Dir Gen., Agricl Markets, 1983–86; Advr to Vice-Pres., 1986–89; Head: Unit for Analysis of Situation of Agricl Holdings, 1989; Unit for Oilseeds and Protein Crops, 1989–93; Director: Internat. affairs relating to agric., 1993–96; orgn of markets in specialised crops, 1996–2001. *Recreations:* chess, travel. *Address:* European Commission, 200 Rue de la Loi, 1049 Brussels, Belgium. *T:* (2) 2953224.

MILEDI, Prof. Ricardo, MD; FRS 1970; Distinguished Professor, University of California, Irvine, since 1984; *b* Mexico City, 15 Sept. 1927; *m* 1955, Ana Carmen (Mela) Garces; one *s*. *Educ:* Univ. Nacional Autónoma, Mexico City. BSc 1945; MD 1955. Research at Nat. Inst. of Cardiology, Mexico, 1952–54; Rockefeller Travelling Fellowship at ANU, 1956–58; research at Dept of Biophysics, UCL, 1958–84. Fellow, Amer. Acad. of Arts and Scis, 1986; Mem., Nat. Acad. of Scis, 1989; Hon. Member: Hungarian Acad. of Scis, 1988; Mexican Acad. of Medicine, 1995; Corresp. Mem., Mexican Acad. of Scis, 1991; Titular Mem., Eur. Acad. of Arts, Scis and Humanities, 1992. Dr *hc* Universidad del País Vasco, Spain, 1992. Luigi Galvani Award, 1987; Internat. Prize for Science, King Faisal Foundn, 1988; Royal Medal, Royal Soc., 1998. *Address:* Laboratory of Cellular and Molecular Neurobiology, Department of Neurobiology and Behavior, University of California, Irvine, CA 92697–4550, USA. *T:* (949) 8245693; *e-mail:* rmiledi@uci.edu; 9 Gibbs Court, Irvine, CA 92612, USA. *T:* (714) 8562677, *Fax:* (949) 8544395.

MILES, Prof. Albert Edward William, LRCP; MRCS; FDS; DSc; Professor of Dental Pathology at The London Hospital Medical College, 1950–76, retired; Hon. Curator, Odontological Collection, Royal College of Surgeons of England, 1955–89; *b* 15 July 1912; *m* 1st, 1939, Sylvia Stuart; one *s* decd; 2nd, 1979, Diana Cross. *Educ:* Stationers' Company Sch.; Charing Cross and Royal Dental Hosps. John Tomes Prize, RCS, 1954–56. Part-time Lectr, Anatomy Dept, London Hosp. Med. Coll., 1977–85; Hon. Researcher, Dept of Palaeontology, Nat. Hist. Museum, 1993–99. Charles Tomes Lecturer, RCS, 1957; Evelyn Sprawson Lectr, London Hosp. Med. Coll., 1977. Hunterian Trustee, 1978–98. Hon. FRSocMed 1988. Howard Mummery Meml Prize, BDA, 1976; Colyer Gold Medal, RCS, 1978; Sir Arthur Keith Medal, RCS, 1990; Wood Jones Medal, RCS, 1993; G. L. Slack Medal, London Hosp. Med. Coll., 1997. Exec. Editor, Archives of Oral Biology, 1969–88. *Publications:* Structural and Chemical Organization of Teeth, 1967; Teeth and Their Origins, 1972; An Early Christian Chapel and Burial Ground in the Outer Hebrides, with a Study of the Skeletal Remains, 1989; (with Caroline Grigson) Colyer's Variations and Diseases of the Teeth in Animals, 1990; contrib. to scientific literature, latterly on physical anthropology. *Address:* 1 Cleaver Square, Kennington, SE11 4DW. *T:* (020) 7735 5350. *Clubs:* Tetrapods, Zoo.

MILES, Anthony John; Executive Publisher, Globe Communications Corporation, Florida, USA, 1985–90; *b* 18 July 1930; *s* of Paul and Mollie Miles; *m* 1975, Anne Hardman. *Educ:* High Wycombe Royal Grammar Sch. On staff of (successively): Middlesex Advertiser; Nottingham Guardian; Brighton Evening Argus. Daily Mirror: Feature writer, 1954–66; Asst Editor, 1967–68; Associate Editor, 1968–71; Editor, 1971–74; Mirror Group Newspapers: Editorial Dir, 1975–84; Dep. Chm., 1977–79 and 1984; Chm., 1980–83. Dir, Reuters Ltd, 1978–84. Member: Press Council, 1975–78; British Exec. Cttee, IPI, 1976–84; Council, CPU, 1983–84; Life Vice-Pres., Newspaper Press Fund (Appeal Chm., 1982–83). *Address:* 197 Friern Barnet Lane, N20 0NN; Millennium Cottage, Dunster, Som TA24 6SY. *Clubs:* Reform, Savile.

MILES, Lieut-Comdr Brian, CBE 1994; RD 1970; FNI; RNR (retired); Director, Royal National Lifeboat Institution, 1988–98; *b* 23 Feb. 1937; *s* of Terence Clifford Miles and Muriel Irene Terry; *m* 1964, Elizabeth Anne Scott; one *s* two *d*. *Educ:* Reed's School, Cobham; HMS Conway; Merchant Navy Cadet School. Master Mariner (Foreign Going Cert. P&O Orient Lines: Cadet, 1954–57; Deck Officer, 1958–64; RNLI: Divl Inspector, 1964–73; Asst to Director, 1974–79; Ops Staff Officer, 1979–81; Dep. Dir, 1982–87. Chm., Poole Arts Trust, 1996–; Member Council: Royal Nat. Mission to Deep Sea Fishermen, 1999– (Dep. Chm., 2001–); Dorset Br., BRCS, 2000–. FNI 1989; CIMgt 1994. Freeman, City of London, 1993; Mem., Master Mariners' Co., 1994–. Younger Brother, Trinity House, 1994. Comdr, Order of Lion (Finland), 1997. *Address:* 8 Longfield Drive, West Parley, Ferndown, Dorset BH22 8TY. *T:* (01202) 571739.

MILES, Mrs Caroline Mary; Chairman, since 1996, and Trustee, since 1999, Ethox, Oxford Institute for Ethics and Communication in Health Care Practice; *b* 30 April 1929; *d* of Brig. A. J. R. M. Leslie, OBE. *Educ:* numerous schools; Somerville Coll., Oxford. HM Treasury, 1953–54; NIESR, 1954–56 and 1964–67; attached to UN Secretariat, NY, 1956–63. Associate Mem., Nuffield Coll., Oxford, 1972–74; Ian Ramsey Fellow, St Cross Coll., Oxford, 1988–94. Market Develt Consultant, Harwell Res. Lab., 1981–86. Chm., Oxfordshire HA, 1984–92. Member: Textile Council, 1968–71; Inflation Accounting Cttee (Sandilands Cttee), 1974–75; Monopolies and Mergers Commn, 1975–84; NEB, 1976–79; Nuffield Council on Bioethics, 1991–96. Trustee: The Tablet, 1982–98; APT Design and Develt, then APT Enterprise Develt Ltd, 1992–2000 (Chm., 1994–98); Radcliffe Medical Foundation: Trustee, 1986–2000; Hon. Treas., 1996–99; Patron, 2000–; Chm. Trustees, Opus Anglicanum Trust. Governor: Ditchley Foundn, 1983–; Oxford Polytechnic, 1988–92. *Publications:* Lancashire Textiles, A Case Study of Industrial Change, 1968; numerous papers and articles. *Recreations:* music, picnics, poohsticks. *Address:* Millbrook, Brookend, Chadlington, Oxford OX7 3NF. *T:* (01608) 676309.

MILES, Prof. Charles William Noel, CBE 1980; Head of Department of Land Management and Development, 1968–81, Dean of Faculty of Urban and Regional Studies, 1972–75, and Professor Emeritus 1981, University of Reading; Chairman, Agricultural Wages Board for England and Wales, 1972–81; *b* 3 Nov. 1915; 2nd *s* of late Lt-Col Sir Charles W. Miles, 5th Bt; *m* 1940, Jacqueline, (Dickie), Cross (*d* 1998); one *d* (one *s* decd). *Educ:* Stowe Sch.; Jesus Coll., Cambridge (MA). FRICS. Army Service, 1939–46; Univ. Demonstrator and Univ. Lectr, Dept of Estate Management, Cambridge, 1946–54; Chief Agent to Meyrick Estates in Hants and Anglesey, 1954–68; Agent to Bisterne Estate, 1957–68. Pres., Chartered Land Agents Soc., 1965–66; Mem., Cambs AEC, 1953–54; Mem., SE Region Adv. Cttee of Land Commn, 1967–70. Mem., Yates Cttee on Recreation Management Trng, 1977–82. Leverhulme Trust Emeritus Fellowship, 1982–84. *Publications:* Estate Finance and Business Management, 1953, 4th edn 1981; Estate Accounts, 1960; Recreational Land Management, 1977, 2nd edn 1992; (co-ed) Walmesley's Rural Estate Management, 6th edn, 1978; Running an Open house, 1986; Going Public, 1991; (jtly) Aspects of Rural Estate Management, 1995. *Recreations:* walking, gardening, theatre. *Address:* Wheelers, Vicarage Lane, Mattingley, Hook, Hants RG27 8LE. *T:* (0118) 932 6357. *Club:* Farmers'.
See also Sir W. N. M. Miles, Bt.

MILES, Prof. Christopher John; film director and producer; *b* 19 April 1939; *s* of late John Miles, MC and Clarice Baskerville (*née* Remnant); *m* 1967, Susan Helen Howard Armstrong; one *d*. *Educ:* Winchester Coll.; Institut des Hautes Etudes Cinématographiques, Paris. Dir, Milesian Film Productions, 1962–; *films* include: Six Sided Triangle, 1963; The Virgin and the Gypsy, 1970 (Best Film Award, US and UK Critics, 1970); Time for Loving, 1972; The Maids, 1974; That Lucky Touch, 1976; Alternative Three, 1977; Priest of Love: life of D. H. Lawrence, 1981; Lord Elgin and some stones of no value, 1985; Cyclone Warning Class 4, 1994; The Clandestine Marriage, 1999; *theatre:* Skin of our Teeth, Chicago, 1973; *television series:* Zinotchka, 1973; Neck, 1978; Love in the Ancient World, 1996. Prof. of Film and Television, RCA, 1989–93. Lecture tours: India, for British Council, 1985; USA, 1986. FRCA 1989. *Publications:* Alternative Three, 1977 (trans. 5 langs); (with John Julius Norwich) Love in the Ancient World, 1996; (contrib.) H of C Report on Film, 1982; contrib. Image et Son, D. H. Lawrence Soc. Jl. *Recreations:* film-making, long walks and sketching in Arcadia. *Address:* Calstone House, Calstone, Calne, Wilts SN11 8PY; Aghios Leos, Methoni, Greece. *Club:* Garrick.

MILES, David, FSA, FSAScot; Chief Archaeologist, English Heritage, since 1999; *b* 6 Dec. 1947; *s* of Tom and Norah Miles; *m* 1969, Gwyn Morgan; one *s* one *d*. *Educ:* St Gregory's Grammar Sch., Huddersfield; King Edward VI Grammar Sch., Nuneaton; Birmingham Univ. (BA Hons). Dir of Excavations, M5 Excavation Cttee, 1970–71; Res. Asst, Bristol Univ., 1971–72; Director of Excavations: Abingdon Excavation Cttee, 1972–73; Upper Thames Excavation Cttee, 1973–74; Dep. Dir, 1974–87, Dir, 1987–99, Oxford Archaeological Unit. FSA 1984; FSAScot 2000. MIFA 1988. *Publications:* (with D. Benson) The Upper Thames Valley, 1974; An Introduction to Archaeology, 1977; (ed) The Romano-British Countryside, 1982; (ed with B. Cunliffe) Aspects of the Iron Age in Central Southern Britain, 1984; (ed with K. Branigan) The Economies of Romano-British Villas, 1987; (jtly) Two Oxfordshire Anglo-Saxon Cemeteries: Berinsfield and Didcot, 1995; (jtly) The Anglo-Saxon Cemetery at Butler's Field, Lechlade, Gloucestershire, 1998; contrib. to learned jls, newspapers and magazines. *Recreations:* reading, gardening, arts. *Address:* 118 Millbank Court, 24 John Islip Street, SW1P 4LQ. *T:* (020) 7828 5781; Pailler de la Devezette, 30460 Lasalle, France; *e-mail:* david.miles@english-heritage.org.uk.

MILES, Dillwyn, FSA, FRGS, FRHistS; The Herald Bard, 1966–96; Director, Dyfed Rural Council, 1975–81; Chairman, National Association of Local Councils, 1977–87, Vice-President, since 1987; *b* 25 May 1916; *s* of Joshua Miles and Anne Mariah (*née* Lewis), Newport, Pembrokeshire; *m* 1944, Joyce Eileen (*d* 1976), *d* of Lewis Craven Ord, Montreal and London; one *s* one *d*. *Educ:* Fishguard County Sch.; University College of Wales, Aberystwyth. Served War of 1939–45, Middle East, Army Captain. National Organiser Palestine House, London, 1945–48; Extra-mural Lectr, Univ. of Wales, 1948–51; Community Centres Officer, Wales, 1951–54; Gen. Sec., Pembrokeshire Community Council, 1954–75. Founder: Jerusalem Welsh Soc., 1940; W Wales Tourist Assoc., 1962; Assoc. of Trusts for Nature Conservation in Wales, 1973; Hon. Sec., W Wales Naturalists Trust, 1958–75 (Vice-Pres., 1975–). Grand Sword Bearer, Gorsedd of Bards of Isle of Britain, 1959–67 (Mem. Bd, 1945–96). Member: Pembrokeshire CC, 1947–63; Cemaes RDC, 1947–52; Newport Parish Council, 1946–52; Haverfordwest Bor. Council, 1957–63; Pembrokeshire Coast Nat. Park Cttee, 1952–75; Exec. Cttee, Council for Protection of Rural Wales, 1946–64; Nature Conservancy's Cttee for Wales, 1966–73; Council, Soc. for Promotion of Nature Reserves, 1961–73; Countryside in 1970 Cttee for Wales, 1969–70; Sports Council for Wales, 1965–69; Mental Health Rev. Tribunal for Wales, 1959–71; Rent Trib. for Wales, 1966–87; Court of Govs, Nat. Libr. for Wales, 1963–64; Court of Govs, Univ. of Wales, 1957–66; Pembroke TA Assoc., 1956–59; Council for Small Industries in Wales, 1968–72; Age Concern Wales, 1972–77; Exec. Cttee, Nat. Council for Social Service, 1978–81; Exec. Cttee, NPFA, 1977–81; Council, Royal Nat. Eisteddfod of Wales, 1967–97; Prince of Wales Cttee, 1971–80 (former Chm., Dyfed Projects Gp); Welsh Environment Foundn, 1971–80; Heraldry Soc., 1974–; Rural Voice, 1980–87. Former Chairman: Further Educn and Libraries and Museums Cttees, Pembs CC; Pembs Cttee, Arthritis and Rheumatism Council; Pembs Jun. Ch. of Commerce; Pembs Community Health Council; Policy and Welsh Cttees,

Nat. Assoc. of Local Councils. Chairman: Wales Playing Fields Assoc., 1965–81; Pembs PO and Telecom Adv. Cttee, 1984–94 (Vice-Chm., 1971–84); Pembs Wildlife Appeal, 1988–89. President: Pembs Histl Soc., 1994–; Haverfordwest Shrievalty Assoc., 1996–99. Editor: The Pembrokeshire Historian, 1955–81; Nature in Wales, 1970–80. Mayor of Newport, Pembs, 1950, 1966, 1967, 1979, and Sen. Alderman. Mayor and Adm. of the Port, Haverfordwest, 1961, Sheriff 1963, Burgess Warden 1974–. FRGS 1946; FSA 1997; FRHistS 2000. Broadcaster, TV and radio, 1936–. *Publications:* (ed) Pembrokeshire Coast National Park, 1973; (jtly) Writers of the West, 1974; The Sheriffs of the County of Pembroke, 1975; The Royal National Eisteddfod of Wales, 1978; A Pembrokeshire Anthology, 1982, 2nd edn 2000; The Castles of Pembrokeshire, 1979, 3rd edn 1988; Portrait of Pembrokeshire, 1984; The Pembrokeshire Coast National Park, 1987; The Secret of the Bards, 1992; The Description of Pembrokeshire, 1994; The Ancient Borough of Newport, 1995; The Lords of Cemais, 1997; A Book on Nevern, 1998; A Mingled Yarn, 2000. *Recreations:* natural history, local history, books, food and wine. *Address:* 9 St Anthony's Way, Haverfordwest, Pembrokeshire SA61 1EL. *T:* (01437) 765275. *Clubs:* Savile, Wig and Pen.

MILES, (Frank) Stephen, CMG 1964; HM Diplomatic Service, retired; *b* 7 Jan. 1920; *s* of Harry and Mary Miles; *m* 1953, Margaret Joy (*née* Theaker); three *d. Educ:* John Watson's Sch., Edinburgh; Daniel Stewart's Coll., Edinburgh; St Andrews Univ. (MA); Harvard Univ. (Commonwealth Fellowship; MPA). Served with Fleet Air Arm, 1942–46 (Lt (A) RNVR). Scottish Home Dept, 1948; FCO (previously CRO), 1948–80; served in: New Zealand, 1949–52; E and W Pakistan, 1954–57; Ghana, 1959–62; Uganda, 1962–63; British Dep. High Commissioner, Tanzania, 1963–65 (Acting High Commissioner, 1963–64); Acting High Commissioner in Ghana, March–April 1966; Consul-Gen., St Louis, 1967–70; Dep. High Comr, Calcutta, 1970–74; High Comr, Zambia, 1974–78; High Comr, Bangladesh, 1978–79. A Dir of Studies, Overseas Services Unit, RIPA, 1980–83. Councillor: Tandridge DC, Surrey, 1982–90; Limpsfield Parish Council, 1983–95 (Chm., 1987–89). *Recreations:* cricket, tennis, golf. *Address:* 25 Sycamore Court, Hoskins Road, Oxted, Surrey RH8 9JQ. *T:* (01883) 713132. *Clubs:* Royal Commonwealth Society, MCC; Tandridge Golf.

MILES, Gwyn; Director of Major Projects, Victoria and Albert Museum, since 1995; *b* 17 Nov. 1947; *d* of Sir Morien Morgan, CB, FRS and of Lady Morgan (*née* Axford); *m* 1969, David Miles; one *s* one *d. Educ:* Bristol Univ. (BSc Physiol.); Bath Univ. (DipEd); Museums Assoc. (Cert. in Conservation). Research Assistant: McGill Univ., Montreal, 1969; Bristol Univ., 1969–70; Science Teacher, St Mary Redcliffe and Temple Sch., Bristol, 1971; Department of Antiquities, Ashmolean Museum, Oxford: Conservator, 1972–82; Head of Conservation, 1982–85; Victoria and Albert Museum: Dep. Keeper of Conservation, 1985–89; Surveyor of Collections, 1989–95. *Publications:* Traditional Knitting in the British Isles, 1979; articles on conservation, collections management and gardening. *Recreations:* arts, architecture, gardening. *Address:* 118 Millbank Court, 24 John Islip Street, SW1P 4LQ. *T:* (020) 7828 5781; Le Pailler de la Devezette, 30460 Lasalle, France.

MILES, Prof. Hamish Alexander Drummond, OBE 1987; Barber Professor of Fine Arts and Director of the Barber Institute, University of Birmingham, 1970–90, Professor at Large and Emeritus Director, 1990–91, Emeritus Professor, since 1992; *b* 19 Nov. 1925; *s* of J. E. (Hamish) Miles and Sheila Barbara Robertson; *m* 1957, Jean Marie, *d* of T. R. Smits, New York; two *s* two *d. Educ:* Douai Sch.; Univ. of Edinburgh (MA); Balliol Coll., Oxford. Served War: Army, 1944–47. Asst Curator, Glasgow Art Gallery, 1953–54; Asst Lectr, then Lectr in the History of Art, Univ. of Glasgow, 1954–66; Vis. Lectr, Smith Coll., Mass, 1960–61; Prof. of the History of Art, Univ. of Leicester, 1966–70. Trustee, National Galleries of Scotland, 1967–87; Mem., Museums and Galleries Commn, 1983–87. *Publications:* (jtly) The Paintings of James McNeill Whistler, 2 vols, 1980; sundry articles and catalogues. *Recreation:* woodland management. *Address:* 31 Drummond Place, Edinburgh EH3 6PW; Burnside, Kirkmichael, Blairgowrie, Perthshire PH10 7NA.

MILES, (Henry) Michael (Pearson), OBE 1989; Chairman, Johnson Matthey PLC, since 1998 (Director, since 1990); Director, ING Baring Holdings Co., since 1995; *b* 19 April 1936; *s* of late Brig. H. G. P. Miles and Margaret Miles; *m* 1967, Carol Jane Berg; two *s* one *d. Educ:* Wellington Coll. National Service, Duke of Wellington's Regt, 1955–57. Joined John Swire & Sons, 1958; Dir, John Swire & Sons (HK) Ltd, 1970–99 (Chm., 1984–88); Managing Director: John Swire & Sons (Japan) Ltd, 1973–76; Cathay Pacific Airways Ltd, 1978–84 (Chm., 1984–88); Chm., Swire Pacific, 1984–88; Exec. Dir, 1988–99, Advr to Board, 1999–, John Swire & Sons Ltd. Director: Baring PLC, 1989–95 (Jt Dep. Chm., 1994–95); Portals Holdings, 1990–95; BP, 1994–; BICC, 1996–. Chm., Hong Kong Tourist Assoc., 1984–88. Vice Pres., China Britain Business Gp, 1995–2000. Gov., Wellington Coll., 1988–. *Recreations:* golf, tennis. *Address:* Shalbourne House, Shalbourne, near Marlborough, Wilts SN8 3QH. *Clubs:* White's; Queen's; Royal and Ancient Golf; Berkshire Golf.

MILES, Jenefer Mary; *see* Blackwell, J. M.

MILES, John Edwin Alfred, CBE 1979 (OBE 1961; MBE 1952); HM Diplomatic Service, retired; *b* 14 Aug. 1919; *s* of late John Miles and late Rose Miles (*née* Newlyn); *m* 1952, Barbara Fergus Ferguson; two *s* one *d. Educ:* Hornsey County Sch. Apptd to Dominions Office, 1937. Served War: joined Queen's Royal West Surrey Regt, 1940; commissioned in N Staffordshire Regt, 1941; attached Royal Indian Army Service Corps, 1942 (Maj. 1943); released, Sept. 1946, and returned to Dominions Office. Served in: Wellington, NZ, 1948–51; Calcutta, 1953–56; CRO, 1957–61; Trinidad (on staff of Governor-Gen.), 1961; Jamaica (Adviser to Governor, and later First Sec. in British High Commission), 1961–64; Wellington, NZ, 1964–68; Counsellor, 1968; Accra, Ghana, 1968–71; Dep. High Comr, Madras, India, 1971–75; High Comr to Swaziland, 1975–79. *Address:* Cartref, Ladyegate Road, Dorking, Surrey RH5 4AR. *T:* (01306) 884346.

MILES, John Richard; Professor of Design, Southampton University, since 2001; *b* 22 June 1944; *s* of Thomas William Miles and Hilda Mary Miles (*née* Davis); *m* 1963, Judith Bud (marr. diss.). *Educ:* Croydon Coll. of Art; Royal Coll. of Art (MDes). Set up design studio, Miles Calver and Pound (now Calver and Pound), 1973–78 (Director); Founder Dir, Peppermint Prints, 1978–82; founded John Miles Partnership, 1996. Head, Textiles and Fashion, Brighton Polytechnic, 1979–85; Design Dir, Courtaulds, 1985–87; Gen. Manager, Next, 1987–89; Prof. of Fashion and Textiles, RCA, 1989–97; Dir of Product Mkting, DMC, France, 1997–2000. Consultant, Studio Claire and Lyn; Dir, Miles Whiston and Wright, 1989–96. Chm., Textile and Fashion Panel, CNAA, 1983–96; Mem., Industrial Lead Body, 1991–95. Governor, Winchester Sch. of Art, 1989–94. Hon. Dr of Design, Southampton, 1998. *Recreations:* gardening, films, cooking, reading. *Address:* 12 Penderyn Way, Carleton Road, N7 0EW.

MILES, John Seeley, FCSD, FSTD; typographer and graphic designer; *b* 11 Feb. 1931; *s* of Thomas William Miles and Winifred (*née* Seeley); *m* 1955, Louise Wilson; one *s* two *d. Educ:* Beckenham and Penge Grammar Sch.; Beckenham School of Art. FCSD (FSIAD 1973); FSTD 1974. UN travelling schol. to Netherlands to practise typography and punch cutting under Jan van Krimpen and S. L. Hartz, 1954–55; Assistant to Hans Schmoller at Penguin Books, 1955–58; joined Colin Banks, *qv*, to form design partnership, Banks and Miles, 1958, Partner, 1958–96; Dir, Parsimony Press, 1999–; Consultant to: Zoological Soc., Regent's Park and Whipsnade, 1958–82; Expanded Metal Co., 1960–83; Consumers' Assoc., 1964–93; British Council, 1968–83; The Post Office, 1972–83; E Midlands Arts Assoc., 1974–79; Curwen Press, 1970–72; Basilisk Press, 1976–79; Enschedé en Zn, Netherlands, 1980–94; British Telecom, 1980–89; British Airports Auth., 1983–87; typographic advisor, HMSO, 1985–96; design advisor: Agricl Inf. Workshop, Udaipur, India, 1973; Monotype Corp., 1985–92; hon. design advisor: UEA, 1990–97; UNHCR, Geneva, 1994–99; Internat. Assoc. Univs, Paris, 2000–; Aston–Mansfield Charities, 2001–. Designed banknote series Netherlands Antilles, 1987. Member: PO Design Adv. Cttee, 1972–76; Icograda Internat. Archive Cttee, 1993–. American Heritage Lectr, New York, 1960; held seminar, Graphic Inst., Stockholm, 1977 and 1986. Chairman: Wynkyn de Worde Soc., 1973–74; Arbitration Cttee, Assoc. Typographique Internationale, 1984–; Mem., Soc. Roy. des Bibliophiles et Iconophiles de Belgique, 1991–94. Governor, Central School of Arts and Crafts, 1978–85; External examiner: London Coll. of Printing, 1984–88; Technische Hoogschool Delft, 1986–87; Reading Univ., 1990–93; De Montfort Univ., 1994–99. Mem. CGLI, 1986. Exhibitions: London, 1971, 1978; Amsterdam and Brussels, 1977; Hamburg, 1991. FRSA 1988. (With Colin Banks) Green Product Award, 1989; BBC Envmtl Award, 1990. *Publications:* Design for Desktop Publishing, 1987; articles and reviews in professional jls. *Recreations:* gardening, painting, reading aloud. *Address:* Pit Cottage, Tunstall Common, Woodbridge, Suffolk IP12 2JR. *T:* (01728) 688889. *Club:* Double Crown.

MILES, Michael; *see* Miles, H. M. P.

MILES, Oliver; *see* Miles, R. O.

MILES, Peter Charles H.; *see* Hubbard-Miles.

MILES, Sir Peter (Tremayne), KCVO 1986; an Extra Equerry to HM the Queen, since 1988; *b* 26 June 1924; *er s* of late Lt-Col E. W. T. Miles, MC; *m* 1956, Philippa Helen Tremlett; two *s* one *d. Educ:* Eton Coll.; RMC, Sandhurst. First The Royal Dragoons, 1944–49; J. F. Thomasson & Co., 1949–59; Gerrard & National Discount Co. Ltd, 1959–80 (Managing Director, 1964–80). Director: P. Murray-Jones Ltd, 1966–75; Astley & Pearce Holdings Ltd, 1975–80 (Chm., 1978–80). Keeper of the Privy Purse and Treas. to the Queen, 1981–87; Receiver-Gen., Duchy of Lancaster, 1981–87; Mem., Prince of Wales' Council, 1981–87. *Clubs:* Cavalry and Guards, Pratt's, White's.

MILES, (Richard) Oliver, CMG 1984; HM Diplomatic Service, retired; Chairman, MEC International Ltd, since 2000 (Director, since 1997); Senior Consultant, mi2g, since 1997; *b* 6 March 1936; *s* of George Miles and Olive (*née* Clapham); *m* 1968, Julia, *d* of late Prof. J. S. Weiner; three *s* one *d. Educ:* Ampleforth Coll.; Merton Coll., Oxford (Oriental Studies). Entered Diplomatic Service, 1960; served in Abu Dhabi, Amman, Aden, Mukalla, Nicosia, Jedda; Counsellor, Athens, 1977–80; Head of Near East and N Africa Dept, FCO, 1980–83; Ambassador to: Libya, 1984; Luxembourg, 1985–88; Under-Sec. on loan to Home CS, 1988–90; Asst Under Sec. of State (Economic), FCO, 1990–91; Dir Gen. of Jt Directorate, Overseas Trade Services, FCO/DTI, 1991–93; Ambassador to Greece, 1993–96. Non-exec. Dir, Vickers Defence Systems, 1990–93. Chm., Host (Hosting for Overseas Students), 1998–; Pres., Soc. for Libyan Studies, 1998–. *Recreations:* bird-watching, playing the flute. *Club:* Travellers.

MILES, Roger Steele, PhD, DSc; freelance museum consultant; Head, Department of Public Services, The Natural History Museum (formerly British Museum (Natural History)), 1975–94; *b* 31 Aug. 1937; *s* of John Edward Miles and Dorothy Mildred (*née* Steele); *m* 1960, Ann Blake; one *s* one *d. Educ:* Malet Lambert High Sch., Hull; King's Coll., Univ. of Durham (BSc, PhD, DSc). Sen. Res. Award, DSIR, 1962–64; Sen. Res. Fellow, Royal Scottish Museum, 1964–66, Sen. Scientific Officer, 1966–68; Sen. Sci. Officer, BM (Nat. Hist.), 1968–71, Principal Sci. Officer, 1971–74. Hon. Fellow, Columbia Pacific Univ., 1983. *Publications:* 2nd edn, Palaeozoic Fishes, 1971 (1st edn, J. A. Moy-Thomas, 1939); (ed, with P. H. Greenwood and C. Patterson) Interrelationships of Fishes, 1973; (ed, with S. M. Andrews and A. D. Walker) Problems in Vertebrate Evolution, 1977; (with others) The Design of Educational Exhibits, 1982, 2nd edn 1988; (ed with L. Zavala) Towards the Museum of the Future, 1994 (trans. Spanish and revised, 1995); papers and monographs on anatomy and palaeontology of fishes, articles on museums, in jls. *Recreations:* music, twentieth century art and architecture. *Address:* 3 Eagle Lane, Snaresbrook, E11 1PF. *T:* (020) 8989 5684.

MILES, Roy; dealer in British fine paintings and writer; Director and proprietor, Roy Miles Gallery, 1975–98; *b* 9 Feb. 1935; *s* of Edward Marsh and Elsa McKinley (who later *m* George Miles); *m* 1970, Christine Rhodes (*d* 1997). *Educ:* Bembridge Sch., Isle of Wight; Sorbonne, Paris. Gold Medal for painting, Liverpool Watercolour Soc., 1945. Set world record prices for British paintings, such as Stubbs and Canaletto, 1970; subseq. instrumental in creation of Victorian art market. First dealer to put on exhibitions of Russian art, early 1980s. Encourages young artists; works with various charities. *Publications:* The Conceit of that Plum: a life in art (autobiog.), 2001; articles in magazines, newspapers and jls. *Recreation:* classical music. *Address:* 10 Ennismore Gardens, SW7 1NP. *T:* (020) 7581 7969.

MILES, Stephen; *see* Miles, F. S.

MILES, Wendy Ann; *see* Henry, W. A.

MILES, William; Chief Executive, West Yorkshire County Council, and Clerk to the Lieutenancy, West Yorkshire, 1984–86; *b* 26 Sept. 1933; *s* of William and Gladys Miles; *m* 1961, Jillian Anne Wilson; three *s. Educ:* Wyggeston School, Leicester; Trinity Hall, Cambridge (MA, LLM). Solicitor. Asst Solicitor, Leicester, Doncaster and Exeter County Boroughs, 1960–66; Asst Town Clerk, Leicester Co. Borough, 1966–69; Dep. Town Clerk, Blackpool Co. Borough, 1969–73; City Legal Adviser, Newcastle upon Tyne, 1973–74; Chief Exec., Gateshead Borough Council, 1974–84. Mem., Local Govt Residuary Body (England), 1995–99. *Recreations:* bridge, hill walking, sport. *Address:* 23 Moor Crescent, Gosforth, Newcastle upon Tyne NE3 4AP. *T:* (0191) 285 1996. *Clubs:* Northumberland Golf; Newcastle Rugby Football.

MILES, Sir William (Napier Maurice), 6th Bt *cr* 1859; retired architect; *b* 19 Oct. 1913; *s* of Sir Charles William Miles, 5th Bt, OBE; *S* father, 1966; *m* 1946, Pamela, *d* of late Capt. Michael Dillon; one *s* two *d. Educ:* Stowe; University of Cambridge (BA). Architectural Assoc. Diploma, 1939; RIBA 1940. Mem., Voluntary Euthanasia Soc. *Recreation:* surviving. *Heir: s* Philip John Miles, *b* 10 Aug. 1953. *Address:* Old Rectory House, Walton-in-Gordano, near Clevedon, North Somerset BS21 7AW. *T:* (01275) 873365.

See also Prof. C. W. N. Miles.

MILFORD, 4th Baron *cr* 1939, of Llanstephan, co. Radnor; **Guy Wogan Philipps;** *b* 25 July 1961; *e s* of 3rd Baron Milford and Hon. Mary Makins (now Viscountess Norwich), *e d* of 1st Baron Sherfield, GCB, GCMG, FRS; *S* father, 1999; *m* 1996, Alice Sherwood; two *s. Educ:* Eton Coll. (KS); Magdalen Coll., Oxford (Roberts-Gawen Scholar; 1st cl. Classical Hon. Mods; 1st cl. Lit. Hum.; MA). Called to the Bar, Inner Temple, 1986; in practice, 1986–. *Heir: er s* Hon. Archie Sherwood Philipps, *b* 12 March 1997. *Address:* 68 Westbourne Park Road, W2 5PJ. *T:* (020) 7229 1844.

MILFORD, John Tillman; QC 1989; a Recorder, since 1985; a Deputy High Court Judge, since 1994; *b* 4 Feb. 1946; *s* of late Dr Roy Douglas Milford, Strathtay, Perthshire, and Jessie Milford (*née* Rhind); *m* 1975, Mary Alice, *d* of late Dr E. A. Spriggs of Wylam, Northumberland; three *d. Educ:* The Cathedral School, Salisbury; Hurstpierpoint; Exeter Univ. (LLB). Called to the Bar, Inner Temple, 1969, Bencher, 1998; in practice on NE Circuit, 1970–. Head, Trinity Chambers, Newcastle upon Tyne, 1985–99. County Chairman: British Field Sports Soc. for South Northumberland, 1996–98; Countryside Alliance for South Northumberland, 1998–99; Regl Chm., Countryside Alliance for NE England, 1999–. Chairman: River Tyne Fishing Festival, 1997; Bywell Country Fair, 1999, 2000; Vice-Chm., Newcastle and Dist Beagles, 1999–. *Recreations:* fishing, shooting, gardening, beagling, collecting. *Address:* (chambers) 12 Trinity Chare, Newcastle upon Tyne NE1 3DF. *T:* (0191) 232 1927; Hill House, Haydon Bridge, Hexham, Northumberland NE47 6HL. *T:* (01434) 684234. *Clubs:* Northern Counties (Newcastle upon Tyne); Durham County (Durham).

MILFORD HAVEN, 4th Marquess of, *cr* 1917; **George Ivar Louis Mountbatten;** Earl of Medina, 1917; Viscount Alderney, 1917; *b* 6 June 1961; *s* of 3rd Marquess of Milford Haven, OBE, DSC, and of Janet Mercedes, *d* of late Major Francis Bryce, OBE; *S* father, 1970; *m* 1989, Sarah Georgina (marr. diss. 1996), *d* of George A. Walker, *qv*; one *s* one *d*, *m* 1997, Clare Wentworth-Stanley. *Heir: s* Earl of Medina, *qv*.

MILIBAND, David Wright; MP (Lab) South Shields, since 2001; *b* 15 July 1965; *s* of late Ralph Miliband and Marion Miliband (*née* Kozak); *m* 1998, Louise Shackelton. *Educ:* Corpus Christi Coll., Oxford (BA 1st Cl. Hons PPE); Massachusetts Inst. of Technol. (Kennedy Schol.; MSC Political Sci.). Res. Fellow, Inst. of Public Policy Res., 1989–94; Head of Policy, Office of Leader of the Opposition, 1994–97; Dir of Policy, 1997, Head, 1998–2001, Prime Minister's Policy Unit. Sec., Commn on Social Justice, 1992–94. *Publications:* (ed) Re-inventing the Left, 1994; (ed jtly) Paying for Inequality: the economic cost of social injustice, 1994. *Recreation:* supporting Arsenal and S Shields FC. *Address:* House of Commons, SW1A 0AA. *Clubs:* Whiteleas Social, Cleadon Social.

MILINGO, Most Rev. Emanuel; Former Archbishop of Lusaka (Archbishop, 1969–83); *b* 13 June 1930; *s* of Yakobe Milingo Chilumbu and Tomaide Lumbiwe Miti; *m* 2001, Maria Sung. *Educ:* Kachebere Seminary, Malawi; Pastoral Inst., Rome; University Coll., Dublin. Curate: Minga Parish, Chipata Dio., 1958–60; St Mary's Parish, 1960–61; Chipata Cathedral, 1963–64; Parish Priest, Chipata Cathedral, 1964–65; Sec. for Communications at Catholic Secretariat, Lusaka, 1966–69. Founder, The Daughters of the Redeemer, Congregation for young ladies, 1971. Dep. Hd, Pontifical Council for Migrants and Itinerants, 1983–99. *Publications:* Amake-Joni, 1972; To Die to Give Life, 1975; Summer Lectures for the Daughters of the Redeemer, 1976; The Way to Daughterhood; My God is a Living God, 1981; Lord Jesus, My Lord and Saviour, 1982; Demarcations, 1982; The Flower Garden of Jesus the Redeemer; My Prayers Are Not Heard; Precautions in the Ministry of Deliverance. *Recreation:* music. *Address:* Via di Porta Angelica 63, 00193 Rome, Italy.

MILKINA, Nina, (Mrs A. R. M. Sedgwick), Hon. RAM; concert pianist; *b* Moscow, 27 Jan. 1919; *d* of Jacques and Sophie Milkine; *m* 1943, Alastair Robert Masson Sedgwick; one *s* one *d. Educ:* privately. Studied in France with Leon Conus of the Moscow Conservatoire, and composition with Alexander Glazunov; also with Profs Harold Craxton and Tobias Matthay in London; first public appearance at age of 11 with Lamoureux Orchestra, Paris, and first compositions published by Boosey and Hawkes in same year; commissioned by BBC to broadcast series of all Mozart's piano sonatas; invited to give Mozart recital for bicentenary celebration of Mozart's birth, Edinburgh Festival. Major works recorded: Mozart piano concertos K271 and K467; Mozart recitals; complete Chopin Mazurkas; Chopin 24 Preludes; Scarlatti Sonatas; Mozart and Haydn Sonatas; works by Rachmaninov, Prokofiev, Scriabin. Widely noted for interpretation of Mozart's piano works. *Recreations:* swimming, chess, fly fishing. *Address:* 17 Montagu Square, W1H 2LE; Casa delle Colonne, San Pietro, Sardinia.

MILL, Douglas Russell; Secretary, Law Society of Scotland, since 1997; *b* 3 Jan. 1957; *s* of Alan M. L. Mill and Anna B. Mill (*née* Russell); *m* 1982, Christine Rankin; two *s* one *d. Educ:* Paisley Grammar Sch.; Glasgow Univ. (LLB, BA, MBA). Apprentice, Wright & Crawford, 1978–80; Partner: Cameron Pinkerton Haggarty, 1980–85; MacFarlane Young & Co., 1985–96. Dep. Dir, Univ. of Strathclyde Centre for Professional Legal Studies, 1993–96. DUniv. *Publication:* Successful Practice Management, 1992. *Recreations:* Rugby, golf. *Address:* Law Society of Scotland, 26 Drumsheugh Gardens, Edinburgh EH3 7YR. *T:* (0131) 226 7411. *Club:* Kingsacre Golf (Edinburgh).

MILL, Ian Alexander; QC 1999; *b* 9 April 1958; *s* of Ronald MacLauchlan Mill and Thelma Anita Mill; *m* 1987, Mary Emma Clayden; two *s. Educ:* Epsom Coll.; Trinity Hall, Cambridge (MA Classics and Law). Called to the Bar, Middle Temple, 1981; in practice at the Bar, 1982–. *Recreations:* cricket, golf, opera, theatre, good food and wine. *Address:* Blackstone House, Temple, EC4Y 9BW. *T:* (020) 7583 1770. *Club:* MCC.

MILL, Robert Duguid Forrest P.; *see* Pring-Mill.

MILLAIS, Sir Geoffroy Richard Everett, 6th Bt *cr* 1885, of Palace Gate, Kensington and Saint Ouen, Jersey; *b* 27 Dec. 1941; *s* of Sir Ralph Regnault Millais, 5th Bt and his 1st wife, Felicity Caroline Mary Ward Robinson (*d* 1994), *d* of Brig.-Gen. W. W. Warner, CMG; *S* father, 1992. *Heir: uncle* Edward Gray St Helier Millais [*b* 15 March 1918; *m* 1947, Rosemary Barbara Lucas; four *s* one *d*].

MILLAN, Rt Hon. Bruce; PC 1975; Member, Commission of the European Communities, 1989–95; *b* 5 Oct. 1927; *s* of David Millan; *m* 1953, Gwendoline May Fairey; one *s* one *d. Educ:* Harris Academy, Dundee. Chartered Accountant, 1950–59. Contested: West Renfrewshire, 1951, Craigton Div. of Glasgow, 1955. MP (Lab): Glasgow, Craigton, 1959–83; Glasgow, Govan, 1983–88; Parly Under-Sec. of State: for Defence, (RAF), 1964–66, for Scotland, 1966–70; Minister of State, Scottish Office, 1974–76; Sec. of State for Scotland, 1976–79; opposition spokesman on Scotland, 1979–83. *Address:* 1 Torridon Avenue, Glasgow G41 5LA. *T:* (0141) 427 6483.

MILLAR, family name of **Baron Inchyra**.

MILLAR, Anthony Bruce; Chairman, Canadian Zinc (formerly San Andreas Resources) Corporation, since 1994; Hon. President, The Albert Fisher Group PLC, since 1992 (Chairman, 1982–92); *b* 5 Oct. 1941; *s* of late James Desmond Millar and of Josephine Georgina Millar (*née* Brice); *m* 1964, Judith Anne (*née* Jester); two *d. Educ:* Haileybury and Imperial Service College. FCA. Asst to Group Management Accountant and Group Treasurer, Viyella Internat. Fedn, 1964–67; United Transport Overseas Ltd, Nairobi, and London (Dep. Group Financial Controller), 1967–72; Finance Dir, Fairfield Property Co. Ltd, 1972–75; Consultant, 1975–77; Managing Dir, Provincial Laundries Ltd, 1977–81; Dep. Chm., Hawley Group, 1981–82. Freeman, City of London, 1993–; Liveryman, Fruiterers' Co., 1993– (Hon Assistant, 2001–). CIMgt; FRSA. *Recreations:* swimming, scuba diving, walking, bridge, travel. *Address:* Frensham Vale House, Lower Bourne, near Farnham, Surrey GU10 3JB. *Club:* Mark's.

MILLAR, Betty Phyllis Joy; Regional Nursing Officer, South Western Regional Health Authority, 1973–84, retired; *b* 19 March 1929; *o d* of late Sidney Hildersly Millar and May Phyllis Halliday. *Educ:* Ursuline High Sch. for Girls; Dumbarton Academy; Glasgow Royal Infirm.; Glasgow Royal Maternity Hosp.; Royal Coll. of Nursing, London. RGN 1950; SCM 1953; NA (Hosp.) Cert. 1961. Theatre Sister, Glasgow Royal Infirm., 1953–54; Ward and Theatre Sister, Henry Brock Meml Hosp., 1954–55; Nursing Sister, Iraq Petroleum Co., 1955–57; Clinical Instructor, Exper. Scheme of Nurse Trng, Glasgow, 1957–60; Admin. Student, Royal Coll. of Nursing, 1960–61; 2nd Asst Matron, Glasgow Royal Infirm., 1961–62; Asst Nursing Officer, Wessex Regional Hosp. Bd, 1962–67; Matron, Glasgow Royal Infirm., 1967–69; Chief Regional Nursing Officer, SW Regional Hosp. Bd, 1969–73. WHO Fellowship to study nursing services in Scandinavia, 1967. Mem. Jt Bd of Clinical Nursing Studies, 1970–82. *Address:* Pinedrift, 45 Stoneyfields, Easton-in-Gordano, Bristol BS20 0LL. *T:* (01275) 372709.

MILLAR, Douglas George; Clerk of Legislation, since 2001, and Departmental Finance Officer, since 1994, House of Commons; *b* 15 Feb. 1946; *s* of late George Millar and Doris Mary Millar (*née* Morris); *m* 1st, 1967, Susan Mary Farrow (marr. diss. 1986); one *s* one *d*; 2nd, 1987, (Jane) Victoria Howard Smith; one *s* one *d. Educ:* City of Norwich Sch.; Bristol Univ. (BA Hons History 1967); Reading Univ. (MA Politics 1968). A Clerk, H of C, 1968–; Clerk of Defence Cttee, 1979–83; Clerk i/c Private Members' Bills and Divs, 1983–87; Clerk of Home Affairs Cttee, 1987–89; Principal Clerk and Clerk of Financial Cttees and Treasury and Civil Service Cttee, 1989–91; Sec. to Public Accounts Commn, 1989–91; Second Clerk, Select Cttees, 1991–94; Clerk of Select Cttees, 1994–97; Prin. Clerk, Table Office, 1998–2001. Jt Sec., Assoc. of Secs Gen. of Parlts, 1971–77. *Publications:* articles and reviews in parly and political jls. *Recreations:* watching Norwich City, family, golf. *Address:* Public Bill Office, House of Commons, SW1A 0AA. *T:* (020) 7219 3255. *Club:* Roehampton.

MILLAR, Prof. Fergus Graham Burtholme, DPhil; DLitt; FSA; FBA 1976; Camden Professor of Ancient History, 1984–Sept. 2002, and Fellow of Brasenose College, Oxford University, since 1984; *b* 5 July 1935; *s* of late J. S. L. Millar and of Jean Burtholme (*née* Taylor); *m* 1959, Susanna Friedmann; two *s* one *d. Educ:* Edinburgh Acad.; Loretto Sch.; Trinity Coll., Oxford (1st Cl. Lit. Hum.; Hon. Fellow, 1992); DPhil 1962, DLitt 1988, Oxon. Fellow: All Souls Coll., Oxford, 1958–64; Queen's Coll., Oxford, 1964–76 (Hon. Fellow, 1999); Prof. of Ancient History, UCL, 1976–84. Conington Prize, 1963. President: Soc. for the Promotion of Roman Studies, 1989–92 (Vice-Pres., 1977–89, 1992–2001); Classical Assoc., 1992–93; Pubns Sec., British Acad., 1997–July 2002. FSA 1978. Corresp. Member: German Archaeolog. Inst., 1978; Bavarian Acad., 1987; Finnish Acad., 1989. Hon. DPhil Helsinki, 1994. Editor, Jl of Roman Studies, 1975–79. *Publications:* A Study of Cassius Dio, 1964; The Roman Empire and its Neighbours, 1967; (ed with G. Vermes) E. Schürer, history of the Jewish people in the age of Jesus Christ (175 BC-AD 135), Vol. I, 1973, Vol. II, 1979, Vol. III, parts 1 and 2 (ed with G. Vermes and M. D. Goodman), 1986–87; The Emperor in the Roman World (31 BC-AD 337), 1977, 2nd edn 1992; (ed with E. Segal) Caesar Augustus: seven aspects, 1984; The Roman Near East, 1993; The Crowd in Rome in the Late Republic, 1998; Rome, the Greek World and the East, vol. I, 2001; The Roman Republic in Political Thought, 2002. *Address:* Brasenose College, Oxford OX1 4AJ; 80 Harpes Road, Oxford OX2 7QL. *T:* (01865) 515782.

MILLAR, Gavin James; QC 2000; *b* 10 July 1959; *s* of Robert and Audrey Millar; partner, Carmel Mary Elizabeth Fitzsimons; one *s* three *d. Educ:* St Peter's Coll., Oxford (BA Jurisprudence). Called to the Bar, Lincoln's Inn, 1981; Founder Mem., Doughty St Chambers, 1990. Mem., Public Affairs Cttee, Bar Council, 1995–97; Vice-Chm., Soc. of Labour Lawyers, 1999–. Mem. (Lab) Westminster CC, 1985–94. *Publication:* (jtly) Media Law and Human Rights, 2001. *Recreations:* family, football, painting. *Address:* Doughty Street Chambers, 10–11 Doughty Street, WC1N 2PL. *T:* (020) 7404 1313. *Club:* Manchester United Football.

MILLAR, George Reid, DSO 1944; MC; farmer and writer; *b* 19 Sept. 1910; 2nd *s* of Thomas Andrew Millar, architect, and Mary Reid Morton; *m* 1945, Isabel Beatriz (*d* 1990), *d* of Montague Paske-Smith, CMG, CBE; no *c. Educ:* Loretto; St John's, Cambridge. Architect, 1930–32; journalist, with Daily Telegraph and Daily Express, 1934–39; Paris correspondent Daily Express, 1939; served War of 1939–45, The Rifle Bde; escaped from German POW camp to England, then served as agent in France; Chevalier de la Légion d'Honneur; Croix de Guerre avec Palmes. Farmer of 1,000 acres, 1962–90. *Publications:* Maquis, 1945; Horned Pigeon, 1946; My Past was an Evil River, 1946; Isabel and the Sea, 1948; Through the Unicorn Gates, 1950; A White Boat from England, 1951; Siesta, 1952; Orellana, 1954; Oyster River, 1963; Horseman, 1970; The Bruneval Raid, 1974; Road to Resistance, 1979. *Recreation:* sailing. *Address:* Uploders Place, Bridport, Dorset DT6 4PF. *T:* (01308) 485653. *Clubs:* Special Forces, Royal Cruising; Royal Yacht Squadron (Cowes).

MILLAR, Rev. Preb. John Alexander Kirkpatrick, (Sandy); Vicar of Holy Trinity Brompton, with St Paul, Onslow Square, since 1985; *b* 13 Nov. 1939; *s* of Maj.-Gen. Robert Kirkpatrick Millar of Orton, CB, DSO and Frances (*née* Beyts); *m* 1971, Annette Fisher; one *s* three *d. Educ:* Eton; Trinity Coll., Cambridge (BA 1962; MA 1966); Univ. of Durham (DipTh). Deacon 1976; priest 1977; Curate, Holy Trinity Brompton, with St Paul, Onslow Square, 1976–85; Area Dean, Chelsea, 1989–94; Prebendary, St Paul's Cathedral, 1997–. *Address:* Holy Trinity Vicarage, 73 Prince's Gate Mews, SW7 2PP. *T:* (020) 7584 8957.

MILLAR, John Stanley, CBE 1979; County Planning Officer, Greater Manchester Council, 1973–83; *b* 1925; *s* of late Nicholas William Stanley Millar and late Elsie Baxter Millar (*née* Flinn); *m* 1st, 1961, Patricia Mary (*née* Land) (*d* 1992); one *d*; 2nd, 1993, Christine (*née* Riley). *Educ:* Liverpool Coll.; Univ. of Liverpool. BArch, DipCD, PPRTPI, RIBA. Planning Asst, then Sen. Asst Architect, City of Liverpool, 1948–51; Sectional Planning Officer, then Dep. Asst County Planning Officer, Lancs CC, 1951–61; Chief Asst Planning Officer, then Asst City Planning Officer, City of Manchester, 1961–64; City Planning Officer, Manchester, 1964–73. *Publications:* papers in professional and technical jls. *Recreations:* walking, listening to music, travel, the sea. *Address:* 55 Stanneylands Drive, Wilmslow, Cheshire SK9 4EU. *T:* (01625) 523616.

MILLAR, Sir Oliver Nicholas, GCVO 1988 (KCVO 1973; CVO 1963; MVO 1953); FBA 1970; Director of the Royal Collection, 1987–88; Surveyor of the Queen's Pictures, 1972–88, Surveyor Emeritus, since 1988; *b* 26 April 1923; *er s* of late Gerald Millar, MC and late Ruth Millar; *m* 1954, Delia Mary (CVO 1996), 2nd *d* of late Lt-Col Cuthbert Dawnay, MC; one *s* three *d*. *Educ:* Rugby; Courtauld Institute of Art, University of London (Academic Diploma in History of Art). Unable, for medical reasons, to serve in War of 1939–45. Asst Surveyor of the King's Pictures, 1947–49, Dep. Surveyor 1949–72. Trustee, Nat. Portrait Gallery, 1972–95. Member: Reviewing Cttee on Export of Works of Art, 1975–87; Exec. Cttee, Nat. Art Collections Fund, 1986–98. Visitor, Ashmolean Mus., 1987–93. Trustee, Nat. Heritage Meml Fund, 1988–92. A Dir, Friends of the Tate Gall., 1989–; Chm., Patrons of British Art, 1989–97. FSA. Corresponding Fellow: Ateneo Veneto, Venice; Koninklijke Academie voor Wetenschappen, Letteren en Schone Kunsten, Belgium. *Publications:* Gainsborough, 1949; William Dobson, Tate Gallery Exhibition, 1951; English Art, 1625–1714 (with Dr M. D. Whinney), 1957; Rubens's Whitehall Ceiling, 1958; Abraham van der Doort's Catalogue, 1960; Tudor, Stuart and Early Georgian Pictures in the Collection of HM the Queen, 1963; Zoffany and his Tribuna, 1967; Later Georgian Pictures in the Collection of HM the Queen, 1969; Inventories and Valuations of the King's Goods, 1972; The Age of Charles I (Tate Gallery Exhibn), 1972; The Queen's Pictures, 1977; Sir Peter Lely (Nat. Portrait Gall. Exhibn), 1978; Van Dyck in England (Nat. Portrait Gall. Exhibn), 1982; Victorian Pictures in the Collection of HM the Queen, 1992; articles in the Burlington Magazine, etc; numerous catalogues, principally for The Queen's Gallery. *Recreations:* grandchildren, drawing, gardening, reading, listening to music. *Address:* The Cottage, Ray's Lane, Penn, Bucks HP10 8LH. *T:* (01494) 812124. *Clubs:* Brooks's, MCC.

MILLAR, Air Vice-Marshal Peter, CB 1998; Chief Operating Officer, Perimele Ltd, since 2000; *b* 20 June 1942; *s* of Air Cdre John Christopher Millar, RAF and Patricia Millar (*née* Allen); *m* 1966, Annette McMillan; one *s* two *d*. *Educ:* Malvern Coll.; RAF Coll., Cranwell. Served RAF: No 20 Sqn, Singapore, 1964–66; No 4 FTS, RAF Valley, 1967–69; Central Flying Sch., RAF Kemble, 1969–71; 560 Trng Sqn, Randolph AFB, Texas, 1971–74; RAF Staff Coll., 1974; Flight Commander: No 20 Sqn, Wildenrath, 1975–77; No 4 Sqn, Gutersloh, 1977–78; MoD, 1978–79; Sqn Comdr, No 233 OCU, RAF Wittering, 1979–82; USAF Air Warfare Coll., Maxwell AFB, Alabama, 1982–83; Brit. Defence Staff, Washington, 1983–84; Stn Comdr, RAF Wittering, 1985–86; RCDS 1987; on staff, UK Mil. Rep., NATO HQ, 1988–90; Dir NATO, MoD, 1990–93; HQ AAFCE, Ramstein AFB, Germany, 1993–95; Administr, Sovereign Base Areas and Comdr, British Forces Cyprus, 1995–98; retd 1998. Dir of Security, Medical World Inc., and Dir, Internat. Admin, Medical Mall Ltd, 1998–99. Mem., RUSI, 1978–. FRAeS 1997; MInstD 1997. *Recreations:* ski-ing, golf, off-shore sailing. *Club:* Royal Air Force.

MILLAR, Peter Carmichael, OBE 1978; Deputy Keeper of HM Signet, 1983–91; *b* 19 Feb. 1927; *s* of late Rev. Peter Carmichael Millar, OBE, DD and of Ailsa Ross Brown Campbell or Millar; *m* 1953, Kirsteen Lindsay Carnegie, *d* of late Col David Carnegie, CB, OBE, TD, DL, Dep. Gen. Manager, Clydesdale Bank; two *s* two *d*. *Educ:* Aberdeen Grammar Sch.; Glasgow Univ.; St Andrews Univ.; Edinburgh Univ. MA, LLB; WS. Served RN, 1944–47. Partner in law firms, Messrs W. & T. P. Manuel, WS, 1954–62; Aitken, Kinnear & Co., WS, 1963–87; Aitken Nairn, WS, 1987–92. Clerk to Soc. of Writers to HM Signet, 1964–83. Chairman: Church of Scotland Gen. Trustees, 1973–85; Mental Welfare Commn for Scotland, 1983–91; (part-time) Medical Appeal Tribunals, 1991–99; Pension Appeal Tribunals, 1992–99. Convener, Scottish Child and Family Alliance, later Children in Scotland, 1992–95. *Recreations:* golf, hill-walking, music. *Address:* 25 Cramond Road North, Edinburgh EH4 6LY. *T:* (0131) 336 2069. *Clubs:* New (Edinburgh); Hon. Co. of Edinburgh Golfers, Bruntsfield Links Golfing Society.

MILLAR, Rev. Preb. Sandy; *see* Millar, Rev. Preb. J. A. K.

MILLARD, Anthony Paul; founded Anthony Millard Consultancy, 2001; Headmaster, Giggleswick School, 1993–2001; *b* 21 Sept. 1948; *s* of Leonard William Millard and Marjorie Ethel Millard (*née* Manley); *m* 1971, Lesley Margaret Baker; one *s* three *d*. *Educ:* Solihull Sch.; LSE (BSc Econ); Balliol Coll., Oxford (PGCE). Teaching in Zambia, 1971–74; Stagiaire (specialist trainee) with EC, 1974–75; Wells Cathedral School: Asst Master, 1975–77; Housemaster, 1977–86; Dep. Headmaster, 1982–86; Headmaster, Wycliffe Coll., Glos, 1987–93. Non-exec. Dir, Servicespan Ltd, 2001–. Chairman: ISIS (Central), 1990–92; Bloxham Project Cttee, 1991–96; Services Cttee, HMC, 1995–2000; Boarding Schs Assoc., 1999–2000 (Mem. Exec. Cttee, 1996–); Mem. Council, ISCO, 1995–98. Contested (C) Wirral South, 2001. FRSA 1986. *Recreations:* squash, travel, mountains. *Address:* Horseshoe Cottage, Westrip, Stroud, Glos GL6 6HA. *Clubs:* East India, Devonshire, Sports and Public Schools.

MILLARD, Sir Guy (Elwin), KCMG 1972 (CMG 1957); CVO 1961; HM Diplomatic Service, retired; *b* 22 Jan. 1917; *s* of Col Baldwin Salter Millard, and Phyllis Mary Tetley; *m* 1st, 1946, Anne, *d* of Gordon Mackenzie; one *s* one *d*; 2nd, 1964, Mary Judy, *d* of late James Dugdale and Pamela Dugdale (*née* Coventry); two *s*. *Educ:* Charterhouse; Pembroke Coll., Cambridge. Served RN, World War II. HM Diplomatic Service, 1939–76: Ambassador to Hungary, 1967–69; Minister, Washington, 1970–71; Ambassador to Sweden, 1971–74; Ambassador to Italy, 1974–76. Chm., British-Italian Soc., 1977–83. Grand Officer, Order of Merit, Italy, 1981. *Address:* Fyfield Manor, Southrop, Glos GL7 3NZ. *T:* (01367) 850234.

MILLEN, Brig. Anthony Tristram Patrick; Defence Advisor to British High Commissioner, Ottawa, Canada, 1980–83, retired; *b* 15 Dec. 1928; *s* of Charles Reginald Millen and Annie Mary Martin; *m* 1954, Mary Alice Featherston Johnston; three *s* two *d* (and two *s* decd). *Educ:* Mount St Mary's Coll. 5th Royal Inniskilling Dragoon Guards, 1948; served in Germany, Korea, Cyprus, N Ireland, Hong Kong, USA. *Publications:* articles in US military jls. *Recreation:* sailing. *Address:* The Manor House, Hutton Sessay, near Thirsk, N Yorks YO7 3BA. *T:* (01845) 501444.

MILLER, family name of **Baronesses Miller of Chilthorne Domer** and **Miller of Hendon.**

MILLER OF CHILTHORNE DOMER, Baroness *cr* 1998 (Life Peer), of Chilthorne Domer in the co. of Somerset; **Susan Elizabeth Miller;** *b* 1 Jan. 1954; *d* of Frederick Oliver Meddows Taylor and Norah Langham; *m* 1980, John Miller (marr. diss. 1998); one *d* (and one *d* decd); *m* 1999, Humphrey Temperley. *Educ:* Sidcot Sch.; Oxford Polytech. David & Charles, Publishers, 1975–77; Weidenfeld & Nicholson, 1977; Penguin Books, 1977–79; bookshop owner, Sherborne and Yeovil, 1979–89. Lib Dem spokesman on rural affairs and agriculture, H of L, 1999. Parish Councillor, Chilthorne Domer, 1987–; Member (Lib Dem): S Somerset DC, 1991– (Leader, 1996–98); Somerset CC, 1997–. *Recreations:* walking, reading, friends. *Address:* House of Lords, SW1A 0PW.

MILLER OF HENDON, Baroness *cr* 1993 (Life Peer), of Gore in the London Borough of Barnet; **Doreen Miller,** MBE 1989; JP; *b* 13 June 1933; *d* of Bernard Henry Feldman and Hetty Feldman; *m* 1955, Henry Miller; three *s*. *Educ:* Brondesbury and Kilburn High Sch.; LSE. Chairman and Managing Director, 1971–88: Universal Beauty Club Ltd (UK); Cosmetic Club International GmbH (Germany); Universal Beauty Club (Pty) Ltd (Australia). Nat. Chm. and Exec. Dir, The 300 Group, 1985–88; Chm., Women Into Public Life Campaign, 1987–; Human Rights Advr, Soroptimist International, 1987–90. A Baroness in Waiting (Govt Whip), 1994–97; an Opposition Whip, 1997–. Crown Agent, 1990–94. Chairman: Barnet FHSA, 1990–94; Nat. Assoc. of Hosp. and Community Friends (formerly Nat. Assoc. of Leagues of Hosp. Friends), 1997–. Mem., Monopolies and Mergers Commn, 1992–93. Trustee, Menerva Educnl Trust, 1992–. Jt Treas., 1990–93, Chm., 1993–96, Pres., 1996–98, Greater London Area, Nat. Union of Conservative & Unionist Party. FRSA. JP Brent, 1971. *Publication:* Let's Make Up, 1975. *Recreations:* politics, reading, football, sitting by sunlit swimming pools given the opportunity. *Address:* House of Lords, SW1A 0PW. *Clubs:* Carlton, St Stephen's Constitutional.

MILLER, (Alan) Cameron, MA; LLB; FCIT; advocate; Tutor at Fettes College, 1974–94; *b* 10 Jan. 1913; *o s* of late Arthur Miller, Edinburgh; *m* 1945, Audrey Main; one *d* (one *s* decd). *Educ:* Fettes Coll.; Edinburgh Univ. MA 1934; LLB 1936. Advocate, 1938; served War of 1939–45, RN. Interim Sheriff-Substitute at Dundee, 1946; Sheriff-Substitute of Inverness, Moray, Nairn, Ross and Cromarty, at Fort William, 1946–52; Legal Adviser (Scotland): British Transport Commn, 1952–62; BR Board, 1962–73. Chm., Inst. of Transport (Scotland), 1971–72. *Recreations:* golf, music. *Address:* 12A Quality Street, North Berwick, Scotland.

MILLER, Alan John McCulloch, DSC 1941, VRD 1950; Chairman, Miller Insulation Ltd, 1975–86; *b* 21 April 1914; *s* of late Louis M. Miller and Mary McCulloch; *m* 1940, Kirsteen Ross Orr; three *s* one *d*. *Educ:* Kelvinside Academy; Strathclyde Univ. CEng, MRINA, MIESS, FBIM, FRSA. Family engrg business, 1933–39. Commnd RNVR (Clyde Div.), 1938; served RN, 1939–45: Far East, Indian Ocean, S Atlantic, HMS Dorsetshire, then destroyers; in comd, HMS Fitzroy, Wolverine, Holderness, St Nazaire, Dieppe raids, Russian convoys, 1943–44; psc 1944. Rejoined family business, 1945, until sold to Bestobell Ltd, 1951; Dir, Bestobell Ltd, 1951–73, Chm. and Man. Dir, 1965–73; Chm. and Man. Dir, Wm Simons & Co. Ltd, Shipbuilders, 1956–60; Dir, Truckline Ferries Ltd, 1972–88; Chairman: Antigua Slipway Ltd, 1966–86; Dev West Ltd, 1973–76; Low & Bonar, 1977–82. Chm., BNEC Southern Africa Cttee, 1970, until abolished. Member: Sports Council, 1973–80; Central Council of Physical Recreation. *Publication:* Over the Horizon 1939–45, 1999. *Recreations:* sailing, golf, ski-ing, shooting. *Address:* Dalruadh, 17 Victoria Terrace, Crieff, Perthshire PH7 4AA. *T:* (01764) 652299. *Clubs:* Royal Thames Yacht, Royal Ocean Racing, Royal Cruising; Western (Glasgow); Royal and Ancient (St Andrews); Helensburgh Golf.

MILLER, Amelia, (Mrs Michael Miller); *see* Freedman, A.

MILLER, Prof. Andrew, CBE 1999; PhD; FRSE; Principal and Vice-Chancellor, University of Stirling, 1994–2001; *b* 15 Feb. 1936; *s* of William Hamilton Miller and Susan Anderson (*née* Auld); *m* 1962, Rosemary Singleton Hannah Fyvie; one *s* one *d*. *Educ:* Beath High Sch.; Edinburgh Univ. (BSc Hons 1958; PhD 1962); Wolfson Coll., Oxford (MA 1967; Hon. Fellow, 1995). Postdoctoral Fellow, CSIRO, Melbourne, 1962–65; Tutor in Chemistry, Ormond Coll., Melbourne Univ., 1963–65; Staff Scientist, MRC Lab. of Molecular Biol., Cambridge, 1965–66; Lectr in Molecular Biophysics, Oxford Univ., 1966–83; Fellow, Wolfson Coll., Oxford, 1967–83; on secondment as Hd, EMBL, Grenoble, 1975–80; Edinburgh University: Prof. of Biochem., 1984–94; on secondment as Dir of Res., European Synchrotron Radiation Facility, Grenoble, 1986–91; Vice-Dean of Medicine, 1991–93; Vice-Provost of Medicine and Veterinary Medicine, 1992–93; Vice-Principal, 1993–94; Chm., Industrial Centre for Math. Scis, 2001–. Leverhulme Emeritus Fellowship, 2001–. Member: Action Gp on Standards in Scottish Schs, DFEE, 1997–99; Scottish Exec. Sci. Strategy Gp, 1999–. Dir, Scottish Knowledge plc, 1997–. Advr, Wellcome Trust, on UK-Wellcome-French-Synchrotron, 1999–2000. Mem. Council, Open Univ., 2001–. FRSE 1986 (Mem. Council, 1997–). *Publications:* (ed jtly) Minerals in Biology, 1984; numerous papers on collagen and muscle in scientific jls incl. Nature, Jl Molecular Biol. *Recreations:* music, walking, reading, wondering. *Address:* 5 Blackford Hill Grove, Edinburgh EH9 3HA.

MILLER, Andrew Peter; MP (Lab) Ellesmere Port and Neston, since 1992; *b* 23 March 1949; *s* of late Ernest William Thomas Miller and of Daphne May Miller; *m* Frances Ewan; two *s* one *d*. *Educ:* Hayling Island Secondary Sch.; LSE (Mature Student; Dip. Indust. Relations 1976). Lab. Technician, Dept of Geology, Portsmouth Poly., specialising in X-RF and X-RD analysis, 1967–76; Divl Officer, ASTMS, subseq. MSF, 1977–92. PPS, DTI, 2001–. Mem., Science and Technol. Select Cttee, 1992–97; Vice Chm., PLP Cttee on Science and Technol., 1993–97; Treas., 1997–2000, Vice Pres., 2000–, Parlt and Sci. Cttee. Ldr, PLP Leadership Campaign Team, 1997–98. Dir, Eur. Informatics Market, 1996–98. Pres., Computing for Labour, 1993–. *Publication:* (jtly) North West Economic Strategy, 1987. *Recreations:* walking, photography. *Address:* Hollytree Cottage, Commonside, Alvanley, Cheshire WA6 9HB. *T:* (01928) 722642; *e-mail:* millera@parliament.uk.

MILLER, Arjay; Dean, and Professor of Management, Graduate School of Business, Stanford University, 1969–79, now Dean Emeritus; Vice-Chairman, Ford Motor Company, 1968–69 (President, 1963–68); *b* 4 March 1916; *s* of Rawley John Miller and Mary Gertrude Schade; *m* 1940, Frances Marion Fearing; one *s* one *d*. *Educ:* University of California at Los Angeles (BS with highest hons, 1937). Graduate Student and Teaching Asst, University of California at Berkeley, 1938–40; Research Technician, Calif. State Planning Bd, 1941; Economist, Federal Reserve Bank of San Francisco, 1941–43. Captain, US Air Force, 1943–46. Asst Treas, Ford Motor Co., 1947–53; Controller, 1953–57; Vice-Pres. and Controller, 1957–61; Vice-Pres. of Finance, 1961–62; Vice-Pres., Staff Group, 1962–63. Mem. Bd of Dirs, Public Policy Inst., Calif; Trustee: Brookings Instn, Washington; Internat. Exec. Service Corps; Urban Inst. Mem. Bd of Dirs, SRI International. Councillor, The Conference Board. Fellow, Amer. Acad. of Arts and Scis, 1990. Hon. LLD: Univ. of California (LA), 1964; Whitman Coll., 1965; Univ. of Nebraska, 1965; Ripon Coll., 1980; Washington Univ., St Louis, 1982. *Address:* 225 Mountain Home Road, Woodside, CA 94062, USA. *Clubs:* Bohemian, Pacific Union (San Francisco).

MILLER, Arthur; playwright; *b* 17 Oct. 1915; *s* of Isadore Miller and Augusta Barnett; *m* 1940, Mary Grace Slattery (marr. diss.); one *s* one *d*; *m* 1956, Marilyn Monroe (marr. diss. 1961; she *d* 1962); *m* 1962, Ingeborg Morath; one *d*. *Educ:* University of Michigan, USA (AB). Pres. of PEN Club, 1965–69. Cameron Mackintosh Prof. of Contemporary Theatre, Oxford Univ., 1995. *Publications:* Honors at Dawn, 1936; No Villains (They Too Arise), 1937; The Pussycat and the Expert Plumber who was a Man, 1941; William Ireland's Confession, 1941; The Man who had all the Luck, 1944; That They May Win, 1944; Situation Normal (reportage), 1944; Focus (novel), 1945; Grandpa and the Statue, 1945; The Story of Gus, 1947; Jane's Blanket, 1963; I Don't Need You Anymore (collected stories), 1967; (jt author) In Russia, 1969; Fame, and the Reason Why, 1970; The Portable Arthur Miller, 1971; (with Inge Morath) In the Country, 1977; (ed Robert

Martin) The Theater Essays of Arthur Miller, 1978; (with Inge Morath) Chinese Encounters, 1979; Salesman in Beijing, 1984; Timebends (autobiog.), 1987; Plain Girl (novel), 1995; *plays:* All My Sons, 1947 (NY Drama Critics Award, 1948); Death of a Salesman (NY Drama Critics Award, Pulitzer Prize), 1949 (filmed 1985); The Crucible, 1953 (filmed 1996); A View from the Bridge, 1955 (filmed 1962); A Memory of Two Mondays, 1955; Collected Plays, 1958; After the Fall, 1963; Incident at Vichy, 1964; The Price, 1968 and 1990; The Creation of the World and Other Business, 1972 (musical version, Up From Paradise, 1974); The American Clock, 1980 (TV version, 1993); Playing for Time (Peabody Award, CBS–TV), 1981; Two Way Mirror, 1985; Danger: Memory!, 1986; Ride Down Mount Morgan, 1990; The Last Yankee, 1992; Broken Glass, 1994; Mr Peter's Connections, 1998; *screenplays:* The Misfits, 1960; Everybody Wins, 1990; contrib. stories and essays to Esquire, Colliers, Atlantic Monthly, etc. *Address:* c/o ICM, 40 W 57th Street, New York, NY 10019, USA.

See also D. Day-Lewis.

MILLER, Hon. (Arthur) Daniel; MLA (NDP) North Coast, since 1986; Minister of Energy and Mines, and Minister responsible for Northern Development, British Columbia, since 1998; *b* 24 Dec. 1944; *s* of Arthur William Miller and Evelyn Estelle Miller (*née* Lewis); *m* 1987, Beverly Gayle Ballard (*née* Bartram); three *s* two *d*. *Educ:* N Vancouver Secondary Sch. Millwright. Former Mem. Council, Prince Rupert City. Minister of: Forests, 1991–93; Skills, Training and Labour, 1993–96; Municipal Affairs, 1996–97; Employment and Investment, 1997–98; Dep. Premier, 1996–99, Premier, 1999–2000. *Address:* Ministry of Energy and Mines, PO Box 9060, Stn Prov Government, Victoria, BC V8W 9E2, Canada.

MILLER, Barry; Director General Service Personnel Policy, Ministry of Defence, since 1999; *b* 11 May 1942; *s* of Lt-Col Howard Alan Miller and Margaret Yvonne Richardson; *m* 1968, Katrina Elizabeth Chandler; one *s* one *d*. *Educ:* Lancaster Royal Grammar Sch. Ministry of Defence: Exec. Officer, RAE Farnborough, 1961; Asst Principal, MoD, London, 1965; Principal: Defence Policy Staff, 1969; Naval Personnel Div., 1969; Equipment Secretariat (Army), 1972; Defence Secretariat, 1973; CSD, 1975; Asst Secretary: Civilian Management, 1977; Defence Secretariat, 1980; RCDS 1984; Asst Sec., Management Services (Organisation), 1985; Director General: Defence Quality Assurance, 1986; Test and Evaluation, 1992; Asst Under Sec. (Finance), PE, 1994; Dir Gen., Finance, 1995; Command Sec. to Second Sea Lord and C-in-C Naval Home Command, and Asst Under-Sec. of State (Naval Personnel), 1996–99. *Address:* Ministry of Defence, St Giles Court, 1-3 St Giles High Street, WC2H 8LD.

MILLER, Sir Bernard; *see* Miller, Sir O. B.

MILLER, Bill; Member (Lab) Scotland, European Parliament, since 1999 (Glasgow, 1994–99); *b* 22 July 1954; *s* of George and Janet Miller; one *s* one *d*. *Educ:* Paisley Coll.; Kingston Poly. (BSc Land Econs). DipTP; ARICS. Surveyor, Glasgow DC, 1978–94. Councillor (Lab) Strathclyde, 1986–94. *Recreations:* record collecting, Kilmarnock Football Club, golf. *Address:* John Smith House, 145-165 West Regent Street, Glasgow G2 4RZ. *T:* (0141) 221 3024, *Fax:* (0141) 221 4912; *e-mail:* bmiller@europarl.eu.int. *Club:* Castlemilk Labour (Glasgow).

MILLER, Bruce; *see* Miller, J. D. B.

MILLER, Cameron; *see* Miller, A. C.

MILLER, Cheryl; *see* Miller, D. C.

MILLER, Colin Brown; Sheriff for South Strathclyde, Dumfries and Galloway, since 1991; *b* 4 Oct. 1946; *s* of late James Miller and Isabella Brown or Miller; *m* 1972, Joan Elizabeth Blyth; three *s*. *Educ:* Paisley Grammar Sch.; Glasgow Univ. (LLB 1967). NP, SSC. Solicitor in private practice, 1969–91. Mem. Council, Law Soc. of Scotland, and Convener of various cttees, 1983–91. Dean, Faculty of Procurators in Paisley, 1991. *Recreations:* walking, family, railways, ships, motor vehicles, photography. *Address:* Sheriffs' Chambers, Wellington Square, Ayr KA7 1EE. *T:* (01292) 268474.

MILLER, Hon. Daniel; *see* Miller, Hon. A. D.

MILLER, David; journalist and author; columnist, Daily Telegraph, since 1997; Chief Sports Correspondent, The Times, 1983–97; *b* 1 March 1935; *er s* of late Wilfred Miller and Everilda Miller (*née* Milne-Redhead); *m* 1957, Marita Marjorie Malyon; one *s* one *d*. *Educ:* Charterhouse; Peterhouse, Cambridge (Nat. Sci. Tripos; CUAFC *v* Oxford, 1954–55). Sub-editor, The Times, 1956–59; Sports Correspondent: Daily Telegraph, 1960–73; Sunday Telegraph, 1961–73; Chief Sports Corresp., Daily Express, 1973–82. Has covered 15 Summer and Winter Olympic Games and 11 Football World Cups. Mem., Press Commn of IAAF, 1988–. Chm., Sports Writers' Assoc. of GB, 1981–84; Mem., Internat. Soc. of Olympic Historians, 1993–. Sports Writer of Year Award, What the Papers Say, 1986; Doug Gardner Award, Sports Writers' Assoc., 2001. *Publications:* Father of Football: biography of Sir Matt Busby, 1970; World Cup, 1970; World Cup, 1974; The Argentina Story, 1978; Cup Magic, 1981; (with Sebastian Coe) Running Free, 1981; The World to Play For, 1982; Coming Back, 1984; England's Last Glory, 1986; Sports Writers' Eye (anthology), 1989; Stanley Matthews, 1990; Born to Run, 1992; (jtly) History of IAAF, 1992; Olympic Revolution: biography of Juan Antonio Samaranch, 1992 (trans. 8 langs); Our Sporting Times, 1996; Official IOC books: Seoul '88; Albertville '92; Lillehammer '94; Atlanta '96; Nagano '98. *Recreations:* sailing, reading. *Address:* Box 14, Holt NR25 7SL. *Fax:* (01263) 588293. *Clubs:* Royal Thames Yacht; Hawks (Cambridge); Achilles; Corinthian Casuals Football; Middlesex Wanderers; Pegasus Football (Oxford).

MILLER, Dr David Andrew Barclay, FRS 1995; W. M. Keck Foundation Professor of Electrical Engineering, since 1997 (Professor of Electrical Engineering, since 1996), Director, E. L. Ginzton Laboratory, and Solid State and Photonics Laboratory, since 1997, Stanford University; *b* 19 Feb. 1954; *s* of Matthew Barclay Miller and Martha Sanders Miller (*née* Dalling); *m* 1976, Patricia Elizabeth Gillies; one *s* one *d*. *Educ:* St Andrews Univ. (BSc Hons 1976); Heriot-Watt Univ. (PhD Phys 1979). FIEEE 1995. Res. Associate, 1979, Lectr, 1980–81, Heriot-Watt Univ.; Technical Staff, 1981–87, Head of Advanced Photonic Res. Dept, 1987–96, AT&T Bell subseq. Bell, Laboratories, Holmdel, NJ. Pres., IEEE Lasers and Electro-Optics Soc., 1995. Fellow: Amer. Phys. Soc.; Optical Soc. of America (Adolph Lomb Medal, 1986; R. W. Wood Prize, 1988); Internat. Prize in Optics, Internat. Commn for Optics, 1991. Hon. Dr Natural and Applied Scis, Free Univ. Brussels, 1997. *Publications:* numerous papers in learned jls. *Recreation:* clarinet and saxophone playing. *Address:* Ginzton Laboratory, 450 Via Palou, Stanford University, Stanford, CA 94305–4085, USA. *T:* (650) 7230111, *Fax:* (650) 7259355; 815 San Francisco Court, Stanford, CA 94305, USA.

MILLER, David Ivimey, OBE 1991; HM Diplomatic Service, retired; Ambassador to Armenia, 1995–97; *b* 26 March 1937; *y s* of late Reginald James Miller and Helen Joyce (*née* Leech), Cambridge; *m* 1966, Caroline Ethel Jackson; two *d*. *Educ:* Aldenham Sch.; Sch. of Slavonic and East European Studies, London Univ.; Magdalen Coll., Oxford. Served FO, subseq. FCO, and Moscow, 1964–72; Berlin, 1972–74; CSCE, Geneva, 1974, Belgrade, 1977; First Sec. and Head of Chancery, Belgrade, 1978–82; seconded to Cabinet Office, 1982–85, to NATO Secretariat, Brussels, 1985–90; Asst Dir of Research, FCO, 1990–95. Associate Fellow, RUSI, 1997. *Address:* The Oast House, Horsmonden, Tonbridge, Kent TN12 8AE.

MILLER, Prof. David Louis, MD; FRCP, FFPHM; Professor of Public Health Medicine, St Mary's Hospital Medical School, University of London, 1983–95, now Emeritus Professor; Hon. Senior Research Fellow, Guy's, King's and St Thomas' Hospitals' Medical and Dental School of King's College London (formerly United Medical and Dental Schools of Guy's and St Thomas' Hospital), since 1995; *b* 16 Sept. 1930; *s* of John Henry Charles Miller and Muriel (*née* Rogers); *m* 1955, Wendy Joy Clark; three *s* one *d*. *Educ:* The Leys, Cambridge; Peddie Sch., Hightstown, NJ, USA; Clare Coll., Cambridge (BA 1952, MA 1955; MB, BChir 1955; MD 1965); St Thomas's Hosp. Med. Sch. (Scholar). DPH 1964; FRCP 1978 (MRCP 1973); FFCM 1972. House Officer, St Thomas' Hosp., 1956–57; MO, RAF, 1957–60; Research Asst, RPMS, 1960–62; Epidemiologist, PHLS, 1962–71; US Public Health Service Internat. Res. Fellow, Johns Hopkins Sch. of Hygiene and Public Health, Md, 1965–66; Prof. of Community Medicine, Middlesex Hosp. Med. Sch., 1972–82. Aneurin Bevan Meml Fellowship, Govt of India, 1981. Pres., Sect. Epidemiology, RSocMed, 1986–88; Acad. Registrar, FPHM, RCP, 1989–94. Life Mem., Soc. of Scholars, Johns Hopkins Univ., 1983. Pres., Central YMCA, 1986– (Chm., 1977–99). *Publications:* (jtly) Lecture Notes on Epidemiology and Public Health Medicine, 1975, 4th edn 1996; Epidemiology of Diseases, 1982; pubns on epidemiology, esp. respiratory infections, vaccines, HIV and health services. *Recreations:* walking, music, youth and community. *Club:* Royal Society of Medicine.

MILLER, David Quentin; His Honour Judge Miller; a Circuit Judge, since 1987; *b* 22 Oct. 1936; *s* of Alfred Bowen Badger and Mair Angharad Evans. *Educ:* Ellesmere Coll., Shropshire; London Sch. of Econs and Pol. Science, London Univ. (LLB Hons 1956). Called to the Bar, Middle Temple, 1958; admitted Barrister and Solicitor of the Supreme Court of NZ, 1959. In practice, SE Circuit, 1960–82; Metropolitan Stipendiary Magistrate, 1982–87; a Recorder, 1986–87. *Recreations:* history, walking, gardening, art, music, Trollope Society. *Address:* 31 Edinburgh Gardens, Windsor, Berks SL4 2AN. *T:* (01753) 866597.

MILLER, Sir Donald (John), Kt 1990; FREng, FIMechE, FIEE; FRSE; Chairman, ScottishPower (formerly South of Scotland Electricity Board), 1982–92; *b* 9 Feb. 1927; *s* of John Miller and Maud (*née* White); *m* 1973, Fay Glendinning Herriot; one *s* two *d*. *Educ:* Banchory Academy; Univ. of Aberdeen. BSc(Eng). FREng (FEng 1981). Metropolitan Vickers, 1947–53; British Electricity Authority, 1953–55; Preece, Cardew and Rider (Consulting Engrs), 1955–66; Chief Engr, North of Scotland Hydro-Electric Bd, 1966–74; Dir of Engrg, then Dep. Chm., SSEB, 1974–82. Chairman: Premium Trust, 1993–98; Nat. Cycle Network Steering Cttee, 1995–2001. Chm., Power Div., IEE, 1979. Hon. Mem., British Nuclear Energy Soc., 1989. DUniv Strathclyde, 1992; Hon. DSc Aberdeen, 1997. *Publications:* papers to IEE. *Recreations:* gardening, hill walking, sailing.

MILLER, (Dorothy) Cheryl; Chief Executive (formerly Head of Paid Service), East Sussex County Council, since 1994; *b* 31 Aug. 1954; *d* of Sidney Radcliffe and Dorothy (*née* Ainsworth); *m* 1976, Graham Edwin Miller; one *s* one *d*. *Educ:* Preston Park Sch., Lancs; Preston Sixth Form Coll.; Manchester Univ. (BA Hons). Admin. Trainee, CSD, 1975–77; HEO(D) and Asst Private Sec. to Lord Privy Seal and Leader of House of Lords, 1977–78; Personnel Policy Br., CSD, 1979–80; Mem., PM's Advr on Efficiency (Lord Rayner) Scrutiny Team, 1980; Cabinet Office: Head, CS Policy on Retirement and Redundancy Conduct and Discipline Br., 1980–84; Head, Constitutional Br., Machinery of Govt Div., 1984–85; Asst Dir, then Dep. Dir, CSSB, 1986–90; Head, Staff Develt, DTI, 1991; County Personnel Officer, 1991–93 and Head, Exec. Office, 1992–93, E Sussex CC. Mem., Royal Commn on Environmental Pollution, 2000–. Non-executive Director: Sussex Enterprise, 1994–; Wired Sussex, 1999–. Chm., ACCE, 2000–01; Mem. Exec. Council, SOLACE, 1996–. *Recreations:* theatre, music, literature, women's equality issues, family activities, cooking, entertaining. *Address:* East Sussex County Council, Pelham House, St Andrew's Lane, Lewes, East Sussex BN7 1UN. *T:* (01273) 481560.

MILLER, Edward, CBE 1988; Director of Education, Strathclyde, 1974–88; *b* 30 March 1930; *s* of Andrew and Elizabeth Miller; *m* 1955; two *s*. *Educ:* Eastbank Academy; Glasgow Univ. (MA, MEd). Taught at Wishaw High Sch., 1955–57 and Whitehill Secondary Sch., 1957–59; Depute Dir of Educn, West Lothian, 1959–63; Sen. Asst Dir of Educn, Stirlingshire, 1963–66; Depute, later Sen. Depute Dir of Educn, Glasgow, 1966–74. Hon. MLitt Glasgow Coll., 1985. *Recreations:* golf, reading, sailing.

MILLER, G(eorge) William; Chairman, G. William Miller & Co., Inc., Merchant Banking, since 1983; *b* Oklahoma, USA, 9 March 1925; *s* of James Dick Miller and Hazle Deane Miller (*née* Orrick); *m* 1946, Ariadna Rogojarsky. *Educ:* Borger High Sch.; Amarillo Junior Coll.; US Coast Guard Acad. (BS 1945); School of Law, Univ. of California, Berkeley (JD 1952). Served as US Coast Guard Officer, Pacific Area, 1945–49, stationed (one year) in China. Admitted to Bar of California, 1952, New York Bar 1953; law practice with Cravath, Swaine & Moore, NYC, 1952–56. Joined Textron Inc., Providence, RI, 1956; Vice-Pres. 1957; Treas. 1958; Pres. 1960; Chief Exec. 1968–78, also Chm., 1974–78; Dir, Federal Reserve Bank of Boston, 1970–78; Chm., Bd of Governors of Federal Reserve System of US, 1978–79; Sec. of the Treasury, USA, 1979–81. Regent Lectr, Univ. of Calif at Berkeley, 1983–84; Lloyd Bentsen Prof. of Govt-Business Relations, Lyndon B. Johnson Sch. of Public Affairs, Univ. of Texas at Austin, 1984; Fannie Wilson Smith Eminent Scholars Chair, Florida State Univ., 1989; Fellow, Univ. of Calif at Berkeley. Chm. and Chief Exec. Officer, Federated Stores, Inc., 1990–92; Director: Repligen Corp.; HomePlace of America, Inc.; Simon Property Gp, Inc.; GS Industries Inc. Chairman: Indust. Adv. Council, President's Cttee on Equal Employment Opportunity, 1963–65; The Conference Board, 1977–78; National Alliance of Business, 1978; US Industrial Payroll Savings Cttee, 1977; President's Cttee on HIRE, 1977; Co-Chairman: US-USSR Trade and Econ. Council; Polish-US Econ. Council; President's Circle, Nat. Acad. of Scis, 1989–92. Mem. Bd, Washington Opera. Treasurer, Amer. Red Cross, 1983–87. Mem., State Bar, California. Phi Delta Phi. *Publication:* (ed) Regrowing the American Economy, 1983. *Recreations:* music, golf. *Address:* 1215 19th Street NW, Washington, DC 20036, USA. *T:* (202) 4291780. *Clubs:* Chevy Chase (Maryland); The Brook (NY); Burning Tree (Bethesda, Md); Acoaxet (Westport, Mass); Sailfish Point Golf (Fla); Lyford Cay (Bahamas).

MILLER, Rt Rev. Harold Creeth; *see* Down and Dromore, Bishop of.

MILLER, Sir Harry, 12th Bt *cr* 1705, of Chichester, Sussex; hill country farmer, New Zealand, 1942–89; *b* 15 Jan. 1927; *yr s* of Sir Ernest Henry John Miller, 10th Bt and Netta Mehalah Miller (*née* Bennett) (*d* 1980); *S* brother, 1995; *m* 1954, Gwynedd Margaret Sheriff; one *s* two *d*. RNZAF 1945 (volunteer pilot). *Recreations:* mountain climbing, golf, forestry management. *Heir:* *s* Anthony Thomas Miller [*b* 4 May 1955; *m* 1990, Barbara Battersby (*née* Kensington); two *s*, and two step *s* one step *d*]. *Address:* 53 Koha Road, Taupo, New Zeland. *T:* (7) 3780905.

MILLER, Sir Hilary Duppa, (Sir Hal), Kt 1988; DL; Chairman, Cosmopolitan Holdings Ltd, since 1991; *b* 6 March 1929; *s* of late Lt-Comdr John Bryan Peter Duppa-Miller, GC; *m* 1st, 1956, Fiona Margaret McDermid; two *s* two *d*; 2nd, 1976, Jacqueline Roe, *d* of T. C. W. Roe and of Lady Londesborough; one *s* one *d*. *Educ:* Eton; Merton Coll., Oxford; London Univ. MA (Oxon) 1956; BSc (Estate Management) (London), 1962. With Colonial Service, Hong Kong, 1955–68. Company Director. Chief Exec., SMMT, 1991–93. Contested: (C), Barrow-in-Furness, 1970; Bromsgrove by-elec. May 1971; MP (C) Bromsgrove and Redditch, Feb. 1974–1983, Bromsgrove, 1983–92. PPS to Sec. of State for Defence, 1979–81, to Chancellor of the Duchy of Lancaster, 1981, resigned; Vice-Chm., Conservative Party Orgn, and PPS to the Chm., 1984–87; Mem., UK delegn to Council of Europe, 1974–76. Jt Chm., All Party Motor Industry Gp, 1978. Fellow, Econ. Develt Inst. of World Bank, Washington. DL Worcs, 2000. *Recreations:* sailing, fell walking, cricket, Rugby. *Address:* Cosmopolitan Holdings Ltd, Road Five, Industrial Estate, Winsford, Cheshire CW7 3QU. *Clubs:* Oxford and Cambridge; Vincent's (Oxford); Aston Fields Royal British Legion (Bromsgrove); Eton Ramblers, Free Foresters, Blackheath Football.

See also Michael Miller.

MILLER, Dr Jacques Francis Albert Pierre, AO 1981; FRS 1970; FAA 1970; Head of Experimental Pathology Unit, Walter and Eliza Hall Institute of Medical Research, 1966–96; Professor of Experimental Immunology, University of Melbourne, 1990–97, now Emeritus; *b* 2 April 1931; French parents; *m* 1956, Margaret Denise Houen. *Educ:* St Aloysius' Coll., Sydney. BSc (Med.) 1953, MB, BS 1955, Sydney; PhD 1960, DSc 1965, London. Sen. Scientist, Chester Beatty Res. Inst., London, 1960–66; Reader, Exper. Pathology, Univ. of London, 1965–66. Croonian Lectr, Royal Soc., 1992. For. Mem., Académie Royale de Médicine de Belgique, 1969; For. Associate, US Nat. Acad. Scis, 1982. Hon. MD Sydney, 1986. Langer-Teplitz Cancer Research Award (USA), 1965; Gairdner Foundn Award (Canada), 1966; Encyclopaedia Britannica (Australia) Award, 1966; Scientific Medal of Zoological Soc. of London, 1966; Burnet Medal, Austr. Acad. of Scis, 1971; Paul Ehrlich Award, Germany, 1974; Rabbi Shai Shacknai Meml Prize, Hadassah Med. Sch., Jerusalem, 1978; Saint-Vincent Internat. Prize for Med. Res., Italy, 1983; first Sandoz Immunology Prize, 1990; first Medawar Prize, Transplantation Soc., 1990; J. Allyn Taylor Internat. Prize for Medicine, John Robarts Res. Inst., 1995; Florey-Faulding Medal and Prize, 2000. *Publications:* over 390 papers in scientific jls and several chapters in books, mainly dealing with thymus and immunity. *Recreations:* music, photography, art, literature. *Address:* Walter and Eliza Hall Institute of Medical Research, Royal Melbourne Hospital PO, Parkville, Victoria 3050, Australia. *T:* (3) 93452555.

MILLER, James, CBE 1986; Chairman, Miller Group Ltd (formerly James Miller & Partners), 1970–99; *b* 1 Sept. 1934; *s* of Sir James Miller, GBE, and Lady Ella Jane Miller; *m* 1st, 1959, Kathleen Dewar; one *s* two *d*; 2nd, 1969, Iris Lloyd-Webb; one *d*. *Educ:* Edinburgh Acad.; Harrow Sch.; Balliol Coll., Oxford (MA Engrg Sci.). Joined James Miller & Partners, 1958; Board Mem., 1960; Man. Dir, 1970–91. Director: Life Assoc. of Scotland, 1981–93; British Linen Bank, 1983–99 (Chm., 1997–99); Britoil, 1988–90; Bank of Scotland, 1993–2000; Mem., Scottish Adv. Bd, British Petroleum, 1990–. Pres., FCEC, 1990–93 (Chm., 1985–86). Dir, Royal Scottish Nat. Orchestra, 1996– (Chm., 1997–). Chm., Court, Heriot-Watt Univ., 1990–96. Hon. Consul for Austria, 1994–; Dean, Consular Corps in Edinburgh, Leith, 1999–2001. *Recreation:* shooting. *Address:* Alderwood, 49 Craigcrook Road, Edinburgh EH4 3PH. *T:* (0131) 332 2222, *Fax:* (0131) 332 1777. *Club:* City Livery.

MILLER, James Francis Xavier; Headmaster, Royal Grammar School, Newcastle upon Tyne, since 1994; *b* 3 March 1950; *yr s* of Lt-Col John Francis Miller and Barbara Mary Miller (*née* Cooke); *m* 1976, Ruth Ellen Rowland (*née* Macbeth); two *s*. *Educ:* Douai Sch.; Merton Coll., Oxford (BA Classical Mods and PPE; MA). Winchester College: Asst Master, 1972–89; Hd of Econs, 1978–82; Housemaster, 1982–89; Headmaster, Framlingham Coll., 1989–94. Chm., study-links.com. Councillor, Winchester CC, 1976–83 (Chm., Health and Works Cttee, 1979–82). FRSA 1994. *Recreations:* golf, cricket, opera, crosswords. *Address:* The Royal Grammar School, Eskdale Terrace, Newcastle upon Tyne NE2 4DX. *T:* (0191) 281 5711. *Clubs:* East India; Free Foresters.

MILLER, Prof. J(ohn) D(onald) Bruce; Executive Director, Academy of the Social Sciences in Australia, 1989–91; Professor of International Relations, Research School of Pacific Studies, Australian National University, 1962–87, now Emeritus; *b* 30 Aug. 1922; *s* of Donald and Marion Miller, Sydney, Australia; *m* 1st, 1943, Enid Huthnance; one *s*; 2nd, 1957, Margaret Martin; one *s*; 3rd, 1990, Judith Bennet. *Educ:* Sydney High Sch.; University of Sydney. BEc, 1944; MEc 1951; MA Cantab 1978. Announcer and Talks Officer, Australian Broadcasting Commission, Sydney and Canberra, 1939–46; Staff Tutor, Department of Tutorial Classes, University of Sydney, 1946–52; Asst Lecturer in Political Science and International Relations, London Sch. of Economics, 1953–55; Lecturer in Politics, University Coll., Leicester, 1955–57; Prof. of Politics, University of Leicester, 1957–62; Dean of Social Sciences, 1960–62; Public Orator, 1961–62. Res. Associate, Chatham House, 1965, 1969, 1973. Visiting Professor: Indian Sch. of International Studies, 1959; Columbia Univ., New York, 1962, 1966, 1981; Yale, 1977; Princeton, 1984, 1986; Overseas Vis. Fellow, St John's Coll., and Smuts Vis. Fellow, Cambridge Univ., 1977–78; Macrossan Lectr, University of Queensland, 1966. Member: Aust. Population and Immigration Council, 1975–81; Aust. Res. Grants Cttee, 1975–81. Joint Editor, Journal of Commonwealth Political Studies, 1961–62; Editor, Australian Outlook, 1963–69; Chm., Editorial Adv. Bd for Austr. documents on foreign relations, 1971–77; Austr. Nat. Commn for UNESCO, 1982–84, 1990–93. Canberra correspondent, The Economist, 1962–87. FASSA 1967 (Treas., 1979–83). *Publications:* Australian Government and Politics, 1954, 4th edn with B. Jinks 1970; Richard Jebb and the Problem of Empire, 1956; Politicians (inaugural), 1958; The Commonwealth in the World, 1958; The Nature of Politics, 1962; The Shape of Diplomacy (inaugural), 1963; Australia and Foreign Policy (Boyer Lectures), 1963; (ed with T. H. Rigby) The Disintegrating Monolith, 1965; Britain and the Old Dominions, 1966; Australia, 1966; The Politics of the Third World, 1966; (ed) India, Japan, Australia: Partners in Asia?, 1968; Survey of Commonwealth Affairs: problems of expansion and attrition 1953–1969, 1974; (ed) Australia's Economic Relations, 1975; The EEC and Australia, 1976; The World of States, 1981; Ideology and Foreign Policy, 1982; Norman Angell and the Futility of War, 1986; (ed) Australians and British, 1987; (ed with L. J. Evans) Policy and Practice, 1987; (ed with R. J. Vincent) Order and Violence, 1990. *Recreation:* staying alive. *Address:* 1 Mountbatten Park, Yarralumla, ACT 2600, Australia. *T:* (2) 62825599.

MILLER, Rt Rev. John Dunlop; Minister, Castlemilk East Parish Church, Glasgow, since 1971; Moderator of the General Assembly of the Church of Scotland, 2001–May 2002 (designation subseq. Very Rev.); *b* 11 Nov. 1941; *s* of Rev. Ian Robert Newton Miller and Dr Jessie Sinclair Miller (*née* Dunlop); *m* 1968, Mary Glen Robertson; one *s* two *d*. *Educ:* Kilmarnock Acad.; Merchant Taylor's Sch.; Corpus Christi Coll., Oxford (BA 1964); New Coll., Edinburgh (BD 1967); Union Theol Seminary, NY (STM 1970). Ordained 1971. Hon DD Glasgow, 2001. *Publications:* Ministry and Mission in Working Class Areas, 1976; Buildings and Mission in Working Class Areas, 1986. *Recreation:* cycling. *Address:* 15 Castlemilk Drive, Glasgow G45 9TL. *T:* (0141) 631 1244.

MILLER, John Harmsworth; architect in private practice; *b* 18 Aug. 1930; *s* of Charles Miller and Brenda Borrett; *m* 1st, 1957, Patricia Rhodes (marr. diss. 1975); two *d*; 2nd, 1985, Su Rogers. *Educ:* Charterhouse; Architectural Assoc. Sch. of Architecture (AA Dip. Hons 1957). ARIBA 1959. Private practice, Colquhoun and Miller, 1961–90, John Miller and Partners, 1990–; works include: Forest Gate High Sch., West Ham (Newham), 1965; Chemistry Labs, Royal Holloway Coll., London Univ., 1970; Melrose Activity Centre, Milton Keynes Develt Corp. (Commendation, Steel Awards, 1975); Pillwood House, Feock, Cornwall (RIBA Regional Award, 1975); housing, Caversham Road/Gaisford Street, Camden, 1978; single person flats, Hornsey Lane, Haringey, 1980; Oldbrook, Milton Keynes (Silver Award, Architectural Design, 1987; Highly Commended, Housing Design and Civic Trust Awards); Whitechapel Art Gall. extension, 1985 (RIBA Regl Award, 1988; Civic Trust Award, 1988); Gulbenkian Gall. for RCA, 1989; Stevens Bldg for RCA, and Nomura Gall. and bookshop for Tate Gall., 1991; Queen's building, UEA (RIBA Nat. Award) and new 20th century galls for Nat. Portrait Gall., 1993; Elizabeth Fry building, UEA, 1995 (RIBA Regl Award); Ramphal building, Warwick Univ., 1996; Serpentine Gall., 1998; Shackleton Meml Library, Scott Polar Res. Inst., Cambridge Univ., 1999 (RIBA Regl Award); Tate Gall. Centenary Develt, Tate Britain, 2001. Exhibition Designs for Arts Council: Dada and Surrealism Reviewed, 1978; Ten Modern Houses, 1980; Picasso's Picassos, 1981; Adolf Loos, 1985. Tutor: RCA and AA, 1961–73; Cambridge Sch. of Arch., 1969–70; Prof. of Environmental Design, RCA, 1975–85, Fellow 1976, Hon. Fellow, 1985. FRSA 1985. Vis. Prof., Sch. of Arch., UC Dublin, 1985. Visiting Critic: Cornell Univ. Sch. of Arch., Ithaca, 1966, 1968 and 1971; Princeton Univ. Sch. of Arch., NJ, 1970; Dublin Univ. Sch. of Arch., 1972–73; Univ. of Toronto, 1985. European Prize for Architecture, 1988. *Publications:* contribs to architect. jls. *Address:* 23 Regent's Park Road, NW1 7TL. *T:* (020) 7267 5800.

MILLER, John Ireland; Vice-President, Methodist Conference of Great Britain, 1973–74; *b* 20 June 1912; *s* of John William Miller and Emma Miller (*née* Minkley); *m* 1943, Vida Bertha Bracher; one *s* one *d*. *Educ:* Hardye's School, Dorchester; Taunton School, Taunton. Admitted Solicitor and Member of Law Society, 1933. HM Coroner: Poole Borough, 1972–74 (Deputy Coroner, 1939–72); East Dorset, 1974–85. *Address:* 24 High Street, Bewdley, Worcs DY12 2DH. *T:* (01299) 405063.

MILLER, Air Vice-Marshal John Joseph, CB 1981; Director of Studies, St George's House, Windsor Castle, 1989–94; *b* 27 April 1928; *s* of Frederick George Miller and Freda Ruth Miller; *m* 1950, Adele Mary Colleypriest; one *s* two *d*. *Educ:* Portsmouth Grammar School. Commissioned RAF, 1947; called to the Bar, Gray's Inn, 1958; CO RAF Support Unit Fontainbleau, 1965; Directing Staff, RAF Staff Coll., 1967; DGPS (RAF) Staff, MoD, 1970; Group Captain Admin., RAF Halton, 1971; Comd Accountant, HQ Strike Comd, 1973; RCDS 1975; Dir, Personnel Management (Policy and Plans) RAF, MoD, 1976; Asst Chief of Defence Staff (Personnel and Logistics), 1978–81; Head of Administrative Branch, RAF, 1979–83; Dir Gen., Personal Services, RAF, 1982–83. Dir, Inst. of Personnel Management, 1983–89. Pres., Eur. Assoc. for Personnel Management, 1987–89. *Recreations:* walking, swimming, theatre, music, collecting (especially antiquarian books). *Address:* 24 Floral Farm, Canford Magna, Wimborne, Dorset BH21 3AU. *T:* (01202) 883701. *Club:* Royal Air Force.

MILLER, Lt-Col Sir John (Mansel), GCVO 1987 (KCVO 1974; CVO 1966); DSO 1944; MC 1944; Crown Equerry, 1961–87, an Extra Equerry since 1987; *b* 4 Feb. 1919; 3rd *s* of Brig.-Gen. Alfred Douglas Miller, CBE, DSO, DL, JP, Royal Scots Greys, and of Ella Geraldine Fletcher, Saltoun, E Lothian. *Educ:* Eton; RMA, Sandhurst. 2nd Lieut Welsh Guards, 1939; Adjt 1942–44; ADC to F-M Lord Wilson, Washington, DC, 1945–47; Regtl Adjt, 1953–56; Brigade Major 1st Guards Brigade, 1956–58; comd 1st Bn Welsh Guards, 1958–61. President: Royal Internat. Horse Show, 1993–; Coaching Club, 1975–82; Hackney Horse Soc., 1978–79, 1994–95; Nat. Light Horse Breeding Soc. (HIS), 1982; British Driving Soc., 1982–; Royal Windsor Horse Show Club, 1985–90; Horse Rangers Assoc., 1985–; Cleveland Bay Horse Soc., 1986–88; BSJA, 1988–93; BHS, 1992–94; Rare Breeds Survival Trust, 1995–; Vice-Pres., Irish Draught Horse Soc., GB, 1990–. Patron: Side Saddle Assoc., 1984–; Coloured Horse and Pony Soc., 1988; Caspian Horse Soc., 1999. President: Wheatley Br, RNLI, 1982–; Wheatley Scouts, 1982–. *Recreations:* hunting, shooting, polo, driving. *Address:* Shotover House, Wheatley, Oxon OX9 1QS. *T:* (018677) 2450. *Clubs:* Pratt's, White's; Constitutional (Windsor).

MILLER, Dr Jonathan Wolfe, CBE 1983; Research Fellow in Neuro-psychology, University of Sussex; *b* 21 July 1934; *s* of late Emanuel Miller, DPM, FRCP; *m* 1956, Helen Rachel Collet; two *s* one *d*. *Educ:* St Paul's Sch.; St John's Coll., Cambridge (MB, BCh 1959; Hon. Fellow 1982). FRCP 1997; FRCPE 1998. Res. Fellow in Hist. of Med., UCL, 1970–73. Associate Director, Nat. Theatre, 1973–75; Artistic Dir, Old Vic, 1988–90. Mem., Arts Council, 1975–76. Vis. Prof. in Drama, Westfield Coll., London, 1977–; Fellow, UCL, 1981–. Co-author and appeared in Beyond the Fringe, 1961–64; stage directing in London and NY, 1965–67; *television:* Editor, BBC Monitor, 1965; directed films for BBC TV (incl. Alice in Wonderland), 1966; Exec. Producer, BBC Shakespeare series, 1979–81; writer and presenter, TV series, including: The Body in Question, 1978; Madness, 1991; Opera Works, 1997; *stage:* School for Scandal, 1968, The Seagull, 1969, The Malcontent, 1973, Nottingham Playhouse; King Lear, The Merchant of Venice, Old Vic, 1970; The Tempest, Mermaid, 1970; Hamlet, Arts Theatre, Cambridge, 1970; Danton's Death, 1971, School for Scandal, 1972, Measure for Measure, 1974, Marriage of Figaro, 1974, The Freeway, 1974, Nat. Theatre; The Taming of the Shrew, 1972, The Seagull, 1973, Chichester; Family Romances, 1974, The Importance of Being Earnest, 1975, All's Well That Ends Well, 1975, Greenwich; Three Sisters, Cambridge, 1976; She Would If She Could, Greenwich, 1979; Long Day's Journey Into Night, Haymarket, 1986; The Taming of the Shrew, RSC, Stratford, 1987, Barbican, 1988; (jtly adapted and directed) The Emperor, Royal Court, 1987 (televised, 1988); Andromache, One Way Pendulum, Bussy D'Ambois, The Tempest, Candide, Old Vic, 1988; King Lear, The Liar, Old Vic, 1989; The Way of the World, Gate Theatre, Dublin, 1992; A Midsummer Night's Dream, Almeida, 1996; As You Like It, Gate Theatre, Dublin, 2000; *film:* Take a Girl Like You, 1970; *operas:* Arden Must Die, Sadler's Wells Theatre, 1974; The Cunning Little Vixen, Glyndebourne, 1975 and 1977; English National Opera: The Marriage of Figaro, 1978; The Turn of the Screw, 1979, 1991; Arabella, 1980; Otello, 1981; Rigoletto, 1982, 1985, 1995; Don Giovanni, 1985; The Magic Flute, 1986; Tosca, 1986; The Mikado, 1986, 1988, 1993; The Barber of Seville, 1987; Der Rosenkavalier, 1994; Carmen, 1995; La Traviata, 1996; Kent Opera: Così Fan Tutte, 1975; Rigoletto, 1975; Orfeo, 1976; Eugene Onegin, 1977; La Traviata, 1979; Falstaff, 1980, 1981; Fidelio, 1982, 1983, 1988; La Scala: La Fanciulla del West, 1991; Manon Lescaut, 1992; Maggio Musicale, Florence: Don Giovanni, 1990; Così fan Tutte, Tosca, 1991; Marriage of Figaro, 1992; Idomeneo, 1996; Metropolitan Opera, New York:

Katya Kabanova, 1991; Pelléas et Mélisande, 1995; Marriage of Figaro, Vienna State Opera, 1991; Roberto Deveureux, Monte Carlo, 1992; Die Gezeichnete, Zürich, 1992; Maria Stuarda, Monte Carlo, 1993; The Secret Marriage, Opera North, 1993; Falstaff, Zürich, 1993; L'Incoronazione di Poppea, Glimmerglass Opera, 1994; Così fan tutti, Royal Opera House, and Rome, 1995; The Beggar's Opera, Wilton's Music Hall, 1999. Nat. Gall. exhibn, Mirror Image: Jonathan Miller on reflection, 1998. Hon. Fellow, RA, 1991; Hon. DLitt: Leicester, 1981; Cambridge, 1996. Silver Medal, Royal TV Soc., 1981; Albert Medal, RSA, 1990. *Publications:* McLuhan, 1971; (ed) Freud: the man, his world, his influence, 1972; The Body in Question, 1978; Subsequent Performances, 1986; (ed) The Don Giovanni Book: myths of seduction and betrayal, 1990; On Reflection, 1998. *Recreation:* deep sleep. *Address:* c/o IMG Artists, Lovell House, 616 Chiswick High Road, W4 5RX.

MILLER, Judith Henderson; author and publishing consultant; Editor, Miller's Guides; *b* 16 Sept. 1951; *d* of Andrew and Bertha Cairns; *m* 1978, Martin John Miller, *qv* (marr. diss. 1992); two *d. Educ:* Galashiels Acad.; Edinburgh Univ. (MA Hons English, 1973). Copywriter, WHT Advertising, Auckland, NZ, 1973–74; Editor, Lyle Publications, Galashiels, 1974–75; Occupational Guidance Officer, Dept of Employment, 1975–79; Man. Dir and Editor, Miller Publications, 1979–; with Martin Miller opened Chilston Park Hotel, 1985; Man. Dir, MJM Publishing Projects, 1985–92; Co-Founder, Miller's Magazine, 1991. Television appearances include The House Detectives, The Art and Antiques Hour, The Antiques Trail. *Publications:* Miller's Antiques and Collectables: the facts at your fingertips, 1993; Miller's Classic Motorcycles Price Guide, annually, 1993–; Miller's Art Nouveau and Art Deco Buyer's Guide, 1995; Miller's Pine and Country Furniture Buyer's Guide, 1995, Period Kitchens, 1995; Period Fireplaces, 1995; How to Make Money out of Antiques, 1995; Period Soft Furnishings, 1996; Country Finishes and Effects, 1997; Miller's Clocks and Barometers Buyer's Guide, 1997; Wooden Houses, 1997; Care and Repair of Antiques and Collectables, 1997; The Style Sourcebook, 1998; Classic Style, 1998; Miller's Antiques Encyclopaedia, 1998; Period Details Sourcebook, 1999; A Closer Look at Antiques, 2000; Colour, 2000; with Martin Miller: Miller's Antiques Price Guide, annually 1979–; The Antiques Directory—Furniture, 1985; Period Details, 1987; Miller's Pocket Antiques Fact File, 1988; Period Style, 1989; Understanding Antiques, 1989; Miller's Collectables Price Guide, annually 1989–; Country Style, 1990; Miller's Collectors Cars Price Guide, annually 1991–; Miller's Art Deco Checklist, 1991; Furniture Checklist, 1991; Period Finishes and Effects, 1992; Victorian Style, 1993. *Recreations:* antiques!, bridge. *Club:* Groucho.

MILLER, Prof. Karl Fergus Connor; Lord Northcliffe Professor of Modern English Literature, University College London, 1974–92; Editor, 1979–92, and Co-Editor, 1989–92, London Review of Books; *b* 2 Aug. 1931; *s* of William and Marion Miller; *m* 1956, Jane Elisabeth Collet; two *s* one *d. Educ:* Royal High School, Edinburgh; Downing Coll., Cambridge. Asst Prin., HM Treasury, 1956–57; BBC TV Producer, 1957–58; Literary Editor, Spectator, 1958–61; Literary Editor, New Statesman, 1961–67; Editor, Listener, 1967–73. FRSL 1992. *Publications:* (ed) Poetry from Cambridge, 1952–54, 1955; (ed, with introd.) Writing in England Today: The Last Fifteen Years, 1968; (ed) Memoirs of a Modern Scotland, 1970; (ed) A Listener Anthology, August 1967–June 1970, 1970; (ed) A Second Listener Anthology, 1973; (ed) Henry Cockburn, Memorials of his Time, 1974; Cockburn's Millennium, 1975; (ed, with introd.) Robert Burns, 1981; Doubles: studies in literary history, 1985; Authors, 1989; Rebecca's Vest (autobiog.), 1993; Boswell and Hyde, 1995; Dark Horses: an experience of literary journalism (autobiog.), 1998. *Recreation:* watching football. *Address:* 26 Limerston Street, SW10 0HH.

MILLER, Dr Kenneth Allan Glen, CBE 1988; FREng, FIMechE; Chairman, PCME Ltd (formerly Pollution Control and Measurement (Europe) Ltd), since 1993; *b* 27 July 1926; *s* of Dr Allan Frederick Miller and Margaret Hutchison (*née* Glen); *m* 1st, 1954, Dorothy Elaine Brown (marr. diss. 1999); three *s*; 2nd, 1999, Betty Nanette Hatton (*née* Bridgwater). *Educ:* Upper Canada Coll., Toronto; Trinity Hall, Cambridge (BA 1946; MA 1950; Hon. Fellow, 1992); PhD Wales, 1949. FIMechE 1965; FREng (FEng 1981). Res. Asst to Prof. of Physics, Aberystwyth, 1946; joined ICI, Billingham, 1949; various posts on production and design, 1949–59; seconded to BTC, 1959–60; Asst Tech. Manager, 1960, Engrg Manager, 1963, Engrg Dir, 1965, HOC Div., ICI; Engrg Advr, ICI, 1971; Managing Director: APV Co., 1974; APV Holdings, 1977–82; Dir-Gen., Engrg Council, 1982–88. Deputy Chairman: ECCTIS 2000 Ltd, 1990–96; standing Conf. on Schs' Sci. and Technology, 1990–96. Member: Cttee for Industrial Technol., 1972–76; UGC, 1981–83; Chm., Steering Cttee for Manufrg Adv. Service, 1977–82. Member Council: Fellowship of Engrg, 1982–85; CRAC, 1987–96. FInstD 1974; CIMgt 1985. *Recreations:* theatre, photography. *Address:* 66 Trematon Place, Broom Road, Teddington, Middx TW11 9RH. *T:* (020) 8943 3561. *Club:* Leander.

MILLER, Kenneth William, FCA; Chairman, Colt Group, since 2000; *b* 4 Feb. 1939; *s* of Albert William Miller and Winifred (*née* Ashworth); *m* 1st, 1964, Carol Susan Hislop (marr. diss. 1987); one *s* one *d*; 2nd, 1988, Jean Helen McPhail McInnes. *Educ:* Surbiton County Grammar Sch. FCA 1961. Company Sec., Hunting Associated Industries, 1965–73; Asst Finance Dir, Hunting Gp, 1969–73; Commercial Dir, E. A. Gibson & Co. Ltd, 1973–78; Hunting Petroleum Services plc: Dir, 1978–87; Man. Dir, 1987–89; Chief Exec., Hunting plc, 1989–2000. *Recreations:* sailing, reading, sport, music. *Address:* Colt Group, New Lane, Havant, Hants PO9 2LY. *T:* (023) 9245 1111. *Club:* Royal Automobile.

MILLER, Prof. Marcus Hay, PhD; Professor of Economics, University of Warwick, 1974; *b* 9 Sept. 1941; *s* of J. Irvine Miller and Rose H. (*née* Moir); *m* 1967, Margaret Ellen Hummel (marr. diss.; she *d* 2001); two *d. Educ:* Price's Sch., Fareham, Hants; University Coll., Oxford (BA 1st Cl. PPE); Yale Univ. (Henry Fellowship, MA, PhD Econ). Lecturer, London School of Economics, 1967–76; Prof. of Economics, Univ. of Manchester, 1976–78. Economist, 1972–73, Houblon-Norman Fellow, 1981–82, Bank of England; Vis. Associate Prof. of Internat. Finance, Univ. of Chicago, 1976; Vis. Prof. of Public and Internat. Affairs, Princeton Univ., 1983; Res. Fellow, Centre for Economic Policy Res., 1983– (Co-Dir, Internat Macroeconomics Prog., 1986–91); Vis. Fellow, Inst. for Internat. Econs, Washington, 1986–. Member, Academic Panel, HM Treasury, 1976– (Chm., 1979–80); Adviser, House of Commons Select Cttee on the Treasury and Civil Service, 1980–81. Mem. Management Cttee, NIESR, 1980–91. *Publications:* joint editor: Monetary Policy and Economic Activity in West Germany, 1977; Essays on Fiscal and Monetary Policy, 1981; Targets and Indicators: a blueprint for the international co-ordination of economic policy, 1993; Exchange Rate Targets and Currency Bands 1992; The Asian Financial Crisis, 1999; articles in professional jls, mainly on domestic and internat. macroecons. *Recreations:* sailboarding, contemporary dance. *Address:* Department of Economics, University of Warwick, Coventry CV4 7AL; *e-mail:* m.h.miller@warwick.ac.uk. *Club:* Reform.

MILLER, Martin John; Chairman, City Diaries, since 1997; Co-Founder and Managing Director, Milroy Estates Ltd, since 1983; *b* 24 Nov. 1946; *s* of Marcus and Phyllis Miller; *m* 1st, 1966, Elaine (marr. diss. 1975); three *d*; 2nd, 1978, Judith Henderson Cairns (*see* J. H. Miller) (marr. diss. 1992); two *d. Educ:* West Tarring Secondary Modern Sch., Worthing. Freelance photographer, 1965–68; Co-Founder, Lyle Publications, 1968–74; semi-retirement, 1974–79; Co-Founder, MJM Publications, 1979; Co-Founder, and Publisher, Miller's Magazine, 1991–95; with Judith Miller opened Chilston Park Hotel, 1985. *Publications: with Judith Miller:* Miller's Antiques Price Guide, annually, 1979–; The Antiques Directory—Furniture, 1985; Period Details, 1987; Miller's Antique Pocket Fact File, 1988; Period Style, 1989; Understanding Antiques, 1989; Miller's Collectables Price Guide, annually 1989–; Country Style, 1990; Miller's Collectors Cars Price Guide, annually 1991–; Miller's Art Deco Checklist, 1991; Furniture Checklist, 1991; Period Finishes and Effects, 1992; Victorian Style, 1993. *Recreations:* shooting, indulging in fine wines and gourmet food. *Address:* (office) 100 Westbourne Grove, W2 5RU. *T:* (020) 7243 2200. *Club:* Groucho.

MILLER, Dame Mary Elizabeth H.; *see* Hedley-Miller.

MILLER, Maurice Solomon, MB; *b* 16 Aug. 1920; *s* of David Miller; *m* 1944, Renée, *d* of Joseph Modlin, Glasgow; two *s* two *d. Educ:* Shawlands Academy, Glasgow; Glasgow University. MB, ChB 1944. Elected Mem. of Glasgow Corporation, 1950; Bailie of Glasgow, 1954–57; JP Glasgow, 1957. MP (Lab): Glasgow Kelvingrove, 1964–74; E Kilbride, 1974–87. Asst Govt Whip, 1968–69. Visited Russia as mem. of medical delegation, 1955. *Publication:* Window on Russia, 1956. *Recreation:* oil painting.

MILLER, Michael, RD 1966; QC 1974; *b* 28 June 1933; 2nd *s* of late John Bryan Peter Duppa-Miller, GC; *m* 1st, 1958, Mary Elizabeth (marr. diss. 1991), *e d* of late Donald Spiers Monteagle Barlow, FRCS; two *s* two *d*; 2nd, 1991, Prof. Barbara Lepine Goodwin (Prof. of Politics, UEA), *d* of late Thomas Goodwin. *Educ:* Dragon Sch., Oxford; Westminster Sch. (King's Scholar); Christ Church, Oxford (Westminster Scholar). BA Lit. Hum. 1955; MA 1958. Ord. Seaman, RNVR, 1950; Sub-Lt 1956; qual. submarines, 1956; Lt-Comdr RNR. Called to Bar, Lincoln's Inn, 1958, Bencher 1984; practice at Chancery Bar, 1958–97; Mem. Bar Council, 1972–74 and 1988–92; Mem. Senate of Inns of Court and Bar, 1974–76. Author and editor of computer programs incl. expert systems; founder of Clarendon Software. *Recreations:* sailing, music, chess, football, gardening. *Address:* Fairfield House, Norwich NR2 2NQ.

See also Sir H. D. Miller.

MILLER, Michael A.; *see* Ashley-Miller.

MILLER, Sir (Oswald) Bernard, Kt 1967; *b* 25 March 1904; *s* of late Arthur Miller and Margaret Jane Miller; *m* 1931, Jessica Rose Marie ffoulkes (*d* 1985); three *s. Educ:* Sloane Sch.; Jesus Coll., Oxford (Stanhope Prize, 1925; BA 1927; MA 1930; Hon. Fellow, 1968). Joined John Lewis Partnership, 1927; Dir, 1935; Chm., 1955–72. Chm., Retail Distributors Assoc., 1953; Member: Council of Industrial Design, 1957–66; Monopolies Commission, 1961–69; EDC for Distributive Trades, 1964–71. Chm. Southern Region, RSA, 1974–80; Mem. Council, RSA, 1977–82. Treasurer, Southampton Univ., 1974–82, Chm. Council, 1982–87, Pro-Chancellor, 1983–90. Hon. LLD Southampton, 1981. *Publication:* Biography of Robert Harley, Earl of Oxford, 1927. *Recreations:* fishing, gardening, opera and theatre. *Address:* 3 Sutton Manor Mews, Sutton Scotney, Hants SO21 3JX. *T:* (01962) 760997.

MILLER, Sir Peter (North), Kt 1988; Chairman, Lloyd's, 1984–87; Chairman, The Miller Insurance Group Ltd (formerly Thos R. Miller & Son (Holdings)), 1971–83 and 1988–96; *b* 28 Sept. 1930; *s* of Cyril Thomas Gibson Risch Miller, CBE and Dorothy Alice North Miller, JP; *m* 1991, Jane Herbertson; one *s* and two *s* one *d* by previous marriage. *Educ:* Rugby; Lincoln Coll., Oxford (MA Hons; Hon. Fellow, 1992); City Univ (DSc). National Service, Intelligence Corps, 1949–50. Joined Lloyd's, 1953; qualified as barrister, 1954; Partner, Thos R. Miller & Son (Insurance), 1959, Sen. Partner, 1971–. Dep. Chm., Lloyd's Insurance Brokers' Asoc., 1974–75, Chm. 1976–77; Mem., Cttee of Lloyd's, 1977–80 and 1982–89 (Mem. Council of Lloyd's, 1983–89); in charge of team responsible for passage of Lloyd's Bill (Fisher), 1980–82. Member: Baltic Exchange, 1966–; Insurance Brokers' Registration Council, 1977–81; Vice-Pres., British Insce Brokers' Assoc., 1978–96; Chm., British Cttee of Bureau Veritas, 1980–. One of HM's Lieutenants for the City of London, 1987–. Mem., Chief Pleas, Sark, 1969–. Commendatore, Ordine al Merito della Repubblica Italiana, 1989. Hon. DSc City, 1987. *Recreations:* all sport (except cricket), including tennis, running, sailing; wine, music, old churches, gardening. *Address:* c/o Miller Insurance Group, Dawson House, 5 Jewry Street, EC3N 2PJ. *Clubs:* Brooks's, City of London; Vincent's (Oxford); Thames Hare and Hounds.

MILLER, Prof. Richard Albert, OBE 1976; FRAeS; Chairman, DGB Sterling (formerly Dinol (GB)) Ltd, since 1998; *b* 12 July 1936; *s* of Albert and Emily Kate Miller; *m* 1959, Beryl Marjorie Thompson; one *s* one *d. Educ:* Northampton Grammar Sch.; Coll. of Art, Nottingham; Open Univ. (DipEd, BA Hons); Poly. of E London (MA, MSc). Royal Air Force, 1956–82, Pilot; Flying Duties, 1957–70; RAF Advanced Staff Course, 1970; MoD, 1971–72; OC 36 Sqn, RAF Lyneham, 1973–75; Station Comdr, RAF Benson and Dep. Captain of Queen's Flight, 1976–78; ADC to the Queen, 1976–78; RAF Diamond Jubilee Fellow, Univ. of S Calif and Fitzwilliam Coll., Cambridge, 1979; Dir, Dept of Air Warfare, RAF Coll., 1980; Dir, Air Staff Briefing, MoD, 1981–82; Dir, PR (RAF), MoD, 1982–84; retired (Air Cdre). Executive Air Weapons, BAe Inc, USA, 1985–86; Dir, Defence Procurement Management Gp, 1986–88, Dean, Continuing Educn, 1987–89, Dir, Sch. of Defence Management, 1988–95, RMCS; Dir of Strategic Mgt, Sch. of Defence Mgt, RMCS, Cranfield Univ., 1995–97. Visiting Professor: Cranfield Univ., 1997–99; Bath Univ., 1999–. FIMgt. Freedom, City of London, 1982. QCVSA 1965, 1970. *Recreations:* reading, significant DIY, computing. *Address:* Barnet House, Faringdon Road, Shippon, Abingdon, Oxon OX13 6LW. *T:* (01235) 522106. *Club:* Royal Air Force.

MILLER, Richard Hugh; QC 1995; *b* 1 Feb. 1953; *s* of Sir Stephen James Hamilton Miller, KCVO, FRCS and Lady (Heather) Miller. *Educ:* Charterhouse; Univ. of Sussex (BSc Chem. Physics). Called to the Bar, Middle Temple, 1976; specialising in patent matters. *Publication:* (ed jtly) Terrell on the Law of Patents, 14th edn 1994, 15th edn 2000. *Recreations:* travel, films. *Address:* 3 New Square, Lincoln's Inn, WC2A 3RS. *T:* (020) 7405 1111.

MILLER, Richard Morgan; Chief Executive, Willis Corroon Group plc, 1990–94; *b* Nashville, Tenn, 1931; *m* 1953, Betty Ruth Randolph; one *s* two *d. Educ:* Montgomery Bell Acad., Nashville; Vanderbilt Univ., Nashville (BA 1953); Wharton Sch., Univ. of Pennsylvania. Served Korean War, 1953–55, Lt US Marine Corps; retired from US Marine Corps Reserve, 1960, Capt. Salesman, Dominion Insce Agency, 1955–58; established Richard M. Miller & Co., 1958, Pres., 1958–70; merger with Synercon Corp., 1970: Founder, Dir, Pres. and Chief Exec. Officer, 1970–76 (also Pres. and Chief Exec. Officer subsid. cos); Synercon Corp. merged into Corroon & Black Corp., 1976: Exec. Vice-Pres., Chief Operating Officer and Dir, 1976–78; Pres., Chief Operating Officer and Dir, 1978–88; Chief Exec. Officer, Pres. and Dir, 1988–89; Chm. Bd, Chief Exec. Officer and Dir, 1990–93; Corroon & Black Corp. merged into Willis Faber plc, 1990. Member, National Associations of: Casualty and Surety Agents; Insurance Brokers; Surety Bond Producers; Mem., Nat. Fedn of Independent Business; Director: Consumer Benefit Life Insce Co.; Meridian Insce Co. (Bermuda); Third Nat. Bank; Third Nat. Corp. Trustee and Member Executive Committee: Insce Inst. of America; Amer. Inst. for Property and Liability Underwriters. *Recreation:* golf. *Clubs:* City Midday, New York Athletic (New York); Belle Meade Country, Cumberland, Nashville City, Tennessee (Nashville, Tennessee); John's Island (Florida); Mid Ocean (Bermuda).

MILLER, Robert Alexander Gavin D.; *see* Douglas Miller.

MILLER, Robin Anthony; a Recorder of the Crown Court, since 1978; *b* 15 Sept. 1937; *s* of William Alexander Miller, CBE, BEM, and Winifred Miller; *m* 1962, Irene Joanna Kennedy; two *s* one *d. Educ:* Devonport High Sch., Plymouth; Wadham Coll., Oxford (MA). Called to the Bar, Middle Temple, 1960. *Address:* St Michael's Lodge, 192 Devonport Road, Stoke, Plymouth, Devon PL1 5RD. *T:* (01752) 564943.

MILLER, Sir Ronald (Andrew Baird), Kt 1993; CBE 1985; CA; *b* 13 May 1937; *m* 1965, Elizabeth Ann Gordon; one *s* one *d. Educ:* Daniel Stewart's Coll.; Univ. of Edinburgh (BSc). With Dawson Internat., 1968–95: Dir, 1976; Chm. and Chief Exec., 1982–91; Exec. Chm., 1991–95. Director: Securities Trust of Scotland, 1983–2001; Christian Salvesen, 1987–97; Aggreko, 1997–; Mem. Bd, Scottish Amicable, 1997– (Dir, Scottish Amicable Life Assce Soc., 1987–97, Dep. Chm., 1994–97). Chairman: British Knitting and Clothing Export Council, 1993–97 (Mem., 1987–98; Vice Pres., 1997–); Scottish Textile Assoc., 1992–95 (Mem., 1992–98); Cttee of Chairmen of Scottish Higher Educn Instns, 1999–2001; Member: N Amer. Adv. Gp, DTI, 1986–96; ScotBIC, 1990–95; Quality Scotland, 1991–95; Scottish Council, CBI, 1992–95; British Apparel and Textile Confedn, 1993–95; SHEFC, 1992–95; Quality Assurance Agency for Higher Educn, 1997– (Chm., Scottish Adv. Cttee, 1998–); Walpole Cttee, 1992–95; SCOTrust, 1994–99. Mem. Court, Napier Univ., 1992–2001 (Chm. Court, 1998–2001). Liveryman, Woolmen's Co., 1992–. FRSA; CIMgt. DSc *hc* Heriot-Watt, 1992. *Address:* 7 Doune Terrace, Edinburgh EH3 6DY.

MILLER, Ronald Kinsman, CB 1989; Solicitor of Inland Revenue, 1986–90, retired; part-time Chairman, VAT and Duties Tribunals, 1991–2001; *b* 12 Nov. 1929; *s* of William Miller and Elsie May Kinsman; *m* 1952, Doris Alice Dew; one *s* one *d. Educ:* Colchester Royal Grammar Sch. Served RN, 1948–50. Called to the Bar, Gray's Inn, 1953. Joined Inland Revenue, 1950; Asst Solicitor, 1971; Law Officers' Dept, 1977–79; Principal Asst Solicitor, 1981–86. *Recreations:* gardening, reading, music. *Address:* 4 Liskeard Close, Chislehurst, Kent BR7 6RT. *T:* (020) 8467 8041. *Club:* Athenæum.

MILLER, Dr Roy Frank; Vice-Principal, 1985–98, Hon. Research Fellow in Physics, since 1998, Royal Holloway and Bedford New College, University of London; *b* 20 Sept. 1935; *s* of Thomas R. Miller and Margaret Ann Tattum; *m* 1961, Ruth Naomi Kenchington; one *s. Educ:* Wembley County Grammar Sch.; University Coll. SW England, Exeter; Royal Holloway Coll. BSc, PhD; CPhys, FInstP. Teacher, Halbutt Secondary Modern Sch., 1957; Royal Holloway College: Demonstrator, 1957, Asst Lectr, 1960, Lectr, 1963, Sen. Lectr, 1973, Physics Dept; Vice-Principal, 1978–81; Acting Principal, 1981–82; Principal, 1982–85; Hon. Fellow, 2000. Research Associate and Teaching Fellow, Case Western Reserve Univ., Ohio, USA, 1967–68. Mem. Senate, Univ. of London, 1981–85; Chm., Bd, Inst. of Classical Studies, Univ. of London, 1983–2001; Trustee and Governor, Strode's Foundn, Strode's Coll., Egham, 1982–. MRI; FRSA. *Publications:* articles in Jl Phys C, Phil. Mag., Vacuum. *Recreations:* mountaineering, squash, music. *Address:* Royal Holloway and Bedford New College, University of London, Egham Hill, Egham, Surrey TW20 0EX. *T:* (01784) 434455. *Club:* Athenæum.

MILLER, Sidney James, MA; Citizens' Advice Bureau Adviser, Bedford, since 1995; *b* 25 Jan. 1943; *s* of Sidney Tomsett Miller and Mary Ada Miller (*née* Marshall); *m* 1971, Judith Branney (*née* Passingham); three *s* one *d. Educ:* Clifton Coll., Bristol; Jesus Coll., Cambridge (MA); Harvard Univ. VIth Form Classical Master and House Tutor, Clifton Coll., Bristol, 1965–68; Asst Master and Classical Tutor, Eton Coll., 1968–73, Head of Classical Dept, 1971–73; Dep. Headmaster (Organisation), Bridgewater Hall, Stantonbury Campus, Milton Keynes, 1974–77; Headmaster, Kingston Grammar Sch., Kingston upon Thames, 1977–86; Head Master, Bedford Sch., 1986–88; Professional Officer, Sch. Exams and Assessment Council, 1988–89; HEO, DES, later DFE, 1989–95. Mem., Gen. Synod of C of E, 1994–95. Dir, Bedford Concern for the Homeless and Rootless, 1996–. *Publications:* (ed jtly) Greek Unprepared Translation, 1968; (ed jtly) Inscriptions of the Roman Empire AD14–117, 1971; article in Didaskalos, 1972. *Recreations:* watching sports, learning languages, walking. *Address:* 43 Waterloo Road, Bedford MK40 3PG. *Clubs:* MCC; Achilles; Bedford Rugby.

MILLER of Glenlee, Sir Stephen (William Macdonald), 8th Bt *cr* 1788, of Glenlee, Kirkcudbrightshire; FRCGP; General Practitioner, since 1986; *b* 20 June 1953; *s* of Sir Macdonald Miller of Glenlee, 7th Bt and of Marion Jane Audrey Pettit, (Audrey, Lady Miller of Glenlee); *S* father, 1991; *m* 1st, 1978, Mary (*d* 1989), *d* of G. B. Owens; one *s* one *d*; 2nd, 1990, Caroline Clark (*née* Chasemore); one step *s* one step *d. Educ:* Rugby Sch.; St Bartholomew's Hosp. MB; FRCS 1981; MRCGP 1986, FRCGP 1995. Surgical Registrar, Sheffield, 1979–81; Orthopaedic Registrar, Newcastle, 1982–84. *Publications:* various papers in med. jls. *Recreations:* gardening, fishing. *Heir: s* James Stephen Macdonald Miller, *b* 25 July 1981. *Address:* The Lawn, Shebbear, Beaworthy, Devon EX21 5RU.

MILLER, Terence George, TD 1960; MA Cantab; Director, Polytechnic of North London, 1971–80; *b* 16 Jan. 1918; *o s* of late George Frederick Miller, Cambridge, and late Marion Johnston, Port William, Wigtownshire; *m* 1944, Inga Catriona, 3rd *d* of Austin Priestman, MD, Folkestone, Kent; one *s* three *d. Educ:* Perse (foundn schol.); Jesus Coll., Cambridge (schol.; Nat. Sci. Tripos, pt 1 cl. 1, pt 2 cl. 1). Wiltshire Prizeman, 1939. Served War of 1939–45: RA, Glider Pilot Regt; RE (TA), 1947–67 (Lt.-Col. 1964). Harkness Scholar, 1948; Research Fellow, Jesus Coll., 1949–54. University Demonstrator, 1948; Lectr in Geology, Univ. of Keele, 1953; Sen. Lectr, 1963, Prof. of Geography, Univ. of Reading, 1965–67; Principal, University Coll. of Rhodesia, 1967–69; Vis. Prof., Reading Univ., 1969–71. *Publications:* Geology, 1950; Geology and Scenery in Britain, 1953; scientific papers in various jls. *Recreations:* trying to understand war, beachcombing, listening. *Address:* Plough House, Docking Road, Sedgeford, Norfolk PE36 5LR.

MILLER, Walter George, CPFA; FCCA; Chief Executive, Bristol City Council, 1990–91 (Acting Chief Executive, 1987–90); *b* 2 March 1932; *s* of Bert and Rosina Miller; *m* 1956, Sheila Mary Daw; one *s* two *d. Educ:* Howardian High Sch., Cardiff. Clerk, City Treasurer's Dept, Cardiff, 1948–50. Served RA, Hong Kong and Korea, 1950–52. Audit Asst, City Treasurer's Dept, Cardiff, 1952–55; Accountant, Treasurer's Dept: Nairobi, 1955–58; Cardiff, 1958–60; Caerphilly, 1960–63; Ilford, 1963–65; Redbridge, 1965; Bromley, 1965–68; Asst Borough Treasurer, Bromley, 1968–72; Bristol: Asst City Treasurer, 1972–73; Dep. City Treasurer, 1973–80; City Treasurer, 1980–90. *Publications:* Morgan at Gatehaven (novel), 1994; contrib. local government and accountancy press. *Recreations:* writing, gardening, walking. *Address:* 21 Heron Gardens, Portishead, Bristol BS20 7DH. *T:* (01275) 818743.

MILLER, William; *see* Miller, G. W.

MILLER, Prof. William Lockley, PhD; FBA 1994; FRSE; Edward Caird Professor of Politics, Glasgow University, since 1985; *b* 12 Aug. 1943; *s* of William Lockley Miller and Florence Ratcliffe; *m* 1967, Fiona Thomson; two *s* one *d. Educ:* Edinburgh Univ. (MA 1st Cl. Maths and Nat. Phil. 1965); Newcastle Univ. (PhD Computing 1970). Lectr in Politics, Sen Lectr and Prof., Strathclyde Univ., 1968–85. Vis. Prof. in Politics, Virginia Tech., Blacksburg, 1983–84. FRSE 1999. *Publications:* Electoral Dynamics, 1977; The End of British Politics?, 1981; The Survey Method, 1983; (with Martin Harrop) Elections and Voters, 1987; Irrelevant Elections?, 1988; (jtly) How Voters Change, 1990; Media and Voters, 1991; (jtly) Alternatives to Freedom, 1995; (jtly) Political Culture in Contemporary Britain, 1996; (jtly) Values and Political Change in Postcommunist Europe, 1998; Models of Local Governance, 2000; A Culture of Corruption?, 2001. *Recreation:* hill walking. *Address:* Department of Politics, Adam Smith Building, The University, Glasgow G12 8RT. *T:* (0141) 339 8855.

MILLER SMITH, Charles; Chairman, Scottish Power plc, since 2000 (Deputy Chairman, 1999–2000); Director, 1994–2001 and Chairman, 1999–2001, Imperial Chemical Industries; *b* 7 Nov. 1939; *s* of William Smith and Margaret Pettigrew Brownlie Wardrope; adopted grandfather's surname, Miller Smith, 1963; *m* 1964, Dorothy Agnes Wilson Adams (*d* 1999); one *s* two *d. Educ:* Glasgow Acad.; St Andrews Univ. (MA). ACCA. Unilever: Financial Dir, Vinyl Products, 1970–73; Head of Planning, 1974; Finance Dir, Walls Meat Co., 1976; Vice-Chm., Hindustan Lever, 1979–81; Speciality Chemicals Group, 1981; Chief Exec., PPF Internat., 1983; Chief Exec., Quest Internat., 1986; Financial Dir, Unilever Board, 1989; Exec., Unilever Foods, 1993–94; Chief Exec., ICI, 1995–99. Non-executive Director: Midland Bank, 1994–96; HSBC Hldgs plc, 1996–. Hon. LLD St Andrews, 1995. *Recreations:* reading, walking. *Address:* Scottish Power plc, 1 Atlantic Quay, Glasgow G2 8SP. *Club:* National.

MILLETT, family name of **Baron Millett**.

MILLETT, Baron *cr* 1998 (Life Peer), of St Marylebone in the City of Westminster; **Peter Julian Millett,** Kt 1986; PC 1994; a Lord of Appeal in Ordinary, since 1998; *b* 23 June 1932; *s* of late Denis Millett and Adele Millett; *m* 1959, Ann Mireille, *d* of late David Harris; two *s* (and one *s* decd). *Educ:* Harrow; Trinity Hall, Cambridge (Schol.; MA; Hon. Fellow, 1994). Nat. Service, RAF, 1955–57 (Flying Officer). Called to Bar, Middle Temple, 1955, *ad eundem* Lincoln's Inn, 1959 (Bencher, 1980), Singapore, 1976, Hong Kong, 1979; at Chancery Bar, 1958–86; QC 1973; a Judge of the High Court of Justice, Chancery Div. 1986–94; a Lord Justice of Appeal, 1994–98. Examnr and Lectr in Practical Conveyancing, Council of Legal Educn, 1962–76. Junior Counsel to Dept of Trade and Industry in Chancery matters, 1967–73. Mem., General Council of the Bar, 1971–75. Outside Mem., Law Commn on working party on co-ownership of matrimonial home, 1972–73; Mem., Dept of Trade Insolvency Law Review Cttee, 1977–82. Pres., West London Synagogue of British Jews, 1991–95. Editor-in Chief, Encyc. of Forms and Precedents, 1988–. Hon. LLD London, 2000. *Publications:* contrib. to Halsbury's Laws of England; articles in legal jls. *Recreations:* philately, bridge, The Times crossword. *Address:* House of Lords, SW1A 0PW; 18 Portman Close, W1H 9HJ. *T:* (020) 7935 1152; St Andrews, Kewhurst Avenue, Cooden, Bexhill-on-Sea, East Sussex TN39 3BH.

MILLETT, Anthea Christine, CBE 2000; Chairman, Wiltshire Health Authority, since 2000; *b* 2 Nov. 1941; *d* of Rupert Millett and Lucy Millett. *Educ:* Erdington Grammar School for Girls, Birmingham; Bedford Coll., Univ. of London (BA Hons). Teacher: Channing School, Highgate, 1963–65; Bournville Grammar Tech. Sch., Birmingham, 1965–67; Solihull High Sch., 1967–71 (Head of Dept); Dep. Head, Tile Hill Comprehensive Sch., Coventry, 1972–77; HM Inspectorate of Schools, subseq. OFSTED, 1978–95: Chief Inspector, 1987–92; Dir of Inspection, 1993–95; Chief Exec., TTA, 1995–99. Mem., Cttee of Enquiry, Management and Government of Schools, 1975–77. Member Council: Commonwealth Inst.; Trustee, Francis Holland Schs. FRGS (Vice-Pres., Educn); FRSA. *Recreations:* travel, walking, gardening, DIY. *Address:* c/o Wiltshire Health Authority, Southgate House, Pans Lane, Devizes, Wilts SN10 5EQ.

MILLGATE, Prof. Michael Henry, PhD; FRSC; FRSL; University Professor of English, Emeritus, Toronto University, since 1994; *b* 19 July 1929; *s* of Stanley Millgate and Marjorie Louisa (*née* Norris); *m* 1960, Jane, *d* of Maurice and Marie Barr. *Educ:* St Catharine's Coll., Cambridge (MA); Michigan Univ.; Leeds Univ. (PhD). FRSC 1982. Tutor-Organizer, WEA, E Lindsey, 1953–56; Lectr in English Lit., Leeds Univ., 1958–64; Prof. of English and Chm. of the Dept, York Univ., Ont, 1964–67; Prof. of English, Toronto Univ., 1967–94 (University Prof., 1987–94). Killam Sen. Res. Schol., 1974–75, Killam Res. Fellow, 1986–88; John Simon Guggenheim Meml Fellow, 1977–78. FRSL 1984. Pierre Chauveau Medal, RSC, 1999. *Publications:* William Faulkner, 1961; (ed) Tennyson: Selected Poems, 1963; American Social Fiction, 1964; (ed jtly) Transatlantic Dialogue, 1966; The Achievement of William Faulkner, 1966; (ed jtly) Lion in the Garden, 1968; Thomas Hardy: his career as a novelist, 1971; (ed jtly) The Collected Letters of Thomas Hardy, vols I-VII, 1978–88; Thomas Hardy: a biography, 1982; (ed) The Life and Work of Thomas Hardy, 1985; (ed) William Faulkner Manuscripts 20, 21, 22 and 23, 1987; (ed) New Essays on Light in August, 1987; (ed) Thomas Hardy: selected letters, 1990; Testamentary Acts: Browning, Tennyson, James, Hardy, 1992; (ed jtly) Thomas Hardy's 'Studies, Specimens &c' Notebook, 1994; (ed) Letters of Emma and Florence Hardy, 1996; Faulkner's Place, 1997; (ed) Thomas Hardy's Public Voice, 2001. *Address:* 1 Balmoral Avenue, Apt 809, Toronto, ON M4V 3B9, Canada. *T:* (416) 920 3717.

MILLICHIP, Sir Frederick Albert, (Sir Bert), Kt 1991; Member of Council, since 1970, and Life Vice President, since 1990, The Football Association (Chairman, 1981–96); *b* 5 Aug. 1914; *s* of late Hugh Bowater Millichip; *m* 1950, Joan Barbara Brown; one *s* one *d. Educ:* Solihull Sch., Warwicks. Qualified as Solicitor, 1950; Sen. Partner, Sharpe & Millichip, subseq. Tyndelwood & Millichip, 1959–88, Consultant, 1988–96; Consultant, Edge & Ellison, 1996–. Served War, 1939–45, in England, N Africa, Sicily and Italy; joined S Staffs Regt as private, commnd RA (Captain). Union of European Football Associations: Chairman: Cttee for Five-a-Side Football, 1988–92; Juridical Cttee, 1992–93; Member: Exec. Cttee, 1988–96 (Advr, 1996–); Organising Cttee for European Championship, 1981–96; Referees' Cttee, 1992–97 (Chm., 1994–96); Hon. Mem., UEFA, 1996. Mem., FIFA Organising Cttee for World Cup, 1983–; Chm., FA Disciplinary Cttee, 1978–81. West Bromwich Albion Football Club: Dir, 1964–84; Chm., 1976–83; Pres., 1984–. Hon. DLitt Loughborough, 1995. Ordre du Mérite, FIFA, 1998. *Recreation:* golf. *Address:* 1 The Woodlands, 1 Fiery Hill, Barnt Green, Birmingham B45 8LB. *T:* (0121) 445 4688. *Club:* Blackwell Golf (Blackwell, Worcs).

MILLIGAN, Rt Hon. Lord; James George Milligan; PC 2000; a Senator of the College of Justice in Scotland, 1988–2001; *b* 10 May 1934; *s* of Rt Hon. Lord Milligan;

m 1st, 1961, Elizabeth Carnegie Thomson (*d* 1982), *e d* of late Hon. Lord Migdale and Louise (*née* Carnegie; later Mrs Thomson); two *s* three *d*; 2nd, 1985, Elizabeth Cynthia Rae Ashworth, *widow* of Rupert S. H. Ashworth, and *y d* of late P. Rae Shepherd. *Educ:* St Mary's Sch., Melrose; Rugby Sch.; Oxford Univ. (BA); Edinburgh Univ. (LLB). Admitted to Faculty of Advocates, 1959; Standing Junior Counsel to the Scottish Home and Health Dept and Dept of Health and Social Security in Scotland; Advocate-Depute, 1971–78; QC (Scot.) 1972; Chm., Med. Appeal Tribunal (Scotland), 1979–88. Chm., RSSPCC Edinburgh, 1978–92. *Publication:* (contrib. small part of) Armour on Valuation for Rating, 3rd edn, 1961. *Recreations:* gardening, golf. *Address:* Parliament House, Edinburgh EH1 1RQ.

MILLIGAN, Eric; JP; Lord Provost and Lord-Lieutenant of the City of Edinburgh (with designation Rt Hon.), since 1996; *b* 27 Jan. 1951; *m* Janis. *Educ:* Tynecastle High Sch.; Napier Coll. Former printer. Member (Lab): Edinburgh DC, 1974–78; Lothian Regl Council, 1978–96 (Chm., Finance Cttee, 1980–82, 1986–90; Convener, 1990–96); Convener, Edinburgh City Council, 1995–96. Pres., COSLA, 1988–90. JP Edinburgh, 1996. Hon. FRCSE 2000. Hon. DBA Napier, 1999. Chevalier, Ordre Nat. du Mérite (France), 1996. *Recreations:* watching football and Rugby as played by Heart of Midlothian FC and Boroughmuir RFC, listening to music. *Address:* City Chambers, High Street, Edinburgh EH1 1YJ. *T:* (0131) 200 2000. *Clubs:* Caledonian; Royal Over-Seas League, Royal Scots, Edinburgh Press (Edinburgh); Boroughmuir Rugby Football.

MILLIGAN, Iain Anstruther; QC 1991; *b* 21 April 1950; *s* of late Wyndham Macbeth Moir Milligan, MBE, TD; *m* 1979, Zara Ann Louise Spearman; one *s* two *d*. *Educ:* Eton; Magdalene College, Cambridge (MA); College of Law. Called to the Bar, Inner Temple, 1973. *Recreations:* farming, forestry, walking. *Address:* 20 Essex Street, WC2R 3AL. *T:* (020) 7583 9294; Dunesslin, Dunscore, Dumfries DG2 0UR. *T:* (01387) 820345.

MILLIGAN, James George; *see* Milligan, Rt Hon. Lord.

MILLIGAN, Terence Alan, (Spike Milligan), Hon. KBE 2000 (Hon. CBE 1992); actor; author; *b* 16 April 1918; *s* of late Captain L. A. Milligan, MSM, RA retd, and Florence Winifred Milligan; *m* (wife *d* 1978); one *s* three *d*; *m* 1983, Shelagh Sinclair. *Educ:* Convent of Jesus and Mary, Poona; Brothers de La Salle, Rangoon; SE London Polytechnic, Lewisham. Lifetime Achievement Award, British Comedy Awards, 1994. Appearances (comedy) as Spike Milligan: *stage:* The Bed-Sitting Room; Son of Oblomov; Ben Gunn, in Treasure Island, Mermaid, 1973, 1974; One man shows, 1979, 1980, 1998, 1999; writer, Ubu Roi, 1980; Spike Milligan and Friends, Lyric, 1982; *radio:* Goon Show (inc. special performance, 1972, to mark 50th Anniversary of BBC); Best British Radio Features Script, 1972; The Milligan Papers, 1987; *TV:* Show called Fred, ITV; World of Beachcomber, BBC; Q5, BBC; Oh in Colour, BBC; A Milligan for All Seasons, BBC, 1972–73; Marty Feldman's Comedy Machine, ITV (writing and appearing; awarded Golden Rose and special comedy award, Montreux, 1972); The Melting Pot, BBC, 1975; Q7, BBC series, 1977; Q8, 1978; Q9, 1979; TV Writer of the Year Award, 1956; *films:* The Magic Christian, 1971; The Devils, 1971; The Cherry Picker, 1972; Digby the Biggest Dog in the World, 1972; Alice's Adventures in Wonderland, 1972; The Three Musketeers, 1973; The Great McGonagall, 1975; The Last Remake of Beau Geste, 1977; The Hound of the Baskervilles, 1978; Monty Python Life of Brian, 1978; History of the World, Part 1, 1980; Yellowbeard, 1983. *Publications:* Dustbin of Milligan, 1961; Silly Verse for Kids, 1963; Puckoon, 1963; The Little Pot Boiler, 1965; A Book of Bits, 1965; Milliganimals, 1968; The Bedside Milligan, 1968; The Bed-Sitting Room (play), 1969; The Bald Twit Lion, 1970; Adolf Hitler, My Part in his Downfall, 1971 (filmed 1973; on record, 1980); Milligan's Ark, 1971; Small Dreams of a Scorpion, 1972; The Goon Show Scripts, 1972; Rommel: Gunner Who?, 1973; (for children) Badjelly the Witch, 1973; (with J. Hobbs) The Great McGonagall Scrapbook, 1975; The Milligan Book of Records, Games, Cartoons and Commercials, 1975; Dip the Puppy, 1975; Transports of Delight, 1975; William McGonagal, the truth at last, 1976; Monty, His Part in my Victory, 1976; Goblins (with Heath Robinson illus), 1978; Mussolini, His Part in my Downfall, 1978; Open Heart University, 1978; Spike Milligan's Q Annual, 1979; Get in the Q Annual, 1980; Unspun Socks from a Chicken's Laundry, 1981; Indefinite Articles and Scunthorpe, 1981; The 101 Best and Only Limericks of Spike Milligan, 1982; (for children) Sir Nobonk and the Terrible, Awful, Dreadful, Naughty, Nasty Dragon (illus. by Carol Barker), 1982; The Goon Cartoons, 1982; More Goon Cartoons, 1983; There's A Lot Of It About, 1983; The Melting Pot, 1983; Spike Milligan's Further Transports of Delight, 1985; Where have all the Bullets Gone? (autobiog.), 1985; Floored Masterpieces with Worse Verse (illus. by Tracey Boyd), 1985; Goodbye Soldier, 1986; The Looney: an Irish fantasy, 1987; The Mirror Running (poetry), 1987; Startling Verse for all the Family (children's poetry), 1987; The Lost Goon Shows, 1987; Milligan's War, 1988; McGonagall Meets George Gershwin, 1988; It Ends With Magic, 1990; Dear Robert, Dear Spike, 1991; Peacework (autobiog.), 1991; Condensed Animals, 1991; Hidden Words (poetry), 1993; (with A. Clare) Depression and How To Survive It, 1993; The Bible According to Spike Milligan, 1993; Lady Chatterly's Lover According to Spike Milligan, 1994; Wuthering Heights According to Spike Milligan, 1995; Fleas, Knees and Hidden Elephants (poetry), 1995; Spike Milligan: a celebration, 1995; D. H. Lawrence's John Thomas and Lady Jane According to Spike Milligan, 1995; The Adventures of Black Beauty According to Spike Milligan, 1996; Frankenstein According to Spike Milligan, 1997; Hounds of the Baskervilles According to Spike Milligan, 1998; Robin Hood According to Spike Milligan, 1998; A Mad Medley of Milligan, 1999; The Family Album–An Illustrated Biography, 1999; A Children's Treasury of Milligan, 1999; Treasure Island According to Spike Milligan, 2000. *Recreations:* restoration of antiques, oil painting, water colours, gardening, eating, drinking, talking, wine, jazz. *Address:* 9 Orme Court, W2 4RL. *T:* (020) 7727 1544.

MILLIGAN, Timothy James; His Honour Judge Milligan; a Circuit Judge, since 1991; *b* 16 March 1940; *s* of Dr Peter James Wyatt Milligan and Rosemary Elizabeth Ann (*née* Dutton); *m* 1976, Sally Marcella (*née* Priest) (marr. diss. 1999); two step *s*. *Educ:* Frilsham House Prep. School; Winchester Coll.; Grenoble Univ. (1st and 2nd Foreigner's Degrees). Articled Clerk, Taylor Garrett, 1960–65; admitted Solicitor, 1967; Asst Solicitor, Leeds Smith, Beds, 1967–69; Asst Solicitor, then Partner, Triggs Turner, Guildford, 1969–73; Solicitor, then Partner, Warner & Richardson, Winchester, 1973–91; HM Coroner, Central Hants, 1982–91; a Recorder of the Crown Court, 1988–91. Hon. Mem., Coroners Soc. of GB, 1991; Mem. of various Old Wykehamist clubs and assocs. Chm. Disciplinary Cttee of Rackets Cttee, Tennis and Rackets Assoc., 1998–. *Recreations:* rackets, cricket, football, reading, music, theatre, cinema. *Address:* 33 East Street, Titchfield, Fareham PO14 4AD. *Clubs:* MCC; Hampshire CC (Mem. Cttee, 1993–); Jesters; Tennis and Rackets Association (Mem., Rackets Cttee, 1988–98).

MILLING, Michael Crowley C.; *see* Crowley-Milling.

MILLING, Peter Francis, MB, BChir, FRCS; formerly: Surgeon, Ear, Nose and Throat Department, University College Hospital; Surgeon in charge, Throat and Ear Department, Brompton Hospital; Consultant Ear, Nose and Throat Surgeon: Epsom District Hospital; Oxted and Limpsfield Cottage Hospital; Visiting Laryngologist Benenden Chest Hospital. *Educ:* Cambridge University. BA Hons, 1937; MRCS, LRCP, 1940; MA, MB, BChir, 1941; FRCS, 1946. Formerly Chief Assistant, Ear, Nose and Throat Department, St Thomas' Hospital; Chief Clinical Assistant and Registrar, Ear, Nose and Throat Department, Guy's Hosp.; Surgical Registrar, Ear, Nose and Throat Dept, Royal Cancer Hospital. Member British Association of Otolaryngologists. *Publications:* contributions to medical text-books and journals. *Address:* Abbotswood House, Crossag Road, Ballasalla, Isle of Man IM9 3DZ. *T:* (01624) 823072.

MILLINGTON, Anthony Nigel Raymond; Director General, Tokyo Office, European Automobile Manufacturers Association, since 1995; *b* 29 Jan. 1945; *s* of Raymond and Nancy Millington; *m* 1969, Susan Carolyn (*née* Steilberg); two *s*. *Educ:* Ipswich School; Univ. of Grenoble; Trinity College, Cambridge (BA); Univ. of Chicago. HM Diplomatic Service, 1968–94: FCO, 1968; Tokyo, 1969–76; FCO, 1976–80; Paris, 1980–84; Japanese National Defence College, 1984–85; Head of Chancery, Tokyo, 1985–88; Head of Far Eastern Dept, FCO, 1989–90; Rolls-Royce PLC, 1990; Pres., Rolls-Royce (Far East) Ltd, 1990–94 (on leave of absence); FCO, 1994. Mem., Japanese Prime Minister's Regulatory Reform Commn, 1998–. Advr to Bd of Dirs, Japan Automobile Importers' Assoc., 2001–; Mem., Internat. Affairs Cttee, Tokyo Chamber of Commerce and Industry, 2001–. *Recreations:* golf, tennis, walking in the countryside. *Address:* c/o European Automobile Manufacturers Association, PO Box 564, Ark Mori Building, 1–12–32 Akasaka, Minato-ku, Tokyo 107–6030, Japan. *T:* (3) 35054963, *Fax:* (3) 35054871; *e-mail:* anrm@miinet.or.jp. *Clubs:* Royal Automobile; Tokyo Lawn Tennis (Director).

MILLINGTON, Christopher James; QC 2001; a Recorder, since 1995; *b* 31 Oct. 1951; *s* of Dennis Millington and Christine Millington; *m* 1976, Jane Elisabeth Bucknell; one *s* one *d*. *Educ:* Birmingham Univ. (LLB, LLM). Called to the Bar, Gray's Inn, 1976; in chambers, Birmingham, 1976–. *Recreations:* tennis, golf, travel, music, especially rock guitar. *Address:* 1 Fountain Court, Steelhouse Lane, Birmingham B4 6DR. *T:* (0121) 236 5721. *Clubs:* Edgbaston Priory Tennis, Moor Hall Golf.

MILLINGTON, Wing Comdr Ernest Rogers, DFC 1945; advisor on training, Youth Training Scheme, 1980–90; Teacher in charge of Teachers' Centre, London Borough of Newham, 1967–80, retired; Founder, and Editor, Project, 1967–80; *b* 15 Feb. 1916; *s* of Edmund Rogers Millington and Emily Craggs; *m* 1st, 1937 (marr. diss. 1974); four *d*; 2nd, 1975, Ivy Mary Robinson. *Educ:* Chigwell Sch., Essex; College of S Mark and S John, Chelsea; Birkbeck Coll., London Univ. Clerk; Accountant; Company Sec.; served War of 1939–45, soldier, gunner officer, pilot RAF, instructor and heavy bomber, CO of a Lancaster Sqdn. MP (Commonwealth) for Chelmsford, 1945–50. Re-joined Royal Air Force, 1954–57. Head of Social Educn, Shoreditch Comprehensive Sch., London, 1965–67. *Publications:* (edited): A Study of Film, 1972; The Royal Group of Docks, 1977; A Geography of London, 1979; National Parks, 1980. *Recreations:* Francophilia, writing. *Address:* Villa Martine, Couze St Front, 24150 Lalinde, France. *T:* 553249431.

MILLINGTON, Tamara; *see* Ingram, T.

MILLION, Clive Ernest; a District Judge, Principal Registry of the Family Division of the High Court, since 1993; a Recorder, since 1999; *b* 7 Sept. 1946; *s* of Arthur Ernest Million and Phyllis May Million; *m* 1975, Pauline Margaret Lock; three *s*. *Educ:* St Dunstan's Coll.; Birmingham Coll. of Art and Design (BA Hons Industrial Design (Engrg) 1969). Called to the Bar, Middle Temple, 1975; an Asst Recorder, 1995–99. *Recreation:* anything legal, but non-legal. *Address:* (office) First Avenue House, 42–49 High Holborn, WC1V 6NP. *T:* (020) 7936 6574.

MILLNER, Ralph; QC 1965; *b* 25 Jan. 1912; *o s* of Ralph Millner, Merchant, Manchester; *m* 1st, 1935, Bruna, *d* of Arturo Rosa, Este, Italy (marr. diss. 1949); one *d* decd; 2nd, 1949, Monica, *d* of Prof. P. W. Robertson, Wellington, NZ; one *s* two *d*. *Educ:* William Hulme's Grammar Sch., Manchester; Clare Coll., Cambridge (MA); Bedford Coll., London (BA, Italian). Called to English Bar, Inner Temple, 1934; Ghana Bar (Gold Coast), 1950; Sierra Leone Bar, 1957; Nigerian Bar and S Cameroons Bar, 1959; Guyana Bar (formerly British Guiana), 1961; has also appeared in courts of Aden and Kenya. Lectr in Italian, QUB, 1972–77. Vis. Lectr in Italian, Univ. of Leicester, 1980–92. Member: Soc. for Italian Studies; Haldane Soc. *Address:* 69 Anson Road, N7 0AS.

MILLON, Charles; Minister of Defence, France, 1995–97; Mayor of Belley, since 1997; *b* Belley, Ain, 12 Nov. 1945; *s* of Gabriel Millon and Suzanne Millon (*née* Gunet); *m* Chantal Delsol; six *c*. *Educ:* Lamartine Instn, Belley; Saint-Marie Sch., Lyon. Asst Lectr, 1969; legal and fiscal consultant, 1969–. Deputy (UDF-PR) for Belley-Gex, elected 1978, 1981, 1986, 1988, 1993, 1995, 1997; Mem., Regl Council for Rhône-Alpes, elected 1981, 1986 (Pres., 1988–98); Mem., Gen. Council of the Ain (Canton of Belley), 1985–88; National Assembly: Vice-Pres., 1986–88; Mem., Foreign Cttee, 1988–; Pres., Parly Gp of UDF, 1989–95. Pres., Departmental Fedn, PR and UDF, 1983–85; Mem., Pol Bd, PR, 1984–95. Pres., Droite libérale Chrétienne, 1999. *Publications:* L'extravagante histoire des nationalisations, 1984; L'alternate-Vérité, 1986; La tentation du conservatisme, 1995; La Paix Civile, 1998. *Address:* National Assembly, 126 rue de l'Université, 75355 Paris, France; Le Mairie de Belley, BP 121, 01306 Belley cedex, France.

MILLS; *see* Platts-Mills.

MILLS, family name of **Viscount Mills**.

MILLS, 3rd Viscount *cr* 1962; **Christopher Philip Roger Mills;** Bt 1953; Baron 1957; Area Manager, Thames Region, Environment Agency, since 1996; *b* 20 May 1956; *s* of 2nd Viscount Mills and Joan Dorothy (*d* 1998), *d* of James Shirreff; *S* father, 1988; *m* 1980, Lesley Alison, *er d* of Alan Bailey. *Educ:* Oundle School; Univ. of London (BSc Hons Biolog. Sciences; MSc Applied Fish Biology); Plymouth Polytechnic. Biologist at Salmon Research Trust of Ireland, 1980–89; National Rivers Authority: Technical Asst, 1989–91; Area Fisheries, Recreation and Ecology Man., NW Region, 1991–95; Area Man., Thames Reg., 1995–96. Member Council: Inst. of Fisheries Mgt, 1993–; RSPB, 1995–2000. *Publications:* papers in Aquaculture, Aquaculture and Fisheries Management, Fish Biology. *Recreations:* flyfishing, fine wines.

MILLS, Dame Barbara (Jean Lyon), DBE 1997; QC 1986; The Adjudicator, since 1999; *b* 10 Aug. 1940; *d* of John and Kitty Warnock; *m* 1962, John Angus Donald Mills; four *c*. *Educ:* St Helen's Sch., Northwood; Lady Margaret Hall, Oxford (Gibbs Scholar, 1961; MA; Hon. Fellow, 1991). Called to the Bar, Middle Temple, 1963, Bencher, 1990; QC (NI) 1991. Jun. Treasury Counsel, Central Criminal Court, 1981–86; a Recorder, 1982–92; Dir, Serious Fraud Office, 1990–92; DPP, 1992–98. Member: Criminal Injuries Compensation Bd, 1988–90; Parole Bd, 1990; Legal Assessor to GMC and GDC, 1988–90. Mem., Gen. Adv. Council, BBC, 1991–92. Chairman: Forum UK, 1999–2001; Women's Liby Council, 2000–. Hon. Vice-Pres., Inst. for Study and Treatment of Delinquency, 1996–. Hon. Fellow, Soc. for Advanced Legal Studies, 1997. CIMgt 1993. Hon. LLD: Hull, 1993; Nottingham Trent, 1993; London Guildhall, 1994. *Recreation:* my family. *Address:* (office) Haymarket House, 28 Haymarket, SW1Y 4SP. *T:* (020) 7930 2292, *Fax:* (020) 7930 2298; *e-mail:* adjudicators@gtnet.gov.uk.

MILLS, Prof. Bernard Yarnton, AC 1976; FRS 1963; FAA 1959; DSc Eng; Professor of Physics (Astrophysics), University of Sydney, 1965–85, Emeritus Professor 1986; *b* 8 Aug. 1920; *s* of Ellice Yarnton Mills and Sylphide Mills. *Educ:* King's Sch., New South Wales; University of Sydney. BSc 1940, DSc Eng 1959 (Sydney). Joined the then Council for Scientific and Industrial Research and worked on Devel of mil. radar systems; after working for many years on radioastronomy he joined Sydney Univ. to form a radioastronomy group in Sch. of Physics, 1960; Reader in Physics, 1960–65; responsible for Mills Cross radio-telescope, near Hoskinstown, NSW. Lyle Medal of Australian Academy of Science, 1957. *Publications:* (jtly) A Textbook of Radar, 1946; many contribs to sci. jls in Australia, England and America, mainly on subjects of radioastronomy and astrophysics. *Address:* 52 Victoria Street, Roseville, NSW 2069, Australia.

MILLS, Vice-Adm. Sir Charles (Piercy), KCB 1968 (CB 1964); CBE 1957; DSC 1953; *b* 4 Oct. 1914; *s* of late Capt. Thomas Piercy Mills, Woking, Surrey; *m* 1944, Anne Cumberlege; two *d. Educ:* RN College, Dartmouth. Joined Navy, 1928; Comdr 1947; Capt. 1953; Rear-Adm. 1963; Vice-Adm. 1966. Served War of 1939–45, Home Waters, Mediterranean and Far East; Korea, 1951–52; Flag Officer, Second in Command, Far East Fleet, 1966–67; C-in-C Plymouth, 1967–69; Lieut-Governor and C-in-C Guernsey, 1969–74. US Legion of Merit, 1955. KStJ 1969. *Recreation:* golf. *Address:* Aldewaye, Aldeburgh, Suffolk IP15 5ER.

MILLS, Eric Robertson, CBE 1981; Registrar of the Privy Council, 1966–83; *b* 27 July 1918; *s* of late Thomas Piercy Mills, Woking, Surrey; *m* 1950, Shirley Manger; two *d. Educ:* Charterhouse; Trinity Coll., Cambridge (BA). Served Royal Artillery, 1939–46; Major 1944. Called to Bar, Inner Temple, 1947; Mem. of Western Circuit. Dep. Judge Advocate, 1955; Chief Clerk, Judicial Cttee of Privy Council, 1963. *Publications:* contribs to legal text books. *Address:* Lamber Green, 10 St Catherines Drive, Guildford, Surrey GU2 4HE. *T:* (01483) 537218.

MILLS, Prof. Eric William, AM 1986; CChem, FRSC; FRACI; Director, South Australian Institute of Technology, 1978–85, retired; *b* 22 April 1920; *s* of William and Lucy Margaret Mills; *m* 1st, 1945, Inge Julia Königsberger (*d* 1986); three *d*; 2nd, 1993, Natalya Bakaeva; one *d. Educ:* Liverpool Institute; Univ. of Liverpool (BSc, PhD). Chemist, British Insulated Cables, 1941–45; Research Chemist, British Oxygen Co., 1948–49; Sen. Lectr, Birmingham College of Advanced Technology, 1949–52; Head of Dept, Rutherford Coll. of Technology, 1952–57; Principal: Carlisle Technical Coll., 1959–60; Chesterfield Coll. of Technology, 1960–63; Asst Dir, SA Inst. of Technology, 1964–77. *Address:* 3 Pam Street, Beaumont, SA 5066, Australia. *T:* (8) 83796674.

MILLS, Sir Frank, KCVO 1983; CMG 1971; HM Diplomatic Service, retired; Chairman of Council, Royal Commonwealth Society for the Blind (Sight Savers), 1985–91; *b* 3 Dec. 1923; *s* of Joseph Francis Mills and Louisa Mills; *m* 1953, Trilby Foster; one *s* two *d. Educ:* King Edward VI Sch., Nuneaton; Emmanuel Coll., Cambridge. RAFVR, 1942–45. CRO, 1948; served in: Pakistan, 1949–51; S Africa, 1955–58; Malaysia, 1962–63; Singapore, 1964–66; India, 1972–75; High Comr, Ghana, 1975–78; Private Sec. to Sec. of State, 1960–62; RCDS, 1971; Dir of Communications, FCO, 1978–81; High Comr, Bangladesh, 1981–83. Chairman: Camberwell HA, 1984–89; Chichester CHC, 1993–95. *Recreations:* golf, water colours, pastels. *Clubs:* Royal Commonwealth Society; Goodwood Golf.

MILLS, Geoffrey Thomas; Headmaster, Latymer School, 1983–98; *b* 13 Nov. 1935; *s* of Thomas Henry Mills and Margaret Jane (*née* Lewington); *m* 1970, Dorothy Anne Williams; one *s* three *d. Educ:* Enfield Grammar Sch.; Clare Coll., Cambridge (MA). Nat. Service, Corporal Clerk, RASC, 1954–56. Foreign lang. asst, Lyons, France, 1960–61; teacher of French and Spanish, Guthlaxton Grammar Sch., Leicester, 1961–62; Hd of Spanish, Sweyne Grammar Tech. Sch., Rayleigh, Essex, 1962–65; Head of Modern Languages: Coborn Sch. for Girls, Bow, 1965–69; Woodhouse Grammar Sch., Finchley, 1969–73; Dir of Studies, Longdean Sch., Hemel Hempstead, 1973–78; Headmaster, Manhood High Sch. and Community Centre, Selsey, W Sussex, 1978–83. Ind. Chm., Standards Cttee, London Borough of Enfield, 1999–. *Recreations:* golf (Blue, 1958), bridge, crosswords, reading. *Address:* 59 Wades Hill, Winchmore Hill, N21 1BD. *T:* (020) 8360 7335. *Club:* Mid Herts Golf (Wheathampstead).

MILLS, Sir (George) Ian, Kt 2001; FCA, FIMC, FIHM; Commissioner, London Region, NHS Executive, Department of Health, since 2001; Member, NHS Appointments Commission, since 2001; *b* 19 Nov. 1935; *s* of George Haxton Mills and Evelyn Mary (*née* Owen); *m* 1968, Margaret Elizabeth Dunstan; one *s* one *d* (and one *s* decd). *Educ:* Taunton's Grammar Sch., Southampton. FCA 1960; FIMC 1964; MHSM (LHSM 1985). Articled to Beal, Young & Booth, Southampton, 1954–60; Price Waterhouse, London, 1960–65; seconded to World Bank team assisting Govt of Pakistan Treasury, 1962; Chief Accountant, Univ. of Ibadan, Nigeria, 1965–68; rejoined Price Waterhouse, 1968; London Office, 1968–70; Newcastle upon Tyne Office, as Manager i/c Northern and Scottish Management Consultancy Ops, 1970–73; Partner, 1973; London Office, 1973–85: i/c Africa Management Consultancy Services, 1975–83; Nat. Dir, Central Govt Services, 1983–85; Nation Health Service Management Board, 1985–89: Dir of Financial Management, 1985–88; Dir of Resource Management, 1988–89; rejoined Price Waterhouse, 1989; Sen. Partner, Business Development Europe, 1989–91. Chairman: Lewisham and N Southwark HA, 1991–93; SE London HA, 1993–96; SE London Commissioning Agency, 1991–93; Lambeth, Southwark and Lewisham Health Commn, then HA, 1993–96; N Thames, then London, Reg., NHS Exec., DOH, 1996–2001. Mem., NHS Policy Bd, then Sec. of State for Health's Regl Chairmen's Adv. Cttee, 1996–2000. Member: Blackheath Preservation Trust Ltd, 1991–; Bd of Govs, UMDS of Guy's and St Thomas' Hosps, 1991–96; IHSM Consultants, 1992–96; Bd of Govs, St Christopher's Hospice, 1993– (Chm., 2000–); Delegacy, KCH Med. Sch., 1993–96. Trustee, SE London Community Foundn, 1995–2000. FRSA. Member: Editl Adv. Bd, Health Services Jl, 1992–96; Editl Bd, British Jl of Health Care Mgt, 1996–. *Publications:* articles in financial, educnl and med. jls. *Recreations:* classical music, photography, travel, heritage. *Address:* 60 Belmont Hill, SE13 5DN. *T:* (020) 8852 2457. *Club:* Royal Commonwealth Society.

MILLS, Maj.-Gen. Giles Hallam, CB 1977; CVO 1984; OBE 1964; retired; *b* 1 April 1922; 2nd *s* of late Col Sir John Digby Mills, TD, Bisterne Manor, Ringwood, Hampshire, and Lady Mills; *m* 1947, Emily Snowden Hallam, 2nd *d* of late Captain W. H. Tuck, Perrywood, Maryland, USA, and Mrs Tuck; two *s* one *d. Educ:* Eton Coll. Served War: 2nd Lieut, KRRC, 1941; 1st Bn, KRRC, N Africa, Italy (Adjt, despatches), 1943–47. Staff Coll., 1951; Armed Forces Staff Coll. (US), 1959; Mil. Asst to CIGS, 1961–63; CO, 2 Green Jackets, KRRC, 1963–65; Admin. Staff Coll., Henley, 1965; Regtl Col, Royal Green Jackets, 1966–67; Comd, 8 Infty Bde, 1968–69; IDC 1970; Comd, British Army Staff and Mil. Attaché, Washington, 1971–73; Divl Brig., The Light Div., 1973–74; Dir of Manning (Army), 1974–77, retd. Major and Resident Governor, HM Tower of London, and Keeper of the Jewel House, 1979–84. *Publications:* Annals of The King's Royal Rifle Corps, vol. VI (with Roger Nixon), 1971, vol. VII, 1979. *Recreations:* gardening, bird-watching, fishing, shooting, history. *Address:* Leeland House, Twyford, Winchester, Hants SO21 1NP. *Club:* Army and Navy.

MILLS, Harold Hernshaw, CB 1995; Chairman, Caledonian MacBrayne Ltd, since 1998; *b* 2 March 1938; *s* of late Harold and Margaret Mills; *m* 1973, Marion Elizabeth Beattie, MA. *Educ:* Greenock High Sch.; Univ. of Glasgow (BSc, PhD). Cancer Research Scientist, Roswell Park Memorial Inst., Buffalo, NY, 1962–64; Lectr, Glasgow Univ., 1964–69; Principal, Scottish Home and Health Dept, 1970–76; Asst Secretary: Scottish Office, 1976–81; Privy Council Office, 1981–83; Scottish Development Dept, 1983–84; Under Sec., Scottish Develt Dept, 1984–88; Prin. Finance Officer, Scottish Office, 1988–92; Sec., Scottish Office Envmt Dept, 1992–95; Sec. and Hd of Dept, Scottish Office Develt Dept, 1995–98. Mem. Bd, Home in Scotland, 1998– (Chm., 2000–). Chairman: LandTrust, 1998–; Edinburgh World Heritage Trust, 1999–; Trustee, Scottish Maritime Mus., 1998–. Gov., Queen Margaret UC, Edinburgh, 1998–. *Publications:* scientific papers in jls of learned socs on the crystal structure of chemical compounds. *Address:* 21 Hatton Place, Edinburgh EH9 1UB. *T:* (0131) 667 7910.

MILLS, Sir Ian; *see* Mills, Sir G. I.

MILLS, Prof. Ian Mark, FRS 1996; Professor of Chemical Spectroscopy, University of Reading, 1966–95, now Emeritus; *b* 9 June 1930; *s* of John Mills, MD and Margheurita Alice Gertrude Mills (*née* Gooding); *m* 1957, Margaret Mary Maynard; one *s* one *d. Educ:* Leighton Park Sch.; Univ. of Reading (BSc); St John's Coll., Oxford (DPhil). Res. Fellow, Univ. of Minnesota, 1954–56; Res. Fellow in Theoretical Chem., Corpus Christi Coll., Cambridge, 1956–57; University of Reading: Lectr in Chemistry, 1957–64; Reader, 1964–66; Leverhulme Emeritus Res. Fellow, 1996–98. Mem. and Chm. of various cttees, IUPAC, 1985–; Royal Society of Chemistry: Vice-Pres., Faraday Div., 1984–86; Mem., British Nat. Cttee for IUPAC, 1992– (Chm., 1998–); Mem. Council, Royal Instn, 2000–. Pres., Consultative Cttee on Units, Bureau Internat. des Poids et Mésures, 1995–; Chm., Cttee on Symbols and Units, BSI, 1996–. Lomb Medal 1960, Fellow 1974, Lippincott Medal 1982, Optical Soc. of America; Spectroscopy Award, RSC, 1990. Editor, Molecular Physics, 1972–77 and 1995–. *Publications:* (ed jtly) Quantities, Units and Symbols in Physical Chemistry, 1988, 2nd edn 1993; papers in learned jls. *Recreations:* walking, sailing. *Address:* 57 Christchurch Road, Reading RG2 7BD. *T:* (0118) 987 2335; Department of Chemistry, University of Reading, RG6 6AD. *T:* (0118) 931 8456.

MILLS, Ivor Henry, FRCP; Professor of Medicine in the University of Cambridge, 1963–88, now Emeritus; Fellow, Churchill College, Cambridge, 1963–88; Hon. Consultant to United Cambridge Hospitals since 1963; *b* 13 June 1921; 3rd *s* of late J. H. W. Mills and late Priscilla Mills; *m* 1947, Sydney Elizabeth Puleston (*née* Roberts); one *s* one *d. Educ:* Selhurst Grammar Sch., Croydon; Queen Mary Coll., London; Trinity Coll., Cambridge. BSc (London) 1942; PhD (London) 1946; BA (Cantab) 1948; MB, BChir Cantab 1951; MRCP 1953; MD Cantab 1956; MA Cantab 1963; FRCP 1964. Pres. Cambridge Univ. Medical Soc., 1947–48; Sen. Schol., Trinity Coll., Cambridge, 1948; MRC (Eli Lilly) Trav. Fellow, 1956; Vis. Scientist, Nat. Inst. of Health, 1957; Lectr in Medicine and Chem. Path., St Thomas's Hosp. Medical Sch., 1954; Reader in Medicine, St Thomas's Hosp. Medical Sch., London, 1962. Vis. Prof. in Physiology and Medicine, N Carolina Med. Sch., USA, 1972. Mem., Hunter Working Party on Medical Administrators, 1970–72. Royal College of Physicians: Mem. Council, 1971–74; Pro-Censor, 1974–75, Censor, 1975–76; Croonian Lectr, 1977; Sec., Soc. for Endocrinology, 1963–71; Chm., Scientific Adv. Cttee, Mason Med. Res. Foundation, 1982–88. Hon. FACP. *Publications:* Clinical Aspects of Adrenal Function, 1964; contrib. Lancet, Science Jl of Endocr., Clin. Science, etc. *Recreations:* gardening, letters to The Times. *Address:* 6 Spinney Drive, Great Shelford, Cambridge CB2 5LY.

MILLS, John Frederick; Chief Executive, Policy and Resources Department, States of Jersey, since 1999; *b* 6 Sept. 1950; *s* of Henry Alfred Mills and Jean Margaret Aitchison; *m* 1974, Jean Marie Correia (*d* 1999); one *s* three *d. Educ:* Highgate Sch.; The Queen's Coll., Oxford (MA, BLitt (Mod. Hist.)); Merton Coll., Oxford (Domus Sen. Schol.). Department of Trade and Industry, 1974–95: Private Sec. to Minister of State for Industry, 1976–78; seconded to Govt of Hong Kong, 1981–85; Hd of Internat. Telecommunications Policy, 1986–89; Mem., Prime Minister's Policy Unit, 1989–92; Under Sec. and Dir of Consumer Affairs, OFT, 1992–95; Chief Exec., Cornwall County Council, 1995–99. Mem., OFT Adv. Panel, 2001–. Gov., Highgate Sch., 1993– (Treasurer and Chm., 1999–). *Address:* Cyril Le Marquand House, PO Box 140, St Helier, Jersey JE4 8QT. *T:* (01534) 603445.

MILLS, Sir John (Lewis Ernest Watts), Kt 1976; CBE 1960; actor, producer, director; *b* 22 Feb. 1908; *m* 1941, Mary Hayley Bell, playwright; one *s* two *d. Educ:* Norwich. 1st appearance, stage, 1929. *Plays:* Cavalcade, London Wall, Words and Music, Five O'clock Girl, Give Me a Ring, Jill Darling, Floodlight, Red Night, We at the Cross Roads, Of Mice and Men, Men in Shadow, Duet for Two Hands, etc.; Old Vic Season, 1938; Top of the Ladder; Figure of Fun, Aldwych; Ross, New York, 1961; Power of Persuasion, Garrick, 1963; Veterans, Royal Court, 1972; At the End of the Day, Savoy, 1973; The Good Companions, Her Majesty's, 1974; Separate Tables, Apollo, 1977; Goodbye, Mr Chips, Chichester Fest., 1982; Little Lies, Wyndham's, 1983; The Petition, NT, (transf. Wyndham's) 1986; Pygmalion, Guildford and NY, 1987; When the Wind Blows (TV play), 1987. *Films:* The Midshipmaid, Britannia of Billingsgate, Brown on Resolution, OHMS, Cottage To Let, The Young Mr Pitt, We Dive at Dawn, In Which We Serve, The Way to the Stars, Great Expectations, So Well Remembered, The October Man, Scott of the Antarctic, The History of Mr Polly, The Rocking Horse Winner, Morning Departure, Mr Denning Drives North, Gentle Gunman, The Long Memory, Hobson's Choice, The Colditz Story, The End of the Affair, Above Us the Waves, Town on Trial, Escapade, Its Great to be Young, The Baby and the Battleship, War and Peace, Around the World in Eighty Days, Dunkirk, Ice Cold in Alex, I Was Monty's Double, Summer of the Seventeenth Doll, Tiger Bay, Swiss Family Robinson, The Singer not the Song, Tunes of Glory, Flame in the Streets, The Valiant, Tiara Tahiti, The Chalk Garden, The Truth about Spring, King Rat, Operation X Bow, Red Waggon, Sky West and Crooked (directed), The Wrong Box, The Family Way, Chuka, Showdown, Oh! What a Lovely War, The Return of the Boomerang, Ryan's Daughter (Best Supporting Actor Award, Oscar Award, 1971), Run Wild, Run Free, Emma Hamilton, Dulcima, Lamb, Young Winston, Oklahoma Crude, Trial by Combat, The Devil's Advocate, Great Expectations, The Big Sleep, Zulu Dawn, The 39 Steps, The Human Factor, Gandhi, Masks of Death, Murder with Mirrors, Who's That Girl?, Frankenstein, the Real Story, Deadly Advice, Hamlet. Tribute to Her Majesty (film documentary), 1986. *TV and TV series:* The Zoo Gang, 1974; Quatermass, 1979; Tales of the Unexpected, 1979, 1980, 1981; Young at Heart, 1980, 1981, 1982; The True Story of Spit MacPhee; A Tale of Two Cities; Ending Up; A Woman of Substance; Harnessing Peacocks, 1993; The Big Freeze; Martin Chuzzlewit, 1994. Member: SFTA (Vice-Pres.); RADA Council, 1965–; Chm., Stars

Organization for Spastics, 1975–79. Pres., Mountview Theatre Sch., 1983–. Vice Pres., Gtr London Fund for Blind, 1998–. Patron Life Mem., Variety Club. *Publications:* Up in the Clouds, Gentlemen Please (autobiog.), 1980; Book of Famous Firsts, 1984; Still Memories (autobiog.), 2000. *Recreations:* ski-ing, golf, painting. *Address:* c/o ICM, 76 Oxford Street, W1N 0AX. *Clubs:* Garrick, St James's.

MILLS, John William, OBE 1945; QC 1962; *b* 24 Oct. 1914; *s* of late John William Mills, OBE and Jessie Mills; *m* 1942, Phyllis Mary, *yr d* of late Arthur Gibson Pears; no *c*. *Educ:* Clifton; Corpus Christi Coll., Cambridge (MA). Called to Bar, Middle Temple, 1938; Bencher, 1968; Treas., 1985; retired 1987. Lt-Col, Royal Signals, 1944; Comdr, Royal Signals, 46 Div., 1944; Hon. Lt-Col 1946. Member: Bar Council, 1961–64; Clifton Coll. Council, 1967–80. *Publication:* (editor/author) Wurtzburg, Law Relating to Building Societies, subseq. Wurtzburg and Mills, Building Society Law, 10th edn 1952 to 14th edn 1988, Ed. Emeritus of 15th edn 1989. *Recreations:* sailing, golf. *Address:* Greenleas, Highleigh, Chichester, Sussex PO20 7NP. *T:* (01243) 641396.

MILLS, Lawrence William Robert; Managing Partner, Oscar, Mills & Associates, since 1994; Institutional/Marketing Advisor, USAID/DAI Market Access Program for West Bank and Gaza Strip, on secondment as Chief Operating Officer, Palestine Trade Center, since 1999; *b* London, 7 May 1934; *m* 1992, Amira Hamdy (*née* Elsayed); one *d* and two *d* by previous marriage. *Educ:* Reigate Grammar Sch., Surrey; MBA. National Service: RN, 1953; Intell. Corps, 1954. Formerly, Jun. Exec., K. F. Mayer Ltd, London. Hong Kong Govt (Mem. of HMOCS): Exec. Officer, Cl. II, 1958; Asst Trade Officer, 1960; Trade Officer, 1964; Sen. Trade Officer, 1968; Principal Trade Officer, 1969; Asst Dir of Commerce and Industry, 1971; Chief Trade Negotiator, 1974–75, 1977–79, 1981–83; Counsellor (Hong Kong Affairs), UK Mission, Geneva, 1976–77; Director of Trade, Hong Kong, 1977–79, 1981–83; Comr of Industry, 1979–81; Regional Sec., Hong Kong and Kowloon, 1983; Official MLC, Hong Kong, 1983; retired from Hong Kong Govt Service, 1983. Chief Exec., Laws Fashion Knitters Ltd, Hong Kong and Sri Lanka, 1983–85; Dir Gen., Fedn of Hong Kong Industries, 1985–89; Chief Exec., Dubai Commerce and Tourism Promotion Board, 1989–93; Sen. Enterprise Advr, UN Develt Prog., China, 1994–97; Gen. Manager, Mohamed Hareb Al Otaiba, Dubai, 1997–98. *Recreation:* music (classical jazz). *Address:* Palestine Trade Center, Green Tower Building, Ramallah, West Bank. *Clubs:* Naval and Military; Hong Kong, Hong Kong Country (Hong Kong).

MILLS, Leif Anthony, CBE 1995; General Secretary, Banking, Insurance and Finance Union (formerly National Union of Bank Employees), 1972–96; Chairman, Covent Garden Market Authority, since 1998; *b* 25 March 1936; *s* of English father and Norwegian mother; *m* 1958, Gillian Margaret Smith; two *s* two *d*. *Educ:* Balliol Coll., Oxford. MA Hons PPE. Commnd in Royal Military Police, 1957–59. Trade Union Official, Nat. Union of Bank Employees, 1960–96: Research Officer, 1960; Asst Gen. Sec., 1962; Dep. Gen. Sec., 1968. Mem. various arbitration tribunals; Member: TUC Non-Manual Workers Adv. Cttee, 1967–72; TUC Gen. Council, 1983–96 (Pres., 1994–95); Office of Manpower Economics Adv. Cttee on Equal Pay, 1971; Cttee to Review the Functioning of Financial Instns, 1977–80; CS Pay Res. Unit Bd, 1978–81; Armed Forces Pay Review Body, 1980–87; Monopolies and Mergers Commn, 1982–91; Financial Reporting Council, 1990–96; Ind. Review Cttee on Higher Educn Pay & Conditions, 1998–99; Chairman: TUC Financial Services Cttee, 1983–96; TUC Educn and Training Cttee, 1989–94. Member: BBC Consultative Gp on Social Effects of Television, 1978–80; Council, NCVQ, 1992–96; Bd, Investors in People, 1992–96; PIA Ombudsman Council, 1994–2000 (Dep. Chm., 1997–2000); Bd, Employment Tribunal Service, 1996–2001; Council, Consumers' Assoc., 1996–. Contested (Lab) Salisbury, 1964, 1965 (by-elecn). Mem. Governing Body, London Business Sch., 1988–92. Trustee, Civic Trust, 1988–96. FRGS 1992. *Publications:* biography (unpublished), Cook: A History of the Life and Explorations of Dr Frederick Albert Cook, SPRI ms 883, Cambridge, 1970; (published) Frank Wild, Antartic explorer, 1999. *Recreations:* rowing, chess. *Address:* 31 Station Road, West Byfleet, Surrey KT14 6DR. *T:* (01932) 342829. *Clubs:* Oxford and Cambridge; Oxford University Boat, Weybridge Rowing.

MILLS, Mary Bell McMillan, (Mrs Ian Mills); *see* MacMurray, M. B. McM.

MILLS, Rt Rev. Murray John; *see* Waiapu, Bishop of.

MILLS, Neil McLay; farmer; *b* 29 July 1923; *yr s* of late L. H. Mills; *m* 1950, Rosamund Mary Kimpton, *d* of Col and Hon. Mrs A. C. W. Kimpton; two *s* two *d*. *Educ:* Epsom Coll.; University Coll. London. Served War, 1940–46: commnd RN; Lieut RNVR; Coastal Forces (mentioned in despatches, 1944). Joined Bland Welch & Co. Ltd, 1948; Exec. Dir, 1955; Chm., 1965–74; Chairman: Bland Payne Holdings Ltd, 1974–79; Sedgwick Group plc, 1979–84. Underwriting Mem. of Lloyd's, 1955–91. Director: Montagu Trust Ltd, 1966–74; Midland Bank Ltd, 1974–79; Wadlow Grosvenor International Ltd, 1984–88; Threadneedle Publishing Co., 1987–93. Vice-President: Insurance Inst. of London, 1971–84; British Insurance Brokers Assoc., 1978–84 (Mem., Internat. Insurance Brokers Cttee); Mem. Cttee, Lloyd's Insurance Brokers Assoc., 1974–77. Member: Church Army Board, 1957–64 (Vice-Chm., 1959–64); Council, Oak Hill Theol Coll., 1958–62. Trustee and Governor, Lord Mayor Treloar Trust, 1975–81. Freeman, City of London, 1984; Liveryman, Insurers' Co., 1984–. *Recreations:* farming, mowing, cooking. *Address:* The Dower House, Upton Grey, near Basingstoke, Hants RG25 2RY. *T:* (01256) 862435, *Fax:* (01256) 862642. *Club:* Pilgrims.

MILLS, Sir Peter (Frederick Leighton), 3rd Bt, *cr* 1921; *b* 9 July 1924; *s* of Major Sir Frederick Leighton Victor Mills, 2nd Bt, MC, RA, MICE, and Doris (*née* Armitage); *S* father 1955; *m* 1954, Pauline Mary, *d* of L. R. Allen, Calverton, Notts; one *s* (one adopted *d* decd). *Educ:* Eastbourne Coll.; Cedara Coll. of Agriculture, University of Natal (BSc Agric.). Served HM Forces, 1943–47. CS, Fedn Rhodesia and Nyasaland, 1953; with Rhodesia Min. of Agric., 1964, Zimbabwe Min. of Agric., 1980–90. *Heir:* *s* Michael Victor Leighton Mills [*b* 30 Aug. 1957; *m* 1981, Susan, *d* of J. Doig, Harare, Zimbabwe]. *Address:* PO Box A474, Avondale, Harare, Zimbabwe.

MILLS, Peter William; QC (Can.) 1985; company director and business consultant, since 1999; *b* 22 July 1942; *s* of Joseph Roger Mills and Jane Eveyln (*née* Roscoe); *m* 1967, Eveline Jane (*née* Black); two *s*. *Educ:* Dalhousie Univ. Law Sch. (LLB); Dalhousie Univ. (BComm). Barrister and solicitor, Ont, Canada; with McInnes, Cooper and Robertson, Halifax, 1967; Solicitor, Canadian Pacific Ltd, Montreal and Toronto, 1967–71; Dir, Cammell Laird Shipbuilders Ltd, 1971–76; Mem. Org. Cttee for British Shipbuilders, 1976–77; Manager, Currie, Coopers & Lybrand Ltd, Toronto, 1977–79; The Woodbridge Co. Ltd: Gen. Counsel, 1980–98; Vice-Pres., 1980–87; Dir, 1982–98; Sen. Vice-Pres., 1988–98. Director: Corporate Develt, FP Publications Ltd, 1979–80; Augusta Newsprint Co., 1981–; Hudson's Bay Co., 1985–; Markborough Properties Inc., 1986–97; Cambridge Shopping Centres Ltd, 1997–2001. *Recreations:* golf, sailing, travel, reading. *Address:* 390 Glencairn Avenue, Toronto, ON M5N 1V1, Canada. *Fax:* (416) 4820754; *e-mail:* pmills@woodbridge.com. *Clubs:* Board of Trade, York Downs Golf and Country (Toronto); Royal Liverpool Golf (Hoylake).

MILLS, Richard Michael; Chairman and Chief Executive, Delfont Mackintosh Theatres Ltd, 1991–96; *b* 26 June 1931; *s* of Richard Henry Mills and Catherine Keeley; *m* 1st, 1960, Lynda Taylor (marr. diss. 1967); one *d*; 2nd, 1983, Sheila White; two *s*. Commenced working in the theatre as an Assistant Stage Manager in 1948, and worked in every capacity, including acting and stage management. Joined Bernard Delfont Ltd, 1962; Dir, 1967; Dep. Chm., 1970–79; Chm., 1979–91; Chief Exec., 1970–91; Managing Director: Prince of Wales Theatre, 1970–96; Prince Edward Theatre, 1978–96. Member: Nat. Theatre Bd, 1976–91; Finance and Gen. Purposes Cttee, NT, 1976–91; Drama Panel, Arts Council of GB, 1976–77; English Tourist Bd, 1982–85. Shows worked on in the West End, 1948–62, include: I Remember Mama, Tuppence Coloured, Medea, Adventure Story, Anne Veronica, The Devil's General, I Capture the Castle, No Escape, Three Times a Day, The Sun of York, To my Love, Be my Guest, Hunter's Moon, The Iceman Cometh, Brouhaha, Detour after Dark, The Ginger Man, Sound of Murder, Will You Walk a Little Faster, Pool's Paradise, Belle, Come Blow your Horn. Whilst Gen. Manager and Dir with Bernard Delfont Ltd: Never Too Late, Pickwick, 1962; Caligula, Maggie May, Little Me, Our Man Crichton, 1963; The Roar of the Greasepaint (NY), Pickwick (NY), Twang, Barefoot in the Park, 1964; The Owl and the Pussycat, The Matchgirls, Funny Girl, Joey Joey, The Odd Couple, 1965; Queenie, Sweet Charity, The Four Musketeers, 1966; Golden Boy, Look Back in Anger (rivival), 1967; Mame, Cat Among the Pigeons, 1968; Carol Channing, Danny La Rue at the Palace, 1969; Kean, Lulu, 1970; Applause, The Unknown Soldier and his Wife, 1971. With Lord Delfont has presented in the West End: The Good Old Bad Old Days, Mardi Gras, Brief Lives, Queen Daniella, Cinderella, Henry IV, Harvey, Sammy Cahn's Songbook, Streetcar Named Desire, Good Companions, It's All Right if I Do It, Charley's Aunt, An Evening with Tommy Steele, Gomes, The Wolf, Danny La Rue Show, Beyond the Rainbow, Dad's Army, Plumber's Progress, Paul Daniels Magic Show, Underneath the Arches, Little Me, and over 100 pantomimes and summer season shows. *Recreations:* golf, poker. *Address:* Sarn, Coombe Park, Kingston Hill, Kingston upon Thames KT2 7JB. *Clubs:* Royal Automobile; Royal Mid-Surrey Golf, Richmond Golf.

MILLS, Robert Ferris; Under Secretary, Department of Finance and Personnel, Northern Ireland, 1990–96, retired; *b* 21 Sept. 1939; *s* of Robert and Rachel Mills; *m* 1st, 1968, Irene Sandra Miskelly (marr. diss. 1978); one *s* one *d*; 2nd, 1984, Frances Elizabeth Gillies; two step *d*. *Educ:* Sullivan Upper School, Holywood, Co. Down; Queen's Univ., Belfast (BA Hons). Inland Revenue, 1961–64; Min. of Commerce, NI, 1964–68; Dept of Housing and Local Govt, 1968–71; Dept of the Environment, NI, 1971–75; Asst Sec., 1975–83, Under Sec., 1983–90, Dept of Health and Social Services, NI. *Recreations:* golf, tennis, travel, the arts. *Address:* 1 Rockport Rise, Craigavad, Co. Down BT18 0EH. *Club:* Helen's Bay Golf.

MILLS, Stratton; *see* Mills, W. S.

MILLS, Rt Hon. Tessa Jane Helen Douglas, (Mrs David Mills); *see* Jowell, Rt Hon. T. J. H. D.

MILLS, (William) Stratton; Senior Partner, 1974–2000, Consultant, since 2000, Mills, Selig, Solicitors, Belfast (Partner, 1959–2000); company director; Chairman, Hampden Group PLC (formerly Hampden Homecare plc), 1992–99; *b* 1 July 1932; *o s* of late Dr J. V. S. Mills, CBE, Resident Magistrate for City of Belfast, and Margaret Florence (*née* Byford); *m* 1959, Merriel E. R. Whitla, *o d* of late Mr and Mrs R. J. Whitla, Belfast; three *s*. *Educ:* Campbell Coll., Belfast; Queen's Univ., Belfast (LLB). Vice-Chm., Federation of University Conservative and Unionist Assocs, 1952–53 and 1954–55; admitted a Solicitor, 1958. MP (UU) Belfast N, Oct. 1959–Dec. 1972; MP (Alliance) Belfast N, Apr. 1973–Feb. 1974; PPS to Parly Sec., Ministry of Transport, 1961–64; Member: Estimates Cttee, 1964–70; Exec. Cttee, 1922 Cttee, 1967–70, 1973; Hon. Sec. Conservative Broadcasting Cttee, 1963–70, Chm., 1970–73; Mem., Mr Speaker's Conference on Electoral Law, 1967. Mem., One Nation Gp, 1972–73. Mem. Adv. Bd, Public Records Office, NI, 1996–. Chm., Ulster Orchestra Soc. Ltd, 1980–90; Mem. Bd, Castleward Opera., 1988–98; Dir, Opera Rara, 1998–. Mem. Council, Winston Churchill Meml Trust, 1990–95. Arnold Goodman Award, for encouragement of business sponsorship of the arts, 1990. *Address:* (office) 21 Arthur Street, Belfast BT1 4GA. *T:* (028) 9024 3878; (home) 17 Malone Park, Belfast BT9 6NJ. *T:* (028) 9066 5210. *Clubs:* Carlton; Reform (Belfast).

MILLSON, John Albert; Assistant Under-Secretary of State, Ministry of Defence, 1972–78; *b* 4 Oct. 1918; *s* of late George Charles Millson and Annie Millson, London; *m* 1953, Megan Laura Woodiss (*d* 1999); one *s* one *d*. *Educ:* St Olave's. Entered Air Min., 1936; Private Sec. to Parly Under-Sec. of State for Air, 1947–50; Principal, Air Min., 1955; Asst Sec., MoD, 1961; Asst Under-Sec. of State, 1972. Chm. of Governors, Homefield Prep. Sch., Sutton, 1975. *Recreations:* walking, listening to music. *Address:* Roseacre, Holly Hill Drive, Banstead, Surrey SM7 2BD. *T:* (01737) 359646.

MILLSON, Tony; HM Diplomatic Service; Counsellor, Foreign and Commonwealth Office, since 2001; *b* 25 Nov. 1951; *s* of Donald Millson and Joan (*née* Whittle). *Educ:* Grimsby Wintringham Grammar Sch. Entered HM Diplomatic Service, 1970; MECAS, 1973; Third Sec. (Commercial), Tripoli, 1974–76; Third, later Second Sec. (Develt), Amman, 1976–80; FCO, 1980–83; Second Sec., BMG Berlin, 1983–86; First Sec., FCO, 1986–88; Hd of Chancery, Kuwait, 1988–90; FCO, 1991–93; Ambassador to Macedonia, 1993–97; Counsellor, FCO, 1997–98; High Comr, The Gambia, 1998–2000; Dep. High Comr, Abuja, 2000–01. *Recreations:* reading, listening to music, bridge. *Address:* c/o Foreign and Commonwealth Office, King Charles Street, SW1A 2AH.

MILMAN, Andrée, (Mrs David Milman); *see* Grenfell, A.

MILMAN, Sir David (Patrick), 10th Bt *cr* 1800, of Levaton-in-Woodland, Devonshire; educational consultant, since 1999; *b* 24 Aug. 1945; *er s* of Lt-Col Sir Derek Milman, 9th Bt and Christine Margaret Milman (*née* Whitehouse); *S* father, 1999; *m* 1969, Christina Hunt; one *s* one *d*. *Educ:* London Univ. (Teacher's Cert. 1st cl. 1968; BEd (Hons) 1969; MA 1976). Headteacher, 1981–89; Headteacher Trng Co-ordinator, ILEA, 1988–89; Asst Dir, Sch. Mgt South, 1989–91; Area Advr, 1991–93, Sen. Area Advr, 1993–98, NW Kent; District Adv. Officer, Dartford, 1998–99. *Publications:* Teachers' Guidelines to Take Part Readers Series, 1973; Take a Look Series, 1974; What do you think?, 1976; Senior Manager's Personal Profile, 1991. *Recreations:* ornithology, reading. *Heir:* *s* Thomas Hart Milman, *b* 7 Oct. 1976. *Address:* 71 Camden Road, Sevenoaks, Kent TN13 3LU. *T:* (01732) 459089.

MILMINE, Rt Rev. Douglas, CBE 1983; an Assistant Bishop, diocese of Chichester, since 1992; *b* 3 May 1921; *s* of Alexander Douglas Milmine and Rose Gertrude Milmine (*née* Moore); *m* 1945, Margaret Rosalind, *d* of Edward and Gladys Whitley, Kilmorie, Meadfoot, Torquay; three *s* one *d*. *Educ:* Sutton Valence School; St Peter's Hall, Oxford (MA 1946); Clifton Theological Coll. RAFVR, 1941–45; POW, 1943–45. Deacon 1947, priest 1948; Curate: SS Philip and James, Ilfracombe, 1947–50; St Paul's, Slough, 1950–53; missionary with South American Missionary Society: Maquehue, Chile, 1954;

Temuco, 1955–60; Santiago, 1961–68; Archdeacon of N Chile, Bolivia and Peru, 1964–68; Hon. Canon of Chile, 1969–72; Midland Area Sec. of SAMS, 1969–72; Bishop in Paraguay, 1973–85; retired 1986. *Publications:* Stiff Upper Smile (autobiog.), 1993; La Comunión Anglicana en América Latina, 1993. *Recreation:* study of current affairs. *Address:* 1c Clive Court, 24 Grand Parade, Eastbourne, East Sussex BN21 3DD. *T:* (01323) 734159.

MILMO, John Boyle Martin; QC 1984; a Recorder of the Crown Court, since 1982; *b* 19 Jan. 1943; *s* of late Dermod Hubert Francis Milmo, MB BCh and Eileen Clare Milmo (*née* White). *Educ:* Downside Sch.; Trinity Coll., Dublin. MA, LLB. Called to the Bar, Lincoln's Inn, 1966, Bencher, 1992. Mem., Bar Council, 1992– (Chm., Legal Aid and Fees Cttee, 1996–97). *Recreations:* opera, discography. *Address:* 1 High Pavement, Nottingham NG1 1HF. *T:* (0115) 941 8218. *Club:* United Services (Nottingham).

MILMO, Patrick Helenus; QC 1985; *b* 11 May 1938; *s* of Sir Helenus Milmo; *m* 1968, Marina, *d* of late Alexis Schiray and of Xenia Schiray, rue Jules Simon, Paris; one *s* one *d*. *Educ:* Downside; Trinity Coll., Cambridge (BA 1961; MA 1997). Harmsworth Scholar; called to the Bar, Middle Temple, 1962, Bencher, 1994. *Recreations:* wine, horse-racing, cinema. *Publication:* (ed jtly) Gatley on Libel and Slander, 9th edn 1998. *Address:* 5 Raymond Buildings, Gray's Inn, WC1R 5BP; 7 Baalbec Road, N5 1QN.

MILNE, family name of **Baron Milne**.

MILNE, 2nd Baron *cr* 1933, of Salonika and of Rubislaw, Co. Aberdeen; **George Douglass Milne,** TD; *b* 10 Feb. 1909; *s* of 1st Baron Milne, GCB, GCMG, DSO, Field Marshal from 1928, and Claire Marjoribanks, MBE, DGStJ (*d* 1970), *d* of Sir John N. Maitland, 5th Bt; *S* father, 1948; *m* 1940, Cicely, 3rd *d* of late Ronald Leslie; two *s* one *d*. *Educ:* Winchester; New Coll., Oxford. Mem., Inst. of Chartered Accountants of Scotland. Partner, Arthur Young McClelland Moores Co., 1954–73; Dir, London & Northern Group Ltd, 1973–87 (Dep. Chm., 1981). Master of the Grocers' Company, 1961–62, Sen. Court Mem., 1984–90. Served War of 1939–45, Royal Artillery (TA); prisoner of war, 1941; NWEF and MEF (wounded, despatches). *Recreation:* art (has exhibited RA, ROI, RP). *Heir: s* Hon. George Alexander Milne, *b* 1 April 1941. *Address:* 33 Lonsdale Road, Barnes, SW13 9JP. *T:* (020) 8748 6421.

MILNE, Alasdair David Gordon; Director-General, BBC, 1982–87; *b* 8 Oct. 1930; *s* of late Charles Gordon Shaw Milne and Edith Reid Clark; *m* 1954, Sheila Kirsten Graucob (*d* 1992); two *s* one *d*. *Educ:* Winchester Coll.; New Coll., Oxford (Hon. Fellow, 1985). Commnd into 1st Bn Gordon Highlanders, 1949. Hon. Mods Oxon 1952; BA Oxon Mod. Langs, 1954. Joined BBC, 1954; Dep. Editor, 1957–61, Editor, 1961–62, of Tonight Programme; Head of Tonight Productions, 1963–65; Partner, Jay, Baverstock, Milne & Co., 1965–67; rejoined BBC, Oct. 1967; Controller, BBC Scotland, 1968–72; Dir of Programmes, 1973–77, Man. Dir, 1977–82, BBC TV, Dep. Dir-Gen., BBC, 1980–82. Chm., Darrell Waters Ltd, 1988–90. Chm., Gaelic Broadcasting Task Force, 1999–2000. Vis. Prof., Univ. of Miami, 1989. Vice-Pres., RTS, 1986–87. Chm., John MacFadyen Meml Trust, 1980–. DUniv Stirling, 1983. Cyril Bennett Award, RTS, 1987. *Publication:* DG: the memoirs of a British broadcaster, 1988. *Recreations:* piping, salmon fishing, golf. *Address:* 30 Holland Park Avenue, W11 3QU. *Club:* Travellers.

MILNE, (Alexander) Berkeley, OBE 1968; HM Diplomatic Service, retired; *b* 12 Feb. 1924; *s* of George and Mary Milne; *m* 1952, Patricia Mary (*née* Holderness); one *s* two *d*. *Educ:* Keith Grammar and Buckie High Schs, Banffshire, Scotland; Univ. of Aberdeen (MA (Hons Mental Phil.) 1943); University Coll., Oxford (BA (Hons Persian and Arabic) 1949). 3/2nd Punjab Regt, Indian Army: service in India and Java, 1943–46. Scarborough Schol., Tehran Univ., 1950–51; Lectr in Persian, Edinburgh Univ., 1951–52. Foreign Office, 1952–53; BMEO, Cyprus, 1953–54; Third, later Second Sec., Tehran, 1954–57; FO, 1958–61; Second, later First Sec., Brussels, 1961–64; FO (later FCO), 1964–65; First Sec., British Residual Mission, Salisbury, Rhodesia, 1966–67; First Sec., Jedda, Saudi Arabia, 1968–70; FCO, 1971–74; Counsellor, Tehran, 1974–77; GCHQ, 1978–83. Consultant, Oman Govt, 1983–86. *Recreations:* gardening, reading; playing chamber music, preferably second violin in string quartets. *Address:* 6 Merestones Close, Cheltenham, Glos GL50 2ST. *T:* (01242) 242370.

MILNE, Berkeley; *see* Milne, A. B.

MILNE, David Calder; QC 1987; FCA; a Recorder, since 1994; *b* 22 Sept. 1945; *s* of late Ernest and of Helena Milne; *m* 1978, Rosemary Bond (marr. diss. 1999); one *d*. *Educ:* Harrow Sch.; Oxford Univ. (MA). ACA 1969; FCA 1974. Articled to Whinney Murray & Co., chartered accountants, 1966–69; called to the Bar, Lincoln's Inn, 1970, Bencher, 1996. *Recreations:* natural history, music, golf, Rugby. *Address:* (chambers) 16 Bedford Row, WC1R 4EB. *T:* (020) 7414 8080. *Clubs:* Garrick, Hurlingham, Gnomes; Walton Heath Golf.

MILNE, Ian Innes, CMG 1965; OBE 1946; a Senior Clerk, House of Commons, 1969–76; *b* 16 June 1912; *e s* of Kenneth John Milne, CBE, and Maud Innes; *m* 1939, Marie Mange (*d* 1989); one *d*. *Educ:* Westminster Sch.; Christ Church, Oxford. Advertising, 1935–40; RE, 1940–46 (Lieut-Col). FO, 1946–68; 2nd Sec., Teheran, 1948–51; 1st Sec., Berne, 1955–56; 1st Sec., Tokyo, 1960–63; retired 1968. US Legion of Merit (Off.), 1946. *Recreations:* gardening, music. *Address:* Red Willows, Urgashay, Yeovil, Somerset BA22 8HH.

MILNE, Maj. Gen. John, CB 2000; Registrar, St Paul's Cathedral, since 2001; *b* 13 Oct. 1946; *s* of Donald William Milne and Evelyn (*née* Ayrer); *m* 1970, Cherrill Rosemary Tookey; two *s* one *d*. *Educ:* Lowestoft Grammar Sch.; Royal Coll. of Defence Studies. Commnd, Royal Artillery, 1966: helicopter pilot, 1970–74; Mil. Asst, CoS Northern Army Gp, 1980–82; Comdr, 2 Field Regt, 1986–88; Dep. Comdr, 7 Armd Bde, Saudi Arabia, 1990; Comdr, 1 Artillery Bde, 1992–93; Dir, Army Recruiting, 1994–97; Dep. Comdr for Logistics, Stabilisation Force, Bosnia Herzegovina, 1997; Dir for Support, Allied Land Forces, Central Europe, 1998–99; COS Kosovo Force, Pristina, 1999–2000. Col Comdt, RA, 2001–. Freeman, City of London, 2001. FInstM 1993. Bronze Star (US), 1991. *Recreations:* tennis, golf, bridge. *Address:* Lloyds TSB, 174 Fleet Road, Fleet, Hants GU13 8DD. *Club:* Army and Navy.

MILNE, Sir John (Drummond), Kt 1986; Chairman, Alfred McAlpine plc, 1992–96; *b* 13 Aug. 1924; *s* of Frederick John and Minnie Elizabeth Milne; *m* 1948, Joan Akroyd; two *s* two *d*. *Educ:* Stowe Sch.; Trinity Coll., Cambridge. Served Coldstream Guards, 1943–47. APCM (now Blue Circle Industries): management trainee, 1948; Asst to Director i/c Overseas Investments, 1953; President, Ocean Cement, Vancouver, 1957; Director, APCM, 1964, Man. Dir and Chief Exec., 1975; Blue Circle Industries: Chm. and Managing Director, 1983; Chm., 1983–90 (non-exec., 1987–90). DRG plc (formerly The Dickinson Robinson Group): Dir, 1973–89; Chm., 1987–89; Director: Royal Insurance, 1982–95; Witan Investment Co., 1988–96; Avon Rubber, 1989–95; Solvay & Cie SA, 1990–96. *Recreations:* golf, shooting. *Address:* Chilton House, Chilton Candover, Hants SO24 9TX. *Clubs:* Boodle's, MCC; Berkshire Golf, Swinley Forest Golf.

MILNE, Judith Frances; Principal, St Hilda's College, Oxford, since 2001; *b* 1 March 1940; *d* of Dr Kenneth James Grant Milne and Dr Constance Nellie Milne; *m* 1973, Ralph Talbot (marr. diss. 2001); two *d*. *Educ:* Notre Dame High Sch., Sheffield (State Schol.); Girton Coll., Cambridge (Crewdson Prize; MA 1963); University Coll. Hosp. Med. Sch., London (MB BChir 1965). MRCP 1968; MRCPsych 1973. Medical house staff posts, Whittington Hosp., Brompton Hosp. and UCH, 1965–67; Lectr in Clinical Immunology, Inst. of Chest Diseases, London Univ., 1967–70; Registrar in Psychiatry, Maudsley Hosp., 1970–74; Fellow in Consultation-Liaison Psychiatry, then Staff Psychiatrist, UCLA, 1974–79; Director, Psychiatric Consultation Service: Boston, VA Med. Center, 1980–95; Chief of Staff, Boston VAMC, New England Med. Center, 1986–93; 1996–2000; Asst Prof. of Psychiatry, Tufts Univ., 1986–2000; Associate Clinical Prof. of Psychiatry, Boston Univ. Sch. of Medicine, 1998–2000. *Publications:* contribs to med. and psychiatric jls. *Recreations:* reading, poetry, dance, cooking. *Address:* Principal's Lodgings, St Hilda's College, Oxford OX4 1DY. *T:* (01865) 276814.

MILNE, Nanette Lilian Margaret, OBE 1994; JP; Councillor, Aberdeen City Council, 1995–99 (City of Aberdeen District Council, 1988–96); *b* 27 April 1942; *d* of Harold G. Gordon and Hannah L. C. Gordon (*née* Stephen); *m* 1965, Alan Ducat Milne; one *s* one *d*. *Educ:* Aberdeen High Sch. for Girls; Univ. of Aberdeen (MB ChB 1965). FFARCS 1969. Medical Officer, Grampian Health Board, later Aberdeen Royal Hospitals NHS Trust: anaesthetics, 1966–73; oncology research, 1980–92. Vice-Chm., Scottish Cons. and Unionist Party, 1989–93. JP Aberdeen, 1993. *Publications:* contrib. to BMJ on cardiovascular effects of laparoscopy and on colorectal cancer. *Recreations:* gardening, sports. *Address:* The Briars, Golfview Road, Bieldside, Aberdeen AB15 9AA. *T:* (01224) 867816.

MILNE, Peter Alexander, PhD; Eur Ing, CEng, FIMechE, FIMarE; engineering consultant, 1996–2000; *b* 23 April 1935; *s* of late Alexander Ogston Milne and of Lilian Winifred Milne (*née* Murray); *m* 1961, Beatrice Taylor Reid; two *d*. *Educ:* Tynemouth Sch.; Harwell Reactor Sch. BSc Marine Engrg Univ. of Durham 1957; PhD Applied Sci. Univ. of Newcastle 1960. Practical experience with apprenticeship at Wallsend Slipway & Engineering and at sea with Union Castle Mail Steamship; Trainee Manager, Swan Hunter Gp, 1961; Technical Dir, Swan Hunter Shipbuilders, 1970–74, Man. Dir, 1974–77; British Shipbuilders HQ at formation of Corp., 1977; Man. Dir, Shipbuilding Ops, 1978–80, Mem. Bd, 1981–90 (Bd Mem. for Engrg, 1981–83, for Merchant Ship and Enginebuilding, 1985–90), Man. Dir, Merchant and Composite Div., 1984, British Shipbuilders; Man. Dir, BMT Cortec, 1990–94; Dir, AMRIE, 1994–96. Director: Vosper Thornycroft, 1978–80; Tyneside Maritime and Engrg, 1996–98. Bd Mem., SMRTB, 1971–75; Chm., BSI Ind. Cttee, 1972–76; Dir, Lloyds Register of Shipping, 1984–91; Chm., Northern Engrg Centre, 1990–94. Vis. Lectr in Marine Engrg, Newcastle Univ., 1970–75. Pres., NECInst, 1986–88. Freeman, City of London, 1984; Liveryman, Shipwrights' Co., 1984–98. *Publications:* papers related to science and industry. *Recreations:* squash, cricket. *Address:* 14 Woodland Close, Earsdon Village, Whitley Bay, Tyne and Wear NE25 9LL. *T:* (0191) 252 2708.

MILNE, Prof. William Ireland, PhD; FIEE; FIM; Professor of Electrical Engineering, University of Cambridge, since 1996; Fellow, Churchill College, Cambridge, since 1977; *b* 15 Feb. 1948; *s* of William Ireland Milne and Jenelia Foy Kelso Milne (*née* Reid); *m* 1st, 1971, Jennifer Stovell (marr. diss. 1991); one *s* one *d*; 2nd, 1992, Catharina Jacqueline Ann Baker; one step *s* one step *d*. *Educ:* Forfar Acad.; St Andrews Univ. (BSc Hons 1970); Imperial Coll., London DIC, PhD 1973). FIEE 1989; FIM 1999. Sen. Scientist, then Principal Scientist, Plessey Res. Centre, Caswell, 1973–76; Engineering Department, University of Cambridge: Asst Lectr, 1976–80; Lectr, 1980–90; Reader, 1990–96. Visiting Professor: Tokyo Inst. of Technol., 1985; Nanyang Technol Univ., Singapore, 1993; Gifu Univ., Japan, 2001. *Recreations:* golf, tennis, travel. *Address:* Engineering Department, Cambridge University, Trumpington Street, Cambridge CB2 1PZ. *T:* (01223) 332757.

MILNE-WATSON, Sir Andrew (Michael), 4th Bt *cr* 1937, of Ashley, Longbredy, co. Dorset; Proprietor, A. D. R. Associates Ltd, since 1993; *b* 10 Nov. 1944; *o s* of Sir Michael Milne-Watson, 3rd Bt, CBE and Mary Lisette Gunion Milne-Watson (*née* Bagnall); *S* father, 1999; *m* 1st, 1970, Beverley Jane Gabrielle Cotton (marr. diss. 1981); one *s* one *d*; 2nd, 1983, Gisella Stafford (*née* Tisdall); one *s*. *Educ:* Eton. Sales and Mgt Trainee, Sidney Flavel & Co. Ltd, 1965–68; Mgt Trainee, E Midlands Gas Bd, 1968–69; Ogilvy & Mather (UK): Trainee, 1969; Account Mgr, 1970; Account Dir, 1973–79; Managing and Client Service Director: Mathers Advertising Ltd, 1979–82; Phoenix Advertising Ltd, 1982–84; Dep. Chm., Lewis Broadbent Advertising Ltd, 1984–87; founded: Minerva Publications Ltd, 1987–89; MW Communications Ltd, 1989–90; Dir of Advertising and Mktg, Inc Publications, 1990–93. Liveryman, Grocers' Co. *Recreations:* cooking, gardening, building renovation. *Heir: s* David Alastair Milne-Watson [*b* 24 Aug. 1971; *m* 2000, Sandra M. Geraldi, Campinas, Brazil]. *Address:* 22 Musgrave Crescent, SW6 4QE. *T:* (020) 7731 4488; The Stables, Oakfield, Mortimer, Berks RG7 3AP. *T:* (01189) 832200. *Club:* Garrick.

MILNER, family name of **Baron Milner of Leeds**.

MILNER OF LEEDS, 2nd Baron *cr* 1951; **Arthur James Michael Milner,** AE 1952; Consultant, Gregory, Rowcliffe & Milners (formerly Milners, Curry & Gaskell), Solicitors, London, since 1988 (Partner, 1953–88); *b* 12 Sept. 1923; *o s* of 1st Baron Milner of Leeds, PC, MC, TD and Lois Tinsdale (*d* 1982), *d* of Thomas Brown, Leeds; *S* father, 1967; *m* 1951, Sheila Margaret (*d* 2000), *d* of Gerald Hartley, Leeds; one *s* one *d* (and one *d* decd). *Educ:* Oundle; Trinity Hall, Cambridge (MA). Served: RAFVR, 1942–46, Flt Lt; 609 (W Riding) Sqn, RAuxAF, 1947–52, Flt Lt. Admitted Solicitor, 1951. Opposition Whip, House of Lords, 1971–74; Member: Jt Cttee on Consolidation Bills, 1982–92; Select Cttees on Private Bills, 1990–96; elected Mem., H of L, 1999. Member: Clothworkers' Co.; Pilgrims; Hon. Treas, Soc. of Yorkshiremen in London, 1967–70. *Heir: s* Hon. Richard James Milner [*b* 16 May 1959; *m* 1988, Margaret, *y d* of G. F. Voisin; two *d*]. *Address:* 2 The Inner Court, Old Church Street, SW3 5BY. *Club:* Royal Air Force.

MILNER, Prof. Arthur David, PhD; FRSE; Professor of Cognitive Neuroscience, University of Durham, since 2000; *b* 16 July 1943; *s* of Arthur Milner and Sarah Ellen Milner (*née* Gaunt); *m* 1965, Christine Armitage; two *s*. *Educ:* Bradford Grammar Sch.; Lincoln Coll., Oxford (Open Schol.; BA 1965; MA 1970); Inst. of Psychiatry, London (DipPsych 1966; PhD 1971). Res. Asst, Inst. of Psychiatry, London, 1966–70; University of St Andrews: Lectr, 1970–82, Sen. Lectr, 1982–85, in Psychology; Reader in Neuropsychology, 1985–90; Prof. of Neuropsychology, 1990–2000; Chm., Dept of Psychology, 1983–88; Dean, Faculty of Science, 1992–94; Head, Sch. of Psychology, 1994–97. Hon. Res. Clin. Psychologist, Tayside Health Bd, 1990–2000. Trustee, Dundee Science Centre, 1998–2000. *Publications:* The Neuropsychology of Consciousness, 1992; The Visual Brain in Action, 1995; Comparative Neuropsychology, 1998; sci. articles in learned jls and books, mainly on brain mechanisms underlying visual perception, visual guidance of movement, and bilateral co-ordination. *Recreations:* walking, cinema, jazz. *Address:* Department of Psychology, University of Durham, Science Laboratories, South Road, Durham DH1 3LE. *T:* (0191) 374 2611.

MILNER, Prof. Arthur John Robin Gorell, FRS 1988; FRSE; Research Professor, since 1999 and Fellow of King's College, since 1995, Cambridge University (Professor of Computer Science, 1995–99); *b* 13 Jan. 1934; *s* of John Theodore Milner and Muriel Emily (*née* Barnes-Gorell); *m* 1963, Lucy Petronella Moor; two *s* one *d*. *Educ:* Eton Coll.; King's Coll., Cambridge (BA Maths, 1957). FRSE 1993. Maths teacher, Marylebone Grammar Sch., 1959–60; Ferranti Ltd, London, 1960–63; Lectr in Maths and Computing, City Univ., London, 1963–68; Research Fellow: University Coll., Swansea, 1968–70; Artificial Intelligence Lab., Stanford Univ., Calif, 1970–72; Edinburgh University: Lectr, 1973–75; Sen. Lectr, 1975–78; Reader, 1978–84; Prof. of Computation Theory, 1984–94. Founder Mem., Academia Europaea, 1988. Hon. DSc(Eng) Chalmers Univ., Gothenburg, Sweden, 1988. A. M. Turing Award, ACM, 1991. *Publications:* Calculus for Communication and Concurrency, 1989; The Definition of Standard ML, 1990, 2nd edn 1997; Commentary on Standard ML, 1990; Communicating and Mobile Systems: the π calculus, 1999; contribs to Computer Science on mechanised logic of computation and on calculus of communicating systems. *Recreations:* music, carpentry, walking. *Address:* 24 Lyndewode Road, Cambridge CB1 2HN.

MILNER, Prof. Brenda (Atkinson), OC 1984; OQ 1985; FRS 1979; FRSC 1976; Professor of Psychology, Department of Neurology and Neurosurgery, McGill University, since 1970; Dorothy J. Killam Professor, Montreal Neurological Institute, since 1993 (Head of Neuropsychology Research Unit, 1970–91); *b* 15 July 1918; *d* of Samuel Langford and Clarice Frances Leslie (*née* Doig). *Educ:* Univ. of Cambridge (BA, MA, ScD); McGill Univ. (PhD). Experimental Officer, Min. of Supply, 1941–44; Professeur Agrégé, Inst. de Psychologie, Univ. de Montréal, 1944–52; Res. Associate, Psychology Dept, McGill Univ., 1952 53; Lectr, 1953–60, Asst Prof., 1960–64, Associate Prof., 1964–70, Dept of Neurology and Neurosurgery, McGill Univ. Hon. LLD: Queen's Univ., Kingston, Ont, 1980; Cambridge, 2000; Hon. DSc: Manitoba, 1982; Lethbridge, 1986; Mount Holyoke, 1986; Toronto, 1987; McGill, 1991; Wesleyan, 1991; Acadia, 1991; St Andrews, 1992; Hartford, 1997; McMaster, 1999; Hon. DScSoc Laval, 1987; Hon. Dr Montreal, 1988; Hon. DHumL Mount St Vincent, 1988. Izaak Walton Killam Prize, Canada Council, 1983; Hermann von Helmholtz Prize, Inst. for Cognitive Neuroscience, USA, 1984; Ralph W. Gerard Prize, Soc. for Neuroscience, 1987; Wilder Penfield Prize, PQ, 1993; Metropolitan Life Foundn award, 1996. Grand Dame of Merit, Order of Malta, 1985. *Publications:* mainly articles in neurological and psychological jls. *Address:* Montreal Neurological Institute, 3801 University Street, Montreal, QC H3A 2B4, Canada. *T:* (514) 3988503, *Fax:* (514) 3988540.

MILNER, Joseph, CBE 1975; QFSM 1962; Chief Officer of the London Fire Brigade, 1970–76; *b* 5 Oct. 1922; *e s* of Joseph and Ann Milner; *m* 1943, Bella Grice (*d* 1976), *e d* of Frederick George Flinton; one *s* one *d*; *m* 1976, Anne Cunningham, *e d* of J. Cunningham. *Educ:* Ladybarn Sch., Manchester. Served King's Regt (Liverpool), 1940–46: India/Burma, 1943–46 (Wingate's Chindits). Nat. Fire Service, 1946–48; North Riding Fire Bde, 1948–50; Manchester Fire Bde, 1950–51; Hong Kong Fire Bde, 1951–60; Dep. Dir, Hong Kong Fire Services, 1961–65; Dir, Hong Kong Fire Services, and Unit Controller, Auxiliary Fire Service, 1965–70. Mem., Hong Kong Council, Order of St John, 1965–70; JP Hong Kong, 1965–70. Regional Fire Commander (designate), London, 1970–76. Mem. Bd, Fire Service College, 1970–76; Mem., Central Fire Brigades Adv. Council, 1970–76; Adviser, Nat. Jt Council for Local Authority Fire Brigades, 1970–76; Chm., London Fire Liaison Panel, 1970–76; Mem., London Local Adv. Cttee, IBA, 1974–78; Fire Adviser, Assoc. of Metrop. Authorities, 1970–76. Vice-President: Fire Services Nat. Benevolent Fund (Chm., 1975–77); GLC Br., Royal British Legion, 1977–. Mem., Caston Parish Council, 1980–; Community Controller, Civil Defence, 1981–; Fellow, Instn of Fire Engineers, 1971; Associate Mem., Inst. of British Engineers, 1953–95; Associate, LCSP, 1987. OStJ 1971. *Publication:* To Blazes with Glory: a Chindit's war, 1995. *Recreations:* walking, poetry, hacking, horse management, remedial therapies, oil painting. *Address:* Lam Low, Caston, Attleborough, Norfolk NR17 1DD. *T:* (01953) 483697. *Club:* Hong Kong (Hong Kong).

MILNER, Ralph; *see* Millner, Ralph.

MILNER, Rt Rev. Ronald James; Bishop Suffragan of Burnley, 1988–93; Hon. Assistant Bishop, diocese of Southwell, since 1994; *b* 16 May 1927; *s* of Maurice and Muriel Milner; *m* 1950, Audrey Cynthia Howard; two *s* two *d* (and one *d* decd). *Educ:* Hull Grammar School; Pembroke Coll., Cambridge (MA); Wycliffe Hall, Oxford. Ordained deacon, 1953, priest, 1954; Succentor, Sheffield Cathedral, 1953–58; Vicar: Westwood, Coventry, 1958–64; St James, Fletchamstead, Coventry, 1964–70; Rector of St Mary's, Southampton, 1970–73; Rector of the Southampton Team Ministry, 1973–83; Archdeacon of Lincoln, 1983–88. *Recreations:* ornithology, walking, music. *Address:* 7 Crafts Way, Southwell, Notts NG25 0BL.

MILNER, Dr Simon Trevor; Secretary of the British Broadcasting Corporation, since 2000; *b* 23 April 1967; *s* of Trevor Winston Milner and Christine Mary Milner; *m* 1991, Sarah Wells; one *s* one *d*. *Educ:* Bradford Grammar Sch.; Wadham Coll., Oxford (BA Hons Hist. and Econs); London Sch. of Econs (MSc Industrial Relns, PhD Industrial Relns 1993). London School of Economics: Res. Officer, Centre for Econ. Performance, 1990–94; Lectr, Dept of Industrial Relns, 1994–95; Sec., Commn on Public Policy and British Business, IPPR, 1995–97; Sen. Advr, Policy and Planning, BBC, 1997–99. *Publication:* New Perspectives on Industrial Disputes, 1993. *Recreations:* children, football. *Address:* c/o BBC, Broadcasting House, Portland Place, W1A 1AA.

MILNER, Sir Timothy William Lycett, (Sir Tim), 10th Bt *cr* 1717, of Nun Appleton Hall, Yorkshire; *b* 11 Oct. 1936; *er s* of Sir (George Edward) Mordaunt Milner, 9th Bt and Barbara Audrey (*d* 1951), *d* of Henry Noel Belsham; *S* father, 1995. *Heir: b* Charles Mordaunt Milner [*b* 18 May 1944; *m* 1965, Lady Charlene French, *e d* of 3rd Earl of Ypres; three *s*]. *Address:* c/o Natte Valleij, Box 4, Klapmuts 7625, South Africa.

MILNES, Rodney; *see* Blumer, Rodney Milnes.

MILNES COATES, Prof. Sir Anthony (Robert), 4th Bt *cr* 1911; BSc, MB BS, MD, FRCPath, FRCP; Professor of Medical Microbiology, St George's Hospital Medical School, since 1990; *b* 8 Dec. 1948; *s* of Sir Robert Edward James Clive Milnes Coates, 3rd Bt, DSO, and of Lady Patricia Ethel, *d* of 4th Earl of Listowel; *S* father, 1982; *m* 1978, Harriet Ann Burton; one *s* two *d*. *Educ:* Eton; BSc London 1970; St Thomas's Hospital, London Univ. (MB BS 1973; MD 1984). MRCS 1973; MRCP 1978, FRCP 1998; FRCPath 1999. MRC Trng Res. Fellow, Dept of Bacteriology, RPMS, 1979–82; Sen. Registrar in Bacteriology, RPMS, 1982–84; Sen. Lectr (Hon. Consultant), Dept of Medical Microbiology, London Hosp. Medical Coll., 1984–90. *Heir: s* Thomas Anthony Milnes Coates, *b* 19 Nov. 1986. *Address:* Hereford Cottage, 135 Gloucester Road, SW7 4TH. *Club:* Brooks's.

MILNOR, (Margaret) Dusa; *see* McDuff, M. D.

MILOSZ, Czeslaw; poet, author; Professor of Slavic Languages and Literatures, University of California, Berkeley, 1961–78, now Emeritus; *b* Lithuania, 30 June 1911; naturalised US citizen, 1970; *s* of Aleksander and Weronika Milosz. *Educ:* High Sch., Wilno; Univ. of Wilno. MJuris 1934. Programmer, Polish Nat. Radio, 1935–39; Mem., Polish diplomatic service, Washington, Paris, 1945–50. Vis. Lectr, Univ. of Calif, Berkeley, 1960–61. Guggenheim Fellow, 1976. Member: Polish Inst. Letters and Scis in America; Amer. Acad. of Arts and Scis; PEN Club in Exile; Amer. Acad. of Arts and Letters. Hon. LittD Michigan, 1977; Hon. doctorates: Catholic Univ. of Lublin, 1981; Harvard Univ., 1989; Jagiellonian Univ., Krakow, 1989; Rome Univ., 1992. Prix Littéraire Européen, Les Guildes du Livre, Geneva, 1953; Neustadt Internat. Prize for Literature, Univ. of Oklahama, 1978; citation, Univ. of Calif, Berkeley, 1978; Nobel Prize for Literature, 1980. Order of White Eagle (Poland), 1994; Order of Gedyminas (Lithuania), 1997. *Publications:* Poemat o czasie zastyglym (Poem on Time Frozen), 1933; Trzy zimy (Three Winters), 1936; Ocalenie (Rescue), 1945; Zniewolony umysl (The Captive Mind), 1953; Zdobycie wladzy, 1953, trans. as The Usurpers (in US as Seizure of Power), 1955; Dolina Issy, 1955, trans. as The Issa Valley, 1981; Swiatlo dzienne (Daylight), 1955; Traktat poetycki (Poetic Treatise), 1957; Rodzinna Europa, 1958, trans. as Native Realm, 1968; Postwar Polish Poetry, 1965; Widzenia nad Zatoka San Francisco (Views from San Francisco Bay), 1969; The History of Polish Literature, 1970; Prywatne obowiazki (Private Obligations), 1972; Selected Poems, 1973, rev. edn 1981; Ziemia Ulro (The Land of Ulro), 1977; Emperor of the Earth, 1977; Bells in Winter, 1978; Hymn o perle, 1982; Visions from San Francisco Bay, 1983; The Witness of Poetry, 1983; Separate Notebooks, 1984; The Land of Ulro, 1985; Unattainable Earth, 1986; Collected Poems, 1988; Provinces, 1991; Beginning With My Streets, 1992; A Year of the Hunter, 1994; Facing the River, 1995; A Book of Luminous Things, 1996; Road-side Dog, 1998. *Address:* Department of Slavic Languages and Literatures, 5416 Dwinelle Hall, University of California, Berkeley, CA 94720, USA.

MILROY, Prof. (Ann) Lesley, PhD; Professor of Linguistics, since 1994, Hans Kurath Collegiate Professor of Linguistics, since 2000, University of Michigan; *b* 5 March 1944; *d* of Thomas Keddie Cross and Janet Elizabeth Cross; *m* 1965, Prof. James R. D. Milroy; three *s*. *Educ:* Univ. of Manchester (BA 1st Cl. Hons English 1965; MA 1967); Univ. of Belfast (PhD 1979). Various lecturing posts, Ulster Poly., 1972–82; Sen. Simon Research Fellow, Univ. of Manchester, 1982–83; University of Newcastle upon Tyne: Lectr in Linguistics, 1983–85; Sen. Lectr, 1985–88; Prof. of Sociolinguistics, 1988–98 (on leave of absence, 1994–98). Vis. Fellow, Univ. of Canterbury, Christchurch, NZ, 1992. *Publications:* Language and Social Networks, 1980, 2nd edn 1987; Observing and Analysing Natural Language, 1987; (with J. Milroy) Authority in Language: investigating language prescription and standardisation, 1987, 3rd edn 1998; (with R. Lesser) Linguistics and Aphasia: psycholinguistic and pragmatic aspects of intervention, 1993; (ed with J. Milroy) Real English: the grammar of English dialects in the British Isles, 1993; (ed with P. Muysken) One Speaker, Two Languages: cross-disciplinary perspectives on codeswitching, 1995; contrib. articles to learned jls. *Recreations:* swimming, walking, reading. *Address:* Program in Linguistics, University of Michigan, 1076 Frieze Building, Ann Arbor, MI 48109–1285, USA.

MILROY, Very Rev. Dominic Liston, OSB; MA; Headmaster, Ampleforth College, 1980–92; *b* 18 April 1932; *s* of Adam Liston Milroy and Clarita Burns. *Educ:* Ampleforth Coll.; St Benet's Hall, Oxford (1st Cl. Mod. Langs, MA). Entered Ampleforth Abbey, 1950; teaching staff, Ampleforth Coll., 1957–74; Head of Mod. Langs, 1963–74; Housemaster, 1964–74; Prior of Internat. Benedictine Coll. of S Anselmo, Rome, 1974–79. Chm., HMC, 1992. *Address:* Ampleforth Abbey, York YO62 4EN. *T:* (01439) 766714.

MILROY, Lesley; *see* Milroy, A. L.

MILSOM, Stroud Francis Charles; QC 1985; FBA 1967; Professor of Law, Cambridge University, 1976–90; Fellow of St John's College, Cambridge, since 1976; *b* 2 May 1923; *yr s* of late Harry Lincoln Milsom and Isobel Vida Collins; *m* 1955, Irène (*d* 1998), *d* of late Witold Szereszewski, Wola Krysztoporska, Poland. *Educ:* Charterhouse; Trinity Coll., Cambridge. Admiralty, 1944–45. Called to the Bar, Lincoln's Inn, 1947, Hon. Bencher, 1970; Commonwealth Fund Fellow, Univ. of Pennsylvania, 1947–48; Yorke Prize, Univ. of Cambridge, 1948; Prize Fellow, Fellow and Lectr, Trinity Coll., Cambridge, 1948–55; Fellow, Tutor and Dean, New Coll., Oxford, 1956–64; Prof. of Legal History, London Univ., 1964–76. Selden Society: Literary Dir, 1964–80; Pres., 1985–88. Mem., Royal Commn on Historical Manuscripts, 1975–98. Vis. Lectr, New York Univ. Law Sch., several times, 1958–70; Visiting Professor: Yale Law Sch., several times, 1968–; Harvard Law Sch. and Dept of History, 1973; Charles Inglis Thomson Prof., Colorado Univ. Law Sch., 1977. Maitland Meml Lectr, Cambridge, 1972; Addison Harris Meml Lectr, Indiana Univ. Law Sch., 1974; Vis. Prof. and Wilfred Fullagar Lectr, Monash Univ., 1981; Ford's Lectr, Oxford, 1986; Carpentier Lectr, Columbia Univ., 1995. Foreign Mem., Amer. Phil Soc., 1984. Hon. LLD: Glasgow, 1981; Chicago, 1985. Ames Prize, Harvard, 1972; Swiney Prize, RSA/RCP, 1974. *Publications:* Novae Narrationes (introd., trans. and notes), 1963; introd. reissue Pollock and Maitland, History of English Law, 1968; Historical Foundations of the Common Law, 1969, 2nd edn 1981; The Legal Framework of English Feudalism, 1976; Studies in the History of the Common Law (collected papers), 1985. *Address:* St John's College, Cambridge CB2 1TP; 113 Grantchester Meadows, Cambridge CB3 9JN. *T:* (01223) 354100. *Club:* Athenæum.

MILSTEIN, César, CH 1995; PhD; FRS 1975; Scientific Staff of Medical Research Council, 1963–95; Fellow, Darwin College, University of Cambridge, 1981–95, now Emeritus; Joint Head, Division of Protein and Nucleic Acid Chemistry, 1981–93, Deputy Director, 1988–95, MRC Laboratory of Molecular Biology; *b* 8 Oct. 1927; *s* of Lázaro and Máxima Milstein; *m* 1953, Celia Prilleltensky. *Educ:* Colegio Nacional de Bahia Blanca; Univ. Nacional de Buenos Aires; Fitzwilliam Coll., Cambridge (Hon. Fellow 1982). Licenciado en Ciencias Quimicas 1952; Doctor en Quimica 1957; PhD Cantab 1960. British Council Fellow, 1958–60; Scientific Staff, MRC, Dept of Biochemistry, Cambridge Univ., 1960–61; Staff of Instituto Nacional de Microbiologia, Buenos Aires, 1957–63; Head of Div. de Biologia Molecular, 1961–63; Staff of MRC Laboratory of Molecular Biology, 1963–95: Mem. Governing Bd, 1975–79; Head of Sub-div. of Protein Chemistry, 1969–80; Head Sub-div. of Molecular Immunobiology, 1980. For. Associate, Nat. Acad. of Scis, USA, 1981; Founding Fellow, Third World Acad. of Scis, 1983. Hon. FRCP, 1983; Hon. FRCPath, 1987; Hon. FRSocMed, 1992. Hon. DSc: Cambridge, 1999; Vigo, Spain, 1999; Helsinki, 2000. Biochem. Soc. Ciba Medal, 1978; Rosenstiel Medal, 1979; Avery-Landsteiner Preis, 1979; Rosenberg Prize, 1979; Mattia Award, 1979; Gross Horwitz Prize, 1980; Koch Preis, 1980; Wolf Prize in Med., 1980; Wellcome Foundn Medal, 1980; Gimenez Diaz Medal, 1981; William Bate Hardy Prize, Camb. Philos. Soc., 1981; Sloan Prize, General Motors Cancer Res. Foundn, 1981; Gairdner Award, Gairdner Foundn, 1981; Royal Medal, Royal Soc., 1982; Nobel Prize for Physiology or Medicine (with Prof. N. Jerne and Dr G. Koehler), 1984; Dale Medal, Soc. for Endicronology, 1984; Galen Medal, Apothecaries' Soc., 1985; Walker Prize, RCS, 1986; Copley Medal, Royal Soc., 1989; Nat. Biotechnology Ventures Award, USA, 1990;

Konex de Brillante Award, Argentina, 1993; Award for Excellence in Res. in Immunology, Duke Univ., USA, 1996; MRC Millennium Medal, 2000. Silver Jubilee Medal, 1977; Orden de Mayo (Argentina), 1999. *Publications:* original papers and review articles on structure, evolution and genetics of immunoglobulins and phosphoenzimes. *Recreations:* open air activities, cooking. *Address:* Medical Research Council Laboratory of Molecular Biology, Hills Road, Cambridge CB2 2QH. *Club:* Sefe (Cambridge).

MILTON, Maj.-Gen. Anthony Arthur, OBE 1995; Director General, Joint Doctrine and Concepts, Ministry of Defence, since 1999; *b* 19 Aug. 1949; *s* of W. W. Milton; *m* 1972, Nova-Mary Biscombe; three *d*. *Educ:* King Edward VI Sch., Chelmsford; St John's Coll., Cambridge (MPhil Internat. Relns). Commnd Royal Marines, 1967; Subaltern, 42, 45 and 40 Commando, serving in Far East, Norway, Caribbean, Cyprus and NI, 1970–76; exchange tour with USMC, 1976–78; CTC, Lympstone, 1978–81; Army Staff Coll., 1982; MoD, 1983–84; Equerry to the Duke of Edinburgh, 1983–84; Co. Comdr, 42 Commando, 1985–86; COS, 3 Commando Bde, 1987–89; MoD, 1991–92; CO, 40 Commando, Norway and NI, 1992–94; rcds 1995; Comdr, 3 Commando Bde, 1995–97; Dir, N Atlantic and Western Europe, 1997–98; ADC to the Queen, 1997–99. FRGS 1992. *Publications:* academic articles. *Recreations:* sailing, music, mountains. *Address:* Joint Doctrine and Concepts Centre, Shrivenham, Swindon, Wilts SN6 8RF. *Clubs:* Army and Navy; Royal Navy and Royal Marines Sailing Association, Royal Navy and Marines Mountaineering.

MILTON, Derek Francis, CMG 1990; HM Diplomatic Service, retired; student of Polish, University of London, since 1999; *b* 11 Nov. 1935; *s* of Francis Henry Milton and Florence Elizabeth Maud Kirby; *m* 1st, 1960, Helge Kahle; two *s*; 2nd, 1977, Catherine Walmsley. *Educ:* Preston Manor County Grammar Sch., Wembley; Manchester Univ. (BA Hons Politics and Modern History, 1959). RAF, 1954–56. Colonial Office, 1959–63; Asst Private Sec. to Commonwealth and Colonial Sec., 1962–64; Commonwealth Prime Ministers' Meeting Secretariat, 1964; First Secretary: CRO (later FO), 1964–67; UK Mission to UN, New York, 1967–71; Rome, 1972–75; FCO, 1975–77; Counsellor: Civil Service Res. Fellow, Glasgow Univ., 1977–78; Caracas, 1978–79; Dept of Trade, 1980–82; Overseas Inspectorate, 1982–84; Minister-Counsellor, Mexico City, 1984–87; RCDS, 1988; High Comr, Kingston, Jamaica, and non-resident Ambassador to Haiti, 1989–95. Americas Res. Gp, Res. Analysts, FCO, 1995–99 (on contract). *Recreations:* QPR Football Club, Poland, swimming. *Address:* 31 Park Road, Beckenham BR3 1QG.

MILTON, Peter James Denis, MD; FRCOG; Consultant Obstetrician and Gynaecologist, Addenbrooke's Hospital, Cambridge, and Associate Lecturer, University of Cambridge, since 1976; *b* 17 Jan. 1938; *s* of James Hugh Milton, CEng, FInstMarE, and Dorothy Winifred Milton (*née* Nelson); *m* 1968, Rosemary Jane Phillips; two *s* one *d*. *Educ:* Merchant Taylors' Sch., Crosby, Liverpool; King's Coll., London; St George's Hosp. Med. Sch., Univ. of London (MB BS; MD 1978); MA Cantab 1978. MRCS, LRCP 1963; DA 1969; MRCOG 1970, FRCOG 1983. Jun. med. and surgical posts, St George's, Winchester, Canterbury and St Thomas' Hosps, 1963–70; Ships Surgeon, Blue Star Line, 1968; Registrar, Obstetrics and Gynaecology, St Thomas' Hosp. and Groote Schuur Hosp., Cape Town, 1970–72; Lectr and Sen. Registrar, St Thomas' Hosp., 1972–76; Res. Associate, Imperial Cancer Res. Lab., Lincoln's Inn, 1972–76. Editor and reviewer, obstetric and gynaecological specialist books and jls. Royal College of Obstetricians and Gynaecologists: Fellows' Rep., Council, 1993–98; Chm., Continuing Med. Educn Cttee, 1995–98; Mem., various cttees; Sen. Vice Pres., 1998–2001. Vice-Pres., Section Obstetrics and Gynaecol., RSocMed, 1993–96 (Hon. Sec., 1992–93). Examiner: RCOG; Univs of Cambridge, London, Edinburgh, Liverpool, Manchester, Colombo and Khartoum. *Publications:* papers and chapters on pre-natal diagnosis, pre-malignant disease, menopause and other obstetric and gynaecol topics in British and overseas specialist jls. *Recreations:* sailing, ski-ing, second-hand bookshops, walking dogs and more distant travel. *Address:* King's Head House, Duxford, Cambridge CB2 4RP. *T:* (01223) 832999. *Clubs:* Athenæum; Royal Harwich Yacht; Aldeburgh Yacht; Island Cruising (Salcombe); Gynaecological Travellers of UK and Ireland.

MILTON-THOMPSON, Surg. Vice-Adm. Sir Godfrey (James), KBE 1988; FRCP; Warden, St Katharine's House, Wantage, 1993–98; Medical Director General (Naval), 1985–90; Surgeon General, Ministry of Defence, 1988–90; *b* 25 April 1930; *s* of Rev. James Milton-Thompson and May LeMare (*née* Hoare); *m* 1952, Noreen Helena Frances, *d* of Lt-Col Sir Desmond Fitzmaurice, CIE; three *d*. *Educ:* Eastbourne Coll.; Queens' Coll., Cambridge (MA); St Thomas' Hosp. (MB BChir); FRCP 1974 (MRCP 1961); DCH 1963. Joined Royal Navy, 1955; after general service and hosp. appts at home and abroad, Cons. Phys., RN Hosp., Plymouth, 1967–70 and 1972–75; Hon. Research Fellow, St Mark's Hosp., London, 1969–71; Prof. of Naval Medicine, 1975–80; RCDS 1981; Dep. Medical Director General (Naval), 1982–84; Surg. Rear-Adm. (Operational Med. Services), 1984–85; Dep. Surg. Gen. (Research and Trng), MoD, 1985–87. QHP, 1982–90. Chm., Cornwall Community Healthcare Trust, 1991–93. Member: Medical Research Soc., 1971–; British Soc. of Gastroenterology, 1972–; Vice Pres., British Digestive Foundn, 1993–. Hon. Col, 211 (Wessex) Field Hosp., RAMC(V), 1990–95. Gov., St Mary's Sch., Wantage, 1995– (Chm., 1996–). Errol-Eldridge Prize, 1974; Gilbert Blane Medal, 1976. KStJ 1989 (Mem., Chapter Gen., 1988–95; Hospitaller, 1991–95; Chm., St John Council, Cornwall, 2000–; Mem., English Priory Chapter, 2000–). *Publications:* on clinical pharmacology of the gastro-intestinal tract and therapy of peptic ulcer, etc, in med. jls. *Recreations:* fishing, paintings and painting, literature. *Address:* Pool Hall, Menheniot, Liskeard, Cornwall PL14 3QT. *Club:* Naval and Military.

MILVERTON, 2nd Baron *cr* 1947, of Lagos and of Clifton; **Rev. Fraser Arthur Richard Richards;** Rector of Christian Malford with Sutton Benger and Tytherton Kellaways, 1967–93; *b* 21 July 1930; *s* of 1st Baron Milverton, GCMG, and Noelle Benda, *d* of Charles Basil Whitehead; *S* father, 1978; *m* 1957, Mary Dorothy, BD, *d* of late Leslie Fly, ARCM, Corsham, Wilts; two *d*. *Educ:* De Carteret Prep. Sch., Jamaica; Ridley Coll., Ontario; Clifton Coll.; Egerton Agric. Coll., Kenya; Bishop's Coll., Cheshunt. Royal Signals, 1949–50; Kenya Police, 1952–53. Deacon 1957, priest 1958, dio. Rochester; Curate: Beckenham, 1957–59; St John Baptist, Sevenoaks, 1959–60; Great Bookham, 1960–63; Vicar of Okewood with Forest Green, 1963–67. Trustee and Dir, Voice (UK) Ltd. Gov., Clifton Coll. *Recreations:* family, reading, current affairs and history; enjoys music and walking; interested in tennis, swimming, cricket and Rugby Union. *Heir:* *b* Hon. Michael Hugh Richards [*b* 1 Aug. 1936; *m* 1960, Edna Leonie, *y d* of Col Leo Steveni, OBE, MC; one *s*].

MILWARD, Prof. Alan Steele, FBA 1987; Professor of Contemporary History, European University Institute, since 1997; Official Historian, Cabinet Office, since 1993; Professor Emeritus of Economic History, London School of Economics, since 1997; *b* 19 Jan. 1935; *s* of Joseph Thomas Milward and Dorothy Milward (*née* Steele); *m* 1st, 1963, Claudine Jeanne Amélie Lemaître (marr. diss. 1994); 2nd, 1998, Frances M. B. Lynch; two *d*; one *d*. *Educ:* University College London (BA 1956); LSE (PhD 1960); MA Manchester 1981. Asst Lectr in Indian Archaeology, Univ. of London, 1959; Lectr in Economic History, Univ. of Edinburgh, 1960; Sen. Lectr in Social Studies, Univ. of East Anglia, 1965; Associate Prof. of Economics, Stanford Univ., 1969; Prof. of European Studies, UMIST, 1971; Prof. of Contemp. Hist., Eur. Univ. Inst., 1983–86; Prof. of Econ. History, LSE, 1986–97. Visiting Professor: Stanford Univ., 1966; Ecole Pratique des Hautes Etudes, 1977, 1990; Univ. of Illinois, 1978; Univ.-Gesamthochschule, Siegen, 1980; Oslo Univ., 1990; Aarhus Univ., 1992; Trondheim Univ., 1993. Hon. Fellow, Royal Norwegian Acad. of Scis and Letters, 1994. *Publications:* The German Economy at War, 1965; The Social and Economic Effects of the Two World Wars on Britain, 1971, 2nd edn 1984; The New Order and the French Economy, 1972; The Fascist Economy in Norway, 1972; (with S. B. Saul) The Economic Development of Continental Europe 1780–1870, 1973; (with S. B. Saul) The Development of the Economies of Continental Europe 1870–1914, 1977; War, Economy and Society, 1977; The Reconstruction of Western Europe 1945–1951, 1984, 2nd edn 1987; (with B. Martin) Landwirtschaft und Ernährung im Zweiten Weltkrieg, 1984; The European Rescue of the Nation-State, 1992; The Frontier of National Sovereignty, 1993; (with G. Brennan) Britain's Place in the World: a historical enquiry into import controls 1945–60, 1996. *Recreations:* theatre, cricket, reading timetables. *Address:* Dipartimento di Storia, Istituto Universitario Europeo, Badia Fiesolana, 50016 San Domenico di Fiesole, Italy. *T:* (55) 4685362; Cabinet Office, Hepburn House, Marsham Street, SW1P 4HW. *T:* (020) 7217 6037.

MIMPRISS, Peter Hugh Trevor, CVO 2001; Partner, Allen & Overy, since 1972; *b* 22 Aug. 1943; *s* of Hugh Trevor Baber Mimpriss and Gwyneth Mary Mimpriss (*née* Bartley); *m* 1st, 1971, Hilary Ann Reed (marr. diss. 1992); two *d*; 2nd, 1992, Elisabeth Lesley Molle. *Educ:* Sherborne Sch. Admitted solicitor, 1967. Joined Allen & Overy, 1968; univ. solicitor, Univ. of London, 1995–. Chairman: Charity Law Assoc., 1992–97; Chariguard Gp of Common Investment Funds, 1994–2000. Director: Leeds Castle Foundn, 1980–; Chatham Historic Dockyard Trust, 1986–2000; Solcare, 1997–; PYBT, 1997–99; Member, Council: Prince's Trust, 1998–; Royal Jubilee Trusts, 2000–; Trustee, Inst. of Philanthropy, 2000–. *Recreations:* maritime history, vintage cars, collecting books, tennis. *Address:* c/o Allen & Overy, One New Change, EC4M 9QQ. *T:* (020) 7330 3000. *Clubs:* Athenæum, Garrick.

MIMS, Prof. Cedric Arthur, MD, FRCPath; Professor of Microbiology, Guy's Hospital Medical School, London, 1972–90; *b* 9 Dec. 1924; *s* of A. H. and Irene Mims; *m* 1952, Valerie Vickery; two *s* two *d*. *Educ:* Mill Hill Sch.; University Coll. London (BSc (Zool)); Middlesex Hosp. Med. Sch. (MB, BS, BSc, MD). Medical Research Officer, East African Virus Research Inst., Entebbe, Uganda, 1953–56; Research Fellow and Professorial Fellow, John Curtin Sch. of Med. Research, Australian Nat. Univ., Canberra, 1957–72; Rockefeller Foundn Fellow, Children's Hosp. Med. Centre, Boston, USA, 1963–64; Visiting Fellow, Wistar Inst., Philadelphia, USA, 1969–70. *Publications:* (jtly) The Biology of Animal Viruses, 1974; Mims' Pathogenesis of Infectious Disease, 1976, 5th edn 2000; (with D. O. White) Viral Pathogenesis and Immunology, 1984; (jtly) Medical Microbiology, 1993, 2nd edn 1998; When We Die, 1998; The War Within Us, 2000; numerous papers on the pathogenesis of virus infections. *Address:* Sheriff House, Hammingden Lane, Ardingly, Sussex RH17 6SR. *T:* (01444) 892243.

MINDHAM, Prof. Richard Hugh Shiels, MD; FRCP, FRCPsych; Nuffield Professor of Psychiatry, 1977–2000, now Emeritus, and Dean, Faculty of Medicine, Dentistry and Health, 1996–99, University of Leeds; *b* 25 March 1935; *s* of Thomas Raper Mindham and Winifred Gertrude Mindham; *m* 1971, Barbara Harris Reid; one *s* one *d*. *Educ:* Guy's Hosp. Medical Sch.; Inst. of Psychiatry, Univ. of London. MD 1974; FRCPsych 1977; FRCPE 1978; FRCP 2000. Nottingham University Medical School: Sen. Lectr in Psychiatry, 1972–76; Reader, 1976–77; Dean of Postgrad. Studies, Univ. of Leeds, 1994–96. Vis. Prof., Johns Hopkins Univ., 1982. Chief Examr, RCPsych, 1995–98. *Publications:* papers on psychiatry, psychopharmacology and Parkinson's disease. *Recreations:* music, architecture, walking; *e-mail:* r.h.s.mindham@leeds.ac.uk. *Club:* Royal Society of Medicine.

MINFORD, Prof. (Anthony) Patrick (Leslie), CBE 1996; Professor of Economics, Cardiff Business School, Cardiff University, since 1997; *b* 17 May 1943; *s* of Leslie Mackay Minford and Patricia Mary (*née* Sale); *m* 1970, Rosemary Irene Allcorn; two *s* one *d*. *Educ:* Horris Hill; Winchester Coll. (scholar); Balliol Coll., Oxford (schol.; BA); London Sch. of Economics (grad. studies; MScEcon, PhD). Economic Asst, Min. of Overseas Development, London, 1966; Economist, Min. of Finance, Malawi, 1967–69; Economic Adviser: Director's Staff, Courtaulds Ltd, 1970–71; HM Treasury, 1971–73, and HM Treasury Delegn in Washington, 1973–74; Visiting Hallsworth Fellow, Manchester Univ., 1974–75; Editor, NIESR Review, 1975–76; Edward Gonner Prof. of Applied Econs, Liverpool Univ., 1976–97. Vis. Prof., Cardiff Business Sch., 1993–97. Dir, Merseyside Develt Corp., 1988–89. Mem., Monopolies and Mergers Commn, 1990–96. Mem., HM Treasury's Panel of Economic Forecasters, 1993–96. Mem. Bd, WNO, 1993–98. *Publications:* Substitution Effects, Speculation and Exchange Rate Stability, 1978; (jtly) Unemployment—Cause and Cure, 1983, 2nd edn 1985; (jtly) Rational Expectations and the New Macroeconomics, 1983; (jtly) The Housing Morass, 1987; The Supply Side Revolution in Britain, 1991; (jtly) The Cost of Europe, 1992; Rational Expectations Macroeconomics, 1993; Markets Not Stakes, 1998; (jtly) Britain and Europe: choices for change, 1999; articles in learned jls on monetary and international economics. *Address:* Cardiff Business School, Cardiff University, Cardiff CF1 3EU.

MINGAY, (Frederick) Ray, CMG 1992; Chief Executive, Trade Development Services, since 1997; consultant to various companies and other organisations; *b* 7 July 1938; *s* of Cecil Stanley and Madge Elizabeth Mingay; *m* 1963, Joan Heather Roberts; three *s* one *d*. *Educ:* Tottenham Grammar Sch.; St Catharine's Coll., Cambridge (Open Exhibnr; MA); London Univ. (Postgrad. Pub. Admin.). Nat. Service, 1959–61: 2nd Lieut RAEC; attached RIF, Kenya. Administration, St Thomas' Hosp., 1961; Min. of Transport, 1962–64; BoT, 1964; Chrysler (UK) Ltd, 1968–70; Consul (Commercial), Milan, 1970–73; Asst Sec., Dept of Trade, 1973–78; Counsellor (Commercial), Washington, 1978–83; Under Secretary: Mechanical and Electrical Engrg Div., DTI, 1983–86; Investment and Develt Div., DTI, 1986–88; Consul-Gen., Chicago, 1988–92; Head of Overseas Trade Div. DTI, 1992–93; Dir-Gen., Export Promotion, DTI, 1993–97 (concurrently Asst Under Sec. of State, FCO (Jt Export Promotion Directorate), 1993–96). Mem., BOTB, 1993–97. Churchill Fellow, Westminster Coll., Fulton, Mo, 1991. FIMgt; MIEx; FRSA. Hon. Public Affairs Advr, John Grooms, 2000–. *Club:* Reform.

MINGHELLA, Anthony, CBE 2001; writer and film director; *s* of Edward and Gloria Minghella; *m* Carolyn Choa; one *s*, and one *d* by previous *m*. *Educ:* Hull Univ. (BA). Lectr in Drama, Hull Univ., 1976–81. *Plays* include: *theatre:* Two Planks and a Passion, Exeter, 1983, Greenwich, 1984; A Little Like Drowning, Hampstead, 1984; Made in Bangkok, Aldwych, 1986; *television* includes: Whale Music; What If It's Raining, 1986; Inspector Morse (various episodes); *films:* (writer and dir) Truly, Madly, Deeply, 1991 (BAFTA and Writers' Guild Awards for best original screenplay, 1992); (dir) Mr Wonderful, 1993; The English Patient (adapted and dir.), 1997 (Academy Award for best dir; BAFTA Award for best adapted screenplay); The Talented Mr Ripley, 2000; *radio:* Hang Up, 1987; Cigarettes and Chocolate, 1988. First Hon. Freeman, IoW, 1997. Hon. DLit Hull, 1997. *Publications:* Whale Music, 1983; Made in Bangkok, 1986; Jim Henson's Storyteller, 1988; Interior—Room; Exterior—City, 1989; Plays: One, 1992; Driven to Distraction: a case for Inspector Morse, 1994; Plays: Two, 1997; The English Patient (screenplay), 1997.

MINGINS, Rev. Canon Marion Elizabeth; Canon Residentiary, since 1993, Canon Pastor, since 1999, St Edmundsbury Cathedral; Chaplain to the Queen, since 1996; *b* 12 July 1952; *d* of George and Marion Mingins. *Educ:* Univ. of Birmingham (BSocSci and Social Admin); Univ. of Leicester (CQSW); Church Army Training Coll. (Cambridge Dip. Religious Studies). Warden, Church Army Old People's Home, 1979; Selection Sec., later Sen. Selection Sec., ACCM, Gen. Synod of C of E, 1983–89; ordained deacon, 1987; Novice, Order of Holy Paraclete, Whitby, 1989; Diocesan Vocations Advr and Asst Diocesan Dir of Ordinands, 1991–92, Diocesan Dir of Ordinands, 1992–99, St Edmundsbury and Ipswich; ordained priest, 1994. *Recreations:* analytical psychology, reading novels, politics. *Address:* 54 College Street, Bury St Edmunds, Suffolk IP33 1NH. *T:* (01284) 753396.

MINGOS, Prof. (David) Michael (Patrick), DPhil; FRS 1992; CChem, FRSC; Principal, St Edmund Hall, Oxford, since 1999; Professor of Chemistry, University of Oxford, since 2000; *b* 6 Aug. 1944; *s* of Vasso Mingos and Rose Enid Billie Hayes (*née* Griffiths); *m* 1967, Stacey Mary Hosken; one *s* one *d*. *Educ:* Univ. of Manchester (BSc); Univ. of Sussex (DPhil). CChem 1983; FRSC 1983. Fulbright Fellow, Northwestern Univ., 1968–70; ICI Fellow, Sussex Univ., 1970–71; Lectr, QMC, 1971–76; University of Oxford: Lectr, 1976–90; Reader, 1990–92; Fellow, Keble Coll., 1976–92 and by special election, 1993 (Hon. Fellow, 1999); Univ. Assessor, 1991–92; Sir Edward Frankland BP Prof. of Inorganic Chemistry, Imperial Coll., Univ. of London, 1992–99; Dean, Royal Coll. of Sci., 1996–99. Dist. Prof., Xi'an Petroleum Inst., China, 1994–; Wilhelm Manchot Res. Prof. and prize, Munich, 1995; Vis. Prof., Imperial Coll., London, 1999–; Univ. of Auckland Foundn Visitor, 2000. Lee Meml Lecture, Univ. of Chicago, 1997. Vice Pres., Dalton Div., RSC, 1993–96. Gov., Harrow Sch., 1994–. Hon. DSc: UMIST, 2000; Sussex, 2001. Corday Morgan Medal, 1980, Tilden Medal, 1988, Chemistry of Noble Metals Award, 1983, RSC; M. J. Collins Prize, for innovation in microwave chemistry, CEM Corp., 1996; Alexander von Humboldt Stiftung Forschungspreis, 1999. Editor, Jl of Organometallic Chem., 1996–; Member, Editorial Board: Transition Metal Chem., 1975–; Structure and Bonding, 1983–; New Jl of Chem., 1986–96; Jl of Organometallic Chem., 1991–; Chemical Soc. Rev., 1992–97; Advances in Inorganic Chem., 1992–; Inorganic Chemistry, 1997–99. *Publications:* Introduction to Cluster Chemistry, 1990; Essentials of Inorganic Chemistry 1, 1995; Essential Trends in Inorganic Chemistry, 1997; (ed) Structural and Electronic Paradigms in Cluster Chemistry, 1997; Essentials of Inorganic Chemistry 2, 1998; (ed) Liquid Crystals, Vols 1 and 2, 1999; contribs to jls of learned socs. *Recreations:* cricket, tennis, walking. *Address:* St Edmund Hall, Oxford OX1 4AR. *T:* (01865) 279003; *e-mail:* michael.mingos@st-edmund-hall.oxford.ac.uk.

MINOGUE, Prof. Kenneth Robert; Professor of Political Science, London School of Economics and Political Science, University of London, 1984–95, now Emeritus; *b* 11 Sept. 1930; *s* of Denis Francis Minogue and Eunice Pearl Minogue (*née* Porter); *m* 1954, Valerie Pearson Hallett; one *s* one *d*. *Educ:* Sydney Boys' High Sch.; Sydney Univ. (BA); London School of Economics (BScEcon). Asst Lectr, Univ. of Exeter, 1955–56; London School of Economics: Asst Lectr, 1956; Sen. Lectr, 1964; Reader, 1971. *Publications:* The Liberal Mind, 1961; Nationalism, 1967; The Concept of a University, 1974; Alien Powers: the pure theory of ideology, 1985; Politics: a very short introduction, 1995; (ed and contrib.) Conservative Realism, 1996; The Silencing of Society, 1997; Waitangi Morality Reality, 1998; numerous contribs to learned jls. *Recreations:* opera, tennis, walking. *Address:* 43 Perrymead Street, SW6 3SN. *T:* (020) 7731 0421. *Club:* Garrick.

MINOGUE, Maj.-Gen. Patrick John O'Brien; retired; *b* 28 July 1922; *s* of Col M. J. Minogue, DSO, MC, late East Surrey Regt, and Mrs M. V. E. Minogue; *m* 1950, June Elizabeth (*née* Morris) (*d* 2000); one *s* two *d*. *Educ:* Brighton Coll.; RMCS. CIMgt, FBCS, FIWSP, FIMH; jssc, psc, ato. Indian Army, 1942–46; East Surrey Regt, 1947; RAOC, 1951; served UK, BAOR, USA, Cyprus; Col, 1969; Brig., 1971; Insp. RAOC, 1971–73; Comdt, Central Ord. Depot, Bicester, 1973–75; Maj.-Gen. 1975; Comdr, Base Orgn, RAOC, 1975–78. Hon. Col, RAOC (TAVR), 1975–78; Col Comdt, RAOC, 1980–87. Group Systems Controller, Lansing Bagnall Ltd, 1978–81; Chm., LT Electronics, 1979–81. Mem., Spanish Golf Fedn, 1982–. *Recreations:* cricket, sailing (Cdre Wayfarer Class, UK, 1975), golf, shooting, gun-dogs, athletics, lawn bowling. *Address:* La Casa Rosada, Apartado 4, Cortijo Grande, Turre, Almeria, Spain. *Clubs:* MCC; Army Sailing Association; Royal Logistic Corps Yacht; Milocarian Athletic; Staff College (Camberley); Cortijo Grande Golf; Cabrera Lawn Bowling (Pres., 1987–92).

MINTER, Graham Leslie, LVO 1983; HM Diplomatic Service; *b* 4 Jan. 1950; *s* of Norman Leslie Minter and Beryl Winifred Minter; *m* 1975, Peter Anne Scott; one *s* one *d*. *Educ:* Orange Hill County Grammar Sch. FCO, 1968–71; Anguilla, 1971–72; Latin American Floater, 1973–75; Asunción, 1975–78; FCO, 1978–79; First Secretary: (Econ.), Mexico City, 1979–84; FCO, 1984–90; Canberra, 1990–94; FCO, 1994–98; Ambassador to Bolivia, 1998–2001. *Recreations:* travel, music, walking, reading, genealogy, birdwatching, table tennis, tennis, football. *Address:* c/o Foreign and Commonwealth Office, King Charles Street, SW1A 2AH.

MINTO, 6th Earl of, *cr* 1813; **Gilbert Edward George Lariston Elliot-Murray-Kynynmound,** OBE 1986 (MBE (mil.) 1955); JP; Bt 1700; Baron Minto, 1797; Viscount Melgund, 1813; late Captain Scots Guards; Vice Lord-Lieutenant, Borders Region (Roxburgh, Ettrick and Lauderdale), since 1992; *b* 19 June 1928; *er s* of 5th Earl of Minto and Marion, OBE (*d* 1974), *d* of G. W. Cook, Montreal; *S* father, 1975; *m* 1st, 1952, Lady Caroline Child-Villiers (from whom he obtained a divorce, 1965), *d* of 9th Earl of Jersey; one *s* one *d*; 2nd, 1965, Mary Elizabeth (*b* 29 Dec. 1936; *d* 24 Jan. 1983), *d* of late Peter Ballantine and of Mrs Ballantine, Gladstone, New Jersey, USA; 3rd, 1991, Mrs Caroline Larlham. *Educ:* Eton; RMA, Sandhurst. Served Malaya, 1949–51; ADC to C-in-C FARELF, 1951, to CIGS, 1953–55, to HE Governor and C-in-C Cyprus, 1955; transferred to RARO, 1956. Lieut, Queen's Body Guard for Scotland (Royal Company of Archers). Director, Noel Penny Turbines Ltd, 1971–92. Regional Councillor (Hermitage Div.), Borders Region, 1974–80, 1986–96; Convener, Borders Regional Council, 1990–96; Mem. Exec., COSLA, 1990–96. Dep. Traffic Comr for Scotland, 1975–81; Property Comr for Local Govt, Scotland, 1995–98. Pres., S of Scotland Chamber of Commerce, 1980–82 (Exec. Vice-Pres., 1978–80). Chm., 1973–87, Pres., 1987–, Scottish Council on Alcohol. JP Roxburghshire, 1961–; DL Borders Region, Roxburgh, Ettrick and Lauderdale, 1983. *Heir: s* Viscount Melgund, *qv*. *Address:* Minto, Hawick, Scotland TD9 8SB. *T:* (01450) 870321.

MINTO, Dr Alfred, FRCPsych; Consultant Psychiatrist (Rehabilitation), Southern Derbyshire Health Authority, 1988–90, retired 1991; *b* 23 Sept. 1928; *s* of Alfred Minto and Marjorie Mavor Goudie Leask; *m* 1949, Frances Oliver Bradbrook; two *s* two *d*. *Educ:* Aberdeen Central Sch.; Aberdeen Univ. (MB ChB 1951); MA History, Univ. of Nottingham, 1996. DPM RCS&P London 1961; MRCPsych 1972, FRCPsych 1974. House Physician, Huddersfield Royal Inf., 1952; Sen. House Officer/Jun. Hosp. Med. Officer, Fairmile Hosp., Wallingford, 1952–56; Sen. Registrar, St Luke's Hosp., Middlesbrough, 1956–59; Sen. Hosp. Med. Officer, 1959–63, Conslt Psychiatrist, 1963, Mapperley Hosp., Nottingham; Conslt Psychiatrist i/c, Alcoholism and Drug Addiction Service, Sheffield RHB, 1963–68; Conslt Psychiatrist, St Ann's and Mapperley Hosps, 1968–81; Med. Dir, Rampton Hosp., 1981–85; Associate Prof. of Psychiatry, Univ. of Calgary, and Clinical Dir of Forensic Psychiatry, Calgary Gen. Hosp., Alberta, 1986–87. Clinical Teacher, Nottingham Univ. Med. Sch., 1971–85; Special Lectr in Forensic Psych., Nottingham Univ., 1982–85. Conslt Psychiatrist, CS Comrs, 1964–85. *Publications:* Key Issues in Mental Health, 1982; papers on alcoholism, community care, toxoplasmosis. *Recreations:* books, people. *Address:* 76 Walsingham Road, Nottingham, NG5 4NR.

MINTOFF, Hon. Dominic, (Dom), BSc, BE&A, MA, A&CE; Prime Minister of Malta, 1971–84; Leader of Malta Labour Party, 1949–84; *b* Cospicua, 6 Aug. 1916; *s* of Lawrence Mintoff and late Concetta (*née* Farrugia); *m* 1947, Moyra de Vere Bentick (decd); two *d*. *Educ:* Govt Elem. Sch., Seminary and Lyceum, Malta; Univ. of Malta (BSc 1937; BE&A, A&CE 1939); Hertford Coll., Oxford (Govt Travelling Scholar; Rhodes Scholar; MA Engrg Science). Practised as civil engineer in Britain, 1941–43, and as architect in Malta, 1943–. Gen. Sec. Malta Labour Party, 1936–37; Mem., Council of Govt and Exec. Council, 1945; MP (Lab) Malta, 1947–98 (did not seek re-election following disagreement with current Lab Party policies); Dep. Prime Minister and Minister for Works and Reconstruction, 1947–49 (resigned); Prime Minister and Minister of Finance, 1955–58; resigned office in 1958 to lead the Maltese Liberation Movement; Leader of Opposition, 1962–71; Minister of Foreign Affairs, 1971–81; Minister of the Interior, 1976–81 and 1983–84. Mem., Labour delegns to UK, 1945, 1947, 1948 and 1949. Negotiated removal of British Military base, 1971 and other foreign mil. bases by 1979. Dr *hc* Univ. of Pol. Studies, Ponterios, Greece, 1976. Order of the Republic, Libya, 1971; Grand Cordon: Order of the Republic, Tunisia, 1973; Order of Oissam Alaouite, 1978. *Publications:* scientific, literary and artistic works. *Recreations:* horse-riding, swimming, water skiing, boċċi. *Address:* The Olives, Tarxien, Malta.

MINTON, Kenneth Joseph, CBE 1995; Executive Chairman, Inveresk plc, since 2001; *b* 17 Jan. 1937; *s* of late Henry Minton and Lilian Minton (*née* Moore); *m* 1961, Mary Wilson; one *s*. *Educ:* Leeds Univ. (BSc 1st cl. Hons Mining Engrg). Management positions with: Unilever, UK and France, 1960–68; Laporte plc, 1968–95 (Chief Exec. and Man. Dir, 1979–95); Chm., SGB Gp plc, 1997–2000; Exec. Chm., Arjo Wiggins Appleton plc, 1997–2001; Director: Caradon plc, 1991–99; Jeyes Gp plc, 1989–98 (Chm., 1993–96); John Mowlem & Co. PLC, 1994–98 (Chm., 1995–98); Solvay SA, 1996–; Sentrachem Ltd, 1996–97. Mem. Bd, CEFIC, 1991–95. Trustee, Industry and Parlt Trust, 1998– (Founder Mem., 1977; Chm., Mgt Council, 1993–96). Pres., SCI, 1996–98. SCI Centenary Medal, 1994. *Recreations:* gardens, fine art, walking, South Africa, charities. *Address:* Inveresk plc, Kilbagie Mills, Alloa, Clackmannanshire FK10 4AE. *T:* (01259) 455000.

MINTON, Yvonne Fay, CBE 1980; mezzo-soprano; *er d* of R. T. Minton, Sydney; *m* 1965, William Barclay; one *s* one *d*. *Educ:* Sydney Conservatorium of Music. Elsa Stralia Scholar, Sydney, 1957–60; won Canberra Operatic Aria Competition, 1960; won Kathleen Ferrier Prize at s'Hertogenbosch Vocal Competition, 1961. Joined Royal Opera House as a Principal Mezzo-Soprano, 1965. Major roles include: Octavian in Der Rosenkavalier; Dorabella in Cosi Fan Tutte; Marina in Boris Godounov; Helen in King Priam; Cherubino in Marriage of Figaro; Orfeo in Gluck's Orfeo; Sextus in La clemenza di Tito; Dido in The Trojans at Carthage; Kundry in Parsifal; Charlotte in Werther; Countess Geschwitz in Lulu. Recordings include Octavian in Der Rosenkavalier, Mozart Requiem, Elgar's The Kingdom, etc. Guest Artist with Cologne Opera Company, Oct. 1969–. Hon. RAM 1975. *Recreations:* reading, gardening. *Address:* c/o Ingpen and Williams, 26 Wadham Road, SW15 2LR. *T:* (020) 8874 3222.

MIQUEL, Raymond Clive, CBE 1981; Chairman and Managing Director, Lees Group Ltd, since 1992; Chairman, Scottish Sports Council, 1987–91; Member, Sports Council, 1988–91; *b* 28 May 1931; *m* 1958; one *s* two *d*. *Educ:* Allan Glen's Sch., Glasgow; Glasgow Technical Coll. Joined Arthur Bell & Sons Ltd as Works Study Engineer, 1956; Production Controller, 1958; Production Director, 1962; Dep. Managing Director, 1965; Man. Dir, 1968–85; Dep. Chairman, 1972; Chm., 1973–85. Chairman: Towmaster Transport Co. Ltd, 1974–86; Canning Town Glass Ltd, 1974–86; Wellington Importers Ltd, USA, 1984–86; Gleneagles Hotels PLC, 1984–86; Chm. and Chief Exec., Belhaven plc, 1986–88. Dir, Golf Fund Plc, 1989–94. Vis. Prof. in Business Develt, Glasgow Univ., 1985–. Member: British Internat. Sports Cttee, 1987–91; CCPR, 1984–. Governor, Sports Aid Foundn, 1979–. CIMgt (CBIM 1981). *Publication:* Business as Usual: the Miquel way (autobiog.), 2000. *Address:* Whitedene, Caledonian Crescent, Gleneagles, Perthshire, Scotland PH3 1NG. *T:* (01764) 662642.

MIRMAN, Sophie, (Mrs R. P. Ross); Joint Managing Director, Trotters Childrenswear and Accessories, since 1990; *b* 28 Oct. 1956; *d* of Simone and Serge Mirman; *m* 1984, Richard Philip Ross; one *s* two *d*. *Educ:* French Lycée, London. Marks & Spencer, 1974–81; Gen. Manager, 1981–82, Man. Dir, 1982–83, Tie Rack; Co-Founder, Sock Shop International, 1983; Chm. and Joint Man. Dir, Sock Shop International plc, 1983–90. *Recreations:* family, sport. *Address:* 34 King's Road, SW3 4UD. *T:* (020) 7259 9622.

MIRREN, Helen; actress; *b* 26 July 1945; *m* 1997, Taylor Hackford. *Theatre includes: RSC:* Troilus and Cressida, Much Ado About Nothing, 1968; Richard III, Hamlet, The Two Gentlemen of Verona, 1970; Miss Julie, 1971; Macbeth, 1974; Henry VI parts I, II and III, 1977; Antony and Cleopatra, The Roaring Girl, 1983; *other:* Teeth 'n' Smiles, Royal Court, 1974; The Bed Before Yesterday, Lyric, 1976; Measure for Measure, Riverside, 1979; The Duchess of Malfi, Manchester Royal Exchange, 1980; Faith Healer, Royal Court, 1981; Extremities, Duchess, 1984; Two Way Mirror, Young Vic, 1988; Sex Please, We're Italian, Young Vic, 1991; A Month in the Country, Albery, and Roundabout, Broadway, 1994; Antony and Cleopatra, RNT, 1998; Collected Stories, Haymarket, 1999; Orpheus Descending, Donmar, 2000; Dance of Death, NY, 2001. *Films include:* Age of Consent, 1969; Savage Messiah, 1971; O Lucky Man, 1973; Caligula, 1977; The Long Good Friday, 1980; Excalibur, 1981; Cal, 1984; 2010, 1985; White Nights, 1986; Heavenly Pursuits, 1986; The Mosquito Coast, 1987; Pascali's Island, 1988; When the Whales Came, 1988; Bethune: The Making of a Hero, 1989; The Cook, The Thief, his Wife and her Lover, 1989; The Comfort of Strangers, 1989; Where Angels Fear to Tread, 1990; The Madness of King George, 1994; Some Mother's Son, 1996; Teaching Mrs Tingle, 1998; Greenfingers, 2001; The Pledge, 2001. *TV includes:* Prime Suspect (5 series), 1991–96; Painted Lady, 1997; Ayn Rand, 1998; Losing Chase; (dir) Happy Birthday (USA). *Address:* c/o Ken McReddie Ltd, 91 Regent Street, W1R 7TB.

MIRRLEES, Sir James (Alexander), Kt 1997; FBA 1984; Professor of Political Economy, University of Cambridge and Fellow of Trinity College, since 1995; *b* 5 July

1936; *s* of late George B. M. Mirrlees; *m* 1961, Gillian Marjorie Hughes (*d* 1993); two *d*; *m* 2001, Patricia Wilson. *Educ:* Douglas-Ewart High Sch., Newton Stewart; Edinburgh Univ.; Trinity Coll., Cambridge. MA Edinburgh Maths, 1957; BA Cantab Maths, 1959; PhD Cantab Econs, 1963. Adviser, MIT Center for Internat. Studies, New Delhi, 1962–63; Cambridge Univ. Asst Lectr in Econs and Fellow of Trinity Coll., 1963, University Lectr, 1965; Adviser to Govt of Swaziland, 1963; Res. Assoc., Pakistan Inst. of Develt Econs, Karachi, 1966–67; Edgeworth Prof. of Econs, and Fellow, Nuffield Coll., Oxford Univ., 1968–95. Visiting Professor: MIT, 1968, 1970, 1976, 1987; Univ. of California, Berkeley, 1986; Yale Univ., 1989. Mem., Treasury Cttee on Policy Optimisation, 1976–78. Econometric Society: Fellow, 1970; Vice-Pres., 1980, Pres., 1982; Chm., Assoc. of Univ. Teachers of Econs, 1983–87; President: Royal Economic Soc., 1989–92; European Economic Assoc., 2000. For. Hon. Mem., Amer. Acad. of Arts and Scis, 1981; Hon. Mem., Amer. Economic Assoc., 1982; Foreign Associate, US Nat. Acad. of Scis, 1999. Hon. FRSE, 1998. Hon. DLitt: Warwick, 1982; Portsmouth, 1997; Oxford, 1998; Hon. DSocSc Brunel, 1997; Hon. DSc Edinburgh, 1997. Nobel Prize for Economics, 1996. *Publications:* (joint author) Manual of Industrial Project Analysis in Developing Countries, 1969; (ed jtly) Models of Economic Growth, 1973; (jt author) Project Appraisal and Planning, 1974; articles in economic jls. *Recreations:* reading detective stories and other forms of mathematics, playing the piano, travelling, listening. *Address:* Trinity College, Cambridge CB2 1TQ.

MIRRLEES, Robin Ian Evelyn Stuart de la Lanne-; Richmond Herald of Arms, 1962–67; *b* Paris, 13 Jan. 1925; grandson of Ambassador La Lanne; godson of 11th Duke of Argyll; one *s*. *Educ:* Merton Coll., Oxford (MA). Several language diplomas. Served India, 1942–46; Captain RA, 1944; Gen. Staff, New Delhi, 1946; Embassy Attaché, Tokyo, 1947; Rouge Dragon Pursuivant of Arms, 1952–62 (and as such attended Coronation). Co-editor, Annuaire de France, 1966–. ADC to HM the King of Yugoslavia, 1963–70. Has raised substantial funds for humanitarian organisations; undertook restoration of Inchdrewer Castle, Scotland, and others; Laird of Island of Bernera, pop. 350. Freeman of City of London, 1960. Patrician of San Marino, 1964. Succeeded to the title of Comte de Lalanne (France), 1962 and titular Prince of Coronata. Various foreign orders of knighthood. *Recreations:* foxhunting, piloting, travelling, painting, sculpture, mystic philosophy. *Address:* Bernera Lodge, Great Bernera Island, by Stornoway, Outer Hebrides, Scotland; Inchdrewer Castle, Banff, Scotland. *Clubs:* Buck's; Travellers (Paris).

MIRSKY, Prof. Rhona Mary, PhD; Professor of Developmental Neurobiology, University College London, since 1990; *b* 29 May 1939; *d* of Thomas Gibson Pearson and Lynda Pearson (*née* Williams); *m* 1963, Jonathan Mirsky (marr. diss. 1985); partner, Kristján R. Jessen. *Educ:* New Hall, Cambridge (BA 1961; PhD 1964). Biochemistry Department, Dartmouth Medical School, USA: Instr, 1966–69; Asst Prof., 1969–73; Res. Associate (Asst Prof.), 1973–75; University College London: Vis. Scientist, 1974, Associate Res. Fellow, 1975–81, MRC Neuroimmunology Project, Dept of Zoology; Lectr, 1981–85, Reader, 1985–90, Dept of Anatomy and Develtl Biology. Mem., MRC, 1998–2001. FMedSci 2001. *Publications:* numerous papers in scientific jls. *Address:* Department of Anatomy and Developmental Biology, University College London, Gower Street, WC1E 6BT. *T:* (020) 7679 3380.

MIRVISH, Edwin, OC 1987; CBE 1989; *b* 24 July 1914; *s* of David and Anna Mirvish; *m* 1941, Anne Maklin; one *s*. *Educ:* Toronto. Proprietor: Ed Mirvish Enterprises and other cos; Honest Ed's World Famous Bargain Shopping Centre; several restaurants; Royal Alexandra Theatre, Toronto; Old Vic Theatre, 1982–98; Princess of Wales Theatre, Toronto, 1993–. Hon. LLD: Trent Univ., 1967; Univ. of Waterloo, 1969; Fellow, Ryerson Technical Inst., 1981. Freeman, City of London, 1984. Award of Merit, City of Toronto. *Recreation:* ballroom dancing. *Address:* 581 Bloor Street West, Toronto, ON M6G 1K3, Canada. *T:* (416) 5372111. *Clubs:* Empire, Canadian, Arts and Letters, Variety (Toronto).

MIRZOEFF, Edward, CVO 1993; CBE 1997; television director, producer and executive producer; *b* 11 April 1936; *s* of late Eliachar Mirzoeff and of Penina (*née* Asherov); *m* 1961, Judith Topper; three *s*. *Educ:* Hasmonean Grammar Sch.; Queen's Coll., Oxford (Open Scholarship in Mod. History). MA Oxon. Market Researcher, Social Surveys (Gallup Poll) Ltd, 1958–59; Public Relns Exec., Duncan McLeish & Associates, 1960–61; Asst Editor, Shoppers' Guide, 1961–63; with BBC Television, 1963–2000: director and producer of film documentaries incl. (with Sir John Betjeman) Metro-land, 1973, A Passion for Churches, 1974, and The Queen's Realm, 1977; Police – Harrow Road, 1975; The Regiment, 1977; The Front Garden, 1979; The Ritz (BAFTA Award for Best Documentary), 1981; The Englishwoman and The Horse, 1981; Elizabeth R (British Video Award), 1992; Torvill and Dean: facing the music, 1994; Treasures in Trust, 1995; Reputations: John Betjeman–the last laugh, 2001; Series Editor: Bird's-Eye View, 1969–71; Year of the French, 1982–83; In At The Deep End, 1983–84; Just Another Day, 1983–85; Real Lives, 1985; Editor, 40 Minutes, 1985–89 (BAFTA Awards for Best Factual Series, 1985, 1989; Samuelson Award, Birmingham Fest., 1988); Executive Producer: Fire in the Blood, Pandora's Box, 1992; The Ark, 1993; True Brits, 1994; Situation Vacant, 1995; The House, 1996 (Royal Philharmonic Soc. Music Award for Radio, TV and Video, 1996; BPG Award for Best Documentary Series, 1996; Internat. Emmy, 1996); Full Circle with Michael Palin, 1997; The 50 Years War: Israel and the Arabs, 1998; Children's Hospital, 1998–2000; Zoo, 1999–2000; Michael Palin's Hemingway Adventure, 1999; Reputations, 2000; Gold Fever, 2000. Trustee: BAFTA, 1999– (Chm., 1995–97; Vice-Chm., TV, 1991–95); Grierson Meml Trust, 1999–. Dir, Dirs' and Producers' Rights Soc., 1999–. BFI TV Award, 1988; Alan Clarke Award for Outstanding Creative Contribn to Television, BAFTA, 1995. *Recreation:* movies, opera, theatre, classical music, art, mowing lawns. *Address:* 9 Westmoreland Road, SW13 9RZ. *T:* (020) 8748 9247.

MISCAMPBELL, Gillian Margaret Mary, OBE 1982; DL; Chairman, Stoke Mandeville Hospital NHS Trust, 1995–2001; *b* 31 Dec. 1935; *d* of late Brig. Francis William Gibb and Agnes Winifred Gibb; *m* 1958, Alexander Malcolm Miscampbell; three *s*. *Educ:* St Leonard's Sch. Member: Area Manpower Bd, 1985–88; Milton Keynes Develt Corp. Bd, 1990–92. Chm., Aylesbury Vale HA, 1981–93; Mem., Bucks HA, 1993–95. Mem. (C), Bucks CC, 1977–93 (Chm., 1989–93; Chm., Educn Cttee, 1985–89). Chm., Aylesbury Cons. Assoc., 1975–78; Vice Chm., Nat. Women's Adv. Cttee, Cons. Party, 1979–80. University of Buckingham: Mem. Council, 1985– (Vice Chm., 1994–); Chm., F and GP Cttee, 1993–98. Dir, Buckinghamshire Foundn, 1999–. DL Bucks, 1993. DUniv Buckingham, 1998. *Address:* Rosemount, 15 Upper Street, Quainton, Aylesbury, Bucks HP22 4AY. *T:* (01296) 655318.

MISCAMPBELL, Norman Alexander; QC 1974; barrister; a Recorder of the Crown Court, 1977–95; *b* 20 Feb. 1925; *s* of late Alexander and Eileen Miscampbell; *m* 1961, Margaret Kendall; two *s* two *d*. *Educ:* St Edward's Sch., Oxford; Trinity Coll., Oxford. Called to Bar, Inner Temple, 1952, Bencher 1983; N Circuit. Mem., Criminal Injuries Compensation Bd, 1993–2000. Mem., Hoylake UDC, 1955–61. Contested (C) Newton, 1955, 1959; MP (C) Blackpool North, 1962–92. *Address:* 1 Temple Gardens, Temple, EC4Y 9BB.

MISCHLER, Norman Martin; Chairman: Hoechst UK Ltd, 1975–84; Hoechst Ireland Ltd, 1976–84; Berger Jenson & Nicholson Ltd, 1979–84; *b* 9 Oct. 1920; *s* of late Martin Mischler and Martha Sarah (*née* Lambert); *m* 1949, Helen Dora Sinclair; one *s* one *d*. *Educ:* St Paul's Sch., London; St Catharine's Coll., Cambridge (MA). Cricket Blue, 1946. Indian Army, 1940; served in Burma Campaign; released, rank of Major, 1946. Joined Burt, Boulton & Haywood, 1947, Vice-Chm. 1963; Dep. Man. Dir, Hoechst UK Ltd, 1966; Chairman: Harlow Chemical Co. Ltd, 1972–74; Kalle Infotec Ltd, 1972–74; Director: Berger, Jenson & Nicholson Ltd, 1975–84; Ringsdorff Carbon Co. Ltd, 1968–84; Vice-Chm., German Chamber of Industry and Commerce in London, 1974–84; Mem. Council, Chemical Industries Assoc. Ltd, 1975–84. Freeman, City of London. Officer's Cross, German Order of Merit, 1985. *Recreations:* cricket, opera, and theatre. *Address:* Scott House, Earsham Street, Bungay, Suffolk NR35 1AF. *Clubs:* Hawks (Cambridge); Norfolk (Norwich).

MISHCON, family name of **Baron Mishcon**.

MISHCON, Baron *cr* 1978 (Life Peer), of Lambeth in Greater London; **Victor Mishcon;** DL; Solicitor; Senior Partner, Mishcon de Reya (formerly Victor Mishcon & Co.), 1988–92, now Consultant; *b* 14 Aug. 1915; *s* of Rabbi Arnold and Mrs Queenie Mishcon; *m* 1976, Joan Estelle Conrad (marr. diss. 2001); two *s* one *d* by previous marr. *Educ:* City of London Sch. Mem. Lambeth Borough Coun., 1945–49 (Chm. Finance Cttee, 1947–49); Mem. London CC for Brixton, 1946–65 (Chairman: Public Control Cttee, 1947–52; Gen. Purposes Cttee, 1952–54; Council, April 1954–55; Supplies Cttee, 1956–57; Fire Brigade Cttee, 1958–65); Mem. GLC for Lambeth, 1964–67 (Chm., Gen. Purposes Cttee, 1964–67); Mem., ILEA, 1964–67. Member: Jt Cttee with House of Commons on Consolidation of Bills, 1983–85; Law Sub-Cttee, House of Lords European Communities Cttee, 1978–86; House of Lords Select Cttee on Procedure, 1981–83; House of Lords Select Cttee on Med. Ethics, 1993; Opposition spokesman, House of Lords, on home affairs, 1983–90, on legal affairs, 1983–92. Vice Chm., Lords and Commons Solicitors Gp, 1983–. Chm. Governors, Cormont and Loughborough Secondary Schools, 1947–60; Governor: Stockwell Manor Sch., 1960–78 (Chm. of Governors, 1960–67, 1970–78); JFS Comprehensive Sch., 1970–85; Philippa Fawcett Coll. of Educn, 1970–80. Member: Standing Joint Cttee, Co. of London Sessions, 1950–65 (Vice-Chm. 1959–61); Nat. Theatre Board, 1965–67, 1968–90; South Bank Theatre Board, 1977–82; London Orchestra Bd, 1966–67; Exec. Cttee, London Tourist Board, 1965–67; Government Cttee of Enquiry into London Transport, 1953–54; Departmental Cttee on Homosexual Offences and Prostitution, 1954–57. Vice-Chm., Council of Christians and Jews, 1976–77; Vice-Pres., Bd of Deputies of British Jews, 1967–73; Hon. President, Brit. Technion Soc.; Vice-Pres. (Past Pres.) Assoc. of Jewish Youth; Pres., British Council of the Shaare Zedek Hosp., Jerusalem. Contested (Lab) NW Leeds, 1950, Bath, 1951, Gravesend, 1955, 1959. DL Greater London, 1954. Hon. QC 1992. Hon. Fellow, UCL, 1993. Hon. LLD Birmingham, 1991. Comdr Royal Swedish Order of North Star, 1954; Star of Ethiopia, 1954; Star of Jordan, 1995. *Address:* House of Lords, SW1A 0PW.

MISKIN, Charles James Monckton; QC 1998; a Recorder, since 1998; *b* 29 Nov. 1952; *s* of Nigel Monckton Miskin and late Hilda Meryl Miskin (*née* Knight); *m* 1982, Karen Elizabeth Booth (marr. diss. 1995); one *s* three *d*. *Educ:* Charterhouse Sch. (Sutton Prizewinner); Worcester Coll., Oxford (Open Exhibnr; BA Hons Juris. 1974; MA 1978). Called to the Bar, Gray's Inn, 1975; in practice as barrister, 1977–; Mem., S Eastern Circuit; Asst Recorder, 1992–98; Standing Counsel to Inland Revenue, 1993–98. Mem., Criminal Bar Assoc., 1977–. Chm., Bar Theatrical Soc., 1976–. Liveryman: Wax Chandlers' Co., 1975–; Armourers' and Braziers' Co., 1986–. *Recreations:* travel, opera, history, the children, laughter. *Address:* 23 Essex Street, WC2R 3AS. *T:* (020) 7413 0353. *Clubs:* Travellers, Hurlingham.

MISKIN, Raymond John, CEng, FIMechE, FIEE, MRAeS, FIQA; Chief Executive, Certification Authority for Dental Laboratories and Suppliers, 1989–93; *b* 4 July 1928; *s* of late Sydney George Miskin and Hilda (*née* Holdsworth); *m* 1st, 1951 (marr. diss. 1981); one *d* (one *s* decd); 2nd, 1991, Brenda (*née* Mills). *Educ:* Woking Grammar Sch.; Southall Technical Coll. The Fairey Aviation Co. Ltd: apprentice, 1945–49; develt engr, 1949–59; Dep. Chief Inspector, 1959–63; Quality Control Manager and Chief Inspector, Graviner Ltd, 1963–69; Sec., Inst. of Qual. Assurance, 1969–73; Dep. Sec., 1973–76, Sec., 1976–87, IProdE; Dir, IPRODE Ltd, 1976–87. Mem. Council and Hon. Treasurer, Inst. of Qual. Assurance, 1963–69; Mem., Bd, Nat. Council for Qual. and Reliability, 1969–81 (Chm., 1975–77). Hon. Mem., Amer. Inst. of Industrial Engrs, 1985. FSME 1994. Hon. FIIPE 1979. Freeman, City of London, 1985. Internat. Industrial Management Award, San Fernando Valley Engineers Council, USA, 1978; Internat. Achievement Award, Los Angeles Council of Engrs, 1981; GTE (Hungary) Technical Achievement Medal, 1984. *Publications:* articles in technical pubns. *Recreation:* golf. *Address:* 36 Hayes Drive, Mosborough, Sheffield S20 4TR. *Club:* Renishaw Park Golf.

MISSELBROOK, (Bertram) Desmond, CBE 1972; FRSE 1978; Chairman, Livingston Development Corporation, 1972–78; *b* 28 May 1913; *s* of late C. J. and E. P. Misselbrook; *m* 1949, Anne, *er d* of late F. O. Goodman; two *s*. *Educ:* Chatham House, Ramsgate; Bristol Univ. Admiralty Psychologist, 1942–45. Lectr in Psychology and Dir, Unit of Applied Psychology, Edinburgh Univ., 1945–49; Senr Res. Fellow in Business Studies, 1970–71, Hon. Fellow, 1971. Personnel Adviser, 1949, Dir. 1955, Dep. Chm. 1963–70, British-American Tobacco Co. Ltd; Chm., Evershed and Vignoles Ltd, 1961–65; Chm., Mardon Packaging International Ltd, 1962–70; Dir, 1963, Dep. Chm. 1966–69, Wiggins Teape Ltd; Dir, Charterhouse Gp Ltd, 1969–72; Deputy Chairman: Standard Life Assurance Co., 1977–80 (Dir, 1970–84); Anderson Mavor Ltd, 1971–74; Chairman: Anderson Strathclyde Ltd, 1974–77; Seaforth Maritime Ltd, 1977–78. Mem. Council, British Inst. of Management, 1967–72 (a Vice-Chm., 1969); Chairman: Bd of Governors, Oversea Service, 1963–70; Construction Ind. Trng Bd, 1970–73; Council, Scottish Business Sch., 1972–77; Economic Development Cttees for Building and Civil Engineering Industries, 1969–72; Member: Adv. Council on Social Work (Scotland), 1970–74; Economic Consultant, Scottish Office, 1970–72. Hon. DSc Edinburgh, 1977. *Address:* Welton House, Coupar Angus, Blairgowrie, Perthshire PH13 9EY. *T:* (01828) 640577. *Recreations:* fishing, gardening, walking.

MISTRY, Dhruva, RA 1991; sculptor; *b* 1 Jan. 1957; *s* of Pramodray and Kantaben Mistry. *Educ:* Maharaja Sayajirao Univ. of Baroda (MA 1981); RCA (British Council schol.; MA 1983). Artist-in-residence, Kettle's Yard, and Fellow of Churchill Coll., Cambridge, 1984–85; Sculptor-in-residence, V&A Mus., 1988. Rep. Britain at 3rd Rodin Grand Prize Exhibn, Japan, 1990. Works of art for Victoria Square, Birmingham, commnd by Birmingham CC. *Recreations:* photography, reading, walking. *Address:* c/o Anthony Wilkinson Gallery, 242 Cambridge Heath Road, E2 9DA.

MITCHELL, family name of **Baron Mitchell**.

MITCHELL, Baron *cr* 2000 (Life Peer), of Hampstead in the London Borough of Camden; **Parry Andrew Mitchell;** Chairman, Syscap plc, since 1992; *b* 6 May 1943; *s* of Leon and Rose Mitchell; *m* 1st, 1972, Doreen Hargreaves (marr. diss.); one *d*; 2nd, 1988, Hannah Ruth Lowy; two *s* (twins). *Educ:* Christ's Coll., Finchley; Univ. of London (BSc ext.); Columbia Univ., NY (MBA). Chm., United Leasing plc, 1976–87. *Recreations:* fiddling with computers, scuba diving, jazz, opera. *Address:* House of Lords, SW1A 0PW. *T:* (020) 7433 3238; *e-mail:* parrym@mac.com. *Clubs:* Groucho; Players' (New York).

MITCHELL, Adrian; writer; *b* 24 Oct. 1932; *s* of James Mitchell and Kathleen Fabian. *Educ:* Greenways Sch.; Dauntsey's Sch.; Christ Church, Oxford. Worked as reporter on Oxford Mail, Evening Standard, 1955–63; subseq. free-lance journalist for Daily Mail, Sun, Sunday Times, New Statesman; Granada Fellow, Univ. of Lancaster, 1968–69; Fellow, Center for Humanities, Wesleyan Univ., 1972; Resident Writer, Sherman Theatre, Cardiff, 1974–75; Vis. writer, Billericay Comp. Sch., 1978–80; Judith E. Wilson Fellow, Cambridge Univ., 1980–81; Resident writer, Unicorn Theatre for Children, 1982–83; Fellow in Drama, Nanyang Univ., Singapore, 1995; Dylan Thomas Fellow, UK Festival of Literature, 1995. Poetry Editor, New Statesman and Society, 1994–96. FRSL 1987. Hon. DArts N London, 1997. *Plays:* Marat/Sade (stage adaptation), RSC, 1964; Tyger, NT Co. at New Theatre, 1971; Man Friday, 7:84 Theatre Co., 1973 (TV 1972, Screenplay 1975); Mind Your Head, Liverpool Everyman, 1973; Daft as a Brush (TV), 1975; A Seventh Man, Hampstead, 1976; White Suit Blues, Nottingham, Edinburgh and Old Vic, 1977; Houdini, Amsterdam, 1977; Glad Day (TV), 1978; Uppendown Mooney, Welfare State Theatre Co., 1978; The White Deer, Unicorn Theatre, 1978; Hoagy, Bix and Wolfgang Beethoven Bunkhaus, King's Head Theatre, 1979; In the Unlikely Event of an Emergency, Bath, 1979; Peer Gynt (adaptation), Oxford Playhouse, 1980; You Must Believe All This (TV), 1981; The Tragedy of King Real, Welfare State Theatre Co., 1982; Mowgli's Jungle, Contact Theatre, Manchester, 1982; A Child's Christmas in Wales (with Jeremy Brooks), Great Lakes Fest., 1983; The Wild Animal Song Contest, Unicorn Theatre, 1983; Life's a Dream (adaptation with John Barton), RSC Stratford, 1983, Barbican, 1984; C'Mon Everybody, Tricycle Theatre, 1984; The Great Theatre of the World (adaptation), Mediaeval Players, 1984; Satie Day/Night, Lyric Studio, Hammersmith, 1986; Mirandolina (adaptation), Bristol Old Vic, 1987; The Last Wild Wood in Sector 88, Rugby Music Centre, 1987; Anna on Anna, Th. Workshop, Edin., 1988; Woman Overboard, The Patchwork Girl of Oz, Palace Th., Watford, 1988; The Snow Queen, NY, 1990; Vasilisa The Fair (adaptation), NY, 1991; Pieces of Peace (TV), 1991; Unicorn Island, Dartington, 1992; The Blue, Walk the Plank, Fitzcarraldo Theatre Ship, Glasson Dock, Lancs and other UK ports, 1992; A New World and The Tears of the Indians (adaptation), Nuffield Theatre, Southampton, 1992; Meet the Baron, Dartington, 1993; Sir Fool's Quest, Dartington and nat. tour, 1994; Tyger Two, Boston, USA, 1995; Tom Kitten and his Friends, Unicorn Th., 1995; The Siege, Nat. Playwright Commissioning Gp, 1996–97; The Little Violin (adaptation), Tricycle Th., 1998; The Lion, the Witch and the Wardrobe (adaptation), RSC, 1998; Start Again, Morecambe, 1998; Jemima Puddleduck and her Friends, Unicorn Th., 1998; The Heroes (trilogy), Kageboushi Th., Japan, 1999; The Mammoth Sails Tonight, Dream Factory, Warwick, 1999; All Shook Up, Tricycle Th., 2001; Alice in Wonderland (adaptation) RSC, 2001; Peter Rabbit and his Friends, Unicorn Th., 2002; National Theatre: The Mayor of Zalamea (adaptation), 1981; Animal Farm (lyrics), 1984; The Government Inspector, 1985; The Pied Piper, 1986; Love Songs of World War Three, 1987; Fuente Ovejuna (adaptation), 1989; Triple Threat, 1989. *Publications: novels:* If You See Me Comin', 1962; The Bodyguard, 1970; Wartime, 1973; *poetry:* Poems, 1964; Out Loud, 1968; Ride the Nightmare, 1971; The Apeman Cometh, 1975; For Beauty Douglas, (Collected Poems 1953–1979), 1982; On the Beach at Cambridge, 1984; Nothingmas Day, 1984; Love Songs of World War Three, 1988; All My Own Stuff, 1991; Adrian Mitchell's Greatest Hits—The Top Forty, 1991; Blue Coffee, 1996; Heart on the Left, 1997; All Shook Up, 2000; (ed) Blackbird Singing: lyrics and poems of Paul McCartney, 2001; *for children:* The Baron Rides Out, 1985; The Baron on the Island of Cheese, 1986; The Baron All At Sea, 1987; Leonardo the Lion from Nowhere, 1987; Our Mammoth, 1987; Our Mammoth Goes to School, 1987; Our Mammoth in the Snow, 1988; The Pied Piper, 1988; Strawberry Drums, 1989; The Thirteen Secrets of Poetry, 1993; (ed) The Orchard Book of Poems, 1993; Maudie and the Green Children, 1996; Gynormous!, 1996; Balloon Lagoon, 1997; Robin Hood and Marian, 1998; Twice My Size, 1998; My Cat Mrs Christmas, 1998; Nobody Rides the Unicorn, 1999; (ed) Dancing in the Street, 1999; Zoo of Dreams, 2001; (ed) A Poem A Day, 2001; also plays. *Address:* c/o Peters, Fraser and Dunlop, Drury House, 34–43 Russell Street, WC2B 5HA. *Club:* Chelsea Arts.

MITCHELL, Alec Burton, MA; CEng, MIMechE, FRINA; Director, Admiralty Marine Technology Establishment, 1977–84, retired; Scientific Adviser to Director General Ships, Ministry of Defence, 1981–84; *b* 27 Aug. 1924; *er s* of Ronald Johnson Mitchell and Millicent Annie Mitchell; *m* 1952, Barbara, *d* of Arthur Edward and Katie Florence Jane Archer; three *s*. *Educ:* Purley County Sch.; St. John's Coll., Cambridge (MA). Mechanical Sciences Tripos, Cambridge, 1944. Aeronautical Engineer with Rolls Royce Ltd, Hucknall, 1944–46; Grad. apprentice and gas turbine design engr with English Electric Co Ltd, Rugby, 1946–48. Joined RN Scientific Service, 1948; Dep. Head of Hydrodynamic Research Div., Admty Research Lab., 1961; promoted Dep. CSO, 1966; Dep. Dir, Admty Research Laboratory, 1973, Dir, 1974–77. *Publications:* numerous scientific papers on hydrodynamics and under-water propulsion systems. *Recreations:* golf, horology, woodwork. *Address:* 32 Ormond Crescent, Hampton, Mddx TW12 2TH.

MITCHELL, Alexander Graham, CBE 1973; DFM 1945; Governor, Turks and Caicos Islands, 1973–75 (Administrator, 1971–73); *b* 2 Nov. 1923; *s* of Alexander Mitchell and Evelyn Mitchell (*née* Green); *m* 1954, Pamela Ann Borman; three *d*. *Educ:* Dulwich College; Downing Coll., Cambridge (Exhibnr). Served RAF, 1942–45. Sudan Government Civil Service, 1951–55; HM Overseas Civil Service, 1955; Western Pacific High Commission: various posts in British Solomon Islands Protectorate and British Residency, New Hebrides, 1955–71; Sec., Financial Affairs, British Residency, 1968–71; retired June 1977. Clerk to Governors, Dame Allan's Schools, Newcastle, 1977–88. *Recreations:* ancient and military history. *Address:* 2 Corchester Towers, Corbridge, Northumberland NE45 5NP. *Club:* Royal Over-Seas League.

MITCHELL, Andrew John Bower; MP (C) Sutton Coldfield, since 2001; Director, Lazard Brothers & Co. Ltd, since 1997; *b* 23 March 1956; *s* of Sir David Bower Mitchell, *qv*; *m* 1985, Sharon Denise (*née* Bennett); two *d*. *Educ:* Rugby; Jesus Coll., Cambridge (MA History). 1st RTR (Short Service (Limited) Commission), 1975; served with UNFICYP. Pres., Cambridge Union, 1978; Chm., Cambridge Univ. Conservatives, 1977; rep. GB in E-SU American debating tour, 1978. Internat. and Corp. business, Lazard Brothers & Co., 1979–87, Consultant, 1987–92. Senior Strategy Adviser: Boots Co., 1997–2001; Accenture (formerly Andersen Consulting), 1997–. Director: Miller Insce Gp, 1997–2001; Commer Gp, 1998–; Financial Dynamics Holdings, 1998–. Advr to Bd, Hakluyt, 1998–2001. Contested (C) Sunderland South, 1983. MP (C) Gedling, 1987–97; contested (C) same seat, 1997. A Vice-Chm., Cons. Party, with special responsibility for candidates, 1992–93; an Asst Govt Whip, 1992–94; a Lord Comr of HM Treasury (Govt Whip), 1994–95; Parly Under Sec. of State, DSS, 1995–97. Sec., One Nation Gp of Conservative MPs, 1989–92. Chairman: Coningsby Club, 1983; Islington North Conservatives, 1983–85 (Pres., 1996–). Vice-Chm., Alexandra Rose Charity, 1998–. Member Council: SOS Sahel, 1991–; GAP, 2000–. *Recreations:* ski-ing, music, travel. *Address:* 30 Gibson Square, N1 0RD. *T:* (020) 7226 5519; 8 Tudor Road, Sutton Coldfield B73 6BA. *T:* (0121) 355 5519. *Clubs:* Carlton; Cambridge Union Society; Carlton and District Constitutional.

MITCHELL, Andrew Robert; QC 1998; a Recorder, since 1999; *b* 6 Aug. 1954; *s* of late Malcolm Mitchell and of Edna Audrey Mitchell; *m* 1st, 1982, Patricia Ann Fairburn (marr. diss. 1991); 2nd, 1992, Carolyn Ann Blore; one *s* one *d*. *Educ:* Haberdashers' Aske's Sch. Called to the Bar, Gray's Inn, 1976; in practice at the Bar, 1976–; Asst Recorder, 1995–99. Head of Chambers, 1990–. Mem. (C) Haringey LBC, 1984–94 (Leader of the Opposition, 1989–91). Contested (C) Islington S and Finsbury, 1987. Gov., Highgate Primary Sch., 1984–99 (Chm. of Govs, 1997–98). *Publications:* Confiscation and Proceeds of Crime, 1993, 2nd edn 1996; Concise Guide to Criminal Procedure Investigations Act 1996, 1997. *Recreations:* playing tennis, refereeing football, watching football and cricket. *Address:* Furnival Chambers, 32 Furnival Street, EC4A 1JQ. *T:* (020) 7405 3232; *e-mail:* arm@furnivallaw.co.uk. *Clubs:* MCC, Royal Automobile.

MITCHELL, Angelica Elizabeth; Her Honour Judge Angelica Mitchell; a Circuit Judge, since 1998; *b* 21 Aug. 1948; *o d* of Sir George Mitchell, CB, QC (Scot.) and Elizabeth Mitchell (*née* Leigh Pemberton); *m* 1981, (James) Nicholas Browne, *qv*; two *d*. *Educ:* Putney High Sch.; Inns of Court Sch. of Law. Called to the Bar, Gray's Inn, 1972; an Asst Recorder, 1992–95; a Recorder, 1995–98. Mem., Steering Gp Adv. Cttee for Diploma in Forensic Psychotherapy, Portman Clinic, 1998–. Mem. Bd, Hampstead Theatre, 1999–. Trustee, Noel Buxton Trust, 1990–. *Recreations:* reading, opera, watching cricket, theatre, being with my family and friends.

See also F. I. Mitchell.

MITCHELL, Angus; *see* Mitchell, J. A. M.

MITCHELL, Anthony Paul; His Honour Judge Tony Mitchell; a Circuit Judge, since 2000; *b* 9 Aug. 1941; *s* of Arthur Leslie Mitchell and Ivy Muriel Mitchell (*née* Simpson); *m* 1st, 1972, Shirley Ann Donovan (marr. diss. 1985); one *s* one *d*, and one step *s* one step *d*; 2nd, 1989, Julia Fryer (*d* 2000); one step *s* one step *d*. *Educ:* Whitgift Sch., Croydon; Coll. of Law, London. Articled, Routh Stacey & Co.; qualified, 1965; admitted Solicitor, 1966; Partner, Toller Hales Collcutt, 1969–2000; Dep. Dist Judge, 1982–2000; Asst Recorder, 1991–95; Recorder, 1995–2000. *Recreations:* music, theatre, cinema, ballet, Rugby, cricket, motor racing, keeping fit, personal development and things spiritual with a small s. *Address:* c/o The Court Service, Midland Circuit, The Priory Courts, 33 Bull Street, Birmingham B4 6DW. *Club:* Lansdowne.

MITCHELL, Air Cdre Sir (Arthur) Dennis, KBE 1977; CVO 1961; DFC 1944, and Bar, 1945; AFC 1943; Founder and Managing Director, Aero Systems SA, since 1972; an Extra Equerry to the Queen since 1962; *b* 26 May 1918; 2nd *s* of Col A. Mitchell, DSO, Carrickfergus, Belfast, N Ireland, and Dorothy (*née* Mitchell), Rathmelton, Co. Donegal; *m* 1949, Comtesse Mireille Caroline Cornet de Ways Ruart (*d* 1999); one *s*. *Educ:* Nautical Coll., Pangbourne; RAF Coll., Cranwell; Army Staff Coll., Camberley; RAF Flying Coll., Manby. Joined RAF, 1936. Served 1938–45, India, Burma, UK and NW Europe; RAF Delegn, Belgium, 1948–49; US Air Force, 1951–53; HQ Allied Air Forces Central Europe, NATO, Fontainebleau, 1953–56; o/c RAF Cottesmore Bomber Comd, 1959–62; Dep. Captain and Captain of the Queen's Flight, 1956–59 and 1962–64; ADC to the Queen, 1958–62. Founder: Brussels Airways; Aero Distributors SA. French Croix de Guerre, 1945. *Recreation:* golf. *Address:* (office) 10 chemin des Chasseurs, 1380 Ohain, Belgium. *T:* (2) 6522222, *Fax:* (2) 6531517; (home) (2) 6531301. *Clubs:* Royal Air Force, Naval and Military.

MITCHELL, Austin Vernon, DPhil; MP (Lab) Great Grimsby, since 1983 (Grimsby, April 1977–1983); *b* 19 Sept. 1934; *s* of Richard Vernon Mitchell and Ethel Mary Mitchell; *m* 1st, Patricia Dorothea Jackson (marr. diss.); two *d*; 2nd, Linda Mary McDougall; one *s* one *d*. *Educ:* Woodbottom Council Sch.; Bingley Grammar Sch.; Manchester Univ. (BA, MA); Nuffield Coll., Oxford (DPhil). Lectr in History, Univ. of Otago, Dunedin, NZ, 1959–63; Sen. Lectr in Politics, Univ. of Canterbury, Christchurch, NZ, 1963–67; Official Fellow, Nuffield Coll., Oxford, 1967–69; Journalist, Yorkshire Television, 1969–71; Presenter, BBC Current Affairs Gp, 1972–73; Journalist, Yorkshire TV, 1973–77; Co- presenter, Target, Sky TV, 1989–98. PPS to Minister of State for Prices and Consumer Protection, 1977–79; Opposition front bench spokesman on trade and industry, 1987–89. Member, Select Committee: on Treasury and Civil Service, 1983–87; on Agric., 1997–. Mem., OT Prophets. Associate Ed., House Magazine. ONZM 2001. *Publications:* New Zealand Politics In Action, 1962; Government By Party, 1966; The Whigs in Opposition 1815–1830, 1969; Politics and People in New Zealand, 1970; Yorkshire Jokes, 1971; The Half-Gallon Quarter-Acre Pavlova Paradise, 1974; Can Labour Win Again, 1979; Westminster Man, 1982; The Case for Labour, 1983; Four Years in the Death of the Labour Party, 1983; Yorkshire Jokes, 1988; Teach Thissen Tyke, 1988; Britain: beyond the blue horizon, 1989; Competitive Socialism, 1989; Accounting for Change, 1993; Election '45, 1995; Corporate Governance Matters, 1996; The Common Fisheries Policy: end or mend?, 1996; (with David Wienir) Last Time: Labour's lessons from the sixties, 1997; (with Anne Tate) Fishermen: the rise and fall of deep water trawling, 1997; Parliament in Pictures, 1999; Farewell My Lords, 1999. *Recreation:* worriting (*sic*). *Address:* 15 New Cartergate, Grimsby, South Humberside DN31 1RB. *T:* (01472) 342145; House of Commons, SW1A 0AA. *T:* (020) 7219 4559; *e-mail:* austin@austinmitchell.co.uk.

MITCHELL, Prof. Basil George, DD; FBA 1983; Nolloth Professor of the Philosophy of the Christian Religion, Oxford University, 1968–84; Fellow of Oriel College, 1968–84, now Emeritus; *b* 9 April 1917; *s* of George William Mitchell and Mary Mitchell (*née* Loxston); *m* 1950, Margaret Eleanor Collin; one *s* three *d*. *Educ:* King Edward VI Sch., Southampton; Queen's Coll., Oxford (Southampton Exhibitioner. 1st cl. Lit Hum 1939). Served Royal Navy, 1940–46; Lt RNVR 1942, Instructor Lt RN 1945. Lectr, Christ Church, Oxford, 1946–47; Fellow and Tutor in Philosophy, Keble Coll., Oxford, 1947–67, Emeritus Fellow, 1981; Sen. Proctor, 1956–57; Hebdomadal Council, 1959–65. Visiting Professor: Princeton Univ., 1963; Colgate Univ., 1976. Lectures: Stanton, in Philosophy of Religion, Cambridge Univ., 1959–62; Edward Cadbury, University of Birmingham, 1966–67; Gifford, Glasgow Univ., 1974–76; Nathaniel Taylor, Yale, 1986; Martin, Univ. of Hong Kong, 1987; Norton, Southern Baptist Theol Seminary, Louisville, 1989; Sarum, Oxford Univ., 1992. Member: C of E Working Parties on Ethical Questions, 1964–78; Doctrine Commn, 1978–84. Hon. DD Glasgow, 1977; Hon. DLitHum Union Coll., Schenectady, 1979. *Publications:* (ed) Faith and Logic, 1957; Law, Morality and Religion in a Secular Society, 1967; Neutrality and Commitment, 1968; (ed) The Philosophy of Religion, 1971; The Justification of Religious Belief, 1973; Morality: Religious and Secular, 1980; How to Play Theological Ping Pong, 1990; Faith and Criticism, 1994; articles in philosophical and theological periodicals. *Recreations:*

gardening, flower arrangement. *Address:* Bartholomew House, 9 Market Street, Woodstock, Oxford OX20 1SU. *T:* (01993) 811265.

MITCHELL, Bob; *see* Mitchell, R. C.

MITCHELL, Bryan James; Head of Cabinet Executive, National Assembly for Wales, since 2000; *b* 1 March 1945; *s* of Herbert Mitchell and Hilda (*née* Grant); *m* (marr. diss.); four *d. Educ:* Robert Clack Technical Sch., Dagenham; Open Univ. (BA). MoT, 1967–74; CSD, 1974–76; DoE, 1976–78; Welsh Office, 1978–86; acting Chief Exec., Cardiff Bay Develt Corp., 1987 (on secondment); Welsh Office, 1988–98; National Assembly for Wales: Project Leader, Office of Presiding Officer and Dep. Clerk, 1998–99; Dir, Personnel and Business Services Gp, 1999–2000. *Address:* c/o National Assembly for Wales, Cardiff Bay, Cardiff CF99 1NA. *T:* (029) 2089 8792.

MITCHELL, Charles Julian Humphrey; *see* Mitchell, Julian.

MITCHELL, Charlotte; Director, Go Organic Ltd, since 1998; organic food consultant, Waitrose plc, since 1998; *b* 3 May 1953; *d* of Dr (John) Angus (Macbeth) Mitchell, *qv* and Ann Katharine (*née* Williamson); *m* 1972 (marr. diss. 2000); one *s* one *d*; partner, Paul Southall. *Educ:* St George's Sch. for Girls, Edinburgh; Birmingham Coll. of Art (DipAD 1974); Dip Wine and Spirits 1991. Exhibn organiser, Scottish Craft Centre, 1974–76; Dir, Real Foods Ltd, 1976–97. Trustee, 1987–, Chm., 1990–97, Soil Assoc. Hon. Mem., BBC Scotland Adv. Council for Rural and Agricl Affairs, 1994–98. *Publication:* The Organic Wine Guide, 1987. *Recreations:* talking, eating, wine. *Address:* 10 Craigleith Gardens, Edinburgh EH4 3JW. *T:* (0131) 332 6421, *Fax:* (0131) 343 1988; *e-mail:* organix@globalnet.co.uk.

See also J. J. Mitchell.

MITCHELL, Sir David (Bower), Kt 1988; DL; *b* June 1928; *er s* of James Mitchell, Naval Architect; *m* 1954, Pamela Elaine Haward (separated); two *s* one *d. Educ:* Aldenham. Farming, 1945–50; businessman, wine merchant, 1951–79. Chm., El Vino Co. Ltd, 1992–. MP (C) Basingstoke, 1964–83, Hampshire North West, 1983–97. An Opposition Whip, 1965–67; PPS to Sec. of State for Social Services, 1970–74; Parly Under Sec. of State, DoI, 1979–81, NI Office, 1981–83, Dept of Transport, 1983–85; Minister of State for Transport, 1986–88. Chm., Cons. Parly Smaller Business Cttee, 1974–79. Founder, 1976, Trustee Mem., 1989–, Small Business Bureau. DL Hants, 1994. *Recreations:* gardening, walking, wine-tasting, travel. *Club:* Carlton.

See also A. J. B. Mitchell.

MITCHELL, David William, CBE 1983; Chairman, Cumbernauld New Town Development Corporation, 1987–97; *b* 4 Jan. 1933; *m* 1965, Lynda Katherine Marion Guy; one *d. Educ:* Merchiston Castle School, Edinburgh. Nat. Service, 1950–52 (commnd RSF; seconded to 4th Nigerian Regt, RWAFF). Western RHB, 1968–75; Jt Man. Dir, M & N Norman (Timber) Ltd, 1992–; Director: Mallinson, Denny (Scotland), 1975–89; Hunter Timber (Scotland), 1989–92. Member: Exec. Cttee, Scottish Council Develt and Industry, 1979–95; Scottish Council, CBI, 1980–85; Scottish Exec. Cttee, Inst. of Directors, 1984–91. President: Timber Trade Benevolent Soc., 1974; Scottish Timber Trade Assoc., 1984. Pres., Scottish Cons. and Unionist Assoc., 1980–82; Treasurer, Scottish Cons. Party, 1990–93, 1998–. Gov., Craighalbert Centre for Children with Motor Neurone Disease, 1992–95. *Recreations:* golf, shooting, fishing. *Address:* Dunmullin House, Blanefield, Stirlingshire G63 9AJ. *T:* (01360) 770885. *Clubs:* Western (Glasgow); Royal and Ancient Golf, Prestwick Golf; Queen's Park Football.

MITCHELL, Sir Dennis; *see* Mitchell, Sir A. D.

MITCHELL, Sir Derek (Jack), KCB 1974 (CB 1967); CVO 1966; Second Permanent Secretary (Overseas Finance), HM Treasury, 1973–77; *b* 5 March 1922; *s* of late Sidney Mitchell, Schoolmaster, and Gladys Mitchell; *m* 1944, Miriam (*d* 1993), *d* of late F. E. Jackson; one *s* two *d. Educ:* St Paul's Sch.; Christ Church, Oxford. Served War of 1939–45: Royal Armoured Corps and HQ London District, 1942–45. Asst Principal HM Treasury, 1947; Private Sec. to Economic Sec., 1948–49; Private Sec. to Permanent Sec. and Official Head of Civil Service (Sir Edward Bridges), 1954–56; Principal Private Secretary to: Chancellor of Exchequer (Mr Reginald Maudling), 1962–63; The Prime Minister (Mr Harold Wilson, previously Sir Alec Douglas-Home), 1964–66; Under-Sec., 1964; Dep. Under-Sec. of State, DEA, 1966–67; Dep. Sec., MAFF, 1967–69; Economic Minister and Head of UK Treasury and Supply Delegn, Washington, (also UK Exec. Dir for IMF and IBRD), 1969–72. Director: Guinness Mahon & Co., 1977–78; Bowater Corp., 1979–84; Bowater Industries, 1984–89; Bowater Inc., 1984–93; Standard Chartered, 1979–89; Indep. Dir, The Observer Ltd, 1981–93; Sen. Advr, Shearson Lehman Brothers Internat., 1979–88; Chm., Jocelyn Burton Silversmith & Goldsmith Ltd, 1991–98. Mem., PLA, 1979–82. Dir, Peter Hall Production Co. Ltd, 1989–90; Mem. Bd, NT, then RNT, 1977–95; Chm., Royal Nat. Theatre Foundn, 1989– (Treas., 1982–89); Bd Mem., French Theatre Season, London 1997, 1996–99. Mem. Council, University Coll. London, 1978–82; Governing Trustee, Nuffield Trust (formerly Nuffield Provincial Hospitals Trust), 1978–98; Trustee, Royal Nat. Theatre Endowment Fund, 1990–2000. *Recreations:* opera, theatre, music, travel, motoring on minor roads. *Address:* 9 Holmbush Road, Putney, SW15 3LE. *T:* (020) 8788 6581. *Club:* Garrick.

MITCHELL, Donald Charles Peter, CBE 2000; PhD; musicologist; Life President and Director, Britten Estate Ltd, since 2000 (Chairman, 1986–2000); Trustee, Britten-Pears Foundation, 1986–2000, now Trustee Emeritus; *b* 6 Feb. 1925; *s* of Frederick George Mitchell and Kathleen Mary Mitchell (*née* Charles); *m* 1956, Kathleen Livingston (*née* Burbidge); one step *s* and two foster *s. Educ:* Brightlands Prep Sch.; Dulwich Coll.; Univ. of Durham (1949–50); Univ. of Southampton (PhD 1977). Advisory Reader (new fiction), Gainsborough Pictures (1928) Ltd, 1942–43; Non-Combatant Corps, 1943–45; Asst Master, Oakfield Sch., London, 1946–48; Founding Editor, Music Survey, 1947, Jt Editor, 1949–52; Music Critic: Musical Times, 1953–57; Musical Opinion, 1953–57; Head of Music Dept, Faber & Faber, 1958; Editor, Tempo, 1958–62; Music Staff, Daily Telegraph, 1959–64; Music Advr, Boosey & Hawkes, 1963–64; Music Critic, Listener, 1964; Man. Dir, Faber Music, 1965–71 (Chm., 1977–86, Pres., 1988–95); founding Prof. of Music, Univ. of Sussex, 1971–76; Executor, Benjamin Britten's estate, 1976. Guest Artistic Dir, Aldeburgh Fest., 1991. Visiting Professor of Music: Univ. of Sussex, 1977; Univ. of York, 1991; KCL, 1995–99; Hon. Res. Fellow, RCM, 2000–. Britten-Pears School for Advanced Musical Studies: Chm., Educn Cttee, 1976; Dir of Study Courses, 1977; Dir of Academic Studies, 1977–90; Hon. Dir, 1995. Director: Performing Right Soc., 1973 (Jt Dep. Chm., 1987–89, Chm., 1989–92, Hon. Mem. Council, 1992); Music Copyright (Overseas) Services Ltd, 1977–92; English Music Theatre, 1973; Nexus Opera, 1986–91; Chm. Exec. Cttee, Mahler Fest., Concertgebouw, Amsterdam, 1995. Member: BBC Central Music Adv. Council, 1967; Council, Aldeburgh Foundn, 1977–94; Adv. Bd, Musical Quarterly, NY, 1985; Adv. Bd, Kurt Weill Edition, NY, 1992; Editl Bd, Muziek & Wetenschap, 1997–. Vice-Pres., CISAC, 1992–94. Gov., 1988, Council of Honour, 2000–, RAM; Gov., NYO, 1989–90. Gustav Mahler Medal of Honor, Bruckner Soc., USA, 1961; Gustav Mahler Medal of Honour, Vienna, 1987; Royal Philharmonic Soc. Award, 1992; Univ. of Toronto Distinguished Visitor Award, 1999. *Publications:* (jtly) Benjamin Britten: a commentary on his works, 1952, 2nd edn 1972; (jtly) The Mozart Companion, 1956, 2nd edn 1965; Gustav Mahler: the early years, 1958, 3rd edn 1995; The Language of Modern Music, 1963, 4th edn 1993; Alma Mahler: Gustav Mahler Memories and Letters, 1968, (jtly) 4th edn 1990; (jtly) The Faber Book of Nursery Songs, 1968; (jtly) The Faber Book of Children's Songs, 1970; Gustav Mahler: the Wunderhorn years, 1975, 2nd edn, 1995; (jtly) Benjamin Britten: pictures from a life 1913–1976, 1978; Britten and Auden in the Thirties: the year 1936, (T. S. Eliot Meml Lectures), 1981; Gustav Mahler: songs and symphonies of life and death, 1985; Benjamin Britten: Death in Venice, 1987; (jtly) Letters from a Life: selected letters and diaries of Benjamin Britten, vols 1 and 2, 1991; Cradles of the New: writings on music 1951–1991, ed Mervyn Cooke, 1995; Gustav Mahler: the world listens, 1995; (jtly) Mahler's Seventh Symphony, facsimile edn 1995; (ed) New Sounds, New Century: Mahler's Fifth Symphony and the Royal Concertgebouw Orchestra, 1997; (jtly) The Mahler Companion, 1999; articles in jls. *Recreations:* travelling, reading, cooking, collecting pottery and paintings, studying the classical music of Thailand. *Address:* 83 Ridgmount Gardens, Torrington Place, WC1E 7AY. *T:* (020) 7580 1241, *Fax:* (020) 7436 7964; Chapel House, Chapel Lane, Horham, Eye, Suffolk IP21 5ES. *T:* (01379) 384242, *Fax:* (01379) 384130. *Club:* Garrick.

MITCHELL, Douglas Svärd; Controller of Personnel and Administrative Services, Greater London Council, 1972–78; *b* 21 Aug. 1918; *er s* of late James Livingstone Mitchell and Hilma Josefine (*née* Svärd); *m* 1943, Winifred Thornton Paterson, *d* of late William and Ellen Paterson; one *s* two *d. Educ:* Morgan Academy, Dundee. Royal Ordnance Factories, 1937–51; Principal, Min. of Supply, 1951–55; Dir of Personnel and Admin., in Industrial, Production and Engineering Groups, UKAEA, 1955–63; Authority Personnel Officer for UKAEA, 1963–64; Dir of Establishments, GLC, 1964–72. *Address:* The Manor House, Horncastle, Lincolnshire LN9 5HF. *T:* (01507) 523553.

MITCHELL, Sir (Edgar) William (John), Kt 1990; CBE 1976; FRS 1986; Fellow of Wadham College, Oxford, 1978–92, now Emeritus Fellow; *b* Kingsbridge, S Devon, 25 Sept. 1925; *s* of late Edgar and Caroline Mitchell; *m* 1985, Prof. Margaret Davies (*née* Brown); one *s* by previous *m. Educ:* Univs of Sheffield (BSc, MSc) and Bristol (PhD). FInstP. Metropolitan Vickers Research Dept, 1946–48, 1950–51; Univ. of Bristol, 1948–50; University of Reading, 1951–78: Prof. of Physics, 1961–78; Dean, Faculty of Science, 1966–69; Dep. Vice-Chancellor, 1976–78; University of Oxford: Dr Lee's Prof. of Experimental Philosophy, 1978–88; Prof of Physics, 1988–89. Science and Engineering Research Council (formerly Science Research Council): Mem., 1970–74, 1982–85; Chm., 1985–90; Mem., 1965–70, Chm., 1967–70, Physics Cttee; Chm., Neutron Beam Res. Cttee, 1966–74 (devised scheme for extensive University use of nuclear res. reactors for condensed matter res.); Mem., Sci. Planning Gp for Spallation Neutron Source, 1978–85; Mem., Sci. Bd (formerly Univ. Sci. and Tech. Bd), 1967–70; Mem., Nuclear Physics Bd, 1980–85. Mem., Management Bd, British National Space Centre, 1986–90. Acting Jt Dir, 1973, Mem., 1973–80, Sci. Council of Inst. Laue-Langevin, Grenoble; Member: Comité de Direction, Solid State Physics Lab., Ecole Normale and Univ. of Paris VI, 1975–79; Exec. Cttee, Univ. Council for Non-Academic Staff, 1979–82; UGC Phys. Sci. Cttee, 1982–85; Council, Inst. of Physics, 1982–86; ABRC, 1985–90; Council, Foundn of Sci. and Technol., 1985–90; Innovation Adv. Bd, DTI, 1988–90; Scientific Adv. Cttee for Nat. Gall., 1988–; Chm., SE Reg. Computing Cttee, 1974–76; Vice-Pres., European Sci. Foundn, 1989–92; Member: Council, CERN, 1985–93 (Vice-Pres., 1990; Pres., 1991–93); CODEST, EEC, 1991–94; ESTA, EU, 1994–97. Mem., Academia Europaea, 1989 (Chm., Physics Section, 1994–96). Hon. DSc: Reading, 1987; Kent, 1988; Budapest, 1988; Birmingham, 1990. Glazebrook Medal, Inst. of Physics, 1995. Officer's Cross, Order of Merit (Germany), 1990. *Publications:* numerous papers on solid state physics. *Recreations:* good food, opera, motoring, physics. *Address:* Wadham College, Oxford OX1 3PN.

MITCHELL, Ewan; *see* Janner, Hon. G. E.

MITCHELL, Fergus Irvine; His Honour Judge Fergus Mitchell; a Circuit Judge, since 1996; *b* 30 March 1947; *s* of Sir George Irvine Mitchell, CB, QC (Scot.) and Elizabeth Mitchell (*née* Leigh Pemberton), JP; *m* 1972, Sally Maureen, *yr d* of Sir Derrick Capper, QPM and Muriel Capper; one *s* one *d. Educ:* Tiffin Boys' Sch., Kingston-upon-Thames. Called to the Bar, Gray's Inn, 1971; Asst Recorder, 1989; Recorder, 1993. Member: Gen. Council of the Bar, 1992–95; Professional Conduct Cttee, 1993–95; Bar Race Relations Cttee, 1994–95. *Recreations:* farm in Aveyron, France, opera. *Address:* Kingston-upon-Thames Crown Court, 6–8 Penrhyn Road, Kingston-upon-Thames, Surrey KT1 2BB.

See also A. E. Mitchell.

MITCHELL, Rear-Adm. Geoffrey Charles, CB 1973; retired 1975; Director, The Old Granary Art and Craft Centre, Bishop's Waltham, Hants, 1975–86; *b* 21 July 1921; *s* of William C. Mitchell; *m* 1st, 1955, Jocelyn Rainger (*d* 1987), Auckland, NZ; one *s* two *d*; 2nd, 1990, Dr Hilary Gardiner. *Educ:* Marlborough College. Joined RN 1940; Captain 1961; Director Officer Recruiting, 1961–63; Captain (F), 2nd Frigate Sqdn, 1963–65; Director Naval Ops and Trade, 1965–67; Comdr, NATO Standing Naval Force Atlantic, 1968–69; Director Strategic Policy, to Supreme Allied Comdr Atlantic, 1969–71; Rear Adm. 1971; Dep. Asst Chief of Staff (Ops), SHAPE, 1971–74; Chm., RNR and Naval Cadet Forces Review Bd, 1974–75. *Recreations:* golf, painting, music, languages, sailing. *Address:* 10 Nelson Close, Stockbridge, Hants SO20 6ES. *T:* (01264) 810365.

MITCHELL, Hon. George John, Hon. GBE 1999; lawyer; *b* 20 Aug. 1933; *s* of George and Mary Mitchell; *m* 1959, Sally L. Heath (marr. diss.); one *d*; *m* 1994, Heather MacLachlan; one *s. Educ:* Bowdoin Coll. (BA 1954); Georgetown Univ. (LLB 1960). Served US Army, 1954–56 (1st Lieut). Admitted to Bar of Maine and of Washington, 1960, to DC Bar, 1960; Trial Attorney, Anti-Trust Div., Dept of Justice, Washington, 1960–62; Exec. Asst to Senator Edmund Muskie, 1962–65; Partner, Jensen, Baird, Gardner, Donovan & Henry, Portland, 1965–77; US Attorney, Maine, 1977–79; US Dist Judge, N Maine, 1979–80; US Senator (Democrat) from Maine, 1980–95; Majority Leader, US Senate, 1988–95. Chm., Irish Peace Talks, 1995–98. Chancellor, QUB, 1999–. Hd, Internat. Adv. Council, Thames Water, 1999–. Hon. LLD QUB, 1997. Presidential Medal of Freedom (USA), 1999. *Publications:* (jtly) Men of Zeal: a candid inside story of the Iran-Contra Hearings, 1988; Making Peace, 1999. *Address:* c/o Verner, Liipfert, Bernhard, 901 15th Street NW #700, Washington, DC 20005, USA. *T:* (202) 3716155.

MITCHELL, Gregory Charles Mathew; QC 1997; PhD; a Recorder, since 2000; *b* 27 July 1954; *s* of John Matthew Mitchell, *qv*; two *s. Educ:* King's Coll., London (BA Hons; PhD); City Univ. (Dip. Law). Called to the Bar, Gray's Inn, 1979. *Recreations:* ski-ing, scuba diving, tennis. *Address:* 3 Verulam Buildings, Gray's Inn, WC1R 5NT. *T:* (020) 7831 8441.

MITCHELL, Harry; QC 1987; Company Secretary, The Wellcome Foundation Ltd, 1976–92, and Wellcome plc, 1985–92; *b* 27 Oct. 1930; *s* of Harry and Lily Mitchell; *m*

1960, Mrs Megan Knill (*née* Watkins); one step *s* one step *d. Educ:* Bolton School; Corpus Christi College, Cambridge (BA). FCIS. Called to the Bar, Gray's Inn, 1968. Asst District Comr, Colonial Service, Sierra Leone, 1954–59; Company Sec., Asbestos Cement, Bombay, 1960–64; Asst Company Sec., British Aluminium Co., 1964–66; Legal Manager/Exec. Dir Legal, Hawker Siddeley Aviation, 1966–76. Chm., Bar Assoc. for Commerce, Finance and Industry, 1984–85 (Vice-Pres., 1986–); Mem. Senate of Inns of Court and Bar and Bar Council, 1978–81, 1983–86; Part-time Immigration Adjudicator, 1992–. Mem., CBI London Regional Council, 1990–92. Mem. Bd, 1994–, Chm., 1995–, Sarsen Housing Assoc., Devizes. Trustee, Migraine Trust, 1995–. *Publications:* articles in New Law Jl and Business Law Review. *Recreations:* playing piano, opera, reading, travel. *Address:* c/o Immigration Appeals, York House, Dukes Green Avenue, Feltham, Middx TW14 0LR. *T:* (020) 8893 1000.

MITCHELL, Helen Josephine, (Mrs Michael Mitchell); *see* Watts, H. J.

MITCHELL, Iain Grant; QC (Scot) 1992; Vice-Chairman: Scottish Lawyers' European Group, since 1998; Scottish Society for Computers and Law, since 2001; *b* 15 Nov. 1951; *s* of late John Grant Mitchell and Isobel (*née* Gilhespie). *Educ:* Perth Acad.; Edinburgh Univ. (LLB Hons 1973). Called to the Scottish Bar, 1976; Temp. Sheriff, 1992–97. Chm., IT Gp, Faculty of Advocates, 1999–; Vice-Chm., Scottish Gp, Soc. for Computers and Law, 1999–2001. Exec. Ed., Scottish Parlt Law Rev., 1999–. Cons. local govt cand. on various occasions, 1973–82; contested (C): Falkirk W, 1983; Kirkcaldy, 1987; Cumbernauld and Kilsyth, 1992; Dunfermline East, 1997; Dundee E, Scottish Parlt, 1999; Scotland, EP elecns, 1999. Edinburgh North & Leith, 2001. Hon. Secretary: Scottish Cons. & Unionist Assoc., 1993–98; Scottish Cons. & Unionist Party, 1998–; Vice-Chm., Edinburgh Central Cons. Assoc., 1994–. Member, Executive Committee: Scottish Council, European Movement, 1992–; Perth Civic Trust, 1999–. Chm., Trust for an Internat. Opera Theatre of Scotland, 1984–; Dir, Scottish Baroque Ensemble Ltd, (Chm., 1999–2001); Trustee, Perthshire Public Arts Trust, 2000–. FSA (Scot) 1974; FRSA 1988. *Recreations:* music and the arts, photography, cinema, walking, travel, finding enough hours in the day. *Address:* Advocates' Library, Parliament House, High Street, Edinburgh EH1 1RF. *T:* (0131) 226 5071.

MITCHELL, James; writer these many years; *b* South Shields, 12 March 1926; *s* of James Mitchell and Wilhelmina Mitchell; *m* 1968, Delia, *d* of Major and Mrs K. J. McCoy; two *s. Educ:* South Shields Grammar Sch.; St Edmund Hall, Oxford (BA 1948, MA 1950); King's Coll., Newcastle upon Tyne, Univ. of Durham (DipEd 1950). Worked in rep. theatre, 1948, then in shipyard, travel agency and Civil Service; taught for some fifteen years in almost every kind of instn from secondary modern sch. to coll. of art. Free-lance writer: novels; more than a hundred television scripts; several screenplays and a theatre play. *Publications:* Here's a Villain, 1957; A Way Back, 1959; Steady Boys, Steady, 1960; Among Arabian Sands, 1963; The Man Who Sold Death, 1964; Die Rich, Die Happy, 1965; The Money that Money can't Buy, 1967; The Innocent Bystanders, 1969; Ilion like a Mist, 1969; A Magnum for Schneider, 1969; The Winners, 1970; Russian Roulette, 1973; Death and Bright Water, 1974; Smear Job, 1975; When the Boat Comes In, 1976; The Hungry Years, 1976; Upwards and Onwards, 1977; The Evil Ones, 1982; Sometimes You Could Die, 1985; Dead Ernest, 1986; Dying Day, 1988; A Woman To Be Loved, 1990; An Impossible Woman, 1992; Leading Lady, 1993; So Far from Home, 1995; Indian Summer, 1996; Dance For Joy, 1997. *Recreations:* travel, military history, aristology. *Club:* Lansdowne.

MITCHELL, James; Social Security Commissioner, 1980–95; a Child Support Commissioner, 1993–95; *b* 11 June 1926; *s* of James Hill Mitchell and Marjorie Kate Mitchell (*née* Williams); *m* 1957, Diane Iris Mackintosh; two *d. Educ:* Merchiston Castle Sch., Edinburgh; Brasenose Coll., Oxford, 1944–45 and 1948–51 (Open Exhibnr, BCL, MA). Served RAFVR, 1945–48. Assistant Master, Edge Grove Preparatory Sch., Herts, 1952–55; called to the Bar, Middle Temple, 1954; private practice as barrister/solicitor, Gold Coast/Ghana, 1956–58; practice as barrister, London, 1958–80. Most Hon. Order of Crown of Brunei, 3rd Cl. 1959, 2nd Cl. 1972. *Recreations:* sailing, walking, railways, the Jacobites.

MITCHELL, Rt Hon. Sir James (Fitz Allen), KCMG 1995; PC 1985; Prime Minister of St Vincent and the Grenadines, 1984–2000; *b* 15 May 1931; *s* of Reginald and Lois Mitchell; *m* (marr. diss.); four *d. Educ:* Imperial College of Tropical Agriculture (DICTA); University of British Columbia (BSA). MIBiol 1965. Agronomist, 1958–65; owner, Hotel Frangipani, Bequia, 1966–, and other cos. MP for Grenadines, 1966–2001; Minister of Trade, Agriculture and Tourism, 1967–72; Premier, 1972–74; Minister of Foreign Affairs, 1984–92; Minister of Finance, 1984–98. Founder and Pres., New Democratic Party, 1975–; Chm., Caribbean Democrat Union, 1991–; Vice-Chm., Internat. Democrat Union, 1992–; Chm., Caribbean Community, 2000. Alumni Award of Distinction, Univ. of BC, 1988. Chevalier d'honneur, Chaîne des Rôtisseurs, 1995. Order of the Liberator (Venezuela), 1972; Order of Propitious Clouds (Taiwan), 1995; Gran Cruz, Order of Infante Dom Henrique (Portugal), 1997; Grand Cross, Order of Knights of Malta, 1998. *Publications:* World Fungicide Usage, 1967; Caribbean Crusade, 1989; Guiding Change in the Islands, 1996; A Season of Light, 2001. *Recreations:* gardening, sailing. *Address:* Bequia, St Vincent, West Indies. *T:* 4573602. *Clubs:* St Vincent Nat. Trust; Bequia Sailing.

MITCHELL, (James Lachlan) Martin, RD 1969; Sheriff of Lothian and Borders (formerly Lothians and Peebles), 1974–95 (as a floating Sheriff, 1974–78, and at Edinburgh, 1978–95); *b* 13 June 1929; *o s* of late Dr L. M. V. Mitchell, OBE, MB, ChB and Harriet Doris Riggall; *m* 1993, Jane Anne, *d* of late Patrick Clement Cox. *Educ:* Cargilfield; Sedbergh; Univ. of Edinburgh. MA 1951, LLB 1953. Admitted Mem. Faculty of Advocates, 1957, in practice, 1957–74; Standing Junior Counsel in Scotland to Admty Bd, 1963–74; Temp. Sheriff, 1971–75 and 1995–98. Hon. Sheriff, Inverness, 1983. Nat. Service, RN, 1954–55; Sub-Lt (S) RNVR 1954; Perm. Reserve, 1956; Comdr RNR 1966, retd 1974. Chm., Lothian Allelon, 1978–2001; Mem. Exec. Cttee, 1978–87, Mem. Main Bd, 1987–88, Scottish Council for Spastics. Gov., Cargilfield Sch., 1966–91. *Recreations:* fishing, photography, listening to music. *Address:* 8 St Colme Street, Edinburgh EH3 6AA. *T:* (0131) 225 3384. *Club:* New (Edinburgh).

MITCHELL, Jeremy George Swale Hamilton; consumer policy adviser; *b* 25 May 1929; *s* of late George Oswald Mitchell and late Agnes Josephine Mitchell; *m* 1st, 1956, Margaret Mary Ayres (marr. diss. 1988); three *s* one *d*; 2nd, 1989, Janet Rosemary Powney. *Educ:* Ampleforth; Brasenose and Nuffield Colls, Oxford (MA). Dep. Research Dir, then Dir of Information, Consumers' Assoc. (Which?), 1958–65; Asst Sec., Nat. Econ. Develt Office, 1965–66; Scientific Sec., then Sec., SSRC, 1966–74; Under Sec., and Dir of Consumer Affairs, Office of Fair Trading, 1974–77; Under Sec. and Dir, Nat. Consumer Council, 1977–86. Member: Economic Develt Cttee for the Distributive Trades, 1981–86; Independent Cttee for Supervision of Telephone Information Services, 1989–97; Direct Mail Services Standards Bd, 1990–95; Bd, PIA, 1994–2000; Scottish Consumer Council, 1995–2000; Vice-Chm., Nat. Council on Gambling, 1981–; Chm., Scottish Adv. Cttee on Telecommunications, 1998–; Comr for Scotland, Broadcasting Standards Commn, 1999–2000. *Publications:* (ed) SSRC Reviews of Research, series, 1968–73; (ed jtly) Social Science Research and Industry, 1971; Betting, 1972; (ed) Marketing and the Consumer Movement, 1978; (ed jtly) The Information Society, 1985; (ed) Money and the Consumer, 1988; Electronic Banking and the Consumer, 1988; The Consumer and Financial Services, 1990; Banker's Racket or Consumer Benefit?, 1991; (ed jtly) Television and the Viewer Interest, 1994. *Recreation:* Swinburne. *Address:* 19 Eglinton Crescent, Edinburgh EH12 5BY.

MITCHELL, Prof. Joan Eileen, (Mrs James Cattermole); Professor of Political Economy, University of Nottingham, 1978–85; *b* 15 March 1920; *d* of late Albert Henry Mitchell, Paper Merchant, and Eva Mitchell; *m* 1956, James Cattermole; one *s* one *d. Educ:* Southend-on-Sea High Sch.; St Hilda's Coll., Oxford. Economist, Min. of Fuel and Power, 1942; Tutor, St Anne's Coll., Oxford, 1945; Economist, BoT, 1947; Research Officer, Labour Party, 1950; Lectr in Econs, Nottingham Univ., 1952, Reader in Econs, 1962. Mem., NBPI, 1965–68; personal economic adviser to Sec. of State for Prices and Consumer Protection, 1974–76. Member: Cttee to Review the Functioning of Financial Institutions, 1977–80 (Chm. Res. Panel); Standing Commn on Pay Comparability, 1979–81. *Publications:* Britain in Crisis 1951, 1963; Groundwork to Economic Planning, 1966; The National Board for Prices and Incomes, 1972; Price Determination and Prices Policy, 1978. *Recreations:* gardening, cooking. *Address:* 15 Ranmoor Road, Gedling, Nottingham NG4 3FW.

MITCHELL, (John) Angus (Macbeth), CB 1979; CVO 1961; MC 1946; Secretary, Scottish Education Department, 1976–84; *b* 25 Aug. 1924; *s* of late John Fowler Mitchell, CIE and Sheila Macbeth, MBE; *m* 1948, Ann Katharine Williamson, MA, MPhil, author; two *s* two *d. Educ:* Marlborough Coll.; Brasenose Coll., Oxford (Junior Hulme Scholar); BA Modern Hist., 1948. Served Royal Armoured Corps, 1943–46: Lieut, Inns of Court Regt, NW Europe, 1944–45; Captain East African Military Records, 1946. Entered Scottish Education Dept, 1949; Private Sec. to Sec. of State for Scotland, 1958–59; Asst Sec., Scottish Educn Dept, 1959–65; Dept of Agriculture and Fisheries for Scotland, 1965–68; Scottish Development Dept, 1968; Asst Under-Secretary of State, Scottish Office, 1968–69; Under Sec., Social Work Services Gp, Scottish Educn Dept, 1969–75; Under Sec., SHHD, 1975–76. Chairman: Scottish Marriage Guidance Council, 1965–69; Working Party on Social Work Services in NHS, 1976; Working Party on Relationships between Health Bds and Local Authorities, 1976; Consultative Cttee on the Curriculum, 1976–80; Stirling Univ. Court, 1984–92; Scottish Action on Dementia, 1985–94; Vice-Convener, Scottish Council for Voluntary Orgs, 1986–91; Member: Commn for Local Authority Accounts in Scotland, 1985–89; Historic Buildings Council for Scotland, 1988–94; Co-ordinator, Recording Scottish Graveyards Project, 1992–99; Sec., Greyfriars Kirkyard Trust, 1992–. Mem., Dementia Services Develt Trust, 1988–2000. Hon. Fellow, Edinburgh Univ. Dept of Politics, 1984–88. Hon. LLD Dundee, 1983; DUniv Stirling, 1992. Kt, Order of Oranje-Nassau (Netherlands), 1946. *Publications:* Procedures for the Reorganisation of Schools in England (report), 1987; Recording of Monumental Inscriptions, 1991. *Recreations:* old Penguins, genealogy, gravestones. *Address:* 20 Regent Terrace, Edinburgh EH7 5BS. *T:* (0131) 556 7671. *Club:* New (Edinburgh).
See also C. Mitchell, J. J. Mitchell.

MITCHELL, John Gall; QC (Scot.) 1970; a Deputy Social Security Commissioner and a Deputy Child Support Commissioner, 1999–2001 (a Social Security (formerly National Insurance) Commissioner, 1979–99; a Child Support Commissioner, 1993–99); *b* 5 May 1931; *s* of late Rev. William G. Mitchell, MA; *m* 1st, 1959, Anne Bertram Jardine (*d* 1986); three *s* one *d*; 2nd, 1988, Margaret, *d* of J. W. Galbraith. *Educ:* Royal High Sch., Edinburgh; Edinburgh Univ. (MA, LLB). Commn, HM Forces, 1954–56 (Nat. Service). Advocate 1957. Standing Junior Counsel, Customs and Excise, Scotland, 1964–70; Chairman: Industrial Tribunals, Scotland, 1966–80; Legal Aid Supreme Court Cttee, Scotland, 1974–79; Pensions Appeals Tribunal, Scotland, 1974–80. Hon. Sheriff: of Lanarkshire, 1970–74; of S Strathclyde, 1975–79. *Address:* Rosemount, Park Road, Dalkeith, Midlothian EH22 3DH.

MITCHELL, John Logan; QC (Scot) 1987; *b* 23 June 1947; *s* of Robert Mitchell and Dorothy Mitchell; *m* 1973, Christine Brownlee Thomson; one *s* one *d. Educ:* Royal High School, Edinburgh (Past Pres., Former Pupils' Club); Edinburgh Univ. (LLB Hons). Called to the Bar, 1974; Standing Junior Counsel: to Dept of Agriculture and Fisheries for Scotland, 1979; Forestry Commission for Scotland, 1979; Advocate Depute, 1981–85. *Recreation:* golf. *Address:* 17 Braid Farm Road, Edinburgh. *T:* (0131) 447 8099. *Club:* Mortonhall Golf.

MITCHELL, John Matthew, CBE 1976; PhD; Assistant Director-General, 1981–84, Senior Research Fellow, 1984–85, British Council; retired; *b* 22 March 1925; *s* of Clifford George Arthur Mitchell and Grace Maud Jamson; *m* 1952, Eva Maria von Rupprecht; three *s* one *d. Educ:* Ilford County High Sch.; Worcester Coll., Oxford; Queens' Coll., Cambridge (MA). PhD Vienna. Served War, RN, 1944–46. British Council: Lectr, Austria, 1949–52 and Egypt, 1952–56; Scotland, 1957–60; Dep. Rep., Japan, 1960–63; Reg. Dir, Zagreb, 1963–66; Reg. Rep., Dacca, 1966–69; Dep. Controller, Home Div., 1969–72; Rep., Federal Republic of Germany, 1973–77; Controller, Educn, Medicine and Sci. Div., 1977–81. Vis. Fellow, Wolfson Coll., Cambridge, 1972–73; former Lectr, univs of Vienna, Cairo and Tokyo. Fellow, Inst. of Linguists (Chm. Council, 1996–99; Vice-Pres., 2000–). *Publications:* International Cultural Relations, 1986; verse, short stories and trans. from German and French. *Recreations:* golf, theatre, cinema, opera. *Address:* The Cottage, Pains Hill Corner, Pains Hill, Limpsfield, Surrey RH8 0RB. *T:* (01883) 723354. *Club:* Tandridge Golf.
See also G. C. M. Mitchell.

MITCHELL, John Wesley, FRS 1956; PhD, DSc; Senior Research Fellow and Emeritus Professor, University of Virginia, since 1979; *b* 3 Dec. 1913; *s* of late John Wesley Mitchell and late Lucy Ruth Mitchell; *m* 1976, Virginia Hill; one step *d* of former marriage. *Educ:* Canterbury University Coll., Christchurch, NZ; Univ. of Oxford. BSc 1934. MSc 1935, NZ; PhD 1938, DSc 1960, Oxford. Reader in Experimental Physics in the Univ. of Bristol, 1945–59; Prof. of Physics, Univ. of Virginia, 1959–63; Dir of the National Chemical Laboratory, Oct. 1963–Aug. 1964; William Barton Rogers Prof. of Physics, Univ. of Virginia, 1964–79. Hon. FRPS 1995. Commonwealth of Virginia Lifetime Achievement Award in Science, 1993; Progress Medal, RPS, 1995. *Publications:* various on photographic sensitivity and on plastic deformation of crystals in scientific journals. *Recreation:* colour photography. *Address:* Department of Physics, University of Virginia, PO Box 400714, Charlottesville, VA 22904–4714, USA. *Clubs:* Athenæum; Cosmos (Washington, DC).

MITCHELL, Jonathan James; QC (Scot) 1992; *b* 4 Aug. 1951; *s* of (John) Angus (Macbeth) Mitchell, *qv* and Ann Katharine (*née* Williamson); *m* 1987, Melinda McGarry; one *s* one *d. Educ:* Marlborough Coll.; New Coll., Oxford (BA); Edinburgh Univ. (LLB). Advocate, 1979; Temp. Sheriff, 1988–95. Dep. Social Security Comr, 1994–. Mem., Scotch Malt Whisky Soc. *Publication:* Eviction and Rent Arrears, 1994. *Address:* 30 Warriston Crescent, Edinburgh EH3 5LB. *T:* (0131) 557 0854, *Fax:* (0131) 557 3210;

e-mail: jonathanmitchell@compuserve.com.
See also C. Mitchell.

MITCHELL, Joseph Rodney; Director General of Defence Accounts, Ministry of Defence, 1973, retired; *b* 11 March 1914; *s* of late Joseph William and Martha Mitchell, Sheffield; *m* 1936, Marian Richardson; two *s* three *d. Educ:* Sheffield Central Secondary School. FCCA, ACMA, ACIS. Works Recorder and Junior Costs Clerk, United Steel Cos Ltd, Sheffield, 1930–35; Senior Accounts Clerk, Cargo Fleet Iron Co. Ltd, Middlesbrough, 1936–39; Royal Ordnance Factories, 1940–55: Chief Exec. Officer, 1951–55; Min. of Supply/Aviation/Technology, 1956–71: Dir of Accounts, 1967–71; Dep. Dir Gen. of Defence Accounts, MoD, 1971–72. *Recreation:* hill-walking. *Address:* 154 Earlsbrook Road, Redhill, Surrey RH1 6HZ.

MITCHELL, Julian; writer; *b* 1 May 1935; *s* of late William Moncur Mitchell and of Christine Mary (*née* Browne). *Educ:* Winchester; Wadham Coll. Oxford. Nat. Service in Submarines, 1953–55; Temp. Acting Sub-Lieut, RNVR. Member: Literature Panel, Arts Council, 1966–69; Welsh Arts Council, 1988–92 (Chm. Drama Cttee, 1989–92). John Llewellyn Rhys Prize, 1965; Somerset Maugham Award, 1966. Television plays include: Shadow in the Sun; A Question of Degree; Rust; Abide With Me (Internat. Critics Prize, Monte Carlo, 1977); Survival of the Fittest; adaptations of: Persuasion; The Alien Corn; Staying On; The Good Soldier; The Mysterious Stranger; The Weather in the Streets; Inspector Morse; series, Jennie, Lady Randolph Churchill, 1974; television documentary: All the Waters of Wye, 1990. Films: Arabesque, 1965; Vincent and Theo, 1990; Wilde, 1997. Theatre: Adelina Patti, 1987. *Publications: novels:* Imaginary Toys, 1961; A Disturbing Influence, 1962; As Far As You Can Go, 1963; The White Father, 1964; A Circle of Friends, 1966; The Undiscovered Country, 1968; *biography:* (with Peregrine Churchill) Jennie: Lady Randolph Churchill, 1974; *translation:* Henry IV (Pirandello), 1979 (John Florio Prize, 1980); *plays:* Half-Life, 1977; The Enemy Within, 1980; Another Country, 1981 (SWET play of the year, 1982; filmed, 1984); Francis, 1983; After Aida (or Verdi's Messiah), 1986; Falling Over England, 1994; August, 1994 (adapted from Chekhov's Uncle Vanya; filmed, 1996); (adapted from Ivy Compton-Burnett): A Heritage and Its History, 1965; A Family and a Fortune, 1975; contribs to: Welsh History Review, The Monmouthshire Antiquary. *Recreations:* local history, fishing. *Address:* 47 Draycott Place, SW3 3DB.

MITCHELL, Katrina Jane, (Katie); freelance director; Associate Director, Royal Court Theatre, since 2001; *b* 23 Sept. 1964; *d* of Michael and Sally Mitchell. *Educ:* Magdalen Coll., Oxford (MA Eng. Lit. and Lang.). Asst Dir, 1989–90, Associate Dir, 1996–98, RSC. Productions directed: Gate Theatre, Notting Hill: Vassa Zheleznova, 1991; Women of Troy, 1991; The House of Bernarda Alba, 1992; Royal Shakespeare Company: The Dybbuk, 1992; Ghosts, 1993; Henry VI, 1995; Easter, 1995; The Phoenician Women, 1996; Beckett Shorts, 1997; Uncle Vanya, 1998; Royal Court: Live Like Pigs, 1993; The Country, 2000; Mountain Language, Ashes to Ashes, 2001; Abbey Theatre, Dublin: The Last Ones, 1993; Iphigenia in Aulis, 2001; Royal National Theatre: Rutherford and Son, 1994; Machine Wreckers, 1995; The Oresteia, 1999; End Game, Donmar Warehouse, 1996; Welsh National Opera: Don Giovanni, 1996; Jenufa, 1998; Katya Kabanova, 2001; The Maids, Young Vic, 1999; television play, Widowing of Mrs Holroyd, 1995. *Recreations:* travel, accordion. *Address:* c/o Sebastian Born, The Agency, 24 Pottery Lane, W11 4LZ.

MITCHELL, Keith Kirkman, OBE 1979; Lecturer in Physical Education, University of Leeds, 1955–90; *b* 25 May 1927; *s* of John Stanley Mitchell and Annie Mitchell; *m* 1950, Hannah Forrest; two *s. Educ:* Loughborough Coll. (Hons Dip. in Physical Educn). Phys. Educn Master, Wisbech Grammar Sch., 1950–52; Dir of Phys. Recreation, Manchester YMCA, 1952–55. Chm. Exec. Cttee, CCPR, 1981–87; Mem., Sports Council, 1976–87. Dir, 1953–84, Pres., 1985–, English Basketball Assoc.; Vice-Pres., Eur. Basketball Fedn, 1994–. *Recreations:* basketball, photography, gardening, golf. *Address:* 7 Park Crescent, Guiseley, West Yorks LS20 8EL. *T:* (01943) 875248.

MITCHELL, Martin; *see* Mitchell, J. L. M.

MITCHELL, Dame Mona (Ann), DCVO 1992 (CVO 1985; LVO 1976); Extra Lady-in-Waiting to HRH Princess Alexandra, the Hon. Lady Ogilvy, since 1968; *b* 20 Feb. 1938; *d* of Maj.-Gen. Francis Neville Mitchell, CB, CBE, DSO and late Ann Christian Mitchell (*née* Livingstone-Learmouth; she *m* 2nd, 1962, Brig. Richard Headlam Keenlyside, CBE, DSO (decd)). *Educ:* North Foreland Lodge. Secretary to: Fulke Walwyn, 1958–62; E. Hardy Amies, 1963–68; Sec., 1968–74, Private Sec., 1974–91, to HRH Princess Alexandra. *Recreations:* gardening, music, the arts in general. *Address:* High House, Harvest Lane, Charlton Horethorne, Sherborne, Dorset DT9 4PH. *T:* (01963) 220441. *Club:* Army and Navy.

MITCHELL, Nicolas John; His Honour Judge Nicolas Mitchell; a Circuit Judge, since 1996; *b* 12 May 1940; *s* of Leslie George Tudor Mitchell and Emma Mitchell; *m* 1962, Marion Davies; two *s. Educ:* Bancroft's Sch. Admitted solicitor, 1962; in private practice, 1962–96; a Recorder, 1992–96. Sheffield Prize, Law Soc., 1962. *Recreations:* walking, gardening, outdoor pursuits, reading, opera. *Address:* c/o Midland and Oxford Circuit Office, The Priory Courts, 33 Bull Street, Birmingham B4 6DW.

MITCHELL, Very Rev. Patrick Reynolds, KCVO 1998; Dean of Windsor, 1989–98; Register, Order of the Garter, 1989–98; Domestic Chaplain to the Queen, 1989–98; *b* 17 March 1930; *s* of late Lt-Col Percy Reynolds Mitchell, DSO; *m* 1st, 1959, Mary Evelyn (*née* Phillips) (*d* 1986); three *s* one *d*; 2nd, 1988, Pamela, *d* of late A. G. Le Marchant and *widow* of Henry Douglas-Pennant; one step *s* one step *d* (and two step *s* decd). *Educ:* Eton Coll.; Merton Coll., Oxford (MA Theol); Wells Theol Coll. Officer in Welsh Guards (National Service), 1948–49. Deacon, 1954; priest, 1955; Curate at St Mark's, Mansfield, 1954–57; Priest-Vicar of Wells Cathedral and Chaplain of Wells Theological Coll., 1957–60; Vicar of St James', Milton, Portsmouth, 1961–67; Vicar of Frome Selwood, Somerset, 1967–73; Dean of Wells, 1973–89; Director of Ordination Candidates for Bath and Wells, 1971–74. Res. Fellow, Merton Coll., Oxford, 1984. Chm., Cathedral Libraries and Archives Assoc., 1997–2001. Member: Adv. Bd for Redundant Churches, 1978–92; Cathedrals Adv. Commn for England, 1981–91. Governor, Wellington Coll., 1994–98. Hon. Freeman, City of Wells, 1986. FSA 1981. *Address:* Wolford Lodge, Dunkeswell, Honiton, Devon EX14 4SQ. *T:* (01404) 841244. *Club:* Oxford and Cambridge.

MITCHELL, Richard Charles, (Bob); Lecturer in Business Studies, Eastleigh College of Further Education, 1984–93; *b* 22 Aug. 1927; *s* of Charles and Elizabeth Mitchell; *m* 1950, Doreen Lilian Gregory; one *s* one *d. Educ:* Taunton's Sch., Southampton; Godalming County Gram. Sch.; Southampton Univ. BSc(Econ) Hons 1951. Bartley County Sec. Sch.: Senior Master and Head of Maths and Science Dept, 1957–65; Dep. Headmaster, 1965–66. MP (Lab) Southampton Test, 1966–70; MP (Lab 1971–81, SDP 1981–83) Southampton, Itchen, May 1971–1983. Contested Southampton, Itchen (SDP) 1983, (SDP/Alliance) 1987. Mem., European Parlt, 1975–79. Member: Bureau of European Socialist Gp, 1976–79; Chairman's Panel, House of Commons, 1979–83. Gov., Itchen Sixth Form Coll., 1984–. *Publication:* (jtly) Public Administration: a casebook approach, 1991. *Recreation:* postal chess (rep. Brit. Correspondence Chess Assoc. against other countries). *Address:* 49 Devonshire Road, Polygon, Southampton SO15 2GL. *T:* (023) 8022 1781.

MITCHELL, Prof. Ross Galbraith, MD, FRCPE, FRCPCH, DCH; Professor of Child Health, University of Dundee and Pædiatrician, Ninewells Hospital, Dundee, 1973–85, now Emeritus; *b* 18 Nov. 1920; *s* of late Richard Galbraith Mitchell, OBE and Ishobel, *d* of late James Ross, Broadford, Skye; *m* 1950, June Phylis Butcher; one *s* three *d. Educ:* Kelvinside Acad.; University of Edinburgh. MB, ChB Edinburgh, 1944. Surg-Lt, RNVR, 1944–47; Jun. hosp. posts, Liverpool, London, Edinburgh, 1947–52; Rockefeller Res. Fellow, Mayo Clinic, USA, 1952–53; Lectr in Child Health, Univ. of St Andrews, 1952–55; Cons. Pædiatrician, Dundee Teaching Hosps, 1955–63; Prof. of Child Health, Univ. of Aberdeen, Pædiatrician, Royal Aberdeen Children's and Aberdeen Maternity Hosps, 1963–72; Univ. of Dundee: Dean, Faculty of Medicine and Dentistry, 1978–81; Mem. Court, 1982–85. Chairman: Scottish Adv. Council on Child Care, 1966–69; Specialist Adv. Cttee on Pædiatrics, 1975–79; Academic Bd, British Pædiatric Assoc., 1975–78; Spastics Internat. Med. Pubns, 1981–85; Mac Keith Press, London, 1986–95; Mem., GMC, 1983–86. President: Harveian Soc., Edinburgh, 1982–83; Scottish Paediatric Soc., 1982–84. For. Corresp. Mem., Amer. Acad. of Cerebral Palsy and Developmental Medicine, 1965–. Jt Editor, Developmental Medicine and Child Neurology, 1968–80. *Publications:* Disease in Infancy and Childhood, (7th edn) 1973; Child Life and Health (5th edn), 1970; Child Health in the Community (2nd edn), 1980; contribs to textbooks of paediatrics, medicine and obstetrics and articles in scientific and medical jls. *Recreations:* Celtic language and literature, fishing. *Address:* Craigard, Abertay Gardens, Broughty Ferry, Dundee DD5 2RR.

MITCHELL, Hon. Sir Stephen (George), Kt 1993; **Hon. Mr Justice Mitchell;** a Judge of the High Court of Justice, Queen's Bench Division, since 1993; *b* 19 Sept. 1941; *s* of Sydney Mitchell and Joan Mitchell (*née* Dick); *m* 1978, Alison Clare (*née* Roseveare) (*d* 1998); two *d. Educ:* Bedford Sch.; Hertford Coll., Oxford (MA). Called to the Bar, Middle Temple, 1964, Bencher, 1993; Second Prosecuting Counsel to the Crown, Inner London Crown Court, 1975; Central Criminal Court: a Junior Prosecuting Counsel to the Crown, 1977; a Senior Prosecuting Counsel to the Crown, 1981–86; QC 1986; a Recorder, 1985–89; a Circuit Judge, 1989–93. Mem., Judicial Studies Bd, 1991–93. *Publications:* (ed) Phipson on Evidence, 11th edn, 1970; (ed) Archbold's Criminal Pleading Evidence and Practice, 1971–88. *Address:* Royal Courts of Justice, Strand, WC2A 2LL.

MITCHELL, Stephen Graham; Head of Radio News, BBC, since 2000; *b* 14 July 1949; *s* of Derek Mitchell and Phyllis Mitchell (*née* Rigden); *m* 1977, Barbara Gilder; one *s* one *d. Educ:* Loughborough Grammar Sch.; Manchester Univ. (BA Hons). Reporter, Thompson Newspapers, Newcastle Jl, S Wales Echo, The Times, 1971–74; BBC: producer, reporter, Radio Newsroom, and Duty Editor, Today prog., 1974–84; Dep. Foreign News Ed., 1985; Ed., Parly Output, 1986–88; Ed., then Man. Ed., Radio Newsroom, 1988–93; Ed., Radio News Progs, 1993–97; Dep. Hd, News Progs (Bimedia), 1997–99. *Recreations:* my family, reading, sailing. *Address:* 30 Amenbury Lane, Harpenden, Herts AL5 2DF.

MITCHELL, Terence Croft; Keeper of Western Asiatic Antiquities, British Museum, 1985–89; *b* 17 June 1929; *s* of late Arthur Croft Mitchell and Evelyn Violet Mitchell (*née* Ware). *Educ:* Holderness School, New Hampshire, USA; Bradfield Coll., Berks; St Catharine's Coll., Cambridge (MA 1956). REME Craftsman, 1947–49. Asst Master, St Catherine's Sch., Almondsbury, 1954–56; Resident Study, Tyndale House, Cambridge, 1956–58; European Rep., Aust. Inst. of Archaeology, 1958–59; Dept of Western Asiatic Antiquities, British Museum, 1959, Dep. Keeper, 1974, Acting Keeper, 1983–85. Chm., Victoria Inst., 1986–; Vice Chm., British Inst. at Amman for Archaeology and History, 1990–93. Lay Chm., Chelsea Deanery Synod, 1981–84. Editor, Palestine Exploration Fund Monograph Series, 1990–. *Publications:* Sumerian Art at Ur and Al-'Ubaid, 1969; (ed) Sir Leonard Woolley, Ur Excavations VIII, The Kassite Period and the Period of the Assyrian Kings, 1965; VII, The Old Babylonian Period, 1976; (ed) Music and Civilization, 1980; chapters on Israel and Judah in Cambridge Ancient History, vol. 3, part 1, 1982, part 2, 1991; The Bible in the British Museum: interpreting the evidence, 1988, rev. edn 1996; articles and reviews. *Recreations:* music, reading, landscape gardening. *Address:* 32 Mallord Street, Chelsea, SW3 6DU. *T:* (020) 7352 3962. *Club:* Athenæum.

MITCHELL, Valerie Joy, OBE 2001; Director-General, English-Speaking Union of the Commonwealth, since 1994; *b* 2 March 1941; *d* of Henry Frederick Twidale and Dorothy Mary (*née* Pierce), MBE; *m* 1st, 1962, Henri Pierre Eschauzier (marr. diss. 1970); two *s*; 2nd, 1972, Graham Rangeley Mitchell; one *d. Educ:* Beaufront Sch., Camberley; McGill Univ., Montreal (BA Hons). PA to Asst Dean of Arts and Sci., McGill Univ., Montreal, 1962–64; PR Consultant to Mayer-Lismann Opera Workshop, 1970–80; English-Speaking Union: Asst, Educn Dept, 1980–83; Dir of Branches and Cultural Affairs, 1983–94; Dep. Dir-Gen., 1989–94; Sec.-Gen., Internat. Council of ESU Worldwide, 1994–. Member: Teaching Socs Cttee, Council for Dance Educn and Trng, 1998–; Internat. Cttee, Shakespeare Globe Centre, 2000–. FRSA 1987. *Recreations:* music, theatre, tennis, walking. *Address:* English-Speaking Union, Dartmouth House, 37 Charles Street, W1J 5ED. *T:* (020) 7529 1550.

MITCHELL, Warren; *b* 14 Jan. 1926; *s* of Montague and Annie Misell, later Mitchell; *m* 1952, Constance Wake; one *s* two *d. Educ:* Southgate Co. Sch.; University Coll., Oxford; RADA. Demobbed RAF, 1946. First professional appearance, Finsbury Park Open Air Theatre, 1950; Theophile in Can-Can, Coliseum, 1954; Crookfinger Jake in The Threepenny Opera, Royal Court and Aldwych, 1956; Mr Godboy in Dutch Uncle, Aldwych, 1969; Satan in Council of Love, Criterion, 1970; Herbert in Jump, Queen's, 1971; Ion Will in The Great Caper, Royal Court, 1974; The Thoughts of Chairman Alf, Stratford E, 1976; Willie Loman in Death of a Salesman, Nat. Theatre, 1979; Ducking Out, Duke of York's, 1983; Harpagon in The Miser, Birmingham Rep, 1986; Max in The Homecoming, 1991; West Yorkshire Playhouse: King Lear, 1996; Visiting Mr Green, 2000; Art, Wyndhams, 2000; *films include:* Diamonds Before Breakfast; Assassination Bureau; Best House in London; Till Death Us Do Part; Moon Zero Two; Whatever Happened to Charlie Farthing; Jabberwocky; Stand Up Virgin Soldiers; Meetings with Remarkable Men; Norman Loves Rose; The Chain; *television:* Alf Garnett in Till Death Us Do Part, BBC, 1966–78, and In Sickness and in Health, BBC, 1985, 1986; The Thoughts of Chairman Alf (series), 1998; Shylock in Merchant of Venice, BBC, 1981; Till Death (series), ITV, 1981; The Caretaker, BBC, 1981; So You Think You've Got Troubles (series), BBC, 1994; Wall of Silence, BBC, 1995; Death of a Salesman, BBC, 1996; Gormenghast, BBC, 2000. TV Actor of the Year Award, Guild of Film and TV Producers, 1966; Actor of Year Award: Evening Standard, 1979; Soc. of West End Theatres, 1979; Plays and Players, 1979. *Recreations:* sailing, tennis, playing clarinet. *Address:* c/o CDA, 19 Sydney Mews, SW3 6HL.

MITCHELL, Sir William; *see* Mitchell, Sir E. W. J.

MITCHELL, Rt Rev. Mgr. William Joseph; Vicar General, Diocese of Clifton, since 1987; Parish Priest, Clifton Cathedral, Bristol, since 1997; *b* 4 Jan. 1936; *s* of late William Ernest and Catherine Mitchell. *Educ:* St Brendan's Coll., Bristol; Corpus Christi Coll., Oxford (MA); Séminaire S Sulpice, Paris; Gregorian Univ., Rome (LCL). Ordained Priest, Pro-Cathedral, Bristol, 1961; Curate, Pro-Cathedral, Bristol, 1963–64; Secretary to Bishop of Clifton, 1964–75; Parish Priest, St Bernadette, Bristol, 1975–78; Rector, Pontifical Beda Coll., Rome, 1978–87; Parish Priest: St John's, Bath, 1988–90; St Antony's, Bristol, 1990–96; St Mary's, Bristol, 1996–97. Prelate of Honour, 1978. *Address:* Cathedral House, Clifton Park, Bristol BS8 3BX. *T:* (0117) 970 6333, *Fax:* (0117) 974 4002; *e-mail:* Mitchell.vg@cliftondiocese.com.

MITCHELL COTTS, Sir Richard Crichton; *see* Cotts.

MITCHELL-INNES, Alistair Campbell; Chairman, Anglo & Overseas Trust PLC, since 1996; *b* 1 March 1934; *s* of Peter Mitchell-Innes and Jocelyn (*née* Ash); *m* 1957, Penelope Ann Hill; one *s* two *d*. *Educ:* Charterhouse; Stanford Business Sch. (Executive Program). Dir, Brooke Bond Gp plc, 1979–84; Chief Exec., Nabisco Gp Ltd, 1985–88; Chief Exec., Isosceles plc, 1991–93; Dep. Chm., H. P. Bulmer (Holdings) plc, 1990–2001; Chm., Sidney C. Banks plc, 1994–2000. Non-exec. Dir, Next plc, 1989–. *Recreations:* golf, cricket, military history. *Address:* Langton Lodge, Station Road, Sunningdale, Berks SL5 0QR. *Clubs:* Caledonian, MCC; Berkshire Golf.

MITCHELL-THOMSON, family name of **Baron Selsdon**.

MITCHINER, Dr John Edward; HM Diplomatic Service; Deputy High Commissioner, Calcutta, since 2000; *b* 12 Sept. 1951; *s* of late Geoffrey Morford Mitchiner and of Ursula Angela Mitchiner (*née* Adolph); *m* 1983, Elizabeth Mary Ford, MA, MNIMH. *Educ:* John Fisher Sch., Purley; Beaumont Coll., Old Windsor; Bristol Univ. (BA 1972); Sch. of Oriental and African Studies, London Univ. (MA 1973; PhD 1977). ACU Res. Fellow, Visva Bharati Univ., Santiniketan, 1977–78; Bipradas Palchaudhuri Fellow, Calcutta Univ., 1978–79; joined FCO, 1980; Third, later Second Sec. (Information), Istanbul 1982–85; FCO, 1985–87; Second Sec. (Develt), New Delhi, 1987–91; Second, later First Sec. (Political), Berne, 1991–95; Head, Japan Section, FCO, 1995–96; Ambassador, Armenia, 1997–99. MRAS. *Publications:* Studies in the Indus Valley Inscriptions, 1978; Traditions of the Seven Rsis, 1982, 2nd edn 2000; The Yuga Purana, 1986; Guru: the search for enlightenment, 1992; contribs to learned jls. *Recreations:* hill farming in Wales, bridge, tennis, family history, karabash. *Address:* c/o Foreign and Commonwealth Office, SW1A 2AH. *Club:* Royal Commonwealth Society.

MITCHISON, Avrion; *see* Mitchison, N. A.

MITCHISON, Prof. Denis Anthony, CMG 1984; Professor of Bacteriology, Royal Postgraduate Medical School, 1971–84, Professor Emeritus, London University, since 1984; at St George's Hospital Medical School, since 1993; Director, Medical Research Council's Unit for Laboratory Studies of Tuberculosis, 1956–84; *b* 6 Sept. 1919; *e s* of Baron Mitchison, CBE, QC, and late Naomi Margaret Mitchison, CBE, writer; *m* 1st, 1940, Ruth Sylvia (*d* 1992), *d* of Hubert Gill; two *s* two *d*; 2nd, 1993, Honora, *d* of Christopher Carlin. *Educ:* Abbotsholme Sch.; Trinity Coll., Cambridge; University Coll. Hosp., London (MB, ChB). House Physician: Addenbrooke's Hosp.; Royal Berkshire Hosp.; Asst to Pathologist, Brompton Hosp.; Prof. of Bacteriology (Infectious Diseases), RPMS, 1968–71. FRCP; FRCPath. *Publications:* numerous papers on bacteriology and chemotherapy of tuberculosis. *Address:* 14 Marlborough Road, Richmond, Surrey TW10 6JR. *T:* (020) 8940 4751.

See also J. M. Mitchison, N. A. Mitchison.

MITCHISON, Prof. John Murdoch, ScD; FRS 1978; FRSE 1966; Professor of Zoology, University of Edinburgh, 1963–88, now Professor Emeritus and Hon. Fellow; *b* 11 June 1922; *s* of Baron Mitchison, CBE, QC, and late Naomi Margaret Mitchison, CBE, writer; *m* 1947, Rosalind Mary Wrong; one *s* three *d*. *Educ:* Winchester Coll.; Trinity Coll., Cambridge. Army Operational Research, 1941–46; Sen. and Research Scholar, Trinity Coll., Cambridge, 1946–50; Fellow, Trinity Coll., Cambridge, 1950–54; Edinburgh University: Lectr in Zoology, 1953–59; Reader in Zoology, 1959–62; Dean, Faculty of Science, 1984–85; Mem. of Court, 1971–74, 1985–88. J. W. Jenkinson Memorial Lectr, Oxford, 1971–72. Member: Council, Scottish Marine Biol. Assoc., 1961–67; Exec. Cttee, Internat. Soc. for Cell Biology, 1964–72; Biol Cttee, SRC, 1972–75; Royal Commn on Environmental Pollution, 1974–79; Science Bd, SRC, 1976–79; Working Gp on Biol Manpower, DES, 1968–71; Adv. Cttee on Safety of Nuclear Installations, Health and Safety Exec., 1981–84. Pres., British Soc. for Cell Biology, 1974–77. Mem., Academia Europaea, 1989. FInstBiol 1963. *Publications:* The Biology of the Cell Cycle, 1971; papers in scientific jls. *Address:* Great Yew, Ormiston, East Lothian EH35 5NJ. *T:* (01875) 340530.

See also D. A. Mitchison, N. A. Mitchison.

MITCHISON, Prof. (Nicholas) Avrion, FRS 1967; Senior Fellow, Department of Immunology, University College London, since 1996; *b* 5 May 1928; 3rd *s* of Baron Mitchison, CBE, QC, and late Naomi Margaret Mitchison, CBE, writer; *m* 1957, Lorna Margaret, *d* of Maj.-Gen. J. S. S. Martin, CSI; two *s* three *d*. *Educ:* Leighton Park Sch.; New Coll., Oxford (MA 1949). Fellow of Magdalen College, 1950–52; Commonwealth Fund Fellow, 1952–54; Lecturer, Edinburgh Univ., 1954–61; Reader, Edinburgh Univ., 1961–62; Head of Div. of Experimental Biology, Nat. Inst. for Med. Research, 1962–71; Jodrell Prof. of Zoology and Comparative Anatomy, UCL, 1970–89 (Hon. Fellow, 1993); Scientific Dir, Deutsches Rheuma-Forschungszentrum Berlin, 1990–96. Hon. MD Edinburgh, 1977. *Publications:* articles in scientific journals. *Address:* 14 Belitha Villas, N1 1PD; Department of Immunology, University College London, Windeyer Building, 46 Cleveland Street, W1P 6DB. *T:* (020) 7380 9349, *Fax:* (020) 7380 9357; *e-mail:* n.mitchison@ucl.ac.uk.

See also D. A. Mitchison, J. M. Mitchison.

MITFORD, family name of **Baron Redesdale**.

MITFORD-SLADE, Patrick Buxton, OBE 2000; Director, SG Hambros Bank & Trust Ltd, since 2001; Partner, Cazenove & Co., 1972–96; *b* 7 Sept. 1936; *s* of late Col Cecil Townley Mitford-Slade and Phyllis, *d* of E. G. Buxton; *m* 1964, Anne Catharine Stanton, *d* of late Major Arthur Holbrow Stanton, MBE; one *s* two *d*. *Educ:* Eton Coll.; RMA Sandhurst. Commissioned 60th Rifles, 1955, Captain; served Libya, NI, Berlin and British Guyana; Adjt, 1st Bn The Royal Green Jackets, 1962–65; Instructor, RMA Sandhurst, 1965–67. Stockbroker, Cazenove & Co., 1968–96; Man. Dir, Cazenove Money Brokers, 1986–96. Chm., London Stock Exchange Retirement Plan Trustees Co., 1995–2000; Director: Clive Securities Group Ltd, 1996–99; John Govett Holdings Ltd, 1996–97; Clive Discount Co. Ltd, 1996–98; AIB Asset Management Hldgs Ltd, 1996–98. Asst Sec., Panel on Takeovers and Mergers, 1970–72; Mem., Stock Exchange, 1972–86, Internat. Stock Exchange, 1986–92 (Mem. Council, 1976–91; Dep. Chm., 1982–85); Chairman: City Telecommunications Cttee, 1983–92; Securities Industry Steering Cttee on Taurus, 1988–90; Money Brokers Assoc., 1990–96; Dep. Chm., Stock Borrowing and Lending Cttee, 1990–98. Chairman: Officers' Assoc., 1985–2000; St Luke's Hosp. for the Clergy, 2001– (Hon. Treas., 1994–2001); Mem., Benevolent and Strategy Cttee, RBL, 1998–; Hon. Treas., British Commonwealth Ex-Services League, 1993–. Gov., Reed's Sch., 2001–. *Recreations:* shooting, fishing. *Address:* Damales House, Borough Court Road, Hartley Wintney, Hook, Hants RG27 8JA. *Club:* City of London.

MITHEN, Dallas Alfred, CB 1983; Chairman, Forestry Training Council, 1984–93; Commissioner for Harvesting and Marketing, Forestry Commission, 1977–83; *b* 5 Nov. 1923; *m* 1st, 1947, Peggy (*née* Clarke) (decd); one *s* one *d*; 2nd, 1969, Avril Teresa Dodd (*née* Stein). *Educ:* Maidstone Grammar Sch.; UC of N Wales, Bangor. BSc (Forestry). Fleet Air Arm, 1942–46. Joined Forestry Commission as District Officer, 1950; Dep. Surveyor, New Forest and Conservator SE (England), 1968–71; Senior Officer (Scotland), 1971–75; Head of Forest Management Div., Edinburgh, 1975–76. Pres., Inst. of Chartered Foresters, 1984–86; Pres., Forestry Section, BAAS, 1985. Trustee, Central Scotland Woodland Trust, 1985–95. *Recreations:* gardening, swimming, walking. *Address:* 12 Stanehead Park, Biggar, South Lanarkshire ML12 6PU. *T:* (01899) 221308.

MITRA, Dr Ashesh Prosad, FRS 1988; FNA; Hon. Scientist of Emminence, National Physical Laboratory, New Delhi; Bhatnagar Fellow, Council of Scientific and Industrial Research, since 1991; *b* 21 Feb. 1927; *s* of late A. C. Mitra and Subarna Prova Mitra; *m* 1956, Sunanda Mitra; two *d*. *Educ:* University of Calcutta (DPhil 1955). FNA 1963. Res. Assistant, Calcutta Univ., 1949–51; Colombo Plan Fellow, CSIRO, Sydney, 1951; Vis. Asst Prof. of Engrg Res., 1952–53, Vis. Prof., 1953–54, Penn. State Univ.; National Physical Laboratory, New Delhi: Sec., Radio Res. Cttee, 1954–56; Head, Radio Propagation Unit, later Radio Sci. Div., 1956–86; Director-level Scientist, 1974–82; Dir., 1982–86; Sec. to Govt of India, Dept of Industrial & Scientific Res., and Dir-Gen., Council of Scientific and Industrial Res., 1986–91. Mem., Indian Acad. of Astronautics, 1974–; Fellow, Third World Acad. of Scis, Trieste, 1988. Hon. DSc Manipur, 1988. *Publications:* (ed) Proceedings of the International Geophysical Year Symposium, vols 1 & 2, 1962; The Chemistry of the Ionosphere, 1970; Advances in Space Exploration, vol. 6, 1979; 50 Years of Radio Science in India, 1984; (ed jtly) Handbook on Radio Propagation for Tropical and Subtropical Countries, 1987; 165 papers. *Recreation:* music. *Address:* National Physical Laboratory, Dr K. S. Krishnan Marg, New Delhi 110012, India. *T:* (11) 5745298. *Clubs:* Delhi Gymkhana (New Delhi); Calcutta (Calcutta).

MITSAKIS, Prof. Kariofilis; Professor of Modern Greek Literature, University of Athens, 1978–99, now Emeritus; *b* 12 May 1932; *s* of Christos and Crystalli Mitsakis; *m* 1966, Anthoula Chalkia; two *s*. *Educ:* Univs of Thessaloniki (BA, PhD), Oxford (MA, DPhil) and Munich. Scientific Collaborator, National Research Foundn of Greece, 1959–62; Associate Prof. of Byzantine and Modern Greek Literature, Univ. of Maryland, 1966–68; Chm. of Dept of Comparative Literature, Univ. of Maryland, 1967–68; Sotheby and Bywater Prof. of Byzantine and Modern Greek Language and Literature, Univ. of Oxford, 1968–72; Prof. of Modern Greek Lit., Univ. of Thessaloniki, 1972–75; Dir, Inst. for Balkan Studies, Thessaloniki, 1972–80. Hon. DLitt and Ph Johannesburgh, 2001. Gottfried Herder Prize, Vienna Univ, 2000. *Publications:* Problems Concerning the Text, the Sources and the Dating of the Achilleid, 1962 (in Greek); The Greek Sonnet, 1962 (in Greek); The Language of Romanos the Melodist, 1967 (in English); The Byzantine Alexanderromance from the Cod. Vindob. theol. gr. 244, 1967 (in German); Byzantine Hymnography, 1971 (in Greek); Petrarchism in Greece, 1973 (in Greek); Introduction to Modern Greek Literature, 1973 (in Greek); Homer in Modern Greek Literature, 1976 (in Greek); George Viziynos, 1977 (in Greek); Modern Greek Prose: the Generation of the '30s, 1978 (in Greek); Modern Greek Music and Poetry, 1979 (in Greek and English); March Through the Time, 1982; The Living Water, 1983; Points of Reference, 1987 (in Greek); The Cycles with their trails that rise and fall, 1991 (in Greek); The Boston Essays, 1993 (in Greek); The Oxford Essays, 1995 (in Greek); The Alexanderromance, 2001 (in Greek); Modern Greek Miscellany, 2001 (in Greek); In Imagination and in Word: studies on the poet C. P. Cavafy, 2001 (in Greek); Pan the Great: studies on the poet A. Sivelianos, 2001 (in Greek); contribs to Balkan Studies, Byzantinisch-Neugriechische Jahrbücher, Byzantinische Zeitschrift, Comparative Literature Studies, Diptycha, Etudes Byzantines-Byzantine Studies, Glotta, Hellenika, Jahrbuch der Oesterreichischen Byzantinischen Gesellschaft, Nea Hestia, etc. *Recreations:* music, travelling. *Address:* 25 Troados Street, 15342 Aghia Paraskevi, Athens, Greece.

MITTAL, Lakshmi Niwas; Chairman and Chief Executive Officer, Ispat International NV, since 1995; *b* 15 June 1950; *s* of Mohan Lal and Guta Mittal; *m* 1971, Usha; one *s* one *d*. *Educ:* commerce degree. Began working in father's steel mill, Calcutta, India, as a teenager; established Ispat Indo, privately owned steel co., Indonesia, 1976; has championed development of integrated mini-mills and use of direct reduced iron (DRI) as scrap substitute for steelmaking. Steelmaker of the Year, New Steel Magazine, 1996; Willy Korf Steel Vision Award, American Metal Market/World Steel Dynamics, 1998. *Recreations:* yoga, swimming. *Address:* Ispat International NV, 7th Floor, Berkeley Square House, Berkeley Square, W1J 6DA. *Club:* Mercantile (Jakarta).

MITTING, Hon. Sir John Edward, Kt 2001; Hon. Mr Justice Mitting; a Judge of the High Court of Justice, Queen's Bench Division, since 2001; *b* 8 Oct. 1947; *s* of late Alison Kennard Mitting and Eleanor Mary Mitting; *m* 1977, Judith Clare (*née* Hampson); three *s*. *Educ:* Downside Sch.; Trinity Hall, Cambridge (BA, LLB). Called to the Bar, Gray's Inn, 1970, Bencher, 1996; QC 1987; a Recorder, 1988–2001. *Recreations:* wine, food, bridge. *Address:* Royal Courts of Justice, Strand, WC2A 2LL.

MITTLER, Prof. Peter Joseph, CBE 1981; MA, PhD, MEd; CPsychol; FBPsS; Professor of Special Education, 1973–95, Professor Emeritus, since 1995, and Dean, Faculty of Education and Director, School of Education, 1991–94, University of Manchester; *b* 2 April 1930; *s* of Dr Gustav Mittler and Gertrude Mittler; *m* 1st, 1955, Helle Katscher (marr. diss. 1997); three *s*; 2nd, 1997, Penelope Anastasia Platt. *Educ:* Merchant Taylors' Sch., Crosby; Pembroke Coll., Cambridge (MA); PhD London; MEd Manchester. Clinical Psychologist, Warneford and Park Hosps, Oxford, 1954–58; Principal Psychologist, Reading Area Psychiatric Services, 1958–63; Lectr in Psychology, Birkbeck Coll., Univ. of London, 1963–68; Manchester University: Dir, Hester Adrian Res. Centre, 1968–82; Dir, Centre for Educnl Guidance and Special Needs, Dept of Educn, 1977–91; Dep. Dir, Sch. of Educn, 1989–91. Vis. Prof., Manchester Metropolitan Univ., 1996–97; Distinguished Vis. Prof., Univ. of Hong Kong, 1997–98; Fellow, Centre for Policy Studies, Dartington, 1995–. Chm., Nat Develt Gp for Mentally Handicapped, 1975–80; Mem., Schs Exams and Assessment Council, 1988–90. Pres., Internat. League of Socs for Persons with Mental Handicap, 1982–86 (Vice-Pres., 1978–82); Mem., Prince of Wales Adv. Gp on Disability, 1984–90; Chm. Trustees and Council, British Inst. of Learning Disabilities, 1995–97; Advr on disability to UN, UNESCO, WHO, ILO. *Publications:* ed, Psychological Assessment of Mental and Physical Handicaps, 1970; The Study of Twins, 1971; ed, Assessment for Learning in the Mentally Handicapped, 1973; ed, Research to Practice in Mental Retardation (3 vols), 1977; People not Patients, 1979; (jtly) Teaching Language and Communication to the Mentally Handicapped, (Schools

Council), 1979; (ed jtly) Advances in Mental Handicap Research, 1980; (ed) Frontiers of Knowledge in Mental Retardation (2 vols), 1981; (ed jtly) Approaches to Partnership: professionals and parents of mentally handicapped people, 1983; (ed jtly) Aspects of Competence in Mentally Handicapped People, 1983; (ed jtly) Staff Training in Mental Handicap, 1987; (jtly) Inset and Special Educational Needs: running short, school-focused inservice courses, 1988; (ed jtly) Special Needs Education (World Yearbook of Education), 1993; Teacher Education for Special Educational Needs, 1993; (jtly) Innovations in Family Support for People with Learning Difficulties, 1994; (ed jtly) Teacher Education for Special Needs in Europe, 1995; (ed) Changing Policy and Practice for People with Learning Disabilities, 1995; (jtly) Disability and the Family, 1995; Working Towards Inclusive Education: social contexts, 2000; papers in psychol and educnl jls. *Recreations:* music, travel. *Address:* 3 Knightsbridge Mews, Manchester M20 6GX. *T:* and *Fax:* (0161) 434 5625.

MIYAKE, Kazunaru, (Issey); fashion designer; *b* 22 April 1938. *Educ:* Tama Art Univ., Tokyo; Chambre Syndicale de la Couture, Paris. Assistant Designer: Guy Laroche, Paris, 1966–68; Hubert de Givenchy, Paris, 1968–69; Designer, Geoffrey Beene, NY, 1969–70; established Miyake Design Studio, Tokyo, 1970; first Paris fashion show, 1973; Founder: Pleats Please, 1993; A-POC, 1999. *Exhibitions:* Bodyworks – Fashion Without Taboos, Tokyo, San Francisco, LA, London, 1985; Musée des Arts Décoratifs, Paris, 1988; Issey Miyake Making Things, Paris, 1998, NY, 1999, Tokyo, 2000. Numerous awards. Hon. Dr: RCA, 1993; Lyon, 1999. Chevalier, Légion d'honneur (France), 1993; Bunka Korosha (Japan), 1998. *Publications:* East Meets West, 1978; Issey Miyake Bodyworks, 1983. *Address:* Issey Miyake Design Studio, 1–23 Oyama-cho, Shibuya-ku, Tokyo 151, Japan.

MKAPA, Benjamin William; President, United Republic of Tanzania, since 1995; *b* 12 Nov. 1938; *s* of William Matwani and Stephania Nambanga; *m* 1966, Anna Joseph Maro; two *s*. *Educ:* Lupaso Primary Sch.; Ndanda Secondary Sch.; Kigonsera Seminary; St Francis Coll., Pugu (Cambridge Sch. Cert.); Makerere UC (BA Hons 1962); Sch. of Internat. Affairs, Columbia Univ. Admin. Officer, subseq. Dist Officer, then Foreign Service Officer, Dodoma, 1962; Managing Editor: The Nationalist and Uhuru, 1966–72; The Daily News, and The Sunday News, 1972–74; Press Sec. to President, 1974–76; Founding Dir, Tanzania News Agency, 1976; High Comr to Nigeria, 1976–77; nominated MP, 1977–82, 1984–85; elected MP for Nanyumbu, 1985, re-elected 1990; Minister for Foreign Affairs, 1977–82, 1984–90; Minister for Information and Culture, 1980–82; High Comr to Canada, 1982–83; Ambassador to USA, 1983–84; Minister for Information and Broadcasting, 1990–92; Minister for Science, Tech. and Higher Educn, 1992–95. Chm., 1996–, Mem., 1977–, Chama cha Mapinduzi (Revolutionary Party). *Address:* Office of the President, PO Box 9120, Dar es Salaam, Tanzania.

MKONA, Callisto Matekenya, Hon. GCVO 1985; Senior Principal Secretary for Home Affairs, Malaŵi, 1994, retired; *b* 4 June 1930; *s* of late Benedicto Mkona and of Martha Matekenya Mkona; *m* 1971, Helen Victoria (*née* Sazuze); two *s* two *d*. *Educ:* Zomba, Malaŵi; Urbanian Univ., Rome (DCL, Dip. Soc. Scis). Secondary School teacher, 1962–64; Mission Educn Liaison Officer, 1964–67; Educn Attaché (First Sec.), Washington and London, 1967–71; Ambassador to Ethiopia, 1971–72; Minister, Washington, 1972–73; High Comr in Zambia, 1973–75; Ambassador in Bonn, 1975–78; Dep. Principal Sec., Min. of External Affairs, 1978–79; Principal Sec., Office of the President and Cabinet, 1979–81; High Comr in London, also concurrently accredited to Denmark, France, Norway, Portugal, Sweden and Switzerland, 1981–87; Chm., Malawi Public Service Commn, 1987–88; High Comr in Nairobi, concurrently accredited to Egypt, Israel and Uganda, 1988–93; Permanent Representative to: UN Centre for Human Settlements (HABITAT), 1988–93; UNEP, 1988–93. Republic of Malaŵi 6th July 1966 Medal, 1966; Malaŵi Silver Jubilee of Independence Award, 1989. *Recreations:* reading, walking, tennis, golf. *Address:* Chigumula, PO Box 5643, Limbe, Malaŵi.

MLINARIC, David; interior decorator and designer, since 1964; founded David Mlinaric Ltd, 1964, became Mlinaric, Henry and Zervudachi Ltd, 1989; *b* 12 March 1939; *s* of Franjo and Mabel Mlinaric; *m* 1969, Martha Laycock; one *s* two *d*. *Educ:* Downside Sch.; Bartlett Sch. of Architecture; University Coll. London. Private and commercial interior designing and decorating, often in historic bldgs. Recent work includes: rooms in Nat. Gall., London, 1986–; Spencer House, London, 1990; Wellcome Building, London, 1992; Royal Opera House, Covent Garden; British Galls, V&A Mus. Hon. Fellow, RCA, 1987. *Recreations:* gardening, sightseeing. *Address:* 38 Bourne Street, SW1W 8JA. *T:* (020) 7730 9072.

MO, Timothy Peter; writer; *b* 30 Dec. 1950; *s* of Peter Mo Wan Lung and Barbara Helena Falkingham. *Educ:* Convent of the Precious Blood, Hong Kong; Mill Hill School; St John's Coll., Oxford (BA; Gibbs Prize 1971). *Publications:* The Monkey King, 1978 (Geoffrey Faber Meml Prize, 1979); Sour Sweet, 1982 (Hawthornden Prize, 1983; filmed, 1989); An Insular Possession, 1986; The Redundancy of Courage, 1991 (E. M. Forster Award, Amer. Acad. and Inst. of Arts and Letters, 1992); Brownout on Breadfruit Boulevard, 1995; Renegade or Halo^2 (James Tait Black Meml Prize), 1999. *Recreations:* scuba diving, weight training, gourmandising. *Address:* BCM Paddleless, WC1N 3XX; *e-mail:* timothymo@eudoramail.com.

MOATE, Sir Roger (Denis), Kt 1993; Director, Robinco Group (Hungary and Czech Republic), since 1997; *b* 12 May 1938; *m* 1st; one *s* one *d*; 2nd, Auriol (*née* Cran); one *d*. *Educ:* Latymer Upper Sch., Hammersmith. Insurance Broker; with J. H. Minet, in S Africa and Kenya, 1957–60; Director: Walker Moate & Co., 1961–66; Alexander Howden Insce Brokers Ltd, 1967–70. Contested (C) Faversham, 1966. MP (C) Faversham, 1970–97; contested (C) Sittingbourne and Sheppey, 1997. Mem., Select Cttee on Agric., 1995–97. Hon. Sec., British-Amer. Parly Gp, 1974–81; Chm., British-Norwegian Parly Gp, 1987–97. Chm., Brentford and Chiswick Young Conservatives; Vice-Chm., Greater London Area Young Conservatives, 1964. Comdr, Royal Norwegian Order of Merit, 1994. *Recreations:* ski-ing, tennis, gardening. *Address:* Calico House, Newnham, Sittingbourne, Kent ME9 0LN. *Club:* Farmers.

MOBBS, Sir (Gerald) Nigel, Kt 1986; Lord-Lieutenant of Buckinghamshire, since 1997; Chairman: Slough Estates plc, since 1976; Bovis Homes Group, since 1996; Director, Barclays Bank PLC, since 1979; *b* 22 Sept. 1937; *s* of Gerald Aubrey Mobbs and Elizabeth (*née* Lanchester); *m* 1961, Hon. Pamela Jane Marguerite Berry, 2nd *d* of 2nd Viscount Kemsley; one *s* twin *d*. *Educ:* Marlborough Coll.; Christ Church, Oxford. Joined Slough Estates plc, 1960; Director, 1963; Man. Dir, 1971; Chief Exec., 1976–96. Director: Barclays Bank Trust Co. Ltd, 1973–86 (Chm., 1985–86); Charterhouse Gp, 1974–84 (Chm., 1977–83); Kingfisher plc (formerly Woolworth Holdings), 1982–96 (Dep. Chm., 1990–95; Chm., 1995–96); Cookson Gp plc, 1985–93; Howard de Walden Estates Ltd, 1989–; Chm., Groundwork Foundn, 1990–94. Chairman: Corporate Health (formerly Slough Occupational Health Service), 1976–; Slough Social Fund, 1975–; Property Services Agency Adv. Bd, 1980–86; Aims of Industry, 1985–; Adv. Panel on Deregulation, DTI, 1988–94. Pres., Slough & Dist Chamber of Commerce, 1969–72; Vice-Pres., Assoc. of British Chambers of Commerce, 1976–90 (Chm. 1974–76); Pres., British Property Fedn, 1979–81. Mem., Cttee on Corporate Governance, 1996–98. Mem., Commonwealth War Graves Commn, 1988–97; Trustee, Nat. Army Mus., 1994–; Comr, Royal Hosp., Chelsea, 2000–. Chm., Wembley Task Force, 1999–. President: Bucks Assoc. of Boys' Clubs, 1984–97; British Council for Offices, 1990–91. Hon. Treas., Cons. Party, 1993–96. Chm., Council, Univ. of Buckingham, 1987–98. CIMgt. Master, Spectacle Makers' Co., 1989. High Sheriff, 1982, DL, 1985, Bucks. Hon. Col No 1 (Royal Bucks Yeomanry) Signal Sqn (Special Communications), 2001–. Hon. Fellow, Coll. of Estate Management, 1978; Hon. Mem., RICS, 1990. Hon. DSc City, 1988; DUniv Buckingham, 1993. Hon. LLD Reading, 2000. KStJ (Pres. Council, Bucks, 1997–). *Recreations:* riding, hunting, ski-ing, golf, travel. *Address:* c/o Slough Estates plc, 234 Bath Road, Slough SL1 4EE. *Clubs:* Brooks's; Toronto (Toronto).

MOBERLY, Sir John (Campbell), KBE 1984; CMG 1976; HM Diplomatic Service, retired; Associate Fellow (formerly Consultant), Middle East Programme, Royal Institute of International Affairs, since 1986; *b* 27 May 1925; *s* of Sir Walter Moberly, GBE, KCB, DSO; *m* 1959, Patience, *d* of Major Sir Richard George Proby, 1st Bt, MC; two *s* one *d*. *Educ:* Winchester College; Magdalen College, Oxford. War Service in Royal Navy, 1943–47 (despatches). Entered HM Foreign (now Diplomatic) Service, 1950; Political Officer, Kuwait, 1954–56; Political Agent, Doha, 1959–62; First Secretary, Athens, 1962–66; Counsellor, Washington, 1969–73; Dir, Middle East Centre for Arab Studies, 1973–75; Ambassador, Jordan, 1975–79; Asst Under-Sec. of State, FCO, 1979–82; Ambassador, Iraq, 1982–85. CStJ 1979. *Recreations:* mountain walking, ski-ing, swimming. *Address:* 35 Pymers Mead, West Dulwich, SE21 8NH. *T:* and *Fax:* (020) 8670 2680; The Cedars, Temple Sowerby, Penrith, Cumbria CA10 1RZ. *T:* (01768) 361437. *Clubs:* Royal Automobile; Leander (Henley-on-Thames).

MOBERLY, Dr Patricia Jane; JP; Chairman, Guy's and St Thomas's Hospital NHS Trust, since 1999; *d* of Capt. Gerald Thomas Coney, RN, OBE, and Margaret Frances Mary Coney; *m* 1959, Rev. Richard Hamilton Moberly; two *s* two *d*. *Educ:* Univ. of Liverpool (BA Hons Eng. Lang. and Lit.); King's Coll., London (PhD 1985). Teacher: Chikola Sch., Zambia, 1964–67; Roan Sch., Greenwich, 1967–68; Mary Datchelor Sch., Camberwell, 1968–74; then Sen. Teacher and Hd, Sixth Form, Pimlico Sch., 1974–98. Mem., Lambeth BC 1971–78. Member: Lambeth Southwark and Lewisham AHA 1976–81; Lambeth DHA, 1981–90. Governor: Maudsley and Bethlem Hosp., 1976–78; UMDS, 1988–90. Mem., Nat. Cttee, Anti-Apartheid Movement. JP Inner London, 1976. *Address:* 24 Wincott Street, SE11 4NT. *T:* (020) 7735 2233.

MOBERLY, Sir Patrick (Hamilton), KCMG 1986 (CMG 1978); HM Diplomatic Service, retired; Ambassador to South Africa, 1984–87; *b* 2 Sept. 1928; *yr s* of G. H. Moberly; *m* 1955, Mary Penfold; two *s* one *d*. *Educ:* Winchester; Trinity Coll., Oxford (MA). HM Diplomatic Service, 1951–88; diplomatic posts in: Baghdad, 1953; Prague, 1957; Foreign Office, 1959; Dakar, 1962; Min. of Defence, 1965; Commonwealth Office, 1967; Canada, 1969; Israel, 1970; FCO, 1974; Asst Under-Sec. of State, 1976–81; Ambassador to Israel, 1981–84. *Recreations:* tennis, opera, canal boating. *Address:* 38 Lingfield Road, SW19 4PZ. *Club:* Oxford and Cambridge.

MOBERLY, Maj.-Gen. Richard James, CB 1957; OBE 1944; retired, 1960, and became Director, Communications Electronic Equipment, War Office, until 1964; *b* 2 July 1906; *o s* of late J. E. Moberly; *m* 1st, 1935, Mary Joyce Shelmerdine (*d* 1964); three *d*; 2nd, 1971, Mrs Vivien Mary Cameron (*d* 1981), *d* of Victor Bayley, CIE, CBE. *Educ:* Haileybury; Royal Military Academy, Woolwich. Commissioned Royal Signals, 1926; India, 1928–35; comd 1st Airborne Div. Signal Regt, 1942–43; CSO 1st Airborne Corps, 1943–45; Comdt Indian Signal Trng Centre, 1946–47; Dep. Comdt, Sch. of Signals, 1949–52; Dep. Dir of Signals, WO, 1952–54; CSO, Northern Army Gp, 1954–57; Signal Officer-in-Chief, WO, 1957–60. Col Comdt, Royal Signals, 1960–66. Comr for Dorset, St John Ambulance, 1968–76. KStJ 1986. *Address:* Galsworthy House, 177 Kingston Hill, Kingston upon Thames, Surrey KT2 7LX. *T:* (020) 8547 2640.

MOCHAN, Charles Francis; HM Diplomatic Service; Ambassador to Republic of Madagascar, since 1999, and concurrently to Federal Islamic Republic of Comoros, since 2001; *b* 6 Aug. 1948; *s* of Charles Mochan and Margaret Mochan (*née* Love); *m* 1970, Ilse Sybilla Carleon Cruttwell; one *s* one *d*. *Educ:* St Patrick's High Sch., Dumbarton. MoD (Navy), 1966; joined FCO 1967; Port Elizabeth, S Africa, 1970–72; Kingston, Jamaica, 1972–74; FCO, 1974–77; Seoul, 1977–80; Second, later First Sec., Helsinki, 1981–84; FCO, 1984–87; Dep. High Comr, Mauritius, 1988–91; FCO, 1991–95; Consul-Gen., Casablanca, 1995–98. *Recreations:* soccer, ornithology, music, walking. *Address:* c/o Foreign and Commonwealth Office, King Charles Street, SW1A 2AH.

MODARRESSI, Anne, (Mrs T. M. Modarressi); *see* Tyler, A.

MODIGLIANI, Prof. Franco; Institute Professor Emeritus, Massachusetts Institute of Technology, since 1988 (Professor of Economics and Finance, 1962–70; Institute Professor, 1970–88); *b* Rome, 1918; *s* of Enrico Modigliani and Olga (*née* Flaschel); *m* 1939, Serena Calabi; two *s*. *Educ:* Univ. of Rome (DJur 1939); DSocSci New Sch. for Social Research, New York, 1944. Instr in Economics and Statistics, New Jersey Coll. for Women, 1942; Instr, Associate in Economics and Statistics, Bard Coll. of Columbia Univ., 1942–44; Lectr, 1943–44, Asst Prof. of Math. Econ. and Econometrics, 1946–48, New Sch. for Social Research; Res. Associate and Chief Statistician, Inst. of World Affairs, NY, 1945–48; Res. Consultant, Cowles Commn for Res. in Economics, Univ. of Chicago, 1949–54; Associate Prof., 1949, Prof. of Economics, 1950–52, Univ. of Illinois; Prof. of Econ. and Indust. Admin, Carnegie Inst. of Technology, 1952–60; Prof. of Economics, Northwestern Univ., 1960–62. Social Science Research Council: Mem., Bd of Dirs, 1963–68; Mem., Cttee on Econ. Stability and Growth, 1970–; Jt Chm., Adv. Sub-Cttee on MIT-Pennsylvania SSRC Model, 1970–81; Mem., Sub-Cttee on Monetary Res., 1970–77. Academic Consultant, Bd of Governors, Federal Reserve System, 1966–; Sen. Adviser, Brookings Panel on Econ. Activity, 1971–; Consultant, Bank of Italy, Rome; Mem., Consiglio Italiano per le Scienze Sociali, 1974–; Perm. Mem., Conf. on Income and Wealth, Nat. Bureau of Econ. Res. Mem., Adv. Bd, Jl of Money, Credit and Banking, 1969–. Mem., Nat. Acad. of Scis, 1973–; Fellow, Econometric Soc., 1949; Fellow, 1960–, Council Mem., 1978–80, Amer. Acad. of Arts and Scis. Numerous hon. degrees. Nobel Prize in Economic Science, 1985. Kt Grand Cross, Italy, 1985. *Publications:* National Incomes and International Trade (with Hans Neisser), 1953; (jtly) Planning Production, Inventories and Work Forces, 1960; (with Kalman J. Cohen) The Role of Anticipations and Plans in Economic Behavior and their Use in Economic Analysis and Forecasting, 1961; (with Ezio Tarantelli) Mercato del Lavoro, Distribuzione del Reddito e Consumi Privati, 1975; (ed with Donald Lessard) New Mortgage Designs for Stable Housing in an Inflationary Environment, 1975; The Collected Papers of Franco Modigliani, vols 1, 2, 3, 1980, vols 4, 5, 1989 (trans. Hungarian, 1988); The Debate Over Stabilization Policy, 1986; Il caso Italia, 1986; Reddito, Interesse, Inflazione, 1987; (with Frank Fabozzi) Capital Markets—Institutions and Instruments, 1991; Consumo, Risparmio, Finanza, 1992; (with Frank Fabozzi) Mortgage and Mortgage Backed Securities Markets, 1992; Avventure di un Economista (autobiog.), 1999 (trans. English, 2001); contribs to Corriere

Della Sera, periodicals and learned jls. *Address:* Massachusetts Institute of Technology, Sloan School of Management, Cambridge, MA 02139, USA.

MODISE, Johannes, (Joe); Minister of Defence, Republic of South Africa, 1994–99; *b* Doornfontein, 23 May 1929. *Educ:* Fred Clark Meml Sch., Nancefield. Commander, Umkhonto we Sizwe, 1963; worked for underground movement and went into exile, 1963; returned to SA, 1990. African National Congress: Mem., NEC, 1963–; Mem., Nat. Wkg Cttee, 1963–; mem., first gp of ANC negotiators to hold talks with Pretoria govt, March 1990; mem., negotiating team of TEC Sub-Council on Defence until elections, April 1994. *Address:* c/o African National Congress, 51 Plein Street, Johannesburg 2001, South Africa.

MOELWYN-HUGHES, Edmwnd Goronwy; Vice Judge Advocate General, since 1994; a Recorder, since 1990; *b* 29 Aug. 1937; twin *s* of late Dr E. A. Moelwyn-Hughes and of Mair Elen Moelwyn-Hughes (*née* Evans); *m* 1964, Carolyn, *o d* of John Sanders and Beryl (*née* Hobday); one *s* two *d*. *Educ:* The Leys Sch., Cambridge; Trinity Hall, Cambridge (MA). Nat. Service, 1956–58, 2nd Lieut Royal Welch Fusiliers. Called to the Bar, Inner Temple, 1968; practised Wales and Chester Circuit, 1968–73. Dep. Judge Advocate, 1973–78; Asst JAG, 1978–94; Standing Civilian Court Magistrate, 1982–96; DJAG, British Forces in Germany, 1989–91. Governor: The Leys Sch., 1996–; St Faith's Sch., Cambridge, 1996–. *Recreations:* reading, music, walking, theatre. *Address:* Office of the Judge Advocate General, 22 Kingsway, WC2B 6LE. *T:* (020) 7218 8092. *Clubs:* Army and Navy, Royal Commonwealth Society.

MOFFAT, Alistair Murray; author and broadcaster; Chairman, Scottish Television Regional Board, since 1999; *b* 16 June 1950; *s* of John and Ellen Moffat; *m* 1976; Lindsay Anne Reid Thomas; one *s* two *d*. *Educ:* Kelso High Sch.; St Andrews Univ. (MA Hons); Edinburgh Univ. (CertEd); London Univ. (MPhil). Administrator, Edinburgh Festival Fringe, 1976–81; Scottish Television, subseq. Scottish Media Group: Arts Corresp., 1981–86; Controller of Features, 1987–90; Dir of Progs, 1990–93; Chief Exec., then Man. Dir, Scottish Television Enterprises, 1993–99. Mem., Scotch Malt Whisky Assoc, 1989–. *Publications:* The Edinburgh Fringe, 1978; Kelsae: a history from earliest times, 1985; Remembering Charles Rennie Mackintosh, 1989; Arthur and the Lost Kingdoms, 1999; The Sea Kingdoms, 2001. *Recreation:* apprentice groom. *Address:* The Henhouse, Selkirk TD7 5EY.

MOFFAT, Sir Brian (Scott), Kt 1996; OBE 1982; Chairman, Corus Group (formerly British Steel), since 1993; a Director, Bank of England, since 2000; *b* 6 Jan. 1939; *s* of Festus and Agnes Moffat; *m* 1964, Jacqueline Mary Cunliffe; one *s* one *d* (and one *s* decd). *Educ:* Hulme Grammar School. FCA. Peat Marwick Mitchell & Co., 1961–68; British Steel Corp., then British Steel plc, now Corus Gp, 1968–; Man. Dir, Finance, 1986–91; Chief Exec., 1991–99. Non-executive Director: Enterprise Oil, 1995–; HSBC Hldgs plc, 1998– (Dep. Chm., 2001–). Hon. DSc Warwick, 1998. *Recreations:* farming, fishing, shooting. *Club:* Flyfishers'.

MOFFAT, Rev. George; Team Rector, Manningham, since 1993; Chaplain to the Queen, since 2000; *b* 31 July 1946; *s* of George and Mary Moffat; *m* 1975, Peta Ollen; two *d*. *Educ:* Edinburgh Theol Coll.; New Coll., Edinburgh (BD 1977); Open Univ. (BA Hons 1987). Ordained deacon, 1972, priest, 1973; Curate: Christ Church, Falkirk, 1973–76; St Peter, Lutton Place, Edinburgh, 1976–81; Anglican Chaplain, Edinburgh Univ., 1977–81; Curate, St Leonard and All Saints, Heston, 1981–84; Vicar, St Mary the Virgin, S Emsall, 1984–93. *Recreations:* country walking, supporting creative modern dance. *Address:* 1 Selborne Grove, Heaton, Bradford, W Yorks BD9 4NL. *T:* (01274) 498566.

MOFFAT, Lt-Gen. Sir (William) Cameron, KBE 1985 (OBE 1975); FRCS; *b* 8 Sept. 1929; *s* of William Weir Moffat and Margaret Garrett; *m* 1953, Audrey Watson; one *s*. *Educ:* King's Park Sch., Glasgow; Univ. of Glasgow, Western Infirmary (MB ChB). DTM&H. House Surgeon, Western Inf., Glasgow, 1952; Ship's Surg., Anchor Line, 1953; MO Seaforth Highlanders, 1954; SMO Edinburgh, 1956–57; Hammersmith Hosp., 1962; Birmingham Accident Hosp., 1964; Surg., RAAF Hosp. Malaya, 1965–67; Cons. Surg., BMH Rinteln, 1968–70; Prof. Military Surgery, RAM Coll. and RCS, 1970–75; CO BMH Rinteln, 1978–80; Comd MED HQ 1 (Br) Corps, 1980–83; PMO, UKLF, 1983–84; Surg. Gen./Dir Gen. Army Med. Servs, MoD, 1985–87, retired. QHS 1984–88. Chief Med. Advr, BRCS, 1988–94. Hon. DSc Glasgow, 1991. CStJ 1985. *Publications:* contribs to surgical text books and jls on missile wounds and their management. *Recreations:* golf, travel, bird-watching. *Address:* Kippax, Pound Green, Freshwater, Isle of Wight PO40 9HH.

MOFFATT, Prof. (Henry) Keith, ScD; FRS 1986; FRSE; Professor of Mathematical Physics, University of Cambridge, since 1980 (Head of Department of Applied Mathematics and Theoretical Physics, 1983–91); Fellow, Trinity College, Cambridge, 1961–76, and since 1980; *b* 12 April 1935; *s* of late Frederick Henry Moffatt and Emmeline Marchant Fleming; *m* 1960, Katharine, (Linty), Stiven, *d* of late Rev. D. S. Stiven, MC, DD; one *s* two *d* (and one *s* decd). *Educ:* George Watson's Coll., Edinburgh; Edinburgh Univ. (BSc); Cambridge Univ. (BA, PhD, ScD). Lecturer in Mathematics, Cambridge Univ., and Director of Studies in Mathematics, Trinity Coll., 1961–76; Tutor, 1971–75; Sen. Tutor, 1975; Professor of Applied Mathematics, Bristol Univ., 1977–80; Dir, Isaac Newton Inst. for Mathematical Scis, Cambridge Univ., 1996–2001. Visiting appts, Stanford Univ. and Johns Hopkins Univ., 1965, Univ. of Paris VI, 1975–76, Institut de Mécanique, Grenoble, 1986, Univ. of California, San Diego, 1987, Santa Barbara, 1991, Ecole Polytechnique Palaiseau, 1992–99, Kyoto Univ., 1993; Blaise Pascal Internat. Chair, Paris, 2001. Co-editor, Journal of Fluid Mechanics, 1966–83. Foreign Mem., Royal Netherlands Acad. of Arts and Scis, 1991; Associé Etranger, Acad. des Sciences, Paris, 1998. MAE 1994. FRSE 1988. *Dhc*: Inst. Nat Polytechnique de Grenoble, 1987; Edinburgh, 2001; Hon. DSc SUNY, 1990. Officier des Palmes Académiques, 1998. *Publications:* Magnetic Field Generation in Electrically Conducting Fluids, 1978; (jt ed) Topological Fluid Mechanics, 1990; Topological Aspects of the Dynamics of Fluids and Plasmas, 1992; papers in fluid mechanics and dynamo theory in Jl Fluid Mech. and other jls. *Address:* Trinity College, Cambridge CB2 1TQ.

MOFFATT, John, MA, DPhil; Provost, The Queen's College, Oxford, 1987–93, Hon. Fellow, 1993; *b* 12 Oct. 1922; *s* of Jacob and Ethel Moffatt; *m* 1949, Una Lamorna Morris (*d* 1992); one *d*. *Educ:* Keighley Boys' Grammar Sch.; Magdalen Coll., Oxford (MA, DPhil). Radar research with British Thomson-Houston Co. Ltd, Rugby, 1942–46; Oxford University: Sen. Res. Officer, Clarendon Lab., 1950; Lectr, Dept of Nuclear Physics, 1965; The Queen's College: Fellow and Praelector in Physics, 1950; Sen. Tutor, 1972–76. *Publications:* articles on physics in various scientific jls. *Address:* 2 Cumnor Rise Road, Cumnor Hill, Oxford OX2 9HD.

MOFFATT, Keith; *see* Moffatt, H. K.

MOFFATT, Laura Jean; MP (Lab) Crawley, since 1997; *b* 9 April 1954; *d* of Stanley and Barbara Field; *m* 1975, Colin Moffatt; three *s*. *Educ:* Hazelwick Comprehensive Sch., Crawley; Crawley Coll. of Technology. SRN, 1975–97. Mem. (Lab), Crawley BC, 1984–97 (Mayor, 1990–91). Contested (Lab) Crawley, 1992. *Recreations:* pets, walking, holidays with family. *Address:* 9 Adrian Court, Chadwick Close, Broadfield, Crawley, Sussex RH11 9LQ. *T:* (01293) 530585.

MOGER, Christopher Richard Derwent; QC 1992; a Recorder, since 1993 (an Assistant Recorder, 1990–93); a Deputy High Court Judge, since 1999; *b* 28 July 1949; *s* of Richard Vernon Derwent Moger and Cecile Eva Rosales Moger (*née* Power); *m* 1st, 1974, Victoria Trollope (marr. diss. 1991); three *s*; 2nd, 1991, Prudence Da Cunha. *Educ:* Sherborne School; Bristol Univ. (LLB Hons). FCIArb 1997. Called to the Bar, Inner Temple, 1972, Bencher, 2001. Member: Western Circuit; London Common Law Bar Assoc.; Commercial Bar Assoc.; Official Referee's Bar Assoc.; Barristers' Overseas Advocacy Cttee. *Recreations:* fishing, walking. *Address:* 4 Pump Court, Temple, EC4Y 7AN. *T:* (020) 7353 2656. *Club:* Garrick.

MOGFORD, Jeremy Lewis; Managing Director: Mogford Ltd, since 1998; Mogford Hotels Ltd, since 1998; Quod Restaurants, since 1999; *b* 9 Oct. 1947; *s* of Peter Charles Mogford and Pamela Margaret Mogford (*née* Bennett); *m* 1971, Hilary Jane Raymond; one *s* one *d*. *Educ:* Canford Sch.; Royal Grammar Sch., High Wycombe; Univ. of Surrey (BSc Hotel and Catering Admin). MHCIMA 1971. Founder, owner and Man. Dir, 1973–97, Consultant, 1997–, Browns Restaurants Ltd; Dir, Peachey Productions, 1998–. Mem. Exec. Cttee, Restaurant Assoc. of GB, 1998–. Dir and Sponsor, Discerning Eye Art Exhibn, 1995–97; Sponsor, Oxford Lit. Fest., 1995. DUniv Oxford Brookes, 2001. Independent Gp Restaurateur of the Year, Caterer and Hotelkeeper mag., 1997. *Recreations:* topiary, fly fishing, 20th century British art. *Address:* c/o Drummonds, 49 Charing Cross, SW1A 2DX. *Clubs:* Groucho, Soho House, Home House.

MOGG; *see* Rees-Mogg, family name of Baron Rees-Mogg.

MOGG, Gen. Sir John, GCB 1972 (KCB 1966; CB 1964); CBE 1960; DSO 1944; Bar, 1944; Deputy Supreme Allied Commander, Europe, 1973–76; *b* 17 Feb. 1913; *s* of late Capt. H. B. Mogg, MC and late Alice Mary (*née* Ballard); *m* 1939, Cecilia Margaret Molesworth; three *s*. *Educ:* Malvern Coll.; RMC Sandhurst. Coldstream Guards, 1933–35; RMC Sandhurst (Sword of Honour) 1935–37; commissioned Oxfordshire and Buckinghamshire Light Infantry, 1937. Served War of 1939–45 (despatches twice, 1944); comd 9 DLI (NW Europe), 1944–45; Instructor, Staff Coll., 1948–50; Commander 10th Parachute Bn, 1950–52; Chief Instructor, School of Infantry, Warminster, 1952–54; Instructor (GSO1), Imperial Defence Coll., 1954–56; Comdr, Commonwealth Brigade Gp, Malaya, 1958–60; Meritorious Medal (Perak, Malaya); Dir of Combat Development, War Office, 1961–62; Comdt, Royal Military Academy, Sandhurst, 1963–66; Comdr 1st (British) Corps, 1966–68; GOC-in-C Southern Comd, 1968; GOC-in-C Army Strategic Comd, 1968–70; Adjutant-Gen., MoD (Army), 1970–73. ADC Gen. to the Queen, 1971–74. Col Comdt: Army Air Corps, 1963–74; The Royal Green Jackets, 1965–73; Hon. Col, 10th Parachute Bn, TA, 1973–78. Kermit Roosevelt Lectr, 1969. President: Army Cricket Assoc.; Army Saddle Club, 1969; Army Boxing Assoc., 1970; Army Parachute Assoc., 1971; BHS, 1972; Ex Services Mental Welfare Soc.; Army Benevolent Fund, 1980– (Chm., 1976); Normandy Veterans Assoc., 1982–; Chairman: Army Free Fall Parachute Assoc., 1970; Army Football Assoc., 1960–63; Royal Soldiers' Daughters Sch., 1976; Operation Drake for Young Explorers, 1978–; Operation Drake Fellowship, 1980–83; Royal Internat. Horse Show, 1979; Vice-Pres., Operation Raleigh. Pres., Council Services Kinema Corp., 1970. Dir, Lloyds Bank S Midland Regional Bd, 1976. Member Council: Wessex TA&VRA, 1976; British Atlantic Cttee, 1977; Fairbridge Drake Soc., 1987. Comr, Royal Hospital Chelsea, 1976. Governor: Malvern College, 1967; Bradfield College, 1977; Chm. of Governors, Icknield Sch., 1981–. Hon. Liveryman, Fruiterers' Co. DL Oxfordshire, 1979, Vice Lord-Lieut, 1979–89. *Recreations:* cricket, most field sports, helicopter pilot. *Address:* Church Close, Watlington, Oxon OX9 5QR. *Clubs:* Army and Navy, Flyfishers', MCC, Cavalry and Guards, Pitt.

MOGG, John Frederick; Director-General, Directorate General Internal Market (formerly Directorate-General XV), European Commission, since 1993; *b* 5 Oct. 1943; *s* of Thomas W. Mogg and Cora M. Mogg; *m* 1967, Anne Smith; one *d* one *s*. *Educ:* Bishop Vesey's Grammar Sch., Sutton Coldfield; Birmingham Univ. (BA Hons). Rediffusion Ltd, 1965–74; Principal: Office of Fair Trading, 1974–76; Dept of Trade (Insurance Div.), 1976–79; First Sec., UK Perm. Representation, Brussels, 1979–82; Department of Trade and Industry: Asst Sec., Minerals and Metals Div., 1982–85; PPS to Sec. of State for Trade and Industry, 1985–86; Under Secretary: European Policy Div., 1986–87; Industrial Materials Market Div., 1987–89; Dep. Hd, European Secretariat, Cabinet Office, 1989–90; Dep. Dir Gen., DGIII, EC, 1990–93. *Address:* European Commission, DG Internal Market, Rue de la loi 200, 1049 Brussels, Belgium.

MOGGACH, Deborah; novelist, journalist and script-writer; *b* 28 June 1948; *d* of late Richard Alexander Hough, writer and of Helen Charlotte (*née* Woodyatt); *m* 1971, Anthony Austin Moggach (marr. diss. 1988); one *s* one *d*. *Educ:* Camden Sch. for Girls; Bristol Univ. (BA Hons English); Inst. of Educn, Univ. of London (BEd English). Mem., Exec. Cttee, English PEN, 1992–95; Chm., Soc. of Authors, 1999– (Mem., Broadcasting Cttee, 1995–97, Mgt Cttee, 1998–). Television includes: Crown Court, 1983; To Have and to Hold, 1986; Stolen, 1990; Goggle Eyes (adaptation; Writers' Guild Award for Best Adapted Serial), 1993; Seesaw, 1998; Close Relations, 1998; Love in a Cold Climate (adaptation), 2001; stage play, Double Take, Liverpool Playhouse, 1990, Chichester Fest. Theatre, 1993. Young Journalist of the Year, Westminster Arts Council, 1975. FRSL 1998. *Publications:* You Must Be Sisters, 1978; Close to Home, 1979; A Quiet Drink, 1980; Hot Water Man, 1982; Porky, 1983; To Have and To Hold, 1986; Smile and other stories, 1987; Driving in the Dark, 1988; Stolen, 1990; The Stand-In, 1991; The Ex-Wives, 1993; Changing Babies, 1995; Seesaw, 1996; Close Relations, 1997; Tulip Fever, 1999; Final Demand, 2001. *Recreation:* walking around London looking into people's windows. *Address:* c/o Curtis Brown, 28–29 Haymarket, SW1Y 4SP. *T:* (020) 7396 6600.

MOGGRIDGE, Harry Traherne, (Hal), OBE 1986; PPLI; FIHort; Consultant, Colvin and Moggridge, Landscape Consultants (established 1922), since 1997 (Partner, 1969–97; Senior Partner, 1981–97); *b* London, 2 Feb. 1936; *s* of late Lt-Col Harry Weston Moggridge, CMG, and Helen Mary Ferrier Taylor; *m* 1963, Hon. Catherine Greville Herbert, *yr d* of 2nd Baron Hemingford; two *s* one *d*. *Educ:* Tonbridge Sch.; Architectural Assoc. (Dip.); evening lectures in landscape design under Prof. P. Youngman. Notts CC, 1960; Asst to Geoffrey Jellicoe, 1961–63; Site architect for Sir Wm Halcrow & Ptrs, Tema Harbour, Ghana, 1964–65; Landscape asst, GLC, 1966–67; own practice; entered into partnership with late Brenda Colvin, CBE, PPILA, 1969, continuing in partnership with Christopher Carter, ALI, and staff of fifteen. Prof. of Landscape Architecture, Univ. of Sheffield, 1984–86. Member: Royal Fine Art Commn, 1988–99; Nat. Trust Architectural Panel, 1991–. Mem. Council, Landscape Inst., 1970–83 (Hon. Sec., Vice Pres., Pres. 1979–81) and 1987–93 (Deleg. to Internat. Fedn of Landscape Architects, 1980–90; Chm., Internat. Cttee, 1986–92); Chm., Landscape Foundn, 1995–99. Landscape works include: Brenig Reservoir, Clwyd; White Horse Hill, a new car park and restoration of grass downland; Gale Common Hill, Yorkshire, woods and fields over 100 million cubic metres of waste ash and shale built over 60 years; quarries; countryside studies; reclamation; public and private gardens; Aldermaston Ct, near Reading, grounds for a new co. headquarters; restoration of historic parks (eg Blenheim, Knole, Castle Hill), creation of new parks and consultancy for Inner Royal Parks of London; master plans for RHS Wisley Gdns and for Middleton Welsh Nat. Botanic Gdns. FRSA. VMH 2000. *Publications:* numerous articles and chapters of books describing works or technical subjects. *Recreations:* looking at pictures, gardens, buildings, towns, landscapes and people in these places; walking, theatre, grandchildren. *Address:* Filkins, Lechlade, Glos GL7 3JQ. *T:* (01367) 860225. *Club:* Farmers.

See also Lady Goodhart.

MOHYEDDIN, Zia; actor; producer and director, Central TV, 1980–94; *b* 20 June 1931. *Educ:* Punjab University (BA Hons). Freelance directing for Aust. broadcasting, 1951–52; RADA, 1953–54; Pakistan stage appearances, 1956–59; UK stage, 1959–71; Dir Gen., Pakistan Nat. Performing Ensemble, to 1977; *stage:* appearances include: A Passage to India, 1960; The Alchemist, 1964; The Merchant of Venice, 1966; Volpone, 1967; The Guide, 1968; On The Rocks, 1969; Measure for Measure, 1981; Film, Film, Film, 1986; *films:* Lawrence of Arabia, 1961; Sammy Going South, 1963; The Sailor from Gibraltar; Khartoum, 1965; Ashanti, 1982; Assam Garden, 1985; Immaculate Conception, 1992; The Odyssey; Doomsday Gun, 1993; L'Enfant des Rues, 1994; *television series:* The Hidden Truth, 1964; Gangsters, 1979; Jewel in the Crown, 1983; King of the Ghetto, 1986; Mountbatten, 1988; Shalom Salaam, 1989; creator, Family Pride, Channel Four, 1990. *Recreations:* reading, bridge, watching cricket. *Address:* c/o Plunket Greene Ltd/ James Sharkey Associates, PO Box 8365 W14 0GL. *T:* (020) 7603 2227, *Fax:* (020) 7603 2221. *Club:* Savile.

MOI, Hon. Daniel arap, EGH, EBS; President of Kenya, since 1978; Minister of Defence, since 1979; *b* Rift Valley Province, 1924. *Educ:* African Inland Mission Sch., Kabartonjo; Govt African Sch., Kapsabet. Teacher, 1946–56. MLC, 1957; Mem. for Baringo, House of Representatives, 1963–78; Minister for Educn, 1961; Minister for Local Govt, 1962–64; Minister for Home Affairs, 1964–67; Vice-Pres. of Kenya, 1967–78. Chm., Kenya African Democratic Union (KADU), 1960; Pres., Kenya African Nat. Union (KANU) for Rift Valley Province, 1966; Pres. of KANU, 1978–. Chm., Rift Valley Provincial Council. Former Member: Rift Valley Educn Bd; Kalenjin Language Cttee; Commonwealth Higher Educn Cttee; Kenya Meat Commn; Bd of Governors, African Girls' High Sch., Kikuyu. *Address:* Office of the President, PO Box 30510, Nairobi, Kenya; State House, PO Box 40530, Nairobi, Kenya.

MOIR, Sir Christopher Ernest, 4th Bt *cr* 1916, of Whitehanger, Fernhurst, co. Sussex; *b* 22 May 1955; *e s* of Sir Ernest Ian Royds Moir, 3rd Bt and of Margaret Hanham, *d* of George Eric Carter; *S* father, 1998; *m* 1983, Mrs Vanessa Kirtikar, *yr d* of V. A. Crosby; twin *s*, and one step *d*. *Educ:* King's College Sch., Wimbledon. FCA 1976. *Heir: er s* Oliver Royds Moir, *b* 9 Oct. 1984. *Address:* Three Gates, 174 Coombe Lane West, Kingston upon Thames, Surrey KT2 7DE.

MOIR, Dorothy Carnegie, MD; FRCP, FFPHM; Director of Public Health and Chief Administrative Medical Officer, Lanarkshire Health Board, since 1994; *b* 27 March 1942; *d* of Charles Carnegie Coull and Jessie Coull (*née* Ritchie); *m* 1970, Alexander David Moir; three *s*. *Educ:* Albyn Sch. for Girls, Aberdeen; Aberdeen Univ. (MB ChB; MD); Open Univ. (MBA). Resident Med. House Officer, Aberdeen Royal Infirmary, 1965–66; Resident Surg. House Officer, Royal Aberdeen Childrens' Hosp., 1966; Res. Fellow in Therapeutics, 1966–69, Lectr in Community Medicine, 1970–79, Univ. of Aberdeen; Community Medicine Specialist, Grampian Health Bd, 1979–88; Unit MO, Acute Services, Aberdeen Royal Infirmary, 1984–88; Dir of Public Health and Chief Admin. MO, Forth Valley Health Bd, 1988–94. *Publications:* (jtly) The Prescription and Administration of Drugs in Hospital: a programmed learning text, 1970, 3rd edn 1988; many articles in med. and pharmaceut. jls. *Address:* 14 Beckford Street, Hamilton ML3 0TA. *T:* (01698) 281313.

MOIR, James William Charles; Controller, BBC Radio 2, since 1995; *b* 5 Nov. 1941; *s* of William Charles Moir and Mary Margaret Moir (*née* Daly); *m* 1966, Julia (*née* Smalley); two *s* one *d*. *Educ:* Gunnersbury Catholic Grammar School; Univ. of Nottingham (BA). Joined BBC TV Light Entertainment Group, 1963; Producer, Light Entertainment, 1970, Exec. Producer, 1979; Head of Variety, 1982–87; Head of Gp, 1987–93; Dep. Dir, Corporate Affairs, BBC, 1993–95. Chm., EBU Working Pty on Light Entertainment, 1992–94. Hon. Mem. Council, NSPCC, 1990–. Mem., Vice Chancellor's Adv. Bd, Univ. of Nottingham, 1990–. Trustee, Symphony Hall, Birmingham, 1996–. FRTS 1990; Fellow, Radio Acad., 1998. *Address:* The Lawn, Elm Park Road, Pinner, Middx HA5 3LE. *Club:* Reform.

MOIR, Judith Patricia; Her Honour Judge Moir; a Circuit Judge, since 1999; *b* 2 Dec. 1954; *d* of Norman and Stephanie Edwardson; *m* 1977, Charles Geoffrey Moir; two *s* one *d*. *Educ:* Central Newcastle High Sch.; Somerville Coll., Oxford (BA Jurisp.). Called to the Bar, Gray's Inn, 1978; in practice at the Bar, NE Circuit, 1978–99. *Recreation:* family. *Address:* Newcastle Combined Court Centre, Quayside, Newcastle upon Tyne NE1 3LA.

MOISEIWITSCH, Prof. Benjamin Lawrence; Professor of Applied Mathematics, Queen's University of Belfast, 1968–93, now Emeritus; *b* London, 6 Dec. 1927; *s* of Jacob Moiseiwitsch and Chana Kotlerman; *m* 1953, Sheelagh Mary Penrose McKeon; two *s* two *d*. *Educ:* Royal Liberty Sch., Romford; University Coll., London (BSc, 1949, PhD 1952). Sir George Jessel Studentship in Maths, UCL, 1949; Queen's University, Belfast: Lectr and Reader in Applied Maths, 1952–68; Dean, Faculty of Science, 1972–75; Hd, Dept of Applied Maths and Theoretical Physics, 1977–89. MRIA 1969. *Publications:* Variational Principles, 1966; Integral Equations, 1977; articles on theoretical atomic physics in scientific jls. *Address:* 21 Knocktern Gardens, Belfast, Northern Ireland BT4 3LZ. *T:* (028) 9065 8332.

MOISEIWITSCH, Tanya, (Mrs Felix Krish), CBE 1976; designer for the theatre; *b* 3 Dec. 1914; *d* of late Benno Moiseiwitsch, CBE, and 1st wife, Daisy Kennedy; *m* 1942, Felix Krish (decd). *Educ:* various private schs; Central School of Arts and Crafts, London; Scenic painting student at Old Vic, London. Abbey Theatre, Dublin, 1935–39; Q. Theatre, 1940; 1st West End prod. Golden Cuckoo, Duchess, 1940; Weekly Repertory, Oxford Playhouse, 1941–44. Stage designs include: Bless the Bride, Adelphi, 1947; Peter Grimes, Covent Garden, 1947; Beggar's Opera, English Opera Group, Aldeburgh Festival, 1948; Treasure Hunt, Apollo, 1949; Home at Seven, Wyndham's, 1950; The Holly and the Ivy, Lyric (Hammersmith) and Duchess, 1950; Captain Carvallo, St James's, 1950; Figure of Fun, Aldwych, 1951. Has designed for Old Vic Company since 1944; at Playhouse, Liverpool, 1944–45; at Theatre Royal, Bristol, 1945–46; productions for Old Vic Company include: (at New Theatre): Uncle Vanya, The Critic, Cyrano de Bergerac, 1945–46, The Cherry Orchard, 1948, A Month in the Country, 1949; (at Old Vic): Midsummer Night's Dream, 1951, Timon of Athens, 1952, Henry VIII, 1953; Two Gentlemen of Verona, 1957. Has designed for Royal Shakespeare Theatre, Stratford upon Avon: Henry VIII, 1950; The History Cycle (assisted by Alix Stone), 1951; Othello, 1954; Measure for Measure, 1956; Much Ado about Nothing (scenery), 1958; All's Well that Ends Well, 1959; also for 1st, and subsequent seasons, Shakespearean Festival, Stratford, Ont, incl. Cymbeline, 1970; The Imaginary Invalid, 1974 (Australian tour for Elizabethan Theatre Trust); All's Well that Ends Well, 1977; Mary Stuart (costumes), 1982; Tartuffe, 1983; (with Polly Scranton Bohdanetzky) The Government Inspector, Stratford, Ont, 1985; consultant to designer, Œdipus Rex, Stratford, Ont, 1997; for The Matchmaker, Edinburgh Festival, 1954, and New York, 1955; for Cherry Orchard, Piccolo Teatro, Milan, 1955; for Merchant of Venice, Habimah Theatre, Israel, 1959; Tyrone Guthrie Theatre, Minneapolis, USA: 1963: Hamlet, The Miser, Three Sisters; 1964: St Joan, Volpone; 1965: The Way of the World; Cherry Orchard; 1966: As You Like It; Skin of our Teeth (with Carolyn Parker); 1967: The House of Atreus; 1973: (with J. Jensen) The Government Inspector (costumes); Metropolitan Opera, New York: Peter Grimes, 1967; Rigoletto, 1977; La Traviata, 1981; National Theatre: Volpone, 1968; The Misanthrope, 1973; Phaedra Britannica, 1975; The Double Dealer, 1978; Macook's Corner, Ulster Players, Belfast, 1969; Caucasian Chalk Circle, Sheffield Playhouse, 1969; Swift, Abbey Theatre, Dublin, 1969; Uncle Vanya, Minneapolis, 1969; The Barber of Seville, Brighton Festival, 1971; The Misanthrope, St James' Theater, NY, 1975; The Voyage of Edgar Allan Poe (world première), Minnesota Opera Co., USA, 1976; Œdipus the King and Œdipus at Colonus (costumes and masks), Adelaide Fest., 1978; Red Roses for Me, Abbey Theatre, Dublin, 1980; The Clandestine Marriage, Compass Theatre Co. tour and Albery, 1984. Cons. designer, Crucible Theatre, Sheffield, 1971–73. For Granada TV, King Lear (costumes), 1983. Assoc. Dir Laureate, Stratford Festival, Canada. Diplôme d'Honneur, Canadian Conference of the Arts; Hon. Fellow, Ontario Coll. of Art, 1979. Hon. DLitt: Birmingham, 1964; Waterloo, Ont, 1977; Minnesota, 1994; Hon. LLD Toronto, 1988. *Address:* 17B St Alban's Studios, St Alban's Grove, W8 5BT.

MOLE, David Richard Penton; QC 1990; a Recorder, since 1995; *b* 1 April 1943; *s* of Rev. Arthur Penton Mole and late Margaret Isobel Mole; *m* 1969, Anu-Reet (*née* Nigol); three *s* one *d*. *Educ:* St John's School, Leatherhead; Trinity College, Dublin (MA); LSE (LLM). City of London College, 1967–74 (Sen. Lectr, 1971); called to the Bar, Inner Temple, 1970; Standing Junior Counsel to Inland Revenue in rating valuation matters, 1984. Jt Hd of Chambers. Part-time cartoonist, 1979–83. *Publications:* contribs to Jl of Planning Law. *Recreations:* sailing, walking, ski-ing, drawing, painting. *Address:* 4-5 Gray's Inn Square, Gray's Inn, WC1R 5AY. *T:* (020) 7404 5252.

MOLESWORTH, family name of **Viscount Molesworth**.

MOLESWORTH, 12th Viscount *cr* 1716 (Ire.); **Robert Bysse Kelham Molesworth;** Baron Philipstown 1716; proprietor, North London Transport, since 1991; *b* 4 June 1959; *s* of 11th Viscount Molesworth and Anne Florence (*née* Cohen; *d* 1983); *S* father, 1997. *Educ:* Cheltenham; Sussex Univ. (BA Philosophy). Admin. and Personnel Officer, 1986–91; established North London Transport, light haulage, transport and removals co., 1991. *Recreations:* carpentry, diving, camping, tennis. *Heir: b* Hon. William John Charles Molesworth, *b* 20 Oct. 1960. *Address:* c/o Garden Flat, 2 Bishopswood Road, Highgate N6 4PR. *T:* (020) 7561 1196.

MOLESWORTH, Allen Henry Neville; management consultant; *b* 20 Aug. 1931; *s* of late Roger Bevil Molesworth (Colonel RA), and of Iris Alice Molesworth (*née* Kennion); *m* 1970, Gail Cheng Kwai Chan. *Educ:* Wellington Coll., Berks; Trinity Coll., Cambridge (MA). FCA, FCMA, FIMC. 2nd Lt, 4th Queen's Own Hussars, Malaya, 1950. Project Accounts, John Laing & Sons (Canada) Ltd, 1954–58; Singleton Fabian & Co., Chartered Accountants, 1959–63; Consultant: Standard Telephones & Cables Ltd, 1963–67; Coopers & Lybrand Associates Ltd, 1967–76: India, 1970; Kuwait, 1971; France, 1972; New Hebrides, 1972; Laos, 1974; Tonga, 1975; Financial and Admin. Controller, Crown Agents, 1976–84; Chief Accountant, British Telecom Property, 1984–90. *Recreations:* shooting, skiing, music, restoring antiques. *Address:* c/o Lloyds TSB, 8–10 Waterloo Place, SW1Y 4BE. *Clubs:* 1900, Coningsby.

MOLESWORTH-ST AUBYN, Sir William, 16th Bt *cr* 1689, of Pencarrow, Cornwall; *b* 23 Nov. 1958; *s* of Sir Arscott Molesworth-St Aubyn, 15th Bt, MBE and of Iona Audrey Armatrude, *d* of Adm. Sir Francis Loftus Tottenham, KCB, CBE; *S* father, 1998; *m* 1988, Carolyn, *er d* of William Tozier; one *s* one *d*. *Educ:* Harrow. Late Captain, The Royal Green Jackets. *Heir: s* Archie Hender Molesworth-St Aubyn, *b* 27 March 1997.

MOLINA, Prof. Mario Jose, PhD; Professor, Department of Earth, Atmospheric and Planetary Sciences, and Department of Chemistry, Massachusetts Institute of Technology, since 1989; *b* 19 March 1943; *s* of Roberto Molina-Pasquel and Leonor Henriquez de Molina; *m* 1973, Luisa Yu Tan; one *s*. *Educ:* Univ. Nacional Autónoma de México (Ingeniero Quimico 1965); Univ. of Calif, Berkeley (PhD 1972). Asst Prof., Univ. Nacional Autónoma de México, 1967–68; Res. Associate, Univ. of Calif, Berkeley, 1972–73; Res. Associate, 1973–74, Asst Prof., 1975–79, Associate Prof., 1979–82, Univ. of Calif, Irvine; Sen. Res. Scientist, Jet Propulsion Lab., Calif, 1983–89. Mem., US Nat. Acad. of Scis, 1993. Tyler Ecology and Energy Prize, USA, 1983; (jtly) Nobel Prize for Chemistry, 1995. *Publications:* articles in jls and chapters in books. *Recreations:* music, tennis. *Address:* Department of Earth, Atmospheric and Planetary Sciences, 54–1814 Massachusetts Institute of Technology, Cambridge, MA 02139, USA.

MOLITOR, Edouard, Hon. KCMG 1976; Grand Officier, Ordre du Mérite (Luxembourg), 1990; Grand Officier, Ordre de la Couronne de Chêne, 1996; Officier, Ordre Civil et Militaire d'Adolphe de Nassau, 1977; Ambassador of Luxembourg to Italy, 1993–96; Permanent Representative to UN Food and Agriculture Organisation, 1993–96; *b* Luxembourg City, 14 Feb. 1931; *s* of Joseph Molitor and Lucie Michels; *m* 1960, Constance Scholtes; three *s*. *Educ:* Univs of Grenoble, Nancy and Paris. Dr en droit. Barrister, Luxembourg, 1955–60; joined Diplomatic Service, 1960 (Political Affairs); First Sec. and Rep. to UNESCO, Paris, 1964–69; Counsellor and Consul-Gen., Brussels, 1969–73; Dir of Protocol and Juridical Affairs, Min. of Foreign Affairs, 1973–78; Mem., Commn de Contrôle, EC, 1973–77; Ambassador to Austria, 1978–89; Perm. Rep. to UNIDO, IAEA, 1978–89; Head of Luxembourg Delegn, MBFR Conf., 1978–89 and at CSCE Conf., Vienna, 1986–89; Ambassador to UK, Ireland and Iceland, and Perm. Rep. to Council of WEU, 1989–92. Mem., Rotary Club, Luxembourg. Foreign Decorations from: Norway, 1964; Italy, W Germany, Belgium, 1973; Greece, 1975; Denmark, Tunisia, Senegal, Netherlands, France, 1978; Vatican, Austria, 1989; Iceland, 1990. *Recreations:* swimming, hiking, ski ing, shooting, music, literature. *Address:* 47 allée Léopold Goebel, 1635 Luxembourg.

MOLLISON, Prof. Patrick Loudon, CBE 1979; MD; FRCP; FRCPath; FRCOG; FRS 1968; Professor of Hæmatology, St Mary's Hospital Medical School, London University, 1962–79, now Emeritus Professor; Hon. Consultant Immunohaematologist, North London Blood Transfusion Centre, since 1983; *b* 17 March 1914; *s* of William Mayhew Mollison, Cons. Surgeon (ENT), Guy's Hospital; *m* 1st, 1940, Dr Margaret D. Peirce (marr. diss., 1964); three *s*; 2nd, 1973, Dr Jennifer Jones. *Educ:* Rugby Sch.; Clare

Coll., Cambridge; St Thomas' Hosp., London. MD Cantab 1944; FRCP 1959; FRCPath 1963; FRCOG *ad eund*, 1980. House Phys., Medical Unit, St Thomas' Hosp., 1939; Medical Officer, S London Blood Supply Depot, 1939–43; RAMC, 1943–46; Dir, MRC Blood Transfusion Res. Unit, Hammersmith Hosp., 1946–60; part-time Dir, MRC Experimental Hæmatology Unit, 1960–79; Hon. Lectr, then Sen. Lectr, Dept of Medicine, Post-grad. Medical Sch., 1948; Consultant Hæmatologist: Hammersmith Hosp., 1947–60; St Mary's Hosp., 1960–79. Hon. FRSocMed 1979; Landsteiner Meml Award, USA, 1960; P. Levine Award, USA, 1973; Oehlecker Medal, Germany, 1974. *Publications:* Blood Transfusion in Clinical Medicine, 1951, 10th edn (jtly) 1997; papers on red cell survival and blood group antibodies. *Recreations:* music, gardening. *Address:* 60 King Henry's Road, NW3 3RR. *T:* (020) 7722 1947.

MOLLO, Joseph Molelekoa Kaibe; Corporate Affairs Manager, Gencor, Johannesburg; *b* 7 May 1944; *s* of Kaibe and Cyrian Mollo; *m* 1972, Makaibe; two *s* two *d*. *Educ:* Univ. of Botswana, Lesotho and Swaziland (BA Admin); Univ. of Saskatchewan (MCEd); Carleton Univ. (working on a Master's degree in Political Science since 1978). Asst Sec., Min. of Finance, 1971; Comr of Co-operatives, 1973; Dep. Perm. Sec., Finance, 1975; High Comr, Canada, 1976; Perm. Sec., Finance, 1980; High Comr in London, 1982–83; Ambassador to Denmark (also accredited to Sweden, Norway, Finland, Iceland, GDR and Poland), 1983–86; Man. Dir, Trading Corp. of Lesotho, 1986–88; Ambassador of Lesotho to Republic of South Africa, 1992–94. Unpublished thesis: Profit versus Co-operation: the struggle of the Western Co-operative College. *Recreations:* jogging, dancing, music, soccer.

MOLLON, Prof. John Dixon, DSc; FRS 1999; Professor of Visual Neuroscience, University of Cambridge, since 1998; Fellow of Gonville and Caius College, Cambridge, since 1996; *b* 12 Sept. 1944; *s* of Arthur Greenwood Mollon and Joyce Dorothy Mollon. *Educ:* Scarborough High Sch.; Hertford Coll., Oxford (BA 1966; DPhil 1970). Sen. Schol., Wadham Coll., Oxford, 1967–69; Post-doctoral Fellow, Bell Telephone Labs, NJ, 1970; Lectr in Psychology, Corpus Christi Coll., Oxford, 1971–72; University of Cambridge: Univ. Demonstrator, 1972–76; Lectr, 1976–93, Reader, 1993–98, in Exptl Psychology. Hon. Sec., Experimental Psychology Soc., 1974–78. Fellow, Optical Soc. of America, 1984. *Publications:* (with H. B. Barlow) The Senses, 1982; (with L. T. Sharpe) Colour Vision: physiology and psychophysics, 1983. *Recreations:* book collecting, historical research. *Address:* Gonville and Caius College, Cambridge CB2 1TA.

MOLLOY, Michael John; writer; *b* 22 Dec. 1940; *s* of John George and Margaret Ellen Molloy; *m* 1964, Sandra June Foley; three *d*. *Educ:* Ealing School of Art. Sunday Pictorial, 1956; Daily Sketch, 1960; Daily Mirror, 1962–85: Editor, Mirror Magazine, 1969; Asst Editor, 1970; Dep. Editor, 1975; Editor, Dec. 1975–1985; Editor, Sunday Mirror, 1986–88; Mirror Group Newspapers: Director, 1976–90; Editor in Chief, 1985–90. *Publications:* The Black Dwarf, 1985; The Kid from Riga, 1987; The Harlot of Jericho, 1989; The Century, 1990; The Gallery, 1991; Sweet Sixteen, 1992; Cat's Paw, 1993; Home Before Dark, 1994; Dogsbody, 1995. *Recreations:* reading, writing. *Address:* 62 Culmington Road, W13 9NH. *Club:* Savile.

MOLONEY, Patrick Martin Joseph; QC 1998; a Recorder, since 2000; *b* 2 July 1953; *s* of late Dr Eamon Moloney and Jean Moloney (*née* Handley). *Educ:* Prior Park Coll., Bath; St Catherine's Coll., Oxford (Open Schol.; BA Hons Jurisp. 1973; BCL 1974). Vis. Asst Prof., Univ. of British Columbia, 1974–75; called to the Bar, Middle Temple, 1976 (Harmsworth Schol.); in practice at the Bar, specialising in libel law, 1978–. Mem. Bar, NI, 1999. *Publication:* (contrib.) Halsbury's Laws of England, 1997. *Recreations:* independent travel, theatre, opera. *Address:* 1 Brick Court, Temple, EC4Y 9BY. *T:* (020) 7353 8845.

MOLONY, Thomas Desmond; 3rd Bt. Does not use the title, and his name is not on the Official Roll of Baronets.

MOLYNEAUX OF KILLEAD, Baron *cr* 1997 (Life Peer), of Killead in the co. of Antrim; **James Henry Molyneaux,** KBE 1996; PC 1983; Leader, Ulster Unionist Party, 1979–95; *b* 27 Aug. 1920; *s* of late William Molyneaux, Seacash, Killead, Co. Antrim; unmarried. *Educ:* Aldergrove Sch., Co. Antrim. RAF, 1941–46. Vice-Chm., Eastern Special Care Hosp. Man. Cttee, 1966–73; Chm. Antrim Br., NI Assoc. for Mental Health, 1967–70; Hon. Sec., S Antrim Unionist Assoc., 1964–70; Vice-Pres., Ulster Unionist Council, 1974–79. MP (UU): Antrim S, 1970–83; Lagan Valley, 1983–97. Leader, UU Party, House of Commons, 1974–95. Mem. (UU) S Antrim, NI Assembly, 1982–86. Dep. Grand Master of Orange Order and Hon. PGM of Canada. JP Antrim, 1957–87; CC Antrim, 1964–73. *Recreations:* gardening, music. *Address:* Aldergrove, Crumlin, Co. Antrim, N Ireland BT29 4AR. *T:* (028) 9442 2545.

MOLYNEUX, Prof. David Hurst, DSc; Professor of Tropical Health Sciences, University of Liverpool, since 1991 (Director, Liverpool School of Tropical Medicine, 1991–2000); *b* 9 April 1943; *s* of Reginald Frank Molyneux and Monica Foden Molyneux; *m* 1969, Anita Elisabeth Bateson; one *s* one *d*. *Educ:* Denstone Coll.; Emmanuel Coll., Cambridge (BA 1965; PhD 1969; MA 1969; DSc 1992). FIBiol 1984. Lectr, Dept of Parasitology, Liverpool Sch. of Tropical Medicine, 1968–77; seconded as Research Officer to Nigerian Inst. for Trypanosomiasis, Kaduna, 1970–72, as Project Manager to UNDP/WHO, Bobo Dioulasso, Burkino Faso, 1975–77; Prof. of Biology, Univ. of Salford, 1977–91. Dir, DFID/Glaxo SmithKline Lymphatic Filariasis Support Centre, 2000–. Member: WHO Cttees incl. Onchocerciasis, Guinea worm, Parasitic Diseases; Internat. Commn on Disease Eradication, 2001–. Mem., Bd of Trustees, BIOSIS, Philadelphia, 1999–. Trustee, Nat. Museums and Galls on Merseyside, 1995–2000. Pres., British Soc. of Parasitology, 1992. Mem., Governing Body, Inst. of Animal Health, 2001–. Chalmers Medal, RSTM&H, 1987; Wright Medal, British Soc. of Parasitology, 1989. *Publications:* The Biology of Trypanosoma and Leishmania: parasites of man and domestic animals (with R. W. Ashford), 1983; numerous contribs to professional jls. *Recreations:* golf, music, travel, primitive art. *Address:* Liverpool School of Tropical Medicine, Pembroke Place, Liverpool L3 5QA. *T:* (0151) 708 9393; Kingsley Cottage, Town Well, Kingsley, Cheshire WA6 8EZ. *T:* (01928) 788397. *Club:* Delamere Forest Golf.

MOLYNEUX, Helena; Human Resources Consultant, Helena Molyneux Consulting, since 2000; *b* 17 Aug. 1948; *d* of Joseph and Mary Molyneux. *Educ:* Manchester Univ. (BSc); Cranfield Inst. of Technol. (MBA). FIPD. United Biscuits, 1969–73; Univ. of Sierra Leone, 1973–76; Bank of America: Personnel Manager, Bank of Amer. Internat., 1979–80; Divl Personnel Manager, NT & SA, San Francisco, 1980–82; Head, Employee Relns and Personnel Planning, Eur., ME and Africa Div., 1982–87; Bankers Trust Co.: Head, Employee Relns and Staffing, Eur., 1987–89; Head, Corporate Personnel, Eur., 1989–93; Dir of Personnel, British Council, 1993–2000. Vice-Chm., Catholic Inst. for Internat. Relations, 1997–. FRSA; FRGS. *Recreations:* music, reading, gardening, Dorset, ski-ing, Africa.

MOLYNEUX, James Robert M.; *see* More-Molyneux.

MONAGHAN, Charles Edward, CA; Chairman, Aegon UK, since 1999; President, Institute of Chartered Accountants of Scotland, 1999–2000; *b* 20 June 1940; *s* of Charles Monaghan and Elspeth Margaret Monaghan; *m* 1971, Dorothy Evelyn Hince; one *s*. *Educ:* Loretto Sch.; Edinburgh Univ. (BSc). CA 1965. Unilever, 1965–98: Ops Mem., E Asia Pacific, 1991–95; Head, Exec. Cttee Secretariat, 1996–98; Chm., Scottish Equitable, 1998. *Recreations:* squash, ski-ing, golf. *Address:* 10 Wool Road, Wimbledon, SW20 0HW. *T:* (020) 8946 8825. *Clubs:* Caledonian, Wimbledon; Royal Wimbledon Golf.

MONCADA, Dr Salvador Enrique, FRCP; FRS 1988; Director, Wolfson Institute for Biomedical Research (formerly Institute for Strategic Medical Research (Cruciform Project)), University College London, since 1996; *b* 3 Dec. 1944; *s* of Dr Salvador Eduardo Moncada and Jenny Seidner; *m* 1st, 1966; one *d*; 2nd, 1998, HRH Princess Esmeralda of Belgium; one *s* one *d*. *Educ:* Univ. of El Salvador (DMS 1970); London Univ. (DPhil 1973; DSc 1983). FRCP 1994. GP, Social Service of El Salvador, 1969; Associate Prof. of Pharmacol. and Physiol., Univ. of Honduras, 1974–75; Wellcome Research Laboratories, 1971–73 and 1975–95: Sen. Scientist, 1975–77; Hd of Dept of Prostaglandin Res., 1977–85; Dir, Therapeutic Res. Div., 1984–86; Dir of Res., Wellcome Foundn, 1986–95. Visiting Professor: KCL, 1988; KCH Sch. of Medicine and Dentistry, 1992. Consultant, Pan Amer. Health Orgn, 1972–. Member, Editorial Board: British Jl of Pharmacol., 1980–85; Atherosclerosis (Jl of Amer. Heart Assoc.), 1980–; European Jl of Clin. Investigation, 1986–; Thrombosis Research, 1989–. Mem., British Pharmacol Soc., 1974. Founder FMedSci 1998. Associate Fellow, Third World Acad. of Sciences, 1988; For. Associate, Nat. Acad. of Scis, USA, 1994. Dr *hc*: Univ. of Complutense de Madrid, 1986; Univ. of Honduras, 1987; Univ. of Cantabria, 1988; Hon. DSc: Sussex, 1994; Mt Sinai Sch. of Medicine, NY, 1995; Nottingham, 1995. Peter Debeye Prize (jtly), Limburg Univ., 1980; Nat. Sci. Prize, Republic of Honduras, 1985; Prince of Asturias Prize for Science and Technology, 1990; Royal Medal, Royal Soc., 1994. *Publications:* (Scientific Ed.) British Medical Bulletin, 39 pt 3: Prostacyclin, Thromboxane and Leukotrienes, 1983; Nitric oxide from L-arginine: a bioregulatory system, 1990; (ed jtly) The Biology of Nitric Oxide, pts 3 and 4, 1994, pt 5, 1996, pt 6, 1998. *Recreations:* music, literature, theatre. *Address:* 16 Park Village East, NW1 7PX. *T:* (020) 7388 8006.

MONCASTER, John Anthony; Master of the Supreme Court, Chancery Division, since 1992; *b* Louth, Lincs, 15 Oct. 1939; *o c* of Jack Moncaster and Muriel, 2nd *d* of Henry Butterick; *m* 1966, Gillian Ann, *o d* of Rev. Royston York; two *s* two *d*. Called to the Bar, Gray's Inn, 1961; practised at Chancery Bar. *Recreation:* books. *Address:* Dukes Farm, Layer Marney, Essex CO5 9UZ. *T:* (01206) 330184.

MONCEL, Lt-Gen. Robert William, OC 1968; DSO 1944; OBE 1944; CD 1944; retired 1966; *b* 9 April 1917; *s* of René Moncel and Edith Brady; *m* 1939, Nancy Allison, *d* of Ralph P. Bell; one *d*. *Educ:* Selwyn House Sch.; Bishop's Coll. Sch. Royal Canadian Regt, 1939; Staff Coll., 1940; Bde Major 1st Armd Bde, 1941; comd 18th Manitoba Dragoons, 1942; GSO1, HQ 2 Cdn Corps, 1943; comd 4th Armd Bde, 1944; Dir Canadian Armd Corps, 1946; Nat. War Coll., 1949; Canadian Jt Staff, London, 1949–54; Comdr 3 Inf. Bde, 1957; QMG, 1960; GOC Eastern Comd, 1963; Comptroller Gen., 1964; Vice-Chief of the Defence Staff, Canada, 1965–66. Col, 8th Canadian Hussars. Chm., Fishermen's Memorial Hosp., 1980–84; Dir, Nova Scotia Rehabilitation Center, 1986–. Mem. Bd of Regents, Mount Allison Univ., 1983–. Croix de Guerre, France, 1944; Légion d'Honneur, France, 1944. Hon. LLD Mount Allison Univ., 1968. *Recreations:* fishing, sailing, golf. *Address:* Windswept, Murder Point, NS B0J 2E0, Canada; Summer Gardens, 1470 Summer Street, Halifax, NS B3H 3A3, Canada. *Club:* Royal Nova Scotia Yacht.

MONCK, family name of **Viscount Monck**.

MONCK, 7th Viscount *cr* 1801; **Charles Stanley Monck;** *S* father, 1982 but does not use the title. *Heir: b* Hon. George Stanley Monck.

MONCK, Elizabeth Mary, (Lady Monck), PhD; Reporting Member, Competition Commission, since 1999; Senior Research Officer, Thomas Coram Research Unit, Institute of Education, since 1997; *b* 7 Aug. 1934; *d* of Geoffrey Dugdale Kirwan and Molly Kirwan (*née* Morrow); *m* 1960, Sir Nicholas Jeremy Monck, *qv*; three *s*. *Educ:* Godolphin Sch., Salisbury; Newnham Coll., Cambridge (MA; Associate, 1997–); UCL (PhD 1996). MRC Social Psychiatry Res. Unit, Inst. Psychiatry, 1957–62; EIU, 1969–73; Research Officer: Centre for Envmtl Studies, 1974–80; Acad. Dept Child Psychiatry, Inst. Child Health, 1980–95. Mem., ILEA, 1986–90. Indep. Mem., Cttee on Chemicals and Materials in Public Water Supply, Drinking Water Inspectorate, 1998–2001. Mem., 1990–93, Chm., 1993–97, Regl Customer Service Cttee (Thames), OFWAT. Trustee, National Gall., 1993–99. *Publications:* books include: (with R. Dobbs) The Great Ormond Street Adolescent Life Events Dictionary of Contextual Threat Ratings, 1985; (ed and contrib.) Emotional and Behavioural Problems in Adolescents: a multi-disciplinary approach to identification and management, 1988; (with A. Kelly) Managing Effective Schools, 1992; (jtly) Child Sexual Abuse: a descriptive and treatment study, 1996. *Recreations:* walking, gardening, listening to music. *Address:* 31 Lady Margaret Road, NW5 2NG.

MONCK, Sir Nicholas (Jeremy), KCB 1994 (CB 1988); international consultant, since 1996; Permanent Secretary, Employment Department Group, 1993–95; *b* 9 March 1935; *s* of Bosworth Monck and Stella Mary (*née* Cock); *m* 1960, Elizabeth Mary Kirwan (*see* E. M. Monck); three *s*. *Educ:* Eton; King's Coll., Cambridge; Univ. of Pennsylvania; LSE. Asst Principal, Min. of Power, 1959–62; NEDO, 1962–65; NBPI, 1965–66; Senior Economist, Min. of Agriculture, Tanzania, 1966–69; HM Treasury, 1969–92: Asst Sec., 1971; Principal Private Sec. to Chancellor of the Exchequer, 1976–77; Under Sec., 1977–84; Dep. Sec. (Industry), 1984–90; Second Perm. Sec. (Public Expenditure), 1990–92. Dir, Standard Life, 1997–. Sen. Associate, Oxford Policy Mgt, 1996–. Member: BSC, 1978–80; IMRO, 1995–2000. Chm., British Dyslexia Assoc., 1995–2000. Mem., Finance Cttee, Nat. Trust, 1990–. Mem., Policy Cttee, Centre for Economic Performance, LSE, 1993–. Gov., NIESR, 1995–. Trustee, Glyndebourne Arts Trust, 1996–. *Address:* 31 Lady Margaret Road, NW5 2NG.

MONCKTON, family name of **Viscount Galway** and **Viscount Monckton of Brenchley**.

MONCKTON OF BRENCHLEY, 2nd Viscount *cr* 1957; **Maj.-Gen. Gilbert Walter Riversdale Monckton,** CB 1966; OBE 1956; MC 1940; DL; FSA; retired, 1967; *b* 3 Nov. 1915; *o s* of 1st Viscount Monckton of Brenchley, PC, GCVO, KCMG, MC, QC, and Mary A. S. (*d* 1964), *d* of Sir Thomas Colyer-Fergusson, 3rd Bt; *S* father, 1965; *m* 1950, Marianna Laetitia (Dame of Honour and Devotion, SMO Malta (also Cross of Merit), OStJ, Pres., St John's Ambulance, Kent, 1975–80, High Sheriff of Kent, 1981–82), 3rd *d* of late Comdr Robert T. Bower; four *s* one *d*. *Educ:* Harrow; Trinity Coll., Cambridge. BA 1939, MA 1942. 2/Lt 5th Royal Inniskilling Dragoon Guards, SR 1938; Reg. 1939; France and Belgium, 1939–40; Staff Coll., 1941; Bde Major Armd Bde, 1942;

Comd and Gen. Staff Sch., USA, 1943; Sqdn Ldr, 3rd King's Own Hussars, 1944, Italy and Syria; Sqdn Ldr, 5th Royal Inniskilling Dragoon Gds, 1945. RAF Staff Coll., 1949; GSO2, 7th Armd Div., 1949; Sqdn Ldr and 2 i/c 5th Royal Inniskilling Dragoon Gds, Korea and Egypt, 1951–52; GSO1, Mil. Ops, WO, 1954–56; Mil. Adv., Brit. Delegn, Geneva Confs on Indo-China and Korea, 1954; transf. 12th Royal Lancers and comd, 1956–58; Comdr Royal Armd Corps, 3rd Div., 1958–60; psc, idc 1961; Dep. Dir, Personnel Admin., WO, 1962; Dir of Public Relations, WO (subseq. MoD), 1963–65; Chief of Staff, HQ BAOR, 1965–67; Col 9th/12th Royal Lancers (Prince of Wales's), 1967–73; Hon. Col, Kent and Sharpshooters Yeomanry Sqdn, 1974–79. President: Kent Assoc. of Boys' Clubs, 1965–78; Inst. of Heraldic and Genealogical Studies, 1965; Kent Archæological Soc., 1968–75; Medway Productivity Assoc., 1968–72; Kent Co. Rifle Assoc., 1970–75; Anglo-Belgian Union, 1973–83; Chm., Thurnham Parish Council, 1968–70. FSA 1987. DL Kent, 1970. Liveryman Broderers' Co. (Master, 1978). KStJ; Chm., Council of Order of St John for Kent, 1969–75; SMO Malta: Bailiff, Grand Cross of Obedience (Chancellor of the British Assoc., 1963–68, Vice-Pres., 1968–74, Pres., 1974–83); Grand Cross of Merit, 1980; Comdr, Order of Crown (Belgium), 1965; Grand Officer, Order of Leopold II (Belgium), 1978. *Recreation:* archaeology. *Heir: s* Hon. Christopher Walter Monckton, *qv*. *Address:* Runhams Farm, Runham Lane, Harrietsham, Maidstone, Kent ME17 1NJ. *T:* (01622) 850313. *Clubs:* Brooks's, MCC; Casino Maltese (Valetta).

See also Hon. D. R. C. Lawson.

MONCKTON, Hon. Christopher Walter; DL; Director, Christopher Monckton Ltd, consultants, since 1987; *b* 14 Feb. 1952; *s* and *heir* of Viscount Monckton of Brenchley, *qv*; *m* 1990, Juliet Mary Anne, *y d* of Jørgen Malherbe Jensen. *Educ:* Harrow; Churchill Coll., Cambridge; University Coll., Cardiff. BA 1973, MA 1977 (Cantab); Dip. Journalism Studies (Wales), 1974. Standing Cttee, Cambridge Union Soc., 1973; Treas., Cambridge Univ. Conservative Assoc., 1973. Reporter, Yorkshire Post, 1974–75, Leader-Writer, 1975–77; Press Officer, Conservative Central Office, 1977–78; Editor-designate, The Universe, 1978, Editor, 1979–81; Managing Editor, Telegraph Sunday Magazine, 1981–82; Leader-Writer, The Standard, 1982; Special Advr to Prime Minister's Policy Unit, 1982–86; Asst Editor, Today, 1986–87; Consulting Editor, 1987–92, Chief Leader-Writer, 1990–92, Evening Standard. Freeman, City of London, and Liveryman, Worshipful Co. of Broderers, 1973–. Member: Internat. MENSA Ltd, 1975–; St John Amb. Brigade (Wetherby Div.), 1976–77; Hon. Soc. of the Middle Temple, 1979–; RC Mass Media Commn, 1979–; Sec. to Econ., Forward Strategy, Health, and Employment Study Gps, Centre For Policy Studies, 1980–82. Vis. Lectr in Business Studies, Columbia Univ., NY, 1980. Editor, Not the Church Times, 1982. Kt SMO, Malta, 1973; OStJ 1973. DL Greater London, 1988. *Publications:* The Laker Story (with Ivan Fallon), 1982; Anglican Orders: null and void?, 1986; The Aids Report, 1987. *Recreation:* romance. *Address:* Crimonmogate, Fraserburgh AB43 8SE. *T:* (01346) 532401, *Fax:* (01346) 532203. *Clubs:* Brooks's, Beefsteak, Pratt's.

MONCKTON-ARUNDELL, family name of **Viscount Galway**.

MONCREIFF, family name of **Baron Moncreiff**.

MONCREIFF, 5th Baron *cr* 1873; **Harry Robert Wellwood Moncreiff;** Bt, Nova Scotia 1626, UK 1871; Lt-Col (Hon.) RASC, retired; *b* 4 Feb. 1915; *s* of 4th Baron Moncreiff and Lucy Vida (*née* Lechmere-Anderson); *S* father, 1942; *m* 1952, Enid Marion Watson (*d* 1985), *o d* of Major H. W. Locke, Belmont, Dollar; one *s*. *Educ:* Fettes Coll., Edinburgh. Served War of 1939–45 (despatches). Retired, 1958. *Recreations:* Rugby football, tennis, shooting. *Heir: s* Hon. Rhoderick Harry Wellwood Moncreiff [*b* 22 March 1954; *m* 1982, Alison Elizabeth Anne, *d* of late James Duncan Alastair Ross; two *s*]. *Address:* Tulliebole Castle, Fossoway, Kinross-shire KY13 7QN. *T:* (01577) 840236.

MONCREIFFE of Moncreiffe, Hon. Peregrine David Euan Malcolm; Chairman, UA Group plc; *b* 16 Feb. 1951; *s* of Sir Iain Moncreiffe of that Ilk, 11 Bt, CVO, DL, QC (Scot) and Countess of Erroll, 23rd in line; *m* 1988, Miranda Fox-Pitt; two *s* four *d*. *Educ:* Eton; Christ Church, Oxford (MA Modern Hist.). Lieut, Atholl Highlanders, 1978. Investment banker: with White Weld & Co. Ltd/Credit Suisse First Boston Ltd, 1972–82; Lehman Brothers Kuhn Loeb/Shearson Lehman, 1982–86; E. F. Hutton & Co., 1986–88; Chief Exec., Buchanan Partners Ltd, 1990–99. Mem., Royal Commn on Ancient and Historical Monuments of Scotland, 1989–94. Chm., Scottish Ballet, 1988–90. Trustee, Save the Rhino, 1991–. Mem., Royal Co. of Archers (Queen's Body Guard for Scotland), 1979–. Freeman, City of London; Liveryman, Co. of Fishmongers, 1987–. *Address:* Easter Moncreiffe, Bridge of Earn, Perth PH2 8QA. *T:* (01738) 812338. *Clubs:* White's, Turf, Pratt's; New (Edinburgh); Leander (Henley); Brook (New York).

MONCTON, Archbishop of, (RC), since 1996; **Most Rev. Ernest Raymond Léger;** *b* 27 Feb. 1944; *s* of Sifroid Léger and Imelda Johnson. *Educ:* Univ. du Sacré Coeur, Bathurst, NB (BA); Univ. de Moncton (BEd); Univ. Laval, Quebec (MTh); Univ. St Paul, Ottawa (LCL). Ordained, 1968; Parish priest, 1968–96: Moncton, 1968–70, 1972–73; St Louis de Kent, 1970–72, 1974–75; St Charles de Kent, 1975–80; Rogersville, 1980–83; Irishtown, 1985–87; St Paul de Kent, 1988–92, 1995–96; Sackville and Dorchester, 1993–95; Judicial Vicar of Marriage Tribunal, Halifax Region, 1985–96; Vicar General, 1992–94, Administrator, 1995–96, Archdio. of Moncton. *Address:* 452 rue Amirault, Dieppe, NB E1A 1G3, Canada. *T:* (506) 8579531.

MOND, family name of **Baron Melchett**.

MONDALE, Walter Frederick; American Ambassador to Japan, 1993–96; *b* Ceylon, Minnesota, 5 Jan. 1928; *s* of Rev. Theodore Sigvaard Mondale and Claribel Hope (*née* Cowan); *m* 1955, Joan Adams; two *s* one *d*. *Educ:* public schs, Minnesota; Macalester Coll., Univ. of Minnesota (BA *cum laude*); Univ. of Minnesota Law Sch. (LLB). Served with Army, 1951–53. Admitted to Minn. Bar, 1956; private law practice, Minneapolis, 1956–60; Attorney-Gen., Minnesota, 1960–65; Senator from Minnesota, 1965–76; Vice-Pres., USA, 1977–81; Counsel with Winston & Strawn, 1981–87; Partner with Dorsey & Whitney, 1987–93. Democratic Candidate for Vice-Pres., USA, 1976, 1980; Democratic Candidate for Pres., USA, 1984. Chm., Nat. Democratic Inst. for Internat. Affairs, 1987–93. Mem., Democratic Farm Labor Party. *Publication:* The Accountability of Power. *Address:* c/o Dorsey & Whitney LLP, 220 South 6th Street, Minneapolis, MN 55402–1498, USA.

MONDS, Prof. Fabian Charles, CBE 1997; PhD; Professor of Information Systems, 1987–2000, and Pro-Vice-Chancellor (Planning), 1993–2000, University of Ulster; Governor for Northern Ireland, BBC, since 1999; *b* 1 Nov. 1940; *s* of Edward James Monds and Mary Brigid (*née* McPoland); *m* 1967, Eileen Joan Graham; two *d*. *Educ:* Queen's Univ., Belfast (BSc; PhD). CEng, MIEE, MBCS. Vis. Asst Prof., Purdue Univ., USA, 1965, 1966; Lectr, 1967–77, Sen. Lectr, 1977–78, Reader, 1978–86, QUB; Dean, Faculty of Informatics, 1989–93, Provost, Magee Coll., Londonderry, 1995–2000, Univ. of Ulster. Chairman: NI Inf. Age Initiative, 1999–; Univ. of Ulster Sci. Res. Parks Ltd, 1999–; NI Industrial Res. and Technol. Unit, 2000–; Omagh 2010 Task Force, 2001–. FIMgt. *Publications:* Minicomputer Systems, 1979; (with R. McLaughlin) An Introduction to Mini and Micro Computers, 1981, 2nd edn 1984; The Business of Electronic Product Development, 1984; two patents; contrib. learned jls. *Recreation:* general aviation (fixed and rotary wing). *Address:* BBC, Broadcasting House, Ormeau Avenue, Belfast BT2 8HQ.

MONE, Rt Rev. John Aloysius; *see* Paisley, Bishop of, (RC).

MONEY, Ernle (David Drummond), CBE 1996; Barrister-at-Law; *b* 17 Feb. 1931; *s* of late Lt-Col E. F. D. Money, DSO, late 4th Gurkha Rifles, and Sidney, *o d* of D. E. Anderson, Forfar; *m* 1st, 1960, Susan Barbara (marr. diss. 1985), *d* of Lt-Col D. S. Lister, MC, The Buffs; two *s* two *d*; 2nd, Bella Maharaj (*d* 1993), barrister-at-law. *Educ:* Marlborough Coll.; Oriel Coll., Oxford (open scholar). Served in Suffolk Regt, 1949–51, and 4th Bn, Suffolk Regt (TA), 1951–56; MA Hons degree (2nd cl.) in mod. hist., 1954. Tutor and lecturer, Swinton Conservative Coll., 1956. Called to Bar, Lincoln's Inn (Cholmeley Scholar), 1958. Mem., Bar Council, 1962–66. MP (C) Ipswich, 1970–Sept. 1974; Opposition Front Bench Spokesman on the Arts, 1974; Sec., Parly Cons. Arts and Amenities Cttee, 1970–73, Vice-Chm., 1974; Vice-Pres., Ipswich Cons. Assoc., 1979–81. Regular columnist, East Anglian Daily Times, for some years. Governor, Woolverstone Hall Sch., 1967–70; co-opted Mem., GLC Arts Cttee, 1972–73; Mem., GLC Arts Bd, 1974–76; Mem., Cttee of Gainsborough's Birthplace, Sudbury. Fine Arts Correspondent, Contemporary Review, 1968–88. Pres., Ipswich Town Football Club Supporters, 1974–80; Vice-Pres., E Suffolk and Ipswich Branch, RSPCA, 1974–77. Mem., Primrose League. *Publications:* (with Peter Johnson) The Nasmyth Family of Painters, 1970; Margaret Thatcher, First Lady of the House, 1975; regular contrib. various periodicals and newspapers on antiques and the arts. *Recreations:* music, pictures and antiques, watching Association football. *Address:* 33a Bishops Road, Highgate Village, N6 4HP. *T:* (020) 8348 5391. *Clubs:* Carlton, Beefsteak, Dinosaurs; Norfolk (Norwich).

MONEY, Hon. George Gilbert, CHB 1986; FCIB; Director, Barclays Bank International Ltd, 1955–81 (Vice-Chairman, 1965–73); *b* 17 Nov. 1914; 2nd *s* of late Maj.-Gen. Sir A. W. Money, KCB, KBE, CSI and late Lady Money (*née* Drummond). *Educ:* Charterhouse Sch. Clerk, L. Behrens & Soehne, Bankers, Hamburg, 1931–32; Clerk, Barclays Bank Ltd, 1932–35, Dir 1972–73; joined Barclays Bank DCO (now Barclays Bank PLC), London, 1935; served in Egypt, Palestine, Cyprus, Ethiopia, Cyrenaica, E Africa, 1936–52; Local Dir, W Indies, 1952; Director: Barclays Bank of California, 1965–75; Bermuda Provident Bank Ltd, 1969–89; Barclays Bank of the Netherlands, Antilles NV, 1970–86; Republic Finance Corp. Ltd, 1972–88; Republic Bank Ltd, 1972–88; Barclays Bank of Jamaica Ltd, 1972–77; Barclays Australia Ltd, 1972–75; New Zealand United Corp., 1972–75; Chairman: Bahamas Internat. Trust Co. Ltd, 1970–72; Cayman Internat. Trust Co. Ltd, 1970–72; Mem., Caribbean Bd, Barclays Bank PLC, 1952–88. *Publication:* Nine Lives of a Bush Banker, 1990. *Recreations:* water ski-ing, fishing, bridge. *Address:* Saltram, St Joseph, Barbados.

MONEY-COUTTS, family name of **Baron Latymer**.

MONEY-COUTTS, Sir David (Burdett), KCVO 1991; Chairman, Coutts & Co., 1976–93; *b* 19 July 1931; *s* of late Hon. Alexander B. Money-Coutts (2nd *s* of 6th Baron Latymer, TD), and Mary E., *er d* of Sir Reginald Hobhouse, 5th Bt; *m* 1958, Penelope Utten Todd; one *s* two *d*. *Educ:* Eton (Hon. Fellow, 1996); New Coll., Oxford (MA). National Service, 1st Royal Dragoons, 1950–51; Royal Glos Hussars, TA, 1951–67. Joined Coutts & Co., 1951; Dir, 1958–96; Man. Dir, 1970–86. Director: National Discount Co., 1964–69; Gerrard Gp (formerly Gerrard & National), 1969–99 (Dep. Chm. 1969–89); United States & General Trust Corp., 1964–73; Charities Investment Managers (Charifund), 1964–2000 (Chm., 1984–2000); Dun & Bradstreet, 1973–87; National Westminster Bank, 1976–90 (Regl Dir, 1969–92, Chm., SE Reg., 1986–88; Chm., S Adv. Bd, 1988–92; Mem., UK Adv. Bd, 1990–92); Phoenix Assurance, 1978–85 (Dep. Chm., 1984–85); Sun Alliance & London Insurance, 1984–90; M & G Gp, 1987–97 (Chm., 1990–97). Member: Kensington and Chelsea and Westminster AHA, 1974–82 (Vice-Chm., 1978–82); Bloomsbury HA, 1982–90 (Vice-Chm., 1982–88); Health Educn Council, 1973–77. Middlesex Hospital: Governor, 1962–74 (Dep. Chm. Governors, 1973–74); Chm., Finance Cttee, 1965–74; Mem., Med. Sch. Council, 1963–88 (Chm., 1974–88; Special Trustee, 1974–2000 (Chm., 1974–97)). Chm., Inst. of Sports Medicine, 1997–. Mem., Council, UCL, 1987–97. Trustee: Multiple Sclerosis Soc., 1967–99; Scout Foundn, 1992– (Chm., 1994–). Hon. Treas., Nat. Assoc. of Almshouses, 1960–92; Hon. Sec., Old Etonian Trust, 1969–76, Chm. Council, 1976–2001; Trustee, Mansfield Coll., Oxford, 1988–95. *Recreations:* odd jobs, living in the country. *Address:* Magpie House, Peppard Common, Henley-on-Thames, Oxon RG9 5JG. *T:* (01491) 628005. *Club:* Leander (Henley-on-Thames).

MONIER-WILLIAMS, His Honour Evelyn Faithfull; a Circuit Judge, 1972–92; continued sitting in Crown and County Courts until 1995; *b* 29 April 1920; *o s* of late R. T. Monier-Williams, OBE, Barrister-at-Law, and Mrs G. M. Monier-Williams; *m* 1948, Maria-Angela Oswald (*d* 1983); one *s* one *d*. *Educ:* Charterhouse; University Coll., Oxford (MA). Admitted to Inner Temple, 1940; served Royal Artillery, 1940–46 in UK, Egypt, Libya, Tunisia, Sicily (8th Army), France, Low Countries and Germany; called to Bar, Inner Temple, 1948; South Eastern Circuit; Master of the Bench, Inner Temple, 1967, Reader, 1987, Treas., 1988; Mem. Senate of Four Inns of Court, 1969–73; Mem. Council, Selden Soc., 1970– (Vice Pres., 1990–96); Mem., Council of Legal Educn, 1971–87, Vice Chm., 1974–87; Mem., Adv. Cttee on Legal Educn, 1979–87; Mem., Council of the Inns of Court, 1987–88. Livery, Glaziers' Company, 1974. *Recreation:* collecting old books. *Address:* Inner Temple, EC4Y 7HL.

MONK, Alec; *see* Monk, D. A. G.

MONK, Rear-Adm. Anthony John, CBE 1973; Appeals Organizer, The Royal Marsden Hospital Cancer Fund, 1984–87; *b* 14 Nov. 1923; *s* of Frank Leonard and Barbara Monk; *m* 1951, Elizabeth Ann Samson; four *s* (one *d* decd). *Educ:* Whitgift Sch.; RNC Dartmouth; RNEC Keyham. MSc, BScEng, CEng, FIMarE, FRAeS, FIMechE. Engr Cadet, 1941; served War of 1939–45, Pacific Fleet; flying trng, Long Air Engrg Course, Cranfield, 1946; RN Air Stn Ford; RNEC Manadon, 1950; Prodn Controller and Man., RN Aircraft Yard, Belfast, 1953–56; Mem. Dockyard Work Measurement Team, subseq. Engr Officer HMS Apollo, Techn. Asst to Dir-Gen. Aircraft, Sqdn Engr Officer to Flag Officer Aircraft Carriers, 1963–65; Asst Dir of Marine Engrg, 1965–68; Dir of Aircraft Engrg, 1968; Comd Engrg Officer to Flag Officer Naval Air Comd; Naval Liaison Officer for NI and Supt RN Aircraft Yard, Belfast, 1970; Port Admiral, Rosyth, 1974–76; Rear-Adm. Engineering to Flag Officer Naval Air Comd, 1976–78. Comdr 1956; Captain 1964; Rear-Adm. 1974. Dir Gen., Brick Develt Assoc., 1979–84. Liveryman, Co. of Engrs, 1998–. MRI. FRSA. *Recreation:* swimming (ASA teacher). *Address:* Morning Glory, Kingsdown, Deal, Kent CT14 8AT.

MONK, Arthur James; Director, Components, Valves and Devices, Ministry of Defence, 1981–84, retired; *b* 15 Jan. 1924; *s* of late Rev. Arthur S. Monk, AKC, and late Lydia E. Monk; *m* 1953, Murial V. Peacock; one *s* two *d*. *Educ:* Latymer Upper School,

Hammersmith; London Univ. BSc Hons Physics 1953; FIEE 1964. Served RAF, 1943–48. Services Electronic Research Labs, 1949–63; Asst Director (Co-ord. Valve Development), MoD, 1963–68; Student, Imperial Defence Coll., 1969; idc 1970; Admiralty Underwater Weapons Establishment, 1970–73; Dep. Director, Underwater Weapons Projects (S/M), MoD, 1973–76; Counsellor, Def. Equipment Staff, Washington, 1977–81. *Publications:* papers on electronics in jls of learned societies. *Recreations:* caravan touring, photography, family history and genealogy. *Address:* 65 Wyke Road, Weymouth, Dorset DT4 9QN. *T:* (01305) 782338.

MONK, (David) Alec (George); Chairman, Charles Wells Ltd, since 1998 (Director, since 1989); *b* 13 Dec. 1942; *s* of Philip Aylmer and Elizabeth Jane Monk; *m* 1965, Jean Ann Searle; two *s* two *d. Educ:* Jesus College, Oxford (Hon. Fellow, 1999). MA (PPE). Research Staff, Corporate Finance and Taxation, Sheffield Univ., 1966 and London Business Sch., 1967; Senior Financial Asst, Treasurer's Dept, Esso Petroleum Co., 1968; various positions with The Rio Tinto-Zinc Corp., 1968–77, Dir, 1974–77; Vice-Pres. and Dir, AEA Investors Inc., 1977–81; Chm. and Chief Exec., The Gateway Corp. (formerly Dee Corp.) PLC, 1981–89; CEO, Tri-Delta Corp. Ltd, 1990–93. Dir, Scottish Eastern Investment Trust, 1985–98. Mem., NEDC, 1986–90. Pres., Inst. of Grocery Distribution, 1987–89. Vis. Indust. Fellow, Manchester Business Sch., 1984. Hon. Fellow, St Hugh's Coll., Oxford, 1985. Hon. LLD Sheffield, 1988. *Publication:* (with A. J. Merrett) Inflation, Taxation and Executive Remuneration, 1967. *Recreations:* sports, reading.

MONK BRETTON, 3rd Baron *cr* 1884; **John Charles Dodson;** DL; *b* 17 July 1924; *o s* of 2nd Baron and Ruth (*d* 1967), 2nd *d* of late Hon. Charles Brand; *S* father, 1933; *m* 1958, Zoë Diana Scott; two *s. Educ:* Westminster Sch.; New Coll., Oxford (MA). DL E Sussex, 1983. *Recreations:* hunting, farming. *Heir: s* Hon. Christopher Mark Dodson [*b* 2 Aug. 1958; *m* 1988, Karen, *o d* of B. J. McKelvain, Fairfield, Conn; two *s* one *d*]. *Address:* Shelley's Folly, Cooksbridge, near Lewes, East Sussex BN8 4SU. *T:* (01273) 400231. *Club:* Brooks's.

MONKS, John Stephen; General Secretary, Trades Union Congress, since 1993; *b* 5 Aug. 1945; *s* of Charles Edward Monks and Bessie Evelyn Monks; *m* 1970, Francine Jacqueline Schenk; two *s* one *d. Educ:* Ducie Technical High Sch., Manchester; Nottingham Univ. (BA Econ). Joined TUC, 1969; Hd of Orgn and Industrial Relns Dept, 1977–87; Dep. Gen. Sec., 1987–93. Member: Council, ACAS, 1979–95; ESRC, 1988–91. Member: EU Competitiveness Council, 1997–; Treasury Preparatory Cttee on Econ. and Monetary Union, 1998–. Trustee, Nat. Museum of Labour History, 1988–. Vis. Prof., Sch. of Mgt, UMIST, 1996–. *Recreations:* squash, hiking, music. *Address:* Congress House, Great Russell Street, WC1 3LS. *T:* (020) 7636 4030; *e-mail:* monks@dircon.co.uk.

MONKSWELL, 5th Baron *cr* 1885; **Gerard Collier;** *b* 28 Jan. 1947; *s* of William Adrian Larry Collier and Helen (*née* Dunbar); *S* to disclaimed barony of father, 1984; *m* 1974, Ann Valerie Collins; two *s* one *d. Educ:* Portsmouth Polytechnic (BSc Mech. Eng, 1971); Slough Polytechnic (Cert. in Works Management 1972). Massey Ferguson Manfg Co. Ltd: Product Quality Engineer, 1972; Service Administration Manager, 1984–89. Mem. (Lab), Manchester City Council, 1989–94. *Recreations:* politics, swimming, movies. *Heir: s* Hon. James Adrian Collier, *b* 29 March 1977.

MONMOUTH, Bishop of; *see* Wales, Archbishop of.

MONMOUTH, Dean of; *see* Fenwick, Very Rev. R. D.

MONRO, family name of **Baron Monro of Langholm**.

MONRO OF LANGHOLM, Baron *cr* 1997 (Life Peer), of Westerkirk in Dumfries and Galloway; **Hector Seymour Peter Monro,** Kt 1981; AE; PC 1995; JP; DL; *b* 4 Oct. 1922; *s* of late Capt. Alastair Monro, Cameron Highlanders, and Mrs Monro, Craigcleuch, Langholm, Scotland; *m* 1st, 1949, (Elizabeth) Anne Welch (*d* 1994), Longstone Hall, Derbs; two *s*; 2nd, 1994, Mrs Doris Kaestner, Baltimore, USA. *Educ:* Canford Sch.; King's Coll., Cambridge. RAF, 1941–46, Flight Lt; RAuxAF, 1946–53 (AE 1953). Mem. of Queen's Body Guard for Scotland, Royal Company of Archers. Dumfries CC, 1952–67 (Chm. Planning Cttee, and Police Cttee). Chm. Dumfriesshire Unionist Assoc., 1958–63. MP (C) Dumfries, 1964–97. Scottish Cons. Whip, 1967–70; a Lord Comr of HM Treasury, 1970–71; Parly Under-Sec. of State, Scottish Office, 1971–74; Opposition Spokesman on: Scottish Affairs, 1974–75; Sport, 1974–79; Parliamentary Under-Secretary of State: (with special responsibility for sport), DoE, 1979–81; Scottish Office, 1992–95. Member, Select Committee: on Scottish Affairs, 1983–86; on Defence, 1987. Chairman: Scottish Cons. Members Cttee, 1983–92; Cons. Parly Cttee on Sport, 1984–85. Vice Chm., Cons. Members Agricl Cttee, 1983–87. Mem. Dumfries T&AFA, 1959–67; Hon. Air Cdre, No 2622 RAuxAF Regt Sqdn, 1982–2000; Hon. Insp. Gen., RAuxAF, 1990–2000. Member: Area Executive Cttee, Nat. Farmers' Union of Scotland; Nature Conservancy Council, 1982–91; Council, Nat. Trust for Scotland, 1983–92. President: Auto-cycle Union, 1983–90; NSRA, 1987–92. JP 1963, DL 1973, Dumfries. *Recreations:* Rugby football (Mem. Scottish Rugby Union, 1958–77, Vice-Pres., 1975, Pres., 1976–77); golf, flying, country sports, vintage sports cars. *Address:* Williamwood, Kirtlebridge, Dumfriesshire DG11 3LN. *T:* (01461) 500213. *Clubs:* Royal Air Force, MCC; Royal Scottish Automobile (Glasgow).

MONRO, (Andrew) Hugh; Master of Wellington College, since 2000; *b* 2 March 1950; *s* of Andrew Killey Monro, FRCS and Diana Louise Rhys; *m* 1974, Elizabeth Clare Rust; one *s* one *d. Educ:* Rugby School; Pembroke College, Cambridge (MA; PGCE). Graduate trainee, Metal Box, 1973; Haileybury College, 1974–79; Noble & Greenough School, Boston, Mass, 1977–78; Loretto School, 1979–86; Headmaster: Worksop College, 1986–90; Clifton College, 1990–2000. *Recreations:* golf, American literature. *Address:* Wellington College, Crowthorne, Berks RG45 7PU. *Club:* Hawks (Cambridge).

MONRO, Hugh; *see* Monro, A. H.

MONRO DAVIES, His Honour William Llewellyn; QC 1974; a Circuit Judge, 1976–99; *b* 12 Feb. 1927; *s* of Thomas Llewellyn Davies and Emily Constance Davies; *m* 1956, Jean, *d* of late E. G. Innes; one *s* one *d. Educ:* Christ Coll., Brecon; Trinity Coll., Oxford (MA, LitHum). Served in RNVR, 1945–48 (Sub-Lt). Called to the Bar, Inner Temple, 1954. Mem., Gen. Council of the Bar, 1971–75. A Recorder of the Crown Court, 1972–76. *Recreations:* the theatre and cinema; watching Rugby football. *Address:* Farrar's Building, Temple, EC4Y 7BD.

MONSON, family name of **Baron Monson**.

MONSON, 11th Baron *cr* 1728; **John Monson;** Bt *cr* 1611; *b* 3 May 1932; *e s* of 10th Baron and of Bettie Northrup (who *m* 1962, Capt. James Arnold Phillips), *d* of late E. Alexander Powell; *S* father, 1958; *m* 1955, Emma, *o d* of late Anthony Devas, ARA, RP; three *s. Educ:* Eton; Trinity Coll., Cambridge (BA). Elected Mem., H of L, 1999. Pres., Soc. for Individual Freedom. *Heir: s* Hon. Nicholas John Monson [*b* 19 Oct. 1955; *m* 1981, Hilary (marr. diss. 1996), *o d* of Kenneth Martin, Nairobi and Diani Beach; one *s* one *d*]. *Address:* The Manor House, South Carlton, Lincoln LN1 2RN. *T:* (01522) 730263.

MONSON, Prof. John Rowat Telford, MD; FRCS, FRCSI; FACS; Professor of Surgery and Head of Department, Academic Surgical Unit, University of Hull, since 1993; *b* 14 Jan. 1956; *s* of Desmond Monson and Ann Monson; *m* 1980, Aideen White, MB; two *s* one *d. Educ:* Sandford Park Secondary Sch., Dublin; Trinity Coll. Dublin (MB BCh, BAO 1979; MD 1987). FRCSI 1983; FRCS 1987; FACS 1992. Pre-registration house officer, Royal City of Dublin Hosp., 1979; pre-Fellowship surgical trng, Dublin, 1980–83; post Fellowship surgical trng, Leeds, 1983–84; Res. Fellow, Univ. of Leeds, 1984–86; Sen. Registrar, Surgical Trng, Dublin, 1986–89; Fellow in Surgical Oncology, Mayo Clinic, USA, 1989–90; Asst Dir and Sen. Lectr in Surgery, St Mary's Hosp. Med. Sch., London, 1990–93. Surgical Res. Soc. Internat. Travelling Fellow, 1986; Edward Halloran Bennett Travelling Fellow in Surgery, 1989; James IV Assoc. Internat. Fellow, 1996. Visiting Professor: UCLA; Univ. of Texas; Univ. of Queensland; Monash Univ. Mem. Council, British Jl of Surgery, 1997–. Vice-Pres., British Assoc. of Surgical Oncology, 1997–; Hon. Sec., Surgical Res. Soc. of GB and Ireland, 1998–; Mem., James IV Assoc. of Surgeons, 1999–. (Dir, 2000–); Mem., Special Adv. Cttee in Gen. Surgery, 2000–. Examiner, Intercollegiate Bd in Gen. Surgery, 2000–; Ext. Examiner, Univ. of Malaysia, 2001. 14th Millin Lectr, RCSI, 1990. Hon. FRCPSGlas, 1998. *Publications:* (ed with A. Darzi) Laparascopic Inguinal Hernia Repair, 1994; (ed jtly) Atlas of Surgical Oncology, 1994; (with A. Darzi) Laparascopic Colorectal Surgery, 1995; (ed jtly) Surgical Emergencies, 1999; numerous contribs on subjects of colorectal surgery, tumour immunology and laparascopic surgery in jls incl. Brit. Jl Surgery and Brit. Jl Cancer. *Recreations:* wine, classic cars, armchair sport, bad golf. *Address:* Academic Surgical Unit, Castle Hill Hospital, Hull, E Yorks HU16 5JQ. *T:* (01482) 623225, *Fax:* (01482) 623274. *Clubs:* Athenæum; Kildare Street and University (Dublin).

MONTAGNIER, Prof. Luc; Head of Viral Oncology Unit, since 1972 and Professor, since 1985, Pasteur Institute, Paris; Director of Research, Centre national de la recherche scientifique, since 1974; *b* 18 Aug. 1932; *s* of Antoine Montagnier and Marianne (*née* Rousselet); *m* 1961, Dorothea Ackermann; one *s* two *d. Educ:* Collège de Châtellerault; Univ. de Poitiers; Univ. de Paris. Asst, 1955–60, Attaché, 1960, Head, 1963, Head of Research, 1967, Faculty of Science, Paris; Head of Lab., Inst. of Radium, 1965–71. Dist. Prof. and Dir, B. and G. Salick Center for Molecular and Cellular Biol., Queens Coll., CUNY, 1997–. Pres., World Foundn for AIDS Res. and Prevention, 1993–. Commandeur: Légion d'honneur; Ordre national du Mérite. *Publications:* Vaincre le Sida, 1986; Des virus et des hommes, 1994; Virus, 2000; scientific papers on research into AIDS virus, molecular biology, virology, etc. *Address:* Pasteur Institute, 28 rue du Docteur-Roux, 75724 Paris Cedex 15, France.

MONTAGU; *see* Douglas-Scott-Montagu.

MONTAGU, family name of **Duke of Manchester, Earl of Sandwich,** and **Baron Swaythling**.

MONTAGU OF BEAULIEU, 3rd Baron *cr* 1885; **Edward John Barrington Douglas-Scott-Montagu;** Chairman, Historic Buildings and Monuments Commission, 1983–92; *b* 20 Oct. 1926; *o s* of 2nd Baron and Pearl (who *m* 2nd, 1936, Captain Hon. Edward Pleydell-Bouverie, RN, MVO, *s* of 6th Earl of Radnor; she *d* 1996), *d* of late Major E. B. Crake, Rifle Brigade, and Mrs Barrington Crake; *S* father, 1929; *m* 1st, 1959, Elizabeth Belinda (marr. diss. 1974), *o d* of late Capt. the Hon. John de Bathe Crossley, and late Hon. Mrs Crossley; one *s* one *d*; 2nd, 1974, Fiona Herbert; one *s. Educ:* St Peter's Court, Broadstairs; Ridley Coll., St Catharines, Ont; Eton Coll.; New Coll., Oxford. Late Lt Grenadier Guards; released Army, 1948. Elected Mem., H of L, 1999. Founded Montagu Motor Car Museum, 1952 and World's first Motor Cycle Museum, 1956; created Nat. Motor Museum Trust, 1970, to administer new Nat. Motor Museum at Beaulieu, opened 1972. Mem., Develt Commn, 1980–84. President: Assoc. of British Transport and Engrg Museums, 1964–; Historic Houses Assoc., 1973–78; Southern Tourist Bd, 1977–; Union of European Historic Houses, 1978–81; Fédération Internationale des Voitures Anciennes, 1980–83; Museums Assoc., 1982–84; Fedn of British Historic Vehicle Clubs, 1989–; Tourism Soc., 1991–2000 (now Pres. Emeritus); UK Vineyards Assoc., 1996–; Millennium Pres., Inst. of Journalists, 2000; Hon. Fellow, Inst. of Motor Industry, 1996; Chancellor, Wine Guild of UK, 1983–; Patron, Assoc. of Independent Museums, 1978–. FRSA 1981. FIPR 1998. Hon. FMA, 1988. Commodore: Nelson Boat Owners' Club; Beaulieu River Sailing Club; Vice Cdre, H of L Yacht Club. Founder and Editor, Veteran and Vintage Magazine, 1956–79. Hon. DTech Nottingham Trent, 1998. *Publications:* The Motoring Montagus, 1959; Lost Causes of Motoring, 1960; Jaguar, A Biography, 1961, rev. edn, 1986; The Gordon Bennett Races, 1963; Rolls of Rolls-Royce, 1966; The Gilt and the Gingerbread, 1967; Lost Causes of Motoring: Europe, vol. i, 1969, vol. ii, 1971; More Equal than Others, 1970; History of the Steam Car, 1971; The Horseless Carriage, 1975; Early Days on the Road, 1976; Behind the Wheel, 1977; Royalty on the Road, 1980; Home James, 1982; The British Motorist, 1987; English Heritage, 1987; The Daimler Century, 1995; Wheels Within Wheels (autobiog.), 2000. *Heir: s* Hon. Ralph Douglas-Scott-Montagu, *b* 13 March 1961. *Address:* Palace House, Beaulieu, Hants SO42 7ZN. *T:* (01590) 612345, *Fax:* (01590) 612623; Flat 11, 24 Bryanston Square, W1H 2DS. *T:* (020) 7262 2603, *Fax:* (020) 7724 3262. *Clubs:* Historical Commercial Vehicle (Pres.), Disabled Drivers Motor (Pres.), and mem. of many historic vehicle clubs.

See also Sir E. John Chichester, Bt, Earl of Lindsay.

MONTAGU, Jennifer Iris Rachel, PhD; FBA 1986; Curator of the Photograph Collection, Warburg Institute, 1971–91, now Hon. Fellow; *b* 20 March 1931; *d* of late Hon. Ewen Edward Samuel Montagu, CBE, QC. *Educ:* Brearley Sch., New York; Benenden Sch., Kent; Lady Margaret Hall, Oxford (BA; Hon. Fellow 1985); Warburg Inst., London (PhD). Assistant Regional Director, Arts Council of Gt Britain, North West Region, 1953–54; Lecturer in the History of Art, Reading Univ., 1958–64; Asst Curator of the Photograph Collection, Warburg Inst., 1964–71. Slade Prof., and Fellow of Jesus Coll., Cambridge, 1980–81; Andrew W. Mellon Lectr, Nat. Gall. of Art, Washington, 1991; Invited Prof., Collège de France, 1994. Member: Academic Awards Cttee, British Fedn of University Women, 1963–89; Executive Cttee, National Art-Collections Fund, 1973–; Consultative Cttee, Burlington Magazine, 1975–; Cttee, The Jewish Museum, 1983–; Reviewing Cttee on Export of Works of Art, 1987–96. Trustee: Wallace Collection, 1989–; BM, 1994–. Hon. Academician, Accademia Clementina, Bologna, 1988. Serena Medal for Italian Studies, British Acad., 1992; Accademica Cultora, Accademia di San Luca, Rome, 2000; Premio Cultore di Roma, 2001; Premio Daria Borghese, 2001. Officier, Ordre des Arts et des Lettres (France), 1991; Chevalier de la Légion d'honneur (France), 1999. *Publications:* Bronzes, 1963; (with Jacques Thuillier) Catalogue of exhibn Charles Le Brun, 1963; Alessandro Algardi, 1985 (special Mitchell Prize); Roman Baroque Sculpture: the industry of art, 1989; The Expression of the Passions, 1994; Gold, Silver and Bronze: metal sculpture of the Roman Baroque, 1996; (ed and contrib.) Algardi: l'altra faccia del Barocco, 1999; articles in learned periodicals.

Address: 10 Roland Way, SW7 3RE. *T:* (020) 7373 6691; Warburg Institute, Woburn Square, WC1H 0AB.

MONTAGU, Sir Nicholas Lionel John, KCB 2001 (CB 1993); Chairman, Board of Inland Revenue, since 1997; *b* 12 March 1944; *s* of late John Eric Montagu and Barbara Joyce Montagu, OBE; *m* 1974, Jennian Ford Geddes, *o d* of Ford Irvine Geddes, *qv*; two *d*. *Educ:* Rugby Sch.; New Coll., Oxford (MA). Asst Lectr 1966–69, Lectr 1969–74, in Philosophy, Univ. of Reading; Department of Social Security (formerly Department of Health and Social Security): Principal, 1974–81 (seconded to Cabinet Office, 1978–80); Asst Sec., 1981–86; Under Sec, 1986–90; Deputy Secretary, 1990 (seconded to Dept of Transport, 1992–95): Public Transport, 1992–94; Infrastructure, 1994–95; Railways, 1995–96; Dir-Gen., Railways, 1996–97; Hd, Econ. and Domestic Secretariat, Cabinet Office, 1997. DUniv Middlesex, 2001. *Publication:* Brought to Account (report of Rayner Scrutiny on National Insurance Contributions), 1981. *Recreations:* cooking, wild flowers. *Address:* Board of Inland Revenue, The Board Room, Somerset House, WC2R 1LB. *T:* (020) 7438 7711.

MONTAGU DOUGLAS SCOTT, family name of **Duke of Buccleuch**.

MONTAGU-DOUGLAS-SCOTT, Douglas Andrew; *see* Scott.

MONTAGU-POLLOCK, Sir Giles Hampden; *see* Pollock.

MONTAGU-STUART-WORTLEY, family name of **Earl of Wharncliffe**.

MONTAGUE, family name of **Baron Amwell**.

MONTAGUE, Adrian Alastair, CBE 2001; Deputy Chairman, Partnerships UK, since 2000; Senior International Adviser, Société Générale, since 2001; *b* 28 Feb. 1948; *s* of late Charles Edward Montague and Olive Montague (*née* Jones); *m* 1st, 1970, Pamela Evans (marr. diss. 1982; she *d* 2000); one *s* two *d*; 2nd, 1986, Penelope Webb; one *s*. *Educ:* Trinity Hall, Cambridge (MA). Admitted Solicitor, 1973; with Linklaters & Paines, Solicitors, 1971–94 (Partner, 1979); Dir, Kleinwort Benson, subseq. Dresdner Kleinwort Benson, 1994–97; Chief Exec., Private Finance Initiative Task Force, HM Treasury, 1997–2000. Dir, Michael Page Internat., 2001–. Mem., Strategic Rail Authy, 2000–01. *Address:* Partnerships UK plc, 10 Great George Street, SW1P 3AE. *T:* (020) 7273 8383. *Club:* Travellers.

MONTAGUE, Robert Joel, CBE 1990; Founder, Chairman and Chief Executive, Axis Intermodal Rental Group, since 1999; *b* 22 June 1948; *s* of Robert and Freda Montague; *m* 1972 (marr. diss.); two *s* one *d*; *m* 1990, Silke Kruse; two *s* one *d*. *Educ:* Bedstone Sch., Shropshire; Caius Sch., Brighton. Esso Petroleum Co. Ltd, 1964–69; Cables Montague Ltd, 1969–80; Founder, Chm. and Chief Exec., Tiphook plc, 1978–94. *Recreations:* children, shooting, fishing, opera, ballet. *Address:* (home) Gill Mill, Stanton Harcourt, Oxon OX8 1AN; (office) 48 Albemarle Street, W1X 3FE.

MONTAGUE, Air Cdre Ruth Mary Bryceson; Director, Women's Royal Air Force, 1989–94; *b* 1 June 1939; *d* of late Griffith John Griffiths and Nancy Bryceson Griffiths (*née* Wrigley); *m* 1966, Roland Arthur Montague. *Educ:* Cavendish Grammar Sch. for Girls, Buxton; Bedford Coll., Univ. of London (BSc). Commissioned RAF, 1962; UK and Far East, 1962–66; UK, 1966–80; HQ Strike Command, 1980–83; RAF Staff Coll., 1983–86; Dep. Dir, WRAF, 1986–89. ADC to the Queen, 1989–94. Mem., Council and F and GP Cttee, RAF Benevolent Fund, 1994–. Mem. Council, Royal Holloway, London Univ., 1994–. FRSA 1993. *Recreations:* cookery, tapestry, gardening, swimming, clay pigeon shooting, world travel. *Address:* c/o National Westminster Bank, PO Box 873, 7 High Street, Marlow, Bucks SL7 1BZ. *Club:* Royal Air Force.

MONTAGUE BROWNE, Sir Anthony (Arthur Duncan), KCMG 2000; CBE 1965 (OBE 1955); DFC 1945; a Managing Director, Gerrard and National PLC, 1970–83 (Director, 1967–70); *b* 8 May 1923; *s* of late Lt-Col A. D. Montague Browne, DSO, OBE, Bivia House, Goodrich, Ross-on-Wye, and Violet Evelyn (*née* Downes); *m* 1st, 1950, Noel Evelyn Arnold-Wallinger (marr. diss. 1970); one *d*; 2nd, 1970, Shelagh Macklin (*née* Mulligan). *Educ:* Stowe; Magdalen Coll., Oxford; abroad. Pilot RAF, 1941–45. Entered Foreign (now Diplomatic) Service, 1946; Foreign Office, 1946–49; Second Sec., British Embassy, Paris, 1949–52; seconded as Private Sec. to Prime Minister, 1952–55; seconded as Private Sec. to Rt Hon. Sir Winston Churchill, 1955–65; Counsellor, Diplomatic Service, 1964; seconded to HM Household, 1965–67. Dir, Columbia (British) Productions, 1967–77; Chm., LandLeisure PLC, 1987–88; Dep. Chm., Highland Participants PLC, 1987–89. Trustee, Winston Churchill Memorial Trust; Vice-Pres., Univs Fedn for Animal Welfare, 1987–93 (Mem., Council, 1985–91); Chm., Internat. Certificate of Deposit Market Assoc., 1980–82. Freeman, City of London, 1987. Hon. DL Westminster Coll., Fulton, Missouri, 1988. *Publication:* Long Sunset: memoirs of Winston Churchill's last Private Secretary, 1995. *Address:* Hawkridge Cottages, Bucklebury, Reading RG7 6EG. *T:* (0118) 971 2578. *Clubs:* Boodle's, Pratt's.

MONTEAGLE OF BRANDON, 6th Baron *cr* 1839; **Gerald Spring Rice;** late Captain, Irish Guards; one of HM Body Guard, Hon. Corps of Gentlemen-at-Arms, 1978–96; *b* 5 July 1926; *s* of 5th Baron and Emilie de Kosenko (*d* 1981), *d* of Mrs Edward Brooks, Philadelphia, USA; *S* father, 1946; *m* 1949, Anne, *d* of late Col G. J. Brownlow, Ballywhite, Portaferry, Co. Down; one *s* three *d* (of whom two are twins). *Educ:* Harrow. Member: London Stock Exchange, 1958–76; Lloyd's, 1978–98. *Heir: s* Hon. Charles James Spring Rice [*b* 24 Feb. 1953; *m* 1987, Mary Teresa Glover; four *d*]. *Address:* Glenamara, Stradbally, Co. Waterford, Ireland. *Clubs:* Cavalry and Guards, Pratt's; Kildare Street and University (Dublin).

MONTEFIORE, Harold Henry S.; *see* Sebag-Montefiore.

MONTEFIORE, Rt Rev. Hugh William, MA, BD; Hon. DD; Hon. Assistant Bishop, Diocese of Southwark, since 1987; *b* 12 May 1920; *s* of late Charles Sebag-Montefiore, OBE, and Muriel Alice Ruth Sebag-Montefiore; *m* 1945, Elisabeth Mary Macdonald Paton (*d* 1999), *d* of late Rev. William Paton, DD, and Mrs Grace Paton; three *d*. *Educ:* Rugby Sch.; St John's Coll., Oxford (Hon. Fellow, 1981). Served during war, 1940–45; Capt. RA (Royal Bucks Yeo). Deacon 1949, priest 1950. Curate, St George's, Jesmond, Newcastle, 1949–51; Chaplain and Tutor, Westcott House, Cambridge, 1951–53; Vice-Principal, 1953–54; Examining Chaplain: to Bishop of Newcastle, 1953–70; to Bishop of Worcester, 1957–60; to Bishop of Coventry, 1957–70; to Bishop of Blackburn, 1966–70; Fellow and Dean of Gonville and Caius Coll., 1954–63; Lectr in New Testament, Univ. of Cambridge, 1959–63; Vicar of Great Saint Mary's, Cambridge, 1963–70; Canon Theologian of Coventry, 1959–70; Hon. Canon of Ely, 1969–70; Bishop Suffragen of Kingston-upon-Thames, 1970–78; Bishop of Birmingham, 1978–87. Mem., Archbishops' Commn on Christian Doctrine, 1967–76; Chm., General Synod Bd for Social Responsibility, 1983–87. Chairman: Indep. Commn on Transport, 1973; Transport 2000, 1987–92; Friends of the Earth Trust, 1992–98; Nat. Trust for the Homeless, 1992–96; Natural Justice, 2000–. Hon. Fellow, Gonville and Caius Coll., Cambridge, 2000. Hon. DD: Aberdeen, 1976; Birmingham, 1985. *Publications:* (contrib.) The Historic Episcopate and the Fullness of the Church, 1954; To Help You To Pray, 1957; (contrib.) Soundings, 1962; Josephus and the New Testament, 1962; (with H. E. W. Turner) Thomas and the Evangelists, 1962; Beyond Reasonable Doubt, 1963; (contrib.) God, Sex and War, 1963; Awkward Questions on Christian Love, 1964; A Commentary on the Epistle to the Hebrews, 1964; Truth to Tell, 1966; (ed) We Must Love One Another Or Die, 1966; (contrib.) The Responsible Church, 1966; Remarriage and Mixed Marriage, 1967; (contrib.) Journeys in Belief, 1968; (ed) Sermons From Great St Mary's, 1968; My Confirmation Notebook, 1968; The Question Mark, 1969; Can Man Survive, 1970; (ed) More Sermons From Great St Mary's, 1971; Doom or Deliverance?, 1972; (ed) Changing Directions, 1974; (ed) Man and Nature, 1976; Apocalypse, 1976; (ed) Nuclear Crisis, 1977; (ed) Yes to Women Priests, 1978; Taking our Past into our Future, 1978; Paul the Apostle, 1981; Jesus Across the Centuries, 1983; The Probability of God, 1985; So Near And Yet So Far, 1986; Communicating the Gospel in a Scientific Age, 1988; God, Sex and Love, 1989; Christianity and Politics, 1990; Reclaiming the High Ground, 1990; (ed) The Gospel and Contemporary Culture, 1992; The Womb and The Tomb, 1992; Preaching for Our Planet, 1992; Credible Christianity, 1994; Oh God, What Next?, 1995; Time to Change, 1996; On Being a Jewish Christian, 1998; contribs to New Testament and Theological jls. *Address:* White Lodge, 23 Bellevue Road, Wandsworth Common, SW17 7EB. *Clubs:* Beefsteak, Royal Commonwealth Society.
See also Ven. M. J. M. Paton.

MONTEITH, Brian; Member (C) Scotland Mid and Fife, Scottish Parliament, since 1999; *b* 8 Jan. 1958; *s* of Donald MacDonald Monteith and Doreen Campbell Monteith (*née* Purves); *m* 1984, Shirley Joyce Marshall; twin *s*. *Educ:* Portobello High Sch.; Heriot Watt Univ. Chm., Fedn of Conservative Students, 1982–83; Public Relations Consultant: Michael Forsyth Associates, London, 1983–84 and 1985–86; Dunseath Stephen Associates, Edinburgh, 1984–85; Man. Dir, Leith Communications Ltd, 1986–91; PR Dir, Forth Mktg Ltd, 1991–94; Scottish Dir, Communication Gp, 1994–96; sole proprietor and Consultant, Dunedin PR, 1996–99. Mem., Tuesday Club. *Recreation:* football. *Address:* Scottish Parliament, Edinburgh EH99 1SP. *T:* (0131) 348 5644. *Club:* Duddingston Golf (Edinburgh).

MONTEITH, Rt Rev. George Rae, BA; Assistant Bishop of Auckland, 1965–76; *b* 14 Feb. 1904; *s* of John Hodge Monteith and Ellen (*née* Hall); *m* 1st, 1931, Kathleen Methven Mules; two *s* one *d*; 2nd, 1982, Hilary Llewellyn Etherington. *Educ:* St John's Coll., Auckland; Univ. of New Zealand. BA 1927. Deacon, 1928; priest, 1929; Curate: St Matthew's, Auckland, 1928–30; Stoke-on-Trent, 1931–33; Vicar of: Dargaville, NZ, 1934–37; Mt Eden, Auckland, NZ, 1937–49; St Mary's Cathedral Parish, Auckland, 1949–69; Dean of Auckland, 1949–69; Vicar-General, 1963–76. *Publications:* Enjoy Europe With Me, 1993; More Travels with Monty and Other Stories, 1996; The Cathedral of the Holy Trinity, Auckland, New Zealand, 1997. *Address:* 10A Mahoe Avenue, Remuera, Auckland 1005, NZ. *T:* (9) 5221188.

MONTEITH, Prof. John Lennox, FRS 1971; FRSE 1972; Emeritus Professor of Environmental Physics, University of Nottingham, 1989; *b* 3 Sept. 1929; *s* of Rev. John and Margaret Monteith; *m* 1955, Elsa Marion Wotherspoon; four *s* one *d*. *Educ:* George Heriot's Sch.; Univ. of Edinburgh (BSc 1951; Hon. DSc 1989); Imperial Coll., London. DIC, PhD; FInstP, FIBiol. Mem. Physics Dept Staff, Rothamsted Experimental Station, 1954–67; Prof. of Environmental Physics, 1967–86, Dean of Faculty of Agricl Sci., 1985–86, Nottingham Univ.; Dir, Resource Management Programme, Internat. Crops Res. Inst. for the Semi-Arid Tropics, 1987–91 (Vis. Scientist, 1984); Sen. Vis. Fellow, NERC, 1992–94. Adjunct Prof., Depts of Agricl Engrg and Agronomy, Univ. of Florida, 1991–; Vis. Prof., Reading Univ., 1992–95; Hon. Prof., Edinburgh Univ., 1992–. Governor: Grassland Res. Inst., 1976–83; Silsoe Res. Inst., 1993–97. Vice Pres., British Ecological Soc., 1977–79; Pres., Royal Meteorol Soc., 1978–80; Fellowship Sec., RSE, 1997–99. Member: NERC, 1980–84; British Nat. Cttee for the World Climate Programme, 1980–86; Lawes Agricl Trust Cttee, 1983–86. Nat. Res. Council Senior Res. Associate, Goddard Space Flight Center, Md, USA, 1985; Clive Behrens Lectr, Leeds Univ., 1986; York Distinguished Lectr, Univ. of Florida, 1991. Buchan Prize, 1962, Symon's Meml Medal, 1995, RMetS; Solco Tromp Award, Internat. Soc. of Biometeorology, 1983; Rank Fund Nutrition Prize, 1989. *Publications:* Instruments for Micrometeorology (ed), 1972; Principles of Environmental Physics, 1973, 2nd edn (with M. H. Unsworth), 1990; (ed with L. E. Mount) Heat Loss from Animals and Man, 1974; (ed) Vegetation and the Atmosphere, 1975; (ed with C. Webb) Soil Water and Nitrogen, 1981; (ed with R. K. Scott and M. H. Unsworth) Resource Capture by Crops, 1994; papers on Micrometeorology and Crop Science in: Quarterly Jl of RMetSoc.; Jl Applied Ecology, etc. *Recreations:* music, photography. *Address:* 34 St Alban's Road, Edinburgh EH9 2LU.

MONTGOMERIE, family name of **Earl of Eglinton**.

MONTGOMERIE, Lord; Hugh Archibald William Montgomerie; Operations Manager, Gander & White Shipping Ltd, since 1996; *b* 24 July 1966; *s* and *heir* of 18th Earl of Eglinton and Winton, *qv*; *m* 1991, Sara Alexandra, *e d* of Niel Redpath. RN officer, 1988–92. *Address:* 17 Ormiston Grove, W12 0JR.

MONTGOMERIE, Colin Stuart, MBE 1998; professional golfer, since 1987; *b* Glasgow, 23 June 1963; *s* of James Montgomerie; *m* 1990, Eimear Wilson; one *s* two *d*. *Educ:* Strathallen Sch., Perth; Baptist Univ., Texas. Wins include: Scottish Amateur Stroke-Play Championship, 1985; Scottish Amateur Championship, 1987; Portuguese Open, 1989; Scandinavian Masters, 1991, 1999; Dutch Open 1993; Volvo Masters, 1993; Spanish Open, 1994; English Open, 1994; German Open, 1994, 1995; Lancôme Trophy, 1995; European Masters, 1996; Dubai Desert Classic, 1996; Irish Open, 1996, 1997, 2001; European Grand Prix, 1997; World Cup (Individual), 1997; World Championship of Golf, 1998; PGA Championship, 1998, 1999, 2000; German Masters, 1998; British Masters, 1998; Benson & Hedges Internat. Open, 1999; Loch Lomond Invitational, 1999; BMW Internat. Open, 1999; Cisco World Matchplay, 1999; French Open, 2000; Australian Masters, 2001; 1st in European Order of Merit, annually, 1993–99. Member: Alfred Dunhill Cup team, 1988, 1991–99; World Cup Team, 1988, 1991–93, 1997–98; Ryder Cup team, 1991–99. *Address:* c/o IMG, Pier House, Strand-on-the-Green, W4 3NN.

MONTGOMERY, family name of **Viscount Montgomery of Alamein**.

MONTGOMERY OF ALAMEIN, 2nd Viscount *cr* 1946, of Hindhead; **David Bernard Montgomery,** CMG 2000; CBE 1975; Chairman, Baring Puma Fund, since 1991; *b* 18 Aug. 1928; *s* of 1st Viscount Montgomery of Alamein, KG, GCB, DSO, and Elizabeth (*d* 1937), *d* of late Robert Thompson Hobart, ICS; *S* father, 1976; *m* 1st, 1953, Mary Connell (marr. diss. 1967); one *s* one *d*; 2nd, 1970, Tessa, *d* of late Gen. Sir Frederick Browning, GCVO, KBE, CB, DSO, and Lady Browning, DBE (Dame Daphne du Maurier). *Educ:* Winchester; Trinity Coll., Cambridge (MA). Shell International, 1951–62; Dir, Yardley International, 1963–74; Man. Dir, Terimar Services (Overseas Trade Consultancy),

1974–99; Dir, Korn/Ferry International, 1977–93; Chm., Antofagasta (Chile) and Bolivia Railway Co., 1980–82; Dir, NEI, 1981–87. Exec. Cttee, British Gp, IPU, 1987–99. Editorial Adviser, Vision Interamericana, 1974–94. Deleg., OSCE Parly Assembly, 1991–2000. Chm., Economic Affairs Cttee, Canning House, 1973–75; Pres., British Industrial Exhibition, Sao Paulo, 1974. Councillor, Royal Borough of Kensington and Chelsea, 1974–78. Hon. Consul, Republic of El Salvador, 1973–77. Pres., Anglo-Argentine Soc., 1977–87; Chairman: Hispanic and Luso Brazilian Council, 1978–80 (Pres., 1987–94); Brazilian Chamber of Commerce in GB, 1980–82; European Atlantic Gp, 1992–94 (Pres., 1994–97); Pres., Anglo-Belgian Soc., 1994–. Patron: D-Day and Normandy Fellowship, 1980–95; 8th Army Veterans Assoc., 1985–. President: Redgrave Theatre, Farnham, 1977–89; Restaurateurs Assoc. of GB, 1982–90 (Patron, 1991–99); Acad. of Food and Wine Service, 1995–98; Centre for International Briefing, Farnham Castle, 1985–. Pres., Amesbury Sch., 1992– (Gov., 1976–92). Gran Oficial: Orden Bernardo O'Higgins (Chile), 1989; Orden Libertador San Martin (Argentina), 1992; Orden Nacional Cruzeiro do Sul (Brazil), 1993; Orden de Isabel la Católica (Spain), 1993; Commander's Cross, Order of Merit (Germany), 1993; Order of Aztec Eagle (Mexico), 1994; Order of Leopold II (Belgium), 1997; Orden de San Carlos (Colombia), 1998; Orden del Libertador (Venezuela), 1999. *Publication:* (with Alistair Horne) The Lonely Leader: Monty 1944–45, 1994. *Heir: s* Hon. Henry David Montgomery [*b* 2 April 1954; *m* 1980, Caroline, *e d* of Richard Odey, Hotham Hall, York; three *d*]. *Address:* 54 Cadogan Square, SW1X 0JW. *T:* (020) 7589 8747. *Clubs:* Garrick, Canning.

MONTGOMERY, Alan Everard, CMG 1993; PhD; HM Diplomatic Service, retired; Trade Policy Adviser, Commonwealth Business Council, 1998–99; *b* 11 March 1938; *s* of Philip Napier Montgomery and Honor Violet Coleman (*née* Price); *m* 1st, 1960, Janet Barton (*d* 1994); one *s* one *d*; 2nd, 1999, Florence Belle Liebst. *Educ:* Royal Grammar Sch., Guildford; County of Stafford Training Coll. (Cert. of Educn); Birkbeck Coll., London (BA Hons, PhD). Served Mddx Regt, 1957–59. Teacher, Staffs and ILEA, 1961–65; Lectr, Univ. of Birmingham, 1969–72; entered FCO, 1972; 1st Secretary: FCO, 1972–75; Dhaka, 1975–77; Ottawa, 1977–80; FCO, 1980–83; Counsellor GATT/UNCTAD, UKMIS Geneva, 1983–87; Counsellor, Consul-Gen. and Hd of Chancery, Jakarta, 1987–89; Head of Migration and Visa Dept, FCO, 1989–92; Ambassador to the Philippines, 1992–95; High Comr to Tanzania, 1995–98. Member: Professional Conduct Cttee, GMC, 2000–; Immigration Services Tribunal, 2001–; Panel of Lay Members, Gen. Council of the Bar, 2001–. Mem. Bd, FARM Africa, 1998–2001. *Publications:* (contrib.) Lloyd George: 12 essays, ed A. J. P. Taylor, 1971; (contrib.) Commonwealth Banking Almanac, 1999; contrib. Cambridge Hist. Jl. *Recreations:* historic buildings, jazz, sailing, theatre, opera, gardening. *Club:* Royal Over-Seas League.

MONTGOMERY, Sir (Basil Henry) David, 9th Bt *cr* 1801, of Stanhope; JP; landowner; Lord-Lieutenant of Perth and Kinross, since 1996; Chairman, Forestry Commission, 1979–89; *b* 20 March 1931; *s* of late Lt-Col H. K. Purvis-Montgomery, OBE, and of Mrs C. L. W. Purvis-Russell-Montgomery (*née* Maconochie Welwood); *S* uncle, 1964; *m* 1956, Delia, *o d* of Adm. Sir (John) Peter (Lorne) Reid, GCB, CVO; one *s* four *d* (and one *s* decd). *Educ:* Eton. National Service, Black Watch, 1949–51. Member: Nature Conservancy Council, 1973–79; Tayside Regional Authority, 1974–79. Comr, Mental Welfare Commn for Scotland, 1990–91. Trustee, Municipal Mutual Insurance Ltd, 1980–96. Hon. LLD Dundee, 1977. DL Kinross-shire, 1960, Vice-Lieutenant 1966–74; JP 1966; DL Perth and Kinross, 1975. *Heir: s* James David Keith Montgomery [*b* 13 June 1957; *m* 1983, Elizabeth, *e d* of late E. Lyndon Evans, Pentyrch, Mid-Glamorgan; one *s* one *d*. Served The Black Watch, RHR, 1976–86]. *Address:* Home Farm, Kinross KY13 8EU. *T:* (01577) 863416.

MONTGOMERY, Clare Patricia; QC 1996; a Recorder, since 2000; *b* 29 April 1958; *d* of Stephen Ross Montgomery and Ann Margaret Barlow; *m* 1991, Victor Melleney; two *d*. *Educ:* Millfield Sch.; UCL (LLB). Called to the Bar, Gray's Inn, 1980. An Asst Recorder, 1999–2000. Mem., Supplementary Panel (Common Law), 1992. *Publication:* (ed) Archbold Criminal Pleading Evidence and Practice, annually, 1993–. *Address:* Matrix Chambers, Gray's Inn, WC1R 5LN. *T:* (020) 7404 3447.

MONTGOMERY, Sir David; *see* Montgomery, Sir B. H. D.

MONTGOMERY, David, CMG 1984; OBE 1972; Foreign and Commonwealth Office, 1987–91; *b* 29 July 1927; *s* of late David Montgomery and of Mary (*née* Walker Cunningham); *m* 1955, Margaret Newman; one *s* one *d*. Royal Navy, 1945–48. Foreign Office, 1949–52; Bucharest, 1952–53; FO, 1953–55; Bonn, 1955–58; Düsseldorf, 1958–61; Rangoon, 1961–63; Ottawa, 1963–64; Regina, Saskatchewan, 1964–65; FCO, 1966–68; Bangkok, 1968–72; Zagreb, 1973–76; FCO, 1976–79; Dep. High Comr to Barbados, 1980–84, also (non-resident) to Antigua and Barbuda, Dominica, Grenada, St Kitts and Nevis, St Lucia, St Vincent and the Grenadines, 1980–84; FCO, 1984–85. *Recreations:* golf, music (light and opera). *Address:* 8 Ross Court, Putney Hill, SW15 3NY. *Club:* Royal Over-Seas League.

MONTGOMERY, David John; Chairman, Mecom, since 2000; *b* 6 Nov. 1948; *s* of William John and Margaret Jean Montgomery; *m* 1st, 1971, Susan Frances Buchanan Russell (marr. diss. 1987); 2nd, 1989, Heidi Kingstone (marr. diss. 1997); 3rd, 1997, Sophie Countess of Woolton, *d* of Baron Birdwood, *qv*. *Educ:* Queen's University, Belfast (BA Politics/History). Sub-Editor, Daily Mirror, London/Manchester, 1973–78; Assistant Chief Sub-Editor, Daily Mirror, 1978–80; Chief Sub-Editor, The Sun, 1980; Asst Editor, Sunday People, 1982; Asst Editor, 1984, Editor, 1985–87, News of the World; Editor, Today, 1987–91 (Newspaper of the Year, 1988); Man. Dir, News UK, 1987–91; Chief Exec., 1991, Dir, 1991–, London Live Television; Chief Exec., Mirror Gp Newspapers, 1992–99. Director: Satellite Television PLC, 1986–91; News Group Newspapers, 1986–91; Caledonian Publishing Co. (Glasgow Herald & Times), 1991–92; Donohue Inc., 1992–95; Newspaper Publishing (The Independent, Independent on Sunday), 1994–98; Scottish Media Gp (formerly Scottish Television), 1995–99; Press Assoc., 1996–99; Chairman: Tri-mex Gp, 1999–; Yava, 2000–; Africa Lakes plc, 2000–. Chm., Integrated Educn Fund Develt Bd (NI), 2000–. *Address:* 15 Collingham Gardens, SW5 0HS.

MONTGOMERY, Prof. Desmond Alan Dill, CBE 1981 (MBE 1943); MD; FRCP, FRCPI; Chairman, Northern Ireland Council for Postgraduate Medical Education, 1979–87; *b* 6 June 1916; 3rd *s* of late Dr and Mrs J. Howard Montgomery, China and Belfast; *m* 1941, Dr Susan Holland, 2nd *d* of late Mr and Mrs F. J. Holland, Belfast; one *s* one *d*. *Educ:* Inchmarlo Prep. Sch.; Campbell Coll.; Queen's Univ., Belfast (3rd, 4th and final yr scholarships; MB, BCh, BAO 1st Cl. Hons 1940; MD (Gold Medal) 1946). Sinclair Medal in Surgery, Butterworth Prize in Medicine, Prize in Mental Disease, QUB. MRCP 1948, FRCP 1964; FRCPI 1975; FRCOG (*ae*) 1981. Served War, RAMC, 1941–46: Temp. Major India Comd; DADMS GHQ India, 1943–45. House Physician and Surgeon, Royal Victoria Hosp., Belfast, 1940–41, Registrar, 1946; Registrar, Royal Postgrad. Med. Sch. and Hammersmith Hosp., and National Heart Hosp., London, 1946–48; Royal Victoria Hosp., Belfast: Sen. Registrar, 1948–51; Consultant Physician, 1951–79, Hon. Consultant 1980–; Physician i/c Sir George E. Clark Metabolic Unit, 1958–79; Endocrinologist, Royal Maternity Hosp., Belfast, 1958–79; Hon. Reader in Endocrinol., Dept of Medicine, QUB, 1969–75, Hon. Prof., 1975–. Hon. Secretary: Royal Victoria Med. Staff Cttee, 1964–66 (Chm., 1975–77); Ulster Med. Soc., 1954–58 (Pres., 1975–76). Member: NI Council for Health and Personal Social Services, 1974–83 (Chm., Central Med. Adv. Cttee, 1974–83, Mem. 1983–87); NI Med. Manpower Adv. Cttee, 1974–83; Distinction and Meritorious Awards Cttee, 1975–87 (Chm., 1982–87); Faculty of Medicine, QUB, 1969–87 (Chm., Ethical Cttee, 1975–81); Senate, QUB, 1979–96; GMC, 1979–84; Pres., QUB Assoc., 1988–89. Member: BMA; Assoc. of Physicians of GB and NI; Eur. Thyroid Assoc.; Corrigan Club (Chm., 1969); Irish Endocrine Soc. (1st Chm., Founder Mem.); Internat. Soc. for Internal Medicine; formerly Mem., Eur. Soc. for Study of Diabetes; Hon. Mem., British Dietetic Assoc. Lectured in USA, India, Greece, Australia and Nigeria; visited Russia on behalf of British Council, 1975. Pres., Belfast City Mission, 1973–92; Mem., Bd of Trustees, Presbyterian Church in Ireland. DSc (*hc*) NUI, 1980. Jt Editor, Ulster Med. Jl, 1974–84. *Publications:* (contrib.) Whitla's Dictionary of Treatment, 1957; (contrib.) Good Health and Diabetes, 1961, 3rd edn 1976; (contrib.) R. Smith, Progress in Clinical Surgery, 1961; (with R. B. Welbourn) Clinical Endocrinology for Surgeons, 1963; (contrib.) Progress in Neurosurgery, 1964; (with R. B. Welbourn) Medical and Surgical Endocrinology, 1975; (contrib.) M. D. Vickers, Medicine for Anaesthetists, 1977; articles in med. jls on endocrinology, diabetes mellitus and related subjects. *Recreations:* travel, photography, music, gardening, philately. *Address:* 59 Church Road, Newtownbreda, Belfast BT8 7AN. *T:* (028) 9064 8326; 15 Carrickmore Road, Ballycastle BT54 6QS. *T:* (028) 2076 2361.

MONTGOMERY, Sir Fergus; *see* Montgomery, Sir W. F.

MONTGOMERY, Hugh Bryan Greville; non-executive Director, Andry Montgomery group of companies (organisers, managers and consultants in exhibitions), since 1994 (Managing Director, 1952–88; Chairman, 1988–94); *b* 26 March 1929; *s* of Hugh Roger Greville Montgomery, MC, and Molly Audrey Montgomery, OBE (*née* Neele). *Educ:* Repton; Lincoln Coll., Oxford (MA PPE; Fleming Fellow, 1996). Founder member, Oxford Univ. Wine and Food Soc. Consultant and adviser on trade fairs and developing countries for UN; Consultant, Internat. Garden Festival, Liverpool, 1984. Chairman: Brit. Assoc. of Exhibn Organisers, 1970; Internat. Cttee, Amer. Nat. Assoc. of Exposition Managers, 1980–82 and 1990–93; British Exhibn Promotion Council, 1982–83; World Trade Centers Assoc., NY, 2000–; Pres., Union des Foires Internat., 1994–97 (Vice Pres., 1987–94). Member: Adv. Bd, Hotel Inst. for Management, Montreux, 1986–; London Regl Cttee, CBI, 1987–90; BOTB, 1991–94. Mem. Council, Design and Industries Assoc., 1983–85. Chm. of Trustees of ECHO (Supply of Equipment to Charity Hosps Overseas), 1978–89; Chairman: The Building Museum, 1988–2000; British Architectural Library Trust, 1989–2000; Interbuild Fund, 1972–; Vice-Pres., Bldg Conservation Trust, 1992–94 (Vice-Chm., 1979–92); Trustee: The Cubitt Trust, 1982–99; Music for the World, 1990–92; Hon. Treas., Contemporary Art Soc., 1980–82; Councillor, Acad. of St Martin-in-the-Fields Concert Soc., 1988–2000. Member Executive Committee: CGLI, 1974–; Nat. Fund for Research into Crippling Diseases, 1970–92. Common Councilman, Dowgate Ward, City of London, 1999–. Mem. Court, Co. of World Traders, 1992– (Master, 1995); Liveryman, 1952, Master, 1980–81, Co. of Tylers and Bricklayers (Trustee, Charitable and Pension Trusts, 1981–2000). Silver Jubilee Medal, 1977; Pro Cultura Hungaria Medal, 1991; Brooch, City of Utrecht, 1992; Gold Medal, Belgrade Fair, 1995; Leadership Award, Internat. Council for Caring Communities, UN, 2000. *Publications:* Industrial Fairs and Developing Countries (UNIDO), 1975; Going into Trade Fairs (UNCTAD/GATT), 1982; Exhibition Planning and Design, 1989 (Russian edn 1991, Chinese edn 2001); The Montgomery Collection at Museum of Fine Art in Budapest, 1999; contrib. to Internat. Trade Forum (ITC, Geneva). *Recreations:* collecting contemporary art, sculpture, wine tasting. *Address:* 11 Manchester Square, W1M 5AB. *T:* (020) 7486 1951; Snells Farm, Amersham Common, Bucks HP7 9QN. *Clubs:* Oxford and Cambridge, City Livery, Guildhall.

MONTGOMERY, John Duncan; JP; Member, Monopolies and Mergers Commission, 1989–95; *b* 12 Nov. 1928; *s* of Lionel Eric Montgomery and Katherine Mary Montgomery (*née* Ambler); *m* 1956, Pauline Mary Sutherland; two *d*. *Educ:* King's College Sch., Wimbledon; LSE (LLB, LLM). Admitted Solicitor 1951; Treasury Solicitor's Dept, 1960–68; Legal Adviser, Beecham Products, 1974–75; Head, Legal Div., Shell UK, 1975–88 and Company Sec., Shell UK, 1979–88. Former Chm., Youth Orgns, Merton. Freeman, City of London, 1987; Mem., Loriners' Co., 1988. JP SW London, 1985. *Recreations:* dinghy sailing, photography. *Address:* 6 White Lodge Close, Sutton, Surrey SM2 5TQ. *Clubs:* MCC; Surrey CC.

MONTGOMERY, John Matthew; Clerk of the Salters' Company, 1975–90; *b* 22 May 1930; *s* of Prof. George Allison Montgomery, QC, and Isobel A. (*née* Morison); *m* 1956, Gertrude Gillian Richards; two *s* one *d*. *Educ:* Rugby Sch.; Trinity Hall, Cambridge (MA). Various commercial appointments with Mobil Oil Corporation and First National City Bank, 1953–74. Member Council: Surrey Trust for Nature Conservation Ltd, 1965–89 (Chm., 1973–83; Vice-Pres., 1983–); Royal Soc. for Nature Conservation, 1980–89; Botanical Soc. of British Isles, 1991–95; Founder Mem., London Wildlife Trust, 1981–. Member, Executive Committee: Nat. Assoc. of Almshouses, 1980–91; Age Concern Gtr London, 1985–96 (Chm., 1988–91; Vice-Pres., 1996–). *Recreations:* various natural history interests. *Address:* 22 Red Lane, Claygate, Esher, Surrey KT10 0ES. *T:* (01372) 464780.

MONTGOMERY, Col John Rupert Patrick, OBE 1979; MC 1943; *b* 25 July 1913; *s* of George Howard and Mabella Montgomery; *m* 1st, 1940, Alice Vyvyan Patricia Mitchell (*d* 1976); one *s* two *d*; 2nd, 1981, Marguerite Beatrice Chambers (*née* Montgomery). *Educ:* Wellington Coll.; RMC, Sandhurst. Commissioned, Oxfordshire and Buckinghamshire LI, 1933; Regimental Service in India, 1935–40 and 1946–47. Served War in Middle East, N Africa and Italy, 1942–45. Commanded 17 Bn Parachute Regt (9 DLI), 1953–56; SHAPE Mission to Portugal, 1956–59; retired, 1962. Sec., Anti-Slavery Soc., 1963–80. Silver Medal, RSA, 1973. *Address:* The Oast House, Buxted, Sussex TN22 4PP. *Club:* Army and Navy.

MONTGOMERY, Sir (William) Fergus, Kt 1985; *b* 25 Nov. 1927; *s* of late William Montgomery and Winifred Montgomery; *m* Joyce, *d* of George Riddle. *Educ:* Jarrow Grammar Sch.; Bede Coll., Durham. Served in Royal Navy, 1946–48; Schoolmaster, 1950–59. Nat. Vice-Chm. Young Conservative Organisation, 1954–57, National Chm., 1957–58; contested (C) Consett Division, 1955; MP (C): Newcastle upon Tyne East, 1959–64; Brierley Hill, April 1967–Feb. 1974; contested Dudley W, Feb. 1974; MP (C) Altrincham and Sale, Oct. 1974–1997. PPS to Sec. of State for Educn and Science, 1973–74, to Leader of the Opposition, 1975–76. Chm., H of C Cttee of Selection, 1992–97; Mem. Exec. Cttee, British American Parly Gp, 1991–97. Mem. Executive, CPA, 1983–97. Councillor, Hebburn UDC, 1950–58. Has lectured extensively in the USA. *Recreations:* bridge, reading, going to theatre. *Address:* 181 Ashley Gardens, Emery Hill Street, SW1P 1PD. *T:* (020) 7834 7905; 6 Groby Place, Altrincham, Cheshire WA14 4AL. *T:* (0161) 928 1983.

MONTGOMERY CAMPBELL, Philip Henry; *see* Campbell.

MONTGOMERY CUNINGHAME, Sir John Christopher Foggo, 12th Bt *cr* 1672, of Corsehill, Ayrshire and Kirktonholm, Lanarkshire; Chairman, Euromax Electronics Ltd, since 1985; Director: Alloy Technology International Inc.; Bedford Capital Finance Corp., and other companies; *b* 24 July 1935; 2nd *s* of Col Sir Thomas Montgomery-Cuninghame, 10th Bt, DSO (*d* 1945), and of Nancy Macaulay (his 2nd wife), *d* of late W. Stewart Foggo, Aberdeen (she *m* 2nd, 1946, Johan Frederik Christian Killander); *b* of Sir Andrew Montgomery-Cuninghame, 11th Bt; *S* brother, 1959; *m* 1964, Laura Violet, *d* of Sir Godfrey Nicholson, 1st Bt; three *d*. *Educ:* Fettes; Worcester Coll., Oxford (MA). 2nd Lieut, Rifle Brigade (NS), 1955–56; Lieut, London Rifle Brigade, TA, 1956–59. *Recreation:* fishing. *Heir:* none. *Address:* The Old Rectory, Brightwalton, Newbury, Berks RG20 7BL.

MONTGOMERY WATT, William; *see* Watt.

MONTI, Dr Mario; a Member, European Commission, since 1995; *b* 19 March 1943; *m*; two *c*. *Educ:* Bocconi Univ. (Dr); Yale Univ. Bocconi University, Italy: Asst, 1965–69; Prof. of Monetary Theory and Policy, 1971–85; Prof. of Economics and Dir, Economics Inst., 1985–94; Founder, Paolo Baffi Centre for Monetary and Financial Economics, 1985; Rector, 1989–94, Pres., 1994, Innocenzo Gasparini Inst. of Economic Res. *Address:* European Commission, 200 rue de la Loi, 1049 Brussels, Belgium.

MONTLAKE, Henry Joseph; solicitor; Senior Partner, H. Montlake & Co., 1954–2000; a Recorder of the Crown Court, 1983–98; *b* 22 Aug. 1930; *s* of Alfred and Hetty Montlake; *m* 1952, Ruth Rochelle Allen; four *s*. *Educ:* Ludlow Grammar Sch., Ludlow; London Univ. (LLB 1951). Law Soc.'s final exam., 1951; admitted Solicitor, 1952. National Service, commnd RASC, 1953. Dep. Registrar of County Courts, 1970–78; Dep. Circuit Judge and Asst Recorder, 1978–83. Pres., West Essex Law Soc., 1977–78. Mem. Ethics Cttee, BUPA Roding Hosp. IVF Unit, 1991–2000. Chm., Ilford Round Table, 1962–63; Pres., Assoc. of Jewish Golf Clubs and Socs, 1984–94 (Sec., 1977–84). Gov., Redbridge Coll. of Further Educn, 1991–92. *Recreations:* golf, The Times crossword, people, travel. *Address:* Chelston, 5 St Mary's Avenue, Wanstead, E11 2NR. *T:* (020) 8989 7228, *Fax:* (020) 8989 5173; *e-mail:* henry@chelston.org. *Clubs:* Wig and Pen; Dyrham Park Golf; Abridge Golf (Chm. 1964, Captain 1965).

MONTMORENCY, Sir Arnold Geoffroy de; *see* de Montmorency.

MONTREAL, Archbishop of, (RC), since 1990; **His Eminence Cardinal Jean-Claude Turcotte;** *b* 26 June 1936. Ordained priest, 1959; consecrated bishop, 1982; Cardinal, 1994. *Address:*; Office of the Archbishop, 2000 Sherbrooke Street West, Montreal, QC H3H 1G4, Canada.

MONTREAL, Bishop of, since 1990; **Rt Rev. Andrew S. Hutchison;** *b* 19 Sept. 1938; *s* of Ralph Burton Hutchison and Kathleen Marian (*née* Van Nostrand); *m* 1960, Lois Arlene Knight; one *s*. *Educ:* Lakefield Coll. Sch.; Upper Canada Coll.; Trinity Coll. Toronto (LTh). Ordained deacon, 1969, priest, 1970; served fifteen years in the dio. of Toronto; Dean of Montreal, 1984–90. Pres., Montreal Diocesan Theol Coll., 1990–; Visitor, Bishops Univ., Lennoxville, 1990–; Chaplain: Canadian Grenadier Guards, 1986–; 6087 and 22 CAR, 1986–; Order of St John of Jerusalem, Quebec, 1987–; Bishop Ordinary, Canadian Forces, 1997–. Trustee, Lakefield Coll. Sch., 1997–. Hon DD: Montreal Diocesan Theol Coll., 1993; Trinity Coll., Toronto, 1994. OStJ 1991. Ecclesiastical Grand Cross, Order of St Lazarus, 1992. *Address:* Bishopscourt, 3630 de la Montagne, Montreal, QC H3G 2A8, Canada. *T:* (514) 849 4089. *Clubs:* Mount Stephen, Montreal Faculty, McGill University (Montreal).

MONTROSE, 8th Duke of, *cr* 1707; **James Graham;** Lord Graham 1445; Earl of Montrose 1505; Bt (NS) 1625; Marquis of Montrose 1644; Duke of Montrose, Marquis of Graham and Buchanan, Earl of Kincardine, Viscount Dundaff, Lord Aberuthven, Mugdock, and Fintrie 1707; Earl and Baron Graham (Eng.) 1722; *b* 6 April 1935; *e s* of 7th Duke of Montrose, and Isobel Veronica (*d* 1990), *yr d* of Lt-Col T. B. Sellar, CMG, DSO; *S* father, 1992; *m* 1970, Catherine Elizabeth MacDonell, *d* of late Captain N. A. T. Young, and of Mrs Young, Ottawa; two *s* one *d*. *Educ:* Loretto. Elected Mem., H of L, 1999. Brig. Royal Company of Archers (Queen's Body Guard for Scotland), 1986 (Mem., 1965–). Area Pres., Scottish NFU, 1986 (Mem. Council, 1982–86 and 1987–90); Pres., RHAS, 1997–98. OStJ 1978. *Heir: s* Marquis of Graham, *qv*. *Address:* Auchmar, Drymen, Glasgow G63 0AG. *T:* (01360) 870307.

MOODY, Ian Charles Hugh, OBE 1996; DL; Commissioner-in-Chief, St John Ambulance, 1991–95; *b* 25 April 1928; *s* of William Thomas Charles Moody and Roberta (*née* Baxter); *m* 1952, Angela de Lisle Carey; one *s* two *d*. *Educ:* Cheltenham Coll.; RMA, Sandhurst. Served RWF, 1947–50. Industrial relations and personnel appointments with: Compania Shell de Venezuela, 1951–54; Shell Trinidad Ltd, 1954–59; Shell BP Nigeria Ltd, 1959–60; PT Shell Indonesia, 1960–64; Pakistan Shell Oil Ltd, 1964–68; Personnel Manager, Shell Nigeria Ltd, 1968–72; Employee Relations, Shell Internat. Petroleum Co. Ltd, 1974–76; Personnel Manager, Shell Internat. Trading Co., 1976–83; retd 1983. St John Ambulance, Devon: Comr, 1983–88; Comdr, 1988–91; Chm., 1995–98. Chm., E Devon Cons. Assoc., 1997–2000. FCIPD. DL Devon, 1991. KStJ 1991. *Recreations:* cricket, sailing, gardening. *Address:* The Queen Anne House, The Strand, Lympstone, Devon EX8 5JW. *T:* (01395) 263189. *Club:* MCC.

MOODY, Leslie Howard; General Secretary, Civil Service Union, 1977–82; *b* 18 Aug. 1922; *s* of George Henry and Edith Jessie Moody; *m* 1944, Betty Doreen Walton; two *s*. *Educ:* Eltham College. Telephone Engineer, General Post Office, 1940–53. Served Royal Signals, Far East, 1944–47. Asst Sec., Civil Service Union, 1953, Dep. Gen. Sec., 1963. A Dep. Chm., Civil Service Appeal Bd, 1990–92. *Recreations:* walking, music, theatre, educating management. *Address:* 9 Lock Chase, Blackheath, SE3 9HB. *T:* (020) 8318 1040. *Club:* Civil Service.

MOODY, Peter Edward, CBE 1981; Director: Prudential Corporation, 1981–91 (Deputy Chairman, 1984–88); The Laird Group, 1981–92; *b* 26 Aug. 1918; *s* of late Edward Thomas Moody and Gladys (*née* Flint); *m* 1945, Peggy Elizabeth *d* of Edward Henry Causer and Elizabeth Theodora (*née* Finke); one *s* one *d*. *Educ:* Christ's Coll., Finchley. FIA. Prudential Assurance Co. Ltd: Dep. Investment Manager, 1960; Jt Sec. and Chief Investment Manager, 1973–80; Jt Sec. and Group Chief Investment Manager, Prudential Corp., 1979–80; Director: Triton Petroleum Ltd, 1971–89; United Dominions Trust, 1972–81; British American and General Trust, 1981–85; Inmos International, 1981–84; 3i Group plc (formerly FFI, then Investors in Industry), 1981–89; Equity Trustee Ltd, 1985–90. Mem., PO Bd, 1981–85. Trustee, Thalidomide Trust, 1984–93. Institute of Actuaries: Hon. Sec., 1968–70; Vice-Pres., 1972–75; Pres., 1978–80; Master, Worshipful Co. of Actuaries, 1988–89. *Publications:* contrib. Jl of Inst. of Actuaries. *Recreation:* golf. *Address:* 46 Brookmans Avenue, Brookmans Park, Herts AL9 7QJ.

MOODY-STUART, Sir Mark, KCMG 2000; PhD; FGS; FRGS; Director, Shell Transport and Trading Company plc, since 1991 (Chairman, 1997–2001); Group Managing Director, 1991–2001, and Chairman, Committee of Managing Directors, 1998–2001, Royal Dutch/Shell Group; *b* 15 Sept. 1940; *s* of Sir Alexander Moody-Stuart, OBE, MC and Judith (*née* Henzell); *m* 1964, Judith McLeavy; three *s* one *d*. *Educ:* Shrewsbury Sch.; St John's Coll., Cambridge (MA, PhD; Hon. Fellow, 2001). Joined Shell, 1966; worked for various Shell companies in: Holland, 1966; Spain, 1967; Oman, 1968; Brunei, 1968–72; Australia, 1972–76; UK, 1977–78; Brunei, 1978–79; Nigeria, 1979–82; Turkey, 1982–86; Malaysia, 1986–89; Holland, 1990–91. Dir, HSBC Hldgs plc, 2001–. Co-Chm., G-8 Task Force on Renewable Energy, 2000–01. Vice-Pres., Liverpool Sch. of Tropical Medicine, 1997–. Gov., Nuffield Hosps, 2001–. Mem., Soc. of Petroleum Engrs, 1990–; FInstPet 1997 (Cadman Medal, 2001); FRGS 1999. Hon. FIChemE 1997. Hon. DBA Robert Gordon, 2000. *Publications:* papers in Geol Mag., Jl of Sedimentary Petrology, Bull. Amer. Assoc. Petrology and Geol., Norsk Polarinstitut. *Recreations:* sailing, travel, reading. *Address:* 9 Gun House, 122 Wapping High Street, E1W 2NL. *Clubs:* Travellers, Cruising Association.

MOOLLAN, Sir (Abdool) Hamid (Adam), Kt 1986; QC (Mauritius) 1976; Chairman, Law Reform Commission, Mauritius, since 1996; *b* 10 April 1933; *s* of Adam Sulliman Moollan and Khatija Moollan; *m* 1966, Sara Sidiot; three *s*. *Educ:* Soonee Surtee Musalman Society Aided School; Royal College School; King's College London (LLB); Faculté de Droit, Univ. de Paris. Called to the Bar, Middle Temple, 1956; joined Mauritian Bar, 1960. Chm., Bar Council, Mauritius, 1970–93. Mem., Presidential Commn for reform of judicial and legal system, Mauritius. *Recreations:* tennis, horse racing, hunting, fishing. *Address:* (home) Railway Road, Phoenix, Mauritius. *T:* 6864983; (chambers) 43 Sir William Newton Street, Port-Louis, Mauritius. *T:* 2083881. *Clubs:* Royal Over-Seas League; Mauritius Gymkhana, Mauritius Turf.

MOOLLAN, Sir Cassam (Ismael), Kt 1982; legal consultant and arbitrator; Chief Justice, Supreme Court of Mauritius, 1982–88, retired; Acting Governor-General, several occasions in 1984, 1985, 1986, 1987, 1988; Commander-in-Chief of Mauritius, 1984; *b* 26 Feb. 1927; *s* of Ismael Mahomed Moollan and Fatimah Nazroo; *m* 1954, Rassoulbibie Adam Moollan; one *s* two *d*. *Educ:* Royal Coll., Port Louis and Curepipe; London Sch. of Econs and Pol. Science (LLB 1950). Called to the Bar, Lincoln's Inn, 1951. Private practice, 1951–55; Dist Magistrate, 1955–58; Crown Counsel, 1958–64; Sen. Crown Counsel, 1964–66; Solicitor Gen., 1966–70; QC (Mauritius) 1969; Puisne Judge, Supreme Court, 1970; Sen. Puisne Judge, 1978. Editor, Mauritius Law Reports, 1982–84. Director: South East Asian Bank, 1990–; Provident Real Estate Fund, 1993–. Chevalier, Légion d'Honneur (France), 1986. *Recreations:* table tennis, tennis, bridge, Indian classical and semi-classical music. *Address:* Chambers, 43 Sir William Newton Street, Port Louis, Mauritius. *T:* 2120794, 2083881, *Fax:* 2088351; 22 Hitchcock Avenue, Quatre Bornes, Mauritius. *T:* 4546949.

MOON, Brenda Elizabeth, FRSE; FLA; University Librarian, University of Edinburgh, 1980–96; *b* 11 April 1931; *d* of Clement Alfred Moon and Mabel (*née* Berks). *Educ:* King Edward's Grammar Sch. for Girls, Camp Hill, Birmingham; St Hilda's Coll., Oxford (MA). MPhil Leeds; FLA 1958; FRSE 1992. Asst Librarian, Univ. of Sheffield, 1955–62; Sub-Librarian, 1962–67, Dep. Librarian, 1967–79, Univ. of Hull. *Publications:* Mycenaean Civilisation: publications since 1935, 1957; Mycenaean Civilisation: publications 1956–1960, 1961; Periodicals for South-East Asian Studies: a union catalogue of holdings in British and selected European libraries, 1979; articles in prof. and other jls. *Recreations:* walking, gardening, cruising on canals. *Address:* 4 Cobden Road, Edinburgh EH9 2BJ. *T:* (0131) 667 0071.

See also M. M. Moon.

MOON, Mary Marjorie; Head Mistress, Manchester High School for Girls, 1983–94; *b* 28 Sept. 1932; *d* of Clement Alfred Moon and Mabel Moon (*née* Berks). *Educ:* King Edward's Grammar Sch. for Girls, Camp Hill, Birmingham; Univ. of Manchester (BA Hons, MEd); Univ. of London Inst. of Education (PGCE). Asst English Teacher, 1955–59, Head of English Dept, 1959–63, Orme Girls' Sch., Newcastle-under-Lyme; Head of English, Bolton Sch. (Girls' Div.), 1963–71; Head Mistress, Pate's Grammar Sch. for Girls, Cheltenham, 1971–83. Mem. Court, Univ. of Manchester, 1985–2000. *Recreations:* photography, sketching, travel. *Address:* 18 South Parade, Bramhall, Stockport, Cheshire SK7 3BH.

See also B. E. Moon.

MOON, Michael, RA 1994; artist; *b* 9 Nov. 1937; *s* of Donald and Marjorie Moon; *m* 1977, Anjum Khan; two *s*. *Educ:* Chelsea Sch. of Art; RCA. One-man shows include: Tate Gall., 1976; Waddington Galls, London, 1969, 1970, 1972, 1978, 1984, 1986, 1992; Macquarie Galls, Sydney, 1982; Christine Abrahams Gall., Melbourne, 1983; Pace Prints, NY, 1987; Kass/Meridien Gall., Chicago, 1988; Linda Goodman Gall., Johannesburg, 1994; Alan Cristea Gall., 1996; Serge Sirocco Gall., San Francisco, 1997; work in public collections include: Tate Gall.; Australian Nat. Gall., Canberra; Mus. of WA, Perth; Art Gall. of NSW, Sydney; Power Inst., Sydney; Walker Art Gall., Liverpool; Birmingham City Art Gall.; V&A Mus. *Address:* 10 Bowood Road, SW11 6PE. *T:* (020) 7228 7358.

MOON, Sir Peter Wilfred Giles Graham-, 5th Bt *cr* 1855; *b* 24 Oct. 1942; *s* of Sir (Arthur) Wilfred Graham-Moon, 4th Bt, and 2nd wife, Doris Patricia, *yr d* of Thomas Baron Jobson, Dublin; *S* father, 1954; *m* 1st, 1967, Sarah Gillian Chater (marr. diss.) (formerly *m* Major Antony Chater; marr. diss. 1966), *e d* of late Lt-Col Michael Lyndon Smith, MC, MB, BS, and Mrs Michael Smith; two *s*; 2nd, 1993, Mrs Terry de Vries, Cape Town, S Africa. *Recreations:* shooting, golf. *Heir: s* Rupert Francis Wilfred Graham-Moon, *b* 29 April 1968. *Clubs:* Cricketers; Royal Cork Yacht.

MOON, Sir Roger, 6th Bt *cr* 1887, of Copsewood, Stoke, Co. Warwick; retired; *b* 17 Nov. 1914; *s* of Jasper Moon (*d* 1975) (*g g s* of 1st Bt) and Isabel (*née* Logan); *S* brother, 1988; *m* 1950, Meg (*d* 2000), *d* of late Arthur Mainwaring Maxwell, DSO, MC; three *d*. *Educ:* Sedbergh. Coffee planter, Kenya, 1933–35; Rubber planter, Malaya, 1939–41 and 1946–63; Oil palms planter, Malaya, 1963–67. *Recreations:* golf, gardening. *Heir: b* Humphrey Moon [*b* 9 Oct. 1919; *m* 1st, 1955, Diana Hobson (marr. diss. 1964); two *d*; 2nd, 1964, Elizabeth Anne (*d* 1994), *d* of late George Archibald Drummond Angus and *widow* of H. J. Butler; one *d*]. *Address:* The Barn House, Wykey, Ruyton-XI-Towns, Shropshire SY4 1JA. *T:* (01939) 260354.

MOONEY, Bel; writer and broadcaster; *b* 8 Oct. 1946; *d* of Edward and Gladys Mooney; *m* 1968, Jonathan Dimbleby, *qv*; one *s* one *d*. *Educ:* Trowbridge Girls' High School; University College London (1st cl. Hons, Eng. Lang. and Lit., 1969; Fellow 1994). Freelance journalist, 1970–79; columnist: Daily Mirror, 1979–80; Sunday Times, 1982–83; The Listener, 1984–86; Ed., Proof mag. (SW Arts), 2000–; *television:* interview series: Mothers By Daughters, 1983; The Light of Experience Revisited, 1984; Fathers By Sons, 1985; Grief, 1995; various series for BBC Radio 4 (Sandford St Martin Trust award for Devout Sceptics, 1994) and films for BBC TV and Channel 4. Mem. Bd, Friends of Gt Ormond St, 1994–98. Governor, Bristol Polytechnic, 1989–91. Hon. DLitt Bath, 1998. *Publications: novels:* The Windsurf Boy, 1983; The Anderson Question, 1985; The Fourth of July, 1988; Lost Footsteps, 1993; Intimate Letters, 1997; The Invasion of Sand, 2002; *for children:* Liza's Yellow Boat, 1980; I Don't Want To!, 1985; The Stove Haunting,

1986; I Can't Find It!, 1988; It's Not Fair!, 1989; A Flower of Jet, 1990; But You Promised!, 1990; Why Not?, 1990; I Know!, 1991; The Voices of Silence, 1994; I'm Scared!, 1994; I Wish!, 1995; The Mouse with Many Rooms, 1995; Why Me?, 1996; The Green Man, 1997; Joining the Rainbow, 1997; I'm Bored, 1997; I Don't Want to Say Yes!, 1998; You Promised You Wouldn't be Cross, 1999; It's Not My Fault, 1999; So What?, 2002; Tough Tim, 2002; *miscellaneous:* The Year of the Child, 1979; Differences of Opinion (collected journalism), 1984; (with Gerald Scarfe) Father Kismass and Mother Claws, 1985; Bel Mooney's Somerset, 1989; From This Day Forward (Penguin Book of Marriage), 1989; Perspectives for Living, 1992. *Recreations:* reading, music, art, churches, friends. *Address:* c/o David Higham Associates, 5 Lower John Street, W1R 3PE. *T:* (020) 7437 7888. *Club:* Groucho.

MOONIE, Lewis George; MP (Lab and Co-op) Kirkcaldy, since 1987; Parliamentary Under-Secretary of State, since 2000, Minister for Veterans Affairs, since 2001, Ministry of Defence; *b* 25 Feb. 1947; *m;* two *c. Educ:* Grove Acad., Dundee; St Andrews Univ. (MB ChB 1970); Edinburgh Univ. (MSc 1981). MRCPsych 1979; MFCM 1984. Psychiatrist, Ciba-Geigy, Switzerland, and Organon Internat., Netherlands; Sen. Registrar (Community Medicine), subseq. Community Medicine Specialist, Fife Health Bd. Mem., Fife Regl Council, 1982–86. Opposition front bench spokesman on technology, 1990–92, on science and technol., 1992–97, and on industry, 1994–97. Member: Social Services Select Cttee, 1987–89; Treasury Select Cttee, 1998; H of C Commn, 1997; Chm., Finance and Services Cttee, 1997. *Address:* House of Commons, SW1A 0AA; 85 Sauchenbush Road, Kirkcaldy, Fife KY2 5RN.

MOONMAN, Eric, OBE 1991; Chairman, Essex Radio Group, since 1991; Visiting Professor of Management, Measurement and Information in Medicine Research Centre, City University, since 1992; *b* 29 April 1929; *s* of late Borach and Leah Moonman; *m* 1962, Jane (marr. diss. 1991); two *s* one *d*; *m* 2001, Gillian Louise Mayer. *Educ:* Rathbone Sch., Liverpool; Christ Church, Southport; Univs of Liverpool and Manchester. Dipl. in Social Science, Liverpool, 1955. Human Relations Adviser, British Inst. of Management, 1956–62; Sen. Lectr in Industrial Relations, SW Essex Technical Coll., 1962–64; Sen. Research Fellow in Management Sciences, Univ. of Manchester, 1964–66. MSc Manchester Univ., 1967. MP (Lab) Billericay, 1966–70, Basildon, Feb. 1974–1979; PPS to Minister without Portfolio and Sec. of State for Educn, 1967–68. Chairman: All-Party Parly Mental Health Cttee, 1967–70 and 1974–79; New Towns and Urban Affairs Cttee, Parly Labour Party, 1974–79. Dir, Centre for Contemporary Studies, 1979–90; Dir, Nat. Hist. Mus. Develt Trust, 1990–91. Sen. Vice-Pres., Bd of Deputies, 1985–91, 1994–99; Pres., Zionist Fedn, 2001– (Chm., 1975–80). Member: Stepney Council, 1961–65 (Leader, 1964–65); Tower Hamlets Council, 1964–67. Chm., Islington HA, 1981–90; Mem., Bloomsbury and Islington HA, 1990–92; Chair, City of Liverpool Continuing Health Care Rev., 1996–. Mem. Adv. Council, Centre for Counter-Terrorism, Washington, 1998–. Mem., Council, Toynbee Hall Univ. Settlement (Chm., Finance Cttee); Governor, BFI, 1974–80. Consultant, Internat. Red Cross (Africa), 1991–95. Trustee: Balfour Diamond Jubilee Trust, 1985–; Winnicott Trust, 1990–94. FRSA. *Publications:* The Manager and the Organization, 1961; Employee Security, 1962; European Science and Technology, 1968; Communication in an Expanding Organization, 1970; Reluctant Partnership, 1970; Alternative Government, 1984; (ed) The Violent Society, 1987. *Recreations:* football (Chm., Everton Supporters' Club London Assoc., 1992–), theatre, music, cinema. *Address:* 1 Beacon Hill, N7 9LY.

MOOR, Philip Drury; QC 2001; *b* 15 July 1959; *s* of Rev. David Drury Moor and late Evangeline Moor (*née* White); *m* 1987, Gillian Stark; two *d. Educ:* Canford Sch., Pembroke Coll., Oxford (MA). Called to the Bar, Inner Temple, 1982. Member: Cttee, Family Law Bar Assoc., 1987– (Actg Treas., 2000–); Gen. Council of the Bar, 1987–89; Council of Legal Educn, 1988–91 (Mem. Bd of Examrs, 1989–92). *Recreations:* cricket, Association football, Rugby football. *Address:* 1 Mitre Court Buildings, Temple, EC4Y 7BS. *T:* (020) 7797 7070, *Fax:* (020) 7797 7435; *e-mail:* moor@1mcb.com. *Club:* MCC (Associate Mem.).

MOOR, Dr Robert Michael, FRS 1994; Head of Protein Function Laboratory, Babraham Institute, 1996–99; *b* 28 Sept. 1937; *s* of Donald C. Moor and Gwendolen (*née* Whitby); *m* 1962, Felicia Alison Elizabeth Stephens; four *d. Educ:* Estcourt, Natal, S Africa; Gonville and Caius Coll., Cambridge Univ. (PhD 1965; ScD). Senior Scientist, ARC Unit of Reproductive Physiology and Biochemistry, 1965–86; Head, Dept of Molecular Embryology, AFRC Inst. of Animal Physiology and Genetics Res., 1986–93; Dep. Dir, Babraham Inst., 1993–97. Hon. Fellow, Italian Vet. Assoc., 1990. Hon. Dr Univ. of Milan, 1990. *Publications:* numerous contribs to learned jls. *Recreations:* mountaineering, music. *Address:* 19 Thornton Close, Cambridge CB3 0NF. *T:* (01223) 276669. *Club:* Alpino Italiano (Milan).

MOORBATH, Prof. Stephen Erwin, DPhil, DSc; FRS 1977; Professor of Isotope Geology, Oxford University, 1992–96, now Emeritus Professor; Professorial Fellow of Linacre College, 1990–96, now Emeritus Fellow (Fellow, 1970–90); *b* 9 May 1929; *s* of Heinz Moosbach and Else Moosbach; *m* 1962, Pauline Tessier-Varlêt; one *s* one *d. Educ:* Lincoln Coll., Oxford Univ. (MA 1957, DPhil 1959). DSc Oxon 1969. Asst Experimental Officer, AERE, Harwell, 1948–51; Undergrad., Oxford Univ., 1951–54; Scientific Officer, AERE, Harwell, 1954–56; Research Fellow: Oxford Univ., 1956–61; MIT, 1961–62; Sen. Res. Officer, 1962–78, Reader in Geology, 1978–92, Oxford Univ. Wollaston Fund, Geol Soc. of London, 1968; Liverpool Geol Soc. Medal, 1968; Murchison Medal, Geol Soc. of London, 1978; Steno Medal, Geol Soc. of Denmark, 1979. *Publications:* contribs to scientific jls and books. *Recreations:* music, philately, travel, linguistics. *Address:* 53 Bagley Wood Road, Kennington, Oxford OX1 5LY. *T:* (01865) 739507.

MOORCOCK, Michael John; author, since 1956; *b* 18 Dec. 1939; *s* of Arthur Moorcock and June Moorcock (*née* Taylor); *m* 1st, 1962, Hilary Bailey (marr. diss. 1978); one *s* two *d*; 2nd, 1978, Jill Riches (marr. diss. 1983); 3rd, 1983, Linda Mullens Steele. *Educ:* Michael Hall, Sussex; Pitman's Coll., Surrey. Ed., Tarzan Adventures, 1956–58; Asst Ed., Sexton Blake Liby, 1959–61; travelled as singer/guitarist in Scandinavia and W Europe, 1961–62; ed. and pamphlet writer for Liberal Party pubns dept, 1962–63; Ed., New Worlds, 1963–80 (Publisher, 1980–); writer and vocalist for Hawkwind, 1971–; writer, vocalist and fretted instruments for Deep Fix; vocalist and instrumentalist for Robert Calvert; writer for Blue Oyster Cult, and associated with various other bands. Has made recordings. *Publications:* books include: Byzantium Endures, 1981; The Laughter of Carthage, 1984; Mother London, 1988; Jerusalem Commands, 1992; Blood, 1994; Fabulous Harbours, 1995; The War Amongst the Angels, 1996; Tales from the Texas Woods, 1997; King of the City, 2000; (with Storm Constantine) Silverheart, 2000; London Bone, 2001; The Dreamthief's daughter, 2001; various omnibus edns of novels; ed numerous anthologies, collections and short stories. *Recreations:* walking, mountaineering, travel. *Address:* PO Box 1230, Bastrop, TX 78602, USA. *T:* (512) 3215000; c/o Nomads Association, 21 Honor Oak Road, Honor Oak, SE23 3SH; c/o Hoffman, 77 Boulevard St Michel, 75005 Paris, France. *Club:* Royal Over-Seas League.

MOORCRAFT, Dennis Harry; Under-Secretary, Inland Revenue, 1975–81; *b* 14 Aug. 1921; *s* of late Harry Moorcraft and Dorothy Moorcraft (*née* Simmons); *m* 1945, Ingeborg Utne (*d* 2000), Bergen, Norway; one *s* one *d. Educ:* Gillingham County Grammar Sch. Tax Officer, Inland Revenue, 1938. RNVR, 1940–46. Inspector of Taxes, 1948; Sen. Inspector of Taxes, 1956; Principal Inspector of Taxes, 1963. *Recreations:* gardening, garden construction, croquet.

MOORE, family name of **Earl of Drogheda** and **Barons Moore of Lower Marsh** and **Moore of Wolvercote**.

MOORE, Viscount; Benjamin Garrett Henderson Moore; *b* 21 March 1983; *s* and *heir* of Earl of Drogheda, *qv.*

MOORE OF LOWER MARSH, Baron *cr* 1992 (Life Peer), of Lower Marsh in the London Borough of Lambeth; **John Edward Michael Moore;** PC 1986; *b* 26 Nov. 1937; *s* of Edward O. Moore; *m* 1962, Sheila Sarah Tillotson; two *s* one *d. Educ:* London Sch. of Economics (BSc Econ). Nat. Service, Royal Sussex Regt, Korea, 1955–57 (commnd). Chm. Conservative Soc., LSE, 1958–59; Pres. Students' Union, LSE, 1959–60. Took part in expedn from N Greece to India overland tracing Alexander's route, 1960. In Banking and Stockbroking instns, Chicago, 1961–65; Democratic Precinct Captain, Evanston, Ill, USA, 1962; Democratic Ward Chm. Evanston, Illinois, 1964; Dir, 1968–79, Chm., 1975–79, Dean Witter Internat. Ltd. An Underwriting Mem. of Lloyds, 1978–92. Councillor (C), London Borough of Merton, 1971–74; Chm., Stepney Green Cons. Assoc., 1968. MP (C) Croydon Central, Feb. 1974–1992. A Vice-Chm., Conservative Party, 1975–79; Parly Under-Sec. of State, Dept. of Energy, 1979–83; HM Treasury: Economic Sec., June–Oct. 1983; Financial Sec., 1983–86; Secretary of State: for Transport, 1986–87; for Social Services, 1987–88; for Social Security, 1988–89. Chairman: Credit Suisse Asset Mgt, 1991–2000; Energy Saving Trust Ltd, 1992–95 (Pres., 1995–2001); Director: Marvin & Palmer Associates Inc., 1989–; Monitor Inc., 1990– (Chm., Monitor Europe, 1990–); Gartmore Investment Management, 1990–92; GTECH Corp., 1992–2001; Swiss American Inc., 1992–96; Blue Circle Industries, 1993–2001; Camelot PLC, 1994–96; Rolls-Royce plc (Dep. Chm., 1996–); BEA Associates, USA, 1996–98; Private Client Partners, Zurich, 1999–. Member: Adv. Bd, Sir Alexander Gibb & Partners, 1990–95; Supervisory Bd, ITT Automotive Europe GmbH (Germany), 1994–97. Mem. Council, Inst. of Dirs, 1991–. Mem. Ct of Governors, LSE, 1977–. *Address:* House of Lords, SW1A 0PW. *Club:* Royal Automobile.

MOORE OF WOLVERCOTE, Baron *cr* 1986 (Life Peer), of Wolvercote in the City of Oxford; **Philip Brian Cecil Moore,** GCB 1985 (KCB 1980; CB 1973); GCVO 1983 (KCVO 1976); CMG 1966; QSO 1986; PC 1977; Private Secretary to the Queen and Keeper of the Queen's Archives, 1977–86; a Permanent Lord-in-Waiting to the Queen, since 1990; *b* 6 April 1921; *s* of late Cecil Moore, Indian Civil Service; *m* 1945, Joan Ursula Greenop; two *d. Educ:* Dragon Sch.; Cheltenham Coll. (Scholar); Oxford Univ. Classical Exhibitioner, Brasenose Coll., Oxford, 1940. RAF Bomber Command, 1940–42 (prisoner of war, 1942–45). Brasenose Coll., Oxford, 1945–46 (Hon. Fellow 1981). Asst Private Sec. to First Lord of Admiralty, 1950–51; Principal Private Sec. to First Lord of Admiralty, 1957–58; Dep. UK Commissioner, Singapore, 1961–63; British Dep. High Comr in Singapore, 1963–65; Chief of Public Relations, MoD, 1965–66; Asst Private Secretary to the Queen, 1966–72, Dep. Private Secretary, 1972–77. Dir, General Accident, Fire and Life Assurance Corp., 1986–91. Chm., King George VI and Queen Elizabeth Foundn of St Catharine's, Cumberland Lodge, 1986–97. Vice-Pres., SPCK. *Recreations:* golf, Rugby football (Oxford Blue, 1945–46; International, England, 1951), hockey (Oxford Blue, 1946), cricket (Oxfordshire). *Address:* Hampton Court Palace, East Molesey, Surrey KT8 9AU. *Club:* MCC.

MOORE, Alan Edward, CBE 1980; Deputy Chairman: Lloyds TSB Group plc, since 1998 (Director, since 1995); Lloyds Bank Plc, since 1998 (Director, since 1989); TSB Bank plc, since 1998; *b* 5 June 1936; *s* of late Charles Edward and Ethel Florence Moore; *m* 1961, Margaret Patricia Beckley; one *s* one *d. Educ:* Berkhamsted Sch. AIB, ACIS, FCT. Glyn Mills & Co., then Williams & Glyn's Bank, London, 1953–74; Dir Gen., Bahrain Monetary Agency, 1974–79; Dir and Treas., Lloyds Bank Internat., 1980–84; Dir of Treasury, Lloyds Bank, 1985–88; Dir of Corporate Banking and Treasury, Lloyds Bank, 1988–94; Dep. Chief Exec. and Treas., Lloyds Bank, 1994–98; Dep. Gp Chief Exec. and Treas., Lloyds TSB Gp plc, 1995–98. *Recreations:* photography, railway history, travel. *Address:* Lloyds TSB Group plc, 71 Lombard Street, EC3P 3BS. *T:* (020) 7626 1500.

MOORE, Alexander Wyndham Hume S.; *see* Stewart-Moore.

MOORE, Anthony Michael Frederick, (Anthony Michaels-Moore); baritone; *b* 8 April 1957; *s* of John Moore and Isabel (*née* Shephard); *m* 1980, Ewa Migocki; one *d. Educ:* Newcastle Univ. (BA Hons 1978); Royal Scottish Acad. of Music and Drama. First British winner, Pavaroti Comp., 1985. *Débuts:* Opera North, 1986; Royal Opera House, Covent Garden, 1987; Vienna State Opera, 1993; La Scala, Milan, 1993; Paris Opera, 1994; Buenos Aires, 1996; Metropolitan, NY, 1996; San Francisco, 1997; Chicago, 2000. *Rôles* include: Marcello, Belcore, Escamillo, Posa, Hamlet, Falke, Lescaut, Simon Boccanegra, Scarpia, Figaro, Orestes, Onegin, Rigoletto, Macbeth, Montforte, Ford, Ezio, Iago. Recordings incl. Carmina Burana, Lucia di Lammermoor, Falstaff, Aroldo, and La Favorite. Royal Philharmonic Soc. Award, 1997. *Recreations:* cricket, swimming, spicy food, computer action games. *Address:* c/o IMG Artists, Media House, 3 Burlington Lane, W4 2TH. *T:* (020) 8233 5800.

MOORE, Prof. Brian Cecil Joseph, PhD; Professor of Auditory Perception, University of Cambridge, since 1995; Fellow of Wolfson College, Cambridge, since 1983; *b* 10 Feb. 1946; *s* of Cecil George Moore and Maria Anna Moore. *Educ:* St Catharine's Coll., Cambridge (BA Nat. Sci. 1968; PhD Exptl Psychol. 1971). Lectr in Psychology, Reading Univ., 1971–77; Vis. Prof., Brooklyn Coll., NY, 1973–74; University of Cambridge: Lectr in Experimental Psychology, 1977–89; Reader in Auditory Perception, 1989–95. FMedSci 2001. Fellow, Acoustical Soc. of America, 1985; Hon. Mem., Belgian Soc. of Audiology, 1997; Hon. Fellow, British Soc. of Hearing Aid Audiologists, 1999. *Publications:* An Introduction to the Psychology of Hearing, 1977, 4th edn 1997; Frequency Selectivity in Hearing, 1986; Perceptual Consequences of Cochlear Damage, 1995; Hearing, 1995; Cochlear Hearing Loss, 1998. *Recreations:* music, playing the guitar, bridge, fixing things. *Address:* Department of Experimental Psychology, University of Cambridge, Downing Street, Cambridge CB2 3EB. *T:* (01223) 333574.

MOORE, Charles Hilary; Editor, The Daily Telegraph, since 1995; *b* 31 Oct. 1956; *s* of Richard and Ann Moore; *m* 1981, Caroline Mary Baxter; twin *s* and *d. Educ:* Eton Coll.; Trinity Coll., Cambridge (BA Hons History). Joined editorial staff of Daily Telegraph, 1979, leader writer, 1981–83; Assistant Editor and political columnist, 1983–84, Editor, 1984–90, The Spectator; weekly columnist, Daily Express, 1987–90; Dep. Editor, Daily Telegraph, 1990–92; Editor, The Sunday Telegraph, 1992–95. Trustee: Prayer Book Soc., 1989–94; Friends of the Union, 1993–. *Publications:* (ed with C. Hawtree) 1936, 1986; (with A. N. Wilson and G. Stamp) The Church in Crisis, 1986; (ed with Simon Heffer)

A Tory Seer: the selected journalism of T. E. Utley, 1989. *Address:* The Daily Telegraph, 1 Canada Square, Canary Wharf, E14 5DT. *T:* (020) 7538 5000. *Club:* Beefsteak.

MOORE, Air Vice-Marshal Charles Stuart, CB 1962; OBE 1945; *b* London, 27 Feb. 1910; *s* of late E. A. Moore and E. B. Moore (*née* Druce); *m* 1st, 1937, Anne (*d* 1957), *d* of Alfred Rogers; 2nd, 1961, Jean Mary (marr. diss. 1993), *d* of John Cameron Wilson; one *d. Educ:* Sutton Valence Sch.; RAF Coll., Cranwell. Commissioned in General Duties Branch, Dec. 1930; served in Egypt, 1932–34 and 1936–41; Sqdn Ldr 1938; Sudan, 1941–42; Wing Comdr 1940; 11 Group, 1943–44; Gp Capt. 1943; OC, OTU, 1944–45; Gp Capt. Org., HQFC, 1945–46; Staff Coll., Bracknell, 1946–47; Dep. Dir Plans, Air Ministry, London, 1947–49; Student, US National War Coll., Washington, 1949–50; Staff of USAF Air War Coll., Alabama, 1950–53; Air Commodore, 1953; AOC 66 Group, 1953–55; Dir of Intelligence, Air Ministry, London, 1955–58; AOA, NEAF, 1958–62; Actg Air Vice-Marshal, 1960; retired, 1962. Joined HM Foreign Service, Oct. 1962; posted to British Embassy, Tehran, Iran; left HM Diplomatic Service, March 1969. *Recreations:* music, photography and travelling. *Address:* Ferndene, The Avenue, Crowthorne, Berks RG45 6PB. *T:* (01344) 772300. *Club:* Royal Air Force.

MOORE, Cicely Frances (Mrs H. D. Moore); *see* Berry, C. F.

MOORE, David James Ladd; Partnership Secretary, Freshfields, 1993–98; *b* 6 June 1937; *s* of James and Eilonwy Moore; *m* 1968, Kay Harrison; two *s. Educ:* King Edward VI Sch., Nuneaton; Brasenose Coll., Oxford (BA). PO, 1961–67 (Asst Principal 1961, Principal 1966); Cabinet Office, 1967–69; HM Treasury, 1969–80 (Asst Sec. 1973); Under Secretary: Cabinet Office, 1980–82; HM Treasury, 1982–83; Inland Revenue (Principal Finance Officer), 1983–85; HM Treasury, 1985–93. *Recreations:* cinema, tennis, history of art. *Address:* 183 Hampstead Way, NW11 7YB.

MOORE, Prof. Derek William, FRS 1990; Professor of Applied Mathematics, Imperial College, London, 1973–96, now Professor Emeritus and Senior Research Fellow; *b* 19 April 1931; *s* of William McPherson Moore and Elsie Marjorie Moore (*née* Patterson). *Educ:* Jesus Coll., Cambridge (MA, PhD). Asst Lectr and Lectr in Maths, Bristol, 1958–64; Sen. Postdoctoral Res. Fellow, Nat. Acad. of Scis, USA, 1964; Imperial College London: Sen. Lectr, Dept of Maths, 1967; Reader in Theoretical Fluid Mechanics, 1968. Sherman Fairchild Dist. Scholar, CIT, 1986. Foreign Hon. Mem., Amer. Acad of Arts and Scis, 1985. *Recreation:* jazz tenor saxophone. *Address:* 71 Boileau Road, W5 3AP. *T:* (020) 8998 8572.

MOORE, Derry; *see* Drogheda, Earl of.

MOORE, Most Rev. Desmond Charles, KBE 1996; Bishop of Alotau (RC); *b* Adelaide, 12 May 1926; *s* of Edwin John Moore and Margaret Mary Leahy. *Educ:* Christian Brothers Sch., Adelaide; Adelaide Univ.; Sacred Heart Monastery, Croydon, Vic. Entered novitiate, 1950, professed mem., 1951–, Congregation of Missionaries of the Sacred Heart of Jesus; ordained priest, 1957; Bursar and Assistant to Novice Master, St Mary's Towers Monastery, Douglas Park, 1958–61; Assistant to Parish Priest, Port Moresby, PNG, 1961–62; first Parish Priest, Boregaina Village, Rigo, 1962–67; Parish Priest, St Joseph's, Boroko, and Religious Superior, Missionaries of the Sacred Heart of Jesus, dio. of Port Moresby, 1967–70; cons. Bishop of Sideia, 1970, name of dio. changed to Alotau, 1977. *Address:* PO Box 107, Alotau, Milne Bay Province, Papua New Guinea. *T:* 6411252, *Fax:* 6411471; *e-mail:* dcmoore@daltron.com.pg.

MOORE, Dudley Stuart John, CBE 2001; actor (stage, films, TV and radio); composer (film music and incidental music for plays, etc); *b* 19 April 1935; *s* of late Ada Francis and John Moore; *m* 1st, 1958, Suzy Kendall (marr. diss.); 2nd, 1975, Tuesday Weld (marr. diss.); one *s*; 3rd, 1988, Brogan Lane (marr. diss.); 4th, 1994, Nicole Rothschild (marr. diss.); one *s. Educ:* County High Sch., Dagenham, Essex; Guildhall Sch.; Magdalen Coll., Oxford (BA, BMus). *Stage:* Beyond the Fringe, 1960–62 (London), 1962–64 (Broadway, New York); Behind the Fridge, 1971–72; Good Evening, NY, 1974; Mikardo (Los Angeles, UK/LA Fest.), 1988; Vic Lewis, John Dankworth Jazz Bands, 1959–60; composed incidental music, Royal Court Theatre (various plays), 1958–60; Play it again Sam, Woody Allen, Globe Theatre, 1970; Behind the Fridge, Cambridge Theatre, 1972–73; Good Evening, Broadway, New York, 1973–74; tour of USA, 1975. *BBC TV:* own series with Peter Cook: Not only . . . but also, 1964, 1966, 1970; *series:* It's Lulu, not to mention Dudley Moore, 1973; in the sixties, *ITV:* Goodbye again; Royal Command Performance; *series:* Orchestra! (co-presenter with Sir Georg Solti), 1991; Concerto!, 1993. Various TV and radio guest spots with Jazz piano trio. *Films:* The Wrong Box, 1966; 30 is a Dangerous Age Cynthia, 1967; Bedazzled, 1968; Monte Carlo or Bust, The Bed-sitting room, 1969; Alice in Wonderland, 1972; The Hound of the Baskervilles, 1977; Foul Play, "10", 1979; Wholly Moses, 1980; Arthur, 1981; Lovesick, Romantic Comedy, 1982; Unfaithfully Yours, Best Defense, 1983; Mickey & Maude, 1984; Santa Claus—The Movie, 1985; Like Father Like Son, 1987; Arthur 2—On The Rocks, 1988; Crazy People, 1990; Blame it on the Bellboy, 1992. *Film music* composed for: Bedazzled, 30 is a dangerous age Cynthia, The Staircase, Inadmissable Evidence, Six Weeks, and various TV films. *Publications:* Dud and Pete: The Dagenham Dialogues, 1971, new edn 1988; Musical Bumps, 1986; The Complete Beyond the Fringe, 1987. *Recreations:* films, theatre, music.

MOORE, Sir Francis Thomas (Sir Frank), Kt 1983; AO 1991; Chairman, Taylor Byrne Tourism Group, since 1990; *b* 28 Nov. 1930; *m* 1972, Norma Shearer; two *s. Educ:* Nudgee Coll. Licensed Valuer, 1952–; Man. Dir, Radio Broadcasting Network of Queensland, 1957–78; Director: Universal Telecasters Qld Ltd, 1961–80; Trust Co. Australia Ltd, 1983–96; Chm., Nature Resorts Ltd, 1997–. Chairman: Queensland Tourist and Travel Corp., 1979–90; Tourism Council of Australia (formerly Australian Tourism Industry Assoc.), 1983–95; Nat. Centre for Studies in Travel and Tourism, 1987–94; Tourism Forecasting Council, 1996–; Co-op. Res. Centre for Sustainable Tourism, 1997–; Mem., World Travel and Tourism Council, 1992–. *Address:* GPO Box 1150, Brisbane, Qld 4001, Australia.

MOORE, George; Chairman, Grayne Marketing Co. Ltd, 1978–95; *b* 7 Oct. 1923; *s* of George Moore and Agnes Bryce Moore; *m* 1946, Marjorie Pamela Davies (*d* 1986); three *s. Educ:* University Coll. and Royal Technical Coll., Cardiff (Jt Engineering Diploma); Hull Univ. (Post Graduate Diploma in Economics). Served War, RN, 1942–46. Graduate Engineer, Electricity Authority, 1948–50; Development Engineer, Anglo-Iranian Oil Co., Abadan, 1950–52; Chief Electrical Engineer, Distillers' Solvents Div., 1952–58; Management Consultant, Urwick, Orr & Partners, 1958–64; Executive Dir, Burton Group, 1964–66; Group Managing Dir, Spear & Jackson International Ltd and Chm., USA Subsidiary, 1966–75; Dir of cos in Sweden, France, India, Australia, Canada, S Africa, 1966–75; Under Sec. and Regional Industrial Dir, NW Regional Office, DoI, 1976–78; Dir, Cordel Corporate Develt Ltd, 1978–95. FIMgt (FBIM 1980); FInstD 1978; MIMC 1990. *Recreations:* golf, sailing. *Address:* Leasgill House, Leasgill, near Milnthorpe, Cumbria LA7 7ET. *Club:* Reform.

MOORE, George, OBE 1994; Member, South Yorkshire County Council, 1974–86 (Chairman, 1978–79); *b* 29 Jan. 1913; *s* of Charles Edward Moore and Edith Alice Moore; *m* 1943, Hannah Kenworthy; two *d. Educ:* Woodhouse, Sheffield. Started work in pit at 14 yrs of age, 1927; worked in hotel business, 1930; publican in own right for several yrs, after which went into fruit and vegetable business, first as retailer and eventually as wholesaler and partner in small co. Served in RAF for short period during war. Barnsley Bor. Council, then Barnsley MBC, 1961–94: served as Vice Chm., Health and Housing Cttee, and Vice Chm., Fire and Licensing Dept; Chairman: Barnsley and Dist Refuse Disposal Cttee, 1959–64; Sanitary Cttee, Barnsley, 1963–73; first Chm., Fire Service Cttee, S Yorks CC, 1974–78. Chm., Barnsley Community Health Council, 1974–92. Chm., Barnsley and Dist, Talking Newspaper for the Blind, 1978–94. *Recreation:* aviculture. *Address:* 34 Derwent Road, Athersley South, Barnsley, S Yorks S71 3QT. *T:* (01226) 206644.

MOORE, (Georgina) Mary, (Mrs Antony Moore); Principal, St Hilda's College, Oxford, 1980–90, Hon. Fellow, 1990; *b* 8 April 1930; *yr d* of late Prof. V. H. Galbraith, FBA, and late Georgina Rosalie Galbraith (*née* Cole-Baker); *m* 1963, Antony Ross Moore, CMG (*d* 2000); one *s. Educ:* The Mount Sch., York; Lady Margaret Hall, Oxford (BA Modern History 1951; MA; Hon. Fellow, 1981). Joined HM Foreign (later Diplomatic) Service, 1951; posted to Budapest, 1954; UK Permanent Delegn to United Nations, New York, 1956; FO, 1959; First Secretary, 1961; resigned on marriage. Mem., Council for Industry and Higher Educn, 1986–90. A Trustee: British Museum, 1982–92; Rhodes Trust, 1984–96; Pilgrim Trust, 1991– (Chm., 1993–). JP Bucks 1977–82. Hon. LLD Mount Holyoke Coll., 1991. Under the name Helena Osborne writes plays for television and radio. *Publications:* (also as Helena Osborne): *novels:* The Arcadian Affair, 1969; Pay-Day, 1972; White Poppy, 1977; The Joker, 1979. *Recreations:* theatre, travel. *Address:* Touchbridge, Brill, Aylesbury, Bucks HP18 9UJ. *T:* and *Fax:* (01844) 238247. *Club:* University Women's.
See also J. H. Galbraith.

MOORE, Graham, QPM 1997; Chief Constable, West Yorkshire Police, since 1998; *b* 15 Jan. 1947; *s* of Graham and Kate Moore; *m* 1965, Susan Fletcher; one *s* one *d. Educ:* Brunts GS, Mansfield; Warwick Univ. (BA Hons Philosophy and Lit. 1975). Professional musician; Police Constable, Birmingham City Police, 1969–72; Inspector of Taxes, Inland Revenue, 1975–77; joined W Midlands Police, 1977; Asst Chief Constable, S Yorks Police, 1991–94; Dep. Chief Constable, Cambs Constabulary, 1994–98. *Recreations:* music, playing saxophone, reading, collecting books, tennis, clay pigeon shooting. *Address:* West Yorkshire Police, PO Box 9, Wakefield, WF1 3QP. *T:* (01924) 292002.

MOORE, Rt Rev. Henry Wylie; General Secretary, Church Missionary Society, 1986–89, retired 1990; *b* 2 Nov. 1923; *m* 1951, Betty Rose Basnett; two *s* three *d. Educ:* Univ. of Liverpool (BCom 1950); Wycliffe Hall, Oxford. MA (Organization Studies) Leeds, 1972. LMS Railway Clerk, 1940–42. Served War with King's Regt (Liverpool), 1942–43; Rajputana Rifles, 1943–46. Curate: Farnworth, Widnes, 1952–54; Middleton, 1954–56; CMS, Khuzistan, 1956–59; Rector: St Margaret, Burnage, 1960–63; Middleton, 1963–74; Home Sec. and later Executive Sec., CMS, 1974–83; Bishop in Cyprus and the Gulf, 1983–86. *Recreation:* family life. *Address:* Fernhill Cottage, Hopesay, Craven Arms, Shropshire SY7 8HD.

MOORE, James Antony Axel Herring, OBE 1998; Executive Director, US-UK Educational Commission (Fulbright Commission), since 1993; *b* 26 April 1940; *s* of late Lieut A. D. W. Moore, RN (killed HMS Audacity, 1941) and Agneta Moore (*née* Wachtmeister); *m* 1964, Marianne Jerlström; two *s* one *d. Educ:* Wellington Coll.; Trinity Coll., Cambridge (MA); London Univ. Inst. of Educn (PGCE). Teacher: Norway, 1962–63; Thailand, 1964–67; British Council: Warsaw, 1967–70; Beirut, 1971–73; Ottawa, 1973–75; London, 1975–80; Chinese lang. trng, 1980–81; Director: Manila, 1981–85; Copenhagen, 1985–89; General Manager, Fellowships and Scholarships, 1990–93. *Recreations:* music, ski-ing, walking, sailing. *Address:* Fulbright House, 62 Doughty Street, WC1N 2LS. *T:* (020) 7539 4411.
See also Vice-Adm. Sir M. A. C. Moore.

MOORE, Rt Rev. James Edward; *see* Connor, Bishop of.

MOORE, Maj.-Gen. Sir Jeremy; *see* Moore, Maj.-Gen. Sir John J.

MOORE, Hon. John Colinton; *b* Rockhampton, Qld, 16 Nov. 1936; *s* of Thomas R. Moore and Doris (*née* Symes); *m* 1st, 1965 (marr. diss.); two *s* one *d*; 2nd, 1980, Jacqueline Sarah, *d* of Hon. Sir William John Farquhar McDonald and Evelyn S. McDonald. *Educ:* Southport Jun. Sch., Qld; Armidale Sch., NSW; Univ. of Queensland (BCom; AAUQ). AASA. Stockbroker, 1960; Mem., Brisbane Stock Exchange, 1962–74. Former Director: Wm Brandt & Sons (Aust.); Phillips; First City; Brandt Ltd (PFCB Ltd); Merrill Lynch, Pierce, Fennell & Smith (Aust.) Ltd; Citi-national Ltd; Agricl Investments Aust. Ltd. MP (L) Ryan, Qld, 1975–2001; Fed. Minister for Business and Consumer Affairs, 1980–82; Opposition spokesman: for Finance, 1983–84; for Communications, 1984–85; for Northern Develt and Local Govt, 1985–87; for Tspt and Aviation, 1987; for Business and Consumer Affairs, 1987–89; for Business Privatisation and Consumer Affairs, 1989–90; Shadow Minister for Industry and Commerce, and Public Admin, 1995–96; Minister for Industry, Sci. and Tourism, 1996–98; Vice-Pres., Exec. Council, 1996–98; Minister for Defence, 1998–2001. Member: various Govt cttees, 1984–96; various internat. delegns. Queensland Liberal Party: Vice-Pres. and Treas., 1967–73; Pres., 1973–76 and 1984–90; Mem., Qld State Exec., Liberal Party of Aust., 1966–91 and 1996–98. Mem. Council, Order of Australia., 1996–98. Mem., Anti-Cancer Council of Qld, 1972. *Recreations:* tennis, cricket, reading, golf. *Clubs:* Queensland, Brisbane, Commonwealth, Tattersall's, Polo (Brisbane); Lord Taverners, Queensland Turf.

MOORE, John David; Headmaster, St Dunstan's College, Catford, 1993–97; *b* 16 Feb. 1943; *s* of John and Hilda Moore; *m* 1966, Ann Medora; one *s* one *d. Educ:* St John's Coll., Cambridge (BA Classics 1965; MA 1969); CertEd Cambridge Univ., 1966. Classics Master, Judd Sch., Tonbridge, 1966–69; trainee commodity trader, Gill and Duffus Ltd, 1969–70; English Master, Skinners' Sch., Tunbridge Wells, 1970–74; Head of General Studies and English Master, King's Sch., Macclesfield, Ches., 1974–80; Dep. Headmaster, Carre's Grammar Sch., Sleaford, Lincs, 1981–86; Headmaster, Ilford County High Sch. for Boys, London Borough of Redbridge, 1986–93. Mem. Cttee, S Lakeland Carers, 1998– (Chm., 1999–). Gov., King's Sch., Macclesfield, 2000– (Mem., Govs' Educn Sub-Gp, 1998–). Freeman, City of London, 1996. *Recreations:* cricket, walking, theatre, music. *Address:* 12 Undercliff Road, Kendal, Cumbria LA9 4PS.

MOORE, Captain John Evelyn, RN; Editor: Jane's Fighting Ships, 1972–87; Jane's Naval Review, 1982–87; *b* Sant Ilario, Italy, 1 Nov. 1921; *s* of William John Moore and Evelyn Elizabeth (*née* Hooper); *m* 1st, 1945, Joan Pardoe; one *s* two *d*; 2nd, Barbara (*née* Kerry). *Educ:* Sherborne Sch., Dorset. Served War: entered Royal Navy, 1939; specialised in hydrographic surveying, then submarines, in 1943. Commanded HM Submarines: Totem, Alaric, Tradewind, Tactician, Telemachus. RN Staff course, 1950–51; Comdr,

1957; attached to Turkish Naval Staff, 1958–60; subseq. Plans Div., Admty; 1st Submarine Sqdn, then 7th Submarine Sqdn in comd; Captain, 1967; served as: Chief of Staff, C-in-C Naval Home Command; Capt. DI3 (Navy), Defence Intell. Staff; retired list at own request, 1972. FRGS 1942. Hon. Professor: Aberdeen Univ., 1987–90; St Andrews Univ., 1990–92. *Publications:* Jane's Major Warships, 1973; The Soviet Navy Today, 1975; Submarine Development, 1976; (jtly) Soviet War Machine, 1976; (jtly) Encyclopaedia of World's Warships, 1978; (jtly) World War 3, 1978; Seapower and Politics, 1979; Warships of the Royal Navy, 1979; Warships of the Soviet Navy, 1981; (jtly) Submarine Warfare: today and tomorrow, 1986; (ed) The Impact of Polaris, 1999. *Recreations:* gardening, archaeology. *Address:* 1 Ridgelands Close, Eastbourne, East Sussex BN20 8EP. *T:* (01323) 638836.

MOORE, Prof. John Halstead Hardman, PhD; FBA 1999; Professor of Economic Theory, London School of Economics, since 1990; Professor of Economics (quarter-time), University of St Andrews, since 1997; Leverhulme Personal Research Professor, since 1998; *b* 7 May 1954; *s* of Frank Moore, OBE and Audrey Jeanne Moore (*née* Halstead); *m* 1986, Dr Susan Mary Hardman, *d* of Bernard Mawson Hardman and Celia June Hardman (*née* Birchall); one *s* one *d*. *Educ:* Dorking County Grammar Sch.; Cambridge Univ. (BA 1st cl. Hons Maths 1976; MA 1983); LSE (MSc 1980; PhD 1984). Exec. Engr, Dundee Telephone Area, 1976–78; Temp. Lectr in Econs, LSE, 1980–81; Lectr, Birkbeck Coll., London Univ., 1981–83; Lectr, 1983–87, Reader, 1987–90, LSE; part-time Professor of Economics: Edinburgh Univ., 1993–95; Heriot-Watt Univ., 1995–97. Vis. Asst Prof., MIT, 1986–87; Vis. Prof., Princeton Univ., 1991–92. Ed., Rev. of Economic Studies, 1987–91. Walras-Bowley Lectr, Econometric Soc., 1996; Clarendon Lectr, Oxford Univ., 2000. Fellow, Econometric Soc., 1989. Yrjö Jahnsson Award, European Econ. Assoc., 1999. *Publications:* contrib. to Amer. Econ. Rev., Econometrica, Jl of Econ. Theory, Jl of Pol Economy, Qly Jl of Econs, Rev. of Econ. Studies and other econs and law jls. *Recreations:* music, mountains. *Address:* 11 McAuley Close, Cosser Street, SE1 7BX; 13 Gloucester Place, Edinburgh EH3 6EE.

MOORE, Maj.-Gen. Sir (John) Jeremy, KCB 1982 (CB 1982); OBE (mil.) 1973; MC 1952, Bar 1962; *b* 5 July 1928; *s* of Lt-Col Charles Percival Moore, MC, and Alice Hylda Mary (*née* Bibby); *m* 1966, Veryan Julia Margaret Acworth; one *s* two *d*. *Educ:* Brambletye Sch.; Cheltenham Coll. Joined RM as Probationary 2/Lt, 1947; training until 1950 (HMS Sirius, 1948); Troop subaltern, 40 Commando RM, 1950–53 (MC Malayan Emergency 1952); Housemaster, RM School of Music, 1954; ADC to MGRM Plymouth Gp, 1954–55; Instructor, NCO's Sch., RM, 1955–57; Adjt, 45 Cdo RM, 1957–59; Instr, RMA Sandhurst, 1959–62; Adjt and Company Comdr, 42 Cdo RM, 1962–63 (Bar to MC Brunei Revolt 1962); Australian Staff Coll., 1963–64; GSO2 Operations, HQ 17 Gurkha Div., 1965; Asst Sec., Chiefs of Staff Secretariat, MoD, 1966–68; HMS Bulwark, 1968–69; Officer Comdg, Officers Wing Commando Trng Centre RM, 1969–71; CO 42 Cdo RM, 1972–73 (OBE operational, NI 1973); Comdt RM School of Music (Purveyor of Music to the Royal Navy), 1973–75; RCDS 1976; Comdr 3rd Cdo Bde RM, 1977–79; Maj. Gen. Commando Forces, RM, 1979–82; Comdr, Land Forces, Falkland Islands, May–July 1982; MoD, 1982–83, retired. Col Comdt, RM, 1990–93. Hon. Col, Wilts ACF, 1991–94. Director-General: Food Manufacturers' Fedn, 1984–85; Food and Drink Fedn, 1984–85. *Recreations:* music (no performing ability except on a gramophone), painting.

MOORE, Sir John (Michael), KCVO 1983; CB 1974; DSC 1944; Chairman, Lymington Harbour Commission, 1993–99 (Deputy Chairman, 1990–93); Second Crown Estate Commissioner, 1978–83; *b* 2 April 1921; *m* 1986, Jacqueline Cingel, MBE. *Educ:* Whitgift Middle Sch.; Selwyn Coll., Cambridge. Royal Navy, 1940–46. Royal Humane Society Bronze Medal, 1942. Ministry of Transport, 1946; Joint Principal Private Sec. to Minister (Rt Hon. Harold (later Lord) Watkinson), 1956–59; Asst Sec., 1959; Under-Sec. (Principal Estabt Officer), 1966; Under-Sec., DoE, 1970–72; Dep. Sec., CSD, 1972–78. *Recreations:* sailing, remembering walking hills and mountains. *Address:* 38 Daniells Walk, Lymington, Hants SO41 3PN. *T:* (01590) 679963. *Club:* Royal Lymington Yacht.

MOORE, Dr John Michael; JP; Headmaster, The King's School, Worcester, 1983–98; *b* 12 Dec. 1935; *s* of late Roy Moore, CBE; *m* 1960, Jill Mary Maycock (*d* 1995); one *s*. *Educ:* Rugby Sch.; Clare Coll., Cambridge (John Stewart of Rannoch Scholar, 1956; George Charles Winter Warr Scholar, 1957; 1st Cl. Hons Classical Tripos; MA; PhD 1960). Asst Master: Winchester Coll., 1960–64; Radley Coll., 1964–83; Jun. Fellow, Center for Hellenic Studies, Washington, DC, 1970–71. Hon. Fellow, Inst. for Advanced Res. in the Humanities, Birmingham Univ., 1986. Governor: Cranleigh Sch., 1998–; Woodhouse Grove Sch., 1999–; Cokethorpe Sch., 1999–. FRSA 1994. JP Worcester City, 1986. Silver Jubilee Medal, 1977. *Publications:* The Manuscript Tradition of Polybius, 1965; (ed with P. A. Brunt) Res Gestae Divi Augusti, 1967, repr. with corrections 1973; (with J. J. Evans) Variorum, 1969; Timecharts, 1969; Aristotle and Xenophon on Democracy and Oligarchy, 1975, 2nd edn 1983; articles and reviews in Gnomon, Jl Soc. for Promotion of Hellenic Studies, Classical Qly, Greek, Roman and Byzantine Studies. *Recreations:* painting, gardening, travel. *Address:* Rattenbury House, Church Lane, Ombersley, Droitwich, Worcs WR9 0ER.

MOORE, John Royston, CBE 1983; BSc, CChem, FRSC; Chairman, Bradford Health Authority, 1982–88; *b* 2 May 1921; *s* of late Henry Roland and Jane Elizabeth Moore; *m* 1947, Dorothy Mackay Hick, *d* of late Charles and Edith Mackay Hick; two *s*. *Educ:* Manchester Central Grammar Sch.; Univ. of Manchester (BSc Hons). War service, research and manufacture of explosives. Lecturer in schools and college, Manchester; Principal, Bradford Technical Coll., 1959–75; Sen. Vice Principal and Dir of Planning and Resources, Bradford Coll., 1975–80, retired. Chm., Wool, Jute and Flax ITB, 1981–83. Leader, Baildon Urban DC, 1965–68; Councillor, West Riding CC, until 1973; West Yorkshire MCC: Member, 1973–86; Leader, 1978–81; Leader of the Opposition, 1981–86. Dir, Yorkshire Enterprise Ltd, 1981–90. President, Yorks Conservative Adv. Cttee on Educn, 1975–89; past Chm., Conservative Nat. Adv. Cttee on Educn. Hon. Mem., and Councillor, City and Guilds of London Inst., 1977–92. Hon. MA Bradford, 1986. *Recreations:* music, history, bridge. *Address:* Bicknor, 33 Station Road, Baildon, Shipley, West Yorkshire BD17 6HS. *T:* (01274) 581777.

MOORE, Jonathan Guy J.; *see* James-Moore.

MOORE, Julian Keith; Head of Management Development Group, Office of Public Service and Science, Cabinet Office, 1992–93; *b* 18 Aug. 1945; *s* of late George H. D. Moore and Amy (*née* Ashwell); *m* 1970, Susan (*née* Dand); one *s* one *d*. *Educ:* St Paul's School; New College, Oxford (Open Scholar, MA). HM Treasury, 1968; Civil Service Dept, 1968–72; Private Sec. to Minister of State, N Ireland Office, 1972–73; Civil Service Dept, 1973–77; Private Sec. to Lord Privy Seal and Leader of House of Lords, 1977–79; Assistant Secretary: CSD, 1979–82; Home Office, 1982–85; Cabinet Office (MPO), 1985–87; Civil Service Comr, 1987–92; Dir, CSSB, 1987–91; Head, Office of Civil Service Comrs, 1991–92. Mem., Careers Adv. Bd, Univ. of London, 1988–92; UK Mem., Bd of Admin, Europ. Inst. of Public Admin, 1993. *Publications:* articles and reviews, Times Literary Supplement. *Recreations:* historical cryptography, walking. *Address:* 6 Priory Crescent, Lewes, E Sussex BN7 1HP. *Club:* Athenæum.

MOORE, Prof. Leslie Rowsell, BSc, PhD, DSc, CEng, FIMinE, FGS; Consultant Geologist; Professor of Geology, University of Sheffield, 1949–77, now Emeritus Professor; *b* 23 June 1912; *m* 1946, Margaret Wilson MacRae (*d* 1985); one *s*. *Educ:* Midsomer Norton Grammar Sch.; Bristol Univ. Univ. of Bristol, 1930–37; Lecturer and Senior Lecturer, Cardiff, 1939–46; Research Dir, Univ. of Glasgow, 1946–48; Reader in Geology, Univ. of Bristol, 1948–49. *Publications:* contributions to: Quarterly Journal Geol; Soc., London; Geological Magazine; S Wales Inst. Engineers. *Recreations:* soccer, cricket, golf. *Address:* c/o 107 Wentworth Road, Harborne, Birmingham B17 9SU.

MOORE, Mary; *see* Moore, G. M.

MOORE, Vice Adm. Sir Michael (Antony Claës), KBE 1997; LVO 1981; Director General, Institution of Mechanical Engineers, since 1998; *b* 6 Jan. 1942; *s* of Lieut A. D. W. Moore, RN (killed HMS Audacity, 1941) and Agneta Moore (*née* Wachtmeister); *m* 1969, Penelope Jane, JP, *d* of Rear-Adm. F. C. W. Lawson, *qv*; one *s* three *d*. *Educ:* Wellington Coll.; RNC Dartmouth. Swedish Naval Interpreter. Joined RN, 1960; served HM Ships Gurkha, Britannia and Ashton, 1963–67; Flag Lieut to Comdr FEF, Singapore, 1967–68; i/c HMS Beachampton, 1969; qualified as Navigator, 1970; HM Ships Tenby, Brighton, Plymouth and Tartar (i/c), 1970–77; Naval Ops, MoD, 1977–79; HMY Britannia, 1979–81; Captain, 1981; Naval Asst to Chief of Fleet Support, MoD, 1981–82; i/c HMS Andromeda, and Capt. 8th Frigate Sqn, 1983–84; i/c Ops, Northwood MHQ, 1985–87; Dir, Naval Warfare, MoD, 1988–90; Rear Adm., 1990; Maritime Advr to SACEUR, 1990–93; Vice Adm. 1994; C of S to Comdr Allied Naval Forces Southern Europe, 1994–97. Dir, Professional Engineering Publications, 1998–. Trustee, Officers' Pension Soc., 1999–. Hon. Fellow, Swedish Royal Soc. of Naval Scis, 1992. Younger Brother, Trinity House, 1988. *Address:* Institution of Mechanical Engineers, 1 Birdcage Walk, SW1H 9JJ. *T:* (020) 7973 1240.

See also J. A. A. H. Moore.

MOORE, Prof. Michael Arthur, DPhil; FRS 1989; Professor of Theoretical Physics, University of Manchester, since 1976; *b* 8 Oct. 1943; *s* of John Moore and Barbara Atkinson; *m* 1967, Susan Eadington; three *s* one *d*. *Educ:* Huddersfield New Coll.; Oriel Coll., Oxford (BA 1964; DPhil 1967). Prize Fellow, Magdalen Coll., Oxford, 1967–71; Res. Associate, Univ. of Illinois, USA, 1967–69; Lectr in Physics, Univ. of Sussex, 1971–76. *Publications:* papers in scientific jls. *Recreation:* tennis. *Address:* The Schuster Laboratory, The University, Manchester M13 9PL.

MOORE, Rt Hon. Michael (Kenneth), ONZ 2000; PC 1990; Director-General, World Trade Organisation, since 1999; *b* 28 Jan. 1949; *m* 1975, Yvonne (*née* Dereany). *Educ:* Dilworth Sch.; Bay of Islands College (only Minister in Labour Govt without a degree). Worked as social worker, builder's labourer, meat freezing worker and printer; MP (Lab) Eden 1972–75 (youngest NZ MP ever elected); MP (Lab) Papanui, later named Christchurch North, then Waimakariri, 1978–99; spokesperson on housing, regional, small town and community development, the environment, tourism, recreation and sport, overseas trade and marketing, external relations and trade, finance; Minister of Foreign Affairs and Trade, 1990; trade missions led incl. Japan, Europe, Soviet Union, Pakistan, Turkey; Prime Minister of NZ, Sept.–Oct. 1990; Leader of the Opposition, 1990–93. *Publications:* On Balance, 1980; Beyond Today, 1981; A Pacific Parliament, 1982; The Added Value Economy, 1984; Hard Labour, 1987; Fighting for New Zealand, 1993; Children of the Poor, 1996; A Brief History of the Future, 1998. *Address:* World Trade Organisation, Centre William Rappard, 154 rue de Lausanne, 1211 Geneva 21, Switzerland.

MOORE, Michael Kevin; MP (Lib Dem) Tweeddale, Ettrick and Lauderdale, since 1997; *b* 3 June 1965; *s* of Rev. (William) Haisley Moore and Geraldine Anne, (Jill), Moore. *Educ:* Strathallan Sch.; Jedburgh Grammar Sch.; Univ. of Edinburgh (MA Jt Hons Politics and Modern Hist.). Research Asst to Archy Kirkwood, MP, 1987–88; with Coopers & Lybrand, Edinburgh, 1988–97 (a Manager, corporate finance). Mem., Select Cttee on Scottish affairs, 1997–99. CA 1991. *Recreations:* jazz, music, films, Rugby, hill-walking. *Address:* Wells Brae Cottage, Innerleithen, Peeblesshire EH44 6HR. *T:* (01896) 830597.

MOORE, Michael Rodney Newton, CBE 1996; Chairman: Quicks Group, since 1993; Linx Printing Technologies, since 1993; Stratus Holdings plc, since 2000; *b* 15 March 1936; *s* of Gen. Sir Rodney Moore, GCVO, KCB, CBE, DSO, PMN and Olive Marion (*née* Robinson); *m* 1986, Jan, *d* of Paul and Lilian Adorian; one *s*. *Educ:* Eton; Magdalen College, Oxford (MA); Harvard Business Sch. (MBA). Nat. Service Commission, Grenadier Guards, 1957–59, serving in Cyprus, Lebanon, UK. Called to the Bar, Gray's Inn, 1961; practised until 1964; joined Hill Samuel & Co., 1966 (Dir, 1970–71); subseq. Chm./Dir, various UK, USA & Swedish cos; Chairman: Tomkins, 1984–95; London Internat. Gp, 1994–99; Jt Dep. Chm., Clerical Medical Investment Gp, 1996–. Chm., Which? Ltd, 1997–; Mem. Council of Mgt, Consumers' Assoc., 1997–. Trustee, Public Concern at Work, 1996–. Chm., NSPCC, 1988–95. *Recreations:* visiting ruins, opera, tennis, reading. *Clubs:* Pratt's, Boodle's, Lansdowne.

MOORE, Michael S.; *see* Stuart-Moore.

MOORE, Noel Ernest Ackroyd; Under-Secretary, Management and Personnel Office (formerly Civil Service Department), 1975–86, and Principal of Civil Service College, 1981–86, retired; *b* 25 Nov. 1928; *s* of late Rowland H. Moore and Hilda Moore (*née* Ackroyd); *m* 1954, Mary Elizabeth Thorpe; two *s*. *Educ:* Penistone Grammar Sch., Yorks; Gonville and Caius Coll., Cambridge (MA; Major Scholar; Half-Blue for chess). Asst Principal, Post Office, 1952; Asst Private Sec. to Postmaster General, 1955–56; Private Sec. to Asst PMG, 1956–57; Principal, 1957; Sec., Cttee of Inquiry on Decimal Currency, 1961–63; Treasury, 1966; Asst Sec., 1967; Sec., Decimal Currency Bd, 1966–72; Civil Service Dept, 1972. Official Side Mem., Civil Service Appeal Bd, 1987–98. Mem., Barking and Havering FHSA, 1992–96. FIPM 1985; FITD 1985. *Publication:* The Decimalisation of Britain's Currency (HMSO), 1973. *Recreations:* wide reading, crosswords, pricing donated books for the local Oxfam shop. *Address:* 30 Spurgate, Hutton, Brentwood, Essex CM13 2LA.

MOORE, (Sir) Norman Winfrid, (3rd Bt *cr* 1919; has established his claim but does not use the title); Senior Principal Scientific Officer, Nature Conservancy Council, 1965–83 (Principal Scientific Officer, 1958–65); Visiting Professor of Environmental Studies, Wye College, University of London, 1979–83; *b* 24 Feb. 1923; *s* of Sir Alan Hilary Moore, 2nd Bt; *S* father, 1959; *m* 1950, Janet, *o d* of late Mrs Phyllis Singer; one *s* two *d*. *Educ:* Eton; Trinity Coll., Cambridge (MA); Univ. of Bristol (PhD). Served War, 1942–45, Germany and Holland (wounded, POW). *Publication:* The Bird of Time, 1987. *Heir: s* Peter Alan Cutlack Moore [*b* 21 Sept. 1951; *m* 1989, Pamela Edwardes; one *s* one *d*. *Educ:* Eton; Trinity Coll., Cambridge (MA); DPhil Oxon]. *Address:* The Farm House, 117 Boxworth End, Swavesey, Cambridge CB4 5RA.

MOORE, Sir Patrick (Alfred) Caldwell-, Kt 2001; CBE 1988 (OBE 1968); free-lance author since 1968; *b* 4 March 1923; *s* of late Capt. Charles Caldwell-Moore, MC, and Gertrude Lilian Moore. *Educ:* privately (due to illness). Served with RAF, 1940–45: Navigator, Bomber Command. Concerned in running of a school, 1945–52; free-lance author, 1952–65; Dir of Armagh Planetarium, 1965–68. TV Series, BBC, The Sky at Night, 1957–; radio broadcaster. Composed and performed in Perseus and Andromeda (opera), 1975, and Theseus, 1982. Pres., British Astronomical Assoc., 1982–84. Honorary Member: Astronomic-Geodetic Soc. of USSR, 1971; Royal Astronomical Soc. of New Zealand, 1983; Royal Astronomical Soc. of Canada, 1994. Editor, Year Book of Astronomy, 1962–. Lorimer Gold Medal, 1962; Goodacre Gold Medal, 1968; Arturo Gold Medal (Italian Astronomical Socs), 1969; Jackson-Gwilt Medal, RAS, 1977; Roberts-Klumpke Medal, Astronom. Soc. of Pacific, 1979. Fellow, QMW. Hon. FRS 2001. Hon. DSc: Lancaster, 1974; Hatfield Polytechnic, 1989; Birmingham, 1990; Leicester, Keele, 1995; Portsmouth, 1998. *Publications:* More than 60 books, mainly astronomical, including The Amateur Astronomer, 1970, rev. edn 1990; Atlas of the Universe, 1970, rev. edn 1995; Guide to the Planets, 1976; Guide to the Moon, 1976; Can You Speak Venusian?, 1977; Guide to the Stars, 1977; Guide to Mars, 1977; (jtly) Out of the Darkness: the Planet Pluto, 1980; The Unfolding Universe, 1982; Travellers in Space and Time, 1983; (jtly) The Return of Halley's Comet, 1984; Stargazing, 1985; Exploring the Night Sky with Binoculars, 1986; The A–Z of Astronomy, 1986; TV Astronomer, 1987; Astronomy for the Under-Tens, 1987; Astronomers' Stars, 1987; (jtly) The Planet Uranus, 1988; The Planet Neptune, 1989; Space Travel for the Under Tens, 1989; Mission to the Planets, 1990; A Passion for Astronomy, 1991; The Earth for Under Tens, 1992; Fireside Astronomy, 1992; The Starry Sky, 1994; The Great Astronomical Revolution, 1994; Stars of the Southern Skies, 1994; Guinness Book of Astronomy, 1995; Teach Yourself Astronomy, 1995; Eyes on the Universe, 1997; Sun in Eclipse, 1999; West Country Eclipse, 1999; Patrick Moore on Mars, 1999; The Wondering Astronomer, 2000; Patrick Moore on the Moon, 2000; The Star of Bethlehem, 2001. *Recreations:* cricket, chess, tennis, music, xylophone playing (composer of music in recordings The Ever Ready Band Plays Music by Patrick Moore, 1979, The Music of Patrick Moore, 1986, Moore Music, 1999). *Address:* Farthings, 39 West Street, Selsey, West Sussex PO19 9AD. *Clubs:* Athenæum, Lord's Taverners; Sussex County Cricket.

MOORE, Sir Patrick (William Eisdell), Kt 1992; OBE 1982; FRCS, FRACS; Consultant Surgeon, Honorary Staff, Auckland Hospital Board, now retired; *b* 17 March 1918; *m* 1942, Doris McBeth (Beth) Beedie; four *s*. *Educ:* Auckland Grammar Sch.; Otago Univ. (MB ChB). DLO. Medical Officer, 28 Bn, 2 NZEF. Consultant Surgeon, Green Lane Hosp., 1951; Reader in Otolaryngology, Auckland Med. Sch., 1975–84. President: Deafness Res. Foundn, 1963–90; NZ Otolaryngological Soc., 1968–70; NZ Hunts Assoc., 1984–89. *Publication:* A Great Run, 1972. *Recreations:* hunting, sketching, writing. *Address:* Binswood, 229 Remuera Road, Auckland 1005, New Zealand. *T:* (9) 5202679.

MOORE, Prof. Peter Gerald, TD 1963; PhD; FIA; Principal, London Business School, 1984–89 (Professor of Statistics, 1965–93, now Emeritus; Fellow, 1993); *b* Richmond, Surrey, 5 April 1928; *s* of late Leonard and Ruby Moore; *m* 1958, Sonja Enevoldson Thomas, Dulwich; two *s* one *d*. *Educ:* King's College Sch., Wimbledon; University Coll. London (BSc (1st Cl. Hons Statistics), PhD; Rosa Morison Meml Medal 1949; Fellow, 1988). Served with 3rd Regt RHA, 1949–51, TA, 1951–65, Major 1963. Lectr, UCL, 1951–57; Commonwealth Fund (Harkness) Fellow, Princeton, NJ, 1953–54; Asst to Economic Adviser, NCB, 1957–59; Head of Statistical Services, Reed Paper Gp, 1959–65; Dep. Principal, London Business Sch., 1972–84. Director: Shell UK, 1969–72; Copeman Paterson Ltd, 1978–87; Martin Paterson Associates, 1984–88; Elf Petroleum UK plc, 1989–94; Partner, Duncan C. Fraser, 1974–77. Consultant, Pugh-Roberts Associates Inc., US, 1989–94. Gresham Prof. of Rhetoric, 1992–95. Member: Review Body on Doctors' and Dentists' Pay, 1971–89; Cttee on 1971 Census Security, 1971–73; UGC, 1979–84 (Vice-Chm., 1980–83); Cons. to Wilson Cttee on Financial Instns, 1977–80. Pres., Royal Statistical Soc., 1989–91 (Mem. Council, 1966–78, 1988–97; Hon. Sec., 1968–74; Guy Medal, 1970; Chambers Medal, 1995); Pres., Inst. of Actuaries, 1984–86 (Mem. Council, 1966–90; Vice-Pres., 1973–76); Member: Internat. Stat. Inst., 1972– (Council, 1985–91); Council, Internat. Actuarial Assoc, 1984–87; Industry and Employment Cttee, ESRC, 1983–88; Jarratt Cttee on Univ. Efficiency, 1984–85; Council, Hong Kong Univ. of Science and Technology, 1986–91; Acad. Council, China Europe Management Inst., Beijing, 1986–94; Univ. of London Senate, 1988–92; Council, UCL, 1989– (Vice-Chm., 1998–2000); Court, Cranfield Inst. of Technology, 1989–96; Court, City Univ., 1990–; Chm., Council of Univ. Management Schs, 1974–76; a Governor: London Business Sch., 1968–89; NIESR, 1985–; Sevenoaks Sch., 1984–90. Freeman, City of London, 1964; Mem., Court of Assts, 1987–, Master, 1994–95, Tallow Chandlers' Co. CIMgt (CBIM 1986). Hon. DSc Heriot-Watt, 1985. J. D. Scaife Medal, Instn of Prodn Engrs, 1964. *Publications include:* Principles of Statistical Techniques, 1958, 2nd edn 1969; (with D. E. Edwards) Standard Statistical Calculations, 1965; Statistics and the Manager, 1966; Basic Operational Research, 1968, 3rd edn 1986; Risk and Business Decisions, 1972; (jtly) Case Studies in Decision Analysis, 1975; (with H. Thomas) Anatomy of Decisions, 1976, 2nd rev. edn 1988; Reason by Numbers, 1980; The Business of Risk, 1983; numerous articles in professional jls. *Recreations:* golf, opera, walking, travel. *Address:* London Business School, Sussex Place, Regent's Park, NW1 4SA. *T:* (020) 7262 5050; 3 Chartway, Sevenoaks, Kent TN13 3RU. *T:* (01732) 451936. *Clubs:* Athenæum; Cordwainer; Knole Park Golf.

MOORE, Philip John, BMus; FRCO; Organist and Master of the Music, York Minster, since 1983; *b* 30 Sept. 1943; *s* of late Cecil and of Marjorie Moore; one *s* two *d*. *Educ:* Maidstone Grammar Sch.; Royal Coll. of Music (ARCM, GRSM). BMus Dunelm; FRCO 1965. Asst Music Master, Eton Coll., 1965–68; Asst Organist, Canterbury Cathedral, 1968–74; Organist and Master of the Choristers, Guildford Cathedral, 1974–83. *Publications:* anthems, services, cantatas, organ music, song cycles, chamber music, orchestral music. *Recreations:* collecting fountain pens, collecting Imari, log fires. *Address:* 1 Minster Court, York YO1 7JJ.

MOORE, Richard Hobart John de Courcy, FCA; Managing Partner, since 1987, and Senior Partner, since 1989, Moore Stephens; *b* 31 Aug. 1949; *s* of late Hobart Harold de Courcy Moore and of Elizabeth Helen Moore; *m* 1977, Lucy Annabelle Sefton-Smith; one *s* one *d*. *Educ:* Stowe Sch. FCA 1979. Partner, Moore Stephens, 1975–. *Recreations:* Real tennis, cricket. *Address:* 11 Chelsea Park Gardens, SW3 6AF. *T:* (020) 7352 7594. *Clubs:* Boodle's, MCC, Hurlingham, Harbour.

MOORE, Richard Valentine, GC 1940; CBE 1963; BSc (Eng); FIMechE; FIEE; retired; Managing Director (Reactor Group), UK Atomic Energy Authority, 1961–76; Member, 1971–76; *b* 14 Feb. 1916; *s* of Randall and Ellen Moore; *m* 1944, Ruby Edith Fair; three *s*. *Educ:* Strand Sch., London; London Univ. County of London Electric Supply Co., 1936–39. RNVR, 1939–46; HMS Effingham, 1939–40; HMS President, 1940–41; HMS Dido, 1942–44; British Admiralty Delegn, Washington, DC, 1944–46; Lieut-Comdr 1944. AERE Harwell, 1946–53; Dept of Atomic Energy, Risley, 1953; Design and Construction of Calder Hall, 1953–57; Chief Design Engineer, 1955; UKAEA, 1955; Dir of Reactor Design, 1958–61. Faraday Lectr, 1966. Hon. DTech Bradford, 1970. *Publications:* various papers to technical institutions. *Recreations:* golf, gardening. *Address:* Culleen House, Cann Lane, Appleton, Ches WA4 5NQ. *T:* (01925) 261023. *Club:* Naval.

MOORE, Robert Jeffery; His Honour Judge Moore; a Circuit Judge, since 1995; Ethnic Minorities Liaison Judge for Sheffield, since 1998; *b* 1947; *s* of Jeffery Moore and Doreen Moore; *m* 1979, Susan Elaine Hatcliffe; two *s*. *Educ:* Loughborough Grammar Sch.; Univ. of Manchester (LLB Hons 1968). Called to the Bar, Gray's Inn, 1970; practised on North Eastern Circuit, from Sheffield, 1971–80 and from 11 Kings Bench Walk, Temple, 1980–95. *Recreations:* my family, Leicester Tigers Rugby club, golf, Italian food. *Address:* The Law Courts, 50 West Bar, Sheffield S3 8PH. *Club:* Sickleholme (Bamford).

MOORE, Roger George, CBE 1999; actor; *b* London, 14 Oct. 1927; *m* 1st, Doorn van Steyn (marr. diss. 1953); 2nd, 1953, Dorothy Squires (marr. diss. 1969; she *d* 1998); 3rd, Luisa Mattioli; two *s* one *d*. *Educ:* RADA. Special Ambassador for UNICEF, 1991–. Golden Globe World Film Favourite Award, 1980. Stage début, Androcles and the Lion. *TV series include:* Ivanhoe, 1958; The Alaskans, 1960–61; Maverick, 1961; The Saint, 1962–69 (dir some episodes); The Persuaders, 1972–73; The Man Who Woundn't Die, 1992; The Quest, 1995; *films include:* The Last Time I Saw Paris, 1954; The Interrupted Melody, 1955; The King's Thief, 1955; Diane, 1956; The Miracle, 1959; Rachel Cade, 1961; Gold of the Seven Saints, 1961; The Rape of the Sabine Women, 1961; No Man's Land, 1961; Crossplot, 1969; The Man Who Haunted Himself, 1970; Live and Let Die, 1973; The Man With The Golden Gun, 1974; Gold, 1974; That Lucky Touch, 1975; Street People, 1975; Shout at the Devil, 1975; Sherlock Holmes in New York, 1976; The Spy Who Loved Me, 1976; The Wild Geese, 1977; Escape to Athena, 1978; Moonraker, 1978; North Sea Hijack, 1979; The Sea Wolves, 1980; Sunday Lovers, 1980; For Your Eyes Only, 1980; The Cannonball Run, 1981; Octopussy, 1983; The Naked Face, 1983; A View to a Kill, 1985; Bed and Breakfast, 1989; Bullseye!, 1989; Fire, Ice and Dynamite, 1990; The Quest, 1997. *Publication:* James Bond Diary, 1973. *Address:* c/o ICM Ltd, 76 Oxford Street, W1N 0AX.

MOORE, Rear-Adm. Simon, CB 2000; Chief Executive, Action Research, since 2001; *b* 25 Sept. 1946; *s* of Ronald and Christine Moore; *m* 1978, Catherine Sarcelet; three *d*. *Educ:* Brentwood Sch. Joined RN 1964; in command, HM Ships: Walkerton, 1974–75; Rhyl, 1983; Berwick, 1984–85; Asst Dir, Defence Policy, MoD, 1988–91; in command, HMS Fearless, 1991–93; Captain, BRNC, Dartmouth, 1993–95; Dir, Intelligence Regl Assessments, 1995–97; ACDS (Ops), MoD, 1997–2000. *Recreations:* music, bellringing, social tennis. *Address:* Action Research, Vincent House, North Parade, Horsham, W Sussex RH12 2DP. *Club:* Naval and Military.

MOORE, Prof. Stuart Alfred; JP; Chairman, Stockport Primary Care Trust, since 2001; Robert Ottley Professor of Quantitive Studies, University of Manchester, 1992–97, now Emeritus Professor; *b* 9 Oct. 1939; *s* of Alfred Moore and Kathleen (*née* Dodd); *m* 1966, Diana Mary Connery; two *s* one *d*. *Educ:* Stockport Sch.; Manchester Univ. (MA Econs 1967). University of Manchester: Computer Asst, 1960–64; Lectr, then Sen. Lectr in Econ. Stats, 1964–92; Dean, Fac. of Econ. and Social Studies, 1980–83; Pro Vice-Chancellor, 1985–90, 1997–; Dep. Vice-Chancellor, 1990–96; Actg Vice-Chancellor, 1990–92; Chm., Central Manchester Healthcare NHS Trust, 1992–2001. JP City of Manchester, 1996. *Publications:* various papers in learned jls. *Recreations:* gardening, photography, travel, thrillers, films. *Address:* Central Manchester Healthcare NHS Trust, Cobbett House, Oxford Road, Manchester M13 9WL. *T:* (0161) 276 4841; 2 Carisbrooke Avenue, Hazel Grove, Stockport SK7 5PL.

MOORE, Terence, CBE 1993; business consultant, since 1995; Group Managing Director and Chief Executive Officer, Conoco Ltd, 1987–95; *b* 24 Dec. 1931; *s* of Arthur Doncaster Moore and Dorothy Irene Gladys (*née* Godwin); *m* 1955, Tessa Catherine (*née* Wynne); two *s* one *d*. *Educ:* Strand Sch., London. BScEcon, Univ. of London; Harvard (AMP). ACII 1958; AICS 1959. Shell Internat. Petroleum Co., 1948–64; Locana Corp. Ltd (investment bank), 1964–65; Conoco Ltd, 1965–95: Dep. Man. Dir, Marketing and Operations, 1975; Man. Dir, Supply and Trading, Europe, 1979. Director: Conoco Pension Trustees Ltd, 1996–; James Fisher & Son plc, 1998–. Hon. Sec., Inst. of Petroleum, 1995–. Gov., Greenwich Theatre, 1991–97 (Vice Chm. Govs, 1992–93). Chm., St Katherines and Shadwell Trust, 1999. *Publications:* articles in industry jls. *Recreations:* music, reading, walking, family and friends. *Address:* 67 Merchant Court, Thorpes Yard, 61 Wapping Wall, E1W 3SJ. *T:* and *Fax:* (020) 7481 0853; *e-mail:* terrymoore@demon.co.uk.

MOORE, Thomas William; JP; Chairman (since inception) of Trojan Metals Ltd, Carseview Holdings Ltd, Dundee Timber Market Ltd, Inverlaw Property Co. Ltd; *b* 9 Aug. 1925; Scottish; *m* 1945, Mary Kathleen Thompson; four *s* two *d*. *Educ:* Stobswell Secondary Sch.; Leicester Coll. of Art and Technology. MIMgt. Contested (Lab), Perth and East Perthshire, 1959. Lord Provost of Dundee, and Lord Lieutenant of County of City of Dundee, 1973–75; Chairman: Tay Road Bridge Jt Cttee, 1973; Tayside Steering Cttee, 1973. FInstD. *Recreations:* golf, reading. *Address:* Cidhmore, 492A Perth Road, Dundee DD2 1LR. *Club:* Royal Automobile.

MOORE, Sir William (Roger Clotworthy), 3rd Bt *cr* 1932; TD 1962; DL; *b* 17 May 1927; *s* of Sir William Samson Moore, 2nd Bt, and Ethel Cockburn Gordon (*d* 1973); *S* father, 1978; *m* 1954, Gillian, *d* of John Brown, Co. Antrim; one *s* one *d*. *Educ:* Marlborough; RMC, Sandhurst. Lieut Royal Inniskilling Fusiliers, 1945; Major North Irish Horse, 1956. Grand Juror, Co. Antrim, 1952–68. Prison visitor, 1968–74. Mem., Parole Bd for Scotland, 1978–80. High Sheriff, Co. Antrim, 1964; DL Co. Antrim, 1990. *Heir:* *s* Richard William Moore [*b* 8 May 1955. *Educ:* Portora; RMA. Lieut Royal Scots, 1974]. *Address:* Moore Lodge, Ballymoney, Co. Antrim, Northern Ireland BT53 7NT. *Club:* Kildare Street and University (Dublin).

MOORE-BICK, Maj. Gen. John David, CBE 1997 (OBE 1991); FICE; General Officer Commanding UK Support Command (Germany), since 2001; *b* 10 Oct. 1949; *s* of late John Ninian Moore-Bick and of Kathleen Margaret Moore-Bick (*née* Beall); *m* 1973, Anne Horton; one *d*. *Educ:* Stonegate Sch.; Skinners'; St Catherine's Coll., Oxford (BA (Forestry), MA). Commissioned RA (V) 1969, regular commission, 1971; transf. to RE, 1972; served 45 Commando Gp, Junior Leaders' Regt RE and 23 Amphibious Engr Sqdn, 1972–79; Führungsakademie der Bundeswehr, 1979–82; HQ UKLF, 1982–84; Falkland Is, 1984–85; 26 Armd Engr Sqdn, 1985–86; Asst to Chm., NATO Mil. Cttee, 1986–88; 21 Engr Regt, Germany, and Gulf War, 1988–91; Chief Engr, Multi National Airmobile Div., 1991; Col Army Plans, MoD, 1991–94; Chief Engr, ARRC, 1994–95 and Implementation Force, Sarajevo, 1995–96; Dir, Army Staff Duties, MoD, 1996–99; Leader, MoD Study into Future of Shrivenham/Watchfield, 1999; MA to High Rep., Sarajevo, 2000. Liveryman, Skinners' Co., 1988– (Extra Mem., Court). Trustee, British German Officers' Assoc. 1st Cl. Service Order (Hungary), 1996. Hon. Col, 39 (Skinners') Signal Regt, 2001–. *Recreations:* Eastern Europe and Germany, Kent and Sussex Weald. *Address:* National Westminster Bank, 1 St James' Square, Wadhurst, Sussex TN5 6BH.

Clubs: Army and Navy; Royal Engineer Yacht (Commodore, 1997–99); British Kiel Yacht (Commodore).
See also Hon. Sir M. J. Moore-Bick.

MOORE-BICK, Hon. Sir Martin (James), Kt 1995; **Hon. Mr Justice Moore-Bick;** a Judge of the High Court of Justice, Queen's Bench Division, since 1995; *b* 6 Dec. 1946; *s* of late John Ninian Moore-Bick and of Kathleen Margaret Moore-Bick (*née* Beall); *m* 1974, Tessa Penelope Gee; two *s* two *d*. *Educ:* The Skinners' Sch., Tunbridge Wells; Christ's Coll., Cambridge (MA). Called to the Bar, Inner Temple, 1969, Bencher, 1992; QC 1986; a Recorder, 1990–95. *Recreations:* early music, gardening, reading. *Address:* Royal Courts of Justice, Strand, WC2A 2LL.
See also Maj. Gen. J. D. Moore-Bick.

MOORE-BRABAZON, family name of **Baron Brabazon of Tara**.

MOORE-WILTON, Maxwell William, AC 2001; Secretary, Department of the Prime Minister and Cabinet, Australia, since 1996; *b* 27 Jan. 1943; *s* of William Moore-Wilton and Cavell Little; *m* 1966, Janette Costin; one *s* one *d*. *Educ:* St Joseph's Coll., Qld; Univ. of Queensland (BEc). Commonwealth Department of Trade, Australia, 1964–78: Minister, Delegn for Trade Negotiations, Geneva, 1974–75; First Asst Sec., Policy Develt/Commodity Policy, 1976–78; Dep. Sec., Commonwealth Dept of Primary Industry, 1979–80; Gen. Manager, Australian Wheat Bd, Melbourne, 1981–83; Man. Dir, Australian Nat. Line, Melbourne, 1984–89; Chief Exec., Maritime Services Bd of NSW, 1989–91; Dir-Gen., NSW Dept of Transport, 1991–94; Chief Exec., Roads and Traffic Authy of NSW, 1994–95; Nat. Dir, Policy Co-ordination and Priorities Rev., Australian Stock Exchange Ltd, 1995–96. *Recreations:* reading, swimming. *Address:* Department of the Prime Minister and Cabinet, 3/5 National Circuit, Barton, ACT 2600, Australia. *T:* (2) 62715200. *Clubs:* Union, Tattersalls (Sydney).

MOORER, Admiral Thomas Hinman; Defense Distinguished Service Medals, 1973 and 1974; Navy DSM 1965, 1967, 1968, 1970; Army DSM 1974; Air Force DSM 1974; Silver Star 1942; Legion of Merit, 1945; DFC 1942; Purple Heart, 1942; Presidential Unit Citation, 1942; Board Member: Blount Inc.; Fairchild Industries; USLICO. CACI; *b* Mount Willing, Alabama, 9 Feb. 1912; *s* of Dr R. R. Moorer and Hulda Hill Hinson, Eufaula, Ala; *m* 1935, Carrie Ellen Foy Moorer; three *s* one *d*. *Educ:* Cloverdale High Sch., Montgomery, Ala; USN Acad.; Naval Aviation Trg Sch.; Naval War Coll. First ship, 1933; serving at Pearl Harbour in Fleet Air Wing, Dec. 1941; Pacific and East Indies areas, 1942; Mining Observer, C-in-C, US Fleet in UK, 1943; Strategic Bombing Survey in Japan, 1945; Naval Aide to Asst Sec. of Navy (Air), 1956; CO, USS Salisbury Sound, 1957; Special Asst to CNO, 1959; Comdr, Carrier Div. Six, 1960; Dir, Long Range Objectives Group, CNO, 1962; Comdr Seventh Fleet, 1964; C-in-C: US Pacific Fleet, 1965; Atlantic and Atlantic Fleet, and Supreme Allied Commander, Atlantic, 1965–67; Chief of Naval Operations, 1967–70; Chm., Jt Chiefs of Staff, USA, 1970–74, retired US Navy 1974. Captain 1952; Rear-Adm. 1958; Vice-Adm. 1962; Adm. 1964. Enshrined in Nat. Aviation Hall of Fame, 1987; introduced into Naval Aviation Hall of Honor, 1988. Gold Medal, Nat. Football Hall of Fame, 1990. Holds seventeen foreign decorations. Hon. LLD Auburn, 1968; Hon. DH Samford, 1970; Hon. Dr Mil. Science, The Citadel, 1983. *Recreations:* golfing, fishing, hunting. *Clubs:* Brook (New York); International, Army-Navy Town (Washington, DC); US Naval Inst. (Annapolis, Md); Chevy Chase (Chevy Chase, Md).

MOORES, Hon. Frank Duff; formerly Chairman, Executive Committee, Government Consultants International; Chairman and Chief Executive Officer, SSF (Holdings) Inc.; Premier of the Province of Newfoundland, 1972–79; *b* 18 Feb. 1933; *s* of Silas Wilmot Moores and Dorothy Duff Moores; *m* 1982, Beth Champion; two *s* six *d* by former marriages. *Educ:* United Church Academy, Carbonear; St Andrew's Coll., Aurora, Ont. MP, Canada, for Bonavista-Trinity-Conception, 1968–71; MHA for Humber W, Newfoundland, 1971; Pres., Progressive Conservative Party in Canada, 1969; Leader, Progressive Conservative Party, Newfoundland, 1970–79. Mem., Royal Commn on Economic Prospects of Newfoundland. Director: Council for Canadian Unity; Atlantic Salmon Fedn (Canada). Gov., Olympia Trust. Is a Freemason. Hon. LLD Meml Univ. of Newfoundland, 1975. *Recreations:* tennis, salmon fishing, golf. *Clubs:* Forest and Stream (Montreal); Mid Ocean (Bermuda); Hobe Sound Golf (Florida).

MOORES, John, CBE 1993; DL; Director, The Littlewoods Organisation, 1950–96; *b* 22 Nov. 1928; *s* of Sir John Moores, CBE; *m* 1st, 1949, Helen Sheila Moore; three *s* one *d*; 2nd, 1963, Jane Staveley-Dick; four *s* one *d*. *Educ:* Eton Coll.; Syracuse Univ., USA. Joined The Littlewoods Organisation, 1946, Dep. Chm., 1968–71; Chm., Littlewoods Equal Opportunities, 1963–96; Chm., Medaillon Mode GmbH, 1968–71. Mem. Council, Britain in Europe, 2000–. Chancellor, Liverpool John Moores Univ., 1994–99 (Sen. Pro-Chancellor, and Chm. Bd of Govs, 1992–94). Chm., Liverpool Motorists' Annual Outing, 1993–; Pres., Roy Castle Lung Cancer Foundn, 1996–2001. DL Merseyside, 1993. Hon. Freeman, City of Liverpool, 1994. *Recreations:* languages, regionalisation, Europe, cattle breeding. *Address:* South Lodge, North Moss Lane, Formby, Liverpool L37 0AQ. *Club:* Boodle's.
See also P. Moores.

MOORES, Peter, CBE 1991; DL; Director, The Littlewoods Organisation, 1965–93 (Chairman, 1977–80); *b* 9 April 1932; *s* of Sir John Moores, CBE; *m* 1960, Luciana Pinto (marr. diss. 1984); one *s* one *d*. *Educ:* Eton; Christ Church, Oxford; Wiener Akademie der Musik und darstellenden Kunst. Worked in opera at Glyndebourne and Vienna State Opera. Founded Peter Moores Foundn, 1964, to support opera, visual arts, educn, health, youth, social and envmtl projects; pioneer of opera recordings in English trans. incl. Der Ring des Nibelungen, Mary Stuart, Julius Caesar (all ENO), Carmen (new critical edn), Il Travatore, Tosca, Der Rosenkavalier; rare 19th century Italian opera in original lang. with Opera Rara, incl. Maria Padilla, Emilia di Liverpool, Rosmonda d'Inghilterra, Ricciardo e Zoraide, Rossini's Otello, Zoraida di Granata; original English lang. recordings incl. Troilus and Cressida, Peter Grimes (Royal Opera). Peter Moores Foundn Scholarships, RNCM, awarded annually to promising young opera singers. Estab. Transatlantic Slave Trade Gallery, Merseyside Maritime Mus., 1994. Endowed Faculty Dirship and Chair of Mgt Studies, Oxford Univ., 1992. Initiated Scotland Beef Project, Barbados, 1993, to encourage agricl land conservation and self-supporting farming practice. Benefactor, Chair of Tropical Horticulture, Univ. of WI, Barbados, 1995. Founded: Compton Verney House Trust, 1993 to house Foundn art collection and other exhibns; Peter Moores Charitable Trust, 1998. Director: Singer & Friedlander, 1978–92; Scottish Opera, 1988–92. Trustee, Tate Gall., 1978–85; Governor of the BBC, 1981–83. DL Lancs, 1992. Hon. RNCM, 1985. Hon. MA Christ Church, 1975. Gold Medal of the Italian Republic, 1974. *Recreations:* opera, shooting. *Address:* Parbold Hall, Parbold, near Wigan, Lancs WN8 7TG. *Club:* Boodle's.
See also John Moores.

MOORES, Dame Yvonne, DBE 1999; Chief Nursing Officer and Director of Nursing, Department of Health, 1992–99; *b* 14 June 1941; *d* of Tom Abraham Quick and late Phyllis Quick (*née* Jeremiah); *m* 1969, Bruce Holmes Ramsden. *Educ:* Itchen Grammar Sch., Southampton; Royal South Hampshire Hosp. (RGN); Southampton Gen. Hosp. (RM). Ward Sister, Whittington Hosp. and Royal Hampshire County Hosp., 1964–70; Principal Nursing Officer: N London HMC, 1971–72; W Manchester, 1973–74; Dist Nursing Officer, N Manchester, 1974–76; Area Nursing Officer, Manchester AHA, 1976–81; Chief Nursing Officer: Welsh Office, 1982–88; Scottish Office, Home and Health Dept, 1988–92. Vice-Chm., NHS Supply Council, 1979–82; Pres., Infection Control Nurses Assoc., 1987–90; Mem., WHO Global Adv. Gp for Nursing and Midwifery, 1992–97; former Vis. Prof., Sheffield Univ., 1996–99. Chm., Macmillan Cancer Unit Appeal, Calderdale, 2000–01. Mem. Council, Southampton Univ. (Chm., 2000–). Hon. Fellow, Coll. of Med., Univ. of Wales, 1995. Hon. FRSH; Hon. FFPHM 1996; Hon. FRCP. Hon. DSc: Portsmouth, 1993; Huddersfield, 1997; Bradford, 1998; DUniv Central England, 2001; Hon. DCL Northumbria, 1995; Hon. MA De Montfort, 1995. *Recreation:* golf. *Address:* Simm Carr Farm, Simm Carr Lane, Shibden, Halifax HX3 7UL.

MOOREY, Adrian Edward; Director of Communications, National Air Traffic Services, since 2001; *b* 4 May 1946; *s* of Edward Alfred Moorey and Lily Elizabeth Moorey; *m* 1st, 1969, Sandra Ann Jeffrey (marr. diss.); one *s*; 2nd, 1987, Lesley Nicola Hancock; one *s* one *d*. *Educ:* Sir Joseph Williamson's Mathematical Sch., Rochester. Advertising and Marketing Asst, Lonsdale-Hands Orgn, 1964–67; Asst Information Officer, 1967–69, Inf. Officer, 1969–72, Home Office; Press Officer, PM's Office, 1973; Department of Employment: Sen. Press Officer, 1974–75; Chief Press Officer, 1976–81; Head of Inf., 1982–86; Director of Information: DTI, 1987–90; Home Office, 1990–94; Dir, Corporate and Govt Affairs, Cable and Wireless plc, 1995–99; Corporate Communications Dir, CAA, 1999–2001. *Recreations:* cricket, golf. *Address:* The Pines, 16 Kent Road, East Molesey, Surrey KT8 9JZ. *T:* (020) 8979 0096.

MOOREY, (Peter) Roger (Stuart), DPhil; FBA 1977; FSA; Keeper, Department of Antiquities, Ashmolean Museum, Oxford, since 1983; Fellow of Wolfson College, since 1976; *b* 30 May 1937; *s* of late Stuart Moorey and Freda (*née* Harris). *Educ:* Mill Hill Sch.; Corpus Christi Coll., Oxford (MA, DPhil). FSA 1967. Nat. Service, 1956–58, Intelligence Corps. Asst Keeper, 1961–73, Sen. Asst Keeper, 1973–82, Ashmolean Museum, Oxford. Editor of Levant, 1968–86. Pres., British Sch. of Archaeology in Jerusalem, 1990–98. *Publications:* Catalogue of the Ancient Persian Bronzes in the Ashmolean Museum, 1971; Ancient Persian Bronzes in the Adam Collection, 1974; Biblical Lands, 1975; Kish Excavations 1923–1933, 1978; Cemeteries of the First Millennium BC at Deve Hüyük, 1980; Excavation in Palestine, 1981; (ed) C. L. Woolley, Ur of the Chaldees, revd edn 1982; (with B. Buchanan) Catalogue of Ancient Near Eastern Seals in the Ashmolean Museum, II, 1984, III, 1988; Materials and Manufacture in Ancient Mesopotamia: the evidence of archaeology and art, 1985; A Century of Biblical Archaeology, 1991; Ancient Mesopotamian Materials and Industries, 1994; museum booklets and articles in learned jls. *Recreations:* travel, walking. *Address:* Ashmolean Museum, Oxford. *T:* (01865) 278019, 278020.

MOORHOUSE, (Cecil) James (Olaf); *b* 1 Jan. 1924; *s* of late Captain Sidney James Humphrey Moorhouse and Anna Sophie Hedvig de Løvenskiold; *m* 1958, Elizabeth Clive Huxtable (marr. diss. 1995), Sydney, Aust.; one *s* one *d*; *m* 1997, Catherine Hamilton Peterson, New Mexico, USA. *Educ:* St Paul's School; King's Coll. and Imperial Coll., Univ. of London. BSc (Eng); DIC (Advanced Aeronautics); CEng. Designer with de Havilland Aircraft Co., 1946–48; Project Engr, BOAC, 1948–53; Technical Advr 1953–68, and Environmental Conservation Advr 1968–72, Shell International Petroleum; Environmental Advr, Shell Group of Companies in UK, 1972–73; Group Environmental Affairs Advr, Rio-Tinto Zinc Corp., 1973–80, Consultant, 1980–84. Dir, Project Development International, 1985–90. Contested (C) St Pancras North, 1966 and 1970. MEP (C 1979–98, Lib Dem 1998–99), London S, 1979–84, London S and Surrey E, 1984–99. European Parliament: spokesman on transport for EDG, 1979–84 and 1987–89; spokesman on external economic relations for EDG, 1984–87 and 1989–92; dep. co-ordinator on external economic relations for EPP, 1992–94; co-ordinator on human rights for EPP and British Cons, 1994–98; spokesman on foreign affairs, defence and human rights for British Cons, 1997–98; Chm., delegn to N Europe and Nordic Council, 1979–84; First Vice-Chm, delegn to EFTA Parliamentarians, 1984–86; Vice-Pres., External Econ. Relations Cttee, 1989–92; Mem., EPP Bureau, 1994–98. Founder Mem., Bow Gp. Jt Founder, Lib Dem Human Rights Gp, 2001. Mem., ESU. Sir Evelyn Wrench Lectr, USA, 1998. Polish Parlt Medal for work on human rights, 1997. *Publications:* (with Anthony Teasdale) Righting the Balance: a new agenda for Euro-Japanese trade, 1987; numerous articles and papers on aviation. *Recreations:* walking, reading, travel, watching cricket, filmgoer. *Address:* 211 Piccadilly, W1J 9HF. *Clubs:* Royal Automobile; Surrey County Cricket.

MOORHOUSE, Geoffrey, FRSL; writer; *b* Bolton, Lancs, 29 Nov. 1931; *s* of William Heald and Gladys Heald (*née* Hoyle, subseq. Moorhouse) and step *s* of Richard Moorhouse; *m* 1st, 1956, Janet Marion Murray; two *s* one *d* (and one *d* decd); 2nd, 1974, Barbara Jane Woodward (marr. diss. 1978); 3rd, 1983, Marilyn Isobel Edwards (marr. diss. 1996). *Educ:* Bury Grammar School. Nat. Service, Royal Navy (Coder), 1950–52; editorial staff: Bolton Evening News, 1952–54; Grey River Argus (NZ), Auckland Star (NZ), Christchurch Star-Sun (NZ), 1954–56; News Chronicle, 1957; (Manchester) Guardian, 1958–70 (Chief Features Writer, 1963–70). FRGS 1972–95; FRSL 1982. *Publications:* in numerous editions and translations: The Other England, 1964; The Press, 1964; Against All Reason, 1969; Calcutta, 1971; The Missionaries, 1973; The Fearful Void, 1974; The Diplomats, 1977; The Boat and The Town, 1979; The Best-Loved Game, 1979 (Cricket Soc. Award); India Britannica, 1983; Lord's, 1983; To the Frontier, 1984 (Thomas Cook Award, 1984); Imperial City: the rise and rise of New York, 1988; At the George (essays), 1989; Apples in the Snow, 1990; Hell's Foundations: a town, its myths and Gallipoli, 1992; Om: an Indian pilgrimage, 1993; A People's Game: the centenary history of Rugby League football 1895–1995, 1995; Sun Dancing: a medieval vision, 1997; Sydney, 1999. *Recreations:* music, gardening, hill-walking, looking at buildings, watching cricket, and Bolton Wanderers FC. *Address:* Park House, Gayle, near Hawes, North Yorkshire DL8 3RT. *T:* and *Fax:* (01969) 667456. *Club:* Lancashire County Cricket.

MOORHOUSE, James; *see* Moorhouse, C. J. O.

MOORHOUSE, (Kathleen) Tessa; a District Judge (formerly Registrar), Family Division of the High Court of Justice, since 1982; *b* 14 Sept. 1938; *d* of late Charles Elijah Hall, MRCVS and Helen Barbara Hall; *m* 1959, Rodney Moorhouse. *Educ:* Presentation Convent, Derbyshire; Leeds Univ.; King's Coll., London. Called to the Bar, Inner Temple, 1971. Asst, Jardine's Bookshop, Manchester, 1953–56; student, Leeds Univ., 1956–59; teacher of educationally subnormal, 1959–61; student, King's Coll., London, 1961–62; Classifier, Remand Home, 1962–64; Lectr in Law, 1964–71; barrister in practice, 1971–82. *Address:* 1st Avenue House, 42–49 High Holborn, WC1V 6NP. *T:* (020) 7947 6000; 4 Brick Court, Temple, EC4Y 9AD. *T:* (020) 7797 7766.

MOORHOUSE, Michael George Currer; His Honour Judge Moorhouse; a Circuit Judge, since 2001; *b* 29 June 1946; *s* of Reginald Currer Moorhouse and Betty Moorhouse; *m* 1970, Jane Mary Ross; one *s* three *d*. *Educ:* Ampleforth Coll. Admitted solicitor, 1970; in private practice, 1970–2001; Partner, R. C. Moorhouse Co., subseq. Keeble Hawson Moorhouse, 1975–2001. *Recreations:* gardening, sport, walking. *Address:* Middlesbrough Combined Court, Russell Street, Middlesbrough TS1 2AE.

MOORHOUSE, Peter William; Chairman, Police Complaints Authority, 1996–99 (Deputy Chairman, 1991–96); *b* 25 Dec. 1938; *s* of Francis and Dorothy Moorhouse; *m* 1962, Jane Catton; two *s* one *d*. *Educ:* Stonyhurst Coll. Joined Schweppes Group, 1961, Divl Dir, 1980–87; Mem., Police Complaints Authy, 1988–2000. Mem., Local Review Cttee, Parole Bd, 1973–88 (Chm., 1977–79, 1986–88). Gov., Stonyhurst Coll., 1991–94. FRSA 1995. *Recreations:* opera, art, walking, inland boating. *Address:* c/o HSBC, 1 High Street, Harpenden, Herts AL5 2RS.

MOORTHY, Arambamoorthy Thedchana; Sri Lanka Foreign Service, retired; private academic research and writing, since 1984; *b* 10 Aug. 1928; *s* of late Mr Arambamoorthy and Mrs Nesamma Arambamoorthy; *m* 1959, Suseela T. Moorthy, *d* of Justice P. Sri Skanda Rajah; one *s* two *d*. *Educ:* BAEcon Hons (Sri Lanka). Called to Bar, Gray's Inn, 1965. Entered Foreign Service of Sri Lanka, 1953; Second Secretary: Indonesia, 1955–57; China, 1957–59; First Secretary: London, 1961–63; Federal Republic of Germany, 1964–66; Chargé d'Affaires, *ai*, Thailand, and Permanent Representative of Sri Lanka to Economic Commn for Asia and Far East, 1969; Chargé d'Affaires, *ai*, Iraq, 1970; Ambassador in Pakistan, 1978–Dec. 1980, and concurrently, Jan-Dec. 1980, Ambassador to Iran with residence in Islamabad; High Comr in London, 1981–84. *Address:* 39 Gladstone Road, Wimbledon, SW19 1QU. *T:* (020) 8544 9537.

MOOSONEE, Bishop of, since 1980; **Rt Rev. Caleb James Lawrence;** *b* 26 May 1941; *s* of James Otis Lawrence and Mildred Viola Burton; *m* 1966, Maureen Patricia Cuddy; one *s* two *d*. *Educ:* Univ. of King's College. BA (Dalhousie Univ.) 1962; BST 1964. Deacon 1963, priest 1965; Missionary at Anglican Mission, Great Whale River, Quebec, 1965–75; Rector of St Edmund's Parish, Great Whale River, 1975–79; Canon of St Jude's Cathedral, Frobisher Bay, Diocese of The Arctic, 1974; Archdeacon of Arctic Quebec, 1975–79; Bishop Coadjutor, Diocese of Moosonee, Jan.-Nov. 1980. Hon. DD, Univ. of King's Coll., Halifax, NS, 1980. *Recreations:* reading, photography. *Address:* The Diocese of Moosonee, Synod Office, Box 841, Schumacher, ON P0N 1G0, Canada. *T:* (705) 2671129.

MORAES, Claude Ajit; Member (Lab) London Region, European Parliament, since 1999; *b* 22 Oct. 1965; *s* of H. I. Moraes and Theresa (*née* Aranha). *Educ:* St Modan's High Sch., Stirling; Univ. of Dundee (LLB 1987); Birkbeck Coll., Univ. of London (MSc 1989). Res. Asst to Rt Hon. Dr John Reid, MP and Paul Boateng, MP, 1987–89; postgrad. study in internat. law, LSE, 1990–91; Nat. Policy Officer, TUC, 1989–92; Dir, Jt Council for Welfare of Immigrants, 1992–98. Comr, CRE, 1998–99. Member: Council, Charter 88, 1997; Council, Liberty, 1997–; London Pol Cttee, AEEU, 1997–. Party spokesman, Employment and Social Affairs Cttee, EP, 1999–. Trustee, Toynbee Hall Charity. Contested (Lab) Harrow W, 1992. FRSA 1999. British Diversity Gold Award for achievement in the voluntary sector, New Impact mag., 1998. *Publications:* (jtly) Social Work and Minorities: European perspectives, 1998; articles on immigration, asylum and European matters in jls and nat. newspapers. *Recreations:* film, Scottish literature, listening to BBC World Service and Radio 5. *Address:* Labour European Office, 16 Charles Square, N1 6HP. *T:* (020) 7253 9615; (Brussels) (2) 2845553.

MORAES, Dom; Indian poet and author; *b* 1938; *s* of Frank Moraes (Editor of the Indian Express and biographer of Nehru); *m* 1970, Leela Naidu. *Educ:* Jesus Coll., Oxford. Read English, 1956–59. Took up residence in England at age of 16, after world-wide travel and a 2–yr stay in Ceylon. *Publications:* A Beginning (poems), 1957 (Hawthornden Prize, 1958); Gone Away (Travel), 1960; Poems, 1960; John Nobody (poems), 1965; The Brass Serpent (trans. from Hebrew poetry), 1964; Poems 1955–65 (collected poems), 1966; My Son's Father (autobiography), 1968; The People Time Forgot, 1972; The Tempest Within, 1972; A Matter of People, 1974; (ed) Voices for Life (essays), 1975; Mrs Gandhi, 1980; Bombay, 1980; Collected Poems 1957–1987, 1988; Serendip (poems), 1990; Never At Home (autobiog.), 1994.

MORAHAN, Christopher Thomas; television, film and theatre director; *b* 9 July 1929; *s* of Thomas Hugo Morahan and Nancy Charlotte Morahan (*née* Barker); *m* 1st, 1954, Joan (*née* Murray) (decd); two *s* (one *d* decd); 2nd, 1973, Anna (*née* Wilkinson, acting name Anna Carteret); two *d*. *Educ:* Highgate; Old Vic Theatre School. Directing for ATV, 1957–61; freelance director in TV for BBC and ITV, 1961–71; Head of Plays, BBC TV, 1972–76; National Theatre, 1977–88 (Dep. to Director, 1979–80); Director, Greenpoint Films, 1983–. *Stage:* Little Murders, RSC, Aldwych, 1967; This Story of Yours, Royal Court, 1968; Flint, Criterion, 1970; The Caretaker, Mermaid, 1972; Melon, Th. Royal, Haymarket, 1987; A Letter of Resignation, Comedy, 1997; Quartet, Albery, 1999; Naked Justice, W Yorks Playhouse, 2001; Chichester Festival: Major Barbara, 1988; The Handyman, 1996; Racing Demon, 1998; The Importance of Being Earnest, Semi-Detached, The Retreat from Moscow, 1999; Heartbreak House, 2000; The Winslow Boy, 2001; for National Theatre: State of Revolution, 1977; Brand, Strife, The Philanderer, 1978; Richard III, The Wild Duck, 1979; Sisterly Feelings, 1980; Man and Superman, 1981; Wild Honey (London Standard, Olivier, British Theatre Assoc. and Plays and Players Awards for Best Dir of the Year), 1984; The Devil's Disciple, 1994; The Importance of Being Earnest, Australia and NZ, 2000; *films:* Clockwise, 1986; Paper Mask, 1990; *television: films:* The Gorge, 1967; In the Secret State, 1985; After Pilkington, 1987 (Special Jury Prize, San Francisco Film Fest., 1987, Prix Italia, 1987); Troubles, 1988; The Heat of the Day, 1989; Old Flames, 1990; Can You Hear Me Thinking?, 1990; Common Pursuit, 1992; The Bullion Boys, 1993 (Internat. Emmy Award, 1994); Summer Day's Dream, 1994; It Might Be You, 1995; Element of Doubt, 1996; *series:* Emergency Ward 10; The Orwell Trilogy; Talking to a Stranger; Fathers and Families; Jewel in the Crown (Internat. Emmy Award, BAFTA Best Series Dir Award, BAFTA Desmond Davis Award, 1984; Peabody Award, 1985; Primetime Emmy Award, 1985); Ashenden, 1991; Unnatural Pursuits, 1992 (Internat. Emmy Award, 1993); Peacock Spring, 1996; A Dance to the Music of Time, 1997. Best Play direction award, SFTA, 1969. *Recreations:* photography, bird watching. *Address:* c/o Whitehall Artists, 125 Gloucester Road, SW7 4TE. *T:* (020) 7244 8466. *Club:* Garrick.

MORAN, 2nd Baron *cr* 1943; **Richard John McMoran Wilson,** KCMG 1981 (CMG 1970); *b* 22 Sept. 1924; *er s* of 1st Baron Moran, MC, MD, FRCP, and Dorothy (*d* 1983), MBE, *d* of late Samuel Felix Dufton, DSc; *S* father, 1977; *m* 1948, Shirley Rowntree Harris; two *s* one *d*. *Educ:* Eton; King's Coll., Cambridge. Served War of 1939–45; Ord. Seaman in HMS Belfast, 1943; Sub-Lt RNVR in Motor Torpedo Boats and HM Destroyer Oribi, 1944–45. Foreign Office, 1945; Third Sec., Ankara, 1948; Tel-Aviv, 1950; Second Sec., Rio de Janeiro, 1953; First Sec., FO, 1956; Washington, 1959; FO 1961; Counsellor, British Embassy in S Africa, 1965; Head of W African Dept, FCO, 1968–73, concurrently Ambassador to Chad (non-resident), 1970–73; Ambassador to Hungary, 1973–76, to Portugal, 1976–81; High Comr in Canada, 1981–84. Cross Bencher, H of L, 1984–; Mem., Industry sub cttee, 1984–86, Envmt sub cttee, 1986–91, Agric. sub cttee, 1991–95, 1997–, EC Cttee; sub cttee on the 1996 Inter-governmental Conf., 1995–96; Mem. Science and Technol. Cttee sub cttees on scientific base of Nature Conservancy Council, 1990, on fish stocks, 1995; Chm., All Party Parly Conservation Gp, 1992–2000 (Vice-Chm., 1989–92); elected Mem., H of L, 1999. Vice-Chm., Atlantic Salmon Trust, 1988–95 (Mem. Management Cttee, 1984–; Vice-Pres., 1995–); Chm., Fisheries Adv. Cttee for Welsh Region, Nat. Rivers Authy, 1989–94; Mem., Regl Fisheries Adv. Cttee, Welsh Water Authority, 1987–89; Pres., Welsh Salmon and Trout Angling Assoc., 1988–95, 2000–; Chm., Salmon and Trout Assoc., 1997–2000 (Exec. Vice Pres., 2000–). Chm., Wildlife and Countryside Link, 1992–95; Pres., Radnorshire Wildlife Trust, 1994–; Vice-Pres., RSPB, 1997–98 (Mem. Council, 1989–94). Grand Cross, Order of the Infante (Portugal), 1978. *Publications:* (as John Wilson): C. B.: a life of Sir Henry Campbell-Bannerman, 1973 (Whitbread Award, 1973); Fairfax, 1985. *Recreations:* fishing, fly-tying, bird-watching. *Heir: s* Hon. James McMoran Wilson [*b* 6 Aug. 1952; *m* 1980, Hon. Jane Hepburne-Scott, *y d* of Lord Polwarth, *qv*; two *s*]. *Address:* House of Lords, SW1A 0PW. *Club:* Flyfishers' (Pres., 1987–88).

See also Baron Mountevans, Hon. G. H. Wilson.

MORAN, Andrew Gerard; QC 1994; a Recorder, since 1997; *b* 19 Oct. 1953; *s* of Francis Michael Moran and Winifrede Moran; *m* 1977, Carole Jane Sullivan; six *s* one *d*. *Educ:* West Park Grammar Sch., St Helens, Lancs; Britannia Royal Naval Coll., Dartmouth; Balliol Coll., Oxford (BA Law). Called to Bar, Gray's Inn, 1976. *Recreations:* family, sport, travel. *Address:* Byrom Chambers, 12 Byrom Street, Manchester M3 4PP. *T:* (0161) 829 2100; 22 Old Buildings, Lincoln's Inn, WC2A 3UJ. *T:* (020) 7831 0222, *Fax:* (020) 7831 2239.

MORAN, Rt Rev. Mgr John, CBE 1985; Principal RC Chaplain and Vicar General (Army), 1981–85; *b* 3 Dec. 1929; *s* of Thomas Moran and Gertrude May (*née* Sheer). *Educ:* De La Salle Coll., Sheffield; Ushaw Coll., Durham. Ordained Priest, Leeds Diocese, 1956; Curate, Dewsbury, 1956–60; Prison Chaplain, Armley, 1960–61; commissioned Army Chaplain, 1961; service in BAOR, Singapore, Malaya, Hong Kong, UK; Chaplain, RMA Sandhurst, 1968–70, Staff Chaplain, 1970–71; Senior Chaplain, HQ BAOR, 1977–79, and HQ UKLF, 1979–80. *Recreations:* music, rivers, clocks.

MORAN, Air Vice-Marshal Manus Francis; Royal Air Force, retired; *b* 18 April 1927; *s* of John Thomas Moran and Katherine Mary (*née* Coyle); *m* 1955, Maureen Elizabeth Martin, *o d* of Martin Dilks; one *s* three *d* (and one *s* decd). *Educ:* Mount St Joseph Abbey, Roscrea; University College Dublin (MB ChB, BAO 1952; MCh 1964); DLO, RCP and RCS, 1963. St Vincent's Hosp., Dublin, 1952; GP, Lutterworth, 1953–54; joined RAF 1954; Department of Otorhinolaryngology: served London, 1955–56; Wroughton, 1956–58; Weeton, 1958–59; Akrotiri, 1959–61; Halton, 1963–65; Consultant in ORL, RAF, 1965; served Changi, Singapore, 1965–68; Vis. Consultant, Johore Bahru Gen. Hosp., 1966–68; Nocton Hall, 1968–75; Wegberg, 1975–78; Wroughton, 1978–83; Consultant Adviser in ORL (RAF), 1983–88; Dean of Air Force Medicine, 1988–90; Sen. Consultant, RAF, 1990–91; Civilian Consultant in ORL, RAF Hosp., Wroughton, 1991–95. QHP, 1988–91. Lectr in ORL, IAM Farnborough, for Dip. in Aviation medicine, RCP, 1983–88. Consultant: Nuffield Hosp., Leicester, 1992–2000; Met. Police, 1994–. Chm., Gen. Cttee, 8th British Acad. Conf. in ORL, 1987–91. Member: Irish Otological Soc.; Midland Inst. of Otology (Vice-Pres., 1971, 1975); Otology Section, RSM (Vice-Pres., Section of Laryngology, 1988–91, Pres., 1991–92); Council, British Assoc. of Otolaryngologists, 1983–88; Joseph Soc., BMA; BS Cttee on Auditory Alarms in med. monitoring equipment, 1983–88; Bd, Co-operation North, 1992–97. Chm., Marston Meysey Charitable Trust, 1989–91 (Vice-Chm., 1987–89); Special Trustee, Royal Nat. Throat, Nose and Ear Hosp., 1993–99. Hon. FRCSI 1991. Liveryman, Apothecaries' Soc. (Chm., Livery Cttee, 1994–96); Freeman, City of London. CStJ 1990. Med. Soc. (UCD) Gold Medal, 1951; Lady Cade Medal, RCS, 1980. *Publications:* Upper Respiratory Problems in Yellow Nail Syndrome (jtly), 1976; contribs to learned jls on ORL applied to aviation medicine, ureamic rhinitis, vestibular dysfunction, acoustic trauma and hearing conservation. *Recreations:* preservation of rural amenities, walking, poetry, theology, power boating. *Address:* The Old Forge House, Marston Meysey, Cricklade, Wilts SN6 6LQ. *T:* (01285) 810511. *Club:* Royal Air Force.

MORAN, Margaret; MP (Lab) Luton South, since 1997; *b* 24 April 1955; *d* of Patrick John, (Jack), Moran and Mary (*née* Murphy). *Educ:* Birmingham Univ. (BSocSc). Dir, Housing for Women, 1987–97. Mem., Lewisham BC, 1984–96 (Chairman: Housing Cttee, 1985–91; Direct Lab. Cttee, 1991; Leader, 1995–96). Dep. Chm., AMA, 1994 (Chm., Housing Cttee, 1992). Contested (Lab) Carshalton and Wallington, 1992. PPS to Minister for Cabinet Office, 1999–. Member: NI Select Cttee, 1997–98; Public Admin. Select Cttee, 1999. *Address:* House of Commons, SW1A 0AA. *T:* (020) 7219 5049.

MORAUTA, Hon. Sir Mekere, Kt 1991; MP (People's Democratic Movement) for Port Moresby North-West, Papua New Guinea, since 1997; Prime Minister, and Minister for Treasury, Papua New Guinea, since 1999; *b* 12 June 1946; *s* of Morauta Hasu and Morikoai Elavo; *m* Roslyn; two *s*. *Educ:* Univ. of Papua New Guinea (BEcon); Flinders Univ., SA. Res. Officer (Manpower Planning), Dept of Labour, 1971; Economist, Office of the Economic Advr, 1972; Sec. for Finance, Govt of PNG, 1973–82; Man. Dir, PNG Banking Corp., 1983–92; Gov., Bank of Papua New Guinea, 1993–94; Executive Chairman: Delta Seafoods, 1994–97; Morauta and Associates (Publishing), 1994–97. Minister: for Planning and Implementation, PNG, 1997–98; for Fisheries and Marine Resources, 1998–99. Chm., Nat. Airline Commn, 1992–94. Mem. Bd, Angco; formerly Director: Highlands Gold (PNG); PNG Associated Industries; Thomas Nationwide Transport (PNG); James Barnes PNG; numerous public and commercial bodies. Former Mem. Fund Raising Cttees, Salvation Army and Red Cross. Hon. DTech Univ. of Technology, PNG, 1987; Hon. DEc PNG, 2001. *Publications:* numerous papers on economic and allied subjects. *Address:* Office of the Prime Minister, PO Box 639, Waigani, NCD, Papua New Guinea. *T:* 3277489, *Fax:* 3277328.

MORAY, 20th Earl of, *cr* 1562; **Douglas John Moray Stuart;** Lord Abernethy and Strathearn, 1562; Lord Doune, 1581; Baron of St Colme, 1611; Baron Stuart (GB), 1796; *b* 13 Feb. 1928; *e s* of 19th Earl of Moray and Mabel Helen Maud Wilson (*d* 1968); *S* father, 1974; *m* 1964, Lady Malvina Murray, *er d* of 7th Earl of Mansfield and Mansfield; one *s* one *d*. *Educ:* Trinity Coll., Cambridge (BA), FLAS 1958. *Heir: s* Lord Doune, *qv*. *Address:* Doune Park, Doune, Perthshire FK16 6HA. *T:* (01786) 841333; Darnaway Castle, Forres, Moray. *Club:* New (Edinburgh).

MORAY, ROSS AND CAITHNESS, Bishop of, since 1999; **Rt Rev. John Michael Crook;** *b* 11 June 1940; *s* of late John Hadley Crook and Ada Crook; *m* 1965, Judith Christine Barber; one *s* three *d*. *Educ:* William Hulme's GS, Manchester; St David's Coll., Lampeter (BA 1962); Coll. of the Resurrection, Mirfield. Ordained deacon, 1964, priest, 1965; Curate: Horninglow, 1964–66; Bloxwich, 1966–70; Rector: St Michael, Inverness, 1970–78; St John, Inverness, 1974–78; Aberfoyle, and Callander, and Doune, 1978–87; Bridge of Allan, 1987–99; Canon, St Ninian's Cathedral, Perth, 1985–99. Diocesan Synod

Clerk, St Andrews, 1997–99. *Recreation:* bird-watching. *Address:* Diocesan Office, 11 Kenneth Street, Inverness IV3 5NR. *T:* and *Fax:* (01463) 226255; 1 Burn Road, Inverness IV2 4NG. *T:* (01463) 231059; *e-mail:* bishop@moray.anglican.org.

MORAY, ROSS AND CAITHNESS, Dean of; *see* Hickford, Very Rev. M. F.

MORCOM, Christopher; QC 1991; *b* 4 Feb. 1939; *s* of late Dr Rupert Morcom and Mary Morcom (*née* Carslake); *m* 1966, Diane, *d* of late Jose Antonio Toledo and Winifred Anne (*née* Wardlaw); one *s* two *d*. *Educ:* Sherborne Sch.; Trinity Coll., Cambridge (BA Hons 1961; MA 1964). Called to the Bar, Middle Temple, 1963 (Cert. Honour, Astbury Scholar; Bencher, 1996); Barrister, Mauritius, 1979–. Member: Senate, Law Soc. Jt Wking Party on Intellectual Property Law, 1976–; Standing Adv. Cttee on Industrial Property, 1990–. Chm., Competition Law Assoc., 1985–99. Pres., Ligue Internationale du Droit de la Concurrence, 1996–98 (Vice Pres., 1994–96; Hon. Pres., 2000). Chm., Bar Musical Soc., 1991–. *Publications:* Service Marks: a guide to the new law, 1987; A Guide to the Trade Marks Act 1994, 1994; (jtly) The Modern Law of Trade Marks, 2000; legal articles in Law Soc. Gazette, Counsel, European Intellectual Property Rev. *Recreations:* music, walking. *Address:* Hogarth Chambers, 5 New Square, Lincoln's Inn, WC2A 3RJ. *T:* (020) 7404 0404. *Club:* Athenæum.

MORDA EVANS, Raymond John; *see* Evans.

MORDAUNT, Sir Richard (Nigel Charles), 14th Bt *cr* 1611; (does not use the title at present); *b* 12 May 1940; *s* of Lt-Col Sir Nigel John Mordaunt, 13th Bt, MBE, and Anne (*d* 1980), *d* of late Arthur F. Tritton; *S* father, 1979; *m* 1964, Myriam Atchia; one *s* one *d*. *Educ:* Wellington. *Heir: s* Kim John Mordaunt, *b* 11 June 1966.

MORDUE, Richard Eric; Director of Economics and Statistics, Ministry of Agriculture, Fisheries and Food, 1989–96, retired; *b* 14 June 1941; *s* of Ralph Yielder Mordue and Helen Mary Mordue; *m* 1979, Christine Phillips; one *s* one *d*. *Educ:* Royal Grammar Sch., Newcastle upon Tyne; King's Coll., Univ. of Durham (BSc); Michigan State Univ. (MS). Joined MAFF as Asst Economist, 1964; Sen. Economic Advr, 1978; Head of Horticulture Div., 1982. *Recreations:* golf, bridge.

MORE, Norman, FRICS; Managing Director, Redditch Development Corporation, 1979–85; *b* 20 Dec. 1921; *s* of Herbert and Anna More; *m* 1952, Kathleen Mary Chrystal; two *s* one *d*. *Educ:* Royal High Sch., Edinburgh; Edinburgh Univ. FRICS 1970 (ARICS 1951). Served in Royal Engineers, Middle East, N Africa, Italy, Greece and Germany, Major, 1941–48. Surveyor, Directorate of Lands and Accommodation, Min. of Works, 1948–58; Sen. Valuer, City Assessor's Office, Glasgow Corporation, 1958–63; Valuation and Estates Officer, East Kilbride Development Corp., 1963–65; Chief Estates Officer, Redditch Development Corp., 1965–79. Consultant Chartered Surveyor, to Grimley J. R. Eve, London and Birmingham, 1985–90. Mem., W Midlands Regl Bd, TSB Gp, 1984–89. Chairman, West Midlands Br., Royal Instn of Chartered Surveyors, 1974–75. Chm., Friendship Project for Children, 1992–99. *Publications:* press articles and contribs to jls. *Recreations:* music, sport. *Address:* Mead Cottage, 192 Loxley Road, Stratford-upon-Avon, Warwickshire CV37 7DU. *T:* (01789) 293763. *Club:* East India, Devonshire, Sports and Public Schools.

MORE-MOLYNEUX, James Robert, OBE 1983; DL; Vice Lord-Lieutenant of Surrey, 1983–96; *b* 17 June 1920; *s* of Brig. Gen. Francis Cecil More-Molyneux-Longbourne, CMG, DSO and Gwendoline Carew More-Molyneux; *m* 1948, Susan Bellinger; one *s*. *Educ:* Eton; Trinity Hall, Cambridge. War service in 4/7th Royal Dragoon Guards and 14th PWO The Scinde Horse, 1941–46; Founder Chm., Guildway Ltd, 1947–85 (introduced first manufactured timber frame houses with brick cladding to UK, 1960); founded Loseley Co-Partnership, 1950; Chm., Loseley Park Farms, 1950–92; opened Loseley House to public, 1950–; founded Loseley Dairy Products, 1967; part-time Dir, Seeboard, 1975–84. Founder: Loseley & Guildway Charitable Trust, 1973; Loseley Christian Trust, 1983. Mem. Exec. Cttee, Industrial Participation Assoc., 1952–77. Lay Pastoral Asst, 1986–. High Sheriff of Surrey, 1974; DL Surrey 1976. Bledisloe Gold Medal for Landowners, RASE, 1984. *Publications:* The Loseley Challenge, 1995; The Spark of God, 2000. *Recreations:* countryside, Christian Healing Ministry, photography, writing. *Address:* Nursery Wing, Loseley Park, Guildford, Surrey GU3 1HS. *T:* (01483) 566090. *Club:* Farmers'.

MOREAU, Jeanne; Officier, Ordre National du Mérite, 1988 (Chevalier, 1970); Officier de la Légion d'Honneur, 1991 (Chevalier, 1975); actress; *b* 23 Jan. 1928; *d* of Anatole-Désiré Moreau and Kathleen Moreau (*née* Buckley); *m* 1949, Jean-Louis Richard (marr. diss.); one *s*; *m* 1977, William Friedkin (marr. diss.). *Educ:* Collège Edgar-Quinet; Conservatoire national d'art dramatique. *Theatre:* Comédie Française, 1948–52; Théâtre National Populaire, 1953; Le Récit de la Servante Zerline, 1986–89; La Celestine, 1989; co-dir, Attila, Paris Opera, 2001; *films* include: Les amants, 1958; Les liaisons dangereuses, 1959; Le dialogue des Carmelites, 1959; Moderato cantabile, 1960; Jules et Jim, 1961; La Baie des Anges, 1962; Journal d'une femme de chambre, 1963; Viva Maria, 1965; Mademoiselle, 1965; The Sailor from Gibraltar, 1965; The Immortal Story, 1966; Great Catherine, 1967; The Bride wore Black, 1967; Monte Walsh, 1969; Chère Louise, 1971; Nathalie Granger, 1972; La Race des Seigneurs, 1974; Mr Klein, 1976; Lumière (also Dir), 1976; Le Petit Théâtre de Jean Renoir, 1976; Madame Rosa, 1978; L'Intoxe, 1980; Querelle, La Truite, 1982; L'Arbre, 1983; Sauve-toi Lola, Le Paltoquet, Le Miracule, 1986; La Nuit de l'Ocean, 1987; Ennemonde, 1988; Jour après Jour, 1988; Nikita, 1989; La Comédie d'un Jour, 1989; Anna Karamazoff, 1989; La Femme Fardée, Until the End of the World, 1990; La Vielle Qui Marchait Dans La Mer, Le Pas Suspendu de la Cigogne, The Map of the Human Heart, L'Amant, 1991; A Demain, L'Absence, 1992; Je m'appelle Victor, 1992; I Love You I Love You Not, 1995; The Proprietor, 1997; *television* plays and series: Huis Clos, BBC, 1984; The Last Seance, Granada, 1984; Le Tiroir Secret, 1985; We Shall Meet Again, BBC, 1992; The Clothes in the Wardrobe, BBC, 1993; A Foreign Field, BBC, 1993; The Great Catherine, 1994. Chm. Jury, Cannes Film Festival, 1995. Commandeur des Arts et des Lettres, 1985 (Chevalier, 1966). *Recreation:* reading. *Address:* Spica Productions, 4 square du Roule, 75008 Paris, France.

MORELAND, Claire Josephine, MA; Principal, Chetham's School of Music, since 1999; *b* 2 Aug. 1958; *d* of late Peter Alfred White and of Eileen Beatrice White (*née* Kidston); *m* 1982, John Moreland (marr. diss. 1999); one *s*. *Educ:* Devonport High Sch. for Girls; St Hugh's Coll., Oxford (MA Modern Langs, PGCE). Asst teacher, Sevenoaks Sch., 1981–84; Hd of German, Croydon High Sch. for Girls, 1984–88; Rugby School: asst teacher, 1988–92; Housemistress, 1992–97; Dep. Head, 1997–99. *Publication:* Schreib mir Bitte, 1982. *Recreations:* literature, music, finding silver linings. *Address:* Chetham's School of Music, Long Millgate, Manchester M3 1SB. *T:* (0161) 834 9644. *Clubs:* University Women's, East India.

MORELAND, Robert John; management consultant; Member, Economic and Social Committee, European Community, 1986–98 (Chairman, Regional Policy and Town and Country Planning Section, 1990–98); *b* 21 Aug. 1941; *s* of late Samuel John Moreland and Norah Mary, (Molly) (*née* Haines). *Educ:* Glasgow Acad.; Dean Close Sch., Cheltenham; Univ. of Nottingham (BA Econs); Inst. of World Affairs, Conn, and Warwick Univ. (postgrad. work). Civil Servant, Govt of NS, Canada, 1966–67, Govt of NB, 1967–72; Sen. Economist, W Central Scotland Planning Study, 1972–74; Management Consultant, Touche Ross and Co., London, 1974–; Consultant: Westminster and City Conferences Ltd, 1985–; Strategy Network Internat., 1988–93; Prima Europe, 1993–98; Sancroft Internat., 1999–. Mem. for Knightsbridge, Westminster City Council, 1990–98 (Chief Whip, 1993–94; Chm. of Envmt, 1994–95; Chm., Planning and Envmt, 1995–97). Contested (C): Pontypool, Oct. 1974; GLA, 2000. Mem. (C) Staffs, European Parlt, 1979–84, contested same seat, 1984; Chm., Eur. Cttee, Bow Gp, 1977–78; Vice-Chm., Conservative Gp for Europe, 1985–88. Dep. Chm., London Europe Soc., 1998–. Dir, Albert Meml Trust, 1997–2000. *Publications:* Climate Change; contrib. to Crossbow. *Recreations:* tennis, ski-ing, watching cricket and Rugby, golf. *Address:* 7 Vauxhall Walk, SE11 5JT. *T:* (020) 7582 2613. *Club:* Royal Automobile.

MORENO RAZO, Alma-Rosa; Ambassador of Mexico to the Court of St James's, since 2001; *b* 9 Jan. 1952; *d* of Eva Razo de Moreno; *m* Alfredo Monreno-Ruiz; three *d*. *Educ:* Instituto Tecnológico Autónomo de México (BA Econs 1972); El Colegio de México (MEc 1977); Univ. of NY. Under-Dir-Gen. for Income Policy, Min. of Finance and Public Credit, 1986–87; Exec. Dir for Reconstruction and Syndicated Loans, Multibanco Comermex, 1987–88; Dir Gen. for Income Policy, Min. of Finance and Public Credit, 1988–93; Dep. Dir for Planning, Promotion and Tech. Assistance, Nat. Bank of Public Works and Services, 1993–95; Ministry of Finance and Public Credit: Adviser: to Minister of State for Income Matters, Feb.–Dec. 1995; to Sec. of State for Finance and Public Credit, 1996–97; Hd, Liaison Unit with Congress, 1997–98; Co-ordinator Gen. for Income and Tax Policy, 1998–99; Pres., Nat. Service for Tax Admin, 1999–2000. Vis. Prof., Centre for Res. and Econ. Studies, Mexico City, 2000–01. *Address:* Mexican Embassy, 42 Hertford Street, Mayfair, W1J 7JR.

MORETON, family name of **Earl of Ducie**.

MORETON, Lord; James Berkeley Moreton; *b* 6 May 1981; *s* and *heir* of 7th Earl of Ducie, *qv*.

MORETON, Sir John (Oscar), KCMG 1978 (CMG 1966); KCVO 1976; MC 1944; HM Diplomatic Service, retired; *b* 28 Dec. 1917; *s* of Rev. C. O. Moreton; *m* 1945, Margaret Katherine, *d* of late Sir John Fryer, KBE, FRS; three *d*. *Educ:* St Edward's Sch., Oxford; Trinity Coll., Oxford (MA). War Service with 99th (Royal Bucks Yeomanry) Field Regt RA, 1939–46: France, Belgium, 1940; India, Burma, 1942–45. Colonial Office, 1946; Private Sec. to Perm. Under-Sec. of State, 1949–50; seconded to Govt of Kenya, 1953–55; Private Sec. to Sec. of State for Colonies (Rt Hon. Alan Lennox-Boyd), 1955–59; transf. to CRO, 1960; Counsellor, British High Commn, Lagos, 1961–64; IDC 1965; Asst Under-Sec. of State, CRO, 1965–66, CO 1966–68, FCO 1968–69; Ambassador to Vietnam, 1969–71; High Comr, Malta, 1972–74; Dep. Perm. Representative, with personal rank of Ambassador, UK Mission to UN, NY, 1974–75; Minister, British Embassy, Washington, 1975–77. Dir, Wates Foundn, 1978–87. Gentleman Usher of the Blue Rod, Order of St Michael and St George, 1979–92. Governor, St Edward's Sch., Oxford, 1980–92. Hon. DL Hanover Coll., Indiana, 1976. *Recreations:* most outdoor activities, formerly athletics (Oxford Blue and International, 880 yds, 1939). *Address:* Weston House, Leigh Place, Cobham, Surrey KT11 2HL. *Club:* Army and Navy.

MOREY, Anthony Bernard Nicholas, CBE 1993; HM Diplomatic Service, retired; *b* 6 Dec. 1936; *s* of late Bernard Rowland Morey and Madeleine Morey; *m* 1961, Agni Campbell Kerr; two *s* one *d*. *Educ:* Wimbledon Coll. Nat. service, 1955–57. FO, 1957–60; Kuwait, 1960–62; FO, 1962–65; Madras, 1965–66; FO, 1966; Tehran, 1967; Kabul, 1968–71; FCO, 1971–72; Washington, 1972–76; Zagreb, 1976–80; Lagos, 1980–83; seconded to Guinness Mahon, 1983–85; Counsellor and Consul General, Moscow, 1985–88; Dep. High Comr, Madras, 1989–91; Ambassador to Mongolia, 1991–93; Dep. High Comr, Calcutta, 1993–96. *Recreations:* gardening, music, cats. *Address:* Lattice House, Castleton, Sherborne, Dorset DT9 3SA. *Clubs:* Royal Commonwealth Society, Oriental; Royal Calcutta Turf.

MORFEY, Dr Kathryn Margaret Victoria; Consultant, Warner Goodman & Streat, since 2000 (Associate Solicitor, 1991–2000); *b* 26 May 1942; *d* of Sidney Charles Waterton and Catherine Margaret Waterton (*née* Lilley); *m* 1963, Christopher Leonard Morfey; one *d* (one *s* decd). *Educ:* Newnham Coll., Cambridge (BA 1963; MA 1968); Univ. of Southampton (PhD 1968; LLB 1977). Admitted Solicitor, 1980. Lecturer: Univ. of Bristol, 1963; Univ. of Southampton, 1967–69; Nat. Childbirth Trust Orgnr, 1970–75; solicitor in private practice, 1980–. Member: Gen. Synod, C of E, 1990–2000; Legal Adv. Commn, C of E, 1991–93; Cathedrals Fabric Commn for England, 1991–96; Cathedrals Statutes Commn, 1996–2000; Vice-Pres., Winchester Diocesan Synod, 1997–. Gov., King Alfred's Coll. of Higher Educn, 1992–99. *Recreations:* visiting other people's gardens, choral music. *Address:* Warner Goodman & Streat, 8 College Place, Southampton SO15 2FF.

MORGAN; *see* Elystan-Morgan.

MORGAN, family name of **Baron Morgan**.

MORGAN, Baron *cr* 2000 (Life Peer), of Aberdyfi in the co. of Gwynedd; **Kenneth Owen Morgan,** FBA 1983; FRHistS; Principal, then Vice-Chancellor, University College of Wales, Aberystwyth and Professor in the University of Wales, 1989–95, Emeritus Professor, 1999 (Research Professor, 1995–99); Vice-Chancellor, then Senior Vice-Chancellor, University of Wales, 1993–95; *b* 16 May 1934; *s* of David James Morgan and Margaret Morgan (*née* Owen); *m* 1973, Jane Keeler (*d* 1992); one *s* one *d*. *Educ:* University College School, London; Oriel College, Oxford (MA, DPhil 1958, DLitt 1985). University College (later University of Wales), Swansea: Lectr in History Dept, 1958–66 (Sen. Lectr, 1965–66); Hon. Fellow, 1985; Hon. Prof., 1995; Fellow and Praelector, Modern Hist. and Politics, Queen's Coll., Oxford, 1966–89 (Hon. Fellow, 1992); Faculty Lectr, 1995–. Supernumerary Fellow, Jesus Coll., Oxford, 1991–92. Amer. Council of Learned Socs Fellow, Columbia Univ., 1962–63; Visiting Professor: Columbia Univ., 1965; Univ. of S Carolina, 1972; Univ. of Witwatersrand, 1997, 1998 and 2000; Vis. Benjamin Meaker Prof., Univ. of Bristol, 2000; Vis. Lectr, Univ. of Texas, 1994, 1999. Neale Lectr, UCL, 1986; BBC (Wales) Lectr, 1995; Prothero Lectr, RHistS, 1996. Member: Bd of Celtic Studies, 1972–; Council, Nat. Library of Wales, 1991–95. Mem., H of L Select Cttee on the Constitution, 2001–. FRHistS 1964 (Mem. Council, 1983–86). Editor, Welsh History Review, 1961–; Jt Editor, 20th Century British History, 1994–99. Hon. Fellow: Univ. of Wales, Cardiff, 1997; Trinity Coll., Carmarthen, 1998. Hon. DLitt: Wales, 1997; Glamorgan, 1997. *Publications:* Wales in British Politics, 1963, 3rd edn 1980; David Lloyd George: Welsh radical as world statesman, 1963, 2nd edn 1982; Freedom or Sacrilege?, 1966; Keir Hardie, 1967; The Age of Lloyd George, 1971, 3rd edn 1978; (ed) Lloyd George: Family Letters, 1973; Lloyd George, 1974; Keir Hardie: radical and socialist, 1975 (Arts Council prize, 1976), 3rd edn 1997; Consensus and Disunity, 1979, 2nd edn 1986; (with Jane Morgan) Portrait of a Progressive, 1980; Rebirth of a Nation: Wales 1880–1980, 1981, 2nd edn 1982 (Arts Council prize, 1982); David Lloyd George, 1981; Labour in Power 1945–1951, 1984, 2nd edn 1985; (ed jtly) Welsh Society and Nationhood, 1984; (ed) The Oxford Illustrated History of Britain, 1984, new rev. edn 1999; (ed) The Sphere Illustrated History of Britain, 1985; Labour People, 1987, new edn 1992; (ed) The Oxford History of Britain, 1988; The Red Dragon and the Red Flag, 1989; The People's Peace: British History 1945–1990, 1991, new edn as The People's Peace: British History since 1945, 2001; Academic Leadership, 1991; Modern Wales: politics, places and people, 1995; Britain and Europe, 1995; Steady As She Goes, 1996; (ed) The Young Oxford History of Britain & Ireland, 1996; Callaghan: a life, 1997; (ed jtly) Crime, Protest and Police in Modern British Society, 1999; The Twentieth Century, 2000; The Great Reform Act, 2001; many articles, reviews etc. *Recreations:* music, architecture, sport, travel. *Address:* The Croft, 63 Millwood End, Long Hanborough, Witney, Oxon OX29 8BP. *T:* (01993) 881341; *e-mail:* k.morgan@online.rednet.co.uk. *Clubs:* Reform, MCC; Yr Academi Gymreig.

MORGAN OF HUYTON, Baroness *cr* 2001 (Life Peer), of Huyton in the County of Merseyside; **Sally Morgan;** Director of Political and Government Relations, Prime Minister's Office, since 2001; *b* 28 June 1959; *d* of Albert Edward Morgan and Margaret Morgan; *m* 1984, John Lyons; two *s*. *Educ:* Belvedere Girls' Sch., Liverpool; Durham Univ. (BA Geog. Hons); Univ. of London (PGCE, MA Educ.). Secondary Sch. Teacher, 1981–85; Labour Party: Student Organiser, 1985–87; Sen. Targetting Officer, 1987–93; Dir, Campaigns and Elecns, 1993–95; Head of Party Liaison for Leader of the Opposition, 1995–97; Pol Sec. to the Prime Minister, 1997–2001; Minister of State, Cabinet Office, 2001. *Recreations:* relaxing with family and friends, cooking, gardening.

MORGAN, Rt Rev. Alan Wyndham; *see* Sherwood, Bishop Suffragan of.

MORGAN, Alasdair Neil; Member (SNP) Galloway & Upper Nithsdale, Scottish Parliament, since 1999; *b* 21 April 1945; *s* of Alexander Morgan and Emily Morgan (*née* Wood); *m* 1969, Anne Gilfillan; two *d*. *Educ:* Breadalbane Acad., Aberfeldy; Univ. of Glasgow (MA Hons 1968); Open Univ. (BA Hons 1990). IT Project Manager, Lothian Reg., 1986–96; IT Consultant, W Lothian Council, 1996–97. Contested (SNP) Dumfries, 1992. MP (SNP) Galloway and Upper Nithsdale, 1997–2001. Mem., Select Cttee on Trade and Industry affairs, 1997–2001. Scottish Parliament: Mem., Rural Affairs Cttee, 1999–2000; Convenor, Justice I Cttee, 2000–01. Scottish National Party: Nat. Treas., 1983–90; Sen. Vice Convenor, 1990–91; Nat. Sec., 1992–97; Vice Pres., 1997–; Leader, Parly Gp, 1999–2001. *Recreation:* hill walking. *Address:* Nether Cottage, Crocketford, Dumfries DG2 8RA. *T:* (office) (01556) 611956.

MORGAN, Anthony Hugh, CMG 1990; HM Diplomatic Service, retired; Consul-General, Zürich, Director of British Export Promotion in Switzerland and Consul-General, Liechtenstein, 1988–91; *b* 27 March 1931; *s* of late Cyril Egbert Morgan and late Muriel Dorothea (*née* Nash); *m* 1957, Cicely Alice Voysey; two *s* one *d*. *Educ:* King's Norton Grammar Sch.; Birmingham Univ. (BA 1952). Served HM Forces (RAF Educn Br.), 1952–55. Joined HM Foreign (later Diplomatic) Service, 1956; Cairo, then Cyprus, 1956; Khartoum, 1957; FO, 1959; Saigon, 1962; Second Sec., 1963; UK Delegn to NATO, 1965; First Sec., 1968; FCO, 1969; First Sec. and Head of Chancery, Calcutta, 1973; FCO, 1976; Dep. Head of Inf. Policy Dept, 1977; Counsellor: (Information), Brussels, 1977–79; (Commercial), Copenhagen, 1979–82; Vienna, 1982–88. Comdr, Order of Dannebrog, Denmark, 1979. *Recreations:* listening to music, looking at pictures. *Club:* Royal Air Force.

MORGAN, Arthur William Crawford, (Tony Morgan); Chief Executive, Industrial Society, 1994–2000; *b* 24 Aug. 1931; *s* of Arthur James and Violet Morgan; *m* 1955, Valerie Anne Williams; three *s*. *Educ:* Hereford High Sch.; Westcliff High Sch. Chm. and Chief Exec. Officer, Purle Bros Holdings, 1964–71; Dep. Chm., Wimpey Waste Management, 1974–81; Dir, Redland plc, 1971–73; Founder and Dir, Morgan Hemingway Investment Bank, 1973–78; working in California for non-profit organisations, incl. Hunger Project and Breakthrough Foundn, 1981–84; Chm., Wistech, 1984–90; Dir, Wraytech UK, 1996–. Governor, BBC, 1972–77. Chm., Fourth Room; non-executive Director, Alexander Corp., 1990–99; Magellan; Quickheart. Sailed Olympic Games, Tokyo; Silver Medal, Flying Dutchman, 1964; Jt Yachtsman of the Year, 1965; Member: British Olympic Yachting Appeal, 1970; Royal Yachting Assoc. Council, 1968–72. Chairman: Hunger Project Trust, 1984–89; Youth at Risk, 1996– (Dir and Trustee). FRSA. *Publications:* various technical papers. *Recreations:* squash, skiing, sailing. *Address:* Bovingdon, Marlow Common, Bucks SL7 2QR. *T:* (01628) 890654; 16 Upper Wimpole Street, W1. *T:* (020) 7486 0674/2597; Haus Arbgrat, Zermatt, Switzerland. *T:* 672395. *Club:* Royal Thames Yacht.

MORGAN, Rt Rev. Barry Cennydd; *see* Llandaff, Bishop of.

MORGAN, Bill; *see* Morgan, J. W. H.

MORGAN, Brian David Gwynne, FRCS, FRCOphth; Hon. Consultant Plastic Surgeon, University College Hospital, London and Mount Vernon Hospital (Consultant Plastic Surgeon, 1972–98); *b* 2 March 1935; *s* of Brig. John Gwynne Morgan and Ethel Lilian (*née* Bloomer); *m* 1962, Sally Ann Lewis; one *s* two *d*. *Educ:* Wycliffe Coll., Glos; University College Hosp., London (MB BS). FRCS 1963; FRCOphth 1995. University College Hospital: pre-registration house appts, 1959–61; Casualty Officer, 1961; Registrar in Surgery, St Richard's Hosp., Chichester, 1962–64; Registrar in Surgery, 1964–66, Sen. Registrar, 1967, UCH; Plastic Surgery Registrar and Sen. Registrar, Mt Vernon Hosp., 1967–70; Consultant Plastic Surgeon, Shotley Bridge, Durham, 1970–72. Mem. Council, RCS, 1991–99. Fellow, UCL, 1992. *Publication:* Essentials of Plastic and Reconstructive Surgery, 1986. *Recreations:* water-colour painting, sailing, jazz trombone. *Address:* Stockers House, Stockers Farm Road, Rickmansworth, Herts WD3 1NZ. *T:* (01923) 773922, *Fax:* (01923) 773754; *e-mail:* bmorgan@mailbox.co.uk.

MORGAN, Rear-Adm. Brinley John, CB 1972; *b* 3 April 1916; *s* of Thomas Edward Morgan and Mary Morgan (*née* Parkhouse); *m* 1945, Margaret Mary Whittles; three *s*. *Educ:* Abersychan Grammar Sch.; University Coll., Cardiff (BSc 1937). Entered Royal Navy as Instr Lt, 1939. Served War of 1939–45: Cruisers Emerald and Newcastle, 1939–41; Aircraft Carrier Formidable, 1941–43; Naval Weather Service (Admty Forecast Section), 1943–45. Staff of C-in-C Medit., 1945–48; HQ, Naval Weather Service, 1948–50; Staff of Flag Officer Trg Sqdn in HM Ships Vanguard, Indefatigable and Implacable, 1950–52; Instr Comdr, 1951; Lectr, RN Coll., Greenwich, 1952–54; Headmaster, RN Schools, Malta, 1954–59; Instr Captain, 1960; Staff of Dir, Naval Educn Service, 1959–61 and 1963–64; Sen. Officers' War Course, 1961; HMS Ganges, 1961–63; Dean, RN Engineering Coll., Manadon, 1964–69; Instr Rear-Adm., 1970; Dir, Naval Educn Service, 1970–75, retired. Freeman, City of London, 1982.

MORGAN, Bruce; District Judge (Magistrates' Courts) (formerly Stipendiary Magistrate), West Midlands, since 1989; *b* 30 March 1945; *s* of Francis William Morgan, DFC, and Phyllis Marie Morgan; *m* 1988, Sandra Joy Beresford; twin *d*. *Educ:* Oswestry School; Open Univ. (BA 1994). Solicitor of Supreme Court. Articled Clerk, Stourbridge, Worcs, 1964–69; Asst Solicitor, London, SE10, 1969–72; Partner with Lickfolds Wiley & Powles, 1973–86. Member: London Criminal Courts Solicitors Assoc. Cttee, 1971–73; Criminal Law Cttee, Westminster Law Soc., 1981–86; No 14 Area Regl Duty Solicitors Cttee, 1986–87; Metropolitan Stipendiary Magistrate, 1987–89. Member: Birmingham Magistrates' Court Cttee, 1990–93; Birmingham Magistrates' Bench Cttee, 1990–; Midland Mem., Nat. Council of Dist Judges (Magistrates' Courts) (formerly Jt Council of Stipendiary Magistrates), 1995–. Member: British Acad. of Forensic Sci., 1970; Legal Medico Soc., 1970–; Our Soc., 1994–. Vice Chm., Cleobury North PCC, 1996–. Mem., Ludlow Rotary Club, 1969–98; Chm., Greenwich Round Table, 1983–84. Governor, Oswestry Sch., 1996– (Vice Chm., 1996–2000). *Publications:* various articles in legal journals. *Recreations:* tennis, cricket, gardening, attending auctions, breeding English butterflies, cooking. *Address:* c/o Birmingham Magistrates' Court, Steelhouse Lane, Birmingham B6 6QJ.

MORGAN, Vice-Adm. Sir (Charles) Christopher, KBE 1996; Director General Chamber of Shipping, since 1997; *b* 11 March 1939; *s* of late Captain Horace Leslie Morgan, CMG, DSO, RN and Kathleen Hilda Morgan; *m* 1970, Susan Caroline Goodbody; three *d*. *Educ:* Clifton College; BRNC Dartmouth. MRIN 1989. Joined RN, 1957; served Brunei, 1962–66; HMS Greatford in Comd, 1966; Specialist Navigation Course, 1967; HMS Eskimo in Comd, 1976; NDC 1978; Comdr Sea Training, 1979; MoD, 1981–83; RCDS, 1984; Captain 5th Destroyer Sqdn (HMS Southampton), 1985–87; Staff, Jt Service Defence Coll., 1987–89; Naval Sec., 1990–92; Flag Officer, Scotland, Northern England and NI, 1992–96. Younger Brother of Trinity House, 1977. Gov., Clifton Coll., 1994–. Chm. Trustees, Royal Naval Benevolent Soc., 1996–; Gov., Tancred Soc., 1996–. Freeman, Co. of Master Mariners, 1999; Liveryman, Shipwrights' Co., 2000. FIMgt; FRIN 1996; MInstD 1996. *Recreations:* golf, tennis, Rugby, wine, gardening. *Address:* Chamber of Shipping, 12 Carthusian Street, EC1M 6EZ; c/o Lloyds TSB, 75 Cheap Street, Sherborne, Dorset. *Clubs:* Army and Navy; Royal North Devon Golf, Sherborne Golf.

MORGAN, Rt Rev. Christopher Heudebourck; *see* Colchester, Area Bishop of.

MORGAN, Clifford Isaac, CVO 1986; OBE 1977; Head of Outside Broadcasts Group, BBC Television, 1975–87; *b* 7 April 1930; *m* 1955, Nuala Martin (*d* 1999); one *s* one *d*. *Educ:* Tonyrefail Grammar School, South Wales. Played International Rugby Union for Wales, British Lions and Barbarians. Joined BBC, 1958, as Sports Organiser, Wales; Editor, Sportsview and Grandstand, 1961–64; Producer, This Week, 1964–66; freelance writer and broadcaster, 1966–72; Editor, Sport Radio, 1972–74; Head of Outside Broadcasts, Radio, 1974–75; Presenter, Sport on 4, 1987–98. President: London Glamorgan Soc., 1974–; Welsh Sports Assoc. for Mental Handicap, 1988–; Wales Council for the Disabled, 1990–; London Welsh Male Voice Choir, 1990–; Welsh Rugby Internats Benevolent Assoc., 2001–; Welsh Pres., Cystic Fibrosis Res. Trust, 1987–97; Vice-President: Sequal, 1976–96; Nat. Children's Home, 1987–; London Welsh Trust, 1999–. Chm., Saints and Sinners Club, 1984–85. Hon. Fellow, Polytechnic of Wales, 1989. Hon. MA Wales, 1988; DUniv: Keele, 1989; Central England, 1998; Hon. LLD Bristol, 1996. *Recreation:* music. *Address:* 34 Kensington Mansions, Trebovir Road, SW5 9TQ.

MORGAN, (David) Dudley; retired from Theodore Goddard & Co., Solicitors, 1983; *b* 23 Oct. 1914; *y s* of Thomas Dudley Morgan; *m* 1948, Margaret Helene, *o d* of late David MacNaughton Duncan, Loanhead, Midlothian; two *d*. *Educ:* Swansea Grammar Sch.; Jesus Coll., Cambridge (MA, LLM). War Service with RAF in Intell. Br., UK, 1940–42 and Legal Br., India, 1942–46; Wing Comdr 1945. Admitted Solicitor, 1939, with Theodore Goddard & Co.; Partner 1948; Senior Partner, 1974–80; Consultant, 1980–83. *Recreation:* gardening. *Address:* St Leonard's House, St Leonard's Road, Nazeing, Waltham Abbey, Essex EN9 2HG. *T:* (01992) 892124. *Club:* Carlton.

MORGAN, David Gethin; County Treasurer, Avon County Council, 1973–94; *b* 30 June 1929; *s* of Edgar and Ethel Morgan; *m* 1955, Marion Brook. *Educ:* Jesus Coll., Oxford (MA Hons English). CPFA, FInstAM(AdvDip). Graduate Accountancy Asst, Staffordshire CC, 1952–58; Computer Systems Officer, Sen. O&M Officer, Cheshire CC, 1958–62; County Management Services Officer, Durham CC, 1962–65; Leicestershire CC: Asst County Treasurer, 1965–68; Dep. County Treasurer, 1968–73. Chm., Local Govt Finance Exec., CIPFA, 1991–92 (Vice Chm., 1987–91); Pres., Soc. of County Treasurers in England and Wales, 1988–89. Mem. Bd, UK Transplant Support Services Authy, 1996–. Hon. Freeman, City of London, 1989. Hon. MA UWE, 1994. *Publication:* Vol. XV Financial Information Service (IPFA). *Recreations:* local history, church architecture, tai chi. *Address:* 6 Wyecliffe Road, Henleaze, Bristol, BS9 4NH. *T:* (0117) 962 9640.

MORGAN, His Honour (David) Glyn; a Circuit Judge, 1984–2001; *b* 31 March 1933; *s* of late Dr Richard Glyn Morgan, MC, and Nancy Morgan; *m* 1959, Ailsa Murray Strang; three *d*. *Educ:* Mill Hill Sch.; Merton Coll., Oxford (MA). Called to Bar, Middle Temple, 1958; practised Oxford Circuit, 1958–70; Wales and Chester Circuit, 1970–84. A Recorder of the Crown Court, 1974–84. 2nd Lieut, The Queen's Bays, 1955; Dep. Col, 1st The Queen's Dragoon Guards, 1976. An Hon. Pres., Royal Nat. Eisteddfod of Wales, Casnewydd, 1988. *Recreations:* fishing, Rugby football, gardening. *Clubs:* Cavalry and Guards; Cardiff and County (Cardiff).

MORGAN, Sir David John H.; *see* Hughes-Morgan.

MORGAN, David Leslie; Chairman, M&G Group plc, 1997–98; *b* 23 Dec. 1933; *s* of Captain Horace Leslie Morgan, CMG, DSO, RN and Kathleen Hilda Morgan (*née* Bellhouse); *m* 1965, Clare Jean Lacy; one *s* one *d*. *Educ:* Clifton Coll., Bristol; University Coll., Oxford (BA Hons PPE 1957). Worked in FE, for Shell, and later stockbroking in Malaysia, 1957–65; banking and investment management, Deltec Internat., London and NY, 1965–70; Dir, E. D. Sassoon, 1970–72; M&G Group, 1972–98: Dir, 1973–91, Man. Dir, 1991–95, Chm., 1995–97, M&G Investment Management; Dep. Gp Man. Dir, 1991–94; Dep. Chm. and Man. Dir, 1994–97. MSI 1993. FRSA 1993. *Recreations:* walking, wine, theatre. *Address:* 6 Palace Green, W8 4QA. *Clubs:* Royal Automobile; Royal North Devon Golf; Royal Mid Surrey Golf.

MORGAN, David Thomas; land and development consultant; *b* 22 Jan. 1946; *s* of Janet Catherine and Noel David Morgan; *m* 1968, Quita Valentine; two *d*. *Educ:* Alleyne's Grammar School, Stevenage; Univ. of Newcastle upon Tyne (BA Hons Land Use Studies 1968). MRTPI 1971. Somerset CC, 1968–70; Worcs CC, 1970–71; Peterborough Develt Corp., 1971–81; Housing Develt Manager, 1981–85, Dir, Planning Services, 1985–87, LDDC; Chief Exec., Black Country Develt Corp., 1987–98. Mem., Inland Waterways Amenity Adv. Council, 1997–. *Recreations:* Rugby football, drama. *Address:* 3 Riverside Court, Caunsall, near Kidderminster, Worcs DY11 5YW. *T:* (01562) 851688.

MORGAN, Prof. David Vernon, PhD, DSc; FREng; Professor of Microelectronics, since 1985, and Head of Cardiff School of Engineering, since 1995, University of Wales Cardiff; *b* 13 July 1941; *s* of late David Vernon Grenville Morgan and Isabel Lovina Benson Williams (formerly Morgan; *née* Emanuel); *m* 1965, Jean Anderson; one *s* one *d*. *Educ:* UCW, Aberystwyth (BSc); Gonville and Caius Coll., Cambridge (PhD); Leeds Univ. (DSc). CPhys, FInstP; FIEE; FREng (FEng 1966). Fellow, Univ. of Wales, at Cavendish Labs, Cambridge, 1966–68; Harwell Fellow, AERE, 1968–70; University of Leeds: Lectr, 1970–77; Sen. Lectr, 1977–80; Reader, 1980–85; Head of Electronics, UWCC, later Univ. of Wales Cardiff, 1988–94. Editor, Solid State Devices and Circuits series, 1975–; Founding Editor, Design and Measurement in Electronic Engineering series, 1986–. FCGI 1998. *Publications:* Channelling Theory Observation and Application, 1971; Solid State Electronics, 1972; An Introduction to Semiconductor Microtechnology, 1983, 2nd edn 1990; more than 200 papers in learned jls. *Recreations:* Rugby, golf, hill walking, yoga. *Address:* Cardiff School of Engineering, Cardiff University, Queen's Buildings, Newport Road, Cardiff CF24 0YF. *T:* (029) 2087 4424.

MORGAN, David Wynn; His Honour Judge David Wynn Morgan; a Circuit Judge, since 2000; *b* 18 April 1954; *s* of Arthur Islwyn Lewis Morgan and Mary Morgan (*née* Wynn); *m* 1982, Marian Eléna Lewis; one *s* one *d*. *Educ:* Kingswood Sch., Bath; Balliol Coll., Oxford (BA Jurisprudence). Called to the Bar, Gray's Inn, 1976; practised on Wales and Chester Circuit, 1977–2000; Asst Recorder, 1991–95, Recorder, 1995–2000. *Recreations:* music, reading, being in Pembrokeshire. *Address:* The Crown Court, Cathays Park, Cardiff CF1 3PG. *Club:* Cardiff Golf.

MORGAN, Derec Llwyd, DPhil, DLitt; Vice-Chancellor and Principal, University of Wales, Aberystwyth, since 1995; Senior Vice-Chancellor, University of Wales, since 2001; *b* 15 Nov. 1943; *s* of Ewart Lloyd Morgan and Margaret Morgan; *m* 1965, Jane Edwards; one *d*. *Educ:* Amman Valley GS; UCNW, Bangor (BA; Hon Fellow, 1996); Jesus Coll., Oxford (DPhil; Hon. Fellow, 1999); DLitt Wales, 1999. Res. Fellow, Univ. of Wales, 1967–69; Lectr, UCW, Aberystwyth, 1969–74; University College of North Wales, Bangor: Lectr, 1975–80, Sen. Lectr, 1980–83, Reader, 1983–89, Dept. of Welsh; Dir, Research Centre Wales, 1985–89; Prof. of Welsh, 1989–95, and Vice-Principal, 1994–95, UCW, Aberystwyth. Supernumerary Fellow, Jesus Coll., Oxford, 1997–98. Member: Bd of Celtic Studies, Univ. of Wales, 1990–96; Court and Council, Nat. Library of Wales, 1995–; Governing Body, Inst. of Grassland and Environmental Res., 1995–. Member: Gen. Adv. Council, BBC, 1984–90; Broadcasting Council for Wales, 1990–95; ITC, 1999–. Royal National Eisteddfod of Wales: Chm. Council, 1979–82, 1985–86; Chm. Exec. Cttee, Ynys Môn, 1983; Pres. Court, 1989–93. Chairman: All-Wales Cultural Forum, 1999; Celtic Film and Television Festival, 2000. Non-executive Director: PO Bd, Wales and the Marches, 1996–2000; Menter a Busnes, 1997–2000. *Publications:* Y Tân Melys, 1966; Pryderi, 1970; Barddoniaeth Thomas Gwynn Jones: astudiaeth, 1972; Kate Roberts, 1974, 2nd edn 1991; (ed) Cerddi '75, 1975; Iliad Homer, 1976; (ed) Adnabod Deg, 1977; Gwna yn Llawen, Wr Ieuanc, 1978; Y Diwygiad Mawr, 1981 (trans., The Great Awakening in Wales, 1988); Williams Pantycelyn, 1983; Pobl Pantycelyn, 1986; (ed) Glas y Nef: cerddi ac emynau John Roberts Llanfwrog, 1987; Cefn y Byd, 1987; (ed) Emynau Williams Pantycelyn, 1991; (ed) Meddwl a Dychymyg Williams Pantycelyn, 1991; Ni cheir byth wir lle bo llawer o feirdd, 1992; Charles Edwards, 1994; Y Beibl a Llenyddiaeth Gymraeg, 1998; John Roberts Llanfwrog: pregethwr, bardd, emynydd, 1999. *Recreations:* cricket, fortunes and misfortunes of Swansea City AFC, reading. *Address:* Plas Penglais, Aberystwyth, Ceredigion SY23 3DF. *Club:* Premier (Glamorgan County Cricket).

MORGAN, Dianne; *see* Edwards, D.

MORGAN, Douglas; IPFA; County Treasurer, Lancashire County Council, 1985–92; *b* 5 June 1936; *s* of late Douglas Morgan and Margaret Gardner Morgan; *m* 1960, Julia (*née* Bywater); two *s*. *Educ:* High Pavement Grammar Sch., Nottingham. IPFA 1963 (4th place in final exam. and G. A. Johnston (Dundee) Prize). Nat. Service, RAF, 1954–56. Nottingham CBC, 1952–61; Herefordshire CC, 1961–64; Berkshire CC, 1964–67; Asst Co. Treas., W Suffolk CC, 1967–70; Asst, later Dep., Co. Treas., Lindsey CC, 1970–73; Dep. Co. Treas., Lancashire CC, 1973–85. Chm., NW & N Wales Region, CIPFA, 1985–86; Pres., NW & N Wales Region, Students' Soc., CIPFA, 1989–90. Treas., Lancs Cttee, Royal Jubilee & Prince's Trust, 1985–92; Hon. Treasurer: Lancs Playing Fields Assoc., 1985–92; NW Region Library System and NW Sound Archive, 1986–92; Mem., Exec. Cttee, Lancs Union of Golf Clubs, 1998–. FRSA. *Publications:* articles for Public Finance & Accountancy and other local govt jls. *Recreations:* golf and "collecting" golf courses, jazz, playing "gypsy" in a motor caravan. *Address:* 8 Croyde Road, St Annes-on-Sea, Lancs FY8 1EX. *T:* (01253) 725808. *Club:* Fairhaven Golf (Centenary Captain, 1995–96).

MORGAN, Dudley; *see* Morgan, David D.

MORGAN, Prof. Edwin (George), OBE 1982; Titular Professor of English, University of Glasgow, 1975–80, now Emeritus; Poet Laureate for Glasgow, since 1999; *b* 27 April 1920; *s* of Stanley Lawrence Morgan and Margaret McKillop Arnott. *Educ:* Rutherglen Academy; High Sch. of Glasgow; Univ. of Glasgow. MA 1st Cl. Hons, Eng. Lang. and Lit., 1947. Served War, RAMC, 1940–46. University of Glasgow: Asst, 1947, Lectr, 1950, Sen. Lectr, 1965, Reader, 1971, in English. Vis. Prof., Strathclyde Univ., 1987–90; Hon. Prof., UCW, 1991–95. Cholmondeley Award for Poets, 1968; Hungarian PEN Meml Medal, 1972; Scottish Arts Council Book Awards, 1968, 1973, 1975, 1977, 1978, 1983, 1985, 1991 and 1992; Soros Translation Award, NY, 1985; Queen's Gold Medal for Poetry, 2000. Visual/concrete poems in many internat. exhibns, 1965–. Opera librettos (unpublished): The Charcoal-Burner, 1969; Valentine, 1976; Columba, 1976; Spell, 1979. HRSA 1997. Hon. DLitt: Loughborough, 1981; Glasgow, 1990; Edinburgh, 1991; St Andrews, 2000; Heriot-Watt, 2000; DUniv: Stirling, 1989; Waikato, 1992; MUniv Open, 1992. Order of Merit (Republic of Hungary), 1997. *Publications: poetry:* The Vision of Cathkin Braes, 1952; The Cape of Good Hope, 1955; (ed) Collins Albatross Book of Longer Poems, 1963; Starryveldt, 1965; Emergent Poems, 1967; Gnomes, 1968; The Second Life, 1968; Proverbfolder, 1969; Penguin Modern Poets 15, 1969; Twelve Songs, 1970; The Horseman's Word, 1970; (co-ed) Scottish Poetry 1–6, 1966–72; Glasgow Sonnets, 1972; Instamatic Poems, 1972; The Whittrick, 1973; From Glasgow to Saturn, 1973; The New Divan, 1977; Colour Poems, 1978; Star Gate, 1979; (ed) Scottish Satirical Verse, 1980; Poems of Thirty Years, 1982; Grafts/Takes, 1983; Sonnets From Scotland, 1984; Selected Poems, 1985; From the Video Box, 1986; Newspoems, 1987; Themes on a Variation, 1988; Tales from Limerick Zoo, 1988; Collected Poems, 1990; Hold Hands Among the Atoms, 1991; (ed) James Thomson, The City of Dreadful Night, 1993; Sweeping out the Dark, 1994; Virtual and Other Realities, 1997; Demon, 1999; New Selected Poems, 2000; *play:* A.D., a Trilogy, 2000; *prose:* Essays, 1974; East European Poets, 1976; Hugh MacDiarmid, 1976; Twentieth Century Scottish Classics, 1987; Nothing Not Giving Messages (interviews), 1990; Crossing the Border: essays in Scottish Literature, 1990; Language, Poetry, and Language Poetry, 1990; Evening Will Come They Will Sew the Blue Sail, 1991; *translations:* Beowulf, 1952; Poems from Eugenio Montale, 1959; Sovpoems, 1961; Mayakovsky, Wi the Haill Voice, 1972; Fifty Renascence Love Poems, 1975; Rites of Passage (selected poetic translations), 1976; Platen: selected poems, 1978; Master Peter Pathelin, 1983; Rostand, Cyrano de Bergerac: a new verse translation, 1992; Collected Translations, 1996; Doctor Faustus, 1999; Phaedra, 2000. *Recreations:* photography, scrapbooks, walking in cities. *Address:* 19 Whittingehame Court, Glasgow G12 0BG. *T:* (0141) 339 6260.

MORGAN, Edwin John; Director, Civil Service Selection Board, 1981–87, retired; *b* 10 Jan. 1927; *s* of Thomas Grosvenor Morgan and Florence (*née* Binmore); *m* 1954, Joyce Beryl, *o d* of Reginald and Gladys Ashurst, Bebington, Wirral; two *s* one *d*. *Educ:* Dauntsey's Sch.; St Edmund Hall, Oxford (Sen. Scholar, BA 1st Cl. Hons 1951). Served Army, Intell. Corps, Palestine and Cyprus, 1944–48. Lecteur d'anglais, Ecole normale supérieure, Paris, 1952; Asst, Dept of French Studies, Glasgow Univ., 1953; Asst Principal, Air Min., 1957, Principal, 1960; MoD, 1965; Registrar, RMCS, 1968; Asst Sec., 1970; CSD, 1971; CS Commn, 1975; Under Sec., 1980; CS Comr, 1980–87. Chm., CS Retirement Fellowship, 1987–92. FIPM 1985. *Recreations:* reading, music, swimming, domesticity. *Address:* Southcote, Petersfield Road, Ropley, Alresford, Hants SO24 0EQ. *T:* (01962) 772321. *Club:* Civil Service.

MORGAN, Eluned; *see* Morgan, M. E.

MORGAN, (Evan) Roger; Senior Clerk, Committee Office, House of Lords, since 1999; *b* 18 April 1945; *s* of late Evan and of Stella Morgan; *m* 1st, 1967 (marr. diss.); one *s* one *d*; 2nd, 1997, Lesley Greene (*née* Smith). *Educ:* Whitgift Sch., South Croydon; Battersea Coll. of Advanced Technol. Career spent within DES, then Dept for Educn, later Dept for Educn and Employment: Under Sec., Further Educn, 1991–94, Internat. Relns and Youth, 1994–95; Asst Dir, Internat. Dept for Educn and Employment, 1995–97. *Recreations:* making music, cycling, gadgets. *e-mail:* morgan.roger@talk21.com.

MORGAN, Francis Vincent; Secretary, Governing Bodies Association and Governing Bodies of Girls' Schools Association, since 1998; *b* 22 June 1936; *s* of Joseph Michael Morgan and Monica Morgan; *m* 1965, Annette Mary Tolhurst; one *s*. *Educ:* St Edward's Coll., Liverpool; Univ. of Liverpool (Oliver Lodge Prize; BSc 1958); St John's Coll., Cambridge (PGCE 1959); Chelsea Coll., Univ. of London (MEd 1974). Asst master, Stonyhurst Coll., 1959–62; various posts, Redrice Sch., Andover, 1962–68; Lectr in Physical Scis, Homerton Coll., Cambridge, 1968–70; Schs Advr, Borough of Southend-on-Sea, 1970–73; Head: Sacred Heart Sch., Tunbridge Wells, 1973–78; St Mary's Catholic Sch., Bishop's Stortford, 1978–84; Schs Officer, Archdio. Westminster, 1984–86; Dir of Educn, RC Dio. Brentwood, 1986–90; Dir, United Westminster Schs and Royal Foundn of Grey Coat Hosp., 1990–98. Mem., Indep. Schs Pension Scheme Cttee, 1996–. Governor: Stonyhurst Coll., 1986–91; New Hall Sch., Chelmsford, 1992–2001 (Chm., 1995–2001); Westminster Cathedral Choir Sch., 1998–; Sutton Valence Sch., 1998–; Trustee: St Mary's Sch., Hampstead, 1992–; United Westminster Schs, 2000–. *Recreations:* books, music, chess, gardening. *Address:* The Ancient Foresters, Bush End, Takeley, Bishop's Stortford, Herts CM22 6NN. *T:* (01279) 870632. *Club:* Athenæum.

See also J. A. Morgan.

MORGAN, (Frank) Leslie, CBE 1988 (MBE 1973); Chairman, Morgan Bros (Mid Wales) Ltd, 1959–2000; Chairman, Development Board for Rural Wales (Mid Wales Development), 1981–89 (Member, 1977–81); *b* 7 Nov. 1926; *s* of Edward Arthur Morgan and Beatrice Morgan; *m* 1962, Victoria Stoker (*née* Jeffery); one *s* two *d*. *Educ:* Llanfair Primary Sch.; Llanfair Grammar Sch.; University College of Wales, Aberystwyth (BA Econ Hons). Post graduate trainee and parts executive in motor industry, 1950–56. Chairman and President, Montgomery Conservative Assoc., 1964–81; Member, Welsh Council, 1970–79; Dep. Chm., Mid Wales New Town Development Corp., 1973–77; Director: Develt Corp. for Wales, 1981–83; Wales Adv. Bd, Abbey National (formerly Abbey National Bldg Soc.), 1982–90; Member: Welsh Development Agency, 1981–89; Wales Tourist Bd, 1982–89; Infrastructure Cttee, BTA, 1982–89; Design Council Welsh Cttee, 1981–85. Pres., Montgomeryshire Agricl Soc., 1986. Pres., Montgomery Cons. Assoc., 1989–92. Chm., Campaign for Montgomeryshire, 1997–98 (Chm. Policy Cttee, 1993–98). *Recreations:* reading, travel, jogging, swimming, cycling. *Address:* Wentworth House, Llangyniew, Welshpool, Powys SY21 9EL. *T:* (01938) 810462.

MORGAN, Gemmell; *see* Morgan, H. G.

MORGAN, Geoffrey Thomas, CB 1991; Adviser, PricewaterhouseCoopers (formerly Coopers & Lybrand), 1991–2000; Under Secretary, Cabinet Office (Office of the Minister for the Civil Service), 1985–91; *b* 12 April 1931; *s* of late Thomas Evan Morgan and Nora (*née* Flynn); *m* 1960, Heather, *d* of late William Henry Trick and of Margery Murrell Wells; two *d*. *Educ:* Roundhay Sch. National Service, Royal Signals, 1950–52; joined Civil Service, 1952; served in Mins of Supply and Aviation, 1952–65; HM Treasury, 1965–68 and 1981–83; CSD, 1968–81; seconded to Arthur Guinness Son & Co., 1970–72; Cabinet Office, 1983–91; Adviser to: World Bank in Washington, 1977–78; UN in NY, 1987–88; official missions to: People's Republic of China in Beijing, 1988, 1991; Govt of Hungary in Budapest, 1990–2000; Govt of Jamaica in Kingston, 1991; South Africa, 1991–95; Czech Republic, 1996–2000; Chile, 1998. Chm., Public Admin Cttee, WEU, 1990–91. Panel Chm., CSSB, 1991–95; Chm. Internat. Adv. Panel, CS Coll., 1998–2001. Trustee, Whitehall and Industry Gp, 1991–94. FRSA 1996. *Recreation:* winding down and spinning out. *Address:* 29 The Green, Twickenham TW2 5TU. *T:* (020) 8894 3858. *Clubs:* Athenæum; Lensbury (Teddington).

MORGAN, George Lewis Bush; Chief Registrar, Bank of England, 1978–83; *b* 1 Sept. 1925; *s* of late William James Charles Morgan and Eva Averill Morgan (*née* Bush); *m* 1949, Mary Rose (*née* Vine); three *s*. *Educ:* Cranbr Sch., Kent. Captain, Royal Sussex Regt, 1943–47. Entered Bank of England, 1947; Asst Chief Accountant, 1966; Asst Sec., 1969; Dep. Sec., 1973. Mem. Bd of Govs, Holmewood House Prep. Sch., Tunbridge Wells, 1983–98 (Chm., 1986–98). *Recreations:* golf, gardening. *Address:* Hill Top House, Five Ashes, Mayfield, East Sussex TN20 6HT. *Club:* Piltdown Golf.

MORGAN, Glyn; *see* Morgan, D. G.

MORGAN, Sir Graham, Kt 2000; Executive Director of Nursing, North West London Hospitals NHS Trust, since 1999; *b* 20 Aug. 1947; *s* of Islwyn and Phyllis Morgan; partner 1967, Raymond Willetts. *Educ:* Treorchy Secondary Modern Sch.; Llandough Hosp. (RGN 1969). Staff Nurse: Llandough Hosp., Cardiff, 1969; Royal Marsden Hosp., 1970–72; Charge Nurse, St Mary's Hosp., Paddington, 1972–74; Nursing Officer, KCH, 1974–83; Asst Dir of Nursing, St Charles' Hosp., 1983–91; Special Nurse Advr, 1991–94, Dir of Nursing and Quality, 1994–99, Central Middlesex Hosp. Consultant in Health Care, Univ. of Nottingham, 1997. Ordained priest, 1984; NSM, Holy Innocents, Hammersmith, 1990–. *Publications:* (with Amanda Layton) Nuts and Bolts of Protocols, 1998; articles in various health care jls. *Recreations:* opera, dining out. *Address:* 24 Charleville Court, Charleville Road, W14 9JG.

MORGAN, Gwyn; *see* Morgan, J. G.

MORGAN, Prof. (Henry) Gemmell; Professor of Pathological Biochemistry, University of Glasgow, 1965–88, now Professor Emeritus, and Hon. Senior Research Fellow, since 1988; *b* 25 Dec. 1922; *s* of John McIntosh Morgan, MC, MD, FRCPE, and Florence Ballantyne; *m* 1949, Margaret Duncan, BSc, MB, ChB; one *d*. *Educ:* Dundee High Sch.; Merchiston Castle Sch., Edinburgh; Univ. of St Andrews at University Coll., Dundee. BSc 1943; MB, ChB (distinction), 1946; FRCPE 1962; FRCPGlas 1968; FRCPath 1970; FRSE 1971. Res. Fellow, Endocrinology, Johns Hopkins Univ., USA, 1956–57. Hon. Consultant, Royal Hosp. for Sick Children, Glasgow, 1965–67. Hon. Consultant and Dir, Inst. of Clin. Biochem., Royal Infirmary, Glasgow, 1966–88; Chm., Med. Cttee, Royal Infirmary, Glasgow, 1984–87. Hon. Life Mem., Assoc. of Clinical Biochemists (UK), 1990 (Chm., 1982–85; Pres., 1985–87); Member: NY Acad. of Scis; British Hyperlipidaemia Assoc. Academic Advr, Univ. of London, 1970–72; External Examiner: in Biochem., Univ. of Dundee, 1974–77; Final in Pathology, Charing Cross and Westminster Med. Sch., 1985–88; UMDS of Guy's and St Thomas' Hosps, London, 1987–89; MSc and PhD Clinical Chemistry, Newcastle, 1972–74, Leeds, 1977–80, Dublin, 1979–82; Examnr in FRCS, RCPGlas, 1970–94. Chm., Scottish Br., Nutrition Soc., 1967–68. Adviser to Greater Glasgow Health Bd and Scottish Health Dept. MInstD. *Publications:* chapters; papers in medical jls on calcium, and lipoproteins. *Recreations:* golf, foreign travel, history. *Address:* Firwood House, 8 Eaglesham Road, Newton Mearns, Glasgow G77 5BG. *T:* (0141) 639 4404; *e-mail:* profmorgan@gem9.demon.co.uk. *Club:* Athenæum.

MORGAN, Hugh Marsden; His Honour Judge Hugh Morgan; a Circuit Judge, since 1995; *b* 17 March 1940; *s* of late Hugh Thomas Morgan, Cyncoed, Cardiff and Irene Morgan (*née* Rees); *m* 1967, Amanda Jane Tapley; two *s* one *d*. *Educ:* Cardiff High Sch.; Magdalen Coll., Oxford (Demy; BCL; MA Jurisp.). Called to the Bar, Gray's Inn, 1964; in practice: Midland Circuit, 1965–71; SE Circuit, 1971–95; Asst Recorder, 1983–87; Recorder, 1987–95. Member: Matrimonial Causes Rule Cttee, 1989–91; Family Proceedings Rule Cttee, 1991–93; Fees and Legal Aid Cttee, Senate and Bar Council, 1976–82. Mem., Wine Cttee, SE Circuit, 1986–88. Mem. Cttee, Family Law Bar Assoc., 1976–89. *Recreations:* gardening, reading, travel, Roman remains. *Address:* c/o Kingston County Court, St James Road, Kingston upon Thames KT1 2AD.

MORGAN, Rt Hon. (Hywel) Rhodri; PC 2000; Member (Lab) Cardiff West, since 1999 and First Minister (formerly First Secretary) for Wales, since 2000, National Assembly for Wales; *b* 29 Sept. 1939; *s* of late Thomas John and of Huana Morgan; *m* 1967, Julie Edwards (*see* Julie Morgan); one *s* two *d*. *Educ:* St John's College, Univ. of Oxford (Hons cl. 2, PPE 1961); Harvard Univ. (Masters in Govt 1963). Tutor Organiser, WEA, S Wales Area, 1963–65; Research Officer, Cardiff City Council, Welsh Office and DoE, 1965–71; Economic Adviser, DTI, 1972–74; Indust. Develt Officer, S Glamorgan County Council, 1974–80; Head of Bureau for Press and Inf., European Commn Office for Wales, 1980–87. MP (Lab) Cardiff West, 1987–2001. Opposition spokesman on: Energy, 1988–92; Welsh Affairs, 1992–97. Sec. for Economic Develt, Nat. Assembly for Wales, 1999–2000. *Publication:* Cardiff: half and half a capital, 1994. *Recreations:* long-distance running, wood carving, marine wildlife. *Address:* Lower House, Michaelston-le-Pit, Dinas Powys, South Glamorgan CF64 4HE. *T:* (home) (029) 2051 4262; (office) (029) 2022 3207. *Address:* National Assembly for Wales, Cardiff Bay, Cardiff CF99 1NA. *T:* (029) 2089 8764.

MORGAN, Janet; *see* Balfour of Burleigh, Lady.

MORGAN, Sir John (Albert Leigh), KCMG 1989 (CMG 1982); HM Diplomatic Service, retired; Chairman: East European Development Trust, since 1994; Gulf International Minerals (Vancouver), since 1997; Director, Japan Discovery Trust, since 1994; *b* 21 June 1929; *s* of late John Edward Rowland Morgan, Bridge, Kent; *m* 1st, 1961, Hon. Fionn Frances Bride O'Neill (marr. diss. 1975), *d* of 3rd Baron O'Neill, Shane's Castle, Antrim; one *s* two *d*; 2nd, 1976, Angela Mary Eleanor, *e d* of Patrick Warre Rathbone, MBE, Woolton, Liverpool; one *s* one *d*. *Educ:* Chingford County High Sch.; London School of Economics (BSc(Econ) Hons Econs and Law; Hon. Fellow, 1984). Served in Army, 1947–49: commnd 1948; interpreter with French Army, 1949. Entered Foreign Service, 1951; FO, 1951–53; 3rd Sec. and Private Sec. to HM Ambassador, Moscow, 1953–56; 2nd Sec., Peking, 1956–58; FO, 1958–63 (attended Geneva Conf. of Foreign Ministers on Berlin, 1959, and on Laos (interpreter in Russian and Chinese), 1961; interpreter for Mr Khrushchev's visit to UK, 1956, for Mr Macmillan's visit to Soviet Union, 1959, and for Summit Conf. in Paris, 1960); 1st Sec., 1960; Head of Chancery, Rio de Janeiro, 1963–64; FO, 1964–65; Chargé d'Affaires, Ulan Bator, 1965; Moscow, 1965–67; Dep. Hd, Econ. Relns Dept, subseq. Export Promotion Dept, FO, 1968; Head of Far Eastern Dept, FCO, 1970–72; Head of Cultural Relations Dept, FCO, 1972–80 (Member: Reviewing Cttee on Export of Works of Art; Fulbright Scholarship Commn; Selection Cttee, US Bicentennial Scholarships Prog.); Ambassador and Consul Gen. to Republic of Korea, 1980–83; Ambassador to Poland, 1983–86; Ambassador to Mexico, 1986–89. Man. Dir (Internat. Relations), Maxwell Communications Corp., 1989–90; Chm., Invesco (formerly Drayton) Korea Trust plc, 1993–99 (Dir, 1991); Director: The European, 1990–91; Christies, 1993–95; Invesco Europe Ltd, 1994–99; Pres., Actions Asie Emergents, Paris, 1996–2001. Pres., IFPI, 1990–93. Served on Earl Marshal's Staff for State Funeral of Sir Winston Churchill, 1965, and for Investiture of Prince of Wales, 1969. Trustee, BM, 1991–99, now Emeritus, (Mem., BM Develt Trust, 1991–). Governor, LSE, 1971–94, 1997–; Chm., LSE Foundn, 1994–97. Chairman: Anglo-Korean Soc., 1990–96; UK-Korea Forum for the Future, 1991–99; Member: Internat. Council, United World Colleges, 1990–; Internat. and Current Affairs Cttee, ESU, 1993–. Royal Philharmonic Orchestra: Dir, 1993–96; Hon. Life Mem. 1979; Chm., Development Trust, 1993–96; Vice Chm., South Bank Foundn Ltd, 1997–. FRSA; Fellow, Royal Asiatic Soc.; Hon. Life Mem., GB-China Centre. Hon. DSc (Politics) Korea Univ., 1983; Hon. LLD Mexico Acad. of Internat. Law, 1987. Order of the Aztec Eagle, 1st cl. (Mexico), 1994; Order of Diplomatic Merit, 1st cl. (Korea), 1999. *Publications:* (contrib.) Travellers' Tales, 1999; (under a pseudonym): various works of French and Chinese literary criticism. *Recreations:* ornithology, oriental art, tennis. *Address:* 41 Hugh Street, SW1V 1QJ. *T:* (020) 7821 1037; Beaumont Cottage, South Brewham, near Bruton, Somerset BA10 0JZ. *T:* (01749) 850606. *Club:* Travellers.

MORGAN, John Alfred; Director, Eleco Holdings plc, since 1997; *b* 16 Sept. 1931; *s* of late Alfred Morgan and of Lydia Amelia Morgan; *m* 1959, Janet Mary Sclater-Jones; one *d*. *Educ:* Rugeley Grammar Sch.; Peterhouse, Cambridge (BA). Investment Research, Cambridge, 1953–59; Investment Manager, S. G. Warburg & Co. Ltd, 1959–67; Director: Glyn, Mills & Co., 1967–70; Williams & Glyn's Bank Ltd, 1970–76; Rothschild Asset Management, 1976–78; Central Trustee Savings Bank Ltd, 1982–86; Zurich Life Assce Co. Ltd, 1970–87; Sealink UK Ltd, 1983–85; Caviapen Investments Ltd, 1993–97; Yamaichi Bank (UK) plc, 1994–98. Gen. Manager, British Railways Pension Funds, 1978–86; Chief Exec., IMRO, 1986–93. Chm., Post Office Users' Nat. Council, 1978–82. *Recreations:* music, contemporary art, fell walking. *Club:* Reform.

MORGAN, John Ambrose; His Honour Judge John Morgan; a Circuit Judge, since 1990; *b* 22 Sept. 1934; *s* of Joseph Michael Morgan and Monica Morgan; *m* 1970, Rosalie Mary Tyson; two *s*. *Educ:* St Edward's Coll., Liverpool; Univ. of Liverpool (Emmott Meml Scholar 1953; Alsopp Prizewinner 1953; LLB 1955). Law Soc. Finals 1957 (Local Govt Prize). Nat. Service, RAF, 1958–60. Admitted Solicitor, 1958; practised in local govt and private practice, 1960–70; called to the Bar, Gray's Inn, 1970; N Circuit, 1970–90; Dep. Stipendiary Magistrate, 1982; Asst Recorder, 1983; Recorder, 1988. Chm. of Govs, St Edward's Coll., Liverpool, 1987–95. *Recreations:* Rugby Union football (Pres., Liverpool RFU, 1980–82), golf, cricket, music, amateur operatics. *Address:* Queen Elizabeth II Law Courts, Derby Square, Liverpool L2 1XA. *T:* (0151) 473 7373. *Clubs:* Athenæum (Liverpool); Liverpool St Helen's RFC, Woolton Golf, Sefton Cricket.
See also F. V. Morgan.

MORGAN, (John) Gwyn(fryn), OBE 1999; private consultant; Head, South-East Asia, Directorate-General of External Relations, European Commission, 1995–99; Head, European Union Election Observation Team, Ivory Coast, 2000; *b* 16 Feb. 1934; *s* of Arthur G. Morgan, coal miner, and Mary Walters; two *s* two *d* from former marriages. *Educ:* Aberdare Boys' Grammar Sch.; UCW Aberystwyth. MA Classics 1957; Dip. Educn 1958. Senior Classics Master, The Regis Sch., Tettenhall, Staffs, 1958–60; Pres., National Union of Students, 1960–62; Sec.-Gen., Internat. Student Conf. (ISC), 1962–65; Head of Overseas Dept, British Labour Party, 1965–69; Asst Gen. Secretary, British Labour Party, 1969–72; Chef de Cabinet to Mr George Thomson, 1973–75; Head of Welsh Inf. Office, EEC, 1975–79; a Dir, Development Corp. for Wales, 1976–81, Hon. Consultant in Canada 1981–83; Head of EEC Press and Inf. Office for Canada, 1979–83; EEC Rep. in Turkey, 1983–86; Hd, Delgn of EEC to Israel, 1987–92; Ambassador-Head of Delegn of EC to Thailand, Vietnam, Laos, Cambodia, Myanmar and Malaysia, 1993–95. Mem., Hansard Commn on Electoral Reform, 1975–76. Head, EU Election Observation Unit, Indonesia, 1999. *Publications:* contribs to numerous British and foreign political jls. *Recreations:* cricket, Rugby football, crosswords, wine-tasting. *Address:* 14 Ravenscroft Road, Chiswick, W4 5EQ. *T:* (020) 8994 4218, *Fax:* (office) (020) 7460 7091. *Clubs:* Reform, Royal Commonwealth Society, MCC; Cardiff and County.

MORGAN, John William Harold, (Bill), CBE 1998; FREng; Chairman, Trafford Park Urban Development Corporation, 1990–98; Director: AMEC plc, 1983–91 (Chairman, 1984–88); Hill Samuel & Co., 1983–89; *b* 13 Dec. 1927; *s* of John Henry and Florence Morgan; *m* 1952, Barbara (*née* Harrison); two *d*. *Educ:* Wednesbury Boys' High Sch.; Univ. of Birmingham (BScEng, 1st Cl. Hons). FIMechE, MIEE. National Service commn with RAF, 1949–51. Joined English Electric Co., Stafford, as design engr, subseq. Chief Development Engr (Machines), 1953; Chief Develt Engr (Mechanical), 1957; Chief Engr (DC Machines), 1960; Product Div. Manager, 1962; Gen. Man., Electrical Machines Gp, 1965; Managing Director, English Electric-AEI Machines Gp (following merger with GEC/AEI), 1968; Asst Man. Dir and main board director, GEC plc, 1973–83. Chm., Staffordshire Cable, 1989–93; Dep. Chm., Petbow Holdings, 1983–86; Director: Simon Engineering, 1983–88; Pitney Bowes, 1989–92; Tekdata, 1989–; UMIST Ventures, 1989–. Additional Mem., Monopolies and Mergers Commn (Electricity Panel), 1992–98. FREng (FEng 1978; Mem. Council, 1987–90). FRSA 1988. Hon. DSc Salford, 1997. S. G. Brown award for an outstanding contrib. to promotion and development of mechanical inventions, Royal Society, 1968. *Recreations:* craft activities, particularly woodworking. *Address:* Mullion, Whitmore Heath, near Newcastle, Staffs ST5 5HT. *T:* (01782) 680 160.

MORGAN, Jonathan; Member (C) South Wales Central, National Assembly for Wales, since 1999; *b* 12 Nov. 1974; *s* of Barrie and Linda Morgan. *Educ:* Bishop of Llandaff Church in Wales Sch., Cardiff; Cardiff Univ. (LLB Hons Law & Politics; MSc Econ European Policy). European Funding Officer, Cardiff Further Educn Coll., 1998–99. FRSA 1999. *Recreations:* theatre, golf, music. *Address:* National Assembly for Wales, Cardiff Bay, Cardiff CF99 1NA. *T:* (029) 2089 8734. *Clubs:* Merthyr Conservative (Merthyr Tydfil); County Conservative (Cardiff).

MORGAN, Julie; MP (Lab) Cardiff North, since 1997; *b* 2 Nov. 1944; *d* of late Jack Edwards and of Grace Edwards; *m* 1967, Rhodri Morgan, *qv*; one *s* two *d*. *Educ:* Howell's Sch., Llandaff; KCL (BA Hons); Manchester Univ.; Cardiff Univ. (DipSocAdmin, CQSW). Sen. Social Worker, Barry, S Glam. Social Services, 1980–83; Principal Officer and Develt Officer, W Glam. CC, 1983–87; Asst Dir, Child Care, Barnados, 1987–97. Member (Lab): S Glam. Council, 1985–96; Cardiff UA, 1996–97. Contested (Lab) Cardiff N, 1992. *Address:* House of Commons, SW1A 0AA; Lower House, Michaelston-le-Pit, Dinas Powys CF64 6HE.

MORGAN, Prof. Keith John, DPhil; FRACI, FRSC; FAIM; Visiting Professor, Hiroshima University, 1995–99; *b* 14 Dec. 1929; *s* of C. F. J. Morgan and Winifred Burman (formerly Morgan, *née* Allen); *m* 1957, Hilary Chapman (marr. diss. 1999); one *d*. *Educ:* Manchester Grammar Sch.; Brasenose Coll., Oxford (MA, BSc, DPhil). Senior Research Fellow, Min. of Supply, 1955–57; ICI Res. Fellow, 1957–58; Lectr, Univ. of Birmingham, 1958–64; AEC Fellow, Purdue Univ., 1960–61; Lectr, Sen. Lectr, Prof., Dept. of Chemistry, Univ. of Lancaster, 1964–86 (Pro-Vice-Chancellor, 1973–78; Sen. Pro-Vice-Chancellor, 1978–86); Vice-Chancellor, Univ. of Newcastle, NSW, 1987–93; Prof., Univ. of Electro-Communications, Tokyo, 1993–95. Chm., Hunter Foundn for Cancer Res., 1992–93; Dep. Chm., Hunter Technol. Develt Centre, 1987–93; Member: Hunter Econ. Develt Council, 1989–93; Hunter Federal Task Force, 1991–93; Hunter Area Health Service Bd, 1992–93; Dir, Hunter Orch., 1991–93. Chm., Regl Council, AIM, 1989–93. Chm. of Govs, Newcastle Grammar Sch., 1991–93; Member: UCNS, 1980–86; Council, Lancashire Polytechnic, 1985–86. Mem., NSW Envmtl Res. Trust, 1990–93. Hon. DSc Newcastle, NSW, 1993. *Publications:* scientific and economic papers in various jls. *Recreations:* mountains, Mozart, cricket. *Address:* 9B Castle Hill, Lancaster LA1 1YS. *T:* (01524) 68619.

MORGAN, Kenneth, OBE 1978; journalist; consultant on Press ethics; Director: Press Council, 1980–90; Press Complaints Commission, 1991; *b* 3 Nov. 1928; *s* of Albert E. and Lily M. Morgan; *m* 1950, Margaret Cynthia, *d* of Roland E. Wilson; three *d*. *Educ:* Stockport Grammar School. Reporter, Stockport Express, 1944; Army, 1946, commissioned, 1947 (served Palestine, Egypt, GHQ MELF); journalism, 1949; Central London Sec., NUJ, 1962; Nat. Organiser, NUJ, 1966; Gen. Sec., NUJ, 1970–77, Mem. of Honour, 1978. Press Council: Consultative Mem., 1970–77; Jt Sec., 1977–78; Dep. Dir and Conciliator, 1978–79; Consultant, Press Complaints Commn, 1992. Director: Journalists in Europe Ltd, 1982–97; Reuters Founder's Share Co., 1984–99. Mem. Exec. Cttee: Printing and Kindred Trades Fedn, 1970–73; Nat. Fedn of Professional Workers, 1970–77; Fedn of Broadcasting Unions, 1970–77; Confedn of Entertainment Unions, 1970–77; Bureau, Internat. Fedn of Journalists, 1970–78. Member: NEDC for Printing and Publishing Industry, 1970; Printing Industries Cttee, TUC, 1974–77; Printing and Publishing Industries Trng Bd, 1975–77; Jt Standing Cttee, Nat. Newspaper Industry, 1976–77; British Cttee, Journalists in Europe, 1977–; C of E General Synod Cttee for Communications Press Panel, 1981–90; CRE Media Gp, 1981–85; Judge, Samuel Storey Editl Awards, 1981–98; Internat. Ombudsman Inst., 1983; Trustee, Reuters, 1984–99.

Consultant: Nat. Media Commn, Ghana, 1995–99; Fiji Media Council, 1998; Media Trust Bd, Mauritius, 1998; (with John Prescott Thomas) conducted Cabinet review of media legislation, Fiji, 1996–97; Advr, Minister of Information and Culture, Sierra Leone, 1998. Vice Pres. (former Chm.), Dulwich UNA, 1989–. Gov., 1992–99, Hon. Sec., 1993–99, ESU. Associate Mem. IPI, 1980; FRSA 1980. Methodist Recorder Lectr, 1989; British Council and Council of Europe lectures in Central and W Africa, Fiji, Spain, Greece, Germany, Russia and Japan. Associate Press Fellow, Wolfson Coll., Cambridge, 1998–. *Publications:* Press Conduct in the Sutcliffe Case, 1983; (with David Christie) New Connexions: the power to inform, 1989; (jtly) Future Media Legislation and Regulation for the Republic of the Fiji Islands, 1996; A Press Council for Mauritius?: freedom, responsibility and redress for Mauritius and its media, 1999; *contributed to:* El Poder Judicial en le Conjunto de los Poderes del Estado y de la Sociedad, 1989; Media Freedom and Accountability, 1989; The Independence of the Journalist, Is de Klant of de Krant Koning, 1990; Beyond the Courtroom: alternatives for resolving press disputes, 1991; Sir Zelman Cowen: a life within the law, 1997; L'Arsenal de la Democratie (Media Accountability Systems), 2001. *Recreations:* theatre, military history, inland waterways, travel. *Address:* 151 Overhill Road, Dulwich, SE22 0PT. *T:* (020) 8693 6585.

MORGAN, Kenneth Smith; Editor of the Official Report (Hansard), House of Commons, 1979–89; *b* 6 Aug. 1925; *er s* of Edward and Florence Morgan; *m* 1952, Patricia Hunt; one *s* one *d.* *Educ:* Battersea and Dartford Grammar Schools. Commissioned Royal West Kent Regt, 1944; Burma, 1944–46. Weekly newspapers, 1947–51; Derby Evening Telegraph, 1951–52; Reuters Parliamentary Staff, 1952–54; joined Official Report, 1954; Dep. Asst Editor, 1972, Dep. Editor, 1978. Founded Commonwealth Hansard Editors Assoc., 1984. *Publication:* The Falklands Campaign: a digest of parliamentary debates on the Falklands, 1982. *Recreations:* Napoleonic warfare history, model soldiers, cricket, bridge. *Address:* 3 Highfield Road, Bexleyheath, Kent DA6 7HX.

MORGAN, Leslie; *see* Morgan, F. L.

MORGAN, Loraine; District Judge (Magistrates' Courts) (formerly Metropolitan Stipendiary Magistrate), since 1995; *b* 2 Dec. 1953; *d* of Enrico Bellisario and late Elizabeth Bellisario (*née* Coyle); *m* 1976, Captain Dai Morgan, RN. *Educ:* St Augustine's Priory, Ealing; Univ. of Exeter; Coll. of Law, Guildford. Admitted Solicitor, 1981; Partner, Reynolds & Hetherington, Fareham, 1982–86, Allsworth & Spears, Fareham, 1986–88; Solicitor Advocate, 1988–95; Co-founder and Dir, Just Advocates Ltd, 1991–95; Plate Judge Advocate, 1996–; Asst Recorder, 1998–2000; a Recorder, 2000. Mem., Crown Court Rules Cttee, 1994. Vice-Pres., Bracton Law Soc., 1974–75; Cttee Mem., Hampshire Inc. Law Soc., 1990–94; Sec. and Chm., Southampton Criminal Courts Solicitors' Assoc., 1990–94; Vice-Chm., Criminal Law Solicitors' Assoc., 1991–94. *Recreations:* good wine, good food, the company of good friends. *Address:* c/o Southampton and New Forest Magistrates' Court, 100 The Avenue, Southampton SO17 1EY. *T:* (023) 8038 4200.

MORGAN, (Mair) Eluned; Member (Lab) Wales, European Parliament, since 1999 (Mid and West Wales, 1994–99); *b* 16 Feb. 1967; *d* of Rev. Bob Morgan and Elaine Morgan; *m* 1996, Dr Rhys Jenkins, one *s.* *Educ:* Atlantic Coll.; Univ. of Hull (BA). Stagiaire with Socialist Gp, Europe. Parlt, 1990; with S4C, 1991; researcher and reporter, Agenda TV, 1992; documentary researcher, BBC TV, 1993. European Parliament: Mem., Cttee on Budgetary Control, 1997–; Substitute Mem., Budgets Cttee, 1997–; spokesperson for Social Group on Budgetary Control, 1999–. *Recreations:* walking, reading. *Address:* Labour European Office, 16 Sachville Avenue, Cardiff CF14 3NY. *T:* (029) 2061 8337, *Fax:* (029) 2061 8226; *e-mail:* emorgan@europe-wales.new.labour.org.uk.

MORGAN, Marilynne Ann, CB 1996; Solicitor to the Departments of Health and for Work and Pensions (formerly of Social Security), and Head of Law and Special Policy Group, Department for Work and Pensions (formerly Department of Social Security), since 1997; *b* 22 June 1946; *d* of late J. Emlyn Williams and Roma Elizabeth Williams (*née* Ellis); *m* 1970, Nicholas Alan, *e s* of Rear-Adm. Sir Patrick Morgan, KCVO, CB, DSC. *Educ:* Gads Hill Place, Higham-by-Rochester; Bedford Coll., Univ. of London (BA Hons History). Called to the Bar, Middle Temple, 1972. Res. Asst, Special Historical Sect., FCO, 1967–71; Department of Health and Social Security: Legal Asst, 1973; Sen. Legal Asst, 1978; Asst Solicitor, 1982; Under Sec. and Principal Asst Solicitor, 1985–91, DSS, 1988–91, DoE, 1991–92; Department of the Environment: Solicitor and Legal Advr, 1992–97; Chm., Departmental Task Force, 1994–95; Sen. Dir, Legal and Corporate Services Gp, 1996–97. Vice-Chm. 1983–84, Chm. 1984–86, Legal Sect. of Assoc. of First Div. Civil Servants. Mem., General Council of the Bar, 1987–92. *Publications:* contributor, Halsbury's Laws of England, 1982, 1986; articles in learned jls. *Recreations:* homely pursuits. *Address:* Department for Work and Pensions, New Court, 48 Carey Street, WC2A 2LS. *Clubs:* Royal Commonwealth Society, University Women's.

MORGAN, Michael David; Development Director, Anglia Housing Association Group, 1993–98; *b* 19 Jan. 1942; *s* of Edward Arthur and Winifred Maud Morgan; *m* 1980, Ljiljana Radojcic; three *d.* *Educ:* Royal Liberty Sch., Romford; Prince Rupert Sch., Wilhemshaven, FRG; Coll. of Estate Management, London Univ. (BSc Est. Man.). FRICS. Sheffield City Council, 1964–67; Derby Borough Council, 1967–70; Telford Develt Corp., 1970–92 (Chief Exec. and Gen. Manager, 1986–92, retd). *Recreations:* cricket, jogging, swimming, gardening. *Address:* Red Roofs, Ashton Road, Kingsland, Shrewsbury SY3 7AP. *T:* (01743) 352800.

MORGAN, Michael Hugh, CMG 1978; HM Diplomatic Service, retired; *b* 18 April 1925; *s* of late H. P. Morgan; *m* 1957, Julian Bamfield; two *s.* *Educ:* Shrewsbury Sch.; Downing College, Cambridge; School of Oriental and African Studies, London Univ. Army Service 1943–46. HMOCS Malaya, 1946–56. Foreign Office, 1956–57; First Secretary, Peking, 1957–60; Belgrade 1960–64; attached to Industry, 1964; First Secretary, FCO, 1964–68; Counsellor and Head of Chancery, Cape Town/Pretoria, 1968–72; Counsellor, Peking, 1972–75; Inspector, FCO, 1975–77; High Comr, Sierra Leone, 1977–81; Ambassador to the Philippines, 1981–85. Consultant, British Rail Engrg, 1986–88; Dir, Swansea Overseas Trust, 1988–91. *Address:* 1 Silkmill Lane, Ludlow, Shropshire SY8 1BJ.

MORGAN, Patrick; HM Diplomatic Service; Ambassador to El Salvador, since 1999; *b* 31 Jan. 1944; *s* of Matthew Morgan and Margaret (*née* Docherty); *m* 1966, Marlene Collins Beaton; two *s* two *d.* *Educ:* St Columba's High Sch., Greenock. BoT, 1963–64; CRO, 1964–65; FCO, 1965–67; British Embassy: Bonn, 1967–69; Kuwait, 1969–71; La Paz, 1972–75; FCO, 1975–79; British Embassy: Washington DC, 1979–83; Jakarta, 1983–86; FCO, 1987–92; Ambassador to Honduras, 1992–95; Counsellor and Dep. Hd of Mission, Abu Dhabi, 1995–98; Counsellor, FCO, 1998–99. Governor, Al Khubairat Community Sch., Abu Dhabi, 1995–98. *Recreations:* swimming, squash, music. *Address:* c/o Foreign and Commonwealth Office, King Charles Street, SW1A 2AH.

MORGAN, Paul Hyacinth; QC 1992; *b* 17 Aug. 1952; *s* of Daniel Morgan and Veronica Mary (*née* Elder); *m* 1980, Sheila Ruth Harvey; three *s.* *Educ:* St Columb's Coll., Londonderry; Peterhouse, Cambridge (BA 1974; MA 1979). Called to the Bar, Lincoln's Inn, 1975. Dep. Chm., Agricl Land Tribunal, 1999–. *Publications:* (ed jtly) Megarry on Rent Acts, 11th edn, 1988; (ed jtly) Woodfall on Landlord and Tenant, 28th edn, 1990; (ed jtly) Gale on Easements, 16th edn, 1997. *Address:* Falcon Chambers, Falcon Court, EC4Y 1AA. *T:* (020) 7353 2484.

MORGAN, Peter John, PhD; Director, Rowett Research Institute, since 1999; *b* 23 Feb. 1956; *s* of Dr John W. W. Morgan and Patricia M. Morgan; *m* 1991, Dr Denise Kelly; one *s* one *d.* *Educ:* Queen Mary Coll., London (BSc); Univ. of Aberdeen (PhD 1981). AFRC post-doctoral res. asst, Dept of Zool., Univ. of Aberdeen, 1981–85; Rowett Research Institute, Aberdeen: SSO, 1985–89; PSO, 1989–; Leader, Molecular Neuroendocrinology Res. Gp, 1991–97; Head, Molecular Neuroendocrinology Unit and Mem., Sen. Mgt Gp, 1997–99. Hon. Prof., Dept of Zoology, Univ. of Aberdeen. *Recreations:* music (pianist), squash, swimming, travel. *Address:* Rowett Research Institute, Greenburn Road, Bucksburn, Aberdeen AB21 9SB. *T:* (01224) 716663.

MORGAN, Peter William Lloyd; External Member of Council, Lloyd's, since 2000; *b* 9 May 1936; *s* of late Matthew Morgan and of Margaret Gwynneth (*née* Lloyd); *m* 1964, Elisabeth Susanne Davis; three *d.* *Educ:* Llandovery Coll.; Trinity Hall, Cambridge. Joined IBM UK Ltd, 1959; Data Processing Sales Dir, 1971–74; Gp Dir of Marketing, IBM Europe, Paris, 1975–80; Director: IBM UK Ltd, 1983–87; IBM UK Holdings Ltd, 1987–89; Dir-Gen., Inst. of Dirs, 1989–94; National Provident Institution: Dir, 1990–94; Dep. Chm., 1995; Chm., 1996–99. Chairman: South Wales Electricity PLC, 1996 (Dir, 1989–95); Pace Micro Technology plc, 1996–2000; KSCL Ltd, 1999–2000; Director: Firth Holdings plc, 1994–; Baltimore Technologies plc (formerly Zergo Holdings), 1994– (Dep. Chm., 1998–2000; Chm., 2000–); IDP (Paris), 2000–; Oxford Instruments plc, 2000–; Assoc. of Lloyd's Mems, 1997–. Mem., Economic and Social Cttee, EU (formerly EC), 1994–. Vice Pres., London Welsh Male Voice Choir, 1993–. Liveryman, Co. of Inf. Technologists, 1992– (Mem., Ct of Assts, 1996–; Warden, 1999). Radical of the Year, Radical Soc., 1990. *Recreations:* music, history, gardening, ski-ing, wine, dog walking. *Address:* 40 Catherine Place, SW1E 6HL. *Club:* Oxford and Cambridge.

MORGAN, Rev. Philip; Minister, St Andrew's United Reformed Church, Frognal, London, 1990–95; *b* 22 June 1930; *s* of David Lewis and Pamela Morgan; *m* 1954, Greta Mary Hanson; one *s* one *d.* *Educ:* Overdale Coll.; Selly Oaks Colls; Univ. of Birmingham (BA Hons Theology). Ordained 1952; Ministries: Aberfan, Godreaman, Griffithstown, Merthyr Tydfil and Treharris, 1952–58; Eltham, London, 1958–62; Leicester and South Wigston, 1962–67; General Secretary, Churches of Christ in GB and Ireland, 1967–80; Gen. Sec., BCC, 1980–90. Moderator, URC, 1984–85. Hon. DD Christian Theological Seminary, USA, 1980. *Recreations:* hill walking, Celtic history, steam railways. *Address:* 1 Ellesmere Avenue, Mill Hill, NW7 3EX.

MORGAN, Piers Stefan; Editor, The Mirror (formerly Daily Mirror), since 1995; *b* 30 March 1965; *s* of Glynne and Gabrielle Pughe-Morgan; *m* 1991, Marion Elizabeth Shalloe; three *s.* *Educ:* Chailey Comprehensive Sch.; Lewes Priory Sixth Form Coll.; Harlow Journalism Coll. With Lloyd's of London, 1985–87; Reporter, Surrey and S London Newspapers, 1987–89; Showbusiness Editor, The Sun, 1989–94; Editor, News of the World, 1994–95. Editor of the Year, Newspaper Focus Awards, 1994. *Publications:* Private Lives of the Stars, 1990; Secret Lives of the Stars, 1991; Phillip Schofield: to dream a dream, 1992; Take That: our story, 1993; Take That: on the road, 1994. *Recreations:* cricket, Arsenal FC. *Address:* The Mirror, 1 Canada Square, Canary Wharf, E14 5AP. *T:* (020) 7293 3000.

MORGAN, Rt Hon. Rhodri; *see* Morgan, Rt Hon. H. R.

MORGAN, Richard Martin, MA; Warden, Radley College, 1991–2000; *b* 25 June 1940; *s* of His Honour Trevor Morgan, MC, QC, and late Leslie Morgan; *m* 1968, Margaret Kathryn, *d* of late Anthony Agutter and of Mrs Launcelot Fleming; three *d.* *Educ:* Sherborne Sch.; Caius Coll., Cambridge (MA, DipEd); York Univ. Assistant Master, Radley Coll., 1963; Housemaster, 1969; Headmaster, Cheltenham College, 1978–90. Member, Adv. Council, Understanding British Industry, 1977–79. JP Glos, 1978–90. *Recreations:* reading, music, games. *Address:* Warmans, Bodenham, Salisbury, Wilts SP5 4EV. *T:* (01722) 333379. *Clubs:* Free Foresters', Jesters'.

MORGAN, Robin Milne; Principal: Daniel Stewart's and Melville College, Edinburgh, 1977–89; The Mary Erskine School, 1979–89; *b* 2 Oct. 1930; *o s* of Robert Milne Morgan and Aida Forsyth Morgan; *m* 1955, Fiona Bruce MacLeod Douglas; three *s* one *d.* *Educ:* Mackie Academy, Stonehaven; Aberdeen Univ. (MA); London Univ. (BA, External). Nat. Service, 2nd Lieut The Gordon Highlanders, 1952–54; Asst Master: Arden House Prep. Sch., 1955–60; George Watson's Coll., 1960–71; Headmaster, Campbell Coll., Belfast, 1971–76. *Recreations:* music, archaeology, fishing, climbing. *Address:* Rose House, High Street, Nawton, Helmsley, York YO6 5TT.

MORGAN, Robin Richard; Editor, The Sunday Times Magazine, since 1995; Contributing Editor, GQ Magazine, since 1999; *b* 16 Sept. 1953; *s* of Raymond Morgan and Jean Edith Bennett; *m* 1977, Ruth Winefride Mary O'Shea; two *s* one *d.* *Educ:* King Edward VI Grammar Sch., Stourbridge, W Midlands. County Express, Stourbridge, 1971–73; Evening Echo, Hemel Hempstead, 1973–79; Sunday Times, London, 1979–89: Reporter, 1979–83; Dep. News Editor, 1983–85; Insight Editor, 1985–87; Features Editor, 1987–89; Editor, Sunday Express, 1989–91; Associate Editor, Sunday Times, 1991–92; Editor, Sunday Times Magazine, 1992–93; Editorial Dir designate, Reader's Digest, 1993–94. Campaigning Journalist of the Year: (commended) 1982; (winner) 1983. *Publications:* (jtly) The Falklands War, 1982; (jtly) Rainbow Warrior, 1986; (jtly) Bullion, 1988; (ed) Manpower, 1988; (jtly) Ambush, 1989. *Recreations:* cinema, US politics, modern American fiction, travel. *Address:* The Sunday Times Magazine, 1 Pennington Street, Wapping, E1 9XW.

MORGAN, Roger; *see* Morgan, E. R.

MORGAN, Roger Hugh Vaughan Charles, CBE 1991; Librarian, House of Lords, 1977–91; *b* 8 July 1926; *s* of late Charles Langbridge Morgan, and Hilda Vaughan, both novelists and playwrights; *m* 1st, 1951, Harriet Waterfield (marr. diss. 1965), *d* of Gordon Waterfield; one *s* one *d* (and one *s* decd); 2nd, 1965, Susan Vogel Marrian, *d* of Hugo Vogel, Milwaukee, USA; one *s.* *Educ:* Downs Sch., Colwall; Phillips Acad., Andover, USA; Eton Coll.; Brasenose Coll., Oxford. MA. Grenadier Guards, 1944–47 (Captain, 1946). House of Commons Library, 1951–63; House of Lords Library, 1963–91. *Recreations:* painting, photography, cooking. *Address:* 30 St Peter's Square, W6 9UH. *T:* (020) 8741 0267, *Fax:* (020) 8563 7881;; Cliff Cottage, Laugharne, Carmarthenshire. *T:* (01994) 427398. *Clubs:* Garrick, Beefsteak, Saintsbury.
See also Marchioness of Anglesey.

MORGAN, Prof. Roger Pearce; External Professor of Political Science, European University Institute, Florence, since 1996; *b* 3 March 1932; *s* of Donald Emlyn Morgan and Esther Mary Morgan (*née* Pearce); *m* 1st, 1957, Annie-Françoise, (Annette) Combes (marr. diss. 1988); three *s* one *d*; 2nd, 1988, Mrs Catherine Howell. *Educ:* Wolverton Grammar Sch.; Leighton Park Sch.; Downing Coll., Cambridge (MA 1957; PhD 1959); Univs of Paris and Hamburg. Staff Tutor, Dept of Extra-Mural Studies, London Univ., 1957–59; Asst Lectr and Lectr in Internat. Politics, UCW, Aberystwyth, 1959–63; Lectr in Hist. and Internat. Relations, Sussex Univ., 1963–67; Asst, then Dep. Dir of Studies, RIIA, 1968–74; Prof. of European Politics, 1974–78, and Dean, Sch. of Human and Environmental Studies, 1976–78, Loughborough Univ.; Head of European Centre for Political Studies, PSI, 1978–86; Vis. Fellow, Centre for Internat. Studies, LSE, 1987–88; Prof. of Political Sci., European Univ. Inst., Florence, 1988–96. Visiting Professor: Columbia Univ., 1965; Johns Hopkins Univ., 1969–70, 1988–89, 1995; Cornell Univ., 1972; Surrey Univ., 1980–84; UCLA, 1993, 2001; Univ. of Bonn, 1996–97; pt-time Prof., Dept of War Studies, KCL, 2000; Res. Associate, Center for Internat. Affairs, Harvard, 1965–66; Visiting Lecturer: Cambridge Univ., 1967; LSE, 1974, 1980–88; Associate Mem., Nuffield Coll., Oxford, 1980–83; Hon. Professorial Fellow, UCW, Aberystwyth, 1980–84, Hon. Prof., 1985–; Sen. Associate Mem., St Antony's Coll., Oxford, 1996–97; Vis. Fellow, European Inst., LSE, 1998–2000. Lectr at RCDS, CS Coll., RNC, etc. Member: Council, RIIA, 1976–85, 1986–92 and 1997–; Academic Council, Wilton Park, 1982–83. Trustee, Gilbert Murray Trust, 1973–88. *Publications:* The German Social Democrats and the First International 1864–72, 1965; Modern Germany, 1966; (ed jtly) Britain and West Germany: changing societies and the future of foreign policy, 1971 (German edn, 1970); West European Politics since 1945, 1972; (ed) The Study of International Affairs, 1972; High Politics, Low Politics: toward a foreign policy for Western Europe, 1973; The United States and West Germany 1945–1973: a study in alliance politics, 1974 (German edn 1975); West Germany's Foreign Policy Agenda, 1978; (ed jtly) Moderates and Conservatives in Western Europe, 1982 (Italian edn 1983); (ed jtly) Partners and Rivals in Western Europe: Britain, France and Germany, 1986; (ed) Regionalism in European Politics, 1986; (ed jtly) New Diplomacy in the Post-Cold War World, 1993; (ed jtly) The Third Pillar of the European Union, 1994; (ed jtly) Parliaments and Parties: the European Parliament in the political life of Europe, 1995; (ed jtly) New Challenges to the European Union: policies and policy-making, 1997; contribs to symposia and jls. *Recreations:* music, travel, watching cricket. *Address:* 29 Burgh Street, N1 8HG. *T:* (020) 7226 4702. *Clubs:* Reform, PEN; Middlesex County Cricket, Surrey County Cricket.

MORGAN, Stephen Peter, OBE 1992; Chairman, Redrow Group plc, 1974–2000; *b* 25 Nov. 1952; *s* of Peter and Mary Morgan; *m* 1973, Pamela Borrett; one *s* one *d*. *Educ:* Colwyn High Sch.; Liverpool Poly (Hon. Fellow). Founded Redrow, 1974. Non-exec. Dir, Devere Gp. Hon. Fellow: John Moores Univ., 1993; NE Wales Inst. of Higher Educn, 1993. *Publication:* The Redrow Way, 1999. *Recreations:* football, Rugby, ski-ing, running, golf.

MORGAN, Most Rev. Thomas Oliver; *see* Saskatoon, Archbishop of.

MORGAN, Tom, CBE 1982; DL; Lord Provost of the City of Edinburgh and Lord Lieutenant of the City and County of Edinburgh, 1980–84; *b* 24 Feb. 1914; *s* of Thomas Morgan; *m* 1940, Mary Montgomery (*d* 1991), *d* of Stephen McLauchlan; two *s*. *Educ:* Longside Public Sch., Aberdeenshire; Aberdeen Univ.; W of Scotland Coll. of Agriculture. Unigate Ltd for 36 yrs (Regional Dir for Scotland). Member, Edinburgh Corp., 1954–71 and Edinburgh DC, 1977–84. Chairman: Edinburgh Festival Soc., 1980–84; Edinburgh Mil. Tattoo Policy Cttee, 1980–84. Formerly: Magistrate; City Treasurer; Curator of Patronage, Univ. of Edinburgh; Governor, George Heriot's Trust; Governor, Edinburgh and E of Scotland Coll. of Agric.; Dir, Edinburgh Chamber of Commerce and Manufactures; Pres., Edinburgh City Business Club; Gen. Comr of Income Tax; Chm., Edinburgh Abbeyfield Soc. DL Edinburgh, 1984. OStJ. *Recreations:* golf, gardening. *Address:* 400 Lanark Road, Edinburgh EH13 0LX. *T:* (0131) 441 3245.

MORGAN, Tony; *see* Morgan, A. W. C.

MORGAN, Rt Rev. Mgr Vaughan Frederick John, CBE 1982; Parish Priest, St Teresa's Charlbury, since 1997; *b* Upper Hutt, New Zealand, 21 March 1931; *o s* of late Godfrey Frederick Vaughan Morgan and Violet (Doreen) Vaughan Morgan. *Educ:* The Oratory Sch., S Oxon; Innsbruck Univ. Ordained, 1957; Archdiocese of St Andrews and Edinburgh, 1959–62; entered Royal Navy as Chaplain, 1962; Prin. RC Chaplain (Naval), and Vicar Gen. for RN, 1979–84; Chaplain, The Oratory Sch., 1984–97. Chaplain to High Sheriff of Oxfordshire, 2000–01. Prelate of Honour to HH Pope John Paul II, 1979. *Publications:* contribs to journals. *Recreations:* music, swimming, painting, heraldry. *Address:* 2 Enstone Road, Charlbury, Oxfordshire OX7 2QR. *T:* (01608) 810576. *Club:* Army and Navy.

MORGAN, Prof. Walter Thomas James, CBE 1959; FRS 1949; Director, Lister Institute of Preventive Medicine, London, 1972–75 (Deputy Director, 1952–68); *b* London, 5 Oct. 1900; *s* of Walter and Annie E. Morgan; *m* 1930, Dorothy Irene Price (*d* 1993); one *s* two *d*. *Educ:* Univ. of London. Grocers' Company Scholar, 1925–27; Beit Memorial Med. Res. Fellow, 1927–28; First Asst and Biochemist, Lister Institute Serum Dept (Elstree), 1928–37; Rockefeller Research Fellow (Eidgenössiche Tech. Hochschule, Zürich), 1937. Reader, 1938–51, Lister Inst.; Prof. of Biochemistry, Univ. of London, 1951–68, now Prof. Emeritus. PhD 1927, DSc 1937, London Univ.; DrSc (Tech.) Zürich, 1938. CChem, FRSC (FRIC 1929). Hon. Secretary: Biochemical Soc., 1940–45; Biological Council, 1944–47. Chm. Bd of Studies, Biochem., Univ. of London, 1954–57; Member: Scientific Advisory Council, 1956–60; MRC, 1966–70. Mem., Lawes Agricl Trust Cttee, 1964–76. Guest Lecturer, 100th meeting of Gesellschaft Deutscher Naturforscher und Ärzte, Germany, 1959; Royal Society: Croonian Lectr, 1959; Vice-Pres., 1961–64; Royal Medal, 1968. Vis. Prof., Japan Soc. for Promotion of Science, 1979. Hon. Member: Biochem. Soc., 1969; Internat. Soc. Blood Transfusion, 1980; British Soc. Blood Transfusion, 1984; Internat. Endotoxic Soc., 1987; Hon. FRCP 1982; Hon. FMedSci 2000. MD *hc* Basel, 1964; DSc *hc* Michigan, 1969. Conway Evans Prize (Royal College of Physicians, London), 1964; (jointly) Landsteiner Memorial Award (USA), 1967; (jointly) Paul Ehrlich and Ludwig Darmstädter Prizes (Germany), 1968; Philip Levine Medal, Amer. Soc. of Clinical Pathologists, 1990. *Publications:* papers on biochemistry, immunology and pathology. *Address:* 57 Woodbury Drive, Sutton, Surrey SM2 5RA. *T:* (020) 8642 2319. *Club:* Athenæum.

MORGAN, Prof. William Basil; Professor of Geography, 1971–92, Professor Emeritus, since 1988, and Head of Geography Department, 1982–87, King's College London; *b* 22 Jan. 1927; *s* of William George Morgan and Eunice Mary (*née* Heys); *m* 1954, Joy Gardner; one *s* one *d*. *Educ:* King Edward's Sch., Birmingham; Jesus Coll., Oxford (MA); PhD Glasgow. Assistant, Glasgow Univ., 1948; Lecturer: University Coll., Ibadan, Nigeria, 1953; Univ. of Birmingham, 1959; Reader in Geography, KCL, 1967. Participant in various UN university res. projects and conferences. *Publications:* (with J. C. Pugh) West Africa, 1969; (with R. J. C. Munton) Agricultural Geography, 1971; Agriculture in the Third World: a spatial analysis, 1978; (with R. P. Moss) Fuelwood and rural energy production and supply in the humid tropics, 1981; contribs to geographical and other learned jls and to various conf. collections. *Recreation:* development geography, walking. *Address:* 57 St Augustine's Avenue, South Croydon, Surrey CR2 6JQ. *T:* (020) 8688 5687, *Fax:* (020) 8667 0201; *e-mail:* william@wmorgan79.freeserve.co.uk.

MORGAN, Air Vice-Marshal William Gwyn, CB 1968; CBE 1960 (OBE 1945); RAF, retired 1969; *b* 13 Aug. 1914; *s* of T. S. Morgan; *m* 1962, Joan Russell. *Educ:* Pagefield Coll., Swansea. Joined Royal Air Force, 1939; Group Capt., 1958; Command Acct, HQ, FEAF, 1962; Air Commodore, 1965; DPS (2), RAF, 1965–66; AOA Technical Training Comd, 1966–68, Training Comd, 1968–69. Air Vice-Marshal, 1967; jssc; psc; FCCA; ACMA. *Recreation:* fell walking. *Address:* c/o Lloyds TSB, 7 Pall Mall, SW1Y 5NH. *Club:* Royal Air Force.

MORGAN-GILES, Rear-Adm. Sir Morgan (Charles), Kt 1985; DSO 1944; OBE 1943 (MBE 1942); GM 1941; DL; *b* 19 June 1914; *e s* of late F. C. Morgan-Giles, OBE, MINA, Teignmouth, Devon; *m* 1946, Pamela (*d* 1966), *d* of late Philip Bushell, Sydney, New South Wales; two *s* four *d*; *m* 1968, Marigold (*d* 1995), *d* of late Percy Lowe. *Educ:* Clifton Coll. Entered Royal Navy, 1932; served on China Station, and in destroyers. War Service: Atlantic convoys and Mediterranean; Tobruk garrison and Western Desert, 1941; with RAF, 1942; Sen. Naval Officer, Vis. (Dalmatia) and liaison with Commandos and Marshal Tito's Partisan Forces, 1943–44. Captain 1953; Chief of Naval Intelligence, Far East, 1955–56; Captain (D) Dartmouth Training Sqdn, 1957–58; HMS Belfast, in command, 1961–62; Rear-Adm. 1962; Adm. Pres., Royal Naval Coll., Greenwich, 1962–64; retd 1964. MP (C) Winchester, May 1964–79. Vice-Chm., Conservative Defence Cttee, 1965–75. Chm., HMS Belfast Trust, 1971–78; Life Vice-Pres., RNLI, 1989. Prime Warden, Shipwrights' Company, 1987–88. DL Hants, 1983. *Recreations:* sailing, country pursuits. *Address:* Anchor House, Little Sodbury Manor, Glos BS37 6QA. *T:* (01454) 327485. *Clubs:* Royal Yacht Squadron; Australian (Sydney).
See also Baron Killearn.

MORGAN HUGHES, David; *see* Hughes.

MORGAN-OWEN, John Gethin, CB 1984; MBE 1945; QC 1981; Judge Advocate General, 1979–84; *b* 22 Aug. 1914; *o s* of late Maj.-Gen. L. I. G. Morgan-Owen, CB, CMG, CBE, DSO, West Dene, Beech, Alton; *m* 1950, Mary, *d* of late F. J. Rimington, MBE, Master Mariner; two *s* one *d*. *Educ:* Shrewsbury; Trinity Coll., Oxford (BA). Called to Bar, Inner Temple, 1938; Wales and Chester Circuit, 1939; practised at Cardiff, 1939–52. 2nd Lieut Suppl. Reserve, S Wales Borderers, 1939; served 2nd Bn SWB, 1939–44: N Norway, 1940; NW Europe, 1944–45; DAA&QMG, 146 Inf. Bde, 1944–45; Hon. Major. Dep. Judge Advocate, 1952: Germany, 1953–56; Hong Kong, 1958–60; Cyprus, 1963–66; AJAG, 1966; DJAG, Germany, 1970–72; Vice JAG, 1972–79. Jt Chm., Disciplinary Appeals Cttee, ICA, 1985–87. *Recreations:* bad tennis, inland waterways, beagling, croquet. *Club:* Army and Navy.

MORIARTY, Gerald Evelyn; QC 1974; a Recorder of the Crown Court, 1976–98; *b* 23 Aug. 1928; *er s* of late Lt-Col G. R. O'N. Moriarty and Eileen Moriarty (*née* Moloney); *m* 1961, Judith Mary, *er d* of Hon. William Robert Atkin; four *s*. *Educ:* Downside Sch.; St John's Coll., Oxford (MA). Called to the Bar, Lincoln's Inn, 1951, Bencher, 1983. *T:* (020) 7727 4593. *Club:* Reform.

MORIARTY, Brig. Joan Olivia Elsie, CB 1979; RRC 1977; Matron-in-Chief and Director of Army Nursing Services, 1976–80; *b* 11 May 1923; *d* of late Lt-Col Oliver Nash Moriarty, DSO, RA, and Mrs Georgina Elsie Moriarty (*née* Moore). *Educ:* Royal Sch., Bath; St Thomas' Hosp. (nursing); Queen Charlotte's Hosp. (midwifery). SRN. VAD, Somerset, 1941–42; joined QAIMNS (R), 1947; Reg. QAIMNS (later QARANC), 1948, retired Jan. 1981; appts incl.: Staff Captain, WO; Instr, Corps Trng Centre; Liaison Officer, MoD; served in UK, Gibraltar, BAOR, Singapore, Malaya, Cyprus; Matron, Mil. Hosp., Catterick, 1973–76; Comdt, QARANC Trng Centre, Aldershot, 1976. Major 1960; Lt-Col 1971; Col 1973; Brig. 1977. QHNS, 1977–80. OStJ 1977.

MORIARTY, Michael John, CB 1988; Deputy Chairman, Radio Authority, 1994–2000 (Member, 1991–2000); Deputy Under-Secretary of State and Principal Establishment Officer, Home Office, 1984–90; *b* 3 July 1930; *er s* of late Edward William Patrick Moriarty, OBE, and May Lilian Moriarty; *m* 1960, Rachel Milward, *d* of late J. S. Thompson and Isobel F. Thompson; one *s* two *d*. *Educ:* Reading Sch., Reading; St John's Coll., Oxford (Sir Thomas White schol.; MA Lit. Hum.). Entered Home Office as Asst Principal, 1954; Private Sec. to Parliamentary Under-Secretaries of State, 1957–59; Principal, 1959; Civil Service Selection Bd, 1962–63; Cabinet Office, 1965–67; Asst Sec., 1967; Private Sec. to Home Sec., 1968; Head of Crime Policy Planning Unit, 1974–75; Asst Under-Sec. of State, 1975–84; seconded to NI Office, 1979–81; Broadcasting Dept, 1981–84. UK Representative, 1976–79, and Chm., 1978–79, Council of Europe Cttee on Crime Problems. Mem. Council, Disasters Emergency Cttee, 1997–98; Sub-Treas., 1991–, Mem. Council, 2001–, Chichester Cathedral; a Church Comr, 1996–98. *Recreations:* music, walking, local interests. *Address:* 22 Westgate, Chichester, West Sussex PO19 3EU. *T:* (01243) 789985.

MORIARTY, Stephen; QC 1999; *b* 14 April 1955; *s* of George William Moriarty and Dorothy Violet Moriarty (*née* Edwards); *m* 1988, Dr Susan Clare Stanford. *Educ:* Chichester High Sch. for Boys; Brasenose Coll., Oxford (BCL, MA; Vinerian Schol. 1978). Univ. Lectr in law, and Fellow and Tutor in Law, Exeter Coll., Oxford, 1979–86; called to the Bar, Middle Temple, 1986; in practice at the Bar, 1986–. *Recreations:* theatre, opera. *Address:* Fountain Court Chambers, Fountain Court, Temple, EC4Y 9DH. *T:* (020) 7583 3335. *Club:* Reform.

MORICE, Prof. Peter Beaumont, DSc, PhD; FREng, FICE, FIStructE; Professor of Civil Engineering, University of Southampton, 1958–91, now Emeritus; *b* 15 May 1926; *o s* of Charles and Stephanie Morice; *m* 1st, 1952, Margaret Ransom (marr. diss. 1986); one *s* two *d*; 2nd, 1986, Rita Corless (*née* Dunk). *Educ:* Barfield Sch.; Farnham Grammar Sch.; University of Bristol; University of London. Surrey County Council, 1947–48; Research Div., Cement and Concrete Assoc., 1948–57. Vis. Prof., Ecole Nat. des Ponts et Chaussées, Paris; Mem. Foundn Cttee, Sultan Qaboos Univ., Oman, 1980–86. FREng (FEng 1989). Compagnon du Beaujolais, 1987. Order of Sultan Qaboos (Oman), 1986. *Publications:* Linear Structural Analysis, 1958; Prestressed Concrete, 1958; papers on structural theory in various learned journals. *Recreations:* sailing, DIY, reading, listening to music. *Address:* 12 Abbotts Way, Highfield, Southampton SO17 1QT. *T:* (023) 8055 7641; Le Coure, La Sauvetat, 32500 Fleurance, France. *T:* 562652175. *Club:* Island Sailing (Cowes).

MORISHIMA, Prof. Michio, FBA 1981; Sir John Hicks Professor of Economics, London School of Economics and Political Science, 1984–88 (Professor of Economics, 1970–84); Emeritus Professor, University of London, 1988; *b* 18 July 1923; *s* of Kameji and Tatsuo Morishima; *m* 1953, Yoko; two *s* one *d*. Assistant Professor: Kyoto Univ., 1950–51; Osaka Univ., 1951–63; Prof., Osaka Univ., 1963–69. *Publications:* Equilibrium, Stability and Growth, 1964; Theory of Economic Growth, 1969; The Working of Econometric Models, 1972; Marx's Economics, 1973; Theory of Demand: real and monetary, 1973; The Economic Theory of Modern Society, 1976; Walras' Economics, 1977; Value, Exploitation and Growth, 1978; Why Has Japan 'Succeeded'?, 1982; The Economics of Industrial Society, 1985; Ricardo's Economics, 1989; Capital and Credit, 1992; Dynamic Economic Theory, 1996; Japan at a Dead Lock, 2000; Collaborative Development in Northeast Asia, 2000. *Address:* Ker, Greenway, Hutton Mount, Brentwood, Essex CM13 2NP. *T:* (01277) 219595.

MORISON, Hon. Lord; Alastair Malcolm Morison; a Senator of the College of Justice, Scotland, 1985–97; *b* 12 Feb. 1931; 2nd *s* of Sir Ronald Peter Morison, QC (Scotland); *m* 1st, 1957, Lindsay Balfour Oatts (marr. diss. 1977); one *s* one *d*; 2nd, 1980, Birgitte Hendil. *Educ:* Cargilfield; Winchester Coll.; Edinburgh Univ. Admitted to Faculty of Advocates, 1956; QC (Scotland) 1968. Chairman: Medical Appeals Tribunal, 1972–85; Performing Right Tribunal, 1984–85. *Recreations:* golf, fishing. *Address:* Parliament House, Edinburgh EH1 1RG. *T:* (0131) 225 2595. *Club:* New (Edinburgh).

MORISON, Hugh; Chief Executive, Scotch Whisky Association, since 1994; *b* 22 Nov. 1943; *s* of Archibald Ian Morison and Enid Rose Morison (*née* Mawer); *m* 1st, 1971, Marion Smithers (marr. diss. 1993); two *d*; 2nd, 1993, Ilona Bellos (*née* Roth). *Educ:* Chichester High School for Boys; St Catherine's Coll., Oxford (MA English Language and Literature; DipEd). Asst Principal, SHHD, 1966–69; Private Sec. to Minister of State, Scottish Office, 1969–70; Principal: Scottish Educn Dept, 1971–73; Scottish Economic Planning Dept, 1973–74; Offshore Supplies Office, Dept of Energy, 1974–75; Scottish Economic Planning Dept, 1975–82, Asst Sec., 1979; Gwilym Gibbon Res, Fellow, Nuffield Coll., Oxford, 1982–83; Scottish Development Dept, 1983–84; Under Secretary: SHHD, 1984–88; Industry Dept for Scotland, subseq. Scottish Office Industry Dept, 1988–93. Dir, The Weir Gp, 1989–93. Member: Health Appts Adv. Cttee (Scotland), 1995–2000; Exec. Cttee, Barony Housing Assoc., 1996–. Chm., Scottish Business and Biodiversity Gp, 1998–. FRSA 1990. *Publications:* The Regeneration of Local Economies, 1987; (with Ilona Bellos) Dauphiné, 1991. *Recreations:* hill walking, cycling, sailing, music, looking at ruins. *Address:* c/o Scotch Whisky Association, 20 Atholl Crescent, Edinburgh EH3 8HF. *T:* (0131) 222 9201. *Clubs:* Royal Commonwealth Society; New (Edinburgh).

MORISON, Niall Maclaine; Chief Executive, General Council of the Bar, since 1994; *b* 3 May 1944; *s* of Dr Neil Morison and Dorothy Morison; *m* 1969, Alison Linda Hill; three *s* one *d*. *Educ:* Edinburgh Academy. Asst Sec., Bar Council, 1973–74; Senate of the Inns of Court and the Bar: Asst Sec., 1974–85; Dep. Sec., 1985–86; Dep. Chief Exec., Gen. Council of the Bar, 1987–94. Governor, Stonegate C of E Primary Sch., 1996–. *Recreations:* family, music, watching Rugby, fishing, ski-ing. *Address:* Bramdean Cottage, Stonegate, Wadhurst, E Sussex TN5 7EP. *T:* (01580) 200142.

MORISON, Air Vice-Marshal Richard Trevor, CBE 1969 (MBE 1944); RAF retired; President, Ordnance Board, 1971–72; *s* of late Oscar Colin Morison and Margaret Valerie (*née* Cleaver); *m* 1964, Rosemary June Brett; one *s* one *d*. *Educ:* Perse Sch., Cambridge; De Havilland Sch. of Aeronautical Engineering. Commnd in RAF, 1940; RAF Staff Coll., 1952; Sen. Techn. Officer, RAF Gaydon, 1955–57; HQ Bomber Comd, 1958–60; STSO HQ 224 Group, Singapore, 1960–61; Dir of Techn. Services, Royal NZ Air Force, 1961–63; Comd Engrg Officer, HQ Bomber Comd, 1963–65; Air Officer i/c Engrg, HQ Flying Training Comd, 1966–68; Air Officer i/c Engrg, HQ Training Comd RAF, 1968–69; Vice-Pres. (Air) Ordnance Bd, 1969–70. *Recreation:* cabinet making. *Address:* Meadow House, Chedgrave, Loddon, Norfolk NR14 6BS.

MORISON, Hon. Sir Thomas (Richard Atkin), Kt 1993; **Hon. Mr Justice Morison;** a Judge of the High Court of Justice, Queen's Bench Division, since 1993; *b* 15 Jan. 1939; *s* of Harold Thomas Brash Morison and Hon. Nancy Morison; *m* 1963, Judith Rachel Walton Morris (marr. diss. 1992); one *s* one *d*; *m* 1993, Caroline Yates. *Educ:* Winchester Coll.; Worcester Coll., Oxford, 1959–62 (MA). Passed final Bar examinations, 1959; called to the Bar, Gray's Inn, 1960, Bencher, 1987; pupil in Chambers, 1962–63; started practice, 1963; QC 1979; a Recorder, 1987–93. *Recreations:* reading, gardening, cooking. *Address:* Royal Courts of Justice, Strand, WC2A 2LL. *Club:* Oriental.

MORLAND, Charles Francis Harold; Chairman, Leonard Cheshire, since 2000; *b* 4 Sept. 1939; *s* of Sir Oscar Morland, GBE, KCMG, and Alice, *d* of Rt Hon. Sir Francis Oswald Lindley, GCMG, PC; *m* 1964, Victoria Longe (*d* 1998); two *s*. *Educ:* Ampleforth Coll.; King's Coll., Cambridge (MA). American Dept, FO, 1963–64; Local Dir, Oxford and Birmingham, Barclays Bank, 1964–79; on secondment as Under Sec. to Dept of Industry, 1979–81; Dir, Barclays Merchant Bank, then Barclays de Zoete Wedd, 1981–87; Man. Dir, Riggs AP Bank, 1987–89; Chm., Belmont Bank, 1991–93. Chm., Oxford Policy Inst., 1996–; Dir, British Inst. in Paris, 1997–. *Recreations:* travel, cooking. *Address:* 63 St Mark's Road, W11 1RE. *T:* (020) 7243 0635. *Club:* Brooks's.

See also M. R. Morland.

MORLAND, Martin Robert, CMG 1985; HM Diplomatic Service, retired; consultant with Hardcastle and Co. Ltd, since 1996; *b* 23 Sept. 1933; *e s* of Sir Oscar Morland, GBE, KCMG and late Alice, *d* of Rt Hon. Sir Francis Oswald Lindley, PC, GCMG; *m* 1964, Jennifer Avril Mary Hanbury-Tracy; two *s* one *d*. *Educ:* Ampleforth; King's Coll., Cambridge (BA). Nat. Service, Grenadier Guards, 1954–56; British Embassy, Rangoon, 1957–60; News Dept, FO, 1961; UK Delegn to Common Market negotiations, Brussels, 1962–63; FO, 1963–65; UK Disarmament Delegn, Geneva, 1965–67; Private Sec. to Lord Chalfont, 1967–68; European Integration Dept, FCO, 1968–73; Counsellor, 1973–77, Rome (seconded temporarily to Cabinet Office to head EEC Referendum Information Unit, 1975); Hd of Maritime Aviation and Environment Dept, FCO, 1977–79; Counsellor and Head of Chancery, Washington, 1979–82; seconded to Hardcastle & Co. Ltd, 1982–84; Under-Sec., Cabinet Office, 1984–86; Ambassador to Burma, 1986–90; Ambassador and UK Perm. Rep. to Office of UN and other internat. orgns, Geneva, 1990–93; Dir, Public Affairs, BNFL, 1994–96. Chm. Govs, Westminster Cathedral Choir Sch., 2001–. *Address:* 50 Britannia Road, SW6 2JP. *Club:* Brooks's.

MORLAND, Hon. Sir Michael, Kt 1989; **Hon. Mr Justice Morland;** a Judge of the High Court of Justice, Queen's Bench Division, since 1989; *b* 16 July 1929; *e s* of Edward Morland, Liverpool, and Jane Morland (*née* Beckett); *m* 1961, Lillian Jensen, Copenhagen; one *s* one *d*. *Educ:* Stowe; Christ Church, Oxford (MA). 2nd Lieut, Grenadier Guards, 1948–49; served in Malaya. Called to Bar, Inner Temple, 1953, Bencher 1979; Northern Circuit; QC 1972; a Recorder, 1972–89; Presiding Judge, Northern Circuit, 1991–95. Mem., Criminal Injuries Compensation Bd, 1980–89. *Address:* Royal Courts of Justice, Strand, WC2A 2LL.

MORLAND, Sir Robert (Kenelm), Kt 1990; non-executive Director, Teddington, Twickenham and Hamptons Primary Care Trust, since 2001; General Manager, Exports: Tate & Lyle Sugars, 1987–93; Tate & Lyle International, 1987–93; Director, Tate & Lyle Norway A/S, 1987–93; *b* 7 April 1935; *s* of late Kenelm and Sybil Morland; *m* 1st, 1960, Eve Charters (marr. diss. 1965); one *s*; 2nd, 1972, Angela Fraser; one *s*. *Educ:* Birkenhead Sch.; Rydal Sch., Colwyn Bay. Joined Tate & Lyle, 1953; held various managerial positions. Member: Cheshire Riverboard Authy, 1962–65; Birkenhead Nat. Assistance Bd, Adv. Cttee, 1962–65. Dir, 1996–98, Associate non-exec. Dir, 1999–2001, Kingston and Richmond HA; Bd Mem., Thames Health Primary Care Gp, 1999–2001. Member: Birkenhead CBC, 1959–65; Richmond upon Thames BC, 1968–71. Contested (C) Birkenhead, 1964. Chairman: Birkenhead Young Conservatives, 1955–58; Kew Conservatives, 1971–74; Richmond and Barnes (now Richmond Park) Cons. Assoc., 1975–79 (Dep. Pres., 1985–98); Cons. Docklands Action Cttee, 1990–92; Greenwich and Lewisham Cons. Action Gp, 1993–94; Dep. Chm., Nat. Trade and Industry Forum, Cons. Party, 1991–96; Vice-President: Gtr London Conservatives, 1990– (Dep. Chm., 1978–81; Jt Hon. Treas., 1981–87; Chm., 1987–90); Newham S Cons. Assoc., 1989–96; Member: Cons. Nat. Union Exec. Cttee, 1978–93; Cons. Bd of Finance, 1981–87. Chm., St Mary's Drama Gp, Hampton, 1999–2001 (Vice Chm., 1996–99). Mem., Glos CCC Exiles Cttee, 1998–. *Recreations:* theatre, travel, cricket, horseriding. *Clubs:* Carlton, Royal Automobile.

MORLEY; *see* Hope-Morley, family name of Baron Hollenden.

MORLEY, 6th Earl of, *cr* 1815; **John St Aubyn Parker,** KCVO 1998; JP; Lt-Col, Royal Fusiliers; Lord-Lieutenant of Devon, 1982–98; Chairman, Plymouth Sound Ltd, 1974–94; *b* 29 May 1923; *e s* of Hon. John Holford Parker (*y s* of 3rd Earl), Pound House, Yelverton, Devon; *S* uncle, 1962; *m* 1955, Johanna Katherine, *d* of Sir John Molesworth-St Aubyn, 14th Bt, CBE; one *s* one *d*. *Educ:* Eton. 2nd Lt, KRRC, 1942; served NW Europe, 1944–45; Palestine and Egypt, 1945–48; transferred to Royal Fusiliers, 1947; served Korea, 1952–53; Middle East, 1953–55 and 1956; Staff Coll., Camberley, 1957; Comd, 1st Bn Royal Fusiliers, 1965–67. Director: Lloyds Bank Ltd, 1974–78; Lloyds Bank UK Management Ltd, 1979–86; Chm., SW Region, Lloyds Bank, 1989–91 (Chm., Devon and Cornwall Regl Bd, 1974–89). Mem., Devon and Co. Cttee, Nat. Trust, 1969–84; President: Plymouth Incorporated Chamber of Trade and Commerce, 1970–; Cornwall Fedn of Chambers of Commerce and Trader Assocs, 1972–79; West Country Tourist Bd, 1971–89. Governor: Seale-Hayne Agric. Coll., 1973–93; Plymouth Polytechnic, 1975–82 (Chm., 1977–82). Pres., Council of Order of St John for Devon, 1979–98. DL 1973, Vice Lord-Lieutenant, 1978–82, Devon. JP Plymouth, 1972. Hon. Colonel: Devon ACF, 1979–87; 4th Bn Devonshire and Dorset Regl, 1987–92. *Heir: s* Viscount Boringdon, *qv*. *Address:* Pound House, Yelverton, Devon PL20 7LJ. *T:* (01822) 853162.

MORLEY, Elliot Anthony; MP (Lab) Scunthorpe, since 1997 (Glanford and Scunthorpe, 1987–97); Parliamentary Secretary, Department for Environment, Food and Rural Affairs, (formerly Ministry of Agriculture, Fisheries and Food), since 1997; *b* 6 July 1952; *m* 1975; one *s* one *d*. *Educ:* St Margaret's C of E High Sch., Liverpool. Remedial teacher, comprehensive sch., Hull; head of individual learning centre, until 1987. Mem., Kingston upon Hull City Council, 1979–85; Chair, Hull City Transport Cttee, 1981–85. Contested (Lab) Beverley, 1983. Opposition front bench spokesman on food, agriculture and rural affairs, 1989–97; Labour spokesperson on animal welfare, 1992–97; Mem., Select Cttee for Agriculture, 1987–90; Dep. Chair, PLP Educn Cttee, 1987–90. Vice-Pres., Wildlife and Countryside Link, 1990–; Member of Council: RSPB, 1989–93; British Trust for Ornithology, 1992–95; Trustee, Birds of the Humber Trust. Hon. Pres., N Lincs RSPCA. Hon. Vice-Pres., Assoc. of Drainage Authorities. Hon. Fellow, Lincs and Humberside Univ. *Recreations:* ornithology, the environment, the countryside. *Address:* House of Commons, SW1A 0AA; 9 West Street, Winterton, Scunthorpe, N Lincs DN15 9QG.

MORLEY, Herbert, CBE 1974; Director and General Works Manager, Samuel Fox & Co. Ltd, 1959–65; Director, United Steel Cos, 1966–70; *b* 19 March 1919; *s* of George Edward and Beatrice Morley; *m* 1st, 1942, Gladys Hardy (*d* 1991); one *s* one *d*; 2nd, 1994, Mrs Frances H. Suagee, Cincinnatti, Ohio. *Educ:* Almondbury Grammar Sch., Huddersfield; Sheffield Univ. (Assoc. Metallurgy); Univ. of Cincinnati (Post-Grad. Studies in Business Admin). Dir and Gen. Man., Steel Peech Tozer, 1965–68; British Steel Corporation: Dir, Northern Tubes Gp, 1968–70; Man. Dir, Gen. Steel Div., 1970–73; Man. Dir, Planning and Capital Develt, 1973–76. Chm., Templeborough Rolling Mills Ltd, 1977–82; Dep. Chm. and Dir, Ellison Circlips Gp Ltd, 1990–92; Director: Ellison-Morlock, 1985–92; Bridon Ltd, 1973–85. *Recreations:* music, cricket lover, weekend golfer. *Address:* 350 Wood Avenue, Cincinnati, OH 45220, USA. *T:* (513) 2216851.

MORLEY, Prof. Leslie Sydney Dennis, DSc; FRS 1992; FREng, FIMA, FRAeS; Hon. Associate Professorial Research Fellow, Institute of Computational Mathematics, Brunel University, since 1998 (Professorial Research Fellow, 1985–98); *b* 23 May 1924; *s* of late Sydney Victor Morley, RN (Chief Petty Officer (Gunnery), HMS Hood, killed in action with the Bismarck, 1941) and of Doris May Huntley (*née* Evans); *m* 1951, Norma Baker; two *s* one *d*. *Educ:* Portsmouth Northern Secondary Sch.; Portsmouth Municipal Tech. Sch.; Southampton Univ. Coll. (HNC 1945); Coll. Aeronautics, Cranfield (DCAe 1948; DSc 1971); Univ. of Cambridge (Post-Grad. Dip. Structures and Materials 1959). FRAeS 1962; FIMA 1964; FREng (FEng 1982). Airspeed Ltd: apprentice toolroom fitter, Portsmouth, 1940–45; Stress Office, Christchurch, 1945–46; Res. Officer, Nat Luchtvartlab., Amsterdam, 1948–49; Tech. Asst, Bristol Aeroplane Co., Filton, 1949–50; Structures Dept, RAE, 1950–84, DCSO, 1976. *Publications:* Skew Plates and Structures, 1963; numerous articles on structural mechanics, esp. finite element method, plate and shell theory, in learned jls in Britain and abroad. *Recreations:* family, British heritage, gardening. *Address:* Institute of Computational Mathematics, Brunel University, Middx UB8 3PH. *T:* (01895) 274000.

MORLEY, Malcolm A.; artist; *b* 1931. *Educ:* Camberwell Sch. of Arts and Crafts; Royal Coll. of Art (ARCA 1957). *One man exhibitions:* Kornblee Gall., NY, 1957, 1964, 1967, 1969; Galerie Gerald Piltzer, Paris, 1973; Stefanotty Gall., NY, 1973, 1974; Clocktower Gall., Inst. for Art & Urban Resources, 1976; Galerie Jurka, Amsterdam, 1977; Galerie Jollenbeck, Cologne, 1977; Nancy Hoffman Gall., NY, 1979; Suzanne Hilberry Gall., Birmingham, Mich, 1979; Xavier Fourcade, NY, 1981, 1982, 1984, 1986; Galerie Nicholine Pon, Zurich, 1984; Fabian Carlsson Gall., London, 1985; Pace Gall., NY, 1988, 1991; Anthony d'Offay Gall., London, 1990; Tate Gall., 1991; Mary Boone Gall., NY, 1993, 1995; retrospective: Whitechapel Art Gall., also shown in Europe and USA, 1983–84; Centre Georges Pompidou, Paris, 1993; Fundacio La Caixa, Madrid, 1995; *major exhibitions:* Wadsworth Atheneum, Hartford, Conn, 1980; Akron Art Mus., 1982; *work in collections:* Met. Mus. of Art, NY; Detroit Inst. of Art; Hirshhorn Mus. and Sculpture Gdn, Washington; Lousiana Mus., Humlebaek, Denmark; Neue Galerie der Stadt Aachen; Mus. of Contemp. Art, Chicago; Munson-Williams-Proctor Inst., Utica, NY; Mus. of Modern Art, NY; Mus. Moderner Kunst, Vienna; Nat. Gall. of Art, Washington; Mus. of Contemp. Art, LA; Wadsworth Atheneum, Hartford; Centre Georges Pompidou, Paris; Nelson-Atkins Mus., Kansas City; Ludwig Forum for Internat. Art, Aachen, Vienna, Budapest; Mus. van Hedendaagse Kunst, Utrecht. First Turner Prize, Tate Gall., 1984; Painting Award, Skowhegan Sch. of Painting and Sculpture, 1992. *Address:* c/o Mary Boone Gallery, 745 Fifth Avenue, New York, NY 10151, USA.

MORLEY, Sheridan Robert; author, journalist and broadcaster; Drama Critic, Spectator, since 1990; London Drama Critic, International Herald Tribune, since 1979; *b* Ascot,

Berks, 5 Dec. 1941; *s* of late Robert Morley, CBE and of Joan Buckmaster; *m* 1st, 1965, Margaret Gudejko (marr. diss. 1990); one *s* two *d*; 2nd, 1995, Ruth Leon. *Educ:* Sizewell Hall, Suffolk; Merton Coll., Oxford (MA (Hons) 1964). Newscaster, reporter and scriptwriter, ITN, 1964–67; interviewer, Late Night Line Up, BBC2, 1967–71; Presenter, Film Night, BBC2, 1972; Dep. Features Editor, The Times, 1973–75; Arts Editor, 1975–88, Drama Critic, 1975–89, Punch; Arts Diarist and TV Critic, The Times, 1989–90; Film Critic, Sunday Express, 1992–95; Regular presenter: Kaleidoscope, BBC Radio 4; Theatreland, LWT, 1995–96; Meridian, BBC World Service; frequent radio and TV broadcasts on the performing arts, incl. Broadway Babes, Song by Song by Sondheim, Morley at the Musicals, and the Arts Programme (Radio 2), Sheridan Morley Meets (BBC1) and Countdown (C4). Mem., Drama Panel, British Council, 1982–89. Narrator: Side by Side by Sondheim, Guildford and Norwich, 1981–82; (also devised): Noël and Gertie (Coward anthology), King's Head, London, 1983, Sonning, 1985, Warehouse, London, 1986, Sydney, 1988, Comedy, London, 1989, NY, 1999; Spread a Little Happiness (Vivian Ellis anthology), King's Head and Whitehall, London, 1992; director: Song at Twilight, Gielgud, 1999; Jermyn Street Revue, 2000, Noel Coward Tonight, 2001, Jermyn Street Theatre; cabaret seasons, Pizza on the Park, 1992, 1994, 1995 and 1998. BP Arts Journalist of the Year, 1989. *Publications:* A Talent to Amuse: the life of Noël Coward, 1969; Review Copies, 1975; Oscar Wilde, 1976; Sybil Thorndike, 1977; Marlene Dietrich, 1977; Gladys Cooper, 1979; (with Cole Lesley and Graham Payn) Noël Coward and his Friends, 1979; The Stephen Sondheim Songbook, 1979; Gertrude Lawrence, 1981; (ed, with Graham Payn) The Noël Coward Diaries, 1982; Tales from the Hollywood Raj, 1983; Shooting Stars, 1983; The Theatregoers' Quiz Book, 1983; Katharine Hepburn, 1984; The Other Side of the Moon, 1985; (ed) Bull's Eyes, 1985; Ingrid Bergman, 1985; The Great Stage Stars, 1986; Spread a Little Happiness, 1986; Out in the Midday Sun, 1988; Elizabeth Taylor, 1988; Odd Man Out: the life of James Mason, 1989; Our Theatres in the Eighties, 1990; Robert My Father, 1993; Audrey Hepburn, 1993; Ginger Rogers, 1995; Faces of the 90s, 1995; Dirk Bogarde: rank outsider, 1996; (with Ruth Leon): Gene Kelly, 1996; Marilyn Monroe, 1998; Hey Mr Producer!: the musicals of Cameron Mackintosh, 1999; Beyond the Rainbow: Judy Garland, 1999; Oberon Theatre Century, 1999; John G: the authorised biography of John Gielgud, 2001; ed, series of theatre annuals and film and theatre studies, incl. Punch at the Theatre, 1980, Methuen Book of Theatrical Short Stories, 1992 and Methuen Book of Movie Stories, 1993; contribs to The Times, Sunday Telegraph, Evening Standard, Radio Times, Mail on Sunday, Playbill (NY), High Life, Sunday Times, Variety, and The Australian. *Recreations:* talking, swimming, eating, narrating Spread a Little Happiness and Noël and Gertie. *Address:* 7 Coral Row, Plantation Wharf, SW11 3UF; (office) 7 Ivory Square, Plantation Wharf, SW11 3UF. *Club:* Garrick.

MORNINGTON, Earl of; Arthur Gerald Wellesley; *b* 31 Jan. 1978; *s* and *heir* of Marquess of Douro, *qv. Educ:* Eton Coll.; Christ Church, Oxford. A Page of Honour to HM Queen Elizabeth the Queen Mother, 1993–95.

MORPETH, Sir Douglas (Spottiswoode), Kt 1981; TD 1959; FCA; Senior Partner, Touche Ross & Co., 1977–85 (Partner, 1958–85); *b* 6 June 1924; *s* of late Robert Spottiswoode Morpeth and Louise Rankine Morpeth (*née* Dobson); *m* 1951, Anne Rutherford, *yr d* of Ian C. Bell, OBE, MC, Edinburgh; two *s* two *d. Educ:* George Watson's Coll., Edinburgh; Edinburgh Univ. (BCom). Commissioned RA; served 1943–47, India, Burma, Malaya. Mem., Inst. of Chartered Accountants in England and Wales, 1952, Fellow, 1957, Pres., 1972. Chm., Clerical Med. and Gen. Life Assce Soc., later Clerical Med. Investment Gp, 1978–94. Chairman: (of Trustees), British Telecom Staff Superannuation Scheme, 1983–92; British Borneo Petroleum Syndicate, 1985–95; Deputy Chairman: Brixton Estate plc, 1983–94; Leslie Langton Hldgs, 1987–91; Director: Allied-Irish Banks, 1986–91; First Ireland Investment Trust, 1992–99 (Chm., 1997–99). Mem., Investment Grants Advisory Cttee, 1968–71; Chm., Inflation Accounting Steering Gp, 1976–80; Vice-Chm., Accounting Standards Cttee, 1970–82. Chm., Taxation Cttee, CBI, 1973–76. Honourable Artillery Company: Member, 1949–; Lt-Col, comdg 1st Regt HAC (RHA), 1964–66; Master Gunner within the Tower of London, 1966–69. Master, Co. of Chartered Accountants in England and Wales, 1977–78. FRCM (Hon. Treasurer, RCM, 1983–96). *Recreations:* golf, gardening. *Address:* Winterden House, Shamley Green, near Guildford, Surrey GU5 0UD. *Clubs:* Athenæum, Caledonian.

MORPHET, David Ian; Director General, The Railway Forum, 1997–2000; *b* 24 Jan. 1940; *s* of late A. Morphet and Sarah Elizabeth Morphet; *m* 1968, Sarah Gillian Sedgwick; two *s* one *d. Educ:* King James's Grammar Sch., Almondbury, Yorks; St John's Coll., Cambridge (History Schol.; English Tripos, class I, Pts I and II). Foreign Office, 1961; Vice Consul, Taiz, 1963; Doha, 1963–64; FO, 1964–66; Asst Private Sec. to Foreign Secretary, 1966–68; First Sec., Madrid, 1969–72; Diplomatic Service Observer, CS Selection Board, 1972–74; transf. to Dept of Energy, 1974; Asst Sec., 1975; Dep. Chm., Midlands Electricity Board (on secondment), 1978–79; Under-Secretary: Electricity Div., 1979–83; Energy Policy Div., 1983–85; Atomic Energy Div., 1985–89; UK Governor: Internat. Energy Agency, Paris, 1983–85; IAEA, Vienna, 1985–89. Director: BICC Cables Ltd, 1981–89; Planning and Develt, Balfour Beatty Ltd, 1989–91; Govt Affairs, BICC plc, 1992–95; Barking Power Ltd, 1993–2001. Chm., Export Finance Cttee, CBI, 1992–96; Mem. Council, CBI, 1995–96 and 1997–2001. Chm., Nat. Schizophrenia Fellowship, 1977–83. *Publication:* Life and Times of Louis Jennings, MP, 1996, rev. edn as Louis Jennings, MP: editor of The New York Times and Tory democrat, 2001. *Recreations:* music, theatre, walking. *Address:* 11 Daisy Lane, SW6 3DD. *Club:* Athenæum.

MORPHET, Richard Edward, CBE 1998; Keeper, Modern Collection, Tate Gallery, 1986–96 (Keeper Emeritus, 1996–98); *b* 2 Oct. 1938; *s* of Horace Taylor Morphet and Eleanor Morphet (*née* Shaw); *m* 1965, Sally Richmond; two *d. Educ:* Bootham Sch., York; London Sch. of Economics (BA Hons History). Fine Arts Dept, British Council, 1963–66; Tate Gallery: Asst Keeper, 1966–73; Dep. Keeper, Modern Collection, 1973–86. Exhibitions (curator and author/editor of catalogue) include: Richard Hamilton, Tate, 1970; Bernard Cohen, Hayward, 1972; William Turnbull, Tate, 1973; Art in One Year: 1935, Tate, 1977; Meredith Frampton, Tate, 1982; Cedric Morris, Tate, 1984; The Hard-Won Image, Tate, 1984; Richard Hamilton, Tate, 1992; R. B. Kitaj, Tate, 1994; Encounters: New Art from Old, National Gallery, 2000; other exhibition catalogues include: Roy Lichtenstein, Tate, 1968; Andy Warhol, Tate, 1971; Howard Hodgkin, Arts Council, 1976; Leonard McComb, Serpentine, 1983; contribs to exhibn catalogues on Late Sickert, Hayward, 1981 and The Art of Bloomsbury, Tate, 1999. *Publications:* contrib. books on Eric Ravilious, 1983, and Anthony Gross, 1992; contrib. Apollo, Burlington Mag., Studio International, TLS, etc. *Fax:* (020) 7820 1610.

MORPURGO, Michael Andrew Bridge, MBE 1999; writer; Joint Founder Director, Farms for City Children, since 1976; *b* 5 Oct. 1943; *s* of Tony Valentine Bridge and late Catherine Noel Kippe (*née* Cammaerts), and step *s* of Jack Eric Morpurgo; *m* 1963, Clare (MBE 1999), *d* of Sir Allen Lane, founder, Penguin Books; two *s* one *d. Educ:* King's Sch., Canterbury; RMA Sandhurst; King's Coll., London (AKC, BA 1967; FKC 2001). Primary school teacher, 1967–75; with Clare Morpurgo founded Farms for City Children and opened Nethercott House farm, 1976; opened Treginnis Isaf, 1989, Wick Court, Glos, 1998. *Publications:* over sixty books for children, including: Friend or Foe, 1978; (jtly) All Around the Year, 1979; The Nine Lives of Montezuma, 1980; The White Horse of Zennor, 1982; War Horse, 1984; Twist of Gold, 1986; Mr Nobody's Eyes, 1989; Why the Whales Came (Silver Pencil award, Holland), 1989 (screenplay, When the Whales Came, 1991); My Friend Walter, 1990 (screenplay, 1994); Little Foxes, 1992; The Marble Crusher, 1992; King of the Cloud Forests, 1992 (Cercle d'Or, Montreuil, 1994; Prix Sorcière, 1995); The War of Jenkins Ear, 1992 (Best Book award, Amer. Liby Assoc., 1996); Blodin the Beast, 1993; Waiting for Anya, 1993; The Sandman and the Turtles, 1994; The Dancing Bear, 1995; The Wreck of the Zanzibar, 1995 (Whitbread Children's Award, and Children's Book Award, Fedn of Children's Books, 1996; IBBY Honour Book, 1998); Arthur High King of Britain, 1995; Sam's Duck, 1996 (screenplay, 1993); Muck and Magic, 1996; The Butterfly Lion, 1996 (Writers' Guild Award, 1996; Smarties Prize, 1997); The Ghost of Grania O'Malley, 1996; Robin of Sherwood, 1997; Farm Boy, 1997; Red Eyes at Night, 1997; Beyond the Rainbow Warrior, 1997; Escape from Shangri-la, 1998; Joan of Arc of Domrémy, 1998; Wartman, 1998; The Rainbow Bear, 1999 (NATE Children's Book Award); Kensuke's Kingdom, 1999 (Children's Book Award, Prix Sorcière, Prix Lire au Collège); Wombat Goes Walkabout, 1999 (Prix Sorcière); Animal Stories, 1999; Dear Olly, 2000; The Silver Swan, 2000; Black Queen, 2000; Tom's Sausage Lion, 2000; From Hereabout Hill, 2000; Billy the Kid, 2000; Classic Boys' Stories, 2000; Toro! Toro!, 2001; More Muck and Magic, 2001; Because a Fire was in my Head, 2001; The Last Wolf, 2002; The Sleeping Sword, 2002; libretti: Solar, 1981; Scarecrow (music by Phyllis Tate), 1982. *Recreation:* dreaming. *Address:* c/o David Higham Associates, 5–8 Lower John Street, Golden Square, W1R 4HA. *Clubs:* Royal Over-Seas League, Two Brydges.

MORPURGO DAVIES, Anna Elbina; *see* Davies.

MORRELL, Prof. David Cameron, OBE 1982; FRCP; FRCGP; Wolfson Professor of General Practice, United Medical and Dental Schools of Guy's and St Thomas' Hospitals, 1974–93, Emeritus Professor of General Practice, 1993; *b* 6 Nov. 1929; *s* of William and Violet Morrell; *m* 1953, Alison Joyce Morrell; three *s* two *d. Educ:* Wimbledon Coll.; St Mary's Hosp. Med. Sch. (MB BS). DObstRCOG; FFPHM. Phys., RAF Med. Br., 1954–57; Principal in Gen. Practice, Hoddesdon, Herts, 1957–63; Lectr in Gen. Practice, Univ. of Edinburgh, 1963–67; Sen. Lectr, then Reader, in Gen. Practice, St Thomas's Hosp. Med. Sch., 1967–74. Pres., BMA, 1994–95. KSG 1982. *Publications:* The Art of General Practice, 1966, 4th edn 1991; An Introduction to Primary Medical Care, 1976, 2nd edn 1981; (with J. Cormack and M. Marinker) Practice: a handbook of general practice, 1976, 2nd edn 1987. *Recreations:* gardening, walking. *Address:* 14 Higher Green, Ewell KT17 3BA. *T:* (020) 8224 5781.

MORRELL, David William James; Scottish Legal Services Ombudsman, 1991–94; *b* 26 July 1933; *s* of Rev. W. W. Morrell, MBE, TD and Grace Morrell; *m* 1960, Margaret Rosemary Lewis; two *s* one *d. Educ:* George Watson's Coll., Edinburgh; Univ. of Edinburgh (MA Hons, LLB). Law Apprentice, Edinburgh, 1954–57; Admin. Asst, Univ. of Durham, 1957–60; Asst Registrar and Graduate Appts Officer, Univ. of Exeter, 1960–64; Sen. Asst Registrar, Univ. of Essex, 1964–66; Academic Registrar, 1966–73, Registrar, 1973–89, Univ. of Strathclyde; Lay Observer for Scotland, 1989–91. OECD Consultant on management in higher educn, 1990. Vice-Chm., Lomond Healthcare NHS Trust, 1995–99 (Chm., 1995–96); Mem., Argyll and Clyde Health Bd, 1999–2001. Governor: Univ. of Paisley (formerly Paisley Coll.), 1990– (Vice-Chm., 1992–97, Chm., 1997–2002); Scottish Centre for Children with Motor Impairments, 1994–97; Chm., Conf. of Scottish Centrally-Funded Colls, 1997–2000. FRSA 1992. *Publications:* papers on higher education and on provision of legal services. *Recreations:* hill-walking, fishing. *Address:* 29 Barclay Drive, Helensburgh, Dunbartonshire G84 9RA. *T:* (01436) 674875.

MORRELL, Frances Maine; Joint Chief Executive, Arts Inform, since 1997 (Chair, 1993–97); *b* 28 Dec. 1937; *d* of Frank and Beatrice Galleway; *m* 1964, Brian Morrell; one *d. Educ:* Queen Anne Grammar Sch., York; Hull Univ. (BA (Hons) English Lang. and Lit.); MA (Distinction) Goldsmiths Coll., Univ. of London 1995. Secondary Sch. Teacher, 1960–69; Press Officer, Fabian Soc. and NUS, 1970–72; Research into MPs' constituency role, 1973; Special Adviser to Tony Benn, as Sec. of State for Industry, then as Sec. of State for Energy, 1974–79. Dep. Leader, 1981–83, Leader, 1983–87, ILEA; Mem. for Islington S and Finsbury, GLC, 1981–86; Sec., Speaker's Commn on Citizenship, 1988–91; Exec. Dir, Inst. for Citizenship Studies, 1992–93; Dir of Studies, Practising Citizenship Project, 1994–98. Sen. Res. Fellow, Federal Trust for Educn and Res., 1993–; Mem., LSE Grad. Sch., 1996–. Member: Oakes Cttee, Enquiry into Payment and Collection Methods for Gas and Electricity Bills (report publ. 1976); Exec., Campaign for Labour Party Democracy, 1979–; Co Founder: Labour Co-ordinating Cttee, 1978; Women's Action Cttee, 1980–. Contested (Lab) Chelmsford, Feb. 1974. Chair: NCVQ Performing Arts Adv. Cttee, 1994–; London Schs Newspaper Project, 1994–; Member: Bd of Dirs, Sadler's Wells Theatre, 1982–88; Bd, King's Head Theatre, 2000–; Bd, Islington Internat. Fest., 2000–. *Publications:* (with Tony Benn and Francis Cripps) A Ten Year Industrial Strategy for Britain, 1975; (with Francis Cripps) The Case for a Planned Energy Policy, 1976; From the Electors of Bristol: the record of a year's correspondence between constituents and their Member of Parliament, 1977; (jtly) Manifesto—a radical strategy for Britain's future, 1981; Children of the Future: the battle for Britain's schools, 1989. *Recreations:* reading, cooking, gardening. *Address:* 91 Hemingford Road, N1 1BY.

MORRELL, Leslie James, OBE 1986; JP; Chairman, Northern Ireland Water Council, 1982–93; *b* 26 Dec. 1931; *s* of James Morrell; *m* 1958, Anne Wallace, BSc; two *s* one *d. Educ:* Portora Royal Sch., Enniskillen; Queen's Univ., Belfast. BAgric 1955. Member: Londonderry CC, 1969–73; Coleraine Bor. Council, 1973–77; Mem. (U) for Londonderry, NI Assembly, 1973–75; Minister of Agriculture, NI Exec., 1973–74; Dep. Leader, Unionist Party of NI, 1974–80. Mem., BBC Gen. Adv. Cttee, 1980–86; Chm., BBC NI Agricl Adv. Cttee, 1986–91. Chm., NI Fedn of Housing Assocs, 1978–80; Hon. Secretary: Oaklee Housing Assoc., 1992– (James Butcher Housing Assoc. (NI), 1981–92 (Chm., 1976–81)); James Butcher Retirement Homes Ltd, 1985–95. Mem. Exec., Assoc. of Governing Bodies of Voluntary Grammar Schs, 1978–84; Chm., Virus Tested Stem Cutting Potato Growers Assoc., 1977–88. JP Londonderry, 1966. *Address:* Dunboe House, Castlerock, Coleraine BT51 4UB. *T:* (028) 7084 8352.

MORRELL, Peter Richard; His Honour Judge Morrell; a Circuit Judge, since 1992; *b* 25 May 1944; *s* of Frank Richard Morrell and Florence Ethel Morrell; *m* 1970, Helen Mary Vint Collins; two *d. Educ:* Westminster Sch.; University, Coll., Oxford (MA). Admitted Solicitor, 1970; called to the Bar, Gray's Inn, 1974; a Recorder, 1990–92. *Recreations:* shooting, fishing, photography. *Address:* Leicester Crown Court, Wellington Street, Leicester LE1 6HG. *T:* (0116) 222 3434.

MORRICE, Jane, (Mrs Paul Robinson); Member (NI Women's Coalition) North Down, since 1998, and Deputy Speaker, since 1999, Northern Ireland Assembly; *b* 11 May 1954; *d* of George Eric Morrice and Irene (*née* Cleland); *m* 1988, Paul Robinson; one *s. Educ:* Univ. of Ulster (BA Hons W Eur. Studies 1977). Journalist, Brussels, specialising in internat. economy and Third World; business and labour relns corresp., 1980–87; BBC TV and Radio in NI, 1987–92; Head, Eur. Commn Office in NI, 1992–97; Mem., Eur. Commn Task Force preparing special support prog. for peace and reconciliation in NI and border counties of Ireland, 1992–97. *Publications:* North/South Dialogue, 1984; The Lomé Convention From Politics to Practice, 1985. *Recreations:* writing, swimming, tennis. *Address:* Parliament Buildings, Stormont BT4 3XX.

MORRICE, Norman; choreographer; Director: the Royal Ballet, 1977–86; Choreographic Studies, Royal Ballet School, since 1987; Royal Ballet Choreographic Group, 1987–96; *b* Mexico, of British parents. *Educ:* Rambert School of Ballet. Joined the Ballet Rambert in early 1950s as a dancer; notably danced Dr Coppélius, in Coppélia, and subseq. also choreographer; first considerable success with his ballet, Two Brothers, in America, and at first London perf., Sept. 1958; première of his 2nd ballet, Hazaña, Sadler's Wells Theatre, 1958; the New Ballet Rambert Company was formed in 1966 and he was Co-Director with Marie Rambert, to create new works by unknown and established choreographers; his ballet, Hazard, was danced at Bath Festival, 1967; he composed 10 new ballets by 1968 and had taken his place with leading choreographers; *ballets include:* 1–2–3, Them and Us and Pastorale Variée, which were staged at the Jeanetta Cochrane Theatre, 1968–69; Ladies, Ladies!, perf. by Ballet Rambert at Young Vic, 1972; Spindrift, at Round House, 1974, etc. Has danced frequently overseas.

MORRICE, Philip; HM Diplomatic Service; Foreign and Commonwealth Office, since 1999; *b* 31 Dec. 1943; *s* of late William Hunter Morrice and Catherine Jane Cowie; *m* 1988, Margaret Clare Bower; one *s* one *d*. *Educ:* Robert Gordon's College, Aberdeen. Entered HM Diplomatic Service, 1963; served Kuala Lumpur, 1964–67; CO, later FCO, 1967–69; Caracas, 1969–72; First Sec., UK Delegn to OECD, Paris, 1973–75; First Sec. (Energy), UK Perm. Rep. to EC, Brussels, 1975–78; FCO, 1978–81; First Sec. (Commercial), later Counsellor (Comm.), Rome, 1981–85; Counsellor (Econ. and Comm.), Lagos, 1986–88; Minister-Counsellor, Consul-Gen. and Dir of Trade Promotion, Brasilia, 1988–92; Director, Anglo-Taiwan Trade Cttee, subseq. British Trade and Cultural Office, Taipei (on secondment), 1992–95; Consul-Gen., Sydney, and Dir Gen. of Trade and Investment Promotion in Australia, 1995–99. *Publications:* The Schweppes Guide to Scotch, 1983; The Whisky Distilleries of Scotland and Ireland, 1987; The Teacher's Book of Whisky, 1993; numerous articles. *Recreations:* travel, tennis, golf. *Address:* c/o Foreign and Commonwealth Office, SW1A 2AH. *Clubs:* Royal Automobile; Union, Tattersall's (Sydney); Royal Sydney Golf.

MORRILL, Rev. Prof. John Stephen, DPhil; FRHistS; FBA 1995; Professor of British and Irish History, University of Cambridge, since 1998; Fellow, since 1975, and Vice Master, since 1994, Selwyn College, Cambridge; *b* 12 June 1946; *s* of William Henry Morrill and Marjorie (*née* Ashton); *m* 1968, Frances Mead; four *d*. *Educ:* Altrincham County Grammar Sch.; Trinity Coll., Oxford (BA 1967; MA, DPhil 1971). FRHistS 1977. Keasbey Lectr in Hist., 1970–71, Jun. Res. Fellow, 1971–74, Trinity Coll., Oxford; Coll. Lectr in Hist., St Catherine's Coll., Oxford, 1973–74; Lectr in Mod. Hist., Univ. of Stirling, 1974–75; Faculty of History, Cambridge University: Asst Lectr and Lectr, 1975–92; Reader in Early Modern Hist., 1992–98; Selwyn College, Cambridge: Dir of Studies in Hist., 1975–91; Tutor, 1979–91; Admissions Tutor, 1983–87; Sen. Tutor, 1987–91. Vice-Pres., RHistS, 1993–. Ordained permanent deacon, RC Ch, 1996. *Publications:* Cheshire 1630–1660, 1974; The Revolt of the Provinces 1630–1650, 1976, rev. edn 1980; The Cheshire Grand Jury 1625–1659, 1976; (with G. E. Aylmer) The Civil Wars and Interregnum: sources for local historians, 1979; Seventeenth-Century Britain, 1980; (ed) Reactions to the English Civil War, 1982; (ed) Land Men and Beliefs, 1985; Charles I, 1989; Oliver Cromwell and the English Revolution, 1990; (ed) The National Covenant in its British Context, 1990; (ed) The Impact of the English Civil War, 1991; (ed) Revolution and Restoration, 1992; The Nature of the English Revolution, 1993; (with P. Slack and D. Woolf) Public Men and Private Conscience in Seventeenth-Century England, 1993; (ed) The Oxford Illustrated History of Tudor and Stuart Britain, 1996; (with B. Bradshaw) The British Problem 1534–1707: state formation in the Atlantic Archipelago, 1996; Revolt in the Provinces: the English people and the tragedies of war, 1998; (jtly) Soldiers and Statesmen of the English Revolution, 1998; contribs to learned jls. *Recreations:* classical music, beer, cricket. *Address:* Selwyn College, Cambridge CB3 9DQ; 1 Bradford's Close, Bottisham, Cambs CB5 9DW. *T:* (01223) 811822.

MORRIS; *see* Temple-Morris, family name of Baron Temple-Morris.

MORRIS, family name of **Barons Killanin, Morris, Morris of Aberavon, Morris of Kenwood, Morris of Manchester** and **Naseby**.

MORRIS, 3rd Baron *cr* 1918; **Michael David Morris;** *b* 9 Dec. 1937; *er* twin *s* of 2nd Baron Morris and Jean Beatrice (later Lady Salmon; she *d* 1989), *d* of late Lt-Col D. Maitland-Makgill-Crichton; *S* father, 1975; *m* 1st, 1959, Denise Eleanor (marr. diss. 1962), *o d* of Morley Richards; 2nd, 1962, Jennifer (marr. diss. 1969), *o d* of Squadron Leader Tristram Gilbert; two *d*; 3rd, 1980, Juliet (marr. diss. 1996), twin *d* of Anthony Buckingham; two *s* one *d*; 4th, 1999, Nicola Mary, *o d* of Colin Morgan Watkins. *Educ:* Downside. *Heir: s* Hon. Thomas Anthony Salmon Morris, *b* 2 July 1982.

MORRIS OF ABERAVON, Baron *cr* 2001 (Life Peer), of Aberavon in the County of West Glamorgan and of Ceredigian in the County of Dyfed; **John Morris,** Kt 1999; PC 1970; QC 1973; Chancellor, University of Glamorgan, since 2001; *b* Nov. 1931; *s* of late D. W. Morris, Penywern, Talybont, Cardiganshire and Mary Olwen Ann Morris (*née* Edwards, later Lewis); *m* 1959, Margaret M., JP, *d* of late Edward Lewis, OBE, JP, of Llandysul; three *d*. *Educ:* Ardwyn, Aberystwyth; University Coll. of Wales, Aberystwyth; Gonville and Caius Coll., Cambridge (LLM); Academy of International Law, The Hague; Holker Senior Exhibitioner, Gray's Inn. Commissioned Royal Welch Fusiliers and Welch Regt. Called to the Bar, Gray's Inn, 1954, Bencher, 1985; a Recorder, 1982–97. MP (Lab) Aberavon, Oct. 1959–2001. Parly Sec., Min. of Power, 1964–66; Jt Parly Sec., Min. of Transport, 1966–68; Minister of Defence (Equipment), 1968–70; Sec. of State for Wales, 1974–79; opposition spokesman on legal affairs and Shadow Attorney Gen., 1983–97; Attorney General, 1997–99. Member: Cttee of Privileges, 1994–97; Select Cttee on Implementation of Nolan Report, 1995–97. Dep. Gen. Sec. and Legal Adviser, Farmers' Union of Wales, 1956–58. Member: UK Delegn Consultative Assembly Council of Europe and Western European Union, 1963–64, 1982–83; N Atlantic Assembly, 1970–74. Chairman: Nat. Pneumoconiosis Jt Cttee, 1964–66; Joint Review of Finances and Management, British Railways, 1966–67; Nat. Road Safety Advisory Council, 1967; Mem. Courts of University of Wales. Pres., London Welsh Trust, 2001–. Hon. Fellow: UCW, Aberystwyth; Trinity Coll., Carmarthen; UC, Swansea. Hon. LLD Wales, 1985. *Address:* House of Lords, SW1A 0PW.
See also D. W. Morris.

MORRIS OF KENWOOD, 2nd Baron *cr* 1950, of Kenwood; **Philip Geoffrey Morris;** JP; Company Director, retired 1990; *b* 18 June 1928; *s* of 1st Baron Morris of Kenwood, and Florence (*d* 1982), *d* of Henry Isaacs, Leeds; *S* father, 1954; *m* 1958, Hon. Ruth, *o d* of late Baron Janner and Lady Janner; one *s* three *d*. *Educ:* Loughborough Coll., Leics. Served RAF, Nov. 1946–Feb. 1949, July 1951–Oct. 1955. JP Inner London, 1967. *Recreations:* tennis, golf, ski-ing. *Heir: s* Hon. Jonathan David Morris [*b* 5 Aug. 1968; *m* 1996, Melanie, *d* of Robin Klein]. *Address:* 35 Fitzjohns Avenue, NW3 5JY. *T:* (020) 7431 6332.

MORRIS OF MANCHESTER, Baron *cr* 1997 (Life Peer), of Manchester in the co. of Greater Manchester; **Alfred Morris;** PC 1979; QSO 1989; *b* 23 March 1928; *s* of late George Henry Morris and Jessie Morris (*née* Murphy); *m* 1950, Irene (*née* Jones); two *s* two *d*. *Educ:* elem. and evening schs, Manchester; Ruskin Coll., Oxford; St Catherine's, Univ. of Oxford (MA); Univ. of Manchester (Postgrad. certif. in Educn). Employed in office of a Manchester brewing firm from age 14 (HM Forces, 1946–48); Teacher and Lectr, Manchester, 1954–56; Industrial Relations Officer, The Electricity Coun., London, 1956–64. Nat. Chm., Labour League of Youth, 1950–52; Observer, Coun. of Europe, 1952–53. Contested Liverpool, Garston, 1951. MP (Lab and Co-op) Manchester, Wythenshawe, 1964–97. PPS to Minister of Agric., Fisheries and Food, 1964–67, and to Lord President of the Council and Leader of House of Commons, 1968–70; Opposition front bench spokesman on social services, specialising in the problems of disabled people, 1970–74 and 1979–92; Parly Under-Sec. of State, DHSS, as Britain's first-ever Minister for the Disabled, 1974–79. Treasurer, British Gp, IPU, 1971–74; Mem., UK Parly Delegn to UN Gen. Assembly, 1966; Chm., Food and Agriculture Gp of Parly Lab. Party, 1971–74; Representative of Privy Council on Council of RCVS, 1969–74; promoted Chronically Sick and Disabled Persons Act, 1970, Food and Drugs (Milk) Act, 1970, Police Act, 1972, as a Private Member; Parly Adviser to the Police Fedn, 1971–74; Chm., Co-operative Parly Group, 1971–72 and 1983–85; Vice-Chm., All-Party Parly Retail Trade Gp, 1972–74; Vice-Pres., Parly and Scientific Cttee, 1991–95 (Chm., 1988–91); Chairman: Managing Trustees, Parly Pensions Fund, 1983–97 (Man. Trustee, 1980–83); Managing Trustees, H of C Members' Fund, 1983–97; Anzac Gp of MPs and Peers, 1982–97 (Pres., 1997–); Jt Treasurer, British-Amer. Parly Gp, 1983–97. Mem., Gen. Adv. Council, BBC, 1968–74, 1983–95; Patron: Disablement Income Group, 1970–; Motability, 1978–; Life Patron, Rehabilitation International (RI), 1999; Mem., Exec. Cttee, Nat. Fund for Research into Crippling Diseases, 1970–74. Chm., World Cttees apptd to draft "Charter for the 1980's" for disabled people worldwide, 1980–81, and "Charter for the New Millennium", 2000; President: N of England Regional Assoc. for the Deaf, 1980–; Co-operative Congress, 1995–96; Soc. of Chiropodists and Podiatrists, 1997–; Haemophilia Soc., 1999–; Vice-Pres., Crisis at Christmas, 1995– (Trustee, 1982–95). FABE 2000. Hon. Fellow, Manchester Metropolitan Univ. (formerly Poly.), 1990. Hon. MA Salford, 1997; Hon. LLD Manchester, 1998. Field Marshal Lord Harding Award, 1971, for services to the disabled; Grimshaw Meml Award of Nat. Fedn of the Blind, 1971; Paul Harris Fellowship, Rotary Internat., for services to the disabled internationally, 1992; AA Award, 1997; Earl Snowdon Award, 1998; Lifetime Achievement Award, People of the Year, 2000; Henry H. Kessler Award, Rehabilitation Internat., 2000. Hon. AO 1991. *Publications:* Value Added Tax: a tax on the consumer, 1970; The Growth of Parliamentary Scrutiny by Committee, 1970; (with A. Butler) No Feet to Drag, 1972; Ed. lectures (Human Relations in Industry), 1958; Ed. Jl (Jt Consultation) publ. Nat. Jt Adv. Coun. Elec. Supply Ind., 1959–61. *Recreations:* gardening, tennis, snooker, chess. *Address:* c/o 20 Hitherwood Drive, SE19 1XB.

MORRIS, Alan Douglas; Global Head of Operations–Legal, PricewaterhouseCoopers, since 2000; *b* 15 Sept. 1956; *s* of Leslie John Morris and Gladys Josephine Morris; *m* 1st, 1984, Barbara Caroline Alexandra Welsh (marr. diss. 1998); two *d*; 2nd, 1999, Anne Marie Stebbings. *Educ:* John Ruskin Grammar Sch., Croydon; Magdalene Coll., Cambridge (MA, LLM). FCMA. Joined Tate & Lyle, 1978; Esso Petroleum, 1981–84; Financial Controller: RBC Systems, 1984–87; MI Group, 1987–88; Simmons & Simmons: Finance Dir, 1988–96; Man. Dir, 1997–99. *Recreations:* cricket, acting, singing, bridge, reading, airport lounges. *Address:* Raggets, Pickwell Lane, Bolney, Sussex RH17 5RH. *T:* (01444) 881149. *Club:* Oxford and Cambridge.

MORRIS, Albert, FCIB; Chairman: Lorien plc, since 1998 (Director, since 1996); Macro 4 plc, since 2000; Director, 1989–94, and Deputy Group Chief Executive, 1992–94, National Westminster Bank; *b* 21 Oct. 1934; *m* 1987, Patricia Lane. *Educ:* Skerry's Coll., Liverpool; City of Liverpool Coll. of Commerce; Admin Staff Coll., Henley; MIT. National Westminster Bank: Head of Money Transmission, 1979–83; Dep. Gen. Manager, 1983–85, Gen. Manager, 1985–88, Management Services Div.; Chief Exec., Support Services, 1989–92. Director: NatWest Estate Management & Development Ltd, 1989–94; National Westminster Life Assce Ltd, 1992–94; Regent Associates, 1995–; Metroline plc (Chm., 1997–2000). Chairman: BACS Ltd, 1985–94; Centre-file Ltd, 1988–94; Founding Mem., 1985–87 and Mem. Council, 1990–94, UK Banking Ombudsman Scheme; Chm., APACS, 1993–94 (Dep. Chm., 1991–93; Dir, APACS Admin Ltd, 1987–94). Mem. Adv. Council, Sema Group, 1995–96; Special Advr, Ibos Ltd, 1995–96; non-exec. Mem., DSS Departmental Bd, 1993–97. Hon. Treas., Kingwood Trust, 1996–2000. CIMgt; FCIB 1984 (Mem. Council, 1989–); FRSA 1989. Court Liveryman, Co. of Information Technologists. *Recreations:* golf, work, politics. *Address:* Stonebridge, 74 West Common, Harpenden, Herts AL5 2LD.

MORRIS, Air Marshal Sir Alec, KBE 1982; CB 1979; FREng; *b* 11 March 1926; *s* of late Harry Morris; *m* 1946, Moyna Patricia (*d* 2000), *d* of late Norman Boyle; one *s* one *d* (twins). *Educ:* King Edward VI Sch., East Retford; King's Coll., Univ. of London; Univ. of Southampton. Commnd RAF, 1945; radar duties, No 90 (Signals) Gp, 1945–50; Guided Weapons Dept, RAE, 1953–56; exchange duty, HQ USAF, 1958–60; space res., Min. of Supply, 1960–63; DS, RAF Staff Coll., 1963–65; OC Eng, No 2 Flying Trng Sch., Syerston, 1966–68; Asst Dir, Guided Weapons R&D, Min. of Tech., 1968–70; OC RAF Central Servicing Devel Estabt, Swanton Morley, 1970–72; SASO, HQ No 90 (Signals) Gp, 1972–74; RCDS, 1974; Dir of Signals (Air), MoD, 1975–76; Dir Gen. Strategic Electronic Systems, MoD (PE), 1976–79; Air Officer Engineering, RAF Strike Command, 1979–81; Chief Engineer, RAF, 1981–83. Exec., BAe, 1983–91, retd. FREng (FEng 1989). *Recreations:* tennis, gardening. *Address:* The Old Rectory, Church Street, Semington, Wilts BA14 6JW. *Clubs:* Royal Air Force; Bath and County (Bath).

MORRIS, Alfred Cosier; Vice Chancellor, University of the West of England, Bristol, since 1992 (Director, Bristol Polytechnic, 1986–92); *b* 12 Nov. 1941; *s* of late Stanley Bernard Morris, Anlaby, E Yorks, and Jennie Fletcher; *m* 1970, Annette, *er d* of Eamonn and May Donovan, Cork, Eire; one *d*. *Educ:* Hymers Coll., Hull (E Riding Scholar); Univ. of Lancaster (MA Financial Control 1970). FCA; FSS. Articled clerk to Oliver Mackrill & Co., 1958–63; Company Sec., Financial Controller and Dir, several cos, 1963–71; Sen. Leverhulme Res. Fellow in Univ. Planning and Orgn, Univ. of Sussex, 1971–74; Vis. Lectr in Financial Management, Univ. of Warwick, 1973; Group Management Accountant, Arthur Guinness Ltd, 1974–76; Management Consultant, Deloitte Haskins & Sells, 1976–77; Financial Adviser, subsids of Arthur Guinness, 1977–80; Dep. Dir, Polytechnic of the South Bank, 1980–85, Acting Dir, 1985–86. Adviser to H of C Select Cttee on Educn, Sci. and Arts, 1979–83. Chm., PCFC Cttee on Performance Indicators in Higher Educn, 1989–90; Member: CNAA, 1988–93; HEFCW, 1992–2000 (Chm., Audit Cttee, 1997–2000); Higher Educn Quality Council, 1992–94; South West Arts,

1994–2000; Bd, Westec, 1995–98; FEFCE, 1997–99 (Chm., Audit Cttee, 1997–99). Dir, Bristol and West, 1992–. Chairman: Bristol Old Vic Trust, 1992–94; Patrons of Bristol Old Vic, 1993–; Mem., SWERDA, 1998–; Trustee: Bristol Cathedral Trust, 1988–; John Cabot's Matthew Trust, 1996–; Mem. Exec. Cttee, Bristol Soc., 1992–. Mem. Council, Clifton High Sch., 1995–. Patron: DAVAR, 1999–; W of England Acad., 2000–; Fast Track Trust, 2000–; Gtr Bristol Foundn, 1999– (Chm., 1999–2000). Hon. Fellow, Humberside Univ., 1990. Hon. LLD Bristol, 1993. *Publications:* (ed jtly and contrib.) Resources and Higher Education, 1982; articles and contribs to jls on higher educn. *Recreations:* sailing, wind-surfing. *Address:* Park Court, Sodbury Common, Old Sodbury BS37 6PX. *T:* (01454) 319900.

MORRIS, Sir Allan Lindsay, 11th Bt *cr* 1806, of Clasemont, Glamorganshire; *b* 27 Nov. 1961; *o s* of Sir Robert Morris, 10th Bt and of Christine Morris (*née* Field); *S* father, 1999; *m* 1986, Cheronne Denise, *e d* of Dale Whitford; two *s* one *d*. *Heir: er s* Sennen John Morris, *b* 5 June 1995. *Address:* Georgetown, Halton Hills, ON, Canada.

MORRIS, Andrew James; HM Diplomatic Service, retired; High Commissioner, Kingdom of Tonga, and Consul for Pacific Islands under American sovereignty South of the Equator, 1994–98; *b* 22 March 1939; *s* of late Albert Morris and of Clara Morris; *m* 1961, Ann Christine Healy; two *s*. *Educ:* Queen's Coll., Oxford. Served Army, 1960–64. Entered FO, 1964; served Kuwait, Salisbury, Sofia, Muscat, and San Francisco, 1965–78; Consul, Los Angeles, 1978–82; FCO, 1982–86; First Sec., Kaduna, 1986–89; Dep. High Comr, Port Moresby, 1989–93; First Sec., FCO, 1993–94. *Recreations:* golf, travel. *Address:* c/o Foreign and Commonwealth Office, SW1A 2AH.

MORRIS, Anthony Paul; QC 1991; a Recorder of the Crown Court, since 1988; *b* 6 March 1948; *s* of late Isaac Morris Morris and Margaret Miriam Morris; *m* 1975, Jennie Foley; two *s*. *Educ:* Manchester Grammar Sch.; Keble Coll., Oxford (MA). Called to the Bar, Gray's Inn, 1970, Bencher, 2001; practising on Northern Circuit, 1970–. *Recreations:* travel, the arts, sport, including cycling across Europe and visiting 'The theatre of dreams'. *Address:* Peel Court Chambers, 45 Hardman Street, Manchester M3 3PL. *Clubs:* Little Ship; Dunham Forest Golf; Bowdon Lawn Tennis (Cheshire).

MORRIS, Air Marshal Sir (Arnold) Alec; *see* Morris, Air Marshal Sir Alec.

MORRIS, Rt Hon. Charles Richard; PC 1978; DL; Deputy Chairman, Ponti Group Ltd, since 1987; *b* 14 Dec. 1926; *s* of late George Henry Morris, Newton Heath, Manchester; *m* 1950, Pauline, *d* of Albert Dunn, Manchester; two *d*. *Educ:* Brookdale Park Sch., Manchester. Served with Royal Engineers, 1945–48. Pres., Clayton Labour Party, 1950–52. Mem. of Manchester Corporation, 1954–64: Chm. of Transport Cttee, 1959–62; Dep. Chm. of Establishment Cttee, 1963–64. Mem., Post Office Workers Union (Mem. Nat. Exec. Council, 1959–63). Contested (Lab) Cheadle Div. of Cheshire, 1959. MP (Lab) Manchester, Openshaw, Dec. 1963–1983; PPS to the Postmaster-General, 1964; Govt Asst Whip, 1966–67; Vice-Chamberlain, HM Household, 1967–69; Treasurer, HM Household (Deputy Chief Whip), 1969–70; PPS to Rt Hon. H. Wilson, MP, 1970–74; Minister of State: DoE, March–Oct. 1974; CSD, 1974–79; Dep. Shadow Leader of the House, 1980–83. Sec., NW Gp of Labour MPs, 1979–83. Chm., Oldham–Rochdale Groundwork Trust, 1984–; Chm., Covent Garden Tenants' Adv. Gp, 1990–; Gov., Disley Sch., 1992–97. DL Greater Manchester, 1985. *Address:* Derwent Reach, Aston Lane, Oker, Matlock DE4 2JP. *T:* (01629) 732738.
See also Rt Hon. E. Morris.

MORRIS, Christopher; Senior Partner, Corporate Recovery, Deloitte & Touche, retired 2000; *b* 28 April 1942; *s* of Richard Archibald Sutton Morris and Josephine Fanny Mary Morris (*née* Galliano); *m* 1968, Isabel Claire Ramsden Knowles (marr. diss.); two *s*. *Educ:* privately. FCA 1967. Partner, Touche Ross & Co., later Deloitte & Touche, 1970–2000; Nat. Dir, Corporate Special Services, 1975; Chm., 1992. Major insolvency assignments: Banco Ambrosiano; Laker Airways; Rush & Tomkins; Polly Peck, BCCI. *Recreations:* racing, music, travel, food and wine, countryside. *Address:* (office) Hill House, Little New Street, EC4A 3TR. *Clubs:* Turf, Garrick, Little House.

MORRIS, Rev. Dr Colin; writer and broadcaster; Director, Centre for Religious Communication, Westminster College, Oxford, 1991–96; *b* 13 Jan. 1929; *o s* of Daniel Manley Morris and Mary Alice Morris, Bolton, Lancs; *m* 1985, Sandy James. *Educ:* Bolton County Grammar Sch.; Lincoln Coll., Oxford; Univ. of Manchester. Served RM, 1947–49. Student, Nuffield Coll., Oxford, 1953–56; ordained into Methodist ministry, 1956; Missionary, Northern Rhodesia, 1956–60; President: United Church of Central Africa, 1960–64; United Church of Zambia, 1965–68; Minister of Wesley's Chapel, London, 1969–73; Gen. Sec., Overseas Div., Methodist Church, 1973–78; Pres. of the Methodist Conference, 1976–77; Hd of Religious Programmes, BBC TV, 1978–84; Dep. Hd, 1978–79, Hd, 1979–87, Religious Broadcasting, BBC; Special Adviser to Dir-Gen., BBC, 1986–87; Controller, BBC NI, 1987–90. Chairman: Community and Race Relations Unit, BCC, 1974–76; Bd of Trustees, Refugee Legal Centre, 1993–95; Mem., Lord Chancellor's Adv. Cttee on Legal Educn and Conduct, 1991–94. Presenter, Sunday, BBC Radio 4, 1994–97. Lectures: Willson, Univ. of Nebraska, 1968; Cousland, Univ. of Toronto, 1972; Voigt, S Illinois Conf. United Methodist Church, 1973; Hickman, Duke University, North Carolina, 1974; Palmer, Pacific NW Univ., 1976; Heslington, Univ. of York, 1983; Hibbert, BBC Radio 4, 1986; William Barclay Meml, Glasgow, 1986; Univ. of Ulster Convocation, 1988; St Cuthbert's, Edinburgh, 1990; Studdert-Kennedy, Univ. of Leeds, 1994; Coll. of Preachers, 1995; Randall Preaching, Toronto, 1996. Select Preacher, Univ. of Cambridge, 1975, Oxford, 1976. Holds several hon. degrees. Officer-Companion, Order of Freedom (Zambia), 1966. *Publications:* Black Government (with President K. D. Kaunda), 1960; Hour After Midnight, 1961; Out of Africa's Crucible, 1961; End of the Missionary, 1961; Church and Challenge in a New Africa, 1965; Humanist in Africa (with President K. D. Kaunda), 1966; Include Me Out, 1968; Unyoung, Uncoloured, Unpoor, 1969; What the Papers Didn't Say, 1971; Mankind My Church, 1971; The Hammer of the Lord, 1973; Epistles to the Apostle, 1974; The Word and the Words, 1975; Bugles in the Afternoon, 1977; Get Through Till Nightfall, 1979; (ed) Kaunda on Violence, 1980; God-in-a-Box: Christian strategy in the TV age, 1984; A Week in the Life of God, 1986; Drawing the Line: taste and standards in BBC programmes, 1987; Starting from Scratch, 1990; Let God be God: TV sermons, 1990; Wrestling with an Angel, 1990; Start Your Own Religion, 1992; Raising the Dead: the art of preacher as public performer, 1996; *relevant publication:* Spark in the Stubble, by T. L. Charlton, 1969. *Recreations:* writing, walking, music. *Address:* Tile Cottage, 8 Houndean Rise, Lewes, E Sussex BN7 1EG.

MORRIS, David; *see* Morris, W. D.

MORRIS, David Elwyn; a District Judge (formerly Registrar) of the Principal Registry of the Family Division of the High Court of Justice, 1976–91; *b* 22 May 1920; *s* of Rev. S. M. Morris and K. W. Morris; *m* 1st, 1947, Joyce Hellyer (*d* 1977); one *s* one *d*; 2nd, 1978, Gwendolen Pearce (*d* 1988), *widow* of Dr John Pearce; 3rd, 1990, Mrs C. M. Tudor. *Educ:* Mill Hill Sch.; Brasenose Coll., Oxford (Hulme Exhibnr; MA). With Friends' Ambulance Unit in China, 1942–44; served British Army in India, 1944–46. Called to Bar, Inner Temple, 1949; admitted Solicitor of the Supreme Court, 1955; Mem., Matrimonial Causes Rule Cttee, 1967–75. Partner, Jaques & Co. until 1975. Adv. Editor, Atkin's Encyclopaedia of Court Forms in Civil Proceedings, 1982–88. *Publications:* China Changed My Mind, 1948; The End of Marriage, 1971; contrib. Marriage For and Against, 1972; Pilgrim through this Barren Land, 1974. *Recreation:* reading. *Address:* 42 Frenchay Road, Oxford OX2 6TG. *T:* (01865) 558390. *Club:* Oxford and Cambridge.

MORRIS, David Griffiths; His Honour Judge David Morris; a Circuit Judge, since 1994; *b* 10 March 1940; *s* of Thomas Griffiths Morris and Margaret Eileen Morris; *m* 1971, Carolyn Mary (*née* Miller); one *s* one *d*. *Educ:* Abingdon Sch.; King's Coll., Univ. of London (LLB Hons). Called to the Bar, Lincoln's Inn, 1965, Bencher, 1999. Pupillage in London (Temple and Lincoln's Inn), 1965–67; Tenant in London Chambers (Temple), 1967–72; Tenant in Cardiff Chambers, 1972–94; Asst Recorder, 1979–84; Local Junior for Cardiff Bar, 1981–87; Head of Chambers, 1984–94; a Recorder, 1984–94. Founder Member: Llantwit Major Round Table and 41 Clubs; Llantwit Major Rotary Club (Pres., 1984–85); Llanmaes Community Council, 1982–84. *Recreations:* Rugby Union football, cricket, swimming, theatre, reading, gardening, family. *Address:* Bryn Hafren, Newport Road, Castleton, Cardiff CF3 2UN. *T:* (01633) 681244. *Clubs:* Cardiff and County, United Services Mess (Cardiff); Pontypool Rugby Football (Pres.).

MORRIS, Rev. David Richard; *b* Llanelli, 28 Jan. 1930. *Educ:* Stebonheath Central Sch., Llanelli; Ruskin Coll., Oxford; University Coll., Swansea; Theological Coll., Aberystwyth. Former foundry labourer; Minister, Mid-Wales and Newport, Presbyterian Church of Wales, 1958–62; former district and county councillor; Educnl Advisor, Gwent CC, 1974–84. Contested (Lab) Brecon and Radnor, 1983. MEP (Lab) Mid and West Wales, 1984–94, South Wales West, 1994–99. Formerly: Member, European Parliament Committees: Social Affairs; Transport and Tourism (substitute); Full Mem., ACP/EEC Assembly; Mem., EU-Romania delegn. Vice-Pres., Welsh Parlt Campaign. Contributor, Low Pay Unit. Member: TGWU; Socialist Educnl Assoc.; Tribune Gp; CND (Chm., CND Wales); Socialist Health Assoc. *Address:* 65 Harlech Crescent, Sketty, Swansea SA2 9LL.

MORRIS, David Richard, CEng, FIMechE; Chairman, Northern Electric plc, 1989–97; *b* 25 July 1934; *s* of Frederick George Morris and Marjorie Amy (*née* Brown); *m* 1961, (Ann) Carole Birch; two *s* one *d*. *Educ:* Imperial College (BSc(Eng)). ACGI. Graduate Engrg apprenticeship, D. Napier & Son, Divl Chief Develt Engr and Gen. Manager, 1956–69, English Electric; Divl Gen. Manager and Divl Dir, General Electric Co., 1969–75; Subsid. Co. Man. Dir, Sears Holdings plc, 1975–80; Delta Group plc: Divl Man. Dir, 1980–84; Gp Exec. Dir, 1984–88. *Recreations:* sailing, golf, tennis, gardening, bridge.

MORRIS, Prof. David William, PhD; FRAgS; sheep farmer, since 1983; agricultural consultant, since 1986; *b* 7 Dec. 1937; *s* of late David William Morris and Mary Olwen Ann Lewis; *m* 1966, Cynthia Cooper; one *s* one *d*. *Educ:* Ardwyn Grammar Sch.; UC of Wales (BSc Agric.); Univ. of Newcastle upon Tyne (PhD). FRAgS 1974. Develt Officer, Agric. Div., ICI, 1963–64; Asst Dir, Cockle Park Exptl Farm, Newcastle upon Tyne Univ., 1964–68; Farms Manager for Marquis of Lansdowne, Bowood, Wilts, 1968–70; Principal, Welsh Agric. Coll., Aberystwyth, 1970–83; Prof. of Agric., UC Wales, Aberystwyth, 1979–83. Churchill Fellowship, 1973. Hon. Life Mem., British Charollais Sheep Soc., 2001. *Publications:* Practical Milk Production, 1976, 3rd edn 1977; (with M. M. Cooper) Grass Farming, 5th edn 1984. *Recreation:* farming. *Address:* Yr Ostrey, St Clears, Carmarthen, Carmarthenshire SA33 4AJ. *T:* (01994) 230240.
See also Baron Morris of Aberavon.

MORRIS, Derek James, MA, DPhil; Chairman, Competition (formerly Monopolies and Mergers) Commission, since 1998 (Member, since 1991; Deputy Chairman, 1995–98); Fellow and Tutor in Economics, Oriel College, Oxford, 1970–98, now Emeritus Fellow; *b* 23 Dec. 1945; *s* of Denis William and Olive Margaret Morris; *m* 1975, Susan Mary Whittles; two *s*. *Educ:* Harrow County Grammar Sch.; St Edmund Hall, Oxford; Nuffield Coll., Oxford. MA (Oxon); DPhil. Research Fellow, Centre for Business and Industrial Studies, Warwick Univ., 1969–70; Tutor and Sen. Tutor, Oxford University Business Summer Sch., 1970–78; Visiting Fellow, Oxford Centre for Management Studies, 1977–81; Economic Dir, Nat. Economic Develt Office, 1981–84; Oxford University: Sir John Hicks Res. Fellow, 1991–92; Chm., Social Studies Bd, 1993–94; Reader in Econs, 1996–98. Vis. Lectr, Univ. of Calif, Irvine, 1986–87. Mem., Cttee of Inquiry into the Future of Cowley, 1990. Gov., NIESR, 1997–. Chm., Oxford Economic Forecasting, 1984–98; Dir, Oxford China Economics Ltd, 1993–97. Member Editorial Board: Oxford Economic Papers, 1984–97; Annual Register of World Events, 1985–97; Asst Editor, Jl of Industrial Economics, 1984–87; Associate Editor, Oxford Review of Economic Policy, 1985–98. *Publications:* (ed) The Economic System in the UK, 1977, 3rd edn 1985; (with D. Hay) Industrial Economics, Theory and Evidence, 1979, 2nd edn 1991; (with D. Hay) Unquoted Companies, 1984; (ed jtly) Strategic Behaviour and Industrial Competition, 1987; (with D. Hay) State-Owned Enterprises and Economic Reform in China 1979–87, 1993; articles on unemployment, trade policy and performance, productivity growth, industrial policy, macroeconomic policy, the Chinese economy, exchange rates, profitability, the stock market and corporate control. *Recreations:* ski-ing, badminton, Rugby, reading history. *Club:* Reform.

MORRIS, Desmond John, DPhil; writer on animal and human behaviour; *b* 24 Jan. 1928; *s* of late Capt. Harry Howe Morris and Dorothy Marjorie Fuller Morris (*née* Hunt); *m* 1952, Ramona Baulch; one *s*. *Educ:* Dauntsey's Sch.; Birmingham Univ. (BSc); Magdalen Coll., Oxford (DPhil). Postdoctoral research in Animal Behaviour, Dept of Zoology, Oxford Univ., 1954–56; Head of Granada TV and Film Unit at Zool. Soc. of London, 1956–59; Curator of Mammals, Zool. Soc. of London, 1959–67; Dir, Inst. of Contemp. Arts, London, 1967–68; Research Fellow, Wolfson Coll., Oxford, 1973–81. Chm. of TV programmes: Zootime (weekly), 1956–67; Life (fortnightly), 1965–68; TV series: The Human Race, 1982; The Animals Roadshow, 1987–89; The Animal Contract, 1990; Animal Country, 1991–95; The Human Animal, 1994; The Human Sexes, 1997; Hon. DSc Reading, 1998. *Publications:* (Jt Ed.) International Zoo Yearbook, 1959–62; The Biology of Art, 1962; The Mammals: A Guide to the Living Species, 1965; (with Ramona Morris) Men and Snakes, 1965; (with Ramona Morris) Men and Apes, 1966; (with Ramona Morris) Men and Pandas, 1966; The Naked Ape, 1967; (ed) Primate Ethology, 1967; The Human Zoo, 1969; Patterns of Reproductive Behaviour, 1970; Intimate Behaviour, 1971; Manwatching: a field guide to human behaviour, 1977; (jtly) Gestures: their origins and distribution, 1979; Animal Days (autobiog.), 1979; The Giant Panda, 1981; The Soccer Tribe, 1981; Inrock (novel), 1983; The Book of Ages, 1983; The Art of Ancient Cyprus, 1985; Bodywatching: a field guide to the human species, 1985; The Illustrated Naked Ape, 1986; Catwatching, 1986; Dogwatching, 1986; The Secret Surrealist, 1987; Catlore, 1987; The Human Nest-builders, 1988; The Animals Roadshow, 1988; Horsewatching, 1988; The Animal Contract, 1990; Animal-Watching, 1990; Babywatching, 1991; Christmas Watching, 1992; The World of Animals, 1993; The Human Animal, 1994; The Naked Ape Trilogy, 1994; Bodytalk: a world guide to gestures, 1994; The Illustrated Catwatching, 1994; Illustrated Babywatching, 1995; Catworld: a feline encyclopedia, 1996; Illustrated Dogwatching, 1996; The Human Sexes, 1997; Illustrated Horsewatching, 1998; Cool Cats: the 100 cat breeds of the world, 1999; Body Guards: protective amulets and charms, 1999; The Naked Eye: travels in search of the human species, 2000; numerous papers in zoological jls. *Recreations:* painting, archæology. *Address:* c/o Jonathan Cape, Random Century House, 20 Vauxhall Bridge Road, SW1V 2SA.

MORRIS, Desmond Victor; HM Diplomatic Service, retired; *b* 26 June 1926; *s* of late John Walter Morris and Bessie (*née* Mason); *m* 1st, 1951, Peggy Iris Mumford; two *d*; 2nd, 1961, Patricia Irene Ward, *d* of Charles Daniel and Emma Camwell; one *d*. *Educ:* Portsmouth Southern Secondary Sch. for Boys; Durham Univ. Served RAF, 1945–48. Joined HM Diplomatic Service, 1948; served at Seattle, Budapest, Saigon, Addis Ababa, Berne, Ankara and Pretoria; Dep. High Comr, Georgetown, 1973–78; Dep. Head of Accommodation and Services Dept, FCO, 1979–82; Consul-Gen. and Counsellor (Administration), Washington, 1982–86. *Recreations:* gardening, music, paintings, travel. *Address:* Grayshott, Green Lane, Axminster, Devon EX13 5TD.

MORRIS, Rt Hon. Estelle; PC 1999; MP (Lab) Birmingham, Yardley, since 1992; Secretary of State for Education and Skills, since 2001; *b* 17 June 1952; *d* of Rt Hon. Charles Richard Morris, *qv* and Pauline Morris. *Educ:* Whalley Range High Sch., Manchester; Coventry Coll. of Educn (TCert); BEd Warwick Univ. Teacher, 1974–92. Councillor, Warwick DC, 1979–91 (Labour Gp Leader, 1981–89). An Opposition Whip, 1994–95; opposition front-bench spokesman on educn, 1995–97; Parly Under-Sec. of State, 1997–98, Minister of State, 1998–2001, DFEE. *Address:* House of Commons, SW1A 0AA. *T:* (020) 7219 3000.

MORRIS, Frederick Reginald; Hon. Mr Justice Morris; President of the High Court, Republic of Ireland, since 1998; *b* 1 Dec. 1929; *s* of Michael Archdale Morris and Mary Archdale Morris (*née* Guiry); *m* 1965, Valerie Rose Farrell; two *d*. *Educ:* Glenstall Abbey Sch.; University Coll., Dublin; King's Inns, Dublin. Called to the Irish Bar, 1959 (Bencher, 1990), Inner Bar, 1973; called to the Bar, Middle Temple, 1969, Hon. Bencher, 1999; Judge, High Court in Ireland, 1990–98. Freeman, City of Waterford, 1963. *Recreations:* sailing, golf, Rugby. *Address:* Beechfield, Monkstown Road, Monkstown, Co. Dublin, Republic of Ireland; Four Courts, Dublin 7, Republic of Ireland. *Clubs:* Royal Irish Yacht (Dun Laoghaire); Milltown Golf (Dublin), Blainroe Golf (Co. Wicklow); University College Dublin Rugby.

MORRIS, Gareth; *see* Morris, John G.

MORRIS, Gareth (Charles Walter); flautist; Professor of the Flute, Royal Academy of Music, 1945–85; *b* Clevedon, Som, 13 May 1920, *e s* of late Walter and Enid Morris; brother of Jan Morris, *qv*; *m* 1954; one *d*; *m* 1975, Patricia Mary, *y d* of Neil and Sheila Murray, Romsey, Hampshire; one *s* two *d*. *Educ:* Bristol Cathedral Sch.; Royal Academy of Music, London. First studied the flute at age of twelve under Robert Murchie and later won a scholarship to RAM. Career since then has been as soloist, chamber music and symphonic player, teacher and lecturer; Principal Flautist, 1949–72, Chm., 1966–72, Philharmonia Orch. Gave first British performances of works by Alwyn, Bowen, Gerhard, Ghedini, Honegger, Ibert, Jacob, Koechlin, Martin, Martinu, Piston, Poulenc, Prokofiev, Rawsthorne, Reizenstein, Roussel, Seiber, Wellesz. Has been mem. Arts Council Music Panel, and Warden of Incorporated Soc. of Musicians Soloists Section; Adjudicator, International Flute playing Competitions, Geneva, 1973, 1978, Munich, 1974, Leeds, 1977, 1980, Ancona, 1978, 1979, 1984. Played at Her Majesty's Coronation in Westminster Abbey in 1953. Gov., RSM; Trustee, Loan Fund for Musical Instruments. Mem. Council of Honour, RAM, 1999–. ARAM 1945; FRAM 1950; FRSA 1967 (Mem. Council, 1977–83; Chm., Music Cttee, 1981–83). *Publication:* Flute Technique, 1991. *Recreations:* reading and collecting books, astronomy, antiquarian horology. *Address:* 4 West Mall, Clifton, Bristol BS8 4BH. *T:* (0117) 973 4966. *Club:* Royal Over-Seas League.

MORRIS, Prof. Howard Redfern, FRS 1988; Professor of Biological Chemistry, Imperial College, University of London, since 1980; *b* 4 Aug. 1946; *s* of Marion Elizabeth and Herbert Morris, Bolton, Lancs; *m* 1st, 1969, Lene Verny Jensen (marr. diss.); two *d*; 2nd, 1988, Maria Panico; one *s* one *d*. *Educ:* Univ. of Leeds (BSc 1967; PhD 1970). SRC Fellow, Cambridge, 1970–72; Scientific Staff, MRC Lab. of Molecular Biol., Cambridge, 1972–75; Imperial College: Lectr, Dept of Biochem, 1975–78; Reader in Protein Chem., 1978–80; Hd, Dept of Biochem., 1985–88; Chm., Div. of Life Sciences, 1985–88. Founder Chm., M-Scan Ltd, analytical chem. consultants, 1979–. Visiting Professor: Univ. of Virginia, 1978; Soviet Acad. of Scis, 1982; Univ. of Naples, 1983; Life Scis Div., E. I. Dupont, USA, 1984–85; Dow Lectr in Analytical Chem., Univ. of British Columbia, 1989–90. Royal Soc. Rep. to Council, Inst. of Cancer Res., 1994–. Mem., EMBO, 1979–. BDH Gold Medal and Prize for analytical biochem., Biochem. Soc., 1978; Medal and Prize for macromolecules and polymers, RSC, 1982; Gold Medal for contribs to biopolymer sequencing and mass spectroscopy, Univ. of Naples/CNR Italy, 1989. *Publications:* (ed) Soft Ionisation Biological Mass Spectrometry, 1981; numerous contribs to learned jls, on enkephalin, SRS-A leukotrienes, interleukin, calcitonin gene related peptide, mass spectrometry, protein and glycoprotein structure elucidation. *Recreations:* fell walking, gardening, guitar. *Address:* Department of Biochemistry, Imperial College, Exhibition Road, SW7 2AZ. *T:* (020) 7594 5221, *Fax:* (020) 7225 0458; *e-mail:* h.morris@ic.ac.uk.

MORRIS, Ian; *see* Morris, James I.

MORRIS, James; *see* Morris, Jan.

MORRIS, Air Vice-Marshal James, CBE 1984 (OBE 1977); Chief Executive, Scottish Society for the Prevention of Cruelty to Animals, 1991–2001; *b* 8 July 1936; *s* of late James and Davina Swann Morris; *m* 1959, Anna Wann Provan; three *s*. *Educ:* Kirkcaldy High Sch.; Edinburgh Univ. (BSc). Commnd RAF, 1957; Flying/Staff Duties, RAF, USN, RN, 1960–72; Sqn Comdr 201 Sqdn, 1975–77; psc 1978; Station Comdr RAF Kinloss, 1981–84; Dir Operational Requirements (Air), MoD, 1986–89; AO Scotland and NI, 1989–91. President: Scottish Area, RAFA, 1991–; Scottish Union Jack Assoc., 1995–. Regl Chm., Scottish and NI Air Cadets, 1995–97. HM Comr, Queen Victoria Sch., Dunblane, 1995–. Member: Governing Bd, Scottish Food Quality Certification Ltd, 1998–; Mgt Bd, RAF Benevolent Fund Home, Alastrean House, 2000–. *Recreations:* sailing, golf. *Address:* c/o Lloyds TSB, George Street, Edinburgh EH2 4TF. *Club:* Royal Air Force.

MORRIS, (James) Ian; His Honour Judge Ian Morris; a Circuit Judge, since 1994; *b* 6 Feb. 1944; *s* of late Thomas Orlando Morris and of Pearl Morris; *m* 1st, 1966, Maureen Burton (marr. diss. 1978); one *s* one *d*; 2nd, 1979, Christine Dyson (*d* 1980); 3rd, 1982, Alison Turner (marr. diss. 1988); 4th, 1998, Jane Boddington. *Educ:* King Henry VIII Grammar Sch., Coventry; Corpus Christi Coll., Oxford (BA Jurisp. 1967; MA 1970). Called to the Bar, Inner Temple, 1968; Asst Recorder, 1984, Recorder, 1988–94, Midland and Oxford Circuit. Chairman: Sandwell AHA Enquiry, 1979; Bromsgrove Hosp. Enquiry, 1982; RHA Counsel, Cttee of Enquiry, Legionnaires' Disease, Stafford, 1985. Founder and first Chm., Birmingham Cancer Support Gp, 1984. *Publication:* contrib. Internat. Jl of Child Abuse and Neglect. *Recreations:* writing poetry and children's stories, music, walking, living. *Address:* c/o Worcester Crown Court, Foregate Street, Worcester.

MORRIS, Sir (James) Richard (Samuel), Kt 1992; CBE 1985; FREng; Chairman and Managing Director, 1980–90, Non-Executive Chairman, 1990–92, Brown and Root Ltd; *b* 20 Nov. 1925; *o s* of James John Morris and Kathleen Mary Morris (*née* McNaughton); *m* 1958, Marion Reid Sinclair; two *s* two *d*. *Educ:* Ardingly Coll.; Birmingham Univ. BSc, 1st cl. hons Chem. Engrg; Vice-Chancellor's Prize, 1955; FIChemE. Captain Welsh Guards, 1944–48. Courtaulds Ltd, 1950–78: Man. Dir, National Plastics Ltd, 1959–64; Dep. Chm., British Cellophane Ltd, 1967–70; Chm., British Celanese Ltd, 1970–72; Chm., Northgate Gp Ltd, 1971–76; Chm., Meridian Ltd, 1972–76; Dir, 1967–78, Gp Technical Dir, 1976–78, Courtaulds Ltd. Chairman: Devonport Management Ltd, 1987–91; Devonport Royal Dockyard plc, 1987–91; UK Nirex, 1989–97; Independent Power Corp. plc, 1996–; Dresser Kellogg Energy Services, 1997–98; Dir, British Nuclear Fuels Ltd, 1971–85; non-exec. Dir, OGC International plc, 1994–96; Chairman: M40 Trains Ltd, 1997–; Spectron Ltd, 1999–; Laing Rail Ltd, 2000–. Vis. Prof. of Chem. Engrg, Univ. of Strathclyde, 1979–88; Pro-Chancellor, 1982–86, Sen. Pro-Chancellor and Chm. of Council, 1986–95, Loughborough Univ. Chm., Cttee of Chairmen of Univ. Councils and Boards, 1991–94. Member: Nuclear Power Adv. Bd, 1973; Adv. Council for Energy Conservation, 1974–80; Adv. Bd for Res. Councils, 1981–90, Dep. Chm., 1988–90; Dep. Chm., NEB, 1978–79; Industrial Adviser to Barclays Bank, 1980–85; Dep. Chm., Foundn for Science and Technology, 1994–98. Mem. Council, 1974, Vice-Pres., 1976, Pres., 1977, IChemE; Vice-Pres., Soc. of Chem. Industry, 1978–81; Hon. Sec., 1979–82, Hon. Sec. for Educn and Training, 1984–91, Vice Pres., 1987–91, Fellowship of Engineering; President: Pipeline Industries Guild, 1983–85; Engrg Sect., BAAS, 1989; Soc. for Underwater Technology, 1989–91; Assoc. of Science Educn, 1990. Chm. British Cttee, Det Norske Veritas, 1983–98. Chm., Bd of Govs, Repton Sch., 1997– (Gov., 1987–97). FRSA 1986. Hon. DSc: Leeds, 1981; Bath, 1981; Birmingham, 1985; Loughborough, 1991. *Recreations:* gardening, music. *Address:* Breadsall Manor, Derby DE21 5LL. *T:* (01332) 831368. *Club:* Athenæum.

MORRIS, James Shepherd, RSA 1989 (ARSA 1975); RIBA, FRIAS; ALI; Partner, Morris & Steedman, Architects and Landscape Architects; *b* 22 Aug. 1931; *s* of Thomas Shepherd Morris and Johanna Sime Malcolm; *m* 1959, Eleanor Kenner Smith; two *s* one *d*. *Educ:* Daniel Stewart's Coll.; Edinburgh Sch. of Architecture (DipArch); Univ. of Pennsylvania (MLA). *Architectural works:* Edinburgh Univ., Strathclyde Univ., Princess Margaret Rose Hosp., Countryside Commn for Scotland. Member, Arts Council of Gt Britain, 1973–80; Vice-Chm., Scottish Arts Council, 1976–80 (Chm., Art Cttee, 1976–80; Mem., Enquiry into Community Arts, 1974); Mem., Council, RSA, 1991–2001 (Hon. Treas., 1992–99); Past Member: Council, RIAS and Edinburgh AA, 1969–71; Council of Cockburn Assoc., Edinburgh; Cttee of Management, Traverse Theatre, Edinburgh. Convenor, Fellowship Cttee, RIAS, 1985–87. Trustee, Nat. Mus. of Antiquities, 1980–86. RIBA Award, 1974; 10 Civic Trust Awards, 1962–75; British Steel Award, 1971; European Architectural Heritage Award, 1975; European Heritage Business & Industry Award, 1975. *Publications:* contribs to RIBA Jl. *Recreations:* golf, tennis, skiing, painting. *Address:* (office) 38 Young Street North Lane, Edinburgh EH2 4JD. *T:* (0131) 226 6563. *Clubs:* New (Edinburgh); Philadelphia Cricket (Philadelphia); Valderrama (Sotogrande, Spain).

MORRIS, Jan, CBE 1999; MA Oxon; FRSL; writer. *Address: b* 2 Oct. 1926. Commonwealth Fellow, USA, 1953; Editorial Staff, The Times, 1951–56; Editorial Staff, The Guardian, 1957–62. Fellow, Yr Academi Gymreig; Mem., Gorsedd of Bards, Nat. Eisteddfod of Wales. Hon. FRIBA 1998. Hon. Fellow, UCW, 1992. Hon. DLitt: Wales, 1993; Glamorgan, 1996. *Publications* (as James Morris or Jan Morris): Coast to Coast, 1956; Sultan in Oman, 1957; The Market of Seleukia, 1957; Coronation Everest, 1958; South African Winter, 1958; The Hashemite Kings, 1959; Venice, 1960, 3rd edn 1993; The Upstairs Donkey, 1962 (for children); The World Bank, 1963; Cities, 1963; The Presence of Spain, 1964, rev. edn (as Spain), 1988; Oxford, 1965, 2nd edn 1986; Pax Britannica, 1968; The Great Port, 1970; Places, 1972; Heaven's Command, 1973; Conundrum, 1974; Travels, 1976; Farewell the Trumpets, 1978; The Oxford Book of Oxford, 1978; Destinations, 1980; My Favourite Stories of Wales, 1980; The Venetian Empire, 1980, 2nd edn 1988; The Small Oxford Book of Wales, 1982; A Venetian Bestiary, 1982; The Spectacle of Empire, 1982; (with Paul Wakefield) Wales, The First Place, 1982; (with Simon Winchester) Stones of Empire, 1983; The Matter of Wales, 1984; Journeys, 1984; Among the Cities, 1985; Last Letters from Hav, 1985; (with Paul Wakefield) Scotland, The Place of Visions, 1986; Manhattan '45, 1987; Hong Kong, 1988, 3rd edn 1996; Pleasures of a Tangled Life, 1989; (with Paul Wakefield) Ireland, Your Only Place, 1990; Sydney, 1992; O Canada!, 1992; Locations, 1992; (ed) Travels with Virginia Woolf, 1993; (with Twm Morys) A Machynlleth Triad, 1994; Fisher's Face, 1995; Fifty Years of Europe: an album, 1997; Lincoln: a foreigner's quest, 1999; (with Twm Morys) Our First Leader, 2000; Trieste and the Meaning of Nowhere, 2001. *Address:* Trefan Morys, Llanystumdwy, Gwynedd, Wales LL52 0LP. *T:* (01766) 522222, *Fax:* (01766) 522426; *e-mail:* janmorris1@msn.com.

MORRIS, Prof. Jeremy Noah, CBE 1972; FRCP; Professor of Public Health, University of London, at London School of Hygiene and Tropical Medicine, 1967–78, Hon. Research Officer, since 1978; *b* 6 May 1910; *s* of Nathan and Annie Morris; *m* 1939, Galina Schuchalter (*d* 1997); one *s* one *d*. *Educ:* Hutcheson's Grammar Sch., Glasgow; Univ. of Glasgow; University Coll. Hosp., London; London School of Hygiene and Tropical Medicine (Hon. Fellow 1979). MA, DSc, DPH. Qual., 1934; hosp. residencies, 1934–37; general practice, 1937–38; Asst MOH, Hendon and Harrow, 1939–41; Med. Spec., RAMC, 1941–46 (Lt-Col 1944–46); Rockefeller Fellow, Prev. Med., 1946–47; Dir, MRC Social Med. Unit, 1948–75; Prof., Social Med., London Hosp., 1959–67. Visiting Professor: Yale, 1957; Berkeley, 1963; Jerusalem, 1968, 1980; Adelaide, 1983. Consultant, Cardiology, WHO, 1960–. Lectures: Ernestine Henry, RCP London; Chadwick Trust; Gibson, RCP Edinburgh; Fleming, RCPS Glasgow; Carey Coombs, Univ. of Bristol; Brontë Stewart, Univ. of Glasgow; St Cyres, Nat. Heart Hosp.; Alumnus, Yale; Delamar, Johns Hopkins Univ.; Wade Hampton Frost, APHA; George Clarke, Univ. of Nottingham. Member: Royal Commission on Penal Reform; Cttee, Personal Social Services, Working Party Med. Admin, 1964–72; Health Educn Council, 1978–80; Chairman: Nat. Adv. Cttee on Nutrition Educn, 1979–83; Fitness and Health Adv. Gp, Sports Council and Health Educn Authority, 1980–. Hon. Member: Amer. Epid. Soc., 1976; Soc. for Social Medicine, 1978; British Cardiac Soc., 1982; Swedish Soc. for Sports Medicine, 1984. JP Middx, 1956–66. Hon. FFCM 1977; Hon. FRSocMed 1991. Hon. MD Edinburgh, 1974; Hon. DSc Hull, 1982. Bisset Hawkins Medal, RCP, 1980; Honor Award, Amer. Coll. of Sports Medicine, 1985; Jenner Medal, RSM, 1987; Alwyn Smith Medal, FPHM, 1996; Internat. Olympic Gold Medal and Prize in Exercise Sci., 1996.

Publications: Uses of Epidemiology, 1957, 3rd edn 1975 (trans. Japanese, Spanish); papers on coronary disease and exercise, and in social medicine. *Recreations:* walking, swimming, piano music. *Address:* 3 Briardale Gardens, NW3 7PN. *T:* (020) 7435 5024.

MORRIS, John Cameron; QC (Scot) 1996; Sheriff of South Strathclyde, Dumfries and Galloway at Airdrie, since 1999; *b* 11 April 1952; *s* of Thomas and Louise Morris. *Educ:* Alan Glens Sch., Glasgow; Strathclyde Univ. Solicitor, Scotland, 1976–84; admitted Advocate, Scottish Bar, 1985; called to the Bar, Inner Temple, 1990. Crown Counsel, Scotland, 1989–92. Temp. Sheriff, 1992–98. *Recreations:* golf, music, reading. *Address:* Sheriff Court House, Graham Street, Airdrie ML6 6EE. *T:* (01236) 751121.

MORRIS, John Evan A.; *see* Artro Morris.

MORRIS, Prof. (John) Gareth, CBE 1994; FRS 1988; FIBiol; Professor of Microbiology, University of Wales, Aberystwyth, 1971–2000, now Emeritus; *b* 25 Nov. 1932; *s* of Edwin Morris and Evelyn Amanda Morris (*née* Griffiths); *m* 1962, Áine Mary Kehoe; one *s* one *d*. *Educ:* Bridgend Grammar Sch.; Univ. of Leeds; Trinity Coll., Oxford. DPhil; FIBiol 1971. Guinness Res. Fellow, Univ. of Oxford, 1957–61; Rockefeller Fellow, Univ. of Calif at Berkeley, 1959–60; Tutor in Biochem., Balliol Coll., Oxford, 1960–61; Lectr, subseq. Sen. Lectr, Univ. of Leicester, 1961–71. Vis. Associate Prof., Purdue Univ., USA, 1965. Member: UGC, 1981–86; Royal Commn on Environmental Pollution, 1991–99. *Publications:* A Biologist's Physical Chemistry, 1968, 2nd edn 1974; contribs on microbial biochemistry and physiology. *Recreations:* gardening, walking. *Address:* Cilgwyn, 16 Lôn Tyllwyd, Llanfarian, Aberystwyth, Dyfed SY23 4UH. *T:* (01970) 612502.

MORRIS, John Michael Douglas; General Secretary, 1986–99 and Company Secretary, 1990–99, Hon. Consultant, since 2000, British Boxing Board of Control; *b* 10 Aug. 1935; *s* of Charles Edward Douglas Morris and Mary Kathleen (*née* Murphy); *m* 1958, Jill Margaret Walker; two *s* two *d*. *Educ:* John Fisher Sch.; Dulwich Coll. Reporter, Northampton Chronicle & Echo, 1953–60; Sports sub-editor, Evening Standard, 1960–67; Gp Sports Editor, United Newspapers, 1967–77; freelance writer and publican, 1977–79; John Morris Sports Agency, Northampton, 1979–86. Co. Sec., European Boxing Union, 1991–99; Mem., Bd of Govs, World Boxing Council, 1986–99 (Consultant, 2000–). Commissioner of the Year: World Boxing Council, 1987, 1989, 1994, and 1997; World Boxing Assoc., 1988. Hon. Organiser, Bromley Th. Guild Full-length Play Fest., 2001–. *Publications:* Play Better Tennis (instructional booklet), 1969; Come in No 3: biography of cricketer David Steele, 1977; Box On: biography of boxing referee Harry Gibbs, 1981. *Recreations:* amateur drama, reading, all sport. *Address:* 1 Parkside, Court Downs Road, Beckenham, Kent BR3 6TN.

MORRIS, Sir Keith (Elliot Hedley), KBE 1994; CMG 1988; HM Diplomatic Service, retired; Chairman, Grahame H. Wills Ltd; *b* 24 Oct. 1934; *m* Maria del Carmen Carratala; two *s* two *d*. Entered Foreign Office, 1959; served Dakar, Algiers, Paris, Bogota; First Sec., FCO, 1971–76; Counsellor (Commercial), Warsaw, 1976–79; Minister-Counsellor, Mexico City, 1979–84; Head of Personnel Policy Dept, FCO, 1984–85; rcds, 1986; Minister (Commercial) and Consul-Gen., Milan, 1987–90; Ambassador to Colombia, 1990–94. Chairman: British and Colombian Chamber of Commerce; Diplomatic Service Appeals Bd. Hon. Res. Fellow, Inst. of Latin American Studies. *Recreations:* history, hill walking, procrastination. *Address:* 72 Farquhar Road, SE19 1LT. *Club:* Polish Hearth.

MORRIS, Kenneth; Managing Director, Nirvana Europe Ltd, Ashington, since 1999; *b* 17 April 1947; *s* of Thomas and Phyllis Morris; *m* 1988, Veronica Ann Young; two *s*. *Educ:* George Stephenson Grammar Sch., West Moor, Newcastle upon Tyne. Group Accountant, Newcastle upon Tyne CBC, 1972; Management Accountant, Tyne and Wear CC, 1974; Chief Accountant, 1976, Dep. Dir of Finance, 1982, Gateshead MBC; County Treasurer, 1988, Man. Dir, 1992–99, Northumberland CC. *Recreations:* sport, reading, music. *Address:* 3 Bank Top, Earsdon, Whitley Bay, Tyne and Wear NE25 9JS. *T:* (0191) 253 4907; (office) Wansbeck Business Centre, Rotary Parkway, Ashington, Northumberland NE63 8QZ. *T:* (01670) 859300.

MORRIS, Mark William; American choreographer and dancer; Founder and Artistic Director, Mark Morris Dance Group, since 1980; *b* Seattle, 29 Aug. 1956; *s* of William Morris and Maxine Crittenden Morris. Dir of Dance, Théâtre Royal de la Monnaie, 1988–91; Jt Founder, White Oak Dance Project, 1990; has choreographed more than 90 modern dance works for Mark Morris Dance Gp, including: L'Allegro, il Penseroso ed il Moderato, 1988; Dido and Aeneas (opera), 1988; The Hard Nut, 1991; Four Saints in Three Acts, 2000; Sang-Froid, 2000; V, 2001; choreography for other companies includes: ballets: Drink to Me Only With Thine Eyes, Amer. Ballet Theatre, 1988; Ein Herz, Paris Opera Ballet, 1990; A Garden, San Francisco Ballet, 2001; Gong, Amer. Ballet Th., 2001; operas: Nixon in China, Houston Grand Opera, 1987; Orfée et Euridice, Seattle Opera, 1988; The Death of Klinghoffer, Théâtre de la Monnaie, 1991; dir, Die Fledermaus, Seattle Opera, 1990; dir and choreographed, Platée, Royal Opera, 1997. *Address:* Mark Morris Dance Group, 3 Lafayette Avenue, Brooklyn, NY 11217, USA.

MORRIS, Max; educational propagandist and reformer; pioneer of the Comprehensive School; Headmaster, Willesden High School, 1967–78, retired; *s* of Nathan and Annie Morris; *m* 1961, Margaret Saunders (*née* Howard), historian. *Educ:* Hutcheson's, Glasgow; Kilburn Grammar Sch., Mddx; University Coll., Univ. of London (BA 1st cl. Hons History); Inst. of Education, Univ. of London (DipEd); LSE. Began teaching, 1936, in Willesden. Served War, 1941–46, demobilised as Captain RASC. Sen. Lectr, Colls of Education, 1946–50; Dep. Head, Tottenham, 1960, after nine years of political discrimination in Middlesex; Headmaster, Chamberlayne Wood Secondary Sch., Willesden, 1962–67. NUT: Mem. Exec., 1966–79; Pres., 1973–74; Chm. Action Cttee, 1976–79. Chairman: Mddx Regional Examining Bd, 1975–79; London Regional Examining Bd, 1979–90; Vice-Chairman: Centre for Information and Advice on Educnl Disadvantage, 1975–80; London and E Anglian Gp, GCSE; Member: Schools Council Cttees, 1967–84; Burnham Cttee, 1970–79; Board of NFER, 1970–80; CLEA/School Teachers Cttee, 1972–79; Schools Broadcasting Council, 1972–80; Nat. Adv. Cttee on Supply and Trng of Teachers, 1973–78; Sub-Cttee on Educn, Labour Party NEC, 1978–83; Council, Inst. of Educn; Jt Council, GCE and CSE Boards; Univ. of London Exams and Assessment Council. Mem. (Lab) Haringey Borough Council, 1984–86. Chm., Socialist Educnl Assoc., 1995–98. *Publications:* The People's Schools, 1939; From Cobbett to the Chartists, 1948; Your Children's Future, 1953; (with Jack Jones) An A to Z of Trade Unionism and Industrial Relations, 1982, 2nd edn 1986; (ed jtly) Education: the wasted years 1973–1986?, 1988; contribs on educnl and historical subjects in newspapers, weeklies and jls. *Recreations:* baiting the Dept of Education and Science; ridiculing Trotskyists and trendies; tasting malt whisky. *Address:* 44 Coolhurst Road, N8 8EU. *T:* (020) 8348 3980.

MORRIS, Michael Sachs; Director-General, British Insurance Brokers' Association, 1980–85; *b* 12 June 1924; *s* of late Prof. Noah Morris, MD, DSc, and Hattie Michaelis; *m* 1952, Vera Leonie, *er d* of late Paul and Lona Heller; one *s* one *d*. *Educ:* Glasgow Acad.; St Catharine's Coll., Cambridge. Wrangler, 1948. Scientific Officer, Admty Signals Estabt, 1943–46; Asst Principal, BoT, 1948; idc 1970; Under Secretary: Insurance Div., DoT, 1973; Shipping Policy Div., DoT, 1978–80. Chm., Consultative Shipping Gp, 1979–80. Mem., Barnet Health Authy, 1985–90. *Recreation:* sitting in the sun. *Address:* 5 Sunrise View, The Rise, Mill Hill, NW7 2LL. *T:* (020) 8959 0837. *Club:* Oxford and Cambridge.

MORRIS, Norma Frances; Research Fellow, University College London, since 1995; *b* 17 April 1935; *d* of Henry Albert Bevis and Lilian Eliza Bevis (*née* Flexon); *m* 1960, Samuel Francis Morris; one *s* two *d*. *Educ:* Ilford County High Sch. for Girls; University College London (BA, MA). Assistante Anglaise, Paris, 1956–57; Asst Lectr, Univ. of Hull, 1959–60; MRC, 1960–95, Admin. Sec, 1989–95. Mem., Nat. Biol Standards Bd, 1990–98. Chm., Gen. Chiropractic Council, 1998–. *Publications:* contribs science policy jls. *Recreations:* canoeing, opera, edible fungi. *Address:* Department of Science and Technology Studies, University College London, Gower Street, WC1E 6BT. *T:* (020) 7419 3703.

MORRIS, Prof. Norman Frederick, MD; FRCOG, FFFP; Director, Department of Postgraduate Medicine, Cromwell Hospital, since 1997; Professor of Obstetrics and Gynæcology, University of London, Charing Cross and Westminster Medical School (formerly Charing Cross Hospital Medical School), 1958–85, now Emeritus; Dean, Faculty of Medicine, University of London, 1971–76; Deputy Vice-Chancellor, University of London, 1976–80; *b* Luton, 26 Feb. 1920; *s* of F. W. Morris, Luton; *m* 1944, Lucia Xenia Rivlin; two *s* two *d*. *Educ:* Dunstable Sch., Dunstable; St Mary's Hospital Medical Sch. MRCS, LRCP 1943; MRCOG 1949; MB, BS (London) 1943; MD (London) 1949; FRCOG 1959; FFFP 1993. House appts St Mary's Hosp., Paddington and Amersham, 1943–44; Res. Obstetrician and Surg. Officer, East Ham Memorial Hosp., E6, 1944–46; Surg. Specialist RAF (Sqdn Ldr), 1946–48; Registrar, St Mary's Hosp., W2, and East End Maternity Hosp., E1, 1948–50; Sen. Registrar (Obst. and Gynæcol.), Hammersmith Hosp., 1950–52; First Asst, Obstetric Unit, Univ. Coll. Hosp., WC1, 1953–56; Reader, Univ. of London in Obst. and Gynæcol., Inst. of Obstetrics and Gynæcology, 1956–58; Med. Dir, IVF Unit, Cromwell Hosp., 1986–97. Dep. Chm., NW Thames RHA, 1974–80; Chm., NW Thames Reg. Res. Cttee, 1981–86. External Examiner, Univs of Sheffield, Leeds, Dundee and Liverpool. President: (founder) Internat. Soc. of Psychosomatic Obstetrics and Gynaecology, 1972–80; Section of Obstetrics and Gynaecology, RSocMed, 1978–79; W London Medico-Chirurgical Soc., 1982; Chairman: Assoc. of Profs of Obstets and Gynaecol. of UK, 1981–86; British Soc. of Psychosomatic Obstets, Gynaecol. and Andrology, 1988–96, now Pres.; Treas., Internat. Soc. for Investigation of Stress, 1990–2000. Mem., Academic Forum, DHSS, 1981–84; Chm., Commonwealth Health Develt Prog., Commonwealth Secretariat, 1990–; Sec. Gen., Commonwealth Health Foundn, 1994–. Mem., Hammersmith and Fulham HA, 1983–84. Mem. Ct and Senate, Univ. of London, 1972–80; Governor: Wye Coll., 1973–76; St Paul's Sch., 1976–91. Trustee, Little Foundn, 1992– (Chm., Scientific Cttee, 1993–). Fellow, Soc. Gyn. et Obst., Italy, 1970–; Hon. FFFP 1993. Formerly Chm., Assoc. of University Clinical Academic Staff. Editor, Midwife and Health Visitor Jl. *Publications:* Sterilisation, 1976; Contemporary Attitudes to Care in Labour (The Psychosomatic Approach), 1986; Factors Influencing Population Control, 1986; articles in medical jls related to obstetric and gynaecological problems, 1952–. *Recreations:* travelling, collecting glass, music. *Address:* Flat 3, The Etons, 13 Eton Avenue, NW3 3EL. *Clubs:* Athenæum, 1942.

MORRIS, Owen Humphrey, CB 1977; CMG 1967; Deputy Under-Secretary of State, Welsh Office, 1974–81, retired; *b* 15 June 1921; *o c* of late David Humphreys Morris, Ton Pentre, Rhondda, Glam., and Mrs Amy Ann Morris (*née* Jones); *m* 1972, Mair Annetta Evans, *d* of late Capt. Daniel Evans, DSC, Tynllys, Morfa Nefyn. *Educ:* Public Elem. Schs; King's Coll. Sch., Wimbledon (Schol.); Balliol Coll., Oxford (Schol.; MA). Served War of 1939–45: The Welch Regt and King's African Rifles, 1941–45 (Capt.). Asst Princ., Colonial Office, 1946; seconded Sierra Leone Administration, 1952–53; Asst Sec., 1955; Dept of Techn. Cooperation, 1962; Min. of Overseas Development, 1964; Min. of Housing and Local Govt, 1966; Welsh Office, 1969; Asst Under-Sec., 1970; Dep. Sec., 1974. Chm., Gwynedd Archaeol Trust, 1984–87. *Address:* Taltreuddyn Fawr, Dyffryn Ardudwy, Gwynedd LL44 2RQ.

MORRIS, Peter Christopher West; solicitor; *b* 24 Dec. 1937; *s* of C. T. R. and L. B. Morris; *m* 1st, 1959, Joy (marr. diss.); two *s* one *d*; 2nd, 1987, Terese; one step *s* two step *d*. *Educ:* Seaford Coll.; Christ's Coll., Cambridge, 1958–61 (MA, LLB). Hockey Blue, 1959, 1960, 1961; Hockey for Wales, 1962–65. National Service, 1956–58. Admitted Solicitor, 1965; Partner with Wild Hewitson & Shaw, 1967; a Recorder of the Crown Court, 1980–84; voluntary removal from Roll of Solicitors, 1982; Barrister, Middle Temple, 1982–84; company dir, 1985–93; name restored to Roll of Solicitors, 1993; Partner with Morris and Rogers. *Recreations:* golf, gardening, cycling. *Address:* 1 Hawthorn Close, Saltdean, Sussex BN2 8HX. *Club:* Hawks (Cambridge).

MORRIS, Sir Peter (John), Kt 1996; FRS 1994; President, Royal College of Surgeons of England, since 2001; Nuffield Professor of Surgery, Chairman, Department of Surgery and Director, Oxford Transplant Centre, Oxford University, 1974–2001, now Emeritus Professor; Fellow of Balliol College, 1974–2001, now Emeritus Fellow; Chairman, Institute of Health Sciences, Oxford University, since 2000; *b* 17 April 1934; *s* of Stanley Henry and Mary Lois Morris; *m* 1960, Mary Jocelyn Gorman; three *s* two *d*. *Educ:* Xavier Coll., Melbourne; Univ. of Melbourne (MB, BS, PhD). FRCS, FRACS, FACS. Jun. surg. appts at St Vincent's Hosp., Melbourne, Postgrad. Med. Sch., London, Southampton Gen. Hosp. and MGH Boston, 1958–64; Research Fellow, Harvard Med. Sch., 1965–66; Asst Prof. in Surgery, Med. Coll. of Virginia, 1967; 2nd Asst in Surgery, Univ. of Melbourne, 1968–69, 1st Asst 1970–71; Reader in Surgery, Univ. of Melbourne, 1972–74. WHO Consultant, 1970–84; Cons. to Walter and Eliza Hall Inst. of Med. Res., 1969–74. President: Transplantation Soc., 1984–86; British Soc. for Histocompatibility and Immunogenetics, 1993–95; Chm., Nat. Kidney Res. Fund, 1986–90; Member: MRC, 1983–87; Oxford RHA, 1988–90; Council, RCS, 1991– (Vice Pres., 2000–01); Council, ICRF, 1995–. President: Eur. Surgical Assoc., 1996–98; Internat. Surgical Soc., 2001–. Hunterian Prof., RCS, 1972. Rudin Prof., Columbia Univ., NY, 1983; USA Nat. Kidney Foundn Prof., 1986; Nimmo Vis. Prof., Univ. of Adelaide, 1993; Ho Tam Kit Hing Vis. Prof., Univ. of Hong Kong, 1994; Walkman Walters Vis. Prof., Mayo Clinic, 1994. Lectures: Champ Lyons, Univ. of Alabama, 1989; Fraser Meml, Univ. of Edinburgh, 1990; Bennett, TCD, 1991; Graham, Washington Univ., 1991; Murdoch Meml, Aberdeen Univ., 1991; Shaw, RCPE, 1991; Pybus Meml, N of Eng. Surg. Soc., 1992; Gallie, Royal Coll. of Physicians and Surgeons, Canada, 1992; Agnew, Univ. of Penn, 1993; Grey Turner, Internat. Surg. Soc., 1993; Belzer, Univ. of Wisconsin, 1998; Martin, Emory Univ., 1999; Cepellini, Eur. Foundn for Immuno-Genetics, 1999; Paul Russell, Harvard Med. Sch., 2000. Governor: PPP Healthcare Med. Trust, 1998–; Garfield Weston Foundn, 1998–; Trustee, Roche Organ Transplantation Res. Foundn, 1998–. Founder FMedSci 1998. Hon. Fellow: Amer. Surgical Assoc., 1982; Asian Surg. Soc., 1989; Hon. FACS 1986; Hon. FRACS, 1995; Hon. FRCSE 1995; Hon. Mem., Amer. Soc. of Transplant Surgeons, 1993. Hon. DSc Hong Kong, 1999. Selwyn Smith

Prize, Univ. of Melbourne, 1971; Cecil Joll Prize, RCS, 1988; Lister Medal, RCS, RCSE, Irish Coll. of Surgeons and Royal Soc., 1997. Editor, Transplantation, 1979–. *Publications:* Kidney Transplantation: principles and practice, 1979, 5th edn 2001; Tissue Transplantation, 1982; Transient Ischaemic Attacks, 1982; (ed jtly) Progress in Transplantation, vol. 1 1984, vol. 2 1985, vol. 3 1986; (ed) Oxford Textbook of Surgery, 1994, 2nd edn 2000; (ed) Transplantation Reviews, 1987–; numerous sci. articles and chapters in books concerned mainly with transplantation and surgery. *Recreations:* golf, tennis, cricket. *Address:* 19 Lucerne Road, Oxford OX2 7QB. *Clubs:* Oxford and Cambridge, MCC; Frilford Heath Golf (Oxford); Oxfordshire County Cricket; St Cyprien Golf (France); Melbourne Cricket (Melbourne).

MORRIS, Sir Richard; *see* Morris, Sir J. R. S.

MORRIS, Richard Francis Maxwell; Chief Executive, Associated Board of the Royal Schools of Music, since 1993; *b* 11 Sept. 1944; *s* of late Maxwell Morris and Frederica (*née* Abelson); *m* 1st, 1974, Sarah Quill (marr. diss. 1978); 2nd, 1983, Marian Sperling; two *d*. *Educ:* Eton Coll.; New Coll., Oxford (MA); Coll. of Law, London. Solicitor, Farrer & Co., 1967–71; Legal Advr and Banker, Grindlay Brandts, 1971–75; Corporate Finance Manager, S. G. Warburg & Co., 1975–79; Hodder and Stoughton: Group Finance Dir, 1979; Man. Dir, Educnl and Acad. Publishing, 1987; Jt Man. Dir, 1989–91; Dir, The Lancet, 1986–91; Man. Dir, Edward Arnold, 1987–91. Director: Invicta Sound, 1984–91; Southern Radio, 1991–92. Mem. Council, Kent Opera, 1985–90; Founder, Almaviva Opera, 1989–. Chm., Music Educn Council, 1998– (Mem. Exec. Cttee, 1995–). Trustee, Council for Dance Educn and Trng, 1999–. Hon. RCM 1994. *Recreations:* singing, visual arts, golf. *Address:* Holdfast House, Edenbridge, Kent TN8 6SJ. *T:* (01732) 862439. *Club:* Athenæum.

MORRIS, Prof. Richard Graham Michael, FRS 1997; Professor of Neuroscience, since 1993, and Chairman, Department of Neuroscience, since 1998, Edinburgh University; *b* 27 June 1948; *s* of Robert Walter and Edith Mary Morris; *m* 1985, Hilary Ann Lewis; two *d*. *Educ:* Trinity Hall, Cambridge (BA 1969; MA 1971); Univ. of Sussex (DPhil 1973). FRSE 1994. Addison Wheeler Fellow, Univ. of Durham, 1973–75; BM (Nat. History), 1975–76; BBC Science and Features Dept, 1977; Lectr, Univ. of St Andrews, 1977–86; Reader, Dept of Pharmacology, Univ. of Edinburgh, 1986–93. Vis. Prof., MIT, 1991; Royal Society Leverhulme Fellow, 1996; Gatsby Res. Fellow, 1997. Member: Neuroscis Grants Cttee, MRC, 1981–85; Neuroscis and Mental Health Bd, MRC, 1993–97; Innovation Bd, MRC, 1997–2000; Strategy Develt Gp, MRC, 2000–. Chm., Brain Res. Assoc., 1990–94; Hon. Sec., Exptl Psychol. Soc., 1985–89. Mem., RYA. Founder FMedSci 1998. *Publications:* contrib. to academic jls and books. *Recreation:* sailing. *Address:* Department of Neuroscience, University of Edinburgh Medical School, 1 George Square, Edinburgh EH8 9JZ. *T:* (0131) 650 3520; *e-mail:* r.g.m.morris@ed.ac.uk.

MORRIS, Richard Keith, FSA; archaeologist, writer, composer; *b* 8 Oct. 1947; *s* of John Richard Morris and Elsie Myra (*née* Wearne); *m* 1972, Jane Whiteley; two *s* one *d*. *Educ:* Denstone Coll., Staffs; Pembroke Coll., Oxford (MA); Univ. of York (BPhil). FSA 1982; MIFA 1986. Musician, 1971–72; Res. Assistant, York Minster Archaeol. Office, 1972–75; Churches Officer, 1975–77, Res. Officer, 1978–88, Council for British Archaeol.; Hon. Lectr, Sch. of History, Univ. of Leeds, 1986–88; Lectr, Dept of Archaeol., Univ. of York, 1988–91; Dir, Council for British Archaeology, 1991–99. Comr, English Heritage, 1996–; Chairman: Ancient Monuments Adv. Cttee for England, 1996–; Historic Settlements and Landscapes Adv. Cttee, 2001–; Bede's World, 2001–. Hon. Vis. Prof., Univ. of York, 1995. Frend Medal, Soc. of Antiquaries of London, 1992. *Publications:* Cathedrals and Abbeys of England and Wales, 1979; The Church in British Archaeology, 1983; Churches in the Landscape, 1989; (jtly) Guy Gibson, 1994; Cheshire, VC, OM, 2000; The Triumph of Time, 2002. *Recreations:* aviation history, natural history, swimming. *Address:* 13 Hollins Road, Harrogate HG1 2JF. *T:* (01423) 817283.

MORRIS, Robert Matthew, CVO 1996; Assistant Under Secretary of State, Home Office, 1983–97; *b* 11 Oct. 1937; *s* of late William Alexander Morris and of Mary Morris (*née* Bryant); *m* 1965, Janet Elizabeth Gillingham; two *s* one *d*. *Educ:* Handsworth Grammar Sch.; Christ's Coll., Cambridge. S Staffords Regt, 1956–58. Joined Home Office, 1961; Asst Private Sec. to Home Sec., 1964–66; CSD, 1969–71; Principal Private Sec. to Home Sec., 1976–78; Sec. to UK Prison Services Inquiry (May Cttee), 1978–79; Head of Crime Policy Planning Unit, 1979–81; Asst Under Sec. of State, Fire and Emergency Planning, 1983, Immigration Policy, Nationality and Passports, 1986, Criminal Justice and Constitutional, 1991; Registrar, Baronetage, 1991–96. Mem. Council, Internat. Social Service UK, 1998–. Hon. Sen. Res. Fellow, Constitution Unit, Sch. of Public Policy, UCL, 1999–. *Address:* 65 Wroughton Road, SW11 6AS.

MORRIS, Rear-Adm. Roger Oliver, CB 1990; FRGS; FRIN; Hydrographer of the Navy, 1985–90; *b* 1 Sept. 1932; *s* of Dr Oliver N. Morris and H. S. (Mollie) Morris (*née* Hudson). *Educ:* Mount House School, Tavistock; Royal Naval College, Dartmouth. Entered Royal Navy, 1946, commissioned 1952; specialized in Hydrographic Surveying, 1956; commanded HM Ships Medusa, Beagle, Hydra, Fawn, Hecla, Hydra, 1964–80; RCDS 1978; Director of Hydrographic Plans and Surveys, 1980–81; Asst Hydrographer, 1982–84. Chm. of Council, Soc. for Nautical Res., 1989–94; Vice-Pres., Royal Inst. of Navigation, 1991–92; Pres., World Ship Soc., 1997–2000. *Publication:* Charts and Surveys in Peace and War, 1995. *Recreations:* heraldry, opera, bird watching. *Address:* Orchard House, Quantock View, Bishops Lydeard, Somerset TA4 3AW. *Club:* Royal Commonwealth Society.

MORRIS, Simon C.; *see* Conway Morris.

MORRIS, Prof. Terence Patrick Michael; JP; Emeritus Professor of Criminology and Criminal Justice, University of London, since 1994 (Professor of Social Institutions, 1981–94); *b* 8 June 1931; *s* of Albert and Norah Avis Morris; *m* 1973, Penelope Jane, *y d* of Stanley and Alexandra Tomlinson. *Educ:* John Ruskin Grammar Sch., Croydon; LSE, Univ. of London (Leverhulme Schol.). BSc (Soc) 1953, PhD (Econ) 1955. Lectr in Sociology, LSE, 1955–63; Reader, 1963–69, Prof., 1969–81, Sociology (with special ref. to Criminology), London Univ.; Founder Dir, Mannheim Centre for Criminology and Criminal Justice, LSE, 1990. Vis. Prof. of Criminology, Univ. of California, 1964–65; Univ. of Manitoba, 1996. Mem., Adv. Mission on Treatment of Offenders (Western Pacific, British Honduras, Bahamas), 1966. Vice-Pres., Howard League for Penal Reform, 1986–; Mem., Magistrates' Assoc. Treatment of Offenders Cttee (co-opted), 1969–77; Founder Mem., Inst. for Study of Drug Dependence. Man. Editor, British Jl of Sociology, 1965–74. JP Inner London, 1967. *Publications:* The Criminal Area, 1957; (with Pauline Morris) Pentonville: a sociological study of an English prison, 1963; (with L. J. Blom-Cooper) A Calendar of Murder, 1964; Deviance and Control: the secular heresy, 1976; Crime and Criminal Justice since 1945, 1989; contribs to Brit. Jl Criminology, Brit. Jl Sociology, Encycl. Britannica, Crim. Law Review. *Recreations:* cycling, photography. *Address:* Christmas Cottage, Lower Road, South Wonston, Winchester, Hants SO21 3ER. *Club:* Cyclists' Touring.

MORRIS, Timothy Colin; HM Diplomatic Service; Counsellor, Tokyo, since 1998; *b* 17 Sept. 1958; *s* of late Maj. Charles Anthony Morris and of Sheila Ann Margaret Morris (*née* Watson); *m* 1996, Patricia Tena; two *s*. *Educ:* Winchester Coll.; Queen's Coll., Oxford (BA 1st Cl. Hons Modern Langs (French and Spanish) 1981). Joined HM Diplomatic Service, 1981; Japanese lang. trng, 1982–84; Second Sec., Commercial, Tokyo, 1984–87; FCO, 1987–89; Head, Exports to Japan Unit, DTI, 1989–91; First Sec. and Head, Political Section, Madrid, 1991–95; Dep. Head, UN Dept, FCO, 1996–98. *Recreations:* music, literature. *Address:* c/o Foreign and Commonwealth Office, King Charles Street, SW1A 2AH. *Club:* Oxford and Cambridge.

MORRIS, Very Rev. Timothy David; Dean of Diocese of Edinburgh, Episcopal Church in Scotland, since 1992; Rector of St Peter's, Galashiels, since 1985; *b* 17 Aug. 1948; *s* of Joseph Ernest and Mabel Elizabeth Morris; *m* 1st, 1972, Dorothy Helen Ralph (marr. diss. 1987); one *d*; 2nd, 1988, Irene Elizabeth Lyness. *Educ:* King Edward's Grammar Sch., Bath; Coll. of Estate Management, London Univ. (BSc Econs); Trinity Coll., Bristol and Bristol Univ. (DipTh). Asst Estate Surveyor, Min. of Public Building and Works, Edinburgh, 1969–72; Curate, St Thomas's Church, Edinburgh, 1975–77; Rector: St James's Episcopal Church, Leith, Edinburgh, 1977–83; St Ninian's, Troon, Ayrshire, 1983–85. *Recreations:* music, Rugby Union, cricket, gardening. *Address:* The Rectory, 6 Parsonage Road, Galashiels, Selkirkshire TD1 3HS. *T:* (01896) 753118.

MORRIS, Sir Trefor (Alfred), Kt 1996; CBE 1992; QPM 1985; HM Chief Inspector of Constabulary, 1993–96; Chairman, Police Information Technology Organisation, 1996–2000; Adviser, British Transport Police Committee, 1996–2000; *b* 22 Dec. 1934; *s* of late Kenneth Alfred Morris and Amy Ursula (*née* Burgess); *m* 1958, Martha Margaret (*née* Wroe); two *d*. *Educ:* Ducie Technical High School, Manchester; Manchester University (Dip. Criminology); Nat. Exec. Inst., USA. Constable to Chief Superintendent, Manchester City Police, Manchester and Salford Police, Greater Manchester Police, 1955–76; Asst Chief Constable, Greater Manchester Police, 1976–79; Dep. Chief Constable, 1979–84, Chief Constable, 1984–90, Herts; HM Inspector of Constabulary, 1990–93. Trustee, Police Foundn, 1993–96. Pres., Police Mutual Assurance Soc., 1994–97. Member: St Albans Diocesan Synod, 1989–96; PCC, St Mary's Church, Abergavenny, 1997–. Vice President: Herts Scouts, 1989–; Police Athletics Assoc.; Pres., Luton, N Herts Inst. of Mgt. Trustee, Hospice of the Marches, 1997–. CIMgt (CBIM 1986). FRSA 1993. OStJ 1984. *Recreations:* music, golf, wine, walking, gardening. *Club:* Royal Over-Seas League.

MORRIS, Prof. Trevor Raymond; Professor of Animal Production, University of Reading, 1984–95, now Professor Emeritus; *b* 11 April 1930; *s* of Ivor Raymond Morris and Dorothy May Morris; *m* 1st, 1954, Elisabeth Jean (*née* Warren) (*d* 1992); three *s* two *d*; 2nd, 1994, Mary (*née* Gillett). *Educ:* Rendcomb Coll., Glos; Reading Univ. (BSc, PhD, DSc). University of Reading: Asst Lectr, 1952–54, 1956–57; Lectr in Agric., 1957–69; Reader in Agric., 1969–81; Prof. of Agriculture, 1981–84; Hd of Dept of Agriculture, 1984–91. *Publications:* over 200 articles in sci. jls. *Recreations:* music, gardening. *Address:* Rowan Trees, Beech Road, Tokers Green, Oxfordshire RG4 9EH. *T:* (0118) 9470758.

MORRIS, Warwick; HM Diplomatic Service; Ambassador to the Socialist Republic of Vietnam, since 2000; *b* 10 Aug. 1948; *e s* of late Clifford Morris and of Patricia Morris (*née* O'Grady), JP; *m* 1972, Pamela Jean Mitchell; one *s* two *d*. *Educ:* Bishop's Stortford Coll. VSO, Cameroon, 1967–68; entered Diplomatic Service, 1969; Third Sec., Paris, 1972–74; Korean lang. trng, Yonsei Univ., Seoul, 1975–76; Second Sec., Seoul, 1977–79; FCO, 1979–83; First Sec., 1982; First Sec. (Commercial), Mexico City, 1984–87; Head of Chancery, Seoul, 1988–91; Dep. Head, Far Eastern Dept, FCO, 1991–93; Counsellor, 1993, Head, 1994, Permanent Under Sec.'s Dept, FCO; Econ. and Commercial Counsellor, New Delhi, 1995–98; RCDS, 1999. *Recreations:* sport, travel, philately. *Address:* c/o Foreign and Commonwealth Office, King Charles Street, SW1A 2AH. *Clubs:* Royal Commonwealth Society, Royal Over-Seas League.

MORRIS, William; General Secretary, Transport and General Workers Union, since 1992 (Deputy General Secretary, 1986–92); a Director, Bank of England, since 1998; *b* 19 Oct. 1938; *s* of William and Una Morris; *m* 1957, Minetta (*d* 1990); two *s*. *Educ:* Mizpah Sch., Manchester, Jamaica; Handsworth Tech. Coll. Hardy Spicer Engineering, 1954. Joined TGWU, 1958: Shop Steward, 1962; Mem. Gen. Exec. Council, 1971–72; Dist Officer, Nottingham, 1973; Dist Sec., Northampton, 1976; Nat. Sec., Passenger Services, 1979–85. Mem., TUC Gen. Council, 1988–. Member: Commn for Racial Equality, 1977–87; IBA Gen. Adv. Council, 1981–86; Road Transport ITB, 1986–92; Prince's Youth Business Trust, 1987–90; BBC General Adv. Council, 1987–88; Employment Appeals Tribunal, 1988–; Economic and Social Cttee, EC, 1990–; NEDC, 1992; Royal Commn on H of L reform, 1999; Commn for Integrated Transport, 1999–. Hon. Prof., Thames Valley Univ., 1997–. Chancellor, Univ. of Technology, Jamaica, 1999–. Member: Governing Body, Atlantic Coll., 1994–; Court: Luton Univ., 1994–; Univ. of Northampton (formerly Nene Coll.), 1996–. Bd of Govs South Bank Univ., 1997–; Univ. Assembly, Greenwich Univ., 1997–. Mem. Trustee Bd, Open Univ. Foundn, 1997–. Hon. FRSA, 1992; Hon. FCGI, 1992. Hon. LLD: South Bank, 1994; Teeside, 1997; DUniv Leeds Metropolitan, 1996; Hon. DBA Greenwich, 1997; Hon. Dr Letters, Westminster, 1997; MUniv Open, 1995. *Recreations:* walking, gardening, watching sports. *Address:* 156 St Agnells Lane, Grove Hill, Hemel Hempstead, Herts HP2 6EG. *T:* (01442) 63110.

MORRIS, Prof. (William) David, PhD, DSc(Eng); Professor of Mechanical Engineering, University of Wales, Swansea (formerly University College of Swansea), since 1985 (Head of Department, 1985–91 and 1995); *b* 14 March 1936; *s* of late William Daniel and Elizabeth Jane Morris; *m* 1959, Pamela Eira Evans; two *s* one *d*. *Educ:* Queen Mary College, London (1st Cl. Hons BSc Eng); UC of Swansea, Wales (PhD); Univ. of London (DSc(Eng)). CEng, FIMechE, FIEE. Bristol Siddeley Engine Co., 1958–60; James Clayton Res. Fellow, Univ. of Wales, Swansea, 1960–63; Lectr, Dept of Mech. Engrg, Univ. of Liverpool, 1963–67; Lectr, 1967–72, Reader, 1972–79, Sch. of Engrg, Univ. of Sussex; J. H. Fenner Prof. of Mech. Engrg and Head, Dept of Engrg Design, Univ. of Hull, 1979–85; Vice Principal, UC Swansea, 1991–93. *Publications:* Differential Equations for Engineers and Applied Scientists, 1979; Heat Transfer and Fluid Flow in Rotating Coolant Channels, 1981. *Recreations:* oil painting, DIY, walking. *Address:* Department of Mechanical Engineering, University of Wales, Swansea, Singleton Park, Swansea SA2 8PP. *T:* (01792) 295534.

MORRIS, Very Rev. William James, KCVO 1995; JP; Minister of Glasgow Cathedral, since 1967; a Chaplain to the Queen in Scotland, 1969–96, an Extra Chaplain, since 1996; Dean of the Chapel Royal in Scotland, 1991–96; *b* Cardiff, 22 Aug. 1925; *o s* of William John Morris and Eliza Cecilia Cameron Johnson; *m* 1952, Jean Daveena Ogilvy Howie, CBE, LLD, *o c* of Rev. David Porter Howie and Veena Christie, Kilmarnock; one *s*. *Educ:* Cardiff High Sch.; Univ. of Wales; Edinburgh Univ. BA 1946, BD 1949, Wales; PhD Edinburgh, 1954. Ordained, 1951. Asst, Canongate Kirk, Edinburgh, 1949–51; Minister, Presbyterian Church of Wales, Cadoxton and Barry Is, 1951–53; Buckhaven (Fife): St David's, 1953–57; Peterhead Old Parish, 1957–67; Chaplain to the Lord High Comr to the General Assembly of the Church of Scotland, 1975–76; Chaplain: Peterhead Prison, 1963–67; Glasgow DC, 1967–; Trades House of Glasgow, 1967–; W of Scotland Engrs Assoc., 1967–; The High Sch. of Glasgow, 1974–76, 1983–; Glasgow Acad., 1976–; Strathclyde Police, 1977–; Queen's Body Guard for Scotland, Royal Co. of Archers, 1994–; Hon. Chaplain, The Royal Scottish Automobile Club; Moderator, Presbytery of Deer, 1965–66; Convener Adv. Bd, Church of Scotland, 1977–80; Vice-Chmn., Bd of Nomination to Church Chairs, Church of Scotland, 1978–81. Mem. IBA, 1979–84 (Chm. Scottish Adv. Cttee). President: Rotary Club of Peterhead, 1965–66; Peterhead and Dist Professional and Business Club, 1967; St Andrew's Soc., Glasgow, 1992– (Vice-Pres., 1967–82); Chairman: Iona Cath. Trust, 1976– (Trustee, 1967); Council, Soc. of Friends of Glasgow Cath., 1967; Club Service Cttee, Dist 101, RIBI, 1964–66; Prison Chaplaincies Bd (Church of Scotland Home Bd), 1969–83; Member: Scottish Cttee, British Sailors' Soc., 1967–83; Bd of Management, W of Scotland Convalescent Home, 1967–; Gen. Convocation, Strathclyde Univ., 1967–; Council of Management, Quarriers' Homes, 1968–88; Bd of Management, Glasgow YMCA, 1973–88; Scottish Council on Crime, 1974–76; Church of Scotland Bd of Practice and Procedure, 1981–85; Bd of Governors, Jordanhill Coll. of Educn, Glasgow, 1983–91; Hon. Pres., Glasgow Soc. of Social Services Inc., 1984–. Hon. Member: Scottish Ambulance Assoc., 1981; Royal Faculty of Procurators in Glasgow, 1997. JP: Co. of Aberdeen, 1963–71; Co. of City of Glasgow, 1971. ChStJ 1991. Hon. LLD Strathclyde, 1974; Hon. DD Glasgow, 1979; FRCPS(Hon.) 1983. Lord Provost's Award, Glasgow, 1996; Paul Harris Fellow, Rotary Internat., 1997. *Publication:* A Walk Around Glasgow Cathedral, 1986. *Recreations:* fishing, gardening. *Address:* 1 Whitehill Grove, Newton Mearns, Glasgow G77 5DH. *T:* (0141) 6396327. *Clubs:* New (Edinburgh); RNVR (Scotland) (Hon.); University of Strathclyde Staff (Hon.); Rotary of Dennistoun (Hon.); Rotary of Glasgow (Hon.).

MORRIS, Wyn, FRAM; conductor; Principal Conductor, New Queen's Hall Orchestra; *b* 14 Feb. 1929; *s* of late Haydn Morris and Sarah Eluned Phillips; *m* 1962, Ruth Marie McDowell; one *s* one *d*. *Educ:* Llanelli Grammar Sch.; Royal Academy of Music; Mozarteum, Salzburg. August Mann's Prize, 1950; Apprentice Conductor, Yorkshire Symph. Orch., 1950–51; Musical Dir, 17th Trg Regt, RA Band, 1951–53; Founder and Conductor of Welsh Symph. Orch., 1954–57; Koussevitsky Memorial Prize, Boston Symph. Orch., 1957; (on invitation George Szell) Observer, Cleveland Symph. Orch., 1957–60; Conductor: Ohio Bell Chorus, Cleveland Orpheus Choir and Cleveland Chamber Orch., 1958–60; Choir of Royal National Eisteddfod of Wales, 1960–62; London debut, Royal Festival Hall, with Royal Philharmonic Orch., 1963; Conductor: Royal Choral Society, 1968–70; Huddersfield Choral Soc., 1969–74; Ceremony for Investiture of Prince Charles as Prince of Wales, 1969; Royal Choral Soc. tour of USA, 1969; former Chief Conductor and Musical Dir, Symphonica of London. FRAM 1964. Specialises in conducting of Mahler; has recorded Des Knaben Wunderhorn (with Dame Janet Baker and Sir Geraint Evans), Das Klagende Lied, Symphonies 1, 2, 5, 8 and 10 in Deryck Cooke's final performing version. Mahler Memorial Medal (of Bruckner and Mahler Soc. of Amer.), 1968. *Recreations:* chess, Rugby football, climbing, cynghanedd and telling Welsh stories. *Address:* Wexham Place, Framewood Road, Fulmer, Bucks SL2 4QS.

MORRIS WILLIAMS, Christine Margaret; *see* Puxon, C. M.

MORRISH, John Edwin, (Jack); school governor and education consultant; Chairman, Northamptonshire Association of School Governing Bodies, 1995–98 (General Secretary, 1992–94; Research Officer, 1994–95); Co-opted Member, Somerset Schools Review Committee, since 2000; *b* 23 Sept. 1915; *s* of Henry Edwin Morrish and Ada Minnie (*née* Tapping); *m* 1st, 1937, Norah Lake (marr. diss.); one *d*; 2nd, 1944, Violet Saunders (marr. diss.); one *s* one *d*; 3rd, 1984, Betty Lupton (*née* Wear) (*d* 1990). *Educ:* Fleet Road, Hampstead, Elem. Sch.; University Coll. Sch.; Northampton Polytechnic, London; various work-faces; MA Leicester, 1991. Post Office Techn. Officer, 1932–54; coalminer, 1944–45. Trade Union Official: Civil Service Union, 1954–72; Soc. of Civil and Public Servants, 1972–76 (Gen. Sec., Customs and Excise Gp). Administrator, Northants Rural Community Council, 1979. Census Officer, 1980–81, 1990–91. Mem. (Lab), Dep. Leader, and Chm., Educn Cttee, Northants CC, 1981–85; Mem. (Lab), Hounslow BC, 1986–90 (Vice-Chm., Educn Cttee). Vice-Chm., E Midlands Further Educn Council, 1982–85; Member: Adv. Cttee, Supply and Educn of Teachers; Assoc. of County Councils, 1981–85; Burnham Cttee on Teachers' Pay, 1983–85, 1986–87; AMA, 1986–90; co-opted Mem., Northants Educn Cttee, 1993–98; Vice-Chm., Nat. Governors' Council, 1994–98. Hon. Chm., Northants Child Poverty Action Gp, 1980–84. Hon. Treas., UK Reading Assoc. (World Congress Local Arrangements Cttee), 1985–86. Chm., Nene Coll. Governors, 1981–85. *Publications:* The Future of Forestry, 1971; contrib. trade union and educn jls. *Recreations:* thinking, pursuit of justice, music, talking. *Address:* 7 De Combe House, Mount Pleasant, Crewkerne, Somerset TA18 7AH. *T:* (01460) 77203. *Club:* Civil Service.

MORRISON, family name of **Viscount Dunrossil** and of **Baron Margadale**.

MORRISON, Alasdair; Member (Lab) Western Isles, Scottish Parliament, since 1999; Deputy Minister for Enterprise and Lifelong Learning and Gaelic, since 2001; *b* 18 Nov. 1968; *m*; one *d*. Former Western Isles correspondent, Reporting Scotland; former Editor, New Gael newspaper. Dep. Minister for Enterprise in the Highlands and Islands and Gaelic, Scottish Exec., 1999–2001. *Address:* Scottish Parliament, Edinburgh EH99 1SP.

MORRISON, Sir (Alexander) Fraser, Kt 1998; CBE 1993; Deputy Chairman, Clydesdale Bank plc, since 1999 (Director, since 1994); Executive Chairman, 1996–2000, and Group Chief Executive, 2000, Morrison (formerly Morrison Construction Group) plc (Managing Director, 1976–96; Chairman, 1984–96); *b* 20 March 1948; *s* of late Alexander Ferrier Sharp Morrison and of Catherine Colina (*née* Fraser); *m* 1972, Patricia Janice Murphy; one *s* two *d*. *Educ:* Tain Royal Acad.; Univ. of Edinburgh (BSc Hons Civil Engrg). CEng, FICE 1993; Eur Ing 1993; MIHT 1982; FCIOB 1995. Joined Morrison Construction Gp Ltd as Dir, 1970; Director: Shand Ltd, 1978–89; Alexander Shand Holdings Ltd, 1982–86. Chm., Highlands & Islands Enterprise, 1992–98. Federation of Civil Engineering Contractors: Chm., Scottish Sect., 1991–92; Chm., Nat. Fedn, 1993–94; Vice Pres., 1994–96. Chairman: Bd of Governors, Univ. of Highlands and Is Project, 1998–2001; Council St Leonard's Sch., St Andrews, 1999–. FRSA 1990; FScotvec 1994. Hon. DTech: Napier, 1995; Glasgow Caledonian, 1997; DUniv Open, 2000. *Recreations:* golf, ski-ing, shooting, opera, art. *Address:* Teasses House, near Ceres, Leven, Fife KY8 5PG. *T:* (01334) 828048.

MORRISON, His Honour Alexander John Henderson; a Circuit Judge, 1980–98; *b* 16 Nov. 1927; *yr s* of late Dr Alexander Morrison and Mrs A. Morrison; *m* 1978, Hon. Philippa, *y d* of 1st Baron Hives. *Educ:* Derby Sch.; Emmanuel Coll., Cambridge. MA, LLB. Called to the Bar, Gray's Inn, 1951. Mem. of Midland Circuit; Dep. Chm., Derbyshire QS, 1964–71; Regional Chm. of Industrial Tribunals, Sheffield, 1971–80; a Recorder of the Crown Court, 1971–80. A Pres., Mental Health Review Tribunals, 1983–98. Pres., Derbys Union of Golf Clubs, 1977–79. *Recreations:* golf, schools football. *Address:* c/o Derby Combined Court, Morledge, Derby DE1 2XE.

MORRISON, (Andrew) Neil, CBE 1997; QFSM 1989; FIFireE; HM Chief Inspector of Fire Services for Scotland, 1994–99; *b* 8 Sept. 1937; *e s* of late Andrew Steel Morrison and Margueritta Wilkin Caird; *m* 1963, Kathleen Rutherford; one *s*. *Educ:* Arbroath High Sch.; Dundee Coll. of Technol. FIFireE 1991. Angus Fire Brigade: Fireman, 1962–70; Leading Fireman, 1970–71; Sub-officer, 1971–74; Station Officer, 1974–75; Tayside Fire Brigade: Station Officer, 1975–76; Asst Divl Officer, 1976; Divl Officer, Grade III, 1976–79; Divl Officer, Grade I, 1979–80; Grampian Fire Brigade: Dep. Firemaster, 1980–85; Firemaster, 1985–93. Hon. DTech Robert Gordon Univ., 1994. *Recreations:* curling, golf, hill-walking, swimming. *Address:* Mill of Cranhill, Banchory-Devenick, Aberdeen AB1 5XR. *T:* (01224) 869800.

MORRISON, Anne Catherine; Controller, Leisure and Factual Entertainment, BBC TV, since 2000; *b* 18 Aug. 1959; *d* of late George Charles Morrison and of Persis Mae Morrison (*née* Ross); *m* 1989, Robert John Jarvis Johnstone; one *d*. *Educ:* Richmond Lodge Sch., Belfast; Churchill Coll., Cambridge (MA Eng. Lit.). Gen. Trainee, BBC, 1981–83; Researcher and Dir, Documentary Features, BBC TV, 1983–87; Prod., Holiday, 1987–88; Series Prod., Crimewatch UK, 1988–90; Chief Assistant, Documentary Features, 1990–92; Exec. Prod., Taking Liberties, and Rough Justice, 1992; Dep. Head, 1992–94, Hd, 1994–96, Features, BBC TV; BBC Production: Head of Consumer and Leisure, 1996–98; Head of Features and Events, 1998–2000. *Recreations:* reading, art history, walking, gardening. *Address:* BBC TV, White City Building, 201 Wood Lane, W12 7TS. *T:* (020) 8752 5909.

MORRISON, Blake; *see* Morrison, P. B.

MORRISON, Hon. Sir Charles (Andrew), Kt 1988; *b* 25 June 1932; 2nd *s* of 1st Baron Margadale, TD; *m* 1st, 1954, Hon. Sara Long (*see* Hon. Sara Morrison) (marr. diss. 1984); one *s* one *d*; 2nd, 1984, Mrs Rosalind Ward (marr. diss. 1999). *Educ:* Eton. Nat. Service in The Life Guards, 1950–52; Royal Wilts Yeo. (TA), 1952–66. County Councillor, Wilts, 1958–65 (Chm., Educn Cttee, 1963–64). MP (C) Devizes, May 1964–1992. Chm., Nat. Cttee for Electoral Reform, 1985–91; Mem. Bd of Dirs, Global Cttee of Parliamentarians on Population and Develt, 1984–91. Chairman: South West Regional Sports Council, 1966–68; Young Volunteer Force Foundn, 1971–74; British Trust for Conservation Volunteers, 1973–78; Game Conservancy, 1987–94; Allerton Res. and Educn Trust, 1994–2001; Population Concern, 1995–2001; Mem., Council, Salmon and Trout Assoc. Chm., Handicapped Anglers Trust, 2000–. A Vice-Chm., 1922 Cttee, 1974–83 (Mem. Exec., 1972). Prime Warden, Fishmongers' Co., 1986–87. DL Hereford and Worcester, 1995–2000. *Recreations:* gardening, shooting, fishing. *Address:* Cowpens, Fonthill Gifford, Salisbury, Wilts SP3 6QJ. *Clubs:* White's, Pratt's.

See also Baron Margadale, Hon. M. A. Morrison.

MORRISON, Chloe Anthony, (Toni); writer; *b* 18 Feb. 1931; *d* of George Wofford and Ella Ramah Wofford (*née* Willis); *m* 1958, Harold Morrison (marr. diss. 1964); two *s*. *Educ:* Howard Univ.; Cornell Univ. (MA 1955). Lectr in English and Humanities: Texas Southern Univ., 1955–57; Howard Univ., 1957–64; Associate Prof. of English, NY State Univ. Coll., Purchase, 1971–72; Professor of Humanities: SUNY, Albany, 1984–89; Princeton Univ., 1989–. An Editor, Random House, NY, 1965. Numerous literary awards, incl Pulitzer Prize for Fiction, 1988; Nobel Prize for Literature, 1993. *Publications:* The Bluest Eye, 1970; Sula, 1974; Song of Solomon, 1977; Tar Baby, 1983; Beloved, 1987; Jazz, 1992; Playing in the Dark: whiteness and the literary imagination, 1992; (ed) Race-ing Justice, En-gendering Power, 1993; (ed jtly) Birth of a Nationhood, 1997; Paradise, 1998. *Address:* c/o Suzanne Gluck, International Creative Management, 40 W 57th Street, New York, NY 10019, USA.

MORRISON, Dennis John; Regional Director, Government Office for the East Midlands, since 1998; Special Professor in Regional Governance and Planning, University of Nottingham, since 2000; *b* 20 May 1942; *s* of Leonard Tait Morrison and Alice Morrison; *m* 1967, Frances Joan Pollard; one *s* one *d*. *Educ:* Ashton-upon-Mersey Boys' School; Lymm Grammar School; Manchester Univ. (BA, DipT&CP). MRTPI. Planning appointments: Lancs CC, 1966–70; Welsh Office, Cardiff, 1970–75; NW Region, DoE, Manchester, 1975–81; Regional Controller, NW Enterprise Unit, DoE, 1981–84; Regional Controller (Urban and Economic Affairs), Merseyside Task Force, Liverpool, 1984–89; Regl Dir, Depts of Envmt and Transport, E Midlands Region, 1989–94; Dir, Envmt and Transport, Govt Office for E Midlands, 1994–97; Regl Dir, Govt Office for Merseyside, 1997–98. FRGS. *Recreations:* antiquarian book collecting, horology, antique barometer restoration, hill walking, gardening, cooking, people watching. *Address:* (office) The Belgrave Centre, Stanley Place, Talbot Street, Nottingham NG1 5GG. *T:* (0115) 971 2750, *Fax:* (0115) 971 2769.

MORRISON, Donald Alexander Campbell; Assistant Under-Secretary of State, Home Office, 1972–76; *b* 30 Nov. 1916; *s* of late George Alexander Morrison, sometime MP for Scottish Univs, and late Rachel Brown Morrison (*née* Campbell); *m* 1st, 1951, Elma Margaret Craig (*d* 1970); one *s* one *d* (and one *s* decd); 2nd, 1973, Jane Margaret Montgomery; one step *s*. *Educ:* Fettes Coll.; Christ Church, Oxford (BA). Home Office, 1939; Asst Sec., 1955. A Senior Clerk (acting), House of Commons, 1976–81. War Service, 1940–45: 79th (Scottish Horse) Medium Regt, RA, 1942–45. *Publications:* Haps and Such (poems), 1986; *children's operas:* The Granite and the Heather, 1990 (perf. Aboyne, 1990); Little Jenny Nobody, 1991 (perf. Aboyne, 1990, Canterbury Fest., 1992); The Golden Slave, 1992 (perf. Aboyne, 1992); Afternoon in Jericho, 1993 (perf. Wingham Fest., 1993); Smugglers at Bay, 1993 (perf. Canterbury Fest., 1993); Remember David, 1995 (perf. Wingham Fest., 1995). *Recreation:* music. *Address:* 27 High Street, Wingham, near Canterbury, Kent CT3 1AW. *T:* (01227) 720774.

MORRISON, Sir Fraser; *see* Morrison, Sir A. F.

MORRISON, Garth; *see* Morrison, W. G.

MORRISON, Graham, RIBA; Partner, Allies and Morrison, Architects, since 1983; *b* 2 Feb. 1951; *s* of Robert Morrison and Robina Sandison Morrison; *m* 1973, Raila Elina Tyrjä (marr. diss. 1993); one *s* one *d*; *m* 2001, Michelle Lovric, novelist. *Educ:* Brighton Coll.; Jesus Coll., Cambridge (MA; DipArch 1975). RIBA 1976. *Projects completed* include: Clove Bldg, London, 1990 (RIBA Award 1991); Sarum Hall Sch., London, 1995 (RIBA Award 1996); Nunnery Square, Sheffield, 1995 (RIBA Award 1996); British Embassy, Dublin, 1995 (RIBA Award 1997); Rosalind Franklin Bldg, Newnham Coll., Cambridge, 1995 (RIBA Award 1996); Abbey Mills Pumping Station, Stratford (RIBA Award), 1997; Rutherford Information Services Bldg, Goldsmiths Coll., London, 1997 (RIBA Award 1998); Blackburn Hse, London, 1999 (RIBA Award 2000). *Exhibitions* include: New British Architecture, Japan, 1994; Allies and Morrison Retrospective, USA Schs of Architecture, 1996–98, Helsinki, Delft and Strasbourg, 1999. Architects to Royal Fest. Hall, 1994–. Lectures in Canada, Finland, India, Ireland, Japan, S Africa, UK, USA. Member: RIBA Council, 1991–94; Architecture Adv. Cttee, Arts Council, 1996–97; Royal Fine Art Commn, 1998–99; Design Review Cttee, Commn for Architecture and the Built Envmt, 2000–; London Adv. Cttee, English Heritage, 2001–. Ext. Examr, Univ.

of Cambridge, 1994–97. Dir, RIBA Jl, 1993–97. *Recreations:* Blues music, Venice. *Address:* Allies and Morrison, 62 Newman Street, W1T 3EE; Oak Yard, The Keep, Blackheath, SE3 0AG. *T:* (020) 8852 6209.

MORRISON, Howard Andrew Clive, OBE 1988; QC 2001; a Recorder, since 1994; *b* 20 July 1949; *s* of Howard Edward Morrison and Roma Morrison (*née* Wilkinson); *m* 1980, Kathryn Margaret Moore; one *s* one *d*. *Educ:* London Univ. (LLB). Volunteer, Ghana, 1968–69, Desk Officer, Zambia and Malawi, 1975–76, VSO. Subaltern, Queen's Regt, 1970–74; Parachute Regt, TAVR and RARO, 1974–99. Called to the Bar, Gray's Inn, 1977; in practice on Midland and Oxford Circuit, 1977–85; Resident Magistrate, then Chief Magistrate, Fiji, 1985–87; concurrently Sen. Magistrate for Tuvalu and locum Attorney Gen. of Anguilla, 1988–89; in practice on Midland and Oxford Circuit, 1989–; engaged in defending in UN War Crime Tribunals, The Hague and Arusha, 1998–. Mem., Race Relations Cttee, Bar Council, 1996–. FRGS 1991. *Publications:* numerous legal articles, mainly on internat. criminal law. *Recreations:* mountain walking, ski-ing, flying, sailing, scuba diving, trying to keep solvent. *Address:* 36 Bedford Row, WC1R 4JH. *T:* (020) 7421 8000.

MORRISON, Sir Howard (Leslie), Kt 1990; OBE 1976; entertainer, self-employed, since 1957; Youth Development Director for Maori Affairs, 1978–91; *b* 18 Aug. 1935; *s* of late Temuera Leslie Morrison and Gertrude Harete Morrison (*née* Davidson); *m* 1957, Rangiwhata Anne (*née* Manahi); two *s* one *d*. *Educ:* Huiarau Primary Sch.; Rotorua Primary Sch.; Rotorua High Sch.; Te Aute College. Surveyor's Asst, 1954–59; performer with Maori concert party groups since childhood; formed Howard Morrison Quartet, 1957 (part-time, later full-time); numerous recordings, TV, national tours; quartet disbanded 1965; solo entertainer, 1965–; tours in NZ, S Pacific, SE Asia; TV and films; Royal Command perfs, 1963, 1974, 1981. Patron, Life Educn Trust, NZ. Entertainer of the Year, 1966, 1990; Life Achievement Award, Entertainer of the Year, 1996. *Recreations:* golf, swimming. *Address:* Korokai Street, Ohinemutu Village, Rotorua, New Zealand. *T:* (7) 3485735, *Fax:* (7) 3480910. *Club:* Carbine (Auckland, NZ).

MORRISON, James, RSA 1992 (ARSA 1973); RSW 1968; painter in oil and water colours; *b* 11 April 1932; *s* of John Morrison and Margaret Thomson; *m* 1955, Dorothy McCormack; one *s* one *d*. *Educ:* Hillhead High Sch., Glasgow; Glasgow Sch. of Art (DA). Vis. Artist, Hospitalfield House, 1962, 1963; Duncan of Jordanstone College of Art, Dundee: Member of Staff, 1965–87; Head of Dept, 1978–87; Mem. Board, 1988–. Council Mem., Soc. of Scottish Artists, 1964–67; Keeper of the Collection, Royal Scottish Acad., 1992–. Mem., Inst. of Contemporary Scotland. Painting in Europe, USA and Canada, 1968–; painting in the High Arctic, 1990–96; painting in Africa, 1998; one-man exhibns, Scotland, London, Italy, Germany, Canada, 1956–; numerous works in public and private collections, UK and overseas. Torrance Award, RGI, 1958; Arts Council Travelling Award, 1968. DUniv Stirling, 1986. *Publication:* Aff the Squerr, 1976, 2nd edn 1990. *Recreation:* playing recorder in a chamber music group. *Address:* Craigview House, Usan, Montrose, Angus DD10 9SD. *T:* (01674) 672639.

MORRISON, Ven. John Anthony; Archdeacon of Oxford and a Residentiary Canon of Christ Church, Oxford, since 1998; *b* 11 March 1938; *s* of Major Leslie Claude Morrison and Mary Sharland Morrison (*née* Newson-Smith); *m* 1968, Angela, *d* of late Major Jonathan Eric Bush; two *s* one *d*. *Educ:* Haileybury; Jesus Coll., Cambridge (BA 1960; MA 1964); Lincoln Coll., Oxford (MA 1968); Chichester Theol Coll. Deacon 1964, priest 1965; Curate: St Peter, Birmingham, 1964–68; St Michael-at-the-Northgate, Oxford, 1968–74; Chaplain, Lincoln Coll., Oxford, 1968–74; Vicar, Basildon, Berks, 1974–82; RD Bradfield, 1978–82; Vicar, Aylesbury, Bucks, 1982–89, Team Rector, 1989–90; RD Aylesbury, 1985–89; Archdeacon of Buckingham, 1990–98. Mem., Gen. Synod, 1980–90, 1998–2000. Mem. Ct of Assts, Spectacle Makers' Co., 1994–. *Address:* Archdeacon's Lodging, Christ Church, Oxford OX1 1DP. *T:* (01865) 204440; *e-mail:* archdoxf@oxford.anglican.org. *Clubs:* Leander (Henley-on-Thames); Vincent's (Oxford).

MORRISON, Sir Kenneth (Duncan), Kt 2000; CBE 1990; Chairman (formerly Chairman and Managing Director), William Morrison Supermarkets plc; *b* 20 Oct. 1931; *m* 1st, Edna (decd); one *s* two *d*; 2nd, Lynne; one *d*. Career in grocery retailing; co. now has over 100 stores. *Address:* William Morrison Supermarkets plc, Hilmore House, Thornton Road, Bradford BD8 9AX.

MORRISON, Hon. Mary Anne, DCVO 1982 (CVO 1970); Woman of the Bedchamber to the Queen since 1960; *b* 17 May 1937; *o d* of 1st Baron Margadale, TD. *Educ:* Heathfield School. *Address:* The Old Rectory, Fonthill Bishop, Salisbury, Wilts SP3 5SF.

See also Baron Margadale, Hon. Sir C. A. Morrison.

MORRISON, Neil; *see* Morrison, A. N.

MORRISON, Nigel Murray Paton; QC (Scot.) 1988; Sheriff of Lothian and Borders at Edinburgh, since 1996; *b* 18 March 1948; *o s* of late David Paton Morrison, FRICS, FLAS and Dilys Trenholm Pritchard or Morrison. *Educ:* Rannoch School. Called to the Bar, Inner Temple, 1972; admitted Scottish Bar, 1975; Asst Editor, Session Cases, 1976–82; Asst Clerk, Rules Council, 1978–84; Clerk of Faculty, Faculty of Advocates, 1979–87; Standing Junior Counsel to Scottish Develt Dept (Planning), 1982–86; Temporary Sheriff, 1982–96; Second (formerly Junior) Counsel to Lord President of Court of Session, 1984–89; First Counsel to Lord President, 1989–96; Counsel to Sec. of State under Private Legislation Procedure (Scotland) Act 1936, 1986–96. Chairman: Social Security Appeal Tribunals, 1982–91; Medical Appeal Tribunals, 1991–96. Trustee, Nat. Library of Scotland, 1989–98; Dir of Judicial Studies, 2000–. Editor: Greens Civil Practice Bulletin, 1995–; Greens Litigation Styles, 1998–. *Publications:* (jtly) Greens Annotated Rules of the Court of Session, 1994 (updated quarterly); (ed jtly) Sentencing Practice, 2000; contribs to Stair Memorial Encyclopaedia of the Laws of Scotland, Macphail on Sheriff Court Practice, 2nd edn. *Recreations:* music, riding, being taken for walks by my dog. *Address:* 9 India Street, Edinburgh EH3 6HA. *T:* (0131) 225 2807. *Club:* New (Edinburgh).

MORRISON, (Philip) Blake, FRSL; poet, novelist and critic; *b* 8 Oct. 1950; *s* of Arthur Blakemore Morrison and Agnes O'Shea; *m* 1976, Katherine Ann Drake; two *s* one *d*. *Educ:* Ermysteds Grammar Sch., Skipton; Nottingham Univ. (BA); McMaster Univ. (MA); University College London (PhD). FRSL 1988. Poetry and fiction editor, TLS, 1978–81; Dep. Literary Editor, 1981–86, Literary Editor, 1987–89, Observer; Literary Editor, 1990–94, Staff writer, 1994–95, Independent on Sunday. Eric Gregory Award, 1980; Somerset Maugham Award, 1984; Dylan Thomas Meml Prize, 1985; E. M. Forster Award, 1988. *Publications:* The Movement: English poetry and fiction of the 1950s, 1980; (ed jtly) The Penguin Book of Contemporary British Poetry, 1982; Seamus Heaney, 1982; Dark Glasses, 1984; The Ballad of the Yorkshire Ripper, 1987; The Yellow House, 1987; And When Did You Last See Your Father, 1993 (Waterstone's/Volvo/Esquire Non-Fiction Award, 1993; J. R. Ackerley Award, 1994); The Cracked Pot, 1995; (ed jtly) Mind Readings, 1996; As If, 1997; Too True, 1998; Dr Ox's Experiment (opera libretto), 1998; Selected Poems, 1999; The Justification of Johann Gutenberg, 2000. *Recreations:* football, tennis, running. *Address:* c/o Peters, Fraser & Dunlop, Drury House, 34–43 Russell Street, WC2B 5HA. *T:* (020) 7344 1000.

MORRISON, Maj.-Gen. Reginald Joseph Gordon, CB 1969; CBE 1959; MD, FRCP; retired; Physician, The Royal Hospital, Chelsea, 1969–79; Director of Medicine, Ministry of Defence (Army), and Consulting Physician to the Army, 1965–68; *b* 29 March 1909; *s* of R. Morrison; *m* 1947, Norma Jacqueline Nicholson; two *s*. *Educ:* Dulwich Coll.; St Joseph's Coll., SE19; St Bartholomew's Hosp. House Phys., St Bart's Hosp., 1934; Res. MO, Hove Gen. Hosp. Commnd RAMC, 1936; served as Med. Specialist, RAMC. Adviser in Medicine, EA Command, 1947–50; OC, Med. Div., QA Mil. Hosp., 1950–56; Cons. Phys., Far East, 1956–59; Prof. of Trop. Med., Royal Army Medical College, 1959–65. QHP 1963–68. *Publications:* (with W. H. Hargreaves) The Practice of Tropical Medicine, 1965; chapter in: Exploration Medicine, 1965; Medicine in the Tropics, 1974; various articles in Lancet, BMJ, Proc. RSM, etc. *Recreations:* rose growing, golf. *Address:* 1 Hollington Court, High Street, Chislehurst, Kent BR7 5AJ.

MORRISON, Richard Duncan; Columnist, The Times, since 1999; *b* 24 July 1954; *s* of Donald and Mary Morrison; *m* 1977, Marian Plant; two *s* one *d*. *Educ:* University Coll. Sch.; Magdalene Coll., Cambridge (MA). Asst Editor, Classical Music magazine, 1977–83; Dep. Editor, Early Music magazine, 1984–88; The Times: Music Critic, 1984–89; Dep. Arts Editor, 1989–90; Arts Editor, 1990–99. FRSA 1995. *Recreations:* walking, organ-playing. *Address:* 11 Sunningfields Crescent, NW4 4RD. *T:* (020) 8202 8028.

MORRISON, Hon. Sara Antoinette Sibell Frances, (Hon. Mrs Sara Morrison); *b* 9 Aug. 1934; *d* of 2nd Viscount Long and of Laura, Duchess of Marlborough; *m* 1954, Hon. Charles Andrew Morrison (*see* Hon. Sir C. A. Morrison) (marr. diss. 1984); one *s* one *d*. *Educ:* in England and France. Gen. Electric Co., 1975–98 (Dir 1980–98); Non-Executive Director: Abbey National plc (formerly Abbey Nat. Building Soc.), 1979–95; Carlton TV, 1992–98; Kleinwort Charter Trust, 1993–. Chairman: Nat. Council for Voluntary Orgns (formerly Nat. Council of Social Service), 1977–81; Nat. Adv. Council on Employment of Disabled People, 1981–84. County Councillor, then Alderman, Wilts, 1961–71; Chairman: Wilts Assoc. of Youth Clubs, 1958–63; Wilts Community Council, 1965–70; Vice-Chairman: Nat. Assoc. Youth Clubs, 1969–71; Conservative Party Organisation, 1971–75; Member: Governing Bd, Volunteer Centre, 1972–77; Annan Cttee of Enquiry into Broadcasting, 1974–77; Nat. Consumer Council, 1975–77; Bd, Fourth Channel TV Co., 1980–85; Video Appeals Cttee (Video Recordings Act, 1984), 1985–; Governing Council, Family Policy Studies Centre, 1983–; Nat. Radiological Protection Bd, 1989–; Council, PSI, 1980–93; Governing Body, Imperial Coll., London, 1986– (Hon. Fellow 1993); UK Round Table on Sustainable Develt, 1995–98; Chm., WWF UK, 1998–. FRSA. Hon. DBA Coventry, 1994; Hon. LLD De Montfort, 1998; Hon. DSc Buckingham, 2000. *Address:* Wyndham's Farm, Wedhampton, Devizes, Wilts SN10 3QE. *T:* (01380) 840221; 16 Groom Place, SW1X 7BA. *T:* (020) 7245 6553.

MORRISON, Stephen Roger; Chief Executive, Granada Media Group, since 1996; *b* 3 March 1947; *s* of Hyman Michael Morrison and Rebecca (*née* Zolkwer); *m* 1979, Gayle Valerie Broughall; three *d*. *Educ:* High Sch., Glasgow; Edinburgh Univ. (MA Hons); Nat. Film Sch., Beaconsfield (ANFS). BBC Scotland (Radio and TV), 1970; Granada Television: Producer/Dir, Northern Documentary Unit, 1974; Ed., Granada Regl Progs, 1977; Hd of Arts and Features, 1981; Dir of Programmes, 1987–92; Man. Dir, Broadcasting, 1992–94; Man. Dir, 1993–94; Man. Dir, LWT, 1994–96. Feature Films Producer: The Magic Toyshop, 1986; The Fruit Machine, 1988; (Exec. Producer) My Left Foot, 1989 (2 Acad. Awards); (Exec. Producer) The Field, 1990; Jack and Sarah, 1995; August, 1996. *Recreations:* walking, reading, films and theatre, talking and dining, touring delicatessens. *Address:* Granada Media Group, London Television Centre, Upper Ground, SE1 9LT. *T:* (020) 7620 1620. *Club:* Garrick.

MORRISON, Dr Stuart Love; Professor of Community Medicine, University of Edinburgh, 1964–75, retired; *b* 25 Nov. 1922; *o s* of late William James Morrison, Ironfounder, Glasgow and late Isabella Murdoch, Edinburgh; *m* 1947, Dr Audrey Butler Lornie; one *d*. *Educ:* Glasgow Acad.; Dundee High Sch.; St Andrews and London Univs. MB, ChB (St Andrews) 1951; DPH (London) 1954; MRCP Edinburgh, 1966; FRCP Edinburgh, 1968; FFCM 1975. Served in RAF, 1939–46; Hosp. and gen. practice, 1951–53; Public Health appts, 1954–56; Mem., Scientific Staff, MRC Social Medicine Research Unit, 1956–62; Vis. Fellow, Epidemiology and Statistics, Univ. of N Carolina, 1961–62; Sen. Lectr in Social Med., Univ. of Edinburgh, 1962–64; Professorial Fellow in Community Medicine, 1976–82 and Dir of Centre for Med. Res., 1979–82, Univ. of Sussex; Vis. Prof. of Community Medicine, LSHTM, 1982–84; Prof. of Community Medicine, Univ. of Malta, 1984–86. *Publications:* (jtly) The Image and the Reality, 1978; contribs to med. jls on epidemiology and medical care, and to Book Collector on bibliography. *Recreation:* book collecting. *Address:* 4 Roselands, Sidmouth, Devon EX10 8PB.

MORRISON, Toni; *see* Morrison, C. A.

MORRISON, William Charles Carnegie, CBE 1993; CA; Member, Scottish Amicable Board, since 1997; UK Deputy Senior Partner, Peat Marwick McLintock, later KPMG Peat Marwick, 1987–93; *b* 10 Feb. 1938; *s* of late William and Grace Morrison; *m* 1st; two *d*; 2nd, 1977, Joceline Mary (*née* Saint). *Educ:* Kelvinside Acad., Lathallan; Merchiston Castle Sch. Thomson McLintock & Co., subseq. KMG Thomson McLintock: qual. CA (with distinction), 1961; Partner, 1966; Jt Sen. Partner, Glasgow and Edinburgh, 1974–80; UK managing partner, 1980–87. Director: Thomas Cook & Son Ltd, 1971–72; Scottish Amicable Life Assce Soc., 1973–87, 1993–97; Securities Trust of Scotland, 1976–80; Brownlee & Co., 1978–80; Bank of Scotland, 1993–97; Chm., British Linen Bank Group Ltd, 1994–97. Pres., Inst. of Chartered Accountants of Scotland, 1984–85 (Vice-Pres., 1982–84). Chairman: Auditing Practices Bd of UK and Ireland, 1991–94; Exec. Cttee, The Accountants' Jt Disciplinary Scheme, 1993–; Mem., Financial Reporting Council, 1991–95. Vice Pres., Scottish Council (Develt and Industry), 1982–93 (mem. various cttees; Fellow, 1993); Member: Scottish Telecommunications Bd, 1978–80; Scottish Cttee, Design Council, 1978–81. Vis. Prof. in Accountancy, Univ. of Strathclyde, 1983. Governor, Kelvinside Acad., 1967–80 (Chm. of Governors, 1975–80); Hon. Treasurer, Transport Trust, 1982–88; Trustee, Indep. Living Funds, 1993–. FRSA 1990. *Publications:* occasional professional papers. *Recreations:* vintage transport, model railways. *Address:* 87 Campden Hill Court, Holland Street, W8 7HW. *T:* (020) 7937 2972. *Clubs:* Caledonian; Royal Scottish Automobile (Glasgow).

MORRISON, (William) Garth, CBE 1994; Chairman, Lothian Primary Care NHS Trust, since 1999; Lord-Lieutenant, East Lothian, since 2001; *b* 8 April 1943; *s* of late Walter Courtenay Morrison and Audrey Elizabeth Morrison (*née* Gilbert); *m* 1970, Gillian Cheetham; two *s* one *d*. *Educ:* Pangbourne Coll.; Pembroke Coll., Cambridge (BA 1966). CEng, MIEE 1973. Service in RN, retiring as Lieut, 1961–73; farming in family partnership, 1973–. Scouting: Area Comr, E Lothian, 1973–81; Chief Comr of Scotland, 1981–88; Chief Scout, 1988–96; Mem., World Scout Cttee, 1991–. Chairman: East and Midlothian NHS Trust, 1994–97; Royal Infirmary of Edinburgh NHS Trust, 1997–99.

Member: Lothian Region Children's Panel, 1976–83; Scottish Community Educn Council, 1988–95 (Fellow, 1995); Nat. Lottery Charities Bd, 1995–99. Chm., SE Regl Cttee, 1996–2000, Pres., 2001–, Scottish Landowners' Fedn. Vice-Pres., Commonwealth Youth Exchange Council, 1997–. Trustee: The MacRobert Trusts, 1998–; Lamp of Lothian Collegiate Trust, 1978– (Chm., 2001–). DL E Lothian, 1984. Hon. DBA Napier, 2001. Argentine Gold Medal, 1962. *Publication:* chapter in The Scottish Juvenile Justice System, 1982. *Recreations:* golf, sailing, scouting. *Address:* West Fenton, North Berwick, East Lothian EH39 5AL. *T:* (01620) 842154. *Club:* Hawks (Cambridge).

MORRISON-BELL, Sir William (Hollin Dayrell), 4th Bt *cr* 1905; solicitor; *b* 21 June 1956; *s* of Sir Charles Reginald Francis Morrison-Bell, 3rd Bt and of Prudence Caroline, *d* of late Lt-Col W. D. Davies, 60th Rifles (she *m* 2nd, Peter Gillbanks); *S* father, 1967; *m* 1984, Cynthia Hélène Marie White; one *s* one *d*. *Educ:* Eton; St Edmund Hall, Oxford. *Heir: s* Thomas Charles Edward Morrison-Bell, *b* 13 Feb. 1985. *Address:* Highgreen, Tarset, Hexham, Northumberland NE48 1RP. *T:* (01434) 240223; 28 Batoum Gardens, W6 7QD. *T:* (020) 7602 1363.

MORRISON-LOW, Sir James; *see* Low.

MORRITT, Rt Hon. Sir (Robert) Andrew, Kt 1988; CVO 1989; PC 1994; Vice-Chancellor of the Supreme Court, since 2000; *b* 5 Feb. 1938; *s* of Robert Augustus Morritt and Margaret Mary Morritt (*née* Tyldesley Jones); *m* 1962, Sarah Simonetta Merton, *d* of John Ralph Merton, *qv*; two *s*. *Educ:* Eton Coll.; Magdalene Coll., Cambridge (BA 1961). 2nd Lieut Scots Guards, 1956–58. Called to the Bar, Lincoln's Inn, 1962, Bencher, 1984; QC 1977. Junior Counsel: to Sec. of State for Trade in Chancery Matters, 1970–77; to Attorney-Gen. in Charity Matters, 1972–77; Attorney General to HRH The Prince of Wales, 1978–88; a Judge of High Court of Justice, Chancery Div., 1988–94; a Lord Justice of Appeal, 1994–2000. Vice-Chancellor of Co. Palatine of Lancaster, 1991–94. Member: Gen. Council of the Bar, 1969–73; Adv. Cttee on Legal Educn, 1972–76; Top Salaries Review Body, 1982–87. Pres., Council of the Inns of Court, 1997–2000. *Recreations:* fishing, shooting. *Address:* Royal Courts of Justice, Strand, WC2A 2LL. *Club:* Garrick.

MORROGH, Henton, CBE 1969; FRS 1964; FREng; Director, BCIRA (formerly British Cast Iron Research Association), 1959–85; *b* 29 Sept. 1917; *s* of Clifford and Amy Morrogh; *m* 1949, Olive Joyce Ramsay; one *d*. Distinguished for his work on the microstructure and solidification of cast iron and for the development of ductile cast iron. Visiting Prof., Dept of Industrial Engineering and Management Univ. of Technology, Loughborough, 1967–72. President: Instn of Metallurgists, 1967–68; Inst. of British Foundrymen, 1972–73; Internat. Cttee of Foundry Technical Assocs, 1978. FREng (FEng 1979). Hon. Member: Japanese Foundrymen's Soc., 1984; Inst. of British Foundrymen, 1986. DSc (*hc*) Univ. of Birmingham, 1965. Iron and Steel Inst. Andrew Carnegie Gold Medal, 1946; E. J. Fox Medal Inst. of Brit. Foundrymen, 1951; McFadden Gold Medal, Amer. Foundrymen's Soc., 1952; Robert Hadfield Medal, Iron & Steel Inst., 1956; Gold Medal, Amer. Gray Iron Founders' Soc., 1961; Bessemer Gold Medal, Metals Soc., 1977. *Address:* Cedarwood, Penn Lane, Tanworth-in-Arden, Warwicks B94 5HH. *T:* (01564) 742414.

MORROW, Cdre Anthony John Clare, CVO 1997; RN; Extra Equerry to the Queen, since 1998; *b* 30 March 1944; *s* of late Capt. John Geoffrey Basil Morrow, CVO, DSC, RN and Dorothy April Bettina (*née* Mather); *m* 1st, 1969 (marr. diss. 1979); two *d*; 2nd, 1982, Julie, *d* of late R. M. Philips and Mrs M. Philips; one *s* one *d*. *Educ:* Summerfields, Oxford; Nautical Coll., Pangbourne; BRNC, Dartmouth. Entered RN, 1962: qualified Signals Officer, HMS Mercury, 1971; Lt-Comdr 1972; on staff of C-in-C Fleet, Signals Officer, HM Yacht Britannia, 1976–78; commanded HMS Lindisfarne, 1978–79; Comdr 1979; on staff, UK Mil. Rep. to NATO, 1980–83; commanded HMS Active, 1983–85; RN Exchange to CNO, US Navy, Washington, 1985–87; MoD, 1987–88; Capt. 1988; Captain, HMS Mercury, 1988–91; commanded Fourth Frigate Sqdn, HMS Active, 1991–93; ACOS, Plans and Policy, CINCHAN, Eastern Atlantic, 1993–94; Commodore Royal Yachts, 1995–98; retired 1998. Gen. Manager, W. & F. C. Bonham & Sons Ltd, 1999. Chm., Assoc. of Royal Yachtsmen, 1998–. Younger Brother, Trinity House, 1996. *Recreations:* outdoor activities, sports. *Clubs:* Bosham Sailing; Imperial Poona Yacht.

MORROW, Graham Eric; QC 1996; a Recorder, since 1997; *b* 14 June 1951; *s* of George Eric Morrow and Freda Morrow; *m* 1987, Rosalind Nola Ellis; one *s*, and two step *d*. *Educ:* Liverpool Coll.; Univ. of Newcastle upon Tyne (LLB). Called to the Bar, Lincoln's Inn, 1974; Asst Recorder, 1990. *Recreations:* cycling, swimming, ski-ing. *Address:* Exchange Chambers, Pearl Assurance House, Derby Square, Liverpool L2 9XX. *T:* (0151) 236 7747.

MORROW, Sir Ian (Thomas), Kt 1973; CA; FCMA, JDipMA, FIMgt; CompIEE; Chairman: MAI (formerly Mills and Allen International) plc, 1974–93 (Director, 1974–94); Additional Underwriting Agencies (No 3) Ltd, since 1985; Scotia Pharmaceuticals Ltd, Scotia (formerly Efamol) Holdings plc, 1986–95; Thurne Group Ltd, 1993–99; *b* 8 June 1912; *er s* of late Thomas George Morrow and Jamesina Hunter, Pilmour Links, St Andrews; *m* 1940, Elizabeth Mary Thackray (marr. diss. 1967); one *s* one *d*; *m* 1967, Sylvia Jane Taylor; one *d*. *Educ:* Dollar Academy, Dollar. Chartered Accountant 1936; FCMA 1945; Asst Accountant, Brocklehurst-Whiston Amalgamated Ltd, 1937–40; Partner, Robson, Morrow & Co., 1942–51; Financial Dir, 1951–52, Dep. Man. Dir, 1952–56, Joint Man. Dir, 1956–57, Man. Dir, 1957–58, The Brush Electrical Engineering Co. Ltd (now The Brush Group Ltd); Jt Man. Dir, H. Clarkson & Co. Ltd, 1961–72; Chairman: UKO International plc (formerly UK Optical & Industrial Holdings Ltd), 1959–86 (former Man. Dir and Chm. of subsidiary cos); Hector Whaling Ltd, 1959–64; Rowe Bros & Co. (Holdings) Ltd, 1960–70; Kenwood Manufacturing Co. Ltd, 1961–68; Crosfield Electronics Ltd, 1963–72; W. M. Still & Sons Ltd, 1964–86; Associated Fire Alarms Ltd, 1965–70; Crane Fruehauf Trailers Ltd, 1969–71; Martin-Black PLC, 1977–86; Collett, Dickenson, Pearce Internat. Ltd, 1979–83; Scotia DAF Trucks Ltd, 1979–83; Agricultural Holdings Co. Ltd, 1981–84; Strong & Fisher (Hldgs), 1981–90 (Dir, 1981–90); Argunex Ltd, 1985–89; Insport Consultants, 1988–93; Beale Dobie & Co. Ltd, 1989–97; Walbrook Insce Co., 1990–92; Brightstone Estates, 1990–92; Deputy Chairman, Rolls Royce Ltd, 1970–71, Rolls Royce (1971) Ltd, 1971–73 (Man. Dir, 1971–72); Director: Hambros Industrial Management Ltd, 1965–91; Hambros PLC, 1972–90 (Dep. Chm., 1983–86); The Laird Gp, 1973–92 (Chm., 1975–87); DAF Trucks (GB), 1977–83; Zeus Management Ltd, 1985–93; Psion PLC, 1987–98; C. E. Heath Public Ltd Co., 1988–97. Led Anglo-American Council on Productivity Team on Management Accounting to US, 1950. Council Member: British Electrical & Allied Manufacturers' Assoc., 1957–58; British Internal Combustion Engine Manufacturers' Assoc., 1957–58; Member: Grand Council, FBI, 1953–58; Council, Production Engineering Research Assoc., 1955–58; Council, Inst. of Cost and Works Accountants (now Inst. of Management Accountants), 1952–70 (Pres. 1956–57, Gold Medallist 1961); Performing Right Tribunal, 1968–74; Council, Inst. of Chartered Accountants of Scotland, 1968–72, 1979–82 (Vice-Pres. 1970–72, 1979–80, 1980–81, Pres., 1981–82); Inflation Accounting Steering Gp, 1976–79; Lay Member, Press Council, 1974–80; Freeman, City of London; Liveryman, Worshipful Co. of Spectaclemakers. DUniv. Stirling, 1979; Hon. DLitt Heriot-Watt, 1982. *Publications:* papers and addresses on professional and management subjects. *Recreations:* reading, music, golf, ski-ing. *Address:* Broadacres, Seven Devils Lane, Saffron Walden CB11 4BB. *T:* (01799) 521358. *Clubs:* National Liberal, Royal Automobile; Royal and Ancient (St Andrews); Saffron Walden Golf.

MORROW, Martin S.; Stipendiary Magistrate, Glasgow, 1972–88; *b* 16 Nov. 1923; *s* of late Thomas Morrow and Mary Lavery; *m* 1952, Nancy May, BMus, LRAM; one *s* two *d*. *Educ:* St Aloysius' Coll., Glasgow; Glasgow Univ. Solicitor. Private practice, 1951–56; Asst Procurator Fiscal, 1956–72. *Recreations:* music, golf, reading. *Address:* 33 Leicester Avenue, Glasgow G12 0LU. *T:* (0141) 334 1324. *Club:* St Mungo (Glasgow).

MORSE, Prof. Christopher George John, (Robin); Professor of Law, King's College London, since 1992; *b* 28 June 1947; *s* of John Morse and Margaret Gwenllian Morse (*née* Maliphant); *m* 1983, Louise Angela Stott; one *s*. *Educ:* Malvern Coll.; Wadham Coll., Oxford (MA, BCL). Called to the Bar, Middle Temple, 1971; King's College London: Lectr in Law, 1971–88; Reader, 1988–92; Hd and Dean, Sch. of Law, 1992–93, 1997–; FKC 2000. Visiting Professor: John Marshall Law Sch., Chicago, 1979–80; Univ. of Leuven, 1982; Dir of Studies, Hague Acad. of Internat. Law, 1990. *Publications:* Torts in Private International Law, 1978; (ed jtly) Dicey and Morris on the Conflict of Laws, 11th edn 1987, 12th edn 1993, 13th edn 2000; (ed jtly) Benjamin's Sale of Goods, 3rd edn 1987 to 5th edn 1997; Public Policy in Transnational Relationships, 1991; (ed jtly) Chitty on Contracts, 27th edn 1994, 28th edn 1999; articles in learned jls and contribs to books. *Recreations:* Swansea City Association Football Club, travel. *Address:* School of Law, King's College London, Strand, WC2R 2LS. *T:* (020) 7848 5454.

MORSE, Sir Christopher Jeremy, KCMG 1975; Warden, Winchester College, 1987–97 (Fellow, 1966–82); Chancellor, Bristol University, since 1989; *b* 10 Dec. 1928; *s* of late Francis John Morse and Kinbarra (*née* Armfield-Marrow); *m* 1955, Belinda Marianne, *d* of Lt-Col R. B. Y. Mills; three *s* one *d* (and one *d* decd). *Educ:* Winchester; New Coll., Oxford (Hon. Fellow, 1979). 1st Class Lit. Hum. 1953. 2nd Lt KRRC, 1948–49. Fellow, All Souls Coll., Oxford, 1953–68, 1983–. Trained in banking at Glyn, Mills & Co., and made a director in 1964; Executive Dir, 1965–72, non-exec. Dir, 1993–97, Bank of England; Lloyds Bank: Dep. Chm., 1975–77; Chm., 1977–93; Lloyds Bank International: Chm., 1979–80; Dep. Chm., 1975–77 and 1980–85; Chm., Lloyds Merchant Bank Hldgs, 1985–88. Alternate Governor for UK of IMF, 1966–72; Chm. of Deputies of Cttee of Twenty, IMF, 1972–74; Chm., Cttee of London Clearing Bankers, 1980–82 (Dep. Chm., 1978–80); Mem., Council of Lloyd's, 1987–98; President: London Forex Assoc., 1978–91; Institut Internat. d'Etudes Bancaires, 1982–83; British Overseas Bankers' Club, 1983–84; BBA, 1984–91 (Vice-Pres., 1991–92); Internat. Monetary Conf., 1985–86; Banking Fedn of EC, 1988–90; CIB, 1992–93 (Vice-Pres., 1991–92); Vice-Pres., BITC, 1992–98. Mem., NEDC, 1977–81. Chm., City Communications Centre, 1985–87; non-executive Director: Alexanders Discount Co. Ltd, 1975–84; Legal & General Assce Soc., 1964 and 1975–87; ICI, 1981–93; Zeneca, 1993–99. Hon. Mem., Lombard Assoc., 1989. Governor, Henley Management Coll., 1966–85. Chairman: Per Jacobsson Foundn, 1987–99; Trustees, Beit Meml Fellowships for Med. Res., 1976–; GBA, 1994–99; Mem., British Selection Cttee, Harkness Fellowships, 1986–90. Freeman, City of London, 1978; Chm., City Arts Trust, 1976–79. FIDE Internat. Judge for chess compositions, 1975–; Pres., British Chess Problem Soc., 1977–79; Hon. Life Mem., British Chess Fedn, 1988. Pres., Classical Assoc., 1989–90. Hon. DLitt City, 1977; Hon DSc Aston, 1984; Hon. LLD Bristol, 1989. *Publication:* Chess Problems: tasks and records, 1995. *Recreations:* poetry, problems and puzzles, coarse gardening, golf. *Address:* 102a Drayton Gardens, SW10 9RJ. *T:* (020) 7370 2265. *Club:* Athenæum.

MORSE, Sir Jeremy; *see* Morse, Sir C. J.

MORSE, Robin; *see* Morse, C. G. J.

MORSON, Basil Clifford, CBE 1987; VRD 1963; MA, DM Oxon; FRCS; FRCPath; FRCP; Civilian Consultant in Pathology to the Royal Navy, 1976–86, now Emeritus; Consulting Pathologist and Research Consultant to St Mark's Hospital, since 1986 (Consultant Pathologist, 1956–86); Director, WHO International Reference Centre for Gastrointestinal Cancer, 1969–86; *b* 13 Nov. 1921; *s* of late A. Clifford Morson, OBE, FRCS; *m* 1st, 1950, Pamela Elizabeth Gilbert (marr. diss. 1982); one *s* two *d*; 2nd, 1983, Sylvia Dutton, MBE. *Educ:* Beaumont Coll.; Wadham Coll., Oxford; Middlesex Hosp. Medical Sch. House Surg., Middlesex Hosp., 1949; House Surg., Central Middlesex Hosp., 1950; Asst Pathologist, Bland-Sutton Institute of Pathology, Middlesex Hosp., 1950. Sub-Lt RNVR, 1943–46; Surgeon-Comdr RNR (London Div.), retd 1972. President: Sect. of Proctology, RSocMed, 1973–74; British Soc. of Gastroenterology, 1979–80 (Hon. Mem., 1987); British Div., Internat. Acad. of Pathology, 1978–; Treas., RCPath, 1983– (Vice-Pres., 1978–81). Vis. Prof. of Pathology, Univ. of Chicago, 1959; Sir Henry Wade Vis. Prof., RCSE, 1970; Vis. Prof of Pathology, Univ. of Texas System Cancer Center, 1980 (Joanne Vandenberg Hill Award); Lectures: Lettsomian, Med. Soc., 1970; Sir Arthur Hurst Meml, British Soc. of Gastroenterology, 1970; Richardson, Massachusetts Gen. Hosp., Boston, 1970; Skinner, RCR, 1983; Shelley Meml, Johns Hopkins Univ., 1983; Kettle, RCPath, 1987. FRCS 1972; FRCP 1979 (MRCP 1973); Hon. Fellow: Amer. Soc. of Colon and Rectal Surgeons, 1974; Amer. Coll. of Gastroenterology, 1978; French Nat. Soc. of Gastroenterology, 1982; RSM, 1989; RAeS, 1990. John Hunter Medal, RCS, 1987; Frederick Salmon Medal, Sect. of Coloproctology, RSM, 1991. *Publications:* Pathology of Alimentary Tract, in Systemic Pathology, ed W. St C. Symmers, 1966, 3rd edn 1987; (ed) Diseases of the Colon, Rectum and Anus, 1969; Textbook of Gastrointestinal Pathology, 1972, 3rd edn 1989; Histological Typing of Intestinal Tumours, 1976; The Pathogenesis of Colorectal Cancer, 1978; Pathology in Surgical Practice, 1985; Colour Atlas of Gastrointestinal Pathology, 1988; numerous articles in medical journals. *Recreations:* gardening, ornithology, travel. *Address:* 14 Crossways Park, West Chiltington, W Sussex RH20 2QZ. *T:* (01798) 813528.

MORT, Rev. (Margaret) Marion; Non-Stipendiary Curate, St Barnabas, Swanmore, since 1997; *b* 10 May 1937; *d* of Rev. Ivan H. Whittaker and Margaret Whittaker; *m* 1959, Colin James Mort; one *s* two *d*. *Educ:* St Mary's Sch., Wantage; Queen's Coll., Harley St; Edinburgh Univ.; Southern Dios MTS. Nat. Sec., World Development Movement, 1970–72; Licensed Lay Reader, 1983–97; Mem. Gen. Synod, 1985–90 (rep. in Partners in Mission consultation for Church in Kenya, 1988). World Develt Educn Adviser, Dio. Portsmouth, 1984–91; Co-ordinator, then Officer, Decade of Evangelism (C of E), 1990–93; Mission and Evangelism Sec., Bd of Mission, Gen. Synod, 1993–94; ordained deacon, 1997, priest, 1998. Dir, Ocean Sound (ILR), 1985–92; Member: Bd of Christian Aid, 1987–90; Gen. Cttee, British and Foreign Bible Soc., 1993–95. Hon. Canon, Portsmouth Cathedral, 2001–. *Publications:* (jtly) Mission Audit, 1983; (jtly) Called to Order, 1988; (jtly) Building Bridges, 1995; (jtly) A Time for Sharing, 1995; church educnl papers; contribs to Church press. *Recreations:* gardening, good beer, good conversation. *Address:* Rivendell, High Street, Shirrell Heath, Southampton SO32 2JN. *T:* and *Fax:* (01329) 832178.

MORT, Timothy James; His Honour Judge Mort; a Circuit Judge, since 1996; *b* 4 March 1950; *s* of Dr Philip Mort and Sybil Mort; *m* 1979, Philippa Mary Brown; one *s* three *d. Educ:* Clifton Coll., Bristol; Emmanuel Coll., Cambridge (Schol.; MA Law Tripos 1971). Called to the Bar, Middle Temple, 1972; in practice, Northern Circuit, 1972–96. *Recreations:* tennis, Real tennis, music. *Address:* c/o Northern Circuit Office, 15 Quay Street, Manchester M60 9FD. *Club:* Manchester Tennis & Racquet.

MORTIMER, Hon. Barry; *see* Mortimer, Hon. J. B.

MORTIMER, Clifford Hiley, DSc, DrPhil; FRS 1958; Distinguished Professor in Zoology, University of Wisconsin-Milwaukee, 1966–81, now Distinguished Professor Emeritus; *b* Whitchurch, Som, 27 Feb. 1911; *er s* of Walter Herbert and Bessie Russell; *m* 1936, Ingeborg Margarete Closs (*d* 2000), Stuttgart, Germany; two *d. Educ:* Sibford and Sidcot Schs; Univ. of Manchester. BSc (Manchester) 1932, DSc (Manchester) 1946; Dr Phil (Berlin) 1935. Served on scientific staff of Freshwater Biological Assoc., 1935–41 and 1946–56. Seconded to Admiralty scientific service, 1941–46. Sec. and Dir, Scottish Marine Biological Assoc., 1956–66; Dir, Center for Great Lakes Studies, Univ. of Wisconsin-Milwaukee, 1966–79. Hon. DSc Wisconsin-Milwaukee, 1985; DèsSc *hc* Ecole Polytechnique Fédérale de Lausanne, 1987. *Publications:* scientific papers on lakes and the physical and chemical conditions which control life in them. *Recreation:* music. *Address:* Milwaukee Catholic Home, 2462 N Prospect Avenue, Milwaukee, WI 53211, USA.

MORTIMER, Hugh Roger, LVO 1992; HM Diplomatic Service; Ambassador to Slovenia, since 2001; *b* 19 Sept. 1949; *s* of Phillip Roger Mortimer and Patricia Henley Mortimer (*née* Moreton); *m* 1974, Zosia Rzepecka (marr. diss. 2000); one *d* (and one *d* decd). *Educ:* Cheltenham Coll.; Univ. of Surrey (BSc Linguistics and Regl Studies); King's Coll., London (MA War Studies). Joined HM Diplomatic Service, 1973: Third Sec., Rome, 1975–78; Third, later Second Sec., Singapore, 1978–81; FCO, 1981–83; Second, later First Sec., UK Mission to UN, NY, 1983–86; FCO, 1986–89; on attachment to German Foreign Ministry, 1990; Dep. Head of Mission, Berlin, 1991–94; FCO, 1994–95; rcds 1996; Dep. Head of Mission, Ankara, 1997–2000. *Recreations:* jogging, squash, sailing, guitar playing. *Address:* c/o Foreign and Commonwealth Office, King Charles Street, SW1A 2AH.

MORTIMER, James Edward; General Secretary of the Labour Party, 1982–85; *b* 12 Jan. 1921; *m*; two *s* one *d. Educ:* Junior Techn. Sch., Portsmouth; Ruskin Coll., Oxford; London Sch. of Economics. Worked in Shipbuilding and Engrg Industries as Ship Fitter Apprentice, Machinist and Planning Engr; TUC Schol., Oxford, 1945–46; TUC Economic Dept, 1946–48; full-time Trade Union Official, Draughtsmen's and Allied Technicians' Assoc., 1948–68. Dir, London Co-operative Soc., 1968–71. Mem., NBPI, 1968–71; Mem., Bd, LTE, 1971–74. Chm., ACAS (formerly Conciliation and Arbitration Service), 1974–81. Member: Wilberforce Ct of Inquiry into the power dispute, 1970; Armed Forces Pay Review Body, 1971–74; EDC for Chemical Industry, 1973–74; Chm. EDC for Mechanical and Electrical Engineering Construction, 1974–82. Vis. Fellow, Admin. Staff Coll., Henley, 1976–82; Sen. Vis. Fellow, Bradford Univ., 1977–82; Vis. Prof., Imperial Coll. of Sci. and Technol., London Univ., 1981–83; Ward-Perkins Res. Fellow, Pembroke Coll., Oxford, 1981. Chm. Editl Cttee, Socialist Campaign Group News, 1987–; Mem. Exec. Cttee, Inst. of Employment Rights, 1989–. Hon. DLitt Bradford, 1982. *Publications:* A History of Association of Engineering and Shipbuilding Draughtsmen, 1960; (with Clive Jenkins) British Trade Unions Today, 1965; (with Clive Jenkins) The Kind of Laws the Unions Ought to Want, 1968; Industrial Relations, 1968; Trade Unions and Technological Change, 1971; History of the Boilermakers' Society, vol. 1, 1973, vol. 2, 1982, vol. 3, 1993; (with Valerie Ellis) A Professional Union: the evolution of the Institution of Professional Civil Servants, 1980; A Life on the Left, 1999. *Address:* 19 Northweald Lane, Kingston-upon-Thames, Surrey KT2 5GL. *T:* (020) 8547 1885.

See also J. E. Mortimer.

MORTIMER, James Edward; Deputy Director and Treasury Officer of Accounts, 1995–2000; *b* 9 Nov. 1947; *s* of James Edward Mortimer, *qv* and Renee Mabel Mortimer (*née* Horton); *m* 1969, Lesley Patricia Young. *Educ:* Latymer Upper Sch.; Wadham Coll., Oxford (MA, BPhil). HM Treasury, 1971–2000: Economic Advr, 1974–81; Principal, 1981–83; Grade 5, 1983–91; Under Sec., 1991–2000; Head of Aid and Export Finance Gp, 1991–95. *Recreations:* football, golf, cricket, birdwatching, cinema. *Address:* 21 Hogarth Way, Hampton, Middlesex TW12 2EL. *Clubs:* Royal Automobile; Old Latymerians Association.

MORTIMER, Hon. (John) Barry; a Non-Permanent Judge, Court of Final Appeal, Hong Kong, since 1997; a Justice of Appeal, 1993–99, a Vice-President, 1997–99, Court of Appeal of the High Court (formerly Supreme Court), Hong Kong; *b* 7 Aug. 1931; *s* of late John William Mortimer and Maud (*née* Snarr) Mortimer; *m* 1958, Judith Mary (*née* Page); two *s* two *d. Educ:* St Peter's School, York (Headmasters' Exhibitioner 1945); Emmanuel College, Cambridge; BA 1955, MA 1959. Commissioned into 4 RTR, 1951; served in Egypt, 1951–52; 45/51 RTR (TA), 1952–57. Called to the Bar, Middle Temple, 1956 (Bencher 1980); Harmsworth Law Scholar 1957; Prosecuting Counsel on NE Circuit: to Post Office, 1965–69; to Inland Revenue, 1969–71; QC 1971; a Recorder, 1972–87; Judge, Supreme Court of Hong Kong, 1985–93. Chancellor, Dio. of Ripon, 1971–85. Chairman: Mental Health Review Tribunal, 1983–85; Overseas Trust Bank (Compensation) Tribunal, 1986–87; Member: Bar Council, 1970–75; Senate, 1979–85; Law Reform Commn, Hong Kong, 1990–99 (Chm., Sub-cttee on Privacy and Data Protection); Judicial Studies Bd, 1996–99; Vice Chm., Advocacy Inst. of Hong Kong, 1997–99; Chm., Criminal Court Users Cttee, 1998–99. Chm., Envmtl Impact Assessment Appeal Bd, Kowloon Canton Railway Corp. Spur Line Appeal, 2001. Dir, City Disputes Panel Ltd, 2000–. Hon. Diplomate, Amer. Bd of Trial Advocates, 1994. *Recreations:* reading, shooting, tennis. *Address:* The Grange, Staveley, Knaresborough, N Yorks HG5 9LD. *Club:* Hong Kong.

MORTIMER, Sir John (Clifford), Kt 1998; CBE 1986; QC 1966; FRSL; barrister; playwright and author; *b* 21 April 1923; *s* of Clifford Mortimer and Kathleen May (*née* Smith); *m* 1st, 1949, Penelope Ruth Fletcher (marr. diss. 1972; she *d* 1999); one *s* one *d*; 2nd, Penelope (*née* Gollop); two *d. Educ:* Harrow; Brasenose Coll., Oxford. Called to the Bar, 1948; Master of the Bench, Inner Temple, 1975. Mem. Nat. Theatre Bd, 1968–88. Chairman: Council, RSL, 1989–99; Royal Court Theatre, 1990–. Pres., Howard League for Penal Reform, 1991–97. Pres., Berks, Bucks and Oxon Naturalists' Trust, 1984–90. Chm., Cttee to advise on vacant plinth, Trafalgar Square, 1999–. FRSL 1973. Hon. DLitt: Susquehanna Univ., 1985; St Andrews, 1987; Nottingham, 1989; Hon. LLD: Exeter, 1986; Brunel, 1990. Won the Italia Prize with short play, The Dock Brief, 1958; another short play What Shall We Tell Caroline, 1958. Full-length plays: The Wrong Side of the Park, 1960; Two Stars for Comfort, 1962; (trans.) A Flea in Her Ear, 1966; The Judge, 1967; (trans.) Cat Among the Pigeons, 1969; Come as You Are, 1970; A Voyage Round My Father, 1970 (filmed, 1982); (trans.) The Captain of Köpenick, 1971; I, Claudius (adapted from Robert Graves), 1972; Collaborators, 1973; Mr Luby's Fear of Heaven (radio), 1976; Heaven and Hell, 1976; The Bells of Hell, 1977; (trans.) The Lady from Maxim's, 1977; (trans.) A Little Hotel on the Side, 1984; opera (trans.) Die Fledermaus, 1988; A Christmas Carol (adapted from Dickens), 1994; Summer of a Dormouse (radio), 1999; Naked Justice, 2001. Film Scripts: John and Mary, 1970; Brideshead Revisited (TV), 1981; Edwin (TV), 1984; Cider with Rosie (TV), 1998; Tea with Mussolini, 1999. British Acad. Writers Award, 1979; Life Achievement Award, Banff Television Fest., 1998. *Publications: novels:* Charade, 1947; Rumming Park, 1948; Answer Yes or No, 1950; Like Men Betrayed, 1953, reissued 1987; Three Winters, 1956; Will Shakespeare: an entertainment, 1977; Rumpole of the Bailey, 1978 (televised; BAFTA Writer of the Year Award, 1980); The Trials of Rumpole, 1979; Rumpole's Return, 1980 (televised); Regina v Rumpole, 1981; Rumpole for the Defence, 1982; Rumpole and the Golden Thread, 1983 (televised); Paradise Postponed, 1985 (televised 1986); Rumpole's Last Case, 1987 (televised); Rumpole and the Age of Miracles, 1988 (televised); Summer's Lease, 1988 (televised 1989); Titmuss Regained, 1990 (televised 1991); Rumpole à la Carte, 1990; Dunster, 1992; Rumpole on Trial, 1992; Under the Hammer, 1994 (televised); Rumpole and the Angel of Death, 1995; Felix in the Underworld, 1997; The Sound of Trumpets, 1998; Rumpole Rests His Case, 2001; *travel:* (in collab. with P. R. Mortimer) With Love and Lizards, 1957; *plays:* The Dock Brief and Other Plays, 1959; The Wrong Side of the Park, 1960; Lunch Hour and Other Plays, 1960; Two Stars for Comfort, 1962; (trans.) A Flea in Her Ear, 1965; A Voyage Round My Father, 1970; (trans.) The Captain of Köpenick, 1971; Five Plays, 1971; Collaborators, 1973; Edwin and Other Plays, 1984; (trans.) Die Fledermaus, 1989; Naked Justice, 2001; *interviews:* In Character, 1983; Character Parts, 1986; *autobiography:* Clinging to the Wreckage (Book of the Year Award, Yorkshire Post), 1982; Murderers and Other Friends, 1994; Summer of a Dormouse, 2000; writes TV plays (incl. six Rumpole series); contribs to periodicals. *Recreations:* working, gardening, going to opera. *Address:* Peters Fraser & Dunlop Group Ltd, Drury House, 34–43 Russell Street, WC2B 5HA. *Club:* Garrick.

MORTIMER, Katharine Mary Hope, (Mrs Robert Dean); Consultant/Financial Adviser, Know How Fund for Eastern Europe, 1990–97; *b* 28 May 1946; *d* of late Rt Rev. Robert Cecil Mortimer and Mary Hope (*née* Walker); *m* 1st, 1973, John Noel Nicholson (marr. diss. 1986); one *s*; 2nd, 1990, Robert Michael Dean. *Educ:* School of SS Mary and Anne, Abbots Bromley; Somerville Coll., Oxford. MA, BPhil Oxon. World Bank, 1969–72; Central Policy Review Staff, 1972–78; N. M. Rothschild Asset Management Ltd, 1978–84; Dir, N. M. Rothschild & Sons (International Corporate Finance, subseq. Internat. Asset Management), 1984–88; seconded as Dir of Policy, SIB, 1985–87; Chief Exec., Walker Books, 1988–89. Member: Bd, Crown Agents, 1990–97; Crown Agents Foundn Council, 1997–; non-executive Director: National Bus Company, 1979–91; Inst. of Development Studies, 1983–95; Mast Develt Co., 1989–93; Crown Agents Financial Services Ltd, 1990–; Crown Agents Asset Mgt Ltd, 1990–; IQI Ltd, 1991–92; British Nuclear Fuels plc, 1993–2000; Pennon Gp plc, 2000–. Member: ESRC, 1983–86; Competition (formerly Monopolies and Mergers) Commn, 1995–. Mem., Royal Commn for Exhibn of 1851, 1988–. Member, Governing Body: Centre for Economic Policy Res., 1986–91; Imperial Coll., 1987–90. Trustee, Inst. for Public Policy Res., 1989–92. *Address:* Lower Corscombe, Okehampton, Devon EX20 1SD.

MORTIMORE, Prof. Peter John, OBE 1994; PhD; FBPsS; Director, Institute of Education, London University, 1994–2000 (Professor of Education, 1990–2000, now Emeritus); Pro-Vice-Chancellor, London University, 1999–2000; *b* 17 Jan. 1942; *s* of late Claude Mortimore and Rose Mortimore; *m* 1965, Jo Hargaden; three *d. Educ:* Chiswick County Grammar Sch.; St Mary's Coll., Strawberry Hill; Birkbeck Coll., London Univ. (BSc; Fellow 2001); Inst. of Education (MSc); Inst. of Psychiatry (PhD). CPsychol 1989; FBPsS 1989. Teacher, Sacred Heart Sch., SE5, 1964–66; Teacher and Head of Dept, Stockwell Manor Sch., SW9, 1966–73; Res. Officer, Inst. of Psychiatry, 1975–78; Mem., HM Inspectorate, 1978; Inner London Education Authority: Dir, Res. and Stats Br., 1979–85; Asst Educn Officer (Secondary Schs), 1985–87; Prof. of Educn, Lancaster Univ., 1988–90; Dep. Dir, London Univ. Inst. of Educn, 1990–94. Member: Educn Res. Bd, SSRC, 1981–82; Educn and Human Devclt Cttee, ESRC, 1982–85; Univ. of London Exams and Assessment Council, 1991; Trustee, VSO, 1992–. Governor: SOAS, 1993–98; Birkbeck Coll., 1998–. Hon. FCP 1994; AcSS 2000. FRSA 1990. Hon. DLitt Heriot-Watt, 1998. *Publications:* (jtly) Fifteen Thousand Hours: secondary schools and their effects on children, 1979; (jtly) Behaviour Problems in Schools, 1984; (jtly) Secondary School Examinations, 1986; (jtly) School Matters: the junior years, 1988; (jtly) The Primary Head: roles, responsibilities and reflections, 1991; The Secondary Head: roles, responsibilities and reflections, 1991; (jtly) Managing Associate Staff, 1994; (jtly) Planning Matters, 1995; (jtly) Living Education, 1997; (jtly) Forging Links, 1997; Road to Improvement, 1998; (jtly) Understanding Pedagogy, 1999; (jtly) Culture of Change, 2000; (jtly) Improving School Effectiveness, 2001. *Recreations:* theatre, art, music, walking. *Address:* c/o Institute of Education, 20 Bedford Way, WC1H 0AL.

MORTIMORE, Simon Anthony; QC 1991; *b* 12 April 1950; *s* of late Robert Anthony Mortimore and Katherine Elizabeth Mackenzie Mortimore (*née* Caine); *m* 1983, Fiona Elizabeth Jacobson; one *s* one *d. Educ:* Westminster School; Exeter Univ. (LLB). Called to the Bar, Inner Temple, 1972. CEDR accredited mediator, 1997–. *Publications:* contribs to Bullen and Leake and Jacobs Precedents of Pleading, 13th edn 1990; Insolvency of Banks, 1996. *Recreations:* opera, general cultural interests, travel, golf. *Address:* 3/4 South Square, Gray's Inn, WC1R 5HP. *T:* (020) 7696 9900. *Clubs:* Hurlingham; Royal Mid Surrey Golf, Royal St George's Golf, Rye Golf.

MORTON, 22nd Earl of, *cr* 1458 (*de facto* 21st Earl, 22nd but for the Attainder); **John Charles Sholto Douglas;** Lord Aberdour, 1458; Lord-Lieutenant of West Lothian, 1985–2001; *b* 19 March 1927; *s* of Hon. Charles William Sholto Douglas (*d* 1960) (2nd *s* of 19th Earl) and Florence (*d* 1985), *er d* of late Major Henry Thomas Timson; *S* cousin, 1976; *m* 1949, Sheila Mary, *d* of late Rev. Canon John Stanley Gibbs, MC, Didmarton House, Badminton, Glos; two *s* one *d*. DL West Lothian, 1982. *Recreation:* polo. *Heir: s* Lord Aberdour, *qv. Address:* Dalmahoy, Kirknewton, Midlothian EH27 8EB. *Clubs:* Farmers'; Edinburgh Polo, Dalmahoy Country.

MORTON, Sir Alastair; *see* Morton, Sir R. A. N.

MORTON, Rev. Andrew Queen; Minister of Culross Abbey, 1959–87; *b* 4 June 1919; *s* of Alexander Morton and Janet Queen; *m* 1948, Jean, *e d* of George Singleton and late Jean Wands; one *s* two *d. Educ:* Glasgow Univ. MA 1942, BD 1947, BSc 1948. Minister of St Andrews, Fraserburgh, 1949–59. Dept of Computer Science, Univ. of Edinburgh, 1965–86. Hon. Res. Fellow, Glasgow Univ., 1990. FRSE 1973. *Publications:* The Structure of the Fourth Gospel, 1961; Authorship and Integrity in the New Testament, 1963; (with G. H. C. Macgregor) The Structure of Luke and Acts, 1965; Paul the Man and the Myth, 1965; (with S. Michaelson) The Computer in Literary Research, 1973; Literary Detection, 1979; (with S. Michaelson and N. Hamilton-Smith) Justice for Helander, 1979; (with James McLeman) The Genesis of John, 1980; (with S. Michaelson) The Cusum Plot, 1990; (with M. G. Farringdon) Fielding and the Federalist, 1990; Proper Words in Proper Places, 1992; The Authorship and Integrity of the New Testament Epistles, 1993; The Making of Mark, 1995; Gathering the Gospels, 1997; A Fresh Look at

Matthew, 1998; Revelation, 1998; contrib. ALLC Jl; TLS. *Recreations:* thinking, talking. *Address:* 4 Upper Adelaide Street, Helensburgh G84 7HT. *T:* (01436) 675152.

MORTON, Admiral Sir Anthony (Storrs), GBE 1982; KCB 1978; DL; King of Arms, Order of the British Empire, 1983–97; Vice Admiral of the United Kingdom, 1990–94; *b* 6 Nov. 1923; *s* of late Dr Harold Morton. *Educ:* Loretto School. Joined RN 1941; war service in Atlantic, Mediterranean and Far East (despatches, HMS Wrangler, 1945); Commander 1956; Comd HMS Appleton and 100th MSS 1957–58; HMS Undine 1960; HMS Rocket 1960–62; Captain 1964; Captain (F) 20th Frigate Squadron, 1964–66; Chief Staff Officer, Plans and Policy, to Commander Far East Fleet, 1966–68; Senior Naval Officer, Northern Ireland, 1968–70; Senior Naval Mem., RCDS, 1971–72; ACDS (Policy), 1973–75; Flag Officer, First Flotilla, 1975–77; Vice-Chief of Defence Staff, 1977–78; Vice-Chief of Naval Staff, 1978–80; UK Mil. Rep. to NATO, 1980–83. Rear Adm. of the UK, 1988–90. Chairman: Govs, Royal Star and Garter Home, 1986–91 (Vice-Pres., 1992–); Trustees, RN Museum, Portsmouth, 1985–94; Vice Pres., King George's Fund for Sailors, 1993– (Chm., 1986–93). DL Hants, 1989. OStJ 1990. *Recreations:* fishing, sailing, shooting, watching Association football. *Address:* c/o Barclays Bank, Winchester, Hants SO23 8RG. *Clubs:* Royal Cruising; Royal Yacht Squadron; Irish Cruising.

MORTON, Christopher; *see* Morton, D. C.

MORTON, (David) Christopher; His Honour Judge Morton; a Circuit Judge, since 1992; *b* 1 Dec. 1943; *s* of Rev. Alexander Francis Morton and Esther Ann Morton; *m* 1970, Sandra Jo Kobes; three *s* one *d. Educ:* Worksop Coll., Notts; Fitzwilliam Coll., Cambridge (BA, LLB). Called to the Bar, Inner Temple, 1968; Wales and Chester Circuit; practised in Swansea, 1969–92. *Recreations:* Welsh affairs, railways, family. *Address:* The Crown Court, St Helens Road, Swansea SA1 4PF. *T:* (01792) 510200. *Club:* Royal Over-Seas League.

MORTON, George Martin; Principal (formerly Senior) Planner, Trafford Borough Council, 1986–99; *b* 11 Feb. 1940; *s* of Rev. Thomas Ralph Morton, DD, and Janet Maclay MacGregor Morton (*née* Baird). *Educ:* Fettes Coll Edinburgh; Edinburgh Coll. of Art; Glasgow Univ. RIBA. Member: Manchester City Council, 1971–74; Greater Manchester Council, 1973–77. Sec., Tameside and Glossop CHC, 1984–86. MP (Lab) Manchester, Moss Side, July 1978–1983; an Opposition Whip, 1979–83. *Address:* 4 St Annes Road, Manchester M21 8TD. *T:* (0161) 881 8195.

MORTON, Prof. John, OBE 1998; PhD; FBPsS; Director, Cognitive Development Unit, Medical Research Council, 1982–98; Hon. Professor, University College London, since 1998; *b* 1 Aug. 1933; *s* of late Winston James Morton and Mary Winifred Morton (*née* Nutter); *m*; one *d*; *m* 3rd, 1985, Guinevere Tufnell. *Educ:* Nelson Grammar Sch.; Christ's Coll., Cambridge (BA, MA); Reading Univ. (PhD 1961). FBPsS 1974 (Hon. FBPsS 1997). Scientist, MRC Applied Psychology Unit, Cambridge, 1960–82. Res. Fellow, Univ. of Michigan, 1967; Res. Associate and Lectr, Yale Univ., 1967–68; Vis. Scientist, MSH Paris, 1974–75; Max Planck Ges., Nijmegen, 1977–80; Visiting Professor: Cornell Univ., 1980; UCL, 1982–98; Vis Fellow, Tokyo Metropolitan Inst. of Gerontology, 1981. Pres., EPsS, 1998–2000. MAE 1990. President's Award, BPsS, 1988. *Publications:* (ed) Biological and Social Factors in Psycholinguistics, 1971; (ed jtly) Psycholinguistics: Developmental and Pathological, Series I, 1977, Series II, 1979; (with M. Johnson) Biology and Cognitive Development, 1991; (ed jtly) Development Neurocognition, 1993; (ed jtly) The Acquisition and Dissolution of Language, 1994; (ed jtly) Cognitive Science: an introduction, 1996; articles in sci. jls. *Recreations:* theatre, cooking, song writing, chocolate, Burnley FC. *Address:* (office) Institute of Cognitive Neuroscience, University College London, Alexandra House, 17–19 Queen Square, WC1N 3AR. *T:* (020) 7391 1156.

MORTON, Kathryn Mary Stuart; Solicitor and Director General, Legal Servies, Department for Environment, Food and Rural Affairs, since 2001; *b* 2 June 1946; *d* of late Samuel Stuart Morton and of Joan Alice Bessie Morton (*née* Tapscott). *Educ:* Ealing Grammar Sch. for Girls; Univ. of Sussex (BA). Admitted Solicitor, 1980. Leverhulme Res. Scholarship, India, 1967–68; Res. Asst, Lancaster Univ., 1969–71; Res. Officer, ODI, 1971–74; Res. Associate, ODI, and free-lance economist, 1974–80; with Bird & Bird, 1978–82; OFT, 1982–85; DTI, 1985–97, Under Sec. (Legal), subseq. Dir, 1992–97; Legal Advr and Solicitor, MAFF, 1997–2001. *Publications:* Aid and Dependence, 1975; (with Peter Tulloch) Trade and Developing Countries, 1977. *Address:* c/o Legal Services, Department for Environment, Food and Rural Affairs, 55 Whitehall, SW1A 2EY. *T:* (020) 7270 8379.

MORTON, Prof. Keith William; Professor of Numerical Analysis, and Professorial Fellow of Balliol College, Oxford University, 1983–97, now Emeritus Professor, Oxford University and Emeritus Fellow, Balliol College; Professor of Mathematics (part-time), University of Bath, since 1998; *b* 28 May 1930; *s* of Keith Harvey Morton and Muriel Violet (*née* Hubbard); *m* 1952, Patricia Mary Pearson; two *s* two *d. Educ:* Sudbury Grammar Sch.; Corpus Christi Coll., Oxford (BA 1952; MA 1954); New York Univ. (PhD 1964). Theoretical Physics Div., AERE, Harwell, 1952–59; Res. Scientist, Courant Inst. of Mathematical Sci., NY Univ., 1959–64; Head of Computing and Applied Maths, Culham Lab., UKAEA, 1964–72; Prof. of Applied Maths, Reading Univ., 1972–83. *Publications:* (with R. D. Richtmyer) Difference Methods for Initial-value Problems, 1967; (ed with M. J. Baines) Numerical Methods for Fluid Dynamics, Vol. I 1982, Vol. II 1986, Vol. III 1988, Vol. IV 1993, Vol. V 1995; (with D. F. Mayers) Numerical Solution of Partial Differential Equations: an introduction, 1994; Numerical Solution of Convection-Diffusion Problems, 1996; numerous articles on numerical analysis and applied maths in learned jls. *Recreations:* reading, Real tennis, walking, gardening, listening to music. *Address:* Roscarrock, 48 Jack Straw's Lane, Headington, Oxford OX3 0DW. *T:* (01865) 768823.

MORTON, Kenneth Valentine Freeland, CIE 1947; OBE 1971; Secretary East Anglian Regional Hospital Board, 1947–72, retired; *b* 13 May 1907; *s* of Kenneth John Morton; *m* 1936, Mary Hadwin Hargreaves (*d* 1996); four *s* one *d. Educ:* Edinburgh Academy; University Coll., Oxford. Joined ICS, 1930; Under-Sec. (Political) Punjab Govt, 1934–36; Deputy Commissioner, 1936–39; Colonisation Officer, 1939–43; Deputy Sec., Development Dept, 1943–46; Sec. Electricity and Industries Depts, 1946–47; retired, 1947. *Address:* Temple End House, 27 Temple End, Great Wilbraham, Cambridge CB1 5JF. *T:* (01223) 880691. *Club:* East India, Devonshire, Sports and Public Schools.

MORTON, Patricia Ann; *see* Jacobs, P. A.

MORTON, Sir (Robert) Alastair (Newton), Kt 1991; Chairman, Strategic Rail Authority, 1999–2001; *b* 11 Jan. 1938; *s* of late Harry Newton Morton and Elizabeth Martino; *m* 1964, Sara Bridget Stephens; one *s* one *d. Educ:* St John's Coll. and Witwatersrand Univ., Johannesburg (BA); Worcester Coll., Oxford (MA; Hon. Fellow, 1994). Special grad. student, MIT, 1964. Anglo American Corp. of SA (mining finance), London and Central Africa, 1959–63; Internat. Finance Corp., Washington, 1964–67; Industrial Reorganisation Corp., 1967–70; Exec. Dir, 117 Group of investment trusts, then Chm., Draymont Securities, 1970–76; Man. Dir, BNOC, 1976–80; Chief Exec., 1982–87, Chm., 1987, Guinness Peat Gp; Co-Chm., Eurotunnel, 1987–96 (Gp Chief Exec., 1990–94). Chairman: Kent TEC, 1990–95; Chancellor's Private Finance Panel, 1993–95; CIT, 1992–94. Mem. Council, RIIA, 1990–96. Chm., NYO of GB, 1994–. Hon. LLD: Bath, 1990; Kent, 1992; DUniv Brunel, 1992; Hon. DSc Warwick, 1994; Cranfield, 1996. Commandeur de la Légion d'Honneur (France), 1994. *Recreations:* sailing, walking, chairing National Youth Orchestra. *Clubs:* University (New York); Itchenor Sailing; Country (Johannesburg).

MORTON JACK, David; His Honour Judge Morton Jack; a Circuit Judge, since 1986; *b* 5 Nov. 1935; *o s* of late Col W. A. Morton Jack, OBE, and late Mrs Morton Jack (*née* Happell); *m* 1972, Rosemary, *o d* of F. G. Rentoul; four *s. Educ:* Stowe (scholar); Trinity Coll., Oxford (Cholmeley Schol., MA). 2nd Lieut, RIrF, 1955–57. Called to the Bar, Lincoln's Inn, 1962; a Recorder of the Crown Court, 1979–86. *Recreations:* country pursuits, sheep-keeping, reading, music, gardens. *Address:* c/o South Eastern Circuit Office, New Cavendish House, 18 Maltravers Street, WC2R 3EU.

MOSAR, Nicolas; barrister; Ambassador from Luxembourg to Italy, 1989–92; *b* Luxembourg, 25 Nov. 1927; *m*; three *c. Educ:* Athénée Grand-Ducal; Faculté de Droit, Paris University. Called to Bar, 1955. Mem. Town Council, Luxembourg, 1959–70, 1975–85. Member of Luxembourg Parliament, 1964–74, 1976–85. Social Christian Party: Sec.-Gen., 1959–72; Chm., 1972–74; Chm., Party Parly Gp, 1979–85. Mem., EEC, 1985–88. *Publications:* political and legal papers. *Address:* (office) 8 rue Notre-Dame, 2240 Luxembourg. *T:* 2280231, *Fax:* 462676.

MOSDELL, Lionel Patrick; Judge of the High Court of Kenya, 1966–72, Tanganyika, 1960–64; *b* 29 Aug. 1912; *s* of late William George Mosdell and late Sarah Ellen Mosdell (*née* Gardiner); *m* 1945, Muriel Jean Sillem; one *s* one *d. Educ:* Abingdon Sch.; St Edmund Hall, Oxford (MA). Solicitor, England, 1938. Served War of 1939–45, Gunner, Sussex Yeomanry RA, 1939–41; Commnd Rifle Bde, 1941; Libyan Arab Force; Force 133; No 1 Special Force; Egypt, Cyrenaica, Eritrea, Abyssinia, Italy (Capt.). Registrar of Lands and Deeds, N Rhodesia, 1946; Resident Magistrate, 1950; Senior Resident Magistrate, 1956; Barrister, Gray's Inn, 1952; Asst Solicitor, Law Soc., 1964–66. Part-time Chairman: Surrey and Sussex Rent Assessment Panel, 1972–82; Nat. Insce Local Tribunal, London S Region, 1974–84; Immigration Appeal Tribunal, 1975–84; Pensions Appeal Tribunals, 1976–86. Volunteer, SSAFA, 1988–. *Recreation:* reading. *Address:* 10 Orpen Road, Hove, East Sussex BN3 6NJ. *Clubs:* Special Forces, Royal Commonwealth Society.

MOSELEY, Elwyn Rhys; Commissioner for Local Administration in Wales (Ombudsman), since 1991; *b* 6 Aug. 1943; *s* of late Rev. Luther Moseley and Megan Eiluned Moseley (*née* Howells); *m* 1968, Annick Andrée Guyomard; two *s* one *d. Educ:* Caterham Sch.; Queens' Coll., Cambridge (MA). Solicitor. Asst Solicitor, Newport CBC, 1969–72; Sen. Asst Solicitor, Cardiff CBC, 1972–74; Cardiff City Council: City Solicitor, 1974–91; Dep. Chief Exec., 1979–91; Dir of Admin. and Legal Services, 1987–91. *Address:* (office) Derwen House, Court Road, Bridgend CF31 1BN. *T:* (01656) 661325, *Fax:* (01656) 658317; *e-mail:* enquiries@ombudsman-wales.org.
See also T. H. Moseley.

MOSELEY, Sir George (Walker), KCB 1982 (CB 1978); Chairman, British Cement Association, 1987–96; *b* 7 Feb. 1925; *o c* of late William Moseley, MBE, and Bella Moseley; *m* 1st, 1950, Anne Mercer (*d* 1989); one *s* one *d*; 2nd, 1990, Madge James. *Educ:* High Sch., Glasgow; St Bees Sch., Cumberland; Wadham Coll., Oxford (MA). Pilot Officer, RAF Levies, Iraq, 1943–48. Asst Principal, Min. of Town and Country Planning, 1950; Asst Private Sec. to Minister of Housing and Local Govt, 1951–52; Private Sec. to Parly Sec., 1952–54; Principal Private Sec. to Minister of Housing and Local Govt, 1963–65; Asst Sec. 1965; Under-Sec. 1970–76; Dep. Sec., DoE, 1976–78, CSD, 1978–80; Second Permanent Sec., DoE, 1980–81, Perm. Sec., 1981–85. Chm., Cement Makers' Fedn, 1987–88. Member: Adv. Council on Public Records, 1989–91; Ancient Monuments Adv. Cttee, 1986–91; Historic Buildings and Monuments Commn for England, 1986–91. Trustee, Civic Trust, 1987–2000 (Chm. Trustees, 1990–2000). *Address:* Churchmead, Church Lane, Widdington, Saffron Walden, Essex CB11 3SF. *Club:* Royal Air Force.

MOSELEY, Joyce; Chief Executive, RPS Rainer, since 1999; *b* 12 Jan. 1947; *d* of late Harry Moseley and Kathleen Moseley (*née* Dalton); *m* 1995, Anthony Allen. *Educ:* Manchester High Sch. for Girls; Bedford Coll., Univ. of London (BScSoc Hons 1968 and Applied Social Studies 1970); Univ. of Surrey (MSc Social Res. 1984). Social worker and Sen. Social Worker, London Borough of Ealing, Sen. Social Worker and Area Manager, London Borough of Islington, 1974-86; Asst Dir, Herts CC, 1986-91; Dir of Social Services, London Borough of Hackney, 1991-97; consultancy, 1997-99. Mem., Youth Justice Bd for England and Wales, 1998-. *Publications:* Other People's Children, 1976; contrib. articles and chapters to social care pubns. *Recreations:* theatre, walking, food and wine. *Address:* RPS Rainer, Rectory Lodge, High Street, Brasted, Kent TN16 1JF. *T:* (01959) 578218. *Club:* Two Brydges.

MOSELEY, (Thomas) Hywel; QC 1985; **His Honour Judge Moseley;** a Circuit Judge, since 1989; *b* 27 Sept. 1936; *s* of late Rev. Luther Moseley and Megan Eiluned Moseley; *m* 1960, Monique Germaine Thérèse Drufin; three *d. Educ:* Caterham Sch.; Queens' Coll., Cambridge (MA, LLM). Called to the Bar, Gray's Inn, 1964; in private practice, Cardiff, 1965–89, and London, 1977–89; a Recorder, 1981–89. Lectr in Law, 1960–65, Prof. of Law, 1970–82, UCW, Aberystwyth. Mem., Insolvency Rules Cttee, 1993–97. *Publication:* (with B. Rudden) Outline of the Law of Mortgages, 4th edn 1967. *Recreation:* bee-keeping. *Address:* Civil Justice Centre, 2 Park Street, Cardiff CF1 1ET. *T:* (029) 2037 6400, *Fax:* (029) 2037 6470.
See also E. R. Moseley.

MOSER, family name of **Baron Moser**.

MOSER, Baron *cr* 2001 (Life Peer), of Regents Park in the London Borough of Camden; **Claus Adolf Moser,** KCB 1973; CBE 1965; FBA 1969; Chairman: British Museum Development Trust, since 1993; Basic Skills Agency, since 1997; Chancellor: University of Keele, since 1986; Open University of Israel, since 1994; Chairman, Askonas Holt (formerly Harold Holt) Ltd, since 1990; *b* Berlin, 24 Nov. 1922; *s* of late Dr Ernest Moser and Lotte Moser; *m* 1949, Mary Oxlin; one *s* two *d. Educ:* Frensham Heights Sch.; LSE, Univ. of London. RAF, 1943–46. London Sch. of Economics: Asst Lectr in Statistics, 1946–49; Lectr, 1949–55; Reader in Social Statistics, 1955–61; Prof. of Social Statistics, 1961–70; Vis. Prof. of Social Statistics, 1970–75; Oxford University: Vis. Fellow, Nuffield Coll., 1972–80; Warden, Wadham Coll., 1984–93 (Hon. Fellow, 1993); Pro-Vice Chancellor, 1991–93. Dir, Central Statistical Office and Hd of Govt Statistical Service, 1967–78. Statistical Adviser, Cttee on Higher Educn, 1961–64. Chm., Economist Intelligence Unit, 1979–83; Director: N. M. Rothschild & Sons, 1978–90 (Vice-Chm.,

1978–84); The Economist Newspaper, 1979–93; Equity & Law Life Assurance Soc., 1980–87; International Medical Statistics Inc., 1982–88; Octopus Books Ltd, 1982–87; Property & Reversionary Investments plc, 1983–86. Chairman: Royal Opera House, 1974–87; Adv. Bd, Music at Oxford, 1985–; Oxford Playhouse, 1992–; Member: Governing Body, Royal Academy of Music, 1967–79; BBC Music Adv. Cttee, 1971–83; Adv. Bd, LSO, 1996–; Pilgrim Trust, 1982–99; Nat. Commission on Educn, 1991–95. Trustee: BM, 1988–; LPO, 1988–94; Glyndebourne Opera Arts Trust, 1989–93; Paul Hamlyn Foundn, 1991–; Soros Foundn, 1993–99; Rayne Foundn, 1995–. President: Royal Statistical Soc., 1978–80; BAAS, 1989–90; British Fedn of Fests for Music, Dance and Speech, 1990–99. Hon. FRAM 1970. Hon. Fellow: LSE, 1976; Inst. of Educn, Univ. of London, 1997; Birkbeck Coll., 1998. Hon. DSocSci Southampton, 1975; Hon. DSc: Leeds, 1977; City, 1977; Sussex, 1980; Wales, 1990; Liverpool, 1991; South Bank, 1994; Hon. DSc(Econ) London, 1991; Hull, 1994; DUniv: Surrey, 1977; Keele, 1979; York, 1980; Open, 1992; Hon. DTech Brunel, 1981; Dr *hc* Edinburgh, 1991; Heriot-Watt, 1995; Hon. DLitt: W of England, 1993; Brighton, 1994; Hon. DCL Northumbria, 1995. Albert Medal, RSA, 1996. Comdr de l'Ordre National du Mérite (France), 1976; Commander's Cross, Order of Merit (FRG), 1985. *Publications:* Measurement of Levels of Living, 1957; Survey Methods in Social Investigation, 1958; (jtly) Social Conditions in England and Wales, 1958; (jtly) British Towns, 1961; papers in statistical jls. *Recreation:* music. *Address:* 3 Regent's Park Terrace, NW1 7EE. *T:* (020) 7485 1619; 7 Ethelred Court, Old Headington, Oxford OX3 9DA. *T:* (01865) 761028. *Club:* Garrick.

MOSER, Dr Michael Edward; Member: Council, English Nature, since 1999; UK Joint Nature Conservation Committee, since 2001; *b* 16 July 1956; *s* of late Roger Michael Moser and of Noreen Moser (*née* Wane); *m* 1983, Joanna Jocelyn Stewart-Smith; three *d*. *Educ:* Shrewsbury Sch.; Durham Univ. (1st cl. Hons. Ecol.; PhD). David Lack Studentship, BOU, 1980–82; British Trust for Ornithology: Estuaries Officer, 1983–86; Dir of Develt, 1986–88; Dir, Internat. Waterfowl and Wetlands Res. Bureau, then Wetlands Internat., 1988–99. *Publication:* (with C. M. Finlayson) Wetlands, 1991. *Recreations:* natural history, travel, fly fishing. *Address:* West Week Farm, Week, Chulmleigh, Devon EX18 7EE; *e-mail:* mike-moser@supanet.com.

MOSES, Rev. Alan; *see* Moses, Rev. L. A.

MOSES, Hon. Sir Alan George, Kt 1996; **Hon. Mr Justice Moses;** a Judge of the High Court, Queen's Bench Division, since 1996; Presiding Judge, South Eastern Circuit, since 1999; *b* 29 Nov. 1945; *s* of Eric George Rufus Moses, *qv*; *m* 1992, Dinah, *d* of Sir Hugh Casson, CH, KCVO, RA and late Margaret MacDonald Casson, architect and designer; two *s* one *d* by a previous marriage. *Educ:* Bryanston Sch.; University Coll., Oxford (Quondam Exhibnr; BA). Called to the Bar, Middle Temple, 1968, Bencher, 1994; Mem., Panel of Junior Counsel to the Crown, Common Law, 1981–90; Junior Counsel to Inland Revenue, Common Law, 1985–90; a Recorder, 1986–96; QC 1990. *Address:* c/o Royal Courts of Justice, Strand, WC2A 2LL. *Club:* Union Socialista La Serra (Italy).

MOSES, Eric George Rufus, CB 1973; Solicitor of Inland Revenue, 1970–79; *b* 6 April 1914; *s* of Michael and Emily Moses; *m* 1940, Pearl Lipton; one *s*. *Educ:* University Coll. Sch., London; Oriel Coll., Oxford. Called to Bar, Middle Temple, 1938, Hon. Bencher, 1979. Served Royal Artillery, 1940–46 (Major). Asst Solicitor, Inland Revenue, 1953–65, Principal Asst Solicitor, 1965–70. *Address:* Broome Cottage, Castle Hill, Nether Stowey, Bridgwater, Somerset TA5 1NB.

See also A. G. Moses.

MOSES, Very Rev. Dr John Henry; Dean of St Paul's, since 1996; Dean, Order of St Michael and St George, and Dean, Order of the British Empire, since 1996; *b* 12 Jan. 1938; *s* of late Henry William Moses and Ada Elizabeth Moses; *m* 1964, Susan Elizabeth; one *s* two *d*. *Educ:* Ealing Grammar School; Nottingham Univ. (Gladstone Meml Prize 1958; BA History 1959; PhD 1965); Trinity Hall, Cambridge (Cert. in Education 1960); Lincoln Theological Coll. Deacon 1964, priest 1965; Asst Curate, St Andrew, Bedford, 1964–70; Rector of Coventry East Team Ministry, 1970–77; Examining Chaplain to Bishop of Coventry, 1972–77; Rural Dean of Coventry East, 1973–77; Archdeacon of Southend, 1977–82; Provost of Chelmsford, 1982–96. Vis. Fellow, Wolfson Coll., Cambridge, 1987. Mem., Gen. Synod, 1985–; a Church Comr, 1988–; Mem., ACC, 1997–. Chm. Council, Centre for Study of Theology, Essex Univ., 1987–96; Rector, Anglia Poly. Univ., 1992–96. Vice-Pres., City of London Fest., 1997–. Freeman, City of London, 1997; Liveryman: Feltmakers' Co., 1998–; Plaisterers' Co., 1999–; Hon. Freeman, Water Conservators' Co., 2000–. Hon. Dr Anglia Poly. Univ., 1997. *Publications:* The Sacrifice of God, 1992; A Broad and Living Way, 1995; The Desert, 1997. *Address:* The Deanery, 9 Amen Court, EC4M 7BU. *T:* (020) 7236 2827, *Fax:* (020) 7332 0298. *Club:* Athenæum.

MOSES, Rev. (Leslie) Alan; Vicar of All Saints', Margaret Street, London, since 1995; *b* 3 Nov. 1949; *s* of Leslie Moses and Edna (*née* Watson); *m* 1971, Theresa Frances O'Connor; one *s* one *d*. *Educ:* Univ. of Hull (BA Hons History); Univ. of Edinburgh (BD Hons); Edinburgh Theol. Coll.; MA Systematic Theol., London Univ., 2001. Ordained deacon 1976, priest 1977; Asst Curate, Old St Paul's, Edinburgh, 1976–79; Rector, St Margaret of Scotland, Leven, 1979–85; Priest-in-Charge, St Margaret of Scotland, Edinburgh, 1986–92; Rector, Old St Paul's, Edinburgh, 1985–95. Area Dean of Westminster, 2001–. Mem., Gen. Synod of C of E, 2001–. Gov., USPG, 1997–. *Recreations:* reading, visiting museums, galleries, churches and other buildings, exploring places. *Address:* The Vicarage, 7 Margaret Street, W1N 8JQ. *T:* (020) 7636 1788, *Fax:* (020) 7436 4470.

MOSEY, Roger; Head of Television News, BBC, since 2000; *b* 4 Jan. 1958; *s* of late Geoffrey Mosey and of Marie Mosey (*née* Pilkington). *Educ:* Bradford Grammar Sch.; Wadham Coll., Oxford (MA Mod. Hist. & Mod. Langs); INSEAD (AMP 1999). Producer, Pennine Radio, 1979; Reporter, BBC Radio Lincolnshire, 1980; Producer: BBC Radio Northampton, 1982; Today programme, BBC Radio Four, 1984; BBC New York office, 1986; Editor: PM prog., 1987; World At One, 1989; Today prog., BBC Radio Four, 1993 (Sony Radio Gold Awards, 1994, 1995); Controller, BBC Radio Five Live, 1996–2000; Acting Dir, BBC Continuous News, 1999. Dir, Parly Broadcasting Unit Ltd, 1999–. Mem., Sony Radio Awards Cttee, 1999, 2000. Member: BAFTA; RTS. Fellow, Radio Acad., 1999. Sony Radio Gold Award for Radio 5 Live, 1998. *Recreations:* America, cinema, music, football. *Address:* BBC Television Centre, W12 7RJ. *T:* (020) 8624 8950; *e-mail:* roger.mosey@bbc.co.uk.

MOSHINSKY, Elijah; Associate Producer, Royal Opera House, since 1979; *b* 8 Jan. 1946; *s* of Abraham and Eva Moshinsky; *m* 1970, Ruth Dyttman; two *s*. *Educ:* Melbourne Univ. (BA); St Antony's Coll., Oxford. Apptd to Royal Opera House, 1973: work includes original productions of: Peter Grimes, 1975; Lohengrin, 1978; The Rake's Progress, 1979; Macbeth, 1981; Samson et Dalila, 1981; Tannhäuser, 1984; Otello, 1987; Die Entführung aus dem Serail, 1987; Attila, 1990; Simon Boccanegra, 1991; Stiffelio, 1993; Aida, 1994; for ENO: Le Grand Macabre, 1982; The Mastersingers of Nuremberg, 1984; The Bartered Bride, 1985, 1986; for Australian Opera: A Midsummer Night's Dream, 1978; Boris Godunov, 1980; Il Trovatore, 1983; Werther, Rigoletto, 1990; Les Dialogues des Carmélites; for Metropolitan Opera, NY: Un Ballo in Maschera, 1980; Samson, 1987; Ariadne auf Naxos, 1993; Otello, 1994; The Makropulos Case, 1996; The Queen of Spades; Samson et Dalila, 1998; other opera productions include: Wozzeck, 1976; Antony and Cleopatra, Chicago, 1990; I Vespri Siciliani, Grand Théâtre, Geneva; La Bohème, 1989, La Forza del Destino, 1990, Scottish Opera; Beatrice and Benedict, 1994, Cavalleria Rusticana and Pagliacci, 1996, WNO; Die Meistersinger von Nürnberg, Holland Fest.; Benvenuto Cellini, 50th Maggio Musicale, Florence, 1987. Producer: Three Sisters, Albery, 1987; Light up the Sky, Globe, 1987; Ivanov, Strand, 1989; Much Ado About Nothing, Strand, 1989; Another Time, Wyndham's, 1989; Shadowlands, Queen's, 1989; Cyrano de Bergerac, Theatre Royal, Haymarket, 1992; Lord of the Flies, 1995, Richard III, 1998, RSC; productions at National Theatre: Troilus and Cressida, 1976; The Force of Habit, 1976; productions for the BBC: All's Well That Ends Well, 1980; A Midsummer Night's Dream, 1981; Cymbeline, 1982; Coriolanus, 1984; Love's Labour's Lost, 1985; Ghosts, 1986; The Rivals, 1987; The Green Man, 1990; Genghis Cohn, 1993; Danton, 1994. Director: Matador, Queen's, 1991; Beckett, Haymarket, 1991; Reflected Glory, Vaudeville, 1992; Old Wicked Songs, Gielgud, 1996; The Female Odd Couple, Apollo, 2001. *Recreations:* telephone conversation, writing film scripts. *Address:* 28 Kidbrooke Grove, SE3 0LG. *T:* (020) 8858 4179. *Club:* Garrick.

MOSIMANN, Anton; Owner: Mosimann's (formerly Belfry Club), since 1988; Château Mosimann, Switzerland, since 2001; Principal, Mosimann Academy, London, since 1996; *b* 23 Feb. 1947; *s* of Otto and Olga Mosimann; *m* 1973, Kathrin Roth; two *s*. *Educ:* private school in Switzerland; youngest Chef to be awarded Chef de Cuisine Diplome; 3 degrees. Served apprenticeship in Hotel Baeren, Twann; worked in Canada, France, Italy, Japan, Sweden, Belgium, Switzerland, 1962–; cuisinier at: Villa Lorraine, Brussels; Les Près d'Eugénie, Eugénie-les-Bains; Les Frères Troisgros, Roanne; Paul Bocuse, Collonges au Mont d'Or; Moulin de Mougins; joined Dorchester Hotel, 1975, Maître Chef des Cuisines, 1976–88. Channel Four TV series: Cooking with Mosimann, 1989; Anton Mosimann Naturally, 1991; Swiss TV series: Healthy Food, 1997; Swiss Regional Cooking, 1998. World Pres., Les Toques Blanches Internationales, 1989–93; Hon. Mem., Chefs' Assoc., Canada, Japan, Switzerland, S Africa. Freeman, City of London, 1999. Royal Warrant Holder to the Prince of Wales, 2000. Johnson & Wales University, RI: Dr of Culinary Arts *hc*, 1990; Restaurateur of the Year, 2000. Numerous Gold Medals in Internat. Cookery Competitions; Chef Award, Caterer and Hotelkeeper, 1985; Personnalité de l'année award, 1986; Glenfiddich Awards Trophy, 1986; Chevalier, Ordre des Coteaux de Champagne, 1990; Grand Cordon Culinaire, Conseil Culinaire Français de Grande Bretagne, 1994; Swiss Ambassador of the Year, Hotel & Restaurant Assoc. of Switzerland, 1995. Le Croix de Chevalier du Mérite Agricole (France), 1988. *Publications:* Cuisine à la Carte, 1981; A New Style of Cooking, 1983; Cuisine Naturelle, 1985; Anton Mosimann's Fish Cuisine, 1988; The Art of Anton Mosimann, 1989; Cooking with Mosimann, 1989; Anton Mosimann Naturally, 1991; The Essential Mosimann, 1993; Mosimann's World, 1996. *Recreations:* jogging, travelling, collecting art. *Address:* c/o Mosimann's, 11B West Halkin Street, SW1X 8JL. *T:* (020) 7235 9625. *Clubs:* Garrick, Reform.

MOSLEY, family name of **Baron Ravensdale**.

MOSLEY, Max Rufus; President, Fédération Internationale de l'Automobile, since 1993; *b* 13 April 1940; *s* of Sir Oswald Mosley, 6th Bt and Hon. Diana, *d* of 2nd Baron Redesdale; *m* 1960, Jean Taylor; two *s*. *Educ:* abroad; Christ Church, Oxford (MA Natural Sciences). Sec., Oxford Union Society, 1961. Called to the Bar, Gray's Inn, 1964; Dir, March Cars, 1969; Legal Adviser, Formula One Constructors' Assoc., 1971; Pres., Fédn Internat. du Sport Automobile, 1991–93 (Pres., Manufacturers' Commn, FISA, 1986–91). Chm., Eur. New Car Assessment Prog., 1997–. Vice Chm., 1999–2001, Chm., 2001–, Supervisory Bd, ERTICO Intelligent Transport Systems Europe. Hon. Pres., Automobile Users' Intergroup, EP, 1994–99. Gold Medal, Castrol/Inst. of Motor Industry, 2000; Quattrovuote Premio Speciale per la Sicurezza Stradale (Italy), 2001; Goldene VdM-Dieselring (Germany), 2001. Grande Ufficiale dell' Ordine al Merito (Italy), 1994; Order of Madarski Konnik, 1st degree (Bulgaria), 2000. *Recreations:* snow-boarding, walking. *Address:* Fédération Internationale de l'Automobile, 8 place de la Concorde, 75008 Paris, France. *T:* 143124455.

MOSLEY, Nicholas; *see* Ravensdale, 3rd Baron.

MOSS, Ann; *see* Moss, J. A.

MOSS, Very Rev. Basil Stanley; Provost of Birmingham Cathedral, 1973–85; Rector, Cathedral parish of St Philip, 1973–85; *b* 7 Oct. 1918; *e s* of Canon Harry George Moss and Daisy Violet (*née* Jolly); *m* 1950, Rachel Margaret, *d* of Dr Cyril Bailey and Gemma (*née* Creighton); three *d*. *Educ:* Canon Slade Grammar Sch., Bolton; The Queen's Coll., Oxford. Asst Curate, Leigh Parish Church, 1943–45; Sub-Warden, Lincoln Theological Coll., 1946–51; Sen. Tutor, St Catharine's Cumberland Lodge, Windsor Gt Pk, 1951–53; Vicar of St Nathanael with St Katharine, Bristol, 1953–60; Dir, Ordination Training, Bristol Dioc., 1956–66; Residentiary Canon of Bristol Cath., 1960–66, Hon. Canon, 1966–72; Chief Secretary, Advisory Council for the Church's Ministry, 1966–72; Chaplain to Church House, Westminster, 1966–72; Examining Chaplain to Bishop of Bristol, 1956–72, to Bishop of Birmingham, 1985–. Chm., Birmingham Community Relations Council, 1973–81. *Publications:* Clergy Training Today, 1964; (ed) Crisis for Baptism, 1966; (contrib.) Living the Faith, 1980. *Recreation:* walking. *Address:* Engelberg, Ash Hill, Compton, Wolverhampton WV3 9DR. *T:* (01902) 420613. *Club:* Stourbridge Rotary.

MOSS, Charles James, CBE 1977; Director, National Institute of Agricultural Engineering, 1964–77; *b* 18 Nov. 1917; *s* of James and Elizabeth Moss; *m* 1939, Joan Bernice Smith; two *d*. *Educ:* Queen Mary Coll., London Univ. (BSc). Rotol Ltd, Gloucester, 1939–43; RAE Farnborough, 1943–45; CIBA Ltd, Cambridge, 1945–51; ICI Ltd, Billingham, 1951–58; Central Engineering Estabt, NCB, Stanhope Bretby, 1958–61; Process Develt Dept, NCB, London, 1961–63; Vis. Prof., Dept of Agric. Engrg, Univ. of Newcastle upon Tyne, 1972–75; Head of Agr. Engineering Dept, Internat. Rice Res. Inst., Philippines, 1977–80; Liaison scientist and agr. engineer, Internat. Rice Res. Inst., Cairo, 1980–81. *Publications:* papers in learned jls, confs., etc. *Recreations:* gardening, walking. *Address:* 1 Laurel Court, Endcliffe Vale Road, Sheffield, South Yorks S10 3DU.

MOSS, Christopher John; QC 1994; a Recorder, since 1993; *b* 4 Aug. 1948; *s* of John (Jack) Gordon Moss and Joyce (Joy) Mirren Moss (*née* Stephany); *m* 1st, 1971, Gail Susan Pearson (marr. diss. 1987); one *s* two *d*; 2nd, 1988, Tracy Louise Levy (marr. diss. 1997); one *s* one *d*; 3rd, 1999, Lisa Annette O'Dwyer; one *d*. *Educ:* Bryanston Sch.; University Coll. London (LLB). Called to the Bar, Gray's Inn, 1972. *Recreation:* playing the piano and accordion. *Address:* 5 Essex Court, Temple, EC4Y 9AH. *T:* (020) 7410 2000.

MOSS, Dr Christopher Michael; TTL Fellow, Liverpool John Moores University, since 2000; *b* 6 Nov. 1946; *s* of Joseph Moss and Hilda Moss (*née* Wilder). *Educ:* Heythrop Coll.

(Bacc Phil 1969; MA Oxon 1972); BD London 1979; MA Cantab; DPhil Sussex 1976. Entered Jesuit Order, 1964; ordained priest, 1979; Staff Mem., Vatican Observatory, Rome and Vatican Observatory Res. Gp, Univ. of Arizona, 1980–85; Dean, 1986–92, Fellow, 1986–97, St Edmund's Coll., Cambridge; Postdoctoral Staff Mem., Inst. of Astronomy, Univ. of Cambridge, 1986–97; Principal, Heythrop Coll., London Univ., 1997–98; Associate Faculty Mem., Univ. of Arizona, 1998–2000; on leave of absence from SJ, 2001–. *Publications:* papers in astrophysical and astronomical jls. *Recreations:* walking, sketching, foreign travel. *Address:* Astrophysics Research Institute, Twelve Quays House, Egerton Wharf, Birkenhead CH41 1LD.

MOSS, David Christopher; Director General (Europe), Railtrack, 1998-2001; *b* 17 April 1946; *s* of Charles Clifford Moss and Marjorie Sylvia Moss (*née* Hutchings); *m* 1971, Angela Mary Wood; one *s*. *Educ:* King's Sch., Chester; Magdalene Coll., Cambridge (BA). Asst Principal, MPBW, 1968; Principal, 1972, DoE, and subseq. Dept of Transport and HM Treasury; Asst Sec., 1980, Dept of Transport and DoE; Under Sec., Internat. Aviation, Dept of Transport, 1988–93; Railtrack: Commercial Dir, 1993–95; European Affairs Dir, 1995–98. Pres, European Civil Aviation Conf., 1990–93; Bd Chm., Jt Aviation Authorities, 1990–93. FCIT. *Recreations:* opera, ecclesiastical architecture, wine. *Club:* Oxford and Cambridge.

MOSS, David John; Chief Executive, Southampton University Hospitals Trust, since 1993; *b* 23 May 1947; *s* of John Henry Moss and Doris (*née* Fenna); *m* 1975, Susan Elizabeth Runnalls; three *s*. *Educ:* Sevenoaks Sch.; St John's Coll., Cambridge (MA); Poly. of Central London (Dip. Management Studies). IPFA; MHSM; FCMA; FIMgt. Management Trainee and Management Accounting, Philips Lamps, 1968–73; Asst Finance Officer, St Thomas' Hosp., 1973–74; Dist Finance Officer, Enfield Health Dist, 1974–79; Dist. Treasurer, E Dorset HA, 1979–86; General Manager: Poole Gen. Hosp., 1986–88; Southampton Gen. Hosp., 1988–91; Southampton Univ. Hosps, 1991–93. Chm., UK Univ. Hosp. Forum, 2001–; Mem., Audit Commn, 2001–. FRSA 1994. *Publications:* (jtly) Managing Nursing, 1984; articles in professional jls. *Recreations:* cricket, golf, tennis, badminton, history, opera, walking.

MOSS, (Sir) David John E.; *see* Edwards-Moss.

MOSS, Sir David Joseph, KCVO 1998; CMG 1989; HM Diplomatic Service, retired; High Commissioner in Kuala Lumpur, 1994–98; *b* 6 Nov. 1938; *s* of Herbert Joseph and Irene Gertrude Moss; *m* 1961, Joan Lillian Moss; one *d* (one *s* decd). *Educ:* Hampton Grammar Sch. CS Commn, 1956; FO, 1957; RAF, 1957–59; FO, 1959–62; Third Sec., Bangkok, 1962–65; FO, 1966–69; First Sec., La Paz, 1969–70; FCO, 1970–73; First Sec. and Head of Chancery, The Hague, 1974–77; First Sec., FCO, 1978–79, Counsellor, 1979–83; Counsellor, Hd of Chancery and Dep. Perm. Rep., UK Mission, Geneva, 1983–87; Asst. Under-Sec. of State, FCO, 1987–90; High Comr, New Zealand, 1990–94. *Recreations:* reading, listening to music. *Club:* Royal Over-Seas League.

MOSS, Elaine Dora; Children's Books Adviser to The Good Book Guide, 1980–86; *b* 8 March 1924; *d* of Percy Philip Levy and Maude Agnes Levy (*née* Simmons); *m* 1950, John Edward Moss, FRICS, FAI; two *d*. *Educ:* St Paul's Girls' Sch.; Bedford Coll. for Women (BA Hons); Univ. of London Inst. of Educn (DipEd); University College London Sch. of Librarianship (ALA). Teacher, Stoatley Rough Sch., Haslemere, 1945–47; Asst Librarian, Bedford Coll., 1947–50; freelance journalist and broadcaster (Woman's Hour, The Times, TES, TLS, The Spectator, Signal, etc.), 1956–; Editor and Selector, NBL's Children's Books of the Year, 1970–79; Librarian, Fleet Primary Sch., ILEA, 1976–82. Eleanor Farjeon Award, 1976. *Publications:* texts for several picture books, incl. Polar, 1976; catalogues for Children's Books of the Year, 1970–79; Picture Books for Young People 9–13, 1981, 3rd edn 1992; Part of the Pattern: a personal journey through the world of children's books 1960–1985, 1986; (with Nancy Chambers) The Signal Companion, 1996. *Recreations:* walking, art galleries, reading, ballet. *Address:* 7 St Anne's Close, N6 6AR.

MOSS, Gabriel Stephen; QC 1989; *b* 8 Sept. 1949; *m* 1979, Judith; one *d*. *Educ:* University of Oxford (Eldon Schol. 1975; BA Jurisprudence, BCL, MA). Lectr, Univ. of Connecticut Law Sch., 1972–73; called to the Bar, Lincoln's Inn, 1974 (Hardwicke Schol., 1971; Cassel Schol., 1975; Bencher, 1998); admitted to the Bar of Gibraltar. Jt DTI Inspector, Bestwood plc, 1989. Formerly (part-time) Lectr/Tutor, Oxford, LSE, Council of Legal Educn. Member: Bd, Insolvency Res. Unit, Univ. of Sussex (formerly at KCL), 1991–; Insolvency Law Sub-Cttee, Consumer and Commercial Law Cttee, Law Soc., 1991–; Insolvency Cttee, Justice, 1993–; Insolvency Lawyers Assoc., 1999–. Fellow, Soc. of Advanced Legal Studies, 1998. Chm. Editl Bd, Insolvency Intelligence, 1994– (Mem., 1992–); Mem. Adv. Editl Bd, Receivers, Administrators and Liquidators Qly, 1993–. *Publications:* (ed with David Marks) Rowlatt on Principal and Surety, 4th edn 1982, 5th edn 1999; (with Gavin Lightman) The Law of Receivers of Companies, 1986, 2nd edn 1994; (with Martin Pascoe) Insolvency chapter, Ryde on Rating, 1990; (ed with Peter Totty) Insolvency, 1996–. *Recreations:* classical music, foreign travel. *Address:* 3/4 South Square, Gray's Inn, WC1R 5HP. *T:* (020) 7696 9900, *Fax:* (020) 7696 9911; *e-mail:* clerks@3/4southsquare.com.

MOSS, James Richard Frederick, OBE 1955; FRINA; RCNC; Founder, Chairman, 1978–94, and President, since 1994, Polynous, Cambridge; Chief Executive, Balaena Structures (North Sea), 1974–77, retired; *b* 26 March 1916; *s* of late Lt-Cdr J. G. Moss, RN, and late Kathleen Moss (*née* Steinberg); *m* 1941, Celia Florence Lucas; three *d*. *Educ:* Marlborough College; Trinity Coll., Cambridge (1st Cl. Hons Mech. Sci. Tripos and Maths Pt I, MA); RCNC, 1941. Constructor Comdr to C-in-C, Far East Fleet, 1949–52; Chief Constructor, HM Dockyard, Singapore, 1955–58; Supt, Naval Construction Research Estab., Dunfermline, 1965–68; Dir, Naval Ship Production, 1968–74. *Recreations:* yachting, music, bell ringing. *Address:* 13 Beaufort Place, Thompsons Lane, Cambridge CB5 8AG. *T:* (01223) 328583. *Club:* Royal Naval Sailing Association.

MOSS, Jane Hope; *see* Bown, J. H.

MOSS, Prof. (Jennifer) Ann, PhD; FBA 1998; Professor of French, University of Durham, since 1996; *b* 21 Jan. 1938; *d* of John Shakespeare Poole and Dorothy Kathleen Beese (*née* Sills); *m* 1960, John Michael Barry Moss (marr. diss. 1966); two *d*. *Educ:* Barr's Hill Grammar Sch., Coventry; Newnham Coll., Cambridge (MA; PhD 1975). Asst Lectr, UCNW, 1963–64; Resident Tutor and part-time Lectr, Trevelyan Coll., Durham, 1966–79; University of Durham: Lectr in French, 1979–85; Sen. Lectr, 1985–88; Reader, 1988–96. *Publications:* Ovid in Renaissance France, 1982; Poetry and Fable, 1984; Printed Commonplace-Books and the Structuring of Renaissance Thought, 1996; Latin Commentaries on Ovid from the Renaissance, 1998. *Recreation:* daughters and grandchildren. *Address:* Department of French, University of Durham, Elvet Riverside, New Elvet, Durham DH1 3JT. *T:* (0191) 374 2722.

MOSS, (John) Michael, CB 1996; Command Secretary to Second Sea Lord and Commander-in-Chief Naval Home Command, 1994–96, and Assistant Under-Secretary of State (Naval Personnel), 1989–96, Ministry of Defence; *b* 21 April 1936; *s* of late Ernest and of Mary Moss. *Educ:* Accrington Grammar Sch.; King's Coll., Cambridge (Foundn Scholar; MA Math. Tripos, Pt I Cl. I, Pt II Wrangler, Pt III Hons with Dist.). National Service, RAF Educn Branch: Pilot Officer 1958; Flying Officer 1959; Flt Lieut 1960; RAF Technical Coll., Henlow, 1959–60. Asst Principal, Air Min., 1960–63; Private Sec. to Air Member for Supply and Orgn, 1962–63; Principal, Air Min., 1963–64, and MoD, 1964–70; Private Sec. to Parly Under-Sec. of State for Defence for the RAF, 1969–70; Asst Sec., MoD, 1971–72; Estab. Officer, Cabinet Office, 1972–75; Sec., Radcliffe Cttee of Privy Counsellors on Ministerial Memoirs, 1975; returned to MoD as Asst Sec., 1976–83; RCDS, 1983; Asst Under-Sec. of State (Air), MoD (PE), 1984–88; Fellow, Center for Internat. Affairs, Harvard Univ., 1988–89. Chm., Greenwich Hosp. Adv. Panel, 1989–96. Hon. Steward, Westminster Abbey, 1996–. *Recreations:* travel, photography, choral singing. *Address:* c/o Royal Bank of Scotland, 119 Blackburn Road, Accrington, Lancs BB5 0AA. *Clubs:* Royal Air Force, Oxford and Cambridge.

MOSS, John Ringer, CB 1972; adviser to companies in Associated British Foods Group, 1980–98; *b* 15 Feb. 1920; 2nd *s* of late James Moss and Louisa Moss; *m* 1946, Edith Bland Wheeler; two *s* one *d*. *Educ:* Manchester Gram. Sch.; Brasenose Coll., Oxford (MA). War Service, mainly India and Burma, 1940–46; Capt., RE, attached Royal Bombay Sappers and Miners. Entered Civil Service (MAFF) as Asst Princ., 1947; Princ. Private Sec. to Minister of Agric., Fisheries and Food, 1959–61; Asst Sec., 1961; Under-Sec., Gen. Agricultural Policy Gp, 1967–70; Dep. Sec., 1970–80. Mem., Economic Devlt Cttee for Agriculture, 1969–70. Specialist Adviser to House of Lords' Select Cttee on European Communities, 1982–90. Chm. Council, RVC, 1983–90. *Recreations:* music, travel. *Address:* 16 Upper Hollis, Great Missenden, Bucks HP16 9HP. *T:* (01494) 862676.

MOSS, Ven. Leonard Godfrey; Archdeacon of Hereford and Canon Residentiary of Hereford Cathedral, 1991–97, now Archdeacon Emeritus; *b* 11 July 1932; *s* of Clarence Walter Moss and Frances Lilian Vera Moss; *m* 1954, Everell Annette (*née* Reed); two *s* one *d*. *Educ:* Regent St Poly., London; King's Coll., London and Warminster (BD, AKC 1959). Quantity Surveyor's Asst, L. A. Francis and Sons, 1948–54; RE (National Service), 1954–56. Ordained: deacon, 1960; priest, 1961; Assistant curate: St Margaret, Putney, 1960–63; St Dunstan, Cheam, 1963–67; Vicar: Much Dewchurch with Llanwarne and Llandinabo, 1967–72; Marden with Amberley and Wisteston, 1972–84; Hereford Diocesan Ecumenical Officer, 1969–83; Prebendary of Hereford Cathedral, 1979–97; Bishop of Hereford's Officer for Social Responsibility and Non-Residentiary Canon of Hereford Cathedral, 1984–91; Priest-in-charge, Marden with Amberley and Wisteston, 1992–94. Proctor in Convocation, 1970–97. *Publications:* (contrib.) The People, the Land and the Church, 1987; articles and reviews in theol jls. *Recreations:* reading, listening to music, walking, folk-dancing. *Address:* 10 Saxon Way, Ledbury, Hereford HR8 2QY.

MOSS, Malcolm Douglas; MP (C) Cambridgeshire North East, since 1987; *b* 6 March 1943; *s* of late Norman Moss and Annie Moss (*née* Gay); *m* 1965, Vivien Lorraine (*née* Peake) (*d* 1997); two *d*. *Educ:* Audenshaw Grammar Sch.; St John's Coll., Cambridge (BA 1965, MA 1968). Teaching Cert 1966. Asst Master, 1966–68, Head of Dept, 1968–70, Blundell's Sch.; Insurance Consultant, 1970–72, Gen. Manager, 1972–74, Barwick Associates; Chairman: Mandrake Gp plc, 1986–88; Mandrake Associates Ltd (formerly Mandrake (Insurance and Finance Brokers)), 1986–93 (Dir, 1974–); Fens Business Enterprise Trust, 1983–87 (Dir, 1983–94). *Recreations:* tennis, ski-ing, amateur dramatics, gardening. *Address:* House of Commons, SW1A 0AA.

MOSS, Martin Grenville, CBE 1975; Director of National Trust Enterprises Ltd, 1985–89; *b* 17 July 1923; *s* of late Horace Grenville Moss and Gladys Ethel (*née* Wootton); *m* 1953, Jane Hope Bown, *qv*; two *s* one *d*. *Educ:* Lancing Coll. Served RAF, 1942–46 (Sqdn Ldr, pilot). Managing Director: Woollands Knightsbridge, 1953–66; Debenham & Freebody, 1964–66; Simpson (Piccadilly) Ltd, 1966–73, 1981–85; Chm. and Chief Exec. Officer, May Department Stores Internat., USA, 1974–80. Member: Export Council of Europe, 1960–64; Design Council, 1964–75 (Dep. Chm., 1971–75); Council, RCA, 1953–58; Royal Fine Art Commn, 1982–84; Council, RSA, 1977–94 (Chm., 1983–85). Formerly Governor: Sevenoaks Sch.; Ravensbourne Coll. of Art and Design; W Surrey Coll. of Art and Design. Order of the Finnish Lion, 1970. *Recreations:* gardening, painting, classic cars. *Address:* Old Mill House, 50 Broad Street, Alresford, Hants SO24 9AN. *T:* (01962) 732419. *Club:* Royal Air Force.

MOSS, Michael; *see* Moss, J. M.

MOSS, Ronald Trevor; His Honour Judge Moss; a Circuit Judge, since 1993; *b* 1 Oct. 1942; *s* of Maurice and Sarah Moss; *m* 1971, Cindy (*née* Fiddleman); one *s* one *d*. *Educ:* Hendon County Grammar School; Nottingham University (Upper Second BA; Hons Law). Admitted Solicitor, 1968; Partner, Moss Beachley, solicitors, 1973–84; Metropolitan Stipendiary Magistrate, 1984–93; Asst Recorder, 1986–90; Recorder, 1990–93. Chm., Inner London Juvenile Courts, subseq. Inner London Youth and Family Panel, 1986–93. Mem. Cttee, London Criminal Courts Solicitors' Assoc., 1982–84. *Recreations:* golf, bridge, Watford Football Club. *Address:* c/o Luton Crown Court, 7 George Street, Luton LU1 2AA. *Club:* Moor Park Golf.

MOSS, Stephen Raymond; writer with The Guardian; *b* 30 July 1957; *s* of Raymond Moss and Catherine Moss (*née* Croome); *m* 1984, Helen Bonnick; one *s*. *Educ:* Balliol Coll., Oxford (BA Modern Hist. 1978); Birkbeck Coll., London (MA in Victorian Studies 1986). Editor with Kogan Page Publishers Ltd, 1979–81; Editor: Managing Your Business, 1981–83; Marketing and Direction, 1983–89; joined The Guardian, 1989: Dep. Arts Ed., 1991–93; Dep. Features Ed., 1994–95; Literary Ed., 1995–98. *Recreations:* opera, cricket, riding, racing. *Address:* c/o The Guardian, 119 Farringdon Road, EC1R 3ER. *T:* (020) 7278 2332; *e-mail:* stephen.moss@guardian.co.uk.

MOSS, Sir Stirling, Kt 2000; OBE 1959; FIE; racing motorist, 1947–62, retired; Managing Director, Stirling Moss Ltd; Chairman, Stirling Finish International Ltd; Director: Hankoe Stove Enamelling Ltd; Stirling Products Ltd; *b* 17 Sept. 1929; *m* 1st, 1957, Kathleen Stuart (marr. diss. 1960), *y d* of F. Stuart Molson, Montreal, Canada; 2nd, 1964, Elaine (marr. diss. 1968), 2nd *d* of A. Barbarino, New York; one *d*; 3rd, 1980, Susan, *y d* of Stuart Paine, London; one *s*. *Educ:* Haileybury and Imperial Service Coll. Brit. Nat. Champion, 1950, 1951, 1952, 1954, 1955, 1956, 1957, 1958, 1959, 1961; Tourist Trophy, 1950, 1951, 1955, 1958, 1959, 1960, 1961; Coupe des Alpes, 1952, 1953, 1954; Alpine Gold Cup (three consecutive wins), 1954. Only Englishman to win Italian Mille Miglia, 1955. Competed in 529 races, rallies, sprints, land speed records and endurance runs, finished in 387 and won 211. Successes include Targa Florio, 1955; Brit. Grand Prix, 1955, 1957; Ital. GP, 1956, 1957, 1959; NZ GP, 1956, 1959; Monaco GP, 1956, 1960, 1961; Leguna Seca GP, 1960, 1961; US GP, 1959, 1960; Aust. GP, 1956; Bari GP, 1956; Pescara GP, 1957; Swedish GP, 1957; Dutch GP, 1958; Argentine GP, 1958; Morocco GP, 1958; Buenos Aires GP, 1958; Melbourne GP, 1958; Villareal GP, 1958; Caen GP, 1958; Portuguese GP, 1959; S African GP, 1960; Cuban GP, 1960; Austrian GP, 1960; Cape GP, 1960; Watkins Glen GP, 1960; German GP, 1961; Modena GP, 1961. Twice voted Driver of the Year, 1954 and 1961. *Publications:* Stirling Moss's Book of Motor

Sport, 1955; In the Track of Speed, 1957; Stirling Moss's Second Book of Motor Sport, 1958; Le Mans, 1959; My Favourite Car Stories, 1960; A Turn at the Wheel, 1961; All But My Life, 1963; Design and Behaviour of the Racing Car, 1964; How to Watch Motor Racing, 1975; Motor Racing and All That, 1980; My Cars, My Career, 1987; (with D. Nye) Fangio: a Pirelli album, 1991; Great Drives in the Lakes and Dales, 1993; (with C. Hilton) Stirling Moss's Motor Racing Masterpieces, 1994; *relevant publications:* Stirling Moss, by Robert Raymond, 1953; Racing with the Maestro, by Karl Ludvigsen; Stirling Moss: the authorised biography, by Robert Edwards, 2001. *Recreations:* subaqua, designing, model making. *Address:* (business) Stirling Moss Ltd, 46 Shepherd Street, W1Y 8JN; (residence) 44 Shepherd Street, W1Y 8JN. *Clubs:* British Racing Drivers', British Automobile Racing, British Racing and Sports Car, Road Racing Drivers of America, 200 mph, Royal Automobile; Internationale des Anciens Pilotes des Grand Prix; Chm. or Pres. of 36 motoring clubs.

MÖSSBAUER, Rudolf L., PhD; Professor of Experimental Physics, Technische Universität München, 1977–97, now Emeritus; *b* Munich, 31 Jan. 1929; *m*; one *s* two *d*. *Educ:* High Sch. and Technische Hochschule, München (equiv. Bachelor's and Master's degrees). PhD (München) 1958. Thesis work, Max Planck Inst., Heidelberg, 1955–57; Research Fellow: Technische Hochschule, München, 1958–59, and at Caltech, 1960–61; Prof. of Physics, CIT, 1962–64; Prof. of Experimental Physics, München, 1965–71; Dir, Institut Max von Laue-Paul Langevin, and French-German-British High-Flux-Reactor at Grenoble, 1972–77. Member: Bavarian Acad. of Sci.; Nat. Acad. of Scis, Washington; Amer. Acad. of Arts and Scis; Pontifical Acad.; Soviet Acad. of Sci.; Acad. Leopoldina, etc. Hon. degrees Oxford, Leuwen, Madrid, Grenoble, etc. Nobel Prize for Physics (jtly), 1961, and numerous other awards. Bavarian Order of Merit, 1962; Order of Merit for Scis and the Arts (Germany), 1996. *Publications:* on gamma resonance spectroscopy (Mössbauer effect) and on neutrino physics. *Recreations:* photography, music, mountaineering. *Address:* Technische Universität München, Physik-Department E 15, James-Franck-Strasse, 85748 Garching, Germany.

MOSSELMANS, Carel Maurits, TD 1961; Chairman: Rothschild International Asset Management, 1989–96; Janson Green Holdings Ltd, 1993–96; Janson Green Ltd, 1993–96 (non-executive Director, 1993–98); *b* 9 March 1929; *s* of Adriaan Willem Mosselmans and Jonkvrouwe Nancy Henriette Mosselmans (*née* van der Wyck); *m* 1962, Hon. Prudence Fiona McCorquodale, *d* of 1st Baron McCorquodale of Newton, KCVO, PC; two *s*. *Educ:* Stowe; Trinity Coll., Cambridge (MA Modern Langs and Hist.). Queen's Bays 2nd Dragoon Guards, 1947–49; City of London Yeomanry (Rough Riders), TA, 1949; Inns of Court and City Yeomanry, 1961; Lt-Col comdg Regt, 1963. Joined Sedgwick Collins & Co., 1952 (Dir, 1963); Director: Sedgwick Forbes Hldgs, 1978; Sedgwick Forbes Bland Payne, 1979; Chm., Sedgwick Ltd, 1981–84; Dep. Chm., 1982–84, Chm., 1984–89, Sedgwick Group plc; Chairman: Sedgwick Lloyd's Underwriting Agents (formerly Sedgwick Forbes (Lloyd's Underwriting Agents)), 1974–89; The Sumitomo Marine & Fire Insurance Co. (Europe), 1981–90 (Dir, 1975–81); Rothschild Asset Management, 1990–93 (Dir, 1989–99); Exco plc, 1991–96; Director: Coutts & Co., 1981–95; Tweedhill Fisheries, 1990–; Chm., Cttee of Mgt, Lionbrook Property Fund 'B' (formerly Five Arrows Property Unit Trust Managers Ltd), 1993–; Mem. Investors' Cttee, Lionbrook Property Partnership, 1997–; Chm., Indoor Golf Clubs plc, 1998–. Vice-Pres., BIIBA, 1987–89. *Recreations:* shooting, fishing, golf, tennis, music. *Address:* 15 Chelsea Square, SW3 6LF. *T:* (020) 7352 0621, *Fax:* (020) 7351 2489. *Clubs:* White's, Cavalry and Guards; Royal St George's Golf; Sunningdale Golf; Swinley Forest Golf; Royal & Ancient Golf (St Andrews).

MOSSON, Alexander Francis; Lord Provost and Lord-Lieutenant of Glasgow, since 1999; *b* 27 Aug. 1940; *m* 1971, Maureen Sweeney; four *s* three *d*. *Educ:* St Patrick's Primary Sch.; St Mungo's Acad. Glasgow Corporation, 1955; apprentice boilermaker, Barclay Curle, 1956; plater, Alexander Stephens, 1959; insulating engineer, 1963. Active Trade Unionist from age of 17; Glasgow City Council: Mem., 1984–: Convener, Environmental Services, 1995–99; Bailie, 1992–99; Dep. Lord Provost, 1996–99. OStJ. *Recreations:* painting with water colours and oils, watching football, researching Scottish and Middle East politics and history. *Address:* Glasgow City Council, City Chambers, George Square, Glasgow G2 1DU. *T:* (0141) 287 4001.

MÖST, Franz W.; *see* Welser-Möst.

MOSTYN, 6th Baron *cr* 1831, of Mostyn, co. Flint; **Llewellyn Roger Lloyd Mostyn;** Bt 1778; *b* 26 Sept. 1948; *o s* of 5th Baron Mostyn, MC and of Yvonne Margaret (*née* Johnson); *S* father, 2000; *m* 1974, Denise Suzanne Duvanel; one *s* one *d*. *Educ:* Eton Coll. Directorate of Army Legal Services, 1974. Called to the Bar, Middle Temple, 1973; in practice, 1975–76 and 1985–89; with Kingsbury and Turner, Solicitors, 1976–78; part-time teacher, Bromley Coll. of Technology, 1981–85. *Recreations:* sport, cinema, theatre, classical music, Rugby, tennis. *Heir: s* Hon. Gregory Philip Roger Lloyd Mostyn, *b* 31 Dec. 1984. *Address:* 9 Anderson Street, SW3 3LU. *Club:* Lansdowne.

MOSTYN, Gen. Sir David; *see* Mostyn, Gen. Sir J. D. F.

MOSTYN, Gen. Sir (Joseph) David (Frederick), KCB 1984 CBE 1974 (MBE 1962); Adjutant General, 1986–88; Aide de Camp General to the Queen, 1987–89; *b* 28 Nov. 1928; *s* of late J. P. Mostyn, Arundel; *m* 1952, Diana Patricia Sheridan; four *s* two *d*. *Educ:* Downside; RMA Sandhurst; psc, rcds. Commnd Oxf. and Bucks LI, 1948; served BAOR, Greece, Cyprus, UK, 1948–58; Canadian Army Staff Coll., 1958; WO, 1959–61; Coy Comdr 1st Green Jackets, Malaya, Brunei, Borneo, 1962–63 (despatches); Instructor, Staff Coll., Camberley, 1964–67; MoD, 1967–69; CO 2 RGJ, BAOR and NI, 1969–71; Comdt Tactics Wing, Sch. of Infantry, 1972; Comdr 8 Inf. Bde, NI, 1972–74; Dep. Dir Army Training, 1974–75; RCDS 1976; BGS, HQ BAOR, 1977; Dir Personal Services (Army), 1978–80; GOC Berlin and Comdt British Sector, 1980–83; Military Sec., 1983–86. Col Commandant: The Light Div., 1983–86; Army Legal Corps, 1983–88. Chm., Army Beagling Assoc., 1979–89; President: Army Boxing Assoc., 1986–89; Army Swimming Assoc., 1986–89. Special Comr, Duke of York's Royal Mil. Sch., Dover, 1989–97. Chairman: Lyme Regis Hosp. Trust, 1990–95; Council, Dorset Respite and Hosp. Trust, 1990–99. President: Uplyme and Lym Valley Soc., 1990–; Devon County Royal British Legion, 1992–98. Kt SMO Malta, 1974. *Recreations:* maintaining a home for the family; all field sports. *Address:* c/o Lloyds TSB Plc, 54 Broad Street, Lyme Regis, Dorset DT7 3QR. *Club:* Army and Navy.

MOSTYN, Nicholas Anthony Joseph Ghislain; QC 1997; a Recorder, since 2000; *b* 13 July 1957; *s* of Jerome John Joseph Mostyn and Mary Anna Bridget Mostyn (now Learoyd); *m* 1981, Lucy Joanna Willis; three *s* one *d*. *Educ:* Ampleforth; Bristol Univ. (LLB). Called to the Bar, Middle Temple, 1980; Asst Recorder, 1997–2000; a Dep. High Court Judge, 2000–. *Publications:* Child's Pay, 1993, 2nd edn 1996; At a Glance 1992, 10th edn 2001. *Recreations:* Wagner, Southampton FC, ski-ing. *Address:* 1 Mitre Court Buildings, Temple, EC4Y 7BS. *T:* (020) 7797 7070. *Club:* MCC.

MOSTYN, Sir William Basil John, 15th Bt *cr* 1670, of Talacre, Flintshire; *b* 15 Oct. 1975; *s* of Sir Jeremy John Anthony Mostyn, 14th Bt and of Cristina, *o d* of Marchese Orengo, Turin; *S* father, 1988. *Heir: uncle* Trevor Alexander Richard Mostyn [*b* 23 May 1946; *m* 1986, Elizabeth Dax (marr. diss. 1988)]. *Address:* The Coach House, Church Lane, Lower Heyford, Oxon OX6 3NZ.

MOTHERWELL, Bishop of, (RC), since 1983; **Rt Rev. Joseph Devine;** *b* 7 Aug. 1937; *s* of Joseph Devine and Christina Murphy. *Educ:* Blairs Coll., Aberdeen; St Peter's Coll., Dumbarton; Scots Coll., Rome. Ordained priest in Glasgow, 1960; postgraduate work in Rome (PhD), 1960–64; Private Sec. to Archbishop of Glasgow, 1964–65; Assistant Priest in a Glasgow parish, 1965–67; Lecturer in Philosophy, St Peter's Coll., Dumbarton, 1967–74; a Chaplain to Catholic Students in Glasgow Univ., 1974–77; Titular Bishop of Voli and Auxiliary to Archbishop of Glasgow, 1977–83. Papal Bene Merenti Medal, 1962. *Recreations:* general reading, music, Association football. *Address:* 22 Wellhall Road, Hamilton ML3 9BG. *T:* (01698) 423058.

MOTION, Prof. Andrew; writer; Professor of Creative Writing, University of East Anglia, since 1995; Poet Laureate, since 1999; *b* 26 Oct. 1952; *s* of Andrew Richard Motion and Catherine Gillian Motion; *m* 1st, 1973, Joanna Jane Powell (marr. diss. 1983); 2nd, 1985, Janet Elisabeth Dalley; two *s* one *d*. *Educ:* Radley Coll.; University Coll., Oxford (BA 1st Cl. Hons, MLitt; Hon. Fellow, 1999). Lectr in English, Univ. of Hull, 1977–81; Editor of Poetry Review, 1981–83; Poetry Editor, 1983–89, Editl Dir, 1985–87, Chatto & Windus. Mem., Arts Council of England, 1996–99 (Chm., Literature Adv. Panel, 1996–). FRSL 1982; FRSA 2000. Hon. DLitt: Hull, 1996; Exeter, 1999; Brunel, 2000. *Publications: poetry:* The Pleasure Steamers, 1978, 4th edn 1999; Independence, 1981; The Penguin Book of Contemporary British Poetry (anthology), 1982; Secret Narratives, 1983; Dangerous Play, 1984 (Rhys Meml Prize); Natural Causes, 1987 (Dylan Thomas Award); Love in a Life, 1991; The Price of Everything, 1994; Salt Water, 1997; Selected Poems, 1998; *criticism:* The Poetry of Edward Thomas, 1981; Philip Larkin, 1982; (ed) William Barnes: selected poems, 1994; Thomas Hardy: selected poems, 1994; *biography:* The Lamberts, 1986 (Somerset Maugham Award, 1987); Philip Larkin: a writer's life, 1993 (Whitbread Award, 1993); Keats, 1997; Wainewright the Poisoner, 2000; *novels:* The Pale Companion, 1989; Famous for the Creatures, 1991. *Address:* c/o Faber & Faber, 3 Queen Square, WC1N 3AU.

MOTSON, John Walker, OBE 2001; BBC Sports Commentator, since 1971; *b* 10 July 1945; *s* of late William and Gwendoline Motson; *m* 1976, Anne Jobling; one *s*. *Educ:* Culford Sch., Bury St Edmunds. Barnet Press, 1963–67; Morning Telegraph, Sheffield, 1967–68; BBC Radio Sport, 1968–71 and 2001–; BBC TV Sport, 1971–. Commentator: 20 FA Cup Finals, 1977–2000; 7 World Cup Series, including 4 Finals, 1974–; 7 European Championships, 1976–2000. *Publications:* Second to None: great teams of post-war soccer, 1972; (with J. Rowlinson) History of the European Cup, 1980; Match of the Day: the complete record, 1992, 1994; Motty's Diary: a year in the life of a commentator, 1996. *Recreation:* running half-marathons. *Address:* c/o Jane Morgan Management, Café Royal, W1R 5EL. *T:* (020) 7287 6045. *Club:* Cricketers'.

MOTT, Gregory George Sidney, CBE 1979; Managing Director, Vickers Shipbuilding and Engineering Ltd, 1979–84, retired; *b* 11 Feb. 1925; *s* of Sidney Cyril George Mott and Elizabeth Rolinda Mott; *m* 1949, Jean Metcalfe. *Educ:* Univ. of Melbourne (BMechE Hons). Trainee Manager, Vickers Armstrong Ltd Naval Yard, 1948–49; Supervising Engr, A. E. Turner and John Coates, London, 1950–52; Sen. Draughtsman, Melbourne Harbour Trust Comrs, 1952–56; joined Vickers Armstrong Ltd, Barrow, trng on submarine construction, 1956; seconded to Naval Section Harwell, for shielding design DS/MP1 (specialised in computer technol.), 1957–59; returned to Barrow as Project Manager, Dreadnought, 1959–61; Technical Manager, Nuclear, 1961–64; Projects Controller, 1964–67; Local Dir, Vickers Ltd Shipbuilding Gp, 1966; responsible for Special Projects Div., incl. Oceanics Dept, 1968–72; Man. Dir, Vickers Oceanics Ltd, on formation of company, 1972–75; Dir, Vickers Ltd Shipbuilding Gp, and Gen. Manager, Barrow Shipbuilding Works (retained directorship, Vickers Oceanics Ltd, resigned later), 1975–77; Dir, Vickers Shipbuilding Gp Ltd, 1977; Gen. Manager and Dir, Barrow Engrg Works, Vickers Shipbuilding Gp Ltd, 1978.

MOTT, John Charles Spencer, FREng; Chairman, William Sindall plc, 1990–94 (Director, 1989–94); *b* Beckenham, Kent, 18 Dec. 1926; *m* 1953, Patricia Mary (*née* Fowler); two *s*. *Educ:* Balgowan Central Sch., Beckenham, Kent; Brixton Sch. of Building; Battersea Polytechnic; Rutherford Coll. of Technology, Newcastle upon Tyne; Wolfson Coll., Cambridge (BA English 1999). FICE, FIStructE. Served war, Lieut, Royal Marines, 1943–46. Indentured as Engr with L. G. Mouchel & Partners, 1949–52; joined Kier Ltd, 1952; Agent on heavy civil engrg contracts, 1952–63; Chairman: French Kier Holdings plc, 1974–86 (Dir, on merger, 1973, Chief Exec., 1974–84); May Gurney Hldgs Ltd, 1986–89. Director: Kier Ltd, 1963; J. L. Kier & Co. Ltd (Holding Co.), 1968; RMC plc, 1986–94. Mem. Council, Fellowship of Engrg, 1983–86; Mem. Council, 1973–75, 1986–87, and Vice Pres., 1986–87, ICE; Mem., Bragg Cttee on Falsework, 1972–74. CIMgt. *Address:* 91 Long Road, Cambridge CB2 2HE. *Club:* Danish.

MOTT, Sir John (Harmar), 3rd Bt *cr* 1930; Regional Medical Officer, Department of Health and Social Security, 1969–84; *b* 21 July 1922; *s* of Sir Adrian Spear Mott, 2nd Bt and Mary Katherine (*d* 1972), *d* of late Rev. A. H. Stanton; *S* father, 1964; *m* 1950, Elizabeth, *d* of late Hugh Carson, FRCS; one *s* two *d*. *Educ:* Radley Coll.; New Coll., Oxford (MA 1948; BM, BCh, 1951). MRCGP 1958. Served War of 1939–45: Pilot, Royal Air Force, 1943–46. Middlesex Hospital: House Physician, 1951; House Surgeon, 1952. *Recreation:* photography. *Heir: s* David Hugh Mott [*b* 1 May 1952; *m* 1980, Amanda Jane, *d* of Lt-Comdr D. W. P. Fryer, RN; two *s*]. *Address:* Staniford, Brookside, Kingsley, Cheshire WA6 8BG. *T:* (01928) 788123.

MOTT, Prof. Martin Gerard, FRCP, FRCPCH; Cancer and Leukemia in Children Professor of Paediatric Oncology, 1990–2000, now Emeritus, and Dean of Clinical Medicine and Dentistry, 1997–2000, University of Bristol; *b* 30 Nov. 1941; *s* of Mervyn Gerard Mott and Frances Emily Davis; *m* 1964, Patricia Anne Green; one *s* two *d*. *Educ:* Wimbledon Coll.; Univ. of Bristol (BSc 1963; MB ChB 1966; DSc 1991). FRCP 1983; FRCPCH 1996. Research Fellow, Univ. of Texas (M. D. Anderson Hosp.), 1972; Vis. Asst Prof., Stanford Univ., 1974–76; Sen. Lectr, then Reader, Univ. of Bristol, 1976–90. Founder Mem., UK Children's Cancer Study Gp, 1977–. International Society of Paediatric Oncology: Hon. Sec., 1979–82; Pres., Eur. Continental Branch, 1999–2000; Mem., GMC, 1999–2000. *Publications:* numerous contribs to learned jls on topics relating to childhood cancer. *Recreations:* music, ornithology. *Address:* 50 Downs Park West, Bristol BS6 7QL. *T:* (0117) 962 1476.

MOTT, Michael Duncan; His Honour Judge Mott; a Circuit Judge, since 1985; *b* 8 Dec. 1940; *s* of Francis J. Mott and Gwendolen Mott; *m* 1970, Phyllis Ann Gavin; two *s*. *Educ:* Rugby Sch.; Caius Coll., Cambridge (Exhibnr, MA). Called to Bar, Inner Temple, 1963; practised Midland and Oxford Circuit, 1964–69; Resident Magistrate, Kenya, 1969–71; resumed practice, Midland and Oxford Circuit, 1972; a Deputy Circuit Judge,

1976–80; a Recorder, 1980–85. *Recreations:* tennis, ski-ing, travel, music. *Address:* c/o Circuit Administrator, Midland and Oxford Circuit, Priory Courts, 33 Bull Street, Birmingham B4 6DW. *Club:* Cambridge Union Society.

MOTT, Philip Charles; QC 1991; a Recorder of the Crown Court, since 1987; a Deputy High Court Judge, since 1998; *b* 20 April 1948; *s* of Charles Kynaston Mott and Elsie (*née* Smith); *m* 1977, Penelope Ann Caffery; two *d*. *Educ:* King's Coll., Taunton; Worcester Coll., Oxford (MA). Called to the Bar, Inner Temple, 1970; in practice on Western Circuit, 1970–. Chm., Mental Health Review Tribunal (Restricted Patients Panel), 2000–. *Recreations:* the countryside, growing trees, sailing. *Address:* 35 Essex Street, Temple, WC2R 3AR. *T:* (020) 7353 6381. *Clubs:* Bar Yacht, Percuil Sailing.

MOTTELSON, Prof. Ben R., PhD; Danish physicist; Professor, Nordic Institute for Theoretical Atomic Physics, Copenhagen, since 1957; *b* Chicago, Ill, USA, 9 July 1926; *s* of Goodman Mottelson and Georgia Mottelson (*née* Blum); *m* 1948, Nancy Jane Reno; three *c*; became a Danish citizen, 1971. *Educ:* High Sch., La Grange, Ill; Purdue Univ. (officers' trng, USN, V12 program; BSc 1947); Harvard Univ. (grad. studies, PhD 1950). Sheldon Trav. Fellowship from Harvard at Inst. of Theoretical Physics, Copenhagen (later, the Niels Bohr Inst.), 1950–51. His Fellowship from US Atomic Energy Commn permitted continuation of work in Copenhagen for two more years, after which he held research position in CERN (European Organization for Nuclear Research) theoretical study group, formed in Copenhagen. Visiting Prof., Univ. of Calif at Berkeley, Spring term, 1959. Mem., Royal Danish Acad. of Scis and Letters, 1958. Nobel Prize for Physics (jtly), 1975; awarded for work on theory of Atomic Nucleus, with Dr Aage Bohr (3 papers publ. 1952–53). *Publications:* Nuclear Structure, vol. I, 1969; vol. II, 1975 (with A. Bohr); contrib. Rev. Mod. Phys (jt), etc. *Address:* Nordisk Institut for Teoretisk Fysik, Blegdamsvej 17, 2100 Copenhagen, Denmark.

MOTTERSHEAD, Frank William, CB 1957; Deputy Secretary, Department of Health and Social Security (formerly Ministry of Health), 1965–71; *b* 7 Sept. 1911; *o s* of late Thomas Hastings and Adeline Mottershead; unmarried. *Educ:* King Edward's Sch., Birmingham; St John's Coll., Cambridge. BA 1933, MA 1973. Entered Secretary's Dept of Admiralty, 1934; Principal Private Sec. to First Lord, 1944–46; idc 1949; Under Sec., 1950; Transferred to Ministry of Defence, 1956; Deputy Sec., 1958; Deputy Under-Sec. of State, 1964. *Address:* Old Warden, Grevel Lane, Chipping Campden, Glos GL55 6HS. *T:* (01386) 840548. *Club:* Oxford and Cambridge.

MOTTISTONE, 4th Baron *cr* 1933, of Mottistone; **David Peter Seely,** CBE 1984; Lord Lieutenant for Isle of Wight, 1986–95; Governor of the Isle of Wight, 1992–95; *b* 16 Dec. 1920; 4th *s* of 1st Baron Mottistone; *S* half brother, 1966; *m* 1944, Anthea, *er d* of T. V. W. McMullan, Cultra, Co. Down, N Ireland; two *s* two *d* (and one *d* decd). *Educ:* RN Coll., Dartmouth. Convoy escorting, Atlantic and Mediterranean, 1941–44; qualified in Communications, 1944; Served in Pacific, 1945; in comd HMS Cossack, FE Flt, 1958–59; in comd HMS Ajax and 24th Escort Sqdn, FE Flt (offensive ops against Indonesian confrontation) (despatches), 1963–65; Naval Advr to UK High Comr, Ottawa, 1965–66; retired at own request as a Captain, 1967. Dir of Personnel and Training, Radio Rentals Gp, 1967–69; Director: Distributive Industry Trng Bd, 1969–75; Cake and Biscuit Alliance, 1975–81; Export Secretary: Biscuit, Cake, Chocolate and Confectionery Alliance, 1981–83. FIEE; FIPD; FIMgt. DL Isle of Wight, 1981. Hon. DLitt Bournemouth, 1993. KStJ 1989. *Recreation:* yachting. *Heir:* *s* Hon. Peter John Philip Seely [*b* 29 Oct. 1949; *m* 1st, 1972, Joyce Cairns (marr. diss. 1975); one *s*; 2nd, 1982, Linda, *d* of W. Swain, Bulphan Fen, Essex; one *s* three *d*]. *Address:* The Old Parsonage, Mottistone, Isle of Wight PO30 4EE. *Clubs:* Royal Commonwealth Society; Royal Yacht Squadron, Royal Cruising, Island Sailing, Royal Navy Sailing Association.

MOTTRAM, Sir Richard (Clive), KCB 1998; Permanent Secretary, Department for Transport, Local Government and the Regions (formerly Department of the Environment, Transport and the Regions), since 1998; *b* 23 April 1946; *s* of John Mottram and Florence Yates; *m* 1971, Fiona Margaret Erskine; three *s* one *d*. *Educ:* King Edward VI Camp Hill Sch., Birmingham; Univ. of Keele (1st Cl. Hons Internat. Relns). Entered Home Civil Service, 1968, assigned to Ministry of Defence: Asst Private Sec. to Sec. of State for Defence, 1971–72; Cabinet Office, 1975–77; Ministry of Defence: Private Sec. to Perm. Under Sec., 1979–81; Private Sec. to Sec. of State for Defence, 1982–86; Asst. Under Sec. of State, 1986–89; Dep. Under Sec. of State (Policy), 1989–92; Permanent Secretary: Office of Public Service and Sci., 1992–95; MoD, 1995–98. Vice Pres., Commonwealth Assoc. for Public Admin and Mgt. Governor: Ditchley Foundn; Ashridge Mgt Coll. AcSS 2000. Hon. DLitt Keele, 1996. *Recreations:* cinema, theatre, tennis. *Address:* Department for Transport, Local Government and the Regions, 6th Floor, Eland House, Bressenden Place, SW1E 5DU.

MOTYER, Rev. John Alexander; Minister of Christ Church, Westbourne, Bournemouth, 1981–89, retired; *b* 30 Aug. 1924; *s* of Robert Shankey and Elizabeth Maud Motyer; *m* 1948, Beryl Grace Mays; two *s* one *d*. *Educ:* High Sch., Dublin; Dublin Univ. (MA, BD); Wycliffe Hall, Oxford. Curate: St Philip, Penn Fields, Wolverhampton, 1947–50; Holy Trinity, Old Market, Bristol, 1950–54; Tutor, Clifton Theol Coll., Bristol, 1950–54, Vice-Principal, 1954–65; Vicar, St Luke's, Hampstead, 1965–70; Dep. Principal, Tyndale Hall, Bristol, 1970–71; Principal and Dean of College, Trinity Coll., Bristol, 1971–81. Vis. Prof. in OT, Reformed Theol Seminary, Jackson, Mississippi, 1999; Jean Alexander Bernhardt Lectr, Lenoir, NC, 2000. DD Lambeth, 1997. *Publications:* The Revelation of the Divine Name, 1959; After Death, 1965, repr. 1997; The Richness of Christ (Epistle to the Philippians), 1966; The Tests of Faith (Epistle of James), 1970, 2nd edn 1975; (Old Testament Editor) New Bible Commentary Revised, 1970, New Bible Commentary 21st Century Edition, 1994; The Day of the Lion (Amos), 1975; The Image of God: Law and Liberty in Biblical Ethics (Laing Lecture), 1976; The Message of Philippians, 1984; The Message of James, 1985; The Prophecy of Isaiah, 1993; A Scenic Route Through the Old Testament, 1994; Look to the Rock: an Old Testament background to our understanding of Christ, 1996; (contrib.) An Exegetical & Expository Commentary: the Minor Prophets, vol. 3, 1998; Isaiah (Tyndale Old Testament Commentaries), 1999; Men with a Message: Old Testament, 2001; contributor: New Bible Dictionary; Expositor's Bible Commentary; Law and Life (monograph); New International Dictionary of New Testament Theology; Evangelical Dictionary of Theology. *Recreations:* reading, odd-jobbing. *Address:* 10 Littlefield, Bishopsteignton, Teignmouth, Devon TQ14 9SG. *T:* (01626) 770986.

MOUATT, (Richard) Brian, CBE 1997; Chief Dental Officer, Deparment of Health, 1991–96; *b* 4 Sept. 1936; *m* 1962, Ursula Wälti; one *s* one *d*. *Educ:* Blundell's Sch.; Edinburgh Univ. (BDS 1960). MGDS RCS 1979; FFGDP (UK) 2001. RAF Dental Branch, 1960–65 (to Sqn Leader); Dept of Public Health, Bournemouth, 1965–68; FCO, Chief Dental Officer to Republic of Zambia under Overseas Aid Scheme contract, 1968–72; gen. dental practice, Dorset, 1972–84; Dept of Health, 1984–96. Hon. Sen. Res. Fellow, Eastman Inst. of Dental Surgery, 1990–; Hon. Sen. Lectr, King's Coll. Sch. of Medicine and Dentistry, 1992–. Chairman: FDI Developing Countries Fund, 1999–; Dental Protection Ltd, 2001–. Mem. Bd, Medical Protection Soc., 1998–. Pres., Commonwealth Dental Assoc., 2000– (Vice-Pres., 1996–2000). Advr to Sec. of State for Educn and Employment on educnl matters for GCC, 1997–. *Recreations:* travel, water colour painting, sailing. *Address:* 30 Crescent Walk, West Parley, Dorset BH22 8PZ. *T:* (01202) 875139; *e-mail:* mouatt@msn.com. *Clubs:* Athenæum; Royal Motor Yacht.

MOULDEN, Peter Ronald; a Vice-President, Immigration Appeal Tribunal, since 2000 (Adjudicator, 1999–2000); *b* 31 Jan. 1945; *s* of Ronald Charles and Kathleen Norah Bell Moulden; *m* 1970, Elaine Williams; one *s* one *d*. *Educ:* Cranleigh Sch. In practice as solicitor, 1969–99. Liveryman, Glass Sellers Co., 1980–. *Recreation:* boating. *Address:* Immigration Appeal Tribunal, Field House, 15 Bream's Buildings, EC4A 1DZ.

MOULE, Rev. Prof. Charles Francis Digby, CBE 1985; FBA 1966; Lady Margaret's Professor of Divinity in the University of Cambridge, 1951–76; Fellow of Clare College, Cambridge, since 1944; Canon Theologian (non-residentiary) of Leicester, 1955–76; Honorary Member of Staff, Ridley Hall, Cambridge, 1976–80; *b* 3 Dec. 1908; *s* of late Rev. Henry William Moule and Laura Clements Pope; unmarried. *Educ:* Weymouth Coll., Dorset; Emmanuel Coll., Cambridge (scholar) (Hon. Fellow 1972); Ridley Hall, Cambridge. 1st Cl. Classical Tripos Part I, 1929; BA (1st Cl. Classical Tripos Part II), 1931; Evans Prize, 1931; Jeremie Septuagint Prize, 1932; Crosse Scholarship, 1933; MA 1934. Deacon, 1933, priest, 1934; Curate, St Mark's, Cambridge, and Tutor of Ridley Hall, 1933–34; Curate, St Andrew's, Rugby, 1934–36; Vice-Principal, Ridley Hall, 1936–44, and Curate of St Mary the Great, Cambridge, 1936–40. Dean of Clare Coll., Cambridge, 1944–51; Faculty Asst Lecturer in Divinity in the Univ. of Cambridge, 1944–47; Univ. Lecturer, 1947–51. Burkitt Medal for Biblical Studies, British Acad., 1970. Hon. DD: St Andrews, 1958; Cambridge, 1988. *Publications:* An Idiom Book of New Testament Greek, 1953; The Meaning of Hope, 1953; The Sacrifice of Christ, 1956; Colossians and Philemon (Cambridge Greek Testament Commentary), 1957; Worship in the New Testament, 1961; The Birth of the New Testament, 1962, 3rd edn 1981; The Phenomenon of the New Testament, 1967; (co-editor) Christian History and Interpretation, 1968; The Origin of Christology, 1977 (Collins Theological Book Prize, 1977); The Holy Spirit, 1978; Essays in New Testament Interpretation, 1982; (co-editor) Jesus and the Politics of His Day, 1984; Forgiveness and Reconciliation and other New Testament Themes, 1998; contrib., Encyclopædia Britannica, Interpreter's Dictionary of the Bible, Biblisch-Historisches Handwörterbuch. *Address:* 1 King's Houses, Pevensey, East Sussex BN24 5JR.

MOULSON, (Roger) Harry; company director; adviser, consultant and lecturer to major firms and universities, on how to run a business, deal with massive change events, culture, and energy, since 1997; *b* 25 Jan. 1944; *s* of Frank and Mary Moulson; *m* Elaine Ann Douthwaite; one *s* one *d*. *Educ:* Harvard Business Sch. (AMP). CEng. British Gas: Engineer, then Manager, 1962–69; Service Management/Dir and Computer Dir, 1971–81; Marketing Dir and New Business Develt Dir, 1981–92; Regl Chm., Wales Reg., 1991–93; Chief Exec., TransCo, 1993–97; Dir, 1995–97. *Recreations:* music, antiques, DIY, sport. *Address:* Sedgecombe House, Broad Campden, Chipping Campden, Glos GL55 6UX.

MOULTON, Alexander Eric, CBE 1976; RDI; FREng; Managing Director, Moulton Developments Ltd, since 1956; *b* 9 April 1920; *s* of John Coney Moulton, DSc, The Hall, Bradford-on-Avon, and Beryl Latimer Moulton. *Educ:* Marlborough Coll.; King's Coll., Cambridge (MA). Bristol Aeroplane Co., 1939–44: Engine Research Dept; George Spencer, Moulton & Co. Ltd, 1945–56; became Techn. Dir; estab. Research Dept (originated work on rubber suspensions for vehicles, incl. own design Flexitor); formed Moulton Developments Ltd, 1956 to do develt work on own designs of rubber suspensions for BLMC incl. Hydrolastic and Hydragas (Queen's Award to Industry, 1967); formed Moulton Bicycles Ltd to produce own design Moulton Bicycle, 1962 (Design Centre Award, 1964); designer of Moulton Coach, 1968–70; Chm., Moulton report on engrg design educn, Design Council, 1975–76; launched Alex Moulton Bicycle, 1983. Dir, SW Regional Bd, National Westminster Bank, 1982–87. RDI 1968 (Master, 1982–83); FRSA 1968; FREng (FEng 1980). Hon. Dr RCA, 1967; Hon. DSc Bath, 1971. SIAD Design Medal, 1976; (jointly): James Clayton Prize, Crompton-Lanchester Medal, and Thomas Hawksley Gold Medal, IMechE, 1979; MacRobert Award (mem., jt winning team), FEng, 1991. *Publications:* numerous articles and papers on engineering and education. *Recreations:* cycling, canoeing, shooting. *Address:* The Hall, Bradford-on-Avon, Wilts BA15 1AJ. *T:* (01225) 862991. *Club:* Brooks's.

MOULTON, Air Vice-Marshal Leslie Howard, CB 1971; DFC 1941; with The Plessey Co., 1971–82, retired; *b* 3 Dec. 1915; *s* of late Peter Moulton, Nantwich, Cheshire; *m* Lesley, *d* of late P. C. Clarke, Ilford; two *s* two *d*. *Educ:* Nantwich and Acton School. Joined RAF, 1932; served War of 1939–45, Pilot; Operations with 14 Sqdn in Africa, 1940–42; CFS, 1942–44; specialised in Signals, 1945; Staff Coll., 1950; USAF, Strategic Air Comd, 1954–56; Dep. Dir Radio, Air Min., 1958–61; Comdt RAF Cosford, 1961–63; CSO Fighter Comd, 1963–65; Min. of Technology, 1965–68. Wing Comdr 1955; Gp Captain 1959; Air Cdre 1964; Air Vice-Marshal 1969; AOC No 90 (Signals) Group, RAF, 1969–71; retired 1971. FIEE, CEng, 1959. *Recreations:* gardening, golf, hill walking. *Address:* No 14 The Paddock, Willaston House, Willaston, Nantwich, Cheshire CW5 7EP. *T:* (01270) 665308. *Club:* Royal Air Force.

MOUND, Laurence Alfred, DSc; FRES; Hon. Research Fellow, CSIRO Entomology (formerly Division of Entomology, Commonwealth Scientific and Industrial Research Organisation), since 1996; Research Associate, Natural History Museum (formerly British Museum (Natural History)), since 1992 (Keeper of Entomology, 1981–92); *b* 22 April 1934; *s* of John Henry Mound and Laura May Cape; *m* 1st, 1958, Agnes Jean Solari (marr. diss. 1985); one *s* two *d*; 2nd, 1987, Sheila Helen Halsey (marr. diss. 1994). *Educ:* Warwick Sch.; Sir John Cass Coll., London; Imperial Coll., London (DIC); DSc London; Imperial Coll. of Tropical Agriculture, Trinidad (DipTropAgric). Nigerian Federal Dept of Agricl Research, 1959–61; Rockefeller Studentship, Washington and Calif, 1961; Empire Cotton Growing Corp., Republic of Sudan, 1961–64; Sen. Scientific Officer, BM (NH), 1964–69; Australian CSIRO Research Award, 1967–68; PSO, 1969–75, Dep. Keeper, Dept of Entomology, BM (NH), 1975–81. Sec., 1976–88, Vice-Chm., 1988–92, Council for Internat. Congresses of Entomology; Consultant Dir, Commonwealth Inst. of Entomology, 1981–92. Hon. Prof., Sch. of Pure and Applied Biology, Univ. of Wales at Cardiff, 1990–96; McMaster Res. Fellow, CSIRO, 1995–96. Editor, Jl of Royal Entomological Soc. of London, 1973–81 (Vice-Pres., RES, 1975–76). Numerous expedns studying thrips in tropical countries. *Publications:* over 190 technical books and papers on biology of thrips and whitefly, particularly in Bull. of BM (NH), incl. Whitefly of the World (with S. H. Halsey), and Thrips of Central and South America (with R. Marullo). *Recreations:* thrips with everything. *Address:* c/o CSIRO Entomology, GPO Box 1700, Canberra, ACT 2601, Australia. *T:* (2) 62464280, *Fax:* (2) 62464264; *e-mail:* laurence@ento.csiro.au.

MOUNT, Air Cdre Christopher John, CBE 1956; DSO 1943; DFC 1940; DL; retired; *b* 14 Dec. 1913; *s* of Capt. F. Mount; *m* 1947, Audrey Mabel Clarke; two *s*. *Educ:* Eton; Trinity Coll., Oxford. Royal Auxiliary Air Force, 1935; Royal Air Force, 1938.

Consultant, Wrights (formerly C. R. Thomas & Son), Solicitors, Maidenhead (partner, 1970–79). DL Berks, 1984. *Address:* Garden House, Bagshot Road, Sunninghill, Ascot, Berks SL5 9JL. *T:* (01344) 622225.

MOUNT, Ferdinand; *see* Mount, W. R. F.

MOUNT, (William Robert) Ferdinand, (3rd Bt *cr* 1921, of Wasing Place, Reading, Berks, but does not use the title); journalist; Editor, Times Literary Supplement, since 1991; *b* 2 July 1939; *s* of Robert Francis Mount (*d* 1969), 2nd *s* of Sir William Arthur Mount, 1st Bt, CBE and his 1st wife, Lady Julia Pakenham (*d* 1956), *d* of 5th Earl of Longford; *S* uncle, 1993; *m* 1968, Julia Margaret, *d* of late Archibald Julian and Hon. Mrs Lucas; two *s* one *d* (and one *s* decd). *Educ:* Eton; Christ Church, Oxford. Has worked for Sunday Telegraph, Conservative Research Dept, Daily Sketch, National Review, Daily Mail, The Times; Political Columnist: The Spectator, 1977–82 and 1985–87; The Standard, 1980–82; Daily Telegraph, 1984–90; Sunday Times, 1997–; Head of Prime Minister's Policy Unit, 1982–83. *Publications:* Very Like a Whale, 1967; The Theatre of Politics, 1972; The Man Who Rode Ampersand, 1975; The Clique, 1978; The Subversive Family, 1982; The Selkirk Strip, 1987; Of Love and Asthma, 1991 (Hawthornden Prize, 1992); The British Constitution Now, 1992; Umbrella, 1994; The Liquidator, 1995; Jem (and Sam): a revenger's tale, 1998; Fairness, 2001. *Heir: s* William Robert Horatio Mount [*b* 12 May 1969; *m* 1997, Deborah Grey; one *s*]. *Address:* 17 Ripplevale Grove, N1 1HS. *T:* (020) 7607 5398.

MOUNT CHARLES, Earl of; Henry Vivian Pierpoint Conyngham; *b* 23 May 1951; *s* and *heir* of 7th Marquess Conyngham, *qv*; *m* 1st, 1971, Juliet Ann, *yr d* of Robert Kitson (marr. diss. 1985); one *s* one *d*; 2nd, 1985, Lady Iona Grimston, *yr d* of 6th Earl of Verulam; one *d*. *Educ:* Harrow; Harvard Univ. Irish Rep., 1976–78, Consultant, 1978–84, Sotheby's; Chairman: Slane Castle Ltd; Slane Castle Productions. Dir, Grapevine Arts Centre, Dublin. Trustee, Irish Youth Foundn. *Heir: s* Viscount Slane, *qv*. *Address:* Slane Castle, Co. Meath, Eire; Beau Parc House, Navan, Co. Meath, Eire. *Club:* Kildare Street and University (Dublin).

MOUNT EDGCUMBE, 8th Earl of, *cr* 1789; **Robert Charles Edgcumbe;** Baron Edgcumbe, 1742; Viscount Mount Edgcumbe and Valletort, 1781; Farm Manager, for Lands and Survey, New Zealand, 1975–84; *b* 1 June 1939; *s* of George Aubrey Valletort Edgcumbe (*d* 1977) and of Meta Blucher, *d* of late Robert Charles Lhoyer; *S* uncle, 1982; *m* 1960, Joan Ivy Wall (marr. diss. 1988); five *d*. *Educ:* Nelson College. Career from farm worker to farm manager, managing first farm, 1960; taking up family seat in Cornwall, 1984. *Recreations:* hunting game, restoring classic cars. *Heir: half-b* Piers Valletort Edgcumbe [*b* 23 Oct. 1946; *m* 1971, Hilda Warn (marr. diss.); two *d*]. *Address:* Empacombe House, Cremyll, Cornwall PL10 1HZ.

MOUNTAIN, Sir Denis Mortimer, 3rd Bt *cr* 1922; Chairman and Managing Director: Eagle Star Insurance Co. Ltd, 1974–85; Eagle Star Holdings plc, 1979–85 (Hon. Pres., 1985–93); Chairman, Eagle Star Insurance Co. of America, 1978–85; *b* 2 June 1929; *er s* of Sir Brian Edward Stanley Mountain, 2nd Bt, and Doris Elsie, *e d* of E. C. E. Lamb; *S* father, 1977; *m* 1958, Hélène Fleur Mary Kirwan-Taylor; two *s* one *d*. *Educ:* Eton. Late Lieut, Royal Horse Guards. Chairman: Australian Eagle Insurance Co. Ltd, 1977–85; South African Eagle Insurance Co. Ltd, 1977–85, and other companies both in UK and overseas; Pres., Compagnie de Bruxelles Risques Divers SA d'Assurances (Belgium), 1977–85; Director: Rank Organisation PLC, 1968–94; Grovewood Securities Ltd, 1969–85 (Dep. Chm.); Philip Hill Investment Trust plc, 1967–86; Bank of Nova Scotia (Toronto), 1978–2000; BAT Industries plc, 1984–85; Allied London Properties, 1986–99, and other UK and overseas companies. *Recreations:* fishing, shooting. *Heir: s* Edward Brian Stanford Mountain [*b* 19 March 1961; *m* 1987, Charlotte Sarah Jesson, *d* of Judge Henry Pownall, *qv*; two *s* one *d*]. *Address:* The Manor, Morestead, Winchester, Hants SO21 1LZ. *T:* (01962) 777237; 12 Queens Elm Square, Old Church Street, Chelsea, SW3 6ED. *T:* (020) 7352 4331.

MOUNTBATTEN, family name of **Marquess of Milford Haven**.

MOUNTBATTEN OF BURMA, Countess (2nd in line) *cr* 1947; **Patricia Edwina Victoria Knatchbull,** CBE 1991; CD; JP; DL; Viscountess Mountbatten of Burma, 1946; Baroness Romsey, 1947; Vice Lord-Lieutenant of Kent, 1984–2000; *b* 14 Feb. 1924; *er d* of Admiral of the Fleet 1st Earl Mountbatten of Burma, KG, GCB, OM, GCSI, GCIE, GCVO, DSO, PC, FRS, and Countess Mountbatten of Burma, CI, GBE, DCVO, LLD (*d* 1960) (Hon. Edwina Cynthia Annette Ashley, *e d* of 1st and last Baron Mount Temple, PC); *S* father, 1979; *m* 1946, Baron Brabourne, *qv*; four *s* two *d* (and one *s* decd). *Educ:* Malta, England and New York City. Served War in WRNS, 1943–46. Colonel-in-Chief, Princess Patricia's Canadian Light Infantry. Chairman: Sir Ernest Cassel Educational Trust; Edwina Mountbatten Trust. President: Friends of Cassel Hosp.; Friends of William Harvey Hosp.; Shaftesbury Homes and Arethusa; Kent Branches of Save the Children and Relate; Dep. Pres., BRCS; Vice-President: NSPCC; FPA; Nat. Childbirth Trust; SSAFA; RLSS; Shaftesbury Soc.; Nat. Soc. for Cancer Relief; Kent Voluntary Service Council; The Aidis Trust; RCN; Royal Nat. Coll. for Blind; Mountbatten Community Trust. Hon. President: Soc. for Nautical Research; British Maritime Charitable Foundn; Patron: Commando Assoc.; Royal Naval Commando Assoc.; Legion of Frontiersmen of the Commonwealth; HMS Cavalier Trust; Foudroyant Trust; HMS Kelly Reunion Assoc.; Safer World Project; VADs (RN); Compassionate Friends; Nurses' Welfare Trust; SOS Children's Villages (UK); Vice-Patron, Burma Star Assoc. Trustee, Kent Community Housing Trust. Gov., Mersham Primary Sch., Kent. JP 1971 and DL 1973, Kent. Hon. DCL Kent, 2000. DStJ 1981. *Heir: s* Lord Romsey, *qv*. *Address:* Newhouse, Mersham, Ashford, Kent TN25 6NQ. *T:* (01233) 503636; 39 Montpelier Walk, SW7 1JH. *T:* (020) 7589 8829.

MOUNTEVANS, 3rd Baron *cr* 1945, of Chelsea; **Edward Patrick Broke Evans;** Assistant Marketing Manager, British Tourist Authority, 1982–89, Advisor, since 1989; *b* 1 Feb. 1943; *s* of 2nd Baron Mountevans and Deirdre Grace (*d* 1997), *d* of John O'Connell, Cork; *S* father, 1974; *m* 1973, Johanna Keyzer, *d* of late Antonius Franciscus Keyzer, The Hague. *Educ:* Rugby; Trinity Coll., Oxford. Reserve Army Service, 1961–66; 74 MC Regt RCT, AER; Lt 1964. Joined management of Consolidated Gold Fields Ltd, 1966; British Tourist Authority, 1972: Manager, Sweden and Finland, 1973; Head of Promotion Services, 1976. *Heir: b* Hon. Jeffrey de Corban Richard Evans [*b* 13 May 1948; *m* 1972, Hon. Juliet, *d* of Baron Moran, *qv*; two *s*].

MOUNTFIELD, Peter; Executive Secretary, Development Committee, World Bank, 1991–95; *b* 2 April 1935; *s* of late Alexander Stuart Mountfield and Agnes Elizabeth (*née* Gurney); *m* 1958, Evelyn Margaret Smithies; three *s*. *Educ:* Merchant Taylors' Sch., Crosby; Trinity Coll., Cambridge (BA); Graduate Sch. of Public Admin, Harvard. RN, 1953–55. Asst Principal, HM Treasury, 1958; Principal, 1963; Asst Sec., 1970; Under Secretary: Cabinet Office, 1977; HM Treasury, 1980–91. *Recreations:* reading, walking, looking at buildings. *Address:* Marchants, Church Street, Seal, Sevenoaks, Kent TN15 0AR. *T:* (01732) 761848.

See also Sir R. Mountfield.

MOUNTFIELD, Sir Robin, KCB 1999 (CB 1988); Permanent Secretary, Cabinet Office, 1998–99; *b* 16 Oct. 1939; *s* of late Alexander Stuart Mountfield and Agnes Elizabeth (*née* Gurney); *m* 1963, Anne Newsham; three *c*. *Educ:* Merchant Taylors' Sch., Crosby; Magdalen Coll., Oxford (BA). Assistant Principal, Ministry of Power, 1961, Principal, 1965; Private Sec. to Minister for Industry, 1973–74; Asst Sec., Dept of Industry, 1974, seconded to Stock Exchange, 1977–78; Under Sec., DoI, later, DTI, 1980–84; Deputy Secretary: DTI, 1984–92; HM Treasury, 1992–95; Permanent Sec., OPS, Cabinet Office, 1995–98. Non-exec. Dir, Innogy Hldgs, 2000–. Chm., St Katharine and Shadwell Trust, 1999–; Trustee, CS Benevolent Fund, 2000–. Member Council: Univ. of Essex, 1999–; BHF, 2000–. *T:* (020) 8293 0359; *e-mail:* rmountfield@hotmail.com.

See also P. Mountfield.

MOUNTFORD, Carol Jean, (Kali); MP (Lab) Colne Valley, since 1997; *b* 12 Jan. 1954; *m*; one *s* one *d*; *m* 1995, Ian Leedham. *Educ:* Crewe and Alsager Coll. (BA SocSc ext.). Civil Service posts, Dept of Employment, 1975–96. Mem., Dept of Employment Exec. Cttee, CPSA, 1986. Mem. (Lab) Sheffield CC, 1992–96. *Address:* House of Commons, SW1A 0AA. *T:* (020) 7219 4507.

MOUNTFORT, Guy Reginald, OBE 1970; retired as Director, Ogilvy & Mather International Inc., New York (1964–66); and as Managing Director, Ogilvy and Mather Ltd, London (1964–66); *b* 4 Dec. 1905; *s* of late Arnold George Mountfort, artist, and late Alice Edith (*née* Hughes); *m* 1931, Joan Hartley (*née* Pink); two *d*. *Educ:* Grammar Sch. General Motors Corporation (France), 1928–38. War service, 1939–46, 12 Regt HAC and British Army Staff (Washington) Lt-Col; service in N Africa, Italy, Burma, Pacific, Germany. Procter & Gamble Inc., USA, 1946–47; Mather & Crowther Ltd, 1947, Dir, 1949; Vice-Chm., Dollar Exports Bd Advertising Cttee, 1948–49. Hon. Sec., Brit. Ornithologists' Union, 1952–62, Pres. 1970–75 (Union Medal, 1967); Leader of scientific expedns to Coto Doñana, 1952, 1955, 1956; Bulgaria, 1960; Hungary, 1961; Jordan, 1963, 1965; Pakistan, 1966, 1967. Vice Pres., World Wildlife Fund (Gold Medal, 1978); Scientific FZS (Stamford Raffles Award, 1969). Medal of Société d'Acclimatation, 1936. Commander, Order of the Golden Ark, Netherlands, 1980. *Publications:* A Field Guide to the Birds of Europe (co-author), 1954, 5th edn, Birds of Britain and Europe, 1994; The Hawfinch, 1957; Portrait of a Wilderness, 1958; Portrait of a River, 1962; Portrait of a Desert, 1965; The Vanishing Jungle, 1969; Tigers, 1973; So Small a World, 1974; Back from the Brink, 1977; Saving the Tiger, 1981; Wild India, 1985; Rare Birds of the World, 1988; Memories of Three Lives, 1991; contribs to ornithological and other scientific jls; television and radio broadcasts on ornithology and exploration. *Recreations:* ornithology, gardening, photography, travel. *Address:* Queensmount, 18 Queens Park West Drive, Bournemouth, Dorset BH8 9DA.

MOUNTGARRET, 17th Viscount *cr* 1550 (Ireland); **Richard Henry Piers Butler;** Baron (UK), 1911; *b* 8 Nov. 1936; *s* of 16th Viscount Mountgarret; *S* father, 1966; *senior known heir* to Earldoms of Ormonde and Ossory and Chief Butler of Ireland; *m* 1st, 1960, Gillian Margaret (marr. diss. 1970), *o d* of Cyril Francis Stuart Buckley, London, SW3; two *s* one *d*; 2nd, 1970, Mrs Jennifer Susan Melville Fattorini (marr. diss. 1983), *yr d* of Captain D. M. Wills, Barley Wood, Wrington, near Bristol; 3rd 1983, Mrs Angela Ruth Waddington, *e d* of Major T. G. Porter, The Croft, Church Fenton, Tadcaster. *Educ:* Eton; RMA, Sandhurst. Commissioned, Irish Guards, 1957; retd rank Capt., 1964. Pres., Yorks CCC, 1984–90. *Recreations:* shooting, stalking, cricket, golf. *Heir: s* Hon Piers James Richard Butler [*b* 15 April 1961; *m* 1995, Laura Brown Gary (marr. diss. 2000), *d* of Albert Dickens Williams, Jr; two *d*]. *Address:* Stainley House, South Stainley, Harrogate, Yorks HG3 3LX. *T:* (01423) 770087. *Clubs:* White's, Pratt's.

MOUNTSTUART, Lord; John Bryson Crichton-Stuart; *b* 21 Dec. 1989; *s* and *heir* of Marquess of Bute, *qv*.

MOWAT, Ashley; *see* Mowat, N. A. G.

MOWAT, David McIvor; JP; consultant, business columnist and commentator; Managing Director, Iatros Ltd, since 1994; Director, St Andrews Golf Club Manufacturing Ltd, since 1994; *b* 12 March 1939; *s* of Ian M. Mowat and Mary I. S. Steel; *m* 1964, Elinor Anne Birtwistle; three *d*. *Educ:* Edinburgh Academy; University of Edinburgh (MA); BA Open Univ., 1984. Chief Executive: Edinburgh Chamber of Commerce and Manufactures, 1967–90; Chamber Developments Ltd, 1971; Edinburghs Capital Ltd, 1986; Who's Who in Business in Scotland Ltd, 1989–90. Dep. Chm., Edinburgh Tourist Gp, 1985–90. Pres., British Chambers of Commerce Execs, 1987–89. JP Edinburgh, 1969. FRSA. *Address:* 37 Orchard Road South, Edinburgh EH4 3JA. *T:* (0131) 332 6865.

MOWAT, Ian Robert Mackenzie, FLA; FRSE; Librarian, University of Edinburgh, since 1997; *b* 20 April 1946; *s* of Robert John Bain Mowat and Violet Mowat (*née* Mackenzie); *m* 1968, Margaret Louise Jackson; one *s* one *d*. *Educ:* Univ. of Aberdeen (MA); Univ. of Sheffield (MA); Univ. of St Andrews (BPhil). FLA 1991. Assistant Librarian: St Andrews Univ., 1970–72; Heriot-Watt Univ., 1972–75; Asst Keeper, Nat. Liby of Scotland, 1975–78; Sub-Librarian, Glasgow Univ., 1978–86; Librarian: Hull Univ., 1986–91; and Keeper, Pybus Collection, Newcastle Univ., 1992–97. FRSE 1998. *Publications:* Easter Ross 1750–1850, 1981; Bibliography of Scotland 1976–77, 1978, 1977–78, 1979; (ed jtly) Networking and the Future of Libraries 2, 1995; (ed with M. Sliwinska) Library Management: East-West relations, 1995; contrib. numerous reports, articles, papers and reviews on librarianship, history and architectural history. *Recreations:* hill-walking, swimming, music, architectural history. *Address:* Main Library, George Square, Edinburgh EH8 9LJ. *T:* (0131) 650 3378.

MOWAT, John Stuart; QC (Scot.) 1988; Sheriff Principal of South Strathclyde, Dumfries and Galloway, 1988–93; *b* 30 Jan. 1923; *s* of George Mowat and Annie Barlow; *m* 1956, Anne Cameron Renfrew; two *s* two *d*. *Educ:* Glasgow High Sch.; Belmont House; Merchiston Castle Sch.; Glasgow Univ. (MA, LLB). Served RAF Transport Comd, 1941–46; Flt-Lt 1944. Journalist, 1947–52; Advocate, 1952; Sheriff-Substitute, then Sheriff, of Fife and Kinross at Dunfermline, 1960–72; Sheriff of Fife and Kinross at Cupar and Kinross, 1972–74; Sheriff of Lanark and Glasgow, subseq. Glasgow and Strathkelvin, 1974–88. Chm., Sheriff Court Rules Council, 1989–92. Contested (L) Caithness and Sutherland, 1955; Office-bearer, Scottish Liberal Party, 1954–58; Life Trustee: Carnegie Dunfermline Trust, 1967–73; Carnegie UK Trust, 1971–73. *Recreations:* golf, curling, watching football. *Address:* Old Mill of Camserney, Camserney, Aberfeldy, Perthshire PH15 2JF. *T:* (01887) 829572.

MOWAT, Mary Jane Stormont; Her Honour Judge Mowat; a Circuit Judge, since 1996; *b* 7 July 1948; *d* of late Duncan McKay Stormont Mowat and Jane Archibald Mowat (*née* Milne); *m* 1973, Dr the Hon. Nicholas Michael John Woodhouse, 2nd *s* of 5th Baron

...errington, DSO, OBE; one *s*. *Educ:* Sherborne [illegible] ...sician and ...Oxford (MA). Called to the Bar, Inner Temple, 197[illegible] ...or Lecturer in ...riding. *Address:* c/o South Eastern Circuit Off[illegible] ...to the Queen in Street, WC2R 3EU.

MOWAT, Dr (Norman) Ashley (Geor[illegible]... ...bella Parker Mowat; *m* Gastroenterologist, Aberdeen Royal [illegible] ...cad.; Aberdeen Univ. (MB Medicine, Aberdeen University Me[illegible] Officer, SHO, then Registrar, Scotland, since 2001; *b* 11 April 1[illegible] ...turer: in Medicine, Aberdeen Univ., 1966, Kathleen Mary Cowie; [illegible] Bartholomew's Hosp., London, 1973–74. ChB). MRCP 1971, FRCP... *Publications:* (ed jtly) Integrated Clinical Sciences: Trng, Aberdeen Teaching... contribs to med. and gastroenterol. jls. *Recreations:* 1972–73; in Gastroente[illegible] *Address:* Gastrointestinal Unit, Aberdeen Royal Vis. Physician to She[illegible] ...deen AB25 2ZN. *T:* (01224) 681818, ext. 52570. Gastroenterology, sailing, photog[illegible] Infirmary, F[illegible]

MOWB[illegible] STO[illegible] ...th Baron *cr* 1283), **SEGRAVE** (27th Baron *cr* 1283), **AND** ...N of Stourton, Co. Wilts (23rd Baron *cr* 1448); **Charles Edward Stourton,** ...2; *b* 11 March 1923; *s* of William Marmaduke Stourton, 25th Baron Mowbray, 26th Baron Segrave and 22nd Baron Stourton, MC, and Sheila (*d* 1975), *er d* of Hon. Edward Gully, CB; *S* father, 1965; *m* 1952, Hon. Jane de Yarburgh Bateson (*d* 1998), *o c* of 5th Baron Deramore, and of Nina Lady Deramore, OBE, *d* of Alastair Macpherson-Grant; two *s*; *m* 1999, Joan, Lady Holland, *widow* of Sir Guy Holland, 3rd Bt. *Educ:* Ampleforth; Christ Church, Oxford. Joined Army, 1942; Commissioned Gren. Guards, 1943; served with 2nd Armd Bn Gren. Gds, as Lt, 1943–44 (wounded, France, 1944; loss of eye and invalided, 1945). Mem. of Lloyd's 1952; Mem. Securicor, 1961–64; Chairman: Ghadeco (UK) Ltd, 1986–; Thames Estuary Airport Co. Ltd, 1993–; Director: Securicor (Scotland) Ltd, 1964–70; General Development Co. Ltd (Ghana), 1980–; EIRC Ghana Ltd, 1982–; EIRC Hldgs Ltd (Jersey), 1986–. Mem., Nidderdale RDC, 1954–58. A Conservative Whip in House of Lords, 1967–70, 1974–78; a Lord in Waiting (Govt Whip), and spokesman for DoE, 1970–74; Dep. Chief Opposition Whip in House of Lords, 1978–79; a Lord in Waiting (Govt Whip), and spokesman for the arts, envt and transport, 1979–80; elected Mem., H of L, 1999. Chm., Govt Picture Buying Cttee, 1972–74; Mem., British Parly Delegn to Bicentennial Celebrations, Washington, 1976. Trustee: College of Arms Trust, 1975–; Church, Convent and Hosp., St John and St Elizabeth. Chancellor, Primrose League, 1974–80, 1981–83. Life Governor, Imperial Cancer Res. Fund, 1983–. Patron, Tayside and Mearns Normandy Veterans Assoc., 1992–. Bicentennial Year Award of Baronial Order of Magna Charta, USA, 1976. Kt of Hon. and Devotion, SMO Malta, 1947. *Recreations:* reading, shooting, gardening. *Heir: s* Hon. Edward William Stephen Stourton [*b* 17 April 1953; *m* 1980, Penelope, *e d* of Dr Peter Brunet; one *s* four *d*]. *Address:* Marcus, by Forfar, Angus DD8 3QH. *T:* (01307) 850219; 23 Warwick Square, SW1V 2AB. *Clubs:* Turf, White's, Pratt's, Beefsteak, Pilgrims, Roxburghe.

MOWBRAY, John; *see* Mowbray, W. J.

MOWBRAY, Sir John, Kt 1983; Chairman, Wellington Diocesan Board of Trustees (Anglican), 1970–95, now Past Chairman; *b* 23 Sept. 1916; *s* of Harry Logan Campbell Mowbray and Therese Josephine Mowbray; *m* 1946, Audrey Burt Steel; two *s* one *d*. *Educ:* King's Coll., Auckland; Auckland University Coll. BCom, Dip. in Banking, Univ. of NZ; FCA NZ 1973. Served War, 2nd NZ Div. Field Artillery, ME, 1940–46 (Lieut). Joined staff of The National Bank of New Zealand, 1934; Gen. Man.'s Asst, 1957; Asst Gen. Man., 1961; Gen. Man. and Chief Exec., 1966–76. Chairman: Develt Finance Corp. of NZ, 1976–85; GEC New Zealand Ltd, 1976–86; Motor Hldgs Ltd, 1980–84; DIC Ltd, 1982–86. Chairman: NZ Bankers' Assoc., 1966, 1972 and 1975; Higher Salaries Cttee in the State Services, 1972–78; Bd of Trustees, NZ Inst. of Econ. Res., 1978–; Asean NZ Business Council, 1984–88; NZ Technol. Advancement Trust, 1984–; Japan/NZ Business Council, 1974–78; NZ Cttee, Pacific Basin Econ. Council, 1972–74. Life Member: NZ Admin. Staff Coll. (formerly Chm.); Arthritis and Rheumatism Foundn of NZ; Barnados NZ. Distinguished Fellow, NZ Inst. of Dirs, 1999. FNZIM 1974; Hon. Fellow, NZ Inst. of Bankers, 1975; FRSA 1970. A Lay Canon Emeritus, Wellington Cathedral. *Recreations:* golf, bridge, gardening. *Address:* 167 Karori Road, Karori, Wellington 5, New Zealand. *T:* 766334. *Clubs:* Wellington (Wellington); Northern (Auckland); Wellington Golf.

MOWBRAY, Sir John Robert, 6th Bt *cr* 1880; DL; *b* 1 March 1932; *s* of Sir George Robert Mowbray, 5th Bt, KBE, and of Diana Margaret, *d* of Sir Robert Heywood Hughes, 12th Bt; *S* father, 1969; *m* 1957, Lavinia Mary, *d* of late Lt-Col Francis Edgar Hugonin, OBE, Stainton House, Stainton in Cleveland, Yorks; three *d*. *Educ:* Eton; New College, Oxford. DL Suffolk, 1993. *Address:* The Hill House, Duffs Hill, Glemsford, Suffolk CO10 7PP. *T:* (01787) 281930.

MOWBRAY, (William) John; QC 1974; *b* 3 Sept. 1928; *s* of James Mowbray, sugar manufr and Ethel Mowbray; *m* 1960, Shirley Mary Neilan; one *s* three *d*. *Educ:* Upper Canada Coll.; Mill Hill Sch.; New Coll., Oxford. BA 1952. Called to Bar, Lincoln's Inn, 1953 (Bencher, 1983); called to Bahamian Bar, 1971, to Eastern Caribbean Bar, 1992. Chairman: Chancery Bar Assoc., 1985–94; Westminster Assoc. for Mental Health, 1981–88, 1999–; Westminster Christian Council, 1986–87 (Vice-Chm., 1984–85). Mem. Editl Bd, The Chase Jl. *Publications:* Lewin on Trusts, 16th edn 1964, 17th edn 2000; Estate Duty on Settled Property, 1969; articles in jls. *Recreations:* music, observing nature in Sussex garden. *Address:* 12 New Square, Lincoln's Inn, WC2A 3SW. *T:* (020) 7419 1212. *Club:* Travellers.

MOWL, Colin John; Director (formerly Deputy Director), Budget and Public Finances, HM Treasury, since 1995; *b* 19 Oct. 1947; *s* of Arthur Sidney and Ada Mowl; *m* 1980, Kathleen Patricia Gallagher; one *s* one *d*. *Educ:* Lawrence Sheriff Sch., Rugby; LSE (BSc Econs, MSc). Econ. Asst, MoT, 1970–72; Sen. Econ. Asst, Econ. Advr, HM Treasury, 1972–83; Res. Manager, Forex Research Ltd, 1983; Sen. Econ. Advr, HM Treasury, 1983–90; Grade 3, and Hd, Econ. Analysis and Forecasting Gp, later Dep. Dir, Macroecon. Policy and Prospects, HM Treasury, 1990–95. *Publications:* various Treasury working papers. *Recreations:* family, visiting France, sport. *Address:* HM Treasury, Parliament Street, SW1P 3AG. *T:* (020) 7270 4419.

MOWLAM, Rt Hon. Marjorie; PC 1997; PhD; journalist and writer; *b* 18 Sept. 1949; *m* 1995, Jon Norton. *Educ:* Coundon Court Comprehensive Sch., Coventry; Durham Univ. (BA Social Anthrop. 1971); Iowa Univ. (MA; PhD 1978). Lecturer: Florida State Univ., 1977–78; Newcastle upon Tyne Univ., 1979–83; Administrator, Northern Coll., Barnsley, 1984–87. MP (Lab) Redcar, 1987–2001. Opposition front bench spokesman on NI, 1988–89 and 1994–97, on city and corporate affairs, 1989–92, on Citizen's Charter and women, 1992–93, on nat. heritage, 1993–94; Mem., Shadow Cabinet, 1992–97; Sec. of State for NI, 1997–99; Minister for the Cabinet Office and Chancellor of the Duchy of Lancaster, 1999–2001. Has held various Labour Party offices at constituency and dist levels; Mem., NEC, 1995–. Mem., Internat. Crisis Gp, 2001–. *Publications:* (ed jtly) Debate on Disarmament, 1982; (contrib.) Over Our Dead Bodies, ed D. Thompson, 1983. *Recreations:* travelling, swimming, jigsaws.

MOWLL, Christopher Martyn; Clerk to The Clothworkers' Company of the City of London and Secretary to The Clothworkers' Foundation, 1978–92; *b* 14 Aug. 1932; *s* of late Christopher Kilvinton Mowll and Doris Ellen (*née* Hutchinson); *m* 1958, Margaret Frances (*née* Laird); four *s*. *Educ:* Epsom Coll.; Gonville and Caius Coll., Cambridge (MA). Admitted Solicitor, 1956. Member: Council, National Library for the Blind, 1964–79; Council, Metropolitan Society for the Blind, 1964– (Chm., 1979–2000); Exec. Council, RNIB, 1982–; Britain-Australia Bicentennial Cttee, 1984–88; Exec. Cttee, Assoc. of Charitable Foundns, 1989–92; Council, Shaftesbury Soc., 1993–98. Mem. Court, Univ. of Leeds, 1979–92, 1995–. Hon. LLD Leeds, 1992. *Address:* 15 West Hill, Sanderstead, South Croydon, Surrey CR2 0SB. *T:* (020) 8657 1207.

MOWLL, Rev. (John) William (Rutley); Chaplain to the Queen, since 2000; Vicar, Boughton-under-Blean with Dunkirk, since 1983, and also Hernhill, since 1989; *b* 24 March 1942; *s* of Wilfred Rutley Mowll and Mary Gifford (*née* Holden); *m* 1966, Susan Frances Lisle Bullen; two *s*. *Educ:* Canterbury Cathedral Choir Sch.; King's Sch., Canterbury; Sarum Theol Coll. Ordained deacon, 1966, priest, 1967; Curate: Church of the Ascension, Oughtibridge, dio. Sheffield, 1966–69; St James, Hill, dio. Birmingham, 1969–72; Industrial Chaplain and Vicar, Upper Arley, 1973–78; Priest-in-Charge, 1978–81, Rector, 1981–83, Upton Snodsbury; Rural Dean, Ospringe, Faversham, 1995–2001; Hon. Minor Canon, Canterbury Cathedral, 1995–; Chaplain to High Sheriff of Kent, 2001–02. Occasional Lectr, Nat. Maritime Mus. Member: Guild of Master Craftsmen, 1984–; Soc. for Nautical Res. (South); Life Mem., HMS Warrior 1860. *Publications:* SS Great Britain: the model ship, 1982; HMS Warrior 1860: building a working model warship, 1997. *Recreations:* practising musician, amateur playwright, engineer in miniature craftwork, specialising in model ships. *Address:* The Vicarage, 101 The Street, Boughton-under-Blean, Faversham, Kent ME13 9BG. *T:* (01227) 751410. *Club:* Faversham Farmers'.

MOWSCHENSON, Terence Rennie; QC 1995; a Recorder, since 2000; *b* 7 June 1953; *s* of Henry and Hanny Mowschenson; *m* 1992, Judith Angela Strang. *Educ:* Eagle Sch., Umtali, Rhodesia; Peterhouse, Marandellas, Rhodesia; Queen Mary Coll., London (LLB Hons 1975); Exeter Coll., Oxford (BCL Hons 1976). FCIArb. Called to the Bar, Middle Temple, 1977; Asst Recorder, 1997–2000. Chm., Barristers' Benevolent Assoc., 1999– (Hon. Sec., 1995–97, Hon. Treas., 1997–99, Benchers' Benevolent Assoc.). *Recreations:* opera, reading, travel. *Address:* Wilberforce Chambers, 8 New Square, Lincoln's Inn, WC2A 3QP. *T:* (020) 7306 0102. *Club:* Royal Automobile.

MOXON, Rt Rev. David John; *see* Waikato, Bishop of.

MOXON, Prof. (Edward) Richard, FRCP; Action Research Professor of Paediatrics, University of Oxford, since 1984; Fellow, Jesus College, Oxford, since 1984; Head, Molecular Infectious Diseases Group, Institute of Molecular Medicine, John Radcliffe Hospital, Oxford, since 1988; Founder and Chairman, Oxford Vaccine Group, since 1994; *b* 16 July 1941; *s* of late Gerald Richard Moxon and of Margaret Forster Mohun; *m* 1973, Marianne Graham; two *s* one *d*. *Educ:* Shrewsbury Sch.; St John's Coll., Cambridge (Keasby Award, 1961; BA 1963); St Thomas' Hosp. (MB, BChir 1966); MA Oxon 1984. MRCP 1968, FRCP 1984; FRCPCH 1997. Surgical House Officer, Kent and Canterbury Hosp., 1966; Medical House Officer, Peace Meml Hosp., Watford, 1966; Pathologist, St Thomas' Hosp., 1967; Sen. House Officer in Paediatrics: Whittington Hosp., 1968; Hosp. for Sick Children, Gt Ormond St, 1969; Children's Hosp. Medical Center, Boston, Mass, USA: Asst Resident in Pediatrics, 1970; Res. Fellow in Infectious Diseases Div., 1971–74; Johns Hopkins Hosp., Baltimore, Md, USA: Asst Prof. in Pediatrics, 1974–80; Associate Prof. in Pediatrics, 1980–84; Chief, Eudowood Div. of Pediatric Infectious Diseases, 1982–84. Vis. Scientist, Washington Univ., St Louis, 1990–91; Burroughs-Wellcome Vis. Prof., Allegheny Univ. of Health Scis, Philadelphia, 1999. Lectures: Mitchell, RCP, 1992; Blackfan, Children's Hosp. Med. Center, Boston, Mass, 1994; Teale, RCP, 1998; Dolman, Univ. of BC, 1999. Convenor, BPA Immunology and Infectious Diseases Gp, 1984–89; Chm., MRC Sub-Cttee, Polysaccharide Vaccines, 1986–90; Member: Steering Gp, Encapsulated Bacteria, WHO, 1987–93. Amer. Soc. Clinical Investigation. Founder FMedSci 1998; Fellow, Infectious Diseases Soc. of America. *Publications:* (with D. Isaacs): Neonatal Infections, 1991; A Practical Approach to Pediatric Infectious Diseases, 1996; Longman Handbook of Neonatal Infections, 1999; contribs to: Mandell's Principles and Practice of Infectious Diseases, 2nd edn 1985, 4th edn 1995; Forfar and Arneil's Textbook of Paediatrics, 4th edn 1992, 5th edn 1998; Oxford Textbook of Medicine, 3rd edn 1996, 4th edn 2000; editorial adviser: Lancet's Modern Vaccines, 1991; Lancet's Vaccine Octet, 1997; Yu, Merigan, Barrière, Antimicrobial Therapy and Vaccines, 1998; Stearns' Evolution in Health and Disease, 1998; many articles in learned jls on molecular microbiol., paediatric vaccines and infectious diseases, esp. relating to *Haemophilus influenzae* and *Neisseria meningitidis*. *Recreations:* tennis, music. *Address:* 17 Moreton Road, Oxford OX2 7AX.

MOXON, Very Rev. Michael Anthony, LVO 1998; Dean and Rector of St Mary's Cathedral, Truro, since 1998; *b* 23 Jan. 1942; *s* of Rev. Canon Charles Moxon and Phyllis Moxon; *m* 1969, Sarah-Jane Cresswell; twin *s* one *d*. *Educ:* Merchant Taylors' Sch., Northwood, Mddx; Durham Univ.; Salisbury Theol Coll.; Heythrop Coll., London (BD 1978; MA 1996). Deacon, 1970; priest, 1971; Curate, Lowestoft gp of parishes, 1970–74; Minor Canon, St Paul's Cathedral, 1974–81; Sacrist of St Paul's, 1977–81; Warden of Coll. of Minor Canons, 1979–81; Vicar of Tewkesbury with Walton Cardiff, 1981–90; Canon, 1990–98, Canon Steward, 1994–97, Canon Treas., 1997–98, St George's Chapel, Windsor; Chaplain in Windsor Great Park, 1990–98. Chaplain to the Queen, 1986–98. Member: Gen. Synod of C of E, 1985–90; Council for the Care of Churches, 1986–90. Chaplain, HQ Cornwall County Fire Brigade, 1998–. *Recreations:* music, reading, cricket. *Address:* The Deanery, Lemon Street, Truro, Cornwall TR1 2PE. *T:* (01872) 272661.

MOXON BROWNE, Robert William; QC 1990; a Recorder, since 1991; a Deputy Judge of the Technology and Construction Court (formerly Deputy Official Referee), since 1992; a Deputy Judge of the High Court, since 1999; *b* 26 June 1946; *s* of Kendall Edward Moxon Browne and Sheila Heron Moxon Browne; *m* 1968, Kerstin Elizabet Warne; one *s* one *d*. *Educ:* Gordonstoun School; University College, Oxford (BA). Called to the Bar, Gray's Inn, 1969; specialises in commercial and insurance law in London and on Western Circuit. *Recreations:* walking, gardening, wine. *Address:* 2 Temple Gardens, EC4Y 9AY. *T:* (020) 7822 1200.

MOYERS, Bill D.; journalist; Executive Editor, Public Affairs Television Inc., since 1987; *b* 5 June 1934; *s* of John Henry Moyers and Ruby Moyers (*née* Johnson); *m* 1954, Judith Suzanne Davidson; two *s* one *d*. *Educ:* High Sch., Marshall, Texas; Univ. of Texas; Univ. of Edinburgh; Southwestern Theological Seminary. BJ 1956; MDiv 1959. Personal Asst to Senator Lyndon B. Johnson, 1959–60; Executive Asst, 1960; US Peace Corps: Associate

Dir, 1961–63; Dep. Dir, 1963. Special Asst to President Johnson, 1963–66; Press Sec., 1965–67; Publisher of Newsday, Long Island, 1967–70; Exec. Ed., Bill Moyers' Jl, Public Broadcasting Service, 1971–76, 1978–81; editor and chief reporter, CBS Reports, 1976–79; Sen. News Analyst, CBS Evening News, 1981–86. Contributing Editor, Newsweek Magazine. Pres., Florence and John Schumann Foundn. Over thirty Emmy Awards, incl. most outstanding broadcaster, 1974; Lowell Medal, 1975; ABA Gavel Award for distinguished service to American system of law, 1974; ABA Cert. of Merit, 1975; Awards for The Fire Next Door: Monte Carlo TV Festival Grand Prize, Jurors Prize and Nymph Award, 1977; Robert F. Kennedy Journalism Grand Prize, 1978, 1988; Christopher Award, 1978; Sidney Hillman Prize for Distinguished Service, 1978, 1981, 1987; Distinguished Urban Journalism Award, Nat. Urban Coalition, 1978; George Polk Award, 1981, 1987; Alfred I. du Pont—Columbia Univ. Award, 1981, 1987, 1988, 1991, 2000; Peabody Award, 1977, 1981, annually 1986–89, 1999, 2000; Overseas Press Award, 1986; Regents Medal of Excellence, 1992; Walter Cronkite Award for Excellence in Journalism, 1995; Nelson Mandela Award for Health and Human Rights, 1996; Charles Frankel Prize in the Humanities, NEH, 1996. *Publications:* Listening to America, 1971; Report from Philadelphia, 1987; The Secret Government, 1988; Joseph Campbell and the Power of Myth, 1988; A World of Ideas, 1989, 2nd edn 1990; Healing and the Mind, 1993; Language of Life, 1995; Genesis, 1996; Fooling With Words, 1999. *Address:* (office) 450 West 33rd Street, New York, NY 10001, USA.

MOYES, James Christopher; Founder and Director, Momart Ltd, Fine Arts Services and Shipping Co., 1971–2000; working artist in all media; *b* 29 April 1943; *s* of Albert Jack Moyes and Catherine Louise Moyes; *m* 1st, 1969, Elizabeth McKee (marr. diss. 1981); one *d*; 2nd, 1987, Joanna Margaret Price (marr. diss. 2000); two *d. Educ:* Univ. of Kent (BA); Slade Sch. of Art (MA 1999). Visiting Lecturer: Essex Univ., 1988–; UEA, 1988–; Associate Vis. Lectr in Mus. Studies, Leicester Univ., 1990–. Vice Chm., Contemporary Arts Soc., 1996–99. Royal Warrant Holder, 1993 (re-assigned to Momart 1999). *Recreation:* rowing. *Address:* Studio #4, Ropewalk Mews, 118 Middleton Road, E8 4LP. *Club:* Quintin Boat.

MOYES, Lt-Comdr Kenneth Jack, MBE (mil.) 1960; RN retd; Under-Secretary, Department of Health and Social Security, 1975–78; *b* 13 June 1918; *s* of Charles Wilfrid and Daisy Hilda Moyes; *m* 1943, Norma Ellen Outred Hillier; one *s* two *d. Educ:* Portsmouth Northern Grammar Sch. FCIS. Royal Navy, 1939–63. Principal, Dept of Health and Social Security, 1963; Asst Secretary, 1970. *Recreations:* gardening, bridge. *Address:* Garden House, Darwin Road, Birchington, Kent CT7 9JL. *T:* (01843) 842015.

MOYLAN-JONES, Rear-Adm. Roger Charles, CEng, FIMechE; Director General Aircraft (Navy), 1992–95; *b* 18 April 1940; *s* of Brian Percy Jameson Moylan-Jones and Louie-Mae (*née* Brown); *m* 1961, Mary Howells; two *s* one *d. Educ:* King Edward VI Grammar Sch., Totnes; BRNC, Dartmouth; RNEC, Manadon (BSc Eng 1964). CEng, FIMechE 1990. Joined BRNC Dartmouth, 1958; service in 766, 890, 360 Sqdns and HMS Ark Royal, 1965–69; HMS Ganges, 1969–71; Air Engineering Officer, 706 Sqdn and 819 Sqdn; Staff of Flag Officer Carriers and Amphibious Ships, 1971–77; ndc 1978; Staff of: Flag Officer, Naval Air Comd, 1979–80; Dep. Chief of Defence Staff (OR), 1981–82; CSO to FONAC, 1983–84; Capt., HMS Daedalus, 1984–86; RCDS 1987; Director: Aircraft Support Policy (Navy), 1988–89; Naval Manning and Trng (Engrg), 1989–91. Capt., RN and Combined Services CC, 1969–73, 1982, 1983; Pres., RNCC, 1993–95 (Chm., 1985–89; Life Vice Pres., 1995). Chm., Devon CCC and Devon Cricket Bd, 1997–; Mem., ECB Mgt Bd, 2000–; Dir, ECB Ltd, 2000–. *Recreations:* cricket, golf. *Clubs:* Army and Navy, MCC; I Zingari, Free Foresters, Forty.

MOYLE, Rt Hon. Roland (Dunstan); PC 1978; barrister-at-law; Deputy Chairman, Police Complaints Authority, 1985–91; *b* 12 March 1928; *s* of late Baron Moyle, CBE; *m* 1956, Shelagh Patricia Hogan; one *s* one *d. Educ:* Infants' and Jun. Elem. Schs, Bexleyheath, Kent; County Sch., Llanidloes, Mont.; UCW Aberystwyth (LLB); Trinity Hall, Cambridge (MA, LLM). Called to the Bar, Gray's Inn, 1954. Commnd in Royal Welch Fusiliers, 1949–51. Legal Dept, Wales Gas Bd, 1953–56; Industrial Relations Executive with Gas Industry, 1956–62, and Electricity Supply Industry, 1962–66. MP (Lab) Lewisham N, 1966–74, Lewisham E, 1974–83; PPS to Chief Secretary to the Treasury, 1966–69, to Home Secretary, 1969–70; opposition spokesman on higher educn and science, 1972–74; Parly Sec., MAFF, 1974; Minister of State: NI Dept, 1974–76; for Health, 1976–79; opposition spokesman on health, 1979–80; deputy foreign affairs spokesman, 1980–83; opposition spokesman on defence and disarmament, 1983. Mem., Select Cttee on Race Relations and Immigration, 1968–72; Vice-Chm., PLP Defence Group, 1968–72; Sec., 1971–74, Mem. Exec. Cttee, 1968–83, British Amer. Parly Gp. *Recreation:* pottering. *Address:* 139 Lee Park, Blackheath, SE3 9HE.

MOYNE, 3rd Baron *cr* 1932, of Bury St Edmunds; **Jonathan Bryan Guinness;** *b* 16 March 1930; *s* of 2nd Baron Moyne and of Hon. Diana (*née* Mitford, now Hon. Lady Mosley); *S* father, 1992; *m* 1st, 1951, Ingrid Wyndham (marr. diss. 1962); two *s* one *d*; 2nd, 1964, Suzanne Phillips (*née* Lisney); one *s* one *d. Educ:* Eton; Oxford (MA, Mod. Langs). Journalist at Reuters, 1953–56. Merchant Banker: trainee at Erlangers Ltd, 1956–59, and at Philip Hill, 1959–62; Exec. Dir, 1962–64, non-exec. Dir, 1964–91, Leopold Joseph; Dir, Arthur Guinness Son & Co. Ltd, 1961–88. CC Leicestershire, 1970–74; Chairman, Monday Club, 1972–74. *Publications:* (with Catherine Guinness) The House of Mitford, 1984; Shoe: the odyssey of a sixties survivor, 1989; Requiem for a Family Business, 1997. *Heir: s* Hon. Jasper Jonathan Richard Guinness [*b* 9 March 1954; *m* 1985, Camilla Alexandra, *d* of Robie David Corbett Uniacke; two *d*]. *Club:* Beefsteak.

See also Hon. D. W. Guinness, Lord Neidpath.

MOYNIHAN, family name of **Baron Moynihan**.

MOYNIHAN, 4th Baron *cr* 1929, of Leeds, co. York; **Colin Berkeley Moynihan;** Bt 1922; Founding Partner, CMA Consultants, since 1994; Director: Ranger Oil & Gas, since 1995; Rowan Companies Inc., since 1996; Independent Power Corporation plc, since 1996; *b* 13 Sept. 1955; *s* of 2nd Baron Moynihan, OBE, TD, and of June Elizabeth (who *m* 1965, N. B. Hayman), *d* of Arthur Stanley Hopkins; *S* half-brother, 1997; *m* 1992, Gaynor-Louise Metcalf; two *s* one *d. Educ:* Monmouth Sch. (Music Scholar); University Coll., Oxford (BA PPE 1977, MA 1982). Pres., Oxford Union Soc., 1976. Personal Asst to Chm., Tate & Lyle Ltd, 1978–80; Manager, Tate & Lyle Agribusiness, resp. for marketing strategy and develt finance, 1980–82; Chief Exec., 1982–83, Chm., 1983–87, Ridgways Tea and Coffee Merchants; external consultant, Tate & Lyle PLC, 1983–87. MP (C) Lewisham East, 1983–92; contested (C) Lewisham East, 1992. Political Asst to the Foreign Sec., 1983; PPS to Minister of Health, 1985, to Paymaster General, 1985–87; Parly Under Sec. of State (Minister for Sport), DoE, 1987–90; Parly Under-Sec. of State, Dept of Energy, 1990–92. Chm., All-Party Parly Gp on Afghanistan, 1986; Vice Chm., Cons. Food and Drinks Sub-Cttee, 1983–85; Sec. Cons. Foreign and Commonwealth Affairs Cttee, 1983–85. Member: Paddington Conservative Management Cttee, 1980–81; Bow Group, 1978–92 (Mem., Industry Cttee, 1978–79, 1985–87); Chm., Trade & Industry Standing Cttee, 1983–87. Elected Mem., H of L, 1999. Mem. Council, Royal Commonwealth Soc., 1980–82. Pres., British Wind Energy Assoc., 1995–. Hon. Sec., Friends of B… Chm., Sydney … 1982–85; Major Sp… Sponsorship of Sport, 1… Oxford Univ. Boat Club, … Women's Boat Club Assoc., … 1980–82. Oxford Double Blue, … for Lightweight Rowing, Internat… Rowing, 1980; World Silver Medal for … Liveryman, Worshipful Co. of Haberdas… Books, music, sport. *Heir: s* Hon. Nicholas E… *Clubs:* Brooks's; Leander (Henley-on-Thames); …

MOYNIHAN, Daniel Patrick; US Senator from New … Oklahoma, 16 March 1927; *s* of John Henry and Margare… 1955, Elizabeth Brennan; two *s* one *d. Educ:* City Coll., NY; … of Law and Diplomacy. MA, PhD. Gunnery Officer, US Navy, … Relations, Internat. Rescue Cttee, 1954; successively Asst to Sec., Asst … to Governor of NY State, 1955–58; Mem., NY Tenure Commn, 1959–60; … Govt Res. Project, Syracuse Univ., 1959–61; Special Asst to Sec. of Labor, … Exec. Asst to Sec., 1962–63, Asst Sec. of Labor, 1963–65; Dir, Jt Center Urban Stud… MIT and Harvard Univ., 1966–69; Prof. of Govt, 1972–77 and Senior Mem., 1966–77, Harvard (Prof. of Education and Urban Politics, 1966–73). Asst to Pres. of USA for Urban Affairs, 1969–70; Counsellor to Pres. (with Cabinet rank), 1969–70; Consultant to Pres., 1971–73; US Ambassador to India, 1973–75; US Permanent Rep. to the UN and Mem. of Cabinet, 1975–76. Ranking Minority Mem., Senate Finance Cttee; Member, Senate Committees: Rules, Envmt and Public Works, (jt) Taxation and Library. Chm., Commn on Protecting and Reducing Govt Secrecy, 1995–97. Member: US delegn 26th Gen. Assembly, UN, 1971; President's Sci. Adv. Cttee, 1971–73. Mem., Usage Panel, Amer. Heritage Coll. Dictionary, 1968–. Member: Amer. Philosophical Soc.; AAAS (formerly Vice-Pres.); Nat. Acad. Public Admin; Fellow, Amer. Acad. Arts and Scis. Hon. Fellow, London Sch. of Economics, 1970. Holds numerous hon. degrees. Meritorius Service Award, US Dept of Labor, 1965; Internat. League for Human Rights Award, 1975; John LaFarge Award for Interracial Justice, 1980; Hubert Humphrey Award, Amer. Pol Sci. Assoc., 1983; Medallion, State Univ. of NY at Albany, 1984; Henry Medal, Smithsonian Instn, 1985; Seal Medallion, CIA, 1986; Meml Sloan-Kettering Cancer Center Medal, 1986; Britannica Award, 1986; AIA Award, 1992; Laetare Medal, Notre Dame Univ., 1992; Thomas Jefferson Medal, Amer. Philosophical Soc., 1993. *Publications:* (co-author) Beyond the Melting Pot, 1963; (ed) The Defenses of Freedom, 1966; (ed) On Understanding Poverty, 1969; Maximum Feasible Misunderstanding, 1969; (ed) Toward a National Urban Policy, 1970; (jt ed) On Equality of Educational Opportunity, 1972; The Politics of a Guaranteed Income, 1973; Coping: On the Practice of Government, 1974; (jt ed) Ethnicity: Theory and Experience, 1975; A Dangerous Place, 1979; Counting Our Blessings, 1980; Loyalties, 1984; Family and Nation, 1986; Came the Revolution, 1988; On the Law of Nations, 1990; Pandaemonium: ethnicity in international politics, 1993; Miles to Go: a personal history of social policy, 1996; Secrecy: the American experience, 1998. *Address:* c/o United States Senate, Washington, DC 20510, USA. *Clubs:* Century, Harvard (NYC); Federal City (Washington).

MOYNIHAN, Martin John, CMG 1972; MC; HM Diplomatic Service, retired; *b* 17 Feb. 1916; *e s* of late William John Moynihan and Phebe Alexander; *m* 1946, Monica Hopwood; one *s* one *d. Educ:* Birkenhead Sch.; Magdalen Coll., Oxford (MA). India Office, 1939. Punjab Frontier Force, IA, N-W Frontier and Burma, 1940–45. Commonwealth Service: Delhi, Madras, Bombay and London, 1946–54; Deputy High Commissioner: Peshawar, 1954–56; Lahore, 1956–58; Kuala Lumpur, 1961–63; Port of Spain, 1964–66; HM Consul-General, Philadelphia, 1966–70; Ambassador to Liberia, 1970–73; High Comr in Lesotho, 1973–76. Administering Officer, Kennedy Meml Trust, 1977–79. Mem., Council, Hakluyt Soc., 1976–90. Associate Mem. in S African Studies, Clare Hall, Cambridge, 1977–78. Hon. Knight Grand Band of Humane Order of African Redemption (Liberia), 1973. *Publications:* The Strangers, 1946; South of Fort Hertz, 1956; The Latin Letters of C. S. Lewis, 1987; Letters: C. S. Lewis and Don Giovanni Calabria, 1988. *Address:* 5 The Green, Wimbledon Common, SW19 5AZ. *T:* (020) 8946 7964. *Clubs:* Athenæum, Travellers.

MOYOLA, Baron *cr* 1971 (Life Peer), of Castledawson; **James Dawson Chichester-Clark;** PC (Northern Ireland) 1966; DL; *b* 12 Feb. 1923; *s* of late Capt. J. L. C. Chichester-Clark, DSO and bar, DL, MP, and Mrs C. E. Brackenbury; *m* 1959, Moyra Maud Haughton (*née* Morris); two *d* one step *s. Educ:* Eton. Entered Army, 1942; 2nd Lieut Irish Guards, Dec. 1942; wounded, Italy, 1944; ADC to Governor-General of Canada (Field-Marshal Earl Alexander of Tunis), 1947–49; attended Staff Coll., Camberley, 1956; retired as Major, 1960. MP (U), S Derry, NI Parlt, 1960–72; Asst Whip, March 1963; Chief Whip, 1963–67; Leader of the House, 1966–67; Min. of Agriculture, 1967–69; Prime Minister, 1969–71. County Derry: DL 1954; Vice Lieut, 1975–93. *Recreations:* shooting, fishing, ski-ing. *Address:* Moyola Park, Castledawson, Co. Derry, N Ireland BT45 8ED.

See also Sir R. Chichester-Clark, P. Hobhouse.

MPALANYI-NKOYOYO, Most Rev. Livingstone; *see* Uganda, Archbishop of.

MPUCHANE, Samuel Akuna; in business in Botswana, since 1991; *b* 15 Dec. 1943; *s* of Chiminya Thompson Mpuchane and Motshidiemang Phologolo; *m* Sisai Felicity Mokgokong; two *s* one *d. Educ:* Univ. of Botswana, Lesotho and Swaziland (BA Govt and Hist.); Southampton Univ. (MSc Internat. Affairs). External Affairs Officer, 1969–70; First Secretary: Botswana Mission to UN, 1970–71; Botswana Embassy, Washington, 1971–74; Under Sec., External Affairs, 1974–76; on study leave, 1976–77; Dep. Perm. Sec., Min. of Mineral Resources and Water Affairs, 1977–79; Admin. Sec., Office of Pres., 1979–80; Perm. Sec., Min. of Local Govt and Lands, 1980–81; High Comr for Botswana in UK, 1982–85; Perm. Sec. for External Affairs, 1986–90. Director, 1991–: Standard Chartered Bank (Botswana); Builders World; Building Materials Supplies; Royal Wholesalers; Parts World; Trade World; Blue Chip Investments; Continental Star Caterers; Botswana Power Corp. *Recreations:* playing and watching tennis, watching soccer.

MSAKA, Bright; High Commissioner of Malaŵi in the United Kingdom, and concurrently Ambassador to Finland, Norway, Portugal, Spain and Sweden, since 1998; *m* Primrose; three *c.* Practised law, specialising in commercial litigation and tort; Lectr in Law, Univ. of Malaŵi; Examr of Co. Law, ACCA. *Address:* Malaŵi High Commission, 33 Grosvenor Street, W1X 0DE.

MSIMANG, Mendi; Order for Meritorious Service (Silver Class), South Africa, 1999; Treasurer-General, African National Congress, since 1998; *b* 1928, Johannesburg; *m* Mantombazana Tshabalala; four *c* from previous *m. Educ:* University Coll. of Roma, Lesotho. Rand Steam Laundries and Organizer, Laundry Workers' Union; Asbestos Assayer, Costa Rican Consulate. Joined ANC; Personal Sec. to Sec.-Gen. Walter Sisulu;

with Nelson Mandela and Oliver Tambo's law practice, until 1960; left for UK, 1960; Rep., ANC Mission to UK and Ireland; Co-Founder, S Africa in Fact (ANC newsletter); Editor, Spotlight on S Africa (ANC jl); Admin. Sec., ANC Nat. Exec. Cttee in Exile, E Africa Br.; collaborated with Oliver Tambo to establish Solomon Mahlangu Freedom Coll., Tanzania; ANC Educn Officer; Admin. Sec. and Treas.-Gen., ANC's Office, Zambia; ANC Chief Rep. to India, 1969, to UK, 1988; returned to SA, 1990; elected Mem., ANC Parly Caucus, 1990; High Comr for S Africa in London, 1995–98. Mem., S African Adv. Council on Nat. Orders, 1998–. *Address:* PO Box 25929, Monument Park, Pretoria 0105, South Africa.

MTESA, Love; High Commissioner for Zambia in South Africa, since 1997; *b* 9 July 1942; *s* of late William Mutesa and Olive Mutesa; *m* Marie Madeleine; two *s* two *d*. *Educ:* Mercy Coll., NY (BSc Pol Sci 1985); Internat. Inst. of Public Relations, Paris (Dipl. Internat. Relations 1994); Univ. of Westminster (MA Diplomatic Studies). Teacher, Ndola, Zambia, 1962–64; 2nd Sec., Zambian Embassy, Kinshasa, 1966–70; 1st Sec., Addis Ababa, 1970–73; Counsellor, Kinshasa, 1974–75; Dir, Africa and Middle East, Foreign Affairs, Lusaka, 1975–79; Dep. High Comr, Harare, 1980–82; Dep. Perm. Rep., UN, NY, 1982–85; resigned from Govt, June 1986; Chm. of Opposition Party, Movement for Multi-Party Democracy for Lusaka Dist, 1990–92; Sec., Internat. Relations Cttee, MMD, 1991–92; High Comr for Zambia in London, 1992–97. *Recreations:* table tennis, watching soccer. *Address:* High Commission of the Republic of Zambia, PO Box 12234, Hartfield, Pretoria 0083, South Africa.

MTETEMELA, Most Rev. Donald Leo; *see* Tanzania, Archbishop of.

MUBARAK, Lt Gen. (Muhammad) Hosni, Hon. GCMG 1985; President of Egypt, since 1981 (Vice President, 1975–81; Prime Minister, 1981–82); *b* 4 May 1928; *m* Suzanne; two *s*. *Educ:* Military Acad.; Air Force Acad. Joined Egyptian Air Force, 1950; Flight Instr., 1952–59, Dir Gen., 1967–69, Air Force Acad.; COS, 1969–72, C-in-C, 1972–75, Air Force; Lt Gen. 1973. Chm., OAU, 1989–90. National Democratic Party: Vice Chm., 1976–81; Sec. Gen., 1981–82; Chm., 1982–. *Address:* Presidential Palace, Abdeen, Cairo, Egypt.

MUCH, Ian Fraser Robert; Chief Executive, De La Rue plc, since 1998; *b* 8 Sept. 1944; *s* of Alan Fraser Much and Helen Isabella Much (*née* Barker); *m* 1978, Perena Amanda Richards; two *d*. *Educ:* Haileybury and ISC; Lincoln Coll., Oxford (MA Jurisp.). The Metal Box Co., 1966–73; Selkirk Metalbestos, 1974–78; Household International Inc., 1978–84; Factory Manager, Nampa, Idaho, 1978–80; Vice-Pres., Gen. Manager, Greensboro, N Carolina, 1980–84; BTR: Man. Dir, Dunlop Aviation Div., 1985–87; Gp Chief Exec., 1987–88; Dir, BTR Industries; T & N: Exec. Dir, 1988–98; Man. Dir, Engineering & Industrial, 1990–91, Bearings and Industrial, 1991–95; Chief Exec., Ops, 1995–96; Chief Exec., 1996–98. Non-exec. Dir, Manchester United plc, 2000–. *Recreations:* ski-ing, tennis, squash, golf, swimming, bridge, theatre, opera. *Address:* De La Rue plc, De La Rue House, Jays Close, Basingstoke, Hampshire RG22 4BS.

MUDD, (William) David; consultant on tourism, transport and communications; *b* 2 June 1933; *o s* of Capt. W. N. Mudd and Mrs T. E. Mudd; *m*; one *s* one *d* (and one step *d*). *Educ:* Truro Cathedral Sch. Journalist, Broadcaster, TV Commentator; work on BBC and ITV (Westward Television). Editor of The Cornish Echo, 1952; Staff Reporter: Western Morning News, 1952–53 and 1959–62; Tavistock Gazette, 1963. Mem., Tavistock UDC, 1963–65. MP (C) Falmouth and Camborne, 1970–92. PPS, Dept of Energy, 1979–81; Mem., Transport Select Cttee, 1982–92. Secretary: Conservative West Country Cttee, 1973–76; Conservative Party Fisheries Sub-Cttee, 1974–75, 1981–82. Patron, Court Interpreters' Assoc., Supreme Court of Hong Kong, 1979–97. *Publications:* Cornishmen and True, 1971; Murder in the West Country, 1975; Facets of Crime, 1975; The Innovators, 1976; Down Along Camborne and Redruth, 1978; The Falmouth Packets, 1978; Cornish Sea Lights, 1978; Cornwall and Scilly Peculiar, 1979; About the City, 1979; Home Along Falmouth and Penryn, 1980; Around and About the Roseland, 1980; The Cruel Cornish Sea, 1981; The Cornish Edwardians, 1982; Cornwall in Uproar, 1983; Around and About the Fal, 1989; Around and About the Smugglers' Ways, 1991; Strange Stories of Cornwall, 1992; Dartmoor Reflections, 1993; The Magic of Dartmoor, 1994; Let the Doors be Lock'd, 2000. *Recreations:* jig-saw puzzles, walking, cycling. *Address:* The Retreat, Down Park Drive, Tavistock, Devon PL19 9AH.

MUDDIMAN, Brig. Noel, CBE 1992 (OBE 1985); Director, Motability, since 1995; *b* 17 Dec. 1943; *s* of Flora Muddiman (*née* Holdsworth), and step *s* of late Arthur George Muddiman; *m* 1969, Patricia Anne Sevage; two *s*. *Educ:* Borden Grammar Sch.; RMA, Sandhurst. Commnd RCT, 1965; regtl posts in Germany, UK, Singapore; Staff Coll., Camberley, 1975; ndc, 1981; CO, 25 Transport and Movements Regt, RCT, 1983–85; Head of Personnel and Logistics, Falkland Islands, 1985–86; Principal Logistic Planner, British Forces Germany, 1987–90; Commander: Transport and Movements, BAOR, 1990–92; Logistic Support Gp (ME), 1991; rcds, 1992; Comdt, Army Sch. of Transport, 1993–95, retd. FIMI 1996. Norwegian Gulf War Medal, 1995. *Publication:* (jtly) Blackadder's War, 1995. *Recreations:* gardening, walking, photography. *Address:* (office) Goodman House, Station Approach, Harlow CM20 2ET. *T:* (01279) 632010. *Club:* New Cavendish.

MUDDIMER, Robert Michael; Deputy Chairman, Tomkins plc, 1996–97 (Director, 1986–97); Chairman, Gates Rubber Co., 1996–97; *b* 30 Jan. 1933; *m* 1959, Marguerite Conroy; two *s* one *d*. *Educ:* Kibworth Grammar Sch.; Univ. of Nottingham (BSc Mech. Eng 1956). FIEE (FIMfgE 1966). Materials Mgt, Lansing Bagnall, 1965–68; Director: BTR Ind. Ltd, 1969–80; Molins Tobacco Ind. Ltd, 1981–86; Chm., Ranks Hovis McDougall, 1992–96. *Recreations:* golf, sailing, wooden clockmaking.

MUDIE, Colin Crichton, RDI 1995; CEng; FRINA, FRIN; Principal Partner, Colin Mudie, Naval Architects and Yacht Designers, since 1958; *b* 11 April 1926; *s* of John Mudie and Janet Somerville Mudie (*née* Jack); *m* 1954, Rosemary Horder; one *s*. *Educ:* George Watson's, Edinburgh; Whitgift Sch.; University Coll., Southampton. CEng 1971; FRINA 1971; FRIN 1972. Design apprentice: British Power Boat Co., Southampton, 1942–46; Laurent Giles & Partners Ltd, 1946–49; various marine projects incl. Sopranino voyage and Small World transatlantic balloon flight, 1949–58. Winston Churchill Fellowship, 1968. Design work includes sail trng vessels, reproduction, expedition and exploration boats, power boats, sailing yachts, motor cruisers, etc; designer of sail trng ship, Young Endeavour, GB's gift to Australia for 1988 Bicentennial. Member: Cttee of Mgt, RNLI, 1987–2001 (Vice-Pres., 1997–2001, now Life Vice-Pres.); Council, RINA, 1988–97. Associate Mem., Acad. de Marinha, Portugal, 1995. FRSA 1996. Award for sail trng brig Royalist, Lloyd's Register of Shipping, 1971; Small Craft Medal, RINA, 1984; Award for sail trng barque Lord Nelson, British Design Council, 1993. *Publications:* Sopranino (with P. Ellam), 1954; Motor Boats and Boating, 1972; Power Boats, 1975; with Rosemary Mudie: The Story of the Sailing Ship, 1975; Power Yachts, 1977; The Sailing Ship, 1984; Sailing Ships, 2000; contrib. papers at various symposia, and articles and illustrations to professional, yachting and other jls. *Recreations:* sailing, motor boating, model making. *Address:* Bywater Lodge, Pierside, Lymington, Hants SO41 5SB. *T:* (01590) 672047. *Clubs:* Royal Ocean Racing; Royal Lymington Yacht, Lymington Town Sailing; Ocean Cruising.

MUDIE, George Edward; MP (Lab) Leeds East, since 1992; *b* 6 Feb. 1945. *Educ:* state schs. Former Mem. (Lab) Leeds CC, and Leader of Council. Treasurer of HM Household (Dep. Chief Govt Whip), 1997–98; Parly Under-Sec. of State, DfEE, 1998–99. *Address:* House of Commons, SW1A 0AA.

MUELLBAUER, Prof. John Norbert Joseph, PhD; FBA 1997; Professor of Economics, University of Oxford, since 1997; Official Fellow in Economics, Nuffield College, Oxford, since 1981; *b* 17 July 1944; *s* of Prof. Norbert J. Muellbauer and Edith Heinz. *Educ:* King's Coll., Cambridge (MA 1965); Univ. of Calif at Berkeley (PhD 1975). Lectr in Economics, Univ. of Warwick, 1969–72; Lectr, 1972–75, Reader, 1975–77, Prof., 1977–81, in Economics, Birkbeck Coll., London Univ. Member: Gp of Outside Ind. Economists advising the Chancellor of the Exchequer, 1989; Retail Price Index Adv. Cttee, 1993–95; Fellow, Econometric Soc., 1976. Medal, Helsinki Univ., 1980. *Publications:* (with Angus Deaton) Economics and Consumer Behaviour, 1980; articles in Financial Times, Observer, Guardian, Amer. Econ. Review, Econometrica, Econ. Jl, etc. *Recreations:* music, tennis. *Address:* Nuffield College, Oxford OX1 1NF. *T:* (01865) 278583.

MUELLER, Rudolf Gottfried, Hon. CBE 1997; Chairman, WJB Chiltern Group plc (formerly Chiltern Group plc), since 1998; *b* 28 May 1934; Swiss national; *m* Christiane Béroud; two *s*. *Educ:* primary and secondary schools, St Gallen, Switzerland; Internat. Management Inst., Geneva. Swiss Fed. Commercial Dip. 1953; grad. 1969 from Univ. of Geneva with dip. equivalent to MBA. James Capel & Co., 1968–77; joined Union Bank of Switzerland, 1977: Exec. Vice-Pres. (UK), 1987–91; Exec. Vice-Pres., Europe, 1991–96; Chief Exec., 1989–93, Chm., 1989–97, UBS Ltd, later UBS Phillips & Drew Ltd, subseq. UBS–UK Gp. Chairman: Lend Lease Europe plc, 1996–; Chelverton Properties Ltd, 1998–; non-exec. Dir, Lend Lease Corp. Ltd, 1996–; TI Gp, 1996–2000. Chm., Swiss Options Financial Futures Exchange, Zürich, 1986–88; Dir, London Stock Exchange, 1991–95 (Mem., 1988). Member of Board: Internat. Management Inst., Kiev, 1993–; Royal Opera House Trust, 1992–97; Dir, Royal Opera House, 1996–98. *Recreations:* golf, ski-ing, hiking, oenology. *Address:* WJB Chiltern Group plc, Sceptre House, 169–173 Regent Street, W1R 7FB.

MUFF, family name of **Baron Calverley**.

MUGABE, Robert Gabriel; President of Zimbabwe, since 1988; President, Zimbabwe African National Union-Patriotic Front, since 1988; *b* Kutama, 1924; *m* 1961, Sarah Francesca Hayfron (*d* 1992); one *s* decd; *m* 1996, Grace Marufu; two *s* one *d*. *Educ:* Kutama Mission School; Fort Hare Univ. (BA (Educ), BSc (Econ)); London Univ. (by correspondence: BSc(Econ); BEd; LLB; LLM; MSc(Econ)); Univ. of S Africa (by correspondence BAdm). Teacher, 1942–58: Kutama, Mapanzure, Shabani, Empandeni Mission, Hope Fountain Mission, Driefontein Mission, Mbizi Govt Sch., Mambo Sch., Chalimbana Trng Coll., Zambia; St Mary's Teacher Trng Coll., Ghana. Publ. Sec. of Nat. Dem. Party, 1960–61; Publicity Sec. and acting Sec.-Gen., Zimbabwe African People's Union, 1961–62. Political detention, 1962; co-founded and became Sec.-Gen. ZANU, Aug. 1963, but in detention in Rhodesia, 1964–74; escaped to Mozambique and led armed struggle from there, 1975–79. Prime Minister 1980–87, Minister of Defence and of Public Service, 1980–84, First Sec. of Politburo, 1984–87, Zimbabwe. Jt Leader (with Joshua Nkomo) of the Patriotic Front, Oct. 1976; Pres., ZANU, 1977–87. Attended Confs: Geneva Constitutional Conf. on Rhodesia, 1976; Malta Conf., 1978; Lancaster House Conf., 1979. Holds hon. degrees from many instns. *Address:* Office of the President, Private Bag 7700, Causeway, Harare, Zimbabwe.

MUGNOZZA, Carlo S.; *see* Scarascia-Mugnozza.

MUHEIM, Franz Emmanuel; President, Swiss Red Cross, since 1996; Vice-President, International Federation of Red Cross and Red Crescent Societies, since 1996; Swiss Ambassador to the Court of St James's, 1989–94; *b* 27 Sept. 1931; *s* of Hans Muheim and Hélène (*née* Ody); *m* 1962, Radmila Jovanovic. *Educ:* Univs of Fribourg (LèsL), Geneva and Paris (arts degree). Joined Swiss Federal Dept of Foreign Affairs, 1960; served successively in Belgrade, Rabat and London, 1961–70; Council of Europe, UN and Internat. Orgns Sect., Dept of Foreign Affairs, Berne, 1971–77; Dep. Head of Mission, Minister Plenipotentiary, Washington, 1978–81; Dep. Dir of Political Affairs and Head of Political Div. Europe and N America, with rank of Ambassador, Berne, 1982–83; Dir, Internat. Orgns, Dept of Foreign Affairs, 1984–89. Head of Swiss delegns to internat. confs, *inter alia* UNESCO, ESA, Red Cross, Non-Aligned Movement. Fellow, Center for Internat. Affairs, Harvard Univ., 1981–82; Prof., Bologna Center, Johns Hopkins Univ., 1995–96. *Publication:* (ed jtly) Einblick in die Schweizerische Aussenpolitik: festschrift für Staatssekretär Raymond Probst, 1984; Multilateralism Today: festchrift zum 70. Geburtstag von a. Ständerat Franz Muheim, 1993. *Recreations:* walking, mountaineering, ski-ing, photography, music. *Address:* Es Chesaux, 1646 Echarlens, Switzerland. *T:* (026) 9152474, *Fax:* (026) 9152450.

MUIR, Prof. Alexander Laird, MD; FRCPE, FRCR, FRCSE; Professor of Postgraduate Medicine, University of Edinburgh, 1993–99; Honorary Consultant Physician, Edinburgh Royal Infirmary, 1974–99; Honorary Physician to the Army in Scotland, 1986–99; *b* 12 April 1937; *s* of Andrew Muir and Helena Bauld; *m* 1968, Berenice Barker Snelgrove, FRCR; one *s* one *d*. *Educ:* Morrisons Acad.; Fettes Coll.; Univ. of Edinburgh. MB ChB; MD 1970; FRCPE 1975 (MRCPE 1967); FRCR 1986; FRCSE 1994. MO, British Antarctic Survey, 1963–65; MRC Fellow, McGill Univ., 1970–71; Consultant Physician, Manchester Royal Infirmary, 1973–74; Edinburgh University: Sen. Lectr in Medicine, 1974; Reader in Medicine, 1981–89; Postgrad. Dean of Medicine, 1990–99. Physician to the Queen in Scotland, 1985–96. Canadian MRC Vis. Scientist, Univ. of British Columbia, 1982. Chm. and Med. Dir, Jt Cttee for Higher Med. Trng, 1998–; Mem., Admin of Radioactive Substances Adv. Cttee, 1986–91. Vice-Pres., RCPE, 1994–97. Founder FMedSci 1998. Member Editorial Board: Thorax, 1981–86; British Heart Jl, 1986–90. *Publications:* contribs on physiology and diseases of heart and lungs to medical books, symposia and jls. *Recreations:* gardening, reading, ski-ing, sailboarding. *Address:* 31/9 Hermitage Drive, Edinburgh EH10 6BY.

MUIR, (Isabella) Helen (Mary), CBE 1981; MA, DPhil, DSc; FRS 1977; Director, Kennedy Institute of Rheumatology, London, 1977–90 (Head of Division of Biochemistry, 1966–86); *b* 20 Aug. 1920; *d* of late G. B. F. Muir, ICS, and Gwladys Muir (*née* Stack). *Educ:* Downe House, Newbury; Somerville Coll., Oxford (Hon. Fellow, 1978). MA 1944, DPhil (Oxon) 1947, DSc (Oxon) 1973. Research Fellow, Dunn's Sch. of Pathology, Oxford, 1947–48; Scientific Staff, Nat. Inst. for Med. Research, 1948–54; Empire Rheumatism Council Fellow, St Mary's Hosp., London, 1954–58; Pearl Research Fellow, St Mary's Hosp., 1959–66; Visiting Professor: Queen Elizabeth Coll., Univ. of London, 1981–85; Newcastle Univ.; Manchester Univ., 1997–. Hon. Prof., Charing Cross and Westminster Med. Sch., 1979–. Scientific Mem. Council, Med. Research

Council (first woman to serve), Oct. 1973–Sept. 1977. Mem., Connective Tissue Res. Adv. Bd, 1971–85; Governor, Strangeways Res. Lab., 1980–90; Trustee, Wellcome Trust, 1982–90. Heberden Orator, London, 1976; Bunim Lectr, US Arthritis Assoc., New Orleans, 1978. Member, Editorial Board: Biochemical Jl, 1964–69; Annals of the Rheumatic Diseases, 1971–77; Connective Tissue Res., 1971–85; Jl of Orthopaedic Res., 1983–. For. Mem., Royal Swedish Acad. of Scis, 1989; Honorary Member: Amer. Soc. of Biological Chemists, 1982; European Soc. of Arthrology, 1988. Hon. DSc: Edinburgh, 1982; Strathclyde, 1983; Brunel, 1990. Feldberg Foundn Award, 1977; Neil Hamilton Fairley Medal, RCP, 1981; Ciba Medal, Biochem. Soc., 1981; Steindler Award, Orthop. Soc., USA, 1982; Ciba Internat. Award, 1993. *Publications:* many scientific papers, mainly on biochem. of connective tissues in reln to arthritis and inherited diseases in Biochem. Jl, Biochim. et Biophys. Acta, Nature, etc; contribs to several specialist books. *Recreations:* gardening, music, horses, natural history and science in general. *Address:* Langlands House, Hornby, Bedale, N Yorks DL8 1NG. *T:* (01677) 450307; School of Biological Sciences, University of Manchester, Stopford Building, Oxford Road, Manchester M13 9PT. *T:* (0161) 275 5074.

MUIR, Sir Laurence (Macdonald), Kt 1981; VRD 1954; company director; Deputy Chairman, National Science and Technology Centre Advisory Committee, 1986–96; Founding Chairman, Canberra Development Board, 1979–86; *b* 3 March 1925; *s* of Andrew Muir and Agnes Campbell Macdonald; two *s* two *d*. *Educ:* Yallourn State Sch.; Scotch Coll., Melbourne; Univ. of Melbourne (LLB). Served RAN, 1942–46 (Lieut); Lt-Comdr, RANR, 1949–65. Admitted Barrister and Solicitor, Supreme Court of Victoria, 1950. Sharebroker, 1950–80; Mem., Stock Exchange of Melbourne, 1960–80; Partner, 1962–80, Sen. Partner, 1976–80, Potter Partners. Director: ANZ Banking Gp, 1980–91; ACI Internat. Ltd (formerly ACI Ltd), 1980–88; Nat. Commercial Union Assce Co. of Aust. Ltd (formerly Commercial Union Assce Co. of Aust.), 1979–91; Wormald Internat. Ltd, 1980–88; Herald and Weekly Times Ltd, 1982–87; ANZ Pensions Ltd, 1982–91; Alcoa of Australia Ltd, 1982–96; Hudson Conway Ltd (formerly Australian Asset Management Ltd), 1987–2000; Templeton Global Growth Fund, 1987–99; Greening Australia, 1985–90; Australian Consolidated Press Group, subseq. Publishing and Broadcasting Ltd, 1992–; Mem. Bd, Focus Books Pty Ltd, 1990–; Chairman: Aust. Biomedical Corp. Ltd, 1983–87; Liquid Air Australia Ltd, 1982–95; Elders Austral Chartering Pty Ltd, 1984–90; University Paton Ltd, 1986–90. Chm., John Curtin Sch. of Medical Res. Adv. Bd, 1982–88; Member: Parlt House Construction Authority (Chm., Artworks Adv. Cttee), 1979–89; Council, Gen. Motors, Aust., 1977–94; L'Air Liquide World Adv. Cttee, 1983–95; Victoria Garden State Cttee; Vic. Appeals Cttee, Anti-Cancer Council; Commn for the Future, 1991–; Consultant, Alfred Hosp. Bd, 1983–88. Patron: Baker Med. Res. Inst.; Microsurgery Foundn; Earthwatch Australia; Trustee and Bd Mem., Sir Robert Menzies Meml Trust, 1984–96; Founder and Trustee, Delta Soc. Aust.; Trustee, Aust. Scout Educn & Trng Foundn; Life Trustee, Cttee for Economic Develt of Aust. Mem. Exec. Cttee, World Athletic Cup 1985; Council Mem., HRH Duke of Edinburgh's 6th Commonwealth Study Conf. (Chm., Aust. Finance Cttee). Fellow: Securities Inst. of Australia, 1962; Australian Inst. of Dirs, 1967; FAIM 1965. *Recreations:* gardening, walking. *Address:* Unit 3, 61 Black Street, Brighton, Vic 3186, Australia. *Clubs:* Melbourne, Melbourne Cricket (Melbourne); Frankston Golf.

MUIR, (Sir) Richard James Kay, (4th Bt *cr* 1892, of Deanston, Perthshire); *S* father, 1994, but does not use the title; *b* 25 May 1939; *s* of Sir John Harling Muir, 3rd Bt, TD and of Elizabeth Mary, *e d* of Frederick James Dundas; *m* 1st, 1965, Susan Elizabeth (marr. diss. 1974), *d* of George A. Gardener; two *d*; 2nd, 1975, Lady Linda Mary Cole, *d* of 6th Earl of Enniskillen, MBE; two *d*. *Heir: b* Ian Charles Muir [*b* 16 Sept. 1940; *m* 1967, Fiona Barbara Elspeth, *d* of Major Stuart Mackenzie; three *d*].

MUIR, Richard John Sutherland, CMG 1994; HM Diplomatic Service; Ambassador to Kuwait, since 1999; *b* 25 Aug. 1942; *s* of John Muir and Edna (*née* Hodges); *m* 1966, Caroline Simpson; one *s* one *d*. *Educ:* The Stationers' Co.'s Sch.; Univ. of Reading (BA Hons). Entered HM Diplomatic Service, 1964; FO, 1964–65; MECAS, Lebanon, 1965–67; Third, then Second Sec. (Commercial), Jedda, 1967–70; Second Sec., Tunis, 1970–72; FCO, 1972–75; First Sec., Washington, 1975–79; seconded to Dept of Energy, 1979–81; Dir-Gen., British Liaison Office, Riyadh, 1981–85; FCO 1985–94: Hd of Information Dept, 1987–90; Principal Finance Officer and Chief Inspector, 1991–94; Ambassador to Oman, 1994–99. *Address:* c/o Foreign and Commonwealth Office, SW1A 2AH.

MUIR, Tom; trade and economic consultant, since 1997; Under Secretary, Textiles and Retailing Division, Department of Trade and Industry, 1992–94; *b* 15 Feb. 1936; *s* of late William and Maria Muir; *m* 1968, Brenda Dew; one *s* one *d*. *Educ:* King Edward VI Sch., Stafford; Leeds Univ. (BA Econs 1962). FCIS 1994. English Electric Co. Ltd, 1954–59; BoT, 1962–68; UK Perm. Delegn to OECD (on secondment to HM Diplomatic Service), 1968–71; DTI, 1972–75; UK Perm. Repn to EC, 1975–79 (on secondment); DoI, 1979–81; Dept of Trade, 1981–83; DTI, 1983–94: Under Sec., Insce Div., 1982–87, Overseas Trade Div. 4, 1987–89, Ext. European Policy, later Internat. Trade Policy Div., 1989–92. Dir, British Retail Consortium, 1995–97. Staff, Competition Commn, 1999–. Chm., Fedn of British Artists (Mall Galls), 1998–2001. FRSA 1992. *Recreations:* walking, reading, looking at buildings and pictures, opera. *Address:* Westhanger Tower, Westbrook Road, Godalming, Surrey GU7 2QH.

MUIR MACKENZIE, Sir Alexander (Alwyne Henry Charles Brinton), 7th Bt *cr* 1805; *b* 8 Dec. 1955; *s* of Sir Robert Henry Muir Mackenzie, 6th Bt and Charmian Cecil de Vere (*d* 1962), *o d* of Col Cecil Charles Brinton; *S* father, 1970; *m* 1984, Susan Carolyn, *d* of John David Henzel Hayter; one *s* one d. *Educ:* Eton; Trinity Coll., Cambridge. *Heir: s* Archie Robert David Muir Mackenzie, *b* 17 Feb. 1989. *Address:* New House Farm, Lydlinch, Sturminster Newton, Dorset DT10 2JB.

MUIR WOOD, Sir Alan (Marshall), Kt 1982; FRS 1980; FREng, FICE; Consultant, Halcrow Group (Partner, 1964–84, Senior Partner, 1979–84, Sir William Halcrow & Partners); *b* 8 Aug. 1921; *s* of Edward Stephen Wood and Dorothy (*née* Webb); *m* 1943, Winifred Leyton Lanagan, (Dr W. L. Wood, mathematician); three *s*. *Educ:* Abbotsholme Sch.; Peterhouse, Cambridge Univ. (MA; Hon. Fellow 1982). FICE 1957. Engr Officer, RN, 1942–46. Asst Engr, British Rail, Southern Reg., 1946–50; Res. Asst, Docks and Inland Waterways Exec., 1950–52; Asst Engr, then Sen. Engr, Sir William Halcrow & Partners, 1952–64. Principally concerned with studies and works in fields of tunnelling, geotechnics, coastal engrg, energy, roads and railways; major projects include: (Proj. Engr) Clyde Tunnel and Potters Bar railway tunnels; (Partner) Cargo Tunnel at Heathrow Airport, and Cuilfail Tunnel, Lewes; studies and works for Channel Tunnel (intermittently, 1958–98); Dir, Orange-Fish Consultants, resp. for 80 km irrigation tunnel. Member: ACARD, 1980–84; SERC, 1981–84; Governing Body, Inst. of Development Studies, 1981–87; Council, ITDG, 1981–84; Chairman: SERC/ESRC Jt Cttee, 1983–85; Res. Councils Individual Merit Promotion Panel, 1989–94. Mem. Council, Royal Soc., 1983–84, a Vice-Pres., 1983–84; President: Internat. Tunnelling Assoc., 1975–77 (Hon. Life Pres., 1977); ICE, 1977–78; FREng (FEng 1977; a Vice-Pres., 1984–87). FIC 1981. Foreign Member, Royal Swedish Acad. of Engrg Sci., 1980; Hon. Fellow, Portsmouth Polytech., 1984. Hon. DSc: City, 1978; Southampton, 1986; Hon. LLD Dundee, 1985; Hon. DEng Bristol, 1991. Telford Medal, ICE, 1976; James Alfred Ewing Medal, ICE and Royal Soc., 1984; Gold Medal, ICE, 1998. *Publications:* Coastal Hydraulics, 1969, (with C. A. Fleming) 2nd edn 1981; Tunnelling: management by design, 2000; papers, mainly on tunnelling, coastal engrg and wider aspects of engrg, in Proc. ICE and elsewhere. *Address:* Franklands, Bere Court Road, Pangbourne, Berks RG8 8JY. *T:* (0118) 984 2833. *Club:* Athenæum.

See also D. Muir Wood.

MUIR WOOD, Prof. David, PhD; FREng; Professor of Civil Engineering, since 1995, and Head, Department of Civil Engineering, since 1997, University of Bristol; *b* 17 March 1949; *s* of Sir Alan Muir Wood, *qv*; *m* 1978, Helen Rosamond Piddington; two *s*. *Educ:* Royal Grammar Sch., High Wycombe; Peterhouse, Cambridge (BA 1970, MA 1974; PhD 1974). FICE 1992; FREng (FEng 1998). University of Cambridge: res. student, Engrg Dept, 1970–73; William Stone Res. Fellow, Peterhouse, 1973–75; Fellow, Emmanuel Coll., 1975–87; Demonstrator/Lectr in Soil Mechanics, Engrg Dept, 1975–87; University of Glasgow: Cormack Prof. of Civil Engrg, 1987–95; Hd, Dept of Civil Engrg, 1991–93; Dean, Faculty of Engrg, 1993–94. Royal Soc. Res. Fellow, Norwegian Geotechnical Inst., Oslo, 1975; Royal Soc. Industry Fellow, Babtie Gp, 1995–96 (Consultant, 1997–). Hon. Editor, Géotechnique, 1991–93. Associate, Geotechnical Consulting Gp, 1983–. Chm., Scottish Geotechnical Gp, 1991–93. Elder, Cairns Ch of Scotland, Milngavie, 1993–98. (Jtly) British Geotechnical Soc. Prize, 1978. *Publications:* (with R. J. Mair) Pressuremeter Testing: methods and interpretation, 1987; Soil Behaviour and Critical State Soil Mechanics, 1990; (jtly) Piled Foundations in Weak Rock, 1999; contrib. numerous papers to professional jls and confs. *Recreations:* hill-walking, music, opera, travel. *Address:* University of Bristol, Department of Civil Engineering, Queen's Building, University Walk, Bristol BS8 1TR. *T:* (0117) 928 7706, *Fax:* (0117) 928 7783; *e-mail:* d.muir-wood@bristol.ac.uk; Leigh Lodge, Church Road, Abbots Leigh, Bristol BS8 3QP. *T:* (01275) 375563.

MUIRHEAD, Geoffrey, FCIT, FICE; Chief Executive, Manchester Airport, since 1993; *b* 14 July 1949; *s* of John Thomas Muirhead and Irene Clarke; *m* 1972, Clare Elizabeth Parker; one *d*. *Educ:* Teeside Polytechnic. FCIT 1994; FICE 1998. Started career with British Steel; subseq. senior positions with William Press, Simon Carves, Fluor and Shand, incl. posts in Saudi Arabia, Belgium, Eire; Manchester Airport: Dir, Develt, 1988; Dir, Business Develt, 1992. Director: Manchester TEC; Marketing Manchester; Piccadilly Radio Ltd. Mem. Organising Council, Manchester 2002 Commonwealth Games. Chm., UK Airport Operators' Assoc.; Vice Pres., Airports Council Internat. Mem. Council, Univ. of Salford. FRSA 1996. *Recreations:* golf, travel. *Address:* Manchester Airport plc, Manchester M90 1QX. *T:* (0161) 489 3701.

MUIRHEAD, Dame Lorna (Elizabeth Fox), DBE 2000; Midwifery Sister, Liverpool Women's Hospital (formerly Liverpool Maternity Hospital), 1966–69 and since 1974; President, Royal College of Midwives, since 1997; *b* 13 Sept. 1942; *d* of Donald Fox and Joan Mary (*née* Harper); *m* 1966, Ronald A. Muirhead; one *s* one *d*. *Educ:* in Shropshire and Warwickshire. SRN 1963; SCM 1965; MTD 1970; FRCOG 2001. Nurse trng, Hallam Hosp., W Bromwich, 1960–63; midwifery trng, Hallam Hosp. and Marston Green Maternity Hosp., 1964–65; Staff Midwife, Liverpool Maternity Hosp., 1965–66; Midwifery Sister Tutor, 1969–71; part-time Lectr, Liverpool Poly., 1975–80; Sen. Lectr, British Shipping Fedn med. course, 1975–85; frequent Lectr at Univ. and Royal Coll. Midwives seminars and study days, 1980–. Fellow, John Moores Univ., 2001. *Publications:* chapter on A Midwife's Role in Epidural Analgesia, in Epidural Analgesia in Obstetrics, ed A. Doughty, 1980. *Recreations:* choral singing, music, poetry, restoration of old furniture. *Address:* 15 Ullet Road, Sefton Gate, Liverpool L17 3BL. *T:* (0151) 733 8710.

MUIRHEAD-ALLWOOD, Sarah Kathryn, FRCS; Consultant Orthopaedic Surgeon: Whittington Hospital, since 1984; Royal National Orthopaedic Hospital, since 1991; King Edward VII's Hospital for Officers, since 1993; *b* 4 Jan. 1947; *c* of late Maj. W. R. Muirhead and of Joyce Muirhead (*née* Forster); *m* 1983; two *s*. *Educ:* Wellington; St Thomas' Hosp. Med. Sch. (BSc, MB BS). MRCS, FRCS, LRCP. St Thomas' Hospital: House Surg., 1971–72; Sen. House Officer, 1972–73; Anatomy Demonstrator, 1973; Sen. House Officer, Stoke Mandeville Hosp., 1973–74; Registrar: UCH, 1974–77; Charing Cross Hosp., 1977–78; Sen. Registrar, Queen Mary's Hosp., Roehampton, Westminster Hosp., Royal Nat. Orthopaedic Hosp., UCH, 1978–84. Hon. Sen. Clin. Lectr, UCL, 1984; Hon. Consultant: St Luke's Hosp. for the Clergy, 1984; Hosp. of St John and St Elizabeth. Member: British Orthopaedic Assoc., 1980; BMA, 1983; British Hip Soc., 1989; European Hip Soc., 1993. *Publications:* contributions to: Joint Replacement—State of the Art, 1990; Recent Advances in Orthopaedic Surgery, 1991; Gray's Anatomy, 1995. *Recreations:* golf, sailing. *Address:* 19 Wimpole Street, W1M 7AD. *T:* (020) 7935 8488.

MUIRHEAD-ALLWOOD, William Forster Gillespie; *see* Muirhead-Allwood, S. K.

MUKARJI, Dr (Satyanand) Daleep; Director, Christian Aid, since 1998; *b* 22 Feb. 1946; *m* Azra Latifi; one *s* two *d*. *Educ:* Christian Med. Coll., Vellore, India (MB BS); London Sch. of Hygiene and Tropical Med. (DTPH); LSE (MSc). Med. Superintendent, Mission Hosp., Andhra Pradesh, India, 1972; MO and Project Dir, Leprosy Hosp., Dichpalli, 1973; Programme Dir, Rural Unit for Health and Social Affairs, Christian Med. Coll., Vellore, 1977–85; Gen. Sec., Christian Med. Assoc. of India, 1985–94; Exec. Sec., Urban Rural Mission, 1994–96, Health, Community and Justice, 1997–98, WCC, Geneva. *Recreations:* music, theatre, cinema. *Address:* Christian Aid, PO Box 100, SE1 7RT; 53 Woodland Rise, N10 3UN.

MUKHAMEDOV, Irek Javdatovich, OBE 2000; ballet dancer; *b* 1960; *s* of Djavdat Rasulievich Mukhamedov and Rashida Nizamovna; *m* 1990, Maria Zubkhova; one *s* one *d*. *Educ:* Moscow Choreographic Inst. Soloist, Moscow Classical Co., 1978–81; Bolshoi Ballet, 1981–90; Principal, 1990–99, Guest Artist, 1999–2001, Royal Ballet Co.; founded Mukhamedov & Co., 1991. *Leading rôles* in ballets including: Spartacus, Ivan the Terrible, Raymonda, La Bayadère, La Fille mal gardée, Manon, Giselle, Mr Worldly Wise, Mayerling, Different Drummer, Fearful Symmetries, Nutcracker, Les Biches, Prodigal Son, Othello, Cheating, Lying, Stealing, L'Après-midi d'un faune, The Crucible. *rôles created* include: Boris in The Golden Age; Vershinin in Winter Dreams; the foreman in the Judas Tree. *Address:* c/o Royal Ballet Company, Royal Opera House, Covent Garden, WC2E 9DD.

MUKHERJEE, Pranab Kumar; Member, Rajya Sabha; Minister of External Affairs, India, 1995–96; *b* 11 Dec. 1935; *s* of Kamda Kinkar Mukherjee, of an illustrious family which was involved actively in the Freedom Movement of India; *m* 1957, Suvra Mukherjee; two *s* one *d*. *Educ:* Vidyasagar Coll., Suri; Calcutta Univ. (MA (Hist. and Pol Sci.); LLB). Elected Mem., W Bengal, Rajya Sabha, 1969, Leader, Rajya Sabha, 1980–85; Dep. Minister, Mins of Industrial Develt and of Shipping and Transport, 1973–74; Minister of State, Finance Min., 1974–77; Cabinet Minister i/c of Mins of Commerce, Steel and Mines, 1980–82; became youngest Minister to hold Finance Portfolio in

Independent India, 1982–85; Commerce Minister, 1993–95. Spokesman, All India Congress Cttee, 1991; Chm., Central Election Campaign Cttee of Congress Party for Lok Sabha Election, 1991. Dep. Chm., Planning Cttee, Govt of India, 1991–93. *Publications:* Crisis in Democracy; An Aspect of Constitutional Problems in Bengal, 1967; Mid-Term Poll, 1969; Beyond Survival: an emerging dimension of Indian economy, 1984; Off the Track: an analysis of Indian economy, 1987. *Recreations:* music, gardening, reading. *Address:* S-22, Greater Kailash, Part II, New Delhi 110048, India. *T:* (home) 6435656, 6474025/6; (office) 3014070, 3011127.

MUKHERJEE, Tara Kumar, FLIA; Managing Director: Owl Financial Services Ltd, since 1988; Greater London Translation Unit, since 1993; President, Confederation of Indian Organisations (UK), since 1975; *b* 20 Dec. 1923; *s* of Sushil Chandra Mukherjee and Sova Moyee Mukherjee; *m* 1951, Betty Patricia Mukherjee; one *s* one *d*. *Educ:* Scottish Church Collegiate Sch., Calcutta, India; Calcutta Univ. (matriculated 1939). Shop Manager, Bata Shoe Co. Ltd, India, 1941–44; Buyer, Brevitt Shoes, Leicester, 1951–56; Sundries Buyer, British Shoe Corp., 1956–66; Prodn Administrator, Priestley Footwear Ltd, Great Harwood, 1966–68; Head Stores Manager, Brit. Shoe Corp., 1968–70; Save & Prosper Group: Dist Manager, 1970–78; Br. Manager, 1978–84; Senior Sales Manager, 1984–85; Br. Manager, Guardian Royal Exchange PFM Ltd, 1985–88. Pres., India Film Soc., Leicester. Chairman: Charter 90 for Asians; Leicester Community Centre Project; Eur. Multicultural Foundn; Member: Brit. Europ. Movement, London; Exec. Council, Leics Europ. Movement; Pres., EC Migrants Forum, Brussels. Dir, Coronary Prevention Gp, 1986–; Trustee, Haymarket Theatre, Leicester. Patron: London Community Cricket Assoc., 1987–; Asha Foundn, 1999–. FRSA. *Recreation:* cricket (1st Cl. cricketer; played for Bihar, Ranji Trophy, 1941; 2nd XI, Leics CCC, 1949). *Address:* Tallah, 51 Viking Way, Pilgrims Hatch, Brentwood, Essex CM15 9HY. *T:* (01277) 263207, *Fax:* (01277) 229946. *Club:* (Gen. Sec.) Indian National (Leicester).

MULCAHY, Sir Geoffrey (John), Kt 1993; Chief Executive, Kingfisher (formerly Woolworth Holdings) plc, since 1995; *b* 7 Feb. 1942; *s* of Maurice Frederick Mulcahy and Kathleen Love Mulcahy; *m* 1965, Valerie Elizabeth; one *s* one *d*. *Educ:* King's Sch., Worcester; Manchester Univ. (BSc); Harvard Univ. (MBA). Esso Petroleum, 1964–74; Norton Co., 1974–77; British Sugar, 1977–83; Woolworth Holdings, subseq. Kingfisher, 1983–: Gp Man. Dir, 1984–86; Chief Exec., 1986–93; Chm., 1990–95. Dir, Bass, 1989–. *Recreations:* sailing, squash. *Clubs:* Lansdowne, Royal Automobile.

MULDOON, Bristow Cook; Member (Lab) Livingston, Scottish Parliament, since 1999; *b* 19 March 1964; *s* of late Bristow Cook Muldoon and of Annie McKenzie Muldoon (*née* McCallum); *m* 1988, Catherine Sloan McMillan; three *s*. *Educ:* Cumbernauld High Sch.; Univ. of Strathclyde (BSc Hons Chem.); Open Univ. (BA Hons). Manager in rail industry, 1986–99; business analyst, Great North Eastern Rly, 1997–99. Member (Lab): Lothian Regl Council, 1994–96 (Vice-Chm., Econ. Develt); West Lothian Council, 1995–99 (Convener, Community Services). Non-exec. Dir, West Lothian NHS Trust, 1997–99. Member: Labour Party; Co-Op Party; TSSA. *Recreations:* golf, music, football, reading. *Address:* Scottish Parliament, Edinburgh EH99 1SP. *T:* (0131) 348 5000; *e-mail:* bristow.muldoon.msp@scottish.parliament.uk. *Club:* Uphall Golf.

MULDOON, Prof. Paul; Professor of Poetry, University of Oxford, since 1999; Fellow, Hertford College, Oxford, since 1999; Howard G. B. Clark Professor in the Humanities, Princeton University, since 1998; *b* Portadown, NI, 20 June 1951; *s* of late Patrick Muldoon and Brigid (*née* Regan); *m* 1987, Jean Hanff Korelitz; one *s* one *d*. *Educ:* St Patrick's Coll., Armagh; Queen's Univ., Belfast (BA Eng. Lang. and Lit. 1973). BBC Northern Ireland: Producer, Arts Progs (Radio), 1973–78, Sen. Producer, 1978–85; TV Producer, 1985–86; Judith E. Wilson Vis. Fellow, Cambridge Univ., 1986–87; Creative Writing Fellow, UEA, 1987; Lecturer: Sch. of the Arts, Columbia Univ., 1987–88; Creative Writing Program, Princeton Univ., 1987–88; Writer-in-residence, 92nd Street Y, NY, 1988; Roberta Holloway Lectr, Univ. of Calif, Berkeley, 1989; Vis. Prof., Univ. of Mass, Amherst, 1989–90; Princeton University: Lectr, 1990–95; Prof., 1995–98; Dir, Creative Writing Program, 1993–; Vis. Prof., Bread Loaf Sch. of English, Middlebury, Vt, 1997–. Pres., Poetry Soc. of GB, 1996–. Mem., Aosdana, 1980–. FRSL 1981; John Simon Guggenheim Meml Fellow, 1990. Readings of work throughout Europe, USA and Canada, Japan and Australia. Eric Gregory Award, 1972; Sir Geoffrey Faber Meml Award, 1980 and 1991; T. S. Eliot Prize for Poetry, 1994; Award in Literature, AAAL, 1996; Poetry Prize, Irish Times, 1997. *Publications: poetry:* Knowing My Place, 1971; New Weather, 1973; Spirit of Dawn, 1975; Mules, 1977; Names and Addresses, 1978; Immram, 1980; Why Brownlee Left, 1980; Out of Siberia, 1982; Quoof, 1983; The Wishbone, 1984; Selected Poems 1968–83, 1986; Meeting the British, 1987; Selected Poems 1968–86, 1987; Madoc: a mystery, 1990; Incantata, 1994; The Prince of the Quotidian, 1994; The Annals of Chile, 1994; Kerry Slides, 1996; New Selected Poems 1968–94, 1996; Hopewell Haiku, 1997; The Bangle (Slight Return), 1998; Hay, 1998; Poems 1968–1998, 2001; *drama:* Monkeys (TV play), 1989; Shining Brow (opera), 1993; Six Honest Serving Men (play), 1995; Bandanna (opera), 1999; *essays:* Getting Round: notes towards an Ars Poetica, 1998; To Ireland, I, 2000; *for children:* The O-O's Party, 1981; The Last Thesaurus, 1995; The Noctuary of Narcissus Batt, 1997; *translations:* The Astrakan Cloak, by Nuala Ni Dhomhnaill, 1993; (with R. Martin) The Birds, by Aristophanes, 1999; *edited:* The Scrake of Dawn, 1979; The Faber Book of Contemporary Irish Poetry, 1986; The Essential Byron, 1989; The Faber Book of Beasts, 1997; contribs to poetry anthologies; works trans. into numerous langs. *Recreations:* tennis, electric guitar. *Address:* c/o Faber & Faber, 3 Queen Square, WC1N 3AU. *Club:* Groucho.

MULDOON, Dame Thea (Dale), DBE 1993; QSO 1986; *b* 13 March 1927; *d* of Stanley Arthur and Annie Eveleen Flyger; *m* 1951, Rt Hon. Sir Robert David Muldoon, GCMG, CH, PC (*d* 1992); one *s* two *d*. *Educ:* Takapuna Grammar Sch. Associated with many charities; Patron: North Shore Hospice; Hibiscus Coast Br., NZ Red Cross Soc.; several horticultural orgns; Vice Patron, NZ Foundn for Conductive Educn. *Recreations:* walking, yoga. *Address:* 4A Ewen Street, Takapuna, Auckland 9, New Zealand. *T:* (9) 4860693.

MULDOWNEY, Diane Ellen, (Mrs Dominic Muldowney); *see* Trevis, D. E.

MULDOWNEY, Dominic John; Music Director, Royal National (formerly National) Theatre, since 1976; *b* 19 July 1952; *s* of William and Barbara Muldowney; *m* 1986, Diane Ellen Trevis, *qv*; one *d*. *Educ:* Taunton's Grammar School, Southampton; York University. BA, BPhil. Composer in residence, Southern Arts Association, 1974–76; composer of chamber, choral, orchestral works, including work for theatre, ballet and TV. *Compositions include:* Piano Concerto, 1983; The Duration of Exile, 1984; Saxophone Concerto, 1985; Sinfonietta, 1986; Ars Subtilior, 1987; Lonely Hearts, 1988; Violin Concerto, 1989; Three Pieces for Orchestra, 1990; Percussion Concerto, 1991; Oboe Concerto, 1992; Trumpet Concerto, 1993; Concerto for 4 Violins, 1994; The Brontës (ballet), 1995; Trombone Concerto, 1996; Clarinet Concerto, 1997; Irish Love Songs, 1998; The Fall of Jerusalem (oratorio), 1999. *Recreation:* driving through France and across America.

MULFORD, Dr David Campbell; Chairman International, Credit Suisse First Boston, since 1999 (Member of Executive Board, since 1992; Chairman Europe, 1993–99); *b* Rockford, Ill, 27 June 1947; *s* of Robert Lewis Mulford and Theodora Henie Moellenhauer Mulford; *m* 1985, Jeannie Louise Simmons; two *s*. *Educ:* Lawrence Univ., Wisconsin (BA Econs *cum laude* 1959); Univ. of Cape Town; Boston Univ. (MA Pol Sci. 1962; Dist. Alumni Award, 1992); St Antony's Coll., Oxford (DPhil 1966). Special Asst to Sec. and Under Sec., US Treasury, 1965–66; Man. Dir and Head, Internat. Finance, White, Weld & Co., Inc., 1966–74; Sen. Investment Advr, Saudi Arabian Monetary Agency, 1974–84, on secondment; Under Sec. and Asst Sec. for Internat. Affairs, US Treasury, 1984–92 (sen. advr on financial assistance to former Soviet Union states; head of internat. debt strategy; led US delegn to negotiate estabt of EBRD). Mem., Council on Foreign Relations, 1972–; Affiliate, Center for Strategic and Internat. Studies, Washington, 1992–. Hon. LLD Lawrence, Wisconsin, 1984. Alexander Hamilton Award, USA, 1992. Légion d'Honneur (France), 1990; Order of May (Argentina), 1993; Officer's Cross, Medal of Merit (Poland), 1995. *Publications:* Northern Rhodesia General Election, 1962; Zambia: the politics of independence, 1967. *Recreations:* golf, running, canoeing. *Address:* Credit Suisse First Boston (International) Ltd, One Cabot Square, E14 4QJ. *T:* (020) 7888 3574, *Fax:* (020) 7888 3501. *Club:* Metropolitan (Washington).

MULGAN, Geoffrey John, PhD; Director, Performance and Innovation Unit, Cabinet Office, since 2000; *b* 28 Aug. 1961; *s* of Anthony Philip Mulgan and Catherine Mulgan (*née* Gough); *m* 1998, Rowena Young. *Educ:* Balliol Coll., Oxford (MA 1982); Central London Poly. (PhD 1990). Investment Exec., Greater London Enterprise, 1984–86; Harkness Fellow, MIT, 1986–87; Consultant, and Lectr in Telecommunications, Central London Poly., 1987–90; Special Advr to Gordon Brown, MP, 1990–92; Fellow, BFI, 1992–93; Co-Founder and Dir, Demos, 1993–99 (Chm., Adv. Council, 1998–); Mem., Prime Minister's Policy Unit, 1997–2000. Vis. Prof., UCL, 1996–. Trustee: Crime Concern, 1996–; Photographers Gall., 1996–; Political Qly, 1995–. *Publications:* Saturday Night or Sunday Morning, 1987; Communication and Control, 1990; Politics in an Antipolitical Age, 1994; (ed) Life After Politics, 1997; Connexity, 1997. *Recreation:* making music. *Address:* 27 Lothair Road South, N4 1EN.

MULGRAVE, Earl of; John Samuel Constantine Phipps; *b* 26 Nov. 1994; *s* and *heir* of Marquis of Normanby, *qv*.

MULHOLLAND, family name of **Baron Dunleath**.

MULHOLLAND, Clare, OBE 1998; Vice Chairman of Council, Independent Media Commission, Bosnia and Herzegovina, since 1998; *b* 17 June 1939; *d* of James Mulholland and Elizabeth (*née* Lochrin). *Educ:* Notre Dame High Sch., Glasgow; Univ. of Glasgow (MA Hons). Gen. trainee, then Press Officer, ICI, 1961–64; Press Officer: Granada Television, 1964–65; TWW, 1965–68; Press Officer, then Educn Officer, HTV, 1968–71; Independent Broadcasting Authority, later Independent Television Commission, 1971–97: Reg. Exec., Bristol, 1971–77; Reg. Officer, Midlands, 1977–82; Chief Asst, Television, 1982–83; Dep. Dir of Television, 1983–91; Dir of Programmes, 1991–96; Dep. Chief Exec., 1996–97. Member: Arts Council of GB, 1986–94; Scottish Film Prodn Fund, 1984–90; Lottery Film Panel, Arts Council of England, 1997–2000. FRTS 1988. *Recreations:* travel, food.

MULKEARNS, Most Rev. Ronald Austin, DD, DCL; Former Bishop of Ballarat (RC); *b* 11 Nov. 1930. *Educ:* De La Salle Coll., Malvern; Corpus Christi Coll., Werribee; Pontifical Lateran Univ., Rome. Ordained, 1956; Coadjutor Bishop, 1968–71; Bishop of Ballarat, 1971–97. *Address:* PO Box 411, Aireys Inlet, Vic 3231, Australia.

MULKERN, John, CBE 1987; JP; FCIT; international airport and aviation consultant, since 1987; *b* 15 Jan. 1931; *s* of late Thomas Mulkern and Annie Tennant; *m* 1954, May Egerton (*née* Peters); one *s* three *d*. *Educ:* Stretford Grammar Sch. Dip. in Govt Admin. Harvard Business Sch. AMP, 1977. FCIT 1973 (Mem. Council, 1979–82). Ministries of Supply and Aviation, Civil Service, 1949–65: Exec. Officer, finally Principal, Audit, Purchasing, Finance, Personnel and Legislation branches; British Airports Authority, 1965–87: Dep. Gen. Man., Heathrow Airport, 1970–73; Dir, Gatwick Airport, 1973–77; Man. Dir and Mem. of Bd, 1977–87. Chairman: British Airports International Ltd, 1978–82; Manchester Handling Ltd, 1988–94; Granik Ltd, 1990–91 (Pres., 1992–94); Director: London Luton Airport Ltd, 1991–2000; Reliance Aviation Security Ltd, 1992–94. President: Western European Airports' Assoc., 1981–83; Internat. Civil Airports Assoc. (Europe), 1986; Chm., Co-ordinating Council, Airports Assocs, 1982; Mem. Bd, Airport Operators Council Internat., 1978–81. Mem., Surrey Probation Cttee, 1996–2001; Trustee: Surrey Springboard, 1997–2001; BAA Pension Trust Co. Ltd, 1997–2000. CIMgt (CBIM 1981); FInstD 1982. JP Surrey, 1988. *Recreations:* family pursuits, opera, classical recorded music.

MULL, Very Rev. Gerald S.; *see* Stranraer-Mull.

MULLALLY, Rev. Sarah Elisabeth; Chief Nursing Officer, Department of Health, since 1999; *b* 26 March 1962; *d* of Michael Frederick Mills Bowser and Ann Dorothy Bowser; *m* 1987, Eamonn James Mullally; one *s* one *d*. *Educ:* Nightingale Sch. of Nursing; S Bank Poly. (BSc Hons Nursing and RGN 1984); MSc Interprofessional Health and Welfare, S Bank Univ., 1992; DipTh Kent 2001. Staff Nurse: St Thomas' Hosp., 1984–86; Royal Marsden Hosp., 1986–88; Ward Sister, Westminster Hosp., 1988–90; Sen. Nurse, Riverside HA, 1990–92; Asst Chief Nurse, Riverside Hosps, 1992–94; Dir of Nursing and Dep. Chief Exec., Chelsea and Westminster Healthcare Trust, 1994–99. Ordained deacon, 2001; NSM, Battersea Fields, 2001–. Hon. Fellow, S Bank Univ., 2000. *Address:* Department of Health, Richmond House, 79 Whitehall, SW1A 2NL.

MULLALY, Terence Frederick Stanley; art historian and critic; *b* 14 Nov. 1927; *s* of late Col B. R. Mullaly (4th *s* of Maj.-Gen. Sir Herbert Mullaly, KCMG, CB, CSI) and Eileen Dorothy (*née* Stanley); *m* 1949, Elizabeth Helen (*née* Burkitt). *Educ:* in India, England, Japan and Canada; Downing Coll., Cambridge (MA). FSA 1977; FRNS 1981 (Mem. Council, 1993–95); FSAScot 1995. Archæological studies in Tripolitania, 1948, and Sicily, 1949; has specialised in study of Italian art, particularly Venetian and Veronese painting of 16th and 17th centuries; lecturer and broadcaster; Art Critic, Daily Telegraph, 1958–86. Vis. Prof., Finch Coll., NY, 1967–72. President: Brit. Section, Internat. Assoc. of Art Critics, 1967–73; British Art Medal Soc., 1986–98 (Vice Chm., 1982–86; Vice-Pres., 1998–); Member: Adv. Cttee, Cracow Art Festival, 1974, Palermo Art Festival, 1976; UK Delgn, Budapest Cultural Forum, 1985; Cttee, FIDEM Congress, 1992; Council: Attingham Summer Sch. Trust, 1984–90; Derby Porcelain Internat. Soc., 1985–; Friends, Univ. of Cyprus, 1995– (Vice Chm., 1998–); Artistic Adviser, Grand Tours, 1974–90; Director: Grand Tours, 1980–90; Specialtours, 1986. Editor, Jl of British–Italian Soc., 1995–. FRSA 1969. Commendatore, Order Al Merito, Italy, 1974 (Cavaliere Ufficiale, 1964); l'Ordre du Mérite Culturel, Poland, 1974; Order of Merit of Poland (Silver Medal), 1978; Bulgarian 1300th Anniversary Medal, 1981; Sacro Militare Ordine Costantiniano di S Giorgio (Silver Medal), 1982; Premio Pietro Torta per il restauro di Venezia, 1983; Socio Straniero, Ateneo Veneto, 1986. *Publications:* Ruskin a Verona,

1966; catalogue of exhibition, Disegni veronesi del Cinquecento, 1971; contrib. to catalogue of exhibition Cinquant' anni di pittura veronese: 1580–1630, 1974; ed and contrib. to catalogue of exhibition, Modern Hungarian Medal, 1984; contrib. to Affreschi del Rinascimento a Verona: interventi di restauro, 1987; Caterina Cornaro, Queen of Cyprus, 1989; Anne Redpath, 1997; The Architecture of Cyprus, 2002; contribs on history of art, to Burlington Magazine, Master Drawings, Arte Illustrata, Arte Documento, Antologia di Belle Arti, The Minneapolis Inst. of Arts Bulletin, Bull. Univ. of New Mexico Art Mus., British Numismatic Jl, Numismatic Chronicle, Jl of British Art Medal Soc., Apollo, etc. *Recreations:* numismatics, Eastern Europe. *Address:* Waterside House, Pulborough, Sussex RH20 2BH. *T:* (01798) 872104.

MULLENS, Lt-Gen. Sir Anthony (Richard Guy), KCB 1989 OBE 1979 (MBE 1973); Associate, Varley Walker & Partners, since 1992; *b* 10 May 1936; *s* of late Brig. Guy John de Wette Mullens, OBE, and Gwendoline Joan Maclean; *m* 1964, Dawn Elizabeth Hermione Pease. *Educ:* Eton; RMA Sandhurst. Commnd 4th/7th Royal Dragoon Guards, 1956; regtl service, BAOR, 1956–58; ADC to Comdr 1st British Corps, 1958–60; Adjt 1962–65; sc 1967, psc; MA to VCGS, MoD, 1968–70; regtl service, 1970–72; Bde Major, 1972–73; Directing Staff, Staff Coll., 1973–76; CO 4/7 DG, BAOR, 1976–78; HQ BAOR, 1978–80; Comdr 7th Armd Bde, 1980–82; MoD (DMS(A)), 1982–85; Comdr 1st Armoured Div., 1985–87; ACDS (Operational Requirements), Land Systems, MoD, 1987–89; DCDS (Systems), MoD, 1989–92, retd. Consultant, BR, 1992–95. Col, Royal Dragoon Guards, 1994–99. Trustee, Army Museums Ogilby Trust, 1997–; Pres., 7th Armoured Div. Officers Club, 2000–. Liveryman: Armourers' and Braziers' Co., 1974 (Mem., Ct of Assts, 1993–97; Renter Warden, 1996–97); Coachmakers' and Coachharness Makers' Co., 1976. Member: Alpheton Parish Council, 2000–; Alpheton PCC, 1989–; Church Warden, Alpheton, 1997–. MInstD 1992. Niedersachsen Verdienstkreuz am Bande, 1982, Erste Klasse, 1987. *Recreations:* travel, riding, shooting, ski-ing. *Address:* The Old Rectory, Alpheton, Sudbury, Suffolk CO10 9BT. *Club:* Cavalry and Guards.

MÜLLER, Alex; *see* Müller, K. A.

MULLER, Franz Joseph; QC 1978; a Recorder of the Crown Court, since 1977; *b* England, 19 Nov. 1938; *yr s* of late Wilhelm Muller and Anne Maria (*née* Ravens); *m* 1985, Helena, *y d* of Mieczyslaw Bartosz; two *s*. *Educ:* Mount St Mary's Coll.; Univ. of Sheffield (LLB). Called to the Bar, Gray's Inn, 1961, Bencher, 1994; called to NI Bar, 1982. Graduate Apprentice, United Steel Cos, 1960–61; Commercial Asst, Workington Iron and Steel Co. Ltd, 1961–63. Commenced practice at the Bar, 1964. Non-Executive Director: Richards of Sheffield (Holdings) PLC, 1969–77; Satinsteel Ltd, 1970–77; Joseph Rodgers and Son Ltd and Rodgers Wostenholm Ltd, 1975–77. Mem., Sen. Common Room, UC Durham, 1981. *Recreations:* the Georgians, fell walking, being in Greece, listening to music. *Address:* Slade Hooton Hall, Laughton en le Morthen, Yorks S25 1YQ; 11 King's Bench Walk, Temple, EC4Y 7EQ. *T:* (020) 7353 3337.

MÜLLER, (Karl) Alex, PhD; FInstP; physicist at IBM Zurich Research Laboratory, since 1963; *b* 20 April 1927. *Educ:* Swiss Federal Institute of Technology, Zürich (PhD 1958). FInstP 1998. Battelle Inst., Geneva, 1958–63; Lectr, 1962, Titular Prof., 1970, Prof., 1987–, Univ. of Zürich; joined IBM Res. Lab, Zurich, 1963; Manager, Physics Dept, 1973; IBM Fellow, 1982–85; researcher, 1985–. Hon. degrees from seventeen European and American univs. Prizes and awards include Nobel Prize for Physics (jtly), 1987. *Publications:* over 400 papers on ferroelectric and superconducting materials. *Address:* Physik-Institut, Universität Zürich-Irchel, Winterthurerstrasse 190, 8057 Zürich, Switzerland.

MULLER, Dr Ralph Louis Junius, FIBiol; Director, International Institute of Parasitology, CAB International, 1981–93; *b* 30 June 1933; *s* of Carl and Sarah Muller; *m* 1st, 1959, Gretta Shearer; one *s* one *d*; 2nd, 1979, Annie Badilla Delgado; one *s* one *d*. *Educ:* Summerhill Sch., Suffolk; London Univ. (BSc, PhD, DSc). Res. Fellow, KCL, 1958–59; ODM, 1959–61; Lectr, Univ. of Ibadan, 1961–66; Sen. Lectr, LSHTM, 1966–80. Pres., European Fedn of Parasitologists, 1988–92; Hon. Sec., British Soc. for Parasitology, 1995–98. Editor: Advances in Parasitology, 1978–; Jl of Helminthology, 1986–95. *Publications:* Worms and Disease, 1975, 3rd edn 2001; Onchocerciasis, 1987; Medical Parasitology, 1989. *Recreations:* beekeeping, writing instruments, sport, photography. *Address:* 22 Cranbrook Drive, St Albans, Herts AL4 0SS. *T:* (01727) 852605, *Fax:* (01727) 856871; *e-mail:* ralphmuller@compuserve.com.

MULLER, Mrs Robert; *see* Whitelaw, Billie.

MULLETT, Aidan Anthony, (Tony), CBE 1993; QPM 1982; Director-General, National Criminal Intelligence Service, 1992–93; *b* 24 May 1933; *s* of Bartholomew Joseph and Mary Kate Mullett; *m* 1957, Monica Elizabeth Coney; one *s* one *d*. *Educ:* Moat Boys' Sch., Leicester. Served Royal Air Force, 1950–56; joined Leicester City Police, 1957; Leicestershire and Rutland Constabulary, 1966, Chief Superintendent, 1973; Asst Chief Constable, W Mercia Constabulary, 1975–82; Dep. Chief Constable, Dyfed Powys Police, 1982–85; Chief Constable, W Mercia Constabulary, 1985–91. Chm., Crime Cttee, ACPO, 1990–91 (Hon. Sec., 1989). *Recreations:* golf, swimming.

MULLETT, Leslie Baden; consultant; *b* 22 Aug. 1920; *s* of Joseph and Edith Mullett; *m* 1st, 1945, Katharine Lear (marr. diss. 1968); no *c*; 2nd, 1971, Gillian Pettit. *Educ:* Gram. Sch., Hales Owen, Worcs; Birmingham Univ. BSc (Hons Physics) 1941. Telecommunications Research Estab., 1941–46; AEA, 1946–60 (Head of Accelerator Div., 1958); Asst Dir, Rutherford High Energy Lab., SRC, 1960–68; on secondment to Res. Gp, Min. of Technology, 1966–68; CSO, Min. of Transport, 1968; CSO, Res. Requirements, DoE, 1970–74; Dep. Dir, Transport and Road Res. Lab., DoE/Dept of Transport, 1974–80. Vis. Prof., Univ. of Reading, 1982–90. *Publications:* A Guide to Transport for Disabled People, 1982; papers in learned jls on particle accelerators and solar energy. *Recreation:* gardening. *Address:* 42 Grosvenor Avenue, Grosvenor Park, Bourne, Lincs PE10 9HU. *T:* (01778) 423054.

MULLETT, Tony; *see* Mullett, A. A.

MULLIGAN, Christopher James; Director General, Passenger Transport Executive, Greater Manchester, since 1991; *b* 24 Feb. 1950; *s* of James Frederick Mulligan and Dorothy Mulligan (*née* Kneill); *m* 1989, Rowena May Burns. *Educ:* Hull Univ. (BA Hons 1971). Mem., CIPFA. Manchester CC, 1971–73; Gtr Manchester CC, 1973–77; Greater Manchester Passenger Transport Executive, 1977–: Dir of Finance, 1987–91. *Recreations:* reading, walking, good food. *Address:* 9 Portland Street, Piccadilly Gardens, Manchester M60 1HX. *T:* (0161) 242 6060.

MULLIGAN, (Margaret) Mary; Member (Lab) Linlithgow, Scottish Parliament, since 1999; *b* Liverpool, 12 Feb. 1960; *m* 1982, John Mulligan; two *s* one *d*. *Educ:* Notre Dame High Sch., Liverpool; Manchester Univ. (BA Hons Econs and Social Studies 1981). Retail and pesonnel mgt, 1981–86. Member (Lab): Edinburgh DC, 1988–95 (Chm., Housing Cttee, 1992–97; City of Edinburgh Council, 1995–99. Chm., Educn, Sports and Culture Cttee, 1999–2000, PPS to First Minister, 2000–, Scottish Parlt. *Recreations:* music, theatre, watching sports. *Address:* Scottish Parliament, Edinburgh EH99 1SP; (constituency office) 62 Hopetoun Street, Bathgate, West Lothian EH48 4PD.

MULLIGAN, Prof. William, FRSE; Professor of Veterinary Physiology, 1963–86, and Vice-Principal, 1980–83, University of Glasgow, now Professor Emeritus; *b* 18 Nov. 1921; *s* of John Mulligan and Mary Mulligan (*née* Kelly); *m* 1948, Norah Mary Cooper one *s* one *d* (and one *d* decd). *Educ:* Banbridge Academy; Queen's Univ. of Belfast (BSc); PhD London. FIBiol 1988. Assistant, Dept of Chemistry, QUB, 1943–45; Demonstrator/Lectr, St Bartholomew's Med. Coll., London, 1945–51; Sen. Lectr, Veterinary Biochemistry, Univ. of Glasgow, 1951–63; McMaster Fellow, McMaster Animal Health Laboratory, Sydney, Aust., 1958–60; Dean of Faculty of Veterinary Medicine, Univ. of Glasgow, 1977–80. Dr. med. vet. *hc* Copenhagen, 1983. *Publications:* (jtly) Isotopic Tracers, 1954, 2nd edn 1959; numerous contribs to scientific jls on immunology and use of radiation and radioisotopes in animal science. *Recreations:* golf, tennis, gardening, pigeon racing, theatre. *Address:* 25 Woodland Way, Wivenhoe, Colchester, Essex CO7 9AT.
See also J. S. Pitt-Brooke.

MULLIN, Christopher John, (Chris); MP (Lab) Sunderland South, since 1987; *b* 12 Dec. 1947; *s* of Leslie and Teresa Mullin; *m* 1987, Nguyen Thi Ngoc, *d* of Nguyen Tang Minh, Kontum, Vietnam; two *d*. *Educ:* Univ. of Hull (LLB). Freelance journalist, travelled extensively in Indo-China and China; sub editor, BBC World Service, 1974–78; Editor, Tribune, 1982–84. Executive Member: Campaign for Labour Party Democracy, 1975–83; Labour Co-ordinating Cttee, 1978–82. Contested (Lab): Devon N, 1970; Kingston upon Thames, Feb. 1974. Parly Under-Sec. of State, DETR, 1999–2001, DFID, 2001. Chm., Home Affairs Select Cttee, 1997–99, 2001–. Chm., All Party Vietnam Gp, 1988–99; Chm., PLP Civil Liberties Gp, 1992–97. Sec., British Cambodia Gp; Hon. Sec., British Tibet Gp. Hon. LLD City, 1992. Editor: Arguments for Socialism, by Tony Benn, 1979; Arguments for Democracy, by Tony Benn, 1981. *Publications: novels:* A Very British Coup, 1982 (televised 1988); The Last Man Out of Saigon, 1986; The Year of the Fire Monkey, 1991; *non-fiction:* Error of Judgement—the truth about the Birmingham bombings, 1986, rev. edn 1997; pamphlets: How to Select or Reselect your MP, 1981; The Tibetans, 1981. *Address:* House of Commons, SW1A 0AA.

MULLIN, Rt Rev. Mgr (John Raymond) Noel, VG 1993; Chaplain, Plater College, since 1998; *b* 21 Dec. 1947. *Educ:* Underley Hall Sch., Kirkby Lonsdale; Upholland Coll., Lancs. Ordained priest, 1972; joined RN as Chaplain, 1978; Prin. RC Chaplain (Naval) and Dir, Naval Chaplaincy Services (Trng and Progs), MoD, 1993–98; served at home and abroad, afloat and ashore, at peace and in conflict. QHC, 1996–98. *Recreations:* Rugby, cricket, fell walking, performing arts, food. *Address:* Plater College, Pullens Lane, Oxford OX3 0DT.

MULLIN, Prof. John William, DSc, PhD; FREng, FRSC, FIChemE; Ramsay Memorial Professor of Chemical Engineering, University College London, 1985–90, now Emeritus Professor; Hon. Research Fellow, University College London, since 1990; *b* Rock Ferry, Cheshire, 22 Aug. 1925; *er s* of late Frederick Mullin and Kathleen Nellie Mullin (*née* Oppy); *m* 1952, Averil Margaret Davies, Carmarthen; one *s* one *d*. *Educ:* Hawarden County Sch.; UCW Cardiff (Fellow, 1981); University Coll. London (Fellow, 1981). 8 yrs in organic fine chemicals industry; University College London: Lectr, 1956; Reader, 1961; Prof., 1969; Dean, Faculty of Engrg, 1975–77; Vice-Provost, 1980–86; Crabtree Orator, 1993; Dean, Faculty of Engrg, London Univ., 1979–85. Vis. Prof., Univ. New Brunswick, 1967. Chm. Bd of Staff Examrs, Chem. Eng, Univ. London, 1965–70. Hon. Librarian, IChemE, 1965–77 (Mem. Council, 1973–76); Mem., Materials Sci. Working Gp, European Space Agency, 1977–81; Founder Mem., Brit. Assoc. for Crystal Growth; Chairman: Process Engrg Gp, SCI, 1996–99; BS and ISO cttees on industrial screens, sieves, particle sizing, etc. Mem., Parly Gp for Engrg Develt, 1994–. Member: Cttee of Management, Inst. of Child Health, 1970–83; Court of Governors, University Coll., Cardiff, 1982–99; Council, Sch. of Pharmacy, Univ. of London, 1983–2000 (Vice-Chm., 1988–2000; Hon. Fellow, 1998). Liveryman, Engineers' Co., 1984–. Moulton Medal, IChemE, 1970; Kurnakov Meml Medal, Inst. of Gen. and Inorganic Chem., USSR Acad. of Scis, 1991. Dr *hc* Inst Nat. Polytechnique de Toulouse, 1989. *Publications:* Crystallization, 1961, 4th edn 2001; (ed) Industrial Crystallization, 1976; papers in Trans IChemE, Chem. Engrg Sci., Jl Crystal Growth, etc. *Address:* 4 Milton Road, Ickenham, Middx UB10 8NQ. *T:* (01895) 634950. *Club:* Athenæum.

MULLIN, Rt Rev. Mgr Noel; *see* Mullin, Rt Rev. Mgr J. R. N.

MULLINS, Rt Rev. Daniel Joseph; *see* Menevia, Bishop of, (RC).

MULLINS, Edwin Brandt; author, journalist and film-maker; *b* 14 Sept. 1933; *s* of late Claud Mullins and Gwendolen Mullins, OBE; *m* 1st, 1960, Gillian Brydone (*d* 1982); one *s* two *d*; 2nd, 1984, Anne Kelleher. *Educ:* Midhurst Grammar Sch.; Merton Coll., Oxford (BA Hons, MA). London Editor, Two Cities, 1957–58; Sub-editor and Art Correspondent, Illustrated London News, 1958–62; Art Critic: Sunday Telegraph, 1962–69; Telegraph Sunday Magazine, 1964–86; contributor, 1962–, to The Guardian, Financial Times, Sunday Times, Director, Apollo, Art and Artists, Studio, Radio Times, TV Times, Country Living. Regular broadcaster on radio and television; scriptwriter and presenter of numerous TV documentaries for BBC, Channel 4 and RM Arts, Munich, incl. 100 Great Paintings, The Pilgrimage of Everyman, Gustave Courbet, Fake?, Prison, The Great Art Collection, A Love Affair with Nature, Masterworks, Paradise on Earth, Montparnasse Revisited, Dürer, Out of the Dark Ages—a tale of four Emperors, Georges de la Tour—Genius Lost and Found. *Publications:* Souza, 1962; Wallis, 1967; Josef Herman, 1967; Braque, 1968; The Art of Elisabeth Frink, 1972; The Pilgrimage to Santiago, 1974, repr. 2001; (ed) Great Paintings, 1981; (ed) The Arts of Britain, 1983; The Painted Witch, 1985; A Love Affair with Nature, 1985; The Royal Collection, 1992; Alfred Wallis: Cornish Primitive, 1994; *novels:* Angels on the Point of a Pin, 1979; Sirens, 1983; The Golden Bird, 1987; The Lands of the Sea, 1988; Dear Venus, 1992; With Much Love, 1993; All My Worldly Goods, 1994; The Outfit, 1995; The Devil's Work, 1996. *Recreations:* everything except football. *Address:* 25 The Crescent, Barnes, SW13 0NN.

MULLIS, Dr Kary Banks; American biochemist; Vice-President and Director of Molecular Biology, Burstein Laboratories, Irvine, California, since 1999; *b* 28 Dec. 1944; *s* of Cecil Banks Mullis and Bernice Alberta Fredericks (*née* Barker); *m* 1963, Richards Train Haley (marr. diss.); one *d*; *m* 1975, Cynthia Gibson (marr. diss.); two *s*; *m* 1998, Nancy Cosgrove. *Educ:* Georgia Inst. of Technol. (BS Chemistry 1966); Univ. of Calif, Berkeley (PhD Biochemistry 1973). Lectr in Biochemistry, Univ. of Calif, Berkeley, 1972; Postdoctoral Fellow: Kansas Med. Sch., 1973–76; Univ. of Calif, San Francisco, 1977–79; Scientist, Cetus Corp., Calif, 1979–86; Dir of Molecular Biology, Xytronyx, Inc., San Diego, 1986–88; Consultant, Specialty Labs Inc., and Amersham Inc., 1988–. Member: American Chemistry Soc.; Inst. of Further Study (Dir, 1983–). Preis Biochemische Analytik, German Soc. Clin. Chemistry, 1990; Allan Award, American Soc. of Human Genetics, 1990; Nat. Biotechnology Award, 1991; Robert Koch Award, 1992; Japan Prize, Japanese Inst. for Sci. and Technology, 1993; (jtly) Nobel Prize for Chemistry,

1993. *Publications:* Dancing Naked in the Mind Field, 1999; articles in prof. jls. *Address:* Apartment 5, 6767 Neptune Place, La Jolla, CA 92031–5924, USA.

MULLIS, Marjorie; *see* Allthorpe-Guyton, M.

MULLOVA, Viktoria; violinist; *b* 27 Nov. 1959; *d* of Juri Mullov and Raisa Mullova; one *s* two *d.* *Educ:* Central Music Sch., Moscow; Moscow Conservatory. First prize, Sibelius Competition, Helsinki, 1980; Gold Medal, Tchaikovsky Competition, Moscow, 1982; left USSR, 1983. Has performed with most major orchestras; many festival appearances. Recordings include: violin concertos: Bach, Brahms, Tchaikovsky, Sibelius, Mendelssohn, Stravinsky, Bartok No 2, Shostakovich No 1, Prokoviev No 2, Paganini No 1; Bach partitas; sonatas for violin and piano: Bach, Janacek, Prokofiev, Debussy, Brahms; Vivaldi, Four Seasons; Through the Looking Glass (arrangements of works by Miles Davis, Weather Report and Youssou N'Dour). *Address:* c/o Askonas Holt, Lonsdale Chambers, 27 Chancery Lane, WC2A 1PF.

MULRONEY, Rt Hon. (Martin) Brian; PC 1984; CC 1998; Senior Partner, Ogilvy, Renault, since 1993; *b* 20 March 1939; *s* of Benedict Mulroney and Irene O'Shea; *m* 1973, Mila Pivnicki; three *s* one *d.* *Educ:* St Francis Xavier Univ. (BA); Université Laval (LLL). Partner, Ogilvy, Renault (Montreal law firm), 1965–76; Pres., Iron Ore Co. of Canada, 1976–83. MP (Progressive Conservative): Central Nova, 1983–84; Manicouagan, 1984–88; Charlevoix, 1988–93. Leader of the Opposition, 1983–84; Prime Minister of Canada, 1984–93. Royal Comr, Cliche Commn investigating violence in Quebec construction industry, 1974. Director: Barrick Gold Corp.; TrizecHahn Corp.; Archer Daniels Midland Co.; Cedant Corp.; Quebecor Inc.; Quebecor World Inc.; Cognicase Inc.; Telesystems Ltd. Member, International Advisory Council: Power Corp. of Canada; Chase Manhattan Corp.; Independent Newspapers plc. Trustee, Montreal Heart Inst. Hon. LLD: St Francis Xavier Univ., 1979; Meml Univ., 1980. *Publication:* Where I Stand, 1983. *Recreations:* tennis, swimming.

MULRYNE, Prof. (James) Ronald, PhD; Professor of English, University of Warwick, since 1977; *b* 24 May 1937; *s* of Thomas Wilfred Mulryne and Mary Mulryne; *m* 1964, Eithne Wallace. *Educ:* St Catharine's Coll., Cambridge (BA 1958; MA 1960; PhD 1962). Fellow, Shakespeare Inst., Univ. of Birmingham, 1960–62; University of Edinburgh: Lectr, 1962–72; Reader in English Lit., 1972–77; Hd, Dept of English Lit., 1976–77; University of Warwick: Pro-Vice-Chancellor, 1982–87; Director: Centre for Study of Renaissance, 1993–; AHRB Centre for Study of Renaissance Elites and Court Cultures, 2000–. Vis. Associate Prof., Univ. of Calif, San Diego, 1970–71; Sen. Vis. Res. Fellow, Jesus Coll., Oxford, 1987; Vis. Fellow, Magdalen Coll., Oxford, 1991. General Editor: Revels Plays, 1979–; Shakespeare's Plays in Performance, 1984–. Founder Dir, Mulryne & Shewring Ltd, Publishers, 1989–. Chm., Drama and Theatre Bd, CNAA, 1972–78; Member: Council of Mgt, UCCA, 1984–87; Drama Panel and Chm., Drama Projects Cttee, Arts Council of GB, 1987–91; Drama and Dance Adv. Cttee, British Council, 1991–97 (Chm., 1993–97); Convener, English Lang. and Lit. Panel, AHRB, 2000–; Res. Cttee, AHRB, 2000–. Mem. Bd of Dirs, Birmingham Rep. Theatre, 1987–95; Governor, RSC, 1998–. Trustee, Shakespeare's Birthplace Trust, 1985–. Gov., 1987–, Trustee, 1998–, King Edward VI Sch., Stratford-upon-Avon (Dep. Chm., 1998–99, Chm., 1999–, of Govs). Chevalier, Ordre des Palmes Académiques (France), 1992. *Publications include:* edited: Thomas Middleton, Women Beware Women, 1975; John Webster, The White Devil, 1970; Thomas Kyd, The Spanish Tragedy, 1970, 2nd edn 1989; edited with Margaret Shewring: Theatre of the English and Italian Renaissance, 1991; Italian Renaissance Festivals and their European Influence, 1992; Theatre and Government Under the Early Stuarts, 1993; Making Space for Theatre, 1995; Shakespeare and the Japanese Stage, 1998; The Cottesloe at the National, 1999; numerous books and articles, mainly on Shakespeare, Elizabethan Drama and W. B. Yeats. *Recreation:* theatre. *Address:* 3 Benson Road, Stratford-upon-Avon CV37 6UU. *T:* (01789) 205774.

MULVANEY, Prof. Derek John, AO 1991; CMG 1982; Professor of Prehistory, Australian National University, 1971–85, now Emeritus; *b* 26 Oct. 1925; *s* of Richard and Frances Mulvaney; *m* 1954, Jean Campbell; four *s* two *d.* *Educ:* Univ. of Melbourne (MA); Clare Coll., Univ. of Cambridge (BA, MA 1959, PhD 1970). FAHA 1970; FSA 1977; Corresp. FBA 1983; FRAI 1996. Navigator, RAAF, 1943–46 (Flying Officer); Lectr and Senior Lectr in History, Univ. of Melbourne, 1954–64; Senior Fellow, ANU, 1965–70; Vis. Prof., Cambridge, 1976–77; Chair of Australian Studies, Harvard, 1984–85; Mem. Council, Aust. Inst. of Aboriginal Studies, 1964–80 (Chm., 1982–84); Australian Heritage Commissioner, 1976–82; Mem., Cttee of Inquiry, Museums and National Collections, 1974–75; Sec., Australian Acad. of Humanities, 1989–96. ANZAAS medal, 1988; Grahame Clark Medal, British Acad., 1999. *Publications:* Cricket Walkabout, 1967, 2nd edn 1988; The Prehistory of Australia, 1969, 2nd edn 1975; Australians to 1788, 1987; Encounters in Place, 1989; Commandant of Solitude, 1992; (ed jtly) My Dear Spencer: the letters of F. J. Gillen to Baldwin Spencer, 1997; (with J. Kamminga) Prehistory of Australia, 1999; numerous excavation reports and historical articles. *Recreation:* gardening. *Address:* 128 Schlich Street, Yarralumla, ACT 2600, Australia. *T:* (2) 62812352.

MULVILLE, James Thomas; Joint Managing Director, Hat Trick Productions, since 1985; *b* 5 Jan. 1955; *s* of James Lawrence Mulville and June Mulville; *m* 1st, 1974, Julia Kelly; 2nd, 1987, Denise O'Donoghue (marr. diss. 1998); 3rd, 1999, Karen Page; one *s* one *d.* *Educ:* Alsop Comprehensive Sch., Liverpool; Jesus Coll., Cambridge (BA Hons; Pres., Cambridge Footlights, 1976–77). With BBC Light Entertainment as writer and producer, 1978–82; co-writer and performer: Who Dares Wins (series), Channel 4, 1983–88; Chelmsford 123, Channel 4, 1987–90; actor: That's Love, 1987–91; GBH, 1991. *Publication:* (jtly) Who Dares Wins, 1986. *Recreations:* my children, family, and friends; films, Everton Football Club. *Address:* c/o Hat Trick Productions, 10 Livonia Street, W1V 3PH. *T:* (020) 7434 2451. *Club:* Royal Automobile.

MUMBENGEGWI, Simbarashe Simbanenduku; High Commissioner for Republic of Zimbabwe in the United Kingdom, and Ambassador to Ireland, since 1999; *b* Chivi, Zimbabwe, 20 July 1945; *s* of late Chivandire Davis Mumbengegwi and Dzivaidzo Shuvai Mumbengegwi; *m* 1983, Emily; one *s* four *d.* *Educ:* Fletcher High Sch., Gweru, Zimbabwe; Monash Univ., Melbourne (BA Gen., BA Combined Hons, DipEd, MEd). Teacher, Dadaya Secondary Sch., Zvishavane, and schools in Melbourne, then Tutor in Politics at colls in Melbourne, 1966–78; MP: Midlands Province, 1980–85; Shurugwi Constituency, Midlands Province, 1985–90; Dep. Speaker and Chm. of Cttees, House of Assembly, Parlt of Zimbabwe, 1980–81; Dep. Minister of Foreign Affairs, 1981–82; Minister: of Water Resources and Develt, 1982; of Nat. Housing, 1982–84; of Public Construction and Nat. Housing, 1984–88; of Transport, 1988–90; Ambassador and Perm. Rep. of Zimbabwe to UN, NY, 1990–95; Vice-Pres., UN Gen. Assembly, 1990–91; Mem., UN Security Council, 1991–92 (Pres. at height of Gulf War, 1991, and 1992); Ambassador to Belgium, Netherlands, Luxembourg and Perm. Rep. to EU, Brussels, 1995; Perm. Rep. to Orgn for Prohibition of Chem. Weapons, The Hague, 1997–99 (Mem. Council, 1997–99). Participated in numerous ministerial confs and Heads of State summits of OAU, 1981–94; Hd of delegns to all annual confs of UN Commn for Human Settlements, 1983–88; served on numerous UN and ACP cttees. Mem., Youth Leagues of Nat. Democratic Party, ZAPU and ZANU, 1960–64; ZANU activist in exile, 1966–72; Zimbabwe African National Union: Dep. Chief Rep., 1973–76, Chief Rep., 1976–78, Australia and Far East; Chief Rep. to Zambia, 1978–80; ZANU-Patriotic Front: Provincial Treas., Midlands Province, 1981–84; Mem., Central Cttee, 1984–94 (Dep. Sec. for Publicity and Inf., 1984–89). *Recreations:* reading, photography, jogging, tennis, golf, swimming. *Address:* Zimbabwe House, 429 Strand, WC2R 0JA. *T:* (020) 7836 7755.

MUMFORD, Prof. Enid; Professor of Organizational Behaviour, Manchester Business School, 1979–88, now Emeritus; *b* 6 March 1924; *d* of Arthur McFarland and Dorothy Evans; *m* 1947, Jim Mumford; one *s* one *d.* *Educ:* Wallasey High Sch.; Liverpool Univ. (BA, MA); Manchester Univ. (PhD). CIPM; FBCS. Personnel Officer, Rotol Ltd, 1946–47; Production Supervisor, J. D. Francis Ltd, 1947–48; Research Associate: Dept of Social Science, Liverpool Univ., 1948–56; Bureau of Public Health Economics, Univ. of Michigan, USA, 1956–57; Res. Lectr, Dept of Social Science, Liverpool Univ., 1957–65; Lectr, then Sen. Lectr and Reader, Manchester Business Sch., 1966–79. LEO Award for Lifetime Exceptional Achievement in Inf. Systems, 1999. *Publications:* Chester Royal Infirmary 1856–1956, 1956; Living with a Computer, 1964; Computers Planning and Personnel Management, 1969; Systems Design for People, 1971; Job Satisfaction: a study of computer specialists, 1972; (with others) Coal and Conflict, 1963; (with O. Banks) The Computer and the Clerk, 1967; (with T. B. Ward) Computers: planning for people, 1968; (with A. Pettigrew) Implementing Strategic Decisions, 1975; (ed, with H. Sackman) Human Choice and Computers, 1975; (ed, with K. Legge) Designing Organizations for Efficiency and Satisfaction, 1978; (with D. Henshall) A Participative Approach to Computer Systems Design, 1978; (with M. Weir) Computer Systems in Work Design, 1979; (ed. with C. Cooper) The Quality of Working Life, 1979; (with others) The Impact of Systems Change in Organizations, 1980; Values, Technology and Work, 1980; Designing Secretaries, 1983; Designing Human Systems for New Technology, 1983; Designing Human Systems for Health Care, 1993; Using Computers for Business Success, 1986; (with W. B. MacDonald) XSEL's Progress, 1989; Tools for Change, 1994; Effective Systems Design and Requirements Analysis, 1995; System Design: ethical tools for ethical change, 1996; Dangerous Decisions: problem solving in tomorrow's world, 1999; contribs to books and journals. *Address:* 4 Windmill Close, Appleton, Warrington, Cheshire WA4 5JS. *T:* (01925) 601039.

MUMFORD, Lady Mary (Katharine), DCVO 1995 (CVO 1982); Lady-in-Waiting to HRH Princess Alexandra, since 1964; *b* 14 Aug. 1940; 2nd *d* of 16th Duke of Norfolk, KG, GCVO, GBE, TD, PC and Lavinia, Duchess of Norfolk, LG, CBE; *heir presumptive* to Lordship of Herries of Terregles; *m* 1986, Gp Captain Anthony Mumford, CVO, OBE. *Address:* North Stoke Cottage, North Stoke, Arundel, West Sussex BN18 9LS. *T:* (01798) 831203; Lantonside, Glencaple, Dumfries DG1 4RQ. *T:* (01387) 770260.

See also Lady Herries of Terregles.

MUMFORD, William Frederick, CB 1989; Deputy Under-Secretary of State for Research Establishments, Ministry of Defence, 1989, retired; Chairman's Panel, Civil Service Selection Board, 1989–95; government departments recruitment consultant; *b* 23 Jan. 1930; *s* of late Frederick Charles Mumford and Hester Leonora Mumford; *m* 1958, Elizabeth Marion, *d* of Nowell Hall; three *s* one *d.* *Educ:* St Albans Sch.; Lincoln Coll., Oxford (MA PPE). Nat. Service commission, Royal Artillery and Herts Yeomanry (TA), 1949–53. Appointed to Home Civil Service, 1953; Asst Principal, 1953–58, Principal, 1958–60, Air Ministry; First Secretary, UK Delegn to NATO, Paris, 1960–65; Principal, 1965–67, Asst Sec., 1967–73, Defence Secretariat, MoD; Dep. Head of UK Delegn to MBFR Exploratory Talks, Vienna, 1973; Principal Private Sec. to Secretaries of State for Defence: Rt Hon. Lord Carrington, 1973–74, Rt Hon. Ian Gilmour, MP and Rt Hon. Roy Mason, MP, 1974–75; Under-Sec., Machinery of Govt Div., CSD, 1975–76; Asst Sec.-Gen. for Defence Planning and Policy, NATO, Brussels, 1976–80; Asst Under-Sec. of State (Material-Naval), MoD, 1980–84; Asst Under-Sec. of State (Estabts and Res.), MoD, 1984–90. Advr to Coopers & Lybrand, management consultants, 1991–95. *Recreations:* antique book collecting, music, swimming.

MUMMERY, Christopher John L.; *see* Lockhart-Mummery.

MUMMERY, Rt Hon. Sir John Frank, Kt 1989; PC 1996; **Rt Hon. Lord Justice Mummery;** a Lord Justice of Appeal, since 1996; *b* 5 Sept. 1938; *s* of Frank Stanley Mummery and Ruth Mummery (*née* Coleman) Coldred, Kent; *m* 1967, Elizabeth Anne Lamond Lackie, *d* of Dr D. G. L. Lackie and Ellen Lackie (*née* Easterbrook), Edinburgh; one *s* one *d.* *Educ:* Oakleigh House, Dover; Dover County Grammar Sch.; Pembroke Coll., Oxford, 1959–63 (MA, BCL; Winter Williams Prize in Law; Hon. Fellow, 1989). National Service, The Border Regt and RAEC, 1957–59. Called to Bar, Gray's Inn (Atkin Schol.), 1964, Bencher, 1985. Treasury Junior Counsel: in Charity Matters, 1977–81; Chancery, 1981–89; a Recorder, 1989; a Judge of the High Court, Chancery Div., 1989–96. President: Employment Appeal Tribunal, 1993–96; Security Services Tribunal, 2000–; Intelligence Services Tribunal, 2000–; Investigatory Powers Tribunal, 2000–. Member, Senate of Inns of Court and Bar, 1978–81; Pres., Council of Inns of Court, 2000–. Member: Justice Cttee on Privacy and the Law, 1967–70; Legal Adv. Commn, Gen. Synod of C of E, 1988–; Council of Legal Educn, 1989–92. Gov., Inns of Court Sch. of Law, 1996–. Hon. Fellow, Soc. for Advanced Legal Studies, 1997. Hon. LLD De Montfort, 1998. *Publication:* (co-ed) Copinger and Skone James on Copyright, 12th edn 1980, 13th edn 1991. *Recreation:* long walks with family, friends and alone. *Address:* Royal Courts of Justice, Strand, WC2A 2LL.

MUNBY, Hon. Sir James (Lawrence), Kt 2000; **Hon. Mr Justice Munby;** Judge of the High Court of Justice, Family Division, since 2000; *b* 27 July 1948; *s* of Denys Lawrence Munby and Mary Munby (*née* Dicks); *m* 1977, Jennifer Anne Lindsay Beckhough; one *s* one *d.* *Educ:* Magdalen College Sch., Oxford; Wadham Coll., Oxford (BA). Called to the Bar, Middle Temple, 1971 (Bencher, 2000); QC 1988. *Address:* c/o Royal Courts of Justice, Strand, WC2A 2LL.

MUNBY, Dr John Latimer, CMG 1997; OBE 1984; Director, British Council, Greece, 1990–97; *b* 14 July 1937; *s* of late Lawrence St John Munby and Jennie Munby; *m* 1961, Lilian Cynthia Hogg; two *s.* *Educ:* King's Sch., Bruton; Lincoln Coll., Oxford (BA Jurisp., MA); Inst. of Educn, London Univ. (PGCE); Univ. of Essex (MA Applied Linguistics, PhD). Nat. service, 2nd Lieut, 1955–57. Educn Officer, Govt of Tanzania, 1961–68; joined British Council, 1969; seconded to Advanced Teachers' Coll., Zaria, then Ahmadu Bello Univ., Nigeria, 1969–72; Director: English Teaching Inf. Centre, 1974–76; English Lang. Consultancies Dept, 1976–78, Representative: Kuwait, 1978–81; Singapore, 1981–85; Dep. Controller, Home Div., 1985–87; Controller, Libraries, Books and Information Div., 1987–90. FRSA 1982. *Publications:* Read and Think, 1968; Communicative Syllabus Design, 1978; contrib. various jls. *Recreations:* music, sport, wine. *Address:* c/o CPS Registry, The British Council, 10 Spring Gardens, SW1A 2BN. *T:* (020) 7930 8466.

MUNDAY, John, FSA; Keeper of Weapons and Antiquities, National Maritime Museum, Greenwich, 1976–84, now Keeper Emeritus; *b* 10 Aug. 1924; *s* of Rodney H. J. Munday and Ethel Emma Cutting; *m* 1953, Brenda Warden; two *s. Educ:* Portsmouth Northern Grammar Sch.; King's Coll., Newcastle; Durham Univ. (BA 1950; MA 1961). FSA 1972. Assistant, Portsmouth Public Libraries and Museums Dept, 1940–42. Served RN, 1942–46; Sub Lieut (Ex. Sp.), RNVR. National Maritime Museum, Greenwich: Asst Keeper, Librarian, 1951; Curator of Presentation, 1964; Dep. Keeper, 1969; Curator of Weapons and Antiquities, 1971. Hon. Vice Pres., Soc. for Nautical Res., 1985 (Hon. Sec., 1979–84); Member: Develt Cttee, SS Great Britain Project, 1980; HMS Victory Adv. Technical Cttee, 1985. *Publications:* For Those in Peril . . . lifesaving, then and now, 1963; Oar Maces of Admiralty, 1966; Dress of the British Sailor, rev. edn 1977; Heads & Tails—the Necessary Seating (with drawings), 1978; Naval Cannon, 1987; E. W. Cooke, RA, FRS: a man of his time, 1996. *Recreations:* painting, collecting, considering. *Address:* Fourteen The Beach, Walmer, Kent CT14 7HE. *T:* (01304) 374493.

MUNDELL, David Gordon; Member (C) South of Scotland, Scottish Parliament, since 1999; *b* 27 May 1962; *s* of Dorah Mundell; *m* 1987, Lynda Jane Carmichael; two *s* one *d. Educ:* Lockerbie Acad.; Edinburgh Univ. (LLB Hons 1984); Univ. of Strathclyde Business Sch. (MBA 1991). Trainee Solicitor, Tindal Oatts, Glasgow, 1985–87; Solicitor, Maxwell Waddell, Glasgow, 1987–89; Sen. Corporate Lawyer, Biggart Baillie & Gifford, Glasgow, 1989–91; Group Legal Advr Scotland, BT, 1991–98; Head of Nat. Affairs, BT Scotland, 1998–99. Member: Law Soc. of Scotland, 1986–; Law Soc., 1992–. *Recreations:* family and friends, travel. *Address:* Scottish Parliament, Edinburgh EH99 1SP. *T:* (0131) 348 5635.

MUNDELL, Prof. Robert Alexander, PhD; Professor of Economics, Columbia University, since 1974; *b* 24 Oct. 1932; *s* of William Campbell Mundell and Lila Teresa Mundell; *m* 1st, 1957, Barba Sheff (*d* 1972); 2nd, 1998, Valerie S. Natsios; one *s. Educ:* Univ. of BC; MIT (PhD); London Sch. of Econs; Univ. of Chicago. Instructor, Univ. of BC, 1957–58; economist, Royal Commn on Price Spreads of Food Products, Ottawa, 1958; Asst Prof. of Econs, Stanford Univ., 1958–59; Prof. of Econs, Johns Hopkins Univ., Sch. of Advanced Internat. Studies, Bologna, 1959–61; Sen. Economist, IMF, 1961-63; Prof. of Internat. Econs, Grad. Inst. Internat. Studies, Geneva, 1965–75; Professor of Economics: Univ. of Chicago, 1966–71; Univ. of Waterloo, Ont., 1972–74. Vis. Prof. of Econs, McGill Univ., 1963–64, 1989–90; First Rockefeller Vis. Res. Prof. of Internat. Econs, Brookings Inst., 1964–65; Guggenheim Fellow, 1971; Annenburg Dist. Schol. in Residence, Univ. of Southern Calif, 1980; Richard Fox Vis. Prof. of Econs, Univ. of Penn, 1990–91. Ed., Jl Pol. Econ., 1966–71. Pres., N American Econ. and Financial Assoc., 1974–78. Hon. Dr: Paris, 1992; People's Univ. of China, 1995. Nobel Prize for Econs, 1999. *Publications:* The International Monetary System: conflict and reform, 1965; Man and Economics, 1968; International Economics, 1968; Monetary Theory: interest, inflation and growth in the world economy, 1971; contrib. learned jls. *Recreations:* painting, tennis, hockey, ski-ing, history. *Address:* 35 Claremont Avenue #5N, New York, NY 10027, USA. *T:* (212) 7490630; Palazzo Mundell, Strada di Santa Columba 2-4, Santa Columba, Siena 53100, Italy. *Club:* Reform.

MUNFORD, William Arthur, MBE 1946; PhD; FLA; Librarian Emeritus, National Library for the Blind; *b* 27 April 1911; *s* of late Ernest Charles Munford and Florence Margaret Munford; *m* 1934, Hazel Despard Wilmer; two *s* one *d. Educ:* Hornsey County Sch.; LSE (BScEcon, PhD). Asst, Hornsey Public Libraries, 1927–31; Chief Asst, Ilford Public Libraries, 1931–34; Borough Librarian, Dover, 1934–45 (Food Exec. Officer, 1939–45); City Librarian, Cambridge, 1945–53; Dir-Gen., Nat. Library for the Blind, 1954–82. Hon. Sec., Library Assoc., 1952–55, Hon. Fellow 1977. Trustee Emeritus, Ulverscroft Foundn. *Publications:* Books for Basic Stock, 1939; Penny Rate: aspects of British public library history, 1951; William Ewart, MP, 1960; Edward Edwards, 1963; (with W. G. Fry) Louis Stanley Jast, 1966; James Duff Brown, 1968; A History of the Library Association, 1877–1977, 1976; (with S. Godbolt) The Incomparable Mac (biog. of Sir J. Y. W. MacAlister), 1983; Who was Who in British Librarianship 1800–1985, 1987; contribs to Librarianship jls, 1933–. *Recreations:* reading, rough gardening, wood sawing, cycling, serendipity. *Address:* 11 Manor Court, Pinehurst, Grange Road, Cambridge CB3 9BE. *T:* (01223) 362962. *Club:* National Liberal.

MUNGLANI, Rajesh, FRCA; Consultant in Pain Management, West Suffolk Hospital, Bury St Edmunds, since 2000; *b* 31 Aug. 1962; *s* of Balwani Rai Munglani and Krishna Gulati; *m* 1989, Dr Jane Bolland; four *d. Educ:* St George's Hosp., Univ. of London (MB BS 1985); DCH 1989. FRCA 1990. Clin Lectr, 1993–96, Lectr in Anaesthesia and Pain Mgt, 1997–2000, Univ. of Cambridge; Consultant in Anaesthesia and Pain Mgt, Addenbrooke's Hosp., Cambridge, 1997–2000. John Farman Prof., RCAnaes, 1997. Mem., St Barnabas' Ch, Cambridge. *Publications:* Pain: current understanding, emerging therapies and novel approaches to drug discovery, 2001; contrib. numerous papers and chapters on scientific basis of chronic pain, spinal pain incl. whiplash and complex regional pain syndromes. *Recreations:* walking in the Lake District, reading. *Address:* BUPA Cambridge Lea Hospital, 30 New Road, Impington, Cambridge CB4 4EL. *T:* (01223) 266927; *e-mail:* rajesh@munglani.com.

MUNIR, (Ashley) Edward, PhD; Barrister; Under Secretary, Ministry of Agriculture, Fisheries and Food, 1982–92; *b* 14 Feb. 1934; *s* of late Hon. Sir Mehmed Munir Bey, Kt, CBE, and late Lady (Vessime) Munir; *m* 1960, Sureyya S. V. Dormen; one *s. Educ:* Brentwood Sch.; St John's Coll., Cambridge (MA 1957); King's Coll., London (PhD 1992). Called to the Bar, Gray's Inn, 1956. Practised as barrister, 1956–60, 1992–; Crown Counsel, 1960–64; entered Govt Legal Service, 1964; Asst Solicitor, MAFF, 1975–82. *Publications:* Perinatal Rights, 1983; Fisheries after Factortame, 1991; Mentally Disordered Offenders, 1993. *Recreations:* walking, music. *Address:* (chambers) 1 Harcourt Buildings, Temple, EC4Y 9DA. *T:* (020) 7353 0375. *Club:* Oxford and Cambridge.

MUNN, Sir James, Kt 1985; OBE 1976; MA; *b* 27 July 1920; *s* of Douglas H. Munn and Margaret G. Dunn; *m* 1946, Muriel Jean Millar Moles; (one *d* decd). *Educ:* Stirling High Sch.; Glasgow Univ. (MA (Hons)). Entered Indian Civil Service, 1941; served in Bihar, 1942–47. Taught in various schools in Glasgow, 1949–57; Principal Teacher of Modern Languages, Falkirk High Sch., 1957–62, Depute Rector, 1962–66; Rector: Rutherglen Acad., 1966–70; Cathkin High Sch., Cambuslang, Glasgow, 1970–83. Univ. Comr, 1988–95; Chairman: Manpower Services Cttee for Scotland, 1984–88; MSC, subseq. Training Commn, 1987–88; Scottish Adv. Bd, Open Coll., 1989–91; Pres., Inst. of Trng and Develt, 1989–92 (Fellow, 1989). Member: Consultative Cttee on Curriculum, 1968–80 (Chm., 1980–87); University Grants Cttee, 1973–82; Chm., Cttee to review structure of curriculum at SIII and SIV, 1975–77. Mem. Court, Strathclyde Univ., 1983–91. Fellow: Paisley Coll. of Technology, 1988; SCOTVEC, 1989; FIPD 1995. Chevalier des Palmes Académiques, 1967. DUniv Stirling, 1978; Hon. LLD Strathclyde, 1988; Hon. DEd Napier Polytechnic, 1989. *Address:* 4 Kincath Avenue, High Burnside, Glasgow G73 4RP. *T:* (0141) 634 4654.

MUNN, Margaret Patricia, (Meg); MP (Lab) Sheffield, Heeley, since 2001; *b* 24 Aug. 1959; *d* of Reginald Edward Munn and Lillian Seward; *m* 1989, Dennis Clifford Bates. *Educ:* Univ. of York (BA Hons Language); Univ. of Nottingham (MA Social Work; CQSW); Open Univ. (Dip. Mgt Studies). Social Work Assistant, Berkshire, 1981–84; Social Worker, 1986–90, Sen. Social Worker, 1990–92, Nottinghamshire; Dist Manager, Barnsley, 1992–96; Children's Service Manager, Wakefield, 1996–99; Asst Dir of Children's Services, Social Services, York, 1999–2000. Mem., Mgt Cttee, Wortley Hall Ltd, 1994–2000; Chm. Cttee, Barnsley Br., CRS Ltd, 1997–2001. *Recreations:* tennis, swimming, gardening. *Address:* House of Commons, SW1A 0AA. *T:* (020) 7219 8316; Barkers Pool House, 2nd Floor, Burgess Street, Sheffield S1 2HF. *T:* (0114) 263 4004.

MUNNS, Victor George; Counsellor (Labour), Washington, 1983–86; *b* 17 June 1926; *s* of Frederick William Munns and Lilian Munns; *m* 1952, Pamela Ruth Wyatt; two *s. Educ:* Haberdashers' Aske's, Hatcham; University Coll., London (BA). Served HM Forces (Army Intell.), 1945–48. Min. of Labour Employment Service, 1951–61; ILO, Trinidad and Belize, 1962–63; Sec., Shipbldg Industry Trng Bd, 1964–66; Res. Staff, Royal Commn on Trade Unions, 1966; Principal, Dept of Employment (Indust. Trng and Indust. Relations), 1967–72; Dep. Chief Officer, Race Relations Bd, 1973–74; Sec., Health and Safety Commn, 1974–77; Asst Sec., Health and Safety Exec., 1977–82. Dir, Nailsworth Festival, 1992–96. *Club:* Royal Over-Seas League.

MUNRO, Sir Alan (Gordon), KCMG 1990 (CMG 1984); HM Diplomatic Service, retired; *b* 17 Aug. 1935; *s* of late Sir Gordon Munro, KCMG, MC and Lilian Muriel Beit; *m* 1962, Rosemary Grania Bacon; twin *s* two *d. Educ:* Wellington Coll.; Clare Coll., Cambridge (MA). MIPM. Mil. Service, 4/7 Dragoon Guards, 1953–55; Middle East Centre for Arab Studies, 1958–60; British Embassy, Beirut, 1960–62; Kuwait, 1961; FO, 1963–65; Head of Chancery, Benghazi, 1965–66 and Tripoli, 1966–68; FO, 1968–73; Consul (Commercial), 1973–74, Consul-Gen., 1974–77, Rio de Janeiro; Head of E African Dept, FCO, 1977–78; Head of Middle East Dept, FCO, 1979; Head of Personnel Ops Dept, FCO, 1979–81; Regl Marketing Dir (ME), MoD, 1981–83; Ambassador to Algeria, 1984–87; Dep. Under-Sec. of State, ME/Africa, FCO, 1987–89; Ambassador to Saudi Arabia, 1989–93. Director: Schroder Asseily & Co. Ltd, 1993–2000; Middle East Internat., 1997–; Dabbagh Gp (Jedda), 1998–2001; Internat. Trade & Investment Missions Ltd, 1998–; Adviser: Tate and Lyle; Nissho IWAI Europe; Vice-Chm., Arab-British Chamber of Commerce, 1993–. Gov., Imperial Coll. Pres., Soc. for Algerian Studies; Chm., Beit Trust for Central Africa; Vice Chm., BRCS, 1994–. *Publication:* An Arabian Affair: politics and diplomacy behind the Gulf War, 1996. *Recreations:* historic buildings, gardening, music, history. *Club:* Travellers.

MUNRO, Dr Alan James; Master, Christ's College, Cambridge, since 1995 (Fellow, since 1962); *b* 19 Feb. 1937; *s* of John Bennet Lorimer Munro, CB, CMG and Gladys, (Pat), Maie Forbes Munro (*née* Simmons); *m* 1960, Mary, *d* of John Gibson Robertson; two *s. Educ:* Edinburgh Acad.; Christ's Coll., Cambridge (BA 1960; MA; PhD 1964). Nat. Service, 2nd Lt Queen's Own Cameron Highlanders, 1955–57; Demonstrator, 1963–67, Lectr, 1967–68, Dept of Biochemistry, Cambridge Univ.; Scientific Officer, MRC Lab. of Molecular Biology, Cambridge, 1968–71; Lectr, 1971–80, Reader, 1980–89, in Immunology, Dept of Pathology, Cambridge Univ.; Jt Founder and Scientific Dir, Cantab Pharmaceuticals plc, 1989–95. Director: Babraham Inst. Ltd, 1996–; Blackwell Science Ltd, 1997–; Genome Research Ltd, 1997–2001; Chm., Lorantis Holdings Ltd, 2000–. Fulbright Travel Schol. and Vis. Scientist, Salk Inst., La Jolla, Calif, 1965–66; Boerhaave Prof., Univ. of Leiden, 1976–77. Chm., Link Cttee on Cell Engrg, DTI, 1994–. Gov., Lister Inst. of Preventive Medicine, 1996–. *Publications:* (jtly) The Immune System, 1981; papers in scientific jls on immunology and molecular biology. *Address:* Master's Lodge, Christ's College, Cambridge CB2 3BU. *T:* (01223) 334940.

MUNRO of Lindertis, Sir Alasdair (Thomas Ian), 6th Bt *cr* 1825; *b* 6 July 1927; *s* of Sir Thomas Torquil Alfonso Munro, 5th Bt and Beatrice Maude (*d* 1974), *d* of Robert Sanderson Whitaker; *S* father, 1985; *m* 1954, Marguerite Lillian, *d* of late Franklin R. Loy, Dayton, Ohio, USA; one *s* one *d. Educ:* Georgetown Univ., Washington, DC (BSS 1946); Univ. of Pennsylvania (MBA 1951); IMEDE, Lausanne. 2nd Lieut, USAF (previously US Army), 1946–53. Senior Vice-Pres., McCann-Erickson, New York, 1952–69; Pres., Jennings Real Estate, Waitsfield, Vermont, 1970–83. Founder, Dir (and Past Pres.), St Andrew's Soc. of Vermont, 1972–; Vice-Chm., Assoc. Bd of Directors, Howard Bank, Waitsfield, 1974–84; Founder, sometime Dir and Pres., Valley Area Assoc., Waitsfield, 1972–80. Chairman: Munro, Jennings & Doig, 1983–90; Highland Develt Gp, 1987–91. *Recreations:* gardening, travel, collector/dealer in Scottish antiques, Scottish heritage matters. *Heir:* s Keith Gordon Munro, *b* 3 May 1959. *Address:* RiverRidge, Box 940, Waitsfield, VT 05673, USA.

MUNRO, Dame Alison, DBE 1985 (CBE 1964); Chairman, Chichester Health Authority, 1982–88; *b* 12 Feb. 1914; *d* of late John Donald, MD; *m* 1939, Alan Lamont Munro (killed on active service, 1941); one *s. Educ:* Queen's Coll., Harley Street; Wynberg Girls' High Sch., South Africa; St Paul's Girls' Sch.; St Hilda's Coll., Oxford (MA). Ministry of Aircraft Production, 1942–45; Principal, Ministry of Civil Aviation, 1945; Asst Sec., 1949; Under-Sec., Ministry of Transport and Civil Aviation, 1958; Under-Sec., Ministry of Aviation, 1960; High Mistress, St Paul's Girls' Sch. Hammersmith, 1964–74. Chm., Merton, Sutton and Wandsworth AHA(T), 1974–82. Chairman: Training Council for Teachers of the Mentally Handicapped, 1966–69; Cttee of Inquiry into Children's Footwear, 1972; Central Transport Consultative Cttee, 1980–85; Maternity Services Adv. Cttee, 1981–85; Code Monitoring Cttee on Infant Formulae, 1985–89; Member: Board, BEA, 1966–73; Board, British Library, 1973–79; British Tourist Authority, 1973–81. Pres., Chichester and Dist Caledonian Soc., 1992–96. Governor: Charing Cross Group of Hospitals, 1967–74; Chichester High Sch. for Girls, 1990–94. Chm., St Richard's Hosp. Equipment Appeal, 1994–98. *Recreations:* gardening, sailing, bridge, Scottish country dancing. *Address:* Harbour Way, Ellanore Lane, West Wittering, West Sussex PO20 8AN. *T:* (01243) 513274. *Clubs:* Civil Service; Goodwood Country; West Wittering Sailing (Cdre, 1986–88).

MUNRO, Colin Andrew; HM Diplomatic Service; Deputy High Representative, Mostar, since 2001; *b* 24 Oct. 1946; *s* of Capt. Frederick Bertram Munro and Jane Eliza (*née* Taylor); *m* 1967, Ehrengard Maria Heinrich; two *s. Educ:* George Watson's Coll., Edinburgh; Edinburgh Univ. (MA Hons Mod. Langs 1968). Asst Principal, Bd of Inland Revenue, 1968–69; FCO, 1969–71; Third, later Second, Sec., Bonn, 1971–73; Second, later First, Sec., Kuala Lumpur, 1973–77; FCO, 1977; Private Sec. to Minister of State, 1979–80; Hd of Chancery, Bucharest, 1981–82; FCO, 1983; Asst Head of W European Dept, 1985–87; Dep. Hd of Mission, E Berlin, 1987–90; Consul Gen., Frankfurt, 1990–93; Hd of OSCE and Council of Europe Dept, FCO, 1993–97; Ambassador to Republic of Croatia, 1997–2000. Mem., Rotary Club. *Publication:* contrib. Jl of Prince Albert Soc. *Recreations:* sports especially hockey, cricket, ski-ing, history, music. *Address:* c/o Foreign and Commonwealth Office, King Charles Street, SW1A 2AH. *Clubs:* Reform; Royal Selangor (Kuala Lumpur).

MUNRO, Colin William Gordon R.; *see* Ross-Munro.

MUNRO, Graeme Neil, FSAScot; Director and Chief Executive, Historic Scotland, since 1991; *b* 28 Aug. 1944; *s* of Daniel Munro and Nancy Kirkwood (*née* Smith); *m* 1972, Nicola Susan Wells (*see* N. S. Munro); one *s* one *d. Educ:* Daniel Stewart's Coll., Edinburgh; Univ. of St Andrews (MA Hons 1967). FSAScot 1990. Joined Scottish Office as Asst Principal, 1968; Scottish Development Department: Housing, 1968; Planning, 1968–70; Private Sec. to Head of Dept, 1971; Principal, Roads, 1972–74; Scottish Home and Health Department: Hosp. Services, 1974–76; Criminal Justice, 1976–79; Asssistant Secrtetary: Dept of Agriculture and Fisheries for Scotland (Fisheries), 1979–83; NHS Funding, Scottish Home and Health Dept, 1983–87; Management and Orgn, Scottish Office Central Services, 1987–90; Dir, Historic Buildings and Monuments, Scotland, 1990–91. FRSA 1999. *Recreations:* gardening, walking, travel, reading. *Address:* (office) Longmore House, Salisbury Place, Edinburgh EH9 1SH. *T:* (0131) 668 8696.

MUNRO, John Farquhar; JP; Member (Lib Dem) Ross Skye and Inverness West, Scottish Parliament, since 1999; *b* 26 Aug. 1934; *m* 1962, Cecilia; one *s* one *d*. *Educ:* Plockton High Sch.; Sea Trng Coll., Gloucester. Merchant Marine Service, 1951–61; Plant Fitter, Kings Road Construction, 1961–65; Manager, contracting co., 1965–75; heavy haulage, bus operation, civil engrg, and quarrying contractor, 1975–93; crofter, 1971–97. Member: Local Council, 1966–74; Skye and Lochalsh DC, 1974–90 (Convenor, 1984–95); Highland Regl Council, 1978–82 (Chair, Gaelic Cttee, 1978–82); Highland Council, 1995–. Chair, Ross, Cromarty and Skye Scottish Liberal Democrats, 1984–98. Non-executive Director: Highland Opportunities Ltd; Acair Publishing; Skye and Lochalsh Enterprise; former Mem., Electricity Consultative Council; Chair: Rail Develt Partnership; Fishery Harbours Mgt; Shipping Service Adv. Cttee, Caledonian MacBrayne. Trustee, Gaelic Coll., Skye. *Recreations:* sailing, fishing, the company of my grandchildren. *Address:* Glomach House, Aultnachruinne, Glenshiel, Kyle of Lochalsh, Wester Ross IV40 8HN. *T:* (01599) 511222.

MUNRO, Kenneth Alexander; Member, Royal Commission on Reform of the House of Lords, 1999; *b* 17 Dec. 1936; *s* of James Gibb Munro and Jean Ralston (*née* McKay); *m* 1961, Elizabeth Coats Forrest McCreanor; two *d*. *Educ:* Hutchesons' Boys' Grammar Sch., Glasgow; Univ. of Glasgow (MA 1963). Served Intelligence Corps, 1955–57. Worked in family business, 1957–59; Scottish American Investment Co. Ltd, 1963–66; Electrical Trades Union, 1966–67; NEDO, 1967–69; Ford Motor Co. Ltd, 1969–74 (on secondment to Pay Bd, 1973–74); European Commission, 1974–98: responsible for employment policy in transport and Asst to Dir Gen. for Transport, Brussels, 1974–82; Press Officer and Dep. Head of Office, London, 1982–88; Head of Commn Office, Edinburgh, 1988–98. Chm., Scottish Centre for Public Policy, 1997–. Member: Equal Opportunities Adv. Cttee for Scotland, 1993–; BP-Amoco Adv. Bd for Scotland, 1997–. Mem. (Lab), Brentwood DC, Essex, 1971–74. Convenor, Children in Scotland, 1999–. Hon. Sec., 1991–2000, Vice Chm., 2000–, Scottish Council, Eur. Movement; Convenor, Scotland in Europe, 2000–. Hon. Fellow, Faculty of Law, Univ. of Edinburgh, 1998. Contested: (Lab) W Aberdeenshire, 1964; (New Scottish Lab) Lothian, Scottish Parlt elecns, 1999. Vice-Chm., John Smith Meml Trust, 1994–. Mem., Campaigning Cttee, Queen Margaret UC, 1999–. *Recreations:* theatre, cinema, swimming, walking. *Address:* 23 Greenhill Gardens, Edinburgh EH10 4BL. *T:* (0131) 447 2284. *Club:* New (Edinburgh).

MUNRO, Sir Kenneth (Arnold William), 16th Bt *cr* 1634, of Foulis-Obsdale, Ross-shire; *b* 26 June 1910; *s* of Arnold Harry Munro (*d* 1968), *g s* of Sir Charles Munro, 9th Bt, and Hilda Marion Smith (*d* 1961); *S* cousin, 1996; *m* 1935, Olive Freda, *d* of Francis Broome; one *s* one *d*. *Heir:* *s* Ian Kenneth Munro; *b* 5 April 1940.

MUNRO, Neil Christopher; Director, Revenue Policy: People and Planning, Board of Inland Revenue, since 2001; *b* 23 July 1947; *s* of late Alan and of Jean Munro; *m* 1967, Caroline Anne Virginia Smith; two *d*. *Educ:* Wallasey Grammar Sch.; St John's Coll., Oxford (BA Hons Mod. Hist., MA). MCIPD (MIPD 1993). Board of Inland Revenue, 1970–: various posts in tax policy and mgt work; seconded to CBI as Head, Taxation Dept, 1978–80; Dep. Dir of Personnel, 1991–94; Director: Mgt Services, 1994–96; Tax Law Rewrite Project, 1996–2001. *Recreations:* modern literature, music, cricket, cooking. *Address:* Board of Inland Revenue, 22 Kingsway, WC2B 6NR. *Club:* MCC.

MUNRO, Nicola Susan; Head of Environment Group, Scottish Executive Rural Affairs Department, since 2000; *b* 11 Jan. 1948; *d* of Ernest Derek Wells and Barbara Gurney Wells; *m* 1972, Graeme Neil Munro, *qv*; one *s* one *d*. *Educ:* Harrogate Grammar Sch.; Univ. of Warwick (BA Hons History). Scottish Office, later Scottish Executive, 1970–: Head of Div. (hosp. services, food, med. educn), Scottish Home and Health Dept, 1986–89; Head of Div. (urban and local economic policy), Scottish Office Industry Dept, 1989–92; Head of Div. (curriculum, assessment, careers service, educn industry links), Scottish Office Educn Dept, 1992–95; Under-Sec., Public Health Policy, Scottish Office, then Scottish Executive, Dept of Health, 1995–2000. FRSA 1996. *Recreations:* reading, travel, gardening, family, friends. *Address:* Scottish Executive, Rural Affairs Department, Victoria Quay, Edinburgh EH6 6QQ.

MUNRO, Sir Sydney Douglas G.; *see* Gun-Munro.

MUNROW, Roger Davis, CB 1993; Chief Master of the Supreme Court of Judicature (Chancery Division), 1986–92, retired (Master, 1985–86); *b* 20 March 1929; *s* of late William Davis Munrow, CBE and Constance Caroline Munrow (*née* Moorcroft); *m* 1957, Marie Jane Beresford (*d* 2001); three *d*. *Educ:* Bryanston School; Oriel College, Oxford. MA; Solicitor. Entered Treasury Solicitor's Dept as Legal Assistant, 1959; Senior Legal Assistant, 1965; Assistant Treasury Solicitor, 1973; Principal Asst Treasury Solicitor, 1981. *Recreations:* swimming, cycling. *Address:* 5 Mallard Close, Harnham, Salisbury, Wilts SP2 8JB.

MURAD, Prof. Ferid, MD, PhD; Professor and Chairman, Department of Integrative Biology, Pharmacology and Physiology, Houston Medical School, since 1997 and Director, Institute of Molecular Medicine, Houston, since 1999, University of Texas; *b* 14 Sept. 1936; *s* of John Murad and Josephine Bowman; *m* 1958, Carol A. Leopold; one *s* four *d*. *Educ:* DePauw Univ. (BA 1958); Sch. of Medicine, Western Reserve Univ. (MD 1965; PhD 1965). University of Virginia: Dir, Clin. Res. Center, Sch. of Medicine, 1971–81; Prof., Depts of Internal Medicine and Pharmacology, 1975–81; Stanford University: Prof., Depts of Internal Medicine and Pharmacology, 1981–88; acting Chm., Dept of Medicine, 1986–88; Adjunct Prof., Dept of Pharmacology, Northwestern Univ., 1988–96. Albert and Mary Lasker Foundn Award for Basic Research, 1996; Nobel Prize in Medicine or Physiology, 1998. *Publications:* papers, published lecture. *Recreations:* golf, carpentry. *Address:* Department of Integrative Biology, Pharmacology and Physiology, University of Texas Medical School-Houston, PO Box 20708, Houston, TX 77225, USA. *Fax:* (713) 5007444, *e-mail:* ferid.murad@uth.tmc.edu.

MURDIN, Paul Geoffrey, OBE 1988; PhD; FInstP; Senior Fellow, Institute of Astronomy, Cambridge University, since 2002; *b* 5 Jan. 1942; *s* of Robert Murdin and Ethel Murdin (*née* Chubb); *m* 1964, Lesley Carol Milburn; two *s* one *d*. *Educ:* Trinity School of John Whitgift; Wadham Coll., Oxford (BA Physics); Univ. of Rochester, NY (PhD Physics and Astronomy). FRAS 1970; FInstP 1992. Res. Associate, Univ. of Rochester, 1970–71; Sen. Res. Associate, Royal Greenwich Observatory, 1971–74; Sen. Res. Scientist, Anglo-Australian Observatory, NSW, 1975–78; Royal Greenwich Observatory: Prin. Sci. Officer, 1979–81; Hd of La Palma Operations, 1981–87; Hd of Astronomy Div., 1987–90; Dir, Royal Observatory, Edinburgh, 1991–93; Head of Astronomy, PPARC, and Dir of Sci., BNSC, 1994–2001. Sen. Mem., Wolfson Coll., Cambridge, 1990–. Mem. Bd of Trustees, Nat. Maritime Museum, 1990–. Pres., Faulkes Telescope Corp., 1999–. Member: Royal Astronomical Soc., 1963– (Councillor, 1997–99; Vice-Pres., 2000–01; Treas., 2001–); European Astronomical Soc., 1991– (Vice-Pres., 1991–93; Pres., 1993–97). *Publications:* The Astronomer's Telescope (with Patrick Moore), 1963; Radio Waves from Space, 1969; (with L. Murdin) The New Astronomy, 1974; (with D. Allen and D. Malin) Catalogue of the Universe, 1980; (with D. Malin) Colours of the Stars, 1985; End in Fire, 1989; Encyclopedia of Astronomy & Astrophysics, 2001; over 150 pubns in astronom. and other sci. jls, principally Monthly Notices of RAS. *Recreations:* writing, music, natural history, history of art. *Address:* Institute of Astronomy, Madingley Road, Cambridge CB3 0HA; *e-mail:* paul@murdin.com.

MURDOCH, Elisabeth, (Mrs M. R. Freud); Chairman and Chief Executive, Shine Entertainment, since 2001; *b* 22 Aug. 1968; *d* of Keith Rupert Murdoch, *qv* and Anna Murdoch Mann (*née* Torv); *m* 1st, 1994, Elkin Kwesi Pianim; two *d*; 2nd, 2001, Matthew Rupert Freud, *qv*; one *d*. *Educ:* Vassar Coll., NY (BA). Dir of Programming, KSTU-TV, 1994–95; Pres. and CEO, EP Communications, 1995–96; Man. Dir, BSkyB Plc, 1996–2001. *Address:* Shine Entertainment, 2 Exmoor Street, W10 6BD.

MURDOCH, Dame Elisabeth (Joy), AC 1989; DBE 1963 (CBE 1961); *b* 8 Feb. 1909; *d* of Rupert Greene and Marie (*née* de Lancey Forth); *m* 1928, Sir Keith (Arthur) Murdoch (*d* 1952); one *s* three *d*. *Educ:* Clyde Sch., Woodend, Victoria. Mem., 1933–65, Pres., 1953–65, Mgt Cttee, Royal Children's Hospital, Melbourne. Trustee: National Gallery, Victoria, 1968–76, now Emeritus Trustee; McClelland Regl Art Gall., 1972. Founding Mem., Bd of Mgt, Victorian Tapestry Workshop, 1976– (Chm., 1986–88). Hon. LLD Melbourne, 1982. *Recreation:* gardening. *Address:* Cruden Farm, Langwarrin, Victoria 3910, Australia. *Clubs:* Alexandra, Lyceum (Melbourne).
See also K. R. Murdoch.

MURDOCH, Gordon Stuart; QC 1995; a Recorder, South Eastern Circuit, since 1995; *b* 7 June 1947; *s* of late Ian William Murdoch and Margaret Henderson McLaren Murdoch; *m* 1976, Sally Kay Cummings; two *s*. *Educ:* Falkirk High Sch.; Sidney Sussex Coll., Cambridge (MA, LLB). Called to the Bar, Inner Temple, 1970. *Recreations:* music, walking. *Address:* 4 Paper Buildings, Temple, EC4Y 7EX. *T:* (020) 7583 0816.

MURDOCH, John Derek Walter; Director, Courtauld Institute Gallery, since 1993; *b* 1 April 1945; *s* of James Duncan and Elsie Elizabeth Murdoch; *m* 1st, 1967, Prue Smijth-Windham (marr. diss. 1986); one *s* two *d*; 2nd, 1990, Susan Barbara Lambert, *qv*. *Educ:* Shrewsbury Sch.; Magdalen Coll., Oxford (BA); King's Coll., London (MPhil). Asst Keeper, Birmingham City Art Gall., 1969–73; Victoria & Albert Museum: Asst, then Dep. Keeper, Dept of Paintings, 1973–86; Keeper of Prints, Drawings, Photographs and Paintings, 1986–89; Asst Dir in charge of Collections, 1989–93. Vis. Fellow, British Art Center, Yale Univ., 1979. Trustee: William Morris Gall., Walthamstow, 1975– (Dep. Chm., 1997–); Dove Cottage, Grasmere, 1982–. *Publications:* David Cox, 1970; Byron, 1974; English Watercolours, 1977; The English Miniature, 1981; Discovery of the Lake District, 1984; A Sort of National Property, 1985; Painters and the Derby China Works, 1986; Seventeenth Century Portrait Miniatures in the Collection of the Victoria and Albert Museum, 1997; contrib. to Rev. of English Studies, Jl of Warburg and Courtauld Insts, Burlington Magazine, Apollo. *Address:* 14 South End Row, W8 5BZ. *T:* (020) 7938 2003.

MURDOCH, (Keith) Rupert, AC 1984; publisher; Chairman, since 1991 and Group Chief Executive, since 1979, The News Corporation Ltd, Australia; Director, News International plc, UK, since 1969 (Chairman, 1969–87 and 1994–95; Chief Executive, 1969–81; Managing Director, 1982–83); *b* 11 March 1931; *s* of late Sir Keith Murdoch and of Dame Elisabeth (Joy) Murdoch, *qv*; *m* Patricia Booker (marr. diss.); one *d*; *m* 1967, Anna Torv (marr. diss. 1999); two *s* one *d*; *m* 1999, Wendi Deng. Chm., News America Publishing Inc.; Dir, Times Newspapers Hldgs Ltd, 1981– (Chm., 1982–90 and 1994–); Chm. and Chief Exec. Officer, Twentieth Century Fox, 1992–, Fox Inc., 1992–; Chm., British Sky Broadcasting, 1999–. KSG 1998. *Address:* 1211 Avenue of the Americas, New York, NY 10036, USA; 1 Virginia Street, E1 9XY.
See also E. Murdoch.

MURDOCH, Rupert; *see* Murdoch, K. R.

MURDOCH, Susan Barbara; *see* Lambert, S. B.

MURE, Kenneth Nisbet; QC (Scot.) 1989; *b* 11 April 1947; *o s* of Robert and Katherine Mure. *Educ:* Cumbernauld JS Sch.; Glasgow High Sch.; Glasgow Univ. (MA, LLB). FTII 1971. Admitted to Scots Bar, 1975; called to English Bar, Gray's Inn, 1990. Lectr, Faculty of Law, Glasgow Univ., 1971–83. Temp. Sheriff, 1983–99. Mem., CICAP, 2000–. *Address:* Advocates' Library, Edinburgh EH1 1RF.

MURERWA, Dr Herbert Muchemwa; Minister of Finance, Zimbabwe, 1996–2000; *b* 31 May 1941; *m* 1969, Ruth Chipo; one *s* four *d*. *Educ:* Harvard University. EdD (Educational Planning). Economic Affairs Officer, UN Economic Commission for Africa, Addis Ababa, 1978–80; Permanent Sec., Min. of Manpower Planning, 1980–81; Permanent Sec., Min. of Labour and Social Services, 1982–84; High Comr for Zimbabwe in UK, 1984–90; Minister for the Envmt and Tourism, 1990–95; Minister of Industry and Commerce, 1995–96. *Address:* c/o Ministry of Finance, Munhumutapa Building, Samora Machel Avenue, Private Bag 7705, Causeway, Harare, Zimbabwe.

MURFIN, Dr David Edward; Principal in general medical practice, Ammanford, since 1974; *b* 15 June 1946; *s* of Leslie Walter Murfin and Elizabeth Ann Murfin; *m* 1972, Ann Margaret Lewis; one *s* one *d*. *Educ:* Gowerton Boys' Grammar Sch.; King's Coll. London; St George's Hosp., London. Adviser to ABPI, 1991–. Mem. Council, RCGP, 1984–90 and 1993–96 (Vice Chm., 1994–96); Mem., Standing Cttee on Medicines, RCPCH, 1996–2001. *Recreations:* reading, walking, cycling. *Address:* Brynteg Surgery, Brynmawr Avenue, Ammanford, Dyfed SA18 2DA. *T:* (01269) 592058.

MURGATROYD, Prof. Walter, PhD; Professor of Thermal Power, Imperial College of Science and Technology, 1968–86, now Professor Emeritus; Rockefeller International Fellow, Princeton University, 1979; *b* 15 Aug. 1921; *s* of Harry G. Murgatroyd and Martha W. Strachan; *m* 1952, Denise Geneviève, *d* of late Robert Adolphe Schlumberger, Paris and Bénouville; one *s* one *d* (and one *s* decd). *Educ:* St Catharine's Coll., Cambridge. BA 1946, PhD 1952. Hawker Aircraft Ltd, 1942–44; Rolls Royce Ltd, 1944–46; Univ. of Cambridge (Liquid Metal and Reactor heat transfer research), 1947–54; UK Atomic Energy Authority, Harwell, 1954–56; Head of Dept of Nuclear Engineering, Queen Mary Coll., Univ. of London, 1956–67, and Dean of Engineering, 1966–67. Member: British-Greek Mixed Commn, 1963–78; British-Belgian Mixed Commn, 1964–78; British-Austrian Mixed Commn, 1965–78. Specialist Adviser to H of C Select Cttee on Energy,

1980–90. *Publications:* contrib. to various scientific and technical journals. *Recreation:* music. *Address:* 7 Currie Hill Close, SW19 7DX. *T:* (020) 8946 0415.

MURIA, Hon. Sir (Gilbert) John Baptist, Kt 1995; Chief Justice, Solomon Islands, since 1993; *b* 2 Feb. 1953; *s* of late John Baptist Manumate and of Adriana Gala; *m* 1982, Rosemary Kekealu; one *s* three *d.* *Educ:* Univ. of Papua New Guinea (LLB). Called to the Bar: PNG, 1980; Solomon Is, 1981. Sen. Crown Counsel, Solomon Is, 1980; Sen. Legal Officer, 1981–83; Chief Legal Officer, 1984–87; Dep. Public Solicitor, 1987–89; Public Solicitor, 1989–91; Actg Attorney Gen., 1989; Puisne Judge, High Court of Solomon Is, 1991–93. *Address:* High Court of Solomon Islands, PO Box G21, Honiara, Solomon Islands. *T:* 21632.

MURIE, John Andrew, MD; FRCSGlas, FRCSE; Consultant Vascular Surgeon, Royal Infirmary of Edinburgh, since 1989; *b* 7 Aug. 1949; *s* of John Andrew Murie and Jessie Murie (*née* Sutherland); *m* 1977, Edythe Munn; one *d.* *Educ:* Univ. of Glasgow (BSc 1st Cl. Hons Biochem. 1971; MB ChB Hons 1975; MD 1984); MA Oxon 1984. FRCSGlas 1979; FRCSE 1993. Clin. Reader in Surgery, Nuffield Dept of Surgery, Univ. of Oxford and Fellow, Green Coll., Oxford, 1984–89; Hon. Consultant Surgeon, John Radcliffe Hosp., Oxford, 1984–89; Clin. Dir, Gen. and Vascular Surgery, Royal Infirmary of Edinburgh, 1995–2000; Hon. Sen. Lectr, Univ. of Edinburgh, 1989–. Mem. Editl Team, 1989-96, Jt Sen. Ed., 1996–, British Jl Surgery. Mem., Nat. Panel of Specialists, NHS Scotland, 2000–. Member of Council: Assoc. of Surgeons of GB and Ireland, 1994–99 (Hon. Editl Sec., 1996–99); Vascular Surgical Soc. of GB and Ireland, 1998–; RCPSG, 1998–. *Publications:* (ed with J. J. Earnshaw) The Evidence for Vascular Surgery, 1999; contrib. numerous chapters in textbooks and papers in learned jls on general theme of surgery (particularly vascular surgery). *Recreations:* golf, running, reading, food and wine. *Address:* Department of Surgery, Royal Infirmary of Edinburgh, 1 Lauriston Place, Edinburgh EH3 9YW. *T:* (0131) 536 1000; 8 Dalhousie Crescent, Eskbank, Edinburgh EH22 3DP. *T:* (0131) 663 5676.

MURLEY, John Tregarthen, CB 1988; DPhil; *b* 22 Aug. 1928; *s* of John Murley and Dorothea Birch; *m* 1954, Jean Patricia Harris; one *d.* *Educ:* University College, London (BA 1st Cl. Hons History); St Antony's Coll., Oxford (DPhil). Entered FO, 1955; Counsellor, Washington, 1976–80. *Publication:* The Origin and Outbreak of the Anglo-French War of 1793, 1959. *Recreations:* tennis, golf, piano.

MURNAGHAN, Dermot John; Presenter, ITV Evening News, since 2001; *b* 26 Dec. 1957; *s* of Vincent Murnaghan and Wendy Murnaghan (*née* Bush); *m* 1989, Maria Keegan; three *d.* *Educ:* Sussex Univ. (BA 1979, MA History 1980); City Univ. (Postgrad. Dip. Journalism, 1983). Presenter, Business Prog., Channel 4, 1984–88; correspondent, EBC Switzerland, 1988–89; presenter: Channel 4 Daily, 1989–92; Lunchtime News, ITN, 1992–99; ITV Nightly News, 1999–2001; presenter: The Big Story, ITV, 1993–97; Britain's Most Wanted, ITV, 1997–. Interview of the Year Award, RTS, 1998; Newscaster of the Year Award, TRIC, 2000. *Recreations:* running, film, football, sailing, chess. *Address:* ITN, 200 Gray's Inn Road, WC1X 8XZ. *T:* (020) 7833 3000.

MURPHY, Andrew John; Sheriff of Tayside Central and Fife at Falkirk, since 1991; *b* 16 Jan. 1946; *s* of Robert James Murphy and Robina Murphy (*née* Scott); *m* 1980, Susan Margaret Thomson; two *s* two *d.* *Educ:* Allan Glen's School, Glasgow; Edinburgh Univ. (MA, LLB). 2nd Lieut RA (V), 1971–73; Flt Lieut RAF, 1973–75. Admitted to Faculty of Advocates, Scottish Bar, 1970; called to Bar, Middle Temple, 1990; Crown Counsel, Hong Kong, 1976–79; Standing Junior Counsel to Registrar General for Scotland, 1982–85; Temporary Sheriff, 1983–85; Sheriff of Grampian, Highland and Islands at Banff and Peterhead, 1985–91. *Address:* c/o Sheriff's Chambers, Court House, Main Street, Camelon, Falkirk FK1 4AR.

MURPHY, Rear-Adm. Anthony Albert, CBE 1976; Special Project Executive, Ministry of Defence, 1977–82; retired, 1983; *b* 19 May 1924; *s* of Albert Edward Murphy and Jennie (*née* Giles); *m* 1954, Antonia Theresa (*née* Rayner); four *s.* *Educ:* Sir George Monoux Grammar Sch. National Provincial Bank, 1940–42; joined RN, 1942; commnd, 1944; Western Approaches, 1944–45; HMS Vanguard (Royal Tour of S Africa), 1945–49; HMS Bulwark (Suez); Comdr 1960; HMS Yarmouth/6th Frigate Sqdn, Kuwait, 1961–63; HMS Eagle, 1965–67; Captain 1967; Dir, Naval Guided Weapons, 1970–73; in comd HMS Collingwood, 1973–76; Rear-Adm. 1977; Vice-Pres., and Senior Naval Mem., Ordnance Board, 1977. *Recreations:* cricket, soccer (Chm. RNFA, 1973–76), country activities.

MURPHY, Brian Gordon; Building Societies' Ombudsman, 1992–99; *b* 18 Oct. 1940; *s* of Albert and Doris Murphy; *m* 1973, Judith Ann Parkinson. *Educ:* Mill Hill Sch. Articled Smiles & Co.; admitted Solicitor, 1966; with Roythorne & Co. and Russell & Dumoulin, Canada; Partner: Knapp Fishers, 1968–87; Farrer & Co., 1987–92. Pt-time Chm., Industrial Tribunals, 1991–92. Vice-Chm., Incorp. Council of Law Reporting for Eng. and Wales, 1992–96; Mem. Council, Law Soc., 1982–93 (Chm., Employment Law Cttee, 1987–90); Pres., Westminster Law Soc., 1983–84. *Recreations:* golf, theatre, photography, travel. *Club:* Phyllis Court (Henley).

MURPHY, Mrs Brian Taunton; *see* Hufton, Prof. Olwen.

MURPHY, Christopher Philip Yorke; Diocesan Secretary, Diocese of Sodor and Man, 1993–2000; *b* 20 April 1947; *s* of Philip John and Dorothy Betty Murphy; *m* 1969, Sandra Gillian Ashton. *Educ:* Devonport High Sch.; The Queen's Coll., Oxford (MA). Formerly Associate Dir, D'Arcy MacManus & Masius. President, Oxford Univ. Conservative Assoc., 1967; held number of Conservative Party offices, 1968–72. Parish Councillor, Windlesham, Surrey, 1972–76. Contested (C): Bethnal Green and Bow, Feb. 1974, Oct. 1974. MP (C) Welwyn Hatfield, 1979–87. Vice-Chairman: Parly Urban and New Town Affairs Cttee, 1980–87; Parly Arts and Heritage Cttee, 1981–86; Mem., Select Cttee on Statutory Instruments, 1980–87 (rep of cttee on Commonwealth Delegated Legislation Cttee, 1980–87); UK Delegate to Council of Europe/WEU, 1983–87 (Hon. Associate, 1988). Vice-President: C of E Artistic Heritage Commn, 1984–87; C of E Youth & Drugs Commn, 1986–87. Member: Nat. Cttee for 900th Anniversary of Domesday Book, 1986; Chief Pleas of Sark (Parlt), 1989–90 (Vice-Pres., Internat. Cttee of Chief Pleas, 1989–90); Arts Council of Bailiwick of Guernsey, 1988–90; Council, Société Guernésiaise, 1988–90. Life Mem., CPA, 1987. Hon. Sec., Société Sercquiaise, 1988–90. Sec., Sodor & Man Diocesan Synod, and Bishop's Advr, 1991–2000; Chapter Clerk, St German's Cathedral, 1992–2000; Secretary: Diocesan Bd of Finance, 1993–2000; Church Comrs for IOM, 1993–2000; Legislative Cttee, 1997–2000; DAC for Care of Churches, 1997–2000. FRSA. Freeman, City of London, 1984. Hon. Citizen, Cork, 1985. *Recreations:* arts, heritage, travel, conservation, walking. *Address:* 26 The Fountains, Ramsey, Isle of Man IM8 1NN. *Club:* Oxford Union Society.

MURPHY, Cornelius McCaffrey, (Neil Murphy), MBE 1982; Chairman, New Life Venues Ltd, 1992–95, retired; *b* 31 May 1936; 2nd *s* of Edward and Annie Murphy, Glasgow; *m* 1992, Carmel Murphy; two *s*; two *d* by previous *m*, and two step *d.* *Educ:* Holyrood Sch.; Univ. of Glasgow (MA 1958). Joined The Builder Group, 1962, following spells of teaching and management trng: Editor, 1974–83, Editor-in-Chief, 1983–87, Building Magazine; Dir, 1979–92; Man. Dir, Building (Publishers) Ltd, 1981–90, Group Man. Dir, 1990–92. *Recreations:* reading, golf.

MURPHY, Denis; MP (Lab) Wansbeck, since 1997; *b* 2 Nov. 1948; *s* of late John Murphy and of Josephine Murphy; *m* 1969, Nancy, *d* of Robert and Annie Moffat; one *s* one *d.* *Educ:* St Cuthbert's Grammar Sch., Newcastle upon Tyne; Northumberland Coll. Apprentice electrician, 1965–69; underground electrician, Ellington Colliery, 1969–94. Mem. (Lab) Wansbeck DC (Leader, 1994–97). *Address:* House of Commons, SW1A 0AA.

MURPHY, Dervla; *b* 28 Nov. 1931; *d* of Fergus Murphy and Kathleen Rochfort-Dowling; one *d.* *Educ:* Ursuline Convent, Waterford. American Irish Foundn Literary Award, 1975; Christopher Ewart-Biggs Meml Prize, 1978; Irish Amer. Cultural Inst. Literary Award, 1985. *Publications:* Full Tilt, 1965, 7th edn 1984; Tibetan Foothold, 1966, 3rd edn 1968; The Waiting Land, 1967, 3rd edn 1969; In Ethiopia with a Mule, 1968, 4th edn 1985; On a Shoe String to Coorg, 1976, 3rd edn 1985; Where the Indus is Young, 1977, 2nd edn 1984; A Place Apart, 1978, 5th edn 1984; Wheels Within Wheels, 1979, 5th edn 1984; Race to the Finish?, 1981; Eight Feet in the Andes, 1983, 2nd edn 1985; Muddling Through in Madagascar, 1985, 3rd edn 1987; Ireland, 1985; Tales from Two Cities, 1987; (ed) Embassy to Constantinople, the Travels of Lady Mary Wortley Montague, 1988; In Cameroon with Egbert, 1989; Transylvania and Beyond, 1992; The Ukimwi Road, 1993; South from the Limpopo, 1997; Visiting Rwanda, 1998; One Foot in Laos, 1999; Bothered in the Balkans, 2002. *Recreations:* reading, music, cycling, swimming, walking. *Address:* Lismore, Co. Waterford, Ireland.

MURPHY, Elaine, MD, PhD; FRCPsych; Chairman, East London and the City Health Authority, since 1999; *b* Nottingham, 16 Jan. 1947; *d* of Roger Lawson and Nell Lawson (*née* Allitt); *m* 1969, John Matthew Murphy (marr. diss. 2001). *Educ:* Univ. of Manchester Med. Sch. (MB, ChB 1971; MD 1979); PhD 2000. FRCPsych 1986. Prof. of Psychiatry of Old Age, UMDS of Guy's and St Thomas' Hosps, 1983–96; Res. Fellow, Wellcome Inst. for Hist. of Medicine, 1996–; Hon. Prof. of Old Age Psychiatry, QMW, 1995–; Dist Gen. Manager, Lewisham and N Southwark HA, 1988–90; Chm., City and Hackney NHS Trust, 1996–99. Vice-Chm., Mental Health Act Commn, 1988–94. *Publications:* Dementia and Mental Illness in Older People, 1986, 2nd edn 1993; Affective Disorders in the Elderly, 1986; After the Asylums, 1991; papers on mental disorder, social policy and social history. *Recreations:* Italy, social history research. *Address:* 382 Lauderdale Tower, Barbican, EC2Y 8NA; The Grange, Brockdish, Norfolk IP21 4JE.

MURPHY, Foster; *see* Murphy, R. S. F.

MURPHY, Rev. Canon Gervase; *see* Murphy, Rev. Canon J. G. M. W.

MURPHY, Ian Patrick; QC 1992; a Recorder, since 1990; *b* 1 July 1949; *s* of Patrick Murphy and Irene Grace (*née* Hooper); *m* 1974, Penelope Gay; two *d.* *Educ:* St Illtyd's Coll., Cardiff; LSE (LLB). Chartering Clerk, Baltic Exchange, 1970–71; called to the Bar, Middle Temple, 1972, Bencher, 2001; Asst Recorder, 1986–90. Asst Comr, Parly Boundary Commn for Wales, 1996–. *Recreations:* golf, ski-ing, cricket. *Address:* 9 Park Place, Cardiff CF10 3DP. *T:* (029) 2038 2731; 3 Llandaff Chase, Llandaff, Cardiff CF5 2NA. *Clubs:* Cardiff County; Royal Porthcawl Golf.

MURPHY, James; MP (Lab) Eastwood, since 1997; *b* 23 Aug. 1967; *s* of Jim Murphy and Anne Murphy. *Educ:* Bellarmine Secondary Sch., Glasgow; Milnerton High Sch., Cape Town; Univ. of Strathclyde. Dir, Endsleigh Insurance, 1994–96; Project Manager, Scottish Lab. Party, 1996–97. PPS to Sec. of State for Scotland, 2001–. Chm., Labour Friends of Israel, 2001–. Pres., NUS, 1994–96. *Address:* House of Commons, SW1A 0AA.

MURPHY, James Joseph, (Jim); Director of Social Services, Manchester City Council, 1995–2000; *b* 11 July 1952; *s* of George Joseph Murphy and Christina Frances Murphy; *m* 1983, Dorothy Anne Lewis; one *s* one *d.* *Educ:* St Bede's Coll., Manchester; Liverpool Univ. (BA Hons 1973; CQSW 1976); Manchester Univ. (MA Econ 1983). Social Worker, Gateshead, 1974–75; Social Worker and Team Leader, Liverpool, 1976–86; Manchester City Council: Team Leader, Social Services Dept, 1986–88; Policy Officer, Chief Exec's Dept, 1988–90; Asst Dir of Recreation, 1991–92; Purchasing Manager, 1992–93, Asst Dir, 1993–95, Social Services Dept; Sen. Manager, Quality Control, Wigan, 1990–91. Trustee and Hon. Treas., Russian European Trust for Welfare Reform, 1997–2000. *Recreations:* reading, travel, family activities.

MURPHY, James Patrick; Sheriff of Glasgow and Strathkelvin, 1989–2001; *b* 24 Jan. 1932; *s* of Henry Francis Murphy and Alice (*née* Rooney); *m* 1956, Maureen Coyne; two *s* one *d.* *Educ:* Notre Dame Convent; St Aloysius' Coll., Glasgow; Univ. of Glasgow (BL 1953). RNVR, 1952–57. Admitted Solicitor, 1953; assumed partner, R. Maguire Cook & Co., Glasgow, 1959; founded, with J. Ross Harper, firm of Ross Harper & Murphy, Glasgow, 1961; Sheriff of N Strathclyde, 1976–89. President: Glasgow Juridical Soc., 1962–63; Glasgow Bar Assoc., 1966–67; Sheriffs' Assoc., 1991–92; Mem. Council, Law Soc. of Scotland, 1974–76. Examnr, Glasgow Univ., 1990–94. Governor, St Aloysius' Coll., Glasgow, 1978–86. *Recreations:* bird watching, tennis, cycling, books, the history of writing, footering. *Address:* 8 Kirklee Gate, Glasgow G12 0SZ.

MURPHY, Rev. Canon (John) Gervase (Maurice Walker), LVO 1987; MA; Chaplain of the Chapel Royal of St Peter ad Vincula, Tower of London, 1991–96; a Chaplain to the Queen, 1987–96, an Extra Chaplain, since 1996; *b* 20 Aug. 1926; *s* of William Stafford and Yvonne Iris Murphy; *m* 1957, Joy Hilda Miriam Livermore; five *d.* *Educ:* Methodist Coll., Belfast; Trinity Coll., Dublin (BA 1952, MA 1955; Rugby football team, 1947–52 (Capt., 1951–52); cricket colours); Birkbeck Coll., Univ. of London (BA Hons Classics, 2000). Guardsman, Irish Guards, 1944–45; commissioned Royal Ulster Rifles, 1945–47. TCD, 1947–52 and Divinity Sch., TCD, 1949–52. Ordained, deacon, 1952, priest, 1953; Curate, Shankill Parish, Lurgan, 1952–55; Royal Army Chaplains' Dept, 1955; served: Korea, 1955–57; Woolwich, 1957–59; Aden, 1959–62; Infantry Junior Leaders, Oswestry, 1962–64; Bagshot, 1964–65; Worthy Down, 1965; Commonwealth Bde Sen. Chaplain, 1965–67; Sen. Chaplain, Guards Depot, Pirbright, 1967–69; DACG, Rhine Area, 1969–72; Sen. Chaplain, RMA Sandhurst, 1972–74; Asst Chaplain General: BAOR, 1974–75; South East, 1975–77; Vicar of Ranworth and RD of Blofield, 1977–79; Chaplain for Holidaymakers on Norfolk Broads, 1977–79; Domestic Chaplain to the Queen, Rector of Sandringham and Leader of Sandringham Group of Parishes, 1979–87; RD of Heacham and Rising, 1985–87; Hon Canon of Norwich Cathedral, 1986, Emeritus, 1987–; Rector, Christ Church Cathedral, Falkland Is, 1987–91; Chaplain, Lord Mayor of London, 1993–94. Vice-Pres., British Assoc. for Physical Trng, 1988– (Hon. Fellow, 1988). Played: Internat. Rugby football for Ireland, 1952, 1954 and 1958; Rugby football for British Army 1957, and for Barbarians, 1958. *Publication:* Christ Church Cathedral, Falkland Islands: its life and times 1892–1992, 1992. *Recreations:* sport, walking, gardening, interior decorating. *Address:* Saffron Close, 17 Ringstead Road, Heacham, Norfolk PE31 7JA. *T:* (01485) 572351. *Clubs:* East India

(Hon. Chaplain), London Irish RFC, Public School Wanderers RFC; Leprechauns Cricket (Ireland); Mid-Ulster Cricket.

MURPHY, (John) Philip; Special Adviser to the Prime Minister, since 2000; *b* 3 June 1958; *s* of Robert Anthony Murphy and Cecily Vaughan Murphy (*née* Nicholson); *m* 1st, 1983, Elizabeth McManus (marr. diss. 1988); 2nd, 1991, Sophie Annabel Davies; one *s* one *d*. *Educ:* St Cuthbert's Grammar Sch., Newcastle upon Tyne; Hertford Coll., Oxford (BA 2nd Cl. Hons French and Latin); City Univ. (Postgrad. Dip. in Practical Journalism); LSE (Dip. Macro- and Micro-Econs). Reporter: Southern Evening Echo, Southampton, 1981–83; and local govt corresp., The Journal, Newcastle upon Tyne, 1983–86; Lobby Corresp., Thomson Newspapers, 1986–87; Political Editor: Yorkshire Post, 1987–96; Press Assoc., 1996–98; Exec. Dir (Communications), Arts Council of England, 1998–99; Asst Gen. Sec. and Dir of Media Communications, Labour Party, 1999–2000. *Publication:* (with R. Caborn) Regional Government for England: an economic imperative, 1995. *Recreations:* football, golf, literature, late 19th and 20th century art, music. *Address:* 10 Downing Street, SW1A 2AA. *T:* (020) 7930 4433.

MURPHY, Laurence; QC (Scot.) 2000; *b* 12 April 1958; *s* of William John Murphy and Alison Boyd Spindlow or Murphy; *m* 1989, Christine Marie Cecile Germaine Boch; one *s* one *d*. *Educ:* Univ. of Glasgow (MA (Hons) 1980; LLB 1982). Solicitor, 1983–89; Advocate, 1990–. *Recreations:* golf, music, travel. *Address:* Advocates' Library, Parliament House, Edinburgh EH1 1RF. *T:* (0131) 226 2881.

MURPHY, Sir Leslie (Frederick), Kt 1978; Chairman, National Enterprise Board, 1977–79 (Deputy Chairman, 1975–77); *b* 17 Nov. 1915; *s* of Frederick Charles and Lillian Annie Murphy; *m* 1st, 1940, Marjorie Iris Cowell (*d* 1991); one *s* one *d*; 2nd, 1993, Dorothy Anne Murray. *Educ:* Southall Grammar Sch.; Birkbeck Coll., Univ. of London. Principal Private Sec. to Minister of Fuel and Power, 1947–49; Asst Sec., Min. of Fuel and Power, 1949–52; Chm., Mobil Supply Co. Ltd and Mobil Shipping Co. Ltd, 1955–59; Finance Dir, Iraq Petroleum Co. Ltd, 1959–64; Director: J. Henry Schroder Wagg & Co. Ltd, 1964–75 (Dep. Chm. 1972–73); Schroders plc, 1979–90 (Dep. Chm., 1973–75); Unigate Ltd, 1968–75; Simon Engrg Ltd, 1980–85; Folksam International Insurance (UK) Ltd, 1980–90; Petroleum Economics Ltd, 1980–94 (Chm., 1980–87). Mem., NEDC, 1977–79. Mem. Royal Commn on Distribution of Income and Wealth, 1974–76; Board Mem., Church Army, 1964–94; Chm., Church Army Housing Ltd, 1973–82, Pres., 1982–84. Trustee, SDP, 1981–90. *Recreations:* music, golf. *Address:* Hedgerley, Barton Common Road, Barton-on-Sea, Hants BH25 5PR.

MURPHY, Michael James, (Mick); Member (SF) South Down, Northern Ireland Assembly, since 1998; *b* Banbridge, 6 Feb. 1942; *s* of Michael and Mary Theresa Murphy; *m* 1965, Carole Trainor; six *d*. *Educ:* Legannay Sch., Leitrim, Co. Down. Publican in Rostrevor, 1978–91. Elected Mem. (SF) Newry and Mourne DC, 1996–; Mem. (SF) NI Forum, 1996–98. Contested (SF) S Down, 2001. *Recreations:* Gaelic games, Irish culture. *Address:* Assembly Building, Stormont, Belfast BT4 3XX. *T:* (028) 9052 1618, *Fax:* (028) 9052 1616.

MURPHY, Michael Joseph Adrian; QC 1993; **His Honour Judge Murphy;** a Circuit Judge, since 1999; *b* 1 Oct. 1949; *s* of Patrick Joseph Murphy, Hirwaun, Mid-Glam, and late Frances Murphy; *m* 1973, Rosemary Dorothy Aitken; three *s* one *d*. *Educ:* Aberdare Grammar Sch., Mid Glam.; Sheffield Univ. (LLB, MA). Called to the Bar, Inner Temple, 1973. A Recorder, 1989–99. *Address:* The Law Courts, 50 West Bar, Sheffield S3 8PH. *T:* (0114) 281 2400.

MURPHY, Neil; *see* Murphy, C. McC.

MURPHY, Patrick James, CMG 1985; HM Diplomatic Service, retired; Regional Director for Poland and the Baltic States, since 1995, Czech and Slovak Republics, since 1997, and Belarus, since 2000, British Executive Service Overseas; *b* 11 March 1931; *e s* of late Dr James Murphy and Cicely Mary (*née* Crowley); *m* 1st, 1959, Barbara May Healey-Purse (marr. diss. 1969); two *s*; 2nd, 1974, Jutta Ulrike Oehlmann; one *s*. *Educ:* Cranbrook School; Gonville and Caius College, Cambridge (BA; Geography Tripos). Served RAF, 1950–52. Oxford and Cambridge Far Eastern Expedition, 1955–56; BBC Gen. Overseas Service, 1956; Joined FO, 1957; Frankfurt, 1958; Berlin, 1959; FO, 1962; Second Sec. (Commercial), Warsaw, 1962; First Sec., FO, 1965; First Sec. (Commercial) and Consul, Phnom Penh, 1966; Consul, Düsseldorf, 1969; Consul, Hamburg, 1971; FCO, 1974; First Sec., Vienna, 1977; Counsellor, FCO, 1981–87. Advr, Sultanate of Oman, 1987–90; Consultant, HM Diplomatic Service, 1990–95. Officer's Cross, Order of Merit (Poland), 2000. *Recreations:* history, travel, wine, boating, Irish life. *Address:* 260 Dacre Park, SE13 5DD. *T:* (020) 8852 2483. *Club:* Royal Air Force.

MURPHY, Patrick Wallace; agricultural consultant, since 1996; Under Secretary, Land Use, Conservation and Countryside Group, Ministry of Agriculture, Fisheries and Food, 1994–96; *b* 16 Aug. 1944; *s* of Lawrence Vincent Murphy and Agnes Dunn; *m* 1972, Denise Lillieth Fullarton-Fullarton; two *s*. *Educ:* St Chad's College, Wolverhampton; Trinity Hall, Cambridge (BA Hons). Joined MAFF, 1966; Asst Private Sec. to Minister of Agriculture, Fisheries and Food, 1970; First Sec. (Agriculture and Commercial), British Embassy, Washington, 1974–78; Controller of Plant Variety Rights, 1978–82; Head, Land Use and Tenure Div., 1982–86; Under Sec., 1986; Head, Milk and Potatoes Gp, 1986–89; Hd of Pesticides, Vet. Medicines, Emergencies and Biotechnol. Gp, 1989–93; Hd of EC Gp, 1993–94. Non-exec. Dir, IDV (UK), 1985–88. *Recreations:* cricket, tennis, gardening.

MURPHY, Rt Hon. Paul (Peter); PC 1999; MP (Lab) Torfaen, since 1987; Secretary of State for Wales, since 1999; *b* 25 Nov. 1948; *s* of late Ronald and Marjorie Murphy. *Educ:* St Francis RC Primary Sch., Abersychan; West Monmouth Sch., Pontypool; Oriel Coll., Oxford (MA; Hon. Fellow, 2000). Management Trainee, CWS, 1970–71; Lectr in History and Govt, Ebbw Vale Coll. of Further Education, 1971–87. Mem., Torfaen Borough Council, 1973–87 (Chm., Finance Cttee, 1976–86); Sec., Torfaen Constituency Labour Party, 1974–87. Opposition front bench spokesman for Wales, 1988–94; on NI, 1994; on for. affairs, 1994–95; on defence, 1995–97; Minister of State, NI Office, 1997–99. *Recreation:* music. *Address:* House of Commons, SW1A 0AA. *T:* (020) 7219 3463. *Clubs:* St Joseph's (St Dials); Fairwater Sports and Social.

MURPHY, Philip; *see* Murphy, J. P.

MURPHY, (Robert Somerville) Foster; Chief Executive, Abbeyfield Society, since 1992; *b* 1 June 1940; *s* of Robert Somerville Foster Murphy and Eva Constance (*née* Harvey); *m* 1964, Patricia Mary Hamilton; one *s* one *d*. *Educ:* Dublin Univ. (MA); Downing Coll., Cambridge (MA); London Univ. (Dip. SocScis (ext.)). Irish Sec., SCM, 1965–67; Youth Sec., BCC, 1967–72; Youth Sec., subseq. Head of Div., then Dep. Dir, NCVO, 1972–81; Dir, Volunteer Centre, UK, 1981–92. Board Member: Innisfree HA, 1993–99; Internat. Assoc. for Homes & Services for the Aging, 1994–; Centre for Policy on Ageing, 1997– (Chm., 2000–). *Publication:* (jtly) Integrating Care, Housing and Community, 1998. *Recreations:* opera, orchids, keeping fit. *Address:* Abbeyfield House, 53 Victoria Street, St Albans, Herts AL1 3UW. *T:* (01727) 857536.

MURPHY, Rory; Joint General Secretary, UNIFI, since 1999; *b* 23 April 1955; *s* of Philip Murphy and Noreen Murphy (*née* Sheahan); *m* 1976, Catherine Deane; two *s*. *Educ:* Bishop Bright RC Grammar Sch., Leamington Spa. Photographer, Pitt Rivers Mus., Oxford, 1972–84 (on secondment as Union Official, 1979–84); Nat. Sec., ASTMS, Ireland, 1984–87; Asst Gen. Sec., ASTMS, later MSF, 1987–89; Chief Exec., Finers, Solicitors, 1989–90; Dir of Industrial Relations, Royal Coll. of Midwives, 1990–95; Gen. Sec., NatWest Staff Assoc., 1995–99. Dir, CARA, 1987–. *Recreations:* football (Arsenal), theatre, art, archaeology. *Address:* UNIFI, Churchill Court, Palmerston Road, Bournemouth, Dorset BH1 4HN. *T:* (01202) 443610. *Club:* Poole Labour.

MURPHY, Dr Simon Francis; Member (Lab) West Midlands Region, European Parliament, since 1999 (Midlands West, 1994–99); *b* 24 Feb. 1962; *s* of Patrick Joseph Murphy and Mary Frances Murphy; *m* 1992, Bridget Lee Brickley. *Educ:* Sacred Heart Coll., Droitwich; N Worcs Coll., Bromsgrove; UCW, Aberystwyth (BSc Econ 1983; PhD 1986). Tutor, Dept of Political Sci., UCW, Aberystwyth, 1984–86; Asst to Leader of Labour Gp, Wolverhampton MBC, 1986–89; Head of Research, Office of John Bird, MEP, 1989–94. Contested (Lab) Wolverhampton SW, 1992. European Parliament: Vice Pres., 1997–99, Leader, 2000–, PSE; Vice Pres., Eurogroup for Animal Welfare & Conservation, 1997–. Dir, W Midlands Develt Agency, 1997. Gov., Univ. of Wolverhampton, 1996–99. *Publication:* (contrib.) chapter in Contemporary Minority Nationalisms, ed M. Watson, 1990. *Recreations:* running, reading, cooking, watching sport. *Address:* West Midlands European Office, AEEU House, 1 George Street, West Bromwich B70 6NT. *T:* (0121) 569 1938, *Fax:* (0121) 569 1935; *e-mail:* smurphy@europarl.eu.int.

MURPHY, Thomas, CBE 1991; Managing Director, Civil Aviation Authority, 1987–95; Director, Parity plc, since 1997; *b* 13 Nov. 1928; *s* of Thomas Murphy and Elizabeth Gray Murphy (*née* Leckie); *m* 1962, Sheila Jean Dorothy Young; one *s* three *d*. *Educ:* St Mirin's Acad., Paisley; Glasgow Univ. (MA Hons). Served Royal Artillery, 1951–53. Marks and Spencer, 1953–55; British Petroleum, 1955–86: appts in Territory of Papua New Guinea, Trinidad, Scotland, Algeria, USA, 1955–68; Asst Gen. Man., BP Tanker Co., 1968–76; Gen. Man., Gp Personnel, 1976–81; Advr, Organisation Planning, 1981–86; Non-Exec. Dir, CAA, 1986–87. Internat. Sen. Managers Programme, Harvard Business Sch., 1973. *Recreations:* walking, coarse golf, destructive gardening. *Address:* Woodruffe, Onslow Road, Sunningdale, Berks SL5 0HW. *T:* (01344) 623261. *Club:* Wentworth.

MURPHY, Thomas A(quinas); Chairman, General Motors Corporation, 1974–80; *b* Hornell, NY, 10 Dec. 1915; *s* of John Joseph Murphy and Alma (*née* O'Grady); *m* 1941, Catherine Rita Maguire; one *s* two *d*. *Educ:* Leo High Sch., Chicago; Univ. of Illinois. US Naval Reserve, 1943–46. Joined General Motors Corporation, 1938; Asst Treas., 1959; Comptroller, 1967; Treas., 1968–70; Vice-Pres. and Gp Exec., Car and Truck Div., 1970–72; Vice-Chm., 1972–74. *Address:* 9 Acacia Drive, Boynton Beach, FL 33436, USA; 21 Lands End Drive, Greensboro, NC 27408, USA.

MURPHY, Thomas James; journalist, The Times, since 1990; singer and actor; *b* 26 June 1956; *s* of James Murphy and Beatrice Murphy (*née* Strand); *m* 1976, Janet Sallis; four *s*. *Educ:* Salesian Sch., Chertsey; Sussex Univ. (BA History); Warwick Univ. (MBA); Royal Acad. of Music (Cert.). Kitchen porter and factory labourer, 1977; trainee journalist, Slough Observer, 1978; Sports editor, Buckinghamshire Advertiser, 1981; Editor: Staines Informer, 1983; East Grinstead Courier, 1984; Sub-editor, The Independent, 1986; Dep. Chief sub-editor, London Evening News, 1987; Editor, The Universe, 1988–90. *Recreation:* swimming. *Address:* 21 Clarke Court, Walsingham Road, Hove, East Sussex BN3 4FW. *T:* (01273) 230436.

MURPHY-O'CONNOR, His Eminence Cardinal Cormac; *see* Westminster, Archbishop of, (RC).

MURRAY; *see* Erskine-Murray.

MURRAY, family name of **Duke of Atholl,** of **Earl of Dunmore,** of **Earl of Mansfield and Mansfield** and of **Baron Murray of Epping Forest.**

MURRAY, Rt Hon. Lord; Ronald King Murray; PC 1974; a Senator of the College of Justice in Scotland, 1979–95; *b* 15 June 1922; *s* of James King Murray, MIEE, and Muriel (*née* Aitken), Glasgow; *m* 1950, Sheila Winifred Gamlin; one *s* one *d*. *Educ:* George Watson's Coll., Edinburgh; Univ. of Edinburgh (MA (1st cl. hons Phil) 1948; LLB 1952); Jesus Coll., Oxford (Hon. Fellow, 1999). Served HM Forces, 1941–46; commnd in REME, 1942; India and SEAC, 1943–46. Asst in Moral Philosophy, Edinburgh Univ., 1949–52; called to Scottish Bar, 1953; QC (Scotland) 1967; Advocate-Depute, 1964–67; Senior Advocate-Depute, 1967–70. MP (Lab) Leith, Edinburgh, 1970–79; Lord Advocate, 1974–79. Vice-Chm., Edinburgh Univ. Court, 1990–93. Mem., Scottish Records Adv. Council, 1987–93. Hon. Pres., Leith Boys' Brigade, 1984–98. Dr *hc* Edinburgh, 1996. *Publications:* articles in various jls. *Recreations:* sailing, astronomy. *Address:* 1 Inverleith Grove, Edinburgh EH3 5PB. *T:* (0131) 551 5330. *Clubs:* Royal Forth Yacht, Forth Corinthian Yacht.

MURRAY OF EPPING FOREST, Baron *cr* 1985 (Life Peer), of Telford in the County of Shropshire; **Lionel Murray,** OBE 1966; PC 1976; General Secretary of the Trades Union Congress, 1973–84; *b* 2 Aug. 1922; *m* 1945, Heather Woolf; two *s* two *d*. *Educ:* Wellington (Salop) Gram. Sch.; QMC, London, 1940–41; NCLC; New Coll., Oxford, 1945–47 (Hon. Fellow, 1975). War Service, KSLI. Economic Dept, TUC, 1947, Head of Dept, 1954–69; Asst Gen. Sec., TUC, 1969–73. Mem., NEDC, 1973–84; Vice-President: ICFTU, 1973; European Trade Union Confedn, 1974. President: Shropshire Soc.; Friends of Epping Forest; Friends of Ironbridge Gorge Museum; Vice-President: Nat. Children's Home; Hearing and Speech Trust; Ironbridge Mus. Trust; Wesley's Chapel; Nat. Youth Theatre. Trustee: NUMAST; ADAPT. Patron, St Clare Hospice; Vice-Patron, Winged Fellowship. Fellow, QMW, 1988; Hon. Fellow, Sheffield City Polytechnic, 1979. Hon. DSc: Aston, 1977; Salford, 1978; Hon. LLD: St Andrews, 1979; Leeds, 1985. *Address:* 29 The Crescent, Loughton, Essex IG10 4PY. *T:* (020) 8508 4425.

MURRAY, Bishop of The, since 1989; **Rt Rev. Graham Howard Walden;** *b* 19 March 1931; *s* of Leonard Howard Walden and Mary Ellen Walden (*née* Cahalane); *m* 1964, Margaret Ann (*née* Brett); two *s* one *d*. *Educ:* Univ. of Queensland (BA 1952; MA 1954); Australian Coll. of Theol. (ThL 1954); Christ Church, Oxford (BLitt 1960; MLitt 1980). Ordained deacon 1954, priest 1955; Assistant Curate: West Hackney, 1954–56; St Saviour's, Poplar, 1957–58; permission to officiate, dio. of Oxford, 1955–59; Mem., Bush Brotherhood of the Good Shepherd, NSW, 1959–63; Vice Principal, Torres Strait Mission Theol Coll., 1963–65; Rector of Mudgee, NSW, 1965–70; Archdeacon of Barker, 1968–70; Archdeacon and Vicar-Gen. of Ballarat, 1970–89; Asst Bishop of Ballarat, 1981–89; Rector of Hamilton and Bishop in Hamilton, 1981–84. Nat. Chm., Anglican Men's Soc., 1983–93 (Vice-Pres., 1993–); Anglican Chm., Jt Anglican RC Diocesan Commn, 1977–89; Vice-Chm., Internat. Bishops' Conf., 1992–95; Member: Gen. Bd of Religious Educn, 1970–81; Anglican Lutheran Conversations constituted by

Gen. Synod of Anglican Church of Australia, 1989– (Co-Chm., 1993–); Gen. Synod Commn on Doctrine, 1989–98 (Chm., 1992–98). *Publications:* contrib. to jls and church papers. *Address:* Bishop's Lodge, 23 Ellendale Avenue, Murray Bridge, SA 5253, Australia. *T:* (8) 85322240; PO Box 269, Murray Bridge, SA 5253, Australia. *T:* (8) 85322270, *Fax:* (8) 85325760.

MURRAY, Alexander, FRHistS; FBA 1995; Fellow and Praelector in Modern History, University College, Oxford, 1980–2001; *b* 14 May 1934; second *s* of late Stephen Hubert Murray and Margaret (*née* Gillett). *Educ:* Bedales Sch., Petersfield; New Coll., Oxford (BA Mod. Hist.; BPhil European Hist.). FRHistS 1971. Served RA, 1953–55. Asst Lectr in Medieval Hist., Univ. of Leeds, 1961–63; University of Newcastle upon Tyne: Lectr, 1963–77; Sen. Lectr, 1977–80; Public Orator, 1973–76; Chm., Faculty of Modern Hist., Univ. of Oxford, 1992–93. Directeur des Etudes Associé, Ecole des Hautes Etudes en Sciences Sociales, Paris, 1986; Vis. Prof. of Medieval Hist., Harvard Univ., 1989–90. Mem., NYO, 1951–53. *Publications:* Reason and Society in the Middle Ages, 1978; The Violent Against Themselves, 1998; The Curse on Self-Murder, 2000; contrib. learned jls and collections. *Recreations:* music, walking.

MURRAY, Dame (Alice) Rosemary, DBE 1977; MA, DPhil; JP; DL; President, New Hall, Cambridge, 1964–81 (Tutor in Charge, 1954–64); Vice-Chancellor, Cambridge University, 1975–77; *b* 28 July 1913; *d* of late Adm. A. J. L. Murray and Ellen Maxwell Spooner. *Educ:* Downe House, Newbury; Lady Margaret Hall, Oxford (Hon. Fellow, 1968). MA (Oxon and Cantab); BSc, DPhil (Oxon). Lecturer in chemistry: Royal Holloway Coll., 1938–41; Sheffield Univ., 1941–42. Served War of 1939–45, Experimental Officer, Admiralty Signals Establishment, 1941; WRNS, 1942–46, Chief Officer. Lectr in Chemistry, Girton Coll., Cambridge, 1946–54, Fellow, 1949, Tutor, 1951, Hon. Fellow, 1976; Demonstrator in Chemistry, Univ. of Cambridge, 1947–52. Dir, Midland Bank Ltd, 1978–84; Independent Dir, The Observer, 1981–93. Member: Lockwood Cttee on Higher Educn in NI, 1963–65; Wages Councils, 1968–93; Council, GPDST, 1969–93; Armed Forces Pay Review Body, 1971–81; Pres., Nat. Assoc. of Adult Educn, 1977–80, Vice-Pres., 1980–83. Governor and Chm., Keswick Coll. of Education, 1953–83; Mem. Delegacy, Goldsmiths' Coll., London Univ., 1986–89; Visitor, Homerton Coll., Cambridge, 1990–. Mem. Council, Toynbee Hall, 1983–89. Liveryman, Goldsmiths' Co., 1978–. JP City of Cambridge, 1953–83; DL Cambs, 1982. Hon. Fellow: LMH, Oxford, 1970; Girton Coll., Cambridge, 1975; New Hall, Cambridge, 1981; Robinson Coll., Cambridge, 1985. Hon. DSc: New Univ. of Ulster, 1972; Leeds, 1975; Pennsylvania, 1975; Wellesley Coll., 1976; Hon. DCL Oxon, 1976; Hon. DL Univ. Southern California, 1976; Hon. LLD: Sheffield, 1977; Cantab, 1988. *Recreations:* gardening, book binding and restoring. *Address:* 3 Oxford Road, Old Marston, Oxford OX3 0PQ.

MURRAY, Andrew Robin; HM Diplomatic Service, retired; Ambassador to Uruguay, 1998–2001; *b* 21 Sept. 1941; *s* of Robert Alexander Murray and Jean Agnes Murray (*née* Burnett); *m* 1965, Irene Dorothy Foy; one *s* one *d*. *Educ:* Trinity Coll., Glenalmond; Edinburgh Univ. (MA Hons 1965). Economist with Govt of Ontario, Canada, 1966; investment analyst, ICFC, 1969; joined HM Diplomatic Service, 1973; First Sec., Islamabad, 1975–78; Head of Chancery, Buenos Aires, 1979–81; FCO, 1982–84; Counsellor, UKMIS to UN, 1984–88; Counsellor and Dep. Head of Mission, Caracas, 1988–91; FCO, 1991–93; Counsellor (Econ. and Commercial), Stockholm, 1993–97. *Recreation:* sporadic sport.

MURRAY, Ann; mezzo-soprano; *b* Dublin, 27 Aug. 1949; *m* 1981, Philip Langridge, *qv*; one *s*. *Educ:* Royal Manchester Coll. of Music. Roles include: *for English National Opera:* Ariodante; Beatrice; Charlotte; Rosina; Xerxes; *for Royal Opera:* Cherubino; Composer; Donna Elvira; Dorabella; Idamante; Oktavian; *other roles:* Cecilio; Cenerentola; Nicklausse; Sextus. Many recitals and concerts (European recital tours, 1990, 1993, 1994); festival appearances incl. Aldeburgh, Edinburgh, Munich, Salzburg. *Address:* c/o Askonas Holt Ltd, Lonsdale Chambers, 27 Chancery Lane, WC2A 1PF.

MURRAY, Sir Antony; *see* Murray, Sir J. A. J.

MURRAY, Athol Laverick, PhD; FRHistS; Keeper of the Records of Scotland, 1985–90; *b* Tynemouth, Northumberland, 8 Nov. 1930; *s* of late George Murray and Margery Laverick; *m* 1958, Irene Joyce Cairns; one *s* one *d*. *Educ:* Royal Grammar Sch., Lancaster; Jesus Coll., Cambridge (BA, MA); Univ. of Edinburgh (LLB, PhD). Research Assistant, Foreign Office, 1953; Assistant Keeper, Scottish Record Office, 1953–83; Deputy Keeper, 1983–84. Consultant Archivist, Jersey Archives Steering Gp, 1990–92. Vice-Pres., Soc. of Antiquaries of Scotland, 1989–92; Chm., Scottish Records Assoc., 1997–2000. FRHistS 1971. *Publications:* The Royal Grammar School, Lancaster, 1951; Castle Tioram: the historical background, 1998; articles in Scottish Historical Review, etc. *Address:* 33 Inverleith Gardens, Edinburgh EH3 5PR. *T:* (0131) 552 4465. *Club:* Civil Service.

MURRAY, Charles Henry; Chairman, National Irish Bank (formerly Northern Bank (Ireland)) Ltd, 1986–89; *b* 29 Jan. 1917; *s* of Charles and Teresa Murray; *m* 1942, Margaret Ryan; one *s* four *d*. *Educ:* Christian Brothers Sch., Synge Street, Dublin; London Univ. (BCom). Asst Secretary, Dept of Finance (Ireland), 1961, Secretary, 1969–76; Dir, 1969–76, Governor, 1976–81, Central Bank of Ireland. Dir, Northern Bank, 1982–88. Hon. LLD, NUI, 1977. *Recreations:* reading, theatre, golf. *Address:* 6 Washington Park, Dublin 14. *T:* 4947781.

MURRAY, Craig John; HM Diplomatic Service; Deputy High Commissioner, Ghana, since 1999; *b* 17 Oct. 1958; *s* of Robert Cameron Brunton Murray and Poppy Katherine Murray (*née* Grice); *m* 1984, Fiona Ann Kennedy; one *s* one *d*. *Educ:* Paston Grammar Sch; Univ. of Dundee (MA Hons). Joined FCO, 1984: Second Sec., Lagos, 1986–89; FCO, 1990–94; First Sec., Warsaw, 1994–98; FCO, 1998–99. *Recreations:* drinking, gossiping, reading, Celtic music, football, cricket. *Address:* c/o Foreign and Commonwealth Office, King Charles Street, SW1A 2AH; 3 Portland Road, Gravesend, Kent DA12 1DL. *Clubs:* National Liberal; Gin Dobry (Poznan).

MURRAY, David Edward; Chairman, Murray International Holdings Ltd, since 1981; director of companies; *b* 14 Oct. 1951; *s* of late David Ian Murray and of Roma Murray; *m* 1972, Louise V. Densley (*d* 1992); two *s*. *Educ:* Fettes Coll.; Broughton High Sch. Formed: Murray International Metals Ltd, 1976; Murray International Holdings Ltd, 1981; Murray Foundn, 1997. Young Scottish Businessman of the Year, 1984. Chairman: UK2000 (Scotland), 1987; Rangers FC, 1988–. Gov., Clifton Hall Sch., 1987. DUniv Heriot-Watt, 1986. *Recreations:* watching sport, wine enthusiast. *Address:* Murray International Holdings, 9 Charlotte Square, Edinburgh EH2 4DR. *T:* (0131) 317 7000.

MURRAY, David Edward, FRICS; management consultant, since 1997; Deputy Chief Executive (Property), Crown Estate, 1993–97; *b* 22 Jan. 1944; *s* of late Thomas and Emily Murray; *m* 1968, Barbara Collins, *d* of late Sir Geoffrey and Lady Collins, Dorset; two *s*. *Educ:* Abbotsholme Sch., Derbys; Manor Park Sch., Hants; Hammersmith Sch. of Art & Building. AIQS 1970; Dip. Contsr. Econs 1975; FRICS 1983. Sir Robert McAlpine & Sons, 1962–67; Planning & Transportation Dept, GLC, 1968–72; Royal County of Berkshire: Gp Quantity Surveyor, 1972–77; Co. Quantity Surveyor, 1977–88; Dir of Property, 1988–93. External Examiner: Coll. of Estate Mgt, 1978–92; Univ. of Portsmouth, 1994–98. Pres., Soc. of Chief Quantity Surveyors in Local Govt, 1979; Royal Institution of Chartered Surveyors: Chm., Quantity Surveyor's R&D Cttee, 1983–84; Mem., Divl Council, 1975–; Regl Trg Advr, 1998–; Mem., several panels and wkg parties. *Publications:* Cost Effectiveness in Property Management, 1984; Artificial Intelligence in Property Portfolio Management, 1988; papers on property mgt and procurement to various UK confs. *Recreations:* sport (especially sailing), reading, music. *Address:* Highcroft, 18 Highclere Drive, Camberley, Surrey GU15 1JY. *T:* (01276) 24345. *Club:* Parkstone Yacht (Dorset).

MURRAY, Rt Rev. David Owen; an Assistant Bishop of Perth, Western Australia, since 1991; *b* 23 Dec. 1940; *s* of George Lawrence Murray and Winifred Eva (*née* Morgan); *m* 1971, Janet Mary Chittleborough; two *s*. *Educ:* Swanbourne State Sch.; Claremont High Sch.; St Michael's House, Crafers, SA (Kelham, Aust.) (ThL 1968). Jun. Postal Officer, 1955; Postal Clerk, 1957–65. Ordained deacon, 1968, priest, 1969; Asst Curate, Bunbury, 1968–70; Rector: Lake Grace, 1970–74; Jerramungup, 1974–79; Mt Barker, 1979–83; Chaplain to the Bishop of Bunbury, 1978–83; Rector: S Perth, 1983–88; Fremantle, 1988–94; Archdeacon of Fremantle, 1988–91. Mem., WA Chamber of Commerce, Fremantle, 1990–. *Recreations:* bagpipe playing, walking, swimming, cycling, caravaning, theatre, concerts, reading, entertaining. *Address:* 6 Donavon Rise, Murdoch, WA 6150, Australia. *T:* (8) 94307224.

MURRAY, Denis James, OBE 1997; Ireland Correspondent, BBC, since 1988; *b* 7 May 1951; *s* of late James and Helen Murray; *m* 1978, Joyce Linehan; two *s* two *d*. *Educ:* St Malachy's Coll., Belfast; Trinity Coll., Dublin (BA Respondency 1993); Queen's Univ., Belfast (HDipEd). Grad. Trainee, then Reporter, Belfast Telegraph, 1975–77; Belfast Reporter, RTE, 1977–82; BBC: Dublin Correspondent, 1982–84; NI Political Correspondent, 1984–88. *Publication:* (contrib.) BBC Guide to 1997 General Election, 1997. *Recreations:* music, reading, sport, family! *Address:* c/o BBC, Ormeau Avenue, Belfast BT2 8HQ. *T:* (028) 9033 8000.

MURRAY, Rt Hon. Sir Donald (Bruce), Kt 1988; PC 1989; a Lord Justice of Appeal, Supreme Court of Northern Ireland, 1989–93; a Judge of the Restrictive Practices Court, 1987–93; *b* 24 Jan. 1923; *y s* of late Charles Benjamin Murray and late Agnes Mary Murray, Belfast; *m* 1953, Rhoda Margaret, *o c* of late Thomas and Anna Parke, Londonderry; two *s* one *d*. *Educ:* Belfast Royal Acad.; Queen's Univ. Belfast (LLB Hons); Trinity Coll. Dublin (BA). 1st Cl., Certif. of Honour, Gray's Inn Prize, English Bar Final Exam., 1944; Called to Bar, Gray's Inn, 1945, Hon Bencher, 1987. Asst Parly Draftsman to Govt of NI, 1945–51; Asst Lectr, Faculty of Law, QUB, 1951–53. Called to NI Bar, 1953, and to Inner Bar, NI, 1964; Bencher, Inn of Court, NI, 1971; Chm., Gen. Council of Bar of NI, 1972–75; Judge of the High Court of Justice, NI, 1975–89. Dep. Chm., Boundary Commn for NI, 1976–84. Chairman: Incorporated Council of Law Reporting for NI, 1974–87 (Mem., 1971); Bd, SLS Legal Publications (NI), 1988–94. Member: UK Delegn to Commn Consultative des Barreaux des Pays des Communautés Européennes, 1972–75; Jt Standing Cttee of Bars of UK and Bar of Ireland, 1972–75; Deptl Cttee on Registration of Title to Land in N Ireland. Chm., Deptl Cttee on Reform of Company Law in NI; Inspector apptd to report on siting of new prison in NI. Mem., Legal Adv. Cttee of Standing Cttee of General Synod of Church of Ireland. Chm., Opera Review Gp, Arts Council of NI, 1998. Hon. LLD QUB, 1996. *Publications:* articles in various legal periodicals. *Recreations:* playing the piano, DXing.

MURRAY, Elaine Kildare, PhD; Member (Lab) Dumfries, Scottish Parliament, since 1999; *b* 22 Dec. 1954; *d* of Kenneth and Patricia Murray; *m* 1986, Jeffrey Leaver; two *s* one *d*. *Educ:* Edinburgh Univ. (BSc 1st Cl. Hons Chemistry); Cambridge Univ. (PhD Physical Chemistry 1980). Res. Fellow, Cavendish Lab., Cambridge, 1979–82; Researcher, Royal Free Hosp., London, 1982–84; SSO, Inst. of Food Res., Reading, 1984–87; Asst to Alex Smith, MEP, 1990–93; Associate Lectr, Open Univ., 1992–99. *Recreations:* spending time with my family and pets, exercise, music, reading. *Address:* Scottish Parliament, Edinburgh EH99 1SP. *T:* (constituency office) (01387) 279205.

MURRAY, George Sargent; Forestry Commissioner, 1981–84; *b* 2 Oct. 1924; *s* of James and Helen Murray; *m* 1951, Anita Garden Fraser; two *s*. *Educ:* Buckie High School. Inland Revenue, 1941–43; Royal Navy, 1943–46; Inland Revenue, 1946–49; Dept of Agriculture and Fisheries for Scotland, 1949–67; Scottish Development Dept, 1967–71; Scottish Economic Planning Dept, Scottish Office, 1971–76; Dept of Agriculture and Fisheries for Scotland, 1976–81. *Recreation:* golf. *T:* (0131) 449 2538.

MURRAY, Gordon; *see* Murray, I. G.

MURRAY, Rev. Gordon, CB 1994; PhD; Methodist Minister, Edinburgh and Forth Circuit, since 1999; Training and Development Officer, Scotland District, Methodist Church, since 1999; *b* 25 Aug. 1935; *s* of late James Murray, Aberdeen, and Annie Hardie (*née* Center); *m* 1964, Janet (*née* Yerrington); two *s* one *d*. *Educ:* Kirkcaldy High Sch.; Edinburgh Univ. (BSc (Hons), PhD). Research Fellow: Atomic Energy of Canada, 1960–62; UKAEA, Harwell, 1962–65; Lectr, Univ. of Manchester, 1965–69; Principal, Scottish Home and Health Dept, 1970–77; Assistant Secretary: Scottish Educn Dept, 1977–79; Central Services, Scottish Office, 1979–86; Dir, Scottish Courts Admin, 1986–95. Ordained, 1992; Methodist Minister, Poole and Swanage Circuit, 1995–99. *Recreations:* reading, hill walking, gardening. *Address:* 12 Liggars Place, Dunfermline, Fife KY12 7XZ. *T:* (01383) 624065.

MURRAY, Iain Richard, OBE 1991; HM Diplomatic Service; Consul-General, Houston, since 2001; *b* 13 Aug. 1944; *s* of William Potts Murray and Barbara (*née* Beard); *m* 1st, 1967, Victoria Crew Gee (marr. diss.); one *s* one *d*; 2nd, 1984, Judith Wilson (marr. diss. 1991); 3rd, 1993, Norma Wisden (*née* Hummel). *Educ:* King Alfred's Grammar Sch., Wantage; Univ. of Kent at Canterbury (BA Hons 1968); Univ. of London (BSc Hons Econs (ext.)). Exec. Officer, CRO, 1963–65; re-joined FCO, 1968: Econ/Commercial Attaché, Accra, 1970–72; Second Sec., Addis Ababa, 1972–75; Vice-Consul (Commercial), Rio de Janeiro, 1975–79; Consul, Oporto, 1979–83; on secondment to Press Office, 10 Downing Street, 1983–85; FCO, 1985–87; Chargé d'Affaires, San Salvador, 1987–91; Asst Hd, Jt Export Promotion Directorate, FCO/DTI, 1992–94; Commercial/Econ. Counsellor, Kuala Lumpur, 1994–96; Consul-Gen., São Paulo, and Dir, Trade Promotion, Brazil, 1997–2000. Mem., Keepers of the Quaich. *Recreations:* hill-walking, history through travel and reading, losing golf balls. *Address:* c/o Foreign and Commonwealth Office, King Charles Street, SW1A 2AH. *Clubs:* Royal Commonwealth Society, Farmers.

MURRAY, Rt Rev. Ian; *see* Argyll and the Isles, Bishop of, (RC).

MURRAY, (Ian) Gordon; Technical Director, McLaren Cars Ltd, since 1990; Director, TAG McLaren Group, since 1990; *b* 18 June 1946; *s* of William and Roma Murray; *m* 1970, Stella Gane; one *s*. *Educ:* Natal Tech. Coll., SA. Moved to England, 1969, to work in motor racing; joined Brabham, 1970: design draughtsman, 1970–73; Chief Designer, 1973–74; Technical Dir, 1974–86 (design innovations incl. fan car, 1978, and hydro-pneumatic suspension, 1981; 22 Grand Prix wins; 2 World Drivers' Formula 1 Championships, first turbo-powered World Championship, 1983); Technical Dir, McLaren Internat., 1986–90 (29 Grand Prix wins; 2 World Drivers' Formula 1 Championships; 2 World Formula 1 Constructors' Championships); McLaren Cars Ltd, 1990–: designed and prod McLaren F1 road car (Fastest Road Car, 1992; GTR version won 2 championships, and Le Mans 1995). *Recreations:* motor-cycles, music, food and fine wine, architecture. *Address:* McLaren Cars Ltd, Unit 12–14, Woking Business Park, Albert Drive, Woking, Surrey GU21 5JY.

MURRAY, Sir James, KCMG 1978 (CMG 1966); HM Diplomatic Service, retired; Ambassador and Permanent UK Representative to UN and other International Organisations at Geneva, 1978–79; *b* 3 Aug. 1919; *er s* of late James Hamilton Murray, King's Cross, Isle of Arran, and Hester Macneill Buie; *m* 1982, Mrs Jill Charmian Chapuisat, *d* of Maj.-Gen. Frederick William Gordon-Hall, CB, CBE; two step *d*. *Educ:* Bellahouston Acad.; Glasgow Univ. Royal Regt of Artillery, 1939; served India and Burma, 1943–45; Staff Coll., Quetta, 1945; Bde Major (RA) 19 Ind. Div.; GSO II (RA) ALFSEA; GSO II War Office. HM Foreign (subseq. Diplomatic) Service, 1947; Foreign Office, 1947–49; First Sec. (Information), HM Embassy, Cairo, 1949–54; Foreign Office, 1954–56; attached National Defence Coll. of Can., 1956–57; First Sec., HM Embassy, Paris, 1957–61; HM Consul in Ruanda-Urundi, 1961–62; Special Ambassador for Independence celebrations in Ruanda, July 1962, and in Burundi, Sept. 1962; Ambassador to Rwanda and Burundi, 1962–63; Deputy Head of UK Delegation to European Communities, 1963–65; Counsellor, Djakarta, 1965–67; Head of Far Eastern Dept, FCO, 1967–70; Consul-Gen., San Francisco, 1970–73; Asst Under-Sec. of State, FCO, 1973–74; Dep. Perm. Representative to UN, 1974–78 (Ambassador, 1976). Special Envoy of 5 Western Govts for negotiations on Namibia, 1979–80. Withrow Prof. of Govt, Deep Springs Coll., Calif, 1990; Adviser: Trade Policy Res. Centre, London, 1981–89; to Chm., Hanson Industries, NY, 1983–92; Nat. Bd of Dirs, Congressional Award Foundn, 1985–; Internat. Advr, Assoc. for a Better New York, 1990–. *Recreations:* horses, lawn tennis. *Address:* 220 Columbia Heights, Brooklyn Heights, New York, NY 11201, USA. *T:* (718) 8523320. *Clubs:* Brooks's, Beefsteak, Pratt's; Brook (New York).

MURRAY, Prof. James Dickson, FRS 1985; FRSE 1979; Professor of Mathematical Biology, 1986–92, now Emeritus Professor, Director, Centre for Mathematical Biology, 1983–92, and Professorial Fellow, Corpus Christi College, 1986–92, now Emeritus Fellow, University of Oxford; *b* 2 Jan. 1931; *s* of Peter and Sarah Murray; *m* 1959, Sheila Todd Murray; one *s* one *d*. *Educ:* Dumfries Acad.; Univ. of St Andrews (BSc 1953; Carstairs Medal; Miller Prize; PhD 1956); Univ. of Oxford (MA 1961; DSc 1968). FIBiol 1988. Lectr, Applied Maths, Kings Coll., Durham Univ., 1955–56; Gordon MacKay Lectr and Res. Fellow, Tutor in Applied Maths, Leverett House, Harvard, 1956–59; Lectr, Applied Maths, UCL, 1959–61; Fellow and Tutor in Maths, Hertford College, Oxford, 1961–63; Res. Associate, Harvard, 1963–64; Prof. of Engineering Mechanics, Univ. of Michigan, 1964–67; Prof. of Maths, New York Univ., 1967–70; Fellow and Tutor in Maths, 1970–85, Sen. Res. Fellow, 1985–86, Corpus Christi Coll., Oxford; Reader in Maths, Univ. of Oxford, 1972–86. Vis. Fellow, St Catherine's Coll., Oxford, 1967; Guggenheim Fellow, Pasteur Inst., Paris, 1968; Visiting Professor: Nat. Tsing Hua Univ., 1975; Univ. of Florence, 1976; MIT, 1979; Winegard Prof., Univ. of Guelph, 1979; Univ. of Utah, 1979, 1985; Ida Beam Prof., Univ. of Iowa, 1980; Univ. of Heidelberg, 1980; CIT, 1983; Univ. of Angers, 1993; La Chaire Européenne, Univ. of Paris, 1994, 1995, 1996; Stan Ulam Vis. Schol., Univ. of Calif. Berkeley's Los Alamos Nat. Lab., 1985; Philip Prof., 1988–94, Boeing Prof., 1997–2000, Prof. Emeritus, 2000, Univ. of Washington; Lectures: Scott Hawkins, Southern Methodist Univ., Dallas, 1984; Landsdowne, Univ. of Victoria, 1990; Pinkham, Swedish Hosp., Seattle, 1992 and 1998; Curle, Univ. of St Andrews, 1994; Smith, St Catherine's Coll., Oxford, 1994; Faculty, Univ. of Washington, 1998. Math. Comr, SERC, 1985–88; Pres., European Soc. for Mathematical and Theoretical Biol., 1991–94; Member: Bd of Dirs, Soc. for Mathematical Biol., USA, 1986–89; ESF Network Cttee, 1991–94. For. Mem., Acad. des Scis, France, 2000. Hon. DSc: St Andrews, 1994; Strathclyde, 1999. Naylor Lect. and Prize in Applied Math., London Math. Soc., 1989. *Publications:* Asymptotic Analysis, 1974, 3rd edn 1996; Nonlinear Differential Equation Models in Biology, 1977 (Russian trans. 1983); (ed with S. Brenner and L. Wolpert) Theories of Biological Pattern Formation, 1981; (ed with W. Jäger) Modelling of Patterns in Space and Time, 1984; Mathematical Biology, 1989, 3rd edn in 2 vols, 2001; (ed with H. G. Othmer and P. K. Maini) Experimental and Theoretical Advances in Biological Pattern Formation, 1993; (ed jtly) The Mathematics of Marriage, 2001; several hundred articles in learned jls on the application of maths in biomed. scis. *Address:* La Combe, 24510 St Laurent des Bâtons, Dordogne, France.

MURRAY, Jennifer Susan, (Jenni), OBE 1999; Presenter, Woman's Hour, since 1987, The Turning World, since 1998, The Message, since 2001, BBC, Radio 4; *b* 12 May 1950; *d* of Alvin Bailey and Win Bailey (*née* Jones); *m* 1971, Brian Murray (marr. diss. 1978); partner, David Forgham-Bailey; two *s*. *Educ:* Barnsley Girls' High Sch.; Hull Univ. (BA Hons French/Drama). BBC Radio Bristol, 1973–78; BBC TV South, 1978–82; BBC Newsnight, 1982–85; BBC Radio 4 Today, 1985–87. Vis. Prof., London Inst., 2000. TV documentaries include: Everyman: Stand By Your Man, 1987, Breaking the Chain, 1988, As We Forgive Them, 1989; The Duchy of Cornwall, 1985, Women in Politics, 1989; Here's Looking At You, 1991; Presenter: Points of View, 1993; This Sunday, 1993–; Dilemmas, 1994. Weekly columnist, The Express, 1998–2000. Vice-Pres., FPA. Hon. DLitt Bradford, 1994; DUniv Open, 1999. *Publications:* The Woman's Hour Book of Humour, 1993; The Woman's Hour: a history of British women 1946–1996, 1996; Is It Me Or Is It Hot In Here, 2001; contrib. to newspapers and periodicals. *Recreations:* reading, theatre, riding. *Address:* c/o Woman's Hour, BBC, Broadcasting House, Portland Place, W1A 1AA. *T:* (020) 7765 4314.

MURRAY, John; *see* Dervaird, Hon. Lord.

MURRAY, Sir (John) Antony (Jerningham), Kt 1987; CBE 1980; Hon. Adviser to Government of Barbados in United Kingdom, since 1961; *b* 21 Jan. 1921; *s* of Captain John Challenger Murray and Cecilia Annette Murray (*née* Jerningham); *m* 1943, Hon. Winifred Mary, *e d* of 2nd Baron Hardinge of Penshurst, PC, GCB, GCVO, MC; one *s*. *Educ:* Eton College; New College, Oxford (2 terms). Grenadier Guards, 1940–46 (Major); Dir, Christmas Island Phosphate Co. Ltd, 1947–51; Mem. Exec. Cttee, West India Cttee, 1957– (Chm., 1963–65; Vice-Pres., 1966–). *Recreation:* fishing. *Address:* Woodmancote Manor Cottage, Cirencester, Glos GL7 7ED. *T:* (01285) 831226. *Clubs:* Boodle's, MCC.

MURRAY, Prof. John Joseph, CBE 1997; PhD; FDSRCS; FMedSci; Dean of Dentistry, University of Newcastle upon Tyne, since 1992; Clinical Director, Dental Hospital, Royal Victoria Infirmary NHS Trust, Newcastle upon Tyne, since 1995; *b* 28 Dec. 1941; *s* of late John Gerald Murray, Bradford, and Margaret Sheila (*née* Parle); *m* 1967, Valerie, *d* of late Harry and Lillie Allen; two *s*. *Educ:* St Bede's Grammar Sch., Bradford; Univ. of Leeds (BChD 1966; MChD 1968; PhD 1970); FDSRCS 1973; MCCDRCS 1989. Res. Fellow in Children's and Preventive Dentistry, Leeds Univ., 1966–70; Sen. Lectr in Children's Dentistry, 1970–75, Reader, 1975–77, Inst. of Dental Surgery, London; University of Newcastle upon Tyne: Prof. of Child Dental Health, 1977–92; Dental Postgrad. Sub-Dean, 1982–92. Chm., Cleft Lip and Palate Cttee, Clinical Standards Adv. Gp, 1998. Chm., Educn Cttee, GDC, 1999–. Founder FMedSci 1998. Hon. MFPHM 1998. H. Trendley Dean Award, Internat. Assoc. Dental Res., 1997. *Publications:* (jtly) The Acid Etch Technique in Paedodontics and Orthodontics, 1985; Fluorides in Caries Prevention, 1976, 3rd edn (jtly) 1991; Appropriate Use of Fluorides for Human Health, 1985; The Prevention of Dental Disease, 1983, 3rd edn 1996 as The Prevention of Oral Disease. *Recreations:* golf, photography. *Address:* Dental School, Framlington Place, Newcastle upon Tyne NE2 4BW. *T:* (0191) 222 8340. *Club:* Ponteland Golf.

MURRAY, Prof. Joseph Edward, MD, DSc; plastic surgeon; Professor of Surgery, Harvard University, since 1970; *b* 1 April 1919; *s* of William Andrew Murray and Mary Murray (*née* DePasquale); *m* 1945, Virginia Link; three *s* three *d*. *Educ:* Holy Cross Coll. (AB 1940); Harvard Univ. (MD 1943). US Army, 1944–47. Chief Plastic Surgeon: Peter Bent Brigham Hosp., 1951–86, Surgeon Emeritus, 1986; Children's Hosp., Boston, 1972–85. Hon. FRCS; Hon. FRCSI; Hon. FRACS. Hon. DSc: Holy Cross Coll., 1965; Rockford Coll., 1966; Roger Williams Coll., 1986. Numerous honours and awards from US sci. instns; (jtly) Nobel Prize for Medicine, 1990. *Address:* 108 Abbott Road, Wellesley Hills, MA 02481, USA.

MURRAY, Sir Kenneth, Kt 1993; PhD; FRCPath; FRS 1979; FRSE; Biogen Professor of Molecular Biology, University of Edinburgh, 1984–98; *b* 30 Dec. 1930; *yr s* of Allen and Elizabeth Ann Murray; *m* 1958, Noreen Elizabeth Parker (*see* N. E. Murray). *Educ:* Birmingham Univ. FRCPath 1991. Dept of Molecular Biology, Univ. of Edinburgh: Sen. Lecturer, 1967–73; Reader, 1973–76; Prof., 1976–. Member: Biochemical Soc.; European Molecular Biology Organisation; Academia Europaea. Chm., Darwin Trust, Edinburgh, 1984– (Founder, 1983). FRSE 1989. *Publications:* papers on nucleic acid biochem., molecular genetics, genetic engineering and viral hepatitis. *Address:* c/o Institute of Cell and Molecular Biology, University of Edinburgh, Edinburgh EH9 3JR. *Clubs:* Athenæum; New (Edinburgh).

MURRAY, Kenneth Alexander George, CB 1977; MA, EdB; Special Adviser to the Home Office on Police Service, Prison Service, and Fire Service selection, 1977–80; Director, Civil Service Selection Board, and Civil Service Commissioner, 1964–77; *b* 16 June 1916; *s* of late George Dickie Murray and Isabella Murray; *m* 1942, Elizabeth Ward Simpson (*d* 1999); one *d*. *Educ:* Skene Street and Central Schools, Aberdeen; Aberdeen Univ. (MA English (1st Cl. Hons), EdB Psychol. (1st Cl. Hons)). RAMC and War Office Selection Bd, 1940–45, Captain. Psychological Adviser, Govt of India, 1945–47; Lectr in Psychology, Univ. of Hull, 1948–50; Principal Psychologist and Chief Psychologist, CS Selection Bd, 1951–63. Adviser to Police Service in high-grade selection, 1963–, also to Fire and Prison Services, to Church of Scotland and C of E; Adviser (earlier) to Govts of Pakistan and Western Nigeria through their Public Service Commns. FBPsS 1984. *Recreations:* reading, walking, bridge, watching cricket and Rugby League. *Address:* 15 Melvinshaw, Leatherhead, Surrey KT22 8SX. *T:* (01372) 372995. *Clubs:* MCC, Royal Commonwealth Society.

MURRAY, Prof. Leo Gerard; Director, Cranfield School of Management, since 1986; *b* 21 May 1943; *s* of Patrick and Teresa Murray; *m* 1970, Pauline Ball; one *s* one *d*. *Educ:* St Aloysius' Coll., Glasgow; Univ. of Rennes; Glasgow Univ. (MA Hons 1965). British Petroleum Co., 1965–67; Courtaulds Gp, 1968–75; A. T. Kearney Ltd, 1975–79; Rothmans International Ltd, 1979–86: Man. Dir, Murray Sons & Co. Ltd, 1979–82; Dir, Overseas Mfg and Licensing, 1982–85; Dir, ME Region, 1985–86. Pro Vice-Chancellor, Cranfield Inst. of Technology, then Univ., 1992–95. Mem., Textile Sector Gp, NEDO, 1987–88. Chairman: ICL Cranfield Business Games Ltd, 1987–92; Cranfield Conference Centre, 1993–; Man. Dir, Cranfield Management Develt Ltd, 1993–; Chm., Fairmays Solicitors, 2001–. Director and Treasurer: Council of Univ. Management Schs, 1987–92; Assoc. of Business Schs, 1992–93 and 1999–; Membre: Conseil d'Orientation, Ecole Internat. d'Affaires, Marseilles, 1988–91; Conseil d'Admin, Univ. Technique de Compiègne, 1996–99. Vice-Pres., Strategic Planning Soc., 1992–99. Trustee, Blind in Business, 1992–. FCIM 1988; FRSA 1989. *Recreations:* family, work, golf. *Address:* The Beeches, 2 Church Lane, Lathbury, Bucks MK16 8JY. *T:* (01908) 615574. *Clubs:* Reform; Woburn Golf and Country.

MURRAY, Leo Joseph, CB 1986; QC (Aust.) 1980; legislation consultant, since 1989; Parliamentary Counsel, Queensland, Australia, 1975–89; *b* 7 April 1927; *s* of William Francis Murray and Theresa Agnes Murray (*née* Sheehy); *m* 1957, Janet Barbara Weir (marr. diss. 1987); two *d*. *Educ:* St Columban's Coll., Brisbane; Univ. of Queensland (BA, LLB). Admitted Barrister, Supreme Court, Queensland, 1951; Asst Crown Prosecutor, 1958; Asst Parly Counsel, 1963. *Recreations:* golf, ski-ing. *Address:* 99 Red Hill Road, Nudgee, Qld 4014, Australia. *T:* (7) 32675786. *Clubs:* Irish, Nudgee Golf (Brisbane); Southern Alps Ski (Sydney).

MURRAY, Leslie Allan, (Les), AO 1989; poet; *b* 17 Oct. 1938; *s* of late Cecil Allan Murray and Miriam Pauline Murray (*née* Arnall); *m* 1962, Valerie Gina Morelli; three *s* two *d*. *Educ:* Univ. of Sydney (BA 1969). Acting Editor, Poetry Australia, 1973–80; Editor, New Oxford Book of Australian Verse, 1985–97; Literary Editor, Quadrant, 1987–. Hon. doctorates from univs of New England, Stirling, NSW, ANU and Sydney. Petrarca Prize, Germany, 1995; T. S. Eliot Prize, 1997; Queen's Gold Medal for Poetry, 1998. *Publications:* Collected Poems, 1976, rev. edn 1998, US edn as The Rabbiters Bounty, 1992; The Boys Who Stole the Funeral (verse novel), 1980; The Paperbark Tree (selected prose), 1991; (ed) Fivefathers, 1995; Subhuman Redneck Poems, 1996; A Working Forest (prose), 1997; Fredy Neptune (verse novel), 1998; Conscious & Verbal (verse), 1999; Learning Human: selected poems (NY Times and Amer. Nat. Liby Assoc. Notable Book award), 2001. *Recreations:* work, gossip, fine coffee, ruminative driving, film-going. *Address:* c/o Margaret Connolly & Associates, 16 Winton Street, Warrawee, NSW 2074, Australia.

MURRAY, Nigel; Master of the Supreme Court, Queen's Bench Division, since 1991, a Recorder, since 1994; *b* 22 Jan. 1944; *s* of late Dr Ronald Ormiston Murray, MBE and Dr Catherine Joan Suzette Gauvain, FFCM; *m* 1970, Shirley Arbuthnot; one *s* one *d*. *Educ:* Stowe. Called to the Bar, Inner Temple, 1965; Mem. of Bar, Republic of Ireland and Sierra Leone; in practice, Western Circuit, specialising in Privy Council Appeals and Commonwealth Law, 1966–90, save when Judge of High Court of Botswana, 1984–87; Asst Recorder, 1982–94. An Editor, Supreme Court Practice, 1991–99. *Recreation:* golf. *Address:* Royal Courts of Justice, Strand, WC2A 2LL. *T:* (020) 7936 6000, *Fax:* (020) 7936 7165. *Clubs:* Garrick; Berkshire Golf, Rye Golf.

MURRAY of Blackbarony, Sir Nigel Andrew Digby, 15th Bt *cr* 1628; farmer; *b* 15 Aug. 1944; *s* of Sir Alan John Digby Murray of Blackbarony, 14th Bt, and of Mabel Elisabeth, *d* of late Arthur Bernard Schiele, Arias, Argentina; *S* father, 1978; *m* 1980, Diana Margaret, *yr d* of Robert C. Bray, Arias, Argentina; one *s* two *d*. *Educ:* St Paul's School, Argentina; Salesian Agricl Sch., Argentina; Royal Agricultural Coll., Cirencester. Farms dairy cattle, store cattle, crops and bees. Holds a private pilot's licence. *Heir: s* Alexander Nigel Robert Murray, *b* 1 July 1981. *Address:* Establecimiento Tinamú, cc 67, 2624 Arias, Provincia de Córdoba, Argentina. *T:* (03468) 440031.

MURRAY, Prof. Noreen Elizabeth, (Lady Murray), PhD; FRS 1982; FRSE; Professor of Molecular Genetics, Institute of Cell and Molecular Biology (formerly Department of Molecular Biology), University of Edinburgh, since 1988; *b* 26 Feb. 1935; *d* of John and Lilian Grace Parker; *m* 1958, Sir Kenneth Murray, *qv*. *Educ:* King's College London (BSc); Univ. of Birmingham (PhD). Research Associate: Stanford Univ., California, 1960–64; Univ. of Cambridge, 1964–67; Mem., MRC Molecular Genetics Unit, Edinburgh, 1968–74; Lectr, 1974, later Sen. Lectr, Reader, 1978–88, Dept. of Molecular Biology, Univ. of Edinburgh; scientist in European Molecular Biol. Lab., Heidelberg, 1980–82. Member: BBSRC, 1994–97; EMBO, 1981–; Pres., Genetical Soc., 1987–90. FRSE 1989. *Publications:* original research papers and reviews in field of genetics and molecular biology. *Recreation:* gardening. *Address:* Institute of Cell and Molecular Biology, University of Edinburgh, Mayfield Road, Edinburgh EH9 3JR. *T:* (0131) 650 5374.

MURRAY, Sir Patrick (Ian Keith), 12th Bt *cr* 1673; *b* 22 March 1965; *s* of Sir William Patrick Keith Murray, 11th Bt, and of Susan Elizabeth (who *m* 1976, J. C. Hudson, PhD), *d* of Stacey Jones; *S* father, 1977. *Educ:* Christ College, Brecon, Powys; LAMDA. *Heir: kinsman* Major Peter Keith-Murray, Canadian Forces [*b* 12 July 1935; *m* 1960, Judith Anne, *d* of late Andrew Tinsley; one *s* one *d*]. *Address:* 12 Burgos Grove, Greenwich, SE10 8LL.

MURRAY, Rev. Paul B.; *see* Beasley-Murray.

MURRAY, Prof. Robin MacGregor, MD; Professor of Psychiatry, University of London, at Institute of Psychiatry, King's College London, since 1999; *b* 31 Jan. 1944; *s* of James Alistair Campbell Murray and Helen Murray; *m* 1970, Shelagh Harris; one *s* one *d*. *Educ:* Royal High Sch., Edinburgh; Glasgow Univ. (MB, ChB 1968; MD 1974). MRCP 1971; MRCPsych 1976; MPhil London, 1976; DSc London, 1989. Registrar, Dept of Medicine, Univ. of Glasgow/Western Infirmary, 1971; Sen. House Officer, successively Registrar and Sen. Registrar, Maudsley Hosp., 1972–76; Vis. Fellow, National Inst. of Health, Washington, DC, 1977; Institute of Psychiatry, 1978–: Sen. Lectr, 1978–82; Dean, 1982–89; Prof. of Psychol Medicine, KCL, 1989–99. Pres., Assoc. of European Psychiatrists, 1995–96. Founder FMedSci 1998. *Publications:* (jtly) Essentials of Postgraduate Psychiatry, 1979; (jtly) Misuse of Psychotropic Drugs, 1981; Lectures on the History of Psychiatry, 1990; Schizophrenia, 1996; Neurodevelopment and Adult Psychopathology, 1997; Psychosis in the Inner City, 1998; (jtly) First Episode Psychosis, 1999; articles on schizophrenia, depression, brain imaging and psychiatric genetics. *Recreations:* Scottish and Jamaican music, swimming, roller blading.

MURRAY, Roger; Chairman: Fuerst Day Lawson Holdings, since 1997; Fleming Emerging Markets plc, since 1997 (Director, since 1993); Pacific Rim Palm Oil Ltd (Mauritius), since 2001; *b* 8 June 1936; *s* of Donald Murray and Nancy (*née* Irons); *m* 1960, Anthea Mary (*née* Turnbull); one *s* three *d*. *Educ:* Uppingham Sch.; Brasenose Coll., Oxford (MA). RNVR (Sub-Lieut), 1954–56. Joined Cargill Inc., Minneapolis, 1959; various positions in Hull and Geneva, 1960–70; President: Cargill Canada, 1973; Cargill Europe Ltd, 1982–97; Chm., Cargill plc, 1982–97; Mem., Management Cttee, Cargill Inc., 1986–97. Mem. Bd, Commonwealth Develt Corp., 1997–2000. Canadian and British citizen. *Recreations:* sailing, ski-ing, mountaineering, golf. *Address:* 11 Pembridge Place, W2 4XB. *T:* (020) 7243 0026.

MURRAY, Ronald King; *see* Murray, Rt Hon. Lord.

MURRAY, Dame Rosemary; *see* Murray, Dame A. R.

MURRAY, Sir Rowland William, 15th Bt *cr* 1630, of Dunerne, Fifeshire; *b* 22 Sept. 1947; *s* of Sir Rowland William Patrick Murray, 14th Bt and Josephine Margaret Murray (*née* Murphy) (*d* 1989); *S* father, 1994; *m* 1970, Nancy Diane, *d* of George C. Newberry; one *s* one *d*. *Educ:* Georgia State Univ. (SB 1974). General Manager, Beverly Hall Furniture Galleries, retail furniture and accessories. *Heir: s* Rowland William Murray IV, *b* 31 July 1979. *Recreations:* golf, gardening, travel. *Address:* 1187 Brookhaven Park Place, Atlanta, GA 30319, USA. *T:* (404) 2662408. *Clubs:* Midtown Atlanta Rotary, Atlanta High Museum of Art, Atlanta Botanical Gardens.

MURRAY, Ruth Hilary; *see* Finnegan, R. H.

MURRAY, Simon Anthony, CEng; Director, Major Projects and Investment, Railtrack plc, 1999–2001; *b* 31 Aug. 1951; *s* of Frank Murray and Barbara (*née* Williams); *m* 1st, 1974, Anne Humphrey (marr. diss. 1982); 2nd, 1983, Lindsay Maxwell; two *s* one *d*. *Educ:* Welbeck Coll.; Imperial Coll., London (BSc). CEng 1978; MICE 1978; FCGI 1999. Ove Arup & Partners: S Africa, 1975–77; Kenya, Zimbabwe, Hong Kong and London, 1977–89; Dir, 1990–94; Man. Dir, Gp Technical Services, BAA plc, 1995–98. Mem., EPSRC, 1998–2001. *Recreations:* jogging, wine, windsurfing. *Address:* 35 Greyladies Gardens, Wat Tyler Road, SE10 8AU. *T:* (020) 8469 2208. *Club:* Whitstable Yacht.

MURRELL, Geoffrey David George, CMG 1993; OBE 1987; HM Diplomatic Service, retired; *b* 19 Dec. 1934; *s* of Stanley Hector Murrell and Kathleen Murrell (Martin); *m* 1962, Kathleen Ruth Berton; one *s* three *d*. *Educ:* Minchenden Grammar School, Southgate; Oxford Univ. BA French and Russian. FCO Research Dept, 1959–61; Moscow, 1961–64; FCO, 1964–68; Moscow, 1968–70; Head, Soviet Section, FCO Research Dept, 1970–75; First Sec., Belgrade, 1975–78; Regional Dir, Soviet and East European Region, Research Dept, 1978–83; Counsellor, Moscow, 1983–87; Counsellor, Res. Dept, FCO, 1987–91; Minister-Counsellor, Moscow, 1991–94. *Publication:* Russia's Transition to Democracy, 1996. *Recreations:* tennis, guitar. *Club:* Oxford and Cambridge.

MURRELL, Prof. John Norman, PhD; FRS 1991; FRSC; Professor of Chemistry, University of Sussex, 1965–99, now Emeritus (Pro-Vice-Chancellor (Science), 1985–88); *b* London, 2 March 1932; *m* 1954, Dr D. Shirley Read; two *s* two *d*. *Educ:* Univ. of London (BSc); Univ. of Cambridge (PhD). University of Sussex: Dean, Sch. of Molecular Scis, 1979–84; Acad. Dir of Univ. Computing, 1984–85; Dean, Chemistry, Physics and Envmtl Sci., 1996–. Chm., Science Bd Computing Cttee, SERC, 1981–84. Hon. DSc Coimbra, Portugal, 1992. *Publications:* Theory of Electronic Spectra of Organic Molecules, 1960; (jointly): Valence Theory, 1965; Semi-empirical Self-consistent-field-molecular Theory of Molecules, 1971; Chemical Bond, 1978; Properties of Liquids and Solutions, 1982; Molecular Potential Energy Surfaces, 1985; Introduction to the Theory of Atomic and Molecular Scattering, 1989. *Address:* School of Molecular Sciences, University of Sussex, Falmer, Brighton BN1 9QJ.

MURRIN, Orlando Richard Charles; journalist; Editor, BBC Good Food Magazine, since 1997; *b* 1 April 1958; *s* of Patrick John Murrin and Patricia Mary, *d* of W. J. Skardon, OBE, MI5. *Educ:* Blundell's Sch., Devon; Magdalene Coll., Cambridge (Exhibnr; BA Hons English). Radio 3 Sub-Editor, Radio Times, 1980–83; Chief Sub Ed., Living mag., 1983–85; Asst Ed., Country Homes and Interiors, 1985–87; advertising copywriter, 1987–90; Dep. Ed., Living mag., 1990–93; Ed., Woman and Home, 1993–96. Clever Cook column, Express, 1997–. Pianist, Kettner's Restaurant, 1983–. *Publication:* The Clever Cookbook, 1999. *Recreations:* cookery (BBC Masterchef semi-finalist), gardening (especially poisonous plants). *Address:* BBC Worldwide, 80 Wood Lane, W12 0TT. *Club:* Soho House.

MURRISON, Dr Andrew William; MP (C) Westbury, since 2001; *b* 24 April 1961; *s* of William Gordon Murrison, RD and Marion Murrison (*née* Horn); *m* 1994, Jennifer Jane Munden; five *d*. *Educ:* Harwich High Sch.; The Harwich Sch.; Bristol Univ. (MB ChB 1984; MD 1996); Hughes Hall, Cambridge (DPH 1996). MFOM 1994. Med. Officer, RN, 1981–2000 (Surgeon Comdr); Consultant Occupational Physician. *Publications:* contribs to various biomed. pubns. *Recreations:* sailing, ski-ing. *Address:* House of Commons, SW1A 0AA.

MURSELL, Very Rev. (Alfred) Gordon; Dean (formerly Provost) of Birmingham, since 1999; *b* 4 May 1949; *s* of late Philip Riley Mursell and Sheena Nicholson Mursell; *m* 1989, Anne Muir. *Educ:* Ardingly Coll.; Brasenose Coll., Oxford (MA 1974; BD 1987). ARCM 1975. Ordained deacon, 1972, priest, 1973; Curate, St Mary Walton, Liverpool, 1973–77; Vicar, St John, E Dulwich, 1977–87; Tutor, Salisbury and Wells Theol Coll., 1987–91; Team Rector, Stafford, 1991–99. *Publications:* Theology of the Carthusian Life, 1988; Out of the Deep: prayer as protest, 1989; The Meditations of Guigo I, Prior of the Charterhouse, 1995; The Wisdom of the Anglo-Saxons, 1997; English Spirituality, 2001; (Gen. Ed.) The Story of Christian Spirituality: two thousand years, from East to West, 2001. *Recreations:* music, hill-walking. *Address:* Birmingham Cathedral, Colmore Row, Birmingham B3 2QB. *T:* (0121) 236 4333, *Fax:* (0121) 212 0868. *Club:* Athenæum.

MURSELL, Sir Peter, Kt 1969; MBE 1941; Vice Lord-Lieutenant, West Sussex, 1974–90; *b* 20 Jan. 1913; *m* 1938, Cicely, *d* of late Mr and Mrs M. F. North; two *s* two *d*. *Educ:* Bedales Sch.; Downing Coll. Cambridge. Fruit growing, 1934. War Service: Air Transport Auxiliary, 1940–44, Sen. Comdr. West Sussex County Council: Mem., 1947–74; Chm., 1962–67 and 1969–74. Member: Cttee on Management in Local Govt, 1965–66; Royal Commn on Local Govt in England, 1966–69; Water Space Amenity Commn, 1973–76; Inland Waterways Amenity Adv. Council, 1974–77. DL West Sussex, 1962. *Recreations:* sailing, mountain walking, ski-ing, squash, canal cruising. *Address:* Taints Orchard, The Street, Washington, West Sussex RH20 4AS. *T:* (01903) 893062.

MURTA, Prof. Kenneth Hall, FRIBA; Professor of Architecture, University of Sheffield, 1974–94, now Emeritus; *b* 24 Sept. 1929; *s* of John Henry Murta and Florence (*née* Hall); *m* 1955, Joan Wilson; two *s* two *d*. *Educ:* Bede Collegiate GS, Sunderland; King's Coll., Univ. of Durham (BArch, DipArch). Architect in private practice and public service, 1954–59; Sen. Lectr, Nigerian Coll. of Arts, Science and Technology, then Ahmadu Bello Univ., 1959–62; University of Sheffield: Lectr, then Sen. Lectr, 1962–74; Dean, Faculty of Architectural Studies, 1974–77, 1984–88. Major designs: Anglican Cathedral, Kaduna, Nigeria; St John, Sheffield Park; All Saints, Denaby Main; St Laurence, Heanor; St Lawrence, Frodingham; Christ Church, Pitsmoor; St Mary the less, St John's Coll., Univ. of Durham; Christ Church, Stannington; St Luke, Lodge Moor, Sheffield; St Leonard, Thrybergh, Rotherham; All Saints, Totley, Sheffield; All Saints, Breadshall, Derbys; Pilgrims, Fordcombe, Kent; Turangi, West Malvern; Clowance, Praze, Cornwall; Stable Block, Brodsworth Hall, Doncaster. Chm., Sheffield Cathedral Fabric Adv. Cttee, 1992–. Mem. and Hon. Officer, ARCUK, 1991–97 (Mem., 1986–97, Vice-Chm., 1990–91, Chm., 1991–97, Bd of Architectural Educn); Chm., RIBA Yorks Reg., 1984–85. Hon. Sec., Ecclesiological Soc., 1991–2000. Editor, The Ecclesiologist, 1991–97. *Publications:* contribs to Architectural Rev., Ecclesiologist, Churchbuilding, Trans RIBA, Architects' Jl, RIBA Jl. *Recreations:* cricket, soccer, churchwatching, travel, walking in cities on Sundays. *Address:* Underedge, Back Lane, Hathersage, Derbyshire S32 1AR. *T:* (01433) 650833. *Clubs:* Royal Over-Seas League; Ford & Hylton Lane Working Men's (Sunderland).

MURTAGH, Miss Marion; Managing Director: Stats (MR) Ltd, 1985–87; CSB Data Processing Ltd, 1985–87; Chairman of both companies, 1970–85. *Educ:* Waverley Gram. Sch., Birmingham. Qualified as: Certified Accountant, 1947; Chartered Secretary, 1948. Proprietor, The Calculating Bureau, 1938–51, Joint Owner, 1951–61. Mem., and Pres., West Midlands Bridge Club. Pres., Dorridge Village Hall Assoc. *Recreation:* bridge. *Address:* 42 Dovehouse Court, Warwick Grange, Solihull, West Midlands B91 1EW. *T:* (0121) 704 0873.

MURTON, family name of **Baron Murton of Lindisfarne**.

MURTON OF LINDISFARNE, Baron *cr* 1979 (Life Peer), of Hexham in the County of Northumberland; **(Henry) Oscar Murton;** PC 1976; OBE 1946; TD 1947 (Clasp 1951); JP; a Deputy Chairman of Committees, since 1981 and a Deputy Speaker, since 1983, House of Lords; *b* 8 May 1914; *o s* of late H. E. C. Murton, and of E. M. Murton (*née* Renton), Hexham, Northumberland; *m* 1st, 1939, Constance Frances (*d* 1977), *e d* of late F. O'L. Connell; one *s* (one *d* decd); 2nd, 1979, Pauline Teresa (Freeman, City of London, 1980), *y d* of late Thomas Keenan, JP. *Educ:* Uppingham Sch. Commissioned, TA, 1934; Staff Capt., 149 Inf. Bde, TA, 1937–39; Staff Coll., Camberley, 1939; tsc; active service, Royal Northumberland Fusiliers, 1939–46; Lt-Col, Gen. Staff, 1942–46 (C-in-C's commendation for special service, 1942, 1944). Managing Dir, Henry A. Murton Ltd, Departmental Stores, Newcastle-upon-Tyne and Sunderland, 1949–57. MP (C) Poole, 1964–79; Sec., Cons. Parly Cttee for Housing, Local Government and Land, 1964–67, Vice-Chm., 1967–70; Chm., Cons. Parly Cttee for Public Building and Works, 1970; PPS to Minister of Local Government and Development, 1970–71; an Asst Govt Whip, 1971–72; a Lord Comr, HM Treasury, 1972–73; Second Dep. Chm., 1973–74, First Dep. Chm., 1974–76, Dep. Speaker and Chm. of Ways and Means, House of Commons, 1976–79. Member: Exec. Cttee, Inter-Parliamentary Union British Group, 1970–71; Panel of Chairmen of Standing Cttees, 1970–71; Jt Select Cttee of Lords and Commons on Private Bill Procedure, 1987–88. Introduced: The Highways (Amendment) Act 1965; The Access to Neighbouring Land Act, 1992. Mem., Poole BC, 1961–63; Pres., Poole Cons. Assoc., 1983–95; a former Vice-Pres., Assoc. of Municipal Corporations; Mem. Herrison (Dorchester) Hosp. Group Management Cttee, 1963–74. Governor, Canford Sch., 1972–76. Chancellor, Primrose League, 1983–88. Freeman, City of London, 1977; Freeman, Wax Chandlers' Co.; Past Master, Clockmakers' Co. JP, Poole, 1963. *Recreations:* sailing, painting. *Address:* 49 Carlisle Mansions, Carlisle Place, SW1P 1HY. *T:* (020) 7834 8226.

MUSEVENI, Lt-Gen. Yoweri Kaguta; President of the Republic of Uganda, since 1986; *b* 1944; *s* of Amos and Esteri Kaguta; *m* 1973, Janet Kataaha; one *s* three *d.* *Educ:* primary and secondary schs in Uganda; Univ. of Dar-es-Salaam, Tanzania (BA). Asst Sec. for Research in President's Office, 1970–71; Hd of Front for National Salvation and anti-Idi Amin armed gp, 1971–79; Minister of Defence, 1979–80, and Vice Chm. of ruling Military Commn; Chm., Uganda Patriotic Movement; Chm., High Comd of Nat. Resistance Army, 1981–. *Publications:* What is Africa's Problem? (essays), 1992; Sowing the Mustard Seed: the struggle for freedom and democracy in Uganda (autobiog.), 1997. *Recreations:* karate, football. *Address:* Office of the President, Parliamentary Buildings, PO Box 25497, Kampala, Uganda. *T:* (41) 234522/234503.

MUSGRAVE, Sir Christopher John Shane, 8th Bt *cr* 1782, of Tourin, Waterford; *b* 23 Oct. 1959; *er s* of Sir Richard Musgrave, 7th Bt and of Maria (*née* Cambanis); *S* father, 2000. *Educ:* Cheltenham. *Heir: b* Michael Shane Musgrave, *b* 30 Jan. 1968.

MUSGRAVE, Sir Christopher (Patrick Charles), 15th Bt *cr* 1611; *b* 14 April 1949; *s* of Sir Charles Musgrave, 14th Bt and of Olive Louise Avril, *o d* of Patrick Cringle, Norfolk; *S* father, 1970; *m* 1st, 1978 (marr. diss. 1992); two *d*; 2nd, 1995, Carol, *d* of Geoffrey Lawson. *Recreations:* drawing, painting, model-making, animals, gardening. *Heir: b* Julian Nigel Chardin Musgrave, *b* 8 Dec. 1951. *Address:* Ranvilles Cottage, 29 Ranvilles Lane, Fareham, Hants PO14 3DX.

MUSGRAVE, Rosanne Kimble, MA; educational consultant, since 2000; Headmistress, Blackheath High School (GDST), 1989–2000; *b* 31 Jan. 1952; *d* of Gp Captain John Musgrave, DSO, and Joanne Musgrave. *Educ:* Cheltenham Ladies' Coll.; St Anne's Coll., Oxford (MA); MA Reading Univ.; PGCE London Univ. Assistant teacher of English: Latymer Grammar Sch., 1976–79; Camden School for Girls (ILEA), 1979–82; Head of English: Channing Sch., Highgate, 1982–84; Haberdashers' Aske's School for Girls, Elstree, 1984–89. Pres., GSA, 1999. Corporate Mem., Cheltenham Ladies' Coll., 1989; Gov., St Albans High Sch., 1996–. FRSA 1994. Freeman, City of London, 1993. *Recreations:* letterpress printing, DIY. *Address:* 14 Fortis Green, N2 9EL.

MUSGRAVE, Thea; composer; *b* 1928; *d* of James P. Musgrave and Joan Musgrave (*née* Hacking); *m* 1971, Peter, *s* of Irving Mark, NY. *Educ:* Moreton Hall, Oswestry; Edinburgh Univ.; Paris Conservatoire; privately with Nadia Boulanger. Dist. Prof., Queens Coll., CUNY, 1987–. *Works include:* Cantata for a summer's day, 1954; The Abbot of Drimock (Chamber opera), 1955; Triptych for Tenor and orch., 1959; Colloquy for violin and piano, 1960; The Phoenix and the Turtle for chorus and orch., 1962; The Five Ages of Man for chorus and orch., 1963; The Decision (opera), 1964–65; Nocturnes and arias for orch., 1966; Chamber Concerto No. 2, in homage to Charles Ives, 1966; Chamber Concerto No 3 (Octet), 1966; Concerto for orchestra, 1967; Music for Horn and Piano, 1967; Clarinet Concerto, 1968; Beauty and the Beast (ballet), 1968; Night Music, 1969; Memento Vitae, a concerto in homage to Beethoven, 1970; Horn concerto, 1971; From One to Another, 1972; Viola Concerto, 1973; The Voice of Ariadne (opera), 1972 73; Rorate Coeli, for chorus, 1974; Space Play, 1974; Orfeo I and Orfeo II, 1975; Mary, Queen of Scots (opera), 1976–77; Christmas Carol (opera), 1979; An Occurrence at Owl Creek Bridge (radio opera), 1981; Peripeteia (orchestral), 1981; Harriet, the Woman called Moses (opera), 1984; Black Tambourine for women's chorus and piano, 1985; Pierrot, 1985; For the Time Being for chorus, 1986; The Golden Echo, 1987; Narcissus, 1988; The Seasons (orchestral), 1988; Rainbow (orchestral), 1990; Simón Bolivar (opera), 1993; Autumn Sonata, 1993; Journey through a Japanese Landscape (marimba concerto), 1993; Wild Winter, 1993; On the Underground (vocal), 1994; Helios (oboe concerto), 1995; Phoenix Rising (orchestral), 1997; Lamenting with Ariadne, 2000. Performances and broadcasts: UK, France, Germany, Switzerland, Scandinavia, USA, USSR, etc, Edinburgh, Cheltenham, Aldeburgh, Zagreb, Venice and Warsaw Festivals. Hon. MusDoc, CNAA. *Address:* c/o Novello & Co. Ltd, 8/9 Frith Street, W1V 5TZ.

MUSGRAVE, Prof. William Kenneth Rodgerson, PhD, DSc (Birmingham); Professor of Organic Chemistry, 1960–81, now Emeritus, and Head of Department of Chemistry, 1968–71, 1974–77, 1980–81, University of Durham; *b* 16 Sept. 1918; *s* of late Charles Musgrave and late Sarah Alice Musgrave; *m* 1944, Joyce Cadman; two *s.* *Educ:* Stanley Grammar Sch., Co. Durham; Univ. of Birmingham. British-Canadian Atomic Energy Project, 1944–45; Univ. of Durham: Lecturer in Chemistry, 1945–56; Senior Lecturer, 1956–60; Personal Readership in Organic Chem., 1960; Second Pro-Vice-Chancellor, 1970–73; Pro-Vice-Chancellor and Sub-Warden, 1973–78; Acting Vice-Chancellor, 1979. *Publications:* (joint) Advances in Fluorine Chemistry, Vol. I, edited by Stacey, Tatlow and Sharpe, 1960; Rodd's Chemistry of Carbon Compounds, vols Ia and IIIa, edited by Coffey; scientific papers in chemical journals. *Recreations:* gardening, rough shooting. *Address:* Apt 14, Pegasus Court, 61–63 Broad Road, Sale, Greater Manchester M33 2ES.

MUSGROVE, Prof. Frank, DLitt; Sarah Fielden Professor of Education, University of Manchester, 1970–82, now Emeritus; Dean of the Faculty of Education, 1976–78; *b* 16 Dec. 1922; *e s* of late Thomas and Fanny Musgrove; *m* Dorothy Ellen (*née* Nicholls); one *d.* *Educ:* Henry Mellish Grammar Sch., Nottingham; Magdalen Coll., Oxford; Empire Air Navigation Sch., Port Elizabeth; Univ. of Nottingham. MA Oxon, PhD Nottingham, MEd Manchester. Served War, RAFVR, 1941–45, Navigator, Bomber Command (commnd), Ops 149 Sqdn (tour of bombing missions completed 1944). Educational appts in England and in the Colonial Educn Service, E Africa, 1947–57; Lectureships in Univs of Leicester and Leeds, 1957–65; Foundn Chair of Research in Educn, Univ. of Bradford, 1965–70. Visiting Professor: of Educn, Univ. of BC, 1965; of Sociology, Univ. of California (Davis), 1969; Guest lectr, Inst. of Sociology, Univ. of Utrecht, 1968; The Chancellor's Lectr, Univ. of Wellington, NZ, 1970; British Council Lectr, Univs of Grenoble, Aix-en-Provence, Nice, Paris, 1972; Raymond Priestley Lectr, Univ. of Birmingham, 1975. Hon. Prof., Univ. of Hull, 1985–88. Co-editor, Research in Education, 1971–76. FRAI 1952; FRSA 1971. DLitt Open, 1982. *Publications:* The Migratory Elite, 1963; Youth and the Social Order, 1964; The Family, Education and Society, 1966; Society and the Teacher's Role (with P. H. Taylor), 1969; Patterns of Power and Authority in English Education, 1971; Ecstasy and Holiness, 1974, new edn 1994; Margins of the Mind, 1977; School and the Social Order, 1979; Education and Anthropology, 1982; The North of England: from Roman to present times, 1990; research papers in: Africa; Sociological Review; Brit. Jl of Sociology; Brit. Jl of Educational Psychology; Economic History Review; Brit. Jl of Social and Clinical Psychology, etc. *Recreations:* fell walking, classical music, fly fishing. *Address:* Dib Scar, The Cedar Grove, Beverley, E Yorks HU17 7EP. *T:* (01482) 868799.

MUSGROVE, Harold John; Chairman, Worcester Acute Hospitals NHS Trust, since 1999; *b* 19 Nov. 1930; *s* of Harold Musgrove; *m* 1959, Jacquelin Mary Hobbs; two *s* two *d.* *Educ:* King Edward Grammar Sch., Birmingham; Birmingham Tech. Coll. Nat. Cert. of Mech. Eng. Apprentice, Austin Motor Co., 1945; held various positions, incl. Chief Material Controller (Commission as Navigator, RAF, during this period); Senior Management, Truck and Bus Group, Leyland Motor Corp., 1963–78; Austin Morris: Dir of Manufacturing, 1978–79; Man. Dir, 1979–80; Chm. and Man. Dir, 1980–81; Chm., Light Medium Cars Group, 1981–82; Chm. and Chief Exec., Austin Rover Gp, 1982–86; Chloride plc: Dir, 1989–92; Chm., Industrial Battery Sector, 1989–91; Chm., Power Supplies and Lighting Gp, 1991–92. Chairman: W Midlands Ambulance Service, 1992–94; Birmingham Heartlands Hosp. NHS Trust, 1994–96; Birmingham Heartlands and Solihull (Teaching) NHS Trust, 1996–99. Pres., Birmingham Chamber of Industry and Commerce, 1987–88. Dir, Metalrax plc, 1986–. Pres., Aston Villa FC, 1986–98. FIMI 1985. DUniv Birmingham, 2000. Midlander of the Year Award, 1980; IProdE Internat. Award, 1981; Soc. of Engineers Churchill Medal, 1982. *Recreations:* golf, soccer. *Address:* The Lodge, Laverton, Broadway, Worcs WR12 7NA.

MUSKERRY, 9th Baron *cr* 1781 (Ire.); **Robert Fitzmaurice Deane;** Bt 1710 (Ire.); *b* 26 March 1948; *s* of 8th Baron Muskerry and Betty Fairbridge, *e d* of George Wilfred Reckless Palmer; *S* father, 1988; *m* 1975, Rita Brink, Pietermaritzburg; one *s* two *d.* *Educ:* Sandford Park School, Dublin; Trinity Coll., Dublin (BA, BAI). *Heir: s* Hon. Jonathan Fitzmaurice Deane, *b* 7 June 1986. *Address:* 725 Ridge Road, Berea, Durban 4001, South Africa.

MUSONDA, Dr Moses; High Commissioner for Republic of Zambia in India, since 2001; *b* 10 March 1937; *s* of William Musonda and Margaret (*née* Mulenga); *m* 1972, Lucy Kawandami; three *s* two *d.* *Educ:* Kent State Univ., Ohio (BA 1967; MA 1968); Bryn Mawr Coll., Penn (PhD 1983). Lectr, then Associate Prof., Univ. of Zambia, 1968–94; on secondment as Dep. Dir-Gen., CICIBA (Internat. Centre for Bantu Civilisations), Gabon, 1986–90; Ambassador of Zambia to China, 1995–97; High Comr for Zambia in UK, 1997–2001. *Publications:* contrib. papers to jls and reviews on educn, language and literature. *Address:* Zambia High Commission, C-79 Anand Niketan, New Delhi 110021, India.

MUSSON, Gen. Sir Geoffrey (Randolph Dixon), GCB 1970 (KCB 1965; CB 1959); CBE 1945; DSO 1944; BA; *b* 9 June 1910; *s* of late Robert Dixon Musson, Yockleton, Shrewsbury; *m* 1939, Hon. Elspeth L. Bailey, *d* of late Hon. Herbert Crawshay Bailey; one *s* (one *d* decd). *Educ:* Shrewsbury; Trinity Hall, Cambridge. 2nd Lt KSLI, 1930. Served War of 1939–45, North Africa and Italy; Comdr 2nd Bn DCLI, 1943–44; Comdr 36th Infantry Bde, 1944–46. Comdr Commonwealth Forces in Korea, 1954–55; Comdt Sch. of Infantry, 1956–58, Comdr 7th Armoured Div., BAOR, 1958; Maj.-Gen. 1958; Comdr, 5th Div., 1958–59. Chief of Staff, GHQ, Near East Land Forces, 1959–62; Vice-Adjutant-Gen., War Office, subseq. Min. of Defence, 1963–64; GOC-in-C, N Command, 1964–67; Adjutant-General, 1967–70, retired. Colonel: King's Shropshire Light Infantry, 1963–68; The Light Infantry, 1968–72. A Vice-Chm., Nat. Savings Cttee, 1970–78; Chairman: HM Forces Savings Cttee, 1970–78; Regular Forces Employment Assoc., 1978–80; Vice-Pres., Royal Patriotic Fund Corporation, 1974–83; Pres., Victory Services Club, 1970–80. *Address:* Barn Cottage, Hurstbourne Tarrant, Andover, Hants SP11 0BD. *T:* (01264) 736354.

MUSSON, Rear Adm. John Geoffrey Robin, CB 1993; Senior Naval Directing Staff, Royal College of Defence Studies, 1990–93; Chief Naval Supply and Secretariat Officer, 1991–93; *b* 30 May 1939; *s* of Geoffrey William Musson and Winifred Elizabeth Musson (*née* Whyman); *m* 1965, Joanna Marjorie Ward; two *s* one *d.* *Educ:* Luton Grammar Sch.; BRNC, Dartmouth. Entered RN, 1957; served HM Ships: Bulwark, 1960–61; Decoy, 1961–62; Cavalier, 1966–67; Forth, 1967–69; Kent, 1975–76; NDC, 1979; MA, VCDS (Personnel and Logistics), 1980–81; Sec. to Chief of Fleet Support, 1982–83; CSO (Personnel and Admin), FONAC, 1984–86; Dir, Naval Officer Appts (Supply and WRNS), 1986–88; Captain, HMS Cochrane, 1988–90; retd, 1993. Admiralty Bd Gov., Royal Naval Benevolent Trust, 1995–. Gov. (formerly Mem. Cttee of Mgt), Royal Hosp. Sch., Holbrook, 1995–. Sec., Salisbury Dio. Sudan Link, 1995–. Freeman, City of London, 1993. *Recreations:* Scottish country dancing, mending things, history, hedge laying.

MUSSON, John Nicholas Whitaker; Warden of Glenalmond College (formerly Trinity College, Glenalmond), 1972–87; *b* 2 Oct. 1927; *s* of late Dr J. P. T. Musson, OBE and Gwendoline Musson (*née* Whitaker); *m* 1953, Ann Preist; one *s* three *d.* *Educ:* Clifton; Brasenose Coll., Oxford (MA). Served with Welsh Guards and Lancs Fusiliers, 1945–48 (commnd); BA Hons Mod. Hist., Oxford, 1951; HM Colonial Service, 1951–59: District Officer, N Nigeria; Lectr, Inst. of Administration, N Nigeria; Staff Dept, British Petroleum, London, 1959–61; Asst Master and Housemaster, Canford Sch., 1961–72. Chm., Scottish Div. HMC, 1981–83; Scottish Dir (formerly Scottish Sec.), ISCO, 1987–93. Governor: Clifton Coll., 1989– (Mem. Council, 1989–95); George Watson's Coll., Edinburgh, 1989–98. Mercy Corps Europe/Scottish European Aid: Dir and Trustee, 1996–2000; Country Dir (Bosnia and Herzegovina), resident in Sarajevo, 1998–99; Vice-Chm., Mercy Corps Scotland, 2000–. *Recreations:* travel, art, Egyptology. *Address:* 47 Spylaw Road, Edinburgh EH10 5BP. *T:* (0131) 337 0089. *Club:* New (Edinburgh).

MUSTILL, family name of **Baron Mustill.**

MUSTILL, Baron *cr* 1992 (Life Peer), of Pateley Bridge in the County of North Yorkshire; **Michael John Mustill,** Kt 1978; PC 1985; FBA 1996; a Lord of Appeal in Ordinary, 1992–97; *b* 10 May 1931; *o s* of late Clement William and Marion Mustill; *m* 1st, Beryl Reid Davies (marr. diss.); 2nd, Caroline Phillips; two *s* and one step *d.* *Educ:* Oundle Sch.; St John's Coll., Cambridge (Hon. Fellow, 1992); LLD Cantab 1992. Royal Artillery, 1949–51 (commissioned, 1950). Called to Bar, Gray's Inn, 1955, Bencher, 1976. QC 1968. Dep. Chm., Hants QS, 1971; a Recorder of the Crown Court, 1972–78; Judge of High Court, QBD, 1978–85; a Lord Justice of Appeal, 1985–92. Presiding Judge, NE Circuit, 1981–84. Chairman: Civil Service Appeal Tribunal, 1971–78; Judicial Studies Board, 1985–89; Deptl Cttee on Law of Arbitration, 1985–90; Adv. Bd, Inst. of Criminology, Cambridge Univ., 1992–. Hon. Prof. of Law, Birmingham Univ., 1995–; Yorke Dist. Vis. Fellow, Cambridge Univ., 1996–. President: British Maritime Law Assoc., 1995–; CIArb, 1995–98; Assoc. of Average Adjusters, 1996–97; London Shipping Law Centre, 1996–; Seldon Soc., 1997–2000; Expert Witness Inst., 1997–; British Br., Internat. Law Assoc., 1997–; Vice-Pres., Court of Arbitration, Internat. Chamber of Commerce, 1997–. Member: Comité Maritime Internat., 1996–; Amer. Law Inst. Hon. LLD Birmingham; DUniv Leeds Metropolitan. *Publications:* The Law and Practice of Commercial Arbitration in England (with S. C. Boyd, QC), 1982, 2nd edn 1989; Anticipatory Breach of Contract, 1990; Joint Editor: Scrutton on Charterparties and Bills of Lading; Arnould on Marine Insurance; articles in legal periodicals. *Address:* 42 Laurier Road, NW5 1SJ. *Club:* Travellers.

MUSTOE, Mrs Anne, MA; travel writer and lecturer; *b* 24 May 1933; *d* of H.W. Revill; *m* 1960, Nelson Edwin Mustoe, QC (*d* 1976). *Educ:* Girton Coll., Cambridge (BA Classical Tripos 1955, MA 1958). DipIPM 1959. Guest, Keen & Nettlefolds Ltd, 1956–60; Head of Classics, Francis Holland School, NW1, 1965–69; independent travel agent, 1969–73; Dep. Headmistress, Cobham Hall, Kent, 1975–78; Headmistress, St Felix School, Southwold, 1978–87. Chm., ISIS, 1986–87; President, Girls' Schools Assoc., 1984–85; Mem., Board of Managers of Girls' Common Entrance Examinations, 1983–86.

Mem., CS Final Selection Bd, 1980–92. Governor: Hethersett Old Hall Sch., 1981–86; Cobham Hall, 1986–99; James Allen's Girls' Sch., 1991–97; Thornton Coll., 1992–97. FRGS 1996. JP Suffolk, 1981–85. *Publications:* A Bike Ride: 12,000 miles around the world, 1991; Escaping the Winter, 1993; Lone Traveller, 1998; Two Wheels in the Dust, 2001. *Recreations:* music, cycling (world cycling tours, 1987–88, 1994–95). *Address:* 12 Melcombe Court, Dorset Square, NW1 6EP. *T:* (020) 7262 1701.

MUSTON, Rt Rev. Gerald Bruce; Bishop of North-West Australia, 1981–92; *b* 19 Jan. 1927; 3rd *s* of Stanley John and Emily Ruth Muston; *m* 1951, Laurel Wright; one *s* one *d*. *Educ:* N Sydney Chatswood High School; Moore Theological College, Sydney. ThL (Aust. Coll. of Theology). Rector, Wallerawang, NSW, 1951–53; Editorial Secretary, Church Missionary Society (Aust.), 1953–58; Rector, Tweed Heads, NSW, 1958–61; Vicar, Essendon, Vic, 1961–67; Rural Dean of Essendon, 1963–67; Rector of Darwin, NT, and Archdeacon of Northern Territory, 1967–69; Federal Secretary, Bush Church Aid Society of Aust., 1969–71; Bishop Coadjutor, dio. Melbourne (Bishop of the Western Region), 1971–81. *Recreations:* golf, reading. *Address:* 17/27 Beddi Road, Duncraig, WA 6023, Australia. *Club:* Melbourne (Melbourne).

MUSTOW, Stuart Norman, CBE 1995; FREng, FICE; consulting engineer, since 1986; Director, W. S. Atkins International, 1986–95; *b* 26 Nov. 1928; *s* of Norman Eric Mustow and Mabel Florence Mustow (*née* Purcell); *m* 1964, Sigrid Hertha Young; two *s* one *d*. *Educ:* Aston Univ. (BSc). FIHT; FREng (FEng 1982). Mil. service, RA; Local Govt Engineering, 1949–69; City Engineer and Surveyor, Stoke on Trent, 1969–74; County Surveyor, W Midlands, responsible for roads, transport planning and Birmingham Airport, 1974–86. Chm., Hazards Forum, 1999–. Mem., Engineering Council, 1995–97. President: Inst. Municipal Engrs, 1980–81; ICE, 1993–94; Vice-Pres., Royal Acad. of Engrg, 1995–99. Hon. DSc Aston, 1994. *Publications:* papers in learned jls. *Recreations:* outdoor life, church, social work. *Address:* 9 Knighton Road, Sutton Coldfield, West Midlands B74 4NY. *T:* (0121) 353 9839.

MUTCH, Dr William Edward Scott, OBE 1989; FRSE; forestry and land use consultant, 1989–99; Member of Board and Chairman, South East Region, Scottish Natural Heritage, 1992–94; *b* 14 Aug. 1925; *s* of Wilfred Ernest Mutch and Helen Anderson Mutch (*née* Bannerman); *m* 1950, Margaret Isobel McKay; one *d*. *Educ:* Royal High Sch., Edinburgh; Edinburgh Univ. (BSc Forestry, PhD); St John's Coll., Oxford. FICFor. Colonial Service Forest Dept, Nigeria, 1946; University of Edinburgh: Lectr in Forestry, 1953; Sen. Lectr, 1963; Head of Dept of Forestry and Natural Resources, 1981–87. Dir, Central Scotland Woodlands Ltd, subseq. Central Scotland Countryside Trust, 1989–97. Member: Countryside Commn for Scotland, 1988–92; Nat. Forestry Res. Adv. Cttee, 1982–96; Nature Conservancy Council, 1989–91; Nature Conservancy Council for Scotland, 1991–92. Institute of Chartered Foresters: Pres., 1982–84; Inst. Medal, 1986. Editor, Scottish Forestry, 1957–62. *Publications:* Public Recreation in National Forests, 1967; The Interaction of Forestry and Farming, 1980; Farm Woodland Management, 1987; Tall Trees and Small Woods, 1998; Steal me a Duchess, 2001; contribs to professional jls. *Recreations:* cabinet making, travel, painting. *Address:* 19 Barnton Grove, Edinburgh EH4 6EQ. *T:* (0131) 339 1400.

MUTI, Riccardo, Hon. KBE 2000; Conductor Laureate, Philadelphia Orchestra, since 1992 (Principal Guest Conductor, 1977–80; Principal Conductor and Music Director, 1980–92); Music Director, La Scala, Milan, since 1986; *b* 28 July 1941; *m* 1969, Cristina Mazzavillani; two *s* one *d*. *Educ:* Diploma in pianoforte, Conservatorio di Napoli; Diploma in conducting and composition, Milan. Principal Conductor, 1973–82, Music Dir, 1979–82, New Philharmonia, later Philharmonia Orchestra, London; Principal Conductor, Orchestra Maggio Musicale Fiorentino, 1969–81. Concert tours in USA with Philadelphia Orch.; concerts at Salzburg, Edinburgh, Lucerne, Flanders, Vienna and Ravenna Festivals; concerts with Berlin Philharmonic, Vienna Philharmonic, Concertgebouw Amsterdam, NY Philharmonic, Bayerisches Rundfunk SO, Filarmonica della Scala, Israel Philharmonic, Boston SO, Chicago SO; opera in Florence, Salzburg, Vienna, Munich, Covent Garden, Milan, Ravenna. Hon. degrees from Univs. of Bologna, Urbino, Milan, Lecce and Tel Aviv, and univs in England and USA. Recording prizes from France, Germany, Italy, Japan and USA. Accademico: dell'Accademia di Santa Cecilia, Rome; dell'Accademia Luigi Cherubini, Florence. Hon. Citizen: Milan; Florence; Sydney; Ravenna. Grande Ufficiale, Repubblica Italiana; Cavaliere, Gran Croce (Italy), 1991; Verdienstkreuz, 1st class (Germany), 1976; KM; Ehrenkreuz (Austria). *Address:* Teatro alla Scala, Via Filodrammtici 2, Milan 20121, Italy.

MUTTER, Anne-Sophie; violinist; *b* Rheinfelden, Baden, 29 June 1963. *Educ:* studied with Prof. Aida Stucki in Switzerland. Début with Herbert von Karajan, Salzburg, 1977; soloist with major orchestras of the world; also plays with string trio and quartet. Guest teacher, RAM, 1985. Hon. Pres., Univ. of Oxford Mozart Soc., 1983. Hon. Mem., Beethoven Soc., 1996. Jugend Musiziert Prize (FRG) for: violin, 1970 and 1974; piano, 1970; Künstler des Jahres Deutscher Schallplattenpreis, 1979; Grand Prix Internat. du Disque, Record Acad. Prize, Tokyo, 1982; Internat. Schallplattenpreis, 1993; Grammy, 1994. Bundesverdienstkreuz (1st Cl.), 1987. *Recreations:* graphic arts, sport. *Address:* Effnerstrasse 48, 81925 Munich, Germany. *T:* (89) 984418, *Fax:* (89) 9827186.

MUTTUKUMARU, Christopher Peter Jayantha; Legal Director (Transport), Department for Transport, Local Government and the Regions, since 2001; *b* 11 Dec. 1951; *y s* of late Maj. Gen. Anton Muttukumaru, OBE and of Margaret Muttukumaru; *m* 1976, Ann Elisabeth Tutton; two *s*. *Educ:* Xavier Coll., Melbourne; Jesus Coll., Oxford (BA, MA). Called to the Bar, Gray's Inn, 1974; in practice at the Bar, 1976–83; Treasury Solicitor's Dept, 1983–88; Law Officers' Dept, 1988–91; Head of Employment Litigation Sect., Treasury Solicitor's Dept, 1991–92; Sec., Scott Inquiry into Export of Defence and Defence-related Equipment to Iraq, 1992–96; Treasury Solicitor's Department: Dep. Legal Advr, MoD, 1996–98; Legal Advr to DCMS, 1998–99; Dir, Legal (Commercial, Envmt, Housing and Local Govt), DETR, 1999–2001. Gov., Eltham Coll., London, 1998–. Mem., Editl Adv. Bd, Nottingham Law Jl. *Recreations:* reading, running, cricket (mostly watching), photography, sunflowers. *Address:* (office) Great Minster House, 76 Marsham Street, SW1P 4DR. *T:* (020) 7944 4770.

MWINYI, Ndugu Ali Hassan; President, United Republic of Tanzania, 1985–95; *b* 8 May 1925; *s* of late Hassan Mwinyi Chande and Asha Mwinyishehe; *m* 1960, Siti A. Mwinyi (*née* Abdulla); five *s* four *d*. *Educ:* Mangapwani Sch. and Dole Sch., Zanzibar; Teachers' Training Coll., Zanzibar; Durham Univ. Inst. of Education. Primary sch. teacher, head teacher, Tutor, Principal, Zanzibar, 1945–64; Acting Principal Sec., Min. of Educn, 1964–65; Dep. Gen. Manager, State Trading Corp., 1965–70; Minister of State, President's Office, Dar es Salaam, 1970–72; Minister for Health, 1972–75; Minister for Home Affairs, 1975–77; Ambassador to Egypt, 1977–81; Minister for Natural Resources and Tourism, 1982–83; Minister of State, Vice-President's Office, 1983; Vice-Pres., Union Govt, 1984. Chama Cha Mapinduzi (Revolutionary Party): Member, 1977; Nat. Exec. Cttee, 1982; Central Cttee, 1984; Vice-Chm., 1984–90; Chm., 1990–; Mem., Afro-Shirazi Party, 1964. Chairman: Zanzibar Film Censorship Bd, 1964–65; E African Currency Bd, Zanzibar, 1964–67; Nat. Kiswahili Council, 1964–77; Tanzania Food and Nutrition Council, 1974–76. Mem.,Univ. Council of Dar es Salaam, 1964–65. *Address:* c/o State House, Dar es Salaam, United Republic of Tanzania.

MYER, Sidney Baillieu, AC 1990; MA Cantab; Chairman, Myer Emporium Ltd, 1978–86 (Director, since 1955); Deputy Chairman, Coles Myer Ltd, 1985–94; Director: Myer Foundation, since 1959 (President, 1992–95; Vice-President, 1959–92); N. M. Rothschild Australia Holdings (formerly N. M. Rothschild & Son (Australia)), since 1993; *b* 11 Jan. 1926; *s* of late Sidney Myer and late Dame (Margery) Merlyn Baillieu Myer, DBE; *m* 1955, Sarah J., *d* of late S. Hordern; two *s* one *d*. *Educ:* Geelong Grammar Sch.; Pembroke Coll., Cambridge (MA). Sub-Lieut, RANVR, 1944–46. Joined Myer Emporium, 1953. Director: Elders IXL Ltd, 1972–82 and 1986–90; Cadbury Schweppes Aust. Ltd, 1976–82; Commonwealth Banking Corp., 1979–83; Network Ten Holdings Ltd and associated Cos, 1985–87; Chm., Nat. Mutual Life Assoc. of Australasia, 1988–92 (Dir, 1978–92). Dir, Howard Florey Inst. of Experimental Physiology and Medicine, 1971– (Pres., 1992–96); Part-time Mem. Executive, CSIRO, 1981–85. Pres., French Chamber of Commerce (Vic), 1962–64; Rep. Chm., Aust.-Japan Foundn, 1976–81; Member: Consultative Cttee on Relations with Japan, 1978–81; Aust.-China Council, 1979–81; Nat. Bicentennial Sci. Centre Adv. Cttee, 1986–89. Councillor: Aust. Conservation Foundn, 1964–73; Vic. Coll. of Arts, 1973–78; Chm., Art Foundn of Vic., 1986–88; Vice-Pres., Nat. Gall. Soc. of Vic., 1964–68; Dir, Tasman Inst., 1990–98; Trustee: Sidney Myer Fund, 1958– (Chm. Trustees, 1958–); Nat. Gall. of Vic., 1973–83 (Vice-Pres., 1977–83); Chm., Commonwealth Research Centres of Excellence Cttee, 1981–82. Hon. LLD Melbourne, 1993. Chevalier de la Légion d'Honneur, 1976. *Address:* Level 45, 55 Collins Street, Melbourne, Victoria 3000, Australia. *Fax:* (3) 98268051. *Clubs:* Naval and Military; Leander (Henley-on-Thames); Australian (Melbourne).

MYERS, Geoffrey, CBE 1984; CEng; FCIT; Chairman, TRANSAID, 1988–95; Vice-Chairman, British Railways Board, 1985–87 (Member, 1980–87); *b* 12 July 1930; *s* of Ernest and Annie Myers; *m* 1959, Patricia Mary (*née* Hall); two *s*. *Educ:* Belle Vue Grammar Sch.; Bradford Technical Coll. (BScEng London). CEng, MICE 1963; FCIT 1973. RE, 1955–57. British Rail: civil engrg positions, 1957–64; Planning Officer, N Eastern Reg., 1964–66; Divl Movements Manager, Leeds Div., 1966–68; Dir of Studies, British Transport Staff Coll., 1968–70; Divl Man., Sheffield, 1970–76; Dep. Gen. Man., Eastern Reg., 1976–77, Gen. Man., 1977–78; Dir of Strategic Develt, 1978–80; Dep. Chief Exec. (Railways), 1983; Jt Managing Dir (Railways), 1984–85. Hon. Lectr, Leeds Univ., 1991–. Pres. Council, CIT, 1986–87. Bd Mem., TRANSAID Worldwide, 1998–2000. Mem. Council, Save the Children (UK), 1993–2000; Pres., White Rose Children's Charity, 1995–. Mem., Carmen's Co., 1983. Hon. DEng Bradford, 1988. OStJ 1979. *Recreations:* golf, walking. *Address:* The Spinney, Lands Lane, Knaresborough, N Yorks HG5 9DE. *T:* (01423) 863719.

MYERS, Geoffrey Morris Price; Under-Secretary, Agricultural and Food Research Council, 1973–87; *b* 8 May 1927. *Educ:* Reigate Grammar Sch.; King's Coll., London. Civil Service, 1950; UKAEA, 1959–67; Nat. Econ. Develt Office, 1967–69; Agric. Research Council, 1970. *Address:* 56 Northampton Road, Croydon CR0 7HT. *T:* (020) 8655 3158.

MYERS, Gordon Elliot, CMG 1979; Under-Secretary, Arable Crops, Pigs and Poultry Group, Ministry of Agriculture, Fisheries and Food, 1984–89, retired; *b* 4 July 1929; *s* of William Lionel Myers and Yvonne (*née* Arthur); *m* 1963, Wendy Jane Lambert; two *s* one *d*. *Educ:* Kilburn Grammar Sch.; University Coll., Oxford (BA 1st Cl. Hons Modern History). Asst Principal, MAFF, 1951; Principal, 1958; Asst Sec., 1966; Head successively of Land Drainage Div., Sugar and Tropical Foods Div., and EEC Div., 1966–74; Under-Sec., MAFF, 1975; Minister (Agriculture), Office of UK Perm. Rep. to EEC, 1975–79; Under-Sec., Food Policy Gp, 1980–85, Cereals and Sugar Gp, 1985–86, MAFF. Mem., Cttee on Simplification of Common Agricl Policy, EEC, 1990–94. Eur. Rep., Caribbean Banana Exporters Assoc., 1993–. *Address:* Woodlands, Nugents Park, Hatch End, Pinner, Middx HA5 4RA. *Club:* Oxford and Cambridge.

MYERS, John David; Chairman of Industrial Tribunals, 1982–97 (Regional Chairman for Newcastle, 1994–97); part-time Chairman of Employment Tribunals, since 1998; *b* 30 Oct. 1937; *s* of Frank and Monica Myers; *m* 1974, Anne McGeough (*née* Purcell), *widow* of J. T. McGeough; one *s*. *Educ:* Marist College, Hull; Hull University. LLB Hons. Called to the Bar, Gray's Inn, 1968. Schoolmaster, 1958–64; University, 1964–67; pupillage with J. D. Walker (later Judge Walker); practice at Hull, 1969–82 (Junior, NE Circuit, 1975–76). *Recreations:* cooking, oenology, bridge. *Club:* Alnmouth Golf.

MYERS, Martin Trevor, FRICS; Chairman and Chief Executive, Mountgrange Ltd, since 2001; *b* 24 Sept. 1941; *s* of Bernard Myers and Sylvia Marjorie Myers (*née* Pearman); *m* 1981, Nicole Josephine Yerna; one *s* one *d*. *Educ:* Arnold House, St John's Wood; Latymer Upper Sch.; Coll. of Estate Management, London Univ. (BSc). FRICS 1975. Jones Lang Wootton, 1965–83: Partner, 1969; Proprietory Partner, 1972; Chm. and Chief Exec., Arbuthnot Properties, 1983; merged with Imry Property Holdings, 1987, and with City Merchant Developers, 1988; Chief Exec. and Man. Dir, Imry Holdings Ltd, 1989–98; Exec. Dep. Chm., Trillium Gp, 1998–2001. *Recreations:* golf, shooting, riding, exercise. *Address:* 1 Durham Place, SW3 4ET; Kingsdown House, Upper Lambourn, Berks RG16 7QU. *Clubs:* Royal Automobile; Wisley Golf (Ripley).

MYERS, Dr Norman, CMG 1998; Managing Director, Norman Myers' Scientific Consultancy, since 1982; *b* 24 Aug. 1934; *s* of John Myers and Gladys Myers (*née* Haworth); *m* 1965, Dorothy Mary Halliman (separated 1992); two *d*. *Educ:* Keble Coll., Oxford (BA 1957; MA 1963); Univ. of Calif, Berkeley (PhD 1973). Dist Officer, Kenya Colonial Admin, 1958–61; high sch. teacher, Nairobi, 1961–65; freelance writer, professional photographer and lectr on African wildlife, Kenya, 1966–69; consultant in envmt and develt, 1972–: projects for develt orgns and res. bodies, incl. World Bank, UN agencies, OECD, EC, US Depts of State and Energy, NASA, US Nat. Acad. of Scis. Hon. Vis. Fellow, Green Coll., Oxford, 1992; Vis. Prof., Univs of Kent, Utrecht, Cape Town, Calif, Texas, Michigan, Cornell, Harvard and Stanford. For. Associate, US NAS, 1994; FWAAS 1989; FAAAS 1990; FRSA 1993; FLS 1993; Fellow, Royal Instn, 1997. Numerous awards for work in environment and development, including Volvo Envmt Prize, 1992; Pew Fellowship in Envmt, 1994; UNEP Sasakawa Envmt Prize, 1995. *Publications:* The Long African Day, 1972; The Sinking Ark, 1979 (trans. Japanese and Hungarian); Conversion of Tropical Moist Forests, 1980; A Wealth of Wild Species, 1983; The Primary Source: tropical forests and our future, 1984, rev. edn 1992; The Gaia Atlas of Planet Management, 1984 (trans. 11 langs), 2nd edn 1993; (ed jtly) Economics of Ecosystem Management, 1985; Future Worlds: challenge and opportunity in an age of change, 1990; Population, Resources and the Environment: the critical challenges, 1991; (ed) Tropical Forests and Climate, 1992; Ultimate Security: the environmental basis of political stability, 1993, 2nd edn 1996; Scarcity or Abundance: a debate on the environment, 1994 (trans. Italian); Environmental Exodus: an emergent crisis in the global arena, 1995; Perverse Subsidies: taxpayer dollars undercutting our economies and environments alike, 1998, and 2001; (jtly) Biodiversity Hotspots, 1999; Towards a New Greenprint for Business and Society, 1999; Food and Hunger in Sub-Saharan Africa, 2001;

contrib. numerous professional papers in scientific jls incl. Science, Nature, Population and Develt Rev., Jl Envmtl Econs & Mgt, Internat. Jl Social Econs. *Recreations:* professional photography, marathon running, mountaineering. *Address:* Upper Meadow, Old Road, Headington, Oxford OX3 8SZ. *T:* (01865) 750387. *Club:* Achilles.

MYERS, Sir Philip (Alan), Kt 1985; OBE 1977; QPM 1972; DL; one of Her Majesty's Inspectors of Constabulary, 1982–93; *b* 7 Feb. 1931; *s* of John and Catherine Myers; *m* 1951, Hazel Gittings; two *s. Educ:* Grove Park, Wrexham. RAF, 1949–50. Shropshire Constabulary, 1950–67; West Mercia Police, 1967–68; Dep. Chief Constable, Gwynedd Constabulary, 1968–70; Chief Constable, North Wales Police, 1970–81. OStJ 1972. DL Clwyd, 1983.

MYERS, Sir Rupert (Horace), KBE 1981 (CBE 1976); AO 1995; FTSE, FAA; Professor Emeritus; Vice-Chancellor and Principal, University of New South Wales, 1969–81; *b* 21 Feb. 1921; *s* of Horace Alexander Myers and Dorothy (*née* Harris); *m* 1944, Io Edwina King (*d* 2001); one *s* three *d. Educ:* Melbourne High Sch.; Univ. of Melbourne (BSc 1942; MSc 1943; PhD 1947). FTSE (FTS 1979); FAA 1997; CPEng, FIMMA, FRACI; FAIM; FAusIMM; FAICD. Commonwealth Res. Fellow, Univ. of Melbourne, 1942–47; Principal Res. Officer, CSIRO, AERE Harwell, 1947–52; University of New South Wales: Foundn Prof. of Metallurgy, 1952–81; Dean, Faculty of Applied Science, 1956–61; Pro-Vice-Chancellor, 1961–69. Chairman: NSW State Pollution Control Commn, 1971–89; Aust. Vice-Chancellors' Cttee, 1977–79; Cttee of Inquiry into Technol Change in Australia, 1979–80; Commonwealth Cttee of Review of Nat. Capital Develt Commn, 1982–83; Consultative Cttee for Nat. Conservation Strategy for Australia, 1983–85; Coastal Council of NSW, 1982–85; Cttee of Review of NZ Univs, 1987–88; Cttee of Review of Aust. Sci. and Technology Council, 1993; Cttee of Review, Co-operative Res. Centres Prog., 1995; Co-operative Res. Centre for Greenhouse Accounting, 1999–. Pres., Aust. Acad. of Technol Scis and Engrg, 1989–94 (Vice-Pres., 1985–88). Director: CSR Ltd, 1982–93; Energy Resources of Australia Ltd, 1982–97; IBM Australia Ltd, 1988–91. Member: Nat. Energy Adv. Cttee, 1980–82; Australian Manufacturing Council, 1980–82. Mem., Sydney Opera House Trust, 1976–83; Foundn Pres., Friends of Royal Botanic Gdns, Sydney, 1982–85. Hon. FIEAust, 1992. Hon. LLD Strathclyde, 1973; Hon. DSc Wollongong, 1976; Hon. DEng Newcastle, 1981; Hon. DLitt NSW, 1981. *Publications:* Technological Change in Australia, 1980; numerous on metallurgy and atomic energy (also patents). *Recreations:* bowls, music, working with silver. *Address:* 135 Neerim Road, Castle Cove, NSW 2069, Australia. *T:* and *Fax:* (2) 94176586. *Club:* Australian (Sydney).

MYERSON, His Honour Arthur Levey; QC 1974; a Circuit Judge, 1978–99; *b* 25 July 1928; *o s* of Bernard and Eda Myerson; *m* 1960, Elaine Shirley Harris; two *s. Educ:* Blackpool Grammar Sch.; Queens' Coll., Cambridge (BA 1950; LLB 1951); BA (Open Univ.) 1985. RAF, 1946–48. Called to the Bar, 1952; a Recorder of the Crown Court, 1972–78; Resident Judge, York Crown Court, 1996–99. Pres., HM Council of Circuit Judges, 1991. *Recreations:* walking, reading, sailing. *Address:* Leeds Combined Court Centre, Oxford Row, Leeds LS1 3BE. *T:* (0113) 283 0040. *Clubs:* Royal Commonwealth Society; Moor Allerton Golf (Leeds).

MYKURA, Janey Patricia Winifred; *see* Walker, J. P. W.

MYLAND, Howard David, CB 1988; Deputy Comptroller and Auditor General, National Audit Office, 1984–89; *b* 23 June 1929; *s* of John Tarrant and Frances Grace Myland; *m* 1951, Barbara Pearl Mills; two *s* one *d. Educ:* Fairfields Schs; Queen Mary's Sch., Basingstoke. Served Intelligence Corps, 1948–50. Entered Exchequer and Audit Dept, 1948; Dep. Dir of Audit, 1972; Dir of Audit, 1977; Dep. Sec. of Dept, 1979; an Asst Auditor Gen., National Audit Office, 1984. Mem., Basingstoke Round Table, 1962–70. *Publication:* Public Audit Law—Key Development Considerations, 1992. *Recreations:* travel, contract bridge.

MYLES, David Fairlie, CBE 1988; tenant hill farmer; *b* 30 May 1925; *s* of Robert C. Myles and Mary Anne S. (*née* Fairlie); *m* 1951, Janet I. (*née* Gall); two *s* two *d. Educ:* Edzell Primary Sch.; Brechin High Sch. National Farmers Union of Scotland: Mem. Council, 1970–79; Convenor of Organisation and Publicity Cttee, 1976–79. MP (C) Banff, 1979–83; Sec., Cons. backbench Cttees on European Affairs and on Agriculture, Fisheries and Food (Jt Sec.); Mem., Select Cttees on Agriculture and on European Legislation. Contested (C) Orkney and Shetland, 1983. Councillor, Angus DC, 1984–96 (Leader, Cons. Gp, 1992–96). Chm., Dairy Produce Quota Tribunal for Scotland, 1984–97; Member: Exec., Angus Tourist Bd, 1984–92; North of Scotland Hydro-Electric Bd, 1985–88; Extra-Parly Panel (Scotland), 1986–95; Potato Marketing Bd, 1988–97. Dean, Guildry of Brechin, 1993–95; Lord Pres., Ct of Deans of Scotland, 1995–96; Session Clerk, Edzell/Lethnot Parish Church, 1996–. *Recreations:* curling, Scottish fiddle music. *Address:* Dalbog, Edzell, Brechin, Angus DD9 7UU; (home) The Gorse, Dunlappie Road, Edzell, Brechin, Angus DD9 7UB. *Clubs:* Farmers'; Brechin Rotary.

MYLES, Lynda Robbie; independent film producer, since 1991; *b* 2 May 1947; *d* of late Alexander Watt Myles and Kathleen Kilgour Myles (*née* Polson); *m* 1972, Dr David John Will (marr. diss. 1978). *Educ:* Univ. of Edinburgh (MA Hons Mental Philosophy). Dir, Edinburgh Internat. Film Fest., 1973–80; Curator of Film, Pacific Film Archive, Univ. of Calif, Berkeley, 1980–82; Film Consultant, Channel Four TV, 1982–83; Producer, Enigma Films, 1983–86; Sen. Vice-Pres., Creative Affairs (Europe), Columbia Pictures, 1986–88; Commng Ed. for Drama, BBC TV, 1989–91. Co-Exec. Dir, East-West Producers' Seminar, 1990–94. Producer: Defence of the Realm, 1986; The Commitments, 1991; The Snapper, 1993; The Van, 1995; The Life of Stuff, 1997; When Brendan Met Trudy, 2000; (jtly) Killing Me Softly, 2001. Mem., Film Policy Rev. Bd, DCMS, 1997–. Gov., BFI, 1993–96. BFI Award, 1981. *Publication:* (with M. Pye) The Movie Brats: how the film generation took over Hollywood, 1978. *Address:* 20 Ossington Street, W2 4LY. *T:* (020) 7243 3013. *Club:* Groucho.

MYLLENT, Peter; *see* Hamylton Jones, K.

MYLNE, Nigel James; QC 1984; a Recorder, since 1985; *b* 11 June 1939; *s* of late Harold James Mylne and Dorothy Evelyn Mylne (later D. E. Hogg); *m* 1st, 1967, Julie Phillpotts (marr. diss. 1977); two *s* one *d*; 2nd, 1979, Judith Hamilton (marr. diss. 1997); one *s. Educ:* Eton College. National Service, 10th Royal Hussars, 1957–59. Called to the Bar, Middle Temple, 1963, Bencher, 1995. Special Adjudicator in Asylum Appeals, 1997–; Pres., Mental Health Review Tribunals, 1999–. *Recreation:* beekeeping. *Address:* Langleys, Brixton Deverill, Wiltshire BA12 7EJ. *T:* (01985) 840992; *e-mail:* nmylneswalker@aol.com. *Clubs:* White's, Pratt's.

MYNERS, Paul; Chairman, Gartmore Investment Management plc, since 1987; *b* 1 April 1948; *s* of late Thomas Russell Myners and of Caroline Molly Myners; *m* 1995, Alison Macleod; one *s* one *d*, and three *d* by a previous marriage. *Educ:* Truro Sch., Cornwall; Univ. of London Inst. of Educn (BEd); Stanford Sch. of Business. Daily Telegraph, 1970–74; N. M. Rothschild & Sons Ltd, 1974–85 (Dir, 1979); Chief Exec., Gartmore plc, 1985–93, 1999–2000. Dep. Chm., PowerGen plc, 1999–2001; Chm., Guardian Media Gp plc, 2000–; non-executive Director: English & Scottish Investors plc, 1986–; Orange plc, 1996–99; Coutts Group, 1997–2000; Guardian Newspapers Ltd, 2001–; BT Wireless, 2001–; Exec. Dir, Nat. Westminster Bank, 1997–2000. Member: Financial Reporting Council, 1995–; Company Law Review Consultative Cttee, 1998–. Chm. Council, Tate St Ives, 2001–. Member: Adv. Council, LSO, 1993–; Adv. Bd, Royal Acad. Trust, 1994– (Trustee, 2000–). Trustee, Nat. and Cornwall Maritime Mus. Trust, 1998–. FRSA 1994. Freeman, City of London, 1996. *Publications:* Developing a Winning Partnership, 1995; Creating Quality Dialogue, 1999; Institutional Investment in the UK: a review for HM Treasury, 2001. *Recreations:* opera, the work of Cornish artists, the countryside, Rugby football. *Address:* (office) Gartmore House, 8 Fenchurch Place, EC3M 4PH. *T:* (020) 7782 2000. *Clubs:* City of London, Oriental; Hong Kong; Royal Cornwall Yacht.

MYNORS, Sir Richard (Baskerville), 2nd Bt *cr* 1964, of Treago, Co. Hereford; landowner; *b* 5 May 1947; *s* of Sir Humphrey Charles Baskerville Mynors, 1st Bt and Lydia Marian (*d* 1992), *d* of Sir Ellis Minns, LittD, FSA, FBA; *S* father, 1989; *m* 1970, Fiona Bridget, *d* of late Rt. Rev. G. E. Reindorp; three *d. Educ:* Marlborough; Royal College of Music (ARCM, ARCO); Corpus Christi Coll., Cambridge (MA). Asst Director of Music, King's School, Macclesfield, 1970–73; Director of Music: Wolverhampton Grammar School, 1973–81; Merchant Taylors' School, Crosby, 1981–88; Belmont Abbey Sch., Hereford, 1988–89. *Heir:* none. *Address:* Treago, St Weonards, Hereford HR2 8QB. *T:* (01981) 580208.

MYNOTT, Dr (Roger) Jeremy; Chief Executive of the Press, Secretary of the Press Syndicate and University Printer, Cambridge University Press, since 1999; Fellow, Wolfson College, Cambridge, since 1999; *b* 15 Feb. 1942; *s* of Clifford Harry Mynott and Margaret Mynott (*née* Ketley); *m* 2000, Diane Speakman. *Educ:* Colchester Royal Grammar Sch.; Corpus Christi Coll., Cambridge (BA 1964; MA 1968; PhD 1968). Schoolmaster, Magdalen Coll. Sch., Oxford, 1964–65; Cambridge University Press, 1966–: sub-editor, 1966–69; editor, 1969–73; sen. editor, 1973–75; Associate Dir, 1975–79; Editl Dir, Humanities and Social Scis, 1979–81; Dir, Publishing Develt, 1981–85; Press Editl Dir Worldwide, 1985–92; Man. Dir, Publishing Div. and Dep. Chief Exec., 1992–99. FRSA 1990. *Publication:* Little Thurlow 2000, 1999. *Recreations:* natural history (especially ornithology), travel, philosophy, sport, vegetable gardening. *Address:* (office) Edinburgh Building, Shaftesbury Road, Cambridge CB2 2RU. *T:* (01223) 325731.

MYRES, Rear-Adm. John Antony Lovell, CB 1993; Hydrographer of the Navy, 1990–94; *b* 11 April 1936; *yr s* of late Dr John Nowell Linton Myres, CBE and Joan Mary Lovell Myres (*née* Stevens); *m* 1965, Alison Anne, *d* of late Lieut David Lawrence Carr, RN and of Mrs James Pertwee; three *s. Educ:* Winchester College. FRICS 1975–95; FRGS 1993–97; FRIN 1994–97. Entered RN 1954; specialised Hydrographic Surveying, 1959; CO HM Ships Woodlark, 1969–71, Fox, 1972–73, Hecla, 1974, 1978–79, 1981–82; Hydrographer, RAustN, 1982–85. Pres., Orders and Medals Res. Soc., 1997–. Younger Brother of Trinity House, 1990. Freeman, City of London, 1990; Liveryman, Chartered Surveyors' Co., 1990–97. Guild Burgess of Preston, 1952. *Publications:* (jtly) British Polar Exploration and Research: a historic and medallic record with biographies, 2000; articles in professional jls. *Recreations:* naval and medallic history, gardening. *Club:* Antarctic.

MYRTLE, Brig. Andrew Dewe, CB 1988 CBE 1979 (MBE 1967); Chief Executive and Secretary, Tennis and Rackets Association, 1989–2001; *b* 17 Dec. 1932; *s* of Lt-Col John Young Elphinstone Myrtle, DSO, KOSB (killed in action in World War II) and late Doreen May Lake; *m* 1973, Mary Rose Ford; two *d. Educ:* Horris Hill Prep. Sch.; Winchester Coll.; RMA, Sandhurst; Army Staff Coll. Co. Comdr, 1 KOSB, 1964–66; Bde Major, 24 Infantry Bde, 1966–68; Co. Comdr, 1 KOSB, 1968–69, CO, 1969–71; MA to Adjt Gen., 1971–74; Comdt, Jun. Div., Staff Coll., 1974–77; Comd 8 Infantry Bde, 1977–79; student, RCDS, 1979; DDMO, MoD, 1980–83; Asst Comdt, RMA, Sandhurst, 1983–85; Comdr Land Forces, Cyprus, 1986–88. ADC to the Queen, 1985–88. *Recreations:* golf, lawn tennis, fly-fishing. *Address:* Pen Guen, Stonor, Henley-on-Thames, Oxon RG9 6HB. *Clubs:* Army and Navy, MCC; Huntercombe Golf; Queen's.

N

NAAS, Lord; Charles Diarmuidh John Bourke; *b* 11 June 1953; *e s* and *heir* of 10th Earl of Mayo, *qv*; *m* 1st, 1975, Marie Antoinette Cronnelly (marr. diss. 1979); one *d*; 2nd, 1985, Marie Veronica Mannion; two *s*. *Educ:* St Aubyn's, Rottingdean; Portora Royal Sch., Enniskillen; QUB; Bolton Street Coll. of Technology, Dublin. *Heir: s* Hon. Richard Thomas Bourke, *b* 7 Dec. 1985. *Address:* Derryinver, Beach Road, Clifden, Co; Galway, Eire.

NABARRO, Prof. Frank Reginald Nunes, MBE 1946; FRS 1971; Professor of Physics, University of the Witwatersrand, 1953–84, now Hon. Professorial Research Fellow; Fellow, South African Council for Scientific and Industrial Research, since 1994; *b* 7 March 1916; *s* of late Stanley Nunes Nabarro and Leah Nabarro; *m* 1948, Margaret Constance (*d* 1997), *d* of late James Dalziel, ARAM; three *s* two *d*. *Educ:* Nottingham High Sch.; New Coll., Oxford (MA, BSc). DSc Birmingham. Sen. Exper. Officer, Min. of Supply, 1941–45; Royal Soc. Warren Research Fellow, Univ. of Bristol, 1945–49; Lectr in Metallurgy, Univ. of Birmingham, 1949–53; University of Witwatersrand: Prof. and Head of Dept of Physics, 1953–77, City of Johannesburg Prof. of Physics, 1970–77; Dean, Faculty of Science, 1968–70; Representative of Senate on Council, 1967–77; Deputy Vice-Chancellor, 1978–80. Vis. Prof., Nat. Research Council, Ottawa, 1956; Republic Steel Vis. Prof., Dept of Metallurgy, Case Inst. of Techn., Cleveland, Ohio, 1964–65; Overseas Fellow of Churchill Coll., Cambridge, 1966–67; Gauss Prof., Akademie der Wissenschaften, Göttingen, 1970; Professeur-associé, Univ. Paris-Sud, 1971, Montpellier II, 1973; Vis. Prof., Dept of Material Science, Univ. of Calif., Berkeley, 1977; Vis. Fellow, Robinson Coll., Cambridge, 1981 and 1999; Vis. Prof., Dept of Materials Engrg, Technion, Haifa, 1983. Founder Mem., Acad. of Sci. of S Africa, 1996; For. Associate, US NAE, 1996. Hon. Member: S African Inst. of Physics, 1992 (Vice-Pres., 1956–57); Microscopy Soc. of S Africa, 1998; Hon. FRSSAf 1973 (Pres., 1989–92). Hon. DSc: Witwatersrand, 1987; Natal, 1988; Cape Town, 1988. Beilby Memorial Award, 1950; South Africa Medal, 1972; De Beers Gold Medal, 1980; Claude Harris Leon Foundn Award of Merit, 1983; J. F. W. Herschel Medal, 1989; R. F. Mehl Award, 1995; Platinum Medal, Inst. of Materials, 1997. *Publications:* Theory of Crystal Dislocations, 1967, repr. 1987; (jtly) Physics of Creep, 1995; scientific papers, mainly on solid state physics. *Recreation:* gardening. *Address:* 32 Cookham Road, Auckland Park, Johannesburg 2092, South Africa. *T:* (11) 7267745.

NADER, Ralph; author, lecturer, lawyer; *b* Winsted, Conn, USA, 27 Feb. 1934; *s* of Nadra Nader and Rose (*née* Bouziane). *Educ:* Gilbert Sch., Winsted; Woodrow Wilson Sch. of Public and Internat. Affairs, Princeton Univ. (AB *magna cum laude*); Harvard Univ. Law Sch. (LLB). Admitted to: Bar of Conn, 1958; Bar of Mass, 1959; US Supreme Court Bar, 1963. Served US Army, 1959. Law practice in Hartford, Conn, 1959–; Lectr in History and Govt, Univ. of Hartford, 1961–63; Lectr, Princeton Univ., 1967–68. Member: Amer. Bar Assoc., 1959–; AAAS, 1964–; Phi Beta Kappa. Has pursued actively better consumer protection and improvement in the lot of the American Indian; lobbied in Washington for safer food, drugs, air, water and against nuclear reactors; played very important role in work for passing of: National Traffic and Motor Vehicle Safety Act, 1966; Wholesome Meat Act, 1967; Occupational Safety and Health Act, 1970; Safe Drinking Water Act, 1974; Freedom of Information Act, 1974; National Cooperative Bank Act, 1978. Niemen Fellows Award, 1965–66; named one of the Ten Outstanding Young Men of the Year by US Jun. Chamber of Commerce, 1967. *Publications:* Unsafe at Any Speed: the designed-in dangers of the American automobile, 1965, rev. edn 1991; (jtly) What to do with Your Bad Car, 1971; Working on the System: a manual for citizen's access to federal agencies, 1972; (jtly) Action for a Change, 1972; (jtly) Whistleblowing, 1972; (jtly) You and Your Pension, 1973; (ed) The Consumer and Corporate Accountability, 1973; (co-ed) Corporate Power in America, 1973; (jtly) Taming the Giant Corporation, 1976; (co-ed) Verdicts on Lawyers, 1976; (jtly) Menace of Atomic Energy, 1977; (co-ed) Who's Poisoning America?, 1981; (jtly) The Big Boys: power and position in American business, 1986; (jtly) Winning the Insurance Game, 1990; (jtly) No Contest, 1996; contrib. articles to many magazines; has weekly syndicated newspaper column. *Address:* PO Box 19367, Washington, DC 20036–9367, USA.

NADESAN, Pararajasingam, CMG 1955; OBE 1954; Governor, Rotary International, District 321; Member, Legislative Council, Rotary International; Director: National Development Bank, since 1995; Cargills (Ceylon) Ltd; Associated Hotels Co. Ltd; Past Chairman: Low Country Products Association; Air Ceylon; *b* 20 Dec. 1917; *s* of Sir Sangarapillai Pararajasingam, and Padmavati, *d* of Sir Ponnambalam Arunachalam; *m* 1st, 1941, Gauri Nair (decd); one *s* one *d*; 2nd, 1953, Kamala Nair; three *d*. *Educ:* Royal College, and Ceylon Univ. Coll.; Univ. of London (BA Hons). Tutor, Ceylon Univ. Coll., 1940; entered Ceylon Civil Service, 1941; held various appts in sphere of provincial administration, 1941–47; Asst Permanent Sec., Min. of Transport and Works, 1948–53; Dir of Civil Aviation in addition to duties as Asst Sec. Min. of Transport and Works, 1954–56; Sec. to the Prime Minister and Information Officer, Ceylon, 1954–56; Member: Ceylon Delegation to the Bandung Conf.; Commonwealth Prime Minister's Conf.; ICAO Gen. Assembly; ILO Cttee on Plantations. Past Mem., Nat. Planning Council. Pres. Emeritus and Life Mem., Ceylon Hotels Assoc.; FHCIMA. FCIT. Past President: Orchid Circle of Ceylon; Sri Lanka Horticultural Soc. Officer Order of Merit (Italy), 1954; Knight Comdr Order of the Crown, Thailand, 1955; Comdr Order of Orange Nassau, Netherlands, 1955; Defence Medal, 1947; Coronation Medal, 1953; Ceylon Armed Services Inauguration Medal, 1956. *Recreations:* golf, tennis, gardening, collecting antiques, stamps and coins. *Address:* 52/1 Flower Road, Colombo 3, Sri Lanka. *T:* 573687. *Clubs:* Colombo, Orient, Rotary (Colombo); Gymkhana.

NAGAI, Kiyoshi, PhD; FRS 2000; Member, MRC Laboratory of Molecular Biology, since 1981; Fellow, Darwin College, Cambridge, since 1993; *b* 25 June 1949; *s* of Prof. Otoji Nagai and Naoko Nagai (*née* Matsumoto); *m* 1974, Yoshiko Majima; one *s* one *d*. *Educ:* Toin High Sch.; Osaka Univ. (BSc 1972; MSc 1974; PhD 1978). Thomas Usher Res. Fellow, Darwin Coll., Cambridge, 1981–83. Mem., EMBO, 2000. Novartis Medal and Prize, Biochem. Soc., 2000. *Publications:* (jtly) RNA: protein interactions, 1994; res. pubns and reviews in scientific jls. *Recreations:* playing cello in chamber groups, reading. *Address:* MRC Laboratory of Molecular Biology, Hills Road, Cambridge CB2 2QH; 100 Mowbray Road, Cambridge CB1 7TG. *T:* (01223) 402292.

NAGANO, Kent George; conductor; Artistic Director, Deutsches Sinfonie–Orchester Berlin, since 2000; Principal Conductor, Los Angeles Opera, since 2001; *b* 22 Nov. 1951; *s* of George Kimiyoshi Nagano and Ruth Okamoto; *m* Mari Kodama; one *d*. *Educ:* Univ. of Calif. Music Dir, Opéra de Lyon, 1989–98; Music Dir, Hallé Orch., 1992–2000. Has performed with: Boston Symphony Orch., 1984; Paris Opera (World Première, St François d'Assise, by Messiaen); Metropolitan Opera, 1994; Salzburg Fest., 1994; Vienna Philharmonic début, 1994; Berlin Philharmonic début, 1997; also World Première, Death of Klinghoffer by John Adams, Brussels, Lyon and Vienna. Gramophone Record of Year, 1990; Gramophone Opera Award, 1993; Grammy Award, 1995, 2001. *Address:* c/o Van Walsum Management Ltd, 4 Addison Bridge Place, W14 8XP. *T:* (020) 7371 4343, *Fax:* (020) 7371 4344.

NAGDA, Kanti; Manager, Sangat Advice Centre, Harrow, since 1998; *b* 1 May 1946; *s* of Vershi Bhoja Nagda and Zaviben Nagda; *m* 1972, Bhagwati Desai; two *s*. *Educ:* City High Sch., Kampala, Uganda; Coll. of Further Educn, Chippenham, Wilts; E African Univ., Uganda; Cassio Coll., Watford. Sec.-Gen., Confedn of Indian Organisations (UK), 1975–98; Manager, Sancroft Community Centre, 1982–98; Pres., Nat. Congress of Gujarati Orgns, 1992–95. Exec. Cttee Member: Harrow Community Relations Council, 1974–76; Gujarati Literary Acad. (GB), 1976–82. President: Uganda Art Circle, 1968–71; Anglo Indian Circle, 1973–82 and 1985–88; Indian Cricket Club, Harrow, 1976–80; Greenford (Willow Tree) Lions Club, 1988–89. Hon. Editorial Consultant, International Asian Guide & Who's Who, 1975–95; Asst Editor, Oshwal News, 1977–84. *Publications:* Muratiyo Ke Nokar (Gujarati novel), Kenya 1967; stories and articles in newspapers and jls. *Recreations:* cricket, photography. *Address:* 170 Tolcarne Drive, Pinner, Middx HA5 2DR. *T:* (020) 8863 9089. *Club:* Greenford Lions.

NAGLE, Terence John, FRICS; Director, Wynnstay Properties plc, since 1998; *b* 10 Nov. 1942; *s* of Richard and Bridget Nagle; *m* 1974, Elizabeth Mary Millett; two *s* two *d*. *Educ:* Ottershaw Sch. FRICS 1964. Property Dir, 1984–93, Man. Dir, 1993–97, Brixton Estate plc. *Recreations:* gardening, tennis, struggling with a theology degree course. *Address:* Pitch Place House, Worplesdon, Guildford, Surrey GU3 3LQ. *T:* (01483) 232036.

NAGLER, Neville Anthony; Director General (formerly Chief Executive), Board of Deputies of British Jews, since 1991; *b* 2 Jan. 1945; *s* of Gerald and Sylvia Nagler; *m* 1971, Judy Mordant; one *s* one *d*. *Educ:* Christ's Coll., Finchley; Jesus Coll., Cambridge (MA); Cert. in Public Services Mgt, 2000. Asst Principal, HM Treasury, 1967–70; Private Sec. to Chancellor of Exchequer, 1970–71; Principal, 1972; transferred to Home Office, 1975; Asst Sec., Race Relations and Equal Opportunities, 1980–83; Head, Drugs and Extradition Div., 1983–88; Asst Sec., Home Office Finance Div., 1988–91. UK Rep. to UN Commn on Narcotic Drugs, 1983–88; Chm., Council of Europe Pompidou Gp, 1984–88. Haldane Essay Prize, Haldane Soc., 1979; Cert. of Appreciation, US Drug Enforcement Admin, 1988. *Publications:* articles in Public Administration and UN Jl of Narcotic Drugs. *Recreations:* wine-making, listening to music, theatre, walking. *Address:* Commonwealth House, 1–19 New Oxford Street, WC1A 1NU. *T:* (020) 7543 5400.

NAHORSKI, Prof. Stefan Ryszard, PhD; FMedSci; Professor of Pharmacology, since 1984 and Head of Department of Cell Physiology and Pharmacology, since 1993, University of Leicester; *b* 10 Dec. 1945; *s* of Stanislaw Nahorski and Linda Nahorska; *m* 1969, Catherine Mary Gower; one *s* two *d*. *Educ:* St Boniface's Coll., Plymouth; Univ. of Southampton (BSc Hons); Portsmouth Sch. of Pharmacy (PhD 1971). Research Asst, Portsmouth, 1968–71; MRC Fellow, Sheffield, 1971–75; University of Leicester: Lectr in Pharmacology, 1976–81; Reader, 1981–84. Founder FMedSci 1998. *Publications:* Pharmacology of Adrenoceptors, 1985; Transmembrane Signalling, 1990; numerous research papers to learned jls. *Recreations:* tennis, badminton, watching (supporting) soccer (especially Leicester FC), sea angling. *Address:* 48 Shanklin Drive, Stoneygate, Leicester LE2 3RG. *T:* (0116) 270 7526.

NAHUM, Peter John; art dealer, Leicester Galleries, London, since 1984; *b* 19 Jan. 1947; *s* of Denis E. Nahum and Allison Faith Nahum (*née* Cooke); *m* 1987, Renate Angelika Meiser. *Educ:* Sherborne. Peter Wilson's Sotheby's, 1966–84; British Paintings Dept, Sotheby's, Belgravia, 1971–84, Sen. Dir, 1977–84; regular contributor to Antiques Road Show, BBC TV, 1980–. *Publications:* Prices of Victorian Paintings, Drawings and Watercolours, 1976; Monograms of Victorian and Edwardian Artists, 1976; Cross Section, British Art in the 20th Century, 1988; British Art in the Twentieth Century, 1989; Burne-Jones, The Pre-Raphaelites & Their Century, 1989; Burne-Jones: a quest for love, 1993; Fairy Folk in Fairy Land, 1997; Pre-Raphaelite . Symbolist . Visionary, 2001. *Recreations:* sailing, photography, gardening, theatre, travel, walking. *Address:* 5 Ryder Street, SW1Y 6PY. *T:* (020) 7930 6059, *Fax:* (020) 7930 4678; *e-mail:* peternahum@leicestergalleries.com.

NAILATIKAU, Brig.-Gen. Ratu Epeli, LVO 1977; OBE 1979; MSD 1988; Interim Deputy Prime Minister, and Minister for Fijian Affairs, Fiji, since 2000; *b* 5 July 1941; *s* of Ratu Sir Edward Cakobau, KBE, MC, ED and Adi Lady Vasamaca Tuiburelevu; *m* 1981, Adi Koila Nailatikau (*née* Mara), *d* of Ratu Sir Kamisese Mara, *qv*; one *s* one *d*. *Educ:* Levuka Public Sch.; Queen Victoria Sch., Fiji; Wadham Coll., Oxford. Enlisted in Royal

Fiji Military Forces, 1962; commnd Fiji Infantry Regt, 1963; seconded to First Bn, Royal NZ Infantry Regt, Malaysia and Borneo, 1966; ADC to Governor of Fiji, 1968–69; Foreign Service Course, Oxford Univ., 1969–70; Second Secretary: Fiji High Commn, Canberra, 1970–72; Fiji Mission to UN, 1973–74; Australian Army Staff Coll., Queenscliffe, 1976 (psc); CO Fiji Bn, Fiji Infantry Regt serving with UNIFIL, 1978–79; Jt Services Staff Coll., Canberra, Australia, 1980 (jssc); Sen. Plans Officer, UNIFIL HQ, 1981; CS, 1981–82, Comdr, 1982–87, Royal Fiji Mil. Forces; Ambassador of Fiji to UK, and concurrently Ambassador to Denmark, Germany, Israel, the Holy See and Egypt, 1988–96; Roving Ambassador to Pacific Island countries, 1998; Perm. Sec. for Foreign Affairs and External Trade, Fiji, 1999. Fiji Equerry: to the Prince of Wales during Fiji Independence visit, 1970; to the Queen during Jubilee visit, 1977. Hon. Col 1st Bn Fiji Infantry Regt, 1996. OStJ 1985. Civil Service Medal (Fiji), 1995. *Recreations:* golf, tennis. *Address:* Office of the Deputy Prime Minister, PO Box 2100, Government Buildings, Suva, Fiji.

NAIPAUL, Sir Vidiadhar Surajprasad, (Sir Vidia), Kt 1990; author; *b* 17 Aug. 1932; *m* 1st, 1955, Patricia Ann Hale (*d* 1996); 2nd, 1996, Nadira Khannum Alvi. *Educ:* Queen's Royal Coll., Trinidad; University Coll., Oxford (Hon. Fellow, 1983). Hon. Dr Letters Columbia Univ., NY, 1981; Hon. LittD: Cambridge, 1983; London, 1988; Oxford, 1992. British Literature Prize, 1993; Nobel Prize for Literature, 2001. *Publications:* The Middle Passage, 1962; An Area of Darkness, 1964; The Loss of El Dorado, 1969; The Overcrowded Barracoon, and other articles, 1972; India: a wounded civilization, 1977; The Return of Eva Perón, 1980; Among the Believers, 1981; Finding the Centre, 1984; A Turn in the South, 1989; India: a million mutinies now, 1990; Beyond Belief: Islamic excursions, 1998; Letters between a Father and Son, 1999; Reading & Writing: a personal account, 2000; *novels:* The Mystic Masseur, 1957 (John Llewelyn Rhys Memorial Prize, 1958); The Suffrage of Elvira, 1958; Miguel Street, 1959 (Somerset Maugham Award, 1961); A House for Mr Biswas, 1961; Mr Stone and the Knights Companion, 1963 (Hawthornden Prize, 1964); The Mimic Men, 1967 (W. H. Smith Award, 1968); A Flag on the Island, 1967; In a Free State, 1971 (Booker Prize, 1971); Guerrillas, 1975; A Bend in the River, 1979; The Enigma of Arrival, 1987; A Way in the World, 1994; Half a Life, 2001. *Address:* c/o Gillon Aitken Associates Ltd, 29 Fernshaw Road, SW10 0TG.

NAIR, Chengara Veetil Devan; President of Singapore, 1981–85; *b* Malacca, Malaysia, 5 Aug. 1923; *s* of Karunakaran Illath Vayalakkara and Devaki Chengara Veetil Nair; *m* 1953, Avadai Dhanam Lakshimi; three *s* one *d*. *Educ:* Victoria Sch., Singapore. Teacher, St Andrew's Sch., 1949–51; Gen. Sec., Singapore Teachers' Union, 1949–51; Convenor, and Mem. Central Exec. Cttee, People's Action Party, 1954–56; Political Sec., Min. of Education, 1959–60; Chm., Singapore Adult Educn Bd, 1961–64; National Trades Union Congress: Sec. Gen., 1962–65, 1969–79; Dir, Res. Unit, 1969–81; Pres., 1979–81; Pres., Asian Regl Orgn, ICFTU, 1976–81. MP Malaysia, 1964–69, Singapore, 1979–81; first Sec. Gen., Democratic Action Party, Malaysia, 1964–69. Member: Nat. Wages Council, 1972–81; Housing and Develt Bd, 1975–81; Presidential Council for Minority Rights, 1979–81; Chm., Singapore Labour Foundn, 1977–81. Mem. Council, Nat. Univ. of Singapore, 1980–81. Life Member: Singapore Cancer Soc.; Ramakrishna Mission; Sri Aurobindo Soc. Hon. DLitt Nat. Univ. of Singapore, 1976. *Publications:* (ed) Who Lives if Malaysia Dies?, 1969; (ed) Singapore: Socialism that Works, 1976; (ed) Tomorrow: the peril and the promise, 1976; (ed) Asian Labour and the Dynamics of Change, 1977; (ed) Not by Wages Alone, 1982. *Address:* 176 Buckingham Drive, Hamilton, Ont L9C 2G7, Canada.

NAIRN, Margaret, RGN, SCM; Chief Area Nursing Officer, Greater Glasgow Health Board, 1974–84; *b* 20 July 1924; *d* of James R. Nairn and Anne G. Nairn. *Educ:* Aberdeen Academy. Nurse Training: general: Aberdeen Royal Infirmary, to 1945 (RGN); midwifery: Aberdeen Maternity Hosp., until 1948 (State Certified Midwife); Health Visitors: Aberdeen Coll. for Health Visitors, until 1952 (Health Visitors Cert.); administrative: Royal Coll. of Nursing, London, to 1959 (Nursing Admin. Cert.); 6 months study in USA as British Commonwealth and Empire Nurses Scholar, 1956. Ward Sister and Night Supt, Aberdeen Maternity Hosp., 1945–52; Director of Nursing Services in Aberdeen and Glasgow, 1952–74. *Publications:* articles in medical and nursing press: A Study of 283 Families with Rent Arrears; Liaison Services between Hospital and Community Nursing Services; Health Visitors in General Practice. *Recreations:* reading, gardening, swimming, travel. *Address:* 12 Countesswells Terrace, Aberdeen AB1 8LQ.

NAIRN, Martin John L.; *see* Lambie-Nairn.

NAIRN, Sir Michael, 4th Bt *cr* 1904; DL; *b* 1 July 1938; *s* of Sir Michael George Nairn, 3rd Bt, TD, and of Helen Louise, *yr d* of Major E. J. W. Bruce, Melbourne, Aust.; *S* father, 1984; *m* 1st, 1972, Diana (*d* 1982), *er d* of Leonard Bligh, NSW; two *s* one *d*; 2nd, 1986, Sally Jane, *d* of Major W. P. S. Hastings. *Educ:* Eton; INSEAD. DL Perth and Kinross, 1996. *Heir: s* Michael Andrew Nairn, *b* 2 Nov. 1973. *Club:* Caledonian.

NAIRN, Sir Robert Arnold S.; *see* Spencer-Nairn.

NAIRN-BRIGGS, Very Rev. George Peter; Dean (formerly Provost) of Wakefield, since 1997; *b* 5 July 1945; *s* of Frederick and Gladys Nairn-Briggs; *m* 1968, Candida Vickery; one *s* one *d*. *Educ:* Slough Tech. High Sch.; King's Coll., London (AKC 1969); St Augustine's Coll., Canterbury. Local authority housing, 1963–64; Press Officer, MAFF, 1964–66; ordained deacon, 1970, priest, 1971; Curate: St Laurence, Catford, 1970–73; St Saviour, Raynes Park, 1973–75; Vicar: Christ the King, Salfords, 1975–81; St Peter, St Helier, dio. Southwark, 1981–87; Bishop's Advr for Social Responsibility, Wakefield, 1987–97; Canon Residentiary, Wakefield Cathedral, 1992–97. *Publications:* Love in Action, 1986; Serving Two Masters, 1988; It Happens in the Family, 1992; contrib. to magazines and jls. *Recreations:* reading, buying antiques, travel. *Address:* The Deanery, 1 Cathedral Close, Margaret Street, Wakefield WF1 2DP. *T:* (01924) 210005; *e-mail:* thedeanofwakefield@hotmail.com.

NAIRNE, Alexander Robert, (Sandy); Director, National Programmes, Tate (formerly Tate Gallery), since 1998; *b* 8 June 1953; *s* of Rt Hon. Sir Patrick Nairne, *qv*; partner since 1981, Sylvia Elizabeth (Lisa) Tickner; one *s* one *d*. *Educ:* Radley Coll.; University Coll., Oxford (BA Modern History and Economics 1974; MA). Asst Dir, Museum of Modern Art, Oxford, 1974–76; Research Asst and Asst Keeper, Tate Gallery, 1976–79; Dir of Exhibitions, Inst. of Contemporary Arts, 1980–83; writer and associate producer, State of the Art, TV series, Channel 4, 1985–87; Dir of Visual Arts, Arts Council, 1987–92; Sen. Res. Fellow, Getty Grant Prog., 1992–93; Dir, Public and Regl Services, Tate Gall., 1994–98. Mem., Fabric Adv. Cttee, St Paul's Cathedral, 1996–. Gov., Middx Univ., 1994– (Dep. Chm., 1999–2000); Mem., Council of Trustees, British Sch. in Rome, 2001–. *Publications:* State of the Art, 1987; Thinking about Exhibitions, 1996. *Recreation:* punting. *Address:* Tate Gallery, Millbank, SW1P 4RG. *Clubs:* Chelsea Arts; Leander (Henley).

NAIRNE, Rt Hon. Sir Patrick (Dalmahoy), GCB 1981 (KCB 1975; CB 1971); MC 1943; PC 1982; Master, St Catherine's College, Oxford, 1981–88 (Hon. Fellow, 1988); Chancellor, Essex University, 1983–97; *b* 15 Aug. 1921; *s* of late Lt-Col C. S. and Mrs E. D. Nairne; *m* 1948, Penelope Chauncy Bridges, *d* of Lt-Col R. F. and Mrs L. C. Bridges; three *s* three *d*. *Educ:* Radley Coll.; University Coll., Oxford (Exhibr; Hon. Fellow, 1981). Seaforth Highlanders, 1941–45 (Capt.). 1st cl. hons Mod. Hist. (Oxon), 1947; MA 1947. Entered Civil Service and joined Admty, Dec. 1947; Private Sec. to First Lord of Admty, 1958–60; Asst Sec., 1960; Private Sec. to Sec. of State for Defence, 1965–67; Assistant Under-Sec. of State (Logistics), MoD, 1967–70; Dep. Under-Sec. of State, MoD, 1970–73; Second Perm. Sec., Cabinet Office, 1973–75; Perm. Sec., DHSS, 1975–81. Mem., Falkland Isles Review Cttee, 1982; Govt Monitor, Hong Kong, 1984; Chm., Commn on Conduct of Referendums, 1996. Central Independent TV: Mem. Bd, 1990–92; Dep. Chm., 1986–90, Chm., 1990–92, W Regl Bd. Church Comr, 1993–98; Chairman: Irene Wellington Educnl Trust, 1987–; Nuffield Council on Bioethics, 1991–96; President: Oxfordshire Craft Guild, 1993–97; Oxford Mus. of Modern Art, 1998– (Chm. Adv. Bd, 1988–98); Vice-President: Soc. for Italic Handwriting, 1987– (Chm., 1981–87); Oxford Art Soc., 1990–; Trustee: Nat. Maritime Museum, 1981–91; Joseph Rowntree Foundn, 1983–96; Nat. AIDS Trust, 1987–95; Oxford Sch. of Drama, 1998–; Member: Radley Coll. Council, 1975–99; Council, Ditchley Foundn, 1988–; President: Assoc. of CS Art Clubs, 1976–89 (Vice-Pres., 1999–); Radleian Soc., 1980–83; Seamen's Hosp. Soc., 1982–. FRSA 1978–2000. Hon. LLD: Leicester, 1980; St Andrews, 1984; DU Essex, 1983. *Recreations:* watercolour painting, calligraphy. *Address:* Yew Tree, Chilson, near Charlbury, Chipping Norton, Oxon OX7 3HU. *Club:* Oxford and Cambridge (Trustee, 1989–95).

See also A. R. Nairne.

NAIRNE, Sandy; *see* Nairne, A. R.

NAIROBI, Archbishop of, (RC), since 1971; **HE Cardinal Maurice Otunga;** *b* Jan. 1923. Priest, 1950; Titular Bishop of Tacape, 1957; Bishop of Kisii, 1960; Titular Archbishop of Bomarzo, 1969; Cardinal 1973. *Address:*; Archbishop's House, PO Box 14231, Nairobi, Kenya.

NAISH, Sir (Charles) David, Kt 1994; DL; FRAgS; President, National Farmers' Union, 1991–98; *b* 28 July 1940; *s* of Charles Naish and Muriel (*née* Turner); *m* 1966, Victoria Cockburn Mattock; two *s* one *d*. *Educ:* Worksop Coll.; RAC, Cirencester (MRAC). Jt Man.-Dir, J. B. Eastwood Ltd, 1969–73; Chm., Thornhill Country Produce Ltd, 1982–85. Dep. Pres., NFU, 1985–91. Chm., Aubourn Farming Ltd, 1998–; Director: Assured British Meat Ltd, 1997–2001; Express Dairies plc, 1998–; Dalgaty Gp Ltd, 1998–; Wilson Gp Ltd, 1997–; Agri-Ex, 2001–. Pres., COPA, 1995–97. FRAgS 1986; FRSA 1992; FIGD 1996. DL Notts, 1991. Hon. DSc De Montfort, 1996; DUniv Essex, 1998. *Recreations:* shooting, vintage motor cars, golf. *Address:* Edwinstowe, Notts NG21 9QE. *Club:* Farmers' (Chm., 1980).

NAISH, Peter; Chief Executive, Wood Green Animal Shelter, 1997; *b* 24 Jan. 1945; *s* of Frederick and Ida Naish; *m* 1970, Janet Kemp (marr. diss. 1996); one *s* two *d*. *Educ:* Hampton Grammar Sch.; King's Coll., London. Area Manager, Notting Hill Housing Trust, 1970–73; Chief Executive: Irwell Valley Housing Assoc., 1973–77; English Churches' Housing Gp, 1971–89; Research and Development for Psychiatry, 1989–91; CLS Care Services, 1991–94; Chief Exec., EOC, 1994–97. *Recreations:* walking, music, poetry. *Address:* c/o Wood Green Animal Shelter, London Road, Godmanchester PE18 8LJ.

NAKAJIMA, Hiroshi, MD, PhD; Director-General of the World Health Organization, 1988–98, now Director-General Emeritus; President, International Research Institute of Health and Welfare, since 1998; *b* Japan, 16 May 1928; *m* Martha Ann (*née* De Witt); two *s*. *Educ:* Nat. Sen. High Sch., Urawa; Tokyo Med. Coll. (MD 1955; PhD 1960); Faculty of Medicine, Univ. of Paris. Research, Nat. Inst. of Health and Med. Res., Paris, 1958–67; Dir of Res. and Admin, Nippon Roche Res. Centre, Tokyo, 1967–73; Scientist, Evaluation and Control of Drugs, 1973–76, Chief, Drug Policies and Management, 1976–79, WHO HQ, Geneva; Regional Dir, Western Pacific Region, WHO, 1979–88. Perm. Hon. Advr, World Fedn of Acupuncture and Moxybustion Socs, Beijing, 1998–. Vis. Prof. in Public Health, Tokyo Med. Coll., 1987; Vis. Prof., Univ. of Tokyo, 1991; Hon. Prof., Universidad Nacional Mayor de San Marcos, Peru, 1992. Corresp. Mem., Acad. de Pharmacie, France, 1988; Assoc. Foreign Mem., Acad. Nat. de Médecine de France, 1989; Hon. Member: Japanese Pharmacological Soc., 1990; Amer. Urological Assoc., 1995; Foreign Mem., Russian Acad. of Med. Scis, 1995; Hon. Foreign Mem., Acad. Royale de Médecine de Belgique, 1991. FCPS(Pak) 1990; Hon. FRCP 1992. DM (*hc*): Med. Univ., Ulan Bator, Mongolia, 1991; Univ. Nat. du Benin, 1997; Hon. DSc Mahidol Univ., Bangkok, 1994; Dr *hc* Bucharest, 1994. Kojima Prize, Japan, 1984; Okamoto Award, Japan, 1989; Polio Eradication Champion Award, Rotary Internat., 1999. First Order of Merit (Japan), 2000; Order of Merit (Poland), 1990; Chevalier de la Légion d'Honneur (France), 1991; Commandeur, Ordre Nat. du Lion (Senegal), 1991; Equestrian Order of St Agatha (San Marino), 1995. *Publications:* articles and reviews in Japanese, French and English pubns. *Address:* International Research Institute of Health and Welfare, Shimato Building, 8-5-34 Akasaka, Tokyo 1070052, Japan. *T:* (3) 5414 6060.

NAKASONE, Yasuhiro; Prime Minister of Japan, 1982–87; Chairman: Institute for International Policy Studies (formerly International Institute for Global Peace), since 1988; Asia Pacific Parliamentary Forum, since 1993; *b* 27 May 1918; 2nd *s* of Matsugoroh Nakasone; *m* 1945, Tsutako Kobayashi; one *s* two *d*. *Educ:* Faculty of Law, Imperial Univ. (graduate). Joined Min. of Home Affairs, 1941; commd as Lt-Comdr, 1945. Elected to House of Representatives (first of 19 consecutive times), 1947; Minister of State, Dir-Gen. of Science and Technology Agency, 1959–60; Minister of Transport, 1967–68; Minister of State, Dir-Gen. of Defence Agency, 1970–71; Minister of Internat. Trade and Industry, 1972–74; Minister of State for Admin. Management Agency, 1980–82. Chm. Exec. Council, 1971–72, Sec. Gen., 1974–76, Liberal Democratic Party. Hon. DHL, Johns Hopkins, 1984. Médaille de la Chancellerie, Univs of Paris. *Publications:* The Ideals of Youth, 1947; Japan Speaks, 1954; The New Conservatism, 1978; Human Cities—a proposal for the 21st century, 1980; Tenchiyujou (auto-biography), 1996. *Address:* Takada 2-18-6, Toshimaku, Tokyo, Japan.

NALL, Sir Edward William Joseph, 3rd Bt *cr* 1954, of Hoveringham, co. Nottingham; *b* 24 Oct. 1952; *er s* of Sir Michael Joseph Nall, 2nd Bt and of Angela Loveday Hanbury (*née* Coryton); *S* father, 2001. *Educ:* Eton. Commnd 13th/18th Royal Hussars (QMO), subseq. Light Dragoons, 1973; Major, 1985; retd, 1993. *Heir: b* Alexander Michael Nall [*b* 3 July 1956; *m* 1982, Caroline Jane Robinson; one *s* one *d*].

NALL-CAIN, family name of **Baron Brocket**.

NAMALIU, Rt Hon. Sir Rabbie (Langanai), KCMG 1996 (CMG 1979); PC 1989; MP for Kokopo (Pangu Pati), Papua New Guinea, since 1982; Minister for Petroleum and Energy, since 1998; *b* 3 April 1947; *s* of Darius Namaliu and Utul Ioan; *m* 1978, Margaret Nakikus (*d* 1993); two *s*, and one step *d*; *m* 1999, Kelin. *Educ:* Univ. of Papua New Guinea

(BA); Univ. of Victoria, BC (MA). Senior Tutor, later Lectr in History, Univ. of Papua New Guinea, 1973; Principal Private Sec. to Chief Minister (Hon. Michael Somare), 1974–75; Vis. Pacific Fellow, Centre for Pacific Studies, Univ. of California, Santa Cruz, 1975; Provincial Comr, East New Britain Province, 1976; Chm., Public Services Commn, 1976–79; Exec. Officer to Leader of the Opposition (Rt Hon. Michael Somare), 1980–81; Minister for Foreign Affairs and Trade, 1982–84, for Primary Industry, 1985; Dep. Leader, 1985–88, Leader, 1988–92, Pangu Pati; Prime Minister, PNG, 1988–92; Leader of the Opposition, and Parly Leader of Pangu Pati, 1992–94; Speaker of Nat. Parlt, 1994–97; Senior Minister of State, 1997–98. Hon. LLD Univ. of Victoria, BC, 1983. *Recreations:* swimming, walking, reading, golf. *Address:* PO Box 6655, Boroko, National Capital District, Papua New Guinea.

NANDY, Dipak; Head of Equal Opportunities, Social Services Department, Nottinghamshire County Council, 1992; *b* 21 May 1936; *s* of B. C. Nandy and Leela Nandy; *m* 1st, 1964, Margaret Gracie (decd); 2nd, 1972, Hon. Luise Byers (marr. diss. 1991); two *d*. *Educ:* St Xavier's Coll., Calcutta; Univ. of Leeds (BA 1st Cl. Hons English Literature, 1960; C. E. Vaughan Research Fellowship, 1960–62). Lectr, English Literature, Univ. of Leicester, 1962–66; Lectr and Fellow of Rutherford College, Univ. of Kent at Canterbury, 1966–68; founder-Director, The Runnymede Trust, 1968–73; Vis. Fellow, Adlai Stevenson Inst. of International Affairs, Chicago, 1970–73; Research Fellow, Social and Community Planning Research, 1973–75; Dep. Chief Exec., Equal Opportunities Commn, 1976–86; Chief Exec., Intermediate Technology Develt Gp, 1986–88; Hon. Lectr in Social Policy, Univ. of Birmingham, 1989–; Financial and Admin. Dir, RSP, Queen Elizabeth House, Oxford, 1991. Member: Cttee of Inquiry into Future of Broadcasting, 1974–77; Council, Nat. Assoc. Citizens' Advice Bureaux, 1983–86; BBC: Chm., Asian Programmes Adv. Cttee, 1983–88; Mem., General Adv. Council. Member: Council, Northern Chamber Orch., 1980–84; Royal Nat. Theatre Bd, 1992–97; Governor, BFI, 1984–87. Trustee, CSV, 1981–91. Hon. Liaison, Employment and Labour Law Sect., Amer. Bar Assoc., 1980–. *Publications:* numerous essays in books, periodicals and newspapers on literature, political thought, race relations, urban problems, equality for women, broadcasting policy and development issues. *Recreations:* collecting records, opera, computing. *Address:* 8 Woodhedge Drive, Thorneywood, Nottingham NG3 6LU. *Club:* National Liberal.

NANKIVELL, Owen; JP; economic and business consultant; Executive Director, Hinksey Network (formerly Hinksey Centre), since 1982; *b* 6 April 1927; *s* of John Hamilton Nankivell and Sarah Ann Mares; *m* 1956, Mary Burman Earnshaw; one *s* two *d*. *Educ:* Torquay Grammar Sch.; Univ. of Manchester. BA (Econ) 1951, MA (Econ) 1963. FRSS. Admty, 1951–52; Colonial Office, 1952–55; Central Statistical Office, 1955–65; DEA, 1965–69; HM Treasury, 1969–72; Asst Dir, Central Statistical Office, 1972–79; Gp Chief Economist, Lucas Industries, 1979–82. JP Worcester, 1983–89, Torbay, 1989. *Publications:* All Good Gifts, 1978; Economics, Society and Values, 1995. *Recreations:* Christian, tennis, choral music, singing. *Address:* 3 Thorne Park Road, Torquay TQ2 6RX. *T:* and *Fax:* (01803) 690147.

NAPIER, family name of **Lord Napier and Ettrick** and **Baron Napier of Magdala.**

NAPIER, 14th Lord *cr* 1627 (Scotland), **AND ETTRICK,** 5th Baron *cr* 1872 (UK); **Francis Nigel Napier,** KCVO 1992 (CVO 1985 LVO 1980); DL; a Bt of Nova Scotia, 1666, 11th Bt of Thirlestane, 22nd of Merchiston; Chief of the Name of Napier; Major, Scots Guards (Reserve of Officers); Treasurer to HRH the Princess Margaret, Countess of Snowdon, since 1998 (Private Secretary, Comptroller and Equerry 1973–98); *b* 5 Dec. 1930; *e s* of 13th Baron Napier and 4th Ettrick, TD, and Muir (*d* 1992), *e d* of Sir Percy Newson, Bt; *S* father, 1954; *m* 1958, Delia Mary, *yr d* of late A. D. B. Pearson; two *s* two *d*. *Educ:* Wellesley House; Eton; RMA, Sandhurst. Commissioned, 1950; served Malaya, 1950–51 (invalided); Adjt 1st Bn Scots Guards, 1955–57. Equerry to His late Royal Highness The Duke of Gloucester, 1958–60, retd, 1960. Deputy Ceremonial and Protocol Secretary, CRO, 1962–66; Purple Staff Officer at State Funeral of Sir Winston Churchill, 1966. A Cons. Whip, House of Lords, 1970–71. On behalf of HM The Queen, handed over Instruments of Independence to Tuvalu (formerly Ellice Is), 1978. Member: Royal Co. of Archers (Queen's Body Guard for Scotland), 1953–; Exec. Cttee, Standing Council of the Baronetage, 1985–; Standing Council of Scottish Chiefs. Mem., Rolls-Royce Enthusiasts Club. Pres., St John Ambulance Assoc. and Brigade for County of London, 1975–83. DL Selkirkshire, 1974, Ettrick and Lauderdale, 1975–94. Freeman, City of London; Liveryman, Worshipful Company of Grocers. Hon. DLitt Napier Univ., 1993. KStJ 1991 (CStJ 1988). *Heir: s* Master of Napier, *qv*. *Address:* Down House, Wylye, Wilts BA12 0QN. *Clubs:* Turf, Pratt's, Pitt; Royal Caledonian Hunt (Edinburgh).

NAPIER OF MAGDALA, 6th Baron *cr* 1868; **Robert Alan Napier;** *b* 6 Sept. 1940; *s* of 5th Baron Napier of Magdala, OBE, and of Elizabeth Marian, *y d* of E. H. Hunt, FRCS; *S* father, 1987; *m* 1964, Frances Clare, *d* of late Alan Frank Skinner; one *s* one *d*. *Educ:* Winchester College; St John's Coll., Cambridge (BA 1st cl. Hons 1962; MA 1966). *Heir: s* Hon. James Robert Napier, *b* 29 Jan. 1966. *Address:* The Coach House, Kingsbury Street, Marlborough, Wilts SN8 1HU. *T:* (01672) 512333. *Club:* Leander (Henley-on-Thames).

NAPIER, Master of; Hon. Francis David Charles Napier; established Napier Garden Planning, 1999; *b* 3 Nov. 1962; *s* and *heir* of 14th Lord Napier (and 5th Baron Ettrick), *qv*; *m* 1993, Zara Jane, *o d* of Hugh McCalmont, Newmarket, Suffolk; one *s* one *d*. *Educ:* Stanbridge Earls School; South Thames Coll., Wandsworth, 1986–87 (City and Guilds Computer Diploma); Otley Coll., Ipswich (Nat. Cert. Hort. Garden Design and Construction, 1999). With a Lloyd's agency, 1984–92; with Heath Bloodstock Ltd, 1992–97. *Recreations:* travelling, horse-racing, Real tennis, squash. *Address:* Gowan Cottage, Westley Waterless, Newmarket, Suffolk CB8 0RQ. *Clubs:* Turf, Pratt's.

NAPIER, Sir Charles Joseph, 6th Bt *cr* 1867, of Merrion Square, Dublin; *b* 15 April 1973; *o s* of Sir Robin Surtees Napier, 5th Bt and of Jennifer Beryl, *d* of H. Warwick Daw; *S* father, 1994. *Educ:* Eton; Univ. of Edinburgh (MA Hons; Fencing Blue). Internat. student fencer (2 caps for Scottish Univs, foil and sabre). Scottish European Aid, 1995–96; Corporate Fundraiser, MIND, 1997–98; Appeal Dir, 1998–99, and Mgt Cttee, Downside Settlement, Bermondsey; public affairs, The Policy Partnership, 1999–. Gov., Peterborough Primary Sch., Fulham. *Recreations:* watching and playing most sports, motorbikes, fishing. *Heir: uncle* John Lennox Napier [*b* 25 Jan. 1934; *m* 1967, Cecily Mary, *d* of late Arthur Mortimer; one *s* one *d*]. *Address:* Flat 10, 2 Cromwell Grove, W6 7RG. *Clubs:* Flyfishers'; Southampton Football.

NAPIER, John, RDI 1996; stage designer; *b* 1 March 1944; *s* of James Edward Thomas Napier and Lorrie Napier (*née* Godbold); *m* 1st, Andreane Neofitou; one *s* one *d*; 2nd, Donna King; one *s* one *d*. *Educ:* Hornsey Coll. of Art; Central Sch. of Arts and Crafts. Designed 1st production, A Penny for a Song, Pheonix, Leicester, 1967; *London productions:* Fortune and Men's Eyes, 1968; The Ruling Class, The Fun War, Muzeeka, George Frederick (ballet), La Turista, 1969; Cancer, Isabel's a Jezebel, 1970; Mister, The Foursome, The Lovers of Viorne, Lear, 1971; Jump, Sam Sam, Big Wolf, 1972; The Devils (ENO), Equus, The Party, 1973; Knuckle, 1974; Kings and Clowns, The Travelling Music Show, 1978; The Devils of Loudon, Lohengrin (Covent Garden); King John, Richard II, Cymbeline, Macbeth, Richard III, 1974; Hedda Gabler, 1975; Much Ado About Nothing, The Comedy of Errors, King Lear, Macbeth, 1976; A Midsummer Night's Dream, As You Like It, 1977; The Merry Wives of Windsor, Twelfth Night, Three Sisters, Once in a Lifetime, 1979; The Greeks, Nicholas Nickleby (SWET award, Tony Award), 1980; Cats (Tony award), 1981; Henry IV Parts I and II, Peter Pan, 1982; Macbeth (Covent Garden), 1983; Starlight Express, 1984 (Tony Award, 1987); Les Misérables, 1985 (Tony Award, 1987); Time, 1986; Miss Saigon, 1989; Children of Eden, 1990; Trelawny of the 'Wells', 1993; Sunset Boulevard, 1993 (Tony Award, 1995); Burning Blue, 1995 (Olivier award, 1996); The Tower, 1995; Jesus Christ Superstar, 1996; Who's Afraid of Virginia Woolf?, 1996; An Enemy of the People, 1997; Peter Pan, 1997; Martin Guerre, 1998; Candide, 1999; *Glyndebourne:* Idomeneo, 1983; *USA:* Siegfried & Roy Show (Las Vegas; also co-dir), 1990; Jane Eyre (NY), 2000; Nabucco (Met. Opera), 2001; film designs incl. Hook, 1991; numerous designs for stage productions in Europe, Japan, Australia, USA and for TV. American Acad. of Achievement, 1994. *Recreation:* photography. *Address:* c/o MLR, Douglas House, 16–18 Douglas Street, SW1P 4PB.

NAPIER, Sir John Archibald Lennox, 14th Bt *cr* 1627 (NS), of Merchistoun; *b* 6 Dec. 1946; *s* of Sir William Archibald Napier, 13th Bt and of Kathleen Mabel, *d* of late Reginald Greaves; *S* father, 1990; *m* 1969, Erica, *d* of late Kurt Kingsfield; one *s* one *d*. *Educ:* St Stithians; Witwatersrand Univ., Johannesburg. MSc(Eng); PhD. *Heir: s* Hugh Robert Lennox Napier, *b* 1 Aug. 1977. *Address:* Merchistoun, PO Box 65177, Benmore 2010, Republic of South Africa.

NAPIER, Maj.-Gen. Lennox Alexander Hawkins, CB 1983; OBE 1970; MC 1957; Vice Lord-Lieutenant of Gwent, since 1995; Inspector of Public Inquiries, 1983–98; *b* 28 June 1928; *s* of Major Charles McNaughton Napier and D. C. Napier; *m* 1959, Jennifer Dawn Wilson; one *s* two *d*. *Educ:* Radley; RMA Sandhurst. Joined Army, 1946; commnd into South Wales Borderers, 1948; commanded 1st Bn S Wales Borderers and 1st Bn Royal Regt of Wales, 1967–70; Instructor, JSSC, 1970–72; served Min. of Defence, 1972–74; Brigade Commander, Berlin Infantry Bde, 1974–76; Prince of Wales's Division: Divisional Brigadier, 1976–80; Col Commandant, 1980–83; GOC Wales, 1980–83. Col, The Royal Regt of Wales, 1983–89; Hon. Col, Cardiff Univ. OTC, 1985–92. Chm., Central Rail Users Cttee, 1985–95. Gwent: DL 1983; High Sheriff 1988. OStJ 1969. *Recreations:* shooting, riding. *Address:* Osbaston Farm, Monmouth, Gwent NP25 5DL.

NAPIER, Michael; *see* Napier, T. M.

NAPIER, Sir Oliver John, Kt 1985; Senior Partner, Napier & Sons, Solicitors, since 1976; Chairman, Standing Advisory Commission on Human Rights, 1988–92; *b* 11 July 1935; *e s* of James J. and Sheila Napier; *m* 1961, Brigid (*née* Barnes); three *s* five *d* (and one *s* decd). *Educ:* Ballycruttle Public Elem. Sch., Downpatrick; St Malachy's Coll., Belfast; Queen's Univ., Belfast (LLB). Qual. Solicitor, NI, 1959; Lectr and Mem. Bd of Examrs, Incorp. Law Soc. of NI, 1965–71. Mem. Exec., Ulster Liberal Party, 1962–69; Founder Mem., New Ulster Movt, 1969; Founder Mem., Alliance Party, 1970, Leader 1973–84, Pres., 1989–92. Mem. (Alliance), E Belfast, NI Assembly, 1973–75; Minister of Legal Affairs, NI Executive, Jan.–May 1974; Mem. (Alliance), N Ireland Constitutional Convention for E Belfast, 1975–76; Mem. (Alliance) Belfast E, NI Assembly, 1982–86. Contested (Alliance): E Belfast, 1979, 1983; N Down, 1997. Councillor for E Belfast, Belfast CC, 1977–89; Mem. for N Down, NI Forum, 1996–98. Mem. (Alliance), Negotiation Team for Good Friday Agreement, 1996–98. Member: Lawyers Insolvency Assoc., 1991–; Council, Soc. of Practitioners of Insolvency, 1993–2000. *Recreations:* many and varied. *Address:* 83 Victoria Road, Holywood, Co. Down BT18 9BG; Napier & Sons, 1–9 Castle Arcade, Belfast BT1 5DF.

NAPIER, Robert Stewart; Chief Executive, WWF–UK, since 1999; *b* 21 July 1947; *s* of Andrew Napier and Lilian V. Napier (*née* Ritchie); *m* 1977, Patricia Stewart; one *d*. *Educ:* Sedbergh School; Sidney Sussex College, Cambridge (BA 1969; MA 1971); Harvard Business School (AMP 1987). RTZ Corp., 1969–73; Brandts, 1973–75; Fisons, 1975–81; Redland: Finance Dir, 1981–87; Man. Dir, 1987–97; Chief Exec., 1991–97. Director: United Biscuits (Hldgs), 1992–2000; Rentokil Initial plc, 1996–99. Pres., Nat. Council of Building Material Producers, 1996–97; Chairman: CBI Transport Policy Cttee, 1995–97; Alliance of Construction Product Suppliers, 1996–97. Governor: Reigate Grammar Sch., 1995–; Sedbergh Sch., 1998– (Chm., 2000–). Trustee: World in Need, 1988–91; ACET, 1991–94; CRASH, 1994–99 (Chm., 1998–99); Baynards Zambia Trust, 1996–. *Recreations:* hill walking, escaping to Scotland, the works of John Buchan. *Address:* Baynards Manor, Rudgwick, W Sussex RH12 3AD.

NAPIER, (Thomas) Michael; Senior Partner, Irwin Mitchell, solicitors, since 1983; President, Law Society, 2000–01; *b* 11 June 1946; *s* of late Montague Keith Napier and Mary Napier; *m* 1969, Denise Christine Willey; one *s* two *d*. *Educ:* Loughborough GS; Manchester Univ. (LLB 1967). Articled clerk, Moss Toone & Deane, Loughborough, 1968–70; admitted Solicitor, 1970; Asst Solicitor, W. H. Thompson, Manchester, 1970–72; Partner, Irwin Mitchell, 1973–; Jt Sen. Partner, Pannone Napier, 1985–94; specialises in personal injury. Mem., Mental Health Act Commn, 1983–92 (Jt Vice-Chm., 1985–88; Chm., NE Reg., 1985–90). Vis. Prof., Nottingham Law Sch., 1992–. Jt Founder, 1990, Pres., 1994–96, Assoc. of Personal Injury Lawyers; Member: Council, Law Soc., 1993– (Vice Pres., 2000); Council, Justice, 1995–; Civil Justice Council, 1998–. Chm., Adv. Cttee, Rampton Hosp., 1992–96. Editorial Consultant: Personal Medical Injuries Law Letter, 1985–; Med. Law Rev., 1994–. Freeman, Co. of Cutlers in Hallamshire, 1992. *Publications:* (jtly) Conditional Fees: a survival guide, 1995; (jtly) Recovering Damages for Psychiatric Injury, 1995; (Ed. in Chief) Litigation Funding, 1999; (contrib.) Blackstones Civil Practice, 2000; contrib. legal books and jls. *Recreation:* mountain biking in Norfolk. *Address:* Irwin Mitchell, St Peter's House, Hartshead, Sheffield S1 2EL. *T:* (0114) 276 7777, *Fax:* (0114) 275 3306; The Manor House, Great Walsingham, Norfolk NR22 6DY, *T:* (01328) 820213; Bridge House, Ford, Ridgeway, Sheffield S12 3YD. *T:* (01246) 433221. *Club:* Athenæum.

NAPOLITAN, Leonard, CB 1970; Director of Economics and Statistics, Ministry of Agriculture, Fisheries and Food, 1965–77; *b* 9 April 1919; *s* of Domenic and Rose G. Napolitan; *m* 1945, Dorothy Laycock; two *d*. *Educ:* Univ. of London (BSc Econ. 1944); LSE (MSc Econ. 1946). Asst Agric. Economist, Univ. of Bristol, 1947–48; joined Min. of Agric. and Fisheries as Agric. Economist, 1948. Pres., Agric. Econs Soc., 1974–75. FRSA. *Address:* 4 Rectory Gardens, Burway Road, Church Stretton, Shropshire SY6 6DP.

NARAIN, Sase, OR 1976; CMG 1969; SC (Guyana) 1985; JP (Guyana); solicitor/attorney-at-law; Speaker of the National Assembly, Guyana, 1971–92; Chairman, National Bank of Industry and Commerce (Guyana), 1986–93; *b* 27 Jan. 1925; *s* of Oudit and Sookdai Naraine; *m* 1952, Shamshun Narain (*née* Rayman); four *s*. *Educ:* Modern Educational Inst.; Gibson and Weldon Law Tutors. Solicitor, admitted in England and Guyana, 1957. Town Councillor, City of Georgetown, 1962–70; Member: History and Arts Council, 1969–; Republic Cttee of Guyana, 1969; Pres., Guyana Sanatan Dharma

Maha Sabha, 1963–94. Comr for Oaths to Affidavits, 1961; Notary Public, 1968. Dep. Chm., Public Service Commn, Guyana, 1966–71; Mem., Police Service Commn, 1966–71. Chm., Berger Paints (Guyana), 1966–78; Dir, Pegasus Hotels of Guyana, 1987–90. Member: Nat. Awards Cttee of Guyana, 1970–92; Bd of Governors, President's Coll., Guyana, 1985–88. JP 1962. *Recreations:* golf, cricket, swimming. *Address:* 217 South Street, Lacytown, Georgetown, Demerara, Guyana. *T:* (2) 66611. *Clubs:* Georgetown Cricket, Everest Cricket (Guyana).

NARASIMHA, Prof. Roddam, FRS 1992; Director, National Institute of Advanced Studies, India, since 1997; Professor Ramanathan Distinguished Professor, since 1995, and Chairman, since 1990, Fluid Mechanics Unit, Jawaharlal Nehru Centre for Advanced Scientific Research (INSA Golden Jubilee Research Professor, 1991–94); *b* 20 July 1933; *s* of Shri R. L. Narasimhaiya and Smt R. N. Leela Devi; *m* 1965, Dr Neelima S. Rao; two *d. Educ:* University Coll. of Engineering, Bangalore (BE 1953); Indian Inst. of Science (DIISc 1955; AIISc 1957); California Inst. of Technology (PhD 1961). Res. Fellow, CIT, 1961–62; Indian Institute of Science: Asst and Associate Prof., 1962–70; Prof., 1970–98, and Chm., 1982–84, Dept of Aerospace Engrg; Dean of Engrg Faculty, 1980–82; Chm., 1982–89, Prof., 1982–98, Centre for Atmospheric Scis; Dir, Nat. Aeronautical Lab., subseq. Nat. Aerospace Labs, Bangalore, 1984–93. Chief Project Co-ordinator, Hindustan Aeronautics Ltd, 1977–79. Clark B. Millikan Vis. Prof., CIT, 1985–; Jawaharlal Nehru Vis. Prof., Cambridge, 1989–90. Member: Sci. Adv. Council to the Prime Minister, 1985–89, to the Cabinet, 1997–; Space Commn, Govt of India, 1989–. Pres., Indian Acad. of Scis, 1992–94. Fellow: Indian Nat. Sci. Acad., 1979; Third World Acad. of Scis, Italy, 1989; Foreign Associate, US Nat. Acad. of Engrg, 1989; Hon. Fellow, Aer. Soc. of India, 1985; Distinguished Alumnus: CIT, 1986; Indian Inst. of Sci., 1988. Bhatnagar Prize in Engrg, CSIR, India, 1976; Gujar Mal Modi Award for Sci., 1990; Srinivasa Ramanujan Medal, Indian Sci. Congress, 1998. Kannada Rajyotsava Award, Karnataka, 1986; Padmabhushan, India, 1987. *Publications:* (ed) Computer Simulation, 1979; (ed) Turbulence Management and Relaminarisation, 1987; (ed) Developments in Fluid Mechanics and Space Technology, 1988; Surveys in Fluid Mechanics, vol. III, 1993; The Monsoon Trough Boundary Layer, 1997; numerous sci. papers in learned jls. *Recreations:* history, walking, music. *Address:* National Institute of Advanced Studies, Indian Institute of Science Campus, Bangalore 560012, India. *T:* (80) 3310969, *Fax:* (80) 3346634.

NARASIMHAN, Chakravarthi Vijayaraghava; Senior Fellow, UN Institute for Training and Research, 1978–93; *b* 21 May 1915; *s* of Chakravarthi V. and Janaki Vijayaraghavachari; *m* 1938, Janaki, *d* of Dr M. T. Chari; two *d. Educ:* University of Madras (BA); Oxford (MA). Indian Civil Service, 1936; Dep. Sec., Development Dept, Government of Madras, 1945–48; Min. of Agriculture, Govt of India, 1950–53; Joint Sec., Economic Affairs Dept, Ministry of Finance, 1953–56; Executive Sec., UN Economic Commission for Asia and Far East, 1956–59; Under-Sec. for Special Political Affairs, UN, 1959–62; Chef de Cabinet of the Sec.-Gen., UN, 1961–73; Under-Sec., 1962–67, Under-Sec.-Gen. 1967–69, for Gen. Assembly Affairs, UN; Dep. Administrator, UN Develt Prog., 1969–72; Under-Sec.-Gen. for Inter-Agency Affairs and Co-ordination, UN, 1973–78; Organizing Exec. Sec., Cotton Develt Internat., UN Develt Programme, 1979–81. Hon. Doctor of Laws, Williams Coll. Williamstown, Mass, 1960; Hon. Dr of Humane Letters, Colgate Univ., 1966. *Publications:* The United Nations: an inside view, 1988; History of United Nations University, 1994; UN at 50: recollections, 1996. *Recreations:* Sanskrit literature, South Indian classical music, tennis. *Address:* 5327 Uppingham Street, Chevy Chase, MD 20815, USA. *T:* (301) 6578571.

NARASIMHAN, Prof. Mudumbai Seshachalu, PhD; FRS 1996; Professor of Geometry, Scuola Internazionale Superiore di Studi Avanzati, Trieste; *b* 7 June 1932; *s* of Seshachalu Iyengar and Padmasani; *m* 1962, Sakuntala Raman; one *s* one *d. Educ:* Madras Univ. (BA Hons); Bombay Univ. (PhD 1960). Tata Institute, Bombay: Associate Prof., 1963–65; Prof., 1965–75; Sen. Prof., 1975–90; Prof. of Eminence, 1990–93; Hon. Fellow, 1994; Dir of Maths, Internat. Centre, subseq. Abdus Salam Internat. Centre, for Theoretical Physics, Trieste, 1992–98. S. S. Bhatnagar Prize in Mathematical Scis, CSIR, 1975; Meghnad Saha Award, Univ. Grants Commn, 1978; Award for Maths, Third World Acad. of Scis, 1987; Srinivasa Ramanujan Medal, INSA, 1988; C. V. Raman Birth Centenary Award, Indian Sci. Congress, 1994. Chevalier, Ordre National du Mérite (France), 1989; Padma Bhushan (India), 1990. *Address:* Scuola Internazionale Superiore di Studi Avanzati, Via Beirut 2-4, 34014 Trieste, Italy. *T:* (40) 2240339.

NARAYANAN, Kocheril Raman; President of India, since 1997 (Vice-President, 1992–97); *b* 27 Oct. 1920; *s* of late Raman Vaidyan Narayanan; *m* 1951, Usha; two *d. Educ:* Travancore Univ. (MA); LSE (BSc 1948; Hon. Fellow, 1972). Lectr, Univ. of Travancore, 1942; journalist, 1944–45; entered Foreign Service, 1949; served Rangoon, Tokyo, London and Min. of External Affairs, 1949–60; Actg High Comr, Australia, 1961–62; Consul-Gen., Hanoi, 1962–63; Dir, China Div., 1963–67; Ambassador to Thailand, 1967–69; Jt Sec. for Policy Planning, 1969–70; Prof., Jawaharlal Nehru Univ., 1970–72; Ambassador to Turkey, 1973–75; Addtl Sec. for Policy Planning Div., 1975–76; Sec. (East), 1976; Ambassador to China, 1976–78; Mem., Indian Delegn to UN Gen. Assembly, 1979; Ambassador to USA, 1980–84; elected MP for Ottapalam, Kerala, Lok Sabha, 1984; Minister of State for: Planning, 1984–85; External Affairs, 1985–86; Atomic Energy, Space, Electronics and Ocean Develt, 1986–87; Sci. and Technol., 1986–89. Hon. Fellow, Centre for Develt Studies, Trivandrum. *Publications:* (jtly) India and America: essays in understanding; Images and Insights; (jtly) Nonalignment in Contemporary International Relations; contribs on internat. relns, Indian politics, and literature. *Address:* Rashtrapati Bhavan, New Delhi 110004, India.

NAREY, Martin James; Director General, HM Prison Service, since 1999; *b* 5 Aug. 1955; *s* of John and Ellenor Narey; *m* 1978, Jan Goudy; one *s* one *d. Educ:* Sheffield Poly. (BA Public Admin). Assistant Governor: HM Young Offender Inst. Deerbolt, 1982–86; Frankland, 1986–90; Gov. IV, Prison Service HQ, 1990–91; Home Office: Private Sec. to Minister of State, 1991–92; Criminal Policy, 1992–94; Co-ordination of Computerisation in the Criminal Justice System Unit, 1994–96; Head of Crime Prevention Agency, 1996; Reviewer of Delay in the Criminal Justice System, 1996–97; Head of Security Policy, 1997–98, Dir of Regimes, 1998–99, HM Prison Service. *Publications:* review of delay in criminal justice system, report on an investigation at the Maze Prison. *Recreations:* planning holidays, watching Middlesbrough FC. *Address:* (office) Cleland House, Page Street, SW1P 4LN. *T:* (020) 7217 6703.

NARJES, Karl-Heinz; Member, Commission of the European Communities, 1981–89 (Vice-President, 1985–89); *b* 30 Jan. 1924; *s* of Heinrich Narjes; *m* 1951, Eva-Maria Rahe; one *s* one *d. Educ:* Hamburg Univ. Entered Foreign Service, 1955; Chef du Cabinet, Pres. of EEC, 1963; Dir-Gen., Press and Inf. Directorate, EEC, 1968–69; Minister of Econs and of Transport, Schleswig-Holstein, 1969–73. Mem., Bundestag, 1972–81; Mem., For. Affairs Cttee, 1976–80; Pres., Econ. Affairs Cttee, 1972–76.

NARUEPUT, Owart S.; *see* Suthiwart-Narueput.

NASEBY, Baron *cr* 1997 (Life Peer), of Sandy in the co. of Bedfordshire; **Michael Wolfgang Laurence Morris;** PC 1994; *b* 25 Nov. 1936; *m* 1960, Dr Ann Appleby (Dr Ann Morris, MB, BS, MRCS, MRCP); two *s* one *d. Educ:* Bedford Sch.; St Catharine's Coll., Cambridge (BA Hons Econs; MA). Trainee to Marketing Manager, UK, India and Ceylon, Reckitt & Colman Gp, 1960–63; Service Advertising Ltd, 1964–68; Marketing Exec. to Account Supervisor, Horniblow Cox-Freeman Ltd, 1968–71, Dir 1969–71; Dir, Benton & Bowles Ltd, 1971–81; Proprietor: A. M. International, 1980–92; Julius International Consultants, 1997–. Non-executive Director: Tunbridge Wells Equitable Friendly Soc., 1992– (Chm., 1998–); Mansell plc, 1998–; Invesco Recovery Trust 2005 plc, 1998–. Contested (C) Islington North, 1966. Islington Council: Councillor, 1968–70; Alderman, 1970–74; Chm. of Housing, 1968; Leader, 1969–71. MP (C) Northampton South, Feb. 1974–1997; contested (C) same seat, 1997. PPS to Minister of State, NI Office, 1979–81; Chm. of Ways and Means and Dep. Speaker, H of C, 1992–97. Member: Public Accounts Cttee, 1979–92; Select Cttee on Energy, 1982–85; Chairman's Panel, 1984–92; Mem. Council, Europe and Western European Union, 1983–91; Chairman: British Sri Lanka Cttee, 1979–92, 1997–; British Singapore Cttee, 1985–92; British Malaysia Cttee, 1987–92; British Burma Cttee, 1989–92; formerly: Vice-Chm., British Indonesia Cttee; Treas., British ASEAN and Thai Cttees; Secretary: British Venezuela Cttee; Cons. Housing and Local Govt Cttee, 1974–76; Cons Trade Cttee, 1974–76; Cons. Environment Cttee, 1977–79; Vice-Chm., Cons. Energy Cttee, 1981–92; Founder, Parly Food and Health Forum. Captain, Parly Golf Soc., 1988–91. Chm., Victoria County History for Northamptonshire, 1994–. Chm., Govs, Bedford Sch., 1989– (Governor, 1982–). *Publications:* (jtly) Helping the Exporter, 1967; (contrib.) Marketing below the Line: Studies in Management, 1972; The Disaster of Direct Labour, 1978. *Recreations:* restoration work, cricket, tennis, golf, budgerigars, forestry. *Address:* Caesar's Camp, Sandy, Beds SG19 2AD. *T:* (01767) 680388. *Clubs:* Carlton, MCC, Lord's Taverners; All England Lawn Tennis and Croquet; George Row, Conservative, Billing Road (Northampton); Royal St George's Golf (Sandwich); John O'Gaunt Golf.

NASH, Prof. Anthony Aubrey, PhD; Professor and Head of Department of Veterinary Pathology, University of Edinburgh, since 1994; *b* 6 March 1949; *s* of Alfred Nash and Mabel Evelyn Nash (*née* Garrett); *m* 1979, Marion Eileen Bazeley; four *d. Educ:* Queen Elizabeth Coll., London (BSc Hons 1970); Univ. of Birmingham (MSc 1971; PhD 1976). Lecturer: in Immunology, Dept of Pathology, Univ. of Cambridge, 1984–94; in Pathology, Newnham Coll., Cambridge, 1987–94. Eleanor Roosevelt Fellow, Dept of Immunology, Scripps Clinic and Res. Foundn, Calif, 1989–90. FMedSci 1999. *Publications:* (jtly) Mims' Pathogenesis of Infectious Disease, 5th edn, 1999; over 100 articles in learned jls. *Recreations:* family, Leicester City Football Club. *Address:* Department of Veterinary Pathology, University of Edinburgh, Summerhall, Edinburgh EH9 1QH. *T:* (0131) 650 6164.

NASH, David John, RA 1999; sculptor, primarily in wood; Research Fellow, University of Northumbria, since 1999; *b* 14 Nov. 1945; *s* of Lt-Col William Charles Nash and Dora Lillian Nash; *m* 1972, Claire Langdown; two *s. Educ:* Brighton Coll.; Kingston Sch. of Art (Higher DipAD); Chelsea Sch. of Art. Has worked in Blaenau Ffestiniog, 1967–; over 100 solo shows world wide; 80 works in internat. public collections incl. Tate Gall., Guggenheim, NY, Nat. Mus. of Wales and Metropolitan Mus., Japan. Hon. Dr, Art and Design, Kingston, 1998. *Publications:* Wood Primer, 1987; Forms into Time, 1996. *Address:* Capel Rhiw, Blaenau Ffestiniog, Gwynedd, N Wales LL41 3NT.

NASH, Ellison; *see* Nash, T. M. E.

NASH, John Edward; Member, Supervisory Board, Bank Winter AG, Vienna, since 1996; Chairman, S. G. Warburg Bank AG, 1980–87 (Director, 1977–87; Deputy Chairman, 1977–80); *b* 25 June 1925; *s* of Joseph and Madeleine Nash; *m* 1947, Ralda Everard Herring; two *s* two *d. Educ:* Univ. of Sydney (BEc); Balliol Coll., Oxford (BPhil). Teaching Fellow in Economics, Sydney Univ., 1947. Exec. Dir, Samuel Montagu & Co. Ltd, 1956; also Director, 1960–73: British Australian Investment Trust; Montagu Trust Ltd; Midland Montagu Industrial Finance Ltd; Capel Court Corp. (in Melb.); resigned all directorships on appt to Brussels, 1973; Dir of Monetary Affairs, EEC, 1973–77; Director: Reckitt & Colman plc, 1966–73 and 1977–86; S. G. Warburg & Co. Ltd, 1977–86; Mem. Adv. Bd, Bank S. G. Warburg Soditic AG, 1987–94. Dir, Oxford Univ. Business Summer Sch., 1965; Research Fellow, Nuffield Coll., Oxford (part-time), 1966–69. Hon. Treasurer, PEP, 1964–73. Mem. Bd of Trustees, WWF Internat., 1979–92, 1993–94 (Hon. Treas., 1985–92). *Recreations:* golf, horse-racing, music. *Address:* Chalet Gstelli, 3785 Gsteig bei Gstaad, Switzerland. *T:* (33) 7551162, *Fax:* (33) 7551132. *Clubs:* Turf, MCC; University (Sydney).

NASH, Philip; Commissioner of Customs and Excise, 1986–90; *b* 14 March 1930; *s* of late John Hollett Nash and Edith Grace Nash (*née* Knee); *m* 1953, Barbara Elizabeth Bangs; one *s. Educ:* Watford Grammar School. National Service, RAF, 1949–50. HM Customs and Excise, 1950–90; on loan to Civil Service College, 1970–73; Asst Sec. and Head of Management Services, 1978–81; Asst Sec., Customs Directorate, 1981–86; Director, Customs, 1986–90. *Recreation:* family history. *Address:* Nutwood, 37 Lower Golf Links Road, Broadstone, Dorset BH18 8BQ. *T:* (01202) 601898.

NASH, Ronald Peter, LVO 1983; HM Diplomatic Service; Ambassador to Nepal, since 1999; *b* 18 Sept. 1946; *s* of John Henry Nash and Jean Carmichael Nash (*née* McIlwraith); *m* 1976, Annie Olsen; three *s. Educ:* Harefield Secondary Modern Sch.; Southall Tech. Sch.; Southall Grammar Tech. Sch.; Manchester Univ. (BA Hons). MIL 1991. FCO, 1970; Moscow, 1974–76; UK Delegn to MBFR, Vienna, 1976–79; FCO, 1979–83; New Delhi, 1983–86; FCO, 1986–87; Dep. Hd of Mission, Vienna, 1988–92; Dep. High Comr, Colombo and (non-res.) Malé, 1992–95; Co-ordinator, Peace Implementation Conf. for Bosnia, 1995; Review of Africa Develt Prog., ODA, 1996; Hd, Human Rights Policy Dept, FCO, 1996–99. Chm. Bd Dirs, Overseas Children's Sch., Colombo, Sri Lanka, 1994–95. *Address:* c/o Foreign and Commonwealth Office, SW1A 2AH. *Club:* Chesham 1879 Lawn Tennis and Squash.

NASH, Stephen Thomas, CMG 2000; HM Diplomatic Service; Ambassador to Latvia, 1999–March 2002; *b* 22 March 1942; *s* of Thomas Gerald Elwin Nash and Gwendolen Selina Nash (*née* Osmaston); *m* 1st, 1967, Rosemarie Bornstrand (marr. diss.); one *s*; 2nd, 1977, Boonying Permkasikam; one *s* three *d. Educ:* Cheltenham Coll.; Pembroke Coll., Cambridge (MA Econs and History); Sch. of Oriental and African Studies (Arabic Studies); Queen's Coll., Oxford (MA Ethnology). Asst Dir, British Council, Baghdad, 1965–67; FCO 1967; served Caracas, Bogotá, Bangkok (SEATO), Guatemala; Dep. High Comr, Belmopan, 1981–82; Head, Indo-China Section, FCO, 1984–86; Chargé d'Affaires, Managua, 1986–88; seconded to British Aerospace, 1989–91; EC Monitor Mission to former Yugoslavia, Zagreb, 1991; Chargé d'Affaires, Tirana, 1993–95; Ambassador to Georgia, 1995–98; Ambassador to Albania, 1998–99. *Recreations:* ski-ing, languages, gardening, viola-playing. *Address:* c/o Foreign and Commonwealth Office, King Charles Street, SW1A 2AH. *Club:* Arts.

NASH, (Timothy Michael) Ellison; His Honour Judge Nash; a Circuit Judge, since 1994; *b* 10 Dec. 1939; *s* of late Denis Frederick Ellison Nash, OBE, AE, FRCS and Joan Mary Andrew; *m* 1965, Gael Nash; one *s* one *d* (and two *s* decd). *Educ:* Dulwich Coll.; St Bartholomew's Hosp. Called to the Bar, Gray's Inn, 1964; Standing Counsel: DHSS, 1974–79; DTI, 1976–91; Asst Recorder, 1987–89; Recorder, 1990–94. Legal Assessor, GMC and Royal Dental Council, 1989–94; Chm., Home Office Police Appeal Tribunals, 1988–94. Metropolitan Police Special Constabulary, 1961–83. Examr, Dio. of Canterbury, 1990–94. *Recreation:* walking round in ever-increasing circles. *Address:* The Law Courts, Chaucer Road, Canterbury, Kent CT1 1ZA.

NASH, Ven. Trevor Gifford; Executive Co-ordinator, Advisers for Churches' Ministry of Healing in England, 1990–97 (Adviser, 1973–97); Hon. Chaplain, Winchester Cathedral, since 1998; *b* 3 May 1930; *s* of Frederick Walter Gifford Nash and Elsie Violet Louise Nash; *m* 1957, Wanda Elizabeth (*née* Freeston); four *d*. *Educ:* Haileybury College, Hertford; Clare Coll., Cambridge (MA); Cuddesdon Coll., Oxford. Curate: Cheshunt, 1955–57; Kingston-upon-Thames, 1957–61; Priest-in-Charge, Stevenage, 1961–63; Vicar, Leagrave, Luton, 1963–67; Senior Chaplain, St George's Hosp. Gp, London, 1967–73; Rector, St Lawrence with St Swithun, Winchester, 1973–82; Priest-in-Charge, Holy Trinity, Winchester, 1977–82; RD of Winchester, 1978–82; Archdeacon of Basingstoke, 1982–90, Archdeacon Emeritus, 1990; Hon. Canon of Winchester, 1980–. Pres., Guild of Health, 1993–97; Warden, Guild of St Raphael, 1995–98. RAChD (TA), 1956–61. *Recreations:* painting, music, walking. *Address:* The Corner Stone, 50B Hyde Street, Winchester, Hants SO23 7DY. *T:* (01962) 861759.

NASHA, Margaret Nnananyana, (Mrs Lawrence Nasha); MP (Democratic Party), Botswana, since 1994; *b* 6 Aug. 1947; *d* of Sadinyana and Motlatshiping Ramontshonyana; *m* 1975, Lawrence Nasha; four *s*. *Educ:* Univ. of Botswana (BA 1976). Several posts as broadcaster, 1968–84; Dir of Information and Broadcasting, Botswana, 1985–89; High Comr in UK, 1989–93. *Recreations:* leisure walks, tennis. *Address:* PO Box 917, Gaborone, Botswana.

NASMITH, Sir James Duncan D.; *see* Dunbar-Nasmith.

NASMYTH, Dr Kim Ashley, FRS 1989; Director, Institute of Molecular Pathology, Vienna, since 1997 (Senior Scientist, 1987–96); *b* 18 Oct. 1952; *s* of James Nasmyth and Jenny Hughes; *m* 1982, Anna Dowson; two *d*. *Educ:* Eton Coll.; York Univ. (BA); Edinburgh Univ. (PhD). Jane Coffin Childs Postdoctoral Fellow, Dept of Genetics, Univ. of Washington, 1978–80; Robertson Fellow, Cold Spring Harbor Lab., NY, 1980–81; Staff Mem., MRC Lab. of Molecular Biol., Cambridge, 1982–87; Unofficial Fellow, King's Coll., Cambridge, 1984–87. Hon. Prof., Univ. of Vienna, 1995–. MAE 1993; Member: EMBO, 1985; Austrian Acad. of Scis, 1999; Foreign Hon. Mem., Amer. Acad. of Arts and Scis, 1999. *Recreations:* climbing, ski-ing. *Address:* Institute of Molecular Pathology, Dr Bohr Gasse 7, 1030 Vienna, Austria. *T:* (1) 79730880; (home) Sonnenfelsgasse 5/13, 1010 Vienna, Austria. *T:* (1) 5124821.

NASON, Justin Patrick Pearse, OBE 1980; HM Diplomatic Service, retired; *b* 29 March 1937; *s* of John Lawrence Nason and Catherine Agnes (*née* McFadden); *m* 2000, Jeannine Dubois. *Educ:* Ampleforth; University Coll., Oxford. National Service, RAF, 1956–58. BICC, 1962–63; entered HM Foreign Service, 1963; FO, 1964–65; Prague, 1965–67; FCO, 1967–71; First Sec., Pretoria and Cape Town, 1971–74; Head of Chancery, Saigon, 1974–75; FCO, 1975–79; Head of Chancery, Kampala, 1979–81; Nat. Defence Coll. of Canada, 1981–82; Dep. High Comr, Colombo, 1982–85; Barclays Bank (on secondment), 1986–87; Minister Counsellor, Mexico City, 1988–90; temp. duty, Accra, 1990–91; Ambassador to Guatemala, 1991–95. *Recreation:* golf. *Club:* Oxford and Cambridge.

NASSAU, Bishop of; *see* West Indies, Archbishop of.

NATHAN, family name of **Baron Nathan**.

NATHAN, 2nd Baron *cr* 1940; **Roger Carol Michael Nathan;** *b* 5 Dec. 1922; *s* of 1st Baron Nathan, PC, TD, and Eleanor Joan Clara (*d* 1972), *d* of C. Stettauer; *S* father, 1963; *m* 1950, Philippa Gertrude, *d* of Major Joseph Bernard Solomon, MC, Pulborough, Sussex; one *s* two *d*. *Educ:* Stowe Sch.; New Coll., Oxford (MA). Served War of 1939–45: Capt., 17/21 Lancers (despatches, wounded twice). Admitted Solicitor (Hons), 1950; Senior Partner, Herbert Oppenheimer Nathan & Vandyk, 1978–86; Consultant, Denton Hall Burgin & Warrens, 1989–92. Chm., Arbitration Panel, The Securities Assoc., 1988–92. Hon. Associate Mem., Bar Assoc. of City of New York. FSA; FRSA; FRGS. Pres., Jewish Welfare Board, 1967–71; Chairman: Central British Fund for Jewish Relief and Rehabilitation, 1971–77 (Hon. Pres., 1977–); Exec. Cttee, Cancer Research Campaign (formerly British Empire Cancer Campaign), 1970–75 (Hon. Treasurer, 1979–87); Working Party on Energy and the Envmt (reported 1974); Animal Procedures Cttee, 1990–93; Wkg Party on Efficiency and Effectiveness in Voluntary Sector, 1989–90; Court of Discipline, Cambridge Univ., 1989–92; Vice Chm., Cttee on Charity Law and Practice (reported 1976); Mem., Royal Commn on Envmtl Pollution, 1979–89. Mem., H of L Select Cttee on European Communities, 1983–88 and 1990–92 (Chm., *ad hoc* Sub-Cttee on European Co. Statute, 1989–90; Chm., Sub-Cttee F (Envmt), 1983–87 and 1990–92), on Science and Technology, 1994–99; Chm., H of L Select Cttee on Murder and Life Imprisonment, 1988–89. Chm., RSA, 1975–77, Vice-Pres., 1977–. Chairman: Inst. of Envmtl Assessment, 1990–91; South Downs Conservation Bd, 1992–97; President: UK Envmtl Law Assoc., 1987–92; Nat. Soc. for Clean Air, 1987–89; Soc. of Sussex Downsmen, 1987–92; Weald and Downland Open Air Mus., 1995–97; Mem., Court and Council, Sussex Univ., 1989–98. Chm., City Festival of Flowers, 1964; Master, Worshipful Company of Gardeners, 1963–64. Hon. LLD Sussex, 1988. *Heir:* *s* Hon. Rupert Harry Bernard Nathan, *b* 26 May 1957. *Address:* Collyers Farm, Lickfold, Petworth, West Sussex GU28 9DU. *T:* (01798) 861284. *Clubs:* Athenæum, Cavalry and Guards.

See also Hon. Lady Waley-Cohen.

NATHAN, Sara Catherine; freelance journalist, since 1997; *b* 16 Feb. 1956; *d* of Derek Nathan and Mary Nathan (*née* Lavine); *m* 1984, Malcolm John Singer; one *s* one *d*. *Educ:* New Hall, Cambridge (BA Hons); Stanford Univ., Calif. (Harkness Fellow). News trainee, 1980–82; with BBC news and current affairs, incl. Results Ed., Election prog., 1992, Newsnight, Breakfast Time/News, Money Prog., 1982–93; Editor: The Magazine, BBC Radio 5, 1993–95; Channel 4 News, 1995–97; columnist, The Scotsman, 1999–2000. Lay Mem., Professional Conduct Cttee, Bar Council, 1998–; Member: HFEA, 1998–; Radio Authy, 1999–; Criminal Injuries Compensation Appeals Panel, 2000–; Gambling Rev. Body, 2000–01. Chm., Children's First Commn, Lambeth, 2000–. Mem., BAFTA. FRSA 1998. *Recreations:* working out, learning Hebrew and Yiddish, cinema, embarassing my children. *Address:* 29 Goldsmith Avenue, W3 6HR. *T:* (020) 8992 2318.

NATHAN, Sellapan Ramanathan; President, Republic of Singapore, since 1999; *b* 3 July 1924; *s* of V. Sellapan and Mme Abirami; *m* 1958, Urmila, (Umi), Nandey; one *s* one *d*. *Educ:* Anglo-Chinese Primary and Middle Sch.; Rangoon Rd Afternoon Sch.; Victoria Sch.; Univ. of Malaya in Singapore (Dip. Social Studies with Dist. 1954). Clerical Service, Johore Govt (Malaya), 1945–55; Almoner, Medical Dept, Gen. Hosp., Singapore, 1955–56; Seamen's Welfare Officer, Min. of Labour, 1956–62; Asst Dir, 1962–63, Dir, 1964–66, Labour Res. Unit; Ministry of Foreign Affairs, Singapore: Asst Sec., 1966; Principal Asst Sec., 1966–67; Dep. Sec., 1967–71; Perm. Sec. (Actg), Min. of Home Affairs, 1971; Dir, Security and Intelligence Div., MoD, 1971–79; First Perm. Sec., Min. of Foreign Affairs, 1979–82; Exec. Chm., Straits Times Press, 1982–88; High Comr to Malaysia, 1988–90; Ambassador to USA, 1990–96; Ambassador-at-Large, Min. of Foreign Affairs, 1996–99; Dir, Inst. of Defence and Strategic Studies, Nanyang Technol Univ., 1996–99. Chm., Mitsubishi Singapore Heavy Industries (Pte) Ltd, 1973–86; Director: Singapore Nat. Oil Co. (Pte), 1980–88; Singapore Mint Pte, 1983–88; Singapore Press Hldgs, 1984–88; Marshall Cavendish, London, 1985–88; Singapore Internat. Media Pte, 1996–99. Chm., Hindu Endowments Bd, 1983–88; Mem. Bd of Trustees, NTUC Res. Unit, 1983–88; Founding Mem. and Trustee, Singapore Indian Develt Assoc., 1997–99. Pro-Chancellor, National Univ. of Singapore, 1996–99. Mem., Bd of Govs, CS Coll., 1997–99. Public Service Star (Singapore), 1964; Public Admin Medal (Silver) (Singapore), 1967; PJG (Meritorious Service Medal) (Singapore), 1974. *Recreations:* walking, reading. *Address:* President's Office, Istana, Orchard Road, Singapore 238823. *T:* 7375522.

NATHAN, Stephen Andrew; QC 1993; a Recorder, since 2000; *b* 30 April 1947; *s* of Frederick Emil Nathan and Margot Sophie Jeanette Nathan (*née* Welch); one *d*; *m* 1999, Colleen Toomey; one *s*. *Educ:* Hall Sch., Hampstead; Cranleigh Sch., Surrey (Schol.); New Coll., Oxford (BA Law 1968; MA 1972). Called to the Bar, Middle Temple, 1969; in practice at the Bar, 1970–; Asst Recorder, 1989–2000. Dep. Chm., Guild of Guide Lectrs, 1975–76; Chm., Ponsonby Residents' Assoc., 1995–99. *Recreations:* tennis, swimming, fine cooking. *Address:* Blackstone Chambers, Blackstone House, Temple, EC4Y 9BW. *T:* (020) 7583 1770. *Clubs:* Royal Automobile; Riverside Tennis.

NATHANSON, Vivienne Hillary; Head, Professional Resources and Research Group, British Medical Association, since 1996; *b* 9 March 1955; *d* of Norman Eric Nathanson and Margaret Nathanson (*née* Milman). *Educ:* Birkenhead High Sch., GDST; Middx Hosp. Med. Sch., Univ. of London (MB BS 1978). Med. Registrar, Glan Clwyd Hosp., 1981–84; British Medical Association: mgt trainee, 1984–86; Hd, Med. Ethics and Internat. Affairs, 1987–90; Scottish Sec., 1990–95. *Recreations:* bridge, opera. *Address:* British Medical Association, BMA House, Tavistock Square, WC1H 9JP. *T:* (020) 7383 6111; 36 Aland Court, Finland Street, SE16 7LA.

NATKIEL, Rod; Chair, West Midlands Arts Board, since 1997; Managing Director and Head of Production, Rod Natkiel Associates, since 1999; *b* 30 Jan. 1952; *s* of late Daniel Natkiel and Marjorie Jessie (*née* Pinkham); *m* 1976, Janet Ruth Sawtell; two *s*. *Educ:* Kingston Grammar Sch.; Univ. of Bristol (BA Drama); Univ. of Birmingham (MBA Dist.). Associate Dir and Resident Musical Dir, Contact Th., Manchester, 1975–78; Dir/Producer, TV Light Entertainment, BBC Scotland, 1978–84; freelance Exec. Producer/Producer/Dir in Entertainment, Drama, News and Current Affairs, 1984–92; Prodn Exec., Birmingham Media Develt Agency, 1992–93; Hd of Network Television, BBC Midlands and E, 1992–96; Hd of Network Prodn, BBC Birmingham, 1996–99. Vis. Prof. in TV Studies, Univ. of Central England, 1993–99. Mem., Arts Council of England, 1997–98. Chm., Variety Club Midlands, 1997–2000. *Recreations:* squash, cricket, theatre, cinema, DIY. *Address:* 5 Vesey Road, Sutton Coldfield, W Midlands B73 5NP. *T:* (0121) 355 2197, *Fax:* (0121) 355 8033; *e-mail:* rod.natkiel@btinternet.com.

NATWAR-SINGH, Kanwar; Padma Bhushan, 1984; MP (Congress Party) Bharatpur, since 1998; Union Minister of State for Foreign Affairs, India, 1986–89; *b* 16 May 1931; *s* of Govind Singh and Prayag Kaur; *m* 1967, Princess Heminder Kumari, *e d* of late Maharaja Yadvindra Singhji of Patiala; one *s* one *d*. *Educ:* St Stephen's Coll., Delhi Univ. (1st cl. hons History 1951); Corpus Christi Coll., Cambridge, 1952–54. Joined Indian Foreign Service, 1953; 3rd Sec., Peking, 1956–58; Under Sec., Ministry of External Affairs, and Private Sec. to Sec. General, 1958–61; Adviser, Indian Delegn to UN, NY, 1961–66; Rapporteur, UN Cttee on Decolonisation, 1962–66; Rapporteur, UN Trusteeship Council, 1965; Alt. Deleg. of India to UN Session for 1962; Rep. of India on Exec. Bd of UNICEF, NY, 1962–66; Dep. Sec. to Prime Minister of India, 1966–67; Dir, Prime Minister's Secretariat, New Delhi, 1967–70; Jt Sec. to Prime Minister, 1970–71; Ambassador to Poland, 1971–73; Dep. High Comr in London, 1973–77; High Comr for India in Zambia and Botswana, 1977–80; Ambassador to Pakistan, 1980–82; Sec., Min. of External Affairs, India, 1982–84; Minister of State for Steel, 1984–85, for Fertilizers, 1985–86. Attended Commonwealth Heads of Govt Meetings: Jamaica, 1975; Lusaka, 1979; Member: Commonwealth Cyprus Cttee, 1977; Indian Delegn to Zimbabwe Indep. Celebrations, 1980; Sec.-Gen., 7th Non-Aligned Summit, New Delhi, 1983; Chief Co-ordinator, Commonwealth Heads of State and Govt Meeting, New Delhi, 1983; Pres., UN Conf. on Disarmament and Develt, 1987; Leader, Indian Delegn to 42nd Session of UN Gen. Assembly, 1987. Dir, Air India, 1982–84. Executive Trustee: UNITAR, 1981–; Jawaharlal Nehru Meml Fund, 1986. Pres., All India Tennis Fedn, 1988. Hon. Res. Fellow, UCL. E. M. Forster Literary Award, 1989. *Publications:* E. M. Forster: A Tribute, 1964; The Legacy of Nehru, 1965; Tales from Modern India, 1966; Stories from India, 1971; Maharaja Suraj Mal, 1707–1763, 1981; Curtain Raisers, 1984; Profiles and Letters, 1997; Magnificent Maharaja, 1998; writes and reviews for national and international papers. *Recreations:* tennis, reading, writing, walking, good conversations followed by prolonged periods of reflective uninterrupted silence. *Address:* 1 Akbar Road, New Delhi 110001, India. *Fax:* (11) 3011102, 6881331. *Clubs:* Garrick, Royal Over-Seas League (Life Mem.); India International Centre (Life Mem.), Gymkhana (Life Mem; Pres., 1984) (Delhi).

NAUGHTIE, (Alexander) James; journalist and broadcaster; Presenter, Today, BBC Radio 4, since 1994; *b* 9 Aug. 1951; *s* of Alexander and Isabella Naughtie; *m* 1986, Eleanor Updale; one *s* two *d*. *Educ:* Keith Grammar Sch.; Aberdeen Univ. (MA Hons); Syracuse Univ., New York (MA). The Press and Journal, 1975–77; The Scotsman, 1977–84; The Guardian, 1984–88, Chief Political Corresp., 1985–88; Presenter: The World at One, BBC Radio 4, 1988–94; Opera News, BBC Radio 3, 1990–93; BBC Proms, 1992–; Bookclub, BBC Radio 4, 1998–. Laurence M. Stern Fellow, Washington Post, 1981. Mem. Council, Gresham Coll., 1997–. Hon. LLD Aberdeen, 1990. Personality of the Year, Sony Radio Awards, 1991. *Publications:* (ed) Playing the Palace: a Westminster collection, 1984; The Rivals: the intimate story of a political marriage, 2001; contribs to newspapers, magazines, journals. *Recreations:* books, opera. *Address:* BBC News Centre, W12 8QT. *Clubs:* Travellers, Garrick.

NAUGHTON, Philip Anthony; QC 1988; *b* 18 May 1943; *s* of Francis and Madeleine Naughton; *m* 1968, Barbara, *d* of Prof. F. E. Bruce; two *s* one *d*. *Educ:* Wimbledon Coll.; Univ. of Nottingham (LLB). Called to the Bar, Gray's Inn, 1970, Bencher, 1997. Marketing and public relations posts with BP Chemicals Ltd and Air Products Ltd,

1964–71; commenced practice as barrister, 1971. *Recreations:* walking with friends, sailing without them. *Address:* 3 Serjeants' Inn, EC4Y 1BQ. *T:* (020) 7353 5537.

NAVARRETE, Jorge Eduardo; Mexican Under-Secretary (Vice-Minister) for Energy, since 1995; Member of South Commission; *b* 29 April 1940; *s* of late Gabriel Navarrete and Lucrecia López; *m* 1st, 1962, María Antonieta Linares (marr. diss. 1973); one *s*; 2nd, 1976, María de Navarrete (*d* 1985); 3rd, 1987, Angeles Salceda (marr. diss. 1994); 4th, 1996, Martha López. *Educ:* Nat. Sch. of Economics, Nat. Autonomous Univ. of Mexico (equivalent BA Econ.); post-graduate studies in internat. economy. Center for Latin American Monetary Studies, Mexico, 1963–65; Nat. Foreign Trade Bank, Mexico, 1966–72; joined Mexican Foreign Service, 1972; Ambassador to: Venezuela, 1972–75; Austria, 1976–77; Yugoslavia, 1977–79; Dep. Perm Rep. to UN, NY, 1979; Under Sec. (Economics), Min. of Foreign Affairs, Mexico, 1979–85; Ambassador: to UK and Republic of Ireland, 1986–89; to China, 1989–93; to Chile, 1993–95. Holds decorations from Argentina, Brazil, Ecuador, Federal Republic of Germany, Italy, Panama, Poland, Sweden, Venezuela. *Publications:* The International Transfer of Technology (with G. Bueno and M. S. Wionczeck), 1969; Mexico's Economic Policy, 2 vols, 1971, 1972; Cancun 1981: the international meeting on co-operation and development, 1982; The External Debt of Latin America: issues and policies, 1987; numerous essays on Mexican and Latin American economic issues, in Mexican and foreign jls. *Recreation:* chess. *Address:* Farallón 121-A, 01900 Mexico City, Mexico.

NAVRATILOVA, Martina; tennis player; *b* Prague, 18 Oct. 1956; *d* of Jana Navratilova. Left Czechoslovakia, 1975; adopted American nationality, 1981. Professional player, 1975–94. Has won 167 singles and 167 doubles titles, including 18 Grand Slam singles titles (a record 9 Wimbledon singles wins) and 37 Grand Slam doubles titles. Pres., Women's Tennis Assoc., 1979–80, 1994–95. *Publications:* Martina (autobiog.), 1985; The Total Zone (novel), 1994; Breaking Point, 1996. *Address:* c/o International Management Group, 1 Erieview Plaza, Cleveland, OH 44114, USA.

NAYAR, Kuldip; syndicated columnist; Mem., Rajya Sabha, since 1999; President: Citizens for Democracy; Transparency International; *b* 14 Aug. 1924; *m* 1949, Bharti; two *s*. *Educ:* Northwestern Univ., USA (BA Hons, LLB, MSc in journalism; Hon. PhD(Phil.) 1998; Alumni Award, 1999). Press Officer to Home Minister, India, 1954–56, to Prime Minister, India, 1960–64; Editor and General Manager, United News of India, 1964–67; Delhi Editor, The Statesman, 1967–75; Editor, Indian Express News Service, 1975–81; syndicated columnist, 1981–; correspondent, The Times, London, 1968–89; High Comr in UK, 1990. Mem., Indian delegn to UN Gen. Assembly, 1996. Numerous journalism and public service awards. *Publications:* Between the Lines, 1967; India: the critical years, 1968; The Supersession of Judges, 1971; Distant Neighbours, 1972; India After Nehru, 1974; The Judgement, 1977; In Jail, 1979; A report on Afghanistan, 1982; The Tragedy of Punjab, 1985; India House, 1992; The Martyr Bhagat Singh: experiments in revolution, 2000. *Recreations:* music (Indian and Western); cricket, hockey. *Address:* D7/2 Vasant Vihar, New Delhi 110057, India.

NAYLER, Georgina Ruth; Director, Pilgrim Trust, since 1996; *b* 16 March 1959; *d* of Dennis Nayler and Yvonne (*née* Loader); partner, Simon Stillwell; one *s* one *d*. *Educ:* Brentwood County High Sch. for Girls; Univ. of Warwick (BA). Joined Nat. Heritage Meml Fund, 1982: Asst Dir, 1987–88; Dep. Dir, 1988–89; Dir, 1989–95. Mem., Historic Bldgs Council for Scotland, 1990–96. *Recreations:* gardening, interior decorating, collecting china and watercolours. *Address:* c/o The Pilgrim Trust, Cowley House, 9 Little College Street, SW1P 3XS.

NAYLOR, Bernard; University Librarian, Southampton University, 1977–2000; President, Library Association, 2001–March 2002; *b* 7 May 1938; *s* of William Edward Naylor and Lilian Naylor (*née* Oakes); *m* 1967, Frances Gemma Trenaman; four *s* one *d*. *Educ:* Balliol Coll., Oxford (BA 1963; MA 1965); Sch. of Librarianship and Archive Administration, University Coll. London (Dip. Lib. 1966). ALA 1969. Asst, Foreign Accessions Dept, Bodleian Liby, 1964–66; Librarian and Bibliographer, Univ. of London Inst. of Latin American Studies, 1966–74; Sec., Library Resources Co-ordinating Cttee, Univ. of London, 1974–77; Co-ordinator of Inf. Services, 1988–93, of Acad. Support Services, 1998–2000, Southampton Univ. Member: British Liby Adv. Cttee on Lending Services, 1978–86 (Chm., 1981–85); Council, Standing Conf. of Nat. and Univ. Libraries, 1979–82, 1984–90 (Vice-Chm., 1984–86; Chm., 1986–88); British Council Libraries Adv. Cttee, 1982–96 (Chm., 1986–95); British Liby Bd, 1995–2001. Chm., Hants Area Tech. Res. Indust. Commercial Service Exec., 1981–2000. Gov., La Sainte Union Coll., Southampton, 1996–97. FRSA 1997. Mem., British Council, 1995. *Publications:* Accounts of Nineteenth Century South America, 1969; Directory of Libraries and Special Collections on Latin America and the West Indies, 1975; articles in liby jls. *Recreations:* playing the piano (in private), making wine, learning foreign languages. *Address:* 12 Blenheim Avenue, Highfield, Southampton SO17 1DU. *T:* (023) 8055 4697.

NAYLOR, (Charles) John, OBE 1993; Secretary and Treasurer, Carnegie United Kingdom Trust, since 1993; *b* 17 Aug. 1943; *s* of late Arthur Edgar Naylor, MBE and Elizabeth Mary Naylor; *m* 1968, Margery Thomson; two *s*. *Educ:* Royal Grammar Sch., Newcastle upon Tyne; Haberdashers' Aske's Sch., Elstree; Clare Coll., Cambridge (MA History). Jun. and sen. exec. posts in industry, 1965–75; Dir, YMCA National Centre, Lakeside, Cumbria, 1975–80; Dep. National Sec., 1980–82, Nat. Sec., 1982–93, National Council of YMCAs; mem. and chm. of YMCA European and world cttees, 1976–92. Vice-Chm., Nat. Council for Voluntary Youth Services, 1985–88; Mem., Nat. Adv. Council for Youth Service, 1985–88. Chairman: Assoc. of Heads of Outdoor Educn Centres, 1979–80; MSC and DES Working Party on Residential Experience and Unemployment, 1980–81; Mem., Scottish Charity Law Review Commn, 2000–01. Chm., Brathay Exploration Gp, 1995–; Trustee, The Tomorrow Project, 2000–. CIMgt; FRSA. *Publications:* contribs on youth, outdoors and grant making to UK periodicals and books. *Recreations:* the outdoors (partic. the mountains), theatre, church. *Address:* Carnegie UK Trust, Comely Park House, Dunfermline, Fife KY12 7EJ. *T:* (office) (01383) 721445.

NAYLOR, Maj.-Gen. David Murray, CB 1992; MBE 1972; DL; Director-General, Territorial Army and Organisation, Ministry of Defence, 1989–92; *b* 5 March 1938; *s* of Thomas Humphrey Naylor and Dorothy Isobel Durning Naylor (*née* Holt); *m* 1965, Rosemary Gillian Hicks Beach; three *s*. *Educ:* Eton Coll. psc, rcds. Joined Scots Guards, 1956; commnd as National Service and later as Regular Officer; commanded: 2nd Bn Scots Guards, 1976–79; 22nd Armoured Bde, 1982–83; Dep. Mil. Sec. (A), 1985–87; GOC NE Dist and Comdr 2nd Inf. Div., 1987–89. Chm., N Yorks Ambulance Service NHS Trust, 1992–97. Mem. (C), N Yorks CC, 1997–. Gov., St Peter's Sch., York, 1991– (Chm. of Govs, 2000–). DL N Yorks, 1994. *Publication:* Among Friends: Scots Guards 1956–1993, 1995. *Recreations:* shooting, walking, tennis, travel. *Address:* Minster Hill, Huttons Ambo, York YO60 7HJ. *T:* (01653) 695008; *e-mail:* cllr.m.naylor@wycc.btinternet.com. *Clubs:* Boodle's, Cavalry and Guards.

NAYLOR, Prof. Ernest, OBE 1998; PhD, DSc; Lloyd Roberts Professor of Marine Zoology (formerly Lloyd Roberts Professor of Zoology), 1982–96, now Professor Emeritus; and Head of School of Ocean Sciences, 1992–96, University College of North Wales, Bangor; *b* 19 May 1931; *s* of Joseph and Evelyn Naylor; *m* 1956, Carol Gillian Bruce; two *d*. *Educ:* Swanwick Hall Grammar Sch.; Univ. of Sheffield (BSc); Univ. of Liverpool (PhD, DSc). FIBiol 1972–96. Commnd RAF, 1954–56 (Educn Br.). Successively Asst Lectr, Lectr, Sen. Lectr and Reader in Zoology, University Coll. of Swansea, Wales, 1956–71; Prof. of Marine Biology, Univ. of Liverpool, 1971–82; Dean of Sci., UCNW, Bangor, 1989–91. Visiting Professor: Duke Univ., USA, 1969, 1970; Univ. of Otago, NZ, 1982. Mem., NERC, 1976–82 (Mem., Marine Sci. and Technol. Bd, 1994–96); Specialist Adviser to H of L Select Sub-Cttee on Marine Sci. and Technology, 1985; Indep. Mem., Co-ordinating Cttee on Marine Sci. and Technology, 1988–91; Indep. Assessor, Inter-Agency Cttee on Marine Sci. and Technol., 1991–98; UK Rep., EC Adv. Cttee for Marine Science and Technol., 1989–96. President: Sect. D (Zoology), BAAS, 1982; Estuarine and Coastal Sciences Assoc., 1986–89 (Hon. Life Mem.); Soc. for Expmtl Biology, 1989–91 (Hon. Life Mem.); Mem. Council, Marine Biol Assoc. of UK, 1977–80, 1982–85. *Publications:* British Marine Isopods, 1972; (co-ed with R. G. Hartnoll) Cyclic Phenomena in Marine Plants and Animals, 1979; over 150 papers in learned jls. *Recreations:* travel, gardening. *Address:* School of Ocean Sciences, University of Wales, Bangor, Gwynedd LL59 5EY. *T:* (01248) 382293, *Fax:* (01248) 382612; *e-mail:* e.naylor@bangor.ac.uk.

NAYLOR, John; *see* Naylor, C. J.

NAYLOR, Prof. Malcolm Neville, RD 1967; DL; BSc, BDS, PhD; FDSRCS; Hon. Senior Research Fellow, Institute of Dental Surgery, since 1991; Professor of Preventive Dentistry, University of London, 1970–91, now Professor Emeritus; Head of Department of Periodontology and Preventive Dentistry, Guy's Hospital Dental School, 1980–91; *b* 30 Jan. 1926; *er s* of late Roland B. Naylor, MBE and Mabel L. (*née* Neville), Walsall, Staffs; *m* 1956, Doreen Mary, *d* of late H. E. Jackson, CBE; one *s*. *Educ:* Queen Mary's Sch., Walsall; Univ. of Glasgow; Univ. of Birmingham (BSc 1951, BDS 1955; Nuffield Scholar, 1949–51); Univ. of London (PhD 1963). FDSRCS 1958; Hon. FDSRCPSGlas 1992. Hosp. appts, Birmingham and Dundee, 1955–59; Guy's Hosp. Dental School: Res. Fellow, 1959–62; Sen. Lectr in Preventive Dentistry, 1962–66; Reader in Preventive Dentistry, 1966–70; Hon. Consultant Dental Surgeon, Guy's Hosp., 1966–91, Consultant Emeritus, 1991. William Waldorf Astor Fellow, USA, 1963. President: British Div., IADR, 1990–92 (Hon. Treas., 1975–90); Odontol Sect., RSocMed, 1984–85; Mem., FDI Commn, 1992–95; Trustee and Treas., Oral and Dental Res. Trust, 1992–; Patron, Soc. of Cosmetic Scientists, 1995–. Served RNVR and RNR, retiring as Surg. Captain (D), 1943–76; Civil Consultant Dental Surgeon, RN, 1974–91; Hon. Dental Surgeon to the Queen, 1976; Hon. Col, Univ. of London OTC, 1979–94; Sec., 1978–82, Chm., 1982–89, COMEC; Pres., 50F (Lambeth) Sqn, ATC, 1999–; Chairman: Mil. Educn Cttee, Univ. of London, 1979–; Sea Cadet Assoc., Sports Council, 1975–94; Mem., Services Liaison Cttee, Sussex Univ., 1988–. Governor: Rochampton Inst. for Higher Educn, 1978–96; Whitelands Coll., 1975–96; Bacons Sch., Bermondsey, 1979–90 (Vice Chm., 1981–90); St Saviour's and St Olave's Sch., 1980– (Chm., 1988–); Wye Coll., Univ. of London, 1992–2000; Member: Council of Govs, UMDS, 1987–91; Ct of Govs, Brunel Univ., 1994–98. Trustee: Sino-British Fellowship Trust, 1978– (Dep. Chm., 1995–98; Chm., 1998–); Walter St John Educn Trust, 1991–; Mem., St Saviour's and St Olave's Foundn, 1991– (Warden, 1997–99). Lay Reader, C of E, 1974–. Mem., Southwark Diocesan Synod, 1983–92. Freeman, City of London, 1983; Liveryman, Bakers' Co., 1983. DL Greater London, 1992 (Rep. DL Lambeth, 1994). Hon. FDSRCPSGlas 1992. Colgate Prize, IADR, 1961; Silver Medal, Soc. of Cosmetics Scientists, 1975; Tomes Medal, BDA, 1987. *Publications:* papers and articles in prof. and scientific jls. *Recreations:* off-shore sailing, music, family and home. *Address:* Carrick Lodge, Roehampton, SW15 5BN. *T:* (020) 8788 5045. *Clubs:* Royal Society of Medicine; Royal Naval Sailing Assoc.

NAYLOR, Maurice; *see* Naylor, W. M.

NAYLOR, Peter Brian, CBE 1987; Representative, British Council, Greece, 1983–86; *b* 10 July 1933; *s* of late Eric Sydney Naylor and Phyllis Marian Jolly; *m* 1958, Barbara Pearson (*d* 1995); two *s* one *d* (and one *s* decd). *Educ:* Grange High Sch., Bradford; Selwyn Coll., Cambridge (Open Exhibnr; BA 1957). Wool Top Salesman, Hirsch, Son & Rhodes, Bradford, 1957; British Council: Asst Rep., Bangkok, 1959; Courses Dept and E Europe Dept, London, 1962; Asst Rep., Warsaw, 1967; Reg. Rep., Dacca, E Pakistan, 1969; Actg Rep., Athens, 1971; Rep., Argentina, 1972, Brazil, 1975; Controller, European Div., 1978–83. *Publication:* contrib. Blood Sweat and Tears, 1992. *Recreations:* reading, writing, drawing, looking. *Address:* 3 Farmadine Court, Saffron Walden, Essex CB11 3HT. *T:* (01799) 527708. *Club:* Saffron Walden Golf.

NAYLOR, Robert Antony; Chief Executive, University College London Hospitals NHS Trust, since 2000; *b* 13 Nov. 1949; *s* of Francis Thomas Naylor and Kathleen Mary (*née* Donellan); *m* 1974, Jane Karen Evans; one *s* one *d*. *Educ:* Presentation Coll., Reading; Thames Poly. (BSc Hons Chem. London). Grad. mgt trainee, King's Fund, 1972–74; Hosp. Sec., National Hosp., Queen Sq., 1974–77; Dist Administrator, Enfield HA, 1977–84; Chief Exec., Birmingham Heartlands and Solihull NHS Trust, 1984–2000. Proprietor, Henley Hotel, 1988–2001. *Recreations:* golf, scuba diving. *Address:* 5 Park Village West, Regent's Park, NW1 4AE. *T:* (020) 7380 9634; *e-mail:* robert.naylor@uclh.org.

NAYLOR, (William) Maurice, CBE 1973; FIHM; JP; Director, National Association of Health Authorities, 1981–84; *b* 20 Dec. 1920; *s* of Thomas and Agnes Naylor; *m* 1948, Maureen Ann, *d* of John and Mary Walsh; one *s* two *d*. *Educ:* St Joseph's Coll., Market Drayton; Manchester Univ. (BA Admin). FIHM (FHSM 1956, Hon. FHSM 1987). War service, 1941–46, RA (FE, POW, 1942–45). Parly Asst, Town Clerk's Office, Manchester, 1950–55; Asst Sec., Manchester RHB, 1955–57; Dep. Sec., 1957–63, Sec., 1963–73, Sheffield RHB; Regl Administrator, Trent RHA, 1973–81. Institute of Health Services Management: Mem., Nat. Council, 1966–86; Chm., 1974; Pres., 1975–76; Chm. Educn Cttee, 1980–86. Member: Cttee on Hosp. Supplies Orgn, 1969; Steering Cttee on Reorgn of NHS, 1973–74; Chm., Patient Transport Services Working Party, 1981; Cornwall AHA, 1982–84. Trustee, NHS Pensioners Trust, 1991–99. Hon. MBA Sheffield, 1982. *Publications:* (contrib.) Challenges for Change, 1971; Organisation of Area Health Services, 1972; (contrib. and Chm., Editl Cttee) Health Care in the United Kingdom: its organisation and management, 1982; contrib. to professional jls. *Address:* 7 Hewitt Drive, Kirby Muxloe, Leicester LE9 2EB. *T:* (0116) 239 2606.

NAYLOR-LEYLAND, Sir Philip (Vyvian), 4th Bt *cr* 1895, of Hyde Park House; Chairman, Milton (Peterborough) Estates Co.; Director: Nantclwyd Farms Ltd; Fitzwilliam Peterborough Properties; Milton Gate Development Co.; *b* 9 Aug. 1953; *s* of Sir Vivyan Edward Naylor-Leyland, 3rd Bt and Hon. Elizabeth Anne Fitzalan-Howard, *yr d* of 2nd Viscount FitzAlan of Derwent, OBE (she *m* 2nd, Sir Stephen Hastings, *qv*, and *d* 1997); *S* father, 1987; *m* 1980, Lady Isabella Lambton, *d* of Viscount Lambton, *qv*; four *s* two *d*. *Educ:* Eton; RMA Sandhurst; NY Univ. Business Sch.; RAC Cirencester. 2nd Lieut, Life Guards, 1973, Lieut, 1975–76. Chm., Peterborough Royal Foxhound Show

Soc., 1995– (Vice-Chm., 1988–95); Pres., Nat. Coursing Club, 1988–. Jt Master, Fitzwilliam Hunt, 1987–. *Heir: s* Thomas Philip Naylor-Leyland, *b* 22 Jan. 1982. *Address:* Milton, Peterborough PE6 7AA; Nantclwyd Hall, Ruthin, Denbighshire LL15 2PR. *Clubs:* White's; Air Squadron; Sunningdale Golf.

NAYSMITH, (John) Douglas, PhD; MP (Lab and Co-op) Bristol North West, since 1997; *b* 1 April 1941; *s* of late James Naysmith and Ina (*née* Vass); *m* 1966, Caroline (separated), *d* of Sidney Hill and late Kate Hill; one *s* one *d*. *Educ:* Musselburgh Burgh Sch.; George Heriot's Sch., Edinburgh; Edinburgh Univ. (BSc, PhD). CBiol 1989, FIBiol 1999. Res. Asst, Edinburgh Univ., 1966–69; Fellow, Yale Univ., 1969–70; Res. Immunologist, Beecham Res. Labs, 1970–72; University of Bristol: Res. Associate, 1972–76; Fellow, 1976–81; Lectr in Immunology, Dept of Pathology, 1981–95; Administrator, Registrar's Office, 1995–97. FRSocMed 1980. *Address:* House of Commons, SW1A 0AA.

NAZARETH, Gerald Paul, GBS 2000; CBE 1985 (OBE 1976); **Hon. Mr Justice Nazareth;** a Non-Permanent Judge, Hong Kong Court of Final Appeal, since 1997; Justice, Bermuda Court of Appeal, since 2001; *b* 27 Jan. 1932; *s* of Vincent Lionel Nazareth and Lily Isabel Monteiro; *m* 1959, Elba Maria Fonseca; three *d*. *Educ:* Nairobi; St Xavier's College, Bombay; LLB Bombay Univ. Called to the Bar, Lincoln's Inn, 1962. Public Prosecutor, and Senior Crown Counsel, Kenya, 1954–63; Solicitor General, British Solomon Islands, 1963–73; Attorney General and Legal Advisor, Western Pacific High Commn, 1973–76; Hong Kong: Law Draftsman, 1976–84; MLC, 1979–84; QC, 1982; Judge of the High Court, 1985–91; Justice of Appeal, 1991–2000 and Vice-Pres., 1994–2000, Court of Appeal. Comr, Supreme Court, Brunei, 1989–93. Member: Law Reform Commn, Hong Kong, 1982–84 (Chm., Sub-Cttee on Copyright Law, 1987–92); Wkg Gp on Sino-British Jt Declaration on Hong Kong, Beijing, 1984. Vis. Fellow, ANU, 1972. Vice-Pres., Commonwealth Assoc. of Legislative Counsel, 1983–90. *Recreations:* music, reading, walking. *Address:* 40 York Avenue, SW14 7LG. *T:* (020) 8274 0730.

NAZIR-ALI, Rt Rev. Dr Michael; *see* Rochester, Bishop of.

NDUNGANE, Most Rev. Winston Hugh Njongonkulu; *see* Cape Town, Archbishop of.

NEAGLE, Lynne; Member (Lab) Torfaen, National Assembly for Wales, since 1999; *b* Merthyr Tydfil, 18 Jan. 1968; *m* 1996, Huw George Lewis, *qv*. *Educ:* Cyfarthfa High Sch., Merthyr Tydfil; Reading Univ. (BA Hons French and Italian). Vol. Housing Rights Worker, Shelter Cymru, 1991–93; Inf. Project Officer, Mid Glam Assoc. of Voluntary Orgns, 1993–94; Res. Asst to Glenys Kinnock, MEP, 1994–97; Carers Develt Officer, Voluntary Action Cardiff, 1997–99. *Recreations:* cinema, reading, swimming. *Address:* (office) 35A Commercial Street, Pontypool, Torfaen NP4 6JQ.

NEAL, Prof. Bernard George, MA, PhD, ScD; FREng; Emeritus Professor, since 1982 and Fellow, since 1986, Imperial College, London University (Professor of Applied Science, 1961–72, of Engineering Structures, 1972–81, of Civil Engineering, 1981–82, and Head of Civil Engineering Department, 1976–82); *b* 29 March 1922; *s* of late Horace Bernard Neal, Wembley, and Hilda Annie Webb; *m* 1948, Elizabeth Ann, *d* of late William George Toller, Woodbridge, and Bertha Catharine Toller; one *s* one *d*. *Educ:* Merchant Taylors'; Trinity College, Cambridge (Schol.). MA Cantab, 1947; PhD Cantab 1948; ScD Cantab 1965; FInstCE 1960; FIStructE 1966; FREng (FEng 1980). Temp. Experimental Officer, Admiralty, 1942–45; Research Student, Univ. of Cambridge, 1945–48; Research Associate, Brown University, USA, 1948–49; Demonstrator, 1949–51, Lecturer, 1951–54, Univ. of Cambridge; Research Fellow, 1947–50, Staff Fellow, 1950–54, Trinity Hall, Cambridge; Prof. of Civil Engineering, University Coll. of Swansea, 1954–61. Pro-Rector, Imperial Coll., London, 1972–74. Dean of City and Guilds Coll., 1964–67; Visiting Prof., Brown Univ., USA, 1959–60. Pres., Welding Inst., 1998–2000 (Chm., Res. Bd, 1974–98; Hon. FWeldI 1996). Vice-Pres., Croquet Assoc., 1995–. Telford Premium, 1951, Manby Premium, 1952, Instn Civil Engineers. *Publications:* The Plastic Methods of Structural Analysis, 1956; Structural Theorems and their Applications, 1964; technical papers on theory of structures, strength of materials. *Recreations:* lawn tennis, croquet. *Address:* Moat Cottage, Kidnappers Lane, Cheltenham GL53 0NR. *T:* (01242) 510624. *Clubs:* All England Lawn Tennis and Croquet (Mem. Cttee, 1982–96; Vice-Pres., 1996–), Hurlingham; Cheltenham Croquet (Pres., 1995–).

NEAL, Prof. David Edgar, FRCS; Professor of Surgery, since 1992, and Director, Medical Research, since 1997, University of Newcastle upon Tyne; *b* 9 March 1951; *s* of Norman and Beth Neal; *m* 1972, Deborah Mary Heyworth; three *d*. *Educ:* University Coll. London (BSc 1st Cl. Hons Anatomy; MB BS, MS). FRCS 1980. Tutor and Lectr in Surgery, Univ. of Leeds, 1981–83; First Asst in Urology, 1983–87, Sen. Lectr in Urological Surgery, 1988–92, Consultant Urologist, 1992–, Freeman Hosp., Newcastle upon Tyne. Mem., King's Fund Mgt Cttee, 1996–. Hon. Mem., Urological Soc. Australia, 1999; Corresp. Mem., Amer. Assoc. Genito-urinary Surgeons, 1999. St Peter's Medal, Brit. Assoc. of Urological Surgeons, 2001. *Publications:* Tumours in Urology, 1994; (jtly) Basic Science in Urology, 1999; contrib. articles to The Lancet, Annals Oncol. *Recreations:* playing the classical guitar, maintenance of classic motor cycles. *Address:* Department of Surgery, University of Newcastle upon Tyne, Newcastle upon Tyne NE2 4HH. *T:* (0191) 222 7073.

NEAL, Sir Eric (James), AC 1988; Kt 1982; CVO 1992; Governor, South Australia, since 1996; *b* 3 June 1924; *s* of James and May Neal; *m* 1950, Thelma Joan, *d* of R. E. Bowden; two *s*. *Educ:* South Australian Sch. of Mines. CEng; FIGasE, FAIM. Boral Ltd: Dir, 1972–92; Chief Exec., 1973–87; Man. Dir, 1982–87; Chairman: Atlas Copco Australia Pty Ltd, 1989–96; Metal Manufacturers Ltd, 1990–96 (Dir, 1987–96); Director: Westpac Banking Corp., 1985–92 (Dep. Chm., 1987–88; Chm., 1989–92); John Fairfax Ltd, 1987–88; BHP Co. Ltd, 1988–94; Coca Cola Amatil Ltd, 1987–96. Mem., Australian Adv. Council, Gen. Motors, 1987–94. Mem., Cttee apptd by Fed. Govt to advise on Higher Defence Orgn, 1982. Member: Amer. Bureau of Shipping, 1976–90; Aust. Gas Assoc. (former Mem. Bd); first Nat. Pres., Aust. Inst. of Co. Dirs, 1990–92. Chm. Exec. Cttee, Duke of Edinburgh's Sixth Commonwealth Study Conf. 1986; Nat. Chm., Duke of Edinburgh's Award Scheme in Australia, 1984–92; Internat. Trustee, Duke of Edinburgh's Award Internat. Assoc., 1986–97. Chief Comr, City of Sydney, 1987–88. Hon. FIEAust 1985; Hon. Fellow, Aust. Inst. of Building, 1998; Emeritus Mem., Aust. Inst. of Mgt, 1998. Hon. DEng Sydney, 1989; DUniv S Australia, 1996. *Recreations:* naval history, travel, reading, shipping. *Address:* Government House, Adelaide, SA 5000, Australia. *T:* (8) 82236166. *Clubs:* Melbourne (Melbourne); Union (Sydney).

NEAL, Frederick Albert, CMG 1990; FIL; aviation consultant; UK Representative on Council of International Civil Aviation Organization, Montreal, 1983–93; *b* 22 Dec. 1932; *s* of Frederick William George Neal and Frances Elizabeth (*née* Duke); *m* 1958, Gloria Maria Moirano. *Educ:* Royal Grammar Sch., High Wycombe; Sch. of Slavonic Studies, Cambridge; Birkbeck Coll., London (BA). FIL 1965. Min. of Supply, 1953; Asst Defence Supply Attaché, Bonn, 1958–64; Principal, Min. of Technology (subseq. DTI), 1967; Asst Sec., DTI, 1974; Counsellor (Economic and Commercial), Ottawa, 1975–80; Asst Sec., Dept of Trade, 1980–83. *Recreations:* golf, bridge, music. *Address:* 2 Hambledon Court, 19B Crescent East, Hadley Wood, Herts EN4 0EY. *Clubs:* Royal Over-Seas League; South Herts Golf; Hadley Wood Golf.

NEAL, (Harry) Morton, CBE 1991; FIC; Chairman, Harry Neal (City) Ltd, since 1987; *b* 21 Nov. 1931; *s* of late Godfrey French Neal and Janet Bryce Morton; *m* 1954, Cecilia Elizabeth Crawford, *d* of late Col M. Crawford, DSO; one *s* three *d*. *Educ:* Uppingham Sch.; London Univ. (BSc(Eng)); City and Guilds Coll. (ACGI). Flying Officer, RAF, 1953. Chm., Connaught Hotel Ltd, 1980–94 (Dir, 1966–97); Dir, Savoy Hotel Ltd, 1982–93; Chm., Harry Neal Ltd, 1985–90. Chm., St Anselm Develt Co. Ltd, 1985–. Member of Lloyd's. Chm., City and Guilds of London Inst., 1979–91 (Vice Pres., 1999–); Member: TEC, then BTEC, 1982–94; Court of City Univ., 1982–91; Delegacy, St Mary's Hosp. Med. Sch., 1993–98; Board of Governors: Imperial Coll., London, 1990–; Willesden Tech. Coll., 1983–86; Francis Holland Sch., 1988– (Vice-Chm., 1996–); Management Cttee, Courtauld Inst. of Art, 1983–99. Trustee: Buckminster Estate, 1969–; Samuel Courtauld Trust, 1989–; Prince of Wales Inst. of Architecture, 1991– (Mem., Bd of Advrs, 1993–). Pres., Greater London Mddx W County (formerly NW County) Scout Council, 1983–. Liveryman, Carpenters' Co., 1955– (Master, 1997–98). High Sheriff, Herts, 1999–2000. FCIOB, FRSA; FCGI 1983. Chevalier de Tastevin, 1981. *Recreations:* gardening, shooting. *Address:* Great Sarratt Hall, Sarratt, Rickmansworth, Herts WD3 4PD.

NEAL, Sir Leonard (Francis), Kt 1974; CBE 1971; FCIT; CIPM; Industrial Relations Consultant to number of industrial and commercial companies; *b* 27 Aug. 1913; *s* of Arthur Henry Neal and Mary Neal; *m* 1939, Mary Lilian Puttock; one *s* one *d*. *Educ:* London School of Economics; Trinity College, Cambridge (MA). Labour Manager, Esso, 1956; Employee Relations Manager, Fawley Refinery, 1961; Labour Relations Adviser, Esso Europe Inc. Mem., British Railways Board, 1967–71; Chm., Commn on Industrial Relations, 1971–74. Prof. (part-time) of Industrial Relations, UMIST, 1970–76; Chairman: MAT International Gp Ltd, 1974–85; Employment Conditions Abroad Ltd, 1977–84; Dir (non-exec.), Pilkington Bros, 1976–83. *Publication:* (with A. Robertson) The Managers Guide to Industrial Relations. *Recreations:* reading, gardening, motoring. *Address:* Towcester, Northants.

NEAL, Michael David; Headmaster, Cranborne Chase School, 1969–83; *b* 27 Jan. 1927; *s* of David Neal, FCA; *m* 1952, Barbara Lisette, *d* of late Harold Carter, MA; two *s* two *d*. *Educ:* Winchester; University Coll., Oxford (BA); BSc Open Univ. 1996. Rifle Bde, 1945–48 (Captain); Asst Master, RNC Dartmouth, 1952–54; Eton Coll., 1954–69 (Housemaster, 1963–69). Mem., Eton UDC, 1960–63. *Address:* Wegnall's Mill, Presteigne, Powys LD8 2LD. *T:* (01544) 267012.

NEAL, Morton; *see* Neal, H. M.

NEALE, Sir Gerrard Anthony, (Sir Gerry), Kt 1990; solicitor; Partner, since 1991, Public and Parliamentary Affairs Department, Radcliffes & Co., Solicitors, Westminster; Director, Commercial Law Affiliates, Minnesota; *b* 25 June 1941; *s* of Charles Woodhouse Neale and Phyllis Muriel Neale; *m* 1965, Deirdre Elizabeth McCann; one *s* two *d*. *Educ:* Bedford Sch. Articled to solicitors, Bedford, 1961; admitted 1966. Director: Telephone Rentals, 1979–89; Cupola (UK) plc. Councillor, Borough of Milton Keynes, 1973–79, Mayor, 1976–77. Chm., Buckingham Constituency Cons. Assoc., 1974–76. Contested (C) N Cornwall, Oct. 1974, 1992; MP (C) N Cornwall, 1979–92. PPS to Minister for Consumer Affairs, 1981–82, to Minister of State for Trade, 1981–83, to Sec. of State for Transport, 1985–86, to Sec. of State for the Environment, 1986–87, to Sec. of State for Defence, 1987–89. *Recreations:* sailing, golf. *Address:* Radcliffes, 5 Great College Street, SW1P 3SJ. *T:* (020) 7222 7040.

NEALE, Rt Rev. John Robert Geoffrey, AKC; Hon. Assistant Bishop: Diocese of Bath and Wells, since 1991; Diocese of Gloucester, since 1996; *b* 21 Sept. 1926; *s* of late Geoffrey Brockman Neale and Stella Beatrice (*née* Wild). *Educ:* Felsted Sch.; King's Coll., London Univ. Served War of 1939–45: Lieut RA; Army, 1944–48. Business, G. B. Neale & Co Ltd, EC2, 1948–51. King's Coll. London, 1951–55 (Jelf Prize, 1954). Deacon, 1955, priest, 1956; Curate, St Peter, St Helier, Dio. Southwark, 1955–58. Chaplain, Ardingly Coll., Sx, 1958–63; Recruitment Sec., CACTM (ACCM), 1963–67; Archbishops' Rep. for ordination candidates, 1967–68; Canon Missioner, Dio. Guildford, Hon. Canon of Guildford Cath. and Rector of Hascombe, Surrey, 1968–74; Suffragan Bishop (later Area Bishop) of Ramsbury, 1974–88; Hon. Canon of Salisbury Cathedral, 1974–88; Archdeacon of Wilts, 1974–80; Sec., Partnership for World Mission, 1989–91. FIC 1991. *Publication:* Ember Prayer, 1965. *Recreation:* horticulture. *Address:* 26 Prospect, Corsham, Wilts SN13 9AF. *T:* (01249) 712557.

NEALE, Keith Douglas; County Treasurer, Essex, since 1987; Treasurer: Essex Police Authority, since 1995; Essex Fire Authority, since 1998; *b* 27 March 1947; *s* of Douglas Jeffrey and Dorothy Neale; *m* 1969, Mary Williamson; one *s* one *d*. East Midlands Electricity Board, 1964; Trainee Accountant, Blackwell RDC, 1965; County Treasurer's Dept, Lindsey CC, Lincs, 1968; Asst Dir of Finance, Humberside CC, 1974; Dep. County Treasurer, Essex, 1982. Treasurer: E Anglia Tourist Bd, 1987–96; E of England Tourist Bd, 1996–. Pres., Soc. of County Treasurers, 1998–99 (Hon. Sec., 1991–97; Vice-Pres., 1997–98); Advr, Policy Cttee, ACC, 1993–97. Member: CIPFA (Mem., Pensions (formerly Superannuation) Panel, 1994–); UK Steering Cttee on Local Govt Pensions (formerly Superannuation), 1991–; Cttee, Nat. Assoc. of Pension Funds Investment, 1995–2000; Public Sector and Not-for-Profit Cttee, Accounting Standards Bd, 1999–. Freeman, City of London, 1999. *Address:* County Treasurer's Department, Essex County Council, County Hall, Chelmsford, Essex CM1 1LX. *T:* (01245) 492211.

NEALE, Kenneth James, OBE 1959; FSA; consultant; author and lecturer; Assistant Under Secretary of State, Home Office, 1976–82; *b* 9 June 1922; *s* of late James Edward and Elsie Neale; *m* 1943, Dorothy Willett; three *s* one *d*. *Educ:* Hackney Downs (Grocers') Sch., London. Entered Civil Service as Clerical Officer, Tithe Redemption Commn, 1939. Lieut, RNVR, 1941–46. Exec. Officer, Min. of Nat. Insce, 1947–51; Asst Princ., 1951–55, Principal, 1955–64, Colonial Office; Sec. for Interior and Local Govt, Cyprus, 1957; Dep. Admin Sec., Cyprus, 1958–59; Central African Office, 1962–64; Asst Sec., Commonwealth Office, and Counsellor, Diplomatic Service, 1964–67; Home Office: Asst Sec., 1967–70; Dir, Industries and Supply, 1970–75; Controller, Planning and Develt, 1976–80; Dir, Regimes and Services, 1980–82. Member: Prisons Bd, 1967–69, 1976–82; European Cttee on Crime Problems, 1976–84; Council of Europe Steering Gp on Reform of the Russian Prison System, 1995–; Chairman: Council of Europe Select Cttee on Standard Minimum Rules for Treatment of Prisoners, 1978–80; Council of Europe Cttee for Co-operation in Prison Affairs, 1981–84; Consultant: Council of Europe, 1984–; Open Univ., 1990–93. Chairman: Essex Archaeol and Historical Congress, 1984–87 (Pres., 1987–90); Friends of Historic Essex, 1986–; Member: Council, Essex Soc. for Archaeol. and Hist. (formerly Essex Archaeol Soc.), 1984–87; Library, Museum and Records Cttee, Essex CC, 1986–96; President: Chingford Hist. Soc., 1971–89; Saffron Walden Hist. Soc., 2000–. Mem. Editl Bd, Essex Jl, 1989–. *Publications:* Discovering Essex in London, 1970, 2nd edn 1986; Victorian Horsham, 1975; Work in Penal Institutions, 1976; Essex in History, 1977, 2nd edn 1997; Her Majesty's Commissioners, 1978; (ed) Strategies for Education within Prison Regimes, 1986; (ed) An Essex Tribute, 1987; (contrib.) Imprisonment: European perspectives, 1991; (ed) Essex Heritage, 1992; (ed) Prison Service People, 1993; (ed jtly) Essex Wills 1558–1603, vols 8–12, 1993–2000; (ed) Essex: 'full of profitable thinges', 1996; various articles and papers on local history, natural history, penology. *Recreations:* reading, local history, natural history. *Address:* Honeysuckle Cottage, Great Sampford, Saffron Walden, Essex CB10 2RW. *T:* (01799) 586304.

NEALE, Mark Frost; Director, Children, Poverty and Housing Costs, Department for Work and Pensions, since 2001; *b* 7 July 1957; *s* of Sir Alan (Derrett) Neale, KCB, MBE and Joan Neale (*née* Frost); *m* 1988, Xanthe Waddington Lunghi; one *s* one *d*. *Educ:* Queen's Coll., Oxford (BA 1st Cl. Hons Modern Hist. 1980). CSD, 1980–83; DES, then DFE, 1983–95; HM Treasury, 1995–98; Head, Structural Unemployment Policy Div., DFEE, 1998–2000; Dir, Finance and Commercial and Corporate Services, Employment Service, 2000–01. *Recreation:* playing with the children. *Address:* 14 Belgrave Road, SW13 9NS. *T:* (020) 8741 8887. *Club:* Reform.

NEALE, Michael Cooper, CB 1987; CEng, FIMechE, FRAeS; *b* 2 Dec. 1929; *s* of late Frank and Edith Kathleen Neale; *m* 1956, Thelma Weare; one *s* two *d*. *Educ:* West Bridgford Grammar Sch., Nottingham; Queen Mary Coll., Univ. of London (BScEng, MScEng). Postgraduate research on fuel injection in diesel engines, 1951–53; Engr Officer, Royal Air Force, 1953–56; joined Civil Service, 1956; Aeroplane and Armament Experimental Estabt, Boscombe Down, 1956–58; joined Nat. Gas Turbine Estabt, Pyestock, 1958; Asst Director of Engine Develt, MoD Headquarters, 1971; Dep. Director (R&D), Nat. Gas Turbine Estabt, 1973–80; Dir Gen. Engines (PE), MoD, 1980–87; Sec., Royal Commn for Exhibn of 1851, 1987–94; non-exec. dir of cos and industrial consultant, 1988–96. Silver medallist, RAeS, 1987. *Publications:* papers in Aeronautical Research Council reports and memoranda series and elsewhere in the technical press, mainly concerning engines. *Recreations:* old railways, cricket. *Address:* Quill Cottage, 32 Hound Street, Sherborne, Dorset DT9 3AA. *T:* (01935) 814332. *Clubs:* Athenæum, Royal Over-Seas League; Somerset CC, Dorset CC.

NEALON, Dr Catherina Theresa, (Rina), CBE 1979; JP; Chairman, Lothian Health Board, 1973–81; *d* of John and Margaret O'Reilly, Glasgow; *m* 1940, James Patrick Nealon (*d* 1989); one *s*. *Educ:* Convent of Mercy, Garnethill, Glasgow. Mem., Edinburgh Town Council for Pilton Ward, 1949–74; served as Magistrate Visiting Prisons, 1954–57; Licensing Court, 1954–57; Judge of Police, 1957–62; Chm., Health Cttee, 1972–73. Member: Educn Cttee, Civil Defence Commn, 1949–73; Royal Infirmary and Associated Hosp's Bd of Management, 1952–56; NHS Exec. Council for City of Edinburgh, 1953–74 (Vice-Chm., May 1966–74); Exec. Cttee of Scottish Assoc. of Exec. Councils, 1967–74 (Vice-Pres., 1971, Pres., 1972); SE Regional Hosp. Bd, Scotland, 1966–74 (Chm., 1969–74); Med. Educn Cttee, 1969–74 (Chm., 1972–74); Livingston New Town Jt Health Service Adv. Cttee, 1969–73; Scottish Health Service Planning Council, 1974–81; Common Services Agency, Management Cttee, and Convenor, Estabt and Accommodation Sub-Cttee, Scottish Health Service, 1974–77; Univ. Liaison Cttee, 1974– (Chm., 1978–81); Edinburgh and SE District Cttee, Scottish Gas Consultative Council, 1967–74 (Chm., 1970–74; Mem. Council, 1969–74); Clean Air Council for Scotland, 1966–75; Nat. Soc. for Clean Air, Scottish Div., 1963– (Vice-Pres., 1970–72, Pres., 1972–74); A&C Whitley Council, 1973–81 (Vice-Chm., 1975–81); Nat. Negotiating Cttee; Ambulance Officers' Negotiating Cttee (Management Side Chm., 1979–81); Gen. Whitley Council (Mem., Gen. Purposes Cttee and Jt Negotiating Cttee, 1980–81); Nat. Appeals Panel; SE Dist Cttee, Gas Consumers' Council, 1981–87; Chm., Scottish Hosp. Supplies Steering Cttee, 1972–74. Former Member: Edin. and Lothian Probation Cttee; Animal Disease Res. Assoc.; Edin. Coll. of Art; Royal Blind Asylum and Sch.; Scottish Accident Prevention Council; Marriage Guidance Council; Nat. Assoc. for Maternal and Child Welfare; Nat. Council on recruitment of Nurses and Midwives; Scottish Assoc. for Mental Health; Assoc. of Sea and Airport Authorities; Edin. and Lothians Tourist Assoc.; Youth Employment Cttee; Extra-Mural Cttee, Edin. Univ., 1960–65; Mem. Bd of Governors: Napier Coll. of Science and Technology, 1964–73 (Vice-Chm., 1971–73); Telford Coll. for Further Education, 1969–72; Moray House Coll. of Educn; Wellington Farm Approved Sch.; Dr Guthrie's Girls' Sch. JP Edinburgh, 1957; Mem. Justices Cttee, 1975; Justice on District Court, 1975–83; Mem. Extra-Parliamentary Panel, 1976–86; Mem., Crossroads Cttee, 1987–98. Attended 25th Anniv. Meeting, President's Cttee on Employment of Handicapped, Washington, 1972. Travelled to many countries with Internat. Hosp. Fedn study tours. Member, Church of Scotland. Dr *hc* Edinburgh, 1977. *Recreation:* reading. *Address:* 34 Learmonth Crescent, Edinburgh EH4 1DE. *T:* (0131) 332 6191.

NEAME, Robert Harry Beale, CBE 1999; DL; Chairman, Shepherd Neame Ltd, brewers, since 1971; *b* 25 Feb. 1934; *s* of Jasper Beale Neame and Violet Evelyn Neame; *m* 1st, Sally Elizabeth Corben; one *s* two *d* (and one *s* decd); 2nd, 1974, Yvonne Mary Mackenzie; one *d*. *Educ:* Harrow (Head of School). Joined Shepherd Neame, 1956; Dir, 1957–. SE Regl Dir, National Westminster Bank, 1982–92; Dir, SE Adv. Bd, Royal Insurance Co., 1988–2000; Director: Folkestone Racecourse, 1985– (Chm., 1988–99); Marr Taverns PLC, 1992–96; non-executive Director: Mendocino Brewing Co. (USA), 1998–; Merrydown plc, 1998–. Chairman: SE England Tourist Bd, 1979–90 (Vice-Pres., 1990–); Gatwick Airport Consultative Cttee, 1990–95; Member: SE RHA, 1977–78; Canterbury and Thanet RHA, 1990–94; Inland Waterways Amenities Adv. Council, 1992–98. Chairman, British Section: IULA, 1986–89; CEMR, 1986–89; Vice Chm., Consultative Council of Regl and Local Authorities, 1989. Mem. (C) for Faversham, Kent CC, 1965–89 (Leader, 1982–84). DL 1992, High Sheriff, 2001, Kent. *Recreations:* cricket, squash, rackets (Army Rackets Champion, 1954), golf, shooting, ski-ing. *Address:* Dane Court Farmhouse, Kits Hill, Selling, Faversham, Kent ME13 9QP. *T:* (01227) 752284. *Clubs:* Press; MCC, Free Foresters, I Zingari, Band of Brothers, Butterflies; Kandahar Ski; Escorts, Jesters; Royal St George's Golf (Sandwich).

NEAME, Ronald, CBE 1996; film producer and director; *b* 23 Apr. 1911; *s* of Elwin Neame and Ivy Close; *m* 1933, Beryl Yolanda Heanly (*d* 1999); one *s*. *Educ:* University College School; Hurstpierpoint College. Entered film industry, 1928; became Chief Cameraman, 1934. In charge of production on: In Which We Serve, This Happy Breed, Blithe Spirit, Brief Encounter, 1942–45; produced: Great Expectations, Oliver Twist, The Magic Box; directed: Take My Life, The Card, 1945–51; The Million Pound Note, 1953; The Man Who Never Was, 1954; Windom's Way, 1957; The Horse's Mouth, 1958; Tunes of Glory, 1960; I Could Go On Singing, 1962; The Chalk Garden, 1963; Mr Moses, 1964; Gambit, 1966; The Prime of Miss Jean Brodie, 1968; Scrooge, 1970; The Poseidon Adventure, 1972; Odessa File, 1973; Meteor, 1978; Hopscotch, 1979; First Monday in October, 1980; Foreign Body, 1985; The Magic Balloon, 1989. *Address:* 2317 Kimridge, Beverly Hills, CA 90210, USA. *Club:* Savile.

NEARS, Colin Gray, CBE 1998; television producer; Member of Council, and Chairman of Advisory Panel on Dance, Arts Council of Great Britain, 1982–90; *b* 19 March 1933; *s* of William Charles Nears and Winifred Mildred Nears (*née* Gray). *Educ:* Ipswich Sch.; King's Coll., Cambridge (MA). Admin. Asst, RIBA, 1956; BBC, 1958–87; Producer: Schools Television, 1960; Music and Arts, 1967; Editor, Review, 1971–72. Author and director of programmes on literature, the visual arts, music and dance. Dir, Royal Opera House, 1995–98 (Mem., 1990–98, Dep. Chm., 1991–98, Ballet Bd); Chm., Birmingham Royal Ballet Bd, 1993–99; Gov., Royal Ballet Sch., 1993–2000; Trustee: Royal Ballet Benevolent Fund, 1992–; Dancers' Resettlement Fund, 1991–; Member Board: Riverside Trust, 1991–93; Rambert Dance Co., 1993–2001. FRSA. BAFTA award for Best Specialised Programme, 1973; Prix Italia music prize, 1982. *Recreations:* reading, gardening, painting. *Address:* 16 Ashchurch Terrace, W12 9SL. *T:* (020) 8749 3615.

NEARY, Martin Gerard James, LVO 1998; conductor and organist; Organist and Master of the Choristers, Westminster Abbey, 1988–98; *b* 28 March 1940; *s* of late Leonard Walter Neary and of Jeanne Marguerite (*née* Thébault); *m* 1967, Penelope Jane, *d* of Sir Brian Warren and Dame Josephine Barnes, DBE; one *s* two *d*. *Educ:* HM Chapels Royal, St James's Palace; City of London Sch.; Gonville and Caius Coll., Cambridge (Organ Schol.; MA Theol. and Music). FRCO. Organist, St Mary's, Hornsey Rise, 1958; St Margaret's, Westminster: Asst Organist, 1963–65; Organist and Master of Music, 1965–71; Prof. of Organ, Trinity Coll., London, 1963–72; Organist and Master of Music, Winchester Cathedral, 1972–87. Organ Advr to dio. of Winchester, 1975–87. Conductor, Twickenham Musical Soc., 1966–72; Founder and Conductor: St Margaret's Westminster Singers, 1967–71; English Chamber Singers; Conductor, Waynflete Singers, 1972–88; Dir, Southern Cathedrals Festival, 1972, 1975, 1978, 1981, 1984, 1987; Conductor, Aspen Music Festival, 1980; Guest Conductor, Australian Youth Choir, 1999–; Vis. Artistic Dir, Paulist Boy Choristers of California, 1999–2000. Consultant, Millennium Youth Choir, RSCM, 1999–. President: Cathedral Organists' Assoc., 1985–88; RCO, 1988–90, 1996–98 (Mem. Council, 1982–; a Vice-Pres., 1990–96); Organists' Benevolent League, 1988–; John Carpenter Club, 1997–98; Chairman: Church Services Cttee, Musicians Benevolent Fund, 1993–; Herbert Howells Soc., 1993–. Many organ recitals and broadcasts in UK, incl. Royal Festival Hall; has conducted many premières of music by British composers incl. John Tavener's Ultimos Ritos, 1979, and Akathist, 1988, Jonathan Harvey's Hymn, 1979, and Passion and Resurrection, 1981; with Martin Neary Singers perf. madrigals and graces at 10 Downing Street, 1970–74. Toured US and Canada, 1963, 1968, 1971, 1973, 1975, 1977, 1979, 1982, 1984, 1986, 1988, 1992, 1996, appearances incl. Carnegie Hall, Lincoln Center, Kennedy Center, Roy Thomson Hall; many European tours, including Russia, 1994, Ukraine, 1996; BBC Promenade Concerts; sometime Conductor with: ECO; LSO; BBCSO; Bournemouth SO and Sinfonietta; Acad. of Ancient Music; Winchester Baroque Ensemble; Orch. of the Age of Enlightenment; Arts Council Contemporary Music Network Tour, 1993; many recordings, incl. Purcell, Music for Queen Mary, and Tavener, Akathist. FRSCM 1997. Hon. FTCL 1969; Hon. RAM 1988. Hon. DMus Southampton, 1997. Hon. Citizen of Texas, 1971. Prizewinner, St Alban's Internat. Organ Festival, 1963; Conducting Scholarship, Berkshire Music Center, USA, 1963; Diploma, J. S. Bach Competn, Leipzig, 1968; UK/USA Bicentennial Fellow, 1979–80; Artist-in-residence, Univ. of California at Davis, 1984. *Compositions* include: What is Man?; May the grace of Christ (Nat. Anthem arr.); responses, descants, carol and hymn arrangements, incl. Make me a channel of your peace. *Publications:* edns of early organ music; contribs to organ jls. *Recreation:* watching cricket. *Address:* 71 Clancarty Road, Fulham, SW6 3BB. *T:* (020) 7736 5268, *Fax:* (020) 7610 6995. *Clubs:* Athenæum, Garrick.

NEARY, Most Rev. Michael; *see* Tuam, Archbishop of, (RC).

NEAVE, Julius Arthur Sheffield, CBE 1978 (MBE (mil.) 1945); JP; DL; General Manager, since 1966, Director since 1977, Mercantile & General Reinsurance Co. Ltd (Managing Director, 1980–82); *b* 17 July 1919; *s* of Col Richard Neave and Helen Mary Elizabeth (*née* Miller); *m* 1951, Helen Margery, *d* of Col P. M. Acton-Adams, DSO, Clarence Reserve, Marlborough, NZ; three *d*. *Educ:* Sherborne School. Joined Mercantile & General Reinsurance Co. Ltd, 1938. Served War, 1939–46: called as Territorial, commnd 13th/18th Royal Hussars, Adjt 3 years, final rank Major (despatches 1945). Returned to Mercantile & General, 1946; Asst Gen. Manager, 1964. Dir, Prudential Corp., 1982–92. (First) Chairman, Reinsurance Offices Assoc., 1969–74, Hon. Pres., 1974–82; Chm., Reinsurance Panel, British Insce Assoc., 1971–82; representative, Gt Britain: Cttee, annual internat. meeting of reinsurers, Monte Carlo, 1969–82; Vice-Pres., Assoc. Internat. pour l'Etude de l'Assurance, Geneva, 1976–83, Pres., 1983. Dir and Governor, Internat. Insce Seminars, 1977–82 (Founder's Gold Medal, 1977); President: Insce Inst. of London, 1976–77, 1983–84; Chartered Insce Inst., 1983–84 (Mem. Council, 1975–); Mem. Court, Insurers' Co., 1979– (Master, 1984–85). Hon. Fellow, RSA, 1975. Essex: JP (Brentwood), 1975; DL, 1983; High Sheriff, 1987–88. OStJ 1988. *Publications:* Speaking of Reinsurance, 1980; Still Speaking of Reinsurance, 1983. *Recreations:* shooting, fishing, golf, needlework. *Address:* Mill Green Park, Ingatestone, Essex CM4 0JB. *T:* (01277) 353036. *Club:* Cavalry and Guards.

NEAVE, Sir Paul (Arundell), 7th Bt *cr* 1795, of Dagnam Park, Essex; Divisional Director, Carr Sheppards Crosthwaite; *b* 13 Dec. 1948; *s* of Sir Arundell Thomas Clifton Neave, 6th Bt and Richenda Alice Ione (*d* 1994), *d* of Sir Robert Joshua Paul, 5th Bt; *S* father, 1992; *m* 1976, Coralie Jane Louise, *e d* of Sir Robin Kinahan, ERD; two *s*. *Educ:* Eton. Mem., Stock Exchange, 1980; formerly Dir, Henderson Crosthwaite Ltd. *Heir: s* Frederick Paul Kinahan Neave, *b* 25 Jan. 1981. *Address:* Queen's House, Monk Sherborne, Hants RG26 5HH.

NEEDHAM, family name of **Earl of Kilmorey**.

NEEDHAM, Karen Ida Boalth; *see* Spärck Jones, K. I. B.

NEEDHAM, Phillip; Chief Executive, ADAS Group (formerly ADAS Agency), 1995–2000; *b* 21 April 1940; *s* of Ephraim and Mabel Jessie Needham; *m* 1962, Patricia Ann (*née* Farr); two *s* two *d*. *Educ:* Dunstable Grammar Sch.; Univ. of Birmingham (BSc); Imperial Coll., London Univ. (MSc, DIC). National Agricultural Advisory Service, subseq. Agricultural Development and Advisory Service, MAFF: Soil Scientist, 1961; Regional Soil Scientist, Reading, 1979; Hd of Soil Science, London, 1982; Sen. Agricl Scientist, 1985; Dep. Dir of R&D, 1987; Dir, Farm and Countryside Service and Commercial Dir, 1988–92; Dir of Ops, 1992–95. *Publications:* contribs to books and jls on various aspects of crop nutrition and soil science. *Address:* 58 Harpsden Road, Henley-on-Thames, Oxon RG9 1EG.

NEEDHAM, Rt Hon. Sir Richard (Francis), (6th Earl of Kilmorey, but does not use the title), Kt 1997; PC 1994; Chairman, BioCompatibles plc, since 2000; Vice Chairman, NEC Europe Ltd, since 1997; Deputy Chairman, Dyson Ltd, since 2000 (Director, since 1995); *b* 29 Jan. 1942; *e s* of 5th Earl of Kilmorey (*d* 1977), and of Helen, *y d* of Sir Lionel Faudel-Phillips, 3rd Bt; *m* 1965, Sigrid Juliane Thiessen-Gairdner, *o d* of late Ernst Thiessen and of Mrs John Gairdner, Hamburg; two *s* one *d*. *Educ:* Eton College. Chm., R. G. M. Print Holdings Ltd, 1967–85. CC Somerset, 1967–74. Contested (C): Pontefract and Castleford, Feb. 1974; Gravesend, Oct. 1974; MP (C): Chippenham,

1979–83; Wilts N, 1983–97. PPS to Sec. of State for NI, 1983–84, to Sec. of State for the Environment, 1984–85; Parly Under-Sec. of State, NI Office, 1985–92 (Minister for Health and Social Security, 1988–89, for Envmt, and for Economy, 1989–92); Minister of State (Minister for Trade), DTI, 1992–95. Mem., Public Accts Cttee, 1982–83. Chairman: GPT Ltd, 1997–98; Intermediate Equity plc, 1999–2000; non-executive Director: GEC plc, 1995–97; Mivan Ltd, 1995–99; Meggitt PLC, 1997–; Tough Glass Ltd, 1997–; MICE plc, 1998–; Tricorder Technology plc, 1999–2001; Zoa plc, subseq. Nyne plc, 2000–; Advr, Amec plc, 1998–. Chm., Gleneagles (UK) Ltd (formerly Nat. Heart Hosp.), 1995–. Pres., British Exporters Assoc., 1998–. Founder Member: Anglo-Japanese 2000 Gp, 1984–; Anglo-Korean Forum for the Future, 1993–2000. Governor, British Inst. of Florence, 1983–85. *Publications:* Honourable Member, 1983; Battling for Peace, 1999. *Heir: s* Viscount Newry and Morne, *qv*. *Address:* Dyson Ltd, Tetbury Hill, Malmesbury, Wilts SN16 0RP. *Clubs:* Pratt's, Beefsteak.

NEEDHAM, Prof. Roger Michael, CBE 2001; FRS 1985; FREng; Managing Director, Microsoft Research Ltd, since 1997; Professor of Computer Systems, 1981–98, now Emeritus, and Fellow of Wolfson College, since 1967, University of Cambridge; *b* 9 Feb. 1935; *s* of Leonard William Needham and Phyllis Mary Needham; *m* 1958, Karen Ida Boalth Spärck-Jones, *qv*. *Educ:* Cambridge Univ. (MA, PhD). FBCS; FREng (FEng 1993). Cambridge University: Sen. Asst in Research, Computer Lab., 1963–64; Asst Dir of Research, 1964–73; Reader in Computer Systems, 1973–81; Hd of Computer Lab., 1980–95; Pro-Vice-Chancellor, 1996–98. Member: UGC, 1985–89; DASC, 1999–. Member: Chesterton RDC, 1971–74; South Cambs DC, 1974–86. Fellow, Assoc. for Computing Machinery, USA, 1994; MAE 1998. Hon. DSc: Kent, 1983; Birmingham, 1995; Twente, 1996; Anglia Poly. Univ., 1998; East Anglia, 1999; Sheffield, 2000; Loughborough, 2001; DUniv N London, 1999. Faraday Medal, IEE, 1998. *Publications:* (with M. V. Wilkes) The Cambridge CAP Computer and its operating system, 1979; (with A. J. Herbert) The Cambridge Distributed Computing System, 1982; contribs to publications on computer operating systems, communications, security and protection. *Recreation:* sailing. *Address:* Microsoft Research Ltd, 7 JJ Thomson Avenue, Cambridge CB3 0FB. *T:* (01223) 479700, *Fax:* (01223) 479999. *Clubs:* Naval; Royal Harwich Yacht.

NEEDLE, Clive; independent public policy advisor, since 1999; Director, European Network of Health Promoting Agencies, Brussels, since 2000. *Educ:* Southend High Sch.; Aston Univ. MEP (Lab) Norfolk, 1994–99; contested (Lab) Eastern Region, 1999. Chm., Labour Party, Norfolk, 1999–. *Address:* 4 Barnham Broom Road, Wymondham, Norfolk NR18 0DF.

NEEL, Janet; *see* Baroness Cohen of Pimlico.

NEELY, William Robert Nicholas; Europe Correspondent, ITN, since 1997; *b* 21 May 1959; *s* of late William John Neely and of Patricia (*née* Larney); *m* 1988, Marion Kerr; two *d*. *Educ:* St Malachy's Coll., Belfast; Queen's Univ., Belfast (BA Jt Hons Eng. Lit. and Hist.). Reporter: BBC NI, 1981–86; BBC Network, 1987–88; Sky TV, Jan.–June 1989; ITN, 1989–90; Washington Correspondent, ITN, 1991–97. *Address:* c/o ITN, 200 Gray's Inn Road, WC1X 8HF; c/o ITN, Boulevard Charlemagne 1/18, 1041 Brussels, Belgium.

NEESON, Liam; *see* Neeson, W. J.

NEESON, Séan; Member (Alliance) Antrim East, Northern Ireland Assembly, since 1998; *b* 6 Feb. 1946; *s* of Patrick and Mary Neeson; *m* 1978, Carol Henderson; two *s* two *d*. *Educ:* Queen's Univ., Belfast (BA); St Joseph's Coll. of Educn, Belfast (Postgrad. Dip. in Educn 1968); Univ. of Ulster, Jordanstown (Postgrad. Dip. in Mktg 1988). Teacher, Head of History Dept, St Comgall's High Sch., Larne, 1968–85; marketing and PR consultant, 1988–98. Mem. (Alliance) Carrickfergus Council, 1977–; Mayor of Carrickfergus, 1993–94; Mem., NI Assembly, 1982–86. Leader, Alliance Party of NI, 1998–2001. Mem. Bd, Nat. Museums and Galleries (NI), 1998–. *Publications:* articles on maritime heritage in jls. *Recreation:* study of British and Irish maritime heritage. *Address:* 44 Milebush Park, Carrickfergus, Co. Antrim BT38 7QR. *T:* (028) 9336 4105; (office) (028) 9052 1314.

NEESON, William John, (Liam), OBE 2000; actor; *b* Ballymena, NI, 7 June 1952; *s* of late Barney Neeson and of Katherine Neeson; *m* 1994, Natasha Jane Richardson, *qv*; two *s*. Winner, NI Youth Heavyweight Boxing Championship. *Theatre* includes: The Risen, Lyric Players' Theatre, Belfast, 1976; Of Mice and Men, Abbey Theatre, Dublin; The Informer, Dublin Theatre Fest.; Translations, NT; The Plough and the Stars, Royal Exchange, Manchester; Anna Christie, Broadway, 1993; The Judas Kiss, Playhouse Theatre, 1998; *films* include: Excalibur, 1981; Krull, 1983; The Bounty, 1984; Duet for One, 1986; Lamb, 1986; The Mission, 1986; A Prayer for the Dying, 1987; Suspect, 1987; The Dead Pool, 1988; The Good Mother, 1988; Darkman, 1990; Crossing the Line, 1990 (retitled The Big Man, 1991); Shining Through, 1992; Under Suspicion, 1992; Leap of Faith, 1992; Husbands and Wives, 1992; Ethan Frome, 1993; Schindler's List, 1994; Nell, 1994; Rob Roy, 1995; Before and After, 1996; Michael Collins, 1996 (Best Actor Award, Venice Film Fest.); Les Misérables, 1998; Star Wars Episode One: the Phantom Menace, 1999; The Haunting, 1999; *television* includes: Arthur the King; Miami Vice; A Woman of Substance; Hold the Dream; Next of Kin; Sweet As You Are. *Address:* c/o ICM, 8942 Wilshire Boulevard, Beverly Hills, CA 90211, USA.

NEGARA BRUNEI DARUSSALAM, HM Sultan of; Hassanal Bolkiah Mu'izzaddin Waddaulah, DKMB, DK, PSSUB, DPKG, DPKT, PSPNB, PSNB, PSLJ, SPMB, PANB; Hon. GCMG; DMN, DK (Kelantan), DK (Johor), DK (Negeri Sembilan), DK (Pahang); Ruler of Negara Brunei Darussalam (formerly Brunei), since 1967; Prime Minister, Negara Brunei Darussalam, since its independence, Jan. 1984; Minister of Defence, since 1986 (Finance and Home Affairs Minister, 1984–86); *b* 15 July 1946; *s* of Sultan Sir Muda Omar 'Ali Saifuddien Sa'adul Khairi Waddien, DKMB, DK, GCVO, KCMG, PSSUB, PHBS, PBLI (*d* 1986); *m* 1st, 1965, Rajah Isteri Anak Saleha; two *s* four *d*; 2nd, 1981, Pengiran Isteri Hajjah Mariam; two *s* two *d*. *Educ:* Victoria Inst., Kuala Lumpur; RMA Sandhurst (Hon. Captain, Coldstream Guards, 1968; Hon. General 1984). Collar of the Supreme Order of the Chrysanthemum; Grand Order of Mugunghwa. *Address:* Istana Nurul Iman, Bandar Seri Begawan, Negara Brunei Darussalam.

NEGUS, Her Honour Norma Florence, (Mrs D. J. Turner-Samuels); a Circuit Judge, 1990–97; *b* 31 July 1932; *d* of late George David Shellabear and Kate (*née* Calvert); *m* 1st, 1956, Richard Negus (marr. diss. 1960); 2nd, 1976, David Jessel Turner-Samuels, *qv*. *Educ:* Malvern Girls' Coll., Malvern, Worcs. Fashion promotion and advertising in UK, Canada and USA, 1950–61; Merchandise Editor, Harper's Bazaar, 1962–63; Asst Promotion Manager, Vogue and House & Garden, 1963–65; Unit Manager, Trends Merchandising and Fashion Promotion Unit, 1965–67; Export Marketing Manager and Advertising Manager, Glenoit (UK) Ltd, 1967–68. Called to the Bar, Gray's Inn, 1970; Mem., Middle Temple, 1984. In practice on SE Circuit, 1971–84; a Metropolitan Stipendiary Magistrate, 1984–90; a Recorder, 1989–90. Member: Parole Bd, 1991–94; Mental Health Review Tribunal, 1996–98. Mem., Central Criminal Court Bar Mess, 1978–84. *Recreations:* reading, writing, theatre, music, travel, swimming. *Address:* c/o Cloisters, 1 Pump Court, Temple, EC4Y 7AA.

NEGUS, Richard; consultant designer; Senior Partner, Negus & Negus, 1967–87; *b* 29 August 1927; *s* of Bertie and Kate Negus; *m* 1949, Pamela Wheatcroft-Hancock (*d* 2000); two *s* one *d*. *Educ:* Battersea Grammar Sch.; Camberwell Sch. of Arts and Crafts. FSTD. Staff designer, Festival of Britain, 1948–51; Partner, Negus & Sharland, 1951–67; Lecturer, Central Sch. of Art, 1951–53. Consultant to: Cotton Board Design Centre, 1960–67; BNEC, 1969–75; British Airways, 1973–84, 1990–; Pakistan Airlines, 1975–79 and 1989–; Rank Organisation, 1979–86; City of Westminster, 1973–75; National Exhibition Centre, 1974–77; Lloyds Bank, 1972–75; Godfrey Davis, 1971–80; John Laing, 1970–73; Andry Montgomery, 1967–; Celltech, 1980–83; Vickers Ltd, 1980–83; SDP, 1981–88; Historic Buildings and Monuments Commn, 1984–; Nat. Maritime Mus., 1984–; Royal Armouries, 1984–; The Emirates (Airline), 1985–88; Tower of London, 1986–91; Science Museum, 1987–; Northern Foods, 1986–91; Waterford/Wedgwood, 1987; DoE Royal Parks, 1987–88; Nature Conservation Council, 1987–89; John Lewis Partnership, 1987–89; Nat. Theatre, 1989–91; Internat. Youth Hostels, 1989; Dubai Tourist Bd, 1990–95; Blue Circle Properties, 1990–92. Member: Design Council Poster Awards Cttee, 1970–72; PO Stamps Adv. Cttee, 1977–; CNAA, 1980–85; Design Council, 1981–86; Art and Design Cttee, Technician Educn Council, 1981–86. Advisor, Norwich Sch. of Art, 1969–71; External Assessor: Birmingham and Bradford Colls of Art, 1969–73; Medway Coll. of Design, 1989–; Governor: Camberwell Sch. of Art, 1964–78; Chelsea Sch. of Art, 1977–85; Mem. Court, RCA, 1979–82. PPCSD (Pres., SIAD, 1977–79, Vice Pres. 1966–68). Hon. RCM 1995. *Publications:* Designing for Export Printing, 1972; Display of Text in Museums, 1989; contribs to: Design Mag., The Designer, Graphis, Gebrauchgraphick, Architectural Review, Rolls Royce Mag., Creative Review, Art and Artists. *Recreations:* the countryside, sailing. *Address:* 15 St Clement's Church, Davey Close, N7 8BT. *T:* (020) 7607 8642; Little Gravenhurst, Bolney, Sussex RH17 5PA. *T:* (01444) 881841.

NEHER, Prof. Dr Erwin; Research Director, Max-Planck-Institut für biophysikalische Chemie, Göttingen, since 1983; *b* 20 March 1944; *s* of Franz Xaver Neher and Elisabeth Neher; *m* 1978, Dr Eva-Maria Ruhr; three *s* two *d*. *Educ:* Technical Univ., Munich (PhD); Univ. of Wisconsin. Research Associate: Max-Planck-Inst. für Psychiatrie, Munich, 1970–72; Max-Planck-Inst. für biophysikalische Chemie, 1972–75 and 1976–83; Yale Univ., 1975–76; Fairchild Scholar, CIT, 1988–89. For. Mem., Royal Soc., 1994. Nat. and internat. sci. awards: (jtly) Nobel Prize in Physiology or Medicine, 1991. *Publications:* Elektronische Messtechnik in der Physiologie, 1974; (ed) Single Channel Recording, 1983. *Address:* Max-Planck-Institut für biophysikalische Chemie, Am Fassberg, 37077 Göttingen, Germany. *T:* (551) 2011675.

NEHRU, Braj Kumar; Padma Vibhushan, 1999; Chairman: Indian Advisory Board, Grindlays Bank, 1988–94; Hindustan Oil Exploration Co. Ltd, 1987–94; Director, East India Hotels Ltd, since 1988; *b* Allahabad, 4 Sept. 1909; *s* of Brijlal and Rameshwari Nehru; *m* 1935, Magdalena Friedmann; three *s*. *Educ:* Allahabad Univ. (BSc); LSE (BSc(Econ); Fellow); Balliol Coll., Oxford. BSc; BSc(Econ.). Called to Bar, Inner Temple. Joined ICS, 1934; Asst Comr, 1934–39; Under-Sec., Dept of Education, Health and Lands, 1939; Mem., Indian Legislative Assembly, 1939; Officer on special duty, Reserve Bank of India, and Under-Sec., Finance Dept, 1940–44; Jt Sec., 1946; Exec. Dir, IBRD (World Bank), and Minister, Indian Embassy, Washington, 1949–54 and 1958–62; Sec., Dept of Econ. Affairs, 1957–58; Comr-Gen. for Econ. Affairs, Min. of Finance, and Ambassador-at-Large, 1958–61; Ambassador to USA, 1961–68; Governor: Assam and Nagaland, 1968–73; Meghalaya, Manipur and Tripura, 1972–73; High Comr in London, 1973–77; Governor: Jammu and Kashmir, 1981–84; Gujarat, 1984–86. Rep. of India: Reparations Conf., 1945; Commonwealth Finance Ministers Confs, UN Gen. Assembly, 1949–52, and 1960; FAO Confs, 1949–50; Sterling Balance Confs, 1946–49; Bandung Conf., 1955; deputed to enquire into Australian Fed. Finance, 1946; Mem., UN Adv. Cttee on Admin and Budgetry Questions, 1951–53; Advr to Sudan Govt, 1955; Mem., UN Investments Cttee, 1962–91 (Chm., 1977–91; Mem. Emeritus, 1991); Vice-Chm., Vienna Inst. for Develt, 1962–90; Mem. Internat. Adv. Council, Vienna Inst. for Develt & Co-operation, 1990–. Mem., Governing Body, Dyal Singh Coll., 1988– (Chm., 1988–97); Trustee: Indira Gandhi Meml Trust, 1986–; Dyal Singh Coll. Trust, 1988– (Pres., 1988–98); Dyal Singh Library Trust, 1988– (Pres., 1988–2000); Tribune Trust, 1988– (Pres., 1996–2000); World Meml Fund for Disaster Relief, 1989–; Soc. for Preservation of Kasauli and its environs, 1991– (Pres., 1991). Hon. LLD Mo Valley Coll.; Hon. LittD Jacksonville; Hon. DLitt Punjab. *Publications:* Australian Federal Finance, 1947; Speaking of India, 1966; Thoughts on the Present Discontents, 1986; Nice Guys Finish Second, 1997. *Recreations:* reading, writing. *Address:* Fair View, Kasauli 173204, India. *T:* (01792) 72189, *Fax:* (01792) 72929. *Clubs:* Gymkhana, India International Centre (Delhi).

NEIDLE, Prof. Stephen, PhD, DSc, CChem, FRSC; Professor of Biophysics, since 1990, Dean, since 1997, Institute of Cancer Research, University of London; *b* 1 July 1946; *e s* of Michael and Hetty Neidle; *m* 1971, Andrea Anne Finn; two *s* one *d*. *Educ:* Hendon County Sch.; Imperial Coll., London (BSc 1967; PhD 1970; DSc 1995). CChem, FRSC 1999. ICI Research Fellow, Univ. of London, 1970–72; Mem., Scientific Staff, Dept of Biophysics, KCL, 1972–85; Reader, Inst. of Cancer Res., 1986–90. Cancer Research Campaign: career develt awardee, 1979–85; Life Fellow, 1985–; Dir, Biomolecular Structure Unit, 1985–. Bristol-Myers Squibb Lectr, SUNY, 1993. Award in Bio-organic and Medicinal Chem., RSC, 1999. *Publications:* DNA Structure and Recognition, 1994; (ed) Oxford Handbook of Nucleic Acid Structure, 1999; numerous papers on nucleic acid structure and on design of anti-cancer drugs. *Recreations:* badminton, film noir, theatre. *Address:* Institute of Cancer Research, Chester Beatty Laboratories, 237 Fulham Road, SW3 6JB. *T:* (020) 7970 6043, *Fax:* (020) 7352 8039.

NEIDPATH, Lord; Hon. James Donald Charteris, Lord Douglas of Neidpath, Lyne and Munard; *b* 22 June 1948; *s* and *heir* of 12th Earl of Wemyss and March, *qv*; *m* 1st, 1983, Catherine Ingrid (marr. diss. 1988), *d* of Baron Moyne, *qv*, and of Mrs Paul Channon; one *s* one *d*; 2nd, 1995, Amanda Claire, *y d* of late Basil Feilding. *Educ:* Eton; University College, Oxford (BA 1969, MA 1974); St Antony's Coll., Oxford (DPhil 1975); Royal Agricultural Coll., Cirencester (Diploma, 1978); ARICS 1983. Page of Honour to HM Queen Elizabeth the Queen Mother, 1962–64. Mem., Royal Co. of Archers (Queen's Body Guard for Scotland), 1978–. Mem. Council, Nat. Trust for Scotland, 1987–92; Chm., Heart of England Reg., Hist. Houses Assoc., 1991–96. *Publication:* The Singapore Naval Base and the Defence of Britain's Eastern Empire 1919–42, 1981. *Heir: s* Hon. Francis Richard Percy Charteris, *b* 15 Sept. 1984. *Address:* Stanway, Cheltenham, Glos GL54 5PQ. *T:* (01386) 584469. *Clubs:* Brooks's, Pratt's, Ognisko Polskie; Puffin's, New (Edinburgh).

NEIGHBOUR, Oliver Wray, FBA 1982; Music Librarian, Reference Division of the British Library, 1976–85; *b* 1 April 1923; *s* of Sydney William Neighbour, OBE, TD, and Gwenydd Joyce (*née* Prentis). *Educ:* Eastbourne Coll.; Birkbeck Coll., London (BA 1950).

Entered Dept of Printed Books, BM, 1946; Asst Keeper in Music Room, 1951; Dep. Keeper, 1976. *Publications:* (with Alan Tyson) English Music Publishers' Plate Numbers, 1965; The Consort and Keyboard Music of William Byrd, 1978; (ed) Music and Bibliography: essays in honour of Alec Hyatt King, 1980; article on Schoenberg in New Grove Dictionary of Music and Musicians, 1980; editor of first publications of works by Schumann, Schoenberg and Byrd. *Recreations:* walking, ornithology. *Address:* 12 Treborough House, 1 Nottingham Place, W1U 5LA. *T:* (020) 7935 1772.

NEIL, Alexander; Member (SNP) Central Scotland, Scottish Parliament, since 1999; *b* 22 Aug. 1951; *s* of late Alexander Neil and of Margaret Gunning Neil; *m* Isabella Kerr; one *s*. *Educ:* Dundee Univ. (MA Hons Econs 1973). Marketing Manager: Digital Equipment Corp., 1979–83; Future Technology Systems, 1983–84; Dir, Cumnock and Doon Enterprise Trust, 1983–88; Economic and Business Advr, 1988–. Dir, Prince's Scottish Youth Business Trust, 1988–90; non-exec. Dir and Chm., Network Scotland Ltd, 1989–96. *Recreations:* reading, travel. *Address:* 26 Overmills Road, Hazelbank, Ayr KA7 3LQ. *T:* (01292) 286675.

NEIL, Andrew Ferguson; publisher, editor, writer, broadcaster and media consultant; Editor-in-Chief, since 1996, and Publisher, since 1999, Press Holdings (formerly European Press Holdings; owner of Sunday Business, The Scotsman, Scotland on Sunday, Edinburgh Evening News, Business Europe.com); *b* Paisley, 21 May 1949; *s* of James and Mary Neil. *Educ:* Paisley Grammar Sch.; Univ. of Glasgow (MA Hons Politics and Economics, 1971). Conservative Res. Dept, 1971–72; joined The Economist, 1973; Correspondent in Belfast, London, NY and Washington, covering politics and business, 1973–82; UK Editor, London, 1982–83; Editor, The Sunday Times, 1983–94; Exec. Editor and Chief Correspondent, Fox Network News, NY, 1994; columnist, The Sunday Times and Daily Mail, 1995–96; Contributing Editor, Vanity Fair, NY, 1995–. Chairman: Sky TV, 1988–90; The Net Media Gp, 1999–; PeopleNews.com, 2000–; Co-Proprietor and Dir, CGA and Country Magazine, 1990–97. Appears regularly on various current affairs television and radio programmes in Britain and America; presenter: television: The Midnight Hour, Westminster On-Line, Is This Your Life?, The Andrew Neil Show, Despatch Box, BBC; Thursday Night Live, ITV; formerly presenter, radio: Sunday Breakfast, BBC. Rector, St Andrews Univ., 1999–. FRSA. *Publications:* The Cable Revolution, 1982; Britain's Free Press: Does It Have One?, 1988; Full Disclosure, 1996; British Excellence, 1998. *Recreations:* dining out in London, New York, Aspen and the Côte d'Azur. *Address:* Glenburn Enterprises Ltd, PO Box 584, SW7 3QY. *T:* (020) 7244 9968. *Club:* Royal Automobile.

NEIL, Matthew, CBE 1976; Secretary and Chief Executive, Glasgow Chamber of Commerce, 1954–83; *b* 19 Dec. 1917; *er s* of John Neil and Jean Wallace. *Educ:* John Neilson High Sch., Paisley; Glasgow Univ. (MA, LLB). Served War, 1939–46: Far East, ME, Mediterranean and Western Europe; RHA, RA and Air Observation Post; RAuxAF, 1950–57. Admitted solicitor, 1947; Hon. Sheriff, Renfrew and Argyll, now N Strathclyde, 1973–. Mem., British Overseas Trade Adv. Council, 1975–82. Hon. LLD Glasgow, 1983. *Recreations:* skiing, golf, music. *Address:* 39 Arkleston Road, Paisley PA1 3TH. *T:* (0141) 889 4975. *Clubs:* East India, Devonshire, Sports and Public Schools; Lamlash Golf, Prestwick Golf.

NEIL, Ronald John Baille, CBE 1999; Chief Executive, BBC Production, 1996–99; *b* 16 June 1942; *s* of John Clark Neil and Jean McMillan Taylor; *m* 1967, Isobel Anne Clark. *Educ:* High Sch. of Glasgow. Reporter, Daily Express, 1961; BBC, 1967–98: Newsreader/Reporter, Reporting Scotland, 1967; Producer, Nationwide and 24 Hours, 1969; Output Editor, Nationwide, 1973; Dep. Editor, Newsnight, 1979; Editor: That's Life, 1981; Newsnight, 1981; Breakfast Time, 1983; Six O'Clock News, 1984; TV News, 1985; Dep. Dir, 1987–88, Dir, 1988–89, News and Current Affairs; Man. Dir, Regl Broadcasting, BBC, 1989. *Recreations:* food, wine. *Club:* Reform.

NEIL, Thomas, CMG 1962; TD 1951; Director, Thomson Foundation, 1963–79; *b* 23 December 1913; *s* of late W. R. Neil; *m* 1939, Phyllis Selina Gertrude Sargeant; one *d*. *Educ:* King's College, University of Durham (now University of Newcastle upon Tyne) (BSc, NDA). Lectr in Agriculture, Devon County Council, 1936–39; Chief Technical Officer, 1946. Colonial Service: District Officer, Kenya, 1947; Assistant Chief Secretary, 1957; Permanent Secretary, 1957; Permanent Secretary, Ministry of State, Kenya, 1959–63. Directed Africanisation of CS. Director, Kenya Famine Relief, 1961–63. Lay Mem., Immigration Appeal Tribunal, 1971–84. Served War of 1939–45 with Devonshire Regiment (TA), Lieutenant-Colonel, in UK, E Africa, Middle East. *Recreation:* country life. *Address:* 5 Cakeham Way, West Wittering, Chichester, W Sussex PO20 8EQ.

NEIL-DWYER, Glenn, FRCS, FRCSE; Consultant Neurosurgeon, Southampton University Hospitals NHS Trust, since 1987; *b* 17 May 1938; *s* of Glen Shamrock Neil-Dwyer and Violet Agatha Hussey; *m* 1966, Jennifer Susan Edith Taylor; three *s*. *Educ:* Ruthin Sch.; St Mary's Hosp., London (MB BS, MS). FRCSE 1967; FRCS 1968. Sen. House Officer, Neurosurgery, Addenbrooke's Hosp., 1968–69; Registrar, then Sen. Registrar, Wessex Neurol Centre, Southampton, 1969–74; Consultant Neurosurgeon: Cornwall Regl Hosp. and UCH (Jamaica), 1974–75; Brook Gen. Hosp., London, 1975–87; Consultant Advr in Neurosurgery to the Army, 1992–. Pres., Soc. of British Neurol Surgeons, 1998–2000; Member, Council: RCS, 1998–2000; Med. Defence Union, 2000–; Sec., Eur. Assoc. Neurosurgical Socs, 1999–. *Publications:* contrib. numerous papers to peer-reviewed jls on neurosurgical topics. *Recreations:* golf, sport, walking, travel, opera. *Address:* Annesley Glade, Bank, Lyndhurst, Hants SO43 7FD. *T:* (023) 8028 3352. *Club:* MCC.

NEILAND, Prof. Brendan Robert, RA 1992; Gallery Artist, Redfern Gallery, since 1992; Keeper of the Royal Academy, since 1998; *b* 23 Oct. 1941; *s* of Arthur Neiland and Joan Agnes Bessie Whiley; *m* 1970, Hilary Vivienne Salter; two *d*. *Educ:* Birmingham Sch. of Art (DipAD Hons); Royal Coll. of Art (MA). RE 1988–92 (Hon. RE 1998). Prof. of Painting, Univ. of Brighton, 1996–98. Vis. Prof. of Fine Art, Loughborough Univ., 1999. Exhibited: Angela Flowers Gall., 1970–78; Fischer Fine Art, 1978–92; Redfern Gall., 1993. Scholar, Crabtree Foundn, 1982. FRSA 1996. Silver Medal, RCA, 1969; John Moores XI Prize, 1978; Daler Rowney Award, RA Summer Exhibn, 1989. *Publication:* Upon Reflection, 1997. *Recreations:* listening to the cricket commentary on Radio 4, drinking fine wines. *Address:* 2 Granard Road, SW12 8UL. *T:* and *Fax:* (020) 8673 4597; Crepe, La Grévé sur le Mignon, 17170 Courçon, France, *T:* 546016297. *Clubs:* Chelsea Arts, Arts.

NEILD, Prof. Robert Ralph; Professor of Economics, University of Cambridge, 1971–84, now Emeritus; Fellow of Trinity College, Cambridge, since 1971; *b* 10 Sept. 1924; *o s* of Ralph and Josephine Neild, Letchmore Heath, Hertfordshire; *m* 1st, 1957, Nora Clemens Sayre (marr. diss. 1961); 2nd, 1962, Elizabeth Walton Griffiths (marr. diss. 1986); one *s* four *d* (incl. twin *d*). *Educ:* Charterhouse; Trinity Coll., Cambridge. Royal Air Force, 1943–44; Operational Research, 1944–45. Secretariat of United Nations Economic Commission for Europe, Geneva, 1947–51; Economic Section, Cabinet Office and Treasury, 1951–56; Lecturer in Economics, and Fellow, Trinity College, Cambridge, 1956–58; National Institute of Economic and Social Research: at first as Editor of its Quarterly Economic Review; then as Deputy Director of the Institute, 1958–64; MIT Center for International Studies, India Project, New Delhi, 1962–63; Economic Adviser to HM Treasury, 1964–67; Dir, Stockholm Internat. Peace Research Inst., 1967–71. Vis. Fulbright Prof., Hampshire Coll. and Five Colls, Amherst, Mass, USA, 1985. Mem., Fulton Cttee on Reform of CS, 1966–68; Vice-Chm., Armstrong Cttee on Budgetary Reform in UK, Inst. for Fiscal Studies, 1979–80. Director: Nat. Mutual Life Assce Soc., 1959–64; Investing in Success Equities Ltd, 1961–64, 1972–87. *Publications:* Pricing and Employment in the Trade Cycle, 1964; (with T. S. Ward) The Measurement and Reform of Budgetary Policy, 1978; How to Make Up Your Mind about the Bomb, 1981; An Essay on Strategy, 1990; (ed with A. Boserup) The Foundations of Defensive Defence, 1990; The English, the French and the Oyster, 1995; various articles. *Recreations:* oysters, painting. *Address:* Trinity College, Cambridge CB2 1TQ.

NEILL, family name of **Baron Neill of Bladen**.

NEILL OF BLADEN, Baron *cr* 1997 (Life Peer), of Briantspuddle in the co. of Dorset; **Francis Patrick Neill,** Kt 1983; QC 1966; Chairman, Committee on Standards in Public Life, 1997–2001; Warden of All Souls College, Oxford, 1977–95; a Judge of the Courts of Appeal of Jersey and Guernsey, 1977–94; *b* 8 Aug. 1926; *s* of late Sir Thomas Neill, JP, and Lady (Annie Strachan) Neill (*née* Bishop); *m* 1954, Caroline Susan, *d* of late Sir Piers Debenham, 2nd Bt, and Lady (Angela) Debenham; three *s* two *d* (and one *s* decd). *Educ:* Highgate Sch.; Magdalen College, Oxford (Hon. Fellow, 1988). Gibbs Law Scholar, 1949; Eldon Law Scholar, 1950. BA 1950; BCL 1951; MA 1972. Served Rifle Brigade, 1944–47 (Captain); GSO III (Training), British Troops Egypt, 1947. Fellow of All Souls Coll., Oxford, 1950–77, Sub-Warden 1972–74, Hon. Fellow, 1997; Lectr in Air Law, LSE, 1955–58; Vice-Chancellor, Oxford Univ., 1985–89. Called to the Bar, Gray's Inn, 1951; Bencher, 1971; Vice-Treas., 1989; Treas., 1990; Member, Bar Council, 1967–71, Vice-Chm., 1973–74, Chm., 1974–75; Chm., Senate of the Inns of Court and the Bar, 1974–75; a Recorder of the Crown Court, 1975–78. Chm., Justice—All Souls Cttee for Rev. of Admin. Law, 1978–87. Chairman: Press Council, 1978–83; DTI Cttee of Inquiry into Regulatory Arrangements at Lloyd's, 1986–87; Feltrim Loss Review Cttee at Lloyd's, 1991–92; first Chm., Council for the Securities Industry, 1978–85; Vice-Chm., CVCP, 1987–89. Independent Nat. Dir, Times Newspaper Hldgs, 1988–97. Hon. Prof. of Legal Ethics, Birmingham Univ., 1983–84. Hon. LLD: Hull, 1978; Buckingham, 1994; Hon. DCL Oxon, 1987. *Publication:* Administrative Justice: some necessary reforms, 1988. *Recreations:* music and forestry. *Address:* 1 Hare Court, Temple, EC4Y 7BE. *Clubs:* Athenæum, Garrick, Beefsteak.

See also Rt Hon. Sir Brian Neill.

NEILL, Alistair, FFA, FIA; General Manager, Scottish Widows' Fund & Life Assurance Society, 1988–92; President, Faculty of Actuaries in Scotland, 1990–92; *b* 18 Nov. 1932; *s* of Alexander Neill and Marion Wilson; *m* 1958, Mary Margaret Hunter; one *s* two *d*. *Educ:* George Watson's Coll., Edinburgh; Univ. of Edinburgh (John Welsh Math. Bursar; MA); Univ. of Wisconsin (Fulbright Grantee; MS); BSc Open Univ. 2001. Instructor Lieut, RN, 1958–60. Actuarial management posts in Scottish Widows' Fund, 1961–92. *Publication:* Life Contingencies, 1977, 5th edn 1989. *Recreations:* golf, model railways. *Address:* 24 Bonaly Crescent, Edinburgh EH13 0EW. *T:* (0131) 441 2038.

NEILL, Rt Hon. Sir Brian (Thomas), Kt 1978; PC 1985; a Lord Justice of Appeal, 1985–96; a Justice of Appeal, since 1997, and President, since 1998, Court of Appeal for Gibraltar; *b* 2 Aug. 1923; *s* of late Sir Thomas Neill and Lady (Annie Strachan) Neill (*née* Bishop); *m* 1956, Sally Margaret, *d* of late Sydney Eric and Marguerite Backus; three *s*. *Educ:* Highgate Sch.; Corpus Christi Coll., Oxford (Hon. Fellow 1986). Rifle Brigade, 1942–46 (Capt.). MA Oxford. Called to the Bar, Inner Temple, 1949, Bencher, 1976. QC 1968; a Recorder of the Crown Court, 1972–78; a Judge of the High Court, Queen's Bench Div., 1978–84. A Judge of the Commercial and Admiralty Courts, 1980–84; a Judge of Employment Appeal Tribunal, 1981–84. Mem., Departmental Cttee to examine operation of Section 2 of Official Secrets Act, 1971; Chairman: Adv. Cttee on Rhodesia Travel Restrictions, 1973–78; IT and the Courts Cttee, 1985–96; Supreme Court Procedure Cttee, 1986–90. Mem., Ct of Assts, 1972–, Master, 1980–81, Turners' Co. Governor, Highgate Sch., 1969–90. *Publication:* (with Colin Duncan) Defamation, 1978, 2nd edn (ed with R. Rampton), 1984. *Clubs:* MCC, Hurlingham.

See also Baron Neill of Bladen.

NEILL, Rev. Bruce Ferguson; Church of Scotland Minister, Maxton and Mertoun with St Boswells, since 1996; *b* 9 Jan. 1941; *s* of Thomas Ferguson Neill and Jane (*née* Bruce); *m* 1966, Ishbel Macdonald; two *s* one *d*. *Educ:* Lesmahagow Primary; Hamilton Academy; Glasgow Univ. and Trinity Coll., Glasgow (MA, BD). Probationer Asst, Drumchapel Old Parish Church, 1964–66; Minister, Dunfermline Townhill Parish Church, 1966–71; commnd as Chaplain, RN, 1971; Naval appts include: HMS Drake, 1972; RM, 1972; HMS Seahawk, 1974; HMS Cochrane, 1976; ships of 1st and 2nd Flotillas, 1979; HMS Dryad, 1981; Britannia RNC, 1983; HMS Cochrane, 1986; ships of Minor War Vessels Flotilla, 1989–91; Prin. Naval Chaplain, Church of Scotland and Free Churches, 1991–96. QHC, 1991–96. *Recreations:* gardening, hill walking, off-shore sailing, woodwork, music, model making. *Address:* The Manse, Main Street, St Boswells, Melrose TD6 0BB. *T:* (01835) 822255.

NEILL, Sir Hugh; *see* Neill, Sir J. H.

NEILL, Major Rt Hon. Sir Ivan, Kt 1973; PC (N Ireland) 1950; *b* Belfast, 1 July 1906; *m* 1928, Margaret Helena Allen. *Educ:* Ravenscroft Nat. Sch., Belfast; Shaftesbury House Tutorial Coll., Belfast; Queen's Univ., Belfast (BSc Econ). FRGS. Served War of 1939–45: RE in UK and FE, 1939–46; Major. MP Ballynafeigh Div. of Belfast, Parlt of Northern Ireland, 1949–73; Government of Northern Ireland: Minister of Labour and National Insurance, 1950–62; Minister of Home Affairs, Aug.-Oct. 1952; Minister of Education, 1962–64; Minister of Finance, 1964–65; Leader of House of Commons, Oct. 1964; resigned from Govt, April 1965; Minister of Develt, Dec. 1968–March 1969; Speaker of House of Commons, 1969–73. Represented N Ireland at Internat. Labour Confs, 1950–61. Councillor and Alderman in Belfast Corp., 1946–50 (specialised in educn, housing and youth welfare). DL Belfast, 1966–86. *Publications:* Travel Experiences, 1991; A Story in Verse, 1995; Church and State, 1995. *Address:* Cranagh Cottage, Warren Road, Donaghadee, Co. Down, Northern Ireland BT21 0PQ.

NEILL, Sir (James) Hugh, KCVO 1996; CBE 1969; TD 1950; JP; Lord-Lieutenant for South Yorkshire, 1985–96; Chairman, James Neill Holdings, 1963–89; *b* 29 March 1921; *o s* of Col Sir Frederick Neill, CBE, DSO, TD, DL, JP, and Lady (Winifred Margaret) Neill (*née* Colver); *m* 1st, 1943, Jane Margaret Shuttleworth (*d* 1980); two *d*; 2nd, 1982, Anne O'Leary; one *s*. *Educ:* Rugby School. War service with RE and Royal Bombay Sappers and Miners, UK, Norway, India, Burma and Germany, 1939–46 (despatches, Burma, 1945). Mem., British Overseas Trade Bd, 1973–78; Pres., European Tool Cttee, 1972–76; Mem., Trent Regional Health Authority, 1974–80; Chm. Exec. Cttee, Sheffield Council for Voluntary Service, 1953–87; Mem. Council, CBI, 1965–83; Chm., E and W

Ridings Regional Council, FBI, 1962–64; Pres., Nat. Fedn of Engrs Tool Manufrs, 1963–65; Pres., Fedn of British Hand Tool Manufrs, 1960–61. Pres., Sheffield Chamber of Commerce, 1984–85. FIMgt. Hon. Col, 3rd Bn Yorks Vol., subseq. 3rd/4th Bn Yorks Vol., later 3rd Bn Duke of Wellington's, 1988–93. Chm., Yorks & Humberside TAVRA, 1991–94. Hon. Fellow, Sheffield City Polytechnic, 1978; Hon. LLD Sheffield, 1982. Master Cutler of Hallamshire, 1958; High Sheriff of Hallamshire, 1971; DL South Yorkshire, 1974, JP 1985. KStJ 1986. *Recreations:* golf, racing. *Address:* Barn Cottage, Lindrick Common, near Worksop S81 8BA. *T:* (01909) 562806. *Clubs:* East India; Lindrick (Worksop); Royal and Ancient (St Andrews); Hon. Co. of Edinburgh Golfers (Muirfield).

NEILL, John Mitchell, CBE 1994; Chief Executive, Unipart Group of Companies, since 1987; a Director, Bank of England, since 1996; *b* 21 July 1947; *s* of Justin Bernard Neill and Johanna Elizabeth Neill; *m* 1975, Jacquelyn Anne, *d* of late Philip Brown; two *s*. *Educ:* George Heriot's Sch., Edinburgh; Univ. of Strathclyde (BA, MBA, DBA). Europe AC Delco: Planning Manager, 1969–71; Marketing Manager, 1972–73; British Leyland: Merchandising Manager, 1974–75, Sales and Marketing Dir, 1976, Parts Div.; Managing Director: Car Parts Div., 1977–78; BL Components, 1979–80; Unipart Gp, 1981–82; Gp Man. Dir, Unipart Gp Ltd, 1983–86. Dir, Charter plc, 1994–. Dir, BITC, 1992–. Vice President: Inst. of Mktg; Inst. of Motor Industry; BEN; Pres., SMMT, 2000–. Trustee, Nat. Motor Mus. *Address:* Unipart Group of Companies Ltd, Unipart House, Cowley, Oxford OX4 2PG.

NEILL, Rt Rev. John Robert Winder; *see* Cashel and Ossory, Bishop of.

NEILL, Robert James Macgillivray; barrister; Member (C) Bexley and Bromley, London Assembly, Greater London Authority, since 2000; *b* 24 June 1952; *s* of John Macgillivray Neill and Elsie May Neill (*née* Chaston). *Educ:* London Sch. of Econs (LLB Hons 1973). Called to the Bar, Middle Temple, 1975; barrister in private practice, 1975–. Member (C): Havering BC, 1974–90 (Chm., Envmt and Social Services Cttees); Romford, GLC, 1985–86; Leader, Cons. Gp, GLA, 2000–. Leader, London Fire and Civil Defence Authy, 1985–87. Regl Chm., Gtr London Cons. Party, 1996–99 (Dep. Chm., 1993–96). Contested (C) Dagenham, 1983 and 1987. *Recreations:* opera, travel, sailing. *Address:* Greater London Authority, Romney House, 43 Marsham Street, SW1P 3PY. *T:* (020) 7983 4354. *Clubs:* Athenæum, Carlton, St Stephen's Constitutional.

NEILSON, Ian (Godfrey), DFC 1944; TD 1951; *b* 4 Dec. 1918; *er s* of James Wilson Neilson, solicitor, Glasgow; *m* 1945, D. Alison St Clair Aytoun, Ashintully; one *s* one *d*. *Educ:* Glasgow Acad.; Glasgow Univ. (BL). Legal Trng, Glasgow, 1935–39; Territorial Army, 1938; War Service, 1939–45: Field Artillery; Air Observation Post, 1941; RA Staff, 1944; Lt-Col comdg War Crimes Investigation Unit, Germany, 1945–46; formed and commanded No 666 (Scottish) Sqdn, RAuxAF, 1948–53. Enrolled Solicitor, 1946. Royal Institution of Chartered Surveyors: Scottish Sec., Edinburgh, 1946–53; Asst Sec., London, 1953–61; Under-Sec., 1961–65; The Boys' Brigade: Brigade Sec., 1966–74; Officer, 5th Mid-Surrey Co., 1972–78; Nat. Hon. Vice-Pres., 1982–; Hon. Vice-Pres., W of England Dist, 1983–; Hon. Vice-Pres., Wilts Bn, 1985–. Clerk to Governors of the Cripplegate Foundn, Cripplegate Educnl Foundn, Trustees of St Giles and St Luke's Jt Parochial Charities, and Governors of the Cripplegate Schs Foundn, 1974–81. Hon. Treasurer, Thames Youth Venture Adv. Council (City Parochial Foundn), 1968–76. Vice-Chm., British Council of Churches Youth Dept, 1971–74; Trustee: St George's Chapel, London Airport, 1978–97 (Chm., 1983–96); Douglas Haig Meml Homes, 1979–96; Mem., Nat. Council for Voluntary Youth Services, 1966–74; Pres., London Br., Glasgow Academical Club, 1977–79; Chm. of Governors, Lucas-Tooth Leadership Training Fund for Boys, 1976–83; Governor, Kingsway-Princeton Coll. of Further Educn, 1977–83. Elder, United Reformed Church, St Andrew's, Cheam, 1972–83; Lay Mem., Provincial Ministerial Cttee, URC, 1974–83; Dir and Jt Sec., URC Trust, 1982–95; Mem. Council: Christchurch, Marlborough, 1984–90, 1992–97; St Peter's and St Paul's Trust, Marlborough, 1985–. BIM: Hon. Sec., City of London Branch, 1976–79, Chm., 1979–81, Vice Pres., 1981–87; Chm., Inner London Branches Area Cttee, 1981–83; FIMgt (FBIM 1980). Sen. Instr, Royal Yachting Assoc., 1977–87; Vice-Pres., Air Observation Post Officers Assoc., 1978–; Chm., Epsom Choral Soc., 1977–81. Mem., Soc. for Army Histl Res., 1997–. Freeman, City of London, 1975; Freeman, GAPAN, 1976–78, Liveryman, 1978–; Chm., Queenhithe Ward Club, 1977–78. Hon. Editor: Tower and Town, Marlborough, 1984–95; Talking Newspaper for the Blind, Marlborough, 1987–. *Recreations:* golf, music, gardening. *Address:* The Paddock, Kingsbury Street, Marlborough, Wilts SN8 1HZ. *T:* (01672) 515114. *Clubs:* Marlborough Golf; Chartered Surveyors' Golfing Society (Hon. Mem.).

NEILSON, John Stuart; Managing Director, Customers and Supply, Office of Gas and Electricity Markets, since 2000; *b* 31 May 1959; *s* of Ian Neilson, ISO, and Dr Betty Neilson (*née* Harley); *m* 1985, Alison Christine Green; one *s* one *d*. *Educ:* St Paul's Sch.; Corpus Christi Coll., Cambridge (BA 1st Cl. Hons 1980; Prize for Mgt Studies, ICE, 1980). Joined Department of Energy, 1980: Second Private Sec. to Sec. of State for Energy, 1983–85; Principal, 1985; on secondment to Econ. Secretariat, Cabinet Office, 1988–89; Principal Private Sec. to Sec. of State for Energy, 1989–92; Department of Trade and Industry: Private Sec. to Minister for Energy, 1992–93; Asst Sec., 1993; Director: UK Communications Policy, 1993–97; Aerospace and Defence Industries Policy, 1997–2000. *Address:* Office of Gas and Electricity Markets, 9 Millbank, SW1P 3GE. *T:* (020) 7901 7035.

NELDER, John Ashworth, DSc; FRS 1981; Visiting Professor, Imperial College of Science, Technology and Medicine (formerly Imperial College of Science and Technology), since 1971; Head of Statistics Department, 1968–84, and of Division of Biomathematics, Jan.-Oct. 1984, Rothamsted Experimental Station; *b* 8 Oct. 1924; *s* of Reginald Charles and Edith May Ashworth Nelder; *m* 1955, Mary Hawkes; one *s* one *d*. *Educ:* Blundell's Sch., Tiverton; Cambridge Univ. (MA); DSc Birmingham. Head, Statistics Section, National Vegetable Research Station, 1950–68. Pres., Royal Statistical Soc., 1985–86. Hon. DSc Paul Sabatier, Toulouse, 1981. *Publications:* Computers in Biology, 1974; (with P. McCullagh) Generalized Linear Models, 1983, 2nd edn 1989; responsible for statistical programs (computer), Genstat and GLIM; numerous papers in statistical and biological jls. *Recreations:* piano-playing, music, natural history. *Address:* Cumberland Cottage, 33 Crown Street, Redbourn, St Albans, Herts AL3 7JX. *T:* (01582) 792907.

NELIGAN, John Oliver; His Honour Judge John Neligan; a Circuit Judge, since 1996; *b* 21 June 1944; *yr s* of late Desmond Neligan, OBE and Penelope Anne Stabb; *m* 1971, Mary Brigid Daniel; one *s* two *d*. *Educ:* Brickwall Sch., Northiam. Admitted Solicitor, 1969; called to the Bar, Middle Temple, 1975; practised on Western Circuit; Recorder, 1994–96. Asst Comr, Boundary Commn for England, 1992–95. *Recreations:* walking, painting, gardening. *Address:* Springfield House, Upton Cheyney, Bitton, Bristol BS30 6LY.

See also M. H. D. Neligan.

NELIGAN, Michael Hugh Desmond; His Honour Judge Neligan; a Circuit Judge, since 1990; *b* 2 Dec. 1936; *s* of late Desmond West Edmund Neligan, OBE and Penelope Anne, *d* of Henry Mason; *m* 1965, Lynn (*née* Maidment); three *d*. *Educ:* Bradfield College; Jesus College, Cambridge. Commissioned Royal Sussex Regt, 1960–62; served East Africa with 23rd and 4th Bns, King's African Rifles. Called to the Bar, Middle Temple, 1965; Prosecuting Counsel to the Crown, 1972; Metropolitan Stipendiary Magistrate, 1987–90. *Recreations:* cabinet making, gardening, dog-walking. *Address:* The Law Courts, Barker Road, Maidstone, Kent ME16 8EQ.

See also J. O. Neligan.

NELIS, Mary Margaret; Member (SF) Foyle, Northern Ireland Assembly, since 1998; *b* 27 Aug. 1935; *d* of Denis Elliott and Catherine Coyle Elliott; *m* 1955, William Nelis; eight *s* one *d* (and one *s* decd). *Educ:* Inch Island Nat. Sch.; St Eugene's Convent Sch., Derry; Univ. of Ulster; Magee Adult Educn Faculty. Factory worker, 1949–56; Teacher, NW Coll. of Technol., Derry, then Derry Youth & Community Workshop, 1975–83. Mem., Sinn Féin, 1980–. Mem. (SF) Derry CC, 1994–. Community develt, 1960–: Literacy trainee and Soc. Mem., Derry Reading Workshop, Cornhill High Sch., Derry, 1974–75; Founder Member: Foyle Hills Tenants' Assoc., 1968–73; Dove House, 1985–90; Founder Mem. and Man. Dir, Templemore Co-op., Derry, 1988–91. *Recreations:* painting, writing, music, children. *Address:* 35 Westland Avenue, Derry City, Co. Londonderry BT48 9JE. *T:* (028) 7128 6453.

NELL, family name of **Baroness O'Neill of Bengarve**.

NELLIST, David; caseworker, Citizens Advice Bureau, since 1997; *b* 16 July 1952; *m* 1984, Jane Warner; one *s* three *d*. Mem., MSF. Welfare Rights Advr, Robert Zara & Co., 1992–97. Member: (Lab) W Midlands CC, 1982–86; (Socialist) Coventry CC, 1998– (Leader, Socialist Gp, 1999–). MP (Lab, 1983–91, Ind. Lab, 1991–92) Coventry SE; contested: (Ind. Lab) Coventry SE, 1992; (Socialist) Coventry S, 1997. Mem. Nat. Cttee, Socialist Party, 1997–; Chm., Socialist Alliance, 1998–. *Address:* 33 Coundon Road, Coventry CV1 4AR. *T:* (024) 7655 2059, *Fax:* (08700) 560199; *e-mail:* dave@nellist.net.

NELMES, Dianne Gwenllian, (Mrs I. McBride); Controller, Documentaries and Features, ITV Network Ltd, since 2000; *b* Windlesham, 6 March 1951; *d* of late James Allen Nelmes and of Celandine Nelmes; *m* 1986, Ian McBride. *Educ:* Holt Co. Girls' Sch., Wokingham; Newcastle upon Tyne Univ. (BA Hons Econs/Politics 1973; Pres., Students' Union, 1973–74). Professional Cert. NCTJ 1978. Thomson grad. trainee journalist (Sen. News Reporter, Municipal corresp.), 1974–78; journalist, on-screen reporter/presenter, BBC TV NE, 1978–83; News Ed., journalist, World in Action, Granada TV, 1983–87; Producer/Dir, Brass Tacks, BBC TV, 1987–88; Granada TV, 1988–98: Launch Ed., This Morning; Exec. Producer, Entertainment (Stars in their Eyes, 1988–89; You've Been Framed!, 1989–90); Ed., World in Action, 1992; Hd, 1993, Controller, 1994–96, Factual Progs; Controller, Lifestyle Progs (launched 5 satellite-digital channels), 1996–98; Controller, Daytime, ITV Network Ltd, 1998–2000. Mem. Council, BAFTA, 2000–. FRTS 1996. *Recreations:* canal boating, travel, cooking, gardening. *Address:* ITV Network Ltd, 200 Gray's Inn Road, WC1X 8HF. *T:* (020) 7843 8090.

NELSON, family name of **Earl Nelson** and **Baron Nelson of Stafford**.

NELSON, 9th Earl *cr* 1805, of Trafalgar and of Merton; **Peter John Horatio Nelson;** Baron Nelson of the Nile and of Hilborough, Norfolk, 1801; Viscount Merton, 1805; *b* 9 Oct. 1941; *s* of Captain Hon. John Marie Joseph Horatio Nelson (*d* 1970) (*y s* of 5th Earl) and of Kathleen Mary, *d* of William Burr, Torquay; *S* uncle, 1981; *m* 1st, 1969, Maureen Diana (marr. diss. 1992), *d* of Edward Patrick Quinn, Kilkenny; one *s* one *d*; 2nd, 1992, Tracy Cowie; one *s*. Chm., Retainacar Ltd, 1988–94. President: Royal Naval Commando Assoc.; Nelson Soc.; Vice-Pres., Jubilee Sailing Trust; Hon. Life Member: Royal Naval Assoc.; Royal Naval Museum. *Heir: s* Viscount Merton, *qv*. *Club:* St James's.

NELSON OF STAFFORD, 3rd Baron, *cr* 1960; **Henry Roy George Nelson;** Bt 1955; Managing Director, TIB Mercantile Ltd, since 1998; *b* 26 Oct. 1943; *er s* of 2nd Baron Nelson of Stafford and Pamela Roy, *yr d* of Ernest Roy Bird, MP; *S* father, 1995; *m* 1968, Dorothy, *yr d* of Leslie Caley; one *s* one *d*. *Educ:* Ampleforth; King's Coll., Cambridge (MA). CEng, FIMechE, MIEE. Joined RHP Bearings, 1970: Gen. Manager, transmission bearings, 1973–78, automotive bearings, 1978–81; Manufacturing Dir, industrial bearings, 1981–83; Man. Dir, Hopkinsons Ltd, 1983–85; Man. Dir, industrial and distribution divs, Pegler-Hattersley plc, 1985–86; Gp Man. Dir, GSPK Ltd, 1986–90; Man. Dir, power transmission div., Fenner plc, 1991–92; Ops Dir, TIB plc, 1993–97 (non-exec. Dir, 1998–2000). Mem., Govt Cttee of Enquiry into Engrng Profession, 1978–80. *Heir: s* Hon. Alistair William Henry Nelson, *b* 3 June 1973. *Address:* Eastlands, Tibthorpe, Driffield, E Yorks YO25 9LD. *Club:* Farmers'.

NELSON, NZ, Bishop of, since 1990; **Rt Rev. Derek Lionel Eaton,** QSM 1985; *b* 10 Sept. 1941; *s* of Henry Jackson Eaton and Ella Barbara (*née* McDouall); *m* 1964, Alice Janice Maslin; two *s* one *d*. *Educ:* Christchurch Boys' High Sch. (NZ); AG Graduate Sch., Missouri (MA *cum laude*); Switzerland (Cert. Française); Univ. of Tunis (Cert. Arabic and Islamics); Missionary Training Coll., Australia (DipTheol): Trinity Theol Coll., Bristol. School teacher, 1964. Missionary with Worldwide Evangelisation Crusade, Tunisia, 1968–78; ordained deacon and priest, 1971; Curate, St Luke's, Bristol, 1971–72; Vicar of Tunis, 1972–78; Hon. Chaplain, British Embassy, Tunis, 1972–78; Provost, Cairo Cathedral, Egypt, 1978–83 (Emeritus, 1984); Hon. Chaplain, British Embassy, Egypt, 1978–83; with Church Missionary Society, 1980–84; Assoc. Vicar, Papanui, Bishopdale, NZ, 1984–85; Vicar, Sumner, Redcliffs, NZ, 1985–90. Hon. Canon, Cairo Cathedral, 1985. *Publications:* After Death What?; contrib. theol and missiological jls. *Recreations:* swimming, golf, reading, tennis. *Address:* Bishopdale, PO Box 100, Nelson, New Zealand. *T:* (3) 5483124.

NELSON, Anthony; *see* Nelson, R. A.

NELSON, Bertram James, OBE 1984; HM Diplomatic Service, retired; Consul-General, Antwerp, 1983–85; *b* 7 Dec. 1925; *s* of Herbert James Nelson and Adelaide Mabel Nelson (*née* Newton); *m* 1958, Constance Dangerfield; one *s* one *d*. *Educ:* North Kensington Central School. Grenadier Guards, 1944–47; Post Office and Cable and Wireless, 1947–54; Foreign Office, 1954; served Cairo, Budapest, Athens, Asunción, Zagreb, DSAO, 1966–69; Vice-Consul, Tokyo, 1969–71; Vice-Consul, Tehran, 1972–75; FCO, 1975–79; First Sec. and Consul, Brussels, 1979–83. *Recreation:* enjoying retirement. *Address:* 2 Hornbeam Close, Aldwick, Bognor Regis, West Sussex PO21 4AH.

NELSON, Eric Victor, LVO 1975; HM Diplomatic Service, retired; *b* 11 Jan. 1927; *s* of Victor H. H. and E. Vera B. Nelson (*née* Collingwood); *m* 1960, Maria Teresa (Marité) Paul; one *d* (and one *d* decd). *Educ:* Western High School; George Washington University, Washington DC. Royal Air Force, 1945–48. Board of Trade, 1949; served FO, later FCO: Athens, Belgrade, Haiphong, Caracas; First Sec., Saigon, 1962; First Sec. and Consul, Bujumbura, 1964 (Chargé d'Affaires *ai*, 1966–67); FO 1968; First Sec. and

Consul, Asunçión, 1971; First Sec., Mexico City, 1974; FCO, 1978; seconded to Brunei Govt Service as Special Adviser to HM Sultan of Brunei, for Establishment of Brunei Diplomatic Service, 1981–84; Consul-Gen., Bordeaux, 1984–87. Order of the Aztec Eagle, Mexico, 1975. *Recreations:* photography, giving illustrated talks, tourism, cartooning, sculpture. *Address:* 8 Purberry Grove, Ewell, Surrey KT17 1LU.

NELSON, Sir Jamie (Charles Vernon Hope), 4th Bt *cr* 1912, of Acton Park, Acton, Denbigh; *b* 23 Oct. 1949; *s* of Sir William Vernon Hope Nelson, OBE and Hon. Elizabeth Ann Bevil Cary, *er d* of 14th Viscount Falkland; *S* father, 1991; *m* 1983, Maralyn Beverly Hedge (*née* Pyatt); one *s*. *Heir:* *b* Dominic William Michael Nelson [*b* 13 March 1957; *m* 1981, Sarah, *e d* of late John Neil Hylton Jolliffe; three *s* one *d*].

NELSON, Prof. Janet Laughland, PhD; FBA 1996; Professor of Medieval History, King's College, London, since 1993; *b* 28 March 1942; *d* of William Wilson Muir and Elizabeth Barnes Muir (*née* Laughland); *m* 1965, Howard George Horatio Nelson; one *s* one *d*. *Educ:* Keswick Sch., Cumbria; Newnham Coll., Cambridge (BA 1964; PhD 1967). King's College, London: Lectr, 1970–87; Reader, 1987–93; Dir, Centre for Late Antique and Medieval Studies, 1994–2000; FKC 2001. Chm., Adv. Bd, Inst. of Histl Res., Univ. of London, 1998–2001. Vice-Pres., British Acad., 1999–2001; FRHistS 1982 (Pres., 2000–); Corresp. Fellow, Medieval Acad. of Amer., 2000. *Publications:* Politics and Ritual in Early Medieval Europe, 1986; The Annals of St-Bertin, 1991; Charles the Bald, 1992; The Frankish World, 1996; Rulers and Ruling Families, 1999; (ed jtly) Rituals of Power, 2000; (ed jtly) The Medieval World, 2001. *Recreations:* music, walking, looking after grandson Elias. *Address:* 71 Oglander Road, SE15 4DD. *T:* (020) 8693 7252.

NELSON, John Graeme; Management Consultant, First Class Partnerships, since 1997; *b* 19 June 1947; *s* of late Charles and of Jean Nelson; *m* 1971, Pauline Dickinson; two *s* one *d*. *Educ:* Aylesbury and Slough Grammar Schs; Univ. of Manchester (BA Econ Hons). Management trainee, BR Western Reg., 1968; Asst Station Man., Liverpool Street, 1971; Area Passenger Man., Shenfield, 1973; Passenger Sales Officer, Leeds, 1977; Passenger Man., Sheffield Div., 1979; Personal Asst, Chief Exec. BRB, 1981; Parcels Man., Southern Reg., 1982; Nat. Business Man., Red Star Parcels, 1984; Gen. Man., BR Eastern Reg., 1987; Man. Dir, Network SouthEast, 1991; Gp Man. Dir, S and E, BR, 1994–97; Dir, London Develt, Railtrack, 1997. Director: First Class Insight Ltd, 1997–; Renaissance Trains Ltd, 1999–; Hull Trains, 1999–; Mem. Bd, M40 Trains Ltd, 1998–. Chm., Tees, E and N Yorks Ambulance Service NHS Trust, 1997–. *Recreations:* piano, football, badminton. *Address:* First Class Partnerships, 32 St Paul's Square, York YO24 4BD. *T:* (01904) 638659, *Fax:* (01904) 635270; *e-mail:* fcp@easynet.co.uk.

NELSON, Michael Edward; Chairman, Reuter Foundation, 1982–90; General Manager, 1976–89, and Deputy Managing Director, 1981–89, Reuters Ltd; *b* 30 April 1929; *s* of late Thomas Alfred Nelson and Dorothy Pretoria Nelson; *m* 1960, Helga Johanna (*née* den Ouden); two *s* one *d*. *Educ:* Latymer Upper School; Magdalen College, Oxford (MA). Joined Reuters, London, as trainee financial journalist, 1952; assignments Asia, 1954–57; returned to London; Manager, Reuters Economic Services, 1962; Chairman, 1987–88: Reuters Asia; Reuters Europe; Reuters Overseas. Trustee: Visnews, 1990–92 (Chm., 1985–89); Internat. Inst. of Communications, 1989–95 (Chm., UK Chapter, 1989–92); Chm. Adv. Council, World Link, 1990–92. Mem., Newspaper Panel, MMC, 1989–95. Trustee, St Bride's Church, 1989–. Hon. Res. Fellow, Univ. of Kent, 1997–. *Publications:* War of the Black Heavens: the battles of western broadcasting in the cold war, 1997; Queen Victoria and the Discovery of the Riviera, 2001. *Recreations:* walking, music, history. *Address:* 21 Lansdowne Road, W11 3AG. *T:* (020) 7727 8533; Domaine de la Rose, 2 Chemin des Restanques, 06650 Opio, France. *T:* 493773232. *Club:* Garrick.

NELSON, Nicholas; Director, Resources and Planning, Design Council; *b* 20 Jan. 1947; *s* of late Peter Nelson and Margaret Nelson; *m* 1972, Charmian Alice (*née* Bell); one *s* two *d*. *Educ:* Pudsey Grammar Sch., Yorkshire; Reading Univ. (BA (Hons) History; CertEd 1992). BOAC: Management Trainee, 1969; Air Cargo Sales Rep., 1971; Cargo Sales Man., Japan/Dep. Marketing Man., Japan, 1973; British Airways: Cargo Manager: Eastern Scotland, 1978; Midlands, 1979; DHL International (UK) Ltd: Gen. Man., 1981; Man. Dir, 1982; Regional Dir (Europe), 1987; Man. Dir, Parcels, PO, then Royal Mail Parcelforce, 1987–91; teacher, 1992–95, Head Teacher, 1995–2000, Queens' Sch., Bushey. *Recreation:* cricket. *Address:* Design Council, 34 Bow Street, WC2E 7DL.

NELSON, Air Marshal Sir Richard; *see* Nelson, Air Marshal Sir S. R. C.

NELSON, (Richard) Anthony; Vice Chairman, Schroder Salomon Smith Barney, since 2000; *b* 11 June 1948; *o s* of late Gp Captain R. G. Nelson, BSc, CEng, FRAeS, MICE, and of Mrs J. M. Nelson; *m* 1974, Caroline Victoria Butler; one *s* one *d*. *Educ:* Harrow Sch. (State scholarship; Head of School; Rothschild Scholar, 1966); Christ's Coll., Cambridge (MA (Hons) Economics and Law). N. M. Rothschild & Sons Ltd, 1969–73; Man. Dir, Salomon Smith Barney, 1997–2000. Mem., Bow Gp Council, 1973. Dir, Chichester Fest. Th., 1983–92. Contested (C) E Leeds, Feb. 1974. MP (C) Chichester, Oct. 1974–97. PPS to Minister for Housing and Construction, 1979–83, to Minister of State for the Armed Forces, 1983–85; Economic Sec., 1992–94, Minister of State, 1994–95, HM Treasury; Minister of State, DTI, 1995–97. Member: Select Cttee on Science and Technology, 1975–79; Select Cttee on Televising of Proceedings of the House, 1988–92. FRSA 1979. *Recreations:* music, Rugby. *Address:* The Old Vicarage, Easebourne, near Midhurst, W Sussex GU29 0AL.

NELSON, Dr (Richard) Stuart, FInstP; Consultant, β Technology Ltd, since 1996; *b* 1 May 1937; *s* of Richard and Winifred Emily Nelson; *m* 1965, Veronica Mary Beck; one *s* two *d*. *Educ:* Univ. of Reading (BSc 1st Cl. Hons Physics, 1958; DSc 1969). FInstP 1968. Joined UKAEA, Harwell, 1958; Div. Head, Materials Develt Div., 1981; Dir, Nuclear Power Res., 1984; Dir, Northern Res. Labs, 1987–90 (including Risley, Springfield and Windscale Labs); Mem. Bd, UKAEA, 1991–96; Man. Dir, Industrial Business Gp, 1991–94, Exec. Dir, Ops, 1994–96, AEA Technology. Vis. Prof., Univ. of Sussex, 1970–. *Publications:* The Observation of Atomic Collisions in Crystalline Solids, 1968; Ion Implantation, 1973; Innovation Business, 1999; 200 papers in scientific jls. *Recreations:* hockey (played for Berkshire), golf (Club Captain, 1998), tennis. *Address:* c/o β Technology Ltd, Barclay Court, Doncaster Carr, Doncaster DN4 5HZ. *T:* (01302) 322633.

NELSON, Hon. Sir Robert (Franklyn), Kt 1996; **Hon. Mr Justice Nelson;** a Judge of the High Court of Justice, Queen's Bench Division, since 1996; *b* 19 Sept. 1942; *s* of late Clarence William and of Lucie Margaret Nelson; *m* 1968, Anne-Marie Sabina Hall; two *s*. *Educ:* Repton; St John's Coll., Cambridge (MA). Called to the Bar, Middle Temple, 1965 (Harmsworth Entrance Exhibn, 1963), Bencher, 1993; QC 1985; a Recorder, 1986–96. *Recreations:* cricket, opera, golf. *Address:* Royal Courts of Justice, Strand, WC2A 2LL.

NELSON, Air Marshal Sir (Sidney) Richard (Carlyle), KCB 1963 (CB 1962); OBE 1949; Director-General, Royal Air Force Medical Services, 1962–67; Director of Research and Medical Services, Aspro-Nicholas Ltd, 1967–72; *b* Ponoka, Alberta, Canada, 14 Nov. 1907; *s* of M. O. Nelson, BA; *m* 1939, Christina Elizabeth Powell; two *s*. *Educ:* University of Alberta (MD). Commissioned in RAF, 1935; served: England 1935–36; Egypt and Western Desert, 1936–42; Fighter Command, 1943; UK Delegation (Canada), 1943–44; British Jt Services Mission (Washington), 1945–48; RAF Staff Coll., 1949; Air Ministry, 1949–52; Comd RAF Hosp., Nocton Hall, 1953–55; SMO British Forces, Arabian Peninsula, 1956–57; PMO Technical Training Comd, 1957–59; Bomber Comd, 1959–62, QHP 1961–67. *Recreations:* fishing, golf. *Address:* Caffyn's Copse, Shappen Hill Lane, Burley, Hants BH24 4EP. *T:* (01425) 403308. *Club:* Royal Air Force.

NELSON, Stuart; *see* Nelson, R. S.

NEPEAN, Lt-Col Sir Evan Yorke, 6th Bt *cr* 1802; late Royal Signals; *b* 23 Nov. 1909; *s* of Sir Charles Evan Molyneux Yorke Nepean, 5th Bt, and Mary Winifred, *o d* of Rev. William John Swayne, formerly Vicar of Heytesbury, Wilts, and Custos of St John's Hospital, Heytesbury; *S* father, 1953; *m* 1940, (Georgiana) Cicely, *o d* of late Major Noel Edward Grey Willoughby, Middlesex Regiment, of Chancel End House, Heytesbury, Wilts; three *d*. *Educ:* Winchester; Downing College, Cambridge (BA 1931; MA 1946). CEng; MIEE. North West Frontier of India (Mohmand), 1935. Served War of 1939–45: GSO3, War Office, 1939–40; with Royal Signals (Lt-Col 1943), UK, and Middle East, Major 1946; on Staff Southern Command, 1947; GSO1 Royal Signals, Ministry of Defence, 1950–53; Lt-Col 1952; GHQ FARELF, Singapore, 1953–55; Cmdg 11 Air Formation Signal Regt, BAOR, 1955–56, retired. Civil Servant, 1957–59; CSO's branch at HQ Southern Command (Retired Officers' Staff appt), 1959–73. Mem., Salisbury Diocesan Guild of Ringers. *Recreations:* bell-ringing, amateur radio. *Heir:* none. *Address:* Elm View, 31 High Street, West Lavington, Devizes, Wilts SN10 4HQ.

NERINA, Nadia, (Mrs Charles Gordon); Prima Ballerina; Ballerina with Royal Ballet, 1951–69; *b* Cape Town, Oct. 1927; *née* Nadine Judd; *m* 1955, Charles Gordon. Joined Sadler's Wells Sch., 1946; after two months joined Sadler's Wells Theatre Ballet; transferred Sadler's Wells Ballet, Royal Opera House (now Royal Ballet), as soloist, 1967. *Rôles:* Princess Aurora in The Sleeping Beauty; Ondine; Odette-Odile in Swan Lake; Swanhilda in Coppelia; Sylvia; Giselle; Cinderella; Firebird; Can Can Dancer in La Boutique Fantasque; Ballerina in Petrushka; Colombine in Carnaval; Mazurka, Little Waltz, Prelude, in Les Sylphides; Mam'zelle Angot; Ballet Imperial; Scènes de Ballet; Flower Festival of Genzano; Les Rendezvous; Polka in Façade; The Girl in Spectre de la Rose; Casse Noisette; Laurentia; Khadra; Vagabonds; The Bride in A Wedding Bouquet; *creations:* Circus Dancer in Mardi Gras; Fairy Spring in Cinderella; Queen of the Earth in Homage to the Queen; Faded Beauty in Noctambules; Variation on a Theme; Birthday Offering; Lise in La Fille Mal Gardée; Electra; The Girl in Home; Clorinda in Tancredi. Appeared with Royal Ballet: Europe; South Africa; USA; Canada; USSR; Bulgaria; Romania. Recital Tours with Alexis Rassine: South Africa, 1952–55; England, 1956–57; concert performances, Royal Albert Hall and Royal Festival Hall, 1958–60. *Guest appearances include:* Turkish Nat. Ballet, 1957; Bolshoi Ballet, Kirov Ballet, 1960; Munich Ballet, 1963; Nat. Finnish Ballet, Royal Danish Ballet, 1964; Stuttgart Ballet, 1965; Ballet Theatre, Opera House Chicago, 1967; Royal Command Variety Performances, 1963–66. Mounted, dir. and prod three Charity Gala performances, London Palladium, 1969, 1971, 1972. Many TV appearances, UK and USA. Hon. Consultant on Ballet, Ohio Univ., 1967–69. British Jury Member: 3rd Internat. Ballet Competition, Moscow, 1977; Benois de la Danse Competition, Moscow, 1993, Paris, 1996. Fellow, 1959, Patron, 1964, Cecchetti Soc. Mem. Council, RSPCA, 1969–74. *Publications:* contrib.: La Fille Mal Gardée, 1960; Ballet and Modern Dance, 1974; *relevant publication:* Ballerina, ed Clement Crisp, 1975.

NESBITT, Dermot William Gibson; Member (UU) South Down, Northern Ireland Assembly, since 1998; *b* 14 Aug. 1947; *s* of William Cromwell Nesbitt and Georgina Nesbitt; *m* 1970, Margaret Oriel Patterson; one *s* one *d*. *Educ:* Queen's Univ., Belfast (BSc 1st cl. Hons Econs). School Teacher, 1969–74; Lectr, Ulster Poly., 1976; Queen's Univ., Belfast, 1976–98 (Sen. Lectr and Head, Dept of Accounting and Finance). Mem., NI Forum for Political Dialogue, 1996–98. Jun. Minister, assisting David Trimble, 1999–. Contested (UU) S Down, 2001. *Publications:* over 20 academic publications. *Recreations:* gardening, ski-ing, Boys' Brigade. *Address:* 21 Downpatrick Road, Crossgar, Downpatrick, Co. Down BT30 9EQ. *T:* (028) 4483 1561.

NESS, Robert; Director, Portugal, British Council, and Cultural Counsellor, Lisbon, since 2000; *b* 30 March 1953; *s* of Robert Mitchell Ness and Mary Ness (*née* Connor); *m* 1985, Geraldine McKendrick; two *s* one *d*. *Educ:* Arbroath High Sch.; Edinburgh Univ. (MA Hons; DipEd); Moray House Coll. of Educn (PGCE). Teacher, Madrid, 1978–80; joined British Council, 1981: English Tuition Co-ordinating Unit, 1981–83; Overseas Educnl Appts Dept, 1983–86; Asst Rep., Austria, 1987–89; English Lang. Div., 1989–92; Dep. Dir, SA, 1992–97; Dir, Cyprus, 1997–2000. *Recreations:* music, especially jazz, running, travel. *Address:* c/o British Council, Rua de São Marcal 174, 1249-062 Lisbon, Portugal. *Clubs:* Royal British, Gremio Literario (Lisbon).

NESTOR, Rt Rev. Donald Patrick; Hon. Assistant Bishop, Diocese of Durham, since 2001; *b* 6 Oct. 1938; *s* of Edwin Roy Nestor and Elsie Myrtle Nestor. *Educ:* Heath Grammar Sch., Halifax, Yorks; Exeter Coll., Oxford (MA); Queen's Coll., Birmingham and Univ. of Birmingham (DipTh). Deacon 1965, priest 1966; Curate: Woodkirk, dio. Wakefield, 1965–68; Forton, dio. Portsmouth, 1968–72; Asst Chaplain, Univ. of Botswana, Lesotho and Swaziland, Roma, 1972–74, Chaplain of Univ. (from 1975 called Nat. Univ. of Lesotho), 1974–79; Warden of Diocesan Seminary, Roma, 1974–79; Suffragan Bishop, Diocese of Lesotho, 1979–92; Priest-in-Charge, Bretherton, 1992–2000; Asst Bp, Dio. of Blackburn, 1992–2000; Diocesan Ecumenical Officer, Blackburn, 1998–2000. *Recreations:* singing, travel. *Address:* SSM, St Antony's Priory, 74 Claypath, Durham DH1 1QT. *T:* (0191) 384 3747.

NETANYAHU, Binyamin; Prime Minister of Israel and Minister of Housing and Construction, 1996–99; *b* 21 Oct. 1949; *s* of Cela and Benzion Netanyahu; *m* (marr. diss.); one *d*; *m* 3rd, 1991, Sara; two *s*. *Educ:* MIT (BA 1976; MBA). Man. Consultant, Boston Consulting Gp, 1976–78; Exec. Dir, Jonathan Inst., Jerusalem, 1978–80; Sen. Manager, Rim Industries, Jerusalem, 1980–82; Dep. Chief of Mission, Washington, 1982–84; Perm. Rep. to UN, 1984–88; Deputy Minister: Ministry of Foreign Affairs, 1988–91; Prime Minister's Office, 1991–92. Leader, Likud, 1993–99. *Publications:* (ed) Self-Portrait of a Hero: the letters of Jonathan Netanyahu, 1981; Terrorism: how the West can win, 1986; A Place Among the Nations: Israel and the world, 1993; Fighting Terrorism, 1996.

NETHERCOT, Prof. David Arthur, PhD, DSc; FREng, FIStructE, FICE; Professor of Civil Engineering, and Head of Department of Civil and Environmental Engineering, Imperial College of Science, Technology and Medicine, University of London, since 1999; *b* 26 April 1946; *s* of late Arthur Owen Martin Nethercot and Dorothy May Nethercot; *m* 1968, Hedd Dwynwen Evans; two *d*. *Educ:* Univ. of Wales Coll. of Cardiff (BSc, PhD, DSc). FIStructE 1989; FICE 1994; FREng (FEng 1993); FCGI 2001. ICI Fellow, Univ. of Wales, 1970–71; Lectr, 1971–81, Sen. Lectr, 1981–86, Reader, 1986–89,

Univ. of Sheffield; Prof. of Civil Engrg, 1989–99, and Hd of Dept, Univ. of Nottingham. Visiting Professor: Japan Soc. for Promotion of Science, Univ. of Nagoya, 1980; Swiss Federal Inst. of Tech., Lausanne, 1990. Vice-Pres., IStructE, 2001– (Mem. Council, 1986–89, 1991–97); Member: Cttee on Structural Use of Steel in Building, BSI, 1986– (Chm., 1995–); Joint Bd of Moderators, 1993–2000 (Chm., 1996–98); Standing Cttee on Structural Safety, 1996–; Council, Royal Acad. of Engrg, 2000–. *Publications:* (jtly) Design for Structural Stability, 1979, 2nd edn 1985; Limit States Design of Structural Steelwork, 1986, 3rd edn 2001; (jtly) Design of Members Subject to Combined Bending and Torsion, 1989; (jtly) Lateral Stability of Steel Beams and Columns: common causes of restraint, 1992; about 300 sci. papers on structural engrg. *Recreation:* sport. *Address:* Department of Civil and Environmental Engineering, Imperial College of Science, Technology and Medicine, Imperial College Road, SW7 2BU. *T:* (020) 7594 6097, *Fax:* (020) 7594 6042.

NETHERTHORPE, 3rd Baron *cr* 1959, of Anston, W Riding; **James Frederick Turner;** *b* 7 Jan. 1964; *s* of 2nd Baron Netherthorpe, and of Belinda, *d* of F. Hedley Nicholson; *S* father, 1982; *m* 1989, Elizabeth Curran Fahan, *d* of Edward Fahan, Connecticut; two *s* two *d*. *Educ:* Heatherdown Prep. School; Harrow School. *Heir: s* Hon. Andrew James Edward Turner, *b* 24 March 1993. *Address:* Boothby Hall, Boothby Pagnell, Grantham, Lincs NG33 4PQ. *T:* (01476) 585374.

NETTEL, Caroline Gillian; *see* Mawhood, C. G.

NEUBERGER, Hon. Sir David Edmond, Kt 1996; **Hon. Mr Justice Neuberger;** a Judge of the High Court of Justice, Chancery Division, since 1996; *b* 10 Jan. 1948; *s* of Prof. Albert Neuberger, CBE, FRS and of Lilian Ida (*née* Dreyfus); *m* 1976, Angela, *d* of Brig. Peter Holdsworth; two *s* one *d*. *Educ:* Westminster; Christ Church, Oxford (MA). N. M. Rothschild & Sons, 1970–73; called to the Bar, Lincoln's Inn, 1974, Bencher, 1993; QC 1987; a Recorder, 1990–96. Chm., Adv. Cttee on Spoliation of Art, 1999–. Gov., London Inst., 2000–. *Address:* Royal Courts of Justice, Strand, WC2A 2LL.
See also M. S. Neuberger.

NEUBERGER, Rabbi Julia Babette Sarah; Chief Executive, The King's Fund, since 1997; a Civil Service Commissioner, since 2001; *b* 27 Feb. 1950; *d* of late Walter and of Alice Schwab; *m* 1973, Anthony John Neuberger; one *s* one *d*. *Educ:* South Hampstead High Sch.; Newnham Coll., Cambridge (BA, MA); Leo Baeck Coll., London (Rabbinic Dip.). Lectr and Associate Fellow, Leo Baeck Coll., 1979–97; Associate, Newnham Coll., Cambridge, 1983–96; Harkness Fellow, Harvard Univ., 1991–92; Associate Fellow, King's Fund Coll., 1993–97. Rabbi, South London Liberal Synagogue, 1977–89; Chm., Rabbinic Conf., Union of Liberal and Progressive Synagogues, 1983–85. Chm., Camden and Islington Community Health Services NHS Trust, 1993–97; Member: Council, N London Hospice Gp, 1984–91; Ethics Adv. Gp, RCN, 1986–93; BMA Ethics Cttee, 1992–94; NHS Health Adv. Service, 1993–97; Council, St George's Hosp. Med. Sch., 1987–93; Chairman: Patients' Assoc., 1988–91; RCN Commn on the Health Service, 1988; Adv. Cttee, UK Clearing House on Health Outcomes, Nuffield Inst., 1992–95; Sainsbury Centre for Mental Health review of training needs of mental health workers. Member: Cttee on Standards in Public Life, 2001–; Interim (formerly Voluntary) Licensing Authority for IVF, 1987–91; Human Fertilization and Embryology Authority, 1990–95; GMC, 1993–; MRC, 1995–2000; Exec., Anchor Housing Assoc. and Trust, 1985–87; Exec., NCVO, 1988–89; Exec., Unicef UK, 1989–91; Council, SCF, 1994–96; Bd, Citizenship Foundn, 1989–92; Council, St George's House, Windsor, 1989–94; Council, Runnymede Trust, 1989–97; Library and Information Commn, 1995–97; DCMS Mem., Review of Funding of BBC, 1999; Governor, British Inst. of Human Rights, 1989–93; Trustee, Imperial War Mus., 1999–. Member: Nat. Cttee, SDP, 1982–88; Policy Cttee, SDP, 1983–85; Convenor, SDP/Liberal Lawyers' Working Party on Legal Services, 1985–87; Mem., Editorial Bd, Political Qly, 1987–93. Presenter, Choices, BBC TV, 1986 and 1987. Chancellor, Univ. of Ulster, 1993–2000. Member Council: RHBNC, 1991–93; UCL, 1993–97; Mem. Visiting Cttee, Meml Church, Harvard Univ., 1994–2000; Governor: James Allen's Girls' Sch., 1994–97; Dulwich Coll. Prep. Sch., 1995–97. Booker Prize Judge, 1994. Hon. FCGI 1997; Hon. Fellow, Mansfield Coll., Oxford, 1998. DUniv: Humberside, 1992; Stirling, 1995; Open, 1997; Hon. DSc: Ulster, 1994; Oxford Brookes, 1995; Hon. DLitt: City, 1994; Teesside, 1995; Hon. LLD; Nottingham, 1996; Hon. Dr QUB, 2000. *Publications:* The Story of Judaism (for children), 1986, 2nd edn 1988; (ed) Days of Decision (4 in series), 1987; Caring for Dying Patients of Different Faiths, 1987, 2nd edn 1994; (ed with John A. White) A Necessary End, 1991; Whatever's Happening to Women?, 1991; Ethics and Healthcare: the role of Research Ethics Committees in the UK, 1992; (ed) The Things That Matter (anthology of women's spiritual poetry), 1993; On Being Jewish, 1995; Dying Well: a guide to enabling a better death, 1999; contribs to various books on cultural, religious and ethical factors in nursing, reviews for variety of jls and newspapers. *Recreations:* riding, sailing, Irish life, opera, setting up the old girls' network, children. *Address:* The King's Fund, 11–13 Cavendish Square, W1G 0AN. *T:* (020) 7307 2400. *Club:* Groucho.

NEUBERGER, Dr Michael Samuel, FRS 1993; Member, Scientific Staff, Medical Research Council Laboratory of Molecular Biology, Cambridge, since 1980; Fellow, Trinity College, Cambridge, since 1985; *b* 2 Nov. 1953; *s* of late Prof. Albert Neuberger, CBE, FRS; and of Lilian Ida (*née* Dreyfus); *m* 1991, Gillian Anne, *d* of late James and Anne Pyman; one *s* two *d*. *Educ:* Westminster Sch.; Trinity Coll., Cambridge (BA 1974; MA); Imperial Coll., University of London (PhD 1978). Res. Fellow, Trinity Coll., Cambridge, 1977–81; SRC Postdoctoral Fellow, Imperial Coll., London, 1977–79; EMBO Postdoctoral Fellow, Inst. of Genetics, Cologne, 1979–80. Internat. Res. Scholar, Howard Hughes Med. Inst., 1992–97. Mem., EMBO, 1989; Founder FMedSci 1998. *Publications:* articles in learned jls on molecular biol. and immunology. *Address:* Medical Research Council Laboratory of Molecular Biology, Hills Road, Cambridge CB2 2QH. *T:* (01223) 248011; Trinity College, Cambridge CB2 1TQ. *T:* (01223) 338400.
See also Hon. Sir D. E. Neuberger.

NEUBERT, Sir Michael (Jon), Kt 1990; *b* 3 Sept. 1933; *s* of Frederick Henry and Mathilda Marie Louise Neubert; *m* 1959, Sally Felicity Bilger; one *s*. *Educ:* Queen Elizabeth's Sch., Barnet; Bromley Grammar Sch.; Royal Coll. of Music; Downing Coll., Cambridge. MA (Cantab) Modern and Medieval Langs. Travel and industrial consultant. Councillor, Borough of Bromley, 1960–63; London Borough of Bromley: Councillor, 1964–68; Alderman, 1968–74; Leader of the Council, 1967–70; Mayor, 1972–73. Contested (C): N Hammersmith, 1966; Romford, 1970. MP (C) Havering, Romford, Feb. 1974–1983, Romford, 1983–97; contested (C) same seat, 1997. PPS to: Minister for Social Security and for the Disabled, 1980; Ministers of State, NI Office, 1981; Minister of State for Employment, 1981–82; Sec. of State for Trade, 1982–83; Asst Govt Whip, 1983–86; a Lord Comr of HM Treasury, 1986–88; Vice-Chamberlain of HM Household, 1988; Parly Under-Sec. of State for the Armed Forces, 1988–89, for Defence Procurement, 1989–90, MoD. Chm., Cons. Back bench Employment Cttee, 1992–95; Joint Chm., Cons. Back bench Educn and Employment Cttee, 1995–97; Mem., 1922 Exec. Cttee, 1992–97. Chm., Bromley Conservative Assoc., 1968–69. Rector's Warden, St Margaret's, Westminster, 1997– (Parly Warden, 1995–97). Chm., IoW Internat. Oboe Competition, 1997–. *Publication:* Running Your Own Society, 1967. *Recreations:* music, literature, cinema, theatre, the countryside. *Club:* Carlton.

NEUMANN, Prof. Bernhard Hermann, AC 1994; FAA 1964; FRS 1959; Hon. Fellow, CSIRO Division of Mathematical and Information Sciences (formerly Mathematics and Statistics), since 2000 (Hon. Research Fellow, 1978–99); *b* Berlin-Charlottenburg, 15 Oct. 1909; *s* of late Richard Neumann and late Else (*née* Aronstein); *m* 1st, 1938, Hanna Neumann (*née* von Caemmerer) (*d* 1971), DPhil, DSc, FAA, formerly Prof. and Head of Dept of Pure Mathematics, Sch. of Gen. Studies, ANU; three *s* two *d*; 2nd, 1973, Dorothea Neumann (*née* Zeim), MA, PhD. *Educ:* Herderschule, Berlin; Univs of Freiburg, Berlin, Cambridge. Dr phil Berlin, 1932; PhD Cambridge 1935; DSc Manchester 1954. FACE 1970. Asst Lectr, University Coll, Cardiff, 1937–40. Army Service, 1940–45. Lectr, University Coll., Hull, 1946–48; Lectr, Senior Lectr, Reader, Univ. of Manchester, 1948–61; Prof. and Hd of Dept of Maths, Inst. of Advanced Studies, ANU, Canberra, 1962–74, Emeritus Prof., 1975–; Sen. Res. Fellow, CSIRO Div. of Maths and Stats, 1975–77. Visiting Lecturer: Australian Univs, 1959; Univ. of Cambridge, 1970; Monash Univ., 1980; Visiting Professor: Tata Inst. of Fundamental Research, Bombay, 1959; New York Univ., 1961–62; Univ. of Wisconsin, 1966–67; Vanderbilt Univ., 1969–70; G. A. Miller Vis. Prof., Univ. of Illinois at Urbana-Champaign, 1975; Univ. of Manitoba, 1979; Vis. Fellow, Fitzwilliam Coll., Cambridge, 1970; SERC Visiting Fellow: Univ. of Glasgow, 1985; Univ. of Wales Coll. of Cardiff, 1991; Deutscher Akademischer Austauschs-Dienst Visitor, Univ. of Bielefeld, 1987; Matthew Flinders Lectr, Aust. Acad. Sci., 1984. Wiskundig Genootschap te Amsterdam Prize, 1949; Adams Prize, Univ. of Cambridge, 1952–53. Mem., Aust. Subcommn, Internat. Commn Math. Instruct., 1967–75 (Chm.), and 1979–83; Mem.-at-large, Internat. Commn Math. Instruct., 1975–82, Mem. Exec. Cttee, 1979–82; Mem., Programme Adv. Cttee, Congress Math. Educn, Karlsruhe, 1976, Berkeley, Calif., 1980, Adelaide, Australia, 1984. Member Council: London Math. Society, 1954–61 (Vice-Pres., 1957–59); Aust. Math. Society, 1963–79 (Vice-Pres., 1963–64, 1966–68, 1971–73, Pres., 1964–66; Hon. Mem. 1981–; Fellow, 1994); Aust. Acad. of Science, 1968–71 (a Vice-Pres., 1969–71). Mem. Aust. Nat. Cttee for Mathematics, 1963–75 (Chm., 1966–75); (Foundation) Pres., Aust. Assoc. Math. Teachers, 1966–68, Vice-Pres., 1968–69, Hon. Mem., 1975–; (Foundn) Pres., Canberra Math. Assoc., 1963–65, Vice-Pres., 1965–66, Hon. Mem., 1975–; Hon. Mem., NZ Math. Soc., 1975–; Member: Acad. Adv. Council, RAN Coll., 1978–87; Sci. and Industry Forum, 1989–93. Chairman: Internat. Math. Olympiad Site Cttee, 1981–83; Aust. Math. Olympiad Cttee, 1980–86. Hon. DSc: Univ. of Newcastle, NSW, 1974; Monash Univ., 1982; Univ. of WA, 1995; Univ. of Hull, 1995; ANU, 2001; Hon. DMath Univ. of Waterloo, 1986; Hon. Dr rer. nat. Humboldt Univ., 1992. Non-res. Fellow (Tutor), Bruce Hall, ANU, 1963–; Hon. Fellow: Inst. of Advanced Studies, Sch. of Mathematical Scis, ANU, 1975–; Inst. of Combinatories and its Applications, 1990–. Pres., Amateur Sinfonia of Canberra Inc., 1978–80, Vice-Pres., 1980–81, 1983–84, Hon. Mem., 1984–85; Vice-Pres., Friends of the Canberra Sch. of Music, 1983– (Hon. Life Mem., 2001); Pres., Woden Valley Chess Club, 1994–95. Hon. Editor, Proc. London Math. Soc., 1959–61; Assoc. Editor, Pacific Jl Math., 1964–92; (Foundation) Editor, Bulletin of Aust. Math. Soc., 1969–79, Hon. Editor, 1979–; Member Editorial Board: Communications in Algebra, 1973–84; Houston Jl Math., 1974–; Mem., Adv. Bd, Zentralblatt Didaktik Math. 1970–84; Editorial Advr, SE Asian Math. Bull., 1987–; Founder Editor and Publisher, IMU Canberra Circular, 1972–99; Hon. Editor, Algebra Colloquium, Beijing, 1994–; Mem. and Regional Chm., IMU Exchange Commn, 1975–78. *Publications:* Appendix to German and Hungarian translations of A. G. Kuroš: Teoriya Grupp, 1953, 1955: Topics in the Theory of Infinite Groups, Bombay, 1961; Special Topics in Algebra, Vol. I: Universal Algebra, Vol. II: Order Techniques, New York, 1962; Selected Works of B. H. Neumann and Hanna Neumann, 6 vols, 1988; papers, mainly on theory of groups, in various mathematical journals. *Recreations:* chess, cycling, music, camping. *Address:* 20 Talbot Street, Forrest, ACT 2603, Australia. *T:* (2) 62733447, *Fax:* (2) 61255549; *e-mail:* bernhard.neumann@maths.anu.edu.au.

NEVILL, family name of **Marquess of Abergavenny**.

NEVILL, Amanda Elizabeth; Head, National Museum of Photography, Film and Television, since 1994; *b* 21 March 1957; *d* of John Henry Howard King and Jill King (*née* Livett); *m* 1980, Dominic John Nevill (marr. diss. 1986); two *d*. *Educ:* Bar Convent, York; British Inst., Paris. Rowan Gall., London, 1978–79; Francis Kyle Gall., London, 1979–80; Bath Internat. Fest. Contemporary Art Fair, 1980–84; Adminr, 1985–90, Sec., 1990–94, Royal Photographic Soc. Hon. FRPS 1994. *Address:* National Museum of Photography, Film and Television, Pictureville, Bradford BD1 1NQ. *T:* (01274) 727488.

NEVILL, Prof. Bernard Richard, FCSD; designer; Professor of Textile Design, Royal College of Art, 1984–89 (Fellow, since 1984); Director, Bernard Nevill Ltd (own furnishing collections), since 1990; *b* 24 Sept. 1934; *s* of R. G. Nevill. *Educ:* privately; St Martin's Sch. of Art; Royal Coll. of Art. FSIA 1970. Designed exhibn, Opera and Ballet, for Cotton Bd, Manchester, 1950; lectured in art, fashion, history of costume, textile design and fashion drawing, Shoreditch Coll., 1954–56 (resp. for first dress show staged at GLC Chm's annual reception, County Hall); Lectr, St Martin's Sch. of Art and RCA, 1959–74 (liaised between Fashion and Textile Schs, devising projs and themes for finale to RCA annual diploma show); lectured in theatre design and book illustration, Central Sch. of Art and Design, 1957–60; freelance illustrator, Good Housekeeping, Woman's Jl, Vogue, Harper's Bazaar, incl. covers for Queen and Sketch, 1956–60; freelance journalist, Vogue, Sketch and textile and fashion periodicals, 1956–66; Art Critic, Vogue, 1965–66; Designer (later Design Dir), Liberty Prints, 1961: for next decade, produced collections which became fashion landmarks and re-estabd Liberty's as major source of fashion textiles worldwide; collections designed: Islamic, 1963 (anticipated Eastern revival in fashion); Jazz, 1964 (first re-appraisal of Art Deco); Tango, 1966; Renaissance, 1967; Chameleon, 1969 (co-ordinated prints); Designer and Design Dir, Ten Cate, Holland, 1969–71; Design Consultant in dress fabrics to Cantoni (founders of cotton industry in Italy), 1971–84: printed velvets and cottons have placed Cantoni in forefront of internat. ready-to-wear; designed printed sheet collection for Cantoni Casa, 1977; textile consultant and designer of dress fabrics, Unitika Ltd, Japan, 1990–; dress fabric collections for KBC, Germany, 1993–; furnishing textile designs commnd by Pierre Frey, France, 1991–; furnishing collections produced by DMC Texunion, France, 1992–; designing own-label home textile and furniture collections, with Hodsoll McKenzie, 1999–; redesign and supervision of restoration of interiors: Lennoxlove Castle, 1988–89; Eastnor Castle, 1989. Designed: two collections for Internat. Wool Secretariat, 1975–77; English Country House Collection for Sekers Internat., 1981–82 (used this collection when redesigning Long Gall., Lutyen's British Embassy, Washington); Collections for Romanex de Boussac, France, 1982–87, including English Gardens, Botanic, Figurative Porcelain Prints and Printed Damasks; furnishing collection for restored Château de Bagnole, France. Designed costumes: films: Genevieve, 1953; Next To No Time, 1955; The Admirable Crichton, 1957; musical: Marigold, 1958; opera: Così fan tutte (Glyndebourne), 1962. Engaged in restoration of Fonthill Abbey and woodlands, 1976–. Mem., Adv. Panel, National Dip. of Design, 1964–66; Governor, Croydon Coll. of Art, 1966–67. FRSA 1966, resigned 1977. Book reviewer, TLS, 1987–. Illustrated articles on his work have appeared in the Press.

Recreations: looking at large well-built walls and buildings; passionate conservationist and environmentalist, collector, bibliophil; tree-worship, chamber music. *Address:* West House, 35 Glebe Place, SW3 5JP; Fonthill Abbey, Fonthill Gifford, near Salisbury, Wilts SP3 6PX.

NEVILL, Maj.-Gen. Cosmo Alexander Richard, CB 1958; CBE 1954; DSO 1944; War Office, 1958–60; Colonel, Royal Fusiliers, 1959–63, retired; *b* 14 July 1907; *s* of late Maj. Cosmo Charles Richard Nevill, DSO, OBE, Eccleston, Leamington Spa; *m* 1934, Grania, *d* of late Maj. G. V. Goodliffe, MC, Birdstown, co. Donegal; one *s* one *d. Educ:* Harrow; Royal Military College. Commissioned as Second Lieutenant, Royal Fusiliers, 1927; served War of 1939–45 (DSO, OBE): on staff, India; commanded 2nd battalion Devonshire Regiment, Normandy; Lieutenant-Colonel, 1944. A General Staff Officer, Military Staff Committee, United Nations, New York, 1946–48; Chief Instr, Sch. of Infantry, 1948–50; commanded 1st battalion Royal Fusiliers, 1950–51; a Brigade Commander, 1951–54; Commandant School of Infantry, 1954–56; Major-General 1957; GOC 2nd Infantry Division, 1956–58. CC West Suffolk, 1962–67. Lay Canon, St Edmundsbury Cathedral, 1979–85. Freeman, City of London, 1962. *Address:* Holt, Edwardstone, Sudbury, Suffolk CO10 5PJ. *T:* (01787) 210428. *Clubs:* Army and Navy; I Zingari.

NEVILLE, family name of **Baron Braybrooke**.

NEVILLE, Prof. Adam Matthew, CBE 1994; TD 1963; FREng; FRSE; arbitrator and consultant on concrete and structural design and failures; Partner (formerly Director), A & M Neville Engineering, since 1975; Principal and Vice-Chancellor, University of Dundee, 1978–87; *b* 5 Feb. 1923; *m* 1952, Dr Mary Hallam Cousins; one *s* one *d. Educ:* Queen Mary Coll., London Univ. (BSc 1st cl. Hons; Hon. Fellow, QMW, 1997); MSc, PhD, DSc (Eng) London; DSc Leeds. FICE, FIStructE; FREng (FEng 1986); FRSE 1979. Served War, Polish Forces under British comd, MC: Major RE (TA), 1950–63. Lectr, Southampton Univ., 1950–51; Engr, Min. of Works, NZ, 1951–54; Lectr, Manchester Univ., 1955–60; Prof. of Civil Engrg, Nigerian Coll. of Technology, 1960–62; Foundn Dean of Engrg, Calgary Univ., 1963–67, also Foundn Dean of Graduate Studies, 1965–66; Vis. Prof., Swiss Federal Inst. of Technology, 1967–68; Prof. and Head of Dept of Civil Engineering, Univ. of Leeds, 1968–78. Chm., Cttee of Principals of Scottish Univs, 1984–86. Former Chm., Permanent Concrete Commn, RILEM (Internat. Union of Testing and Res. Labs for Materials and Structures); Dir, Petroleum Recovery Res. Inst.; Advr to Canadian Govt on management of concrete research. Member Council: Concrete Soc., 1968–77, (Pres., 1974–75); IStructE, 1976–79; Faculty of Building, 1976–80; Royal Acad. (formerly Fellowship) of Engrg, 1989–95 (Vice-Pres., 1991–95); Open University, 1979–87; Council of Europe Standing Conference on Univ. Problems, 1980–87 (Pres., 1984–86); Member: Bd, Architectural Educn, ARC, 1980–87; Exec. Cttee, IUPC, 1979–90 (Vice-Chm., 1983–85); British Library Adv. Council, 1989–94; SERC Envmt Cttee, 1988–91; Athlone-Vanier Fellowships Bd, 1990–96; NAPAG, 1992–97. Mem. Editorial Boards of various technical jls. Fellow: Amer. Concrete Inst., 1973 (Hon. Mem., 1986); Concrete Soc., 1994 (Hon. Mem., 2000); Hon. Fellow: Inst. of Concrete Technology, 1976; Singapore Concrete Inst., 1987; Hon. For. Mem., Académie Royale des Sciences d'Outre-Mer, Belgium, 1974. Hon. LLD: St Andrews, 1987; Dundee, 1998; Hon. DAppSci Sherbrooke, Quebec, 1999. IStructE Research Award, 1960; Reinforced Concrete Assoc. Medal, 1961; Senior Research Fellowship, Nat Research Council of Canada, 1967; Stanton Walker Award (US) 1968; Medal of Univ. of Liège (Belgium), 1970; Arthur R. Anderson Award, 1972, Turner Medal, 2001, Amer. Concrete Inst.; President's Medal, Soc. of Engrs, 1985; Silver Medal, Inst. of Concrete Technology, 1993. OStJ 1983. *Publications:* Properties of Concrete, 1963, 4th edn 1995, trans. into 13 languages; (with J. B. Kennedy) Basic Statistical Methods, 1964, 3 edns; Creep of Concrete: plain, reinforced and prestressed, 1970; (with A. Ghali) Structural Analysis: a unified classical and matrix approach, 1971, 4th edn 1997, trans. into Chinese; Hardened Concrete: physical and mechanical aspects, 1971; High Alumina Cement Concrete, 1975; (with W. H. Dilger and J. J. Brooks) Creep of Plain and Structural Concrete, 1983; (with J. J. Brooks) Concrete Technology, 1987; numerous research papers on concrete and concrete structures. *Recreations:* ski-ing, travel (Travelers' Century Club Plaque, 1990). *Address:* 24 Gun Wharf, 130 Wapping High Street, E1 9NH. *T:* (020) 7265 1087. *Clubs:* Athenæum; New (Edinburgh).

NEVILLE, Prof. (Alexander) Munro, MD; FRCPath; Associate Director (formerly Administrator) and Research Secretary, Ludwig Institute for Cancer Research, since 1985; *b* 24 March 1935; *s* of Alexander Munro and Georgina Neville; *m* 1961, Anne Margaret Stroyan Black; one *s* one *d. Educ:* Hillhead High Sch.; Univ. of Glasgow (MB ChB 1959; PhD 1965; MD 1969); Harvard Med. Sch.; DSc London, 1985. MRCPath 1969, FRCPath 1981. Med. appts, Glasgow Royal and Victoria Infirmaries, 1960–65; Res. Fellow, Harvard Med. Sch., 1965–67; Sen. Lectr in Pathology, Univ. of Glasgow, 1967–70; Hon. Consultant Pathologist, Royal Marsden Hosp., 1970–85; Prof. of Experimental Pathology, Univ. of London, 1972–85; Dean, Inst. of Cancer Research, 1982–84; Dir, Ludwig Inst. for Cancer Research, London Branch, 1975–85. Vis. Prof. of Pathol., RPMS, 1992–. Hon. Treas., RCPath, 1993–98. *Publications:* The Human Adrenal Cortex, 1982; numerous papers on oncology and pathology in primary jls. *Recreations:* golf, gardening. *Address:* (office) Glen House, Stag Place, SW1E 5AG. *T:* (020) 7828 0202, *Fax:* (020) 7828 5427; 6 Woodlands Park, Tadworth, Surrey KT20 7TL, *T:* (01737) 844113, *Fax:* (01737) 844287. *Clubs:* Athenæum; Banstead Downs.

NEVILLE, John, OBE 1965; actor, stage and film; Hon. Professor in Drama, Nottingham University, since 1967; Artistic Director, Festival Theatre, Stratford, Ontario, 1985–89; *b* Willesden, 2 May 1925; *s* of Reginald Daniel Neville and Mabel Lillian (*née* Fry); *m* 1949, Caroline Hooper; three *s* three *d. Educ:* Willesden and Chiswick County Schools; Royal Academy of Dramatic Art. Worked as a stores clerk before studying at RADA. First appearance on stage, walking-on part in Richard II; subseq. parts at Open Air Theatre, in repertory at Lowestoft, and with Birmingham Repertory Co.; Bristol Old Vic Co., 1950–53; Old Vic Co., London, 1953–61; Nottingham Playhouse, 1961–63; Theatre Director, Nottingham Playhouse, 1963–68; Dir, Park Theatre Co., Fortune, 1969; Theatre Director: Citadel Theatre, Edmonton, Canada, 1973–78; Neptune Theatre, Halifax, NS, 1978–83. Parts with Old Vic include: Ferdinand in The Tempest, Macduff, Richard II, Orlando in As You Like It, Henry Percy in Henry IV, Part I, Mark Antony; during Old Vic tour of Europe, 1958, Hamlet, Sir Andrew Aguecheek. Played lead in Irma La Douce, Lyric, 1959–60; produced Henry V, Old Vic, 1960; The Lady From the Sea, Queen's, 1961; The School for Scandal, Haymarket, 1962; Alfie, Mermaid and Duchess, 1963. Acted in: The Chichester Festival Theatre, 1962; Beware of the Dog, St Martin's, 1967; Iago in Othello, Nottingham Playhouse, 1967; Mr and Mrs, Palace, 1968; The Apple Cart, Mermaid, 1970; The Beggar's Opera, The Doctor's Dilemma, Chichester, 1972; Sherlock Holmes, NY, 1975; Happy Days, Nat. Theatre, 1977; Grand Theatre, London, Ontario: acted in Dear Antoine and Arsenic and Old Lace, directed Hamlet, 1983; Stratford, Ontario: acted in Loves Labours' Lost, 1983, Merchant of Venice, 1984, Intimate Admiration, 1987, My Fair Lady, 1988; directed Mother Courage, and Othello, 1987, Three Sisters, 1989; acted in: The School for Scandal, NT, 1990; The Dance of Death, Almeida, 1995; Beethoven's Tenth, Chichester, 1996; Krapp's Last Tape, Nottingham Playhouse, 1999. Tour W Africa (Jt Dir and acting), 1963. *Films:* Oscar Wilde; Topaze; Billy Budd; A Study in Terror; Adventures of Baron Munchausen; The X-Files. Has appeared on television, incl. The First Churchills, series for BBC 2. Hon. Dr Dramatic Arts Lethbridge Univ., 1979; Hon. DFA Nova Scotia Coll. of Art and Design, 1981; Hon. LLD Ryerson Univ., 1999. *Address:* 139 Winnett Avenue, Toronto, ON M6C 3L7, Canada. *Clubs:* Royal Over-Seas League; Arts and Letters (Toronto).

NEVILLE, (John) Oliver, MA, PhD; Principal, Royal Academy of Dramatic Art, 1984–93; *b* 14 Aug. 1929; *s* of Frederick and Ethel Neville; *m* 1st, 1952, Shirley Hall; one *s* one *d*; 2nd, 1964, Pat Heywood. *Educ:* Price's Sch., Fareham; King's Coll., Cambridge (Le Bas Student; BA Eng. Lit., MA, PhD). After National Service, engaged in following with ultimate aim of becoming a theatre director: studied theatre design under Reginald Leefe, 1949–51; joined Old Vic Co., walking on in Tyrone Guthrie's Tamburlaine, with Donald Wolfit, 1951; studied singing with Clive Carey and Frank Titterton; seasons of rep. at York, Scarborough, Worthing, Bristol, Birmingham and Manchester, 1952–58; re-joined Old Vic Co., 1958 (roles included Warwick in Henry VI Trilogy and Claudius in Hamlet); toured America, Poland, Russia, India, Pakistan, Ceylon, with Old Vic and Bristol Old Vic, as stage dir, actor and dir; Associate Dir, Old Vic Co., 1960–62 (directed Macbeth and The Tempest); Director: Library Theatre, Manchester, 1963–66; Arts Theatre, Ipswich, 1966–69; Mature Student, Cambridge, 1969–76 (PhD on Ben Jonson's Masques and Poetry); Caroline Spurgeon Res. Fellow, Bedford Coll., London, 1977–79; Sen. Lectr in Drama, Univ. of Bristol, 1979–84. *Recreations:* mediaeval church architecture and stained-glass, gardening. *Address:* c/o Peters, Fraser & Dunlop, Drury House, 34–43 Russell Street, WC2B 5HA.

NEVILLE, Munro; *see* Neville, A. M.

NEVILLE, Air Vice-Marshal Patrick, CB 1988; OBE 1976; AFC 1960; Chief of Air Staff, Royal New Zealand Air Force, 1986–89, retired; *b* 23 Sept. 1932; *s* of Patrick Joseph Neville and Helena Neville; *m* 1954, Barbara Howell; one *s* one *d. Educ:* Purbrook Park County High Sch. (SchCert). Commnd 1951; Navigator: RAF, 1951–55; RNZAF, 1955; CO No 14 Sqdn RNZAF, 1966–69; Base Comdr, RNZAF Base Ohakea, NZ, 1969–70; Hon. ADC to Gov. Gen., 1972; Sen. ASO, Air HQ, ANZUK Force Singapore; later, Dep. Comdr NZ Force SE Asia in Singapore, 1973–75; RNZAF Air Staff, 1975–77; Base Comdr, RNZAF Base Auckland, 1978–79; AOC RNZAF Support Gp, 1980–82; Asst CDS for Operations and Plans, Defence HQ, Wellington, 1982–83; Hd of NZ Defence Liaison Staff, London, 1984–86. Gp Captain 1973, Air Cdre 1980, Air Vice-Marshal 1986. FNZIM; FRAeS. *Recreations:* golf, fishing. *Address:* 12 Mark Place, Lynmore, Rotorua, New Zealand. *T:* (7) 3459650. *Club:* Rotorua Golf.

NEVILLE, Sir Roger (Albert Gartside), Kt 1994; VRD 1965; FCA; Group Chief Executive, Sun Alliance Group, 1987–94 (Director, 1979–96); *b* 23 Dec. 1931; *s* of Geoffrey Graham Gartside Neville and Veronica Lily Neville; *m* 1957, Brenda Mary Parke Hamilton; one *s* three *d.* Royal Navy, 1950–52; joined Sun Alliance Insurance, 1962; General Manager, 1977; Dep. Chief General Manager, 1984. Chm., Eyretel Ltd, 1995–; Dir, Equitas Holdings Ltd, 1996–99. Chairman: Policyholders Protection Bd, 1991–94; Pool RE, 1993–96. *Recreations:* sailing, fly fishing, cabinet making. *Address:* Possingworth Manor, Blackboys, near Uckfield, East Sussex TN22 5HE. *Clubs:* Royal Automobile, Royal Ocean Racing.

NEVILLE-JONES, Dame (Lilian) Pauline, DCMG 1996 (CMG 1987); a Governor, BBC, since 1998; *b* 2 Nov. 1939; *d* of Roland Neville-Jones and Dr Cecilia Emily Millicent Winn. *Educ:* Leeds Girls' High Sch.; Lady Margaret Hall, Oxford (BA Hons Mod. History). Harkness Fellow of Commonwealth Fund, USA, 1961–63; HM Diplomatic Service, 1963–96: Third Sec., Salisbury, Rhodesia, 1964–65; Third, later Second Sec., Singapore, 1965–68; FCO, 1968–71; First Sec., Washington, 1971–75; FCO, 1975–77; Mem. Cabinet, later Chef de Cabinet to Christopher Tugendhat, European Comr for Budget, Financial Control, Financial Instns and Taxation, 1977–82; Vis. Fellow, RIIA, and Inst. français des relations internationales, 1982–83; Head of Planning Staff, FCO, 1983–87; Minister (Econ.), 1987–88, Minister, 1988–91, Bonn; Dep. Sec., Cabinet Office (on secondment), 1991–94; Chm., Jt Intelligence Cttee, Cabinet Office, 1993–94; Political Dir and Dep. Under-Sec. of State, FCO, 1994–96; Sen. Advr to High Rep. for Bosnia (on secondment), 1996. Man. Dir, and Hd of Global Business Strategy, NatWest Markets, 1996–98; Vice Chm., Hawkpoint Partners Ltd, 1998–2000. FRSA 1986. DUniv Open, 1998; Hon. DSc (Econ) London, 1999. *Recreations:* antiques, cooking, gardening. *T:* (020) 7352 0610; *e-mail:* gdr57@dial.pipex.com.

NEVILLE-ROLFE, Lucy Jeanne, (Lady Packer); Director of Corporate Affairs, Tesco plc, since 1997; *b* 2 Jan. 1953; *d* of Edmund and Margaret Neville-Rolfe; *m* Sir Richard John Packer, *qv*; four *s. Educ:* Somerville Coll., Oxford (BA PPE; MA). Joined MAFF, 1973; Pvte Sec. to Minister of Agric., Fisheries and Food, 1977–79; EC Sheepmeat and Milk, 1979–86; Land Use, 1986–88; Food Safety Act, 1988–90; Head of Personnel, 1990–92; Mem., Prime Minister's Policy Unit, 1992–94; Under Sec., 1994; Dir, Deregulation Unit, DTI, then Better Regulation Unit, Cabinet Office, 1995–97. Non-executive Director: John Laing Construction, 1991–92; Bd of Mgt, FCO, 2000–. British Retail Consortium: Bd of Mgt, 1998–; Chairman: Eur. Gp, 1998–99; Property, Envmt, Transport and Safety Steering Gp, 1999–; Confederation of British Industry: Mem., Econs and Eur. Cttees, 1998–; Vice Pres., Eur. Commerce Steering Cttee, 1998–; Mem., UNICE Task Force on Enlargement, 1999–. *Recreations:* cricket, racing, gardening, art, architecture, theatre. *Address:* Tesco plc, Tesco House, Delamare Road, Cheshunt, Herts EN8 9SL. *T:* (01992) 632222, *Fax:* (01992) 623371.

See also M. T. Neville-Rolfe.

NEVILLE-ROLFE, Marianne Teresa, CB 2000; Chief Executive, North East Manchester Ltd, since 2000; *b* 9 Oct 1944; *d* of Edmund Neville-Rolfe and Margaret (*née* Evans); *m* 1972, David William John Blake (marr. diss. 1992). *Educ:* St Mary's Convent, Shaftesbury; Lady Margaret Hall, Oxford (BA). CBI, 1965–73 (Head, Brussels Office, 1971–72); Principal, DTI, 1973, Asst Sec., 1982, Under Sec., Internal European Policy Div., 1987; Chief Exec., CS Coll., and Dir, Top Management Prog., OMCS, then OPSS, Cabinet Office, 1990–94; Regl Dir, Govt Office for NW, 1994–99. Mem., ESRC. *Recreations:* travel, opera. *Address:* (office) 17 Stilton Drive, Beswick Shopping Centre, Manchester M11 3SB. *T:* (0161) 230 2109.

See also L. J. Neville-Rolfe.

NEVIN, Prof. Norman Cummings, MD; FRCP, FRCPE, FRCPath, FFPHM; Professor of Medical Genetics, Queen's University of Belfast, 1975–2000, now Emeritus; (Personal Chair, 1975–78); Consultant Clinical Geneticist and Head, Northern Ireland Regional Genetics Service, Belfast City Health Trust, 1968–2000; *b* 10 June 1935; *s* of Joseph and Sarah Nevin; *m* 1961, Jean Hamilton; one *s* one *d. Educ:* Queen's Univ. of Belfast (BSc, MB BCh, BAO; MD 1964). FRCPE 1976; FFPHM 1981; FRCPath 1981; FRCP 1990. House physician and surgeon, Royal Victoria Hosp., Belfast, 1960–61; John

Dunville Fellow in Pathology, QUB, 1961–64; Registrar in Medicine, Royal Victoria Hosp., 1964–65; MRC Fellow, MRC Clinical Genetics Unit, Inst. of Child Health, London and MRC Population Genetics Res. Unit, 1965–67; Lectr in Human Genetics, QUB, 1967–75. Mem., Gene Therapy Adv. Cttee, 1993– (Chm., 1996–). Mem., Assoc. Physicians of GB and Ireland, 1986–. President: Clinical Genetics Soc., 1991–92; Ulster Paediatric Soc., 1989. *Publications:* numerous contribs on congenital abnormalities in learned medical jls. *Recreations:* walking (hill), painting, medical ethics. *Address:* 17 Ogles Grove, Hillsborough, Co. Down, Northern Ireland BT28 6RS.

NEW, Maj.-Gen. Sir Laurence (Anthony Wallis), Kt 1990; CB 1986; CBE 1980; Lieutenant Governor of the Isle of Man, and President of the Tynwald Court, 1985–90; International President, Association of Military Christian Fellowships, since 1991; *b* 25 Feb. 1932; *s* of Lt-Col S. W. New, MBE and Mrs C. M. New; *m* 1956, Anna Doreen Verity; two *s* two *d*. *Educ:* King William's College, Isle of Man; RMA Sandhurst, 1950–52; commissioned, RTR, 1952; service in Hong Kong, Germany, Malaya, Borneo; CO 4 RTR, 1971–73; Bde Major, 20th Armd Bde, 1969–70; Sec., Defence Policy Staff, 1970–71; Defence and Military Attaché, Tel Aviv, 1974–77; Col GS, MoD, 1977–79; Brig. GS, MoD, 1981–82; ACGS (Op. Reqs), 1983–84; ACDS (Land Systems), MoD, 1984–85; graduate Staff Coll., JSSC, RCDS. Col Comdt, RTR, 1986–93; Vice Pres., TA&VRA, 1985–90; Hon. Col I of M ACF, 1998–. Gen. Sec., Officers' Pensions Soc., 1990–95; Campaign Dir, War and Service Widows Pensions Campaign, 1994–95. Consultant, Lagan Gp of Cos, 1998–; Dir, Charles Brand (IOM) Ltd, 1999–. Lectr, City Univ. Business Sch., 1992–. Licenced Reader, C of E; Church Warden, St Peter upon Cornhill, 1986–95; Pres., Soldiers' and Airmen's Scripture Readers Assoc., 1985–99; Vice Pres., Officers' Christian Union, 1988–93. President: Manx Music Fest., 1985–90; Mananan Internat. Fest. of Music and the Arts, 1987–; Manx Nat. Youth Band, 1995–; Mannin Art Gp, 1996–; Friends of the Gaiety Theatre, 1996–. County Pres., St John Ambulance Brigade and Assoc., 1985–90, and 1999–; Patron: I of M Red Cross, 1985–90; Burma Star Assoc. (I of M), 1995–; Pres., Normandy Veterans Assoc. (I of M), 1997–; Vice-Pres., 4/7th RTR and Comrades, 1997–. Pres., Fishermen's Mission, 1998–; Vice Patron, Royal Nat. Mission to Deep Sea Fishermen, 1999–; Patron: Ramsey Life Boat, 1999–; Choice of Living in Community Homes, 1999–; Friends of Chernobyl's Children, 1999–. Chairman: Bishop Barrow's Trustees, 1985–90; Royal Jubilee and Prince's Trust (I of M), 1986–90; Pres., White House School, Wokingham, 1985–. Freeman, City of London, 1985. CIMgt (FBIM 1979; CBIM 1986). KStJ 1986. Internat. Centurion Award, Washington, 2000. *Recreations:* family, music, water colour painting. *Address:* Ballaquark, Laxey, Isle of Man IM4 7PH. *Fax:* (01624) 861933; *e-mail:* generalnew@manx.net. *Club:* Army and Navy.

NEW WESTMINSTER, Bishop of, since 1994; **Rt Rev. Michael Ingham;** *b* 25 Aug. 1949; *s* of Herbert and Dorothy Ingham; *m* 1982, Gwen Robbins; two *d*. *Educ:* Univ. of Edinburgh (MA 1970; BD 1973 (First Class Hons)). Ordained deacon and priest, 1974; Asst Curate, St John the Evangelist, Ottawa, Ontario, 1974–76; Rector: Christ the King, Burnaby, BC, 1976–80; St Francis-in-the-Wood, W Vancouver, 1980–89; Principal Sec. to the Primate, Toronto, 1989–92; Dean of Christ Church Cathedral, Vancouver, 1992–94. Hon. DD Vancouver Sch. of Theol., 1998. *Publications:* Rites for a New Age, 1985, 2nd edn 1990; Mansions of the Spirit, 1997. *Recreations:* sailing, squash. *Address:* #580–401 West Georgia Street, Vancouver, BC V6B 5A1, Canada. *T:* (604) 6846306.

NEW ZEALAND, Primate and Presiding Bishop of, since 1998; **Most Rev. John Campbell Paterson;** Bishop of Auckland, since 1995; *b* 4 Jan. 1945; *s* of Thomas Paterson and Lucy Mary Paterson; *m* 1968, Marion Reid Anderson; two *d*. *Educ:* King's Coll., Auckland; Auckland Univ. (BA); St John's Coll., Auckland (LTh (Hons)); Dip. Public Speaking (NZ Speech Bd), 1969. Ordained, deacon, 1969, priest, 1970; Assistant Curate, Whangarei, 1969–71; Vicar, Waimate North Maori Pastorate, 1971–76; Co-Missioner, Auckland Maori Mission, 1976; Chaplain, Queen Victoria Sch., 1976–82; TF Chaplain, 1976–84; Sec., Te Pihopatanga o Aotearoa, 1978–86; Provincial Sec., Church of the Province of NZ, 1986–92; Gen. Sec., Anglican Church in Aotearoa, NZ and Polynesia, 1992–95. Vice-Chm., ACC, 1996– (Mem., 1990–96). *Publication:* (ed) He Toenga Whatiwhatinga, 1983. *Recreations:* music, sport, literature. *Address:* PO Box 37–242, Parnell 1033, Auckland, New Zealand. *T:* (9) 3027202.

NEWALL, family name of **Baron Newall.**

NEWALL, 2nd Baron *cr* 1946; **Francis Storer Eaton Newall;** DL; company director and Chairman of several companies; Chairman, British Greyhound Racing Board, 1985–97; *b* 23 June 1930; *o s* of 1st Baron (Marshal of the RAF Lord) Newall, GCB, OM, GCMG, CBE, AM; *S* father, 1963; *m* 1956, Pamela Elizabeth, *e d* of E. H. L. Rowcliffe, Pinkney Park, Malmesbury, Wilts; two *s* one *d*. *Educ:* Eton College; RMA Sandhurst. Commissioned into 11th Hussars (Prince Albert's Own), 1950; served in: Germany, 1950–53; Malaya, 1953–55; on staff of GHQ FarELF, Singapore, 1955–56; Adjt Royal Gloucestershire Hussars, 1956–58; retired 1961. Introduced Farriers Registration Acts and Betting Gaming and Lotteries Amendment Acts (Greyhound Racing) in House of Lords. Cons. Whip and front bench spokesman, 1976–79; Founder Mem., House of Lords all party Defence Study Group; official visits to NATO, SHAPE, Norway, Morocco, Bonn, Cyprus, BAOR, Qatar, Oman, Bahrain and Romania; Deleg. to Council of Europe and WEU, 1983–97. Mem., Select Cttee on Laboratory Animals Protection Bill. Pres., Soc. for Protection of Animals Abroad. Chm, British Moroccan Soc. Mem., Merchant Taylors' Co (Master, 1985–86). DL Greater London, 1988. *Recreations:* sport, travel, meeting people. *Heir:* *s* Hon. Richard Hugh Eaton Newall [*b* 19 Feb. 1961; *m* 1996, Keira, *d* of Robert Glen; one *d*]. *Address:* Wotton Underwood, Aylesbury, Bucks HP18 0RZ. *Club:* Cavalry and Guards.

NEWALL, Sir Paul (Henry), Kt 1994; TD 1967; JP; DL; Lord Mayor of London, 1993–94; *b* 17 Sept. 1934; *s* of late Leopold Newall and Frances Evelyn Newall (*née* Bean); *m* 1969, Penelope Moyra, *o d* of Sir Julian Ridsdale, *qv* and Lady Ridsdale (*see* V. E. P. Ridsdale); two *s*. *Educ:* Harrow; Magdalene Coll., Cambridge (MA Econs). Nat. Service, commnd Royal Fusiliers, 1953–55; TA 1955–70, Major. Partner, Loeb Rhoades & Co. (mem., NY Stock Exchange), 1971; Overseas Director: Shearson Loeb Rhoades Inc., 1978; Shearson Lehman American Express (UK) Hldgs, 1981; Exec. Dir, Lehman Brothers Securities, 1990; Dir, Lehman Brothers Ltd (formerly Shearson Lehman International Ltd), 1985–94 (Sen. Advr, 1993–98); non-exec. Dir, Guardian Royal Exchange plc, 1995–99. Member: Adv. Cttee, Energy Internat. NV, 1978–98; Asia Pacific Advisers Gp, and Korea Advisers Gp, Trade Partners UK; UK–Japan 21st Century Gp. Vice-Pres., Inst. of Export, 1995–. City of London: Mem., Court of Common Council (Ward of Cripplegate), 1980–81; Alderman, Ward of Walbrook, 1981–; Sheriff, 1989–90; Chm., City of London TAVRA, 1986–89; Vice-Chm., TA&VRA for Gtr London, 1989; Hon. Col, The London Regt, 1995–2001; Master, Bakers' Co., 1990–91; Founder Master, Guild of Internat. Bankers, 2001; Member: Guild of Freemen, 1988– (Court, 1988–91); Court, HAC, 1980–; Incorp. of Bakers of Glasgow, 1995–; Liveryman, Gold and Silver Wyre Drawers' Co., 1980–; Hon. Liveryman, Marketors' Co., 1995; Hon. Freeman, Fuellers' Co., 1995. Vice-Pres., City of London Sector, British Red Cross, 1986–; Member: Friends of St Paul's Cathedral; City Heritage Soc.; Samuel Pepys Club; Pro-Chancellor and Chm. Council, City Univ., 1997–; Governor: MENCAP City Foundn, 1982–97; City of London Freemen's Sch., 1987–88; City of London Girls' Sch., 1997–98; City of London Boys' Sch., 1999–; Trustee: Morden Coll., 1991–; City of London Endowment Trust for St Paul's Cathedral, 1996–; Temple Bar Trust, 1996–; Exec. Trustee, Army Benevolent Fund, 1998–. Patron: Samaritans Nat. Appeal, 1989–98; Internat. Centre for Child Studies, 1989–93. Hon. Rep., City of Seoul, 1996–; Chm., UK-Korea Forum for the Future, 1999–. Churchwarden, St Stephen's, Walbrook. Burgess, City of Glasgow, 1995. One of HM Lieutenants of City of London, 1975–; DL Gtr London, 1977; JP City of London, 1981; Hon. Vis. Magistrate, HM Tower of London, 1988–. Hon. DLitt City, 1993. KStJ 1993. Order of Diplomatic Merit (First Class) (Korea), 1999. *Publication:* Japan and the City of London, 1996. *Recreations:* fencing, fly fishing, shooting, water-skiing, tennis, trees. *Address:* PO Box 270, Guildhall, EC2V 2EJ. *Clubs:* East India, City Livery, United Wards, Walbrook Ward (Pres.), MCC, Pilgrims.

NEWARK, Archdeacon of; *see* Peyton, Ven. N.

NEWBERRY, Raymond Scudamore, OBE 1989; Director, Brazil, British Council, 1990–93; *b* 8 Feb. 1935; *s* of James Henry Newberry and late Doris Ada Newberry; *m* 1967, Angelina Nance; one *s* one *d*. *Educ:* Bristol Grammar Sch.; Selwyn Coll., Cambridge (BA); Univ. of Leeds (DipESL); Univ. of Bristol (DipEd). National Service, 1953–55. Lectr, Coll. of Arts, Baghdad Univ., 1959–62; British Council posts, 1962–94: Lectr, Teheran, 1963–64; Educn Officer, Calcutta, 1964–66; Head of English Dept, Advanced Teacher Trng Coll., Winneba, Ghana, 1966–70; Advr on English Lang., Min. of Educn, Singapore, 1970–74; Rep., Colombia, 1975–80; Director: North and Latin American Dept, 1980–82; America and Pacific Dept, 1982–84; Rep., Australia, 1984–89. Consultant, London Film Commn, 1996–99. *Publication:* (with A. Maley) Between You and Me, 1974. *Recreations:* bookbinding, golf. *Address:* Silverwood, Wildwood Close, Woking, Surrey GU22 8PL. *T:* (01932) 341826.

NEWBERY, Prof. David Michael Garrood, FBA 1991; Professor of Economics and Director of Department of Applied Economics, Cambridge, since 1988; Fellow, Churchill College, Cambridge, since 1966; *b* 1 June 1943; *s* of late Alan James Garrood Newbery, OBE, RN, and of Betty Amelia Newbery; *m* 1975, Dr Terri Eve Apter; two *d*. *Educ:* Portsmouth Grammar Sch.; Trinity Coll., Cambridge (BA, MA, PhD). Economist, Treasury, Tanzania, 1965–66; Cambridge University: Asst Lectr, 1966–71; Lectr, 1971–86; Reader, 1986–88. Associate Prof., Stanford Univ., 1976–77; Div. Chief, World Bank, Washington, 1981–83; Fellow, Centre for Economic Policy Res., 1984–; Vis. Prof., Princeton, 1985; Vis. Scholar, IMF, 1987; Ford Vis. Prof., Univ. of California, Berkeley, 1987–88; Sen. Res. Fellow, Inst. for Policy Reform, Washington, DC, 1990–. Mem., Competition (formerly Monopolies and Mergers) Commn, 1996–. Pres., European Economic Assoc., 1996 (Vice-Pres., 1994); Mem. Council, REconS, 1984–89; Fellow, Econometric Soc., 1989 (Frisch Medal, 1990). Bd Mem, Review of Economic Studies, 1968–79; Associate Editor: Economic Jl, 1977–; European Economic Review, 1988–93. *Publications:* Project Appraisal in Practice, 1976; (with J. E. Stiglitz) The Theory of Commodity Price Stabilization, 1981; (with N. H. Stern) The Theory of Taxation for Developing Countries, 1987; (with I. P. Székely) Hungary: an economy in transition, 1992; Tax and Benefit Reform in Central and Eastern Europe, 1995; Privatization, Restructuring and Regulation of Network Utilities, 2000; articles in learned jls. *Recreation:* ski-ing. *Address:* 9 Huntingdon Road, Cambridge CB3 0HH. *T:* (01223) 360216.

NEWBIGGING, David Kennedy, OBE 1982; DL; Chairman, Friends' Provident PLC (formerly Life Office), since 1998 (Director, since 1993; Deputy Chairman, 1996–98); *b* 19 Jan. 1934; *s* of late David Locke Newbigging, CBE, MC, and Lucy Margaret; *m* 1968, Carolyn Susan (*née* Band); one *s* two *d*. *Educ:* in Canada; Oundle Sch., Northants. Joined Jardine, Matheson & Co. Ltd, Hong Kong, 1954; Dir, 1967; Man. Dir, 1970; Chm. and Sen. Man. Dir, 1975–83; Chairman: Hongkong & Kowloon Wharf & Godown Co. Ltd, 1970–80; Jardine Matheson & Co. Ltd, 1975–83; Jardine Fleming Holdings Ltd, 1975–83; Hongkong Land Co. Ltd, 1975–83; Hongkong Electric Holdings Ltd, 1982–83 (Dir, 1975–83); Rentokil Gp plc, 1987–94 (Dir, 1986–94); Redfearn PLC, 1988; NM UK Ltd 1990–93; Ivory & Sime plc, 1992–95 (Dir, 1987–95); Maritime Transport Services Ltd, 1993–95; Faupel Trading Gp plc, 1994– (Dir, 1989–); Equitas Holdings Ltd, 1995–98; Thistle Hotels plc, 1999–; Deputy Chairman: Provincial Gp plc, 1985–91 (Dir, 1984–91); Benchmark Gp plc, 1996–; Director: Hongkong & Shanghai Banking Corp., 1975–83; Hong Kong Telephone Co., 1975–83; Safmarine and Rennies Holdings Ltd (formerly Rennies Consolidated Holdings), 1975–85; Provincial Insurance, 1984–86; Provincial Life Insurance Co., 1984–86; CIN Management, 1985–87; PACCAR (UK) Ltd, 1986–97; Internat. Financial Markets Trading Ltd, 1986–93; United Meridian Corp., USA, 1987–98; Wah Kwong Shipping Hldgs Ltd (Hong Kong), 1992–99; Market Bd, Corp. of Lloyd's, 1993–95; Merrill Lynch & Co. Inc., USA, 1997–; Ocean Energy Inc., USA, 1998–; PACCAR Inc., USA, 1999–. Dir, British Coal Corp. (formerly NCB), 1984–87. Mem., Internat. Council, Morgan Guaranty Trust Co. of NY, 1977–85; Mem. Supervisory Bd, DAF Trucks NV, 1997–2000. Chm. of Council, Mission to Seafarers (formerly Missions to Seamen), 1993–. Chm. of Trustees, Wilts Community Foundn, 1991–97; Trustee, King Mahendra UK Trust for Nature Conservation, 1988–. Member: Hong Kong Exec. Council, 1980–84; Hong Kong Legislative Council, 1978–82. Chairman: Hong Kong Tourist Assoc., 1977–82; Hong Kong Gen. Chamber of Commerce, 1980–82; Steward, Royal Hong Kong Jockey Club, 1975–84. JP (unofficial) Hong Kong, 1971; DL Wilts, 1993. *Recreations:* most outdoor sports; Chinese art. *Address:* 15 Old Bailey, EC4M 7AP. *T:* (020) 7506 1000. *Clubs:* Boodle's; Hongkong (Hong Kong).

NEWBOLD, Yvette Monica, (Yve); Chair, Ethical Trading Initiative, since 2000; *b* 6 July 1940; *d* of late Thomas Peter Radcliffe and of Anne Gertrude Radcliffe (*née* Flynn); *m* 1958, Anthony Patrick Newbold; three *s* one *d*. *Educ:* Blessed Sacrament Convent, Brighton; LLB London; Solicitor, 1970. Staff Counsel: IBM, 1968–71; Rank Xerox, 1972–79; Internat. Counsel, Xerox (USA), 1979–82; European Counsel, Walt Disney Productions, 1983–85; Co. Sec., Hanson, 1986–95; Chief Exec., Pro-Ned, 1995–97; Partner, Heidrick & Struggles, 1998–2000. Non-executive Director: BT, 1991–97; Coutts & Co., 1994–98. Member: Royal Commn on Criminal Justice, 1991–93; Sen. Salaries Rev. Body, 1994–97; Adv. Bd, Inst. of Global Ethics, 1997–. Governor, London Business Sch., 1990–. *Address:* Ethical Trading Initiative, 2nd Floor, Cromwell House, 14 Fulwood Place, WC1V 6HZ.

NEWBOROUGH, 8th Baron *cr* 1776 (Ire.), of Bodvean; **Robert Vaughan Wynn;** Bt 1742; landowner and organic farmer; *b* 11 Aug. 1949; *o s* of 7th Baron Newborough, DSC and Rosamund Lavington Wynn (*née* Barbour); *S* father, 1998; *m* 1st, 1981, Sheila Christine Massey (marr. diss. 1988); one *d*; 2nd, 1988, Susan Elizabeth Hall (*née* Lloyd); one step *s*. *Educ:* Milton Abbey. Chm. and Man. Dir, Wynn Electronics, 1982–89; Dir, Country Wide Communications, 1992–. *Recreations:* ski-ing, sailing, golf, tennis. *Heir:* *uncle* Hon. Charles Henry Romer Wynn [*b* 25 May 1923; *m* 1947, Hon. Angela Hermione

Ida Willoughby, *er d* of 11th Baron Middleton, KG, MC, TD; two *s*]. *Address:* Peplow Hall, Peplow, Market Drayton, Shropshire TF9 3JP. *T:* (01952) 840230.

NEWBURGH, 12th Earl of, *cr* 1660 (Scot.); **Don Filippo Giambattista Francesco Aldo Maria Rospigliosi;** Viscount Kynnaird, Baron Levingston, 1660; 11th Prince Rospigliosi (Holy Roman Empire), 11th Duke of Zagarolo, 14th Prince of Castiglione, Marquis of Giuliana, Count of Chiusa, Baron of La Miraglia and Valcorrente, Lord of Aidone, Burgio, Contessa and Trappeto, and Conscript Roman Noble, Patrician of Venice, Genoa and Pistoia; *b* 4 July 1942; *s* of 11th Earl of Newburgh and of Donna Giulia, *d* of Don Guido Carlo dei Duchi Visconti di Mondrone, Count of Lonate Pozzolo; *S* father, 1986; *m* 1972, Baronessa Donna Luisa, *d* of Count Annibale Caccia Dominioni; one *d*. *Heir: d* Princess Donna Benedetta Francesca Maria Rospigliosi, *b* 4 June 1974. *Address:* Piazza Sant'Ambrogio 16, 20123 Milan, Italy.

NEWBY, family name of **Baron Newby**.

NEWBY, Baron *cr* 1997 (Life Peer), of Rothwell in the co. of West Yorkshire; **Richard Mark Newby,** OBE 1990; Director, Flagship Group, since 1999; Chairman, Reform Publications Ltd, since 1993; *b* 14 Feb. 1953; *s* of Frank and Kathleen Newby; *m* 1978, Ailsa Ballantyne Thomson; two *s*. *Educ:* Rothwell Grammar Sch.; St Catherine's Coll., Oxford (MA). HM Customs and Excise: Administration trainee, 1974; Private Sec. to Permanent Sec., 1977–79; Principal, Planning Unit, 1979–81; Sec. to SDP Parly Cttee, 1981; joined SDP HQ Staff, 1981; Nat. Sec., SDP, 1983–88; Exec., 1988–90, Dir of Corporate Affairs, 1991, Rosehaugh plc; Dir, Matrix Public Affairs Consultants, subseq. Matrix Communications Consultancy Ltd, 1992–99. Dep. Chm., Lib Dem Gen. Election Team, 1995–97; Chief of Staff to Rt Hon. Charles Kennedy, 1999–. Lib Dem spokesman on Treasury affairs, H of L, 1998–. Member: Select Cttee on Monetary Policy Cttee of Bank of England, 1998–2000; Select Cttee on Economic Affairs, 2001–. Trustee: Centre for Reform, 1998–; Aviation Health Inst., 1998–. *Recreations:* family, football, cricket. *Address:* House of Lords, SW1A 0PW. *Clubs:* Reform, MCC.

NEWBY, (George) Eric, CBE 1994; MC 1945; FRSL 1972; FRGS 1975; writer; *b* 6 Dec. 1919; *o s* of George Arthur Newby and Hilda Pomeroy, London; *m* 1946, Wanda, *d* of Viktor Skof and Gisella Urdih, Trieste; one *s* one *d*. *Educ:* St Paul's School. With Dorland Advertising, London, 1936–38; apprentice and ord. seaman, 4-masted Finnish barque, Moshulu, 1938–39; served War of 1939–45, Special Boat Section, POW 1942–45; Women's Fashion Business, 1946–56 (with Worth Paquin, 1955–56); explored in Nuristan and made unsuccessful attempt to climb Mir Samir, Afghan Hindu Kush, 1956; with Secker & Warburg, 1956–59; with John Lewis Partnership (Central Buyer, Model Dresses), 1959–63; descended Ganges with wife, 1963. Travel Editor, The Observer, and Gen. Editor, Time Off Books, 1964–73. Mem., Assoc. of Cape Horners. Hon. DLitt Bournemouth, 1994; DUniv Open, 1996. *Publications:* The Last Grain Race, 1956; A Short Walk in the Hindu Kush, 1958; Something Wholesale, 1962; Slowly Down the Ganges, 1966; Time Off in Southern Italy, 1966; Grain Race: Pictures of Life Before the Mast in a Windjammer, 1968; (jointly) The Wonders of Britain, 1968; (jointly) The Wonders of Ireland, 1969; Love and War in the Apennines, 1971; (jointly) The World of Evelyn Waugh, 1973; Ganga (with photographs by Raghubir Singh), 1973; World Atlas of Exploration, 1975; Great Ascents, 1977; The Big Red Train Ride, 1978; A Traveller's Life, 1982; On the Shores of the Mediterranean, 1984; A Book of Travellers' Tales, 1985; Round Ireland in Low Gear, 1987; What the Traveller Saw, 1989; A Small Place in Italy, 1994; A Merry Dance Around the World, 1995; Learning the Ropes, 1999; Departures and Arrivals, 1999; Around the World in Eighty Years, 2000. *Recreations:* walking, cycling, gardening. *Address:* Pine View House, 4 Pine View Close, Chilworth, Surrey GU4 8RS. *T:* (01483) 571430. *Clubs:* Garrick, Travellers (Hon. Mem.).

NEWBY, Sir Howard (Joseph), Kt 2000; CBE 1995; Chief Executive, Higher Education Funding Council for England, since 2001; *b* 10 Dec. 1947; *s* of Alfred Joseph Newby and Constance Annie (*née* Potts); *m* 1970, Janet Elizabeth (*née* Craddock); two *s*. *Educ:* John Port Grammar Sch., Etwall, Derbyshire; Atlantic Coll., St Donat's, Glamorgan; Univ. of Essex (BA, PhD). University of Essex: Lectr in Sociology, 1972–75; Sen. Lectr, 1975–79; Reader, 1979–83; Prof. of Sociology, 1983–88; Dir, Data Archive, 1983–88, Chm. and Chief Exec., 1988–94, ESRC; Vice-Chancellor, Southampton Univ., 1994–2001. Prof. of Sociology and Rural Sociology, Univ. of Wisconsin-Madison, 1980–83; visiting appointments: Univ. of NSW, 1976; Sydney, 1976; Newcastle upon Tyne, 1983–84. Chm., CEST, 1995–99; Pres., CVCP, 1999–2001. Member: UFC, 1991–93; Rural Develt Commn, 1991–99; South and West RHA, 1994–96; ESTA, 1997–98. Hon. Fellow, Univ. of Wales, Cardiff, 1996. Hon. DLitt: City of London Poly., 1991; South Bank Univ., 1992; Surrey, 1992; Portsmouth, 1992 (Hon. Fellow, Portsmouth Poly., 1991); Ulster, 1994; DU Essex, 2000. *Publications:* (jtly) Community Studies, 1971; The Deferential Worker, 1977; (jtly) Property, Paternalism and Power, 1978; Green and Pleasant Land?, 1979, 2nd edn 1985; (jtly) The Problem of Sociology, 1983; (jtly) Approximación Teoretica a la Sociologia Rural, 1983; Country Life, 1987; The Countryside in Question, 1988; (jtly) Social Class in Modern Britain, 1988; *edited jointly:* The Sociology of Community, 1974; Doing Sociological Research, 1977; International Perspectives in Rural Sociology, 1978; The Rural Sociology of the Advanced Societies, 1980; Political Action and Social Identity, 1985; Restructuring Capital, 1985; The National Trust: the next hundred years, 1995; over 50 papers in learned jls. *Recreations:* family life, gardening, Derby County and railway enthusiasms. *Address:* The Old Mill, Mill Lane, Corston, Malmesbury, Wilts SN16 0HH. *Club:* Athenæum.

NEWCASTLE, Bishop of, since 1997; **Rt Rev. (John) Martin Wharton;** *b* 6 Aug. 1944; *s* of John and Marjorie Wharton; *m* 1970, Marlene Olive Duckett; two *s* one *d*. *Educ:* Van Mildert Coll., Durham (BA 1969); Linacre Coll., Oxford (BA 1971; MA 1976); Ripon Hall, Oxford, 1969. Ordained: deacon, 1972, priest, 1973; Assistant Curate: St Peter, Birmingham, 1972–75; St John the Baptist, Croydon, 1975–77; Dir of Pastoral Studies, Ripon Coll., Cuddesdon, 1977–83; Asst Curate, Cuddesdon, 1979–83; Exec. Sec., Bd of Ministry and Training, dio. of Bradford, 1983–91; Hon. Canon, Bradford Cathedral, 1984; Bishop's Officer for Ministry and Training, 1992; Residentiary Canon, Bradford Cathedral, 1992; Area Bishop of Kingston-upon-Thames, 1992–97. *Recreation:* sport. *Address:* Bishop's House, 29 Moor Road South, Newcastle upon Tyne NE3 1PA.

NEWCASTLE, NSW, Bishop of, since 1993; **Rt Rev. Roger Adrian Herft;** *b* 11 July 1948; *s* of Richard Clarence and Esmie Marie Herft; *m* 1976, Cheryl Oranee Jayasekera; two *s*. *Educ:* Royal College, Colombo; Theological Coll. of Lanka. BTh, BD (Serampore). Employed at Carson Cumberbatch & Co. Ltd, 1966–69; theol coll., 1969–73; deacon 1972, priest 1973; Assistant Curate: Holy Emmanuel Church, Moratuwa, 1972; St Luke's Church, Borella, with chaplaincy to Colombo Prison, 1973; Vicar: Holy Emmanuel, Moratuwa, 1976; SS Mary and John Nugegoda, 1979; Parish Consultant, Diocese of Waikato, 1983; Bishop of Waikato, 1986–93. Chaplain, Lambeth Conf. of Bishops, 1998. *Publications:* (co-ed) Encounter with Reality, 1971; Christ's Battlers, 1997. *Recreations:* reading, avid follower of cricket. *Address:* Bishopscourt, PO Box 980, Newcastle, NSW 2300, Australia. *T:* (2) 49262767, *Fax:* (2) 49252526; Bishop's Registry, PO Box 817, Newcastle, NSW 2300, Australia, *T:* (2) 49263733, *Fax:* (2) 49261968.

NEWCASTLE, Dean of; *see* Coulton, Very Rev. N. G.

NEWDEGATE; *see* FitzRoy Newdegate, family name of Viscount Daventry.

NEWELL, Christopher William Paul; Director, Casework, Crown Prosecution Service, since 1998; *b* 30 Nov. 1950; *s* of Nicolas Gambier Newell and Edith Alice Newell (*née* Edgill). *Educ:* Wellington College; Southampton Univ. (LLB Hons). Called to the Bar, Middle Temple, 1973; Department of Director of Public Prosecutions: Legal Asst, 1975–78; Sen. Legal Asst, 1978–79; Law Officers' Dept, 1979–83; Sen. Legal Asst, DPP, 1983–86; Asst DPP, 1986; Branch Crown Prosecutor, Crown Prosecution Service, 1986–87; Asst Legal Sec., Law Officers' Dept, 1987–89; Crown Prosecution Service: Dir of HQ Casework, 1989–93; Dir (Casework), 1993–96; Dir, Casework Evaluation, 1996–98. *Recreations:* sport, travel. *Address:* Crown Prosecution Service, 50 Ludgate Hill, EC4M 7EX. *T:* (020) 7796 8553. *Club:* Royal Automobile.

NEWELL, David Richard; Director, Newspaper Society, since 1997; *b* 21 Sept. 1951; *s* of late Dick Newell and Davida Newell (*née* Juleff); *m* 1978, Cora Sue Feingold; one *d*. *Educ:* Shrewsbury Sch.; Birmingham Univ. (LLB Hons 1973); Southampton Univ. (MPhil 1976). US, UK and British Council res. grants, 1974–81. Admitted Solicitor, 1978; Lawford & Co., 1976–78; Lectr in Law, Leicester Univ., 1978–86 (Postgrad. Tutor, 1979–84; Dir, Employment Law Postgrad. prog., 1983–86); Hon. Legal Advr, Leicester Legal Advice Centre, 1979–84; Hd of Govt and Legal Affairs, 1984–96, Dep. Dir, 1992–97, Newspaper Soc. Sec., Parly and Legal Cttee, Guild of Editors, 1984–97; Member: Cttee of Advertising Practice, 1984–; Advertising Assoc. Cttees, 1984–; Council, Campaign for Freedom of Information, 1990– (Award for campaigning against official secrecy, 1989); Employment and Media Cttees, Law Soc., 1990–97; Advertising Law Gp, 1995–; UK Assises Gp, 1995–; Confedn of Communication and Inf. Industries, 1984–; CPU, 1997–; Council, World Assoc. of Newspapers, 1997–; Chm., Legal Framework Cttee, 1995–98, Bd Mem., 1996–, European Newspaper Publishers' Assoc. Director: ABC, 1997–; Press Standards Bd of Finance, 1997–; Advertising Standards Bd of Finance, 1998–; Publishers NTO, 2001–. Mem., CBI Council, 1999–. Press Awards Judge, 1999–. Special Award, UK Press Gazette, 1988. *Publications:* The New Employment Legislation: a guide to the Employment Acts 1980 and 1982, 1983; Understanding Recruitment Law, 1984; (jtly) How to Study Law, 1986, 4th edn 2000; (jtly) Financial Advertising Law, 1989; (jtly) Aspects of Employment Law, 1990; (jtly) Law for Journalists, 1991; (jtly) Tolleys Employment Law, 1994, 2nd edn 2000; (jtly) The Law of Journalism, 1995; (contrib.) Copinger on Copyright, 1998; research papers and articles on employment law, media and legal policy issues. *Recreations:* country and seaside walks, sailing, tennis. *Address:* Newspaper Society, Bloomsbury House, 74–77 Great Russell Street, WC1B 3DA. *T:* (020) 7636 7014; *e-mail:* ns@newspapersoc.org.uk.

NEWELL, Donald, FRICS; Co-Chairman, Europe Middle East Africa Division, CB Richard Ellis Services Inc., USA, 1998–2000; *b* 31 Aug. 1942; *s* of Stephen Newell and Ida Laura Newell (*née* Hatch); *m* 1968, Rosemary Litler-Jones; one *s* two *d*. *Educ:* Cheshunt Grammar Sch. FRICS 1968. Lander Bedells & Crompton, 1961–68; Hillier Parker May & Rowden, Chartered Surveyors, 1968–98: Partner, 1973–98; Man. Partner, 1986–90; Sen. Partner, 1990–98. Director: Oncor Internat., USA, 1995–98; CB Hillier Parker, 1998–2000; non-exec. Dir, London Merchant Securities PLC, 1998–. Pres., Brit. Council for Offices, 1991–92. Liveryman, Company of: Pattenmakers, 1979; Chartered Surveyors, 1993–. *Recreations:* sport, farming. *Address:* 73 Sussex Square, W2 2SS. *T:* (020) 7262 6440. *Clubs:* Buck's, MCC.

NEWELL, Rev. Canon Edmund John, DPhil; Canon Residentiary of St Paul's Cathedral, since 2001; *b* 9 Sept. 1961; *s* of Kenneth Ernest Newell and late Mary Newell (*née* James); *m* 1989, Susan Georgina Greer. *Educ:* Ilfracombe Sch.; University Coll. London (BSc(Econ) 1983); Nuffield Coll., Oxford (DPhil 1988; MA 1989); Oxford Ministry Course; Ripon Coll., Cuddesdon. Prize Res. Fellow, 1987, British Acad. Postdoctoral Fellow, 1989, Nuffield Coll., Oxford. Ordained deacon, 1994, priest, 1995; Curate, Deddington with Barford, Clifton and Hempton, 1994–98; Domestic Chaplain and Res. Asst to Bp of Oxford, 1998–2001; Chaplain, Headington Sch., Oxford, 1998–2001. FRHistS 1998. *Publications:* contribs to books, articles in learned jls and newspapers. *Recreations:* cricket, running, badminton, music. *Address:* 6 Amen Court, EC4M 7BU.

NEWELL, Michael Cormac; film director; *b* 28 March 1942; *s* of Terence William Newell and Mollie Louise Newell; *m* 1979, Bernice Stegers; one *s* one *d*. *Educ:* St Albans Sch.; Magdalene Coll., Cambridge (MA). Television dir, Granada TV, 1964–70: Ready When You Are Mr Magill; Baa Baa Black Sheep; Charm; freelance television dir, 1970–80: Melancholy Hussar; Just Your Luck; Destiny; Mr and Mrs Bureaucrat; Gift of Friendship; *films* include: Man in the Iron Mask, 1976; The Awakening, 1979; Dance with a Stranger, 1984 (Prix de la Jeunesse, Cannes); Good Father, 1986 (Prix Italia); Sweet and Sour, 1988; Into the West, 1992; Four Weddings and a Funeral, 1994 (Best Dir, BAFTA Awards, 1995); An Awfully Big Adventure, 1995; Donnie Brasco, 1997; Pushing Tin, 1999; executive producer, Photographic Fairies, 1997; Best Laid Plans, 200 Cigarettes, 1999; High Fidelity, Traffic, 2000. *Recreations:* walking, reading (anything but fiction). *Address:* Fifty Cannon Entertainment, c/o ICM, Oxford House, 76 Oxford Street, W1N 0AX.

NEWELL, Rt Rev. Phillip Keith, AO 1993; Bishop of Tasmania, 1982–2000; *b* 30 Jan. 1930; *s* of Frank James and Ada Miriam Newell; *m* 1959, Merle Edith Callaghan; three *s*. *Educ:* Univ. of Melbourne; Trinity Coll., Melbourne. BSc 1953; DiplEd(Hons) 1954; ThL(Hons) 1959; BEd 1960; MEd 1969; FACE 1990. Mathematics Master: Melbourne High School, 1954–56; University High School, 1957–58; Tutor in Physics, Secondary Teachers' Coll., 1957; Assistant Curate: All Saints, East St Kilda, Melbourne, 1960–61; S Andrew's, Brighton, Melbourne, 1962–63; Asst Priest, S James, King Street, Sydney, 1963–67; Chaplain, Sydney Hosp., 1963–67; Rector, Christ Church, St Lucia, Brisbane, 1967–82; Residentiary Canon, S John's Cathedral, Brisbane, 1973–82; Archdeacon of Lilley, Brisbane, 1976–82. CGSJ (KStJ 1981); ChLJ. *Publications:* Body Search, 1993; A Pocket Lent Book, 1996. *Recreations:* education, music (classical and light opera), singing, choral conducting, wine making, travel, cricket (spectator), tennis (occasional game). *Address:* 4 Howley Court, Howrah, Tas 7018, Australia. *T:* and *Fax:* (3) 6247 1706. *Club:* Tasmanian (Hobart).

NEWELL, Robert Fraser, LVO 2000; Director-General, Royal Over-Seas League, since 1991; *b* 3 May 1943; *m* 1969, Shahnaz Bakhtiar; two *d*. *Educ:* University Coll. Sch. MHCIMA 1986, FHCIMA 1997. Hotel mgt positions in London, Iran and Kenya, 1965–75; Dir of Admin, Kenya Utalii Coll., Nairobi, 1975–79; Gen. Manager, Royal Over-Seas League, 1979–91. Vis. Lectr in Hotel Financial Mgt, Ecole Hotelière de Lausanne, 1983–. Chm., Assoc. of London Clubs, 1992–95; Member: Club Secs and Managers Assoc., 1982–; Jt Commonwealth Socs Council, 1991–; Cttee, Eur. Atlantic Gp, 1993–; Cttee, Kenya Soc., 1996–. Fellow, Brit. Assoc. Hotel Accountants, 1997; FIMgt 1983. *Recreations:* tennis, teaching. *Address:* Royal Over-Seas League, Over-Seas House, Park Place, St James's Street, SW1A 1LR. *T:* (020) 7408 0214.

NEWENS, (Arthur) Stanley; *b* 4 Feb. 1930; *s* of Arthur Ernest and Celia Jenny Newens, Bethnal Green; *m* 1st, 1954, Ann (*d* 1962), *d* of J. B. Sherratt, Stoke-on-Trent; two *d*; 2nd, 1966, Sandra Christina, *d* of J. A. Frith, Chingford; one *s* two *d*. *Educ:* Buckhurst Hill County High Sch.; University Coll., London (BA Hons History); Westminster Training Coll. (Post-Graduate Certificate of Education). Coal face worker in N Staffs mines, 1952–55. Secondary Sch. Teacher, 1956–65, 1970–74. MP (Lab) Epping, 1964–70 (NUT sponsored); MP (Lab and Co-op) Harlow, Feb. 1974–1983; contested (Lab) Harlow, 1983 and 1987; MEP (Lab) London Central, 1984–99. Chairman: Eastern Area Gp of Lab. MPs, 1974–83; Tribune Gp of MPs, 1982–83 (Vice-Chm., 1981–82); PLP Foreign Affairs Gp, 1982–83 (Vice-Chm., 1976–77); Dep. Leader, British Lab. Gp of MEPs, 1988–89 (Chm., 1985–87); Pres., EP Central Amer. and Mexico Delegn, 1994–96; Vice-Chm., Labour Action for Peace. Active Member: Labour Party, holding numerous offices, 1949–; NUM, 1952–55; NUT, 1956–. Pres., Liberation (Movement for Colonial Freedom), 1992– (Chm., 1967–92). Dir, London Co-operative Soc., 1971–77 (Pres., 1977–81); Mem., Central Exec., Co-op. Union, 1974–80. Sec., Harlow Council for Voluntary Service, 1983–84. Chairman: Harlow Civic Soc., 1999–; Gibberd Garden Trust, 1999–. *Publications:* The Case Against NATO (pamphlet), 1972; Nicolae Ceausescu, 1972; Third World: change or chaos, 1977; A History of North Weald Bassett and its People, 1985; A Short History of the London Co-op Society Political Committee, 1988; (with Ron Bill) Leah Manning, 1991; The Kurds, 1994; Pathfinders, 1998; pamphlets and articles. *Recreations:* local historical research, family, reading. *Address:* The Leys, 18 Park Hill, Harlow, Essex CM17 0AE. *T:* (01279) 420108.

NEWEY, Guy Richard; QC 2001; *b* 21 Jan. 1959; *s* of His Honour John Henry Richard Newey, QC and of Mollie Patricia Newey (*née* Chalk); *m* 1986, Angela Clare Neilson; one *s* three *d*. *Educ:* Tonbridge Sch.; Queens' Coll., Cambridge (MA 1st Cl., LLM 1st Cl.); Council of Legal Educn (1st Cl. in Bar Exams). Called to the Bar, Middle Temple, 1982; in practice at Chancery Bar, 1983–; Jun. Counsel to the Crown, Chancery, and A Panel, 1990–2001; Jun. Counsel to Charity Comrs, 1991–2001. Gov., New Beacon Educnl Trust Ltd, 2001–. *Publications:* (contrib.) Directors' Disqualification, 2nd edn 1998; (contrib.) Civil Court Service, 1999. *Address:* Maitland Chambers, 7 Stone Buildings, Lincoln's Inn WC2A 3SZ. *T:* (020) 7406 1200.

NEWEY, Sidney Brian; consultant in transport; Assistant to Chief Executive, Railways, British Rail, 1990–93, retired; *b* 8 Jan. 1937; *s* of Sidney Frank Newey and Edith Mary Newey; *m* 1967, Margaret Mary Stevens (*d* 1996); one *s*. *Educ:* Burton upon Trent Grammar Sch.; Worcester Coll., Oxford (MA Mod. History). MCIT. British Rail: Traffic apprentice, Western Region, 1960; Stationmaster, Southall, Mddx, 1964; Freight Marketing Manager, Western Region, 1971; Divl Manager, Birmingham, 1978; Dep. General Manager, London Midland Region, 1980; Gen. Manager, Western Region, 1985–87; Director, Provincial, 1987–90. *Recreations:* fell walking, history, reading, village and church affairs. *Address:* Chestnut Cottage, The Green South, Warborough, Oxon OX10 7DN. *T:* (01865) 858322.

NEWFOUNDLAND, CENTRAL, Bishop of, since 2000; **Rt Rev. Donald Arthur Young;** *b* 11 Nov. 1944; *s* of Harold and Frances Young; *m* 1966, Sylvia Joan Spurrell; one *s* three *d*. *Educ:* Univ. of Newfoundland; Atlantic Sch. of Theology; Queen's Coll., St John's, Nfld (LTh). Ordained deacon, 1977, priest, 1977; Deacon in charge, Buchans, 1977; Rector: Buchans, 1977–81; Port Rexton, 1981–89; Diocesan Progs and Exec. Officer, Central Newfoundland, 1989–2000. *Address:* 34 Fraser Road, Gander, NF A1V 2E8, Canada. *T:* (709) 2562372, *Fax:* (709) 2562396; *e-mail:* bishopcentral@nfld.net.

NEWFOUNDLAND, EASTERN, AND LABRADOR, Bishop of, since 1993; **Rt Rev. Donald Frederick Harvey;** *b* St John's, Newfoundland, 13 Sept. 1939; *s* of Robert Joseph and Elsie May Harvey (*née* Vaters); *m* 1964, Gertrude, *d* of George and Jessie Hiscock. *Educ:* St Michael's Sch., 1956; Memorial Univ. (BA 1985; MA 1987); Queen's Theol Coll. (MDiv 1986). Sch. teacher, 1956–57; ordained deacon, 1963, priest, 1974; served in parishes: Portugal Cove, 1963–64, 1973–76; Twillingate, 1965; King's Cove, 1965–68; Happy Valley, Labrador, 1968–73; St Michael & All Angels, St John's, 1976–83; Anglican Chaplain, Meml Univ. of Newfoundland, 1984–87; Rector, and Dean, Cathedral of St John the Baptist, St John's, 1989–92. Rural Dean of Labrador, 1968–73. Lectr in Pastoral Theol., Queen's Coll., 1984–; Sessional Lectr, English, Meml Univ. of Newfoundland, 1985–89. Hon. DD Huron Coll., 1996. *Address:* (office) 19 King's Bridge Road, St John's, NF A1C 3K4, Canada; (home) 22 Church Hill, St John's, NF A1C 3Z9, Canada.

NEWHAM, Prof. Dianne Jane, PhD; Professor of Physiotherapy, since 1993, and Head of Applied Biomedical Research Group, since 2000, King's College, London; *b* 31 July 1949; *d* of Geoffrey Newham and Denise Millicent Newham; partner, Terry N. Williams; one *s*. *Educ:* Nairobi Convent Sch., Kenya; Ockbrook Moravian Sch.; Prince of Wales Sch. of Physiotherapy (MCSP, SRP 1976); UCL (MPhil 1982); North London Poly. (PhD 1985). Lab. Asst, Boots Co. Ltd, 1967–70; VSO, Nigeria, 1970–72; University College London: Physiotherapist, 1976–79; Res. Physiotherapist, Dept of Medicine, 1979–82; Associate Res. Fellow, Medicine and Surgery, 1985–87; Lectr in Physiology, 1987–89; King's College, London: Reader, 1989–93; Hd of Physiotherapy, 1989–2000. Mem., Working Gp on estabt of UK Acad. of Med. Scis, 1996–98. *Publications:* chapters on human muscle pain, skeletal muscle function and fatigue; original research papers in jls of physiology, physiotherapy and rehabilitation. *Recreations:* travel, gardening, food and wine. *Address:* Physiotherapy Division, King's College London, Shepherd's House, Guy's Hospital Campus, SE1 1UL. *T:* (020) 7848 6320.

NEWING, John Frederick, CBE 1999; QPM 1988; DL; Chief Constable, Derbyshire Constabulary, 1990–2000; *b* 1 March 1940; *s* of Frederick George Newing and Emily Beatrice Newing (*née* Bettles); *m* 1963, Margaret May Kilborn; two *s* one *d*. *Educ:* Kettering Grammar Sch.; Leeds Univ. (BA Hons Social and Public Administration). Joined Metropolitan Police, 1963; Police Staff Coll., 1967–68; Bramshill Scholarship, Leeds Univ., 1969–72; Community Relations Bd, 1974; Staff Officer to Commissioner, 1977; Chief Supt i/c Marylebone Div., 1980; Senior Command Course, Police Staff Coll., 1981; Comdr, Community Relations, 1982, Public Order Branch, 1984; Dep. Asst Comr i/c W London Area, 1985–87; seconded to Home Office Science and Technology Gp, 1987–90. Pres., ACPO, 1998–99. DL Derbyshire, 2000. *Publications:* articles in Policing and other professional jls. *Recreations:* reading, walking, voluntary youth work, such sports as age allows. *Address:* Glapwell, Derbys.

NEWING, Rt Rev. Dom Kenneth Albert, OSB; *b* 29 Aug. 1923; *s* of Albert James Pittock Newing and Nellie Louise Maude Newing; unmarried. *Educ:* Dover Grammar School; Selwyn College, Cambridge (MA); Theological College, Mirfield, Yorks. Deacon, 1955; priest, 1956; Assistant Curate, Plymstock, 1955–63; Rector of Plympton S Maurice, Plymouth, 1963–82; Archdeacon of Plymouth, 1978–82; Bishop Suffragan of Plymouth, 1982–88; joined Order of St Benedict, 1988; solemn (life) profession, 1989. *Address:* Elmore Abbey, Church Lane, Speen, Newbury, Berks RG14 1SA. *T:* (01635) 33080.

NEWINGTON, Sir Michael (John), KCMG 1993 (CMG 1982); HM Diplomatic Service, retired; Ambassador to Brazil, 1987–92; *b* 10 July 1932; *er s* of late J. T. Newington, Spalding, Lincs; *m* 1956, Nina Gordon-Jones; one *s* one *d*. *Educ:* Stamford Sch.; St John's Coll., Oxford. MA. RAF, 1951–52, Pilot Officer. Joined Foreign Office, 1955; Economic Survey Section, Hong Kong, 1957–58; resigned 1958. ICI, 1959–60. Rejoined FO, 1960; Second, later First Sec. (Economic), Bonn, 1961–65; First Sec., Lagos, 1965–68; Asst Head of Science and Technology Dept, FCO, 1968–72; Counsellor (Scientific), Bonn, 1972–75; Counsellor and Consul-Gen., Tel Aviv, 1975–78; Head of Republic of Ireland Dept, FCO, 1978–81; Consul-Gen., Düsseldorf, 1981–85; Ambassador to Venezuela and concurrently (non-resident) to Dominican Republic, 1985–87. *Recreations:* golf, gardening, cultivating olives. *Address:* Mas Bomuré, 83460 Taradeau, France; 2 Church Street, St Clements, Sandwich, Kent CT13 9EH.

NEWIS, Kenneth, CB 1967 CVO 1970 (MVO 1958); FRSAMD; *b* 9 Nov. 1916; *o s* of late H. T. and G. Newis, Manchester; *m* 1943, Kathleen, *o d* of late John Barrow, Davenport, Cheshire; two *d*. *Educ:* Manchester Grammar Sch.; St John's Coll., Cambridge (Scholar). BA 1938, MA 1942. Entered HM Office of Works, 1938; Private Sec. to Minister of Works (Rt Hon. C. W. Key), 1948–49; Asst Sec., 1949; Under-Sec., 1959; Dir of Management Services, MPBW, 1969–70; Under-Sec., Scottish Devel Dept, 1970–73, Sec., 1973–76. Hon. Pres., Queen's Hall (Edinburgh) Ltd, 1991– (Chm., 1977–91). Vice-Chm., Cockburn Assoc., 1986–94; Member: Historic Buildings Council for Scotland, 1978–88; Bd, Methodist Homes for the Aged, and Vice-Chm., MHA Housing Assoc., 1977–91; Bd, RSAMD, 1977–88 (FRSAMD 1995); Scottish Churches' Council, 1984–87 (Chm., Friends of Scottish Churches' Council, 1984–87). Conservator of Wimbledon and Putney Commons, 1963–70. Governor: Farrington's School, 1964–70; Richmond College, 1964–70. *Recreation:* music. *Address:* 10/9 St Margaret's Place, Thirlestane Road, Edinburgh EH9 1AY. *T:* (0131) 447 4138. *Club:* New (Edinburgh).

NEWLAND, Prof. David Edward, MA; ScD; FREng, FIMechE, FIEE; Professor of Engineering (1875), since 1976, Head, Engineering Department, since 1996, and a Deputy Vice-Chancellor, since 1999, University of Cambridge; Fellow, Selwyn College, Cambridge, since 1976; consulting engineer (part-time), since 1963; *b* 8 May 1936; *s* of late Robert W. Newland and Marion A. Newland (*née* Dearman); *m* 1959, Patricia Frances Mayne; two *s*. *Educ:* Alleyne's Sch., Stevenage; Selwyn Coll., Cambridge (Lyttleton Scholar, 1956; Mech. Sciences Tripos: Rex Moir Prize, 1956, Ricardo Prize, 1957; MA 1961; ScD 1990); Massachusetts Inst. of Technol. (ScD thesis on nonlinear vibrations, 1963). English Electric Co., 1957–61; Instr and Asst Prof. of Mech. Engrg, MIT, 1961–64; Lectr and Sen. Lectr, Imperial Coll. of Science and Technol., 1964–67; Prof. of Mech. Engrg, Sheffield Univ., 1967–76. Mem., Royal Commn on Envmtl Pollution, 1984–89. Visitor, Transport and Road Res. Lab., 1990–92; non-exec. Dir, Cambridge-MIT Inst., 2000–. Past or present mem., cttees of IMechE, DTI, BSI, SERC, Design Council, Engrg Council and Royal Academy (formerly Fellowship) of Engineering, including: Mem., Editorial Panel, 1968–82 and Consultant Editor, 1983–87, Jl Mech. Engrg Sci., Proc. IMechE, Part C; Engrg Awards Panel, Design Council, 1977–79; Council, Fellowship of Engrg, 1985–88; Working Party on Engineers and Risk Issues, Engrg Council, 1990–94; Member: SRC Transport Cttee, 1969–72; Mech. Engrg and Machine Tools Requirements Bd, 1977, 1978; Chm., BSI Tech. Cttee on bellows expansion jts, 1976–85. Technical witness, Flixborough Inquiry, 1974–75, and other legal cases; Engrg Advr, London Millennium Bridge Trust, 2000–01. Governor, St Paul's Schs, 1978–93. Freeman, City of London, 2000; Liveryman, Engrs' Co., 2001. Churchwarden, Ickleton, 1979–87. Distinguished Alumni Lectr, MIT, 1999. FREng (FEng 1982). Hon. DEng Sheffield, 1997. Charles S. Lake award, 1975, and T. Bernard Hall prize, IMechE, 1991, for papers in IMechE Procs. *Publications:* An Introduction to Random Vibrations and Spectral Analysis, 1975, 3rd edn, as Random Vibrations, Spectral and Wavelet Analysis, 1993; Mechanical Vibration Analysis and Computation, 1989; technical papers, mostly in British and Amer. engrg jls. *Recreations:* music, jogging, golf, bell ringing. *Address:* c/o University Engineering Department, Trumpington Street, Cambridge CB2 1PZ. *T:* (01223) 332670. *Club:* Athenæum.

NEWLANDS, David Baxter; Chairman: Tomkins plc, since 2000 (Director, since 1999); Britax International plc, since 2000 (Director, since 1999); Paypoint, since 1998; *b* 13 Sept. 1946; *s* of George Frederick Newlands and Helen Frederica Newlands; *m* 1973, Susan Helena Milne; two *s* two *d*. *Educ:* Edinburgh Acad. FCA 1969. Deloitte & Touche, 1963–86, Partner, 1977–86; Gp Finance Director: Saatchi & Saatchi, 1986–89; General Electric Co., 1989–97. Non-executive Director: Weir Gp, 1997–; Global Software Services, 1998–; Standard Life Assce Co., 1999–; London Regl Transport, 1999–; non-exec. Chm., Prospect Investment Mgt, 1999–. *Recreations:* golf, Rugby, bridge. *Address:* Lane End, Chucks Lane, Walton-on-the-Hill, Surrey KT20 7UB. *T:* (01737) 812582. *Clubs:* Royal Automobile; Walton Heath Golf; Sutton and Epsom Rugby (Cheam).

NEWLANDS, Rev. Prof. George McLeod, PhD; Professor of Divinity, since 1986, and Director, Centre for Theology, Literature and the Arts, since 1999, University of Glasgow (Dean, Faculty of Divinity, 1988–90); *b* 12 July 1941; *s* of George and Mary Newlands; *m* 1967, Mary Elizabeth Wallace; three *s*. *Educ:* Perth Acad.; Univ. of Edinburgh (MA 1st Cl. Classics (Vans Dunlop Scholar, 1963); BD 1st Cl. Eccles. Hist. (Cunningham Fellow, 1966); PhD); Univ. of Heidelberg; Univ. of Zürich; Churchill Coll., Cambridge (MA). Ordained minister, C of S, 1970, and priest, C of E, 1982. Asst Minister, Muirhouse, Edinburgh, 1969–70; Lectr in Divinity, Univ. of Glasgow, 1969–73; Cambridge University: Lectr in Divinity, 1973–86; Fellow, Wolfson Coll., 1975–82; Fellow and Dean, Trinity Hall, 1982–86; Principal, Trinity Coll., Glasgow, 1991–97. Hensley Henson Lectr, Oxford, 1995. Vis. Prof., Univ. of Mainz, 1999. Member: Doctrine Commn, C of E, 1983–86; Convener, Panel on Doctrine, C of S, 1995–. Member: Eur. Cttee, World Alliance of Reformed Churches, 1987–95; Church and Nation Cttee, C of S, 1992–96; Unity, Faith and Order Commn, Action for Churches Together in Scotland, 1995–; Scottish Churches Initiative for Unity, 1995–; HEFCE RAE Panel for Theology and Religious Studies, 1996, 2001; Center of Theol Inquiry, Princeton, 1998; Netherlands RAE Panel, 1999. Mem. Edtl Bd, Theology in Scotland, 1996–. *Publications:* Hilary of Poitiers, 1978; Theology of the Love of God, 1980; (ed) Explorations in Theology 8, 1981; The Church of God, 1984; Making Christian Decisions, 1985; God in Christian Perspective, 1994; Generosity and the Christian Future, 1997; (ed jtly) Scottish Christianity in the Modern World, 2000; contribs to theol pubns. *Recreations:* music, walking, commuting. *Address:* Faculty of Divinity, University of Glasgow, Glasgow G12 8QQ. *T:* (0141) 330 5297, 6525, *Fax:* (0141) 330 4943; (home) 2/19 Succoth Court, Edinburgh EH12 6BZ, *T:* (0131) 337 4941. *Club:* New (Edinburgh).

NEWMAN, Dr Barry Hilton; Director, Propellants, Explosives and Rocket Motor Establishment, and Head of Rocket Motor Executive, Ministry of Defence, 1980–84, retired; *b* 16 Sept. 1926; *s* of Charles Ernest Newman and Kathleen (*née* Hilton); *m* 1950, Dorothy Ashworth Truesdale; one *s* one *d*. *Educ:* Bishop Vesey's Grammar Sch., Sutton Coldfield; Univ. of Birmingham (BSc (Hons) 1947, PhD 1950). Joined Scientific Civil Service, 1950; Explosives R&D Estabt, 1950–63; Defence Research Staff, Washington,

1963–66; Supt Explosives Br., Royal Armament R&D Estabt, 1966–71; Asst Dir, Directorate General Weapons (Army), 1971–72; Dir, Research Armaments, 1972–74; RCDS 1975; Head of Terminal Effects Dept, RARDE, 1976–77; Dep. Dir, RARDE, 1977–80. *Publications:* official reports. *Recreations:* France, cricket, bridge, history, theatre. *Address:* c/o Barclays Bank, 80 High Street, Sevenoaks, Kent. *Club:* MCC.

NEWMAN, Catherine Mary; QC 1995; a Recorder, since 2000; *b* 7 Feb. 1954; *d* of Dr Ernest Newman and Josephine (*née* McLaughlin); *m* 1982, Ian James Gouldsbrough; one *s* one *d. Educ:* University Coll. London (LLB 1st Cl. Hons 1978). Called to the Bar, Middle Temple, 1979 (Harmsworth Schol.); in practice in business and commercial fields, Chancery Div., 1980–; Dep. Registrar in Bankruptcy, 1991–; an Asst Recorder, 1998–2000. Member: Bar Council, 1987–90; Public Interest Adv. Panel, Legal Services Commn, 2000–. *Publications:* Bar Finals Guide, 1980, 3rd edn 1987; Insolvency Issues, 1999. *Recreation:* family life. *Address:* Maitland Chambers, 7 Stone Buildings, Lincoln's Inn, WC2A 3SZ. *T:* (020) 7406 1200.

NEWMAN, Edward; *b* 14 May 1953; *m;* three *c.* Formerly in light engineering, cable making; postal worker, Manchester. Mem., Manchester CC, 1979–85. MEP (Lab) Greater Manchester Central, 1984–99. *Address:* 234 Ryebank Road, Chorlton cum Hardy, Manchester M21 1LU.

NEWMAN, Sir Francis (Hugh Cecil), 4th Bt *cr* 1912, of Cecil Lodge, Newmarket; *b* 12 June 1963; *s* of Sir Gerard Robert Henry Sigismund Newman, 3rd Bt and of Caroline Philippa, *d* of late Brig. Alfred Geoffrey Neville, CBE, MC; *S* father, 1987; *m* 1990, Katharine, *d* of Timothy Edwards; two *s* one *d. Educ:* Eton; Univ. of Pennsylvania (BA Econs). *Recreations:* family, collecting, field sports. *Heir: s* Thomas Ralph Gerard Newman, *b* 7 Jan. 1993. *Address:* Burloes Hall, Royston, Herts SG8 9NE. *Clubs:* Turf; Eton Vikings.

NEWMAN, Frederick Edward Fry, CBE 1986; MC 1945; Chairman: Dan-Air Services, 1953–89; Davies & Newman Holdings, 1971–90; *b* 14 July 1916; *s* of Frank Newman and Katharine Newman; *m* 1947, Margaret Helen (*née* Blackstone); two *s* one *d. Educ:* The Leys School, Cambridge. Joined Davies & Newman, 1937; served HAC and 9th Field Regt, RA, 1939–46; formed Dan-Air Services, 1953. *Address:* Cranstone, Hook Heath Road, Woking, Surrey GU22 0DT. *T:* (01483) 772605.

NEWMAN, Sir Geoffrey (Robert), 6th Bt *cr* 1836; Director, Blackpool Sands (Devon) Utilities Co. Ltd, since 1970; *b* 2 June 1947; *s* of Sir Ralph Alured Newman, 5th Bt, and of Hon. Ann Rosemary Hope, *d* of late Hon. Claude Hope-Morley; *S* father, 1968; *m* 1980, Mary, *y d* of Colonel Sir Martin St John Valentine Gibbs, KCVO, CB, DSO, TD; one *s* three *d. Educ:* Heatherdown, Ascot; Kelly Coll., Tavistock. 1st Bn, Grenadier Guards, 1967–70. Vice Chm. and Dir, Dartmouth Tourist Inf. Centre, 1995–; Mem., Devon Assoc. of Tourist Attractions, 1995–. Chm., Dartmouth Swimming Pool, 1999–. Walk Leader/Guide, Wayfarers, 1991–. Pres., Dartmouth and Kingswear Soc., 2001–; Trustee, Marine Conservation Soc., 2001–. FRGS. *Recreations:* sub-aqua, sailing, all sports. *Heir: s* Robert Melvil Newman, *b* 4 Oct. 1985.

NEWMAN, Hon. Sir George (Michael), Kt 1995; **Hon. Mr Justice Newman;** a Judge of the High Court of Justice, Queen's Bench Division, since 1995; *b* 4 July 1941; *s* of late Wilfred James Newman and Cecilia Beatrice Lily Newman; *m* 1966, Hilary Alice Gibbs (*née* Chandler); two *s* one *d. Educ:* Lewes County Grammar Sch.; St Catharine's Coll., Cambridge (Squire Schol.; BA Law). Called to the Bar, Middle Temple, 1965 (Blackstone Scholar; Bencher, 1989), Trinidad and Tobago, 1979, St Kitts and Nevis, 1989. QC 1981; a Recorder, 1985–95. Counsel and Constitutional Advr to Gov. Gen. of Fiji, 1987; Constitutional Advr to Pres. of Fiji, 1988–90. Fellow, Inst. of Advanced Legal Studies, 1999. FRSA 1991. *Publications:* (jtly) contribs to Halsbury's Laws of England, 4th edn. *Recreations:* tennis, golf, ski-ing, the countryside. *Address:* Royal Courts of Justice, Strand, WC2A 2LL. *Club:* Royal Ashdown Forest.

NEWMAN, John Arthur, FSA; Reader, Courtauld Institute of Art, University of London, 1987–2001; *b* 14 Dec. 1936; *s* of Arthur Charles Cecil Newman and late Wynifred Kate Newman (*née* Owles); *m* 1965, Margaret Banner; two *d. Educ:* Dulwich Coll.; University Coll., Oxford (MA); Courtauld Inst. of Art, London Univ. (Academic Dip. 1965). Lectr, Courtauld Inst. of Art, 1966–87. Mem., Historic Buildings Council for England, 1977–84; Comr, English Heritage, 1986–89; Chm., Adv. Bd for Redundant Churches, 2000–; Mem., Royal Commn on Ancient and Historical Monuments of Wales, 2000–. Pres., Soc. of Architectural Historians of GB, 1988–92. *Publications:* Buildings of England series: Kent (2 vols), 1969; (with Nikolaus Pevsner) Dorset, 1972; (contrib.) The History of the King's Works, vol. V, 1975; (ed with Howard Colvin) Roger North on Architecture, 1981; (contrib.) The History of the University of Oxford, vol. III, 1986, vol. IV, 1997; Buildings of Wales series: Glamorgan, 1995; Gwent/Monmouthshire, 2000. *Address:* 31 Gordon Road, Sevenoaks, Kent TN13 1HE.

NEWMAN, Sir Kenneth (Leslie), GBE 1987; Kt 1978; QPM 1982; Commissioner of the Metropolitan Police, 1982–87; non-executive director of various companies; *b* 15 Aug. 1926; *s* of John William Newman and Florence Newman; *m* 1949, Eileen Lilian. *Educ:* London Univ. (LLB Hons). Served War, RAF, 1942–46. Palestine Police, 1946–48; Metropolitan Police, 1948–73; Comdr, New Scotland Yard, 1972; Royal Ulster Constab., 1973–79; Sen. Dep. Chief Constable, 1973; Chief Constable, 1976–79; Comdt, Police Staff Coll., and HM Inspector of Constabulary, 1980–82. Vis. Prof. of Law, Bristol University, 1987–88. Registrar, Imperial Soc. of Knights Bachelor, 1991–98. Chairman: Disciplinary Cttee, Security Systems Inspectorate, British Security Industry Assoc., 1987–97; Assoc. for Prevention of Theft in Shops, 1987–91; Pres., Assoc. of Police and Public Security Suppliers, 1993–2000; Vice Pres., Defence Manufacturers Assoc., 1987–2000. Trustee: Police Foundn, 1982– (Chm., Res. Cttee, 1991–98); Community Action Trust (Crime Stoppers), 1987–; World Humanity Action Trust, 1993–98. CIMgt (FBIM 1977). Freeman of the City of London, 1983. KStJ 1987 (CStJ 1984). Communicator of the Year, BAIE, 1984. Order of: Bahrain, Class 2, 1984; the Aztec Eagle, Cl. 2, Mexico, 1985. King Abdul Aziz, Cl. 1, Saudi Arabia, 1987; Grand Officer: Order of Orange-Nassau, Netherlands, 1982; Grand Order of the Lion, Malaŵi, 1985; Order of Ouissam Alouite, Morocco, 1987; Commander: National Order of Legion of Honour, France, 1984; Order of Military Merit, Spain, 1986; Kt Comdr, Order of Merit, West Germany, 1986; Medal of Merit, Cl. 1, Qatar, 1985. *Recreations:* walking, reading, bridge.

NEWMAN, Kevin; Global Delivery Director, Citibank, 1997; *b* 28 June 1957; *s* of John and Valerie Newman; *m* 1983, Catherine Stewart-Murray; two *s* one *d. Educ:* Keele Univ. (BA Amer. Studies and Politics); Essex Univ. (US Govt and Politics). Mars Gp Services, 1981–85; Inf. Centre Manager, Business Systems Manager and Management Inf. Systems Dir, Woolworth, 1985–89; First Direct: joined 1989; Ops Dir, 1990; Chief Exec., 1991–97. *Recreations:* squash, tennis, ski-ing, golf, gym workout, American football, family.

NEWMAN, Dr Lotte Therese, (Mrs N. E. Aronsohn), CBE 1998 (OBE 1991); general practitioner since 1958; President, Royal College of General Practitioners, 1994–97; *b* 22 Jan. 1929; *d* of Dr George Newman and Dr Tilly Newman; *m* 1959, Norman Edward Aronsohn; three *s* one *d. Educ:* North London Collegiate Sch.; Univ. of Birmingham; King's College London and Westminster Hosp. Med. Schs. BSc 1951, MB BS 1957; LRCP, MRCS 1957; FRCGP 1977. Casualty Officer, Westminster Hosp.; Paediatric House Officer, Westminster Children's Hosp.; gen. medicine, St Stephen's Hosp. Director: Private Patients Plan, 1983–96; Private Patients Plan (Lifetime) plc, 1991–96; Gov., PPP Medical Trust, 1997–99. Mem. Council, 1980–94, Vice-Chm., 1987–89, former Provost, NE London Faculty and former Examr, RCGP; Hon. Sec., 1981–86, Pres. elect, 1986–87, Pres., 1987–88, Medical Women's Fedn; Pres., Internat. Soc. of Gen. Practice, 1988–90; Europ. Regl Vice-Pres., World Orgn of Nat. Colls, Acads and Academic Assocs of GPs/Family Physicians, 1992–94; Member: GMC, 1984–99 (Chm., Registration Cttee, 1997–98); Council, BMA, 1985–89 (Member: Med. Ethics Cttee; General Med. Services Cttee, 1983–86 and 1988–91; Private Practice and Prof. Fees Cttee, 1985–89; Forensic Medicine Sub-Cttee, 1985–89; Visitor to Council, 1996–97); Adv. Cttee on Breast Cancer Screening, 1998–; Home Office Misuse of Drugs Tribunal, 1993–; Disability Benefits Forum, 1998–99; Chm., Camden and Islington Local Med. Cttee, 1986–89 (Vice-Chm., 1983–86); Chm., Regional Co-ordinating Cttee of Area Local Med. Cttees, 1985–87; Lectr, Royal Army Med. Coll., 1976–89 (first woman to give Sir David Bruce Lecture in Gen. Practice, 1989); temp. Adviser, WHO; formerly UK rep., OECD and Mem., Expert Cttees studying Primary Health Care in Germany, Switzerland, Sweden. Med. Advr, St John Ambulance, 1999–. Mem., Parole Bd, 1992–94. Mackenzie Lectr, RCGP, 1991; Dame Hilda Rose Lectr, Med. Women's Fedn, 1994. Member: Hunterian Soc.; Hampstead Medical Soc.; Assurance Med. Soc., 1987–. FRSocMed 1977; Fellow: BMA, 1998; Royal NZ Coll. of Gen. Practitioners, 1998. Freeman, City of London; Liveryman, Apothecaries' Soc. of London. Sir David Bruce Medal, RAMC, 1990; Purkinje Medal for Services to Medicine, Czech Soc. of Gen. Practice, 1985. *Publications:* papers on: women doctors; multidisciplinary training and courses of Primary Health Care Team; breast feeding; ENT conditions and management of mental health handicap in gen. practice. *Recreations:* listening, music, boating. *Address:* The White House, One Ardwick Road, NW2 2BX. *T:* (020) 7435 6630, *Fax:* (020) 7435 6672. *Clubs:* Royal Automobile, City Livery, Little Ship.

NEWMAN, Malcolm, CPFA; Director, Carlisle Partnerships, since 1997; *b* 2 April 1946; *s* of John George and Elizabeth Newman; *m* 1980, Marilyn Wilson; one *s* one *d. Educ:* Jarrow Grammar Sch. Clerk, Hebburn UDC, 1962–66; Newcastle upon Tyne City Council: various positions, 1966–71; Sen. Audit Asst, 1971–72; Sen. Management Accountant, 1972–73; Chief Accountant, 1973–77; Asst City Treas. (Accounting), 1977–79; Man. (Cons.) and Gen. Man., Wilson Johnson, 1979–80; Asst Finance Officer (Audit and Tech.), Sefton MDC, 1980–82; Hd of Financial Services 1982–85, Bor. Treas. 1985–87, London Borough of Southwark; City Treas., 1987–97, Dep. Chief Exec., 1990–97, Sheffield City Council. Director: Hallamshire Investments plc, 1988–; Northern Gen. Hosp. NHS Trust, 1997–; Chm., START Fedn, 1994–. Governor: Sheffield Hallam Univ. (formerly Sheffield Poly.), 1989–94; Silverdale Sch., 1993–97. *Recreations:* outdoors, jogging, Newcastle United, learning about myself. *Address:* 113 Knowle Lane, Sheffield S11 9SN.

NEWMAN, Nanette, (Mrs Bryan Forbes); actress and writer; *b* 29 May 1934; *d* of Sidney and Ruby Newman; *m* 1955, Bryan Forbes, *qv*; two *d. Educ:* Sternhold Coll., London; Italia Conti Stage Sch.; RADA. Appeared as a child in various films for Children's Film Foundn; other film appearances include: The L-Shaped Room, 1962; The Wrong Arm of the Law, 1962; Seance on a Wet Afternoon, 1963; The Wrong Box, 1965; The Whisperers, 1966; Deadfall, 1967; The Madwoman of Chaillot, 1968; The Raging Moon, 1971 (Variety Club Best Film Actress Award); The Stepford Wives, 1974; International Velvet, 1978 (Evening News Best Film Actress Award); The Mystery of Edwin Drood, 1992; *television:* Call My Bluff, What's My Line, London Scene, Stay with me till Morning, Jessie (title role), Let There Be Love, A Breath of Fresh Air, Late Expectations, The Endless Game, The Mixer; own series: The Fun Food Factory; Newman Meets; Celebrations; Patten on a Plate, 2001. *Publications:* God Bless Love, 1972 (repr. 16 times); Lots of Love, 1973 (repr. 7 times); Vote for Love, 1976 (repr. 4 times); All Our Love, 1978; Fun Food Factory, 1976 (repr. twice); Fun Food Feasts, 1978; The Root Children, 1978; The Pig Who Never Was, 1979; Amy Rainbow, 1980; The Facts of Love, 1980; That Dog, 1980; Reflections, 1981; The Dog Lovers Coffee Table Book, 1982; The Cat Lovers Coffee Table Book, 1983; My Granny was a Frightful Bore, 1983; A Cat and Mouse Love Story, 1984; Nanette Newman's Christmas Cook Book, 1984; Pigalev, 1985; The Best of Love, 1985; The Summer Cookbook, 1986; Archie, 1986; Small Beginnings, 1987; Bad Baby, 1988; Entertaining with Nanette Newman and her Daughters Sarah and Emma, 1988; Sharing, 1989; Charlie the Noisy Caterpillar, 1989; ABC, 1990; 123, 1991; Cooking for Friends, 1991; Spider the Horrible Cat, 1992; There's a Bear in the Bath, 1993; There's a Bear in the Classroom, 1996; The Importance of Being Ernest the Earwig, 1996; Take 3 Cooks, 1996; Up to the Skies and Down Again, 1999; To You With Love, 1999. *Recreation:* needlepoint. *Address:* c/o Lloyds Private Banking, 50 Grosvenor Street, W1X 9FH. *Fax:* (01344) 845174.

NEWMAN, Paul; American actor and director; *b* 26 Jan. 1925; *s* of Arthur Newman and Theresa (*née* Fetzer); *m* 1st, 1949, Jacqueline Witte; two *d* (one *s* decd); 2nd, 1958, Joanne Woodward; three *d. Educ:* Kenyon Coll. (BA); Yale Drama Sch. Mil. Service, USNR, 1943–46. Chairman: Newman's Own; Salad King. Team owner, and formerly driver, IndyCar racing. *Stage appearances include:* Picnic, 1953–54; Sweet Bird of Youth, 1959; *films include:* Somebody Up There Likes Me, 1956; Cat on a Hot Tin Roof, 1958; The Hustler, 1961; Sweet Bird of Youth, 1962; Hud, 1963; Torn Curtain, 1966; Cool Hand Luke, 1967; Butch Cassidy and the Sundance Kid, 1969; The Sting, 1973; Drowning Pool, 1975; Quintet, 1979; Fort Apache, the Bronx (also dir), 1980; Absence of Malice, 1981; The Verdict, 1982; Harry and Son (also wrote and directed), 1984; The Color of Money, 1986 (Academy Award, 1987); Blaze, 1990; Shadow Makers, 1990; Mr and Mrs Bridge, 1991; The Hudsucker Proxy, 1994; Nobody's Fool, 1995; Twilight, 1998; Message in a Bottle, 1999; Where the Money Is, 2000; *films directed include:* Rachel, Rachel, 1968; When Time Ran Out, 1980; The Glass Menagerie, 1987. Hon. Academy Award for career achievement, 1986. *Address:* Newman Haas Racing, 500 Tower Parkway, Lincolnshire, IL 60069, USA.

NEWMAN, Prof. Ronald Charles, PhD; FRS 1998; FInstP; Professor of Physics, University of London, 1989–99, now Emeritus; Senior Research Fellow, Centre for Semiconductor Materials and Devices, Department of Physics, Imperial College of Science, Technology and Medicine, since 1999; *b* 10 Dec. 1931; *s* of Charles Henry Newman and Margaret Victoria May Newman (*née* Cooper); *m* 1956, Jill Laura Weeks; two *d. Educ:* Imperial Coll. of Sci. and Technol. (BSc 1st Cl. Hons, ARCS; DIC 1954; PhD 1955). FInstP 1971. Research scientist, AEI Central Res. Lab., Aldermaston Court, 1955–63; Sen. Res. Scientist, AEI Rugby, 1963–64; University of Reading: Lectr, Dept of Physics, 1964–69; Reader, 1969–75; Prof., 1975–89; Vis. Prof., 1989–; Associate Dir, IRC for Semiconductor Materials, ICSTM, 1989–99. Vis. Prof., Dept of Electrical Engrg and Electronics, UMIST, 2000–. Has held numerous consultancies. *Publications:* Infra-Red Studies of Crystal Defects, 1973; (contrib.) Semiconductors and Semimetals, 1993; (contrib.) Handbook on Semiconductors, 1994; numerous contribs to learned jls. *Recreations:* music, foreign travel. *Address:* 23 Betchworth Avenue, Earley, Reading, Berks RG6 7RH. *T:* (0118) 966 3816.

NEWMAN, Vice Adm. Sir Roy (Thomas), KCB 1992 (CB 1991); JP; DL; Flag Officer Plymouth, and Commander Central Sub Area Eastern Atlantic, 1992–96; *b* 8 Sept. 1936; *s* of Mr and Mrs T. U. Newman; *m* 1960, Heather (*née* Macleod); four *s*. *Educ:* Queen Elizabeth's Grammar Sch., Barnet, Herts. Joined RN, 1954; specialised in anti-submarine warfare, 1963; joined Submarine Service, 1966; Comdr 1971, Captain 1979; commanded: HMS Onyx, 1970–71; HMS Naiad, 1978–79; First Submarine Sqn and HMS Dolphin, 1981–83; Seventh Frigate Sqn and HMS Cleopatra, 1984–85; Dir of Naval Warfare, 1986–88; Flag Officer Sea Trng, 1988–89; COS to C-in-C Fleet and Dep. Comdr Fleet, 1990–92. Pres., Royal Naval Assoc., 1996–2001. Chm., Trustees, RN Submarine Mus., 1999–. Younger Brother, Trinity House, 1997. Liveryman, Shipwrights' Co., 1997. JP SE Hants, 1996; DL Hants, 2001. *Recreations:* cricket, golf, music, reading. *Club:* Army and Navy.

NEWMAN, Col Sir Stuart (Richard), Kt 1993; CBE 1984; TD 1952; *b* 13 June 1919; *e s* of late Capt. Thomas Pacey Newman, MC, DCM, and Dorothy, *y d* of Richard Booth Beverley. *Address:* 47 Gilkes Crescent, Dulwich Village, SE21 7BP.

NEWMAN TAYLOR, Prof. Anthony John, OBE 1992; FRCP; FFOM; Consultant Physician, since 1977, Medical Director, since 1994, Director of Research, since 1997, Royal Brompton Hospital (Acting Chief Executive, 1996); Professor of Occupational and Environmental Medicine, National Heart and Lung Institute, Imperial College School of Medicine, University of London, since 1992; *b* 11 Dec. 1943; *s* of Reginald John Newman Taylor and Violet Anne (*née* Hilliard); *m* 1st, 1968, Gillian Frances Crick (marr. diss.); two *s* one *d*; 2nd, 1986, Frances Victoria Costley; one *s*. *Educ:* Radley Coll.; St Bartholomew's Hosp. Med. Coll. (MB BS 1970; MSc 1979). FRCP 1986; FFOM 1987; FMedSci 1999. Postgrad. trng, St Bartholomew's and Brompton Hosps, 1970–77. Civilian Advr in Chest Medicine to RAF, 1983–. Chm., Industrial Injuries Adv. Council, 1996– (Mem., 1983–; Chm., Res. Wkg Gp, 1984–96); Mem., MRC Cttee on toxic hazards in envmt and workplace, 1982–90. Advr in occupational medicine, Nat. Asthma Campaign, 1994–. WHO Advr to Minister of Health, India on long term consequences of methyl isocyane exposure to population of Bhopal, 1985; Advr to Dept of Health, Valencia on epidemic of lung disease in textile spray workers, 1994. Chm., Coronary Artery Disease Res. Assoc., 1998–. Gov., Royal Brompton Hosp., 1994–. Gov., Chislehurst C of E Primary Sch., 1995–99. *Publications:* chapters in textbooks on respiratory disease and occupational and environmental lung disease; papers in Lancet, BMJ, Thorax, Amer. Jl of Respiratory Disease and Critical Care Medicine; Jl of Allergy and Clinical Immunology, etc. *Recreations:* history and politics, cricket. *Address:* 11 Waldegrave Road, Bickley, Kent BR1 2JP. *Clubs:* Athenæum, MCC.

NEWMARCH, Michael George, (Mick); Chief Executive, Prudential Corporation plc, 1990–95; *b* 19 May 1938; *s* of late George Langdon Newmarch and Phyllis Georgina Newmarch; *m* 1959, Audrey Clarke; one *s* two *d*. *Educ:* Univ. of London (BSc (Econs) external). Joined Prudential, 1955, Econ. Intelligence Dept; Exec. Dir, Prudential Corp., 1985–95; Chairman: Prudential Money Funds, 1983–95; Prudential Holborn, 1986–89; Prudential Financial Services, 1987–95 (Chief Exec., 1987–89); Prudential Currency Fund, 1987–95; Prudential Assce Co., 1990–95; Prudential Portfolio Managers, 1990–95 (Chief Exec., 1982–89); Prudential Nominees, 1990–95; Prudential Services, 1990–95; Mercantile and Gen. Gp., 1990–95. Non-exec. Chm., Transacsys, 2000–; Chm., Weston Medical, 2001–; non-exec. Dir, Celltech Gp (formerly Celltech plc), 1996–. Vice-Chm., Princess Royal Trust for Carers, 1989–; Chm. of Trustees, Berks Community Foundn, 1998–. Member: Adv. Bd, Orchestra of the Age of Enlightenment, 1992–; Council, Univ. of Reading, 1999–. *Recreations:* salmon and trout fishing, flytying, bridge, theatre, concerts. *Clubs:* Flyfishers', Royal Automobile.

NEWPORT, Viscount; Alexander Michael Orlando Bridgeman; *b* 6 Sept. 1980; *s* and *heir* of 7th Earl of Bradford, *qv*.

NEWPORT, Dr Ronald William; Head of Daresbury Laboratory, Council for the Central Laboratory of the Research Councils, 1995–96; *b* 3 Nov. 1933; *s* of Thomas Prescott Newport and Elsie Newport; *m* 1959, Joan Margaret Williams; one *s* one *d*. *Educ:* Nantwich and Acton County Grammar Sch.; Univ. of Liverpool (BSc 1955; PhD 1960). Res. Physicist, British Nat. Hydrogen Bubble Chamber, 1960–62; Science Research Council, subseq. Science and Engineering Council, later Engineering and Physical Sciences Research Council: Rutherford High Energy Laboratory, later Rutherford Appleton Laboratory: Res. Physicist, 1962–79; Div. Manager, Technol. Dept, 1979–81; Dep. Div. Head, Instrumentation Div., 1981–84; Project Manager, James Clerk Maxwell Telescope, 1981–87; Associate Dir for Technol., 1987–88; Head of Science Div., 1988–91, Associate Dir Progs, 1991–94, SERC; Dep. Dir, Daresbury and Rutherford Appleton Lab., 1994–95. Member: Steering Cttee, Institut Laue Langevin, 1989–92; Council, European Synchroton Radiation Facility, 1989–92 (Chm., 1993–95). MRI 1995; FRSA 1997. MacRobert Award, for James Clerk Maxwell Telescope, Fellowship of Engineering, 1988. *Publications:* various papers, mainly on instrumentation. *Recreations:* reading, walking, photography, travel. *Address:* 5 Chapel Lane, Sutton Courtenay, Abingdon, Oxon OX14 4AN. *T:* (01235) 848424.

NEWRY AND MORNE, Viscount; Robert Francis John Needham; Director: Collabra Net Solutions Ltd, since 2000; Morne Consultancy Ltd, since 2000; *b* 30 May 1966; *s* and *heir* to Earl of Kilmorey (*see* Rt Hon. Sir R. F. Needham); *m* 1991, Laura Mary, *o d* of Michael Tregaskis; one *s* one *d*. *Educ:* Sherborne Prep. School; Eton College; Lady Margaret Hall, Oxford (BA); Imperial Coll., London (MBA 1993). Management trainee, Benjamin Priest, 1988–90; Sales Man., Lewmar Marine Ltd, 1991–92; Asst Man., Business Develt, Inchcape Pacific Ltd, 1994–95; Business Develt Manager, Inchcape NRG, 1995–97; Dir, Ops, Inchcape NRG HK, 1998–2000; Exec. Dir, NRG Solutions, 1997–2000. Mem., Chichester Fest. Theatre Soc. *Recreations:* squash, theatre, travelling. *Heir:* *s* Hon. Thomas Francis Michael Needham, *b* 25 Sept. 1998. *Address:* 6 Lattimer Place, Chiswick, W4 2UA. *Club:* Pratt's.

NEWSAM, Sir Peter (Anthony), Kt 1987; Chief Adjudicator, School Organisation and Admissions, since 1999; Director, University of London Institute of Education, 1989–94; *b* 2 Nov. 1928; *s* of late W. O. Newsam and of Mrs D. E. Newsam; *m* 1st, 1953, Elizabeth Joy Greg (marr. diss. 1987); four *s* one *d*; 2nd, 1988, Sue Addinell; one *d*. *Educ:* Clifton Coll.; Queen's Coll., Oxford (MA, DipEd). Asst Principal, BoT, 1952–55; teacher, 1956–63; Asst Educn Officer, N Riding of Yorks, 1963–66; Asst Dir of Educn, Cumberland, 1966–70; Dep. Educn Officer: W Riding of Yorks, 1970–72; ILEA, 1972–76; Educn Officer, ILEA, 1977–82; Chm., CRE, 1982–87; Sec., ACC, 1987–89; Dep. Vice-Chancellor, Univ. of London, 1992–94. *Address:* Ivy House, Thornton Dale, N Yorks YO18 7QW.

NEWSOM-DAVIS, Prof. John Michael, CBE 1996; MD; FRCP; FRS 1991; Professor of Clinical Neurology, University of Oxford, 1987–98, now Emeritus; *b* 18 Oct. 1932; *s* of John Kenneth and late Dorothy Eileen Newsom-Davis; *m* 1963, Rosemary Elisabeth (*née* Schmid); one *s* two *d*. *Educ:* Sherborne Sch.; Pembroke Coll., Cambridge (BA 1957 Nat. Scis); Middlesex Hosp. Med. Sch. (MB BChir 1960, MD 1966); FRCP 1973. RAF, 1951–53 (Pilot). Lectr, Univ. Dept of Clinical Neurology, Nat. Hosp. for Nervous Diseases, 1967–69; Neurological Research Fellow, Cornell Med. Center, New York Hosp., 1969–70; Consultant Neurologist, Royal Free Hosp. and Nat. Hosp. for Nervous Diseases, 1970–80; MRC Clinical Res. Prof. of Neurology, Royal Free Hosp. Med. Sch. and Inst. of Neurology, 1980–87; Hon. Consultant, Nat. Hosp. for Nervous Diseases, 1987–. Department of Health: consultant advr in neurology, 1985–94; Mem., Central R & D Cttee, 1991–95. Mem., MRC, 1983–87 (Mem., Neurosciences Grants Cttee, 1978–80; Mem., 1980–83, 1992–, Chm., 1983–85, Neuroscis Bd); President: Biomedical Section, BAAS, 1982–83; Assoc. of British Neurologists, 1999– (Hon. Sec., 1981–84); Vice-Pres., Internat. Soc. for Neuroimmunology, 1987–95; Chairman: Med. Adv. Cttee, British Council, 1995–99; Chairs and Prog. Grants Cttee, BHF, 1996–97; Med. Res. Cttee, Muscular Dystrophy Group UK, 1996–99. Mem. Council, Royal Soc., 1996–97. Founder FMedSci 1998. Corr. Mem., Amer. Acad. of Neurology. Editor, Brain, 1997–; Mem. Editorial Bds of Jl of Neurological Sci., Jl of Neuroimmunology. *Publications:* (with E. J. M. Campbell and E. Agostoni) Respiratory Muscles: mechanics and neural control, 1970; numerous papers in Neurol. and Immunol. jls. *Recreation:* music. *Address:* Department of Clinical Neurology, University of Oxford, Radcliffe Infirmary, Oxford OX2 6HE.

NEWSOME, David Hay, MA; LittD Cantab 1976; FRSL 1981; Master of Wellington College, 1980–89; *b* 15 June 1929; *s* of Captain C. T. Newsome, OBE; *m* 1955, Joan Florence (*d* 1999), *d* of Lt-Col L. H. Trist, DSO, MC; four *d*. *Educ:* Rossall Sch., Fleetwood; Emmanuel Coll., Cambridge (Scholar). First Cl. in Hist. Tripos Parts I and II, 1952, 1953. Asst Master, Wellington Coll., 1954–59 (Head of History Dept, 1956–59); Fellow of Emmanuel Coll., Cambridge, 1959–70; Asst Lectr in Ecclesiastical History, Univ. of Cambridge, 1961–66; Univ. Lectr, 1966–70; Sen. Tutor, Emmanuel Coll., Cambridge, 1965–70; Headmaster of Christ's Hospital, 1970–79. Lectures: Gore Memorial, Westminster Abbey, 1965; Bishop Westcott Memorial, Cambridge, 1968; Birkbeck, Univ. of Cambridge, 1972. Council of: Ardingly Coll., 1965–69; Eastbourne Coll., 1966–70; Epsom Coll., 1966–70. FRHistS, 1970. *Publications:* A History of Wellington College, 1859–1959, 1959; Godliness and Good Learning, Four Studies in a Victorian Ideal, 1961; The Parting of Friends, a study of the Wilberforces and Henry Manning, 1966; Bishop Westcott and the Platonic Tradition, 1969; Two Classes of Men: Platonism and English Romantic Thought, 1974; On the Edge of Paradise: A. C. Benson the Diarist, 1980 (Whitbread Book of the Year Award); (ed) Edwardian Excursions, 1981; The Convert Cardinals: Newman and Manning, 1993; The Victorian World Picture, 1997; articles in Jl of Theological Studies, Jl of Ecclesiastical History, Theology, History Today, Historical Jl, Recusant History. *Recreations:* music, fell-walking. *Address:* The Retreat, Thornthwaite, Keswick, Cumbria CA12 5SA. *T:* (017687) 78372. *Club:* East India.

NEWSOME, William Antony; Director-General, Association of British Chambers of Commerce, 1974–84; *b* 8 Nov. 1919; *s* of William F. Newsome and Elizabeth (*née* Thompson); *m* 1951, Estella Ann (*née* Cope); one *s*. *Educ:* King Henry VIII Sch., Coventry; Bedford Modern Sch. Student Engineer, W. H. Allen, Sons & Co. Ltd, Bedford, 1937–40. Served War, Royal Engineers: N Africa, Sicily, Italy campaigns, 1940–47. Engrg Dept, Crown Agents for Oversea Governments and Administrations, 1949–61; Principal: Home Office, 1961–64; Min. of Technology, 1964–70; Dept of Trade and Industry, 1970–71; Asst Sec., Dept of Trade, 1971–74. Member: SITPRO, 1972–84; Production Statistics Adv. Cttee, 1975–84; Home Office Standing Cttee on Crime Prevention, 1978–84. *Recreations:* photography, swimming, golf. *Address:* Bourdon Lacey, Old Woking Road, Woking, Surrey GU22 8HR. *T:* (01483) 762237.

NEWSON, Prof. Linda Ann, PhD; FBA 2000; Professor of Geography, King's College, London, since 1994; *b* 2 Aug. 1946; *d* of Donald George Newson and Evelyn Maud Newson (*née* Lee). *Educ:* Grey Coat Hosp., Westminster; University Coll. London (BA 1967; PhD 1972). King's College, London: Lectr, 1971–87; Reader, 1987–94; Hd, Sch. of Humanities, 1997–2000; FKC 2001. Vis. Prof., Univ. of Calif, Berkeley, 1989. Fellow, Newberry Liby, Chicago, 1985 and 2000. C. O. Sauer Award, Conf. of Latin Americanist Geographers, USA, 1992; Back Award, RGS, 1993. *Publications:* Aboriginal and Spanish Colonial Trinidad: a study in culture contact, 1976; The Cost of Conquest: Indian societies in Honduras under Spanish rule, 1986; Indian Survival in Colonial Nicaragua, 1987; Patterns of Life and Death in Early Colonial Ecuador, 1995. *Address:* Department of Geography, King's College London, Strand, WC2R 2LS. *T:* (020) 7848 2364.

NEWSON-SMITH, Sir Peter (Frank Graham), 3rd Bt *cr* 1944, of Totteridge, co. Hertford; Director of Music, Clayesmore Preparatory School, since 1979; *b* 8 May 1947; *s* of Sir John Newson-Smith, 2nd Bt and of Vera, Lady Newson-Smith; *S* father, 1997; *m* 1974, Mary Ann Owens (*née* Collins); one *s* one *d*, and two step *s*. *Educ:* Dover Coll.; Trinity Coll. of Music, London. GTCL; LT (MusEd). Asst Dir of Music, Dover Coll. Jun. Sch., 1969–73; Director of Music: Westbourne House, Chichester, 1973–78; Hazelwood, Limpsfield, 1978–79. Freeman, City of London, 1969; Liveryman, Musicians' Co., 1969–. *Recreations:* travel, DIY, gardening. *Heir:* *s* Oliver Nicholas Peter Newson-Smith, *b* 12 Nov. 1975. *Address:* Lovells Court, Marnhull, Sturminster Newton, Dorset DT10 1JJ.

NEWSTROM, Prof. David Graham L.; *see* Lloyd-Newstrom.

NEWSUM, Jeremy Henry Moore, FRICS; Group Chief Executive, Grosvenor (formerly Chief Executive, Grosvenor Estate Holdings), since 1989; *b* 4 April 1955; *s* of Neill Henry Hillas Newsum and late Jane Ridsdale Newsum (*née* Moore); *m* 1979, Gillian Lucy Ratcliff; three *d*. *Educ:* Rugby; Reading Univ. (BSc Estate Mgt). With: Grosvenor Estate Holdings, 1976–78; Savills, 1979–85; London Partner, Bidwells, 1985–87; with Grosvenor (formerly Grosvenor Estate Hldgs), 1987–. A Church Comr, 1993–2000. Trustee, Grosvenor Estate, 1993–. *Recreation:* any sport. *Address:* Priory House, Swavesey, Cambs CB4 5QJ. *T:* (01954) 232084.

NEWTON, family name of **Baron Newton of Braintree**.

NEWTON, 5th Baron *cr* 1892, of Newton-in-Makerfield, Co. Lancaster; **Richard Thomas Legh;** *b* 11 Jan. 1950; *er s* of 4th Baron Newton and of Priscilla Egerton-Warburton; *S* father, 1992; *m* 1978, Rosemary Whitfoot, *yr d* of Herbert Clarke; one *s* one *d*. *Educ:* Eton; Christ Church, Oxford (MA). Solicitor, May May & Merrimans, 1976–79. General Comr for Income Tax, 1983–. Mem., Wealden DC, 1987–99. Mem., Sussex Downs Conservation Bd, 1992–95, 1997–98. *Recreation:* bridge. *Heir:* *s* Hon. Piers Richard Legh, *b* 25 Oct. 1979. *Address:* Laughton Park Farm, Laughton, Lewes, East Sussex BN8 6BU. *T:* (01825) 840627. *Clubs:* Pratt's, MCC.

NEWTON OF BRAINTREE, Baron *cr* 1997 (Life Peer), of Coggeshall in the co. of Essex; **Antony Harold Newton,** OBE 1972; PC 1988; economist; Chairman, North East Essex Mental Health NHS Trust, since 1997; *b* Aug. 1937; *m* 1st, 1962, Janet Huxley (marr. diss. 1986); two *d*; 2nd, 1986, Mrs Patricia Gilthorpe; one step *s* two step *d. Educ:* Friends' Sch., Saffron Walden; Trinity Coll., Oxford. Hons PPE. President: OU Conservative Assoc., 1958; Oxford Union, 1959. Formerly Sec. and Research Sec., Bow Group. Head of Conservative Research Dept's Economic Section, 1965–70; Asst Dir, Conservative Research Dept, 1970–74. Chm. Coningsby Club, 1965–66. Contested (C) Sheffield, Brightside, 1970. MP (C) Braintree, Feb. 1974–1997; contested (C) same seat, 1997. An Asst Govt Whip, 1979–81; a Lord Comr of HM Treasury, 1981–82; Parly Under-Sec. of State for Social Security, 1982–84, and Minister for the Disabled, 1983–84, Minister of State (Minister for Social Security and the Disabled), 1984–86, Minister of State (Minister for Health) and Chm., NHS Management Bd, 1986–88, DHSS; Chancellor of Duchy of Lancaster and Minister of Trade and Industry, 1988–89; Sec. of State for Social Security, 1989–92; Lord Pres. of the Council and Leader of H of C, 1992–97. Vice-Chm., Fedn of Univ. Conservative and Unionist Assocs, 1959. Mem., FEFC, 1998– (Chm., E Region Cttee, 1998–). Professional Standards Dir, Inst. of Dirs, 1998–. Chair, Standing Conf. on Drug Abuse, 1997–; Chm., E Anglia's Children's Hospices, 1998–. Gov., Felsted Sch. Interested in taxation and social services. *Address:* House of Lords, SW1A 0PW.

NEWTON, Air Vice-Marshal Barry Hamilton, CB 1988; OBE 1975; a Gentleman Usher to The Queen, since 1989; *b* 1 April 1932; *s* of late Bernard Hamilton Newton, FCA and Dorothy Mary Newton; *m* 1959, Constance Lavinia, *d* of late Col J. J. Aitken, CMG, DSO, OBE; one *s* one *d. Educ:* Highgate; RAF College Cranwell. Commissioned 1953; 109 Sqn, 1954; 76 Sqn, Australia and Christmas Island, 1956; Flying Instr, RAF Coll. and No 6 Flying Trng Sch., 1959–63; HQ Flying Trng Comd, 1964; Staff Coll., Bracknell, 1966; Personal Staff Officer to Comdr, Second Allied Tactical Air Force, 1967; OC Ops Wing, RAF Cottesmore, 1969; Air Warfare Course, 1971; Defence Policy Staff, 1972; Cabinet Office, 1975; Asst Dir, Defence Policy, 1978; Cabinet Office, 1979; Air Cdre Flying Trng, HQ RAF Support Comd, 1982; Sen. Directing Staff (Air), RCDS, 1984; Comdt, JSDC, 1986–88; Special Project Officer, RCDS, 1988—89. Mem. Council, TA&VRA, 1989–99. Hon. Air Cdre, No 606 (Chiltern) (formerly Helicopter Support) Sqn, RAuxAF, 1997–; Hon. Inspector-Gen., RAuxAF, 2000–. *Recreations:* military history, walking, philately. *Address:* c/o National Westminster Bank, Blue Boar Row, Salisbury, Wilts SP1 1DF. *Club:* Royal Air Force.

NEWTON, Sir (Charles) Wilfrid, Kt 1993; CBE 1988; FCIT; Chairman: London Regional Transport, 1989–94 (Chief Executive, 1989–94); London Underground Ltd, 1989–94; *b* 11 Dec. 1928; *s* of late Gore Mansfield Newton and Catherine Knox Newton; *m* 1954, Felicity Mary Lynn Thomas; two *s* two *d. Educ:* Orange Grove Prep. Sch.; Highlands North High Sch.; Univ. of Witwatersrand, Johannesburg. FCIT 1989. Chartered Accountant (South Africa). Chartered Accountant, Saml Thomson & Young, 1947–55; Territory Accounting and Finance Manager, Mobil Oil Corp., S Africa, 1955–62; Controller, Mobil Sekiyu KK, Tokyo, 1962–63; Financial Manager/Dep. Gen. Manager, Mobil Oil, E Africa, Nairobi, 1963–65; Finance Dir, Mobil Sekiyu KK, Tokyo,, 1965–68; Turner & Newall: Finance Dir, 1968; Man. Dir of Finance and Planning, 1974, of Plastics, Chemicals and Mining, 1976; Gp Man. Dir, 1979; Gp Man. Dir and Chief Exec., 1982; Chairman: Mass Transit Railway Corp., Hong Kong, 1983–89; Hong Kong Futures Exchange Ltd, 1987–89; non-executive Chairman: Raglan Properties plc, 1994–99; Jacobs Holdings PLC, 1994–; Guy Maunsell Internat. Ltd, 1996–99; non-executive Director: Hongkong & Shanghai Banking Corp., 1986–90; Sketchley PLC, 1990–99; MetroPower Ltd, 1990–94; HSBC Hldgs plc, 1990–99; Midland Bank, 1992–99; Mountcity Investments Ltd, 1994–. CIMgt (CBIM 1974); FRSA 1990. Hon. FREng (Hon. FEng 1993); Hon. FHKIE 1994. JP Hong Kong, 1986–89. *Recreations:* sailing, reading. *Address:* Newtons Gate, 12 Ramley Road, Pennington, Lymington, Hants SO41 8GQ. *T:* (01590) 679750; 7A Balmoral House, Windsor Way, Brook Green, W14 0UF. *T:* (020) 7602 4996. *Clubs:* Carlton; Wanderers (Johannesburg); Hong Kong, Aberdeen Boat, Royal Hong Kong Yacht (Hong Kong); Royal Lymington Yacht.

NEWTON, Clive Trevor, CB 1991; Independent Chairman, Disciplinary Committee, National Association of Funeral Directors, since 1995; *b* 26 Aug. 1931; *s* of late Frederick Norman and Phyllis Laura Newton; *m* 1961, Elizabeth Waugh Plowman; one *s* one *d. Educ:* Hove Grammar School for Boys. LLB London; called to Bar, Middle Temple, 1969; certified accountant, 1962–2000. Examiner, Insolvency Service, Board of Trade, 1952, Sen. Examiner, 1963, Asst Official Receiver, 1967; Principal, Marine Div., BoT, 1969; Sen. Principal, Marine Div., Dept of Trade, 1973; Asst Director of Consumer Credit, Office of Fair Trading, 1974; Asst Sec., Regional Development Grants Div., Dept of Industry, 1978; Dir of Consumer Affairs, OFT, 1980; Under Sec., Head of Consumer Affairs Div., DTI, 1986–91. Member: Legislation Cttee, Nat. Fedn of Consumer Gps, 1991–2001 (Vice Chm., 1993–96); E Sussex Valuation Tribunal, 1998–. Chartered Association of Certified Accountants, subseq. Association of Chartered Certified Accountants: Mem., 1983–92, Chm., 1987–91, and 1997–99, Disciplinary Cttee; Chm., Authorisation Appeal Cttee, 1994–97, 1999–2000. Lay Performance Assessor, GMC, 1997–2001; Ind. Chm. Disciplinary Cttee, Nat. Assoc. for Pre-Paid Funeral Plans, 1995–2001; Chm., Compliance Cttee, Funeral Planning Authy, 2001–. Dir, Concordia (YSV) Ltd, 1994–99. Vice Chm., Sussex Area Cttee, Sanctuary Housing Assoc., 1999–. *Recreations:* golf, watching cricket and football. *Clubs:* Royal Automobile; Surrey County Cricket (Mem. Gen. Cttee, 2000–), East Brighton Golf.

NEWTON, David Alexander; Chairman, Carr's Milling Industries, since 1997 (Director, since 1996); *b* 6 Oct. 1942; *s* of Alexander and Hazel Newton; *m* 1965, Kathleen Mary Moore; one *s* one *d. Educ:* Morecambe Grammar Sch.; Wyvern Coll. Mgt trainee, J. Bibby & Sons Ltd, UK, 1964–67; Area Manager, Cobb Breeding Co., 1967–69; Gen. Manager and Dir, Anglian Food Gp, 1969–72; Agricl Dir, Sovereign Chicken Ltd, 1972–82; Ops Dir, Ross Poultry Ltd, 1982–84; Chief Exec. Officer and Dir, Buxted Poultry Ltd, 1984–85; Hillsdown Holdings: Dir, 1985–96; Chief Operating Officer, 1992–93; Chief Exec. Officer, 1993–96; Chm., Maple Leaf Mills Ltd, Toronto, 1987–90; Pres. and Chief Exec. Officer, Canada Packers Inc., 1990–92. Director: Bernard Matthews, 1996–; Bodfari, 1996–; MRCT, 1997–; Chm., Firstan Ltd. FIMgt (FBIM 1984); FInstD 1984. *Recreations:* golf, music, watching sports. *Address:* Carr's Milling Industries, Old Croft, Stanwix, Carlisle CA3 9BA. *T:* (01228) 528291. *Club:* Diss Golf (Norfolk).

NEWTON, Derek Henry; Chairman, C. E. Heath plc, 1984–87; *b* 14 March 1933; *s* of Sidney Wellington Newton and Sylvia May Newton (*née* Peacock); *m* 1957, Judith Ann (*d* 1995), *d* of Roland Hart, Kingston, Surrey; two *d. Educ:* Emanuel School. FCII. Commissioned Royal Artillery, 1952–54 (Lieut). Clerical, Medical & General Life Assurance Society, 1954–58; C. E. Heath Urquhart (Life & Pensions), 1958–83, Chm., 1971–84; Dir. C. E. Heath, 1975, Dep. Chm., 1983–84; Director: Glaxo Insurance (Bermuda), 1980–93; Glaxo Trustees, 1980–92; Clarges Pharmaceutical Trustees, 1985–92. Governor, BUPA Med. R&D, 1981–94. *Recreations:* cricket, golf. *Address:* Pantiles, Meadway, Oxshott, Surrey KT22 0LZ. *T:* (01372) 842273. *Clubs:* Royal Automobile, MCC; Surrey County Cricket (Chm. 1979–94).

NEWTON, Sir (Harry) Michael (Rex), 3rd Bt *cr* 1900; *b* 7 Feb. 1923; 2nd and *e* surv. *s* of Sir Harry K. Newton, 2nd Bt, OBE, DL, and Myrtle Irene (*d* 1977), *e d* of W. W. Grantham, Balneath Manor, Lewes; *S* father, 1951; *m* 1958, Pauline Jane, *o d* of late R. J. F. Howgill, CBE; one *s*; three adopted *d. Educ:* Eastbourne College. Served War of 1939–45, with KRRC, in 8th Army and Middle East, 1941–46 (wounded). Master, Girdlers' Company, 1975–76; Freeman of City of London. *Recreation:* sailing (winner of 1953 Fastnet Race). *Heir: s* Rev. George Peter Howgill Newton [*b* 26 March 1962; *m* 1988, Jane, twin *d* of John Rymer; two *d*]. *Address:* Cliff House, Old Lyme Road, Charmouth, Dorset DT6 6BW. *T:* (01297) 560704. *Club:* Royal Ocean Racing.

NEWTON, Ian; *see* Newton, R. E. I.

NEWTON, Prof. Ian, OBE 1999; FRS 1993; FRSE; Head, Avian (formerly Vertebrate) Ecology Section, NERC Institute of Terrestrial Ecology, 1989–99, now Fellow, NERC Centre for Ecology and Hydrology; *b* 17 Jan. 1940; *s* of Haydn Edwin Newton and Nellie Newton (*née* Stubbs); *m* 1962, Halina Teresa Bialkowska; two *s* one *d. Educ:* Bristol Univ. (BSc Zoology 1961); Worcester Coll., Oxford (DPhil Ornithology 1964; DSc 1982). FRSE 1994. Dept of Zoology, Oxford, 1964–67; Nature Conservancy, Edinburgh, 1967–73; Institute of Terrestrial Ecology, Natural Environment Research Council: Edinburgh, 1973–79; Huntingdon, 1979–99; research on avian population ecology, incl. finches, waterfowl, birds of prey, impact of pesticides. President: BOU, 1999– (Vice-Pres., 1989–93); British Ecological Soc., 1994–95. Hon. Mem., Amer. Ornith. Union. Union Medal, BOU, 1988; President's Medal, British Ecological Soc., 1989; Gold Medal, RSPB, 1991; Elliot Coue's Award, Amer. Ornith. Union, 1995; Marsh Award in Conservation Biology, Zool Soc. of London, 1995. *Publications:* Finches, 1972; Population Ecology of Raptors, 1979; The Sparrowhawk, 1986; (ed) Lifetime Reproduction in Birds, 1989; Population Limitation in Birds, 1998; papers in sci. jls. *Recreations:* apple growing, walking. *Address:* NERC Centre for Ecology and Hydrology, Monks Wood, Abbots Ripton, Huntingdon, Cambs PE17 2LS. *T:* (01487) 773381.

NEWTON, Jeremy; Chief Executive, National Endowment for Science, Technology and the Arts, since 1998; *b* 14 June 1955; *s* of Arthur James Newton and Dorothy Burton Newton; *m* 1978, Mary Rose Colleran; one *s* one *d. Educ:* Manchester GS; St John's Coll., Cambridge (MA Hons Mod. and Medieval Langs). FCA 1989. Audit Supervisor, Coopers & Lybrand, 1976–80; Dep. Dir, 1980–84, Dir, 1984–90, Chief Exec., 1990–94, Eastern Arts Assoc., then Eastern Arts Bd; Nat. Lottery Dir, Arts Council of England, 1994–98. *Recreations:* theatre, cinema, chess, lacrosse, stand-up comedy. *Address: e-mail:* jeremy.newton@nesta.org.uk.

NEWTON, Rev. Dr John Anthony, CBE 1997; Associate Tutor, Wesley College, Bristol, since 1995; *b* 28 Sept. 1930; *s* of late Charles Victor Newton and of Kathleen Marchant; *m* 1963, Rachel, *d* of late Rev. Maurice H. Giddings and of Hilda Giddings, Louth, Lincs; four *s. Educ:* Grammar School, Boston, Lincs; University Coll., Hull; London Univ.; Wesley House, Cambridge. BA, PhD (Lond), MA (Cantab). Jun. Research Fellow, Inst. of Historical Research, London Univ., 1953–55, Housemaster and [illegible] Chaplain, Kent Coll., Canterbury, 1955–56; trained for Methodist Ministry, Wesley House, 1956–58; Asst Tutor, Richmond Coll., Surrey, 1958–61, having been ordained, 1960; Circuit Minister at Louth, Lincs, 1961–64, and Stockton-on-Tees, 1964–65; Tutor at Didsbury Coll. (from 1967, Wesley Coll.), Bristol, 1965–72; taught Church History, St Paul's United Theolog. Coll., Limuru, Kenya, and Univ. of Nairobi, 1972–73; Principal of Wesley Coll., Bristol, 1973–78; Superintendent Minister, London Mission (W London) Circuit, 1978–86; Chm., Liverpool Dist of Methodist Church, 1986–95; Warden, John Wesley's Chapel, Bristol, 1995–2000. President of the Methodist Conference, 1981–82; Jt Pres., Merseyside and Region Churches' Ecumenical Assembly, 1987–95; Moderator, Free Church Federal Council, 1989–90 and 1993–94; a Pres., Churches Together in England, 1990–94. Hon. Canon, Lincoln Cathedral, 1988. Chm. of Governors, Westminster Coll., Oxford, 1979–88; Trustee, Wesley House, Cambridge, 1979–88. President: Chesterton Soc., 1991–; Wesley Historical Soc., 1996–. Governor, Rydal School, Colwyn Bay, 1986–95. Hon. Fellow, Liverpool John Moores Univ., 1993. Hon. DLitt Hull, 1982; DD Lambeth, 1995. *Publications:* Methodism and the Puritans, 1964; Susanna Wesley and the Puritan Tradition in Methodism, 1968; The Palestine Problem, 1972; Search for a Saint: Edward King, 1977; The Fruit of the Spirit in the Lives of Great Christians, 1979; A Man for All Churches: Marcus Ward, 1984; The Wesleys for Today, 1989; Heart Speaks to Heart: ecumenical studies in spirituality, 1994. *Recreations:* music, walking, book-collecting. *Address:* 3 College Road, Westbury-on-Trym, Bristol BS9 3EJ. *T:* (0117) 959 3225.

NEWTON, Prof. John Michael, DSc; Professor of Pharmaceutics, School of Pharmacy, University of London, 1984–2001; (Fellow, School of Pharmacy, 2000); *b* 26 Dec. 1935; *s* of Richard and Dora Newton; *m* 1959, Janet Hinninghan (marr. diss. 1986); one *s* two *d. Educ:* Leigh Grammar Sch., Lancs; Sch. of Pharmacy, Univ. of London (BPharm; DSc 1990); Univ. of Nottingham (PhD). FRPharmS. Apprentice pharmacist, Royal Albert Edward Infirmary, Wigan, 1953–55; Demonstrator, Univ. of Nottingham, 1958–62; Sen. Lectr, Sunderland Polytechnic, 1962–64; Lectr, Univ. of Manchester, 1964–67; Sen. Scientist, Lilly Research Centre Ltd, 1968–71; Lectr, Univ. of Nottingham, 1972–78; Prof. of Pharmaceutics, Univ. of London, at Chelsea College, 1978–83. Mem., Medicines Commn, 1996–2000. Dist. Lectr, Nagai Foundn, Tokyo, 1997. Hon. Dr Uppsala, 1995. Harrison Meml Medal, RPSGB, 1996. *Publications:* numerous articles in sci. jls associated with pharmaceutical technology. *Recreations:* fell walking, long distance running (Belgrave Harriers), gardening. *Address:* School of Pharmacy, 29–39 Brunswick Square, WC1N 1AX. *T:* (020) 7753 5869.

NEWTON, (John) Nigel; Founder, Chairman and Chief Executive, Bloomsbury Publishing Plc, since 1986; *b* 16 June 1955; *s* of Peter Leigh Newton and Anne St Aubyn Newton; *m* 1981, Joanna Elizabeth Hastings-Trew; one *s* two *d. Educ:* Deerfield, Mass; Selwyn Coll., Cambridge (BA 1976; MA). Asst to Sales Dir, Macmillan Ltd, 1976–78; Dep. Man. Dir, Sidgwick & Jackson Ltd, 1978–86. *Recreations:* walking, tennis, riding, great views. *Address:* (office) 38 Soho Square, W1D 3HB. *T:* (020) 7494 2111; *e-mail:* nigel_newton@bloomsbury.com. *Clubs:* Garrick, MCC, Hurlingham.

NEWTON, Rt Rev. Keith; *see* Richborough, Bishop Suffragan of.

NEWTON, Sir Kenneth (Garnar), 3rd Bt *cr* 1924; OBE 1970 (MBE 1944); TD; Chairman, Garnar Booth plc, 1972–87 (Managing Director, 1961–83); *b* 4 June 1918; *s* of Sir Edgar Henry Newton, 2nd Bt, and Gladys Maud (*d* 1966), *d* of late Sir James Garnar; *S* father, 1971; *m* 1944, Margaret Isabel (*d* 1979), *d* of Rev. Dr George Blair, Dundee; two *s. Educ:* Wellington College, Berks. Served War of 1939–45 (MBE); Lt-Col, RASC (TA). Chm. Governors, Colfe's Sch., 1982–93. Pres., Internat. Council of Tanners, 1972–78; Past President, British Leather Federation (1968–69); Liveryman and Member of Court of Assistants, Leathersellers' Company (Master, 1977–78) and Feltmakers' Company (Master,

1983–84). *Heir: s* John Garnar Newton [*b* 10 July 1945; *m* 1972, Jacynth A. K. Miller; three *s* (incl. twins)]. *Address:* Oaklands, Harborough Gorse, West Chiltington, West Sussex RH20 2RU.

NEWTON, Leslie; Her Honour Judge Newton; a Circuit Judge, since 2001; *b* 4 April 1955; *d* of Archie Newton and Joan Newton (*née* Robinson); *m* 1987, David Anthony Hernandez; one *s* one *d*. *Educ:* Univ. of Manchester (LLB 1976). Called to the Bar, Middle Temple, 1977; barrister on N Circuit, 1978–2001; Head, Young Street Chambers, Manchester, 1997–2001. *Address:* Preston Crown Court, The Ringway, Preston PR1 2LL. *T:* (01772) 832300.

NEWTON, Margaret; Schools Officer, Diocese of Oxford, 1984–88, retired; *b* 20 Dec. 1927; 2nd *d* of F. L. Newton, KStJ, MB, ChB, and Mrs A. C. Newton, MBE, BA. *Educ:* Sherborne School for Girls; St Andrews Univ.; Oxford University. MA Hons St Andrews, 1950; Educn Dip. Oxon 1951. Asst Mistress, King Edward VI Grammar School, Handsworth, Birmingham, 1951–54; Classics Mistress, Queen Margaret's Sch., York, 1954–60 (House Mistress, 1957); House Mistress, Malvern Girls' College, 1960–64 (Head of Classics Dept, 1962); Headmistress, Westonbirt Sch., 1965–80; Gen. Sec., Friends of the Elderly, 1981–83. *Address:* 14 Lygon Court, Fairford, Glos GL7 4LX.

NEWTON, Sir Michael; *see* Newton, Sir H. M. R.

NEWTON, Nigel; *see* Newton, J. N.

NEWTON, Peter Marcus; HM Diplomatic Service, retired; Executive Director, Canada UK Chamber of Commerce, since 2000; *b* 16 Sept. 1942; *s* of Leslie Marcus Newton and Edith Mary Newton; *m* 1972, Sonia Maria; two *s* one *d*. *Educ:* Hamilton Academy; Glasgow Univ. (MA Hons); McGill Univ. (postgrad. studies). Third Sec., CRO, later CO, 1965; Kinshasa, 1967; Lima, 1968; First Sec., FCO, 1972; First Sec. (Econ.), Tokyo, 1975; First Sec. and Head of Chancery, Caracas, 1979; FCO, 1981; Counsellor, FCO, 1985–87; Consul-Gen., Montreal, 1987–89; Dep. High Comr, Ottawa, 1989–92; Head of S Atlantic and Antarctic Dept, FCO, 1992–95; Ambassador to Guatemala, 1995–98.

NEWTON, Richard James; Chairman, National and Provincial Building Society, 1988–93; *b* 17 Nov. 1927; *s* of Alfred Richard Newton and Rosamond Newton (*née* Tunstill); *m* 1961, Elizabeth Seraphine Meuwissen (*d* 1986); four *s*. *Educ:* Clifton; St John's College, Cambridge (MA). Managerial positions at: Courtaulds, 1951–58; Midland Silicones, 1959–62; Chemstrand, 1963–66; Keith Shipton & Co., 1967–69; Man. Dir, Bury & Masco (Holdings), 1970–77; non-executive Director: Sketchley, 1978–87 (Chm., 1983–87); National & Provincial Building Soc., 1985–93. Fellow and Bursar, Trinity Hall, Cambridge, 1977–89. Gov., Clifton Coll., 1990– (Mem. Council, 1993–98). *Recreations:* music, fell-walking, playing the piano. *Address:* 15 Valiant House, Vicarage Crescent, Battersea, SW11 3LU.

NEWTON, (Robert Edward) Ian; OFSTED inspector and educational consultant, since 1995; Yachtmaster instructor, since 1999; *b* 4 Aug. 1946; *o s* of John Newton and Ethel Albiston; *m* 1969, Fiona Olive Pallant; one *s* one *d*. *Educ:* Dulwich Coll.; Oriel Coll., Oxford (BA Hons Nat. Sci. (Physics) 1967; MA 1973); Inst. of Education, London Univ. (Postgrad. CertEd 1968). Rugby School: Physics Teacher, 1968; Sixth Form girls' housemaster, 1976; Head of Physics, 1991; Headmaster, Bedales Sch., 1992–94. Admin. Officer, HMC/GSA Wkg Party on Univ. Admission, 1996–98; Charter Mark Award assessor, 1996–97. Chm., Edward Barnsley Educnl Trust and Workshop Co., 1997–2000. Mem., RGS. CFM 1983. *Publication:* Wave Physics, 1990. *Recreations:* sailing, playing the bassoon, walking. *Address:* 10 Linley Road, Southam, Warwicks CV47 0JY. *T:* (01926) 817067. *Club:* Royal Naval Sailing Association.

NEWTON, Trevor, OBE 1991; Deputy Chairman 1990–96, and Group Managing Director 1991–96, Yorkshire Water plc; *b* 22 Sept. 1943; *m* 1968, Christine Diane Bingham. *Educ:* Acklam Hall Grammar Sch., Middlesbrough; Manchester Univ. (BA Hons Econs). CIPFA 1970. Local Government Finance: Middlesbrough, 1966–71; Coventry, 1971–73; Bradford, 1973–76; Yorkshire Water Authority: Asst Finance Dir, 1976–83; Finance Dir, 1983–89; Finance Dir, Yorks Water plc, 1989–90. *Publication:* Cost-Benefit Analysis in Administration, 1971. *Recreation:* gardening. *Address:* Upper Park House, 5 Park House Road, Low Moor, Bradford, W Yorks BD12 0QD. *T:* (01274) 677189. *Club:* Naval and Military.

NEWTON, Sir Wilfrid; *see* Newton, Sir C. W.

NEWTON-CLARE, Herbert Mitchell, (Bill), CBE 1976; MC 1943; Executive Chairman, Albemarle Group PLC; *b* 5 May 1922; *s* of Herbert John and Eileen Margaret Newton-Clare; *m*; three *d*; *m* 1992, Harriet Mary Sheila Stormonth-Darling. *Educ:* Cheltenham Coll. TA, Middlesex Regt, 1938; served War of 1939–45: mobilised, 1939; commnd, Wiltshire Regt, 1941; wounded, Normandy, 1944; demobilised, 1945 (Major). Joined Bowyers (Wiltshire) Ltd, as trainee, 1945; Factory Manager, 1955, Gen. Manager, 1957, Man. Dir, 1960, Chm., 1966; following take-over by Unigate of Scot Bowyers (formerly Bowyers (Wiltshire) Ltd), became Director of Unigate, 1973, Vice-Chm., 1974–76; Dir, FMC Ltd, and ancillary cos, 1976–77. Chm., Meat Manufrs Assoc., 1970–82; Member: Exec. and Council, Food Manufrs Fedn, 1970–82; Food and Drink Industries Fedn, 1970–82; Exec. Centre de Liaison des Industries Transformatrice de Viandes de la Commune Européenne, 1970–82. *Recreations:* golf, tennis, swimming, fishing. *Address:* Fallowfield, Hightown Hill, Ringwood, Hants BH24 3HE. *T:* (01425) 476011. *Club:* Sunningdale Golf.

NEWTON DUNN, William Francis; Member, East Midlands Region, European Parliament (C, 1999–2000; Lib Dem, since 2000); *b* 3 Oct. 1941; *s* of late Lt-Col Owen Newton Dunn, OBE, and Barbara (*née* Brooke); *m* 1970, Anna Terez Arki; one *s* one *d*. *Educ:* Marlborough Coll. (scholar); Gonville and Caius Coll., Cambridge (MA); INSEAD Business Sch., Fontainebleau (MBA). With Fisons Ltd (Fertilizer Division), 1974–79. MEP (C) Lincolnshire, 1979–94; contested (C) Lincolnshire and Humberside S, 1994. European Parliament: Cons. Spokesman: on Transport, 1984–87; on Rules of Procedure, 1987–89; on Political Affairs, 1989–91; Chm., 1979 Cttee (Cons. backbench MEPs), 1983–88; Mem. Bureau, Cons. MEP Gp, 1988–94; Dep. Leader, EDG, 1991–93; Chm., British Cons. MEP Section, Eur. People's Party, 1993–94. Contested (C): general elections: Carmarthen, Feb. 1974; Cardiff West, Oct. 1974. *Publications:* Greater in Europe, 1986; Big Wing: biography of Air Chief Marshal Sir Trafford Leigh-Mallory, 1992; The Man Who Was John Bull: biography of Theodore Hook, 1996; The Devil Knew Not (novel), 2000; several pamphlets on the EU's democratic deficit. *Recreations:* walking, writing. *Address:* 10 Church Lane, Navenby, Lincoln LN5 0EG. *T:* (01522) 810812; *e-mail:* wnewton@europarl.eu.int.

NGAIZA, Christopher Pastor; Chairman and Managing Director, PES Consultants Ltd, Tanzania, since 1986; *b* 29 March 1930; parents decd; *m* 1952, Thereza; three *s* two *d* (and one *s* decd). *Educ:* Makerere University Coll.; Loughborough Co-operative College. Local Courts Magistrate, 1952–53; Secretary/Manager, Bahaya Co-operative Consumer Stores, 1955–57; Loughborough Co-operative Coll., 1957–59; Auctioneer and Representative of Bukoba Native Co-operative Union, Mombasa, 1959–61; joined Tanzanian Foreign Service, 1961; Counsellor, Mission to UN, 1961–62; Counsellor, Tanganyika High Commn, London, 1962–63; High Commissioner for United Republic of Tanganyika and Zanzibar in London, 1964–65; Tanzanian Ambassador: to Netherlands, 1965–67, to Arab Republic of Egypt, 1972–77; Mem., E African Common Market Tribunal, 1968–69; Tanzania's first High Comr to Zambia, 1969–72; Special Personal Assistant to Pres. of Tanzania, 1977–83; Comr for Kagera River Basin Orgn, 1978–83. *Recreations:* music, tennis. *Address:* PES Consultants Ltd, PO Box 4647, Dar es Salaam, Tanzania.

NGALI, Mwanyengela; Permanent Secretary, Ministry of Energy, Kenya, since 1999; *b* 1 Jan. 1947; *s* of Ngali Maganga and Ruth Mkandoo; *m* 1970, Elizabeth Wuganga; two *s* three *d*. *Educ:* Alliance High Sch., Kikuyu, Kenya; Univ. of Nairobi (BCom). Sales exec., Voice of Kenya, 1971–72; sales rep., Esso Standard Kenya Ltd, 1972–73; joined Kenyan Diplomatic Service, 1974: Commercial Attaché: Washington, 1974–81; London, 1981–82; First Sec. and Actg High Comr, Kampala, 1983–84; Counsellor, Jeddah and Riyadh, 1984–87; Under-Sec., Min. of Commerce, 1987–92; Dir, Political Affairs, Min. of Foreign Affairs and Internat. Co-operation, 1992; Counsellor and Actg High Comr, London, 1992–93; High Comr, Canada, 1993–95; High Comr, London, and Ambassador to Republic of Ireland and Switzerland, 1996–99. *Publication:* Mwana Taabu na Michezo Mingine ya Kuigiza, 1970. *Recreations:* walking, tennis, cycling, reading. *Address:* Ministry of Energy, Nyayo House, Kenyatta Avenue, POB 30582, Nairobi, Kenya. *T:* (2) 330048, *Fax:* (2) 228314.

NGATA, Sir Henare Kohere, KBE 1982 (OBE); chartered accountant, retired; *b* Waiomatatini, 19 Dec. 1917; *s* of Sir Apirana Ngata and Arihia, *d* of Tuta Tamati; *m* 1940, Rora Lorna, *d* of Maihi Rangipo Mete Kingi; one *s*. *Educ:* Waiomatatini Sch.; Te Aute Coll., Victoria Univ. of Wellington, BA; BCom; FCA (NZ Soc. of Accountants). Served 28th Maori Bn, 1939–45: POW, Greece; Germany, 1941–45. Director: Fieldair Ltd, 1960–79; Gisborne Sheepfarmers Mercantile Co. Ltd; Gisborne Sheepfarmers Freezing Co. Ltd. Member: Gisborne Reg. Commn, NZ Historic Places Trust, 1962–70; NZ Maori Council, 1962–85; C of E Provincial Commn on Maori Schs, 1964–66; Gisborne/East Coast Regional Develt Council, 1973–78; Finance Cttee, Bishopric of Aotearoa. Nat. Pres., 28th Maori Bn Assoc., 1964–66. Vice-Pres., NZ Nat. Party, 1967–69. Hon. LLD, Victoria Univ. of Wellington, 1979. *Address:* 10 Grant Road, Gisborne, New Zealand.

NIAGARA, Bishop of, since 1997; **Rt Rev. (David) Ralph Spence;** *b* 1942; *m* Carol Anne Spence; three *c*. *Educ:* Univ. of Guelph (BA 1964); Wycliffe Coll. (LTh 1968). Ordained priest, 1968; Asst Curate, St George's, Guelph, 1968–70; Rector: St Bartholomew, Hamilton, 1970–74; St John, Thorold, 1974–82; Archdeacon of Trafalgar, 1992–97. *Address:* Cathedral Place, 252 James Street, N Hamilton, ON L8R 2L3, Canada. *T:* (905) 5271278, *Fax:* (905) 5271281.

NIBLETT, Prof. (William) Roy, CBE 1970; BA, MLitt; Professor of Higher Education, University of London, 1967–73, now Professor Emeritus; *b* 25 July 1906; *m* 1938, Sheila Margaret (*d* 1997), OBE 1975, *d* of A. C. Taylor, Peterborough; one *s* one *d*. *Educ:* Cotham Sch., Bristol; University of Bristol (1st cl. hons English; DipEd 1st cl.; John Stewart Schol.); St Edmund Hall, Oxford. Sen. English Master, Doncaster GS, 1930–34; Lectr in Educn, King's Coll., Newcastle, 1934–45 (Registrar, Durham Univ., 1940–44); Prof. of Educn, University Coll., Hull, 1945–47; Prof. of Education, and Dir, Inst. of Education, Univ. of Leeds, 1947–59; Dean, Univ. of London Inst. of Education, 1960–68. Hibbert Lectr, 1965; Fulbright Schol. (Harvard) and Kellogg International Fellow, 1954; sometime Visiting Professor, Universities of California, Otago and Japanese Govt Vis. Prof., Univs of Japan; Nuffield Fellow, Univ. of Melbourne, 1960. Mem., UGC, 1949–59; Chairman: UGC Sub-Cttee on Halls of Residence, 1956 (Report 1957); Educn Dept, BCC, 1965–71; Higher Educn Policy Gp, 1969–72; Cttee on Future of Ministry of URC, 1973–75; President: European Assoc. for Res. in Higher Educn, 1972; Higher Educn Foundn, 1984–97 (Chm. Trustees, 1980–81). Vice-President: World Univ. Service (UK), 1963–90; Soc. for Res. in Higher Educn, 1978–. Member: Nat. Advisory Coun. on Trng and Supply of Teachers, 1950–61; Council on Army Educn, 1961–70; Council, Royal Holloway College, 1963–76; Council, Cheltenham Ladies' College, 1967–79; Trustee, Westhill Coll., Birmingham, 1979–91. FSRHE 1992. Chm., Editorial Bd, Studies in Higher Education, 1975–82. *Publications:* Education and the Modern Mind, 1954; Christian Education in a Secular Society, 1960; (ed) The Expanding University, 1962; (ed) Moral Education in a Changing Society, 1963; (ed) Higher Education: Demand and Response, 1969; (ed with R. F. Butts) World Year Book of Education, 1972–73; Universities Between Two Worlds, 1974; (with D. Humphreys and J. Fairhurst) The University Connection, 1975; (ed) The Sciences, The Humanities and the Technological Threat, 1975; (contrib.) International Encyclopedia of Higher Education, 1977; (contrib.) The Study of Education, 1980; (contrib.) Validation in Higher Education, 1983; (contrib.) Academic Community: discourse or discord?, 1994; (contrib.) Christian Thinking and Social Order, 1999; Life, Education, Discovery, 2001. *Recreations:* theology, music. *Address:* Moreton Hill Farm, Stonehouse, Glos GL10 3BZ. *T:* (01453) 826000.

NICE, Geoffrey; QC 1990; a Recorder, since 1987; *b* 21 Oct. 1945; *s* of William Charles Nice and Mahala Anne Nice (*née* Tarryer); *m* 1974, Philippa Mary Gross; three *d*. *Educ:* St Dunstan's College, Catford; Keble College, Oxford. Called to the Bar, Inner Temple, 1971, Bencher, 1996. Member: CICB, 1995–; Bd, Indict, 2001–. Sen. Trial Attorney, Internat. Criminal Tribunal for Former Yugoslavia, 1998–2001. Contested (SDP/Liberal Alliance) Dover, 1983, 1987. *Address:* Temple Gardens, Temple, EC4Y 9BB. *T:* (020) 7583 1315.

NICHOL, Comdt (Daphne) Patricia, CBE 1986; Director, Women's Royal Naval Service, 1982–86; *b* 25 Sept. 1932; *d* of Captain Ralph Geoffrey Swallow, RN and Daphne Lucy Regina Swallow (*née* Parry); *m* 1991, Capt. Peter Dale Nichol, RN. *Educ:* St George's Sch., Ascot; Portsmouth Polytechnic (Hon. Fellow, 1983). Joined WRNS as Signal Wren, 1950; qualified as WRNS Communications Officer, 1955; served in HMS Drake and Malta, 1956–58; Oslo, Portsmouth, HMS Mercury, Northwood and Gibraltar, 1958–67; HMS Pembroke and HMS Heron, 1968–71; passed Naval Staff Course, 1972; HMS Dauntless, 1973–74; Staff of C-in-C Naval Home Comd and MoD, 1974–76; National Defence College Latimer Course, 1976–77; Staff of Naval Secretary, 1977; Command Personnel Officer to C-in-C Naval Home Comd, 1977–79; Dep. Dir, WRNS, 1979–81; Staff Officer Training Co-ordination and Comd WRNS Officer to C-in-C Naval Home Comd, 1981–82; Hon. ADC to the Queen, 1982–86. Asst Sec., Benevolent Dept, Officers' Assoc., 1987–89; Case Sec., DGAA, 1989–90. Member: Nat. Exec. Cttee, Forces Help Soc. and Lord Roberts Workshops, 1986–95; Council and Exec. Cttee, Shipwrecked Fishermen and Mariners Royal Benevolent Soc., 1991–96, 1998–; Council, Soc. of Friends of RN Mus. and HMS Victory, Portsmouth, 1994–97. Hon. Fellow, Univ. of Portsmouth, 1993. *Recreations:* tennis, dressmaking and needlework, reading, theatre, opera, music. *Address:* c/o Lloyds TSB, 23 Elm Grove, Hayling Island, Hants PO11 9EA.

NICHOL, Sir Duncan (Kirkbride), Kt 1993; CBE 1989; Hon. Professorial Fellow of International Health Care Management, Health Services Management Unit, University of Manchester, since 1999 (Professor and Director, Health Services Management Unit, 1994–98); *b* 30 May 1941; *s* of James and Mabel Nichol; *m* 1972, Elizabeth Wilkinson; one *s* one *d*. *Educ:* Bradford Grammar Sch.; St Andrews Univ. (MA Hons). AHSM (AHA 1967); FFPHM 1991. Asst Gp Sec. and Hosp. Sec. to Manchester Royal Infirmary, 1969–73; Dep. Gp Sec. and Actg Gp Sec., Univ. Hosp. Management Cttee of S Manchester, 1973–74; Dist Administrator, Manchester S Dist, 1974–77; Area Administrator, Salford AHA(T), 1977–81; Regional Administrator, 1981–84, Regional Gen. Manager, 1984–89, Mersey RHA; Chief Exec., NHS Management Executive, 1989–94. Non-executive Director: HM Prison Service, 1994–; BUPA, 1994–; Chm., B Plan Information Systems, 1999–. Member: Central Health Services Council, 1980–81; NHS Training Authy, 1983–85. Chm., Jt Prison and Probation Services Accreditation Panel for Offending Behaviour Progs, 1999–. Pres., Inst. of Health Services Management, 1984–85; Chm., Educn Cttee, King Edward's Hosp. Fund for London, 1987–94. *Publications:* contributed: Health Care in the United Kingdom, 1982; Management for Clinicians, 1982; Working with People, 1983; Managers as Strategists, 1987. *Recreations:* walking, golf, squash. *Address:* Health Services Management Unit, University of Manchester, Devonshire House, Precinct Centre, Oxford Road, Manchester M13 9PL. *Club:* Athenæum.

NICHOL, Prof. Lawrence Walter, DSc; FAA; Vice-Chancellor, Australian National University, 1988–93; *b* 7 April 1935; *s* of Lawrence Gordon Nichol and Mavis Lillian Nichol (*née* Burgess); *m* 1963, Rosemary Esther (*née* White); three *s*. *Educ:* Univ. of Adelaide (BSc 1956, Hons 1957; PhD 1962; DSc 1974). Postdoctoral Fellow, Clark Univ., Mass, 1961–62; Res. Fellow, ANU, 1963–65; Sen. Lectr, then Reader, Univ. of Melbourne, 1966–70; Prof. of Phys. Biochem., ANU, 1971–85; Vice-Chancellor, Univ. of New England, 1985–88. FRACI 1971–94; FAA 1981; Fellow, Royal Soc. of NSW, 1986. David Syme Res. Prize, 1966; Lemberg Medal, Aust. Biochem. Soc., 1977. *Publications:* Migration of Interacting Systems, 1972; Protein-Protein Interactions, 1981; over 100 papers in internat. sci. jls. *Recreations:* philately, cinema, art, Spanish language. *Address:* Unit 36, 171 Walker Street, North Sydney, NSW 2060, Australia.

NICHOL, Comdt Patricia; *see* Nichol, Comdt D. P.

NICHOLAS, (Angela) Jane (Udale), OBE 1990; Dance Director, Arts Council of Great Britain, 1979–89, retired; *b* 14 June 1929; *d* of late Bernard Alexander Royle Shore, CBE; *m* 1964, William Alan Nicholas. *Educ:* Norland Place Sch.; Rambert Sch. of Ballet; Arts Educnl Trust; Sadler's Wells Ballet Sch. Founder Mem., Sadler's Wells Theatre Ballet, 1946–50; Mem., Sadler's Wells Ballet at Royal Opera House, 1950–52; freelance dancer, singer, actress, 1952–60; British Council Drama Officer, 1961–70; Arts Council of Great Britain: Dance Officer, 1970–75; Asst Dance Dir, 1975–79. Member: Exec. Cttee, Dance UK, 1989–98; Creative Dance Artists Trust, 1990–93; Riverside Arts Trust, 1991–97; Benesh Inst. Endowment Fund, 1992–; Bd, Birmingham Royal Ballet, 1993–. FRSA 1990. *Recreations:* pruning, weeding, collecting cracked porcelain. *Address:* 21 Stamford Brook Road, W6 0XJ. *T:* (020) 8741 3035.

NICHOLAS, Barry; *see* Nicholas, J. K. B. M.

NICHOLAS, Sir David, Kt 1989; CBE 1982; Chief Executive, 1977–91, Chairman, 1989–91, Independent Television News; *b* 25 Jan. 1930; *m* 1952, Juliet Davies; one *s* one *d*. *Educ:* Neath Grammar School; University Coll. of Wales, Aberystwyth. BA (Hons) English. National Service, 1951–53. Journalist with Yorkshire Post, Daily Telegraph, Observer; joined ITN, 1960; Deputy Editor, 1963–77; Editor, 1977–89. Produced ITN General Election Results, Apollo coverage, and ITN special programmes. Dir, Channel Four TV, 1992–97. Chm., Sports News TV, 1996–. Visiting Editor: Graduate Sch. of Journalism, Berkeley, Calif, 1993; Sch. of Journalism, Univ. of Colorado, 1994. Chm., Deptford Challenge Trust, 1996–. Mem. Council, Goldsmiths Coll., 1996–. FRTS 1980. Fellow, UC Aberystwyth, 1990. Hon. LLD Wales, 1990; Hon. DHL Southern Illinois, 2000. Producers' Guild Award 1967, on return of Sir Francis Chichester; Cyril Bennett Award, RTS, 1985; Judges' Award, RTS, 1991. *Recreations:* walking, sailing, golf. *Clubs:* Garrick, Reform.

NICHOLAS, Jane; *see* Nicholas, A. J. U.

NICHOLAS, (John Keiran) Barry (Moylan), FBA 1990; Principal of Brasenose College, Oxford, 1978–89 (Fellow, 1947–78; Hon. Fellow, 1989); *b* 6 July 1919; *s* of Archibald John Nicholas and Rose (*née* Moylan); *m* 1st, 1948, Hildegart (*d* 1995), *d* of Prof. Hans Cloos, Bonn; one *s* one *d*; 2nd, 1998, Rosalind, *widow* of Prof. Alan Williams, FRS. *Educ:* Downside; Brasenose Coll., Oxford (Scholar). 1st cl. Class. Mods, 1939 and Jurisprudence, 1946. Royal Signals, 1939–45: Middle East, 1941–45; Major, 1943. Called to Bar, Inner Temple, 1950, Hon. Bencher, 1984. Tutor, 1947–71 and Vice-Principal, 1960–63, Brasenose Coll.; All Souls Reader in Roman Law, Oxford Univ., 1949–71; Prof. of Comparative Law, Oxford, 1971–78; Mem., Hebdomadal Council, 1975–83. Visiting Professor: Tulane Univ., 1960; Univ. of Rome, 1964, 1993; Fordham Univ., 1968, 1985; Georgetown Univ., 1990; Univ. of Florida, 1997. UK Deleg. to UN Conf. on Internat. Sales Law, 1980. Mem., Louisiana State Law Inst., 1960. Dr *hc* Paris V, 1987. *Publications:* Introduction to Roman Law, 1962; (trans. Spanish, 1987, Chinese, 2000); Jolowicz's Historical Introduction to Roman Law, 3rd edn 1972; French Law of Contract, 1982, 2nd edn 1992. *Address:* 18A Charlbury Road, Oxford OX2 6UU. *T:* (01865) 558512.

NICHOLAS, Sir John (William), KCVO 1981; CMG 1979; HM Diplomatic Service, retired; *b* 13 Dec. 1924; *m* 1944, Rita (*née* Jones) (*d* 2000); two *s*. *Educ:* Birmingham Univ. Served 7th Rajput Regt, Indian Army, 1944–47; joined Home Civil Service, 1949; War Office, 1949–57; transf. to CRO 1957; First Sec., Brit. High Commn, Kuala Lumpur, 1957–61; Economic Div., CRO, 1961–63; Dep. High Comr in Malawi, 1964–66; Diplomatic Service Inspector, 1967–69; Dep. High Comr and Counsellor (Commercial), Ceylon, 1970–71; Dir, Establishments and Finance Div., Commonwealth Secretariat, 1971–73; Hd of Pacific Dependent Territories Dept, FCO, 1973–74; Dep. High Comr, Calcutta, 1974–76; Consul Gen., Melbourne, 1976–79; High Comr to Sri Lanka and (non-resident) to Republic of the Maldives, 1979–84.

NICHOLAS, Michael Bernard, FRCO; organist, choral director and composer; *b* 31 Aug. 1938; *s* of Bernard Victor Herbert Nicholas and Dorothy (*née* Gilfillan); *m* 1975, Heather Grant Rowdon; two *s*. *Educ:* City of London Sch.; Jesus Coll., Oxford (MA). FRCO 1958. Organist and Choirmaster: Louth Parish Church, Lincs, 1960–64; St Matthew's Ch., Northampton, 1965–71; Organist and Master of Choristers, Norwich Cathedral, 1971–94; (part-time) Lectr in Music, UEA, 1971–94; Chief Exec., RCO, 1994–97. Conductor: Louth Choral and Orchestral Soc., 1960–64; Northampton Bach Choir and Orch., 1965–71; Norwich Philharmonic Chorus, 1972–94; Musical Dir, Allegri Singers, 1994–2000; Organist and Dir of Music, All Saints' Church, Blackheath, 1995–99; Dir of Music, St Mary-le-Tower, Ipswich, 1999–. Exams Sec., Guild of Church Musicians, 1997–. Hon. FGCM, 1995. Hon. DMus UEA, 1995. *Publications:* Sightsinging, 1966; Muse at St Matthew's, 1968; various choral and organ compositions. *Recreations:* bridge, walking in East Suffolk, real ale. *Address:* Cansell Grove Farmhouse, Poy Street Green, Rattlesden, Bury St Edmunds, Suffolk IP30 0SR. *Clubs:* Athenæum; Ipswich and Suffolk (Ipswich).

NICHOLAS, William Ford, OBE 1954; Director, London Chamber of Commerce and Industry, 1974–84; *b* 17 March 1923; *s* of William and Emma Nicholas; *m* 1954, Isobel Sybil Kennedy; two *s*. *Educ:* Stockport Grammar School. Called to Bar, Middle Temple, 1965. Joined S Rhodesia Civil Service, 1947; Private Sec. to Prime Minister, S Rhodesia, 1950; Private Sec. to Prime Minister, Fedn of Rhodesia and Nyasaland, 1953; Counsellor, High Comr's Office, London, 1960; retd 1963. Dir, UK Cttee, Fedn of Commonwealth Chambers of Commerce, 1964; Dep. Dir, London Chamber of Commerce, 1966. *Address:* 2 Lime Close, Frant, Tunbridge Wells, Kent TN3 9DP. *T:* (01892) 750428.

NICHOLL, Anthony John David; His Honour Judge Nicholl; a Circuit Judge, since 1988; *b* 3 May 1935; *s* of late Brig. and Mrs D. W. D. Nicholl; *m* 1961, Hermione Mary (*née* Landon); one *s* two *d*. *Educ:* Eton; Pembroke Coll., Oxford. Called to Bar, Lincoln's Inn, 1958. Practised in London, 1958–61, in Birmingham, 1961–88; Head of Chambers, 1976–87; Chm., Fountain Court Chambers (Birmingham) Ltd, 1984–88. A Recorder, 1978–88. *Recreations:* history, gardening and other rural pursuits. *Address:* c/o Birmingham Crown Court, Newton Street, Birmingham B4 6NE.

NICHOLL, Air Vice-Marshal Steven Mark, CB 2001; CBE 1991; AFC 1981; FRAeS; Capability Manager (Strike), Ministry of Defence, 1998–2001; *b* 15 Nov. 1946; *s* of Capt. Jack Nicholl, BOAC and Berry Nicholl; *m* 1974, Suzanne Tucker; two *s* one *d*. *Educ:* Abingdon Sch.; Pembroke Coll., Oxford (BA Eng.). FRAeS 1993. RAF university cadetship, 1965; flying/staff duties, 1970–88; Gp Capt. Plans, HQ RAF Germany, 1989–91; OC RAF Leuchars, 1992–93; rcds 1994; Dir Air Ops, Dir Air Plans, ACDS OR Air, MoD, 1995–2001. *Recreations:* family, golf, ski-ing, hang-gliding, reading. *Address:* The Barn, Heath Park Road, Leighton Buzzard, Beds LU7 8BB. *Clubs:* Royal Air Force; Leighton Buzzard Golf.

NICHOLLS, family name of **Baron Nicholls of Birkenhead**.

NICHOLLS OF BIRKENHEAD, Baron *cr* 1994 (Life Peer), of Stoke D'Abernon in the County of Surrey; **Donald James Nicholls,** Kt 1983; PC 1986; a Lord of Appeal in Ordinary, since 1994; *b* 25 Jan. 1933; *yr s* of William Greenhow Nicholls and late Eleanor Jane; *m* 1960, Jennifer Mary, *yr d* of late W. E. C. Thomas, MB, BCh, MRCOG, JP; two *s* one *d*. *Educ:* Birkenhead Sch.; Liverpool Univ.; Trinity Hall, Cambridge (Foundn Schol.; Hon. Fellow, 1986). LLB 1st cl. hons Liverpool, BA 1st cl. hons with dist., Pt II Law Tripos Cantab, LLB 1st cl. hons with dist. Cantab. Certif. of Honour, Bar Final, 1958; called to Bar, Middle Temple, 1958, Bencher, 1981, Treas., 1997; in practice, Chancery Bar, 1958–83; QC 1974; Judge of High Court of Justice, Chancery Div., 1983–86; a Lord Justice of Appeal, 1986–91; Vice-Chancellor, Supreme Court, 1991–94; a Non-permanent Judge, Hong Kong Court of Final Appeal, 1998–. Chairman: Lord Chancellor's Adv. Cttee on Legal Educn and Conduct, 1996–97; Jt Parly Cttee on Party Privilege, 1997–99; Mem., Senate of Inns of Court and the Bar, 1974–76. Patron, Cayman Is Law Sch., 1994–. Pres., Birkenhead Sch., 1986–. Hon. LLD Liverpool, 1987. *Recreations:* walking, history, music. *Address:* House of Lords, SW1A 0PW. *Club:* Athenæum (Trustee, 1998–).

NICHOLLS, Brian; Director, John Brown Engineering, 1979–91; *b* 21 Sept. 1928; *s* of late Ralph and Kathleen Nicholls; *m* 1961, Mary Elizabeth Harley; one *s* two *d*. *Educ:* Haberdashers' Aske's Sch., Hampstead; London Univ. (BSc Econ); Harvard Business Sch. George Wimpey & Co., 1951–55; Constructors John Brown Ltd, 1955–75; Director: CJB Projects Ltd, 1972–75; CJB Pipelines Ltd, 1974–75; Dep. Chm., CJB Mohandessi Iran Ltd, 1974–75; Industrial Adviser, Dept of Trade, 1975–78; Director: John Brown Engrg Gas Turbines, 1979–91; Rugby Power Co., 1990–91; Vice Pres., John Brown Power Ltd, 1987–90; consultant, Scottish Enterprise, 1991–98. Member: Council, British Rly Industry Export Gp, 1976–78; Overseas Projects Bd, 1976–78; BOTB, 1978. Member: Council, British Chemical Engineering Contractors Assoc., 1973–75; Trade and Industry Cttee, British Algerian Soc., 1974–75; Scottish Council (Develt and Industry), 1983–98 (Vice Pres., 1991–98; Fellow 1998). Dir, Scottish Opera, 1993–99. Freeman Mem., Incorp. of Coopers of Glasgow, 1991; Mem., Trades House of Glasgow, 1990. *Recreations:* writing, walking, music. *Address:* Blairlogie Park, Blairlogie, by Stirling FK9 5PY. *T:* (01259) 761497. *Clubs:* Western (Glasgow); Royal Northern and Clyde Yacht (Rhu).

NICHOLLS, Christine Stephanie, DPhil; writer; *b* 23 Jan. 1943; *d* of Christopher James Metcalfe, Mombasa, Kenya, and Olive Metcalfe (*née* Kennedy); *m* 1966, Anthony James Nicholls, *s* of Ernest Alfred Nicholls, Carshalton; one *s* two *d*. *Educ:* Kenya High School; Lady Margaret Hall, Oxford (BA); St Antony's Coll., Oxford (MA, DPhil). Henry Charles Chapman Res. Fellow, Inst. of Commonwealth Studies, London Univ., 1968–69; freelance writer for BBC, 1970–74; res. asst, 1975–76; Jt Editor, 1977–89, Editor, 1989–95, DNB; Editor, Sutton Pocket Biographies, 1996–. *Publications:* The Swahili Coast, 1971; (with Philip Awdry) Cataract, 1985; Power: a political history of the 20th Century, 1990; The Dictionary of National Biography: 1961–70, 1981; 1971–80, 1986; 1981–85, 1990; Missing Persons, 1993; 1986–90, 1996; (ed) The Hutchinson Encyclopedia of Biography, 1996; David Livingstone, 1998; The History of St Antony's College, Oxford, 1950–2000, 2000; Elspeth Huxley: a biography, 2002. *Recreations:* reading novels, playing the flute. *Address:* 27 Davenant Road, Oxford OX2 8BU. *T:* (01865) 511320.

NICHOLLS, Clive Victor; QC 1982; a Recorder, 1984–99; *b* 29 Aug. 1932; twin *s* of late Alfred Charles Victor Nicholls and of Lilian Mary (*née* May); *m* 1960, Alison Virginia, *d* of late Arthur and Dorothy Oliver; three *s* three *d*. *Educ:* Brighton Coll.; Trinity Coll., Dublin (MA, LLB); Sidney Sussex Coll., Cambridge (BA *ad eund*; LLM). Called to the Bar: Gray's Inn, 1957 (Bencher, 1990); Australian Capital Territories, 1991. Trustee, Bob Champion Cancer Trust, 1994– (Chm. Trustees, 1982–94). *Recreations:* sailing, fishing. *Address:* 3 Raymond Buildings, Gray's Inn, WC1R 5BH. *T:* (020) 7831 3833. *Clubs:* Garrick; Royal Western Yacht (Plymouth).

See also C. A. A. Nicholls.

NICHOLLS, Colin Alfred Arthur; QC 1981; a Recorder, 1984–99; *b* 29 Aug. 1932; twin *s* of late Alfred Charles Victor Nicholls and of Lilian Mary (*née* May); *m* 1976, Clarissa Allison Spenlove, *d* of late Clive and of Theo Dixon; two *s*. *Educ:* Brighton Coll.; Trinity Coll., Dublin. MA, LLB. Called to the Bar, Gray's Inn, 1957 (Albion Richardson Schol.), Bencher, 1989. Auditor, 1956, and Hon. Mem., 1958–, TCD Historical Soc. Commonwealth Lawyers Association: Mem. Council, 1987–; a Vice Pres., 1990–96; Hon. Treas., 1996–; Hon. Sec., 1999–. Fellow, Soc. of Advanced Legal Studies, 1998. Chm., Friends' Cttee, Mall Galls; Gov., FBA, 2001. *Recreation:* painting (exhib. RHA). *Address:* 3 Raymond Buildings, Gray's Inn, WC1R 5BH. *T:* (020) 7831 3833. *Club:*

Garrick.
See also C. V. Nicholls.

NICHOLLS, David Alan, CB 1989; CMG 1984; defence consultant; Senior Political-Military Associate, Institute for Foreign Policy Analysis, Cambridge, Mass, USA, since 1991; *s* of Thomas Edward and Beatrice Winifred Nicholls; *m* 1955, Margaret (*née* Lewis); two *d. Educ:* Cheshunt Grammar School; St John's Coll., Cambridge (Schol., Wright's Prizeman 1952, 1953; BA Hons 1954; MA 1989). Served RAF (Flying Officer), 1950–51. Admiralty, 1954–64; Asst Principal, 1954; Private Sec. to Parliamentary Sec., 1958–59; Principal, 1959; MoD, 1964–75; Private Sec. to Minister of Defence for Admin, 1968–69; Asst Sec., 1969; Cabinet Office, 1975–77; Asst Under-Sec. of State, MoD, 1977–80; Asst Sec., Gen. for Defence Planning and Policy, NATO, 1980–84; Dep. Under Sec. of State (Policy), MoD, 1984–89. Vis. Fellow, Magdalene Coll., Cambridge, 1989–90; Associate Fellow, RIIA, 1990–93; Hon. Fellow, Graduate Sch. of Internat. Studies, Univ. of Birmingham, 1992–. Chm., Defence and Security Cttee, London Chamber of Commerce and Industry, 1994– (Mem., 1991–). Chm., Soc. for Italic Handwriting, 1987–97. Mem., Visiting Cttee, RCA, 1991–92. *Recreations:* sketching, printmaking. *Address:* c/o HSBC, Church Stretton, Shropshire SY6 6BT. *Club:* National Liberal.

NICHOLLS, Rt Rev. John; *see* Sheffield, Bishop of.

NICHOLLS, John; *see* Nicholls, R. J.

NICHOLLS, Prof. John Graham, FRS 1988; Professor of Biophysics, International School for Advanced Studies, Trieste, since 1998; *b* 19 Dec. 1929; *s* of late Dr Nicolai and of Charlotte Nicholls; *m* (marr. diss.); two *s. Educ:* Berkhamsted Sch.; Charing Cross Hosp.; King's Coll. and University Coll., London. BSc (1st cl. Hons); PhD; MB, BS. Research and teaching in Neurobiology at: Oxford, 1962; Harvard, 1962–65; Yale, 1965–68; Harvard, 1968–73; Stanford, 1973–83; Biocenter, Basel, 1983–98. *Publications:* From Neuron to Brain (with S. Kuffler), 1976, 3rd edn 1992; The Search for Connections, 1987. *Recreations:* Latin American history, music. *Address:* Scuola Internazionale Superiore di Studi Avanzati, via Beirut 2, Trieste 34014, Italy.

NICHOLLS, Air Marshal Sir John (Moreton), KCB 1978; CBE 1970; DFC 1953; AFC 1965; non-executive Director, James Paget Hospital NHS Trust, 1993–95; *b* 5 July 1926; *s* of Alfred Nicholls and Elsie (*née* French); *m* 1st, Enid Jean Marjorie Rose (*d* 1975); two *d;* 2nd, Shelagh Joyce Hall (*née* Strong). *Educ:* Liverpool Collegiate; St Edmund Hall, Oxford. RAF Coll., 1945–46; No 28 Sqdn and No 257 Sqdn; 335th Ftr Sqdn USAF, Korea, 1952; Fighter Leader Sch.; 435th and 83rd Ftr Sqdns USAF, 1956–58; attached British Aircraft Co., Lightning Project, 1959–61; psa 1961; Comd, Air Fighting Develt Sqdn; jssc 1964; MoD; comd RAF Leuchars, 1967–70; idc 1970; SASO 11 Gp, 1971; Principal Staff Officer to CDS, 1971–73; SASO, Strike Comd, 1973–75; ACAS (Op. Requirements), 1976–77; Air Mem. for Supply and Orgn, 1977–79; Vice-Chief of the Air Staff, 1979–80. Dir i/c, British Aircraft Co. (British Aerospace), Saudi Arabia, 1980–82. CIMgt. DFC (USA) and Air Medal (USA), 1953. *Club:* Royal Air Force.

NICHOLLS, Michael William Newbery; FRCPath; Vice-President, since 1998, and Hon. Treasurer, since 2000, Fellowship of Postgraduate Medicine (President, 1993–98); *b* 22 May 1931; *s* of William Stanley Nicholls, MBE and Florence May (*née* King); *m* 1957, Pamela Winifred Hemer (*d* 1997); two *s. Educ:* Xaverian Coll., London; UCL; UCH Med. Sch. (MB, BS). MRCS, LRCP; FRCPath 1980. Resident hosp. posts and general practice, 1955–61; Asst Microbiologist and Registrar, UCH, 1961–70; Consultant Microbiologist, Chichester and Worthing HAs, 1972–90; Dean of Postgrad. Medicine, SE Thames Reg., Univ. of London, 1990–95; Chief Exec., Centre for Educn R and D, 1990–94; Hon. Sen. Lectr in Med. Microbiology, UMDS, 1991–95. Mem., Worthing HA, 1982–90. Freeman, City of London, 1984; Mem., Livery Cttee, Soc. of Apothecaries, 1994. *Publications:* various contribs, usually of new or creatively provocative material on med. microbiol., med. educn and the needed reforms in postgrad. and continuing med. educn. *Recreations:* sailing, singing, chamber music, 19th and 20th Century Arabic history. *Address:* Creekside, Greenacres, Birdham, Chichester, W Sussex PO20 7HL. *T:* (01243) 512937, *Fax:* (01243) 511087. *Clubs:* Athenæum; Offshore Cruising (Southampton).

NICHOLLS, Sir Nigel (Hamilton), KCVO 1998; CBE 1982; Clerk of the Privy Council, 1992–98; *b* 19 Feb. 1938; *s* of late Bernard Cecil Hamilton Nicholls and Enid Kathleen Nicholls (*née* Gwynne); *m* 1967, Isobel Judith, *d* of Rev. Canon Maurice Dean; two *s. Educ:* King's School, Canterbury; St John's College, Oxford (BA 1962; MA 1966). Asst Principal, Admiralty, 1962, MoD, 1964; Asst Private Sec. to Minister of Defence for RN, 1965–66; Principal, 1966; Directing Staff, RCDS, 1971–73; Asst Private Sec. to Sec. of State for Defence, 1973–74; Asst Sec., 1974; Defence Counsellor, UK Delegation to MBFR Talks, Vienna, 1977–80; Asst Under-Sec. of State, MoD, 1984; Under Sec., Cabinet Office, 1986–89; Asst Under-Sec. of State (Systems), MoD, 1989–92. Mem. Council, Malvern Girls' Coll., 1999–. Freeman, City of London, 1999; Liveryman, Woolmen's Co., 1999–. Companion, IMM, 1999. *Recreations:* choral singing, genealogy, walking. *Address:* Loddiswell, 28 Avenue Road, Great Malvern, Worcs WR14 3BG. *Club:* Oxford and Cambridge.

NICHOLLS, Patrick Charles Martyn; Partner, Dunn & Baker, solicitors; *b* 14 Nov. 1948; *s* of late Douglas Charles Martyn Nicholls and Margaret Josephine Nicholls; *m* 1976, Bridget Elizabeth Fergus Owens; one *s* two *d. Educ:* Redrice Sch., Andover. Qualified solicitor, 1974. joined Dunn & Baker as Partner, 1976. Mem., E Devon District Council, 1980–84. MP (C) Teignbridge, 1983–2001; contested (C) same seat, 2001. PPS to Ministers of State: Home Office, 1984–86; MAFF, 1986–87; Parliamentary Under-Secretary of State: Dept of Employment, 1987–90; DoE, 1990; Opposition spokesman on health, 1997–98, on agric., 1998–99. Vice Chm., Social Security Select Cttee, 1990–93. Vice-Chm., Cons. Party, 1993–94. Vice Chm., Soc. of Cons. Lawyers, 1986–87. Steward, British Boxing Bd of Control, 1985–87. Freeman, City of London, 1996. *Recreations:* theatre, opera, historical research, ski-ing. *Address:* Dunn & Baker, 21–22 Southernhay East, Exeter EX1 1QQ. *T:* (01392) 250041. *Club:* Carlton.

NICHOLLS, Philip, CB 1976; *b* 30 Aug. 1914; *yr s* of late W. H. Nicholls, Radlett; *m* 1955, Sue, *yr d* of late W. E. Shipton; two *s. Educ:* Malvern; Pembroke Coll., Cambridge. Asst Master, Malvern, 1936; Sen. Classical Master, 1939; resigned, 1947. Served in Army, 1940–46: 8th Bn, The Worcestershire Regt; HQ, East Africa Command; Allied Commn for Austria. Foreign Office (German Section), 1947; HM Treasury, 1949; a Forestry Commissioner (Finance and Administration), 1970–75, retired. Mem. Council, Malvern Coll., 1960–90 (Vice-Chm., 1963–88). *Address:* Barnards Green House, Barnards Green, Malvern, Worcs WR14 3NQ. *T:* (01684) 574446.

NICHOLLS, Prof. (Ralph) John; Consultant Surgeon, since 1978, Clinical Director, since 1997, St Mark's Hospital, London; *b* 20 May 1943; *s* of Clifton Wilson Nicholls and Muriel Morten Nicholls (*née* Heathcote); *m* 1966, Stella Mary McBride; two *s* one *d* (and one *d* decd). *Educ:* Felsted Sch., Essex; Gonville and Caius Coll., Cambridge (BA 1964; MB 1968, BChir 1967, MChir 1978; MA 1999); London Hosp. Med. Coll. London Hosp. trng posts, 1966–78; MRC Res. Fellow, 1971–72; Alexander von Humboldt Fellow, 1976–77; Consultant Surgeon, St Thomas' Hosp., 1982–93; Hon. Prof. of Colorectal Surgery, ICSM, 1997–. Hon. Civilian Consultant in Colorectal Surgery to RAF, 1999–. Ed., Colorectal Disease, 1999–. Mem., Specialist Adv. Cttee in Gen. Surgery, Jt Cttee for Higher Surgical Trng, 1997–. Pres., Assoc. of Coloproctology of GB and Ireland, 1999–2000; Sec., Div. of Coloproctology, Sect. of Surgery, Union Européene des Médecins Specialists, 1997–. Fellow, Amer. Soc. Colon and Rectal Surgeons, 1993. Hon. FRCPSGlas 1992; Hon. Fellow: Brazilian Soc. Surgery, 1982; Swiss Soc. Gastroenterol., 1990. Mem. d'Honneur, Assoc. Française de Chirurgie, 1997. *Publications:* (ed jtly) Restorative Proctocolectomy, 1993; (ed with R. R. Dozois) Colorectal Surgery, 1997; contribs to learned jls incl. Lancet, BMJ, British Jl Surgery, Annals of Surgery. *Recreations:* languages, travel, history. *Address:* 24 St Mark's Crescent, NW1 7TU. *T:* (020) 7267 4433. *Club:* Athenæum.

NICHOLLS, Robert Michael, CBE 1995; health care management consultant, since 1996; Health Sector Reform Adviser, British Council, since 1997; *b* 28 July 1939; *s* of late Herbert Edgar Nicholls and of Bennetta L'Estrange (*née* Burges); *m* 1961, Dr Deírín Deirdre (*née* O'Sullivan); four *s. Educ:* Hampton Sch.; University Coll. of Wales (BA 1961); Univ. of Manchester (DSA 1962). FHSM (AHA 1963; FHA 1993). Asst Sec., Torbay Hosp., 1964; House Governor, St Stephen's Hosp., Chelsea, 1966; Asst Clerk to the Governors, St Thomas' Hosp., 1968; Dep. Gp Sec., Southampton Univ. Hosp. Management Cttee, 1972; Dist Administrator, Southampton and SW Hampshire Health Dist, 1974; Area Administrator, Newcastle upon Tyne AHA(T), 1977; Regl Administrator, SW RHA, 1981; Dist Gen. Man., Southmead DHA, 1985; Regl Gen. Man., later Chief Exec., Oxford RHA, 1988–93; Exec. Dir, London Implementation Gp, NHS Mgt Exec., 1993–96. Sen. non-exec. Dir, Nestor Healthcare Gp plc, 1997–. Member: Health Educn Council, 1984–87; CMO's Med. Educn Wkg Pty, 1992–93; GMC, 1996– (Chm., PPC, 2000–). National Council, Inst. of Health Service Management (formerly IHA): Mem., 1976–86; Pres., 1983–84. Associate Fellow, Templeton Coll., Oxford, 1996–2001. *Publications:* (contrib.) Resources in Medicine, 1970; (contrib.) Working with People, 1983; (contrib.) Rationing of Healthcare in Medicine, 1993. *Recreations:* bird-watching, jazz, opera, sport. *Address:* Charlton on Otmoor, Oxon.

NICHOLS, Rt Rev. Anthony Howard; *see* Australia, North-West, Bishop of.

NICHOLS, Dinah Alison, CB 1995; Director General, Environment, Department for Environment, Food and Rural Affairs, since 2001; *b* 28 Sept. 1943; *d* of late Sydney Hirst Nichols and of Freda Nichols. *Educ:* Wyggeston Girls' Grammar Sch., Leicester; Bedford Coll., Univ. of London (Reid Arts Schol.; BA Hons History, 1965; Hon. Fellow, RHBNC, 1997). Ministry of Transport: Asst Principal, 1965–69; Asst Private Sec. to Minister, 1969–70; Principal, 1970–74; Cabinet Office, 1974–77; Asst Sec., DoE, 1978–83; Principal Private Sec. to Sec. of State for Transport, 1983–85; Under Sec., DoE, 1985–91; Dep. Sec., DoE, then DETR, now DEFRA, 1991–; Dir Gen., Envmtl Protection, 1996–2001. Director: John Laing ETE, 1987–90; Anglian Water plc, 1992–95; Shires Smaller Companies plc, 1999–. Sec. of State for the Envmt's Rep., Commonwealth War Graves Commn, 1993–97. Dir, Cities in Schs, 1996–2000; Mem. Bd, Toynbee Housing Assoc., 1996–. Winston Churchill Meml Fellow, 1969. *Recreations:* fell walking, choral singing, music, theatre. *Address:* Department for Environment, Food and Rural Affairs, Ashdown House, 123 Victoria Street, SW1E 6DE. *T:* (020) 7944 3050. *Club:* Swiss Alpine.

NICHOLS, Jeremy Gareth Lane, MA; Headmaster, Stowe School, since 1989; *b* 20 May 1943; *yr s* of late Derek Aplin Douglas Lane Nichols and of Ruth Anne Baiss (formerly Nichols); *m* 1972, Patricia Anne, *d* of Cdre Alan Swanton, DSO, DFC and bar, RN; one *s* three *d. Educ:* Lancing Coll., Sussex; Fitzwilliam Coll., Cambridge (BA English Lit. 1966; MA); Perugia Univ. Assistant Master: Livorno Naval Acad., 1965; Rugby Sch., 1966–67; Eton Coll., 1967–89, House Master, 1981–89; Gilman Sch., Baltimore, USA, 1979–80. Chm., Assoc. of Educnl Guardians for Internat. Students. Founding Mem. Bd and Pres., Model EP, 1997–. Advr Trustee, Manor Charitable Trust, 1989–. Governor: Wellesley House Sch., 1985–; Papplewick Sch., 1988–; Aysgarth Sch., 1990–. FCT (FCollP 1997); FRSA. *Recreations:* outdoor pursuits, sport, music, old cars. *Address:* Kinloss, Stowe, Buckingham MK18 5EH. *Clubs:* East India, Lansdowne; Hawks (Cambridge); I Zingari, Free Foresters, Corinthian Casuals.

NICHOLS, John Roland; HM Diplomatic Service; Deputy Chief Executive, International Financial Services (on secondment), since 2000; *b* 13 Nov. 1951; *s* of Richard Alan Nichols and Katherine Louisa Nichols (*née* Barham); *m* 1983, Suzanne, *d* of James Harry Davies, MBE, RA retd, and Helen Christine Davies, JP (*née* Berry); one *s* one *d. Educ:* Latymer Upper Sch., Hammersmith; Univ. of Surrey (BSc Hons). Admitted as solicitor, 1977; entered FCO, 1977: First Secretary: Budapest, 1979–82; FCO, 1982–85; Brasilia, 1985–89; FCO, 1989–93; Counsellor and Dep. High Comr, Dhaka, 1993–95; Consul-Gen., Geneva, 1995–97; Dep. Hd of Mission, Dir of Trade Promotion and Consul-Gen., Berne, 1997–2000; Counsellor, FCO, 2000. *Recreations:* food and wine, DIY, cycling, gardening, opera, theatre. *Address:* c/o Foreign and Commonwealth Office, King Charles Street, SW1A 2AH.

NICHOLS, John Winfrith de Lisle, BSc (Eng); CEng; FIEE; retired; Director: National Maritime Institute, 1976–79; Computer Aided Design Centre, Cambridge, 1977–79; *b* 7 June 1919; *er s* of late John F. Nichols, MC, PhD, FRHistS, FSA, Godalming; *m* 1942, Catherine Lilian (*d* 1984), *er d* of Capt. A. V. Grantham, RNR, Essex; two *s* two *d. Educ:* Sir Walter St John's Sch., Battersea; London Univ. Royal Navy, 1940–46; GPO, Dollis Hill, 1946–47; RN Scientific Service, 1947–55; Chief Research Officer, Corp. of Trinity House, 1955–59; UKAEA, 1959–65; Min. of Technology, later DTI and Dept of Industry, 1965–; Under-Sec., and Chm., Requirement Bd for Computers, Systems and Electronics, 1972–74; Under Sec., Research Contractors Div., DoI, 1974–76. *Recreations:* gardening, sailing, caravanning. *Address:* Flat 8, Lords Bridge Court, Shepperton, Middx TW17 9HE.

NICHOLS, Peter Richard, FRSL 1983; playwright since 1959; *b* 31 July 1927; *s* of late Richard George Nichols and Violet Annie Poole; *m* 1960, Thelma Reed; one *s* two *d* (and one *d* decd). *Educ:* Bristol Grammar Sch.; Bristol Old Vic Sch.; Trent Park Trng College. Actor, mostly in repertory, 1950–55; worked as teacher in primary and secondary schs, 1958–60. Mem., Arts Council Drama Panel, 1973–75. Playwright in residence, Guthrie Theatre, Minneapolis, 1976. *TV plays:* Walk on the Grass, 1959; Promenade, 1960; Ben Spray, 1961; The Reception, 1961; The Big Boys, 1961; Continuity Man, 1963; Ben Again, 1963; The Heart of the Country, 1963; The Hooded Terror, 1963; The Brick Umbrella, 1964; When the Wind Blows, 1964 (later adapted for radio); Daddy Kiss It Better, 1968; The Gorge, 1968; Hearts and Flowers, 1971; The Common, 1973; Greeks Bearing Gifts (Inspector Morse series), 1991; *films:* Catch Us If You Can, 1965; Georgy Girl, 1967; Joe Egg, 1971; The National Health, 1973; Privates on Parade, 1983; *stage plays:* A Day in The Death of Joe Egg, 1967 (Evening Standard Award, Best Play; Tony

Award, Best Revival, 1985); The National Health, 1969 (Evening Standard Award, Best Play); Forget-me-not Lane, 1971; Chez Nous, 1973; The Freeway, 1974 (radio broadcast, 1991); Privates on Parade, 1977 (Evening Standard Best Comedy, Soc. of West End Theatres Best Comedy and Ivor Novello Best Musical Awards); Born in the Gardens, 1979 (televised 1986); Passion Play, 1980 (Standard Best Play award, 1981); A Piece of My Mind, 1986; Blue Murder, 1995; So Long Life, 2000; *musical:* Poppy, 1982 (SWET Best Musical Award). *Publications:* Feeling You're Behind (autobiog.), 1984; Diaries 1969–1977, 2000; some TV plays in anthologies; all above stage plays published separately and in 2 vols, Nichols: Plays One and Two, 1991. *Recreations:* listening to jazz, looking at cities. *Address:* c/o Alan Brodie Representation, 211 Piccadilly, W1V 9LD.

NICHOLS, Sir Richard (Everard), Kt 1998; Partner, Sedgwick Kelly Solicitors, since 1996; Lord Mayor of London, 1997–98; *b* 26 April 1938; *s* of late Guy Everard Nichols and of Patricia Mary (*née* Hurst); *m* 1966, Shelagh Mary Loveband; two *s* one *d. Educ:* Christ's Hosp., Horsham. Nat. Service, commnd RE, 1956–58. Admitted solicitor, 1963; Asst Solicitor, Gunston & Smart, Hong Kong, 1963–64; Partner, 1965, Sen. Partner, 1976–96, Kelly Nichols & Blayney. Almoner, Christ's Hosp., 1984–; Gov., City Literary Inst., 1990–95. Alderman, Ward of Candlewick, 1984–; Sheriff, City of London, 1994–95. Master, Salters' Co., 1988. KStJ 1997. *Recreations:* wine, travel, coarse gardening. *Address:* Newhall Farm, Bucks Hill, Kings Langley, Herts WD4 9AH. *T:* (01923) 269882. *Club:* East India.

NICHOLS, Most Rev. Vincent Gerard; *see* Birmingham, Archbishop of, (RC).

NICHOLS, William Henry, CB 1974; *b* 25 March 1913; *s* of William and Clara Nichols. *Educ:* Owens School. Entered Inland Revenue, 1930; Exchequer and Audit Dept, 1935, Secretary, 1973–75, retired. *Address:* 23 Church View, Haughley, Stowmarket, Suffolk IP14 3NU.

NICHOLS, William Reginald, CBE 1975; TD; MA; Clerk of the Worshipful Company of Salters, 1946–75, Master, 1978–79; *b* 23 July 1912; *s* of late Reginald H. Nichols, JP, FSA, Barrister-at-Law; *m* 1946, Imogen (*d* 2001), *d* of late Rev. Percy Dearmer, DD, Canon of Westminster, and late Nancy (who *m* 1946, Sir John Sykes, KCB; he died, 1952); one *s* one *d. Educ:* Harrow; Gonville and Caius Coll., Cambridge (Sayer Classical Scholar). MA 1938. Called to the Bar, Gray's Inn, 1937. Served War of 1939–45 with Hertfordshire Regt (despatches) and on staff 21st Army Group. Former Jt Hon. Sec., CGLI; Governor of Christ's Hospital; former Governor of Grey Coat Hospital Foundation. *Address:* The Farriers Cottage, St Nicholas-at-Wade, Birchington, Kent CT7 0NR.

NICHOLSON OF WINTERBOURNE, Baroness *cr* 1997 (Life Peer), of Winterbourne in the Royal County of Berkshire; **Emma Harriet Nicholson;** Member (Lib Dem) South East Region, England, European Parliament, since 1999; *b* 16 Oct. 1941; *d* of Sir Godfrey Nicholson, 1st Bt and late Lady Katharine Constance Lindsay, 5th *d* of 27th Earl of Crawford; *m* 1987, Sir Michael Harris Caine (*d* 1999); one adopted *s* two step *c. Educ:* St Mary's School, Wantage; Royal Academy of Music. LRAM, ARCM. Computer Programmer, Programming Instructor, Systems Analyst, ICL, 1962–66; Computer Consultant, John Tyzack & Partners, 1967–69; Gen. Management Consultant and Computer Consultant, McLintock Mann and Whinney Murray, 1969–74; joined Save the Children Fund, 1974, Dir of Fund Raising, 1977–85, Pres., Hatherleigh Dist Br. MP Devon West and Torridge (C, 1987–95, Lib Dem, 1995–97). PPS to Minister of State, Home Office, 1992–93, MAFF, 1993–95, to Financial Sec. to HM Treasury, 1995–. Founder and Jt Chm., All Party Parly Gp for Romanian Children; formerly Chm., All Party Parly Gp for Iraqi-Shias; Vice Chm., All Party Gp on Penal Affairs, 1992; Mem., Select Cttee on Employment, 1990–91; formerly Member: British-Turkish, Franco-British, British-Japanese, and Anglo-Botswana Parly Gps; All Party Parly Gp on AIDS; All Party Gp on Child Abduction; All Party Conservation Gp; All Party Jazz Gp; Parly Panel, RCN, 1990–92. Alternate Mem., UK Delegn to WEU and Council of Europe, 1990–92. Sec. then Chm., Cons. Backbench Envmt Cttee, 1990–91; Vice-Chm., Cons. Party, 1983–87; formerly Vice-President: Cons. Technol. Forum; Cons. Disability Gp; Western Area Young Conservatives; Mem., Tony Green Initiative. Contested (C) Blyth Valley, 1979. Vis. Parly Fellow, St Antony's Coll., Oxford, 1995–96 (Sen. Associate Mem., 1997–98, 1998–99). Vice-Moderator, Movement for Ordination of Women, 1991–93. Dir, Shelter; Member: Exec. Bd, UNICEF UK; MRC; Mgt Bd, European Movement (Vice-Chm.); POW Adv. Trust on Disability; Council, PITCOM; Centre for Policy Studies; RIIA; Adv. Bd, Women of Tomorrow Awards; RAM Appeal Cttee; Editl Panel, 300 Gp Newsletter. Fellow, Industry and Parliament Trust. Vice President: Small Farmers' Assoc.; Assoc. of Dist Councils. Deputy Chairman: Duke of Edinburgh's Award 30th Anniv. Tribute Project, 1986–88; Duke of Edinburgh's Internat. Project '87, 1987–88. President: Plymouth and W Devon Cassette, Talking Newspaper; W Regl Assoc. for the Deaf; Patron: Hospice Care Trust, N Devon; CRUSAID; Devon Care Trust; Chm. Adv. Cttee, Carnegie UK Trust Venues Improvement Programmes. *Publications:* Why does the West forget?, 1993; Secret Society, 1996; contrib. various periodicals. *Recreations:* music, chess, reading, walking. *Address:* House of Lords, SW1A 0PW. *Clubs:* Reform, National Liberal.

NICHOLSON, Air Commodore Angus Archibald Norman, CBE 1961; AE 1945; Deputy Secretary-General, International Shipping Secretariat, 1971–80; *b* 8 March 1919; *s* of Major Norman Nicholson and Alice Frances Nicholson (*née* Salvidge), Hoylake, Cheshire; *m* 1943, Joan Mary, *d* of Ernest Beaumont, MRCVS, DVSM; one *s* one *d. Educ:* Eton; King's Coll., Cambridge. Cambridge Univ. Air Sqn, 1938–39; commissioned, 1939. Served War 1939–45: flying duties in Bomber Command and Middle East. Air Cdre, 1966; Dir of Defence Plans (Air), Min. of Defence, 1966–67; Defence Adviser to British High Comr in Canada and Head of British Defence Liaison Staff, 1968–70; retired from RAF, 1970. FIMgt (MBIM 1967, FBIM 1980). *Recreations:* sailing, music. *Address:* 8 Courtenay Place, Lymington, Hants. *Clubs:* Army and Navy; Leander (Henley); Royal Lymington Yacht.

See also Air Vice-Marshal A. A. Nicholson.

NICHOLSON, Air Vice-Marshal Antony Angus, CBE 1997; LVO 1980; FRAeS; Eurofighter International Ltd, since 2000; *b* 27 June 1946; *s* of Air Cdre Angus Archibald Norman Nicholson, *qv*; *m* 1980, Fenella Janet Fraser; one *s* one *d*, and one step *s. Educ:* Eton Coll.; Churchill Coll., Cambridge (MA). FRAeS 1998. Joined RAF, 1968: helicopter pilot, 28 Sqn (Hong Kong), 3 Sqn SOAF (Oman), and 230 Sqn (UK), 1970–75; OC 3 Sqn SOAF, 1975–77; Equerry to HRH Duke of Edinburgh, 1978–80; OC 72 Sqn, 1981–83; MoD, 1984–86; RAF Instr, Army Staff Coll., 1986–88; Stn Comdr, RAF Shawbury, 1988–90; rcds 1991; Air Cdre Flying Trng, 1993–96; Dir, Operational Requirements (Air), 1996–98; Dir Gen. Air Systems 1, Defence Procurement Agency, 1998–2000. DSM (Oman), 1977. *Recreations:* squash, hill walking, Gloucester RFC. *Address:* c/o Barclays Bank, High Street, Odiham, Hants RG25 1LL. *Club:* Army and Navy.

NICHOLSON, Brian Thomas Graves, CBE 1998; Chairman, Advertising Standards Board of Finance, 1989–99; *b* 27 June 1930; *s* of late Ivor Nicholson, CBE, and Mrs Alan McGaw; *m* Henrietta, *d* of late Nevill Vintcent, OBE, DFC, and Mrs Ralph Dennis; two *s* (and one *s* decd). *Educ:* Charterhouse. Reporter, Newcastle Evening Chronicle, 1949–53; Montreal Star, Toronto Telegram, and Victoria Times, 1953–54; Manchester Evening Chronicle, 1954–56; Sunday Graphic, 1956–57; Advertisement Manager, Sunday Times, 1957–65; Director: Sunday Times, 1963–65; Beaverbrook Newspapers, 1967–77; Man. Dir, Evening Standard, 1972–77; Jt Man. Dir, Observer, 1977–84; Hd of Public Affairs, Lloyd's of London, 1990–92; Director: CompAir, 1977–85; Center for Communication (USA), 1981–95; Lloyd's of London Press, 1982–93; London Broadcasting Co., 1983–90; Royal Opera House Covent Garden, 1984–89; Royal Ballet, 1984–92 (Mem., Bd of Govs, 1995–); News (UK), 1985–87; CCA Galleries, 1986–89; Logie Bradshaw Media, 1986–97; Messenger Newspapers Gp, 1986–89; Aurora Productions, 1987–91; Messenger Television Ltd, 1989–; Whitespace Software Ltd, 1990–; Home Counties Newspaper Holdings plc, 1991–98; Messenger Leisure Ltd, 1994–; Benesh Inst., 1995–98; Birmingham Royal Ballet, 2001–; Chairman: Audit Bureau of Circulation, 1975–77; Marlar Internat. Ltd, 1985–90; Carthusian Trust, 1987–2000; SE Arts Bd (formerly Assoc.), 1989–95; Publicitas Hldg (UK) Ltd, 1989–99; Adv. Cttee on Advertising, COI, 1993–98; Charterhouse Sports Centre Ltd, 1995–; Dance Teachers' Benevolent Fund, 1999–. Vice President: CAM Foundn, 1975–2000; Royal Gen. Theatrical Fund Assoc., 1986– (Vice-Chm., 1996–2000); Member: Council of Commonwealth Press Union, 1975–99; Adv. Bd, New Perspective Fund (USA), 1984–97; Trustee, Glyndebourne Opera Co., 1977–2000; Gov., British Liver Foundn, 1989–99. Mem., Editorial Adv. Bd, Focus in Education Ltd, 1986–90. Churchwarden, St Bride's Church, Fleet Street, 1978–. Mackintosh Medal, 2000. *Recreations:* travelling, listening, playing games. *Address:* 6 Laxford House, Cundy Street, SW1W 9JU. *Clubs:* Beefsteak, Brooks's, Pratt's, MCC; Piltdown Golf; Wentworth Golf.

NICHOLSON, Sir Bryan Hubert, Kt 1987; Chairman: British United Provident Association, 1992–2001; Cookson Group, since 1998; *b* 6 June 1932; *s* of late Reginald Hubert and Clara Nicholson; *m* 1956, Mary Elizabeth, *er d* of A. C. Harrison of Oxford; one *s* one *d* (and one *s* decd). *Educ:* Palmers School, Grays, Essex; Oriel College, Oxford (MA PPE; Hon. Fellow, 1989). 2nd Lieut, RASC, 1950–52; Unilever Management Trainee, 1955–58; Dist. Manager, Van den Berghs, 1958–59; Sales Manager, Three Hands/Jeyes Group, 1960–64; Sperry Rand: Sales Dir, UK, Remington Div., 1964–66; Gen. Manager, Australia, Remington Div., 1966–69; Managing Dir, UK and France, Remington Div., 1969–72; Dir, Ops, Rank Xerox (UK), 1972–76; Dir, Overseas Subsidiaries, Rank Xerox, 1976; Exec. Main Bd Dir, Rank Xerox, 1976–84; Chm., Rank Xerox (UK) and Chm., Rank Xerox GmbH, 1979–84; Chm., MSC, 1984–87; Chm. and Chief Exec., PO, 1987–92; Chm., Varity Hldgs, later Varity Europe Ltd, 1993–96. Non-executive Director: Rank Xerox, 1984–87; Baker Perkins Holdings, 1982–84; Evode, 1981–84; Internat. Post Corp. SA, 1988–92; GKN, 1991–2000; Varity Corp., USA, 1993–96; LucasVarity, 1996–99; Equitas Hldgs Ltd, 1996–; Action Centre for Europe Ltd, 1996–; Newsquest plc, 1997–99. Chm., Financial Reporting Council, 2001– (Dir and Dep. Chm., 1993–96; Mem., 1996–98); Dir, Accountancy Foundn, 2000–. Confederation of British Industry: Mem. Council, 1987–; Mem., President's Cttee, 1990–98; Dep. Pres., 1993–94, 1996–97; Pres., 1994–96; Chairman: Task Force on Vocational Educn and Training, 1988–89; Educn and Training Affairs Cttee, 1990–93; Global Counsellor, Conf. Bd, 1994–; Chairman: CNAA, 1988–91; NICG, 1988–90; NCVQ, 1990–93; Interchange Panel, 1996–97; Pres., N of England Educn Conf., 1996. Department of Employment: Member: Adv. Cttee on Women's Employment, 1985–87; Women's Issues Wkg Gp, 1992–93; Race Relns Adv. Gp, 1985–87; Member: NEDC, 1985–92; Council, Inst. of Manpower Studies, 1985–93; Governing Council, Business in the Community, 1985–93; Council, Prince's Youth Business Trust, 1986–; Council, Industrial Soc., 1988– (Chm., 1990–93); Adv. Council, Economic and Regional Analysis, 1998–; Prime Minister's Adv. Cttee on Business Appointments, 1998–; Editl Bd, European Business Jl, 1988–; Adv. Bd, Britain in Europe, 1999–; Council, Atlantic Coll., 1999–. President: Involvement and Participation Assoc., 1990–94; ACFHE, 1992–93; AFC, 1993–94; Vice President: SRHE, 1992–; Re-Solv (Soc. for Prevention of Solvent Abuse), 1985–; NCH Action for Children (formerly Nat. Children's Home), 1989–. Chancellor, Sheffield Hallam Univ., 1992–2001; Pro Chancellor and Chm. Council, Open Univ., 1996–. Pres., Oriel Soc., 1988–92; Patron, Rathbone Community Industry (formerly Rathbone Soc.), 1987–; Vice Pres., Industrial Trust, 1999–; Trustee, Babson Coll., Mass, USA, 1990–96. Pres., Wakefield Trinity Wildcats, 2000–. UK Hon. Rep. for W Berlin, 1983–84. CIMgt (CBIM 1985); Hon. CIPD 1994. FCGI (CGIA 1988); FCIM 1990; FRSA 1985. Freeman, City of London, 1988. Hon. Fellow: Manchester Metropolitan Univ. (formerly Polytechnic), 1990; SCOTVEC, 1994. Hon. DEd CNAA, 1992; DUniv Open, 1994; Hon. DLitt Glasgow Caledonian, 2000. *Recreations:* tennis, bridge, opera, political history. *Address:* c/o Cookson Group plc, The Adelphi, 1-11 John Adam Street, WC2N 6HJ. *Club:* Oxford and Cambridge (Chm., 1995–97).

NICHOLSON, Sir Charles (Christian), 3rd Bt *cr* 1912, of Harrington Gardens, Royal Borough of Kensington; *b* 15 Dec. 1941; *s* of Sir John Norris Nicholson, 2nd Bt, KBE, CIE and Vittoria Vivien (*d* 1991), *y d* of Percy Trewhella; *S* father, 1993; *m* 1975, Martha Don, *d* of Stuart Warren Don and *widow* of Niall Anstruther-Gough-Calthorpe; one step *s* one step *d. Educ:* Ampleforth; Magdalen Coll., Oxford. *Heir: b* James Richard Nicholson [*b* 24 Oct. 1947; *m* 1980, Sarah Hazel, *d* of Richard Alan Budgett; one *s* one *d*]. *Address:* Turners Green Farm, Elvetham, Hartley Wintney, Hants RG27 8BE. *Clubs:* Brooks's, Pratt's; Royal Yacht Squadron.

See also Sir E. H. Anstruther-Gough-Calthorpe.

NICHOLSON, (Charles) Gordon (Brown); QC (Scot.) 1982; Sheriff Principal of Lothian and Borders and Sheriff of Chancery, since 1990; *b* 11 Sept. 1935; *s* of late William Addison Nicholson, former Director, Scottish Tourist Board, and Jean Brown; *m* 1963, Hazel Mary Nixon; two *s. Educ:* George Watson's Coll., Edinburgh; Edinburgh Univ. (Hon. Fellow, Faculty of Law, 1988). MA Hons (English Lit.) 1956, LLB 1958. 2nd Lieut Queen's Own Cameron Highlanders, 1958–60. Admitted Faculty of Advocates, Edinburgh, 1961; in practice at Bar; Standing Junior Counsel, Registrar of Restrictive Trading Agreements, 1968; Advocate-Depute, 1968–70; Sheriff of: South Strathclyde, Dumfries and Galloway, 1970–76; Lothian and Borders, 1976–82; Mem., Scottish Law Commn, 1982–90. Vice-Pres., Sheriffs' Assoc., 1979–82 (Sec., 1975–79); Convener, Sheriffs Principal, 1991–. Member: Scottish Council on Crime, 1972–75; Dunpark Cttee on Reparation by Offenders, 1974–77; May Cttee of Inquiry into UK Prison Service, 1978–79; Kincraig Review of Parole in Scotland, 1988–89; Judicial Studies Cttee, 1997–; Criminal Justice Forum, 2000–. Hon. President: Victim Support Scotland (formerly Scottish Assoc. of Victim Support Schemes), 1989– (Chm., 1987–89); Scottish Assoc. for Study of Delinquency, 1988– (Chm., 1974–79; Hon. Vice-Pres., 1982–88); Jt Patron, British Juvenile and Family Courts Soc., 1995–. Chm., Edinburgh CAB, 1979–82. Comr, Northern Lighthouse Bd, 1990– (Vice Chm., 1993–94; Chm., 1994–95). *Publications:* The Law and Practice of Sentencing in Scotland, 1981, 2nd edn 1992; (ed jtly) Sheriff Court Practice by I. Macphail, 2nd edn 1999; contrib. to legal periodicals. *Recreation:* music.

Address: Back o'Redfern, 24C Colinton Road, Edinburgh EH10 5EQ. *T:* (0131) 447 4300, *Fax:* (0131) 447 3274. *Club:* New (Edinburgh).

NICHOLSON, David; former racehorse trainer, National Hunt; *b* 19 March 1939; *s* of Herbert Charles Denton Nicholson (Frenchie) and Diana Nicholson; *m* 1962, Dinah Caroline Pugh; two *s*. *Educ:* Oakley Hall Prep. Sch.; Haileybury Coll. Professional National Hunt jockey, 1951–74 (won Whitbread Gold Cup, 1967, with Mill House); racehorse trainer, 1968–99 (won Gold Cup, 1988, with Charter Party); Champion National Hunt Trainer, seasons 1993–94, 1994–95. *Recreation:* watching sport. *Address:* Halloween Cottage, Nether Westcote, Chipping Norton, Oxon OX7 6SD. *T:* (01993) 830297, *Fax:* (01993) 831573. *Clubs:* MCC; Gloucester County Cricket.

NICHOLSON, David John; public affairs consultant, Butler-Kelly Ltd, since 1998; *b* 17 Aug. 1944; *s* of late John Francis Nicholson and of Lucy Warburton Nicholson (*née* Battrum); *m* 1981, Frances Mary, *d* of late Brig. T. E. H. Helby, MC; two *s* one *d*. *Educ:* Queen Elizabeth's Grammar School, Blackburn; Christ Church, Oxford (MA Hons Mod. Hist.). Dept of Employment, 1966; Research Fellow, Inst. of Historical Res., 1970; Cons. Res. Dept, 1972 (Head, Political Section, 1974–82); Assoc. of British Chambers of Commerce, 1982–87 (Dep. Dir-Gen., 1986–87). MP (C) Taunton, 1987–97; contested (C) same seat, 1997. PPS to Minister for Overseas Develt, 1990–92. Member: Select Cttee on Parly Comr for Admin, 1992–97; Public Accounts Cttee, 1992–94; Select Cttee on Employment, 1994–96; Select Cttee on Educn and Employment, 1996–97; Jt Sec., All-Party Parly Gp for Population and Develt, 1990–94; Treasurer: All-Party Parly Gp on Water, 1993–97; All-Party Parly Gp on Waste Management, 1995–97; Sec., Cons. Backbench Social Services Cttee, 1988–90; Chm., Cons. W Country Mems Cttee, 1994–95 (Vice-Chm., 1992–93); Sec., Cons. Backbench Agriculture Cttee, 1995–97. *Publication:* (ed with John Barnes) The Diaries of L. S. Amery: vol. I, 1896–1929, 1980; vol. II, The Empire at Bay, 1929–45, 1988. *Recreations:* travel, gardening, music, the country. *Address:* Allshire, near Brushford, Somerset EX16 9JG.

NICHOLSON, (Edward) Max, CB 1948; CVO 1971; Chairman, Land Use Consultants, 1966–89; *b* 12 July 1904; *m* 1st, 1932, Eleanor Mary Crawford (marr. diss., 1964); two *s*; 2nd, Marie Antoinette Mauerhofer; one *s*. *Educ:* Sedbergh; Hertford Coll., Oxford (Hon. Fellow, 1993). Head of Allocation of Tonnage Division, Ministry of War Transport, 1942–45; Secretary of Office of The Lord President of the Council, 1945–52. Member Advisory Council on Scientific Policy, 1948–64; Dir-Gen., Nature Conservancy, 1952–66; Convener, Conservation Section, Internat. Biological Programme, 1963–74; Secretary, Duke of Edinburgh's Study Conference on the Countryside in 1970, 1963; Albright Lecturer, Univ. of California, 1964; a Dir and Managing Editor, Environmental Data Services Ltd, 1978–80. President: RSPB, 1980–85; Trust for Urban Ecology (formerly Ecological Parks Trust), 1987–88 (Chm., 1977–87); New Renaissance Gp, 1998–2000 (Chm., 1996–98); Vice-President: RSA, 1978–82; Wildfowl and Wetlands Trust; WWF, UK; Trustee, Earthwatch Europe, 1985–93; Member: Council, Internat. Inst. of Environment and Develt, 1972–88; Internat. Council, WWF, 1983–86. Chairman: Environmental Cttee, London Celebrations for the Queen's Silver Jubilee, 1976–77; London Looks Forward Conf., 1977; UK Standing Cttee for World Conservation Strategy Prog., 1981–83. Hon. Member: IUCN; British Ecol Soc.; WWF; RTPI. Hon. Fellow: American Ornithologists' Union; RIBA; RGS 2001. Hon. LLD Aberdeen, 1964; Hon. Dr, RCA, 1970; Hon. DL Birmingham, 1983. John C. Phillips Medallist International Union for Conservation of Nature and Natural Resources, 1963; Europa Preis für Landespflege, 1972; Stamford Raffles Award, Zool Soc., 1999. Comdr, Order of Golden Ark, Netherlands, 1973. *Publications:* Birds in England, 1926; How Birds Live, 1927; Birds and Men, 1951; Britain's Nature Reserves, 1958; The System, 1967; The Environmental Revolution, 1970 (Premio Europeo Cortina-Ulisse, 1971); The Big Change, 1973; The New Environmental Age, 1987; (ed jtly) The Birds of the Western Palearctic, Vol. I, 1977, Vol. II, 1980, Vol. III, 1983, Vol. IV, 1985, Vol. V, 1988, Vol. VI, 1992, Vol. VII, 1993, Vol. VIII and Vol. IX, 1994, and other books, scientific papers and articles. *Address:* 13 Upper Cheyne Row, SW3 5JW. *Club:* Athenæum.

NICHOLSON, Rev. Prof. Ernest Wilson, DD; FBA 1987; Provost of Oriel College, Oxford, since 1990; Pro-Vice-Chancellor, University of Oxford, since 1993; *b* 26 Sept. 1938; *s* of Ernest Tedford Nicholson and Veronica Muriel Nicholson; *m* 1962, Hazel (*née* Jackson); one *s* three *d*. *Educ:* Portadown Coll.; Trinity Coll., Dublin (Scholar; BA 1960; MA 1964; Hon. Fellow, 1992); Glasgow Univ. (PhD 1964). MA (by incorporation) 1967, BD 1971, DD 1978, Cambridge; DD Oxford (by incorporation) 1979. Lectr in Hebrew and Semitic Languages, TCD, 1962–67; Univ. Lectr in Divinity, Cambridge Univ., 1967–79; Fellow: University Coll. (now Wolfson Coll.), Cambridge, 1967–69 (Hon. Fellow, 1992); Pembroke Coll., Cambridge, 1969–79; Chaplain, Pembroke Coll., Cambridge, 1969–73, Dean, 1973–79; Oriel Prof. of the Interpretation of Holy Scripture, and Fellow of Oriel Coll., Oxford Univ., 1979–90. At various times vis. prof. at univs and seminars in Europe, USA, Canada and Australia. Pres., SOTS, 1988. Chm., Jardine Foundn, 1993–2000. Hon. Fellow, St Peter's Coll., Oxford, 1994. Comdr, Order of Merit (Italian Republic), 1990. *Publications:* Deuteronomy and Tradition, 1967; Preaching to the Exiles, 1971; Exodus and Sinai in History and Tradition, 1973; (with J. Baker) The Commentary of Rabbi David Kimḥi on Psalms 120–150, 1973; Commentary on Jeremiah 1–25, 1973; Commentary on Jeremiah 26–52, 1975; God and His People: covenant and theology in the Old Testament, 1986; The Pentateuch in the Twentieth Century: the legacy of Julius Wellhausen, 1997; articles in biblical and Semitic jls. *Recreations:* music, the English countryside. *Address:* Oriel College, Oxford OX1 4EW.

NICHOLSON, Frank; DL; Managing Director, Vaux Breweries Ltd, 1984–99; Director, Swallow Group plc (formerly Vaux Group), 1987–99; *b* 11 Feb. 1954; 5th *s* of late Douglas Nicholson, TD and Pauline Nicholson; *m* 1986, Lavinia Stourton; three *s*. *Educ:* Harrow Sch.; Magdalene Coll., Cambridge (MA). FRICS 1977. Assistant, Debenham, Tewson and Chinnocks, 1976–81; Tied Trade Dir, Vaux Breweries Ltd, 1981–84. Dir, Washington Develt Corp., 1985–88; Chairman: Sunderland Youth Enterprise Trust, 1986–; Wearside Opportunity, 1988–92; City of Sunderland Partnership, 1992–. Dep. Chm., Sunderland Univ. (formerly Poly.), 1991– (Hon. Fellow, 1991). Gov., Durham Sch., 1999–. DL 1995, High Sheriff, 1999–2000, Co. Durham. Prince of Wales Community Ambassador's Award, 1995. *Recreation:* country sports. *Address:* Cocken House, Chester-le-Street, Co. Durham DH3 4EN. *T:* (0191) 388 0505. *Clubs:* Royal Automobile; Northern Counties (Newcastle); Pallion Workingmen's (Co. Durham).
See also Sir P. D. Nicholson.

NICHOLSON, Gordon; *see* Nicholson, C. G. B.

NICHOLSON, Dr Howard, FRCP; Physician, University College Hospital, since 1948; Physician, Brompton Hospital, 1952–77, retired; Fellow of University College, London, since 1959; *b* 1 Feb. 1912; *s* of Frederick and Sara Nicholson; *m* 1941, Winifrid Madeline Piercy (*d* 2001). *Educ:* University Coll., London, and University Coll. Hospital. MB, BS, London, 1935; MD London 1938; MRCP 1938, FRCP 1949. House appointments and Registrarship, UCH, 1935–38; House Physician at Brompton Hosp., 1938. Served War, 1940–45, RAMC; Physician to Chest Surgical Team and Officer i/c Medical Div. (Lt-Col). Registrar, Brompton Hosp., and Chief Asst, Inst. of Diseases of Chest, 1945–48. Goulstonian Lecturer, RCP, 1950. *Publications:* sections on Diseases of Chest in The Practice of Medicine (ed J. S. Richardson), 1961, and in Progress in Clinical Medicine, 1961; articles in Thorax, Lancet, etc. *Recreations:* reading, going to the opera. *Address:* Chelwood, Laughton, Lewes, E Sussex BN8 6BE.

NICHOLSON, Jack; American film actor, director and producer; *b* 22 April 1937; *s* of John and Ethel May Nicholson; *m* 1961, Sandra Knight (marr. diss. 1966); one *d*. *Films include:* Cry-Baby Killer, 1958; Studs Lonigan, 1960; The Shooting (also produced); Easy Rider, 1969; Five Easy Pieces, 1970; The Last Detail, 1973; Chinatown, 1974; One Flew Over the Cuckoo's Nest, 1975 (Acad. Award for Best Actor, 1976); The Passenger, 1975; The Shining, 1980; The Postman Always Rings Twice, 1981; Reds, 1981; Terms of Endearment (Acad. Award for Best Supporting Actor), 1984; Prizzi's Honor, 1985; Heartburn, 1986; The Witches of Eastwick, 1986; Ironweed, 1987; Batman, 1988; The Two Jakes, 1991 (also dir.); A Few Good Men, 1992; Man Trouble, 1993; Hoffa, 1993; Wolf, 1994; The Crossing Guard, 1996; Mars Attacks!, 1997; Blood & Wine, 1997; As Good as it Gets (Acad. Award for Best Actor), 1998; The Pledge, 2001. *Address:* c/o Bresler Kelly & Associates, 11500 West Olympic Boulevard, Suite 510, Los Angeles, CA 90064–1529, USA.

NICHOLSON, James Frederick; farmer; Member (UU), Northern Ireland, European Parliament, since 1994 (OUP, 1989–94); *b* 29 Jan. 1945; *s* of Thomas and Matilda Nicholson; *m* 1968, Elizabeth Gibson; six *s*. *Educ:* Aghavilly Primary Sch. Member: Armagh Dist Council, 1975–97 (Chm., 1994–95; Mayor of Armagh, March–June 1995); Southern Health and Social Services Bd, 1977–. Mem. (OU) Newry and Armagh, NI Assembly, 1982–86. Contested (OUP) Newry and Armagh, 1987. MP (OU) Newry and Armagh, 1983–85. *Address:* European Office, 3 Glengall Street, Belfast BT12 5AE. *T:* (028) 9043 9431, *Fax:* (028) 9024 6738; *e-mail:* j_nicholson@uup.org.

NICHOLSON, Rt Hon. Sir (James) Michael (Anthony), Kt 1988; PC 1995; **Rt Hon. Lord Justice Nicholson;** a Lord Justice of Appeal, Supreme Court of Judicature, Northern Ireland, since 1995; *b* 4 Feb. 1933; *s* of late Cyril Nicholson, QC, DL and late Eleanor Nicholson (*née* Caffrey); *m* 1973, Augusta Mary Ada, *d* of late Thomas F. Doyle and of Mrs Elizabeth Doyle, Co. Cork; one *s* two *d*. *Educ:* Downside; Trinity College, Cambridge (MA). Called to the Bar of N Ireland, 1956; to English Bar, Gray's Inn, 1963 (Hon. Bencher, 1995); to Bar of Ireland, 1975; QC (NI), 1971; Bencher, Inn of Court of NI, 1978; Chm., Exec. Council of Inn of Court of NI and of Bar Council, 1983–85; High Court Judge, NI, 1986–95. Chm., Mental Health Review Tribunal (NI), 1973–76; Mem., Standing Adv. Commn for Human Rights (NI), 1976–78. High Sheriff, Co. Londonderry, 1972. President: Irish Cricket Union, 1978; NW ICU, 1986–93. *Recreations:* cricket, chess. *Address:* Royal Courts of Justice, Chichester Street, Belfast, Northern Ireland BT1 3JF. *Club:* MCC.

NICHOLSON, Jeremy Mark; QC 2000; *b* 21 March 1955; *s* of Eric Day Nicholson and Joy Nicholson; *m* 1987, Elizabeth Brooke-Smith; two *s*. *Educ:* Rugby Sch.; Trinity Hall, Cambridge (MA). Called to the Bar, Middle Temple, 1977 (Harmsworth Schol.); in practice at the Bar, 1978–. *Recreations:* sailing, walking, pursuing superficial interests. *Address:* 4 Pump Court, Temple, EC4Y 7AN. *T:* (020) 7842 5555. *Club:* Royal Automobile.

NICHOLSON, Lindsay, (Mrs John Merritt); Editor-in-Chief, Good Housekeeping magazine, since 1999; *b* 7 Aug. 1956; *d* of late Anthony Cuthbertson-Nicholson and of Sheila (*née* Pigram); *m* 1981, John Merritt (*d* 1992); one *d* (and one *d* decd). *Educ:* University Coll. London (BSc Hons Astronomy and Physics). Editl trng scheme, Mirror Gp Newspapers, 1978–80; worked on magazines: Woman's Own, 1981–83; Honey, 1983–84; Living, 1984–85; Best, 1987–89; Woman, 1992–95; Editor-in-Chief, Prima (incl. Launch of Prima Baby and Your Home), 1995–99. Editor of Year, PPA, 1999. *Recreations:* riding, theatre. *Address:* National Magazine Company, 72 Broadwick Street, W1V 2BP. *T:* (020) 7439 5247. *Clubs:* Groucho; Royal Corinthian Yacht (Burnham-on-Crouch).

NICHOLSON, Margaret Beda; *see* Yorke, M.

NICHOLSON, Martin Buchanan, CMG 1997; HM Diplomatic Service, retired; Associate Fellow, Royal Institute of International Affairs, 1999–March 2002; *b* 12 Aug. 1937; 2nd *s* of late Carroll and Nancy Nicholson; *m* 1964, Raili Tellervo Laaksonen; one *s* one *d*. *Educ:* Oundle Sch.; St Catharine's Coll., Cambridge (BA 1961; MA 1964); Moscow Univ. (Post-grad.). Entered Foreign Office, 1963; served Moscow, 1965–68 and 1971; Prague, 1972–75; Research Dept, FCO, 1975–78 and 1981–86; Mem., UK Delegn to MBFR, Vienna, 1978–81; Advr on Soviet, later Russian, Affairs, Cabinet Office (on secondment), 1987–94; Minister-Counsellor, Moscow, 1994–97. Res. Associate, IISS, 1998–99. *Publications:* Towards a Russia of the Regions, 1999; articles on Soviet and Russian affairs in The World Today and Internat. Affairs. *Recreations:* gardening, playing the flute. *Address:* 13 Riverdale Gardens, Twickenham TW1 2BX. *T:* (020) 8892 8214.
See also Sir Robin Nicholson.

NICHOLSON, Max; *see* Nicholson, E. M.

NICHOLSON, Hon. Sir Michael; *see* Nicholson, Hon. Sir J. M. A.

NICHOLSON, Michael Constantine; a Recorder of the Crown Court, 1980–95; *b* 3 Feb. 1932; *m* 1960, Kathleen Mary Strong; two *d*. *Educ:* Wycliffe Coll., Stonehouse; University Coll. of Wales, Aberystwyth (LLB). Called to the Bar, Gray's Inn, 1957; Crown Counsel, Nyasaland, 1960–63; Wales and Chester circuit, 1963–94. *Recreations:* opera, cinema, theatre. *Address:* c/o 33 Park Place, Cardiff CF10 3TN.

NICHOLSON, Michael Thomas, OBE 1992; reporter and presenter, Tonight programme, ITV; *b* 9 Jan. 1937; *s* of Major Allan Nicholson and Doris Alice (*née* Reid); *m* 1968, Diana Margaret Slater; two *s*, and two adopted *d*. *Educ:* Leicester Univ. (BA). Joined ITN, 1963: News Editor, 1965–66; War Correspondent, 1968–94: Nigeria, Biafra, Beirut, Jordan, Cyprus, Congo, Israel, Indo-Pakistan, Rhodesia, Angola, Falklands, Gulf, Bosnia, Croatia; Southern Africa Corresp., 1977–81; Newscaster, 1982–86; Washington Corresp., Channel 4, 1989–90; Sen. Foreign Correspondent, ITN, 1991. Campaign Medal: Falklands War, 1982; Gulf War, 1991. *Publications:* Partridge Kite, 1976; Red Joker, 1978; December Ultimatum, 1981; Pilgrims Rest, 1983; Across the Limpopo, 1986; A Measure of Danger, 1991; Natasha's Story, 1993. *Recreations:* sailing, walking. *Address:* Grayswood, Surrey. *Clubs:* Reform, Groucho.

NICHOLSON, Sir Paul (Douglas), Kt 1993; Chairman, Vaux Group, 1976–99 (Managing Director, 1971–92); Lord-Lieutenant, County Durham, since 1997; *b* 7 March 1938; *s* of late Douglas Nicholson, TD and Pauline Nicholson; *m* 1970, Sarah, *y d* of Sir Edmund Bacon, Bt, KG, KBE, TD; one *d*. *Educ:* Harrow; Clare College, Cambridge (MA). FCA. Lieut, Coldstream Guards, 1956–58; joined Vaux Breweries, 1965. Chm., Northern Investors Co., 1984–89; Director: Tyne Tees Television, then Yorkshire-Tyne

Tees Television Hldgs, 1981–97; Northern Development Co., 1986–2000; Northern Electric, 1990–97; Scottish Investment Trust plc, 1998–; Steelite International plc, 2000–. Chm., Urban Develt Corp. for Tyne and Wear, 1987–98; Chm., N Region, CBI, 1977–79; Chm., N Regional Bd, British Technology Group, 1979–84. Chm., Brewers and Licensed Retailers Assoc. (formerly Brewers' Soc.), 1994–96; Pres., NE Chamber of Commerce, 1995–96. High Sheriff, Co. Durham, 1980–81; DL Co. Durham, 1980. *Recreations:* deerstalking, driving horses (Pres., Coaching Club, 1990–97). *Address:* Quarry Hill, Brancepeth, Durham DH7 8DW. *T:* (0191) 3780275. *Clubs:* Boodle's; Northern Counties (Newcastle upon Tyne).

See also F. Nicholson.

NICHOLSON, Ralph Lambton Robb; Secretary, United Kingdom Atomic Energy Authority, 1984–86; *b* 26 Sept. 1924; *s* of Ralph Adam Nicholson and Kathleen Mary Nicholson (*née* Robb); *m* 1951, Mary Kennard; one *s* two *d.* *Educ:* Sherborne School; Cambridge Univ.; Imperial College, London (BSc; ACGI). FIChemE. Royal Engineers, 1943–47. Chemical engineer, Distillers Co., 1950–51; Wellcome Foundation, 1951–54; Fisons, 1954–58; planning and commercial manager, UKAEA, 1958–67; Dir, Min. of Technology Programmes Analysis Unit, 1967–71; Principal Programmes and Finance Officer, UKAEA, 1971–84. *Publications:* contribs to energy and management jls. *Recreations:* gardening, music, canals. *Address:* The Garth, Midgham, Reading, Berks RG7 5UJ. *T:* (0118) 971 2211.

NICHOLSON, Robert; publisher, designer, artist; *b* Sydney, Australia, 8 April 1920; *m* 1951 (marr. diss. 1976); one *s* one *d*; *m* 1989. *Educ:* Troy Town Elementary Sch., Rochester; Rochester Tech. Sch.; Medway Sch. of Art. Served 1939–45, RAMC. Responsible with brother, Roger Nicholson, for major design projects during post-war design boom, 1945–55, including Festival of Britain Exhibition in Edinburgh, 1951 and Design Centre, London, 1956. Writer and publisher of guide books including: Nicholson's London Guide; Street Finder; Guide to Great Britain, guides to the Thames, the canals, etc. Benjamin Franklin medal, 1960. Exhibns of landscape painting in London, Spain, France, and annually in Kent and Sussex. Lives in Winchelsea, Sussex.

NICHOLSON, Robin Alaster, CBE 1999; Director, Edward Cullinan Architects, since 1989 (Partner, 1979–89); *b* 27 July 1944; *s* of late Gerald Hugh Nicholson and Margaret Evelyn Nicholson (*née* Hanbury); *m* 1969, Fiona Mary Bird; three *s.* *Educ:* Magdalene Coll., Cambridge (MA); University Coll. London (MSc 1969). RIBA 1989. Architect: Evan Walker Associates, Toronto, 1966; James Stirling, Chartered Architects, 1969–76; Boza Lührs Muzard, Santiago, Chile, 1973; Tutor in Architecture: UCL, 1974–76; Poly of N London, 1976–79. Vis. Fellow, Univ. of Wales, 1984. Dir, RIBA Journals Ltd, 1993–97. Mem. Council, 1991–97, Vice Pres., 1992–94, RIBA; Chm., Construction Industry Council, 1998–2000; Mem. Bd, Movement for Innovation, 1998–; Mem., DETR, subseq. DTLR, Urban Sounding Bd, 2001–. FRSA 1995. *Recreations:* gardening, building. *Address:* (office) 1 Baldwin Terrace, N1 7RU. *T:* (020) 7704 1975. *Club:* The Edge.

NICHOLSON, Sir Robin (Buchanan), Kt 1985; PhD; FRS 1978; FREng; Chairman, Pilkington Optronics Ltd, since 1991; *b* 12 Aug. 1934; *s* of late Carroll and Nancy Nicholson; *m* 1st, 1958, Elizabeth Mary Caffyn (*d* 1988); one *s* two *d*; 2nd, 1991, Yvonne, *d* of late Arthur Appleby and of Gwendoline Appleby. *Educ:* Oundle Sch.; St Catharine's Coll., Cambridge (BA 1956; PhD 1959; MA 1960). FIM; MInstP; FREng (FEng 1980). University of Cambridge: Demonstrator in Metallurgy, 1960; Lectr in Metallurgy, 1964; Fellow of Christ's Coll., 1962–66, Hon. Fellow 1984; Prof. of Metallurgy, Univ. of Manchester, 1966. Inco Europe Ltd: Dir of Research Lab., 1972; Dir, 1975; Man. Dir, 1976–81; Co-Chm., Biogen NV, 1979–81. Chief Scientific Advr to Cabinet Office, 1983–85 (Central Policy Review Staff, 1981–83). Director: Pilkington Brothers, then Pilkington, plc, 1986–96; Rolls-Royce plc, 1986–; BP plc, 1987–. Chairman: CEST, 1987–90; ACOST, 1990–93. Member: SERC (formerly SRC), 1978–81; Council for Sci. and Technol., 1993–. Mem. Council: Royal Soc., 1983–85; Fellowship of Engrg, 1986–89; Pres., Inst. of Materials, 1997–98. Foreign Associate, Nat. Acad. of Engrg, USA, 1983. CIMgt. Hon. FIChemE; Hon. Fellow UMIST, 1988. Hon. DSc: Cranfield, 1983; Aston, 1983; Manchester, 1985; Hon. DMet Sheffield, 1984; Hon. DEng Birmingham, 1986; DUniv Open, 1987. Rosenhain Medallist, Inst. of Metals, 1971; Platinum Medal, Metals Soc., 1982. *Publications:* Precipitation Hardening (with A. Kelly), 1962; (jtly) Electron Microscopy of Thin Crystals, 1965; (ed and contrib. with A. Kelly) Strengthening Methods in Crystals, 1971; numerous papers to learned jls. *Recreations:* family life, gardening, music. *Address:* c/o Pilkington Optronics Ltd, Glascoed Road, St Asaph, Denbighshire LL17 0LL. *T:* (01745) 588003. *Club:* MCC.

See also M. B. Nicholson.

NICKELL, Prof. Stephen John, FBA 1993; School Professor of Economics, London School of Economics, since 1998; *b* 25 April 1944; *s* of John Edward Hilary Nickell and Phyllis Nickell; *m* 1976, Susan Elizabeth (*née* Pegden); one *s* one *d.* *Educ:* Merchant Taylors' Sch.; Pembroke Coll., Cambridge (BA); LSE (MSc). Maths teacher, Hendon County Sch., 1965–68; London School of Economics: Lectr, 1970–77; Reader, 1977–79; Prof. of Economics, 1979–84; Dir, Inst. of Econs and Stats, Prof. of Econs, and Fellow of Nuffield Coll., Oxford Univ., 1984–98. Member: Academic Panel, HM Treasury, 1981–89; ESRC, 1990–94. Mem., Monetary Policy Cttee, Bank of England, 2000–. President: Eur. Assoc. of Labour Economists, 1999–Sept. 2002; REconS, 2001– (Mem. Council, 1984–94). Fellow, Econometric Soc., 1980. Hon. Mem., Amer. Economic Assoc., 1997. *Publications:* The Investment Decisions of Firms, 1978; (with R. Layard and R. Dornbusch) The Performance of the British Economy, 1988; (with R. Jackman and R. Layard) Unemployment, 1991; (with R. Jackman and R. Layard) The Unemployment Crisis, 1994; The Performance of Companies, 1995; articles in learned jls. *Recreations:* reading, riding, cooking; *e-mail:* s.j.nickell@lse.ac.uk.

NICKLAUS, Jack William; professional golfer, 1961–2000; *b* 21 Jan. 1940; *s* of Louis Charles Nicklaus and Helen (*née* Schoener); *m* 1960, Barbara Jean Bash; four *s* one *d.* *Educ:* Upper Arlington High Sch.; Ohio State Univ. Won US Amateur golf championship, 1959, 1961; became professional golfer, 1961; designs golf courses in USA, Europe, and Far East; Chm., Golden Bear Internat. Inc. Captained US team which won 25th Ryder Cup, 1983. *Major wins include:* US Open, 1962, 1967, 1972, 1980; US Masters, 1963, 1965, 1966, 1972, 1975, 1986; US Professional Golfers' Assoc., 1963, 1971, 1973, 1975, 1980; British Open, 1966, 1970, 1978, and many other championships in USA, Europe, Australia and Far East. Hon. Dr Athletic Arts Ohio State, 1972; Hon. LLD St Andrews, 1984. *Publications:* My 55 Ways to Lower Your Golf Score, 1962; Take a Tip from Me, 1964; The Greatest Game of All, 1969 (autobiog.); Lesson Tee, 1972; Golf My Way, 1974; The Best Way to Better Your Golf, vols 1–3, 1974; Jack Nicklaus' Playing Lessons, 1976; Total Golf Techniques, 1977; On and Off the Fairway, 1979 (autobiog.); The Full Swing, 1982; My Most Memorable Shots in the Majors, 1988; Jack Nicklaus: my story, 1997. *Address:* (office) 11780 US Highway #1, North Palm Beach, FL 33408, USA.

NICKLESS, Edmund Francis Paul, CGeol, FGS; Executive Secretary, Geological Society of London, since 1997; *b* 25 Jan. 1947; *e s* of Philip Wilfred Nickless and Gabrielle Frances Nickless (*née* Hughes); *m* 1970, Elisabeth Deborah Pickard; two *d.* *Educ:* Salvatorian Coll., Harrow; Queen Mary Coll., Univ. of London (BSc). FGS 1971; CGeol 1990. Various posts with British Geol Survey, London and Edinburgh, 1968–83; Sec., Earth Scis Directorate, NERC, Swindon, 1983–89; Envmtl Advr, Sci. and Technol. Secretariat, Cabinet Office, 1989–91; Asst Dir, British Geol Survey, 1991–97. FRSA 1998. *Publications:* various papers on geology in learned jls and official pubns of British Geol Survey. *Recreations:* listening to music, gardening, walking. *Address:* Ringrose House, Main Street, Belton-in-Rutland LE15 9LB. *T:* (01572) 717324; Geological Society of London, Burlington House, Piccadilly, W1V 0JU. *Club:* Athenæum.

NICKOLS, Herbert Arthur; Headmaster, Westonbirt School, Tetbury, Gloucestershire, 1981–86; *b* 17 Jan. 1926; *s* of Herbert and Henrietta Elizabeth Nickols; *m* 1953, Joyce Peake; two *s* one *d.* *Educ:* Imperial Coll., Univ. of London (BSc). ACGI. Res. Demonstrator, Imperial Coll., 1947–49; Housemaster, Sen. Science Master and later Dep. Headmaster, St Edmund's Sch., Canterbury, Kent, 1949–81. *Recreations:* music, travel, cricket. *Address:* 146 New Dover Road, Canterbury, Kent CT1 3EJ. *T:* (01227) 452605.

NICKSON, family name of **Baron Nickson.**

NICKSON, Baron *cr* 1994 (Life Peer), of Renagour in the District of Stirling; **David Wigley Nickson,** KBE 1987 (CBE 1981); FRSE; Vice Lord-Lieutenant of Stirling and Falkirk, since 1997; *b* 27 Nov. 1929; *s* of late Geoffrey Wigley Nickson and Janet Mary Nickson; *m* 1952, Helen Louise Cockcraft; three *d.* *Educ:* Eton; RMA, Sandhurst. Commnd Coldstream Guards, 1949–54. Joined Wm Collins, 1954; Dir, 1961–85; Jt Man. Dir, 1967; Vice Chm., 1976–83; Gp Man. Dir, 1979–82; Chm., Pan Books, 1982. Director: Scottish United Investors plc, 1970–83; General Accident plc, 1971–98 (Dep. Chm., 1993–98); Scottish & Newcastle (formerly Scottish & Newcastle Breweries) plc, 1981–95 (Dep. Chm., 1982–83; Chm., 1983–89); Clydesdale Bank, 1981–89 (Dep. Chm., 1990–91; Chm., 1991–98); Radio Clyde PLC, 1982–85; Edinburgh Investment Trust plc, 1983–94; Hambro's PLC, 1989–98; National Australia Bank Ltd, 1991–96. Chm., Top Salaries, then Sen. Salaries, Rev. Body, 1989–95; Chairman: SDA, 1989–90, Scottish Enterprise, 1990–93; CBI in Scotland, 1979–81; Pres., CBI, 1986–88 (Dep. Pres., 1985–86). Member: Scottish Indust. Develt Adv. Bd, 1975–80; Scottish Econ. Council, 1980–94; NEDC, 1985–88; Scottish Cttee, Design Council, 1978–81; Nat. Trng Task Force, 1989–91. Chairman: Countryside Commn for Scotland, 1983–85; Scottish Adv. Cttee, ICRF, 1994–2001; Atlantic Salmon Trust, 1989–96 (Mem., Council of Management, 1982–; Vice-Pres., 1996–); Conon Dist Salmon Fishery Bd, 1994–; Sec. of State for Scotland's Atlantic Salmon Task Force, 1996; Pres., Assoc. of Scottish Dist Salmon Fishery Bds, 1996– (Vice Chm., 1989–92); Dir, Countryside Alliance, 1998–2000. Chm., Loch Lomond Shores Trust, 1999–. Trustee: Game Conservancy, 1988–91; Prince's Youth Business Trust, 1987–90; Princess Royal's Trust for Carers, 1990–94. Chancellor, Glasgow Caledonian Univ., 1993–. Brig., Queen's Body Guard for Scotland, Royal Co. of Archers. Freeman, City of London, 1999; Hon. Freeman, Fishmongers' Co., 1999. DL Stirling and Falkirk, 1982. CIMgt (CBIM 1980); FRSE 1987. Hon. Fellow, Paisley Coll., subseq. Univ. of Paisley, 1992. DUniv Stirling, 1986; Hon. DBA Napier Polytechnic, 1990; DUniv Glasgow Caledonian, 1993. *Recreations:* fishing, shooting, bird watching, the countryside. *Clubs:* Boodle's, Flyfishers', MCC.

NICOL, family name of **Baroness Nicol.**

NICOL, Baroness *cr* 1982 (Life Peer), of Newnham in the County of Cambridgeshire; **Olive Mary Wendy Nicol;** FRGS; *b* 21 March 1923; *d* of James and Harriet Rowe-Hunter; *m* 1947, Alexander Douglas Ian Nicol (CBE 1985); two *s* one *d.* Civil Service, 1943–48. Opposition Whip, 1983–87, Opposition Dep. Chief Whip, 1987–89, Dep. Speaker, 1995–, H of L; Member: H of L Science and Technol. Select Cttee, 1990–93; Envmt and Social Affairs sub-cttee, European Communities Cttee, 1993–95; Sustainable Develt Select Cttee, 1994–95; Select Cttee on Animals in Scientific Procedures, 2001–; Member: Ecclesiastical Cttee, 1989–95; Sci. and Technol. Subcttee on Disposal of Nuclear Waste, 1998–99; Bd Mem., Parly OST, 1998–99. Trustee, Cambridge United Charities, 1967–86; Director, Cambridge and District Co-operative Soc., 1975–81, Pres. 1981–85; Member: Supplementary Benefits Tribunal, 1976–78; Cambridge City Council, 1972–82; Assoc. of District Councils, Cambridge Branch, 1974–76 and 1980–82; various school Governing Bodies, 1974–80; Council, Granta Housing Soc., 1975–; Careers Service Consultative Group, 1978–81. JP Cambridge City, 1972–86. FRGS 1990. *Recreations:* reading, walking. *Address:* c/o House of Lords, SW1A 0PW.

NICOL, Andrew George Lindsay; QC 1995; a Recorder, since 2000; *b* 9 May 1951; *s* of late Duncan Rennie Nicol and Margaret (*née* Mason); two *s.* *Educ:* Selwyn Coll., Cambridge (BA, LLB); Harvard Law Sch. (LLM). Harkness Fellow, 1973–75; Special Assistant: to Dir of Housing and Community Develt, California, 1975–76; Allen Allen and Hemsley, solicitors, Sydney, NSW, 1976–77; Lectr in Law, LSE, 1977–87; called to the Bar, Middle Temple, 1978; barrister, 1979–; an Asst Recorder, 1998–2000. Chm., Immigration Law Practitioners' Assoc., 1997–2000. *Publications:* (with G. Robertson) Media Law, 1984, revd edn 1992; (with A. Dummett) Subjects, Citizens, Aliens and Others, 1990; (with G. Millar and A. Sharland) Media Law and Human Rights, 2001. *Recreations:* family, walking. *Address:* Doughty Street Chambers, 10 Doughty Street, WC1N 2PL. *T:* (020) 7404 1313, *Fax:* (020) 7404 2283.

NICOL, (Andrew) William; JP; BSc; FICE, FIMechE, FIEE; Chairman, 1987–93, and Chief Executive, 1990–93, South Western Electricity plc; *b* 29 April 1933; *s* of Arthur Edward Nicol and Ethel Isabel Gladstone Nicol (*née* Fairley); *m* 1960; Jane Gillian Margaret Mann; one *s.* *Educ:* King's College School, Wimbledon; Durham Univ. (BSc). W. S. Atkins & Partners, 1960–67; Electricity Council, 1967–69; London Electricity Board, 1969–81; Dep. Chm., SE Electricity Board, 1981–87. Chairman: Trustees, NICEIC Pension Fund, 1986–93; South Western Enterprises, 1992–93. JP Surrey 1976. *Recreation:* Honourable Artillery Company. *Club:* Caledonian.

NICOL, Angus Sebastian Torquil Eyers; barrister; a Recorder of the Crown Court, 1982–98; *b* 11 April 1933; *s* of late Henry James Nicol and Phyllis Mary Eyers; *m* 1968, Eleanor Denise Brodrick; two *d.* *Educ:* RNC, Dartmouth. Served RN, 1947–56. Called to the Bar, Middle Temple, 1963. A Chairman: Disciplinary Cttee, Potato Marketing Bd, 1988–96; VAT and Duties (formerly VAT) Tribunal, 1988–; Adjudicator and Special Adjudicator, Immigration Appellate Authy, 1998–. Founder Vice-Chm. and Mem. Council, Monday Club, 1961–68. Lectr in Gaelic, Central London Adult Educn Inst., 1983–96; Sen. Steward, Argyllshire Gathering, 1983, 1998; Dir, 1981–, and Jt Sec., 1984–, Highland Soc. of London; Conductor, London Gaelic Choir, 1985–91; Chieftain of Clan MacNicol and Comr for all Territories of GB south of River Tweed, 1988–. FSA (Scot.). *Publications:* Gaelic poems and short stories in Gairm, etc. *Recreations:* music, Gaelic language and literature, shooting, fishing, sailing, gastronomy. *Address:* 5 Paper Buildings, Temple, EC4Y 7HB. *T:* (020) 7353 8494. *Club:* Royal Highland Yacht.

NICOL, Prof. Donald MacGillivray, FBA 1981; FKC 1980; Koraës Professor of Modern Greek and Byzantine History, Language and Literature, University of London,

King's College, 1970–88, now Emeritus; Vice Principal, King's College, 1980–81 (Assistant Principal, 1977–80); *b* 4 Feb. 1923; *s* of late Rev. George Manson Nicol and Mary Patterson (*née* MacGillivray); *m* 1950, Joan Mary Campbell, *d* of Sir Walter Campbell, KCIE; three *s*. *Educ:* King Edward VII Sch., Sheffield; St Paul's Sch., London; Pembroke Coll., Cambridge (MA, PhD). Friends' Ambulance Unit, 1942–46; Scholar at British Sch. of Archæology, Athens, 1949–50; Lectr in Classics, University Coll., Dublin, 1952–64; Vis. Fellow, Dumbarton Oaks, Washington, DC, 1964–65; Vis. Prof. of Byzantine History, Indiana Univ., 1965–66; Sen. Lectr and Reader in Byzantine History, Univ. of Edinburgh, 1966–70. Dir, Gennadius Library, Athens, 1989–92. Birkbeck Lectr, Cambridge, 1976–77. Pres., Ecclesiastical Hist. Soc., 1975–76. MRIA 1960; FRHistS 1971. Hon. Citizen of Arta, Greece, 1990. Editor, Byzantine and Modern Greek Studies, 1973–83. *Publications:* The Despotate of Epiros, 1957; Meteora, the Rock Monasteries of Thessaly, 1963, rev. edn, 1975; The Byzantine Family of Kantakouzenos (Cantacuzenus) ca 1100–1460: a genealogical and prosopographical study, 1968; The Last Centuries of Byzantium, 1261–1453, 1972, 2nd edn 1993; Byzantium: Its Ecclesiastical History and Relations with the Western World, 1972; Church and Society in the Last Centuries of Byzantium, 1979; The End of the Byzantine Empire, 1979; The Despotate of Epiros 1267–1479: a contribution to the history of Greece in the middle ages, 1984; Studies in Late Byzantine History and Prosopography, 1986; Byzantium and Venice: a study in diplomatic and cultural relations, 1988; Joannes Gennadios—The Man: a biographical sketch, 1990; A Biographical Dictionary of the Byzantine Empire, 1991; The Immortal Emperor: the life and legend of Constantine Palaiologos, last Emperor of the Romans, 1992; The Byzantine Lady: ten portraits 1250–1500, 1994; The Reluctant Emperor: a biography of John Cantacuzene, Byzantine emperor and monk, *c* 1295–1383, 1996; (ed and trans.) Theodore Spandounes, On the Origin of the Ottoman Emperors, 1997; articles in Byzantine, classical and historical jls. *Recreation:* bookbinding. *Address:* 4 Westberry Court, Pinehurst, Grange Road, Cambridge CB3 9BG. *T:* (01223) 360955.

NICOL, Dr Joseph Arthur Colin, FRS 1967; Professor of Zoology, University of Texas Institute of Marine Science, 1967–80, now Professor Emeritus; *b* 5 Dec. 1915; *s* of George Nicol and Noele Petrie; *m* 1941, Helen Wilhelmina Cameron; one *d*. *Educ:* Universities of McGill, Western Ontario and Oxford. BSc (hons Zool.) 1938, McGill; MA 1940, Western Ontario; DPhil 1947, DSc 1961, Oxford. Canadian Army, RCCS, 1941–45. Asst Professor in Zoology, University of British Columbia, 1947–49; Experimental Zoologist, Marine Biological Assoc., UK, 1949 (research on marine animals, comparative physiology, luminescence, vision, at Plymouth Laboratory, 1949–66). Guggenheim Fellow, Scripps Inst. Oceanography, 1953–54. Vis. Prof., Univ. of Texas, 1966–67. *Publications:* Biology of Marine Animals, 1960; Eyes of Fishes, 1989; papers on comparative physiology and anatomy in Jl Marine Biol. Assoc. UK, Proc. Royal Soc, Jl Exp. Biol., Biol. Review, etc. *Recreation:* English literature. *Address:* Ribby, Lerryn, Lostwithiel, Cornwall PL22 0PG. *T:* (01208) 872319.

NICOL, Dr Richard Charles, FREng, FIEE; Head of Research, BTexact Technologies (formerly British Telecommunications), since 1998; *b* 14 July 1948; *s* of George Nicol and Alice (*née* Ardley); *m* 1974, Rosemary Jane Greaves; one *s* one *d*. *Educ:* University Coll. London (BSc Eng; PhD 1976). FIEE 1994. Joined Post Office Res., 1970; British Telecommunications: Hd, Digital TV Res. Gp, 1976–80; Section Hd, Digital TV, 1980–88; Manager, Univ. Res. Prog., 1988–92; Divl Manager, Visual Telecomms, BT Labs, 1992–95. Dir, Suffolk Develt Agency, 2000–; Mem. Bd, Suffolk Learning and Skills Council, 2001–. Corp. Mem., Suffolk Coll., 1990. FREng 2000. *Recreations:* gardening, caravanning, football (Ipswich Town). *Address:* High Storrs, Hall Lane, Witnesham, Ipswich IP6 9HN. *T:* (01473) 785710. *Club:* Ipswich and Suffolk.

NICOL, William; *see* Nicol, A. W.

NICOLI, Eric Luciano; Chairman: EMI Group plc, since 1999; Tussauds Group, since 2001 (Director, since 1999); HMV Media Group plc, since 2001; *b* 5 Aug. 1950; *s* of Virgilio and Ida Nicoli; *m* 1977, Rosalind West; one *s* one *d*. *Educ:* Diss Grammar Sch.; King's College London (BSc Hons 1st class Physics). Marketing, Rowntree Mackintosh, 1972–80; United Biscuits: Marketing, 1980–83; Business Planning, 1984; Managing Dir, Frozen Food Div., 1985, Biscuit and Confectionery Div., 1986–88; Chief Exec., Europe, 1989–90; Gp Chief Exec., 1991–99. Dir, EMI Gp plc (formerly Thorn EMI plc), 1993–. Dep. Chm., BITC, 1991–. Chm., Per Cent Club, 1994–. Trustee, Comic Relief, 1999–. CIMgt. *Recreations:* music, sport, food. *Address:* EMI Group plc, 4 Tenterden Street, Hanover Square, W1A 2AY.

NICOLL, Douglas Robertson, CB 1980; retired; *b* 12 May 1920; *s* of James George Nicoll and Mabel Nicoll (*née* Styles); *m* 1st, 1949, Winifred Campion (*d* 1987); two *s*; 2nd, 1992, Mrs Cathryn Sansom. *Educ:* Merchant Taylors' School; St John's College, Oxford (MA 1946). FO (Govt Code & Cipher Sch., Bletchley Pk, deciphering German Enigma machine), 1941–45; FCO (GCHQ), 1946–80; Joint Services' Staff College, 1953; Under Secretary, 1977–80; Cabinet Office, 1980–81. *Publications:* contrib. to DNB and New DNB. *Recreations:* chess, bridge, National Hunt racing, politics. *Address:* c/o National Westminster Bank, 31 The Promenade, Cheltenham, Glos GL50 1LH. *Club:* Travellers.

NICOLL, Sir William, KCMG 1992 (CMG 1974); a Director General, Council of European Communities, 1982–91; *b* 28 June 1927; *s* of Ralph Nicoll and Christina Mowbray Nicoll (*née* Melville); *m* 1954, Helen Morison Martin; two *d*. *Educ:* Morgan Acad., Dundee; St Andrews Univ. Entered BoT, 1949; British Trade Comr, India, 1955–59; Private Sec. to Pres. of BoT, 1964–67; Commercial Inspector, FCO, 1967–69; DTI, 1969–72; Office of UK Perm. Rep. to European Communities, 1972–75; Under Sec., Dept of Prices and Consumer Protection, 1975–77; Dep. UK Rep. to EEC, 1977–82. Fulbright Fellow, George Mason Univ., Va, USA, 1991–92. Editor, European Business Jl, 1993–. Hon. LLD Dundee, 1983. *Publications:* (ed and contrib.) Competition Policy Enquiry, 1988; (with T. C. Salmon) Understanding the European Communities, 1990; (with T. C. Salmon) Understanding the New European Community, 1993; (ed jtly) Perspectives on European Business, 1995, 2nd edn 1998; (ed jtly) Europe 2000, 1996; Building European Union, 1997; Europe Beyond 2000, 1998; (with T. C. Salmon) Understanding European Union, 2000; contributed to: Government and Industry, ed W. Rodgers, 1986; The State of the EC, ed G. Rosendahl, 1993; Margaret Thatcher, Prime Minister Indomitable, ed W. Thompson, 1994; Maastricht and Beyond, ed A. N. Duff, 1994; The Council of the EU, ed M. Westlake, 1996; Britain, the Commonwealth and Europe, ed A. May; contribs to various jls on European subjects. *Address:* Outback, Nackington Road, Canterbury, Kent CT4 7AX. *T:* (01227) 456495.

NICOLLE, Anthony William, OBE 1991; consultant on banking supervision; *b* 13 April 1935; *s* of late Roland Nicolle and Dorothy May Pearce; *m* 1960, Josephine Anne (*née* Read); one *s* one *d*. *Educ:* Tiffin Sch.; King's Coll., London (LLB). Served RA, 1956–58. Joined Bank of England, 1958; seconded to NEDO, 1968–70; Econ. Intelligence Dept, 1970–77; seconded to Royal Commn on Distribn of Income and Wealth, 1974–75; banking supervision, 1977–80; Banking Dept, 1980–83; banking supervision, 1983–87; Comr of Banking, Hong Kong, 1987–91; Gen. Man. for Hong Kong and China, Standard Chartered Bank, 1991–94. Trustee, Psychiatry Res. Trust. *Recreations:* walking (a little), gardening (occasionally). *Address:* Upper Folds, Little Bognor, Fittleworth, Pulborough, W Sussex RH20 1JT. *Club:* Oriental.

NICOLLE, Frederick Villeneuve; FRCSCan; Consultant Plastic Surgeon, Hammersmith Hospital, since 1970; Senior Lecturer, University of London and Royal Postgraduate Medical School, since 1970; *b* 11 March 1931; *s* of Arthur Nicolle and Alice Nicolle (*née* Cobbold); *m* 1957, Helia Immaculata Stuart-Walker; one *s* two *d*. *Educ:* Eton; Trinity Coll., Cambridge (BA; MB BChir 1956; MChir 1970). FRCSCan 1963. McLaughlin Travelling Fellow, Canada, 1964; Consultant Plastic Surgeon, Montreal Gen. Hosp. and Montreal Children's Hosp., 1964–69; Lectr, McGill Univ., 1964–69; returned to UK, 1970; in private practice in aesthetic and reconstructive plastic surgery, 1970–. Vis. Prof. in Plastic Surgery, China, Syria, S America, SA, Australia, NZ and guest lectr in many countries. President: Brit. Assoc. Aesthetic Plastic Surgery, 1984–86 (Mem., 1980–); Chelsea Clinical Soc., 1986; Internat. Alpine Surgical Soc., 1996, 1997; Treas., Internat. Soc. Aesthetic Plastic Surgery, 1986–94 (Trustee, 1992–94); Member: Brit. Assoc. Plastic Surgery, 1966; Internat. Soc. Plastic Surgery, 1971; Amer. Soc. Aesthetic Plastic Surgery, 1982. *Publications:* The Care of the Rheumatoid Hand, 1975; Aesthetic Rhinoplasty, 1996; chaps in numerous text books of plastic and reconstructive surgery; contrib. British Jl Plastic Surgery and Jl Aesthetic Surgery. *Recreations:* painting, ski-ing, shooting, fishing, tennis. *Address:* 56 Eaton Place, SW1X 8AT. *T:* (020) 7235 6572. *Club:* White's.

NICOLLE, Dr Hilary Ann; JP; education management consultant, since 1998; Schools Adjudicator, Department for Education and Employment, since 1999; *b* 12 April 1945; *d* of A. H. and E. V. Upton; *m* 1st, 1970, Noël Leo Nicolle; two *s*; 2nd, 1985, Paul Newman Hudson Clokie; one step *s* one step *d*. *Educ:* Bromley High Sch.; St Hilda's Coll., Oxford (BA 1st Class Hons; MA); LSE (PhD); London Univ. (PGCE 1977). HM Diplomatic Service, 1967–70; PhD research and univ. lecturing, 1970–76; school teacher, 1977–82; Headmistress, Tiffin Girls' Sch., Kingston upon Thames, 1982–88; Dep. Dir of Educn, London Borough of Wandsworth, 1988–92; Chief Exec., Sch. Examinations and Assessment Council, 1992–93; Dir of Educn, London Bor. of Islington, 1993–98. JP Kent, 1999. *Recreations:* history, choral music, National Trust, gardening. *Address:* Gibbet Oak, Appledore Road, Tenterden, Kent TN30 7DH.

NICOLLE, Stéphanie Claire; QC (Jersey) 1995; HM Solicitor General for Jersey, since 1994; *b* 11 March 1948; *d* of Walter Arthur Nicolle and Madeleine Claire Nicolle (*née* Vitel). *Educ:* Convent of the Faithful Companions of Jesus, Jersey; St Aidan's Coll., Univ. of Durham. Called to the Bar, Gray's Inn, 1976; called to the Jersey Bar, 1978; Crown Advocate, 1986–94. *Publications:* (with P. Matthews) The Jersey Law of Property, 1991; The Origin and Development of Jersey Law, 1998. *Address:* Solicitor General's Chambers, Morier House, Halkett Place, St Helier, Jersey, Channel Islands JE1 1DD.

NICOLSON, family name of **Baron Carnock**.

NICOLSON, Nigel, OBE 2000 (MBE 1945); FSA; FRSL; author; Director of Weidenfeld and Nicolson Ltd, 1948–92; *b* 19 Jan. 1917; 2nd *s* of late Hon. Sir Harold Nicolson, KCVO, CMG and Hon. V. Sackville-West, CH; *heir-pres.* to 4th Baron Carnock, *qv*; *m* 1953, Philippa Janet (marr. diss. 1970; she *d* 1987), *d* of Sir Gervais Tennyson d'Eyncourt, 2nd Bt; one *s* two *d*. *Educ:* Eton Coll.; Balliol Coll., Oxford. Capt. Grenadier Guards. Served War of 1939–45 in Tunisian and Italian Campaigns (MBE). Contested (C) NW Leicester, 1950, and Falmouth and Camborne, 1951; MP (C) Bournemouth East and Christchurch, Feb. 1952–Sept. 1959. Chm. Exec. Cttee, UNA, 1961–66. Columnist: The Spectator, 1992–95; Sunday Telegraph, 1995–. *Publications:* The Grenadier Guards, 1939–45, 1949 (official history); People and Parliament, 1958; Lord of the Isles, 1960; Great Houses of Britain, 1965, revd edn 1978; (editor) Harold Nicolson: Diaries and Letters, 3 vols, 1966–68; Great Houses, 1968; Alex (FM Alexander of Tunis), 1973; Portrait of a Marriage, 1973; (ed) Letters of Virginia Woolf, 1975–80 (6 vols); The Himalayas, 1975; Mary Curzon, 1977 (Whitbread Award); Napoleon: 1812, 1985; (with Adam Nicolson) Two Roads to Dodge City, 1986; Kent, 1988; The World of Jane Austen, 1991; Vita and Harold: the letters of Vita Sackville-West and Harold Nicolson 1910–1962, 1992; Long Life (autobiog.), 1997; Virginia Woolf, 2000; Fanny Burney, 2002. *Recreation:* archæology. *Address:* Sissinghurst Castle, Cranbrook, Kent TN17 2AB. *T:* (01580) 714239. *Club:* Beefsteak.

NICOLSON, Roy Macdonald; Chief Executive, Scottish Amicable Life plc, since 1997; *b* 12 June 1944; *s* of Alan Neil Nicolson and Mary Nicolson; *m* 1972, Jennifer Margaret Miller; one *s* one *d*. *Educ:* Paisley Grammar School. FFA, FPMI. Joined Scottish Amicable, 1960; Asst London Secretary, 1971; Asst Actuary, 1973; Pensions Manager (Operations), 1976; Asst Gen. Manager (Pensions), 1982; Gen. Manager (Systems), 1985; Dep. Chief Gen. Manager, then Man. Dir, 1990. Director: J. Rothschild Assurance Hldgs, 1991–; St James's Place Capital, 1997–; Prudential Assurance Co., 1997–. Chm., Associated Scottish Life Offices, 1998–. *Recreations:* golf, bridge. *Address:* Scottish Amicable, Craigforth, PO Box 25, Stirling FK9 4UE; Ardgarten, Doune Road, Dunblane, Perthshire FK15 9HR. *T:* (01786) 823849.

NIEDUSZYŃSKI, Anthony John; Secretary to Monopolies and Mergers Commission, 1993–96; *b* 7 Jan. 1939; *er s* of Tadeusz Adolf Antoni Nieduszyński, LLD and Madaleine Gladys Lilian (*née* Huggler); *m* 1980, Frances, *yr d* of Wing Comdr Max Oxford, OBE; one *d*. *Educ:* St Paul's School (Foundation Scholar); Merton College, Oxford (Postmaster; 1st cl. Hon. Mods 1959; 1st cl. Lit Hum 1961; MA). Board of Trade, 1964; Private Sec. to Pres. of BoT, 1967–68; Principal Private Sec. to Minister for Trade and Consumer Affairs, 1972–74 and to Sec. of State for Trade, 1974; Asst Sec., Dept of Prices and Consumer Protection, 1974, Dept of Industry, 1977, Home Office, 1982; Under Sec., DTI, 1985–93; Head: of Radiocommunications Div., 1985; of Air Div., 1988; of Business Task Forces Div. 2, 1990; of Aerospace Div., 1992. *Recreations:* gardening, fell walking, linguistics, opera. *Address:* 8 Walpole Gardens, Twickenham, Mddx TW2 5SJ.

NIELSEN, Aksel Christopher W.; *see* Wiin-Nielsen.

NIELSEN, Hon. Erik H., DFC; PC (Can.) 1984; QC (Can.) 1962; Principal, Solar Electric Engineering Distributors, Canada, since 1992; President: Solar Electric Engineering Hawaii Inc., since 1993; Electricycle Inc., since 1994; *b* 24 Feb. 1924; *m* 1st, Pamela Hall (*d* 1969); three *c*; 2nd, 1983, Shelley Coxford. *Educ:* Dalhousie Univ. (LLB). Royal Canadian Air Force, 1942–51; flew Lancaster bombers, War of 1939–45. Called to the Bar of Nova Scotia, 1951; legal practice in Whitehorse, Yukon, 1952–. MP (PC) Yukon, 1957–87; Minister of Public Works, 1979–80; Dep. Opposition House Leader, Opposition House Leader, Leader of the Opposition, and Dep. Leader of the Opposition, 1980–84; Dep. Leader, Progressive Cons. Party, 1983; Dep. Prime Minister and Pres. of the Queen's Privy Council for Canada, 1984–85; Minister of Nat. Defence, 1985–86. Pres., Canadian Transport Commn, 1987; Chm., Nat. Transportation Agency of Canada, 1987–92. Dep. House Leader, 1980–81; Opposition appts, 1981–83. Caucus Chm., Cttee on Govt Planning and Orgn, 1983–84. Chm., Ministerial Task Force on Program Review (report published, 1985). Member: Canadian Bar Assoc; Yukon Law Soc.; NS Barristers' Soc.; Hon. Mem., Whitehorse Chamber of Commerce; Hon. Life Mem., Yukon

Chamber of Mines. *Publication:* The House is Not a Home, 1989. *Address:* MSPO PO Box 31024, Whitehorse, YT Y1A 5P7, Canada.

NIELSON, Poul; Member, European Commission, since 1999; *b* 11 April 1943; *s* of Svend and Esther Nielson; *m* 1967, Anne-Marie Jørgensen; one *s* two *d*. *Educ:* Århus Univ. (Masters degree in Political Sci. 1972). Nat. Chm., Social Democratic Student Movt, 1966–67; Chm., Foreign Affairs Cttee, SDP, 1974–79. MP (SDP) Denmark, 1971–73, 1977–84, 1986–99; Minister of Energy, 1979–82; Minister for Develt Co-operation, 1994–99. Head of Section, Min. of Foreign Affairs, 1974–79, 1984–85; Cons. in Public Mgt, Danish Admin. Sch., 1985–86; Investment Cons., Danish Wage Earner Pensions Fund, 1985–88; Man. Dir, LD Energi A/S, 1988–94; Mem., Bd of Dirs, Denerco, Danop, Vestas and other cos, 1986–94. Polio Eradication Champion Award, Rotary Internat., 1999. *Publications:* Power Play and Security, 1968; The Company Act and the Wage Earners, 1974; Politicians and Civil Servants, 1987. *Recreations:* photography, literature, music, gardening. *Address:* c/o European Commission, Rue de la Loi 200, 1049 Brussels, Belgium.

NIEMEYER, Oscar; architect; *b* Rio de Janeiro, 15 Dec. 1907; *s* of Oscar Niemeyer Soares; *m* Anita Niemeyer; one *d*. *Educ:* Escola Nacional de Beles Artes, Univ. of Brazil. Joined office of Lúcio Costa, 1935; worked on Min. of Education and Health Building, Rio de Janeiro, Brazilian Pavilion, NY World Fair, etc., 1936–41. Major projects include: Pamphulha, Belo Horizonte, 1941–43; also Quintandinha, Petrópolis; Exhibition Hall, São Paulo, 1953; Brasilia (Dir of Architecture), 1957–. Brazilian Rep., UN Bd of Design Consultants, 1947. Lenin Peace Prize, 1963; Prix Internat. de l'Architecture Aujourd'hui, 1966; Royal Gold Medal for Architecture, RIBA, 1998. *Publication:* The Curves of Time: the memoirs of Oscar Niemeyer, 2001. *Address:* 3940 avenida Atlântica, Rio de Janeiro, Brazil.

NIENOW, Prof. Alvin William, FREng; Professor of Biochemical Engineering, University of Birmingham, since 1989; *b* 19 June 1937; *o s* of late Alvin William Nienow and Mary May Nienow (*née* Hawthorn); *m* 1959, Helen Mary Sparkes; two *s* one *d*. *Educ:* St Clement Danes Grammar Sch.; University Coll. London (BSc Eng, 1st Cl. Hons; PhD; DSc Eng). FIChemE; CEng, FREng (FEng 1985). Industry, 1958–61; Lectr and Sen. Lectr, 1963–80, Hon. Res. Fellow, 1980–, Dept of Chem. and Biochem. Engineering, UCL; University of Birmingham: Prof. of Chem. Engineering, 1980–89; Dir, SERC, later BBSRC, Centre for Biochem. Engrg, 1989–2000. Vis. Prof., Fellow and Lectr, China and Japan; Eminent Speaker, IEAust, 1999. Member: AFRC, 1987–90; Biotechnol. Directorate, SERC, 1990–93; Engrg Bd, SERC, then EPSRC, 1991–94; Planning and Resources Bd, BBSRC, 1994–96; Council, IChemE, 1984–89; Scientific Adv. Cttee, EFCE, 1987–94; Standing Cttee for Engrg, Royal Acad. of Engrg, 1996–98; Internat. Adv. Bd, Inst. of Chemical Process Fundamentals, Acad. of Scis, Czech Republic, 1996–; numerous other scientific and engrg bodies. Consultant: BHR Gp Fluid Mixing Processes, 1985–; Rhône-Poulenc Conseil Technologique, 1988–2000 (Pres., 1998–2000). Mem., Governing Body, Silsoe Res. Inst., 1996–98. Ed. (Europe and Africa), Jl Chem. Engrg, Japan, 2001. Moulton Medal, 1984, Donald Medal, 2000, IChemE; Jan E. Purkyne Medal, Czech Acad. of Science, 1993. *Publications:* (jtly) Mixing in the Process Industries, 1985, 2nd edn revised 1997; (ed) 3rd International Conference on Bioreactor and Bioprocess Fluid Dynamics, 1993, 4th International Conference, 1997; numerous papers on mixing, fluidisation and biochem. engrg in learned jls. *Recreations:* sport, travel, dancing, music, real ale. *Address:* School of Chemical Engineering, University of Birmingham, Edgbaston, Birmingham B15 2TT. *T:* (0121) 414 5325. *Clubs:* Athenæum, MCC; Edgbaston Priory, Reading Cricket.

NIGERIA, Metropolitan Archbishop and Primate of, since 1988; **Most Rev. Joseph Abiodun Adetiloye;** Bishop of Lagos, since 1985. *Educ:* Melville Hall, Ibadan; King's Coll., London (BD); Wycliffe Hall, Oxford. Ordained, dio. of Lagos, 1954; Bossey Ecumenical Inst., 1961–62; Lectr, 1962, Vice Principal, 1963–66, Immanuel Coll., Ibadan; Provost, Ibadan Cathedral, 1966–70; Bishop of Ekiti, 1970–85. Mem., Eames Commn; Chm., Anglican Encounter in the South, 1994–. DD Gen. Theol. Seminary, NY, 1993. *Address:* PO Box 13 (Bishopscourt, 29 Marina), Lagos, Nigeria. *Fax:* (1) 2636026, 2635681.

NIGHTINGALE, Benedict; *see* Nightingale, W. B. H.

NIGHTINGALE, Sir Charles (Manners Gamaliel), 17th Bt *cr* 1628; Grade 7, Department of Health, since 1996; *b* 21 Feb. 1947; *s* of Sir Charles Athelstan Nightingale, 16th Bt, and Evelyn Nadine Frances (*d* 1995), *d* of late Charles Arthur Diggens; *S* father, 1977. *Educ:* St Paul's School. BA Hons Open Univ., 1990. Entered DHSS as Executive Officer, 1969; Higher Executive Officer, 1977; Sen. Exec. Officer, DoH, 1989. *Heir: cousin* Edward Lacy George Nightingale, *b* 11 May 1938. *Address:* 16 Unity Grove, Harrogate HG1 2AQ.

NIGHTINGALE, Sir John (Cyprian), Kt 1975; CBE 1970; BEM 1941; QPM 1965; DL; Chief Constable, Essex, 1962–69 and 1974–78, retired (Essex and Southend-on-Sea Joint Constabulary, 1969–74); *b* 16 Sept. 1913; *s* of Herbert Paul Nightingale, Sydenham, London; *m* 1947, Patricia Mary, *d* of Norman Maclaren, Glasgow University. *Educ:* Cardinal Vaughan Sch., Kensington; University Coll., London. Joined Metropolitan Police, 1935; Asst Chief Constable, Essex, 1958. Chm., Police Council, 1976–78; Mem., Parole Bd, 1978–82. Served with RNVR, 1943–45. DL Essex 1975. *Publications:* various police pubns. *Address:* The Hoppet Barn, Chapel Lane, Little Baddow, Essex CM3 4BD.

NIGHTINGALE, Nicholas John; Secretary General, World Alliance of YMCAs, since 1999; *b* 29 Aug. 1942; *s* of late Christopher, (Toby), and of Muriel, (Buster), Nightingale; *m* 1968, Sue Lyth (Rev. Sue Nightingale); one *s* two *d* (and one *d* decd). *Educ:* Brighton, Hove and Sussex GS; Trinity Coll., Dublin (BA, LLB 1964); Harvard Business Sch. (AMP 1983). Qualified as solicitor, 1968; Solicitor, Slaughter & May, 1970–74; Partner, Patterson Glenton & Stracey, 1974; Solicitor and Co. Sec., Rowntree Mackintosh, 1975–85; Exec. Dir, Rowntree plc, 1985–89; Co. Sec., Tate & Lyle, 1989–93; Nat. Sec., YMCA England (formerly Nat. Council, YMCAs), 1993–98. Director: Tom Smith Crackers, 1983–85; Original Cookie Co., 1985–89; Cookie Jar, 1989–98; Ellis Patents, 1990–. Chm., Service 9, Bristol Council of Social Service, 1966–70; Treas., YMCA Metropolitan Reg., 1992–93. Vice Chm., Yorks Rural Community Council, 1985–89. *Recreations:* family life, walking, cycling, gardening, tennis. *Address:* World Alliance of YMCAs, 12 Clos-Belmont, 1208 Geneva, Switzerland. *T:* (22) 8495112.

NIGHTINGALE, Roger Daniel; economist and strategist; *b* 5 June 1945; *s* of Douglas Daniel John Nightingale and Edna Kathleen Vincent; one *s* three *d*. *Educ:* Welwyn Garden City Grammar Sch.; Keele Univ. (BA double hons Maths and Econs); University Coll. London (MSc Stats). Economist, Hoare & Co., 1968; Datastream, 1972, Dir, 1975; Hoare Govett, 1976, Dir, 1980; Head of Economics and Strategy Dept, Smith New Court, 1988–90; founded Roger Nightingale & Associates, consultancy firm, 1990. *Publications:* articles in financial magazines and newspapers. *Recreations:* snooker, collecting dictionaries, European history. *Address:* 22 Lonsdale Road, Chiswick, W4 1ND. *Club:* Reform.

NIGHTINGALE, (William) Benedict (Herbert); theatre critic, The Times, since 1990; *b* 14 May 1939; *s* of late Ronald Nightingale and Hon. Evelyn Nightingale, *d* of 1st Baron Burghclere; *m* 1964, Anne Bryan Redmon; two *s* one *d*. *Educ:* Charterhouse Sch.; Magdalene College, Cambridge (BA Hons); Univ. of Pennsylvania. General writer and northern drama critic, The Guardian, 1963–66; Literary Editor, New Society, 1966–68; theatre critic, New Statesman, 1968–86; Sunday theatre critic, New York Times, 1983–84; Prof. of English, Theatre and Drama, Univ. of Michigan, 1986–89. Mem., Drama Panel, and New Writing Cttee, Arts Council, 1975–80. Gov., Goldsmiths' Coll., 1978–81. *Publications:* Charities, 1973; Fifty Modern British Plays, 1981; Fifth Row Center, 1985; The Future of the Theatre, 1998. *Address:* 40 Broomhouse Road, SW6 3QX. *Club:* Garrick.

NIKLASSON, Birgit, (Fru Bertil Niklasson); *see* Nilsson, B.

NIKOLAYEVA-TERESHKOVA, Valentina Vladimirovna; *see* Tereshkova.

NILSSON, Birgit, (Fru Bertil Niklasson); Swedish operatic soprano; *b* Karup, Kristianstadslaen, 17 May 1918; *d* of Nils Svensson; *m* 1948, Bertil Niklasson. *Educ:* Stockholm Royal Academy of Music. Debut as singer, 1946; with Stockholm Opera, 1947–51. Has sung at Glyndebourne, 1951; Bayreuth, 1953, 1954, 1957–70; Munich, 1954; Hollywood Bowl, Buenos Aires, Florence, 1956; La Scala, Milan, 1958; Covent Garden, 1957, 1960, 1962, 1963, 1973 and 1977; Edinburgh, 1959; Metropolitan, New York, 1959; Moscow, 1964; also in most leading opera houses and festivals of the world. Particularly well-known for her Wagnerian rôles. Austrian Kammersängerin, 1968; Bavarian Kammersängerin, 1970. Hon. Professor: Swedish Govt, 1998; Royal Music Sch., Stockholm, 2000. Hon. RAM, 1970; Hon. Mem., Vienna Philharmonic Orch., 1999. Hon. Dr: Andover Univ., Mass, 1970; Manhattan Sch. of Music, NY, 1982; East Lansing Univ. of Fine Arts, Mich, 1982; Sibelius Acad., Helsinki, 1997. Swedish Royal Acad. of Music's Medal for Promotion of Art of Music, 1968; Swedish Golden Medal (cl. 18 *illis quorum*) (only lady to be so honoured). Comdr of the Vasa Order (1st cl.), Sweden, 1974. Comdr des Arts et des Lettres, France, 1991. *Address:* Box 527, 10130 Stockholm, Sweden.

NIMMO SMITH, Hon. Lord; William Austin Nimmo Smith; a Senator of the College of Justice in Scotland, since 1996; *b* 6 Nov. 1942; *s* of Dr Robert Herman Nimmo Smith and Mrs Ann Nimmo Smith; *m* 1968, Jennifer Main; one *s* one *d*. *Educ:* Eton Coll. (King's Scholar, 1956); Balliol Coll., Oxford (BA Hons Lit. Hum. 1965); Edinburgh Univ. (LLB 1967). Admitted to Faculty of Advocates, 1969; Standing Junior Counsel to Dept of Employment, 1977–82; QC (Scot.) 1982; Advocate-Depute, 1983–86; Temp. Judge, Court of Session, 1995–96. Chairman: Medical Appeal Tribunals, 1986–91; Vaccine Damage Tribunals, 1986–91; Mem. (part-time), Scottish Law Commn, 1988–96. Chm. Council, Cockburn Assoc. (Edinburgh Civic Trust), 1996–2001. *Recreations:* mountaineering, music. *Address:* Parliament House, Parliament Square, Edinburgh EH1 1RQ. *Club:* New (Edinburgh).

NIND, Philip Frederick, OBE 1979; TD 1946; Director, Foundation for Management Education, 1968–83; Secretary, Council of Industry for Management Education, 1969–83; *b* 2 Jan. 1918; *s* of W. W. Nind, CIE; *m* 1944, Fay Allardice Crofton (*née* Errington) (*d* 1991); two *d*. *Educ:* Blundell's Sch.; Balliol Coll., Oxford (MA). War service, 1939–46, incl. Special Ops in Greece and Albania (despatches), 1943–44, Mil. Govt Berlin, 1945–46 (Major). Shell Gp of Cos in Venezuela, Cyprus, Lebanon, Jordan and London, 1939–68. Educn and Trng Cttee, CBI (formerly FBI), 1961–68; OECD Working Gp on Management Educn, 1966–69; Nat. Adv. Council on Educn for Industry and Commerce, 1967–70; UGC Management Studies Cttee, 1968–83; NEDO Management Educn Trng and Develt Cttee, 1968–83; Chm., NEDO Management Teacher Panel, 1969–72; Member: Council for Techn. Educn and Trng for Overseas Countries, 1970–75; CNAA Management Studies Bd, 1971–83; Vice-Pres., European Foundn for Management Develt, 1978–83. Member: Oxford Univ. Appts Cttee, 1967–83; Grand Council, Royal Academy of Dancing, 1988– (Mem. Exec. Cttee, 1970–88); Governor: Univ. of Keele, 1961–; Bedford Coll., London Univ., 1967–85. Hon. Fellow, London Business School, 1988. FRSA. Chevalier, Order of Cedars of Lebanon, 1959; Grand Cross, Orders of St Mark and Holy Sepulchre, 1959. *Publications:* (jtly) Management Education and Training Needs of Industry, 1963; Fourth Stockton Lecture, 1973; A Firm Foundation, 1985; Never a Dull Moment, 1991; articles in various jls. *Club:* Special Forces.

NINEHAM, Rev. Prof. Dennis Eric, DD (Oxon); BD (Cantab); Hon. DD (Birmingham); Hon. DD (BDS Yale); Professor of Theology and Head of Theology Department, Bristol University, 1980–86, now Emeritus; Honorary Canon of Bristol Cathedral, 1980–86, now Emeritus; *b* 27 Sept. 1921; *o c* of Stanley Martin and Bessie Edith Nineham, Shirley, Southampton; *m* 1946, Ruth Corfield, *d* of Rev. A. P. Miller; two *s* two *d*. *Educ:* King Edward VI Sch., Southampton; Queen's Coll., Oxford (Hon. Fellow, 1991). Asst Chaplain of Queen's Coll., 1944; Chaplain, 1945; Fellow and Praelector, 1946; Tutor, 1949; Prof. of Biblical and Historical Theology, Univ. of London (King's Coll.), 1954–58; Prof. of Divinity, Univ. of London, 1958–64; Regius Prof. of Divinity, Cambridge Univ., and Fellow, Emmanuel Coll., 1964–69; Warden of Keble Coll., Oxford, 1969–79, Hon. Fellow, 1980. FKC 1963. Examining Chaplain: to Archbishop of York and to Bishop of Ripon; to Bishop of Sheffield, 1947–54; to Bishop of Norwich, 1964–73; to Bishop of Bristol, 1981–. Select Preacher to Univ. of Oxford, 1954–56, 1971, 1990, 1992, 1994, and to Univ. of Cambridge, 1959; Proctor in Convocation of Canterbury: for London Univ., 1955–64; for Cambridge Univ., 1965–69. Mem. General Synod of Church of England for Oxford Univ., 1970–76; Mem., C of E Doctrine Commn, 1968–76. Roian Fleck Resident-in-Religion, Bryn Mawr Coll., Pa, 1974; Provost's Visitor, Trinity Coll., Toronto, 1992; Vis. Prof., Rikkyo Univ., Tokyo, 1994. Governor of Haileybury, 1966–93. *Publications:* The Study of Divinity, 1960; A New Way of Looking at the Gospels, 1962; Commentary on St Mark's Gospel, 1963; The Use and Abuse of the Bible, 1976; Explorations in Theology, no 1, 1977; Christianity Mediaeval and Modern, 1993; (Editor) Studies in the Gospels: Essays in Honour of R. H. Lightfoot, 1955; The Church's Use of the Bible, 1963; The New English Bible Reviewed, 1965; contrib. to: Studies in Ephesians (editor F. L. Cross), 1956; On the Authority of the Bible, 1960; Religious Education, 1944–1984, 1966; Theologians of Our Time, 1966; Christian History and Interpretation, 1967; Christ for us To-day, 1968; Christian Believing, 1976; The Myth of God Incarnate, 1977; Imagination and the Future, 1980; God's Truth, 1988; A Dictionary of Biblical Interpretation, 1990; Resurrection, 1994. *Recreations:* reading, walking. *Address:* 9 Fitzherbert Close, Iffley, Oxford OX4 4EN. *T:* (01865) 715941.

See also Very Rev. J. H. Drury.

NINIS, Ven. Richard Betts; Archdeacon of Lichfield (formerly Stafford) and Treasurer of Lichfield Cathedral, 1974–98; *b* 25 Oct. 1931; *s* of late George Woodward Ninis and Mary Gertrude Ninis; *m* 1967, Penelope Jane Harwood; two *s* one *d*. *Educ:* Lincoln Coll., Oxford (MA); Bishop's Hostel, Lincoln (GOE). Curate, All Saints, Poplar, 1955–62; Vicar of: St Martins, Hereford, 1962–71; Bullinghope and Dewsall with Callow, 1966–71. Diocesan Missioner for Hereford, 1971–74. Chm., USPG, 1988–91. Chm., Derbyshire

Coll. of Higher Educn, 1978–90; Vice Chm., Univ. of Derby, 1992–98. Hon. Dr Derby, 1999. *Recreations:* gardening, travel. *Address:* Hillview, 32 Robert Street, Williton, Taunton, Som TA4 4QA.

NIRENBERG, Dr Marshall Warren; Research Biochemist; Chief, Laboratory of Biochemical Genetics, National Heart, Lung and Blood Institute, National Institutes of Health, Bethesda, Md, since 1966; *b* New York, 10 April 1927; *m* 1961, Perola Zaltzman; no *c. Educ:* Univs of Florida (BS, MS) and Michigan (PhD). Univ. of Florida: Teaching Asst, Zoology Dept, 1945–50; Res. Associate, Nutrition Lab., 1950–52; Univ. of Michigan: Teaching and Res. Fellow, Biol Chemistry Dept, 1952–57; Nat. Insts of Health, Bethesda: Postdoctoral Fellow of Amer. Cancer Soc., Nat. Inst. Arthritis and Metabolic Diseases, 1957–59, and of Public Health Service, Section of Metabolic Enzymes, 1959–60; Research Biochemist, Section of Metabolic Enzymes, 1960–62 and Section of Biochem. Genetics, 1962–66. Member: Amer. Soc. Biol Chemists; Amer. Chem. Soc.; Amer. Acad. Arts and Sciences; Biophys. Soc.; Nat. Acad. Sciences; Washington Acad. Sciences; Sigma Xi; Soc. for Study of Development and Growth; (Hon.) Harvey Soc.; Leopoldina Deutsche Akademie der Naturforscher; Neurosciences Research Program, MIT; NY Acad. Sciences; Pontifical Acad. Science, 1974. Robbins Lectr, Pomona Coll., 1967; Remsden Mem. Lectr, Johns Hopkins Univ., 1967. Numerous awards and prizes, including Nobel Prize in Medicine or Physiology (jtly), 1968. Hon. Dr Science: Michigan, Yale, and Chicago, 1965; Windsor, 1966; Harvard Med. Sch., 1968; Hon. PhD, Weitzmann Inst. of Science, Israel, 1978. *Publications:* numerous contribs to learned jls and chapters in symposia. *Address:* NIH Laboratory of Biochemical Genetics, Building 36, Bethesda, MD 20892, USA; 7001 Orkney Parkway, Bethesda, MD, USA.

NISBET, Prof. Hugh Barr; Professor of Modern Languages, University of Cambridge, since 1982; Professorial Fellow, Sidney Sussex College, since 1982; *b* 24 Aug. 1940; *s* of Thomas Nisbet and Lucy Mary Hainsworth; *m* 1st, 1962, Monika Luise Ingeborg Uecker (marr. diss. 1981); two *s*; 2nd, 1995, Angela Maureen Parker (*née* Chapman). *Educ:* Dollar Acad.; Univ. of Edinburgh. MA, PhD 1965. University of Bristol: Asst Lectr in German, 1965–67; Lectr, 1967–72; Reader, 1972–73; Prof. of German Lang. and Lit., Univ. of St Andrews, 1974–81. Mem., Gen. Teaching Council for Scotland, 1978–81. Pres., British Soc. for Eighteenth Century Studies, 1986–88. Governor, Dollar Acad., 1978–81. Jt Editor, Cambridge Studies in German, 1983–; Germanic Editor, 1973–80, Gen. Editor, 1981–84, Modern Language Rev. *Publications:* Herder and the Philosophy and History of Science, 1970; (ed with Hans Reiss) Goethe's Die Wahlverwandtschaften, 1971; Goethe and the Scientific Tradition, 1972; (ed) German Aesthetic and Literary Criticism: Winckelmann to Goethe, 1985; (ed with Claude Rawson) Cambridge History of Literary Criticism, 9 vols, 1989–; (ed with John Hibberd) Texte, Motive und Gestalten der Goethezeit, 1989; (ed with D. E. D. Beales) Sidney Sussex College, Cambridge: historical essays, 1996; (ed with Laurence Dickey) Hegel's Political Writings, 1999; *translations:* Kant, Political Writings, 1970, 2nd edn 1991; Hegel, Lectures on the Philosophy of World History, 1975, 2nd edn 1980; Hegel, Elements of the Philosophy of Right, 1991; Hegel, Political Writings, 1999; articles and reviews on German literature and thought. *Recreations:* music, art history. *Address:* Sidney Sussex College, Cambridge CB2 3HU. *T:* (01223) 338877.

NISBET, Prof. John Donald, OBE 1981; MA, BEd, PhD; FEIS; Professor of Education, Aberdeen University, 1963–88; *b* 17 Oct. 1922; *s* of James Love Nisbet and Isabella Donald; *m* 1952, Brenda Sugden; one *s* one *d. Educ:* Dunfermline High Sch.; Edinburgh Univ. (MA, BEd); PhD (Aberdeen); Teacher's Certif. (London). FEIS 1975; Royal Air Force, 1943–46. Teacher, Fife, 1946–48; Lectr, Aberdeen Univ., 1949–63. Editor: British Jl of Educnl Psychology, 1967–74; Studies in Higher Education, 1979–84; Chairman: Educnl Research Bd, SSRC, 1972–75; Cttee on Primary Educn, 1974–80; Scottish Council for Research in Educn, 1975–78; President: British Educnl Research Assoc., 1975; Scottish Inst. of Adult and Continuing Educn, 1991. *Publications:* Family Environment, 1953; Age of Transfer to Secondary Education, 1966; Transition to Secondary Education, 1969; Scottish Education Looks Ahead, 1969; Educational Research Methods, 1970; Educational Research in Action, 1972; Impact of Research, 1980; Towards Community Education, 1980; (ed) World Yearbook of Education, 1985; Learning Strategies, 1986; Curriculum Reform: assessment in question, 1993; Educational Disadvantage, 1994; Pipers and Tunes: a decade of educational research in Scotland, 1995; papers in jls on educnl psychology and curriculum develt. *Recreations:* golf, orienteering. *Address:* 7 Lawson Avenue, Banchory AB31 5TW. *T:* (01330) 823145.

See also S. D. Nisbet.

NISBET, Prof. Robin George Murdoch, FBA 1967; Corpus Christi Professor of Latin, Oxford, 1970–92; Fellow of Corpus Christi College, Oxford, 1952–92, Hon. Fellow 1992; *b* 21 May 1925; *s* of R. G. Nisbet, Univ. Lecturer, and A. T. Husband; *m* 1969, Anne, *d* of Dr J. A. Wood. *Educ:* Glasgow Academy; Glasgow Univ.; Balliol Coll., Oxford (Snell Exhibitioner; Hon. Fellow, 1989). Tutor in Classics, Corpus Christi College, Oxford, 1952–70. Kenyon Medal, British Acad., 1997. *Publications:* Commentary on Cicero, *in Pisonem*; 1961; (with M. Hubbard) on Horace, *Odes I*, 1970; *Odes II*, 1978; Collected Papers on Latin Literature, 1995. *Recreation:* 20th century history. *Address:* 80 Abingdon Road, Cumnor, Oxford OX2 9QW. *T:* (01865) 862482.

NISBET, Prof. Stanley Donald; Professor of Education, University of Glasgow, 1951–78; *b* 26 July 1912; *s* of Dr J. L. and Isabella Nisbet; *m* 1942, Helen Alison Smith; one *s* one *d. Educ:* Dunfermline High Sch., Edinburgh Univ. MA (1st Cl. Hons Classics), 1934; Diploma in Education, 1935; BEd (with distinction in Education and Psychology), 1940. Taught in Moray House Demonstration Sch., Edinburgh, 1935–39. Served War in RAF, 1940–46; research officer at Air Ministry, 1944–46. Lecturer in Education, Univ. of Manchester, Feb.-Sept. 1946; Prof. of Education, Queen's Univ. of Belfast, 1946–51. FRSE 1955; FEIS 1976. *Publications:* Purpose in the Curriculum, 1957; (with B. L. Napier) Promise and Progress, 1970; articles in psychological and educational journals. *Recreations:* walking, sailing, Esperanto. *Address:* 6 Victoria Park Corner, Glasgow G14 9NZ.

See also J. D. Nisbet.

NISBET-SMITH, Dugal, CBE 1996; Director, Newspaper Society, 1983–97; *b* 6 March 1935; *s* of David and Margaret Homeward Nisbet-Smith; *m* 1959, Dr Ann Patricia Taylor; one *s* two *d. Educ:* Southland Boys' High Sch., Invercargill, NZ. Journalist on Southland Daily News, NZ, 1952–56; Features writer and reporter, Beaverbrook Newspapers, London, 1956–60; variously Asst Editor, Gen. Manager and Man. Dir, Barbados Advocate Co., Barbados, WI, Gen. Manager, Sierra Leone Daily Mail Ltd, W Africa, Dep. Gen. Manager, Trinidad Mirror Co., 1960–66; Sen. Industrial Relations Manager, Mirror Gp Newspapers, London, 1966–68; Develt Manager, 1969–71, Production Dir, 1971–73, Man. Dir, 1974–78, Scottish Daily Record and Sunday Mail Ltd, Glasgow; joined Bd, Mirror Gp Newspapers, 1976; Dir/General Manager, 1978–80, Man. Dir, 1980–81, Times Newspapers Ltd; Publishing Advr to HH the Aga Khan, Aiglemont, France, 1981–83. *Recreations:* travel, sculpture, painting. *Address:* The Butterfly, Borough Lane, Great Finborough, Stowmarket, Suffolk IP14 3AS. *T:* (01449) 774286.

NISSAN, Prof. Alfred Heskel, PhD, DSc (Chem. Eng, Birmingham), FIChemE, FAIChE, FAIC; Member Sigma XI; Consultant to WESTVACO (formerly West Virginia Pulp and Paper), New York (Vice-President, 1967–79, and Corporate Director of Research, 1962–79); Professor, College of Environmental Science and Forestry, Syracuse, New York, since 1979; *b* 14 Feb. 1914; *s* of Heskel and Farha Nissan, Baghdad, Iraq; *m* 1940, Zena Gladys Phyllis, *o d* of late Phillip and Lillian Frances Pursehouse-Ahmed, Birmingham; one *d. Educ:* The American Sch. for Boys, Baghdad, Iraq; Univ. of Birmingham. Instn of Petroleum Scholarship, 1936; first cl. Hons BSc 1937; Sir John Cadman Medal, 1937; Instn of Petroleum Medal and Prize and Burgess Prize, 1937; Research Fellow, 1937, Lectr, 1940, Univ. of Birmingham; Head of Central Research Laboratories, Bowater Paper Corporation Ltd, 1947; Technical Director in charge of Research, Bowaters Development and Research Ltd, 1950; Research Prof. of Wool Textile Engineering, the Univ. of Leeds, 1953; Prof. of Chemical Engineering, Rensselaer Polytechnic Inst., Troy, NY, USA, 1957. Hon. Vis. Prof., Uppsala Univ., 1974; ERCO Res. Fellow, Univ. of Toronto, 1987. Schwarz Memorial Lectr, Amer. Soc. of Mech. Engrs, 1967; Dow Dist. Lectr, Univ. of British Columbia, 1989. Member: Adv. Council for Advancement of Industrial R&D, State of NY, 1965–; Board of Directors: Technical Assoc. of Pulp & Paper Industry, 1968–71 (R&D Div. Award, 1976); Industrial Res. Inst., 1973–77. Bd of Trustees, Amer. Inst. of Chemists Foundn, 1989–91. Alexander Mitscherlich Medal, Zellcheming, W Germany, 1980; Gold Medal, Technical Assoc. of Pulp and Paper Industry, 1982. *Publications:* (ed) Textile Engineering Processes, 1959; (ed) Future Technical Needs and Trends in the Paper Industry, 1973; Lectures on Fiber Science in Paper, 1977; papers on physical chemistry and chemical engineering problems of petroleum, paper and textile technology in scientific jls. *Address:* 6A Dickel Road, Scarsdale, NY 10583, USA.

NISSEN, David Edgar Joseph, CB 1999; Solicitor and Director General Legal Services, Department of Trade and Industry, since 1997; *b* 27 Nov. 1942; *s* of Tunnock Edgar Nissen and Elsie Nissen (*née* Thorne); *m* 1969, Pauline Jennifer (*née* Meaden); two *d. Educ:* King's School, Chester; University College London (LLB). Solicitor, admitted 1969. Asst Solicitor, W Midlands Gas Board, 1969–70; Prosecuting Solicitor, Sussex Police Authority, 1970–73; HM Customs and Excise, 1973–90: Asst Solicitor, 1983–87; Principal Asst Solicitor, 1987–90; Legal Advr to Dept of Energy (Principal Asst Treasury Solicitor), 1990–92; Solicitor to HM Customs and Excise, 1992–95; Legal Advr to Home Office, 1995–97. *Recreations:* photography, music, gardening. *Address:* c/o Department of Trade and Industry, 10 Victoria Street, SW1H 0NN.

NISSEN, George Maitland, CBE 1987; Chairman, Book Guild Ltd, since 1993; *b* 29 March 1930; *s* of Col Peter Norman Nissen, DSO, and Lauretta Maitland; *m* 1956, Jane Edmunds, *d* of late S. Curtis Bird, New York; two *s* two *d. Educ:* Eton; Trinity Coll., Cambridge (MA). National Service, KRRC, 1949–50, 2/Lieut. Sen. Partner, Pember & Boyle, Stockbrokers, 1982–86; Chairman: Foreign & Colonial Emerging Markets Trust (formerly CDFC Trust) plc, 1987–99; Liberty Syndicate Management Ltd, 1997–; Director: Morgan Grenfell Gp, 1984–87 (Advr, 1987–92); Festiniog Rly, 1993–. Mem., Stock Exchange, 1956–92 (Dep. Chm., 1978–81; Mem. Council, 1973–91); Chairman: Gilt-Edged Market Makers Assoc., 1986–92; IMRO, 1989–92; Dir, The Securities Assoc., 1986–89; Mem., Inflation Accounting Steering Gp, 1976–80. Non-exec. Dir, Ealing, Hammersmith and Hounslow HA, 1993–96. Mem. Council, GDST (formerly GPDST), 1993–. Gov., Godolphin and Latymer School, Hammersmith; Trustee, Lucy Cavendish Coll., Cambridge, 1994–97; Pres., Reed's Sch., Cobham, 1995–. Chm. of Trustees, CPRW, 1991–. Hon. FRAM 1994. *Recreations:* railways, music. *Address:* Swan House, Chiswick Mall, W4 2PS. *T:* (020) 8994 8203.

NITTVE, (Arvid) Lars (Olov); Director, Moderna Museet, Stockholm, since 2001; *b* 17 Sept. 1953; *s* of Bengt and Ulla Nittve; *m* 1988, Anna Olsson (marr. diss. 1999); one *s. Educ:* Stockholm Univ. (MA 1978). Res. Asst and Lectr, Dept of Art History, Stockholm Univ., 1978–85; Art Critic, Svenska Dagbladet, Stockholm, 1979–85; Sen. Curator, Moderna Museet, Stockholm, 1986–90; Director: Rooseum-Center for Contemporary Art, Malmö, 1990–95; Louisiana Mus. of Modern Art, Humleback, Denmark, 1995–98; Tate Gall. of Modern Art, subseq. Tate Modern, 1998–2001. *Publications* include: Svenska Valaffischer, 1979; Ola Billgren, 1985; Jan Håfström: grammaticus, 1990; Ulrik Samuelson: exit, 1987; Landskapet i nytt lijus, 1987; The Sublime – Walter De Maria, 1992; Truls Melin, 1992; Rolf Hanson, 1995. *Address:* Moderna Museet, Skeppsholmen, Box 16382, 103 27 Stockholm, Sweden. *T:* (020) 7401 5221.

NIVEN, Alastair Neil Robertson, OBE 2001; PhD; Principal, King George VI and Queen Elizabeth Foundation of St Catharine's, Cumberland Lodge, since 2001; *b* 25 Feb. 1944; *s* of late Harold Robertson Niven and Elizabeth Isobel Robertson Niven (*née* Mair); *m* 1970, Helen Margaret Trow; one *s* one *d. Educ:* Dulwich Coll.; Gonville and Caius Coll., Cambridge (MA); Univ. of Ghana (Commonwealth Schol.; MA); Univ. of Leeds (PhD). Lecturer in English: Univ. of Ghana, 1968–69; Univ. of Leeds, 1969–70; Lectr in English Studies, Univ. of Stirling, 1970–78; Dir Gen., Africa Centre, London, 1978–84; Chapman Fellow 1984–85, Hon. Fellow 1985, Inst. of Commonwealth Studies; Special Asst to Sec. Gen., ACU, 1985–87; Lit. Dir, Arts Council of GB, then of England, 1987–97; Dir of Literature, British Council, 1997–2001. Visiting Professor: Univ. of Aarhus, 1975–76; Sheffield Hallam Univ., 1998–; Vis. Fellow, Aust. Studies Centre, Univ. of London, 1985; Hon. Lectr, SOAS, 1979–85; Hon. Fellow, Univ. of Warwick, 1988. Editor, Jl of Commonwealth Literature, 1979–92. Chairman: Public Schools Debating Assoc. of Eng. and Wales, 1961–62; Literature Panel, GLAA, 1981–84; Welfare Policy Cttee, 1983–87, Exec. Cttee, 1987–92, UK Council for Overseas Student Affairs; Southern Africa Book Develt Educn Trust, 1997–; Sec. and Treas., Assoc. for Commonwealth Lit. and Lang. Studies, 1986–89; Member: Public Affairs Cttee, Royal Commonwealth Soc., 1979–99; Laurence Olivier Awards Theatre Panel, 1989–91; British Library Adv. Cttee for the Centre for the Book, 1990–97; Home Office Standing Cttee on Arts in Prisons, 1995–97. Trustee, Millennium Liby Trust, 1998–. Judge: Booker Prize, 1994; Forward Poetry Prizes, 1996; David Cohen British Literature Prize, 2000 (deviser of Prize, 1992); The Independent Foreign Fiction Prize, 2001; Chairman of Judges: Eurasia Reg., 1994, 1995, Adv. Cttee, 1996–, Commonwealth Writers' Prize; Stakis Prize for Scottish Writer of Year, 1998; ESU Marsh Prize for Biography, 1999–2001. Mem. Editorial Bd, Annual Register, 1988–. *Publications:* The Commonwealth Writer Overseas (ed), 1976; D. H. Lawrence: the novels, 1978; The Yoke of Pity: the fiction of Mulk Raj Anand, 1978; D. H. Lawrence: the writer and his work, 1980; (with Sir Hugh W. Springer) The Commonwealth of Universities, 1987; (ed) Under Another Sky: the Commonwealth Poetry Prize anthology, 1987; (ed jtly) Enigmas and Arrivals: an anthology of Commonwealth writing, 1997; articles in Afr. Affairs, Ariel, Brit. Book News, Jl of Commonwealth Lit., Jl of Indian Writing in English, Jl of RSA, Lit. Half-Yearly, Poetry Review, TES, THES, World Lit. Written in English, etc; study guides on Elechi Amadi, Wm Golding, R. K. Narayan, Raja Rao. *Recreations:* theatre, travel. *Address:* Eden House, 28 Weathercock Lane, Woburn Sands, Bucks MK17 8NT. *T:*

(01908) 582310. *Clubs:* Garrick, Royal Commonwealth Society.
See also C. H. R. Niven, P. A. R. Niven.

NIVEN, Dr Colin Harold Robertson; Headmaster, Alleyn's School, Dulwich, 1992–Aug. 2002; *b* 29 Sept. 1941; *s* of late Harold Robertson Niven and Elizabeth Isobel Robertson Niven (*née* Mair). *Educ:* Dulwich Coll. (Capt. of School); Gonville and Caius Coll., Cambridge (MA); Brasenose Coll., Oxford (DipEd); Nancy Univ. (LèsL); Lille Univ. (Dr de l'Univ.). Lycée Mixte, Châlons-sur-Marne, 1963–64; Samuel Pepys Comprehensive Sch., 1964; Sedbergh Sch., 1964; Fettes Coll., 1965–73 (Housemaster, 1971–73); Head of Mod. Langs, Sherborne Sch., 1973–83; Principal: Island Sch., Hong Kong, 1983–87; St George's English Sch., Rome, 1988–91; Vis. Fellow, Westminster Coll., Oxford, 1991; Dir of Internat. Liaison, Sherborne Internat. Study Centre, 1992. Chm., European Div., 1990–91, Chm., London Div., 1998, HMC. Pres., Marlowe Soc., 1996–; Trustee, Dulwich Picture Gall., 1996–99. Vice-Pres., Rugby Fives Assoc., 2001–. Gov., Portsmouth GS, 1999–; Member: Council, King's Coll., Madrid, 1999–; Educn Cttee, ESU, 1999–. Patron, Ind. Schs MLA, 1998–. FRSA. CCF Medal 1983. *Publications:* Voltaire's Candide, 1978; Thomas Mann's Tonio Kröger, 1980; Vailland's Un jeune homme seul (critical edn), 1983; Island School: the first twenty years, 1987. *Recreations:* theatre, sport, foreign travel, cats, opera (Mem. choir, Dorset Opera). *Address:* (until Aug. 2002) Alleyn's School, Dulwich, SE22 8SU; 8 Dulwich Village, SE21 7AL. *T:* (020) 8693 2983. *Clubs:* East India, Royal Over-Seas League, Royal Commonwealth Society, English-Speaking Union.
See also A. N. R. Niven, P. A. R. Niven.

NIVEN, Ian; *see* Niven, J. R.

NIVEN, John Robertson, (Ian); Under-Secretary, Department of the Environment, formerly Ministry of Housing and Local Government, 1974–79; *b* 11 May 1919; *s* of Robert Niven and Amelia Mary Hill; *m* 1946, Jane Bicknell; three *s*. *Educ:* Glasgow Academy; Jesus Coll., Oxford. Entered Min. of Town and Country Planning, 1946; Sec., Royal Commn on Local Govt in Greater London, 1957–60. *Address:* White Gates, Parham, Woodbridge, Suffolk IP13 9AA.

NIVEN, Peter Ashley Robertson, FRCS, FRCOG; Consultant Obstetrician and Gynaecologist, United Bristol Hospitals, since 1976; *b* 3 March 1938; *s* of late Harold Robertson Niven and Elizabeth Isobel Robertson Niven (*née* Mair); *m* 1964, Sarah Peta Callaway; three *s*. *Educ:* Dulwich Coll.; Gonville and Caius Coll., Cambridge (Open Exhibnr 1955; BA 1959; MA 1963); St Bartholomew's Hosp. (MB BChir 1962). FRCS 1966; MRCOG 1969, FRCOG 1981. Eden Travelling Fellow, RCOG, 1972; Purdue Frederick Award, Amer. Coll. of Obstetricians and Gynecologists, 1975; Sen. Registrar, St Bartholomew's Hosp., 1971–74; Consultant, Newcastle Gen. and Hexham Gen. Hosps, 1975–76. Chm., Higher Trng Cttee, and Mem. Council, RCOG, 1992–95; Pres., SW Obstetrical and Gynaecol Soc., 1997–98; Mem., Gynaecol Vis. Soc. of GB and Ireland, 1978. FRSocMed 1971. *Recreations:* ski-ing, golf, Rugby, cricket, history, travel, long distance walking. *Address:* 21 Clifton Park, Clifton, Bristol BS8 3BZ. *T:* (0117) 973 8446. *Club:* Royal Over-Seas League.
See also A. N. R. Niven, C. H. R. Niven.

NIVISON, family name of **Baron Glendyne**.

NIX, Prof. John Sydney; Emeritus Professor, University of London, since 1989 (Professor of Farm Business Management, 1982–89, and Head, Farm Business Unit, 1974–89, Wye College); *b* 27 July 1927; *s* of John William Nix and Eleanor Elizabeth (*née* Stears); *m* 1950, Mavis Marian (*née* Cooper); one *s* two *d*. *Educ:* Brockley County Sch.; University Coll. of the South-West. BSc Econ (London), MA Cantab. Instr Lieut, RN, 1948–51. Farm Economics Branch, Sch. of Agriculture, Univ. of Cambridge, 1951–61; Wye College: Farm Management Liaison Officer and Lectr, 1961–70; Sen. Tutor, 1970–72; Sen. Lectr, 1972–75; Reader, 1975–82; apptd to personal chair, the first in Farm Business Management in UK, 1982; Fellow, 1995. Founder Mem., Farm Management Assoc., 1965; formerly Member: Study Groups etc. for Natural Resources (Tech.) Cttee; Agric. Adv. Council; ARC Tech. Cttee; ADAS Exptl and Develt Cttee; Meat and Livestock Commn; Countryside Commn. Programme Advr, Southern Television, 1966–81; Specialist Advr, Select Cttee on Agric., 1990–91. British Institute of Management: Chm., Jl Cttee of Centre of Management of Agric., 1971–96; Chm., Bd of Farm Management, 1979–81; Nat. Award for outstanding and continuing contrib. to advancement of management in agric. industry, 1982 (1st recipient). President: Agricl Economics Soc., 1990–91; Kingshay Farming Trust, 1991–96; Assoc. of Indep. Crop Consultants, 1993–97; Guild of Agricl Journalists., 2000–March 2002. CIMgt (CBIM 1983). FRSA 1984; FRAgS 1985; FIAgrM 1993. Liveryman, Farmers' Co., 1999–. Agricl Communicators Award (1st recipient), Hydro Agri (UK), 1999. *Publications:* Farm Management Pocketbook, 1966, 32nd edn 2001; (with C. S. Barnard) Farm Planning and Control, 1973, 2nd edn 1979, Spanish edn 1984; (with W. Butterworth) Farm Mechanisation for Profit, 1983; (with G. P. Hill and N. T. Williams) Land and Estate Management, 1987, 3rd edn 1999; articles in Jl of Agricl Econs, Jl of RASE, Farm Management, etc. *Recreations:* Rugby, cricket, old films, reading the papers. *Address:* Imperial College at Wye, Wye, Ashford, Kent TN25 5AH. *T:* (01233) 812401. *Club:* Farmers'.

NIXON, Anthony; Chairman for the NHS Executive (Complaints Procedure), North West Region, Department of Health, since 1998; Business and Management Consultant, A. & M. Nixon Enterprises, since 1992; *b* 25 Nov. 1932; *s* of late Aitzad and Hydray Nixon; *m* 1975, Marion Audrey Farr; one *s* four *d*. *Educ:* Univ. of Peshawar (BA 1955); Univ. of Karachi (DipM 1959; MA Econ. 1960); UCW, Aberystwyth (MSc Pol Econ. 1986); Leeds Poly.; Salford Univ.; Manchester Univ. ACP 1958. Local Govt Officer, Lancs CC, 1968–71; Chief College Librarian and Lectr, Burnley Coll. of Further and Higher Educn, 1972–93 (Mem., Acad. Bd and Bd Cttees); Chm. and Man. Dir, A. & M. Nixon Enterprises Ltd, 1990–91; Man. Dir, Costcutter Nixon Supermkt, 1993–96. Columnist, New Life (London weekly mag.), 1987–88. Probation Officer Volunteer and Exec. Cttee Mem., Rossendale Probation and Aftercare Service, 1975–81; Mem. Bd, Nat. Probation Service, Lancs, 2001–; Lay Assessor, Inspection Unit, Social Services, Lancs CC, 2000–. Mem., Community Relns Council, 1980–92, Chm., Employment Panel, 1987–88, Hyndburn and Rossendale. Dir, Exec. Trustee and Sec., Bd of Dirs, BHAF Ltd, Manchester, 1998– (Chm., Finance Cttee). Business Advr and Mentor, Prince's Business Trust, 1999–. Travelled extensively in Russian Fedn and Republics of Latvia, Estonia and Lithuania and met prominent govt and religious leaders, industrialists, trade union officials, etc in order to promote goodwill between Britain and former Soviet Union, 1987; organised exchange visits between British and Soviet families for first time during Soviet rule, 1987–91. Consultant: Collective Farm, Piraviena, Rumsiskes, Lithuania, 1988–90; Pedagogical Univ., Vilnius, Lithuania, 1997. Has given talks on local radio in Lancs on various Russian, Lithuanian, Estonian and Latvian radio and TV stations. *Publications:* South Asia: detente and co-operation or confrontation?, 1982; (contrib.) Day of Peace 1917–87, 1987; Meeting People through Russia to the Baltics, 1990; contrib. articles to Sunday Times, New Scientist and British and foreign jls. *Recreations:* discussing politics and philosophising on national and international economic and social issues; travelling, reading, country walks, picnics. *Address:* The Oak, 7 Flax Close, Helmshore, Rossendale, Lancs BB4 4JL. *Club:* Inter-Varsity (Manchester).

NIXON, Sir Edwin (Ronald), Kt 1984; CBE 1974; DL; Deputy Chairman, National Westminster Bank PLC, 1987–96 (Director, 1975–96); Chairman: Amersham International plc, 1988–96 (Director, 1987–96); Natwest Pension Trustees Ltd, 1992–98; Leicester BioSciences Ltd, 1997–2000; *b* 21 June 1925; *s* of William Archdale Nixon and Ethel (*née* Corrigan); *m* 1st, 1952, Joan Lilian (*née* Hill) (*d* 1995); one *s* one *d*; 2nd, 1997, Bridget Diana, *er d* of late Reginald and of Lenna Rogers. *Educ:* Alderman Newton's Sch., Leicester; Selwyn Coll., Cambridge (MA; Hon. Fellow 1983). Man. Accountant, Dexion Ltd, 1950–55; IBM United Kingdom Ltd, 1955–90; Chm., IBM UK Hldgs Ltd, 1986–90 (Man. Dir, 1965–78; Chm. and Chief Exec., 1979–86); Director: Royal Insurance PLC, 1980–88; International Westminster Bank PLC, 1987–96; UK-Japan 2000 Gp Ltd, 1987–96; Partnership Sourcing, 1990–96; Natwest Bancorp Inc., 1991–96; Natwest Bank USA, 1992–96; Alternate Dir, BCH Property Ltd, 1988–96. Member Council: Foundn for Automation and Employment, 1967–77; Electronic Engineering Assoc., 1965–76; CBI, 1971–96 (Chm. Standing Cttee on Marketing and Consumer Affairs, 1971–78; Mem., Cttee on Industrial Policy, 1978–85; President's Cttee, 1986–88); Foundn for Management Educn, 1973–84. Member: British Cttee of Awards for Harkness Fellowships, 1976–82; Adv. Council, Business Graduates Assoc., 1976–87; Board of Governors, United World Coll. of Atlantic, 1977–; Bd of Trustees, Internat. Inst. for Management Develt, 1990–96; Chm. Council, Leicester Univ., 1992–98; Member Council: Manchester Business Sch., 1974–86 (Chm., 1979–86); Business in the Community, 1981–88 (Companion, 1992); Westfield Coll., London, 1969–82 (Vice Chm., 1980–82; Hon. Fellow 1983); William Temple Coll., Manchester, 1972–80; Oxford Centre for Management Studies, 1973–83; Open Univ., 1986–92. Member: The Civil Service Coll., 1979–91; Adv. Council, New Oxford English Dictionary, 1985–89; Council for Industry and Higher Educn, 1986–97. Trustee, Inst. of Econ. Affairs, 1986–92 (Hon. Trustee, 1992). Member: Chichester Cathedral Develt Trust, 1986–96; The Prince's Youth Business Trust, 1987–; Lloyd's of London Tercentary Foundn, 1987–. Pres., Nat. Assoc. for Gifted Children, 1980–91 (Hon. Mem., 1991); Vice-Pres., Opportunities for People with Disabilities (formerly Opportunities for the Disabled), 1980–; Chm., Jt Bd for Pre-Vocational Educn, 1983–87; Mem., Study Commn on the Family, 1979–83. Chm. of Bd of Trustees and a Dir, Royal Opera House, Covent Garden, 1984–87 (Trustee, 1980–87); Chm., Bd of Trustees, Monteverdi Choir and Orch., 1988–2001 (Trustee, 1980–); Vice-Pres., London Internat. String Quartet Competition. Patron, Assoc. Internationale des Etudiantes en Sciences Economiques et Commerciales, 1980–. DL Hampshire, 1987. Hon. Fellow: Inst. of Marketing, 1982 (Hon. Vice-Pres., 1980–96); Portsmouth Polytechnic, subseq. Portsmouth Univ., 1986; Leeds Polytechnic, subseq. Leeds Metropolitan Univ., 1991. Hon. DSc Aston, 1985; DUniv Stirling, 1985; Hon. DTech Brunel, 1986; Hon. LLD: Manchester, 1987; Leicester, 1990; Hon. DTech CNAA, 1991. *Recreations:* music, golf, reading. *Address:* Starkes Heath, Rogate, Petersfield, Hants GU31 5EJ. *T:* (01730) 821504. *Club:* Athenæum.

NIXON, Prof. John Forster, FRS 1994; Professor of Chemistry, University of Sussex since 1986; *b* 27 Jan. 1937; *s* of late Supt Edward Forster Nixon, MBE and Mary Nixon (*née* Lytton); *m* 1960, Dorothy Joan (Kim) Smith; one *s* one *d*. *Educ:* Univ. of Manchester (BSc 1st Cl. Hons Chem. 1957, MSc 1958; PhD 1960; DSc 1973). Research Associate in Chem., Univ. of Southern Calif., LA, 1960–62; ICI Fellow, Inorganic Chem. Dept, Univ. of Cambridge, 1962–64; Lectr in Inorganic Chem., Univ. of St Andrews, 1964–66; University of Sussex: Lectr in Chem., 1966–76; Reader, 1976–86; Subject Chm. in Chem., 1981–84; Dean, Sch. of Chem. and Molecular Scis, 1989–92. Vis. Associate Prof. in Chem., Univ. of Victoria, BC, Canada, 1970–71; Vis. Prof., Simon Fraser Univ., BC, 1976; Alexander von Humboldt Res. Fellow, 2001–Dec. 2002. Mem., Editl Bd, Phosphorus, Sulfur and Silicon, 1989–. Mem. Bd of Dirs, Internat. Council for Main Gp Chem., 2000– (Chm., 2000). Member: Internat. Cttee on Phosphorus Chem., 1983, 2000; IUPAC Commn on Inorganic Nomenclature, 1985–87; Inorganic Chem. Panel, SERC Cttee, 1986–89; EPSRC Cttee, 1997–98. Royal Soc. Leverhulme Trust Sen. Res. Fellow, 1993. Mem. Council, Dalton Div., RSC, 1994–99. Corday-Morgan Medal and Prize, Chem. Soc., 1973; Main Gp Element Medal, 1985, Tilden Lectr and Medal, 1992, RSC. FRSA 1992. *Publications:* (jtly) Phosphorus: the carbon copy, 1998; numerous papers in various learned jls. *Recreations:* walking, playing squash, tennis, badminton, watching cricket, theatre. *Address:* School of Chemistry, Physics and Environmental Science, University of Sussex, Brighton, Sussex BN1 9QJ. *T:* (01273) 678536; Juggs Barn, The Street, Kingston, Lewes, Sussex BN7 3PB. *T:* (01273) 483993.

NIXON, Patrick Michael, CMG 1989; OBE 1984; HM Diplomatic Service; Ambassador to the United Arab Emirates, since 1998; *b* 1 Aug. 1944; *s* of John Moylett Gerard Nixon and late Hilary Mary (*née* Paterson); *m* 1968, Elizabeth Rose Carlton; four *s*. *Educ:* Downside; Magdalene Coll., Cambridge. Joined HM Diplomatic Service, 1965; MECAS, Lebanon, 1966; Cairo, 1968; Lima, 1970; FCO, 1973; Tripoli, Libya, 1977; British Inf. Services, New York, 1980; Asst, later Hd, Near East and N Africa Dept, FCO, 1983; Ambassador and Consul-Gen. at Doha, Qatar, 1987–90; Counsellor, FCO, 1990–93; High Comr to Zambia, 1994–97; Dir, FCO, 1997–98. *Address:* c/o Foreign and Commonwealth Office, SW1A 2AH.

NIXON, Rev. Rosemary Ann; Vicar of Cleadon, since 1999; *b* 25 May 1945; *d* of Edwin Nixon and Dorothy Hall. *Educ:* Bishop Grosseteste Coll. of Educn (CertEd); Trinity Coll., Bristol (DipTh (London); BD Hons (London)); Durham Univ. (MA); Edinburgh Univ. (MTh). School teacher, Denton, Manchester, 1966–69; Parish Worker, St Luke's, West Hampstead, 1973–75; Tutor, St John's Coll., Durham and Dir of St John's Coll. Extension Prog., 1975–89; ordained deacon, 1987, priest, 1994; Team Vicar and Dir of the Urban Studies Unit, Parish of Gateshead, 1990–92; Staff Mem., Edinburgh Theol Coll., 1992–95; Principal, Theol Inst., Scottish Episcopal Church, 1995–99. Hon. Canon, St Mary's Cathedral, Edinburgh, and Pantonian Prof. of Theol., Edinburgh, 1996–99. *Publications:* Who's the Greatest?: Sunday schools today, 1984; Jonah: working with the word, 1986; articles in theol dictionaries and periodicals. *Recreations:* music, hill walking, photography, friends. *Address:* 5 Sunderland Road, Cleadon, Sunderland SR6 7UR. *T:* (0191) 536 7147.

NIXON, Sir Simon (Michael Christopher), 5th Bt *cr* 1906, of Roebuck Grove, Milltown, co. Dublin and Merrion Square, City of Dublin; *b* 20 June 1954; *s* of Major Cecil Dominic Henry Joseph Nixon, MC (*d* 1994), and of Brenda Nixon (*née* Lewis); *S* uncle, 1997. *Heir:* *b* Michael David Hugh Nixon, *b* 19 May 1957.

NIZAMI, Farhan Ahmad, DPhil; Founder Director, Oxford Centre for Islamic Studies, since 1985; Prince of Wales Fellow, Magdalen College, Oxford, since 1997; *b* 25 Dec. 1956; *s* of late Prof. Khaliq Nizami and of Razia Nizami; *m* 1983, Farah Deba Ahmad; one *s* one *d*. *Educ:* Aligarh Muslim Univ., India (BA Hons History, 1st cl., 1977; Nat. Schol., 1977–79; MA, 1st cl., 1979); Wadham Coll., Oxford (Oxford Overseas Schol.; Frere Exhibnr; DPhil 1983). Rothman's Fellow in Muslim Hist., 1983–85, Fellow, 1985–97,

Emeritus Fellow, 1997, St Cross Coll., Oxford. Member: Academic Council, Wilton Park, 2000–; Court, Oxford Brookes Univ., 2000–. Founder Editor, Jl of Islamic Studies, 1990–. *Recreations:* reading, cricket. *Address:* Oxford Centre for Islamic Studies, George Street, Oxford OX1 2AR. *T:* (01865) 278731.

NOAKES, Baroness *cr* 2000 (Life Peer), of Goudhurst in the co. of Kent; **Sheila Valerie Masters,** DBE 1996; non-executive Director: Carpetright plc, since 2001; Solutions in Staffing and Software plc, since 2001; *d* of Albert Frederick Masters and Iris Sheila Masters (*née* Ratcliffe); *m* 1985, Colin Barry Noakes. *Educ:* Eltham Hill Grammar Sch.; Univ. of Bristol (LLB). FCA. Joined Peat Marwick Mitchell & Co., 1970; seconded to HM Treasury, 1979–81; seconded to Dept of Health as Dir of Finance, NHS Management Exec., 1988–91; Partner, Peat Marwick Mitchell & Co., subseq. KPMG Peat Marwick, then KPMG, 1983–2000; a Dir, Bank of England, 1994–2001 (Chm., Cttee of non-exec. Dirs, 1998–2001). Comr, Public Works Loan Bd, 1995–; Member: Council, ICAEW, 1987– (Pres., 1999–2000); Inland Revenue Management Bd, 1992–99; NHS Policy Bd, 1992–95; Chancellor of Exchequer's Private Finance Panel, 1993–97; Bd of Companions, Inst. of Mgt, 1997–; Public Services Productivity Panel, 1998–2000; Council, Inst. of Business Ethics, 1998–. Trustee, Reuters Founders Share Co., 1998–. Mem. Bd, ENO, 2000–. Governor: London Business Sch., 1998–; Eastbourne Coll., 2000–; Marlborough Coll., 2000–. CIMgt. Hon. DBA London Guildhall, 1999; Hon. LLD Bristol, 2000; Hon. DSc Buckingham, 2001. *Recreations:* ski-ing, horse racing, opera, early classical music. *Address:* House of Lords, SW1A 0PW. *T:* (020) 7219 5353. *Club:* Farmers'.

NOAKES, Rt Rev. George; Archbishop of Wales, 1987–91; Bishop of St Davids, 1982–91; *b* 13 Sept. 1924; *s* of David John and Elizabeth Mary Noakes; *m* 1957, Jane Margaretta Davies. *Educ:* Tregaron Secondary School; University Coll. of Wales, Aberystwyth (BA); Wycliffe Hall, Oxford. Curate of Lampeter, 1950–56; Vicar: Eglwyswrw, 1956–59; Tregaron, 1959–67; Dewi Sant, Cardiff, 1967–76; Rector of Aberystwyth, 1976–79; Canon of St Davids Cathedral, 1977–79; Archdeacon of Cardigan, 1979–82; Vicar of Llanychaearn, 1980–82. Hon. DD Wales, 1989. *Recreations:* cricket, angling. *Address:* Hafodlon, Rhydargaeau, Carmarthen, Dyfed SA32 7DT. *T:* (01267) 253302.

NOAKES, John Edward, OBE 1993; FRCGP; Partner, group medical practice in Harrow, 1961–99; *b* 27 April 1935; *s* of Edward and Mary Noakes; *m* 1960, Margaret Ann Jenner; two *s* one *d*. *Educ:* Wanstead County High Sch.; Charing Cross Hospital Medical Sch. (MB BS); DObstRCOG. Trainer, Gen. Practice Vocational Trng Scheme, Northwick Park Hosp., 1974–82. Member: Brent Harrow Local Med. Cttee, 1972–97; Harrow HA, 1982–90; CMO's Wkg Gp on Health of Nation, 1990–98; Chm., Brent Harrow Med. Audit Adv. Gp, 1992–95. Non-exec. Director: HEA, 1995–2000; HDA, 2000–. Mem. Council, RCGP, 1989–94 (Vice-Chm., 1990–92; Chairman: NW London Faculty, 1989–91; Maternity Care Task Gp, 1994). *Recreations:* music (mainly opera), horticulture (Alpine plants), exploring Britain's canal system in own Narrow Boat. *Address:* Old Church Cottage, Chapel Lane, Long Marston, Herts HP23 4QT.

NOAKES, Michael, PPROI, RP; portrait and landscape painter; *b* 28 Oct. 1933; *s* of late Basil and Mary Noakes; *m* 1960, Vivien Noakes (*née* Langley), DPhil, FRSL, writer; two *s* one *d*. *Educ:* Downside; Royal Academy Schs, London. Nat. Dipl. in Design, 1954; Certificate of Royal Academy Schools, 1960. Commnd: National Service, 1954–56. Has broadcast and appeared on TV on art subjects in UK and USA; Art Correspondent, BBC TV programme Town and Around, 1964–68; subject of BBC films: (with Eric Morley) Portrait, 1977, 1978; (with JAK) Changing Places, 1989. Member Council: ROI, 1964–78 (Vice-Pres. 1968–72; Pres., 1972–78; Hon. Mem. Council, 1978–); RP, 1969–71, 1972–74, 1978–80, 1993–95; NS, 1962–76 (Hon. Mem., 1976–); Chm., Contemp. Portrait Soc., 1971; a Dir, Fedn of British Artists, 1981–83 (a Governor, 1972–83). Freeman, City of London; Liveryman, Co. of Woolmen. *Exhibited:* Royal Acad.; Royal Inst. Oil Painters; Royal Soc. Portrait Painters; Contemp. Portrait Soc.; Nat. Society; Young Contemporaries, Grosvenor Galleries, Upper Grosvenor Galls, Woodstock Galls, Royal Glasgow Inst. of Fine Arts, Nat. Portrait Gall.; Roy. Soc. of British Artists; Grafton Gall.; New Grafton Galls; Art Exhibitions Bureau, touring widely in Britain, USA and Canada. Judge, Miss World Contest, 1976. Platinum disc, 1977 (record sleeve design Portrait of Sinatra). *Portraits include:* The Queen (unveiled Silver Jubilee year, for Manchester; Queen's Lancs Regt); Queen Elizabeth The Queen Mother (as Chancellor, Univ. of London; as Patron, RADAR); Prince of Wales (for 2nd KEO Gurkhas; as Patron, RCPsych); Princess Anne (for Saddlers' Co.; Royal Signals); Duke and Duchess of York; Duchess of Kent; Lord Aberconway; Lord Aldington; Lord Amory; Princess Ashraf; Sir Michael Atiyah; Lord Benson; Lord Barnetson; Sir Christopher Benson; Lord Boothby; Lord Bowden; Lord Boyd; Rt Rev. Mgr Christopher Budd, Bishop of Plymouth; Lord Butterfield; Lord Carr; FM Lord Carver; Sir John Chalstrey, Lord Mayor of London; Lord Charteris; Lord Chuter-Ede; President Clinton; Lord Craigmyle; Lord Denning; Paul Dirac; Lord Elwyn-Jones; Archbishop Lord Fisher; Dom Charles Fitzgerald-Lombard, Abbot of Downside; Lord Fulton; Sir Alec Guinness; Gen. Sir John Hackett; Gilbert Harding; Robert Hardy; Sir Denys Henderson; Sir Alan Hodgkin; Dr David Hope, Bishop of London; Robert Horton; Cardinal Hume; Lord Kingsdown; Lord Kings Norton; AF Lord Lewin; Amb. John J. Louis, USA; Very Rev. Michael Mayne, Dean of Westminster; Cliff Michelmore; Eric Morley; Robert Morley; Malcolm Muggeridge; Sir Gerald Nabarro; Sir David Napley; Rev. Prof. Ernest Nicholson; Max Perutz; Earl of Powis; Ambassador Charles Price, USA; J. B. Priestley; Valerie Profumo; Lord Pym; Sir Ralph Richardson; Dom John Roberts, Abbot of Downside; Sir Martin Roth; Edmund de Rothschild; Lord Runcie; Dame Margaret Rutherford; Lord Selwyn-Lloyd; Sir Roland Smith; Very Rev. M. Sullivan; Margaret Thatcher (as Prime Minister); Lord Todd; Sir Peter Walters; Dennis Wheatley; Sir Mortimer Wheeler; Sir Frank Whittle; Lord Wolfenden; Sir Donald Wolfit; Prof. Graham Zellick; *major group portraits:* Royal Family, with Lord and Lady Mayoress, for Guildhall; Members and Officers, Metropolitan Water Board (47 figures); Lords of Appeal in Ordinary (for Middle Temple); Queen Elizabeth the Queen Mother opening Overlord Embroidery to public view, with Princess Alice, Lord Mountbatten, Duke of Norfolk, etc; Company of Woolmen showing Princess Royal. *Represented in collections:* The Queen, for Royal Collection Windsor; The Prince of Wales; British Mus.; Nat. Portrait Gall. (incl. Hugill Fund Purchase, RA, 1972); numerous Oxford and Cambridge colleges; County Hall, Westminster; various livery companies and Inns of Court; House of Commons; Univs of London, Nottingham, East Anglia; City Univ.; Frank Sinatra. Designed £5 coin for 50th birthday of the Prince of Wales, 1998. *Publications:* A Professional Approach to Oil Painting, 1968; (with Vivien Noakes) The Daily Life of The Queen, 2000; contributions to various art journals. *Recreation:* idling. *Address:* 146 Hamilton Terrace, St John's Wood, NW8 9UX. *T:* (020) 7328 6754, *Fax:* (020) 7625 1220. *Club:* Garrick.

NOAKES, Philip Reuben, OBE 1962; HM Diplomatic Service, retired; *b* 12 Aug. 1915; *y s* of late Charles William and Elizabeth Farey Noakes; *m* 1940, Moragh Jean Dickson; two *s*. *Educ:* Wyggeston Grammar Sch.; Wycliffe Coll.; Queens' Coll., Cambridge (Open Schol.). Mod. Langs Tripos Part I, Hist. Tripos Part II; BA 1937; MA 1945; Pres., Cambridge Union Soc., 1937. Served War, 1940–46; Capt.-Adjt 2nd Fife and Forfar Yeomanry, RAC (despatches). Public Relations Officer, Royal Over-Seas League, 1947–48; Sen. Information Officer, Colonial Office, 1948; Prin. Information Officer, CO, 1953; Information Adviser to Governor of Malta, 1960–61; Chief Information Officer, CO, 1963–66; Commonwealth Office, 1967; Counsellor (Information), Ottawa, 1967–72; Consul-Gen., Seattle, 1973–75. *Recreations:* bird-watching, protection of country living and wildlife. *Club:* Royal Over-Seas League.

NOBAY, Prof. (Avelino) Robert, PhD; Senior Research Associate, Financial Markets Group, London School of Economics and Political Science, since 1996; Brunner Professor of Economic Science, University of Liverpool, 1980–96; *b* 11 July 1942; *s* of Theodore Anastasio Nobay and Anna Gracia D'Silva; *m* 1st, 1965; two *s*; 2nd, 1987, Carole Ann McPhee. *Educ:* Univ. of Leicester (BA); Univ. of Chicago; PhD Southampton. Jun. Economist, Electricity Council, London, 1964–66; Res. Officer, NIESR, 1966–70; Sen. Lectr, Univ. of Southampton, 1970–80. Vis. Associate Prof., Univ. of Chicago, 1977–79; Adjunct Prof., Centre for Internat. Econ. Studies, Univ. of Adelaide, 2001–. *Publications:* (with H. G. Johnson) The Current Inflation; (with H. G. Johnson) Issues in Monetary Economics. *Recreations:* sailing, golf, music.

NOBBS, David Gordon; writer; *b* 13 March 1935; *s* of Gordon and Gwen Nobbs; *m* 1st, 1968, Mary Blatchford (marr. diss. 1998); two step *s* one step *d*; 2nd, 1998, Susan Sutcliffe; one step *d*. *Educ:* Marlborough; St John's Coll., Cambridge (BA English). Wrote scripts for: That Was the Week That Was, BBC TV, 1963; The Frost Report, The Two Ronnies, The Fall and Rise of Reginald Perrin, 1976–78; BBC TV: The Hello Goodbye Man, 1984; Dogfood Dan and The Carmarthen Cowboy, 1988; Love on a Branch Line, 1994; Gentlemen's Relish, 2000; Yorkshire TV: Sez Les; Cupid's Darts, 1981; A Bit of a Do, 1989, 1990; Rich Tea and Sympathy, 1991; Stalag Luft, 1993; Granada: Our Young Mr Wignall, 1976; The Glamour Girls, 1980, 1982; Channel 4: Fairly Secret Army, 1984, 1986; The Life and Times of Henry Pratt, 1992. *Publications:* The Itinerant Lodger, 1965; Ostrich Country, 1968; A Piece of the Sky is Missing, 1969; The Fall and Rise of Reginald Perrin, 1975; The Return of Reginald Perrin, 1977; The Better World of Reginald Perrin, 1978; Second From Last in the Sack Race, 1983; A Bit of a Do, 1986; Pratt of the Argus, 1988; Fair Do's, 1990; The Cucumber Man, 1994; The Legacy of Reginald Perrin, 1995; The Reginald Perrin Omnibus, 1999; Going Gently, 2000. *Recreations:* cricket, football, bird-watching, travel, food, drink, bridge, theatre, weeding. *Address:* c/o Jonathan Clowes, Iron Bridge House, Bridge Approach, NW1 8BD. *Club:* Hereford United Football.

NOBES, (Charles) Patrick; retired Headmaster and teacher of English; *b* 17 March 1933; *o c* of Alderman Alfred Robert Nobes, OBE, JP, and Marguerite Violet Vivian (*née* Fathers), Gosport, Hants; *m* 1958, Patricia Jean (*née* Brand); three *s*. *Educ:* Price's Sch., Fareham, Hants; University Coll., Oxford. MA. With The Times, reporting and editorial, 1956–57; Head of English Dept, King Edward VI Grammar Sch., Bury St Edmunds, 1959–64; Head of English and General Studies and Sixth Form Master, Ashlyns Comprehensive Sch., Berkhamsted, 1964–69; Headmaster: The Ward Freman Sch., Buntingford, Herts, 1969–74; Bedales Sch., 1974–81; Weymouth Grammar Sch., 1981–85, later The Budmouth Sch., 1985–86; St Francis' Coll., Letchworth, 1986–87. Chairman: HMC Co-ed Schs Gp, 1976–80; Soc. of Headmasters of Independent Schs, 1978–80; Mem., SHA Council, 1985–86. Pres., Soc. of Old Priceans, 1999–. General Editor and adapter, Bulls-Eye Books (series for adults and young adults with reading difficulties), 1972–. *Recreations:* writing, cricket and hockey, King Arthur, Hampshire, music, First World War. *Address:* 73 Exeter Street, Salisbury, Wilts SP1 2SE. *T:* (01722) 504473.

NOBLE, Adrian Keith; Artistic Director, Royal Shakespeare Company, since 1991; *b* 19 July 1950; *s* of late William John Noble and of Violet Ena (*née* Wells); *m* 1991, Joanne Elizabeth Pearce; one *s* one *d*. *Educ:* Chichester High Sch. for Boys; Bristol Univ. (BA); Drama Centre, London. Associate Dir, Bristol Old Vic, 1976–79; Resident Dir, RSC, 1980–82; Guest Dir, Royal Exchange Theatre, Manchester, 1980–81; Associate Dir, RSC, 1982–90. *Stage productions include:* Ubu Rex, A Man's A Man, 1977; A View from the Bridge, Titus Andronicus, The Changeling, 1978; Love for Love, Timon of Athens, Recruiting Officer (Edinburgh Fest.), 1979; Duchess of Malfi, 1980, Paris 1981; Dr Faustus, The Forest, A Doll's House, 1981; King Lear, Antony and Cleopatra, 1982; A New Way to Pay Old Debts, Comedy of Errors, Measure for Measure, 1983; Henry V, The Winter's Tale, The Desert Air, 1984; As You Like It, 1985; Mephisto, The Art of Success (and NY, 1989), Macbeth, 1986; Kiss Me Kate, 1987; The Plantagenets, 1988; The Master Builder, 1989; The Three Sisters, 1990; Henry IV, parts 1 and 2, 1991; The Thebans, 1991; Hamlet, Winter's Tale, 1992; King Lear, Travesties, Macbeth, 1993; A Midsummer Night's Dream, 1994; Romeo and Juliet, The Cherry Orchard, 1995; Little Eyolf, 1996; Cymbeline, Twelfth Night, 1997; The Tempest, The Lion, the Witch and the Wardrobe, 1998; The Family Reunion, 1999; The Seagull, 2000; The Secret Garden, 2000; *opera:* Don Giovanni, Kent Opera, 1983; The Fairy Queen, 1989, Il Ritorno d'Ulisse in Patria, 2000, Aix-en-Provence Fest.; *film:* A Midsummer Night's Dream, 1996. Hon. DLitt: Birmingham, 1994; Bristol, 1996; Exeter, 1999. *Address:* Barbican Theatre, EC2Y 8BQ.

NOBLE, Alistair William; Sheriff of Glasgow and Strathkelvin, since 1999; *b* 10 Jan. 1954; *s* of late William Alexander Noble and Alexanderina Noble (*née* Fraser); *m* 1986, Olga Helena Marr Wojtas. *Educ:* Aberdeen Grammar Sch.; Aberdeen Univ. (LLB). Admitted Advocate, 1978; Temporary Sheriff, 1986; Sheriff of N Strathclyde at Dunoon, 1992–99. *Recreation:* reading. *Address:* Sheriff's Chambers, Sheriff Court House, 1 Carlton Place, Glasgow G5 9DA. *T:* (0141) 429 8888.

NOBLE, Barrie Paul; Chairman and Assessor, Civil Service Selection Board Preliminary (Disabled) Interview Board, 1997–99; *b* 17 Oct. 1938; *s* of late Major and Mrs F. A. Noble; *m* 1965, Alexandra Helene Giddings; one *s*. *Educ:* Hele's, Exeter; New Coll., Oxford (BA Jurisprudence); Univ. of Dakar. RAF, 1957–59. HM Diplomatic Service, 1962–93: Third, later Second Sec., (Leopoldville) Kinshasa, 1965–67; Second Sec. (Commercial), Kaduna, 1967–69; FCO, 1969–72; First Sec., 1972–75 and Head of Chancery, 1975, Warsaw; FCO, 1976–80; Counsellor, UK Mission to UN, Geneva, 1980–84; Counsellor: FCO, 1984–89; Paris, 1989–93; Chm., CSSB Panel, 1993–97. Mem., British–Polish Council, 1996–. *Publication:* Droit Coutumier, Annales Africaines, 1965. *Recreations:* grass cutting, bridge, skiing. *Clubs:* Royal Air Force, Ski Club of Great Britain; Rolls-Royce Enthusiasts'.

NOBLE, Rt Rev. Brian Michael; *see* Shrewsbury, Bishop of, (RC).

NOBLE, David, WS, JP; Sheriff of North Strathclyde at Oban and Fort William, 1983–95; *b* 11 Feb. 1923; *s* of late Donald Noble, Solicitor, Inverness, and Helen Kirk Lynn Melville or Noble; *m* 1947, Marjorie Scott Smith or Noble; two *s* one *d*. *Educ:* Inverness Royal Academy; Edinburgh Univ. (MA, LLB *summa cum laude*). Royal Air Force Bomber Command, 1942–46. Partner in Miller Thomson & Robertson, WS, Edinburgh, 1953–82. JP Midlothian, 1970. *Address:* Woodhouselee, North Connel, Argyll PA37 1QZ. *T:* (01631) 710678.

NOBLE, David, CBE 1989; Under Secretary and Head of Administrative Division, Medical Research Council, 1981–89, retired; *b* 12 June 1929; *s* of late William Ernest Noble and Maggie (*née* Watt); *m* 1969, Margaret Patricia Segal. *Educ:* Buckhurst Hill County High Sch., Essex; University Coll., Oxford (BA Hons English, 1952). Admin. Assistant, UCH, 1952–58; Mem., Operational Res. Unit, Nuffield Provincial Hosps Trust, 1958–61; Project Sec., Northwick Park Hosp. and Clinical Res. Centre, NW Thames RHA and MRC, 1961–68; Medical Research Council: Principal, 1968–72; Asst Sec., 1972–81. Member: Nat. Biological Standards Bd, 1983–90; PHLS Bd, 1990–97 (Dep. Chm., 1996–97). *Publications:* contribs to literature on operation and design of hosps and res. labs. *Recreations:* music, reading, travel. *Address:* 173 Bittacy Hill, NW7 1RT. *T:* (020) 8346 8005.

NOBLE, Sir David (Brunel), 6th Bt *cr* 1902, of Ardmore and Ardadan Noble, Cardross, Co. Dunbarton; sales consultant, Allied Maples Group Ltd, 1989–97; *b* 25 Dec. 1961; *s* of Sir Marc Brunel Noble, 5th Bt, CBE and of Jennifer Lorna, *d* of late John Mein-Austin; *S* father, 1991; *m* 1st, 1987, Virginia Ann (marr. diss. 1993), *yr d* of late Roderick Wetherall; two *s*; 2nd, 1993, Stephanie (*née* Digby); one *s* one *d* (and one *s* decd). *Educ:* Eton Coll.; Cambridge Tutors, Croydon; Canterbury Coll.; Greenwich Univ. Sales Exec., Gabriel Communications Ltd, 1986–88. Patron, Special Needs Children, 1997–. *Recreations:* golf, photography, gardening. *Heir: s* Roderick Lancaster Brunel Noble, *b* 12 Dec. 1988. *Address:* 3 Oast Cottages, Breach Lane, Upchurch, Sittingbourne, Kent ME9 7PH. *Club:* HAC.

NOBLE, Prof. Denis, CBE 1998; FMedSci; FRS 1979; Burdon Sanderson Professor of Cardiovascular Physiology, Oxford University, since 1984; Tutorial Fellow, 1963–84, Professorial Fellow, since 1984, Balliol College, Oxford; *b* 16 Nov. 1936; *s* of George and Ethel Noble; *m* 1965, Susan Jennifer Barfield, BSc, BA, DPhil; one *s* one *d*. *Educ:* Emanuel Sch., London; University Coll. London (BSc, MA, PhD; Fellow 1985). Asst Lectr, UCL, 1961–63; Tutor in Physiology, Balliol Coll., and Univ. Lectr, Oxford Univ., 1963–84; Praefectus of Holywell Manor (Balliol Graduate Centre), 1971–89; Vice-Master, Balliol Coll., 1983–85. Founder Dir, Physiome Scis Inc., 1994–. Visiting Professor: Alberta, 1969–70; Univs of BC, Calgary, Edmonton, and SUNY at Stonybrook, 1990; Univ. of Auckland, 1990. Lectures: Darwin, British Assoc., 1966; Nahum, Yale, 1977; Bottazzi, Pisa, 1985; Ueda, Tokyo, 1985; Lloyd Roberts, London Med. Soc., 1987; Allerdale Wyld, Northern Industrial and Technical Soc., 1988; Bowden, UMIST, 1988; Annual, Internat. Science Policy Foundn, 1993; Rijlant, Internat. Congress of Electrocardiology, Japan, 1994. Chm., Jt Dental Cttee (MRC, SERC, Depts of Health), 1985–90. Hon. Sec., 1974–80, Foreign Sec., 1986–92, Hon. Mem., 1997, Physiol Soc.; Founder Mem., Save British Science; Pres., Med. Section, BAAS, 1991–92; Sec. Gen., IUPS, 1994–. Chm., IUPS Congress, Glasgow, 1993. Founder FMedSci 1998; Hon. MRCP 1988; Hon. FRCP 1994; Mem., Academia Europaea, 1989; Correspondent Etranger (Fellow), Royal Acad. of Medicine, Belgium, 1985; Hon. Member: Amer. Physiol. Soc., 1996; Japanese Physiol Soc., 1998. Editor, Progress in Biophysics, 1967–. Scientific Medal, Zoolog. Soc., 1970; Gold Medal, British Heart Foundn, 1985; Pierre Rijlant Prize, Belgian Royal Acad., 1991. *Publications:* Initiation of the Heartbeat, 1975, 2nd edn, 1979; Electric Current Flow in Excitable Cells, 1975; Electrophysiology of Single Cardiac Cells, 1987; Goals, No Goals and Own Goals, 1989; Sodium-Calcium Exchange, 1989; Ionic Channels and the Effect of Taurine on the Heart, 1993; The Logic of Life, 1993; papers mostly in Jl of Physiology; contribs on sci. res. and funding to New Scientist, nat. press, radio and TV. *Recreations:* Indian and French cooking, Occitan language and music, classical guitar. *Address:* 49 Old Road, Oxford OX3 7JZ. *T:* (office) (01865) 272533.

NOBLE, Sir Fraser; *see* Noble, Sir T. A. F.

NOBLE, Gillian Mae, CB 1999; Director (formerly Deputy Director) (Law and Order, Health and Local Government), HM Treasury, 1995–2001; *b* Edinburgh, 18 Nov. 1947; *d* of John Noble and Jessie Mae Noble (*née* Bonnington). *Educ:* Aberdeen Univ. (MA Hons Econ. Sci. 1969); University Coll. London (MSc Public Sector Econs 1974). Joined MoT, subseq. DoE, as econ., 1969; transf. to HM Treasury, 1976; various posts dealing with: planning and control of public expenditure, 1976–84; pensions and social security, 1984–87; Asst Sec., 1986; Head: Banking Div., 1987–92; Educn Sci. and Nat. Heritage Div., 1992; Under Sec., 1993; Hd, Health, Social Services and Territorial Depts Gp, 1993–95. Trustee, Meningitis Trust, 1996–. *Recreations:* listening to music, visiting heritage properties.

NOBLE, Sir Iain (Andrew), 3rd Bt *cr* 1923, of Ardkinglas and Eilean Iarmain; OBE 1988; businessman and entrepreneur; Proprietor, Fearann Eilean Iarmain estate, Isle of Skye, since 1972; Chairman, Pràban na Linne Ltd (The Gaelic Whiskies), since 1976; Chairman and Chief Executive, Sir Iain Noble & Partners Ltd, since 2000; Founder and Director, Independent Insurance Group PLC (formerly New Scotland Insurance Group), since 1986; Director, Premium Investment Trust PLC, since 1993; *b* 8 Sept. 1935; *s* of Sir Andrew Napier Noble, 2nd Bt, KCMG and of Sigrid, 2nd *d* of Johan Michelet, Norwegian Diplomatic Service; *S* father, 1987; *m* 1990, Lucilla Charlotte James, *d* of late Col H. A. C. Mackenzie, OBE, MC, TD, DL, JP, Dalmore. *Educ:* China, Argentina and England (Eton); University Coll., Oxford (MA 1959). Matthews Wrightson, London, 1959–64; Scottish Council (Develt and Industry), Edinburgh, 1964–69; Jt Founder and Jt Man. Dir, Noble Grossart Ltd, merchant bankers, Edinburgh, 1969–72; Jt Founder and Chm., Seaforth Maritime Ltd, Aberdeen, 1972–78; Chairman: Lennox Oil Co. plc, Edinburgh, 1980–85; Noble Gp Ltd, merchant bankers, 1980–2000; Skye Bridge Ltd, 1994–96; Founder and Dir, Adam and Co. plc, Edinburgh, 1983–93. Dep. Chm., Traverse Theatre, Edinburgh, 1966–68; Mem., Edinburgh Univ. Court, 1970–73; Founder, first Chm., 1973–74, and Trustee, 1974–84, College of Sabhal Mor Ostaig, Isle of Skye; Trustee, Nat. Museums of Scotland, 1987–91 (Trustee, Charitable Trust, 1991–). Chm., Scots Australian Council, 1991–99; Pres., Saltire Soc., 1992–96. Keeper of the Quaich, 2000–. Scotsman of the Year Award, 1981. *Publication:* Sources of Finance, 1968. *Recreations:* Comhradh, beul-aithris is ceol le deagh chompanaich. *Heir: b* Timothy Peter Noble [*b* 21 Dec. 1943; *m* 1976, Elizabeth Mary, *d* of late Alexander Wallace Aitken; two *s* one *d*]. *Address:* 20 Great Stuart Street, Edinburgh EH3 7TN; An Lamraig, Eilean Iarmain, An t-Eilean Sgitheanach IV43 3QR; 20 Great Stuart Street, Edinburgh EH3 7TN. *T:* (offices) (01471) 833266 and (0131) 220 2400. *Club:* New (Edinburgh).

NOBLE, Rt Rev. John Ashley; an Assistant Bishop, since 1993, and Director of Ministries Development and Theological Education, since 1999, Diocese of Brisbane; *b* 30 March 1944; *s* of Mowbray Lloyd Noble and Norma June (*née* Shucksmith); *m* 1969, Lorene May Christine Wardrop; one *s* one *d*. *Educ:* St Francis Theological Coll., Brisbane (ThL 1965); Univ. of Queensland (BA 1973); Mt Gravatt Teachers' Coll., Brisbane (Cert. in Teaching, Secondary 1973). Deacon 1965, priest 1968; Asst Curacies, 1965–69; History Subject Master, Queensland Dept of Educn, 1974–78; Asst Chaplain, St Peter's Coll., Adelaide, 1979–81; Chaplain, St Paul's Sch., Brisbane, 1981–82; Diocese of Brisbane: Rector, St John's, Dalby, 1982–84; Rector, St Barnabas', Sunnybank, 1984–88; Lectr, St Francis Theol Coll., 1989–93; Bishop of the Northern Region, 1993–99. *Recreations:* reading, music, computers. *Address:* St Martin's House, 373 Ann Street, Brisbane, Qld 4000, Australia. *T:* (7) 38352213; 9 Fisher Lane, East Brisbane, Qld 4169, Australia.

NOBLE, Sir (Thomas Alexander) Fraser, Kt 1971; MBE 1947; Principal and Vice-Chancellor, University of Aberdeen, 1976–81, now Principal Emeritus; *b* 29 April 1918; *s* of late Simon Noble, Grantown-on-Spey and Jeanie Graham, Largs, Ayrshire; *m* 1945, Barbara A. M. Sinclair, Nairn; one *s* one *d*. *Educ:* Nairn Acad; Univ. of Aberdeen. After military service with Black Watch (RHR), entered Indian Civil Service, 1940. Served in NW Frontier Province, 1941–47, successively as Asst Comr, Hazara; Asst Polit. Agent, N Waziristan; Controller of Rationing, Peshawar; Under-Sec., Food Dept and Develt Dept; Sec., Home Dept; Joint Dep. Comr, Peshawar; Civil Aide to Referendum Comr. Lectr in Political Economy, Univ. of Aberdeen, 1948–57; Sec. and Treas., Carnegie Trust for Univs of Scotland, 1957–62; Vice-Chancellor, Leicester Univ., 1962–76. Mem. and Vice-Chm., Bd of Management, Aberdeen Mental Hosp. Group, 1953–57. Sec., Scottish Economic Soc., 1954–58; Vice-Pres., 1962–. Chm., Scottish Standing Conf. of Voluntary Youth Organisations, 1958–62; Vice-Chm., Standing Consultative Council on Youth Service in Scotland, 1959–62. Mem., Departmental Cttee on Probation Service, 1959–62; Chairman: Probation Advisory and Training Board, 1962–65; Television Research Cttee, 1963–69; Advisory Council on Probation and After-Care, 1965–70; Univs Council for Adult Education, 1965–69; Min. of Defence Cttee for Univ. Assistance to Adult Educn in HM Forces, 1965–70; Advisory Board, Overseas Students' Special Fund, 1967–71, Fees Awards Scheme, 1968–75; Cttee of Vice-Chancellors and Principals of Univs of UK, 1970–72; British Council Cttee on Exchanges between UK and USSR, 1973–78; Scottish Council for Community Educn, 1979–80. Member: Academic Advisory Cttee, Univs of St Andrews and Dundee, 1964–66; E Midlands Economic Planning Council, 1965–68; Council, Assoc. Commonwealth Univs, 1970–79; Exec. Cttee, Inter-Univ. Council for Higher Educn Overseas, 1972–79; Exec. Cttee, British Council, 1973–79; British Council Cttee for Commonwealth Univ. Interchange, 1973–79; US-UK Educnl Commn, 1973–76. Hon. LLD: Aberdeen, 1968; Leicester, 1976; Glasgow, 1981; Washington Coll., Maryland, 1981. *Publications:* Something in India (autobiog.), 1997; articles in economic journals and on education. *Recreation:* golf. *Address:* Hedgerley, Victoria Street, Nairn IV12 4HH. *Club:* Nairn Golf.

NOBLETT, Ven. William Alexander; Chaplain-General and Archdeacon to HM Prisons, since 2001; *b* Dublin, 16 April 1953; *s* of Joseph Henry and Hilda Florence Noblett; *m* 1986, Margaret Armour; one *s*. *Educ:* High Sch., Dublin; Salisbury and Wells Theol Coll.; Univ. of Southampton (BTh 1978); MTh Oxford 1999. Ordained deacon, 1978, priest, 1979; Curate, Sholing, Southampton, 1978–80; Rector, Ardamine Union, 1980–82; Chaplain, RAF, 1982–84; Vicar, Middlesbrough St Thomas, 1984–87; Chaplain of HM Prison: Wakefield, 1987–93; Norwich, 1993–97; Full Sutton, 1997–2001. Canon and Prebend, York Minster, 2001–. *Publication:* Prayers for People in Prison, 1998. *Recreations:* family life, running, reading, squash, music. *Address:* Room 621 Horseferry House, Dean Ryle Street, SW1P 2AW.

NODDER, Timothy Edward, CB 1982; Deputy Secretary, Department of Health and Social Security, 1978–84; *b* 18 June 1930; *s* of Edward Nodder. *Educ:* St Paul's Sch.; Christ's Coll., Cambridge. Under-Sec., DHSS, 1972. *Recreation:* natural history. *Address:* 83 Oakley Street, SW3 5NP.

NOEL, family name of **Earl of Gainsborough**.

NOEL, Geoffrey Lindsay James; Metropolitan Stipendiary Magistrate, 1975–93; *b* 19 April 1923; *s* of Major James Noel and Maud Noel; *m* 1st, 1947; two *d*; 2nd, 1966, Eileen Pickering (*née* Cooper); two step *s*. *Educ:* Crewkerne Sch., Somerset. Enlisted Royal Regt of Artillery, 1941; commnd, 1942; attached 9th Para Bn, 6 Airborne Div., 1944, Captain; POW Oflag 79; RWAFF; Major 1957; retd 1960. Called to Bar, Middle Temple, 1962; practised London and SE circuit. Chm., Juvenile Courts, 1977–79; Dep. Circuit Judge, 1980–82. *Recreations:* gardening, golf. *Address:* Loja, Albourne Road, Hurstpierpoint, Hassocks, W Sussex BN6 9ES.

NOEL, Hon. Gerard Eyre Wriothesley, FRSL; author, publisher and lecturer; Editor, Catholic Herald, 1971–76 and 1982–84, Editorial Director, 1976–81 and since 1984; *b* 20 Nov. 1926; *s* of 4th Earl of Gainsborough, OBE, TD, and Alice (*née* Eyre); *m* 1958, Adele, *d* of Major V. N. B. Were and Dr Josephine Were (*née* Ahern), OBE; two *s* one *d*. *Educ:* Georgetown, USA; Exeter Coll., Oxford (MA, Modern History). Called to Bar, Inner Temple, 1952. Director: Herder Book Co., 1959–66; Search Press Ltd, 1972–. Literary Editor, Catholic Times, 1958–61; Asst Editor, Catholic Herald, 1968–71. Sen. Res. Fellow, St Anne's Coll., Oxford, 1993–. Lects and lect. tours, UK, USA, Ireland and Spain; Vis. Lectr, Oxford Centre for Jewish Studies, 1992–93. Mem. Exec. Cttee, 1974–, Hon. Treasurer, 1979–81, Council of Christians and Jews. Contested (L) Argyll, 1959. FRSL 1999. Liveryman, Co. of Stationers and Newspapermakers. Freeman, City of London. Gold Staff Officer at Coronation, 1953. *Publications:* Paul VI, 1963; Harold Wilson, 1964; Goldwater, 1964; The New Britain, 1966; The Path from Rome, 1968; Princess Alice: Queen Victoria's Forgotten Daughter, 1974; contrib. The Prime Ministers, 1974; The Great Lock-Out of 1926, 1976; The Anatomy of the Roman Catholic Church, 1980; Ena: Spain's English Queen, 1984; Cardinal Basil Hume, 1984; (jtly) The Anatomy of the Catholic Church: before and after Pope John Paul II, 1994; Stranger than Truth: life and its fictions, 1996; Sir Gerard Noel, MP, 2001; Inner and Middle: a portrait of the Temple, 2002; *translations:* The Mystery of Love, 1960; The Way to Unity after the Council, 1967; The Holy See and the War in Europe (Official Documents), 1968; articles in: Church Times, Catholic Times, Jewish Chronicle, Baptist Times, Catholic Herald, Literary Review, European, International Mind. *Recreations:* travel, exploring London. *Address:* (office) Herald House, Lamb's Passage, EC1Y 8TQ; Westington Mill, Chipping Campden, Glos GL55 6EB. *Clubs:* Beefsteak, Garrick, White's.
See also R. J. B. Noel.

NOEL, Lynton Cosmas; barrister, retired 1994; *b* 25 Oct. 1928; *m* 1962, Teresa Angela Diamonda; one *s* one *d*. *Educ:* St Joseph's RC Sch., Grenada; Polytechnic/Holborn Coll. of Law, Languages and Commerce; Inns of Court Sch. of Law (LLB). Called to the Bar, Lincoln's Inn, 1976. Asst Head Teacher, 1956–60; Telephone Engr, GPO, 1960–67; practised law, 1976–84; Lectr in Law, Coll. of Law Studies, 1984; 1st Sec., Grenada High Commn, London, 1984–85; Chargé d'Affaires, Caracas, 1985–90; High Comr for Grenada in London, 1990–92; returned to practice at the Bar, 1992. *Recreations:* music, chess.

NOEL, Robert John Baptist; Lancaster Herald of Arms, since 1999; *b* 15 Oct. 1962; *s* of Hon. Gerard Eyre Wriothesley Noel, *qv*. *Educ:* Ampleforth; Exeter Coll., Oxford (MA Hebrew); St Edmund's Coll., Cambridge (MPhil Internat. Relns). Baltic Exchange, 1984–85; Christie's, 1988–91; Bluemantle Pursuivant, 1992–99. Vice-Chm., White Lion Soc., 1998–. Fellow, Purchase Soc., 1998. Officer of Arms Attendant, Imperial Soc. of Kts Bach., 2001–. *Address:* College of Arms, 130 Queen Victoria Street, EC4V 4BT. *T:* (020) 7332 0414, *Fax:* (020) 7248 6448. *Clubs:* Brooks's, Beefsteak, Garrick, Pratt's.

NOEL-BAKER, Hon. Francis Edward; Director, North Euboean Enterprises Ltd, since 1973; *b* 7 Jan. 1920; *o s* of Baron Noel-Baker, PC, and late Irene, *o d* of Frank Noel, British landowner, of Achmetaga, Greece; *m* 1957, Barbara Christina, *yr d* of late Joseph Sonander, Sweden; four *s* one *d* (and one *s* decd). *Educ:* Westminster Sch.; King's Coll., Cambridge (Exhibitioner; 1st cl. hons History). Founder and Chm., CU Lab. Club, 1939; left Cambridge to join Army, summer 1940, as Trooper, Royal Tank Regt; Commissioned in Intelligence Corps and served in UK, Force 133, Middle East (despatches). Editor, United Nations World/World Horizon, 1945–47, Go! magazine, 1947–48; BBC European Service, 1950–54. MP (Lab) Brentford and Chiswick Div. of Mddx, 1945–50; PPS Admiralty, 1949–50; MP (Lab) Swindon, 1955–68; sent by Prime Minister to mediate in Cyprus, 1956; Sec., 1955–64, Chm., 1964–68, UN Parly Cttee; resigned from Lab. Party, 1969; Vice-Chm., Lab. Cttee for Europe, 1976–78; Member: SDP 1981–83; Conservative Party, 1984–; NUJ, 1946–81. Chm., Advertising Inquiry Council, 1951–68. Chairman: North Euboean Foundation Ltd, 1965–; Candili Craft Centre, Philip Noel-Baker Centre, Euboea, 1983–; Dir, Fini Fisheries, Cyprus, 1976–90; Founder Pres., European Council for Villages and Small Towns, 1984–; Pres., Internat. Campaign for Environmental Health, 1985–; Hon. Pres., Union of Forest Owners of Greece, 1968–. Member: Parochial Church Council, St Martin in the Fields, 1960–68; Freedom from Hunger Campaign UK Cttee Exec. Cttee, 1961; Ecology Party, 1978–; Soil Assoc., 1979–. Governor, Campion Sch., Athens, 1973–78. Archives Fellow Commoner, Churchill Coll., Cambridge, 1989. Wine Constable, Guyenne, 1988–. *Publications:* Greece, the Whole Story, 1946; Spanish Summary, 1948; The Spy Web, 1954; Land and People of Greece, 1957; Nansen, 1958; Looking at Greece, 1967; My Cyprus File, 1985; Book Eight: a taste of hardship, 1987; Three Saints and Poseidon, 1988. *Recreation:* gardening. *Address:* Achmetaga Estate, 340–04 Procopi, Greece. *T:* (227) 41204, *Fax:* (227) 41190; 74 Westbourne Terrace, W2 6QR. *T:* (020) 7262 8400, *Fax:* (020) 7402 4278. *Clubs:* Travellers, Special Forces.
See also M. E. F. Chance.

NOEL-BUXTON, family name of **Baron Noel-Buxton**.

NOEL-BUXTON, 3rd Baron *cr* 1930; **Martin Connal Noel-Buxton;** *b* 8 Dec. 1940; *s* of 2nd Baron Noel-Buxton and Helen Nancy (*d* 1949), *yr d* of late Col K. H. M. Connal, CB, OBE, TD; *S* father, 1980; *m* 1st, 1964, Miranda Mary (marr. diss. 1968), *er d* of H. A. Chisenhale-Marsh; 2nd, 1972, Sarah Margaret Surridge (marr. diss. 1982), *o d* of N. C. W. Barrett, TD; one *s* one *d*; 3rd, 1986, Abigail Marie, *yr d* of E. P. R. Clent; one *d*. *Educ:* Bryanston School; Balliol College, Oxford (MA). Admitted a Solicitor, 1966. *Heir: s* Hon. Charles Connal Noel-Buxton, *b* 17 April 1975.

NOEL-PATON, Hon. (Frederick) Ranald; Chairman: Pacific Assets Trust plc, since 1998 (Director, 1986–98); Murray Global Return plc, since 2000 (Director, 1998–2000); *b* 7 Nov. 1938; *s* of Baron Ferrier, ED and Joane Mary, *d* of Sir Gilbert Wiles, KCIE, CSI; *m* 1973, Patricia Anne Stirling; four *d*. *Educ:* Rugby School; McGill Univ. (BA). Various posts, British United Airways, 1965–70; various sen. exec. posts, British Caledonian Airways, 1970–86; John Menzies Plc: Gp Man. Dir, 1986–97; Dep. Chm., 1997–98; Director: General Accident plc, 1987–98; Macallan-Glenlivet plc, 1990–96; Royal Bank of Scotland Gp, 1991–93. Hon. DBA Napier, 1992. *Recreations:* fishing, walking, gardening, bird watching, the arts. *Address:* Easter Dunbarnie, Bridge of Earn, Perthshire PH2 9ED. *Clubs:* Royal Perth Golfing Soc. and County and City; Shek-O Country, Hong Kong (Hong Kong).

NOEST, Peter John, FRICS; Managing Director: P. H. Gillingham (Investments) Ltd, since 1987; Capital Consultancy Group, since 1993; Cotswold Land and Estates Ltd; *b* 12 June 1948; *s* of Major A. J. F. Noest and Mrs M. Noest-Gerbrands; *m* 1st, 1972, Lisabeth Penelope Moody (marr. diss. 1993); one *s* one *d*; 2nd, 1993, Jocelyn Claire, *yr d* of late A. D. Spencer; one *s*. *Educ:* St George's Coll., Weybridge; Royal Agricl Coll., Cirencester. FRICS 1978 (ARICS 1973). Joined Knight Frank & Rutley, 1971; Partner i/c Dutch office, Amsterdam, 1972; London Partner, 1977; full equity Partner, 1981; Consultant, 1983, full equity Partner, 1984, Hampton & Sons; Dir, Hampton & Sons Holdings, 1987 (subseq. merged with Lambert Smith to form Lambert Smith Hampton); Dir, Lambert Smith Hampton, 1988–92. *Publication:* (contrib.) Office Development, 1985. *Recreations:* hunting, shooting, photography, travel. *Address:* Manor Farmhouse, Withington, Cheltenham, Glos GL54 4BG. *Club:* Turf.

NOGUEIRA, Albano Pires Fernandes; Ambassador of Portugal; *b* 8 Nov. 1911; *m* 1937, Alda Maria Marques Xavier da Cunha (*d* 1998). *Educ:* Univ. of Coimbra. 3rd Sec., Washington, 1944; 2nd Sec., Pretoria, 1945; 1st Sec., Pretoria, 1948; Head of Mission, Tokyo, 1950; Counsellor, London, 1953; Consul-Gen., Bombay, 1955; Consul-Gen., NY, 1955; Dep. Perm. Rep. UN, NY, 1955; Asst Dir-Gen., Econ. Affairs, Lisbon, 1959; Dir Gen., Econ. Affairs, Lisbon, 1961; Ambassador to: European Communities, Brussels, 1964; NATO, 1970; Court of St James's, 1974–76; Sec.-Gen., Ministry for Foreign Affairs, 1977. Vis. Prof., Univ. of Minho, Braga, 1979, 1980. Mem., Internat. Assoc. of Literary Critics, 1981–. Grand Cross: Merito Civil (Spain), 1961; Order of Infante Dom Henrique (Portugal), 1964; Isabel la Católica (Spain), 1977; Merit (Germany), 1977; St Olav (Norway), 1978; Christ (Portugal), 1981; the Flag with golden palm (Yugoslavia), 1978; Grand Officer: Cruzeiro do Sul (Brazil), 1959; White Elephant (Thailand), 1960. *Publications:* Imagens em Espelho Côncavo (essays); Portugal na Arte Japonesa (essay); Uma Agulha no Céu (novel); contribs to: NATO and the Mediterranean, 1985; NATO's Anxious Birth—the Prophetic Vision of the 1940s, 1985; contrib. leading Portuguese papers and reviews. *Recreations:* reading, writing. *Address:* Avenida Gaspar Corte-Real 18, Apt 4D, 2750 Cascais, Portugal. *T:* (21) 4868264; Rua Alberto de Oliveira 5–3-Esc., 3000-016 Coimbra, Portugal. *T:* (239) 715035. *Clubs:* Grémio Literário, Automóvel de Portugal (Lisbon).

NOLAN, family name of **Baron Nolan**.

NOLAN, Baron *cr* 1994 (Life Peer), of Brasted in the County of Kent; **Michael Patrick Nolan,** Kt 1982; PC 1991; DL; a Lord of Appeal in Ordinary, 1994–98; *b* 10 Sept. 1928; *yr s* of James Thomas Nolan and Jane (*née* Walsh); *m* 1953, Margaret, *yr d* of Alfred Noyes, CBE, and Mary (*née* Mayne); one *s* four *d*. *Educ:* Ampleforth; Wadham Coll., Oxford (Hon. Fellow, 1992). Served RA, 1947–49; TA, 1949–55. Called to Bar, Middle Temple, 1953 (Bencher, 1975); QC 1968; called to Bar, NI, 1974; QC (NI) 1974; a Recorder of the Crown Court, 1975–82; Judge, High Court of Justice, QBD, 1982–91; Presiding Judge, Western Circuit, 1985–88; a Lord Justice of Appeal, 1991–93. Member: Bar Council, 1973–74; Senate of Inns of Court and Bar, 1974–81 (Treasurer, 1977–79). Mem., Sandilands Cttee on Inflation Accounting, 1973–75; Chairman: Cttee on Standards in Public Life, 1994–97; Review on Child Protection in the Catholic Church in England and Wales, 2000–. Chm. Bd, Inst. of Advanced Legal Studies, 1994–2000. DL Kent, 2001. Mem. Governing Body, Convent of the Sacred Heart, Woldingham, 1973–83; Governor, Combe Bank Sch., 1974–83. Chancellor, Essex Univ., 1997–. DU Essex, 1996; DUniv Surrey, 1996; Hon. LLD: Warwick, 1998; Exeter, 1998; Bournemouth, 2000; DU Middlesex, 1999. *Recreation:* fishing. *Address:* House of Lords, SW1A 0PW. *Clubs:* Army and Navy, Boodle's, MCC.

NOLAN, Benjamin; QC 1992; a Recorder, since 1989; a Deputy High Court Judge; *b* 19 July 1948; *s* of Benjamin Nolan and Jane Nolan (*née* Mercer); *m* 1973, Noreen Frances Kelly; two *d*. *Educ:* St Joseph's Coll., Blackpool; Newcastle upon Tyne Polytechnic; LLB London, 1970. Called to the Bar, Middle Temple, 1971. *Recreations:* travel, cooking, walking, gardening, swimming. *Address:* Mercury Chambers, 33–35 Clarendon Road, Leeds LS2 9NZ. *T:* (0113) 234 2265.

NOLAN, Brig. Eileen Joan, CB 1976; Director, Women's Royal Army Corps, 1973–77; *b* 19 June 1920; *d* of late James John and Ethel Mary Nolan. *Educ:* King's Norton Grammar Sch. for Girls. Joined ATS, Nov. 1942; commissioned, 1945. Lt-Col, 1967; Col, 1970; Brig., 1973. Hon. ADC to the Queen, 1973–77; Chm., NATO Senior Women Officers' Cttee, 1975–77; Dep. Controller Comdt, WRAC, 1977–84. *Address:* c/o Barclays Bank, High Street, Crowthorne, Berkshire.

NOLAN, Prof. Peter Hugh, PhD; Sinyi Professor of Chinese Management, Judge Institute of Management Studies, University of Cambridge, since 1997; Fellow, Jesus College, Cambridge, since 1979; *b* 28 April 1949; *s* of Charles Patrick Nolan and Barbara Vere Nolan; *m* 1975, Siobāin Suzanne Mulligan; one *s* one *d*. *Educ:* St Boniface's Coll., Plymouth; Fitzwilliam Coll., Cambridge (Open Schol.; BA 1970); SOAS, Univ. of London (MSc 1971; PhD 1981). Res. Fellow, Contemporary China Inst., SOAS, Univ. of London, 1971–75; Lectr, Dept of Economic History, Univ. of NSW, 1976–78; Res. Officer, Inst. of Commonwealth Studies, Oxford Univ., 1978–79; Cambridge University: Asst Lectr, 1979–84, Lectr, 1984–97, Faculty of Econs and Politics; Dir of Studies in Econs, Jesus Coll., 1980–97; Chair, Develt Studies Cttee, 1995–. *Publications:* (jtly) Inequality: India and China compared 1950–1970, 1976; Growth Processes and Distributional Change in a South Chinese Province: the case of Guangdong, 1983; (ed jtly) Re-thinking Socialist Economics, 1986; The Political Economy of Collective Farms: an analysis of China's post-Mao rural economic reforms, 1988; (ed jtly) Market Forces in China: competition and small business—the Wenzhou debate, 1989; (ed jtly) The Chinese Economy and Its Future, 1990; State and Market in the Chinese Economy: essays on controversial issues, 1993; (ed jtly) China's Economic Reforms in the 1980s: the costs and benefits of incrementalism, 1994; (ed jtly) The Transformation of the Communist Economies: against the mainstream, 1995; China's Rise, Russia's Fall: politics and economics in the transition from Stalinism, 1995; Indigenous Large Firms in China's Economic Reforms: the case of Shougang Iron and Steel Corporation, 1998; Coca-Cola and the Global Business Revolution, 1999; China and the Global Economy, 2001; China and the Global Business Revolution, 2001. *Recreations:* swimming, music, playing recorder. *Address:* Jesus College, Cambridge CB5 8BL. *T:* (01223) 339477.

NOLAN, Philip Michael Gerard, PhD; Chief Executive, Lattice Group plc, since 2000; *b* 15 Oct. 1953; *m* 1978, Josephine Monaghan; two *s*. *Educ:* Queen's Univ., Belfast (BSc Geol. 1976; PhD 1980); London Business Sch. (MBA 1991). Lectr in Geol., Ulster Poly., 1979–81; joined BP, 1981: geologist, holding posts in exploration, appraisal and develt, in UK, US and Australia, 1981–87; BP Exploration, London: commercial and planning posts, Head Office, 1987–93; Manager, Acquisitions and Disposals, 1993–95; on secondment as Man. Dir, Interconnector (UK) Ltd, 1995–96; joined BG, 1996; Dir, East Area, 1996–97, Man. Dir, 1997–99, Chief Exec., 1999–2001, Transco; Dir, BG, 1999–2000. Non-exec. Dir, De la Rue plc, 2000–. *Recreations:* golf, watching football and Rugby, walking, listening to music, reading. *Address:* (office) 130 Jermyn Street, SW1Y 4UR. *T:* (020) 7389 3202.

NOON, Paul Thomas; Joint General Secretary, Prospect, since 2001 (General Secretary, Institution of Professionals, Managers and Specialists, 1999–2001); *b* 1 Dec. 1952; *s* of Thomas Noon and Barbara Noon (*née* Grocott); *m* 1977, Eileen Elizabeth Smith; two *d*. MoD, 1971–74; Institution of Professional Civil Servants: Asst Negotiations Officer, 1974–77; Negotiations Officer, 1977–81; Asst Sec., 1981–89; Asst Gen. Sec., 1989–99. Board Member: Unions Today, 1999–; Trade Union Fund Managers, 2001–. Vice-Chm., Civil Service Housing Assoc., 1999–. Trustee, Learning Through Life Foundn, 1999–. *Recreations:* reading, politics, family. *Address:* 3 Warwick Close, Bexley, Kent DA5 3NL. *T:* (01322) 550968, *Fax:* (01322) 550309; Prospect, 75–79 York Road, SE1 7AQ. *T:* (020) 7902 6704, *Fax:* (020) 7902 6667.

NOONEY, David Matthew; Director, Modernising Government Programme, Lord Chancellor's Department, since 1999; *b* 2 Aug. 1945; *m* 1973, Maureen Georgina Revell; one adopted *d*. *Educ:* St Joseph's Acad., Blackheath. FICMA. HM Treasury, 1965–86; on loan to Lord Chancellor's Dept as Management Accounting Advr, 1986–88, transf. to the Dept, 1989; Head, Resources Div., 1988–91; Head, Civil Business, 1991–93; Head, Legal Services and Agencies Div., 1993; Prin. Estabt and Finance Officer, then Dir, Corporate Services, CPS, 1993–98; on secondment to Welsh Office, 1998–99. *Recreations:* sport, theatre, crosswords, poetry. *Address:* Lord Chancellor's Department, Selborne House, 54/60 Victoria Street, SW1E 6QW.

NORBURN, Prof. David, PhD; Director, The Management School, Imperial College of Science, Technology and Medicine, and Professor of Management, University of London, since 1987; *b* 18 Feb. 1941; *s* of late Richard Greville and Constance Elizabeth Norburn; *m* 1st, 1962, Veronica Ellis (marr. diss. 1975); one *s* one *d*; 2nd, 1975, Prof. Susan Joyce Birley, *qv*. *Educ:* Bolton Sch.; LSE (BSc); City Univ. (PhD). Salesman, Burroughs Corp., 1962–66; Management Consultant, Price Waterhouse, 1966–67; Sen. Lectr, Regent Street Polytechnic, 1967–70; Sen. Res. Fellow, City Univ., 1970–72; Lectr, Sen. Lectr, Dir, MBA programme, London Business Sch., 1972–82; Inaugural Chairholder, Franklin D. Schurz Prof. in Strategic Management, Univ. of Notre Dame, Indiana, 1982–85; Prof. of Strategic Management, Cranfield Inst. of Technology, 1985–87. Director: Newchurch & Co., 1985–97; Whurr Publishing Co. Ltd, 1994–; Com. Medica Ltd, 1999–; Management Diagnostics Ltd, 2001–. Director: Strategic Mgt Soc., 1993–; Bd of Companions, Inst. of Mgt, 1994–97. Freeman, Clockmakers' Co. CIMgt, FRSA. Editor, European Business Journal, 1988–. *Publications:* British Business Policy (with D. Channon and J. Stopford), 1975; (jtly) Globalisation of Telecommunications, 1994; (jtly) Fusion in Home Automation, 1994; (with Sir William Nicoll and R. Schoenberg) Perspectives on European Business, 1995; articles in professional jls. *Recreations:* antiquarian horology, competitive tennis, carpentry. *Address:* The Management School, Imperial College of Science, Technology and Medicine, 53 Prince's Gate, SW7 2PG. *T:* (020) 7589 5111. *Club:* Athenæum.

NORBURN, Susan Joyce, (Mrs David Norburn); *see* Birley, S. J.

NORBURY, 7th Earl of, *cr* 1827 (Ire.); **Richard James Graham-Toler;** Baron Norwood 1797; Baron Norbury 1800; Viscount Glandine 1827; *b* 5 March 1967; *o s* of 6th Earl of Norbury and of Anne, *d* of Francis Mathew; *S* father, 2000.

NORBURY, Brian Martin; Chairman, Board of Visitors, Pentonville Prison, since 2000 (Member of Board, since 1994); *b* 2 March 1938; *s* of Robert Sidney Norbury and Doris Lilian (*née* Broughton). *Educ:* Churcher's Coll., Petersfield; King's Coll., London (BA; AKC 1959). National Service, RAEC, 1959–61. Asst Principal, WO, 1961; Private Sec.

to Under Sec. of State for War, 1962; Asst Private Sec. to Dep. Sec. of State for Defence, 1964; Principal, MoD, 1965, Cabinet Office, 1969; Private Sec. to Sec. of the Cabinet, 1970–73; Asst Sec., MoD, 1973; Principal Private Sec. to Sec. of State for Defence, 1979–81; Under Sec., MoD, 1981, DES, later Dept for Educn, 1984–94. Lay Mem., Special Educnl Needs Appeals Tribunal, 1994–. FRSA 1992. *Recreation:* riding on top of Routemaster buses. *Address:* 6 The Red House, 49–53 Clerkenwell Road, EC1M 5RS. *Club:* Reform.

NORCROSS, Lawrence John Charles, OBE 1986; Headmaster, Highbury Grove School, 1975–87; *b* 14 April 1927; *s* of Frederick Marshall Norcross and Florence Kate (*née* Hedges); *m* 1958, Margaret Wallace; three *s* one *d*. *Educ:* Ruskin Coll., Oxford; Univ. of Leeds (BA Hons English). Training Ship, Arethusa, 1941–42; RN, 1942–49 (E Indies Fleet, 1944–45); clerical asst, 1949–52; Asst Teacher: Singlegate Sch., 1957–61; Abbey Wood Sch., 1961–63; Housemaster, Battersea County Sch., 1963–74; Dep. Headmaster, Highbury Grove Sch., 1974–75. Member: NAS/UWT, 1970–86; Secondary Heads' Assoc., 1975–87; HMC, 1985–87; Trustee and Mem. Exec. Cttee, Nat. Council for Educnl Standards, 1976–89; Trustee: Educnl Res. Trust, 1986–; Ind. Primary and Secondary Educn Trust, 1987–93; Grant Maintained Schools Trust, 1988–; Nat. Cttee for Educnl Standards, 1997–; Director: Choice in Educn, 1989–94; Grant-Maintained Schs Foundn, 1994–; Member: Educn Study Gp, Centre for Policy Studies, 1980–; Univ. Entrance and Schs Examinations Council, Univ. of London, 1980–84; Steering Cttee, Campaign for a Gen. Teaching Council. Mem., Adv. Council, Educn Unit, IEA, 1986–90. Founder and Hon. Sec., John Ireland Soc., 1960–; former Chm., Contemp. Concerts Co-ordination. *Publications:* (with F. Naylor) The ILEA: a case for reform, 1981; (with F. Naylor and J. McIntosh) The ILEA after the Abolition of the GLC, 1983; (contrib.) The Wayward Curriculum, 1986; GCSE: the Egalitarian Fallacy, 1990; occasional articles. *Recreations:* talking to friends, playing bridge badly, watching cricket, listening to music. *Address:* Crockwell Cottage, Crockwell Street, Long Compton, Warwicks CV36 5JN. *T:* (01608) 684662; 3 St Nicholas Mansions, 6–8 Trinity Crescent, SW17 7AF. *T:* (020) 8767 4299. *Clubs:* St Stephen's Constitutional; Surrey County Cricket.

NORDEN, Denis, CBE 1980; scriptwriter and broadcaster; *b* 6 Feb. 1922; *s* of George Norden and Jenny Lubell; *m* 1943, Avril Rosen; one *s* one *d*. *Educ:* Craven Park Sch., London; City of London Sch. Theatre Manager, 1939–42; served RAF, 1942–45; staff-writer in Variety Agency, 1945–47. With Frank Muir, 1947–64: collaborated for 17 years writing comedy scripts, including: (for radio): Take It From Here, 1947–58; Bedtime with Braden, 1950–54; (for TV): And So To Bentley, 1956; Whack-O!, 1958–60; The Seven Faces of Jim, 1961, and other series with Jimmy Edwards; resident in TV and radio panel-games; collaborated in film scripts, television commercials, and revues; joint Advisors and Consultants to BBC Television Light Entertainment Dept, 1960–64; jointly received Screenwriters Guild Award for Best Contribution to Light Entertainment, 1961; together on panel-games My Word!, 1956–93, and My Music, 1967–. Since 1964, solo writer for television and films; Looks Familiar (Thames TV), 1973–87; It'll Be Alright on the Night (LWT), 1977–97; It'll be Alright on the Day, 1983; In On The Act, 1988; Pick of the Pilots, 1990; Denis Norden's Laughter File, 1991; Denis Norden's Trailer Cinema, 1992; Laughter by Royal Command, 1993; 40 Years of ITV Laughter, 1995; Legends of Light Music, 1995. Film Credits include: The Bliss of Mrs Blossom; Buona Sera, Mrs Campbell; The Best House in London; Every Home Should Have One; Twelve Plus One; The Statue; The Water Babies. Variety Club of GB Award for Best Radio Personality (with Frank Muir), 1978; Male TV Personality of the Year, 1980; Lifetime Achievement Award: Writers' Guild of GB, 1999; RTS, 2000. *Publications:* (with Frank Muir): You Can't Have Your Kayak and Heat It, 1973; Upon My Word!, 1974; Take My Word for It, 1978; The Glums, 1979; Oh, My Word!, 1980; The Complete and Utter My Word Stories, 1983; Coming to You Live! behind-the-screen memories of 50s and 60s Television, 1986; You Have My Word, 1989. *Recreations:* reading, loitering. *Address:* c/o April Young, 11 Woodlands Road, Barnes, SW13 0JZ. *Club:* Saturday Morning Odeon.

NORDMANN, François; Mission to International Organisations, Geneva, since 2000; *b* 13 May 1942; *s* of Jean and Bluette Nordmann; *m* 1980, Miriam Bohadana. *Educ:* Univ. de Fribourg (licencié en droit). Private Sec. to Foreign Minister, Switzerland, 1975–80; Counsellor and Perm. Observer, Mission to UN, NY, 1980–84; Ambassador to Guatemala, El Salvador, Honduras, Nicaragua, Costa Rica and Panama, 1984–87; Ambassador and Head of Swiss Perm. Delegn to UNESCO, Paris, 1987–92; Ambassador and Dir, Directorate of Internat. Orgns, Swiss Foreign Min., Berne, 1992–94; Ambassador to UK, 1994–99. *Recreations:* reading, theatre, walking, golf. *Address:* Mission to International Organisations, 9–11 rue de Varenba, PO Box 194, 1211 Geneva 20, Switzerland. *Club:* Cercle de l'Union Interalliée (Paris).

NORELL, Dr Jacob Solomon, (Jack), FRCGP; principal in general practice, 1956–90; *b* 3 March 1927; *s* of Henry (formerly Habib) Norell and Malka Norell; *m* 1948, Brenda Honeywell (marr. diss. 1973); three *s*. *Educ:* South Devon Technical Coll.; Guy's Hosp. Med. Sch. (MB, BS 1953). MRCS, LRCP 1953; LMSSA 1952; MRCGP 1972, FRCGP 1982. Dean of Studies, RCGP, 1974–81; Exec. Officer, Jt Cttee on Postgrad. Educn for Gen. Practice, 1976–81. Mem. Council, RCGP, 1984–90; Pres., Section of Gen. Practice, RSM, 1989–90. Pres., Balint Soc., 1984–87, Internat. Balint Fedn, 1989–93, ambassadorial rôle in Eastern Europe, 1994–. William Pickles Lectr, RCGP, 1984. Editor, The Practitioner, 1982–83. *Publications:* (co-ed) Six Minutes for the Patient, 1973; Entering General Practice, 1981; papers and chapters on general practice topics: the Balint philosophy, consultation, practice orgn, postgrad. educn, women doctors, measuring quality of med. care, professional self-regulation, doctor-patient relationship. *Recreations:* rural walks, driving open-topped cars, spotting unclad emperors. *Address:* 50 Nottingham Terrace, York Gate, Regent's Park, NW1 4QD. *T:* (020) 7486 2979.

NORFOLK, 17th Duke of, *cr* 1483; **Miles Francis Stapleton Fitzalan-Howard,** KG 1983; GCVO 1986; CB 1966; CBE 1960; MC 1944; DL; Royal Victorian Chain, 2000; Earl of Arundel, 1139; Baron Beaumont, 1309; Baron Maltravers, 1330, Earl of Surrey, 1483; Baron FitzAlan, Clun, and Oswaldestre, 1627; Earl of Norfolk, 1644; Baron Howard of Glossop, 1869; Earl Marshal and Hereditary Marshal and Chief Butler of England; Premier Duke and Earl; *b* 21 July 1915; *s* of 3rd Baron Howard of Glossop, MBE, and Baroness Beaumont (11th in line), OBE; *S* to barony of mother, 1971, and of father, 1972, and to dukedom of cousin, 1975; *m* 1949, Anne Mary Teresa, CBE, *e d* of late Wing Commander Gerald Joseph Constable Maxwell, MC, DFC, AFC; two *s* three *d*. *Educ:* Ampleforth Coll.; Christ Church, Oxford (MA; Hon. Student, 1983). 2nd Lieut, Grenadier Guards, 1937. Served War of 1939–45, France, North Africa, Sicily, Italy (despatches, MC), NW Europe. Appointed Head of British Military Mission to Russian Forces in Germany, 1957; Commanded 70 Bde KAR, 1961–63; GOC, 1 Div., 1963–65 (Maj.-Gen.); Dir, Management and Support Intelligence, MoD, 1965–66; Director, Service Intelligence, MoD, 1966–67; retd 1967. Chm., Arundel Castle Trustees, Ltd, 1976–. Pres., Building Socs Assoc., 1982–86. Prime Warden, Fishmongers' Co., 1985–86. Hon. Fellow, St Edmund's House, Cambridge, 1983; Hon. Bencher, Inner Temple, 1984. DL West Sussex, 1977. Knight, SMO Malta; Kt Grand Cross, Order of Pius IX. *Heir:* *s* Earl of Arundel and Surrey, *qv*. *Address:* Arundel Castle, Sussex BN18 9AB. *T:* (01903) 882173; Carlton Towers, Goole, North Humberside DN14 9LZ. *T:* (01405) 860 243. *Address:* Bacres House, Hambleden, Henley-on-Thames, Oxfordshire RG9 6RY. *T:* (01491) 571350. *Club:* Pratt's.

See also Lord Michael Fitzalan-Howard, Sir D. P. Frost.

NORFOLK, Archdeacon of; *see* Handley, Ven. A. M.

NORFOLK, Ven. Edward Matheson; Archdeacon of St Albans, 1982–87, Emeritus since 1987; *b* 29 Sept. 1921; *s* of Edward and Chrissie Mary Wilson Norfolk; *m* 1947, Mary Louisa Oates; one *s* one *d* (and one *s* decd). *Educ:* Latymer Upper School; Leeds Univ. (BA); College of the Resurrection, Mirfield. Deacon, 1946; priest, 1947; Assistant Curate: Greenford, 1946–47; King Charles the Martyr, South Mymms, 1947–50; Bushey, 1950–53; Vicar: Waltham Cross, 1953–59; Welwyn Garden City, 1959–69; Rector, Great Berkhamsted, 1969–81; Vicar, King's Langley, 1981–82. Hon. Canon of St Albans, 1972–82. *Recreations:* walking, bird-watching. *Address:* 5 Fairlawn Court, Sidmouth, Devon EX10 1UR.

NORFOLK, Leslie William, CBE 1973 (OBE 1944); TD 1946; CEng; Chief Executive, Royal Dockyards, Ministry of Defence, 1969–72; *b* 8 April 1911; *e s* of late Robert and Edith Norfolk, Nottingham; *m* 1944, A. I. E. W. (Nancy) Watson (then WRNS), *d* of late Sir Hugh Watson, IFS (retd); two *s* one *d*. *Educ:* Southwell Minster Grammar Sch., Notts; University Coll., Nottingham (BSc). MICE; MIMechE; MIEE. Assistant and later Partner, E. G. Phillips, Son & Norfolk, consulting engineers, Nottingham, 1932–39. 2nd Lieut 1931, 5 Foresters TA, transferred and served with RE, France, Gibraltar, Home Forces, 1939–45, Lt-Col. Engineer, Dyestuffs Div., ICI Ltd, 1945–53; Resident Engineer, ICI of Canada, Kingston, Ont., 1953–55; Asst Chief Engr, Metals Div., ICI Ltd, 1955–57; Engineering Manager, Severnside Works, ICI Ltd, 1957–59; Engineering Director, Industrias Quimicas Argentinas Duperial SAIC, Buenos Aires, 1959–65; Director, Heavy Organic Chemicals Div., ICI Ltd, 1965–68; retired from ICI, 1968. *Recreations:* home workshop, industrial archaeology. *Address:* Beechwoods, Beechwood Road, Combe Down, Bath, Avon BA2 5JS. *T:* (01225) 832104. *Club:* Bath & County (Bath).

NORGARD, John Davey, AO 1982; Chairman, Australian Broadcasting Commission, 1976–81; retired as Executive General Manager, Operations, BHP Co. Ltd, and as Chairman, Associated Tin Smelters, 1970; *b* 3 Feb. 1914; *s* of John Henry and Ida Elizabeth Norgard; *m* 1943, Irena Mary Doffkont; one *s* three *d*. *Educ:* Adelaide Univ. (BE); SA Sch. of Mines (FSASM). Part-time Chm., Metric Conversion Bd, Australia, 1970–81; Chairman: Commonwealth Employment Service Review, 1976–77; Pipeline Authority, 1976–81; Mem., Nat. Energy Adv. Cttee, 1977–80. Dep. Chancellor, La Trobe Univ., 1972–75. Chm., Grad. Careers Council of Australia, 1979–86. *Recreation:* golf. *Address:* 29 Montalto Avenue, Toorak, Victoria 3142, Australia. *T:* (3) 98274937. *Clubs:* Australian, Royal Melbourne Golf, Royal Society of Victoria (Melbourne).

NORGROVE, Michael William; Commissioner, since 1998, and Executive Director, since 2000, HM Customs and Excise; *b* 16 Dec. 1952; *s* of Walter and Nell Norgrove; *m* 1977, Lalita (*née* Shiner); one *s* one *d*. *Educ:* Palmer's Boys' Sch., Grays, Essex; Bedford Coll., London (BA 1974); King's Coll. London (MA 1975); St John's Coll., Oxford (PGCE 1978). Joined HM Customs and Excise as Exec. Officer, 1978, Admin trainee, 1981; seconded to HM Treasury, 1985–87; Principal, 1986; seconded to UK Permanent Repn, Brussels, 1988–93; Asst Sec., 1992; Head, Financial Mgt Div., 1993–98, Dir Ops (Compliance), 1998–2000, HM Bd of Customs and Excise. *Recreations:* bird-watching, golf, jazz. *Address:* HM Customs and Excise, New King's Beam House, Upper Ground, SE1 9PJ. *T:* (020) 7865 5020.

NORLAND, Otto Realf; London representative, Deutsche Schiffsbank (formerly Deutsche Schiffahrtsbank) AG, 1984–2000; Chairman, Otto Norland Ltd, 1984–2000; *b* 24 Feb. 1930; *s* of Realph I. O. Norland and Aasta S. Sæther; *m* 1955, Gerd Ellen Andenæs; two *d* (one *s* decd). *Educ:* Norwegian University College of Economics and Business Administration, Bergen. FCIB. Hambros Bank Ltd, 1953–84, Dir, 1964–84. Director: Alcoa of Great Britain Ltd, 1968–84 (Chm., 1978–84); Banque Paribas Norge A/S, Oslo, 1986–88; Northern Navigation International Ltd, USA, 1991–. Dir, Aluminium Fedn Ltd, 1979–84 (Pres., 1982). *Recreations:* tennis, ski-ing, books (polar explorations). *Clubs:* Den Norske; Norske Selskab (Oslo).

NORMAN, Andrew John; international sports marketing consultant, since 1994; *b* 21 Sept. 1943; *m* 1997, Fatima Whitbread, MBE; one *s*. Metropolitan Police Officer, 1962–84; Promotions Dir, British athletics, BAAB, 1984–91, British Athletics Fedn, 1991–94; agent for many top British athletes, 1994–. Principal Dir, European Athletics Championships, Budapest, 1998; Consultant, S African Athletics Fedn, 1994–; Special Projs Consultant, Eur. Athletics Assoc., 1999–; Competition Develt Consultant, IAAF, 2000–. Member: Grand Prix Commn, and Mkting Commn, IAAF, 1984–99; Mkting Commn, European Athletics Assoc., 1992–99. *Recreations:* sport, theatre. *Address:* Javel Inn, Mill Hill, Shenfield, Essex CM15 8EU. *T:* (01277) 213957.

NORMAN, Rear-Adm. Anthony Mansfeldt, CB 1989; Bursar and Fellow, St Catharine's College, Cambridge, 1989–97; *b* 16 Dec. 1934; *s* of Cecil and Jean Norman; *m* 1961, Judith Pye; one *s* one *d*. *Educ:* Royal Naval Coll., Dartmouth. Graduate ndc. Various sea/shore appts, 1952–73; Staff of Dir Underwater Weapons, 1973–74; student ndc, 1974–75; CO HM Ships Argonaut and Mohawk, 1975–76; Fleet Anti-Submarine Warfare Officer, 1976–78; CO (Captain), HMS Broadsword, 1978–80; Asst Dir Naval Plans, MoD, 1980–83; Captain: 2nd Frigate Sqdn, HMS Broadsword, 1983–85; Sch. of Maritime Ops, HMS Dryad, 1985–86; Dir Gen., Naval Personal Services, MoD (Navy), 1986–89. *Recreations:* tennis, hill walking, travel. *Address:* c/o National Westminster Bank, 208 Piccadilly, W1A 2DG. *Club:* Army and Navy.

NORMAN, Archibald John; MP (C) Tunbridge Wells, since 1997; *b* 1 May 1954; *s* of Dr Archibald Percy Norman, *qv*; *m* 1983, Vanessa Mary Peet; one *d*. *Educ:* Univ. of Minnesota; Emmanuel Coll., Cambridge (BA Hons Econs, MA); Harvard Business Sch. (MBA 1979). Citibank NA, 1975–77; McKinsey & Co. Inc., 1979–86, Principal 1984; Gp Finance Dir, Woolworth Holdings plc, later Kingfisher plc, 1986–91; Gp Chief Exec., 1991–96, Chm., 1996–99, Asda Group plc. Chairman: Chartwell Land plc, 1987–91; French plc, 1999–2001; non-exec. Dir, Geest plc, 1988–91; Member: British Railways Bd, 1992–94; Railtrack Gp Bd, 1994–2000. Member: DTI Deregulation Taskforce, 1993–97; Anglo-German Deregulation Taskforce, 1995. Chief Exec. and Dep. Chm., Cons. Party, 1998–99 (a Vice-Chm., 1997–98). Opposition front bench spokesman on the envmt, transport and the regions, 2000–01. Fellow, Marketing Soc. Hon. Dr Leeds Metropolitan Univ., 1995. Yorkshire Business Man of the Year, 1995; NatWest Retailer of the Year, 1996. *Recreations:* farming, opera, music, fishing, ski-ing, tennis. *Address:* House of Commons, SW1A 0AA. *T:* (020) 7219 3000. *Club:* Vanderbilt.

NORMAN, Archibald Percy, MBE 1945; MD; FRCP, FRCPCH, FRCPI; Physician, Hospital for Sick Children, 1950–77, then Hon. Physician; Paediatrician, Queen

Charlotte's Maternity Hospital, 1951–77, then Hon. Paediatrician; *b* 19 July 1912; *s* of Dr George Percy Norman and Mary Margaret MacCallum; *m* 1950, Aleida Elisabeth M. M. R. Bisschop; five *s*. *Educ:* Charterhouse; Emmanuel Coll., Cambridge. FRCP 1954; FRCPI 1995; FRCPCH 1996. Served War of 1939–45, in Army, 1940–45. Chairman: Med. and Res. Cttee, Cystic Fibrosis Res. Trust, 1976–84; E Surrey Cttee, Mencap Homes Foundn, 1987–92; Mem., Attendance Allowance Appeals Bd, 1978–84. Mem., Bd of Trustees, Children's Trust, 1987–98 (Chm., 1991–93). *Publications:* (ed) Congenital Abnormalities, 1962, 2nd edn 1971; (ed) Moncreiff's Nursing and Diseases of Sick Children, 1966; (ed) Cystic Fibrosis, 1983; contributions to medical journals. *Address:* White Lodge, Heather Close, Kingswood, Surrey KT20 6NY. *T:* (01737) 832626.

See also A. J. Norman.

NORMAN, Sir Arthur (Gordon), KBE 1969 (CBE 1966); DFC 1943 (and Bar 1944); Chairman, The De La Rue Company, 1964–87; *b* N Petherton, Som, 18 Feb. 1917; *m* 1944, Margaret Doreen Harrington (*d* 1982); three *s* two *d*. *Educ:* Blundell's Sch. Joined Thomas De La Rue & Co., 1934. RAF, 1939–45; Wing-Comdr, 1943. Rejoined Thomas De La Rue & Co., 1946; Director, 1951; Managing Director, 1953–77. Vice-Chm., Sun Life Assurance Society, 1984–87 (Dir, 1966–87); Director: SKF (UK) Ltd, 1970–87; Kleinwort, Benson, Lonsdale plc, subseq. Kleinwort Benson Gp, 1985–88. Pres., CBI, 1968–70. Bd mem., Internat. Inst. for Environment and Develt, 1982–92; Chairman: WWF UK, 1977–84, 1987–90; UK CEED, 1984–96; Mem., Nature Conservancy Council, 1980–86. *Recreations:* golf, country life. *Address:* Fir Tree Cottage, Hammoon, Sturminster Newton, Dorset DT10 2DB.

NORMAN, Barry (Leslie), CBE 1998; author, journalist and broadcaster; *b* 21 Aug. 1933; *s* of late Leslie and Elizabeth Norman; *m* 1957, Diana, *o d* of late A. H. and C. A. Narracott; two *d*. *Educ:* Highgate Sch. Entertainments Editor, Daily Mail, 1969–71, then made redundant; writer and presenter of Film 1973–81, and Film 1983–98, BBC1; presenter of: Today, Radio 4, 1974–76; Going Places, Radio 4, 1977–81; Breakaway, Radio 4, 1979–80; Omnibus, BBC1, 1982; The Chip Shop, Radio 4, 1984; How Far Can You Go?, Radio 4, 1990; writer and presenter of: The Hollywood Greats, BBC1, 1977–79, 1984, 1985; The British Greats, 1980; Talking Pictures (series), BBC1, 1988; Barry Norman's Film Night, BSkyB, 1998–2001. Weekly columnist: The Guardian, 1971–80; Radio Times. Gov., BFI, 1996–. Hon. LittD: UEA, 1991; Hertfordshire, 1996. Richard Dimbleby Award, BAFTA, 1981; Columnist of the Year, 1991; Special Award: London Film Critics' Circle, 1995; Guild of Regl Film Writers, 1995. *Publications:* The Matter of Mandrake, 1967; The Hounds of Sparta, 1968; Tales of the Redundance Kid, 1975; End Product, 1975; A Series of Defeats, 1977; To Nick a Good Body, 1978; The Hollywood Greats, 1979; The Movie Greats, 1981; Have a Nice Day, 1981; Sticky Wicket, 1984; The Film Greats, 1985; Talking Pictures, 1988; The Birddog Tape, 1992; 100 Best Films of the Century, 1993; The Mickey Mouse Affair, 1995; Death on Sunset, 1998. *Recreation:* playing village cricket. *Address:* c/o Curtis Brown Ltd, Haymarket House, 28–29 Haymarket, SW1Y 4SP. *T:* (020) 7396 6600.

NORMAN, David Mark; Chairman, Norlan Resources Ltd, since 1998; *b* 30 Jan. 1941; *s* of late Mark Richard Norman, CBE and of Helen Norman (*née* Bryan); *m* 1966, Diana Sheffield; one *s* three *d*. *Educ:* Eton Coll.; McGill Univ. (BA); Harvard Business Sch. (MBA). Norcros Ltd, 1967–77, Dir of Ops and Main Bd Dir, 1975–77; Russell Reynolds Associates Inc., 1977–82: Exec. Dir, 1977–78; Man. Dir, 1978–82; Chairman: Norman Resources Ltd. 1982–83; Norman Broadbent Internat. Ltd, 1983–98; Chm. and Chief Exec., 1987–97, non-exec. Chm., 1997–98, BNB Resources plc. Chm., Royal Ballet Sch., 2000–. *Recreations:* golf, tennis, rackets, classical music, opera, ballet. *Address:* Norlan Resources Ltd, 54 St James's Street, SW1A 1JT. *T:* (020) 7495 4666, *Fax:* (020) 7495 4667; Burkham House, Alton, Hants GU34 5RS. *T:* (01256) 381211. *Clubs:* Boodle's; Queen's, All England Lawn Tennis; New York Racquet and Tennis.

NORMAN, Desmond; *see* Norman, N. D.

NORMAN, Rev. Canon Edward Robert; Canon Residentiary, since 1995, and Chancellor, since 1999, York Minster; *b* 22 Nov. 1938; *o s* of Ernest Edward Norman and Yvonne Louise Norman. *Educ:* Chatham House Sch.; Monoux Sch.; Selwyn Coll., Cambridge (MA, PhD, DD). FRHistS. Lincoln Theological Coll., 1965. Deacon, 1965; Priest, 1971. Asst Master, Beaconsfield Sec. Mod. Sch., Walthamstow, 1957–58; Fellow of Selwyn Coll., Cambridge, 1962–64; Fellow of Jesus Coll., Cambridge, 1964–71; Lectr in History, Univ. of Cambridge, 1965–88; Dean of Peterhouse, Cambridge, 1971–88 (Emeritus Fellow); Dean of Chapel, Christ Church Coll., Canterbury, 1988–95; Wilkinson Prof. of Church History, Wycliffe Coll., Univ. of Toronto, 1981–82; Associated Schol., Ethics and Public Policy Center, Washington, 1986–; Hon. Prof., Univ. of York, 1996–. NATO Res. Fellow, 1966–68. Asst Chaplain, Addenbrooke's Hosp., Cambridge, 1971–78. Lectures: Reith, 1978; Prideaux, 1980; Suntory-Toyota, LSE, 1984. Six Preacher in Canterbury Cathedral, 1984–90. FRSA. *Publications:* The Catholic Church and Ireland, 1965; The Conscience of the State in North America, 1968; Anti-Catholicism in Victorian England, 1968; The Early Development of Irish Society, 1969; A History of Modern Ireland, 1971; Church and Society in Modern England, 1976; Christianity and the World Order, 1979; Christianity in the Southern Hemisphere, 1981; The English Catholic Church in the Nineteenth Century, 1983; Roman Catholicism in England, 1985; The Victorian Christian Socialists, 1987; The House of God: church architecture, style and history, 1990; Entering the Darkness: Christianity and its modern substitutes, 1991; An Anglican Catechism, 2001; Out of the Depths, 2001. *Recreation:* watching television. *Address:* 1 Precentor's Court, York YO1 7EJ. *Club:* Athenæum.

NORMAN, Gailene Patricia S.; *see* Stock-Norman.

NORMAN, Ven. Garth; Archdeacon of Bromley, since 1994; *b* 26 Nov. 1938; *s* of Harry and Freda Norman; *m* 1977, Jacqueline Elisabeth (*née* Junge-Bateman); one *s*. *Educ:* Henry Mellish Grammar Sch., Nottingham; Univ. of Durham (BA Hons Theol, DipTh, MA); Univ. of East Anglia (MEd); Univ. of Cambridge (PGCE). Deacon 1963, priest 1964; Curate, St Anne's, Wandsworth, 1963–66; Team Vicar, Trunch, Norfolk, 1966–71; Rector of Gimingham, 1971–77; Team Rector of Trunch, 1977–83; RD, Repps, 1975–83; Principal, Chiltern Christian Trng Scheme, Dio. of Oxford, 1983–88; Dir of Training, Dio. of Rochester, 1988–94; Hon. Canon of Rochester Cathedral, 1991–. *Recreations:* walking, music. *Address:* 6 Horton Way, Farningham, Kent DA4 0DQ. *T:* (01322) 864522.

NORMAN, Geoffrey, OBE 1995; Deputy Secretary of Commissions (Training), Lord Chancellor's Department, 1990–95; *b* 25 March 1935; *s* of late William Frederick Trafalgar Norman and of Vera May Norman (*née* Goodfellow); *m* 1958, Dorothy Frances King (*d* 1978); two *s* two *d*. *Educ:* Harrow County Sch.; Brasenose Coll., Oxford (MA). Admitted Solicitor, 1959. Deputy Clerk to the Justices, Uxbridge, 1961–66; Clerk to the Justices, N Hertfordshire and Stevenage, 1966–77; Sec., Magistrates' Assoc., 1977–86; Asst Sec. of Commns (Trng), Lord Chancellor's Dept, 1986–90. Member: Duty Solicitor Scheme-making Cttee, 1984–86; Magisterial Cttee, Judicial Studies Bd, 1986–95; Magistrates' Courts Rules Cttee, 1989–93. JP Inner London, 1982–90. Freeman, City of London, 1981; Liveryman, Curriers' Co., 1983. *Publications:* The Magistrate as Chairman (with Lady Ralphs), 1987; Benchmarks, 1997. *Address:* Easter Cottage, Gosmore, Hitchin, Herts SG4 7QH. *T:* (01462) 450783.

NORMAN, George Alfred B.; *see* Bathurst Norman.

NORMAN, Geraldine Lucia; Executive Director, Hermitage Development Trust, since 1999; UK Representative, State Hermitage Museum, St Petersburg, since 2001; *b* 13 May 1940; *d* of Harold Hugh Keen and Catherine Eleanor Lyle Keen (*née* Cummins); *m* 1971, Frank Norman (*d* 1980). *Educ:* St Mary's Sch., Calne; St Anne's Coll., Oxford (MA). Teaching Asst, UCLA, 1961–62; Statistician, The Times, 1962–66; Econ. Writer, FAO, Rome, 1966–67; Sale Room Corresp., The Times, 1969–87; Art Market Corresp., The Independent, 1987–95. News Reporter of Year, British Press Awards, 1976. *Publications:* (as Geraldine Keen) The Sale of Works of Art, 1971; Nineteenth Century Painters and Painting: a dictionary, 1977; (with Tom Keating and Frank Norman) The Fake's Progress, 1977; (as Florence Place) Mrs Harper's Niece, 1982; Biedermeier Painting, 1987; (with Natsuo Miyashita) Top Collectors of the World, 1993; The Hermitage: the biography of a great museum, 1997. *Recreations:* transcendental meditation, reading detective stories. *Address:* 5 Seaford Court, 220 Great Portland Street, W1N 5HH. *T:* (020) 7387 6067.

See also M. H. Keen.

NORMAN, Gregory John, AM; golfer; *b* 10 Feb. 1955; *s* of M. Norman; *m* 1981, Laura Andrassy; one *s* one *d*. *Educ:* Townsville Grammar Sch.; High Sch., Aspley, Queensland. Professional golfer, 1976–; tournament wins include: Open, Turnberry, 1986; Open, Royal St George's, 1993; Australian Open, 1980, 1985, 1987; US PGA, 1993, 1994; Players' Championship, 1994; numerous awards and other wins in Australia, S Africa, USA. *Publications:* My Story, 1983; Shark Attack, 1988; Greg Norman's Better Golf, 1994. *Address:* Great White Shark Enterprises Inc., PO Box 1189, Hobe Sound, FL 33475–1189, USA.

NORMAN, (Herbert) John (La French), FIMIT, FISOB; writer and organ consultant; *b* 15 Jan. 1932; *s* of late Herbert La French Norman, Hon. RCO, FRSA, and Hilda Caroline (*née* West); *m* 1956, Jill Frances Sharp; one *s* two *d*. *Educ:* Tollington Sch.; Imperial Coll., London (BSc 1953). ARCS 1953. Wm Hill & Son and Norman & Beard Ltd (organbuilders by appt to HM Queen), 1953–74; Dir, 1960–74; Man. Dir, 1970–74; Exec., IBM UK Ltd, 1974–90. Work on organs in cathedrals in Gloucester, Norwich, Lichfield, Southwell Minster, Chelmsford and Brisbane, Australia; also Bath Abbey and RCO. Organ Advr, Dio. London, 1975–; Organ Consultant to: Harrow Sch.; Lancing Coll.; Mill Hill Sch.; English and American Ch, Den Haag; Sherborne Abbey; Gibraltar Cathedral; Liberal Jewish Synagogue, St John's Wood; St Margaret's, Westminster; St Mary's Pro-cathedral, Dublin; Pershore Abbey; St Helen's, Bishopsgate; Chapel of St Mary Undercroft, Houses of Parliament; Mullingar Cathedral, Ireland; St Lawrence, Whitchurch (Handel organ); Parish Churches of Oakham, Westbourne, Ashton-on-Ribble, Baldock and Donaghadee (NI); Armenian Ch, Kensington; St Botolph, Aldersgate. Founding Editor: Musical Instrument Technol., 1969–; The Organbuilder, 1983–2000; In Sight, 1991–95; Columnist, Organists' Rev., 1980–. Member: St Albans Diocesan Synod, 1980–86; Organs Cttee, Council for Care of Churches, 1987–2001; London DAC for Care of Churches, 1989–; Cathedrals Fabric Commn for England, 1991–2001. Mem., Panel of Assessors, Arts Council of England Lottery Fund, 1996–. Mem., Musical Instrument Technol. Adv. Bd, London Guildhall Univ. (formerly City of London Polytechnic), 1990–. Past Pres., Inst. of Musical Instrument Technol. Freeman, City of London; Liveryman, Musicians' Co., 1972–. *Publications:* (with Herbert Norman) The Organ today, 1966, 2nd edn 1980; The Organs of Britain, 1984. *Recreations:* writing, music, architecture, travel. *Address:* 15 Baxendale, Whetstone, N20 0EG. *T:* (020) 8445 0801.

NORMAN, Jessye; soprano, concert and opera singer; *b* Augusta, Ga, USA, 15 Sept. 1945; *d* of late Silas Norman Sr and Janie King Norman. *Educ:* Howard Univ., Washington, DC (BM *cum laude*). Peabody Conservatory, 1967; Univ. of Michigan, 1967–68 (MMus). Operatic début, Deutsche Oper, Berlin, 1969; La Scala, Milan, 1972; Royal Opera House, Covent Garden, 1972; NY Metropolitan Opera, 1983; American début, Hollywood Bowl, 1972; Lincoln Centre, NYC, 1973. Tours include North and South America, Europe, Middle East, Australia, Israel, Japan. Many international festivals, including Aix-en-Provence, Aldeburgh, Berlin, Edinburgh, Flanders, Helsinki, Lucerne, Salzburg, Tanglewood, Spoleto, Hollywood, Ravinia. Hon. Fellow: Newnham Coll., Cambridge, 1989; Jesus Coll., Cambridge, 1989. Hon. DMus: Howard Univ., 1982; Univ. of the South, Sewanee, 1984; Boston Conservatory, 1984; Univ. of Michigan and Brandeis Univ., Mass, 1987; Harvard Univ., 1988; Cambridge, 1989; Hon DHL Amer. Univ. of Paris, 1989. Hon. RAM 1987. Musician of the Year, Musical America, 1982; prizes include: Grand Prix du Disque (Acad. du Disque Français), 1973, 1976, 1977, 1982, 1984; Grand Prix du Disque (Acad. Charles Cros), 1983; Deutscher Schallplattenpreis, 1975, 1981; Cigale d'Or, Aix-en-Provence Fest., 1977; IRCAM record award, 1982; Grammy, 1984, 1988. Commandeur de l'Ordre des Arts et des Lettres, France, 1984. *Address:* c/o Raymond Zagorski, L'Orchidée, PO Box S, Crugers, NY 10521, USA. *T:* (914) 2712037, *Fax:* (914) 2712038.

NORMAN, John; *see* Norman, H. J. La F.

NORMAN, Prof. Kenneth Roy, FBA 1985; Professor of Indian Studies, University of Cambridge, 1990–92, Emeritus Professor 1992; *b* 21 July 1925; *s* of Clement and Peggy Norman; *m* 1953, Pamela Raymont; one *s* one *d*. *Educ:* Taunton School; Downing College, Cambridge (MA 1954). Fellow and Tutor, Downing College, Cambridge, 1952–64; Lectr in Indian Studies (Prakrit), 1955–78, Reader, 1978–90, Univ. of Cambridge. Foreign Mem., Royal Danish Acad. of Sciences and Letters, 1983. *Publications:* Elders' Verses I (Theragāthā), 1969; Elders' Verses II (Therīgāthā), 1971; (trans.) Jain Cosmology, 1981; Pāli Literature, 1983; The Group of Discourses (Sutta-nipāta), Vol. I, 1984, Vol. II, 1992; Collected Papers: Vol. I, 1990, Vol. II, 1991, Vol. III, 1992, Vol. IV, 1993, Vol. V, 1994, Vol. VI, 1996, Vol. VII, 2001; Poems of Early Buddhist Monks, 1997; The Word of the Doctrine (Dhammapada), 1997; A Philological Approach to Buddhism, 1997; (with W. Pruitt) The Pātimokkha, 2001; (ed) Pāli Tipitakam Concordance, Vol. II 4–9, 1963–73; (ed) Critical Pāli Dictionary Vol. II 11–17, 1981–90. *Recreation:* reading. *Address:* 6 Huttles Green, Shepreth, Royston, Herts SG8 6PR. *T:* (01763) 260541.

NORMAN, Sir Mark (Annesley), 3rd Bt *cr* 1915; DL; farmer; *b* 8 Feb. 1927; *s* of Sir Nigel Norman, 2nd Bt, CBE, and Patricia Moyra (*d* 1986) (who *m* 2nd, 1944, Sir Robert Perkins), *e d* of late Colonel J. H. A. Annesley, CMG, DSO; *S* father, 1943; *m* Joanna Camilla, *d* of late Lt-Col I. J. Kilgour; two *s* one *d*. *Educ:* Winchester Coll.; RMC. Coldstream Guards, 1945–47; Flying Officer, 601 (County of London) Sqdn, RAuxAF, 1953–56. Hon. Air Cdre, No 4624 (County of Oxford) Movements Sqdn, RAuxAF, 1984–2000. Chm., Anglo-US Cttee, RAF Upper Heyford, 1984–91. Director: Gotaas-Larsen Shipping Corp., 1979–88. Chm., IU Europe Ltd, 1973–87. Mem., Council, St Luke's, Oxford, 1985–91 (Chm., 1986–88). Patron and Churchwarden, St Peter's,

Wilcote, 1972–. High Sheriff, 1983–84, DL 1985, Oxon. *Recreations:* gardening, workshop, offshore cruising. *Heir: s* Nigel James Norman, late Major 13/18th Royal Hussars (Queen Mary's Own) [*b* 5 Feb. 1956; *m* 1994, Mrs Juliet Marriott, *e d* of R. Baxendale; two *s* one *d*]. *Address:* Wilcote Manor, Wilcote, Chipping Norton, Oxon OX7 3EB. *T:* (01993) 868357. *Fax:* (01993) 868032. *Clubs:* White's, Pratt's, Royal Air Force, MCC; St Moritz Tobogganing; Royal Southern Yacht, Royal London Yacht.

See also N. D. Norman.

NORMAN, (Nigel) Desmond, CBE 1970; CEng; FRAeS; Chairman and Managing Director, AeroNorTec Ltd, since 1988; *b* 13 Aug. 1929; 2nd *s* of Sir Nigel Norman, 2nd Bt (*d* 1943), CBE, and Patricia Moyra (*d* 1987) (who *m* 2nd, 1944, Sir Robert Perkins); *m* 1st, Anne Fogg-Elliott; two *s*; 2nd, 1965, Mrs. Boel Elizabeth Holmsen; two *s* two *d*. *Educ:* Eton; De Havilland Aeronautical Technical Sch. (1946–49). RAF GD Pilot, thereafter 601 Sqdn, RAuxAF Fighter Sqdn, until disbandment, 1948–57. Export Asst at SBAC, 1951–53; Founder of Britten-Norman Ltd with F. R. J. Britten, 1954. *Recreations:* aviation, sailing, shooting. *Address:* Flat 4, 73 Duke Street, W1M 5DH; Le Palland, 87400 St Leonard de Noblat, France. *Clubs:* Royal Air Force, Royal Yacht Squadron.

See also Sir Mark Norman, Bt.

NORMAN, Sir Robert (Henry), Kt 1989; OBE 1957; Chairman, Cairns Campus Co-ordinating Committee, James Cook University of North Queensland, since 1987; *b* 30 Jan. 1914; *s* of Robert Moreton Norman and Dora Muriel Hoole; *m* 1942, Betty Merle Kimmins; one *s* three *d*. *Educ:* Christian Brothers' Coll. Joined RAAF, 1941; Dep. Flt Lieut, 1942; 459 Sqdn, 1943; discharged, 1945. Founded Bush Pilot Airways, 1952, retd 1984. Cairns Centenary Co-ordinator, 1976. Past Pres., Rotary Club of Cairns, Marlin Coast; Dist Gov., Dist 9550, Rotary Internat., 1991–92. Hon. DLitt James Cook Univ. of N Qld, 1994. *Publication:* Bush Pilot, 1976. *Recreations:* motoring, reading. *Address:* Unit 14, Woodward Retirement Village, 82 McManus Street, Whitfield, Qld 4870, Australia; PO Box 133H, Edge Hill, Qld 4870, Australia.

NORMAN, Sir Ronald, Kt 1995; OBE 1987; DL; CEng; Chairman, Priority Sites, since 1997; *b* 29 April 1937; *s* of Leonard William Norman and Elsie Louise Norman (*née* Cooke); *m* 1st, 1961, Jennifer Mansfield (marr. diss. 1972); two *s* one *d*; 2nd, 1975, Joyce Lyons. *Educ:* Dulwich Coll.; King's Coll., London (BSc Eng.). CE; CEng, MICE 1966. Man. Dir, then Chm., Cecil M. Yuill Ltd, Developers, Hartlepool, 1965–86; Chm., R. Norman Ltd, Developers, Durham, 1986–93. Chm., Teesside Develt Corp., 1987–98. DL Cleveland, 1996. *Recreations:* mountain climbing, book collecting. *Address:* Sparrow Hall, Dalton-Piercy, Cleveland TS27 3HY. *T:* (01429) 273857.

NORMAN, Susan Elizabeth, (Mrs J. C. Sheridan); Chief Executive and Registrar, United Kingdom Central Council for Nursing, Midwifery and Health Visiting, since 1995; *b* 9 Aug. 1946; *d* of late Dr J. M. Norman and of Betty Norman (*née* Colyer); *m* 1983, John Christopher Sheridan. *Educ:* St Nicholas Sch., Fleet, Hants; Dartington Hall, Devon; St Thomas' Hosp. (RGN); Bedford Coll., London (RNT); South Bank Univ. (BEd Hons). Student nurse, St Thomas' Hosp., 1965–69; Dist Nurse, RBK&C, 1969–71; Staff Nurse, Royal Marsden Hosp., 1972; Nursing Officer (Dist Nursing), Kensington and Chelsea, 1972–73; Staff Nurse, Montreal Gen. Hosp., 1974–75; Tutor Student, London Univ., 1975–77; Tutor and Sen. Tutor, Nightingale Sch., 1977–87; Principal Nursing Officer (Asst Sec.), DoH, London and Leeds, 1990–93. *Publication:* Nursing Practice and Health Care, 1989, 3rd edn 1998. *Recreations:* music (singing and opera), walking, UK and France, eating out. *Address:* UKCC, 23 Portland Place, W1N 4JT. *T:* (020) 7333 6527.

NORMANBY; 5th Marquis of, *cr* 1838; **Constantine Edmund Walter Phipps**. Baron Mulgrave (Ire.) 1767; Baron Mulgrave (GB) 1794; Earl of Mulgrave and Viscount Normanby 1812; *b* 24 Feb. 1954; *e s* of 4th Marquis of Normanby KG, CBE and of Hon. Grania Guinness (OBE 2000), *d* of 1st Baron Moyne; *S* father, 1994; *m* 1990, Mrs Nicola St Aubyn, *d* of Milton Shulman, *qv* and Drusilla Beyfus, *qv*; two *s* one *d*. *Educ:* Eton; Worcester Coll., Oxford; City Univ. *Publications:* Careful with the Sharks, 1985; Among the Thin Ghosts, 1989. *Heir: s* Earl of Mulgrave, *qv*. *Address:* Mulgrave Castle, Whitby, N Yorks YO21 3RJ. *Clubs:* Travellers, Garrick.

NORMANTON, 6th Earl of, *cr* 1806; **Shaun James Christian Welbore Ellis Agar;** Baron Mendip, 1794; Baron Somerton, 1795; Viscount Somerton, 1800; Baron Somerton (UK), 1873; Royal Horse Guards, 1965; Blues and Royals, 1969; left Army, 1972, Captain; *b* 21 Aug. 1945; *er s* of 5th Earl of Normanton; *S* father, 1967; *m* 1970, Victoria Susan (marr. diss. 2000), *o d* of late J. H. C. Beard; one *s* two *d*. *Educ:* Eton. *Recreations:* shooting, skiing, scuba diving, motor boating. *Heir: s* Viscount Somerton, *qv*. *Address:* Somerley, Ringwood, Hants BH24 3PL. *T:* (01425) 473253. *Clubs:* White's; Royal Yacht Squadron.

NORMINGTON, David John, CB 2000; Permanent Secretary, Department for Education and Skills (formerly for Education and Employment), since 2001; *b* 18 Oct. 1951; *s* of late Ronald Normington and of Kathleen Normington (*née* Towler); *m* 1985, Winifred Anne Charlotte Harris. *Educ:* Bradford Grammar Sch.; Corpus Christi College, Oxford (BA Hons Mod. Hist.). Department of Employment, subseq. Department for Education and Employment: joined 1973; Private Sec. to Perm. Sec., 1976–77; Principal Private Sec. to Sec. of State for Employment, 1984–85; Employment Service Regional Dir for London and SE Region, 1987–89; Hd of Strategy and Employment Policy Div., 1990–92; Dir of Personnel and Develt, 1992–95, of Personnel and Support Services, 1995–97; Dir Gen., Strategy, Internat. and Analytical Services, 1997–98; Dir Gen. for Schs, 1998–2001. *Recreations:* gardening, ballet, theatre, cricket. *Address:* Department for Education and Employment, Sanctuary Buildings, Great Smith Street, SW1P 3BT. *T:* (020) 7925 6236.

NORREYS, Lord; Henry Mark Willoughby Bertie; *b* 6 June 1958; *s* and *heir* of the Earl of Lindsey (14th) and Abingdon (9th), *qv*; *m* 1989, Lucinda, *d* of Christopher Moorsom; two *s*. *Educ:* Eton; Univ. of Edinburgh. Kt of Honour and Devotion, SMO Malta, 1995; Kt of Justice, Constantinian Order of St George, 1998; Kt, Order of St Maurice and St Lazarus, 1999. *Heir: s* Hon. Willoughby Henry Constantine St Maur Bertie, *b* 15 Jan. 1996. *Address:* c/o Gilmilnscroft, Sorn, Mauchline, Ayrshire KA5 6ND. *Clubs:* Pratt's; Puffin's (Edinburgh).

NORRIE, family name of **Baron Norrie**.

NORRIE, 2nd Baron *cr* 1957; **George Willoughby Moke Norrie;** *b* 27 April 1936; *s* of 1st Baron Norrie, GCMG, GCVO, CB, DSO, MC, and Jocelyn Helen (*d* 1938), *d* of late R. H. Gosling; *S* father, 1977; *m* 1st, 1964, Celia Marguerite, JP (marr. diss. 1997), *d* of John Pelham Mann, MC; one *s* two *d*; 2nd, 1997, Mrs Pamela Ann McCaffry, *d* of Sir Arthur Ralph Wilmot, 7th Bt. *Educ:* Eton College; RMA Sandhurst. Commissioned 11th Hussars (PAO), 1956; ADC to C-in-C Middle East Comd, 1960–61; GSO 3 (Int.) 4th Guards Brigade, 1967–69; retired, 1970. Underwriting Mem. of Lloyd's, 1977–97. Director: Fairfield Nurseries (Hermitage) Ltd, 1976–89; International Garden Centre (British Gp) Ltd, 1984–86; Conservation Practice Ltd, 1989–91; Hilliers (Fairfield) Ltd, 1989–97; Advisor to: S Grundon (Waste) Ltd, 1991–2001; CH2M Hill Ltd (London), 1994–96. Mem., EC Cttee, Sub Cttee F (Environment), H of L, 1988–92. President: British Trust for Conservation Volunteers, 1987–; Internat. Cultural Exchange, 1988–2000; Commercial Travellers Benevolent Instn, 1992–; Royal British Legion (Newbury Branch), 1971–96; Nat. Kidney Fedn, 1994–2001; Vice President: Tree Council, 1990–; Council for Nat. Parks, 1990–. Mem. Council, Winston Churchill Meml Trust, 1993–. Patron: Age Resource, 1991–; Faure-Alderson Romanian Appeal, 1993–2001; Janki Foundn, 1997–; UK Patron, RLSS, 1994– (Mem., Commonwealth Council, 1999–). Gov., Dunstan Park Sch., Thatcham, 1989–94. Mem., British Soc. of Dowsers, 1999–. Sponsored: Swimming and Water Safety Bill, 1993 (enacted under statutory order, 1994); Nat. Parks Bill, 1993 (incorp. in Envmt Act, 1995). Green Ribbon Political Award for services to the envmt, H of L, 1993. *Recreations:* fishing, golf, Real tennis. *Heir: s* Hon. Mark Willoughby John Norrie [*b* 31 March 1972; *m* 1998, Carol, *e d* of Michael Stockdale; one *s*]. *Address:* Chapel on the Water, Ramsbury, Marlborough, Wilts SN8 2QN. *T:* (01672) 521180. *Clubs:* Cavalry and Guards, White's, MCC.

NORRIE, Marian Farrow, (Mrs W. G. Walker); Her Honour Judge Norrie; a Circuit Judge, since 1986; *b* 25 April 1940; *d* of Arthur and Edith Jackson; *m* 1st, 1964, two *d*; 2nd, 1983, William Guy Walker, *qv*; one step *s* two step *d*. *Educ:* Manchester High Sch. for Girls; Nottingham Univ. (LLB). Admitted Solicitor of Supreme Court, 1965; a Recorder, 1979–86. Consultant, Norrie, Bowler & Wrigley, Solicitors, Sheffield, 1983–86 (Sen. Partner, 1968–83). Member: Parole Bd, 1983–85; Appts Commn, Press Council, 1985. *Address:* The Family Centre, Brighton County Court, 1 Edward Street, Brighton BN2 2JD.

NORRINGTON, Humphrey Thomas, OBE 2001; Vice Chairman, Barclays Bank, 1991–93; *b* 8 May 1936; *s* of Sir Arthur Norrington and Edith Joyce, *d* of William Moberly Carver; *m* 1963, Frances Guenn Bateson; two *s* two *d*. *Educ:* Dragon School, Oxford; Winchester; Worcester College, Oxford (MA). Barclays Bank: joined, 1960; general management, 1978–87; Dir, 1985–93; Exec Dir, Overseas Ops, 1987–91. Chm., Exec. Cttee, British Bankers' Assoc., 1990–91. Chm., Southwark Cathedral Develt Trust, 1986–93; Director: City Arts Trust, 1988–93; Mildmay Mission Hosp., 1992–; World Vision UK, 1991–. Member, Archbishops' Commission: on Rural Areas, 1988–90; on Orgn of the C of E, 1994–95. Chm., Christian Media Trust. Hon. Treasurer: RSPB, 1996–; RCM, 1997–. *Recreations:* music, countryside. *Address:* Hill House, Frithsden Copse, Berkhamsted, Herts HP4 2RQ. *T:* (01442) 871855. *Club:* Oxford and Cambridge.

See also Sir R. A. C. Norrington.

NORRINGTON, Sir Roger (Arthur Carver), Kt 1997; CBE 1990 (OBE 1980); Chief Conductor: Radio Sinfonie Orchester Stuttgart, since 1998; Camerata Academica Salzburg, since 1997; *b* 16 March 1934; *s* of late Sir Arthur Norrington and Edith Joyce, *d* of William Moberly Carver; *m* 1st, 1964, Susan Elizabeth McLean May (marr. diss. 1982); one *s* one *d*; 2nd, 1986, Karalyn Mary Lawrence; one *s*. *Educ:* Dragon Sch., Oxford; Westminster; Clare Coll., Cambridge (BA; Hon. Fellow, 1991); Royal Coll. of Music. Freelance singer, 1962–72. Principal Conductor: Kent Opera, 1966–84; Bournemouth Sinfonietta, 1985–89; Music Director: Orch. of St Luke's, NY, 1990–94; Schütz Choir of London, 1962–82; London Classical Players, 1978–98; Prince Consort Prof., RCM, 1997. Guest conducts many British, European and American orchestras, appears at Covent Garden, Coliseum, Proms and festivals; broadcasts regularly at home and abroad. Débuts: British, 1962; BBC Radio, 1964; TV 1967; Germany, Austria, Denmark, Finland, 1966; Portugal, 1970; Italy, 1971; France and Belgium, 1972; USA, 1974; Holland, 1975; Switzerland, 1976. Many gramophone recordings. Hon. RAM 1988. FRCM 1992. DUniv York, 1991; Hon. DMus Kent, 1994. Cavaliere, Orden al Merito (Italy), 1981; Ehrenkreuz, 1st cl. (Austria), 1999. *Publications:* occasional articles in various musical journals. *Recreations:* gardening, reading, walking.

See also H. T. Norrington.

NORRIS, Brig. (Alaric) Philip, OBE 1982; **His Honour Judge Norris;** a Circuit Judge, since 1995; *b* 20 Sept. 1942; *yr s* of late Charles Henry Norris and Maud Frances Norris (*née* Neild); *m* 1967, Pamela Margaret Parker; three *s*. *Educ:* Sir William Turner's Sch., Coatham, Redcar; Queens' Coll., Cambridge (MA); Dip. in Law and Amer. Studies, Univ. of Virginia, USA, 1979. Admitted Solicitor, 1968; commnd Army Legal Services, 1970; served MoD, SHAPE, BAOR, Berlin, NEARELF, NI, UKLF/Land Comd, USA and Geneva; retired, in rank of Brig., 1995. *Recreations:* a bit of all sorts, but not golf. *Address:* c/o Woolwich Crown Court, 2 Belmarsh Road, SE28 0EY.

NORRIS, Alastair Hubert; QC 1997; FCIArb; **His Honour Judge Norris;** a Circuit Judge, since 2001; *b* 17 Dec. 1950; *s* of Hubert John Norris and Margaret Murray (*née* Savage); *m* 1982, Patricia Lesley Rachel White; one *s* two *d*. *Educ:* Pate's Grammar Sch., Cheltenham; St John's Coll., Cambridge (MA). FCIArb 1991. Called to the Bar, Lincoln's Inn, 1973; an Asst Recorder, 1998–2000; a Recorder 2000–01. *Recreation:* sailing. *Address:* The Priory Courts, 33 Bull Street, Birmingham B4 6DS. *Clubs:* Gloucestershire County Cricket; Marlow Sailing, Teifi Boating.

NORRIS, Air Chief Marshal Sir Christopher Neil F.; *see* Foxley-Norris.

NORRIS, Dan; MP (Lab) Wansdyke, since 1997; an Assistant Government Whip, since 2001; *b* 28 Jan. 1960; *s* of David Norris and June Norris (*née* Allen). *Educ:* Chipping Sodbury Comprehensive Sch.; Univ. of Sussex (MSW). Researcher and author. Member (Lab): Bristol CC, 1989–92, 1995–97; Avon CC, 1994–96. Contested (Lab): Northavon, 1987; Wansdyke, 1992. Member: Lab. Leadership Campaign Team, 1998–2000; Lab. Parly Campaign Team, 2000–01. Founder, Kidscape SW, 2000. Hon. Fellow, Sch. of Cultural and Community Studies, Univ. of Sussex, 1989. Mem., GMB. Ed., Liberal Demolition (qly jl). *Publications:* Violence Against Social Workers: the implications for practice, 1990; contribs to learned jls and newspaper articles. *Recreations:* smoking, drinking, gambling, hunting, shooting. *Address:* House of Commons, SW1A 0AA. *Club:* Radstock Working Men's.

NORRIS, Rt Rev. Mgr David Joseph; Protonotary Apostolic to the Pope; Vicar General of Westminster Diocese, 1972–99; General Secretary to RC Bishops' Conference of England and Wales, 1967–83; *b* 17 Aug. 1922; *s* of David William and Anne Norris. *Educ:* Salesian Coll., Battersea, St Edmund's Coll., Ware; Christ's Coll., Cambridge (MA). Priest, 1947; teaching at St Edmund's Coll., Ware, 1948–53; Cambridge, 1953–56; Private Secretary to Cardinal Godfrey, 1956–64; National Chaplain to Catholic Overseas Students, 1964–65; Private Secretary to Cardinal Heenan, 1965–72. *Recreations:* reading, music, sport. *Address:* Cathedral Clergy House, 42 Francis Street, SW1P 1QW. *T:* (020) 7798 9055.

NORRIS, David Owen, FRAM, FRCO; pianist and broadcaster; *b* 16 June 1953; *s* of Albert Norris and Margaret Norris (*née* Owen); two *s*. *Educ:* Royal Academy of Music (FRAM 1986); Keble Coll., Oxford (MA). FRCO 1972. Repetiteur, Royal Opera House, 1977–80; Asst Mus. Dir, RSC, 1977–79; Prof., Royal Acad. of Music, 1977–89; Dir, Petworth Fest., 1986–92; Artistic Dir, Cardiff Fest., 1992–95; Gresham Prof. of

Music, 1993–97; AHRB Fellow in Performing Arts, Southampton Univ., 2000–. Chm., Steans Inst. for Singers, Chicago, 1992–98. Concerts world-wide; tours of Australia, USA, Canada; radio and TV progs in GB and N America. Gilmore Artist, 1991. *Address:* c/o Clarion/Seven Muses, 47 Whitehall Park, N19 3TW.

NORRIS, Sir Eric (George), KCMG 1969 (CMG 1963); HM Diplomatic Service, retired; Director: Inchcape & Co., 1977–88 (Deputy Chairman, 1981–86); London Sumatra Plantations Ltd, 1978–88; Gray Mackenzie Ltd, 1978–88; *b* 14 March 1918; *s* of late H. F. Norris, Bengeo, Hertford; *m* 1941, Pamela Crane; three *d. Educ:* Hertford Grammar Sch.; St Catharine's Coll., Cambridge. Served Royal Corps of Signals, 1940–46 (Major). Entered Dominions Office, 1946. Served in British Embassy, Dublin, 1948–50; UK High Commission in Pakistan, 1952–55; UK High Commission in Delhi, 1956–57; Dep. High Commissioner for the UK, Bombay, 1957–60; IDC 1961; British Dep. High Comr, Calcutta, 1962–65; Commonwealth Office, 1966–68; High Comr, Kenya, 1968–72; Dep. Under Sec. of State, FCO, 1972–73; High Comr, Malaysia, 1974–77. Chm., Royal Commonwealth Soc., 1980–84. PMN (Malaysia), 1974. *Address:* Tilings, Goring Road, Steyning, W Sussex BN44 3GF. *T:* (01903) 879064. *Clubs:* East India, Royal Commonwealth Society.

NORRIS, Geoffrey; Chief Music Critic, Daily Telegraph, since 1995; *b* 19 Sept. 1947; *s* of Leslie and Vera Norris. *Educ:* Univ. of Durham (BA); Inst. Teatra, Muzyki i Kinematografii, Leningrad; Univ. of Liverpool. ARCM 1967. Lectr in Music History, RNCM, 1975–77; Commning Editor, Scholarly Music Books, OUP, 1977–83; Music Critic: The Times, 1983; Daily Telegraph, 1983–95. *Publications:* Rakhmaninov, 1976, 2nd edn, Rachmaninoff, 1993; (with Robert Threlfall) A Catalogue of the Compositions of S. Rachmaninoff, 1982; contribs to New Grove Dictionary of Music and Musicians, Oxford Companion to Music. *Recreation:* Italy. *Address:* The Daily Telegraph, 1 Canada Square, Canary Wharf, E14 5DT. *T:* (020) 7538 7622.

NORRIS, Gilbert Frank; Chief Road Engineer, Scottish Development Department, 1969–76; *b* 29 May 1916; *s* of Ernest Frank Norris and Ada Norris; *m* 1941, Joan Margaret Catherine Thompson; one *s. Educ:* Bemrose Sch., Derby; UC Nottingham. FICE. Served with Notts, Bucks and Lindsey County Councils, 1934–39; Royal Engineers, 1939–46; Min. of Transport: Highways Engr in Nottingham, Edinburgh and Leeds, 1946–63; Asst Chief Engr, 1963–67; Dep. Chief Engr, 1967; Dir, NE Road Construction Unit, 1967–69. *Address:* Woodhead Lee, Lamlash, Isle of Arran KA27 8JU.

NORRIS, Col Graham Alexander, OBE (mil.) 1945; JP; Vice Lord-Lieutenant of County of Greater Manchester, 1975–87; *b* 14 April 1913; *er s* of late John O. H. Norris and Beatrice H. Norris (*née* Vlies), Manchester; *m* 1st, 1938, Frances Cicely, *d* of late Walter Gorton, Minchinhampton, Glos; one *d*; 2nd, 1955, Muriel, *d* of late John Corris, Manchester. *Educ:* William Hulme's Grammar Sch.; Coll. of Technology, Manchester; Regent St Polytechnic, London; Merchant Venturers Techn. Coll., Bristol. CEng, FIMechE. Trng as automobile engr, Rolls Royce Ltd, Bristol Motor Co. Ltd; Joseph Cockshoot & Co. Ltd: Works Man., 1937, Works Dir 1946, Jt. Man. Dir 1964, Chm. and Man. Dir, 1968; Dir, Lex Garages Ltd, 1968–70; Dir, Red Garages (N Wales) Ltd, 1973–88. War service, RAOC and REME, UK, ME and Italy, 1940–46 (Lt-Col); Comdr REME 22 (W) Corps Tps (TA), 1947–51; Hon. Col, 1957–61. Mem., NEDC for Motor Vehicle Distrib. and Repair, 1966–74; Pres., Motor Agents Assoc., 1967–68; Vice-Pres., Inst. of Motor Industry, 1973–76; Mem., Industrial Tribunal Panel, 1976–82. Pres., Manchester and Dist Fedn of Boys' Clubs, 1968–74; Vice-Pres., NABC, 1972–98; Chm. Council, UMIST, 1971–83; Member Court: Univ. of Manchester; UMIST. Master, Worshipful Co. of Coachmakers and Coach Harness Makers, 1961–62; Freeman, City of London, 1938. JP, Lancashire 1963; DL Co. Palatine of Lancaster, 1962. *Recreations:* walking, social service activities. *Address:* c/o Croft of Greenbog, Glenkindle, Alford, Aberdeenshire AB3 8SE.

NORRIS, John Hallam Mercer, CBE 1987; Crown Estate Commissioner, 1991–99; Vice Lord-Lieutenant of Essex, since 1992; *b* 30 May 1929; *s* of late William Hallam Norris and Dorothy Edna Norris (*née* Mercer); *m* 1954, Maureen Joy Banyard; two *d. Educ:* Brentwood School. Mem., BSES Expedn, Newfoundland, 1947. Partner, W. H. Norris & Sons, 1963–. Chm., Essex River Authy, 1971–74; Member: Anglian Water Authy, 1974–85; Adv. Cttee, 1988, Board, 1989–94, NRA; Adv. Cttee, Envmt Agency, 1994–96; Founder Mem., Envmt Agency Bd, 1996–97; Chairman: Essex Land Drainage Cttee, 1974–89; Crouch Harbour Authy, 1981–88. President: CLA, 1985–87 (Mem., Exec. Cttee, 1973–; Chm., 1983–85); Essex Agricl Soc., 1989. Chm., Chelmsford Cathedral Council, 2000–. FRAgS 1992; Hon. FIWEM 1992. DL Essex, 1989. *Recreations:* fishing, sailing. *Address:* Mountnessing Hall, Brentwood, Essex CM13 1UN. *T:* (01277) 352152. *Clubs:* Boodle's, Farmers'.

NORRIS, John Robert, CBE 1991; PhD, DSc; Director, Group Research, Cadbury Schweppes Ltd, 1979–90; *b* 4 March 1932; *s* of Albert Norris and Winifred May Perry; *m* 1st, 1956, Barbara Jean Pinder (*d* 1994); two *s* one *d* (and one *s* decd); 2nd, 1998, Pauline Mary Corrigan. *Educ:* Depts of Bacteriology and Agriculture, Univ. of Leeds (BSc 1st Cl. Hons 1954, PhD 1957, DSc 1987). Lectr in Bacteriology, Univ. of Glasgow, 1957–63; Microbiologist, Shell Research Ltd, 1963–73 (Dir, Borden Microbiol Lab., 1970–73); Dir, Meat Res. Inst., ARC, 1973–79. Editor, Methods in Microbiology, 1969–92. *Publications:* papers in microbiol jls. *Recreations:* walking, wood carving, Yoga. *Address:* Langlands, 10 Langley Road, Bingley, West Yorks BD16 4AB. *T:* (01274) 510301. *Club:* Farmers'.

NORRIS, Philip; *see* Norris, A. P.

NORRIS, Stephen Anthony; British Film Commissioner, since 1998; *b* 14 June 1959; *s* of Roy Anthony Norris and Brenda Winifred Norris; *m* 1986, Susan Jennifer Boyle; two *s* one *d. Educ:* St Nicholas Grammar Sch. Warner Bros Productions, London, 1979–82; European Production, Warner Bros, LA, 1982–84; Dir of Ops, Enigma Productions, 1984–86; Sen. Vice Pres., Columbia Pictures, LA, 1986–88; Man. Dir, Enigma Productions Ltd, 1989–97. Dir, British Film and TV Producers Assoc., 1989–91; Vice Chm., Producers Alliance for Cinema and TV, 1991–93; Council Member: British Screen Adv. Council, 1998–; BAFTA, 1999–. Associate Producer/Producer: Memphis Belle, 1990; Being Human, 1993; War of the Buttons, 1994; Le Confessional (Best Film, Canadian Acad., 1995); My Life So Far, 1998. *Recreations:* cinema, Rugby, my family. *Address:* (office) 10 Little Portland Street, W1W 7JG. *T:* (020) 7861 7905. *Club:* Groucho.

NORRIS, Steven John; Board Member, Transport for London, since 2000; Consultant, Citigate, since 2000; *b* 24 May 1945; *s* of John Francis Birkett Norris and Eileen Winifred (*née* Walsh); *m* 1969, Peta Veronica Cecil-Gibson (marr. diss.); two *s*; *m* 2000, Emma Courtney; one *s. Educ:* Liverpool Institute; Worcester College, Oxford. MA. Private company posts, 1967–90; Dir-Gen., Road Haulage Assoc., 1997–2000. Mem., Berks CC, 1977–85. Mem., Berks AHA, 1979–82; Vice-Chm., W Berks District HA, 1982–85. Contested (C) Oxford E, 1987. MP (C): Oxford E, 1983–87; Epping Forest, Dec. 1988–1997. PPS to Hon. William Waldegrave, MP, Minister of State, DoE, 1985–87, to Rt Hon. Nicholas Ridley, Sec. of State for Trade and Industry, 1990, to Rt Hon. Kenneth Baker, Home Sec., 1991–92; Parly Under-Sec of State, Dept of Transport, 1992–96. Vice Chm., Cons. Party, 2000–. Chairman: Grant Maintained Schools Trust, 1988–89; Crime Concern Trust, 1988–91; Alcohol and Drug Addiction Prevention and Treatment, 1990–92; Prince Michael Road Safety Awards Scheme, 1997–. FCIT 1997; FIMI 1997; FIHT 1997; Hon. CompICE 1996. Freeman, City of London, 1985; Liveryman: Coachmakers' and Coach-Harness Makers' Co., 1985–; Watermen and Lightermen's Co., 1997–; Co. of Carmen, 1998–. *Publication:* Changing Trains, 1996. *Recreations:* reading, not walking. *Address:* Citigate Public Affairs, 26 Grosvenor Gardens, SW1W 0GT. *Clubs:* Brooks's, Royal Automobile.

NORRIS, Sydney George, CB 1996; Director of Finance, Prison Service, Home Office, 1996–97; *b* 22 Aug. 1937; *s* of late George Samuel Norris, FCA and Agnes Rosa Norris; *m* 1965, Brigid Molyneux FitzGibbon; two *s* one *d. Educ:* Liverpool Inst. High Sch. for Boys; University Coll., Oxford (MA); Trinity Hall and Inst. of Criminology, Cambridge (Dip. in Criminology); Univ. of California, Berkeley (MCrim). Intelligence Corps, 1956–58; Home Office, 1963–97; Private Sec. to Parly Under Sec. of State, 1966; Harkness Fellow, 1968–70; Sec., Adv. Council on Penal System, 1970–73; Principal Private Sec. to Home Sec., 1973–74; Asst Sec., 1974; seconded to HM Treasury, 1979–81; Asst Under Sec. of State, 1982; seconded to NI Office as Principal Estabt and Finance Officer, 1982–85; Dir of Operational Policy, Prison Dept, 1985–88; Police Dept, 1988–90; Principal Finance Officer, 1990–96. *Recreations:* running, fell walking, gardening, choral singing, piano. *Address:* 58 East Sheen Avenue, SW14 8AU. *Club:* Thames Hare and Hounds.

NORRIS, William John; QC 1997; *b* 3 Oct. 1951; *s* of Dr John Phillips Norris, QGM and Dr Joan Hattersley Norris; *m* 1987, Lesley Jacqueline Osborne; two *d. Educ:* Sherborne Sch.; New Coll., Oxford (MA). Called to the Bar, Middle Temple, 1974 (Benefactors' Scholarship). *Recreations:* sailing, cricket, shooting, racing. *Address:* Farrar's Building, Temple, EC4Y 7BD. *T:* (020) 7583 9241. *Clubs:* Royal Cruising, Royal Lymington Yacht.

NORRISS, Air Marshal Sir Peter (Coulson), KBE 2000; CB 1996; AFC 1977; defence consultant; *b* 22 April 1944; *s* of Arthur Kenworthy Norriss and Marjorie Evelyn Norriss; *m* 1971, Lesley Jean McColl; two *s* one *d. Educ:* Beverley Grammar Sch.; Magdalene Coll., Cambridge (MA 1970). Joined RAF, 1966; flying trng, 1966–68; Flying Instruction RAF Coll., Cranwell, 1969–71; Buccaneer Pilot, 1972–76; RAF Staff Coll., 1977; on Staff of RAF Minister, 1977–79; OC, No 16 Sqn, 1980–83; Head, RAF Presentation Team, 1984; Station Comdr, RAF Marham, 1985–87; ADC to the Queen, 1985–87; Higher Comd and Staff Course, 1988; on Staff, Operational Requirements, 1988–91; Dir Gen. Aircraft 2, 1991–95; Dir Gen. Air Systems 1, MoD (PE), 1995–98; Controller Aircraft, 1996–2000, and Dep. Chief of Defence Procurement (Ops), 1998–2000, MoD (PE, subseq. Defence Procurement Agency). Non-exec. Dir, DERA, 1999–2000. Mem. Council, RAeS, 1997– (Vice-Pres., 1999–). *Recreations:* golf, ski-ing. *Address:* c/o RAF Personnel Management Agency, RAF Innsworth, Glos GL3 1EZ. *Club:* Royal Air Force.

NORTH, family name of **Earl of Guilford**.

NORTH, Prof. Douglass Cecil, PhD; Professor of Economics, Washington University, since 1983; *b* 6 Nov. 1920; *s* of Henry North and Edith Saitta; *m* 1st, 1944, Lois Heister; three *s*; 2nd, 1972, Elisabeth Case. *Educ:* Univ. of California at Berkeley (BA, PhD). Acting Asst Prof., Asst Prof. and Associate Prof., Univ. of Washington, Seattle, 1950–83; Henry R. Luce Prof. of Law and Liberty and Prof. of Econs and of History, Washington Univ., St Louis, 1983. Peterkin Prof. of Political Economy, Rice Univ., 1979; Pitt Prof. of American Instns, Cambridge, 1981–82. Fellow, Amer. Acad. of Arts and Scis.; Corresp. FBA, 1996. Hon. degrees: Cologne 1988; Zürich 1993; Stockholm 1994. (Jtly) Nobel Prize for Economics, 1993. *Publications:* The Economic Growth of the United States 1790–1860, 1961; Growth and Welfare in the American Past, 1966; (with Roger Miller) The Economics of Public Issues, 1971; (with Lance Davis) Institutional Change and American Economic Growth, 1971; (with Robert Thomas) The Rise of the Western World, 1973; Structure and Change in Economic History, 1981; Institutions, Institutional Change and Economic Performance, 1990. *Recreations:* tennis, hiking, music, photography. *Address:* Economics Department, Washington University, Campus Box 1208, 1 Brookings Drive, St Louis, MO 63130–4899, USA.

NORTH, Prof. John David; Professor of History of Philosophy and the Exact Sciences, University of Groningen, Netherlands, 1977–99, now Emeritus; *b* 19 May 1934; *s* of late J. E. and G. A. North, Cheltenham; *m* 1957, Marion Pizzey; one *s* two *d. Educ:* Grammar Sch., Batley; Merton Coll., Oxford (BA 1956, MA 1960, DPhil 1964, DLitt 1993); London Univ. (BSc 1958). University of Oxford: Nuffield Foundn Res. Fellow, 1963–68; Asst Curator, Mus. of Hist. of Sci., 1968–77; University of Groningen, 1977–: Dean, Central Inter-Faculty, 1981–84; Dean of Faculty, 1991–93. Vis. Prof., Univs in Germany, Denmark and USA. Member: Council, Mus. Boerhaave, Leiden, 1986–94; Comité Scientifique, CNRS, Paris, 1985–99; Acad. internat. d'histoire des scis, 1967– (Hon. Permanent Sec., 1983–); IAU, 1977 (Pres., Hist. Commn, 1988–92). Member: Royal Netherlands Acad., 1985 (Mem Council, 1990–93); Acad. Leopoldina, 1992; Corresp. Fellow, British Acad., 1992; Foreign Mem., Royal Danish Acad., 1985. Editor: Archives internat. d'hist. des scis, 1971–84; Travaux de l'Académie, 1984–97. Kt, Order of Netherlands Lion, 1999. *Publications:* The Measure of the Universe, 1965, 2nd edn 1990; Isaac Newton, 1967; (ed) Mid-Nineteenth Century Scientists, 1969; Richard of Wallingford, 3 vols, 1976; (ed with J. Roche) The Light of Nature, 1985; Horoscopes and History, 1986; Chaucer's Universe, 1988, 2nd edn 1990; Stars, Minds and Fate, 1989; The Universal Frame, 1989; Fontana History of Astronomy and Cosmology, 1994; Stonehenge, 1996; The Ambassadors' Secret, 2001. *Recreation:* archaeology. *Address:* 28 Chalfont Road, Oxford OX2 6TH. *T:* (01865) 558458.

NORTH, John Joseph; Associate, Department of Land Economy, University of Cambridge, since 1992 (Senior Visiting Fellow, 1985–92); *b* 7 Nov. 1926; *s* of Frederick James North and Annie Elizabeth North (*née* Matthews); *m* 1958, Sheila Barbara Mercer; two *s. Educ:* Rendcomb College; Univ. of Reading (BSc, DipAgric); Univ. of California (MS). FIBiol 1972. Agricultural Adviser, Nat. Agricultural Advisory Service, 1951; Kellogg Fellowship, USA, 1954–55; Regional Agricultural Officer, Cambridge, 1972; Senior Agricultural Officer, 1976; Chief Agricl Officer, ADAS, MAFF, 1979. *Recreations:* golf, gardening. *Address:* 28 Hauxton Road, Little Shelford, Cambridge CB2 5HJ. *T:* (01223) 843369.

NORTH, Sir Jonathan; *see* North, Sir W. J. F.

NORTH, Sir Peter (Machin), Kt 1998; CBE 1989; DCL; FBA 1990; Principal of Jesus College, Oxford, since 1984; Pro-Vice-Chancellor, University of Oxford, 1988–93, and since 1997 (Vice-Chancellor, 1993–97); *b* Nottingham, 30 Aug. 1936; *o s* of late Geoffrey Machin North and Freda Brunt (*née* Smith); *m* 1960, Stephanie Mary (OBE 2000; JP, DL), *e d* of T. L. Chadwick; two *s* one *d. Educ:* Oakham Sch.; Keble Coll., Oxford (BA 1959, BCL 1960, MA 1963, DCL 1976; Hon. Fellow, 1984). National Service, Royal Leics

Regt, 2nd Lieut, 1955–56. Teaching Associate, Northwestern Univ. Sch. of Law, Chicago, 1960–61; Lecturer: University Coll. of Wales, Aberystwyth, 1961–63; Univ. of Nottingham, 1963–65; Tutor in Law, 1965–76, Fellow, 1965–84, Keble Coll., Oxford. Mem., Hebdomadal Council, 1985–. A Law Comr, 1976–84; called to the Bar, Inner Temple, 1992 (Hon. Bencher, 1987). Vis. Professor: Univ. of Auckland, 1969; Univ. of BC, 1975–76; Dir of Studies, Hague Acad. of Internat. Law, 1970 (general course in private internat. law, 1990); Lectures: Hague Acad. of Internat. Law, 1980; Horace Read Meml, Dalhousie Univ., 1980; Colston, Bristol Univ., 1984; Frances Moran Meml, TCD, 1984; Philip James, Leeds Univ., 1985; James Smart, 1988; MacDermott, QUB, 1991; Graveson, KCL, 1992; Douglas McK. Brown, Univ. of BC, 1998; F. A. Mann, 2000. Chairman: Road Traffic Law Review, 1985–88; Conciliation Project Adv. Cttee, 1985–88; Management Cttee, Oxford CAB, 1985–88; Appeal Cttee, Assoc. of Certified Accountants, 1990–93 (Mem., 1987–93); Ind. Review of Parades and Marches in NI, 1996–97; Ind. Cttee for Supervision of Standards of Telephone Inf. Services, 1999–; Member: Lord Chancellor's Adv. Cttee on Legal Educn, 1973–75; Social Scis and the Law Cttee, ESRC (formerly SSRC), 1982–85; Govt and Law Cttee, ESRC, 1985–87; Council, British Inst. of Internat. and Comparative Law, 1986– (Chm., Private Internat. Law Section, Adv. Bd, 1986–92); Council, Univ. of Reading, 1986–89; Council, British Acad., 1996–99; Adv. Develt Council, Nat. Fisheries Mus., 1996–2000. Pres., Oxford Inst. of Legal Practice, 1999–; Mem., Inst. of Internat. Law, 1985; Mem., Internat. Acad. of Comparative Law, 1990. Hon. QC 1993. Hon. Fellow: UCNW, Bangor, 1988; Trinity Coll., Carmarthen, 1995; Univ. of Wales, Aberystwyth, 1996. Hon. LLD: Reading, 1992; Nottingham, 1996; Aberdeen, 1997. Mem., Editorial Cttee, British Yearbook of Internat. Law, 1983–; General Editor, Oxford Jl of Legal Studies, 1987–92. *Publications:* (ed jtly) Chitty on Contracts, 23rd edn 1968 - 26th edn 1989; Occupiers' Liability, 1971; The Modern Law of Animals, 1972; Private International Law of Matrimonial Causes, 1977; Cheshire and North's Private International Law, 13th edn 1999; Contract Conflicts, 1982; (with J. H. C. Morris) Cases and Materials on Private International Law, 1984; Private International Law Problems in Common Law Jurisdictions, 1993; Essays in Private International Law, 1993; articles and notes in legal jls. *Recreations:* children, grandchildren, gardening, cricket (both playing and sleeping through). *Address:* Jesus College, Oxford OX1 3DW. *T:* (01865) 279701.

NORTH, Prof. Richard Alan, PhD; FRS 1995; Professor of Molecular Physiology, Institute of Molecular Physiology, Department of Biomedical Sciences, University of Sheffield, since 1998; *b* 20 May 1944; *s* of Douglas Abram North and Constance (*née* Ramsden); *m* 1st, 1969, Jean Valerie Aitken Hall (marr. diss. 1982); two *d*; 2nd, 1991, Annmarie Surprenant; two *s*. *Educ:* Univ. of Aberdeen (BSc; MB, ChB 1969; PhD 1973). Asst and Associate Prof., Dept of Pharmacol., Loyola Univ., Chicago, 1975–81; Massachusetts Institute of Technology: Associate Prof., Dept of Nutrition and Food Sci., 1981–84; Prof. of Neuropharmacol., Dept of Applied Biol Scis, 1984–86; Sen. Scientist, Vollum Inst., Oregon Health Scis Univ., Portland, 1987–93; Prin. Scientist, Geneva Biomedical Res. Inst., Glaxo Wellcome R&D (formerly Glaxo Inst. for Molecular Biol.), 1993–98. Visiting Professor: Flinders Univ., 1983; Bogomoletz Inst., 1984; Frankfurt Univ., 1988. Gaddum Lecture, British Pharmacol Soc., 1988. *Publications:* original res. papers in jls of physiol., pharmacol., neuroscience and biochem. *Recreation:* mountaineering. *Address:* Department of Biomedical Sciences, Alfred Denny Building, University of Sheffield, Western Bank, Sheffield S10 2TN. *T:* (0114) 222 4668, *Fax:* (0114) 222 2360; *e-mail:* R.A.North@sheffield.ac.uk.

NORTH, Robert, (Robert North Dodson); Artistic Director, Scottish Ballet, since 1999; freelance choreographer; *b* 1 June 1945; *s* of Charles Dodson and Elizabeth Thompson; *m* 1st, 1978, Janet Smith (marr. diss.); 2nd, 1999, Sheri Cook. *Educ:* Pierrepont Sch. (A levels in Maths, Physics and Art); Central Sch. of Art; Royal Ballet Sch. Dancer and choreographer, London Contemporary Dance Co., 1966–81 (Jt Artistic Dir, 1980–81); seasons with Martha Graham Dance Co., 1967 and 1968; Teacher of Modern Dance, Royal Ballet Sch., 1979–81; Artistic Dir, Ballet Rambert, 1981–86; freelance work, Europe and USA, 1986–90; Ballet Dir, Teatro Regio, Turin, 1990–91; Artistic Dir, Gothenburg Ballet, 1991–96; Dir, Corps de Ballet, Arena di Verona, 1997–99. Has choreographed ballets for dance companies throughout the world, including: Royal Ballet; English National Ballet; Dance Theatre of Harlem; Royal Danish Ballet; San Francisco Ballet; Oakland Ballet; Finnish Nat. Ballet; Batsheva; Janet Smith and Dancers; La Scala, Milan; Rome Opera; Staatsoper Dresden; Györ Ballett; *ballets choreographed* include: Troy Game; Death and the Maiden; The Annunciation; A Stranger I Came; Running Figures; Pribaoutki; Colour Moves; Entre dos Aguas; full-length ballets: Carmen; Elvira Madigan; Romeo & Juliet; Living in America; Prince Rama and the Demons; Life, Love & Death; The Russian Story; The Snowman; The Cradle Will Rock; Eva; Ragazzi Selvaggi; Orlando; also choreography for films, television (incl. Lonely Town, Lonely Street), theatre and musicals (incl. For My Daughter). *Address:* c/o Val West, 49 Springcroft Avenue, N2 9JH.

NORTH, Sir Thomas (Lindsay), Kt 1982; FAIM, FRMIA; Chairman, G. J. Coles & Coy Limited, Melbourne, Australia, 1979–83, Hon. Chairman, 1983–84; *b* 11 Dec. 1919; *s* of John North and Jane (*née* Irwin); *m* 1944, Kathleen Jefferis; two *d*. *Educ:* Rutherglen, Vic. FAIM 1972. Joined G. J. Coles & Co. Ltd, 1938; Gen. Man., 1966; Dep. Man. Dir, 1969; Man. Dir, 1975–79; Dir, various G. J. Coles subsid. cos. Dep. Chm., KMart (Australia) Ltd, 1975–; Chairman: Island Cooler Pty Ltd, 1985–; Smurfit Australia Pty Ltd. 1986–. *Recreations:* horse racing, swimming. *Address:* Chiltern, 5/627 Toorak Road, Toorak, Vic 3142, Australia. *T:* (3) 98223161. *Clubs:* Athenæum, Royal Automobile Club of Victoria (Melbourne); Australian Armoured Corps (Sydney); Victorian Amateur Turf (Dep. Chm.), Victoria Racing Club, Moonee Valley Race; Melbourne Cricket.

NORTH, Sir (William) Jonathan (Frederick), 2nd Bt *cr* 1920; *b* 6 Feb. 1931; *s* of Muriel Norton (*d* 1989), 2nd *d* of Sir William Hicking, 1st Bt, and Hon. John Montagu William North (marr. diss. 1939; he *d* 1987), 2nd *s* of 8th Earl of Guilford; *S* grandfather, 1947 (under special remainder); *m* 1956, Sara Virginia, *d* of Air Chief Marshal Sir Donald Hardman, GBE, KCB, DFC; one *s* two *d*. *Educ:* Marlborough Coll. *Heir:* *s* Jeremy William Francis North [*b* 5 May 1960; *m* 1986, Lucy, *d* of G. A. van der Meulen, Holland; two *s* two *d*]. *Address:* Frogmore, Weston-under-Penyard, Herefordshire HR9 5TQ.

NORTHAMPTON, 7th Marquess of, *cr* 1812; **Spencer Douglas David Compton;** DL; Earl of Northampton, 1618; Earl Compton, Baron Wilmington, 1812; *b* 2 April 1946; *s* of 6th Marquess of Northampton, DSO, and Virginia (*d* 1997), *d* of Lt-Col David Heaton, DSO; *S* father, 1978; *m* 1st, 1967, Henriette Luisa Maria (marr. diss. 1973), *o d* of late Baron Bentinck; one *s* one *d*; 2nd, 1974, Annette Marie (marr. diss. 1977), *er d* of C. A. R. Smallwood; 3rd, 1977, Hon. Mrs Rosemary Dawson-Damer (marr. diss. 1983); one *d*; 4th, 1985, Hon. Mrs Michael Pearson (marr. diss. 1988); one *d*; 5th, 1990, Pamela Martina Raphaela Kyprios. *Educ:* Eton. DL Northants 1979. *Recreation:* freemasonry (Pro Grand Master, United Lodge of England, 2001). *Heir:* *s* Earl Compton, *qv*. *Address:* Compton Wynyates, Tysoe, Warwicks CV35 0UD. *T:* (01295) 680629. *Club:* Turf.

NORTHAMPTON, Bishop of, (RC), since 2001; **Rt Rev. Kevin John Patrick McDonald;** *b* 18 Aug. 1947. *Educ:* St Joseph's Coll., Stoke; Birmingham Univ. (BA Latin); Ven. English Coll., Rome; Gregorian Univ. (STL); Angelicum Univ. (STD). Ordained priest, 1974; Asst Priest, All Saints, Stourbridge, 1975–76; Lectr in Moral Theol., St Mary's Coll., Oscott, 1976–85; official with resp. for Anglican and Methodist relns, Pontifical Council for Promoting Christian Unity, Rome, 1985–93; Parish Priest, English Martyrs, Sparkhill, Birmingham, 1993–98; Rector, Oscott Coll., 1998–2001. Chairman: Ecumenical Commn, Archdio. Birmingham, 1980–85; Archdiocesan Commn for Inter-Religious Dialogue, 1998–2001. Canon, St Chad's Cathedral, Birmingham, 1998–2001. *Recreations:* music, reading, walking. *Address:* Bishop's House, Marriott Street, Northampton NN2 6AW.

NORTHAMPTON, Archdeacon of; *see* Chapman, Ven. M. R.

NORTHARD, John Henry, CBE 1987 (OBE 1979); FREng; Hon. FIMM; Director of Operations, 1985–88, Deputy Chairman, 1988–92, British Coal Corporation; Chairman, British Coal Enterprise Ltd, 1991–93; *b* 23 Dec. 1926; *s* of William Henry Northard and Nellie Northard; *m* 1952, Marian Josephine Lay; two *s* two *d*. *Educ:* St Bede's Grammar School, Bradford; Barnsley Mining and Technical College (Certificated Colliery Manager, first class). CEng, FREng (FEng 1983). Colliery Manager, Yorks, 1955–57, Leics, 1957–63; Group Manager, Leics Collieries, 1963–65; Dep. Chief Mining Engineer, NCB, Staffs Area, 1965–70; Area Dep. Dir (Mining), NCB, N Derbyshire Area, 1970–73; Area Dir, NCB, N Derbyshire Area, 1973–81, Western Area, 1981–85; Bd Mem., NCB, 1986–92. Pres., IMinE, 1982. CIMgt. SBStJ 1981. *Publications:* contribs to mining engineering instns and tech. jls. *Address:* Rydal, 196 Ashgate Road, Chesterfield, Derbyshire S40 4AL. *T:* (01246) 232260.

NORTHBOURNE, 5th Baron *cr* 1884; **Christopher George Walter James,** Bt 1791; DL; FRICS; Chairman: Betteshanger Farms Ltd, since 1975; Betteshanger Investments Ltd; *b* 18 Feb. 1926; *s* of 4th Baron Northbourne and Katherine Louise (*d* 1980), *d* of late George A. Nickerson, Boston, Mass; *S* father, 1982; *m* 1959, Aliki Louise Hélène Marie Sygne, *e d* of Henri Claudel, Chatou-sur-Seine, and *g d* of late Paul Claudel; three *s* one *d*. *Educ:* Eton; Magdalen Coll., Oxford (MA). Director: Anglo Indonesian Corp., 1971–96; Plantation & General (formerly Chillington Corp.) PLC, 1986–96; Center Parcs PLC, 1988–96 (Dep. Chm., 1988–96). Elected Mem., H of L, 1999. DL Kent, 1996. *Heir:* *s* Hon. Charles Walter Henri James [*b* 14 June 1960; *m* 1987, Catherine Lucy, *d* of Ralph Burrows; two *s* one *d*]. *Address:* 11 Eaton Place, SW1X 8BN. *T:* (020) 7235 6790; Coldharbour, Northbourne, Deal, Kent CT14 0NT. *T:* (01304) 611277. *Clubs:* Brooks's, Royal Yacht Squadron.

NORTHBROOK, 6th Baron *cr* 1866; **Francis Thomas Baring;** Bt 1793; Director, Mars Asset Management Ltd, since 1996; *b* 21 Feb. 1954; *s* of 5th Baron Northbrook and of Rowena Margaret, 2nd *d* of Brig.-Gen. Sir William Manning, GCMG, KBE, CB; *S* father, 1990; *m* 1987, Amelia Sarah Elizabeth, *er d* of Dr Reginald Taylor; three *d*. *Educ:* Winchester Coll.; Bristol Univ. (BA Hons 1976). Trainee accountant, Dixon Wilson & Co., 1976–80; Baring Brothers and Co. Ltd, 1981–89; Sen. Investment Man., Taylor Young Investment Management Ltd, 1990–93; Investment Man., Smith and Williamson Securities, 1993–95. Elected Mem., H of L, 1999; an Opposition Whip, 1999–2000. Trustee, Winchester Medical Trust, 1991–96. *Heir:* (to baronetcy) *kinsman* Peter Baring [*b* 12 Sept. 1939; *m* 1973, Rose, *d* of George Nigel Adams; one *s*]. *Address:* House of Lords, SW1A 0PW. *Club:* White's.

NORTHCOTE, family name of **Earl of Iddesleigh**.

NORTHCOTE, Prof. Donald Henry, FRS 1968; Fellow of Sidney Sussex College, Cambridge, since 1992 (Master, 1976–92); Professor of Plant Biochemistry, University of Cambridge, 1972–89 (Reader, 1965–72), Emeritus Professor, 1989; *b* 27 Dec. 1921; *m* Eva Marjorie Mayo; two *d*. *Educ:* Sir George Monoux Grammar Sch., London; London Univ.; Cambridge Univ. Fellow, St John's College, Cambridge, 1960–76. Hon. Fellow, Downing Coll., Cambridge, 1976. *Publications:* 300 pubns in scientific jls on plant cell differentiation. *Recreations:* sitting and chatting; strolling about. *Address:* Sidney Sussex College, Cambridge CB2 3HU. *T:* (01223) 338821; *e-mail:* dhn21@cam.ac.uk; (home) 100 North Street, Burwell, Cambs CB5 0BB. *T:* (01638) 743924. *Club:* Oxford and Cambridge.

NORTHCOTE, His Honour Peter Colston; a Circuit Judge 1973–89; *b* 23 Oct. 1920; *s* of late William George Northcote and late Edith Mary Northcote; *m* 1947, Patricia Bickley; two *s*. *Educ:* Ellesmere Coll.; Bristol Univ. Called to Bar, Inner Temple, 1948. Chm., Nat. Insce Tribunal; Chm., W Midland Rent Tribunal; Dep. Chm., Agric. Land Tribunal. Commnd KSLI, 1940; served 7th Rajput Regt, Far East (Major). *Recreations:* music, travel, ski-ing. *Address:* Pendil House, Pendil Close, Wellington, Salop TF1 2PQ. *T:* (01952) 641160. *Club:* Army and Navy.

NORTHCOTT, Prof. Douglas Geoffrey, MA, PhD, Cambridge; FRS 1961; Town Trust Professor of Mathematics, University of Sheffield, 1952–82, now Emeritus; *b* London, 1916; *m* 1949, Rose Hilda Austin, Twickenham, Middlesex; two *d*. *Educ:* Christ's Hospital; St John's Coll., Cambridge; Princeton Univ., USA. *Publications:* Ideal Theory, 1953; An Introduction to Homological Algebra, 1960; Lessons on Rings, Modules and Multiplicities, 1968; A First Course of Homological Algebra, 1973; Finite Free Resolutions, 1976; Affine Sets and Affine Groups, 1980; Multilinear Algebra, 1984. *Address:* 25 Parkhead Road, Sheffield S11 9RA.

NORTHERN, Richard James, MBE 1982; HM Diplomatic Service; Director General for Trade and Investment in Italy, and Consul General, Milan, since 2001; *b* 2 Nov. 1954; *s* of James Wilfred Northern and Margaret Northern (*née* Lammie); *m* 1981, Linda Denise Gadd; two *s* one *d*. *Educ:* Bedford Sch.; Jesus Coll., Cambridge (BA 1976; MA 1979). Joined HM Diplomatic Service, 1976: FCO, 1976–78; MECAS, Beirut and London, 1978–80; Third Sec. and Vice Consul, Riyadh, 1980–83; Second, later First, Sec. (Political/Inf.), Rome, 1983–87; First Secretary: FCO, 1987–92; (Economic), Ottawa, 1992–94; Dep. Consul Gen. and Dep. Dir for Trade and Investment, Toronto, 1994–97; Counsellor (Econ./Commercial), Riyadh, 1997–2000; Counsellor, FCO, 2000–01. *Recreations:* tennis, music, languages. *Address:* c/o Foreign and Commonwealth Office, King Charles Street, SW1A 2AH. *Club:* Royal Over-Seas League.

NORTHERN ARGENTINA, Bishop of, since 1990; **Most Rev. Maurice Walter Sinclair;** Presiding Bishop (Primate) of the Province of the Southern Cone of America, 1995–2001; *b* 20 Jan. 1937; *s* of Maurice and Dorothea Sinclair; *m* 1962, Gillian (*née* Spooner); four *s*. *Educ:* Chigwell Sch.; Nottingham Univ. (BSc 1959); Leicester Univ. (PGCE 1960); Tyndale Hall, Bristol. Asst Master, Brays Grove County Secondary Sch., Harlow, Essex, 1960–62. Ordained, 1964; Asst Curate, St John's Church, Boscombe, 1964–67; Missionary, South American Missionary Soc., serving in Argentina, 1967–78; Personnel Sec., 1979–83, Asst Gen. Sec., 1983–84, South American Missionary Soc.; Principal, Crowther Hall, Selly Oak Colls, 1984–90. Ibo chief, Nigeria, 1987. *Publications:*

Green Finger of God, 1980; Ripening Harvest Gathering Storm, 1988. *Recreations:* gardening, hill walking, veteran football. *Address:* Iglesia Anglicana, Casilla 187, CP 4400 Salta, Argentina. *T:* (87) 310167.

NORTHERN TERRITORY (AUSTRALIA), Bishop of the, since 1999; **Rt Rev. Philip Leslie Freier,** PhD; *b* 9 Feb. 1955; *m* 1976, Joy Launder; two *s*. *Educ:* Qld Inst. of Technol. (BAppSc 1975); Univ. of Qld (DipEd 1976); St John's Coll., Morpeth (Associate Dip. in Theol 1984); Melbourne Coll. of Divinity (BD 1984); Univ. of Newcastle (MEdSt 1984); James Cook Univ., Townsville (PhD 2000). Teacher, Qld Educn Dept, 1976–81. Ordained deacon, 1983, priest, 1984; Deacon in Charge, Ch of the Ascension, Kowanyama, 1983–84, Priest in Charge, 1984–88; Rector: St Oswald, Banyo, 1988–93; Christ Ch, Bundaberg, 1993–99; Area Dean: Brisbane N, 1992–93; the Burnett, 1995–98; Examining Chaplain to Archbp of Brisbane, 1993–99. Member: Diocesan Council, Dio. Carpentaria, 1986–88; Gen Synod, 1987–98 (Mem., Missionary and Ecumenical Commn, 1995–98); Provincial Synod, 1987–98 (Mem., Standing Cttee, 1988–); Diocesan Council, Dio. Brisbane, 1991–94. *Publications:* Thaw Pathn a Palal Nguwl, 1978; (with E. J. Freier) Kupmari, A Picture Book, 1978; Science Program for Aboriginal Community Schools, 1980; (jtly) Mathematical Program for Schools in Aboriginal and Torres Strait Islander Communities, 1983; articles in jls. *Address:* Anglican Diocesan Office, Corner Smith Street & The Esplanade, Darwin, NT 0801, Australia. *T:* (8) 89417440, *Fax:* (8) 89417446; *e-mail:* dio.nt@octa4.net.au; GPO Box 2950, Darwin, NT 0801, Australia. *T:* (8) 89417226, *Fax:* (8) 89417227; *e-mail:* philipfreier@optusnet.com.au.

NORTHESK, 14th Earl of *cr* 1647; **David John MacRae Carnegie;** Lord Rosehill and Inglismaldie 1639; estate manager/owner; *b* 3 Nov. 1954; *s* of 13th Earl of Northesk, and Jean Margaret (*d* 1989), *yr d* of Captain (John) Duncan George MacRae; *S* father, 1994; *m* 1979, Jacqueline Reid, *d* of Mrs Elizabeth Reid, Sarasota, Florida, USA; three *d* (one *s* decd). *Educ:* West Hill Park, Titchfield; Eton; Brooke House, Market Harborough; UCL. Elected Mem., H of L, 1999; an Opposition Whip, 1999. *Heir: kinsman* Patrick Charles Carnegy, *b* 23 Sept. 1940. *Address:* House of Lords, SW1A 0PW.

NORTHFIELD, Baron *cr* 1975 (Life Peer), of Telford, Shropshire; **(William) Donald Chapman;** Chairman: Telford Development Corporation, 1975–87; Consortium Developments Ltd, 1986–92; *b* 25 Nov. 1923; *s* of Wm H. and Norah F. E. Chapman, Barnsley. *Educ:* Barnsley Grammar Sch.; Emmanuel Coll., Cambridge, MA (1st Cl. Hons) Economics, also degree in Agriculture; Senior Scholar of Emmanuel Coll. Research in Agric. Economics, Cambridge, 1943–46. Cambridge City Councillor, 1945–47; Sec., Trades Council and Labour Party, 1945–57; MP (Lab) Birmingham (Northfield), 1951–70. Research Sec. of the Fabian Soc., 1948–49, Gen. Sec., 1949–53. Gwilym Gibbon Fellow, Nuffield Coll., Oxford, 1971–73; Vis. Fellow, Centre for Contemporary European Studies, Sussex Univ., 1973–79. Special Adviser to EEC Commn, 1978–84; Chairman: Rural Develt Commn, 1974–80; Inquiry into recent trends in acquisition and occupancy of agric. land, 1977–79. *Publications:* The European Parliament: the years ahead, 1973; The Road to European Union, 1975; articles and Fabian pamphlets. *Recreation:* travel. *Address:* House of Lords, SW1A 0PW.

NORTHLAND, Viscount; title of heir to Earldom of Ranfurly.

NORTHOLT, Archdeacon of; *see* Chessun, Ven. C. T. J.

NORTHOVER, Baroness *cr* 2000 (Life Peer), of Cissbury in the co. of West Sussex; **Lindsay Patricia Granshaw,** PhD; Member, Liberal Democrats' Health Team, House of Lords, since 2000; *b* 21 Aug. 1954; *d* of Maurice Colin Charles Granshaw and Patricia Winifred Granshaw (*née* Jackson); *m* 1988, John Martin Alban Northover; two *s* one *d*. *Educ:* Brighton and Hove High Sch.; St Anne's Coll., Oxford (exhibitioner; MA Modern History); Bryn Mawr Coll.; Univ. of Pennsylvania (MA History and Philosophy of Sci. 1978; PhD 1981). Res. Fellow, UCL and St Mark's Hosp., 1980–83; Fellow, St Thomas's Hosp. Med. Sch., 1983–84; Lectr, Wellcome Inst. for the History of Medicine and UCL, 1984–91. Mem., cttee negotiating Liberal and SDP merger, 1987–88; Chair: SDP Health and Welfare Assoc., 1987–88; SDP Parly Cands' Assoc., 1987–88; Lib Dem Parly Cands' Assoc., 1988–91; Mem., Lib Dem Federal Exec. Cttee, 1988–, Federal Conference Cttee, 1988–, Federal Policy Cttee, 1998–; Chair, Women Liberal Democrats, 1992–95. Contested: (SDP/Alliance) Welwyn, Hatfield, 1983 and 1987; (Lib Dem) Basildon, 1997. *Publications:* St Mark's Hospital, London: a social history of a specialist hospital 1835–1985, 1985; contribs to academic jls and books. *Address:* House of Lords, SW1A 0PW.

NORTHUMBERLAND, 12th Duke of, *cr* 1766; **Ralph George Algernon Percy;** DL; Bt 1660; Earl of Northumberland, Baron Warkworth 1749; Earl Percy 1766; Earl of Beverley 1790; Lord Lovaine, Baron of Alnwick 1784; Chairman, since 1992, and President, since 1995, Northumberland Estates; *b* 16 Nov. 1956; 2nd *s* of 10th Duke of Northumberland, KG, GCVO, TD, PC, FRS and of Lady Elizabeth Diana Montagu-Douglas-Scott, *er d* of 8th Duke of Buccleuch and Queensberry, KT, GCVO, PC; *S* brother, 1995; *m* 1979, Isobel Jane Miller, *d* of John W. M. M. Richard; two *s* two *d*. *Educ:* Eton; Oxford Univ. ARICS 1986. Land Agent with: Cluttons, 1979–82; Humberts, 1982–86; Northumberland Estates, 1986–96. DL Northumberland, 1997. *Recreations:* tennis, fishing, shooting, painting. *Heir: s* Earl Percy, *qv*. *Address:* Alnwick Castle, Alnwick, Northumberland NE66 1NG. *T:* (01665) 602456; Syon House, Brentford, Middlesex TW8 8JF. *T:* (020) 8560 2353.

NORTHUMBERLAND, Archdeacon of; *see* Elliott, Ven. P.

NORTHWAY, Eileen Mary, CBE 1990; RRC 1982 (ARRC 1969); Principal Nursing Officer and Matron-in-Chief, Queen Alexandra's Royal Naval Nursing Service, 1986–90, retired; *b* 22 July 1931; *d* of Ernest and Margaret Northway. *Educ:* St Michael's Convent, Newton Abbot. SRN 1952, SCM 1954; joined QARNNS 1956. QHNS, 1986–90. OStJ 1985. *Recreations:* gardening, reading.

NORTON; *see* Hill-Norton.

NORTON, family name of **Barons Grantley** and **Rathcreedan**.

NORTON, 8th Baron *cr* 1878; **James Nigel Arden Adderley;** *b* 2 June 1947; *er s* of 7th Baron Norton, OBE and of Betty Margaret, *o d* of James McKee Hannah; *S* father, 1993; *m* (marr. diss.); one *s* one *d*; *m* 1997, Frances Elizabeth Prioleau, *yr d* of George Frederick Rothwell. *Educ:* Downside. FCA 1970. *Heir: s* Hon. Edward James Arden Adderley, *b* 19 Oct. 1982. *Address:* Fillongley Hall, Coventry, Warwicks CV7 8EH.

NORTON OF LOUTH, Baron *cr* 1998 (Life Peer), of Louth in the co. of Lincolnshire; **Philip Norton,** PhD; Professor of Government, since 1986 and Director, Centre for Legislative Studies, since 1992, University of Hull; *b* 5 March 1951; *y s* of late George E. Norton and of Ena D. Norton. *Educ:* Univ. of Sheffield (BA 1st cl. Hons; Nalgo Prize 1972; PhD); Univ. of Pennsylvania (MA; Thouron Scholar). Lectr, 1977–82, Sen. Lectr, 1982–84, Reader, 1984–86, Univ. of Hull. Member: Exec. Cttee, Study of Parlt Gp, 1981–93 (Acad. Sec., 1981–85); Exec. Cttee, British Politics Gp (USA), 1982–95 (Pres., 1988–90); Exec. Cttee, Political Studies Assoc. of UK, 1983–89; Society and Politics Res. Develt Gp, ESRC, 1987–90; Council, Hansard Soc., 1997–. Chm., H of L Select Cttee on the Constitution, 2001–. Chairman: Cons. Pty Commn to Strengthen Parlt, 1999–2000; Standards Cttee, Kingston-upon-Hull City Council, 1999–. Co-Chm., Res. Cttee of Legislative Specialists, Internat. Political Sci. Assoc., 1994–. Pres., Politics Assoc., 1993–. Governor, King Edward VI Grammar Sch., Louth, 1988– (Warden, 1990–93). FRSA 1995. Assoc. Ed., Political Studies, 1987–93; Ed., Jl of Legislative Studies, 1995–. *Publications:* Dissension in the House of Commons 1945–74, 1975; Conservative Dissidents, 1978; Dissension in the House of Commons 1974–79, 1980; The Commons in Perspective, 1981; (jtly) Conservatives and Conservatism, 1981; The Constitution in Flux, 1982; The British Polity, 1984, 4th edn 2001; Law and Order and British Politics, 1984; (ed) Parliament in the 1980s, 1985; (ed jtly) The Political Science of British Politics, 1986; (ed) Legislatures, 1990; (ed) Parliaments in Western Europe, 1990; (ed) New Directions in British Politics, 1991; (ed jtly) Parliamentary Questions, 1993; (jtly) Back from Westminster, 1993; Does Parliament Matter?, 1993; (jtly) Politics UK, 1991, 4th edn 2000; (ed) National Parliaments and the European Union, 1996; (ed jtly) The New Parliaments of Central and Eastern Europe, 1996; (ed) The Conservative Party, 1996; (ed) Legislatures and Legislators, 1998; (ed) Parliaments and Governments in Western Europe, 1998; (ed) Parliaments and Pressure Groups in Western Europe, 1999; (ed jtly) Parliaments in Asia, 1999. *Recreations:* table-tennis, walking. *Address:* Department of Politics, University of Hull, Hull, East Yorkshire HU6 7RX. *T:* (01482) 465863. *Clubs:* Royal Over-Seas League, Royal Commonwealth Society.

NORTON, Donald; Regional Administrator, Oxford Regional Health Authority, 1973–80, retired; *b* 2 May 1920; *s* of Thomas Henry Norton and Dora May Norton (*née* Prentice); *m* 1945, Miriam Joyce, *d* of Herbert and Florence Mann; two *s* one *d*. *Educ:* Nether Edge Grammar Sch., Sheffield; Univs of Sheffield and London. LLB, DPA; FHA. Senior Administrator Sheffield Regional Hosp. Bd, 1948–51; Sec. Supt, Jessop Hosp. for Women and Charles Clifford Dental Hosp., Sheffield, 1951–57; Dep. Sec., Archway Gp of Hosps, London, 1957–60; Gp Sec., Dudley Road Gp of Hosps, Birmingham 1960–70; Sec., Oxford Regional Hosp. Bd, 1970–73. *Recreations:* marriage, golf, gardening. *Address:* The Squirrels, 14 Pullens Field, Headington, Oxford OX3 0BU. *T:* (01865) 767291. *Clubs:* Victory; Frilford Heath.

NORTON, Captain Gerard Ross, VC 1944; MM; 1/4th Hampshire Regiment; *b* S Africa, 7 Sept. 1915; *m* 1942, Lilia Morris, East London, S Africa; three *d*. *Educ:* Selborne Coll., East London, S Africa. Bank clerk. *Recreations:* Rugger-provincial, tennis, cricket. *Address:* Annandale Farm, Box 112, Banket, Zimbabwe.

NORTON, Hilary Sharon Braverman; *see* Blume, H. S. B.

NORTON, Hugh Edward; Director: Inchcape plc, since 1995; Standard Chartered plc, since 1995; Lasmo plc, since 1997; *b* 23 June 1936; *s* of late Lt-Gen. Edward F. Norton, CB, DSO, MC and I. Joyce Norton; *m* 1965, Janet M. Johnson (*d* 1993); one *s*; *m* 1998, F. Joy Harcup; one *d*. *Educ:* Winchester Coll.; Trinity Coll., Oxford (BA Hons Lit.Hum.). British Petroleum Co., 1959–95: Chief Exec., BP Exploration Co., 1986–89; Man. Dir, 1989–95. *Recreations:* painting, ornithology, tennis, travel. *Club:* Athenæum.

NORTON, James, FCIS; General Secretary, Arthritis and Rheumatism Council for Research, 1981–98; *b* 12 July 1931; *s* of James and May Norton; *m* 1956, Dora Ashworth; one *s*. *Educ:* West Hill Sch., Stalybridge. FCIS 1972. Stalybridge, Hyde, Mossley and Dukinfield Tspt Bd, 1947–60; Wing Comdr, RAF, 1961–81. *Recreations:* walking, cricket, Manchester United. *Address:* 665 Chatsworth Road, Chesterfield S40 3PA. *T:* (01246) 566160. *Club:* Royal Air Force.

NORTON, Jim; *see* Norton, M. J.

NORTON, John Lindsey; Chairman, National Society for Prevention of Cruelty to Children, 1995–2001 (Hon. Treasurer, 1991–95); *b* 21 May 1935; *s* of Frederick Raymond Norton and Doris Ann Norton; *m* 1959, Judith Ann Bird; three *d*. *Educ:* Winchester College; Cambridge Univ. (MA). Blackburn Robson Coates & Co., 1959–63; BDO Binder Hamlyn, later Binder Hamlyn, 1963–96: Nat. Man. Partner, 1983–88; Chm., BDO Binder, 1988–92; Sen. Partner, Binder Hamlyn, 1993–96. Chm., Barking Power Ltd, 1995–; Non-executive Director: Thames Valley Power Ltd, 1995–; H. P. Bulmer Hldgs plc, 1997–. *Recreations:* walking, gardening, golf. *Address:* The Old Rectory, Holwell, Sherborne, Dorset DT9 5LB. *Club:* Army and Navy.

NORTON, Marjorie; *see* Mowlam, M.

NORTON, Michael James, (Jim); Head of Electronic Business Policy, Institute of Directors, since 1999; *b* 15 Dec. 1952; *s* of Christopher Stephen Norton and Lilian Ivy Norton; *m* 1976, Barbara Foster; one *s*. *Educ:* Roan Sch., Blackheath; Sheffield Univ. (BEng Hons (Electronic Engrg) 1974; Mappin Medal, 1974). AMIEE 1974, FIEE 1997. Post Office (Telecommunications), later British Telecommunications, 1970–87 (lastly, Sen. Man., Internat. Business); Practice Dir, Butler Cox plc, 1987–90; Marketing Dir, Cable & Wireless (Europe), 1990–93; Chief Exec., Radiocoms Agency, DTI, 1993–98; Dir, Electronic Commerce Team, Performance and Innovation Unit, Cabinet Office, 1999. Non-executive Director: Securicor plc; Telemetrix plc; 3i European Technology Trust. Vis. Prof. of Electronic Engrg, Univ. of Sheffield, 1998–. FRSA 1993. *Recreations:* reading, music, amateur radio. *Address:* Institute of Directors, 120 Pall Mall, SW1Y 5EA. *T:* (020) 7451 3126.

NORTON-GRIFFITHS, Sir John, 3rd Bt *cr* 1922; FCA; President and Chief Executive Officer, Main Street Data Services Inc.; *b* 4 Oct. 1938; *s* of Sir Peter Norton-Griffiths, 2nd Bt, and Kathryn (*d* 1980), *e d* of late George F. Schrafft; *S* father, 1983; *m* 1964, Marilyn Margaret, *er d* of Norman Grimley. *Educ:* Eton. FCA 1966. Lately Sub Lieutenant RN. *Heir: b* Michael Norton-Griffiths [*b* 11 Jan. 1941; *m* 1965, Ann, *o d* of late Group Captain Blair Alexander Fraser; one *s*].

NORWICH, 2nd Viscount *cr* 1952, of Aldwick; **John Julius Cooper,** CVO 1993; FRSL, FRGS, FSA; writer and broadcaster; *b* 15 Sept. 1929; *s* of 1st Viscount Norwich, PC, GCMG, DSO, and Lady Diana Cooper (*d* 1986), *d* of 8th Duke of Rutland; *S* father, 1954; *m* 1st, 1952, Anne (Frances May) (marr. diss. 1985), *e d* of late Hon. Sir Bede Clifford, GCMG, CB, MVO; one *s* one *d*; 2nd, 1989, Mollie Philipps, *e d* of 1st Baron Sherfield, GCB, GCMG, FRS. *Educ:* Upper Canada Coll., Toronto, Canada; Eton; University of Strasbourg; New Coll., Oxford. Served 1947–49 as Writer, Royal Navy. Entered Foreign Office, 1952; Third Secretary, British Embassy, Belgrade, 1955–57; Second Secretary, British Embassy, Beirut, 1957–60; worked in Foreign Office (First Secretary from 1961) and in British Delegation to Disarmament Conference, Geneva, from 1960 until resignation from Foreign Service 1964. Chairman: British Theatre Museum, 1966–71; Venice in Peril Fund, 1970–; Colnaghi, 1992–96; Chm., World Monuments Fund in Britain; Member: Exec. Cttee, National Trust, 1969–95 (Properties Cttee, 1970–87); Franco-British Council, 1972–79; Bd, English Nat. Opera, 1977–81.

Curator, Sovereign Exhibn, London, 1992. Has made some thirty documentary films for television, mostly on history and architecture. Commendatore, Ordine al Merito della Repubblica Italiana. *Publications:* (as John Julius Norwich): Mount Athos (with Reresby Sitwell), 1966; The Normans in the South (as The Other Conquest, US), 1967; Sahara, 1968; The Kingdom in The Sun, 1970; (ed) Great Architecture of the World, 1975; A History of Venice: vol. I, The Rise to Empire, 1977: vol. II, The Greatness and the Fall, 1981; Christmas Crackers: being ten commonplace selections, 1970–79, 1980; (ed) Britain's Heritage, 1982; (ed) The Italian World: history, art and the genius of a people, 1983; Fifty Years of Glyndebourne, 1985; A Taste for Travel (anthology), 1985; The Architecture of Southern England, 1985; Byzantium: vol. 1, The Early Centuries, 1988; vol. 2, The Apogee, 1991; vol. 3, The Decline and Fall, 1995; More Christmas Crackers 1980–89, 1990; Venice: a traveller's companion, 1990; (ed) The Oxford Illustrated Encyclopaedia of the Arts, 1990; (with Quentin Blake) The Twelve Days of Christmas, 1998; Shakespeare's Kings, 1999; Still More Christmas Crackers, 2000. *Recreations:* sight-seeing, piano-playing, walking at night through Venice. *Heir: s* Hon. Jason Charles Duff Bede Cooper, *b* 27 Oct. 1959. *Address:* 24 Blomfield Road, W9 1AD. *T:* (020) 7286 5050, *Fax:* (020) 7266 2561. *Club:* Beefsteak.

See also A. J. Beevor, Baron Milford.

NORWICH, Bishop of, since 1999; **Rt Rev. Graham Richard James;** *b* 19 Jan. 1951; *s* of late Rev. Lionel Dennis James and of Florence Edith May James (*née* James); *m* 1978, Julie Anne Freemantle; one *s* one *d* (and one *d* decd). *Educ:* Northampton Grammar Sch.; Univ. of Lancaster (BA 1972); Univ. of Oxford (DipTh 1974); Cuddesdon Theological Coll. Deacon 1975, priest 1976; Asst Curate, Christ the Carpenter, Peterborough, 1975–78; Priest-in-charge, later Team Vicar, Christ the King, Digswell, 1979–83; Selection Sec. and Sec. for Continuing Ministerial Educn, ACCM, 1983–85; Sen. Selection Sec., ACCM, 1985–87; Chaplain to Archbishop of Canterbury, 1987–93; Bishop Suffragan of St Germans, 1993–99. Hon. Canon, St Matthew's Cathedral, Dallas, Texas, 1989–; Hon. Canon, Truro Cathedral, 1993–99. Vice-Moderator, Churches Commn on Inter-Faith Relations, 1993–99; Chm., Rural Bishops Panel, C of E, 2001–; Mem., Gen. Synod of C of E, 1995–. Mem. Bd, Countryside Agency, 2001–. *Publications:* (contrib.) Say One for Me, 1992; (ed) New Soundings, 1997; contribs to Theology. *Recreations:* theatre, discovering secondhand bookshops. *Address:* Bishop's House, Norwich NR3 1SB. *T:* (01603) 629001. *Club:* Athenæum.

NORWICH, Dean of; *see* Platten, Very Rev. S. G.

NORWICH, Archdeacon of; *see* Offer, Ven. C. J.

NORWOOD, Mandi, (Mrs M. Kelly); Editor-in-Chief, Mademoiselle, 2000–01; *b* 9 Oct. 1963; *m* 1995, Martin Kelly; two *d.* Sub-editor, Look Now, 1983–84; Features Editor, Clothes Show, 1986; Dep. Editor, More!, 1986–90; Editor: Looks, 1989–90; Company, 1990–95; Cosmopolitan, 1995–2000. Editor of Year, British Press Awards, 1993. *Address:* Condé Nast Publications Inc., 4 Times Square, New York, NY 10036, USA. *Club:* Groucho.

NORWOOD, Her Honour Suzanne Freda, (Mrs John Lexden Stewart); a Circuit Judge, 1973–95; *b* 24 March 1926; *d* of late Frederic Francis Norwood and of Marianne Freda Norwood (*née* Thomas); *m* 1954, John Lexden Stewart (*d* 1972); one *s. Educ:* Lowther Coll., Bodelwyddan; St Andrews Univ. MA English, MA Hons History. Called to Bar, Gray's Inn, 1951; practised at Bar, SE Circuit. Member: Parole Bd, 1976–78; Mental Health Review Tribunal, 1983–98 (Chm., Oxford and Anglia Area, 1994–98). Member: Greenwich and Bexley AHA, 1979–82; Greenwich DHA, 1982–85; Bexley DHA, 1985–90. Pres., Medico-Legal Soc., 1990–92. Hon. LLD St Andrews, 1996. *Recreations:* walking, housekeeping, opera. *Address:* 69 Lee Road, SE3 9EN.

NOSS, John Bramble; HM Diplomatic Service, retired; *b* 20 Dec. 1935; *s* of John Noss and Vera Ethel (*née* Mattingly); *m* 1957, Shirley May Andrews; two *s* one *d. Educ:* Portsmouth Grammar School. Foreign Office, 1954; RAF, 1955–57; served FO, Beirut, Copenhagen, FCO; Russian language training, 1965; Moscow, 1965–68; Santiago, 1968–70; FCO, 1970–73; First Sec. (Economic), Pretoria, 1974–77; First Sec. (Commercial), Moscow, 1977–78; FCO, 1978–81; Consul (Inward Investment), New York, 1981–85; High Comr, Solomon Is, 1986–88; Dep. Hd of Mission and Commercial Counsellor, Helsinki, 1988–91; Consul-Gen., Perth, 1991–93; Internat. Primary Aluminium Inst., 1994–97 (Dep. Sec. Gen., 1996–97). *Recreations:* photography, reading, golf. *Address:* 8 Hither Chantlers, Langton Green, Tunbridge Wells, Kent TN3 0BJ. *T:* (01892) 862157.

NOSSAL, Sir Gustav (Joseph Victor), AC 1989; Kt 1977; CBE 1970; FRS 1982; FAA; Director, The Walter and Eliza Hall Institute of Medical Research, Melbourne, 1965–96; Professor of Medical Biology, University of Melbourne, 1965–96, now Professor Emeritus; *b* Austria, 4 June 1931; *m* 1955, Lyn B. Dunnicliff; two *s* two *d. Educ:* Sydney Univ. (1st Cl. Hons BScMed (Bacteriology), 1952; 1st Cl. Hons MB, BS 1954 (Mills Prize)); Melbourne Univ. (PhD 1960). FAA 1967; FRACP 1967; Hon. FRCPA 1971; FRACMA 1971; FRCP 1980; FTS 1981; Hon. FRSE 1983. Jun., then Sen. Resident Officer, Royal Prince Alfred Hosp., Sydney, 1955–56; Res. Fellow, Walter and Eliza Hall Inst. of Med. Res., 1957–59; Asst Prof., Dept of Genetics, Stanford Univ. Sch. of Medicine, Calif, 1959–61; Dep. Dir (Immunology), Walter and Eliza Hall Inst. of Med. Res., 1961–65. Vis. scientist and vis. professor to several univs and res. insts; has given many lectures to learned societies, assocs and univs. Dir, CRA Ltd, 1977–97. World Health Organisation: Member: Expert Adv. Panel on Immunology, 1967; Adv. Cttee Med. Res., 1973–80; Special Consultant, Tropical Disease Res. Prog., 1976; Chm., Global Programme for Vaccines and Immunization, 1993–. Chm., West Pac Adv. Co. Med. Res., 1976–80; Member: Aust. Science and Technol. Council, 1975–83; Bd, CSIRO, 1987–94; Prime Minister's Sci. and Engrg Council, 1989–98. Chairman: Felton Bequests' Cttee, 1977–; Vic. Health Promotion Foundn, 1987–96. President: Internat. Union of Immunological Socs, 1986–89; Australian Acad. of Science, 1994–98. Mem., Aust. Soc. of Immunology; Hon. Mem., Amer. (1975), French (1979), Indian (1976), Soc. of Immunology; Foreign Hon. Mem., Amer. Acad. of Arts and Scis, 1974. For. Associate, US Nat. Acad. of Scis, 1979; Fellow, New York Acad. of Scis, 1977; For. Fellow, Indian Nat. Sci. Acad., 1980. Hon. MD Johannes Gutenberg Univ., Mainz, 1981. Emil von Behring Prize, Philipps Univ., Marburg, Germany, 1971; Rabbi Shai Shacknai Memorial Prize, Univ. of Jerusalem, 1973; Ciba Foundn Gold Medal, 1978; Burnet Medal, Aust. Acad. of Sci., 1979; Robert Koch Gold Medal, Univ. of Bonn, 1996. Mem. Editorial Bd of several med. jls. *Publications:* Antibodies & Immunity, 1968 (rev. edn 1977); Antigens Lymphoid Cells & The Immune Response, 1971; Medical Science & Human Goals, 1975; Nature's Defences (Boyer Lectures), 1978; Reshaping Life: key issues in genetic engineering, 1984. *Recreations:* golf, literature. *Address:* Department of Pathology, University of Melbourne, Parkville, Vic 3052, Australia. *T:* (3) 93446946. *Clubs:* Melbourne (Melbourne); National, Cape Schanck.

NOTLEY, Maj.-Gen. Charles Roland Sykes, CB 1994; CBE 1991; President of the Ordnance Board, 1992–94; *b* 5 May 1939; *s* of late Major Henry Sykes Notley, 3rd Carabiniers, and Mrs Stephanie Paterson-Morgan; *m* 1965, Katherine Sonia Bethell; two *d. Educ:* Winchester Coll. Commnd 3rd Carabiniers, 1959; Command, Royal Scots Dragoon Guards, 1979–82; Dir, Op. Requirements (Land), MoD, 1986–89; Dir, Logistic Ops (Army), MoD, 1989–90; Vice-Pres., Ordnance Board, 1991–92. *Recreations:* equitation, sailing. *Address:* c/o Royal Bank of Scotland, 62 Threadneedle Street, EC2R 8LA. *Clubs:* Royal Ocean Racing; Royal Yacht Squadron (Cowes).

NOTT, Rt Hon. Sir John (William Frederic), KCB 1983; PC 1979; Farmer, Trewinnard Farms Ltd; *b* 1 Feb. 1932; *s* of Richard Nott, Bideford, Devon, and Phyllis (*née* Francis); *m* 1959, Miloska Sekol, Maribor, Slovenia; two *s* one *d. Educ:* King's Mead, Seaford; Bradfield Coll.; Trinity Coll., Cambridge. Lieut, 2nd Gurkha Rifles (regular officer), Malayan emergency, 1952–56; Trinity Coll., Cambridge, 1957–59 (BA Hons Law and Econs); Pres., Cambridge Union, 1959; called to the Bar, Inner Temple, 1959; Gen. Manager, S. G. Warburg & Co. Ltd, Merchant Bankers, 1959–66. MP (C) Cornwall, St Ives, 1966–83; Minister of State, HM Treasury, 1972–74; Cons. front bench spokesman on: Treasury and Economic Affairs, 1974–76; Trade, 1976–79; Sec. of State for Trade, 1979–81; Sec. of State for Defence, 1981–83. Chm and Chief Executive, Lazard Brothers & Co. Ltd, 1985–90 (Dir, 1983–90); Chm., Hillsdown Hldgs plc, 1993–99 (Dir, 1991–99). Chairman: Etam plc, 1991–95; Maple Leaf Foods Inc., Canada, 1993–95; Dep. Chm., Royal Insurance PLC, 1986–91 (Dir, 1985–91); Director: AMEC plc, 1991–93; Apax Partners & Co. Capital Ltd, 1996–; Apax Partners & Co. Asset Mgt Ltd, 1997–; BOE Investment Mgt Ltd, 1999–; Chiswell Associates Ltd, 1999–; Adviser: Apax Partners, 1990–98; Freshfields, 1991–95. *Recreations:* farming, fishing, shooting, golf, boating. *Address:* 31 Walpole Street, SW3 4QS. *T:* (020) 7730 2351, *Fax:* (020) 7730 9859. *Clubs:* Buck's, Pratt's, Beefsteak.

NOTT, Rt Rev. Peter John; Bishop of Norwich, 1985–99; Hon. Assistant Bishop, Diocese of Oxford, since 1999; *b* 30 Dec. 1933; *s* of Cecil Frederick Wilder Nott and Rosina Mabel Bailey; *m* 1961, Elizabeth May Maingot; one *s* three *d. Educ:* Bristol Grammar School; Dulwich Coll.; RMA Sandhurst; Fitzwilliam House, Cambridge; Westcott House, Cambridge (MA). Curate of Harpenden, 1961–64; Chaplain of Fitzwilliam Coll., Cambridge, 1964–69; Fellow of Fitzwilliam Coll., 1967–69, Hon. Fellow, 1993; Chaplain of New Hall, Cambridge, 1966–69; Rector of Beaconsfield, 1969–77; Bishop Suffragan of Taunton, 1977–85. Archbishop's Adviser to HMC, 1980–85; President: SW Region, Mencap, 1978–84; Somerset Rural Music Sch., 1981–85; Royal Norfolk Agricl Assoc., 1996. Vice-Chm., Archbishops' Commn for Rural Areas, 1988–90. Trustee, Nat. Army Mus., 2001–. Dean, Priory of England, Order of St John of Jerusalem, 1999–. KStJ 1999. *Address:* Ickford End, Limes Way, Shabbington, Bucks HP18 9HB. *T:* (01844) 201551.

NOTT, Roger Charles L.; *see* Lane-Nott.

NOTTAGE, Raymond Frederick Tritton, CMG 1964; Chairman, Bobath Centre for Children with Cerebral Palsy, since 1987; Deputy Chairman, Association of Lloyd's Members, 1985–91; Treasurer, Arkwright Arts Trust, Hampstead, 1975–92; *b* 1 Aug. 1916; *s* of Frederick and Frances Nottage; *m* 1941, Joyce Evelyn, *d* of Sidney and Edith Philpot; three *d. Educ:* Hackney Downs Secondary Sch. Civil servant, Post Office Headquarters, 1936–49; Editor of Civil Service Opinion, and Member Exec. Cttee, Soc. of Civil Servants, 1944–49; Dir-Gen., RIPA, 1949–78. Mem. Hornsey Borough Council, 1945–47. Mem. Cttee on Training in Public Admin. for Overseas Countries, 1961–63; Vice-Pres. Internat. Inst. of Admin. Sciences, 1962–68; Mem. Governing Body, Inst. of Development Studies, Univ. of Sussex, 1966–76; travelled abroad as Consultant and Lectr. *Publications:* Sources of Local Revenue (with S. H. H. Hildersley), 1968; Financing Public Sector Pensions, 1975; (with Gerald Rhodes) Pensions: a plan for the future, 1986; articles on public administration. *Recreations:* music, swimming.

NOTTINGHAM, Bishop of, (RC), since 2000; **Rt Rev. Malcolm Patrick McMahon,** OP; *b* 14 June 1949; *s* of Patrick McMahon and Sarah McMahon (*née* Watson). *Educ:* St Aloysius Coll., Highgate; Univ. of Manchester Inst. of Sci. and Technol. (BSc); Blackfriars, Oxford; Heythrop Coll., London Univ. (BD; MTh). Pres., Students' Union, UMIST, 1970–71; contracts engr, London Transport, 1971–76; joined Dominican Order, 1976; ordained priest, 1982; Student Chaplain, Leicester Univ., 1982–85; Prior and Parish Priest, St Dominic's Priory, NW5, 1985–92; Prior Provincial, English Province of Order of Preachers (Dominican Order), 1992–2000; Prior of Blackfriars, Oxford, 2000. *Publications:* contrib. articles and reviews in New Blackfriars, Dominican Ashram and Signum. *Recreations:* walking, golf, reading thrillers. *Address:* Bishop's House, 27 Cavendish Road East, The Park, Nottingham NG7 1BB.

NOTTINGHAM, Archdeacon of; *see* Ogilvie, Ven. G.

NOULTON, John David; Director of Public Affairs, Eurotunnel, since 1992; *b* 5 Jan. 1939; *s* of John Noulton and Kathleen (*née* Sheehan); *m* 1961, Anne Elizabeth Byrne; three *s* one *d. Educ:* Clapham Coll. MCIT 1988; ComplCE 1994. Asst Principal, Dept of Transport, 1970–72; Principal, DoE, 1972–78; Pvte Sec. to Minister of State, DoE, 1976–78; Asst Sec., Depts of the Environment and of Transport, 1978–85; Under Sec., Dept of Transport, 1985–89. British Co-Chm., Channel Tunnel Intergovtl Commn, 1987–89; Dir, Transmanche Link, 1989–92. Chm., Council for Travel and Tourism, 2001–. *Recreations:* boating, swimming, walking, reading. *Address:* 12 Ladderstile Ride, Coombe, Surrey KT2 7LP. *T:* (020) 8546 3855.

NOURSE, Rt Hon. Sir Martin (Charles), Kt 1980; PC 1985; a Lord Justice of Appeal, 1985–2001; Vice-President, Court of Appeal (Civil Division), 2000–01; Acting Master of the Rolls, 2000; *b* 3 April 1932; *yr s* of late Henry Edward Nourse, MD, MRCP, of Cambridge, and Ethel Millicent, *d* of Rt Hon. Sir Charles Henry Sargant, Lord Justice of Appeal; *m* 1972, Lavinia, *yr d* of late Comdr D. W. Malim; one *s* one *d. Educ:* Winchester (Fellow, 1993–); Corpus Christi Coll., Cambridge (Hon. Fellow, 1988). National Service as 2nd Lieut, Rifle Bde, 1951–52; Lieut, London Rifle Bde Rangers (TA), 1952–55. Called to Bar, Lincoln's Inn, 1956, Bencher, 1978, Treas., 2001; Mem., General Council of the Bar, 1964–68; a Junior Counsel to BoT in Chancery matters, 1967–70; QC 1970; Attorney Gen., Duchy of Lancaster, 1976–80; a Judge of the Courts of Appeal of Jersey and Guernsey, 1977–80; Judge of the High Court of Justice, Chancery Div., 1980–85. Pres., Council of Inns of Court, 1992–95. *Address:* Dullingham House, Dullingham, Newmarket, Cambs CB8 9UP.

NOVA SCOTIA, Archbishop of, since 1997; **Most Rev. Arthur Gordon Peters;** Metropolitan of the Ecclesiastical Province of Canada; *b* 21 Dec. 1935; *s* of William Peters and Charlotte Peters (*née* Symes); *m* 1962, Elizabeth Baert; one *s* two *d. Educ:* High School, North Sydney, NS; Univ. of King's College, Halifax, NS (BA 1960, BST 1963, BD 1973). Student, Parish of Waverley, 1961–63; deacon 1962, priest 1963, Nova Scotia; Morris Scholar, 1963, at Canterbury (Eng.), Geneva, Jerusalem, Norton (dio. Durham, Eng.); Rector: Weymouth, NS, 1964–68; Annapolis-Granville, NS, 1968–73; Christ Church, Sydney, NS, 1973–82; Bishop Coadjutor of Nova Scotia, 1982–84; Bishop of Nova Scotia, 1984–. Hon. DD Univ. of King's College, 1982. *Recreations:* swimming, ski-ing, reading, skating, photography. *Address:* 5732 College Street, Halifax, NS B3H 1X3, Canada. *T:* (902) 4200717.

NOWELL-SMITH, Prof. Patrick Horace, AM (Harvard); MA (Oxon); Professor of Philosophy, York University, Toronto, 1969–85, now Emeritus; *b* 17 Aug. 1914; *s* of Nowell Charles Smith; *m* 1st, 1946, Perilla Thyme (marr. diss. 1968), *d* of Sir Richard Vynne Southwell; three *s* one *d*; 2nd, 1968, Felicity Margret (marr. diss. 1986), *d* of Dr Richard Leonard Ward; two *d*. *Educ:* Winchester Coll.; New College, Oxford. Commonwealth Fellow, Harvard Univ., 1937–39. Served War of 1939–45, in Army, 1939–45. Fellow and Lecturer, Trinity Coll., Oxford, 1946–57, Estates Bursar, 1951–57; Professor of Philosophy: University of Leicester, 1957–64; University of Kent, 1964–69. *Publications:* Ethics, 1954; articles in Mind, Proc. Aristotelian Soc., Theoria, etc. *Address:* 7 Wyndham House, Plantation Road, Oxford OX2 6JJ.

See also Sir S. S. T. Young.

NOYER, Christian; Vice President, European Central Bank, since 1998; *b* 6 Oct. 1950. *Educ:* Univ. of Rennes (lic. en droit 1971); Univ. of Paris (DèS droit 1972); Inst d'Etudes Politiques, Paris (Dip. 1972); Ecole Nat. d'Admin. Entered Treasury, Min. of Finance, France, 1976; Financial Attaché, Perm. Repn to EEC, Brussels, 1980–82; French Treasury: Chief of Banking Office and of Export Credit Office, 1982–85; Advr to Minister for Econ. Affairs and Finance, 1986–88; Dep. Dir in charge of internat. multilateral issues, 1988–90; Dep. Dir in charge of debt mgt, monetary and banking issues, 1990–92; Dir responsible for public hldgs and public financing, 1992–93; Chief of Staff to Minister for Economic Affairs, 1993; Dir, Treasury, 1993–95; Chief of Staff to Minister for Econ. Affairs and Finance, 1995–97; Dir, Min. for Econ. Affairs, Finance and Industry, 1997–98. Member: European Monetary Cttee, 1993–95, 1998 (Alternate Mem., 1988–90); Econ. and Financial Cttee, 1999–; OECD Working Party, 1993–95; Alternate Mem., G7 and G10, 1993–95. Alternate Gov., IMF and World Bank, 1993–95. Chm., Paris Club of Creditor Countries, 1993–97. Chevalier: Ordre Nat. du Mérite (France), 1994; Légion d'Honneur (France), 1998; Comdr, Ordre Nat. du Lion (Senegal), 1995. *Publications:* Banks: the rules of the game, 1990; articles in jls. *Address:* European Central Bank, Kaiserstrasse 29, 60311 Frankfurt am Main, Germany. *T:* (69) 13447340.

NSEKELA, Amon James, OURT 1985; Director: Tanzania–Zambia Railway Authority, since 1982; Computers and Telecoms Systems, since 1993; *b* 4 Jan. 1930; *s* of Ngonile Reuben Nsekela and Anyambilile Nsekela (*née* Kalinga); *m* 1957, Christina Matilda Nsekela (*née* Kyusa); two *s*. *Educ:* Rungwe Dist Sch.; Malangali Secondary Sch.; Tabora Govt Sen. Sec. Sch.; Makerere UC (DipEd); Univ. of Pacific (Scholar, MA). Schoolteacher, Rungwe Middle Sch. and Alliance Secondary Sch., 1954–57; entered Civil Service as DO, Moshi, 1960; Perm. Sec., Min. of External Affairs and Defence, 1963; Perm. Sec. to Min. of Commerce, 1964; Prin. Sec. to Treasury (also ex-officio Paymaster Gen.), 1966–67. MP 1973–75, and Mem. E African Legis. Assembly, 1967–70. High Comr, UK, 1974–81, and Ambassador Extraordinary and Plenipotentiary to Ireland, 1980–81. Chm. or Dir of many cos and corporations, 1967–, incl.: Chm., Nat. Insurance Corp. of Tanzania, 1967–72; Chm. and Man. Dir, Nat. Bank of Commerce, 1967–74 and 1981–94; Chm., Tanzania Investment Bank, 1982–91; Director: Nat. Develt Corp. (past Chm. when Tanganyika Develt Corp.); Bd of Internal Trade; E African Airways Corp.; Bd, African Medical Res. Fund, 1986–. Mem./Sec., Presidential Commn on Estabt of Democratic One-Party State in Tanzania; Mem., Internat. Council of Trustees, Internat. Defence and Aid Fund for Southern Africa, 1985–. Chairman: Council, Inst. of Finance Management, 1971–; Inst. of Develt Management, 1982–; Public Service Salaries Review Commn, 1985–86. Pres., Tanzania Soc. for Internat. Develt; Past Pres., Economic Assoc. of Tanzania; Chm., Britain–Tanzania Soc., 1982–. Mem., TANU, 1955. Mem., NEC, Chama Cha Mapinduzi, 1987–. Chm. Council, Univ. of Dar es Salaam; Vice-Chm., Council, Sokoine Univ. of Agriculture, 1982–. *Publications:* Minara ya Historia ya Tanganyika: Tanganyika hadi Tanzania, 1965, new edns 1966 and 1971; Demokrasi Tanzania, 1973; (with A. L. Nhonoli) The Development of Health Services in Mainland Tanzania: Tumetoka Mbali, 1976; Socialism and Social Accountability in a Developing Nation, 1978; (ed) Southern Africa: toward economic liberation, 1981; Towards Rational Alternatives, 1984; A Time to Act, 1984; contribs to Jl of Administration Overseas (ODM), African Review, Development Dialogue. *Recreations:* swimming, darts, reading, writing. *Address:* 9 Lupa Way, Box 722, Mbeya, Tanzania.

NUGEE, Christopher George; QC 1998; *b* 23 Jan. 1959; *s* of Edward George Nugee, *qv* and Rachel Elizabeth Nugee, *qv*; *m* 1991, Emily Thornberry; two *s* one *d*. *Educ:* Radley Coll.; Corpus Christi Coll., Oxford (BA 1st Cl. Hons Lit. Hum 1981); City Univ. (Dip. Law (Distinction) 1982). Called to the Bar, Inner Temple, 1983 (Queen Elizabeth Schol., 1983; Eldon Law Schol., 1984); in practice at the Bar, 1984–. Member: Bar Council, 1991–93 (Mem., Professional Conduct Cttee, 1992–96); Cttee, Assoc. of Pension Lawyers, 1998–. *Recreations:* cycling, the family. *Address:* Wilberforce Chambers, 8 New Square, Lincoln's Inn, WC2A 3QP. *T:* (020) 7306 0102.

NUGEE, Edward George, TD 1964; QC 1977; *b* 9 Aug. 1928; *o s* of late Brig. George Travers Nugee, CBE, DSO, MC, RA, and Violet Mary (*née* Richards, later Brooks); *m* 1955, Rachel Elizabeth Makower (*see* R. E. Nugee); four *s*. *Educ:* Brambletye; Radley Coll. (Open Scholar); Worcester Coll., Oxford (Open Exhibnr; Law Mods, Distinction, 1950; 1st Cl. Hons Jurisprudence, 1952; Eldon Law Scholar, 1953; MA 1956). National Service, RA, 1947–49 (Office of COS, GHQ, FARELF); service with 100 Army Photographic Interpretation Unit, TA, 1950–64 (retd Captain, Intell. Corps, 1964). Read as pupil with Lord Templeman and Lord Brightman; called to the Bar, Inner Temple, 1955, Bencher 1976, Treas. 1996; *ad eundem* Lincoln's Inn, 1968. Jun. Counsel to Land Commn (Chancery and Conveyancing), 1967–71; Counsel for litigation under Commons Registration Act, 1965, 1968–77; Conveyancing Counsel to Treasury, WO, MAFF, Forestry Commn, MoD (Admiralty), and DoE, 1972–77; Conveyancing Counsel of Court, 1976–77. Poor Man's Lawyer, Lewisham CAB, 1954–72. Member: CAB Adv. Cttee, Family Welfare Assoc., 1969–72; Management Cttee, Greater London Citizens Advice Bureaux Service Ltd, 1972–74; Man. Cttee, Forest Hill Advice Centre, 1972–76; Bar Council, 1962–66 (Mem., External Relations Cttee, 1966–71); Council of Legal Educn, 1967–90 (Vice-Chm. 1976–82, and Chm. of Bd of Studies, 1976–82); Adv. Cttee on Legal Educn, 1971–90; Common Professional Exam. Bd, 1976–89 (Chm., 1981–87); Lord Chancellor's Law Reform Cttee, 1973–; various working parties and consultative groups of Law Commn, 1966–; Inst. of Conveyancers, 1971– (Pres., 1986–87); Chm., Cttee of Inquiry into Management Problems of Privately Owned Blocks of Flats, 1984–85. Church Comr, 1990–2001 (Mem., Bd of Govs, 1993–2001); Mem., C of E Legal Adv. Commn, 2001–. Chm. Governors, Brambletye Sch., 1972–77; Mem. Council, Radley Coll., 1975–95. *Publications:* (jtly) Nathan on the Charities Act 1960, 1962; (ed jtly) Halsbury's Laws of England, titles Landlord and Tenant (3rd edn 1958), Real Property (3rd edn 1960 to 5th edn 1998); contribs to legal jls. *Recreations:* travel, cooking, church and family life. *Address:* Wilberforce Chambers, 8 New Square, Lincoln's Inn, WC2A 3QP. *T:* (020) 7306 0102; 10 Heath Hurst Road, Hampstead, NW3 2RX. *T:* (020) 7435 9204.

See also C. G. Nugee.

NUGEE, Rachel Elizabeth, MA; *b* 15 Aug. 1926; *d* of John Moritz Makower and Adelaide Gertrude Leonaura Makower (*née* Franklin); *m* 1955, Edward George Nugee, *qv*; four *s*. *Educ:* Roedean Sch., Brighton; Lady Margaret Hall, Oxford; MA (EngLang and Lit); Reading Univ. (Dip. Soc. Studies). Joined Mothers' Union, 1956; Diocesan Pres., London Dio., 1974–76; Central Pres., 1977–82; MU rep. on Women's Nat. Commn, 1983–88. Chm., Edmonton Area Social Responsibility Policy Cttee, 1987–90; Member: Royal Free Hosp. (Hampstead Gen. Hosp.) House Cttee and Patients' Services Cttee, 1961–72; London Diocesan Bd for Social Responsibility, 1984–85, 1987–90; Law of Marriage Gp, General Synod, 1985–88; Lord Chancellor's Adv. Cttee on Conscientious Objectors, 1986–. Trustee: One plus One – the Marriage and Partnership res. charity, 1984–94; King's Cross Furniture Project, 1996–98; Voluntary Worker, Witness Service, CCC, Old Bailey, 1997–2000. JP Inner London (Thames), 1971–96; Dep. Chm. of Bench, 1985–91; Court Chm., Inner London Family Panel, 1991–96. *Publications:* several religious articles and booklets. *Recreations:* active support of Church and family life, reading, especially history, visiting friends, criminal and family law. *Address:* 10 Heath Hurst Road, Hampstead, NW3 2RX. *T:* (020) 7435 9204, *Fax:* (020) 7435 9204.

See also C. G. Nugee.

NUGENT, family name of **Earl of Westmeath.**

NUGENT, Rear Adm. James Michael B.; *see* Burnell-Nugent.

NUGENT, Sir John (Edwin Lavallin), 7th Bt *cr* 1795; *b* 16 March 1933; *s* of Sir Hugh Charles Nugent, 6th Bt, and of Margaret Mary Lavallin, *er d* of late Rev. Herbert Lavallin Puxley; *S* father, 1983; *m* 1959, Penelope Anne, *d* of late Brig. Richard Nigel Hanbury, CBE, TD; one *s* one *d*. *Educ:* Eton. Short service commn, Irish Guards, Lieut, 1953–56. PA to William Geoffrey Rootes (later 2nd Baron Rootes), Chm. of Rootes Gp, 1957–59; joined board of Lambourn group of cos, 1959, Chm., 1980–90. High Sheriff of Berks, 1981–82; JP Berks, 1962–87. *Recreations:* garden and fishing. *Heir: s* Nicholas Myles John Nugent, *b* 17 Feb. 1967. *Address:* Ballinlough Castle, Clonmellon, Navan, Co. Meath, Ireland. *T:* (046) 33135, *Fax:* (046) 33331.

NUGENT, Sir Peter Walter James, 5th Bt *cr* 1831; *b* 26 Jan. 1920; *s* of Sir Walter Richard Nugent, 4th Bt and of Aileen Gladys, *y d* of late Middleton Moore O'Malley, JP, Ross, Westport, Co. Mayo; *S* father, 1955; *m* 1947, Anne Judith, *o d* of Major Robert Smyth, Gaybrook, Mullingar, Co. Westmeath; two *s* two *d*. *Educ:* Downside. Served War of 1939–45; 2nd Lieut, Hampshire Regt, 1941; Major, 1945. *Heir: s* Walter Richard Middleton Nugent [*b* 15 Nov. 1947; *m* 1985, Okabe Kayoko]. *Address:* Bay Bush, Straffan, Co. Kildare, Eire.

NUGENT, Sir Robin (George Colborne), 5th Bt *cr* 1806; *b* 11 July 1925; *s* of Sir Guy Nugent, 4th Bt and Maisie, Lady Nugent (*d* 1992), *d* of J. A. Bigsby; *S* father, 1970; *m* 1st, 1947, Ursula Mary (marr. diss. 1967), *d* of late Lt-Gen. Sir Herbert Fothergill Cooke, KCB, KBE, CSI, DSO; two *s* one *d*; 2nd, 1967, Victoria Anna Irmgard, *d* of late Dr Peter Cartellieri. *Educ:* Eton; RWA School of Architecture. Lt Grenadier Guards, 1943–48; served Italy, 1944–45. ARIBA 1959. *Recreation:* fishing. *Heir: s* Christopher George Ridley Nugent [*b* 5 Oct. 1949; *m* 1985, Jacqueline Vagba; three *s*].

NUNAN, Manus; lecturer; *b* 26 March 1926; *s* of Manus Timothy Nunan, Dist Justice, and Nan (*née* FitzGerald); *m* 1987, Valerie (*née* Robinson); one *s* one *d* by previous marriages. *Educ:* St Mary's Coll., Dublin; Trinity Coll., Dublin (BA, LLB). Called to the Irish Bar, King's Inns, 1950; called to the English Bar, Gray's Inn, 1956. Asst d'Anglais, Lycée Masséna, Nice, 1949–50; practised at Irish Bar, 1950–53; entered Colonial Legal Service, 1953; Crown Counsel, Nigeria, 1953–62; Solicitor-Gen., Northern Nigeria, 1962–64; Minister of Govt, Northern Nigeria, 1962; QC (Nigeria) 1962; practised at English Bar, 1965–85; a Recorder, 1978–84; since 1985 has lectured throughout English-speaking world on the life and trials of Oscar Wilde, Dr Samuel Johnson and his circle, Talleyrand, Bernard Shaw, Oliver Gogarty; autobiog. lect., Never Listen to an Irishman; Evelyn Wrench Lectr, E-SU of USA, 1988; Vis. Lectr, Broward Community Coll., Fla, 1989; Lecturer: Amer. Irish Historical Soc., NY, 1990; Nat. Portrait Gall., 1991–94; Bournemouth Internat. Festival, QE2, Oxford Univ. E-SU Soc., and Mus. of Modern Art, Oxford, 1992; Shirley Soc., Cambridge Univ., 1993; Centre Culturel Irlandais, Paris, 1994. *Club:* Kildare Street and University (Dublin).

NUNBURNHOLME, 6th Baron *cr* 1906; **Stephen Charles Wilson;** *b* 29 Nov. 1973; *o s* of 5th Baron Nunburnholme and of Linda Kay (*née* Stephens); *S* father, 2000. *Educ:* Nottingham Univ. *Heir: half-b* Hon. David Mark Wilson [*b* 5 Aug. 1954; *m* 1983, Amanda Christian Hayward (marr. diss. 1989)].

NUNN, Imogen Mary; *see* Stubbs, I. M.

NUNN, John Francis, PhD, DSc, MD; FRCS, FRCA; FGS; Head of Division of Anaesthesia, Medical Research Council Clinical Research Centre, 1968–91; *b* 7 Nov. 1925; *s* of late Francis Nunn, Colwyn Bay; *m* 1949, Sheila, *d* of late E. C. Doubleday; one *s* two *d*. *Educ:* Wrekin Coll.; Birmingham Univ. (MD(Hons) 1970; PhD 1959; DSc 1992). FRCA (FFARCS 1955); FRCS 1983. MO, Birmingham Univ. Spitzbergen Expedition, 1948; Colonial Med. Service, Malaya, 1949–53; University Research Fellow, Birmingham, 1955–56; Leverhulme Research Fellow, RCS, 1957–64; Part-time Lectr, Postgrad. Med. Sch., Univ. of London, 1959–64; Consultant Anæsth., Hammersmith Hosp., 1959–64; Prof. of Anaesthesia, Univ. of Leeds, 1964–68. Member: Council, RCS, 1977–82 (Mem. Board, Faculty of Anaesthetists, Vice-Dean, 1977–79, Dean, 1979–82); Council, Assoc. of Anaesthetists, 1973–76 (Vice Pres., 1988–90); Pres., Sect. Anaesthesia, RSM, 1984–85. Hunterian Professor, RCS, 1960; Visiting Professor to various American Universities, 1960–98; British Council Lecturer: Switzerland, 1962; USSR, 1963; Czechoslovakia, 1969; China, 1974. Joseph Clover Lectr, RCS, 1968. Mem., Egypt Exploration Soc. FGS 2001. Hon. FFARCSI 1985; Hon. FRSocMed 1992; Hon. FANZCA 1993 (Hon. FFARACS); Hon. FRCA 1993. Hon. Dr: Turin, 1993; Uppsala, 1996. (1st) Sir Ivan Magill Gold Medal, Assoc. of Anaesthetists of GB and Ireland, 1988; Richardson Award, Geologists' Assoc., 1999. *Publications:* Applied Respiratory Physiology, 1969, 4th edn 1993; (ed jtly) General Anaesthesia, 3rd edn 1971, 5th edn 1989; Ancient Egyptian Medicine, 1996; several chapters in medical text-books, and publications in Journal Appl. Physiol., Lancet, Nature, British Journal Anæsth., etc. *Recreations:* Egyptology, model engineering, ski-ing. *Address:* 3 Russell Road, Moor Park, Northwood, Mddx HA6 2LJ. *T:* (01923) 826363.

NUNN, Rear-Adm. John Richard Danford, CB 1980; Bursar and Official Fellow, Exeter College, Oxford, 1981–88, retired; *b* 12 April 1925; *s* of Surg. Captain Gerald Nunn and Edith Florence (*née* Brown); *m* 1951, Katharine Mary (*née* Paris); three *d*. *Educ:* Epsom Coll. CEng, FIMechE; MPhil Cantab, 1981; MA Oxon, 1982. Entered RN, 1943; RN Engrg Coll., Keyham, 1943–47; HMS Devonshire, Second Cruiser Sqdn, 1945; HMS Vengeance, 1947; Advanced Engineering Course, RNC Greenwich, 1949–51. HMS Amethyst, Korea, 1952–53; HMS Tiger, 1957–59; Commander, 1960; HMS Glamorgan, 1967–68; Captain, 1969; Sea Dart and Seaslug Chief Engineer, 1970–72;

Cabinet Office, 1973–74; Staff of SACLANT, 1975–77; Rear-Adm., 1978; Port Adm., Rosyth, 1977–80. Fellow Commoner, Downing Coll., Cambridge, 1980–. Vice Chm. of Govs, Peter Symonds VI Form Coll., Winchester, 1996–99. Editor, The Naval Review, 1980–83. *Recreations:* sailing, tennis, gliding, travel. *Address:* Warner's Cottage, Corhampton, Hants SO3 1LL. *Clubs:* Naval; Royal Naval Sailing Association (Portsmouth).

NUNN, Trevor Robert, CBE 1978; Artistic Director, Royal National Theatre, since 1997; *b* 14 Jan. 1940; *s* of late Robert Alexander Nunn and of Dorothy May (*née* Piper); *m* 1st, 1969, Janet Suzman, *qv* (marr. diss. 1986); one *s*; 2nd, 1986, Sharon Lee Hill (marr. diss. 1991); two *d*; 3rd, 1994, Imogen Stubbs, *qv*; one *s* one *d*. *Educ:* Northgate Grammar Sch., Ipswich; Downing Coll., Cambridge (BA). Producer, Belgrade Theatre, Coventry; Royal Shakespeare Company: Chief Exec., 1968–86; Artistic Dir, 1968–78; Jt Artistic Dir, 1978–86; Dir Emeritus, 1986–. Mem., Arts Council of England, 1994–96. Hon. MA: Newcastle upon Tyne, 1982; Warwick. *Address:* Royal National Theatre, Upper Ground, South Bank, SE1 9PX.

NUNNELEY, Charles Kenneth Roylance, CA; Chairman: Nationwide Building Society, since 1996 (Director, since 1994; Deputy Chairman, 1995–96); National Trust, since 1996; *b* 3 April 1936; *s* of Robin Michael Charles Nunneley and late Patricia Mary (*née* Roylance); *m* 1961, Catherine Elizabeth Armstrong Buckley; one *s* three *d*. *Educ:* Eton Coll. CA 1961. Robert Fleming (merchant bankers), 1962–96: Dir, 1968–96; Dep. Chm., 1986–96; Chairman: Save & Prosper Gp, 1989–96; Fleming Income & Capital Investment Trust plc, 1992–; IMRO Ltd, 1992–97 (Dir, 1986–97); Monks Investment Trust plc, 1996– (Dir, 1977–); Dep. Chm., Clerical Medical & General Life Assurance Soc., 1978–96 (Dir, 1974–96); Dir, Macmillan Ltd, 1982–96. Chm., Instnl Fund Managers' Assoc., 1989–92. National Trust: Member: Council, 1992–; Exec. Cttee, 1991–; Chm., Finance Cttee, 1991–96. Mem. Court, Grocers' Co., 1975– (Master, 1982–83). Governor, Oundle Schs, 1975–. *Recreations:* walking, shooting, photography. *Address:* Nationwide Building Society, 136 High Holborn, WC1V 6PX.

NUNNELEY, John Hewlett, MBE 2001; Chairman, AMF Microflight Ltd, 1987–93; *b* Sydney, NSW, 26 Nov. 1922; *o s* of Wilfrid Alexander Nunneley and Audrey Mary (*née* Tebbitt); *m* 1945, Lucia, *e d* of Enrico Ceruti, Milan, Italy; one *s* one *d*. *Educ:* Lawrence Sheriff Sch., Rugby. Served War of 1939–45: Somerset LI, seconded KAR; Abyssinia, Brit. Somaliland, 1942; Burma campaign, 1944 (wounded, despatches); Captain and Adjt. Various management posts in aircraft, shipping, printing and publishing industries, 1946–55. Exec., Beaverbrook Newspapers, 1955–62; joined BTC, 1962: Chief Publicity Officer, 1962–63; Chief Development Officer (Passenger) BR Bd, 1963–64; Chief Passenger Manager, 1964–69; Pres. and Chm., BR-Internat. Inc., New York, USA, 1966–69; Man. Dir, British Transport Advertising Ltd, 1969–87. Principal Advertising Consultant, Hong Kong Govt, 1981–83. Member: Passenger Co-ordination Cttee for London, 1964–69; Outdoor Advertising Council, 1969–88. Pres., European Fedn of Outdoor Advertising (FEPE), 1984–87. Introduced BR Corporate Identity, 1964 and Inter-City concept, 1965. Hon. Mem., All-Burma Veterans Assoc. of Japan, 1991; Chm., Burma Campaign Fellowship Gp, 1996–. Freeman, GAPAN, 1990. City of Paris Medal, 1986. *Publications:* Tales from the King's African Rifles, 1997; (ed) Tales from the Burma Campaign 1942–1945, 1998; (with K. Tamayama) Tales by Japanese Soldiers, 2000; numerous articles on aviation, transport and advertising subjects. *Recreations:* gliding (FAI Gold C and Two Diamonds), powered flight. *Address:* 6 Ashfield Close, Petersham, Surrey TW10 7AF.

NURSAW, Sir James, KCB 1992 (CB 1983); QC 1988; HM Procurator General and Treasury Solicitor, 1988–92; Counsel to Chairman of Committees, House of Lords, since 1993; *b* 18 Oct. 1932; *s* of William George Nursaw (*d* 1994); *m* 1959, Eira, *yr d* of late E. W. Caryl-Thomas, MD, BSc, Barrister-at-law; two *d*. *Educ:* Bancroft's School; Christ's Coll., Cambridge (Schol.; MA, LLB). Called to Bar, Middle Temple, 1955 (Blackstone Entrance Schol. and Prize, Harmsworth Schol.), Bencher 1989. Senior Research Officer, Cambridge Univ. Dept of Criminal Science, 1958. Joined Legal Adviser's Branch, Home Office, 1959; Principal Asst Legal Advr, HO and NI Office, 1977–80; Legal Secretary, Law Officers' Dept, 1980–83; Legal Adviser, Home Office and NI Office, 1983–88. Liveryman, Loriners' Co. *Clubs:* Oxford and Cambridge, MCC.

NURSE, Sir Paul (Maxime), Kt 1999; PhD; FRS 1989; Director General, Imperial Cancer Research Fund, since 1996 (Director of Laboratory Research, 1993–96); *b* 25 Jan. 1949; *s* of Maxime Nurse and Cissie Nurse (*née* White); *m* 1971, Anne Teresa (*née* Talbott); two *d*. *Educ:* Harrow County Grammar Sch.; Univ. of Birmingham (BSc): Univ. of East Anglia (PhD). Research Fellow, Univ. of Edinburgh, 1973–79; SERC Advanced Fellow and MRC Sen. Fellow, Univ. of Sussex, 1979–84; Hd of Cell Cycle Control Laboratory, Imp. Cancer Res. Fund, London, 1984–87; Oxford University: Fellow, 1987–93, Hon. Fellow, 1993–, Linacre Coll.; Iveagh Prof. of Microbiology, 1987–91; Royal Soc. Napier Res. Prof., 1991–93. MAE 1992; Foreign Associate US NAS, 1995. Fleming Lectr, 1984, Marjory Stephenson Lectr, 1990, Soc. of Gen. Microbiology; Florey Lectr, Royal Soc., 1990; Wenner-Gren Lectr, Stockholm, 1993; Dunham Lectr, Harvard, 1994. Pres., Genetical Soc., 1990–94. Founder FMedSci 1998. Ciba Medal, Biochemical Soc., 1991; Feldberg Foundn Prize, 1991; (jtly) Louis Jeantet Prize for Medicine, Geneva, 1992; Gairdner Foundn Internat. Jt Award, 1992; Royal Soc. Wellcome Medal, 1993; Jimenez Diaz Meml Award, Madrid, 1993; Rosenstiel Award, Brandeis Univ., 1993; Pezcoller Award for Oncology Res., Trento, 1995; Royal Soc. Royal Medal, 1995; Dr Josef Steiner Prize, Steiner Cancer Foundn, Bern, 1996; Dr H. P. Heineken Prize, Netherlands, 1996; Alfred P. Sloan Jr Prize and Medal, General Motors Cancer Res. Foundn, 1997; Judd Award, Meml Sloan-Kettering Cancer Center, NY, 1998; Lasker Award, Albert and Mary Lasker Foundn, NY, 1998; (jtly) Nobel Prize for Physiology or Medicine, 2001. *Publications:* numerous, in sci. jls, concerned with cell and molecular biology. *Recreations:* gliding, astronomy, talking. *Address:* Imperial Cancer Research Fund, PO Box 123, Lincoln's Inn Fields, WC2A 3PX.

NURSTEN, Prof. Harry Erwin, PhD, DSc; CChem, FRSC; FIFST; FSLTC; Professor of Food Science, Reading University, 1976–92, Professor Emeritus 1992; *s* of Sergius Nursten and Helene Nursten; *m* 1950, Jean Patricia Frobisher. *Educ:* Ilkley Grammar Sch.; Leeds Univ. (BSc 1st Cl. Hons Colour Chemistry, 1947; PhD 1949; DSc 1973). FRIC 1957; FIFST 1972; FSLTC 1986. Bradford Dyers Assoc. Res. Fellow, Dept of Colour Chem. and Dyeing, Leeds Univ., 1949–52; Lectr in Textile Chem. and Dyeing, Nottingham and Dist Tech. Coll., 1952–54; Lectr 1955–65, Sen. Lectr 1965–70, and Reader 1970–76, Procter Dept of Food and Leather Science, Leeds Univ.; Head of Dept of Food Sci., 1976–86, Head of Dept of Food Science and Technology, 1986–89, Head of Sub-Dept of Food Sci., 1989–91, Reading Univ. Res. Associate, Dept of Nutrition, Food Science and Technol., MIT, 1961–62; Visiting Professor: Univ. of Calif, Davis, 1966; Univ. of Zimbabwe, 1994. Chief Examiner, Mastership in Food Control, 1982–90. Pres., Soc. of Leather Technologists and Chemists, 1974–76. Bill Littlejohn Memorial Medallion Lectr, Brit. Soc. of Flavourists, 1974; Sen. Medal, Food Chemistry Gp, RSC, 1996. *Publications:* (ed jtly) Progress in Flavour Research, 1979; (contrib.) Rothe and Kruse, Aroma, Perception, Formation, Evaluation, 1995; (contrib.) Schubert and Spiro, Chemical and Biological Properties of Tea Infusions, 1997; (ed jtly) The Maillard Reaction in Foods and Medicine, 1998; (contrib.) Caffeinated Beverages: health benefits, physiological effects, and chemistry, 2000; (jtly) Capillary Electrophoresis for Food Analysis: method development, 2000; (contrib.) Rothe, Flavour 2000: perception, release, evaluation, formation, acceptance, nutrition/health, 2001; papers mainly in Jl Sci. Food Agric. and Jl Chromatog. *Address:* School of Food Biosciences, University of Reading, Whiteknights, PO Box 226, Reading RG6 6AP. *T:* (0118) 931 6725.

NÜSSLEIN-VOLHARD, Christiane, PhD; Director of Department of Genetics, Max Planck Institute for Developmental Biology, since 1990; *b* 20 Oct. 1942; *d* of Rolf Volhard and Brigitte Volhard (*née* Haas). *Educ:* Univ. of Tübingen. Res. Associate, Max Planck Institute for Virus Research, 1972–74; EMBO Fellow: Biozentrum Basel Lab., 1975–76; Univ. of Freiberg, 1977; Head of Gp, European Molecular Biology Lab., Heidelberg, 1978–80; Gp Leader, Friedrich Miescher Lab., 1981–85, Scientific Mem., 1985–90, Max Planck Ges. (Jtly) Nobel Prize for Physiology or Medicine, 1995. *Publications:* articles in learned jls. *Address:* Max-Planck-Institut für Entwicklungsbiologie, Spemannstraße 35/III, 72076 Tübingen, Germany.

NUTBEAM, Prof. Donald, PhD; Head of Public Health, Department of Health, since 2000; *b* 18 May 1955; *s* of late Walter Charles Nutbeam and of Ada Rose Nutbeam; *m* 1978, Sarah Choules; one *s* one *d*. *Educ:* St Bartholomew's Grammar Sch., Newbury; Univ. of Southampton (MA; PhD 1988). Health Educn Officer, Portsmouth Health Dist, 1978–81; Res. Assistant, Wessex RHA, 1981–83; Res. Fellow in Health Promotion, Southampton Univ., 1983–85; Hd of Res., Welsh Heart Prog., Univ. of Wales Coll. of Medicine, 1985–88; Dir, Res. and Policy, Health Promotion Authy, Wales, 1988–90; University of Sydney, Australia: Prof. of Public Health, 1990–2001; Hd, Dept. of Public Health and Community Medicine, 1997–2000; Associate Dean of Medicine, 1999–2000. Vis. Prof., LSHTM, 2001–. *Publications:* numerous contribs to scientific jls and texts. *Recreations:* sport, singing. *Address:* 4 Reidon Hill, Bisley, Surrey GU21 2SH.

NUTMAN, Dr Phillip Sadler, FRS 1968; Head of Department of Soil Microbiology, Rothamsted Experimental Station, Harpenden, 1957–79; *b* 10 Oct. 1914; *s* of John William Nutman and Elizabeth Hester Nutman (*née* Hughes); *m* 1940, Mary Meta Stanbury; two *s* one *d*. *Educ:* Teignmouth Grammar Sch.; Imperial Coll., London Univ. Research Asst, Rothamsted Experimental Station, 1940; Senior Research Fellow, Canberra, Australia, 1953–56; Rothamsted, 1956–79; Hannaford Res. Fellow, Waite Inst., Adelaide, 1980. Huxley Medal, 1959. *Publications:* research papers in plant physiological, genetical and microbiological journals. *Recreations:* music, woodworking. *Address:* Melbury, Hensleigh Drive, St Leonards, Exeter EX2 4NZ. *T:* (01392) 276877.

NUTT, Prof. David John, DM; FRCPsych; Director, Psychopharmacology Unit, since 1988, Professor of Psychopharmacology, since 1994, and Head of Clinical Medicine, since 1997, University of Bristol; *b* 16 April 1951; *s* of R. J. (Jack) Nutt and Eileen M. (*née* Baber); *m* 1979, Diana Margaret Sliney; two *s* two *d*. *Educ:* Bristol GS; Downing Coll., Cambridge (MB BChir); Guy's Hosp.; Lincoln Coll., Oxford (DM 1983). MRCP 1977; FRCPsych 1983. Oxford University: Clinical Scientist, MRC Clinical Pharmacology Unit, 1978–82; Lectr, Dept of Psychiatry, 1982–84; Wellcome Sen. Fellow in Clinical Sci., 1985–86; Head, Section of Clinical Sci., Nat. Inst. of Alcohol Abuse and Alcoholism, NIH, 1986–88; Head, Div. of Psychiatry, Bristol Univ., 1995–97. Chm., Tech. Cttee, Adv. Council on the Misuse of Drugs, 2000–; Member: Ind. Inquiry into Misuse of Drugs Act 1971, 1997–2000 (reported, 2000); Cttee on the Safety of Medicines, 2001–. *Publications:* Inverse Agonists, 1994; (with W. B. Mendelson) Hypnotics and Anxiolytics, 1995; (jtly) Depression, Anxiety and the Mixed Conditions, 1997; (jtly) Panic Disorder: clinical diagnosis, management and mechanisms, 1998; (jtly) Atlas of Psychiatric Pharmacotherapy, 1999. *Recreations:* golf, Austin Healeys. *Address:* School of Medical Sciences, University Walk, University of Bristol, Bristol BS8 1TD. *T:* (0117) 925 3066.

NUTTALL, Prof. Anthony David, FBA 1997; Professor of English, Oxford University, since 1992 (Reader, 1990–92); Fellow of New College, Oxford, since 1984; *b* 25 April 1937; *s* of Kenneth and Hilda Mary Nuttall; *m* 1960, Mary Donagh; one *s* one *d*. *Educ:* Hereford Cathedral Sch.; Merton Coll., Oxford. Sussex University: Asst Lectr, 1962–70; Reader in English, 1970–73; Prof. of English, 1973–84; Pro-Vice-Chancellor, 1978–81. *Publications:* Shakespeare: The Winter's Tale, 1966; Two Concepts of Allegory, 1967; A Common Sky: philosophy and the literary imagination, 1974; Dostoevsky's Crime and Punishment: murder as philosophical experiment, 1978; Overheard by God, 1980; A New Mimesis, 1983; Pope's Essay on Man, 1984; Timon of Athens, 1989; The Stoic in Love, 1989; Openings, 1992; Why Does Tragedy Give Pleasure?, 1996; The Alternative Trinity: Gnostic heresy in Marlowe, Milton and Blake, 1998. *Recreations:* walking, looking at architecture. *Address:* New College, Oxford OX1 3BN.

NUTTALL, Christopher Peter; consultant to Government of Barbados on criminal justice research, information and policy, since 2000; Director of Research and Statistics, Home Office, 1989–99; *b* 20 April 1939; *s* of Barbara Goodwin and David Nuttall; *m* 1966, Caryn Thomas; two *s*. *Educ:* Queen Elizabeth Grammar Sch., Wakefield; Univ. of Keele (BA); Univ. of California at Berkeley (MA). Home Office Res. Unit, 1963–75 (Principal Res. Officer, 1971–75); Dir of Res., 1975–80, Dir Gen., Res. and Stats, 1980–82, Min. of Solicitor Gen., Ottawa; Asst Dep. Solicitor Gen. of Canada, 1982–89; Asst Under-Sec. of State, Home Office, 1989. UN Human Rights Fellow, 1967–68. *Publications:* Parole in England and Wales, 1977; articles on parole, deterrence, crime prevention and imprisonment. *Recreations:* The United States, motorcycling, taking baths, books. *Address:* 17 Rowans, St George, Barbados.

NUTTALL, Rev. Derek, MBE 1990; Minister, United Reformed Church, Windsor, since 1990; *b* 23 Sept. 1937; *s* of Charles William Nuttall and Doris Nuttall; *m* 1965, Margaret Hathaway Brown (*d* 1993); two *s* one *d*; *m* 2000, Doreen Margaret Fox. *Educ:* Ironville Sch.; Somercotes Sch.; Overdale Coll., Selly Oak (Diploma). Semi-skilled worker in industry, 1953–60; office clerk, 1960–61; college, 1961–65; ministry in Falkirk, 1965–67; ordained, 1967; ministry and community work in Aberfan, 1967–74; Gen. Sec., Community Assoc.; mem., church and community cttees; Nat. Organiser, 1974–78, Dir, 1978–90, Cruse—the Nat. Orgn for the widowed and their children, subseq. Cruse—Bereavement Care. Member: Exec., Internat. Fedn of Widow/Widower Orgns, 1980–90; Internat. Workgroup on Death and Dying, 1980–90; Internat. Liaison Gp on Disasters, 1986–90; Sec., Wkg Party on Social and Psychological Aspects of Disasters, 1989–91. Chm., Churches Together in Windsor, 1992–95; Convenor, Reading and Oxford Dist URC Pastoral Cttee, 1995–98. Chaplain: King Edward VII Hosp., Windsor, 1991–; Thames Valley Hospice, Windsor, 1993–. *Publications:* The Early Days of Grieving, 1986; (contrib.) Interpreting Death, 1997; articles and papers on bereavement and on needs of widows, widowers and bereaved children. *Recreations:* music, reading, golf, keeping up with the family's activities, writing a weekly story for my grandchildren! *Address:* The Manse, 10 Clifton Rise, Windsor, Berks SL4 5TD. *T:* (01753) 854558.

NUTTALL, Dr Geoffrey Fillingham, FBA 1991; Ecclesiastical historian, retired; Visiting Professor, King's College, London, 1977–80; *b* Colwyn Bay, Wales, 8 Nov. 1911; *s* of Harold Nuttall and Muriel Fillingham (*née* Hodgson); *m* 1944, Mary (*née* Preston) (*d* 1982), *widow* of George Philip Powley. *Educ:* Bootham Sch., York; Balliol Coll., Oxford (MA 1936); Mansfield Coll., Oxford (BD 1938, DD 1945). Ordained Congregational Minister, 1938; Warminster, Wilts, 1938–43; Fellow, Woodbrooke, Selly Oak Colls, Birmingham, 1943–45; Lectr in Church Hist., New Coll. (Sch. of Divinity), London Univ., 1945–77; Chm., Bd of Studies in Theol., Univ. of London, 1957–59; Dean, Faculty of Theol., 1960–64; FKC 1977. University Preacher: Leeds, 1950; Cambridge, 1958; London, 1968; Oxford, 1972, 1980. Lectures: Friends of Dr Williams's Library, 1951; Drew, New Coll., London, 1956; Hibbert, 1962; W. M. Llewelyn, Memorial Coll., Swansea, 1966; Charles Gore, Westminster Abbey, 1968; Owen Evans, Aberystwyth, 1968; F. D. Maurice, King's Coll., London, 1970; R. T. Jenkins, Bangor, 1976; Ethel M. Wood, London, 1978; Dr Williams Meml, Swansea, 1978. External Examiner: Belfast, Birmingham, Cambridge, Canterbury, Durham, Edinburgh, Leeds, McMaster, Manchester, Nottingham, Oxford, Salford, St Andrews, Wales. President: Friends' Hist. Soc., 1953; Congregational Hist. Soc., 1965–72; London Soc. for Study of Religion, 1966; Eccles. History Soc., 1972; United Reformed Church History Soc., 1972–77. Trustee, Dr Daniel Williams's Charity, 1948–98. A Vice-Pres., Hon. Soc. of Cymmrodorion, 1978–. Mem., Adv. Editorial Bd, Jl of Eccles. History, 1950–86. For. Hon. Mem., Kerkhistorisch Gezelschap, 1981–. Hon. DD Wales, 1969. *Publications:* (ed) Letters of John Pinney 1679–1699, 1939; The Holy Spirit in Puritan Faith and Experience, 1946 (2nd edn 1947; 3rd edn (with new foreword), 1992); The Holy Spirit and Ourselves, 1947 (2nd edn 1966); Studies in Christian Enthusiasm illustrated from Early Quakerism, 1948; (ed) Philip Doddridge 1702–1751: his contribution to English religion, 1951; Richard Baxter and Philip Doddridge: a study in a tradition, 1951; The Reality of Heaven, 1951; James Nayler: a fresh approach, 1954; (contrib.) Studies in Christian Social Commitment, 1954; Visible Saints: the Congregational Way 1640–1660, 1957; The Welsh Saints 1640–1660: Walter Cradock, Vavasor Powell, Morgan Llwyd, 1957; Christian Pacifism in History, 1958 (2nd edn 1971); (ed with Owen Chadwick) From Uniformity to Unity 1662–1962, 1962; Better Than Life: the lovingkindness of God, 1962; (contrib.) Man's Faith and Freedom: the theological influence of Jacobus Arminius, 1962; (contrib.) The Beginnings of Nonconformity, 1964; (contrib.) Choose your Weapons, 1964; Richard Baxter (Leaders of Religion), 1965; Howel Harris 1714–1773: the last enthusiast, 1965; The Puritan Spirit: essays and addresses, 1967; Congregationalists and Creeds, 1967; (contrib.) A Declaration of Faith (Congregational Church in England and Wales), 1967; The Significance of Trevecca College 1768–91, 1969; The Faith of Dante Alighieri, 1969; Christianity and Violence, 1972; (contrib.) Violence and Oppression: a Quaker Response, 1973; New College, London and its Library, 1977; The Moment of Recognition: Luke as story-teller, 1978; contrib. Studies in Church History: Vol. VII, 1971; Vol. X, 1973; (contrib.) Pietismus und Réveil, 1978; (ed) Calendar of the Correspondence of Philip Doddridge, DD 1702–1751, 1979; (contrib.) Philip Doddridge, Nonconformity and Northampton, 1981; Handlist of the Correspondence of Mercy Doddridge 1751–1790, 1984; (with J. van den Berg) Philip Doddridge (1702–1751) and the Netherlands, 1987; (ed with N. H. Keeble) Calendar of the Correspondence of Richard Baxter, 1991; contrib. to Festschriften for: Gordon Rupp, 1975; Martin Schmidt, 1975; C. W. Dugmore, 1979; A. G. Dickens, 1980; R. Buick Knox, 1985; R. Tudur Jones, 1986; J. van den Berg, 1987; H. Barbour, 1992; B. R. White, 1999; contrib. Dict. of Nat. Biog., Encyc. Brit., Dict. d'Histoire et de Géog. Ecclés., Evang. Kirchenlexikon; articles and revs in Jl Eccles. History and Jl Theol Studies; *Festschrift:* Reformation, Conformity and Dissent: essays in honour of Geoffrey Nuttall, 1977. *Recreations:* walking, genealogy, languages. *Address:* Burcot Grange, Bromsgrove, Worcs B60 1BJ. *T:* (0121) 445 2700.

NUTTALL, Rt Rev. Michael; Bishop of Natal, 1982–2000; *b* 3 April 1934; *s* of Neville and Lucy Nuttall; *m* 1959, Dorris Marion Meyer; two *s* one *d*. *Educ:* Maritzburg Coll. (matric. 1951); Univ. of Natal (BA 1955); Rhodes Univ. (BA Hons in History 1956); MA (Cantab); MA, DipEd (Oxon); BD Hons (London). Teacher at Westville High Sch., Natal, 1958; Lectr in History, Rhodes Univ., 1959–62; Theological Student, St Paul's Coll., Grahamstown, 1963–64; ordained deacon, 1964, priest, 1965; Assistant Priest, Cathedral of St Michael and St George, Grahamstown, 1965–68; Lectr in Ecclesiastical History, Rhodes Univ., 1969–74; Dean of Grahamstown, 1975; Bishop of Pretoria, 1976–81. Hon. DTheol Western Cape, 1998; Hon. DLitt Natal, 2000. *Publications:* chapters in: Better Than They Knew, Volume 2 (ed R. M. de Villiers), 1974; Authority in the Anglican Communion (ed Stephen W. Sykes), 1987; Change and Challenge (ed J. Suggit and M. Goedhals), 1998; articles in Dictionary of S African Biography. *Recreations:* walking, bird watching. *Address:* 5 River Glen, 124 Chase Valley Road, Pietermaritzburg, 3201, South Africa.

NUTTALL, Sir Nicholas Keith Lillington, 3rd Bt *cr* 1922; *b* 21 Sept. 1933; *s* of Lieut-Colonel Sir E. Keith Nuttall, 2nd Bt, RE (who died on active service, Aug. 1941), and Gytha Primrose Harrison (*d* 1967), *e d* of Sidney H. Burgess, of Heathfield, Bowdon, Cheshire; *S* father, 1941; *m* 1st, 1960, Rosemary Caroline (marr. diss. 1971), *e d* of Christopher York, *qv*; one *s* one *d*; 2nd, 1971, Julia Jill Beresford (marr. diss. 1975), *d* of Thomas Williamson; 3rd, 1975, Miranda (marr. diss. 1983), *d* of Richard St John Quarry and Diana Elizabeth (who *m* subseq. 2nd Baron Mancroft, KBE, TD); three *d*; 4th, 1983, Eugenie Marie Alicia, *e d* of William Thomas McWeeney; one *s*. *Educ:* Eton; Royal Military Academy, Sandhurst. Commissioned Royal Horse Guards, 1953; Captain, 1959; Major 1966; retd 1968. *Heir:* *s* Harry Nuttall [*b* 2 Jan. 1963; *m* 1996, Kelly Marie, *o d* of Anthony E. Allen, Raleigh, N Carolina]. *Address:* PO Box N7776, Nassau, Bahamas. *T:* (809) 3267938. *Club:* White's.

NUTTALL, Peter Francis; a District Judge (Magistrates' Courts) (formerly Stipendiary Magistrate), Nottinghamshire, since 1991; *b* 20 Feb. 1944; *s* of Francis Nuttall and Dorothy May Nuttall (*née* Horning); *m* 1965, Wendy Anna Ida Griffiths; one *s* two *d*. *Educ:* Lewes County Grammar Sch. for Boys; Coll. of Law, Guildford and London. Articled Clerk, Uckfield, 1961, Harrow, 1964; Asst to Justices' Clerk, 1964–68; Dep. Clerk to Justices, Watford, 1968–73; Clerk to Justices, Pendle and Ribble Valley, 1973–85; Clerk to Bradford Justices, 1985–90. Chm., Yorks Region Mental Health Review Tribunal, 1986–90. *Recreations:* dinghy sailing, fruit growing, photography, painting, Morgan owner, committed francophile. *Address:* Court House, Carrington Street, Nottingham NG2 1EE. *T:* (0115) 955 8235.

NUTTALL, Simon James; Visiting Professor, since 1995, and Member of the Academic Council, since 1997, College of Europe, Bruges; *b* 6 Oct. 1940; *s* of John C. Nuttall and Amy L. Nuttall. *Educ:* Glossop Grammar Sch.; St John's Coll., Oxford (MA). HM Diplomatic Service, 1963–71; Office of Clerk of the Assembly, Council of Europe, 1971–73; Eur. Commn, 1973–95. Vis. Fellow, 1995–97, Acad. Visitor, 2000–, LSE. *Publications:* European Political Co-operation, 1992; European Foreign Policy, 2000; articles on European foreign policy. *Recreation:* strolling in the mountains. *Address:* 14 Lesley Court, Strutton Ground, SW1P 2HZ; Duck House, South Street, Sherborne, Dorset DT9 3LT. *Club:* Oxford and Cambridge.

NUTTER, Most Rev. Harold Lee, CM 1997; DD; Archbishop of Fredericton and Metropolitan of the Ecclesiastical Province of Canada, 1980–89, retired (Bishop of Fredericton, 1971, Bishop Emeritus, 1992); Vice-Chairman, New Brunswick Police Commission, 1988–98; *b* 29 Dec. 1923; *s* of William L. Nutter and Lillian A. Joyce; *m* 1946, Edith M. Carew; one *s* one *d*. *Educ:* Mount Allison Univ. (BA 1944); Dalhousie Univ. (MA 1947); Univ. of King's College (MSLitt 1947). Rector: Simonds and Upham, 1947–51; Woodstock, 1951–57; St Mark, Saint John, NB, 1957–60; Dean of Fredericton, 1960–71. Co-Chairman, NB Task Force on Social Development, 1970–71; Mem., Adv. Cttee to Sec. of State for Canada on Multi-culturalism, 1973. Member: Bd of Governors, St Thomas Univ., 1979–89; Bd of Regents, Mount Allison Univ., 1978–84; Vice-Chm., Bd of Governors, Univ. of King's Coll., 1971–89. Pres., Atlantic Ecumenical Council, 1972–74, 1984–86. Co-Chm., Dialogue New Brunswick, 1989–90. Hon. DD: Univ. of King's College, 1960; Montreal Diocesan Coll., 1982; Wycliffe Coll., 1983; Trinity Coll., Toronto, 1985; Hon. LLD, Mount Allison Univ., 1972. *Publication:* (jointly) New Brunswick Task Force Report on Social Development, 1971. *Address:* 21 Cedar Ridge Drive, Douglas, NB E3A 7X2, Canada.

NUTTGENS, Patrick John, CBE 1983; Director, Leeds Polytechnic, 1969–86; *b* 2 March 1930; 2nd *s* of late Joseph Edward Nuttgens, stained glass artist, and Kathleen Mary Nuttgens (*née* Clarke); *m* 1954, Bridget Ann Badenoch; six *s* three *d*. *Educ:* Ratcliffe Coll., Leicester; Univ. of Edinburgh; Edinburgh Coll. of Art. MA, PhD, DA (Edin), ARIBA. Lectr, Dept of Architecture, Univ. of Edinburgh, 1956–61; Dir, Inst. of Advanced Architectural Studies, Univ. of York, 1962–68; Prof. of Architecture, Univ. of York, 1968–69; Hoffman Wood Prof. of Architecture, Univ. of Leeds, 1968–70. Member: Royal Commn on Ancient and Historical Monuments of Scotland, 1967–76; Ancient Monuments Bd, 1975–78; Royal Fine Art Commn, 1983–90; Yorks Sculpture Park, 1964–65; Chairman: BBC North Region Adv. Council, 1970–75; BBC Continuing Educn Adv. Council, 1977–82; CNAA Cttee for Art and Design, 1981–84; Cttee, Employment of People with Disabilities (Leeds/York), 1992–94; Educn Cttee, Nat. Mus. of Film and Photography, 1963–73; Trustee, Leonard Cheshire Foundn, 1993–2000 (Chm. Bldg Rev. Team, 1993–98). Chm. Bd, York Theatre Royal, 1990–96. President: York Georgian Soc.; York Univ. of Third Age. Trustee, Selby Abbey, 1997–. Hon. Prof., York Univ., 1986–. Hon. Fellow, Leeds Polytechnic. DUniv: York, 1986; Open, 1986; Leeds Metropolitan, 1998; Hon. DLitt: Sheffield, 1987; Heriot-Watt, 1990. Television includes: In Search of the City (series on Leeds), 1973; York: a journey, 1975; A Full Life and an Honest Place (on arts and crafts movement), 1975; Edwin Lutyens: last architect of the age of humanism, 1981; Five Meditations for Holy Week, 1985; The Flight from Utopia (series), 1985; The Home Front (series), 1989; radio: (contributor) A Word in Edgeways, Round Britain Quiz. *Publications:* Reginald Fairlie, a Scottish Architect, 1959; York, City Building Series, 1971; The Landscape of Ideas, 1972; (contrib.) Spirit of the Age, 1975; York: the continuing city, 1976, 2nd edn 2000; Leeds, Old and New, 1976; Leeds, 1979; Yorkshire section, Shell Guide to English Villages, 1980; Pocket Guide to Architecture, 1980; (Gen. Editor) World's Great Architecture, 1980; (contrib.) Study Service, 1982; The Story of Architecture, 1983, 2nd edn 1997; What should we teach and How should we teach it?, 1988; Understanding Modern Architecture, 1988; The Home Front, 1989; The Art of Learning, 2000; regular contributor to jls on architecture, planning, education and environmental studies. *Recreations:* drawing, painting, broadcasting. *Address:* Roselea Cottage, Terrington, York YO60 6PP.

NUTTING, Sir John (Grenfell), 4th Bt *cr* 1903, of St Helens, Booterstown, co. Dublin; QC 1995; a Recorder of the Crown Court, since 1986; a Judge, Courts of Appeal of Jersey and Guernsey, since 1995; a Deputy High Court Judge, since 1998; *b* 28 August 1942; *s* of Rt Hon. Sir Anthony Nutting, 3rd Bt, PC and of Gillian Leonora (*née* Strutt); *S* father, 1999; *m* 1974, Diane, Countess Beatty, *widow* of 2nd Earl Beatty, DSC; one *s* one *d*, and one step *s* one step *d*. *Educ:* Eton Coll.; McGill Univ. (BA 1964). Called to the Bar, Middle Temple, 1968, Hon. Bencher 1991; Jun. Treasury Counsel, 1981; First Jun. Treasury Counsel, 1987–88; Sen. Treasury Counsel, 1988–93; First Sen. Treasury Counsel, 1993–95. Mem., Bar Council, 1976–80, 1986–87; Chm., Young Bar, 1978–79; Vice Chm., Criminal Bar Assoc., 1995. Member: Lord Chancellor's Adv. Cttee on Legal Educn and Conduct, 1997–99; Appts Panel, Ind. Supervisory Authy for Hunting, 2001–. Chm., Helmsdale River Bd, and Helmsdale Dist Salmon Fishery Bd, 2001–. Pres., NE Milton Keynes Conservative Assoc., 1990–93. A Patron, Philharmonia Orch., 2001–. FRPSL 1970. *Recreations:* shooting, stalking, fishing, stamp collecting. *Heir:* *s* James Edward Sebastian Nutting, *b* 12 Jan. 1977. *Address:* Chicheley Hall, Newport Pagnell, Bucks MK16 9JJ; K3 Albany, Piccadilly, W1V 9RQ; Achentoul, Kinbrace, Sutherland KW11 6UB; (chambers) 3 Raymond Buildings, Grays Inn, WC1R 3BH. *Clubs:* White's, Pratt's, Mark's.

NYAKYI, Anthony Balthazar; Tanzanian Ambassador to Burundi, since 1998; *b* 8 June 1936; *m* 1969, Margaret Nyakyi; two *s* two *d*. *Educ:* Makerere Coll., Univ. of E Africa (BA Gen.). Admin. Office, Prime Minister's Office and Min. of Educn, Tanzania, 1962–63; Head of Political Div., Foreign Service Office, 1963–68; Ambassador for Tanzania: to the Netherlands, 1968–70; to Fed. Republic of Germany, 1970–72; Principal Sec., Foreign Affairs, 1972–78; Principal Sec., Defence, 1978–80; High Comr to Zimbabwe, 1980–81, in London, 1981–89; Permanent Tanzanian Rep. to UN, 1989–94; Special Rep. of UN Sec. Gen. in Liberia, 1994–98. *Address:* Tanzanian Embassy, BP 1653, Bujumbura, Burundi.

NYE, Prof. John Frederick, FRS 1976; Melville Wills Professor of Physics, University of Bristol, 1985–88 (Professor of Physics, 1969–88), now Professor Emeritus; *b* 26 Feb. 1923; *s* of Haydn Percival Nye and Jessie Mary, *d* of Anderson Hague, painter; *m* 1953, Georgiana Wiebenson; one *s* two *d*. *Educ:* Stowe; King's Coll., Cambridge (Maj. Schol.; MA, PhD 1948). Research, Cavendish Laboratory, Cambridge, 1944–49; Univ. Demonstrator in Mineralogy and Petrology, Cambridge, 1949–51; Bell Telephone Laboratories, NJ, USA, 1952–53; Lectr, 1953, Reader, 1965, Univ. of Bristol; Visiting Professor: in Glaciology, California Inst. of Technol., 1959; of Applied Sciences, Yale Univ., 1964; of Geophysics, Univ. of Washington, 1973. President: Internat. Glaciological Soc., 1966–69; Internat. Commn of Snow and Ice, 1971–75. For. Mem., Royal Swedish Acad. of Scis, 1977. Kirk Bryan Award, Geol. Soc. of Amer., 1961; Seligman Crystal, Internat. Glaciol Soc., 1969; Antarctic Service Medal, USA, 1974; NPL Metrology Award, 1986; Charles Chree Medal, Inst. of Physics, 1989. *Publications:* Physical Properties of Crystals, 1957, rev. edn 1985; Natural Focusing and Fine Structure of Light, 1999; papers on physics of crystals, glaciology, optics, microwaves, and applications of catastrophe theory in scientific jls. *Address:* 45 Canynge Road, Bristol BS8 3LH. *T:* (0117) 973 3769.

See also P. H. Nye.

NYE, Ven. Nathaniel Kemp; retired; *b* 4 Nov. 1914; *s* of Charles Frederick and Evelyn Nye; *m* 1941, Rosa Jackson; two *s* one *d*. *Educ:* Merchant Taylors' Sch.; King's College London (AKC 1935); Cuddesdon College, Oxford. Ordained 1937 to St Peter's, St Helier Estate, Morden, Surrey; Chaplain RAF, 1940–46 (POW 1941–43; escaped from Italy at liberation); Rector, Holy Trinity, Clapham, 1946–54; Vicar, St Peter's, St Helier Estate,

1954–60; Vicar, All Saints, Maidstone (Parish Church), Canon, and Rural Dean, 1960–66; Tait Missioner, Canterbury Diocese, 1966–72; Archdeacon of Maidstone, 1972–79; Archdeacon Emeritus, dio. Canterbury, 1982. Hon. Canon of Canterbury, 1960; Canon Emeritus, 1979. *Recreations:* woodcraft, sailing, travel, family life! *Address:* Appledore, Ashley, Box, Wilts SN13 8AQ. *T:* (01225) 743933.

NYE, Peter Hague, FRS 1987; Reader in Soil Science, University of Oxford, 1961–88; Fellow of St Cross College, Oxford, 1966–88 (Senior Fellow, 1982–83), now Emeritus Fellow; *b* 16 Sept. 1921; *s* of Haydn Percival Nye and Jessie Mary (*née* Hague); *m* 1953, Phyllis Mary Quenault; one *s* two *d*. *Educ:* Charterhouse; Balliol Coll., Oxford (MA, BSc (Domus Exhibnr)); Christ's Coll., Cambridge. Agricl Chemist, Gold Coast, 1947–50; Lectr in Soil Science, University Coll. of Ibadan, Nigeria, 1950–52; Sen. Lectr in Soil Science, Univ. of Ghana, 1952–60; Res. Officer, Internat. Atomic Energy Agency, Vienna, 1960–61. Vis. Professor, Cornell Univ., 1974, 1981, Messenger Lectures, 1989; Commonwealth Vis. Prof., Univ. of Western Aust., 1979; Vis. Prof., Royal Vet. and Agricl Univ., Copenhagen, 1990; Hon. Res. Prof., Scottish Crops Res. Inst., 1995–2000. Pres., British Soc. Soil Science, 1968–69; Mem. Council, Internat. Soc. Soil Science, 1968–74. Governor, Nat. Vegetable Res. Station, 1972–87. *Publications:* (with D. J. Greenland) The Soil under Shifting Cultivation, 1961; (with P. B. Tinker) Solute Movement in the Soil-Root System, 1977, 2nd edn as Solute Movement in the Rhizosphere, 2000; articles, mainly in Jl of Soil Science, Plant and Soil, Jl of Agricl Science. *Recreations:* computing; formerly cycling, cricket, tennis, squash. *Address:* Hewel Barn, Common Road, Beckley, Oxon OX3 9UR. *T:* (01865) 351607.

See also J. F. Nye.

NYE, Robert; writer; *b* 15 March 1939; *s* of Oswald William Nye and Frances Dorothy Weller; *m* 1st, 1959, Judith Pratt (marr. diss. 1967); three *s*; 2nd, 1968, Aileen Campbell; one *d*. *Educ:* Southend High School, Essex. Freelance writer, 1961–. FRSL 1977. *Publications: poetry:* Juvenilia 1, 1961; Juvenilia 2, 1963 (Eric Gregory Award, 1963); Darker Ends, 1969; Agnus Dei, 1973; Two Prayers, 1974; Five Dreams, 1974; Divisions on a Ground, 1976; A Collection of Poems 1955–1988, 1989; 14 Poems, 1994; Henry James and Other Poems, 1995; Collected Poems, 1995; *fiction:* Doubtfire, 1967; Tales I Told My Mother, 1969; Falstaff, 1976 (The Guardian Fiction Prize, 1976; Hawthornden Prize, 1977); Merlin, 1978; Faust, 1980; The Voyage of the Destiny, 1982; The Facts of Life and Other Fictions, 1983; The Memoirs of Lord Byron, 1989; The Life and Death of My Lord Gilles de Rais, 1990; Mrs Shakespeare: the complete works, 1993; The Late Mr Shakespeare, 1998; *plays:* (with Bill Watson) Sawney Bean, 1970; The Seven Deadly Sins: A Mask, 1974; Penthesilea, Fugue and Sisters, 1976; *children's fiction:* Taliesin, 1966; March Has Horse's Ears, 1966; Wishing Gold, 1970; Poor Pumpkin, 1971; Out of the World and Back Again, 1977; Once Upon Three Times, 1978; The Bird of the Golden Land, 1980; Harry Pay the Pirate, 1981; Three Tales, 1983; Lord Fox and Other Spine-Chilling Tales, 1997; *translation:* Beowulf, 1968; *editions:* A Choice of Sir Walter Ralegh's Verse, 1972; William Barnes: Selected Poems, 1973; A Choice of Swinburne's Verse, 1973; The English Sermon 1750–1850, 1976; The Faber Book of Sonnets, 1976; PEN New Poetry 1, 1986; (jtly) First Awakenings: the early poems of Laura Riding, 1992; A Selection of the Poems of Laura Riding, 1994; contribs to British and American periodicals. *Recreation:* gambling. *Address:* Thornfield, Kingsland, Ballinhassig, Co. Cork, Ireland.

NYE, Roderick Christopher; Director, Conservative Research Department, since 1999; *b* 28 Feb. 1967; *s* of late Bertram Edward Nye and of Elsie Doreen Nye; *m* 1994, Diana Grace, *d* of John and Priscilla Douglas. *Educ:* Norton Knatchbull Sch., Ashford; American Univ., Washington; Univ. of Leeds (BA Hons 1989). Policy Advr to David Owen, 1989–90; Journalist, VNU Business Publications, 1990–92; Dep. Dir, 1992–95, Dir, 1995–99, Social Market Foundn. Mem. (C), Westminster CC, 1998–. *Publications:* Welfare to Work: the 'America Works' experience, 1996; (ed) The Future of Welfare, 1997. *Recreations:* United States, reading, sport (watching), Chelsea FC. *Address:* Conservative Central Office, 32 Smith Square, SW1P 3HH. *T:* (020) 7222 9000. *Club:* Sam's.

NYMAN, Michael; composer; *b* 23 March 1944; *s* of Mark and Jeanette Nyman; *m* 1970; two *d*. *Educ:* Royal Academy of Music; King's College London (BMus); Conservatorul Ciprian Porumbescu, Bucharest. FRAM 1991. Music critic, Spectator, New Statesman, The Listener, 1968–78; formed Michael Nyman Band, 1977. *Film scores include:* The Draughtsman's Contract, 1982; Drowning by Numbers, 1988; The Cook, The Thief, His Wife and Her Lover, 1989; Monsieur Hire, 1989; The Hairdresser's Husband, 1990; Prospero's Books, 1991; The Piano, 1992; Carrington, 1994; The Diary of Anne Frank, 1995; The Ogre, 1996; Gattaca, 1997; Ravenous, 1998; Wonderland, 1999; The End of the Affair, 1999; Act Without Words, 2000; The Claim, 2001; *other compositions:* A Broken Set of Rules, Royal Ballet, 1983; The Man Who Mistook his Wife for a Hat (opera), 1986; String Quartets, 1985, 1988, 1990, 1995; Six Celan Songs, 1990–91; Noises, Sounds and Sweet Airs (opera), 1991; Where the Bee Dances, for saxophone and orch., 1991; Songs for Tony, 1993; The Piano Concerto, 1993; MGV (Musique à Grand Vitesse), 1993; Harpsichord Concerto, 1995; Trombone Concerto, 1995; After Extra Time, 1996; Double Concerto for Saxophone and Cello, 1997; Cycle of Disquietude, 1998; The Commissar Vanishes, 1999; Facing Goya (opera), 2000; Concerto for Saxophone Quartet and Orch., 2001; ballet scores. *Publication:* Experimental Music: Cage and Beyond, 1974, 2nd edn 1999. *Recreation:* QPR. *Address:* Michael Nyman Ltd, 83 Pulborough Road, SW18 5UL. *Club:* Groucho.

O

OAKELEY, Sir John (Digby Atholl), 8th Bt *cr* 1790, of Shrewsbury; Director, Dehler Yachts UK, since 1988; *b* 27 Nov. 1932; *s* of Sir Atholl Oakeley, 7th Bt and of Mabel, (Patricia), *d* of Lionel H. Birtchnell; *S* father, 1987; *m* 1958, Maureen Frances, *d* of John and Ellen Cox; one *s* one *d*. *Educ:* private tutor. Own charter business, 1958–61; Contracts Manager, Proctor Masts, 1961–72; Managing Director: Freedom Yachts Internat. Ltd, 1981–88; Miller & Whitworth, 1972–81. *Publications:* Winning, 1968; Sailing Manual, 1980; Downwind Sailing, 1981. *Recreation:* yachting (holder of national, international, European and world titles; twice represented Great Britain in Olympic Games). *Heir: s* Robert John Atholl Oakeley [*b* 13 Aug. 1963; *m* 1989, Catherine Amanda, *d* of late William Knowles; one *s* one *d*]. *Address:* 10 Bursledon Heights, Long Lane, Bursledon, Hants SO3 8DB. *Club:* Warsash Sailing (Warsash, Hants).

OAKES, Sir Christopher, 3rd Bt *cr* 1939; *b* 10 July 1949; *s* of Sir Sydney Oakes, 2nd Bt, and Greta (*d* 1977), *yr d* of Gunnar Victor Hartmann, Copenhagen, Denmark; *S* father, 1966; *m* 1978, Julie Dawn, *d* of Donovan Franklin Cowan, Regina, Canada; one *s* one *d*. *Educ:* Bredon, Tewkesbury; Georgia Mil. Acad., USA. *Heir: s* Victor Oakes, *b* 6 March 1983.

OAKES, Rt Hon. Gordon James; PC 1979; *b* 22 June 1931; *o s* of late James Oakes and Florence (*née* Hewitt), Widnes, Lancs; *m* 1952, Esther O'Neill (*d* 1998), *e d* of late Councillor Joseph O'Neill; three *s*. *Educ:* Wade Deacon Gram. Sch., Widnes; Univ. of Liverpool. BA (Hon.) English, 1952; Admitted Solicitor, 1956. Entered Widnes Borough Council, 1952 (Mayor, 1964–65). Chm. Widnes Constituency Labour Party, 1953–58; contested (Lab): Bebington, 1959; Moss Side (Manchester) by-election, 1961; MP (Lab): Bolton West, 1964–70; Widnes, Sept. 1971–1983; Halton, 1983–97. PPS, Home Office, 1966–67, DES, 1967–70; Front Bench Opposition spokesman on local govt and the environment, 1970–74; Parly Under-Secretary of State: DoE, 1974–76; Dept of Energy, 1976; Minister of State, DES, 1976–79; Front Bench Opposition spokesman on Environment, 1979–83. British Deleg., NATO Parliamentarians, 1967–70; Member: Select Cttee on Race Relations, 1969–70; Executive, NW Region of Labour Party, 1971–73; Exec. Cttee, CPA, 1979–97; Chairman: All-Party Energy Efficiency Gp, 1980–97; All-Party Chem. Industry Gp, 1990–97 (Vice-Chm., 1982–90); Jt Chm., All-Party Gp for the Licensing Trade, 1986–97. Vice-President: Rural District Councils Assoc., 1972–74; County Councils Assoc., 1982–97; Environmental Officers' Assoc. (formerly Inst. of Public Health Inspectors), 1973–97; Building Societies Assoc., 1984–89; Jt Chm., Nat. Waste Management Adv. Council, 1974–76. Gov., Commonwealth Inst., 1992–97. Hon. Alderman and Hon. Freeman, Borough of Halton. *Publications:* The Management of Higher Education in the Maintained Sector, 1978; various articles. *Recreations:* conversation, caravanning, maps. *Address:* Upton Bridle Path, Widnes, Cheshire WA8 9HB.

OAKES, Joseph Stewart; barrister-at-law; *b* 7 Jan. 1919; *s* of Laban Oakes and Mary Jane Oakes; *m* 1950, Irene May Peasnall (*d* 1995). *Educ:* Royal Masonic Sch., Bushey; Stretford Grammar Sch.; Manchester Univ., 1937–40 (BA Hons). Royal Signals, 1940–48, Captain. Called to Bar, Inner Temple, 1948; practised on Northern Circuit, 1948–91; a Recorder, 1975–82. Presiding Legal Mem., Mental Health Review Tribunal, 1971–91. *Recreations:* horticulture, photography, music, freemasonry. *Address:* 38 Langley Road, Sale, Greater Manchester M33 5AY. *T:* (0161) 962 2068.

OAKESHOTT, family name of **Baron Oakeshott of Seagrove Bay**.

OAKESHOTT OF SEAGROVE BAY, Baron *cr* 2000 (Life Peer), of Seagrove Bay in the co. of Isle of Wight; **Matthew Alan Oakeshott;** Joint Managing Director: OLIM Ltd, since 1986; Value and Income Trust plc, since 1986; *b* 10 Jan. 1947; *o s* of Keith Robertson Oakeshott, CMG and Jill Oakeshott; *m* 1976, Dr Pippa Poulton; two *s* one *d*. *Educ:* Charterhouse (Sen. Foundn Scholar); University Coll. and Nuffield Coll., Oxford (BA 1st cl. Hons PPE). ODI/Nuffield Fellow, Kenya Ministry of Finance and Planning, 1968–70; Special Advr to Rt Hon. Roy Jenkins, MP, 1972–76; Investment Mgr, then Dir, Warburg Investment Management, 1976–81; Investment Mgr, Courtaulds Pension Fund, 1981–85; founded OLIM Ltd (Independent Investment Managers), 1986. Mem. (Lab) Oxford City Council, 1972–76 (Vice Chm., Finance Cttee; Mem., Housing and Planning Cttee). Member: SDP Nat. Cttee, 1981–82; SDP Nat. Economic Policy Cttee, 1981–83. Contested: (Lab) Horsham and Crawley, Oct. 1974; (SDP/Alliance) Cambridge, 1983. *Publication:* (contrib.) By-Elections in British Politics, 1973. *Recreations:* music, elections, watching Arsenal FC. *Address:* Pollen House, 10–12 Cork Street W1X 1PD. *T:* (020) 7439 4400.

OAKHAM, Archdeacon of; *see* Painter, Ven. D. S.

OAKLEY, Brian Wynne, CBE 1981; *b* 10 Oct. 1927; *s* of Bernard and Edna Oakley; *m* 1953, Marian Elizabeth (*née* Woolley); one *s* three *d*. *Educ:* Exeter Coll., Oxford. MA. FInstP, FBCS. Telecommunication Res. Establishment, 1950; Head, Industrial Applications Unit, RRE, 1966–69; Head, Computer Systems Branch, Min. of Technology, 1969–72; Head, Res. Requirements Div., DTI, 1972–78; Sec., SRC, later SERC, 1978–83; Dep. Sec., DTI, and Dir, Alvey Programme, 1983–87. Dir, Logica (Cambridge) Ltd. Pres., BCS, 1988. DUniv York, 1988. *Publication:* (with Kenneth Owen) Alvey, 1990. *Recreations:* theatre, sailing. *Address:* 120 Reigate Road, Ewell, Epsom, Surrey KT17 3BX. *T:* (020) 8393 4096.

OAKLEY, Christopher John, CBE 1999; Chief Executive, Regional Independent Media, since 1998; *b* 11 Nov. 1941; *s* of late Ronald Oakley and Joyce Oakley; *m* 1st, 1962, Linda Margaret Viney (marr. diss. 1986); one *s* two *d*; 2nd, 1990, Moira Jean Martingale; one *s*, and two adopted *d*. *Educ:* Skinners' School, Tunbridge Wells. Kent and Sussex Courier, 1959; Bromley and Kentish Times, 1963; Kent and Sussex Courier, 1963; Evening Argus, Brighton, 1966; Evening Echo, Basildon, 1969; Evening Post, Leeds, 1970; Dep. Editor, Yorkshire Post, 1976; Editor, Lancashire Evening Post, 1981; Dir, Lancashire Evening Post, 1981–83; Editor, Liverpool Echo, 1983–89; Dir, Liverpool Daily Post and Echo Ltd, 1984–89; Editor-in-Chief, 1989–91, Man. Dir, 1990–93, Chm., 1993–97, Birmingham Post & Mail; Gp Chief Exec., Midland Ind. Newspapers plc, 1991–97. Chairman: Coventry Newspapers, 1991–97; Midland Weekly Media, 1997; Man. Dir, Mirror Regl Newspapers, 1997–98. Pres., Newspaper Soc., 1997–98; Hon. Vice Pres., Soc. of Editors. Nat. Appeals Chm., Newspaper Press Fund, 2000–. Non-executive Chairman: atmyside, 2000–; Venturedome, 2000–; non-exec. Dir, Teamtalk, 2000–. Hon. Fellow, Univ. of Central Lancashire, 1998. *Address:* Regional Independent Media, Wellington Street, Leeds LS1 1RR.

OAKLEY, John Davidson, CBE 1981; DFC 1944; Chairman: Grosvenor Development Capital, 1981–92; Grosvenor Technology Ltd, 1986–91; Gardners Transformers Ltd, 1986–91 (Deputy Chairman, 1984–86; Director, 1982–91); Third Grosvenor Ltd, 1987–91; *b* 15 June 1921; *s* of Richard Oakley and Nancy Davidson; *m* 1943, Georgina Mary Hare; two *s*. *Educ:* Green Lane Sch. Joined Briggs Motor Bodies Ltd, 1937. Served War in RAF, 1941–46: commissioned 1942; Flt Lt 1943; actg Sqdn Leader 1944; apptd to Air Min. Directorate Staff, 1945. Engrg Buyer, Briggs Motor Bodies Ltd, 1946–53; Dep. Purchase Manager, Body Div., Ford Motor Co. Ltd, 1953–56; Production Dir/General Manager, Standard Triumph (Liverpool) Ltd, until 1962; Managing Director: Copeland & Jenkins Ltd, 1963–71; R. Woolf & Co. Ltd, 1964–67; Gp Man. Dir, L. Sterne & Co., 1967–69; Chairman: General Electric & Mechanical Systems Ltd, 1970–73; Berwick Timpo Ltd, 1970–82; Edgar Allen Balfour Ltd, 1974–79; Australian British Trade Assoc., 1977–81 (Vice-Pres., British Council, 1981); BOTB Adv. Gp Australia and NZ, 1977–81; Mem., British Overseas Trade Adv. Council, 1977–83. Director: Blairs Ltd, 1976–82; Eagle & Globe Steel Ltd, NSW, 1978–79; Ionian Securities Ltd, 1978–88; Nexos Office Systems Ltd, 1981–82; Isis Gp PLC (formerly Industrial Services plc), 1982; Beau Brummel Ltd, 1972–85; Robert Jenkins (Hldgs) Ltd, 1976–92 (Dep. Chm., 1978–83, Chm., 1983–90). Oxford Univ. Business Summer School: Dir for 1978; Mem., Steering Cttee, 1981, Chm., 1984–87. Cons. Mem., Essex CC, 1982–85. Member: Glovers' Co.; Cutlers' Co. in Hallamshire; Inst. of British Carriage & Automobile Manufacturers. CIMgt; FIPS. FRSA. *Recreations:* golf, tennis, walking, bridge. *Address:* 25 Manor Links, Bishop's Stortford, Herts CM23 5RA. *T:* (01279) 507552. *Clubs:* Reform, Royal Air Force; Bishop's Stortford Golf (Bishop's Stortford, Herts).

OAKLEY, Robin Francis Leigh, OBE 2001; European Political Editor, CNN, since 2000; *b* 20 Aug. 1941; *s* of Joseph Henry Oakley, civil engineer and Alice Barbara Oakley; *m* 1966, Carolyn Susan Germaine Rumball; one *s* one *d*. *Educ:* Wellington College; Brasenose College, Oxford (MA). Liverpool Daily Post, 1964–70; Sunday Express, 1970–79; Assistant Editor: Now! magazine, 1979–81; Daily Mail, 1981–86; Political Editor: The Times, 1986–92; BBC, 1992–2000. Presenter, The Week in Westminster, BBC Radio. Turf columnist, Spectator, 1995–. Trustee, Thomson Foundn, 2001–. Dir, Epsom Trng and Develt Fund (Charity), 2000–; Mem., Epsom Race Cttee, 2001. *Publications:* Valley of the Racehorse: a year in the life of Lambourn, 2000; Inside Track: the political correspondent's life, 2001. *Recreations:* theatre, horse racing, sports, bird watching. *Address:* 46 Cleaver Square, Kennington, SE11 4EA. *Club:* Royal Automobile.

OAKLEY, Dame Susan (Elizabeth Anne); *see* Devoy, Dame S. E. A.

OAKSEY, 2nd Baron *cr* 1947 (properly **TREVETHIN,** 4th Baron *cr* 1921, **AND OAKSEY); John Geoffrey Tristram Lawrence,** OBE 1985; Racing Correspondent to Daily Telegraph, 1957–94; racing commentator: ITV, since 1970; Channel Four Racing, since 1984; *b* 21 March 1929; *o s* of 1st Baron Oaksey and 3rd Baron Trevethin and Marjorie (*d* 1984), *d* of late Commander Charles N. Robinson, RN; *S* father, 1971; *m* 1st, 1959, Victoria Mary (marr. diss. 1987), *d* of late Major John Dennistoun, MBE; one *s* one *d*; 2nd, 1988, Rachel Frances Crocker, *d* of late Alan Hunter. *Educ:* Horris Hill; Eton; New College, Oxford (BA); Yale Law School. Racing Correspondent: Horse and Hound, 1959–88; Sunday Telegraph, 1960–88; columnist, Racing Post, 1988–90. Director: HTV, 1980–91; Elite Racing Club, 2000–. JP Malmesbury, 1978–99. *Publications:* History of Steeplechasing (jointly), 1967; The Story of Mill Reef, 1974; Oaksey on Racing, 1991. *Recreations:* skiing, riding. *Heir: s* Hon. Patrick John Tristram Lawrence [*b* 29 June 1960; *m* 1987, Lucinda, *e d* of Demetri Marchessini and Mrs Nicholas Peto; one *s* two *d*]. *Address:* Hill Farm, Oaksey, Malmesbury, Wilts SN16 9HS. *T:* (01666) 577303, *Fax:* (01666) 577962. *Club:* Brooks's.

OAKSHOTT, Hon. Sir Anthony (Hendrie), 2nd Bt *cr* 1959; *b* 10 Oct. 1929; *s* of Baron Oakshott, MBE (Life Peer), and Joan (*d* 1986), *d* of Marsden Withington; *S* to baronetcy of father, 1975; *m* 1965, Mrs Valerie de Pret-Roose (marr. diss. 1981; she *d* 1988), *d* of Jack Vlasto. *Educ:* Rugby. *Heir: b* Hon. Michael Arthur John Oakshott [*b* 12 April 1932; *m* 1st, 1957, Christina Rose Methuen (*d* 1985), *d* of late Thomas Banks; three *s*; 2nd, 1988, Mrs (Helen) Clare Jones, *d* of late Edward Ravell]. *Address:* 1 High Street, Fifield, Oxon OX7 6HL. *Club:* White's.

OATEN, Mark; MP (Lib Dem) Winchester, since 1997; *b* 8 March 1964; *s* of Ivor Condell Oaten and Audrey Oaten; *m* 1992, Belinda Fordham; one *d*. *Educ:* Hatfield Poly. (BA Hons 1986); Hertfordshire Coll. of FE, Watford (Dip in Public Relns 1989). Consultant, Shandwick Public Affairs, 1990–92; Consultant, 1992–95, Man. Dir, 1995–97, Westminster Public Relations. Dir, Oasis Radio, 1995–96. Mem. (Lib Dem) Watford BC, 1986–94. Contested (Lib Dem) Watford, 1992. PPS to Leader of Liberal Democrat Party, 1999–2001. Lib Dem spokesman: on disabilities, 1997–99; on foreign affairs and defence, 1999–2001; on Cabinet Office, 2001–. Mem., Select Cttee on Public Admin, 1999–2001.

Chm., All-Pty Prisoners of War Gp, 1998–2000; Sec., All-Pty EU Accession Gp, 2000–; Co-Chm., All-Pty Adoption Gp, 2000–. Treas., Human Rights Gp, 2000–. Chm., Lib Dem Parly Pty, 2001–. *Recreations:* gardening, cinema, swimming, football. *Address:* House of Commons, SW1A 0AA. *T:* (020) 7219 3000, *Fax:* (020) 7219 2389; *e-mail:* oatenm@parliament.uk.

OATES, Prof. (Edward Ernest) David (Michael), FSA; FBA 1974; Professor of Western Asiatic Archaeology, University of London, 1969–82; *b* 25 Feb. 1927; *s* of Thomas Oates and Dora B. Strike; *m* 1956, Joan Louise Lines; one *s* two *d*. *Educ:* Callington County Sch.; Oundle Sch.; Trinity Coll., Cambridge (BA, MA). Fellow of Trinity Coll., Cambridge, 1951–65; British School of Archaeology in Iraq: Dir, 1965–69; Chm., 1988–96; Vice Pres., 1997–2000; Pres., 2000–; Gertrude Bell Meml Medal, 1997. Director, British Archaeological Expedition to Tell Brak, Syria, 1976–. FSA 1954. *Publications:* (contrib.) The Great Palace of the Byzantine Emperors, ed D. Talbot Rice, 1958; (contrib.) The Dark Ages, ed D. Talbot Rice, 1965; Studies in the Ancient History of N Iraq, 1968; (with J. Oates) The Rise of Civilisation, 1976; The Excavations at Tell al Rimah: the pottery, 1998; Excavations at Tell Brak, Vol. 1: the Mitanni and Old Babylonian periods, 1998, Vol. 2: Nagar in the 3rd Millennium, 2001; (with J. Oates) Numrud Ancient Kalḫu: an Assyrian Imperial City, 2001; Papers of the British School at Rome, Iraq, etc. *Recreations:* history, carpentry. *Address:* 86 High Street, Barton, Cambridge CB3 7BG. *T:* (01223) 262273.

See also Sir Thomas Oates.

OATES, Rev. Canon John; Rector of St Bride's Church, Fleet Street, 1984–2000; Prebendary, St Paul's Cathedral, 1997, Prebendary Emeritus, 2001; *b* 14 May 1930; *s* of John and Ethel Oates; *m* 1962, Sylvia Mary, *d* of Herbert Charles and Ada Harris; three *s* one *d*. *Educ:* Queen Elizabeth School, Wakefield; SSM, Kelham. Curate, Eton College Mission, Hackney Wick, 1957–60; Development Officer, C of E Youth Council and mem. staff, Bd of Education, 1960–64; Development Sec., C of E Council for Commonwealth Settlement, 1964–65, Gen. Sec. 1965–70; Sec., C of E Cttee on Migration and Internat. Affairs, Bd for Social Responsibility, 1968–71; Vicar of Richmond, Surrey, 1970–84; RD, Richmond and Barnes, 1979–84; Area Dean, City of London, 1997–2000. Commissary: of Archbishop of Perth and Bishop of NW Australia, 1968–; to Archbishop of Jerusalem, 1969–75; to Bishop of Bunbury, 1969–. Hon. Canon, Bunbury, 1969–. Mem., Unilever Central Ethical Compliance Gp, 1991–97; Consultant, Creative Visions (USA), 2001–. Chapter Clerk, London City Deanery, 1994–97. Chaplain: Inst. of Journalists, 1984–2000 (Life FCIJ 1995); Inst. of Public Relations, 1984–2000; Publicity Club of London, 1984–2000; London Press Club, 1984–2000; Co. of Marketors, 1984–2000; Co. of Stationers and Newspapermakers, 1989–2000; Co. of Turners, 1995–2001. Freeman, City of London, 1985; Hon. Liveryman: Marketors' Co., 1999–; Turners' Co., 2000–. *Recreations:* broadcasting, walking, exploring, squash. *Address:* Flat 7, King's Court, Deer Park Close, Kingston upon Thames KT2 7RJ. *T:* (020) 8974 8821; *e-mail:* john@joates.co.uk. *Club:* Athenæum.

OATES, (John) Keith; Deputy Chairman, 1994–99 and Managing Director, 1991–99, Marks and Spencer plc; a Governor of the BBC, 1988–93; *b* 3 July 1942; *s* of late John Alfred Oates and Katherine Mary (*née* Hole); *m* 1968, Helen Mary (*née* Blake); one *s* three *d*. *Educ:* King's Sch., Chester; Arnold Sch., Blackpool; London School of Economics (BScEcon); Univ. of Manchester Inst. of Sci. and Technology (DipTech Industrial Admin); Bristol Univ. (MSc Management Accounting). FCT 1982. Work Study trainee, Reed Paper Gp, 1965–66; Budgets and Planning Man., IBM (UK) Ltd, 1966–73; Gp Financial Controller, Rolls Royce (1971) Ltd, 1973–74; Controller, Black and Decker Europe, 1974–78; Vice Pres., Finance, Thyssen Bornemisza NV, 1978–84; Finance Dir, Marks and Spencer plc, 1984–91: Founder Chm., Marks and Spencer Financial Services. Non-executive Director: John Laing plc, 1987–89; British Telecom, 1994–2000; Guinness, 1995–97; MCI, 1996–; Diageo, 1997–; Coutts Bank, Monaco, 2001–. Member: Council, CBI, 1988–2000; Bd, London First, 1993–96; Sports Council of GB, 1993–97; English Sports Council, 1997–99; Chm., Quality, Efficiency and Standards Team, 1999–2000. Chm., Europ. Council of Financial Execs, 1984; Member: 100 Gp Chartered Accountants, 1985–93; FSA, 1998–2001. Pres., UMIST Assoc., 1996–97. Mem. Council, Wycombe Abbey Sch., 1995–. Patron: Campaign for Resource, Bristol Univ., 1996–; London Christies Against Cancer, 1999–. DTI Innovation Lecture, 1997. CIMgt 1992. FRSA 1993. Hon. LLD Bristol, 1998; Hon. DSc UMIST, 1998. *Recreations:* music, travel, salmon fishing, ski-ing, spectator sports (esp. Association Football, athletics and cricket). *Address:* 9 Kensington Gate, W8 5NA.

OATES, Laurence Campbell; Official Solicitor to the Supreme Court, since 1999; Public Trustee, since 2001; *b* 14 May 1946; *s* of Stanley Oates and late Norah Christine Oates (*née* Meek); *m* 1968, Brenda Lilian Hardwick; one *s* one *d*. *Educ:* Beckenham and Penge Grammar School; Bristol Univ. (LLB 1967). Called to the Bar, Middle Temple, 1968; Dept. of Employment, 1976–80; Law Officers' Dept, 1980–83; Asst Treasury Solicitor, Dept of Transport, 1983–88; Lord Chancellor's Department: Under Sec. and Hd of Legislation Gp, 1988–92; Circuit Administrator, Midland and Oxford Circuit, 1992–94; Assoc. Head of Policy Gp, 1995–96; Dir, Magistrates' Courts' Gp, 1996–99. *Recreations:* music, golf. *Address:* (office) 81 Chancery Lane, WC2A 1DD.

OATES, Sir Thomas, Kt 1972; CMG 1962; OBE 1958 (MBE 1946); Governor and Commander-in-Chief of St Helena, 1971–76; *b* 5 November 1917; *er s* of late Thomas Oates, Wadebridge, Cornwall; unmarried. *Educ:* Callington Grammar School, Cornwall; Trinity College, Cambridge (MA). Mathematical Tripos (Wrangler). Admiralty Scientific Staff, 1940–46; HMS Vernon, Minesweeping Section, 1940–42; British Admiralty Delegn, Washington, DC, 1942–46; Temp. Lieut, RNVR. Colonial Administrative Service, Nigeria, 1948–55; seconded to HM Treasury, 1953–55; Adviser to UK Delegn to UN Gen. Assembly, 1954. Financial Sec. to Govt of: British Honduras, 1955–59, Aden, 1959–63; Dep. High Comr, Aden, 1963–67; Permanent Sec., Gibraltar, 1968–69; Dep. Governor, Gibraltar, 1969–71. *Recreation:* reading. *Address:* Tristan, Trevone, Padstow, Cornwall PL28 8QX. *Clubs:* East India, Devonshire, Sports and Public Schools, Royal Commonwealth Society.

See also E. E. D. M. Oates.

OATLEY, Brian; Chairman, Invicta Community Care NHS Trust, 1997–2001; *b* 1 June 1935; *s* of Arnold and Vivian Oatley. *Educ:* Bolton School; King's College, Cambridge. BA, PGCE. Teacher, North Manchester Grammar School, 1959–64; Assistant, Senior Assistant and Deputy County Education Officer, Kent County Council, 1964–84, County Educn Officer, 1984–88. Chm., Maidstone Priority Care NHS Trust, 1991–97. Member: RHS; Kent Trust for Nature Conservation; Bearsted Choral Soc., Maidstone. Gov., Kent Inst. of Art and Design, 1989–98. *Recreations:* music, travel, gardening. *Address:* 45 Beresford Road, Aylesford, Maidstone, Kent ME20 7EP.

OATLEY, Michael Charles, CMG 1991; OBE 1975; Deputy Chairman, Ciex Ltd, since 2001 (Managing Director, 1994–98; Chairman, 1998–2001); *b* 18 Oct. 1935; *s* of Sir Charles Oatley, OBE, FRS and Lady Oatley (*née* Enid West); *m* 1st, Pippa Howden; two *s* one *d*; 2nd, Mary Jane Laurens; one *s*. *Educ:* The Leys Sch.; Trinity Coll., Cambridge. Served HM Foreign, later Diplomatic, Service, 1959–91; a Man. Dir, Kroll Associates, 1991–94. *Address:* Manor Farmhouse, Caundle Marsh, Sherborne, Dorset DT9 5LX. *Club:* Oriental.

OBAN (St John's Cathedral), Provost of; *see* MacCallum, Very Rev. N. D.

OBASANJO, Gen. Olusegun; President of Nigeria, since 1999; Nigerian Head of State, Head of the Federal Military Government and Commander-in-Chief of the Armed Forces, Nigeria, 1976–79; Member, Advisory Council of State, since 1979; farmer; *b* Abeokuta, Ogun State, Nigeria, 5 March 1937; *m*; two *s* three *d*. *Educ:* Abeokuta Baptist High Sch.; Mons Officers' Cadet Sch., England. Entered Nigerian Army, 1958; commission, 1959; served in Zaire (then, the Congo), 1960. Comdr, Engrg Corps, 1963; Comdr of 2nd (Rear) Div. at Ibadan; GOC 3rd Inf. Div., 1969; Comdr, 3rd Marine Commando Div.; took surrender of forces of Biafra, in Nigerian Civil War, 1969–70; Comdr Engrg Corps, 1970–75. Political post as Federal Comr for Works and Housing, Jan.–July 1975. Chief of Staff, Supreme HQ, July 1975–Feb. 1976. Mem., Internat. Indep. Commn on Disarmament and Security. Part-time Associate, Univ. of Ibadan. *Publications:* My Command (autobiog.), 1980; Africa in Perspective: myths and realities, 1987; Nzeognu, 1987; Africa Embattled, 1988; Constitution for National Integration and Development, 1989; Not My Will, 1990; Challenge of Leadership in African Development, 1990; Impact of Europe in 1992 on West Africa, 1990; Leadership Challenge of Economic Reforms in Africa, 1991; Challenge of Agricultural Production and Food Security in Africa, 1992. *Recreations:* squash, table tennis, billiards, snooker. *Address:* Office of the President, Abuja, Nigeria.

OBASI, Godwin Olu Patrick, OFR 1983; Secretary-General, World Meteorological Organization, since 1984; *b* 24 Dec. 1933; *s* of Albert B. Patrick Obasi and Rhoda A. Akande; *m* 1967, Winifred O. Akande; one *s* five *d*. *Educ:* McGill Univ., Canada (BSc Hons Maths and Physics); Massachusetts Inst. of Technology (MSc, DSc Meteorology). Mem., Inst. of Statisticians. University of Nairobi: WMO/UNDP Expert and Sen. Lectr, 1967–74; Acting Head of Dept of Meteorology, 1972–73; Dean, Faculty of Science, Prof. of Meteorology and Chm., Dept of Meteorology, 1974–76; Adviser in Meteorology to Nigerian Govt and Head of Nigerian Inst. for Met. Res. and Training, 1976–78; Dir, Educn and Training Dept, WMO, 1978–83. Chm., New Sun Foundn. Cons. Ed., Weatherwise (Amer. Met. Soc.). Fellow: African Acad. of Scis, 1993; Third World Acad. of Scis, 1996 (Vice-Pres., 1999); Internat. Energy Foundn, 1998; FSS; meteorol socs of USA, Africa, Nigeria, Dominican Republic, Ecuador and Colombia. Hon. Fellow, meteorol socs of India, Cuba and Burkina Faso; Hon. Member: Acad. of Agricl and Forestry Scis, Romania, 1995; Kenya Meteorol Soc. Dr of Physics *hc* Bucharest, 1991; Hon. LLD Philippines, 1992; Hon DSc: Federal Univ. of Technology, Akure, Nigeria, 1992; Alpine Geophys. Res. Inst., Nal-Chik, 1993; Nairobi, 1998. Carl Rossby Award, MIT, 1963; Gold plaque merit award medal, Czechoslovakian Acad. of Sciences, 1986; Medal, Inst. of Meteorol. and Water Management, Poland, 1989; Ogori Merit Award, Nigeria, 1991; Climate Inst. Award, Washington, 1990; Direccion Nacional de Aeronautica Civil Honour of Merit Award, Paraguay, 1992; Gold Medal Award, African Meteorological Soc., 1993; Medal of Merit, Slovak Hydrometeorol Inst., 1994; Gold Medal, Balkan Physical Union, 1997; Award for Promotion of Hydromet., Viet Nam, 1998; Gold Medal, Govt of Paraguay, 1988; Air Force Cross, Venezuela, 1989; Freedom of Ho Chi Minh City, Viet Nam, 1990; Commander, National Order: Côte d'Ivoire, 1992; Niger, 1994; Senegal, 1995; Benin, 1997; Burkina Faso, 1997. *Publications:* numerous contribs to learned jls. *Recreations:* tennis, gardening. *Address:* Chemin en Vuaracaux, 1297 Founex, Vaud, Switzerland. *T:* (22) 762825.

O'BEIRNE RANELAGH, John, (John Ranelagh), PhD; Consultant, TV 2 Norway, since 1991; Member, Independent Television Commission, 1994–99; *b* 3 Nov. 1947; *o s* of late James O'Beirne Ranelagh and Elaine Lambert O'Beirne Ranelagh; *m* 1974, Elizabeth Grenville, *y d* of Sir William Hawthorne, *qv*. *Educ:* St Christopher's Sch.; Cambridgeshire Coll. of Arts and Technology; Christ Church, Oxford (MA); Eliot Coll., Univ. of Kent (PhD). Chase Manhattan Bank, 1970; Campaign Dir, Outset Housing Assoc., 1971; Univ. of Kent Studentship, 1972–74; BBC TV, 1974; Conservative Res. Dept, 1975–79; Associate Producer, Ireland: a television history, BBC TV, 1979–81; Commissioning Editor, Channel Four TV Co., 1981–88 (Sec. to the Bd, 1981–83); Dep. Chief Exec. and Dir of Programmes, TV2 Denmark, 1988; Exec. Producer and writer, CIA, BBC TV/NRK/Primetime, 1989–92; Associate, Hydra Associates, 1989–91; Consultant, TVI Portugal, 1992–94; Director: Kanal Kaks, Estonia, 1995–97; TMS Ltd, 1999–; Barnimagen, 2000–. Dir, Broadcasting Research Unit, 1988–90 (Mem., Exec. Cttee, 1984–87). Mem., Political Cttee, UNA, 1978–90. Governor, Daneford Sch., 1977–81. *Publications:* Science, Education and Industry, 1978; (with Richard Luce) Human Rights and Foreign Policy, 1978; Ireland: an illustrated history, 1981; A Short History of Ireland, 1983, 2nd edn 1995; The Agency: the rise and decline of the CIA, 1986 (Nat. Intelligence Book Award, and New York Times Notable Book of the Year, 1987); (contrib.) Freedom of Information, ed by Julia Neuberger, 1987; (contrib.) The Revolution in Ireland 1879–1923, ed D. G. Boyce, 1988; Den Anden Kanal, 1989; Thatcher's People, 1991; CIA: a history, 1992; (contrib.) In the Name of Intelligence: essays in honor of Walter Pforzheimer, 1994. *Recreations:* old Bentley motor cars, quarter horses. *Address:* The Garner Cottages, Mill Way, Grantchester, Cambridge CB3 9NB. *Clubs:* Travellers; Metropolitan (Washington).

OBOLENSKY, Sir Dimitri, Kt 1984; MA, PhD, DLitt; FBA 1974; FSA; FRHistS; Emeritus Professor, University of Oxford, since 1985 (Professor of Russian and Balkan History, 1961–85, and Student of Christ Church, 1950–85, Emeritus Student, since 1985); *b* Petrograd, 1 April 1918; *s* of late Prince Dimitri Obolensky and late Countess Mary Shuvalov; *m* 1947, Elisabeth Lopukhin (marr. diss. 1989). *Educ:* Lycée Pasteur, Paris; Trinity College, Cambridge (Hon. Fellow, 1991). Cambridge: 1st Class Modern and Medieval Langs Tripos Parts I and II; Amy Mary Preston Read and Allen Schol.; Fellow of Trinity Coll., 1942–48; Faculty Asst Lecturer, 1944; Lecturer, Trinity Coll., 1945; Univ. Lecturer in Slavonic Studies, 1946; Reader in Russian and Balkan Medieval History in Univ. of Oxford, 1949–61. Sen. Associate Mem., St Antony's Coll., Oxford, 1993–. Vis. Schol., Dumbarton Oaks Center for Byzantine Studies, Harvard Univ., 1952, 1964, 1977, Vis. Fellow, 1981–82; Vis. Prof. of Russian History, Yale Univ., 1957; Vis. Prof. of European Hist., Univ. of California, Berkeley, 1973, Davis Prof. in Slavic Studies, Wellesley Coll., Mass, 1982; Vis. Mellon Prof., Inst. for Advanced Study, Princeton, 1985–86; Birkbeck Lecturer in Ecclesiastical History, Trinity Coll., Cambridge, 1961; Raleigh Lectr, British Acad., 1981. Vice-Pres., British Acad., 1983–85. Gen. Sec. Thirteenth Internat. Congress of Byzantine Studies, Oxford, 1966; British Co-Chairman: Anglo-Bulgarian Conf. of Historians, 1973; Anglo-Romanian Conf. of Historians, 1975; Chm., British Nat. Cttee, Association Internationale d'Etudes du Sud-Est Européen, 1985–93. Corresp. Mem., Acad. of Athens; Foreign Member: Serbian Acad. of Scis and Arts, 1988; Amer. Philosophical Soc., 1990; Russian Acad. of Scis, 1994. Hon. Dr Univ: Paris, Sorbonne, 1980; Sofia, 1989; Hon. DLitt Birmingham, 1988. *Publications:* The Bogomils, A Study in Balkan Neo-Manichaeism, 1948; (ed) The Penguin Book of Russian Verse, 1962; (jointly) The Christian Centuries, vol. 2: The Middle Ages, 1969;

Byzantium and the Slavs, 1971; The Byzantine Commonwealth, 1971; (ed jtly) Companion to Russian Studies, 3 vols, 1976–80; The Byzantine Inheritance of Eastern Europe, 1982; Six Byzantine Portraits, 1988. *Address:* 29 Belsyre Court, Woodstock Road, Oxford OX2 6HU. *T:* (01865) 556496. *Club:* Athenæum.

OBOTE, Dr (Apollo) Milton; President of Uganda and Minister of Foreign Affairs, 1980–85; former Leader, Uganda People's Congress Party; *b* 1924; *m*; three *s*. Migrated to Kenya and worked as labourer, clerk and salesman, 1950–55; Founder Mem., Kenya Africa Union. Mem., Uganda Nat. Congress, 1952–60; Mem., Uganda Legislative Council, 1957–71; Founder and Mem., Uganda People's Congress, 1960–71; Leader of the Opposition, 1961–62; Prime Minister, 1962–66; Minister of Defence and Foreign Affairs, 1963–65; President of Uganda, 1966–71 (deposed by military coup); in exile in Tanzania, 1971–80; returned to Uganda, 1980.

O'BRIEN, family name of **Baron Inchiquin**.

O'BRIEN, Basil Godwin, CMG 1996; High Commissioner of the Bahamas to the United Kingdom, and Ambassador to the European Union, Belgium, France, Germany and Italy, since 1999; *b* 5 Dec. 1940; *s* of late Cyril O'Brien and Kathleen O'Brien (*née* Brownrigg); *m* 1967, Marlene Devika Chand. *Educ:* St John's Coll., Nassau; Univ. Tutorial Coll., London; London Inst. of World Affairs (Dip. Internat. Affairs, London Univ.). HEO, Min. of Ext. Affairs, Bahamas, 1969–70; Asst Sec., later Dep. Perm. Sec., Cabinet Office, 1970–78; Permanent Secretary: Min. of Tourism, 1978–86; Min. of Foreign Affairs, 1986–89; Min. of Agriculture, Trade and Ind., 1989–93; Min. of Educn, 1993–94; Sec. to Cabinet and Hd, Public Service, 1994–99. Formerly: Director: Bahamas Hotel Trng Coll.; Bahamasair Hldgs Co. Past Chm., Bd of Govs, St John's Coll., Nassau. Past Mem., Anglican Central Educn Authy. *Recreations:* walking, swimming, gardening. *Address:* Bahamas High Commission, Bahamas House, 10 Chesterfield Street, W1X 8AH. *Club:* Skal.

O'BRIEN, Brian Murrough Fergus; Deputy Special Commissioner of Income Tax since 1991; *b* 18 July 1931; *s* of late Charles Murrough O'Brien, MB, BCh and Elizabeth Joyce O'Brien (*née* Peacocke). *Educ:* Bedford Sch.; University Coll., Oxford (BA 1954, MA 1959). Nat. Service, Royal Inniskilling Fusiliers, 1950–51. Called to the Bar, Lincoln's Inn, 1955; Office of Solicitor of Inland Revenue, 1956–70; Asst Solicitor, Law Commn, 1970–80; Secretary, Law Commn, 1980–81. Special Comr of Income Tax, 1981–91. Mem., Senate of Inns of Court and Bar Council, 1977–80; Hon. Gen. Sec., 1962–67 and Chm., 1974–76, CS Legal Soc.; Chm., Assoc. of First Div. Civil Servants, 1979–81. Lay Chm., Westminster (St Margaret's) Deanery Synod, 1978–82. Trustee, St Mary's, Bourne St (Chm. Trustees, 1968–92). *Recreations:* music, travel, light-hearted bridge. *Address:* Rathkeale Cottage, Castlematrix, Rathkeale, Co. Limerick, Ireland. *T:* (69) 64234. *Clubs:* Reform; Kildare Street and University (Dublin).

O'BRIEN, Charles Michael, MA; FIA, FPMI; General Manager (formerly Manager), and Actuary, 1955–84, Council Member, 1984–99, Royal National Pension Fund for Nurses; *b* 17 Jan. 1919; *s* of late Richard Alfred O'Brien, CBE, MD, and Nora McKay; *m* 1950, Joy, *d* of late Rupert Henry Prebble and Phyllis Mary Langdon; two *s*. *Educ:* Westminster Sch.; Christ Church, Oxford (MA). Commissioned, Royal Artillery, 1940 (despatches, 1945). Asst Actuary, Equitable Life Assce Soc., 1950; Asst Manager, Royal National Pension Fund for Nurses, 1953. Director: M & G Assurance Gp Ltd, 1984–91; M & G Life Assurance Co. Ltd, 1991–94. Institute of Actuaries: Fellow, 1949; Hon. Sec., 1961–62; Vice-Pres., 1965–68; Pres., 1976–78. Mem., Governing Body, 1970–95, Hon. Fellow, 1998, Westminster Sch. *Address:* The Boundary, Goodley Stock, Crockham Hill, Edenbridge, Kent TN8 6TA. *T:* (01732) 866349.

O'BRIEN, Conor Cruise; Contributing Editor, The Atlantic, Boston; Editor-in-Chief, The Observer, 1979–81; Pro-Chancellor, University of Dublin, since 1973; *b* 3 November 1917; *s* of Francis Cruise O'Brien and Katherine Sheehy; *m* 1st, 1939, Christine Foster (marr. diss. 1962); one *s* one *d* (and one *d* decd); 2nd, 1962, Máire Mac Entee; one adopted *s* one adopted *d*. *Educ:* Sandford Park School, Dublin; Trinity College, Dublin (BA, PhD). Entered Department of External Affairs of Ireland, 1944; Counsellor, Paris, 1955–56; Head of UN section and Member of Irish Delegation to UN, 1956–60; Asst Sec., Dept of External Affairs, 1960; Rep. of Sec.-Gen. of UN in Katanga, May-Dec. 1961; resigned from UN and Irish service, Dec. 1961. Vice-Chancellor, Univ. of Ghana, 1962–65; Albert Schweitzer Prof. of Humanities, New York Univ., 1965–69. TD (Lab) Dublin North-East, 1969–77; Minister for Posts and Telegraphs, 1973–77. Mem. Senate, Republic of Ireland, 1977–79. Vis. Fellow, Nuffield Coll., Oxford, 1973–75; Fellow, St Catherine's Coll., Oxford, 1978–81; Vis. Prof. and Montgomery Fellow, Dartmouth Coll., USA, 1984–85; Sen. Res. Fellow, Nat. Humanities Center, N Carolina, 1993–94. Member: Royal Irish Acad.; Royal Soc. of Literature. Hon. DLitt: Bradford, 1971; Ghana, 1974; Edinburgh, 1976; Nice, 1978; Coleraine, 1981; QUB, 1984. Valiant for Truth Media Award, 1979. *Publications:* Maria Cross (under pseud. Donat O'Donnell), 1952 (reprinted under own name, 1963); Parnell and his Party, 1957; (ed) The Shaping of Modern Ireland, 1959; To Katanga and Back, 1962; Conflicting Concepts of the UN, 1964; Writers and Politics, 1965; The United Nations: Sacred Drama, 1967 (with drawings by Felix Topolski); Murderous Angels, 1968; (ed) Power and Consciousness, 1969; Conor Cruise O'Brien Introduces Ireland, 1969; (ed) Edmund Burke, Reflections on the Revolution in France, 1969; Camus, 1969; A Concise History of Ireland, 1972; (with Máire Cruise O'Brien) The Suspecting Glance, 1972; States of Ireland, 1972; Herod, 1978; Neighbours: the Ewart-Biggs memorial lectures 1978–79, 1980; The Siege: the saga of Israel and Zionism, 1986; Passion and Cunning, 1988; God Land: reflections on religion and nationalism, 1988; The Great Melody: a thematic biography and commented anthology of Edmund Burke, 1992; Ancestral Voices, 1994; On the Eve of the Millennium, 1996; The Long Affair: Thomas Jefferson and the French Revolution, 1996; Memoir: my life and themes, 1998. *Recreation:* travelling. *Address:* Whitewater, Howth Summit, Dublin, Ireland. *T:* (1) 8322474. *Club:* Athenæum.

O'BRIEN, David P.; Director, since 1995, Chairman, President and Chief Executive Officer, since 1996, Canadian Pacific Ltd; *b* 9 Sept. 1941; *s* of John L. O'Brien and Ethel (*née* Cox); *m* 1968, Gail Baxter Corneil; one *s* two *d*. *Educ:* Loyola Coll. (BA Hons Econs 1962); McGill Univ. (BCL 1965). Associate and Partner, Ogilvy Renault (law firm), 1967–77; various mgt posts, 1978–85, Exec. Vice Pres., 1985–89, Petro-Canada; Pres. and CEO, Noverco Inc., 1989; Dir, 1990–, Chm., 1992–, PanCanadian Petroleum Ltd (Pres. and CEO, 1990–95); Pres. and Chief Operating Officer, Canadian Pacific Ltd, 1995–96. Director: Fording Coal Ltd, 1995–; Royal Bank of Canada, 1996–; Inco Ltd, 1996–; Air Canada, 1998–. Chm., Business Council on Nat. Issues, 1999–; Director: Conf. Bd of Canada, 1995–; C. D. Howe Inst. Mem. Bd of Govs, Univ. of Calgary, 1997–. *Recreations:* tennis, biking. *Address:* 1800 Bankers Hall East, 855 2nd Street SW, Calgary, Alta T2P 4Z5, Canada. *T:* (403) 2188000. *Clubs:* Calgary Petroleum, Calgary Golf and Country, Glencoe Golf and Country (Calgary).

O'BRIEN, Prof. Denis Patrick, FBA 1988; Professor of Economics, University of Durham, 1972–97, now Emeritus; *b* Knebworth, Herts, 24 May 1939; *s* of Patrick Kevin O'Brien and Dorothy Elizabeth Crisp; *m* 1st, 1961, Eileen Patricia O'Brien (*d* 1985); one *s* two *d*; 2nd, 1993, Julia Stapleton; one *d*. *Educ:* Douai Sch.; University Coll. London (BSc (Econ) 1960); PhD Queen's Univ., Belfast, 1969. In industry, 1960–62; Queen's University, Belfast: Assst Lectr, 1963–65; Lectr, 1965–70; Reader, 1970–72. *Publications:* (with D. Swann) Information Agreements, 1969; J. R. McCulloch, 1970; Correspondence of Lord Overstone, 3 vols, 1971; (jtly) Competition in British Industry, 1974; (ed) J. R. McCulloch: Treatise on Taxation, 1975; The Classical Economists, 1975; Competition Policy, Profitability and Growth, 1979; (with J. Presley) Pioneers of Modern Economics in Britain, 1981; (with A. C. Darnell) Authorship Puzzles in the History of Economics, 1982; (with J. Creedy) Economic Analysis in Historical Perspective, 1984; Lionel Robbins, 1988; Thomas Joplin and Classical Macroeconomics, 1993; Methodology, Money and the Firm, 2 vols, 1994. *Recreation:* the violin.

O'BRIEN, Dermod Patrick; QC 1983. a Recorder of the Crown Court, since 1978; *b* 23 Nov. 1939; *s* of Lieut D. D. O'Brien, RN, and Mrs O'Brien (*née* O'Connor); *m* 1974, Zoë Susan Norris; two *s*. *Educ:* Ampleforth Coll., York; St Catherine's Coll., Oxford. BA (Jurisprudence); MA. Called to Bar, Inner Temple, 1962, Bencher, 1993; joined Western Circuit, 1963. Head of Chambers, 1999–. Governor, Milton Abbey Sch., 1992–. *Recreations:* fishing, shooting, ski-ing. *Address:* Little Daux Farm, Billingshurst, West Sussex RH14 9DB. *T:* (01403) 784800; (chambers) 2 Temple Gardens, Temple, EC4Y 9AY. *T:* (020) 7822 1200. *Club:* Boodle's.

O'BRIEN, Edna; writer; *b* Ireland; marr. diss.; two *s*. *Educ:* Irish convents; Pharmaceutical Coll. of Ireland. Yorkshire Post Novel Award, 1971. *Publications:* The Country Girls, 1960 (screenplay for film, 1983); The Lonely Girl, 1962; Girls in Their Married Bliss, 1963; August is a Wicked Month, 1964; Casualties of Peace, 1966; The Love Object, 1968; A Pagan Place, 1970; (play) A Pagan Place, 1971; Night, 1972; (short stories) A Scandalous Woman, 1974; Mother Ireland, 1976; Johnnie I hardly knew you, 1977; Mrs Reinhardt and other stories, 1978; Virginia (play), 1979; The Dazzle, 1981; Returning, 1982; A Christmas Treat, 1982; A Fanatic Heart (selected stories), 1985; Tales for the Telling, 1986; Flesh and Blood (play), 1987; Madame Bovary (play), 1987; The High Road, 1988; Lantern Slides (short stories), (Los Angeles Times Award) 1990; Time and Tide, 1992 (Writers' Guild Award, 1993); House of Splendid Isolation, 1994; Down by the River, 1997; James Joyce, 1999; Wild Decembers, 1999. *Recreations:* walking, reading, meditating. *Address:* c/o David Godwin Associates, 55 Monmouth Street, WC2H 9DG. *T:* (020) 7240 9992.

O'BRIEN, Sir Frederick (William Fitzgerald), Kt 1984; QC (Scotland) 1960; Sheriff Principal of Lothian and Borders, 1978–89; Sheriff of Chancery in Scotland, 1978–89; Hon. Sheriff at Edinburgh and Paisley, since 1990; *b* 19 July 1917; *s* of Dr Charles Henry Fitzgerald O'Brien and Helen Jane; *m* 1950, Audrey Muriel Owen; two *s* one *d*. *Educ:* Royal High Sch.; Univ. of Edinburgh; MA 1938; LLB 1940. Admitted Faculty of Advocates, 1947. Comr, Mental Welfare Commission of Scotland, 1962–65; Home Advocate Depute, 1964–65; Sheriff-Principal of Caithness, Sutherland, Orkney and Shetland, 1965–75; Interim Sheriff-Principal of Aberdeen, Kincardine and Banff, 1969–71; Sheriff Principal of N Strathclyde, 1975–78; Interim Sheriff Principal of S Strathclyde, 1981. Hon. Mem., Sheriffs' Assoc., 1990–. Member: Scottish Medical Practices Cttee, 1973–76; Scottish Records Adv. Council, 1974–83; Convener of Sheriffs Principal, 1972–89; Chm., Sheriff Court Rules Council, 1975–81. Chm., Northern Lighthouse Bd, 1983–84 and 1986–87. Convener, Gen. Council Business Cttee, Edinburgh Univ., 1980–84. Hon. Pres., Royal High Sch. Former Pupils Club, 1982–92 (Pres. 1975–76); Chm., Edinburgh Sir Walter Scott Club, 1989–92. *Recreations:* golf, music. *Address:* 22 Arboretum Road, Edinburgh EH3 5PN. *T:* (0131) 552 1923. *Clubs:* New, Scottish Arts (Edinburgh); Bruntsfield Golf (Hon. Mem.).

See also S. J. O'Brien.

O'BRIEN, Rt Rev. James Joseph; Auxiliary Bishop of Westminster, (RC), and Titular Bishop of Manaccenser, since 1977; *b* 5 Aug. 1930; *s* of John and Mary Elizabeth O'Brien. *Educ:* St Ignatius College, Stamford Hill; St Edmund's Coll., Ware. Priest, 1954; Assistant, St Lawrence's, Feltham, 1954–62; Catholic Missionary Society, 1962–68; Director of Catholic Enquiry Centre, 1967–68; Rector of Allen Hall, 1968–77; Bishop in Hertfordshire, 1977–2001. Bishops' Conference of England and Wales: Chm., Dept for Internat. Affairs, 1984–88; Chm., Cttee for Ministerial Formation, 1988–. Prelate of Honour, 1969. *Address:* The Gate House, All Saints Pastoral Centre, London Colney, St Albans, Herts AL2 1AG. *T:* (01727) 824664.

O'BRIEN, Prof. John W., PhD; Rector Emeritus, Concordia University (incorporating Loyola College and Sir George Williams University, Montreal), since 1984 (Rector and Vice-Chancellor, 1969–84; Professor of Economics, 1965–96); *b* 4 Aug. 1931; *s* of Wilfred Edmond O'Brien and Audrey Swain; *m* 1956, Joyce Helen Bennett; two *d*. *Educ:* McGill Univ., Montreal, Que. BA 1953, MA 1955, PhD 1962. Sir George Williams Univ.: Lectr in Economics, 1954; Asst Prof. of Economics, 1957; Associate Prof. of Economics and Asst Dean, 1961; Dean, Faculty of Arts, 1963; Vice-Principal (Academic), 1968–69. Hon. DCL Bishop's Univ., 1976; Hon. LLD McGill Univ., 1976. *Publication:* Canadian Money and Banking, 1964 (2nd edn, with G. Lermer, 1969). *Address:* 38 Holton Avenue, Westmount, QC H3Y 2E8, Canada.

O'BRIEN, Most Rev. Keith Michael Patrick; *see* St Andrews and Edinburgh, Archbishop of, (RC).

O'BRIEN, Rt Rev. Kevin; *see* O'Brien, Rt Rev. T. K.

O'BRIEN, Michael; MP (Lab) Warwickshire North, since 1992; *b* 19 June 1954; *s* of Timothy Thomas and Mary O'Brien; *m* 1987, Alison Munro; one *d*. *Educ:* Worcester Tech. Coll.; North Staffs Poly. (BA Hons Hist. and Pol.). Lectr in Law, Colchester Inst., 1981–87; solicitor, 1987–92. Opposition spokesperson: HM Treasury, 1995–96; City, 1996–97; Parly Under-Sec. of State, Home Office, 1997–2001. Member: Home Affairs Select Cttee, 1992–94; Treasury Select Cttee, 1994–95. Chm., Lab. Home Affairs Cttee, 1995–96. Parly Advr, Police Fedn, 1993–96. *Address:* House of Commons, SW1A 0AA. *Clubs:* Bedworth Ex-Service Men's (Bedworth); Wood End Social (Kingsbury, N Warwicks).

O'BRIEN, (Michael) Vincent; racehorse trainer, 1943–94, retired; *b* 9 April 1917; *s* of Daniel P. O'Brien and Kathleen (*née* Toomey); *m* 1951, Jacqueline (*née* Wittenoom), Perth, Australia; two *s* three *d*. *Educ:* Mungret Coll., Ireland. Started training in Co. Cork, 1944; moved to Co. Tipperary, 1951. Champion trainer: Nat. Hunt, 1952–53 and 1954–55; Flat, 1966 and 1967. Won all major English and Irish hurdle and steeple-chases, incl. 3 consecutive Grand Nationals, Gold Cups and Champion Hurdles. From 1959 concentrated on flat racing and trained winners of 44 Classics, incl. 6 Epsom Derbys, 6 Irish Derbys and 1 French Derby; also 3 Prix de l'Arc de Triomphe, Breeders Cup Mile, and Washington International; trainer of Nijinsky, first triple crown winner since 1935. Hon. LLD NUI, 1983; Hon. DSc Ulster, 1995. *Recreations:* fishing, golf. *Address:* Ballydoyle House, Cashel, Co. Tipperary, Ireland. *T:* (62) 61222, *Fax:* (62) 61677.

O'BRIEN, Prof. Patrick Karl, DPhil; FBA 1990; Professor of Economic History, University of London, 1990–98, now Emeritus; Senior Research Fellow and Convenor of the Programme in Global History, Institute of Historical Research, since 1998 (Director, 1990–98); *b* 12 Aug. 1932; *s* of William O'Brien and Elizabeth Stockhausen; *m* 1959, Cassy Cobham; one *s* two *d. Educ:* London Sch. of Economics (Lilian Knowles Schol.; BSc 1958); Nuffield Coll., Oxford (DPhil). London University: Res. Fellow, 1960–63; Lectr, 1963–70; Reader in Econs and Econ. Hist., 1967–70; Oxford University: Univ. Lectr in Econ. Hist., 1970–84; Reader, 1984–90; Faculty Fellow, 1970–84, Professorial Fellow, 1984–90, Emeritus Fellow, 1991, St Antony's Coll. Centennial Prof. of Econ. History, LSE, 1999–. Pres., Econ. Hist. Soc., 1999–2001. *Publications:* The Revolution in Egypt's Economic System, 1966; The New Economic History of the Railways, 1977; (with C. Keyder) Economic Growth in Britain and France 1780–1914, 1978; (ed jtly) Productivity in the Economies of Europe in the 19th and 20th Centuries, 1983; (ed) Railways and the Economic Development of Western Europe 1830–1914, 1983; (ed) International Productivity Comparisons 1750–1939, 1986; The Economic Effects of the Civil War, 1988; (ed jtly) The Industrial Revolution and British Society, 1993; (ed) Industrialization: perspectives on the international economy, 1998; contribs to many learned jls. *Recreations:* theatre, Western art, tennis, squash, walking. *Address:* 66 St Bernards Road, Oxford OX2 6EJ. *T:* (01865) 512004.

O'BRIEN, Patrick William; His Honour Judge O'Brien; a Circuit Judge, since 1991; *b* 20 June 1945; *s* of William C. O'Brien and Ethel M. O'Brien; *m* 1970, Antoinette Wattebot; one *s* two *d. Educ:* St Joseph's Academy, Blackheath; Queens' College, Cambridge (MA, LLM). Called to the Bar, Lincoln's Inn, 1968; practised SE Circuit; a Recorder, 1987. *Recreations:* cricket, choral singing, musical theatre. *Address:* Cambridge County Court, Bridge House, Bridge Street, Cambridge CB2 1UA. *Club:* MCC.

O'BRIEN, Raymond Francis, CBE 2000; DL; Chairman: Speke/Garston Development Company Ltd, since 1995; Liverpool Development Co. Ltd, since 2001; *b* 13 Feb. 1936; *s* of Ignatius and Anne O'Brien; *m* 1959, Mary Agnes, (Wendy), *d* of late James and of Agnes Alcock; two *s* two *d. Educ:* St Mary's Coll., Great Crosby, Liverpool; St Edmund Hall, Oxford (BA Hons 1959; MA 1962). IPFA. Accountant, Cheshire CC, 1959–65; Head of Data Processing, Staffs CC, 1965–67; Asst County Treas., Notts CC, 1967–70; Dep. Clerk, Notts CC, 1970–73; Clerk of CC and Chief Executive, Notts, 1973–77; Chief Exec., Merseyside MCC, 1978–86; Chief Exec. and Bd Mem., Severn-Trent Water Authy, 1986–87; Chief Exec., FIMBRA, 1987–90. Consultant, Information Corp (UK) Ltd, 1993. Mem., Merseyside Area Bd, MSC, 1980–86; Director: Merseyside Economic Development Co. Ltd, 1981–86; Merseyside Cablevision Ltd, 1982–86; Anfield Foundation, 1983–92. Chm., Midlands Reg. Electricity Consumers Cttee, 1996–2000. DL Merseyside, 1980. *Recreations:* sports critic, gardening, music, reading. *Address:* 80 Broad Oaks Road, Solihull, West Midlands B91 1HZ. *T:* (0121) 682 6030, *Fax:* (0121) 682 6890.

O'BRIEN, Sir Richard, Kt 1980; DSO 1944, MC 1942 (Bar 1944); Chairman, Manpower Services Commission, 1976–82; *b* 15 Feb. 1920; *s* of late Dr Charles O'Brien and of Marjorie Maude O'Brien; *m* 1951, Elizabeth M. D. Craig; two *s* three *d. Educ:* Oundle Sch.; Clare Coll., Cambridge (MA). Served, 1940–45, with Sherwood Foresters and Leicesters, N Africa, ME, Italy and Greece; Personal Asst to Field Marshal Montgomery, 1945–46. Develt Officer, Nat. Assoc. of Boys' Clubs, 1946–48; Richard Sutcliffe Ltd, Wakefield (latterly Prodn Dir), 1948–58; Dir and Gen. Man., Head Wrightson Mineral Engrg Ltd, 1958–61; Dir, Industrial Relns, British Motor Corp., 1961–66; Industrial Adviser (Manpower), DEA, 1966–68; Delta Metal Co. Ltd (subseq. Dir of Manpower, and Dir 1972–76), 1968–76. Chairman: CBI Employment Policy Cttee, 1971–76; Crown Appointments Commn, 1979; Engineering Industry Trng Bd, 1982–85; Archbishop's Commn on Urban Priority Areas, 1983–85; Industrial Participation Assoc., 1983–86; Policy Studies Inst., 1984–90 (Jt Pres., 1991–98); Employment Inst. and Charter for Jobs, 1985–87; Community Educn Develt Centre, 1989–94; People for Action, 1991– (Pres., 1994–); Deputy Chairman: AMARC, 1988–91; Church Urban Fund, 1988–94. Member: NEDC, 1977–82; Engrg Council, 1985–88; President: British Inst. of Industrial Therapy, 1982–87; Inst. of Trng and Develt, 1983–84; Nat. Assoc. of Colls of Further and Higher Educn, 1983–85; Concordia (Youth Service Volunteers), 1987– (Chm., 1981–87); Campaign for Work, 1988–92; Employment Policy Inst., 1992–95. Mem. Bd, Community Industry, 1991–96; Member Council: Industrial Soc., 1962–86; Univ. of Birmingham, 1969–88; Hymns Ancient & Modern, 1984–2000. Mem. Ct of Governors, ASC, 1977–83. Chm., Chiswick House Friends, 1997–2000. Hon. DSc Aston, 1979; Hon. LLD: Bath, 1981; Liverpool, 1981; Birmingham, 1982; Hon. DLitt: Warwick, 1983; CNAA (Coll. of St Mark and St John), 1988; DCL Lambeth, 1987; Hon. Fellow Sheffield City Polytech., 1980. JP Wakefield, 1955–61. *Publications:* contrib: Conflict at Work (BBC pubn), 1971; Montgomery at Close Quarters, 1985; Seekers and Finders, 1985; articles in various jls. *Recreations:* reading, theatre, cinema. *Address:* 53 Abingdon Villas, W8 6XA. *T:* (020) 7937 8944.

O'BRIEN, Air Vice-Marshal Robert Peter, CB 1997; OBE 1983; FRAeS; Air Secretary, 1994–97, and Chief Executive, RAF Personnel Management Agency, 1997–98; *b* 1 Nov. 1941; *s* of Major Thomas Joseph O'Brien, MC, RE and Doris Winifred O'Brien; *m* 1964, Carole Evelyn Anne Wallace; two *s. Educ:* Salesian College, Farnborough; RAF College, Cranwell. BA (External) London. FRAeS 1997. Commissioned 1962; Pilot 31 Sqn (Canberras), 1963–66; Central Flying Sch./4FTS (Gnats), 1966–67; ADC to AOC 38 Gp, 1967–70; Flt Comdr, 15 Sqn (Buccaneers), 1970–73; Army Staff Coll., 1974; HQ RAF Germany, 1975–77; OC London UAS (Bulldogs), 1977–79; Chief Instr/TTTE (Tornados), 1980–83; Stn Comdr, RAF Marham, 1983–85; Air Staff, MoD, 1985–87; Dep. Comdr/COS HQ BF Cyprus, 1988–91; Dir of Infrastructure (RAF), MoD, 1991–92; Comdt, JSDC, 1992–94. ADC to the Queen, 1983–85. *Recreations:* tennis, golf, walking. *Address:* c/o Lloyds TSB, Cox's and King's Branch, PO Box 1190, 7 Pall Mall, SW1Y 5NA. *Club:* Royal Air Force.

O'BRIEN, (Robert) Stephen, CBE 1987; Chief Executive: London First, and London First Centre, since 1992; London Forum, 1993–94; *b* 14 Aug. 1936; *s* of Robert Henry and Clare Winifred O'Brien; *m* 1st, 1958, Zoë T. O'Brien (marr. diss. 1989); two *s* two *d*; 2nd, 1989, Meriel Barclay. *Educ:* Sherborne Sch., Dorset. Joined Charles Fulton & Co. Ltd, 1956; Dir, 1964; Chm., 1973–82; Chief Exec., 1983–92, Vice-Chm., 1992–, BITC. Chm., Cranstoun, 1969–83 (Pres., 1983–88); Dir, Kirkland-Whittaker Co. Ltd, 1980–82. Chairman: Foreign Exchange and Currency Deposit Brokers Assoc., 1968–72; Project Fullemploy, 1973–91; Home Sec.'s Adv. Bd on Community Radio, 1985–86. Ordained Deacon, 1971; Hon. Curate, St Lawrence Jewry, 1973–80; Chm., Christian Action, 1976–88. Vice-Chm., Church Urban Fund, 1994–. Pres., Esher Assoc. for Prevention of Addiction, 1979–90. Chm., UK 2000, 1988–92 (Mem. Bd, 1986–92); Director: Cities in Schools, 1989–95; Prince of Wales' Business Leaders Forum, 1990–; Member: Administrative Council, Royal Jubilee Trusts, 1984–89; Management Cttee, Action Resource Centre, 1986–91; Council, RSA, 1987–91; Trustee: Learning from Experience Trust, 1986–94; Immigrants Aid Trust, 1997–; PYBT, 1987–99; Chm., Prince's Trust Regl Council for London, 2000–. Chm. Govs, Univ. of E London, 1999–. Hon. LLD Liverpool, 1994; Hon DSc City, 2000. *Recreations:* causes, gentle gardening. *Address:* 177 Pierpoint, 16 Westferry Road, E14 8NQ.

O'BRIEN, Stephen Rothwell; MP (C) Eddisbury, since July 1999; *b* Tanzania, 1 April 1957; *s* of David and Rothy O'Brien; *m* 1986, Gemma Townshend; two *s* one *d. Educ:* Sedbergh Sch.; Emmanuel Coll., Cambridge (MA); Chester Coll. of Law. Solicitor, Freshfields, 1981–88; Gp Sec. and Gp Internat. Dir, Redland plc, 1988–98; Dep. Chm., Redland Tile & Brick Ltd, NI, 1995–98. Mem., Govt trade mission to Argentine and Brazil, 1994. PPS to Opposition spokesman on foreign affairs, 2000, to Chm. of Cons. Pty, 2000–01; an Opposition Whip, 2001–. Member, Select Committee: on Educn and Employment, 1999–2001; on Envmt, Food and Rural Affairs, 2001–. All Party Groups: Jt Vice Chairman: Tanzania; Uganda; Jt Treas., Jubilee 2000 Coalition. Introduced Private Members Bill on Honesty in Food Labelling, 2001. Mem., Cons. Nat. Membership Cttee, 1999–2001; Secretary: Cons. Trade and Industry Cttee, 1999–2001; Cons. NI Cttee, 1999–. Mem., British-Irish Inter-Parly Body, 2000–. Member: Council, ScotBIC, 1995–98; Internat. Investment Panel, and Mem., SE Regl Council, CBI, 1995–98. UK Building Materials Producers, then Construction Products Association: Chm., Public and Parly Affairs Cttee, 1995–99; Member: Cttee of Mgt; Pres.'s Strategy Cttee; Econ. and Market Forecasting Panel, 1989–95. FCIS 1997 (Parly Advr, 2000–). Director: Cambridge Univ. Careers Service, 1992–99; City of London Sinfonia, 2001–. Trustee, Reigate Priory Mus., 1992–98. Chm., Chichester Cons. Assoc., 1998–99. *Recreations:* music (piano, conducting), fell-walking, golf. *Address:* House of Commons, SW1A 0AA. *T:* (020) 7219 6315. *Clubs:* Carlton; Winsford Constitutional and Conservative (Cheshire).

O'BRIEN, Susan Joyce; QC (Scot.) 1998; *b* 13 Aug. 1952; *d* of Sir Frederick O'Brien, *qv*; *m* 1978, Peter Ross, Professor of Evolutionary Computing, Napier Univ.; two *d. Educ:* St George's Sch., Edinburgh; Univ. of York (BA Hons 1973; BPhil 1976); Univ. of Edinburgh (LLB 1978). Admitted Solicitor, Scotland, 1980; Asst Solicitor, Shepherd & Wedderburn WS, 1980–86; WS 1983; admitted to Faculty of Advocates, 1987; Standing Junior Counsel to: Registrar Gen., 1991; Home Office, 1992–97; Keeper of the Registers, 1998; Temp. Sheriff, 1995–99. Part-time Chm., Employment Tribunal, 2000–. Reporter, Scottish Legal Aid Bd, 1999–. *Recreation:* bringing up the children. *Address:* 21 Nile Grove, Edinburgh EH10 4RE. *T:* (0131) 446 9210.

O'BRIEN, Terence John, CMG 1971; MC 1945; HM Diplomatic Service, retired; *b* 13 Oct. 1921; *s* of Joseph O'Brien; *m* 1950, Phyllis Mitchell (*d* 1952); *m* 1953, Rita Emily Drake Reynolds; one *s* two *d. Educ:* Gresham's Sch., Holt; Merton Coll., Oxford. Ayrshire Yeo., 1942–45. Dominions Office, 1947; CRO, 1947–49; British High Comr's Office, Ceylon, 1950–52; Princ., Treasury, 1953–56; 1st Sec. (Financial), Canberra, 1956–58; Planning Officer, CRO, 1958–60; 1st Sec., Kuala Lumpur, 1960–62; Sec. to Inter-Governmental Cttee, Jesselton, 1962–63; Head of Chancery, New Delhi, 1963–66; Imp. Def. Coll., 1967; Counsellor, FCO (formerly FO), 1968–70; Ambassador: Nepal, 1970–74; Burma, 1974–78; Indonesia, 1978–81. *Address:* Beaufort House, Woodcutts, Dorset SP5 5RP. *T:* (01725) 552234.

O'BRIEN, Rt Rev. (Thomas) Kevin; Auxiliary Bishop of Middlesbrough, (RC), and Titular Bishop of Ard Carna, 1981–98; *b* Cork City, Republic of Ireland, 18 Feb. 1923; *s* of Jack and Mary O'Brien. *Educ:* Christian Brothers Coll., Cork. Ordained, All Hallows College, Dublin, 1948; Curate at Batley, Yorks, 1948–51, and St Anne's Cathedral, Leeds, 1951–56; Catholic Missionary Society, 1956–71, Superior 1960–71; Vicar General, Diocese of Leeds, 1971–81; Parish Priest: St Patrick's, Huddersfield, 1971–79; St Francis, Bradford, 1979–81. Chm., Home Mission Cttee of Bishops' Conference, 1983–; Mem., Co-ordinating Gp for Evangelisation, Churches Together in England, 1986–. Hon. DD Hull, 1998. *Address:* Mount St Joseph's, Shire Oak Road, Headingley, Leeds LS6 2DE.

O'BRIEN, Timothy Brian, RDI 1991; designer; Hon. Associate Artist, Royal Shakespeare Company, since 1988 (Associate Artist, 1966–88); *b* 8 March 1929; *s* of Brian Palliser Tiegue O'Brien and Elinor Laura (*née* Mackenzie). *Educ:* Wellington Coll.; Corpus Christi, Cambridge (MA); Yale Univ. Design Dept, BBC TV, 1954; Designer, Associated Rediffusion, 1955–56; Head of Design, ABC Television, 1956–66 (The Flying Dutchman, 1958); partnership in stage design with Tazeena Firth, 1961–79; output incl.: The Bartered Bride, The Girl of the Golden West, 1962; West End prodns of new plays, 1963–64; London scene of Shakespeare Exhibn, 1964; Tango, Days in the Trees, Staircase, RSC, and Trafalgar at Madame Tussaud's, 1966; All's Well that Ends Well, As You Like It, Romeo and Juliet, RSC, 1967; The Merry Wives of Windsor, Troilus and Cressida (also Nat. Theatre, 1976), The Latent Heterosexual, RSC, 1968; Pericles (also Comédie Française, 1974), Women Beware Women, Bartholomew Fair, RSC, 1969; 1970: Measure for Measure, RSC; Madame Tussaud's in Amsterdam; The Knot Garden, Royal Opera; 1971: Enemies, Man of Mode, RSC; 1972: La Cenerentola, Oslo; Lower Depths, The Island of the Mighty, RSC; As You Like It, OCSC; 1973: Richard II, Love's Labour's Lost, RSC; 1974: Next of Kin, NT; Summerfolk, RSC; The Bassarids, ENO; 1975: John Gabriel Borkman, NT; Peter Grimes, Royal Opera (later in Göteborg, Paris); The Marrying of Ann Leete, RSC; 1976: Wozzeck, Adelaide Fest.; The Zykovs, RSC; The Force of Habit, NT; 1977: Tales from the Vienna Woods, Bedroom Farce, NT; Falstaff, Berlin Opera; 1978: The Cunning Little Vixen, Göteborg; Evita, London (later in Australia, Austria, USA); A Midsummer Night's Dream, Sydney Opera House; 1979: The Rake's Progress, Royal Opera; 1981: Lulu, Royal Opera; 1982: La Ronde, RSC; Le Grand Macabre, ENO; 1983: Turandot, Vienna State Opera; 1984: The Mastersingers of Nuremberg, ENO; Tannhäuser, Royal Opera; 1985: Samson, Royal Opera; Sicilian Vespers, Grande Théâtre, Geneva; Old Times, Haymarket; Lucia di Lammermoor, Köln Opera; 1986: The Threepenny Opera, NT; Die Meistersinger von Nürnberg, Netherlands Opera; The American Clock, NT; 1987: Otello (revived 1990), and Die Entführung aus dem Serail, Royal Opera; 1988: Three Sisters, RSC; 1989: Cymbeline, RSC; Exclusive, Strand; 1990: King, Piccadilly; Love's Labours Lost, RSC; 1991: Twelfth Night, Tartuffe, Playhouse; War and Peace, Kirov, Leningrad; Beauty and the Beast, City of Birmingham Touring Opera; 1992: Christopher Columbus, RSC; 1993: Eugene Onegin, Royal Opera; Misha's Party, RSC; 1994: On Approval, Playhouse; The Clandestine Marriage, Queen's; 1995: The Merry Wives of Windsor, NT; The Merry Wives of Windsor, Oslo; 1996: Outis, La Scala, Milan; 1997: A Christmas Carol, Clwyd; 1998: Evita, US tour; 1999: Twelfth Night, Macbeth, Clwyd; 2001: Bedroom Farce, Clwyd. Chm., Soc. of British Theatre Designers, 1984–91; Master, Faculty of RDI, 1999–2001. (Jtly) Gold Medal for Set Design, Prague Quadriennale, 1975; (jtly) Golden Triga, for Best Nat. Exhibit, Prague Quadriennale, 1991. *Recreation:* sailing. *Address:* 33 Lansdowne Gardens, SW8 2EQ. *T:* (020) 7622 5384, *Fax:* (020) 7720 5348.

O'BRIEN, Sir Timothy John, 7th Bt *cr* 1849; *b* 6 July 1958; *s* of John David O'Brien (*d* 1980) and of Sheila Winifred, *o d* of Sir Charles Arland Maitland Freake, 4th Bt; *S* grandfather, 1982; *m* 2000, Susannah, *yr d* of Bryan Farr. *Educ:* Millfield; Univ. of Hartford, Conn. *Heir: b* James Patrick Arland O'Brien [*b* 22 Dec. 1964; *m* 1992, Lianna Mace; two *s*].

O'BRIEN, Vincent; *see* O'Brien, M. V.

O'BRIEN, William; JP; MP (Lab) Normanton, since 1983; *b* 25 Jan. 1929; *m* Jean; three *d. Educ:* state schools; Leeds Univ. Coalminer, 1945–83. Wakefield DC: Mem., 1973–83; former Dep. Leader and Chm., Finance and Gen. Purposes Cttee. Mem., NUM, 1945–; Local Branch Official, 1956–83. Opposition front bench spokesman on the Environment, 1987–92, for Northern Ireland, 1992–96. Member: Public Accounts Cttee, 1983–88; Energy Select Cttee, 1986–88; Envmt, Transport and Regions Select Cttee, 1997–; Public Accounts Commn, 1997. JP Wakefield, 1979. *Recreations:* reading, organising. *Address:* House of Commons, SW1A 0AA. *T:* (020) 7219 3000; 29 Limestrees, Ferrybridge Road, Pontefract WF8 2QB.

O'BRIEN, Adm. Sir William (Donough), KCB 1969 (CB 1966); DSC 1942; Commander-in-Chief, Western Fleet, Feb. 1970–Sept. 71, retd Nov. 1971; Vice-Admiral of the United Kingdom and Lieutenant of the Admiralty, 1984–86; *b* 13 Nov. 1916; *s* of late Major W. D. O'Brien, Connaught Rangers and I. R. Caroe (*née* Parnis); *m* 1943, Rita Micallef, Sliema, Malta; one *s* two *d. Educ:* Royal Naval Coll., Dartmouth. Served War of 1939–45: HM Ships Garland, Wolsey, Witherington, Offa, 1939–42; Cottesmore i/c, 1943–44; Arakan Coast, 1945. HMS Venus i/c, 1948–49; Commander 1949; HMS Ceylon, 1952; Admiralty, 1953–55; Captain, 1955; Captain (D) 8th DS in HMS Cheviot, 1958–59; HMS Hermes i/c, 1961–64; Rear-Admiral 1964; Naval Secretary, 1964–66; Flag Officer, Aircraft Carriers, 1966–67; Comdr, Far East Fleet, 1967–69; Admiral 1969. Rear-Admiral of the UK, 1979–84. Chairman: Kennet and Avon Canal Trust, 1974–91; King George's Fund for Sailors, 1974–86. Pres., Assoc. of RN Officers, 1973–88. *Address:* The Black Barn, Steeple Ashton, Trowbridge, Wilts BA14 6EU. *T:* (01380) 870496. *Club:* Army and Navy.

O'BRIEN QUINN, James Aiden; *see* Quinn.

O'CATHAIN, Baroness *cr* 1991 (Life Peer), of The Barbican in the City of London; **Detta O'Cathain,** OBE 1983; Managing Director, Barbican Centre, 1990–95; *b* 3 Feb. 1938; *d* of late Caoimhghin O'Cathain and Margaret O'Cathain; *m* 1968, William Bishop (*d* 2001). *Educ:* Laurel Hill, Limerick; University College, Dublin (BA). Aer Lingus, Dublin, 1961–66; Group Economist, Tarmac, 1966–69; Economic Advr, Rootes Motors, 1969–72; Sen. Economist, Carrington Vyella, 1972–73; Economic Advr, British Leyland, 1973–74; Dir, Market Planning, Leyland Cars, 1974–76; Corporate Planning Exec., Unigate, 1976–81; Milk Marketing Board: Head of Strategic Planning, 1981–83; Dir and Gen. Manager, 1984; Man. Dir Milk Marketing, 1985–88. Advr on Agricl Marketing to Minister of Agriculture, 1979–83. Non-executive Director: Midland Bank, 1984–93; Channel 4, 1985–86; Tesco, 1985–2000; Sears, 1987–94; British Airways, 1993–; BET, 1994–96; BNP Paribas (formerly BNP) UK Holdings Ltd, 1995–; Thistle Hotels, 1996–; South East Water plc, 1998–; William Baird Plc, 2000–; Allders plc, 2000–. FCIM 1987 (Pres., 1998–2001); FRSA 1986. *Recreations:* music, reading, walking, gardening. *Address:* Eglantine, Tower House Gardens, Arundel, W Sussex BN18 9RU. *T:* (01903) 883775.

OCEAN, Humphrey; *see* Butler-Bowdon, H. A. E.

OCKELTON, (Christopher) Mark (Glyn); Deputy President, Immigration Appeal Tribunal, since 2000; *b* 11 July 1955; *s* of Denis William Ockelton and Elvire Mabel Louise Jeanne (*née* May); *m* 1992, Brigid Joan Oates; one step *s* one step *d. Educ:* Winchester Coll.; Peterhouse, Cambridge (BA 1976; MA 1980); BD London 1989. Called to the Bar, Lincoln's Inn, 1977 (Bencher, 2001); Lectr in Law, 1979–93, Sen. Lectr, 1993–96, Univ. of Leeds; Immigration Adjudicator, 1992–96; Chm., 1996–2000, Vice-Pres., Jan.–May 2000, Immigration Appeal Tribunal. Vis. Prof. of Law, Univ. of Louisville, 1984–85; Vis. Lectr, Univ. du Maine, France, 1989. Parish Clerk, St Mary's Ch, Whitby, 1994–. Mem., Ancient Soc. of Coll. Youths, 1974–. Hon. Col, Commonwealth of Ky, 1985. *Publications:* The Tower, Bells and Ringers of Great St Mary's, Cambridge, 1981; Trusts for Accountants, 1987; Heydon and Ockelton's Evidence: cases and materials, 4th edn 1996; contrib. articles and reviews in legal, philosophical, antiquarian and campanological jls. *Recreations:* books, bells, ecclesiology, looking at architecture. *Address:* Immigration Appeal Tribunal, Field House, 15–25 Bream's Buildings, EC4A 1DZ. *Club:* Athenæum.

OCKENDON, Dr John Richard, FRS 1999; University Lecturer in Applicable Mathematics, Oxford University, since 1976; Fellow, St Catherine's College, Oxford, since 1965; Research Director, Oxford Centre for Industrial and Applied Mathematics, 1989–99; *b* 13 Oct. 1940; *s* of George and Doris Ockendon; *m* 1967, Hilary Mason; one *d. Educ:* Dulwich Coll.; St John's Coll., Oxford (MA; DPhil 1965). Lectr, Christ Church, Oxford, 1963–65. *Publications:* (with C. Elliott) Free Boundary Problems, 1981; (with H. Ockendon) Viscous Flow, 1997; (jtly) Applied Partial Differential Equations, 1999. *Recreations:* mathematical modelling, bird watching, Hornby-Dublo, old sports cars. *Address:* St Catherine's College, Oxford OX1 3UJ. *T:* (01865) 270513.

O'CONNELL, Desmond Henry, Jr; Group Managing Director, BOC Group, 1986–90; *b* 22 Feb. 1936; *s* of Desmond H. and Rosemary O'Connell; *m* 1964, Roberta M. Jaeger; two *s* one *d. Educ:* University of Notre Dame, Indiana; Harvard Business School. BS Elec. Eng., MBA. McKinsey & Co., Chicago, 1962–69; Walsh, Killian & Co., 1969–70; Baxter Travenol Labs, Deerfield, 1970–80; Airco, Montvale, NJ, 1980–86. Non-exec. Dir, Lucas Industries, 1988. *Recreations:* golf, ski-ing. *Address:* 971 South Lagoon Lane, Mantoloking, NJ 08738, USA. *Clubs:* East India; Leander; Indian Hill Country (Winnetka, Ill); Ridgewood Country (Ridgewood, NJ); Harvard (New York); Bay Head Yacht (Bay Head, NJ).

O'CONNELL, Sir Maurice (James Donagh MacCarthy), 7th Bt *cr* 1869, of Lakeview, Killarney and Ballybeggan, Tralee; *b* 10 June 1958; *s* of Sir Morgan Donal Conail O'Connell, 6th Bt and of Elizabeth, *o d* of late Major John MacCarthy O'Leary; *S* father, 1989; *m* 1993, Francesca, *d* of Clive Raleigh. *Heir: b* John Morgan Ross MacCarthy O'Connell, *b* 17 April 1960. *Address:* Lakeview House, Killarney, Co. Kerry, Ireland.

O'CONNOR, Surgeon Rear-Adm. Anthony, LVO 1967; Director, Red Cross Blood Transfusion Service, Western Australia, 1981–84 (Deputy Director, 1975–81); *b* 8 Nov. 1917; *s* of Armel John O'Connor and Lucy Violet O'Connor (*née* Bullock-Webster); *m* 1946, Catherine Jane (*née* Hayes); three *d. Educ:* Kings Coll., Strand, London; Westminster Hosp. Med. Sch. MRCS, LRCP, MB, BS, FFARCS, MFCM. Qualified Medical Practitioner, 1941; joined Royal Navy (RNVR), 1942; Permanent Commn, 1945; Dep. Medical Director General (Naval), 1969; MO i/c, Inst. of Naval Med. and Dean of Naval Med., 1972–75. QHP 1970–75. *Recreations:* gardening, photography. *Address:* c/o Lloyds TSB, Ludlow, Shropshire SY8 1NQ.

O'CONNOR, Rev. Canon (Brian) Michael (McDougal); Dean of Auckland, New Zealand, 1997–2000; *b* 20 June 1942; *s* of Brian McDougal O'Connor and Beryl O'Connor; *m* 1968, Alison Margaret Tibbutt; two *s. Educ:* Lancing Coll.; St Catharine's Coll., Cambridge (BA, MA); Cuddesdon Coll., Oxford. Admitted Solicitor, 1964; Asst Curate, St Andrew, Headington, 1969–72; Sec., Oxford Dio. Pastoral Cttee, 1972–79; Vicar, Rainham, Kent, 1979–97; Rural Dean of Gillingham, 1981–88. Hon. Canon: of Rochester Cathedral, 1988–97; of Auckland Cathedral, 2000–. Church Com[illegible] Member: General Synod, 1975–90 (Mem., Standing Cttee, 1985–90); Appointments Commn, 1987–90; ACC, 1988–92. Deleg., WCC Assembly, Ca[illegible] 1991. Commissary for Bishop: of Auckland, NZ, 1996–97; of Newcastle, NSW, 19[illegible] Exec. Officer, Ecclesiastical Law Soc., 2001–. *Address:* Woolgrove House, Duns Te[illegible] Road, Hempton, Banbury, Oxon OX15 0QZ. *T:* (01869) 337626; *e-mail:* canonmichaeloc@cs.com. *Club:* Northern (Auckland).

O'CONNOR, His Eminence Cardinal Cormac M.; *see* Murphy-O'Connor.

O'CONNOR, Professor Daniel John; Professor of Philosophy, University of Exeter, 1957–79, now Emeritus; *b* 2 April 1914; *m* 1948, Kathleen Kemsley; no *c. Educ:* Birkbeck Coll., University of London. Entered Civil Service, 1933; Commonwealth Fund Fellow in Philosophy, University of Chicago, 1946–47; Professor of Philosophy, University of Natal, SA, 1949–51; Professor of Philosophy, University of the Witwatersrand, Johannesburg, 1951–52; Lecturer in Philosophy, Univ. Coll. of North Staffordshire, 1952–54; Professor of Philosophy, University of Liverpool, 1954–57. Visiting Professor, University of Pennsylvania, 1961–62. *Publications:* John Locke, 1952; Introduction to Symbolic Logic (with A. H. Basson), 1953; Introduction to the Philosophy of Education, 1957; A Critical History of Western Philosophy (ed), 1964; Aquinas and Natural Law, 1968; Free Will, 1971; (ed jtly) New Essays in the Philosophy of Education, 1973; The Correspondence Theory of Truth, 1975; various papers in philosophical journals. *Address:* 101a Pennsylvania Road, Exeter EX4 6DT.

O'CONNOR, Deirdre Frances; Hon. Justice O'Connor; Judge, Federal Court of Australia, since 1990; President, Administrative Appeals Tribunal, 1990–94 and since 1999; *b* 5 Feb. 1941; *d* of D. A. Buff; *m* 1974, Michael Joseph, SC; five *s. Educ:* Bethlehem Coll., Ashfield; Sydney Univ. (BA; LLB 1st Cl. Hons); DipEd New England. Lectr in Law, Univ. of NSW, 1974–75; Sen. Lectr in Law, Macquarie Univ., 1975–78; part-time Lectr on media and law, Aust. Film and TV Sch., 1975–80; admitted NSW Bar, 1980; Comr, NSW Law Reform Commn, 1983–85; Chm., Aust. Broadcasting Tribunal, 1986–90. President: Nat. Native Title Tribunal, 1993–94; Aust. Industrial Relns Commn, 1994–97. Mem., Aust. Inst. Judicial Admin, 1992–. Trustee, Internat. Inst. of Communications, 1989–92. Member, Council: Order of Australia, 1990–96; Univ. of Canberra, 1992–95. *Recreations:* reading, antiques. *Address:* Federal Court of Australia, Level 16, Law Courts Building, Queens Square, Sydney, NSW 2000, Australia.

O'CONNOR, Denis Francis, QPM 1996; Chief Constable, Surrey Police, since 2000; *b* 21 May 1949; *m* 1972, Louise (*née* Harvey); one *s* two *d. Educ:* Le Sante Union Coll.; Southampton Univ. (BEd Hons 1974); Cranfield Inst. of Tech. (MSc 1985). Chief Supt, Notting Hill, 1990; Asst Chief Constable, Surrey Police, 1991; Dep. Chief Constable, Kent Constabulary, 1993; Asst Comr, SW Area, later S London, Metropolitan Police, 1997–2000. Former Member: Criminal Justice Wkg Gp, Adv. Council on Misuse of Drugs; DoH Task Force on Effectiveness of Drugs Services; Mem., Indep. Inquiry into the Misuse of Drugs Act 1971, 1997–2000. *Publications:* Developing a Partnership Approach for Drugs Education, 1992; Management by Objectives on Trial, 1992; Community Policing: are good intentions enough?, 1994; Increasing Community Safety from Drug Related Crime, 1995; Criminal Justice: what works?, 1995; Drugs: partnerships for policy, prevention and education, 1998. *Recreations:* reading, running, gardening. *Address:* Surrey Police HQ, Mount Browne, Sandy Lane, Guildford GU3 1HQ.

O'CONNOR, Desmond Bernard, (Des); entertainer and singer; *b* 12 Jan. 1932; *m* 1st, Phyllis; one *d*; 2nd, Gillian Vaughan; two *d*; 3rd, Jay; one *d*. Served RAF. Former Butlin's Red Coat, Filey; professional début, Palace Theatre, Newcastle upon Tyne, 1953; one-man shows, UK, Canada and Australia, 1980–; Royal Variety Show appearances, incl. compère, 1997. *Television includes:* Spot the Tune, 1958; Sunday Night at the London Palladium; Take Your Pick, 1992, 1994, 1996; Pot of Gold, 1993, 1995; own shows: Des O'Connor Tonight, 1977–; The Des O'Connor Show; Des O'Connor Now, 1985; Fame in the Family, 2000–. Has made over 1,000 appearances at the London Palladium. No 1 single, I Pretend, 1968. Male TV Personality, TV Times, annually 1969–73; Lifetime Achievement Award, Nat. TV Awards, 2001. *Publication:* Bananas Can't Fly (autobiog.), 2001. *Address:* c/o Lake-Smith Griffin Associates, 15 Maiden Lane, WC2E 7NG

O'CONNOR, Gillian Rose; mining correspondent, Financial Times, since 1999; *b* 11 Aug. 1941; *d* of Thomas McDougall O'Connor and Kathleen Joan O'Connor (*née* Parnell). *Educ:* Sutton High School for Girls; St Hilda's College, Oxford. Editor, Investors Chronicle, 1982–94; Personal Finance Ed., FT, 1994–98. *Publication:* A Guide to Stockpicking, 1996. *Address:* Financial Times, Number One, Southwark Bridge, SE1 9HL.

O'CONNOR, Rev. Canon Michael; *see* O'Connor, Rev. Canon B. M. McD.

O'CONNOR, Patrick Michael Joseph; QC 1993; *b* 7 Aug. 1949; *s* of Denis Bellew O'Connor and Ingelore Biegel; *m* 1986, Gillian Denise Brasse; two *d. Educ:* St Francis Xavier's Grammar Sch., Liverpool; UCL (LLB Hons). Called to the Bar, Inner Temple, 1970. *Publications:* articles in Criminal Law Review and other academic and professional jls. *Address:* Doughty Street Chambers, 10–11 Doughty Street, WC1N 2PL. *T:* (020) 7404 1313.

O'CONNOR, Ronald; Director of Social Work Services, Glasgow City Council, since 1999; *b* 1 Dec. 1950; *s* of John O'Connor and Mary O'Connor (*née* McDermott); *m* 1992, Marie Harvey Milne; one *s. Educ:* Stirling Univ. (BA (Hons), Dip Ed). Teacher, modern langs, Belmont Acad., Ayr, 1977; Principal Teacher, modern langs, 1981, Asst Head, 1983, Garnock Acad.; Educn Officer, 1988, Asst Dir of Educn, 1993, Strathclyde Regl Council; Sen. Depute Dir of Educn, Glasgow CC, 1995. *Recreations:* golf, football, reading. *Address:* Nye Bevan House, 2 India Street, Glasgow G2 4PF. *T:* (0141) 287 8853.

O'CONNOR, Rory, CBE 1991; Member, Gibraltar Court of Appeal, 1991–97; Judge of the High Court of Hong Kong, 1977–90; *b* Co. Down, 26 Nov. 1925; *s* of late James O'Connor and Mary (*née* Savage); *m* 1963, Elizabeth, *d* of late Frederick Dew; one *s* two *d. Educ:* Blackrock Coll., Dublin; Univ. Coll., Dublin (BCom). Called to Irish Bar, King's Inns, 1949. Resident Magistrate, Kenya, 1956–62; Hong Kong: Magistrate, 1962–70; District Judge, 1970–77. *Address:* 12 Windermere Crescent, Bangor, Co. Down, N Ireland BT20 4QH.

O'CONNOR, Sandra Day; Associate Justice of the Supreme Court of the United States, since 1981; *b* 26 March 1930; *d* of Harry and Ada Mae Day; *m* 1952, John Jay O'Connor III; three *s. Educ:* Stanford Univ. (BA 1950; LLB 1952). Legal appts in Calif and Frankfurt, 1952–57; in private practice, 1959–60; Asst Attorney-Gen., Arizona, 1965–69; Judge: Maricopa County Superior Ct, 1975–79; Arizona Ct of Appeals, 1979–81. Mem. Senate, Arizona, 1969–75 (majority leader, 1972–75). Director: Nat. Bank of Arizona, Phoenix, 1971–74; Blue Cross/Blue Shield, Arizona, 1975–79. Chm., Maricopa County Juvenile Detention Home, 1963–64; Pres., Heard Museum, Phoenix, 1968–74, 1976–81; Mem. Nat. Bd, Smithsonian Assocs, 1981–. Trustee, Stanford Univ., 1976–81. Hon. Bencher,

Gray's Inn, 1982. *Address:* Supreme Court Building, 1 First Street NE, Washington, DC 20543, USA.

O'CONNOR HOWE, Mrs Josephine Mary; HM Diplomatic Service, retired; *b* 25 March 1924; *d* of late Gerald Frank Claridge and late Dulcie Agnes Claridge (*née* Waldegrave); *m* 1947, John O'Connor Howe (decd); one *d.* *Educ:* Wychwood Sch., Oxford; Triangle Coll. (course in journalism). Inter-Allied Information Cttee, later, United Nations Information Office, 1942–45; Foreign Office: The Hague, 1945–46; Internat. News Service and freelance, 1946–50; FO, 1952; Counsellor, FCO, 1974–1979. Reader's Digest, 1979–83; Dir, Council for Arms Control, 1983–84; Exec. Editor, Inst. for the Study of Conflict, 1985–89; Freelance Editor specialising in internat. affairs, arms control, etc., 1985–. *Publication:* (ed) Armed Peace—the search for world security, 1984. *Recreations:* theatre, gardening, grandchildren. *Address:* Dering Cottage, Little Chart, Ashford, Kent TN27 0PT. *T:* (01233) 840328.

ODDIE, Bill; *see* Oddie, W.

ODDIE, His Honour Christopher Ripley; a Circuit Judge, 1974–94, sitting at Mayor's and City of London Court, 1989–94; *b* Derby, 24 Feb. 1929; *o s* of Dr and Mrs J. R. Oddie, Uttoxeter, Staffs; *m* 1957, Margaret Anne, *d* of Mr and Mrs J. W. Timmis; one *s* three *d.* *Educ:* Giggleswick Sch.; Oriel Coll., Oxford (MA). Called to Bar, Middle Temple, 1954, Oxford Circuit. Contested (L) Ludlow, Gen. Election, 1970. A Recorder of the Crown Court, 1972–74. Chm., County Court Rule Cttee, 1985–87 (Mem., 1981–87). Member: Judicial Studies Bd, 1989–91; Cttee, Council of Her Majesty's Circuit Judges, 1989–91. Mem. Council, St Mary's Hosp. Med. Sch., 1980–88. Gen. Editor, Butterworth's County Court Precedents and Pleadings, 1988–92. *Recreations:* reading, opera, walking. *Address:* 89 The Vineyard, Richmond, Surrey TW10 6AT. *T:* (020) 8940 4135; Lower Riddings, Woodside, Clun, Shropshire SY7 0JE. *Club:* Reform.

ODDIE, Prof. Guy Barrie, BArch; Robert Adam Professor of Architecture, 1968–82, now Emeritus, and Head of Department of Architecture, 1968–80, University of Edinburgh; *b* 1 Jan. 1922; *o s* of Edward Oddie and Eleanor Pinkney; *m* 1952, Mabel Mary Smith (*d* 1990); two step *d.* *Educ:* state schools in London and Co. Durham; King's Coll., Univ. of Durham (now Univ. of Newcastle upon Tyne). Local Defence Volunteer, later Home Guard, 1939–45 (Hon. Lieut). Demonstrator, Univ. of Newcastle upon Tyne, 1944–45; Asst, public offices, Glasgow and Coventry, 1945–47; Research Architect, Building Res. Stn, 1947–50; Sen. Lectr, Birmingham Sch. of Architecture, 1950–52; Develt Gp, Min. of Educn, 1952–58; Staff architect, UGC, 1958–63; Consultant to OECD, 1963–66; Dir, Laboratories Investigation Unit, DES, 1966–68. Sen. Advr to OECD Prog. on Educnl Bldg, 1972–84. Participant in and advocate for 1950's architectural movement led by school-designers and aimed at producing quality buildings on time, in the number needed and at a politically acceptable cost. *Publications:* School Building Resources and their Effective Use, 1966; Development and Economy in Educational Building, 1968; Industrialised Building for Schools, 1975; contrib. Architects Jl, Architectural Rev., RIBA Jl. *Recreations:* dry-fly fishing, writing light verse, company of friends. *Address:* 29 The Causeway, Edinburgh EH15 3QA.

ODDIE, William Edgar, (Bill); writer, actor and broadcaster; *b* 7 July 1941; *m* 1st, Jean Hart (marr. diss.); two *d*; 2nd, Laura Beaumont; one *d.* *Educ:* Halesowen Grammar Sch.; King Edward's Sch., Birmingham; Pembroke Coll., Cambridge (BA 1963; MA 1967). Mem. Council, RSPB. *Theatre* includes: writer and performer, Cambridge Circus (revue), Cambridge Footlights, transf. London, then NZ and Australia; performer: Tommy; Mikado, Coliseum, 1988; The Ghost Train, Lyric, Hammersmith, 1992; *TV* includes: joint writer: Doctor in the House; Doctor at Large; Astronauts; writer and actor: TW3; BBC3; The Goodies (eight series), 1970–81; presenter: Ask Oddie; wildlife programmes incl. Birding With Bill Oddie (three series); *Radio* includes: jt writer, I'm Sorry I'll Read That Again; presenter, Breakaway. *Publications:* Little Black Bird Book, 1982; Gone Birding, 1983; (jtly) Big Bird Race, 1983; (jtly) The Toilet Book, 1986; Bird Watching With Bill Oddie, 1988; Bird Watching for Under Tens; Bill Oddie's Colouring Guides, 1991–92; Follow That Bird!, 1994; (jtly) Bird in the Nest, 1995; (jtly) Birding With Bill Oddie, 1997; Bill Oddie's Gripping Yarns: tales of birds & birding, 2000; articles in jls. *Address:* c/o London Management, 2–4 Noel Street, W1V 3RB. *T:* (020) 7287 9000.

ODDIE, Dr William John Muir; Editor, Catholic Herald, since 1998; *b* 1 June 1939; *s* of John Male and Irene Oddie; *m* 1969, Cornelia; one *s* two *d.* *Educ:* Silcoates Sch., Yorks; Trinity Coll., Dublin (BA 1964; MA 1980); Leicester Univ. (PhD 1970); St Stephen's House, Oxford (MA Oxon 1981). Sec., Ancient Monuments Soc., 1970–72; ordained deacon, 1977, priest 1978; Asst Curate, Holy Trinity, Westbury on Trym, Bristol, 1978–80; Bp's Chaplain to Graduates, Oxford Univ., 1980–85; Librarian, Pusey House, Oxford, 1980–85; Fellow, St Cross Coll., Oxford, 1981–85; Rector, St Andrew's, Romford, 1985–87; received into RC Church, 1991; freelance journalist, Sunday Telegraph, Daily Telegraph, Daily Mail, Sunday Times, etc, 1987–98. *Publications:* Dickens and Carlyle: the question of influence, 1972; After the Deluge: essays towards the desecularisation of the Church, 1987; What will Happen to God? feminism and the reconstruction of Christian belief, 1989; The Crockford's File: Gareth Bennett and the death of the Anglican mind, 1989; The Roman Option: crisis and the realignment of English-speaking Christianity, 1996. *Recreations:* reading, music, travel, domestic pursuits. *Address:* 6 Sunningwell Road, Oxford OX1 4SX. *T:* (01865) 439473; (office) (0171) 558 3101. *Club:* Athenæum.

ODDSSON, Davíd, Hon. KBE; MP (Ind) Reykjavík, since 1991; Prime Minister of Iceland, since 1991; *b* 17 Jan. 1948; *s* of Oddur Ólafsson and Ingibjörg Kristín Lúdvíksdóttir; *m* 1970, Ástrídur Thorarensen; one *s.* *Educ:* Univ. of Iceland (grad. Lawyer). Reykjavík Theatre Co., 1970–72; Morgunbladid Daily, 1973–74; Almenna Bókafélagid Publishing House, 1975–76; Office Manager, 1976–78, Man. Dir. 1978–82, Reykjavík Health Fund; Mayor of Reykjavík, 1982–91. Hon. LLD Manitoba, 2000. Grand Cross, Order of Merit (Luxembourg). *Publications:* (trans.) Estonia: a study of imperialism, by Anders Küng, 1973; Róbert Elíasson Returns from Abroad (TV drama), 1977; A Policy of Independence, 1981; Stains on the White Collar (TV drama), 1981; Everything's Fine (TV drama), 1991; A Couple of Days without Gudny (short stories), 1997. *Recreations:* bridge, forestry, angling. *Address:* Prime Minister's Office, Stjórnarrádshúsinu, 150 Reykjavík, Iceland. *T:* 5609400.

ODDY, Andrew; *see* Oddy, W. A.

ODDY, Christine Margaret; freelance lecturer and consultant; *b* 20 Sept. 1955; *d* of Eric Lawson Oddy and Audrey Mary Oddy. *Educ:* Stoke Park Sch., Coventry; University Coll. London (LLB Hons); Licence Spéciale en droit européen, Inst. d'Etudes européennes, Brussels; Birkbeck Coll., London (MSc (Econ)). Stagiaire (grad. trainee) in EC, 1979–80; Articled Clerk, Clifford Turner, 1980–82; admitted Solicitor, 1982; Lectr in Law, City of London Poly., 1984–89. MEP (Lab) Midlands Central, 1989–94, Coventry and N Warwicks, 1994–99; European Parliament: Member: Legal Affairs Cttee, 1989–99; Social Affairs Cttee, 1989–99; Women's Rights Cttee, 1989–99; Central America Delegn, 1989. Sec., Anti-Racism Wkg Gp, 1989–99, and Treas., Eur. Parly Labour Pty, 1994–99. Member: RIIA, 1990; Law Soc., 1982 (Mem., Employment Law Cttee); ESU, 1987; Inst. for Employment Rights. FRSA 1992. *Recreations:* travel, wine, theatre, cinema. *Address:* 33 Longfellow Road, Coventry CV2 5HD. *T:* (024) 7645 6856.

ODDY, Revel, FSA; Keeper, Department of Art and Archaeology, Royal Scottish Museum, Edinburgh, 1974–83; *b* 11 April 1922; *s* of Sidney Oddy and Muriel Barnfather; *m* 1949, Ariadne Margaret, *d* of late Sir Andrew Gourlay Clow, KCSI, CIE; two *s* two *d.* *Educ:* Worksop Coll.; Pembroke Coll., Cambridge (MA). FSA 1982. Served War, Loyal Regt and King's African Rifles, 1941–46. Mod. langs master, Dr Challoner's Grammar Sch., Amersham, 1949; Res. Asst, V&A Mus., London, 1950–55; Asst Keeper, Royal Scottish Mus., Edinburgh, 1955–74. *Recreations:* mild gardening, reading. *Address:* 44 Findhorn Place, Edinburgh EH9 2NT. *T:* (0131) 667 5815. *Club:* Civil Service.

ODDY, (William) Andrew, DSc; FSA; Keeper of Conservation, British Museum, 1985–2002; *b* 6 Jan. 1942; *s* of late William T. Oddy and of Hilda F. Oddy (*née* Dalby); *m* 1965, Patricia Anne Whitaker; one *s* one *d.* *Educ:* Bradford Grammar Sch.; New Coll., Oxford (BA 1964; BSc 1965; MA 1969; DSc 1994). FSA 1973; FIIC 1974. Joined British Museum Research Lab., 1966, research into conservation and ancient technology; Head of Conservation, 1981. Member: Scientific Cttee, Internat. Congress on Deterioration and Preservation of Stone, 1976–91; Dept of Transport Adv. Cttee on Historic Wrecks, 1981–91; Council, Textile Conservation Centre, 1985–99; Cons. Cttee, Council for Care of Churches, 1985–90; Cons. Cttee, Cons. Unit, Mus. and Gall. Commn, 1987–92; Science-based Archaeol. Cttee, SERC, 1990–93; Council, Internat. Inst. for Conservation of Historic and Artistic Works, 1990–96; Fabric Adv. Cttee, Cathedral and Abbey Church of St Alban, 1991–. Trustee, Anna Plowden Trust, 1998–. Hon. Res. Fellow, UCL, 1992–2001. Lectures: Chester Beatty, RSA, 1982; Leventritt, Harvard Univ. Art Mus., 1996; Forbes Prize, Internat. Inst. for Conservation, 1996. Freeman, Goldsmiths' Co., 1986. *Publications:* editor: Problems in the Conservation of Waterlogged Wood, 1975; Aspects of Early Metallurgy, 1980; Scientific Studies in Numismatics, 1980; Metallurgy in Numismatics II, 1988; The Art of the Conservator, 1992; Restoration: is it acceptable?, 1994; joint editor: Conservation in Museums and Galleries, 1975; Metallurgy in Numismatics I, 1980; Aspects of Tibetan Metallurgy, 1981; A Survey of Numismatic Research 1978–1984, 1986; Metallurgy in Numismatics IV, 1998; Reversibility: does it exist?, 1999; Past Practice - Future Prospects, 2001; (jtly) Romanesque Metalwork: copper alloys and their decoration, 1986; papers in learned jls. *Recreation:* travel. *Address:* 6 Ashlyns Road, Berkhamsted, Herts HP4 3BN.

O'DEA, Sir Patrick Jerad, KCVO 1974; retired public servant, New Zealand; Extra Gentleman Usher to the Queen, since 1981; *b* 18 April 1918; 2nd *s* of late Patrick O'Dea; *m* 1945, Jean Mary, *d* of Hugh Mulholland; one *s* three *d.* *Educ:* St Paul's Coll. and Univ. of Otago, Dunedin, NZ; Victoria Univ., Wellington, NZ. Joined NZ Public Service, 1936; served in Agriculture Dept, 1936–47. Served War in Royal New Zealand Artillery of 2 NZEF, 1941–45. With Industries and Commerce Dept, 1947–49; subseq. served with Dept of Internal Affairs in various posts interrupted by 2 years' full-time study at Victoria Univ. of Wellington (DPA). Group Exec. Officer, Local Govt, 1950–61, Dep. Sec., 1964–67; Sec. for Internal Affairs, NZ, 1967–78; formerly Sec. for: Local Govt; Civil Defence; Sec. of Recreation and Sport; Clerk of the Writs; NZ Sec. to the Queen, 1969–78, reapptd 1981, for visit of Queen and Duke of Edinburgh to NZ. Nat. Co-ordinator and Chm., Duke of Edinburgh Award in NZ, 1975–90; Chm., Duke of Edinburgh NZ Foundn, 1988–92; Mem., Vicentian Foundn. *Publications:* several papers on local govt in New Zealand. *Recreations:* gardening, golf, bowls. *Address:* 8 Cranbrook Grove, Waikanae, Kapiti Coast, New Zealand. *T:* (4) 2931235. *Club:* Waikanae Golf.

ODELL, John William, (Jack), OBE 1969; Chairman, Lledo (London) Ltd, since 1982. Joint Vice-Chairman, Lesney Products & Co. Ltd, Diecasting Engineers, London E9, 1981–82 (Joint Managing Director, 1947–73; Deputy Chairman, 1973–81). *Address:* Lledo (London) Ltd, Woodhall Road, South Street, Ponders End, Enfield, Middx EN3 4ND.

O'DELL, Mrs June Patricia, OBE 1990; Chair, Probus Women's Housing Society Ltd, since 1998 (Member Board, 1993); *b* 9 June 1929; *d* of Leonard Vickery, RN and Myra Vickery; *m* 1951 (marr. diss. 1963); one *s* two *d.* *Educ:* Edgehill Girls College; Plymouth Technical College. Estate Agent. Dir, Eachdale Developments Ltd. Nat. Pres., Fedn of Business and Professional Women, 1983–85; Chm., Employment Cttee, Internat. Fedn of Business Professional Women, 1983–87; Dep. Chm., EOC, 1986–90; Member: Women's Nat. Commn, 1983–85; European Adv. Cttee for Equal Treatment between Women and Men, 1986–90; Authorised Conveyancing Practitioners Bd, 1991–95; Legal Aid Adv. Cttee, 1993–94. Non-exec. Dir, Aylesbury Vale Community Healthcare NHS Trust, 1991–98. FRSA 1986 (Mem. Council, 1992–97). *Recreations:* music, particularly opera and choral; writing, literature, the countryside, equestrian events. *Address:* Gable End, High Street, Great Missenden, Bucks HP16 9AA. *Club:* University Women's.

ODELL, Prof. Peter Randon; Professor Emeritus, Erasmus University, Rotterdam (Director, Centre for International Energy Studies, 1981–90); *b* 1 July 1930; *s* of late Frank James Odell and late Grace Edna Odell; *m* 1957, Jean Mary McKintosh; two *s* two *d.* *Educ:* County Grammar Sch., Coalville; Univ. of Birmingham (BA, PhD); Fletcher Sch. of Law and Diplomacy, Cambridge, Mass (AM). FInstPet 1973. RAF 1954–57. Economist, Shell International Petroleum Co., 1958–61; Lectr, LSE, 1961–65; Sen. Lectr, LSE, 1965–68; Prof. of Economic Geography, Erasmus Univ., 1968–81. Visiting Professor: LSE, 1983–; College of Europe, Bruges, 1983–90; Plymouth Univ., 1996–; Scholar in Residence, Rockefeller Centre, Bellagio, 1984; Killam Vis. Scholar, Univ. of Calgary, 1989; Vis. Scholar, Univ. of Cambridge, 1996–99. Stamp Meml Lectr, London Univ., 1975. Canadian Council Fellow, 1978. Adviser, Dept of Energy, 1977–78. Contested (Lib Dem) Suffolk, EP elecns, 1989. European Editor, Energy Jl, 1988–90. FRSA 1983; FRGS 1995. Internat. Assoc. for Energy Econs Prize, for outstanding contribns to energy econs and its literature, 1991; RSGS Centenary Medal, 1993. *T:* and *Fax:* An Economic Geography of Oil, 1963; Natural Gas in Western Europe, 1969; Oil and World Power, 1970, 8th edn 1986; (with D. A. Preston) Economies and Societies in Latin America, 1973, 2nd edn 1978; Energy: Needs and Resources, 1974, 2nd edn 1977; (with K. E. Rosing) The North Sea Oil Province, 1975; The West European Energy Economy: the case for self-sufficiency, 1976; (with K. E. Rosing) The Optimal Development of the North Sea Oilfields, 1976; (with L. Vallenilla) The Pressures of Oil: a strategy for economic revival, 1978; British Oil Policy: a Radical Alternative, 1980; (with K. E. Rosing) The Future of Oil, 1980–2080, 1980, 2nd edn 1983; (ed with J. Rees) The International Oil Industry: an interdisciplinary perspective, 1986; Global and Regional Energy Supplies: recent fictions and fallacies revisited, 1991; Europe's Energy: resources and choices, 1998; Fossil Fuel Resources in the 21st Century, 1999; Global Oil and Gas Issues, 2001; The Evolution of the European Energy Economy 1960–2000, 2001. *Address:* 22A Compton Road, N1 2PB. *T:* (020) 7359 8199; *e-mail:* peter@odell.u-net.com.

ODELL, Sir Stanley (John), Kt 1986; Chairman, Bedfordshire and Luton Community Health Care NHS Trust, since 1999; *b* 20 Nov. 1929; *s* of George Frederick Odell and

Florence May Odell; *m* 1952, Eileen Grace Stuart; four *d. Educ:* Bedford Modern School. Chairman: Mid Beds Young Conservatives, 1953–59; Mid Beds Cons. Assoc., 1964–69 (Pres., 1991–); Beds Cons. European Constituency Council, 1979; E of England Provincial Council, Cons. Party, 1983–86 (Pres., 1991–93); Nat. Union of Cons. and Unionist Assocs, 1989–90 (Vice Chm., 1986–89). Chm., S Beds Community Health Care NHS Trust, 1994–99. Chm., Anglo-American Cttee, RAF Chicksands, 1987–96. Mem. Ct, Luton Univ., 1994–. Churchwarden, Campton Parish Church, 1993–. *Recreations:* politics, shooting. *Address:* Woodhall Farm, Campton, Shefford, Beds SG17 5PB. *T:* (01462) 813230. *Club:* Farmers'.

ODGERS, Sir Graeme (David William), Kt 1997; Chairman, Locate in Kent, since 1998; *b* 10 March 1934; *s* of late William Arthur Odgers and Elizabeth Minty (*née* Rennie); *m* 1957, Diana Patricia Berge; one *s* two *d* (and one *d* decd). *Educ:* St John's Coll., Johannesburg; Gonville and Caius Coll., Cambridge (Mech. Scis Tripos); Harvard Business Sch. (MBA, Baker Scholar). Investment Officer, Internat. Finance Corp., Washington DC, 1959–62; Management Consultant, Urwick Orr and Partners Ltd, 1962–64; Investment Executive, Hambros Bank Ltd, 1964–65; Director: Keith Shipton and Co. Ltd, 1965–72; C. T. Bowring (Insurance) Holdings Ltd, 1972–74; Chm., Odgers and Co. Ltd (Management Consultants), 1970–74; Dir, Industrial Develt Unit, DoI, 1974–77; Assoc. Dir (Finance), General Electric Co., 1977–78; Gp Finance Dir, 1979–86, Gp Man. Dir, 1983–86, Tarmac; British Telecommunications: pt-time Mem. Bd, 1983–86; Govt Dir, 1984–86; Dep. Chm. and Chief Finance Officer, 1986–87; Gp Man. Dir, 1987–90; Chief Exec., Alfred McAlpine plc, 1990–93; Chm., Monopolies and Mergers Commn, 1993–97. Non-executive Director: Dalgety, 1987–93; Nat. & Provincial Bldg Soc., 1990–93; Scottish and Southern Energy, 1998–. Mem., Kent Ambassadors, 1998–. *Recreation:* golf. *Address:* 5 The Coach House, Springwood Park, Tonbridge, Kent TN11 9LZ. *Clubs:* Carlton; Wildernesse (Sevenoaks).

ODGERS, Paul Randell, CB 1970; MBE (mil.) 1945; TD 1949; Deputy Secretary, Department of Education and Science, 1971–75; *b* 30 July 1915; *e s* of late Dr P. N. B. Odgers and Mrs M. A. Odgers (*née* Higgins); *m* 1944, Diana, *d* of late R. E. F. Fawkes, CBE; one *s* one *d. Educ:* Rugby; New Coll., Oxford. Entered CS, Board of Education, 1937. Army Service, UK, Malta, Sicily, Italy, NW Europe, 1939–45 (despatches three times). Asst Secretary: Min. of Educn, 1948; Cabinet Office, 1956; Under-Secretary: Min. of Educn, 1958; Office of First Secretary of State, 1967; Office of Lord President of the Council, 1968; Office of Sec. of State for Social Services, 1968; Cabinet Office, 1970. Hon. Vice-Pres., Soc. for Promotion of Roman Studies; Mem. Council, GPDST, 1976–89. *Address:* Stone Walls, Aston Road, Haddenham, Bucks HP17 8AF. *T:* (01844) 291830. *Club:* Oxford and Cambridge.

See also C. D. Compston.

ODLING, Thomas George, CB 1974; *b* 18 Sept. 1911; *yr s* of late Major W. A. Odling, Paxford, Glos and late Mary Bennett Odling (*née* Case); *m* 1st, Camilla Haldane Paterson (marr. diss.); two *s*; 2nd, Hilary Katharine, *d* of late W. J. Palgrave-Ker, Lilliput, Dorset. *Educ:* Temple Grove; Rugby Sch.; New Coll., Oxford (MA). House of Commons: Asst Clerk, 1935; Clerk of Private Bills, Examr of Petitions for Private Bills and Taxing Officer, 1961–73; Clerk of Select Cttee on Parly Comr for Admin, 1969–73; Clerk of Committees, 1974–76, retired 1976. Temp. attached to Consultative Assembly of Council of Europe during 1949 and later sessions. *Recreations:* music, gardening. *Address:* Paxford, Campden, Glos GL55 6XQ. *Clubs:* Athenæum, MCC.

ODLING-SMEE, John Charles; Director, European II Department, International Monetary Fund, since 1992; *b* 13 April 1943; *s* of late Rev. Charles William Odling-Smee and Katharine Hamilton Odling-Smee (*née* Aitchison); *m* 1996, Carmela Veneroso. *Educ:* Durham School; St John's College, Cambridge. BA Cantab 1964, MA Oxon 1966. Junior Research Officer, Dept of Applied Economics, Cambridge, 1964–65; Asst Research Officer, Inst. of Economics and Statistics, Oxford, 1965–66; Fellow in Economics, Oriel College, Oxford, 1966–70; Research Officer, Inst. of Economics and Statistics, Oxford, 1968–71 and 1972–73; Economic Research Officer, Govt of Ghana, 1971–72; Senior Research Officer, Centre for Urban Economics, LSE, 1973–75; Economic Adviser, Central Policy Review Staff, Cabinet Office, 1975–77; Senior Economic Adviser, HM Treasury, 1977–80; Senior Economist, IMF, 1981–82; Under-Sec., HM Treasury, 1982–89; Dep. Chief Economic Advr, HM Treasury, 1989–90; Sen. Advr, IMF, 1990–91. *Publications:* (with A. Grey and N. P. Hepworth) Housing Rents, Costs and Subsidies, 1978, 2nd edn 1981; (with R. C. O. Matthews and C. H. Feinstein) British Economic Growth 1856–1973, 1982; articles in books and learned jls. *Address:* 3506 Garfield Street NW, Washington, DC 20007, USA. *T:* (202) 6238308.

ODONE, Cristina; Deputy Editor, The New Statesman, since 1998; *b* 11 Nov. 1960; *d* of Augusto and Ulla Odone. *Educ:* Worcester Coll., Oxford (MA). Freelance journalist, 1983–84; journalist: Catholic Herald, 1985–86; The Times diary, 1987; Vice-Pres., Odone Associates, Washington, 1988–92; Editor, The Catholic Herald, 1992–96; television reviewer, The Daily Telegraph, 1996–98. Mem. Adv. Bd, Citizens' Service Scheme, 1995–. FRSA 1996. *Publications:* novels: The Shrine, 1996; A Perfect Wife, 1997. *Recreations:* writing, reading, walking, travelling. *Address:* Capel & Land, 29 Wardour Street, W1D 6PS. *T:* (020) 7734 2414.

O'DONNELL, Augustine Thomas, CB 1994; Head of Government Economic Service, since 1998, and Managing Director, Macroeconomic Policy and International Finance, since 2000, HM Treasury; *b* 1 Oct. 1952; *s* of Helen O'Donnell (*née* McClean) and James O'Donnell; *m* 1979, Melanie Joan Elizabeth Timmis; one *d. Educ:* Univ. of Warwick (BA Hons); Nuffield Coll., Oxford (MPhil). Lectr, Dept of Political Economy, Univ. of Glasgow, 1974–79; Economist, HM Treasury, 1979–85; First Sec. (Econ.), British Embassy, Washington, 1985–88; Sen. Economic Adviser, 1988–89, Press Sec., 1989–90, HM Treasury; Press Sec. to Prime Minister, 1990–94; Under Sec., Monetary Gp, HM Treasury, 1994–95; Dep. Dir, Macroeconomic Policy and Prospects Directorate, HM Treasury, 1995–96; Minister (Economic), British Embassy, Washington, and UK Exec. Dir, IMF and World Bank, 1997–98; Dir, Macroeconomic Policy and Prospects Directorate, HM Treasury, 1998–2000. *Publications:* articles in economic jls. *Recreations:* football, cricket, golf. *Address:* HM Treasury, Parliament Street, SW1P 3AG. *Club:* Old Salesians FC.

O'DONNELL, Prof. Barry, FRCS, FRCSI; President, Royal College of Surgeons of Ireland, 1998–2000; Professor of Paediatric Surgery, Royal College of Surgeons in Ireland, 1986–93, now Professor Emeritus; Consultant Paediatric Surgeon, Our Lady's Hospital for Sick Children, Dublin, 1957–93; *b* 6 Sept. 1926; *e s* of Michael J. O'Donnell and Kathleen O'Donnell (*née* Barry); *m* 1959, Mary Leydon, BA, BComm, BL, *d* of John Leydon, LLD, KCSG; three *s* one *d. Educ:* Christian Brothers College, Cork; Castleknock College, Dublin; University College, Cork (MB Hons 1949). MCh NUI, 1954. FRCS 1953, FRCSI 1953; FRCSEd *ad hominem* 1992; FRCPSGlas *qua surgeon* 1999. Ainsworth Travelling Scholar, Boston (Lahey Clinic and Boston Floating Hosp., 1955–56); Sen. Registrar, Hosp. for Sick Children, London, 1956–57. Vis. Prof. at many US univs, incl. Harvard, Columbia, Johns Hopkins, Michigan, Pennsylvania; Hunterian Prof., RCS, 1986. Jt Pres., British, Canadian and Irish Med. Assocs, 1976–77; President: British Assoc. of Paediatric Surgeons, 1980–82; Surgical Sect., Royal Acad. of Medicine of Ireland, 1990–92; Mem. Council, RCSI, 1972–77 and 1993–96 (Vice Pres., 1996–98); Chm., Jl Cttee, BMA, 1982–88. Dir, West Deutsche Landesbank, 1990–96. Hon. Fellow: Amer. Acad. of Pediatrics, 1974; New England Surgical Assoc., 1996; Amer. Surgical Assoc., 1998; Coll. of Medicine of S Africa, 2001; Hon. FACS 1999; Hon. Mem., Boston Surgical Soc., 2000. People of the Year Award, New Ireland Insce Co., 1984; Denis Browne Gold Medal, British Assoc. of Paediatric Surgeons, 1989. *Publications:* Essentials of Paediatric Surgery, 1961, 4th edn 1992; Abdominal Pain in Children, 1985; (ed jtly) Paediatric Urology, 3rd edn 1997. *Recreations:* telling old stories to new audiences, golf. *Address:* 28 Merlyn Road, Ballsbridge, Dublin 4, Ireland. *T:* and *Fax:* 2694000. *Clubs:* Royal Ocean Racing; Royal Irish Yacht; Portmarnock Golf.

O'DONNELL, Christopher John; Chief Executive, Smith & Nephew plc, since 1997; *b* 30 Oct. 1946; *s* of Anthony John O'Donnell and Joan Millicent O'Donnell; *m* 1971, Maria Antonia Wallis; three *s* one *d. Educ:* Imperial Coll., London (BSc Eng Hons); London Business Sch. (MSc Econ). Man. Dir, Vickers Ltd Medical Engineering, 1974–79; Area Vice Pres., Europe, C. R. Bard, Inc., 1979–88; Man. Dir, Smith & Nephew Medical Ltd, 1988–93; Gp Dir, Smith & Nephew plc, 1993–97. *Recreations:* tennis, golf. *Address:* Swanland, E Yorks.

O'DONNELL, James Anthony, FRCO, FRSCM; Organist and Master of the Choristers, Westminster Abbey, since 2000; *b* 15 Aug. 1961; *s* of Dr James Joseph Gerard O'Donnell and Dr Gillian Anne O'Donnell (*née* Moody). *Educ:* Westcliff High Sch., Essex; Jesus Coll., Cambridge (Organ Scholar and Open Scholar in Music; BA 1982, MA). Westminster Cathedral: Asst Master of Music, 1982–88; Master of Music, 1988–99. Lectr in Church Music Studies, 1992–, Prof. of Organ, 1997–, RAM. FRCO 1983 (Performer of the Year, 1987; Mem. Council, 1989–); FRSCM 2000. Hon. FGCM 2001. Has made many recordings with Westminster Cathedral Choir: Gramophone Record of the Year and Best Choral Recording awards, 1998 for masses by Martin and Pizzetti; Royal Philharmonic Soc. award, 1999. KCSG 1999. Hon. RAM 2001. *Recreations:* opera, food, wine. *Address:* c/o The Chapter Office, 20 Dean's Yard, Westminster Abbey, SW1P 3PA. *Club:* Athenæum.

See also D. K. Womersley.

O'DONNELL, Dr Michael; author and broadcaster; *b* 20 Oct. 1928; *o s* of late James Michael O'Donnell and Nora (*née* O'Sullivan); *m* 1953, Catherine Dorrington Ward; one *s* two *d. Educ:* Stonyhurst; Trinity Hall, Cambridge (Lane Harrington Schol.); St Thomas's Hosp. Med. Sch., London (MB, BChir). FRCGP 1990. Editor, Cambridge Writing, 1948; Scriptwriter, BBC Radio, 1949–52. General Medical Practitioner, 1954–64. Editor, World Medicine, 1966–82. Member: GMC, 1971–97 (Chm., Professional Standards Cttee, 1995–97); Longman Editorial Adv. Bd, 1978–82. Mem., Alpha Omega Alpha Honor Med. Soc., 1995–. Inaugural lecture, Green Coll., Oxford, 1981. John Rowan Wilson Award, World Medical Journalists Assoc., 1982; John Snow Medal, Assoc. of Anaesthetists of GB and Ireland, 1984. Scientific Adviser: O Lucky Man (film), 1972; Inside Medicine (BBC TV), 1974; Don't Ask Me (Yorkshire TV), 1977; Don't Just Sit There (Yorkshire TV), 1979–80; Where There's Life (Yorkshire TV), 1981–83. *Television plays:* Suggestion of Sabotage, 1963; Dangerous Reunion, 1964; Resolution, 1964; *television documentaries:* You'll Never Believe It, 1962; Cross Your Heart and Hope to Live, 1975; The Presidential Race, 1976; From Europe to the Coast, 1976; Did History Really Happen?, 1977, 1998; Chasing the Dragon, 1979; Second Opinion, 1980; Judgement on Las Vegas, 1981; Is Your Brain Really Necessary, 1982; Plague of Hearts, 1983; Medical Express, 1984; Can You Avoid Cancer?, 1984; O'Donnell Investigates... booze, 1985; O'Donnell Investigates ... food, 1985; O'Donnell Investigates ... the food business, 1986; O'Donnell Investigates ... age, 1988; Health, Wealth and Happiness, 1989; What is this thing called health, 1990; The Skin Trade, 1991; Whose Blue Genes?, 1992; Out of Town, Out of Mind, 1993; Beyond belief, 1994; Way beyond belief, 1995; Dads, 1995; Still Beyond Belief, 1996; New Age Superstition, 1999; *radio:* contributor to Stop the Week (BBC), 1976–92; Chm., My Word (BBC), 1983–92; Presenter: Relative Values (BBC), 1987–97; The Bhamjee Beat, 1995; Utopia and Other Destinations, 1996–98; Murder, Magic and Medicine, 1998–. Medical Journalists Assoc. Award, 1973, 1982, 1990, 1996; British Science Writers' Award, 1979. *Publications:* Cambridge Anthology, 1952; The Europe We Want, 1971; My Medical School, 1978; The Devil's Prison, 1982; Doctor! Doctor! an insider's guide to the games doctors play, 1986; The Long Walk Home, 1988; Dr Michael O'Donnell's Executive Health Guide, 1988; A Sceptic's Medical Dictionary, 1997; contrib. Punch, New Scientist, The Listener, The Times, The Guardian, Daily Telegraph, Daily Mail. *Recreations:* walking, listening to music, loitering (with and without intent). *Address:* Handon Cottage, Markwick Lane, Loxhill, Godalming, Surrey GU8 4BD. *T:* (01483) 208295. *Club:* Garrick.

O'DONNELL, Rt Hon. Turlough; PC 1979; Lord Justice of Appeal, Supreme Court of Northern Ireland, 1979–89; *b* 5 Aug. 1924; *e s* of Charles and Eileen O'Donnell; *m* 1954, Eileen McKinley; two *s* two *d. Educ:* Abbey Grammar Sch., Newry; Queen's Univ., Belfast (LLB). Called to Bar of Northern Ireland, 1947; called to Inner Bar, 1964; Puisne Judge, NI, 1971–79. Chairman: NI Bar Council, 1970–71, Council of Legal Educn, NI, 1980–90. *Recreations:* golf, folk music. *Address:* c/o Royal Courts of Justice (Ulster), Belfast BT1 3JF.

O'DONOGHUE, Denise, OBE 1999; Managing Director, Hat Trick Productions, since 1986; *b* 13 April 1955; *d* of late Micheal O'Donoghue and Maura O'Donoghue; *m* 1987, James Mulville, *qv* (marr. diss. 1998). *Educ:* St Dominic's Girls' Sch.; York Univ. (BA Hons). Coopers & Lybrand, 1979–81; Dir, IPPA, 1981–83; Holmes Associates, 1983–86; Man. Dir, Hat Trick Films, 1995–. FRTS 1998; CIMgt 1998. Awards from RTS, BAFTA, and Press Guild; Emmy Awards. *Address:* Hat Trick Productions, 10 Livonia Street, W1V 8AF. *T:* (020) 7434 2451.

O'DONOGHUE, Lt-Gen. Kevin, CBE 1996; UK Military Representative to NATO and the European Union, since 2001; *b* 9 Dec. 1947; *s* of Phillip James O'Donoghue and Winifred Mary O'Donoghue; *m* 1973, Jean Monkman; three *d. Educ:* Eastbourne Coll.; UMIST (BSc 1st Cl. Hons). Commnd RE, 1969; Instructor, RMA Sandhurst, 1976; Staff Coll., Canada, 1978; Mil. Ops, MoD, 1979; MA to CGS, 1980; OC 4 Field Sqdn, 1982; Directing Staff, Staff Coll., Camberley, 1984; Dep. ACOS, HQ UKLF, 1988; Higher Comd and Staff Course, 1990; Comdr Corps RE, 1 (BR) Corps, 1990; Comd Engr, ACE Rapid Reaction Corps, 1992; NATO Defence Coll., 1993; Dir, Staff Ops, SHAPE, 1993; COS HQ QMG, 1996–99; ACGS, 1999–2001. *Recreations:* military history, furniture restoration, gardening. *Address:* Royal Bank of Scotland, Holt's, Farnborough, Hants GU14 7NR. *Club:* National Liberal.

O'DONOGHUE, His Honour Michael; a Circuit Judge, 1982–94; *b* 10 June 1929; *s* of late Dr James O'Donoghue, MB, ChB and Vera O'Donoghue (*née* Cox). *Educ:* Rhyl Grammar School; Univ. of Liverpool. LLB (Hons) 1950. Called to the Bar, Gray's Inn, 1951; National Service as Flying Officer, RAF, 1951–53; practised at the Chancery Bar, 1954–82; Lectr in Law (part time), Univ. of Liverpool, 1966–82. Mem. (part-time), Lands

Tribunal, 1990–94. *Recreations:* music, sailing, photography. *Clubs:* Athenæum (Liverpool); Royal Welsh Yacht (Caernarfon) (Commodore, 1980–82; Pres., 1994–).

O'DONOGHUE, Rt Rev. Patrick; *see* Lancaster, Bishop of, (RC).

O'DONOGHUE, Philip Nicholas, CBiol, FIBiol; General Secretary, Institute of Biology, 1982–89; *b* 9 Oct. 1929; *s* of Terence Frederick O'Donoghue and Ellen Mary (*née* Haynes); *m* 1955, Veronica Florence Campbell; two *d. Educ:* East Barnet Grammar Sch.; Univ. of Nottingham (BSc; MSc 1959). FIBiol 1975. Experimental Officer, ARC's Field Stn, Compton, 1952–55 and Inst. of Animal Physiology, Babraham, 1955–61; Scientific Officer, National Inst. for Res. in Dairying, Shinfield, 1962–66; Lectr in Exptl Vet. Science and later Sen. Lectr in Lab. Animal Science, Royal Postgrad. Med. Sch., Univ. of London, 1966–82. Hume Meml Lect., UFAW, 1990. Vice-Pres., Inst. of Animal Technicians, 1969–2001; Hon. Sec., Inst. of Biology, 1972–76; Member: TEC, 1973–79 (Chm., Life Sciences Cttee, 1973–80); Council, Section of Comparative Medicine, RSM, 1983–96 (Pres., 1985–86); President: Lab. Animal Sci. Assoc., 1989–91; Fedn of European Lab. Animal Sci. Assocs, 1990–95. Editor, Laboratory Animals, 1967–82. Lab. Animal Sci. Assoc. Award, 1994. *Publications:* editor of books and author of articles chiefly on the law relating to and the effective use and proper care of laboratory animals. *Recreations:* music, local history, talking, limited gardening. *Address:* 21 Holyrood Road, New Barnet, Herts EN5 1DQ. *T:* (020) 8449 3692. *Clubs:* Athenæum, Royal Society of Medicine.

O'DONOVAN, Kathleen Anne; Finance Director, Invensys plc (formerly BTR, then BTR Siebe), since 1991; *b* Warwicks, 23 May 1957. *Educ:* University Coll. London (BSc Econs). Joined Turquands Barton Mayhew, subseq. Ernst & Young, 1975; Partner, 1989–91. Non-exec. Dir, EMI Gp, 1997–; Mem. Court, Bank of England, 1999–. *Address:* Invensys plc, Carlisle Place, SW1P 1BX.

O'DONOVAN, Rev. Canon Oliver Michael Timothy, DPhil; FBA 2000; Regius Professor of Moral and Pastoral Theology, University of Oxford, since 1982; Canon of Christ Church, Oxford, since 1982; *b* 28 June 1945; *s* of Michael and Joan M. O'Donovan; *m* 1978, Joan Elizabeth Lockwood; two *s. Educ:* University Coll. Sch., Hampstead; Balliol Coll., Oxford (MA, DPhil); Wycliffe Hall, Oxford; Princeton Univ. Ordained deacon 1972, priest 1973, dio. of Oxford. Tutor, Wycliffe Hall, Oxford, 1972–77; Prof. of Systematic Theology, Wycliffe Coll., Toronto, 1977–82. McCarthy Vis. Prof., Gregorian Univ., Rome, 2001. Member: C of E Bd for Social Responsibility, 1976–77, 1982–85; ARCIC, 1985–90; Anglican-Orthodox Jt Doctrinal Discussions, 1982–84. Pres., Soc. for the Study of Christian Ethics, 1997–2000. Hulsean Lectr, Cambridge Univ., 1993–94. *Publications:* The Problem of Self-Love in Saint Augustine, 1980; Begotten or Made?, 1984; Resurrection and Moral Order, 1986; On the Thirty Nine Articles, 1986; Peace and Certainty, 1989; The Desire of the Nations, 1996; (with Joan Lockwood O'Donovan) From Irenaeus to Grotius, 1999; contrib. Jl of Theol Studies, Jl of Religious Ethics, Ethique and Studies in Christian Ethics. *Address:* Christ Church, Oxford OX1 1DP.

O'DOWD, Sir David (Joseph), Kt 1999; CBE 1995; QPM 1988; HM Chief Inspector of Constabulary, since 1996; *b* 20 Feb. 1942; *s* of late Michael Joseph O'Dowd and Helen (*née* Merrin); *m* 1963, Carole Ann Watson; one *s* one *d. Educ:* Gartree High Sch., Oadby, Leics; Univ. of Leicester (Dip. Social Studies); Open Univ. (BA); Univ. of Aston (MSc); FBI Nat. Acad., USA. Sgt, Inspector and Chief Inspector, CID, Leicester City Police, 1961–77; Supt, W Midlands Police, Coventry and Birmingham, 1977–84; Hd, Traffic Policing, Dir, Complaints and Discipline Investigation Bureau and Hd, Strategic Planning and Policy Analysis Unit, Metropolitan Police, 1984–86; Chief Constable, Northants Police, 1986–93; HM Inspector of Constabulary, 1993–96. British Chief Constables' Rep., Nat. Exec. Inst., FBI Acad., Washington, 1988. Dir, police extended interview scheme, 1992–93. Vis. Teaching Fellow, Mgt Centre, Univ. of Aston, Birmingham, 1988. Fellow, Nene Coll., Northants, 1993. CIMgt 1988. OStJ 1997. *Recreations:* golf, gardening. *Address:* Home Office, Queen Anne's Gate, SW1H 9AT. *Club:* Northamptonshire County Golf (Church Brampton, Northants).

O'DRISCOLL, Most Rev. Percival Richard; Archbishop of Huron and Metropolitan of Ontario, 1993–2000; Bishop of Huron, 1990–2000; *b* 4 Oct. 1938; *s* of T. J. O'Driscoll and Annie O'Driscoll (*née* Copley); *m* 1965, Suzanne Gertrude Savignac; one *s* one *d. Educ:* Bishop's Univ., Lennoxville, Quebec (BA, STB); Huron Coll., London, Ont. (DD). Ordained deacon 1964, priest 1966; Assistant Curate: St Matthias, Ottawa, 1965–67; St John Evan, Kitchener, 1967–70; Religious Educn Dir, St Paul's Cathedral and Bishop Cronyn Memorial, London, 1970; Rector: St Michael & All Angels, London, 1970–75; St Batholomew's, Sarnia, 1975–80; Rector, St Paul's Cathedral, and Dean of Huron, 1980–87; Suffragan Bishop of Huron, 1987; Coadjutor Bishop, 1989. *Recreations:* camping, hiking, photography. *Address:* c/o One London Place, Suite 903, 255 Queens Avenue, London, ON N6A 5R8, Canada. *T:* (519) 4330299, *Fax:* (519) 6734151. *Club:* London (Ontario).

ÖE, Kenzaburo; Japanese writer; *b* 31 Jan. 1935; *m* 1960, Yukari Itami; two *s* one *d. Educ:* Tokyo Univ. (BA French Lit. 1959). Visited Russia and Western Europe to research and write series of essays on Youth in the West, 1961. Shinchosa Lit. Prize, 1964; Tanizaka Prize, 1967; Nobel Prize for Literature, 1994. *Publications* include: The Catch, 1958 (Akutagawa Prize); Nip the Buds, Shoot the Kids, 1958; Our Age, 1959; Screams, 1962; The Perverts, 1963; Hiroshima Notes, 1963; Adventures in Daily Life, 1964; A Personal Matter, 1964; The Silent Cry (original title, Football in the First Year of the Man'en Era), 1967; Teach us to Outgrow our Madness: four short novels, 1978; (ed) Fire from the Ashes: short stories about Hiroshima and Nagasaki, 1985; The Treatment Tower, 1990; Japan, the Ambiguous and Myself (lectures), 1995; A Quiet Life, 1998. *Address:* Marion Boyars Publishers Ltd, 24 Lacy Road, SW15 1NL; 585 Seijo-Machi, Setagaya-Ku, Tokyo, Japan.

OEHLERS, Maj.-Gen. Gordon Richard, CB 1987; Director, Corps of Commissionaires, 1994–99; *b* 19 April 1933; *s* of late Dr Roderic Clarke Oehlers and Hazel Ethne Oehlers (*née* Van Geyzel); *m* 1956, Doreen, (Rosie), Gallant; one *s* one *d. Educ:* St Andrews School, Singapore. CEng, FIEE. Commissioned Royal Corps of Signals, 1958; UK and Middle East, 1958–64; Adjutant, 4th Div. Signals Regt, 1964–66; Instructor, School of Signals, 1966–68; OC 7th Armd Bde HQ and Signals Sqdn, 1968–70; GSO2 (Weapons), 1970–72; CO 7th Signal Regt, 1973–76; Commander Corps Royal Signals, 1st (British) Corps, 1977–79; Dir, Op. Requirements 4 (Army), 1979–84; ACDS (Comd Control, Communications and Inf. Systems), 1984–87. Dir of Security and Investigation, British Telecom, 1987–94. Col Comdt, RCS, 1987–93; Hon. Col 31st (Greater London) Signal Regt (Volunteers), 1988–94. Chm., Royal Signals Instn, 1990–93. Pres., British Wireless Dinner Club, 1986–87. *Recreations:* interested in all games esp. badminton (Captain Warwicks County Badminton Team, 1954–56), lawn tennis (Chm., Army Lawn Tennis Assoc., 1980–86), golf. *Address:* c/o National Westminster Bank, 4 High Street, Petersfield, Hants GU32 3JF. *Club:* Liphook Golf (Captain, 1998–99).

OESTERHELT, Dr Jürgen; Ambassador of Germany to the Holy See, since 1997; *b* 19 Aug. 1935; *s* of Dr Egon Oesterhelt and Trude (*née* Pfohl); *m* 1964, Katharina Galeiski; one *s* one *d. Educ:* Munich Univ. (LLD 1959); State Bar Exam. 1962; Columbia Univ., NY (Master of Comparative Law 1963). Internat. lawyer in Paris, 1963–64; joined German Diplomatic Service, 1964; Moscow, 1965–66; UN, NY, 1967–71; Sofia, 1971–74; German Foreign Office, 1974–77; Athens, 1977–80; Foreign Office: Hd of Div., Legal Dept, 1980–85; Dir, Political Dept, 1985–86; Dir Gen., Legal Dept and Legal Advr to Foreign Minister, 1986–92; Ambassador to Turkey, 1992–95; Ambassador to the UK, 1995–97. Commander's Cross: Order of Merit (Germany), 1997 (Cross, 1988); Order of Phoenix (Greece), 1982; Order of White Rose (Finland), 1989; Grand Cross, Order of Merit (Austria), 1990. *Recreations:* sport (ski-ing, tennis), music. *Address:* German Embassy, Via di Villa Sacchetti 4-6, 00197 Rome, Italy.

OESTREICHER, Rev. Canon Paul; Director of the International Ministry of Coventry Cathedral, 1986–97; Canon Residentiary of Coventry Cathedral, 1986–97, now Canon Emeritus; Hon. Consultant in International Ministry, since 1997; Member of the Society of Friends (Quakers), since 1982; journalist; *b* Germany, 29 Sept. 1931; *s* of Paul Oestreicher and Emma (*née* Schnaus); *m* 1958, Lore Feind (*d* 2000); one *s* two *d* (and one adopted *s* decd). *Educ:* King's High Sch., Dunedin; Otago and Victoria Univs, NZ; Lincoln Theol College. BA Mod. Langs Otago 1953; MA Hons Polit. Sci. Victoria 1955. Ordained 1959. Fled to NZ with refugee parents, 1939; Editor, Critic (Otago Univ. newspaper), 1952–53; subseq. free-lance journalist and broadcaster; returned to Europe, 1955. Humboldt Res. Fellow, Bonn Univ., 1955–56, Free Univ. of Berlin, 1992–93; fraternal worker with German Lutheran Church at Rüsselsheim, trng in problems of industrial soc. (Opel, Gen. Motors), 1958–59; Curate, Dalston, E London, 1959–61; Producer, Relig. Dept, BBC Radio, 1961–64; Assoc. Sec., Dept of Internat. Affairs, Brit. Council of Churches with special resp. for East-West Relations, 1964–69; Vicar, Church of the Ascension, Blackheath, 1968–81; Asst Gen. Sec. and Sec. for Internat. Affairs, BCC, 1981–86; Dir of (Lay) Trng, Dio. Southwark, 1969–72; Hon. Chaplain to Bp of Southwark, 1975–81; Public Preacher in Dio. Southwark, 1981–86; Hon. Canon of Southwark Cathedral, 1978–83, Canon Emeritus 1983–86. Member: Gen. Synod of C of E, 1970–86, 1996–97; Internat. Affairs Cttee, C of E, 1965–2001. Member: Brit. Council of Churches working parties on Southern Africa and Eastern Europe; Anglican Pacifist Fellowship, 1960– (Counsellor, 1998–); Exec. Cttee, Christian Peace Conf., Prague, 1964–68; Exec. Mem., Christian Concern for Southern Africa, 1978–81; Chm. of Trustees, Christian Inst. (of Southern Africa) Fund, 1984–95; Chairman: British Section, Amnesty International, 1974–79; Christians Aware, 1999–2000. Mem. Council, Keston Coll. (Centre for the Study of Religion and Communism), 1976–82. Vice-Chm., Campaign for Nuclear Disarmament, 1980–81, Vice-Pres. 1983–; Mem. Alternative Defence Commn, 1981–87; Vice-Chm., Ecumenical Commn for Church and Society in W Europe (Brussels), 1982–86. Trustee, Dresden Trust, 1993–. Shelley Lectr, Radio NZ, 1987. Freeman, Meiningen, Germany, 1995. Hon. DLitt Coventry Polytechnic, 1991. Prize for Promotion of European Unity, Wartburg Foundn, 1997. Order of Merit, 1st Cl. (Germany), 1995. *Publications:* (ed English edn) Helmut Gollwitzer, The Demands of Freedom, 1965; (trans.) H. J. Schultz, Conversion to the World, 1967; (ed, with J. Klugmann) What Kind of Revolution: A Christian-Communist Dialogue, 1968; (ed) The Christian Marxist Dialogue, 1969; (jtly) The Church and the Bomb, 1983; The Double Cross, 1986. *Address:* 20 Styvechale Avenue, Coventry CV5 6DX. *T:* and *Fax:* (024) 7667 3704.

O'FARRELL, Declan Gerard, CBE 2000; FCCA; Chief Executive, Metroline plc, since 1994; *b* 10 Feb. 1949; *s* of Bartholomew and Mary Carmel O'Farrell; *m* 1971, Jennie; one *s* three *d. Educ:* Finchley Catholic Grammar Sch. FCCA 1973. With British Tissues, 1967–81 (mgt trainee to Gp Mgt Accountant); financial analyst, Express Dairies, 1981; various financial posts with Express Foods Gp (Financial Controller, Distribn Div., until 1986); joined LT bus operations, 1986; Man. Dir, Metroline (new bus co. subsid.), 1989–94. Dir, NW London TEC, 1990–2001 (Chm., 1993–96); Founder Mem., London TEC Council. Chm., Business Link London, 1997–2001. CIMgt; FRSA. *Recreations:* gardening, golf.

O'FERRALL, Very Rev. Basil Arthur, CB 1979; MA; Dean of Jersey, and Rector of St Helier, Jersey, 1985–93; Hon. Canon of Winchester, 1986–93, now Emeritus; *b* 25 Aug. 1924; *s* of Basil James and Mabel Violet O'Ferrall, Dublin; *m* 1952, Joyce Forbes (*née* Taylor); one *s* two *d. Educ:* St Patrick's Cathedral Gram. Sch., Dublin; Trinity Coll., Dublin (BA 1948, MA 1966). Curate Assistant, St Patrick's, Coleraine, 1948; Chaplain RN, 1951; served: HMS Victory, 1951; Ganges, 1952; Gambia, 1952–54; Curlew, 1955; Daedalus, 1956; Amphibious Warfare Sqdn, 1956–58; HMS Adamant, 1958–60 (3rd Submarine Sqn); 40 Commando, RM, 1960–62; RN Hosp., Bighi, 1962; HMS Victorious, 1963–64; Condor, 1964–66; HMS Maidstone, 1966–68 (3rd and 10th Submarine Sqns); St Vincent, 1968; Commando Training Centre, RM, 1969–71; HM Naval Base, Portsmouth, 1971–74; CTC, RM, 1975; Chaplain of the Fleet and Archdeacon of the Royal Navy, 1975–80; Vicar of Ranworth wih Panxworth and Woodbastwick (Norwich) and Bishop's Chaplain for the Broads, 1980–85; Chaplain to the Queen, 1980–85. Hon. Canon of Gibraltar, 1977–80. Anglican Advr, Channel TV, 1985–93. QHC 1975–80. Mem., Gen. Synod of C of E, 1990–93. Pres., Jersey Br., Missions to Seamen, 1987–93. *Recreations:* sailing, ornithology. *Address:* The Stone House, Barrack Square, Winchelsea, East Sussex TN36 4EG. *T:* (01797) 223458.

O'FERRALL, Rev. Patrick Charles Kenneth, OBE 1989; Curate (Ordained Local Minister), SS Peter and Paul, Godalming, since 2000; *b* 27 May 1934; *s* of late Rev. Kenneth John Spence O'Ferrall and Isoult May O'Ferrall; *m* 1st, 1960, Mary Dorothea (*d* 1997), 4th *d* of late Maj. C. E. Lugard and Mrs K. I. B. Lugard; one *s* two *d*; 2nd, 1999, Wendy Elizabeth Barnett (*née* Gilmore). *Educ:* Winchester Coll.; New Coll., Oxford (BA Lit.Hum. 1958; MA); Harvard Business Sch. (AMP 1983). Nat. Service, 1952–54, 2nd Lieut, Royal Fusiliers. Iraq Petroleum and associated cos, 1958–70; BP, 1971–73; Total CFP Paris (Total Moyen Orient), 1974–77; Total Oil Marine, London: Commercial Manager, 1977–82; Dir, Gas Gathering Pipelines (N Sea) Ltd, 1977–78; Project Co-ordination Manager, Alwyn N, 1983–85; Projects Co-ordination Manager, 1985–90; Dep. Chm., 1991–93, Chm., 1993–99, Lloyd's Register of Shipping. Mem., Offshore Industry Adv. Bd, 1992–94. Chm., City of London Outward Bound Assoc., 1993–97. Mem., Court of Common Council, Corp. of London, 1996–2001. Liveryman, Co. of Shipwrights, 1992–; Master, Coachmakers' and Coach Harness Makers' Co., 1993–94. FRSA 1993; CIMgt 1994. Hon. FREng 2000. Lay Reader, 1961–2000; ordained deacon, 2000, priest, 2001. *Recreations:* music (playing violin and singing), tennis, wine, crosswords, travel. *Address:* Catteshall Grange, Catteshall Road, Godalming, Surrey GU7 1LZ. *T:* (01483) 410134, *Fax:* (01483) 414161; *e-mail:* pof59@hotmail.com. *Clubs:* MCC, Aldgate Ward (Pres., 1998).

OFFER, Prof. Avner, DPhil; FBA 2000; Chichele Professor of Economic History, University of Oxford, since 2000; Fellow, All Souls College, Oxford, since 2000; *b* 15 May 1944; *s* of Zvi and Ivriyah Offer; *m* 1966, Leah Koshet; one *s* one *d. Educ:* Western Valley Sch., Yif'at, Israel; Hebrew Univ. (BA 1973); St Antony's Coll., Oxford; Merton

Coll., Oxford (MA 1976; DPhil 1979). Mil. service, Israel, 1962–65; Kibbutz mem., 1965–67; Conservation Officer, Israel, 1967–69; Jun. Res. Fellow, Merton Coll., Oxford, 1976–78; Lectr in Econ. and Social Hist., 1978–90, Reader, 1990–91, Univ. of York; Reader in Recent Social and Econ. Hist., Univ. of Oxford, and Fellow, Nuffield Coll., 1992–2000. Hartley Fellow, Univ. of Southampton, 1981–82; Vis. Associate, Clare Hall, Cambridge, 1984; Res. Fellow, Inst. Advanced Study, ANU, 1985–88; Sen. Fellow, Rutgers Univ., 1991–92; Sen. Vis. Fellow, Remarque Inst., NY Univ., 1999. *Publications:* Property and Politics 1870–1914: landownership, law, ideology and urban development in England, 1981; The First World War: an agrarian interpretation, 1989; (ed) In Pursuit of the Quality of Life, 1996; articles on land, law, empire, consumption and quality of life. *Recreations:* reading, classical music, visual arts. *Address:* 15 Hamilton Road, Oxford OX2 7PY. *T:* (01865) 553380.

OFFER, Ven. Clifford Jocelyn; Archdeacon of Norwich and Canon Residentiary (Cathedral Librarian) of Norwich Cathedral, since 1994; *b* 10 Aug. 1943; *s* of late Rev. Canon Clifford Jesse Offer and Jocelyn Mary Offer; *m* 1980, Dr Catherine Mary Lloyd; two *d*. *Educ:* King's Sch., Canterbury; St Peter's Coll., Oxford (sent down); Exeter Univ. (BA 1967); Westcott House, Cambridge. Ordained deacon, 1969, priest, 1970; Curate, St Peter and St Paul, Bromley, 1969–74; Team Vicar, Southampton City Centre, 1974–83; Team Rector, Hitchin, 1983–94. Vice Chm., then Chm., St Albans ABM, 1989–94; Chairman: Norwich Diocesan Adv. Bd for Mission and Ministry (formerly ABM), 1994–99, 2000–; Norwich Course Mgt Cttee, 1999–; Warden of Readers, dio. Norwich, 1994–. Mem., Council for E Anglia Studies. FRSA 1997. *Publication:* King Offa in Hitchin, 1992. *Recreations:* collecting naval buttons, ship-modelling, growing chrysanthemums. *Address:* 26 Cathedral Close, Norwich, Norfolk NR1 4DZ. *T:* (01603) 620375.

OFFNER, Gary John; Official Representative of New South Wales Government in United Kingdom and Europe, since 1997; *b* 26 Oct. 1961; *s* of John Frederick Offner and Dorothy Offner; *m* 1993, Beth Frances Hickey. *Educ:* Christian Brothers Coll., Sutherland; Barristers' Admission Board (Dip. Law 1988); Univ. of Technology, Sydney (MBA 1993). Joined NSW Public Sector, 1980; admitted to NSW Bar, 1988; Advr to Minister for Natural Resources, 1988–89; Manager, Internat. Div., NSW Dept of State and Regl Develt, 1990–97; Dir, NSW Govt Trade and Investment Office, 1997–. Mem., British Cook Soc. *Recreations:* golf, cricket, Rugby. *Address:* The Australia Centre, Strand, WC2B 4LG. *T:* (020) 7887 5871. *Clubs:* Royal Over-Seas League; Sydney Cricket Ground.

OFILI, Christopher; artist; *b* Manchester, 1968. *Educ:* Thameside Coll. of Technol.; Chelsea Sch. of Art (BA); Hochschule der Kunst, Berlin; Royal Coll. of Art (MA). Travelling Scholarship, Zimbabwe, 1993. Solo exhibitions include: Kepler Gall., London, 1991; Victoria Miro Gall., London, 1996; Contemporary Fine Art, Berlin, 1997; Southampton City Art Gall., 1998; Serpentine Gall., London, 1998; Whitworth Art Gall., Manchester, 1998–99. Group exhibitions include: Cornerhouse Gall., Manchester, 1993; MOMA, Oxford, 1996; ICA, 1997; Mus. of Contemp. Art, Sydney, 1997; RA, 1997; Walker Art Gall., Liverpool, 1997; Tate Gall., London, 1998; British Council touring exhibn, incl. Finland, Sweden, Russia and Czech Republic, 1997–99. Turner Prize, 1998. *Address:* c/o Victoria Miro Gallery, 21 Cork Street, W1X 1HB.

O'FLAHERTY, Prof. Coleman Anthony, AM 1999; writer; Deputy Vice-Chancellor, University of Tasmania, Australia, 1991–93, Professor Emeritus 1993; *b* 8 Feb. 1933; *s* of Michael and Agnes O'Flaherty; *m* 1957, Nuala Rose Silke (*d* 1999). *Educ:* Nat. Univ. of Ireland (BE); Iowa State Univ. (MS, PhD). FICE; FIEI; FIE(Aust); FIHT; FCIT. Engineer: Galway Co. Council, Ireland, 1954–55; Canadian Pacific Railway Co., Montreal, 1955–56; M. W. Kellogg Co., USA, 1956–57; Asst Prof., Iowa State Univ., 1957–62; Leeds University: Lectr, 1962–66; Prof. of Transport Engineering, Inst. for Transport Studies and Dept of Civil Engineering, 1966–74; First Asst Comr (Engineering), Nat. Capital Develt Commn, Canberra, 1974–78; Dir and Principal, Tasmanian Coll. of Advanced Educn, subseq. Tasmanian State Inst. of Technology, 1978–90. Chairman: Tasmanian Liby Adv. Bd, 1997–; Tasmania State Liby and Archives Trust, 1997–. Vis. Prof., Univ. of Melbourne, 1973. Hon. LLD Tasmania, 1994. *Publications:* Highways, 1967, vol. I of 4th edn (Transport Planning and Traffic Engineering), 1997, vol. II of 4th edn (Highway Engineering), 2000; (jtly) Passenger Conveyors, 1972; (jtly) Introduction to Hovercraft and Hoverports, 1975; contribs to professional jls. *Recreation:* walking. *Address:* 22 Beach Road, Legana, Tasmania 7277, Australia. *T:* and *Fax:* (3) 63301990. *Club:* Launceston.

O'FLYNN, Rt Hon. Francis Duncan, (Frank); PC 1987; QC 1968; Chairman, Community Trust, Trust Bank, Wellington, 1988–94 (Director, Trust Bank, 1988–91); *b* 24 Oct. 1918; *s* of Hon. Francis E. O'Flynn, MLC; *m* 1942, Sylvia Elizabeth Hefford; one *s* three *d*. *Educ:* Christchurch Boys' High School; Victoria University of Wellington (BA, LLM). Flight Lieut, RNZAF, 1942–46; Flying Instructor, NZ and 6 Flying Boat Sqdn, Pacific. Barrister and Solicitor, 1948; in practice on own account, 1954–78. MP (Lab): Kapiti, 1972–75; Island Bay, 1978–87. Minister of State and of Defence, and Dep. Minister of Foreign Affairs, NZ, 1984–87. Member: Otaki Borough Council, 1968–71; Wellington City Council, 1977–83. Mem. Council, Wellington District Law Soc., 1970–74. *Recreation:* reading. *Address:* 11 Rosetta Road, Raumati South, Wellington, New Zealand. *T:* (4) 9021669.

of MAR, family name of **Countess of Mar**.

OGATA, Prof. Sadako; United Nations High Commissioner for Refugees, 1991–2000; *b* 1927; *m*. *Educ:* Univ. of the Sacred Heart, Tokyo (BA); Georgetown Univ. (MA); PhD California (Berkeley). Director of Internat. Relations, Sophia Univ., Japan, later Dean, Faculty of Foreign Studies, to 1990; Minister, Perm. Mission of Japan to UN, 1976–78; Chm. Exec. Bd, UNICEF, Japanese Rep. to UN Commn on Human Rights, 1982–85. Hon. DCL Oxon, 1998; Hon. LLD Cantab, 1999. *Address:* c/o United Nations High Commission for Refugees, Casa Postale 2500, 1211 Genève 2 dépôt, Switzerland.

OGDEN, Sir (Edward) Michael, Kt 1989; QC 1968; barrister, 1950–97; a Recorder (formerly Recorder of Hastings), 1971–97; a Deputy High Court Judge, 1977–96; *b* 9 April 1926; *er s* of late Edward Cannon Ogden and Daisy (*née* Paris); *m* 1951, Joan Kathleen, *er d* of late Pius Charles Brodrick and Kathleen (*née* Moran); two *s* two *d*. *Educ:* Downside Sch.; Jesus Coll., Cambridge (MA). FCIArb 1990; Fellow, Singapore Inst. of Arbitrators, 1996. Served in RAC (Royal Glos Hussars and 16th/5th Lancers), 1944–47 (Capt.); Inns of Court Regt (TA) 1950–56. Jesus Coll., Cambridge, 1948–49; called to Bar, Lincoln's Inn, 1950 (Bencher, 1977; Treasurer, 1998); Dep. Recorder, Southend-on-Sea, 1964–71; Dep. Official Referee, 1996–97. Leader, SE Circuit, 1975–78. Mem. Bar Council, 1960–64, 1966–70, 1971–78 (responsible for fee negotiations, 1968–72, Treas., 1972–74, Chm., Internat. Relns Cttee, 1974–75); Mem. Senate of the Inns of Court, 1966–70, 1972–78. Member: Council of Union Internationale des Avocats, 1962–83; Council of Legal Educn, 1969–74; Council, Internat. Bar Assoc., 1983–87. Chairman: Criminal Injuries Compensation Bd, 1975–89 (Mem., 1968–89); Wkg Party publishing Actuarial Tables for Personal Injury and Fatal Accident Cases (4th edn 2000; Ogden Tables enacted Civil Evidence Act 1995); Disciplinary Appeal Cttee, ICAEW, 1993–98; Mem., Lord Chancellor's Adv. on Legal Education, 1972–74. Dir, Internat. Assoc. of Crime Victim Compensation Bds, 1978–89 (Co-Chm. 1983–87). The Independent Assessor for Home Sec. of compensation for miscarriages of justice, 1978–89, and for Minister of Defence, 1986–89. Pres., Sea Fish Licence Tribunal, 1993–94. Proponent, Criminal Procedure (Right of Reply) Act, 1964. Mem. Bd, Internat. and Comparative Corp. Law Jl, 1998–. Hon. Fellow, Soc. of Advanced Legal Studies, 1998; Hon. FIA 1999; Hon. Mem., Litigation Section, Amer. Bar Assoc., 1979. *Address:* 1 Paper Buildings, Temple, EC4Y 7ET. *T:* (020) 7797 8100, *Fax:* (020) 7797 8101.

OGDEN, Sir Michael; *see* Ogden, Sir E. M.

OGILVIE, (Dame) Bridget (Margaret), (Dr Bridget Ogilvie), DBE 1997; FMedSci; Director, Wellcome Trust, 1991–98; Director, AstraZeneca (formerly Zeneca Group plc), since 1997; High Steward of University of Cambridge, since 2001; *b* 24 March 1938; *er d* of late John Mylne Ogilvie and Margaret Beryl (*née* McRae). *Educ:* New England Girls' Sch., Armidale, NSW; Univ. of New England, Armidale (BRurSc 1960; Distinguished Alumni Award, 1994). PhD 1964, ScD 1981, Cambridge. FIBiol 1985. Parasitology Div., Nat. Inst. for Med. Res., London, 1963–81; Ian McMaster Fellow, CSIRO Div. of Animal Health, Australia, 1971–72; with Wellcome Trust, 1979–98: Co-ordinator, Tropical Med. Prog., 1979–81; Dep. Sec. and Asst Dir, 1981–84; Dep. Dir, Science, 1984–89; Dir, Science Progs, 1989–91. Director: Lloyds Bank, 1995–; Lloyds TSB Gp, 1996–2000. Visiting Professor: Dept of Biology, Imperial Coll., London, 1985–92; UCL, 1998–. Member: Council for Science and Technol., 1993–2000; Commonwealth Scholarship Commn, 1993–2000; Adv. Council for Chemistry, Univ. of Oxford, 1997–2001; Australian Health and Med. Res. Strategic Review, 1998–99; Chairman: COPUS, 1998–; AstraZeneca Sci. Teaching Trust, 1998–; Medicines for Malaria Venture, 1999–; Adv. Cttee for Sci., Technol., Business, British Liby, 2000–. Non-executive Director: Scottish Sci. Trust, 1999–; Manchester Technol. Fund, 1999–. Trustee: Sci. Mus., London, 1992–Feb. 2002; RCVS Trust Fund, 1998–2001; NESTA, 1998–; CRC, 2001–. Chm. Governing Body, Inst. for Animal Health, 1997–. Founder FMedSci 1998. Hon. Member: British Soc. for Parasitology, 1990; Amer. Soc. of Parasitologists, 1992; BVA, 1998; Hon. FRCP 1996 (Hon. MRCP 1992); Hon. FRACP 1998; Hon. ARCVS 1993. Hon. Fellow: UCL, 1993; Girton Coll., Cambridge, 1993; St Edmund's Coll., Cambridge, 1999; Hon. FRVC 1994; Hon. FIBiol 1998; Hon. FRSocMed 1999. Hon. DSc: Nottingham, Salford, Westminster, 1994; Glasgow, Bristol, ANU, 1995; Buckingham, Dublin, Trent, Oxford Brookes, 1996; Greenwich, 1997; Auckland, NZ, Durham, Kent, 1998; Exeter, Imperial Coll., London, 1999; Leicester, 2000; Manchester, St Andrews, 2001; Hon. LLD: TCD, 1996; Dundee, 1998; Hon. MD Newcastle, 1996; Dr *hc* Edinburgh, 1997. Lloyd of Kilgerran Prize, Foundn for Sci. and Technology, 1994; Wooldridge Meml Medal, BVA, 1998; Australian Soc. for Medical Res. Medal, 2000. *Publications:* contrib. scientific papers to parasitological and immunological jls. *Recreations:* the company of friends, looking at landscapes, music, gardening. *Address:* c/o Medical School Administration, University College London, Gower Street, WC1E 6BT. *T:* (020) 7679 4538. *Clubs:* Reform; Queen's (Sydney).

OGILVIE, Ven. Gordon; Archdeacon of Nottingham, since 1996; *b* 22 Aug. 1942; *s* of late Gordon Ogilvie and Eliza J. Ogilvie (*née* Cullen); *m* 1967, Sylvia Margaret, *d* of late Rankin and Jessie Weir; one *s* one *d*. *Educ:* Hillhead High Sch., Glasgow; Glasgow Univ. (MA 1964); London Coll. of Divinity (ext. BD London Univ., 1967). Ordained deacon, 1967, priest, 1968; Asst Curate, Ashtead, 1967–72; Vicar, St James, New Barnet, 1972–80; Dir, Pastoral Studies, Wycliffe Hall, Oxford, 1980–87; Priest-in-charge, 1987–89, Team Rector, 1989–96, Harlow Town Centre with Little Parndon; Chaplain, Princess Alexandra Hosp., Harlow, 1988–96. Hon. Canon, Chelmsford Cathedral, 1993–96. *Recreations:* cricket, piano, photography. *Address:* (office) Dunham House, Westgate, Southwell, Notts NG25 0JL. *T:* (01636) 814490, *Fax:* (01636) 815882; 2b Spencer Avenue, Mapperley, Nottingham NG3 5SP. *T:* (0115) 967 0875, *Fax:* (0115) 967 1014.

OGILVIE-GRANT, family name of **Earl of Seafield**.

OGILVIE-LAING of Kinkell, Gerald, NDD; FRBS 1993 (ARBS 1987); sculptor; *b* 11 Feb. 1936; *s* of Gerald Francis Laing and Enid Moody (*née* Foster), and *g s* of Capt. Gerald Ogilvie Laing; adopted name of Ogilvie-Laing by Deed Poll, 1968; *m* 1st, 1962, Jenifer Anne Redway; one *d*; 2nd, 1969, Galina Vassilovna Golikova; two *s*; 3rd, 1988, Adaline Havemeyer Frelinghuysen; two *s*. *Educ:* Berkhamsted Sch.; RMA, Sandhurst; St Martin's Sch. of Art, London (NDD) 1964). Served Royal Northumberland Fusiliers, 1955–60, resigned; lived in NYC, 1964–69; Pop painting, 1962–65, abstract sculpture, 1965–69; Artist in Residence, Aspen Inst., 1966; restored Kinkell Castle, Scotland, 1969–70 (Civic Trust Award, 1971); established Tapestry Workshop, 1970–74; changed to figurative sculpture, 1973. Vis. Prof. of Painting and Sculpture, Univ. of New Mexico, 1976–77; Prof. of Sculpture, Columbia Univ., 1986–87. Installed: Callanish sculpture, Strathclyde Univ., 1971; Frieze of Wise and Foolish Virgins, Edinburgh, 1979; Fountain of Sabrina, Bristol, 1980; Conan Doyle Meml, and Axis Mundi, Edinburgh, 1991; Bank station Dragons, 1995; four figures on Rowland Hill Gate, Twickenham Rugby Stadium, 1996; St George and Dragon sequence, Harrow, 1996; Cricketer, Wormsley, Bucks, 1998; Fire Icon, Bluewater, Kent, 1999; Glass Virgins, Edinburgh, and Fifth Fusilier Meml, Badajoz, Spain, 2000; Batsman, MCC, Lord's Ground, 2001; exhibits frequently; work in many public and private collections worldwide, including Tate Gall., V&A, Nat. Portrait Gall., London and Edinburgh, Nat. Gall. (portrait bust of Sir Paul Getty, 1997), Scottish Nat. Gall. of Modern Art, Mus. of Modern Art, NY, Whitney Mus., NY, and Smithsonian Instn. Member: Art Cttee, Scottish Arts Council, 1978–80; Royal Fine Art Commn for Scotland, 1987–95. Chm., Black Isle Civic Trust, 1991–93. *Publication:* Kinkell—the Reconstruction of a Scottish castle, 1974, 2nd edn 1984. *Address:* Kinkell Castle, Ross and Cromarty IV7 8AT. *T:* (01349) 861485. *Clubs:* Chelsea Arts, Academy.

OGILVIE THOMPSON, Julian; Chairman: Anglo American plc, 1999–May 2002 (Chief Executive, 1999–2000); Anglo American Corporation of SA Ltd, 1990–May 2002; Deputy Chairman, De Beers Consolidated Mines Ltd, 1982–85 and since 1998 (Chairman, 1985–97); *b* 27 Jan. 1934; *s* of late Hon. N. Ogilvie Thompson, formerly Chief Justice of S Africa, and of Eve Ogilvie Thompson; *m* 1956, Hon. Tessa Mary Brand, *yr* surv. *d* of 4th Viscount Hampden, CMG and Leila, Viscountess Hampden; two *s* two *d*. *Educ:* Diocesan Coll., Rondebosch; Univ. of Cape Town; Worcester Coll., Oxford. MA. Diocesan Coll. Rhodes Scholar, 1953. Joined Anglo American Corp. of SA Ltd, 1956; Dir, 1970; Exec. Dir, 1971–82; Chairman: Anglo American Gold Investment Co. Ltd, 1976–90; Minorco SA (formerly Minerals and Resources Corp. Ltd), 1982–99; Vice Chairman: First Nat. Bank Ltd, 1977–90; Urban Foundn, 1986–95. Hon. LLD Rhodes, 1986. Comdr, Order of the Crown (Belgium), 1993; Grand Official, Order of Bernardo O'Higgins (Chile), 1996; Presidential Order of Honour (Botswana), 1997. *Recreations:* shooting, fishing, golf. *Address:* Froome, Froome Street, Athol Extension 3, Sandton, Transvaal, S Africa. *T:* (11) 8843925. *Clubs:* White's; Rand (Johannesburg); Kimberley

(Cape Province); The Brook (NY).
See also Baroness Dacre.

OGILVY, family name of **Earl of Airlie**.

OGILVY, Lord; David John Ogilvy; Managing Director, Richard L. Feigen UK Ltd, Art Dealers; *b* 9 March 1958; *s* and *heir* of 13th Earl of Airlie, *qv*; *m* 1st, 1981, Hon. Geraldine Harmsworth (marr. diss. 1991), *d* of 3rd Viscount Rothermere; one *d*; 2nd, 1991, Tarka Kings; three *s*. *Educ:* Eton and Oxford (MA). *Heir: s* Master of Ogilvy, *qv*. *Address:* Airlie Castle, Kirriemuir, Angus DD8 5NG.

OGILVY, Master of; David Huxley Ogilvy; *b* 11 Dec. 1991; *s* and *heir* of Lord Ogilvy, *qv*.

OGILVY, Rt Hon. Sir Angus (James Bruce), KCVO 1989; PC 1997; *b* 14 Sept. 1928; *s* of 12th (*de facto* 9th) Earl of Airlie, KT, GCVO, MC and Lady Alexandra Marie Bridget Coke, *d* of 3rd Earl of Leicester, GCVO, CMG; *m* 1963, HRH Princess Alexandra of Kent; one *s* one *d*. *Educ:* Eton Coll.; Trinity Coll., Oxford (MA). Scots Guards, 1946–48; Mem., HM Body Guard for Scotland (The Royal Company of Archers). Chm. Adv. Council, Prince's Trust (formerly Chm. Adv. Council, PYBT). President: Imperial Cancer Res. Fund, 1964–94; Youth Clubs UK (formerly NAYC), 1969–89 (Chm. 1964–69); Carr-Gomm Soc., 1983–; Vice-President: Friends of the Elderly & Gentlefolk's Help, 1969– (Treas., 1952–63; Chm., 1963–69); Gtr London Fund for the Blind, 1999–; Patron: Arthritis Care (formerly British Rheumatism and Arthritis Soc.), 1978– (Chm. 1963–69; Pres., 1969–78); Scottish Wildlife Trust, 1974–90 (Pres., 1969–74); Friends of Youth Clubs UK, 1993–; Vice-Patron, NCH Action for Children (formerly Nat. Children's Homes), 1986–. Mem., Governing Council, Society for Promoting Christian Knowledge, 1984–94. Dir, various public cos. Trustee, Leeds Castle Foundn, 1975–. *Recreations:* architecture, reading, music. *Address:* Thatched House Lodge, Richmond Park, Surrey TW10 5HP. *T:* (020) 8546 8833. *Club:* White's.
See also J. D. D. Ogilvy, and under Royal Family.

OGILVY, Sir Francis (Gilbert Arthur), 14th Bt *cr* 1626 (NS), of Inverquharity, Forfarshire; Chartered Surveyor; *b* 22 April 1969; *s* of Sir David John Wilfrid Ogilvy, 13th Bt and of Penelope Mary Ursula, *d* of Captain Arthur Lafone Frank Hills, OBE; *S* father, 1992; *m* 1996, Dorothy, *e d* of Rev. Jock Stein and Rev. Margaret Stein; two *s*. *Educ:* Edinburgh Acad.; Glenalmond; RAC, Cirencester (BSc Hons). MRICS (ARICS 1995). *Heir: s* Robert David Ogilvy, *b* 8 July 1999. *Address:* Winton House, Pencaitland, E Lothian EH34 5AT.

OGILVY, Hon. James (Donald Diarmid); Chairman, Foreign & Colonial Management Ltd, 1998 (Chief Executive, 1988–97); *b* 28 June 1934; *y s* of 12th Earl of Airlie, KT, GCVO, MC and Lady Alexandra Marie Bridget Coke, *d* of 3rd Earl of Leicester, GCVO, CMG; *m* 1st, 1959, June Ducas (marr. diss. 1978); two *s* two *d*; 2nd, 1980, Lady Caroline (*née* Child-Villiers), *d* of 9th Earl of Jersey. *Educ:* Eton Coll. Clerk, Panmure Gordon, 1957–58; Partner, Rowe & Pitman, 1959–86; Vice Chm., Mercury Asset Management plc, 1986–88. Chm., Sutherlands (Holdings), 1998–2000; Director: Foreign & Colonial Emerging Markets, 1995–; Berkshire Capital Corp. UK, 1998–. Grand Official, Nat. Order of the Southern Cross (Brazil), 1993. *Recreations:* shooting, golf. *Address:* Sedgebrook Manor, Sedgebrook, Grantham, Lincs NG32 2EN. *T:* (01949) 842337; Flat D, 51 Eaton Square, SW1W 9BE. *T:* (020) 7235 7595. *Clubs:* White's, Pratt's.
See also Rt Hon. Sir A. J. B. Ogilvy.

OGILVY-WEDDERBURN, Sir Andrew John Alexander, 13th and 7th Bt *cr* 1704 and 1803; *b* 4 Aug. 1952; *s* of Sir (John) Peter Ogilvy-Wedderburn, 12th and 6th Bt, and of Elizabeth Katharine, *e d* of late John A. Cox, Drumkilbo; *S* father, 1977; *m* 1984, Gillian Meade, *yr d* of Richard Adderley, Pickering, N Yorks; two *s* (twins) one *d* (and one *s* decd). *Educ:* Gordonstoun. *Heir: s* Peter Robert Alexander Ogilvy-Wedderburn, *b* 20 April 1987. *Address:* Silvie, Alyth, Perthshire PH11 8NA.

OGLESBY, Peter Rogerson, CB 1982; *b* 15 July 1922; *s* of late Leonard William Oglesby and late Jessie Oglesby (*née* Rogerson); *m* 1947, Doreen Hilda Hudson; three *d*. *Educ:* Woodhouse Grove Sch., Apperley Bridge. Clerical Officer, Admlty, 1939–47; Exec. Officer, Min. of Nat. Ins., 1947–56; Higher Exec. Officer, MPNI, 1956–62, Principal 1962–64; Principal Private Secretary: to Chancellor of Duchy of Lancaster, 1964–66; to Minister without Portfolio, 1966; to First Sec. of State, 1966–68; to Lord President, 1968; Asst Sec., Cabinet Office, 1968–70, Asst Sec., DHSS, 1970–73; Sec., Occupational Pensions Bd, 1973–74; Under Sec., 1974–79; Dep. Sec., 1979–82, DHSS. Dir, Regency Final Gp, 1983–91. *Address:* 41 Draycot Road, Wanstead, E11 2NX. *T:* (020) 8989 5526.

OGLEY, William David; Chief Executive, Hertfordshire County Council, since 1996; *b* 26 May 1955; *s* of Thomas William and Olive Ogley; *m* 1976, Anne Dolores Walker; two *d*. *Educ:* Manchester Univ. (BA Hons Physics and Psych.); CIPFA (prize winner). Derbyshire CC, 1976–83 (to Principal Accountant, 1980–83); Group Accountant, Oxfordshire CC, 1983–85; Hertfordshire County Council: Sen. Asst. County Treasurer, 1985–88 (Educn and Social Services); Dep. County Treasurer, 1988–90; Dir, Inf. Systems, 1990–91; Dir of Finance, 1991–93; Dep. Controller and Dir of Resources, Audit Commn, 1993–96. Mem. Council, Herts Learning and Skills Council, 2001–; Director: Herts TEC, 1996–2001; Herts Business Link, 1996–. *Recreations:* tennis, gardening, sailing, family, reading. *Address:* County Hall, Hertford SG13 8DE.

OGMORE, 2nd Baron *cr* 1950, of Bridgend; **Gwilym Rees Rees-Williams;** *b* 5 May 1931; *er s* of 1st Baron Ogmore, PC, TD, and Constance (*d* 1998), *er d* of W. R. Wills; *S* father, 1976; *m* 1967, Gillian Mavis, *d* of M. K. Slack; two *d*. *Educ:* Mill Hill School. *Heir: b* Hon. Morgan Rees-Williams [*b* 19 Dec. 1937; *m* 1st, 1964, Patricia (marr. diss. 1970), *o d* of C. Paris Jones; 2nd, 1972, Roberta (marr. diss. 1976), *d* of Captain Alec Cunningham-Reid, DFC; 3rd, 1990, Beata, *o d* of Z. Solski; two *s*]. *Address:* 12 Lavant Road, Summersdale, Chichester, West Sussex PO19 4RQ.

OGNALL, Hon. Sir Harry Henry, Kt 1986; DL; a Judge of the High Court of Justice, Queen's Bench Division, 1986–2000; *b* 9 Jan. 1934; *s* of Leo and Cecilia Ognall; *m* 1977, Elizabeth Young; two step *s* and two *s* one *d* of former marriage. *Educ:* Leeds Grammar Sch.; Lincoln Coll., Oxford (MA (Hons)); Univ. of Virginia, USA (LLM). Called to Bar (Gray's Inn), 1958; Bencher, 1983. Joined NE Circuit; a Recorder, 1972–86; QC 1973. Member: Criminal Injuries Compensation Bd, 1976; Planning Cttee, Senate of Inns of Court and Bar, 1980–83; Professional Conduct Cttee, 1985; Judicial Studies Bd (Chm., Criminal Cttee), 1986–89; Parole Bd, 1989–91 (Vice-Chm., 1990–91); a Judicial Mem., Proscribed Orgns Appeal Commn, 2001–. Arbitrator, Motor Insurers' Bureau Agreement, 1979–85. Exec. Chm., eWitness Ltd, 2000–. DL W Yorks, 2000. *Recreations:* golf, music, travel. *Address:* The Coach House, LS29 9JR. *Clubs:* Ganton Golf, Ilkley Golf, Ilkley Bowling.

O'GRADY, Prof. Francis William, CBE 1984; TD 1970; MD, MSc; FRCP, FRCPath, FFPM; Foundation Professor of Microbiology, University of Nottingham, 1974–88, now Emeritus; *b* 7 Nov. 1925; *s* of Francis Joseph O'Grady and Lilian Maud Hitchcock; *m* 1951, Madeleine Marie-Thérèse Becquart; three *d*. *Educ:* Middlesex Hosp. Med. Sch., London (BSc 1st Cl. Hons; MB, BS Hons; MSc; MD). FRCP 1976; FRCPath 1972; FFPM 1989. House Physician, Mddx and North Mddx Hosps, 1951; Asst Pathologist, Bland-Sutton Inst. of Pathol., Mddx Hosp., 1952–53, 1956–58 and 1961–62; Pathologist, RAMC, 1954–55, AER, 1956–72; Asst Prof. of Environmental Medicine, Johns Hopkins Univ., Baltimore, 1959–60; Reader, 1962–66, and Prof. of Bacteriology, 1967–74, Univ. of London; Bacteriologist, St Bartholomew's Hosp., 1962–74; Chief Scientist, DHSS, subseq. DoH, 1986–90. Hon. Consultant Microbiologist, PHLS, 1974–96. Mem., MRC, 1980–84, 1986–90; Chm., MRC Physiol Systems and Disorders Bd, 1980–82 (Mem., 1977–80; Mem., Grants Cttee, 1975–76); Chm., MRC Cttee on Hosp. Infection, 1977–80 (Mem., 1967–77). Member: Antibiotics Panel, Cttee on Med. Aspects of Food Policy, 1968–72; Sub-Cttee on Toxicity, Clin. Trials and Therapeutic Efficacy, 1971–75, and Sub-Cttee on Biol Substances, 1971–81, Cttee on Safety of Medicines; Jt Sub-Cttee on Antimicrobial Substances, Cttee on Safety of Medicines and Vet. Products Cttee, 1973–80; Cttee on Rev. of Medicines, 1975–81; Public Health Lab. Service Bd, 1980–86, 1993–96; Nat. Biological Standards Bd, 1983–87. Hon. Consultant Microbiologist to the Army, 1982–91. William N. Creasy Vis. Prof. of Clin. Pharmacology, Duke Univ., NC, 1979. Erasmus Wilson Demonstrator, RCS, 1967; Foundn Lectr, Univ. of Hong Kong, 1974; Sydney Watson Smith Lectr, RCPE, 1975; Jacobson Vis. Lectr, Univ. of Newcastle upon Tyne, 1979; Berk Lectr, British Assoc. of Urol Surgeons, 1980; Garrod Lectr, British Soc. for Antimicrobial Chemotherapy, 1983; Jenner Lectr, St George's Hosp. Med. Sch., 1988. Pres. Council, British Jl of Exper. Pathol., 1980–91 (Mem., 1968–80); Mem. Editorial Boards: Jl of Med. Microbiol., 1970–75; Pathologie Biologie, 1973–78; British Jl of Clin. Pharmacol., 1974–84; Drugs, 1976–88; Gut, 1977–83; Jl of Infection, 1978–83; Revs of Infectious Diseases, 1979–88. *Publications:* Airborne Infection: transmission and control, 1968; Antibiotic and Chemotherapy, 1968, 7th edn 1997; (ed) Urinary Tract Infection, 1968; (ed) Microbial Perturbation of Host Defences, 1981; papers on clin. and exper. infection and on antimicrobial chemotherapy. *Address:* 32 Wollaton Hall Drive, Nottingham NG8 1AF.

OGSTON, Prof. Derek, CBE 1995; MD, PhD, DSc; FRCP; FRSE 1982; Professor of Medicine, 1983–97, and Vice Principal, 1987–97, University of Aberdeen; *b* 31 May 1932; *s* of Frederick John Ogston and Ellen Mary Ogston; *m* 1963, Cecilia Marie Clark; one *s* two *d*. *Educ:* King's Coll. Sch., Wimbledon; Univ. of Aberdeen (MA, MD, PhD, DSc; MLitt 1999). FRCP Edin 1973; FRCP 1977; FIBiol 1987. University of Aberdeen: Res. Fellow, 1959–62; Lectr in Medicine, 1962–69; Sen. Lectr in Med., 1969–75; Reader in Med., 1975–76; Regius Prof. of Physiology, 1977–83; Dean, Faculty of Medicine, 1984–87. MRC Trav. Fellow, 1967–68. Vice-Chm., Grampian Health Bd, 1993–97 (Mem., 1991–97); Mem., GMC, 1984–94. Member: Governing Body, Rowett Res. Inst., 1977–92; Court, Univ. of Aberdeen, 1998–. *Publications:* Physiology of Hemostasis, 1983; Antifibrinolytic Drugs, 1984; Venous Thrombosis, 1987; The Life and Work of George Smith, RSA, 2000; scientific papers on haemostasis. *Recreation:* travel. *Address:* 64 Rubislaw Den South, Aberdeen AB15 4AY. *T:* (01224) 316587.

OGUS, Prof. Anthony Ian; Professor of Law, University of Manchester, since 1987; *b* 30 Aug. 1945; *s* of Samuel Joseph Ogus and Sadie Phyllis Ogus (*née* Green); *m* 1980, Catherine Klein (*d* 1998); *m* 2001, Helen Margaret Legard Owens. *Educ:* St Dunstan's Coll.; Magdalen Coll., Oxford (BA 1966; BCL 1967; MA 1970). Asst Lectr in Law, Univ. of Leicester, 1967–69; Tutorial Fellow in Law, Mansfield Coll., Oxford, 1969–75; Sen. Res. Fellow, Centre for Socio-Legal Studies, Wolfson Coll., Oxford, 1975–78; Prof. of Law, Univ. of Newcastle, 1978–87. Res. Prof., Univ. of Maastricht, 1997–. Mem., Social Security Adv. Cttee, 1994–. Hamlyn Trustee, 1979–2001. *Publications:* Law of Damages, 1973; (jtly) Law of Social Security, 1978, 4th edn 1995; (jtly) Policing Pollution, 1983; (jtly) Readings in the Economics of Law and Regulation, 1984; Regulation: legal form and economic theory, 1994; (jtly) Controlling the Regulators, 1998; articles in legal periodicals. *Recreations:* theatre, opera, concerts, reading, walking. *Address:* School of Law, University of Manchester, Oxford Road, Manchester M13 9PL. *T:* (0161) 275 3572. *Club:* Oxford and Cambridge.

O'HAGAN, 4th Baron *cr* 1870; **Charles Towneley Strachey;** *b* 6 Sept. 1945; *s* of Hon. Thomas Anthony Edward Towneley Strachey (*d* 1955; having assumed by deed poll, 1938, the additional Christian name of Towneley, and his mother's maiden name of Strachey, in lieu of his patronymic) and Lady Mary (who *m* 1981, St John Gore, *qv*; she *d* 2000), *d* of 3rd Earl of Selborne, PC, CH; *S* grandfather, 1961; *m* 1995, Mrs Elizabeth Lesley Eve Macnamara (*née* Smith); two *d* from previous marriages. *Educ:* Eton; (Exhibitioner) New College, Oxford. Page to HM the Queen, 1959–62. Independent Member, European Parliament, 1973–75; Junior Opposition Whip, House of Lords, 1977–79; MEP (C) Devon, 1979–94. *Heir: brother* Hon. Richard Towneley Strachey [*b* 29 Dec. 1950; *m* 1983, Sally Anne, *yr d* of Frederick Cecil Cross]. *Address:* Heath Barton, Beacon Heath, Exeter, Devon EX4 8QW. *Clubs:* Beefsteak, Pratt's.

O'HAGAN, Dr Dara; Member (SF) Upper Bann, Northern Ireland Assembly, since 1998; *b* 29 Aug. 1964; *d* of Joseph and Bernadette O'Hagan; *m* 1990, Thomas Mulholland. *Educ:* Univ. of Ulster (BA Hons Hist. and Politics 1991); Queen's Univ., Belfast (MSSc 1994; PhD 1998). Contested (SF) Upper Bann, 2001. *Address:* (constituency office) 77 North Street, Lurgan, Co. Armagh BT67 9AH. *T:* (028) 3834 9675, *Fax:* (028) 3832 2610.

O'HAGAN, Desmond, CMG 1957; *b* 4 Mar. 1909; *s* of Captain Claud O'Hagan, Nyeri, Kenya and Eva O'Hagan (*née* Napier Magill); *m* 1942, Pamela, *d* of Major A. H. Symes-Thompson, DSO, Kiambu, Kenya; one *s* two *d*. *Educ:* Wellington Coll.; Clare Coll., Cambridge. Entered Colonial Administrative Service, Kenya, 1931. Called to Bar, Inner Temple, 1935. Private Secretary to British Resident, Zanzibar, 1937; served with E African Forces in N Province, Kenya, 1940–42; Native Courts Adviser, 1948–51; Provincial Commissioner, Coast Province, Kenya, 1952–59; Chairman, Transport Licensing Authority, Tanganyika, 1959–63. *Recreations:* bridge, golf. *Address:* Kianjibbi, Box 68, Kiambu, Kenya. *Clubs:* East India, Devonshire, Sports and Public Schools; Muthaiga, Nairobi (life mem.).

O'HANLON, Michael David Peter, PhD; Director, Pitt Rivers Museum, Oxford, since 1998; Professorial Fellow, Linacre College, Oxford, since 1998; *b* 2 July 1950; *s* of late Michael Charles O'Hanlon, Kitale, Kenya, and of Rosemary Alice Sibbald; *m* 1981, Linda Helga Elizabeth, *d* of (Anthony) Noble Frankland, *qv*; one *d*. *Educ:* Kenya; Plymouth Coll., Devon; Pembroke Coll., Cambridge (MA); University Coll. London (PhD 1985). Field res., Wahgi Valley, PNG Highlands, 1979–81; Curator, Pacific collections, Ethnography Dept, BM, 1983–98. Mem. Council, 1994–97, Hon. Sec., 1997–98, RAI. Reviews Editor, MAN, 1988–90; Member, Editorial Board: Jl Material Culture, 1996–; Ethnos, 1997–; Jl RAI, 1999–. *Publications:* Reading the Skin, 1989; Paradise: portraying the New Guinea Highlands, 1993; (ed with E. Hirsch) The Anthropology of Landscape, 1995; (ed with Robert L. Welsch) Hunting the Gatherers: ethnographic collectors, agents and agency in Melanesia 1870s–1930s, 2000; contrib. articles and reviews in professional jls. *Address:* c/o Pitt Rivers Museum, South Parks Road, Oxford OX1 3PP.

O'HARA, Bill; JP; National Governor of the BBC for Northern Ireland, 1973–78; *b* 26 Feb. 1929; *s* of William P. O'Hara and Susanna Agnes O'Hara (*née* Gill); *m* 1953, Anne Marie Finn; two *s* two *d. Address:* Summer Cottage, 12 Raglan Road, Bangor, Co. Down, N Ireland BT20 3TL. *Clubs:* Royal Ulster Yacht, Royal Belfast Golf.

O'HARA, Edward; MP (Lab) Knowsley South, since Sept. 1990; *b* 1 Oct. 1937; *s* of Robert Edward O'Hara and Clara O'Hara (*née* Davies); *m* 1962, Lillian Hopkins; two *s* one *d. Educ:* Magdalen Coll., Oxford (MA 1962); PGCE 1966, DipED (Adv.) 1970, London. Assistant Teacher: Perse Sch., Cambridge, 1962–65; Birkenhead Sch., 1966–70; Lectr and Principal Lectr, C. F. Mott Coll. of Educn, 1970–74; Principal Lectr and Sen. Tutor, Dean of Postgrad. Studies, City of Liverpool Coll. of Higher Educn, 1974–83; Head of Curriculum Studies, Sch. of Educn and Community Studies, Liverpool Polytechnic, 1983–90. Knowsley Borough Council: Mem., 1975–91; Mem., all Standing Cttees; Chairman: Youth Cttee, 1977–79 and 1981–82; Educn Cttee, 1978–79 and 1987–90; Econ. Develt and Planning Cttee, 1990–91. Mem., Educn Cttee, 1978–79 and 1987–90, Planning and Develt Cttee, 1990–91, AMA. Mem., Speaker's Panel of Chairmen, 1993–. Co-Chm., All Pty Gp on Ageing and Older People, 1997–; Chairman: All Pty MV Derbyshire Gp, 1997–; British-Greek Gp, IPU, 1997–. Member: Bd of Management, NFER, 1986–90; European Assoc. of Teachers; Socialist Educn Assoc.; Hon. Mem. and former Parly Advr, Assoc. of Chief Educn Social Workers; Member: Labour Movement in Europe; Perm. Cttee of Assembly of European Regions, 1989–90; Merseyside Rep., Régions Européennes de Tradition Industrielle, 1989–90; Deleg., Council of Europe and WEU, 1997–. Member: Fabian Soc.; Co-op Party; Socialist Educn Assoc. Mem., Bd of Management, Royal Liverpool Philharmonic Soc., 1987–90; Corresp. Mem., Foundn for Hellenic Culture. Trustee, Community Develt Foundn (Chm., 1997–); Vice-Chm., Develt Trust Bd, Nat. Wildflower Centre, 1996–. Vice-Pres., TS Iron Duke, Huyton. Governor: Knowsley Community Coll.; Prescot Co. Primary Sch. Pres., Knowsley South Jun. FC. *Recreations:* music (classical, jazz, folk, esp. Rembetiko), reading, theatre, travel, Greek language and culture. *Address:* 69 St Mary's Road, Huyton, Merseyside L36 5SR. *T:* (0151) 489 8021. *Clubs:* Halewood Labour, Lyme Grove Labour (Knowsley).

O'HARA, Prof. Michael John, PhD; FRS 1981; FRSE 1969; Distinguished Research Professor, University of Wales College of Cardiff, since 1994; *b* 22 Feb. 1933; *s* of Michael Patrick O'Hara, OBE, and Winifred Dorothy O'Hara; *m* 1st, 1962, Janet Tibbits; one *s* two *d*; 2nd, 1977, Susan Howells; two *s* one *d. Educ:* Dulwich Coll. Prep. Sch.; Cranleigh; Peterhouse, Cambridge (MA, PhD). Asst, Lectr, Reader and Prof. (1971), Edinburgh Univ., 1958–78; Prof. of Geology, Univ. of Wales, Aberystwyth, 1978–93. Principal Investigator, NASA Lunar Science Prog., 1968–75; Prof. of Geology, Sultan Qaboos Univ., Oman, 1988–90. Sherman-Fairchild Vis. Scholar, Calif Inst. of Technology, 1984–85; Vis. Prof., Harvard Univ., 1986. Member: Council, NERC, 1986–88; UGC, 1987–89. Associate Mem., Geol Soc. of France; Geochemistry Fellow, Geochemical Soc. and Eur. Assoc. for Geochem., 1997. Murchison Medal, Geol Soc., 1983; Bowen Award, Amer. Geophys. Union, 1984. *Publications:* numerous in learned jls. *Recreation:* mountaineering. *Address:* Department of Earth Sciences, University of Wales College of Cardiff, PO Box 914, Cardiff CF1 3YE. *T:* (029) 2087 4830.

O'HARE, John Edward; Master of Supreme Court Costs (formerly Taxing) Office, since 1995; *b* 26 Feb. 1949; *s* of Kevin Mark Plunkett O'Hare and Kathleen Mary O'Hare; *m* 1st, 1970, Vivien Eleanor Harwood; one *s*; 2nd, 1993, Alison Jane Springett; one *s. Educ:* Bromley Boys' GS; Leicester Univ. (LLB). Called to the Bar, Lincoln's Inn, 1972; College of Law: Lectr, 1974–78; Sen. Lectr, 1978–85; Principal Lectr, 1985–95. *Publications:* Civil Litigation, 1980, 10th edn 2001; White Book, 2001. *Recreations:* bridge, cycling. *Address:* Supreme Court Costs Office, Clifford's Inn, Fetter Lane, EC4A 1DQ.

O'HEAR, Prof. Anthony, PhD; Professor of Philosophy, University of Bradford, since 1985; Director, Royal Institute of Philosophy, since 1994; *b* 14 Jan. 1942; *s* of Hugo O'Hear and Ann Margery Hester O'Hear (*née* Gompertz); *m* 1981, Patricia Catherine Mary Patterson (Patricia Linton, in ballet); one *s* two *d. Educ:* St Ignatius' Coll., Tottenham; Heythrop Coll.; Warwick Univ. (MA 1968; PhD 1971). Lecturer in Philosophy: Univ. of Hull, 1971–75; Univ. of Surrey, 1975–84. Ed., Philosophy, 1995–. Member: CATE, 1990–94; SCAA, 1993–97; TTA, 1994–97. *Publications:* Karl Popper, 1980; Education, Society and Human Nature, 1981; Experience, Explanation and Faith, 1984; What Philosophy Is, 1985; The Element of Fire, 1988; Introduction to the Philosophy of Science, 1989; Jesus for Beginners, 1993; Beyond Evolution, 1997; After Progress, 1999; Philosophy in the New Century, 2001. *Recreations:* music, visual arts, skiing, tennis, Rugby. *Address:* Department of Interdisciplinary Human Studies, University of Bradford, Bradford BD7 1DP. *T:* (01274) 233985.

O'HIGGINS, Prof. Paul; Fellow, Christ's College, Cambridge, since 1959 (Vice-Master, 1992–95); Professor of Law, King's College London, 1987–92, now Emeritus; *b* 5 Oct. 1927; *s* of Richard Leo O'Higgins, MC, MRCVS and Elizabeth O'Higgins, MA (*née* Deane); *m* 1952, Rachel Elizabeth Bush; one *s* three *d. Educ:* St Ignatius' Coll., Galway; St Columba's Coll., Rathfarnham; Trinity Coll., Dublin (MA, LLB, LLD; Hon. Fellow, 1996); MA, PhD, LLD Cantab. MRIA 1986. Called to the Bar, King's Inns, 1957, and Lincoln's Inn, 1959. University of Cambridge: Dir of Studies in Law, Peterhouse, 1960–74; Steward, Christ's Coll., 1964–68; Tutor for Advanced Students, Christ's, 1970–79; University Lectr, 1965–79; Reader in Labour Law, 1979–84; Regius Prof. of Laws, TCD, 1984–87 (Hon. Prof., 1992–). Co-founder, Cambridge Law Surgery, 1969. Lectr in Labour Law, Inns of Court Sch. of Law, 1976–84; Visiting Professor: Univ. of Kent at Canterbury, 1973–74; City Univ., 1992–96. Mem. Bureau, European Inst. of Social Security, 1970–95; Mem., Staff Side Panel, Civil Service Arbitration Tribunal, 1972–84; Vice-Pres., Inst. of Shops, Health and Safety Acts Admin, 1973–; Pres., Irish Soc. for Labour Law, 1985–87 (Hon. Life Mem., 1997); Mem., Exec. Cttee, Internat. Soc. for Labour Law and Social Security, 1985–. Patron, Cambridge Univ. Graduate Union, 1973–84; Trustee, Cambridge Union Soc., 1973–84; Vice-Pres., Haldane Soc., 1976–; Pres., Ireland Br., Cambridge Soc., 1999–; Gov., British Inst. of Human Rights, 1988–; Vice-Pres., Inst. of Employment Rights, 1989–; Mem., Acad. of European Private Lawyers, 1994. Hon. Treas., Alan Bush Music Trust, 1997–. Mem. Editl Bd, Bibliography of Nineteenth Century Legal Lit., 1991–. Hon. Mem., Grotian Soc., 1968. Gilbert Murray Prize (jt), 1968; Joseph L. Andrews Bibliographical Award, Amer. Assoc. of Law Libraries, 1987. Grand Consul honorifique du consulat de la Vinée de Bergerac, 1983. *Publications:* Bibliography of Periodical Literature relating to Irish Law, 1966, 2nd supp. 1983; (with B. A. Hepple) Public Employee Trade Unionism in the UK: the legal framework, 1971; (with B. A. Hepple) Employment Law, 1971, 4th edn 1981; Censorship in Britain, 1972; Workers' Rights, 1976, 2nd edn 1986; Cases and Materials on Civil Liberties, 1980; Bibliography of Irish Trials, 1986; (with A. D. Dubbins and J. Gennard) Fairness at Work: even-handed industrial relations, 1986; (with M. Partington) Bibliography of Social Security Law, 1986; (ed jtly) The Common Law Tradition: Essays in Irish Legal History, 1990; (ed jtly) Lessons from Northern Ireland, 1991; British and Irish Labour Law, 1979–88: a bibliography, 1993. *Recreations:* wine, talking and travelling, particularly in France and Italy. *Address:* Christ's College, Cambridge CB2 3BU. *T:* (01223) 232659. *Club:* Royal Dublin Society (Dublin).

O'HIGGINS, Hon. Thomas Francis; SC (Ireland) 1954; a Judge of the European Court of Justice, 1985–92; *b* 23 July 1916; *e s* of Dr Thomas F. O'Higgins and Agnes McCarthy; *m* 1948, Thérese Keane; five *s* two *d. Educ:* St Mary's Coll., Rathmines, Clongowes Wood Coll.; University Coll., Dublin (BA); King's Inns, Dublin (BL). Called to Irish Bar, 1938; Bencher of King's Inns, 1967; Judge of High Court, 1973; Chief Justice of Ireland, 1974–85. Elected to Dail Eireann, 1948; Minister for Health, 1954; contested Presidency, 1966 and 1973. *Recreations:* fishing, golf. *Address:* Glenville Cottage, 75 Monkstown Road, Monkstown, Co. Dublin. *T:* (1) 2809119. *Clubs:* Stephen's Green (Dublin); Royal Irish Yacht.

OHLSON, Sir Brian (Eric Christopher), 3rd Bt *cr* 1920; money broker, retired; *b* 27 July 1936; *s* of Sir Eric James Ohlson, 2nd Bt, and of Marjorie Joan, *d* of late C. H. Roosmale-Cocq; *S* father, 1983. *Educ:* Harrow School; RMA Sandhurst. Commissioned into Coldstream Guards, 1956–61. Started money broking, 1961. *Recreations:* sport of kings, cricket, bowls, safaris, bridge, Real tennis. *Heir: b* Peter Michael Ohlson [*b* 18 May 1939; *m* 1968, Sarah, *o d* of Maj.-Gen. Thomas Brodie, CB, CBE, DSO]. *Address:* 1 Courtfield Gardens, SW5 0PA. *Clubs:* MCC, Hurlingham, Queen's.

OISTRAKH, Igor Davidovich; Soviet violinist and conductor; Professor, Royal Conservatoire, Brussels, since 1996; *b* Odessa, 27 April 1931; *s* of late David Oistrakh; *m* 1960, Natalia Nikolaevna Zertsalova, Soviet pianist; one *s. Educ:* Music Sch. and State Conservatoire, Moscow. FRCM. Many foreign tours (USSR, Europe, the Americas, Japan); many gramophone recordings. Prof., Internat. Summer Acad., Belgium, 1997–. 1st prize, Violin Competition, Budapest, 1949; 1st prize, Wieniawski Competition, Poznan, 1952; People's Artist of USSR, 1989. Pres., César Franck Soc., Liège; Hon. Pres., Russian Br., Europ. String Teachers Assoc.; Hon. Member: Beethoven Soc., Bonn; Ysaye Foundn, Liège. Mem. jury of major violin competitions; Igor Oistrakh internat. violin competition established Iserlohn, Germany.

OKA, Prof. Takeshi, PhD; FRS 1984; FRSC 1977; Professor of Chemistry, Astronomy and Astrophysics, since 1981, and Robert A. Millikan Distinguished Service Professor, since 1989, University of Chicago; *b* 10 June 1932; *s* of Shumpei and Chiyoko Oka; *m* 1960, Keiko Nukui; two *s* two *d. Educ:* University of Tokyo. BSc, PhD. Fellow, Japanese Soc. for Promotion of Science, 1960–63; National Research Council of Canada: Postdoctorate Fellow, 1963–65; Asst Research Physicist, 1965–68; Associate Research Physicist, 1968–71; Senior Research Physicist, 1971–75; Herzberg Inst. of Astrophysics, 1975–81. Centenary Lectr, Royal Soc., 1982; Chancellor's Distinguished Lectr, Univ. of California, 1985–86. Fellow, Amer. Acad. of Arts and Scis, 1987. Steacie Prize, Steacie Fund, NRSC, 1972; Earle K. Plyler Prize, Amer. Physical Soc., 1982; William F. Meggers Award, 1997, Ellis R. Lippincott Award, 1998, Optical Soc. of America. *Address:* Department of Chemistry, University of Chicago, 5735 S Ellis Avenue, Chicago, IL 60637, USA.

O'KEEFE, John Harold; TV consultant; *b* 25 Dec. 1938; *s* of Terence Harold O'Keefe and Christian Frances (*née* Foot); *m* 1959, Valerie Anne Atkins; two *s* two *d. Educ:* Acton County Grammar School. Dir, Newspaper Publishers Assoc., 1974; Hd of Industrial Relations, 1974–81, Production Dir, Central London, 1981, Thames TV, 1982; Man. Dir, Limehouse Studios, 1982–86. *Address:* The White House, Dymock, Glos GL18 2AQ.

O'KEEFFE, (Peter) Laurence, CMG 1983; CVO 1974; HM Diplomatic Service, retired; *b* 9 July 1931; *s* of Richard O'Keeffe and Alice (*née* Chase); *m* 1954, Suzanne Marie Jousse; three *d. Educ:* St Francis Xavier's Coll., Liverpool; University Coll., Oxford (schol.). HM Customs and Excise, 1953–62; 2nd, later 1st Sec. (Economic), Bangkok, 1962–65; FO, 1965–68; 1st Sec. and Head of Chancery, Athens, 1968–72; Commercial Counsellor, Jakarta, 1972–75; Head of Hong Kong and Indian Ocean Dept, FCO, 1975–76; Dir-Gen., British Information Services, and Dep. Consul General (Information), New York, 1976–78; Counsellor, Nicosia, 1978–81; Research Associate, Inst. for the Study of Diplomacy, Georgetown Univ., Washington, DC, 1981–82; Ambassador to Senegal, 1982–85, and concurrently (non-resident) to Guinea, Guinea-Bissau, Mali, Mauritania and Cape Verde, 1982–85; Diplomatic Service Chm., CSSB, 1985–86; Head, British Delegn to CSCE Rev. Conf., Vienna, 1986–88; Ambassador to Czechoslovakia, 1988–91. *Publications:* (as Laurence Halley): Simultaneous Equations (novel), 1975; Ancient Affections, 1985; Abiding City (novel), 1986. *Recreations:* gardening, church recording, lecturing. *Address:* Wylye Cottage, Great Wishford, Salisbury, Wilts SP2 0PD.

O'KELLY, Surgeon Rear-Adm. Francis Joseph, OBE 1965; Royal Navy, retired 1980; Occupational Health Consultant, Medical and Health Department, Government of Hong Kong, 1980–86; *b* 24 Dec. 1921; *s* of Francis John O'Kelly and Elizabeth Mary O'Kelly (*née* Rogan); *m* 1954, Winifred Mary Teresa Henry; one *s* three *d. Educ:* St Patrick's Coll., Cavan; University Coll., Dublin. MB, BCh 1945; FFCM, FFOM (RCPI), MFOM (RCPE); Hon. FACOM; DPH, DIH. Hosp. appts in Dublin, 1946–48; joined RN 1948; served with RM Commandos, Middle and Far East, 1948–52; HM Ships Unicorn, St Bride's Bay and Centaur, RNB Chatham and RN Air Station, Brawdy, 1952–63; Naval MOH appts, Far East Fleet, Scotland and NI Comd, Portsmouth and Chatham Comd, 1963–72; Dep. Dir, Health and Research, 1972–74; MO i/c RN Hosp. Gibraltar, 1974–77; Surgeon Rear-Adm. (Ships and Establishments), 1977–78; Surg. Rear-Adm. (Naval Hosps), 1978–80; QHP 1977–80. Adviser in Preventive and Industrial Medicine to Med. Dir Gen. (Naval), 1972–77, in Community Medicine, 1977–80. *Publications:* articles in med jls. *Recreations:* reading and travel. *Address:* Large Barn, North Bersted Street, Bognor Regis, W Sussex PO22 9AH.

O'KENNEDY, Michael E., SC; TD (FF) Tipperary North, 1969–80, 1982–93 and since 1997; *b* Nenagh, Co. Tipperary, 21 Feb. 1936; *s* of Éamonn and Helena O'Kennedy; *m* 1965, Breda, *d* of late Andrew Heavey and of Mary Heavey; one *s* two *d. Educ:* St Flannan's College, Ennis, Co. Clare; St Patrick's Coll., Maynooth, Co. Kildare; Univ. Coll., Dublin. MA 1957. Called to Irish Bar, 1961; Bencher, King's Inns, Dublin, 1998; Senior Counsel 1973. Mem., Irish Senate, 1965–69, 1993–97; Mem., Oireachtas Select Constitutional Cttee, 1966; Parly Sec. to Minister for Educn, 1970–72; Minister without Portfolio, Dec. 1972–Jan. 1973; Minister for Transport and Power, Jan.–March 1973; Opposition spokesman on Foreign Affairs (incl. Anglo-Irish Affairs), 1973–77; Minister for Foreign Affairs, 1977–79; Pres., Council of Ministers of the European Communities, July–Dec. 1979; Minister for Finance, 1979–81; Pres., Bd of Govs, EIB, 1979; opposition spokesman on finance, 1983–87; Minister for Agriculture and Food, 1987–92; Pres., Council of Agriculture Ministers, EC, Jan.–June 1990. Mem., Commn of the European Communities, 1981–82. Personal Rep. of An Taoiseach, Eur. Convention for Charter of Fundamental Human Rights, 1999–. Co-Chm., British-Irish Parly Body, 1997–. Non-executive Director: Hanzard Europe Ltd; Tradewise Underwriting Agencies Ltd.

OKEOVER, Sir Peter Ralph Leopold W.; *see* Walker-Okeover.

OKINE, Most Rev. Robert Garshong Allotey; *see* West Africa, Archbishop of.

OKOGIE, Most Rev. Anthony Olubunmi; *see* Lagos, Archbishop of, (RC).

OKOTH, Rt Rev. Yona; Archbishop of Uganda and Bishop of Kampala, 1984–94; *b* 15 April 1927; *s* of Nasanairi Owora and Tezira Akech; *m* Jessica Naome Okoth (*d* 2001); four *s* five *d*. Bishop's clerk, 1947; Ordination Class, 1953–54 (certificate); deacon 1954, priest 1955; Parish Priest, Nagongera, 1956–60; St Augustine's Coll., Canterbury, 1963 (Diploma); Diocesan Treasurer, Mbale Diocese, 1961–65; Provincial Sec., Kampala, 1965–66; studies, Wycliffe Coll., Toronto Univ., 1966–68 (Dip. and LTh); Provincial Sec., Kampala, 1968–72; Diocesan Bishop of Bukedi, 1972–83. Hon. DD Wycliffe Coll., Toronto, 1978. *Recreation:* interest in farming. *Address:* c/o PO Box 255, Tororo, Uganda.

OKRI, Ben, OBE 2001; FRSL; writer; *b* 15 March 1959; *s* of Silver and Grace Okri. *Educ:* Univ. of Essex. Poetry Editor, West Africa, 1983–86; broadcaster and presenter, BBC, 1983–85; Fellow Commoner in Creative Arts, Trinity Coll., Cambridge, 1991–93. Mem. Bd, RNT, 1999–. Mem., Soc. of Authors, 1986–. FRSL 1998. Hon. DLitt Westminster, 1997. Crystal Award, World Econ. Forum, Switzerland, 1995. *Publications:* Flowers and Shadows, 1980; The Landscapes Within, 1982; Incidents at the Shrine, 1986 (Commonwealth Prize for Africa, 1987; Paris Review Aga Khan Prize for fiction, 1987); Stars of the New Curfew, 1988; The Famished Road, 1991 (Booker Prize, 1991; Premio Letterario Internazionale Chianti-Ruffino-Antico Fattore, 1993; Premio Grinzane Cavour, 1994); An African Elegy, 1992; Songs of Enchantment, 1993; Astonishing the Gods, 1995; Birds of Heaven, 1995; Dangerous Love, 1996 (Premio Palmi, 1999); A Way of Being Free, 1997; Infinite Riches, 1998; Mental Fight, 1999. *Recreations:* music, chess, theatre, art, good conversation, walking, silence. *Address:* c/o Orion Books Ltd, Orion House, 5 Upper St Martin's Lane, WC2H 9EA. *Club:* PEN International (Vice-Pres., English Centre, 1997).

OLAH, Prof. George Andrew, PhD; Distinguished Professor of Chemistry and Director, Loker Hydrocarbons Research Institute, University of Southern California, since 1977; *b* 22 May 1927; *s* of Julius Olah and Magda Krasznai; *m* 1949, Judith Lengyel; two *s*. *Educ:* Technical Univ. of Budapest (PhD Chemistry 1949). Faculty Mem., Technical Univ. of Budapest, 1950–55; Associate Dir for Organic Chem., Central Res. Inst., Hungarian Acad. of Scis, 1955–56; Res. Scientist, Dow Chemical Co., Ontario, 1957–65; Prof. and Chm., Dept of Chem., Case Western Reserve Univ., Cleveland, Ohio, 1965–77. For. Mem., Royal Soc., 1997. Numerous hon. doctorates. Nobel Prize in Chemistry, 1994; numerous awards. *Publications:* Theoretical Organic Chemistry, 2 vols, 1954; (ed) Friedel-Crafts and Related Reactions, 4 vols, 1963–65; (ed jtly) Carbonium Ions, 5 vols, 1968–75; Friedel-Crafts Chemistry, 1973; Carbocations and Electrophilic Reactions, 1973; Halonium Ions, 1975; (jtly) Superacids, 1985; (jtly) Hypercarbon Chemistry, 1987; (jtly) Nitration: methods and mechanism, 1989; (ed) Cage Hydrocarbons, 1990; (ed jtly) Electron Deficient Boron and Carbon Clusters, 1991; (ed jtly) Chemistry of Energetic Materials, 1991; (ed jtly) Synthetic Fluorine Chemistry, 1992; (jtly) Hydrocarbon Chemistry, 1994; A Life of Magic Chemistry, 2001; numerous scientific papers and 100 patents. *Address:* Loker Hydrocarbons Research Institute, University of Southern California, Los Angeles, LA 90089, USA. *T:* (213) 7405976.

OLANG', Most Rev. Festo Habakkuk; *b* 11 Nov. 1914; *m* 1937, Eseri D. Olang'; four *s* eight *d*. *Educ:* Alliance High School. Teacher, 1936–43; ordained 1945; consecrated Assistant Bishop of Mombasa in Namirembe Cathedral, by Archbishop of Canterbury, 1955; Bishop of Maseno, 1961; Bishop of Nairobi, 1970; Archbishop of Kenya, 1970–79. Hon. DD Univ. of the South Sewanee, USA. *Address:* PO Box 1, Maseno, Kenya.

OLAYAN, Suliman Saleh, Hon. KBE 1987; Founder and Chairman, The Olayan Group, since 1947; *b* 5 Nov. 1918; *s* of Saleh Olayan and Haya Al Ghanim; *m* 1974, Mary Perdikis; one *s* three *d*. *Educ:* Bahrain. Founding Chairman: Arab Commercial Enterprises, 1950–84; Nat. Gas Co., 1951–54; Saudi British Bank, 1978–89; Saudi Spanish Bank, 1979–84; Director: Al Khobar Power Co., 1950–54; Riyad Bank, 1963–78; Saudi Arabian Airlines, 1965–81; Mobil Corp., 1980–83; CS First Boston, 1988–95. Member: Internat. Council of Morgan Guaranty Trust Co., 1979–90; Internat. Adv. Bd, Amer. Internat. Gp, 1982–99; Adv. Bd, Energy Internat. NV, 1983–92. Chairman: Riyadh Chamber of Commerce and Industry, 1981–89; Council of Saudi Chambers of Commerce and Industry, 1984–87. Member: Internat. Industrial Conf., 1961–; Gp of Thirty, 1984–87; Bd, Inst. for Internat. Econs, 1987–; Internat. Council, INSEAD, 1991–97. Mem., Rockefeller Univ. Council, 1974–87 (Alumnus Mem., 1987–). Founding Vice Chm., Handicapped Children's Assoc., Riyadh, 1983–88. Medal of Honour, Madrid Chamber of Commerce and Industry, 1985. Great Cross, Order of Merit (Spain), 1984; Comdr First Class, Royal Order of Polar Star (Sweden), 1988. *Publications:* contribs to Washington Qly, Fortune, Wall Street Jl, Financial Times. *Address:* PO Box 8772, Riyadh, Saudi Arabia. *Clubs:* Royal Automobile; Equestrian (Riyadh); Knickerbocker, New York Athletic (New York); Pacific–Union, Bohemian (San Francisco).

OLDENBOURG-IDALIE, Zoë; Chevalier, Légion d'Honneur, 1980; Officier du Mérite des Arts et des Lettres, 1978; writer (as Zoë Oldenbourg); *b* 31 March 1916; *d* of Sergius Oldenbourg, writer and historicist, and of Ada (*née* Starynkevitch); *m* 1948, Heinric Idalie; one *s* one *d*. *Educ:* Lycée Molière, Paris; Sorbonne, Paris. Prix Fémina, 1953. *Publications:* Argile et cendres, 1946 (The World is Not Enough, 1949); La Pierre angulaire, 1953 (The Cornerstone, 1954); Réveillés de la Vie, 1956 (The Awakened, trans. E. Hyams, 1957); Les Irréductibles, 1958 (The Chains of Love, 1959); Bûcher de Montségur, 1959 (Massacre at Montségur, 1962); Les Brûlés, 1961 (Destiny of Fire, trans. P. Green, 1961); Les Cités charnelles, 1961 (Cities of the Flesh, 1963); Les Croisades: un essai historique, 1963 (The Crusades, trans. Anne Carter, 1966); Catherine de Russie, 1965 (Catherine the Great, 1965); Saint Bernard, 1969; La Joie des pauvres, 1970 (The Heirs of the Kingdom, trans. Anne Carter, 1972); L'Epopée des cathédrales, 1973; Que vous a donc fait Israël?, 1974; Visages d'un autoportrait (autobiog.), 1977; La Joie-Souffrance, 1980; Le Procès du Rêve, 1982; Que nous est Hécube?, 1984; Les Amours égarées, 1987; Déguisements, 1989; Aliénor, 1992. *Recreation:* painting. *Address:* 4 rue de Montmorency, 92100 Boulogne, France.

OLDENBURG, Claes Thure; artist; *b* Stockholm, 28 Jan. 1929; *s* of Gosta Oldenburg and Sigrid Elisabeth (*née* Lindfors); *m* 1st, 1960, Pat Muschinski (marr. diss. 1970); 2nd, 1977, Coosje van Bruggen. *Educ:* Yale Univ. (BA 1951); Art Inst. Chicago. Apprentice reporter, City News Bureau, Chicago, 1950–52; became American citizen, 1953. First gp exhibn at Club St Elmo, Chicago, 1953; subseq. at local shows, Chicago and Evanston, 1953–56; moved to NY, 1956; has participated in numerous gp exhibns of contemp. art in USA and Europe, including: Dallas Mus. Contemp. Art, 1961, 1962; ICA, 1963; Mus. Mod. Art, NY, 1963, 1988, 1990, 1991; Washington Gall. Mod. Art, 1963; Tate Gall., 1964; Metropolitan Mus. Art, NY, 1969; one-man shows in USA and Europe, including: Reuben Gall., NY, 1960; Sidney Janis Gall., NY, 1964–70; travelling exhibitions: Tate Gall. and other European galls, 1970; Musée d'Art Moderne, Paris, 1977; Nat. Gall. of Art, Washington, 1995; Solomon R. Guggenheim Mus., NY, and galls in London, LA and Bonn, 1995–96; numerous commnd works in permanent collections in USA and Europe, incl. Centre Georges Pompidou, Paris, Museums of Contemp. Art, Chicago and LA, Tate Gall.; numerous outdoor works in corporate and private collections. Member: AAIL, 1975; Amer. Acad. Arts and Scis, 1978. Awards include: Brandeis Award for Sculpture, 1971; Medal, Amer. Inst. Architects, 1977; Wilhelm-Lehmbruck Sculpture Award, Duisburg, 1981; Wolf Foundn Prize, Israel, 1989; Lifetime Achievement Award, Internat. Sculpture Centre, 1994. *Publications:* Spicy Ray Gun, 1960; Ray Gun Poems, 1960; More Ray Gun Poems, 1960, 2nd edn 1973; Injun and Other Histories, 1960; Store Days, 1967; Notes, 1968; Constructions, Models and Drawings, 1969; Notes in Hand, 1971; Raw Notes, 1973; Log, May 1974–August 1976, 1976; (jtly) Il Corso del Coltello: Menu, 1985 (trans. Italian 1985); (jtly) Sketches and Blottings toward the European Desktop, 1990 (trans. Italian 1990); Multiples in Retrospect, 1991; (with Coosje van Bruggen) Large-Scale Projects, 1994; exhibn catalogues; contribs to books and jls. *Address:* c/o Pace Gallery, 32 E 57th Street, New York, NY 10022–2513, USA.

See also R. E. Oldenburg.

OLDENBURG, Richard Erik; Hon. Chairman, Sotheby's North and South America, since 2000 (Chairman, 1995–2000); *b* 21 Sept. 1933; *s* of Gösta Oldenburg and Sigrid Elisabeth (*née* Lindforss); *m* 1960, Harriet Lisa Turnure (*d* 1998). *Educ:* Harvard Coll. (AB 1954). Manager, Design Dept, Doubleday & Co., NYC, 1958–61; Man. Editor, Trade Div., Macmillan Co., NYC, 1961–69; Dir, Publications, 1969–72, Dir, 1972–94, Museum of Modern Art, NYC. *Address:* c/o Sotheby's, 1334 York Avenue, New York, NY 10021, USA.

See also C. T. Oldenburg.

OLDFATHER, Irene; Member (Lab) Cunninghame South, Scottish Parliament, since 1999; *b* 6 Aug. 1954; *d* of Campbell and Margaret Hamilton; *m* 1978, Rodrick Oldfather; one *s* one *d*. *Educ:* Univ. of Strathclyde (BA Hons Politics 1976; MSc Res. 1983). Lectr in US Politics, Univ. of Arizona, 1978–79; Policy Planner, Glasgow CC, 1980–90; Political Researcher, MEP, 1990–97; freelance journalist, European affairs, 1994–98; part-time Lectr, Paisley Univ., 1996–98. Scottish Parliament: Vice Convenor, Cross Party Gp on Tobacco Control; Member: Eur. Cttee, 1999–; Health and Community Care Cttee, 1999–2001. *Publication:* res. paper for Scotland Europa. *Recreations:* going to ballet, reading, children, pets. *Address:* Scottish Parliament, Edinburgh EH99 1SP. *T:* (0131) 348 5769; (constituency office) Sovereign House, Academy Road, Irvine KA12 8RL. *T:* (01294) 313078, *Fax:* (01294) 313605.

OLDFIELD, Bruce, OBE 1990; designer; *b* 14 July 1950; parents unknown; brought up by Dr Barnardo's, Ripon, Yorks. *Educ:* Ripon Grammar School; Sheffield City Polytechnic (Hon. Fellow 1987); Ravensbourne College of Art; St Martin's College of Art. Established fashion house, 1975; produced designer collections of high fashion clothes for UK and overseas; began exporting clothes worldwide, 1975; began making couture clothes for individual clients, 1981; opened first Bruce Oldfield retail shop, selling ready to wear and couture to international clientèle, 1984. Exhibitor: British Design Exhibn, Vienna, 1986; Australian Bicentennial Fashion Show, Sydney Opera House, 1988. Lectures: Fashion Inst., NY, 1977; Los Angeles County Museum, 1985; Internat. Design Conf., Aspen, Colorado, 1986 (Speaker and show). Vice Pres., Barnardo's. Trustee, Royal Acad., 2000–. Gov., London Inst. Hon. Fellow RCA, 1990. Hon. DCL Northumbria at Newcastle, 2001. Designed for films: Jackpot, 1974; The Sentinel, 1976. *Publication:* (with Georgina Howell) Bruce Oldfield's Season, 1987. *Recreations:* music, reading, driving, working. *Address:* 27 Beauchamp Place, SW3 1NJ. *T:* (020) 7584 1363.

OLDFIELD, Michael Gordon, (Mike); musician and composer; *b* 15 May 1953; *s* of Dr Raymond Henry Oldfield and Maureen Bernadine Liston; three *s* two *d*. *Educ:* St Edward's, Reading; Presentation Coll., Reading. Records include: Tubular Bells, 1973 (over 16 million copies sold to date); Hergest Ridge; Ommadawn; Incantations; Platinum; QE2, 1980; Five Miles Out, 1982; Crises, 1983; Discovery, 1984; The Killing Fields (film sound track), 1984; Islands, 1987; The Wind Chimes (video album), 1988; Earthmoving, 1989; Amarok, 1990; Heaven's Open, 1991; Tubular Bells II, 1992; The Songs of Distant Earth, 1994; Voyager, 1996; Tubular Bells III, 1998. Extensive world wide concert tours, 1979–. Mem., Assoc. of Professional Composers. Freeman, City of London, 1982. Hon. Pict. *Recreations:* helicopter pilot, squash, ski-ing, cricket. *Address:* c/o Ross, Bennet-Smith, 112 Jermyn Street, SW1Y 6LS. *Club:* Jacobs Larder (Ealing).

OLDHAM, Prof. (Charles Herbert) Geoffrey, CBE 1990; Professorial Fellow, Science Policy Research Unit, University of Sussex, 1966–97, now Hon. Professor (Director, 1980–92); Science Adviser to President, International Development Research Centre, Ottawa, on secondment, 1992–96; *b* 17 Feb. 1929; *s* of Herbert Cecil Oldham and Evelyn Selina Oldham (*née* Brooke); *m* 1951, Brenda Mildred Raven; two *s* one *d* (and one *s* decd). *Educ:* Bingley Grammar Sch.; Reading Univ. (BSc Hons); Toronto Univ. (MA, PhD). Research geophysicist, Chevron Research Corp., 1954–57; Sen. Geophysicist, Standard Oil Co. of California, 1957–60; Fellow, Inst. of Current World Affairs, studying Chinese lang. and sci., 1960–66; Scientific Directorate, OECD, 1965–66; Dep. Dir, Science Policy Res. Unit, 1966–80; Associate Dir, Internat. Develt Res. Centre, Ottawa, 1970–80. Vis. Prof., Stanford Univ., 1979; Vis. Researcher, Aust. Sci. and Tech. Adv. Council, 1988. Chm., UN Adv. Cttee on Sci. and Tech. for Develt, 1991–92; UK Mem., UN Commn on Sci., Technol. and Develt, 1993–97. *Publications:* articles in jls on science, technology and Chinese development. *Recreations:* travel, esp. long distance train journeys, golf. *Address:* Science Policy Research Unit, University of Sussex, Brighton, E Sussex BN1 9RF; Buff Cottage, Firle Road, Seaford, E Sussex BN25 2HU.

OLDMAN, Gary; actor; *b* 21 March 1958; *m* 1st, Lesley Manville (marr. diss.); one *s*; 2nd, 1991, Uma Thurman (marr. diss. 1993); 3rd, Donya Fiorentino; one *s*. *Educ:* South East London Sch. for Boys; Rose Bruford Coll. of Speech and Drama (BA Theatre Arts 1979). *Theatre* includes: Greenwich Young People's Theatre; Theatre Royal, York; Glasgow Citizens' Theatre: Massacre at Paris, A Waste of Time, Desperado Corner, Chinchilla, 1980 (toured Europe and S America); Royal Court Theatre: Rat in the Skull, 1984; The Pope's Wedding, 1984; Women Beware Women, 1986; Serious Money, 1987; Royal Shakespeare Company: The Desert Air, 1985; The War Plays, 1985; Real Dreams, 1986; The Country Wife, Royal Exchange, Manchester, 1986; Entertaining Mr Sloane, Oldham Rep. Co., 1987; *films* include: Sid and Nancy, 1986; Prick Up Your Ears, 1987; Track 29, 1988; Paris By Night, 1989; State of Grace, 1990; JFK, Chattahoochee, 1991; Bram Stoker's Dracula, 1992; True Romance, 1993; Romeo is Bleeding, Immortal Beloved, The Professional, 1994; Murder in the First, The Scarlet Letter, 1995; The Fifth Element, Air Force One, 1997; Lost in Space, Nil By Mouth, 1998 (writer and dir; BAFTA Award for best original screenplay); Hannibal, The Contender, 2001; *television* includes: Remembrance, 1982; Meantime, 1984; Heading Home, 1991; Fallen Angels: dead end for Delia, 1993. *Address:* c/o ICM, Oxford House, 76 Oxford Street, W1N 0AX; c/o Douglas Management Inc., 515 N Robertson Boulevard, Los Angeles, CA 90048-1730, USA.

O'LEARY, John; *see* O'Leary, M. J.

O'LEARY, Michael; barrister; *b* 8 May 1936; *s* of John O'Leary and Margaret McCarthy; unmarried. *Educ:* Presentation Coll., Cork; University Coll., Cork; Columbia Univ., NY. Called to the Bar, King's Inns, Dublin, 1979. Educn Officer, Irish TUC, 1962–65. TD: (Lab) Dublin N Central, 1965–82; (FG) Dublin SW, 1982–87; Minister for Labour, 1973–77; Dep. Leader, Labour Party, 1977–81, Leader, 1981–82 (resigned); Tánaiste (Dep. Prime Minister) and Minister for Industry and Energy, 1981–82; joined Fine Gael, 1982. President, ILO, 1976. Mem. for Ireland, European Parlt, 1979–81. *Address:* Áras Uí Dhálaigh, Inns Quay, Dublin 7, Ireland.

O'LEARY, (Michael) John; Education Editor, The Times, since 1993; *b* 11 Dec. 1951; *s* of Captain Daniel Joseph O'Leary, RN, and Sylvia Jane O'Leary; *m* 1977, Susan Berenice Whittingham; two *s* one *d*. *Educ:* Taunton Sch.; Sheffield Univ. (BA Politics 1973; Pres., Students' Union, 1973–74). Reporter, Evening Chronicle, Newcastle upon Tyne, 1975–78; Reporter/news editor, 1978–85, Dep. Editor, 1985–90, THES; Educn Corresp., The Times, 1990–93. Mem., Govt Inquiry into Primary Sch. Test Standards, 1999. *Publication:* The Times Good University Guide, 1993–. *Recreations:* squash, tennis, travel, watching Arsenal. *Address:* The Times, 1 Pennington Street, E98 1TF. *T:* (020) 7782 5788. *Club:* Woodford Wells (Woodford).

O'LEARY, Peter Leslie; Under-Secretary, Inland Revenue, 1978–84; *b* 12 June 1929; *s* of Archibald and Edna O'Leary; *m* 1960, Margaret Elizabeth Debney; four *d*. *Educ:* Portsmouth Southern Grammar Sch.; University Coll., London (BA). Joined Inland Revenue as Inspector, 1952; Sen. Principal Inspector, 1974. *Recreations:* horology, gardening, wine-making. *Address:* 17 Sleaford Road, Heckington, Sleaford, Lincs NG34 9QP. *T:* (01529) 461213.

O'LEARY, Terence Daniel, CMG 1982; MA; HM Diplomatic Service, retired 1988; *b* 18 Aug. 1928; 2nd *s* of late Daniel O'Leary and Mary (*née* Duggan); *m* 1960, Janet Douglas Berney (*d* 1997), *d* of Dr H. B. Berney, Masterton, NZ; twin *s* one *d*. *Educ:* Dulwich; St John's Coll., Cambridge (MA). Army, commnd Queen's Royal Regt, 1946–48. Commerce, 1951–53; Asst Principal, CRO, 1953; 2nd Sec., British High Commn, Wellington, 1956–58; Principal, PSO's Dept, CRO, 1958; 1st Sec., New Delhi, 1960–63; 1st Sec., Dar es Salaam, 1963–64; CRO, 1964–65; 1st Sec. and Defence Sec., Canberra, 1965–68; Actg Head, S Asia Dept, FCO, 1969; Asst Sec., Cabinet Office, 1970–72; Counsellor, Pretoria/Cape Town, 1972–74; Dep. High Comr, Wellington, 1974–78; Senior Civil Mem., Directing Staff, Nat. Defence Coll., 1978–81; High Comr in Sierra Leone, 1981–84; High Comr in New Zealand and concurrently to Western Samoa, and Governor of Pitcairn, 1984–87. Mem., EC Monitoring Mission, Yugoslavia, 1991–92. Parish Councillor (Ind.), Petworth, 1993–97. *Recreations:* cutting grass, croquet. *Address:* Glebe Cottage, Bartons Lane, Petworth, W Sussex GU28 0DA. *T:* (01798) 344137. *Clubs:* Travellers; Wellington (NZ).

OLINS, Wallace, (Wally), CBE 1999; MA Oxon; FCSD; Founder, Wolff Olins; *b* 19 Dec. 1930; *s* of Alfred Olins and Rachel (*née* Muscovitch); *m* 1st, 1957, Maria Renate Olga Laura Steinert (marr. diss. 1989); two *s* one *d*; 2nd, 1990, Dornie Watts; one *d*. *Educ:* Highgate Sch.; St Peter's Coll., Oxford (Hons History, MA). National Service, Army, in Germany, 1950–51. S. H. Benson Ltd, London, 1954–57; Benson, India, 1957–62; Caps Design Group, London, 1962–65; Wolff Olins, London, 1965–2001. Vis. Lectr, Design Management, London Business Sch., 1984–89; Visiting Professor, Management School: Imperial Coll., 1987–89; Lancaster Univ., 1992–; Visiting Professor: Copenhagen Business Sch., 1993; DUXX (formerly Centro de Excelencia Empresarial), Mexico, 1995–. Non-exec. Dir, HEA, 1996–99; Dir, Glasgow Year of Design and Architecture, 1999. Vice-Pres., SIAD, 1982–85. Chm., Design Dimension Educnl Trust, 1987–93; Mem. Develt Trust, RPO, 1994–99. Mem., Council, RSA, 1989–95. Bicentenary Medal, RSA, 2000. *Publications:* The Corporate Personality, 1978; The Wolff Olins Guide to Corporate Identity, 1983; The Wolff Olins Guide to Design Management, 1985; Corporate Identity, 1989; International Corporate Identity, vol. 1, 1995; The New Guide to Identity, 1996; Trading Identities, 1999; numerous articles in Design and Management publications. *Recreations:* looking at buildings, shopping for books, theatre. *Address:* Grahamsfield, Goring-on-Thames, Reading RG8 9AD. *Club:* Groucho.

OLIPHANT, Air Vice-Marshal David Nigel Kington B.; *see* Blair-Oliphant.

OLIPHANT, Tuelonyana Rosemary D.; *see* Ditlhabi Oliphant.

OLIVE, Prof. David Ian, FRS 1987; Research Professor of Physics, University of Wales Swansea (formerly University College of Swansea), since 1994; *b* 16 April 1937; *s* of Ernest Edward Olive and Lilian Emma Olive (*née* Chambers); *m* 1963, Jenifer Mary Tutton; two *d*. *Educ:* Royal High Sch., Edinburgh; Univ. of Edinburgh (MA); Univ. of Cambridge (BA, PhD). Fellow of Churchill Coll., 1963–70; Lectr, Univ. of Cambridge, 1965–71; Staff Mem., CERN, 1971–77; Imperial College: Lectr, 1977; Reader, 1980; Prof. of Theoretical Physics, 1984–92; Res. Prof. of Maths, Univ. Coll. of Swansea, 1992–94. Visiting Professor: Univ. of Virginia, 1982–83; Univ. of Geneva, 1986; Inst. for Advanced Studies, Princeton, 1987–88; Newton Inst. for Math. Scis, Cambridge, 1992, 1997; Kramers Prof., Univ. of Utrecht, 2000. Dirac Medal and Prize, Abdus Salam Internat. Centre for Theoretical Physics, Trieste, 1997. *Publications:* (jtly) The Analytic S-Matrix, 1966; (jtly) Kac-Moody and Virasoro Algebras, 1988; (jtly) Paul Dirac: the man and his work, 1998; many articles on theoretical physics in learned jls. *Recreations:* listening to music, golf. *Address:* Department of Physics, University of Wales Swansea, Singleton Park, Swansea SA2 8PP. *T:* (01792) 295842. *Club:* Pennard Golf.

OLIVER, family name of **Baron Oliver of Aylmerton**.

OLIVER OF AYLMERTON, Baron *cr* 1986 (Life Peer), of Aylmerton in the County of Norfolk; **Peter Raymond Oliver,** Kt 1974; PC 1980; a Lord of Appeal in Ordinary, 1986–92; *b* 7 March 1921; *s* of David Thomas Oliver, Fellow of Trinity Hall, Cambridge, and Alice Maud Oliver; *m* 1st, 1945, Mary Chichester Rideal (*d* 1985), *d* of Sir Eric Keightley Rideal, MBE, FRS; one *s* one *d*; 2nd, 1987, Wendy Anne, *widow* of I. Lewis Lloyd Jones. *Educ:* The Leys, Cambridge; Trinity Hall, Cambridge (Hon. Fellow, 1980). Military Service, 1941–45, 12th Bn RTR (despatches). Called to Bar, Lincoln's Inn, 1948, Bencher 1973; QC 1965; Judge of the High Ct of Justice, Chancery Div., 1974–80; a Lord Justice of Appeal, 1980–86. Mem., Restrictive Practices Court, 1976–80; Chm., Review Body on Chancery Div. of High Court, 1979–81. Hon. LLD: City of London Poly., 1989; UEA, 1991; Cambridge, 1995. *Recreations:* gardening, music. *Address:* House of Lords, SW1A 0PW.

See also Hon. D. K. R. Oliver.

OLIVER, Prof. (Ann) Dawn (Harrison), PhD; Professor of Constitutional Law, University College London, since 1993; *b* 7 June 1942; *d* of Gordon and Mieke Taylor; *m* 1967, Stephen John Lindsay Oliver, *qv*; one *s* two *d*. *Educ:* Newnham Coll., Cambridge (BA 1964; MA 1967; PhD 1993; Associate Fellow, 1996–99). Called to the Bar, Middle Temple, 1965 (Harmsworth Schol.; Bencher, 1996); in practice at the Bar, 1965–69; Consultant, Legal Action Gp, 1971–76; University College London: Lectr in Law, 1976–87; Sen. Lectr, 1987–90; Reader in Public Law, 1990–93; Dean, Faculty of Laws, and Head of Law Dept, 1993–98; Hon. Fellow, 2001. Hon. Fellow, Soc. of Advanced Legal Studies, 1997–. Member: Commn on Election Campaigns, 1990–91, Res. and Academic Panel, 1995–, Hansard Soc.; Wkg Party on Noise, DoE, 1990–91; Study of Parlt Gp, 1991–; Adv. Bd, Constitution Unit, 1995–; Labour and Liberal Democrats Jt Consultative Cttee on Constitutional Reform, 1996–97; Royal Commn on Reform of the H of L, 1999; Trustee, Citizenship Foundn, 1990–94 (Mem., Adv. Bd, 1994–). Editor, Public Law, 1993–. *Publications:* (ed jtly) The Changing Constitution, 1985, 4th edn 2000; (ed jtly) New Directions in Judicial Review, 1988; (ed jtly) Economical with the Truth: the press in a democratic society, 1990; Government in the United Kingdom: the search for accountability, effectiveness and citizenship, 1991; (jtly) The Foundations of Citizenship, 1994; (jtly) Public Service Reform: issues of accountability and public law, 1996; (ed jtly) Halsbury's Laws of England on Constitutional Law and Human Rights, 1996; (ed jtly) The Law and Parliament, 1998; Common Values and the Public-Private Divide, 1999; articles on constitutional and admin. law. *Recreations:* walking, London, Aldeburgh, travel. *Address:* Faculty of Laws, University College London, Bentham House, Endsleigh Gardens, WC1H 0EG. T: (020) 7391 1409.

OLIVER, Benjamin Rhys; Stipendiary Magistrate for Mid-Glamorgan, 1983–95; a Recorder of the Crown Court, 1972–93; *b* 8 June 1928; *m* 1955; one *s* one *d*. *Educ:* Llandovery and Aberystwyth. Called to the Bar, Inner Temple, 1954. An Asst Recorder, Swansea, Cardiff and Merthyr Tydfil QS, 1967–71. A Chm., Med. Appeal Tribunals and Vaccine Damage Tribunals, 1981–83. *Recreation:* golf.

OLIVER, Hon. David Keightley Rideal; QC 1986; *b* 4 June 1949; *o s* of Baron Oliver of Aylmerton, *qv*; *m* 1st, 1972, Marisa Mirasierras (marr. diss. 1987); two *s*; 2nd, 1988, Judith Britannia Caroline Powell; two *s*. *Educ:* Westminster School; Trinity Hall, Cambridge; Institut d'Etudes Européennes, Brussels. Called to the Bar, Lincoln's Inn, 1972, Bencher, 1994; Junior Counsel to Dir-Gen. of Fair Trading, 1980–86. *Recreations:* gardening, bird watching, shooting. *Address:* Erskine Chambers, 30 Lincoln's Inn Fields, WC2A 3PF. *T:* (020) 7242 5532.

OLIVER, Dawn; *see* Oliver, A. D. H.

OLIVER, Dame Gillian (Frances), DBE 1998; Director of Service Development, Macmillan Cancer Relief, since 2000; *b* 10 Oct. 1943; *d* of Frank Joseph Power and Ethel Mary Power; *m* 1966, Martin Jeremy Oliver; three *d*. *Educ:* Brentwood County High Sch., Essex; Middlesex Hosp., London (RN); Open Univ. (BA 1979). Night Sister and Ward Sister, Clatterbridge Centre for Oncology, 1978–87; Advr in Oncology Nursing, RCN, 1987–89; Regl Nurse, Cancer Services, Mersey RHA, 1989–90; Dir of Patient Services, Clatterbridge Centre for Oncology, 1990–2000. *Recreations:* travel, music, literature. *Address:* 1 Well Close, Ness, S Wirral, Cheshire CH64 4EE.

OLIVER, Comdr James Arnold, RN; Clerk, Ironmongers' Company, since 1990 (Deputy Clerk, 1989–90); *b* 10 Aug. 1941; *s* of Capt. Philip Daniel Oliver, CBE, RN and Audrey Mary Oliver (*née* Taylor); *m* 1973, Anne Elise de Burgh Sidley. *Educ:* Sedbergh Sch.; BRNC. Joined RN, 1959; seaman officer, 1959–88; navigation specialist, 1969; Divl Officer, Dartmouth, 1971–73; served in minesweepers, frigates and HM Ships Ark Royal, 1973–74, Sheffield, 1976–78, and Fearless, 1984–86; CO, Barbados Coastguard, 1981–83. FIMgt 1994. *Recreations:* cruising under sail, riding, country life.

See also S. J. L. Oliver.

OLIVER, (James) Michael (Yorrick); Director, Investment Funds, Scottish Widows Investment Partnership (formerly Hill Samuel Asset Management Ltd), since 1996; Lord Mayor of London, 2001–Nov. 2002; *b* 13 July 1940; *s* of George Leonard Jack Oliver and Patricia Rosamund Oliver (*née* Douglas); *m* 1963, Sally Elizabeth Honor Exner; two *d*. *Educ:* Brunswick Sch.; Wellington Coll. AIIMR 1978; MSI 1992. Rediffusion Ltd, 1959–63; Manager, Helios Ltd, 1965–70; Kitcat & Aitken, 1970–86 (Partner, 1977–86); Dir, Kitcat & Aitken & Co., 1986–90; Man. Dir, Carr Kitcat & Aitken, 1990–93; Dir, Lloyds Investment Managers Ltd, 1994–96. Director: Garbhaig Hydro Power Co., 1988–; German Investment Trust, 1994–97; German Smaller Cos Investment Trust, 1994–; Central and Eastern European Fund Ltd, 1995–; Euro Spain Fund Ltd, 1996–; Portugal Growth Fund, 1996–2000; European Growth Fund, 2001–; Hill Samuel UK Emerging Cos Investment Trust plc, 1996–2000. Dir, Centrepoint Soho, 1992–96. Trustee: UK Growth & Income Fund; Income Plus Fund, 1992–. Vice-Chm., St John Ambulance, City of London Centre, 1994– (Chm., 1998–99). Governor: Bishopsgate Foundn, 1983– (Chm., 1985–88); King Edward's Sch., Witley, 1992–; Univ. of East London, 1999–. Chm., Steering Cttee for Mus. of Port of London and Docklands, 1993– (Chm., Trustees, 1996–98); Mem., Mus. of London Develt Council, 1991–96; Trustee, Geffrye Mus., 1992–97. Common Councilman, City of London Corp., 1980–87; Alderman, Ward of Bishopsgate, 1987–; Sheriff, City of London, 1997–98. Liveryman, Ironmongers' Co., 1962– (Master, 1991–92). FRGS 1962. JP City of London, 1987. CStJ 1998 (OStJ 1989). *Recreations:* archaeology, travel. *Address:* 3a Oliver's Wharf, Wapping High Street, E1 9PJ. *T:* (020) 7247 7546; Paradise Barns, Bucks Lane, Cambridge CB3 7HL. *T:* (01223) 263303. *Club:* City Livery.

OLIVER, Dr John Andrew, CB 1968; *b* 25 Oct. 1913; *s* of Robert John Oliver, Limavady, Co. Londonderry and Martha Sherrard, Magilligan, Co. Londonderry; *m* 1943, Stella Ritson; five *s*. *Educ:* Royal Belfast Academical Institution; Queen's Univ., Belfast; Bonn Univ.; Königsberg Univ.; Zimmern School of International Studies, Geneva; Imperial Defence Coll., London. BA 1936; DrPhil, 1951; IDC, 1954. Ministry of Development, NI: Second Sec., 1964–71; Permanent Sec., 1971–74; Permanent Sec., Housing, Local Govt and Planning, NI, 1974–75; Chief Adviser, NI Constitutional Convention, 1975–76. Hon. Sec., Assoc. of Governing Bodies of Voluntary Grammar Schs in NI, 1964–77; Chm., Bd of Governors, Royal Belfast Academical Instn, 1970–77. UK Election Supervisor, Que Que, Rhodesia, 1980. Chm. Management Review, Royal Victoria Hosp. Gp, Belfast, 1981–82. Chm., S Lakeland Council for Voluntary Action, 1980; Vice-Chm., Voluntary Action Cumbria, 1980–. Proposer and interim Governor, new Dallam Schs, Cumbria, 1983–84. Retired deliberately from all cttees and exec. positions on reaching 70, to make way for younger people. Hon. MRTPI, 1964; Hon. Member, Assoc. for Housing and Town Planning, W Germany, 1966. Rhodesia Medal, 1980; Zimbabwe Independence Medal, 1980. *Publications:* Ulster Today and Tomorrow, 1978; Working at Stormont, 1978; Aspects of Ulster (essays), 1994; short stories; many articles in learned jls on Ulster Admin and on family history. *Recreations:* swimming, maps, languages, family history. *Address:* Laundry Cottage, Hale, Milnthorpe, Cumbria LA7 7BL. *T:* (015395) 62698. *Club:* Royal Over-Seas League.

OLIVER, Rt Rev. John Keith; *see* Hereford, Bishop of.

OLIVER, John Laurence; Journalist; *b* 14 Sept. 1910; *s* of late Harold and Teresa Oliver; *m* 1946, Renée Mary Webb; two *s*. *Educ:* Haberdashers' Aske's Hampstead School. Publicity Manager, The Book Society, 1934; Art Editor, The Bystander, 1935–39. War of 1939–45: served in the Field Security Corps; commissioned 1941, The Suffolk Regt (transferred The Cambridgeshire Regt). Joined staff of The Sphere, 1946; Art Editor, 1947; Assistant Editor, 1956; Editor, 1960–64; Editor, The Tatler, 1961–65. *Publications:* Saint John's Wood Church (with Rev. Peter Bradshaw), 1955; Malcolm Morley at the Everyman, 1977; occasional short stories and articles. *Recreations:* reading, theatre going, watching cricket. *Address:* 10 Wellington Place, NW8 9JA. *T:* (020) 7286 5891. *Clubs:* Garrick, MCC.

OLIVER, Ven. John Michael; Archdeacon of Leeds, since 1992; *b* 7 Sept. 1939; *s* of Frederick and Mary Oliver; *m* 1964, Anne Elizabeth Barlow; three *d*. *Educ:* Ripon Grammar Sch.; St David's Coll., Lampeter (BA 1962); Ripon Hall, Oxford. Ordained deacon, 1964, priest 1965; Asst Curate, St Peter, Harrogate, 1964–67; Senior Curate, Bramley, Leeds, 1967–72; Vicar: St Mary, Harrogate, 1972–78; St Mary with St David, Beeston, Leeds, 1978–92. Ecumenical Officer for Leeds, 1980–86; Rural Dean of Armley, 1986–92; Hon. Canon of Ripon, 1987–92. *Recreations:* cricket, theatre, cooking, a reluctant gardener. *Address:* 3 West Park Grove, Roundhay, Leeds LS8 2HQ. *T:* and *Fax:* (home) (0113) 269 0594, *T:* (office) (0113) 248 7487; *e-mail:* john.anne@archdeaconleeds.freeserve.co.uk.

OLIVER, Kaye Wight, CMG 2001; OBE 1994; HM Diplomatic Service; High Commissioner to Lesotho, since 1999; *b* 10 Aug. 1943. Joined Dept of Customs and Excise, 1962; entered Diplomatic Service, 1965; served FCO, Kuala Lumpur, Lilongwe and Paris; First Sec., Nairobi, 1983–84; Head of Chancery and Consul, Yaoundé, 1984–87; FCO, 1987–90; Consul and Dep. Head of Mission, later Chargé d'Affaires, Kinshasa, Burundi and Rwanda, 1990–94; on secondment to ODA, 1994–95; Ambassador to Rwanda, 1995–98 and (non-resident) to Burundi, 1996–98. *Address:* c/o Foreign and Commonwealth Office, SW1A 2AH.

OLIVER, Michael; *see* Oliver, J. M. Y.

OLIVER, Michael Edgar; writer and broadcaster; *b* 20 July 1937; *s* of Alan Oliver and Marguerite (*née* Moore). *Educ:* St Clement Danes GS; Isleworth Poly.; London Sch. of Printing. Work in librarianship, publishing and business, 1953–73; Presenter: BBC Radio London, 1970–75; BBC Radio: Kaleidoscope, 1974–87; Music Weekly, 1975–90; Soundings, 1990–92; contributor, Record Review, 1973–. Reviewer, Gramophone, 1973–; contributor: Classic CD, 1990–; Classic FM mag., 1996–; Internat. Record Review, 2000–. *Publications:* Igor Stravinsky, 1995; Benjamin Britten, 1996; Settling the Score, 1999. *Recreation:* travel. *Address:* 129 Crouch Hill, N8 9QH; via Castello 34, 06066 Oro, Piegaro, Italy.

OLIVER, Prof. Michael Francis, CBE 1985; MD; FRCP, FRCPEd, FFPHM; FRSE; Professor Emeritus, University of Edinburgh, since 1990; *b* 3 July 1925; *s* of late Captain Wilfrid Francis Lenn Oliver, MC (DLI), and Cecilia Beatrice Oliver (*née* Daniel); *m* 1st; two *s* one *d* (and one *s* decd); 2nd, Helen Louise Daniel. *Educ:* Marlborough Coll.; Univ. of Edinburgh. MB, ChB 1947, MD (Gold Medal) 1957. Edinburgh University: Consultant Physician, Royal Infirmary and Sen. Lectr in Medicine, 1961; Reader in Medicine, 1973; Personal Prof. of Cardiology, 1977; Duke of Edinburgh Prof. of Cardiology, 1979–89. Dir, Wynn Inst. for Metabolic Res., 1989–93; Hon. Prof., Nat. Heart and Lung Inst., 1989–93. Mem., Cardiovascular Panel, Govt Cttee on Medical Aspects of Food Policy, 1971–74, 1982–84; UK Rep, Mem. Adv. Panel for Cardiovascular Disease, WHO, 1972–2001; Chm., BBC-Medical Adv. Gp in Scotland, 1975–81; Mem. Scientific Bd, Internat. Soc. of Cardiology, 1968–78 (Chm., Council on Atherosclerosis and Ischaemic Heart Disease, 1968–75); Chairman: Brit. Atherosclerosis Gp, 1970–75; Science Cttee, Fondation Cardiologique Princess Lilian, Belgium, 1976–85; MoT Panel on driving and cardiovascular disease, 1985–90; Jt Cttee on Higher Medical Training, 1987–90. Convener, Cardiology Cttee, Scottish Royal Colls, 1978–81; Council Mem., Brit. Heart Foundn, 1976–85. Pres., British Cardiac Soc., 1981–85; Pres., RCPEd, 1986–88. FRSE 1987. Hon. FRCPI 1988; Hon. FRACP 1988. Hon. Fellow, Amer. Coll. of Cardiology, 1973. Hon. MD: Karolinska Inst., Stockholm, 1980; Univ. Bologna, 1985. Purkinje Medal, 1981; Polish Cardiac Soc. Medal, 1984. *Publications:* Acute Myocardial Infarction, 1966; Intensive Coronary Care, 1970, 2nd edn 1974; Effect of Acute Ischaemia on Myocardial Function, 1972; Modern Trends in Cardiology, 1975; High-Density Lipoproteins and Atherosclerosis, 1978; Coronary Heart Disease in Young Women, 1978; Strategy for Screening of Coronary Heart Disease, 1986; contribs to sci. and med. jls on causes of coronary heart disease, biochemistry of fats, myocardial metabolism, mechanisms of sudden death, clinical trials of drugs, and population studies of vascular diseases. *Recreations:* Italy and the Italians. *Address:* Keepier Wharf, 12 Narrow Street, E14 8DH; Apecolle, Spedalicchio, 06019 Umbertide (Pg), Italy. *T:* (020) 7722 4460. *Clubs:* Athenæum; New (Edinburgh).

OLIVER, Pauline Ann, (Mrs D. D. Walker); Director of Social Services, Lancashire County Council, since 1990; *b* 17 Nov. 1947; *d* of Percy Leonard Parsons and Doreen Maud Parsons; *m* 1991, David Douglas Walker. *Educ:* Rosebery County Grammar Sch., Epsom; Univ. of Surrey (BSc Hons Human Relns); Goldsmiths' Coll., Univ. of London (CQSW 1972, Dip. Applied Social Studies 1972). Asst Housemother, London Borough of Wandsworth, 1966–67; Social Worker, Surrey CC, 1970–73; social work and managerial posts, London Borough of Lewisham, 1973–83; London Borough of Bexley: Asst Chief Social Services Officer, 1983–87; Chief Social Services Officer, 1987–88; Dep. Dir of Social Services, Lancs CC, 1988–90. Member: Social Care Assoc.; British Agencies for Adoption and Fostering; Assoc. of Women Sen. Managers (Personal Social Services). MIMgt. *Recreations:* reading, antiques, gardening. *Address:* Social Services Department, East Cliff County Offices, Preston, Lancs PR1 3EA. *T:* (01772) 264390.

OLIVER, Peter Richard, CMG 1965; HM Diplomatic Service, retired; Ambassador to Uruguay, 1972–77; *b* 3 June 1917; *yr s* of William Henry Oliver and Muriel Daisie Elisabeth Oliver (*née* Widdicombe); *m* 1940, Freda Evelyn Gwyther; two *s* two *d*. *Educ:* Felsted Sch.; Hanover; Berlin; Trinity Hall, Cambridge. Indian Civil Service, 1939–47; served in Punjab and Bahawalpur State. Transferred to HM Foreign (subsequently Diplomatic) Service, 1947; served in Karachi, 1947–49; Foreign Office, 1949–52; The Hague, 1952–56; Havana, 1956–59; Foreign Office, 1959–61; Djakarta, 1961–64; Bonn, 1965–69; Dep. High Comr, Lahore, 1969–72. *Recreations:* publisher-hunting, Bumbloclasm. *Address:* Apt 5, Annethy Lowen, Sarah's Lane, Padstow, Cornwall PL28 8EL. *T:* (01841) 532558. *Clubs:* Royal Commonwealth Society; Hawks (Cambridge); Union (Cambridge).

OLIVER, Maj.-Gen. Richard Arthur, CB 1999; OBE 1986; Chief Executive, Year Out Group, since 2000; *b* 16 July 1944; *s* of late Arthur R. L. and Betty Oliver; *m* 1972, Julia Newsum; three *s*. *Educ:* Repton Sch.; RMA, Sandhurst; RMCS (psc†). GSO2, Exercise Planning Staff, HQ BAOR, 1977–79; OC, 25 Field Sqdn Regt, 1979–81; GSO2, Exercise Planning Staff, HQ 3rd Armoured Div., 1981; Chief Logistic Plans, HQ 1st (Br.) Corps, 1982–83; CO, 36 Engr Regt, 1983–85; Col, Army Staff Duties 2, MoD (Army), 1985–88; hcsc, Army Staff Coll., 1988; Comdr, Berlin Infantry Bde, 1988–90; rcds 1991; Brig., AQ, HQ 1st (Br.) Corps, 1992; Deputy Chief of Staff: G1/G4 HQ Allied Comd Europe, Rapid Reaction Corps, 1992–94; HQ Land Comd, 1994–96; COS HQ Adjutant Gen. (PTC), 1996–99. Business Develt Advr, Granada Food Services, 1999–2000. Member: Nat. Bd, Race for Opportunity, BITC, 1998–99; Council, Cranstoun Drug Services, 2000– (Chm., 2001–). FInstD 1998; FIMgt 1997. *Publications:* (contrib.) The British Army and the Operational Level of War, 1989; contrib. RUSI Jl. *Recreations:* gardening, fishing, shooting, indoor rowing, reading, water colours. *Address:* Queensfield, 28 Kings Road, Easterton, Devizes, Wilts SN10 4PX. *T:* (01380) 812368. *Club:* Army and Navy.

OLIVER, Prof. Roland Anthony, MA, PhD (Cantab); FBA 1993; Professor of the History of Africa, London University, 1963–86; *b* Srinagar, Kashmir, 30 March 1923; *s* of late Major D. G. Oliver and Lorimer Janet (*née* Donaldson); *m* 1st, 1947, Caroline Florence (*d* 1983), *d* of late Judge John Linehan, KC; one *d*; 2nd, 1990, Suzanne Doyle, *widow* of Brig. Richard Miers. *Educ:* Stowe; King's Coll., Cambridge. Attached to Foreign Office, 1942–45; R. J. Smith Research Studentship, King's Coll., Cambridge, 1946–48; Lecturer, School of Oriental and African Studies, 1948–58, Hon. Fellow, 1992; Reader in African History, University of London, 1958–63. Francqui Prof., University of Brussels, 1961; Visiting Professor: Northwestern Univ., Illinois, 1962; Harvard Univ., 1967; travelled in Africa, 1949–50 and 1957–58; org. international Conferences on African History and Archæology, 1953–61. President: African Studies Assoc., 1967–68; British Inst. in Eastern Africa, 1981–93. Vice-Pres., Royal African Soc., 1965– (Mem. Council, 1959–65); Mem., Perm. Bureau, Internat. Congress of Africanists, 1973–78; Chm., Minority Rights Group, 1973–91. Corresp. Member, Académie Royale des Sciences d'Outremer, Brussels. Editor (with J. D. Fage) Jl of African History, 1960–73. Haile Selassie Prize Trust Award, 1966; Distinguished Africanist Award, American African Studies Assoc., 1989. *Publications:* The Missionary Factor in East Africa, 1952; Sir Harry Johnston and the Scramble for Africa, 1957; (ed) The Dawn of African History, 1961; (with J. D. Fage) A Short History of Africa, 1962; (ed with Gervase Mathew) A History of East Africa, 1963; (with A. E. Atmore) Africa since 1800, 1967; (ed) The Middle Age of African History, 1967; (with B. M. Fagan) Africa in the Iron Age, 1975; (with A. E. Atmore) The African Middle Ages, 1400–1800, 1981; The African Experience, 1991; In the Realms of Gold: pioneering in African history, 1997; (with A. E. Atmore) Medieval Africa, 2001; Gen. Editor (with J. D. Fage), Cambridge History of Africa, 8 vols, 1975–86. *Address:* Frilsham Woodhouse, Thatcham, Berks RG18 9XB. *T:* (01635) 201407.

OLIVER, Dr Ronald Martin, CB 1989; RD 1973; FRCP; Deputy Chief Medical Officer (Deputy Secretary), Department of Health and Social Security, 1985–89, retired; *b* 28 May 1929; *s* of late Cuthbert Hanson Oliver and Cecilia Oliver; *m* 1957, Susanna Treves Blackwell; three *s* one *d*. *Educ:* King's Coll. Sch., Wimbledon; King's Coll., London; St George's Hosp. Med. Sch. (MB, BS 1952). MRCS, LRCP 1952; DCH 1954; DPH 1960; DIH 1961; MD London 1965; MFOM 1978; FRCP 1998 (MRCP 1987); MFCM 1987. Served RNR: Surg. Lieut, 1953–55; Surg. Lt-Comdr, retd 1974. St George's Hosp., London: House Surgeon and Physician, 1952–53; Resident Clin. Pathologist, 1955–56; trainee asst, gen. practice, 1956–57; Asst County MO, Surrey CC, 1957–59; MO, London Transport Exec., 1959–62; MO, later SMO, Treasury Med. Service (later CS Med. Adv. Service), 1962–74; seconded Diplomatic Service as Physician, British Embassy, Moscow, 1964–66; SMO, 1974–79, SPMO, 1979–85, DHSS; Chief Med. Advr, ODA, 1983–85. Gov., Manor House Sch., Little Bookham, 1991–99 (Chm., 1995–99). *Publications:* papers in med. jls on epidemiology of heart disease, public health, toxicology, and health service admin. *Recreations:* golf, sailing, gardening, bad bridge. *Address:* Greenhill House, 5 Mayfield, Leatherhead, Surrey KT22 8RS. *T:* (01372) 362323. *Club:* Effingham Golf.

OLIVER, Rev. Canon Stephen John; Canon Residentiary, St Paul's Cathedral, since 1997; *b* 7 Jan. 1948; *s* of John Oliver and Nora Oliver (*née* Greenhalgh); *m* 1969, Hilary Joan Barkham; two *s*. *Educ:* St Augustine's Coll., Canterbury; King's Coll. London (AKC 1970). Ordained deacon, 1971, priest, 1972; Asst Curate, Clifton, Nottingham, 1970; Vicar, Christ Church, Newark on Trent, 1975; Rector, St Mary Plumtree, Nottingham, 1979; Producer, Religious Programmes, BBC, 1985, Chief Producer, 1987; Rector of Leeds, 1991–97. Mem., Liturgical Commn, Gen. Synod of C of E, 1991–2001. Hon. Canon, Ripon Cathedral, 1996. Chm., Praxis, 1997–2001; Member: Elida Gibbs Ethics Cttee, 1994–96; W Yorks Playhouse Community and Educn Cttee, 1991–96; Leeds Common Purpose Adv. Gp, 1994–96; Unilever Central Ethical Compliance Gp, 1997–. Chairman, Governors: Leeds Girls' High Sch., 1993–96; Agnes Stewart High Sch., 1993–96. Pres., Leeds Church Inst., 1991–96. *Publications:* Why Pray?, 1993; (ed) Pastoral Prayers, 1996. *Recreations:* reading, theatre, flying. *Address:* 3 Amen Court, EC4M 7BU. *T:* (020) 7248 2559.

OLIVER, Stephen John Lindsay; QC 1980; Presiding Special Commissioner, and President, VAT and Duties (formerly Value Added Tax) Tribunals, since 1992; *b* 14 Nov. 1938; *s* of late Philip Daniel Oliver and Audrey Mary Oliver; *m* 1967, Anne Dawn Harrison Taylor (*see* A. D. H. Oliver); one *s* two *d*. *Educ:* Rugby Sch.; Oriel Coll., Oxford (MA Jurisprudence). National Service, RN, 1957–59: served submarines; Temp. Sub-Lieut. Called to the Bar, Middle Temple, 1963; Bencher, 1987; a Recorder, 1989–91; Circuit Judge, 1991–92. Asst Boundary Comr, Parly Boundary Commn, 1977. Chm. Blackheath Concert Halls Charity, 1986–92; Mem. Council, London Sinfonietta, 1993–. Trustee, Britten-Pears Foundn, 2001–. *Recreations:* music, golf. *Address:* 15–19 Bedford Avenue, WC1B 3AS. *T:* (020) 7631 4242.

See also J. A. Oliver.

OLIVER-JONES, Stephen, QC 1996; **His Honour Judge Oliver-Jones;** a Circuit Judge, since 2000; *b* 6 July 1947; *s* of Arthur William Jones and Kathleen Jones; *m* 1972, Margaret Anne Richardson; one *s* one *d*. *Educ:* Marling Sch., Stroud; UC, Durham Univ. (BA Hons). Lectr in Law, Durham Tech. Coll., 1968–70. Called to the Bar, Inner Temple, 1970; Mem., Oxford, later Midland and Oxford, Circuit; an Asst Recorder, 1988–93; a Recorder, 1993–2000. Pres., Mental Health Rev. Tribunal, 2000–. *Recreations:* fly fishing, postal history. *Address:* Nottingham Crown Court, Canal Street, Nottingham NG1 7EJ.

OLIVIER, Lady, (Joan); *see* Plowright, Joan.

OLLARD, Richard Laurence, FRSL, FSA; author and editor; *b* 9 Nov. 1923; *s* of Rev. Dr S. L. Ollard and Mary Ollard (*née* Ward); *m* 1954, Mary, *d* of Sir Walter Buchanan Riddell, 12th Bt; two *s* one *d*. *Educ:* Eton College; New College, Oxford. MA. Lectr in History and English, Royal Naval College, Greenwich, 1948–59; Senior Editor, Collins, 1960–83. Caird Medal, Nat. Maritime Mus., 1992; (jtly) Heywood Hill Lit. Prize, 1998. *Publications:* The Escape of Charles II, 1966; Man of War: Sir Robert Holmes and the Restoration Navy, 1969; Pepys: a biography, 1974, 2nd edn 1991; This War Without an Enemy, 1976; The Image of the King: Charles I and II, 1979; An English Education: a perspective of Eton, 1982; (ed jtly) For Veronica Wedgwood These: studies in Seventeenth-Century History, 1986; Clarendon and his Friends, 1987; (ed) Clarendon's Four Portraits, 1989; Fisher and Cunningham: a study in the personalities of the Churchill era, 1991; Cromwell's Earl: a life of Edward Mountagu, 1st Earl of Sandwich, 1994; Dorset: a Pimlico county history guide, 1995; The Sayings of Samuel Pepys, 1996; A Man of Contradictions: a life of A. L. Rowse, 1999. *Address:* Norchard Farmhouse, Morcombelake, Bridport, Dorset DT6 6EP; c/o Curtis Brown Ltd, 28–29 Haymarket, SW1 4SP. *Club:* Brooks's.

OLLERENSHAW, Eric, OBE 1991; Member (C), London Assembly, Greater London Authority, since 2000 (Deputy Leader, Conservative Group, since 2000); *b* 26 March 1950; *s* of Eric and Barbara Ollerenshaw. *Educ:* London Sch. of Economics and Political Science (BSc Econs). History teacher, Northumberland Park Sch., Tottenham, Hendon Sch., Barnet, and Tom Hood Sch., Leytonstone, 1973–2000. Member (C): ILEA, 1986–90 (Leader, Conservative Gp, 1988–90); Hackney LBC, 1990– (Leader, Conservative Gp, 1996–). *Recreations:* reading, listening to music. *Address:* 36 Clissold Court, Greenway Close, N4 2EZ. *T:* (020) 8800 6057.

OLLERENSHAW, Dame Kathleen (Mary), DBE 1971; DL; MA, DPhil; FIMA, FCP, CMath; Freeman of the City of Manchester, 1984; Chairman, Council for St John Ambulance in Greater Manchester, 1974–89; Member, Manchester City Council, 1956–80, Leader of Conservative Opposition, 1977–79; Alderman, 1970–74, Hon. Alderman since 1980; Lord Mayor, 1975–76, Deputy Lord Mayor, 1976–77; *b* 1 Oct. 1912; *d* of late Charles Timpson, JP, and late Mary Elizabeth Timpson (*née* Stops); *m* 1939, Robert Ollerenshaw (*d* 1986); (one *s* one *d* decd). *Educ:* Ladybarn House Sch., Manchester; St Leonards Sch., St Andrews; (open schol. in maths) Somerville Coll., Oxford (BA (Hons) 1934, MA 1943, DPhil 1945; Hon. Fellow, 1978). Foundation Fellow, Institute of Mathematics and its Applications (FIMA), 1964 (Mem. Council, 1973–94, Vice-Pres., 1976–77, Pres., 1978–79; Hon. Fellow 1986). Research Assistant, Shirley Institute, Didsbury, 1937–40. Hon. Res. Fellow, Dept of Computer Sci., Univ. of Manchester, 1999–. Chairman: Educn Cttee, Assoc. of Municipal Corporations, 1968–71; Assoc. of Governing Bodies of Girls' Public Schs, 1963–69; Manchester Educn Cttee, 1967–70 (Co-opted Mem., 1954–56); Manchester Coll. of Commerce, 1964–69; Council, Science and Technology Insts, 1980–81; first Chm., Court, Royal Northern Coll. of Music, Manchester, 1971–86 (CRNCM 1978); Member: Central Adv. Council on Educn in England, 1960–63; CNAA, 1964–74; SSRC, 1971–75; Tech. Educn Council, 1973–75; (Vice-Pres.) British Assoc. for Commercial and Industrial Educn (Mem. Delegn to USSR, 1963); Exec., Assoc. of Educn Cttees, 1967–71; Nat. Adv. Council on Educn for Industry and Commerce, 1963–70; Gen. Adv. Council of BBC, 1966–72; Schools Council, 1968–71; Management Panel, Burnham Cttee, 1968–71; Nat. Foundn of Educnl Res., 1968–71; Layfield Cttee of Inquiry into Local Govt Finance, 1974–76; Court, Univ. of Salford, 1967– (Mem. Council, 1967–89; a Pro-Chancellor, 1983–89); Court, Univ. of Manchester, 1964–; Manchester Polytechnic, 1968–86 (first Chm., 1969–72; Dep.-Chm., 1972–75; Hon. Fellow, 1979); Court, UMIST, 1971–87 (Vice-Pres., 1976–86; Hon. Fellow, 1987); Court, Lancaster Univ., 1991– (Mem. Council, 1975–91; a Dep. Pro-Chancellor, 1978–91); Council, CGLI, 1972–84 (Hon. Fellow, 1978; Vice-Pres., 1979–84); Rep. Governor, Royal Coll. of Advanced Technol., Salford, 1959–67; Governor: St Leonard's Sch., St Andrews, 1950–72 (Pres., 1980–); Manchester High Sch. for Girls, 1959–69; Ladies' Coll., Cheltenham, 1966–68; Chetham's Hosp. Sch., Manchester, 1967–77; Further Educn Staff Coll., Blagdon, 1960–74. Sen. Res. Fellow (part-time), 1972–75, Hon. Res. Fellow, 1975–77, Lancaster Univ.; Hon. Res. Fellow, Dept of Computer Science, Univ. of Manchester, 1998–2001. Member: Manchester Statistical Soc., 1950– (Mem. Council, 1977–; Vice-Pres., 1977, Pres., 1981–83); Manchester Astronomical Soc., 1990– (Hon. Vice-Pres., 1994–); Hon. Member: Manchester Technology Assoc., 1976– (Pres., 1982); Manchester Literary and Philosophical Soc., 1982–; Hon. Col, Manchester and Salford Univs OTC, 1977–81; Mem., Mil. Educn Cttee, 1979–. Dir, Greater Manchester Independent Radio, Ltd, 1972–83. Winifred Cullis Lecture Fellow to USA, 1965; Fourth Cockroft Lecture, UMIST and Manchester Tech. Assoc., 1977. DStJ 1983 (CStJ 1978) (Mem., Chapter Gen., 1974–96). Hon. LLD CNAA, 1975; Hon. DSc Salford, 1975; Hon LLD Manchester, 1976; Hon. DSc Lancaster, 1992; Hon. LLD Liverpool, 1994. DL Greater Manchester, 1987. Mancunian of the Year, Jnr Chamber of Commerce, 1977. *Publications:* Education of Girls, 1958; Education for Girls, 1961; The Girls' Schools, 1967; Returning to Teaching, 1974; The Lord Mayor's Party, 1976; First Citizen, 1977; (with Prof. David Brée) Most-Perfect Pandiagonal Magic Squares: their construction and enumeration, 1998; papers in mathematical journals, 1945–54 and 1977–, incl. Proc. RI 1981 (on form and pattern), Phil. Trans Royal Soc. 1982 (on magic squares), and Proc. Royal Soc. 1986 (on pandiagonal magic squares); articles on education and local govt in national and educational press. *Recreations:* research mathematics, astronomy. *Address:* 2 Pine Road, Didsbury, Manchester M20 6UY. *T:* (0161) 445 2948. *Club:* English-Speaking Union.

OLNER, William John; MP (Lab) Nuneaton, since 1992; *b* 9 May 1942; *s* of Charles William Olner, miner and Lillian Olner; *m* 1962, Gillian Everitt. *Educ:* Atherstone Secondary Modern Sch.; North Warwicks Tech. Coll. Engineer, Rolls Royce, 1957–92. Nuneaton and Bedworth Borough Council: Cllr, 1972–92; Leader, 1982–87; Mayor, 1987–88; Chm., Envmtl Health Cttee, 1990–92. Member: Envmt, Transport and the Regions (formerly Envmt) Select Cttee, 1995–2001; Foreign Affairs Select Cttee, 2001–. *Recreations:* hospice movement, walking, current affairs. *Address:* c/o House of Commons, SW1A 0AA.

O'LOGHLEN, Sir Colman (Michael), 6th Bt *cr* 1838; *b* 6 April 1916; *s* of Henry Ross O'Loghlen (*d* 1944), 6th *s* of 3rd Bt, and of Doris Irene, *d* of late Major Percival Horne, RA; *S* uncle, 1951; *m* 1939, Margaret, *d* of Francis O'Halloran, Melbourne, Victoria; six *s* two *d*. *Educ:* Xavier Coll., Melbourne; Melbourne Univ. (LLB). Formerly Captain AIF. Sometime Magistrate and Judge of Supreme Court, PNG. *Heir: s* Michael O'Loghlen, *b* 21 May 1945. *Address:* Qld 4078, Australia.

OLSEN, Hon. John Wayne; MP (L) Kavel, South Australia, since 1992; Premier of South Australia, since 1996; Minister for State Development, and for Multicultural (formerly Multicultural and Ethnic) Affairs, since 1996; *b* 7 June 1945; *s* of S. J. Olsen; *m* 1968, Julie, *d* of G. M. Abbott; two *s* one *d*. *Educ:* Kadina Memorial High Sch.; Sch. of Business Studies, SA. Managing Dir, J. R. Olsen & Sons Pty Ltd, 1968–79. Pres., S Australia Liberal Party, 1976–79; MP (L): Rocky River, 1979–85; Custance, 1985–90; Chief Sec. and Minister of Fisheries, SA, 1982; Leader of the Opposition, 1982–90; Senator for SA, 1990–92; Shadow Minister of Industry, Trade, Regl Develt, Public Works and Small Business, 1992–93; Minister for Industry, Mfrg, Small Business, Regl Develt and Minister for Infrastructure, 1993–96. *Recreation:* barefoot water ski-ing. *Address:* GPO Box 2343, Adelaide, SA 5001, Australia. *Club:* West Adelaide Football.

OLSSON, Curt Gunnar; Chairman, Skandinaviska Enskilda Banken, 1984–96; *b* 20 Aug. 1927; *s* of N. E. and Anna Olsson; *m* 1954, Asta Engblom; two *d*. *Educ:* Stockholm Sch. of Econs (BSc Econs 1950). Managing Director, Stockholm Group: Skandinaviska Banken, 1970–72; Skandinaviska Enskilda Banken, 1972–76; Man. Dir and Chief Exec., Head Office, 1976–82, and first Dep. Chm., 1982–84, Skandinaviska Enskilda Banken. Dir, Fastighets AB Hufvudstaden, 1983–. Hon. Consul Gen. for Finland, 1989–99. Hon. DEcon, Stockholm, 1992. Kt Order of Vasa, Sweden, 1976; King Carl XVI Gustaf's Gold Medal, Sweden, 1982; Comdr, Royal Norwegian Order of Merit, 1985; Comdr, Order of the Lion, Finland, 1986. *Address:* c/o Skandinaviska Enskilda Banken, 106 40 Stockholm, Sweden. *T:* (8) 221900.

OLSWANG, Simon Myers; Chairman, Olswang, solicitors, since 1998; *b* 13 Dec. 1943; *s* of Simon Alfred Olswang and Amelia Olga Olswang; *m* 1969, Susan Jane Simon; one *s* two *d*. *Educ:* Bootham Sch., York; Newcastle upon Tyne Univ. (BAEcon). Admitted solicitor, 1968; Attorney at Law, California State Bar, 1978. Trainee, Asst Solicitor, then Partner, Brecher & Co., 1966–81; Founder, 1981, Sen. Partner, 1981–98, Simon Olswang & Co., subseq. Olswang. Member: Entertainments Symposium Adv. Bd, UCLA, 1982–88; British Screen Adv. Council, 1985– (Chm., Wkg Party on Convergence); non-exec. Dir, Press Assoc., 1995–97; Council, BFI, 1998–99; Bd, BL, 2001– (Chm., Think Tank, 1999–2001). Chm. Govs and Trustee, Langdon Coll. of Further (Special) Educn, 1992–. *Publications:* (contrib.) Accessright: an evolutionary path for copyright into the digital era, 1995; (contrib.) Masters of the Wired World, 1988. *Recreations:* family, friends, sailing, ski-ing, theatre, travel. *Address:* Olswang, 90 Long Acre, WC2E 9TT. *T:* (020) 7208 8700. *Clubs:* Garrick; Royal Yacht Motor (Poole).

OLSZEWSKI, Jan; MP Poland 1991–93 and since 1997; Chairman, Movement for Reconstruction of Poland, since 1995; *b* Warsaw, 20 Aug. 1930. *Educ:* Warsaw Univ. Mem., underground Boy Scouts during German occupation. Res. Asst, Legal Scis Dept, Polish Acad. Scis, 1954–56; Mem., editorial staff, Po Prostu, 1956–57 (periodical then closed down by authorities); subseq. banned from work as journalist; apprenticeship in legal profession, 1959–62; practised as trial lawyer, specialising in criminal law; served as defense counsel in political trials; suspended from the Bar, 1968, for defending students arrested for anti-communist demonstrations; returned as attorney, 1970. Founder (with Zdzisław Najder), Polish Independence Alliance, 1975–81; Co-Founder, Workers' Defense Cttee, 1976–77; co-author of statute of Free Trade Unions, 1980, which he personally delivered to Gdansk shipyard; involved in formation of Solidarity, and legal advr, 1980; defense counsel at trials of Solidarity activists (incl. Lech Wałęsa), 1980–89; attorney for family of Fr Jerzy Popiełuszko at trial of his assassins, 1985; Mem., President Lech Wałęsa's Adv. Cttee, Jan.–Nov. 1991; Prime Minister of Poland (first non-communist govt), 1991–92. *Address:* Ruch Odbudowy Polski, ul. Piekna 22 M 7, 00549 Warsaw, Poland; Biuro Koła Parlamentarnego ROP, Sejm RP, ul. Wiejska 4/6/8, 00902 Warsaw, Poland.

OLVER, Richard Lake; Managing Director, Exploration and Production, BP plc (formerly British Petroleum Co. PLC, then BP Amoco plc), since 1998; *b* 2 Jan. 1947; *s* of Graham Lake Olver and Constance Evelyn Olver; *m* 1968, Pamela Kathleen Larkin; two *d*. *Educ:* City Univ. (BSc 1st Cl., Civil Eng); Univ. of Virginia Business Sch. MICE. British Petroleum: joined Engineering Dept, 1973, UK and overseas; Vice-Pres., BP Pipeline Inc., 1979; Divl Manager, New Technology, 1983; Divl Manager, Corporate Planning, 1985; Man. Dir, Central North Sea Pipelines, 1988; Gen. Manager, BP Gas Europe, 1988; Chief of Staff, BP, and Head, Corporate Strategy, 1990; Chief Exec., BP Exploration, USA, and Exec. Vice-Pres., BP America, 1992; Dep. CEO, BP Exploration, 1995; CEO, BP Exploration, 1998; Chm., BP Amer. Adv. Bd, 1998. Non-exec. Dir, Reuters, 1997–. *Recreations:* sailing, downhill ski-ing, ballet, fine art. *Address:* BP plc, 1 Finsbury Circus, EC2M 7BA. *T:* (020) 7496 4714.

OLVER, Sir Stephen (John Linley), KBE 1975 (MBE 1947); CMG 1965; HM Diplomatic Service, retired; *b* 16 June 1916; *s* of late Rev. S. E. L. Olver and Mrs Madeleine Olver (*née* Stratton); *m* 1953, Maria Morena, Gubbio, Italy; one *s*. *Educ:* Stowe. Indian Police, 1935–44; Indian Political Service, Delhi, Quetta, Sikkim and Bahrain, 1944–47; Pakistan Foreign Service, Aug.–Oct. 1947; Foreign Service, Karachi, 1947–50; Foreign Office, 1950–53; Berlin, 1953–56; Bangkok, 1956–58; Foreign Office, 1958–61; Washington, 1961–64; Foreign Office, 1964–66; The Hague, 1967–69; High Comr, Freetown, 1969–72; High Comr, Nicosia, 1973–75. *Recreations:* photography, painting. *Address:* 6 Saffrons Court, Compton Place Road, Eastbourne, Sussex BN21 1DX.

OLYOTT, Ven. Leonard Eric; Archdeacon of Taunton and Prebendary of Milverton, 1977–92, Archdeacon Emeritus, 1992; *b* 11 Jan. 1926; *s* of Thomas Olyott and Maude Ann Olyott (*née* Purser); *m* 1951, Yvonne Winifred Kate Keele; two *s* one *d*. *Educ:* Colchester Royal Grammar School; London Univ. (BA 1950); Westcott House, Cambridge. Served RNVR, 1944–47; commissioned, 1945. Asst Curate, St George, Camberwell, 1952–55; Priest-in-Charge, St Michael and All Angels, Birchwood, Hatfield, Herts, 1955–60; Vicar of Chipperfield, Herts, 1960–68; Vicar of Crewkerne, 1968–71; Rector of Crewkerne with Wayford, 1971–77; Rural Dean of Crewkerne, 1972–77; Prebendary of Timberscombe, 1976. Hospital Chaplains Adviser to Bishop of Bath and Wells, 1983–92. *Recreations:* sailing, gardening, music, genealogy. *Address:* 5 Greendale, Ilminster, Somerset TA19 0EB.

O'MALLEY, Stephen Keppel; His Honour Judge O'Malley; DL; a Circuit Judge, since 1989; *b* 21 July 1940; *s* of late D. K. C. O'Malley and Mrs R. O'Malley; *m* 1963, Frances Mary, *e d* of late James Stewart Ryan; four *s* two *d*. *Educ:* Ampleforth Coll.; Wadham Coll., Oxford (MA). Called to Bar, Inner Temple, 1962; Mem. Bar Council, 1968–72; Co-Founder, Bar European Gp, 1977; a Recorder, Western Circuit, 1978–89. Wine Treasurer, Western Circuit, 1986–89. DL Somerset, 1998. *Publications:* Legal London, a Pictorial History, 1971; European Civil Practice, 1989. *Address:* Heale House, Curry Rivel, Langport, Som TA10 0PN. *T:* (01458) 251220.

OMAN, Julia Trevelyan, (Lady Strong), CBE 1986; RDI 1977; designer; Director, Oman Productions Ltd; *b* 11 July 1930; *d* of late Charles Chichele Oman and Joan Trevelyan; *m* 1971, Sir Roy Colin Strong, *qv*. *Educ:* Royal College of Art, London (Royal Scholar, 1953; Silver Medal, 1955). Designer: BBC Television, 1955–67. Designer: *theatre:* Brief Lives, London and NY, 1967; Country Dance, London and Edinburgh, 1967; 40 Years On, 1968; The Merchant of Venice, NT, 1970; Othello, RSC, 1971; Getting On, Queen's, 1971; The Importance of Being Earnest, Vienna, 1976; Hay Fever and The Wild Duck, Lyric, Hammersmith, 1980; The Shoemakers' Holiday, NT, 1981; Mr and Mrs Nobody, Garrick, 1986; A Man for All Seasons, Chichester and Savoy, 1987; The Best of Friends, Apollo, 1988; Beatrix, Chichester, 1996; *opera:* Mefistofele, WNO, 1957; Eugene Onegin, Covent Garden, 1971; Un Ballo in Maschera, Hamburgische Staatsoper, 1973; La Bohème, Covent Garden, 1974, 1995; Die Fledermaus, Covent Garden, 1977; Die Csardasfürstin, Kassel, 1982; Otello, Stockholm, 1983; Arabella, Glyndebourne, 1984, 1985, 1989, 1996; The Consul, Connecticut Grand Opera, USA, 1985; *ballet:* Enigma Variations, Royal Ballet, 1968, Birmingham Royal Ballet, 1994; A Month in the Country, Royal Ballet, 1976, Nat. Ballet of Canada, 1995; Sospiri, 1980; Swan Lake, Boston, 1981; The Nutcracker, 1984; *films:* Alice in Wonderland (BBC TV), 1966 (Designer of the Year Award, 1967); (Art Dir (England)) The Charge of the Light Brigade, 1967; (Art Dir) Laughter in the Dark, 1968; (prodn designer) Julius Caesar, 1969; The Straw Dogs, 1971; *television:* Hay Fever, 1979; Separate Tables, 1982; *exhibitions:* Samuel Pepys, Nat. Portrait Gall., 1971; Mme Tussaud's hist. tableaux, 1979; The Bear's Quest for Ragged Staff, Warwick Castle, 1981. Mem., DES Vis. Cttee for RSA, 1981–85. DesRCA (1st cl.), 1955; FCSD. Hon. DLitt Bristol, 1987. Award for Cable Excellence, for best art direction, NCTA, 1983. *Publications:* Street Children (photographs by Julia

Trevelyan Oman; text by B. S. Johnson), 1964; (with Roy Strong) Elizabeth R, 1971; (with Roy Strong) Mary Queen of Scots, 1972; introd. The Merchant of Venice, Folio Soc. edn, 1975; (with Roy Strong) The English Year, 1982; (with Roy Strong) A Celebration of Gardens, 1991; (with Roy Strong) A Country Life, 1994; (with Roy Strong) On Happiness, 1998; (with Roy Strong) Garden Party, 2000; contrib. Architectural Review (photographs), Vogue (text and photographs). *Address:* c/o Oman Productions Ltd, The Laskett, Much Birch, Hereford HR2 8HZ.

OMAND, Sir David (Bruce), KCB 2000; Chairman, Centre for Management and Policy Studies, Cabinet Office, since 2001; *b* 15 April 1947; *s* of late J. Bruce Omand, JP, and of Esther Omand; *m* 1971, Elizabeth, *er d* of late Geoffrey Wales, RE, ARCA; one *s* one *d*. *Educ:* Glasgow Acad.; Corpus Christi Coll., Cambridge (BAEcon). Ministry of Defence: Asst Principal, 1970; Private Sec. to Chief Exec. (PE), 1973; Asst Private Sec. to Sec. of State, 1973–75, 1979–80; Principal, 1975; Asst Sec., 1981; Private Sec. to Sec. of State, 1981–82; on loan to FCO as Defence Counsellor, UK Delegn to NATO, Brussels, 1985–88; Asst Under Sec. of State (Management Strategy), 1988–91, (Programmes), 1991–92; Dep. Under Sec. of State (Policy), MoD, 1992–96; Dir, GCHQ, 1996–97; Permanent Under-Sec. of State, Home Office, 1998–2001. *Recreations:* opera, hill-walking. *Address:* c/o Centre for Management and Policy Studies, Admiralty Arch, The Mall, SW1A 2WH. *Club:* Reform.

O'MARA, Margaret; Associate Director, Policing and Security, Northern Ireland Office, since 2000; *b* 10 May 1951; *d* of Thomas Patrick and Madge O'Mara. *Educ:* St Hilda's Coll., Oxford (1st Cl. Hons Lit.Hum.); University Coll. London (MSc Econs of Public Policy). Entered HM Treasury, 1973; Private Sec. to Chancellor of Exchequer, 1982–85; Head: Economic Briefing Div., 1985–87; Monetary Policy Div., 1987–90; Public Expenditure Div., monitoring Dept of Employment, 1990–92; Arts Gp, then Libraries, Museums and Galls Gp, Dept of Nat. Heritage, 1992–95; Dir, Personnel and Support, then Personnel, Accommodation and Information Services, HM Treasury, 1995–2000. *Recreations:* walking, cooking. *Address:* c/o Northern Ireland Office, Stormont House, Stormont Estate, Belfast BT4 3ST.

O'MORCHOE, David Nial Creagh, CB 1979; MBE 1967; (The O'Morchoe); Chief of O'Morchoe; *b* 17 May 1928; *s* of Nial Creagh O'Morchoe and Jessie Elizabeth, *d* of late Charles Jasper Joly, FRS, FRIS, MRIA, Astronomer Royal of Ireland; *S* father as Chief of the Name (O'Morchoe, formerly of Oulartleigh and Monamolin), 1970; *m* 1954, Margaret Jane, 3rd *d* of George Francis Brewitt, Cork; two *s* one *d*. *Educ:* St Columba's Coll., Dublin (Fellow 1983; Chm. of Fellows, 1989–99); RMA Sandhurst. Commissioned Royal Irish Fusiliers, 1948; served in Egypt, Jordan, Gibraltar, Germany, Kenya, Cyprus, Oman; psc 1958, jssc 1966; CO 1st Bn RIrF, later 3rd Bn Royal Irish Rangers, 1967–68; Directing Staff, Staff Coll., Camberley, 1969–71; RCDS 1972; Brigade Comdr, 1973–75; Brig. GS, BAOR, 1975–76; Maj.-Gen. 1977; Comdr, Sultan of Oman's Land Forces, 1977–79, retired. Dep. Col, 1971–76, Col 1977–79, The Royal Irish Rangers. Pres., Republic of Ireland Dist, RBL, 1999–; Chm., Republic of Ireland Br., SSAFA Forces Help (formerly SSAFA/Forces Help Soc.), 1982–; Mem. Council, Concern, Dublin, 1984– (Sec., 1989–98). Member: Church of Ireland Gen. Synod, 1993–; Rep. Church Body, 1994–. Founder Mem., Standing Council of Irish Chiefs and Chieftans, 1992 (Chm., 1994–98). *Recreations:* sailing and an interest in most sports. *Heir:* *s* Dermot Arthur O'Morchoe, *b* 11 Aug. 1956. *Address:* c/o Ulster Bank, Patrick Street, Cork; *e-mail:* omor@[illegible]. *Clubs:* Friendly Brothers (Dublin); Irish Cruising.

OÑATE, Santiago; Ambassador of Mexico to the Netherlands, since 2001; *b* 24 May 1949; *s* of Santiago Oñate and Clara Laborde; *m* 1981, Laura Madrazo; three *d*. *Educ:* Universidad Nacional Autónoma de México (LLB 1972); postgrad. studies at Università degli Studi di Pavia, LSE and Univ. of Wisconsin-Madison. Prof. of Law, Universidad Autónoma Metropolitana-Azcapotzalco, Mexico, 1976–81; Vis. Prof., Law Sch., Univ. of Wisconsin-Madison, 1981–82. Mem. Congress, Chamber of Deputies, Mexico, 1985–88; Mem., Representative Assembly of Federal Dist, Mexico, 1988–91; Ambassador, Permanent Rep. to OAS, Washington, 1991–92; Attorney Gen. for Protection of Envmt, 1992–94; COS, President's Office, 1994; Sec. of State for Labour, 1994–95; Pres., Nat. Exec. Cttee, Partido Revolucionario Institucional, 1995–96; Ambassador to UK, 1997–2001. *Publications:* La Acción Procesal en la Doctrina y el Derecho Positivo Mexicano, 1972; El Estado y el Derecho, 1977; Legal Aid in Mexico, 1979; Los Trabajadores Migratorios Frente a la Justicia Norteamericana, 1983. *Recreations:* theatre, music, walking, nature protection. *Address:* Burgemeester Patijnlaan 1930, 2585 CB The Hague, Holland. *Club:* University (Mexico).

ONDAATJE, Christopher; *see* Ondaatje, P. C.

ONDAATJE, Michael; writer; *b* 12 Sept. 1943; *s* of Philip Mervyn Ondaatje and Enid Doris Gratiaen. *Educ:* Dulwich Coll.; Univ. of Toronto; Queen's Univ., Canada. *Publications: poetry:* The Dainty Monsters, 1967; The Man with Seven Toes, 1968; There's a Trick I'm Learning to Do, 1979; Secular Love, 1984; The Cinnamon Peeler, 1991; (ed) The Long Poem Anthology, 1979; Handwriting, 1998; *prose:* Leonard Cohen (criticism), 1968; The Collected Works of Billy the Kid (poetry and prose), 1970; (ed) The Broken Ark, 1971; How to Train a Bassett, 1971; Rat Jelly, 1973; Coming Through Slaughter, 1976; Running in the Family (autobiog.), 1982; In the Skin of a Lion, 1987 (Trillium Award); (ed) From Ink Lake: an anthology of Canadian stories, 1990; Elimination Dance, 1991 (trans. French); The English Patient, 1992 (jt winner, Booker Prize; Trillium Award; filmed, 1997); Anil's Ghost, 2000. *Address:* 2275 Bayview Avenue, Toronto, ON N4N 3M6, Canada.

See also P. C. Ondaatje.

ONDAATJE, (Philip) Christopher, OC 1993; CBE 2000; President, Ondaatje Foundation, since 1975; *b* 22 Feb. 1933; *s* of Philip Mervyn Ondaatje and Enid Doris Gratiaen; *m* 1959, Valda Bulins; one *s* two *d*. *Educ:* Blundell's Sch., Tiverton; LSE. National and Grindlays Bank, London, 1951–55; Burns Bros, & Denton, Toronto, 1955–56; Montrealer Mag. and Canada Month Mag., 1956–57; Maclean-Hunter Publishing Co. Ltd, Montreal, 1957–62; Financial Post, Toronto, 1963–65; Pitfield Mackay, Ross & Co. Ltd, Toronto, 1965–69; Founder: Pagurian Corp. Ltd, 1967–89; Loewen, Ondaatje, McCutcheon & Co. Ltd, 1970–88. Mem., Adv. Bd, Royal Soc. of Portrait Painters, 1998–. Mem., Canada's Olympic Bob-Sled Team, 1964. FRGS 1992. Hon. LLD Dalhousie, 1994. *Publications:* Olympic Victory, 1964; The Prime Ministers of Canada (1867–1967), 1967, rev. edn (1867–1985), 1985; Leopard in the Afternoon, 1989; The Man-Eater of Punanai, 1992; Sindh Revisited: a journey in the footsteps of Sir Richard Francis Burton, 1996; Journey to the Source of the Nile, 1998. *Recreations:* tennis, golf, adventure, photography. *Address:* Glenthorne, Countisbury, near Lynton, N Devon EX35 6NQ. *T:* (01598) 741385. *Clubs:* Travellers; Somerset County Cricket (Life Mem., Patron); Mid Ocean Golf (Bermuda); Toronto Golf.

See also M. Ondaatje.

O'NEIL, Roger; non-executive Board Member: Enterprise Oil plc, since 1997; Clearvision International Ltd, since 1997; *b* 22 Feb. 1938; *s* of James William O'Neil and Claire Kathryn (*née* Williams); *m* 1976, Joan Mathewson; one *s* one *d*. *Educ:* Univ. of Notre Dame (BS Chemical Engrg, 1959); Cornell Univ. (MBA 1961). Joined Mobil Corp., New York, 1961; Various staff and exec. positions in Japan, Hong Kong, Australia, Paris, Cyprus, London and New York, 1963–73; Chm., Mobil cos in SE Asia, Singapore, 1973–78; Manager, Planning, Mobil Europe Inc., London, 1978–81; Manager, Corporate Econs and Planning, Mobil Corp., New York, 1981–82; Gp Vice Pres., Container Corp. of America, Chicago, 1982–84; Pres., Mobil Oil Italiana SpA, Rome, 1984–87; Chm. and Chief Exec., Mobil Oil Co., London, 1987–91; Dir and Vice Pres., Mobil Europe, 1991–92; Exec. Vice Pres. and Mem. Exec. Cttee, Statoil, 1992–97. Sen. Oil and Gas Advr, Dresdner Kleinwort Benson, 1997–. Vice-Pres., Inst. of Petroleum, 1989– (FInstPet 1988). Member: President's Council, Asia Soc., NY, 1982–; Adv. Bd, Johnson Business Sch., Cornell Univ., 1990–. FRSA 1988. *Recreations:* archæology, ski-ing, tennis. *Address:* 3 Ormonde Gate, SW3 4EU. *Clubs:* Royal Automobile, Hurlingham.

O'NEIL, William Andrew, CM 1995; Secretary-General, International Maritime Organization, since 1990; *b* Ottawa, 6 June 1927; *s* of Thomas Wilson and Margaret O'Neil (*née* Swan); *m* 1950, Dorothy Muir; one *s* two *d*. *Educ:* Carleton Univ.; Univ. of Toronto (BASc Civil Engrg 1949). Engrg posts with Fed. Dept of Transport, 1949–55; Div. Engr, Regl Dir and Dir of Construction, St Lawrence Seaway Authy, 1955–71; Federal Department of Transport: Dep. Administrator, Marine Services, 1971–80; also Comr, Canadian Coast Guard, 1975–80; St Lawrence Seaway Authority, 1980–90: Pres. and Chief Exec. Officer; Dir, Canarctic Shipping Co.; Pres., Seaway Internat. Bridge Corp. Council of International Maritime Organization: Canadian Rep., 1972–90; Chm., 1980–90. Chm., Canadian Cttee, Lloyd's Register of Shipping, 1987–88; Mem. Bd, Internat. Maritime Bureau, 1991–. Chm., Governing Bd, Internat. Maritime Law Inst., Malta, 1991–. Chancellor, World Maritime Univ., 1991–. Member: Assoc. of Professional Engrs of Ont; ASCE; Engrg Alumni Hall of Dist., Univ. of Toronto, 1996. FILT (FCIT 1994); FRSA 1992; Foreign Mem., Royal Acad. of Engrg, 1994. Hon. Titulary Mem., Comité Martitime Internat., 2001. Hon. LLD: Univ. of Malta, 1993; Meml Univ. of Newfoundland, Canada, 1996; Hon. DSc Nottingham Trent, 1994. Engrg Medal, 1972, Gold Medal, 1995, Assoc. of Professional Engrs of Ont; Distinguished Public Service Award, USA, 1980; Admirals' Medal, Admirals' Medal Foundn, Canada, 1994; NUMAST Award, 1995; Seatrade Personality of the Year Award, 1995; Silver Bell Award, Seamen's Church Inst., NY, 1997; Cdre Award, Conn Maritime Assoc., USA, 1998; Dioscuri Prize, Italian Naval League, 1998; Vice-Adm. Jerry Land Medal, Soc. of Naval Architects and Marine Engrs, USA, 1999; Halert C. Shepheard Award, Chamber of Shipping of America, 2000. Ordre Nat. des Cèdres (Lebanon), 1995; Grand Cross, Order of Vasco Nuñez de Balboa (Panama), 1998. *Address:* (office) 4 Albert Embankment, SE1 7SR. *T:* (020) 7587 3100; 15 Ropers Orchard, SW3 5AX.

O'NEILL, family name of **Barons O'Neill** and **Rathcavan**.

O'NEILL, 4th Baron *cr* 1868; **Raymond Arthur Clanaboy O'Neill,** TD 1970; Lord-Lieutenant of County Antrim, since 1994; *b* 1 Sept. 1933; *s* of 3rd Baron and Anne Geraldine (she *m* 2nd, 1945, 2nd Viscount Rothermere, and 3rd, 1952, late Ian Fleming, and *d* 1981), *e d* of Hon. Guy Charteris; *S* father, 1944; *m* 1963, Georgina Mary, *er d* of Lord George Montagu Douglas Scott; three *s*. *Educ:* Eton; Royal Agricultural Coll. 2nd Lieut, 11th Hussars, Prince Albert's Own; Major, North Irish Horse, AVR; Lt-Col, RARO; Hon. Colonel: NI Horse Sqn, RYR, 1986–91; 69 Signal Sqn, NI Horse, 1988–93. Chairman: Ulster Countryside Cttee, 1971–75; NI Museums Council, 1993–98; Vice-Chm., Ulster Folk and Transport Mus., 1987–90 (Trustee, 1969–90); Member: NI Tourist Bd, 1973–80 (Chm., 1975–80); NI Nat. Trust Cttee, 1980–91 (Chm., 1981–91); Museums and Galleries Commn, 1987–94; President: Youth Action (formerly NI Assoc. of Youth Clubs), 1965–; Royal Ulster Agricl Soc., 1984–86 (Chm. Finance Cttee, 1974–83). DL Co. Antrim, 1967. *Recreations:* vintage motoring, railways, gardening. *Heir:* *s* Hon. Shane Sebastian Clanaboy O'Neill [*b* 25 July 1965; *m* 1997, Celia, *e d* of Peter Hickman; one s]. *Address:* Shanes Castle, Antrim, N Ireland BT41 4NE. *T:* (028) 9446 3264. *Club:* Turf.

See also Sir J. A. L. Morgan.

O'NEILL OF BENGARVE, Baroness *cr* 1999 (Life Peer), of The Braid in the County of Antrim; **Onora Sylvia O'Neill,** CBE 1995; PhD; FBA 1993; Principal, Newnham College, Cambridge, since 1992; *b* 23 Aug. 1941; *d* of Hon. Sir Con O'Neill, GCMG and of Rosemary Margaret (*née* Pritchard) (now Lady Garvey); *m* 1963, Edward John Nell (marr. diss. 1976); two *s*. *Educ:* St Paul's Girls' Sch.; Somerville Coll., Oxford (BA, MA; Hon. Fellow, 1993); Harvard Univ. (PhD). Asst, then Associate Prof., Barnard Coll., Columbia Univ., 1970–77; University of Essex: Lectr, 1977–78; Sen. Lectr, 1978–83; Reader, 1983–87; Prof. of Philosophy, 1987–92. Member: Animal Procedures Cttee, 1990–94; Nuffield Council on Bioethics, 1991–98 (Chm., 1996–98); Human Genetics Adv. Commn, 1996–99. Chm., Nuffield Foundn, 1998– (a Trustee, 1997–). Fellow, Wissenschaftskolleg, Berlin, 1989–90. Pres., Aristotelian Soc., 1988–89. Foreign Hon. Mem., Amer. Acad. of Arts and Scis, 1993. *Publications:* Acting on Principle, 1976; Faces of Hunger, 1986; Constructions of Reason, 1989; Towards Justice and Virtue, 1996; numerous articles on philosophy, esp. political philosophy and ethics in learned jls. *Recreations:* walking, talking. *Address:* Newnham College, Cambridge CB3 9DF. *T:* (01223) 335821.

O'NEILL, Alan Dennis; Chairman and Managing Director, Kodak Ltd, 1998–2001; *b* 2 March 1945; *s* of Dennis O'Neill and Audrey Florence O'Neill; *m* 1969, Susan Fearnley; one *s* two *d*. *Educ:* King George V Sch., Southport; Bishopshalt Sch., Hillingdon; Univ. of Birmingham (BSc Hons Physics 1966). Joined Kodak Ltd as res. scientist, 1966; Dir and Manager, Manufacturing Ops, 1991–96; Chief Purchasing Officer and Vice-Pres., Eastman Kodak Co., 1996–98. *Recreations:* bee-keeping, running, golf. *Address:* St Michael's Croft, Woodcock Hill, Berkhamsted, Herts HP4 3TR.

O'NEILL, Brendan Richard, PhD; FCMA; Chief Executive, ICI plc, since 1999 (Chief Operating Officer, 1998–99); *b* 6 Dec. 1948; *s* of John Christopher O'Neill and Doris O'Neill (*née* Monk); *m* 1979, Margaret Maude; one *s* two *d*. *Educ:* West Park GS, St Helens; Churchill Coll., Cambridge (MA Nat. Sci. 1972); Univ. of East Anglia (PhD Chemistry 1973). FCMA (FCIMA 1983). Ford Motor Co., 1973–75; British Leyland, 1975–81; BICC plc, 1981–83; Gp Financial Controller, Midland Bank, 1983–87; Guinness plc: Dir of Financial Control, 1987; Finance Dir, 1988–90, Man. Dir, Internat. Reg., 1990–92, United Distillers; Man. Dir, Guinness Brewing Worldwide, 1993–97; Chief Exec., Guinness, Diageo plc, 1997–98. Director: Guinness plc, 1993–97; EMAP plc, 1995–; Diageo plc, 1997–98; ICI plc, 1998–. Mem. Council, 2000–, Finance Cttee, 1994–2000, ICRF. *Recreations:* music, reading, family. *Address:* ICI plc, 9 Millbank, SW1P 3JF. *T:* (020) 7834 4444.

O'NEILL, Dennis James, CBE 2000; operatic tenor; *b* 25 Feb. 1948; *s* of late Dr William P. O'Neill and of Eva A. O'Neill (*née* Rees); *m* 1st, 1970, Ruth Collins (marr. diss. 1987); one *s* one *d*; 2nd, 1988, Ellen Folkestad. *Educ:* Gowerton Boys' Grammar Sch. FTCL 1969; ARCM 1971. Specialist in Italian repertoire and works of Verdi in particular; Début: Royal Opera House, Covent Garden, 1979; Vienna State Opera, 1981; Hamburg

State Opera, 1981; San Francisco Opera, 1984; Chicago Lyric Opera, 1985; Paris Opera, 1986; Metropolitan Opera, NY, 1986; Bayerische Staatsoper, Munich, 1992; has performed worldwide in opera and concerts. Many recordings. Presenter, Dennis O'Neill, BBC TV, 1987, 1988, 1989. Hon. Fellow, Univ. of Wales, 1997; Hon. FWCMD, 1993. *Recreations:* dinner parties, Verdi. *Address:* c/o Ingpen & Williams, 26 Wadham Road, SW15 2LR. *T:* (020) 8874 3222.

O'NEILL, Martin (John); MP (Lab) Ochil, since 1997 (Stirlingshire, East and Clackmannan, 1979–83; Clackmannan, 1983–97); *b* 6 Jan. 1945; *s* of John and Minnie O'Neill; *m* 1973, Elaine Marjorie Samuel; two *s. Educ:* Trinity Academy, Edinburgh; Heriot Watt Univ. (BA Econ.); Moray House Coll. of Education, Edinburgh. Insurance Clerk, Scottish Widows Fund, 1963–67; Asst Examiner, Estate Duty Office of Scotland, 1971–73; Teacher of Modern Studies: Boroughmuir High School, Edinburgh, 1974–77; Craigmount High School, Edinburgh, 1977–79; Social Science Tutor, Open Univ., 1976–79. Opposition spokesman on Scottish affairs, 1980–84, on defence matters, 1984–88, on energy, 1992–95; chief opposition spokesman on defence, 1988–92. Mem., Select Cttee, Scottish Affairs, 1979–80; Chm., Select Cttee on Trade and Industry, 1995–. Member: GMB; EIS. FRSA. *Recreations:* watching football, reading, listening to jazz, the cinema. *Address:* House of Commons, SW1A 0AA. *T:* (020) 7219 5059; 19 Mar Street, Alloa, Clackmannanshire FK10 1HR. *T:* (01259) 721536.

O'NEILL, Prof. Patrick Geoffrey, BA, PhD; Professor of Japanese, School of Oriental and African Studies, University of London, 1968–86, now Emeritus; *b* 9 Aug. 1924; *m* 1951, Diana Howard; one *d. Educ:* Rutlish Sch., Merton; Sch. of Oriental and African Studies, Univ. of London. Lectr in Japanese, Sch. of Oriental and African Studies, Univ. of London, 1949. Vis. Prof., Univ. of Michigan, 1961–62. Chm., Organizing Cttee, Eur. Assoc. for Japanese Studies, 1973 (Sec., 1974–79); Pres., British Assoc. for Japanese Studies, 1980–81. First Sakura Award, Nihon Zenkoku Gakushikai, 1976. Order of the Rising Sun (Japan), 1987. *Publications:* A Guide to Nō, 1954; Early Nō Drama, 1958; (with S. Yanada) Introduction to Written Japanese, 1963; A Programmed Course on Respect Language in Modern Japanese, 1966; Japanese Kana Workbook 1967; A Programmed Introduction to Literary-style Japanese, 1968; Japanese Names, 1972; Essential Kanji, 1973; (ed) Tradition and Modern Japan, 1982; (with H. Inagaki) A Dictionary of Japanese Buddhist Terms, 1984; A Reader of Handwritten Japanese, 1984; (trans.) Japan on Stage, by T. Kawatake, 1990; annotated plate supplement, in H. Plutschow, Matsuri, 1996; P. G. O'Neill—Collected Writings, 2001. *Address:* 44 Vine Road, East Molesey, Surrey KT8 9LF.

O'NEILL, Paul Henry; Secretary of the Treasury, USA, since 2001; *b* 4 Dec. 1935; *m* 1955, Nancy Jo Wolfe; one *s* three *d. Educ:* Fresno State Coll., Calif (BA Econs); Indiana Univ. (MPA). Computer analyst, Veterans Admin, 1961–66; Asst Dir, Associate Dir and Dep. Dir, Office of Mgt and Budget, 1967–77; Vice-Pres., 1977–85, Pres., 1985–87, Internat. Paper Co.; Chm. and CEO, 1987–99, Chm., 1999–2000, Alcoa. *Recreation:* painting. *Address:* Department of the Treasury, 1500 Pennsylvania Avenue NW, Washington, DC 20220, USA. *T:* (202) 6221100.

O'NEILL, Robert James, CMG 1978; HM Diplomatic Service, retired; *b* 17 June 1932; *m* 1958, Helen Juniper; one *s* two *d. Educ:* King Edward VI Sch., Chelmsford; Trinity Coll., Cambridge (Schol.). 1st cl. English Tripos Pts I and II. Entered HM Foreign (now Diplomatic) Service, 1955; FO, 1955–57; British Embassy, Ankara, 1957–60; Dakar, 1961–63; FO, 1963–68, Private Sec. to Chancellor of Duchy of Lancaster, 1966, and to Minister of State for Foreign Affairs, 1967–68; British Embassy, Bonn, 1968–72; Counsellor Diplomatic Service, 1972; seconded to Cabinet Office as Asst Sec., 1972–75; FCO, 1975–78; Dep. Governor, Gibraltar, 1978–81; Under Sec., Cabinet Office, 1981–84; Asst Under-Sec. of State, FCO, 1984–86; Ambassador to Austria, and concurrently Head of UK Delegn, MBFR, Vienna, 1986–89; Ambassador to Belgium, 1989–92; EC Presidency Rep. for Macedonia, 1992. EU Rep., OSCE Bosnia elections Task Force, 1995. *Recreations:* local government, diplomatic history, hill-walking. *Address:* 4 Castle Street, Saffron Walden, Essex CB10 1BP. *T:* (01799) 520291. *Clubs:* Travellers, Royal Anglo-Belgian.

O'NEILL, Prof. Robert John, AO 1988; FASSA; FRHistS; Chairman, Australian Strategic Policy Institute, Canberra, since 2000; Chichele Professor of the History of War, and Fellow of All Souls College, University of Oxford, 1987–2001, now Emeritus Fellow; *b* 5 Nov. 1936; *s* of Joseph Henry and Janet Gibbon O'Neill; *m* 1965, Sally Margaret Burnard; two *d. Educ:* Scotch Coll., Melbourne; Royal Military Coll. of Australia; Univ. of Melbourne (BE); Brasenose Coll., Oxford (MA, DPhil 1965; Hon. Fellow, 1990). FASSA 1978; FIE(Aust) 1981–96; FRHistS 1990. Served Australian Army, 1955–68; Rhodes Scholar, Vic, 1961; Fifth Bn Royal Australian Regt, Vietnam, 1966–67 (mentioned in despatches); Major 1967; resigned 1968. Sen. Lectr in History, Royal Military Coll. of Australia, 1968–69; Australian National University: Sen. Fellow in Internat. Relations, 1969–77, Professorial Fellow, 1977–82; Head, Strategic and Defence Studies Centre, 1971–82; Dir, IISS, 1982–87; Dir of Graduate Studies, Modern History Faculty, Univ. of Oxford, 1990–92. Adjunct Prof., Strategic and Defence Studies Centre, ANU, 2001–. Official Australian Historian for the Korean War, 1969–82. Dir, Shell Transport and Trading, 1992–. Chairman: Management Cttee, Sir Robert Menzies Centre for Australian Studies, Univ. of London, 1990–95; Bd, Centre for Defence Studies, KCL, 1990–95; Chm. Council, IISS, 1996–2001 (Mem. Council, 1977–82, 1992–, Vice-Chm. Council, 1994–96). Governor: Ditchley Foundn, 1989–; Internat. Peace Acad., 1990–; Salzburg Seminar, 1992–97; Trustee: Imperial War Museum, 1990– (Chm. Trustees, 1998–2001); Commonwealth War Graves Commn, 1991–2001; Mem., Rhodes Trust, 1995–. Mem., Adv. Bd, Investment Co. of America, 1988–; Dir, two Mutual Funds, Capital Group, LA, 1992–. Chm., Round Table Moot, 1986–92. Hon. Col 5th (Volunteer) Royal Green Jackets, 1993–99. Hon. DLitt ANU, 2001. *Publications:* The German Army and the Nazi Party 1933–1939, 1966; Vietnam Task, 1968; General Giap: politician and strategist, 1969; (ed) The Strategic Nuclear Balance, 1975; (ed) The Defence of Australia: fundamental new aspects, 1977; (ed) Insecurity: the spread of weapons in the Indian and Pacific Oceans, 1978; (ed jtly) Australian Dictionary of Biography, Vols 7–14, 1979–97; (ed with David Horner) New Directions in Strategic Thinking, 1981; Australia in the Korean War 1950–1953, Vol. 1, Strategy and Diplomacy, 1981, Vol. II, Combat Operations, 1985; (ed with David Horner) Australian Defence Policy for the 1980s, 1982; (ed) Security in East Asia, 1984; (ed) The Conduct of East-West Relations in the 1980s, 1985; (ed) New Technology and Western Security Policy, 1985; (ed) Doctrine, the Alliance and Arms Control, 1986; (ed) East Asia, the West and International Security, 1987; (ed) Security in the Mediterranean, 1989; (ed with R. J. Vincent) The West and the Third World, 1990; (ed with Beatrice Heuser) Securing Peace in Europe 1945–62, 1992; (ed jtly) War, Strategy and International Politics, 1992; (ed with John Baylis) Alternative Nuclear Futures, 1999; articles in many learned jls. *Recreations:* local history, walking. *Club:* Garrick.

O'NEILL, Sally Jane; QC 1997; a Recorder, since 2000; *b* 30 Sept. 1953; *d* of late Maj. John O'Neill, RA retd and of Frances Agnes O'Neill (*née* Riley); *m* 1986, David Bloss Kingsbury. *Educ:* St Joseph's Convent, Stafford; Alleyne's Grammar Sch., Uttoxeter; Mid-Essex Technical Coll. (LLB 1975). Called to the Bar, Gray's Inn, 1976; in practice at the Bar, 1976–. An Asst Recorder, 1997–2000. *Recreations:* gardening, tennis, ski-ing, sailing, bull dogs. *Address:* Furnival Chambers, 32 Furnival Street, EC4A 1JQ. *T:* (020) 7405 3232.

O'NEILL, William Alan; Executive Vice President, News Corporation, since 1990; Director, News International plc, since 1995; *b* 22 May 1936; *s* of John O'Neill and Martha O'Neill (*née* Kitson); *m* 1962, Alene Joy Brown; one *s* one *d. Educ:* Sydney Tech. Coll. Gp Employee Relns Manager, News Ltd (Australia), 1977–80; Gen. Manager, 1981, Dir, 1981–90, Times Newspapers Ltd; Vice-Pres. (Personnel), News America Publishing, 1984–85; Exec. Vice-Pres., and Gen. Manager, New York Post, 1985–86, and Vice-Pres. (Human Resources), News Corp., 1986; Man. Dir, News Internat. Newspapers, 1987–90; Director: News Corp., 1987–90; News Gp Newspapers Ltd, 1987–90; Director and Executive Vice-President: News America Inc., 1990–; News America Publishing Inc., 1990–; CEO, News Internat. plc, 1995. Chm., Convoys Ltd, 1987–89; Dep. Chm., Townsend Hook, 1987–89; Director: Sky TV; Eric Bemrose Ltd. *Recreations:* travelling, genealogy. *Address:* News Corporation, 1211 Avenue of the Americas, New York, NY 10036, USA. *T:* (212) 8527193; (home) 31 Wolfeton Way, San Antonio, TX 78218, USA. *T:* (210) 8058871.

ONG Teng Cheong; Chairman, Ong & Ong Architects, since 1999; President of Singapore, 1993–99; *b* 22 Jan. 1936; *m* 1963, Ling Siew May (*d* 1999); two *s. Educ:* Chinese High Sch.; Univ. of Adelaide (BArch 1961); Univ. of Liverpool (MCD 1967). Architect, Adelaide and Singapore, 1962–65; town planner in Singapore CS, 1967–71; architect and town planner in private sector, 1971–75. MP: for Kim Keat, 1972–88; Toa Payoh Gp, 1988–93; Sen. Minister of State for Communications, 1975–78; Minister for Communications, 1978–83; Actg Minister for Culture, 1978–80; Minister for Labour, 1980–83; Minister Without Portfolio, 1983–85; 2nd Dep. Prime Minister, 1985–90; Dep. Prime Minister, 1990–93. Chm., People's Action Party Central Exec. Cttee, 1981–93. Sec.-Gen., NTUC, 1983–93. *Address:* Ong & Ong Architects, 510 Thomson Road, 11-00 SLF Building, Singapore 298135.

ONIONS, Jeffery Peter; QC 1998; *b* 22 Aug. 1957; *s* of Derrick and Violet Onions; *m* 1987, Sally Louise Hine; one *d. Educ:* St Alban's Sch.; St John's Coll., Cambridge (BA 1979, MA 1983); LLM (LLB 1980); hockey blue 1977–79). Called to the Bar, Middle Temple, 1981 (Astbury Schol.); in practice at the Bar, 1981–. Mem., Bar Council, 1987–89. Mem., Royal Opera House Trust. *Recreations:* cricket, wine, opera. *Address:* 1 Essex Court, Temple, EC4Y 9AR. *T:* (020) 7583 2000. *Clubs:* MCC, Middlesex CC, Surrey CC; 1890.

O'NIONS, Sir (Robert) Keith, Kt 1999; PhD; FRS 1983; Chief Scientific Adviser, Ministry of Defence, since 2000; Professor of the Physics and Chemistry of Minerals, University of Oxford, since 1995 (on leave of absence); Fellow of St Hugh's College, Oxford, since 1995; *b* 26 Sept. 1944; *s* of William Henry O'Nions and Eva O'Nions; *m* 1967, Rita Margaret Bill; three *d. Educ:* Univ. of Nottingham (BSc 1966); Univ. of Alberta (PhD 1969). Post-doctoral Fellow, Oslo Univ., 1970; Demonstr in Petrology, Oxford Univ., 1971–72, Lectr in Geochem., 1972–75; Associate Prof., then Prof., Columbia Univ., NY, 1975–79; Royal Soc. Res. Prof., 1979–95, and Fellow, Clare Hall, 1980–95, Cambridge Univ.; Head, Dept of Earth Scis, Oxford Univ., 1995–99. Hon. Fellow, Indian Acad. of Scis, 1998; For. Fellow, Nat. Indian Sci. Acad., 2000; Mem., Norwegian Acad. of Sciences, 1980. Macelwane Award, Amer. Geophys. Union, 1979; Bigsby Medal, Geol. Soc. London, 1983; Holmes Medal, Eur. Union of Geosciences, 1995; Lyell Medal, Geol Soc. of London, 1995; Urey Medal, 2001. *Publications:* contrib. to jls related to earth and planetary sciences. *Address:* Ministry of Defence, Whitehall, SW1A 2HB.

ONIONS, Robin William; His Honour Judge Onions; a Circuit Judge, since 2000; *b* 12 April 1948; s of late Ernest Onions, DFC, and Edith Margaret Onions; *m* 1970, Catherine Anne Graham; two *s. Educ:* Prestfelde Sch., Shrewsbury; Priory Grammar Sch., Shrewsbury; London Sch. of Econs (LLB 1970). Articled clerk, Royal Borough of Kingston upon Thames, 1971–73; admitted solicitor, 1973; J. C. H. Bowdler & Sons, Shrewsbury, subsequently Lanyon Bowdler: solicitor, 1974–76; Partner, 1977–2000; Sen. Partner, 1993–2000. *Recreations:* football, cricket, travel, gardening, keeping fit? *Address:* Stoke Combined Court Centre, Bethesda Street, Hanley, Stoke-on-Trent ST1 3BP. *T:* (01782) 854000.

ONSLOW, family name of **Earl of Onslow**.

ONSLOW, 7th Earl of, *cr* 1801; **Michael William Coplestone Dillon Onslow;** Bt 1660; Baron Onslow, 1716; Baron Cranley, 1776; Viscount Cranley, 1801; *b* 28 Feb. 1938; *s* of 6th Earl of Onslow, KBE, MC, TD, and Hon. Pamela Louisa Eleanor Dillon (*d* 1992), *o d* of 19th Viscount Dillon, CMG, DSO; *S* father, 1971; *m* 1964, Robin Lindsay, *o d* of Major Robert Lee Bullard III, US Army, and of Lady Aberconway; one *s* two *d. Educ:* Eton; Sorbonne. Life Guards, 1956–60, served Arabian Peninsula. Farmer; director, various cos. Governor, Royal Grammar Sch., Guildford; formerly Governor, University Coll. at Buckingham. High Steward of Guildford. Elected Mem., H of L, 1999. *Heir: s* Viscount Cranley, *qv. Address:* Temple Court, Clandon Park, Guildford, Surrey GU4 7RQ. *Clubs:* White's, Beefsteak.

ONSLOW, Sir John (Roger Wilmot), 8th Bt *cr* 1797; Captain, Royal Yacht of Saudi Arabia; *b* 21 July 1932; *o s* of Sir Richard Wilmot Onslow, 7th Bt, TD, and Constance (*d* 1960), *o d* of Albert Parker; *S* father, 1963; *m* 1955, Catherine Zoia (marr. diss. 1973), *d* of Henry Atherton Greenway, The Manor, Compton Abdale, near Cheltenham, Gloucestershire; one *s* one *d*; *m* 1976, Susan Fay (*d* 1998), *d* of E. M. Hughes, Frankston, Vic, Australia. *Educ:* Cheltenham College. *Heir: s* Richard Paul Atherton Onslow, *b* 16 Sept. 1958.

ONTARIO, Bishop of, since 1992; **Rt Rev. Peter Ralph Mason;** *b* 30 April 1943; *s* of late Ralph Victor Mason and of Dorothy Ida Mullin; *m* 1965, Carmen Ruth Ruddock; one *s* two *d. Educ:* McGill Univ., Montreal (BA 1964; BD 1967; MA 1971); Princeton Univ. (DMin 1983). Ordained, deacon, 1967, priest, 1968; Asst Curate, St Matthew's, Montreal, 1967–69; Incumbent, parish of Hemmingford, 1969–71; Rector: St Clement's, Montreal, 1971–74; St Peter's, Montreal, 1975–80; St Paul's, Halifax, NS, 1980–85; Principal, Wycliffe Theol Coll., Univ. of Toronto, 1985–92. Hon. DD Montreal Diocesan Theol Coll., 1987; Hon. DD: Trinity Coll., Toronto, 1992; Wycliffe Coll., Toronto, 1994. *Recreations:* golf, sailing, ski-ing, opera. *Addresses:* (office) 90 Johnson Street, Kingston, ON K7L 1X7, Canada. *T:* (613) 5444774; (home) 73 Seaforth Road, Kingston, ON K7M 1E1, Canada. *e-mail:* pmason@ontario.anglican.ca.

OPENSHAW, Caroline Jane, (Mrs C. P. L. Openshaw); *see* Swift, C. J.

OPENSHAW, (Charles) Peter (Lawford), QC 1991; DL; **His Honour Judge Openshaw;** a Senior Circuit Judge, since 1999; *b* 21 Dec. 1947; *s* of late Judge William Harrison Openshaw and Elisabeth Joyce Emily Openshaw; *m* 1979, Caroline Jane Swift, *qv*; one *s* one *d. Educ:* Harrow; St Catharine's College, Cambridge (MA). Called to the

Bar, Inner Temple, 1970; practising on Northern Circuit, Junior 1973; Assistant Recorder, 1985; a Recorder, 1988–99; Hon. Recorder of Preston, 1999–. DL Lancs 2000. *Recreations:* fishing, gardening, village life. *Address:* Preston Law Courts, Openshaw Place, The Ring Way, Preston PR1 2LL. *Club:* Oxford and Cambridge.

OPIE, Alan John; baritone; *b* 22 March 1945; *s* of Jack and Doris Winifred Opie; *m* 1970, Kathleen Ann Smales; one *s* one *d*. *Educ:* Truro Sch.; Guildhall Sch. of Music (AGSM); London Opera Centre. Principal rôles include: Papageno in The Magic Flute, Sadler's Wells Opera, 1969; Tony in the Globolinks, Santa Fé Opera, 1970; Officer in the Barber of Seville, Covent Garden, 1971; Don Giovanni, Kent Opera, and Demetrius, English Opera Gp, 1972; Prin. Baritone with ENO, 1973–96; *English National Opera:* Figaro; Papageno; Gugliemo; Beckmesser; Valentin; Lescaut in Manon; Eisenstein and Falke in Die Fledermaus; Danilo; Silvio; Junius in Rape of Lucretia; Cecil in Gloriana; Faninal in Der Rosenkavalier; Germont in La Traviata; Marcello and Schaunard in La Bohème; Kovalyov in The Nose; Strephon in Iolanthe; Grosvenor in Patience; Tomsky in Queen of Spades; Paolo in Simon Boccanegra; Harlequin in Ariadne auf Naxos; Dr Faust by Busoni; Sharpless in Madame Butterfly; Fiddler in Königskinder; Sancho in Don Quixote, 1994; Alfonso in Cosí fan Tutte, and Falstaff, 1997; Don Carlo in Ernani, 2000; *Royal Opera, Covent Garden:* Hector in King Priam, 1985; Ping in Turandot, 1986; Mangus in The Knot Garden, 1988; Falke in Die Fledermaus, 1989; Paolo in Simon Boccanegra; rôles in Death in Venice, 1992; Sharpless in Madame Butterfly, 1993; Faninal in Der Rosenkavalier, 1995; Germont in La Traviata, 2001; *Glyndebourne Festival Opera:* Sid in Albert Herring, 1985, 1990; rôles in Death in Venice, 1989; Figaro in Le Nozze di Figaro, 1991; Balstrode in Peter Grimes, 1992; *Scottish Opera:* Baron in La Vie Parisienne, 1985; Storch in Intermezzo, 1986; Forester in Cunning Little Vixen, 1991; *Opera North:* Diomede in Troilus and Cressida, 1995; *Metropolitan Opera, NY:* Balstrode in Peter Grimes, 1994; Sharpless in Madama Butterfly, 1997; *La Scala, Milan:* title role, Outis, by Berio, world première 1996; has also appeared at Bayreuth Fest., Berlin (Unter den Linden, Berlin Staatsoper, 1990) and in Amsterdam and Munich (rôles include Beckmesser), and at Buxton Fest. and in Brussels, Chicago, Vienna, Paris, Dallas, Sydney. *Address:* Quanda, Old Court, Ashtead, Surrey KT21 2TS. *T:* (01372) 274038.

OPIE, Geoffrey James; freelance lecturer on 19th and 20th century art and design; *b* 10 July 1939; *s* of Basil Irwin Opie and Florence Mabel Opie (*née* May); *m* 1st, 1964, Pamela Green; one *s* one *d*; 2nd, 1980, Jennifer Hawkins; one *s*. *Educ:* Humphry Davy Grammar School, Penzance; Falmouth Sch. of Art (NDD); Goldsmiths' Coll., London (ATC). Asst Designer, Leacock & Co., 1961; Curator, Nat. Mus. of Antiquities of Scotland, 1963; Designer, Leacock & Co., 1967; Curator, Victoria and Albert Mus., 1969, Educn Dept, 1978–89, Head of Educn Services, 1983–89. *Publications:* The Wireless Cabinet 1930–1956, 1979; (contrib.) Encyclopedia of Interior Design, 1997; contribs to various jls. *Recreations:* painting, literature, music, motorcycling. *Address:* 130 Kingston Road, Teddington, Middx TW11 9JA.

OPIE, Iona Margaret Balfour, CBE 1999; FBA 1998; folklorist; *b* 13 Oct. 1923; *d* of late Sir Robert Archibald, CMG, DSO, MD, and of Olive Cant; *m* 1943, Peter Mason Opie (*d* 1982); two *s* one *d*. *Educ:* Sandecotes Sch., Parkstone. Served 1941–43, WAAF meteorological section. Hon. Mem., Folklore Soc., 1974. Coote-Lake Medal (jtly with husband), 1960. Hon. MA: Oxon, 1962; OU, 1987; Hon. DLitt: Southampton, 1987; Nottingham, 1991; DUniv Surrey, 1997. *Publications:* (with Peter Opie or using material researched with him): I Saw Esau, 1947, 2nd edn (illus. Maurice Sendak), 1992; The Oxford Dictionary of Nursery Rhymes, 1951, 2nd edn 1997; The Oxford Nursery Rhyme Book, 1955; The Lore and Language of Schoolchildren, 1959; Puffin Book of Nursery Rhymes, 1963 (European Prize City of Caorle); Children's Games in Street and Playground, 1969 (Chicago Folklore Prize); The Oxford Book of Children's Verse, 1973; Three Centuries of Nursery Rhymes and Poetry for Children (exhibition catalogue), 1973, enl. edn 1977; The Classic Fairy Tales, 1974; A Nursery Companion, 1980; The Oxford Book of Narrative Verse, 1983; The Singing Game, 1985 (Katharine Briggs Folklore Award; Rose Mary Crawshay Prize; Children's Literature Assoc. Book Award); Babies: an unsentimental anthology, 1990; Children's Games with Things, 1997; edited jointly: The Treasures of Childhood, 1989; A Dictionary of Superstitions, 1989; sole author: Tail Feathers from Mother Goose, 1988; The People in the Playground, 1993; My Very First Mother Goose (illus. Rosemary Wells), 1996; Here Comes Mother Goose (illus. Rosemary Wells), 1999. *Recreation:* opsimathy. *Address:* Mells House, Farnham Road, Liss, Hants GU33 6JQ. *T:* (01730) 893309.

ÖPIK, Lembit; MP (Lib Dem) Montgomeryshire, since 1997; *b* 2 March 1965; *s* of Uno and Liivi Öpik. *Educ:* Royal Belfast Academical Instn; Bristol Univ. (BA Hons Philosophy). Pres., Univ. of Bristol Students' Union, 1985–86; Mem., Nat. Exec., NUS, 1987–88. Procter and Gamble Ltd, 1988–97: Brand Asst, 1988–89; Asst Brand Manager, 1989–91; Corporate Trng and Orgn Develt Manager, 1991–96; Global Human Resources Trng Manager, 1996–97. Mem., Newcastle upon Tyne CC, 1992–97. Mem., Lib Dem Federal Exec., 1991–. Lib Dem spokesman for Young People, and NI, 1997–, for Wales, 2001–; Mem., Welsh Affairs team, 1997–. Leader, Welsh Liberal Democrats, 2001–. *Recreations:* aviation, astronomy, motorcycling, windsurfing, military history. *Address:* House of Commons, SW1A 0AA. *T:* (020) 7219 1144; *e-mail:* opikl@parliament.uk; Montgomeryshire Liberal Democrats, 3 Park Street, Newtown, Powys SY16 1EE. *T:* (01686) 625527.

OPPÉ, Prof. Thomas Ernest, CBE 1984; FRCP; Professor of Paediatrics, University of London at St Mary's Hospital Medical School, 1969–90, now Emeritus Professor; *b* 7 Feb. 1925; *s* of late Ernest Frederick Oppé and Ethel Nellie (*née* Rackstraw); *m* 1948, Margaret Mary Butcher; three *s* one *d*. *Educ:* University Coll. Sch., Hampstead; Guy's Hosp. Med. Sch. (MB BS, hons dist. in Medicine, 1947). DCH 1950; FRCP 1966. Sir Alfred Fripp Meml Fellow, Guy's Hosp., 1952; Milton Res. Fellow, Harvard Univ., 1954; Lectr in Child Health, Univ. of Bristol, 1956–60; Consultant Paediatrician, United Bristol Hosps, 1960; Asst Dir, 1960–64, Dir, 1964–69, Paediatric Unit, St Mary's Hosp. Med. Sch.; Consultant Paediatrician, St Mary's Hosp., 1960–90. Consultant Adviser in Paediatrics, DHSS, 1971–86; Member, DHSS Committees: Safety of Medicines, 1974–79; Med. Aspects of Food Policy, 1966–88 (Chm., Panel on Child Nutrition); Child Health Services, 1973–76. Royal College of Physicians: Chm., Cttee on Paediatrics, 1970–74; Pro-Censor and Censor, 1975–77; Sen. Censor and Sen. Vice-Pres., 1983–84; University of London: Mem., Bd of Studies in Medicine, 1964–90 (Chm., 1978–80); elected Mem. of Senate, 1981–89; Dean, Faculty of Medicine, 1984–86; Mem. of Court, 1984–89. Member: BMA (Dep. Chm., Bd of Sci. and Educn, 1974–82); British Paediatric Assoc. (Hon. Sec., 1960–63); European Soc. for Paediatric Res., 1969–; GMC, 1984–88; sometime Mem., Governing Bodies, St Mary's Hosp., Inst. of Med. Ethics, Paddington Coll.; Examiner in Paediatrics, Univs of Glasgow, Leicester, Liverpool, London, Sheffield, Wales, Colombo, Singapore. *Publications:* Modern Textbook of Paediatrics for Nurses, 1961; Neurological Examination of Children (with R. Paine), 1966; chapters in books and papers on paediatrics and child health. *Address:* 2 Parkholme Cottages, Fife Road, Sheen Common, SW14 7ER. *T:* (020) 8392 1626.

OPPENHEIM, Sir Duncan (Morris), Kt 1960; Adviser to British-American Tobacco Co. Ltd, 1972–74 (Chairman 1953–66, President, 1966–72); Chairman, Tobacco Securities Trust Co. Ltd, 1969–74; Deputy Chairman, Commonwealth Development Finance Co., 1968–74; *b* 6 Aug. 1904; *s* of Watkin Oppenheim, BA, TD, and Helen, 3rd *d* of Duncan McKechnie, JP; *m* 1st, 1932, Joyce Mary (*d* 1933), *d* of Stanley Mitcheson; no *c*; 2nd, 1936, Susan May (*d* 1964), *e d* of Brig.-Gen. E. B. Macnaghten, CMG, DSO; one *s* one *d*. *Educ:* Repton Sch. Admitted Solicitor of the Supreme Court, 1929; Messrs Linklaters & Paines, London, Assistant Solicitor, 1929–34; joined British-American Tobacco Ltd group as a Solicitor, 1934; Director: British-American Tobacco Co. Ltd, 1943; Lloyds Bank Ltd, 1956–75; Equity and Law Life Assurance Society, 1966–80. Chairman: Council, Royal College of Art, 1956–72; Council of Industrial Design, 1960–72 (Mem. 1959); British Nat. Cttee of Internat. Chamber of Commerce, 1963–74; Overseas Investment Cttee CBI, 1964–74; RIIA (Chatham House), 1966–71; Member: Adv. Council, V&A Mus., 1967–79 (Chm. V&A Associates, 1976–81); Crafts Council (formerly Crafts Adv. Cttee), 1972–83 (acting Chm., 1977; Dep. Chm., 1978); Trustee and Mem., Council, 1973–94, Chm. of Council, 1990–, St John's, Smith Square. Governing Body of Repton School, 1959–79; Chm. Court of Governors, Admin. Staff Coll., 1963–71. Pt-time Civil Defence, City of Westminster, 1938–45; pictures painted of air-raid incidents in Westminster in archives of Imperial War Mus. Exhibitor: London Gp, 1954; RA Summer Exhibns, 1957, 1962–1982; one-man shows: Upper Grosvenor Galls, 1971; Spinks, 1980, 1983; New Grafton Gall., 1985, 1988, 1992. Hon. Dr and Senior Fellow, Royal College of Art; Hon. FCSD (Hon. FSIAD 1972). Bicentenary Medal, RSA, 1969. *Recreations:* painting, sailing. *Address:* 43 Edwardes Square, Kensington, W8 6HH. *T:* (020) 7603 7431. *Clubs:* Athenæum; Royal Yacht Squadron.

OPPENHEIM, Hon. Phillip Anthony Charles Lawrence; author; columnist, The Sunday Times; Managing Director, Cubana Ltd; *b* 20 March 1956; *s* of late Henry Oppenheim and of Baroness Oppenheim-Barnes, *qv*. *Educ:* Harrow; Oriel College, Oxford. BA Hons. MP (C) Amber Valley, 1983–97; contested (C) same seat, 1997. PPS to Sec. of State for Health, 1988–90, to Sec. of State for Educn and Sci., 1990–92, to Home Sec., 1992–93, to Chancellor of the Exchequer, 1993–94; Parliamentary Under-Secretary of State: Dept of Employment, 1994–95; DTI, 1995–96; Exchequer Sec. to HM Treasury, 1996–97. Co-editor, What to Buy for Business, 1980–85. *Publications:* A Handbook of New Office Technology, 1982; Telecommunications: a user's handbook, 1983; A Word Processing Handbook, 1984; The New Masters: can the West match Japan?, 1991; Trade Wars: Japan versus the West, 1992. *Recreations:* Rugby, tennis, travel, ski-ing, tropical plants. *Address:* 29 Redburn Street, SW3 4DA.

OPPENHEIM-BARNES, Baroness *cr* 1989 (Life Peer), of Gloucester in the county of Gloucestershire; **Sally Oppenheim-Barnes;** PC 1979; *b* 26 July 1930; *d* of Mark and Jeanette Viner; *m* 1st, 1949, Henry M. Oppenheim (*d* 1980); one *s* two *d*; 2nd, 1984, John Barnes. *Educ:* Sheffield High Sch.; Lowther Coll., N Wales. Formerly: Exec. Dir, Industrial & Investment Services Ltd; Social Worker, School Care Dept, ILEA. Trustee, Clergy Rest House Trust. MP (C) Gloucester, 1970–87. Vice Chm., 1971–73, Chm., 1973–74, Cons. Party Parly Prices and Consumer Protection Cttee; Opposition Spokesman on Prices and Consumer Protection, 1974–79; Mem. Shadow Cabinet, 1975–79; Min. of State (Consumer Affairs), Dept of Trade, 1979–82. Chairman: Nat. Consumer Council, 1987–89; Council of Management, Nat. Waterways Museums Trust, 1988–89. Non-executive Director: and Mem., Main Bd, Boots Co., 1982–93; Fleming High Income Trust, 1989–97; HFC Bank, 1989–98. *Recreations:* tennis, bridge. *Address:* c/o House of Lords, Westminster, SW1A 0AA.

See also Hon. P. A. C. L. Oppenheim.

OPPENHEIMER, (Lætitia) Helen, (Lady Oppenheimer); writer on moral and philosophical theology; *b* 30 Dec. 1926; *d* of Sir Hugh Lucas-Tooth (later Munro-Lucas-Tooth), 1st Bt; *m* 1947, Sir Michael Oppenheimer, Bt, *qv*; three *d*. *Educ:* Cheltenham Ladies' Coll.; Lady Margaret Hall, Oxford (Schol.; BPhil, MA). Lectr in Ethics, Cuddesdon Theological Coll., 1964–69. Served on: Archbp of Canterbury's Gp on the law of divorce (report, Putting Asunder, 1966); C of E Marriage Commn (report, Marriage, Divorce and the Church, 1971); Wkg Party, ACCM (report, Teaching Christian Ethics, 1974); C of E Wkg Party on Educn in Personal Relationships (Chm.), 1978–82; Inter-Anglican Theol and Doctrinal Commn (report, For the Sake of the Kingdom, 1986); General Synod Wkg Party on the law of marriage (report, An Honourable Estate, 1988). Pres., Soc. for the Study of Christian Ethics, 1989–91. Lectures: John Coffin Meml, London Univ., 1977; First Mary Sumner, Mothers' Union, 1978; Larkin-Stuart, Trinity Coll., Toronto, 1997; preached University Sermon, Oxford, 1979, Cambridge, 1983. DD Lambeth, 1993. *Publications:* Law and Love, 1962; The Character of Christian Morality, 1965, 2nd edn 1974; Incarnation and Immanence, 1973; The Marriage Bond, 1976; The Hope of Happiness: a sketch for a Christian humanism, 1983; Looking Before and After: The Archbishop of Canterbury's Lent Book for 1988; Marriage, 1990; Finding and Following, 1994; contributor: New Dictionary of Christian Theology, 1983; New Dictionary of Christian Ethics, 1986; Companion Encyclopedia of Theology, 1996; Dictionary of Ethics, Theology and Society, 1996; Making Good: creation, tragedy and hope, 2001; articles in Theology, Religious Studies, Studies in Christian Ethics, etc, and in various collections of essays. *Address:* L'Aiguillon, Grouville, Jersey, CI JE3 9AP. *Club:* Victoria (Jersey).

OPPENHEIMER, Michael Anthony; His Honour Judge Oppenheimer; a Circuit Judge, since 1991; *b* 22 Sept. 1946; *s* of Felix Oppenheimer and Ingeborg Hanna Oppenheimer; *m* 1973, Nicola Anne Brotherton (*see* N. A. Oppenheimer); one *s* one *d*. *Educ:* Westminster Sch.; LSE (LLB). Called to the Bar, Middle Temple, 1970 (Blackstone Exhibnr 1970); Asst Recorder, 1985–89; Recorder, 1989–91. Chm., Bar Disciplinary Tribunal, 1999–. *Recreations:* cinema, theatre, wine and food, performing and listening to music. *Club:* Athenæum.

OPPENHEIMER, Sir Michael (Bernard Grenville), 3rd Bt *cr* 1921; *b* 27 May 1924; *s* of Sir Michael Oppenheimer, 2nd Bt, and Caroline Magdalen (who *m* 2nd, 1935, Sir Ernest Oppenheimer; she *d* 1972), *d* of Sir Robert G. Harvey, 2nd Bt; *S* father, 1933; *m* 1947, Laetitia Helen Lucas-Tooth (*see* L. H. Oppenheimer); three *d*. *Educ:* Charterhouse; Christ Church, Oxford (BLitt, MA). Served with South African Artillery, 1942–45. Lecturer in Politics: Lincoln Coll., Oxford, 1955–68; Magdalen Coll., Oxford, 1966–68. *Publication:* The Monuments of Italy, 6 vols, 2000. *Heir:* none. *Address:* L'Aiguillon, Grouville, Jersey, CI JE3 9AP. *Clubs:* Victoria (Jersey); Kimberley (Kimberley).

OPPENHEIMER, Nicholas Frank; Chairman: Anglo-American Gold Investment Co., since 1990; De Beers Consolidated Mines Ltd, since 1998; *b* Johannesburg, 8 June 1945; *s* of late Harry Frederick Oppenheimer, and Bridget (*née* McCall); *m* 1968, Orcillia Lasch; one *s*. *Educ:* Harrow Sch.; Christ Church, Oxford (BA PPE, MA). Joined Anglo-American Corp., 1968; Dir, 1974; Deputy Chairman: Anglo-American plc, 1974–; Anglo American Corp. of SA Ltd; De Beers Consolidated Mines Ltd, 1985–97; Dep. Chm., 1990, subseq. Chm., De Beers Centenary AG; Chairman: Central Selling Orgn, 1985–; Anglogold, 1997–2000. Director: De Beers Hldgs Ltd, 1983–; De Beers Industrial Corp.

Ltd; Minorco, 1989; E. Oppenheimer & Son (Pty) Ltd; Vaal Reefs Exploration and Mining Co. Ltd. *Address:* PO Box 61631, Marshalltown 2107, South Africa.

OPPENHEIMER, Nicola Anne; Partner, Odgers Ray & Berndtson, since 2001; *b* 30 Sept. 1950; *d* of Basil Vincent Brotherton and Joan Pamela Brotherton; *m* 1973, Michael Anthony Oppenheimer, *qv*; one *s* one *d*. *Educ:* St Margaret's Sch., Bushey; Queen's Coll., London; Queen Mary Coll., London Univ. (LLB). Called to the Bar, Middle Temple, 1972. Lord Chancellor's Department, 1973–96: Judicial Appts Div., 1985; Head of Personnel Management, 1987; Head of Legal Services and Agencies Div., 1991; Cabinet Office: Prin. Estabt and Finance Officer, 1993–96; Cabinet Office: Prin. Estabt and Finance Officer, 1996–2000; Fellow, Knowledge Mgt Centre for Mgt and Policy Studies, 2000–01. Chairman, Trustees: King's Consort, 1998–2000; Orchestra of St John, 2000–01; Trustee: Classical Opera Co., 1999–; Gabrieli Consort and Players, 2000–; Member, Development Board: RAM, 1996–; LAMDA, 1999–. *Recreations:* early music, theatre, ski-ing, walking. *Address:* Odgers Ray & Berndtson, 11 Hanover Square, W1S 1JJ. *T:* (020) 7529 1111; *e-mail:* nicky.oppenheimer@odgers.com.

OPPENHEIMER, Peter Morris; Student of Christ Church, Oxford, since 1967; President, Oxford Centre for Hebrew and Jewish Studies, since 2000; *b* 16 April 1938; *s* of late Friedrich Rudolf and Charlotte Oppenheimer; *m* 1964, Catherine, *er d* of late Dr Eliot Slater, CBE, FRCP, and Dr Lydia Pasternak; two *s* one *d*. *Educ:* Haberdashers' Aske's Sch.; The Queen's Coll., Oxford (BA 1961). National Service, RN, 1956–58. Bank for International Settlements, Basle, 1961–64; Research Fellow, Nuffield Coll., Oxford, 1964–67; Univ. Lectr in Econs, 1967–2000; on secondment as Chief Economist, Shell Internat. Petroleum Co., 1985–86. Vis. Prof., London Graduate Sch. of Business Studies, 1976–77; Temp. Econ. Attaché, British Embassy, Moscow, 1991. Mem., Gen. Bd of Faculties, Oxford Univ., 1989–97. Director: Panfida plc (formerly Investing in Success Equities Ltd), 1975–92; Target Hldgs, 1982–84; J. Rothschild Investment Management, 1982–86; Jewish Chronicle Ltd, 1986– (Chm., 2001–); Delbanco, Meyer and Co. Ltd, 1986–2001; Dixons Group plc, 1987–93 (Chm., Audit Cttee, 1987–92); OAO Purneftegaz, Russia, 1998–; OAO Tomskueft of VNK, Russia, 1999; Far Eastern Shipping Co., Russia, 1999–2000; VSMPO, Russia, 1999–2001. Chm., Caminus Energy Ltd, 1991–93. Delegate, OUP, 1987–97 (Mem., Finance Cttee, 1989–97). Specialist Advr, H of C Expenditure Cttee, 1975–76. Mem., Royal Commn on Legal Services, 1976–79. Mem. Council, Trade Policy Research Centre, 1976–89, and co-Editor, The World Economy, 1977–89; Member: Internat. Econs Steering Gp, and Energy and Envmt Steering Gp, RIIA, 1989–; Editl Bd, International Affairs, 1989–; Mem. Bd, Jewish Policy Res. (formerly Inst. of Jewish Affairs), 1991–; Renewable Energy Adv. Gp, Dept of Energy, 1991–92; Academic Adv. Council, World ORT Union, 1992–; Spoliation Adv. Panel, DCMS, 2000–. Governor: St Edward's Sch., Oxford, 1979–; St Clare's, Oxford, 1985– (Chm., 1993–); Haberdashers' Monmouth Schs, 1987–. Freeman, Haberdashers' Co., 1987. Presenter: (BBC radio): File on 4, 1977–80; Third Opinion, 1983; Poles Apart, 1984; (BBC TV) Outlook, 1982–85; (Granada TV) Under Fire, 1988; (participant) Round Britain Quiz, Radio 4, 1979–96. *Publications:* (ed) Issues in International Economics, 1980; (ed with B. Granville and contrib.) Russia's Post-Communist Economy, 2001; contribs to symposia, conference procs, prof. jls, bank reviews, etc. *Recreations:* music, opera, amateur dramatics, swimming, ski-ing. *Address:* 6 Linton Road, Oxford OX2 6UG. *T:* (01865) 558226.

O'RAHILLY, Prof. Stephen, MD; FRCP, FRCPI, FMedSci; Professor of Metabolic Medicine, Departments of Medicine and Clinical Biochemistry, University of Cambridge, since 1996; Fellow of Churchill College, Cambridge, since 1992; *b* 1 April 1958; *s* of Patrick Francis O'Rahilly and Emer (*née* Hyland); *m* 1990, Suzy Oakes. *Educ:* Beneavin Coll., Finglas, Dublin; University Coll., Dublin (MB Bch BAO 1981; MD 1987). FRCP 1996; FRCPI 1996. House Officer, Mater Hosp., Dublin, 1981–82; Senior House Officer: St Bartholomew's Hosp., London, 1982–83; Hammersmith Hosp., 1983–84; Res. Fellow, Nuffield Dept of Medicine, Diabetes Res. Lab., Univ. of Oxford, 1984–87; Registrar in Diabetes and Endocrinology, Oxford HA, 1987–89; MRC Travelling Fellow, Harvard Med. Sch., Boston, 1989–91; Wellcome Trust Sen. Fellow in Clinical Sci., Univ. of Cambridge, 1991–96. British Diabetic Association: Redcliffe-Maud Fellow, 1986–87; R. D. Lawrence Lectr, 1996. Lectures: Clinical Endocrinology Trust, 1999; Rufus Cole, Rockefeller Univ., 2000; McCallum, Univ. of Toronto, 2000; Andrew Marble, Joslin Clinic, Boston, USA, 2001. FMedSci 1999. Medal, Soc. of Endocrinology, 2000; Graham Bull Prize, RCP, 2000; Novaltis Award, 2001; European Jl of Endocrinology Prize, 2001. *Publications:* papers on: pathophysiol. and genetics of non-insulin-dependent diabetes; mechanism of insulin action; molecular and cell biol. of human fat cells; molecular basis for human obesity. *Recreations:* literature, music, food and wine and good company, tennis, Manchester United. *Address:* University of Cambridge, Departments of Medicine and Clinical Biochemistry, Box 157, Addenbrooke's Hospital, Hills Road, Cambridge CB2 2QQ.

ORAMO, Sakari; Music Director, City of Birmingham Symphony Orchestra, since 1999 (Principal Conductor and Artistic Adviser, 1998–99); Chief Conductor designate, Finnish Radio Symphony Orchestra; *b* Finland, 1965; *m* Anu Komsi, soprano; two *c*. *Educ:* musical training as violinist; Sibelius Acad., Helsinki (conducting, under Jorma Panula). Formerly violinist, Avanti! Chamber Orch.; Concert Master, 1992–94, Co-Principal Conductor, 1994, Finnish Radio SO (professional conducting début, 1993); Artistic Dir, Finland 75 SO, 1995–98. Débuts include: CBSO, 1995; Henry Wood Promenade Concert, 1999. Guest Conductor: LA Philharmonic Orch.; Berlin Philharmonic; NHK SO, Japan; Oslo Philharmonic Orch. *Address:* City of Birmingham Symphony Orchestra, CBSO Centre, Berkeley Street, Birmingham B1 2LF; c/o Harrison Parrott Ltd, 12 Penzance Place, W11 4PA.

ORANMORE and BROWNE, 4th Baron *cr* 1836 (Ireland); **Dominick Geoffrey Edward Browne;** Baron Mereworth of Mereworth Castle (UK) 1926; *b* 21 Oct. 1901; *e s* of 3rd Baron and Lady Olwen Verena Ponsonby (*d* 1927), *e d* of 8th Earl of Bessborough; *S* father, 1927; *m* 1st, 1925, Mildred Helen (who obtained a divorce, 1936; she *d* 1980), *e d* of Hon. Thomas Egerton; two *s* one *d* (and two *d* decd); 2nd, 1936, Oonagh (marr. diss., 1950; she *d* 1995), *d* of late Hon. Ernest Guinness; one *s* (and two *s* decd); 3rd, 1951, Sally Gray, 5b Mount Street, London, W. *Educ:* Eton; Christ Church, Oxford. *Heir: s* Hon. Dominick Geoffrey Thomas Browne [*b* 1 July 1929; *m* 1957, Sara Margaret (marr. diss. 1974), *d* of late Dr Herbert Wright, 59 Merrion Square, Dublin, and late Mrs C. A. West, Cross-in-Hand, Sussex]. *Address:* 52 Eaton Place, SW1X 8AL.

ORCHARD, Edward Eric, CBE 1966 (OBE 1959); *b* 12 Nov. 1920. *Educ:* King's Sch., Grantham; Jesus Coll., Oxford (MA). War Service, 1941–46; FO and HM Embassy, Moscow, 1948–51; Lectr in Russian, Oxford, 1951–52; HM Embassy Moscow and FCO, 1953–76 (Dir of Research, 1970–76). Mem., Waverley Borough Council, 1978–87; Mayor, Haslemere, 1987. *Publications:* articles and reviews. *Recreations:* swimming, gardening, local government and welfare. *Address:* Sturt Meadow House, Haslemere, Surrey GU27 3RT. *T:* (01428) 643034.

ORCHARD, Stephen Michael, CBE 1999; Chief Executive, since 1989, and Member, since 1992, Legal Services Commission (formerly Legal Aid Board); *b* 5 Aug. 1944; *s* of Stephen Henry Orchard and Ellen Frances Orchard; *m*; one *s* one *d*. *Educ:* Swanage Grammar School. Lord Chancellor's Dept, 1961–89. *Recreations:* walking, food and wine. *Address:* Legal Services Commission, 85 Gray's Inn Road, WC1X 8TX. *T:* (020) 7759 0000.

ORCHARD, Susan Kathleen; *see* Doughty, S. K.

ORCHARD-LISLE, Brig. Paul David, CBE 1988; TD 1961; DL; Chairman, Healey & Baker Investment Advisors Inc., since 1999; *b* 3 Aug. 1938; *s* of Mervyn and late Phyllis Orchard-Lisle. *Educ:* Marlborough College; Trinity Hall, Cambridge (MA; Hon. Fellow, 1999). FRICS. Nat. Service, RA, 1956–58. Joined Healey & Baker, 1961; Sen. Partner, 1988–99. RA (TA), 1958–88; ADC (TA), 1985–87; Brig. (TA), UKLF, 1985; Chm., TAVRA Greater London, 1988–91. Pres., RICS, 1986–87. Hon. Fellow, Coll. of Estate Management, 1985–. Dep. Chm., Slough Estates plc, 1993– (non-exec. Dir, 1984–). Commonwealth War Graves Comr, 1998–. Chm., RA Mus., 2000–. Pres. of Council, Reading Univ., 1994– (Mem. Council, 1989–94); Mem. Council, Marlborough Coll., 1991–; Governor: West Buckland Sch., 1986– (Chm., 2000–); Harrow Sch., 1988–99; Nottingham Trent Univ., 1992–94. Hon. DSc City, 1998. DL Gtr London, 1987. *Recreations:* golf, squash. *Address:* 30 Mount Row, W1Y 5DA. *Club:* Athenæum.

ORD, Andrew James B.; *see* Blackett-Ord.

ORD, Jeffrey, QFSM 1995; Firemaster, Strathclyde Fire Brigade, since 1999; *b* 22 June 1949; *s* of Stanley and Alice Ord; *m* 1970, Beryl Dobinson; one *s*. *Educ:* Realby Sch., Sunderland. Joined Fire Service, 1967: Sunderland Fire Bde, 1967–86; on secondment as Tutor and Course Dir, Fire Service Coll., 1983–86; Comdr, N Div., 1986–87, Hd of Ops (Asst Chief Officer), 1987–88, Kent Fire Bde; Northumberland Fire and Rescue Service: Chief Fire Officer, 1988–92; Dir, Protective Services, Chief Fire Officer and Co. Emergency Planning Officer, 1992–96; Chief Fire Officer, S Yorks Fire and Rescue Service, 1996–99. JP Kent, 1971. DUniv Glasgow, 2001. OStJ 1994. *Recreations:* walking, tennis, avid Sunderland Football supporter. *Address:* Strathclyde Fire Brigade, Bothwell Road, Hamilton ML3 0EA. *T:* (01698) 338240.

ORDE, Denis Alan; His Honour Judge Orde; a Circuit Judge, since 1979; *b* 28 Aug. 1932; *s* of late John Orde, CBE, Littlehoughton Hall, Northumberland, and Charlotte Lilian Orde, County Alderman; *m* 1961, Jennifer Jane, *d* of late Dr John Longworth, Masham, Yorks; two *d*. *Educ:* Oxford Univ. (MA Hons). Served Army, 1950–52, 2nd Lieut 1951; TA, 1952–64 (RA), Capt. 1958. Pres., Oxford Univ. Conserv. Assoc., 1954; Mem. Cttee, Oxford Union, 1954–55; Vice-Chm., Fedn of Univ. Conserv. Assocs., 1955. Called to Bar, Inner Temple, 1956; Pupil Studentship, 1956; Profumo Prize, 1959; Bencher, 1998. Assistant Recorder: Kingston upon Hull, 1970; Sheffield, 1970–71; a Recorder of the Crown Court, 1972–79; Liaison Judge to Magistrates, 1983–97; Dep. High Court Judge (Civil), 1983–; Resident Judge, Crown Court, 1986–; sits in NE and London. Mem., Mental Health Review Tribunal, 2001–. Chairman: Criminal Justice Liaison Cttee, Cos of Northumberland, Tyne and Wear and Durham, 1995–2000; Criminal Justice Strategy Cttee for Durham Co., 2000–; Mem., Lord Chancellor's County Adv. Cttee, 1987–. Contested (C): Consett, 1959; Newcastle upon Tyne West, 1966; Sunderland South, 1970. Rep. for NE, Bow Gp, 1962–70. Mem., Chollerton PCC, 1980–91. Vice-Pres., Northumberland LTA, 1982–. Gov., Christ's Hospital, Sherburn, 1993–98. *Publications:* Nelson's Mediterranean Command, 1997; (contrib.) New DNB. *Recreations:* listening to music, cricket, family history, biography. *Address:* Chollerton Grange, Chollerton, near Hexham, Northumberland NE46 4TG; Aristotle Court, 75 Plater Drive, Oxford Waterside, Oxford OX2 6QT. *Club:* Northern Counties (Newcastle).

ORDE, Sir John (Alexander) Campbell-, 6th Bt *cr* 1790, of Morpeth; *b* 11 May 1943; *s* of Sir Simon Arthur Campbell-Orde, 5th Bt, TD, and Eleanor (*d* 1996), *e d* of Col Humphrey Watts, OBE, TD, Haslington Hall, Cheshire; *S* father, 1969; *m* 1973, Lacy Ralls (marr. diss. 1991), *d* of Grady Gallant, Nashville, USA; one *s* three *d*. *Educ:* Gordonstoun. *Heir: s* John Simon Arthur Campbell-Orde, *b* 15 Aug. 1981. *Address:* PO Box 22974, Nashville, TN 37202, USA. *Clubs:* Caledonian, Lansdowne.

ORDE-POWLETT, family name of **Baron Bolton.**

O'REGAN, Sister Pauline Margaret, DCNZM 2001; CBE 1990; writer; *b* 28 June 1922; *d* of John Joseph O'Regan and Mary Margaret O'Regan (*née* Barry). *Educ:* Cronadun Primary Sch., W Coast, NZ; St Mary's High Sch., Greymouth; Univ. of Canterbury, Christchurch (MA Hist.). Entered Order of Sisters of Mercy, 1942; professed as Sister of Mercy, 1944; teacher, St Mary's Coll., Christchurch, 1945–49; Principal: Villa Maria Coll., Christchurch, 1950–66; Mercy Coll., Timaru, 1967–68; teacher, Aranui High Sch., Christchurch, 1973–77; community worker, Aranui, 1978–. Winston Churchill Fellow, 1979. Mem., Winston Churchill Meml Trust Bd, NZ, 1985–90. *Publications:* A Changing Order, 1986, 2nd edn 1995; (jtly) Community, 1989; Aunts and Windmills, 1991; There is Hope for a Tree, 1995. *Recreations:* walking, films, reading. *Address:* Christchurch 9, New Zealand.

O'REGAN, Sir Stephen Gerard, (Sir Tipene), Kt 1994; Ngai Tahu tribal leader; company director; *b* 23 Sept. 1939; *s* of Rolland O'Regan and Rena Ruhia O'Regan (*née* Bradshaw); *m* 1963, Sandra Anne McTaggart; one *s* four *d*. *Educ:* Marist Brothers Primary Sch.; St Patrick's Coll.; Victoria Univ. (BA (Hons) Pol Sci. and Hist.); Wellington Teachers' Coll. Sen. Lectr and Head of Dept of Social Studies and Maori, Wellington Teachers' Coll., 1968–83; founded Aoraki Consultant Services, 1983, now Principal Dir. Maori Fisheries Negotiator with Crown, 1987–92. Gp Chm., Sealord Group (formerly Sealord Products) Ltd, 1993–; Director: Whalewatch Kaikoura Ltd, 1988–; Moana Pacific Fisheries Ltd, 1990–95; Ngai Tahu Property Group Ltd, 1993–. QEII Postgrad. Schol. in Maori, 1977–78; Ngai Tahu Fellow (History), Canterbury Univ., 1977–78; Lansdowne Fellow, Univ. of Victoria, BC, 1994; Visiting Lecturer: Classics, 1983–84, Zoology, 1986–88, Victoria Univ.; Southampton Univ., 1986; NZ History, Canterbury Univ., 1989–. Chairman: Ngai Tahu Maori Trust Bd, 1983–96 (Mem., 1974–96); Ngai Tahu Negotiating Gp, 1990–; Maori Fisheries Commn, 1990–93; Treaty of Waitangi Fisheries Commn, 1993–; Ngai Tahu Charitable Trust, 1996–; Ngai Tahu Holding Corp., 1996–; Dep. Chm., Fedn of Maori Authorities, 1986–88 (Exec. Mem., 1988–97); Member: Maori Adv. Cttee, NZ Historic Places Trust, 1977–90; NZ Geographic Bd, 1983–; Bd of Trustees, Nat. Mus. of NZ, 1984–94; NZ Conservation Authy, 1990–96; Bd, Law of the Sea Inst., 1995–. Writer and presenter, Manawhenua: the Natural World of the Maori (TV documentary series), 1987. Hon. DLitt Canterbury, 1992. *Publications:* contribs to numerous books, articles in jls, reports, etc. *Address:* PO Box 6346, Te Aro, Wellington, New Zealand.

O'REILLY, Sir Anthony (John Francis), Kt 2001; PhD; Executive Chairman, Independent News & Media, since 2000; Chairman: Independent Newspapers PLC, since

1980; Waterford Wedgwood PLC, since 1993; *b* Dublin, 7 May 1936; *o c* of J. P. O'Reilly, former Inspector-General of Customs; *m* 1962, Susan (marr. diss.), *d* of Keith Cameron, Australia; three *s* three *d* (of whom two *s* one *d* are triplets); *m* 1991, Chryss Goulandris. *Educ:* Belvedere Coll., Dublin; University Coll., Dublin (BCL 1958); Bradford Univ. (PhD 1980). Admitted Solicitor, 1958. Industrial Consultant, Weston Evans UK, 1958–60; PA to Chm., Suttons Ltd, Cork, 1960–62; Chief Exec. Officer, Irish Dairy Bd, 1962–66; Man. Dir, Irish Sugar Bd, 1966–69; Man. Dir, Erin Foods Ltd, 1966–69; Jt Man. Dir, Heinz-Erin, 1967–70; Man. Dir, H. J. Heinz Co. Ltd, UK, 1969–71; H. J. Heinz Co.: Sen. Vice-Pres., N America and Pacific, 1971–72; Exec. Vice-Pres. and Chief Op. Off., 1972–73; Pres. and Chief Operating Officer, 1973–79; Pres., 1979–96; CEO, 1979–98; Chm., 1987–2000. Lectr in Business Management, UC Cork, 1960–62. Director: Robt McCowen & Sons Ltd, 1961–62; Agricl Credit Corp. Ltd, 1965–66; Nitrigin Eireann Teoranta, 1965–66; Allied Irish Investment Bank Ltd, 1968–71; Thyssen-Bornemisza Co., 1970–72; Independent Newspapers (Vice Chm., 1973–80); Nat. Mine Service Co., 1973–76; Mobil, 1979–88; Bankers Trust Co., 1980–90; Allegheny Internat. Inc., 1982–87; Washington Post, 1987–94; GEC, 1990–92; Chairman: Fitzwilliam Securities Ltd, 1971–77; Fitzwilton Ltd, 1978– (Dep. Chm., 1972–78); Atlantic Resources PLC, 1981–. Member: Incorp. Law Soc.; Council, Irish Management Inst.; Hon. LLD: Wheeling Coll., 1974; Rollins Coll., 1978; Trinity Coll., 1978; Allegheny Coll., 1983. *Publications:* Prospect, 1962; Developing Creative Management, 1970; The Conservative Consumer, 1971; Food for Thought, 1972. *Recreations:* Rugby (played for Ireland 29 times), tennis. *Address:* Independent News & Media, 2023 Bianconi Avenue, City West, Dublin 24, Ireland; Castlemartin, Kilcullen, Co. Kildare, Ireland. *Clubs:* Reform, Annabel's; Stephen's Green (Dublin); Duquesne, Allegheny, Fox Chapel, Pittsburgh Golf (Pittsburgh); Carlton (Chicago); Lyford Cay (Bahamas).

O'REILLY, Most Rev. Colm; *see* Ardagh and Clonmacnoise, Bishop of, (RC).

O'REILLY, Francis Joseph; Chancellor, University of Dublin, Trinity College, 1985–98 (Pro-Chancellor, 1983–85; Hon. Fellow, 1999); Chairman, Ulster Bank Ltd, 1982–89 (Deputy Chairman, 1974–82; Director, 1961–90); Director, National Westminster Bank, 1982–89; *b* 15 Nov. 1922; *s* of Lt-Col Charles J. O'Reilly, DSO, MC, MB, KSG and Dorothy Mary Martin; *m* 1950, Teresa Mary, *e d* of Captain John Williams, MC; three *s* seven *d*. *Educ:* St Gerard's Sch., Bray; Ampleforth Coll., York; Trinity Coll., Dublin (BA, BAI). Served HM Forces, RE, 1943–46. John Power & Son, 1946–66 (Dir, 1952–66, Chm., 1955–66); Chm., Player & Wills (Ire.) Ltd, 1964–81; Chm., 1966–83, Dir, 1983–88, Irish Distillers Gp. President: Marketing Inst. of Ireland, 1983–85; Inst. of Bankers in Ireland, 1985–86. President: Equestrian Fedn of Ireland, 1963–79; Royal Dublin Soc., 1986–89 (Mem. Cttees, 1959–80; Chm. of Soc., 1980–86); Chm., Collège des Irlandais, Paris, 1987–. Hon. Life Delegate, Fédn Equestre Internationale, 1979–. MRIA 1987–. LLD *hc*: Univ. of Dublin, 1978; NUI, 1986. GCLJ 1992. *Recreations:* fox-hunting, racing, gardening. *Address:* Rathmore, Naas, Co. Kildare, Ireland. *T:* (45) 862136. *Clubs:* Kildare Street and University (Dublin); Irish Turf (The Curragh, Co. Kildare).

O'REILLY, Most Rev. Leo; *see* Kilmore, Bishop of.

O'REILLY, Air Vice-Marshal Patrick John, CB 1999; CEng, FIEE, FRAeS; Director of Operations Support Chain Management Division, Claverham Group Ltd, since 2000; *b* 26 April 1946; *s* of John Francis O'Reilly and Elizabeth O'Reilly (*née* Hammond); *m* 1974, Christine Adair Williamson; two *s*. *Educ:* Ryland Bedford Sch., Sutton Coldfield; Aston Univ. (BSc). Joined RAF 1969; numerous aircraft engrg appts in UK, Germany and the Falkland Is involving fast-jet and rotary aircraft; rcds 1991; Air Officer Wales, 1992–94; Dir Gen. Technical Services, and Pres. of Ordnance Bd, 1996–98, retd 1999. Pres., RAF Basketball, 1994–98. *Recreation:* shooting. *Address:* Seend, Wilts. *Clubs:* Royal Air Force; Bath and County.

O'REILLY, William John, CB 1981; OBE 1971; FCPA; Commissioner of Taxation, Australian Taxation Office, 1976–84, retired; *b* 15 June 1919; *s* of William O'Reilly and Ruby (*née* McCrudden). *Educ:* Nudgee Coll., Brisbane, Qld; Univ. of Queensland (AAUQ 1950). FCPA 1990 (FASA 1983). Served RAAF, 1942–44. Joined Australian Public Service, 1946; Australian Taxation Office: Brisbane, 1946–55; Melbourne, 1955–61; Canberra, 1961–84; Asst Comr of Taxation, 1963; First Asst Comr of Taxation, 1964; Second Comr of Taxation (Statutory Office), 1967. *Recreations:* reading, walking. *Address:* 7/48 Glen Road, Toowong, Qld 4066, Australia. *T:* (7) 33710641. *Clubs:* Commonwealth, Canberra (Canberra).

OREJA AGUIRRE, Marcelino; Member, European Commission, 1995–99; *b* 13 Feb. 1935; *m* 1967, Silvia Arburua; two *s*. *Educ:* Univ. of Madrid (LLD). Prof. of Internat. Affairs, Diplomatic Sch., Madrid, 1962–70; Dir of Internat. Service, Bank of Spain, 1970–74; Minister of Foreign Affairs, 1976–80; Governor-Gen., Basque Country, 1980–82; Sec. Gen., Council of Europe, 1984–89; Mem. (Partido Popular) European Parlt, 1989–94 (Chm., Institutional Affairs Cttee, 1989–94). *Address:* 81 Nunez de Balboa, 28006 Madrid, Spain. *T:* (1) 5759101.

ORGAN, Diana Mary; MP (Lab) Forest of Dean, since 1997; *b* 21 Feb. 1952; *d* of Jack Stanley Pugh and Vera Lillian Pugh; *m* 1975, Richard Thomas Organ; two *d*. *Educ:* Church of England Coll., Edgbaston; St Hugh's Coll., Oxford (BA Hons 1973); Bath Univ. (CertEd 1974). Special Needs Teacher, High Heath Special Sch., 1975; Remedial Teacher, Cardiff, 1976; Special Needs Teacher, Plymouth, 1977–78; Dep. Head, St German's Primary Sch., 1978–79; Head, Special Needs Units, Shepton Mallet, 1979–82; special needs posts, Somerset, 1982–92; Lab Gp policy researcher, Oxfordshire CC, 1993–95. *Recreations:* gardening, cinema, sailing, ski-ing. *Address:* (constituency) St Annals House, Belle Vue Centre, Belle Vue Road, Cinderford, Glos GL14 1AB.

ORGAN, (Harold) Bryan; painter; *b* Leicester, 31 Aug. 1935; *o c* of late Harold Victor Organ and Helen Dorothy Organ; *m* (marr. diss. 1981); *m* 1982, Sandra Mary Mills. *Educ:* Wyggeston Sch., Leicester; Coll. of Art, Loughborough; Royal Academy Schs, London. Lectr in Drawing and Painting, Loughborough Coll. of Art, 1959–65. One-man exhibns: Leicester Museum and Art Gallery, 1959; Redfern Gallery, 1967, 1969, 1971, 1973, 1975, 1978, 1980; Leicester 1973, 1976; New York, 1976, 1977; Turin, 1981. Represented: Kunsthalle, Darmstadt, 1968; Mostra Mercatao d'Arte Contemporanea, Florence, 1969; 3rd Internat. Exhibn of Drawing, Germany, 1970; Sao Paolo Museum of Art, Brazil; Baukunst Gallery, Cologne, 1977. Works in public and private collections in England, USA, Germany, France, Canada, Italy. Portraits include: Malcolm Muggeridge, 1966; Sir Michael Tippett, 1966; David Hicks, 1968; Mary Quant, 1969; Nadia Nerina, 1969; Princess Margaret, 1970; Dr Roy Strong, 1971; Elton John, 1973; Lester Piggott, 1973; Lord Ashby, 1975; Sir Rex Richards, 1977; Harold Macmillan, 1980; Prince of Wales, 1981; Lady Diana Spencer, 1981; Lord Denning, 1982; Jim Callaghan, 1982; Duke of Edinburgh, 1983. Hon. MA Loughborough, 1974; Hon. DLitt: Leicester, 1985; Loughborough, 1992. *Address:* c/o Redfern Gallery, 20 Cork Street, W1X 2HL. *T:* (020) 7734 1732.

ORGEL, Prof. Leslie Eleazer, DPhil Oxon, MA; FRS 1962; Senior Fellow and Research Professor, Salk Institute, La Jolla, California, USA, and Adjunct Professor, University of California, San Diego, Calif, since 1964; *b* 12 Jan. 1927; *s* of Simon Orgel; *m* 1950, Hassia Alice Levinson; two *s* one *d*. *Educ:* Dame Alice Owen's Sch., London. Reader, University Chemical Laboratory, Cambridge, 1963–64, and Fellow of Peterhouse, 1957–64. Fellow, Amer. Acad. of Arts and Sciences, 1985; Mem., Nat. Acad. of Scis, USA, 1990. *Publications:* An Introduction to Transition-Metal Chemistry, Ligand-Field Theory, 1960; The Origins of Life: molecules and natural selection, 1973; (with Stanley L. Miller) The Origins of Life on the Earth, 1974. *Address:* Salk Institute, PO Box 85800, San Diego, CA 92186–5800, USA. *T:* (619) 4534100, ext. 1321, *Fax:* (619) 5587359; *e-mail:* orgel@salk.edu.

ORGILL, Richard Michael James; Global Head of Corporate and Institutional Banking, HSBC Holdings plc, 1998–2001; *b* 14 Oct. 1938; *m* 1968, Anne Whitley; two *s* one *d*. *Educ:* Bryanston Sch. FCIB 1989. Gen. Manager and Chief Exec. Officer, Hongkong and Shanghai Banking Corp., Malaysia, 1985–89; Gen. Manager Internat., Hongkong and Shanghai Banking Corp., Hong Kong, 1989–90; Gen. Manager and Chief Exec. Officer, Hongkong Bank of Australia Ltd, 1990–93; Chief Operating Officer, 1993–94, Dir and Dep. Chief Exec., 1994–98, Midland Bank plc. Director: HSBC (formerly Midland) Bank plc, 1994–2001; Hongkong and Shanghai Banking Corp. Ltd, 1999–2001; HSBC Investment Bank Hldgs plc, 1999–2001.

ORHNIAL, Anthony Joseph Henry; Director, Personal Tax, Board of Inland Revenue, since 2000; *b* 31 Oct. 1947; *s* of Antoine Orhnial and Hilda Orhnial (now Mell); *m* 1982, Gertrud Wienecke; one *d*. *Educ:* St Edward's Coll., Malta; St Benedict's Sch., Ealing; London Sch. of Economics (BSc (Econ), MSc (Econ)). Research Asst, RTZ Services Ltd, 1970–71; Kingston Polytechnic, Kingston on Thames: Lectr, 1971–74; Sen. Lectr, 1974–84; Principal Lectr in Economics, 1984–88; Principal: Inland Revenue, 1988–91; HM Treasury, 1991–93; Asst Dir, Personal Tax, Inland Revenue, 1993–2000. Vis. Lectr in Economics, Konstanz Univ., Germany, 1979–80. *Publications:* Limited Liability and the Modern Corporation, 1982; articles in Economica, Jl of Accounting Research, British Review of Economics. *Recreations:* travel, reading, cookery, carpentry. *Address:* Board of Inland Revenue, New Wing, Somerset House, Strand, WC2R 1LB. *T:* (020) 7438 6546.

O'RIORDAN, Rear-Adm. John Patrick Bruce, CBE 1982; DL; Chief Executive, St Andrew's Group of Hospitals, Northampton, 1990–2000; *b* 15 Jan. 1936; *yr s* of Surgeon Captain Timothy Joseph O'Riordan, RN and Bertha Carson O'Riordan (*née* Young); *m* 1959, Jane, *e d* of John Alexander Mitchell; one *s* two *d*. *Educ:* Kelly College. Nat. Service and transfer to RN, 1954–59; served in submarines, Mediterranean, Home and Far East; HM Ships Porpoise (i/c) and Courageous, NDC, HMS Dreadnought (i/c), MoD, 1960–76; Captain (SM), Submarine Sea Training, 1976–78; RCDS, 1979; HMS Glasgow (i/c), 1980–81; ACOS (Policy), Saclant, USA, 1982–84; Dir, Naval Warfare, MoD, 1984–86; Mil. Dep. Comdt, NATO Defence Coll., Rome, 1986–89. Consultant, Spencer Stuart and Associates, 1989. Director: Workbridge Enterprises Ltd, 1990–2000; Indep. Healthcare Assoc., 1993–2000; NXD O'Riordan Bond, 1999–. Chairman: SSAFA Forces Help (formerly SSAFA) Northants, 1996–2000; SSAFA Forces Help, Dumfriesshire and the Stewartry, 2000–. JP S Northants, 1991–2000; DL Northants, 1997. FIMgt. *Recreations:* sailing, Rugby football, stalking, fishing, painting. *Address:* Nether Crae, Mossdale, Kirkcudbrightshire DG7 2NL. *T:* (01644) 450644; 45 Church Lane, Kislingbury, Northampton NN7 4AD. *T:* (01604) 833493. *Clubs:* Army and Navy, Royal Navy of 1765 and 1785; Royal Yacht Squadron, Royal Naval Sailing Association.
See also Sir J. A. N. Graham.

O'RIORDAN, Marie; Editor, Marie Claire, since 2001; *b* 3 April 1960; *d* of Michael and Maura O'Riordan. *Educ:* University Coll. Dublin (BA English and Hist.; MA Modern English and American Lit.). More! magazine: Prodn Editor, 1990–92; Dep. Editor, 1992–94; Editor, 1994–96; Editor, Elle magazine, 1996–99; Gp Publishing Dir, EMAP Elan, 1999–2001. EMAP Editor of Year, 1996. *Recreations:* reading, movies, walking, partying! *Address:* Marie Claire, European Magazines Ltd, 2 Hatfields, SE1 9PG. *Club:* Soho House.

O'RIORDAN, Prof. Timothy; DL; FBA 1999; Professor of Environmental Sciences, University of East Anglia, since 1980; *b* 21 Feb. 1942; *s* of late Kevin Denis O'Riordan and Norah Joyce O'Riordan (*née* Lucas); *m* 1967, Ann Morison Philip (*d* 1992); two *d*. *Educ:* Univ. of Edinburgh (MA 1963); Cornell Univ. (MS 1965); Univ. of Cambridge (PhD 1967). Asst Prof. and Associate Prof., Dept of Geography, Simon Fraser Univ., Canada, 1967–74; Reader, Sch. of Environmental Scis, UEA, 1974–80. Chm., Envmt Cttee, Broads Authy, 1989–98; Mem., UK Sustainable Develt Commn, 2000–; Advr, Envmtl Res. Directorate, EC, 1996–97; Member, Environmental Advisory Council: Dow Chemicals, 1992–98; Eastern Group plc, 1995–. FRSA. DL Norfolk, 1998. Gill Meml Award, RGS, 1982. *Publications:* Environmentalism 1976, 2nd edn 1981; (jtly) Countryside Conflicts, 1986; (jtly) Sizewell B: an anatomy of the inquiry, 1987; (ed) Environmental Science for Environmental Management, 1994, 2nd edn 1999; (ed jtly) Interpreting the Precautionary Principle, 1994; (ed) The Politics of Climate Change in Europe, 1996; (ed) Ecotaxation, 1997; (ed jtly) The Transition to Sustainability, 1998; Globalism, Localism and Identity, 2000; (ed jtly) Reinterpreting the Precautionary Principle, 2001. *Recreation:* classical double bass playing. *Address:* Wheatlands, Hethersett Lane, Colney, Norwich NR4 7TT. *T:* (01603) 810534; *e-mail:* t.oriordan@uea.ac.uk.

ORKNEY, 9th Earl of *cr* 1696; **Oliver Peter St John;** Lord Dechmont, Viscount Kirkwall, 1696; Professor of Political Studies, University of Manitoba, since 1998 (Associate Professor, 1972–98); *b* Victoria, BC, 27 Feb. 1938; *s* of Lt-Col Frederick Oliver St John, DSO, MC (*d* 1977; *g s* of 5th Earl of Orkney) and of Elizabeth, *d* of E. H. Pierce; *S* kinsman, 1998; *m* 1st, 1963, Mary Juliet (marr. diss. 1985), *d* of W. G. Scott-Brown, CVO, MD, FRCS, FRCSE; one *s* three *d* (and one *d* decd); 2nd, 1985, Mrs Mary Barbara Huck (*née* Albertson); one step *s* three step *d*. *Educ:* Woodbridge Sch.; Univ. of British Columbia (BA 1960); LSE (MSc 1963); PhD London Univ. 1972. Lecturer: UCL, 1963–64; Univ. of Manitoba, 1964–66; Asst Prof., Univ. of Manitoba, 1966–72. Visiting Professor: Carleton Univ., 1981–82; Canadian Armed Forces, W Germany, 1985 and 1990–91; Univ. of Victoria, 1986; USAF Special Ops Sch., Florida, 1993–. Member: RIIA, 1962; Canadian Inst. of Internat. Affairs, 1964–. Regular radio and TV commentaries, Canada and USA. Outreach Award, Univ. of Manitoba, 1996; Stanton Award for Excellence in Teaching, 1997. *Publications:* Fireproof House to Third Option, 1977; Mackenzie King to Philosopher King, 1984; Air Piracy, Airport Security and International Terrorism: winning the war against hijackers, 1991; numerous contribs to jls. *Recreations:* swimming, squash, tennis, photography, touring, farming. *Heir:* *s* Oliver Robert St John [*b* 19 July 1969; *m* Consuela Davies]. *Address:* 595 Gertrude Avenue, Winnipeg, MB R3L 0M9, Canada. *T:* (204) 2841089, *Fax:* (204) 4533615; *e-mail:* pstjohn@cc.umanitoba.ca.

ORMAN, Stanley, PhD; Chief Executive Officer, Orman Associates Inc., Maryland, since 1996; Vice President, Employment Solutions Inc., Maryland, since 1998; *b* 6 Feb. 1935; *s* of Jacob and Ettie Orman; *m* 1960, Helen (*née* Hourman); one *s* two *d*. *Educ:* Hackney

Downs Grammar School; King's College London. BSc (1st Cl. Hons) 1957; PhD (Organic Chem.) 1960. MICorr; FRIC 1969. Research Fellowship, Brandeis Univ., 1960–61; AWRE Aldermaston, research in corrosion and mechano-chemical corrosion, 1961–74, project work, 1974–78; Director Missiles, 1978–81, Chief Weapon System Engineer Polaris, 1981–82, MoD; Minister-Counsellor, Hd of Defence Equip. Staff, British Embassy, Washington, 1982–84; Dep. Dir, AWRE, MoD, 1984–86; Dir Gen., SDI Participation Office, MoD, 1986–90; Chief Exec. Officer, General Technology Systems Inc., 1990–95. Founder Chm., Reading Ratepayers' Assoc., 1974; Pres., Reading Hebrew Congregation, 1970–74. *Publications:* Faith in G.O.D.S.: stability in the nuclear age, 1991; numerous papers on free radical chemistry, materials science, mechano-chemical corrosion and ballistic missile defence, in learned jls. *Recreations:* sporting—originally athletics, now tennis and badminton; designing bow ties, woodwork. *Address:* 17825 Stoneridge Drive, Gaithersburg, MD 20878, USA. *T:* (301) 6700685, *Fax:* (301) 8403901; *e-mail:* or2withdog@aol.com.

ORME, Baron *cr* 1997 (Life Peer), of Salford in the co. of Greater Manchester; **Stanley Orme;** PC 1974; *b* 5 April 1923; *s* of Sherwood Orme, Sale, Cheshire; *m* 1951, Irene Mary, *d* of Vernon Fletcher Harris, Worsley, Lancashire. *Educ:* elementary and technical schools; National Council of Labour Colleges and Workers' Educational Association classes. Warrant Officer, Air-Bomber Navigator, Royal Air Force Bomber Command, 1942–47. Joined the Labour party, 1944; Member of Sale Borough Council, 1958–65; contested (Lab) Stockport South, 1959. MP (Lab) Salford West, 1964–83, Salford East, 1983–97. Minister of State: NI Office, 1974–76; DHSS, 1976; Minister of State for Social Security, 1976–77, Minister for Social Security, and Mem. Cabinet, 1977–79; Opposition Spokesman on Health and Social Services, June 1979–Dec. 1980, on Industry, 1980–83, on Energy, 1983–87; Chm., PLP, 1987–92. Member: AEU; District Committee, Manchester; shop steward. Hon. DSc Salford, 1985. *Address:* House of Lords, SW1A 0PW; 8 Northwood Grove, Sale, Cheshire M33 3DZ.

ORME, Jeremy David, FCA; Adviser, Financial Services Authority, since 2001 (Head, Financial Crime Liaison Unit, 1998–2001); *b* 27 Dec. 1943; 2nd *s* of John Samuel Orme, CB, OBE, and of Jean Esther (*née* Harris); *m* 2001, Jennifer Anne Page, *qv*; two *s* from former marriage. *Educ:* Winchester Coll.; Christ Church, Oxford (MA). Robson Rhodes, chartered accountants, 1966–87, Man. Partner, 1982–87; Asst Sec. (on secondment), Dept of Transport, 1979–81; SIB, 1987–98 (investigations and enforcement roles). Member: National Bus Co., 1984–86 (Dep. Chm. 1985–86); Audit Commn for Local Authorities and NHS in England and Wales, 1989–2000 (Dep. Chm., 1997–2000); Chm., Financial Fraud Information Network, 1997–2000.

ORME, Prof. Michael Christopher L'Estrange, MD; FRCP; Professor of Pharmacology and Therapeutics, Liverpool University, since 1984; *b* 13 June 1940; *s* of Christopher Robert L'Estrange Orme and Muriel Evelyn Janet Orme; *m* 1967, Joan Patricia Abbot; one *s*. *Educ:* Sherborne Sch.; Sidney Sussex Coll., Cambridge (MB BChir 1964; MA 1965; MD 1975); King's Coll. Hosp. FRCP 1980; FFPM 1989; FFFP 1994; FFPHM 2000. House Officer and Registrar posts, KCH, Hammersmith Hosp., Brompton Hosp. and St Mary's Hosp., 1965–69; Sen. Registrar, Hammersmith Hosp., 1970–73; Wellcome Fellowship, Karolinska Inst., Stockholm, 1973–74; Liverpool University: Sen. Lectr, 1975–81; Reader in Clinical Pharmacology, 1981–84; Dean, Faculty of Medicine, 1991–96. Hon. Consultant Physician, Royal Liverpool and Broadgreen Univ. Hosps NHS Trust, 1975–; Dir of Educn and Trng, NW Regl Office, NHS Exec., 1996–2001. Secretary: Clin. Sect., British Pharmacol Soc., 1982–88; Clin.. Sect., Internat. Union of Pharmacol., 1987–93; Eur. Assoc. of Clin. Pharmacol. and Therapeutics, 1991–; Pres., Liverpool Medical Inst., 1994–95; Chm., Specialist Adv. Cttee on Clin. Pharmacol. and Therapeutics, 1991–93; Member: Internat. Adv. Bd, World Conf. on Clin. Pharmacol. and Therapeutics, 1989, 1992, 1996, 2000; WHO Scientific Working Gp on Drugs in Breast Milk, and on Filariasis, 1981–. Gov., Birkenhead Sch., Wirral, 1990–. Founder FMedSci 1998. Hon. FRCGP 1998. Hon. DSc Salford, 2000. Paul Martini Prize, Paul Martini Stiftung, Germany, 1974. *Publications:* Self Help Guide to Medicine, 1988; (ed) Therapeutic Drugs, 1991; contribs to learned jls. *Recreations:* sailing, astronomy, cooking, walking. *Address:* 80 Brimstage Road, Heswall, Wirral CH60 1XG. *T:* (0151) 342 3269, *Fax:* (0151) 342 8154.

ORME, Robert Thomas Neil; His Honour Judge Orme; a Circuit Judge, since 1992; *b* 25 Jan. 1947; *s* of Thomas Elsmore Orme and Iris Marguerita Orme; *m* 1971, Angela Mary Stokes; one *s* one *d*. *Educ:* Denstone Coll., Staffs; University Coll. London (LLB Hons). Called to the Bar, Gray's Inn, 1970; Midland and Oxford Circuit; Asst Recorder, 1984–88; Recorder, 1988–92. Chm., Moseley Soc., 1993–. *Recreations:* opera, theatre, visiting France, keen interest in conservation. *Address:* Queen Elizabeth II Law Courts, Birmingham B4 7NA. *T:* (0121) 681 3300.

ORMEROD, Alec William; District Judge (Magistrates' Courts) (formerly Metropolitan Stipendiary Magistrate), since 1988; Chairman, Family Court, since 1991; Assistant Judge Advocate General, since 1996; Judge, Summary Appeals Court, since 2000; *b* 19 July 1932; *s* of William and Susan Ormerod; *m* 1976, Patricia Mary Large. *Educ:* Nelson Grammar Sch.; Christ's Coll., Cambridge (Major Scholar; MA, LLM). Solicitor. Mil. Service, Staff of GOC London Dist, 1956–58. Asst Lectr in Law, Burnley Coll., 1953–55; Local Govt Service, 1958–64; Sen. Partner, Boyle and Ormerod, Solicitors, Aylesbury, 1964–88. Councillor, Aylesbury Borough Council, 1966–72. Freeman, City of London, 1973. *Recreations:* travel, fine art, gardening. *Address:* c/o South Western Magistrates' Court, 176A Lavender Hill, SW11 1JU. *Club:* Naval and Military.

ORMEROD, Mark Edward; with Lord Chancellor's Department; *b* 3 Aug. 1957; *s* of Dr Thomas Edward Ormerod and Dr June Anne (*née* Vaux). *Educ:* Oundle Sch.; Leeds Univ. (BA); Univ. de Tours (MèsL). Trainee accountant, Whinney Murray, 1980–81; joined Lord Chancellor's Department, 1981: Inner London Crown Court, 1981–83; posts at HQ, 1983–93; Private Sec. to Lord Chancellor, 1993–96; Head: of Magistrates' Courts Div., 1996–97; of Criminal Justice Div., 1997–99; Dir, Criminal Justice, 1999–2001; sabbatical, 2001–02. *Recreations:* sailing, ski-ing, gardening. *Address:* c/o Lord Chancellor's Department, Selborne House, 54–60 Victoria Street, SW1E 6QW. *T:* (020) 7210 8809.

ORMEROD, Pamela Catherine, (Mrs P. A. Ormerod); *see* Meadows, P. C.

ORMESSON, Comte Jean d'; Chevalier des Palmes académiques 1962; Commandeur des Arts et Lettres 1973; Officier de la Légion d'honneur 1988; Officier de l'Ordre national du Mérite, 1978; Membre Académie française 1973; President, International Council for Philosophy and Humanistic Studies (UNESCO), since 1992 (Secretary-General, 1971–92); writer and journalist; *b* 16 June 1925; 2nd *s* of Marquis d'Ormesson, French diplomat and Ambassador; *m* 1962, Françoise Béghin; one *d*. *Educ:* Ecole Normale Supérieure. MA (History), Agrégé de philosophie. Mem. French delegns to various internat. confs, 1945–48; Mem. staff of various Govt Ministers, 1958–66; Mem. Council ORTF, 1960–62; Mem. Control Cttee of Cinema, 1962–69; Mem. TV Programmes Cttee, ORTF, 1973–74. Mem., Brazilian Acad. of Letters, 1979. Diogenes: Dep. Editor, 1952–72; Mem. Managing Cttee, 1972–80; Editor, 1980–82; Editor-in-Chief, 1982–; Le Figaro: Dir, 1974–77; Editor-in-Chief, 1975–77. *Publications:* L'Amour est un plaisir, 1956; Du côté de chez Jean, 1959; Un amour pour rien, 1960; Au revoir et merci, 1966; Les Illusions de la mer, 1968; La Gloire de l'Empire, 1971 (Grand Prix du Roman de l'Académie française), Amer. edn (The Glory of the Empire), 1975, Eng. edn 1976; Au Plaisir de Dieu, 1974, Amer. edn (At God's Pleasure), 1977, Eng. edn 1978; Le Vagabond qui passe sous une ombrelle trouée, 1978; Dieu, sa vie, son œuvre, 1981; Mon dernier rêve sera pour vous, 1982; Jean qui grogne et Jean qui rit, 1984; Le Vent du soir, 1985; Tous les hommes en sont fous, 1986; Le Bonheur à San Miniato, 1987; Garçon de quoi écrire, 1989; Histoire du Juif errant, 1991; Tant que vous penserez à moi, 1992; articles and essays, columns in Le Figaro, Le Monde, Le Point, La Revue des Deux Mondes, La Nouvelle Revue Française. *Recreation:* ski-navigation. *Address:* CIPSH-UNESCO, 1 rue Miollis, 75732 Paris Cedex 15, France. *T:* 45682685; (home) 10 avenue du Parc Saint-James, 92200 Neuilly-sur-Seine, France.

ORMOND, Richard Louis, CBE 2001; Director, National Maritime Museum, 1986–2000 (Head of Picture Department, 1983–86); *b* 16 Jan. 1939; *s* of late Conrad Eric Ormond and Dorothea (*née* Gibbons); *m* 1963, Leonée Jasper; two *s*. *Educ:* Oxford University. MA. Assistant Keeper, 1965–75, Dep. Director, 1975–83, Nat. Portrait Gallery. *Publications:* J. S. Sargent, 1970; Catalogue of Early Victorian Portraits in the National Portrait Gallery, 1973; Lord Leighton, 1975; Sir Edwin Landseer, 1982; The Great Age of Sail, 1986; F. X. Winterhalter and the Courts of Europe, 1987; (jtly) Frederic, Lord Leighton, 1996; (jtly) Sargent Abroad, 1997; (jtly) John Singer Sargent: the early portraits, 1998; (jtly) John Singer Sargent (catalogue of exhibn at Tate Gallery), 1998. *Recreations:* cycling, opera, theatre. *Address:* 8 Holly Terrace, N6 6LX. *T:* (020) 8340 4684. *Club:* Garrick.

ORMSBY GORE, family name of **Baron Harlech**.

O'RORKE, Richard Charles Colomb; His Honour Judge O'Rorke; a Circuit Judge, since 1994; *b* 4 June 1944; *s* of late Charles Howard Colomb O'Rorke and Jacqueline O'Rorke; *m* 1966, Jane Elizabeth Phoebe Harding; one *s* three *d*. *Educ:* Blundell's Sch.; Exeter Coll., Oxford. Called to the Bar, Inner Temple, 1968; Recorder, Midland and Oxford Circuit, 1987–94. *Recreations:* Japanese literature and culture, gardening. *Address:* c/o Midland and Oxford Circuit Office, 33 Bull Street, Birmingham B4 6DW.

O'ROURKE, Andrew; Ambassador of Ireland, retired; *b* 7 May 1931; *s* of Joseph O'Rourke and Elizabeth (*née* O'Farrell); *m* 1962, Hanne Stephensen; one *s* two *d*. *Educ:* Trinity Coll., Dublin (BA, BComm). Joined diplomatic service, 1957; Third Sec., Berne, 1960; First Sec., London, 1964; First Sec., later Counsellor, Dept of Foreign Affairs, Dublin, 1969–73; Counsellor, later Dep. Perm. Rep., Perm. Rep. of Ireland to EEC, 1973–78; Sec.-Gen., Dept of For. Affairs, 1978–81; Perm. Rep. to EEC, 1981–86; Ambassador to: France, OECD and UNESCO, 1986–87; UK, 1987–91; Denmark, Norway and Iceland, 1991–96. Grand Cross: Order of Civil Merit, Spain, 1985; OM, Luxembourg, 1986; OM, Portugal, 1987. *Recreations:* walking, golf, European affairs. *Address:* 2 Sorrento Lawn, Dalkey, Co. Dublin, Ireland. *Club:* Kildare Street and University (Dublin).

O'ROURKE, Patrick Jake; journalist, since 1970; author; *b* 14 Nov. 1947; *s* of Clifford Bronson O'Rourke and Delphine O'Rourke (*née* Loy); *m* 1st, 1990, Amy Lumet (marr. diss.); 2nd, 1995, Christina Mallon; two *d*. *Educ:* Miami Univ. (BA); Johns Hopkins Univ. (MA). Free-lance writer and ed., miscellaneous small press publications, 1970–73; National Lampoon: writer/editor, 1973–75; Man. Editor, 1975–77; Editor-in-Chief, 1977–81; free-lance writer, 1981–85; Foreign Corresp., Rolling Stone, 1986–. *Publications:* Modern Manners, 1983; The Bachelor Home Companion, 1987; Republican Party Reptile, 1987; Holidays in Hell, 1988; Parliament of Whores, 1991; Give War a Chance, 1992; All the Trouble in the World, 1994; Age and Guile Beat Youth, Innocence and a Bad Haircut, 1995; Eat the Rich, 1998; The CEO of the Sofa, 2001. *Address:* c/o Grove/Atlantic Press, 841 Broadway, New York, NY 10003, USA.

O'ROURKE, Sarah Louise E.; *see* Evans O'Rourke.

ORR, Prof. Christopher John, RA 1995; RE 1990; artist; Professor and Course Director of Printmaking, Royal College of Art, since 1998; *b* 8 April 1943; *s* of Ronald Orr and Violet (*née* Townley); *m* 1984, Catherine Terris; one *s* one *d*. *Educ:* Royal Coll. of Art (MA; RCA 1967). Artist and teacher, 1967–. One man touring exhibitions: The Complete Chris Orr, 1976; Many Mansions, 1990. Work in public collections: British Council; Arts Council; V&A Mus.; Science Mus. *Publications:* Many Mansions, 1990; The Small Titanic, 1994; Happy Days, 1999; Semi-Antics, 2001. *Address:* 7 Bristle Hill, Buckingham MK18 1EZ. *T:* (01280) 815255; *e-mail:* chrisorr@aol.com. *Club:* Chelsea Arts.

ORR, Sir David (Alexander), Kt 1977; MC and bar 1945; LLB; Chairman, Unilever Ltd, 1974–82; *b* 10 May 1922; *s* of late Canon Adrian William Fielder Orr and Grace (*née* Robinson); *m* 1949, Phoebe Rosaleen Davis; three *d*. *Educ:* High Sch., Dublin; Trinity Coll., Dublin (Hon. LLD 1978). Served Royal Engineers attached QVO Madras Sappers and Miners, 1941–46. With various Unilever companies, 1948–82; Hindustan Lever, 1955–60; Mem. Overseas Cttee, Unilever, 1960–63; Lever Bros Co., New York, 1963, Pres. 1965–67; Dir, 1967–82, Vice-Chm. 1970–74, Unilever Ltd; Vice-Chm., Unilever NV, 1974–82; Chm., 1983–86, 1991–92, Inchcape (Dep. Chm., 1986–91); Director: Rio Tinto-Zinc Corp., 1981–92; Shell Transport & Trading Co., 1982–92; Mem. Court, Bank of Ireland, 1982–90. Chm., British Council, 1985–92. Chm., Armed Forces Pay Review Body, 1982–84; Member: Cttee to Review Functioning of Financial Instns, 1977–80; Top Salaries Review Body, 1982–85; Adv. Cttee on Business Appointments of Crown Servants, 1984–92. Chairman: Leverhulme Trust, 1982–92; Shakespeare Globe Theatre Trust, 1982–93; Charles Wallace (India) Trust, 1991–98; Jt Chm., Anglo-Irish Encounter, 1983–87. Dir, Five Arrows Chile Fund, 1990–96; Pres., Children's Medical Charity, 1991–96. Chancellor, QUB, 1992–99; President: Liverpool Sch. of Tropical Medicine, 1981–89; Coll. of Speech Therapists, 1992–96; Governor, LSE, 1980–96. FRSA. Hon. LLD: TCD, 1978; Liverpool, 1989; NUI, 1993; DUniv Surrey, 1981. Comdr, Order of Oranje Nassau, 1979. *Recreations:* golf, Rugby, travel. *Address:* 81 Lyall Mews West, SW1X 8DJ; Home Farm House, Shackleford, near Godalming, Surrey GU8 6AH. *Clubs:* Athenæum; Sunningdale Golf.

ORR, Iain Campbell; HM Diplomatic Service; Deputy High Commissioner, Ghana, 1998–2000; *b* 6 Dec. 1942; *s* of late Rev. David Campbell Orr and Hilda Dora Moore; *m* 1978, Susan Elizabeth Gunter; one *s* one *d*. *Educ:* Kirkcaldy High Sch.; St Andrews Univ. (MA); Linacre Coll., Oxford (BPhil). Asst Lectr, Dept of Politics, Glasgow Univ., 1967–68; entered HM Diplomatic Service, 1968; language student, Hong Kong, 1969–71; Second, later First Sec., Peking, 1971–74; FCO, 1974–78; Asst Political Adviser, Hong Kong, 1978–81; Dublin, 1981–84; FCO, 1984–87; Consul-Gen., Shanghai, 1987–90. Dep. High Comr, Wellington, 1991–94; Counsellor, FCO, 1994–98. *Recreations:* natural history, islands, anthologies, reading poetry. *Address:* c/o Foreign and Commonwealth Office, SW1A 2AH.

ORR, James Bernard Vivian, CVO 1968 (MVO 1962); Secretary, Medical Commission on Accident Prevention, 1970–82; *b* 19 Nov. 1917; *s* of Dr Vivian Bernard Orr and Gladys Constance Orr (*née* Power); unmarried. *Educ:* Harrow; Gordonstoun; RMC, Sandhurst. British South Africa Police, Southern Rhodesia, 1939–46. Attached occupied Enemy Territory Administration in Ethiopia and Eritrea Police Forces, 1941–49; Kenya Police, 1954–57. Private Secretary to HRH The Duke of Edinburgh, 1957–70, an Extra Equerry, 1970–. *Recreations:* horse racing, watching cricket. *Address:* 10 Mulberry Trees, Shepperton, Mddx TW17 8JN. *T:* (01932) 885034.

ORR, Dr James Henry; consultant in forensic psychiatry, 1982–98; *b* 2 Feb. 1927; *s* of Hubert Orr and Ethel Maggs; *m* 1950, Valerie Elizabeth Yates; two *s* one *d*. *Educ:* Bristol Grammar Sch.; Bristol Univ. (MB, ChB 1955). DPM; FRCPsych. Enlisted, 1944; commnd RE, 1947; demobilised, 1949. Hosp. appts, 1955–56; gen. practice, 1956–58; Medical Officer, HM Prison: Leeds, 1958; Winchester, 1962; Lincoln, 1966; SMO, Leeds, 1967; Asst Dir, Prison Med. Services, 1973; Dir, Prison Med. Services, and Mem., Prisons Bd, 1976–82; Mem., Parole Bd, 1983–86. *Recreation:* gardening.

ORR, Sir John, Kt 2001; OBE 1992; QPM 1997; DL; Chief Constable of Strathclyde Police, 1996–2001; *b* 3 Sept. 1945; *s* of Samuel Orr and Margaret Orr (*née* Walker); *m* 1966, Joan Underwood; two *s* one *d*. *Educ:* James Hamilton Acad., Kilmarnock; Open Univ. (BA 1983); Glasgow Univ. (DipFM 1987). Cadet, Renfrew & Bute Constab., 1961–64; Kilmarnock Burgh Police, 1964–66; Cumbria Constab., 1966–69; Ayrshire Constab., 1969–75; Strathclyde Police, 1975–87; Detective Chief Supt and Jt Head, Strathclyde Police CID, 1987–90; Dep. Chief Constable, Dumfries and Galloway Constab., 1990–94; Asst Insp. of Constab. for Scotland, 1994–95. Pres., ACPO in Scotland, 1997–98; Chm. Crime Cttee, ACPO, 1998–2001; Mem., Scottish Crime Prevention Council, 1997–2001. Graduate, FBI Nat. Exec. Inst., Washington, 1997. Hon. Pres., Glasgow Bn, Boy's Bde, 1997–. DL Dumfries, 2001. CIMgt 1996 (FBIM 1988). Hon. LLD Glasgow Caledonian, 1998. Paul Harris Fellow, Rotary Internat., 1997. Lord Provost of Glasgow's Award for Public Service, 1998. *Recreations:* football, reading, hillwalking. *Address:* c/o Clydesdale Bank, Lainshaw Street, Stewarton, Kilmarnock KA3 5BY. *Club:* Royal Scottish Automobile (Glasgow).

ORR, John Carmichael; Chairman: Molins plc, 1991–99; Waddington plc, 1997–99; *b* 19 Aug. 1937; *s* of John Washington Orr and Nora Margaret Orr (*née* Carmichael); *m* 1967, Janet Sheila Grundy; one *s* one *d*. *Educ:* King Edward's Sch., Birmingham; Trinity Hall, Cambridge (MA). Industrial & Commercial Finance Corporation Ltd, 1960–68; S. G. Warburg & Co. Ltd, 1969–81 (Dir, 1972–81); Finance Dir, Grand Metropolitan plc, 1981–87; Man. Dir, Merrill Lynch Europe Ltd, 1987–90. Non-executive Director: Sketchley plc, 1990–99; Throgmorton Trust plc, 1990–; Marston, Thompson & Evershed plc, 1992–96; Govett Strategic Investment Trust plc, 1992–97; Granada Group plc, 1992–; W. H. Smith Group plc, 1993–; Lazard Brothers & Co. Ltd, 1993–. Trustee, Liver Res. Trust, 1999–. *Recreations:* tennis, golf, opera, theatre. *Address:* 24 Denbigh Gardens, Richmond, Surrey TW10 6EL. *T:* (020) 8948 1563. *Clubs:* Roehampton; Frilford Heath Golf.

ORR, Prof. Robin, (Robert Kemsley Orr), CBE 1972; MA, MusD (Cantab); FRCM; Hon. RAM; Hon. FRSAMD; Hon. DMus, Hon. LLD; Composer; Professor of Music, Cambridge University, 1965–76, now Professor Emeritus; Fellow of St John's College, Cambridge, 1965–76, Hon. Fellow 1987; *b* Brechin, Scotland, 2 June 1909; *s* of Robert Workman Orr and Florence Mary Kemsley; adopted, additionally, Swiss nationality, 1995; *m* 1st, 1937, Margaret (marr. diss. 1979), *er d* of A. C. Mace; one *s* one *d* (and one *d* decd); 2nd, 1979, Doris Winny-Meyer, *d* of Leo Meyer-Bechtler, Zürich. *Educ:* Loretto Sch.; Royal Coll. of Music; Pembroke Coll., Cambridge (Organ Scholar; Hon. Fellow, 1988); Accademia Musicale Chigiana, Siena. Studied privately with Casella and Nadia Boulanger. Dir of Music, Sidcot Sch., Somerset, 1933–36; Asst Lecturer in Music, Univ. of Leeds, 1936–38. Served War of 1939–45, RAFVR, Photographic Intelligence (Flight Lieut). Organist and Dir of Studies in Music, St John's Coll., 1938–51, and Fellow, 1948–56, Univ. Lecturer in Music, 1947–56, Cambridge; Prof. of Theory and Composition, RCM, 1950–56; Gardiner Prof. of Music, Univ. of Glasgow, 1956–65. Mem., Carl Rosa Trust, 1953–70; Chm., Scottish Opera, 1962–76; Director: Arts Theatre, Cambridge, 1970–75; Welsh Nat. Opera, 1977–83. Mem., Assoc. Suisse des Musiciens, 1997. Compositions include: Sonatina for violin and piano, 1941; Three Chinese Songs, 1943; Sonata for viola and piano, 1947; Winter's Tale (Incidental Music), BBC, 1947; Overture, The Prospect of Whitby, 1948; Oedipus at Colonus (Cambridge Univ. Greek Play), 1950; Four Romantic Songs (for Peter Pears), 1950; Festival Te Deum, 1950; Three Pastorals for soprano, flute, viola and piano, 1951; Deirdre of the Sorrows (Incidental Music), BBC, 1951; Italian Overture, 1952; Te Deum and Jubilate in C, 1953; Motet, I was glad, 1955; Spring Cantata, 1955; Sonata for violin and clavier, 1956; Rhapsody for string orchestra, 1956; Antigone (Bradfield College Greek Play), 1961; Symphony in one movement, 1963; Full Circle (opera), 1967; From the Book of Philip Sparrow, 1969; Journeys and Places (mezzo-sop. and strings), 1971; Symphony No 2, 1971; Hermiston (opera), 1975; Symphony No 3, 1978; Versus from Ogden Nash for medium voice and strings, 1978; Songs of Zion (choir), 1978; On the Razzle (opera), 1986; Sinfonietta Helvetica, 1990; Rondeau des Oiseaux for recorder, 1993; Three Lyric Pieces for piano, 1994; O Gracious Light (choir), 1999. Hon. DMus Glasgow, 1972; Hon. LLD Dundee, 1976. *Publication:* Musical Chairs (autobiog.), 1998. *Recreations:* gardening, mountain walks. *Address:* 16 Cranmer Road, Cambridge CB3 9BL. *T:* (01223) 352858.

ORR-EWING, Hon. Sir (Alistair) Simon, 2nd Bt *cr* 1963, of Hendon, co. Middlesex; *b* 10 June 1940; *e s* of Baron Orr-Ewing, OBE and of Joan Helen Veronica Orr-Ewing (*née* McMinnies); *S* to Btcy of father, 1999; *m* 1968, Victoria, *er d* of Keith Cameron; two *s* one *d*. *Educ:* Harrow; Grenoble Univ.; Trinity Coll., Oxford (BA Hons PPE). FRICS 1972. Trainee surveyor, 1968–72. Dir various private cos. Mem. (C), RBK&C Council, 1982–90 (Chm., Planning Cttee, 1986–88). *Recreations:* ski-ing, shooting, tennis. *Heir: er s* Archie Cameron Orr-Ewing [*b* 29 March 1969; *m* 1999, Nicola de Selincourt; one *s*]. *Address:* The Old Farmhouse, Fifield, Chipping Norton, Oxon OX7 6HJ. *T:* (01993) 830305. *Clubs:* Boodle's, Queen's, MCC.

ORR EWING, Major Edward Stuart; landowner and farmer, since 1969; Lord-Lieutenant of Wigtown, since 1989; *b* 28 Sept. 1931; *s* of late Captain David Orr Ewing, DSO, DL and of Mary Helen Stuart Orr Ewing (*née* Noaks); *m* 1st, 1958, Fiona Anne Bowman (*née* Farquhar) (marr. diss. 1981); one *s* two *d*; 2nd, 1981, Diana Mary Waters. *Educ:* Sherborne; Royal Military Coll. of Science. Regular soldier, The Black Watch, 1950–69. DL Wigtown, 1970. *Recreations:* country sports, ski-ing, painting. *Address:* Dunskey, Portpatrick, Wigtownshire DG9 8TJ. *T:* (01776) 810211. *Club:* New (Edinburgh).

ORR-EWING, Hamish; Chairman, Rank Xerox Ltd, 1980–86; *b* 17 Aug. 1924; *o s* of Hugh Eric Douglas Orr-Ewing and Esme Victoria (*née* Stewart), Strathgarry, Killiecrankie, Perthshire; *m* 1st, 1947, Morar Margaret Kennedy; one *s* (one *d* decd); 2nd, 1954, Ann Mary Teresa Terry. *Educ:* Heatherdown, Ascot; Eton. Served War, Captain Black Watch. Salesman, EMI, 1950; Ford Motor Co., 1954; Ford Light Car Planning Manager, 1959–63; Leyland Motor Corp. Ltd, 1963–65; joined Rank Xerox, 1965; apptd to Bd as Dir of Product Planning, 1968; Dir of Personnel, 1970; Man. Dir, Rank Xerox (UK) Ltd, 1971; Reg. Dir for Rank Xerox Ops in UK, France, Holland, Sweden and Belgium, 1977; Chairman: Jaguar plc, 1984–85; White Horse Hldgs, 1987–91; Dir, Tricentrol PLC, 1975–86. Chairman: Work and Society, 1982–85; European Govt Business Relations Council, 1980–84; Member: MSC, 1983–85; Engrg Council, 1984–87; Envmt Awards Panel, RSA, 1987–94; President: Inst. of Manpower Studies, 1986–89; Inst. of Training and Develt, 1987–89. CBI: Member: Bd, Educn Foundn (UBI), 1982–87; Council, 1985–87; Chm., Educn and Trng Cttee, 1985–87. Trustee: Shaw Trust, 1985–; Roman Res. Trust, 1990–97. Governor: Interphil, 1985–94; New Coll., Swindon, 1984–95 (Chm. of Govs, 1986–92); Bradon Forest Sch., 1989–92. CIMgt (CBIM 1981). *Recreations:* anything mechanical, country life, the Roman Empire. *Address:* Fox Mill Farm, Purton, near Swindon, Wilts SN5 9EF. *T:* (01793) 770496.

ORR EWING, Major Sir Ronald Archibald, 5th Bt *cr* 1886; Major (retired) Scots Guards; *b* 14 May 1912; *e s* of Sir Norman Orr Ewing, 4th Bt, CB, DSO, and Lady Orr Ewing (*née* Robarts), Tile House, Buckingham; *S* father, 1960; *m* 1938, Marion Hester (*d* 1997), *yr d* of late Colonel Sir Donald Walter Cameron of Lochiel, KT, CMG, and of Lady Hermione Cameron of Lochiel, *d* of 5th Duke of Montrose, KT; two *s* two *d*. *Educ:* Eton; RMC, Sandhurst. Scots Guards, 1932–53, Major. Served War of 1939–45, Middle East (POW 1942). JP Perthshire, 1956; DL Perthshire, 1963. Grand Master Mason of Scotland, 1965–69. *Recreation:* forestry. *Heir: s* Archibald Donald Orr Ewing [*b* 20 Dec. 1938; *m* 1st, 1965, Venetia Elizabeth (marr. diss. 1972), *y d* of Major and Mrs Richard Turner, Co. Dublin; 2nd, 1972, Nicola Jean-Anne, *d* of Reginald Baron Black, Fovant, near Salisbury; one *s*]. *Address:* Cardross, Port of Menteith, Kippen, Stirling FK8 3JY. *T:* (01877) 385220. *Club:* New (Edinburgh).

ORR-EWING, Hon. Sir Simon; *see* Orr-Ewing, Hon. Sir A. S.

ORREGO-VICUÑA, Prof. Francisco; Professor of International Law, School of Law and Institute of International Studies, University of Chile, since 1969; President, Chilean Council on Foreign Relations, 1989–2000; *b* 12 April 1942; *s* of Fernando Orrego Vicuña and Raquel Vicuña Viel; *m* 1965, Soledad Bauzá; one *s* two *d*. *Educ:* Univ. of Chile (Degree in Law); LSE (PhD). Admitted to legal practice, 1965. Sen. Legal Advisor, OAS, 1965–69 and 1972–74; Dir, Inst. of Internat. Studies, Univ. of Chile, 1974–83; Ambassador of Chile to UK, 1983–85. Advisor on legal matters, 1974–83, Mem. Adv. Council on Foreign Policy, 1997–, Min. of Foreign Affairs. Judge, 1992–, and Pres., 2001–, World Bank Admin. Tribunal (Vice-Pres., 1995–2001). Mem. Panel of Arbitrators and Councillors, ICSID, 1995–; Pres. Panel, UN Compensation Commn, 1998–2001. *Publications:* Derecho de la Integraciòn Latinoamericana, 1969; Los Fondos Marinos, 1976; Antarctic Resources Policy, 1983; The Exclusive Economic Zone, 1984; Antarctic Mineral Exploration, 1988; The Exclusive Economic Zone in International Law, 1989; The Changing International Law of High Seas Fisheries, 1999; contrib. Amer. Jl of Internat. Law and Annuaire Français de Droit Internat. *Recreations:* golf, ski-ing. *Address:* Institute of International Studies, University of Chile, PO Box 14187, Suc. 21, Santiago 9, Chile. *T:* (2) 2745377. *Club:* Athenæum.

ORRELL, James Francis Freestone; His Honour Judge Orrell; a Circuit Judge, since 1989; *b* 19 March 1944; *s* of late Francis Orrell and Marion Margaret Orrell; *m* 1970, Margaret Catherine Hawcroft; two *s*. *Educ:* Ratcliffe; Univ. of York (BA History). Called to the Bar, Gray's Inn, 1968; Recorder, Midland and Oxford Circuit, 1988. *Address:* c/o Derby Combined Court Centre, Morledge, Derby DE1 2XE.

ORRELL-JONES, Keith; Chairman: Smiths Group (formerly Smiths Industries) plc, since 1998; FKI plc, since 1999; *b* 15 July 1937; *m* 1961, Hilary Kathleen Pegram; four *s*. *Educ:* Newcastle-under-Lyme High Sch.; St John's Coll., Cambridge (BA 1961; MA 1967). Tarmac Civil Engineering, 1961–64; RMC plc, 1964–70; Marley plc, 1970–72; Area Manager, ARC, 1972–81; Pres., ARC America, 1981–87; Chief Exec., ARC, 1987–89; Dir, Consolidated Gold Fields, 1989; Pres., Blue Circle America, and Dir, Blue Circle Industries plc, 1990–92; Gp Chief Exec., Blue Circle Industries, 1992–99. Dir, Smiths Industries plc, 1992–98. FRSA 1989; CIMgt 1992. *Address:* Smiths Group plc, 765 Finchley Road, NW11 8DS. *Club:* Royal Automobile.

ORSON, Rasin Ward, CBE 1985; CompIEE; consultant; Member, The Electricity Council, 1976–89; *b* 16 April 1927; *s* of Rasin Nelson Orson and Blanche Hyre; *m* 1st, 1950, Marie Goodenough; two *s*; 2nd, 1979, Lesley Jean Vallance. *Educ:* Stratford Grammar Sch.; London School of Economics (BScEcon 1948). Asst Statistician, Min. of Civil Aviation, 1948, Statistician, 1953; Electricity Council: Head of Economics and Forecasting Branch, 1963; Dep. Commercial Adviser, 1968; Commercial Adviser, 1972. Dir, Chloride Silent Power, 1974–89. *Recreations:* music, photography. *Address:* The Old Garden, Dunorlan Park, Tunbridge Wells, Kent TN2 3QA. *T:* (01892) 524027.

ORTIZ DE ROZAS, Carlos; career diplomat, retired; Professor of International Relations, University of Belgrano, Buenos Aires, since 1995; *b* 26 April 1926; *m* 1952, María del Carmen Sarobe. *Educ:* School of Diplomacy, Min. of Foreign Affairs, Buenos Aires (grad. 1949). Lawyer, Faculty of Law, Univ. of Buenos Aires, 1950. Entered Argentine Foreign Service, 1948; served Bulgaria, Greece, UAR and UK (Minister); Ambassador to Austria, 1967–70; Permanent Rep. to UN, 1970–77; Pres. UN Security Council, 1971–72; Chairman: First (Polit. and Security) Cttee of 29th Gen. Assembly, 1974; Preparatory Cttee of Special Session on Disarmament, 1977–78; Cttee on Disarmament, Geneva, 1979; Mem. Adv. Bd on Disarmament Studies, New York, 1978–92; Ambassador to UK, 1980–82; Head, Argentine Special Mission to the Holy See, 1982–83; Ambassador to France, 1984–89; Dep. Foreign Minister, 1990; Ambassador to USA, 1991–93; retd Foreign Service, 1994. Universidad del Salvador, Buenos Aires: Prof. of History and Constitutional Law, and Prof. of Political Science, Faculty of Law, 1958–80; Prof. of Internat. Relations, School of Political Sciences, and at School of Diplomacy, 1962–80. Mem. Bd of Dirs, Bunge and Born SA, 1995–99; President: Bunge and Born Foundn, 1994–99; Alliance Française, Buenos Aires, 2000–. Holds many foreign decorations incl. Grand Cross, Order of Pius IX, 1985, and Commandeur, Légion d'Honneur, 1985. *Address:* Gelly y Obes 2263, 1425 Buenos Aires, Argentina. *Clubs:* Jockey, Círculo de Armas (Buenos Aires); Cercle de l'Union Interalliée (Paris).

ORTOLI, François-Xavier; Hon. Chairman, Total, since 1990 (Président Directeur Général, 1984–90); *b* 16 Feb. 1925. *Educ:* Hanoi Faculty of Law; Ecole Nationale d'Administration. Inspector of Finances, 1948–51; Tech. Adv., Office of Minister of Econ. Affairs and Information, 1951–53; Asst Dir to Sec. of State for Econ. Affairs and Sec.-Gen., Franco-Italian Cttee of EEC, 1955; Head, Commercial Politics Service of Sec. of State for Econ. Affairs, 1957; Dir-Gen., Internal Market Div., EEC, 1958; Sec.-Gen., Inter-Ministerial Cttee for Questions of European Econ. Co-operation, Paris, 1961–; Dir of Cabinet to Prime Minister, 1962–66; Comr-Gen. of the Plan, 1966–67; Minister: of Works, 1967–68; of Educn, 1968; of Finance, 1968–69; of Industrial and Scientific Develt, 1969–72; Pres., EEC, 1973–76, a Vice-Pres., with responsibility for econ. and financial affairs, 1977–84. Hon. Fellow, Worcester Coll., Oxford, 1991. Hon. DCL Oxon, 1975;

Hon Dr Sch. of Political Scis, Athens, 1975. Grand Officier de la Légion d'Honneur; Médaille Militaire; Croix de Guerre, 1945; Médaille de la Résistance. *Address:* 18 rue de Bourgogne, 75007 Paris, France.

ORTON, Peter Charles; Founder, 1989, and Executive Chairman, since 2001, HIT Entertainment plc (Chief Executive, 1989–2001); *b* 17 June 1943; *s* of Harold Charles Orton and Eva Lillian Orton; *m* 1972, Susan Virginia Stevenson; one *s*. *Educ:* Portsmouth Tech. Coll.; Westlane Grammar Sch. Gen. salesman, Scholl Medical Co., 1962–67; Programme Exec., TIE, 1967–69; Internat. Dir of Programming, Children's TV Workshop, NY, 1969–72; Founder, Sport on TV (TV Sports Packaging Co.), 1972–74; Vice-Pres., Worldwide Distribn, Children's TV Workshop, NY, 1974–82; CEO, Henson Internat. TV, 1982–89. *Recreations:* breeding steeplechase race horses, shooting, golf, most other country pursuits. *Address:* HIT Entertainment, The Pump House, 13/16 Jacob's Well Mews, W1H 5PD; Lower Greenhill Farm, Wootton Bassett, Wilts SN4 7QP. *T:* (01793) 853837. *Clubs:* White's, Turf; Wootton Bassett Rugby.

ORWIN, Peter David, OBE 1991; MC 1966; HM Diplomatic Service, retired; Security and Business Risks Adviser, Syngenta (formerly Zeneca Agrochemicals), since 1999; *b* 20 Dec. 1944; *s* of late John Antony Arnold Orwin and of Catherine Mary Orwin (*née* Rutherford); *m* 1977, Pamela Jane Heath; one *s* two *d*. *Educ:* Peter Symonds Sch.; RMA, Sandhurst. Commnd into Prince of Wales's Own Regt of Yorkshire, 1964; served Berlin, 1965; Aden, 1965–67; UK, 1968–69; Cyprus, 1969–70; UK/MoD, 1970–74; retd 1975; entered HM Diplomatic Service, 1975: First Secretary: Athens, 1977–84; Brasilia, 1984–87; FCO, 1987–89; First Sec., then Counsellor, Tel Aviv, 1989–93; Counsellor, FCO, 1993–96; Counsellor, The Hague, 1996–99. Associate Mem., IoD. *Recreations:* country pursuits, travel, dinghy sailing, tennis. *Address:* Byeways, Broad Oak, East Sussex TN21 8UR. *Club:* Mayfield Tennis.

OSBALDESTON, Michael David; Director of Global Learning, Shell International Ltd, since 2000; *b* 12 Feb. 1949; *s* of Richard Grahame Osbaldeston and Betty Osbaldeston (*née* Mackenzie); *m* 1974, Valerie Davies; one *s* one *d*. *Educ:* Bishop Vesey's Grammar Sch.; Liverpool Univ. (BSc Hons); Liverpool Univ. Business Sch. (MBA). FCIPD (FIPD 1985). Consultant, Merrett Cyriax Associates, 1971–73; Researcher, Ashridge Res. Unit, 1973–76; Ashridge Management College, 1976–2000: Programme Dir, 1977–81; Dir, Ext. Relns, 1982–84; Dir of Studies, 1985–87; Dean, 1988–90; Chief Exec., 1990–2000. Non-exec. Dir, Chartwell Ltd, 1997–. Vice-President: Strategic Planning Soc., 1995–2000; Eur. Foundn for Mgt Develt, 1997. CIMgt 1991; FRSA 1991. *Publications:* The Way We Work: a European study of changing practice in job design, 1979; (contrib.) Redesigning Management Development in The New Europe, 1998; contrib. numerous articles and papers in mgt jls. *Recreations:* sailing, theatre, France. *Address:* The Old Barns, High Street, Whitchurch, Aylesbury, Bucks HP22 4JA. *T:* (01296) 641671; Shell Centre, Belvedere Road, SE1 7NA. *Club:* Athenæum.

OSBORN, Frederic Adrian, (Derek), CB 1991; Chairman, United Nations Environment and Development Forum, since 1996; *b* 14 Jan. 1941; *s* of late Rev. George R. Osborn and E. M. Osborn, MBE; *m* 1971, Caroline Niebuhr Tod; one *d* one *s*. *Educ:* Leys School, Cambridge; Balliol College, Oxford (BA Maths 1963; BPhil 1965). Min. of Housing and Local Govt, 1965–75; Dept of Transport, 1975–77; Department of the Environment, 1977–95: Under Sec., Finance, 1982–86, Housing Gp, 1986–87; Dep. Sec., Local Govt and Finance, 1987–89; Dir Gen., Envmtl Protection, 1990–95. Chm., EEA, 1995–2000; Co-Chm., UN Special Session, 1997; Bd Mem. for England and Wales, Envmt Agency, 1996–98; Special Advr, H of C Envmtl Audit Cttee, 1998–99; Chairman: Internat. Inst. for Envmt and Develt, 1998–; Joseph Rowntree Foundn Steering Gp on Reconciling Envmtl and Social Objectives, 1998–; UK Round Table on Sustainable Develt, 1999–. Mem. Bd, Severn Trent Plc, 1998–; Chm., Jupiter Global Green Investment Trust, 2001–. Vis. Fellow, Green Coll., Oxford, 1996–97; Vis. Prof., Sch. of Public Policy, UCL, 1998–. Mem. Council, RSPB, 1996–. *Publications:* Earth Summit II, 1998; contribs to Jl of Envmtl Law, Pol Qly. *Recreations:* music, reading, chess.

OSBORN, Sir John (Holbrook), Kt 1983; semi-retired scientist, soldier, industrialist and politician; *b* 14 Dec. 1922; *s* of late Samuel Eric Osborn and Aileen Decima, *d* of Colonel Sir Arthur Holbrook, KBE, MP; *m* 1st, 1952, Molly Suzanne (*née* Marten) (marr. diss.); two *d*; 2nd, 1976, Joan Mary MacDermot (*née* Wilkinson) (*d* 1989); 3rd, 1989, Patricia Hine (*née* Read). *Educ:* Rugby; Trinity Hall, Cambridge. MA Cantab; Part 2 Tripos in Metallurgy; Diploma in Foundry Technology, National Foundry Coll., 1949. Served in Royal Corps of Signals, 1943–47 (West Africa, 1944–46; Captain); served in RA (TA) Sheffield, 1948–55, Major. Joined 1947, and Technical Dir, 1951–79, Samuel Osborn & Co. Ltd, and associated companies. Chairman, Hillsborough Divisional Young Conservative and Liberal Association, 1949–53. MP (C) Hallam Div. of Sheffield, 1959–87 (NL and U, 1959–64); PPS to the Secretary of State for Commonwealth Relations and for the Colonies, 1963–64. Chairman: Cons. Parly Transport Cttee, 1970–74; Anglo-Swiss Parly Gp, 1981–87; (or Vice-Chm.) Anglo-Soviet Parly Gp, 1968–87; Vice Chm., Parly and Scientific Cttee, 1963–66, 1982 (Officer, 1959–87; Life Mem., 1987); Jt Sec., 1922 Cttee, 1968–87; Member: Science and Technol. Select Cttee, 1970–73; Educn, Science and Arts Select Cttee, 1979–83; Chm., All Party Channel Tunnel Gp, 1985–87; Individual Mem., Parly Gp for Energy Studies, 1987– (Chm., 1985–87; Vice-Chm., Cons. Parly Energy Cttee, 1979–81). Mem., UK Delegn to Council of Europe and WEU, 1973–75, 1980–87 (Hon. Associate, Council of Europe, 1987–, WEU, 1990–); Council of Europe: Vice Chm., Science and Technol. Cttee, 1981–87; Chm., Eur. Scientific Contact Gp, 1982–87. Chm., Econ. Affairs and Develt Sub-Cttee (North/South: Europe's role), 1985–87. Mem., European Parlt, 1975–79. Life Member, British Branch: CPA, 1987 (Mem., 1959–87); IPU, 1987 (Mem. Exec., 1968–75, 1979–83). Mem. Cttee, European Atlantic Gp, 1990–. Mem., Interim (formerly Voluntary) Licensing Authy, MRC/RCOG, 1987–91. Chairman: Friends of Progress, 1989–95; Business and Develt Cttee, UK Chapter, Soc. for Internat. Develt, 1990–95. Mem., RIIA, 1985–. Freeman Co. of Cutlers in Hallamshire, 1987 (Asst Searcher, 1951–65; Searcher, 1965–70 and 1973–87). Fellow, Institute of British Foundrymen, 1948–72 (Member Council, Sheffield Branch, 1954–64); FIM 1986 (MISI 1947); Fellow, Institute of Directors; Member Council: Sheffield Chamber of Commerce, 1956–89 (Hon. Life Mem., 1989); Assocs British Chambers of Commerce, 1960–62 (Hon. Secretary, 1962–64); British Iron and Steel Res. Association, 1965–68; CBI and Yorks and WR Br., CBI, 1968–79; Industrial Soc., 1963–79 (Life Mem.). Hon. Patron, Sheffield Inst. of Advanced Motorists, 1996– (Pres., 1960–96); Chm., H of C Motor Club, 1979–84. Mem., Court and Council Sheffield Univ., 1951–79. Trustee: Talbot Trust, 1950–98; Zackery Merton Trust, 1951– (Chm., 1988–98). FRSA 1966. Travelled widely in business and politics. *Recreations:* golf, photography, gardening, gymnasium, swimming. *Address:* Newlands, 147 Hawton Road, Newark, Notts NG24 4QG. *T:* (01636) 704480. *Club:* Carlton.

OSBORN, Sir Richard (Henry Danvers), 9th Bt *cr* 1662, of Chicksands Priory, Co. Bedford; fine art consultant; *b* 12 Aug. 1958; surv. *s* of Sir Danvers Lionel Rouse Osborn, 8th Bt, and Constance Violette, JP, OStJ (*d* 1988), *d* of late Major Leonard Frank Rooke, KOSB and RFC; *S* father, 1983. *Educ:* Eton. Christie's, 1978–83; Consultant to P & D Colnaghi Ltd, 1984–86. Dir, Paul Mitchell Ltd (antique frames and picture conservation), 1991–. *Recreations:* cricket, tennis, squash, horse racing, Real tennis. *Heir: kinsman* William Danvers Osborn [*b* 4 June 1909; *m* 1939, Jean Burns, *d* of R. B. Hutchinson, Vancouver; one *d*]. *Address:* 25 Queens Gardens, W2 3BD. *Clubs:* Pratt's, MCC, Turf, Queen's.

OSBORNE, Rt Hon. Lord; Kenneth Hilton Osborne; PC 2001; a Senator of the College of Justice in Scotland, since 1990; *b* 9 July 1937; *s* of Kenneth Osborne and Evelyn Alice (*née* Hilton); *m* 1964, Clare Ann Louise Lewis; one *s* one *d*. *Educ:* Larchfield Sch., Helensburgh; Merchiston Castle Sch., Edinburgh; Edinburgh Univ. (MA, LLB). Admitted to Faculty of Advocates in Scotland, 1962; QC (Scotland) 1976. Standing Junior Counsel to Min. of Defence (Navy) in Scotland, 1974–76; Advocate-Depute, 1982–84. Chairman: Disciplinary Cttee, Potato Marketing Bd, 1975–90; (part-time), VAT Tribunals, 1985–90; Medical Appeal Tribunals, 1987–90; Mem., Lands Tribunal for Scotland, 1985–87. Chm., Local Govt Boundary Commn for Scotland, 1990–2000. *Recreations:* ski-ing, fishing, gardening, music, cooking. *Address:* 42 India Street, Edinburgh EH3 6HB. *T:* (0131) 225 3094; Primrose Cottage, Bridgend of Lintrathen, by Kirriemuir, Angus. *T:* (01575) 560316. *Club:* New (Edinburgh).

OSBORNE, Anthony David, CB 1995; Chief Executive, Government Property Lawyers, 1993–95; *b* 21 March 1935; *s* of Frederick Charles Osborne and Eva Mary Osborne (*née* Tutt); *m* 1958, Ethelwyn Grieve; two *s* one *d*. *Educ:* Brighton College. Articled: Aldrich and Crowther, Brighton; Ashurst, Morris, Crisp & Co., London; admitted Solicitor, 1958; private practice, London, 1958–65; joined Treasury Solicitor's Dept, 1965; Asst Treasury Solicitor, 1975; Solicitor to Health and Safety Commn and Health and Safety Exec., 1985–90; Principal Asst Treasury Solicitor, 1990; Head of Property Div., Taunton, 1990–93. *Recreations:* music, theatre, travel, photography.

OSBORNE, Rt Rev. Basil; *see* Sergievo, Bishop of.

OSBORNE, Rev. Canon Brian Charles; Vicar of Holy Trinity, Skirbeck, Boston, Lincolnshire, since 1980; Chaplain to the Queen, since 1997; *b* 17 May 1938; *s* of Walter and Gweneth Osborne; *m* 1968, Kathryn Ruth Grant; two *d*. *Educ:* St Andrews Univ. (MA Hons Classics); DipTh London Univ. 1980; Clifton Theol Coll. Ordained deacon, 1963, priest, 1964; Asst Curate, Holy Trinity, Boston, 1963–68; Priest-in-charge, 1968–71, Incumbent, 1971–75, St John's, New Clee, Grimsby; Vicar, St Augustine's, Derby, 1975–80. Pt-time Chaplain, Pilgrim Hosp., Boston, 1984–88. Rural Dean, Holland East, 1985–94; Hon. Canon of Lincoln, 1992–. *Recreations:* golf, squash, long walks, reading. *Address:* The Vicarage, 64 Spilsby Road, Boston, Lincs PE21 9NS. *T:* (01205) 363657. *Clubs:* Boston Squash; Kirton Holme Golf.

OSBORNE, Charles (Thomas), FRSL; author and critic; *b* 24 Nov. 1927; *s* of Vincent Lloyd Osborne and Elsa Louise Osborne; *m* 1970, Marie Korbelářová (marr. diss. 1975). *Educ:* Brisbane State High Sch. Studied piano and voice, Brisbane and Melbourne; acted in and directed plays, 1944–53; wrote poetry and criticism, published in Aust. and NZ magazines; co-owner, Ballad Bookshop, Brisbane, 1947–51; actor, London, provincial rep. and on tour, also TV and films, 1953–57; Asst Editor, London Magazine, 1958–66; Asst Lit. Dir, Arts Council of GB, 1966–71, Lit. Dir, 1971–86; Chief Theatre Critic, The Daily Telegraph, 1987–91. Broadcaster, musical and literary progs, BBC, 1957–; Dir, Poetry International, 1967–74; Sec., Poetry Book Soc., 1971–84; opera critic, Jewish Chronicle, 1985–. Mem. Editorial Board: Opera, 1970–; Annual Register, 1971–87. Vice Pres., Richard Strauss Soc., 1994–. FRSL 1996. DUniv Griffith Univ., Australia, 1994. Gold Medal, Amici di Verdi, 1993. *Publications:* (ed) Australian Stories of Today, 1961; (ed) Opera 66, 1966; (with Brigid Brophy and Michael Levey) Fifty Works of English Literature We Could Do Without, 1967; Kafka, 1967; Swansong (poems), 1968; The Complete Operas of Verdi, 1969 (Italian trans. 1975, French trans. 1989); Ned Kelly, 1970; (ed) Australia, New Zealand and the South Pacific, 1970; (ed) Letters of Giuseppe Verdi, 1971; (ed) The Bram Stoker Bedside Companion, 1973; (ed) Stories and Essays by Richard Wagner, 1973; The Concert Song Companion, 1974; Masterpieces of Nolan, 1976; Masterpieces of Drysdale, 1976; Masterpieces of Dobell, 1976; Wagner and his World, 1977 (USA 1977; trans. Spanish 1985); Verdi, 1977 (trans. Spanish 1985); (ed) Dictionary of Composers, 1977; The Complete Operas of Mozart, 1978 (trans. Ital. 1982); (ed) Masterworks of Opera: Rigoletto, 1979; The Opera House Album, 1979 (trans. Dutch 1981); W. H. Auden: the Life of a Poet, 1980; (ed with Kenneth Thomson) Klemperer Stories, 1980 (trans. German 1981); The Complete Operas of Puccini, 1981; The Life and Crimes of Agatha Christie, 1982, 2nd edn 1999; The World Theatre of Wagner, 1982; How to Enjoy Opera, 1983 (trans. Spanish 1985); The Dictionary of Opera, 1983 (trans. Finnish 1984; trans. Portuguese 1987); Letter to W. H. Auden and Other Poems, 1984; Schubert and his Vienna, 1985 (trans. German 1986); Giving It Away (memoirs), 1986; (ed) The Oxford Book of Best-Loved Verse, 1986; Verdi: a life in the theatre, 1987; The Complete Operas of Richard Strauss, 1988; Max Oldaker: last of the matinée idols, 1988; The Complete Operas of Wagner, 1990; The Bel Canto Operas, 1993; The Oxford Opera Guide, 1998; The Pink Danube (novel), 1998; novels, adapted from plays by Agatha Christie: Black Coffee, The Unexpected Guest, 1998; Spider's Web, 2000; The Importance of Being Earnest (novel, adapted from play by Oscar Wilde), 1999; poems in: The Oxford Book of Australian Verse, 1956; Australian Poetry, 1951–52, etc; The Queensland Centenary Anthology, 1959; Australian Writing Today, 1968; various jls; contrib.: TLS, Observer, Sunday Times, Times, Guardian, New Statesman, Spectator, London Mag., Encounter, Opera, Chambers Encyc. Yearbook, and Enciclopedia dello spettacolo; also cassettes. *Recreations:* travelling, planning future projects. *Address:* 125 St George's Road, SE1 6HY. *T:* (020) 7928 1534. *Club:* Savile.

OSBORNE, David Allan; HM Diplomatic Service; Ambassador to Honduras, since 1998; *b* 31 Aug. 1942; *s* of Donald Stewart Osborne and Caroline Susie Osborne (*née* Stanbury); *m* 1966, Joan Marion Duck; one *s* two *d*. *Educ:* St Albans Grammar Sch.; Central London Poly. (DMS). Joined Commonwealth Relations Office, 1961; Accra, 1963–65; FCO, 1966–68; Guatemala City, 1968–73; Bonn, 1973–74; Valletta, 1974–77; sabbatical, 1977–78; First Sec., FCO, 1978–79; Mexico City, 1979; San José (concurrently accredited to Managua and San Salvador), 1980–84; FCO, 1984–88; Dep. Consul Gen., São Paulo, 1988–91; EU Monitor, Croatia, 1991–92; FCO, 1992–94; Santiago, 1994–95; FCO, 1995–96; Chargé d'Affaires, Managua, 1997. EU Monitor Medal, 1992. *Recreations:* reading, walking, chess, indigenous cultures in Latin America, various sports. *Address:* c/o Foreign and Commonwealth Office, King Charles Street, SW1A 2AH.

OSBORNE, Denis Gordon, CMG 1990; adviser on governance, development and training, since 1992; *b* 17 Sept. 1932; *s* of A. Gordon Osborne and Frances A. Osborne (*née* Watts); *m* 1970, Christine Susannah, *d* of P. Rae Shepherd and C. Elaine Shepherd; two *d*. *Educ:* Dr Challoner's Grammar Sch., Amersham; University Coll., Durham (BSc 1st Cl. Hons Physics, PhD). FInstP 1966. Lectr in Physics, Univ. of Durham, 1957; Lectr, Fourah Bay Coll., Sierra Leone, 1957–58; Lectr, 1958–63, Sen. Lectr, 1963–64, Univ. of Ghana; Reader in Physics, 1964–66, Prof., 1966–71, Dean of Science, 1968–70, Univ. of Dar es Salaam; Res. Fellow, UCL, 1971–72; Cons. for World Bank missions to Malaysia and Ethiopia, 1971, 1972; Overseas Development Administration: Principal, 1972;

Multilateral Aid Dept, 1972–75; Mediterranean and Near East Dept, 1975–77; Sci. and Technology Dept, 1977–80; Asst Sec., 1980; Hd of Dept in Natural Resources Div., 1980–84; Hd of E and W Africa Dept, 1984–87; HM Diplomatic Service, High Comr in Malaŵi, 1987–90; RIPA Internat., 1990–92. Reader, C of E, 1975–, at St Barnabas, Dulwich, 1980–. *Publications:* Way Out: some parables of science and faith, 1977; research papers on develt and governance, and until 1978 on geophysics, particularly the equatorial ionosphere. *Recreations:* reading, writing, attempts at windsurfing. *Address:* 112 Dulwich Village, SE21 7AQ; *e-mail:* do@governance.org.uk. *Club:* Athenæum.

OSBORNE, Douglas Leonard, FCIS; Chief Executive, Leukaemia Research Fund, since 1989; *b* 19 Oct. 1940; *s* of Leonard Osborne and Gladys Ellen (*née* Ward); *m* 1969, Barbara Helen Bartrop; one *s* one *d. Educ:* Royal Masonic Sch. ACIS 1967, FCIS 1985. London Association for the Blind: Asst Sec., 1965–75; Asst Dir, 1975–79; Dir, 1979–83; Administrator, Leukaemia Res. Fund, 1983–89. Mem. Council, Metropolitan Soc. for the Blind, 1979–. *Publication:* (ed jtly) Charities Administration, 1986, and Supplements, 1987–. *Recreations:* listening to music, cooking, travel. *Address:* (office) 43 Great Ormond Street, WC1N 3JJ. *T:* (020) 7405 0101.

OSBORNE, George Gideon Oliver; MP (C) Tatton, since 2001; *b* 23 May 1971; *s* and *heir* of Sir Peter George Osborne, Bt, *qv*; *m* 1998, Hon. Frances Victoria, *d* of Baron Howell of Guildford, *qv*; one *s. Educ:* St Paul's Sch., London; Davidson Coll., N Carolina (Dean Rusk Schol.); Magdalen Coll., Oxford (MA Hons Mod. Hist.). Freelance journalist, 1993; Hd, Pol Sect., Cons. Res. Dept, 1994–95; Special Advr, MAFF, 1995–97; Pol Office, 10 Downing St, 1997; Pol Sec. to Leader of Opposition, 1997–2001; Sec. to Shadow Cabinet, 1997–2001. Mem., Public Accounts Cttee, H of C, 2001–. *Recreations:* walking, ski-ing, theatre, observing American politics. *Address:* House of Commons, SW1A 0AA. *T:* (020) 7219 8329. *Clubs:* Beefsteak; Wilmslow Conservative, Cheshire Pitt.

OSBORNE, Ven. Hayward John; Archdeacon of Birmingham, since 2001; *b* 16 Sept. 1948; *s* of Ernest and Frances Joy Osborne; *m* 1973, Sandra Julie Hollander; two *s* three *d. Educ:* Sevenoaks Sch.; New Coll., Oxford (BA 1970, MA 1973); King's Coll., Cambridge (PGCE); Westcott House Theol Coll., Cambridge. Ordained deacon, 1973, priest, 1974; Curate, Bromley Parish Ch, 1973–77; Team Vicar, Halesowen, 1977–83; Team Rector, St Barnabas, Worcester, 1983–88; Vicar, St Mary, Moseley, Birmingham, 1988–2001; Area Dean, Moseley, 1994–2001. Mem., Gen. Synod of C of E, 1998–. Hon. Canon, Birmingham Cathedral, 2000. *Recreations:* music, theatre, computing. *Address:* Diocesan Office, 175 Harborne Park Road, Birmingham B17 0BH. *T:* (0121) 426 0400.

OSBORNE, Helena; *see* Moore, G. M.

OSBORNE, Jana; General Secretary, National Federation of Women's Institutes, since 1996; *b* 11 Jan. 1953; *d* of Jan Koutny' and Miloslava Koutna'; *m* 1978, Graeme Stephen Osborne. *Educ:* Charles Univ., Prague (BA Hons Modern Langs 1978); Poly. of Central London (Postgrad. Personnel Mgt Course). MIPD 1989. Journalist and interpreter, Nikon Denpa News, Prague, 1974–79; Personnel Officer, Bowater Industrial plc, 1987–88; Office Manager, Thorpac Gp plc, 1988–89; National Federation of Women's Institutes: Personnel Officer, 1989–92; Head of Personnel, 1992–95; Gen. Manager, 1995–96. *Recreations:* cycling, walking, classical music, literature, gardening. *Address:* (office) 104 New Kings Road, SW6 4LT. *T:* (020) 7371 9300.

OSBORNE, Kenneth Hilton; *see* Osborne, Rt Hon. Lord.

OSBORNE, Prof. Michael John, FAHA; FAIM; Vice-Chancellor, since 1990, and President, La Trobe University, Australia; *b* 25 Jan. 1942; *s* of Samuel Osborne and Olive May Osborne (*née* Shove); *m* 1978, Dawn Brindle. *Educ:* Eastbourne Grammar Sch.; Christ Church, Oxford (MA); Catholic Univ. of Leuven (DPhil and Lett.). Lectr, Dept of Classics, Bristol, 1966–67; Lectr, then Sen. Lectr, Dept of Classics and Archaeology, Univ. of Lancaster, 1967–82; University of Melbourne: Prof. and Chm., Dept of Classical and Near Eastern Studies, 1983–90, now Prof. Emeritus; Dep./Associate Dean, Faculty of Arts, 1985–89; Pro-Vice-Chancellor and Vice-Pres., Academic Bd, 1989. Mem., Inst. for Advanced Study, Princeton, 1978–79; Visiting Professor: Maximilians Univ., Munich, 1973; Leuven, 1975, 1988; Vis. Fellow, other univs, 1972–85; Hon. Professor: Yunnan Univ., China, 1994; Kunming Med. Coll., China, 1995; Yunnan Normal Univ., China, 1997. Chm., Victorian Vice-Chancellors' Cttee, 1993–94; Member: Bd of Dirs, Australian Vice-Chancellors' Cttee, 1994–96 (Chm., Students and Scholarships Cttee, 1995–96; Chm., Standing Cttee for Internat. Affairs, 1996–; Leader, delegn to Hungary, Czech and Slovak Republics, 1993, to S Africa, 1994); Business/Higher Educn Round Table (Mem., Task Force on Higher Educn, 1996–; Mem. Bd of Dirs, 1996–); Res. Cttee, Cttee for Econ. Develt of Australia, 1993–96; Bd of Dirs, Internat. Develt Program, 1996–99; Bd of Dirs, Grad. Careers Council of Australia, 1996–98. Co-Chm. Planning Cttee, Australian Educn Internat., 2000–. President: Univ. Mobility in Asia Pacific Scheme, 2000–; Internat. Network of Univs, 2000–. FAHA 1985; FAIM 2000. Laureate, Royal Acad. of Sci., Letters and Fine Arts, Belgium, 1980; Hon. Fellow, Hungarian Acad. of Engrg, 1998; Corresp. Mem., Acad. of Athens, 1998. Aristotle Award, Greece, 1998; Hon. Distinction, Hellenic Republic of Cyprus, 2000. *Publications:* Naturalization in Athens, 4 vols, 1981–83; Lexicon of Greek Personal Names, vol. II: Attica, 1994; The Foreign Residents of Athens, Studia Hellenistica Vol. 33, 1995; numerous articles in learned jls on Greek history, Greek epigraphy and Greek archaeology. *Recreations:* tennis, travel, Australian Rules football. *Address:* Office of the Vice-Chancellor, La Trobe University, Bundoora, Vic 3086, Australia. *T:* (3) 94792000. *Club:* Essendon Football.

OSBORNE, Prof. Nigel; composer; Reid Professor of Music, Edinburgh University; *b* 1948. *Educ:* St Edmund Hall, Oxford; studied at Warsaw Acad. and Polish Radio Exptl Studio. FRCM 1996. Staff of Music Dept, Nottingham Univ., 1978; Co-Editor-in-Chief, Contemporary Music Review. Initiator of programme of rehabilitation for refugee children in Balkans and Caucasus, 1992–. Queen's Award, Edinburgh Univ., 1997. *Compositions include:* Seven Words, 1971 (Radio Suisse Romande Prize); Heaventree, 1973 (Gaudeamus Prize); Kinderkreuzzug, 1974; I am Goya, 1977 (Radcliffe Award); Orlando Furioso, 1978; In Camera, 1979; Sinfonia, 1982; Sinfonia II, 1983; Zansa, 1985; The Electrification of the Soviet Union (opera), 1987; Violin Concerto, 1990; Terrible Mouth, 1991; The Sun of Venice, 1993; Art of Fugue, 1993; Sarajevo (opera), 1994; Evropa (first opera of war in Sarajevo), 1995; Oboe Concerto, 1998; String Quartet no 1, 1999; Widows (opera), 2000; orchestral, choral, instrumental, ballet and electronic music; numerous recordings. *Address:* c/o Faculty of Music, Edinburgh University, 12 Nicolson Square, Edinburgh EH8 9DF.

OSBORNE, Sir Peter (George), 17th Bt *cr* 1629; Chairman and Managing Director, Osborne & Little plc (design company), since 1967; *b* 29 June 1943; *s* of Lt-Col Sir George Osborne, 16th Bt, MC, and Mary (Grace) (*d* 1987), *d* of C. Horn; *S* father, 1960; *m* 1968, Felicity Alexandra, *d* of Grantley Loxton-Peacock; four *s. Educ:* Wellington Coll., Berks; Christ Church Coll., Oxford. *Heir: s* George Gideon Oliver Osborne, *qv. Address:* 67 Lansdowne Road, W11 2LG. *Club:* White's.

OSBORNE, Richard Ellerker; author and broadcaster; *b* 22 Feb. 1943; *s* of late William Harold Osborne and Georgina Mary Osborne (*née* Farrow); *m* 1985, Hailz-Emily Wrigley; one *s. Educ:* Worksop Coll.; Univ. of Bristol (BA, MLitt). Asst Master, Bradfield Coll., 1967–88 (Head of Sixth Form Gen. Studies, 1978–88; Head of English, 1982–88); presenter and contrib., BBC Radio 3, 1969–; Music Critic, The Oldie, 1991–. Mem., Critics' Panel, Gramophone, 1974–; Chm., Music Section, Critics' Circle, 1984–87. *Publications:* Rossini, 1985; Conversations with Karajan, 1989; Herbert von Karajan: a life in music, 1998; contribs to newspapers, jls, music dictionaries and guides. *Recreations:* hill-walking, food and wine, reading in the garden, watching cricket. *Address:* 2 Vaughan Copse, Eton, Berks SL4 6HL. *T:* (01753) 671368, *Fax:* (01753) 621580.

OSBORNE, Col Robert; Director, Tree Council, 1991–2001; *b* 14 March 1936; *s* of Kenneth George Hulbert Osborne and Mary Irene (*née* Daymond); *m* 1st, 1961, Sybil Kathi Gisela Hudson (*née* von Knobloch) (marr. diss. 1988); two *s*; 2nd, 1988, Claudia Downing (*née* Radok); one step *d. Educ:* Cheltenham Coll.; RMA, Sandhurst. Commnd RTR, 1955; served BAOR and UK, 1956–72; Staff Coll., Camberley, 1968; US Army, 1972–75; UN Force in Cyprus, 1977–80; Defence and Military Attaché, Cairo, 1983–86; NATO Defence Coll., Rome, 1987; HQ NATO, Brussels, 1987–90, retd. Hon. Citizen, State of Texas, USA, 1974. *Recreations:* antiquities, the countryside, plain cookery. *Address:* Unwin's House, Waterbeach Road, Landbeach, Cambridge CB4 8EA. *T:* (01223) 861243.

OSBORNE, Roy Paul; HM Diplomatic Service; Deputy Head, Overseas Territories Department, since 2001; *b* 13 July 1951; *s* of Gilbert William Osborne and Jean Mary Osborne; *m* 1977, Vivienne Claire Gentry; two *d. Educ:* St Christopher's Junior Sch., Cowley; Magdalen Coll. Sch., Oxford. Entered FCO, 1970; served Oslo, Islamabad and Rome; FCO, 1981–85, Asst Private Sec. to Minister of State, 1983–85; Second Sec., Commercial/Aid, later First Sec., Head of Chancery and Consul, Yaoundé, 1985–89; First Sec., Press and Inf., Madrid, 1989–93; Section Head, Drugs and Internat. Crime, FCO, 1993–97; Ambassador to Nicaragua, 1997–2000. *Recreations:* birdwatching, wild life conservation, gardening, tennis, jogging. *Address:* c/o Foreign and Commonwealth Office, SW1A 2AH.

OSBORNE, Sandra Currie; MP (Lab) Ayr, since 1997; *b* 23 Feb. 1956; *d* of Thomas Clark and Isabella Clark; *m* 1982, Alastair Osborne; two *d. Educ:* Camphill Sen. Secondary Sch., Paisley; Anniesland Coll.; Jordanhill Coll.; Strathclyde Univ. (MSc). Community Worker, Glasgow; Women's Aid. Mem. (Lab), S Ayrshire Council, 1991–97. *Address:* House of Commons, SW1A 0AA.

OSBORNE, Trevor, FRICS; Chairman, Trevor Osborne Property Group Ltd, since 1973; *b* 7 July 1943; *s* of Alfred Osborne and Annie Edmondson; *m* 1969, Pamela Ann Stephenson; one *s* one *d. Educ:* Sunbury Grammar School. South Area Estate Manager, Middx County Council, 1960–65; Partner, A. P. C., 1966–67; Principal, Private Property Interests, 1967–73; Chm., 1973–93, Chief Exec., 1981–93, Speyhawk plc; Chairman: St George, 1985–96; Hawk Development Management, 1992–98; Lucknam Park Ltd, 1991–95; Building & Property Management Services, 1993–96; non-exec. Dir, Redland, 1989–92. Pres., British Property Fedn, 1991–93 (Mem. Council, 1985–92); BPF Vis. Fellow, Land Management, Reading Univ., 1987–90; Founder Mem. and Chm., POW Urban Villages Forum, 1992–99; Member: Royal Opera House Develt Bd, 1987–94 (Chm., ROH Development Ltd, 1994); Council of Advrs, Prince of Wales Inst. of Architecture (Trustee, 1991–93); Council, City Property Assoc, 1987–94; Royal Fine Art Commn, 1994–99. Formerly Mem., Wokingham DC (Leader, 1980–82); Trustee, Wokingham Cons. Assoc., 1982–91. Pres., Windsor Arts Centre; Chm., St Sebastian's Playing Field Trust; Dir, London First, 1992–95. Freeman, City of London; Liveryman, Chartered Surveyors' Co. Fellow, Duke of Edinburgh Award World Fellowship; FRSA. *Recreations:* travel, walking, art, theatre, opera, tennis. *Address:* Trevor Osborne Property Group Ltd, 70 Conduit Street, W1S 2GF. *Clubs:* Athenæum, Carlton, Arts.

O'SHEA, David Michael; Solicitor to the Metropolitan Police, 1982–87, retired; *b* 27 Jan. 1927; *s* of late Francis Edward O'Shea and Helen O'Shea; *m* 1953, Sheila Winifred Polkinghorne; two *s. Educ:* St Ignatius Coll., London; King's Coll., London Univ. (LLB). Served RN, 1946–48. Articled H. C. L. Hanne & Co., London, 1949–52; admitted solicitor, 1952; in practice with H. C. L. Hanne & Co., 1952–56; joined Solicitor's Dept, Metropolitan Police Office, 1956; Dep. Solicitor, 1976–82. *Recreation:* travel. *Address:* c/o Solicitor's Department, New Scotland Yard, SW1H 0BG.

O'SHEA, Michael Kent; Director, Engineering Industries, Department of Trade and Industry, since 1998; *b* 12 March 1951; *s* of Donovan Henry Victor and Joan O'Shea; *m* 1988, Linda Beata Szpala. *Educ:* Bristol Grammar Sch.; Corpus Christi Coll., Cambridge (BA 1st Cl. Hons History). Department of Trade and Industry, 1973–: Under Sec., Finance and Resource Mgt, 1992–96; Dir, Engrg Automotive and Metals, 1996–98. *Recreations:* watching cricket, football and National Hunt racing, listening to Wagner, walking, drinking good beer and wine. *Address:* (office) 151 Buckingham Palace Road, SW1W 9SS. *Club:* Gloucestershire CC.

O'SHEA, Prof. Michael Roland, PhD; Director, BBSRC Sussex Centre for Neuroscience, University of Sussex, since 1991; *b* 5 April 1947; *s* of Capt. Jack Arthur O'Shea and Ellen O'Shea (*née* Hughes); *m* 1977, Barbara Moore (marr. diss. 1991); (one *d* decd). *Educ:* Forest Hill Sch., London; Univ. of Leicester (BSc 1st Cl. Hons Biol Scis 1968); Univ. of Southampton (PhD Neurobiol. 1971). University of California, Berkeley: NATO Fellow, 1971–73; NIH Fellow, 1973–75; SRC Fellow, Univ. of Cambridge, 1975–77; Asst Prof., Univ. of Southern Calif., LA, 1977–79; Associate Prof., Brain Research Inst., Univ. of Chicago, 1979–85; Professor of: Neurobiol., Univ. of Geneva, 1985–88; Molecular Cell Biol., RHBNC, Univ. of London, 1988–91. *Publications:* numerous papers on neuroscience in learned jls. *Recreations:* classical music, mountaineering, modern poetry, triathlons, restoration of classic Lotus. *Address:* 29 Eldred Avenue, Brighton BN1 5EB. *T:* (01273) 678508; Sussex Centre for Neuroscience, School of Biological Sciences, University of Sussex, Brighton BN1 9QG.

O'SHEA, Prof. Timothy Michael Martin, PhD; Master of Birkbeck College and Professor of Information and Communication Technologies, since 1998, Pro-Vice-Chancellor, since 2001, University of London; *b* 28 March 1949; *s* of John Patrick O'Shea and Elisabeth Hedwig Oberhof; *m* 1982, Prof. Eileen Scanlon; two *s* two *d. Educ:* Royal Liberty Sch., Havering; Sussex Univ. (BSc); Leeds Univ. (PhD). Postgrad. res., Univs of Texas at Austin and Edinburgh; Open University: founder, Computer Assisted Learning Res. Gp, 1978; Lectr, 1980–82, Sen. Lectr, 1983–87, Inst. of Educnl Technol.; Prof. of IT and Educn, 1987–97; Pro-Vice-Chancellor for QA and Res., 1994–97; Vis. Res. Prof., 1997–. Vis. Scientist, Xerox PARC, and Vis. Schol., Univ. of Calif, Berkeley, 1986–87. Chm., NATO prog. on Advanced Educnl Technol., 1988–90. Chairman: London Metropolitan Network Ltd, 1999–; HERO Ltd, 2000–. Director: Edexcel Foundn, 1998–2001 (Mem., Exec. Cttee, 1998–2001); Univs and Colls Staff Develt Agency, 1999–2000. Chm., Inf. Systems Sector Gp, CVCP, 1999–. Pres., Psychol. Sect., BAAS, 1991–92; Chm., Artificial Intelligence Soc., 1979–82. Trustee, Eduserv, 1999–2000.

Curator, Sch. of Advanced Study, London Univ., 1999–; Provost, Gresham Coll., 2000–; Mem. Council, RCM, 2001–; Governor: City Lit. Inst., 1998–2000; SOAS, 1998–; St George's Med. Sch., London Univ., 2000–. Presenter and author, The Learning Machine (TV series), 1985. *Publications* include: Self-improving teaching systems, 1979; (jtly) Learning and Teaching with Computers, 1983; (jtly) Artificial Intelligence: tools, techniques and applications, 1984; (ed) Advances in Artificial Intelligence, 1985; (ed jtly) Intelligent Knowledge-based Systems: an introduction, 1987; (ed jtly) Educational Computing, 1987; (ed jtly) New Directions in Educnl Technology, 1992; contrib. learned jls. *Address:* Birkbeck College, Malet Street, WC1E 7HX.

OSHEROFF, Prof. Douglas Dean, PhD; Professor of Physics and Applied Physics, Stanford University, since 1987; *b* 1 Aug. 1945; *s* of William and Bessie Anne Osheroff; *m* 1970, Phyllis Shih-Kiang Liu. *Educ:* California Inst. of Technology (BSc Physics 1967); Cornell Univ. (PhD Physics 1973). AT&T Bell Laboratories: Mem., technical staff, 1972–81; Hd, Solid State and Low Temp. Physics Res., 1981–87; Chm., Dept of Physics, Stanford Univ., 1993–96. MNAS, 1987; Mem., Amer. Acad. Arts and Scis, 1982. Fellow, APS. Sir Francis Simon Meml Award, 1976; Oliver E. Buckley Condensed Matter Physics Prize, 1981; Macarthur Prize Fellow Award, 1981; (jtly) Nobel Prize for Physics, 1996. *Publications:* contrib. chapters in books; numerous papers and articles in jls incl. Phys Rev., Phys Rev. Letters, Jl Low Temp. Phys. *Recreations:* photography, hiking, travel, music. *Address:* Department of Physics, Stanford University, Stanford, CA 94305–4060, USA.

OSIFELO, Sir Frederick (Aubarua), Kt 1977; MBE 1972; Speaker of Legislative Assembly, Solomon Islands, 1974–78; Chairman: Public Service Commission, since 1975; Police and Prison Service Commission, since 1977; Member, Judicial and Legal Service Commission, since 1977; *b* 15 Oct. 1928; *s* of late Paul Iromea and Joy Ngangale Iromea; *m* 1949, Margaret Tanai; three *s* three *d*. *Educ:* Torquay Technical Coll., England (Dip. Public Admin). Office cleaner, 1945; clerk, 1950; 1st Cl. Magistrate, 1967; Admin. Officer, Cl. B, 1967; Admin. Officer, Cl. A, 1972; District Comr, Eastern Solomons, 1972; Sen. Sec., 1973; Comr of Lands, 1974. Chairman: Cttee of Prerogative of Mercy, 1979; ad hoc cttee on Solomon Islands Honours and Awards, 1979. Pres., Amateur Sports Assoc., 1975–. Lay Canon, 1977. *Address:* PO Box 548, Honiara, Solomon Islands. *T:* (office) 21529, (home) 22018.

OSLER, Douglas Alexander; HM Senior Chief Inspector of Education, Scottish Executive, since 2001; *b* 11 Oct. 1942; *s* of Alexander Osler and Jane Brown; *m* 1973, Wendy Cochrane; one *s* one *d*. *Educ:* Univ. of Edinburgh (MA Hons Hist.); Moray House Coll. of Educn (Teaching Cert.). Teacher, Liberton High Sch., Edinburgh, 1965; Principal Teacher, History, Dunfermline High Sch., 1969; HM Inspector, Chief Inspector, Depute Sen. Chief Inspector of Schools, Scottish Office, 1974–95. HM Sen. Chief Inspector of Schls, Scottish Office, then Scottish Exec., 1996–2001. ESU Fellowship, 1966; Internat. Vis. Fellowship, USA, 1989. KSG. *Recreations:* golf, gardening, reading, Rotary International. *Address:* Scottish Executive, Saughton House, Edinburgh EH11 3XD. *T:* (0131) 244 7106, *Fax:* (0131) 244 7124.

OSMAN, Dr Mohammad Kheir; Member of Foundation Committee, 1981–86, Professor and Dean of Students, 1985–98, and Educational Advisor to the Vice-Chancellor, 1994–98, Sultan Qaboos University, Muscat, Sultanate of Oman; *b* Gedarif, Sudan; *s* of Osman Khalifa Taha and Khadija Al Shareef; *m* 1953, Sara Ahmed. *Educ:* Khartoum Univ. (BA); London Univ. (PGCE; AcDip; MA); UCLA (PhD). Director: Educational Research and Planning, 1970–71; Sudan/ILO Mgt and Productivity Centre, Khartoum, 1972; Minister of Education, 1972–75; Mem., Sudan Nat. Assembly, 1972–75; Ambassador to UK, 1975–76; Manager, UNDP/UNESCO Educnl Project, Oman, 1977–84; Adviser to Min. of Educn, Oman, 1984–85. Professional interests include Western educnl experience and indigenous Afro/Arab conditions, and the problems of change through institutional educnl systems; keen interest in nature, and developing countries' adjustment of educn to globalization, information and technology. Constitution Decoration, 1973; Two-Niles Decoration for Public Service, 1979; Sultan Qaboos Decoration, 1986. *Address:* PO Box 948 code 132, Al Khod, Sultanate of Oman.

OSMOND, Prof. Charles Barry, PhD; FRS 1984; FAA; President and Executive Director, Biosphere 2 Center, Columbia University, since 2001; *b* 20 Sept. 1939; *s* of Edmund Charles Osmond and Joyce Daphne (*née* Krauss); *m* 1st, 1962, Suzanne Alice Ward; one *s* one *d* (and two *s* decd); 2nd, 1983, Ulla Maria Cornelia Gauhl (*née* Büchen). *Educ:* Morisset Central Sch.; Wyong High Sch.; Univ. of New England, Armidale (University Medal in Botany, 1961; BSc 1961, MSc 1963); Univ. of Adelaide (PhD 1965). FAA 1978. Post-doctoral Res. Associate, Botanical Sciences Dept, Univ. of Calif, LA, 1965; Royal Commn for Exhibn of 1851 and CSIRO Fellow, Botany Sch., Cambridge Univ., 1966; successively Res. Fellow, Fellow and Sen. Fellow, Dept of Environmental Biol., ANU, Canberra, 1967–78, Prof. of Biology, 1978–87; Exec. Dir, Biol Sciences Center, Desert Res. Inst., Reno, 1982–86; Arts and Scis Prof., Duke Univ., USA, 1987–91; Prof., 1991–2001, and Dir, 1991–98, Res. Sch. of Biol Scis, ANU, Canberra. Fulbright Sen. Scholar, Univ. of Calif, Santa Cruz, 1973–74; Carnegie Instn Fellow (Plant Biol.), Stanford, 1973–74; Richard Mereton Guest Prof., Technical Univ., Munich, 1974; Overseas Fellow, Churchill Coll., Cambridge, 1980. Goldacre Award, Aust. Soc. of Plant Physiologists, 1972; Edgeworth David Medal, Royal Soc. of NSW, 1974; Forschungspreis, Alexander von Humboldt Foundn, 1997; Clarke Medal, Royal Soc. of NSW, 1998. *Publications:* (ed jtly) Photosynthesis and Photorespiration, 1971; (ed jtly) Photorespiration in Marine Plants, 1976; (jtly) Physiological Processes in Plant Ecology, 1980; (ed jtly) Encyclopedia of Plant Physiology, Vols 12 A-D, Physiological Plant Ecology, 1981–83; (ed jtly) Photoinhibition, 1987; (ed jtly) New Vistas in Measurement of Photosynthesis, 1989; (ed jtly) Plant Biology of the Basin and Range, 1990; (ed jtly) Water and Life, 1992; (ed jtly) Nurturing Creativity in Research, 1997; articles on plant metabolic biology and its ecological implications in learned jls. *Recreations:* biological research, social cricket, music of romantic composers, confections of Continental Europe. *Address:* Biosphere 2 Center, PO Box 689, Oracle, AZ 85623, USA. *T:* (520) 8965096, *Fax:* (520) 8966429.

OSMOND, Sir Douglas, Kt 1971; CBE 1968 (OBE 1958); QPM 1962; DL; Chief Constable, Shropshire, 1946–62, Hampshire, 1962–77; *b* 27 June 1914. *Educ:* University Coll., London. Metropolitan Police Coll., Metropolitan Police, RN, Control Commn for Germany (Public Safety Branch); Dep. Asst Inspector Gen., 1944–46. Pres., Assoc. of Chief Police Officers of England and Wales, 1967–69; Chm., Police Council for UK, 1972, 1974; Provincial Police Representative, Interpol, 1968–70; Member: Inter-Deptl Cttee on Death Certification and Coroners, 1964–71; Bd of Governors, Police Coll., 1968–72 (Adv. Cttee, 1959–77); Royal Commn on Criminal Procedure, 1978–81. DL Hants, 1981. OStJ 1971. *Address:* 12 Hays Park, Sedgehill, Shaftesbury, Dorset SP7 9JR. *T:* (01747) 830881.

OSMOND, Michael William Massy, CB 1977; Solicitor to the Department of Health and Social Security, and to the Office of Population Censuses and Surveys, and the General Register Office, 1974–78; *b* 1918; *s* of late Brig. W. R. F. Osmond, CBE, and Mrs C. R. E. Osmond; *m* 1943, Jill Ramsden (*d* 1989); one *s* one *d*. *Educ:* Winchester; Christ Church, Oxford. 2nd Lieut Coldstream Guards, 1939–40. Called to Bar, Inner Temple, 1941; Asst Principal, Min. of Production, 1941–43; Housemaster, HM Borstal Instn, Usk, 1943–45; Legal Asst, Min. of Nat. Insce, 1946; Sen. Legal Asst, 1948; Asst Solicitor, Min. of Pensions and Nat. Insce, 1958; Principal Asst Solicitor, DHSS, 1969. *Recreation:* music. *Address:* Waylands, Long Newnton, near Tetbury, Glos GL8 8RN. *T:* (01666) 503308. *Club:* Oxford and Cambridge.

OSMOND, Richard George; consultant, since 1997; *b* 22 Jan. 1947; *s* of late Lt-Col Clifford George Osmond, OBE, RE and Florence Rose Osmond (*née* Baker). *Educ:* Merchant Taylors' Sch. (Exhibr); Univ. of Exeter. FCIPD (FIPD 1988). Post Office, 1967–97: Dep. Sec., 1985; Controller, Corporate Personnel, 1986; Head of Community Affairs, 1989; Dir, Group Personnel, 1993; Secretary, 1995–97. Dir, Headteachers into Industry, 1990–96; Mem., Adv. Bd, Centre for Educn and Industry, Univ. of Warwick, 1992–98, Hon. Associate Fellow, 1998–2001; Chm., Policy Adv. Cttee, Sch. Curriculum and Industry Partnership, 1995–97. Vis. Fellow, Inst. of Educn, London Univ., 1997–99. Diocesan Gov., King Alfred's Coll., Winchester, 1999–; Chm. of Governors, Peter Symonds' Coll., Winchester, 2000–. Vice Pres., ACRE, 1997–. FRSA 1990 (Member: Early Learning Study, 1993–94; Educn Adv. Gp, 1996–). Mem. Council, Friends of Cathedral Music, 1977–83. Freeman, City of London, 1989; Liveryman, Musicians' Co., 1990–. *Recreations:* church music, bird watching. *Address:* 10 Hazel Grove, Badger Farm, Winchester SO22 4PQ. *T:* and *Fax:* (01962) 850818. *Club:* Athenæum.

OSMOTHERLY, Edward Benjamin Crofton, CB 1992; Chairman, Commission for Local Administration in England, 1994–2001; *b* 1 Aug. 1942; *s* of Crofton and Elsie Osmotherly; *m* 1970, Valerie (*née* Mustill); one *d* one *s*. *Educ:* East Ham Grammar School; Fitzwilliam College, Cambridge (MA). Asst Principal, Ministry of Housing and Local Govt, 1963–68 (Private Sec. to Parly Sec., 1966–67, to Minister of State, 1967–68); Principal, 1968–76; Harkness Fellow, 1972–73 (Guest Scholar, Brookings Instn, Washington DC; Exec. Fellow, Univ. of California at Berkeley); Asst Sec., DoE, 1976–79; seconded to British Railways Bd, 1979; Head of Machinery of Govt Div., CSD, 1980–81; Under Sec. (Railways), Dept of Transport, 1982–85; Under Sec., Dir of Personnel, Management and Training, Depts of the Environment and of Transport, 1985–89; Dep. Sec., Public Transport and Res. Dept, 1989–92, Prin. Establishment and Finance Officer, 1992–93, Dept of Transport; Local Govt Ombudsman, 1993–2001. Chm., Ind. Review of Govt Business Statistics, 1996. Chm., British and Irish Ombudsman Assoc, 1998–2001. *Recreation:* reading.

OSOLA, (Victor) John, (Väinö Juhani), CBE 1980; FREng, FIMechE; Chairman, John Osola & Associates Ltd, 1983–98; *b* 24 Jan. 1926; *s* of Väinö Kaarlo Osola and Violet Agenoria (*née* Jones); *m* 1948, Brenda Lilian Davison; two *s* one *d*. *Educ:* Hymers Coll., Hull; Sunderland Technical Coll., Univ. of Durham (BSc). FIMechE 1966; FREng (FEng 1979); Life Fellow ASME. Technical Commn, RE, 1945–48. Gas Turbine Res. Engr, C. A. Parsons & Co. Ltd, 1951–52; Sen. Proj. Design Engr, Procter & Gamble Ltd, 1952–57; Chief Engr, Lankro Chemicals Ltd, 1957–65; Technical Director: Fibreglass Ltd, 1965–72; Triplex Safety Glass Co. Ltd, 1972–79; Chm., Fibreglass Pilkington Ltd, Bombay, 1967–72; Director: Triplex Ireland Ltd, 1976–79; Triclover Safety Glass Co. Ltd, 1976–79; (non-exec.) Kongsberg Systems Technology Ltd, 1983–85; Cranfield Precision Engrg Ltd, 1990–95; Mem., Pilkington Brothers European Safety Glass Bd, 1977–79; Group Chief Exec., Redman Heenan Internat. plc, 1979–82, non-exec. Dir, 1982–84. Pres., IMechE, 1982–83; Ind. Mem., Mech. Engrg and Machine Tool Requirements Bd, Dept of Industry, 1974–77, Chm. 1977–79; Chm., NEDO Adv. Manufacturing Systems Cttee, 1983–86; Member: Parly and Scientific Cttee, 1983–89; (Founder), Parly Gp for Engrg Develt, 1985–89; Court of Cranfield Inst. of Technol., 1979–85; Policy Bd, Cranfield Product Engrg Centre, 1980–85; Chm., Engrg Doctorate Prog., Cranfield Univ., 1994–98. Sec., Fellowship of Engrg, 1983–89; Chm., Royal Acad. of Engrg MacRobert Award Trust, 1994–98; Trustee and Dir, 1996–2001, Chm., 1998–2001, Smallpeice Trust. Foreign Mem., Finnish Nat. Acad. of Technology, 1989. Associate, St George's House, Windsor, 1980–; Governor, Malvern Coll., 1981–. Freeman, City of London, 1984; Liveryman, Worshipful Co. of Engineers, 1984–. FRSA 1976. Hon. Fellow, Humberside Coll. of Higher Educn, 1986. MacRobert Award, 1978. *Publications:* papers in specialised engrg jls. *Recreations:* offshore sailing (BoT yachtmaster), music. *Address:* Whiddon End, Yarhampton Cross, near Stourport-on-Severn, Worcs DY13 0UY. *T:* (01299) 896293. *Clubs:* Army and Navy; Royal Dee Yacht (Cheshire); Royal Irish Yacht (Dublin); North West Venturers Yacht (Beaumaris).

OST, Michael Stuart; Director (non-executive): Lex Service plc, since 1993; Porvair plc, since 1999; *b* 29 Oct. 1944; *s* of Peter Stuart Ost and Betty Constance Ost; *m* 1977, Judith Ann Latham; one *s*. *Educ:* Scarborough High Sch. for Boys; London School of Economics (BSc Econ). Univ. Apprentice, Rolls-Royce Aero Engines Ltd, 1963–67; Singer Co.: Corporate Auditor, NY, 1968–70; Financial Controller, Thailand, 1970–72; Mktg Dir, Brazil, 1972–75; Gen. Manager, Turkey, 1975–77; Vice Pres., Far East, Getz Corp., 1978–82; President: Singer Brazil, 1982–83; Latin America Div., Singer, 1983–84; Exec. Vice Pres., Carrier International, 1984–85; Pres., ETO Carrier, 1985–87; Group Chief Executive: McKechnie plc, 1987–97; Coats Viyella plc, 1997–99. Non-exec. Dep. Chm., MG plc, 1999–2000. FRSA 1993; CIMgt 1994. *Recreations:* golf, bridge, reading. *Clubs:* Savile, Royal Automobile; Landings (Savannah, USA); Worplesdon Golf, Little Aston Golf.

OSTLERE, Dr Gordon; *see* Gordon, Richard.

OSTROWSKI, Joan Lorraine; *see* Walley, J. L.

O'SULLEVAN, Sir Peter (John), Kt 1997; CBE 1991 (OBE 1977); Racing Correspondent: Daily Express, 1950–86; Today, 1986–87; BBC Television Commentator, 1946–97; *b* 3 March 1918; *o s* of late Col John Joseph O'Sullevan, DSO, formerly Resident Magistrate, Killarney, and Vera, *o d* of Sir John Henry, DL, JP; *m* 1951, Patricia, *o d* of Frank Duckworth, Winnipeg, Manitoba, Canada. *Educ:* Hawtreys; Charterhouse; Collège Alpin, Switzerland. Specialised in ill-health in early life and not accepted for fighting forces in 1939–45 war, during which attached to Chelsea Rescue Services. Subsequently worked for John Lane, the Bodley Head, on editorial work and MSS reading. Joined Press Assoc. as Racing Correspondent, 1945, until appointed Daily Express, 1950, in similar capacity. Race-broadcasting 1946–97 (incl. Australia, S Africa, Italy, France, USA); in 1953 became first regular BBC TV and horse-racing commentator to operate without a race-reader; commentated: first television Grand National, 1960; world's first televised electronic horse race from Atlas computer at Univ. of London, transmitted by BBC TV Grandstand, 1967; first horse race transmitted live via satellite, from NY, to invited audience in London, 1980. Director: Internat. Racing Bureau, 1979–93; Racing Post Ltd, 1985–95. Mem., Jockey Club, 1986–. Chm., Osborne Studio Gall., 1999–. Patron: Brooke Hosp. for Animals; Internat. League for Protection of Horses; Thoroughbred Rehabilitation Centre. Derby Award for Racing Journalist of the Year, 1971 (with late Clive Graham), 1986; Racehorse Owner of the Year Award, Horserace Writers' Assoc., 1974; Clive Graham Meml Award for services to racing, Press Club, 1978, 1985; Evening News Sports Commentator of the Year, 1978; William Hill

Golden Spurs for services to racing, 1985; Par Excellence Award, Racing Club of Ireland, 1993; Sport on TV Award, Daily Telegraph, 1994; Media Award, Variety Club of GB, 1995; Services to Racing Award, Daily Star, 1995; Lesters Award, Jockeys' Assoc., 1996; TV Sports Award, RTS, 1996; George Ennor Trophy, Horserace Writers and Photographers Assoc., 1997; Special Award, TRIC, 1998. *Publication:* Calling the Horses: a racing autobiography, 1989. *Recreations:* racehorse owning, in minor way (happiest broadcasting experience commentating success of own horses, Be Friendly, 1966–67, and Attivo, 1974); travel, reading, art, food and wine. *Address:* 37 Cranmer Court, SW3 3HW. *T:* (020) 7584 2781.

O'SULLIVAN, (Carrol Austin) John (Naish), CB 1973; LLB (London); Public Trustee, 1971–75; *b* Plaistow, 24 Jan. 1915; *s* of late Dr Carrol Naish O'Sullivan and late Stephanie O'Sullivan (*née* Manning); *m* 1939, Lillian Mary (*d* 2000), *y d* of Walter Frank Yate Molineux, Ulverston; one *s* one *d*. *Educ:* Mayfield College. Admitted Solicitor, 1936. Served War of 1939–45, Gordon Highlanders and HQ Special Force SEAC (Captain). Joined Public Trustee Office, 1945; Chief Administrative Officer, 1963–66; Asst Public Trustee, 1966–71. Pres., Holborn Law Soc., 1965–66. Chm. of Governors of St Thomas More High Sch. for Boys, Westcliff-on-Sea, 1964–66. *Publications:* articles in legal jls; short stories. *Recreations:* television, reading, The Times crosswords. *Address:* 62 Hullbridge Road, South Woodham Ferrers, Chelmsford, CM3 5LJ. *T:* (01245) 322749.

O'SULLIVAN, David; Secretary-General, European Commission, since 2000; *b* 1 March 1953; *s* of Gerald and Philomena O'Sullivan; *m* 1984, Agnes O'Hare; one *s* one *d*. *Educ:* St Mary's Coll., Rathmines, Dublin; Trinity Coll. Dublin (MA 1975); Coll. of Europe, Bruges. Irish Diplomatic Service, 1977–79; entered European Commission, 1979: First Sec., Delegn to Tokyo, 1981–84; Mem., Cabinet of Comr Peter Sutherland, 1985–89; Hd, Educn and Trng Unit, 1989–93; Dep. Hd, Cabinet of Comr Padraig Flynn, 1993–96; Dir, Eur. Social Fund, 1996–99; Dir-Gen., Educn, Trng and Youth, Feb.–May 1999; Hd, Cabinet of Pres. Romano Prodi, 1999–2000. *Recreations:* tennis, music, cinema. *Address:* Rue Langeveld 87, 1180 Brussels, Belgium. *T:* (2) 2950948.

O'SULLIVAN, John; *see* O'Sullivan, C. A. J. N.

O'SULLIVAN, Michael Joseph; Director, British Council, China, since 2000; *b* 21 Dec. 1958; *s* of Patrick Joseph O'Sullivan and Mary Elizabeth O'Sullivan (*née* Herbert); *m* 1989, Moira Helen Grant; one *s* two *d*. *Educ:* Brasenose Coll., Oxford (BA Hons German and French); Wolfson Coll., Cambridge (MPhil Linguistics). VSO Teacher of English, Xiangtan, Hunan, China, 1982–84; joined British Council, 1985: E Europe and N Asia Dept, 1985–87; Asst Dir, China, 1987–90; UK planner, Corporate Affairs, 1991–93; Dir, S China (Hong Kong), 1993–95; Hd, Corporate Planning, 1995–97; Policy Dir, Asia Pacific, 1997–2000. *Recreations:* music, football. *Address:* Cultural and Education Section, British Embassy, Beijing, People's Republic of China.

O'SULLIVAN, Prof. Patrick Edmund, OBE 1988; PhD; CEng; FInstE; Haden-Pilkington Professor of Environmental Design and Engineering (formerly of Environmental Design), and Dean, Faculty of the Built Environment, University College London, since 1989, (Head of Bartlett School, 1989–99); *b* 28 March 1937; *s* of Daniel O'Sullivan and Margaret Cecilia (*née* Mansfield); *m* 1963, Diana Grimshaw; three *s* one *d*. *Educ:* Finchley Catholic Grammar Sch.; Leeds Univ. (BSc), Durham Univ. (PhD). FCIBSE 1975. University of Newcastle upon Tyne: DSIR Post-Doctoral Res. Fellow, 1963–64; Sen. Res. Fellow in Bldg Sci., 1964–66; Lectr, 1966–70; Sen. Lectr, 1970; Prof. of Architectural Sci., UWIST, 1970–89. Chm., Bldg Regulation Adv. Cttee, DETR, 2000–01. Hon. FRIBA; Hon. FCIBSE 2000. MIOA 1975. Gold Medal, RSH, 1999. *Publications:* Insulation and Fenestration, 1967; Global Warming and the Built Environment, 1994; articles in learned jls. *Recreations:* swimming, riding, walking, theatre, bridge. *Address:* The Bartlett School of Graduate Studies, University College London, Gower Street, WC1E 6BT. *T:* (020) 7679 5916. *Club:* Farmers.

O'SULLIVAN, Sally Angela; Chief Executive, Cabal Communications, since 1998; *b* 26 July 1949; *d* of Lorraine and Joan Connell; *m* 1st, 1973, Thaddeus O'Sullivan (marr. diss.); 2nd, 1980, Charles Martin Wilson, *qv*; (marr. diss. 2001) one *s* one *d*. *Educ:* Ancaster House Sch.; Trinity Coll., Dublin (BA). Dep. Editor, Woman's World, 1977–78; Women's Editor: Daily Record, 1980; Sunday Standard, 1981; Editor, Options, 1982–88; Launch Editor, Country Homes & Interiors, 1986; Editor: She, 1989; Harpers & Queen, 1989–91; Editor-in-Chief: Good Housekeeping, 1991–95; Ideal Home, Homes & Ideas, Woman & Home, Homes & Gardens, Country Homes & Interiors, Beautiful Homes, Living, etc, 1996–98. Non-executive Director: London Transport, 1995–2000; Anglian Water, 1996–. Member: Broadcasting Standards Council, 1994–; Foresight Retail and Consumer Services Panel, 1999–. Magazine Editor of the Year, 1986 and 1994. *Recreations:* family, horses, farming. *Address:* Cabal Communications, 374 Euston Road, NW1 3BL. *T:* (020) 7554 5700.
See also Sir M. B. Connell.

O'SULLIVAN, Hon. Victoria; *see* Glendinning, Hon. V.

OSWALD, Prof. Andrew John, DPhil; Professor of Economics, Warwick University, since 1996; *b* 27 Nov. 1953; *s* of Ian Oswald and late Joan Oswald (*née* Thomsett); *m* 1975, Coral Simpson; two *d*. *Educ:* Hollywood High Sch., Perth, Aust.; Currie High Sch., Edinburgh; Stirling Univ. (BA); Strathclyde Univ. (MSc); Nuffield Coll., Oxford (DPhil 1980). Lectr, Balliol Coll., Res. Officer at Inst. of Econs and Stats, and Jun. Res. Fellow, St John's Coll., Oxford Univ., 1979–82; Vis. Lectr, Princeton Univ., 1983–84; Jun. Res. Fellow, St John's Coll., Oxford, 1985–86; Sen. Res. Fellow, Centre for Lab Econs, LSE, 1987–98; De Walt Ankeny Prof. of Econs, Dartmouth Coll., USA, 1989–91; Sen. Res. Fellow, Centre for Econ. Performance, LSE, 1992–95. Tassie Medallion, Stirling Univ., 1975; Lester Prize, Princeton Univ., 1995; Medal, Univ. of Helsinki, 1996. *Publications:* (with A. Carruth) Pay Determination and Industrial Prosperity, 1989; (with D. Blanchflower) The Wage Curve, 1994; contrib. numerous articles to jls. *Recreations:* walking, racquet sports. *Address:* Economics Department, Warwick University, Coventry CV4 7AL. *T:* (024) 7652 3510.

OSWALD, Lady Angela Mary Rose, CVO 2001 (LVO 1993); Woman of the Bedchamber to HM Queen Elizabeth the Queen Mother, since 1983; *b* 21 May 1938; *d* of 6th Marquess of Exeter, KCMG, and Lady Mary Burghley, *d* of 7th Duke of Buccleuch, KT; *m* 1958, Sir (William Richard) Michael Oswald, *qv*; one *s* one *d*. *Educ:* Winceby House Sch., Bexhill. Extra Woman of the Bedchamber to HM Queen Elizabeth the Queen Mother, 1981–83. Freeman, City of London, 1995. *Address:* The Old Rectory, Weasenham St Peter, King's Lynn, Norfolk PE32 2TB. *T:* (01328) 838311.

OSWALD, Adm. of the Fleet Sir (John) Julian (Robertson), GCB 1989 (KCB 1987); Director: James Fisher & Sons plc, since 1993; Marine and General Mutual Life Assurance, since 1994; Chairman: Aerosystems International, since 1995; Green Issues Communications, since 1999; *b* 11 Aug. 1933; *s* of George Hamilton Oswald and Margaret Elliot Oswald (*née* Robertson), Newmore, Invergordon; *m* 1958, Veronica Therese Dorette Thompson; two *s* three *d*. *Educ:* Beaudesert Park, Minchinhampton; Britannia RNC, Dartmouth. Junior Officer, 1951; served in HM Ships Devonshire, Vanguard, Verulam, Newfoundland, Jewel, Victorious, Naiad; specialised in Gunnery, 1960; Commanded HMS Yarnton, 1962–63, HMS Bacchante, 1971–72; MoD, 1972–75; RCDS, 1976; Commanded HMS Newcastle, 1977–79; RN Presentation Team, 1979–80; Captain, Britannia RNC, 1980–82; ACDS (Progs), 1982–84; ACDS (Policy and Nuclear), 1985; Flag Officer, Third Flotilla, and Comdr, Anti-Submarine Warfare, Striking Fleet, 1985–87; C-in-C, Fleet, Allied C-in-C, Channel, and C-in-C, E Atlantic, 1987–89; First Sea Lord and Chief of Naval Staff, and First and Principal Naval ADC to the Queen, 1989–93. Vice-Chm., S and W RHA, 1993–96. Vice President: RUSI, 1992–; World Ship Trust, 1997–; Mem., European Atlantic Gp, 1988–. Chairman: Nat. Historic Ships Cttee, 1995–; Ends of the Earth, 1996–; Maritime Trust, 1994–; Naval Rev., 1999–. Trustee, Nat. Maritime Mus., 1995–. President: Jellicoe Sea Cadets, Newcastle, 1979–96; Invergordon Br., RBL, 1992–; Assoc. of Royal Naval Officers, 1993–; Sea Cadet Assoc., 1994–; Trident Trust, 1993–; Officers' Assoc., 1994–; Frinton Soc., 1993–99. Member: Mensa, 1964–; Catholic Union, 1987–. Book reviewer for various publications. FRSA 1995. Hon. DBA CNAA, 1992; Hon. LLD Portsmouth, 2000. *Publications:* The Royal Navy—Today and Tomorrow, 1993; articles on strategy and defence policy. *Recreations:* tennis, gliding, walking, stamp collecting, family, fishing. *Address:* c/o Naval Secretary, Victory Building, HM Naval Base, Portsmouth PO1 3LS.

OSWALD, Sir Michael; *see* Oswald, Sir W. R. M.

OSWALD, Dr Neville Christopher, TD 1946; MD Cantab 1946; FRCP 1947; retired 1975; formerly: Consultant Physician: St Bartholomew's Hospital; Brompton Hospital; King Edward VII's Hospital for Officers, London; King Edward VII's Hospital, Midhurst; *b* 1 Aug. 1910; *s* of late Col Christopher Percy Oswald, CMG; *m* 1st, 1941, Patricia Rosemary Joyce Cooke (*d* 1947); one *s* one *d*; 2nd, 1948, Marjorie Mary Sinclair; one *d*. *Educ:* Clifton Coll.; Queens' Coll., Cambridge. Research Fellow, USA, 1938–39. Royal Army Medical Corps, 1939–45. Hon. Physician to the Queen, 1956–58; Hon. Consultant in Diseases of the Chest to the Army, 1972–75. Hon. Col, 17th (London) General Hospital RAMC (TA), 1963–70, 217 (Eastern) General Hospital RAMC (V), 1967–70. President: British Tuberculosis Assoc., 1965–67; Thoracic Soc., 1974. DL Greater London, 1973–78. RCP: Mitchell Lectr; Tudor Edwards Lectr. *Publications:* Recent Trends in Chronic Bronchitis, 1958; Diseases of the Respiratory System, 1962; many articles upon respiratory diseases. *Recreations:* travel, golf. *Address:* 4 St Martins Square, Chichester, West Sussex PO19 1NT. *T:* (01243) 784457.

OSWALD, Richard Anthony; Deputy Health Service Commissioner, 1989–96; *b* 12 Jan. 1941; *s* of late Denis Geoffrey Oswald and Dorothy Lettice Oswald (*née* Shaw); *m* 1963, Janet Iris Penticost; three *s* one *d* (and one *d* decd). *Educ:* The Leys School, Cambridge. DipHSM, MHSM, 1966. NHS admin. posts, 1961–77; Dist Administrator, Leeds West, 1977–84; Gen. Manager, Leeds Western HA, 1985–89. Trustee, CHASE Children's Hospice Service. *Recreations:* acting, bird-watching, DIY. *Address:* Wymarks Cottage, Brighton Road, Shermanbury, Horsham, W Sussex RH13 8HQ. *T:* (01403) 711961.

OSWALD, Sir (William Richard) Michael, KCVO 1998 (CVO 1988 LVO 1979); Racing Manager for Queen Elizabeth the Queen Mother, since 1970; *b* 21 April 1934; *s* of Lt-Col William Alexander Hugh Oswald, ERD and Rose-Marie (*née* Leahy); *m* 1958, Lady Angela Mary Rose Cecil, (*see* Lady A. M. R. Oswald); one *s* one *d*. *Educ:* Eton; King's College, Cambridge (MA). 2nd Lieut The King's Own Royal Regt, 1953; Captain, Royal Fusiliers (TA), 1957. Manager, Lordship and Egerton Studs, 1962–70; Manager, 1970–97, Dir, 1998–99, Royal Studs. Mem. Council, Thoroughbred Breeders' Assoc., 1964–2001 (Pres., 1996–2001); Chm., Bloodstock Industry Cttee, Animal Health Trust, 1989–; Trustee, British Equine Veterinary Assoc. Trust, 1998–. Mem., Jockey Club. Hon. DSc De Montfort, 1997. *Recreations:* shooting, painting, military history. *Address:* The Old Rectory, Weasenham St Peter, King's Lynn, Norfolk PE32 2TB. *T:* (01328) 838311, *Fax:* (01328) 838264; The Royal Studs, Sandringham, Norfolk PE35 6EF. *T:* (01485) 540588. *Club:* Army and Navy.
See also Major Sir F. J. Matheson of Matheson, Bt.

OTAKA, Tadaaki, Hon. CBE 1997; Music Advisor and Chief Conductor, Sapporo Symphony Orchestra, since 1998; Music Advisor and Principal Conductor, Kioi Sinfonietta, Tokyo, since 1995; Director, Britten Pears Orchestra, since 1998; *b* 8 Nov. 1947; *s* of Hisatada and Misaoko Otaka; *m* 1978, Yukiko. *Educ:* Toho Music Coll., Tokyo; Vienna Acad. Chief Conductor, Tokyo Philharmonic Orch., 1974–91, now Conductor Laureate; Conductor, Sapporo SO, 1981–86; Principal Conductor, BBC Nat. Orch. of Wales, 1987–95, now Conductor Laureate; Chief Conductor, Yomiuri Nippon SO, 1992–98. Suntory Award (Japan), 1992. *Recreations:* fishing, cooking, computer. *Address:* c/o Askonas Holt Ltd, Lonsdale Chambers, 27 Chancery Lane, WC2A 1PF. *T:* (020) 7400 1700.

O'TOOLE, Dr Barbara Maria; Member (Lab) North East Region, European Parliament, since 1999; *b* 24 Feb. 1960. *Educ:* Convent of the Sacred Heart, Fenham, Newcastle upon Tyne; Newcastle upon Tyne Poly. (BA Hons 1983); Univ. of Newcastle upon Tyne (PhD 1994). Lecturer: Postgrad. Sch. For Advanced Urban Studies, Univ. of Bristol, 1991–94; in Politics, Univ. of Newcastle upon Tyne, 1994–97; Hd, Policy Promotion, Local Govt Internat. Bureau, 1997–99. *Publications:* Prélèvement Obligatoire: a transitional comparison of European local taxation systems, 1991; Rebuilding the City: property led regeneration in the UK, 1992; An Evaluation of the Castlemilk Initiative for the Scottish Office, 1995; Regulation Theory and the British State, 1996. *Address:* (office) 7 Palmersville, Newcastle upon Tyne NE12 9HN. *T:* (0191) 256 6066; (office) European Parliament, Rue Wiertz, 1047 Brussels, Belgium. *T:* (2) 2845362.

O'TOOLE, (Seamus) Peter; actor; *b* 2 Aug. 1932; *s* of Patrick Joseph O'Toole; *m* 1960, Sian Phillips, *qv* (marr. diss. 1979); two *d*; *m* 1983, Karen Brown (marr. diss.); one *s*. *Educ:* Royal Academy of Dramatic Art. With Bristol Old Vic Company, 1955–58; first appearance on London stage as Peter Shirley in Major Barbara, Old Vic, 1956. Associate Dir, Old Vic Co., 1980. *Plays include:* Oh, My Papa!, Garrick, 1957; The Long and the Short and the Tall, Royal Court and New, 1959; season with Shakespeare Memorial Theatre Company, Stratford-on-Avon, 1960; Baal, Phœnix, 1963; Hamlet, National Theatre, 1963; Ride a Cock Horse, Piccadilly, 1965; Juno and the Paycock, Man and Superman, Pictures in the Hallway, Gaiety, Dublin, 1966; Waiting for Godot, Happy Days (dir.), Abbey, Dublin, 1969; Uncle Vanya, Plunder, The Apple Cart, Judgement, Bristol Old Vic, 1973; Uncle Vanya, Present Laughter, Chicago, 1978; Macbeth, Old Vic, 1980; Man and Superman, Haymarket, 1982; Pygmalion, Shaftesbury, 1984, Yvonne Arnaud, Guildford, and NY, 1987; The Apple Cart, Haymarket, 1986; Jeffrey Bernard is Unwell, Apollo, 1989, Shaftesbury, 1991, Old Vic, 1999; Our Song, Apollo, 1992. *Films include:* Kidnapped, 1959; The Day They Robbed the Bank of England, 1959; The Savage Innocents, 1960; Lawrence of Arabia, 1962; Becket, 1963; Lord Jim, 1964; What's New, Pussycat, 1965; How to Steal a Million, 1966; The Bible . . . in the Beginning, 1966; The Night of the Generals, 1967; Great Catherine, 1968; The Lion in Winter, 1968; Goodbye Mr Chips, 1969; Brotherly Love, 1970; Murphy's War, 1971; Under Milk Wood, 1971;

The Ruling Class, 1972; Man of La Mancha, 1972; Rosebud, 1975; Man Friday, 1975; Foxtrot, 1975; The Stunt Man, 1977; Coup d'Etat, 1977; Zulu Dawn, 1978; Power Play, 1978; The Antagonists, 1981; My Favorite Year, 1981; Supergirl, 1983; Club Paradise, 1986; The Last Emperor, 1987; High Spirits, 1988; Creator, 1990; King Ralph, 1991; Wings of Fame, 1991; Rebecca's Daughters, 1992; Fairytale: the true story, 1997; *television:* Rogue Male, 1976; Strumpet City, 1979; Masada, 1981; Svengali, 1982; Pygmalion, 1983; Kim, 1983; Banshee, 1986; The Dark Angel, 1989; Civvies, 1992; Coming Home (serial), 1998. *Publications:* Loitering With Intent: the Child (autobiog.), 1992; Loitering With Intent: the Apprentice, 1996. *Address:* c/o William Morris Agency, Stratton House, Stratton Street, W1X 5FE. *Club:* Garrick.

OTTAWA, Archbishop of, (RC), since 1989; **Most Rev. Marcel Gervais;** *b* 21 Sept. 1931; *s* of Frédéric Pierre Gervals and Marie-Louise Beaudry. *Educ:* St Peter's Seminary, London, Ont.; Angelicum Athenæum Pontifical Inst., Rome; Pontifical Biblical Inst., Rome; Ecole Biblique et Archéologique Française de Jérusalem. Ordained priest, 1958; Prof. of Sacred Scriptures, St Peter's Seminary, London, 1962–76; Dir of Divine Word Internat. Centre of Religious Educn, London, 1974–80; Auxiliary Bishop of London, Ontario, 1980–85; Bishop of Sault Sainte-Marie, 1985–89; Coadjutor Archbishop of Ottawa, June–Sept. 1989. Pres., Canadian Conf. of Catholic Bishops, 1991. *Address:* Archbishop's Residence, 1247 Kilborn Place, Ottawa, ON K1H 6K9, Canada. *T:* 7385025.

OTTAWA, Bishop of; since 1999; **Rt Rev. Peter Robert Coffin;** *b* 31 May 1946; *s* of Gerald R. A. Coffin and Jean Mary Thorburn Coffin (*née* Edwards); *m* 1972, Deborah Creighton; one *d. Educ:* Univ. of King's Coll., Halifax, NS (BA); Trinity Coll., Toronto (STB); Carleton Univ., Ottawa (MA Internat. Affairs). Ordained deacon, 1971, priest 1971; Asst Curate, St Matthew's, Ottawa, 1971–73; Lectr, House of the Epiphany, Kuching, Sarawak, E Malaysia, 1973–76; Incumbent, Parish of Hull, Quebec, 1976–84; Archdeacon of W Quebec, 1978–84; Incumbent, Christ Church, Bell's Corners, Ottawa (Nepean), 1984–90; Archdeacon of Carleton, 1986–90; Rector of Christ Church Cathedral, Ottawa and Dean of Ottawa, 1990–99. Hon. DD Univ. of King's Coll., Halifax, NS, 1998. *Address:* 71 Bronson Avenue, Ottawa, ON K1R 6G6, Canada. *T:* (613) 2337741. *Club:* National Press (Ottawa).

OTTAWAY, Richard Geoffrey James; MP (C) Croydon South, since 1992; *b* 24 May 1945; *s* of late Professor Christopher Ottaway, PhD, FRCVS and Grace Ottaway; *m* 1982, Nicola E. Kisch. *Educ:* Backwell Secondary Modern School, Somerset; Bristol University. LLB (Hons). Entered RN as an Artificer apprentice, 1961; commissioned and entered RNC, Dartmouth, 1966; served with Western Fleet, HM Ships Beechampton, Nubian and Eagle, 1967–70; Bristol Univ., 1971–74; articled to Norton Rose Botterell & Roche, 1974; admitted Solicitor, 1977; specialist in international, maritime and commercial law; Partner, William A. Crump & Son, 1981–87. Dir, Coastal Europe Ltd, 1990–95. MP (C) Nottingham N, 1983–87; contested (C) same seat, 1987. PPS to Ministers of State, FCO, 1985–87, to Pres. of BoT, 1992–95, to Dep. Prime Minister, 1995; an Asst Govt Whip, 1995–96; a Lord Comr of HM Treasury (Govt Whip), 1996–97; an Opposition Whip, 1997; front bench opposition spokesman: local govt and London, 1997–98; defence, 1999–2000; Treasury, 2000–01. Chm., All-Party Parly Gp on Population and Development, 1992–95. A Vice-Chm., Cons. Party, 1998–99. *Publications:* (jtly) Road to Reform, 1987; papers on combating internat. maritime fraud, on financial matters and on the environment. *Recreations:* jazz, ski-ing, yacht racing. *Address:* c/o House of Commons, SW1A 0AA. *Club:* Royal Corinthian Yacht.

OTTEWILL, Prof. Ronald Harry, OBE 1989; PhD; FRS 1982; FRSC; Leverhulme Professor of Physical Chemistry, 1982–92, now Emeritus, and Senior Research Fellow, since 1996, University of Bristol; *b* 8 Feb. 1927; *m* Ingrid Geraldine Roe; one *s* one *d. Educ:* Southall Grammar Sch.; Queen Mary Coll., London (BSc 1948; PhD 1951); Fitzwilliam Coll., Cambridge (MA 1955; PhD 1956). Sen. Asst in Res., 1955–58, Asst Dir of Res., 1958–63, Dept of Colloid Sci., Cambridge Univ.; Bristol University: Lectr, 1964–66; Reader, 1966–70; Prof. of Colloid Science, 1970–82; Head of Dept of Physical Chem., 1973–92; Dean, Faculty of Science, 1988–90; Head, Sch. of Chem., 1990–92. Chm., SERC Neutron Beam Res. Cttee, 1982–85. Vice Pres., Faraday Soc., 1986–89, 1991–99 (Pres., 1989–91; Hon. Treas., 1985–89). Lectures: A. E. Alexander, RACI, 1982; Liversidge, RSC, 1985–86; Canadian High Polymer Forum, 1987; Langmuir, ACS, 1988; Rideal, RSC/SCI, 1990. Medal for Surface and Colloid Chemistry, RSC, 1972; Wolfgang Ostwald Medal, Kolloid Gesellschaft, W Germany, 1979; Bude Medal, Collège de France, Paris, 1981; Colloid and Interface Science Gp Medal, Faraday Div., RSC, 1993. *Publications:* contribs to learned jls. *Address:* School of Chemistry, The University, Bristol BS8 1TS.

OTTON, Sir Geoffrey (John), KCB 1981 (CB 1978); Second Permanent Secretary, Department of Health and Social Security, 1979–86, retired; *b* 10 June 1927; *s* of late John Alfred Otton and Constance Alma Otton; *m* 1952, Hazel Lomas (*née* White); one *s* one *d. Educ:* Christ's Hosp.; St John's Coll., Cambridge (MA). Home Office, 1950–71: (seconded to Cabinet Office, 1959–61; Principal Private Sec. to Home Sec., 1963–65); Dept of Health and Social Security, 1971–86. *Recreation:* music. *Address:* 72 Cumberland Road, Bromley, Kent BR2 0PW. *T:* (020) 8460 9610.

OTTON, Rt Hon. Sir Philip (Howard), Kt 1983; PC 1995; a Lord Justice of Appeal, 1995–2001; *b* 28 May 1933; *o s* of late Henry Albert Otton and Leah Otton, Kenilworth; *m* 1965, Helen Margaret, *d* of late P. W. Bates, Stourbridge; two *s* one *d. Educ:* Bablake School, Coventry; Birmingham Univ. LLB 1954. 2nd Lieut, 3rd Dragoon Guards, 1955–57. Called to the Bar, Gray's Inn, 1955, Bencher 1983; QC 1975. Dep. Chm., Beds QS, 1970–72; Junior Counsel to the Treasury (Personal Injuries), 1970–75; a Recorder of the Crown Court, 1972–83; Judge of the High Court, QBD, 1983–95; Presiding Judge, Midland and Oxford Circuit, 1986–88; Judge in Charge of Official Referees Courts, 1991–95. Chairman: Royal Brompton and National Heart and Lung Hospitals SHA, 1991–94; Royal Brompton and Harefield (formerly Royal Brompton Hosp.) NHS Trust, 1994–; Nat. Heart and Lung Inst., 1991–95. President: Soc. of Construction Law, 1995–; Bar Disability Panel, 1996–; Professional Negligence Bar Assoc., 1997–; Personal Injury Bar Assoc., 2000–. Mem., Transitional Med. Bd, Imperial Coll. Sch. of Medicine, 1995–. Governor, Nat. Heart and Chest Hosps, 1979–85. Trustee, Migraine Trust, 1992–98. Pres., Holdsworth Club, Birmingham Univ., 2000–. Fellow: Inst. of Advanced Legal Studies, 1999; Amer. Law Inst., 2000; Hon. Fellow, Inst. of Judicial Admin, Birmingham Univ., 1995. Hon. Mem., Amer. Bar Assoc. FCIArb 1994; FRSocMed 1998. Hon. LLD Nottingham Trent, 1997. *Recreations:* theatre, opera, music. *Address:* c/o Royal Courts of Justice, Strand, WC2A 2LL. *Clubs:* Garrick, Pilgrims.

OTTON-GOULDER, Catharine Anne; QC 2000; a Recorder, since 2000; *b* 9 April 1955; *e d* of Prof. Michael Douglas Goulder, DD and Alison Clare (*née* Gardner). *Educ:* Somerville Coll., Oxford (BA 1st Cl. Hons Lit. Hum. 1977). Admitted as solicitor, 1980; called to the Bar, Lincoln's Inn, 1983; Mem., Brick Court Chambers, 1984–; Asst Recorder, 1997–2000. Reader, C of E, 1998–. *Address:* Brick Court Chambers, 7–8 Essex Street, WC2R 3LD.

OTUNGA, HE Cardinal Maurice; *see* Nairobi, Archbishop of, (RC).

OUELLET, Hon. André; PC (Can.) 1972; QC (Can.) 1992; President and Chief Executive Officer, Canada Post Corporation, since 1999 (Chairman, 1996–99); *b* St Pascal, Quebec, 6 April 1939; *s* of Albert Ouellet and Rita Turgeon; *m* 1965, Édith Pagé; two *s* two *d. Educ:* Univ. of Ottawa (BA 1960); Univ. of Sherbrooke (LLL 1963). Called to the Bar. MP (L): Montreal-Papineau, 1967–84; Papineau-St-Michel, 1988–96; PMG, 1972–74; Minister: for Consumer and Corporate Affairs, 1974–76; of Urban Affairs, 1976–78; of Public Works, 1978–79; PMG 1980–84, and Minister for Consumer and Corporate Affairs, 1980–83; Minister of Labor, 1983–84; Minister of State for Regl Economic Develt, 1984; Pres., Privy Council and Govt Leader in H of C, 1984; Minister of Foreign Affairs, 1993–96. Hon. Dr Ottawa, 1995. *Recreations:* tennis, ski-ing, reading, theatre. *Address:* Canada Post Corporation, 2701 Riverside Drive, Suite N1250, Ottawa, ON K1A 0B1, Canada.

OUGHTON, John Raymond Charles; Deputy Under-Secretary of State, since 1998, Deputy Chief of Defence Logistics, since 1999, Ministry of Defence; *b* 21 Sept. 1952. *Educ:* Reading Sch.; University Coll., Oxford (BA Mod. Hist. 1974). Joined MoD, 1974; Mem. UK Delegn, UN Law of Sea Conf., 1978; Asst Pvte Sec. to Minister of State for Defence, 1978–80; Principal, 1980; on secondment to Canadian Govt, 1980–81; Sales Policy, 1981–83; Office of Personal Advr to Sec. of State for Defence, 1984; Pvte Sec. to Minister for the Armed Forces, 1984–86; Sen. Principal, Directorate of Procurement Policy, 1986–87; Asst Sec., Dir of Procurement Policy, 1988–89; Head of Resources and Progs (Navy), 1990–93; Office of Public Service, Cabinet Office: Under Sec. and Head, Govt Efficiency Unit, 1993–98; Dir, Efficiency and Effectiveness Gp, 1996–98; Hd, Chief of Defence Logistics Implementation Team, MoD, 1998–99. FRSA. *Recreations:* squash, tennis, travel, watching cricket and football. *Address:* HQ Defence Logistics Organisation, Ministry of Defence, Management Suite, Block E, Ensleigh, Bath BA1 5AB. *T:* (01225) 467125, *Fax:* (01225) 467764. *Clubs:* Oxford and Cambridge; Tottenham Hotspur Football, Middlesex CC.

OULTON, Sir (Antony) Derek (Maxwell), GCB 1989 (KCB 1984; CB 1979); QC 1985; MA, PhD; Permanent Secretary, Lord Chancellor's Office, and Clerk of the Crown in Chancery, 1982–89; barrister-at-law; Life Fellow, Magdalene College, Cambridge, since 1995 (Fellow, 1990–95); *b* 14 Oct. 1927; *y s* of late Charles Cameron Courtenay Oulton and Elizabeth, *d* of T. H. Maxwell, KC; *m* 1955, Margaret Geraldine (*d* 1989), *d* of late Lt-Col G. S. Oxley, MC, 60th Rifles; one *s* three *d. Educ:* St Edward's Sch., Oxford; King's Coll., Cambridge (scholar; BA (1st Cl.), MA; PhD 1974). Called to Bar, Gray's Inn, 1952, Bencher, 1982; in private practice, Kenya, 1952–60; Private Sec. to Lord Chancellor, 1961–65; Sec., Royal Commn on Assizes and Quarter Sessions, 1966–69; Asst Solicitor, 1969–75. Dep. Sec., 1976–82, and Dep. Clerk of the Crown in Chancery, 1977–82, Lord Chancellor's Office. Vis. Prof. in Law, Bristol Univ., 1990–91. Chm., Mental Health Foundn Cttee on the Mentally Disordered Offender, 1989–92. Trustee, Nat. Gallery, 1989–96. Pres., Electricity Arbitration Assoc., 1990–. Mem., Adv. Council, Inst. of Criminology, Cambridge, 1992–. *Publications:* (jtly) Legal Aid and Advice, 1971; (ed) Lewis, We the Navigators, 2nd edn 1994; contrib. New DNB. *Address:* Magdalene College, Cambridge CB3 0AG. *T:* (01223) 332100.

OULTON, Claire Marion, MA; Headmistress, Benenden School, since 2000; *b* 23 July 1961; *d* of Prof. L. Zisman and S. Zisman; *m* 1986, Nicholas Oulton; two *d. Educ:* Somerville Coll., Oxford (BA Hons History 1983; MA 1994); KCL (PGCE 1984). Teacher of History, Benenden Sch., 1984–88; Head of History, Charterhouse, 1988–94; Headmistress, St Catherine's Sch., Guildford, 1994–2000. *Address:* Benenden School, Benenden, Cranbrook, Kent TN17 4AA. *T:* (01580) 240592.

OUNSTED, John, MA Cantab; HM Inspector of Schools, 1971–81, retired; *b* London, 24 May 1919; *e s* of late Rev. Laurence J. Ounsted, Dorchester Abbey, Oxon (ordained 1965; formerly with Sun Life Assurance) and Vera, *d* of E. S. Hopkins, India Office; *m* 1940, Irene, 3rd *d* of late Rev. Alfred Newns; one *s* four *d. Educ:* Winchester (Scholar); Trinity College, Cambridge (Major Scholar). Math. Tripos Part I, 1st Class; Science Tripos Part II, 1st Class; Senior Scholarship, Trinity College. Assistant Master, King Edward's School, Birmingham, 1940–48; Headmaster, Leighton Park School, 1948–70. First layman ever to be Select Preacher, Oxford Univ., 1964. Page Scholarship to visit USA, 1965. Vice-Pres., Botanical Soc. of British Isles, 1989–93 (Hon. Mem., 1997). Liveryman, Worshipful Company of Mercers (Trustee, Educnl Trust Fund, 1957–). *Publications:* verses from various languages in the 2 vols of Translation, 1945 and 1947; contributions to Watsonia, The Proceedings of the Botanical Society of the British Isles, and various other educational and botanical periodicals. *Recreations:* botany, camping, being overtaken when motoring. *Address:* Apple Tree Cottage, Woodgreen Common, Fordingbridge, Hants SP6 2BD. *T:* (01725) 512271.

OUSELEY, Baron *cr* 2001 (Life Peer), of Peckham Rye in the London Borough of Southwark; **Herman George Ouseley,** Kt 1997; Managing Director, Different Realities Partnership Ltd, since 2000; Director, Focus Consultancy Ltd, since 2000; *b* 24 March 1945. Various public service posts, 1963–86; Race Relations Adviser: Lambeth BC, 1979–81; GLC, 1981–84; Dir of Educn, 1986–88, Chief Exec., 1988–90, ILEA; Chief Exec., London Borough of Lambeth, 1990–93; Chm., CRE, 1993–2000. Chair, Policy Res. Inst. on Ageing and Ethnicity, Univ. of Bradford, 1997–. Council Member: Inst. of Race Relations, 1990–; Inst. of Educn, Univ. of London, 1995–; Adv. Council Mem., Prince's Youth Business Trust, 1993–; Chair: Presentation Educn and Employment Charitable Trust, 1997–; Caribbean Adv. Gp, 2000; Kick It Out, 2000; Patron, Presentation Housing Assoc., 1990–. Non-exec. Dir, Brooknight Security, 1995–. *Publications:* The System, 1981; pamphlets and articles on local government, public services, employment, training and race equality issues. *Address:* (office) Different Realities Partnership, Brooknight Group, 254 High Street, Croydon, Surrey CR0 1NF.

OUSELEY, Hon. Sir Duncan (Brian Walter), Kt 2000; **Hon. Mr Justice Ouseley;** a Judge of the High Court, Queen's Bench Division, since 2000; *b* 24 Feb. 1950; *s* of late Maurice and Margaret Ouseley; *m* 1974, Suzannah Price; three *s. Educ:* Trinity Sch., Croydon; Fitzwilliam Coll., Cambridge (MA); University Coll. London (LLM). Called to the Bar, Gray's Inn, 1973 (Atkin Scholar 1972); Bencher 2000; Junior Counsel to the Crown, Common Law, 1986–92; QC 1992; a Recorder, 1994–2000; QC (NI) 1997; Jt Hd of Chambers, 2000. Chairman, Examination in Public Shropshire Structure Plan, 1985, Hampshire Structure Plan, 1991. Vice-Chm. Planning and Envmt, Bar Assoc., 2000. *Recreations:* family, sport, music, wine. *Address:* Royal Courts of Justice, Strand, WC2A 2LL.

OUTRAM, Sir Alan James, 5th Bt *cr* 1858; MA; *b* 15 May 1937; *s* of late James Ian Outram and late Evelyn Mary Littlehales; *S* great-uncle, 1945; *m* 1976, Victoria Jean, *d* of late George Dickson Paton, Bexhill-on-Sea; one *s* one *d. Educ:* Spyway, Langton Matravers, Swanage; Marlborough College, Wilts; St Edmund Hall, Oxford. Harrow School: Asst Master, 1961–98; Housemaster, 1979–91; Under Master, 1992–96. Lt-Col TAVR. Pres., Dorset LTA, 1995–. *Recreations:* golf, bridge. *Heir: s* Douglas Benjamin

James Outram, *b* 15 March 1979. *Address:* Chase House, Moorside, Sturminster Newton, Dorset DT10 1HQ. *Club:* Vincent's (Oxford).

OVENDEN, John Frederick; County Councillor, Kent, since 1985 (Leader, Labour Group, 1994–97); *b* 17 Aug. 1942; *s* of late Richard Ovenden and Margaret Louise Ovenden (*née* Lucas); *m* 1963, Maureen (*née* White); one *d. Educ:* Salmestone County Primary Sch., Margate; Chatham House Grammar Sch., Ramsgate. Asst Exec. Engr, Post Office, 1961–74. MP (Lab) Gravesend, Feb. 1974–1979. Contested (Lab) Gravesham, 1983. Manager, Post Office, subseq. British Telecom, 1979–90. *Recreations:* football (Gillingham FC), cricket (Kent), theatre, gardening, books. *Club:* Gillingham Labour (Gillingham).

OVERALL, Sir John (Wallace), Kt 1968; CBE 1962; MC and Bar; architect, town planner and company director; *b* 15 July 1913; *s* of late W. Overall, Sydney; *m* 1943, Margaret J. (*d* 1988), *d* of C. W. Goodman; four *s. Educ:* Sydney Techn. College. AIF, 1940–45: CO, 1 Aust. Para. Bn (Lt-Col). Chief Architect, S Australian Housing Trust, 1946–48; private practice, Architect and Town Planner, 1949–52; Dir of Architecture, Commonwealth Dept of Works, 1952–57; Comr, Nat. Capital Develt Commn, 1958–72; Chm., Nat. Capital Planning Cttee, 1958–72; Comr, Cities Commn (Chm., Adv. Cttee), 1972–73; Principal, John Overall and Partners, 1973–81; Director: Lend Lease Corp. Ltd, 1973–83; General Property Trust, 1975–83; Alliance Holdings Ltd, 1975–83 (Chm., 1980–83); CSR Ltd, 1973–85. Mem., Parliament House Construction Authority (Commonwealth Govt of Australia), 1979–85; Chm. Assessors, Parlt House Design Competition, 1979–80. Chm. of Olympic Fine Arts Architecture and Sculpture Exhibn, Melb., 1956. Life Fellow, RAIA and API; Hon. Fellow, AIA, 1984; Pres., Austr. Inst. of Urban Studies, 1970–71. Past Pres., Canberra Legacy Club. Sydney Luker Meml Medal, 1970; Sir James Barrett Medal, 1970; Gold Medal, RAIA, 1982. *Publications:* Observations on Redevelopment Western Side of Sydney Cove, 1967; Canberra: yesterday, today and tomorrow, 1995; sundry papers to professional jls. *Recreations:* golf, tennis. *Address:* Unit 1, Kingston Tower, 9 Jardine Street, Kingston, ACT 2604, Australia. *Club:* Commonwealth (Canberra).

OVERBURY, (Henry) Colin (Barry), CBE 1993 (OBE (mil.) 1974); independent lecturer in EC Law, since 1993; Consultant in EC Law, Allen & Overy, Solicitors, since 1993; *b* 13 Jan. 1931; *s* of Stanley and Daisy Overbury; *m* 1st, 1954, Dawn Rhodes Dade (marr. diss. 1981); three *s*; 2nd, 1989, Louise Jane Rosewarne. *Educ:* Dragon Sch., Oxford; Eastbourne Coll.; Law Society's Coll. of Law. Admitted Solicitor of the Supreme Court, 1955. HM Army Legal Services, 1955–74: progressively, Captain, Major, Lt-Col; Retired List, Lt-Col, 1974. European Commission: Prin. Administrator, 1974–82; Adviser, 1982–84; Hd of Div., 1984–86; Dir, Directorate-Gen. for Competition, 1986–93, retd; Hon. Dir Gen., 1993. Sen. Fellow of the Salzburg Seminar, 1984. *Publications:* articles in Common Market Law Rev., 1977, Fordham Univ. Law Inst. Jl, 1984, 1989. *Recreations:* travel, boating, good living. *Clubs:* Lansdowne; Cercle Royal Gaulois (Brussels); Royal Harwich Yacht.

OVEREND, Prof. (William) George; Professor of Chemistry in the University of London, 1957–87, now Professor Emeritus; Master, Birkbeck College, 1979–87 (Vice-Master, 1974–79; Hon. Fellow, 1988); *b* 16 Nov. 1921; *e s* of late Harold George Overend, Shrewsbury, Shropshire; *m* 1949, Gina Olava, *y d* of late Horace Bertie Cadman, Birmingham; two *s* one *d. Educ:* Priory School, Shrewsbury; Univ. of Birmingham. BSc (Hons) 1943, PhD 1946, DSc 1954, Birmingham; CChem; FRSC (FRIC 1955). Asst Lecturer, Univ. Coll., Nottingham, 1946–47; Research Chemist with Dunlop Rubber Co. Ltd and subsequently British Rubber Producers' Assoc., 1947–49; Hon. Research Fellow, 1947–49, Lecturer in Chemistry, 1949–55, Univ. of Birmingham; Vis. Associate Prof., Pennsylvania State Univ., 1951–52; Reader in Organic Chemistry, Univ. of London, 1955–57; Hd of Dept of Chem., Birkbeck Coll., London, 1957–79. Univ. of London: Mem., Academic Council, 1963–67, 1976–79 and 1984–87; Mem., Collegiate Council, 1979–87; Mem., University Entrance and Schools Examination Council, 1966–67 and 1985–87; Mem., F and GP Cttee, 1976–87; Mem., External Cttee, 1984–87; Chm., Bd of Studies in Chemistry, 1974–76; Mem., Senate, 1976–87; Mem., Jt Cttee of Court and Senate for collective planning, 1976–79; Dean, Faculty of Science, 1978–79; Chm., Acad. Adv. Bd in Sci., 1978–79; Mem., Extra-Mural Council, 1979–87, Chm., 1983–84; Chm., Cttee for Extra-Mural Studies, 1984–87. Mem. Council, Inst. of Educn, 1979–82; Leverhulme Emeritus Fellow, 1987–89. Member Council: National Inst. of Adult Continuing Educn, 1983–88; London and E Anglian Gp for GCSE, 1986–87; Mem. Chem. Bd, 1981–84, Mem. Adv. Bd on Credit Accumulation and Transfer, 1986–87, CNAA. Rep. of South Bank Poly, Assoc. of Colls of Further and Higher Educn, 1981–91. Royal Institute of Chemistry: Examiner, 1958–62; Assessor, 1959–72; Mem., Institutions and Examinations Cttee, 1969–75 (Chm., 1976–85); Mem. Council, 1977–80; Mem. Qual. and Admissions Cttee, 1977–80; Mem. Qual. and Exam. Bd, RSC, 1980–85; Chemical Society (subseq. Royal Society of Chemistry): Mem. Council, 1967–70, 1972–77; Mem. Publications Bd, 1967–78; Hon. Sec. and Hon. Treasurer, Perkin Div., 1972–75; Vice-Pres., 1975–77; Mem., Interdivisional Council, 1972–75; Mem., Educn and Trng Bd, 1972–78; Soc. of Chemical Industry: Mem., Council, 1955–65; Mem., Finance Committee, 1956–65; Mem., Publications Cttee, 1955–65 (Hon. Sec. for publications and Chairman of Publications Committee, 1958–65); Member: Brit. Nat. Cttee for Chemistry, 1961–66, 1973–78; Brit. Nat. Cttee for Biochemistry, 1975–81; Chemical Council, 1960–63 and 1964–69 (Vice-Chm. 1964–69); European Cttee for Carbohydrate Chemists, 1970–85 (Chm.); Hon. Sec., Internat. Cttee for Carbohydrate Chemistry, 1972–75 (Pres., 1978–80); Mem., Jt IUPAC-IUB Commn on Carbohydrate Nomenclature, 1971–. Jubilee Memorial Lecturer, Society of Chemical Industry, 1959–60; Lampitt Medallist, Society of Chemical Industry, 1965; Member: Pharmacopœia Commission, 1963–81; Home Office Poisons Board, 1973–94. Governor: Polytechnic of the South Bank, 1970–91 (Chm., 1980–89; Hon. Fellow 1989); Thomas Huxley Coll., 1971–77; Mem., Council of Governors, Queen Elizabeth Coll., Univ. of London, 1983–85. Mem., Cttee of Management, Inst. of Archaeology, 1980–86. FIMgt (FBIM 1988). Hon. FCollP 1986. DUniv Open, 1988. *Publications:* The Use of Tracer Elements in Biology, 1951; papers in Nature, and Jl of Chemical Soc. *Recreation:* gardening (rose grower). *Address:* The Retreat, Nightingales Lane, Chalfont St Giles, Bucks HP8 4SR. *Clubs:* Athenæum, Royal Automobile.

OVERY, Prof. Richard James, PhD; FRHistS; FBA 2000; Professor of Modern History, King's College, London, since 1992; *b* 23 Dec. 1947; *s* of James Herbert Overy and Margaret Grace Overy (*née* Sutherland); *m* 1992, Kim Turner; two *d*, and one *s* two *d* from previous marriage. *Educ:* Sexey's Grammar Sch., Som; Gonville and Caius Coll., Cambridge (BA 1969; MA 1972; PhD 1977). Cambridge University: Res. Fellow, Churchill Coll., 1972–73; Lectr, Queens' Coll., 1973–79; Asst Univ. Lectr, 1976–79; King's College, London: Lectr, 1980–88; Reader, 1988–92. Trustee, RAF Mus. FRHistS 1997. *Publications:* William Morris, Viscount Nuffield, 1976; The Air War 1939–45, 1980; The Nazi Economic Recovery, 1982, 2nd edn 1996; Goering: the Iron Man, 1984, 2nd edn 2000; The Origins of the Second World War, 1987, 2nd edn 1998; The Road to War, 1989, 2nd edn 1999; War and Economy in the Third Reich, 1994; The Interwar Crisis 1919–1939, 1994; Why the Allies Won, 1995; The Penguin Atlas of the Third Reich, 1996, 2nd edn 2000; The Times Atlas of the Twentieth Century, 1996, 2nd edn 1999; Bomber Command 1939–45, 1997; Russia's War, 1998; (Gen. Ed.) The Times History of the World, 1999; The Battle, 2000; Interrogations: the Nazi elite in Allied hands 1945, 2001; contrib. to Econ. Hist. Rev., Jl of Strategic Studies, Past and Present, English Histl Rev., etc. *Recreations:* tennis, running, football. *Address:* Department of History, King's College London, Strand, WC2R 2LS. *T:* (020) 7848 1080. *Club:* Academy.

OWEN, family name of **Baron Owen**.

OWEN, Baron *cr* 1992 (Life Peer), of the City of Plymouth; **David Anthony Llewellyn Owen,** CH 1994; PC 1976; European Union Co-Chairman, International Conference on Former Yugoslavia, 1992–95; Chairman, Middlesex Holdings, since 1995; *b* Plympton, South Devon, 2 July 1938; *s* of Dr John William Morris Owen and Mary Llewellyn; *m* 1968, Deborah Schabert; two *s* one *d. Educ:* Bradfield College; Sidney Sussex College, Cambridge (Hon. Fellow, 1977); St Thomas' Hospital. BA 1959; MB, BChir 1962; MA 1963. St Thomas' Hospital: house appts, 1962–64; Neurological and Psychiatric Registrar, 1964–66; Research Fellow, Medical Unit, 1966–68. Contested (Lab) Torrington, 1964; MP (Lab 1966–81, SDP, 1981–92) Plymouth Sutton, 1966–74, Plymouth Devonport, 1974–92. PPS to Minister of Defence, Administration, 1967; Parly Under-Sec. of State for Defence, for RN, 1968–70; Opposition Defence Spokesman, 1970–72, resigned over EEC, 1972; Parly Under-Sec. of State, DHSS, 1974; Minister of State: DHSS, 1974–76; FCO, 1976–77; Sec. of State for Foreign and Commonwealth Affairs, 1977–79; Opposition spokesman on energy, 1979–80. Sponsored 1973 Children's Bill; ministerially responsible for 1975 Children's Act. Co-founder, SDP, 1981; Chm., Parly Cttee, SDP, 1981–82; Dep. Leader, SDP, 1982–83; Leader, SDP, 1983–87, resigned over issue of merger with Liberal Party, re-elected, 1988–92. Chm., New Europe, 1999–. Chm., Decision Technology Internat., 1970–72. Director: New Crane Publishing, 1992–; Coats Viyella plc, 1994–2001; Abbott Laboratories Inc., 1996–2001; Europe Steel.com, 2000–. Member: Independent Commn on Disarmament and Security Issues, 1980–89; Ind. Commn on Internat. Humanitarian Issues, 1983–88; Carnegie Commn on Preventing Deadly Conflict, 1994–; Eminent Persons Gp on Curbing Illicit Trafficking in Small Arms and Light Weapons, 1999–. Chm., Humanitas, 1990–2001. Governor of Charing Cross Hospital, 1966–68; Patron, Disablement Income Group, 1968–. Chancellor, Liverpool Univ., 1996–. *Publications:* (ed) A Unified Health Service, 1968; The Politics of Defence, 1972; In Sickness and in Health, 1976; Human Rights, 1978; Face the Future, 1981; A Future That Will Work, 1984; A United Kingdom, 1986; Personally Speaking to Kenneth Harris, 1987; Our NHS, 1988; Time to Declare (autobiog.), 1991; (ed) Seven Ages (anthology of poetry), 1992; Balkan Odyssey, 1995; articles in Lancet, Neurology, Clinical Science, and Foreign Affairs. *Recreation:* sailing. *Address:* 78 Narrow Street, Limehouse, E14 8BP. *T:* (020) 7987 5441, (office) (020) 7787 2751, *Fax:* (01442) 876108.

OWEN, Albert; MP (Lab) Ynys Môn, since 2001; *b* 10 Aug. 1959; *s* of late William Owen and Doreen Owen (*née* Woods); *m* 1983, Angela Margaret Magee; two *d. Educ:* Holyhead Comprehensive Sch.; Coleg Harlech; Univ. of York (BA Hons Politics 1997). Merchant seafarer, 1975–92; full-time educn, 1992–97; Manager, Centre for the Unwaged (advice, trng and information centre), 1997–2001. *Recreations:* travel by train, cooking, gardening, walking, running, cycling. *Address:* House of Commons, SW1A 0AA; (constituency office) Ty Cledwyn, 18 Thomas Street, Holyhead, Anglesey LL65 1RR. *T:* (01407) 765750.

OWEN, (Alfred) David, OBE 1997; Group Chairman, Rubery Owen Holdings Ltd, since 1975; *b* 26 Sept. 1936; *m* 1966, Ethne (*née* Sowman); two *s* one *d. Educ:* Brocksford Hall; Oundle; Emmanuel Coll., Cambridge Univ. (MA). Joined Rubery Owen Gp, 1960; Gen. Man., Rubery Owen Motor Div., 1962–67; Dep. Man. Dir, Rubery Owen & Co. Ltd, 1967; Acting Chm. and Man. Dir, Rubery Owen Holdings Ltd, 1969; Director: Brooke Industrial Holdings (formerly Brooke Tool Engineering (Holdings)) plc, 1968–2000; Severn Valley Railways (Holdings) plc, 1984–; Blackwell Science Ltd, 1993–. Warden, Birmingham Assay Office, 1999–. Member: Council, Univ. of Aston, 1981–; Bd, British Library, 1982–90; Bd, Nat. Exhibn Centre, 1982–; Bd, Castle Vale Housing Action Trust, 1993–2000. President: Comité de Liaison Eur. de la Distrib. Ind. de Pièces de rechange et équipements pour Autos, 1988–90; Comité de Liaison de la Construction de Carrosseries et de Remorques, 1998–99; Commercial Trailer Assoc., 1992–. Hon. DSc Aston, 1988; DUniv Central England, 2000. *Recreations:* walking, photography, music, industrial archaeology, local history, collecting books. *Address:* Mill Dam House, Mill Lane, Aldridge, Walsall, West Midlands WS9 0NB. *T:* (office) (0121) 526 3131. *Club:* National.

OWEN, Alun, MC 1945; retired; Under-Secretary, Land Use Planning Group, Welsh Office, 1975–79; *b* 14 March 1919; *m* 1946, Rhona Evelyn Griffiths; one *s* four *d. Educ:* West Monmouth Grammar Sch.; Bridgend Grammar Sch.; LSE (BScEcon). Mil. Service, 1939–46: Ches. Regt, 1940–46 (Captain) (despatches, Normandy, 1944); Civil Service, Min. of Labour NW Region, 1946–48; Min. of Fuel and Power, 1948–50; Customs and Excise, 1950–59; Welsh Office, Min. of Housing and Local Govt, 1959–62; Welsh Bd of Health, 1962–69; Welsh Office, 1969–79. *Address:* 12 Knowbury Avenue, Penarth, South Glam CF64 5RX.

OWEN, His Honour Aron, PhD; a Circuit Judge, 1980–92 (Resident Judge, Clerkenwell County Court, 1986–92); Deputy Judge, Clerkenwell County Court, and Family Division, Royal Courts of Justice, 1992–94; *b* 16 Feb. 1919; *m* 1946, Rose (*née* Fishman), JP; one *s* two *d. Educ:* Tredegar County Grammar Sch.; Univ. of Wales (BA Hons, PhD). Called to the Bar, Inner Temple, 1948. Freeman, City of London, 1963. *Recreations:* travel, gardening. *Address:* 44 Brampton Grove, Hendon, NW4 4AQ. *T:* (020) 8202 8151.

OWEN, Arthur Leslie, (Les); Group Chief Executive, Axa Asia Pacific Holdings, since 2000 (Board Member, since 1998); *b* 6 Feb. 1949; *s* of Arthur Llewellyn Owen and Annie Louise Owen (*née* Hegarty); *m* 1972, Valerie Emmott; three *d. Educ:* Holt High Sch., Liverpool; Univ. of Manchester (BSc Hons Maths). FIA 1975. Joined Sun Life Corp., 1971: Chief Gen. Manager, 1992–95; Gp Man. Dir, 1995–97; Chief Exec., Axa Sun Life plc, 1997–99; Board Member: Sun Life & Provincial Holdings plc, 1996–2000; Axa Nichidan, Japan, 1999–; Alliance Capital Management (Australia & NZ), 2000–. Member Board: Western TEC, 1994–98; PIA, 1997–99. *Recreations:* sport, soccer, cricket, golf, gardening, reading. *Address:* Broadway Lea, Broadway, Shipham, Somerset BS25 1UE.

OWEN, Bernard Laurence; a Chairman of Industrial Tribunals, 1982–95; *b* 8 Aug. 1925; *s* of Albert Victor Paschal Owen and Dorothy May Owen; *m* 1950, Elsie Yarnold; one *s* two *d. Educ:* King Edward's School, Birmingham; solicitor. Commissioned Royal Warwickshire Regt, 1945, service in Sudan, Eritrea, Egypt; staff appts in GHQs Middle East and Palestine, 1946–47; retired 1947 (Major); qualified as solicitor, 1950; a Senior Partner, C. Upfill Jagger Son & Tilley, 1952–82. *Recreations:* gardening, photography, bird watching.

OWEN, David; *see* Owen, A. D.

OWEN, David Harold Owen, OBE 1998; Registrar of the Privy Council, 1983–98; *b* 24 May 1933; *er* twin *s* of late Lloyd Owen Owen and Margaret Glyn Owen, Machynlleth, Powys; *m* 1st, 1961, Ailsa Ransome Wallis (*d* 1993); three *d*; 2nd, 1995, Julia (*née* Beck), *widow* of W. M. Lowe. *Educ:* Harrow Sch.; Gonville and Caius Coll., Cambridge. Called to the Bar, Gray's Inn, 1958. Served Royal Welch Fusiliers, 1951–53 (2nd Lieut). Campbell's Soups Ltd, King's Lynn, 1958–68; Lord Chancellor's Dept, 1969–80 (Private Sec. to Lord Chancellor, 1971–75); Chief Clerk, Judicial Cttee of Privy Council, 1980–83. *Recreations:* music, travel. *Address:* Whitelea, Stoney Lane, Bovingdon, Herts HP3 0DP. *Club:* Reform.

OWEN, Rt Rev. Edwin, MA; Bishop of Limerick and Killaloe, 1976–81; *b* 3 Nov. 1910; *s* of late William Rowland Owen; *m* 1940, Margaret Mary Williams, BA; one *s* one *d*. *Educ:* Royal School, Armagh; Trinity College, Dublin (MA). Deacon 1934, priest 1935, Dublin; Curate of Glenageary, 1934–36; Christ Church, Leeson Park, Dublin, 1936–38; Minor Canon of St Patrick's Cathedral, Dublin, 1935–36; Chancellor's Vicar, 1936–38; Succentor, 1938–42; Incumbent of Birr with Eglish, 1942–57; Canon, Killaloe Cathedral, 1954–57; Rector of Killaloe and Dean of Killaloe Cathedral, 1957–72; Diocesan Secretary of Killaloe and Kilfenora, 1957–72; Bishop of Killaloe, Kilfenora, Clonfert and Kilmacduagh, 1972–76, when diocese amalgamated with Limerick, Ardfert and Aghadoe, and Emly. *Recreation:* classical music. *Address:* 4 Cypress, Hazeldene, Anglesea Road, Dublin 4.

OWEN, Dr Gareth, CBE 1988; DSc; MRIA; CBiol, FIBiol; Principal, University College of Wales, Aberystwyth, 1979–89; Vice-Chancellor, University of Wales, 1985–87; *b* 4 Oct. 1922; *s* of J. R. and B. M. Owen; *m* 1953, Beti Jones; one *s* two *d*. *Educ:* Pontypridd Boys' Grammar Sch.; University Coll., Cardiff (BSc 1950; Fellow, 1982). DSc Glasgow, 1959. FIBiol 1964. Served War, RAF Pilot, 1942–47. Lectr in Zoology, Univ. of Glasgow, 1950–64; Prof. of Zool., 1964–79, and Pro-Vice-Chancellor, 1974–79, Queen's Univ. of Belfast. Welsh Supernumerary, Jesus Coll., Oxford, 1981–82 and 1986–87. Mem., Nature Conservancy Council, 1984–91 (Chm., Adv. Cttee for Wales, 1985–91). Pres., Welsh Centre of Internat. Affairs, 1989–93. Mem., RSPB Adv. Cttee for Wales, 1991–97. MRIA 1976. Hon. Fellow: UCW, Cardiff, 1982; AFRC Inst. for Grassland and Envmtl Res., 1991. Hon. Mem. of the Gorsedd, 1983. Hon. DSc QUB, 1982; Hon. LLD Wales, 1989. *Publications:* contrib. Trans Royal Soc., Proc. Malacol. Soc. London, Jl Mar. Biol. Soc., and Qly Jl Micro. Sci. *Recreation:* photography. *Address:* 6A St Margaret's Place, Whitchurch, Cardiff CF14 7AD. *T:* (029) 2069 2199.

OWEN, Sir Geoffrey (David), Kt 1989; Senior Fellow, Inter-disciplinary Institute of Management, London School of Economics and Political Science, since 1998; *b* 16 April 1934; *s* of late L. G. Owen and Violet Owen (*née* Chamberlain); *m* 1st, 1961, Dorothy Jane (*d* 1991); two *s* one *d*; 2nd, 1993, Miriam Marianna Gross, *qv*. *Educ:* Rugby Sch.; Balliol Coll., Oxford (MA). Joined Financial Times, 1958, feature writer, industrial correspondent; US Correspondent, 1961; Industrial Editor, 1967; Executive, Industrial Reorganisation Corp., 1967–69; Dir of Admin, Overseas Div., 1969, Dir of Personnel and Admin, 1972, British Leyland Internat.; Dep. Editor, 1974–80, Editor, 1981–90, Financial Times; Dir, Business Policy Prog., Centre for Econ. Performance, LSE, 1991–98. Dir, Laird Gp, 2000–. Chm., Wincott Foundn, 1998–. *Publications:* Industry in the USA, 1966; From Empire to Europe, 1999. *Address:* London School of Economics and Political Science, Houghton Street, WC2A 2AE.

OWEN, Gerald Victor; QC 1969; a Recorder of the Crown Court, 1979–95; *b* London, 29 Nov. 1922; *m* 1946, Phyllis (*née* Ladsky); one *s* one *d*. *Educ:* Kilburn Grammar Sch.; St Catharine's Coll., Cambridge. Exhibr, St Catharine's Coll., Cambridge, 1940; Drapers' Company Science Schol., Queen Mary Coll., London, 1940. 1st cl. Maths Tripos I, 1941; Senior Optimes Tripos II, 1942; BA 1943, MA 1946, Cantab; Royal Statistical Soc. Certif., 1947; LLB London (Hons) 1949. Research Ballistics, Min. of Supply, 1942–45; Statistical Officer, LCC, 1945–49. Called to Bar, Gray's Inn, 1949; *ad eundem* Inner Temple, 1969. A Dep. Circuit Judge, 1971. Chairman: Dairy Produce Quota Tribunal, 1984–85; Medical Appeals Tribunal, 1984–94. Member, Cttees of Justice on: Legal Aid in Criminal Cases; Complaints against Lawyers, 1970; False Witness, the problem of perjury, 1973. *Address:* 11 Wellington House, Eton Road, NW3 4SY. *T:* (020) 7797 7000.

OWEN, Gillian Frances, PhD; energy and environment policy consultant, since 1988; Member, Competition (formerly Monopolies and Mergers) Commission, since 1996; *b* 26 May 1954; *d* of Iorwerth Ellis Owen and Edith Maud Owen; *m* 1980, David Ian Green. *Educ:* Newcastle upon Tyne (BA Librarianship/Social Scis 1976); Birkbeck Coll., Univ. of London (PhD Public Policy 1994). Asst Cataloguer, Clwyd CC, 1976–77; Asst Librarian, Coll. of Librarianship, Wales, 1978; Energy Advice Officer, City of Newcastle upon Tyne, 1979–81; Information and Develt Officer, 1981–84, Chief Officer, 1984–88, Nat. Energy Action. Specialist Advr, Envmt Select Cttee, 1993–95; Expert Advr, Economic and Social Cttee, EC, 1996; Special Advr, Energy Services Assoc. Member: Bedfordshire Police Authy, 1994–; Adv. Bd, Ofgem, 1999–2000; Vice Chm., Consumer Congress, 1987; Chm., Public Utilities Access Forum, 1995–. *Publication:* Public Purpose or Private Benefit: the politics of energy conservation, 1999. *Recreations:* travel, walking, cycling, art, design and architecture, theatre, cinema. *Address:* Energy Services Association, 1 Charlotte Square, Newcastle upon Tyne NE1 4XF. *T:* (01234) 358163.

OWEN, Gordon Michael William, CBE 1991; Chairman: Energis plc (formerly Energis Communications Ltd), since 1993; NXT plc, since 2001; Yeoman Group plc, since 1996; Waste Gas Technology, since 1997; *b* 9 Dec. 1937; *s* of Christopher Knowles Owen and late Mrs Margaret Joyce Milward (*née* Spencer); *m* 1963, Jennifer Pearl, (Jane), Bradford; one *s* one *d*. *Educ:* Cranbrook Sch. Cable & Wireless, 1954–91: Dir, 1986–91; Jt Man. Dir, 1987–88; Dep. Chief Exec., 1988–90; Gp Man. Dir, 1990–91; Chairman: Mercury Communications Ltd, 1990–91 (Man. Dir, 1984–90); Peterstar Communications, St Petersburg, 1992–94; Utility Cable plc, 1994–98; Acorn (formerly Acorn Computer) Group, 1996–; Director: Portals Gp, 1988–95; London Electricity, 1989–97; Olivetti SpA, 1996–. Chm., MacIntyre Care, 1993–. Vice-Chm. Academy Concerts Soc., Council of Mgt of Acad. of St Martin in the Fields Orch., 1994–. Chm. Bd of Govs, St Michael's Sch., Otford, 1994–. *Recreations:* beekeeping, stamp collecting, sailing, bad golf. *Address:* Sutton End House, Sutton, Pulborough RH20 1PY.

OWEN, Griffith; *see* Owen, S. G.

OWEN, Sir Hugh (Bernard Pilkington), 5th Bt *cr* 1813; *b* 28 March 1915; *s* of Sir John Arthur Owen, 4th Bt and Lucy Fletcher (*d* 1985), *e d* of F. W. Pilkington; *S* father, 1973. *Educ:* Chillon Coll., Switzerland. *Heir:* none. *Address:* 63 Dudsbury Road, Ferndown, Dorset BH22 8RD.

OWEN, Sir Hugo Dudley C.; *see* Cunliffe-Owen.

OWEN, Idris Wyn; a director of a company in the construction industry; *b* 1912; *m*. *Educ:* Stockport Sch. and Coll. of Technology; Manchester Sch. of Commerce. Contested (C): Manchester Exchange, 1951; Stalybridge and Hyde, 1955; Stockport North 1966; MP (C) Stockport North, 1970–Feb. 1974; contested (C) Stockport North, Oct. 1974. Member, Stockport Borough Council, 1946; Mayor, 1962–63. Vice-Pres., Nat. Fedn of Building Trades Employers, 1965. FCIOB. *Address:* 3 Prestbury Court, Castle Rise, Prestbury, Macclesfield, Cheshire SK10 4UR.

OWEN, Ivor Henri, CBE 1992; CEng, FIMechE; Director General, Design Council, 1988–93; *b* 14 Nov. 1930; *s* of Thomas and Anne Owen; *m* 1954, Jane Frances Graves; two *s* one *d*. *Educ:* Liverpool College of Technology; Manchester College of Science and Technology. Engineering apprentice, later design engineer, Craven Bros (Manchester), Stockport, 1947–57; Manufacturing Develt Engr, Steam Turbine Div., English Electric, Rugby, 1957–62; Manager, Netherton Works, English Electric, Bootle, 1962–66 (hydro electric plant, steam turbine components, condensers, nuclear equipment); Manager, English Electric Computers, Winsford, 1966–69; Manager, Winsford Kidsgrove Works, ICL, 1969–70; Man. Dir, RHP Bearings, 1970–81; Thorn EMI: Chief Exec., Gen. Engineering Div., 1981–83; Chm., Appliance and Lighting Group, 1984–87; Dir, 1984–87. Chm., Ball Roller Bearing Manufrs Assoc., 1978–80; Vice-Pres., Fedn European Bearing Manufrs Assoc., 1978–80. Royal Acad. of Engrg Vis. Prof., Univ. of Bath, 1994–97. FRSA. *Recreations:* theatre, reading, running, gardening, motor cycling. *Address:* Linden House, Back Ends, Chipping Campden, Glos GL55 6AU.

OWEN, Hon. Sir John (Arthur Dalziel), Kt 1986; a Judge of the High Court of Justice, Queen's Bench Division, 1986–2000; Master of the Faculty Office, 1980–2000; *b* 22 Nov. 1925; *s* of late R. J. Owen and Mrs O. B. Owen; *m* 1952, Valerie, *d* of W. Ethell; one *s* one *d*. *Educ:* Solihull Sch.; Brasenose Coll., Oxford (MA, BCL 1949); LLM Wales, 1996. RN, 1944; commnd 2nd King Edward VII's Own Goorkha Rifles, 1946. Called to Bar, Gray's Inn, 1951, Bencher, 1980. Dep. Chm., Warwickshire QS, 1967–71; QC 1970; a Recorder, 1972–84; Dep. Leader, Midland and Oxford Circuit, 1980–84; a Circuit Judge, CCC, 1984–86; a Presiding Judge, Midland and Oxford Circuit, 1988–92. Mem. Senate of the Inns of Court and the Bar, 1977–80. Chm., West Midlands Area Mental Health Review Tribunal, 1972–80. Mem., General Synod of Church of England, Dio. Coventry, 1970–80; Chancellor, Dio. Derby, 1973–80, Dio. Coventry, 1973–80, Dio. Southwell, 1979–80; Dean, Arches Court of Canterbury and Auditor, Chancery Court of York, 1980–2000. DCL Lambeth, 1993. *Club:* Garrick.

See also Baroness Seccombe.

OWEN, John Aubrey; Senior Partner, Inside Advice (Consultancy Services), since 2001; *b* 1 Aug. 1945; *s* of late Prebendary Douglas Aubrey Owen and Patricia Joan Owen; *m* 1971, Julia Margaret Jones; one *s* one *d*. *Educ:* City of London Sch., St Catharine's Coll., Cambridge (MA). Joined Min. of Transport, 1969; Asst Private Sec. to Minister for Transport Industries, 1972; DoE, 1973–75; Dept of Transport, 1975–78; seconded to Cambridgeshire CC, 1978–80; DoE, 1980–2001: Regional Dir, Northern Regional Office, Depts of the Environment and Transport, 1987–91; Dir, Personnel Management, 1991–95. Dir, Regeneration, then Skills, Educn and Regeneration, later Skills, Enterprise and Communities, Govt Office for London, 1995–2001. FRSA; MInstD. *Recreations:* gardening, opera, reading. *Address:* 33 Valley Road, Welwyn Garden City, Herts AL8 7DH. *T:* (01707) 321768; *e-mail:* john.owen@insideadvice.co.uk.

OWEN, John Gethin M.; *see* Morgan-Owen.

OWEN, John Halliwell, OBE 1975; HM Diplomatic Service, retired; *b* 16 June 1935; *e s* of late Arthur Llewellyn Owen, OBE and Doris Spencer (*née* Halliwell); *m* 1st, 1963 (marr. diss. 1971); one *s* one *d*; 2nd, 1972, Dianne Elizabeth (*née* Lowry); one *d*. *Educ:* Sedbergh School; The Queen's Coll., Oxford (Hastings Scholar). MA. 2nd Lieut, RA, 1954–56; HMOCS, Tanganyika Govt Service, 1960; Dist Officer, Provincial Administration, 1960–61; Dist Comr, 1962; Dist Magistrate and Regional Local Courts Officer, 1963–65; HM Foreign Service, 1966; Second Sec., Dar-es-Salaam, 1968–70; FCO, 1970–73; First Sec., Dacca, 1973–75; FCO 1976; First Sec., Accra, 1976–80; FCO, 1980–82; Counsellor, Pretoria, 1982–86; Counsellor, FCO, 1986–90. *Recreations:* music, travel, wildlife, gardening. *Club:* Dar es Salaam Yacht.

OWEN, Prof. John Joseph Thomas, FRS 1988; Visiting Scholar, Stanford University, USA, since 2000; Sands Cox Professor and Head of Department of Anatomy, University of Birmingham, 1978–2001; *b* 7 Jan. 1934; *s* of Thomas and Alice Owen; *m* 1961, Barbara Schofield Forster (marr. diss. 1992); two *s*. *Educ:* Univ. of Liverpool (BSc, MD); MA Oxon 1963. Lecturer: Univ. of Liverpool, 1960–63; Univ. of Oxford, 1963–72; Fellow, St Cross Coll., Oxford, 1968–72; Sen. Scientist, Imperial Cancer Res. Fund's Tumour Immunology Unit, UCL, 1972–74; Prof. of Anatomy, Univ. of Newcastle upon Tyne 1974–78. Medical Research Council: Mem., Physiol Systems and Disorders Bd, 1978–83; Chm., Grants Cttee, B, 1980–83; Mem., Cell Bd, 1991–94; Member: Wellcome Trust's Biochemistry and Cell Biology Panel, 1987–90; Council, Nat. Kidney Res. Fund, 1987–90; Council, Royal Soc., 1991–93. Founder FMedSci 1998. *Publications:* numerous contribs to sci. literature. *Recreations:* sport, travel. *Address:* 6 Birch Hollow, Egbaston, Birmingham B15 2QE.

OWEN, Prof. John V.; *see* Vallance-Owen.

OWEN, John Wyn, CB 1994; Secretary, Nuffield Trust, since 1997; *b* 15 May 1942; *s* of late Idwal Wyn Owen and of Myfi Owen (*née* Hughes); *m* 1967, Elizabeth Ann (*née* MacFarlane); one *s* one *d*. *Educ:* Friars School, Bangor; St John's Coll., Cambridge (BA 1964, MA 1968); Hosp. Admin. Staff Coll. (DipHA 1967). Trainee, King Edward VII's Hosp. Fund for London, 1964–66; Dep. Hosp. Sec., West Wales Gen. Hosp., Carmarthen, 1966–67; Hosp. Sec., Glantawe HMC, Swansea, 1967–70; Staff Training Officer, Welsh Hosp. Bd, Cardiff, 1968–70; Divl Administrator, Univ. of Wales, Cardiff, HMC, 1970–72; St Thomas' Hospital: Asst Clerk, and King's Fund Fellow, 1972–74; Dist Administrator, St Thomas' Health Dist, Teaching, 1974–79; Trustee, Refresh, 1976–78; Hon. Tutor, Med. Sch., 1974–79; Praeceptor, Sch. of Health Administration, Univ. of Minnesota, 1974–79; Exec. Dir, United Medical Enterprises, London, 1979–85; Dir, NHS Wales, Welsh Office, 1985–94; Chm., Welsh Health Common Services Authy, 1985–94; Dir Gen., NSW Health Dept, Sydney, 1994–97. Chairman: Olympic Health and Med. Working Cttee, 1994–; DoH Change Mgt Gp on Nurse Regulation, 1999–; Member: Strategic Planning and Evaluation Cttee, Nat. Health and MRC, 1994–; Australian Health Ministers' Adv. Council, 1994–97 (Chm., 1995–97); Health Adv. Bd, 1994–97; Public Health Assoc., 1994; Mgt Cttee, Nat. Breast Cancer Centre, 1995–97. Sen. Associate, Judge Inst. of Mgt Studies, Univ. of Cambridge, 1997–; Visiting Fellow: Univ. of NSW, 1979; LSE, 1997–. Trustee, Florence Nightingale Museum Trust, 1983–90; Chm., Health Bldg Educn Gp, British Consultants' Bureau, 1983–85; Mem. Adv. Forum, Personnel Lead Body, 1992–94. Founder Mem., Med. Chapter, Australian Opera, 1995–97; Mem., NSW Cambridge Soc. Cttee, 1996–; Sec., London Cambridge Soc., 1997–. Member: Court, Univ. of Wales, 1998–; Council, Univ. of Wales Coll. of Medicine, 1997–. FRGS 1968; FRSA 1998; FHSM 1992; FACHSE 1994; FRSocMed 1997; Hon. FFPHM 1991. Mem., Inst. of Medicine, NAS, USA, 1998. Hon. Fellow: UCW, Aberystwyth, 1991; UCW, Bangor, 1992. Hon. Mem., Gorsedd of Bards, 2000.

DUniv Glamorgan, 1999. *Publications:* contribs to professional jls. *Recreations:* organ playing, opera, travel. *Address:* Newton Farm, Newton, Cowbridge CF71 7RZ. *T:* (01446) 775113. *Club:* Athenæum.

OWEN, John Wynne, CMG 1998; MBE 1979; HM Diplomatic Service, retired; Chairman (non-executive), CLS Fabrication Ltd, since 1989; Director (non-executive), Scimitar Advisers, since 1999; *b* 25 April 1939; *s* of Thomas David Owen and Mair Eluned Owen; *m* 1st, 1962, Thelma Margaret Gunton (*d* 1987); one *s* two *d*; 2nd, 1988, Carol Edmunds; one step *d*. *Educ:* Gowerton Grammar Sch.; Westminster Coll., London. FO 1956; 2nd Lieut Royal Signals, 1958–60; served Djakarta, Saigon, Paris, San Salvador, to 1967; resigned 1967; business, 1967–70; reinstated 1970; FCO, 1970–73; Tehran, 1973–77; São Paulo, 1978–80; Peking, 1980–82; FCO, 1983; special leave, 1985; Chm., Gunham, Holdings Ltd, 1985–89; Counsellor, FCO, 1989–92; Consul Gen., Boston, 1992–95; Governor, Cayman Is, 1995–99. Chm., British Laminated Plastics Fabricators' Assoc., 1987–90. Trustee, Grandparents Fedn, 2000. Freeman, City of London, 1978; Liveryman, 1978–, Mem., Ct of Assts, 1999–, Loriners' Co. FIMgt. *Recreations:* walking, art, reading, fly-fishing. *Clubs:* Royal Automobile, City Livery.

OWEN, Les; *see* Owen, A. L.

OWEN, Dr Myrfyn; Director General, Wildfowl and Wetlands Trust, 1992–97; ecological consultant, since 1997; *b* 8 April 1943; *s* of William Owen and Anne Mary Owen; *m* 1967, Lydia Marian Vaughan (*née* Rees); two *d*. *Educ:* Sir Hugh Owen Grammar Sch.; University Coll., Aberystwyth (BSc 1964); Univ. of Leeds (PhD 1967). Wildfowl Trust, later Wildfowl and Wetlands Trust: Ecologist, 1967; Conservation Res. Officer, 1974; Asst Dir (Res.), 1979; Head of Res., 1988; Dir, 1991–92. *Publications:* Wildfowl of Europe, 1976; Wild Geese of the World, 1980; Wildfowl in Great Britain, 1986; Waterfowl Ecology, 1990; numerous scientific papers. *Recreations:* gardening, cookery, cycling, wildlife. *Address:* Woodleigh House, 62 Woodmancote, Dursley, Glos GL11 4AQ. *T:* (01453) 543244.

OWEN, Nicholas David Arundel; Presenter and Correspondent, Independent Television News, since 1984; *b* 10 Feb. 1947; *m* 1983, Brenda (*née* Firth); one *s* one *d*, and one step *s* one step *d*. Journalist, 1964; BBC TV, 1981–83. *Publications:* History of the British Trolleybus, 1970; The Brighton Belle, 1972; Diana, The People's Princess, 1997. *Recreations:* reading, walking, golf. *Address:* Independent Television News, 200 Gray's Inn Road, WC1X 8XZ. *T:* (020) 7430 4750.

OWEN, Patricia, (Mrs Peter Owen); *see* Hodge, P.

OWEN, Peter Francis, CB 1990; Executive Director, Institute of Chartered Accountants in England and Wales, since 1998; *b* 4 Sept. 1940; *s* of Arthur Owen and Violet (*née* Morris); *m* 1963, Ann Preece; one *s* one *d*. *Educ:* The Liverpool Inst.; Liverpool Univ. (BA French). Joined MPBW, 1964; Cabinet Office, 1971–72; Private Sec. to successive Ministers of Housing and Construction, 1972–74; Asst Sec., Housing Policy Review, 1975–77, Local Govt Finance, 1977–80; Under Sec. and Regional Dir of Northern and Yorks and Humberside Regs, Depts of the Environment and of Transport, 1980–82; Under Secretary: Rural Affairs, DoE, 1983; Local Govt Finance Policy, DoE, 1984–86; Dep. Sec., Housing and Construction, DoE, 1986–90; Head of Econ. and Domestic Affairs Secretariat, Cabinet Office, 1990–94; Dep. Sec., Sch. Curriculum and Teachers, DFE, 1994–95; Dir Gen. for Schools, DfEE, 1995–98. *Recreations:* reading, gardening, French, classical guitar. *Address:* Institute of Chartered Accountants in England and Wales, PO Box 433, Chartered Accountants' Hall, Moorgate Place, EC2P 2BJ.

OWEN, Philip W.; *see* Wynn Owen.

OWEN, Richard Wilfred, FCA; retired from Touche Ross, 1993; *b* 26 Oct. 1932; *s* of Wilfred Owen and Ivy (*née* Gamble); *m* 1966, Sheila Marie Kerrigan; three adopted *s* one adopted *d*, and one foster *s* one foster *d*. *Educ:* Gunnersbury Catholic Grammar Sch. Lloyds Bank, 1949–51; RAF Russian translator, 1951–53; accountancy articles, 1953–58; Thomson McLintock, 1958–62; Crompton Parkinson, 1962–64; Touche Ross & Co., Chartered Accountants and Management Consultants, 1964–93: admitted to Partnership, 1969; seconded to Treasury, 1971; Partner-in-Charge, Management Consultancy, 1974–87, Nat. Dir, Personnel, 1987–93; UK Chm., 1988–90; Europ. Dir, Management Consultancy, 1990–92. Pres., Management Consultancies Assoc., 1987. Chm., Cardinal Hume Centre, 1996–; Trustee, Isabel Hospice, 1994–2000. KSG 1997. *Address:* 25 Gainsborough House, Frognal Rise, Hampstead Village, NW3 6PZ.

OWEN, Robert Frank; QC 1996; a Recorder, since 2000; *b* 31 May 1953; *s* of Tudor Owen and Pat Owen; *m* 1980, Anna Shaw; three *s*. *Educ:* Prestatyn High Sch.; Poly. of Central London (LLB Hons). Called to the Bar, Gray's Inn, 1977. *Recreations:* coastal walking, sport. *Address:* 24 The Ropewalk, Nottingham NG1 5EF.

OWEN, Robert John Richard; Deputy Chairman, Nomura International (Hong Kong) Ltd, since 1993; Director, European Capital Co. Ltd, since 1992; *b* 11 Feb. 1940; *s* of Richard Owen and Margaret Owen (*née* Fletcher); *m* (marr. diss.); two *s* one *d*. *Educ:* Repton School; Oxford University. Foreign Office, 1961–68, incl. HM Embassy, Washington, 1965–68; HM Treasury, 1968–70; Morgan Grenfell & Co., 1970–79 (Dir, 1974); Lloyds Bank International, 1979–85 (Dir); Chm. and Chief Exec., Lloyds Merchant Bank, 1985–88; Comr for Securities, Hong Kong, 1988–89; Chm., Securities and Futures Commn, Hong Kong, 1989–92. Director: Internat. Securities Consultancy Ltd, 1995–; Regent Pacific Gp Ltd, 1998–; ECK & Partners Ltd, 1999–; TechPacific Ltd, 1999–. Mem. Council and Mem. UK Regulatory Bd, Lloyd's of London, 1993–95. *Recreations:* oriental paintings, mountain walking. *Address:* c/o European Capital Co. Ltd, 3 Lombard Street, EC3V 9AA.

OWEN, Hon. Sir Robert (Michael), Kt 2000; **Hon. Mr Justice Owen;** a Judge of the High Court, Queen's Bench Division, since 2001; *b* 19 Sept. 1944; *s* of Gwynne Llewellyn Owen and Phoebe Constance Owen; *m* 1969, Sara Josephine Rumbold; two *s*. *Educ:* Durham Sch.; Exeter Univ. (LLB). Called to Bar, Inner Temple, 1968, Bencher, 1995; QC 1988. Judicial Mem., Transport Tribunal, 1985–97; a Recorder, 1987–2000; a Dep. High Court Judge, 1994–2000. DTI Inspector, 1991–92. Chm., Gen. Council of the Bar, 1997. Chm., London Common Law and Commercial Bar Assoc., 1994–95. Gov., Coll. of Law, 1998–. FRSA 1997. *Address:* Royal Courts of Justice, Strand, WC2A 2LL. *T:* (020) 7797 7500. *Clubs:* Travellers, Les Six.

OWEN, Robert Penrhyn; Director and Secretary, The Water Companies' Association, 1974–83, retired; *b* 17 Dec. 1918; *s* of late Captain Richard Owen; *m* 1949, Suzanne, *d* of late L. H. West; one *s* one *d*. *Educ:* Friar's School. War service in Royal Welch Fusiliers, 1939–46, in Madagascar, India, The Arakan and North and Central Burma. Admitted Solicitor, 1947. Asst Solicitor: Berks CC, 1948–50; Leics CC, 1950–54; Chief Asst Solicitor, Lancs CC, 1954–60; 2nd Dep. Clerk and 2nd Dep. Clerk of the Peace, Lancs CC, 1960–63; Gen. Manager, Telford Develt Corp. (New Town), 1963–69; Sec., Chief Exec. Officer and Solicitor, Thames Conservancy, 1969–74. *Recreations:* all sport, gardening, reading. *Address:* Pilgrims Wood, Three Gables Lane, Streatley, Reading RG8 9LJ. *T:* (01491) 874294. *Clubs:* MCC; Phyllis Court (Henley-on-Thames).

OWEN, (Samuel) Griffith, CBE 1977; MD, FRCP; Second Secretary, Medical Research Council, 1968–82, retired; *b* 3 Sept. 1925; *e s* of late Rev. Evan Lewis Owen and of Marjorie Lawton; *m* 1954, Ruth, *e d* of late Merle W. Tate, Philadelphia, Pa, USA; two *s* two *d*. *Educ:* Dame Allen's Sch.; Durham Univ. MB, BS Dunelm 1948; MRCP 1951; MD Dunelm 1954; FRCP 1965; clinical and research appts at Royal Victoria Infirmary, Newcastle upon Tyne, 1948–49 and 1950–53; RAMC, SMO, HM Troopships, 1949–50; Med. Registrar, Nat. Heart Hosp., 1953–54; Instr in Pharmacology, Univ. of Pennsylvania Sch. of Med., 1954–56; Reader in Med., Univ. of Newcastle upon Tyne, 1964–68 (First Asst, 1956, Lectr, 1960, Sen. Lectr, 1961); Hon. Cons. Physician, Royal Victoria Infirmary, Newcastle upon Tyne, 1960–68; Clin. Sub-Dean of Med. Sch., Univ. of Newcastle upon Tyne, 1966–68 (Academic Sub-Dean, 1964–66); Examr in Med., Univ. of Liverpool, 1966–68; Examr in Membership, RCP, 1967–68 and Mem., Research Cttee, RCP, 1968–76; Member: Brit. Cardiac Soc., 1962–82; Assoc. of Physicians of GB, 1965–; European Molec. Biol. Conf., 1971–82; European Molec. Biol. Lab., 1974–82; Exec. Council, European Science Foundn, 1974–78; Comité de la Recherche Médicale et de la Santé Publique, EEC, 1977–82; Scientific Coordinating Cttee, Arthritis and Rheumatism Council, 1978–82; NW Thames RHA, 1978–82. Consultant to WHO, SE Asia, 1966 and 1967–68; Commonwealth Fund Fellow, Univ. of Illinois, 1966; Fellow, Hunterian Soc., 1978. Chm., Feldberg Foundn, 1974–78; Governor, Queen Charlotte's Hosp. for Women, 1979–82. Liveryman, Soc. of Apothecaries, 1976–. *Publications:* Essentials of Cardiology, 1961 (2nd edn 1968); Electrocardiography, 1966 (2nd edn 1973); contribs to med. jls on heart disease, cerebral circulation, thyroid disease, med. research, etc. *Recreations:* gastronomy, music, theatre. *Address:* Flat 17, 9 Devonhurst Place, Heathfield Terrace, Chiswick, W4 4JB. *T:* (020) 8995 3228. *Club:* Royal Society of Medicine.

OWEN, Tim; QC 2000; *b* 11 Jan. 1958; *s* of Meurig Wynn Owen and Thelma Owen (*née* Parry); *m* 1992, Jemma Redgrave; two *s*. *Educ:* Atlantic Coll.; London Sch. of Economics (BA 1st Cl. Hons History 1979); PCL (Dip. Law 1982). Campaign Co-ordinator, Radical Alternatives to Prison, 1979–81; called to the Bar, Middle Temple, 1983; in practice at the Bar, 1984–; called to the Bar of Antigua and Barbuda, 1994. *Publication:* (jtly) Prison Law, 1993, 2nd edn 1999. *Recreations:* film, travel. *Address:* Matrix Chambers, Griffin Building, Gray's Inn, WC1R 5LN. *T:* (020) 7404 3447.

OWEN, Trevor Bryan, CBE 1987; Chairman: Bethlem Royal and Maudsley Special Health Authority, 1988–94; Committee of Management, Institute of Psychiatry, 1990–97; *b* 3 April 1928; *s* of Leonard Owen, CIE and Dilys (*née* Davies Bryan); *m* 1955, (Jennifer) Gaie (*née* Houston); one *s* one *d*. *Educ:* Rugby Sch.; Trinity Coll., Oxford (Scholar; MA). Sch. Student, British Sch. of Archaeology, Athens, 1953–54; ICI, 1955–78: wide range of jobs culminating in, successively: Chm., J. P. MacDougall Ltd; Dir, Paints, Agricl and Plastics Divs; Co. Personnel Manager; Man. Dir, Remploy Ltd, 1978–88. Member: Higher Educn Review Gp, Govt of NI, 1979–81; CNAA, 1973–79; Continuing Educn Adv. Council, BBC, 1977–83; Council, CBI, 1982–88; Council, Industrial Soc., 1987–88; Council, Inst. of Manpower Studies, 1975–88 (Chm., 1977–78); Chm. Bd of Governors, Nat. Inst. for Social Work, 1985–91 (Mem., 1982–97; Mem., Working Party on Role and Tasks of Social Workers, 1981–82). Chm., Phab, 1988–91. *Publications:* Business School Programmes—the requirements of British manufacturing industry (with D. Casey and N. Huskisson), 1971; Making Organisations Work, 1978; The Manager and Industrial Relations, 1979; articles in jls. *Address:* 8 Rochester Terrace, NW1 9JN.

OWEN, Ursula Margaret; Editor and Chief Executive, Index on Censorship, since 1993; *b* 21 Jan. 1937; *d* of Emma Sophie Sachs (*née* Boehm) and Werner Sachs; *m* 1960, Edward Roger John Owen (marr. diss.); one *d*. *Educ:* Putney High Sch.; St Hugh's Coll., Oxford (BA Hons Physiol.); Bedford Coll., London (Dip. Soc. Studies). Lectr, English Lang., Amer. Univ. in Cairo, 1962–63; research work in mental health and physical disabilities, 1964–67; Editor, Frank Cass, 1971–73; Sen. Editor, Barrie & Jenkins, 1973–75; Virago Press: Co-founder, 1974; Director, 1974–; Editl Dir, 1974–90; Jt Man. Dir, 1982–90; Dir, Paul Hamlyn Fund, 1990–92. Cultural Policy Advr to Lab. Party, 1990–92. Dir, New Statesman and Society, 1983–90. Chm., Educn Extra, 1993–; Mem., Royal Literary Fund Cttee, 1989–94. Gov., Parliament Hill School, 1991–. *Publications:* (ed) Fathers: Reflections by Daughters, 1983; (ed with Mark Fisher) Whose Cities?, 1991. *Recreations:* music, reading, film, travel. *Address:* Index, 33 Islington High Street, N1 9LH. *T:* (020) 7278 2313. *Club:* Groucho.

OWEN, Prof. Walter Shepherd, PhD, DEng; Professor Emeritus of Materials Science, Massachusetts Institute of Technology; *b* 13 March 1920; *s* of Walter Lloyd and Dorothea Elizabeth Owen; *m*; one *d*. *Educ:* Alsop High Sch.; University of Liverpool. Metallurgist, D. Napier and Sons and English Electric Co., 1940–46; Asst Lecturer and Lecturer in Metallurgy, Univ. of Liverpool, 1946–54; Commonwealth Fund Fellow, Metallurgy Dept, Mass Inst. of Technol., 1951–52; on research staff, 1954–57, and Henry Bell Wortley Professor of Metallurgy, 1957–66, Univ. of Liverpool; Thomas R. Briggs Prof. of Engineering and Dir of Materials Science and Engineering, Cornell Univ., 1966–70; Dean of Technological Inst., Northwestern Univ., 1970–71; Vice Pres. for Science and Research, Northwestern Univ., 1971–73; Head of Dept, 1973–82, and Prof. of Physical Metallurgy, 1973–85, Mass Inst. of Technol. Mem., Nat. Acad. of Engineering, USA, 1977. *Publications:* papers in British and American journals on aspects of physical metallurgy. *Recreation:* walking. *Address:* 1 Marine Terrace, Porthmadog, Gwynedd LL49 9BL. *Club:* St Botolph (Boston).

OWEN-JONES, Lindsay Harwood, CBE 2000; Chairman and Chief Executive Officer, L'Oréal, since 1988; *b* 17 March 1946; *s* of Hugh A. Owen-Jones and Esmee Owen-Jones (*née* Lindsay); *m*; one *d*; *m* 1994, Cristina Furno. *Educ:* Oxford Univ. (BA); European Inst. of Business Admin. Product Manager, L'Oréal, 1969; Head, Public Products Div., Belgium, 1971–74; Manager, SCAD (L'Oréal subsid.), Paris, 1974–76; Marketing Manager, Public Products Div., Paris, 1976–78; Gen. Manager, SAIPO (L'Oréal subsid.), Italy, 1978–81; Pres., 1981–83, Chm., 1991–, COSMAIR (L'Oreal agent), USA; Vice-Pres., L'Oréal Man. Cttee and Mem. Bd of Dirs, 1984; Pres. and Chief Operating Officer, 1984–88. Director: Banque Nationale de Paris, 1989–; LAFARGE, 1993–; Air Liquide, 1994–. Officier, Légion d'Honneur (France), 1998. *Recreation:* private helicopter pilot. *Address:* L'Oréal, 41 rue Martre, 92117 Clichy, France. *T:* 47567000.

OWENS, Bernard Charles; Director, British Jewellery and Giftware Federation, 1987–96 (Vice-President, 1990–91; President, 1991–92; Deputy President, 1992–93); *b* 20 March 1928; *s* of late Charles A. Owens and Sheila (*née* O'Higgins); *m* 1954, Barbara Madeline Murphy; two *s* four *d*. *Educ:* Solihull Sch.; London Sch. of Econs and Pol Science. Commnd 2nd Lieut, RASC, 1947; transf. RARO, 1949 (Lieut). Managing Director: Stanley Bros, 1962–67; Coronet Industrial Securities, 1965–67; Chairman: Unochrome Industries, 1964–79; Silverthorne Group, 1972–79; Director: Hobbs Savill & Bradford, 1957–62; Trinidad Sugar Estates, 1965–67; Cornish Brewery, 1987–93; Local Dir, Alexander Stenhouse UK (formerly Reed Stenhouse UK), 1980–87. Mem. of Lloyd's,

1978–. Mem., Monopolies and Mergers Commn, 1981–93. Chm., Metal Finishing Assoc., 1982–85 (Vice-Chm., 1981–82; Dep. Chm., 1985–88); Treas. and Trustee, British Jewellery Giftware and Leathergoods Benevolent Soc., 1992–96; Member: Cttee, Nat. Clayware Fedn, 1962–67; Council, Zoological Society, 1987–90. Mem., Solihull Council, 1953–63 (Chm., Finance Cttee, 1957–63); contested (C) Birmingham, Small Heath, 1959 and March 1961. Freeman, City of London, 1981; Liveryman: Co. of Gardeners, 1982; Basketmakers' Co., 1994; Mem., HAC, 1984–. Life Governor, RNLI, 1984. FRSA 1972. Mem., SMO Malta, 1979. *Recreations:* cruising, fine food and wine. *Address:* The Vatch House, Stroud, Glos GL6 7JY. *T:* (01453) 763402. *Clubs:* MCC, City Livery Yacht (Cdre, 1995–97), Wig and Pen.

OWENS, John Ridland; Chairman: Owens Associates, independent consultancy specialising in strategic advice and government relations, since 1993; Do It Even Better Ltd, since 2001; *b* 21 May 1932; *s* of Dr Ridland Owens and late Elsie Owens; *m* 1st, 1958, Susan Lilian (*née* Pilcher); two *s* one *d*; 2nd, 1985, Cynthia Rose (*née* Forbes); one *s*. *Educ:* Merchant Taylors' Sch.; St John's Coll., Oxford (MA). National Service, RA (Lieut), 1951–52. ICI, 1955–67; Managing Dir, Cape Asbestos Fibres, 1967–73; Dir Gen., Dairy Trade Fedn, 1973–83; Dep. Chm., Assilec, Paris, 1973–83; Exec. Dir, Nat. Dairy Council, 1975–83; Dep. Dir Gen., CBI, 1983–90; Dir Gen., Building Employers Confederation, 1990–92; Dir, UK Skills Ltd, 1990–92. Chm., Haringey Healthcare NHS Trust, 1993–99. Vice-Chm., EEC Adv. Cttee on Milk and Milk Products; Member: Food and Drink Industry Council, 1973–83; RSA Industry Cttee for Industry Year, 1986; Council, Assoc. of Business Sponsorship of the Arts, 1985–94; Exec. Cttee, PRO NED, 1983–90; Council, CBI, 1990–92; NHS Supplies Policy Steering Gp, 1995–97; Mem. Trust Council, 1995–97, Chm., Procurement and Facilities Mgt Gp, 1995–97, NAHAT, then NHS Confedn. Member: Council, CGLI, 1988–93; Court, City Univ., 1988–. Founder: Stokesley Soc.; Civil Trust for NE; Nat. Mus. of Dairying. FRSA (Mem. Council, 1995–). Mem. Court, Merchant Taylors' Co., 1982–. Governor: Merchant Taylors' Sch., 1996– (Vice-Chm. Govs, 1999–); Middx Univ., 1999–. *Publications:* Marketing for the NHS —Putting Patients First, 1993; Strategic Procurement for the NHS: working with suppliers, 1996; articles for The Times Review of Industry. *Recreations:* painting, music, walking. *Address:* 40 Blenheim Terrace, NW8 0EG. *T:* (020) 7372 7783, *Fax:* (020) 7372 1114; *e-mail:* jowensoa@aol.com. *Club:* Reform.

OWENS, Dr Susan Elizabeth, OBE 1998; Reader in Environment and Policy, Department of Geography, University of Cambridge, since 2000; Fellow of Newnham College, Cambridge, since 1981; *b* 24 Jan. 1954; *d* of Alfred Raymond Penrose and Patricia Mary Penrose (*née* Dorrell); *m* 1976. *Educ:* Stevenage Girls' Sch.; Univ. of East Anglia (BSc Hons, PhD). Res. Officer, Energy Panel, SSRC, 1979; Res. Fellow, Inst. of Planning Studies, Univ. of Nottingham, 1980–81; University of Cambridge: Asst Lectr in Geography, 1981–86; Lectr, 1986–2000. Global Envmtl Change Programme Res. Fellow, ESRC, 1993–94. Member: UK Round Table on Sustainable Develt, 1995–98; Countryside Commn, 1996–99; Govt Adv. Panel on Integrated Transport Policy, 1997–98; Royal Commn on Envmtl Pollution, 1998– (Special Advr, 1992–94). Back Award, RGS (with IBG), 1999. *Publications:* Energy, Planning and Urban Form, 1986; (jtly) Environment, Resources and Conservation, 1990; (ed jtly) Britain's Changing Environment from the Air, 1991; (jtly) Land Use Planning Policy and Climate Change, 1992; contrib. learned jls, incl. Trans Inst. of British Geographers, Land Use Policy, Town Planning Review, Political Qly. *Recreations:* walking, literature. *Address:* Department of Geography, University of Cambridge, Downing Place, Cambridge CB2 3EN. *T:* (01223) 333362, 333399.

OWER, Dr David Cheyne, TD 1975; Senior Principal Medical Officer, Department of Health and Social Security, 1976–87; *b* 29 July 1931; *s* of Ernest Ower and Helen Edith Cheyne (*née* Irvine); *m* 1954, June Harris; two *s* two *d*. *Educ:* King's Coll. Sch., Wimbledon; King's Coll., London; King's Coll. Hosp. Med. Sch. (MB, BS 1954). DObstRCOG 1959; FFPHM (FFCM 1983; MFCM 1976). Jun. hosp. appts, King's Coll. Hosp. and Kingston Hosp., 1955; RAF Med. Br., 1956–58; gen. practice, 1959–64; DHSS (formerly Min. of Health) Med. Staff, 1965–87. T&AVR, and RAMC(V), 1962–; Lt-Col RAMC(V); CO 221 (Surrey) Field Amb., 1973–75. *Recreations:* music, bridge, thinking about playing golf. *Address:* Merlewood, 94 Coombe Lane West, Kingston-upon-Thames, Surrey KT2 7DB. *T:* (020) 8942 8552.

OWERS, Anne Elizabeth, CBE 2001; HM Chief Inspector of Prisons for England and Wales, since 2001; *b* 23 June 1947; *d* of William Spark and Anne Smailes Spark (*née* Knox); *m* 1968 (marr. diss.); two *s* one *d*. *Educ:* Washington Grammar Sch., Co. Durham; Univ. of Cambridge (BA Hons). Research and teaching in Zambia, 1968–71; work at JCWI, 1981–92 (Gen. Sec., 1986–92); Dir, Justice, 1992–2001. Chm. Bd of Trustees, Refugee Legal Centre, 1994–98; Member: Lord Chancellor's Adv. Cttee on Legal Educn and Conduct, 1997–99; Home Office Task Force on Human Rights, 1999–2001; Legal Services Consultative Panel, 2000–. *Publications:* (ed jtly) Economic, Social and Cultural Rights, 1999; chapters and papers on immigration and nationality matters. *Recreations:* theatre, music, friends, family. *Address:* HM Inspectorate of Prisons, Home Office, 50 Queen Anne's Gate, SW1H 9AT.

OXBURGH, family name of **Baron Oxburgh**.

OXBURGH, Baron *cr* 1999 (Life Peer), of Liverpool in the county of Merseyside; **Ernest Ronald Oxburgh,** KBE 1992; PhD; FRS 1978; Rector, Imperial College of Science, Technology and Medicine, 1993–2001; *b* 2 Nov. 1934; *m* Ursula Mary Brown; one *s* two *d*. *Educ:* Liverpool Inst.; University Coll., Oxford (BA 1957, MA 1960); Univ. of Princeton (PhD 1960). Departmental Demonstrator, 1960–61, Lectr in Geology, 1962–78, Univ. of Oxford; Fellow of St Edmund Hall, Oxford, 1964–78, Emeritus Fellow, 1978, Hon. Fellow, 1986; University of Cambridge: Prof. of Mineralogy and Petrology, 1978–91; Hd of Dept of Earth Scis, 1980–88; Fellow of Trinity Hall, 1978–82, Hon. Fellow, 1983; Queens' College: Pres., 1982–89; Professorial Fellow, 1989–91; Hon. Fellow, 1992; Chief Scientific Advr, MoD, 1988–93. Vis. Professor: CIT, 1967–68; Stanford and Cornell Univs, 1973–74; Sherman Fairchild Distinguished Vis. Scholar, CIT, 1985–86. Trustee, Natural History Mus., 1993– (Chm. Trustees, 1999–). Chm., H of L Select Cttee on Sci. and Technol., 2001–. Member: SERC, 1988–93; Hong Kong UGC, 1988–; Nat. Cttee of Inquiry into Higher Educn (Dearing Cttee), 1996–97. President: Eur. Union of Geosciences, 1985–87 (Hon. Fellow 1993); BAAS, 1995–96. FGS (Pres., 2000–); Fellow: Geol. Soc. of America; Amer. Geophys. Union. Hon. Mem., Geologists' Assoc.; Foreign Corresp., Geologische Bundesanstalt, Austria and of Geological Soc. of Vienna; For. Mem., Venezuelan Acad. of Scis, 1992; Deutsche Acad. der Naturforscher Leopoldina, 1994; Corresp. Mem., Australian Acad. of Sci., 1999; For. Associate, US Acad. of Scis, 2001. Hon. FIMechE 1993; Hon. FCGI 1996. Hon. Fellow, Univ. Coll., Oxford, 1983. DSc (*hc*): Univ. of Paris, 1986; Leicester, 1990; Loughborough, 1991; Edinburgh, 1994; Birmingham, 1996; Liverpool, 1996. Bigsby Medal, Geol Soc., 1979. Officier, Ordre des Palmes Académiques (France), 1995. *Publications:* contribs to Nature, Jl Geophys Res., Phil Trans Royal Soc., Annual Reviews, Science, Bull. Geol Soc. America, Jl Fluid Mechanics, Jl Geol Soc. London. *Recreations:* mountaineering, orienteering, reading, theatre. *Address:* c/o House of Lords, SW1A 0PW.

OXBURY, Harold Frederick, CMG 1961; Deputy Director-General, British Council, 1962–66 (Assistant Director-General, 1959); *b* 11 Nov. 1903; *s* of Fredric Thomas Oxbury; *m* 1st, 1928, Violet Bennets (*d* 1954); one *s* one *d*; 2nd, 1954, Helen Shipley (*d* 1975), *d* of Amos Perry, FLS, VMH. *Educ:* Norwich Sch.; Trinity Coll., Cambridge (Senior Scholar). Entered Indian Civil Service, 1928; Chief Collector of Customs, Burma, 1940; in charge of civilian evacuation from N Burma, 1942; Government of Burma Representative, Burma Office, 1942–44; Dep. Controller Finance (Colonel), Military Administration, Burma, 1945; Finance Secretary, Government of Burma, 1946; British Council: Director, Colonies Dept, 1947; Controller Finance, 1956. *Publications:* Great Britons: twentieth century lives, 1985; contrib. number of articles to Dictionary of National Biography, and compiled epitomes for 1961–1985 in Concise edn, 3 vols, 1992. *Recreations:* writing, painting. *Address:* 122B Woodstock Road, Oxford OX2 7NF.

OXENBURY, Helen Gillian; children's writer and illustrator; *b* Suffolk, 2 June 1938; *d* of Thomas Bernard Oxenbury and Muriel (*née* Taylor); *m* 1964, John Burningham, *qv*; one *s* two *d*. *Educ:* Ipswich Sch. of Art; Central Sch. of Art. Stage designer, Colchester, 1960, Tel-Aviv, 1961; TV designer, London, 1963. *Publications: author and illustrator:* Number of Things, 1967; ABC of Things, 1971; Pig Tale, 1973; (with F. Maschler) A Child's Book of Manners: Verses, 1978; The Queen and Rosie Randall, 1979; 729 Curious Creatures, 1980; 729 Merry Mixips, 1980; 729 Puzzle People, 1980; 729 Animal Allsorts, 1980; Crazy Creatures, 1980; Assorted Animals, 1980; Bill and Stanley, 1981; Bedtime, 1982; Monkey See, Monkey Do, 1982; Holidays, 1982; Helping, 1982; Mother's Helper, 1982; Animals, 1982; Beach Day, 1982; Shopping Trip, 1982; Good Night, Good Morning, 1982; The Birthday Party, 1983; The Dancing Class, 1983; Eating Out, 1983; The Car Trip, 1983; The Drive, 1983; The Checkup, 1983; First Day of School, 1983; First Day at Playschool, 1983; Playschool, 1983; Grandma and Grandpa, 1984; Our Dog, 1984; The Important Visitor, 1984; Helen Oxenbury Nursery Story Book, 1985; Tom and Pippo Go Shopping, 1988; Tom and Pippo's Day, 1988; Tom and Pippo in the Garden, 1988; Tom and Pippo Go for a Walk, 1988; Tom and Pippo Make a Mess, 1988; Tom and Pippo Read a Story, 1988; Tom and Pippo See the Moon, 1988; Tom and Pippo and the Washing Machine, 1988; Pippo Gets Lost, 1989; Tom and Pippo and the Dog, 1989; Tom and Pippo in the Snow, 1989; Tom and Pippo Make a Friend, 1989; Tom and Pippo on the Beach, 1993; It's My Birthday, 1994; First Nursery Stories, 1994; *illustrator:* The Great Big Enormous Turnip, 1968; The Quangle-Wangle's Hat, 1969; Letters of Thanks, 1969; The Dragon of an Ordinary Family, 1969; The Hunting of the Snark, 1970; Meal One, 1971; Cakes and Custard: Children's Rhymes, 1974; Balooky Klujypop, 1975; Animal House, 1976; Tiny Tim: Verses for Children, 1981; We're Going on a Bear Hunt, 1989; Farmer Duck, 1992; The Three Little Wolves and The Big Bad Pig, 1993; So Much, 1994; Alice in Wonderland, 1999. *Address:* c/o Greene and Heaton Ltd, 37 Goldhawk Road, W12 8QQ.

OXENBURY, Dame Shirley (Ann), DBE 1992 (OBE 1987); Personal Assistant to Rt Hon. Christopher Patten, 1997–2000; *b* 4 July 1936. *Educ:* Ensham County Sch., London, SW17. PA to Harold Fielding, 1965–70; Personal Assistant (at Conservative Central Office) to Chairman of the Conservative Party: Katharine Macmillan, Sara Morrison, Baroness Young, 1970–75; Lord Thorneycroft, 1975–81; Cecil Parkinson, 1981–83; John Gummer, 1983–85; Norman Tebbit, 1985–87; Peter Brooke, 1987–89; Kenneth Baker, 1989–90; Christopher Patten, 1990–92; Norman Fowler, 1992–94; Jeremy Hanley, 1994–95; Brian Mawhinney, 1995–97. Women's Transport Service (FANY), 1979–87. *Recreations:* tennis, swimming, arts, learning languages. *T:* (020) 7821 1051.

OXFORD, Bishop of, since 1987; **Rt Rev. Richard Douglas Harries;** *b* 2 June 1936; *s* of late Brig. W. D. J. Harries, CBE and Mrs G. M. B. Harries; *m* 1963, Josephine Bottomley, MA, MB, BChir, DCH; one *s* and *d*. *Educ:* Wellington Coll.; RMA, Sandhurst; Selwyn Coll., Cambridge (MA 1965; Hon. Fellow, 1998); Cuddesdon Coll., Oxford. Lieut, Royal Corps of Signals, 1955–58. Curate, Hampstead Parish Church, 1963–69; Chaplain, Westfield Coll., 1966–69; Lectr, Wells Theol Coll., 1969–72; Warden of Wells, Salisbury and Wells Theol Coll., 1971–72; Vicar, All Saints, Fulham, 1972–81; Dean, King's Coll., London, 1981–87. GOE examnr in Christian Ethics, 1972–76; Dir, Post Ordination Trng for Kensington Jurisdiction, 1973–79. Chm., C of E Bd for Social Responsibility, 1996–2001; Vice-Chairman: Council of Christian Action, 1979–87; Council for Arms Control, 1982–87; Member: Home Office Adv. Cttee for reform of law on sexual offences, 1981–85; ACC, 1994–; Bd, Christian Aid, 1994–; Royal Commn on H of L reform, 1999; Chairman: Southwark Ordination Course, 1982–87; Shalom; ELTSA (End Loans to Southern Africa), 1982–87; CCJ, 1992–2001. Pres., Johnson Soc., 1988–89. Consultant to Archbishops of Canterbury and York on Interfaith Relns, with special resp. for Jewish Christian relns, 1986–92 (Sir Sigmund Sternberg Award, 1989). Radio and TV work. Lectures: Hockerill, and Drawbridge, London, 1982; Stockton, London Business Sch., 1992; Pall Mall, Inst. of Dirs, 1993; Theological, QUB, 1993; Heslington, York, 1994. FKC 1983; FRSL 1996. Hon. DD London, 1994. *Publications:* Prayers of Hope, 1975; Turning to Prayer, 1978; Prayers of Grief and Glory, 1979; Being a Christian, 1981; Should Christians Support Guerillas?, 1982; The Authority of Divine Love, 1983; Praying Round the Clock, 1983; Prayer and the Pursuit of Happiness, 1985; Morning has Broken, 1985; Christianity and War in a Nuclear Age, 1986; C. S. Lewis: the man and his God, 1987; Christ is Risen, 1988; Is There a Gospel for the Rich?, 1992; Art and the Beauty of God, 1993; The Real God, 1994; Questioning Belief, 1995; A Gallery of Reflections: the Nativity of Christ, 1995; In the Gladness of Today, 1999; *edited:* (jtly) Seasons of the Spirit, 1984; The One Genius; Through the Year with Austin Farrer, 1987; (jtly) Two Cheers for Secularism, 1998; *edited and contributed:* What Hope in an Armed World?, 1982; Reinhold Niebuhr and the Issues of Our Time, 1986; *contributed to:* Stewards of the Mysteries of God, 1979; Unholy Warfare, 1983; The Cross and the Bomb, 1983; Dropping the Bomb, 1985; Julian, Woman of our Time, 1985; If Christ be not raised, 1986; The Reality of God, 1986; A Necessary End, 1991; articles in Theology, The Times, The Observer and various other periodicals. *Recreations:* theatre, literature, walking, lecturing on cruises. *Address:* Diocesan Church House, North Hinksey, Oxford OX2 0NB. *T:* (01865) 244566.

OXFORD, Archdeacon of; *see* Morrison, Ven. J. A.

OXFORD AND ASQUITH, 2nd Earl of, *cr* 1925; **Julian Edward George Asquith,** KCMG 1964 (CMG 1961); Viscount Asquith, *cr* 1925; Governor and Commander-in-Chief, Seychelles, 1962–67; Commissioner, British Indian Ocean Territory, 1965–67; *b* 22 April 1916; *o s* of late Raymond Asquith and Katharine Frances (*d* 1976), *d* of late Sir John Horner, KCVO; *S* grandfather, 1928; *m* 1947, Anne Mary Celestine, CStJ (*d* 1998), *d* of late Sir Michael Palairet, KCMG; two *s* three *d*. *Educ:* Ampleforth; Balliol Coll., Oxford (Scholar), 1st Class Lit. Hum., 1938. Lieut, RE, 1941; Assistant District Commissioner, Palestine, 1942–48; Dep. Chief Secretary, British Administration, Tripolitania, 1949; Director of the Interior, Government of Tripolitania, 1951; Adviser to Prime Minister of Libya, 1952; Administrative Secretary, Zanzibar, 1955; Administrator

of St Lucia, WI, 1958. KStJ. *Heir:* s Viscount Asquith, *qv.* *Address:* The Manor House, Mells, Frome, Somerset BA11 3PN. *T:* (01373) 812324. *Club:* Naval and Military.
See also Hon. D. A. G. Asquith, Baron Hylton.

OXFUIRD, 13th Viscount of, *cr* 1651; **George Hubbard Makgill,** CBE 1997; Bt 1627; Lord Macgill of Cousland, 1651; *b* 7 Jan. 1934; *s* of Richard James Robert Haldane Makgill, RNZAF (*d* 1948) (*yr s* of 11th Bt) and Elizabeth Lyman (*d* 1981), *d* of Gorham Hubbard, Boston, USA; *S* uncle, 1986; *m* 1st, 1967, Alison Campbell (marr. diss. 1977), *er d* of late Neils Max Jensen, Randers, Denmark; three *s* (inc. twin *s*); 2nd, 1980, Venetia Cunitia Mary, *o d* of Major Charles Anthony Steward, Crondall, Farnham, Surrey; one *s*. *Educ:* St Peter's School, Cambridge, NZ; Wanganui Collegiate School. Commissioned RAF, 1955–58. Overseas Exec., Lansing Bagnall Ltd, 1964–92. A Deputy Speaker, House of Lords, 1990–; Vice-Chm., Assoc. of Cons. Peers, 1993–; Mem., Jt Cttee on Statutory Instruments, 1991–97; Mem., Hybrid Bills Cttee, 1995–, Offices Cttee, 1995–97, H of L; elected Mem., H of L, 1999. *Recreations:* fishing, gardening, shooting. *Heir:* s Master of Oxfuird, *qv.* *Address:* House of Lords, SW1A 0PW. *Club:* Caledonian.

OXFUIRD, Master of; Hon. Ian Arthur Alexander Makgill, MA; *b* 14 Oct. 1969; *s* and *heir* of 13th Viscount of Oxfuird, *qv.*

OXLADE, Zena Elsie, CBE 1984; SRN, RNT; Regional Nursing Officer, East Anglian Regional Health Authority, 1981–87, retired; *b* 26 April 1929; *d* of James and Beatrice May Oxlade. *Educ:* Latymer Grammar Sch., N9. SRN 1950; RNT (London Univ.). Ward Sister, 1952; Theatre Sister 1953; Night Sister, 1954; Sister Tutor, 1956; Principal Tutor, 1963; Principal Nursing Officer, 1969; Chief Nursing Officer, 1973; District Nursing Officer, 1974; Area Nursing Officer, Suffolk AHA, 1978–81. Chm., GNC, 1977–83 (Mem., 1975–83; Chm., GNC Trust, 1983–); Mem., UK Council for Nurses, Midwives and Health Visitors, 1983–89. DUniv Surrey, 1993. *Publication:* Ear, Nose and Throat Nursing, 1972. *Recreations:* motoring, reading, handicrafts. *Address:* 5 Morgan Court, Claydon, Suffolk IP6 0AN. *T:* (01473) 831895.

OXLEY, Humphrey Leslie Malcolm, CMG 1966; OBE 1956; HM Diplomatic Service, retired; *b* 9 Oct. 1909; *s* of W. H. F. Oxley, MRCS, LRCP, FRCOG, and Lily Malcolm; *m* 1945, Frances Olga, *d* of George Bowden, San Jose, Costa Rica; twin *s*. *Educ:* Epsom Coll. Admitted Solicitor, 1933; Junior Legal Assistant, India Office, 1933; Commissioner for Oaths, 1934; Assistant Solicitor, 1944; Commonwealth Relations Office, 1947; Assistant Legal Adviser, 1961; Legal Counsellor, Commonwealth Office, 1965–67; HM Diplomatic Service, 1967; Dep. Legal Adviser, FCO, 1967–69. Legal Consultant to HM Comr, Magistrate, various legal appts, Anguilla, 1971–72. *Recreation:* gardening. *Address:* Sandpipers, Crooked Lane, Birdham, Chichester, West Sussex PO20 7ET. *Club:* Civil Service.

OXLEY, James Keith R.; *see* Rice-Oxley.

OXLEY, Julian Christopher; Director, Heatherwood and Wexham Park Hospitals NHS Trust, since 1999; *b* 23 Nov. 1938; *s* of Horace Oxley and Lilian Oxley (*née* Harris); *m* 1979, Carol (née Heath); one *d*; one *s* two *d* from previous marr. *Educ.* Clifton Coll., Bristol; Oriel Coll., Oxford (Organ Scholar, MA). FCA. Dir and Sec., Williams & James plc, 1970–84; Guide Dogs for the Blind Association: Dir and Sec., 1984–89; Dir-Gen., 1989–96; Chm., Internat. Fedn of Guide Dog Schs, 1990–97. Mem. Council, Gloucester Civic Trust, 1972–75. Chm. of Govs, Selwyn Sch., Gloucester, 1980–84. *Recreations:* music, old furniture, railway signalling. *Address:* Applecroft, Upper Basildon, Berks RG8 8NT. *T:* (01491) 671415; *e-mail:* julian.oxley@btinternet.com.

OXMANTOWN, Lord; Laurence Patrick Parsons; Leasing and PR Manager, East Lake Villas, Beijing; *b* 31 March 1969; *s* and *heir* of Earl of Rosse, *qv.* *Educ:* Aiglon Coll., Switzerland; Univ. of Beijing Language Inst. *Address:* Beijing, China.

OZ, Amos; Professor of Hebrew Literature, Ben-Gurion University of the Negev, since 1987 (Agnon Professor in Modern Hebrew Literature, 1993); *b* Jerusalem, 4 May 1939. *Educ:* Hebrew Univ. of Jerusalem (BA Hebrew Literature and Philosophy 1965). Teacher of Literature and Philosophy, Hulda High Sch. and Regl High Sch., Givat Brenner, 1963–86. Vis. Fellow, St Cross Coll., Oxford, 1969–70; Writer in Residence: Hebrew Univ. of Jerusalem, 1975–76, 1990; Tel Aviv Univ., 1996; Visiting Professor: Univ. of Calif at Berkeley, 1980; Oxford Univ., 1998; Writer in Residence and Visiting Professor of Literature: Boston Univ., 1987; Princeton Univ., 1997. Member: Peace Now, 1977–; Catalan Acad. of Mediterranean, 1989; Acad. of Hebrew Language, 1991. Hon Dr: Hebrew Union Coll., Cincinnati and Jerusalem, 1988; Western New England Coll., Mass, 1988; Tel Aviv, 1992; Brandeis, 1998. Bernstein Prize, 1983; Bialik Prize, 1986; Internat. Peace Prize, German Publishers' Union, 1992; Israel Prize for Literature, 1998. Officier de l'Ordre des Arts et des Lettres, 1984, Chevalier de la Légion d'Honneur, 1997, (France). *Publications: stories:* Where the Jackal Howls, 1965; *novels:* Elsewhere Perhaps, 1966; My Michael, 1968 (elected one of 100 masterpieces of the 20th century, Bertelsmann Club, Germany, 1999; elected one of best foreign bks in China, 1999); Touch the Water, Touch the Wind, 1973; A Perfect Peace, 1982; Black Box, 1987 (Prix Femina Etranger, Wingate Prize, 1988); To Know a Woman, 1989; The Third Condition, 1991; Don't Call it Night, 1994; Panther in the Basement, 1995; The Same Sea, 1999; *for children:* Soumchi, 1977 (Ze'ev Award, Hans Christian Andersen Medal, 1978; Luchs Prize, Germany, Hamore Prize, France, 1993); *novellas:* Unto Death, 1971; The Hill of Evil Counsel, 1976; *anthology:* Other People, 1974; *essays:* Under This Blazing Light, 1978; In the Land of Israel, 1983; The Slopes of Lebanon, 1987; Report of the Situation, 1992; The Silence of Heaven, 1993; Israel, Palestine and Peace, 1994; The Real Cause of My Grandmother's Death, 1994; The Story Begins, 1996; All Our Hopes, 1998; work translated into 33 languages; articles on literary, political and ideological topics in jls.

OZAWA, Seiji, Japanese conductor; Music Director: Boston Symphony Orchestra, 1973–summer 2002; Vienna State Opera, from autumn 2002; *b* Shenyang, China, 1 Sept. 1935; *m* 1st, Kyoko Edo; 2nd, Vera Ilyan; one *s* one *d*. *Educ:* Toho School of Music, Tokyo; studied with Hideo Saito, Eugène Bigot, Herbert von Karajan, Leonard Bernstein. Won Besançon Internat. Comp., 1959, Koussevitzky Meml Scholarship, 1960. Asst Conductor, NY Philharmonic Orch., 1961–62 and 1964–65; music dir, Ravinia Fest., Chicago, 1964–68; conductor, Toronto Symph. Orch., 1965–69; music dir, San Francisco Symph. Orch., 1970–76, music advisor, 1976–77; Artistic Advr, Tanglewood Fest., 1970–73. Tours with Boston Symphony Orchestra: Europe, 1976, 1988, 1993; Japan, 1978; China (musical and cultural exchange), 1979; European music festivals, 1979, 1984, 1991; 14 USA cities (orchestra's hundredth birthday), 1982; Japan, 1982 and 1986; Far East, 1989, 1994; S America, 1992; tours with Vienna Philharmonic: Asia, 1993, 1996, 2000; Europe, 1997, 1998, 2000, 2001; Berlin Philharmonic: regular concerts; tours incl. US/Asia, 1993; Guest conductor with major orchestras in Canada, Europe, Far East and USA; Conductor: Saito Kinen Orch., Japan (European tours, 1987, 1989, 1991; Carnegie Hall NY, 1991; Saito Kinen Fest., 1992–); Salzburg Fest. Opera highlights: La Scala, Milan; Covent Garden, London; Paris Opera (incl. world première of Messiaen's Saint François d'Assise); Vienna State Op. début, Eugene Onegin, 1988; many recordings (awards). Evening at Symphony, PBS television series with Boston Symphony Orch. (Emmy award). Hon. DMus: Univ. of Mass; New England Conservatory of Music; Wheaton Coll., Norton, Mass. Seiji Ozawa Hall inaugurated at Tanglewood, Mass, 1994. Inouye Award (first), for lifetime achievement in the arts, Japan, 1994. *Address:* c/o Columbia Artists Management Inc., 165 West 57th Street, New York, NY 10019, USA.

P

PACEY, Stephen James; Social Security and Child Support Commissioner, since 1996; *b* 5 July 1949; *s* of Randall Brown Pacey and May Pacey (*née* Oldknow); *m* 1978, Jessica Susan Turley; one *s*. *Educ:* Kimberley County Secondary Modern Sch.; Beeston Coll.; Trent Poly. (LLB 1971). Admitted Solicitor, 1975 (Wolverhampton Law Soc. Centenary Prizeman, 1975). Directorate of Legal Affairs, CBI, 1971–72; Lectr in Law, Isleworth Poly., 1972–73; solicitor in private practice, 1975–87; consultant planning inspector, 1989–91; Chm., Independent Tribunal Service, 1991–96; Dep. Social Security and Child Support Comr, 1993–96. Chairman (part-time): Social Security Appeal Tribunals, 1984–91; Med. Appeal Tribunals, 1987–91; Industrial Tribunals, 1988–91; Registered Homes Appeal Tribunals, 1992–96; pt-time Immigration Adjudicator, 1998. Freeman, City of London. *Recreations:* photography, literature, performing arts. *Address:* Office of the Social Security and Child Support Commissioners, Harp House, 83–86 Farringdon Street, EC4A 4DH. *T:* (020) 7395 3347.

PACINO, Alfredo James, (Al); actor; *b* New York, 25 April 1940; *s* of Salvatore Pacino and late Rosa Pacino; one *d* by Jan Tarrant. *Educ:* High Sch. of Performing Arts, NY; Actors Studio, NY. Has worked as mail delivery boy, messenger, cinema usher and bldg supt; actor, dir and writer, NY theatres; appeared in première of The Indian Wants the Bronx, Waterford, Conn, 1966, and NY, 1968; Broadway début, Does a Tiger Wear a Necktie?, 1969 (Tony Award, best supporting actor); film début, Me, Natalie, 1969; *theatre includes:* Camino Real, Lincoln Center Rep. Theater, 1970; The Basic Training of Pavlo Hummel, 1972, (title rôle) Richard III, 1973, Boston Theater Co.; Arturo Ui, 1975; Jungle of Cities, 1979; American Buffalo, 1981, transf. UK, 1984; Julius Caesar, 1988; Salome, 1992; Circle in the Square, 1992; Hughie (also dir), 1996; *films include:* Panic in Needle Park, 1971; The Godfather, 1972 (Best Actor Award, Nat. Soc. of Film Critics, USA); Scarecrow, 1973; Serpico, The Godfather Part II, 1974; Dog Day Afternoon, 1975; Bobby Deerfield, 1977; And Justice for All, 1979; Cruising, 1980; Author! Author!, 1982; Scarface, 1983; Revolution, 1985; The Local Stigmatic, 1989 (also play, Actors Playhouse, NY, 1969); Sea of Love, The Godfather Part III, 1990; Frankie and Johnny, 1991; Glengarry Glen Ross, Scent of a Woman (Acad. Award for best actor, 1993), 1992; Carlito's Way, Two Bits, 1994; City Hall, Heat, 1995; Donny Brasco, Looking for Richard (also writer, prod. and dir), 1996; Devil's Advocate, 1997; Man of the People, 1999; Any Given Sunday, Insider, Chinese Coffee (also dir), 2000. Co-artistic Dir, Actors Studio Inc., NY, 1982–83; Mem., Artistic Directorate, Globe Theatre, 1997–. Cecil B. DeMille award for lifetime achievement, Golden Globe Awards, 2001. *Address:* c/o CAA, 9830 Wilshire Boulevard, Beverly Hills, CA 90212, USA.

PACK, Prof. Donald Cecil, CBE 1978 (OBE 1969); MA, DSc; CMath, FIMA; FEIS, FRSE; Professor of Mathematics, University of Strathclyde, Glasgow, 1953–82, Hon. Professor, 1982–86, Professor Emeritus, 1986 (Vice-Principal, 1968–72); *b* 14 April 1920; *s* of late John Cecil and late Minnie Pack, Higham Ferrers; *m* 1947, Constance Mary Gillam; two *s* one *d*. *Educ:* Wellingborough School; New Coll., Oxford. Lecturer in Mathematics, University College, Dundee, University of St Andrews, 1947–52; Visiting Research Associate, University of Maryland, 1951–52; Lecturer in Mathematics, University of Manchester, 1952–53. Guest Professor: Technische Universität, Berlin, 1967; Bologna Univ. and Politecnico Milano, 1980; Technische Hochschule Darmstadt, 1981; other vis. appts at Warsaw Univ., 1977, Kaiserslautern, 1980, 1984; DERA Vis. Fellow, 1999–. Member: Dunbartonshire Educn Cttee, 1960–66; Gen. Teaching Council for Scotland, 1966–73; Chairman: Scottish Certificate of Educn Examn Bd, 1969–77; Cttee of Inquiry into Truancy and Indiscipline in Schools in Scotland, 1974–77; Member: various Govt Scientific Cttees, 1952–84; Defence Scientific Adv. Council, 1975–80; British Nat. Cttee for Theoretical and Applied Mechanics, 1973–78; Internat. Adv. Cttee on Rarefied Gas Dynamics Symposia, 1976–88; Council, Gesellschaft für Angewandte Mathematik und Mechanik, 1977–83; Council, RSE, 1960–63; Scottish Arts Council, 1980–85; Hon. Mem., European Consortium for Mathematics in Industry, 1988. Founder Chm., NYO of Scotland, 1978–88 (Hon. Pres., 1988–); Mem., European Music Year UK Cttee (Chm., Scottish Sub-Cttee), 1982–86; First Hon. Treasurer, IMA, 1964–72; Governor, Hamilton Coll. of Education, 1977–81; Pres., Milngavie Music Club, 1983–93 (Hon. Pres., 1994–). *Publications:* papers on fluid dynamics. *Recreations:* music, gardening, golf. *Address:* 18 Buchanan Drive, Bearsden, Glasgow G61 2EW. *T:* (0141) 942 5764.

PACK, Maj.-Gen. Simon James, CB 1997; CBE 1994 (OBE 1990); Royal Marines, retired; International Teams Director, England and Wales Cricket Board, 1997–2000; *b* 10 July 1944; *s* of Captain A. J. James Pack, OBE, RN and Eloise Pack; *m* 1970, Rosemary-Anne Fuller; one *s* one *d*. *Educ:* Fernden Prep. Sch.; Hurstpierpoint Coll. Commnd into RM, 1962; served Malaya, Sarawak, HMS Zulu, 1963–68; ADC to Governor of Queensland, 1969–70; Malta, Army Sch. of Infantry, Norway, Hong Kong, MoD, 1971–80; Directing Staff, Army Staff Coll., 1981–83; MoD, 1984–87; CO 45 Commando Group, 1987–89; COS, HQ Commando Forces, 1989–90; Commitments Staff, MoD, 1990–94; Comdr, British Forces, Gibraltar, 1994–97. ADC to the Queen, 1991–94. Gov., Oratory Sch., Reading, 1991–. FIMgt 1997. *Recreations:* cricket, golf, current affairs, heritage, gardening, music. *Address:* The Oast House, Chawton, Alton, Hants GU34 1SJ; 10 Berisford Mews, St Ann's Crescent, SW18 2LW.

PACKER, Rt Rev. John Richard; *see* Ripon and Leeds, Bishop of.

PACKER, Prof. Kenneth John, PhD; FRS 1991; CChem, FRSC; Research Professor in Chemistry, Nottingham University, 1993–2001; *b* 18 May 1938; *s* of late Harry James Packer and Alice Ethel Packer (*née* Purse); *m* 1962, Christine Frances Hart; one *s* one *d*. *Educ:* Harvey Grammar Sch., Folkestone; Imperial Coll., London (BSc Hons Chemistry, 1st cl., 1959); Cambridge Univ. (PhD 1962). CChem 1985, FRSC 1985. Post-doctoral Res. Fellow, Central Res. Dept, E. I. duPont de Nemours, Wilmington, USA, 1962–63; University of East Anglia: SERC Res. Fellow, 1963–64; Lectr in Chemistry, 1964–71; Sen. Lectr, 1971–78; Reader, 1978–82; Prof., 1982–84; BP Research: Sen. Res. Associate, Spectroscopy, 1984–87; Prin. Res. Associate, 1987–90; Chief Res. Associate, Analytical Res. Div., 1990–92; Chief Scientist, Gp Res. and Engrg, BP Internat., 1992–93. Visiting Professor in Chemistry: UEA; Southampton Univ.; KCL; Imperial Coll., London, 1985–92. Science and Engineering Research Council: Member: Physical Chem. Cttee, 1976–81; Chem. Cttee, 1979–82; Sci. Bd, 1988–91; Chm., Central Services Panel, 1980–82; Cttee Mem. and Sec., British Radiofrequency Spectroscopy Gp; Mem. Council, Faraday Div., 1988–91, Mem. Scientific Affairs Bd, 1992–, RSC; Hon. Sec., Royal Instn of GB, 1993–98. Gov., Hampton Sch., Hanworth, 1990–93. Ed., Molecular Physics, 1982–88. *Publications:* NMR Spectroscopy of Solid Polymers, 1993; contrib. approx. 150 papers on topics involving develt and application of NMR spectroscopy to internat. jls. *Recreations:* fly-fishing, ski-ing, gardening, music. *Address:* The Beeches, 68 Cawston Road, Aylsham, Norwich NR11 6ED. *T:* (01263) 731728.

PACKER, Kerry Francis Bullmore, AC 1983; Chairman, Consolidated Press Holdings Ltd, since 1974; *b* 17 Dec. 1937; *s* of late Sir Douglas Frank Hewson Packer, KBE, and Lady (Gretel Joyce) Packer (*née* Bullmore); *m* 1963, Roslyn Redman Weedon; one *s* one *d*. *Educ:* Cranbrook Sch., Sydney, NSW; Geelong C of E Grammar Sch., Vic. Largest shareholder in: Publishing and Broadcasting Ltd (publisher of magazines; major TV broadcaster). *Recreations:* golf, tennis, cricket, polo. *Address:* 54 Park Street, Sydney, NSW 2000, Australia. *T:* (2) 92828000. *Clubs:* Athenæum (Melbourne); Royal Sydney Golf, Australian Golf, Elanora Country, Tattersall's (NSW).

PACKER, Lucy Jeanne, (Lady Packer); *see* Neville-Rolfe, L. J.

PACKER, Sir Richard (John), KCB 2000; consultant; Permanent Secretary, Ministry of Agriculture, Fisheries and Food, 1993–2000; *b* 18 Aug. 1944; *s* of late George Charles Packer and Dorothy May Packer (*née* Reynolds); *m* 1st, Alison Mary Sellwood; two *s* one *d*; 2nd, Lucy Jeanne Blackett-Ord (*see* L. J. Neville-Rolfe); four *s*. *Educ:* City of London School; Manchester Univ. (BSc 1965, MSc 1966). Ministry of Agriculture, Fisheries and Food, 1967–2000: on secondment as 1st Sec., Office of Perm Rep. to EEC, 1973–76; Principal Private Sec. to Minister, 1976–78; Asst Sec., 1979; Under Sec., 1985–89; Dep. Sec. (Agricl Commodities, Trade and Food Prodn), 1989–93. *Recreations:* ideas, sport. *Address:* 113 St George's Road, SE1 6HY.

PACKER, William John; painter and critic; art critic, Financial Times, since 1974; *b* 19 Aug. 1940; *o s* of late Rex Packer and Evelyn Mary Packer (*née* Wornham); *m* 1965, Clare, *er d* of late Thomas Winn and Cecily Philip; three *d*. *Educ:* Windsor Grammar Sch.; Wimbledon Sch. of Art (NDD 1963); Brighton Coll. of Art (ATC 1964). Teaching full-time, 1964–67, part-time in art schs, 1967–77; external assessor, 1980–2000. First exhibited, RA, 1963 and continues to exhibit widely; one-man exhibn, Piers Feetham Gall., 1996, 2001. Member: Fine Art Board, CNAA, 1976–83; Adv. Cttee, Govt Art Collection, 1977–84; Crafts Council, 1980–87; Cttee, Nat. Trust Foundn for Art, 1986–. Exhibn selector, incl. first British Art Show, 1979–80. London corresp., Art & Artists, 1969–74. Inaugural Henry Moore Lectr, Florence, 1986. Ballinglen Artist Fellow, Ballinglen Foundn, Co. Mayo, 1995. Hon. Fellow, RCA, 1988; Hon. RBA 1992; Hon. RBS. *Publications:* The Art of Vogue Covers, 1980; Fashion Drawing in Vogue, 1983; Henry Moore: a pictorial biography, 1985; Carl Erickson, and René Bouët-Willaumez, 1989. *Recreations:* hockey, Venice. *Address:* 39 Elms Road, Clapham, SW4 9EP. *T:* (020) 7622 1108. *Clubs:* Chelsea Arts, Academy.

PACKSHAW, Robin David; Chairman, International City Holdings, Money and Securities Brokers, 1985–89; *b* 20 March 1933; *s* of late Savil Packshaw and Fay Mary Packshaw; *m*; three *s* one *d*. *Educ:* Diocesan Coll., Cape Town; Bradfield Coll., Berks. Served RM, 1951–53; commnd and served in Special Boat Service; RMFVR, 1953–58. Iraq Petroleum Co. Ltd, 1953–63; Long Till and Colvin Ltd, 1963–69; founded Packshaw & Associates Ltd, Sterling Money Brokers, 1969, became Fulton Packshaw Ltd, 1973; Chairman: Charles Fulton (UK) Ltd, Internat. For. Exch. and Currency Deposit Brokers, 1982; Manex Sterling Brokers Ltd, 1993; Consultant: BITC, 1990–92; London First, 1992–93; Sterling, then Sterling Internat., Brokers Ltd, 1993–99. Dep. Chm., Partners in the Countryside, 1996–2001. Chm., Radionic Assoc., 1991–99. Chm., Stours Br., N Dorset Conservation Assoc., 1989–95. Church Warden, All Saints, Stour Row, Dorset, 1984–95. Gov., Stower Provost Co. Primary Sch., 1992–95. Freeman, City of London, 1983; Life Mem., Guild of Freemen of City of London. FZS 1972; FRGS 1997; FRSA 1997. Hon. Fellow, Radionic Assoc., 1999. *Recreations:* travel, people, voluntary work. *Address:* 5 Hurlingham Court, Ranelagh Gardens, SW6 3SH. *T:* (020) 7736 6832, *Fax:* (020) 7371 7576.

PADFIELD, Nicholas David; QC 1991; a Recorder, since 1995; *b* 5 Aug. 1947; *s* of David Padfield and Sushila, *d* of Sir Samuel Runganadhan; *m* 1st, 1978, Nayana Parekh (*d* 1983); one *d*; 2nd, 1986, Mary Barran, JP, *d* of Sir Edward Playfair, KCB; two *s*. *Educ:* Dragon Sch., Charterhouse; University Coll., Oxford (Open Scholar, MA; hockey blue; England hockey internat.); Trinity Hall, Cambridge (LLM Internat Law). FCIArb. Called to the Bar, Inner Temple, 1972, Bencher, 1995; called to various overseas Bars; Mem. Panel, Treasury Counsel (Common Law), 1985–90. Mem., Panel of Lloyd's Arbitrators, 1991–. Dep. Chm., Cons. Party Ethics and Integrity Cttee. Trustee and Dir, Lord Glynn Eur. Law Foundn. Mem. Cttee, London Oratory Appeal, 1990–95. *Address:* 6 New Square, Lincoln's Inn, WC2A 3QS. *T:* (020) 7242 6105. *Clubs:* Garrick, Buck's, MCC; Vincent's (Oxford).

PADMORE, Elaine Marguirite; Director of Opera, Royal Opera House, Covent Garden, since 2000; *b* Haworth, Yorks, 3 Feb. 1947; *d* of Alfred and Florence Padmore. *Educ:* Newland High Sch., Hull; Arnold Sch., Blackpool; Birmingham Univ. (MA;

BMus); Guildhall Sch. of Music; LTCL. Liberal Studies Lectr, Croydon and Kingston Colls of Art, 1968–70; Books Editor, OUP Music Dept, 1970–71; Producer, BBC Music Div., 1971–76; Announcer, Radio 3, 1982–90. Major BBC Radio 3 series include: Parade, Music of Tchaikovsky's Russia, England's Pleasant Land, Journal de mes Mélodies; Presenter of numerous programmes, incl. Festival Comment, Edinburgh Fest., 1973–81; Chief Producer, Opera, BBC Radio, 1976–83: series incl. complete operas of Richard Strauss and first performances of works by Delius and Havergal Brian; formerly active as professional singer (soprano), particularly of opera; Lectr in Opera, RAM, 1979–87; Artistic Director: Classical Prodns, London, 1990–92; Wexford Festival Opera, 1982–94; DGOS Opera Ireland, 1989–90 and 1991–93; Artistic Consultant, 1992 London Opera Fest.; Dir, Royal Danish Opera, Copenhagen, 1993–2000. Hon. ARAM. Hungarian Radio Pro Musica Award for prog. Summertime on Bredon, 1973; Prix Musical de Radio Brno for prog. The English Renaissance, 1974; Sunday Independent Award for services to music in Ireland, 1985. Kt, Order of Dannebrog (Denmark), 1994. *Publications:* Wagner (Great Composers' Series), 1970; Music in the Modern Age: chapter on Germany, 1973; contributor to: New Grove Dict. of Music, Proc. of Royal Musical Assoc., Music and Letters, The Listener. *Recreations:* gardening, travel, art exhibitions. *Address:* Royal Opera House, Covent Garden, WC2E 9DD.

PADOA-SCHIOPPA, Tommaso; banker and economist; Member, Executive Board, European Central Bank, since 1998; *b* Belluno, Italy, 23 July 1940. *Educ:* Luigi Boccini Univ., Milan; Massachusetts Inst. Technol. (MSc). C. & A. Brenninkmeyer, 1966–68; Economist, Res. Dept, Banca d'Italia, 1970–79; Dir Gen. for Econ. and Financial Affairs, CEC, Brussels, 1979–83; Central Dir for Econ. Res., 1983, Dep. Dir Gen., 1984–97, Banca d'Italia; Pres., Commissione Nazionale per le Società e la Borsa, 1997–98. Mem., Bd of Dirs, EIB, 1979–83. Jt Sec., Delors Cttee for Study of Eur. Econ. and Monetary Union, 1988–89; Chm., Banking Adv. Cttee, CEC, 1988–91; Member: G-7 Deputies; G-10 Deputies; G-20 Deputies; Chairman: Eur. Regl Cttee, IOSCO, 1997–98; FESCO, 1997–98; Mem., Wkg Party 3, Econ. Policy Cttee, OECD. Hon. Prof., Univ. of Frankfurt am Main, 1999. Alternate Mem. Council, Eur. Monetary Inst., 1995–97; Member, Advisory Board: Inst. for Internat. Econs; Eur. Univ. Inst. Hon. Dr Trieste, 1999. *Publications:* include: (with F. Modigliani) The Management of an Open Economy with 100% plus Wage Indexation, 1978; (with F. Padoa-Schioppa) Agenda e Non-Agenda: limiti o crisi della politica economica?, 1984; Money, Economic Policy and Europe, 1985; Efficiency, Stability and Equity: a strategy for the evolution of the economic system of the European Community, 1987; La moneta e il sistema dei pagamenti, 1992; The Road to Monetary Union in Europe: The Emperor, the Kings and the Genies, 1994; Europe: the impossible status quo, 1997; Il governo dell'economia, 1997; Che cosa ci ha insegnato l'avventura europea, 1998. *Address:* European Central Bank, Kaiserstrasse 29, 60311 Frankfurt am Main, Germany. *T:* (69) 13447170, *Fax:* (69) 13447163.

PADOVAN, John Mario Faskally; Chairman, Williams Lea Group, since 2000 (Director, 1992–2000); *b* 7 May 1938; *s* of Umberto Mario Padovan and Mary Nina Liddon Padovan; *m* 1964, Sally Kay (*née* Anderson); three *s*. *Educ:* St George's College, Weybridge; King's College London (LLB); Keble College, Oxford (BCL). FCA. County Bank, 1970–84: Dir, 1971; Dep. Chief Exec., 1974; Chief Exec., 1976; Chm., 1984; Dep. Chm., Hambros Bank and Dir, Hambros, 1984–86, Chm., Merchant Banking Div., Barclays de Zoete Wedd Gp, 1986–91; Dep. Chm., Barclays de Zoete Wedd, 1989–91; Dep. Chm., 1992, Chm., 1993–95, AAH; Dir, 1989–91, Chm., 1991–95, Mabey Hldgs. Chairman: Gardner Merchant, 1993–95; Furniture Village, 1998–; Schroder Split Fund, 2000– (Dir, 1992–); Director: Tesco, 1982–94; Whitbread, 1992–; Interserve; HFC Bank, 1997–. Mem. Court, Drapers' Co., 1991– (Master, 1999–2000). *Recreations:* golf, walking, contemporary art. *Address:* 15 Lord North Street, SW1P 3LD. *T:* (020) 7222 3261. *Clubs:* Royal St George's Golf, West Surrey Golf.

PAGE, family name of **Baron Whaddon.**

PAGE, Adrienne May, (Mrs A. C. Waldeck); QC 1999; a Recorder, since 1999; *b* 14 July 1952; *d* of Gwythian Lloyd Page and Betty Page (*née* Spring); *m* 1983, Anthony Crichton Waldeck; one step *s* one step *d*. *Educ:* Godolphin Sch., Salisbury; Univ. of Kent at Canterbury (BA Social Sci.). Called to the Bar, Middle Temple, 1974; Asst Recorder, 1995–99. *Recreations:* sailing, gardening. *Address:* 5 Raymond Buildings, Gray's Inn, WC1R 5BP. *T:* (020) 7242 2902. *Clubs:* Royal Southampton Yacht, Beaulieu River Sailing.

PAGE, Annette, (Mrs Ronald Hynd); Ballerina of the Royal Ballet until retirement, 1967; Ballet Mistress, Ballet of the Bayerischestaatsoper, Munich, 1984–86; *b* 18 Dec. 1932; *d* of James Lees and Margaret Page; *m* 1957, Ronald Hynd, *qv*; one *d*. *Educ:* Royal Ballet School. Audition and award of scholarship to Roy. Ballet Sch., 1944. Entry into touring company of Royal Ballet (then Sadler's Wells Theatre Ballet), 1950; promotion to major Royal Ballet Co. (Sadler's Wells Ballet), 1955. Mem., Arts Council of GB, 1976–79. *Roles included:* The Firebird, Princess Aurora in Sleeping Beauty, Odette-Odile in Swan Lake, Giselle, Lise in La Fille Mal Gardée, Juliet in Romeo and Juliet, Cinderella. *Recreations:* music, books, gardening.

PAGE, Anthony (Frederick Montague); stage, film and television director; *b* India, 21 Sept. 1935; *s* of Brig. F. G. C. Page, DSO, OBE, and P. V. M. Page. *Educ:* Oakley Hall, Cirencester; Winchester Coll. (Schol.); Magdalen Coll., Oxford (Schol., BA); Neighborhood Playhouse Sch. of the Theater, NY. Asst, Royal Court Theatre, 1958: co-directed Live Like Pigs, directed The Room; Artistic Dir, Dundee Repertory Theatre, 1962; The Caretaker, Oxford and Salisbury; Women Beware Women, and Nil Carborundum, Royal Shakespeare Co., 1963; BBC Directors' Course, then several episodes of Z-Cars, Horror of Darkness and 1st TV prodn Stephen D; Jt Artistic Dir, Royal Court, 1964–65; directed Inadmissible Evidence (later Broadway and film), A Patriot for Me, 1st revival of Waiting for Godot, Cuckoo in the Nest; Diary of a Madman, Duchess, 1966; Artistic Dir, two seasons at Royal Court: Uncle Vanya, 1970; Alpha Beta (also film); Hedda Gabler; Krapp's Last Tape; Not I; Cromwell; other plays transf. from Royal Court to West End: Time Present; Hotel in Amsterdam; revival, Look Back in Anger; West of Suez; directed Hamlet, Nottingham, 1970; Rules of the Game, Nat. Theatre; King Lear, Amer. Shakespeare Fest., 1975; Cowardice, Ambassadors, 1983; Heartbreak House, Broadway, 1984 (televised); Mrs Warren's Profession, RNT, 1985; Three Tall Women, Wyndham's, 1994; Absolute Hell, RNT, 1995; The Doll's House, Playhouse, 1996, NY, 1997 (Tony Award); A Delicate Balance, Theatre Royal, Haymarket, 1997; The Forest, Sleep With Me, 1999; Finding the Sun, Marriage Play, 2001, RNT; Cat on a Hot Tin Roof, Lyric, 2001; *television:* The Parachute; Emlyn; Hotel in Amsterdam; Speaking of Murder; You're Free; The Changeling; Headmaster; Sheppey; Absolute Hell, 1991; Middlemarch, 1994; in USA: Missiles of October; Pueblo Incident; FDR, the Last Year; Bill (starring Mickey Rooney (Golden Globe Award); Johnny Belinda; Bill on His Own; The Nightmare Years; Patricia Neal Story; Murder by Reason of Insanity; Second Serve; Pack of Lies; Chernobyl: The Final Warning, 1990; Guests of the Emperor; The Human Bomb; *films:* Inadmissible Evidence; I Never Promised You a Rose Garden; Absolution; Forbidden. Directors' and Producers' Award for TV Dir of Year, 1966. *Recreations:* movies, reading, travelling. *Address:* c/o ICM, Oxford House, Oxford Street, W1N 0AX.

PAGE, Sir (Arthur) John, Kt 1984; Chairman, Three Valleys Water, 1986–2001; *b* 16 Sept. 1919; *s* of Sir Arthur Page, QC (late Chief Justice of Burma), and Lady Page, KiH; *m* 1950, Anne, *d* of Charles Micklem, DSO, JP, DL, Longcross House, Surrey; four *s*. *Educ:* Harrow, Magdalene College, Cambridge. Joined RA as Gunner, 1939, commissioned, 1940; served War of 1939–45, Western Desert (wounded), France, Germany; demobilised as Major, comdg 258 Battery Norfolk Yeomanry, 1945; various positions in industry and commerce, 1946–. Chm. Bethnal Green and E London Housing Assoc., 1957–70; contested (C) Eton and Slough, Gen. Election, 1959. MP (C) Harrow W, March 1960–1987. PPS to Parly Under-Sec. of State, Home Office, 1961–63; Conservative Parly Labour Affairs Cttee: Sec., 1960–61, 1964–67, Vice-Chm., 1964–69, Chm., 1970–74; Sec., Conservative Broadcasting Cttee, 1974–76. Pres., Cons. Trade Unionists Nat. Adv. Council, 1967–69; Member: Parly Select Cttee on Race Relations and Immigration, 1970–71; British Delegn to Council of Europe and WEU, 1972–87 (Chm. Budget Cttee, 1973–74, Social and Health Cttee, 1975–78). Mem. Exec., IPU, British Gp, 1970 (Treasurer, 1974–77; Vice-Chm., 1977–79; Chm., 1979–82); Acting Internat. Pres., IPU, 1984 (Dep. Internat. Pres., 1982–84). Vice-Pres., British Insurance Brokers Assoc., 1980–; President: Water Companies Assoc., 1986–89 (Dep. Pres., 1984–86); Independent Schools Assoc., 1971–78; Chm., Council for Indep. Educn, 1974–80. *Recreations:* painting, politics, defending the Monarchy. *Address:* Hitcham Lodge, Taplow, Maidenhead, Berks SL6 0HG. *T:* (01628) 605056. *Clubs:* Brooks's, MCC.

PAGE, Ashley John; Principal Dancer, Royal Ballet, and choreographer, since 1984; *b* 9 Aug. 1956; named Ashley Laverty; *s* of John Henry Laverty and Sheila Rachel Laverty. *Educ:* St Andrew's Sch., Rochester; Royal Ballet Schs. Joined Royal Ballet at Covent Garden, 1976; Soloist, 1980, Principal 1984. Works choreographed for: Royal Ballet; Ballet Rambert, subseq. Rambert Dance Co.; Dutch Nat. Ballet; Dance Umbrella Fest. and other cos in GB and abroad. *Recreations:* interest in all the arts, travel. *Address:* c/o Royal Ballet, Royal Opera House, Covent Garden, WC2E 9DD.

PAGE, Bruce; journalist; *b* 1 Dec. 1936; *s* of Roger and Beatrice Page; *m* 1969, Anne Louise Darnborough; one *s* one *d*. *Educ:* Melbourne High Sch.; Melbourne Univ. The Herald, Melbourne, 1956–60; Evening Standard, 1960–62; Daily Herald, 1962–64; Sunday Times, 1964–76; Daily Express, 1977; Editor, The New Statesman, 1978–82. Dir, Direct Image Systems and Communications Ltd, 1992–95. *Publications:* (jtly) Philby, 1968, 3rd edn 1977; (jtly) An American Melodrama, 1969; (jtly) Do You Sincerely Want to be Rich?, 1971; (jtly) Destination Disaster, 1976; contrib. Ulster, 1972; The Yom Kippur War, 1974; The British Press, 1978. *Recreations:* sailing, reading. *Address:* Beach House, Shingle Street, Shottisham, Suffolk IP12 3BE. *T:* (01394) 411427; 32 Lauderdale Tower, Barbican, EC2Y 8BY. *T:* (020) 7628 3847; *e-mail:* bruce@pages [illegible].co.uk.

PAGE, Dr Christopher Howard, Senior Research Fellow, Sidney Sussex College, Cambridge, since 1985; Reader in Medieval Literature and Music, University of Cambridge, since 1997; Director, Gothic Voices, since 1982; *b* 8 April 1952; *s* of Ewart Lacey Page and Marie Victoria (*née* Graham); *m* 1975, Régine Fourcade. *Educ:* Sir George Monoux Grammar Sch.; Balliol Coll., Oxford (BA English 1974; MA); Univ. of York (DPhil). Jun. Res. Fellow, Jesus Coll., Oxford, 1977–80; Lecturer in English: New Coll., Oxford, 1980–85; Univ. of Cambridge, 1989–97. Editor, Plainsong and Medieval Music, 1991–. Presenter, Spirit of the Age, Radio 3, 1992–. Fellow, Fellowship of Makers and Restorers of Historical Instruments, 1982. Former Chm., Plainsong and Medieval Music Soc. Dent Medal, Royal Musical Assoc., 1991. *Publications:* Voices and Instruments of the Middle Ages, 1987; The Owl and the Nightingale, 1989; the *Summa Musice*, 1991; Discarding Images, 1993; Songs of the Trouvères, 1995; Latin Poetry and Conductus Rhythm in Medieval France, 1997; articles in Early Music, Galpin Soc. Jl, Plainsong and Medieval Music, Musical Times. *Address:* Sidney Sussex College, Cambridge CB2 3HU. *T:* (01223) 338800.

PAGE, Cyril Leslie, OBE 1965; Controller, Personnel, Television, BBC Television Service, 1971–76, retired; *b* 20 Oct. 1916; *s* of Cyril Herbert Page and Rosamund Clara Page; *m* 1939, Barbara Mary Rowland; one *s* one *d*. *Educ:* Sherborne Sch. Royal Air Force, 1936–46 (Wing Comdr). British Broadcasting Corporation, 1946–: Asst, Appts Dept, 1947; Asst Admin. Officer, Overseas Services, 1949; Asst Head of TV Admin., 1951; Estabt Officer, TV, 1958; Head of TV Estabt Dept, 1961; Asst Controller, TV Admin., 1964. Consultant, Osborne Management Ltd, 1998– (Dir, 1984–98; Chm., 1984–92). Mem. Council, Royal Postgrad. Med. Sch., 1975–Sept. 1989. *Recreations:* reading, gardening. *Address:* 95 Fountain Gardens, Windsor, Berks SL4 3SU.

PAGE, David John, FCCA; Deputy Chief Executive, Leeds City Council, since 2001; *b* 24 Feb. 1954; *s* of Clifford Page and Evelyn Page (*née* Banks); *m* 1976, Carole Watson; one *s* one *d*. *Educ:* W Leeds Boys' High Sch.; Leeds Poly. FCCA 1976. Trainee accountant, CEGB, 1972–74; Leeds City Council, 1974–: Chief Accountant, 1985–88; Asst Dir of Finance, 1988–89; Sen. Asst Dir of Finance, 1989–92; Dir of Finance, 1992–99; Exec. Dir (Resources), 1999–2001. Dir, Educn Leeds. Gov., Ossett Sch. *Recreations:* music, all sports, caravanning, quizzes. *Address:* 3 Stonegate, Ossett, Wakefield, WF5 0JD. *T:* (01924) 279875, *Fax:* (01924) 216465; *e-mail:* david.page2@which.net.

PAGE, Rt Rev. Dennis Fountain; *b* 1 Dec. 1919; *s* of Prebendary Martin Fountain Page and Lilla Fountain Page; *m* 1946; Margaret Bettine Clayton; two *s* one *d*. *Educ:* Shrewsbury Sch.; Gonville and Caius Coll., Cambridge (MA); Lincoln Theological Coll.; BSc Open Univ., 1996. Curate, Rugby Parish Church, 1943; Priest-in-Charge, St George's Church, Hillmorton, Rugby, 1945; Rector of Hockwold, Vicar of Wilton and Rector of Weeting, Norfolk, 1949; Archdeacon of Huntingdon and Vicar of Yaxley, 1965–75; Hon. Canon of Ely Cathedral, 1968; Bishop Suffragan of Lancaster, 1975–85. *Publication:* Reflections on the Reading for Holy Communion in the Alternative Service Book 1980, 1983. *Recreations:* music, astronomy, gardening. *Address:* Larkrise, Hartest Hill, Hartest, Bury St Edmunds, Suffolk IP29 4ES.

PAGE, Prof. Edward Charles, PhD; FBA 2001; Sidney and Beatrice Webb Professor of Public Policy, London School of Economics, since 2001; *b* London, 19 Oct. 1953; *s* of Edward Charles Page and Winifred Victoria Page; *m* 1975, Christine Mary Batty; one *s* two *d*. *Educ:* Kingston Poly. (BA (CNAA) German and Politics 1976); Univ. of Strathclyde (MSc Politics 1978; PhD Politics 1982). Lectr in Politics, Univ. of Strathclyde, 1978-81; University of Hull: Lectr, 1981-89; Sen. Lectr, 1989-92; Reader, 1992-95; Prof., 1995-2001. Vis. Associate Prof., Texas A&M Univ., 1986-87. Dir, ESRC Res. Prog. on Future Governance: Lessons from Comparative Public Policy, 1998-. Co-Ed., Eur. Jl Political Res., 2000-. *Publications:* (ed with R. Rose) Fiscal Stress in Cities, 1982; Political Authority and Bureaucratic Power, 1985, 2nd edn 1992; (ed with M. Goldsmith) Central and Local Government Relations: a comparative analysis of West European Unitary States, 1987; Centralism and Localism in Europe, 1992; (ed with J. Hayward) Governing the New Europe, 1995; People Who Run Europe, 1997; (ed with V. Wright)

Bureaucratic Elites in Western Europe, 1999; Governing by Numbers: delegated legislation and everyday policy making, 2001; contrib. to jls incl. British Jl Pol Sci., Eur. Jl Pol Res., Govt and Policy, W Eur. Politics, Jl Public Policy, Jl Theoretical Politics, Leviathan, Local Govt Studies, Pol Studies, Politique et Management Publique, Pouvoirs, Public Admin, Urban Affairs Qly. *Recreations:* jazz, cooking. *Address:* Department of Government, London School of Economics, Houghton Street, WC2A 2AE. *T:* (020) 7849 4629.

PAGE, Ewan Stafford, PhD, MA, BSc; Vice-Chancellor, University of Reading, 1979–93; *b* 17 Aug. 1928; *s* of late Joseph William Page and Lucy Quayle (*née* Stafford); *m* 1955, Sheila Margaret Smith; three *s* one *d. Educ:* Wyggeston Grammar Sch., Leicester; Christ's Coll., Cambridge (MA, PhD, Raleigh Prize 1952); Univ. of London (BSc). Instr, RAF Techn. Coll., 1949–51; Lectr in Statistics, Durham Colls, 1954–57; Director: Durham Univ. Computing Lab., 1957–63; Newcastle Univ. Computing Lab., 1963–78; Visiting Prof., Univ. of N Carolina, Chapel Hill, USA, 1962–63; University of Newcastle upon Tyne: Prof. of Computing and Data Processing, 1965–78; Pro-Vice Chancellor, 1972–78 (Actg Vice-Chancellor, 1976–77). Member: Newcastle AHA, 1976–79; Berks AHA, 1980–82; Oxford RHA, 1982–84; West Berks DHA, 1984–93; Berks HA, 1993–96. Mem. Bd, Aycliffe and Peterlee Develt Corp., 1969–78. Chairman: Food Adv. Cttee, 1988–94; Univs' Authorities Panel, 1988–93. Pres., British Computer Soc., 1984–85 (Dep. Pres., 1983–84); Member: Gen. Optical Council, 1984– (Vice-Chm., 1989–); Bd, Optical Consumer Complaints Service, 1999–; Hon. Treasurer, Royal Statistical Soc., 1983–89. CIMgt (CBIM 1986); Hon. Fellow, Amer. Statistical Assoc., 1974; Hon. FBCS, 1976; Hon. Fellow, Northumbria Univ. (formerly Newcastle upon Tyne Poly.), 1979. Hon. DSc Reading, 1993. Chevalier, l'Ordre des Palmes Académiques (France), 1991. *Publications:* (jtly) Information Representation and Manipulation in a Computer, 1973, 2nd edn 1978; (jtly) Introduction to Computational Combinatorics, 1978; papers in statistical and computing jls. *Recreations:* golf, music, reading, Freemasonry. *Address:* High View, Charlcombe Lane, Bath BA1 5TT.

PAGE, Sir Frederick (William), Kt 1979; CBE 1961; FRS 1978; FREng, Hon. FRAeS; Member of the Board, British Aerospace PLC, 1977–83; Chairman and Chief Executive, Aircraft Group of British Aerospace PLC, 1977–82; retired 1983; *b* 20 Feb. 1917; *s* of Richard Page and Ellen Potter; *m* 1940, Kathleen Edith de Courcy; three *s* one *d. Educ:* Rutlish Sch., Merton; St Catharine's Coll., Cambridge (MA). Hawker Aircraft Co., 1938; English Electric, 1945; Chief Engr, 1950, and Dir and Chief Exec. (Aircraft), English Electric Aviation, 1959; Managing Dir, Mil. Aircraft Div. of BAC, 1965–72, Chm., 1967; apptd Managing Dir (Aircraft), BAC, and Chm., Commercial Aircraft Div., 1972. Jt Chm. of SEPECAT, the Anglo-French co. formed for management of Jaguar programme, 1966–73; apptd to Bd of Panavia Aircraft GmbH, 1969, Chm. 1977; apptd Chm. BAC Ltd (a co. of Brit. Aerospace), 1977. Mem. Council, Soc. of Brit. Aerospace Cos Ltd; apptd to Bd of BAC (Operating) Ltd, 1963; Dir, BAC (USA) Inc., 1975–77. FRAeS, 1951–80, Hon. FRAeS, 1980 (Gold Medal, 1974); FREng (FEng 1977). Hon. Fellow, UMIST, 1970. Hon. DSc Cranfield, 1979. British Gold Medal for Aeronautics, 1962. *Recreation:* gardening. *Address:* 28 Farm Lane, Mudeford, Christchurch, Dorset BH23 4AH. *T:* (01425) 280024.

PAGE, Howard William Barrett; QC 1987; *b* 11 Feb. 1943; *s* of Leslie Herbert Barrett Page and Phyllis Elizabeth Page; *m* 1969, Helen Joanna Shotter (LVO 1996); two *s* one *d. Educ:* Radley Coll.; Trinity Hall, Cambridge (BA, LLB). Called to the Bar, Lincoln's Inn, 1967 (Mansfield Schol.); Bencher, 1994. *Recreations:* music, walking. *Address:* 6 New Square, Lincoln's Inn, WC2A 3QS.

PAGE, Jennifer Anne, CBE 1994; Chief Executive, New Millennium Experience Company Ltd, 1997–2000; *b* 12 Nov. 1944; *d* of Edward and Olive Page; *m* 2001, Jeremy David Orme, *qv. Educ:* Barr's Hill Grammar School, Coventry; Royal Holloway College, Univ. of London (BA Hons). Entered Civil Service, 1968; Principal, DoE, 1974; Asst Sec., Dept of Transport, 1980; seconded BNOC, 1981; LDDC, 1983; Senior Vice-Pres., Pallas Invest SA, 1984–89; Chief Executive: English Heritage (Historic Buildings and Monuments Commn), 1989–95; Millennium Commn, 1995–97. Member, Board: Railtrack Group, 1994–2001; Equitable Life Assurance Soc., 1994–2001.

PAGE, Sir John; *see* Page, Sir (Arthur) John and Page, Sir John (Joseph Joffre).

PAGE, John Brangwyn; Chairman, Agricultural Mortgage Corporation, 1982–85; Director: Standard Chartered Bank, 1982–89; Nationwide Building Society, 1982–92; *b* 23 Aug. 1923; *s* of late Sidney John Page, CB, MC; *m* 1948, Gloria Vail; one *s* one *d. Educ:* Highgate Sch. (Foundation Schol.); King's Coll., Cambridge (BA). RAF, 1942–46; Cambridge, 1946–48; Bank of England, 1948; seconded to IMF, 1953; Chief Cashier, 1970–80; Exec. Dir, 1980–82. FCIB; CIMgt; FRSA. *Recreations:* gardening, music, travel.

PAGE, Maj.-Gen. John Humphrey, CB 1977; OBE 1967; MC 1952; *b* 5 March 1923; *s* of late Captain W. J. Page, JP, Devizes and late Alice Mary Page (*née* Richards); *m* 1956, Angela Mary Bunting; three *s* one *d. Educ:* Stonyhurst. Commnd into RE, 1942; served in NW Europe, India, Korea, Middle East and UK, 1942–60; Instr, Staff Coll., Camberley, 1960–62; comd 32 Armd Engr Regt, 1964–67; idc 1968; CCRE 1st Br. Corps, 1969–70; Asst Comdt, RMA Sandhurst, 1971–74; Dir of Personal Services (Army), MoD, 1974–78, retd. Col Comdt, RE, 1980–85. Dir, London Law Trust, 1979–88. Dir, RBM (Holdings), 1980–86. Member Council: REOWS, 1980–92 (Chm., 1990–92; Chm. Investment Cttee, 1990–95); Officers' Pension Soc., 1979–96; Vice-Chm., SSAFA, 1983–87. Chm. Trustees, Home-Start Consultancy, 1982–90; Mem., Management Cttee, Stackpole Trust, 1981–92; Chm. for Wilts, Winged Fellowship Trust, 1997–2000; Chm., The Trust For Devizes, 1999–. Chm., Bd of Governors, St Mary's Sch., Shaftesbury, 1985–93 (Trustee, St Mary Sch. Shaftesbury Trust, 1990–99); Mem., Bd of Governors, Stonyhurst Coll., 1980–90 (Trustee, Stonyhurst Charitable Fund, 1983–97). KSG 1993. *Address:* c/o Lloyds TSB, Devizes, Wiltshire.

PAGE, Sir John (Joseph Joffre), Kt 1979; OBE 1959; Chairman, Christie Hospital NHS Trust, 1991–92; *b* 7 Jan. 1915; 2nd *s* of late William Joseph and Frances Page; *m* 1939, Cynthia Maynard, *d* of late L. M. Swan, CBE; two *s. Educ:* Emanuel School. RAF, 1933–38 and 1939–46 (despatches, 1943); Group Captain. Iraq Petroleum Group of Cos, 1938–39 and 1946–70; served in Palestine, Jordan, Lebanon, Syria, Iraq, Qatar, Bahrain and Abu Dhabi; Head Office, London, 1958–61; Gen. Man., 1955–58; Chief Representative, 1961–70. Chm., 1972–77 and 1980–84, Chief Exec., 1975–77, Mersey Docks and Harbour Co.; Dep. Chm., British Ports Assoc., 1974–77; Chm., Nat. Ports Council, 1977–80. Chairman: Chester DHA, 1981–82; North Western RHA, 1982–88. Hon. Fellow, Manchester Metropolitan Univ., 1993. *Recreations:* photography, fishing, music. *Address:* The Cottage, Hockenhull Lane, Tarvin, Chester CH3 8LB. *Clubs:* Oriental, Royal Air Force, MCC.

PAGE, Prof. John Kenneth; energy and environmental consultant; (part-time) Senior Research Fellow, Department of Physics, University of Manchester Institute of Science and Technology, since 2000; Professor of Building Science, University of Sheffield, 1960–84, now Emeritus; *b* 3 Nov. 1924; *s* of late Brig. E. K. Page, CBE, DSO, MC; *m* 1954, Anita Bell Lovell; two *s* two *d. Educ:* Haileybury College; Pembroke College, Cambridge. Served War of 1939–45, Royal Artillery, 1943–47. Asst Industrial Officer, Council of Industrial Design, 1950–51; taught Westminster School, 1952–53; Sen. Scientific Officer, Tropical Liaison Section, Building Research Station, 1953–56; Chief Research Officer, Nuffield Div. for Architectural Studies, 1956–57; Lecturer, Dept. of Building Science, Univ. of Liverpool, 1957–60. Chm., Environmental Gp, and Mem., Econ. Planning Council, Yorks and Humberside Region, 1965–78; Founding Chm., UK Section, Internat. Solar Energy Soc.; Initiating Dir, Cambridge Interdisciplinary Envmtl Centre, 1990–92. Consultant author working with UN internat. agencies on energy use in Third World and on environmental health in tropical bldgs. Farrington Daniels Internat. Award, for distinguished contribs to solar energy studies, 1989. *Publications:* 200 papers on Energy policy, Environmental Design and Planning, Environmental Management, Building Climatology and Solar Energy. *Address:* 15 Brincliffe Gardens, Sheffield S11 9BG. *T:* (0114) 255 1570.

PAGE, Oliver; Director, Major Financial (formerly Complex) Groups Division, Financial Services Authority, since 1998; *b* 29 April 1946; *s* of Sir Harry Robertson Page and Lady Elsie Page (*née* Dixon); *m* 1968, Jennifer Jane Murphy; one *d. Educ:* Trinity Coll., Cambridge (MA; DipEcon). Bank of England, 1968–98: posts included: Chief Manager, Reserves Management, 1984–90; Dep. Dir, Supervision and Surveillance, 1996–98. UK Alternate Dir, EIB, 1989–95. *Address:* Financial Services Authority, 25 The North Colonnade, Canary Wharf, E14 5HS.

PAGE, Piers John B.; *see* Burton-Page.

PAGE, Prof. Raymond Ian, LittD; Fellow, Corpus Christi College, Cambridge, since 1962; Elrington and Bosworth Professor of Anglo-Saxon, University of Cambridge, 1984–91, now Professor Emeritus; *b* 25 Sept. 1924; *s* of Reginald Howard Page and Emily Louise Page; *m* 1953, Elin Benedicte Hustad, *d* of Tormod Kristoffer Hustad and Anne Margarethe Hustad, Oslo; two *d* (one *s* decd). *Educ:* King Edward VII Sch., Sheffield; Rotherham Technical Coll.; Univ. of Sheffield. LittD Cambridge 1974. Assistant Lecturer and Lecturer, Univ. of Nottingham, 1951–61; Cambridge University: successively Lectr, Reader and Professor, Dept of Anglo-Saxon, Norse and Celtic, 1961–91; Sandars Reader in Bibliography, 1989–90; Corpus Christi College: Librarian, 1965–91; Dir, Leverhulme Trust Res. Gp on MS Evidence, Parker Liby, 1989–94. Special Prof. in Anglo-Saxon Studies, Univ. of Nottingham, 1992–97; Hon. Professorial (formerly Hon. Sen.) Res. Fellow, Dept of Eng. Lang., Univ. of Glasgow, 1993–. Hon. LittD Sheffield, 1994; Hon. Dr philos Trondheim, 1996. Dag Strömbäck prize, Royal Gustav Adolfs Acad., Uppsala, 1995. *Address:* Ashton House, Newnham Road, Cambridge CB3 9EY.

PAGE, Richard Lewis; MP (C) Hertfordshire South West, since Dec. 1979; *b* 22 Feb. 1941; *s* of Victor Charles and Kathleen Page; *m* 1964, Madeleine Ann Brown; one *s* one *d. Educ:* Hurstpierpoint Coll.; Luton Technical Coll. Apprenticeship, Vauxhall Motors, 1959–64; HNC Mech. Engineering; dir of family co., 1964–95. Young Conservatives, 1964–66; Councillor, Banstead UDC, 1968–71; contested (C) Workington, Feb. and Oct. 1974; MP (C) Workington, Nov. 1976–1979; PPS: to Sec. of State for Trade, 1981–82; to Leader of the House, 1982–87; Parly Under-Sec. of State, DTI, 1995–97; opposition front-bench spokesman on trade and industry, 2000–01. Mem., Public Accounts Cttee, 1987–95, 1997–2000; Vice-Chairman: Cons. Trade and Industry Cttee, 1988–95; All Party Engrg Gp, 1997–; Jt Chm., All Party Racing and Bloodstock Industries Cttee, 1998–. Vice Chm., Chemical Industry Council, 1997–. Mem. Investment Cttee, Leukaemia Res. Fund, 1991–95, 1997– (Hon. Treas., 1987–95). *Recreation:* most sport. *Address:* House of Commons, SW1A 0AA.

PAGE, Simon Richard; District Judge (formerly Registrar), Guildford, Epsom and Reigate County Courts, and High Court of Justice, 1980–2000; a Recorder of the Crown Court, 1980–99; *b* 7 March 1934; *s* of Eric Rowland Page and Vera (*née* Fenton); *m* 1st, 1963, (marr. diss. 1977); three *s* one *d*; 2nd, 1984. *Educ:* Lancing; LSE (LLB External, 1956). Admitted solicitor (hons), 1957. National Service, Second Lieut RA, 1957–59. Private practice as solicitor, 1959–75; Pres., West Surrey Law Soc., 1972–73; Registrar, Croydon County Court, 1975–80; Pres., Assoc. of County Court and District Registrars, 1983–84. *Recreations:* squash racquets, cricket, bridge. *Address:* c/o The Law Courts, Mary Road, Guildford GU1 4PS.

PAGE WOOD, Sir Anthony John, 8th Bt *cr* 1837; *b* 6 Feb. 1951; *s* of Sir David (John Hatherley) Page Wood, 7th Bt and of Evelyn Hazel Rosemary, *d* of late Captain George Ernest Bellville; *S* father, 1955; *m* 1997, Kristine Louise, *d* of John Ernest Scott. *Educ:* Harrow. *Heir: kinsman* Matthew Wakefield Drury Evelyn-Wood [*b* 9 July 1917; *m* 1st, 1939, Marjorie Longmire (*d* 1963); one *s*; 2nd, 1967, Phyllis Margaret Chavasse Whateley (*née* Holder)]. *Address:* 77 Dovehouse Street, SW3 6JZ.

PAGEL, Prof. Bernard Ephraim Julius, FRS 1992; Professor of Astrophysics, NORDITA (Nordic Institute for Theoretical Physics), Copenhagen, 1990–98; Visiting Professor of Astronomy, University of Sussex, since 1970; *b* 4 Jan. 1930; *s* of Walter T. U. Pagel and Magdalene M. E. Pagel; *m* 1958, Annabel Ruth Tuby; two *s* one *d. Educ:* Merchant Taylors' Sch., Northwood; Sidney Sussex Coll., Cambridge (MA, PhD). Res. Fellow, Sidney Sussex Coll., 1953–56; Radcliffe Student, Pretoria, 1955; PSO, Royal Greenwich Observ., 1955–61; Astrophysicist, Sacramento Peak Observ., New Mexico, 1960; SPSO, 1961–71, DCSO, 1971–89, Royal Greenwich Observ. Vis. Reader in Astronomy, Univ. of Sussex, 1966–70. Kelvin Lectr, BAAS, 1962; Vice-Pres. and For. Corresp., RAS, 1974–75. Gold Medal, RAS, 1990. *Publications:* Théorie des Atmosphères Stellaires, 1971; Nucleosynthesis and Chemical Evolution of Galaxies, 1997; articles in Nature, Encycl. Britannica, Monthly Notices of RAS, New Scientist, and procs of astronomical confs. *Recreations:* music, ski-ing, bicycling. *Address:* Groombridge, Lewes Road, Ringmer, East Sussex BN8 5ER. *T:* (01273) 812729.

PAGET, family name of **Marquess of Anglesey**.

PAGET DE BEAUDESERT, Lord; Benedict Dashiel Paget; *b* 11 April 1986; *s* and *heir* of Earl of Uxbridge, *qv*.

PAGET, David Christopher John, QC 1994; **His Honour Judge Paget;** a Circuit Judge, since 1997; *b* 3 Feb. 1942; *s* of late Henry Paget and of Dorothy Paget (*née* Colenutt), Johannesburg, S Africa; *m* 1968, Dallas Wendy (*née* Hill); two *d. Educ:* St John's Coll., Johannesburg; Inns of Court Sch. of Law. Called to Bar, Inner Temple, 1967; Jun. Prosecuting Counsel to the Crown, 1982–89, Sen. Prosecuting Counsel, 1989–94, CCC; a Recorder, 1986–97. Freeman, City of London, 1999; Liveryman, Co. of Coopers, 1999–. *Recreations:* walking, bird watching, listening to music. *Address:* Central Criminal Court, Old Bailey, EC4M 7EH. *T:* (020) 7248 3277.

PAGET, Lt-Col Sir Julian (Tolver), 4th Bt *cr* 1871; CVO 1984; an Extra Gentleman Usher to the Queen, since 1991 (Gentleman Usher, 1971–91); author; *b* 11 July 1921; *s* of General Sir Bernard Paget, GCB, DSO, MC (*d* 1961) (*g s* of 1st Bt), and Winifred (*d*

.631

1986), *d* of Sir John Paget, 2nd Bt; *S* un… 3rd Bt, 1972; *m* 1954,
Diana Frances, *d* of late F. S. H. F… …adley College; Christ
Church, Oxford (MA). Joined C… …ed North West Europe,
1944–45; retired as Lt-Col, 1968… …–93. *Publications:* Counter-
Insurgency Campaigning, 1967; …1969; The Story of the Guards,
1976; The Pageantry of Britai… …uard, 1984; Discovering London's
Ceremonial and Tradition… Peninsular War: the battles and
battlefields, 1990; Hougou… …ory at Waterloo, 1992; No Problem Too
Difficult, 1999; (ed) T… …s 1650–2000, 2000. *Recreations:* fishing,
shooting, travel, writin… …es Paget [*b* 2 Feb. 1959; *m* 1993, Mrs Margrete
Varvill (*née* Lynner)… Cavalry and Guards, Flyfishers'.
See also N. J. Co…

PAGET, Sir R… …rt), 4th Bt *cr* 1886, of Cranmore Hall, Co. Somerset; independent …sultant; *b* 17 Feb. 1957; *s* of Sir John Starr Paget, 3rd Bt and Nancy Mar… …of Francis Parish, DSO, MC; *S* father, 1992; *m* 1985, Richenda Rachel, *d* …eb. J. T. C. B. Collins; three *d*. *Educ:* Eton Coll. AES, 1983–87; Nixdorf… …s, 1987–88; Inforem plc, 1988–89; Sales Manager, SAS Inst., 1989–95; Outpl… Councillor, Encos, 1995–97; Empathy Audit Manager, Harding and Yorke Ltd …99; Business Develt Manager, UMTC3, 1999–; non-exec. Dir, SFM Technol. …99–. Mem. Ct, Russia Co. Pres., Paget Gorman Signed Speech Soc. *Recreations:* …age driving, cricket, tennis. *Heir: b* David Vernon John Paget [*b* 26 March 1959; *m* …990, Cluny Macpherson; one *s* two *d*]. *Address:* Burridge Heath Farm, Little Bedwyn, Marlborough, Wilts SN8 3JR; *e-mail:* rpaget@netcomuk.co.uk.

PAGET-WILKES, Ven. Michael Jocelyn James; Archdeacon of Warwick, since 1990; *b* 11 Dec. 1941; *s* of Arthur Hamilton Paget-Wilkes and Eleanor Bridget Paget-Wilkes; *m* 1969, Ruth Gillian Macnamara; one *s* two *d*. *Educ:* Harper Adams Agricultural Coll. (NDA); London Coll. of Divinity (ALCD). Agricultural Extension Officer, Tanzania, 1964–66; attended London Coll. of Divinity, 1966–69; Curate, All Saints', Wandsworth, 1969–74; Vicar: St James', Hatcham, New Cross, 1974–82; St Matthew's, Rugby, 1982–90. *Publications:* The Church and Rural Development, 1968; Poverty, Revolution and the Church, 1981. *Recreations:* squash, tennis, music, ski-ing, gardening. *Address:* 10 Northumberland Road, Leamington Spa, Warwicks CV32 6HA.

PAGETT, Nicola Mary; actress; *b* 15 June 1945; *d* of Barbara Scott and H. W. F. Scott; took stage name of Pagett; *m* 1977, Graham Swannell; one *d*. *Educ:* St Maurs Convent, Yokohama; The Beehive, Bexhill; RADA. *Stage:* Voyage Round My Father, Haymarket, 1971; Ophelia in Hamlet, Greenwich, 1974; Yahoo, Queen's, 1976; Taking Steps, Lyric, 1980; The Trojan War will not take place, NT, 1983; School for Scandal, Duke of York's, 1984; Aren't We All?, Haymarket, 1984; Old Times, Haymarket, 1985; The Light of Day, Hammersmith, 1987; The Rehearsal, Garrick, 1990; Party Time, Almeida, 1991; The Rules of the Game, Almeida, 1992; What the Butler Saw, NT, 1995; *films:* Seven Men at Daybreak, 1974; Oliver's Story, 1978; Privates on Parade, 1982; *television series:* Upstairs, Downstairs, 1972; Napoleon in Love, 1974; Anna Karenina, 1977; Scoop, 1987; A Bit of a Do, 1988–90; Ain't Misbehavin, 1994–95. *Publication:* Diamonds Behind My Eyes, 1997. *Address:* c/o Gavin Barker Associates, 45 South Molton Street, W1Y 1HD.

PAGNAMENTA, Peter John; independent television producer, Pagnamenta Associates Ltd, since 1997; *b* 12 April 1941; *s* of Charles Francis Pagnamenta and Daphne Pagnamenta; *m* 1966, Sybil Healy; one *s* one *d*. *Educ:* Shrewsbury; Trinity Hall, Cambridge (MA). Joined BBC, 1965; Prodn Asst, Tonight and 24 Hours, 1965–67; Asst Editor, 24 Hours, 1967; New York office, 1968–71 (Producer, US Election coverage and Apollo flights); Editor: 24 Hours, 1971; Midweek, 1972–75; Panorama, 1975–77; Dir of News and Current Affairs, Thames Television, 1977–80; Exec. Producer, All Our Working Lives (eleven part series), BBC2, 1984; Editor, Real Lives (documentary strand), BBC 1, 1984–85; Head of Current Affairs Gp, BBC TV, 1985–87; Exec. Producer, BBC TV Documentary Dept, 1981–85, 1987–92; Executive Producer: Nippon (eight parts), BBC 2, 1990; People's Century (26 parts), BBC 1, 1995–96; Bubble Trouble (three parts), BBC 2, 2000. *Publication:* (with Richard Overy) All Our Working Lives, 1984. *Recreations:* walking, fishing. *Address:* 145 Elgin Crescent, W11 2JH. *T:* (020) 7727 9960.

PAIBA, His Honour Denis Anthony; a Circuit Judge, 1982–98; *b* 10 Dec. 1926; *e s* of late Geoffrey Paiba and Geraldine Paiba; *m* 1955, Lesley Patricia Dresden; two *s*. *Educ:* University Coll. Sch. (Junior); Magdalen Coll. Sch., Oxford; Jesus Coll., Cambridge. 44 Royal Marine Commando, 1945–47. Financial Times, 1957–58. Called to the Bar, Gray's Inn, 1958; a Recorder of the Crown Court, 1980–82. *Recreations:* theatre, music, gardening, study of English ceramics up to 1850, watching Rugby and cricket, wining and dining. *Address:* 11 Angel Mews, Roehampton High Street, SW15 4HU. *T:* and *Fax:* (020) 8788 4674; *e-mail:* denpaib@tinyonline.co.uk.

PAICE, Clifford, FCIT; Member and Group Director, Economic Regulation, Civil Aviation Authority, 1989–97; *b* 26 Feb. 1938; *s* of Owen Edward and Dorothy Paice; *m* 1968, Elisabeth Marlin (*see* E. W. Paice); one *s* two *d*. *Educ:* Cambridgeshire High Sch.; LSE (BSc Econ.). FCIT 1990. Joined Civil Service, 1959: War Office, 1959–61; MoD, 1962–65; Min. of Econ. Affairs, 1965–68; Treasury, 1968–72; Head, Econ. Divs, CAA, 1972–89. FRSA 1997. *Address:* 142 Cromwell Tower, Barbican, EC2Y 8DD. *T:* (020) 7628 5228.

PAICE, Elisabeth Willemien, FRCP; Dean Director, London Department of Postgraduate Medical and Dental Education, NHS Executive, since 2001; *b* 23 April 1945; *d* of Ervin Ross, (Spike), Marlin and Hilda van Stockum, HRHA; *m* 1968, Clifford Paice, *qv*; one *s* two *d*. *Educ:* Trinity Coll., Dublin (MB, BCh, BAO, MA); Dundee Univ. (Dip. Med. Ed.). FRCP 1989. Clinical training, Westminster Hosp.; Senior Registrar in Rheumatology: Stoke Mandeville Hosp., 1977–79; UCH, 1979–82; Consultant Rheumatologist, Whittington Hosp. NHS Trust, 1982–95; Associate Dean, N Thames E, 1992–95, Dean Dir, N Thames, 1995–2000, Postgrad. Medicine. *Publications:* Delivering the New Doctor, 1998; contrib. various articles on rheumatology and postgrad. med. educn. *Address:* London Deanery, 20 Guilford Street, WC1N 1DZ. *T:* (020) 7692 3355.

PAICE, James Edward Thornton; MP (C) Cambridgeshire South East, since 1987; *b* 24 April 1949; *s* of late Edward Paice and of Winifred Paice; *m* 1973, Ava Barbara Patterson; two *s*. *Educ:* Framlingham College, Suffolk; Writtle Agricultural College. Farm Manager, 1970–73; farmer, 1973–79; Framlingham Management and Training Services Ltd: Training Officer, 1979–82; Training Manager, 1982–85; Gen. Manager/Exec. Dir, 1985–87; Non-Exec. Dir, 1987–89; Non-Exec. Dir, United Framlingham Farmers, 1989–94. PPS to Minister of State, 1989–91, to Minister, 1991–93, MAFF, to Sec. of State for the Envmt, 1993–94; Parly Under-Sec. of State, DFE, then DFEE, 1994–97; opposition front bench spokesman on agriculture, 1997–2001. Mem., Select Cttee on Employment, 1987–89. Chm., All Party Racing and Bloodstock Cttee, 1992–94. Gov., Writtle Agricl Coll., 1991–94. *Recreations:* shooting, windsurfing. *Address:* House of Commons, SW1A 0AA.

PAICE, Karlo Bruce; Assistant Under-Secretary of State, Home Office, 1955–66; *b* 18 August 1906; *s* of H. B. Paice, Horsham, Sussex; *m* 1st, 1935, Islay (*d* 1965), *d* of late Paymaster Comdr Duncan Cook; four *s*; 2nd, 1966, Mrs Gwen Morris (*née* Kenyon) (*d* 1991). *Educ:* Collyer's School, Horsham; Jesus Coll., Cambridge (MA). Second Clerk, Metropolitan Police Courts, 1928; Assistant Principal, Home Office, 1929; Asst Sec. to the Poisons Bd, 1933–35; Private Sec. to successive Parliamentary Under-Secretaries of State for Home Affairs, 1935–39. Principal, 1936; Assistant Secretary, 1941, serving in London Civil Defence Region, Fire Service Department, and Aliens Department. Secretary to the Prison Commission and a Prison Commissioner, 1949–55. *Recreations:* history, music. *Address:* 38 Gretton Court, Girton, Cambridge CB3 0QN. *T:* (01223) 277442.

PAIGE, Deborah Penrose; freelance theatre director; *b* 7 Feb. 1950; *d* of David and Barbara Dunhill; *m* 1969, John Paige (marr. diss. 1985); two *d*. *Educ:* Godalming County Grammar Sch.; Dartington Hall Sch.; Bristol Old Vic Theatre Sch. Actress, 1970–84; Asst Dir, Bristol Old Vic, 1986–87; Associate Dir, Soho Theatre Co., 1988–90; Artistic Director: Salisbury Playhouse, 1990–94; Sheffield Theatres, 1995–2000. *Recreations:* walking, music, reading.

PAIGE, Prof. Edward George Sydney, PhD; FRS 1983; Professor of Electrical Engineering, and Fellow of St John's College, University of Oxford, 1977–97, now Emeritus Professor of Engineering Science and Emeritus Fellow; *b* 18 July 1930; *s* of Sydney and Maude Paige; *m* 1953, Helen Gill; two *s* two *d*. *Educ:* Reading University (BSc, PhD). FInstP. Junior Research Fellow to DCSO, Royal Radar Establishment, Malvern, 1955–77. *Address:* c/o Department of Engineering Science, University of Oxford, Parks Road, Oxford OX1 3PJ. *T:* (01865) 273110.

PAIGE, Elaine, OBE 1995; actress and singer; *b* 5 March 1948; *d* of Eric Bickerstaff and Irene Bickerstaff. *Educ:* Southaw Sch. for Girls, Barnet. *Theatre:* The Roar of the Greasepaint, the Smell of the Crowd, UK tour, 1964; Rock Carmen, Maybe That's Your Problem, Alexandra, Birmingham, 1966; Nuts, Stratford East, 1967; Maybe That's Your Problem, Roundhouse; West End début, Hair, Shaftesbury, 1969; Jesus Christ Superstar, Palace, 1971; Sandy in Grease, New London, 1973; Rita in Billy, Drury Lane, 1974; Eva Perón in Evita, Prince Edward, 1978 (Best Actress in a Musical, SWET, 1978); Grizabella in Cats, New London, 1981; Carabosse in Abbacadabra, Lyric Hammersmith, 1983; Florence Vassey in Chess, Prince Edward, 1986; Reno Sweeney in Anything Goes, Prince Edward, 1989 (co-producer); Edith Piaf in Piaf, Piccadilly, 1993; Norma Desmond in Sunset Boulevard, Adelphi, 1994 and 1995, NY, 1996; Célimène in The Misanthrope, Piccadilly, 1998; Anna in The King and I, London Palladium, 2000; has appeared in four Royal Variety Performances; *television:* Phyllis Dixey, Ladykillers, 1980; Ladybirds, 1980; Elaine Paige in Concert, 1985; A View of Harry Clark (play), 1988; Showstoppers: In Concert at the White House, 1988; Unexplained Laughter (play), 1989; Elaine Paige in Concert, 1991; South Bank Show: the faces of Elaine Paige, 1996; Boston Pops Opening, 1997; concert tours in UK, Europe, ME, Australia, NZ and FE. Has made numerous recordings (8 consecutive gold albums, incl. 4 multi-platinum). Variety Club Awards: Showbusiness Personality of Year, 1978; Recording Artiste of Year, 1986; Best Actress, 1995; Gold Badge of Merit, BASCA, 1993; Lifetime Achievement Award, HMV, 1996; Lifetime Achievement Award, NODA, 1999. *Recreations:* antiques, ski-ing, gardening, tennis. *Address:* E. P. Records, Sanctuary House, 45–53 Sinclair Road, W14 0NS. *T:* (020) 7300 1865, *Fax:* (020) 7300 1864. *Clubs:* Mosimann's, Monte's.

PAIGE, Victor Grellier, CBE 1978; Chairman, National Health Service Management Board, and Second Permanent Secretary, Department of Health and Social Security, 1985–86; *b* 5 June 1925; *s* of Victor Paige and Alice (*née* Grellier); *m* 1948, Kathleen Winifred, 3rd *d* of Arthur and Daisy Harris; one *s* one *d*. *Educ:* East Ham Grammar Sch.; Univ. of Nottingham. CIPD, FCIT, CIMgt, FAIM. Roosevelt Mem. Schol. 1954. Dep. Personnel Manager, Boots Pure Drug Co. Ltd, 1957–67; Controller of Personnel Services, CWS Ltd, 1967–70; Dir of Manpower and Organisation, 1970–74, Exec. Vice-Chm. (Admin), 1974–77, Nat. Freight Corp.; Dep. Chm., Nat. Freight Corp., later Nat. Freight Co., 1977–82; Dir, 1977–88 (non.-exec., 1985–88), and Dep. Chm., 1982–85, Nat. Freight Consortium; Chm., Iveco (UK), 1984–85. Chm., PLA, 1980–85; Member: Manpower Services Commn, 1974–80; Thames Water Authy, 1983–85. Member: Notts Educn Cttee, 1957–63; Secondary Schs Examn Council, 1960–63; UK Adv. Council for Educn in Management, 1962–65; Careers Adv. Bd, Univ. of Nottingham, 1975–81; Chairman: Regional Adv. Council for Further Educn, E Mids, 1967; Exec. Council, British Assoc. for Commercial and Industrial Educn, 1974 (Vice-Pres. 1980); Pres., Inst. of Admin. Management, 1984–90; Vice-Pres., Chartered Inst. of Transport, 1984–85 (Mem. Council, 1976–79); Mem. Council, CBI, 1983–85 (Chm., Educn and Trng Cttee, 1983–85). Mem. Court, Henley, The Management College, 1985–94. Governor, British Liver Trust, 1990–98. Vice-Pres., London Fedn of Boys' Clubs. Freeman, Co. of Watermen and Lightermen of the River Thames; Freeman, City of London, 1981. Commander, Order of Orange Nassau, The Netherlands, 1982. *Publications:* contrib. techn. press on management. *Recreations:* reading, sport generally, athletics in particular (Pres. Notts Athletic Club, 1962–67). *Address:* 7 Benningfield Gardens, Castle Village, Berkhamsted, Herts HP4 2GW. *T:* (01442) 865030. *Club:* MCC.

PAIN, Barry Newton, CBE 1979; QPM 1976; Commandant, Police Staff College, Bramshill, and HM Inspector of Constabulary, 1982–87, retired; *b* 25 Feb. 1931; *s* of Godfrey William Pain and Annie Newton; *m* 1952, Marguerite Agnes King; one *s* one *d*. *Educ:* Waverley Grammar Sch., Birmingham. Clerk to Prosecuting Solicitor, Birmingham, 1947–51; 2nd Lieut (Actg Captain) RASC, Kenya, 1949–51. Birmingham City Police, 1951–68; Staff Officer to HM Inspector of Constabulary, Birmingham, 1966–68; Asst Chief Constable, Staffordshire and Stoke-on-Trent Constabulary, 1968–74; Chief Constable of Kent, 1974–82; JSSC 1970. Adviser to Turkish Govt on Reorganization of Police, 1972. Pres., Assoc. of Chief Police Officers, 1981–82. *Recreations:* golf, shooting, boating.

PAIN, Gillian Margaret; Chief Reporter, Scottish Office Inquiry Reporters Unit, 1993–96; *b* 29 May 1936; *d* of late Geoffrey Ernest Pain and Florence Agnes Pain (*née* Marshall). *Educ:* Felixstowe Coll., Suffolk; Univ. of St Andrews (MA 1957); University Coll. London (DipTP 1965). MRTPI. Asst Teacher of Geography, Northfield Sch., Watford, 1957–58; Photogrammetrist, Hunting Aero Surveys, 1958–60; Asst Map Res. Officer, Directorate of Mil. Surveys, 1960–62; posts with Essex Co. Planning Dept, 1962–73, Asst Chief County Planning Adviser, 1970–73; Department of the Environment: Sen. Housing and Planning Inspector, 1973–77; Principal Planning Inspector, 1977–86; Asst Chief Planning Inspector, 1986–93. Pres., Town and Country Planning Summer Sch., 1992–94. *Publication:* Planning and the Shopkeeper, 1967. *Recreations:* sailing, ski-ing, classical music. *Club:* Blackwater Sailing (Past Commodore) (Essex).

PAIN, Lt-Gen. Sir (Horace) Rollo (Squarey), KCB 1975 (CB 1974); MC 1945; late 4th/7th Royal Dragoon Guards; Head of British Defence Staff, Washington, 1975–78, retired; *b* 11 May 1921; *s* of late Horace Davy Pain, Levenside, Haverthwaite, Ulverston, and late Audrey Pain (*née* Hampson); *m* 1950, Denys Sophia (*née* Chaine-Nickson); one *s* two *d*. Commissioned into Reconnaissance Corps during War of 1939–45: served NW Europe (MC). After War, served for two years in E Africa and Brit. Somaliland before joining 4th/7th Royal Dragoon Gds in Palestine, 1947; attended Staff Coll., Camberley, 1951; subseq. served in Mil. Ops Directorate, in War Office; served with his Regt in BAOR, 1955–56; Mem. Directing Staff, Staff Coll., Camberley, 1957; GSO1, Brit. Army Staff, Washington, DC, 1960; commanded his Regt in BAOR, 1962; commanded one of the three divs, Staff Coll., Camberley, 1964; commanded 5 Inf. Bde in Borneo, 1965; IDC, 1968; ADC to the Queen, 1969; BGS, HQ, BAOR, 1969–70; GOC 2nd Div., 1970–72; Dir of Army Training, MoD, 1972–75; Col Comdt, Mil. Provost Staff Corps, 1974–83; Col. 4th/7th Royal Dragoon Guards, 1979–83. *Address:* Eddlethorpe Hall, Malton, North Yorkshire YO17 9QS. *T:* (01653) 658218. *Club:* Cavalry and Guards.

PAIN, Jacqualyn Christina Mary; Head, Henrietta Barnett School, since 2000; *b* 31 Aug. 1957; *d* of J. K. and J. W. Pain. *Educ:* Sch. of St Helen and St Katharine, Abingdon; St David's UC, Lampeter (MA); Birkbeck Coll., London Univ. (MA); Univ. of Leicester (MBA); NPQH 2001. Teacher: Tiffin Girls' Sch., 1981–83; Old Palace Sch., 1983–84; James Allen's Girls' Sch., 1984–96 (on secondment to Inst. of Educn, Univ. of London), 1992–94; Dep. Head, Northwood Coll., 1996–2000. *Recreations:* running, woodwork, philosophy, cooking. *Address:* Henrietta Barnett School, Central Square, Hampstead Garden Suburb, NW11 7BN. *T:* (020) 8458 8999. *Clubs:* University Women's, International Rescue.

PAIN, Hon. Sir Peter (Richard), Kt 1975; a Judge of the High Court of Justice, Queen's Bench Division, 1975–88; *b* 6 Sept. 1913; *s* of Arthur Richard Pain and Elizabeth Irene Pain (*née* Benn); *m* 1941, Barbara Florence Maude Riggs; two *s*. *Educ:* Westminster; Christ Church, Oxford. Called to the Bar, Lincoln's Inn, 1936, Bencher 1972. QC 1965. Chairman: Race Relations Board Conciliation Cttee for Greater London, 1968–71; South Metropolitan Conciliation Cttee, 1971–73; Mem., Parole Bd, 1978–80. Pres., Holiday Fellowship, 1977–83. *Publications:* Manual of Fire Service Law, 1951; The Law Relating to the Motor Trade (with K. C. Johnson-Davies), 1955. *Recreations:* forestry, cricket, mountain walking. *Address:* Loen, St Catherine's Road, Frimley, Surrey GU16 7NJ. *T:* (01252) 835639.

PAIN, Sir Rollo; *see* Pain, Sir H. R. S.

PAINE, Sir Christopher (Hammon), Kt 1995; DM; FRCP, FRCR; Consultant in Radiotherapy and Oncology, Churchill Hospital, Oxford, 1970–95; President, British Medical Association, 2000–01; *b* 28 Aug. 1935; *s* of late Major John Hammon Paine and Hon. Mrs Joan Frances Shedden, MBE; *m* 1959, Susan Martin; two *s* two *d*. *Educ:* Eton Coll.; Merton Coll., Oxford (BM, BCh 1961; DM 1981); St Bartholomew's Hosp. Med. Sch. FRCP 1976; FRCR (FFR 1969). Junior med. posts, Oxford, London, Paris, 1962–70; Oxford University: Lectr in Radiotherapy and Oncology, 1972–95; Dir of Clinical Studies (clinical dean), 1982–85; Dist Gen. Manager, Oxfordshire HA, 1984–88; Chm., Oxford Med. Staff Council, 1991–92. Med. Dir, Adv. Cttee for Distinction Awards, 1994–99. Pres., British Oncological Assoc., 1989–91; Royal College of Radiologists: Dean, Faculty of Clinical Oncology, 1990–92; Vice-Pres., 1991–92; Pres., 1992–95. Pres., RSocMed, 1996–98. *Publications:* papers on interstitial and other aspects of radiation therapy. *Recreation:* gardening. *Address:* Kings Farm, Withypool, near Minehead, Somerset TA24 7RE. *T:* (01643) 831381. *Club:* Farmers'.

PAINE, Surg. Rear Adm. Michael Patrick William Halden, FRCS; Medical Director General (Naval), 1997–99; *b* 18 March 1939; *s* of Comdr Geoffrey W. W. H. Paine, RN and Eileen Paine (*née* Irwin); *m* 1972, Thayer Clark. *Educ:* Downside Sch.; London Hosp. Med. Coll. (MB BS 1963); Southampton Univ.; Edinburgh Univ. FRCS 1976. Joined Royal Navy, 1963; HMS Plymouth, 1965–66; HMS Repulse (SSBN), 1967–68; surgical trainee, RN Hosp. Haslar, 1969–75; PMO, HMS Bulwark, 1975–76; RN Hosp. Plymouth, 1977–79; Orthopaedic Senior Registrar: Southampton Gen. and Lord Mayor Treloar's Hosps, 1979; RN Hosp. Haslar, 1980; Cons. Orth. Surg., RN Hosp. Plymouth, 1981–82; HMS Illustrious, 1982–84; Cons. Orth. Surg., RN Hosp. Haslar, 1984–88; RAMC Sen. Officers' Course (Course Medal), 1986; Defence Med. Services Directorate, MoD, 1988–90 (Mem., Thompson Rev. of Service Hosps); Fleet MO, 1990–92; ACOS (Med. and Dental), C-in-C Fleet, 1992–97. QHS 1994–99. *Recreation:* sailing. *Address:* RR1, Box 73, Canaan, NH 03741, USA.

PAINE, Peter Stanley, CBE 1981; DFC 1944; Chairman, Oracle Teletext Ltd, 1984–93; *b* 19 June 1921; *s* of Arthur Bertram Paine and Dorothy Helen Paine; *m* 1st, 1942, Sheila Mary (*d* 1994), *d* of Frederick Wigglesworth, MA; two *s* two *d*; 2nd, 1999, Marion Dyason Strong (*née* Hunter). *Educ:* King's Sch., Canterbury. Served 1940–46, 2 Gp RAF (Flt-Lt). Worked in Punch Publishing Office, 1945–47; Sales Promotion Man., Newnes Pearson, 1948–52, Odhams Press, then Sales Dir and Dir of Tyne Tees Television, 1958–67; Sales Dir and Dir of Yorkshire Television, 1967–74; Managing Director: Tyne Tees Television, 1974–83; Tyne Tees Television Holdings, 1981–84. Director: Trident Television, 1970–81; Independent Television News Ltd, 1982–83; Independent Television Publications Ltd, 1977–83; Broadcasters Audience Res. Bd, 1980–86; Member: Council, Independent Television Companies Assoc., 1974–83 (4 yrs Chm. Marketing Cttee); Cable Authority, 1984–90. *Recreations:* golf, fishing, theatre, music, reading. *Address:* Briarfield, Ashwood Road, Woking, Surrey GU22 7JW. *T:* (01483) 773183. *Club:* Worplesdon Golf.

PAINE, Roger Edward; management coach and consultant; Vice President, Solace Enterprises Ltd, since 2001 (Executive Director, 1996–99; Managing Director, 1999–2001); *b* 20 Oct. 1943; *s* of Ethel May Jones and Edward Paine. *Educ:* Stockport Sch.; Univ. of Wales (BA Hons); Univ. of Manchester (part time; Dip TP); Univ. of Birmingham (MSocSci). Town Planner: Lancs CC, 1964–66; Stockport CB, 1966–68; Lancs CC, 1968–70; Salford City, 1970; Stockport Borough: Corporate Planner, 1971–73; Head of Corporate Planning, 1973–75; Co-ordinator of Central Units, 1975–77; Dep. Chief Exec., Camden, 1977–80; Chief Executive: Wrekin Council, 1980–88; Cardiff CC, 1988–94. Pres., Solace, 1992–93. Hon. Fellow, Inst. of Local Govt Studies, Birmingham. *Recreations:* music, travel, sport. *Address:* Pilgrims House, Barksdale, Winchcombe, Cheltenham, Glos GL54 5QW.

PAINES, Nicholas Paul Billot; QC 1997; *b* 29 June 1955; *s* of Anthony John Cooper Paines and Anne Paines; *m* 1985, Alison Jane Sargent Roberts; one *s* three *d*. *Educ:* Downside Sch.; New Coll., Oxford (BA 1977; MA 1984); Université Libre de Bruxelles (Licence speciale en droit européen). Called to the Bar, Gray's Inn, 1978; in practice at the Bar, 1980–; called to the Bar, NI, 1996; Mem., Supplementary Panel of Jun. Counsel to the Crown (Common Law), 1993–97. Mem., Bar Council, 1991–96; Chm., Bar European Gp, 1996–98. Mem. Council, St Christopher's Fellowship, 1983–. Jt Editor, Common Market Law Reports, 1996–. *Publications: contributions to:* Halsbury's Laws of England, 3rd edn, 1986; Vaughan, Law of the European Communities, 1986; Bellamy and Child, Common Market Law of Competition, 4th edn, 1993. *Recreation:* family life. *Address:* Monckton Chambers, 4 [illegible] 7405 7211.

PAINTAL, Prof. Autar Singh, Padma[illegible] FRSE; Director-General, Indian Council [illegible] 24 Sept. 1925; *s* of Dr Man Singh and Raj[illegible] Ashima Anand. *Educ:* SSBS Khalsa High Sch., [illegible] Lucknow Univ. (MB, BS, MD); Edinburgh Univ[illegible] George's Med. Coll., Lucknow Univ., 1949; Rocke[illegible] Edinburgh Univ., 1951; Control Officer, Technical D[illegible] Kanpur, 1952–54; Prof. of Physiology, All-India Inst. [illegible] 1958–64; Prof. of Physiology and Dir, Vallabhbhai Pat[illegible] 1964–90 (Asst Dir, 1954–56); Dean, Faculty of Med. Scien[illegible] Associate Prof., Albert Einstein Coll. of Medicine, New York, [illegible] of Physiol., Univ. of Utah, 1957; Commonwealth Vis. Prof., St [illegible] Med. Sch., London, 1966. FRSE 1966; Fellow: Indian Acad. of [illegible] Indian National Science Acad., 1971 (Vice Pres., 1981–83; Pres., 19[illegible] Nat. Coll. of Chest Physicians, 1981–86; Indian Sci. Congress, 1984–85; [illegible] Soc., UK, 1953 (Hon. Mem., 1988); Ergonomics Res. Soc., UK, 1954; Fo[illegible] USSR Acad. of Scis, 1988; Hon. Mem., Amer. Physiol. Soc., 1990. B. C. Ro[illegible] New Delhi, 1973; Sharpey-Schafer Lectr, Univ. of Edin., 1981; Dr Zakir Husain [illegible] Lectr, Jawaharlal Nehru Univ., 1984. Hon. FRCP, 1987. Hon. DSc: Benares [illegible] Univ., 1982; Delhi Univ., 1984; Aligarh Muslim Univ., 1986; N Bengal Univ., 1990; Guru Nanak Dev Univ., 1996; Lucknow Univ., 1996; Punjabi Univ., Patiala, 1997. Basanti Devi Amir Chand Prize, 1967; Silver Jubilee Res. Award, 1978; Barclay Medal, Asiatic Soc., 1982; R. D. Birla Award, 1982; Nehru Sci. Award, 1983; Maharishi Dayanand Centenary Gold Medal, 1983; Acharya J. C. Bose Medal, Bose Inst., 1985; C. V. Raman Medal, Indian Nat. Sci. Acad., 1994; Ashutosh Mukherjee Medal, Indian Science Congress Assoc., 1994. *Publications:* (ed) Morphology and Mechanisms of Chemoreceptors, 1976; (ed) Respiratory Adaptations, Capillary Exchange and Reflex Mechanisms, 1977; Respiratory Control Mechanisms and Sensations, 1998; papers in Jl of Physiol. and in other physiol jls. *Recreations:* swimming, rowing, bird watching. *Address:* DST Centre for Visceral Mechanisms, Vallabhbhai Patel Chest Institute, Delhi University, PO Box 2101, Delhi 110007, India. *T:* (11) 7667749, (11) 7667856. *Club:* Roshanara (Delhi).

PAINTER, Ven. David Scott; Archdeacon of Oakham, since 2000; Canon Residentiary of Peterborough Cathedral, since 2000; *b* 3 Oct. 1944; *s* of Frank Painter and Winifred Ellen Painter (*née* Bibbings). *Educ:* Queen Elizabeth's Sch., Crediton; Trinity Coll. of Music (LTCL 1965); Worcester Coll., Oxford (BA 1968; MA 1972); Cuddesdon Theol Coll. Ordained deacon, 1970, priest, 1971; Curate, St Andrew, Plymouth, 1970–73; Chaplain, Plymouth Poly., 1971–73; Curate, All Saints, St Marylebone, 1973–76; Domestic Chaplain to Archbishop of Canterbury, 1976–80; Vicar, Holy Trinity, Roehampton, 1980–91; RD, Wandsworth, 1985–90; Canon Residentiary and Treas., Southwark Cathedral, and Dio. Dir of Ordinands, Southwark, 1991–2000. *Recreations:* music, country walking, crossword puzzles. *Address:* 7 Minster Precincts, Peterborough, Cambs PE1 1XS. *T:* (01733) 891360, *Fax:* (01733) 554524; *e-mail:* david.painter@peterborough-cathedral.org.uk.

PAINTER, George Duncan, OBE 1974; biographer and incunabulist; Assistant Keeper in charge of fifteenth-century printed books, British Museum, 1954–74; *b* Birmingham, 5 June 1914; *s* of George Charles Painter and Minnie Rosendale (*née* Taylor); *m* 1942, Isabel Joan, *d* of Samuel Morley Britton, Bristol; two *d*. *Educ:* King Edward's Sch., Birmingham; Trinity Coll., Cambridge (Schol.). Bell Exhibr; John Stewart of Rannoch Schol.; Porson Schol.; Waddington Schol.; 1st cl. hons Class. Tripos pts I and II; Craven Student; 2nd Chancellor's Class. Medallist, 1936; MA Cantab 1945. Asst Lectr in Latin, Univ. of Liverpool, 1937; joined staff of Dept of Printed Books, BM, 1938. FRSL 1965. Hon. DLitt Edinburgh, 1979. *Publications:* André Gide, A Critical Biography, 1951, rev. edn 1968; The Road to Sinodun, Poems, 1951; André Gide, Marshlands and Prometheus Misbound (trans.), 1953; Marcel Proust, Letters to his Mother (trans.), 1956; Marcel Proust, A Biography, vol. 1, 1959, vol. 2, 1965 (Duff Cooper Memorial Prize), rev. and enl. edn in 1 vol., 1989, new edn 1996; The Vinland Map and the Tartar Relation (with R. A. Skelton and T. E. Marston), 1965, rev. edn 1996; André Maurois, The Chelsea Way (trans.), 1966; William Caxton, a Quincentenary Biography, 1976; Chateaubriand, A Biography, vol. 1, The Longed-for Tempests, 1977 (James Tait Black Meml Prize); Studies in Fifteenth-Century Printing, 1984; articles on fifteenth-century printing in The Library, Book Collector, Gutenberg-Jahrbuch. *Recreations:* family life, gardening, music. *Address:* 10 Mansfield Road, Hove, East Sussex BN3 5NN. *T:* (01273) 416008.

PAINTER, Terence James, CB 1990; a Deputy Chairman and Director General, Board of Inland Revenue, 1986–93; *b* 28 Nov. 1935; *s* of late Edward Lawrence Painter and Ethel Violet (*née* Butler); *m* 1959, Margaret Janet Blackburn; two *s* two *d*. *Educ:* City of Norwich Sch.; Downing Coll., Cambridge (BA (History)). Nat. Service Commn, Royal Norfolk Regt, 1958–59. Entered Inland Revenue as Asst Principal, 1959; Principal, 1962; seconded to Civil Service Selection Bd, 1967–68; Asst Sec., 1969; seconded to HM Treasury, 1973–75; Under-Sec., 1975–86. *Recreations:* music, books, walking. *Club:* Reform.

PAISLEY, Bishop of, (RC), since 1988; **Rt Rev. John Aloysius Mone;** Auxiliary Bishop of Glasgow, 1984–88; *b* 22 June 1929; *s* of Arthur Mone and Elizabeth Mone (*née* Dunn). *Educ:* Holyrood Secondary School, Glasgow; Séminaire Saint Sulpice, Paris; Institut Catholique, Paris (Faculty of Social Studies). Ordained Priest, Glasgow, 1952; Assistant Priest: St Ninian's, Knightswood, Glasgow, also hosp. and sch. chaplain, 1952–74; Our Lady and St George's, Glasgow, 1975–79; Parish Priest, St Joseph's, Tollcross, Glasgow, 1979–84. Episcopal Vicar, Marriage, 1981–83; Dir, Ministry to Priests Prog., 1982–84. Scottish National Chaplain, Girl Guides, 1971–; Chm., Scottish Catholic Internat. Aid Fund, 1974–75, Pres./Treas., 1985–; Chm., Scottish Catholic Marriage Advisory Council, 1982–84; President: Scottish Justice and Peace Commn, 1987–; Pastoral and Social Care Commn, 1996–. *Recreations:* watching soccer (attending if possible), playing golf (when time!), playing the piano. *Address:* 107 Corsebar Road, Paisley, Renfrewshire PA2 9PY. *T:* (0141) 889 7200, *Fax:* (0141) 849 6053.

PAISLEY, Rev. Ian Richard Kyle; MP (DemU) North Antrim, since 1974 (ProtU 1970–74) (resigned seat Dec. 1985 in protest against Anglo-Irish Agreement; re-elected Jan. 1986); Member (DemU) Northern Ireland, European Parliament, since 1979; Member (DemU) Antrim North, Northern Ireland Assembly, since 1998; Minister, Martyrs Memorial Free Presbyterian Church, Belfast, since 1946; *b* 6 April 1926; 2nd *s* of late Rev. J. Kyle Paisley and Mrs Isabella Paisley; *m* 1956, Eileen Emily Cassells; two *s* three *d* (incl. twin *s*). *Educ:* Ballymena Model Sch.; Ballymena Techn. High Sch.; S Wales Bible Coll.; Reformed Presbyterian Theol. Coll., Belfast. Ordained, 1946. Moderator, Free Presbyterian Church of Ulster, 1951; Pres., Whitefield Coll. of the Bible, 1979–. Commenced publishing The Protestant Telegraph, 1966. Contested (Prot U) Bannside,

NI Parlt, 1969; MP (Prot U), Bannside, Co. Antrim, NI Parlt, 1970–72; Leader of Opposition, 1972; Chm., Public Accounts Cttee, 1972. Co-Founder, Democratic Unionist Party, NI, 1972. Mem. (Democratic Unionist), N Antrim, NI Assembly, 1973–75; Mem. (UUUC), N Antrim, NI Constitutional Convention, 1975–76; Mem. (DemU) N Antrim, NI Assembly, 1982–86. Hon. DD Bob Jones Univ., SC. FRGS. Mem., Internat. Cultural Soc., Korea, 1977. *Publications:* History of the 1859 Revival, 1959; Christian Foundations, 1960; Ravenhill Pulpit, Vol. 1, 1966, Vol. 2, 1967; Exposition of the Epistle to the Romans, 1968; Billy Graham and the Church of Rome, 1970; The Massacre of St Bartholomew, 1972; America's Debt to Ulster, 1976; (jtly) Ulster—the facts, 1981; No Pope Here, 1982; Dr Kidd, 1982; Those Flaming Tennents, 1983; Mr Protestant, 1985; Be Sure, 1986; Paisley's Pocket Preacher, 1987, vol. II, 1988, vol. III, 1989, vol. IV, 1990; Jonathan Edwards: the theologian of revival, 1987; Union with Rome, 1989; The Soul of the Question, 1990; The Revised English Bible: an exposure, 1990; What a Friend We Have in Jesus, 1994; Understanding Events in Northern Ireland: an introduction for Americans, 1995; Ian Paisley Library, 10 vols, 1997–99. *Address:* House of Commons, SW1A 0AA; The Parsonage, 17 Cyprus Avenue, Belfast BT5 5NT.

See also I. R. K. Paisley.

PAISLEY, Ian Richard Kyle; Member (DemU) Antrim North, Northern Ireland Assembly, since 1998; *b* 12 Dec. 1966; *s* of Rev. I. R. K. Paisley, *qv*; *m* 1990, Fiona Margaret Elizabeth Currie; two *d. Educ:* Shaftesbury House Coll.; Methodist Coll.; Queen's Univ., Belfast (BA Hons Modern History; MSSc Irish Politics 1995). Res. Asst for Dr Ian Paisley, MP, MEP, H of C, 1989–. Mem., NI Forum for Political Dialogue, 1996–98. Justice spokesman, DUP, 1992–. Fellow, Sch. of Leadership, Maryland State Univ., 1997. Royal Humane Soc. Testimonial, 1999. *Publications:* Reasonable Doubt: the case for the UDR Four, 1991; Echoes: Protestant identity in Northern Ireland, 1994; Peace Deal?, 1998; articles in jls. *Recreations:* my children, Chinese food, cinema, Rugby, motorcycling. *Address:* Parliament Buildings, Stormont, Belfast BT4 3ST; 256 Ravenhill Road, Belfast BT6 8GJ; 46 Hill Street, Ballymena BT43 6BH.

PAJARES, Ramón, OBE 2000; Director and Advisor, Como Hotels and Investments Co. Ltd, since 2000; *b* 6 July 1935; *s* of Juan Antonio Pajares Garcia and Rosario Salazar; *m* 1963, Jean Kathleen Porter; one *s* two *d. Educ:* Madrid Inst. of Hotel and Tourism Studies. Nat. Service, Spanish Navy, 1955–57. Hotel posts: Ritz, Barcelona, 1954–55; San Jorge, Playa de Aro, 1957; Pargue, Llavaneras, 1957–59; Mansion, Eastbourne, 1959–61; Kleiner Reisen, Koblenz, Germany, 1961; Feldbergerhof, Feldberg, 1961–62; Le Vieux Manoir, Morat, Switzerland, 1962; Reina Isabel, Canary Is, 1963–69; Food and Beverage Dir, Inn on the Park, London, 1969–71; Gen. Manager, San Antonio, Lanzarote, Canary Is, 1972–74; Gen. Manager and Vice-Pres., Inn on the Park, later Four Seasons, 1975–94; Man. Dir, Savoy Gp of Hotels and Restaurants, 1994–99. Member: Assoc. Culinaire Française, 1971; Cookery and Food Assoc., 1973; Gp Bd, Leading Hotels of the World, 2000–. Pres., BHA, 2000. FHCIMA 1982. Freeman, City of London, 1988. Hotelier of Year Award, Brit. Hotel and Catering Ind., 1984; Personalité de l'année for Hotel Ind., 1986; Catey Special Award, 1997; Lifetime Achievement Award, Eur. Hotel Design and Develt Awards, 1998; British Travel Industry Hall of Fame, 1998; Spanish Govt Silver Medal, for services to tourism, 2000. Medals: Mérito Civil (Spain), 1984; Oficial de la Orden de Isabel la Católica (Spain), 1989. *Recreation:* classical music. *Club:* Les Ambassadeurs.

PAKENHAM, family name of **Earl of Longford**.

PAKENHAM, Elizabeth; *see* Longford, Countess of.

PAKENHAM, Henry Desmond Verner, CBE 1964; HM Diplomatic Service, retired; *b* 5 Nov. 1911; *s* of Hamilton Richard Pakenham and Emilie Willis Stringer; *m* 1st, 1946, Crystal Elizabeth Brooksbank (marr. diss., 1960); one *s* one *d* (and one *s* decd); 2nd, 1963, Venetia Maude; one *s* one *d. Educ:* Monkton Combe; St John Baptist College, Oxford. Taught modern languages at Sevenoaks School, 1933–40. Served in HM Forces, 1940–45. Entered Foreign Service, 1946; served in Madrid, Djakarta, Havana, Singapore, Tel Aviv, Buenos Aires and Sydney; retired 1971. Chm., Suffolk Preservation Soc., 1979–82. Asst Editor, Satow's Guide to Diplomatic Practice, 5th edn, 1979. *Address:* The Mill House, Lavenham, Suffolk CO10 9RD.

PAKENHAM, Hon. Michael Aidan, CMG 1993; HM Diplomatic Service; Ambassador to Poland, since 2001; *b* 3 Nov. 1943; *s* of 7th Earl of Longford, KG, PC, and Countess of Longford, *qv*; *m* 1980, Meta (Mimi) Landreth Doak, *d* of William Conway Doak of Maryland, USA; two *d* two step *d. Educ:* Ampleforth College (schol.); Trinity College, Cambridge (schol.; MA Classics); Rice University, Texas (exchange fellow). Washington Post, 1965; Foreign Office, 1965; Nairobi, 1966; Warsaw, 1967; FCO, 1970; Asst Private Sec., later Private Sec. to Chancellor of Duchy of Lancaster (European Community Affairs), on secondment to Cabinet Office, 1971–74; Geneva (CSCE), 1974; New Delhi, 1974; Washington, 1978; Head of Arms Control and Disarmament Dept, FCO, 1983–87; Counsellor (External Relations), UK Perm. Rep. to EC, Brussels, 1987–91; Ambassador and Consul-Gen., Luxembourg, 1991–94; Minister, Paris, 1994–97; Cabinet Office (on secondment): Dep. Sec. (Overseas and Defence), 1997–99; Chm., Jt Intelligence Cttee, 1997–2000 and Intelligence Co-ordinator, 1999–2000. Freeman of City of London, 1992. *Recreations:* tennis, golf, reading history, museums. *Address:* c/o Foreign and Commonwealth Office, King Charles Street, SW1A 0AA. *Clubs:* Garrick, Pilgrims, MCC; Vanderbilt Racquets; First Warsaw Golf; Rye Golf.

PAKENHAM, Thomas Frank Dermot; writer; *b* 14 Aug. 1933; *e s* of 7th Earl of Longford, KG, PC, and of Countess of Longford, *qv*; *S* father, 2001, but does not use the title; *m* 1964, Valerie, *d* of Major R. G. McNair Scott; two *s* two *d. Educ:* Dragon School, Oxford; Belvedere Coll., Dublin; Ampleforth Coll., York; Magdalen Coll., Oxford (BA Greats 1955). Travelled, Near East and Ethiopia, 1955–56 (discovered unrecorded medieval Ethiopian church at Bethlehem, Begemdir, 1956). Free-lance writing, 1956–58. Editorial staff: Times Educational Supplement, 1958–60; Sunday Telegraph, 1961; The Observer, 1961–64. Founder Mem. 1958, and Member Cttee 1958–64, Victorian Soc.; Founder Mem., and Mem. Cttee 1968–72, Historic Irish Tourist Houses and Gardens Assoc. (HITHA); Treas., British-Irish Assoc., 1972–; Sec. (co-founder), Christopher Ewart-Biggs Memorial Trust, 1976–; Founder and Chm., Irish Tree Soc., 1990–. Chm., Ladbroke Assoc., 1988–91. Sen. Associate Mem., St Antony's Coll., Oxford, 1979–81. Hon. DLitt Ulster, 1992. *Publications:* The Mountains of Rasselas: an Ethiopian adventure, 1959, 1998; The Year of Liberty: the story of the Great Irish Rebellion of 1798, 1969; The Boer War, 1979 (Cheltenham Prize, 1980); (selected and introd with Valerie Pakenham) Dublin: a travellers' companion, 1988; The Scramble for Africa, 1991 (W. H. Smith Prize, 1992; Alan Paton Meml Prize, 1992); Meetings with Remarkable Trees, 1996. *Recreation:* water. *Address:* 111 Elgin Crescent, W11 2JF. *T:* (020) 7727 7624; Tullynally, Castlepollard, Westmeath, Ireland. *T:* (044) 61159. *Clubs:* Beefsteak; Stephen's Green (Dublin).

PAKENHAM-WALSH, John, CB 1986; Standing Counsel to Gen. Synod of C of E, 1988–2000; *b* 7 Aug. 1928; *s* of late Rev. W. P. Pakenham-Walsh, formerly ICS, and Guendolen (*née* Elliott); *m* 1951, Deryn, *er d* of late Group Captain R. E. G. Fulljames, MC, and Mrs Muriel Fulljames; one *s* four *d. Educ:* Bradfield Coll.; University Coll., Oxford (MA). Called to the Bar, Lincoln's Inn, 1951. Crown Counsel, Hong Kong, 1953–57; Parly Counsel, Fedn of Nigeria, 1958–61; joined Legal Adviser's Br., Home Office, 1961; Under Sec. (Legal), Home Office, 1980–87. Hon. QC 1992. *Address:* 2 Roberts Close, Burton Bradstock, Bridport, Dorset DT6 4ST. *T:* (01308) 897651; *e-mail:* john.pw@linesne.net.

PAKINGTON, family name of **Baron Hampton**.

PALADE, Prof. George Emil, scientist, USA; Professor, Department of Cellular and Molecular Medicine and Dean for Scientific Affairs, School of Medicine, University of California at San Diego, 1990–2000, Emeritus Professor and Emeritus Dean for Scientific Affairs, since 2001; *b* Iassy, Romania, 19 Nov. 1912; *s* of Emil Palade and Constanta Cantemir; *m* 1st, 1941, Irina Malaxa (decd); one *s* one *d*; 2nd, 1970, Dr Marilyn Farquhar. *Educ:* Liceul Al. Hasdeu, Buzau, Romania; Med. Sch., Univ. of Bucharest (MD). Arrived in US, 1946; naturalized US citizen, 1952. Instructor, Asst Prof., then Lectr in Anatomy, Sch. of Med., Univ. of Bucharest, 1940–45; Visiting Investigator, Rockefeller Inst. for Med. Research, 1946–48; continuing as an Assistant (later the Inst. became Rockefeller Univ., NYC); promoted to Associate, 1951, and Associate Mem., 1953; Prof. of Cell Biology, Rockefeller Univ. and full Member of Rockefeller Inst., 1956; Prof. of Cell Biology, Yale Univ. Med. Sch., 1973; Sen. Res. Scientist, Yale Univ., 1983–90. Fellow, Amer. Acad. of Arts and Sciences; Member: Nat. Acad. of Sciences; Pontifical Acad. of Sciences; Leopoldina Acad.; Romanian Acad.; For. Mem., Royal Soc., 1984. Awards include: Albert Lasker Basic Research, 1966; Gairdner Award, 1967; Hurwitz Prize, 1970; Nobel Prize for Medicine, 1974; Nat. Medal of Science, USA, 1986. *Publications:* Editor: Annual Review of Cell Biology, 1985–95; Jl of Cell Biology (co-founder); Jl of Membrane Biology; numerous contribs med. and sci. jls on structure, biochemistry and function of sub-cellular components. *Address:* School of Medicine, University of California, San Diego, La Jolla, CA 92093–0602, USA. *T:* (858) 5347708, *Fax:* (858) 5346573.

PALETHORPE-TODD, Richard Andrew; *see* Todd.

PALETTE, John, OBE 1986; Director of Personnel, British Rail, 1982–86; *b* 19 May 1928; *s* of Arthur and Beatrice Palette; *m* 1950, Pamela Mabel Palmer; three *s. Educ:* Alexandra Sch., Hampstead. MCIT. Gen. Railway Admin, 1942–69; Divl Manager, Bristol, 1969–72; Asst Gen. Manager, Western Region, 1972–74; Divl Manager, Manchester, 1974–76; Gen. Manager, Scottish Region, 1976–77, Southern Region, 1977–82, British Railways. Chm., British Transport Ship Management (Scotland) Ltd, 1976. *Recreations:* walking, reading, gardening, watching sport. *Address:* 90 Wargrave Road, Twyford, Reading, Berks RG10 9PJ. *T:* (0118) 934 0965.

PALIN, Michael Edward, CBE 2000; writer and actor; *b* 5 May 1943; *s* of late Edward and Mary Palin; *m* 1966, Helen M. Gibbins; two *s* one *d. Educ:* Birkdale Sch., Sheffield; Shrewsbury; Brasenose Coll., Oxford (BA 2nd Cl. Hons Mod. Hist.). Pres., Transport 2000. Actor and writer: Monty Python's Flying Circus, BBC TV, 1969–74; Ripping Yarns, BBC TV, 1976–80; actor: Three Men in a Boat, BBC, 1975; GBH, Channel 4, 1991; writer: East of Ipswich, BBC TV, 1987; Number 27, BBC1, 1988; *stage play:* The Weekend, Strand, 1994. *Films:* actor and jt author: And Now for Something Completely Different, 1970; Monty Python and the Holy Grail, 1974; Monty Python's Life of Brian, 1978; Time Bandits, 1980; Monty Python's "The Meaning of Life," 1982; American Friends, 1991; actor, writer and co-producer: The Missionary, 1982; actor: Jabberwocky, 1976; A Private Function, 1984; Brazil, 1985; A Fish Called Wanda, 1988 (Best Supporting Film Actor, BAFTA Award, 1988); Fierce Creatures, 1997. *Television* series: contributor, Great Railway Journeys of the World, BBC, 1980; retraced Phileas Fogg's journey for Around the World in Eighty Days, BBC, 1989; travelled from North to South Pole for Pole to Pole, BBC, 1992; circumnavigated the Pacific Ocean for Full Circle, BBC, 1995–96; Michael Palin's Hemingway Adventure, BBC, 1999. *Publications:* Monty Python's Big Red Book, 1970; Monty Python's Brand New Bok, 1973; Dr Fegg's Encyclopeadia of *All* World Knowledge, 1984; Limericks, 1985; Around the World in Eighty Days, 1989; Pole to Pole, 1992 (Travel Writer of the Year, British Book Awards, 1993); Pole to Pole: the photographs, 1994; Hemingway's Chair (novel), 1995; Full Circle, 1997; Michael Palin's Hemingway Adventure, 1999; *for children:* Small Harry and the Toothache Pills, 1981; (with R. W. Seymour and Alan Lee) The Mirrorstone, 1986; The Cyril Stories, 1986. *Recreations:* reading, running, railways—preferably all three in a foreign country. *Address:* (office) 34 Tavistock Street, WC2E 7PB.

PALIN, Air Chief Marshal Sir Roger Hewlett, KCB 1989; OBE 1978; Controller, Royal Air Force Benevolent Fund, 1993–98; *b* 8 July 1938; *m* 1967, Kathryn Elizabeth Pye; two *d. Educ:* Canford Sch.; St John's Coll., Cambridge (BA 1967; MA 1979); psc. FRAeS; FIPD. Commnd KRRC, 1958; served 3 Para. Bn, 1958–59, 10 Para. Bn (TA), 1959–62; Flight Lieut, 1964; Sqn Leader, 1970; Wing Comdr, 1975; Group Captain, 1980; ADC to the Queen, 1981–82; Air Cdre, 1984; Dir of Defence Policy, MoD, 1984–85; Air Vice-Marshal, 1986; ACDS (Progs), 1986–87; AOC No 11 Gp, 1987–89; Air Marshal, 1989; C-in-C, RAF Germany and Comdr Second Allied Tactical Air Force, 1989–91; Air Chief Marshal, 1991; Air Mem. for Personnel, 1991–93; Air ADC to the Queen, 1991–93; retired 1993. Guest Schol., Woodrow Wilson Internat. Center for Scholars, Washington, 1980; Res. Associate, IISS, 1993. *Recreations:* sport, travel, international relations, defence studies.

PALING, Her Honour Helen Elizabeth, (Mrs W. J. S. Kershaw); a Circuit Judge, 1985–2000; *b* 25 April 1933; *o d* of A. Dale Paling and Mabel Eleanor Thomas; *m* 1961, William John Stanley Kershaw, PhD; one *s* three *d. Educ:* Prince Henry's Grammar Sch., Otley; London Sch. of Economics. LLB London 1954. Called to Bar, Lincoln's Inn, 1955; a Recorder, 1972–85. *Address:* c/o Quayside Law Courts, Newcastle upon Tyne NE1 2LA. *T:* (0191) 201 2000.

PALLEY, Dr Claire Dorothea Taylor, OBE 1998; Constitutional Adviser, Republic of Cyprus, 1980–94 and since 1999; Principal of St Anne's College, Oxford, 1984–91, Hon. Fellow, 1992; *b* 17 Feb. 1931; *d* of Arthur Aubrey Swait, Durban; *m* 1952, Ahrn Palley (marr. diss. 1985; he *d* 1993); five *s. Educ:* Durban Girls' Coll.; Univs of Cape Town and London. BA 1950, LLB 1952, Cape Town; PhD London 1965; MA Oxon 1984. Called to Bar, Middle Temple. Queen's University, Belfast: Lectr, 1966–67; Reader, 1967–70; Prof. of Public Law, 1970–73; Dean of Faculty of Law, 1971–73; Prof. of Law, 1973–84, and Master of Darwin Coll., 1974–82, Univ. of Kent. Member: Council, Minority Rights Group, 1975–94; UN Sub-Commn on Prevention of Discrimination and Protection of Minorities, 1988–98. Hon. LLD QUB, 1991. *Publications:* The Constitutional History and Law of Southern Rhodesia, 1966; The United Kingdom and Human Rights, 1991; contrib. learned jls. *Address:* 13 Nikou Sophocleous Avenue, Pachna, 4700 Limassol, Cyprus.

PALLISER, Rt Hon. Sir (Arthur) Michael, GCMG 1977 (KCMG 1973; CMG 1966); PC 1983; HM Diplomatic Service, retired; Vice-Chairman, Board of Salzburg Seminar, since 1995; *b* 9 April 1922; *s* of late Admiral Sir Arthur Palliser, KCB, DSC, and Lady Palliser (*née* Margaret Eva King-Salter); *m* 1948, Marie Marguerite (*d* 2000), *d* of late Paul-Henri Spaak; three *s*. *Educ:* Wellington Coll.; Merton Coll., Oxford (Hon. Fellow 1987). Served with Coldstream Guards, 1942–47 (despatches); Capt. 1944. Entered HM Diplomatic Service, 1947; SE Asia Dept, Foreign Office, 1947–49; Athens, 1949–51; Second Sec., 1950; Foreign Office: German Finance Dept, 1951–52; Central Dept, 1952–54; Private Sec. to Perm. Under-Sec., 1954–56; First Sec., 1955; Paris, 1956–60; Head of Chancery, Dakar, 1960–62 (Chargé d'Affaires in 1960, 1961 and 1962); Counsellor, and seconded to Imperial Defence College, 1963; Head of Planning Staff, Foreign Office, 1964; a Private Sec. to PM, 1966; Minister, Paris, 1969; Ambassador and Head of UK Deleg. to European Communities, Brussels, 1971; Ambassador and UK Permanent Representative to European Communities, 1973–75; Permanent Under-Sec. of State, FCO and Head of Diplomatic Service, 1975–82. Chm., Samuel Montagu & Co., 1984–85, 1986–93 (Dir, 1983–96; Vice Chm., 1988, 1993–96); Deputy Chairman: Midland Montagu (Hldgs), 1987–93; Midland Bank, 1987–91. Director, 1983–92: BAT Industries plc; Booker plc; Eagle Star Hldgs; Shell Transport & Trading Co. plc; Director: United Biscuits (Hldgs), 1983–89; Arbor Acres Farm Inc., 1985–91; UK–Japan 2000 Gp, 1987–96; XCL Ltd, 1994–2000. Dep. Chm., BI (formerly BIEC), 1987–95. Pres., China-Britain Trade Gp, 1992–96; Member: Council, IISS, 1982–91 (Chm., 1983–90; Vice-Pres., 1999–); Trilateral Commn, 1982–96; Security Commn, 1983–92; Council, British N American Cttee and Res. Assoc., 1987–95 (British Chm., 1990–92); BOTB, 1993–96; Adv. Bd, RAND Europe, 1995–; Adv. Council, British Consultants Bureau, 1997–. Mem., Royal Nat. Theatre Bd, 1988–96. Pres., Internat. Social Service of UK, 1982–96; Chairman: City and E London Confedn of Medicine and Dentistry, 1989–95; Major Projects Assoc., 1994–98. Trustee, The Tablet, 1989–. Governor, Wellington Coll., 1982–92. FRSA 1983. Hon. Fellow, QMW, 1990. Chevalier, Order of Orange Nassau, 1944; Commandeur, Légion d'Honneur, 1996 (Chevalier, 1957). *Address:* 12B Wedderburn Road, NW3 5QG. *T:* (020) 7794 0440, *Fax:* (020) 7916 2163. *Club:* Buck's.

PALLOT, Arthur Keith, CB 1981; CMG 1966; Secretary and Director-General, Commonwealth War Graves Commission, 1975–82 (Director of Finance and Establishments, 1956–75); *b* 25 Sept. 1918; *s* of Harold Pallot, La Tourelle, Jersey; *m* 1945, Marjorie, *d* of J. T. Smith, Rugby; two *d*. *Educ:* Newton College. Royal Navy, 1936; retired as Lt-Comdr, 1947. Commonwealth War Graves Commission, 1947. Awarded the Queen's Commendation for brave conduct, 1958.

PALMAR, Sir Derek, Kt 1986; FCA; President, Bass PLC, 1987–89 (Chairman, 1976–87; Chairman and Chief Executive, 1976–84; Director, 1970–76); Chairman: Yorkshire Television, 1981–93; Yorkshire–Tyne Tees Television Holdings, 1992–93; Vice President, Brewers' Society, since 1982 (Chairman, 1980–82); *b* 25 July 1919; *o s* of late Lt-Col Frederick Palmar and Hylda (*née* Smith); *m* 1st, 1946, Edith Brewster (*d* 1990); one *s* one *d*; 2nd, 1992, Shuna, *o d* of late Keith Pyman and Peggy (*née* Hare). *Educ:* Dover College. FCA 1957 (ACA 1947). Served RA and Staff, 1941–46; psc; Lt-Col 1945. Peat, Marwick, Mitchell & Co., 1937–57; Director: Hill Samuel Group, 1957–70; Grindlays Bank, 1970–85. Adviser, Dept of Economic Affairs, 1965–67; Mem., British Railways Bd, 1969–72; Chm., BR Southern Regional Adv. Bd, 1972–79. Chm., Readyhigh, 1986–94; Director: Drayton Consolidated Trust, 1982–93; Consolidated Venture Trust, 1984–93; CM Group Holdings, 1985–92; United Newspapers, 1986–93; Chm., NEDC for Food and Drink Packaging Equipment, 1986–87. Chairman: Zool Soc. of London Develt Trust, 1986–89; Leeds Univ. Foundn, 1986–89; Member: Accounting Standards Cttee, 1982–84; Alcohol Educn and Res. Council, 1982–87. Director: Business in the Community, 1984–; Centre for Policy Studies, 1983–88; Mem., Adv. Council, Prince's Trust, 1984–. Trustee, Develt Trust, Queen Elizabeth's Foundn for Disabled People, 1993–96. Freeman, City of London; Mem., Ct, Brewers' Co., 1982–89. *Recreation:* gardening. *Address:* Church Farm, Naunton, Cheltenham, Glos GL54 3AJ.

PALMER, family name of **Earl of Selborne, Baron Palmer** and **Baron Lucas of Crudwell**.

PALMER, 4th Baron *cr* 1933, of Reading; **Adrian Bailie Nottage Palmer;** Bt 1916; *b* 8 Oct. 1951; *s* of Col the Hon. Sir Gordon Palmer, KCVO, OBE, TD, MA, FRCM and of the Hon. Lady Palmer, DL; *S* uncle, 1990; *m* 1977, Cornelia Dorothy Katherine, *d* of R. N. Wadham, DFC, Exning, Newmarket; two *s* one *d*. *Educ:* Eton; Edinburgh Univ. Mem., Exec. Council, HHA, 1981–99; Chm., HHA for Scotland, 1994–99 (Mem., Exec. Council, 1980–99; Vice Chm., 1993). Elected Mem., H of L, 1999. Mem., Queen's Body Guard for Scotland (Royal Company of Archers), 1992–96. Scottish Rep. to European Landowning Orgn, 1986–92. Pres., British Assoc. for Biofuels and Oils. Sec., The Royal Caledonian Hunt, 1989–. *Recreations:* gardening, shooting, hunting. *Heir:* *s* Hon. Hugo Bailie Rohan Palmer, *b* 5 Dec. 1980. *Address:* Manderston, Duns, Berwickshire TD11 3PP. *T:* (01361) 883450. *Clubs:* Pratt's, MCC; New (Edinburgh).

PALMER, Adrian Oliver; QC 1992; a Recorder, since 1992; *b* 20 Aug. 1950; *s* of Richard Gilbert Palmer and Patricia Mary Palmer; *m* 1974, Rosemary Shaw; one *s* one *d*. *Educ:* Clifton Coll., Bristol; St John's Coll., Cambridge (MA). Called to the Bar, Middle Temple, 1972. *Recreations:* gardens, sheep, walking. *Address:* Guildhall Chambers, 23 Broad Street, Bristol BS1 2HG. *T:* (0117) 927 3366.

PALMER, Prof. Andrew Clennel, PhD; FRS 1994; FREng, FICE; Jafar Research Professor in Petroleum Engineering, Cambridge University, since 1996; Fellow, Churchill College, Cambridge, since 1996; *b* 26 May 1938; *s* of Gerald Basil Coote Palmer and Muriel Gertrude Palmer (*née* Howes); *m* 1963, Jane Rhiannon Evans; one *d*. *Educ:* Cambridge Univ. (BA, MA); Brown Univ. (PhD). FICE 1986; FREng (FEng 1990). Lectr, Liverpool Univ., 1965–67; Cambridge University: Sen. Asst in Res., 1967–68; Lectr, 1968–75; Fellow, Churchill Coll., 1967–75; Chief Engr, R. J. Brown and Associates, 1975–79; Prof. of Civil Engrg, UMIST, 1979–82; Vice-Pres. Engrg, R. J. Brown and Associates, 1982–85; Man. Dir, Andrew Palmer and Associates, 1985–93; Technical Dir, SAIC Ltd, 1993–2000. Pres., Pipeline Industries Guild, 1998–2000. *Publications:* Structural Mechanics, 1976; articles and papers in scientific and engrg jls. *Recreations:* travel, glass-blowing, cooking, languages. *Address:* University Engineering Department, Trumpington Street, Cambridge CB2 1PZ. *T:* (01223) 332718; *e-mail:* acp24@eng.cam.ac.uk; (home) 49 Ashley Gardens, Ambrosden Avenue, SW1P 1QF. *T:* (020) 7828 8843. *Club:* Athenæum.

PALMER, Andrew Eustace, CMG 1987; CVO 1981; HM Diplomatic Service, retired; An Extra Equerry to the Duke of Kent, since 1996; *b* 30 Sept. 1937; *s* of late Lt-Col Rodney Howell Palmer, MC, and of Mrs Frances Pauline Ainsworth (*née* Gordon-Duff); *m* 1962, Davina, *d* of Sir Roderick Barclay, GCVO, KCMG; two *s* one *d*. *Educ:* Winchester Coll.; Pembroke Coll., Cambridge (MA). Second Lieut. Rifle Bde, 1956–58. Joined HM Foreign (later Diplomatic) Service, 1961; American Dept, FO, 1962–63; Third, later Second, Secretary (Commercial), La Paz, 1963–65; Second Sec., Ottawa, 1965–67; Treasury Centre for Administrative Studies, 1967–68; Central Dept, FO, later Southern European Dept, FCO, 1968–72; First Sec. (Information), Paris, 1972–76; Asst Head of Defence Dept, FCO, 1976–77; RCDS 1978; Counsellor, Head of Chancery and Consul-Gen., Oslo, 1979–82; Hd, Falkland Is Dept, FCO, 1982–85; Fellow, Harvard Center for Internat. Affairs, 1985–86; Ambassador to Cuba, 1986–88; seconded as Pvte Sec. to the Duke and Duchess of Kent, 1988–90; Ambassador to the Holy See, 1991–95. Local organiser, Bilderberg Conf., Turnberry, 1998. Mem. Council, Reading Univ., 1996– (Mem. Standing Cttee, 1997–). *Recreations:* fishing, tennis, following most sports, photography, ornithology. *Address:* Town Farm Cottage, Little Missenden, Amersham, Bucks HP7 0QX. *Clubs:* Brooks's, MCC, Vanderbilt.

See also Viscount Garmoyle.

PALMER, Angela, (Mrs J. D. F. Palmer); freelance journalist; *b* 27 March 1957; *m* 1988, Jeremy David Fletcher Palmer, *er s* of Maj.-Gen. Sir (Joseph) Michael Palmer, *qv*; two *s* one *d*. *Educ:* George Watson's Ladies' Coll., Edinburgh. Trainee, Evening News, Edinburgh, 1979–82; Peterborough Column, Daily Telegraph, 1982–84; Editor, PHS, The Times, 1984–86; News Editor, Observer, 1986–88; Editor: Observer Mag., 1988–92; Elle, 1992–93. Appears on radio and television. Journalist of the Year, Scotland, 1980. *Recreations:* family, painting, tennis. *Club:* Reform.

PALMER, Maj. Gen. Anthony Malcolm Douglas, CBE 1995; Chief Executive, Army Training and Recruiting Agency, since 1999; *b* 13 March 1949; *s* of late Lt-Col A. G. D. Palmer and Joan Palmer (*née* Wintour); *m* 1972, Harriet Ann Jardine; two *s* one *d*. *Educ:* Woodcote House; Winchester Coll. Commnd RGJ, 1969; despatches, 1972, 1990; BAOR, 1969–70; NI, 1970–71; Shorncliffe, 1971–73; Catterick, 1973–74; Warminster, 1974–76; 2nd Bn RGJ, 1976, Ops Officer, 1978–80; Trng Co. Cmdr, Winchester, 1980–81; Staff Coll., Pakistan, 1981; Co. Cmdr, 3rd Bn RGJ, 1983–85; MoD, 1985–87; Directing Staff, Camberley, 1987–89; CO, 2nd Bn RGJ, 1989–91; Col, MoD, 1991; Comdr, 8 Inf. Bde, 1993; rcds 1995; Dir, Army Plans, 1996–99. Mem. Bd, Prince's Trust Volunteers, 1999–. *Recreations:* music, bridge, golf, tennis, fishing. *Address:* Trenchard Lines, Upavon, Pewsey, Wilts SN9 6BE. *T:* (01980) 615001; *e-mail:* hqatra@gtnet.gov.uk. *Club:* Royal Green Jackets.

PALMER, Anthony Thomas Richard; *see* Palmer, Tony.

PALMER, Anthony Wheeler; QC 1979; a Recorder of the Crown Court, since 1980; *b* 30 Dec. 1936; *s* of late Philip Palmer and of Doris Palmer; *m* Jacqueline, *d* of Reginald Fortnum, Taunton; one *s* two *d*. *Educ:* Wrekin Coll., Salop. Called to the Bar, Gray's Inn, 1962. *Address:* 17 Warwick Avenue, Coventry CV5 6DJ.

PALMER, Arnold Daniel; professional golfer since 1954; golf course designer; *b* 10 Sept. 1929; *s* of Milfred J. and Doris Palmer; *m* 1954, Winifred Walzer (*d* 1999); two *d*. *Educ:* Wake Forest Univ. Winner of numerous tournament titles, including: British Open Championship, 1961, 1962; US Open Championship, 1960; Masters Championship, 1958, 1960, 1962, 1964; Spanish Open Championship, 1975; Professional Golfers' Assoc. Championship, 1975; Canadian PGA, 1980; USA Seniors' Championship, 1981. Hon. Dr of Laws: Wake Forest; Nat. Coll. of Educn; Hon. DHum: Thiel Coll.; Florida Southern College; St Vincent Coll. Hon. Member: Royal and Ancient Golf Club, 1979; Troon Golf Club, 1982; Royal Birkdale Golf Club, 1983. *Publications* (all jointly): Arnold Palmer Golf Book, 1961; Portrait of a Professional Golfer, 1964; My Game and Yours, 1965; Situation Golf, 1970; Go for Broke, 1973; Arnold Palmer's Best 54 Golf Holes, 1977; Arnold Palmer's Complete Book of Putting, 1986; Play Great Golf, 1987; Arnold Palmer, A Personal Journey, 1994; A Golfer's Life, 1999. *Recreations:* aviation (speed record for flying round world in twin-engine jet, 1976), bridge, hunting, fishing. *Address:* PO Box 52, Youngstown, Pa 15696, USA. *T:* (724) 5377751. *Clubs:* (Owner and Pres.) Latrobe Country; (Pres. and Part-Owner) Bay Hill (Orlando, Fla); (Tournament Professional) Laurel Valley Golf; (Hon. Life Mem., 1992–) Carnoustie Golf; numerous other country, city, golf.

PALMER, Bernard Harold Michael, OBE 1989; MA; Editor of the Church Times, 1968–89; *b* 8 Sept. 1929; *e s* of late Christopher Harold Palmer; *m* 1954, Jane Margaret, *d* of late E. L. Skinner; one *s* one *d*. *Educ:* St Edmund's School, Hindhead; Eton (King's Scholar); King's College, Cambridge. BA 1952; MA 1956. Member of editorial staff, Church Times, 1952–89; Managing Director, 1957–89; Editor-in-Chief, 1960–68; Chm., 1962–89. DLitt Lambeth, 1988. *Publications:* Gadfly for God: a history of the Church Times, 1991; High and Mitred: a study of prime ministers as bishop-makers, 1992; Reverend Rebels: five Victorian clerics and their fight against authority, 1993; Men of Habit: the Franciscan ideal in action, 1994; A Class of Their Own: six public-school headmasters who became Archbishop of Canterbury, 1997; Imperial Vineyard: the Anglican church in India under the Raj from the Mutiny to Partition, 1999; Willingly to School: a history of St Edmund's, Hindhead, 2000. *Recreations:* cycling, penmanship. *Address:* Three Corners, 15 East Hill, Charminster, Dorchester, Dorset DT2 9QL. *T:* (01305) 260948. *Club:* Royal Commonwealth Society.

PALMER, Brian Desmond; formerly Under Secretary, Northern Ireland Office; *b* 1 May 1939; *m* 1964, Hilary Eileen Latimer; one *s* one *d*. *Educ:* Royal Belfast Academical Instn; Queen's Univ. of Belfast (LLB 1962). Joined Northern Ireland Civil Service, 1957: Estate Duty Office, 1957–62; Min. of Home Affairs, 1962–65; Dept of the Environment, 1965–77; Head of Central Secretariat, 1977–81. *Recreation:* golf.

PALMER, Caroline Ann, (Cally), (Mrs I. J. Palmer-Makowski); Chief Executive, Royal Marsden NHS Trust, since 1998; *b* 12 Jan. 1958; *d* of Christopher and Ann Palmer; *m* 1986, Ian Julian Makowski; two *s* one *d*. *Educ:* Woking Girls Grammar Sch.; Westfield Coll., London Univ. (BA 1979); London Business Sch. (MSc 1995). MHSM 1983; DipHSM. Gen. mgt trng scheme, 1980–83; Asst Unit Adminr, St Luke's Hosp., 1983–85; Royal Free Hospital, subseq. Royal Free Hampstead NHS Trust: Associate Unit Adminr, 1985–87; Dep. Manager, 1987–90; Gen. Manager, 1990–94; Dep. CEO, 1994–98. *Recreations:* history of art, ballet. *Address:* Royal Marsden NHS Trust, Fulham Road, SW3 6JJ.

PALMER, Sir (Charles) Mark, 5th Bt *cr* 1886; *b* 21 Nov. 1941; *s* of Sir Anthony Frederick Mark Palmer, 4th Bt, and of Henriette (*see* Lady Abel Smith); *S* father, 1941; *m* 1976, Hon. Catherine Elizabeth Tennant, *y d* of 2nd Baron Glenconner; one *s* one *d*. *Heir:* *s* Arthur Morris Palmer, *b* 9 March 1981. *Address:* Mill Hill Farm, Sherborne, Northleach, Glos GL54 3DU. *T:* (01451) 844395.

PALMER, David Erroll Prior; Chairman, Independent Newspapers (Ireland), since 1999 (Managing Director, 1994–98); *b* 20 Feb. 1941; *s* of Sir Otho Prior-Palmer, DSO, and Sheila Peers (*née* Weller-Poley), OBE; *m* 1974, Elizabeth Helen Young; two *s* one *d*. *Educ:* Eton; Christ Church, Oxford (MA PPE). Joined Financial Times, 1964: New York Correspondent, 1967; Management Editor, 1970; News Editor, 1972; Foreign Editor, 1979; Dep. Editor, 1981; Gen. Manager and Dir, 1983; Dep. Chief Exec., 1989; Chief Exec., 1990–93; Chm., South-West Sussex Radio, 1995–. First British finisher, seventh over-all, Observer Singlehanded Transatlantic Race, 1976. *Publication:* The Atlantic

Challenge, 1977. *Recreations:* sailing, travelling. *Address:* Independent Newspapers, 1–2 Upper Hatch Street, Dublin 2, Ireland. *Clubs:* Royal Yacht Squadron (Cowes); Itchenor Sailing (near Chichester); Royal St George Yacht, Fitzwilliam Lawn Tennis (Dublin).

PALMER, David Vereker; DL; Chairman, 1982–88, and Chief Executive, 1978–88, Willis Faber plc; Chairman, Syndicate Capital Trust plc, 1993–96; *b* 9 Dec. 1926; *s* of late Brig. Julian W. Palmer and Lena Elizabeth (*née* Vereker); *m* 1950, Mildred Elaine O'Neal; three *d. Educ:* Stowe. ACII 1950. Commnd The Life Guards, 1944; served as regular officer in Europe and ME, 1944–49; joined Edward Lumley & Sons, 1949; Manager, New York office, 1953–59; joined Willis, Faber & Dumas Ltd, 1959; Dir, 1961. Mem. Lloyd's, 1953. Chm., British Insurance & Investment Brokers Assoc., 1987–90 (Dep. Chm., 1984–87); Pres., Insurance Inst. of London, 1985–86. Commissioner, Royal Hosp. Chelsea, 1982–88. Mem. Council, St George's House, Windsor. Trustee, Tower Hill Improvement Trust. Master, Worshipful Co. of Insurers, 1982. High Sheriff, Bucks, 1993–94, DL Bucks, 1995. *Recreations:* farming, shooting. *Address:* Burrow Farm, Hambleden, near Henley-on-Thames, Oxon RG9 6LT. *T:* (01491) 571256. *Clubs:* City of London, Cavalry and Guards.

PALMER, Rev. Canon Derek George; Chaplain to the Queen, 1990–98; Team Rector of Dronfield with Holmesfield, 1987–95; *b* 24 Jan. 1928; *s* of late George Palmer, MBE and Edna Palmer; *m* 1952, June Cecilie Goddard; two *s* two *d. Educ:* Clifton Coll.; Selwyn Coll., Cambridge (MA); Wells Theological Coll. Deacon 1952, priest 1953; Priest in Charge, Good Shepherd, Bristol, 1954–58; first Vicar of Hartcliffe, 1958–68; Vicar of Christ Church, Swindon, 1968–77; Archdeacon of Rochester and Canon Residentiary of Rochester Cathedral, 1977–83; Home Secretary, Bd for Mission and Unity, 1983–87. Mem., General Synod, 1971–81. Hon. Canon: Rochester Cathedral, 1983–87; Derby Cathedral, 1992–. Chm., Christian Enquiry Agency, 1988–99; Ecumenical Officer, Bucks, 1995–. *Publications:* All Things New, 1963; Quest, 1971; Strangers No Longer, 1990. *Recreation:* canals. *Address:* 124 Bath Road, Banbury, Oxon OX16 0TR.

PALMER, Edward Hurry, CB 1972; retired Civil Servant; *b* 23 Sept. 1912; *s* of late Harold G. Palmer and late Ada S. Palmer; *m* 1940, Phyllis Eagle; no *c. Educ:* Haileybury. Dep. Chief Surveyor of Lands, Admty, 1942; Chief Surveyor of Lands, Admty, 1950; Chief Surveyor of Defence Lands, MoD, 1964; Comptroller of Defence Lands and Claims, MoD, 1968–72; Property Services Agency, DoE: Dir, Defence Lands Services, 1972–73; Dir, Estate Surveying Services, 1973–74. *Recreation:* walking. *Address:* 4 Barrowdene Close, Pinner, Middlesex HA5 3DD. *T:* (020) 8866 5961.

PALMER, Felicity Joan, CBE 1993; mezzo-soprano. *Educ:* Erith Grammar Sch.; Guildhall Sch. of Music and Drama. AGSM (Teacher/Performer), FGSM. Kathleen Ferrier Meml Prize, 1970; major appearances at concerts in Britain, America, Belgium, France, Germany, Italy, Russia and Spain, firstly as soprano and then as mezzo-soprano; début as soprano, Dido in Dido and Aeneas, Kent Opera, 1972; début in USA, Marriage of Figaro, Houston, 1973; soprano roles included: Pamina in The Magic Flute, ENO, 1975; Cleopatra in Julius Caesar, Herrenhausen Hanover, and Frankfurt Opera, 1978; title role, Alcina, Bern Opera, 1978; Elektra in Idomeneo, Zurich Opera, 1980; the Countess in The Marriage of Figaro, ENO; Elvira in Don Giovanni, Scottish Opera and ENO; Marguerite in Damnation of Faust, ENO; mezzo-soprano roles include: ENO: Tristan und Isolde, 1981; Rienzi, 1983; Mazeppa, 1984; Herodias in Salome, and The Witch in Hansel and Gretel, 1987; Orfeo, Opera North, 1984; King Priam, Royal Opera, 1985; Albert Herring, Glyndebourne, 1985; Tamburlaine, Opera North, 1985; Katya Kabanova, Chicago Lyric Opera, 1986; début at La Scala, Milan, as Marguerita in world première of Riccardo III by Flavio Testi, 1987; Last Night of the Proms, 1987; début, Netherlands Opera, as Kabanicha in Katya Kabanova, 1988, same role, Glyndebourne, 1988; Mistress Quickly in Falstaff, 1988 and 1990, Marcellina in The Marriage of Figaro, 1989, Glyndebourne; world première of Tippett's New Year, Houston, USA, 1989; The Marriage of Figaro and The Gambler (Prokofiev), Chicago, 1991; Klytemnestra in Elektra, WNO, 1992, La Scala, Milan and Japan, 1995, Royal Opera, 1997; Orlando, Aix-en-Provence, 1993; Dialogue des Carmelites, Geneva, 1993; La Fille du Régiment, San Francisco, 1993; Ariodante, WNO, 1994; The Rake's Progress, Chicago, 1994; Ballo in Maschera, Catania, 1995; Countess in The Queen of Spades, Glyndebourne, 1995; Juno/Ino in Semele, Royal Opera, 1996; Mahagonny, Paris, 1997, Chicago, 1998; Frika in The Ring, Munich, 1997 and 1999, Canaries, 1999, Met. Opera House, NY, 2000; recitals in Amsterdam, Paris, Vienna, 1976–77, Tokyo, 1991; concert tours with BBC SO, Europe, 1973, 1977 and 1984, Australasia, Far East and Eastern Europe, 1977–; ABC tour of Australia, 1978. Recordings include: Poèmes pour Mi, with Pierre Boulez; Holst Choral Symphony, with Sir Adrian Boult; title role in Gluck's Armide; Elektra in Idomeneo, with Nikolaus Harnoncourt; The Music Makers; Sea Pictures; Britten's Phaedra; recitals, with John Constable, of songs by Poulenc, Ravel and Fauré, and of Victorian ballads. *Address:* c/o Askonas Holt Ltd, Lonsdale Chambers, 27 Chancery Lane, WC2E 1PF.

PALMER, Rev. Preb. Francis Harvey; Prebendary of Sawley in Lichfield Cathedral, 1986–89; Prebendary Emeritus since 1989; *b* 13 Jan. 1930; *s* of Harry Hereward North Palmer and Ada Wilhelmina Annie Utting; *m* 1955, Mary Susan Lockhart; three *d. Educ:* Nottingham High Sch.; Jesus Coll., Cambridge (Exhibr); Wycliffe Hall, Oxford. MA. Deacon, 1955; Priest, 1956. Asst Curate: Knotty Ash, Liverpool, 1955–57; St Mary, Southgate, Crawley, 1958–60; Chaplain, Fitzwilliam House, Cambridge, 1960–64; Vicar of Holy Trinity, Cambridge and Chaplain to Cambridge Pastorate, 1964–71; Principal, Ridley Hall, Cambridge, 1971–72; Rector of Worplesdon, Surrey, 1972–80; Diocesan Ecumenical Officer, Guildford, 1974–80; Diocesan Missioner, Lichfield, 1980–89. *Publication:* (contrib.) New Bible Dictionary, 1959. *Address:* The Old Vicarage, Claverley, Wolverhampton WV5 7DT.

PALMER, Prof. Frank Robert, FBA 1975; Professor and Head of Department of Linguistic Science, University of Reading, 1965–87; *b* 9 April 1922; *s* of George Samuel Palmer and Gertrude Lilian (*née* Newman); *m* 1948, Jean Elisabeth Moore; three *s* two *d. Educ:* Bristol Grammar Sch.; New Coll., Oxford (Ella Stephens Schol., State Schol.) 1942–43 and 1945–48; Merton Coll., Oxford (Harmsworth Sen. Schol.) 1948–49. MA Oxon 1948; Craven Fellow, 1948. Served war, E Africa, 1943–45. Lectr in Linguistics, Sch. of Oriental and African Studies, Univ. of London, 1950–60 (study leave in Ethiopia, 1952–53); Prof. of Linguistics, University Coll. of N Wales, Bangor, 1960–65; Dean of Faculty of Letters and Social Sciences, Univ. of Reading, 1969–72. Linguistic Soc. of America Prof., Buffalo, 1971; Distinguished Visiting Professor: Foreign Languages Inst., Beijing, 1981; Univ. of Delaware, 1983. Professional visits to Canada, USA, Mexico, Venezuela, Peru, Chile, Argentine, Uruguay, Brazil, India, Japan, China, Indonesia, Morocco, Tunisia, Uganda, Kuwait and most countries of Europe. MAE 1991. Hon. DLitt Reading, 1996. *Publications:* The Morphology of the Tigre Noun, 1962; A Linguistic Study of the English Verb, 1965; (ed) Selected Papers of J. R. Firth, 1968; (ed) Prosodic Analysis, 1970; Grammar, 1971, 2nd edn 1984; The English Verb, 1974, 2nd edn 1987; Semantics, 1976, 2nd edn 1981; Modality and the English Modals, 1979, 2nd edn 1990; Mood and Modality, 1986, 2nd edn 2001; Grammatical Roles and Relations, 1994; articles and reviews on Ethiopian langs, English and linguistic theory, in learned jls. *Recreations:* gardening, crosswords. *Address:* Whitethorns, Roundabout Lane, Winnersh, Wokingham, Berks RG41 5AD. *T:* (0118) 978 6214.

PALMER, Geoffrey; actor; *b* 4 June 1927; *m* 1963, Sally Green; one *s* one *d. Educ:* Highgate Sch. *Theatre* includes: Difference of Opinion, Garrick; West of Suez, Royal Court, 1971; Private Lives, Globe, 1973; Eden End, NT, 1974; St Joan, Old Vic, 1977; Tishoo, Wyndham's, 1979; Kafka's Dick, Royal Court, 1986; Piano, NT, 1990; *television* includes: The Fall and Rise of Reginald Perrin, 1976–78; Butterflies; The Last Song; Absurd Person Singular, 1984; Insurance Man, 1985; Fairly Secret Army, 1985; Seasons Greetings, 1986; As Time Goes By, 1992–; The Savages, 2001; *films include:* O Lucky Man!, 1973; The Honorary Consul, 1982; A Zed and Two Noughts, 1985; Clockwise, 1986; A Fish Called Wanda, 1988; The Madness of King George, 1994; Mrs Brown, 1997; Tomorrow Never Dies, 1998; Anna and the King, 1999. *Address:* c/o Marmont Management, Langham House, 308 Regent Street, W1R 5AL.

PALMER, Sir Geoffrey (Christopher John), 12th Bt *cr* 1660; *b* 30 June 1936; *er s* of Lt-Col Sir Geoffrey Frederick Neill Palmer, 11th Bt, and Cicely Katherine (who *m* 1952, Robert W. B. Newton; she *d* 1989), *o d* of late Arthur Radmall, Clifton, nr Watford; *S* father, 1951; *m* 1957, Clarissa Mary, *er d* of Stephen Villiers-Smith, Knockholt, Kent; four *d. Educ:* Eton. Agent for Burberrys, Norway, Sweden, Finland, 1971–94. *Recreations:* golf, crossword puzzles, shooting. *Heir: b* Jeremy Charles Palmer [*b* 16 May 1939; *m* 1968, Antonia, *d* of late Ashley Dutton; two *s*]. *Address:* Carlton Curlieu Hall, Leicestershire LE8 0PH. *T:* (0116) 259 2656. *Clubs:* MCC, I Zingari, Free Foresters, Eton Ramblers, Butterflies, Gentlemen of Leicestershire, Lincolnshire Gentlemen's Cricket, Derbyshire Friars, XL, Frogs, Old Etonian Golfing Society, Old Etonian Racquets and Tennis, Northants Amateurs' CC.

PALMER, Rt Hon. Sir Geoffrey (Winston Russell), AC 1991; KCMG 1991; PC 1985; Partner, Chen & Palmer, barristers and solicitors, Wellington, since 1995; Professor of Law, Victoria University of Wellington, New Zealand, 1974–79, and since 1991; *b* 21 April 1942; *s* of Leonard Russell and Jessie Patricia Palmer; *m* 1963, Margaret Eleanor Hinchcliff; one *s* one *d. Educ:* Nelson Coll.; Victoria Univ. of Wellington (BA; LLB); Univ. of Chicago (JD). Barrister and Solicitor, High Court of New Zealand. Prof. of Law, Univ. of Iowa, 1969–73, and 1991–95. Vis. Professor of Law, Univ. of Virginia, 1972–73. MP (Lab) Christchurch Central, NZ, 1979–90; Dep. Prime Minister, 1984–89; Attorney-Gen., 1984–89; Minister of Justice, 1984–89; Minister for the Environment, 1987–90; Prime Minister, 1989–90. *Publications:* Unbridled Power?—an interpretation of New Zealand's constitution and government, 1979, 2nd edn 1987; Compensation for Incapacity—a study of law and social change in Australia and New Zealand, 1979; Environmental Politics—a greenprint for New Zealand, 1990; New Zealand's Constitution in Crisis, 1992; Environment—the international challenge, 1995; Bridled Power, 1997. *Recreations:* cricket, golf, playing the trumpet. *Address:* 63 Roxburgh Street, Mount Victoria, Wellington, New Zealand. *T:* (4) 8015185; 6th Floor, NGC House, 22 The Terrace, Wellington, New Zealand.

PALMER, His Honour Henry; *see* Palmer, His Honour R. H. S.

PALMER, Horace Anthony, (Tony); Chairman, Meyer International, 1997–99 (Director, 1995–99); *b* 20 Feb. 1937; *s* of Horace Charles and Violet Victoria Palmer; *m* 1961, Beryl Eileen Freakley; two *d. Educ:* Pinner County Grammar School; Hammersmith Sch. of Building. FRICS; FCIOB. Trainee Quantity Surveyor, 1954; joined Taylor Woodrow, 1954; Contracts Manager, 1970; Subsidiary Dir, 1974; Subsidiary Man. Dir, 1987; Man. Dir, 1989; Chief Exec., 1990–97. Chairman: High Point Rendel Gp plc; Monacon Hldgs Ltd; Parker Plant Ltd; Pilkington Tiles, 1998–; Galliford, 1999–; non-exec. Dir, Berkeley Gp, 1997–. *Recreations:* sports, reading biography.

PALMER, Howard William Arthur; QC 1999; *b* 24 June 1954; *s* of William Alexander Palmer, CBE, DL and Cherry Ann Palmer (*née* Gibbs); *m* 1983, Catherine Margaret Jackson; one *s* three *d. Educ:* Eton Coll.; University Coll., Oxford (MA Juris). Called to the Bar, Inner Temple, 1977; Lectr, KCL, 1977–78; barrister in private practice, 1978–. *Recreations:* cricket, golf, fieldsports, theatre, enjoying the countryside. *Address:* 2 Temple Gardens, EC4Y 9AY. *T:* (020) 7822 1200. *Clubs:* MCC; Berkshire County Cricket.

PALMER, Joe; *see* Palmer, T. J.

PALMER, John, CB 1986; Chairman, European Passenger Services, British Rail, 1990–94; *b* 13 Nov. 1928; 2nd *s* of late William Nathaniel Palmer and Grace Dorothy May Palmer (*née* Procter); *m* 1958, Lyliane Marthe Jeanjean; two *d. Educ:* Heath Grammar Sch., Halifax; The Queen's Coll., Oxford (Lit. Hum.) (MA). Entered Min. of Housing and Local Govt, 1952; Cabinet Office, 1963–65; Asst Sec., 1965; Under Secretary: DoE, 1971; Dept of Transport, 1976–82; Dep. Sec., Dept of Transport, 1982–89. Liveryman, Carmens' Co., 1987. *Address:* 72 College Road, SE21 7LY. *Club:* Oxford and Cambridge.

PALMER, Sir John (Chance), Kt 1979; solicitor; Consultant, Bevan Ashford; Vice Lord-Lieutenant of Devon, 1991–95; *b* 21 March 1920; *s* of Ernest Clephan Palmer and Claudine Pattie Sapey; *m* 1945, Mary Winifred, *d* of Arthur Sidney Ellyatt, OBE, and Winifred Mary Ellyatt (*née* East); four *s. Educ:* St Paul's Sch.; St Edmund Hall, Oxford (MA). Served War, RNVR, Atlantic and Mediterranean, 1939–46. Admitted a Solicitor, 1948; Elected Council of Law Society, 1963, President, 1978–79; Member: Criminal Injuries Compensation Board, 1981–92; SW Region Mental Health Tribunal, 1983–92. Governor, Coll. of Law, 1965–83; Pres., Devon and Exeter Law Society, 1972; Pres., S Western Law Societies, 1973; Chm., Governors of Blundells Sch., 1980–91; Chm., Exmoor Calvert Trust, 1991–94; Chm. Trustees, London Sailing Project, 1982–92;Chm., Internat. Technol Univ., 1988–95; Mem. Council, Exeter Univ., 1983–96. Hon. Member: Amer. Bar Assoc., 1978; Canadian Bar Assoc., 1979; Florida Defence Lawyers Assoc., 1981. Hon. Sec., Soc. for Protection of Animals in N Africa, 1989–98. Freeman, City of London, 2000. Hon. Citizen, Texas, 1980. DL Devon, 1984. Hon. LLD Exeter, 1980. *Recreations:* gardening, woodland, boats. *Address:* Lower Withleigh Farmhouse, Tiverton, Devon EX16 8JJ. *T:* (01884) 252959. *Clubs:* Athenæum, Royal Over-Seas League, Naval; Western (Glasgow); Royal Yacht Squadron.

PALMER, Sir John (Edward Somerset), 8th Bt *cr* 1791; retired; Director, W. S. Atkins Agriculture, 1979–88; *b* 27 Oct. 1926; *e s* of Sir John A. Palmer, 7th Bt; *S* father, 1963; *m* 1956, Dione Catharine Skinner; one *s* one *d. Educ:* Canford School; Cambridge Univ. (MA); Durham Univ. (MSc). Colonial Service, Northern Nigeria, 1952–61. R. A. Lister & Co. Ltd, Dursley, Glos, 1962–63; Min. Overseas Develt, 1964–68. *Recreations:* fishing, sailing. *Heir: s* Robert John Hudson Palmer [*b* 20 Dec. 1960; *m* 1990, Lucinda Margaret Barker]. *Address:* Court Barton, Feniton, Honiton, Devon EX14 3BD. *T:* (01404) 851020.

PALMER, Maj.-Gen. Sir (Joseph) Michael, KCVO 1985; Chairman, Copley Marshall & Co. Ltd, since 1980; *b* 17 Oct. 1928; *s* of late Lt-Col William Robert Palmer, DSO, and late Joan Audrey Palmer (*née* Smith); *m* 1953, Jillean Monica Sherston; two *s* one *d. Educ:* Wellington College. Commissioned 14th/20th King's Hussars, 1948; Adjutant

14th/20th King's Hussars, 1953–55; Adjutant Duke of Lancaster's Own Yeomanry, 1956–59; psc 1960; jssc 1965; CO 14th/20th King's Hussars, 1969–72; Comdr RAC 1st (BR) Corps, 1974–76; Asst Chief of Staff, Allied Forces Central Europe, 1976–78; Director, Royal Armoured Corps, 1978–81; Defence Services Sec., 1982–85. Col, 14th/20th King's Hussars, 1981–92; Hon. Col, Duke of Lancaster's Own Yeomanry, 1988–92. Director: Alexanders, Laing & Cruickshank Service Co., 1986–89; Credit Lyonnais Construction Co., 1988–90. Chm. of Governors, Sandroyd Sch., 1984–99. Liveryman, Salters' Co., 1965 (Master, 1989–90). FIMgt. *Recreations:* riding, shooting, music, reading. *Club:* Cavalry and Guards.

See also Angela Palmer.

PALMER, Prof. Marilyn, PhD; FSA 1991; Professor of Industrial Archaeology, and Head, School of Archaeology and Ancient History, Leicester University, since 2000; *b* 30 April 1943; *d* of Joseph Henry Allum and Mary Winifred Allum; *m* 1965, David Palmer (marr. diss. 1991). *Educ:* St Anne's Coll., Oxford (BA Hons Modern History 1965; MA 1969); Leicester Univ. (PGCE (Distinction) 1966; Postgrad. Cert. in British Archaeol. (Distinction) 1973; PhD 1976). History Teacher, Loughborough High Sch., 1966–69; Lectr, 1969–72, Sen. Lectr, 1972–77, Loughborough Coll. of Educn; Lectr, 1977–80, Sen. Lectr, 1980–83, Head, 1983–88, History Dept, Loughborough Univ.; Sen. Lectr in History, 1988–98, Reader in Industrial Archaeol., and Hd, Archaeol. Div., 1998–2000, Leicester Univ.; adult educn lectr on indust. archaeology, 1973–. Member: Royal Commn on Historical Monuments of England, 1993–99; Archael. Panel, and Industrial Archael. Adv. Cttee, NT, 1999–; Industrial Archael. Adv. Panel, English Heritage, 2001– (Mem., Ancient Monuments Adv. Cttee, 1999–2001); Pres., Assoc. for Indust. Archaeology, 1986–89 (Mem. Council, 1980–). Jt Editor, Industrial Archaeology Review, 1984–. *Publications:* (with P. A. Neaverson) Industrial Landscapes of the East Midlands, 1992; Industry in the Landscape, 1994; Industrial Archaeology: principles and practice, 1998; articles in jls. *Recreations:* hill walking, folk dancing, travelling—and industrial archaeology! *Address:* School of Archaeological Studies, University of Leicester, Leicester LE1 7RH. *T:* (0116) 252 2821.

PALMER, Sir Mark; *see* Palmer, Sir C. M.

PALMER, Maj.-Gen. Sir Michael; *see* Palmer, Maj.-Gen. Sir J. M.

PALMER, Michael Julian Barham, CMG 1990; writer; Chairman, East-West Committee, European League for Economic Co-operation, since 1996; *b* 2 Feb. 1933; *s* of Cecil Barham Palmer and Phyllis Palmer; *m* 1983, Dr Karin Reichel. *Educ:* Corpus Christi College, Oxford (MA). Research Officer, Political and Economic Planning, 1957–61; Sec., Political Cttee, Council of Europe, 1961–66; Councillor for Defence and Armaments, WEU, 1966–68; Dir of Cttees, N Atlantic Assembly, 1968–72; Dir-Gen. of Research European Parlt, 1972–90. Jean Monnet Prof., European Univ. Inst., Florence, 1989. Economic Consultant, Inst. for East-West Studies, NY and Prague, 1992–98. Advr to the Gov., Luxembourg Central Bank, 2000–. Austrian Order of Merit, 1990; Order of Oak Leaf Crown (Luxembourg), 1990. *Publications:* European Organisations, 1959; European Unity, 1968; Prospects for a European Security Conference, 1971; The European Parliament, 1981; From Ensor to Magritte, 1994; Belgian paintings in the Simon collection, 1997; Liliane Heidelberger-Sculptrice, 1999; The Central Bank of Luxembourg, 2001; Belgian Art 1940–2000, 2002; articles in The World Today, Foreign Policy, The Times, Christie's International, EIU publications. *Recreations:* music, art, cooking, climbing. *Address:* 8 rue des Franciscaines, 1539 Luxembourg Grand Duchy.

PALMER, Monroe Edward, OBE 1982; FCA; chartered accountant; *b* 30 Nov. 1938; *s* of William and Sybil Polikoff; *m* 1962, Susette Sandra (*née* Cardash); two *s* one *d. Educ:* Orange Hill Grammar Sch. FCA 1963. Chm., Hendon CAB, 1981–83; Vice-Chm., Barnet CAB, 1986–88; Treasurer: Disablement Assoc., London Borough of Barnet, 1971–88; Liberal Parly Party, 1977–83; Jt Treasurer, Liberal Party, 1977–83; Chm., Lib Dem Friends of Israel, 1987–. Councillor (L, then Lib Dem) London Borough of Barnet, 1986–94 and 1998– (Leader, Lib Dem Gp, 1999–; Cabinet Lead Mem. for develt and regeneration, 1999–). Contested: (L) Hendon South, 1979, 1983, 1987; (Lib Dem) Hastings and Rye, 1992, 1997. *Recreations:* politics, fishing, horse riding. *Address:* 31 The Vale, NW11 8SE. *T:* (020) 8455 5140. *Club:* National Liberal.

PALMER, Nicholas Douglas; MP (Lab) Broxtowe, since 1997; *b* 5 Feb. 1950; *s* of late Reginald Palmer and Irina Palmer (*née* Markin). *Educ:* Copenhagen Univ. (MSc equivalent); Birkbeck Coll., London (PhD Maths 1975). Computer scientist: Ciba-Geigy, Switzerland, 1977–82 and 1985–97; MRC London, 1982–85. Member: European Scrutiny Select Cttee, 1998–99; NI Select Cttee, 1999–2001; HM Treasury Select Cttee, 2001–. Contested (Lab): Chelsea, 1983; E Sussex and S Kent, EP elecn, 1994. *Publications:* The Comprehensive Guide to Board Wargaming, 1973; The Best of Board Wargaming, 1980. *Recreation:* games played by post. *Address:* House of Commons, SW1A 0AA. *T:* (020) 7219 4197, (office) (020) 7219 2397; *e-mail:* palmern@parliament.uk.

PALMER, Prof. Nigel Fenton, DPhil; FBA 1997; Professor of German Medieval and Linguistic Studies, University of Oxford, since 1992; Professorial Fellow, St Edmund Hall, Oxford, since 1992; *b* 28 Oct. 1946; *s* of James Terence Palmer and Constance May Palmer (*née* Fenton); *m* 1974, Susan Patricia Aldred; one *s* one *d. Educ:* Hyde County Grammar Sch.; Worcester Coll., Oxford (MA, DPhil). Lectr in German, Durham Univ., 1970–76; University of Oxford: Univ. Lectr in Medieval German, 1976–90; Reader in German, 1990–92; Fellow, Oriel Coll., 1976–92. Fellow, Humboldt Foundn, 1982. *Publications:* Visio Tnugdali, 1976; Tondolus der Ritter, 1980; (with K. Speckenbach) Träume und Kräuter, 1990; Die Blockbücher der Berlin-Breslauer Sammelbandes, 1992; German Literary Culture in the Twelfth and Thirteenth Centuries, 1993; Zisterzienser und ihre Bücher, 1998. *Address:* St Edmund Hall, Oxford OX1 4AR. *T:* (01865) 510487.

PALMER, Prof. Norman Ernest; barrister; Professor of Commercial Law (formerly Rowe & Maw Professor of Commercial Law), University College London, since 1991; *b* 16 Aug. 1948; *s* of Norman George Palmer and Muriel (*née* Walker); *m* 1970, Judith Ann Weeks (marr. diss.); one *d*; 1994, Ruth Redmond-Cooper. *Educ:* Palmer's Endowed Sch., Grays Thurrock; Magdalen Coll., Oxford (BA Jurisp. 1969; BCL 1971; MA 1974). Called to the Bar, Gray's Inn, 1973; Head of Chambers, 1992–99. Lectr and Sen. Lectr in Law, Univs of Liverpool, Tasmania and Manchester, 1971–81; Professor of Law: Univ. of Reading, 1981–84 (Head of Dept, 1982–84); Univ. of Essex, 1984–90 (Dean of Faculty, 1985–88); Prof. of English Law, Univ. of Southampton, 1990–91 (Dep. Dean of Faculty). Sec. and a Dir, Internat. Cultural Property Soc., 1990–95 (Editor, Jl, 1991–95). Chairman: Treasure Valuation Cttee, 2001– (Mem., 1996–); Ministerial Adv. Panel on Illicit Trade in Cultural Objects, 2000–; Wkg Gp on Human Remains in Mus. Collections, 2001–. Mem., Standing Conf. for Portable Antiquities, 1995–. Principal Academic Advr, Inst. of Art and Law. Editor, Art, Antiquity and Law, 1996–. *Publications:* (ed with E. L. G. Tyler) Crossley Vaines on Personal Property, 5th edn, 1973; Bailment, 1979, 2nd edn 1991; (ed jtly) Emden's Construction Law, 1990; (with C. J. Miller) Business Law, 1992; (ed jtly) Interest in Goods, 1993, 2nd edn 1998; (with E. McKendrick) Product Liability in the Construction Industry, 1993; Art Loans, 1997; The Recovery of Stolen Art, 1998; Museums and the Holocaust, 2000; Halsbury's Laws of England, 4th edn and re-issue: (ed with H. Street) Titles on Tort; (ed with A. Powell) Bailment; (ed with W. J. Swadling) Carriers; (ed with A. H. Hudson) Confidence and Data Protection; (ed with N. Bamforth et al) Libraries and Other Scientific and Cultural Institutions. *Recreations:* literature, biography, travel, antique motor cars, collecting tombstone verse. *Address:* 2 Field Court, Gray's Inn, WC1R 5BB. *T:* (020) 7405 6114.

PALMER, Most Rev. Norman Kitchener, CMG 1981; MBE 1975; *b* 2 Oct 1928; *s* of Philip Sydney and Annie Palmer; *m* 1960, Elizabeth Lucy Gorringe; three *s* one *d. Educ:* Kokeqolo, Pawa, Solomon Is; Te Aute, NZ; Ardmore, NZ (Teachers' Cert,); St John's Theological Coll., NZ (LTh; ordained deacon, 1964). Appts in Solomon Islands: Deacon/Teacher, Pawa Secondary (Anglican), 1966; priest, Pawa, 1966; Priest/Headmaster: Alangiala Primary, 1967–69; St Nicholas Primary, 1970–72; Dean, St Barnabas Cathedral, 1973–75; Bishop of Central Melanesia, 1975–87; Archbishop of Melanesia, 1975–87. Member, Public Service Advisory Bd, 1971–75. *Address:* Varei Village, Bauro District, General Post Office, Kira Kira, Makira Province, Solomon Islands.

PALMER, Penelope Jane; *see* Dash, P. J.

PALMER, Sir Reginald (Oswald), GCMG 1992; MBE 1973; Governor General, Grenada, 1992–96; *b* 15 Feb. 1923; *m* 1954, Judith Juliana Parke; two *s* five *d. Educ:* St George's RC Boys' Sch.; Govt Teachers' Trng Coll., Trinidad; Univ. of Birmingham (CertEd); Univ. of Calgary (BEd 1971). Pupil Teacher, 1939–41; pupil teacher scholarship, 1941; Asst Teacher, 1945–56; Headteacher, 1956–68; Tutor, Grenada Teachers' Coll., 1968–72; Asst Educn Officer, 1972–73; Principal, Grenada Teachers' Coll., 1973–74; Chief Educn Officer, 1974–80, retd. Manager, Grenada Teachers' Sch. Supplies Ltd, 1980–87; Pres., Grenada Employers' Fedn, 1987–89. Dir, Grenada Bank of Commerce, 1990–92. Foundn Mem., Grenada Teachers' Social Security and Welfare Assoc. (Sec. 1951–69); Pres., Grenada Union of Teachers, 1962–63. Member: Public Service Commn, 1983–87; Local Adv. Council, Sch. of Continuing Educn, 1978– (Pres. 1989–98). Chm., Grenada Drug Avoidance Cttee, 1988–92. Dir, Richmond Fellowship of Grenada, 1991–92. *Recreations:* reading, backyard gardening, walking, sea-bathing. *Address:* Mount Parnassus, PO Box 884, St George's, Grenada, West Indies.

PALMER, Richard William, OBE 1987; Executive Vice President, British Olympic Association, since 1997 (Secretary General, 1977–97); *b* 13 April 1933; *s* of late Richard Victor Palmer and Mary Ellen Palmer (*née* Sambrook). *Educ:* Haverfordwest Grammar Sch.; Trinity Coll., Carmarthen; The College, Chester (Dip PE); Univ. of Leicester (MEd). Head, PE Dept, Windsor Grammar Sch., 1961–64; Sec., UAU, 1964–69; Gen. Sec., British Univs Sports Fedn, 1969–74; Dep. Sec. Gen., British Olympic Assoc., 1975–77. Vice Pres., European Olympic Cttees, 1993–97; Pres., British Inst. of Sports Administrators, 1997–; Chm., Confedn of British Sport, 1998–99. Gen. Sec., Commonwealth Games Council for England, 1977–86; Dep. Chef de Mission, GB, 1976, Chef de Mission, GB, 1980, 1984, 1988, 1992, 1996, Olympic Games and Olympic Winter Games; Gen. Team Manager, England, Commonwealth Games, 1978, 1982, 1986. FRSA 1998. Freeman of Pembroke, 1990. Prix de Merit, Assoc. of Nat. Olympic Cttees, 1990; Olympic Order, IOC, 1998. *Recreations:* golf, sailing, Rugby Union, gardening, fishing. *Address:* British Olympic Association, 1 Wandsworth Plain, SW18 1EH. *T:* (020) 8871 2677. *Clubs:* Scribes, East India; Haverfordwest and Fulwell Golf; Llangwm Boat.

PALMER, His Honour (Robert) Henry (Stephen); a Circuit Judge, 1978–93; *b* 13 Nov. 1927; *s* of Henry Alleyn Palmer and Maud (*née* Obbard); *m* 1955, Geraldine Elizabeth Anne Evens; one *s* two *d. Educ:* Charterhouse; University Coll., Oxford. Called to the Bar, 1950. Dep. Chm., Berks QS, 1970. A Recorder of the Crown Court, 1972–78. Resident Judge: Acton Crown Court, 1987–91; Harrow Crown Court, 1991–93; Pres., 1983–98, S Thames Regl Chm., 1993–99, Mental Health Rev. Tribunal. Dir of Appeals, Specialist Trng Authy, Med. Royal Colls, 1997–99. *Publications:* Harris's Criminal Law, 1960; Guide to Divorce, 1965. *Recreation:* self-sufficiency.

PALMER, Prof. Stuart Beaumont, PhD; FREng; Professor of Experimental Physics, since 1987, Deputy Vice-Chancellor, since 2001, University of Warwick; *b* 6 May 1943; *s* of Frank Beaumont Palmer and Florence Beryl Palmer (*née* Wilkinson); *m* 1966, Susan Mary Clay; two *s* one *d. Educ:* Ilkeston Grammar Sch.; Sheffield Univ. (BSc 1964; PhD 1968; DSc 1986). CPhys, FInstP, 1981; FInstNDT 1989; CEng, FIEE, 1992. University of Hull: Asst Lectr, 1967–70; Lectr, 1970–78; Sen. Lectr, 1978–83; Reader, 1983–87; University of Warwick: Chair, Physics Dept, 1989–2001; Pro-Vice-Chancellor, 1995–99; Sen. Pro-Vice-Chancellor, 1999–2000; Actg Vice-Chancellor, 2001. Vis. Prof., Univ. of Grenoble, 1982–83; Vis. Scientist, Queen's Univ., Kingston, Canada, 1986. Chm., Standing Conf. of Profs of Physics, 2001–; chm. and mem., various SERC and EPSRC cttees and working gps. FREng 2000. *Publications:* (with M. Rogalski) Advanced University Physics, 1995; (with M. Rogalski) Quantum Physics, 1999; (with M. Rogalski) Solid State Physics, 2000; over 250 contribs to learned scientific jls in magnetism, ultrasound and non destructive testing. *Recreations:* tennis, sailing, flying, ski-ing. *Address:* University of Warwick, Coventry CV4 7AL. *T:* (024) 7657 4004; Max Gate, Forrest Road, Kenilworth CV8 1LT. *Clubs:* Athenæum; Hull Sailing; Warwick Boat; Coventry Flying.

PALMER, Thomas Joseph, (Joe), CBE 1990; Chairman, Personal Investment Authority, 1993–2000; *b* 11 Sept. 1931; *m* 1955, Hilary Westrup; two *s* two *d. Educ:* King's School, Bruton; Trinity College, Cambridge. MA. Asst Gen. Man. (Planning), Legal and General Assurance Soc., 1969–72, Dir and Gen. Man. (Admin.), 1972–78; Legal & General Group plc: Dir, 1978–91; Gen. Man. (Internat.), 1978–83; Group Chief Exec., 1984–91. Chm., Laser Richmount, 1991–93; Director: SIB, 1991–93; Halifax BS, 1991–93; National Power plc, 1991–96; Sedgwick Gp, 1992–93; ProShare, 1992–94. Chairman: London Business Sch. Assoc., 1974–78; Assoc. of British Insurers, 1989–91; Pres., Insurance Inst. of London, 1982–83; Dir, Investors' Compensation Scheme, 1992–93. Gov., King's Sch., Bruton, 1989–. Hon. Fellow, London Business Sch., 1990. *Recreations:* gardening, long-distance walking, cross country ski-ing.

PALMER, Tony; *see* Palmer, H. A.

PALMER, Tony; film, television and theatre director; author; brought up by godparents, late Bert Spencer (railway engineer) and Elsie Spencer; *m* 2001, Michela Antonello. *Educ:* Lowestoft Grammar Sch. Presenter, Night Waves, R3, 1994–98 (Sony Award, 1996). FRGS 1993. *Films include:* All My Loving, 1968; Farewell Cream, 1968; 200 Motels, 1971 (Gold Record); Rory Gallagher Irish Tour, 1974 (Platinum Record); All This & World War Two, 1976 (Gold Record); A Time There Was, 1979 (Italia Prize); At the Haunted End of the Day, 1980 (Italia Prize); Once at a Border, 1981 (Special Jury Prize, San Francisco); Wagner, 1982 (Best Drama, NY Film and TV Fest.); God Rot Tunbridge Wells, 1985 (Best Drama, NY); Maria, 1986 (Gold Medal, NY); Testimony, 1987 (Fellini Prize); The Children, 1989 (Best Director, NY); Menuhin, 1990 (Grand Award, NY); The Symphony of Sorrowful Songs, 1993 (platinum CD; Jury Prize, Chicago Film Fest.);

England, My England, 1995 (Best Dir, NY); Parsifal, 1998 (1st prize, Casta Diva, Moscow; Golden Mask, Russia); The Harvest of Sorrow, 1999; *theatre:* John Osborne's Deja Vu, Comedy, 1992; dir operas, Berlin, Karlsruhe, Munich, Hamburg, Zürich, Augsburg, St Petersburg, Savonlinna, Moscow, Ravello, Helsinki. Numerous BAFTA and Emmy awards. *Publications:* Born Under a Bad Sign, 1970; Trials of Oz, 1971; Electric Revolution, 1972; Biography of Liberace, 1976; All You Need is Love, 1976; Charles II, 1979; A Life on the Road (biog. of Julian Bream), 1982; Menuhin: a family portrait, 1991. *Recreation:* walking. *Address:* Nanjizal, St Levan, Cornwall TR19 6JH. *Club:* Garrick.

PALMER, Maj.-Gen. Tony Brian, CB 1984; CEng, FIMechE; conducted a study on maintenance philosophy and organisation in the Army, 1986; retired 1986; *b* 5 Nov. 1930; *s* of Sidney Bernard Palmer and Ann (*née* Watkins); *m* 1953, Hazel Doris Robinson; two *s*. *Educ:* Wolverton Technical College; Luton College of Technology; General Motors Inst. of Technology, USA. General Motors UK, 1948–51 and 1953–54; commissioned REME 1954; RMCS, 1960–62; Tank Gunnery Trials, Infantry Workshop, staff duties MoD, JSSC, Ops and Plans MoD, 1962–70; Head, DG FVE Secretariat, 1970–72; Comdr REME, 3 Div., 1972–74; Head, Tech. Intell. (Army), 1974–76; Dir, Elect. and Mech. Engineering (Organisation and Training), 1977–79; Comdt, REME Training Centre, 1979–83; Dir-Gen. of Elect. and Mech. Engrg, MoD (Army), 1983–85. Col Comdt, REME, 1986–91. Vice-Pres., S Region, British Sports Assoc. for Disabled, 1980–96; Chairman: Somerset Br., Army Benevolent Fund, 1988–; Dorset Cttee for Employment of Disabled People, 1989–91; Somerset Cttee for Employment of People with Disabilities, 1991–94. Mem., Parish Council, Stoke St Gregory, 1995– (Chm., 1999–2001); Gov., Stoke St Gregory Primary Sch., 1997–2001. MIMgt. *Recreations:* history, gardening. *Address:* Little Deer Leaps, Windmill, Stoke St Gregory, Taunton, Somerset TA3 6EL.

PALMER-MAKOWSKI, Caroline Ann; *see* Palmer, C. A.

PALMES, Peter Manfred Jerome; Principal Assistant Director, Public Prosecutions Department, 1979–81; *b* 28 Feb. 1920; *s* of late Manfred Palmes and Gwendoline Robb; *m* 1st, 1945, Sylvia Theodor (decd); 2nd, 1969, Brenda Laban; one step *d*. *Educ:* Charterhouse; Worcester Coll., Oxford. Served War of 1939–45: Oxford and Bucks LI and 1/8th Gurkha Rifles, 1940–45. Called to Bar, Inner Temple, 1948. Public Prosecutions Dept: Legal Assistant, 1948; Sen. Legal Asst, 1958; Asst Solicitor, 1969; Asst Director, 1977. Jubilee Medal, 1977. *Address:* Chapel Lodge, Cross Colwood Lane, Bolney, West Sussex RH17 5RY.

PÁLSSON, Thorsteinn; Ambassador of Iceland to the Court of St James's, since 1999; *b* 29 Oct. 1947; *s* of Pall Sigurdsson and Ingigerdur Thorsteinsdottir; *m* 1973, Ingibjórg Rafnar; one *s* two *d*. *Educ:* Commercial Coll., Reykjavik; Univ. of Iceland (law degree). Journalist, Morgunbladid, 1974–75; Editor-in-Chief, Visir, 1975–79; Admin. Dir, Confedn of Icelandic Employers, 1979–83; MP (Independence) Southland, Iceland, 1983–99; Minister: of Finance, 1985–87; of Industry, 1987; Prime Minister, 1987–88; Minister: of Fisheries, 1991–99; of Justice and Ecclesiastical Affairs, 1991–99. Chm., Independence Party, 1983–91. *Address:* Embassy of Iceland, 2A Hans Street, SW1X 0JE.

PALTROW, Gwyneth; actress; *b* Los Angeles, 29 Sept. 1973; *d* of Bruce W. Paltrow and Blythe Katharine Danner. *Educ:* Spence Sch., New York; Univ. of Calif, Santa Barbara. Williamstown Theater, Mass. acting début, Picnic (with Blythe Danner); Rosalind, in As You Like It, 1999; other plays include: The Adventures of Huck Finn; Sweet Bye and Bye; The Seagull. Film début, Shout, 1991; films include: Moonlight and Valentino; Seven, 1995; Emma, 1996; Great Expectations, Sliding Doors (Best Actress, Golden Globe Awards, 1999), Hush, A Perfect Murder, 1998; Shakespeare in Love (Academy Award for Best Actress, 1999); The Talented Mr Ripley, 1999; Duets, 2000; Bounce, 2001. *Address:* c/o CAA, 9830 Wilshire Boulevard, Beverly Hills, CA 90212, USA.

PALUMBO, family name of **Baron Palumbo**.

PALUMBO, Baron *cr* 1991 (Life Peer), of Walbrook in the City of London; **Peter Garth Palumbo,** MA; Chairman, Arts Council of Great Britain, 1989–94; *b* 20 July 1935; *s* of late Rudolph and of Elsie Palumbo; *m* 1st, 1959, Denia (*d* 1986), *d* of late Major Lionel Wigram; one *s* two *d*; 2nd, 1986, Hayat, *er d* of late Kamel Morowa; one *s* two *d*. *Educ:* Eton College; Worcester College, Oxford. MA Hons Law. Governor, London School of Economics and Political Science, 1976–94; Chairman: Tate Gallery Foundn, 1986–87; Painshill Park Trust Appeal, 1986–96; Serpentine Gall., 1994–; Trustee: Mies van der Rohe Archive, 1977–; Tate Gallery, 1978–85; Whitechapel Art Gallery Foundation, 1981–87; Natural History Mus., 1994–; Trustee and Hon. Treas., Writers and Scholars Educnl Trust, 1984–99; Mem. Council, Royal Albert Hall, 1995–99. Chancellor, Portsmouth Univ., 1992–. Liveryman, Salters' Co., 1965–. Hon. FRIBA 1986; Hon. FFB 1994; Hon. FIStructE 1994. Hon. DLitt Portsmouth, 1993. Nat. Order of Southern Cross (Brazil), 1993. *Recreations:* music, travel, gardening, reading. *Address:* 2 Astell Street, SW3 3RU. *T:* (020) 7351 7371. *Clubs:* Athenæum, White's, Pratt's, Garrick.

PAMPLIN, Elizabeth Ann, FCIPD; human resources and corporate ethics consultant, since 1999; Chief Executive, Liberal Democrats, 1998–99; *b* 13 April 1940; *d* of Richard Thomas Webb and Hilda Ethel Webb (*née* Teague); *m* 1969, Terence Michael Pamplin; twin *d*. *Educ:* Rosebery GS; St Hugh's Coll., Oxford (BA PPE 1962; DPSA 1963). FCIPD (FIPD 1991). Clarks Ltd, 1963–66; Industrial Trng Service, 1966–71; Sen. Lectr, Personnel Mgt and Trng, Slough Coll. of HE, 1973–75; human resource management and consultancy: MSC, 1975–77; Petroleum Industry Trng Bd, 1977–82; RBK&C, 1983–91; P & L Associates, 1991–93; DoT, 1993–96; Cabinet Office, 1996–97. Examr in personnel mgt, PCL, then Univ. of Westminster, 1985–98; Nat. Examr, IPD, now CIPD, 1996–. Gov., Lord Mayor Treloar Sch., 2000. Contested (SDP), 1983, (SDP/L Alliance), 1987, Reigate. Freeman, City of London, 1997; Liveryman, Co. of Musicians, 1997–. FRGS 2000. *Publications:* reports and articles. *Recreations:* music, early dance, walking, countryside conservation. *Address:* Little Critchmere, Manor Crescent, Haslemere, Surrey GU27 1PB.

PANAYIDES CHRISTOU, Tasos, Hon. GCVO 1990; Chairman, AVRA Shipmanagement SA, since 1997; *b* 9 April 1934; *s* of Christos Panayides and Efrosini Panayides; *m* 1969, Pandora Constantinides; two *s* one *d*. *Educ:* Paphos Gymnasium; Teachers' Training Coll.; Univ. of London (Diploma in Education); Univ. of Indiana, USA (MA Political Science, Diploma in Public Administration). Teacher, 1954–59; First sec. to Pres., 1960–63; Director, President's Office, 1963–69; Ambassador of Cyprus to Federal Republic of Germany, Switzerland, Austria, and Atomic Energy organisation, Vienna, 1969–78; High Comr in UK, and Ambassador to Sweden, Norway, Denmark and Iceland, 1979–90; Doyen of the Diplomatic Corps in London and Sen. High Comr, 1988–90; Permanent Sec., Min. of Foreign Affairs, Cyprus, 1990–94; Ambassador to Sweden, Finland, Norway, Denmark, Latvia, Lithuania and Estonia, 1994–96. Chairman: Commonwealth Foundn Grants Cttee, 1985–88; Commonwealth Fund Tech. Co-operation Bd of Reps, 1986–89; Commonwealth Steering Cttee of Sen. Officials, 1994–95. Hon. Fellow, Ealing Coll. of Higher Educn, 1983. Freeman, City of London, 1984. Hon. LLD Birmingham, 1991. 1st Cl., Grand Order and Grand Cross with Star and Sash, Federal Republic of Germany, 1978; Grand Cross in Gold with Star and Sash, Austria, 1979; Golden Cross of the Archdiocese of Thyateira and Great Britain, 1981; Grand Cross in Gold of Patriarchate of Antioch, 1984. *Publications:* articles in newspapers and magazines. *Recreations:* swimming, reading books. *Address:* (office) 116 Kolokotroni Street, 185–35 Piraeus, Greece.

PANDOLFI, Filippo Maria; a Vice-President of the Commission of the European Communities, 1989–92; *b* 1 Nov. 1927; *m* 1963, Carola Marziani; three *s* one *d*. *Educ:* Catholic Univ. of Milan (BA in philosophy). Member, Italian Parliament (Christian Democrats), 1968–88; Under Secretary of State, Min. of Finance, 1974–76; Minister of Finance, 1976–78; Minister of the Treasury, 1978–80; Chm. of Interim Cttee of IMF, 1979–80; Minister of Industry, 1980–82; Minister of Agriculture, 1983–88. *Recreations:* music, classical Greek, rock climbing.

PANFORD, Frank Haig; QC 1999; *b* 23 Jan. 1949; *s* of Frank Essandoh Martin Panford and Susanna Panford (*née* Holdbrook-Smith); *m* 1st, 1979, Hilary Ann Luper (marr. diss. 1986); one *d*; 2nd, 1994, Najma Khanzada; two *s*. *Educ:* Holborn Coll. of Law (LLB Hons London 1971); Hague Acad. Internat. Law (Diplôme de Droit Privé 1976); Wolfson Coll., Cambridge (LLB 1979). Called to the Bar, Middle Temple, 1972; Lectr in Law, Poly. of Central London, 1974–92; Legal Advr and Sen. Film Examr, BBFC, 1984–90; in practice at the Bar, 1992–; called to Gibraltar Bar, 1994. Mem., Charter 88, 1998–99. *Recreations:* African politics, music, cooking, travel. *Address:* Doughty Street Chambers, 11 Doughty Street, WC1N 2PL. *T:* (020) 7404 1313.

PANK, Dorian Christopher L.; *see* Lovell-Pank.

PANK, Maj.-Gen. (John) David (Graham), CB 1989; Chief Executive, Newbury Racecourse plc, 1990–98; *b* 2 May 1935; *s* of late Edward Graham Pank and Margaret Sheelah Osborne Pank; *m* 1963, Julia Letitia Matheson; two *s* one *d*. *Educ:* Uppingham Sch. Commnd KSLI, 1958; served in Germany, Borneo, Singapore and Malaya; commanded: 3rd Bn The Light Infantry, 1974–76; 33rd Armoured Bde, 1979–81; Dir Gen. of Personal Services, Army, 1985–88; Dir of Infantry, 1988–90. Col, The LI, 1987–90. President: Army Cricket Assoc., 1987–89; Combined Services Cricket Assoc., 1988. Dir, Racecourse Assoc., 1994–98. *Recreations:* racing, fishing, cricket. *Address:* c/o Royal Bank of Scotland, London Drummonds Branch, 49 Charing Cross, SW1A 2DX. *Clubs:* Army and Navy, Victory Services; Mounted Infantry; Free Foresters, I Zingari, Mount Cricket.

PANNETT, Juliet Kathleen, MBE 1993; FRSA; portrait artist; *b* Hove, 15 July 1911; 2nd *d* of Charles Somers and May (*née* Brice); *m* 1938, Major M. R. D. Pannett (*d* 1980), late the Devonshire Regt; one *s* one *d*. *Educ:* Wistons Sch., Brighton; Brighton College of Art. Special Artist to Illustrated London News, 1957–64. *Exhibitions:* Royal Festival Hall, 1957, 1958; Qantas Gallery, 1959; New York, 1960; Cleveland, Ohio, 1960; Cooling Gallery, London, 1961; Coventry Cathedral Festival, 1962; Gloucester Three Choirs Festival, 1962; Brighton Corporation Gallery, Rottingdean, 1967; Arun Art Centre, 1967, 1969, 1972; Fine Art Gall., London, 1969, Mignon Gall., Bath, 1970; Brotherton Gall., London, 1980; Pacific and Fringe Clubs, Hong Kong, 1986; Wigmore Hall, 1989, 1991; RNCM, 1989; Stamford Arts Centre, 1995. Exhibitor: Royal Academy; Royal Society of Portrait Painters; Royal Inst. of Painters in Watercolours, etc. Official Artist on several Qantas and Air Canada inaugural flights. Freeman: City of London, 1960; Painter Stainers' Company, 1960 (Gold Medal, 1995). *Work in Permanent Collections:* 22 portraits in National Portrait Gall.; Bodleian Library; Ashmolean Mus.; Oxford and Cambridge colls; RCM; Painter Stainers' Hall, London; Edinburgh Univ.; D Day painting for Devon and Dorset Regt, 1963; Commemorative Stained Glass Window (St Alban), Garrison Church, Munster, 1967; painting of Duke of Kent presenting new colours to Devon and Dorset Regt, 1982; Portraits, many for official bodies, include: HM The Queen (twice); HRH Princess Alexandra, 1984; HRH Prince Andrew, HRH Prince Edward, for HM The Queen, 1974; HRH Princess Marina, Duchess of Kent, 1968; Field Marshal Viscount Alanbrooke; Louis Armstrong; Dame Peggy Ashcroft; Earl Attlee; W. H. Auden; Prof. A. J. Ayer; Gp Capt. Sir Douglas Bader; David Ben-Gurion; Sir Adrian Boult; Sir Benjamin Britten; Lord Callaghan; Pablo Casals; Lord David Cecil; Gp Capt. Leonard Cheshire; Sir Winston Churchill; Jean Cocteau; Sir Colin Davis; Walter de la Mare; Victoria de los Angeles; Lord Denning; Sir Alec Douglas-Home; Jacqueline du Pré; Duke Ellington; Gracie Fields; Sir Ranulph Fiennes; Lord Grimond; Lord Hailsham; Michael Heseltine; Cardinal Basil Hume; Augustus John; Colonel 'H' Jones, VC; Otto Klemperer; C. S. Lewis; Sophia Loren; Humphrey Lyttelton; Sir Neville Marriner; Golda Meir; Yehudi Menuhin; Naomi Mitchison; Field Marshal Lord Montgomery; Patrick Moore; Lord Mountbatten of Burma; Dame Marie Rambert; Ginger Rogers; Sir Malcolm Sargent; Sir Harry Secombe; Igor Stravinsky; A. J. P. Taylor; Lady Thatcher; Sir Wilfred Thesiger; Sir Michael Tippett; Sir Laurens van der Post; Sir William Walton; Sir Ralph Vaughan Williams; Sir Harold Wilson, and many other members of the political, legal, military, academic, musical, artistic and literary professions. Has broadcast on art subjects on TV in UK and USA. *Publications:* cover portraits for books by Sir Thomas Beecham, Charles Causley, Henry Cecil, Canon John Collins, Mary Drewery, Louis Golding, Gerald Pawle and Cyril Scott; drawings reproduced in The Times, Daily Telegraph, Birmingham Mail, Radio Times, The Lancet, Leisure Painter, The Artist, Law Guardian, Guardian Gazette, etc. *Recreation:* water colour painting, esp. landscapes and old buildings. *Address:* Pound House, Roundstone Lane, Angmering Village, Sussex BN16 4AL. *T:* (01903) 784446.

PANNICK, David Philip; QC 1992; Fellow of All Souls College, Oxford, since 1978; a Recorder, since 1995; *b* 7 March 1956; *s* of late Maurice Pannick and of Rita Pannick; *m* 1978, Denise Sloam (*d* 1999); two *s* one *d*. *Educ:* Bancroft's Sch., Woodford Green, Essex; Hertford Coll., Oxford (MA, BCL). Called to the Bar, Gray's Inn, 1979, Bencher, 1998. Jun. Counsel to the Crown (Common Law), 1988–92; Dep. High Court Judge, 1998–. Columnist, The Times, 1991–. Mem., Editl Bd, Public Law, 1990–. Hon. LLD Hertfordshire, 1998. *Publications:* Judicial Review of the Death Penalty, 1982; Sex Discrimination Law, 1985; Judges, 1987; Advocates, 1992; (ed with Lord Lester of Herne Hill) Human Rights Law and Practice, 1999. *Recreations:* travel, supporting Arsenal FC, musicals. *Address:* Blackstone Chambers, Blackstone House, Temple, EC4Y 9BW. *T:* (020) 7583 1770.

PANNONE, Rodger John; DL; Senior Partner, Pannone & Partners (formerly Pannone March Pearson), Solicitors, since 1991; President of the Law Society of England and Wales, 1993–94; *b* 20 April 1943; *s* of late Cyril John Alfred Pannone and Violet Maud (*née* Weeks); *m* 1966, Patricia Jane Todd; two *s* one *d*. *Educ:* St Brendan's Coll., Bristol; Coll. of Law, London; Law Sch., Manchester. Articled to Casson & Co., Salford, 1966–69; Asst Solicitor and Partner, W. H. Thompson, 1969–73; Partner, Pannone March Pearson, subseq. Pannone & Partners, 1973–. Member: Lord Chancellor's Adv. Cttee on Civil Justice, 1986–89; Council, Law Soc., 1979–96 (Vice-Pres., 1992–93). Gov., Coll. of Law, 1990– (Chm., 1999–); Mem. Council, Manchester Univ., 1996– (Chm., 2000–). Vice-Pres., British Acad. of Experts, 1994–. Chm., Manchester Concert Hall Ltd, 1993–; Vice-Pres., Gtr Manchester Community Trust, 1992–. FRSA 1992. DL Greater Manchester, 1999. Hon. Life Mem., Canadian Bar, 1993. Hon. Fellow: Manchester Metropolitan Univ., 1994; Birmingham Univ., 1998. Hon. DLitt Salford,

1993; Hon. LLD Nottingham Trent, 1993. *Publications:* numerous legal pubns. *Recreations:* the Lake District, walking slowly, food and wine. *Address:* 5 Darley Avenue, West Didsbury, Manchester M20 2XE. *T:* (0161) 909 3000; 123 Deansgate, Manchester M3 2BU. *Clubs:* St James's (Manchester); Wyresdale Anglers.

PANTLIN, Sir Dick (Hurst), Kt 1993; CBE 1977 (OBE 1970); Partner, 1946–52, Co-Managing Director, 1952–68, Henrijean International Insurance Brokers; *b* 8 Dec. 1919; *s* of Albert Ralph Pantlin and Gwendolyn Clara Thomas; *m* 1946, Janine Henrijean; two *s*. *Educ:* Felsted; Alliance Française, Paris. ACIB. War service, Royal Marines, 1940–46, Major (despatches 1944). Founder and Chairman: British Sch., Brussels, 1969–95 (Hon. Pres., 1995–); Council of British Indep. Schs in EC, 1980–95 (Hon. Pres., 1995–); Trustee, St George's English Sch., Rome, 1988–97; Pres., British Chamber of Commerce, Belgium and Luxembourg, 1975–77; Vice-Pres., Royal Belgo-British Union, 1975–; Founder and first Pres., Council of British Chambers of Commerce in Continental Europe, 1975–78. Chevalier: Ordre de la Couronne (Belgium), 1959; Ordre de Léopold (Belgium), 1969. *Publications:* articles for expatriates on educn, British nationality and voting legislation. *Recreations:* golf, travel, politics, ancestral research. *Address:* 11 Avenue de Mercure, Brussels B1180, Belgium. *T:* and *Fax:* (2) 3752721; *e-mail:* dick.pantlin@freeworld.be. *Clubs:* Army and Navy; Royal Golf de Belgique.

PANTLING, Mary; *see* Allen, M.

PANTON, Air Cdre Alastair Dyson, CB 1969; OBE 1950; DFC 1939; Provost Marshal and Director of RAF Security, 1968–71; retired. *Educ:* Bedford School; RAF Coll., Cranwell. Pilot Officer, No 53 Sqdn RAF, 1937; POW 1940–45; OC, Nos 58 and 540 Sqdns, 1946–47; Air Staff, Hong Kong, 1948–50; Wing Comdr Flying, RAF Coningsby, 1951–53; Staff Coll., 1953–54; Air Ministry, 1954–57; Station Comdr, RAF Cranwell, 1957–60, RAF Bircham Newton, 1961–62, RAF Tern Hill, 1963–64; HQ Far East Air Force, 1965–67. *Recreations:* sleeping, reading. *Address:* Bridge House, Bankwell Road, Giggleswick, Settle, N Yorks BD24 0AN.

PANTON, (Elizabeth) Jane; Headmistress, Bolton School Girls' Division, since 1994; *b* 20 June 1947; *d* of Richard Henry Panton and Constance Doreen Panton. *Educ:* Clayton Hall Grammar Sch., Newcastle; Merchant Taylors' Sch. for Girls, Liverpool; St Hugh's Coll., Oxford (MA Hons History); West Midlands Coll. of Educn, Walsall (PGCE). Teacher, Moreton Hall, near Oswestry, 1972–73; Third Mistress, Shrewsbury High Sch., 1973–83; Head of History and of Sixth Form, Clifton High Sch., Bristol, 1983–88; Headmistress, Merchant Taylors' Sch. for Girls, Crosby, Liverpool, 1988–94. Member: ISC (formerly HMC/GSA) Assisted Places Working Party, 1992–; GSA Professional Develt Cttee, 1992–96; ISIS North Cttee, 1993– (Chm., 1997–99); Chm., GSA NW, 2000–. Mem., Sefton FHSA, 1990–92. Mem. Council, Liverpool Univ., 1990–94. *Recreations:* fell walking, UK and abroad, birdwatching, foreign travel, music, art, reading. *Address:* Bolton School Girls' Division, Chorley New Road, Bolton BL1 4PB. *T:* (01204) 840201.

PANTON, Dr Francis Harry, CBE 1997 (MBE (mil.) 1948); Consultant, Ministry of Defence, 1984–99; Director, Royal Armament Research and Development Establishment, Ministry of Defence, 1980–83; *b* 25 May 1923; 3rd *s* of George Emerson Panton and Annie Panton; *m* 1st, 1952, Audrey Mary Lane (*d* 1989); two *s*; 2nd, 1995, Pauline Joyce Dean. *Educ:* City Sch., Lincoln; University College and Univ. of Nottingham; PhD (Chem.) Nottingham, 1952; PhD (History) Kent, 1999. Served War of 1939–45: commissioned, Bomb Disposal, Royal Eng., 1943–47. Pres., Univ. of Nottingham Union, 1950–51; Vice-Pres., Nat. Union of Students, 1952–54; Technical Officer, ICI, Billingham, 1952–53; Permanent Under-Secretary's Dept, FO, 1953–55; Office of Political Adviser, Berlin, 1955–57; Dep. Head, Technical Research Unit, MoD, 1957–58; Attaché, British Embassy, Washington, DC, 1958–59; Technical Adviser, UK Delegn to Conf. on Discontinuance of Nuclear Tests, Geneva, 1959–61; Permanent Under-Secretary's Dept, FO, 1961–63; Counsellor (Defence), British Embassy, Washington, DC, 1963–66; Head of Defence Science 6, MoD, 1966–68; Asst Chief Scientific Adviser (Nuclear), MoD, 1969–76; Dir Gen., Estabs, Resources and Programmes (B), MoD, April-Sept. 1976; Dir, Propellants, Explosives and Rocket Motor Estabt, and Head, Rocket Motor Exec., MoD, 1976–80. Consultant, Cabinet Office, 1985–97. Chairman: Mgt Cttee, Canterbury Archaeol Trust, 1985–2000; Dover Bronze Age Boat Trust, 1995–; Mem. Council, Kent Archaeol Soc., 1990– (Hon. Librarian, 1999–). FRSC (FRIC 1961); FRSA 1973; FRAeS 1982. *Recreations:* archaeology, local history. *Address:* Grove End, Tunstall, Sittingbourne, Kent ME9 8DY. *T:* (01795) 472218. *Club:* Reform.

PANTON, Jane; *see* Panton, E. J.

PANTRIDGE, Prof. (James) Frank, CBE 1978; MC 1942; *b* 3 Oct. 1916. *Educ:* Queen's Univ., Belfast (MD). FRCP 1957; FACC 1967. Research Fellow, Univ. of Mich, 1948–49; Dir, Regional Medical Cardiology Centre, NI, 1977–82; Hon. Prof. of Cardiol., QUB. Canadian Heart Foundn Orator; St Cyres Orator, National Heart Hosp., London. Chm., British Cardiac Soc., 1978. Developer of the Portable Defibrillator, and initiator (with J. S. Geddes) of pre-hospital coronary care. Hon. FRCPI. DUniv Open, 1981; Hon. DSc NUU, 1981. *Publications:* The Acute Coronary Attack, 1975; An Unquiet Life (autobiog), 1989, 4th edn 1995. *Recreation:* fishing. *Address:* Hillsborough, Co. Down, N Ireland BT26 6EH. *T:* (028) 9268 9976.

PAOLETTI, (Romano) Roland, CBE 2000; RIBA; architect. *Educ:* Manchester Univ. (DipArch 1970). Projects incl. Metro, Hong Kong; Architect-in-Chief, Jubilee Line extension, London, 1999 (Millennium Bldg of Year Award, 2000). *Address:* 11 Pear Tree Lane, Wapping, E1 9SR.

PAOLOZZI, Sir Eduardo (Luigi), Kt 1989; CBE 1968; RA 1979 (ARA 1972); sculptor; HM Sculptor in Ordinary for Scotland, since 1986; Visiting Professor, Royal College of Art, since 1989 (Tutor in Ceramics, 1968–89); *b* 7 March 1924; *s* of Rudolpho Antonio Paolozzi and Carmella (*née* Rossi), both Italian; *m* (marr. diss.) three *d*. *Educ:* Edinburgh School of Art; Slade Sch. Worked in Paris, 1947–50; Instructor, Central School of Arts and Crafts, London, 1950–55; Lecturer, St Martin's School of Art, 1955–56; Prof. of Ceramics at Fachhochschule, Cologne, 1977–81; Prof. of Sculpture, Akad. der Bildenden Künste, Munich, 1981–91. Trustee, Nat. Portrait Gall., 1988–. Fellow, UCL, 1986. Hon. Dr RCA, 1979; Hon. RSA; Hon. DLitt: Glasgow, 1980; Heriot-Watt, 1987; London, 1987; St Andrews, 1994; Cambridge, 1995; Birmingham, 1996. British Critics Prize, 1953; David E. Bright Foundn Award, 1960; Watson F. Blaire Prize, 1961; Purchase Prize, Internat. Sculpture Exhibn at Solomon R. Guggenheim Mus., 1967; First Prize for Sculpture, Carnegie Internat. Exhibn, 1967; Sculpture Prize, European Patent Office, Munich, 1978; First Prize, Rhinegarten Cologne comp., 1981; Grand Prix d'Honneur, Print Biennale at Ljubljana, Yugoslavia, 1983. *One-man exhibitions include:* first in London, Mayor Gallery, 1947; first in New York, Betty Parsons Gallery, 1960, also 1962; Tate Gallery, 1971, 1996; V&A Mus., 1973, 1977 (print retrospective); Nationalgal., W Berlin, 1975; Fruit Market Gall., Edinburgh, 1976; Kassel, Germany, 1978; Glasgow League of Artists, 1979; Edinburgh Univ., 1979; Cologne, Germany, 1979; Museum for Künste und Gewerbe, Hamburg, 1982; Aedes Gall., Berlin, 1983; Architectural Assoc., London; Royal Scottish Acad., Stadische Galerie im Lenbachhaus, Munich; Mus. Ludwig, Cologne; De Beyerd Mus., Breda, Holland; Contemporary Art Centre, Lyon, France; Ivan Dougherty Gall., Sydney, Aust., 1985; Cork, Ireland, 1985; Mus. of Mankind, 1986; RA, 1986; Serpentine Gall., 1987; Nat. Portrait Gall., 1988; Talbot Rice Art Gall., Edinburgh, 1989; Goethe Inst., London, 1991; Fitzwilliam Mus., Cambridge, 1992, 1996; Jason and Rhodes, London, 1996; Hayward Gall., 1996. Invited artist, 6th Internat. Drawing Biennale, Cleveland (UK), 1983. Designed: glass mosaics for Tottenham Ct Road Underground Station, London; film sets for Percy Adlon's Herschel and the Music of the Stars, 1984–85. Work in permanent collections: Tate Gallery; Contemporary Art Society; Museum of Modern Art, New York; Kowloon Park, Hong Kong, etc. Work exhibited in: British Pavilion, Venice Biennale, 1952; Documenta 2, Kassel, 1959; New Images of Man, New York, 1959; British Pavilion, 30th Venice Biennale; Open Air Sculpture, Battersea Park, London; British Sculpture in the Sixties, Tate Gallery. Corresponding Mem., Bayerische Akad. der Schöner Künste, 1990. Hon. Member: AA, 1980; RGI, 1993; Hon. RIAS, 1991. Eduardo Paolozzi Art Sch. inaugurated at Ipswich Sch., 1987. Goethe Medal, 1991. Cavalieri Ufficiale, Ordine al Merito (Italy), 1991. *Relevant publication:* Eduardo Paolozzi, by Winfried Konnertz, 1984. *Recreation:* music. *Clubs:* Athenæum, Chelsea Arts.

PAPANDREOU, George Andreas; MP; Minister of Foreign Affairs, Greece, since 1999; *b* St Paul, Minn, 16 June 1952; *m* 1989, Ada Papapanou; one *s* one *d*. *Educ:* King City Secondary Sch., Toronto; Amherst Coll., Massachusetts (BA Sociol.); Stockholm Univ. (undergrad. studies Sociol.); LSE (MSc Sociol. and Develt). Member of Parliament: Achaia (Patras) Dist, 1981–96; 1st Dist, Athens, 1996–. Under Sec. for Cultural Affairs, Ministry of Culture, 1985–87; Minister of Educn and Religious Affairs, 1988–89, 1994–96; Dep. Minister of Foreign Affairs, 1993–94; Alternate Minister of Foreign Affairs, 1996–99. Chm., Parly Cttee of Educn, 1981–85; Vice-Chm., cross-party Parly Cttee for Free Radio, 1987; in charge, Parly Cttee for Culture and Educn, 1989–93; Panhellenic Socialist Movement: Member: Central Cttee, 1984–; Exec. Office, 1987–88, 1996–; Pol Bureau, 1996–; Sec., Cttee on Greek Diaspora, 1990–93. Founding Member: Helsinki Citizens Assembly, Prague, 1990; Lagonisi Initiative on Co-operation in Balkans, 1994; Member Board: Foundn of Mediterranean Studies (Mem., Res. Teams); Foundn for Res. and Self-Educn. Fellow, Center for Internat. Affairs, Harvard Univ., 1992–93. Botsis's Foundn for the Promotion of Journalism Award, 1988; SOS against Racism, and Affiliated Orgns Cttee Award, 1996; Abdi Ipekci Special Award for Peace and Friendship, 1997. *Address:* Ministry of Foreign Affairs, Odos Zalakosta 2, 10671 Athens, Greece.

PAPANDREOU, Vasso; MP (Pasok) Athens, since 1993; Minister of the Interior, Public Administration and Decentralisation, Greece, since 1999; *d* of Andreas and Anastasia Papandreou. *Educ:* Athens Economic Univ. (BSc 1969); London Univ. (MSc 1971); Reading Univ. (PhD 1980). Economics Tutor, Exeter Univ., 1971–73; Res. Asst, Oxford Univ., 1973–74; Lectr, High Business and Econs Sch., Athens, 1981–85; MP, Greece, 1985–89; Dep. Minister, 1985–86; Alternate Minister: for Industry, Energy and Technology, 1986–87; for Trade, 1988–89; Minister of Develt, 1996–99. Mem., CEC, 1989–92. Vice President: Parly Assembly, Council of Europe, 1995–96; Parly Assembly, WEU, 1995–96. Panhellenic Socialist Movement: Mem., Central Cttee, 1981–85; Mem., Exec. Bureau of Central Cttee, 1984–88. Dir, Hellenic Orgn for Small and Medium Size Firms, 1981–85. Mem., Bd of Dirs, Commercial Bank of Greece, 1982–85. Hon. DEd CNAA, 1992; Hon. DLitt Sheffield, 1992; Dr *hc* Paul Sabatier Univ., Toulouse, 1993. Chevalier, Legion of Honour (France), 1993; Grand Cross, Order of Leopold II (Belgium), 1993. *Publications:* Multinational Companies and Less Developed Countries: the case of Greece, 1981; numerous papers and articles. *Address:* 15 Omirou Street, 10672 Athens, Greece.

PAPOULIAS, George Dimitrios; Commander, Order of Phoenix; Order of George I; Ambassador to the Court of St James's and (non-resident) to Iceland, 1990–93; *b* 19 May 1927; *s* of Dimitrios G. Papoulias and Caterina Kontopoulou; *m* 1974, Emily Pilavachi; one *d*. *Educ:* Athens Univ. (Law degree; Econ. and Comm. Scis degree). Military service, 2nd Lieut, 1950–51. Entered Greek Diplomatic Service, 1955; served Athens, New Delhi, Bonn; Dep. Perm. Deleg. to UN and to Internat Orgns, Geneva, 1964–69; Counsellor, 1967; Dir, Political Affairs, Min. of N Greece, 1969–70; Minister, Paris and Perm. Rep. to Unesco, 1971–74; Mem., Bd of Dirs, Resettlement Fund, Council of Europe, 1971–74; Ambassador to UN, NY, 1975–79, to Turkey, 1979–83, to USA, 1983–89; Alternate Minister and Minister for Foreign Affairs, 1989, 1990; special envoy of Greek govt to UN talks on former Yugoslav Republic of Macedonia, 1993. Holds foreign orders and decorations. *Recreations:* archaeology, history. *Address:* Rigillis 16, Athens 10674, Greece. *T:* 7229888. *Clubs:* Brooks's; Athenian (Greece).

PAPOUTSIS, Christos; economist; Member, European Commission, 1995–99; *b* 11 April 1953; *m*; one *d*. Pres., Nat. Students' Orgn, Students of Greece, 1978–80. Special Advr, Min. of Presidency of Govt, Greece, 1981–84; European Parliament: Mem., 1984–95; Vice Chm., Socialist Gp; Mem. Cttees on Foreign Affairs, Security and Defence; Mem., Budgets and Budgetary Control Cttees, 1989–94; Vice-Chm., Canada Delegn, 1984–89; Mem., USA Delegn, 1989–94. Mem., Central Cttee, Pan-Hellenic Socialist Movt (PASOK) (Dep. Sec. Youth, 1978–81; Internat. Sec., 1988–94). *Publication:* European Journeys, 1994. *Address:* Filikis Etairids 21, 10673 Athens, Greece.

PAPP, Helen Richenda; *see* Wallace, H. R.

PAPPANO, Antonio; conductor and pianist; Music Director, Théâtre Royal de la Monnaie, Brussels, since 1992; Music Director, Royal Opera House, from Sept. 2002; *b* London. *Educ:* studied under Norma Verrilli, Arnold Franchetti and Gustav Meier, USA. Has worked as pianist and assistant conductor with: NY City Opera; Gran Teatro del Liceo, Barcelona; Frankfurt Opera; Lyric Opera of Chicago; Bayreuth Fest.; former Music Dir, Norwegian Opera. Principal Guest Conductor, Israel Philharmonic Orch., 1997–. Conducting débuts include: Royal Opera House, 1990; Vienna Staatsoper, 1993; Bavarian Radio SO, 1999; Boston SO, 1999; has conducted orchs in Europe and USA, incl. ENO and LSO. Recordings include: La Bohème, 1996; Don Carlos, 1996; La Rondine, 1997; Il Trittico, 1999; Werther, 1999; The Turn of the Screw, 1999. *Address:* c/o IMG Artists, Hovell House, 616 Chiswick High Road, W4 5RX.

PAPPENHEIM, Karin; Chief Executive, Haemophilia Society, since 1998; *b* 11 Dec. 1954; *d* of Wolfgang and Joy Pappenheim; one *s* one *d*. *Educ:* St Paul's Girls' Sch.; Sussex Univ. (BA Hons Intellectual Hist.); London Coll. of Printing; Université de Toulouse; Goldsmiths' Coll. (Post grad. dip. in communicns). Weidenfeld & Nicolson, Publishers, 1977–79; Camden Social Services, 1980–82; Greater London Assoc. for Disabled People, 1982–84; Alcohol Concern, 1984–89; FPA, 1989–95; Dir, Nat. Council for One Parent Families, 1995–97. *Recreations:* family and friends, travel in France. *Address:* Haemophilia Society, Chesterfield House, 385 Euston Road, NW1 3AU.

See also M. Pappenheim.

PAPPENHEIM, Mark; arts journalist; *b* 25 May 1956; *s* of Wolfgang and Joy Pappenheim; *m* 1988, Katie Tearle; two *s*. *Educ:* St Paul's Boys' Sch.; Merton Coll., Oxford (BA Hons Lit. Hum., MA); City Univ., London (Cert. Arts Admin). Box-office manager, Buxton Fest. and Opera Hse, 1979–80; Asst Hd of Educn, WNO, 1980–81; Fest. Administrator, Vale of Glamorgan Fest., 1982; Asst Administrator, Live Music Now, 1982–83; Pubns Ed., Opera North, 1983–84; Radio Ed., Radio Times, 1984–90; with The Independent, 1990–98, Arts Editor, 1996–98; Opera Critic, The Daily Express, 1998–. Editor: Glyndebourne Touring Opera programme books, 1986–88; BBC Proms programmes, 1998–; BBC Proms Guide, 2000, 2001. *Publications:* numerous articles; essays; programme/notes, incl. BBC Proms, Edinburgh Internat. Fest., Royal Opera, Glyndebourne Fest. Opera, South Bank Centre, EMI Records, Warner Vision; contrib. BBC Music Mag., Classic FM Mag., Internat. Record Review. *Address:* 42 Ferrers Road, Lewes, E Sussex BN7 1PZ. *T:* (01273) 483546.

See also K. Pappenheim.

PAPPS, Alastair Harkness; Associate Director, International Consultancy Group, Civil Service College (on secondment), 1999–April 2002; *b* 28 April 1942; *s* of Osborne Stephen Papps and Helen Papps (*née* Harkness); *m* 1963, Marian Caroline Clayton; two *s* one *d*. *Educ:* King Edward's Sch., Birmingham; St Catharine's Coll., Cambridge (MA); Univ. of Newcastle upon Tyne (Dip. in Applied Social Studies 1970). Joined HM Prison Service, 1965; Prison Service Staff Coll., Wakefield, 1965–66; Asst Gov., Huntercombe Borstal, 1966–69; Tutor, Prison Service Staff Coll., Wakefield, 1970–73; Asst Gov., 1973–75, Dep. Gov., 1975–77, Wakefield Prison; Personnel Div., Prison Service HQ, 1977–80; Governor: Acklington Prison, 1980–83; Durham Prison, 1983–87; Frankland Prison, 1987–89; Dep. Dir, subseq. Dir, North Regl Office, 1989–90; Area Manager, North East, 1990–95; Dir of Ops–North, and Mem., Prisons Bd, 1995–99. Ed., Prison Service Jl, 1987–89. *Publications:* articles in jls. *Recreations:* reading, theatre, cinema, travel, observing politics. *Address:* (until April 2002) Civil Service College, 11 Belgrave Road, SW1V 1RB. *T:* (office) (01344) 634408, *Fax:* (01344) 634451; Ratcheugh, Longhoughton, Alnwick, Northumberland NE66 3AE. *Club:* Travellers.

PAPUA NEW GUINEA, Archbishop of, since 1996; **Most Rev. James Simon Ayong;** Primate of the Anglican Church of Papua New Guinea, since 1996; Bishop of Aipo Rongo, since 1995; *b* 3 Sept. 1944; *s* of Julius and Margaret Ayong; *m* 1967, Gawali Susuwa; one *d*, and one adopted *s*. *Educ:* Martyrs' Sch.; Newton Theol Coll. (DipTh); Martin Luther Seminary (BTh). Govt Administrative Officer, 1964–71; Church Purchasing Officer and Radio Operator, 1976–79. Ordained deacon, 1982, priest, 1984; asst priest, Resurrection parish, Popondetta, 1985–86; Lectr, 1987–88, Principal, 1989–93, Newton Theol Coll.; locum at Burgess Hill, Sussex, UK, and student at Chichester Theol Coll., 1993–94; Parish priest, Gerehu, Port Moresby, 1994–95. *Recreations:* reading, watching Rugby football. *Address:* PO Box 893, Mount Hagen, Western Highlands Province, Papua New Guinea. *T:* 5421131, *Fax:* 521181.

PAQUET, Dr Jean-Guy, CC 1994 (OC 1984); FRSC; President and Chief Executive Officer, National Optics Institute, since 1994; *b* Montmagny, Qué, 5 Jan. 1938; *s* of Laurent W. Paquet and Louisianne Coulombe. *Educ:* Université Laval (BSc Engrg Physics, 1959; DSc Elec. Engrg, 1963); Ecole Nat. Sup. de l'Aéronautique, Paris (MSc Aeronautics, 1960). FRSC 1978; FAAAS 1981. Université Laval: Asst Prof. of Elec. Engrg, 1962; Associate Prof., 1967; Head, Elec. Engrg Dept, 1967–69; Vice-Dean (Research), Faculty of Science, 1969–72; Prof. of Elec. Engrg, 1971; Vice-Rector (Academic), 1972–77; Rector, 1977–87; Pres., La Laurentienne Vie Inc., 1987–94. Fellowships: French Govt, 1959; NATO, 1962; Nat. Science Foundn, 1964; Québec Govt, 1965. Def. Res. Bd of Canada Grant, 1965–76. National Research Council of Canada: Fellowship, 1961; Grant, 1964–77; Mem., Associate Cttee on Automatic Control, 1964–70; Special Asst to Vice-Pres. (Scientific), 1971–72. Pres., Conf. of Rectors and Principals of Univs of Prov. of Québec, 1979–81. Member: Council, Univs of Prov. of Qué, 1973–77; Bd, Assoc. of Scientific, Engrg and Technol Community of Canada, 1970–77 (Pres., 1975–76); Bd, French Canadian Assoc. for Advancement of Science, 1969–71; Canadian Assoc. of Univ. Res. Administrators; Special Task Force on Res. and Develt, Science Council of Canada, 1976; Order of Engrs, Qué; Amer. Soc. for Engrg Educn; Amer. Management Assoc., 1980; Soc. for Res. Administrators. Member Board: Interamerican Univs Assoc., 1980–87; Assoc. des universités partiellement ou entièrement de langue française, 1981–87 (Vice-Pres., 1983); Assoc. of Commonwealth Univs, 1981–87; Founding Mem., Corporate Higher Educn Forum. Pres., Selection Cttee, Outstanding Achievement Awards, Canada, 1984 (Mem., 1983). DSc *hc* McGill Univ., 1982; DLaw *hc*, York Univ., 1983. *Publications:* (with P. A. Roy) Rapport d'études bibliographiques: l'automation dans la production et la distribution de l'énergie électrique, 1968; (with J. F. Le Maître) Méthodes pratiques d'étude des oscillations non-linéaires: application aux systèmes par plus-ou-moins, 1970; more than fifty pubns in scientific jls, on control systems engrg; articles on research, develt and scientific policy. *Recreations:* jogging, travels, golf. *Address:* National Optics Institute, 2740 rue Einstein, Sainte-Foy, Québec, QC G1P 4S4, Canada. *T:* (418) 6577006, *Fax:* (418) 6577088. *Clubs:* Cercle de la Garnison de Québec, Club de Golf Royal Québec (Québec).

PARAGUAY, Bishop of, since 1988; **Rt Rev. John Alexander Ellison;** *b* 24 Dec. 1940; *s* of Alexander and Catherine Ellison; *m* 1964, Judith Mary Cox; one *s* two *d*. *Educ:* London College of Divinity (ALCD); Borough Road College (Teacher's Cert.). Secondary school teacher, 1961–64. Deacon 1967, priest 1968; Curate, St Paul, Woking, 1967–71; missionary, church planter, evangelist; Bible school/Bible institute lecturer, 1971–79; Asst to Archdeacon, St Saviour, Belgrano, Dio. Argentina, 1979–82; Rector, Aldridge, Dio. Lichfield, 1983–88. *Recreations:* walking, gardening, family, dining out, club. *Address:* Diocesan Office, Casilla de Correo 1124, Asunción, Paraguay. *Club:* Garden (Asunción).

PARASKEVA, Janet; Chief Executive, Law Society of England and Wales, since 2000; *b* 28 May 1946; *d* of Antonis Paraskeva and Doris Amanda Paraskeva (*née* Fowler); *m* 1967, Alan Richard Derek Hunt (marr. diss. 1983); two *d*, and two step *s*. *Educ:* Open Univ. (BA Social Scis 1983). HM Inspector of Schs, DES, 1983–88; Dir, Nat. Youth Bureau, 1988–91; Chief Exec., Nat. Youth Agency, 1991–95; Dir, England, Nat. Lotteries Charities Bd, 1995–2000. *Publications:* articles in youth and educn periodicals and in TES. *Recreations:* golf, riding, gardening. *Address:* Law Society, 113 Chancery Lane, WC2A 1PL.

PARAYRE, Jean-Paul Christophe; Officier de la Légion d'Honneur; Commandeur, l'Ordre National du Mérite, 1991; Chairman, Vallourec, since 2000 (Member, Supervisory Board, 1989–2000); Member, Supervisory Board, Peugeot SA, since 1984; *b* Lorient, 5 July 1937; *s* of Louis Parayre and Jehanne Malarde; *m* 1962, Marie-Françoise Chaufour; two *s* two *d*. *Educ:* Lycées in Casablanca and Versailles; Ecole Polytechnique, Paris; Ecole Nationale des Ponts et Chaussées. Engr, Dept of Highways, 1963–67; Technical Adviser: Min. of Social Affairs, 1967; Min. of Economy and Finance, 1968; Dir of Mech. Industries, Min. of Industry and Res., 1970–74; Chief Adviser to Pres. and Gen. Man., Banque Vernes et Commerciale de Paris, 1974; Manager of Planning, Automobile Div. of Peugeot, 1975; Manager, Automobile Div., Peugeot-Citroën, 1976; Chm., Peugeot SA, 1977–84; Mem., Supervisory Bd, 1977–84, Dir-Gen., 1984–88, Chm. and Chief Exec. Officer, 1988–90, Dumez SA; Vice-Chm. and Chief Operating Officer, Bolloré, 1994–99 (Dir, 1994–2000); Chm. and CEO, Saga, 1996–99. Chm., GIE Trans-Manche Construction, 1986–92; Vice-Chm., Lyonnaise des Eaux-Dumez, 1990–92; Mem., Board of Directors: Crédit National, then Natexis, 1978–97; Valeo, 1986–91; GTM, 1986–92; LVMH, 1987–89; Jean Lefebvre, 1988–92; McAlpine, 1990–92; Inchcape plc, 1991–94; Indosuez, 1991–94; Bolloré (formerly Albatros) Investissement, 1994–; Coflexip, 1995–2000; Delmas, 1995–99; Stena International BV, 1995–; Tarmac plc, 1995–99; Financière de l'Odet, 1997–2000; Financière Moncey, 1997–99; Stena UK, 1999–; Carillion plc, 1999–. *Recreations:* tennis, golf. *Address:* 31/32 Ennismore Gardens, SW7 1AE. *Clubs:* Polo de Paris, Golf de Morfontaine; Wisley Golf.

PARBO, Sir Arvi (Hillar), AC 1993; Kt 1978; non-executive Chairman, WMC (formerly Western Mining Corporation) Ltd, 1990–99 (Chairman and Managing Director, 1974–86; Executive Chairman, 1986–90); *b* 10 Feb. 1926; *s* of Aado and Hilda Parbo; *m* 1953, Saima Soots; two *s* one *d*. *Educ:* Clausthal Mining Acad., Germany; Univ. of Adelaide (BE Hons). Western Mining Corporation: Underground Surveyor, 1956; Underground Manager, Nevoria Mine, 1958–60; Techn. Asst to Man. Dir, 1960–64; Dep. Gen. Supt, WA, 1964–68; Gen. Manager, 1968–71 (Dir, 1970–); Dep. Man. Dir, 1971; Man. Dir, 1971. Director: Aluminium Co. of America, 1980–98; Hoechst Australia (formerly Hoechst Australian Investments Pty) Ltd, 1981–97; Chase AMP Bank Ltd, 1985–91; Sara Lee Corp., 1991–; Chairman: Munich Reinsurance Company of Australia Ltd, 1984–98 (Dir, 1983–); Zurich Insurance Australian Group, 1985–98; Alcoa of Australia Ltd, 1978–96; The Broken Hill Pty Co. Ltd, 1989–92 (Dir, 1987–92). Member: Chase Internat. Adv. Bd; Degussa AG Supervisory Bd, 1988–93. Hon. DSc: Deakin, 1989; Curtin, 1989; Hon. DEng Monash, 1989; DUniv Flinders, 1991. Comdr, Order of Merit, Germany, 1979; Grand Cordon, Order of the Sacred Treasure, Japan, 1990; Australian Achiever, 1990. *Recreations:* reading, carpentry. *Address:* Level 23, HWT Tower, 40 City Road, Southbank, Vic 3006, Australia. *T:* (3) 96740412. *Clubs:* Melbourne, Australian (both Melbourne); Weld (Perth); Commonwealth (Canberra); Hannans (Kalgoorlie); Duquesne (Pittsburgh, USA).

PARDOE, Alan Douglas William; QC 1988; a Recorder, since 1990; *b* 16 Aug. 1943; *s* of William Pardoe and Grace Pardoe, DSc, FRSC; *m* 1st, 1972, Mary Ensor (marr. diss. 1976); 2nd, 1991, Catherine Williams (marr. diss. 1994). *Educ:* Oldbury Grammar Sch.; St Catharine's Coll., Cambridge (MA, LLB). Called to the Bar, Lincoln's Inn, 1971, Bencher, 1998. Asst Lectr and Lectr in Law, Univ. of Exeter, 1965–70; Vis. Lectr in Law, Univ. of Auckland, NZ, 1970; Lectr in Law, Univ. of Sussex, 1970–74; began practice at the Bar, 1973. *Publications:* A Practical Guide to the Industrial Relations Act 1971, 1972; articles in legal periodicals. *Recreations:* mountain-walking, cooking. *Address:* 50 Northumberland Place, W2 5AS; Devereux Chambers, Devereux Court, Temple, WC2R 3JJ. *T:* (020) 7353 7534. *Club:* Travellers.

PARDOE, John George Magrath, CBE 1975; FRAeS; Director-General, Airworthiness, Civil Aviation Authority, 1972–79. *Educ:* Coll. of Aeronautical Engineering. Entered design work in Aircraft Industry, 1935; joined Accidents Inspection Br. of Air Ministry, 1942; joined Staff, Air Registration Bd, 1945; Chief Technical Officer, 1969. Médaille de l'aéronautique, 1980.

PARDOE, John Wentworth; Chairman, Sight and Sound Education Ltd, 1979–89; *b* 27 July 1934; *s* of Cuthbert B. Pardoe and Marjorie E. W. (*née* Taylor); *m* 1958, Joyce R. Peerman; two *s* one *d*. *Educ:* Sherborne; Corpus Christi Coll., Cambridge (MA). Television Audience Measurement Ltd, 1958–60; Osborne Peacock Co. Ltd, 1960–61; Liberal News, 1961–66. MP (L) Cornwall N, 1966–79; Treasurer of the Liberal Party, 1968–69. Presenter, Look Here, LWT, 1979–81. Sen. Res. Fellow, PSI, 1979–81. Consultant to Nat. Assoc. of Schoolmasters, 1967–73. Director: William Schlackman Ltd, 1968–71; Gerald Metals, 1972–83; Mem. London Metal Exchange, 1973–83. Mem., Youth Trng Bd, 1985–89. *Recreations:* walking, reading, music, carpentry. *Address:* 18 New End Square, NW3 1LN.

PAREKH, family name of **Baron Parekh.**

PAREKH, Baron *cr* 2000 (Life Peer), of Kingston upon Hull, in the East Riding of Yorkshire; **Bhikhu Chhotalal Parekh;** Professor of Political Theory, University of Hull, since 1982; *b* 4 Jan. 1935; *s* of Chhotalal Parekh and Gajaraben Parekh; *m* 1959, Pramila (*née* Dalal); three *s*. *Educ:* Univ. of Bombay (BA 1954, MA 1956); Univ. of London (PhD 1966). Tutor, LSE, 1962–63; Asst Lectr, Univ. of Glasgow, 1963–64; Lectr, Sen. Lectr and Reader, Hull Univ., 1964–82. Vice-Chancellor, Univ. of Baroda, 1981–84. Visiting Professor: Univ. of BC, 1967–68; Concordia Univ., 1974–75; McGill Univ., 1976–77; Harvard Univ., 1996; Inst. of Advanced Study, Vienna, 1997; Univ. of Pompeu Fabra, Barcelona, 1997; Univ. of Pennsylvania, 1998; Ecole des Hautes Etudes en Sciences Sociales, Paris, 2000. Mem., Rampton/Swann Cttee of Inquiry into Educnl Problems of Ethnic Minority Children, 1978–82; Mem. Council, PSI, 1985–90; Vice Pres., UK Council for Overseas Students Affairs, 1989–; Chm., British Assoc. of S Asia Scholars, 1989–91. Dep. Chm., CRE, 1985–90; Member: Commn on Rise of Neo-Fascism in Europe, 1992–; Nat. Commn on Equal Opportunities, CVCP, 1994–99; Chm., Commn on Future of Multi-Ethnic Britain, 1998–2000. Trustee: Runnymede Trust, 1986–; Inst. for Public Policy Res., 1988–95; Gandhi Foundn, 1988– (Vice-Pres., 1996–); Anne Frank Educnl Trust, 1992–. FRSA 1988. British Asian of the Year, Asian Who's Who, 1991; Special Lifetime Achievement Award for Asians, BBC, 1999. *Publications:* Politics and Experience, 1968; Dissent and Disorder, 1971; The Morality of Politics, 1972; Knowledge and Belief in Politics, 1973; Bentham's Political Thought, 1973; Colour, Culture and Consciousness, 1974; Jeremy Bentham: ten critical essays, 1974; The Concept of Socialism, 1975; Hannah Arendt and the Search for a New Political Philosophy, 1981; Karl Marx's Theory of Ideology, 1982; Contemporary Political Thinkers, 1982; Political Discourse, 1986; Gandhi's Political Philosophy, 1989; Colonialism, Tradition and Reform, 1989; Jeremy Bentham: critical assessments (4 vols), 1993; The Decolonisation of Imagination, 1995; Crisis and Change in Contemporary India, 1995; Gandhi, 1997; Rethinking Multiculturalism, 2000; articles in learned jls incl. Political Studies, British Jl of Political Science, Social Research, Jl of History of Ideas, Indian Jl of Social Science, Ethics, Hist. of Pol Thought, TLS, Canadian Jl of Philosophy, Radical Philosophy. *Recreations:* reading, music. *Address:* 211 Victoria Avenue, Hull HU5 3EF.

PARENT, Hon. Gilbert; Speaker of the House of Commons, Canada, 1994–2001; *b* 25 July 1935; *s* of Joseph Nelson Parent and Marie Delina (*née* Boulanger); *m*; four *d*. *Educ:* St Joseph's Coll., Rensselear, Ind. (BSc); Niagara Univ., NY (MA); State Univ. of NY (MEd). French teacher: Notre Dame High Sch., Welland, Ont, 1957–59; Dennis Morris High Sch., St Catharines, Ont, 1959–70; Vice-Principal, Thorold Secondary Sch., 1970–74; history teacher, Niagara South Bd of Educn, 1985–89. MP (L) Welland-St Catharines-Thorold, 1974–85 and 1988–2001. Hon. LLD: St Joseph's Coll., Ind., 1995; Niagara Univ., NY, 1995; Brock Univ., Ont, 1996. *Recreations:* reading, playing golf, spending time with grand-children, promoting greater awareness of Parliament among young people. *Address:* c/o House of Commons, Centre Block, Ottawa, ON K1A 0A6, Canada.

PARFIT, Derek Antony, FBA 1986; Senior Research Fellow, All Souls College, Oxford, since 1984; *b* 11 Dec. 1942; *s* of Norman and Jessie Parfit. *Educ:* Eton; Balliol College, Oxford. BA Modern History, 1964. Fellow of All Souls, 1967–. *Publication:* Reasons and Persons, 1984. *Recreation:* architectural photography. *Address:* All Souls College, Oxford OX1 4AL. *T:* (01865) 279282.

PARFITT, Andrew John; Controller, BBC Radio 1, since 1998; *b* 24 Sept. 1958; *s* of John Raymond Parfitt and Jeanne Parfitt; *m* 1996, Laura Druce; two *d. Educ:* Bristol Old Vic Theatre Sch. Asst stage manager, Bristol Arts Centre, 1978; studio manager, BBC, 1979–84; programme presenter, British Forces Broadcasting Service, 1984; BBC: educn producer, 1985; producer, features and magazines, Radio 4, 1986–91; Breakfast Show Editor, Radio 5, 1991–93; Radio 1: Editor, 1993–95; Managing Editor, 1995–98. *Recreations:* running, playing the trumpet. *Address:* BBC Radio 1, Yalding House, 152–156 Great Portland Street, W1N 4DJ.

PARFITT, David John; film producer; Director: Renaissance Theatre Company, since 1987; Trademark Films, since 1999; *b* 8 July 1958; *s* of late William Arnold Parfitt and of Maureen Parfitt (*née* Collinson); *m* 1st, 1988, Susan Coates (marr. diss. 1993); two *s*; 2nd, 1996, Elizabeth Barron; two *s. Educ:* Bede Grammar Sch., Sunderland; Barbara Speake Stage Sch., London. Actor, 1970–88; producer, 1985–: productions include: *theatre*: Tell Me Honestly, 1985, John Sessions at the 11th Hour, 1986, Donmar Warehouse; Romeo and Juliet, 1986, Public Enemy, 1987, Lyric Hammersmith; Napoleon, Albery, 1987; Much Ado About Nothing, As You Like It, and Hamlet, Phoenix, 1988; Look Back in Anger, Lyric, 1989; A Midsummer Night's Dream, King Lear, Dominion, 1990; Scenes from a Marriage, Wyndhams, 1990; Travelling Tales, Haymarket, 1991; Uncle Vanya, Lyric Hammersmith, 1991; Coriolanus, Chichester Fest. Th., 1992; *television:* Twelfth Night, 1988; Look Back in Anger, 1989; *films:* Henry V, 1988; Peter's Friends, 1992; Swan Song, 1992; Much Ado About Nothing, 1993; Mary Shelley's Frankenstein, 1994; The Madness of King George, 1995; Twelfth Night, 1996; The Wings of the Dove, 1997; Shakespeare in Love, 1998; (consultant) Gangs of New York, 2002; I Capture the Castle, 2002. Mem. Council, BAFTA, 2000–. Mem. Bd, London Film Commn, 1999–. Trustee, Chicken Shed Th. Co., 1997–; Patron, Royalty Th., Sunderland, 1999–. Hon. DA Sunderland, 1999; Hon. Dr Drama RSAMD, 2001. *Address:* Trademark Films, New Ambassadors Theatre, West Street, WC2H 9ND. *T:* (020) 7240 5585, *Fax:* (020) 7240 5586; *e-mail:* mail@trademarkfilms.co.uk.

PARGETER, Rt Rev. Philip; Auxiliary Bishop of Birmingham, (RC), and Titular Bishop of Valentiniana, since 1989; *b* 13 June 1933; *s* of Philip William Henry Pargeter and Ellen Pargeter. *Educ:* St Bede's Coll., Manchester; Oscott Coll., Sutton Coldfield. Priest, 1959; on staff of Cotton College, 1959–85; Administrator, St Chad's Cathedral, Birmingham, 1985–90; Canon, 1986. *Recreations:* reading, listening to music, walking. *Address:* Grove House, 90 College Road, Sutton Coldfield B73 5AH. *T:* (0121) 354 4363.

PARHAM, Philip John; HM Diplomatic Service; Commercial Counsellor, Saudi Arabia, since 2000; *b* 14 Aug. 1960; *s* of John Carey Parham and Christian Mary Parham (*née* Fitzherbert); *m* 1985, Anna Catherine Astrid Louise, (Kasia), Giedroyc; five *s* two *d. Educ:* Eton Coll.; Christ Church, Oxford (MA Lit.Hum.). Morgan Grenfell, 1983–89 (Sen. Asst Dir, 1988); Barclays de Zoete Wedd Ltd, 1989–93 (Dir, 1993); joined FCO, 1993; FCO, 1993–96 (Private Sec. to Parly Under-Sec. of State, 1995); First Sec. (Chancery), Washington, 1996–2000. *Recreations:* children, tennis, researching the parentage of Mary Anne Smythe. *Address:* c/o Foreign and Commonwealth Office, King Charles Street, SW1A 2AH. *Club:* Wadi (Riyadh).

PARHAM, Richard David; Managing Director, Peugeot Motor Company (formerly Peugeot Talbot Motor Company) PLC, 1994–99; *b* 17 Nov. 1944; *s* of James Parham and Lily Elizabeth Parham; *m* 1967, Janet Burton; one *s* one *d. Educ:* Royal Liberty Sch., Romford; Barking Coll. of Technol. Ford Motor Co., 1961–67; Rootes Motors, 1967–69; Chrysler UK, then Chrysler UK/Talbot Motor Co., 1969–81: Profit Analysis Manager, then Finance Manager, Hills Precision Ltd, 1969–72; Manager, Product and Pricing Analysis, then Pricing and Investment, 1972–76; Co. Comptroller, 1976–77; Dir of Finance, 1977–80; Asst Man. Dir, Peugeot Talbot Motor Co. PLC, 1981–94. *Recreations:* Rugby, cricket, music, reading.

PARIS, Archbishop of; *see* Lustiger, His Eminence Cardinal J.-M.

PARIS, Prof. Jeffrey Bruce, PhD; FBA 1999; Professor of Mathematics, Manchester University, since 1984; *b* 15 Nov. 1944; *s* of George William and Marie Eileen Paris; *m* 1st, 1967, Malvyn Loraine Blackburn (marr. diss. 1983); two *d*; 2nd, 1983, Alena Vencovská; three *s* one *d. Educ:* Manchester Univ. (BSc 1st Cl. Maths 1966; PhD Mathematical Logic 1969). Manchester University: Lectr, Dept of Maths, 1969–74; Reader, 1974–84. Junior Whitehead Prize, London Mathematical Soc., 1983. *Publications:* The Uncertain Reasoner's Companion, 1994; numerous research papers in learned jls. *Recreations:* football, angling, painting, pop music. *Address:* Department of Mathematics, The University, Manchester M13 9PL. *T:* (0161) 275 5880.

PARISH, Neil Quentin Gordon; Member (C) South West Region, England, European Parliament, since 1999; *b* 26 May 1956; *s* of Reginald Thomas Parish and Kathleen Susan Mari Parish; *m* 1981, Susan Gail; one *s* one *d. Educ:* Brymore Sch., Somerset. Left sch. at 16 to run farm of 100 acres; farm increased to 300 acres, dairy and arable, 1990. Member (C): Sedgemoor DC, 1983–95 (Dep. Leader, 1989–95); Somerset CC, 1989–93; Parish Council, 1985–. Contested (C) Torfaen, 1997. *Recreations:* swimming, walking. *Address:* Bridgwater Conservative Office, 16 Northgate, Bridgwater, Som TA6 3EU.

PARISH, Richard, CBiol; FRSH; Chief Executive, Health Development Agency, since 2000; *b* 11 Oct. 1951; *s* of Leslie Thomas Parish, FCCA and Winifred Alice Parish; *m* 1976, Joan Margaret Shepherd; one *s* one *d. Educ:* Univ. of London (BSc ext. 1975); South Bank Poly. (PDipHEd 1978); Huddersfield Univ. (MEd). CBiol 1989; MIBiol 1989. Dir of Health Promotion, Stockport HA, 1980–85; Head of Progs, 'Heartbeat Wales', and Sen. Lectr, Welsh Nat. Sch. of Medicine, 1985–87; Dir of Ops, Health Promotion Authy for Wales, 1987–90; Principal and Chief Exec., Humberside Coll. of Health, 1990–96; Dir, Health and Community Studies, and Prof. of Public Health, Sheffield Hallam Univ., 1996–97; Hd, Health Studies, and Prof., Univ. of York, 1997–99; Regl Dir, Educn and Trng, NHS Eastern Reg., 1999. FRSH 1988. MIPR 1989; MHSM 1991. Hon. MFPHM 2001. *Publications:* contribs on health promotion and health policy, incl. for WHO. *Recreations:* photography, rambling, cycling. *Address:* Health Development Agency, Trevelyan House, 30 Great Peter Street, SW1P 2HW. *T:* (020) 7413 1946.

PARISOT, Pierre Louis André; Chevalier de l'Ordre du Mérite; Chevalier de la Légion d'Honneur; Chairman and Chief Executive, Omnium de Traitement et de Valorisation, since 1997; Chairman, Transmanche-Link (TML), since 1991; *b* Ambacourt, France, 9 Jan. 1940; *s* of Louis Parisot and Marie (*née* Boye); *m* 1963, Evelyne Treilhou; two *s* two *d. Educ:* Ecole Polytechnique; Ecole Nationale des Ponts et Chaussées; Institut d'Etudes Politiques de Paris. Assistant to the Director, Civil Works Department: Réunion Island, 1966–72; Morbihan, Brittany, 1973–76; Dep. Dir, Personnel Policy and Mod. Management Methods, Min. of Civil Works, Transport and Envmt, 1976–77; Technical Advr, French Home Office Cabinet, 1977–80; Internat. Dir, St Gobain subsid., SOBEA, 1980–84; Dir Gen., SOGEA (Gp Générale des Eaux), 1985–90; Chm., Supervisory Bd, Société des Tuyaux Bonna (Gp Générale des Eaux, now Vivendi), 1990–; Dep. Man. Dir, Société Générale d'Entreprises, 1991–97; Chm. and Chief Exec., Consortium Stade de France SA, 1995. *Recreations:* sailing, ski-ing. *Address:* Omnium de Traitement et de Valorisation, L'Aquarène, 1 place Montgolfier, 94417 Saint-Maurice Cedex, France. *T:* 145115741.

PARIZEAU, Jacques, PhD; Member, Québec National Assembly (Parti Québécois) for Assomption, 1976–84 and 1989–96; Prime Minister of Québec, 1994–96; *b* Montreal, 9 Aug. 1930; *s* of Gerard Parizeau and Germaine Parizeau (*née* Biron); *m* 1st, 1956, Alicja Poznanska (decd); one *s* one *d*; 2nd, 1992, Lisette Lapointe. *Educ:* Ecole des Hautes Etudes Commerciales, Montreal; Institut d'Etudes Politiques, Paris (Dip. 1952); London Sch. of Econs (PhD 1955). Prof., Ecole des Hautes Etudes Commerciales, Montreal, 1955–65, 1967–76 and 1985–89 (Dir, Applied Econs Inst., 1973–75). Econs and financial advr to Prime Minister and Cabinet of Québec, 1961–69; Minister of Finance, 1976–84; also Pres., Treasury Bd and Minister of Revenue and of Financial Instns; Leader, Official Opposition, 1989–94. Parti Québécois: Mem., 1969–; Chm., Nat. Exec., 1970–73; Pres., 1988–. Pres., Québec Financial Instns Task Force, 1967–69; Chm., Québec Municipalities Study Commn, 1985. *Publications:* The Terms of Trade of Canada, 1956; Initiation à l'économie du Québec, 1975; Pour un Québec souverain, 1997; numerous articles. *Recreations:* reading, music, gardening. *Address:* 40 avenue Robert, Outremont, Québec, QC H3S 2P2, Canada.

PARK, family name of **Baroness Park of Monmouth**.

PARK OF MONMOUTH, Baroness *cr* 1990 (Life Peer), of Broadway in the County of Hereford and Worcester; **Daphne Margaret Sybil Désirée Park,** CMG 1971; OBE 1960; HM Diplomatic Service, retired; Principal of Somerville College, Oxford, 1980–89; *b* England, 1 Sept. 1921; British parents; unmarried. *Educ:* Rosa Bassett Sch.; Somerville Coll., Oxford (Hon. Fellow, 1990). WTS (FANY), 1943–47 (Allied Commn for Austria, 1946–48). FO, 1948; UK Delegn to NATO, 1952; 2nd Sec., Moscow, 1954; FO, 1956; Consul and 1st Sec., Leopoldville, 1959; FO, 1961; Lusaka, 1964; FO, 1967; Consul-Gen., Hanoi, 1969–70; Hon. Res. Fellow, Univ. of Kent, 1971–72, on sabbatical leave from FCO; Chargé d'Affaires *ai*, Ulan Bator, Apr.–June 1972; FCO, 1973–79. Gov., BBC, 1982–87. Chm., Legal Aid Adv. Cttee to the Lord Chancellor, 1985–91. Chm., RCHM, 1989–94. Member: British Library Bd, 1983–89; Sheffield Develt Corp. Bd, 1989–92; RIIA; Royal Asiatic Soc.; Forum UK; Mem. Council, VSO, 1981–84; Mem. Council, GB–Sasakawa Foundn, 1994–2001; Dir, Zoo Develt Trust, 1989–90. Pro-Vice-Chancellor, Univ. of Oxford, 1985–89. Pres., Soc. for Promotion of Training of Women, 1995–. Mem., Thatcher Foundn, 1992–; Trustee: Royal Armouries Develt Trust, 1991–92; Jardine Educnl Trust, 1991–98. Vice-Patron, Atlantic Council Appeal, 2001–. MRSA. Hon. LLD: Bristol, 1988; Mount Holyoke Coll., 1992. *Recreations:* good talk, politics, and difficult places. *Address:* House of Lords, SW1A 0PW. *Clubs:* Oxford and Cambridge, Naval and Military, Royal Commonwealth Society, Special Forces.

PARK, Hon. Sir Andrew (Edward Wilson), Kt 1997; **Hon. Mr Justice Park;** a Judge of the High Court of Justice, Chancery Division, since 1997; *b* 27 Jan. 1939; *m* 1962, Ann Margaret Woodhead; two *s* one *d* (and one *s* decd). *Educ:* Leeds Grammar Sch.; University Coll., Oxford. Winter Williams Law Schol., 1959; BA (Jurisp.) 1960, MA 1964. FTII 1990. Various academic posts in UK and abroad, 1960–68. Called to the Bar, Lincoln's Inn, 1964, Bencher, 1986; QC 1978; QC (NI) 1992; a Recorder, 1989–94; practice at Revenue Bar, 1965–97. Chairman: Taxation and Retirement Benefits Cttee of the Bar Council, 1978–82; Revenue Bar Assoc., 1987–92; Treasurer, Senate of the Inns of Court and Bar, 1982–85. *Publications:* The Sources of Nigerian Law, 1963; various articles, notes and reviews in legal periodicals, mainly concerning taxation. *Recreations:* tennis, golf. *Address:* Royal Courts of Justice, Strand, WC2A 2LL.

PARK, Graham; *see* Park, J. G.

PARK, Ian Grahame, CBE 1995; Chairman, Northcliffe Newspapers Group Ltd, since 1995 (Managing Director, 1982–95); Director, Daily Mail and General Trust plc, since 1994; *b* 15 May 1935; *s* of William Park and Christina (*née* Scott); *m* 1965, Anne Turner; one *s. Educ:* Lancaster Royal Grammar Sch.; Queens' Coll., Cambridge. 1st Bn Manchester Regt, Berlin (Nat. Service Commn), 1954–56. Trainee Journalist, Press and Journal, Aberdeen, 1959; Asst Lit. Editor, Sunday Times, 1960–63; various management posts, Thomson Newspapers, 1963–65; Liverpool Daily Post and Echo, 1965–, Man. Dir and Editor in Chief, 1972–82; Dir, Associated Newspaper Holdings Ltd, 1983–95. Mem. Council, Newspaper Soc., 1967– (Pres., 1980–81); Dir, Press Assoc., 1973–83 (Chm., 1978–79 and 1979–80); Dir, Reuters, 1978–82, 1988–94. Mem. Newspaper Panel, Monopolies and Mergers Commn, 1986–95. Dir, Radio City (Sound of Merseyside Ltd), 1973–82; Dir, Liverpool Playhouse, 1973–80; Trustee, Blue Coat Soc. of Arts, Liverpool, 1973–82. FRSA. Gov. and Trustee, Dr Johnson's House Trust, 1996–. *Recreations:* eighteenth-century English pottery, twentieth-century English pictures. *Address:* (office) 31 John Street, WC1N 2QB. *Club:* Reform.

PARK, (Ian) Michael (Scott), CBE 1982; Consultant, Paull & Williamsons, Advocates, Aberdeen, since 1991 (Partner, 1964–91); *b* 7 April 1938; *m* 1964, Elizabeth Mary Lamberton Struthers, MBE, BL; one *s* (and one *s* decd). *Educ:* Aberdeen Grammar Sch.; Aberdeen Univ. (MA, LLB). Admitted Mem. Soc. of Advocates, Aberdeen, 1962 (Treas., 1991–92; Pres., 1992–93). Temp. Sheriff, 1976–94; Hon. Sheriff at Aberdeen, 1997–. Law Society of Scotland: Mem. Council, 1974–85; Vice-Pres., 1979–80; Pres., 1980–81. A Chm., Med. Appeal Tribunals, 1991–96; Member: Criminal Injuries Compensation Bd, 1983–2000; Criminal Injuries Compensation Appeals Panel, 1996–. Chm., Aberdeen Citizens Advice Bureau, 1976–88. Frequent broadcaster on legal topics. *Recreations:* golf, gardening, cheating Parkinson's Disease. *Address:* Beechwood, 46 Rubislaw Den South, Aberdeen AB15 4AY. *T:* (01224) 313799. *Club:* New (Edinburgh).

PARK, (James) Graham, CBE 1995; Senior Partner, H. L. F. Berry & Co. Solicitors, since 1983; Compliance Officer, since 1999, and Chairman, Constitutional Committee, since 2000, Conservative Party; *b* 27 April 1941; *s* of late Alderman James Park, OBE and Joan Park (*née* Sharp); *m* 1969, Susan Don; one *s. Educ:* Malvern Coll., Worcs; Manchester Univ. (LLB Hons). Articled, 1965; admitted as solicitor, 1968; Partner, H. L. F. Berry & Co. Solicitors, 1969–83. Member: Parole Bd, 1996–; Criminal Injuries Compensation Appeals Panel, 2000–. Chairman, Constituency Conservative Association: Knutsford, 1982–83; Altrincham and Sale, 1983–87; Chm., NW Area Cons. Assoc., 1992–95; Vice-Pres., 1996–98, Pres., 1998, Nat. Union of Cons. and Unionist Assocs; Pres., Nat. Cons. Convention and Mem., Bd of Mgt, Cons. Party, 1998–99. Contested (C): Crewe, Feb. and Oct. 1974; Middleton and Prestwich, 1979. Mem. Court, Salford Univ., 1989–97.

Recreations: cricket, motor-racing, cycling. *Address:* (office) 758 Oldham Road, Failsworth, Manchester M35 9XB. *T:* (0161) 681 4005.

PARK, Dame Merle (Florence), (Dame Merle Bloch), DBE 1986 (CBE 1974); Principal, Royal Ballet; Director, Royal Ballet School, 1983–98; *b* Salisbury, S Rhodesia, 8 Oct. 1937; *d* of P. J. Park, Eastlea, Salisbury, S Rhodesia, C Africa; *m* 1st, 1965, James Monahan, CBE (marr. diss. 1970; he *d* 1985); one *s*; 2nd, 1971, Sidney Bloch (*d* 2000). *Educ:* Elmhurst Ballet Sch. Founder, Ballet Sch., St Peter's Sq., W6, 1977–83. Joined Sadler's Wells Ballet, 1955; first rôle, a Mouse (Sleeping Beauty prologue); first solo, Milkmaid (Façzce); principal soloist, 1959. First danced: Blue Bird (Act III, Sleeping Beauty), 1956; Swanhilda (Coppelia), Mamzelle Angot (Mamzelle Angot), 1958; Lise (Fille Mal Gardée), 1960; Cinderella, 1962; Juliet (Romeo and Juliet), 1965; Giselle, Celestial (Shadow Play), 1967; Clara (Nutcracker), Aurora (Sleeping Beauty), 1968; Odette (Swan Lake), 1971; A Walk to Paradise Garden, 1972; Firebird, Odette/Odile (Swan Lake), Dances at a Gathering, 1973; Manon, Emilia (The Moor's Pavane), Aureole, Terpsichore (Apollo), Elite Syncopations, 1974; Lulu, 1976; Kate (The Taming of the Shrew), La Bayadère, Tuesday's Child (Jazz Calendar), Triad, Symphonic Variations, Waltzes of Spring (in Royal Opera Fledermaus), Le Papillon, 1977; Countess Larisch (Mayerling), 1978; La Fin du Jour, 1979; Mary Vetsera (Mayerling), Natalia (A Month in the Country), Adieu, 1980; Chloë (Daphnis and Chloë), Isadora, 1981; Raymonda, 1983. Queen Elizabeth Award, Royal Acad. of Dancing, 1982. *Recreations:* gardening, coaching professionals, reading. *Address:* c/o Royal Ballet School, 144 Talgarth Road, W14 9DE.

PARK, Michael; *see* Park, I. M. S.

PARK, Nicholas Wulstan, CBE 1997; director and animator of 3D stop motion films; Partner, Aardman Animations Ltd, since 1995; *b* 6 Dec. 1958. *Educ:* Sheffield Poly., Faculty of Art and Design; National Film and TV Sch. Films include: A Grand Day Out, 1989 (BAFTA award for Best Animated Short, 1990); Creature Comforts, 1990 (Acad. Award for Best Animated Short, 1990); The Wrong Trousers, 1993 (Acad. Award and BAFTA award for Best Animated Short Film, 1993); A Close Shave, 1995 (Acad. Award and BAFTA award for Best Animated Film, 1995; Emmy for Best Popular Arts Programme, 1996); Chicken Run, 2000. *Address:* Aardman Animations Ltd, Gas Ferry Road, Bristol BS1 6UN. *T:* (0117) 984 8485, *Fax:* (0117) 984 8486.

PARK, Stephen H., FCA, FCT; Finance Director, Defence Evaluation and Research Agency, since 1997; *b* 7 Aug. 1952; *m* Linda Susan; three *s* one *d*. *Educ:* Essex Univ. FCA 1977; FCT 1992. Articled clerk, Alliott Peirson & Co., 1972–77; Audit Sen., Arthur Andersen & Co., 1977–80; Financial Planning and Analysis Manager, Data Gen. Ltd, 1980–81; Hanson plc, 1981–92 (Associate Dir and Asst to Chm. and Chief Exec.); Gp Finance Dir, Sears plc, 1992–94; Dep. Finance Dir, Allders plc, 1995–97. *Address:* Room 2012, Cody Building, Defence Evaluation and Research Agency, Ively Road, Farnborough, Hants GU14 0LX.

PARKE, Prof. Dennis Vernon William, PhD, DSc; CChem, FRSC, FIBiol, FRCPath; (first) Professor and Head of Department of Biochemistry, University of Surrey, 1967–87; University Professor of Biochemistry, 1986–90; Emeritus Professor, since 1990; *b* London, 15 Nov. 1922; *e s* of William Parke and Florence Parke; *m* 1943, Doreen Joan Dunn; two *s* one *d*. *Educ:* West Ham Municipal Secondary Sch. (Gurney Scholar); Chelsea and University Colls, Univ. of London 1940–48 (MBBS 1943; BSc Special (1st cl. hons Chemistry) 1948); BS (Stanford) 1945; St Mary's Hosp. Med. Sch., London (PhD, DSc). War Service, RA RAMC, 1942–47. Head, Dept of Microbiol Chem., Glaxo Labs Ltd, 1948–49; St Mary's Hosp. Med. Sch., Univ. of London: Res. Asst to Prof. R. T. Williams, FRS, 1949–52; Lectr in Biochem., 1952–58, Sen. Lectr, 1958–62; Reader in Biochem., 1962–67; Dean, Faculty of Biol and Chem. Sciences, Univ. of Surrey, 1971–75. Visiting Professor: Univ. of Calif, Davis, 1978; Edmonton, Canada, 1984. Sometime Examnr, Univs of Dublin (Trinity), Edinburgh, Glasgow, Liverpool, London, Newcastle upon Tyne, Reading, Strathclyde, Wales, Auckland, Ibadan, Nairobi, Singapore, Sydney and Wellington. Sigma Xi Lectr, Univ. of Calif (Davis), 1978. Member: Cttee on Safety of Drugs, 1968–70; Cttee on Safety of Medicines, 1970–83; Cttee on Med. Aspects of Chemicals in Food and Environment, DHSS, 1972–86; Food Additives and Contaminants Cttee, MAFF, 1972–80; WHO Expert Panel on Food Additives, 1975–88; WHO Sci. Gp on Toxicity Evaluation of Chemicals, 1975; WHO Cons. in Indust. Toxicol., 1974, 1979, 1981, 1983; Sci. Dir, NATO Workshop on Ecotoxicology, July–Aug. 1977; Consultant to Environmental Protection Agency, Washington, 1985. Dir, Food and Veterinary Labs Ltd, 1988–92. Mem., Internat. Acad. of Environmental Safety. Editor, Xenobiotica, 1970–93. Hon. FRCP 1998; Hon. Member: Polish Soc. of Toxicology, 1984; Biochemical Soc., 1991; Soc. of Toxicology, USA, 1996; Hon. Fellow, Polish Soc. of Occupational Medicine, 1984. MD *hc* Lødz, 1995. Nobel Laureate, Medicine, 1989; Scheele Lectr and Medal, Uppsala, 1989. *Publications:* The Biochemistry of Foreign Compounds, 1968; (ed) Enzyme Induction, 1975; Drug Metabolism from Microbe to Man, 1977; Mucus in Health and Disease, 1977; Immunotoxicology, 1983; The Future of Predictive Safety Evaluation, 1987; Food, Nutrition and Chemical Toxicity, 1993; chapters in books and res. papers in biochem., pharm., toxicol. and med. jls. *Recreations:* landscape gardening, music. *Address:* Trevelen, 11 Poyle Road, Guildford, Surrey GU1 3SL. *T:* (01483) 573667.

PARKER, family name of **Earls of Macclesfield** and **Morley**.

PARKER, Alan; Senior Partner, Brunswick Group Ltd, since 1987; *b* 3 May 1956; *s* of Sir Peter Parker, *qv*.*m* 1977, Caroline Louise, *d* of Thaddeus Gordon; one *s* three *d*. Dep. Man. Dir, Broad St Associates, 1982–87. Freeman, City of London. Governor: RSC; Holland Park Sch.; Trustee, Demos. *Recreation:* friends. *Address:* Brunswick Group Ltd, 16 Lincoln's Inn Fields, WC2A 3ED. *T:* (020) 7404 5959, *Fax:* (020) 7831 2823.

PARKER, Alan Frank Neil; Director of Education, London Borough of Ealing, since 1997; *b* 24 July 1953; *s* of Frank Parker, ISO and Joan Parker; *m* 1983, Valerie Shawcross, *qv* (separated 1998). *Educ:* Leicester Poly. (BA Hons 1977); Inst. of Education, London Univ. (MA Educn 1984). UK Council for Overseas Student Affairs, 1977–83; Sen. Adminr (Educn), ACC, 1984–85; Principal Officer (Colls), Surrey CC, 1986–89; Asst Sec. (Educn), 1990–92, Educn Officer, 1992–97, AMA. Vice-Pres., 2001–02, Pres., 2002–, Soc. of Educn Officers. FRSA 1996. *Publications:* (contrib.) Visions of Post-Compulsory Education, 1992; pamphlets. *Recreations:* outdoor activities, visual and performing arts. *Address:* Education Department, London Borough of Ealing, Perceval House, 14–16 Uxbridge Road, W5 2HL.

PARKER, Alan William, CBE 1995; film director and writer; Chairman, Film Council, since 1999; *b* 14 Feb. 1944; *s* of William and Elsie Parker; *m* 1966, Annie Inglis (marr. diss. 1992); three *s* one *d*. *Educ:* Owen's Sch., Islington. Advertising Copywriter, 1965–67; Television Commercials Director, 1968–78. Wrote screenplay, Melody, 1969; wrote and directed: No Hard Feelings, 1972; Our Cissy, 1973; Footsteps, 1973; Bugsy Malone, 1975; A Turnip Head's Guide to the British Cinema, 1985; Angel Heart, 1987; Come See the Paradise, 1990; Evita, 1996; Angela's Ashes, 2000; directed: The Evacuees, 1974; Midnight Express, 1977; Fame, 1979; Shoot the Moon, 1981; The Wall, 1982; Birdy, 1984; Mississippi Burning, 1989; The Commitments, 1991; The Road to Wellville, 1995. Vice-Chm., Directors Guild of Great Britain, 1982–86; Chm., BFI, 1998–99. BAFTA Michael Balcon Award for Outstanding Contribution to British Film, 1985. *Publications: novels:* Bugsy Malone, 1976; Puddles in the Lane, 1977; *cartoons:* Hares in the Gate, 1983; Making Movies, 1998; *non-fiction:* The Making of Evita, 1997.

PARKER, Cameron Holdsworth, OBE 1993; JP; Lord-Lieutenant of Renfrewshire, since 1998; Vice-Chairman, Lithgows Ltd, 1991–97 (Managing Director, 1984–92); *b* 14 April 1932; *s* of George Cameron Parker and Mary Stevenson Parker; *m* 1st, 1957, Elizabeth Margaret Thomson (*d* 1985); three *s*; 2nd, 1986, Marlyne Honeyman, JP, FSI. *Educ:* Morrison's Acad., Crieff; Glasgow Univ. (BSc Hons). John G. Kincaid & Co. Ltd, Greenock: Asst Manager, 1958; Asst Gen. Man., 1961; Dir, 1963; Man. Dir, 1967; Chm., 1976; Chm. and Chief Exec., Scott Lithgow Ltd, Port Glasgow, 1980–83. Bd Mem., British Shipbuilders, 1977–80, 1981–83. Director, 1984–94 (Chairman, 1984–92): Campbeltown Shipyard Ltd; J. Fleming Engrg Ltd; Glasgow Iron & Steel Co. Ltd; Landcatch Ltd; Lithgow Electronics Ltd; Malakoff & Wm Moore Ltd; McKinlay & Blair Ltd; Prosper Engrg Ltd; Director: Lithgows Pty Ltd, 1984–94; Scottish Homes, 1992–96; Clyde Shaw Ltd, 1992–94. Mem. Scottish Council, CBI, 1986–92. Mem., Argyll and Clyde Health Bd, 1991–95. Pres., SSAFA, Renfrewshire, 1998–. Hon. Pres., Accord Hospice, Paisley, 1998–. Freeman, City of London, 1981; Liveryman, Co. of Shipwrights, 1981–. DL 1993, JP 1998, Renfrewshire. *Recreation:* golf. *Address:* Heath House, Rowantreehill Road, Kilmacolm, Renfrewshire PA13 4PE. *T:* (01505) 873197. *Club:* Royal Scottish Automobile (Glasgow).

PARKER, Charles George Archibald; DL; Vice Lord-Lieutenant for Oxfordshire, 1996–99; *b* 30 Jan. 1924; *s* of late Capt. Charles Edward Parker, MC, and Hilda Margaret, *o d* of Sir John Starkey, 1st Bt, DL; *m* 1958, Shirley, *d* of late Col Frank Follett Holt, TD, and of Yvonne (*née* duMont); one *d*. *Educ:* Eton; New Coll., Oxford (MA). Served War, 1942–46, Rifle Bde (Capt.), NW Europe. Times Publishing Co., NW Europe, 1949–56; Charringtons, 1956–61; BMA Pubns, 1961–76; Chm., R. Hazell & Co., 1976–. Pres., ALPSP, 1978–99. Chm., Tower Hill Improvement Trust, 1987–. Chm., Anglo-US Cttee, RAF Upper Heyford, 1991–94. FRGS 1958; FRSA 1969. Liveryman, Co. of Stationers, 1964. JP: W Central Div., London, 1978–89; Oxford City, 1990–94; High Sheriff 1989–90, DL 1992, Oxon. KStJ 1996 (Chm., St John Council, Oxon, 1989–95; Chapter-Gen., 1994–99). *Address:* The White House, Nuffield, Oxon RG9 5SR. *T:* (01491) 641289; 19 Lennox Gardens, SW1X 0DB. *T:* (020) 7589 2645. *Clubs:* Beefsteak, Garrick, White's.

PARKER, Charles Herbert; Clerk to the Worshipful Company of Mercers, since 1998; *b* 26 July 1953; *e s* of Capt. Herbert Blake Parker, RN and Diana Katharine Parker (*née* Barnwell); *m* 1977, Victoria Kathleen Scott; two *s* one *d* (and one *d* decd). *Educ:* Winchester Coll.; Trinity Coll., Oxford (MA 1979); Insead (MBA 1982). Commercial Dir, Charter plc, 1990–96. Director: Johnson Matthey plc, 1990–93; Cape plc, 1990–96. Clerk: Govs, St Paul's Schs, 1998–; Jt Grand Gresham Cttee, 1998–. Gov., Royal Ballet Sch., 2000–. *Recreations:* sailing, shooting, cricket. *Address:* Mercers' Hall, Ironmonger Lane, EC2V 8HE. *Club:* Boodle's.

PARKER, Christopher Stuart, CBE 1999; Headmaster, Nottingham High School, since 1995; *b* 16 Feb. 1947; *s* of Gerald Stuart Parker and Brenda Mary Parker (*née* Briggs); *m* 1969, Margaret, *er d* of late Charles Godfrey Hannant and Frances Hannant; two *s*. *Educ:* Windsor Grammar Sch.; Bristol Univ. (BA 1968); St Catharine's Coll., Cambridge (PGCE 1969). Asst Master, Bedford Modern Sch., 1969–72; Head of Geography, Bradford Grammar Sch., 1972–78; Dep. Head, Goffs Sch., 1978–86; Headmaster, Batley Grammar Sch., 1986–95. HMC–OFSTED Lead Insp., 1995–; Member, Admiralty Interview Bd, 1990–97; Assisted Places Cttee, ISC, 1995–; Jt Chair, HMC/GSA/Ind. Schs Bursars' Assoc. Assisted Places Wkg Party, 1996–98; Chairman: Assisted Places Cttee, 1996–, Bridges and Partnerships Cttee, 1998–99, HMC; Govt Adv. Gp on Independent/State Sch. Partnerships, 1997–. Gov., Nottingham Trent Univ., 1996–99. FRSA 1994. *Publications:* articles in American Jl of Geography, Envmt and Planning. *Recreations:* watching sport, keeping fit, escaping to France when possible. *Address:* Nottingham High School, Waverley Mount, Nottingham NG7 4ED. *T:* (0115) 978 6056. *Club:* East India.

PARKER, Christopher William Oxley, MA; JP; DL; *b* 28 May 1920; *s* of late Lieut-Col John Oxley Parker, TD, and Mary Monica (*née* Hills); *m* 1947, Jocelyn Frances Adeline, *d* of late Colonel C. G. Arkwright, Southern Rhodesia; one *s* two *d*. *Educ:* Eton; Trinity Coll., Oxford. Served War of 1939–45, 147th Field Regt (Essex Yeomanry) RA, 1939–42. Director: Strutt and Parker (Farms) Ltd; Local Dir, Chelmsford Bd, Barclays Bank, 1951–83. Mem., Nat. Trust Properties Cttee, 1974–89; Mem. Exec. Cttee, CLA, 1959–73; Pres., Essex CLA, 1987–. JP Essex, 1952; High Sheriff of Essex, 1961; DL Essex 1972. *Recreations:* golf, estate management. *Address:* Faulkbourne Hall, Witham, Essex CM8 1SP. *T:* (01376) 513385.

PARKER, (Diana) Jean, CBE 1989; Director, Goldsborough Healthcare plc, 1994–97; *b* 7 June 1932; *d* of Lewis William Reeve Morley and Amy (*née* Southwood); *m* 1959, Dudley Frost Parker (*d* 1971); one *s* one *d*. *Educ:* Kesteven and Grantham Girls' Sch.; Birmingham Univ. (BCom). CIMgt (CBIM 1986). Director: Vacu-Lug Traction Tyres Ltd, 1957–; Central Independent Television Plc, 1982–97; British Steel (Industry) Ltd, 1986–90; Grantham and Dist Hosp. NHS Trust, 1995–98; Chm., Middle England Fine Food Ltd, 1995–. Mem. Bd, E Midlands Electricity, 1983–90; Mem., E Midlands, later Eastern Adv. Bd, National Westminster Bank, 1985–92; Chm., Lincs Jt Develt Cttee, 1983–97; Chm., CBI Smaller Firms Council, 1986–88. Chm., N Lincs HA, 1987–90; Non-exec. Dir, Lincs Ambulance and Health Service Trust, 1991–92.

PARKER, Sir Douglas D.; *see* Dodds-Parker.

PARKER, Sir Eric (Wilson), Kt 1991; FCA; Chairman, Caradon plc, 1998–99 (Director, Metal Box plc, then MB-Caradon, now Caradon plc, 1985–99); *b* 8 June 1933; *s* of late Wilson Parker and Edith Gladys (*née* Wellings); *m* 1955, Marlene Teresa (*née* Neale); two *s* two *d*. *Educ:* The Priory Grammar Sch. for Boys, Shrewsbury. FCA 1967 (ACA 1956); CIMgt (CBIM 1983). Articled Clerk with Wheeler, Whittingham & Kent, Shrewsbury, 1950–55; National Service, Pay Corps, 1956–58; Taylor Woodrow Gp, 1958–64; Trafalgar House Gp, 1965–93: Finance/Admin Dir, 1969; Dep. Man. Dir, 1973; Gp Man. Dir, 1977; Chief Exec., 1983–92; Dep. Chm., 1988–93; Chm., Graham Consulting, 1993–97. Non-executive Director: European Assets Trust NV, 1972–85; Sealink UK Ltd, 1979–81; British Rail Investments Ltd, 1980–84; Evening Standard Co. Ltd, 1982–85; Touche Remnant Hldgs Ltd, 1985–89; The Royal Automobile Club (formerly The Automobile Pty Ltd), 1986–95; Hardy Oil & Gas, later British Borneo, plc, 1989–2000; Criterion Properties plc, 1998–; Job Partners Ltd, 2000–. Advr, Phoenix Develt Capital Fund, 1992–97; Mem. Adv. Bd, QMG, MoD, 1997–2000. Director: British Horseracing Bd, 1999–; Horserace Betting Levy Bd, 2000–; Pres., Race Horse Owners' Assoc., 1998– (Dir, 1994–99). Proprietor, Crimbourne Stud, 1991–. Patron, Teenage Cancer Trust. *Recreations:* sports (including golf and horseracing), wines. *Address:* Crimbourne House,

Crimbourne Lane, Wisborough Green, Billingshurst, W Sussex RH14 0HR. *Clubs:* Royal Automobile, MCC; West Sussex Golf; Dartmouth Golf and Country.

PARKER, Frederick John, (Jack), FICE, FIStructE, FIHT; Chief Highway Engineer (Under Secretary), Department of Transport, 1988–91; *b* 6 Sept. 1927; *s* of Charles Fred Parker and Eleanor Emily (*née* Wright); *m* 1955, Ann Shirley Newnham; three *d. Educ:* Shene Grammar School; Univ. of Liverpool (BEng 1948; MEng 1951). Engineer with Scott, Wilson, Kirkpatrick & Partners in London, Hong Kong and elsewhere, 1952–65; Sen. Engineer, then Partner, with Husband & Co., 1965–78; Director, W. S. Atkins & Partners, 1978–88. Institution of Highways and Transportation: Chm., Greater London Br., 1975–77; Vice-Pres., 1985; Pres., 1988. Vice-Chm., Brit. Nat. Cttee of Permanent Internat. Assoc of Road Congresses, 1988–91. *Publications:* professional papers in engineering jls. *Recreations:* athletics (Olympics 1952 and 1956, European silver medallist 1954); local affairs, music. *Address:* 43 York Avenue, East Sheen, SW14 7LQ. *T:* (020) 8876 1059. *Club:* South London Harriers.

PARKER, Geoffrey; *see* Parker, James G. and Parker, N. G.

PARKER, Prof. Geoffrey Alan, FRS 1989; Derby Professor of Zoology, School of Biological Sciences, University of Liverpool, since 1996; *b* 24 May 1944; *s* of late Dr Alan Parker and G. Ethel Parker (*née* Hill); *m* 1967, Susan Mary Wallis (*d* 1994); one *s* one *d*; *m* 1997, Carol Elizabeth Emmett; one step *d. Educ:* Stockton Heath Primary Sch.; Lymm Grammar Sch.; Univ. of Bristol (BSc (1st Cl. Hons Zoology; Rose Bracher Prize for Biology); PhD); Univ. of Cambridge (MA). Asst Lectr 1968, Lectr 1969, Sen. Lectr 1976, Reader 1980, Prof. in Dept of Envmtl and Evolutionary Biol, 1989–96, Univ. of Liverpool. Fellow of King's Coll., Cambridge, 1978–79; Nuffield Sci. Res. Fellow, 1982–83; BBSRC (formerly SERC) Sen. Res. Fellow, 1990–95. *Publications:* (jtly) Evolution of Sibling Rivalry, 1997; many scientific papers in learned jls. *Recreations:* playing jazz in local bands (clarinet), mainly Dixieland; breeding, showing and judging exhibition bantams (Hon. Sec./Treasurer, Partridge & Pencilled Wyandotte Club, 1987–94; Mem. Council, Poultry Club, 1986–90; Supreme Champion, Nat. Poultry Club GB Show, 1997). *Address:* Saunton, The Runnel, Neston, South Wirral, Cheshire L64 3TG. *T:* (0151) 336 4202.

PARKER, Geoffrey John, CBE 1985; Deputy Chairman, Maritime Transport Services Ltd, 1997–98 (Chief Executive, 1989–97); Chairman, Thamesport (London) Ltd, 1997–98; *b* 20 March 1937; *s* of Stanley John Parker and Alice Ellen Parker; *m* 1957, Hazel Mary Miall; two *s* two *d. Educ:* County Grammar Sch., Hendon. Commercial Dir, Townsend Car Ferries Ltd, 1972–74; Man. Dir, Atlantic Steam Navigation Co., 1974–87; Man. Dir, 1976–87, Chm., 1983–87, Felixstowe Dock & Rly Co.; Chairman: Larne Harbour Bd, 1983–87; European Ferries PLC, 1986–87; Chief Exec., Highland Participants, 1987–89. Mem., Nat. Bus Co., 1980–87. FCIT 1982. *Recreation:* golf. *Address:* 101 Valley Road, Ipswich, Suffolk IP1 4NF. *T:* (01473) 216003. *Club:* Ipswich Golf (Purdis Heath, Ipswich).

PARKER, Herbert John Harvey; *see* Parker, John.

PARKER, Hugh; Industrial Liaison Officer, Massachusetts Institute of Technology, since 1996; *b* 12 June 1919; *s* of Ross Parker and Ruth Baker Parker; *m* 1957, Elsa del Carmen Mijares Osorio; one *s* one *d. Educ:* Tabor Academy; Trinity Hall, Cambridge; Massachusetts Inst. of Technology. North Carolina Shipbuilding Co., 1941–43; General Electric Co., 1945–46; Ludlow Manufacturing Co., 1947–50; McKinsey & Co. Inc., 1951–84 (Sen. Dir, 1974–84). Pres., American Chamber of Commerce (UK), 1976–79. Vis. Lectr, Sloan Sch. of Mgt, MIT, 1992–96. Governor, Ditchley Foundn. *Publications:* Letters to a New Chairman, 1979; numerous articles on management and corporate governance. *Recreations:* reading, writing, cooking. *Address:* Zero Redstone Lane, Marblehead, MA 01945, USA. *Clubs:* Oxford and Cambridge; Leander; Eastern Yacht (Mass).

PARKER, Jack; *see* Parker, F. J.

PARKER, (James) Geoffrey, CBE 1996; High Master, Manchester Grammar School, 1985–94; Chairman, Teacher Training Agency, 1994–97; *b* 27 March 1933; *s* of late Ian Sutherland Parker and Kathleen Lilian Parker; *m* 1956, Ruth Major; two *d. Educ:* Alderman Newton's Sch., Leicester; Christ's Coll., Cambridge (Exhibnr); Wadham Coll., Oxford. National Service, RA, 1954–56. Asst Master, Bedford Modern Sch., 1957–66; Head of History Dept, Tonbridge Sch., 1966–75; Headmaster, Queen Elizabeth Grammar Sch., Wakefield, 1975–85. Chairman: HMC, 1991; ISIS, 1994–97. Gov., Charterhouse, 1993–; Trustee: St George's English Sch., Rome, 1992–97; Berlin British Sch., 1994–. *Recreation:* sailing. *Address:* Ty Mawr, Carno, Powys SY17 5LL. *T:* (01686) 420276.

PARKER, Dr James Gordon; Registrar of Public Lending Right, since 1991; *b* 1 June 1952; *s* of James Frank Taylor Parker and Mary Hutchison Gordon; *m* 1975, Catherine Ann Hyndman; one *s* one *d. Educ:* Stranraer High Sch.; Edinburgh Univ. (MA 1st Cl. Hons History 1974; PhD 1977). Vans Dunlop Res. Schol., Edinburgh Univ., 1974–77; Carnegie Travelling Schol. to India, 1976. Royal Commission on Historical Manuscripts: Res. Asst, 1977–87; Asst Keeper, resp. for Nat. Register of Archives, 1987–91. Mem., PLR Adv. Cttee, 1991–. *Publications:* (contrib.) The Scots Abroad, 1985; Bibliographies of British Statesmen No 5 (Lord Curzon), 1991; (contrib.) International Directory of Company Histories, vol. 4, 1991; Library & Information Briefings Series No 51 (on PLR), 1994; (ed) Proceedings of the First International Conference on Authors' Lending Right, 1996; (ed) Whose Loan is it Anyway?: essays in celebration of PLR's 20th anniversary, 1999; reviews and contribs to learned jls. *Recreations:* golf, squash, gardening, family. *Address:* Public Lending Right, Richard House, Sorbonne Close, Stockton-on-Tees, Cleveland TS17 6DA; 14 Ash Grove, Kirklevington, Yarm, Cleveland TS15 9NQ. *T:* (01642) 791445.

PARKER, James Mavin, (Jim Parker); composer and conductor; *b* Hartlepool, 18 Dec. 1934; *s* of James Robertson Parker and Margaret Mavin; *m* 1969, Pauline George; two *d*; one *d* by a previous marriage. *Educ:* various grammar schools; Guildhall Sch. of Music (AGSM 1959; Silver Medal; Hon. GSM 1986). LRAM 1959. Professional oboeist, 1959; joined the Barrow Poets, 1963. Wrote musical settings of Sir John Betjeman's poems, Banana Blush, 1973 (recorded these and subsequent settings with Sir John as speaker); wrote music for Chichester Theatre, 1974–77; music for television and films, 1977–, includes: Credo; Another Six English Towns; Good Behaviour; Wynne and Penkovsky; Mapp and Lucia; Time After Time; Betjeman's Britain; Late Flowering Love; The Miser; España Viva; The Blot (silent film made in 1921); Girl Shy (Harold Lloyd silent film); Wish Me Luck; House of Cards; Parnell and the Englishwoman; The House of Eliott; Soldier Soldier; Body and Soul; To Play the King; Goggle Eyes; Late Flowering Lust; Moll Flanders; Tom Jones; A Rather English Marriage. BAFTA awards for best television music, 1993, 1996, 1997, 1998. *Compositions* include: with William Bealby-Wright: Moonshine Rock, 1972; Mister Skillicorn Dances, 1974; with Cicely Herbert: Mayhew's London, 1978; La Comédie Humaine, 1986; (with John Betjeman) Poems (ballet), 1981; In The Gold Room (words by Oscar Wilde), 1983; (with Jeremy Lloyd) The Woodland Gospels, 1984, re-written as Heaven's Up, 1990; (with John Edmunds) Pelican Five, 1986. Recordings with Barrow Poets, Keith Michell, Peter Sellers, Harry Secombe, Twiggy, etc. *Publications:* (with Wally K. Daly) Follow the Star, 1975; (with Jeremy Lloyd) Captain Beaky, 1977; with Tom Stanier: The Shepherd King, 1979; The Burning Bush, 1980; All Aboard, 1983; Blast Off, 1986; A Londoner in New York (suite for brass), 1986; (with Tom Stanier and Chris Ellis) BabylonTimes, 1988; English Towns (for flute and piano), 1988; Mississippi Five (woodwind quintet), 1991; Lullingstone (for concert band), 1986; The Golden Section (brass quintet), 1993; Concerto for clarinet and strings, 1994; (with Alan Platt) The Happy Prince (one act opera), 1995. *Recreations:* literature, 20th Century art. *Address:* 16 Laurel Road, Barnes, SW13 0EE. *T:* (020) 8876 8442.

PARKER, James Roland Walter, CMG 1978; OBE 1968; HM Diplomatic Service, retired; Governor and Commander-in-Chief, Falkland Islands and Dependencies, and High Commissioner, British Antarctic Territory, 1976–80; *b* 20 Dec. 1919; *s* of late Alexander Roland Parker, ISM; *m* 1941, Deirdre Mary Ward (*d* 2001). Served War of 1939–45: 1st London Scottish, 1940–41. Ministry of Labour, 1938–57; Labour Attaché, Tel Aviv, 1957–60; Labour Adviser: Accra, 1960–62; Lagos, 1962–64; seconded to Foreign Office, 1965–66; Dep. High Comr, Enugu, 1966–67; Commonwealth Office (later FCO), 1968–70; Head of Chancery, Suva, Fiji, 1970–71; High Comr in The Gambia, 1972–75; Consul-Gen., Durban, 1976. *Address:* 1 St Edmund's Court, St Edmund's Terrace, NW8 7QL.

PARKER, Jean; *see* Parker, D. J.

PARKER, Sir John; *see* Parker, Sir T. J.

PARKER, Sir John; *see* Parker, Sir W. J.

PARKER, Comdr (John) Michael (Avison), CVO 1957 (MVO 1953); AM 1995; RN (retired); *b* 23 June 1920; *s* of late Capt. C. A. Parker, CBE, Royal Australian Navy, Melbourne; *m* 1st, 1943, Eileen Margaret Anne (*née* Allan) (marr. diss. 1958); one *s* one *d*; 2nd, 1962, Carol (marr. diss.; she *d* 1977); one *d* (one *s* decd); 3rd, 1976, Mrs Jean Lavinia Grice Ramsay. *Educ:* Xavier College, Melbourne, Australia. Royal Navy, 1938–47. Equerry-in-Waiting to Princess Elizabeth and the Duke of Edinburgh, 1947–52; Private Sec. to Duke of Edinburgh, 1947–57. Dir, Brain Behavioural Res. Cttee, La Trobe Univ., 1984–. Chm., Australian Dredging and Gen. Services Co., 1987–; Director: Spoerry, Australia, 1975– (Rep., Spoerry, port and town planners, France, 1980–); Spacelift Australia, 1999–. Member: Aust.-Britain Soc. (Vice-Pres.); Navy League; RSL; Australian Ballet Trust; Victorian Harbour Corp.; Chairman: Royal Navy Assoc.; Trustees, Melbourne Maritime Trust; Trustee: World Wildlife Australia; The World Ship Trust (UK). Chm., Plain English Foundn, Aust.; Dir, Day Cttee, Melbourne Foundn, 1996–. *Recreations:* painting, tennis, golf, sailing. *Address:* Santosa, 33 Albany Road, Toorak, Vic 3142, Australia. *Clubs:* Melbourne; Sandringham Yacht (Melbourne); Robe Golf (SA).

PARKER, Prof. John Stewart, DPhil; Director, Botanic Garden, and Professor of Plant Cytogenetics, since 1996, Curator, Herbarium, since 2001, University of Cambridge; Fellow, St Catharine's College, Cambridge, since 1997; *b* 12 July 1945; *s* of George Parker and Helen Parker (*née* Teare); *m* 1970, Iris Veronica Berry (marr. diss.); two *s*; *m* 1999, Mary Elizabeth Edmunds. *Educ:* Birkenhead Sch.; Christ Church, Oxford (BA 1966; MA 1970; DPhil 1971). Lectr, 1969–90, Reader, 1990–92, QMC; Prof. of Botany, Univ. of Reading, 1992–96. Member Council: RHS, 1998–99; NIAB, 1998–2001. Trustee: Royal Botanic Gardens, Kew, 1996–; Brogdale Horticultural Trust, 1999–; Science and Plants for Schs, 1998–. Hon. Res. Fellow, Natural History Mus., 1995–98. *Publications:* numerous papers in scientific jls. *Recreations:* church architecture, bird watching, landscape history, gardening, apples and cheese. *Address:* University of Cambridge Botanic Garden, Cory Lodge, Bateman Street, Cambridge CB2 1JF. *T:* (01223) 336265.

PARKER, Rt Hon. Sir Jonathan (Frederic), Kt 1991; PC 2000; **Rt Hon. Lord Justice Parker;** a Lord Justice of Appeal, since 2000; *b* 8 Dec. 1937; *s* of late Sir (Walter) Edmund Parker, CBE and late Elizabeth Mary Butterfield; *m* 1967, Maria-Belen Burns; three *s* one *d. Educ:* Winchester College; Magdalene College, Cambridge (MA). Called to Bar, Inner Temple, 1962, Bencher, 1985; practising member of the Bar, 1962–91; QC 1979; a Recorder, 1989–91; Attorney Gen. of Duchy of Lancaster, 1989–91; Judge of the High Court of Justice, Chancery Div., 1991–2000; Vice Chancellor, Co. Palatine of Lancaster, 1994–98. *Recreations:* painting, gardening. *Address:* Royal Courts of Justice, Strand, WC2A 2LL. *Club:* Garrick.

PARKER, Keith John, OBE 1993; Managing Director, Shropshire Newspapers, since 1996; Editor, Shropshire Magazine, since 1997; *b* 30 Dec. 1940; *s* of late Sydney John Parker and Phyllis Mary Parker; *m* 1962, Marilyn Ann Edwards; one *s*. Various editorial appointments; Editor, Shropshire Star, 1972–77; Editor, 1977–95, Gen. Manager, 1995, Express and Star, Wolverhampton. Director: Midland News Assoc. Ltd, 1996–; Telford Radio Ltd, 1998–. President: Guild of British Newspaper Editors, 1987–88 (Vice-Pres., 1986–87; Chm., Parly and Legal Cttee, 1991–94); Midlands Newspaper Soc., 1999–2000; Member: Press Complaints Commn, 1992–94; Data Protection Tribunal, 1996–; Parly, Editl and Regulatory Cttee (formerly Govt and Legal Affairs Cttee), Newspaper Soc., 1997–. Dir, Shropshire Chamber of Commerce, Trng and Enterprise, 2000–01. Trustee, Ironbridge Gorge Mus. Develt Trust, 2000–. *Recreations:* reading, travel. *Address:* 94 Wrottesley Road, Tettenhall, Wolverhampton, West Midlands WV6 8SJ. *T:* (01902) 758595.

PARKER, Kenneth Blades; QC 1992; a Recorder, since 2000; *b* 20 Nov. 1945; *s* of Rudolph Parker, Capt., Argyll and Sutherland Highlanders and Catherine (*née* Boyd); *m* 1967, Margaretha Constance Beyerman; three *s* one *d. Educ:* Kettering Grammar Sch.; Exeter Coll., Oxford (Class. Schol.; 1st cl. Lit. Hum. 1968; 1st cl. BCL 1973; Vinerian Schol.). Lectr in Law, Univ. of Oxford and Fellow, Exeter Coll., Oxford, 1973–76; called to the Bar, Gray's Inn, 1975; Arbitrator, Lloyd's, 1988–. Specialist Advr, H of C Select Cttee for Trade and Ind., 1991. *Publications:* (Asst Ed.) Chitty on Contracts, 23rd edn, 1972; (contrib.) Common Market Law of Competition, 1987. *Recreations:* tennis, ski-ing. *Address:* 4 Raymond Buildings, Gray's Inn, WC1R 5BP. *T:* (020) 7405 7211.

PARKER, Lyn; HM Diplomatic Service; High Commissioner to Cyprus, since 2001; *b* 25 Nov. 1952; *s* of Ronald Arthur Parker and Tjardina Torrenga; *m* 1991, Jane Elizabeth Walker; two *d. Educ:* King's Sch., Canterbury; Magdalen Coll., Oxford (BA Jurisprudence); Manchester Univ. (MA European Community Studies). Lectr in Law, Manchester Univ., 1975–78; joined HM Diplomatic Service, 1978; Second, later First, Sec., Athens, 1980–84; FCO, 1984–88; Cabinet Office, 1989–91; Head of Chancery and Political Counsellor, New Delhi, 1992–95; Counsellor (Political), UK Perm. Repn to EU, Brussels, 1995–99; Hd, Whitehall Liaison Dept, FCO, 1999–2001. *Recreations:* music, sailing, walking. *Address:* c/o Foreign and Commonwealth Office, King Charles Street, SW1A 2AH.

PARKER, (Lynda) Tanya; Social Security and Child Support Commissioner, since 2000; *d* of Sidney Sansom and Olive May (*née* Hudson); *m* 1968, Prof. David Francis Parker; two *c*. *Educ:* Manchester Univ. (LLB); Univ. of Calif, Berkeley (LLM). Called to the Bar, Gray's Inn, 1966. Regl Chm., Appeals Service, 1991–2000. *Recreations:* friends, travel, performing and visual arts. *Address:* (office) 23 Melville Street, Edinburgh EH3 7PH. *T:* (0131) 225 2201. *Club:* Royal Over-Seas League.

PARKER, Margaret Annette McCrie Johnston, (Margaret Johnston); actress; *d* of James and Emily Dalrymple Johnston; *m* 1946, Albert E. W. Parker (*d* 1974). *Educ:* North Sydney and Neutral Bay High School; Sydney University, Australia. Student, RADA; studied with Dr Stefan Hock; in repertory and acted as understudies. *Plays:* Murder without Crime, 1943; Fifth Column, 1944; Last of Summer, 1944; Time of Your Life, 1946; Shouting Dies, 1946; Barretts of Wimpole Street, 1947; Always Afternoon, 1949; Summer and Smoke, 1950; Second Threshold, 1951; The Dark is Light Enough, 1954; Sugar in the Morning, 1959; The Ring of Truth, 1959; Masterpiece, 1961. Stratford Memorial Theatre, 1956 season: Othello, The Merchant of Venice, Measure for Measure; Chichester Festival Theatre, 1966 Season: Lady Macbeth. *Films:* Rake's Progress, 1945; Man About the House, 1946; Portrait of Clare, 1949; Magic Box, 1951; Knave of Hearts, 1953; Touch and Go, 1955; Nose on her Face; Life at the Top, 1965; Psychopath; Sebastian. Television plays.

PARKER, Comdr Michael; *see* Parker, Comdr J. M. A.

PARKER, His Honour Michael Clynes; QC 1973; a Circuit Judge, 1978–94; *b* 2 Nov. 1924; *s* of Herbert Parker and Elsie Vera Parker (sometime Pres., NUT); *m* 1950, Molly Leila Franklin; one *s* two *d*. *Educ:* City of London Sch.; Pembroke Coll., Cambridge (BA, LLB). Sec., Cambridge Union, 1943. Flt-Sgt/Air Gunner, RAF, 1943–47. Called to Bar, Gray's Inn, 1949; practised in London and SE Circuit; a Recorder of the Crown Court, 1972–78. Contested (Lab) S Kensington, 1951. *Recreations:* theatre, watching cricket. *Address:* 22 Priory Avenue, W4 1TY. *Clubs:* Oxford and Cambridge, MCC.
See also B. Tizard.

PARKER, Major Sir Michael (John), KCVO 2000 (CVO 1991); CBE 1996 (MBE (mil.) 1968); Producer: Royal Tournament, 1974–99; Edinburgh Tattoo, 1991–94; *b* 21 Sept. 1941; *s* of Capt. S. J. Wilkins and V. S. M. Wilkins (*née* Parker); name changed by Deed Poll, 1959. *Educ:* Dulwich Coll. Prep. Sch.; Hereford Cathedral Sch.; RMA Sandhurst. Captain, Queen's Own Hussars, 1961–71 (produced Berlin Tattoo, 1965, 1967 and 1971); Major, TA, Special List, attached QOH, 1973–. Producer of international events, 1972–: Berlin Tattoo, 1972–88, Bandanza, 1990; Last Tattoo, 1992; Aldershot Army Display, 1974–83; Queen's Bonfire, Windsor and others, Queen's Silver Jubilee, 1977; Wembley Musical Pageant, 1979, 1981, 1985; Great Children's Party for Internat. Year of the Child, 1979; Carols for the Queen, 1979; Royal Fireworks (Prince of Wales's wedding), 1981; Heart of the Nation, son et lumière, Horse Guards, 1983, 1985; America's Cup, Newport, 1983; Great St John Party (180,000 children), Hyde Park, 1985; King Hussein of Jordan's 50th Birthday Celebration, 1985; Finale, Christmas Horse Show, Olympia, 1986–; Jordanian Royal Wedding, 1987, 1993; Coronation Anniversary Celebration, Jordan, 1988; Joy to the World, Royal Albert Hall, 1988–; Royal Equestrian Day, Oman, 1990; Fortress Fantasia, Gibraltar, 1990; Queen Mother's 90th Birthday Celebration, Horse Guards, 1990; Opening Ceremony, World Equestrian Games, 1990; Economic Summit Spectacular, Buckingham Palace, 1991; British Nat. Day Expo '92, Seville, 1992; The Queen's 40th Anniversary Celebration, 1992; Memphis in May Internat. Tattoo, 1992–94; King Hussein of Jordan's 40th Anniversary Celebrations, Unveiling of Queen Elizabeth Gate in Hyde Park, 1993; Channel Tunnel Gala Fireworks Display, D-Day Celebrations in Portsmouth, Normandy Veterans, RAH, Army Benevolent Fund, Drumhead Service, Royal Hosp. Chelsea, Pavarotti, Internat. Horse Show Modena Italy, P&O ship naming, China, 1994; P&O ship naming, Portsmouth, VE Day Celebrations in Hyde Park and Buckingham Palace, VJ Celebrations on Horse Guards, Jersey Liberation Fireworks, Horse Show in Los Angeles, 1995; Oriana Gala, Sydney, 1996; Dawn Princess Naming, Fort Lauderdale, and The Countryside Rally, Hyde Park, 1997; Fireworks, Royal Windsor Horse Show, 1998; re-opening of Albert Memorial, Hyde Park, 1998; Centenary Celebrations for King Abdul Aziz al Saud, Saudi Arabia, 1999; Royal Mil. Tattoo, Horse Guards, 2000; Queen Mother's 100th birthday celebrations, Horse Guards, 2000. Vice-Pres., Morriston Orpheus Choir; Vice-Patron, Internat. Music Centre for Blind Children, Luberadz, Poland. KStJ 1985 (OStJ 1982). Grand Officer, Order of al Istiqlal (Jordan), 1987. *Publication:* The Awful Troop Leaders Gunnery Crib, 1969. *Recreations:* painting, antiques, giving parties. *Club:* Cavalry and Guards.

PARKER, Michael Joseph Bennett; Managing Director, 1970–80, and Chairman, 1980–98, Favor Parker Ltd; *b* 22 June 1931; *s* of Henry Gordon Parker and Alice Rose Parker; *m* 1960, Tania Henrietta Tiarks; two *s* one *d*. *Educ:* Eton; Magdalene Coll., Cambridge (BA Agric., MA). Chm., Favor Parker Gp, 1977–98. Chm., Land Settlement Assoc., 1982–85; Mem., UKAEA, 1985–88. *Recreations:* country sports, wind-surfing, lying in the sun. *Address:* Gooderstone Manor, King's Lynn, Norfolk PE33 9BP. *T:* (01366) 328255.

PARKER, Michael St J.; *see* St John Parker.

PARKER, Prof. (Noel) Geoffrey, PhD, LittD; FBA 1984; Andreas Dorpalen Professor of History, Ohio State University, since 1997; *b* 25 Dec. 1943; *s* of late Derek Geoffrey Parker and Kathleen Betsy Symon; *m* 1st, Angela Maureen Chapman; one *s* one *d*; 2nd, Jane Helen Ohlmeyer; two *s*. *Educ:* Nottingham High Sch.; Christ's Coll., Cambridge (BA 1965; MA; PhD 1968; LittD 1981). Fellow of Christ's Coll., Cambridge, 1968–72; Lectr in Mod. Hist., 1972–78, Reader in Mod. Hist., 1978–82, and Prof. of Early Mod. Hist., 1982–86, St Andrews Univ. Charles E. Nowell Dist. Prof. of History, Univ. of Illinois at Urbana-Champaign, 1986–93 (Dept Chair, 1989–91); Robert A. Lovett Prof. of Military and Naval Hist., Yale Univ., 1993–96. British Acad. Exchange Fellow, Newberry Library, Chicago, 1981; J. S. Guggenheim Foundn Fellow, 2001–02; Visiting Professor: Vrije Universiteit, Brussels, 1975 (Dr phil and letters *hc*, 1990); Univ. of BC, Vancouver, Canada, 1979–80; Keio Univ., Tokyo, 1984. Lees Knowles Lectr in Mil. Hist., Univ. of Cambridge, 1984. Television scripts and broadcasts. Corres. Fellow, Spanish Royal Acad. of History, 1988–. Samuel E. Morison Prize, Soc. for Mil. Hist., 1999. Order of Isabel the Catholic (Spain), Kt Grand Cross, 1992 (Encomienda, 1988); Order of Alfonso the Wise (Spain), Kt Grand Cross, 1996. *Publications:* The Army of Flanders and the Spanish Road 1567–1659, 1972, 3rd edn 1990; The Dutch Revolt, 1977, 3rd edn 1985; Philip II, 1978, 3rd edn 1995; Europe in Crisis 1598–1648, 1979, 2nd edn 2001; Spain and the Netherlands 1559–1659, 1979, 2nd edn 1990; The Thirty Years' War, 1984, 2nd edn 1996; (ed) The World: an illustrated history, 1986, 3rd edn 1995; The Military Revolution: military innovation and the rise of the West 1500–1800, 1988, 3rd edn 1996 (Dexter Prize, 1987–90); (with Colin Martin) The Spanish Armada, 1988, 3rd edn 1999; (ed) Cambridge Illustrated History of Warfare, 1995; (ed) The Times Compact Atlas of World History, 1995, 2nd edn 2001; (ed with Robert C. Cowley) The Reader's Companion to Military History, 1996; The Grand Strategy of Philip II, 1998; edited numerous other works; articles and reviews. *Recreations:* travel, archaeology. *Address:* History Department, Ohio State University, 230 West 17th Avenue, Columbus, OH 43210–1367, USA. *T:* (614) 2926721, *Fax:* (614) 2922282.

PARKER, Sir Peter; *see* Parker, Sir W. P. B.

PARKER, Sir Peter, KBE 1993; Kt 1978; LVO 1957; Chairman, Mitsubishi Electric Europe BV, since 1996; *b* 30 Aug. 1924; *s* of late Tom and Dorothy S. Parker; *m* 1951, Gillian Rowe-Dutton, *d* of late Sir Ernest Rowe-Dutton, KCMG, CB, and of Lady Rowe-Dutton; three *s* one *d*. *Educ:* Bedford Sch.; London Univ.; Lincoln Coll., Oxford (Hon. Fellow, 1980). Major, Intelligence Corps, 1943–47. Commonwealth Fund Fellowship to Cornell and Harvard, 1950–51. Contested (Lab) Bedford, 1951. Phillips Electrical, 1951–53; Head of Overseas Dept, Industrial Soc. 1953–54; Sec., Duke of Edinburgh's Study Conf. on Human Problems of Industry, 1954–56 (Vice-Chm., UK Trustees, Commonwealth Study Confs, 1986–); joined Booker McConnell Ltd, 1956; Dir, Booker Bros McConnell & Co. Ltd, 1960–70; Chairman: Bookers Engineering & Industrial Holdings Ltd, 1966–70; Associated British Maltsters Ltd, 1971–73; Curtis Brown Ltd, 1971–76; Victoria Deep Water Terminal Ltd, 1971–76; Dawnay Day Group, 1971–76; British Railways Bd, 1976–83; Mitsubishi Electric UK Ltd, 1984–96; Whitehead Mann Gp plc, 1984–2000; Horace, Holman Gp Ltd, 1988–93; Evered, subseq. Bardon Gp, 1989–94; Apricot Computers, 1990–99; Arcadian Internat., 1990–98; Accuread, 1996–; Vice-Chm., H. Clarkson & Co. (Hldgs), 1984–93 (Dir, 1976–93; Chm., 1975–76); Director: Rockware Gp, 1976–92 (Chm., 1971–76, and 1983–92); Group 4 Securitas (UK), 1984–2000. Chairman: Clothing EDC, 1971–78; DETR (formerly DoE) Adv. Cttee on Packaging, 1996–; Nat. Steering Gp, DTI Nat. Langs for Export Campaign, 1993–. Member: British Tourist Authy Bd, 1969–75; British Airways Bd, 1971–81; Royal Nat. Theatre Bd, 1986–91; Political and Econ. Planning Exec. (Vice-Chm., 1969–70; Hon. Treasurer, 1973–78); Council, BIM (Chm., 1984–86); Engineering Industries Council, 1975–76; NEDC, 1980–83. Dir, UK-Japan 21st Century Gp, 1986–; Chm., Japan Fest. 1991. Founder Mem., Council of Foundn for Management Educn; Chairman: Westfield College, 1969–76 (Hon. Fellow, 1979); Ct of Governors, LSE, 1988–98; Dep. Chm., Ct of London Univ., 1970–. Mem. Council, Oxford Mus. of Modern Art, 1984–; Trustee, British Architecture Library Trust, 1984; Chm., Young Vic, 1993–96; Pres., Industry Council for Packaging and Envmt, 1990–99. Dimbleby Lecture, BBC TV, 1984. Hon. Patron, Langs NTO. Hon. Fellow: SIAD; SOAS, 1991; London Business Sch., 1991; LSE,1999. Hon. LLD: London, 1981; Manchester Polytechnic, 1981; Bath, 1983; Birmingham, 1991; Hull, 1996; Westminster, 1996; Hon. DBA Robert Gordon, 1997. Communicator of the Year Award, British Assoc. of Indust. Editors, 1981; Bicentenary Medal, RSA, 1990. CStJ 1983. Grand Cordon of Order of Sacred Treasure (Japan), 1991. *Publication:* For Starters (autobiog.), 1989. *Recreations:* Rugby (played for Bedford and E Mids); swimming, browsing. *Address:* 20–23 Lincoln's Inn Fields, WC2A 3ED. *T:* (020) 7936 8233.
See also Alan Parker.

PARKER, Philip Laurence; QC 2000; *b* 10 Aug. 1953; *s* of Robert Bernard Parker and Barbara Doherty Parker; *m* 1980, Mel Frisby Treacy; three *d*. *Educ:* Prior Park Coll., Bath; King Edward's Sch., Birmingham; Mathew Boulton Tech. Coll., Birmingham; Univ. of Birmingham (LLB). Called to the Bar, Middle Temple, 1976. *Recreation:* golf. *Address:* 3 Fountain Court, Steelhouse Lane, Birmingham B4 6DR. *T:* (0121) 236 5854.

PARKER, Sir Richard (William) Hyde, 12th Bt *cr* 1681; DL; *b* 5 April 1937; *o s* of Sir William Stephen Hyde Parker, 11th Bt, and Ulla Ditlef (*d* 1998), *o d* of C. Ditlef Nielsen, Dr of Philosophy, Copenhagen; *S* father, 1951; *m* 1972, Jean, *d* of late Sir Lindores Leslie, 9th Bt; one *s* three *d* (incl. twin *d*). *Educ:* Millfield; Royal Agricultural College. High Sheriff and DL, Suffolk, 1995. *Heir:* *s* William John Hyde Parker, *b* 10 June 1983. *Address:* Melford Hall, Long Melford, Suffolk CO10 9AA.

PARKER, Robert Christopher Towneley, FBA 1998; DPhil; Wykeham Professor of Ancient History, and Fellow of New College, University of Oxford, since 1996; *b* 19 Oct. 1950; *s* of Geoffrey Parker and Janet Parker (*née* Chidley); *m* 1979, Joanna Hilary Martindale; one *d*. *Educ:* St Paul's Sch., London; New Coll., Oxford (MA, DPhil). CUF Lectr in Greek and Latin Languages and Literature, Oxford Univ., and Fellow of Oriel Coll., Oxford, 1976–96. *Publications:* Miasma, 1983; Athenian Religion: a history, 1996. *Recreation:* gardening. *Address:* New College, Oxford OX1 3BN.

PARKER, Robert Stewart, CB 1998; Parliamentary Counsel, since 1992; *b* 13 Jan. 1949; *o s* of Robert Arnold Parker and Edna Parker (*née* Baines). *Educ:* Brentwood School; Trinity College, Oxford (Scholar; First in Mods; MA 1974). Called to the Bar, Middle Temple, 1975 (Harmsworth Exhibnr; Astbury Senior Law Scholarship); Lincoln's Inn *ad eundem*, 1977. Classics Master, Brentwood School, 1971–74; in practice at the Bar, 1975–80; Office of Parly Counsel, 1980; Law Commn, 1985–87; Dep. Parly Counsel, 1987–92. Freeman, City of London, 1984; Liveryman, Wheelwrights' Co., 1984. Mem., Horation Soc.; Royal Soc. of St George. MIMgt (MBIM 1984); FRSA 2000. *Publications:* Cases and Statutes on General Principles of Law (with C. R. Newton), 1980; (contrib.) The Best of Days? (Brentwood School Millennium book), 2000. *Recreations:* the Livery, cricket, bridge, books, music. *Address:* Office of the Parliamentary Counsel, 36 Whitehall, SW1A 2AY. *Clubs:* Athenæum, City Livery, Langbourn Ward.
See also E. Blackburn.

PARKER, Rt Hon. Sir Roger (Jocelyn), Kt 1977; PC 1983; a Lord Justice of Appeal, 1983–92; *b* 25 Feb. 1923; *s* of Captain Hon. T. T. Parker, DSC, RN (Retired) and Marie Louise Leonie (*née* Kleinwort); *m* 1948, Ann Elizabeth Frederika (*née* White); one *s* three *d*. *Educ:* Eton; King's Coll., Cambridge. Served Rifle Bde, 1941–46. Called to Bar, Lincoln's Inn, 1948, Bencher, 1969; QC 1961. Dep. Chm., Herts QS, 1969–71; Judge of the Courts of Appeal, Jersey and Guernsey, 1974–83; a Judge of the High Court, QBD, 1977–83. Member, Bar Council, 1968–69, Vice-Chm., 1970–72, Chm., 1972–73. Vice-Pres., Senate of Four Inns of Court, 1972–73. Treas., Lincoln's Inn, 1990–91. Conducted Windscale Nuclear Fuel Reprocessing Inquiry, 1977. Chm., Court of Inquiry into Flixborough Explosion, 1974. *Clubs:* Lansdowne; Leander.

PARKER, Prof. Roger Leslie, PhD; Professor of Music, University of Cambridge, since 1999; Fellow, St John's College, Cambridge, since 1999; *b* 2 Aug. 1951; *m* 1972, Lynden Cranham; two *s* one *d*. *Educ:* Goldsmiths' Coll., London (BMus 1973); King's Coll., London (MMus 1975; PhD 1981). Associate Prof., Cornell Univ., 1982–93; Oxford University: Lectr in Music, 1994–97; Prof. of Music, 1997–99; Fellow, St Hugh's Coll., 1994–99. Jt Gen. Ed., Donizetti Critical Edn, 1987–. Premio Giuseppe Verdi, Istituto nazionale di studi verdiani, 1985; Dent Medal, Royal Musical Assoc., 1991. *Publications:* (ed jtly) Reading Opera, 1988; (ed) Oxford Illustrated History of Opera, 1994; (ed) Oxford History of Opera, 1996; Leonora's Last Act, 1997. *Address:* St John's College, Cambridge CB2 1TP.

PARKER, Tanya; *see* Parker, L. T.

PARKER, Sir (Thomas) John, Kt 2001; DSc; FREng; Chairman, Lattice Group plc, since 2000; Deputy Chairman, 2001–May 2002, Chairman, from May 2002, RMC Group; *b* 8 April 1942; *s* of Robert Parker and Margaret Elizabeth Parker (*née* Bell); *m* 1967, Emma Elizabeth (*née* Blair); one *s* one *d*. *Educ:* Belfast Coll. of Technology; Queen's Univ. Belfast (DSc (Eng) 1985). FREng (FEng 1983); FRINA; FIMarE. Harland & Wolff, Belfast: Student Apprentice Naval Architect, 1958–63; Ship Design Staff, 1963–69 (Nat. Physical Lab. (Ship Hydrodynamics), 1964); Numerical Applications Manager, 1969–71; Prodn Drawing Office Manager, 1971–72; Gen. Manager, Sales and Projects, 1972–74; Man. Dir, Austin-Pickersgill Ltd, Sunderland, 1974–78; British Shipbuilders: Dir of Marketing, 1977–78; Bd Mem. for Shipbuilding, 1978–83; Dep. Chief Exec., 1980–83; Chm. and Chief Exec., Harland and Wolff, 1983–93; Dep. Chm. and Chief Exec., 1993–94, Chm., 1994–2000, Babcock Internat. Gp. Mem., British Coal Corp., 1986–93; Dep. Chm., 1999–, Chm., 2001–, Firth Rixson; non-executive Director: GKN, 1993–; BG plc, 1997–. Member: Council, RINA, 1978–80, 1982– (Pres., 1996–99); Bd of Governors, Sunderland Polytechnic, 1976–81; Internat. Cttee, Bureau Veritas, Paris, 1979–83; Gen. Cttee, Lloyd's Register of Shipping, 1983– (Chm. Tech. Cttee, 1996); Industrial Develt Bd of NI, 1983–87. Hon. ScD Trinity Coll. Dublin, 1986; Hon. DSc: Ulster, 1992; Abertay Dundee, 1997. *Publications:* papers to Trans IES, RINA. *Recreations:* reading, ships, sailing, music. *Address:* Lattice Group plc, 130 Jermyn Street, SW17 4UR.

PARKER, Vice-Adm. Sir (Wilfred) John, KBE 1969 (OBE 1953); CB 1965; DSC 1943; *b* 12 Oct. 1915; *s* of Henry Edmond Parker and Ida Mary (*née* Cole); *m* 1943, Marjorie Stuart Jones (*d* 1999), Halifax, NS, Canada; two *d*. *Educ:* RN College, Dartmouth. Joined Royal Navy, 1929; War Service in N Atlantic, N Russia, Mediterranean, Pacific, Korea (OBE); sunk in HMS Edinburgh and HMS Trinidad; mined in HMS Sheffield; torpedoed in HMS Newfoundland; DSC (Capture of Sicily); twice mentioned in despatches (HMS Edinburgh on N Russian convoys, and destruction of an Italian convoy, HMS Aurora 1942); Imperial Defence College, 1957; Commodore West Indies, 1958–60; Captain RNC Dartmouth, 1961–63; an Asst Chief of Defence Staff, Min. of Defence, 1963–66; Flag Officer, Medway, and Adm. Supt HM Dockyard, Chatham, 1966–69, retd 1969. Pres., RN Communication Chief Petty Officers Assoc., 1969–94. *Recreation:* 7 grandchildren (3 Mayo, 3 Panton, 1 Polak). *Address:* Flint Cottage, East Harting, Petersfield, Hants GU31 5LT. *Club:* Royal Navy.

PARKER, Sir (William) Peter (Brian), 5th Bt *cr* 1844, of Shenstone Lodge, Staffordshire; FCA; Partner, Stephenson Nuttall & Co., chartered accountants, Newark, since 1988; *b* 30 Nov. 1950; *s* of Sir (William) Alan Parker, 4th Bt and of Sheelagh Mary, *o d* of late Dr Sinclair Stevenson; *S* father, 1990; *m* 1976, Patricia Ann, *d* of R. Filtness and Mrs D. Filtness; one *s* one *d*. *Educ:* Eton. FCA 1974. *Heir: s* John Malcolm Parker, *b* 14 May 1980. *Address:* Apricot Hall, Sutton-cum-Beckingham, Lincoln LN5 0RE.

PARKER-BROWN, Hazel Christine; Director of Human Resources, Department for Transport, Local Government and the Regions (formerly Department of the Environment, Transport and the Regions), since 1999; *m*; two *s* one *d*. Head, Finance Policy (formerly Public Expenditure) Div., 1990–94, Head, Finance, Strategy and Audit Div., 1994–95, PSA; Head, Office Services Div., DoE, 1995–97; Dir, Human Resource Services, Highways Agency, DETR, 1998–99. *Address:* Department for Transport, Local Government and the Regions, 4/05A Great Minster House, 76 Marsham Street, SW1P 4DR. *T:* (020) 7944 6050; *e-mail:* hazelparker-brown@dtlr.gsi.gov.uk.

PARKER-JERVIS, Roger; DL; Deputy Chairman, CGA plc, 1982–90; *b* 11 Sept. 1931; *s* of George Parker-Jervis and late Ruth, *d* of C. E. Farmer; *m* 1958, Diana, *d* of R. St V. Parker-Jervis; two *s* one *d*. *Educ:* Eton; Magdalene College, Cambridge. Served Rifle Brigade, 1950–51, Queen Victoria Rifles, 1951–54; ADC to Governor of Tasmania, 1954–56. Bucks County Council: Mem., 1967–93; Chm., 1981–85. Mem., Milton Keynes Develt Corp., 1975–92; Pres., Timber Growers of England and Wales, 1981–83; Vice-Chm., Forestry Cttee of GB, 1981–83. Chm., Bucks Historic Buildings Trust, 1983–98; Mem., Thames and Chiltern Regl Cttee, NT, 1987–94. High Sheriff of Bucks, 1973–74, DL Bucks, 1982. *Publication:* Down the Rhône, 1997. *Recreations:* barging and caravanning in France, painting. *Address:* The Old Schoolhouse, The Green, Brill, Bucks HP18 9RU. *T:* (01844) 238025. *Clubs:* Farmers', Greenjackets.

PARKES, Sir Edward (Walter), Kt 1983; DL; FREng; Vice-Chancellor, University of Leeds, 1983–91; Chairman, Committee of Vice-Chancellors and Principals of the Universities of the United Kingdom, 1989–91 (Vice-Chairman, 1985–89); *b* 19 May 1926; *o s* of Walter Frederick Parkes; *m* 1950, Margaret Parr (*see* Margaret Parkes); one *s* one *d*. *Educ:* King Edward's, Birmingham; St John's College, Cambridge; Scholar; 1st cl. hons Mech. Sci. Tripos, 1945; MA, PhD, ScD; FIMechE. At RAE and in the aircraft industry, 1945–48; research student and subsequently Univ. Lecturer, Cambridge, 1948–59; Fellow and Tutor of Gonville and Caius College; Vis. Prof., Stanford Univ., 1959–60; Head of the Department of Engineering, Univ. of Leicester, 1960–65; Prof. of Mechanics, Cambridge, and Professorial Fellow, Gonville and Caius Coll., 1965–74 (Mem. Gen. Bd, Dep. head of Dept of Engineering); Vice-Chancellor, City Univ., 1974–78; Chm., UGC, 1978–83. Member: Brynmor Jones Cttee, 1964–65; Adv. Bd for Res. Councils, 1974–83; University and Polytechnic Grants Cttee for Hong Kong, 1974–96; Chm., Clinical Academic Staff Salaries Cttee, 1985–90. Chm., Adv. Panel on Limestone Workings in the W Midlands, 1983–95. DL W Yorks, 1990. Hon. FIMechE 1992. Hon. DTech Loughborough, 1984; Hon. DSc: Leicester, 1984; City, 1988; Hon. LLD Wales, 1984. Silver Bauhinia Star (Hong Kong), 1999. *Publications:* Braced Frameworks, 1965, 2nd edn 1974; papers on elasticity, dynamic plasticity or thermal effects on structures in Proc. and Phil. Trans. Royal Society and other jls. *Address:* The Cottage, Headington Hill, Oxford OX3 0BT. *Club:* Athenæum.

PARKES, John Alan, CBE 1996; DL; financial consultant; Chief Executive, Humberside County Council, and Clerk to Humberside Lieutenancy, 1988–96; Director, EMIH Ltd, since 1998; *b* 18 Jan. 1939; *s* of Arthur and Alice Parkes:; *m* 1963, Margaret Jill (*née* Clayton); two *d*. *Educ:* Nottingham High Sch.; Oriel Coll., Oxford (MA). IPFA 1965 (Gold Medal, 1965). Various posts from graduate traineeship, Council Finance, Derbyshire, 1961–68; Asst County Treasurer, Glos, 1968–71; Dep., then County Treasurer, Lindsey, 1971–74; Dir of Finance, Humberside, 1974–88. Member: Phildrew Ventures Adv. Cttee, 1986–96; Financial Reporting Council, 1990–95. Advr, ACC, 1976–96; Sec., 1980–86, Pres., 1987–88, Soc. of County Treasurers; Dir, Humberside TEC, 1990–96. A Public Works Loan Comr, 1996–. Mem., ERHHA, 2000–. Mem. Council, Univ. of Hull, 1996– (Treas., 2001–). Freeman, City of London, 1988. Hon. Fellow, Univ. of Humberside, 1991. DL E Riding of Yorks, 1997. *Publications:* articles on local govt finance in prof. jls. *Recreations:* walking, cars, railways. *Address:* 2 Burton Road, Beverley HU17 7EH. *T:* (01482) 881228. *Club:* Royal Over-Seas League.

PARKES, John Hubert, CB 1984; Permanent Secretary, Department of Education, Northern Ireland, 1979–90; *b* 1 Oct. 1930; 2nd *s* of Frank Hubert Parkes and Mary Edith (*née* Barnes), Birmingham; *m* 1956, Elsie Griffiths Henderson; two *s*. *Educ:* George Dixon Sch., Birmingham; Magdalen Coll., Oxford (MA). Joined NI Civil Service, 1953; Asst Sec. 1966; RCDS 1972; Dep. Sec., 1973. Hon. DLitt Ulster, 1991. *Address:* The New House, Boreham Street, Hailsham, E Sussex BN27 4SF. *Club:* Oxford and Cambridge.

PARKES, Prof. Malcolm Beckwith, DLitt; FSA; FRHistS; FBA 1993; Professor of Palaeography, University of Oxford, 1996–97, now Emeritus; Lyell Reader in Bibliography, Oxford, 1998–99; Fellow, Keble College, Oxford, 1965–97, now Emeritus; *b* 26 June 1930; *s* of Edward James Lennard Parkes and Clara Parkes (*née* Beckwith); *m* 1954, Ann Winifred Dodman; two *s*. *Educ:* Colfe's Grammar Sch.; Strasbourg Univ.; Hertford Coll., Oxford (BA Eng. Lang. and Lit. 1953; MA 1957; BLitt 1959; Gordon-Duff Prize 1959; DLitt 1985). FSA 1971; FRHistS 1977. Archivist, Lambeth Palace Library, 1957–58; Lectr in English Lang., Keble and Mansfield Colls, Oxford, 1961–65; Tutor in Eng. Lang., Keble Coll., Oxford, 1965–97; Lectr, Faculty of English, 1964–71, Lectr in Palaeography, 1971–93, Reader, 1993–96, Univ. of Oxford. Vis. Prof., Universität Konstanz, 1974 and 1980; James J. Hill Prof., Univ. of Minn (Twin Cities), 1991; Vis. Prof. of Latin, Harvard, 1998; Vis. Fellow, Princeton Univ., 1996; Mem., Inst. for Advanced Study, Princeton, 1997. Special Lecturer: in Palaeography and Diplomatic, Univ. of Durham, 1972; in Palaeography, Univ. of London, 1976; Lectures: Jarrow, 1982; Mont Follick, Univ. of Manchester, 1986; Robert F. Metzdorf, Univ. of Rochester, NY, 1987; James L. Rosier, Univ. of Pennsylvania, 1995; Fellows', Medieval Acad. of America, 2000. Mem., Standing Conf. of Nat. and Univ. Libraries, Adv. Cttee on MSS, 1977–86. Member: Wolfenbütteler Mediävistischen Arbeitskreis, 1986–; Comité Internat. de Paléographie Latine, 1986–; Council, EETS, 1995–. Corresp. Fellow, Medieval Acad. of America, 1992. *Publications:* English Cursive Book Hands 1250–1500, 1969, rev. edn 1979; (ed with A. G. Watson) Medieval Scribes, Manuscripts and Libraries: essays presented to N. R. Ker, 1978; Medieval Manuscripts of Keble College, Oxford, a descriptive catalogue, 1979; Scribes, Scripts and Readers, 1991; Pause and Effect: an introduction to the history of punctuation in the West, 1992; introductions to facsimile edns of various manuscripts; articles and chapters on topics in palaeography, book production and ownership, and history of reading in learned jls and series. *Recreation:* growing fuchsias. *Address:* Keble College, Oxford OX1 3PG. *T:* (01865) 272727.

PARKES, Margaret, (Lady Parkes), CBE 1990; JP; President, Christian Education Movement, since 1992; a Governor of the BBC, 1984–89; *b* 26 Sept. 1925; *d* of John and Dorothy Parr; *m* 1950, Sir Edward Walter Parkes, *qv*; one *s* one *d*. *Educ:* Perse School for Girls, Cambridge; Leicester Univ. (MEd). Homerton Coll., Cambridge, 1965–74. Pres., Leeds Marriage and Personal Counselling Service, 1987–91; Chairman: London Diocesan Bd of Educn, 1976–80; Colleges Adv. Cttee, Gen. Synod Bd of Educn, 1982–86; Radio London Adv. Council, 1979–83; Ripon Diocesan Bd of Educn, 1988–91; Leeds Parish Church Commn, 1988. Member: Press Council, 1978–84; Secondary Exams Council, 1983–88; Voluntary Sector Consultative Council, 1984–88; Chairman: Design and Technology Wkg Gp for Nat. Curriculum, 1988–89; NCET, 1991–92. Chm. of Governors, Whitelands Coll., London, 1981–87. JP Inner London, 1977. *Address:* The Cottage, Headington Hill, Oxford OX3 0BT.

PARKES, Terence, (Larry); freelance cartoonist, since 1957; *b* 19 Nov. 1927; *s* of Walter Thomas Parkes and Alice Parkes (*née* Hirons); *m* 1952, Jean Pauline Woodward; one *s* one *d*. *Educ:* Handsworth Grammar Sch., Birmingham; Birmingham Coll. of Art (Art Teacher's Dip.). Regular contributor to Punch, 1954–92; contrib. Private Eye, 1962–94; illustrations in Observer and Daily and Sunday Telegraph; worked for Joan Littlewood's Theatre Workshop, 1973–74; contrib. HMSO and FO pubns. Fellow, Univ. of W Midlands (formerly Birmingham Poly.), 1991. *Publications:* Man in Apron, 1959; Man in Office, 1961; Man at Work, 1962; Man at Large, 1964; Man and Dog, 1965 (US); Man in Garden, 1966; Man and Wife, 1966 (US); Large Economy Man, 1967 (US); Private Eye Cartoon Library, 1974; Art Collection, 1982; Best of Larry, 1985; Larry on Art, 1986; Larry's Great Western, 1987; Garden Lot, 1988; DIY Man, 1989; Larry on Larry (autobiog.), 1994. *Recreations:* ceramic sculpture, black Labrador dog walking. *Address:* 20 West Street, Stratford-upon-Avon, Warwickshire CV37 6DW. *T:* (01789) 293547; Flat 4, 4 Payton Street, Stratford-upon-Avon, Warwickshire CV37 6VA. *T:* (01789) 292900.

PARKHOUSE, James, MD, FFARCS; Hon. Assistant Director, Medical Careers Research Group, Oxford, since 1989 (Director, 1984–89); *b* 30 March 1927; *s* of Charles Frederick Parkhouse and Mary Alice Sumner; *m* 1952, Hilda Florence Rimmer; three *s* two *d*. *Educ:* Merchant Taylors' Sch., Great Crosby; Liverpool Univ. (MD 1955). MB ChB, 1950; MA Oxon 1960; MSc Manchester 1974. DA; FFARCS 1952. Anaesthetist, RAF Med. Br., 1953–55. Sen. Resident Anaesth., Mayo Clinic, 1957–58; First Asst, Nuffield Dept of Anaesths, Oxford, and Hon. Cons. Anaesth., United Oxford Hosps, 1958–66; Prof. and Head of Dept of Anaesths, Univ. of Manitoba, and Chief Anaesth., Winnipeg Gen. Hosp., 1967–68; Postgrad. Dean, Faculty of Med., Sheffield Univ., and Hon. Cons. Anaesth., United Sheffield Hosps, 1969–70; Prof. of Anaesths, Manchester Univ., and Hon. Cons. Anaesth., Manchester and Salford AHAs (Teaching), 1970–80; Prof. of Postgraduate Med. Educn, Univ. of Newcastle upon Tyne, and Postgrad. Dean and Dir, Northern Postgrad. Inst. for Medicine and Dentistry, 1980–84. Consultant, postgrad. med. trng, WHO, 1969–89; Specialist Adviser, H of C Social Services Cttee, 1980–81, 1984. Member: Sheffield Reg. Hosp. Bd, 1969–70; Bd, Faculty of Anaesthetists, 1971–82; Neurosciences Bd, MRC, 1977–80; GMC, 1979–89; Nat. Trng Council, NHS, 1981–84; North Tyneside HA, 1982–84. *Publications:* A New Look at Anaesthetics, 1965; Medical Manpower in Britain, 1979; Doctors' Careers, 1991; contrib. to The Lancet, BMJ and specialist jls. *Recreations:* music, golf. *Address:* 145 Cumnor Hill, Oxford OX2 9JA. *Club:* Royal Birkdale Golf.

PARKHOUSE, Nicholas, DM; FRCS; Consultant Plastic Surgeon: Queen Victoria Hospital, East Grinstead, since 1994; King Edward VII Hospital Sister Agnes (formerly King Edward VII Hospital for Officers), since 1998; *b* 7 Aug. 1957; *s* of late David Parkhouse and of Eileen Croxford, pianist; *m* 1986, Helen, *d* of late Austin and of Margaret Fitzmaurice; two *s* two *d*. *Educ:* St Paul's Sch.; Oriel Coll., Oxford (Open Exhibnr; BA 1978); Middx Hosp. Med. Sch. (MB BS 1981); DM 1990, MCh 1991, Oxon. FRCS 1985. Surgical trng at John Radcliffe Hosp., Oxford, Wexham Park, Orsett and Basildon Hosp., E Grinstead, Mt Vernon and UCH, 1982–91; Consultant Plastic Surgeon, Mt Vernon Hosp., 1991–94; Director: Rainsford Burn Centre, 1991–94; McIndoe Burns Centre, E Grinstead, 1994–97. Hunterian Prof., RCS, 1989; Visiting Professor: USC, 2001; Mayo Clinic, Minn, 2001. Ed., British Jl Plastic Surgery, 1997–. Mem. Council, British Assoc. Plastic Surgeons, 1997–. Freeman, City of London, 1998; Liveryman, GAPAN, 1998. De Havilland Trophy, 1990. *Publications:* contrib. chapters on burn injury; contrib. scientific jls on reconstructive surgery and restoration of function. *Recreations:* flying, fishing, family. *Address:* 149 Harley Street, W1G 6BN. *T:* (020) 7935 2550; The McIndoe Surgical Centre, E Grinstead, W Sussex RH19 3EB. *T:* (01342) 330364; Chelworth House, Chelwood Gate, W Sussex RH17 7JZ. *T:* (01825) 740615. *Clubs:* Vincent's (Oxford); Leander (Henley); Houghton (Stockbridge).

PARKHOUSE, Peter; Chairman, Severn NHS Trust, 1992–95; *b* 22 July 1927; *s* of late William Richard Parkhouse, MBE, and late Alice Vera Parkhouse (*née* Clarke); *m* 1st, 1950, Mary Alison Holland (*d* 1987); one *s* one *d*; 2nd, 1994, Sally Isabel Squires. *Educ:*

Blundell's Sch.; Peterhouse, Cambridge (organist, 1944–45; BA 1947; MA 1951). Instr Lieut, RN, 1947–50; Cologne Univ., 1950–51; Asst Master, Uppingham Sch., 1951–52; Asst Principal, Min. of Food, 1952; transf. to MAFF, 1955; served in private office of successive Ministers and Parly Secs, 1954–58; Principal 1958; Principal Private Sec. to Minister, 1966–67; Asst Sec. 1967; Under-Sec. 1973; Dir in Directorate-Gen. for Agriculture, Commn of European Communities, 1973–79; Under-Sec., 1979–84. Mem., EDC for Agriculture, 1982–84. Mem., Mgt Cttee, Cheltenham Internat. Fest. of Music, 1992–95. Trustee, Tetbury Hosp. Trust Ltd, 1992–93 and 1996–; Gov., Barnwood House Trust, 1996–. Dir, Nat. Star Centre, Coll. of Further Educn, Cheltenham, 1997–. *Recreations:* music (sub-organist of Tetbury Parish Church), fishing. *Address:* Stafford House, The Chipping, Tetbury, Glos GL8 8ET. *T:* (01666) 502540. *Club:* Oxford and Cambridge.

PARKIN, Prof. David John, PhD; FBA 1993; Professor of Social Anthropology, Oxford University and Fellow of All Souls College, Oxford, since 1996; *b* 5 Nov. 1940; *s* of Cecil Joseph Parkin and Rose May Parkin (*née* Johnson); *m* 1962, Monica Ann Lacey; two *s* one *d*. *Educ:* London Univ. (BA 1st cl. Hons African Studies 1962); SOAS (PhD Social Anthropol. 1965). FRAI 1966. Res. Associate, E African Inst. of Social Res., Makerere Univ. Coll., Kampala, Uganda, 1962–64 and 1966–67; School of Oriental and African Studies, University of London: Asst Lectr, 1964–65; Lectr, 1965–71; Lecturer: Sussex Univ., 1971–72; SOAS, 1972–76; Reader in Anthropol., 1976–81, Prof. of Anthropology with ref. to Africa, 1981–96, SOAS. University of Nairobi: Sen. Res. Fellow, Lang. Survey Unit, 1968–69; Sen. Res. Associate, 1977–78; Vis. Prof., Univ. of Calif, Berkeley, 1980; Directeur d'études Associé, Ecole des Hautes Etudes en Sciences Sociales, Paris, 1986, 1987 and 1993; Chercheur Associé, CNRS, Paris, 1992–93. Hon. Dir, Internat. African Inst., 1992–95. Chm., Assoc. of Social Anthropologists of GB and Commonwealth, 1989–93. MAE 1993. Rivers Meml Medal, RAI, 1985. *Publications:* Neighbours and Nationals in an African City Ward, 1969; Palms, Wine and Witnesses, 1972; (ed) Town and Country in Central and Eastern Africa, 1975; The Cultural Definition of Political Response, 1978; The Sacred Void, 1991; edited: Semantic Anthropology, 1982; The Anthropology of Evil, 1985; Swahili Language and Society, 1985; Transformations of African Marriage, 1987; Social Stratification in Swahili Society, 1989; Bush, Base, Forest, Farm, 1992; Continuity and Autonomy in Swahili Communities, 1994; The Politics of Cultural Performance, 1996; Autorité et Pouvoir chez les Swahili, 1998; Islamic Prayers Across the Indian Ocean, 2000; Anthropologists in a Wider World, 2000. *Recreations:* music, voyaging, swimming, squash. *Address:* All Souls College, Oxford OX1 4AL.

PARKIN, John Mackintosh; Administrator, Royal Courts of Justice, 1982–85, retired; *b* 18 June 1920; *s* of Thomas and Emily Cecilia Parkin; *m* Biancamaria Giuganino, Rome; two *d*. *Educ:* Nottingham High Sch.; Emmanuel Coll., Cambridge (Sen. Schol.; MA). Royal Artillery, 1939–46 (Captain). Asst Principal, WO, 1949; Registrar, RMCS, 1957–60; Principal Private Sec. to Sec. of State for War, 1960–62; Asst Sec. 1962; Sen. Fellow, Harvard Univ., 1966–67; Comd Sec., BAOR, 1967–70; Asst Under-Sec. of State, MoD, 1974–80. Mem., Royal Patriotic Fund Corpn, 1977–80. *Recreation:* history of architecture and art. *Address:* 18 Dulwich Mead, 48–50 Half Moon Lane, SE24 9HS. *T:* (020) 7274 7581.

PARKIN, Sara Lamb, OBE 2001; Programme Director, Forum for the Future, since 1994; *b* 9 April 1946; *d* of late Dr George Lamb McEwan and of Marie Munro Rankin; *m* 1969, Dr Donald Maxwell Parkin; two *s*. *Educ:* Barrs Hill School, Coventry; Edinburgh Royal Infirmary (RGN). Ward Sister, Royal Infirmary, Edinburgh, and Res. Asst, Nursing Res. Unit, Univ. of Edinburgh, 1973–74; Council Mem., Brook Adv. Centre, 1974–76; Family Planning Nurse, Leeds AHA, 1976–80. Green Party, UK: Internat. Liaison Sec., 1983–90; Speaker, 1989–92; Chair, Executive, 1992; Co-Sec., European Green Co-ordination, 1985–90. Mem. Bd, Envt Agency, 2000–. Mem., Population Concern, 1995–; Trustee, Friends of the Earth Trust, 1995–. CompICE, 1996. *Publications:* Green Parties: an international guide, 1989; Green Futures: agenda for the twenty first century, 1991; Green Light on Europe, 1991; The Life and Death of Petra Kelly, 1994. *Recreations:* reading, films, theatre, opera, walking. *Address:* (office) 227a City Road, EC1V 1JT.

PARKINS, Graham Charles; QC 1990; a Recorder, since 1989; *b* 11 Nov. 1942; *s* of John Charles Parkins and Nellie Elizabeth Parkins; *m* 1st, 1964, Carole Ann Rowe (marr. diss. 1977); two *s* one *d*; 2nd, 1977, Susan Ann Poole (*d* 1994); two *d*; 3rd, 1995, Linda Smith. *Educ:* Harwich County High Sch.; Mid-Essex Coll. of Law; LLB Hons London. Called to the Bar, Inner Temple, 1972; an Asst Recorder, 1986–89. Mem., FB Soc., Norwich. *Recreations:* golf, relaxing. *Address:* Nuestra, 14 Heathfields, Eight Ash Green, Colchester CO6 3QP. *Club:* North Countryman's (Colchester).

PARKINSON, family name of **Baron Parkinson.**

PARKINSON, Baron *cr* 1992 (Life Peer), of Carnforth in the County of Lancashire; **Cecil Edward Parkinson;** PC 1981; chairman and director of companies; *b* 1 Sept. 1931; *s* of Sidney Parkinson, Carnforth, Lancs; *m* 1957, Ann Mary, *d* of F. A. Jarvis, Harpenden, Herts; three *d*. *Educ:* Royal Lancaster Grammar Sch., Lancaster; Emmanuel Coll., Cambridge (BA 1955; MA 1961). Joined Metal Box Company as a Management Trainee; joined West, Wake, Price, Chartered Accountants, 1956; qualified 1959; Partner, 1961–71; founded Parkinson Hart Securities Ltd, 1967; Director of several cos, 1965–79, 1984–87, 1992–. Constituency Chm., Hemel Hempstead Conservative Assoc.; Chm., Herts 100 Club, 1968–69; contested (C) Northampton, 1970. MP (C) Enfield West, Nov. 1970–74, Hertfordshire South, 1974–83, Hertsmere, 1983–92. PPS to Minister for Aerospace and Shipping, DTI, 1972–74; an Asst Govt Whip, 1974; an Opposition Whip, 1974–76; Opposition Spokesman on trade, 1976–79; Minister for Trade, Dept of Trade, 1979–81; Paymaster General, 1981–83; Chancellor, Duchy of Lancaster, 1982–83; Sec. of State for Trade and Industry, June–Oct. 1983, for Energy, 1987–89, for Transport, 1989–90. Sec., Cons. Parly Finance Cttee, 1971–72; Chm., Anglo-Swiss Parly Gp, 1979–82; Pres., Anglo-Polish Cons. Soc., 1986–98. Chm., Cons. Party, 1981–83 and 1997–98. *Publication:* Right at the Centre: an autobiography, 1992. *Recreations:* reading, opera, golf, ski-ing; ran for combined Oxford and Cambridge team against Amer. Univs, 1954 and 1955; ran for Cambridge against Oxford, 1954 and 1955. *Address:* House of Lords, SW1A 0PW. *Clubs:* Beefsteak, Garrick, Pratt's; Hawks (Cambridge).

PARKINSON, Ewart West, BSc, DPA, CEng, FICE, PPRTPI, FIMunE; OStJ; development adviser in urban regeneration; Director of Environment and County Engineer, County of South Glamorgan, 1973–85; *b* 9 July 1926; *s* of Thomas Edward Parkinson and Esther Lilian West; *m* 1948, Patricia Joan Wood; two *s* one *d*. *Educ:* Wyggeston Sch., Leicester; Coll. of Technology, Leicester (BSc, DPA). Miller Prize (bridge design), Instn CE, 1953. After working with Leicester, Wakefield, Bristol and Dover Councils, he became Dep. Borough Engr, Chelmsford, 1957–60; Dep. City Surveyor Plymouth, 1960–64; City Planning Officer, Cardiff, 1964–73, specialising in reconstruction of war damaged cities and urban regeneration. Mem. Council, RTPI, 1971–83 (Vice-Pres., 1973–75, Pres., 1975–76, Chm. Internat. Affairs Bd, 1975–80); Member: Sports Council for Wales, 1966–78 (Chm., Facilities Cttee); Internat. Soc. of City and Regional Planners, 1972; Govt Deleg. to UN Conf. on Human Settlements, 1976; Watt Cttee for Energy, 1977–83 (Chm., Working Gp on Energy and Envt, 1980–83); UK mem., Internat. Wkg Party on Urban Land Policy, Internat. Fedn for Housing and Planning, 1979–85; Chairman: Internat. Wkg Party on Energy and the Environment, Internat. Fedn for Housing and Planning, 1982–85 (Life Mem. 1986); Wkg Party on Land Policy, Royal Town Planning Inst., 1983–85; Development Advisor: to Mayor of Sanya Hainan, China, 1999–2001; to cities of Nanjing and Xiamen, China, 2001; led Study Tours to Soviet Union, 1977, India and Bangladesh, 1979, China, 1980, Kenya, Zimbabwe and Tanzania, 1981; lecture visits to People's Republic of China at invitation of Ministry of Construction, 1982, 1986, 1989, 1990, 1991, 1996, 1997. Chm., Ind. Commn on Councillors' Allowances, Cardiff, 1999. Director: Moving Being Theatre Co., 1986–90; W. S. Atkins (Wales), 1988–; Pontypridd Market Co., 1988–. Chairman: STAR Community Trust Ltd, 1979–95; Intervol, 1985–89; Wales Sports Centre for the Disabled Trust, 1986–; Norwegian Church Preservation (formerly Rebuilding) Trust, 1992– (Man. Trustee, 1988); Roald Dahl Arts Project Trust, 1995–; Dir, Cardiff Action for the Single Homeless, 1988–; Vice-Pres., Wales Council for the Disabled, 1982–. Diamond Jubilee Silver Medal, Nat. Housing and Town Planning Council, 1978; many urban design awards, from Prince of Wales Cttee, Civic Trust, Concrete Soc., and Cardiff 2000. OStJ 1980 (S Glamorgan Council, 1975–). *Publications:* The Land Question, 1974; And Who is my Neighbour?, 1976; articles in prof. jls on land policy, energy and the environment, and public participation. *Recreations:* working, travelling, being with family, talking with friends. *Address:* 42 South Rise, Llanishen, Cardiff CF14 0RH. *T:* (029) 2075 6394.

PARKINSON, Graham Edward, CBE 2001; a District Judge (Magistrates' Courts) (formerly Metropolitan Stipendiary Magistrate), since 1982; Chief Metropolitan Stipendiary Magistrate, 1997–2000; a Recorder, since 1989; a Chairman, Inner London Youth, and City and Family Proceedings Court; *b* 13 Oct. 1937; *s* of Norman Edward Parkinson and late Phyllis (*née* Jaquiss); *m* 1963, Dinah Mary Pyper; one *s* one *d*. *Educ:* Loughborough Grammar Sch. Admitted Solicitor of the Supreme Court, 1961. Articled to J. Tempest Bouskell, Leicester, 1955–60; Asst Solicitor: Slaughter & May, 1961–63; Amery Parkes & Co., 1963–67; Partner, Darlington and Parkinson, Ealing, 1967–82. Pres., Central and S Mddx Law Soc., 1978–79; Mem. Cttee, London Criminal Courts Solicitors Assoc., 1978–80; Chm., Legal Cttee, Magistrates' Assoc., 1992–97; Mem., Lord Chancellor's Adv. Cttee for Inner London, 1997–99. *Recreations:* opera, reading, playing piano and church organ. *Address:* Bow Street Magistrates' Court, Bow Street, WC2E 7AS.

PARKINSON, Howard, CVO 1998; HM Diplomatic Service; Deputy High Commissioner, Mumbai (Bombay), since 2000; *b* 29 March 1948; *s* of Ronald Parkinson and Doris (*née* Kenyon); *m* 1974, Linda Wood; one *s* one *d*. *Educ:* Openshaw Tech. High Sch., Manchester. BoT, 1967–69; joined HM Diplomatic Service, 1969; Latin American Floater, 1972–74; Vice Consul: Tegucigalpa, 1974–75; Buenos Aires, 1975–78; Second Sec., Maputo, 1978–81; Second, later First Sec., FCO, 1981–85; First Sec. (Commercial), Lisbon, 1985–89; on loan to British Gas, 1989–91; Asst Hd, Migration and Visa Dept, FCO, 1991–94; Consul Gen., Washington, 1994–96; Commercial and Econ. Counsellor, Kuala Lumpur, 1997–2000. *Recreations:* travel, music, reading. *Address:* c/o Foreign and Commonwealth Office, King Charles Street, SW1A 2AH.

PARKINSON, Dr James Christopher, MBE 1963; TD 1962; Deputy Director, Brighton Polytechnic, 1970–83, retired; *b* 15 Aug. 1920; *s* of late Charles Myers Parkinson, Pharmacist, Blackburn, Lancs; *m* 1950, Gwyneth Margot, *d* of late Rev. John Raymond Harrison, Macclesfield, Ches; three *s*. *Educ:* Queen Elizabeth's Gram. Sch., Blackburn; Univ. Coll., Nottingham. BPharm, PhD (London), FRPharmS. Served in Mediterranean area, Parachute Regt, 1943–46; Parachute Regt TA: 16 AB Div. and 44 Parachute Bde, 1949–63 (Major). Lectr, Sch. of Pharmacy, Univ. of London, 1948–54; Head of Sch. of Pharmacy, Brighton Coll. of Technology, 1954–64; Dep. Sec., Pharmaceutical Soc. of Gt Britain, 1964–67; Principal, Brighton Coll. of Technology, 1967–70. Mem. various pharmaceutical cttees of British Pharmacopœia, British Pharmaceutical Codex and British Veterinary Codex, 1956–64; Examr, Pharmaceutical Soc. of Gt Britain, 1954–64; Mem. Bds of Studies in Pharmacy and Librarianship, CNAA, 1965–75. Mem., Mid-Downs DHA, 1984–87. Member, Gen. Synod of Church of England, 1970–85. *Publications:* research papers on applied microbiology in Jl Appl. Bact. and Jl Pharm. (London) and on pharmaceutical education in Pharm. Jl. *Recreation:* do-it-yourself. *Address:* 5 Marchants Close, Hurstpierpoint, West Sussex BN6 9XB. *T:* (01273) 833369.

PARKINSON, Michael, CBE 2000; interviewer, television presenter, writer; *b* 28 March 1935; *m* Mary Heneghan; three *s*. *Educ:* Barnsley Grammar School. Journalist on local paper; The Guardian; Daily Express; columnist on Sunday Times; radio work; has written for Punch, The Listener, New Statesman; Columnist: Daily Mirror, 1986–90; Daily Telegraph, 1991–; Editor, Catalyst, 1988–; Producer and interviewer: Granada's Scene; Granada in the North; World in Action; What the Papers Say; reporter on 24 Hours (BBC); Exec. producer and presenter, London Weekend Television, 1968; Presenter: Cinema, 1969–70; Tea Break, Where in the World, The Movie Quiz, 1971; host of own chat show, Parkinson, 1971–82 and 1998–; TV-am, 1983–84; Parkinson in Australia, 1979–84; The Boys of '66, 1981 (documentary); Give Us a Clue, 1984–92; All Star Secrets, 1984–86; The Skag Kids, 1985; Parkinson One-to-One, 1987–88; Desert Island Discs, BBC Radio 4, 1986–88; LBC Radio, 1990; Help Squad, 1991–92; Ghostwatch, 1992; Surprise Party, 1993; A League Apart: 100 years of Rugby League, BBC2, 1995; Going for a Song, BBC1, 1995–99; Parkinson on Sport, R5, 1994–97; Parkinson's Sunday Supplement, R2, 1996–. Founder-Director, Pavilion Books, 1980–97. Fellow, BFI, 1998. Hon. Dr: Lincs, 1999; Humberside, 1999. Sports Feature Writer of the Year, British Sports Journalism Awards, 1995; Sony Radio Award, 1998; Sports Writer of the Year, British Press Awards, 1998; Media Personality of the Year, Variety Club, 1998; Most Popular Talk Show, Nat. TV Awards, 1998, 1999; Best Light Entertainment, BAFTA, 1999; Media Soc. annual award, 2000. *Publications:* Football Daft, 1968; Cricket Mad, 1969; (with Clyde Jeavons) Pictorial History of Westerns, 1972; Sporting Fever, 1974; (with Willis Hall) Football Classified, 1974; George Best: an intimate biography, 1975; (with Willis Hall) A-Z of Soccer, 1975; Bats in the Pavilion, 1977; The Woofits, 1980; Parkinson's Lore, 1981; The Best of Parkinson, 1982; Sporting Lives, 1992; Sporting Profiles, 1995; Michael Parkinson on Golf, 1999. *Address:* c/o Stella Management Ltd, 74 Wimpole Street, W1M 7DD.

PARKINSON, Sir Nicholas (Fancourt), Kt 1980; consultant; *b* 5 Dec. 1925; *s* of late Rev. C. T. Parkinson, MA Oxon, and Dorothy Fancourt (*née* Mitchell); *m* 1952, Roslyn Sheena Campbell; two *d*. *Educ:* King's Sch., Parramatta, NSW; Univ. of Sydney (BA). Entered Aust. Foreign Service, 1951; Third Sec., Cairo, 1953–56; First Sec., Hong Kong, 1958–61; Counsellor, Moscow, Wellington, Kuala Lumpur, 1963–67; Chm., Jt Intell. Cttee, Dept of Defence, Canberra, 1967–70; High Comr, Singapore, 1970–74; Dep. Sec., Dept of For. Affairs, Canberra, 1974–76; Ambassador to the US, 1976–77 and 1979–82; Sec., Dept of For. Affairs, Canberra, 1977–79. Dir, Sears World Trade (Australia),

1983–86. Mem., ABC Adv. Council, 1991–93. *Recreation:* bridge. *Address:* 62 Collings Street, Pearce, ACT 2607, Australia. *T:* (2) 62861004. *Club:* Commonwealth (Canberra).

PARKINSON, Ronald Dennis; Assistant Curator, Victoria and Albert Museum, 1978–98; *b* 27 April 1945; *s* of Albert Edward Parkinson and Jennie Caroline Clara Meager. *Educ:* St Dunstan's Coll.; Clare Coll., Cambridge (MA). Res. Assistant: Paul Mellon Foundn for British Art, 1971–72; V&A Mus., 1972–74; Asst Keeper, Tate Gall., 1974–78. *Publications:* (ed jtly) Richard Redgrave, 1988; Catalogue of British Oil Paintings 1820–1860 in the Victoria and Albert Museum, 1990; British Watercolours at the Victoria and Albert Museum, 1998; Constable, the man and his art, 1998; articles in Apollo, Burlington Mag., Cambridge Res., Connoisseur, Country Life, Times Higher Educn Sup. *Recreations:* reading, shopping. *Address:* 13 Childebert Road, SW17 8EY. *Club:* Algonquin.

PARKINSON, Stephen Lindsay; Deputy Legal Secretary to Law Officers, since 1999; *b* 15 June 1957; *s* of late Rev. Edward James Parkinson and of Dr Mary Vere Parkinson (*née* Young); *m* 1982, Penelope Jane Venvell; one *s* two *d*. *Educ:* Hampton Grammar Sch.; Chippenham Sch.; University Coll. London (LLB 1979). Called to the Bar, Lincoln's Inn, 1980; pupillage, 1980–82; sub-editor, Butterworths Legal Publishers, 1982–84; Legal Asst, Dept of DPP, 1984–86; Sen. Crown Prosecutor, then Asst Br. Crown Prosecutor, CPS, 1986–88; Law Officers' Dept, 1988–91; Hd, Internat. Co-operation Unit, CPS, 1991–92; Asst Solicitor, DTI, 1992–96; Hd, Company/Chancery Litigation Gp, Treasury Solicitor's Dept, 1996–99. *Recreations:* reading, music, walking. *Address:* Legal Secretariat to the Law Officers, 9 Buckingham Gate, SW1E 6JP.

PARKS, Timothy Harold; author; *b* 19 Dec. 1954; *s* of late Harold James Parks and of Joan Elizabeth Parks (*née* MacDowell); *m* 1979, Rita Maria Baldasarre; one *s* one *d*. *Educ:* Westminster City Sch.; Downing Coll., Cambridge (BA 1977); Harvard Univ. Mktg Exec., Tek Translation and Internat. Print, 1979–80; freelance teacher and translator, Verona, 1981–85; Lectr, Univ. of Verona, 1985–. Vis. Lectr, Istituto Universitario di Lingue Moderne, Milan, 1992–. Mem., Soc. of Authors, 1986–. *Publications: fiction:* Tongues of Flames, 1985 (Somerset Maugham Award, Betty Trask Award); Loving Roger, 1986 (John Llewellyn Rhys Award); Home Thoughts, 1987; Family Planning, 1989; Goodness, 1991; Shear, 1993; Mimi's Ghost, 1995; Europa, 1997; Destiny, 1999; as John MacDowell: Cara Massimina, 1990; *essays:* Adultery and Other Diversions, 1998; Hell and Back, 2001; *non-fiction:* Italian Neighbours, 1992; An Italian Education; Translating Style, 1997; translations from Italian of books by several authors, incl. Calasso, Calvino, Moravia, and Tabucchi; contribs to short story and essay collections, conf. proceedings and jls. *Address:* c/o Antony Harwood Ltd, Office 109, Riverbank House, 1 Putney Bridge Approach, SW6 3JD. *T:* (020) 7384 9209.

PARKYN, Brian (Stewart); General Manager, Training Services, British Caledonian Airways Ltd, 1981–88; *b* 28 April 1923; *o s* of Leslie and Gwen Parkyn, Whetstone, N20; *m* 1951, Janet Anne, *o d* of Charles and Jessie Stormer, Eastbourne; one *s* one *d*. *Educ:* King Edward VI Sch., Chelmsford; technical colleges. Principal, Glacier Inst. of Management (Associated Engineering Ltd), 1976–80. Director: Scott Bader Co. Ltd, 1953–83; Hunting Industrial Plastics Ltd, 1979–83; Halmatic Ltd, 1983–88. British Plastics Federation: Chm., Reinforced Plastics Gp, 1961–63; Mem. Council, 1959–75. Vice Pres., Rubber and Plastics Inst., 1972–75. Has travelled widely and lectured in N and S America, Africa, Australasia, India, Japan, USSR and China, etc.; Plastics Lectr, Worshipful Co. of Horners, 1967. Contested (Lab) Bedford, 1964; MP (Lab) Bedford, 1966–70; Mem., Select Cttee on Science and Technology, 1967–70; Chm., Sub-Cttee on Carbon Fibres, 1969; contested (Lab) Bedford, Oct. 1974. Member: Council, 1970–94, Ct, 1970–, Cranfield Univ. (formerly Inst. of Technology); Council, RSA, 1976–82 (Hon. Treas., 1977–82). FIM. *Publications:* Democracy, Accountability and Participation in Industry, 1979; various papers and books on polyester resins and reinforced plastics. *Recreations:* writing, industrial democracy. *Address:* 4 Meadow Road, Southam, Warwicks CV47 1EN. *T:* (01926) 815133.

PARMINTER, Kathryn Jane, (Kate); Director, Council for the Protection of Rural England, since 1998; *b* 24 June 1964; *d* of James Henry Parminter and June Rose Parminter (*née* Cayless); *m* 1994, Neil Sherlock; one *d*. *Educ:* Millais Sch.; Collyer's Sixth Form Coll., Horsham; Lady Margaret Hall, Oxford (MA Theol.). Graduate trainee, Nestlé Co., 1986–88; Parly researcher for Simon Hughes, MP, 1988–89; Sen. Account Exec., Juliette Hellman Public Relns, 1989–90; Royal Society for the Prevention of Cruelty to Animals: Public Relations Officer, 1990–92; Head: Campaigns and Events, 1992–95; Public Affairs, 1995–96; Press and Public Affairs, 1996–98. Mem. (Lib Dem), Horsham DC, 1987–95. Chm., Campaign for Protection of Hunted Animals, 1997–98. *Publications:* (contrib.) Working For and Against Government, in Pressure Group Politics in Modern Britain, 1996; (contrib.) The Progressive Century: the future of the Centre Left in Britain. *Recreations:* pre-Raphaelite paintings, walking. *Address:* 12 Binscombe Lane, Farncombe, Godalming, Surrey GU7 3PN. *T:* (01483) 428184. *Club:* National Liberal.

PARMOOR, 4th Baron *cr* 1914; **Milo Cripps;** *b* 18 June 1929; *s* of 3rd Baron Parmoor, DSO, TD, DL, and Violet Mary Geraldine, *d* of Sir William Nelson, 1st Bt; *S* father, 1977. *Educ:* Ampleforth; Corpus Christi College, Oxford. *Heir: cousin* Michael Leonard Seddon Cripps, *qv*. *Address:* Dairy, Sutton Veny, Wilts BA12 7AL.

PARNABY, Dr John, CBE 1987; FREng; Group Director, LucasVarity plc, 1996–98; Director and Chief Executive Officer, Geared Systems Inc., 1996–98; Chairman and Chief Executive Officer, BPSE Ltd, since 1998; *b* 10 July 1937; *s* of John Banks Parnaby and Mary Elizabeth Parnaby; *m* 1959, Lilian Armstrong; three *s* one *d*. *Educ:* Durham Univ. (BSc Mech. Engrg, 1961); Glasgow Univ. (PhD Control Systems Engrg, 1966). MIEE 1966 (Hon. FIEE 1989). FIProdE 1978; FIMechE 1978 (Hon. FIMechE 1998). FREng (FEng 1986). Technical Apprentice, 1954–58, Ironworks Develt Engr, 1961–62, United Steel Co.; Res. Asst, Univ. of Durham, 1962–63; Lectr in Mech. Engrg, Univ. of Glasgow, 1963–66; Sen. Projects Engr, Albright & Wilson Ltd, 1966–67; Works Man., Solway Chemicals Ltd, 1967–70; University of Bradford: Sen. Lectr, 1970–73; Prof. of Manufg Systems Design, 1973–80 (Chm., Sch. of Manufacturing Systems Engrg, 1975–80); Technical and Marketing Dir, subseq. Jt Man. Dir, Rieter Scragg Ltd, 1980–82; Gen. Man., Dunlop Ltd, 1982–83; Gp Dir, Technology, Lucas Industries, 1983–90; Man. Dir and CEO, Lucas Electronic Systems Products (formerly Lucas Applied Technology Sector), 1990–96; Chairman: Lucas Metier, later Lucas Mgt Systems, 1990–96; Lucas Engrg and Systems Ltd, 1990; Lucas Gp Dir, Develt, 1995–96; Knowledge Process Software plc, 2000–; Think Digital Solutions plc, 2001–. Director: Scottish Power plc, 1994–; Molins plc, 1998–99; Jarvis plc, 1999–2001. Chm., Anglo-German Res. Cttee, British Council, 1990–. Chm., Link Bd, DTI/OST, 1993–96; Mem., DTI/EPSRC Innovative Manufg Initiative Mgt Cttee, 1998–. Vis. Hon. Prof. of Manufacturing Systems Engrg, Univ. of Birmingham, 1984–2000; Vis. Hon. Prof. of Engrg, Univ. of Cambridge, 1999–. Pres., IProdE, 1989; Pres., IEE, 1995–96 (Dep. Pres., 1993–95); Mem. Council, Royal Acad. of Engrg, 1997–; Senator, Engrg Council, 1997–. Mem. Queen's Anniversary Award Cttee, 1996–. Mem. Council, Univ. of Aston, 1999–. Hon. FIMechE; Hon. FIEE. Hon. Fellow: Coventry Poly., 1989; Sheffield Poly., 1991; Univ. of Wales, 1995. Hon. DTech: Liverpool Poly., 1990; CNAA 1990; Loughborough, 1991; Napier, 1997; Hon. DSc Hull, 1991; DUniv Open, 1992; Hon. DEng: Bradford, 1993; Newcastle, 2000. Gold Medal, Instn of Manufg Engrs, 1987; Silver Medal, 1990, Faraday Medal, 1994, IEE. *Publications:* Minicomputers and Microcomputers in Engineering and Manufacture, 1986; Manufacturing Systems Engineering Miniguide Handbook, 1989, 2nd edn 1992; over 40 papers in engrg and management jls on manufg systems, control engrg, process engrg, business process systems engrg and machinery design. *Recreations:* hockey, sailing, golf. *Address:* Crest Edge, Beechnut Lane, Solihull, W Midlands B91 2NN. *T:* (0121) 705 4348; *e-mail:* drjparnaby@aol.com.

PARNELL, family name of **Baron Congleton**.

PARR, John Robert; Chairman, Airline-Consumer Forum, International Air Transport Association, Geneva, 1995–99; *b* 25 Sept. 1934; *s* of Henry George Parr and Hilda Frances Parr (*née* Pattison); *m* 1993, Prof. Margaret Dolores O'Reilly. *Educ:* Dulwich Coll.; Merton Coll., Oxford (Postmaster; MA). MCIT 1996. British Iron and Steel Fedn, 1959–65 (incl. Dep. Sec., 1963); Principal, Industrial Policy Div., Dept of Economic Affairs, 1965–68; British Steel Corp., 1968–73; Dir-Gen., British Footwear Manufacturers Fedn, 1973–76; Divl Head, Gen. Secretariat, Council of Ministers of EC, 1976–89, Hon. Dir, 1989; Dir-Gen., Air Transport Users Council, 1989–96. Mem., Labour Party. *Recreations:* political history of 19th and 20th centuries, opera and other forms of classical music, Irish country life. *Address:* 41 Albany Court, 56 Vincent Square, SW1P 2NE.

PARR, Martin; freelance photographer and film-maker; *b* 23 May 1952; *s* of Donald Parr and Joyce Parr (*née* Watts); *m* 1980, Susan P. Mitchell; one *d*. *Educ:* Manchester Poly. (1st cl. Creative Photography 1973). Freelance photographer, 1973–; Mem., Magnum, photo co-operative, 1994–; freelance TV film-maker, 1996–; Vis. Prof. of Photography, Univ. of Industrial Arts, Helsinki, 1990–92; Visiting Lecturer: Nat. Coll. of Art and Design, Dublin, and Chelsea Sch. of Art, 1975–82; Sch. of Documentary Photography, Newport, 1982–84; W Surrey Coll. of Art and Design, 1983–. Exhibitions worldwide, including: Photographer's Gall., 1977, 1981, 1982, 1987, 1995; Whitechapel Art Gall., 1978; Hayward Gall., 1979; Serpentine Gall., 1986; Nat. Centre of Photography, Paris, 1987, 1995; RA, 1989; RPS, 1989; Janet Borden Gall., NY, 1991, 1992, 1996; Nat. Mus. of Photography, Bradford, 1998; retrospective exhibn, Barbican Gall., 2002. Work in permanent collections incl. V&A Mus., MOMA, NY, Walker Art Gall., Liverpool. Arts Council of GB Photography Award, 1975, 1976, 1979. *Publications:* Bad Weather, 1982; A Fair Day, 1984; (with Ian Walker) The Last Resort: photographs of New Brighton, 1986, 2nd edn 1998; (jtly) The Actual Boot: the photographic postcard 1900–1920, 1986; The Cost of Living, 1989; Signs of the Times, 1992; Home and Abroad, 1993; From A to B, 1994; Small World, 1995; West Bay, 1997; Flowers, 1999; Common Sense, 1999; Boring Postcards, 1999; Auto Portrait, 2000; Think of England, 2000; Boring Postcards USA, 2000; Boring Postcards Germany, 2001. *Recreation:* working! *Address:* c/o Magnum, 5 Old Street, EC1V 9HL. *T:* (020) 7490 1771.

PARR, (Thomas) Donald, CBE 1986; Chairman, William Baird PLC, 1981–98; *b* 3 Sept. 1930; *s* of Thomas and Elizabeth Parr; *m* 1954, Gwendoline Mary Chaplin; three *s* one *d*. *Educ:* Burnage Grammar Sch. Own business, 1953–64; Chm., Thomas Marshall Investments Ltd, 1964–76; Director: William Baird PLC, 1976–; Vendôme Luxury Gp (formerly Dunhill Holdings) PLC, 1986–98; Hepworth PLC, 1989–98; Kwik Save Group, 1991–98. Chm., British Clothing Industry Assoc., 1987–91; Member: NW Industrial Develt Bd, 1975–87; Ct of Governors, UMIST, 1984–. *Recreation:* sailing. *Address:* Homestead, Homestead Road, Disley, Stockport, Cheshire SK12 2JP. *T:* (01663) 765211. *Clubs:* Boodle's, Royal Ocean Racing; Royal Yacht Squadron (Cowes).

PARRINDER, Prof. (Edward) Geoffrey (Simons); Professor of Comparative Study of Religions, University of London, at King's College, 1970–77, Professor Emeritus, 1977; *b* 30 April 1910; *s* of William Patrick and Florence Mary Parrinder; *m* 1936, Esther Mary Burt; two *s* one *d*. *Educ:* private sch.; Richmond Coll., London Univ.; Faculté libre de théologie protestante, Montpellier. MA, PhD, DD London. Minister of Methodist Church, Dahomey and Ivory Coast, 1933; ordained 1936; Principal, Séminaire Protestant, Dahomey, 1936–40, 1945–46; Methodist Church: Redruth, 1940; Dahomey, 1943; Guernsey, 1946; Lectr in Religious Studies, 1949, Sen. Lectr, 1950–58, UC Ibadan; Reader in Comparative Study of Religions, Univ. of London, 1958–70; Dean, Faculty of Theology, KCL, 1972–74. Hon. Sec., Internat. Assoc. for History of Religions, British Br., 1960–72, Pres., 1972–77; President: London Soc. for Study of Religion, 1980–82; London Soc. of Jews and Christians, 1981–90 (Hon. Life Pres., 1990). Lectures: Charles Strong (Australian Church), 1964; Wilde, in Natural and Comparative Religion, Oxford Univ., 1966–69; Teape, Delhi, Madras, 1973. Vis. Prof., Internat. Christian Univ., Tokyo, 1977–78; Vis. Lectr, Surrey Univ., 1978–83. FKC 1972; Hon. DLitt Lancaster, 1975. *Publications:* West African Religion, 1949; Bible and Polygamy, 1950; West African Psychology, 1951; Religion in an African City, 1953; African Traditional Religion, 1954; Story of Ketu, 1956; Introduction to Asian Religions, 1957; Witchcraft, 1958; (ed) African Ideas of God, 1961; Worship in the World's Religions, 1961; Comparative Religion, 1962; Upanishads, Gītā and Bible, 1962; What World Religions Teach, 1963; The Christian Debate, 1964; The World's Living Religions, 1965; A Book of World Religions, 1965; Jesus in the Qur'ān, 1965; African Mythology, 1967; Religion in Africa, 1969, repr. as Africa's Three Religions, 1976; Avatar and Incarnation, 1970; Dictionary of Non-Christian Religions, 1971; (ed) Man and his Gods, 1971, repr. as Illustrated History of the World's Religions, 1983; The Indestructible Soul, 1973; Themes for Living, 1973; The Bhagavad Gita, a Verse Translation, 1974; Something after Death?, 1974; The Wisdom of the Forest, 1975; Mysticism in the World's Religions, 1976; The Wisdom of the Early Buddhists, 1977; Sex in the World's Religions, 1980; Storia Universale delle Religioni, 1984; Encountering World Religions, 1987; A Dictionary of Religious and Spiritual Quotations, 1989; The Sayings of the Buddha, 1991; Son of Joseph, 1992; A Concise Encyclopedia of Christianity, 1998; The Wisdom of Jesus, 2000; In the Belly of the Snake, 2000; articles and reviews in jls of theology, African and Asian religions and Annual Register, 1958–. *Recreations:* travel, gardening, literature. *Address:* 31 Charterhouse Road, Orpington, Kent BR6 9EJ. *T:* (01689) 823887.

See also D. M. Boston.

PARRIS, Matthew Francis; author, journalist and broadcaster; *b* 7 Aug. 1949; *s* of Leslie Francis Parris and Theresa Eunice Parris (*née* Littler). *Educ:* Waterford School, Swaziland; Clare Coll., Cambridge (BA Hons); Yale Univ., USA (Paul Mellon Fellowship). Foreign Office, 1974–76; Conservative Research Dept, 1976–79; MP (C) West Derbyshire, 1979–86; Presenter, Weekend World, LWT, 1986–88. Mem., Broadcasting Standards Council, 1992–97. Various journalistic awards. *Publications:* Inca-Kola: a traveller's tale of Peru, 1990; So Far So Good, 1991; Look Behind You!, 1993; (ed) Scorn, 1994; Great Parliamentary Scandals, 1995; (ed) Scorn with Added Vitriol, 1995; (ed jtly) Read My Lips: a treasury of things politicians wish they hadn't said, 1996; I Couldn't Possibly Comment: parliamentary sketches, 1997; The Great Unfrocked: two thousand years of church scandal, 1998; (ed) Scorn with Extra Bile, 1999. *Address:* c/o The Times, Pennington Street, E98 1DD.

PARROTT, Andrew Haden; conductor and musicologist; Music Director, London Mozart Players, since 2000; *b* 10 March 1947. *Educ:* Merton Coll., Oxford (schol.; BA 1969). Dir of Music, Merton Coll., Oxford, 1969–71; formerly musical assistant to Sir Michael Tippett. Founded Taverner Choir, 1973, then Taverner Consort and Taverner Players, for performance of music ranging from medieval to late 18th century. Débuts: BBC Prom. concerts, 1977; EBU, 1979; La Scala, 1985; Salzburg, 1987; Guest Conductor worldwide of symphony and chamber orchs, opera and contemporary music. Over 50 recordings. Hon. Res. Fellow, Royal Holloway, Univ. of London, 1995–; Hon. Sen. Res. Fellow, Univ. of Birmingham, 2000–. *Publications:* (ed jtly) New Oxford Book of Carols, 1992; The Essential Bach Choir, 2000; contrib. learned jls. *Address:* c/o Allied Artists, 42 Montpelier Square, SW7 1JZ.

PARROTT, Brian Robert; Director of Social Services, Surrey County Council, since 1995; *b* 24 Sept. 1949; *s* of late Derek Charles Parrott and Lilian Esme Parrott (*née* Thoy); *m* 1974, Pamela Elizabeth Rigby; two *s*. *Educ:* Bedford Modern Sch.; Downing Coll., Cambridge (BA 1971; MA 1974); Univ. of Kent (CQSW 1973). Social Worker, Camden LBC, 1973–76; Sen. Social Worker, Notts CC, 1976–81; Area Officer, Haringey LBC, 1981–85; an Asst Dir, 1985–90, First Asst Dir, 1990–95, Social Services, Suffolk CC. Mem., Exec. Council, 1999–, Chm., Resources Cttee, 2000–, Assoc. of Dirs of Social Services. FRSA 1999. *Publications:* (jtly) A Unitary Approach to Social Work: application in practice, 1981; contribs to social work and local govt publications and jls. *Recreations:* mountain walking, running, sport. *Address:* 3 Jervis Close, Holbrook, Ipswich, Suffolk IP9 2RR. *T:* (01473) 328056.

PARROTT, Jasper William; Director, since 1969, Chairman and Managing Director, since 1987, Harrison/Parrott Ltd; *b* 8 Sept. 1944; *s* of Sir Cecil Parrott, KCMG, OBE and of Lady (Ellen) Parrott; *m* 1974, Cristina Ortiz, pianist; two *d*. *Educ:* Tonbridge Sch.; Peterhouse, Cambridge (MA). With Ibbs and Tillett, concert mgt, 1965–69. *Publications:* Beyond Frontiers, 1984 (trans German, Japanese, French, Russian, Norwegian, Finnish and Icelandic). *Recreations:* books, tennis, languages, gardens. *Address:* c/o Harrison/Parrott Ltd, 12 Penzance Place, W11 4PA. *T:* (020) 7229 9166.

PARROY, Michael Picton; QC 1991; a Recorder, since 1990; *b* 22 Oct. 1946; *s* of Gerard May and Elizabeth Mary Parroy; *m* 1978, Susan Patricia Blades (*née* Winter). *Educ:* Malvern College; Brasenose College, Oxford (MA). Called to the Bar, Middle Temple, 1969, Bencher, 2001. Trustee, Wincanton Recreational Trust, 2000–. *Publication:* Road Traffic, in Halsbury's Laws of England, 4th edn. vol. 40, 1983. *Recreations:* gardening, food and wine, dog walking. *Address:* First Floor, 3 Paper Buildings, Temple, EC4Y 7EU.

PARRY; *see* Jones Parry and Jones-Parry.

PARRY, family name of **Baron Parry**.

PARRY, Baron *cr* 1975 (Life Peer), of Neyland, Dyfed; **Gordon Samuel David Parry;** DL; President, Milford Docks Company, since 1991 (Chairman, 1984–91); *b* 30 Nov. 1925; *s* of Thomas Lewis Parry and Anne Parry (*née* Evans); *m* 1948, Glenys Parry (*née* Incledon); one *d*. *Educ:* Neyland Board Sch.; Pembroke County Intermediate Sch.; Trinity Coll., Carmarthen; Univ. of Liverpool (Dipl. Advanced Educn). Teacher: Coronation Sch., Pembroke Dock, 1945–46; Llanstadwell Voluntary Primary Sch., Neyland, 1946–47; Barn St Voluntary Sch., Haverfordwest, 1947; County Primary Sch., Neyland, 1947–52; Librarian, Housemaster, County Sec. Sch., Haverfordwest, 1952–62 and 1963–68; Inst. of Educn, Univ. of Liverpool, 1962–63; Warden, Pembs Teachers' Centre, 1969–78. Former member: Welsh Develt Authority; Gen. Adv. Council, IBA; Welsh Arts Council; Schs Council Cttee for Wales; Member: Fac. of Educn, Univ. Coll. of Wales Aberystwyth; Council, Open Univ. (Chm., Adv. Cttee on Studies in Educn, 1978–83); British Tourist Authority, 1978–84; President: Pembs Br., Multiple Sclerosis Soc.; Pembs Spastics Soc.; Spastics Soc., Wales; Commonwealth Games Appeal Cttee for Wales, 1979; Keep Wales Tidy Cttee, 1979– (Chm., 1979–86); BICSc, 1981–91; Tidy Britain (formerly Keep Britain Tidy) Gp, 1991–96 (Chm., 1986–91); Chairman: Wales Tourist Bd, 1978–84; British Cleaning Council, 1983–87; Keep Britain Beautiful Campaign, 1986–96; Clean World Internat., 1991–96; British Travel Educn Trust; Vice President: Nat. Chamber of Trade, 1980; Internat. Year of Disabled People in Wales, 1979; Nat. Soc. for Mentally Handicapped Children, S Wales Region; Soc. of Handicapped Drivers in Wales; Welsh Nat. Council of YMCAs. Chm., Taylorplan Services, 1987–96; Non-exec. Bd Mem., Marriott Services UK Ltd, 1996–. Contested (Lab) Monmouth 1959, Pembroke 1970, and Feb. and Oct. 1974. Writer, broadcaster, and TV panel Chm. President: Neyland Ladies' Choir, 1991–; Côr Meibion De Cymru (S Wales Male Choir), 1998–. Burgess, Guild of Freemen of Haverfordwest. FRSA; Fellow: Tourism Soc., 1979; HCIMA, 1980; BICSc, 1981; James Cook Univ., N Qld, Aust, 1989. DL Dyfed, 1993. Hon. Fellow: Trinity Coll., Carmarthen, 1990; Polytechnic of Wales, 1991; Pembrokeshire Coll., 1998. Hon. Fellow, Inst. of Wastes Management. Hon. DEd Wales, 1992. *Publication:* Trinity '43–'45: a legacy for life (autobiog.), 1996. *Recreations:* travel; watching Welsh Rugby XV win the Grand Slam; reading. *Address:* Willowmead, 52 Port Lion, Llangwm, Haverfordwest, Pembrokeshire, Dyfed SA62 4JT. *T:* (01646) 600667.

PARRY, Alan; President, Johnson & Higgins Ltd, 1989–97 (Chairman, 1987–89); *b* 30 Oct. 1927; *s* of George Henry James Edgar Parry and Jessica Cooke; *m* 1954, Shirley Yeoman; one *s* one *d*. *Educ:* Reedham School. Leonard Hammond Ltd, 1941; Sedgwick Collins Ltd, 1948, Dir, 1960; Dir, Man. Dir, Dep. Chm. and Chm., Sedgwick companies and subsidiaries, to 1981; Chm., Carter Brito e Cunha, 1982–87. Mem., Lloyd's Insurance Brokers' Assoc., 1961–64, 1970–73, 1975–78 (Chm., 1977); Mem. Council, BIBA, and LIBA and BIBA rep. on Cttee on Invisible Exports, 1977; Mem., Cttee of Lloyd's, 1979–82, 1985–88 (Dep. Chm., 1987–88). *Recreations:* flyfishing, drama. *Address:* The Quarry, Firtoll Road, Mayfield, East Sussex TN20 6NG.

PARRY, Anthony Joseph, QFSM 1990; County Fire Officer, 1985–90, and Chief Executive, County Fire Service, 1986–90, Greater Manchester; *b* 20 May 1935; *s* of Henry Joseph Parry and Mary Elizabeth McShane; *m* 1959, Elizabeth Therese Collins; three *s* one *d*. *Educ:* St Francis Xavier's Coll., Liverpool. MIFireE. Liverpool Fire Bde, 1958; Fire Service Technical Coll., 1967; Gloucestershire Fire Service, 1969; Avon Fire Service, 1974; Lancashire County Fire Service, 1975. Long Service and Good Conduct Medal, 1978. *Address:* 10 Oakenclough Drive, Bolton BL1 5QY.

PARRY, David Johnston; His Honour Judge Parry; a Circuit Judge, since 1995; *b* 26 Aug. 1941; *s* of Kenneth Johnston Parry and Joyce Isobel Cooper (formerly Parry); *m* Mary Harmer; one *s* three *d*. *Educ:* Merchant Taylors' Sch., Northwood; St Catharine's Coll.; Cambridge (MA Hons). Admitted Solicitor, 1969; Partner, later Jt Sen. Partner, Dixon Ward, Richmond, 1969–95; Asst Recorder, 1986–91; Recorder, 1991–95. Co-Chm., Richmond Legal Advice Service, 1969–95; Administrator, Richmond Duty Solicitors' Scheme, 1990–95; part-time Chm., Independent Tribunal Service, 1993–96. Member: Law Society; London Criminal Courts Solicitors' Assoc. *Recreations:* family activities, reading, music, television, DIY, sport, lying on a beach, relaxing in the sun, travel. *Address:* 16 The Green, Richmond, Surrey TW9 1QD. *T:* (020) 8940 4051. *Club:* Old Merchant Taylors'.

PARRY, Prof. Eldryd Hugh Owen, OBE 1982; MD, FRCP; Chairman, Tropical Health and Education Trust, since 1989; *b* 28 Nov. 1930; *s* of Dr Owen Parry and Dr Constance Parry (*née* Griffiths); *m* 1960, Helen Madeline, *d* of Humphry and Madeline House; one *s* three *d*. *Educ:* Shrewsbury; Emmanuel Coll., Cambridge; Welsh Nat. Sch. of Medicine (BChir 1955; MA; MD). FWACP. Junior posts, Cardiff Royal Infirmary, Nat. Heart Hosp., Hammersmith Hosp., 1956–65; seconded to UCH, Ibadan, 1960–63; Associate Prof., Haile Selassie I Univ., Addis Ababa, 1966–69; Prof. of Medicine, Ahmadu Bello Univ., 1969–77; Foundn Dean, Faculty of Health Sciences, Univ. of Ilorin, Nigeria, 1977–80; Dean and Prof. of Medicine, Sch. of Med. Scis, Kumasi, 1980–85; Dir, Wellcome Tropical Inst., 1985–90; Sen. Res. Fellow, 1990–95, Vis. Prof., 1996–, Hon. Fellow, 1997, LSHTM. Special Prof., Dept of Med., Univ. of Nottingham, 1997–. Albert Cook Meml Lectr, Kampala, 1974. Member: Med. and Dental Council, Ghana, 1980–85; Council, All Nations Christian Coll., 1986–99. Hon. FRSTM&H 1993 (Donald Mackay Medal, 1998). Frederick Murgatroyd Prize, RCP, 1973. *Publications:* Principles of Medicine in Africa, 1976; papers on medicine in the tropics in med. jls. *Recreations:* tennis, Wales, old Welsh furniture. *Address:* 21 Edenhurst Avenue, SW6 3PD.

See also J. P. H. House.

PARRY, Emyr Owen; solicitor; a Recorder of the Crown Court, 1979–99; District Judge at the Caernarfon Group of County Courts and the District Registry of the High Court at Llangefni, Caernarfon and Rhyl, since 1992; *b* 26 May 1933; *s* of Ebenezer Owen Parry and Ellen Parry; *m* 1959, Enid Griffiths; one *s* one *d*. *Educ:* Caernarfon Grammar Sch.; University Coll. of Wales, Aberystwyth (LLB Hons Wales, 1954). Admitted solicitor, 1957. Estabd own practice in Llangefni, Anglesey, 1958; formed partnership (Emyr Parry & Davies) with Mrs Elinor C. Davies, 1964; Dep. Circuit Judge, 1975. Chairman: Social Security (formerly National Insurance) Appeals Tribunal, Holyhead Area, 1969–92; Medical Appeal Tribunal, 1986–92; Solicitor Mem., Lord Chancellor's County Court Rule Cttee, 1975–80. *Recreations:* cricket, music, theatre.

PARRY, John Alderson, CBE 1985; BBC National Governor for Wales, 1986–91; *b* 3 Jan. 1934; *s* of Albert Parry and Mary Parry (*née* Alderson); *m* 1st, 1959, Joan Rathbone (marr. diss. 1992); one *s* one *d*; 2nd, 1998, Ruth Tomkins-Russell (*d* 2001). *Educ:* Leighton Park, Reading; Christ's College, Cambridge (MA, Vet MB). MRCVS; FRAgS 1986. Veterinary practice, Brecon, 1958–96. Mem., Agricl Adv. Council, 1969–73; Chairman: Hill Farming Res. Orgn, 1981–87 (Mem., 1971–85); Welsh Agricl Adv. Cttee, BBC, 1978–85; Welsh Office Hydatid Control Steering Cttee, 1981–96; Member: Sec. of State for Wales' Agricl Adv. Cttee, 1978–94; AFRC, 1982–92 (Chm., Animals Res. Cttee, 1983–87); Develt Bd for Rural Wales, 1985–88; Council, Royal Welsh Agricl Soc., 1986–; Dir, Animal Disease Res. Assoc., 1987–92. President: BVA, 1976–77; RCVS, 1986–87. Chm., Governing Body, Inst. of Grassland and Animal Prodn, AFRC, 1987–94; Gov., McCauley Land Use Res. Inst., 1987–94. Freeman, City of London; Liveryman, Co. of Farriers. *Recreations:* field sports. *Address:* Trefin, Cradoc Road, Brecon, Powys LD3 9PF. *T:* (01874) 622649. *Clubs:* Oxford and Cambridge, Farmers'; Hawks (Cambridge); Cardiff & County (Cardiff).

PARRY, Prof. Jonathan Patrick, PhD; FBA 2001; Professor of Anthropology, London School of Economics and Political Science, since 1993; *b* 10 Sept. 1943; *s* of Dennis Arthur Parry and Kathleen Aroma Parry (*née* Forbes); *m* 1972, Margaret Dickinson; one *s* one *d*. *Educ:* King's Coll., Cambridge (BA 1965; PhD 1971). Lectr, Dept of Social Anthropol., Univ. of Edinburgh, 1971–74; Lectr, 1974–84, Sen. Lectr, 1984–86, Reader, 1986–93, Dept of Social Anthropol., subseq. Dept of Anthropol., LSE. *Publications:* Caste and Kinship in Kangra, 1979; (ed with M. Bloch) Death and the Regeneration of Life, 1982; (ed with M. Bloch) Money and the Morality of Exchange, 1989; Death in Banaras, 1994; (ed with J. Breman) The World of Indian Industrial Labour, 1999; (ed with R. Guha) Institutions and Inequalities, 1999. *Recreations:* reading novels, cinema. *Address:* Department of Anthropology, London School of Economics and Political Science, Houghton Street, WC2A 2AE.

PARRY, Margaret Joan; Headmistress of Heathfield School, Ascot, 1973–82; *b* 27 Nov. 1919; *d* of W. J. Tamplin, Llantrisant, Glamorgan; *m* 1946, Raymond Howard Parry; two *s* one *d*. *Educ:* Howell's Sch., Llandaff, Cardiff; Univ. of Wales. Hons English Cl I. Married to a schoolmaster at Eton; taught and coached interesting people from time to time; Examiner for: Civil Service, LCC, Schools Examination Boards. Patron, Univ, of Buckingham, 1983. *Recreations:* books, music, tapestry. *Address:* Carreg Gwaun, 23a Murray Court, Ascot, Berks SL5 9BP. *T:* (01344) 626299.

PARRY, Rev. Canon Marilyn Marie, PhD; Canon Residentiary of Christ Church, Oxford and Diocesan Director of Ordinands, Oxford, since 2001; *b* 24 Aug. 1946; *d* of Robert Warren Fortey and Jane Carolyn (*née* Turner); *m* 1969, Rev. David Thomas Newton Parry; one *s* one *d*. *Educ:* Western Coll., Oxford, Ohio (BA Maths, Theol. and Philos. 1968); Univ. of Manchester (MA Theol. 1977, PhD 2000); Gilmore Scheme (IDC 1978). Diocese of Manchester: Accredited Lay Worker, 1978; ordained deaconess, 1979, deacon, 1987, priest, 1994; Curate, St Peter, Westleigh, 1978–85 and C of E Chaplain, Leigh Infirmary, 1983–85; Chaplain's Asst, N Manchester Gen. Hosp., 1985–90 and Chaplaincy Team Leader, Booth Hall Children's Hosp., 1989–90; Northern Ordination Course: New Testament Tutor, 1990–97; Dir of Studies, 1991–97; Nat. Advr for Pre-Theol Educn and Selection Sec., Ministry Div., Archbishops' Council, 1997–2001. *Recreations:* playing clarinet (chamber music), walking, conversation with friends. *Address:* Diocesan Church House, North Hinksey, Oxford OX2 0NB. *T:* (01865) 208289.

PARRY, Prof. Martin Lewis, OBE 1998; PhD; Professor of Environmental Management, Department of Geography, since 1994, and Director, Jackson Environment Institute, since 1996, University College London; *b* 12 Dec. 1945; *s* of John Fyson Parry and Frances Joan (*née* Stewart); *m* 1968, Cynthia Jane Mueller; two *d*. *Educ:* Univ. of Durham (BA Hons); Univ. of West Indies (MSc); Univ. of Edinburgh (PhD). Lectr, Univ. of Edinburgh, 1972–73; University of Birmingham: Lectr, 1973–86; Sen. Lectr, 1986–88; Reader, 1988–89; Prof. of Envmtl Management, 1989–91; Prof. of Envmtl Management, and IBM Dir, Envmtl Change Unit, Oxford Univ., 1991–94. *Publications:* Climatic Change, Agriculture and Settlement, 1976; The Impact of Climatic Variations on Agriculture, Vol. 1 1988, Vol. 2 1989; Climate Change and World Agriculture, 1990; Economic Implications of Climate Change in Britain, 1995. *Recreations:* riding, ski-ing, sailing. *Address:* Department of Geography, University College London, Gower Street, WC1E 6BT.

PARRY, Richard Hawley Grey, PhD, ScD; FICE; civil engineering consultant, since 1967; Secretary General, International Society for Soil Mechanics and Geotechnical Engineering, 1981–99; *b* 27 April 1930; *s* of late Joseph Grey Parry and Ena Rachel (*née* Hawley); *m* 1954, Frances Irene McPherson; three *s* one *d*. *Educ:* Swinburne Technical Coll.; Melbourne Univ. (BCE 1951; MEngSc 1954; MEng 1963); Imperial Coll., London (PhD 1957); MA 1967, ScD 1983, Cantab. Res. Student and Sen. Demonstrator,

Melbourne Univ., 1952–54; Shell Res. Student, Imperial Coll., London, 1954–56; Engr, Soil Mechanics Ltd, 1956–57; Res. Officer, CSIRO, 1957–60; Dir, Foundation Engineering (Aust.) Pty Ltd, 1960–67; Colombo Plan consultant on bridge sites, Sarawak, 1963–64; Lectr, Engrg Dept, Cambridge Univ., 1967–90; Fellow, Pembroke Coll., Cambridge, 1970–90, now Fellow Emeritus. MASCE (Life Mem.). Prize, 1978, Skempton Gold Medal, 1999, British Geotechnical Soc. *Publications:* (ed) Stress-Strain Behaviour of Soils, 1971; Mohr Circles, Stress Paths and Geotechnics, 1995; technical papers in learned jls and proceedings. *Recreations:* archaeology, history of civil engineering, allotment, golf. *Address:* 5 Farm Rise, Whittlesford, Cambridge CB2 4LZ. *T:* (01223) 832024. *Club:* Gog Magog Golf.

PARRY, Richard James; Director of Education, City and County of Swansea, since 1998; *b* 4 Oct. 1953; *s* of John and Margaret Parry; *m* 1st, 1981, Barbara Parish; one *s* one *d*; 2nd, 1991, Gwyneth Selby; one *d*. *Educ:* Emmanuel Coll., Cambridge (BA, MA). Teacher, 1976–88: Head of Maths, Hatfield Sch., 1979–82; Head of Maths, Fearnhill Sch., Letchworth, 1983–88; Maths Adv. Teacher, Herts, 1985–88; Maths Advr, 1988–93, Chief Advr, 1993–96, W Glam; Asst Dir of Educn, 1996–97, acting Chief Educn Officer, 1997–98, City and County of Swansea. *Recreations:* golf, sport generally. *Address:* c/o Education Department, County Hall, Swansea SA1 3SN. *T:* (01792) 636351.

PARRY, Victor Thomas Henry, MA Oxon; FLA; Director of Central Library Services and Goldsmiths' Librarian, University of London, 1983–88; *b* 20 Nov. 1927; *s* of Thomas and Daisy Parry; *m* 1959, Mavis K. Russull; two *s* one *d*. *Educ:* St Julian's High Sch., Newport; St Edmund Hall, Oxford (MA); University College, London (DipLib). FLA 1959. Manchester Public Libraries, 1950–56; Colonial Office and CRO Library, 1956–60; Librarian, Nature Conservancy, 1960–63; British Museum (Natural History), 1963–74; Chief Librarian and Archivist, Royal Botanic Gdns, Kew, 1974–78; Librarian, SOAS, Univ. of London, 1978–83. Sen. Examiner, LA, 1959–68. Chm., Circle of State Librarians, 1966–68; Mem., Adv. Cttee, British Library Dept of Humanities and Social Scis (formerly Reference Div.), 1983–90; Council Member: Sir Anthony Panizzi Foundn, 1983–89; London Soc., 1984–88. Chm., Friends of Univ. of London Liby, 1998–. FRAS 1981; FRSA 1985. *Publications:* contrib. prof. books and jls. *Recreations:* ball games, books, bridge, railways. *Address:* 69 Redway Drive, Twickenham TW2 7NN. *T:* (020) 8894 0742. *Club:* Surrey CC.

PARRY, Prof. William, PhD; FRS 1984; Professor of Mathematics, University of Warwick, 1970–99, now Emeritus; *b* 3 July 1934; *s* of late Richard Parry and Violet Irene Parry; *m* 1958, Benita (*née* Teper); one *d*. *Educ:* University Coll. London (BSc 1956); Univ. of Liverpool (MSc 1957); Imperial Coll. of Science and Technol., London (PhD 1960). Lectr, Univ. of Birmingham, 1960–65; Sen. Lectr, Univ. of Sussex, 1965–68; Reader, Univ. of Warwick, 1968–70. Member: Labour Party; NCCL. *Publications:* Entropy and Generators in Ergodic Theory, 1969; Topics in Ergodic Theory, 1981; (with S. Tuncel) Classification Problems in Ergodic Theory, 1982; articles in Trans Amer. Math. Soc., Amer. Jl of Maths, and Annals of Maths. *Recreations:* theatre, concerts, walking. *Address:* Manor House, High Street, Marton CV23 9RR. *T:* (01926) 632501.

PARRY BROWN, Arthur Ivor; *see* Brown.

PARRY-EVANS, Air Chief Marshal Sir David, GCB 1991 (KCB 1985); CBE 1978; Royal Air Force, retired; *b* 19 July 1935; *s* of late Group Captain John Parry-Evans, MRCS, LRCP, DLO, and Dorothy Parry-Evans; *m* 1960, Ann, 2nd *d* of late Charles Reynolds and Gertrude Reynolds; two *s*. *Educ:* Berkhamsted School. Joined RAF, 1956; served FEAF, Coastal Command, United States Navy, RN Staff Coll., 1958–70; Headquarters Strike Command, 1970–74; OC 214 Sqn, 1974–75; OC RAF Marham, 1975–77; MoD, 1977–81 (Director of Defence Policy, 1979–81); Comdt, RAF Staff Coll., 1981–82; AOC Nos 1 and 38 Groups, RAF Strike Comd, 1982–85; C-in-C RAF Germany, and Comdr, Second ATAF, 1985–87; Dep. Chief of Defence Staff (Progs and Personnel), 1987–89; Air Mem. for Personnel, 1989–91. Chief Comdr, St John Ambulance, 1992–98. Gov., Royal Star and Garter Home, 1991–99 (Chm., 1996–99). KStJ 1992. *Address:* c/o National Westminster Bank, 26 Spring Street, W2 1WE. *Club:* Royal Air Force.

PARRY EVANS, Mary Alethea, (Lady Hallinan); a Recorder of the Crown Court, 1978–97; *b* 31 Oct. 1929; *o c* of Dr Evan Parry Evans, MD, JP, and Dr Lilian Evans; *m* 1955, Sir (Adrian) Lincoln Hallinan (*d* 1997); two *s* two *d*. *Educ:* Malvern Girls' Coll.; Somerville Coll., Oxford (BCL, MA). Called to Bar, Inner Temple, 1953; Wales and Chester Circuit. Member: Cardiff City Council, 1961–70; S Glamorgan CC, 1972–81; S Glamorgan Health Authority, 1977–81. Lady Mayoress of Cardiff, 1969–70. *Address:* (chambers) 33 Park Place, Cardiff CF1 3BA. *T:* (029) 2023 3313.

PARRY JONES, Terence Graham; *see* Jones, Terry.

PARSLOE, Prof. Phyllida; Chairman, North Bristol NHS Trust, since 1999; Professor of Social Work, Bristol University, 1978–96, now Emeritus Professor and Senior Research Fellow; *b* 25 Dec. 1930; *d* of late Charles Guy Parsloe and Mary Zirphie (*née* Munro). *Educ:* Bristol Univ. (BA, PhD); London Univ. (Cert. in Mental Health). Probation Officer, Devon CC, 1954–59; Psychiatric Social Worker, St George's Hospital, 1959–65; Lectr, London Sch. of Economics, 1965–70; Associate Prof., Sch. of Law, Indiana Univ., 1970–73; Prof. of Social Work, Univ. of Aberdeen, 1973–78; Pro-Vice Chancellor, 1988–91, Warden of Wills Hall, 1991–97, Bristol Univ. Member: Central Council for Educn and Training in Social Work, 1986–; Commonwealth Scholarships Commn. *Publications:* The Work of the Probation and After Care Officer, 1967; Juvenile Justice in Britain and America, 1978; (with Prof. O. Stevenson) Social Service Teams: the practitioner's view, 1978; Social Service Area Teams, 1981; report to the Sec. of State for Scotland on Social Work in Prisons, 1987; (with S. Macara *et al*) Data Protection in Health and Social Services, 1988; Aiming for Partnership, 1990; (ed) Risk Assessment in Social Care and Social Work, 1999; contribs to: British Jl of Social Work, Community Care, Social Work Today, British Jl Criminology. *Recreations:* hill walking, crafts, gardening. *Address:* School for Policy Studies, 8 Woodland Road, Bristol BS8 1TN; Lion House, 9 Castle Street, Thornbury, S Glos BS35 1HA.

PARSONS, family name of **Earl of Rosse**.

PARSONS, Adrian; *see* Parsons, C. A. H.

PARSONS, Alan; *see* Parsons, T. A.

PARSONS, Alfred Roy, AO 1986; High Commissioner for Australia in the UK, 1984–87, retired; *b* 24 May 1925; *s* of W. G. R. Parsons and R. E. Parsons; *m* 1958, Gillian Tryce Pigot; two *s* one *d*. *Educ:* Hobart High School; Univ. of Tasmania (postgraduate research; BCom); Canberra University College. Dept of Foreign Affairs, 1947; Djakarta, 1950–53, Rangoon, 1956–58, Berlin, 1961–62; Aust. Mission to UN, NY, 1962–64; Counsellor, Djakarta, 1964–66; High Comr, Singapore, 1967–70; First Asst Sec., Canberra, 1970–73; High Comr, Kuala Lumpur,1973–76; Dep. Sec., periodically Acting Sec., Dept of Foreign Affairs, 1978–83. Chm., Commonwealth Observer Gp on Namibia, 1989. Member: Australia Japan Foundn, 1978–83; Australia China Council. Pres., ACT Br., Lord's Taverners Australia. *Recreations:* golf, reading. *Address:* 11 Hotham Crescent, Deakin, Canberra, ACT 2600, Australia. *Clubs:* Commonwealth (Canberra); Royal Canberra Golf, Canberra Wine and Food.

PARSONS, (Charles) Adrian (Haythorne); Consultant to National Solicitors Network; consultant to solicitors on charity matters; *b* 15 June 1929; *s* of Dr R. A. Parsons and Mrs W. S. Parsons (*née* Haythorne); *m* 1951, Hilary Sharpe; one *d*. *Educ:* Bembridge Sch.; Wadham Coll., Oxford. Called to Bar, Gray's Inn, 1964. Coutts & Co., Bankers, 1952–64; joined Charity Commn, 1964; Dep. Comr, 1972; Comr, 1974–89; Head of Legal Staff, 1981; Unit Trust Ombudsman, 1989–90; National Solicitors Network Ombudsman, 1989–94. *Address:* 6 Garrick Close, The Green, Richmond, Surrey TW9 1PF. *T:* (020) 8940 3731. *Club:* Oxford and Cambridge.

See also Sir R. E. C. F. Parsons.

PARSONS, Colin James, FCA; Group Chairman, Taylor Woodrow plc, 1992–99 (Director, since 1987; Chief Executive, 1997–98); *b* Neath, Wales, 15 Jan. 1934; *s* of Ivor Parsons and Elsie (*née* Price); *m* 1960, Alice McAuley; two *s*. *Educ:* Haverfordwest and Neath Grammar Schs. CA 1955; FCA 1991. Peat Marwick Mitchell, Toronto, 1957–59; Monarch Development Corp., 1959–99: Pres., 1977–92; Chm., 1992–99. Dir, Trow Engrg (Canada), 1999–. Pres. and Chm., London Chamber of Commerce and Industry, 1998–2000; Pres., Canada-UK Chamber of Commerce, 1998–99. Dir, Foundn for Canadian Studies in UK, 1997–. *Recreations:* running, golf. *Address:* 42 Teal Court, Star Place, St Katharine by the Tower, E1W 1AB. *Clubs:* Brooks's; Albany, Granite, Donalda (Toronto).

PARSONS, David; *see* Parsons, J. D.

PARSONS, John Christopher, CVO 1998 (LVO 1992); Deputy Keeper of the Privy Purse and Deputy Treasurer to the Queen, since 1988; *b* 21 May 1946; *s* of late Arthur Christopher Parsons and of Veronica Parsons; *m* 1982, Hon. Anne Manningham-Buller, *d* of 1st Viscount Dilhorne, PC; two *s* one *d*. *Educ:* Harrow; Trinity College, Cambridge. BA (Mech. Scis) 1968. FCA, FIMC. Dowty Group Ltd, 1968–72; Peat, Marwick, Mitchell & Co., 1972–85; Asst Treas. to the Queen, 1985–87; Dep. Dir (Finance), Royal Collection, 1992–93. *Address:* The Old Stables, Kensington Palace, W8 4PU. *Clubs:* Brooks's, Pratt's.

PARSONS, Prof. (John) David, DSc; FREng, FIEE; independent consultant, since 1998; David Jardine Professor of Electrical Engineering, 1982–98, and Head, Department of Electrical Engineering and Electronics, 1983–86 and 1996–98, University of Liverpool; *b* 8 July 1935; *s* of Oswald Parsons and Doris Anita (*née* Roberts); *m* 1969, Mary Winifred Stella Tate. *Educ:* University College of Wales, Cardiff (BSc); King's College London (MSc (Eng), DSc (Eng)). FIEE 1986; FREng (FEng 1988). GEC Applied Electronics Labs, 1959–62; Regent Street Poly., 1962–66; City of Birmingham Poly., 1966–68; Lectr, Sen. Lectr and Reader in Electronic Engrg, Univ. of Birmingham, 1969–82; University of Liverpool: Dean, Faculty of Engrg, 1986–89; Pro-Vice-Chancellor, 1990–96. Vis. Prof., Univ. of Auckland, 1982; Vis. Res. Engr, NTT, Japan, 1987. UN Expert in India, 1977; Hon. SPSO, RSRE, Malvern, 1978–82. Member Council: IERE, 1985–88; IEE, 1988–89. *Publications:* Electronic and Switching Circuits, 1975; Mobile Communication Systems, 1989; The Mobile Radio Propagation Channel, 1992, 2nd edn 2000; many papers on radio communication systems and radio propagation in learned jls. *Recreations:* golf, bridge, ski-ing. *Address:* 46 Green Lane, Formby, Merseyside L37 7BH.

PARSONS, Sir (John) Michael, Kt 1970; Deputy Chairman and Chief Executive, 1979–81, Senior Managing Director, 1976–81, Director, 1971–81, Inchcape & Co. Ltd; *b* 29 Oct. 1915; *s* of late Rt Rev. Richard Godfrey Parsons, DD, Bishop of Hereford; *m* 1st, 1946, Hilda Mary Frewen (marr. diss. 1964); one *s* two *d*; 2nd, 1964, Caroline Inagh Margaret Frewen. *Educ:* Rossall Sch.; University Coll., Oxford. Barry & Co., Calcutta, 1937. Served in Royal Garhwal Rifles (Indian Army), 1939–45: Bde Major, 1942; POW, Singapore, 1942. Macneill & Barry Ltd, Calcutta, 1946–70; Chm. & Managing Dir, 1964–70; Chm., Macdonald Hamilton & Co. Pty Ltd, 1970–72; Chairman and Director: Assam Investments, 1976–81; Paxall Investments Ltd, 1982–84; Dep. Chm. and Dir, Inchcape Insurance Hldgs Ltd, 1979–83; Dir, Commonwealth Develt Finance Co. Ltd, 1973–86. Vice-Chm., Indian Jute Mills Assoc., 1960–61; President: Bengal Chamber of Commerce, 1968–69; Associated Chambers of Commerce of India, 1969; Chm., UK Cttee, Fedn of Commonwealth Chambers of Commerce, 1974; Mem., Advisory Council on Trade, Bd of Trade, India, 1968–69. Chm. Council, Royal Commonwealth Soc., 1976–80, Vice Pres., 1980–; Pres., India, Pakistan and Bangladesh Assoc., 1973–78, Vice Pres., 1978. Dep. Chm., Internat. Bd, United World Colls, 1981–86. *Recreation:* golf. *Address:* Tall Trees, Warren Hill Lane, Aldeburgh, Suffolk IP15 5QB. *T:* (01728) 452917. *Club:* Oriental.

PARSONS, Sir Michael; *see* Parsons, Sir J. M.

PARSONS, Nicholas; actor, presenter and solo performer; *b* 10 Oct. 1928; *s* of late Dr Paul Frederick Nigel Parsons and Nell Louise Parsons (*née* Maggs); *m* 1st, 1954, Denise Pauline Rosalie Bryer (marr. diss. 1989); one *s* one *d*; 2nd, 1995, Ann Reynolds. *Educ:* St Paul's Sch.; Univ. of Glasgow. *Theatre* includes: The Hasty Heart, Aldwych, 1945; Charley's Aunt, Palace, 1947; Arsenic and Old Lace (tour); in rep., Bromley, 1949–51; cabaret and revues, 1951–65; Swing Along with Arthur Haynes, Palladium, 1963; Boeing Boeing, Duchess, 1967; Say Who You Are, Vaudeville, 1968; Uproar in the House, Whitehall, 1968; Charlie Girl, Victoria Palace and tour, 1986–87; Into the Woods, Phoenix, 1990; Rocky Horror Show, Duke of York's, 1994 and 1995 (tours 1996, 1998–99 and 2000); numerous pantomimes and one-man shows incl. Nicholas Parsons' Happy Hour, Edinburgh Fringe, 2000, 2001; *television* includes: straight man in partnership with Arthur Haynes, 1956–66; Last Train to Surbiton (series), 1966; Benny Hill Show, 1969–70; host: Sale of the Century, 1971–84; The Alphabet Game, 1988; Laughlines, 1990; Just a Minute, 1994, 1995 and 1999; *films* include: Brothers-in-Law, Carlton-Browne at the FO, Happy is the Bride, Upstairs Downstairs, Too Many Crooks, Eyewitness, Carry on Regardless; *radio* includes: host, Just a Minute, 1966–2001. Rector, St Andrews Univ., 1988–91. Barker, Variety Club of GB, 1975–2001; Trustee: Lord's Taverners, 1979–2001 (Pres., 1998–2000); Aspire Deaf-Blind UK, 1999–; Gov., NSPCC, 1977–2001. Hon. LLD St Andrews, 1991. Radio Personality of Year, Variety Club, 1967. *Publications:* Egg on the Face, 1985; The Straight Man; my life in comedy, 1994. *Recreations:* cricket, golf, gardening, photography. *Address:* c/o London Management, 2–4 Noel Street, W1V 3RB. *T:* (020) 7287 9000, *Fax:* (020) 7287 3036.

PARSONS, Air Comdt Dame Pauline, (formerly **Air Comdt Dame Pauline Giles**), DBE 1967; RRC; Matron-in-Chief, Princess Mary's Royal Air Force Nursing Service, 1966–70, retired; *b* 17 Sept. 1912; *m* 1987, Daniel G. Parsons, OBE. *Educ:* Sheffield. Joined PMRAFNS, Nov. 1937; later appointments included Principal Matron for Royal

Air Force Command in Britain and Western Europe; became Matron-in-Chief, PMRAFNS, Sept. 1966. *Address:* 3 School View, Wraxall, N Somerset BS48 1HG.

PARSONS, Prof. Peter John, FBA 1977; Regius Professor of Greek, University of Oxford, since 1989; Student of Christ Church, Oxford, since 1964; *b* 24 Sept. 1936; *s* of Robert John Parsons and Ethel Ada (*née* Frary). *Educ:* Raynes Park County Grammar Sch.; Christ Church, Oxford (MA 1961). Oxford University: Craven Scholar, 1955; 1st Cl. Hons Mods and de Paravicini Scholar, 1956; Chancellor's Prize for Latin Verse and Gaisford Prize for Greek Verse, 1st Cl. Lit. Hum., Derby Scholar, Dixon and Sen. Scholar of Christ Church, 1958; Passmore Edwards Scholar, 1959; Lectr in Documentary Papyrology, 1960–65; Lectr in Papyrology, 1965–89. J. H. Gray Lectr, Univ. of Cambridge, 1982; Heller Lectr, Univ. of Calif, Berkeley, 1988. Hon. PhD: Bern, 1985; Athens, 1995; Hon. DLitt Milan, 1994. *Publications:* (jtly) The Oxyrhynchus Papyri XXXI, 1966, XXXIII and XXXIV, 1968, LIV, 1987, LIX, 1992, LX, 1994, LXVI, 1999; The Oxyrhynchus Papyri XLII, 1973; (with H. Lloyd-Jones) Supplementum Hellenisticum, 1983; articles in learned jls. *Recreations:* music, cinema, cooking and eating. *Address:* Christ Church, Oxford OX1 1DP. *T:* (01865) 276223.

PARSONS, Sir Richard (Edmund Clement Fownes), KCMG 1982 (CMG 1977); HM Diplomatic Service, retired; Ambassador to Sweden, 1984–87; *b* 14 March 1928; *s* of Dr R. A. Parsons; *m* 1960, Jenifer Jane Mathews (*d* 1981); three *s*. *Educ:* Bembridge Sch.; Brasenose Coll., Oxford. Served in Army, 1949–51; joined HM Foreign (subseq. Diplomatic) Service, 1951; FO, 1951–53; 3rd Sec., Washington, 1953–56; 2nd Sec., Vientiane, 1956–58; FO, 1958–60; 1st Sec., Buenos Aires, 1960–63; FO, 1963–65; 1st Sec., Ankara, 1965–67; FO, 1967–69; Counsellor, Lagos, 1969–72; Head of Personnel Ops Dept, FCO, 1972–76; Ambassador to: Hungary, 1976–79; Spain, 1980–84. Plays produced in London, Edinburgh and Brighton. *Publications:* The Moon Pool, 1988; Mortmain and other plays, 1993; *as John Haythorne:* None of Us Cared for Kate, 1968; The Strelsau Dimension, 1981; Mandrake in Granada, 1984; Mandrake in the Monastery, 1985. *Recreations:* reading, writing, music, travel. *Address:* 152 De Beauvoir Road, N1 4DJ. *Club:* Garrick.

See also C. A. H. Parsons.

PARSONS, Roger, PhD, DSc; FRS 1980; FRSC; Professor of Chemistry, University of Southampton, 1985–92, now Emeritus; *b* 31 Oct. 1926; *s* of Robert Harry Ashby Parsons and Ethel Fenton; *m* 1953, Ruby Millicent Turner; three *s* one *d*. *Educ:* King Alfred Sch., Hampstead; Strathcona High Sch., Edmonton, Alta; Imperial Coll. of Science and Technol., (BSc, PhD). DSc Bristol 1962; ARCS 1946; FRIC 1962. Asst Lectr, Imp. Coll. of Science and Technol., 1948–50; Deedes Fellow, UC Dundee, St Andrews Univ., 1950–54; Lectr, then Reader in Electrochem., Bristol Univ., 1954–79; Dir, Lab. d'Electrochimie Interfaciale, Centre Nat. de la Recherche Scientifique, Meudon, France, 1977–84. Unesco Specialist, Buenos Aires, 1961; Vis. Prof., Calif Inst. of Technol., 1966–67. Editor, Jl of Electroanal. Chem., 1962–99. Royal Society of Chemistry: Pres., Faraday Div., 1991–93 (Vice-Pres., 1984–91, 1993–99); Liversidge Lectr, 1989–90. Hon. Fellow, Polish Chem. Soc., 1981. Palladium Medal, US Electrochem. Soc., 1979; Bruno Breyer Medal, Electrochem. Div., RACI, 1980; Prix Paul Pascal de l'Acad. des Scis, 1983; Galvani Medal, Electrochem. Div., Italian Chem. Soc., 1986; Franklin Meml Medal, Internat. Soc. of Electrochem., 2000. DUniv Buenos Aires, 1997. *Publications:* Electrochemical Data, 1956; (with J. Lyklema) Electrical Properties of Interfaces, 1983; (ed jtly) Standard Potentials in Aqueous Solution, 1985; (ed with R. Kalvoda) Electrochemistry in Research and Development, 1985; *circa* 200 papers in scientific jls. *Recreations:* listening to music, going to the opera. *Address:* 16 Thornhill Road, Bassett, Southampton SO16 7AT.

PARSONS, Susie; independent management consultant; *b* 29 April 1950; *d* of Alfred and Dorothy Parsons; partner, Dave Perry; one *s*. *Educ:* E Grinstead Co. Grammar Sch.; Univ. of Lancaster (BA Hons French Studies); King's Coll. London (PGCE). Teacher of French, John Kelly Girls' High Sch., LB of Brent, 1973–74; Dir, Community Educn, Shelter, 1974–77; Housing Projects Officer, N Kensington Law Centre, 1977–81; Sec., Paddington and N Kensington CHC, 1981–84; Gen. Manager, London Energy and Employment Network, 1984–87; Hd, Press and Publicity, London Borough of Hackney, 1987–94; Exec. Dir, 1994–97, Chief Exec., 1997–99, London Lighthouse; Chief Exec., CRE, 1999–2001. *Publications:* Workout, 1979; contrib. numerous articles on subjects ranging from educn to energy efficiency, women in mgt, health and social care and race equality. *Recreations:* friendship, swimming, voluntary work, the arts. *Address:* 228a Ladbroke Grove, W10 5LT. *T:* (020) 8969 7415, *Fax:* (020) 8964 0236; *e-mail:* susieparsons@228a.fsnet.co.uk.

PARSONS, (Thomas) Alan, CB 1984; LLB; Chief Adjudication Officer, Department of Health and Social Security, 1984–86; *b* 25 Nov. 1924; *s* of late Arthur and Laura Parsons; *m* 1st, 1947, Valerie Vambeck; one *s*; 2nd, 1957, Muriel Lewis; two *s*. *Educ:* Clifton Coll.; Bristol Univ. (LLB). Called to the Bar, Middle Temple, 1950. Served, Royal Marines, 1943–46. Legal Asst, Min. of Nat. Insurance, 1950; Sen. Legal Asst, Min. of Pensions and Nat. Insurance, 1955; Asst Solicitor,1968, Principal Asst Solicitor, 1977, DHSS. *Recreations:* walking, listening to music. *Address:* 11 Northiam Street, Pennethorne Place, E9 7HX. *T:* (020) 8986 0930.

PÄRT, Arvo; free-lance composer, since 1982; *b* Estonia, 11 Sept. 1935; *s* of August Pärt and Linda Anette Pärt (*née* Mäll); *m* 1st, 1959, Hille Aasmäe (marr. diss.); one *d*; one *d* by Marina Nestieva; 2nd, 1972, Nora Supina; two *s*. *Educ:* composition studies with Heino Eller, Conservatory of Music, Tallinn, Estonia. Sound Engr, Estonian broadcasting station, Tallinn, 1958–67; free-lance composer, Tallinn, 1967–80; emigrated to Vienna, 1980; became Austrian citizen, 1981; Scholar, Deutscher Akademischer Austauschdienst, Berlin, 1981. Hon. Mem., Amer. Acad. of Arts and Letters, 1996. Hon. PhD: Acad. of Music, Tallinn, 1990; Royal Swedish Music Acad., 1991; Hon. DMus Sydney, 1996; Hon. Dr Univ. of Tartu, Estonia, 1998. Triumph award, Russia, 1997; Culture Prize, Estonia, 1998; Herder Award, Germany, 2000. Order of the Nat. Coat of Arms, 2nd class (Estonia), 1998; Commandeur de l'Ordre des Arts et des Lettres (France), 2001. *Compositions* include: Sinfonie No 1, 1963; Sinfonie No 2, 1966; Credo, 1968; Sinfonie No 3, 1971; Fratres (variations for ensembles, orchestra and various instruments), 1977, 1980, 1983, 1985, 1989, 1990, 1991, 1992; Tabula Rasa (double violin concerto), 1977; Sarah was Ninety Years Old, 1977, 1990; Passio, 1982; Stabat Mater, 1985; Te Deum, 1985; Miserere, 1989; Berliner Messe (choir, soloists and organ), 1990; Berliner Messe (choir, soloists and string orch.), 1991; Sieben Magnificat-Antiphonen, 1991; Litany (soloists, choir and orch.), 1994; Kanon Pokajanen (choir a cappella), 1997; Como anhela la Cierva (solo soprano and orch.), 1999; Cantique des Degrés (choir and orch.), 1999; Orient et Occident (orch.), 2000; Cecilia, Vergine Romana (choir and orch.), 2000. *Address:* c/o Universal Edition Ltd, 48 Great Marlborough Street, W1V 2BN.

PARTHIER, Prof. Benno; Director, Institut für Pflanzenbiochemie, Halle, 1990–98, now Emeritus; President, Deutsche Akademie der Naturforscher Leopoldina, since 1990; *b* 21 Aug. 1932; *s* of Hermann and Helene Parthier; *m* 1967, Christiane Luecke; one *s* two *d*. *Educ:* Martin Luther Univ., Halle-Wittenberg (Dip. Biol. 1958; Dr rer. nat. 1961; Dr habil. 1967). Asst, Botanical Inst., Univ. Halle, 1958–65; Head, Dept of Molecular Biol., Inst. of Plant Biochemistry, Acad. of Scis, GDR, 1967–90. Mem., learned socs, Germany and overseas. *Publications:* (with R. Wollgiehn) Von der Zelle zum Molekül, 1971 (Polish edn 1976); (with L. Nover and M. Luckner) Zell differenzierung, Molekulare Grundlagen und Probleme, 1978 (English edn 1982); numerous papers in sci. jls; Editor or co-Editor 10 sci. jls. *Recreations:* gardening, travelling. *Address:* Deutsche Akademie der Naturforscher Leopoldina, August-Bebel Strasse 50a, 06019 Halle, Germany. *T:* (345) 4723910.

PARTINGTON, Ven. Brian Harold; Archdeacon of Man, since 1996; Vicar of St George's, Douglas, since 1996; *b* 31 Dec. 1936; *s* of Harold Partington and Edith (*née* Hall); *m* 1962, Valerie Nurton; two *s* one *d*. *Educ:* Burnage Grammar Sch., Manchester; St Aidan's Coll., Birkenhead. Nat. Service, RAF, 1955–57; local govt officer, Manchester Corp., 1953–59. Ordained deacon, 1963, priest, 1964; Assistant Curate: Emmanuel Church, Didsbury, Manchester, 1963–66; St Mary's, Deane, Bolton, 1966–68; Vicar: Kirk Patrick, Sodor and Man, 1968–96; Foxdale, 1977–96; St John's, 1977–96. Bishop's Youth Officer, 1968–77; Rural Dean of Peel, 1976–96; Canon of St Patrick, St German's Cathedral, 1985–96. Vice-Pres., Hospice Care, 1996– (Chm., 1988–96). Exec. Chm., IOM Sports Council, 1990–; Vice-Chm., Internat. Island Games Orgn, 2001–; President: IOM Hockey Assoc., 1997–; IOM Cricket Assoc., 1998–. Mem., Douglas Rotary Club. *Recreations:* cricket, golf, travel. *Address:* St George's Vicarage, Devonshire Road, Douglas, Isle of Man IM2 3RB. *T:* (01624) 675430. *Clubs:* Royal Commonwealth Society; St John's Cricket; Peel Golf.

PARTINGTON, Gillian Doreen, (Mrs W. D. Partington); *see* Ruaux, G. D.

PARTINGTON, Prof. Thomas Martin; Professor of Law, Bristol University, since 1987; a Law Commissioner, since 2001; *b* 5 March 1944; *s* of Thomas Paulett Partington and Alice Emily Mary Partington; *m* 1st, 1970, Marcia Carol Leavey (marr. diss.); one *s*; 2nd, 1978, Daphne Isobel Scharenguivel; one *s* one *d*. *Educ:* King's Sch., Canterbury; Peterhouse, Cambridge (BA 1965; LLB 1966). Called to the Bar, Middle Temple, 1984. Asst Lectr, Bristol Univ., 1966–69; Lectr, Warwick Univ., 1969–73, LSE, 1973–80; Prof. of Law, Brunel Univ., 1980–87 (Dean, Faculty of Soc. Scis, 1985–87); Dean, Faculty of Law, 1988–92, Pro-Vice-Chancellor, 1995–99, Bristol Univ. Visiting Professor: Osgoode Hall Law Sch., Canada, 1976; Univ. of NSW, 1983. Chm., Cttee of Heads of Univ. Law Schools, 1990–92. Vice-Chm., Legal Action Gp, 1982–83; Member: Lord Chancellor's Adv. Cttee on Legal Aid, 1988–91; Law Society's Trng Cttee, 1989–92; Law Society's Academic Consultative Cttee, 1989–92; Judicial Studies Bd, 1992–95 (Mem., Tribunals Cttee, 1988–95); Trng Cttee, Indep. Tribunal Service Bd, 1990–94; Council on Tribunals, 1994–2000; Civil Justice Council, 1998–; Bd, United Bristol Healthcare NHS Trust, 1998–2001; Adv. Cttee, Leverhulme Trust Res. Awards, 1999–; External Adviser, Educn and Trng Cttee, Inst. of Housing, 1985–89. Part time Chairman: Soc. Security Appeals Tribunal, 1990–94; Med. Appeals Tribunal, 1992–94; Disability Appeals Tribunal, 1992–94. Expert Consultant, Leggatt Review of Tribunals, 2000–01. Barrister, Chambers of A. Arden, QC, 1993–. Chm., Socio-Legal Studies Assoc., 1993–95. Gen. Editor, Anglo-American Law, now Common Law World, Review, 1984–. FRSA 1999. *Publications:* Landlord and Tenant, 1975; Claim in Time, 1978; (with A. Arden) Housing Law, 1983; (with P. O'Higgins) Bibliography of Social Security Law, 1986; Secretary of State's Powers of Adjudication in Social Security Law, 1990; (with J. Hill) Housing Law: cases, materials and commentary, 1991; United Kingdom: Social Security Law, 1998; (with M. Harris) Administrative Justice in the 21st Century, 1999; English Legal System: an introduction, 2000; articles on public law, housing law, social security law, legal educn, Legal Aid and Legal Services. *Recreations:* playing the violin, reading fiction, cooking. *Address:* First Floor Flat, 8/9 Clifton Hill, Bristol BS8 1BN. *T:* (0117) 973 6294. *Club:* Reform.

PARTON, Prof. John Edwin; Professor of Electrical Engineering, University of Nottingham, 1954–78, now Emeritus; *b* Kingswinford, Staffordshire, 26 Dec. 1912; *s* of Edwin and Elizabeth Parton; *m* 1940, Gertrude Brown (*d* 1998); one *s* one *d*. *Educ:* Huntington Church of England Sch.; Cannock Chase Mining Coll.; University of Birmingham. BSc (1st Class Hons), 1936, PhD, 1938, Birmingham; DSc Glasgow, 1971. Training: Littleton Collieries, 1934; Electrical Construction Co., 1935; Asst Engineer, PO Engineering Dept, Dollis Hill Research Station, 1938–39; Part-time Lecturer: Cannock Chase Mining Coll., 1931–38; Northampton Polytechnic, 1938–39. Served RNVR Electrical Branch, Sub-Lt, 1939, to Lt-Comdr, 1943–45. Sen. Sci. Officer, British Iron and Steel Research Assoc., 1946; Lecturer, 1946–54, Senior Lecturer, 1954, University of Glasgow. Sen. Vis. Scientist, Nat. Sci. Foundn at Univ. of Tennessee, 1965–66; Vis. Prof., Univ. of W Indies, Trinidad, 1979, 1980. Chairman, East Midland Centre Institution of Electrical Engineers, 1961–62. FIEE 1966; Life MIEEE 1990; FIMechE 1967. *Publications:* Applied Electromagnetics (jtly), 1975; papers in Proc. IEE, Trans.'FEE, Trans. IES, Instrument Practice, International Journal of Electrical Engineering Education, etc. *Recreations:* golf, gardening, bowls, bridge. *Address:* Bramcote House Nursing Home, Town Street, Bramcote, Nottingham NG9 3DP. *T:* (0115) 922 7877.

PARTRIDGE, Bernard B.; *see* Brook-Partridge.

PARTRIDGE, Derek William, CMG 1987; HM Diplomatic Service, retired; *b* 15 May 1931; *o s* of late Ernest and Ethel Elizabeth Partridge (*née* Buckingham), Wembley. *Educ:* Preston Manor County Grammar Sch., Wembley. Entered Foreign Service (later Diplomatic Service), 1949. Royal Air Force, 1949–51. Served: Foreign Office, 1951–54; Oslo, 1954–56; Jedda, 1956; Khartoum, 1957–60; Sofia, 1960–62; Bangkok, 1962; Manila, 1962–65; Djakarta, 1965–67; FCO, 1967–70; Diplomatic Service Inspectorate, 1970–72; British Consul-General, Brisbane, 1972–74; First Sec. (Economic and Commercial), Colombo, 1974–77; FCO, 1977–86: Counsellor and Head of Migration and Visa Dept, 1981–83; Counsellor and Head of Nationality and Treaty Dept, 1983–86; High Comr, Sierra Leone, 1986–91. Mem. (Lib Dem) Southwark BC, 1994–. Mem., Royal African Soc. *Address:* 16 Wolfe Crescent, Rotherhithe, SE16 6SF. *T:* and *Fax:* (020) 7231 2759. *Club:* National Liberal.

PARTRIDGE, Frances Catherine, CBE 2000; FRSL; writer and literary journalist; *b* 15 March 1900; *d* of William Cecil Marshall, architect, and Margaret Anna Marshall (*née* Lloyd); *m* 1933, Major Reginald Sherring Partridge, (Ralph Partridge), MC and Bar, Croix de Guerre (*d* 1960); one *s* (Lytton Burgo Partridge, *d* 1963). *Educ:* Bedales Sch.; Newnham Coll., Cambridge (BA). Antiquarian bookseller, 1922–28; translator of numerous books from French and Spanish, to 1965. Hon. DLit London, 2000. *Publications:* (ed with husband) The Greville Memoirs (diaries), 8 vols, 1938; A Pacifist's War: diaries 1939–45, 1978; Memories (memoirs), 1981; Julia, 1983; Everything to Lose: diaries 1945–60, 1986; Friends in Focus (photographs), 1987; Hanging On: diaries 1960–63, 1990; The Pasque Flower, 1990; Other People: diaries 1963–66, 1993; Good Company: diaries 1967–70, 1994; Life Regained: diaries 1970–72, 1998. *Recreations:* music, reading, botany. *Address:* c/o Rogers, Coleridge & White, 20 Powis Mews, W11 1JN. *T:* (020) 7221 3717; 15 West Halkin Street, SW1X 8JL. *Club:* International PEN.

PARTRIDGE, Ian Harold, CBE 1992; concert singer (tenor); *b* 12 June 1938; *s* of late Harold Partridge and Ena Stinson; *m* 1959, Ann Glover; two *s*. *Educ:* New Coll., Oxford (chorister); Clifton Coll. (music scholar); Royal Coll. of Music; Guildhall Sch. of Music (LGSM, singing and teaching). Began as piano accompanist, although sang tenor in Westminster Cath. Choir, 1958–62; full-time concert singer, 1963–; performs in England and all over the world, both in recitals (with sister Jennifer) and in concerts; has worked with many leading conductors, incl. Stokowski, Boult, Giulini, Boulez and Colin Davis. Opera debut at Covent Garden as Iopas in Berlioz, Les Troyens, 1969. Title role, Britten's St Nicolas, Thames Television (Prix Italia, 1977). Over 150 records, *including:* Bach, St John Passion; Handel, Chandos Anthems, and Esther; Schubert, Die Schöne Müllerin, Die Winterreise; Schumann, Dichterliebe; Beethoven, An die ferne Geliebte; Vaughan-Williams, On Wenlock Edge; Warlock, The Curlew; Fauré and Duparc Songs; Britten, Serenade and Winter Words; Lord Berners, Complete Songs; as conductor (of Pro Cantione Antiqua), The Triumphs of Oriana. Innumerable radio broadcasts, many TV appearances. Prof., RAM, 1996–. Chm., Royal Soc. of Musicians, 1999– (Gov., 1995–99); Pres., ISM, 1996–97; Dir, Performing Artists' Media Rights Assoc., 1996–. Governor, Clifton Coll., 1981–. Sir Charles Santley Meml Gift, Musicians' Co., 1992. Hon. RAM 1996. Harriet Cohen Award, 1967. *Recreations:* bridge, horse racing, theatre, cricket. *Address:* 127 Pepys Road, SW20 8NP. *Club:* Garrick.

PARTRIDGE, John Albert, CBE 1981; RA; FRIBA; architect in private practice; a Senior and Founder Partner, Howell, Killick, Partridge & Amis (HKPA), 1959–95, now Consultant; *b* 26 Aug. 1924; *s* of George and Gladys Partridge; *m* 1953, Doris (*née* Foreman); one *s* one *d*. *Educ:* Shooter's Hill Grammar Sch., Woolwich; Polytechnic School of Architecture, Regent Street. FRIBA 1966 (ARIBA 1951); RA 1988 (ARA 1980). London County Council Housing Architects Dept, 1951–59; Design Tutor, Architectural Assoc., 1958–61. The work of HKPA includes universities, colleges, public buildings, housing and leisure buildings; principal commissions include: Wolfson, Rayne and Gatehouse building, St Anne's Coll., Oxford; New Hall and Common Room building, St Antony's Coll., Oxford; Wells Hall, Reading Univ.; Middlesex Polytechnic College of Art, Cat Hill; Medway Magistrates' Court; The Albany, Deptford; Hall of Justice, Trinidad and Tobago; Warrington Court House; Basildon Magistrates' Courthouse; Berlin Mineral Spa Project; Haywards Heath Magistrates' Courthouse; Japanese University Chaucer Coll., Univ. of Kent, Canterbury. RIBA: Vice-Pres., 1977–79; Hon. Librarian, 1977–81; Chm. Res. Steering Gp, 1977–84. Vice-Pres., Concrete Soc., 1979–81. External Examiner in Architecture: Bath Univ., 1975–78, 1992; Thames Polytechnic, 1978–86; Cambridge Univ., 1979–81; Manchester Univ., 1982; South Bank Polytechnic, 1982–86; Brighton Polytechnic, 1987–90; RCA, 1991–93. Governor, Building Centre Trust, 1982–96; Chm., Assoc. of Consultant Architects, 1983–85. Mem., NEDO Construction Res. Strategy Cttee, 1983–86; Architect Mem., FCO Adv. Bd on the Diplomatic Estate, 1985–92. *Publications:* articles in technical press. *Recreations:* looking at buildings, travel, sketching and taking photographs. *Address:* Cudham Court, Cudham, near Sevenoaks, Kent TN14 7QF. *T:* (01959) 571294. *Club:* Arts.

PARTRIDGE, Prof. Linda, FRS 1996; FRSE; Weldon Professor of Biometry, since 1994 and NERC Research Professor, 1997–July 2002, University College London; *b* 18 March 1950; *d* of George and Ida Partridge; *m* 1st, 1983, Dr V. K. French (marr. diss. 1992); 2nd, 1996, Prof. Michael John Morgan. *Educ:* Convent of the Sacred Heart, Tunbridge Wells; St Anne's Coll., Oxford (MA); Wolfson Coll., Oxford (DPhil 1974). FRSE 1992. Post-doctoral Fellow, York Univ., 1974–76; Edinburgh University: Lectr, 1976–87; Reader in Zoology, 1987–92; Prof. of Evolutionary Biol., 1992–93. Mem., BBSRC, 1998–2001. President: Internat. Soc. for Behavioural Ecology, 1990–92; Assoc. for Study of Animal Behaviour, 1995–97; Genetical Soc., 1999–. *Publications:* on evolutionary biology in scientific jls. *Recreations:* tennis, hill walking, gardening. *Address:* Department of Biology, University College London, Wolfson House, 4 Stephenson Way, NW1 2HE.

PARTRIDGE, Sir Michael (John Anthony), KCB 1990 (CB 1983); Permanent Secretary, Department of Social Security, 1988–95; *b* 29 Sept. 1935; *s* of late Dr John Henry Partridge, DSc, PhD, and Ethel Green; *m* 1968, Joan Elizabeth Hughes; two *s* one *d*. *Educ:* Merchant Taylors'; St John's Coll., Oxford (BA (1st Cl. Hons Mods and Lit Hum) 1960, MA 1963; Hon. Fellow, 1991). Entered Home Civil Service (Min. of Pensions and Nat. Insce), 1960; Private Sec. to Permanent Sec., 1962–64; Principal, 1964–71 (MPNI, Min. of Social Security and DHSS); DHSS: Asst Sec., 1971–76; Under Sec., 1976–81; Dep. Sec., 1981–83; Dep. Under-Sec. of State, Home Office, 1983–87; Second Permanent Sec., DHSS, 1987–88. Non-executive Director: Norwich Union, 1996–2000; Epworth Investment Mgt Ltd, 1996–; The Stationery Office, 1997–; CGNU, 2000–; Harefield Res. Foundn, 2001–. Senior Treasurer, Methodist Ch. Finance Div., 1980–96. Trustee: Harefield Hosp. Heart Transplant Trust, 1991–; Methodist Ministers' Pensions Trust, 1993–. Mem. Court, Univ. of York, 1991–95. Governor: Middlesex Univ., 1992– (Chm., 1997–); Merchant Taylors' Sch., 1992–99. CIMgt (CBIM 1988). Liveryman, Merchant Taylors' Co., 1987. *Recreations:* Do-it-Yourself, classical sites, reading, ski-ing. *Address:* 27 High View, Pinner, Middlesex HA5 3NZ. *T:* (020) 8868 0657. *Club:* Oxford and Cambridge.

PASCALL, David Lewis, CBE 1993; European Transaction Director, Principal Finance Group, Nomura International plc, since 2000; *b* 5 Feb. 1949; *s* of Robert Lewis Pascall and Dorothy Pascall (*née* Smith); *m* 1980, Carolyn Judith White; one *s* two *d*. *Educ:* Queen Mary's Grammar Sch., Basingstoke; Univ. of Birmingham (BSc 1st Cl. Hons Chem. Engrg 1970); INSEAD, Fontainebleau (MBA Dist. 1979). With British Petroleum Co. plc, 1967–93: posts in oil refining, trading, finance and business management in UK and, 1974–79, Germany and France; Divl Manager, BP Finance Internat., 1986–89; Manager: BP Share Sale, 1987; Project 1990 (cultural change prog.), 1989–93; Finance Dir, 1993–94, Chief Exec., Asia Pacific, 1994–95, MAI plc; Finance Dir to Hon. Sir Rocco Forte, 1996–98. On secondment to: Central Policy Rev. Staff, Cabinet Office, 1982–83; No 10 Policy Unit, 1983–84. Non-exec. Dir, Colt Gp Ltd, 1999–2000. Advr, MoD Defence Costs Review, 1994. Mem., 1990–91, Chm., 1991–93, Nat. Curriculum Council; Mem. Exec. Cttee, Field Studies Council, 1993–99. Foundn Gov., Sir John Cass and Redcoat Comprehensive Sch., Stepney, 1995–2001. Mem., Nat Soc., 1994–2000. FRSA 1993. *Recreations:* my family, current affairs, golf. *Address:* 31 Lanchester Road, N6 4SX. *T:* (020) 8883 7708; *e-mail:* david.pascall@nomura.co.uk. *Club:* Carnegie; Highgate Golf.

PASCO, Adam Gerhold; Editor, BBC Gardeners' World magazine, since 1991; *b* 11 Jan. 1957; *s* of Cecil Filmer Pasco and Sheila Mary Pasco (*née* Gerhold); *m* 1992, Jayne Petra Fisher; one *s* one *d*. *Educ:* North East Surrey Coll. of Tech. (HND Applied Biology 1977); Univ. of Nottingham (BSc Horticulture 1982). Technical Editor, 1982–84, Editor, 1984–88, Garden Answers magazine; Editor, Garden News, 1988–90. Gardening Correspondent, Daily Telegraph, 1995–. *Publications:* Collins Complete Garden Manual, 1998; Greenfingers Book, 1999; Collins Gardeners' Calendar, 2000. *Recreations:* gardening, writing, walking, travel, family life. *Address:* 43 Latham Avenue, Orton Longueville, Peterborough PE2 7AD. *T:* (01733) 237613.

PASCO, Richard Edward, CBE 1977; actor; Hon. Associate Artist, Royal Shakespeare Company; *b* 18 July 1926; *s* of Cecil George Pasco and Phyllis Irene Pasco; *m* 1st, Greta (*née* Watson) (marr. diss.); one *s*; 2nd, 1967, Barbara Leigh-Hunt, *qv*. *Educ:* Colet Court; King's Coll. Sch., Wimbledon; Central Sch. of Speech and Drama (Gold Medallist). Served HM Forces, 1944–48. 1st stage appearance, She Stoops to Conquer, 1943; 1st London appearance, Zero Hour, Lyric, 1944; 1st New York appearance, The Entertainer, 1958. London appearances include: leading roles, English Stage Co., Royal Court, 1957; The Entertainer, Palace, 1957; The Lady from the Sea, Queen's, 1961; Teresa of Avila, Vaudeville, 1961; Look Homeward, Angel, Phoenix, 1962; The New Men, Strand, 1962; The Private Ear and the Public Eye, Globe, 1963; Bristol Old Vic: Henry V (title role), Berowne in Love's Labour's Lost, 1964; Peer Gynt (title role), Angelo in Measure for Measure, Hamlet (title role), 1966 (and world tour); Ivanov, Phoenix, 1965; The Italian Girl, Wyndham's, 1968. Joined RSC, 1969; leading roles include: Becket, Murder in the Cathedral, Aldwych, 1972; (alternated with Ian Richardson) Richard and Bolingbroke in Richard II, Stratford-on-Avon, 1973, and Stratford and Aldwych, 1974; Jacques in As You Like It, 1973; tour of Amer. univs; Jack Tanner in Man and Superman, Malvern Festival, tour and Savoy, 1977; Timon in Timon of Athens, Clarence in Richard III, Arkady Schatslivtses in The Forest, Stratford, 1980–81; La Ronde, Aldwych, 1982; Soren in The Seagull, Stratford, tour and Barbican, 2000; National Theatre: The Father in Six Characters in Search of an Author, Pavel in Fathers and Sons, 1987; Rt Rev. Charlie Allen in Racing Demon, 1990, 1993; Sir Peter Edgecombe in Murmuring Judges, 1991, 1993; Birling in An Inspector Calls, 1992; Malcolm Pryce in Absence of War, 1993; Boss Findley in Sweet Bird of Youth, 1994. Many foreign tours; accompanied HSH Princess Grace of Monaco at Edinburgh, Stratford and Aldeburgh Festivals and on tour of USA, 1977–78. Frequent appearances at Aldeburgh, Brighton, Windsor and Harrogate festivals, Stratford-upon-Avon Poetry Festival etc. Recent films: A Watcher in the Woods; Wagner; Mrs Brown. Countless TV and radio appearances; recent television series: Sorrell & Son; Drummonds; Hannay; Inspector Morse; Absence of War; Kavanagh QC, Hetty Wainthrop Investigates, etc. Many recordings of poems, plays, recitals, etc. Life Trustee, Shakespeare Birthplace Trust, 1992. *Publications:* (contrib.) Shakespeare in Perspective, 1982; (contrib.) Time and Concord: Aldeburgh Festival recollections, 1997; (contrib.) Acting in Stratford, 1997. *Recreations:* music, gardening, reading. *Address:* c/o Michael Whitehall Ltd, 10 Lower Common South, SW15 1BP. *Club:* Garrick.

PASCO, Rowanne, (Mrs William FitzGerald); writer and broadcaster; *b* 7 Oct. 1938; *d* of John and Ann Pasco; *m* 1994, Rev. William FitzGerald. *Educ:* Dominican Convent, Chingford; Ursuline Convent, Ilford; Open Univ. (BA). Reporter, 1956–57, Editor, 1957–58, Chingford Express; Publicity Officer, NFU, 1958–59; Account Exec., Leslie Frewin PR, 1959–60; Travel Rep., Horizon Holidays, 1960–64; Publicity Asst, Paramount Pictures Corp., Hollywood, 1964–66; Publicity Officer, Religious Progs, Radio and TV, BBC, 1966–71; Reporter, BBC Radio London, 1971–72; TV Editor, Ariel, BBC Staff Newspaper, 1972–74; Radio 4 Reporter, 1974–76; Researcher, Religious Progs, BBC TV, 1976–77; Producer and Presenter, Religious Progs, BBC Radio, 1977–78; Dep. Editor, 1979–81, Editor, 1981–87, The Universe; Religious Editor, TV-am, 1987–92; religious correspondent, GMTV, 1993–94; Editl Advr, CCJ, 1994–. Mem., Blockley Parish Council, 1999–. *Publications:* (ed with Fr John Redford) Faith Alive, 1988, New Catechism edn, 1994; Answers to One Hundred & One Questions on the Catechism, 1995; Why I am a Catholic, 1995. *Recreations:* gardening, Italy, creative cooking. *Address:* 12 The Dell, Blockley, Glos GL56 9DB.

PASCOE, Alan Peter, MBE 1975; Chairman, Fast Track, since 1998; *b* 11 Oct. 1947; *s* of Ernest George Frank Pascoe and Joan Rosina Pascoe; *m* 1970, Della Patricia (*née* James); one *s* one *d*. *Educ:* Portsmouth Southern Grammar Sch.; Borough Road Coll. (Cert. in Educn); London Univ. (Hons degree in Educn). Master, Dulwich Coll., 1971–74; Lectr in Physical Educn, Borough Road Coll., Isleworth, 1974–80. Dir, 1976–83, Man. Dir, 1983, Chm., 1985–98, CEO, 1994–98, Alan Pascoe Associates Ltd, then API Gp of Cos; Chm., Carat Sponsorship, 1987–92; Dir, WCRS, then Aegis Gp, 1986–92. Member: Sports Council, 1974–80; Minister for Sport's Working Party on Centres of Sporting Excellence; BBC Adv. Council, 1975–79. European Indoor Champion, 50m Hurdles, 1969; Europ. Games Silver Medallist, 110m Hurdles, 1971; Silver Medal, Olympic Games, Munich, 4×400m Relay, 1972; Europa Gold Cup Medallist, 400m Hurdles, 1973; Commonwealth Games Gold Medal, 400m Hurdles, and Silver Medal, 4×400m Relay, 1974; Europ. Champion and Gold Medallist in both 400m Hurdles and 4×400m Relay, 1974; Europa Cup Gold Medallist, 400m Hurdles, 1975; Olympic Finalist (injured), Montreal, 1976; Europe's Rep., World Cup Event, 1977. DUniv Brunel, 1997. *Publication:* An Autobiography, 1979. *Recreations:* theatre, sport. *Address:* Fast Track, 192 Sloane Street, SW1X 9QX.

PASCOE, Dr Michael William; Head of Science, Camberwell College of Arts (formerly Camberwell School of Arts and Crafts), 1981–90; *b* 16 June 1930; *s* of Canon W. J. T. Pascoe and Mrs D. Pascoe; *m* 1st, 1956, Janet Clark (marr. diss. 1977); three *d*; 2nd, 1977, Brenda Hale Reed; one *d*. *Educ:* St John's, Leatherhead; Selwyn Coll., Cambridge (BA, PhD). MInstP. Res. Student (Tribology), Cambridge, 1951–55; Physicist: Mount Vernon Hosp., Northwood, 1956–57; British Nylon Spinners Ltd, 1957–60; Chemist/Physicist, ICI Paints Div., 1960–67; Lectr (Polymer Science), Brunel Univ., 1967–77; Principal Scientific Officer, 1976–79, Keeper of Conservation and Technical Services, 1979–81, British Museum. Tutor and Counsellor, Open Univ., 1971–76. Occasional Lectr: Winchester Coll., 1989–90; Univ. of Stirling, 1991–; Camberwell Coll. of Arts; Vis. Lectr in Materials, Univ. of Brunel, 1995 and 1999. Consultant to: Royal Acad. of Arts (Great Japan exhibn), 1982–; Mary Rose Trust, 1978–83; Council for the Care of Churches, 1980–91; Public Record Office (Domesday exhibn), 1986; Science Museum, 1988; Parliament of Guyana, 1991–; Govt and cultural instns of Guatemala on conservation matters, 1996–. FRSA. *Publications:* contrib. to books on polymer tribol. and technol.; articles in scientific, engrg and conservation jls on tribol., materials technol. and on conservation methods. *Recreations:* painting and drawing *inter alia*. *Address:* 15 Parkfield Road, Ickenham, Uxbridge UB10 8LN. *T:* (01895) 674723.

PASCOE, Nigel Spencer Knight; QC 1988; a Recorder of the Crown Court, since 1979; *b* 18 Aug. 1940; *er s* of late Ernest Sydney Pascoe and of Cynthia Pascoe; *m* 1964, Elizabeth Anne Walter; two *s* four *d*. *Educ:* Epsom Coll. Called to the Bar, Inner Temple, 1966, Bencher, 1996; Leader, Western Circuit, 1995–98. Chm., Bar Public Affairs Cttee, 1996–98. County Councillor for Lyndhurst, Hants, 1979–84. Founder and Editor, All England Qly Law Cassettes, 1976–85; Chm., Editl Bd, Counsel. *Publications:* The Trial of Penn and Mead, 1985; The Nearly Man, 1994; Pro Patria, 1996; Who Killed William Rufus?, 2000; articles in legal jls. *Recreations:* theatre, devising and presenting with Elizabeth Pascoe legal anthologies, after-dinner speaking, cricket, play writing. *Address:* 3 Pump Court, Temple, EC4 7AJ. *T:* (020) 7353 0711. *Club:* Garrick.

PASCOE, Gen. Sir Robert (Alan), KCB 1985; MBE 1968; Adjutant General, 1988–90; Aide de Camp General to the Queen, 1989–91, retired; *b* 21 Feb. 1932; *er s* of late C. and Edith Mary Pascoe; *m* 1955, Pauline (*née* Myers); one *s* three *d*. *Educ:* Tavistock Grammar Sch.; RMA, Sandhurst. rcds, psc. Commissioned Oxford and Bucks LI, 1952; served with 1 Oxf. Bucks, 1 DLI and 4 Oxf. Bucks (TA), 1953–57; Middle East Centre for Arab Studies, Lebanon, 1958–59; 1st Cl. Interpretership (Arabic); GSO2 Land Forces Persian Gulf, 1960–62; sc Camberley, 1963; Co. Comd 2RGJ, UK and Malaysia, 1964–66 (despatches (Borneo) 1966); GSO2 HQ 2 Div. BAOR, 1967–68; Co. Comd 1RGJ, UK and UNFICYP, 1968–69; Second in Comd 2RGJ, BAOR, 1969; MA to QMG, 1970–71; Comd 1RGJ, 1971–74, BAOR and NI (despatches (NI) 1974); Col General Staff HQ UKLF, 1974–76; Comd 5 Field Force BAOR, 1976–79; rcds 1979; Asst Chief of Gen. Staff (Operational Requirements), MoD, 1980–83; Chief of Staff, HQ, UKLF, 1983–85; GOC Northern Ireland, 1985–88. Rep. Col Comdt, RGJ, 1988–90; Colonel Commandant: 1st Bn Royal Green Jackets, 1986–91; Army Legal Corps, 1988–90. Hon. Col, Oxfordshire ACF, 1991–. Chm., Belautruche (UK) plc, 1997–2000; non-exec. Dir, Belautruche NV, 1997–2000. Chairman of Governors: Royal Sch., Bath, 1988–96 (Governor, 1981–96); Royal High Sch., Bath, 1996–. Mem. Council, King Edward VII's Hosp., London, 1995–. President: Army LTA, 1986–91; Army Boxing Assoc., 1989–90; Reg. Forces Employment Assoc., 1997–99 (Chm., 1994–97); Chm., Ex-Services Resettlement Gp, 1994–98. Mem. and Vice Pres., Royal Patriotic Fund Corp., 1992–; Patron, Retired Officers Assoc., 1991–2001. Chairman: 43rd and 52nd Club, 1992–; Oxford and Bucks LI Mus. Trustees, 1992–. Freeman, City of London, 1992; Hon. Liveryman, Fruiterers' Co., 1992. *Recreations:* gardening, golf, fishing, tennis, ski-ing. *Clubs:* Army and Navy; Queen's.

PASHLEY, Prof. Donald William, FRS 1968; Professor of Materials, Imperial College of Science, Technology and Medicine, 1979–92, now Professor Emeritus and Senior Research Fellow; *b* 21 April 1927; *s* of late Harold William Pashley and Louise Pashley (*née* Clarke); *m* 1954, Glenys Margaret Ball; one *s* one *d*. *Educ:* Henry Thornton Sch., London; Imperial Coll., London (BSc). 1st cl. hons Physics, 1947; PhD 1950. Research Fellow, Imp. Coll., 1950–55; TI Res. Labs, Hinxton Hall: Res. Scientist, 1956–61; Gp Leader and Div. Head, 1962–67; Asst Dir, 1967–68; Dir, 1968–79 (also Dir of Research, TI Ltd, 1976–79); Imperial College: Hd, Dept of Materials, 1979–90; Dean, Royal Sch. of Mines, 1986–89; Mem. Governing Body, 1986–89. Mem. Council, Royal Soc., 1981–83. Rosenhain Medal, Inst. of Metals, 1968. *Publications:* (jtly) Electron Microscopy of Thin Crystals, 1965; numerous papers on electron microscopy and diffraction, thin films and epitaxy in Phil. Mag., Proc. Roy. Soc., etc. *Address:* 11 The Gables, Oxshott, Leatherhead, Surrey KT22 0SD. *T:* (01372) 844518; Department of Materials, Imperial College, SW7 2AZ.

PASLEY, Sir (John) Malcolm (Sabine), 5th Bt *cr* 1794; FBA 1991; Emeritus Fellow, Magdalen College, Oxford; *b* 5 April 1926; *s* of Sir Rodney Marshall Sabine Pasley, 4th Bt, and Aldyth Werge Hamber (*d* 1983); *S* father, 1982; *m* 1965, Virginia Killigrew Wait; two *s*. *Educ:* Sherborne Sch.; Trinity Coll., Oxford (MA). War service, Royal Navy, 1944–46. Laming Travelling Fellow, Queen's Coll., Oxford, 1949–50; Lectr in German, Brasenose and Magdalen Colls, 1950–58; Fellow and Tutor, 1958–86, Vice-Pres., 1979–80, Magdalen Coll. Mem., Deutsche Akademie für Sprache und Dichtung, 1983–. Hon. DPhil Giessen, 1986. Austrian Ehrenkreuz für Wissenschaft und Kunst, 1st cl., 1987. *Publications:* (co-author) Kafka-Symposion, 1965; (ed) Germany: A Companion to German Studies, 1972, 2nd edn 1982; (trans.) Kafka Shorter Works, vol. 1, 1973; (ed) Nietzsche: Imagery and Thought, 1978; (ed) Franz Kafka, Das Schloss, 1982; (ed) Max Brod, Franz Kafka, Reiseaufzeichnungen, 1987; Briefwechsel, 1989; (ed) Franz Kafka, Der Process, 1990; (trans.) Franz Kafka, The Transformation and other stories, 1992; (ed) Franz Kafka, Nachgelassene Schriften und Fragmente I, 1993; Die Schrift ist unveränderlich: Essays zu Kafka, 1995. *Heir: s* Robert Killigrew Sabine Pasley, *b* 23 Oct. 1965. *Address:* 25 Lathbury Road, Oxford OX2 7AT.

PASQUA, Charles Victor; President, General Council for Hauts-de-Seine, 1973–76 and since 1988; Member (RPF) for France, European Parliament, since 1999; *b* 18 April 1927; *s* of late André Pasqua and Françoise (*née* Rinaldi); *m* 1947; one *s*. *Educ:* Grasse High Sch.; Law Inst., Nice; Univ. of Aix-en-Provence (degree in Law). Sales Rep., then Sales Dir, 1962–63; Dir for sales in France and exports, 1963–68. Deputy (UDR) for Hauts-de-Seine, 1968–73; President: Centre National de la Libre Enterprise; Amicale Parlementaire Présence et Action du Gaullisme, 1972–73; Nat. Sec., then Dep. Gen. Sec., UDR, 1974–76; Senator (RPR) for Hauts-de-Seine, 1977–86, 1988–93 and 1995–99; Pres., RPR in Senate, 1981–86 and 1988–93; Minister of Interior, 1986–88; Minister of State and Minister for the Interior and Town and Country Planning, 1993–95. Pres., Union pour l'Europe des Nations Gp, EP, 1999–. Jt Founder and Pres., RPF, 1999–. Croix du Combattant volontaire de la Résistance; Médaille de la France Libre; Officier de la Légion d'Honneur. *Publications:* La Libre entreprise un état d'esprit, 1964; L'ardeur nouvelle, 1985; Que demande le peuple, 1992. *Recreation:* travel. *Address:* Conseil Général des Hauts-de-Seine, Hôtel du Département, 2/16 Boulevard Soufflot, 92015 Nanterre, France.

PASSLEY, Patrick Derek; Law Lecturer, Barnet College, since 1991; Member, Commission for Racial Equality, since 1999; *b* London, 10 Oct. 1965; *s* of Ivan Augustus Passley and Lurline Isamanda Passley; *m* 1991, Jean Francis; two *d*. *Educ:* Poly. of E London (LLB Hons); Middlesex Univ. (CertEd; Assessors Trainers Award Cert.). Managing Director: Paralegal Charity, 1994–; Diversity +, 2001–. Chm., Nat. Sports Cttee, CRE, 2001–; Official CRE Observer on Disability Rights Commn, 2000–. Mem. Council, Prince's Trust, 2001–. Member: Equity Sub-gp, Sport England, 2000–; Adult Learning Cttee, Nat. Learning and Skills Council, 2001–; London E Local Learning Skills Council, 2001–. Sec., African and Caribbean Finance Forum, 2001–. Mem. Mgt Cttee, Jt Council for Anglo-Caribbean Churches, 1997–. FRSA 2001. *Recreations:* amateur boxing (former Nat. Amateur Boxing Champion and Commonwealth Rep. for England at Super Heavyweight, 1989–90), cinema, current affairs. *Address:* Commission for Racial Equality, Elliot House, 10/12 Allington Street, SW1E 5EH. *T:* (020) 7932 5347.

PASTINEN, Ilkka; KCMG (Hon.) 1976; Finnish Ambassador to the Court of St James's, 1983–91; *b* 17 March 1928; *s* of Martti and Ilmi Pastinen; *m* 1950, Eeva Marja Viitanen; two *d*. Entered Diplomatic Service, 1952; served Stockholm, 1955; Perm. Mission to UN, 1957–60; Peking, 1962–64; London, 1966–69; Ambassador and Dep. Representative of Finland to UN, 1969–71; Special Representative of Sec. Gen. of UN to Cttee of Disarmament, 1971–75; Ambassador and Perm. Representative of Finland at UN, NY, 1977–83. Kt Comdr of Order of White Rose of Finland, 1984. *Address:* Maneesikatu 1–3B, Helsinki, Finland. *Clubs:* Athenæum, Travellers; Swinley Forest Golf.

PASTON-BEDINGFELD, Sir Edmund George Felix, 9th Bt *cr* 1661; Major late Welsh Guards; Managing Director, Handley Walker (Europe) Ltd, 1969–80; *b* 2 June 1915; *s* of Sir Henry Edward Paston-Bedingfield, 8th Bt and Sybil (*d* 1985), *e d* of late H. Lyne Stephens of Grove House, Roehampton; *S* father, 1941; *m* 1st, 1942, Joan Lynette (*née* Rees) (*d* 1965); one *s* one *d*; 2nd, 1957, Agnes Kathleen (*d* 1974), *d* of late Miklos Gluck, Budapest; 3rd, 1975, Mrs Peggy Hannaford-Hill (*d* 1991), Fort Victoria, Rhodesia; 4th, 1992, Sheila Riddell (*née* Finlayson Douglas). *Educ:* Oratory School; New College, Oxford. Under-Sec., Head of Agricultural Div., RICS, 1966–69. Liveryman, Bowyers' Co., 1988–. *Heir: s* Henry Edgar Paston-Bedingfeld, *qv*. *Address:* The Old Stables, Livermere Road, Great Barton, Bury St Edmunds, Suffolk IP35 2RZ. *T:* (01284) 788160. *Clubs:* Naval and Military, New Cavendish.

PASTON-BEDINGFELD, Henry Edgar; York Herald of Arms, since 1993; *b* 7 Dec. 1943; *s* and *heir* of Sir Edmund Paston-Bedingfeld, Bt, *qv*; *m* 1968, Mary Kathleen, *d* of Brig. R.D. Ambrose, CIE, OBE, MC; two *s* two *d*. *Educ:* Ampleforth College, York. Chartered Surveyor. Rouge Croix Pursuivant of Arms, 1983–93. Genealogist, British Assoc. of SMO Malta, 1995–2000. Founder Chairman, Norfolk Heraldry Soc., 1975–80, Vice-Pres. 1980–; Member Council: Heraldry Soc., 1976–85, and 1990–99; Norfolk Record Soc., 1986–; Royal Soc. of St George, 2000–; Sec., Standing Council of the Baronetage, 1984–88; Vice-President: Cambridge Univ. Heraldic and Genealogical Soc., 1988–; Suffolk Family Hist. Soc., 1991–. Rep. of Duke of Norfolk, Commn d'Inf. et de Liaison des Assocs Nobles d'Europe, 1994. Freeman of the City of London; Liveryman: Scriveners' Co; Bowyers' Co. Kt of Sovereign Mil. Order of Malta. *Publications:* Oxburgh Hall, The First 500 Years, 1982; (jtly) Heraldry, 1993. *Address:* The College of Arms, Queen Victoria Street, EC4V 4BT. *T:* (020) 7236 6420; Oxburgh Hall, Norfolk PE33 9PS. *T:* (01366) 328269. *Club:* Boodle's.

PATAKI, George Elmer; Governor, New York State, since 1995; *b* 24 June 1945; *s* of Louis Pataki and Margaret Pataki; *m* Elizabeth (Libby) Rowland; two *s* two *d*. *Educ:* Peekskill High Sch.; Yale Univ. (BA 1967); Columbia Univ. Sch. of Law (JD 1970). Associate, Dewey, Ballantine, Bushby, Plamer and Wood, 1970–74; Partner, Plunkett & Jaffe, 1974–89. Mem., State Assembly 91st AD, 1985–92; Ranking Minority Member: Assembly Envmtl Conservation Cttee, 1987–90; Assembly Educn Cttee, 1991–92; Mem., State Senate 37th SD, 1993–95; Chm., State Ethics Cttee, 1993–95. Mayor, Peekskill, Westchester City, 1982–84. Co-proprietor, Pataki Farm, Peekskill, NY. *Recreations:* hiking in the woods, ski-ing, basketball, working on the family farm. *Address:* Executive Chamber, State Capitol, Albany, NY 12224, USA. *T:* (518) 4748418.

PATE, Prof. John Stewart, FRS 1985; FAA 1980; FLS; Professor of Botany, University of Western Australia, since 1974; *b* 15 Jan. 1932; *s* of Henry Stewart Pate and Muriel Margaret Pate; *m* 1959, Elizabeth Lyons Sloan, BSc; three *s*. *Educ:* Campbell College; Queen's Univ., Belfast (BSc, MSc, PhD, DSc). FLS 1990. Lectr, Sydney Univ., 1956–60; Lectr, Reader, Personal Chair in Plant Physiology, Queen's Univ. Belfast, 1960–73. Vis. Fellow, Univ. of Cape Town, 1973. Individual Excellence Award, AMEEF, 1998. *Publications:* (ed with J. F. Sutcliffe) Physiology of the Garden Pea, 1977; (ed with A. J. McComb) Biology of Australian Plants, 1981; (with K. W. Dixon) Tuberous, Cormous and Bulbous Plants, 1983; (ed with J. S. Beard) Kwongan: plant life of the sandplain, 1984; (ed with K. A. Meney) Australian Rushes: biology, indentification and conservation of restionaceae and allied families, 1999; (ed jtly and contrib.) Agriculture as a Mimic of Natural Ecosystems, 1999; reviews on carbon:nitrogen metabolism and biology of Australian flora. *Recreations:* music, nature study, hobby farming. *Address:* 83 Circe Circle, Dalkeith, WA 6009, Australia. *T:* (8) 93866070.

PATEL, family name of **Barons Patel** and **Patel of Blackburn**.

PATEL, Baron *cr* 1999 (Life Peer), of Dunkeld in Perth and Kinross; **Narendra Babubhai Patel,** Kt 1997; FRCOG; consultant obstetrician, Tayside Teaching Hospitals NHS Trust, Dundee; Hon. Professor, University of Dundee, since 1974; *b* 11 May 1938; *m* 1970, Dr Helen Dally; twin *s* one *d*. *Educ:* Univ. of St Andrews (MB, ChB 1964). MRCOG 1969, FRCOG 1988; FRCPE 1997; FRCSE 1997; FRCPGlas 1998; FRCS 1998; FRSE 1999. Consultant obstetrician, Dundee, 1974–. Chairman: Acad. of Med. Royal Colls, Scotland, 1994–95; Acad. of Med. Royal Colls, UK, 1996–98; Specialist Trng Authority, 1998–; Clinical Standards Bd for Scotland, 1999–. Pres., RCOG, 1995–98 (Hon. Sec., 1987–92; Vice-Pres., 1992–95). FACOG 1996; FSOGC 1997; FSACOG 1997; FICOG 1997; FSLCOG 1998; FRANZCOG 1998; Founder FMedSci 1998; FRCPI. Hon. Mem., German, Finnish, Argentinian and Italian Socs of Obstetrics and Gynaecology. Hon. DSc: Napier, 1996; Aberdeen, 2001; Hon. MD Stellenbosch, 2001. *Publications:* books and articles on pre-term labour, foetal monitoring, birth handicap, obstetrics, etc. *Recreations:* occasional golf, walking. *Address:* Department of Obstetrics, University of Dundee, Dundee DD1 4HN. *T:* (01382) 632959.

PATEL OF BLACKBURN, Baron *cr* 2000 (Life Peer), of Langho in the co. of Lancashire; **Adam Hafejee Patel;** *b* Gujarat, India, 7 June 1940; *m* 1964, Ayesha; four *s*; four *d*. *Educ:* Maharaja Sayajirao Univ. of Baroda, India (BCom). Accountant with chartered accountants Ivan Jacques, Blackburn and S. & R. D. Thornton, Preston, 1967–74; Chief Internal Auditor, Zamtan, Lusaka, Zambia, 1975–76; Man. Dir, Comet Cash and Carry Co. Ltd, Blackburn, 1977–97. Mem., Labour Party, 1966–. Founder Mem., Blackburn Community Relns Council, later Blackburn with Darwen Racial Equality Council (Hon. Vice Pres.; former Treas., Vice-Chm. then Chm.); Chm., Blackburn and Dist Commonwealth Friendship Soc., 1966–67; founder Gen. Sec., Blackburn Indian Workers Assoc., 1967–74 (Pres., 1977–). Mem., Home Secretary's Race Relns Adv. Forum. Founder Director: Lancs TEC; Blackburn Partnership. Jt Chm., Christian/Muslim Inter-Faith Forum; Member: Muslim Council of Britain; Lancs CC Standing Adv. Council on Religious Educn. Chm. and Trustee, W Brookhouse Community Centre, Blackburn. JP Blackburn, 1984–95. *Recreations:* community and social work, gardening, football, cricket. *Address:* Snodworth Hall, Snodworth Road, Langho, Lancs BB6 8DS.

PATEL, Indraprasad Gordhanbhai, Hon. KBE 1990; PhD; Director, London School of Economics and Political Science, 1984–90 (Hon. Fellow, 1990); *b* 11 Nov. 1924; *s* of F. Patel Gordhanbhai Tulsibhai and M. Patel Kashiben Jivabhai; *m* 1958, Alaknanda Dasgupta; one *d*. *Educ:* Bombay Univ. (BA Hons); King's Coll., Cambridge (BA, PhD; Hon. Fellow, 1986). Prof. of Economics and Principal, Baroda Coll., Maharaja Sayajirao Univ. of Baroda, 1949; Economist, later Asst Chief, IMF, 1950–54; Dep. Economic Adviser, Min. of Finance, India, 1954–58; Alternate Exec. Dir for India, IMF, 1958–61; Chief Economic Adviser, Min. of Finance and Planning Commn, 1962–64, 1965–67; Special Sec. and Sec., Dept of Economic Affairs, 1967–72; Dep. Administrator, UN Develt Programme, 1972–77; Governor, Reserve Bank of India, 1977–82; Dir, Indian Inst. of Management, Ahmedabad, 1982–84. Chm., Bd of Dirs, Hindustan Oil Exploration Co. Ltd, 1999–; Member: Bd of Dirs, State Bank of India, 1995–; Prime Minister's Econ. Adv. Council, 1998–. Vis. Prof., Delhi Univ., 1964. Hon. Prof., Jawaharlal Nehru Univ., New Delhi, 2000–. Chairman: Bd of Govs, Indian Inst. of Mgt, 1996–; Indian Council for Res. in Internat. Economic Relations, 1997–; Mem., Bd of Govs, Mahindra United World Coll. of India, 1996–. Hon. DLitt: Sardar Patel Univ.; Maharaja Sayajirao Univ. of Baroda, 1993; Hon. DCL Univ. of Mauritius, 1990. Padma Vibhushan, 1991; Hon. DPhil Roorkee, 1997. *Publications:* Essays in Economic Policy and Economic Growth, 1986; Economic Reform and Global Change, 1998; articles in IMF staff papers etc. on inflation, monetary policy, internat. trade. *Recreations:* music, reading, watching cricket. *Address:* 12 Amee Co-operative Housing Society, Diwali Pura, Old Padra Road, Vadodara 390015, India.

PATEL, Praful Raojibhai Chaturbhai; Company Director; Investment Adviser in UK, since 1962; Hon. Secretary, All-Party Parliamentary Committee on UK Citizenship, since 1968; *b* Jinja, Uganda, 7 March 1939; *s* of Raojibhai Chaturbhai Patel, Sojitra, Gujarat, India, and Maniben Jivabhai Lalaji Patel, Dharmaj, Gujarat; unmarried. *Educ:* Government Sec. Sch., Jinja, Uganda; London Inst. of World Affairs, attached to University Coll., London (Extra Mural Dept). Sec., Uganda Students Union, 1956–58; Deleg. to Internat. Youth Assembly, New Delhi, 1958; awarded two travel bursaries for visits to E, Central and S Africa, and Middle East, to study and lecture on politics and economics; arrived in Britain as student, then commenced commercial activities, 1962; increasingly involved in industrial, cultural and educational projects affecting immigrants in Britain. Spokesman for Asians in UK following restriction of immigration resulting from Commonwealth Immigrants Act 1968; Council Mem., UK Immigrants Advisory Service, 1970–79; Mem., Uganda Resettlement Bd, 1972–74; Hon. Sec., Uganda Evacuees Resettlement Advisory Trust, 1974; Pres., Nava Kala India Socio-Cultural Centre, London, 1962–75; Chm. Bd of Trustees, Swaminarayan Hindu Mission, UK, 1970–76; Jt Convener, Asian Action Cttee, 1976; Convener, Manava Trust, 1979–. Contested (Lab) Brent North, 1987. *Publications:* articles in newspapers and journals regarding immigration and race relations. *Recreations:* cricket; campaigning and lobbying; current affairs; and inter-faith co-operation. *Address:* 60 Bedford Court Mansions, Bedford Avenue, WC1B 3AD. *T:* (020) 7580 0897; Taj Mahal Hotel, Apollo Bunder, Mumbai 400001, India. *Fax:* (22) 2872711.

PATEMAN, Jack Edward, CBE 1970; FREng; Chairman, Kent County Engineering Society, 1989–96; *b* 29 Nov. 1921; *s* of William Edward Pateman and Lucy Varley (*née* Jetten); *m* 1949, Cicely Hope Turner; one *s* one *d.* *Educ:* Gt Yarmouth Grammar Sch. Served War of 1939–45, RAF, 1940–46. Research Engineer: Belling & Lee, 1946–48; Elliott Bros (London) Ltd, 1948–51; formed Aviation Div. of EBL at Borehamwood, 1951–62; Dep. Chm. and Jt Man. Dir, Elliott Flight Automation Ltd, 1962–71; Man. Dir, 1971–86, Dep. Chm., 1986–87, GEC Avionics; Director: Canadian Marconi Co., 1971–87; GEC Computers Ltd, 1971–89 (Chm., 1978–82); Elliott Brothers (London) Ltd, 1979–89; Marconi Electronic Devices, 1980–87; GEC Avionics Projects Ltd, 1980–89; GEC Information Systems, 1982–86; GEC Avionics Projects (UK) Ltd, 1984–89; General Electric Co. Plc, 1986–88. GEC-Marconi Ltd, 1987–89. FREng (FEng 1981). British Gold Medal, RAeS, 1981. *Recreation:* sailing. *Address:* Spindles, Ivy Hatch, Sevenoaks, Kent TN15 0PG. *T:* (01732) 810364.

PATEMAN, Prof. John Arthur Joseph, FRS 1978; FRSE 1974; Emeritus Professor of Genetics, Australian National University; *b* 18 May 1926; *s* of John and Isobel May Pateman; *m* 1952, Mary Phelps; one *s* two *d.* *Educ:* Clacton County High Sch., Essex; University Coll., Leicester. BSc, PhD(Lond); MA(Cantab). Lectr, Univ. of Sheffield, 1954–58; Sen. Lectr, Univ. of Melbourne, Australia, 1958–60; Lectr, Univ. of Cambridge, 1960–67; Prof., Flinders Univ., S Australia, 1967–70; Prof. of Genetics, Univ. of Glasgow, 1970–79; Prof. of Genetics, ANU, 1979–88 (Exec. Dir, Centre for Recombinant DNA Res., 1982–88). Fellow, Churchill Coll., Cambridge, 1961–67. *Publications:* scientific papers in genetical, biochemical and microbiological jls. *Recreations:* reading, music, walking. *Address:* 1 Abberbury Road, Oxford OX4 4ET. *T:* (01865) 748275. *Club:* Oxford and Cambridge.

PATERSON, Alasdair Talbert; Librarian, University of Exeter, since 1994; *b* 22 Oct. 1947; *s* of Talbert Robertson Paterson and Alys Morton Paterson (*née* Campbell); *m* 1st, 1967, Corinne Brenda Norton (marr. diss. 1975); one *s*; 2nd, 1976, Ann Mary Cecilia Mulheirn; one *s* one *d.* *Educ:* Leith Acad.; Royal High Sch., Edinburgh; Univ. of Edinburgh (MA 1st cl. Hons 1970); Univ. of Sheffield (MA 1972). ALAI 1990. Asst Librarian, Univ. of Liverpool, 1972–86; Deputy Librarian: UC Cork, 1986–89; Univ. of Sheffield, 1989–94. Mem., Devon and Exeter Instn, 1994–. Eric Gregory Award, Soc. of Authors, 1975. *Publications:* Bibliography of Studies in Regional Industrial Development, 1978; The Floating World, 1984; Brief Lives, 1987; articles in prof. jls. *Recreations:* literature, the arts, travel, gardening, walking, watching sport, boules. *Address:* Taddyforde House North, New North Road, Exeter EX4 4AT. *T:* (01392) 430498. *Club:* Isca Pétanque (Exeter).

PATERSON, Alexander Craig, (Alastair), CBE 1987; FREng; Senior Partner, Bullen and Partners, Consulting Engineers, 1969–88, retired (Partner 1960–69); *b* 15 Jan. 1924; *s* of Duncan McKellar Paterson and Lavinia (*née* Craig); *m* 1947, Betty Hannah Burley; two *s* two *d.* *Educ:* Glasgow High Sch.; Royal Coll. of Science and Technol. (ARCST); Glasgow Univ. (BSc). FICE 1963; FIMechE 1964; FIStructE 1970; FREng (FEng 1983); FCIArb 1968. Commd REME, 1944; served India and Burma, attached Indian Army, 1944–47. Engineer: with Merz and McLellan, 1947–58; with Taylor Woodrow, 1958–60. Mem., Overseas Projects Bd, 1984–87. Institution of Structural Engineers: Mem. Council, 1976–89; Vice Pres., 1981–84; Pres., 1984–85; Institution of Civil Engineers: Mem. Council, 1978–81 and 1982–91; Vice-Pres., 1985–88; Pres., 1988–89. Pres., British Section, Société des Ingénieurs et Scientifiques de France, 1980; Chm., British Consultants Bureau, 1978–80; Member: Council, British Bd of Agrément, 1982–95; Engrg Council, 1987–90. Mem. Court, Cranfield Inst. of Technol., 1970–80. Hon. DSc Strathclyde, 1989. *Publications:* professional and technical papers in engrg jls. *Recreations:* sailing, gardening. *Address:* Willows, The Byeway, West Wittering, Chichester, West Sussex PO20 8LJ. *T:* (01243) 514199. *Club:* Caledonian.

PATERSON, Dame Betty (Fraser Ross), DBE 1981 (CBE 1973); DL; Chairman: NW Thames Regional Health Authority, 1973–84; National Staff Advisory Committee for England and Wales (Nurses and Midwives), 1975–84; *b* 14 March 1916; *d* of Robert Ross Russell and Elsie Marian Russell (*née* Fraser); *m* 1940, Ian Douglas Paterson; one *s* one *d.* *Educ:* Harrogate Coll.; Western Infirmary, Glasgow. Mem. Chartered Soc. of Physiotherapy (MCSP). County Comr, Herts Girl Guides, 1950–57. Member: Herts CC, 1952–74 (Alderman 1959–74; Chm., 1969–73); NE Metropolitan Regional Hosp. Bd, 1960–74; Governing Body, Royal Hosp. of St Bartholomew, 1960–74; Commn for the New Towns, England and Wales, 1961–75 (Dep. Chm., 1971–75); Governing Body, Bishop's Stortford Coll., 1967–81; Central Health Services Council, 1969–74; Gen. Council, King Edward's Hosp. Fund for London, 1975–84 (Management Cttee, 1975–80); Chm. Trustees, NHS Pensioners' Trust, 1991–96; Pres., Herts Assoc. of Local Councils, 1980–90; Vice-Pres., Herts Magistrates' Assoc., 1987–. JP Herts, 1950–86 (Chm. Bishop's Stortford Bench, 1978–86); DL Herts, 1980. *Recreations:* family, current affairs, music, talking books. *Address:* 52 Free Trade Wharf, The Highway, E1W 9ES. *T:* (020) 7791 0367.

PATERSON, Bill; *see* Paterson, W. T.

PATERSON, Prof. Sir Dennis (Craig), Kt 1976; MB, BS 1953, MD 1983; FRCS, FRACS; Director and Chief Orthopaedic Surgeon, Adelaide Children's Hospital, 1970–95; Consultant Orthopaedic Surgeon, Queen Victoria Hospital, 1968–95; Clinical Associate Professor, University of Adelaide, since 1990; *b* 14 Oct. 1930; *s* of Gilbert Charles Paterson and Thelma Drysdale Paterson; *m* 1955, Mary, *d* of Frederick Mansell Hardy; one *s* three *d.* *Educ:* Collegiate Sch. of St Peter; Univ. of Adelaide (MB, BS 1953; MD 1983). FRCS 1958, FRACS 1961. Res. Med. Officer: Royal Adelaide Hosp., 1954; Adelaide Children's Hosp., 1955; Registrar, Robert Jones & Agnes Hunt Orthop. Hosp., Oswestry, Shropshire, 1958–60; Royal Adelaide Hospital: Sen. Registrar, 1960–62; Cons. Orthop. Surg., 1964–86; Cons. Orthop. Surg., Repatriation Gen. Hosp., Adelaide, 1962–70; Adelaide Children's Hospital: Asst Hon. Orthop. Surg., 1964–66; Sen. Hon. Orthop. Surg., 1966–70; Mem. Bd of Management, 1976–84; Chm., Med. Adv. Cttee, 1976–84; Chm., Med. Staff Cttee, 1976–84. Amer./British/Canadian Trav. Prof., 1966. Chairman: Trauma Systems Cttee for SA, 1994–2001; SA Road Safety Consultative Council, 1994–98; Southern Partnership, 1998–. Archbishop's Appeal Cttee, 1994–; Member: Nat. Road Trauma Adv. Council, 1990–95; Bd of Management, McLaren Vale and Fleurieu Visitors Centre, 1995– (Chm., 1998–). Royal Australasian Coll. of Surgeons: Mem., Bd of Orthop. Surg., 1974–82, 1984–85 (Chm., 1977–82); Mem., Court of Examnrs, 1974–84; Mem., SA Cttee, 1974–78; Fellow: British Orthopaedic Assoc.; RSocMed; Member: Aust. Orthopaedic Assoc. (Censor-in-Chief, 1976–80; Dir, Continuing Educn, 1982–85); AMA; Internat. Scoliosis Res. Soc.; SICOT (Aust. Nat. Delegate, 1975–84, First Vice-Pres., 1984–87; Pres., 1987–90); Paediatric Orthopaedic Soc.; W Pacific Orthopaedic Soc.; Hon. Mem., American Acad. of Orthopaedic Surgeons, 1981. Pres., Crippled Children's Assoc. of South Australia Inc., 1970–84 (Mem. Council, 1966–70). Life Mem., S Aust. Cricket Assoc. Queen's Jubilee Medal, 1977. *Publications:* over 80 articles in Jl of Bone and Joint Surg., Clin. Orthopaedics and Related Res., Aust. and NZ Jl of Surg., Med. Jl of Aust., Western Pacific Jl of Orthop. Surg. *Recreations:* tennis, golf, gardening, vigneron. *Address:* 31 Myall Avenue, Kensington Gardens, SA 5068, Australia. *T:* (8) 83310890. *Clubs:* Adelaide, Royal Adelaide Golf (Adelaide).

PATERSON, Douglas McCallum; Chief Executive, Aberdeen City Council, since 1995; *b* 20 Nov. 1949; *s* of Douglas James Paterson and Violet Joan Paterson (*née* McCallum); *m* 1971, Isobel Stewart Beaton; two *d.* *Educ:* Aberdeen Univ. (MA Hons Econs 1971; DipEd 1976; MEd Hons 1981); Aberdeen Coll. of Educn (PGCE Dist. 1976); Robert Gordon Univ. (Dip Mgt 1990, DipM 1990). Manager, John Wood Gp, 1971–75; Grampian Regional Council: teacher, then head teacher, 1976–86; Advr in Educn, 1986–90; Depute Dir of Educn, 1990–92; Sen. Depute Dir of Educn, 1992–94; Dir of Educn, 1994–95. *Recreations:* walking, theatre, local history and culture, music, D-I-Y. *Address:* (office) Town House, Broad Street, Aberdeen AB10 1FY. *T:* (01224) 522500.

PATERSON, Francis, (Frank), FCIT, FILT; General Manager, Eastern Region, British Rail, York, 1978–85; Member, British Railways (Eastern) Board, 1978–85; Chairman, North Yorkshire Family Practitioner Committee, 1987–91; *b* 5 April 1930; *s* of Francis William Paterson and Cecilia Eliza Reid Brownie; *m* 1950, Grace Robertson (*d* 1996); two *s* two *d.* *Educ:* Robert Gordon's Coll., Aberdeen. Joined LNER as Junior Clerk, 1946; clerical and supervisory positions in NE Scotland; management training, Scotland, 1956–59; various man-management, operating and marketing posts, Scotland, Lincs and Yorks, 1960–66; Operating Supt, Glasgow North, 1967–68; Sales Manager, Edinburgh, 1968; Asst Divl Manager, S Wales, 1968–70; Dir, United Welsh Transport, 1968–70; Harbour Comr, Newport Harbour, 1968–70; Divl Manager, Central Div., Southern Region, 1970–75; Director: Southdown Motor Services Ltd, 1970–73; Brighton, Hove & District Omnibus Co., 1970–73; Dep. Gen. Man., Southern Region, 1975–77; Chief Freight Manager, British Railways Bd, 1977–78. Dir, N Yorks Moors Rly plc, 1993–2000. Vice-Chm., Nat. Railway Mus. Cttee, 1984– (Mem., 1978–); Member: CBI Southern Regional Council, 1975–77; CBI Transport Policy Cttee, 1977–78; BBC NE Adv. Council, 1987–91; Chm., BBC Local Radio Adv. Council, Radio York, 1987–91. Pres., St Andrews Soc. of York, 1989–90. Trustee, Friends of Nat. Railway Museum, 1988–. Mem. Court, Univ. of York, 1981–92. OStJ 1980. FCIT 1978 (Mem. Council, CIT, 1979–84); FILT 1999. *Publications:* papers to transport societies. *Recreations:* transport, travel, hill walking, country pursuits, Scottish culture, enjoying grandchildren. *Address:* Alligin, 97 Main Street, Askham Bryan, York YO23 3QS. *T:* (01904) 708478.

PATERSON, His Honour Frank David; a Circuit Judge (formerly County Court Judge), 1968–93; *b* 10 July 1918; *yr s* of late David Paterson and Dora Paterson, Liverpool; *m* 1953, Barbara Mary, 2nd *d* of late Oswald Ward Gillow and Alice Gillow, Formby; one *s* two *d.* *Educ:* Calderstones Preparatory Sch. and Quarry Bank High Sch., Liverpool; Univ. of Liverpool (LLB). Called to Bar, Gray's Inn, 1941; Warden, Unity Boys' Club, Liverpool, 1941; Asst Warden, Florence Inst. for Boys, Liverpool, 1943. Practised on Northern Circuit. Chairman: Min. of Pensions and Nat. Insce Tribunal, Liverpool, 1957; Mental Health Review Tribunal for SW Lancashire and Cheshire, 1963. Asst Dep. Coroner, City of Liverpool, 1960. Pres., Merseyside Magistrates' Assoc., 1978–93. Hon. LLD Liverpool, 1993. *Address:* Vailima, 2 West Lane, Formby, Liverpool L37 7BA. *T:* (01704) 874345. *Club:* Athenæum (Liverpool).

PATERSON, Gil; Member (SNP) Central Scotland, Scottish Parliament, since 1999; *b* 1942; *m*; one *s.* *Educ:* Possilpark Secondary Sch. Company owner and director. Mem., Strathclyde Regl Council, 1975–78. Contested (SNP): Glasgow Central, June 1980; Strathkelvin and Bearsden, 1987. *Address:* Scottish Parliament, Edinburgh EH99 1SP.

PATERSON, James Rupert; HM Diplomatic Service, retired; *b* 7 Aug. 1932; *s* of late Major Robert Paterson, MC, Seaforth Highlanders and Mrs Josephine Paterson; *m* 1956, Kay Dineen; two *s* two *d.* *Educ:* Nautical Coll., Pangbourne; RMA, Sandhurst. Commnd RA, 1953 (Tombs Meml Prize); Staff Coll., Camberley, 1963; retd from Army with rank of Major, 1970; joined FCO, 1970; First Sec., Pakistan, 1972; Dep. High Comr, Trinidad and Tobago, 1975; Ambassador to the Mongolian People's Republic, 1982; Consul-General, Istanbul, 1985, Geneva, 1989–92. *Recreations:* reading, travel, golf. *Address:* c/o Barclays Bank, Deal, Kent CT14 6EP.

PATERSON, James Veitch; Sheriff of the Lothian and Borders (formerly Roxburgh, Berwick and Selkirk) at Jedburgh, Selkirk and Duns, 1963–2000; *b* 16 April 1928; *s* of late John Robert Paterson, ophthalmic surgeon, and Jeanie Gouinlock; *m* 1956, Ailie, *o d* of Lt-Comdr Sir (George) Ian Clark Hutchison, *qv*; one *s* one *d.* *Educ:* Peebles High School; Edinburgh Academy; Lincoln College, Oxford; Edinburgh University. Admitted to Faculty of Advocates, 1953. *Recreations:* fishing, shooting, gardening. *Address:* Sunnyside, Melrose, Roxburghshire TD6 9BE. *T:* (01896) 822502. *Club:* New (Edinburgh).

PATERSON, Most Rev. John Campbell; *see* New Zealand, Primate and Presiding Bishop of.

PATERSON, Very Rev. John Munn Kirk; Minister Emeritus of St Paul's Parish Church, Milngavie (Minister, 1970–87); Moderator of the General Assembly of the Church of Scotland, 1984–85; *b* 8 Oct. 1922; *s* of George Kirk Paterson and Sarah Ferguson Paterson (*née* Wilson); *m* 1946, Geraldine Lilian Parker; two *s* one *d.* *Educ:* Hillhead High School, Glasgow; Edinburgh Univ. MA, BD. RAF, 1942–46 (Defence and Victory medals, Italy Star, 1945). Insurance Official, 1940–58 (ACII 1951); Assistant

Minister, 1958–64; Ordained Minister of Church of Scotland, 1964–. Hon. DD Aberdeen, 1986. *Recreations:* fishing, hill walking. *Club:* Royal Over-Seas League (Edinburgh).

PATERSON, Very Rev. John Thomas Farquhar; Dean of Christ Church, Dublin, since 1989; *b* Portadown, Co. Armagh, 21 Dec. 1938; *s* of Henry Paterson and Margreta Elizabeth Paterson (*née* Bell); *m* 2001, Patricia Bray (*née* Daniel); two step *s*. *Educ:* Portadown College; Trinity College, Dublin (BA, MA, BD). Curate-Assistant: Drumglass (Dungannon), 1963; St Bartholomew, Dublin, 1966; Priest-in-charge, St Mark, Dublin and Asst Chaplain, TCD, 1968; Vicar, St Bartholomew with Christ Church, Leeson Park, Dublin, 1972; Dean and Rector of Kildare, 1978. Lectr in Pastoral Liturgy, Church of Ireland Theol Coll., 1984–91. Hon. Sec., Gen. Synod, Church of Ireland, 1985–91. *Publications:* (jtly) A Parish Education Handbook, 1987; Mary in the Church, 1990; All Sorts and Conditions: a history of the laity in the Church of Ireland, 2002; articles in Irish theological jls (Search, The Furrow, Doctrine and Life). *Recreations:* travel, reading, music. *Address:* The Deanery, St Werburgh Street, Dublin 8, Ireland. *T:* (1) 4781797, (cathedral) (1) 6778099, *Fax:* (1) 4753442, (cathedral) (1) 6798991; *e-mail:* paterson@iol.ie. *Club:* Kildare Street and University (Dublin).

PATERSON, Owen William; MP (C) North Shropshire, since 1997; *b* 24 June 1956; *s* of late Alfred Paterson and of Cynthia Owen; *m* 1980, Rose Ridley; two *s* one *d*. *Educ:* Radley Coll.; Corpus Christi Coll., Cambridge (BA Hist.). British Leather Co.: Sales Dir, 1980; Man. Dir, 1993–97. Pres., European Tanners' Confedn, 1996–97. Contested (C) Wrexham, 1992. *Recreations:* travel, history, trees, riding, hunting, racing, poultry. *Address:* House of Commons, SW1A 0AA.

PATERSON, William Alexander; *see* Alexander, Bill.

PATERSON, Prof. William Edgar, OBE 1999; PhD; FRSE; Director, Institute for German Studies, and Professor of German Politics, University of Birmingham, since 1994; *b* Blair Atholl, Perthshire, 26 Sept. 1941; *s* of late William Paterson, FRICS, FLAS, Land Agent, and of Winnie Paterson (*née* McIntyre); *m* 1st, 1964, Jacqueline Cramb (*d* 1974); two *s*; 2nd, 1979, Phyllis MacDowell; one *d*, and one step *s* one step *d*. *Educ:* Morrison's Acad.; Univ. of St Andrews (MA, Class Medallist); London Sch. of Econs (S. H. Bailey Schol.; MSc, PhD 1973). FRSE 1994. Lectr in Internat. Relns, Univ. of Aberdeen, 1967–70; University of Warwick: Volkswagen Lectr in German Politics, 1970–75; Sen. Lectr, 1975–82; Reader, 1982–89; Prof. and Chm. of Dept, 1989–90; Salvesen Prof. of Eur. Insts, and Dir, Europa Inst., Univ. of Edinburgh, 1990–94. Jt Ed., German Politics; Member, Editorial Board: Jl Common Mkt Studies, 1991–; Internat. Affairs, 1993–. Mem., ESRC Res. Priorities Bd, 1995–99. Mem., Königswinter Conf. Steering Cttee, 1994. Chairman: Assoc. for Study of German Politics, 1974–76; Univ. Assoc. for Contemporary Eur. Studies, 1989–94; Vice-Chm., German-British Forum, 1999. Mem., Adv. Bd, Centre for British Studies, Humboldt Univ., Berlin, 1997. Associate Fellow, RIIA, 1994; AcSS 2000. FRSA 1998. Officer's Cross, Order of Merit (FRG), 1999. *Publications:* The SPD and European Integration, 1974; *jointly*: Social Democracy in Post-War Europe, 1974; The Federal Republic of Germany and the European Community, 1987; Government and the Chemical Industry, 1988; Governing Germany, 1991; A History of Social Democracy in Post-War Europe, 1991; Developments in German Politics, 1992; Developments in German Politics II, 1996; The Kohl Chancellorship, 1998; The Future of the German Economy, 2000; Germany's European Diplomacy, 2000; *edited jointly:* Social and Political Movements in Western Europe, 1976; Social Democratic Parties in Western Europe, 1977; Foreign Policy Making in Western Europe, 1978; Sozialdemokratische Parteien in Europa, 1978; The West German Model, 1981; The Future of Social Democracy, 1986; Developments in West German Politics, 1989; Politics in Western Europe Today, 1990; El Futuro de la Social Democracia, 1992; Rethinking Social Democracy in Western Europe, 1993; contrib. over 100 articles to edited collections and learned jls. *Recreation:* walking. *Address:* Institute for German Studies, University of Birmingham, Pritchatts Road, Edgbaston, Birmingham B15 2TT. *T:* (0121) 414 7182; 220 Myton Road, Warwick CV34 6PS. *T:* and *Fax:* (01926) 492492; 6 Port Road, Pacnackie, Dumfriesshire DG7 1PQ. *T:* and *Fax:* (01556) 600395. *Club:* Royal Over-Seas League.

PATERSON, William Tulloch, (Bill); actor since 1968; *b* 3 June 1945; *s* of late John Paris Paterson and of Ann Tulloch Paterson; *m* 1984, Hildegard Bechtler; one *s* one *d*. *Educ:* Whitehill Sen. Secondary Sch., Glasgow; RSAMD. First professional engagement, Glasgow Citizens' Theatre, 1968; Asst Dir, Citizens' Theatre for Youth, 1970–72; Founder Mem., 7:84 (Scotland) Theatre Co. *Stage:* The Cheviot, the Stag and the Black Black Oil, 1973; Writer's Cramp, 1977; Whose Life is it Anyway?, Savoy, 1978; Guys and Dolls, NT, 1982; Schweyk, NT, 1983; Death and the Maiden, Royal Court, 1992; Misery, Criterion, 1993; Mongrel's Heart, Edinburgh, 1994; Ivanov, Almeida, 1997; Marriage Play, RNT, 2001; *films:* Comfort and Joy, 1984; The Killing Fields, 1984; Defence of the Realm, 1985; A Private Function, 1986; The Adventures of Baron Munchausen, 1987; The Witches, 1989; Truly Madly Deeply, 1991; Chaplin, 1992; Richard III, 1996; Hilary and Jackie, 1998; Complicity, 2000; Crush, 2001; *television series and serials:* Smiley's People, 1981; Auf Wiedersehen Pet, 1986; The Singing Detective, 1987; Traffik, 1989; Tell Tale Hearts, 1992; Hard Times, 1993; The Writing on the Wall, 1995; The Crow Road, 1996; Wives and Daughters, 1999; Rebel Heart, 2000; The Whistleblower, 2001. *Address:* c/o Gordon and French, 12–13 Poland Street, W1V 3DE.

PATERSON-BROWN, Dr June, CBE 1991; JP; Lord-Lieutenant of Roxburgh, Ettrick and Lauderdale, since 1998; Chief Commissioner, Girl Guides Association, and Commonwealth Chief Commissioner, 1985–90; *b* 8 Feb. 1932; *d* of Thomas Clarke Garden and Jean Martha (*née* Mallace); *m* 1957, Dr Peter N. Paterson-Brown; three *s* one *d*. *Educ:* Esdaile Sch.; Edinburgh Univ. (MB, ChB). MO in Community Health, 1960–85. Scottish Chief Comr, Girl Guides Assoc., 1977–82; Vice-Pres., Guide Assoc., 1992–; Pres., Roxburghshire, Guide Assoc., 1993–. Non-exec. Dir, Border Television, 1980–2000; Chm., Borders Children's Panel Adv. Cttee, 1982–85; Trustee: Prince's Trust, 1982–94 (Vice-Chm., 1982–92); MacRobert's Trust, 1987–; Chm., Scottish Standing Conf. Voluntary Youth Organisations, 1982–85. Chm. Cttee, Duke of Edinburgh's Award Scheme, Roxburgh, 1970–85. DL 1990, JP 1999, Roxburgh, Ettrick and Lauderdale. Paul Harris Fellow, Rotary Internat., 1990. Silver Jubilee Medal, 1977. *Recreations:* ski-ing, golfing, fishing, tennis, music, reading. *Address:* Norwood, Hawick, Roxburghshire TD9 7HP. *T:* (01450) 372352. *Club:* Lansdowne.

PATEY, Very Rev. Edward Henry; Dean of Liverpool, 1964–82, now Dean Emeritus; *b* 12 Aug. 1915; *s* of Walter Patey, MD, and Dorothy Patey; *m* 1942, Margaret Ruth Olivia Abbott, OBE; one *s* three *d*. *Educ:* Marlborough College; Hertford College, Oxford; Westcott House, Cambridge. Assistant Curate, St Mary-at-the-Walls, Colchester, 1939; MA (Oxon) 1941; Assistant Curate Bishopwearmouth Parish Church, Sunderland, 1942; Youth Chaplain to the Bishop of Durham, 1946; Vicar of Oldland, with Longwell Green, Bristol, 1950; Secretary, Youth Department, The British Council of Churches, 1952; Assistant Gen. Secretary, The British Council of Churches, 1955; Canon Residentiary of Coventry Cathedral, 1958. Hon. LLD Liverpool, 1980. *Publications:* Religion in the Club, 1956; Boys and Girls Growing Up, 1957; Worship in the Club, 1961; A Doctor's Life of Jesus, 1962; Young People Now, 1964; Enquire Within, 1966; Look out for the Church, 1969; Burning Questions, 1971; Don't Just Sit There, 1974; Christian Lifestyle, 1975; All in Good Faith, 1978; Open the Doors, 1978; Open the Book, 1981; I Give You This Ring, 1982; My Liverpool Life, 1983; Becoming An Anglican, 1985; Preaching on Special Occasions, 1985; Questions For Today, 1986; For the Common Good, 1989; Faith in a Risk-Taking God, 1991. *Recreations:* reading, listening to music, walking. *Address:* 139 High Street, Malmesbury, Wilts SN16 9AL.

PATEY, William Charters; HM Diplomatic Service; Head of Middle East Department, Foreign and Commonwealth Office, since 1999; *b* 11 July 1953; *s* of William Maurice Patey and Christina Kinnell (*née* Hastie); *m* 1978, Vanessa Carol Morrell; two *s*. *Educ:* Trinity Acad., Edinburgh; Univ. of Dundee (MA Hons). Joined FCO, 1975; MECAS, 1977–78; Commercial Attaché, Abu Dhabi, 1978–81; Second Sec., Tripoli, 1981–84; FCO, 1984–88; First Sec. (Political), Canberra, 1988–92; Dep. Head, UN Dept, 1992–93, Inspector, 1994–95, FCO; Dep. Head of Mission and Consul-Gen., Riyadh, 1995–98. Trustee: Bahrain-Britain Foundn, 1999–; Anglo-Omani Soc., 2001. Mem., Oxford Energy Policy Club, 2000–. Hon. Pres., St Margaret's Film Soc., 1996. *Recreations:* tennis, theatre, acting, golf. *Address:* c/o Foreign and Commonwealth Office, King Charles Street, SW1A 2AH.

PATHAK, Raghunandan Swarup; Member: Indian Council of Arbitration, since 1991; Permanent Court of Arbitration, The Hague, since 1997; *b* 25 Nov. 1924; *s* of Gopal Swarup Pathak and Prakashwati; *m* 1955, Asha Paranjpe; three *s*. *Educ:* St Joseph's Coll., Allahabad; Ewing Christian Coll., Allahabad; Allahabad Univ. (BSc 1945; LLB 1947; MA (Pol. Sci.) 1948; Sastri Medal in Internat. Law, 1947). Enrolled Advocate: Allahabad High Court, 1948; Supreme Court of India, 1957; Additional Judge, 1962, Judge, 1963, Allahabad High Court; Chief Justice, Himachal Pradesh High Court, 1972; Judge, Supreme Court of India, 1978; Chief Justice of India, 1986–89; Judge, Internat. Court of Justice, The Hague, 1989–91. Chm., All India Univ. Professors' Internat. Law Res. Gp, 1969–89; Visitor, Nat. Law Sch. of India, Bangalore, 1986–89; Pro-Chancellor, Univ. of Delhi, 1986–89; Distinguished Vis. Prof., Inst. of Advanced Studies in the Humanities, Edinburgh Univ. President: Indian Law Inst., 1986–89; Indian Council of Legal Aid and Advice; Indian Soc. of Internat. Law, 1989–93; International Law Association, London: Mem., 1952–; Pres., India Regl Br., 1986–89; Mem., Cttee on Space Law, and Cttee on Enforcement of Human Rights; Vice-Pres., Indian Acad. of Environmental Law and Research; Pres., Centre for Res. on Envmt, Ecol. and Develt, New Delhi, 1995–. Chairman: World Congress on Law and Medicine, New Delhi, 1985; Indian Nat. Steering Cttee, Leadership in Envmt and Develt Prog., 1991–; Indian Nat. Cttee for Promotion of Social and Economic Welfare; Sarvodaya Internat. Trust, Bangalore. Member: Indo-Soviet Internat. Law Confs; Indo-W German Internat. Law Colloquia; UN Univ. project on Internat. Law, Common Patrimony and Intergenerational Equity; UN Univ. project on Internat. Law and Global Change, 1989; UN High-level Adv. Bd on Sustainable Develt, 1993–95. Hon. Mem., Indian Social Security Foundn. Mem., Internat. Council of Arbitration for Sport, 1991–; Court of Arbitration for Sport *ad hoc* Division: Co-Pres., Olympic Games, Atlanta, 1996, Nagano, 1998; Pres., Commonwealth Games, Kuala Lumpur, 1998. Pres., Nehru Trust for Indian Collections at V & A Mus. (London), India, 1991–; Trustee, Bd of Trustees, The Tribune, Chandigarh, 1994–. Mem. Exec. Council, Univ. of Delhi. Lectures worldwide on human rights, envmtl law and sustainable develt, commercial arbitration, constitutional law, internat. law. Hon. Bencher, Gray's Inn, 1988. Hon. LLD: Agra; Panjab; Hon. DLitt Kashi Vidyapeeth, Varanasi. *Publications:* papers on internat. law, law of the sea, etc, in learned jls. *Recreations:* golf, photography. *Address:* 7 Sardar Patel Marg, New Delhi 110021, India. *T:* (11) 3017161, *Fax:* (11) 3017170. *Clubs:* Delhi Gymkhana, India International Centre, Delhi Golf (New Delhi).

PATIENCE, Adèle; *see* Williams, J. A.

PATIENCE, Andrew, QC 1990; **His Honour Judge Patience;** a Circuit Judge, since 1999; *b* 28 April 1941; *s* of late William Edmund John Patience and Louise Mary Patience; *m* 1975, Jean Adèle Williams, *qv*; one *s* one *d*. *Educ:* Whitgift School, Croydon; St John's College, Oxford (MA). Called to the Bar, Gray's Inn, 1966; a Recorder, 1986–99; Resident Judge, Maidstone Crown Court, 2000–. *Recreations:* mimicry, complaining, African politics. *Address:* The Law Courts, Barker Road, Maidstone, Kent ME16 8EQ. *Club:* Oxford and Cambridge.

PATMORE, Prof. (John) Allan, CBE 1993; Professor of Geography, University of Hull, 1973–91, Professor Emeritus, since 1991; Vice-Chairman, Sports Council, 1988–94 (Member, 1978–94); *b* 14 Nov. 1931; *s* of John Edwin Patmore and Marjorie Patmore; *m* 1956, Barbara Janet Fraser; one *s* two *d*. *Educ:* Harrogate Grammar Sch.; Pembroke Coll., Oxford (MA, BLitt). Served RAF, Educn Br., 1952–54. Department of Geography, University of Liverpool: Tutor, 1954–55; Asst Lectr, 1955–58; Lectr, 1958–69; Sen. Lectr, 1969–73; University of Hull: Dean of Social Science, 1979–81; Pro-Vice-Chancellor, 1982–85. Visiting Professor: Univ. of Southern Illinois, 1962–63; Univ. of Canterbury, NZ, 1978. Pres. 1979–80, Trustee 1979–88, Hon. Mem., 1991, Geographical Assoc.; Pres., Sect. E, BAAS, 1987–88. Pres., N Yorks Moors Assoc., 1993–2000; Member: N York Moors National Park Cttee, 1977–92; Nat. Parks Review Panel, 1990–91; Countryside Commn, 1992–98; Inland Waterways Amenity Adv. Council, 1993–94; Bd, Nat. Lottery New Opportunities Fund, 1998–. Chm., Friends of Nat. Railway Mus., 1992–; Mem. Adv. Cttee, Nat. Railway Mus., 1988–. JP Hull, 1975–2001. Hon. DLitt Loughborough, 1993. *Publications:* Land and Leisure, 1970; People, Place and Pleasure, 1975; Recreation and Resources, 1983; Leisure and Mission, 2000. *Recreations:* pursuing railway history, enjoying the countryside. *Address:* 4 Aston Hall Drive, North Ferriby, East Yorkshire HU14 3EB. *T:* (01482) 632269.

PATNICK, Sir (Cyril) Irvine, Kt 1994; OBE 1980; Chairman, Keyturn Solutions Ltd, since 1997; *b* Oct. 1929; *m* 1960, Lynda Margaret (*née* Rosenfield); one *s* one *d*. *Educ:* Sheffield Poly. FCIOB. Member: Sheffield City Council, 1967–70; Sheffield MDC, 1971–88; S Yorks CC, until abolition in 1986 (Opposition Leader, 1973–86); Dep. Chm., S Yorks Residuary Body, 1985–87; Chm., Cons. Party Local Govt Adv. Cttee, 1989–90. Contested (C) Sheffield, Hillsborough, 1970, 1979. MP (C) Sheffield, Hallam, 1987–97; contested (C) same seat, 1997. An Asst Govt Whip, 1989–90; a Lord Comr of HM Treasury (Govt Whip), 1990–94. Member: Envmt Select Cttee, 1994–97; Cttee of Selection, 1997; Dep. Chm., Channel Tunnel Rail Link Bill Select Cttee, 1995–96. Vice-Chm., Cons. Party Back Bench Envmt Cttee, 1988–89. Member: Council of Europe, 1995–97; WEU, 1995–97. Mem., Cons. Party NEC, 1987–89. Chm., Yorks and Humberside Council for Sport and Recreation, 1979–85; Member: Sheffield Community Health Council, 1974–75; Yorks and Humberside Tourist Bd, 1977–79; Governor, Sports Aid Foundn, Yorks and Humberside, 1980–85. Freeman, City of London, 1996. *Address:* Keyturn Solutions Ltd, 20 Crown Passage, Pall Mall, SW1Y 6PP. *T:* (020) 7839 8882.

PATON, Hon. Lady; Ann Paton; a Senator of the College of Justice in Scotland, since 2000; *d* of James McCargow and Ann Dunlop or McCargow; *m* 1974, Dr James Y. Paton;

no *c*. *Educ:* Laurel Bank Sch.; Univ. of Glasgow (MA 1972; LLB 1974). Admitted to the Scottish Bar, 1977. Standing Junior Counsel: to the Queen's and Lord Treasurer's Remembrancer (excluding *Ultimus Haeres*), 1979; in Scotland to Office of Fair Trading, 1981; QC (Scot.) 1990; Advocate Depute, 1992–94. Mem., Criminal Injuries Compensation Bd, 1995–2000. Dir, Scottish Council of Law Reporting, 1995–2000. *Publications:* Map of Sheriffdoms and Sheriff Court Districts in Scotland, 1977, 2nd edn 1980; (Jt Asst Editor) Gloag and Henderson, Law of Scotland, 8th edn 1980, to 10th edn 1995; (with R. G. McEwan) A Casebook on Damages in Scotland, 1983, 2nd edn as Damages in Scotland (sole author), 1989, re-titled Damages for Personal Injuries in Scotland, 1997; Faculty Digest Supplement 1971–1980, 1995; contrib. Scottish Current Law Statutes, Session Cases, Scots Law Times, and Green's Reparation Bulletin. *Recreations:* sailing, tennis, cycling. *Address:* Parliament House, Parliament Square, Edinburgh EH1 1RQ. *Club:* Grange Tennis.

PATON, Alasdair Chalmers, CEng, FICE, FCIWEM; Chief Executive, Scottish Environment Protection Agency, 1995–2000; *b* Paisley, 28 Nov. 1944; *o s* of David Paton and Margaret Elizabeth Paton (*née* Chalmers); *m* 1969, Zona Gertrude Gill; one *s* one *d*. *Educ:* John Neilson Instn, Paisley; Univ. of Glasgow (BSc). Assistant Engineer: Clyde Port Authy, 1967–71; Dept of Agric. and Fisheries for Scotland, 1971–72; Sen. Engineer, Scottish Develt Dept, 1972–77; Engineer, Public Works Dept, Hong Kong Govt, 1977–80; Scottish Development Department: Sen. Engineer, 1980–84; Principal Engineer, 1984–87; Dep. Chief Engineer, 1987–91; Dir and Chief Engineer, Water and Waste Directorate, Scottish Office Envmt Dept, 1991–95. *Recreations:* Rotary, sailing, golf. *Address:* Oriel House, Academy Square, Limekilns, Fife KY11 3HN.

PATON, Ann; *see* Paton, Hon. Lady.

PATON, Douglas Shaw F.; *see* Forrester-Paton.

PATON, Maj.-Gen. Douglas Stuart, CBE 1983 (MBE 1961); FFPHM; Commander Medical HQ BAOR, 1983–85; retired 1986; *b* 3 March 1926; *s* of Stuart Paton and Helen Kathleen Paton (*née* Hooke); *m* 1957, Jennifer Joan Land; two *d*. *Educ:* Sherborne; Bristol University. MB ChB 1951; FFPHM 1989 (FFCM 1982, MFCM 1973). Commissioned RAMC, 1952; served Middle East (Canal Zone), Malaya, Hong Kong and UK, 1952–61; 16 Para Bde, 1961–66; jssc 1966; CO BMH Terendak, Malaysia, 1967–70; MoD, 1970–73; CO Cambridge Mil. Hosp., Aldershot, 1973–76; rcds 1977; DDMS HQ 1 (BR) Corps, 1978–81; Dep. Dir-Gen., Army Med. Services, MoD, 1981–83. QHP 1981–86. Hon. Col 221 (Surrey) Field Amb. RAMC(V), TA, 1988–92. Chm., RAMC Assoc., 1988–98. Mem. Bd of Governors, Moorfields Eye Hosp., 1988–91. CStJ 1986. *Publications:* contribs to Jl RAMC. *Recreations:* golf, skiing, travel, opera, gardening. *Address:* Brampton, Springfield Road, Camberley, Surrey GU15 1AB.

PATON, Hon. (Frederick) Ronald N.; *see* Noel-Paton.

PATON, Ven. Michael John Macdonald; Archdeacon of Sheffield, 1978–87, Archdeacon Emeritus since 1988; *b* 25 Nov. 1922; *s* of late Rev. William Paton, DD, and Grace Mackenzie Paton (*née* Macdonald); *m* 1952, Isobel Margaret Hogarth; one *s* four *d*. *Educ:* Repton School; Magdalen Coll., Oxford (MA). Indian Army, 1942–46; HM Foreign Service, 1948–52; Lincoln Theological Coll., 1952–54; Deacon 1954, priest 1955; Curate, All Saints', Gosforth, Newcastle upon Tyne, 1954–57; Vicar, St Chad's, Sheffield, 1957–67; Chaplain, United Sheffield Hosps, 1967–70; Vicar, St Mark's, Broomhill, Sheffield, and Chaplain, Weston Park Hosp., 1970–78. *Publications:* contrib. to: Essays in Anglican Self-criticism, 1958; More Sermons from Great St Mary's, 1971; Religion and Medicine, 1976; Mud and Stars, 1991. *Recreations:* hill walking, music, birdwatching. *Address:* 947 Abbeydale Road, Sheffield S7 2QD. *T:* (0114) 236 6148.
See also Rt. Rev. H. W. Montefiore.

PATON, William; Director, TÜV Suddeutschland, since 2001; *b* 29 Nov. 1941; *s* of Matthew and Elizabeth Harrison; *m* 1964, Elizabeth Anne Marr; two *s*. *Educ:* Douglas Ewart Sch., Newton Stewart; Univ. of Glasgow (BSc Hons Physics). Seismologist, SSL Ltd, 1964; Mgt Trainee, Colvilles Ltd, 1965; National Engineering Laboratory: scientific posts, 1965–80; Dir of Ops, 1990–95; Dir, 1995–97; Chief Exec., TÜV Product Service Ltd, 1997–2001. Dir and Sen. Exec., Nat. Engrg Assessment Gp, 1997–. Patents relating to improvements in carbon fibre processing technol., engrg designs and sports equipment. *Publications:* various articles in technical jls. *Recreations:* golf, travel. *Address:* 2 Wester Balrymonth, St Andrews, Fife KY16 8NN. *T:* (01334) 472131.

PATON WALSH, Jill, CBE 1996; self-employed author, since 1966; *b* 29 April 1937; *d* of John Llewelyn Bliss and Patricia Paula DuBern; *m* 1961, Antony Paton Walsh (separated); one *s* two *d*. *Educ:* St Michael's Convent, Finchley; St Anne's Coll., Oxford (BA English; MA; DipEd). Schoolteacher, Enfield Girls' Grammar Sch., 1959–62. Arts Council Creative Writing Fellowship, Brighton Poly., 1976–77, 1977–78; Gertrude Clark Whitall Meml Lectr, Library of Congress, 1978; vis. faculty mem., Center for Children's Lit., Simmons Coll., Boston, Mass, 1978–86. A Judge, Whitbread Lit. Award, 1984; Chm., Cambridge Book Assoc., 1987–89; former Mem., Management Cttee, Soc. of Authors; Member: Cttee, Children's Writers' and Illustrators' Gp; Adjunct British Bd, Children's Literature New England. FRSL 1996. *Publications: fiction:* Farewell, Great King, 1972; Lapsing, 1986; A School for Lovers, 1989; The Wyndham Case, 1993; Knowledge of Angels, 1994; A Piece of Justice, 1995; The Serpentine Cave, 1997; Thrones, Dominations (completion of novel by Dorothy L. Sayers), 1998; A Desert in Bohemia, 2000; *for children:* The Island Sunrise: pre-historic Britain, 1975; *fiction:* Hengest's Tale, 1966; The Dolphin Crossing, 1967; (with Kevin Crossley-Holland) Wordhoard, 1969; Fireweed (Book World Fest. Award), 1970; Goldengrove, 1972; Toolmaker, 1973; The Dawnstone, 1973; The Emperor's Winding Sheet (jtly, Whitbread Prize), 1974; The Butty Boy, 1975 (US edn as The Huffler); Unleaving (Boston Globe/Horn Book Award), 1976; Crossing to Salamis, The Walls of Athens, and Persian Gold, 1977–78 (US combined edn as Children of the Fox, 1978); A Chance Child, 1978; The Green Book, 1981 (re-issued as Shine, 1988); Babylon, 1982; Lost & Found, 1984; A Parcel of Patterns (Universe Prize), 1984; Gaffer Samson's Luck, 1985 (Smarties Prize Grand Prix, 1984); Five Tides, 1986; Torch, 1987; Birdy and the Ghosties, 1989; Grace, 1991; When Grandma Came, 1992; Matthew and the Sea-Singer, 1992; Pepi and the Secret Names, 1994; When I Was Little Like You, 1997. *Recreations:* photography, gardening, reading. *Address:* c/o David Higham Associates, 5–8 Lower John Street, Golden Square, W1R 4HA. *T:* (020) 7437 7888.

PATRIARCA, Stephen Richard; Headmaster, William Hulme's Grammar School, Manchester, since 2000; *b* 3 May 1953; *s* of Ronald and Maureen Patriarca. *Educ:* Sweyne Sch., Rayleigh; UC of Swansea (BA Hons 1995). Asst English Master, 1978–95, Dep. Headmaster, 1995–2000, Hulme GS, Oldham. *Recreations:* travel, music, art, cooking, wine. *Address:* William Hulme's Grammar School, Spring Bridge Road, Manchester M16 8PR. *T:* (0161) 226 2054. *Club:* East India.

PATRICK, Gail; *see* Patrick, L. G.

PATRICK, Graham McIntosh, CMG 1968; CVO 1981; DSC 1943; Under Secretary, Department of the Environment, 1971–81, retired; *b* 17 Oct. 1921; *m* 1945, Barbara Worboys; two *s*. *Educ:* Dundee High Sch.; St Andrews Univ. RNVR (Air Branch), 1940–46. Entered Ministry of Works, 1946; Regional Director: Middle East Region, 1965–67; South West Region, DoE, 1971–75; Chm., South West Economic Planning Bd, 1971–75; Dir, Scottish Services, PSA, 1975–81. *Address:* 20 Woodlands, Budleigh Salterton, Devon EX9 6AT.

PATRICK, (Lilian) Gail; Sheriff of Tayside, Central and Fife at Kirkcaldy, since 1991; *b* 24 Dec. 1941; *d* of Alexander Findlay McFadzean, MA, LLB and Elizabeth Fullerton McFadzean (*née* Fenton); *m* 1967, Spencer Francis Rodger, LLB, WS, *s* of Francis and Isabel Patrick; one *s* three *d*. *Educ:* Radleigh Sch., Glasgow; Marr Coll., Troon; St Andrews Univ. (MA); Edinburgh Univ. (LLB). Enrolled as solicitor, 1966; pt-time practice, 1967–79; Lecturer and Tutor: Glasgow Univ., 1967–82; Edinburgh Univ., 1980–82, 1985–90; pt-time Procurator Fiscal Depute, 1979–80; admitted to Faculty of Advocates, 1981; Standing Jun. Counsel, Scottish Educn Dept, 1986–91; Chm., Social Security Appeal Tribunal, 1986–91; Reporter, Scottish Legal Aid Bd, 1986–91; Temp. Sheriff, 1988–91; called to the Bar, Lincoln's Inn, 1990. *Recreations:* golf, hill-walking, cycling, fishing, music. *Address:* 13 Succoth Place, Edinburgh EH12 6BJ. *Clubs:* Murrayfield Golf (Edinburgh); Ladies' Golf (Troon); Bonar Bridge and Ardgay Golf (Bonar Bridge, Sutherland).

PATRICK, Margaret Kathleen, OBE 1976; District/Superintendent Physiotherapist, Central Birmingham Health Authority (Teaching) (formerly United Birmingham Hospitals Hospital Management Committee), 1951–88, retired; *b* 5 June 1923; *d* of late Roy and Rose Patrick. *Educ:* Godolphin and Latymer Sch., London; Guy's Hosp. Sch. of Physiotherapy. BA, Open Univ., 1980. MCSP (Hon. FCSP). Chm. Physio. Adv. Cttee, and Mem. Health Care Planning for Elderly, Birmingham AHA (T). Member: Exec., Whitley Council PTA, 1960–75 (Chm., PTA Cttee C, 1960–75); Tunbridge Cttee on Rehab. Services, 1971–72; Hosp. Adv. Service on Geriatrics, 1972; DHSS Working Party on Stat. Data in Physio., 1969–76; Council, Chartered Soc. of Physio., 1953–75 (Exec. Mem., 1960–75; Vice Chm., 1971–75); Birmingham AHA (Teaching), 1979–82; Vice-Chm., Bromsgrove and Redditch HA, 1982–90. Assoc. of Supt Chartered Physiotherapists: Chm., 1964–75; Pres., 1971–72. *Publications:* Ultrasound Therapy: a textbook for physiotherapists, 1965; (contrib.) Physiotherapy in some Surgical Conditions, ed Joan Cash, 1977, 2nd edn 1979; contrib. Physiotherapy, and articles on ultrasound therapy, geriatric care, and paediatrics. *Recreation:* gardening.

PATTEN, family name of **Baron Patten**.

PATTEN, Baron *cr* 1997 (Life Peer), of Wincanton in the co. of Somerset; **John Haggitt Charles Patten,** PC 1990; Senior Advisor, Charterhouse Development Capital Ltd, since 2001; *b* 17 July 1945; *s* of late Jack Patten and Maria Olga (*née* Sikora); *m* 1978, Louise Alexandra Virginia Charlotte Rowe (*see* Lady Patten); one *d*. *Educ:* Wimbledon Coll.; Sidney Sussex Coll., Cambridge (PhD 1972). University Lectr, 1969–79, Fellow, Hertford Coll., 1972–94, Univ. of Oxford. Oxford City Councillor, 1973–76. MP (C) City of Oxford, 1979–83; Oxford W and Abingdon, 1983–97. PPS to the Ministers of State at the Home Office, 1980–81; Parliamentary Under-Secretary of State: NI Office, 1981–83; DHSS, 1983–85; Minister of State for Housing, Urban Affairs and Construction, DoE, 1985–87; Minister of State, Home Office, 1987–92; Sec. of State for Educn, 1992–94. Advr, 1997–2000, non-exec. Dep. Chm., 2000–01, Charterhouse plc; non-executive Director: Energy Power Resources Ltd, 1997–; Amey plc, 1999–; Lockheed Martin UK Ltd, 1999–. UK Advr, Lockheed Martin, 1997–; Advr, Thomas Goode & Co. Ltd, 1997–. Hon. Fellow, Harris Manchester Coll., Oxford, 1996. *Publications:* The Conservative Opportunity (with Lord Blake), 1976; English Towns, 1500–1700, 1978; Pre-Industrial England, 1979; (ed) The Expanding City, 1983; (with Paul Coones) The Penguin Guide to the Landscape of England and Wales, 1986; Things to Come: the Tories in the 21st Century, 1995. *Recreation:* talking to my wife and daughter. *Address:* House of Lords, SW1A 0PW.

PATTEN, Lady; Louise Alexandra Virginia Charlotte Patten; Adviser, Bain & Co. Inc., since 1997; *b* 2 Feb. 1954; *d* of late John Rowe and Claire Rowe; *m* 1978, John Haggitt Charles Patten (*see* Baron Patten); one *d*. *Educ:* St Paul's Girls' Sch., Hammersmith; St Hugh's Coll., Oxford (MA Hons). Manager, Citibank NA, 1977–81; Resident Vice Pres., Wells Fargo Bank NA, 1981–85; Partner: PA Consulting Gp, 1985–93; Bain & Co. Inc., 1994–97. Director: Hilton Gp plc, 1993–; Harveys Furnishings plc, 1993–2000; Gt Universal Stores plc, 1997–; Somerfield plc, 1998– (Actg Chm., 1999–2000); Brixton plc, 2001–. *Recreations:* talking with my husband, our daughter and her ponies. *Address:* c/o Bain & Co. Inc., 40 Strand, WC2N 5HZ. *T:* (020) 7969 6000.

PATTEN, Brian; poet; *b* 7 Feb. 1946. Regents Lectr, Univ. of Calif (San Diego), 1985. *Publications: poetry:* Penguin Modern Poets, 1967; Little Johnny's Confession, 1967; Notes to the Hurrying Man, 1969; The Irrelevant Song, 1971; The Unreliable Nightingale, 1973; Vanishing Trick, 1976; The Shabby Angel, 1978; Grave Gossip, 1979; Love Poems, 1981; Clare's Countryside: a book on John Clare, 1982; New Volume, 1983; Storm Damage, 1988; Grinning Jack (Selected Poems), 1990; Armada, 1996; The Blue and Green Ark, 1999; *novel:* Mr Moon's Last Case, 1975 (Mystery Writers of Amer. Special Award, 1976); *for younger readers:* The Elephant and the Flower, 1969; Jumping Mouse; 1971; Emma's Doll, 1976; The Sly Cormorant and the Fish: adaptations of The Aesop Fables, 1977; (ed) Gangsters, Ghosts and Dragonflies, 1981; Gargling with Jelly, 1985; Jimmy Tag-along, 1988; Thawing Frozen Frogs, 1990; (ed) The Puffin Book of Twentieth Century Children's Verse, 1991; Grizzelda Frizzle, 1992; The Magic Bicycle, 1993; Impossible Parents, 1994; The Utter Nutters, 1994; (ed) The Puffin Book of Utterly Brilliant Poetry, 1998; Beowulf and the Monster, 1999; Juggling with Gerbils, 2000; Little Hotchpotch, 2000; Impossible Parents Go Green, 2000; The Story Giant, 2001; *plays:* The Pig And The Junkle, 1975; (with Roger McGough) The Mouth Trap, 1982; Blind Love, 1983; Gargling with Jelly, 1989; *recordings:* Brian Patten Reading His Own Poetry, 1969; British Poets Of Our Time, 1974; Vanishing Trick, 1976; The Sly Cormorant, 1977; Grizzelda Frizzle and other stories, 1995; The Mersey Sound, 1997. *Address:* c/o Puffin Books, 27 Wrights Lane, W8 5TZ. *Club:* Chelsea Arts.

PATTEN, Rt Hon. Christopher (Francis), CH 1998; PC 1989; Member, European Commission, since 1999; *b* 12 May 1944; *s* of late Francis Joseph Patten and Joan McCarthy; *m* 1971, Mary Lavender St Leger Thornton; three *d*. *Educ:* St Benedict's School, Ealing; Balliol College, Oxford (Hon. Fellow, 1999). Conservative Research Dept, 1966–70; Cabinet Office, 1970–72; Home Office, 1972; Personal Asst to Chairman of Conservative Party, 1972–74; Director, Conservative Research Dept, 1974–79. Governor and C-in-C, Hong Kong, 1992–97; Chm., Ind. Commn on Policing for NI, 1998–99. MP (C) Bath, 1979–92; Contested (C) Bath, 1992. PPS to Chancellor of Duchy of Lancaster and Leader of House of Commons, 1979–81, to Secretary of State for Social Services, 1981; Parly Under-Sec. of State, NI Office, 1983–1985; Minister of State, DES, 1985–86; Minister of State (Minister for Overseas Develt), FCO, 1986–89; Sec. of State for the Envmt, 1989–90; Chancellor of Duchy of Lancaster, 1990–92; Chm. of Cons.

Party, 1990–92. Vice Chm., Cons. Parly Finance Cttee, 1981–83; Mem., Select Cttees on Defence and Procedure, 1982–83. Dir, Independent Newspapers, 1998–99. Chancellor, Newcastle Univ., 1999–. Hon. FRCPE 1994. Hon Djur: Massachusetts, 1999; Birmingham, 2001; Hon. DCL Newcastle, 1999; Hon. DLitt Sydney, 2001. *Publications:* The Tory Case, 1983; East and West, 1998. *Recreations:* reading, tennis, gardening. *Address:* European Commission, 200 Rue de la Loi, 1049 Brussels, Belgium; c/o Coutts & Co., Campbells Office, 440 Strand, WC2R 0QS. *Clubs:* Beefsteak, Royal Automobile.

PATTEN, Louise Alexandra Virginia Charlotte; *see* Lady Patten.

PATTEN, Hon. Sir Nicholas (John), Kt 2000; **Hon. Mr Justice Patten;** a Judge of the High Court of Justice, Chancery Division, since 2000; *b* 7 Aug. 1950; *s* of late Peter Grenville Patten and of Dorothy Patten (*née* Davenport); *m* 1984, Veronica Mary Schoeneich (marr. diss. 1998); two *s* one *d*. *Educ:* Tulse Hill Sch.; Christ Church, Oxford (Open Schol.; MA; BCL (1st Cl. Hons Jurisprudence)). Called to the Bar, Lincoln's Inn, 1974, Bencher, 1997; QC 1988; a Dep. High Court Judge, 1998–2000. Chm., Chancery Bar Assoc., 1997–99. *Recreations:* gardening, ski-ing, motor cars. *Address:* Royal Courts of Justice, Strand, WC2A 2LL.

PATTENDEN, Prof. Gerald, FRS 1991; Sir Jesse Boot Professor of Organic Chemistry, since 1988, and Pro-Vice-Chancellor, since 1997, Nottingham University; *b* 4 March 1940; *s* of Albert James and Violet Eugene Pattenden; *m* 1969, Christine Frances Doherty; three *d*. *Educ:* Brunel Univ. (BSc); Queen Mary College London (PhD, DSc). CChem, FRSC. Lectr, UC, Cardiff, 1966–72; Nottingham University: Lectr, 1972–75; Reader, 1975–80; Prof., 1980–88; Hd of Dept of Org. Chem., 1988–96. Chm., Org. Chem. Cttee, SERC, 1992–94. Royal Society of Chemistry: Pres., Perkin Div., 1995–97 (Scientific Ed., Perkin Trans); Corday-Morgan Medal and Prize, 1975; Simonsen Lect. and Medal, 1987; Tilden Lect. and Medal, 1991; Award for Synthetic Organic Chem., 1992; Pedler Lect. and Medal, 1993; Award for Heterocyclic Chem., 1994; Award for Natural Product Chemistry, 1997. *Publications:* editor of several books and jls. *Recreations:* sport, entertainment, gardening. *Address:* Chemistry Department, The University, Nottingham NG7 2RD. *T:* (0115) 951 3530, *Fax:* (0115) 951 3535; *e-mail:* gp@nottingham.ac.uk.

PATTERSON, Ben; *see* Patterson, G.B.

PATTERSON, (Constance) Marie, (Mrs Barrie Devney), CBE 1978 (OBE 1973); National Officer, Transport and General Workers' Union, 1976–84 (National Woman Officer, 1963–76); Member of General Council of TUC 1963–84 (Chairman, 1974–75 and 1977); *b* 1 April 1934; *d* of Dr Richard Swanton Abraham; *m* 1st, 1960, Thomas Michael Valentine Patterson (marr. diss. 1976); 2nd, 1984, Barrie Devney. *Educ:* Pendleton High Sch.; Bedford Coll., Univ. of London (BA). Member: Exec., Confedn of Shipbuilding and Engrg Unions, 1966–84 (Pres., 1977–78); Hotel and Catering Trng Bd, 1966–87; Equal Opportunities Commn, 1975–84; Central Arbitration Commn, 1976–94; Legal Aid Adv. Cttee, 1988–90; Council, Office of Banking Ombudsman, 1992–. Dir of Remploy, 1966–87. Lay Mem., Press Council, 1964–70. Chm. Council, Queen's Coll., Harley St, 1994–2000; Mem. Council, LSE, 2000–. Chm., Galleon Trust, 1998–. FRSA 2000. Hon. DSc Salford, 1975. *Recreations:* sight-seeing, jig-saws.

PATTERSON, Eric, MBE 1970; HM Diplomatic Service, retired; Consul-General, 1982–88 and Counsellor (Commercial), 1986–88, Auckland; *b* 2 May 1930; *s* of Richard and Elizabeth Patterson; *m* 1953, Doris (*née* Mason); two *s*. *Educ:* Hookergate Grammar Sch., Co. Durham. Served Royal Signals, 1948–50. Local govt service, 1947–50; Lord Chancellor's Dept, 1950–52; BoT, 1952–62; Asst Trade Comr, Halifax, NS, 1962–67; Second Sec. (Commercial), Khartoum, 1967–70; First Sec. (Commercial), The Hague, 1970–74; FCO, 1974–76; First Sec. (Commercial), Warsaw, 1976–80; FCO, 1980–82. *Recreations:* golf, sailing, photography, fly-fishing. *Address:* 45A Bleakhouse Road, Howick, Auckland, New Zealand. *Clubs:* Auckland, Auckland Golf (Auckland).

PATTERSON, Frances Silvia; QC 1998; a Recorder, since 2000; *m* 1980, Dr Graham Nicholson; three *s*. *Educ:* Queen's Sch., Chester; Leicester Univ. Called to the Bar, Middle Temple, 1977; Asst Recorder, 1997–2000. *Address:* 40 King Street, Manchester M2 6BA. *T:* (0161) 832 9082.

PATTERSON, George Benjamin, (Ben); Principal Administrator, Economic Affairs (formerly Internal Market) Division, Directorate General for Research, European Parliament, since 1994; *b* 21 April 1939; *s* of late Eric James Patterson and Ethel Patterson; *m* 1970, Felicity Barbara Anne Raybould; one *s* one *d*. *Educ:* Westminster Sch.; Trinity Coll., Cambridge (MA); London Sch. of Economics. Lecturer, Swinton Conservative Coll., 1961–65; Editor (at Conservative Political Centre), CPC Monthly Report, 1965–74; Dep. Head, London Office of European Parlt, 1974–79. MEP (C) Kent W, 1979–94; contested (C) Kent W, Eur. Parly elecns, 1994. MInstD. *Publications:* The Character of Conservatism, 1973; Direct Elections to the European Parliament, 1974; Europe and Employment, 1984; Vredeling and All That, 1984; VAT: the zero rate issue, 1988; A Guide to EMU, 1990; A European Currency, 1994; Options for a Definitive VAT System, 1995; The Co-ordination of National Fiscal Policies in the Context of Monetary Union, 1996; The Social and Economic Consequences of Abolishing Duty Free Within the EU, 1997; Adjusting to Asymmetric Shocks, 1998; The Feasibility of a Tobin Tax, 1999; The Determination of Interest Rates, 1999; Exchange Rates and Monetary Policy, 2000. *Recreation:* reading science fiction. *Address:* Elm Hill House, High Street, Hawkhurst, Kent TN18 4XU. *T:* (01580) 752780; 32 rue de la Corniche, 5956 Itzig, Luxembourg. *T:* 26360622.

PATTERSON, Harry; novelist; *b* 27 July 1929; *s* of Henry Patterson and Rita Higgins Bell; *m* 1st, 1958, Amy Margaret Hewitt (marr. diss. 1984); one *s* three *d*; 2nd, 1985, Denise Lesley Anne Palmer. *Educ:* Roundhay Sch., Leeds; Beckett Park Coll. for Teachers; London Sch. of Economics as external student (BSc(Hons) Sociology). FRSA. NCO, The Blues, 1947–50. 1950–58: tried everything from being a clerk to a circus tent-hand; 1958–72: variously a schoolmaster, Lectr in Liberal Studies, Leeds Polytechnic, Sen. Lectr in Education, James Graham Coll. and Tutor in Sch. Practice, Leeds Univ.; since age of 41, engaged in full-time writing career. Dual citizenship, British/Irish. *Publications include:* (as Jack Higgins): Prayer for the Dying, 1973 (filmed 1985); The Eagle has Landed, 1975 (filmed 1976); Storm Warning, 1976; Day of Judgement, 1978; Solo, 1980; Luciano's Luck, 1981; Touch the Devil, 1982; Exocet, 1983; Confessional, 1985 (filmed 1985); Night of the Fox, 1986 (filmed 1989); A Season in Hell, 1989; Cold Harbour, 1990; The Eagle Has Flown, 1990; Angel of Death, 1995; Drink with the Devil, 1996; Day of Reckoning, 2000; Edge of Danger, 2001; (as Harry Patterson): The Valhalla Exchange, 1978; To Catch a King, 1979 (filmed 1983); Dillinger, 1983; Walking Wounded (stage play), 1987; and many others (including The Violent Enemy, filmed 1969, and The Wrath of God, filmed 1972) under pseudonyms (Martin Fallon, Hugh Marlowe, Henry Patterson); some books trans. into 42 languages. DUniv Leeds Metropolitan, 1995. *Recreations:* tennis, old movies. *Address:* c/o Ed Victor Ltd, 6 Bayley Street, WC1B 3HB.

PATTERSON, John Allan, CB 1989; Panel Chairman, Recruitment and Assessment Services, since 1992; *b* 10 Oct. 1931; *s* of William Gilchrist Patterson and May (*née* Eggie); *m* 1956, Anne Marie Lasson; one *s* one *d* (and one *d* decd). *Educ:* Epsom Coll.; Clare Coll., Cambridge (Major Scholar in Classics, Stewart of Rannoch Scholar; BA 1954); Open Univ. (Dip. German, 2000). HM Diplomatic Service, 1954–65: served in Bangkok, 1957–61 and in Rome, 1961–64 (Private Sec. to the Ambassador); HM Treasury, 1965–81 (on loan to Cabinet Office, 1974–78); Dep. Dir of Savings, Dept for Nat. Savings, 1981–86; Dir of Savings and Head, Dept for Nat. Savings, 1986–91. Chm., Money Management Council, 1991–94; Mem., SW Surrey CHC, 1997–2000. Lay Mem., Guildford Primary Care Gp, 1999–2000. FRSA 1989. *Recreations:* gardening, walking, languages, church. *Address:* 5 Nelson Gardens, Guildford GU1 2NZ. *T:* (01483) 564369.

PATTERSON, Marie; *see* Patterson, C. M.

PATTERSON, Dr Mark Jonathan Lister; Hon. Consultant Haematologist, Manchester Royal Infirmary, since 1997; Consultant Haematologist, Mid Cheshire NHS Trust, since 1996; *b* 2 March 1934; *s* of Alfred Patterson and Frederica Georgina Mary Lister Nicholson; *m* 1958, Jane Teresa Scott Stokes; one *s* two *d*. *Educ:* privately; St Bartholomew's Hosp. Med. Coll., Univ. of London (MB 1959). MRCP. Jun. hosp. appts at St Bartholomew's Hosp., Royal Postgrad. Med. Sch., and MRC Exptl Haematol. Unit; Consultant Haematologist to Nat. Heart and Chest Hosps, 1967–84. Mem., GLC, 1970–73 and 1977–81; contested (C) Ealing N, Feb. 1974. *Recreations:* medicine, politics. *Address:* Wolverton Manor, Shorwell, Newport, Isle of Wight PO30 3JS. *T:* (01983) 740609.

PATTERSON, Paul Leslie; composer; Manson Professor of Composition, Royal Academy of Music, since 1997; Artistic Director, Park Lane Group Young Composer Forum, since 1998; formed: Manson Ensemble, 1968; The Patterson Quintet, 1982; *b* 15 June 1947; *s* of Leslie and Lilian Patterson; *m* 1981, Hazel Wilson; one *s* one *d*. *Educ:* Royal Academy of Music. FRAM 1980. Freelance composer, 1968–; Arts Council Composer in Association, English Sinfonia, 1969–70; Director, Contemporary Music, Warwick Univ., 1974–80; Prof. of Composition, and Hd of Composition and Twentieth Century Music, RAM, 1985–97; Composer in Residence: SE Arts Assoc., 1980–82; Bedford School, 1984–85; Southwark Fest., 1989–91; James Allen School, Dulwich, 1990–91; Three Spires Fest., Truro, 1992–94; NYO, 1997–; Guest Prof., Yale Univ., 1989–90; Vis. Prof. of Composition, Univ. of Canterbury, Christchurch, 2000–. Artistic Dir, Exeter Fest., 1991–97; Artistic Advr, N Devon Fest., 1999–. Chm., Mendelssohn Scholarship, Royal Schs of Music, 1997–. Member: Exec. Cttee, Composers Guild, 1972–75; Council, SPNM, 1975–81, 1985–; Adv. Council, BBC Radio London, 1986–; Adv. Cttee, Arts Council's Recordings Panel, 1986–; Artistic Director of RAM Festivals: Lutosławski, 1984; Penderecki, 1986; Messiaen, 1987; Henze, 1988; Berio, 1989; Carter, 1990; Da Capo, 1993; Schnittke, 1994. Featured Composer at: Three Choirs Fest., Patterson at South Bank Fest., 1988; Cheltenham Fest., 1988, 1990; Peterborough Fest., 1989; Exeter Fest., 1991; Presteigne Fest., 2001. Performances world wide by leading orchestras and soloists and ensembles; also film and TV music. Numerous recordings. Pres., RAM Club, 1993–94. FRSA 1989. Hon. FLCM 1998. Lesley Boosey Award, Royal Philharmonic Soc., 1996. OM, Polish Ministry of Culture, 1987. *Publications:* Rebecca, 1968; Trumpet Concerto, 1969; Time Piece, 1972; Kyrie, 1972; Requiem, 1973; Comedy for Five Winds, 1973; Requiem, 1974; Fluorescences, 1974; Clarinet Concerto, 1976; Cracowian Counterpoints, 1977; Voices of Sleep, 1979; Concerto for Orchestra, 1981; Canterbury Psalms, 1981; Sinfonia, 1982; Mass of the Sea, 1983; Deception Pass, 1983; Duologue, 1984; Mean Time, 1984; Europhony, 1985; Missa Brevis, 1985; Stabat Mater, 1986; String Quartet, 1986; Magnificat and Nunc Dimittis, 1986; Propositions, 1987; Trombone Quartet, 1987; Suite for Cello, 1987; Sorriest Cow, 1987; Tides of Mananan, 1988; Te Deum, 1988; Tunnel of Time, 1989; White Shadows, 1989; Symphony, 1990; The End, 1990; Mighty Voice, 1991; Violin Concerto, 1992; Little Red Riding Hood, 1992; Magnificat, 1993; Music for Opening Channel Tunnel, 1994; Overture: Songs of the West, 1995; Soliloquy, 1996; Rustic Sketches, 1997; Hell Angels, 1998; Gloria, 1999; Western Winds, 1999; Millennium Mass, 2000; Deviations, 2001; Cello Concerto, 2002. *Recreations:* sailing, croquet, swimming, computing. *Address:* 31 Cromwell Avenue, Highgate, N6 5HN. *T:* (020) 8348 3711, *Fax:* (020) 8340 6489.

PATTERSON, Rt Hon. Percival (Noel James); PC 1992; QC 1984; MP (PNP) South East Westmoreland, 1972–80 and since 1989; Prime Minister of Jamaica, since 1992; Minister of Defence, since 1992; *b* 10 April 1935; *s* of Henry Patterson and Ina James; *m* (marr. diss.); one *s* one *d*. *Educ:* Somerton Primary; St James Calabar High Sch., Kingston; Univ. of the West Indies (BA Hons English 1959); LSE (LLB 1963). Called to the Bar, Middle Temple, 1963; admitted to Jamaican Bar, 1963; private legal practice, Kingston. Senator, Leader of Opposition Business, 1969–70; Minister of Industry and Tourism, 1972–77; Dep. Prime Minister and Minister of Foreign Affairs and Foreign Trade, 1978–80; Minister of Develt Planning and Production, 1989–90; Minister of Finance and Planning, 1990–91. Order of Liberator Simon Bolivar (Venezuela), 1st Class, 1992; Order of San Martin (Argentina), 1992. *Recreations:* music (jazz/Jamaican), sports (cricket, boxing, track and field, tennis). *Address:* c/o Jamaica House, Hope Road, Kingston 6, Jamaica. *T:* 9279941, 9267863.

PATTERSON, Rev. Canon William James, CBE 1991; Dean of Ely, 1984–90; Vicar of Abbotsley, Everton and Waresley, 1990–93; *b* 25 Sept. 1930; *s* of William Moscrop and Alice Patterson; *m* 1955, Elisabeth Roederer; one *s* two *d*. *Educ:* Haileybury; Balliol College, Oxon. MA. Asst Curate of St John Baptist, Newcastle upon Tyne, 1955–58; Priest-in-Charge, Rio Claro with Mayaro, Dio. Trinidad, 1958–65; Rector of Esher, 1965–72; RD of Emly, 1968–72; Rector of Little Downham, 1972–80; Priest-in-Charge of Coveney, 1978–80; Archdeacon of Wisbech, 1979–84; Vicar of Wisbech St Mary, 1980–84. Hon. Canon, Ely Cathedral, 1990–. *Recreation:* cycling. *Address:* 1 Watledge Close, Tewkesbury, Glos GL20 5RJ.

PATTIE, Rt Hon. Sir Geoffrey (Edwin), Kt 1987; PC 1987; Senior Partner, Terrington Management, since 1999; Chairman, GEC-Marconi, 1996–99 (Joint Chairman, 1991–96); *b* 17 Jan. 1936; *s* of late Alfred Edwin Pattie, LDS, and Ada Clive (*née* Carr); *m* 1960, Tuëma Caroline (*née* Eyre-Maunsell); one *s* (one *d* decd). *Educ:* Durham Sch.; St Catharine's Coll., Cambridge (MA). BA Cantab 1959. Called to Bar, Gray's Inn, 1964. Served: Queen Victoria's Rifles (TA), 1959–61; (on amalgamation) Queen's Royal Rifles (TA), now 4th Royal Green Jackets, 1961–65; Captain, 1964, Hon. Col, 1996–99, Dep. Col Comdt (TA and Cadets), 1999–. Mem. GLC, Lambeth, 1967–70; Chm. ILEA Finance Cttee, 1968–70. Marketing Dir, 1997–98, Dir of Communications, 1998–99, GEC. Contested (C) Barking, 1966 and 1970. MP (C) Chertsey and Walton, Feb. 1974–1997. Parly Under Sec. of State for Defence for the RAF, 1979–81, for Defence Procurement, 1981–83; Minister of State: for Defence Procurement, 1983–84; DTI (Minister for IT), 1984–87; Vice-Chm., Cons. Party, 1990–97. Sec., Cons. Parly Aviation Cttee, 1974–75, 1975–76, Vice Chm., 1976–77, 1977–78; Jt Sec., Cons. Parly Defence Cttee, 1975–76, 1976–77, 1977–78, Vice Chm.,

1978–79; Mem., Cttee of Public Accounts, 1976–79; Vice-Chm., All Party Cttee on Mental Health, 1977–79. Mem. General Synod of Church of England, 1970–75. Chm., Intellectual Property Inst., 1994–99. Chm. of Governors, London Coll. of Printing, 1968–69. Trustee, Excalibur Scholarship Scheme, 1992–. FRSA 1990. *Publications:* Towards a New Defence Policy, 1976; (with James Bellini) A New World Role for the Medium Power: the British Opportunity, 1977. *Recreations:* opera, theatre, following Middlesbrough Football Club. *Address:* Terrington Management, 45 St Peter Street, SW1P 3LT. *Clubs:* Reform, Royal Green Jackets, MCC.

PATTINSON, Rev. Sir Derek; *see* Pattinson, Rev. Sir W. D.

PATTINSON, Rev. Sir (William) Derek, Kt 1990; Secretary-General, General Synod of Church of England, 1972–90; *b* 31 March 1930; *s* of late Thomas William and Elizabeth Pattinson. *Educ:* Whitehaven Grammar Sch.; Queen's Coll., Oxford (Stanhope Historical Essay Prize, 1951; BA 1952; MA 1956); St Deiniol's Liby, Hawarden; Coll. of Resurrection, Mirfield. Entered Home Civil Service, 1952; Inland Revenue Dept, 1952–62 and 1965–68; HM Treasury, 1962–65 and 1968–70; Assoc. Sec.-Gen., General Synod, 1970–72. Chm., William Temple Assoc., 1966–70; Member: Archbishops' Commn on Church and State, 1966–70; British Council of Churches, 1972–90; London Diocesan Synod, 1972–91. Ordained deacon, 1991, priest, 1992; Asst Curate, St Gabriel's Pimlico, 1991–2000. Principal, Soc. of the Faith, 1992–. Vice-Chm., Grosvenor Chapel Cttee, 1973–81; Vice-Pres., SPCK; Chm. of Governors, Liddon House, 1972–; Chm., English Friends of Anglican Centre in Rome, 1985; Gov., Sir John Cass Foundn, 1973–92; Vice Chm., Greycoat Hosp., 1988–97. Freeman, City of London, 1973; Mem., Parish Clerks' Co. (Master, 1986–87). Member: Alcuin Club; Nikaean Club. Parish Clerk, St Luke's, Old Street, 1972–; Churchwarden, St Michael's Cornhill, 1988–91. *Address:* 9 Strutton Court, Great Peter Street, SW1P 2HH. *T:* (020) 7222 6307.

PATTISON, David Arnold, PhD; Director, David A. Pattison Associates, 1998–2000; *b* 9 Feb. 1941; *s* of David Pattison and Christina Russell Bone; *m* 1967, Anne Ross Wilson; two *s* one *d*. *Educ:* Glasgow Univ. (BSc 1st Cl. Hons, PhD). Planning Assistant, Dunbarton County Council, 1966–67; Lecturer, Strathclyde Univ., 1967–70; Head of Tourism Division, Highlands and Islands Development Board, 1970–81; Chief Exec., Scottish Tourist Board, 1981–85; Dir of Leisure and Tourism Consulting, Arthur Young Group, 1985–90; Principal Associate: Cobham Resource Consultants, 1990–96; Scott Wilson Resource Consultants, 1996–98. Best Value Inspector, Audit Commn, 2000–. Mem. Council, Inland Waterways Amenity Adv. Council, 2001–. Hon. Prof., Queen Margaret Coll., Edinburgh, 1992. Hon. Pres., Scottish YHA, 1995–. *Publications:* Tourism Development Plans for: Argyll, Bute, Ayrshire, Burgh of Ayr, Ulster. *Recreations:* reading, watching soccer and Rugby, golf, gardening. *Address:* 7 Cramond Glebe Gardens, Cramond, Edinburgh EH4 6NZ.

PATTISON, Rev. Dr George Linsley; Dean of Chapel, King's College, Cambridge, since 1991; *b* 25 May 1950; *s* of George William Pattison and Jean Pattison; *m* 1971, Hilary Christine Cochrane; one *s* two *d*. *Educ:* Perse Sch., Cambridge; Edinburgh Univ. (MA, BD); Durham Univ. (PhD). Ordained deacon, 1977, priest, 1978; Curate, St James' Church, Benwell, Newcastle upon Tyne, 1977–80; Priest-in-charge, St Philip and St James' Church, Kimblesworth, Co. Durham, 1980–83; Res. Student, Durham Univ., 1980–83; Rector, Badwell Ash, Great Ashfield, Hunston and Stowlangtoft with Langham, Suffolk, 1983–91. Vis. Res. Prof., Univ. of Copenhagen, 1997, 2000. Vice-Pres., Modern Churchpeople's Union, 1999–. Has broadcast on BBC Radio 3, Radio 4 and World Service on subjects of art and religion. Editor, Modern Believing, 1994–98. *Publications:* Art, Modernity and Faith, 1991, 2nd edn 1998; Kierkegaard: the aesthetic and the religious, 1992, 2nd edn 1999; (ed) Kierkegaard on Art and Communication, 1993; (with Sister Wendy Beckett) Pains of Glass, 1995; (with S. Platten) Spirit and Tradition, 1996; Agnosis: theology in the void, 1996; Kierkegaard and the Crisis of Faith, 1997; (ed with S. Shakespeare) Kierkegaard: the self in society, 1998; The End of Theology and the Task of Thinking About God, 1998; Poor Paris!, 1998; Anxious Angels, 1999; The Later Heidegger, 2000; A Short Course in the Philosophy of Religion, 2001; articles on theology, philosophy of religion and the arts in specialist and non-specialist jls. *Recreations:* family life, music, films, theatre, visiting cities. *Address:* King's College, Cambridge CB2 1ST. *T:* (01223) 331100.

PATTISON, Sir John (Ridley), Kt 1998; DM; FRCPath, FMedSci; Director of Research and Development, Department of Health and National Health Service, since 1999 (on secondment); Professor of Medical Microbiology, University College London, since 1984; *b* 1 Aug. 1942; *s* of Tom Frederick and Elizabeth Pattison; *m* 1965, Pauline Evans; one *s* two *d*. *Educ:* Barnard Castle Sch.; University Coll., Oxford (BSc, MA; BM, BCh 1968; DM 1975); Middlesex Hosp. Med. Sch. FRCPath 1985. Asst Lectr in Pathology, then Lectr in Virology, Middx Hosp. Med. Sch., 1970–75; Lectr, then Sen. Lectr in Virology, St Bartholomew's and London Hosp. Med. Colls, 1976–77; Prof. of Medical Microbiol., KCH Med. Sch., 1977–84; Dean, UCL Med. Sch., 1990–98; Vice-Provost, UCL, 1994–99. Hon. NHS Consultant, UCH, subseq. UCL Hosps NHS Trust, 1984–; Hon. Consultant, PHLS, 1980– (Board Mem., 1989–95); Sen. Med. Advr, MRC, 1996–99. Mem., MRC, 1992–95, 1999– (Mem., Grants Cttee, 1985–87, Systems Bd, 1988–92; Chm., Physiol Medicine and Infection Bd, 1992–95); Chm., Spongiform Encephalopathy Adv. Cttee, 1995–99 (Mem., 1994–95). Mem. Council, Soc. of Gen. Microbiol., 1981–87. Member of Board: LSHTM, 1989–92; Inst. of Child Health, 1992–96; Inst. of Neurology, 1995–97. Member: Mgt Cttee, King's Fund, 1993–99 (Dep. Chm., 1994–99); King's Fund London Commn, 1994–95. Editor-in-Chief, Epidemiology & Infection, 1980–94; Mem. Council, Internat. Jl Exptl Pathology, 1979–. Founder FMedSci 1998. *Publications:* (ed jtly) Principles & Practice of Clinical Virology, 1987, 4th edn 1999; (ed jtly) Practical Guide to Clinical Virology, 1989; (ed jtly) Practical Guide to Clinical Bacteriology, 1995; papers and reviews on aspects of medical virology, esp. rubella virus and parvovirus infections. *Recreations:* family, windsurfing, music, reading, theatre. *Address:* Department of Health, Richmond House, 79 Whitehall, SW1A 2NS. *T:* (020) 7210 5556.

PATTISON, Michael Ambrose, CBE 1996; Director, Sainsbury Family Charitable Trusts, since 1995; *b* 14 July 1946; *s* of late Osmond John Pattison and Eileen Susanna Pattison (*née* Cullen); *m* 1975, Beverley Jean, *d* of Genevieve and Hugh Webber, Florida, USA; one *d*. *Educ:* Sedbergh School; University of Sussex (BA Hons 1968). Min. of Overseas Develt, 1968; Asst Private Sec. to Minister, 1970; seconded to HM Diplomatic Service as First Sec., Perm. Mission to UN, New York, 1974; ODA, 1977; Private Sec. to successive Prime Ministers, 1979–82; ODA, 1982, Establishment Officer, 1983–85; Chief Exec. and Sec. Gen., RICS, 1985–95; Dir, Surveyors Holdings Ltd, 1985–95. Mem. Council, British Consultants Bureau, 1985–95. Non-exec. Dir, Ordnance Survey, 1997–2001. Dir, Battersea Axs Centre Trust, 1988–94. Mem., Cambridge Univ. Careers Service Syndicate, 1989–93; Pro-Chancellor, Greenwich Univ., 1994–97 (Gov., 1989–97, when Thames Poly.). Vis. Fellow, City Univ., 1990–. FRSA 1990. *Recreations:* cricket, Real tennis, golf, local history, countryside. *Address:* (office) 9 Red Lion Court, EC4A 3EF. *T:* (020) 7410 0330. *Clubs:* Athenæum; Warwickshire CC.

PATTISON, Stephen Dexter, DPhil; HM Diplomatic Service; Head, United Nations Department, Foreign and Commonwealth Office, since 2000; *b* 24 Dec. 1953; *s* of George Stanley and May Elizabeth Pattison; *m* 1987, Helen Chaoushis; one *d*. *Educ:* Sir George Monoux Sch.; Queens' Coll., Cambridge (BA 1976); Wadham Coll., Oxford (DPhil 1980). Joined FCO, 1981: Second Sec., Nicosia, 1983–86; FCO, 1986–89; First Sec., Washington, 1989–94; Dep. Hd, Non-Proliferation Dept, FCO, 1994–96; Dir of Trade Promotion and Consul-Gen., Warsaw, 1997–2000. *Recreations:* the arts, cricket. *Address:* c/o Foreign and Commonwealth Office, King Charles Street, SW1A 3AH.

PATTON, Joseph Alexander, CBE 1982; FRAgS; farmer; *b* 17 Jan. 1936; *s* of Marshall Lyons and Bessie Robinson Patton; *m* 1967, Mary Morton Kirkpatrick; one *s* two *d*. Member: Milk Marketing Board, NI, 1982–; Council, Food From Britain, 1983–; Broadcasting Council of NI, 1982–84. President: Young Farmers' Clubs of Ulster, 1969–71; Ulster Farmers' Union, 1980–81. FRAgS 1984. *Address:* Roseyards, 107 Kirk Road, Ballymoney, Co. Antrim, Northern Ireland BT53 8HN. *T:* (028) 2074 1263.

PATTULLO, Sir (David) Bruce, Kt 1995; CBE 1989; Governor, Bank of Scotland, 1991–98 (Group Chief Executive, 1988–96); *b* 2 Jan. 1938; *s* of late Colin Arthur Pattullo and Elizabeth Mary Bruce; *m* 1962, Fiona Jane Nicholson; three *s* one *d*. *Educ:* Rugby Sch.; Hertford Coll., Oxford (BA). FCIBS. Commnd Royal Scots and seconded to Queen's Own Nigeria Regt. Gen. Man., Bank of Scotland Finance Co. Ltd, 1973–77; Chief Exec., British Linen Bank Ltd, 1977–78 (Dir, 1977–98); Bank of Scotland: Dep. Treas., 1978; Treas. and Gen. Manager (Chief Exec.), 1979–88; Dir, 1980–98; Dep. Governor, 1988–91. Director: Melville Street Investments, 1973–90; Bank of Wales, 1986–98; NWS Bank plc, 1986–98; Standard Life Assurance Co., 1985–96. Chm., Cttee, Scottish Clearing Bankers, 1981–83, 1987–89; Pres., Inst. of Bankers in Scotland, 1990–92 (a Vice-Pres., 1977–90). First Prizeman (Bilsland Prize), Inst. of Bankers in Scotland, 1964. FRSE 1990. Hon. LLD Aberdeen, 1995; DUniv Stirling, 1996; Hon. DBA Strathclyde, 1998. *Recreations:* tennis, hill walking. *Address:* 6 Cammo Road, Edinburgh EH4 8EB. *Clubs:* Caledonian; New (Edinburgh).

PAUFFLEY, Anna Evelyn Hamilton; QC 1995; a Recorder, since 1998; *b* 13 Jan. 1956; *d* of Donald Eric Hamilton Pauffley and Josephine Sybil Pauffley; *m* 2001, Frank Harris. *Educ:* Godolphin Sch., Salisbury; London Univ. (BA Hons). Called to the Bar, Middle Temple, 1979. *Address:* 4 Paper Buildings, Temple, EC4Y 7EX. *T:* (020) 7583 0816.

PAUK, György; Order of the Hungarian Republic, 1998; international concert violinist; Professor at Guildhall School of Music and Drama; Professor, Royal Academy of Music, since 1987; *b* 26 Oct. 1936; *s* of Imre and Magda Pauk; *m* 1959, Susanne Mautner; one *s* one *d*. *Educ:* Franz Liszt Acad. of Music, Budapest. Toured E Europe while still a student; won three internat. violin competitions, Genoa 1956, Munich 1957, Paris 1959; soon after leaving Hungary, settled in London, 1961, and became a British citizen. London début, 1961; seasonal appearances there and in the provinces, with orchestra, in recital and chamber music; also plays at Bath, Cheltenham and Edinburgh Fests and London Promenade Concerts; performs in major European music venues; US début, under Sir George Solti, with Chicago Symph. Orch., 1970, followed by further visits to USA and Canada to appear with major orchs; holds master classes in many US univs, major music schs in Japan and Internat. Mozart Acad., Prague; Vis. Prof., Winterthur Conservatorium, Switzerland, 1996; plays regularly in Hungary following return in 1973; overseas tours to Australia, NZ, S America, S Africa, Middle and Far East; many performances for BBC, incl. Berg and Bartók concertos, with Boulez. As conductor/soloist, has worked with the English, Scottish and Franz Liszt chamber orchs and London Mozart Players; guest dir, Acad. of St Martin-in-the-Fields; with Peter Frankl and Ralph Kirshbaum, formed chamber music trio, 1973; performances at major fests; public concerts in GB have incl. complete Brahms and Beethoven Cycles; the trio has also made many broadcasts for the BBC. First performances: Penderecki's Violin Concerto, Japan, 1979, UK, 1980; Tippett's Triple Concerto, London, 1980; Lutosawski's Chain 2, with composer conducting, Britain, The Netherlands and Hungary, 1986–87; Sir Peter Maxwell Davies' Violin Concerto, Switzerland, 1988; William Mathias' Violin Concerto, Manchester, 1991. Has made many recordings including: Bartok Sonatas (among top records in US, 1982), and Bartok's music for solo violin, with piano, for two violins and violin concertos; Tippett Concerto (Best Gramophone Record Award, 1983); Berg Concerto (Caecilia Prize, Belgium, 1983); complete sonatas for violin and harpsichord by Handel; all violin concertos and orch. works by Mozart; Brahms Sonatas. Hon. GSM 1980. Hon. RAM 1990.

PAUL, family name of **Baron Paul**.

PAUL, Baron *cr* 1996 (Life Peer), of Marylebone in the City of Westminster; **Swraj Paul;** Padma Bhushan; Chairman: Caparo Group Ltd, since 1978; Caparo Industries Plc, since 1981; Caparo Inc., USA, since 1988; *b* 18 Feb. 1931; *s* of Payare and Mongwati Paul; *m* 1956, Aruna Vij; three *s* one *d* (and one *d* decd). *Educ:* Punjab Univ. (BSc); Mass Inst. of Technol. (BSc, MSc (Mech. Engrg)). Began work as Partner in family-owned Apeejay Surrendra Gp, India, 1953; came to UK in 1966 and estabd first business, Natural Gas Tubes Ltd; Caparo Group Ltd formed in 1978 as holding co. for UK businesses involved in engrg, hotel and property develt, investment; Caparo Industries Plc (engrg, metals) formed in 1981. Founder Chm., Indo-British Assoc., 1975–. Chancellor, Univ. of Wolverhampton, 1999–; Pro-Chancellor, Thames Valley Univ., 1998–. Pres., Family Service Unit, 1997–. Trustee, Police Foundn, 1997–. Chm., Fundraising Cttee, Zool Soc. of London, 1997–. FRSA. Padma Bhushan (equivalent to British Peerage), 1983. Hon. PhD Amer. Coll. of Switzerland, Leysin, 1986; Hon. DSc (Econ) Hull, 1992; Buckingham, 1999; DUniv: Bradford, 1997; Central England, 1999; Hon. DLitt Westminster, 1997. Corporate Leadership Award, MIT, 1987. Freeman, City of London, 1998. *Publications:* Indira Gandhi, 1984, 2nd edn 1985; Beyond Boundaries, 1998. *Address:* Caparo House, 103 Baker Street, W1U 6LN. *T:* (020) 7486 1417. *Clubs:* MCC, Royal Automobile; Royal Calcutta Turf, Royal Calcutta Golf (Calcutta); Cricket of India (Bombay).

PAUL, Alan Roderick, CMG 1997; HM Diplomatic Service; Senior Representative (with personal rank of Ambassador), Sino-British Joint Liaison Group, Hong Kong, 1997–2000; *b* 13 May 1950; *s* of late Roderick Ernest Paul and of Hilda May Paul (*née* Choules); *m* 1979, Rosana Yuen-Ling Tam; one *s* one *d*. *Educ:* Wallington High Sch. for Boys; Christ Church, Oxford (Scholar; MA Modern Langs, 1st class Hons). FCO, 1972–73; language training, Univs of Cambridge and Hong Kong, 1973–75; FCO, 1975–77; Peking, 1977–80; FCO, 1980–84; Head of Chancery, The Hague, 1984–87; Asst Head, 1987–89, Head, 1989–91, Hong Kong Dept, FCO; Counsellor and Dep. Sen. Rep., Jt Liaison Gp, Hong Kong, 1991–97. *Recreations:* gardening, genealogy, philately, music. *Address:* c/o Foreign and Commonwealth Office, King Charles Street, SW1A 2AH.

PAUL, Geoffrey David, OBE 1991; Consultant, Sternberg Foundation, since 1996; *b* 26 March 1929; *s* of Reuben Goldstein and Anne Goldstein; *m* 1st, 1952, Joy Stirling (marr. diss. 1972); one *d*; 2nd, 1974, Rachel Mann; one *s*. *Educ:* Liverpool, Kendal, Dublin.

Weekly newspaper and news agency reporter, 1947–57; asst editor, Jewish Observer and Middle East Review, 1957–62; Jewish Chronicle, 1962–96: successively sub-editor, foreign editor, Israel corresp., deputy editor; Editor, 1977–90; US Affairs Editor, 1991–96. Dir, Anglo-Israel Assoc., 2001–. FRSA 1998. *Publication:* Living in Jerusalem, 1981. *Address:* 1 Carlton Close, West Heath Road, NW3 7UA.

PAUL, George William; DL; Deputy Chairman, CGNU, since 2000; *b* 25 Feb. 1940; *s* of William Stuart Hamilton Paul and Diana Violet Anne Martin; *m* 1st, 1963, Mary Annette Mitchell (*d* 1989); two *s* one *d*; 2nd, Margaret J. Kilgour (*née* Hedges). *Educ:* Harrow; Wye Coll., Univ. of London (BSc Agric Hons). Pauls & Whites Foods: Marketing Dir, 1968; Managing Dir, 1972; Pauls & Whites: Dir, 1972; Group Managing Dir, 1982; Chm., Pauls, 1985; Harrisons & Crosfield: Dir, 1985; Jt Chief Exec., 1986; Chief Exec., 1987–94; Chm., 1994–97; Norwich Union: Dir, 1990–2000; Vice-Chm., 1992–94; Chm., 1994–2000. Director: Notcutts Ltd, 1998–; Fleming Overseas Investment Trust plc, 1998–; Chairman: Agricola Holdings Ltd, 1998–2000; Agricola Gp Ltd, 2000–. Mem., Jockey Club; Chm., Jockey Club Estates Ltd, 1991–. High Sheriff, Suffolk, 1990, DL Suffolk, 1991. *Recreations:* theatre, country sports, sailing. *Clubs:* Boodle's, Farmers'.

PAUL, Air Cdre Gerard John Christopher, CB 1956; DFC 1944; MA; *b* 31 Oct. 1907; *s* of E. W. Paul, FRCS; *m* 1st, 1937, Rosemary (*d* 1975), *d* of Rear-Admiral H. G. E. Lane, CB; two *s* one *d*; 2nd, 1987, Mollie Denise Samuels, *d* of Joseph Samuels, MM. *Educ:* Cheltenham Coll.; St John's Coll., Cambridge. Entered Royal Air Force, 1929; Fleet Air Arm, 1931–36; served War of 1939–45 in England and N.W. Europe; Commandant, Central Flying School, 1954–56; retired, 1958. Secretary-General of the Air League, 1958–71. Life Vice-Pres., RAF Gliding and Soaring Assoc.; Pres., Popular Flying Assoc., 1969–78. Croix de Guerre avec Palme (Belgium), 1944; Military Cross (Czechoslovakia), 1945. *Recreations:* dogs, garden. *Address:* Wearne House, Old Alresford, Hants SO24 9DH. *Club:* Royal Air Force.

PAUL, Hugh Glencairn B.; *see* Balfour-Paul.

PAUL, Dame Janet (Elaine), DNZM 1997; painter and writer; *b* 9 Nov. 1919; *d* of Alfred Harry Wilkinson and Eleanor Sinton; *m* 1945, David Blackwood Paul (*d* 1965); four *d* (one *s* decd). *Educ:* Wanganui Girls' Coll.; Victoria Univ. of Wellington (BA Hons 1943). Teacher, 1937–40; Locomotive plan tracer, Railways Dept, Wellington, 1941; Researcher, Historical Br., Dept of Internal Affairs, 1942–45; publishing under imprints: Paul's Book Arcade, Blackwood and Janet Paul, 1945–68; Square and Circle, 1970–73; Art Librarian, Alexander Turnbull Liby, Wellington, 1971–80; occasional lectures in art history, Victoria Univ. of Wellington, and painting, Maroota, NSW, 1985–91. Hon. DLitt Victoria Univ. of Wellington, 1992. *Exhibitions* include: Auckland City Art Gall., 1957, 1958–59, 1962, 1963; Qantas Gall., London, 1964; Victoria Univ. of Wellington Liby, 1971; Arteder '82, Bilbao, Spain, 1982; Wellington City Art Gall., 1983; Loft Gall., Wellington, 1992; Akaroa Art Gall., 1993; Landmarks in NZ Publishing, Nat. Liby Gall., Wellington, 1995; *solo exhibitions:* Galerie Legard, Wellington, 1981, 1983, 1985; Brooker Gall., Wellington, 1987, 1988, 1990; *work represented in collections:* Auckland City Art Gall.; Waikato Art Mus.; Nat. Art Gall., Wellington; Alexander Turnbull Liby; Victoria Univ. of Wellington; Foreign Affairs Dept; Hocken Liby, Univ. of Otago. *Publications:* (contrib.) Women in New Zealand Society, 1981; (ed jtly) A Musician's Journal, 1986; (contrib.) Beyond Expectations, 1986; Mrs Hobson's Album 1840–1845, 1989; biographies in exhibn catalogues; contribs to Landfall, Turnbull Liby Record, Art NZ, NZ Nature Heritage, Bulletin of NZ Art History. *Recreations:* gardening, drawing, grandchildren. *Address:* 24 Ascot Street, Wellington, New Zealand. *T:* (4) 722928.

PAUL, Rev. Canon John Douglas; Dean of Moray, Ross and Caithness, 1991–92, retired; *b* 13 Sept. 1928; *s* of George Anson Moncreiff Paul and Vivian (*née* Ward); *m* 1969, Mary Susan Melody Woodhouse. *Educ:* Winchester Coll.; Edinburgh Univ. (MA); Ely Theol Coll. Asst Curate, Portsmouth, 1954–56; Missionary Priest, Mozambique, 1956–70; Archdeacon, Mozambique, 1965–70; Rector: Castle Douglas, 1970–75; Portobello, 1975–80; Holy Trinity, Elgin, with St Margaret's, Lossiemouth, 1980–92. Hon. Canon and Synod Clerk, Dio. of Moray, Ross and Caithness, 1989–91; Hon. Canon, St Andrew's Cathedral, Inverness, 1992–. *Publication:* Mozambique: Memoirs of a Revolution, 1975. *Recreation:* travel. *Address:* 2 The Avenue, Gifford EH41 4QX. *T:* (01620) 810547. *Club:* Royal Scots (Edinburgh).

PAUL, Sir John (Warburton), GCMG 1965 (KCMG 1962); OBE 1959; MC 1940; Lieutenant Governor, Isle of Man, 1974–80; *b* 29 March 1916; 2nd *s* of Walter George Paul and Phoebe (*née* Bull), Weymouth; *m* 1946, Kathleen Audrey, CStJ 1962, *d* of Dr A. D. Weeden, Weymouth; three *d*. *Educ:* Weymouth Coll., Dorset; Selwyn Coll., Cambridge (MA; Hon. Fellow, 1982). Secretary, Maddermarket Theatre, Norwich, 1936. Commissioned Royal Tank Regt (Suppl. Res.), 1937; regular commission, RTR, 1938; BEF 1940 (despatches, prisoner-of-war); ADC and Private Secretary to Governor of Sierra Leone, 1945 (seconded). Called to the Bar, Inner Temple, 1947. Colonial Administrative Service, Sierra Leone, 1947; District Commissioner, 1952; Permanent Secretary, 1956; Provincial Commissioner, 1959; Secretary to the Cabinet, 1960; Governor and C-in-C, The Gambia, 1962–65; Governor-General of The Gambia, 1965–66; Governor and C-in-C: British Honduras, 1966–72; The Bahamas, 1972–73; Governor-General, The Bahamas, July–Oct. 1973. Dir, Overseas Relns, St John Ambulance, 1981–89. Member Board, West African Airways Corporation, 1954–56. Chm., St Christopher Motorists' Security Assoc., and associated cos, 1980–93. A Patron, Pain Relief Foundn, 1980–97. Mem., Bd of Governors, Pangbourne Coll., 1981–86. KStJ 1962 (Member: Chapter-Gen., 1981–91; St John Council, Hants, 1990–96). *Recreation:* painting. *Address:* Sherrens Mead, Sherfield-on-Loddon, Hampshire RG27 0ED. *Clubs:* MCC; Hawks (Cambridge).

PAUL, Noël Strange, CBE 1978; Director, Press Council, 1976–79 (Assistant Secretary, 1964, Secretary, 1968–76), retired; *b* 1914; *y s* of late S. Evan Paul, SSC, and Susan, *d* of Dr Henry Habgood; *m* 1950, Mary (*d* 1998), *yr d* of Philip J. Bone, FRSA, MRST, Luton. *Educ:* Kingston Grammar School. Journalist, Press Assoc., 1932; served War of 1939–45, Iran and Italy, Major seconded RAF (despatches). Home Counties Newspapers, 1949; Liverpool Daily Post, 1958. Mem., Steering Cttee on the Mass Media, Council of Europe, 1976–82; Governor, English-Speaking Union, 1980–82. *Publications:* Self-regulation of the Press, 1982; Principles for the Press, 1985. *Recreations:* sailing, photography. *Address:* The Lodge, St Catherine's, Strachur, Argyllshire PA25 8AZ. *T:* (01499) 302208.

PAUL, Robert Cameron, CBE 1996; FREng; Chief Executive, Albright & Wilson plc, 1995–97; *b* 7 July 1935; *m* 1965, Diana Kathleen Bruce (*d* 2001); two *d*. *Educ:* Rugby Sch.; Corpus Christi Coll., Cambridge (BA 1958; MEng 1992). Nat. Service, 2nd Lieut RE, 1953–55. Chemical Engineer, ICI, Runcorn, 1959; Dir, ICI Fibres, 1976; Dep. Chm., Mond Div., ICI, 1979; Dep. Chm. and Man. Dir, Albright & Wilson, 1986–95. Non-exec. Dir, Courtaulds plc, 1994–98. President: IChemE, 1990–91; Chemical Industries Assoc., 1995–97. FREng (FEng 1990). Hon DEng Birmingham, 1990. *Recreations:* music (piano), golf. *Address:* 2 Devonshire Place, Kensington, W8 5UD.

PAUL, Air Marshal Sir Ronald Ian S.; *see* Stuart-Paul.

PAULET, family name of **Marquess of Winchester**.

PAULIN, Prof. Roger Cole, DrPhil, LittD; Schröder Professor of German, University of Cambridge, since 1989; Fellow, Trinity College, Cambridge since 1989; *b* 18 Dec. 1937; *s* of Thomas Gerald Paulin and Paulina (*née* Duff); *m* 1966, Traute Fielitz; one *s* one *d*. *Educ:* Otago Boys' High Sch., Dunedin, NZ; Univ. of Otago (MA); Heidelberg Univ. (DrPhil); MA, LittD (Cantab). Asst Lectr, Univ. of Birmingham, 1963–64; Lectr, Univ. of Bristol, 1965–73; Fellow and Coll. Lectr in German, Trinity Coll., Cambridge, 1974–87; Univ. Lectr, Univ. of Cambridge, 1975–87; Henry Simon Prof. of German, Univ. of Manchester, 1987–89. Mem., Editl Bd, Literatur-Lexikon, 1988–93. *Publications:* Ludwig Tieck: a literary biography, 1985, 2nd edn 1986 (trans. German, 1988); The Brief Compass, 1985; Ludwig Tieck, 1987; Theodor Storm, 1991; Wilhelm Jerusalem, 1999. *Recreation:* gardening. *Address:* 45 Fulbrooke Road, Cambridge CB3 9EE. *T:* (01223) 322564.

PAULIN, Thomas Neilson; poet and critic; G. M. Young Lecturer in English Literature, University of Oxford, since 1994; Fellow, Hertford College, Oxford, since 1994; *b* 25 Jan. 1949; *s* of Douglas and Mary Paulin; *m* 1973, Munjiet Kaur Khosa; two *s*. *Educ:* Hull Univ. (BA); Lincoln Coll., Oxford (BLitt). English Department, University of Nottingham: Lectr, 1972–89; Reader in Poetry, 1989–94; Prof. of Poetry, 1994. NESTA Fellow, 2000–. Hon. DLitt: Saskatchewan, 1987; Stafford, 1995; Hull, 2000. *Publications:* Thomas Hardy: the poetry of perception, 1975; A State of Justice, 1977; The Strange Museum, 1980; Liberty Tree, 1983; The Riot Act, 1985; Ireland and the English Crisis, 1985; The Faber Book of Political Verse, 1986; The Hillsborough Script, 1987; Fivemiletown, 1987; Seize the Fire, 1989; The Faber Book of Vernacular Verse, 1990; Minotaur: poetry and the nation state, 1992; Walking a Line, 1994; Writing to the Moment: selected critical essays, 1996; The Day-Star of Liberty: William Hazlitt's radical style, 1998; The Wind Dog, 1999. *Address:* c/o Faber & Faber, 3 Queen Square, WC1N 3AU.

PAULUSZ, Jan Gilbert; a Recorder of the Crown Court, since 1980; *b* 18 Nov. 1929; *s* of Jan Hendrik Olivier Paulusz and Edith (*née* Gilbert); *m* 1973, Luigia Maria Attanasio. *Educ:* The Leys Sch., Cambridge. Called to the Bar, Lincoln's Inn, 1957; South Eastern Circuit, 1959–. *Recreations:* mountain walking, photography. *Address:* (chambers) 8 King's Bench Walk, Temple, EC4Y 7DU; 50 Royston Gardens, Redbridge, Ilford, Essex IG1 3SY.

PAUNCEFORT, Bernard Edward, OBE 1983; HM Diplomatic Service, retired 1986; Administrator, Tristan da Cunha, South Atlantic, 1989–92; *b* 8 April 1926; *o s* of Frederick George Pauncefort and Eleanor May (*née* Jux); *m* 1956, Patricia Anne, *yr d* of Charles Ernest Leah and Alice (*née* Kendal-Banks). *Educ:* Wandsworth School. RAFVR 1942–44; Royal Fusiliers, 1944–48. Metropolitan Police Civil Staff, 1948–53; HM Colonial Service, 1953; Malaya, 1953–56; Tanganyika, 1956–63; CRO, 1963–67; First Sec., Zambia, 1967–68; Consul, Cape Town, 1969–72; Lord Pearce's staff, Rhodesia, 1971–72; Head of Chancery, Madagascar, 1972–73; FCO, 1973–76; Sec. to Seychelles Electoral Review Commn, 1976; Head of Chancery, Burma, 1976–78; Dir, British Inf. Services, S Africa, 1978–80; Lord Soames' staff, Rhodesia-Zimbabwe, 1979–80; Administrator, Ascension Island, 1980–82; FCO, 1982–83; Counsellor and Chief Sec., Falkland Is, 1983–85; Counsellor, FCO, 1985–86; Under-Sec., Govt of the Turks & Caicos Is. W Indies, 1986–88. Zimbabwe Medal, 1980. *Recreations:* dogs, birds, waterways. *Address:* 10 New Church Road, Uphill, Weston-super-Mare BS23 4UY.

PAUNCEFORT-DUNCOMBE, Sir Philip; *see* Duncombe.

PAVAROTTI, Luciano; Italian tenor; *b* 12 Oct. 1935; *s* of Fernando Pavarotti and Adele (*née* Venturi); *m* 1961, Adua Veroni; three *d*. *Educ:* Istituto Magistrale. Teacher, 1955–57. Professional début, Teatro Municipale, Reggio Emilia, 1961; sang throughout Europe, 1961–64; US début and Australian tour 1965; rôles include Rodolfo in La Bohème, Cavaradossi in Tosca, Duke of Mantua in Rigoletto, Radames in Aïda, Ernani, Alfredo in La Traviata, Manrico in Il Trovatore, Rodolfo in Luisa Miller, Arturo in I Puritani, Elvino in La Sonnambula, Nemorino in L'Elisir d'Amore, Idomeneo, Enzo in La Gioconda, Riccardo (Gustavo) in Un Ballo in Maschera, Don Carlos, etc. Chevalier des Grieux in Manon. Grammy Award for best classical vocal soloist, 1978, 1979, 1981, 1988, 1990. *Publications:* (jtly) Pavarotti: my own story, 1981; Grandissimo Pavarotti, 1986; (jtly) Pavarotti: My World, 1995. *Address:* c/o Herbert Breslin, 119 West 57th Street, New York, NY 10019, USA.

PAVEY, Martin Christopher; educational consultant; *b* 2 Dec. 1940; *s* of Archibald Lindsay Pavey and Margaret Alice Pavey (*née* Salsbury); *m* 1969, Louise Margaret (*née* Bird); two *s*. *Educ:* Magdalen College Sch., Oxford; University Coll., London (Hons English); Nottingham Univ. (MA English); Univ. of Cambridge (Dip. Educn). Wigglesworth & Co., London and E. Africa (Shipping and Finance), 1956–62; Assistant Master: King's Sch., Ely, 1962–64; Lancing Coll., 1968–71; Fairham Comprehensive School, Nottingham: Head of English, 1971–75; Dep. Headmaster, 1975–76; Headmaster, 1976–81; Headmaster: Cranbrook School, 1981–88; Latymer Upper School, Hammersmith, 1988–91. *Recreations:* art architecture, cinema. *Address:* 5 Vineyards, Bath, Avon BA1 5NA.

PAVORD, Anna, (Mrs T. D. O. Ware); Gardening Correspondent, The Independent, since 1986; *b* 20 Sept. 1940; *d* of Arthur Vincent Pavord and Christabel Frances (*née* Lewis); *m* 1966, Trevor David Oliver Ware; three *d*. *Educ:* Univ. of Leicester (BA Hons English). PA/Dir, Line Up, BBC2, 1963–70; contributor, Observer Mag., 1970–92; writer and presenter, Flowering Passions, Channel 4 TV, 1991–92. Associate Editor, Gardens Illustrated, 1993–. Member: NT Gardens Panel, 1996– (Chm., 2002–); English Heritage Parks and Gardens Panel, 2001–. *Publications:* Foliage, 1990; The Flowering Year, 1991; Gardening Companion, 1992; Hidcote, 1993; The Border Book, 1994; The New Kitchen Garden, 1996; The Tulip, 1999; Plant Partners, 2001. *Recreations:* sailing, walking, gardening, visiting Guyana. *Address:* c/o The Independent, Independent House, 191 Marsh Wall, E14 9RS. *T:* (020) 7005 2000.

PAWLEY, Prof. Godfrey Stuart, PhD; FRS 1992; FRSE; Professor of Computational Physics, University of Edinburgh, 1985–Sept. 2002; *b* 22 June 1937; *s* of George Charles Pawley and Winifred Mary (*née* Wardle); *m* 1961, Anthea Jean Miller; two *s* one *d*. *Educ:* Bolton Sch.; Corpus Christi Coll., Cambridge (MA, PhD 1962). Chem. Dept, Harvard Univ., 1962–64; University of Edinburgh: Lect, 1964–69; Reader, 1970–85. Guest Prof., Chem. Dept, Århus Univ., Denmark, 1969–70. Principal Investigator, EPSRC Colloidal Hydrodynamics Computational Grand Challenge, 1995–99. FRSE 1975. *Publications:* (contrib.) An Introduction to OCCAM 2 programming, 2nd edn, 1989; numerous scientific papers. *Recreations:* choral singing, mountain walking. *Address:* 26 Relugas Road, Edinburgh EH9 2ND. *T:* (0131) 667 2122.

PAWLEY, (Robert) John; Director of Professional Services, Valuation Office Agency, 1995–99; *b* 10 Sept. 1939; *s* of Frederick Clifford and Marjorie Pawley; *m* 1965, Simone

Elizabeth Tayar; two *s.* *Educ:* Plymouth Coll.; Exeter Univ. (BA). Private practice, Plymouth, 1962–71; joined Valuation Office, 1972; Dist Valuer, Waltham Forest, 1977, Haringey, 1978–81; Suptg Valuer, Chief Valuer's Office, London, 1981–84, Cambridge, 1984–87; Asst Chief Valuer, 1987–88; Dep. Chief Valuer, Inland Revenue Valuation Office, later Dep. Chief Exec. (Technical), Valuation Office Agency, 1989–95. *Recreations:* 18th century English naval history and exploration, period model boats, antiques.

PAWSEY, James Francis; non-executive Director, Autobar Group Ltd, since 1983; *b* 21 Aug. 1933; *s* of William Pawsey and Mary Mumford; *m* 1956, Cynthia Margaret Francis; six *s* (including twins twice). *Educ:* Coventry Tech. School; Coventry Tech. Coll. Director: (non-exec.) St Martins Hosps Ltd, 1989–; Love Lane Investments, 1995–; (non-exec.) Opinion Res. Business, 1997–; Keyturn, 1997–. MP (C) Rugby, 1979–83, Rugby and Kenilworth, 1983–97; contested (C) Rugby and Kenilworth, 1997. Parliamentary Private Secretary: DES, 1982–83; DHSS, 1983–84; to Minister of State for NI, 1984–86. Member: Parly Scientific Cttee, 1982–97; Select Cttee of Parly Comr for Admin, 1983–97 (Chm., 1993); Select Cttee on Standing Orders, 1987–97; Exec., 1922 Cttee, 1989–97; Liaison Cttee, 1993–97; Ct of Referees, 1993–97; Chm., Cons Parly Educn Cttee, 1985–97; Mem. Exec., IPU, 1984–97; Sec., Cons. Back Bench Social Services and Educn Cttees, 1982–83; Chm., W Midlands Gp of Cons. MPs, 1993–97. Member: Rugby RDC, 1965–73; Rugby Borough Council, 1973–75; Warwickshire CC, 1974–79; former Chm. and Pres., Warwickshire Assoc. of Parish Councils. MInstD. KLJ. *Publication:* The Tringo Phenomenon, 1983. *Address:* Shilton House, Shilton, near Coventry CV7 9HT.

PAWSON, Prof. Anthony James, PhD; OC 2000; FRS 1994; FRSC 1994; Senior Scientist, Samuel Lunenfeld Research Institute, Mount Sinai Hospital, Toronto, since 1985; Professor, Department of Molecular and Medical Genetics, University of Toronto, since 1985; *b* 18 Oct. 1952; *s* of Henry Anthony Pawson, OBE and Hilarie Anne Pawson (*née* Bassett); *m* 1975, Margaret Anne Luman; two *s* one *d.* *Educ:* Clare Coll., Cambridge (BA); London Univ. (PhD). Grad. Student, ICRF, London, 1973–76; Postdoctoral Fellow, Univ. of Calif, Berkeley, 1976–80; Asst Prof., Univ. of BC, 1981–85. Terry Fox Cancer Res. Scientist, Nat. Cancer Inst. of Canada, 1988–98; Internat. Res. Schol., Howard Hughes Med. Inst., 1991–; Apotex Prof. of Molecular Oncology, Mt Sinai Hosp., 1991–. Gairdner Foundn Internat. Award, 1994; Amer. Assoc. for Cancer Res. Inc./Pezcoller Internat. Award, 1998; Dr H. P. Heineken Prize for Biochem. and Physics, Royal Netherlands Acad. of Arts and Scis, 1998; Flavelle Medal, RSC, 1998; Dist. Scientist Award, MRC of Canada, 1998; Killam Prize for Health Scis, 2000; J. Allyn Taylor Internat. Prize in Medicine, 2000. *Publications:* papers in Nature, Cell, Science, Molecular and Cell Biol., Proc. Nat. Acad. of Sci. (USA), Jl Virology, EMBO Jl, Jl Biol Chem., Oncogene and other learned jls. *Recreations:* reading, theatre, fly-fishing, ski-ing, baseball. *Address:* Samuel Lunenfield Research Institute, Mount Sinai Hospital, 600 University Avenue, Toronto, ON M5G 1X5, Canada. *T:* (416) 5868262; 34 Glenwood Avenue, Toronto, ON M6P 3C6, Canada. *T:* (416) 7632266.

PAWSON, Anthony John Dalby; Director General Defence Export Services, Ministry of Defence, since 1998; *b* 14 Oct. 1946; *s* of Donald Pawson and Kathleen (*née* Goodwin); *m* 1969, Kathleen Chisholm; one *s* one *d.* *Educ:* Kent Coll., Canterbury; City Univ. (BSc 1st Class Hons Computer Science). MoD 1967; Private Sec. to Chief of Air Staff, 1978–80; First Sec., UK Delgn to NATO, Brussels, 1981–83; Private Sec. to Sec. of State for NI, 1990–92; RCDS 1992; Asst Under-Sec. of State (Fleet Support), MoD, 1993–95; Under-Sec. (Overseas and Defence), Cabinet Office, 1995–97; Dir Gen. Marketing, MoD, 1997–98. *Recreations:* Rugby, cricket. *Address:* Ministry of Defence, St Christopher House, Southwark Street, SE1 0TD. *Clubs:* Civil Service; Tunbridge Wells Rugby Football; Borderers' Cricket.

PAXMAN, Jeremy Dickson; journalist, author and broadcaster; *b* 11 May 1950; *s* of Arthur Keith Paxman and Joan McKay Dickson; partner, Elizabeth Ann Clough; one *s* two *d* (of whom one *s* one *d* are twins). *Educ:* Malvern College; St Catharine's College, Cambridge (Exhibnr; Hon. Fellow, 2000). Reporter: N Ireland, 1974–77; BBC TV Tonight, 1977–79; Panorama, 1979–85; The Bear Next Door; presenter: Breakfast Time, 1986–89; Newsnight, 1989–; Did You See?, 1991–93; You Decide—with Paxman, 1995–96; Start The Week, R4, 1998–; Chairman: University Challenge, 1994–; Times Past, Times Present, R4, 1996. Hon. Fellow, St Edmund Hall, Oxford, 2000. Hon. LLD Leeds, 1999; Hon. DLitt Bradford, 1999. Award for Internat. Current Affairs, RTS, 1985; Award for best personal contribution to television, Voice of Viewer and Listener, 1993, 1998; Richard Dimbleby Award, BAFTA, 1996, 2000; Interview of the Year, RTS, 1997 and 1998; BPG Award, 1998; Variety Club Media Personality of the Year, 1999. *Publications:* (jtly) A Higher Form of Killing: the secret story of gas and germ warfare, 1982; Through the Volcanoes: a Central American journey, 1985; Friends in High Places: who runs Britain?, 1990; Fish, Fishing and the Meaning of Life, 1994; The Compleat Angler, 1996; The English: a portrait of a people, 1998. *Recreations:* food, books, fishing. *Address:* c/o Capel and Land, 29 Wardour Street, W1D 6PS.

See also T. G. Paxman.

PAXMAN, Timothy Giles, LVO 1989; HM Diplomatic Service; Counsellor (Political Affairs), UK Permanent Representation to the European Union, Brussels, since 1999; *b* 15 Nov. 1951; *s* of Arthur Keith Paxman and Joan McKay Paxman (*née* Dickson); *m* 1980, Segolene Claude Marie Cayol; three *d.* *Educ:* Malvern Coll.; New Coll., Oxford. DoE, 1974–76; Dept of Transport, 1976–78; Ecole Nat. d'Admin, Paris, 1978–79; joined FCO, 1980: 1st Secretary: UK Perm. Rep. to EC, 1980–84; FCO, 1984–88; Head of Chancery, Singapore, 1988–92; on secondment to Cabinet Office, 1992–94; Counsellor (Econ. and Commercial), Rome, 1994–98. *Recreations:* tennis, ski-ing, jazz and blues music, cinema, golf. *Address:* c/o Foreign and Commonwealth Office, King Charles Street, SW1A 2AH.

See also J. D. Paxman.

PAXTON, John; author, also writing as Jack Cherrill; Editor, The Statesman's Year-Book, 1969–90; *b* 23 Aug. 1923; *m* 1950, Joan Thorne; one *s* one *d.* Head of Economics department, Millfield, 1952–63. Joined The Statesman's Year-Book, 1963, Dep. Ed., 1968; Consultant Editor, The New Illustrated Everyman's Encyclopaedia, 1981–84. Jt Treas., English Centre, Internat. PEN, 1973–78; Chm., West Country Writers' Assoc., 1993–95. *Publications:* (with A. E. Walsh) Trade in the Common Market Countries, 1965; (with A. E. Walsh) The Structure and Development of the Common Market, 1968; (with A. E. Walsh) Trade and Industrial Resources of the Common Market and Efta Countries, 1970; (with John Wroughton) Smuggling, 1971; (with A. E. Walsh) Into Europe, 1972; (ed) Everyman's Dictionary of Abbreviations, 1974, 2nd edn 1986, as Penguin Dictionary of Abbreviations, 1989; World Legislatures, 1974; (with C. Cook) European Political Facts 1789–1999, 3 vols, 1975–2000; The Statesman's Year-Book World Gazetteer, 1975, 4th edn, 1991; (with A. E. Walsh) Competition Policy: European and International Trends and Practices, 1975; The Developing Common Market, 1976; A Dictionary of the European Economic Community, 1977, 2nd edn, A Dictionary of the European Communities, 1982; (with C. Cook) Commonwealth Political Facts, 1979; (with S. Fairfield) Calendar of Creative Man, 1980; Companion to Russian History, 1984, 2nd edn as Encyclopedia of Russian History, 1993; Companion to the French Revolution, 1988; The Statesman's Year-Book Historical Companion, 1988; (with G. Payton) Penguin Dictionary of Proper Names, 1991; European Communities (a bibliography), 1992; Calendar of World History, 1999; (with W. G. Moore) Penguin Encyclopedia of Places, 1999; Imperial Russia: a reference handbook, 2000; Dictionary of Financial Abbreviations, 2002; contrib. to Keesing's Contemporary Archives, Children's Britannica, TLS. *Address:* Moss Cottage, Hardway, Bruton, Somerset BA10 0LN. *T:* (01749) 813423.

PAXTON, Peter James, FCIS; FCCA; FCIB; Chief Executive Officer, Cambridge and District Co-operative Society Ltd, 1972–86; *b* 27 April 1923; *m* 1st, 1947, Betty Jane Madden (marr. diss. 1980); one *s* one *d*; 2nd, 1985, Sylvia June Stock. *Educ:* Lawrence Sherriff Sch., Rugby. Served RAF, 1941–46. Accountant, Rugby Co-operative Society Ltd, 1949–55; Chief Accountant, Cambridge and District Co-operative Society Ltd, 1955; Chairman: CWS, 1980–86; Co-operative Bank, 1980–86; First Co-op. Finance, 1980–86; Co-op. City Investments, 1983–86; Dep. Chm., Co-op. Insce Soc., 1983–86. *Address:* Westwood House, Westwood, Broadclyst, Exeter, Devon EX5 3DH. *T:* (01404) 822821.

PAXTON, (Peter) Robin; Managing Director, Walt Disney Television International (Asia Pacific), since 1999 (Managing Director, Broadcasting and Production, 1997–99); *b* 14 April 1951; *s* of late Richard Gordon Paxton and of Marion Paxton; *m* 1987, Linda Jane French; two *s.* *Educ:* Leighton Park Sch.; Sussex Univ. (BA Hons); LSE (MScEcon); Nuffield Coll., Oxford. Joined London Weekend Television, 1977; Managing Director: LWT Broadcasting Ltd, 1993–94; Carlton Television (India), 1995–97. *Address:* Walt Disney Studios (Asia Pacific) Ltd, 19th Floor, Shell Tower, Times Square, Causeway Bay, Hong Kong. *T:* 22032323, *Fax:* 22031313.

PAYE, Jean-Claude; Chevalier de la Légion d'Honneur; Commandeur de l'Ordre National du Mérite; Chevalier de l'Ordre National du Mérite agricole; Croix de la Valeur militaire; Member, Conseil d'Etat, France, 1996–2000; *b* 26 Aug. 1934; *s* of late Lucien Paye and of Suzanne Paye (*née* Guignard); *m* 1963, Laurence Hélène Marianne Jeanneney; two *s* two *d.* *Educ:* Lycée Bugeaud, Algiers; Lycée Carnot, Tunis; Faculté de droit, Tunis; Institut d'Etudes Politiques, Paris; Ecole Nationale d'Administration. Government service, 1961–64; Technical Adviser to: Sec. of State for Scientific Research, 1965; Minister of Social Affairs, 1966; Chief Adviser to Vice-Pres., EEC, 1967–73; Adviser, Embassy, Bonn, 1973; Asst Principal Private Sec. to Minister of Foreign Affairs, 1974–76; Diplomatic Advr to Prime Minister, 1976–79; Head of Economic and Financial Affairs, Ministry of Foreign Affairs, 1979–84; Pres., Exec. Cttee in special Session, 1980–84, Sec-Gen., 1984–96, OECD. *Address:* 1 Place A. Deville, 75006 Paris, France.

PAYKEL, Prof. Eugene Stern, FRCP, FRCPE, FRCPsych; Professor of Psychiatry, 1985–2001, now Emeritus, and Head of Department, 1985–2000, University of Cambridge; Professorial Fellow, Gonville and Caius College, Cambridge, 1985–2001, now Emeritus Fellow; *b* 9 Sept. 1934; *s* of late Joshua Paykel and Eva Stern Paykel; *m* 1969, Margaret, *d* of late John Melrose and Joan Melrose; two *s.* *Educ:* Auckland Grammar Sch.; Univ. of Otago (MB ChB, MD; Stuart Prize, Joseph Pullar Schol., 1956); DPM London. Maudsley Hosp., 1962–65; Asst Prof. of Psychiatry and Co-Dir/Dir, Depression Res. Unit, Yale Univ., 1966–71; Consultant and Sen. Lectr, 1971–75, Reader, 1975–77, Prof. of Psychiatry, 1977–85, St George's Hosp. Med. Sch., Univ. of London. Chief Scientist's Adviser and Mem., Mental Illness Res. Liaison Gp, DHSS, 1984–88; Chm., Jt Cttee on Higher Psychiatric Trng, 1990–95. Previously examiner Univs of Edinburgh, Nottingham, Manchester, London, and RCPsych. Mem., Neurosciences Bd, MRC, 1981–85, 1995–99. Mem., Bethlem Royal and Maudsley Hosp. SHA, 1990–94. Vice Pres., RCPsych, 1994–96 (Chm., Social and Community Psych. Sect., 1984–88); Zonal Rep., World Psychiatric Assoc., 1993–99 (Chm., Pharmaco-psychiatry Sect., 1993–98); Hon. Mem., British Assoc. for Psychopharmacology, 1991 (Pres., 1982–84); President: Marce Soc., 1992–94; Collegium Internat. Neuropsychophamacologicum, 2000–June 2002. Trustee, Mental Health Foundn, 1988–95. Founder FMedSci 1998; Hon. FRCPsych 2001. Foundations Fund Prize for Res. in Psychiatry, 1978; BMA Film Competition Bronze Award, 1981; Anna Monika Stiftung 2nd Prize, 1985; Eur. Coll. of Neuropsychopharmacol.-Lilly Award for Clin. Neurosci., 2001. Jt Editor, Jl of Affective Disorders, 1979–93; Editor, Psychological Medicine, 1994–; Member, Editorial Board: Social Psychiatry; Psychopharmacology; Jl of Affective Disorders; Acta Psychiatrica Belgica, etc. *Publications:* The Depressed Woman, 1974; Psychopharmacology of Affective Disorders, 1979; Monoamine Oxidase Inhibitors: the state of the art, 1981; Handbook of Affective Disorders, 1982, 2nd edn 1992; Community Psychiatric Nursing for Neurotic Patients, 1983; papers on depression, psychopharmacology, social psychiatry, life events, evaluation of treatment. *Recreations:* opera, music, theatre. *Address:* Department of Psychiatry, University of Cambridge, Douglas House, 18E Trumpington Road, Cambridge CB2 2AH. *T:* (01223) 741928.

PAYNE, Alan Jeffrey, CMG 1988; HM Diplomatic Service, retired; *b* 11 May 1933; *s* of Sydney Ellis Payne and Lydia Payne; *m* 1959, Letitia Freeman; three *s.* *Educ:* Enfield Grammar Sch.; Queens' Coll., Cambridge (Exhibnr). FIL 1962. RN, 1955–57. EMI, London, later Paris, 1957–62; Secretariat, NATO, Paris, 1962–64; joined Diplomatic Service, 1965; Commonwealth Relations Office (later FCO), 1965–67; British High Commn, Kuala Lumpur, 1967–70; FCO, 1970–72; British Embassy, Budapest, 1972–75; Counsellor, Mexico City, 1975–79; FCO, 1979–82; Consul-General, Lyons, 1982–87; High Comr, Jamaica, and Ambassador (non-resident) to Haiti, 1987–89. Sec. Gen., Internat. Primary Aluminium Inst., 1989–97. *Recreations:* music, theatre, growing trees, restoring old cars. *Club:* Royal Automobile.

PAYNE, Anthony Edward; freelance composer and writer; *b* 2 Aug. 1936; *s* of Edward Alexander Payne and Muriel Margaret Elsie Payne (*née* Stroud); *m* 1966, Jane Marian Manning, *qv.* *Educ:* Dulwich Coll.; Durham Univ. (BA Hons Music 1961). Composition Tutor: London Coll. of Music, 1983–85; Sydney Conservatorium, 1986; Univ. of W Australia, 1996; Vis. Milhaud Prof., Mills Coll., Calif, 1983. Contributor: Daily Telegraph, 1964–; Times, 1964–; Independent, 1986–; Country Life, 1995–. Hon. DMus Birmingham, 2001. *Compositions:* principal works include: Paraphrases and Cadenzas, 1969; Phoenix Mass, 1972; Paean, 1971; Concerto for Orchestra, 1974; The World's Winter, 1976; String Quartet, 1978; The Stones and Lonely Places Sing, 1979; Song of the Clouds, 1980; Springs Shining Wake, 1981; A Day in the Life of a Mayfly, 1981; Evening Land, 1981; The Spirit's Harvest, 1985; The Song Streams in the Firmament, 1986; Half Heard in the Stillness, 1987; Sea Change, 1988; Time's Arrow, 1990; Symphonies of Wind and Rain, 1991; Orchestral Variations, 1994; completion of Elgar's Third Symphony, 1997; Piano Trio, 1998; Scenes from the Woodlanders, 1999; Of Knots and Skeins, 2000; Visions and Journeys, 2002. *Publications:* Schoenberg, 1968; Frank Bridge—Radical and Conservative, 1976, 2nd edn 1984; Elgar's Third Symphony: the story of the reconstruction, 1998; articles in learned jls, incl. Musical Times, Tempo, Listener, etc, 1962–. *Recreations:* cinema, English countryside. *Address:* 2 Wilton Square, N1 3DL. *T:* (020) 7359 1593, *Fax:* (020) 7226 4369; *e-mail:* tony@wiltonsq.demon.uk.

PAYNE, Arthur Stanley, OBE 1977; HM Diplomatic Service, retired; Director, then Chief Executive, Southern Africa Association, 1988–92; *b* 17 Nov. 1930; *s* of late Arthur and Lilian Gertrude Payne; *m* 1964, Heather Elizabeth Cavaghan; one *d.* *Educ:* Chatham

Tech. Sch.; Gillingham Grammar Sch.; Nat. Defence Coll. HM Forces, 1949–50. Joined BoT, 1949; Raw Materials Dept, Washington, 1951–52; Min. of Materials, London, 1953–55; British Trade Commns, New Delhi, Bombay, Port of Spain, and Georgetown (First Sec.), 1956–67; joined HM Diplomatic Service, 1965; First Sec. (Inf.), Auckland, 1967–70; FCO, 1971–74; Dacca, 1974–76; Bonn, 1976–78; FCO, 1978–79; Dep. High Comr and Head of Chancery, Gabarone, 1980–83; Dep. Hd of Mission, Counsellor and Hd of Commercial Dept, Manila, 1983–87. Hon. Consultant, Southern Africa Business Assoc., 1995–2001. *Recreations:* bridge, music, computing, cooking. *Address:* Hoders Gate, Woodhurst Park, Oxted, Surrey, RH8 9HA.

PAYNE, Prof. Christopher Charles, OBE 1997; Professor of Horticulture and Landscape, University of Reading, since 1999; *b* 15 May 1946; *s* of Rupert George Payne and Evelyn Violet (*née* Abbott); *m* 1969, Margaret Susan Street; one *s* one *d*. *Educ:* Wadham Coll., Oxford (MA, DPhil). CBiol, FIBiol 1995; FIHort 1991. Post-Doctoral Fellow, Univ. of Otago, NZ, 1972; SSO, NERC, Oxford, 1973–77; PSO, 1977–83, Head, Entomology Dept, 1983–86, Glasshouse Crops Res. Inst., Littlehampton; Head, Crop Protection Div., Inst. of Horticultural Res., E Malling, 1987–90; Chief Exec., Horticulture Research Internat., 1990–99. Hon. Professor: Univ. of Warwick, 1991–99; Univ. of Birmingham, 1995–99. Editor in Chief, Biocontrol Science and Technology, 1991–2000. FRSA 1997. *Publications:* (with R. Hull and F. Brown) Virology: directory and dictionary of animal, bacterial and plant viruses, 1989; numerous contribs to books and learned jls. *Recreations:* gardening, walking, cycling. *Address:* Old Thatch, 15 North Street, Marcham, Oxon OX13 6NG. *T:* (01865) 391185; *e-mail:* chris@chapelst.demon.co.uk. *Club:* Farmers'.

PAYNE, Christopher Frederick, CBE 1987; QPM 1975; DL; Chief Constable of Cleveland Constabulary, 1976–90; *b* 15 Feb. 1930; *o s* of late Gerald Frederick Payne, OBE, BEM, QPM, and Amy Florence Elizabeth Payne (*née* Parker); *m* 1952, Barbara Janet Saxby; one *s* three *d*. *Educ:* Christ's Coll., Finchley; Hendon Technical Coll. CIMgt (CBIM 1987). Joined Metropolitan Police, 1950; Sen. Comd. course, 1965; Home Office R&D Br., 1968–70; Comdr 'X' Div., 1971–74; Comdr Airport Div., 1974–76. Dep. Chm., Metrop. Police Friendly Soc., 1971–76; Police Advr to ACCs' Social Services Cttee, 1979–90; Chm., Public Order Sub-Cttee, ACPO, 1981–88; Pres., Chief Constables' Club, 1989–90. Sen. Vis. Res. Fellow, Univ. of Bradford, 1991–2001. Adviser to: Chemical Hazards Unit, Qld Govt, 1989–90; UN Disaster Relief Org. External Services, 1990–96; Emergency Planning Advr, BRCS, Cleveland, 1990–94. County Dir, St John Ambulance, 1978–85, Comdr, SJAB, 1985–89, Chm., St John Council, 1986–89, Cleveland. Chm., Cleveland Mental Health Support Gp, 1981–86; Vice-Pres., Cleveland Youth Assoc., 1983–; Vice Chm., Royal Jubilee and Prince's Trusts Cttee for Durham and Cleveland, 1984–90. Chm., Castlegate Quay Trust, 1991–2001. Chm. Mgt Devclt Cttee and Mem. Exec. Bd, Inst. of Mgt, 1998–2001. Freeman, City of London, 1988. DL Cleveland, 1983, N Yorks, 1996. CStJ 1985 (OStJ 1980). *Publications:* various articles on contingency planning and management. *Recreations:* painting, philately, gardening. *Address:* c/o The Chief Constable's Office, PO Box 70, Ladgate Lane, Middlesbrough TS8 9EH. *Club:* Cleveland (Middlesbrough).

PAYNE, Prof. David Neil, FRS 1992; Director, Optoelectronics Research Centre, since 1995 (Deputy Director, 1989–95), and Pirelli Professor of Photonics, since 1991, University of Southampton; *b* 13 Aug. 1944; *s* of Raymond and Maisie Payne. *Educ:* Univ. of Southampton (BSc, PhD). Commissioning Engineer, English Electric Co., 1962; University of Southampton: Research Asst, 1969; Jun. Res. Fellow, 1971; Pirelli Res. Fellow, 1972, Sen. Res. Fellow, 1978, Principal Res. Fellow, 1981; Pirelli Reader, 1984. Fellow, Optical Soc. of America, 1995. Awards include: Rank Prize for Optoelectronics, 1991; IEEE/OSA John Tyndall Award, 1991; Computers and Communications Prize, Foundn for Computer and Communications Promotion in Japan, 1993; Franklin Medal, Franklin Inst., 1998. *Publications:* numerous contribs to learned jls. *Recreations:* squash, cooking, scuba diving, motorcycling, gardening. *Address:* Optoelectronics Research Centre, The University, Southampton SO17 1BJ. *T:* (023) 8059 3583.

PAYNE, Donald Hedley; Chief Executive, Willis Corroon, 1992–95; *b* 14 Nov. 1938; *s* of Norman Kingsley and Elizabeth Payne; *m* 1965, Leonore Maria Beatrice Skjoldebrand; one *s* one *d*. *Educ:* Christ's Hosp.; Durham Univ. (BSc Hons). ACII. Director: Bland Payne Ltd, 1965–79; Willis Faber PLC, 1979–90; Willis Corroon PLC, 1992–95. *Recreations:* travel, opera, ski-ing. *Club:* Royal Automobile.

PAYNE, (Geoffrey John) Nicholas; General Director, English National Opera, since 1998; *b* 4 Jan. 1945; *s* of John Laurence Payne and Dorothy Gwendoline Payne (*née* Attenborough); *m* 1986, Linda Jane Adamson; two *s*. *Educ:* Eton Coll. (King's Schol.); Trinity Coll., Cambridge (BA Eng Lit). Finance Assistant, Royal Opera House, 1968–70; Subsidy Officer, Arts Council, 1970–76; Financial Controller, Welsh National Opera, 1976–82; Gen. Adminr, Opera North, 1982–93; Dir, Royal Opera, Covent Garden, 1993–98. *Address:* English National Opera, London Coliseum, St Martin's Lane, WC2N 4ES.

PAYNE, Henry Salusbury Legh D.; *see* Dalzell Payne.

PAYNE, Ian; barrister; *b* 15 July 1926; *s* of late Douglas Harold Payne and of Gertrude (*née* Buchanan); *m* 1st, 1951, Babette (marr. diss. 1975), *d* of late Comte Clarence de Chalus; four *s* two *d*; 2nd, 1977, Colette Eugénie, *d* of late Marinus Jacobus van der Eb, Rotterdam. *Educ:* Wellington Coll. Commnd 60th Rifles, 1944–48. Called to the Bar, Lincoln's Inn, 1953, Hong Kong, 1981; Dep. Recorder of Derby, 1969–72; a Recorder, 1972–81. *Clubs:* Hong Kong; Refreshers Cricket.

PAYNE, Rev. James Richmond, MBE 1982; ThL; JP; General Secretary, Bible Society in Australia, 1968–88; Chairman, United Bible Societies World Executive Committee, 1976–88; *b* 1 June 1921; *s* of late R. A. Payne, Sydney, New South Wales; *m* 1943, Joan, *d* of late C. S. Elliott; three *s*. *Educ:* Drummoyne High School; Metropolitan Business College, Moore Theological College, Sydney. Served War of 1939–45: AIF, 1941–44. Catechist, St Michael's, Surry Hills, NSW, 1944–47; Curate, St Andrew's, Lismore, NSW, 1947–50; Rector, St Mark's, Nimbin, NSW, 1950–52; Chaplain, RAAF, Malta and Amberley, Qld, 1952–57; Rector, St Stephen's, Coorparoo, Qld, 1957–62; Dean of Perth, Western Australia, 1962–68. Hon. Commissary in Australia for Anglican Bp of Central Tanganyika, E Africa, 1988–. JP, ACT, 1969. *Publications:* Around the World in Seventy Days, 1965; And Now for the Good News, 1982. *Recreations:* sport, walking, reading, family. *Address:* 10/42 Jinka Street, Hawker, ACT 2614, Australia. *T:* (2) 62546722.

PAYNE, Jane Marian, (Mrs A. E. Payne); *see* Manning, J. M.

PAYNE, Keith; VC 1969; *b* 30 Aug. 1933; *s* of Henry Thomas Payne and Remilda Payne (*née* Hussey); *m* 1954, Florence Catherine Payne (*née* Plaw); five *s*. *Educ:* State School, Ingham, North Queensland. Soldier, Department of Army, Aug. 1951–75; 1 RAR, Korea, 1952–53; 3 RAR, Malaya, 1963–65; Aust. Army Trng Team, Vietnam, 1969 (Warrant Officer; awarded VC after deliberately exposing himself to enemy fire while trying to cover his outnumbered men); WO Instructor: RMC, Duntroon, ACT, 1970–72; 42 Bn, Royal Qld Regt, Mackay, 1973–75; Captain, Oman Army, 1975–76. Member: VC and GC Assoc.; Legion of Valour, USA; Aust. Army Training Team Vietnam Assoc.; Life Member: Totally and Permanently Disabled Soldiers' Assoc. (Mackay Centre); Korea & SE Asia Forces Assoc.; Special Operations Assoc., USA; RSL (also Sarina Sub Br.). Patron, TRY-Sponsored Aust. Cadet Corp Units (Victoria). Freeman City of Brisbane and of Shire of Hinchinbrook. Vietnamese Cross of Gallantry, with bronze star, 1969; US Meritorious Unit Citation; Vietnamese Unit Citation Cross of Gallantry with Palm; DSC (US); SSM (US). *Recreations:* football, fishing, hunting. *Address:* 1 Forest Court, Andergrove, Mackay, Qld 4740, Australia. *T:* (7) 49552794.

PAYNE, Leonard Sidney, CBE 1983; Director, J. Sainsbury Ltd, 1974–86; Adviser on Distribution and Retailing, Coopers & Lybrand, since 1986; *b* 16 Dec. 1925; *s* of Leonard Sydney Payne and Lillian May Leggatt; *m* 1944, Marjorie Vincent; two *s*. *Educ:* Woodhouse Grammar School. FCCA, CIMgt, FCIT. Asst Accountant, Peek Frean & Co. Ltd, 1949–52; Chief Accountant, Administrator of various factory units, head office appts, Philips Electrical Industries, 1952–62; Dep. Gp Comptroller, Morgan Crucible Co. Ltd, 1962–64; British Road Services Ltd: Finance Dir, 1964–67; Asst Man. Dir, 1967–69; Man. Dir, 1969–71; Dir of Techn. Services and Develt, Nat. Freight Corp., 1971–74, Vice-Chm. Executive 1974. President: Freight Transport Assoc., 1980–82; Chartered Inst. of Transport, 1983–84. Chm., CBI Transport Policy Cttee, 1980–86. *Recreations:* gardening, swimming, squash, chess. *Address:* Apartment 5, Evenholme, Green Walk, Bowdon, Altrincham, Cheshire WA14 2SL.

PAYNE, Nicholas; *see* Payne, G. J. N.

PAYNE, Sir Norman (John), Kt 1985; CBE 1976 (OBE 1956; MBE (mil.) 1944); FREng; Chairman, BAA plc (formerly British Airports Authority), 1977–91 (Chief Executive, 1972–77); *b* 9 Oct. 1921; *s* of late F. Payne, Folkestone; *m* 1946, Pamela Vivien Wallis (separated); four *s* one *d*. *Educ:* John Lyon Sch., Harrow; City and Guilds Coll., London. BSc Eng Hons; FCGI, FICE, FCIT; FREng (FEng 1984). Royal Engrs (Captain), 1939–45 (despatches twice); Imperial Coll. of Science and Technology London (Civil), 1946–49; Sir Frederick Snow & Partners, 1949, Partner 1955; British Airports Authority: Dir of Engrg, 1965; Dir of Planning, 1969, and Mem. Bd 1971. Pres., West European Airports Assoc., 1975–77; Chairman: Airports Assoc. Co-ordinating Council, 1976; Aerodrome Owners' Assoc., 1983–84. Chm., British Sect., Centre for European Public Enterprise, 1979–82. Chm., NICG, 1982–83; Comr, Manpower Services Commn, 1983–85. Pres., CIT, 1984–85. CBIM (FBIM 1975); RAeS 1987. FIC 1989; FRSA 1990. Hon. FIStructE, 1988; Hon. FRIBA 1991. Hon. DTech Loughborough, 1985. *Publications:* various papers on airports and air transport. *Recreations:* travel, gardening. *Address:* L'Abri, La route des Merriennes, St Martin, Guernsey, CI GY4 6NS.

PAYNE, Peter Charles John, PhD; MSc(AgrEng); farmer, 1975–2000; *b* 8 Feb. 1928; *s* of late C. J. Payne, China Clay Merchant, and Mrs F. M. Payne; *m* 1961, Margaret Grover; two *s* one *d*. *Educ:* Plymouth Coll.; Teignmouth Grammar School; Reading University. BSc Reading 1948; Min. of Agriculture Scholar, Durham Univ., MSc(AgrEng) 1950; Scientific Officer, Nat. Institute of Agricultural Engineering, 1950–55; PhD Reading 1954; Lecturer in Farm Mechanisation, Wye College, London Univ., 1955–60; Lecturer in Agricultural Engineering, Durham Univ., 1960–61; Principal, Nat. Coll. of Agricultural Engineering, Silsoe, 1962–75 (Hon. Fellow, 1980); Visiting Professor: Univ. of Reading, 1969–75; Cranfield Inst. of Technology, 1975–80. Chm., Agricl Panel, Intermed. Technol. Develt Gp, 1979–86; Mem., British Inst. of Agricl Consultants, 1978. Vice-Pres., Section III, Commn Internationale du Génie Rural, 1969. FIAgrE 1968; FRAgSs 1971; CEng 1980. *Publications:* various papers in agricultural and engineering journals. *Recreation:* sailing. *Address:* 21 Arwenack Avenue, Falmouth TR11 3JW. *T:* (01326) 219359.

PAYNE, Most Rev. (Sidney) Stewart; Metropolitan of the Ecclesiastical Province of Canada and Archbishop of Western Newfoundland, 1990–97; *b* 6 June 1932; *s* of Albert and Hilda Payne; *m* 1962, Selma Carlson Penney, St Anthony, Newfoundland; two *s* two *d*. *Educ:* Elementary and High School, Fogo, Newfoundland; Memorial Univ. of Newfoundland (BA); Queen's Coll., Newfoundland (LTh); BD(General Synod). Incumbent of Mission of Happy Valley, 1957–65; Rector, Parish of Bay Roberts, 1965–70; Rector, Parish of St Anthony, 1970–78; Bishop of Western Newfoundland, 1978–97. DD *hc* Univ. of King's Coll., Halifax, NS, 1981. *Address:* PO Box 2255, RR1 Stn Main, Corner Brook, NF A2H 2N2, Canada.

PAYNE, (Trevor) Ian; *see* Payne, I.

PAYNE-BUTLER, George William; County Treasurer, Surrey County Council, 1973–79 (Assistant, 1962; Deputy, 1970); *b* 7 Oct. 1919; *s* of late George and Letitia Rachel Payne; *m* 1947, Joyce Louise Cockburn; one *s* two *d*. *Educ:* Woking Sch. for Boys. Joined Surrey CC, 1937. Served War, RAF, 1940–45. Chartered Municipal Treasurer, 1950 (CIPFA). *Recreations:* gardening, handicraft work in wood, reading. *Address:* Janston, Hillier Road, Guildford, Surrey GU1 2JQ. *T:* (01483) 565337.

PAYNE-GALLWEY, Sir Philip (Frankland), 6th Bt *cr* 1812; Director, British Bloodstock Agency plc, 1968–97; *b* 15 March 1935; *s* of late Lt-Col Lowry Philip Payne-Gallwey, OBE, MC and Janet (*d* 1996), *d* of late Albert Philip Payne-Gallwey; *S* cousin, 1964. *Educ:* Eton; Royal Military Academy, Sandhurst. Lieut, 11th Hussars, 1957. *Recreations:* hunting, shooting, golf. *Heir:* none. *Address:* The Little House, Boxford, Newbury, Berks RG20 8DP. *T:* (01488) 608315; 160 Cranmer Court, Whiteheads Grove, SW3 3HF. *T:* (020) 7589 4231. *Clubs:* Cavalry and Guards, White's.

PAYNTER, Alan Guy Hadley; Commissioner, 1997–2000, and Director, Corporate Services, 1999–2000, HM Customs and Excise; *b* 5 Nov. 1941; *s* of Leslie Alan Paynter and Dorothy Victoria Paynter (*née* Voak); *m* 1964, Mary Teresa Houghton; two *d*. *Educ:* East Ham Grammar Sch.; Central London Poly. (Post-grad. DMS 1972). EO, then HEO, MPBW, 1960–72 (Asst Private Sec. to Minister of Public Bldg and Works, 1968–71); HM Customs and Excise: Sen. Exec. Officer, 1972; Principal, 1978; on secondment to Overseas Containers Ltd, 1981–83; Sen. Principal, Computer Services, 1983–87; Asst Sec., 1987; Head, 1989–93, Dir, 1993–99, Information Systems; Mem. of Board, 1993–2000. *Recreations:* golf, bowling, reading, theatre, gardening.

PAYNTER, Prof. John Frederick, OBE 1985; Professor of Music, 1982–97, and Head of Department of Music, 1983–94, University of York, now Professor Emeritus; *b* 17 July 1931; *s* of late Frederick Albert Paynter and late Rose Alice Paynter; *m* 1956, Elizabeth Hill (*d* 1998); one *d*. *Educ:* Emanuel Sch., London; Trinity Coll. of Music, London (GTCL 1952). DPhil York, 1971. Teaching appts, primary and secondary schs, 1954–62; Lectr in Music, City of Liverpool C. F. Mott Coll. of Educn, 1962–65; Principal Lectr (Head of Dept of Music), Bishop Otter Coll., Chichester, 1965–69; Lectr, Dept of Music, Univ. of York, 1969, Sen. Lectr, 1974–82. Composer and writer on music-educn. Dir, Schs

Council Proj., Music in the Secondary School Curriculum, 1973–82. Gen. Editor, series, Resources of Music, 1969–93; Jt Editor, British Jl of Music Educn, 1984–97. FRSA 1987. Hon. GSM 1985. Leslie Boosey Award, Royal Philharmonic Soc./PRS, 1998. *Publications:* (with Peter Aston) Sound and Silence, 1970; Hear and Now, 1972; (with Elizabeth Paynter) The Dance and the Drum, 1974; All Kinds of Music, vols 1–3, 1976, vol. 4, 1979; Sound Tracks, 1978; Music in the Secondary School Curriculum: trends and developments in class music teaching, 1982; Sound and Structure, 1992; editor and contributor to: A Companion to Contemporary Musical Thought, 1992; Between Old Worlds and New: occasional writings on music by Wilfrid Mellers, 1997; contributor to: How Music Works, 1981; Musik og Skola, 1981; Musikalische Erfahrung: Wahrnehmen, Erkennen, Aneignen, 1992; Zwischen Aufklärung & Kulturindustrie, 1993; Music Education: international viewpoints, 1994; Powers of Being: David Holbrook and his work, 1995; articles in Internat. Jl of Music Educn, British Jl of Music Educn, La Discussione, Popular Music, Música Arte y Proceso, beQuadro; scripts and commentaries for radio and TV; *musical compositions:* choral and instrumental works including: Landscapes, 1972; The Windhover, 1972; May Magnificat, 1973; God's Grandeur, 1975; Sacraments of Summer, 1975; Galaxies for Orchestra, 1977; The Voyage of St Brendan, 1978; The Visionary Hermit, 1979; The Inviolable Voice, 1980; String Quartet no 1, 1981; Cantata for the Waking of Lazarus, 1981; The Laughing Stone, 1982; Contrasts for Orchestra, 1982; Variations for Orchestra and Audience, 1983; Conclaves, 1984; Piano Sonata, 1987; Time After Time, 1991; String Quartet no 2, 1991; Four Sculptures of Austin Wright (for solo violin and orch.), 1991–94; Melting (for solo piano), 1997; Holding On (for viola and piano), 1998; Breakthrough (double piano duet), 2000; Memorials (unacc. choir), 2000. *Address:* Westfield House, Newton upon Derwent, E Yorks YO41 4DA.

PAYTON, Stanley Walden, CMG 1965; Chief of Overseas Department, Bank of England, 1975–80, retired; *b* 29 May 1921; *s* of late Archibald Walden Payton and late Ethel May Payton (*née* Kirtland); *m* 1941, Joan (*née* Starmer); one *s* one *d*. *Educ:* Monoux School. Fleet Air Arm, 1940–46; Entered Bank of England, 1946; UK Alternate on Managing Board of European Payments Union, Paris, 1957–59; First Governor of Bank of Jamaica, 1960–64.

PEACE, David Brian, MBE 1977; FSA; glass engraver; town planner, 1947–82; *b* 13 March 1915; *y s* of Herbert W. F. Peace, Sheffield, and Mabel Peace (*née* Hammond); *m* 1939, Jean Margaret, ARCA (*d* 1989), *d* of Rev. McEwan and Margaret Lawson, Mill Hill; two *d*. *Educ:* Mill Hill; Univ. of Sheffield. ARIBA, FRTPI. RAF Airfield Construction Service, 1942–46, Sqdn Leader. Glass engraver, 1935–; presentation glass, 1952–; 11 one-man shows, retrospective exhibn, Ruskin Gall., Sheffield, 1990; work in 16 public collections, including: V&A (4); Kettle's Yard, Cambridge (7); Nat. Glass Mus., Stourbridge (2); Keatley Trust (10); Fitzwilliam Mus. (2); Turner Glass Mus., Sheffield (5); Corning Mus., USA; windows, screens and doors since 1956 in churches and colleges, incl. St Nicholas Liverpool, St Albans Cathedral, Manchester Cathedral, St Botolph Aldgate, St Nicholas Whitehaven; Royal Acad. of Music, Waltham Abbey, Gray's Inn Chapel, Great St Mary's, Cambridge, Chapel Royal, Brighton, St Anthony-in-Meneage; meml inscriptions to G. M. Hopkins and John Betjeman, Westminster Abbey, 1996; with Sally Scott: Westminster Abbey, Norwich Cathedral, Lancaster and Sheffield Univs, Lincoln Coll., Oxford, and St John's Coll., Cambridge, Burwell Church, Cambs, Christ the Cornerstone, Milton Keynes, St Michael and All Angels, Northampton, St Andrew, Headington, St Alban, Romford, Ealing Green Chapel, St Augustine, Wisbech, St Mary's, Newick, All Saints, Holbeach, Bollington Arts Centre, Cheshire, St Lalluwy, Menheniot, St James, Hanslope, St George, Methwold (RAF Meml). Master, Art Workers Guild, 1973; Guild of Glass Engravers: first Chm., 1975; Pres., 1980–86; Liveryman, Glaziers' Co., 1977. Town Planner: Staffs CC, 1948–61; Cambs CC, Dep. County Planning Officer, 1961–75, then head of envtl planning, 1975–80 (MBE); DoE appeals inspectorate, 1980–82. Member: Council for Visual Education, 1960–80; Council, RTPI, 1961–62, 1972–73; Council for British Archæology, 1965–85. President: Surveyors Club, 1984; ASCHB, 1994; Vice Pres., Betjeman Soc., 1996; Member: Ely DAC for Care of Churches, 1966–98; Council, Artists Gen. Benevolent Inst., 1994–96. Hon. DSc (Tech.) Sheffield Univ., 1991. *Publications:* Glass Engraving: lettering and design, 1985; The Engraved Glass of David Peace: the architecture of lettering, 1990; Eric Gill, the Inscriptions: a descriptive catalogue, 1994; originator of A Guide to Historic Buildings Law, 1965 (The Cambridgeshire Guide); Historic Buildings: maps and guides to the Peak District and N Wales. *Recreations:* townscape, heraldry. *Address:* Abbots End, High Street, Hemingford Abbots, Huntingdon PE28 9AA. *T:* (01480) 462472. *Club:* Arts.

See also David Davies.

PEACE, John Wilfred; Chief Executive, Great Universal Stores plc, since 2000; *b* 2 March 1949; *m* 1971, Christine Blakemore; three *d*. *Educ:* Sandhurst. Experian (formerly CCN): Founding Dir, 1980; Man. Dir, 1991–96; Chief Exec., 1996–2000. *Recreations:* horse riding, golf. *Address:* (office) Leconfield House, Curzon Street, W1Y 7FL. *T:* (020) 7495 0070.

PEACH, Ceri; *see* Peach, G. C. K.

PEACH, Prof. (Guthlac) Ceri (Klaus), DPhil; Professor of Social Geography, Oxford University, since 1992; Fellow and Tutor, St Catherine's College, Oxford, since 1969; *b* 26 Oct. 1939; *s* of Wystan Adams Peach and Charlotte Marianne (*née* Klaus); *m* 1964, Susan Lesley Godfrey; two *s* one *d*. *Educ:* Howardian High Sch., Cardiff; Merton Coll., Oxford (MA, DPhil). Oxford University: Demonstrator, 1964–66; Faculty Lectr in Geography, 1966–92; Hd of Dept, Sch. of Geography, 1995–98; St Catherine's College: Dean, 1971–73; Sen. Tutor, 1973–77; Finance Bursar, 1981–84; Domestic Bursar, 1986–89; Vice-Master, 1990–92; Pro-Master, 1993–94. Mem., Hebdomadal Council, Oxford Univ., 1996–. Visiting Fellow: Dept of Demography, ANU, 1972; Dept of Sociology, Yale Univ., 1977; Visiting Professor: Dept of Geog., Univ. of BC, 1998; Dept of Sociology, Harvard Univ., 1998; Fulbright Vis. Prof., Dept of Geog., Univ. of Calif, Berkeley, 1985. *Publications:* West Indian Migration to Britain: a social geography, 1968; Urban Social Segregation, 1975; (ed jtly) Ethnic Segregation in Cities, 1981; (ed jtly) Geography and Ethnic Pluralism, 1984; (ed jtly) South Asians Overseas, 1990; The Caribbean in Europe, 1991; The Ethnic Minority Populations of Great Britain, 1996; (ed jtly) Islam in Europe, 1997. *Recreations:* travelling, reading, computing. *Address:* St Catherine's College, Oxford OX1 3UJ.

PEACH, Sir Leonard (Harry), Kt 1989; a Civil Service Commissioner, 1995–2000; *b* 17 Dec. 1932; *s* of late Harry and Beatrice Peach; *m* 1958, Doreen Lilian (*née* Barker); two *s*. *Educ:* Queen Mary's Grammar Sch., Walsall; Pembroke Coll., Oxford (MA; Hon. Fellow, 1996); LSE (Dip. Personnel Management). Research Asst to Randolph S. Churchill, 1956; personnel management posts, 1956–62; IBM UK Ltd: personnel management posts, 1962–71; Dir of Personnel, 1971–72; Gp Dir, Personnel, IBM Europe, Africa, Middle East (based Paris), 1972–75; Dir, Personnel and Corporate Affairs, 1975–85 and 1989–92; seconded to DHSS, 1985–89: Dir, Personnel, NHS Management Bd, 1985; Chief Exec., NHS Management Bd, 1986–89 (in rank of 2nd Perm. Sec.); Chairman: NHS Training Authy, 1986–91; Skillbase Ltd, 1990–94; Standards Develt Cttee, Management Charter Initiative, 1989–97; Development Partnership Consultancy, 1993–; Mgt Verification Consortium Bd, 1995–99; UKCC Commn on Educn and Trng of Nurses, Midwives and Health Visitors, 1998–99 (report Fitness for Practice, 1999); Member: Data Protection Tribunal, 1985–99; Civilian Trng Bd and Personnel Bd, MoD, 1992–2000; Forensic Science Service Remuneration Cttee, 1999–. Chm., Police Complaints Authy, 1992–95; Comr for Public Appts, 1995–99; Comr for Public Appts in NI, 1995–99. Non-exec. Dir, Royal London Hosp., 1991–94. Chm., PSI, 1991–. Dep. Chm., Nationwide Pension Fund, 1992–; Director: IBM UK Rentals, 1971–76; IBM UK Holdings, 1976–85, and 1989–92; IBM UK Pensions Trust, 1989–92; IBM UK Trust, 1989–92; PIA, 1993–97 (Dep. Chm., Memship and Discipline Cttee, 1996–); non-exec. Director: Nationwide Anglia Bldg Soc, 1990–93; Coutts Consulting plc, 1993–99. Pres., IPM, and Chm., IPM Services Ltd, 1983–85 and 1991–98 (President's Gold Medal, 1988); Chm., Inst. of Continuing Professional Develt, 1998–; President: Manpower Soc., 1991–97; Assoc. of Business Schs, 1993–99. Vice-President: British Sports Assoc. for Disabled, 1988–; Industrial Participation Soc., 1989–. Chm., Remuneration and Succession Cttee, SCOPE, 1996–. Chairman: Quentin Hogg Trust, 1999–; Regent Street Poly. Trust, 1999–. Chm., Univ. of Westminster, 1993–99; Vice-Chm., Morley Coll., 1993–99; Gov., Portsmouth Grammar Sch., 1976–. CIMgt; CIPM; FRSA. Hon. FFOM, RCP, 1994. Hon. Fellow, Thames Polytechnic, 1990. Hon. DSc: Aston, 1991; UWE, 2000; Hon. DLitt Westminster, 1998; Hon. DCL Huddersfield, 2000. *Publications:* report on appt processes of judges and QCs in England and Wales, 1999; articles on personnel management and social responsibility. *Recreations:* opera, theatre, cricket, gardening. *Address:* Crossacres, Meadow Road, Wentworth, Virginia Water, Surrey GU25 4NH. *T:* (01344) 842258. *Clubs:* Oxford & Cambridge University; Wentworth Golf.

PEACOCK, Prof. Sir Alan (Turner), Kt 1987; DSC 1945; MA; FBA 1979; FRSE; Hon. Research Professor in Public Finance, Heriot-Watt University, since 1987; *b* 26 June 1922; *s* of late Professor A. D. Peacock, FRSE and of Clara Mary (*née* Turner); *m* 1944, Margaret Martha Astell Burt; two *s* one *d*. *Educ:* Grove Acad.; Dundee High School; University of St Andrews (1939–42, 1945–47). Royal Navy, 1942–45 (Lieut RNVR). Lecturer in Economics: Univ. of St Andrews, 1947–48; London Sch. of Economics, 1948–51 (Hon. Fellow, 1980); Reader in Public Finance, Univ. of London, 1951–56; Prof. of Economic Science, Univ. of Edinburgh, 1957–62; Prof. of Economics, Univ. of York, 1962–78; Prof. of Economics, and Principal-designate, University Coll. at Buckingham, 1978–80, Principal, 1980–83; Vice-Chancellor, Univ. of Buckingham, 1983–84, Professor Emeritus, 1985–; Exec. Dir, David Hume Inst., Edinburgh, 1985–90. Seconded from Univ. of York as Chief Economic Adviser, Depts of Industry and Trade, 1973–76. Visiting Prof. of Economics, Johns Hopkins Univ., 1958. Keynes Lectr, British Acad., 1994. Mem., 1959–87, Chm., 1991–93, Adv. Council, IEA (Trustee, 1987–93; Hon. Fellow, 1994); Member: Commission of Enquiry into land and population problems of Fiji, 1959; Departmental Committee on Electricity in Scotland, 1961; Council, REconS, 1961–78; Cttee of Enquiry on impact of rates, 1964; Commn on the Constitution, 1970–73; SSRC, 1972–73; Cttee of Inquiry on Retirement Provision, 1984; Chm., Rowntree Inquiry into Corporate Takeovers, 1990–91. Chm., UN Adv. Mission to Russian Fedn on Social Protection, 1992. Pres., Internat. Inst. of Public Finance, 1966–69. Mem., Arts Council, 1986–92; Chairman: Arts Council Enquiry on Orchestral Resources, 1969–70; Cttee on Financing the BBC, 1985–86; Scottish Arts Council, 1986–92. Non-exec. Director: Economist Intelligence Unit Ltd, 1977–84; Caledonian Bank plc, 1991–96. FRSE 1989. Corr. Fellow, Accademia Nazionale dei Lincei, Rome, 1996. Hon. Mem., Royal Soc. of Musicians, 1996. DUniv: Stirling, 1974; Brunel, 1989; York, 1997; Hon. DEcon Zürich, 1984; Hon. DSc: Buckingham, 1986; Edinburgh, 1990; Hon. LLD: St Andrews, 1990; Dundee, 1990; Dr *hc:* Catania, 1991; Lisbon, 1999. *Publications:* Economics of National Insurance, 1952; (ed) Income Redistribution and Social Policy 1954; National Income and Social Accounting (with H. C. Edey), 1954, 3rd imp. 1967; The National Income of Tanganyika (1952–54) (with D. G. M. Dosser), 1958; The Growth of Public Expenditure in the UK, 1890–1955 (with J. Wiseman), 1961; Economic Theory of Fiscal Policy (with G. K. Shaw), 1971, 2nd edn, 1976; The Composer in the Market Place (with R. Weir), 1975; Welfare Economics: a liberal re-interpretation (with C. K. Rowley), 1975; Economic Analysis of Government, 1979; (ed and contrib.) Structural Economic Policies in West Germany and the UK, 1980; (ed jtly) Political Economy of Taxation, 1981; (ed and contrib.) The Regulation Game, 1984; (ed jtly) Public Expenditure and Government Growth, 1985; Waltz Contrasts (for piano solo), 1988; Public Choice Analysis in Historical Perspective, 1992; (with G. Bannock) Corporate Takeovers and the Public Interest, 1991; Paying the Piper, 1993; (ed jtly) Cultural Economics and Cultural Policies, 1994; Political Economy of Economic Freedom, 1997; (ed) The Political Economy of Heritage, 1998; (with B. Main) What Price Civil Justice?, 2000; Calling the Tune, 2001; articles on applied economics in Economic Jl, Economica and other journals. *Recreations:* trying to write music, wine spotting. *Address:* 5/24 Oswald Road, Edinburgh EH9 2HE. *T:* (0131) 667 5677; *e-mail:* peacock@ebs.hw.ac.uk. *Clubs:* Reform; New (Edinburgh).

PEACOCK, Hon. Andrew (Sharp), AC 1997; Australian Ambassador to the United States of America, 1997–2000; *b* 13 Feb. 1939; *s* of late A. S. Peacock and Iris Peacock. *Educ:* Scotch Coll., Melbourne, Vic; Melbourne Univ. (LLB). Former Partner, Rigby & Fielding, Solicitors; Chm., Peacock and Smith Pty Ltd, 1962–69. Army Reserve (Captain), 1966–94. Pres., Victorian Liberal Party, 1965–66; MP (L) Kooyong, Australia, 1966–94; Minister for Army and Minister assisting Prime Minister, 1969–71; Minister for Army and Minister asstg Treasurer, 1971–72; Minister for External Territories, Feb.-Dec. 1972; Mem., Opposition Exec., 1973–75; Oppos. Shadow Minister for For. Affairs, 1973–75, 1985–87; Minister for: Foreign Affairs, 1975–80; Industrial Relns, 1980–81; Industry and Commerce, 1982–83; Leader of the Parly Liberal Party, and of the Opposition, 1983–85; Dep. Leader, Liberal Party and Dep. Leader, Opposition, 1987–89; Leader, Parly Liberal Party, and of the Opposition, 1989–90; Shadow Attorney-Gen. and Shadow Minister for Justice, 1990–92; Shadow Minister: for Trade, 1992–93; for Foreign Affairs, 1993–94. Chm., Internat. Democrat Union, 1989–92. *Recreations:* horse racing, sailboarding, Australian Rules football. *Address:* 48 Berry Street, East Melbourne, Vic 3002, Australia. *Clubs:* Melbourne, Melbourne Cricket, Victoria Racing, Victoria Amateur Turf (Melbourne); Moonee Valley Racing.

PEACOCK, Elizabeth Joan; JP; DL; *b* 4 Sept. 1937; *d* of late John and Dorothy Gates; *m* 1963, Brian David Peacock; two *s*. *Educ:* St Monica's Convent, Skipton. Asst to Exec. Dir, York Community Council, 1979–83; Administrator, four charitable trusts, York, 1979–83. County Councillor, N Yorks, 1981–84. MP (C) Batley and Spen, 1983–97; contested (C) same seat, 1997, 2001. PPS to Minister of State, Home Office, 1991–92, to Minister for Social Security and disabled people, 1992. Mem., Select Cttee on Employment, 1983–87. Chairman: All Party Trans Pennine Gp, 1988–94; All Party Wool Textile Gp, 1989–97. Hon. Sec., Yorks Cons. MPs, 1983–88; Vice Chm., Cons. Backbench Party Organisation Cttee, 1985–87; Mem. Exec. Cttee, 1922 Cttee, 1987–91; Mem. Exec., CPA, 1987–92. Mem., BBC Gen. Adv. Council, 1987–93. Vice Pres., Yorks Area Young Conservatives, 1984–87; Pres., Yorks Area Cons. Trade Unionists,

1991–98 (Vice Pres., 1987–91). FRSA 1990. JP Macclesfield, 1975–79, Bulmer East 1983; DL W Yorks, 1998. *Recreations:* reading, motoring. *Address:* Spen House, 87 George Lane, Notton, Wakefield, W Yorks WF4 2NQ.

See also J. D. Peacock.

PEACOCK, Geraldine, CBE 2001; Chief Executive, Guide Dogs for the Blind Association, since 1997; *b* 26 Jan. 1948; *d* of Sidney Peter Watkins Davies and Joyce Irene Davies (*née* Pullin); *m* 1971, John Howard Peacock (marr. diss. 1988); three *s*. *Educ:* Redland High Sch., Bristol; Durham Univ. (BA Hons Sociology 1969); Univ. of California; Univ. of Newcastle upon Tyne (CQSW 1981; post-grad. dip. in Applied Social Work Studies 1981). Teaching Asst, Univ. of California, and Heroin Addiction Counsellor, San Bernadino State Prison, 1969–70; Med. Social Worker, Durham Hosp. Bd, 1970–72; Lectr in Social Admin, Teesside Poly., 1972–75; Social Worker: Thalidomide Children's Trust, 1975–85; Lady Hoare Trust for Handicapped Children, 1975–79; part-time Lectr in Community Issues, Univ. of Newcastle upon Tyne, 1979; part-time Course Tutor, 1973–86, Course Co-ordinator, 1978–80, Open Univ.; part-time Lectr in Social Policy, Glasgow Univ., 1973–86; Lectr in Social Work, Queen's Coll., Glasgow, 1983–86; Dep. Dir, London Boroughs Training Cttee, 1986–89; Chief Exec., Nat. Autistic Soc., 1989–97. A Civil Service Comr, 2001–. Member: Exec. Cttee, ACENVO, 1994– (Chm., 1996–2000); Council, Industrial Soc., 1996–; Social Investment Taskforce, HM Treasury, 2000–; Vice-Chm., Internat. Fedn of Guide Dog Schs for the Blind, 2001–. Trustee, NCVO, 1999–. *Publications:* (jtly) Social Work and Received Ideas, 1988; (ed jtly) The Haunt of Misery: essays in helping and caring, 1989; Appraising the Chief Executive, 1996. *Recreations:* theatre, cinema, art, literature, cooking, family. *Address:* (office) Hillfields, Burghfield Common, Reading, Berks RG7 3YG. *T:* (0118) 983 5555. *Club:* New Cavendish.

PEACOCK, Ian Douglas, OBE 1998; Chief Executive, Lawn Tennis Association, 1986–96; *b* 9 April 1934; *s* of Andrew Inglis Peacock and Minnie Maria (*née* King); *m* 1962, Joanna Hepburn MacGregor; one *s* one *d*. *Educ:* Sevenoaks Sch. Pilot Officer, RAF, 1953–54. Slazengers Ltd, 1955–83, Man. Dir 1976–83; Sports Marketing Surveys Ltd, 1984–85. Pres., British Sports & Allied Industry Fedn, 1984–85; Director: Golf Foundn, 1982– (Chm., 1996–; Chm., Golf Ball Cttee, 1976–96); LTA Trust, 1988–96; Queen's Club Ltd, 1993–96; Wembley Nat. Stadium Ltd, 1998–; British Tennis Foundn, 1998–. Trustee: Torch Trophy Trust, 1993– (Chm., 1998–); English Nat. Stadium Trust, 1998–. *Recreations:* golf, ski-ing, painting. *Address:* Moat End House, Church Lane, Burstow, Surrey RH6 9TG. *T:* (01342) 842262. *Clubs:* Queen's, Royal Air Force; All England Lawn Tennis and Croquet; Royal Ashdown Forest Golf (Forest Row).

PEACOCK, (Ian) Michael; Chairman: UBC Media Group plc, since 2000; The Michael Peacock Charitable Foundation, since 1990; *b* 14 Sept. 1929; *e s* of Norman Henry and Sara Barbara Peacock; *m* 1956, Daphne Lee; two *s* one *d* *Educ:* Kimball Union Academy, USA; Welwyn Garden City Grammar School; London School of Economics (BSc Econ.). BBC Television: Producer, 1952–56; Producer Panorama, 1956–58; Asst Head of Television Outside Broadcasts, 1958–59; Editor, Panorama, 1959–61; Editor, BBC Television News, 1961–63; Chief of Programmes, BBC-2, 1963–65; Controller, BBC-1, BBC Television Service, 1965–67; Managing Dir, London Weekend Television Ltd, 1967–69; Chm., Monitor Enterprises Ltd, 1970–89; Man. Dir, Warner Bros TV Ltd, 1972–74; Exec. Vice-Pres., Warner Bros Television Inc., 1974–76. Dir, Video Arts Ltd, 1972–89; Pres., Video Arts Inc., 1976–78; Man. Dir, Dumbarton Films Ltd (formerly Video Arts Television), 1978–87; Chairman: Video Answers, 1989–90; Unique Broadcasting Co. Ltd, 1989–2000; Publishing Projects plc, 1990–92. Dep. Chm., Piccadilly Radio, 1988–89. IPPA: First Chm., 1981–82; Mem. Council, 1983–88. Mem., Ct of Governors, LSE, 1982– (Chm., Media @ LSE Adv. Panel, 1999–). *Recreation:* sailing. *Address:* 21 Woodlands Road, Barnes, SW13 0JZ. *T:* (020) 8876 2025. *Clubs:* Savile, Royal Thames Yacht, Royal Ocean Racing.

PEACOCK, Ian Rex; Chairman, MFI Furniture Industries plc, since 2000; *b* 5 July 1947; *s* of Mervyn (George) and Evelyn (Joyce) Peacock; *m* 1973, Alyanee Chya-Rochana; one *s*. *Educ:* Kingswood Grammar Sch.; Trinity Coll., Cambridge (MA). Economist: Unilever Plc, 1968–73; Cripps Warburg Ltd, 1973–75; Kleinwort Benson Gp, 1975–94 (Gp Dir, 1990–94); Co Head, Merchant Banking Div., USA, 1994–97, Chief Operating Officer, Investment Banking, 1997–98, BZW Ltd; Special Advr, Bank of England, 1998–2000. Non-exec. Dir, Norwich & Peterborough Bldg Soc., 1997–; Director: Lombard Risk Mgt, 2000–; i-documentsystems, 2000–. *Recreations:* music, particularly opera, squash, gardening, travel. *Address:* 65 Park Road, Chiswick, W4 3EY. *T:* (020) 8995 3923; 30 West 90th Street (#9c), New York, NY 10024, USA. *Club:* Oxford and Cambridge.

PEACOCK, Jonathan David; QC 2001; *b* 21 April 1964; *s* of Brian David Peacock and Elizabeh Joan Peacock, *qv*; *m* 1997, Charlotte Ann Cole; one *d*. *Educ:* King's Sch., Macclesfield; Nunthorpe Grammar Sch., York; Corpus Christi Coll., Oxford (MA Juris 1st Cl.). Called to the Bar, Middle Temple, 1987 (Sen. Schol.). *Recreation:* cricket. *Address:* 11 New Square, Lincoln's Inn, WC2A 3QB. *T:* (020) 7242 4017. *Clubs:* United and Cecil; Brigands (Hants).

PEACOCK, Michael; *see* Peacock, I. M.

PEACOCK, Peter James, CBE 1998; Member (Lab) Highland and Islands, Scottish Parliament, since 1999; Deputy Minister for Finance and Local Government, since 2000; *b* 27 Feb. 1952; *m*; two *s*. *Educ:* Hawick High Sch.; Jordanhill Coll. of Educn (Dip. Youth Work and Community Studies 1973). Community Educn Officer, Orkney CC, 1973–75; Area Officer for Highland, Grampian, Tayside, Orkney, Shetland and Western Isles, and Central Policy Advr, Scottish Assoc. of CABx, 1975–87; Partner, The Apt Partnership, 1987–96. Member: Highland Regl Council (Dep. Leader; Chm. Finance Cttee), 1982–96; (Lab) Highland Council, 1995–99 (Leader/Convenor; Chm., Policy and Resources Cttee). Dep. Minister for Children and Educn, Scottish Exec., 1999–2000. Vice Pres., COSLA. Former Member: Bd, Scottish Natural Heritage; European Cttee of Regions; Scottish Economic Council; Bd, Scottish Post Office; Bd, Cairngorm Partnership. Chm., Scottish Library and Information Council, 1991–94; former Chairman: Moray Firth Community Radio; Community Work North; former Member: Scottish Valuation Adv. Council; Centres for Highlands and Islands Policy Studies. *Address:* 68 Braeside Park, Balloch, Inverness IV2 7HN. *T:* (01463) 790371.

PEACOCK, Dr William James, AC 1994; BSc, PhD; FRS 1982; FAA; Chief, Division of Plant Industry, Commonwealth Scientific and Industrial Research Organization, since 1978; *b* 14 Dec. 1937; *m* 1961, Margaret Woodward; one *s* two *d*. *Educ:* Katoomba High Sch.; Univ. of Sydney (BSc, PhD). FAA 1976. CSIRO Postdoctoral Fellow, 1963 and Vis. Associate Prof. of Biology, 1964–65, Univ. of Oregon; Res. Consultant, Oak Ridge National Lab., USA, 1965; res. staff, Div. of Plant Industry, CSIRO, 1965–. Adjunct Prof. of Biology, Univ. of Calif, San Diego, 1969; Vis. Prof. of Biochem., Stanford Univ., 1970; Vis. Distinguished Prof. of Molecular Biol., Univ. of Calif, LA, 1977. For. Associate, US Nat. Acad. of Scis, 1990; For. Fellow, Indian Nat. Science Acad., 1990. FTSE (FTS 1988); FAIAST (FAIAS 1989). Edgeworth David Medal, Royal Soc. of NSW, 1967; Lemberg Medal, Aust. Biochem. Soc., 1978; BHP Bicentennial Prize for Pursuit of Excellence in Science and Technol., 1988; CSIRO Medal for Leadership of Div. of Plant Industry, 1989; Burnet Medal, Aust. Acad. of Sci., 1989; (jtly) Prime Minister's Prize for Science (inaugural winner), 2000. *Publications:* editor of 5 books on genetics and molecular biology; approx. 250 papers. *Recreations:* squash, sailing, bush-walking. *Address:* 16 Brassey Street, Deakin, ACT 2600, Australia. *T:* (home) (2) 62814485, (office) (2) 62465250, *Fax:* (2) 62465530.

PEACOCKE, Rev. Canon Arthur Robert, MBE 1993; DSc, ScD, DD; SOSc; Hon. Canon, Christ Church Cathedral, Oxford, since 1995 (Hon. Chaplain, 1988–96); Director, Ian Ramsey Centre, Oxford, 1985–88, and 1995–99; *b* 29 Nov. 1924; *s* of Arthur Charles Peacocke and Rose Elizabeth (*née* Lilly); *m* 1948, Rosemary Winifred Mann; one *s* one *d*. *Educ:* Watford Grammar Sch.; Exeter Coll., Oxford (Scholar; BA Chem., BSc 1946; MA, DPhil 1948); DSc Oxon, 1962; ScD Cantab (incorp.), 1973; DD Oxon, 1982; DipTh 1960, BD 1971, Birmingham. Asst Lectr, Lectr and Sen. Lectr in Biophys. Chemistry, Univ. of Birmingham, 1948–59; Lectr in Biochem., Oxford Univ., and Fellow and Tutor in Chem., subseq. in Biochem., St Peter's Coll., 1959–73; Lectr in Chem., Mansfield Coll., Oxford, 1964–73; Dean and Fellow, Clare Coll., Cambridge, 1973–84; Fellow, St Cross Coll., 1985–88; Catechist, Exeter Coll., Oxford, 1989–93. Rockefeller Fellow, Univ. of Calif at Berkeley, and Univ. of Wis, 1951–52; Vis. Fellow, Weizmann Inst., Israel, 1956; Prof. of Judeo-Christian Studies, Tulane Univ., 1984; J. K. Russell Fellow in Religion and Science, Center for Theology and Natural Sci., Berkeley, 1986; Royden Davis Prof., Georgetown Univ., 1994; Select Preacher, Oxford Univ., 1973, 1985; Hulsean Preacher, Cambridge Univ., 1976; Lectures: Bampton, Oxford Univ., 1978; Bishop Williams Meml, Rikkyo (St Paul's) Univ., Japan, 1981; Shann, Univ. of Hong Kong, 1982; Mendenhall, DePauw Univ., Indiana, 1983; McNair, Univ. of N Carolina, 1984; Nina Booth Bricker Meml, Tulane Univ., 1986, 1989; Norton, Southern Baptist Seminary, Louisville, 1986; Sprigg, Virginia Theol Seminary, 1987; Rolf Buchdahl, N Carolina State Univ., 1987; Drawbridge, KCL, 1987; Alister Hardy Meml, 1989; Gifford, St Andrews Univ., 1993; Idreos, Oxford, 1997; Witherspoon, Princeton Center of Theol Inquiry, 1999. Lay Reader, Oxford Dio., 1960–71; ordained, 1971; Mem., Archbps' Commn on Christian Doctrine, 1969–76 (Mem. sub-gp on Man and Nature, 1972–74); Chm., Science and Religion Forum, 1972–78 (Vice-Pres., 1981–95, Hon. Pres., 1995–); Vice-Pres., Inst. of Religion in an Age of Science, USA, 1984–87 (Academic Fellow, 1987); Warden, SOSc, 1987–92, now Emeritus. Judge, Templeton Foundn Prize, 1979–82. Meetings Sec., Sec. and Chm., Brit. Biophys. Soc., 1965–69. Mem. Editorial Bd, Biochem. Jl, and Biopolymers, 1966–71, Zygon, 1973–; Editor, Monographs in Physical Biochemistry (OUP), 1967–82. Hon. DSc DePauw Univ., Indiana, 1983; Hon. DLitHum Georgetown Univ., Washington, 1991. Lecomte du Noüy Prize, 1973; Templeton Prize for Progress in Religion, 2001. *Publications:* Molecular Basis of Heredity (with J. B. Drysdale), 1965 (repr. 1967); Science and the Christian Experiment, 1971; (with M. P. Tombs) Osmotic Pressure of Biological Macromolecules, 1974; (with J. Dominian) From Cosmos to Love, 1977; Creation and the World of Science, 1979; (ed) The Sciences and Theology in the Twentieth Century, 1982; The Physical Chemistry of Biological Organization, 1983; Intimations of Reality, 1984; (ed) Reductionism in Academic Disciplines, 1985; God and the New Biology, 1986; (ed with G. Gillett) Persons and Personality, 1987; (ed with S. Andersen) Evolution and Creation: a European perspective, 1987; Theology for a Scientific Age, 1990, new edn 1993 (Templeton Prize, 1995); (ed with R. Russell and N. Murphy) Chaos and Complexity, 1995; From DNA to Dean, 1996; God and Science, 1996; Paths from Science towards God, 2001; articles and papers in scientific and theol jls, and symposia vols. *Recreations:* piano, music, walking, churches. *Address:* 55 St John Street, Oxford OX1 2LQ; Exeter College, Oxford OX1 3DP. *T:* (01865) 512041, *Fax:* (01865) 554791; *e-mail:* arthur.peacocke@theology.oxford.ac.uk.

See also C. A. B. Peacocke.

PEACOCKE, Prof. Christopher Arthur Bruce, FBA 1990; Professor of Philosophy, New York University, since 2000; *b* 22 May 1950; *s* of Rev. Dr Arthur Robert Peacocke, *qv*; *m* 1980, Teresa Anne Rosen; one *s* one *d*. *Educ:* Magdalen College Sch., Oxford; Exeter Coll., Oxford (MA, BPhil, DPhil). Kennedy Schol., Harvard Univ., 1971; Sen. Schol., Merton Coll., Oxford, 1972; Jun. Res. Fellow, Queen's Coll., Oxford, 1973; Prize Fellow, All Souls Coll., Oxford, 1975; Fellow and Tutor, New Coll., Oxford, and CUF Lectr in Philosophy, 1979–85; Susan Stebbing Prof. of Philosophy, KCL, 1985–88; Waynflete Prof. of Metaphysical Philosophy, Univ. of Oxford and Fellow of Magdalen Coll., Oxford, 1989–2000. Visiting Professor: Berkeley, 1975; Ann Arbor, 1978; UCLA, 1981; Maryland, 1987; NY Univ., 1996–97; Vis. Fellow, ANU, 1981; Fellow, Center for Advanced Study in the Behavioral Sciences, Stanford, 1983; Vis. Res. Associate, Center for Study of Language and Information, Stanford, 1984; Leverhulme Personal Res. Professorship, 1996–2000. Whitehead Lectr, Harvard, 2001. Pres., Mind Assoc., 1986; Mem., Steering Cttee, European Soc. for Philosophy and Psychology, 1991–95. *Publications:* Holistic Explanation: action, space, interpretation, 1979; Sense and Content, 1983; Thoughts: an essay on content, 1986; A Study of Concepts, 1992; Being Known, 1999; papers on philosophy of mind and language, and philosophical logic, in Jl of Philosophy, Philosophical Rev., etc. *Recreations:* music, visual arts. *Address:* Department of Philosophy, New York University, Main Building, 100 Washington Square East, New York, NY 10003-6688, USA. *T:* (212) 998 3559.

PEAKE, family name of **Viscount Ingleby**.

PEAKE, David Alphy Edward Raymond; Chairman, BNP Paribas (formerly Banque Nationale de Paris) UK Hldgs Ltd, since 1997 (Director, since 1974); Director, BNP Paribas (formerly Banque Nationale de Paris) SA, since 1998; *b* 27 Sept. 1934; *s* of Sir Harald Peake, AE and Mrs Resy Peake, OBE; *m* 1962, Susanna Kleinwort; one *s* one *d*. *Educ:* Ampleforth Coll.; Christ Church, Oxford (MA History, 1958). 2nd Lieut Royal Scots Greys, 1953–55. Banque Lambert, Brussels, 1958–59; J. Henry Schroder Wagg & Co. Ltd, 1959–63; Kleinwort Benson Ltd, 1963–93: Dir, 1971–93; Vice-Chm., 1985–87; Chm., 1988–89; Chm., Kleinwort Benson Group plc, 1989–93 (Dir, 1986–96); Hargreaves Group, 1964–86: Dir, 1964–86; Vice-Chm., 1967–74; Chm., 1974–86; Dir, M&G Gp, 1979–87. Pt-time Mem. of Bd, British Liby, 1990–96. Chairman: City and Inner London N TEC, 1990–93; 21st Century Learning Initiative (UK) (formerly Educn 2000 Trust), 1994–; Mem., BOTB, 1993–96. Chm., Chipping Norton Theatre Ltd, 1995–. Trustee, Harefield Hosp. Fund, 1994–95. Mem. Council, Goldsmiths Coll., Univ. of London, 1997–. Mem. Ct of Assts, Goldsmiths' Co., 1992–. *Recreations:* reading, country sports. *Address:* 15 Ilchester Place, W14 8AA. *T:* (020) 7602 2375. *Clubs:* Brooks's, Pratt's, Cavalry and Guards.

PEAKE, Air Cdre (retired) Dame Felicity (Hyde), (Lady Peake), DBE 1949 (MBE 1941); AE; *b* 1 May 1913; *d* of late Colonel Humphrey Watts, OBE, TD, and Mrs Simon Orde; *m* 1st, 1935, John Charles Mackenzie Hanbury (killed on active service, 1939); no *c*; 2nd, 1952, Sir Harald Peake, AE (*d* 1978); one *s*. *Educ:* St Winifreds, Eastbourne; Les Grands Huguenots, Vaucresson, Seine et Oise, France. Joined ATS Company of the RAF, April 1939; commissioned in the WAAF, Aug. 1939; served at home and in the Middle

East; Director, Women's Auxiliary Air Force, 1946–49; Director Women's Royal Air Force, from its inception, 1949, until her retirement, 1950; Hon. ADC to King George VI, 1949–50. Member Advisory Cttee, Recruitment for the Forces, 1958. Trustee: Imperial War Museum, 1963–85 (Chm., 1986–88, Pres., 1988–92, Friends of Imperial War Museum); St Clement Danes church, 1989–. Governor, London House, 1958–76, 1978–92; Mem. Council, RAF Benevolent Fund, 1946–96 (a Vice-Pres., 1978–); Mem. Council, Union Jack Club, 1950–78. Patron, WAAF Assoc., 1997. *Publication:* Pure Chance (memoirs), 1993.

PEAKE, John Fordyce; consultant; Associate Director (Scientific Development), Natural History Museum, 1989–92; *b* 4 June 1933; *s* of late William Joseph Peake and of Helena (*née* Fordyce); *m* 1963, Pamela Joyce Hollis; two *d. Educ:* City of Norwich Grammar Sch.; University Coll. London (BSc). National Trust, 1955–56; Norwich Technical Coll., 1956–58; Nature Conservancy Studentship, 1958–59; British Museum (Natural History): Research Fellow, 1959–61; Sen. Scientific Officer, 1961–69; PSO, 1969–71; Dep. Keeper, 1971–85; Keeper of Zoology, 1985–89. Hon. Research Associate, Bernice P. Bishop Mus., Honolulu, 1972–. Royal Society: Member: Aldabra Research Cttee, 1972–77; Southern Zones Cttee, 1982–86; Unitas Malacologica: Treas. 1962–63, Mem. Council, 1963–75; Vice Pres., Malacological Soc. of London, 1976–78; Council Mem., Zoological Soc. of London, 1985–88. *Publications:* (editor and contributor with Dr V. Fretter) Pulmonates, 3 vols, 1975–79; papers on taxonomy, biogeography and ecology of terrestrial molluscs in sci. jls. *Recreation:* gardening. *Address:* Crows Nest, Back Lane, Blakeney, Holt, Norfolk NR25 7NP. *T:* (01263) 740388.

PEAKE, John Morris, CBE 1986; Chairman: Cambridgeshire Careers Guidance Ltd, 1995–98; Careers Services National Association, 1997–98; *b* 26 Aug. 1924; *s* of late Albert Edward Peake and Ruby Peake (*née* Morris); *m* 1953, Elizabeth Rought; one *s* one *d. Educ:* Repton School; Clare College, Cambridge (Mech. Scis Tripos; MA 1949); Royal Naval College, Greenwich (Dip. Naval Arch.). CEng, FIMechE; CMath, FIMA; CIMgt. Royal Corps of Naval Constructors, 1944–50; Personnel Administration Ltd, 1950–51; Baker Perkins (BP): joined 1951; Dir, parent co., 1956; Jt Man. Dir, BP Ltd, 1963–66; Man. Dir, BP Pty, 1969–74, in Australia; Pres., BP Inc., 1975–77, in USA; Dep. Man. Dir, BP Holdings, 1978–79, Man. Dir, 1980–85; Chm., Baker Perkins PLC, 1984–87. Member: Chemicals and Minerals Requirements Bd, 1978–81; Council, CBI, 1980–89 (Chairman: Overseas Schols Bd, 1981–87; Educn and Trng Cttee, 1986–88); Council, BTEC, 1986–89 (Chm., Bd for Engineering, 1985–91); MSC, subseq. Trng Commn, 1986–88; RSA Examinations Bd, 1987–93 (Chm., 1989–93); RSA Council, 1989–93; Adv. Council, British Library, 1989–92; Design Council, 1991–93 (Chm. Educn Cttee, 1990–94); Chm., Greater Peterborough Partnership, 1994–95; Vice Chm., Gtr Peterborough TEC, 1990–94. Chm., Nene Park Trust, 1988–93. Hockey Silver Medal, London Olympics, 1948. FRSA. Hon. DTech CNAA, 1986. *Recreations:* sport, travel. *Address:* Old Castle Farmhouse, Stibbington, Peterborough PE8 6LP. *T:* (01780) 782683. *Clubs:* East India, MCC; Hawks (Cambridge).

PEAKER, Prof. Malcolm, DSc, PhD; FRS 1996; FZS, FLS, FIBiol, FRSE; Director, Hannah Research Institute, Ayr, since 1981; Hannah Professor, University of Glasgow, since 1981; *b* 21 Aug. 1943; *s* of Ronald Smith Peaker and Marian (*née* Tomasin); *m* 1965, Stephanie Jane Large; three *s. Educ:* Henry Mellish Grammar Sch., Nottingham; Univ. of Sheffield (BSc Zoology; DSc); Univ. of Hong Kong (SRC NATO Scholar; PhD). FZS 1969; FIBiol 1979; FRSE 1983; FLS 1989. Inst. of Animal Physiology, ARC, 1968–78; Head, Dept of Physiol., Hannah Res. Inst., 1978–81. Chm. Bd, London Zoo, 1992–93; Vice-Pres., Council, Zoological Soc. of London, 1992–94; Mem. Council, RSE, 1999–. Mem., Rank Prize Funds Adv. Cttee on Nutrition, 1997–. Scientific Governor, British Nutrition Foundn, 1997–. Raine Distinguished Visitor, Univ. of WA, 1998. Munro Kerr Lecture, Munro Kerr Soc., 1997; Annual Lecture, Edinburgh Centre for Rural Res./RSE/Inst. of Biol., 2000; Dist. Lectr, Univ. of Hong Kong, 2000. Hon. DSc Hong Kong, 2000. Mem. Editorial Board: Jl of Dairy Science, 1975–78; Internat. Zoo Yearbook, 1978–82; Jl of Endocrinology, 1981–91; Procs of RSE, 1989–92; Endocrine Actions, 1991–; Mammary Gland Biology and Neoplasia, 1993–2000; Editor: British Jl of Herpetology, 1977–81; Internat. Circle of Dairy Research Leaders, 1982–. *Publications:* Salt Glands in Birds and Reptiles, 1975; (ed) Avian Physiology, 1975; (ed) Comparative Aspects of Lactation, 1977; (ed jtly) Physiological Strategies in Lactation, 1984; (ed jtly) Intercellular Signalling in the Mammary Gland, 1995; (ed jtly) Biological Signalling and the Mammary Gland, 1997; papers in physiol, endocrinol, zool, biochem., vet. and agricl science jls. *Recreations:* vertebrate zoology, natural history, golf, grumbling about bureaucrats. *Address:* Hannah Research Institute, Ayr KA6 5HL. *T:* (01292) 674000. *Clubs:* Farmers'; Royal Troon Golf.

PEARCE, Andrew; Deputy Head of Distributive Trades Unit, European Commission, Brussels, since 1994; *b* 1 Dec. 1937; *s* of late Henry Pearce, Liverpool cotton broker, and Evelyn Pearce; *m* 1966, Myra Whelan; three *s* one *d. Educ:* Rydal School, Colwyn Bay; University of Durham. BA. Formerly in construction industry; in Customs Dept, EEC, Brussels, 1974–79. Contested (C) Islington North, 1969 and 1970; Mem. (C) Cheshire W, Eur. Parlt, 1979–89; contested: (C) Cheshire W, EP elecn, 1989; (C) Ellesmere Port and Neston, 1992; (Pro Euro C) NW Reg., EP elecn, 1999. Founder and Vice-Pres., British Cons. Assoc. in Belgium; Vice-Pres., Consultative Assembly of Lomé Convention, 1980–89. Chm., Internat. Trade Cttee, British Retail Consortium, 1990–93; Vice Chm., European Business Develt Gp, Liverpool Chamber of Commerce, 1991–93. Governor: Archway Comprehensive School, 1967–70; Woodchurch High Sch., Birkenhead, 1985–90; Nugent Sch., Liverpool, 1992–94. *Address:* Laurel Cottage, 59 Stanley Lane, Eastham, Wirral CH62 0AQ.

PEARCE, (Ann) Philippa, (Mrs M. J. G. Christie), OBE 1997; freelance writer of children's fiction, since 1967; *b* 23 Jan. 1920; *d* of Ernest Alexander Pearce and Gertrude Alice (*née* Ramsden); *m* 1963, Martin James Graham Christie (decd); one *d. Educ:* Perse Girls' Sch., Cambridge; Girton Coll., Cambridge (MA Hons English Pt I, History Pt II). Temp. civil servant, 1942–45; Producer/Scriptwriter, Sch. Broadcasting, BBC Radio, 1945–58; Editor, Educn Dept, Clarendon Press, 1958–60; Children's Editor, André Deutsch Ltd, 1960–67. Also lectures. FRSL 1994. Hon. DLitt Hull, 1995. *Publications:* Minnow on the Say, 1955 (3rd edn 1974); Tom's Midnight Garden, 1958 (3rd edn 1976; Carnegie Medal, 1959; filmed and staged, 2000); Mrs Cockle's Cat, 1961 (2nd edn 1974); A Dog So Small, 1962 (2nd edn 1964); (with Sir Harold Scott) From Inside Scotland Yard, 1963; The Strange Sunflower, 1966; (with Sir Brian Fairfax-Lucy) The Children of the House, 1968 (2nd edn 1970) (reissued as The Children of Charlecote, 1989); The Elm Street Lot, 1969 (enlarged edn, 1979); The Squirrel Wife, 1971 (2nd edn 1992); What the Neighbours Did and other stories, 1972 (2nd edn 1974); (ed) Stories from Hans Christian Andersen, 1972; Beauty and the Beast (re-telling), 1972; The Shadow Cage and other stories of the supernatural, 1977; The Battle of Bubble and Squeak, 1978 (Whitbread Award, 1978); Wings of Courage (trans. and adapted from George Sand's story), 1982; The Way to Sattin Shore, 1983; Lion at School and other stories, 1985; Who's Afraid? and other strange stories, 1986; The Toothball, 1987; Emily's Own Elephant, 1987; Freddy, 1988; Old Belle's Summer Holiday, 1989; Here comes Tod, 1992; (ed) Dread and Delight: a century of children's ghost stories (anthology), 1995; The Rope and other stories, 2000; reviews in TLS and Guardian. *Address:* c/o Viking-Kestrel Books, 27 Wright's Lane, W8 5TZ. *T:* (020) 7938 2200.

PEARCE, Sir Austin (William), Kt 1980; CBE 1974; PhD; FREng; Chairman, Oxford Instruments Group, 1987–91; *b* 1 Sept. 1921; *s* of William Thomas and Florence Annie Pearce; *m* 1st, 1947, Maglona Winifred Twinn (*d* 1975); three *d*; 2nd, 1979, Dr F. Patricia Grice (*née* Forsythe) (*d* 1993). *Educ:* Devonport High Sch. for Boys; Univ. of Birmingham (BSc (Hons) 1943; PhD 1945; Cadman Medallist). Joined Agwi Petroleum Corp., 1945 (later Esso Petroleum Co., Ltd): Asst Refinery Manager, 1954–56; Gen. Manager Refining, 1956–62; Dir, 1963; Man. Dir, 1968–71; Chm., 1972–80; Chm., British Aerospace, 1980–87; Director: Esso Europe Inc., 1972–80; Esso Africa Inc., 1972–80; Pres., Esso Holding Co. UK Inc., 1971–80; Chairman: Esso Pension Trust Ltd, 1972–80; Irish Refining Co. Ltd, 1965–71; Director: Williams & Glyn's Bank, 1974–85 (a Dep. Chm., 1980–83; Chm., 1983–85); Royal Bank of Scotland Gp (formerly Nat. & Commercial Banking Gp), 1978–92 (a Vice-Chm., 1985–92); Pearl Assurance PLC, 1985–91; Jaguar PLC, 1986–93; Smiths Ind. PLC, 1987–92; Home Group Ltd, 1998–2001. Part-time Mem., NRDC, 1973–76; Member: Adv. Council for Energy Conservation, 1974–79; Energy Commn, 1977–79; British Aerospace, 1977–87 (Mem., Organising Cttee, 1976); Standing Commn on Energy and the Environment, 1978–81; Takeover Panel, 1987–92. Chm., UK Petroleum Industry Adv. Cttee, 1977–80; Pres., UK Petroleum Industry Assoc. Ltd, 1979–80; CBI: Chm., Industrial Policy Cttee, 1982–85; Chm., Industrial Steering Policy Gp, 1985–86. President: Inst. of Petroleum, 1968–70; The Pipeline Industries Guild, 1973–75; Oil Industries Club, 1975–77; Pres., SBAC, 1982–83. Mem., Bd of Governors, English-Speaking Union, 1974–80; Chm., Bd of Trustees, Science Museum, 1986–95. Treas., RSA, 1988–93. Chairman: Warden Housing Assoc., 1994–2001; Martlets Hospice Ltd, 1994–98; Sussex Victim Support, 1999–2000. Mem. Council, Surrey Univ., 1981–93 (Pro-Chancellor, 1986–93; Pro Chancellor Emeritus, 1994–). FREng (FEng 1978). Hon. DSc: Southampton, 1978; Exeter, 1985; Salford, 1987; Cranfield, 1987; Hon. DEng Birmingham, 1986; DUniv Surrey, 1993. *Recreations:* golf, woodwork. *Address:* Treeps House, 2 High Street, Hurstpierpoint, Hassocks, W Sussex BN6 9TY.

PEARCE, Brian; *see* Pearce, J. B.

PEARCE, Sir (Daniel Norton) Idris, Kt 1990; CBE 1982; TD 1972; DL; Deputy Chairman, English Partnerships, 1993–2001; *b* 28 Nov. 1933; *s* of late Lemuel George Douglas Pearce and Evelyn Mary Pearce; *m* 1963, Ursula Helene Langley (marr. diss. 1997); two *d. Educ:* West Buckland Sch.; College of Estate Management. FRICS. Commnd RE, 1958; comd 135 Field Survey Sqdn, RE(TA), 1970–73. Joined Richard Ellis, 1959: Partner, 1961–92; Man. Partner, 1981–87; Consultant, 1992–2000. Chairman: English Estates, 1989–94; Flexit Cos, 1993–98; Varsity Funding, 1995–2000; Redburgh Ltd, 1996–2000; Director: The Phoenix Initiative, 1991; ITC, 1992–94; Nat. Mortgage Bank, 1992–97; Swan Hill (formerly Higgs & Hill), 1993–; Dusco UK Ltd, 1993–; Innisfree, 1996–; Millennium & Copthorne Hotels, 1996–; Regalian, 1998–; Resolution, 1998–. Royal Instn of Chartered Surveyors: Member: Gen. Council, 1980–94; Management Bd, 1984–91; Chm., Parly and Public Affairs Cttee, 1984–89; Vice Pres., 1986–90; Pres., 1990–91. Chm., Internat. Assets Valuation Standards Cttee, 1981–86. Member: Adv. Panel for Instnl Finance in New Towns, 1974–80; Sec. of State for Health and Social Security Inquiry into Surplus Land in the NHS, 1982; PSA Adv. Bd, 1981–86; FCO Adv. Panel on Diplomatic Estate, 1985–97; Financial Reporting Review Panel, 1991–93; Bd, London Forum, 1993–; Property Advr, NHS Management Bd, 1985–90; Dep. Chm., Urban Regeneration Agency, 1993–2001; Dir, London First Centre, 1995–2001. Chm., Higher Educn Funding Council for Wales, 1992–96; Member: UFC, 1991–93; HEFCE, 1992–96. Vice Chm., Greater London TA&VRA, 1991–94 (Mem. 1970–98; Chm., Works and Bldgs Sub-Cttee, 1983–90). Chm. Develt Bd, Nat. Art-Collections Fund, 1988–92. Member: Court, City Univ., 1987–2000; Council, Univ. of Surrey, 1993– (Pro-Chancellor, 1994–; Chm., 1998–2001); Council, Reading Univ., 1997–2000; Comr, Royal Hosp., 1995–. Chm. Governors, Stanway Sch., Dorking, 1982–85. Trustee, Rochester Bridge Trust, 1991–94. Governor: Peabody Trust, 1992–; RCA, 1997–. Contested (C) Neath, 1959. DL Greater London, 1986. Hon. Fellow: Coll. of Estate Management, 1987; Univ. of Wales Cardiff, 1997; Centenary Fellow, Thames Poly., 1991; Companion, De Montfort Univ., 1992. Hon. Col, 135 Indep. Topographic Sqn, RE(V), TA, 1989–94. FRSA 1989. Hon. DSc: City, 1990; Oxford Poly., 1991; Salford Univ., 1991; Hon. DEng West of England, 1994; Hon. DTech E London, 1999. *Publications:* A Call to Talent, 1993; various articles on valuation and property matters. *Recreations:* reading, opera, ballet, travel. *Clubs:* Brooks's, City of London.

PEARCE, Prof. David William, OBE 2000; Professor of Environmental Economics, University College London, since 1983; *b* 11 Oct. 1941; *s* of William Henry and Gladys Muriel Pearce; *m* 1966, Susan Mary Reynolds; two *s. Educ:* Lincoln Coll., Oxford (BA, MA). Lectr in Econs, Lancaster Univ., 1964–67; Sen. Lectr in Econs, Southampton Univ., 1967–74; Dir, Public Sector Econs Res. Centre, 1974–77; Prof. of Political Economy, Univ. of Aberdeen, 1977–83; Dir, 1991–96, Associate Dir, 1996–, Centre for Social and Econ. Res. on the Global Envmt, UCL and UEA. Global 500 Award for services to world envmt, UN, 1989. *Publications:* books include: (jtly) Blueprint for a Green Economy, 1989, rev. edn 1999; (jtly) The Economics of Natural Resources and the Environment, 1990; (jtly) Blueprint 2: Greening the World Economy, 1991; (jtly) World Without End: economics, environment and sustainable development, 1993; Economic Values and the Natural World, 1993; (jtly) Environmental Economics: an elementary introduction, 1993; Blueprint 3: Measuring Sustainable Development, 1993; (jtly) Project and Policy Appraisal: integrating economics and environment, 1994; (jtly) The Causes of Tropical Deforestation, 1994; Blueprint 4: Sustaining the Earth—Capturing Global Value, 1995; (jtly) Blueprint 5: The Social Costs of Road Transport, 1996; (ed jtly) Acid Rain: counting the cost, 1997; (jtly) Measuring Sustainable Development: macroeconomics and the environment, 1997; Economics and the Environment: essays in ecological economics and sustainable development, 1999; (jtly) Blueprint for a Sustainable Economy, 2000; numerous papers in refereed jls. *Recreations:* tending seven acres of wild land, drinking wine, birdwatching in Africa. *Address:* Department of Economics, University College London, Gower Street, WC1E 6BT. *T:* (020) 7679 5258.

PEARCE, Edward Robin; author and political commentator; Commissioning Editor, Punch, since 2000; *b* 28 March 1939; *s* of late Frank Pearce and Olive Pearce (*née* Johnson); *m* 1966, Deanna Maria Stanwell (*née* Singer); one *d. Educ:* Queen Elizabeth Grammar Sch., Darlington; St Peter's Coll., Oxford (MA); Univ. of Stockholm. Res. Asst, Labour Party, Transport Hse, 1964–66; Res. Officer, Police Fedn, 1966–68; with Douglas Mann & Co., solicitors, 1968–70; teacher, S Shields, 1970–75; contributor, Sunday Express, 1975–77; Leader-writer, Daily Express, 1977–79; Parliamentary sketch-writer: Daily Telegraph, 1979–87; The Express, 1998–; freelance career, 1987–: columnist: Sunday Times, 1987–90; The Guardian, 1990–95; The Scotsman, 1998–2000; contrib. Punch, Sunday Telegraph, Daily Mail, The Herald (Glasgow), Evening Standard, Wall St Jl, Sunday Tribune (Dublin), New Statesman, Spectator, History Today, Encounter,

Tatler, New Republic (Washington), London Rev. of Books, Lit. Rev., TLS, Prospect, etc. Panel Member: The Moral Maze, Radio 4, 1991–95; Dateline, BBC World Service TV, 1997–; contrib. News Talk, LBC, 1989–92. Columnist of Year Award, What the Papers Say, 1987; Peter Wilson Award, League Against Cruel Sports, 1993. *Publications:* The Senate of Lilliput, 1983; Hummingbirds and Hyenas, 1985; Looking Down on Mrs Thatcher (collected Commons sketches), 1987; The Shooting Gallery, 1989; The Quiet Rise of John Major, 1990; Election Rides, 1992; Machiavelli's Children, 1993; The Lost Leaders, 1997; Lines of Most Resistance: the Lords, the Tories and Ireland 1886–1914, 1999; Denis Healey: a life in our times, 2001. *Recreations:* listening to classical music, esp. Schubert, watching cricket, esp. Lancashire, and football, esp. Oldham Athletic, reading history, esp. 18th Century, travel, esp. Italy, wandering around old towns, esp. ones with bookshops. *Address:* Ryedale House, Thormanby, York YO61 4NN. *Club:* Reform.

PEARCE, Most Rev. George; former Archbishop of Suva; *b* 9 Jan. 1921; *s* of George H. Pearce and Marie Louise Duval. *Educ:* Marist Coll. and Seminary, Framingham Center, Mass, USA. Entered Seminary, 1940; Priest, 1947; taught in secondary sch. in New England, USA, 1948–49; assigned as missionary to Samoa, 1949; consecrated Vicar Apostolic of Samoa, 1956; first Bishop of Apia, 1966; Archbishop of Suva, 1967–76, retired 1976. *Address:* Cathedral Rectory, 30 Fenner Street, Providence, RI 02903, USA. *T:* (401) 3312434.

PEARCE, Howard John Stredder, CVO 1993; HM Diplomatic Service; High Commissioner, Malta, since 1999; *b* 13 April 1949; *s* of late Ernest Victor Pearce and Ida (*née* Booth). *Educ:* City of London Sch.; Pembroke Coll., Cambridge (MA, LLB). Joined HM Diplomatic Service, 1972; FCO, 1972–74; Third Sec., Buenos Aires, 1975–78; FCO, 1978–83; First Sec. and Hd of Chancery, Nairobi, 1983–87; FCO, 1987–90; Sen. Associate Mem., St Antony's Coll., Oxford, 1990–91; Dep. Hd of Mission, Budapest, 1991–94; Fellow, Center for Internat. Affairs, Harvard Univ., 1994–95; Hd, Central European Dept, FCO, 1996–99. Mem., Exec. Cttee, VSO, 1988–90. Officer's Cross, Republic of Hungary, 1999. *Recreations:* classical music, opera, reading, travel. *Address:* c/o Foreign and Commonwealth Office, King Charles Street, SW1A 2AH. *Club:* Oxford and Cambridge.

PEARCE, Howard Spencer; Director for Wales, Property Services Agency, Department of Environment, 1977–85; *b* 23 Sept. 1924; *m* 1951, Enid Norma Richards (*d* 1994); one *s*. *Educ:* Barry County Sch.; College of Estate Management. ARICS. Armed Services, Major RE, 1943–47. Ministry of Works: Cardiff, 1953–61; Salisbury Plain, 1961–64; Ministry of Public Building and Works: Hong Kong, 1964–67; Abingdon, 1967–70; Area Officer, Abingdon, 1970–72; Regional Works Officer, SW Region, Bristol, PSA, Dept of Environment, 1972–77. *Recreations:* music, playing golf and watching Rugby football. *Address:* 2 Longhouse Close, Lisvane, Cardiff CF14 0XR. *T:* (029) 2076 2029. *Club:* Cardiff Golf.

PEARCE, Sir Idris; *see* Pearce, Sir D. N. I.

PEARCE, Jessica Mary, (Mrs R. W. Hand); HM Diplomatic Service; Deputy Head, Non-Proliferation Department, Foreign and Commonwealth Office, since 1999; *b* 1 Sept 1957; *d* of William Evan Pearce and Mary Elizabeth Pearce (*née* Pimm); *m* 1999, Major Robert Wayne Hand, US Army. *Educ:* Aberdeen Univ. (MA Jt Hons, French and Internat. Relations). Sec. to Dir, NERC Research Vessel Base, Barry, 1976–78; sales co-ordinator for wine co., Cardiff, 1983–85; joined FCO, 1985; Second Sec., FCO, 1985–87; Dakar, Senegal, 1987–90; First Sec., UN Dept, 1990–92, African Dept (Southern), 1992–94, FCO; lang. trng, 1994–95; Ambassador to Belarus, 1996–99. *Recreations:* campanology, walking, reading, cooking, music (classical, jazz and anything to dance to). *Address:* c/o Foreign and Commonwealth Office, SW1A 2AH.

PEARCE, (John) Brian, OBE 2000; Director, The Inter Faith Network for the United Kingdom, since 1987; *b* 25 Sept. 1935; *s* of late George Frederic Pearce and Constance Josephine Pearce; *m* 1960, Michelle Etcheverry; four *s*. *Educ:* Queen Elizabeth Grammar Sch., Wakefield; Brasenose Coll., Oxford (BA). Asst Principal: Min. of Power, 1959; Colonial Office, 1960; Private Sec. to Parly Under-Sec. of State, 1963; Principal: Colonial Office, 1964; Dept of Economic Affairs, 1967; Principal Private Sec. to Sec. of State for Economic Affairs, 1968–69; Asst Sec., Civil Service Dept, 1969, Under-Sec., 1976; Under-Sec., HM Treasury, 1981–86, retd. MLitt Lambeth, 1993. *Recreations:* comparative theology, music, architecture. *Address:* 124 Court Lane, SE21 7EA.

PEARCE, Maj.-Gen. Leslie Arthur, CB 1973; CBE 1971 (OBE 1964; MBE 1956); Chief of General Staff, NZ Army, 1971–73, retd; *b* 22 Jan. 1918; British parents; *m* 1944, Fay Mattocks, Auckland, NZ; two *s* one *d*. *Educ:* in New Zealand. Joined Army, 1937; served War: Greece, Western Desert, Italy, 1939–45. Staff Coll., Camberley, 1948. Directing Staff, Australia Staff Coll., 1958–59; Commandant, Army Schools, NZ, 1960; Comdg Officer, 1 NZ Regt, in NZ and Malaysia, 1961–64; Dep. QMG, NZ Army, 1964–65; Dir of Staff Duties, NZ Army, 1966; IDC, 1967; QMG, 1968–69; Dep. Chief of Defence Staff, 1970. Chm., Vocational Training Council, 1975–81. Company director. Dep. Chm., NZ Council for Educnl Res., 1983–85 (Mem., 1977–85). *Recreations:* golf, fishing, gardening; Provincial and Services Rugby representative, in youth. *Address:* Apt 218 Park Lane Village, 106 Becroft Drive, Forrest Hill, Auckland, New Zealand.

PEARCE, Rev. Neville John Lewis; Priest-in-charge, Swainswick/Woolley, Diocese of Bath and Wells, 1993–98; Chief Executive, Avon County Council, 1982–89; *b* 27 Feb. 1933; *s* of John and Ethel Pearce; *m* 1958, Eileen Frances Potter; two *d*. *Educ:* Queen Elizabeth's Hosp., Bristol; Silcoates Sch., Wakefield; Univ. of Leeds (LLB Hons 1953, LLM 1954); Trinity Theol Coll., Bristol. Asst Solicitor: Wakefield CBC, 1957–59; Darlington CBC, 1959–61; Chief Asst Solicitor, Grimsby CBC, 1961–63, Dep. Town Clerk, 1963–65; Dep. Town Clerk, Blackpool CBC, 1965–66; Town Clerk, Bath CBC, 1967–73; Dir of Admin and County Solicitor, Avon CC, 1973–82. Ordained (C of E), 1991; Asst Curate, St Swithin, Walcot, Bath, 1991–93. *Recreations:* family, philately, a West Highland terrier, Anglican church affairs. *Address:* Penshurst, Weston Lane, Bath BA1 4AB. *T:* (01225) 426925.

PEARCE, Peter Huxley; Director, Landmark Trust, since 1995; *b* 16 May 1956; *s* of Dr Alan John Pearce and Marion Joyce (*née* Wright); *m* 1983, Christina Zalichi; two *s*. *Educ:* Reading Univ. (BSc Hons Rural Estate Mgt). FRICS 1981. National Trust: Man. Land Agent, E Midlands Reg., 1982–87, Southern Reg., 1988–95; Dir, Uppark Repair Project, 1989–95. *Recreations:* historic buildings, music, fishing, landscape and conservation, family life. *Address:* The Landmark Trust, Shottesbrooke, Maidenhead, Berks SL6 3SW. *T:* (01628) 825920.

PEARCE, Philippa; *see* Pearce, A. P.

PEARCE, Prof. Robert Penrose, FRMetS; FRSE; Professor of Meteorology and Head of Department of Meteorology, University of Reading, 1970–90, now Emeritus Professor; *b* 21 Nov. 1924; *s* of Arthur Penrose Pearce and Ada Pearce; *m* 1951, Patricia Frances Maureen Curling; one *s* two *d*. *Educ:* Bishop Wordsworth Sch., Salisbury; Imperial Coll., London (BSc, ARCS, DIC, PhD). Asst, Meteorological Office, 1941–43. Served RAF, 1943–47 (commnd 1945). Lectr, then Sen. Lectr in Mathematics, Univ. of St Andrews, 1952–66; Reader in Phys. Climatology, Imperial Coll., 1966–70. Pres., Royal Meteorological Soc., 1972–74; Chm., World Meteorol Org. Working Gp in Trop. Meteorology, 1978–90. *Publications:* Observer's Book of Weather, 1980; (co-ed) Monsoon Dynamics, 1981; sci. papers in meteorol jls. *Recreations:* walking, gardening, bridge, music. *Address:* Schiehallion, 27 Copped Hall Way, Camberley, Surrey GU15 1PB. *T:* (01276) 501523.

PEARCE-HIGGINS, Daniel John; QC 1998; a Recorder, since 1999; *b* 26 Dec. 1949; *m*. *Educ:* St Paul's Sch., London; Univ. of Bristol (BSc Philosophy and Politics). Called to the Bar, Middle Temple, 1973; Asst Recorder, 1995–99. Mem., Mental Health Review Tribunal, 2000–. CEDR accredited mediator, 1999–. FCIArb 1999. *Address:* 2 Temple Gardens, EC4Y 9AY. *T:* (020) 7822 1200.

PEARCEY, Oliver Henry James; Director of Conservation, English Heritage, since 1997; *b* 13 June 1951; *s* of Lawrence Henry Victor Pearcey and Gladys Winifred Pearcey (*née* Bond); *m* 1979, Elizabeth Platts; two *d*. *Educ:* Westminster Sch.; Univ. of Sussex (BSc Biochem). Department of the Environment: Admin trainee, 1972–78; Principal, 1978–85; on secondment to GLC, 1981–83; English Heritage: Team Leader, 1985–88, Head, 1988–91, Historic Bldgs Div.; Dir, Conservation, Midlands Reg., 1991–94; Dep. Dir, Conservation, 1994–97. Mem., IHBC, 1998. *Recreations:* industrial archaeology, English salt-glaze stoneware, reading voraciously. *Address:* 48 Westville Road, W12 9BD. *T:* (020) 8749 2793.

PEARL, David Stephen, PhD; **His Honour Judge Pearl;** a Circuit Judge, since 1994; *b* 11 Aug. 1944; *s* of late Chaim Pearl and of Anita (*née* Newman); *m* 1st, 1967, Susan Roer (marr. diss.); three *s*; 2nd, 1985, Gillian Maciejewska; one step *s* one step *d*. *Educ:* George Dixon Grammar Sch., Birmingham; Westminster City Sch.; Birmingham Univ. (LLB); Queens' Coll., Cambridge (Sen. Scholar; LLM, MA, PhD). Called to the Bar, Gray's Inn, 1968; Cambridge University: Asst Lectr in Law, 1967–72; Lectr, 1972–89; Res. Fellow, Queens' Coll., 1967–69; Fellow and Dir of Studies in Law, Fitzwilliam Coll., Cambridge, 1969–89 (Life Fellow, 1989); Prof. of Law and Dean, Sch. of Law, UEA, 1989–94, Hon. Prof., 1995–; a Recorder, 1992–94. Vis. Prof., KCL, 1995–. Immigration Appeals Adjudicator, 1980–92; Chm., 1992–97, Pres., 1998–99, Immigration Appeal Tribunal; Chief Immigration Adjudicator, 1994–98. Judicial Studies Board: Member: Civil and Family Cttee, 1994–96; Tribunals Cttee, 1996–99; Dir of Studies, 1999–2001. Vice-Pres., Internat. Soc. for Family Law, 1991–97. Yorke Prize, Cambridge, 1972; Shaw Prize, Boston Coll. Law Sch., 1985; Van Heyden de Lancy Prize, Cambridge, 1991. *Publications:* A Textbook on Muslim Law, 1979, 3rd edn as Muslim Family Law (with W. Menski), 1998; Interpersonal Conflict of Laws in India, Pakistan and Bangladesh, 1980; (with K. Gray) Social Welfare Law, 1980; (with B. Hoggett) Family Law and Society, 1983, 4th edn 1996; Family Law and Immigrant Communities, 1986; (with A. Grubb) Blood Testing AIDS and DNA Profiling, 1990; (jtly) Butterworth's Immigration Law Service, 1991–. *Recreations:* helping my wife with the horses and chickens, painting, drawing. *Address:* Judicial Studies Board, 9th Floor, Millbank Tower, Millbank SW1P 4QU. *T:* (020) 7217 4708.

PEARL, Valerie Louise, DPhil; FRHistS; President, New Hall, Cambridge, 1981–95; *b* 31 Dec. 1926; *d* of late Cyril Raymond Bence, sometime MP and Florence Bence; *m* 1949, Morris Leonard Pearl (*d* 2000); one *d*. *Educ:* King Edward VI High Sch., Birmingham; St Anne's Coll., Oxford (Exhibnr; Hon. Fellow, 1994). BA Hons Mod. History; MA, DPhil (Oxon). Allen Research Studentship, St Hugh's Coll., Oxford, 1951; Eileen Power Studentship, 1952; Sen. Research Studentship, Westfield Coll., London, 1962; Leverhulme Research Award, 1962; Graham Res. Fellow and Lectr in History, Somerville Coll., Oxford, 1965; Reader in History of London, 1968–76, Prof. of History of London, 1976–81, University College London. Convenor of confs to found The London Journal, Chm. of Editorial Bd, Editor-in-Chief, 1973–77; McBride Vis. Prof., Cities Program, Bryn Mawr Coll., Pennsylvania, 1974; Lectures: Woodward, Yale Univ., New Haven, 1974; Indian Council for Soc. Sci., Calcutta, New Delhi, 1977; John Stow Commem., City of London, 1979; James Ford Special, Oxford, 1980; Sir Lionel Denny, Barber Surgeons' Co., 1981. Literary Dir, Royal Historical Soc., 1975–77; Pres., London and Mddx Archaeol. Soc., 1980–82; Governor, Museum of London, 1978; Comr, Royal Commn on Historical MSS, 1983; Syndic: Cambridge Univ. Library, 1982; Cambridge Univ. Press, 1984. Trustee, Henry and Procter Fellowships, 1985. FSA 1976. *Publications:* London and the Outbreak of the Puritan Revolution, 1625–43, 1961; Change and Stability in 17th Century London (inaugural lecture, Univ. of London), 1978; (ed jtly) History and Imagination: essays for Hugh Trevor-Roper, 1981; (ed) J. Stow, The Survey of London, 1987; Studies in Social Change in Puritan London, Parts 1, 2 (trans. Japanese, ed S. Sugawara), 1994; contributor to: Studies in London History (ed W. Kellaway, A. Hollaender), 1969; The Interregnum (ed G. Aylmer), 1972; Puritans and Revolutionaries (ed K. Thomas, D. Pennington), 1978; The Tudor and Stuart Town (ed J. Barry), 1990; also to learned jls and other works, including Trans Royal Hist. Soc., Eng. Historical Rev., History of English Speaking Peoples, Past and Present, Archives, Economic Hist. Rev., History, Jl of Eccles. History, Times Literary Supplement, The London Journal, London Rev. of Books, Albion, Listener, BBC, Rev. of English Studies, (jtly) Proc. Mass. Hist. Soc., DNB Missing Persons, Urban History, Encyclopedia Americana. *Recreations:* walking and swimming.

PEARLMAN, Valerie Anne; Her Honour Judge Pearlman; a Circuit Judge, since 1985; *b* 6 Aug. 1936; *d* of late Sidney and Marjorie Pearlman; *m* 1972; one *s* one *d*. *Educ:* Wycombe Abbey Sch. Called to the Bar, Lincoln's Inn, 1958; a Recorder, 1982–85. Member: Parole Bd, 1989–94; Civil and Family Cttee, Judicial Studies Bd, 1992–97; Chm., Home Sec's Adv. Bd on Restricted Patients, 1991–98; Mem., Cttee on Mentally Disordered Offenders, Mental Health Foundn, 1992–95. Mem., Council of Circuit Judges, 1998–2000; Vice-Pres., Inner London Magistrates' Assoc., 1999–. Patron, British Juvenile and Family Courts Soc., 2000–. Member: Council, Marlborough Coll., 1989–97; Governing Body, Godolphin and and Latymer Sch., 1998–. Patron, Suzy Lamplugh Trust, 1987–. *Recreations:* gardening, reading. *Address:* Crown Court at Southwark, English Grounds, SE1 2HU.

PEARMAN, Hugh Geoffrey; architecture and design critic, Sunday Times, since 1986; *b* 29 May 1955; *s* of late Douglas Pearman and of Tegwyn Pearman (*née* Jones); partner, Kate Hobson; two *s* two *d*. *Educ:* Skinners' Sch., Tunbridge Wells; St Chad's Coll., Durham Univ. (BA Hons Eng. Lang. and Lit.). Asst Editor, Building Design Magazine, 1978–82; Communications Editor, BDP, 1982–86. Contributor, Guardian and Observer, 1984–87. Member: Envmtl and Arts Panel, South Bank Employers' Gp, 1990–; Architectl Adv. Panel, Arts Council of GB, then of England, 1992–95; Chm., Art for Architecture Adv. Panel, RSA, 2000–. Advr, Calmann and King, 1996–. Curator, British Council internat. touring exhibn, 12 for 2000: Building for the Millennium, 1998–2000. Vis. teacher in architecture, Univ. of Greenwich, 1999–2000. Founder and Juror: Sunday Times/Royal Fine Art Commn Annual Architecture Award, 1989–95; Stirling Prize for

Architecture, 1996–98; judge of numerous competitions in architecture, design and public art. FRSA 1990. Hon. FRBS 1996; Hon. FRIBA 2001. Frequent contributor to television and radio. *Publications:* Excellent Accommodation, 1984; Rick Mather: urban approaches, 1992; The Ark, London, 1993; Contemporary World Architecture, 1998; Equilibrium: the work of Nicholas Grimshaw and Partners, 2000; (introd.) Ten Years, Ten Cities: Terry Farrell and Partners 1991–2001, 2001; (introd.) 30 Bridges, 2002; articles in newspapers, magazines and periodicals. *Recreation:* escaping. *Address:* 29 Nelson Road N8 9RX. *T:* (020) 8348 4838; *e-mail:* hughpear@aol.com.

PEARS, David Francis, FBA 1970; Student of Christ Church, Oxford, 1960–88, now Emeritus; Professor of Philosophy, Oxford University, 1985–88; *b* 8 Aug. 1921; *s* of late Robert and Gladys Pears; *m* 1963, Anne Drew; one *s* one *d*. *Educ:* Westminster Sch.; Balliol Coll., Oxford. Research Lecturer, Christ Church, 1948–50; Univ. Lectr, Oxford, 1950–72, Reader, 1972–85; Fellow and Tutor, Corpus Christi Coll., 1950–60. Visiting Professor: Harvard, 1959; Univ. of Calif, Berkeley, 1964; Rockefeller Univ., 1967; UCLA, 1979; Hill Prof., Univ. of Minnesota, 1970; Humanities Council Res. Fellow, Princeton, 1966. Mem., l'Inst. Internat. de Philosophie, 1978– (Prés., 1988–90); For. Corresp. Fellow, Amer. Acad. of Arts and Scis. *Publications:* (trans. with B. McGuinness), Wittgenstein, Tractatus Logico-Philosophicus, 1961, repr. 1975; Bertrand Russell and the British Tradition in Philosophy, 1967, 2nd edn 1972; Ludwig Wittgenstein, 1971; What is Knowledge?, 1971; (ed) Russell's Logical Atomism, 1973; Some Questions in the Philosophy of Mind, 1975; Motivated Irrationality, 1984; The False Prison: a study of the development of Wittgenstein's philosophy, vol. I, 1987, vol. II, 1988; Hume's System, 1990. *Address:* 7 Sandford Road, Littlemore, Oxford OX4 4PU. *T:* (01865) 778768.

PEARS, Mary Madeline; *see* Chapman, M. M.

PEARSE, Prof. Anthony Guy Everson, MA, MD (Cantab); FRCP, FRCPath; DCP (London); Professor of Histochemistry, University of London, Royal Postgraduate Medical School, 1965–81, now Emeritus; *b* 9 Aug. 1916; *o s* of Captain R. G. Pearse, DSO, MC, Modbury, Devon, and Constance Evelyn Steels, Pocklington, Yorks; *m* 1947, Elizabeth Himmelhoch, MB, BS (Sydney), DCP (London); one *s* three *d*. *Educ:* Sherborne Sch.; Trinity Coll., Cambridge. Kitchener Scholar. Posts, St Bart's Hospital, 1940–41; Surg.-Lt, RNVR, 1941–45 (21st and 24th Destroyer Flotillas). Registrar, Edgware General Hospital, 1946; Asst Lecturer in Pathol., PG Med. School, London, 1947–51, Lecturer, 1951–57; Cons. Pathol., Hammersmith Hospital, 1951; Fulbright Fellow and Visiting Prof. of Path., University of Alabama, 1953–54; Guest Instructor in Histochemistry: University of Kansas, 1957, 1958; Vanderbilt Univ., 1967; Reader in Histochemistry, University of London, 1957–65; Middleton Goldsmith Lectr, NY Path. Soc., 1976; Feulgen Lectr, Deutsch Ges. Histochem., 1983, Hon. Mem., 1986. Member: Path. Society (GB), 1949 (Hon. Mem., 1990); Biochem. Society (GB), 1957; European Gastro Club, 1969; Hon. Member or Member various foreign societies incl. Deutsche Akademie der Naturforscher Leopoldina, 1973 and Amer. Assoc. Endocrine Surgeons, 1981; Corresp. Mem., Deutsche Gesellschaft für Endokrinologie, 1978; Hon. Fellow, Royal Microscop. Society, 1964 (Vice-Pres., 1970–72; Pres., 1972–74). Hon. Mem., Mark Twain Soc., 1977. Hon. MD: Basel, 1960; Krakow, 1978. Raymond Horton-Smith Prize, Univ. of Cambridge, 1950; John Hunter Medal and Triennial Prize, RCS, 1976–78; Ernest Jung Foundn Prize and Medal for Medicine, 1979; Fred W. Stewart Medal and Prize, Sloan-Kettering Cancer Center, NY, 1979; Jan Swammerdam Medal, Soc. for Advancement of Nat. Scis, Amsterdam, 1988; Schleiden Medal, Deutsche Akademie der Naturforscher Leopoldina, 1989. Member Editorial Board: Histochemie, 1958–73; Jl Histochem. Cytochem., 1959–68; Enzymol. biol. clin., 1961–67; Jl of Royal Microscopical Soc., 1967–69; Histochemical Jl, 1968–; Brain Research, 1968–76; Cardiovascular Research, 1968–75; Virchow's Archiv 'B', 1968–91; Jl Microscopy, 1969–81; Jl of Neuro-visceral Relations, 1969–73; Jl of Molecular and Cellular Cardiology, 1970–79; Scand. Jl Gastroenterol., 1971–81; Jl Neural Transmission, 1973–76; Jl of Pathology, 1973–83; Progress in Histochem. Cytochem., 1973–; Histochemistry, 1974–91; Mikroscopie, 1977–88; Basic and Applied Histochem., 1979–90; Acta Histochem., 1980–; Europ. Jl of Basic and Applied Histochem., 1991–92; European Jl of Hystochem., 1993–; Editor, Medical Biology, 1974–84. *Publications:* Histochemistry Theoretical and Applied, 1953, 2nd edn, 1960; 3rd edn, vol. I, 1968, vol. II, 1972; 4th edn vol. I, 1980, vol. II, 1984, vol. III (ed with P. J. Stoward), 1991; numerous papers on theoretical and applied histochemistry, esp. endocrinology (The Neuroendocrine System). *Recreations:* horticulture (plant hybridization, Liliaceae, Asclepiadaceae); ship modelling, foreign touring. *Address:* Church Cottage, Church Lane, Cheriton Bishop, Exeter EX6 6HY. *T:* (01647) 24231. *Club:* Naval.

PEARSE, Barbara Mary Frances, (Mrs M. S. Bretscher), PhD; FRS 1988; Staff Scientist, Medical Research Council Laboratory of Molecular Biology, Cambridge, since 1981; *b* 24 March 1948; *d* of Reginald William Blake Pearse and Enid Alice (*née* Mitchell); *m* 1978, Mark Steven Bretscher, *qv*; one *s* one *d*. *Educ:* The Lady Eleanor Holles Sch., Hampton, Mddx; University Coll. London (BSc Biochemistry, PhD; Fellow, 1996). MRC Res. Fellowship, 1972–74; Beit Meml Fellowship, 1974–77; SRC Advanced Fellowship, 1977–82; CRC Internat. Fellowship Vis. Prof., Stanford Med. Centre, USA, 1984–85. Mem., EMBO, 1982–. EMBO Medal, 1987. *Publications:* contribs to sci. jls. *Recreations:* wild flowers, planting trees, fresh landscapes. *Address:* Ram Cottage, 63 Commercial End, Swaffham Bulbeck, Cambridge CB5 0ND. *T:* (01223) 811276.

PEARSE, Sir Brian (Gerald), Kt 1994; FCIB; Deputy Chairman, Britannic Assurance Plc, since 1997; Chief Executive, Midland Bank, 1991–94; *b* 23 Aug. 1933; *s* of Francis and Eileen Pearse; *m* 1959, Patricia M. Callaghan; one *s* two *d*. *Educ:* St Edward's Coll., Liverpool. Martin's Bank Ltd, 1950; Barclays Bank, 1969–91: Local Dir, Birmingham, 1972; Gen. Man., 1977; Chief Exec. Officer, N America, 1983; Finance Dir, 1987–91; Dir, Midland Bank, 1994–95. Chm., Lucas Industries, later LucasVarity, PLC, 1994–98; non-executive Director: Smith & Nephew, 1993–; HSBC plc, 1992–94. Chm., Assoc. for Payments Clearing Services, 1987–91. Director: British American Chamber of Commerce, 1987–98; Private Finance Panel, 1993–95; BOTB, 1994–97. Chairman: Young Enterprise, 1992–95; British Invisibles, 1994–97; Housing Corp., 1994–97. Chm. Council, Centre for Study of Financial Innovation, 1998–. Member: Council for Industry of Higher Educn, 1994–98; City Promotion Panel, 1995–97; Bd of Banking Supervision, 1998–. Treas., KCL, 1992–99 (FKC 1996). Pres., CIB, 1993–94. Trustee, Charities Aid Foundn, 1995–99. Gov., Univ. of Plymouth, 1997– (Vice Chm. Govs, 1999–). FRSA 1991. CIMgt (CBIM 1992). *Recreations:* Rugby football, opera. *Address:* Flat 7, 14 Gloucester Street, SW1V 2DN. *Club:* Royal Automobile.

PEARSE, Rear-Adm. John Roger Southey G.; *see* Gerard-Pearse.

PEARSON, family name of **Viscount Cowdray** and **Baron Pearson of Rannoch**.

PEARSON OF RANNOCH, Baron *cr* 1990 (Life Peer), of Bridge of Gaur in the district of Perth and Kinross; **Malcolm Everard MacLaren Pearson;** Chairman, PWS Holdings plc, 1970–86, and since 1988 (Deputy Chairman, 1987); *b* 20 July 1942; *s* of Col John MacLaren Pearson; *m* 1st, 1965, Francesca Frua De Angeli (marr. diss. 1970); one *d*; 2nd, 1977, Hon. Mary (marr. diss. 1995), *d* of Baron Charteris of A GCVO, QSO, OBE, PC; two *d*; 3rd, 1998, Caroline, *d* of Major Hugh Vincent Rose. *Educ:* Eton. Founded Pearson Webb Springbett, now PW reinsurance brokers, 1964. Member: H of L Select Cttee on Eur. Communities, Sub-cttee C on Envmt and Social Affairs, 1992–95. founded Rannoch Trust, 1984 Trustee). Mem., CNAA, 1983–93 (Hon. Treas., 1986–93). Hon. Pres., Nat. Soc Mentally Handicapped People in Residential Care (Rescare), 1994–. Patron, Brit Register of Chinese Herbal Medicine, 1998–. *Recreations:* stalking, fishing, golf. *Address:* House of Lords, SW1A 0AA. *Clubs:* White's; Swinley Forest Golf.

PEARSON, Anthony James; Director of Security, Prison Service, 1993–99; *b* 2 Nov. 1939; 2nd *s* of Leslie Pearson and Winifred Pearson (*née* Busby); *m* 1964, Sandra Lowe; two *d*. *Educ:* Saltley Grammar Sch., Birmingham; Exeter Univ. (BA Hons 1961); Oxford Univ. (Dip. Soc. and Public Admin 1962). Prison Governor: Gartree, 1977–81; Brixton, 1981–85; HM Dep. Chief Inspector of Prisons, 1985–87; Prison Service Headquarters: Hd of Div., 1987–89; Hd, Directorate of Telecommunications, 1989–91; Area Manager, 1991–93. Trustee: CCJS, 1998–; Butler Trust, 1999–. *Recreations:* Rugby, cricket (armchair expert).

PEARSON, Rev. Canon Brian William; Diocesan Ordained Local Ministry Officer, and Priest-in-charge, Leek Wootton, diocese of Coventry, since 2000; *b* 18 Aug. 1949; *s* of Victor William Charles Pearson and Florence Irene (*née* Webster); *m* 1974, Althea Mary Stride; two *s*. *Educ:* Roan Sch. for Boys, Blackheath; Brighton Polytechnic (BSc Hons); City Univ. (MSc); Ordination Training (Southwark Ordination Course); MTh Oxford 1994. CEng; MBCS; FHSM. Systems Engineer: IBM UK, 1967–71; Rohm and Haas UK, 1971–72; Lectr, Thames Polytechnic, 1972–81; College Head of Dept, Northbrook Coll., W Sussex, 1981–88; Bishop's Research Officer and Communications Officer, Bath and Wells, 1988–91; Archbishop's Officer for Mission and Evangelism and Tait Missioner, dio. of Canterbury, 1991–97; Hon. Canon, Canterbury Cathedral, 1992; Gen. Dir, CPAS, 1997–2000. Trustee, Christians in Sport, 1996–2001. Director: Trinity Coll., Bristol, 1997–2000; Christian Research, 2000–. *Publications:* Yes Manager: Management in the local church, 1986; (with George Carey) My Journey, Your Journey, 1996; How to Guide: managing change, 1996. *Recreations:* cricket, theatre, cinema, music, learning more about life through the experiences of two energetic sons, travel, enjoying the humour God has placed in His world. *Address:* The Vicarage, Leek Wootton, Warks CV35 7QL.

PEARSON, David Compton Froome; Deputy Chairman, Robert Fleming Holdings Ltd, 1986–90 (Director, 1974–90); *b* 28 July 1931; *s* of late Compton Edwin Pearson, OBE and of Marjorie (*née* Froome); *m* 1st, 1966, Venetia Jane Lynn (marr. diss. 1994); two *d*; 2nd, 1997, Mrs Bridget Thomson. *Educ:* Haileybury; Downing Coll., Cambridge (MA). Linklaters & Paines, Solicitors, 1957–69 (Partner, 1961–69); Dir, Robert Fleming & Co. Ltd, 1969–90; Chairman: The Fleming Property Unit Trust, 1971–90; Gill & Duffus Group Plc, 1982–85 (Dir, 1973–85); Robert Fleming Securities, 1985–90; River & Mercantile Investment Management Ltd, 1994–96; Dep. Chm., Austin Reed Group Plc, 1977–96 (Dir, 1971–96); Director: Blue Circle Industries Plc, 1972–87; Lane Fox and Partners Ltd, 1987–91; Fleming Income & Growth Investment Trust plc (formerly River & Mercantile Trust Plc), 1994–2001; Chesterton International Plc, 1994–98. Mem., Finance Act 1960 Tribunal, 1978–84. *Recreations:* gardening, walking. *Address:* The Manor, Berwick St John, Shaftesbury, Dorset SP7 0EX. *T:* (01747) 828363. *Clubs:* Brooks's, Army and Navy.

PEARSON, Derek Leslie, CB 1978; Deputy Secretary, Overseas Development Administration (formerly Ministry of Overseas Development), 1977–81; *b* 19 Dec. 1921; *s* of late George Frederick Pearson and Edith Maud Pearson (*née* Dent); *m* 1956, Diana Mary, *d* of late Sir Ralph Freeman; no *c*. *Educ:* William Ellis Sch.; London Sch. of Economics. BSc (Econ). Served War of 1939–45; Lieut (A) (O) RNVR. Colonial Office, 1947; seconded to Kenya, 1954–56; Principal Private Sec. to Sec. of State for Colonies, 1959–61; Dept of Technical Cooperation, 1961; Asst Sec., 1962; ODM, 1964; Under Secretary: CSD, 1970–72; Min. of Overseas Develt, 1972–75; Dep. Sec., Cabinet Office, 1975–77. *Address:* Langata, Little London Road, Horam, Heathfield, East Sussex TN21 0BG. *Clubs:* Naval, Civil Service.

PEARSON, (Edward) John (David); Hon. Director General, European Commission, since 2001; *b* 1 March 1938; *s* of Sydney Pearson and Hilda Beaumont; *m* 1963, Hilary Stuttard; three *s* two *d*. *Educ:* Huddersfield Coll.; Emmanuel Coll., Cambridge (MA). Admin. Trainee, London Transport Exec., 1959; Asst Principal, MoT, 1960, Principal 1965; Sen. Principal, DoE, 1971; Commission of the European Communities: Head of Div., Transport Directorate-Gen., 1973–81; Dir, Fisheries Directorate-Gen., 1981–91; Dir, Regl Policy and Cohesion Directorate-Gen., 1991–98; Dep. Financial Controller, EC, 1999–2001 (Acting Financial Controller, July–Aug. 2000). *Recreation:* orienteering (Pres., Belgian Orienteering Assoc., 1982–87; Chm., Develt and Promotion Cttee, 1986–88, Mem. Council, 1988–94, Internat. Orienteering Fedn). *Address:* Rue du Repos 56, 1180 Brussels, Belgium. *T:* (2) 3751182.

PEARSON, Sir (Francis) Nicholas (Fraser), 2nd Bt *cr* 1964, of Gressingham, Co. Palatine of Lancaster; *b* 28 Aug. 1943; *s* of Sir Francis Fenwick Pearson, 1st Bt, MBE and of Katharine Mary, *d* of Rev. D. Denholm Fraser; *S* father, 1991; *m* 1978, Henrietta Elizabeth, *d* of Comdr Henry Pasley-Tyler. *Educ:* Radley Coll. Commnd The Rifle Brigade, 1961; ADC to: Army Comdr, Far East, 1967; C-in-C, Far East, 1968. Dir, Hill & Delamain Ltd, 1970–75; Dep. Chm., Claughton Manor Brickworks, 1978; Chm., Turner Gp Ltd, 1979; Director: Intercontinental Hotel Group Ltd, 1989–92; Virgin Atlantic Airlines, 1989–92; Saison Hldgs BV, 1990–93. Trustee: Ruskin Foundn; Temenos Foundn. Prospective Parly Cand. (C), Oldham West, 1976–79. *Recreations:* shooting, fishing. *Heir:* none. *Address:* c/o National Westminster Bank, 55 Main Street, Kirkby Lonsdale, Cumbria. *Club:* Carlton.

PEARSON, Dr Graham Scott, CB 1990; CChem, FRSC; Hon. Visiting Professor of International Security, Department of Peace Studies, University of Bradford, since 1996; Assistant Chief Scientific Adviser (Non-Proliferation), Ministry of Defence, 1995–96; *b* 20 July 1935; *s* of Ernest Reginald Pearson and Alice (*née* Maclachlan); *m* 1960, Susan Elizabeth Meriton Benn; two *s*. *Educ:* Woodhouse Grove Sch., Bradford; St Salvator's Coll., Univ. of St Andrews (BSc 1st Cl. Hons Chemistry, 1957; PhD 1960). Postdoctoral Fellow, Univ. of Rochester, NY, USA, 1960–62; joined Scientific Civil Service, 1962; Rocket Propulsion Estab., 1962–69; Def. Res. and Develt Staff, Washington, DC, 1969–72; PSO to Dir Gen. Res. Weapons, 1972–73; Asst Dir, Naval Ordnance Services/Scientific, 1973–76; Technical Adviser/Explosives, Materials and Safety (Polaris), 1976–79; Principal Supt, Propellants Explosives and Rocket Motor Estab., Westcott, 1979–80; Dep. Dir 1, 1980–82 and Dep. Dir 2, 1982–83, RARDE, Fort Halstead; Dir Gen., ROF (Res. and Develt), 1983–84; Dir, Chemical Defence Estabt, later Dir Gen., Chemical and Biol Defence Estabt, Porton Down, 1984–95. FRSA 1989. *Publications:* (ed jtly) Strengthening the Biological Weapons Convention, 1996; The UNSCOM Saga: chemical and biological weapons non-proliferation, 1999; contributor to: Advances in Photochemistry, vol. 3, 1964; Advances in Inorganic and Radio Chemistry, vol. 8, 1966;

Oxidation and Combustion Reviews, vol. 3, 1968 and vol. 4, 1969; Biological Weapons: Weapons of the Future?, 1993; Non-Conventional Weapons Proliferation in the Middle East, 1993; Verification after the Cold War, 1994; Weapons Proliferation in the 1990s, 1995; Verification 1997, 1997; Biological Weapons: limiting the threat, 1999; Biological Warfare: modern offense and defense, 2000; articles on combustion, and on chemical and biological defence and arms control, in scientific jls; official reports. *Recreations:* long distance walking, photography, reading, gardening. *Address:* Department of Peace Studies, University of Bradford, Bradford, W Yorks BD7 1DP. *T:* (01274) 234188.

PEARSON, Ian Phares, PhD; MP (Lab) Dudley South, since 1997 (Dudley West, Dec. 1994–1997); an Assistant Government Whip, since 2001; *b* 5 April 1959; *m* Annette Pearson; one *s* two *d*. *Educ:* Brierley Hill GS; Balliol Coll., Oxford (BA Hons PPE); Warwick Univ. (MA, PhD). Mem. (Lab) Dudley MBC, 1984–87. Local Govt Policy Res. Officer, Lab. Party, 1985–87; Dep. Dir, Urban Trust, 1987–88; business and economic develt consultant, 1988–91; Jt Chief Exec., W Midlands Enterprise Bd, 1991–94. *Address:* House of Commons, SW1A 0AA.

PEARSON, John; *see* Pearson, E. J. D.

PEARSON, Captain John William, CBE 1981; Regional Administrator, Mersey Regional Health Authority, 1977–81; *b* 19 Sept. 1920; *s* of Walter and Margaret Jane Pearson; *m* 1945, Audrey Ethel Whitehead; two *s*. *Educ:* Holloway Sch. FCIS, FHA, FCCA, IPFA. Served War, RA (Field), 1939–46. Hospital Service, LCC, 1947–48; NW Metropolitan Regional Hosp. Bd, 1948–49; Northern Gp, HMC, Finance Officer, 1949–62; Treasurer: St Thomas' Bd of Governors, 1962–73; Mersey Regional Health Authority, 1973–77. Pres., Assoc. of Health Service Treasurers, 1970–71. *Recreations:* tennis, golf, gardening, snooker. *Address:* 20 Weare Gifford, Shoeburyness, Essex SS3 8AB. *T:* (01702) 585039.

PEARSON, Keith Philip, MA; FRSE; Headmaster, George Heriot's School, Edinburgh, 1983–97; *b* 5 Aug. 1941; *s* of Fred G. and Phyllis Pearson; *m* 1965, Dorothy (*née* Atkinson); two *d*. *Educ:* Madrid Univ. (Dip. de Estudios Hispanicos); Univ. of Cambridge (MA; Cert. of Educn). FRSE 1995. Teacher, Rossall Sch., 1964–72 (Head of Mod. Langs, 1968–72); George Watson's College: Head of Mod. Langs, 1972–79; Dep. Principal, 1979–83. *Recreations:* sport, mountains, music, DIY. *Address:* 11 Pentland Avenue, Edinburgh EH13 0HZ. *T:* (0131) 441 2630.

PEARSON, Sir Nicholas; *see* Pearson, Sir F. N. F.

PEARSON, Maj.-Gen. Ronald Matthew, CB 1985; MBE 1959; Director Army Dental Service, 1982–85, retired; *b* 25 Feb. 1925; *s* of Dr John Pearson and Sheila Pearson (*née* Brown); *m* 1956, Florence Eileen Jack; two *d*. *Educ:* Clifton Hall Sch., Ratho, Midlothian; Glasgow Acad.; Glasgow Univ./Glasgow Dental Hosp. LDS RFPS(Glas) 1948; FBIM 1979. Civilian Dental Practice, 1948–49. Commnd RADC, 1949; served: RWAFF, 1950–53; UK, 1953–57; BAOR, 1957–60; UK, 1961–67; CO No 1 Dental Gp, BAOR, 1967–70; CO Army Dental Centres, Cyprus, 1970–73; CO No 8 Dental Gp, UK, 1973–75; CO No 4 Dental Gp, UK, 1975–76; Dep. Dir Dental Service, UKLF, 1976–78; Dep. Dir Dental Service, BAOR, 1978–82. QHDS, 1978–85. CStJ 1983. *Recreations:* trout fishing, photography, gardening, caravanning.

PEARSON, Sybil Angela Margaret, (Mrs Michael Pearson); *see* Jones, S. A. M.

PEARSON, Gen. Sir Thomas (Cecil Hook), KCB 1967 (CB 1964); CBE 1959 (OBE 1953); DSO 1940, and Bar, 1943; DL; retired 1974; *b* 1 July 1914; *s* of late Vice-Admiral J. L. Pearson, CMG; *m* 1947, Aud, *d* of late Alf Skjelkvale, Oslo; two *s*. *Educ:* Charterhouse; Sandhurst. 2nd Lieutenant Rifle Bde, 1934. Served War of 1939–45, M East and Europe; CO 2nd Bn The Rifle Bde, 1942; Dep. Comdr 2nd Independent Parachute Bde Gp 1944; Dep. Comdr 1st Air-landing Bde 1945; GSO1 1st Airborne Div. 1945; CO 1st Bn The Parachute Regt 1946; CO 7th Bn The Parachute Regt 1947; GSO1 (Land Air Warfare), WO, 1948; JSSC, GSO1, HQ Malaya, 1950; GSO1 (Plans), FARELF, 1951; Directing Staff, JSSC, 1953; Comdr 45 Parachute Bde TA 1955; Nat. Defence Coll., Canada, 1956; Comdr 16 Indep. Parachute Bde 1957; Chief of Staff to Dir of Ops Cyprus, 1960; Head of Brit. Mil. Mission to Soviet Zone of Germany, 1960; Major-General Commanding 1st Division, BAOR, 1961–63; Chief of Staff, Northern Army Group, 1963–67; Comdr, FARELF, 1967–68; Military Sec., MoD, 1968–72; C-in-C, Allied Forces, Northern Europe, 1972–74; psc 1942; jssc 1950; ndc Canada 1957. ADC Gen. to the Queen, 1974. Col Comdt, the Royal Green Jackets, 1973–77. Fisheries Mem., Welsh Water Auth., 1980–83. DL Hereford and Worcester, 1983. Haakon VII Liberty Cross, 1948; Medal of Honour, Norwegian Defence Assoc., 1973. *Recreations:* field sports, yachting. *Clubs:* Naval and Military; Kongelig Norsk Seilforenning.

PEART, Brian; Under-Secretary, Ministry of Agriculture, Fisheries and Food, 1976–85; *b* 17 Aug. 1925; *s* of late Joseph Garfield Peart and Frances Hannah Peart (*née* English); *m* 1952, Dorothy (*née* Thompson); one *s* one *d*. *Educ:* Wolsingham Grammar Sch.; Durham Univ. (BA). Served War, RAF, 1943–47. Agricultural Economist, Edinburgh Sch. of Agric., 1950–57; Sen. Agricultural Economist, 1957–64; Regional Farm Management Adviser, MAFF, West Midlands Region, 1964–67; Chief Farm Management Adviser, MAFF, 1967–71; Regional Manager, MAFF, Yorks/Lancs Region, 1971–74; Head of Intelligence and Trng Div., 1974–76; Chief Administrator, ADAS, 1976–80; Under Sec., Lands Gp, MAFF, 1980–85. *Recreations:* golf, genealogy, bridge, The Times crossword. *Address:* 18 Derwent Close, Claygate, Surrey KT10 0RF. *Club:* Farmers'.

PEART, Michael John, CMG 1995; LVO 1983; HM Diplomatic Service, retired; *b* 15 Dec. 1943; *s* of Joseph Albert William Peart and Thelma Theresa Peart (*née* Rasmussen); *m* 1968, Helena Mary Stuttle; one *s* (one *d* decd). *Educ:* Gillingham County Grammar Sch., Kent. Prison Dept, Home Office, 1960–65; FCO 1966–69; served Blantyre, 1969–71; Warsaw, 1972–75; Mexico City, 1975–80; FCO, 1980–83; Dhaka, 1983–86; FCO, 1987–91; Ambassador, Lithuania, 1991–94; Ambassador, later High Comr, Fiji, and High Comr, Kiribati, Nauru and Tuvalu, 1995–97. Mem. Council, Pacific Is Soc. of UK and Ire., 1999–; Chm., British-Lithuanian Soc., 2000–. Mem. Cttee, Foreign and Commonwealth Assoc., 1999–. Mem., Meopham Parish Council, 1999–. *Recreations:* music, reading, walking. *Address:* Kyalami, Whitepost Lane, Culverstone, Kent DA13 0TJ.

PEART, Prof. Sir (William) Stanley, Kt 1985; MD; FRS 1969; Professor of Medicine, University of London, at St Mary's Hospital Medical School, 1956–87, now Emeritus; *b* 31 March 1922; *s* of J. G. and M. Peart; *m* 1947, Peggy Parkes; one *s* one *d*. *Educ:* King's College School, Wimbledon; Medical School, St Mary's Hospital. MB, BS (Hons), 1945; FRCP 1959; MD (London), 1949. Lecturer in Medicine, St Mary's Hospital, 1950–56. Master, Hunterian Inst., RCS, 1988–92. Wellcome Trust: Trustee, 1975–94; Dep. Chm., 1991–94; Consultant, 1994–98; Beit Trustee, 1986–. Goulstonian Lectr, 1959, Croonian Lectr, 1979, RCP. Founder FMedSci 1998. Hon. For. Mem., Académie Royale de Médicine de Belgique, 1984. Hon. FIC 1988; Hon. FRCA 1991; Hon. FRCS 1995; Hon. Fellow, UCL, 1997. Hon. DSc Edinburgh, 1993. Stouffer Prize, Amer. Heart Assoc., 1968. *Publications:* chapters in: Cecil-Loeb, Textbook of Medicine; Renal Disease; Biochemical Disorders in Human Disease; articles in Biochemical Journal, Journal of Physiology, Lancet. *Recreations:* ski-ing, reading, tennis. *Address:* 17 Highgate Close, N6 4SD.

PEASE, family name of **Barons Gainford** and **Wardington**.

PEASE, Sir (Alfred) Vincent, 4th Bt *cr* 1882; *b* 2 April 1926; *s* of Sir Alfred (Edward) Pease, 2nd Bt (*d* 1939), and his 3rd wife, Emily Elizabeth Pease (*d* 1979); *S* half-brother, 1963; unmarried. *Educ:* Bootham School, York; Durham Sch. of Agric., Houghall. *Heir:* *b* Joseph Gurney Pease [*b* 16 Nov. 1927; *m* 1953, Shelagh Munro, *d* of C. G. Bulman; one *s* one *d*]. *Address:* 149 Aldenham Road, Guisborough, Cleveland TS14 8LB. *T:* (01287) 636453.

PEASE, Dr (Rendel) Sebastian, FRS 1977; Programme Director for Fusion, UKAEA, 1981–87; *b* 1922; *s* of Michael Stewart Pease and Helen Bowen (*née* Wedgwood); *m* 1st, 1952, Susan Spickernell (*d* 1996); two *s* three *d*; 2nd, 1998, Jean Frances White (*d* 2000). *Educ:* Bedales Sch.; Trinity Coll., Cambridge (MA, ScD). Scientific Officer, Min. of Aircraft Prodn at ORS Unit, HQ, RAF Bomber Comd, 1942–46; research at AERE, Harwell, 1947–61; Div. Head, Culham Lab. for Plasma Physics and Nuclear Fusion, UKAEA, 1961–67; Vis. Scientist, Princeton Univ., 1964–65; Asst Dir, UKAEA Research Gp, 1967; Dir, Culham Lab., UKAEA, 1968–81. Gordon Godfrey Vis. Prof. of Theoretical Physics, Univ. NSW, 1984, 1988 and 1991; Visitor, Blackett Lab., Imperial Coll., London, 1992–. Chairman: Adam Hilger Ltd, 1976–77; Plasma Physics Commn, Internat. Union of Pure and Applied Physics, 1975–78; Internat. Fusion Res. Council, Internat. Atomic Energy Agency, 1976–83; British Pugwash Gp, 1988–April 2002 (Mem., Pugwash Council, 1992–). Member: Council, Royal Soc., 1985–87 (a Vice-Pres., 1986–87); Fabian Soc., 1942–; Inst. of Physics (Vice-Pres., 1973–77; Pres., 1978–80); Amer. Inst. of Physics, 1961–; IEE, 1979–; Eur. Atlantic Gp, 1996–. Mem., West Ilsley Parish Council, 1987–2000 (Chm., 1997–2000). Hon. MINucE 1984. Hon. Fellow, European Nuclear Soc., 1990. DUniv Surrey, 1973; Hon. DSc: Aston, 1981; City Univ., 1987. *Publications:* articles in physics jls, and Pugwash Confs on Science and World Affairs. *Recreation:* music. *Address:* The Poplars, West Ilsley, Newbury, Berks RG20 7AW.

PEASE, Sir Richard Thorn, 3rd Bt *cr* 1920; DL; Chairman, Yorkshire Bank, 1986–90 (Director, since 1977; Deputy Chairman, 1981–86); *b* 20 May 1922; *s* of Sir Richard Arthur Pease, 2nd Bt, and Jeannette Thorn (*d* 1957), *d* of late Gustav Edward Kissel, New York; *S* father, 1969; *m* 1956, Anne, *d* of late Lt-Col Reginald Francis Heyworth; one *s* two *d*. *Educ:* Eton. Served with 60th Rifles, Middle East, Italy and Greece, 1941–46 (Captain). Director: Owners of the Middlesbrough Estate Ltd, 1954–86; Barclays Bank, 1964–89; Bank of Scotland, 1977–85; Grainger Trust PLC, 1986–94; Vice-Chairman: Barclays Bank Ltd, 1970–82; Barclays Bank UK Management, 1971–82; Chm., Foreign and Colonial High Income Trust, 1990–92. DL Northumberland, 1990. *Heir:* *s* Richard Peter Pease, *b* 4 Sept. 1958. *Address:* Hindley House, Stocksfield-on-Tyne, Northumberland NE43 7SA.

PEASE, Robert John Claude; HM Diplomatic Service, retired; Counsellor (Administration) and Consul-General, British Embassy, Moscow, 1977–80; *b* 24 April 1922; *s* of Frederick Robert Hellier Pease and Eileen Violet Pease (*née* Beer); *m* 1945, Claire Margaretta Whall; one *s* two *d*. *Educ:* Cattedown Road Sch., Plymouth; Sutton High Sch., Plymouth. Served War of 1939–45; Telegraphist, RN, 1942; commnd Sub Lt RNVR, 1944. Clerk, Lord Chancellor's Dept, Plymouth County Court, 1939, Truro County Court, 1946; Foreign Office, 1948; Moscow, 1952; HM Consul, Sarajevo, 1954; 2nd Sec., Bangkok, 1958; HM Consul, Gdynia, 1959, Düsseldorf, 1961; 1st Sec., Pretoria, 1964, Bombay, 1966; FCO, 1969; Dep. High Commissioner, Mauritius, 1973. *Recreations:* golf, opera. *Address:* 4 Kiln Close, Prestwood, Bucks, HP16 9DG.

PEASE, Rosamund Dorothy Benson; Under Secretary, Department of Health, 1989–95; *b* 20 March 1935; *d* of Helen Bowen (*née* Wedgwood) and Michael Stewart Pease; one *s*. *Educ:* Chester Sch., Nova Scotia; Perse Sch., Cambridge; Mount Sch., York; Newnham Coll., Cambridge (BA Classical Tripos). Asst Principal, Min. of Health, 1958; Principal, 1965; Asst Sec., Pay Board, 1973; Office of Manpower Economics, 1974; Cabinet Office, 1975–76; DHSS, 1976; Office of Population Censuses and Surveys, 1983; Under Sec., NI Office, 1985. *Recreations:* gardening, family.

See also R. S. Pease.

PEASE, Sebastian; *see* Pease, R. S.

PEASE, Sir Vincent; *see* Pease, Sir A. V.

PEAT, Adam Erskine; Director, Local Government and Housing (formerly Local Government) Group, National Assembly for Wales, since 1999; *b* 30 Nov. 1948; *s* of late Raymond Basil Peat and Cynthia Elisabeth Peat; *m* 1973, Christine Janet Champion; one *s* one *d*. *Educ:* Stowmarket Co. Grammar Sch.; Pembroke Coll., Oxford (MA). Joined Welsh Office, 1972: Principal, 1977; Private Sec. to Sec. of State for Wales, 1983–84; Asst Sec., 1984–89; Chief Exec., Tai Cymru, 1989–98; Gp Dir, Welsh Office, 1998–99. *Recreations:* music, walking, ski-ing. *Address:* National Assembly for Wales, Cathays Park, Cardiff CF1 3NQ. *T:* (029) 2082 5565.

PEAT, Sir Gerrard (Charles), KCVO 1988; FCA; Partner, KPMG Peat Marwick (formerly Peat Marwick Mitchell) & Co., Chartered Accountants, 1956–87; Auditor to the Queen's Privy Purse, 1980–88 (Assistant Auditor, 1969–80); *b* 14 June 1920; *s* of Charles Urie Peat, MC, FCA, sometime MP and Ruth (*née* Pulley); *m* 1949, Margaret Josephine Collingwood; one *s*. *Educ:* Sedbergh Sch. FCA 1961. Served War, RAF and ATA (pilot), 1940–45 (Service Medals); Pilot, 600 City of London Auxiliary Sqdn, 1948–51. Underwriting Mem. of Lloyd's, 1973–; Member: Cttee, Assoc. of Lloyd's Members, 1983–89; Council of Lloyd's, 1989–92. Member: Corp. of City of London, 1973–78; Worshipful Co. of Turners, 1970–. Hon. Treasurer, Assoc. of Conservative Clubs, 1971–78. Jubilee Medal, 1977. *Recreations:* travel, shooting, fishing, golf. *Address:* (office) Britannia House, Glenthorne Road, W6 0LF. *T:* (020) 8748 9898; Flat 10, 35 Pont Street, SW1X 0BB. *T:* (020) 7245 9736; Home Farm, Upper Basildon, Pangbourne, Berks RG8 8ND. *T:* (01491) 671241. *Clubs:* Boodle's, MCC.

PEAT, Ven. Lawrence Joseph; Archdeacon of Westmorland and Furness, 1989–95, now Emeritus; *b* 29 Aug. 1928; *s* of Joseph Edward and Lilian Edith Peat; *m* 1953, Sheila Shipway; three *s* three *d*. *Educ:* Lincoln Theological College. Curate of Bramley, Leeds, 1958–61; Rector of All Saints', Heaton Norris, Stockport, 1961–65; Vicar of Bramley, Leeds, 1965–73; Team Rector of Southend-on-Sea, 1973–79; Vicar of Skelmsmergh, Selside and Longsleddale, Cumbria, 1979–86; RD of Kendal, 1984–88; Team Vicar of Kirkby Lonsdale, 1986–88. Canon of Carlisle Cathedral, 1988–95, now Emeritus. *Recreations:* walking, music. *Address:* 32 White Stiles, Kendal, Cumbria LA9 6DJ. *T:* (01539) 733829.

PEAT, Sir Michael (Charles Gerrard), KCVO 1998 (CVO 1994); FCA; Keeper of the Privy Purse, Treasurer to the Queen, and Receiver-General of the Duchy of Lancaster, since 1996; *b* 16 Nov. 1949; *m* 1976, Deborah Sage (*née* Wood); two *s* two *d* (and one *s* decd). *Educ:* Eton; Trinity Coll., Oxford (MA); INSEAD, Fontainebleau (MBA). FCA 1975. KPMG Peat Marwick, 1972–93; Dir, Finance and Property Services, HM Household, 1990–96. *Recreations:* sport, history, literature.

PEATTIE, Catherine; Member (Lab) Falkirk East, Scottish Parliament, since 1999; *b* 24 Nov. 1951; *d* of Ian Roxburgh and late Catherine Cheape (*née* Menzies); *m* 1969, Ian Peattie; two *d*. *Educ:* Moray Secondary Sch., Grangemouth. Shop worker, 1966–68; factory worker, 1968–69; Trng Supervisor, 1970–75; Field Worker and Trng Officer, SPPA, 1980–86; Develt worker, Volunteer Network, Falkirk, 1986–90; Community Develt worker, Langlees Community Flat, Falkirk, 1990–91; Manager, Community Outreach, 1991–93; Dir, Falkirk Voluntary Action Resource Centre, 1993–99. Scottish Parliament: Dep. Convener, Educn, Culture and Sport Cttee (Mem., 1999–); Mem., Equal Opportunities Cttee. *Address:* Scottish Parliament, Edinburgh EH99 1SP.

PEATTIE, Charles William Davidson; freelance cartoonist, since 1985; *b* 3 April 1958; *s* of Richard Peattie and Frances Peattie; *m* 1988, Siobhan Clark; two *d*. *Educ:* Charterhouse; St Martin's Sch. of Art (BA Fine Art). Portrait painter, 1980–85; artist: Alex cartoon (written with Russell Taylor) in: London Daily News, 1987; The Independent, 1987–91; Daily Telegraph, 1992–; Celeb cartoon (written with Mark Warren and Russell Taylor) in Private Eye, 1987–. *Publications:* (with Mark Warren) Dick, 1987; (co-designed with Phil Healey) Incredible Model Dinosaurs, 1994; with Russell Taylor: Alex, 1987; The Unabashed Alex, 1988; Alex II: Magnum Force, 1989; Alex III: Son of Alex, 1990; Alex IV: The Man with the Golden Handshake, 1991; Celeb, 1991; Alex V: For the Love of Alex, 1992; Alex Calls the Shots, 1993; Alex Plays the Game, 1994; Alex Knows the Score, 1995; Alex Sweeps the Board, 1996; Alex Feels the Pinch, 1997; The Full Alex, 1998; The Alex Technique, 1999. *Recreations:* drawing, skating, gossiping. *Address:* c/o Alex Cartoons, 6 Market Place, W1N 7AH. *T:* (020) 7636 5007. *Clubs:* Groucho, Cobden, Soho House.

PÉBEREAU, Michel; Chairman and Chief Executive Officer, Banque Nationale de Paris, since 1993; Chairman, Paribas, since 1999. *Educ:* Ecole Polytechnique; Ecole Nationale d'Administration. Inspecteur Général des Finances. Rep., later Tech. Advr, Cabinet of Minister of Econ. and Finance, 1970–74; Rep., Sub-Dir, Asst Dir and Hd of Service, Treasury Directorate, Ministry of Econ. and Finances, 1971–82; Dir, then Rep., Cabinet of Minister of Econ., 1978–81; Crédit Commercial de France: Man. Dir, 1982–87; Chm. and Chief Exec. Officer, 1987–93. Director, numerous companies, including: Banque Nationale de Paris; Société Anonyme des Galeries Lafayette; Elf; Renault; Financière BNP; BNP UK Hldgs Ltd. Institute of Political Studies, Paris: Master of Confs, 1967–78; Prof., 1980–; Mem., Mgt Cttee, 1984–; Master of Confs, Nat. Sch. of Statistic and Econ. Admin, 1968–79. Officer, Legion of Honour; Kt, Nat. Order of Merit (France). *Publications:* La Politique Economique de France, 3 Vols; science fiction book reviews for La Recherche. *Address:* c/o Banque Nationale de Paris, 16 boulevard des Italiens, 75009 Paris, France.

PECK, David Arthur; Clerk to Merchant Taylors' Company, since 1995; *b* 3 May 1940; *s* of Frank Archibald Peck and late Molly Peck (*née* Eyels); *m* 1968, Jennifer Mary Still; one *s* two *d*. *Educ:* Wellingborough Sch.; St John's Coll., Cambridge (MA). Admitted Solicitor, 1966; Partner, Birkbeck Julius Coburn & Broad, 1967; Sen. Partner, Birkbeck Montagu's, 1985–91; Partner, Penningtons, 1991–95. Mem. Council, Radley Coll., 1993–. *Recreations:* golf, ski-ing, cinema. *Address:* Merchant Taylors' Hall, 30 Threadneedle Street, EC2R 8JB. *T:* (020) 7588 7606. *Clubs:* MCC (Mem. Cttee, 1998–); Hawks (Cambridge).

See also Maj.-Gen. R. L. Peck.

PECK, His Honour David (Edward); a Circuit Judge (formerly Judge of County Courts), 1969–85; *b* 6 April 1917; *m* 1st, 1950, Rosina Seton Glover Marshall (marr. diss.); one *s* three *d*; 2nd, 1973, Frances Deborah Redford (*née* Mackenzie) (marr. diss.); one *s*; 3rd, 1983, Elizabeth Charlotte Beale (*née* Boost). *Educ:* Charterhouse School; Balliol College, Oxford. Served Army (Cheshire Regiment), 1939–46. Called to Bar, Middle Temple, 1949. Mem., County Court Rule Cttee, 1978–84 (Chm., 1981–84); Jt Editor, County Court Practice, 1982–90. *Address:* 2/3 Gray's Inn Square, WC1R 5JH.

PECK, Sir Edward (Heywood), GCMG 1974 (KCMG 1966; CMG 1957); HM Diplomatic Service, retired; *b* 5 Oct. 1915; *s* of Lt-Col Edward Surman Peck, IMS, and Doris Louise Heywood; *m* 1948, Alison Mary MacInnes; one *s* two *d* (and one *d* decd). *Educ:* Clifton College; The Queen's College, Oxford. 1st Cl. Hons (Mod. Langs), 1937; Laming Travelling Fellow, 1937–38. Entered Consular Service, 1938; served in Barcelona, 1938–39; Foreign Office, 1939–40; Sofia, 1940; Ankara, 1940–44; Adana, 1944; Iskenderun, 1945; Salonica, 1945–47; with UK Deleg. to UN Special Commn on the Balkans, 1947; Foreign Office, 1947–50; seconded to UK High Commissioner's Office, Delhi, 1950–52; Counsellor, Foreign Office, 1952–55; Dep. Comdt, Brit. Sector, Berlin, 1955–58; on staff of UK Commissioner-General for S-E Asia, 1959–60; Assistant Under-Secretary of State, Foreign Office, 1961–66; British High Commissioner in Kenya, 1966–68; Dep. Under-Secretary of State, FCO, 1968–70; British Perm. Rep. to N Atlantic Council, 1970–75. Dir, Outward Bound (Loch Eil), 1976–90; Mem. Council, Nat. Trust for Scotland, 1982–87. Hon. Vis. Fellow in Defence Studies, Aberdeen Univ., 1976–85. Hon. LLD Aberdeen, 1997. *Publications:* North-East Scotland (Bartholomew's Guides Series), 1981; Avonside Explored, 1983; The Battle of Glenlivet, 1994. *Recreations:* hill-walking, travel, reading history. *Address:* Easter Torrans, Tomintoul, Banffshire AB37 9HJ. *Club:* Alpine.

PECK, Gregory; film actor, US, since 1943; *b* 5 April 1916; *s* of Gregory P. Peck and Bernice Ayres; *m* 1st, 1942, Greta Konen Rice (marr. diss. 1954); two *s* (and one *s* decd); 2nd, 1955, Veronique Passani; one *s* one *d*. *Educ:* Calif Public Schools; Univ. of Calif (BA). Broadway stage, 1941–43. *Films:* Days of Glory, 1943; Keys of the Kingdom, Valley of Decision, 1944; Spellbound, 1945; Duel in the Sun, The Yearling, 1946; The Macomber Affair, Gentlemen's Agreement, 1947; The Paradine Case, 1948; Yellow Sky, The Great Sinner, Twelve O'Clock High, 1949; The Gun Fighter, 1950; Only the Valiant, Captain Horatio Hornblower, David and Bathsheba, 1951; The World in his Arms, 1952; The Snows of Kilimanjaro, 1952; Roman Holiday, 1953; The Million Pound Note, 1953; Night People, 1954; The Purple Plain, 1954; The Man in the Grey Flannel Suit, 1956; Moby Dick, 1956; Designing Woman, 1957; The Bravados, 1958; The Big Country (co-producer), 1958; Pork Chop Hill, 1959; On the Beach, 1959; Guns of Navarone, 1960; Cape Fear, 1961; To Kill a Mocking Bird, 1962 (Academy Award for best performance); Captain Newman, MD, 1963; Behold a Pale Horse, 1964; Mirage, 1965; Arabesque, 1965; Mackenna's Gold, 1967; The Chairman, 1968; The Stalking Moon, 1968; Marooned, 1970; I Walk the Line, 1971; Shoot Out, 1971; The Trial of the Catonsville Nine, 1972; Billy Two-Hats, 1974; The Boys From Brazil, 1978; The Sea Wolves, 1980; Amazing Grace and Chuck, 1987; Old Gringo, 1989; Other People's Money, 1991; Cape Fear, 1991; *television:* The Blue and the Gray, 1982; The Scarlet and the Black, 1983; (also producer) The Portrait, 1993; *produced:* The Dove, 1974; The Omen, 1976; MacArthur, 1977. Nat. Chm., Amer. Cancer Soc., 1966. Mem., Nat. Council on Arts, 1965–67, 1968–; Pres., Acad. Motion Picture Arts and Sciences, 1967–70; Chm., Board of Trustees, Amer. Film Inst., 1967–69. Medal of Freedom Award, 1969; Jean Hersholt Humanitarian Award, Acad. of Motion Picture Arts and Sciences, 1968; Nat. Medal of the Arts, 1998. *Recreations:* riding, swimming, bicycling, gardening. *Address:* c/o CAA, 9830 Wilshire Boulevard, Beverly Hills, CA 90212–1825, USA. *Club:* Players (New York).

PECK, Maj.-Gen. Richard Leslie, CB 1991; FRGS; CEng, FICE; Director, The Churches Conservation Trust (formerly Redundant Churches Fund), 1992–97; *b* 27 May 1937; *s* of Frank Archibald Peck and late Molly Peck (*née* Eyels); *m* 1962, Elizabeth Ann, *d* of late Major Denis James Bradley and of Barbara Edith Amy Bradley (*née* Metcalfe); two *s* one *d*. *Educ:* Wellingborough Sch.; Royal Mil. Acad., Sandhurst; Royal Mil. Coll. of Science, Shrivenham. BScEng. Commnd RE, 1957; served Cyprus, Libya, Germany, UK; psc 1969; Bde Major 5 Inf. Bde, 1969–71; Sqn Comd BAOR, 1972–73; Directing Staff, Staff Coll., 1973–77; CO 21 Engr Regt, 1977–79; Asst Mil. Sec., 1979–81; Comd 19 Inf. Bde, 1981–83; RCDS 1984; Dir Army Service Conditions, MoD, 1985; Dir Personnel, Staff of CDS, 1985–87; Engr-in-Chief (Army), 1988–91. Mem., Lord Kitchener Nat. Meml Fund, 1992– (Treas., 1999–). Col Comdt, RE, 1991–97; Col, Queen's Gurkha Engineers, 1991–96. Freeman, City of London, 1991; Mem., Engineers' Co, 1990–. *Recreations:* Association football, cricket, golf, shooting, ski-ing, Rugby football. *Clubs:* MCC; I Zingari, Free Foresters, Band of Brothers, Cryptics; Royal Mid-Surrey Golf.

See also D. A. Peck.

PECK, Stanley Edwards, CBE 1974; BEM 1954; QPM 1964; DL; HM Inspector of Constabulary, 1964–78; *b* 1916; *er s* of late Harold Edwards Peck, Edgbaston and Shanghai; *m* 1st, 1939, Yvonne Sydney Edwards (*d* 1994), *er d* of late John Edwards Jessop, LDS; two *s* two *d*; 2nd, 1996, Elizabeth Beddows. *Educ:* Solihull School; Birmingham University. Served with RAF, 1941–45 (Flt-Lt). Joined Metropolitan Police, 1935; Chief Inspector and Supt, New Scotland Yard, 1950–54; Asst Chief Constable, Staffs, 1954–61; Chief Constable, Staffs, 1961–64. DL Staffs, 1962. Pres., Royal Life Saving Soc., UK, 1969–74 (Chm., East Midlands Region, RLSS, 1968–80). OStJ. *Recreations:* golf and dog walking. *Address:* Lodge Gardens, Walnut Grove, Radcliffe-on-Trent, Nottinghamshire NG12 2AD. *Club:* Royal Air Force.

PECKFORD, Hon. (Alfred) Brian; PC (Can.) 1982; Premier of the Province of Newfoundland and Labrador, 1979–89; *b* Whitbourne, Newfoundland, 27 Aug. 1942; *s* of Ewart Peckford and Allison (*née* Young), St John's; *m* 1st, 1969, Marina Dicks; three *d*; 2nd, 1986, Carol Ellsworth; one *s*. *Educ:* Lewisporte High Sch.; Memorial Univ. of Newfoundland (BAEd). Schoolmaster, 1962–63 and 1966–72. MHA (Progressive C) Green Bay, 1972–89; Special Asst to Premier, 1973; Minister: of Dept of Municipal Affairs and Housing, 1974; of Mines and Energy, 1976, also of Rural Development, 1978. Leader of Progressive Cons. Party, Newfoundland and Labrador, 1979–89. President: Peckford Consulting Ltd (formerly Peckford Inc.), 1989–; Ming Financial Corp., Vancouver. Hon. LLD Meml Univ. of Newfoundland, 1986. *Recreations:* reading, sport, swimming, ski-ing. *Address:* 441 West Crescent Road, Qualicum Beach, British Columbia V9K 1J5, Canada.

PECKHAM, Arthur John; UK Permanent Representative, Food and Agriculture Organisation, Rome, 1977–80; *b* 22 Sept. 1920; *s* of Richard William Peckham and Agnes Mercy (*née* Parker); *m* 1949, Margaret Enid Quirk; two *s* one *d*. *Educ:* The Judd Sch., Tonbridge. RAF (Pilot), 1942–46, 59 Sqdn Coastal Command. Cadet, Min. of Labour and Nat. Service, 1948; Colonial Office: Asst Principal, 1950; Private Sec. to Perm. Under-Sec., 1952; Principal, 1954; Counsellor (Technical Assistance), Lagos, 1964; Asst Sec., Min. of Overseas Develt, 1966; Minister, FAO, Rome, 1977. *Recreation:* gardening. *Address:* 147A Newmarket Road, Norwich NR4 6SY.

PECKHAM, Prof. Catherine Stevenson, CBE 1998; MD, FRCP, FRCOG, FRCPath, FFPHM; Professor of Paediatric Epidemiology, Institute of Child Health, University of London, since 1985; Hon. Consultant, Hospital for Sick Children, Great Ormond Street, since 1985; *b* 7 March 1937; *d* of Alexander King, *qv*; *m* 1958, Sir Michael John Peckham, *qv*; three *s*. *Educ:* St Paul's Girls' Sch.; University Coll., London (MB BS, MD). FFPHM (FFPM 1980); FRCP 1988; FRCPath 1991; FRCOG 1994. Reader in Community Medicine and Head of Dept, Charing Cross Hosp. Med. Sch., 1980–85. Member: Standing Med. Adv. Cttee, DoH, 1992–; Health Adv. Cttee, British Council, 1992–95; Bd, PHLS, 1989–92; Children Nationwide, Scientific Adv. Cttee, 1994–; Chairman: Steering Cttee on Epidemiol Res., Surveillance and Forecasting, WHO Global Prog. on AIDS, 1991–93; Exec. Cttee, British Paediatric Surveillance Unit, 1993–. Member: Fulbright Commn, 1987–95; Bd of Govs, St Paul's Sch., 1992–; UK Women's Forum, 1990–; ASA, 1993–. Founder FMedSci 1998. Harding Award, Action Research, 1993. *Publications:* The Peckham Report: national immunization study, 1989; chapters and papers on infections in pregnancy and early childhood, national cohort studies and epidemiology of common childhood conditions. *Recreation:* flute.

PECKHAM, Sir Michael (John), Kt 1995; FRCP, FRCS, FRCR, FRCPath; Founder, and Director, School of Public Policy, University College London, 1996–2000; *b* 2 Aug. 1935; *s* of William Stuart Peckham and Gladys Mary Peckham; *m* 1958, Catherine Stevenson King (*see* Prof. C. S. Peckham); three *s*. *Educ:* St Catharine's Coll., Cambridge (MA; Hon. Fellow, 1998); University College Hosp. Med. Sch., London (MD). MRC Clin. Res. Schol., Inst. Gustav Roussy, Paris, 1965–67; Institute of Cancer Research, London: Lectr, 1967–71; Sen. Lectr, 1971–74; Prof. of Radiotherapy, 1974–86; Dean, 1984–86; Dir, BPMF, 1986–90; Dir, R&D, DoH, 1991–95. Consultant: Royal Marsden Hosp., 1971–86; to Royal Navy, 1974–86. Mem., MRC, 1991–95; Mem., MRC Cell Biology and Disorders Bd, 1977–81. Member, Special Health Authority: Gt Ormond St Hosp., 1988–90; Brompton Nat. Heart and London Chest Hosps, 1986–90; Hammersmith and Queen Charlotte's Hosps, 1989–90. President: European Soc. of Therapeutic Radiology and Oncology, 1983–85; British Oncological Assoc., 1986–88; Fedn of European Cancer Socs, 1989–91; Mem., British Council Scientific Adv. Cttee, 1988–92. Vice-Chm., Council, ICRF, 1988–91. Chairman: BUPA Foundn, 1996–; Nat. Educn Res. Forum, 1999–; Develt Forum, 2000–. Founder: Bob Champion Cancer Trust, 1983; British Oncological Assoc., 1985; Co-founder, European Soc. of Therapeutic Radiology and Oncology, 1988. Mem., Inst. of Medicine, Nat. Acad. of Scis, Washington, 1995. Trustee: Louise Buchanan Meml Trust, 1973–99; Guy's and St Thomas' Charitable Foundn, 1996–2000. Editor-in-Chief, European Jl of Cancer, 1989–95. Artist; one-man exhibitions: Oxford, 1965; London, 1970, 1976, 1982, 1989, 1992, 1997; Edinburgh, 1989. Fellow: UCL, 1995; UCL Hosps, 1998; Inst. of Cancer Res., 1999. Founder FMedSci 1998. Dr *hc*: Univ. de Franche-Comté at Besançon, 1991; Catholic Univ. of Louvain, 1993; Hon. DSc: Loughborough, 1992; Exeter, 1996. *Publications:* Management of Testicular Tumours, 1981; (jtly) The Biological Basis of Radiotherapy, 1983; (jtly) Primary Management of Early Breast Cancer, 1985; (jt sen. editor) Oxford Textbook of Oncology, 1995; (with M. Marinker) Clinical Futures, 1998; A Model for Health: innovation and the future of health services, 1999. *Address:* 9 Ennismore Mews, SW7 1AP. *Club:* Reform.

PECKOVER, Dr Richard Stuart; Director of Safety and Environment (formerly Corporate Director of Safety), UK Atomic Energy Authority, since 1992; *b* 5 May 1942;

s of Rev. Cecil Raymond Peckover and Grace Lucy (*née* Curtis). *Educ:* King Edward VII Sch., King's Lynn; Wadham Coll., Oxford (MA); Corpus Christi Coll., Cambridge (PhD). FInstP, FIMA, FRMetS, FRAS, FSaRS. United Kingdom Atomic Energy Authority: Res. Scientist, Culham Lab., 1969–81; Res. Associate, MIT, 1973–74; Safety and Reliability Directorate, 1982, Br. Head, 1983–87; Asst Dir, AEE Winfrith, 1987, Dep. Dir, 1989, Sites Dir, 1990. Mem., Amer. Nucl. Soc. *Recreations:* walking, talking, listening to music. *Address:* Winfrith Technology Centre, Dorchester, Dorset DT2 8DH. *T:* (01305) 251101. *Club:* Oxford and Cambridge.

PEDDER, Air Marshal Sir Ian (Maurice), KCB 1982; OBE 1963; DFC 1949; international aviation consultant, since 1992; *b* 2 May 1926; *s* of Maurice and Elsie Pedder; *m* 1949, Jean Mary (*née* Kellett); one *s* two *d*. *Educ:* Royal Grammar Sch., High Wycombe; Queen's Coll., Oxford. Service in Nos 28, 60, 81, 213 Sqdns, CFS, and with Burma Air Force, 1946–59; Staff Coll., Andover, and MoD, 1959–62; Far East, 1962–64; Staff appts, 1965–70; RCDS, 1971; Comdg RAF Chivenor, 1972–74; Nat. Air Traffic Services, 1974–84, Dep. Controller, 1977–81, Controller and Mem. CAA, 1981–84. Dep. Chm., 1986–89, Chm., 1989–90, Dan-Air Services; Dir, Davies & Newman plc, 1989–92. *Publications:* contribs to Service and aviation jls, UK, US and EU. *Recreations:* study of Victorian times, photography, riding (a bicycle). *Address:* The Chestnuts, Cheddar, Somerset. *Clubs:* Royal Air Force, Victory Services.

PEDDIE, Hon. Ian James Crofton; QC 1992; a Recorder, since 1997; *b* 17 Dec. 1945; *s* of Baron Peddie, MBE, JP, LLD and Hilda Mary Alice (*née* Bull), (Lady Peddie); *m* 1976, Susan Renée Howes; two *s* two *d*. *Educ:* Gordonstoun Sch.; University Coll. London (LLB Hons). Called to the Bar, Inner Temple, 1971; Asst Recorder, 1992–97. *Recreations:* family life, classic cars. *Address:* One Garden Court, Temple, EC4Y 9BJ. *T:* (020) 7797 7900, *Fax:* (020) 7797 7929.

PEDDIE, Peter Charles, CBE 1983; Adviser to the Governor, and Head of Legal Unit, Bank of England, 1992–96; *b* 20 March 1932; *s* of Ronald Peddie and Vera Peddie (*née* Nicklin); *m* 1960, Charlotte Elizabeth Ryan; two *s* two *d*. *Educ:* Canford Sch., Wimborne; St John's Coll., Cambridge (BA 1954; MA 1977). Admitted Solicitor, 1957; Freshfields: articled, 1954–57; Asst Solicitor, 1957–60; Partner, 1960–92; Consultant, 1992. Mem., Standing Cttee on Company Law, Law Soc., 1972–92. Mem. Council, Middlesex Hosp. Med. Sch., 1977–88; Special Trustee, Middlesex Hosp., 1977–92. Gov., Canford Sch., 1981–94. Hon. QC 1997. *Recreations:* gardening, foreign travel. *Address:* Bannisters Farmhouse, Mattingley Green, Hook, Hants RG27 8LA. *T:* (0118) 932 6570. *Clubs:* Athenæum, City of London.

PEDELTY, Mervyn Kay, FCA, FCIB; Chief Executive, Co-operative Bank, since 1997; *b* 16 Jan. 1949; *s* of late William Hopper Pedelty and of Muriel Pedelty; *m* 1st, 1983, Carol (decd); 2nd, 1998, Jill Wesson (*née* Hughes); one *s*, and one step *d*. *Educ:* Felixstowe GS; AMP, Harvard Business Sch. ACA 1971, FCA 1976. Scrutton, Goodchild & Sanderson, 1966–71; Whinney Murray & Co., 1971–73; British Leyland Ltd, 1973–76; Divl Finance Dir, 1976–80, Divl Man. Dir, 1980, Plantation Hldgs, then Phicom plc; Divl Man. Dir, Gould Inc., 1981–83; Finance Dir and Asst Man. Dir, Abacus Electronics Hldgs plc, 1983–87; Finance Dir, TSB Banking and Insurance, 1987–92; Chief Exec., Commercial Ops, TSB Gp plc, 1992–95; Partner, LEK Consulting, 1995–97. Dir and Dep. Chm., Unity Trust Bank plc, 1997–; Exec. Cttee, Co-operative Gp (CWS) Ltd, 1997–; Dir, Co-operative Insurance Soc. Ltd, 1990–. Mem., The Co-operative Commn, 2000–. Chairman: Sustainability NW, 1998–; Manchester Investment and Development Agency Service, 1999–; Director: NW Business Leadership Team, 1997–; Manchester Enterprises Ltd, 2000–. Vice-Pres., Community Foundn for Gtr Manchester, 2000–. Trustee: Triumph over Phobia, 1995–; Symphony Hall, Birmingham, 1996–. FCIB 1992; FRSA 1997. *Recreations:* charity and community work, the countryside and the environment, music, art, ski-ing. *Address:* The Co-operative Bank plc, 1 Balloon Street, Manchester M60 4EP. *T:* (0161) 832 3456. *Club:* Royal Automobile.

PEDERSEN, Prof. (Knud) George, OC 1993; OOnt 1994; PhD; FCCT; FRSA; Professor, The University of Western Ontario, 1985–96 (President and Vice-Chancellor, 1985–94); Chancellor, University of Northern British Columbia, since 1998; *b* 13 June 1931; *s* of Hjalmar Nielsen Pedersen and Anna Marie (*née* Jensen); *m* 1st, 1953, Joan Elaine Vanderwarker (*d* 1988); one *s* one *d*; 2nd, 1988, Penny Ann Jones. *Educ:* Vancouver Normal Sch. (Dip. in Teaching 1952); Univ. of BC (BA History and Geography, 1959); Univ. of Washington (MA 1964); Univ. of Chicago (PhD 1969). FCCT 1977; FRSA 1983. Schools in North Vancouver: Teacher, Highlands Elem. Sch., 1952–56; Vice-Principal, North Star Elem. Sch., 1956–59; Principal, Carisbrooke Elem. Sch., 1959–61; Vice-Principal, Handsworth Sec. Sch., 1961–63; Principal, Balmoral Sec. Sch., 1963–65; Univ. of Chicago: Teaching Intern, 1966; Staff Associate, Midwest Admin Center, 1965–66, Res. Associate (Asst Prof.), 1966–68; Asst Prof., Ontario Inst. for Studies in Educn and Univ. of Toronto, 1968–70; Asst Prof. and Associate Dir, Midwest Admin Center, Div. of Social Sciences, Univ. of Chicago, 1970–72; Faculty of Educn, Univ. of Victoria: Associate Prof., 1972–75; Dean, 1972–75; Vice-Pres. (Academic), and Prof., Univ. of Victoria, 1975–79; Pres. and Prof., Simon Fraser Univ., 1979–83; Pres. and Prof., Univ. of British Columbia, 1983–85; Interim Pres., Univ. of Northern BC, 1995; Pres., Royal Roads Univ., 1995–96. Universities Council of British Columbia: Mem., Prog. Co-ordinating Cttee, 1975–78; Mem., Business Affairs Cttee, 1975–78; Mem., Long-range Planning Cttee, 1979–85. Chm., Adv. Cttee on Educnl Planning, Min. of Educn (Prov. of BC), 1977–78; Member: Jt Bd of Teacher Educn, Prov. of BC, 1972–75; Planning Cttee, Canadian Teachers' Fedn, 1974; Planning Cttee, 1973–74, and Bd of Dirs, 1974–75 and 1979–80, BC Council for Leadership in Educn; Interior Univ. Progs Bd, Min. of Educn, 1977–78. Member, Board of Directors: Assoc. of Univs and Colls of Canada, 1979–84 (Mem., Adv. Cttee, Office of Internat. Develt, 1979–83); Public Employers' Council of BC, 1979–84; Vancouver Bd of Trade, 1983–85; Pulp and Paper Res. Inst. of Canada, 1983–85; President: N Vancouver Teachers' Assoc., 1962–63; N Vancouver Principals' and Vice-Principals' Assoc., 1963–64; Vice-Pres., Inter-American Orgn for Higher Educn, 1992– (Mem. Bd of Dirs, 1979–85); Sec.-Treasurer, Canadian Assoc. of Deans and Directors of Educn, 1972–73 and 1973–74. Mem., Bd of Dirs, Corporate and Higher Educn Forum, 1988–94. Member: BoT, Vancouver, 1983–85; Nat. Council, Canadian Human Rights Foundn, 1984–. Mem., Bd of Dirs, MacMillan Bloedel Ltd, 1984–86. Member, Board of Governors: Arts, Sciences and Technol. Centre, 1980–85; Leon and Thea Koerner Foundn, 1981–85; Mem., Bd of Trustees, Discovery Foundn, 1980–85; Pres., Bill Reid Foundn, 2000–. Consultant, Salzburg Seminar, Austria, 1999–2000. Hon. LLD McMaster, 1996. Confedn of Canada 125th Anniversary Medal, 1992. *Publications:* The Itinerant Schoolmaster: a socio-economic analysis of teacher turnover, 1973; chapters in books on educn; articles in Administrator's Notebook (Univ. of Chicago), selected articles for Elem. Sch. Principals, Res. in Educn, Educn and Urban Soc., Educn Canada, Teacher Educn, Resources in Educn, Elem. Sch. Jl, Jl of Educnl Admin, and Canadian Jl of Univ. Continuing Educn; book reviews; proc. of confs and symposia; governmental and institutional studies and reports. *Address:* 2232 Spruce Street, Vancouver, BC V6H 2P3, Canada. *T:* (604) 7332400. *Clubs:* Blaine (Washington); Semiahmoo Golf and Country.

PEDLEY, Alan Sydney, DFC 1946; Lord Mayor of Leeds, 1975–1976; District Insurance Manager, 1974–82, retired; *b* 16 Aug. 1917; *s* of Herbert Leonard Pedley and Edith Mary (*née* Skipsey); *m* 1st, 1949, Evelyn Anderson (*née* Scott) (*d* 1977); 2nd, 1981, Shirley Elizabeth (*d* 1995), *widow* of Reg Howard. *Educ:* Leeds Modern Sch. Entered Insurance, 1934; retd (Commercial Union), 1971; joined Barclays Insurance Services Co. Ltd, 1971. Member: Leeds City Council, 1951–81; W Yorkshire Metropolitan CC, 1973–81; Dep. Lord Mayor, 1971–72. Hon. Alderman, City of Leeds, 1993. FCII 1949. *Recreations:* cricket, Association football, Rugby League, music, theatre, the Arts, after dinner speaking. *Address:* Whitelea, 8 Bentcliffe Close, Leeds LS17 6QT. *T:* (0113) 268 5424.

PEDLEY, Rt Rev. (Geoffrey) Stephen; *see* Lancaster, Bishop Suffragan of.

PEDLEY, Prof. Timothy John, PhD, ScD; FRS 1995; G. I. Taylor Professor of Fluid Mechanics, since 1996, and Head of Department of Applied Mathematics and Theoretical Physics, since 2000, University of Cambridge; Fellow of Gonville and Caius College, Cambridge, 1973–89 and since 1996; *b* 23 March 1942; *s* of Richard Rodman Pedley and Jean Mary Mudie Pedley (*née* Evans); *m* 1965, Avril Jennifer Martin Uden; two *s*. *Educ:* Rugby Sch.; Trinity Coll., Cambridge (BA 1963; MA, PhD 1967; ScD 1982). Post-doctoral Fellow, Johns Hopkins Univ., 1966–68; Res. Associate, then Lectr, Physiol. Flow Studies Unit and Dept of Maths, Imperial Coll. London, 1968–73; Department of Applied Mathematics and Theoretical Physics, University of Cambridge: Asst Dir of Res., 1973–77; Lectr, 1977–89; Reader in Biolog. Fluid Dynamics, 1989; Prof. of Applied Maths, Univ. of Leeds, 1990–96. EPSRC Sen. Res. Fellow, 1995–2000. Foreign Associate, US NAE, 1999. *Publications:* (ed) Scale Effects in Animal Locomotion, 1977; (jtly) The Mechanics of the Circulation, 1978; The Fluid Mechanics of Large Blood Vessels, 1980; (ed with C. P. Ellington) Biological Fluid Dynamics, 1995; numerous articles in fluid mechanics and biomechanics jls. *Recreations:* bird-watching, running, reading. *Address:* Oakhurst Farm, 375 Shadwell Lane, Leeds LS17 8AH; Department of Applied Mathematics and Theoretical Physics, Silver Street, Cambridge CB3 9EW. *T:* (01223) 339842.

PEEBLES, Prof. Phillip James Edwin, FRS 1982; Professor of Physics, since 1965, and Albert Einstein Professor of Science, since 1984, Princeton University; *b* Winnipeg, 25 April 1935; *s* of Andrew Charles Peebles and Ada Marian (*née* Green); *m* 1958, Jean Alison Peebles; three *d*. *Educ:* Univ. of Manitoba (BSc 1958); Princeton Univ. (Ma 1959; PhD 1962). Member: Amer. Phys. Soc.; Amer. Astron. Soc.; AAAS; Internat. Astron. Union; Fellow: Amer. Physical Soc.; Amer. Acad. of Arts and Scis; Royal Soc. of Canada. Hon. DSc: Univ. of Toronto, 1986; Univ. of Chicago, 1986; McMaster Univ., 1989; Univ. of Manitoba, 1989. *Publications:* Physical Cosmology, 1971; The Large Scale Structure of the Universe, 1979; (ed jtly) Objects of High Redshift, 1980; Quantum Mechanics, 1992; Principles of Physical Cosmology, 1993. *Address:* 24 Markham Road, Princeton, NJ 08540, USA; Joseph Henry Laboratory, Princeton University, Princeton, NJ 08544, USA.

PEEK, Vice-Adm. Sir Richard (Innes), KBE 1972 (OBE 1944); CB 1971; DSC 1945; *b* 30 July 1914; 2nd *s* of late James Norman and Kate Ethel Peek; *m* 1943, Margaret Seinor (*née* Kendall) (*d* 1946); one *s*; *m* 1952, Mary Catherine Tilley (*née* Stops); two *d*. *Educ:* Royal Australian Naval College. Joined RAN, 1928; served War of 1939–45 in HMS Revenge, HMAS Cerberus, Hobart, Australia, Navy Office; Korean War Service in HMAS Tobruk, 1951; Flag Officer Comdg HMA Fleet, 1967–68; Chief of Naval Staff, Australia, 1970–73. Legion of Merit (US), 1951. *Recreations:* gardening, golf. *Address:* 10 Galway Place, Deakin, ACT 2600, Australia. *Clubs:* Royal Automobile (Sydney); Royal Commonwealth Society (Canberra).

PEEK, Sir William Grenville, 5th Bt *cr* 1874, of Rousden, Devon; *b* 15 Dec. 1919; *s* of Captain Roger Grenville Peek, 9th Lancers (*d* 1921) and Hon. Joan Penelope Sclater-Booth (*d* 1976), *d* of 2nd Baron Basing; *S* cousin, 1996; *m* 1950, Lucy Jane, *d* of Maj. Edward Dorrien-Smith, DSO; one *s* three *d*. *Educ:* Eton. Served War 1939–45 (despatches). Captain late 9th Lancers. *Heir:* *s* Richard Grenville Peek, *b* 3 Feb. 1955.

PEEL, family name of **Earl Peel**.

PEEL, 3rd Earl *cr* 1929; **William James Robert Peel,** Bt 1800; Viscount Peel, 1895; Viscount Clanfield, 1929; DL; Lord Warden of the Stannaries, Duchy of Cornwall, since 1994; *b* 3 Oct. 1947; *s* of 2nd Earl Peel and Kathleen (*d* 1972), *d* of Michael McGrath; *S* father, 1969; *m* 1st, 1973, Veronica Naomi Livingston (marr. diss. 1987), *d* of Alastair Timpson; one *s* one *d*; 2nd, 1989, Hon. Mrs Charlotte Hambro, *yr d* of Baron Soames, PC, GCMG, GCVO, CH, CBE and of Lady Soames, *qv*; one *d*. *Educ:* Ampleforth; University of Tours; Cirencester Agric. Coll. Mem., Nature Conservancy Council for England, then English Nature, 1991–96; Chm., 1994–2000, Pres., 2000–, Game Conservancy Trust. Mem., Prince's Council, Duchy of Cornwall, 1993–. President: Yorks Wildlife Trust, 1989–96; Gun Trade Assoc., 1993–99. Elected Mem., H of L, 1999–. DL N Yorks, 1998. *Heir:* *s* Viscount Clanfield, *qv*. *Address:* Eelmire, Masham, Ripon, N Yorks HG4 4PF.

PEEL, Catherine Anne; *see* Mackintosh, C. A.

PEEL, David Alexander Robert; Reference Secretary, Competition (formerly Monopolies and Mergers) Commission, since 1996; *b* 12 Nov. 1940; *s* of late Maj. Robert Edmund Peel and Sheila Mary (*née* Slattery); *m* 1971, Patricia Muriel Essery; two *s*. *Educ:* St Edmund's Coll., Ware; University Coll., Oxford. Building labourer, New Scotland Yard develt, 1963; joined MoT, 1964; Private Sec. to Minister of State, 1967; Principal, 1968; DoE, 1970; First Sec., UK Perm. Repn to EC, Brussels, 1972; Private Sec. to Minister for Transport, 1975; Asst Sec., Depts of Transport and the Environment, 1976–90: Nat. Roads Prog. and Highway Policy, 1982; Okehampton Bypass (Confirmation of Orders) Act, 1985; Interdeptl Review on Using Private Enterprise in Govt, 1986; Office Services, 1987–90; Under Sec., Dir of Admin Resources, DoE, 1990–96. *Recreations:* allotment gardening, ballet, baroque architecture.

PEEL, Sir John; *see* Peel, Sir W. J.

PEEL, John; *see* Ravenscroft, J. R. P.

PEEL, Prof. John David Yeadon, FBA 1991; Professor of Anthropology and Sociology, with reference to Africa, School of Oriental and African Studies, University of London, since 1989; *b* 13 Nov. 1941; *e s* of late Prof. Edwin Arthur Peel and Nora Kathleen Yeadon; *m* 1969, Jennifer Christine Ferial (marr. diss. 2000), *d* of K. N. Pare, Leicester; three *s*. *Educ:* King Edward's Sch., Birmingham; Balliol Coll., Oxford (Scholar; BA 1963, MA 1966); LSE (PhD 1966); DLit London 1985. Asst Lectr, then Lectr in Sociology, Nottingham Univ., 1965–70; Lectr in Sociology, LSE, 1970–73; Charles Booth Prof. of Sociology, 1975–89, Dean, Faculty of Social and Envmtl Studies, 1985–88, Univ. of Liverpool; Dean of Undergraduate Studies, SOAS, 1990–94. Vis. Reader in Sociology and Anthropology, Univ of Ife, Nigeria, 1973–75; Vis. Prof. in Anthropology and Sociology, Univ. of Chicago, 1982–83; Marett Lectr, 1993, Associate, Inst. of Develt Studies, 1973–94. Pres., African Studies Assoc. of UK, 1996–98; Vice-Pres., British Acad.,

1999–2000. Editor, Africa, and Officer, Internat African Inst., 1979–86; Gen. Editor, Internat. African Library, 1986–. Frazer Lectr, 2000, Univ. of Oxford. Amaury Talbot Prize for African Anthropology, 1983; Herskovits Award, African Studies Assoc., USA, 1984. *Publications:* Aladura: a religious movement among the Yoruba, 1968; Herbert Spencer: the evolution of a sociologist, 1971; (ed) Herbert Spencer on Social Evolution, 1972; Ijeshas and Nigerians, 1983; Religious Encounter and the Making of the Yoruba, 2000; articles in anthropological, sociological and Africanist jls. *Recreations:* gardening, fell-walking, old churches. *Address:* 80 Archway Road, N19 3TT. *T:* (020) 7272 9487.

PEEL, Sir John (Harold), KCVO 1960; MA, BM, BCh; FRCP 1971; FRCS 1933; FRCOG 1944; Surgeon-Gynæcologist to the Queen, 1961–73; Consulting Obstetric and Gynæcological Surgeon, King's College Hospital, since 1969; Emeritus Consulting Gynæcologist, Princess Beatrice Hospital, since 1965; *b* 10 December 1904; *s* of Rev. J. E. Peel; *m* 1st, 1936, Muriel Elaine Pellow; one *d*; 2nd, 1947, Freda Margaret Mellish (*d* 1993); 3rd, 1995, Sally Barton. *Educ:* Manchester Grammar Sch.; Queen's Coll., Oxford. MA, BM, BCh Oxon 1932. King's College Hospital Med. Sch., qualified 1930; MRCS, LRCP. Obstetric and Gynæcological Surgeon: King's Coll. Hosp., 1936–69; Princess Beatrice Hosp., 1937–65; Queen Victoria Hosp., East Grinstead, 1941–69; Surgeon EMS, 1939–45. Director of Clinical Studies, King's College Hospital Medical School, 1948–67. Mem., Economic and Social Cttee, EEC, 1973–78. Litchfield Lecturer, Oxford University, 1961 and 1969; Sir Kadar Nath Das Lecturer, Bengal O and G Soc., 1962; Sir A. Mudaliar Lecturer, Madras Univ., 1962; Vis. Prof., Cape Town Univ., 1963; Travelling Prof., S African Council, RCOG, 1968. Past Examiner, Universities of Oxford, Cambridge, London, Liverpool, Bristol, Glasgow, Newcastle, Nat. Univ. of Ireland, Birmingham, Dundee, Sheffield, Conjoint Board, RCOG and CMB. Nuffield visitor to Colonies, 1950 and 1953. President, RCOG, 1966–69 (Hon. Treasurer, 1959–66, Councillor, 1955–); President: Internat. Fedn of Obstetrics and Gynæcology, 1970–73; Chelsea Clinical Society, 1960; BMA 1970 (Chm., Bd of Science and Educn, 1972–76); Family Planning Assoc., 1971–74; Chm., DHSS Cttees of Enquiry: Domiciliary Midwifery and Bed Needs, 1971; The Use of Fetus and Fetal Material for Research, 1972. FKC 1980; Hon. Fellow: American Association of Obstetricians and Gynæcologists, 1962 (Joseph Price Oration, 1961); Edinburgh Obstetrical Soc., 1971; RSM, 1973; Hon. Member: Canadian Assoc. of O and G, 1955; Italian Assoc O and G, 1960; Hon. Treas., GMC, 1972–75; Hon. FRCS (Canada), 1967; Hon. FCOG (SA), 1968; Hon. MMSA 1970; Hon. FACS 1970; Hon. FACOG 1971; Hon. Fellow, American Gynæcological Soc., 1974. Hon. DSc Birmingham, 1972; Hon. DM Southampton, 1974; Hon. DCh Newcastle, 1980. *Publications:* Textbook of Gynæcology, 1943; Lives of the Fellows of Royal College of Obstetricians and Gynaecologists 1929–69, 1976; Biography of William Blain-Bell, 1986; numerous contributions to Medical Journals. *Recreations:* fishing, gardening. *Address:* 11 Harnwood Road, Harnham, Salisbury SP2 8DD. *T:* (01722) 334892. *Club:* Naval and Military.

PEEL, Jonathan Sidney, CBE 1994; MC 1957; Vice Lord-Lieutenant of Norfolk, since 1981; Director, Norwich Union Insurance Group, 1973–98; *b* 21 June 1937; *s* of Major D. A. Peel (killed in action 1944) and Hon. Mrs David Peel (*née* Vanneck); *m* 1965, Jean Fulton Barnett, *d* of Air Chief Marshal Sir Denis Barnett, GCB, CBE, DFC; one *s* four *d*. *Educ:* Norwich Sch.; Eton; St John's Coll., Cambridge (BA Land Economy; MA 1970). Commnd, Rifle Bde, Royal Green Jackets, 1956; served Malaya, 1956–57; UN forces, Congo (Zaire), 1960–61; Cyprus, 1962–63; resigned, 1966. Chm., Pleasureworld plc, 1986–89. Vice Pres., Norfolk Naturalists Trust, 1984–; National Trust: Mem. Exec. Cttee, 1982–; Mem. Council, 1984–; Dep. Chm., 1992–; Chm., Cttee for East Anglia, 1981–90; Chm., Properties Cttee, 1990–2000. Norfolk Scouts Association: Dist Comr, 1971–75; Comr for Norwich, 1975–77; County Comr, 1977–81. Chairman: E Anglian Br., Royal Forestry Soc., 1979–81; Norfolk Police Authority, 1983–89; Norfolk Churches Trust, 1983–85; The Broads Authority, 1985–97; Norwich Sch., 1985–; How Hill Trust, 1987–; Pres., Norfolk Assoc. for the Advancement of Music, 1978–93. Mem., Norfolk CC, 1973–97 (Chm., Planning and Transportation Cttee, 1990–93). JP North Walsham, 1973–86. High Sheriff, Norfolk, 1984. Ordained deacon, C of E, 2000. *Publication:* (with M. J. Sayer) Towards a Rural Policy for Norfolk, 1973. *Recreations:* forestry, music. *Address:* Barton Hall, Barton Turf, Norwich NR12 8AU. *T:* (01692) 536250. *Clubs:* Boodle's; Norfolk (Norwich).

PEEL, Robert Edmund Guy, FHCIMA; Chairman, Peel Hotels plc, since 1998; *b* 13 March 1947; *s* of John and Joanna Peel. *Educ:* Eton Coll. FHCIMA 1985. Various hotel appts, Europe, 1964–66; Queen Anne's Hotels & Properties, then Trust Houses Ltd, later Trust House Forte plc, 1966–76; Dir, 1976–98, Chief Exec., 1977–97, Mount Charlotte Investments, later Thistle Hotels plc. Director: Brierley Investments Ltd, 1992–96; Ivory & Sime Discovery Trust; Peel Hunt & Co. (Stockbrokers). Dir, London Tourist Bd, 1994–98. *Recreations:* deep sea fishing, marine biology, tennis, gardening. *Address:* (office) 19 Warwick Avenue, Maida Vale, W9 2PS. *Club:* White's.

PEEL, Sir (William) John, Kt 1973; *b* 16 June 1912; *s* of late Sir William Peel, KCMG, KBE, and Violet Mary Drake, *er d* of W. D. Laing; *m* 1936, Rosemary Mia Minka, *er d* of Robert Readhead; one *s* three *d*. *Educ:* Wellington College; Queens' College, Cambridge. Colonial Administrative Service, 1933–51; on active service, 1941–45; British Resident, Brunei, 1946–48; Res. Comr, Gilbert and Ellice Is Colony, 1949–51. Personal Asst to Man. Dirs of Rugby Portland Cement Co. Ltd, 1952–54. Contested (C) Meriden Division of Warwickshire, 1955; MP (C) Leicester SE, 1957–Feb. 1974; Parliamentary Private Secretary: to Economic Secretary to the Treasury, 1958–59; to Minister of State, Board of Trade, 1959–60; Asst Govt Whip (unpaid), 1960–61; a Lord Comr of the Treasury, Nov. 1961–Oct. 1964. Parly Delegate to: Assemblies of Council of Europe, 1961–74; WEU 1961–74 (Vice-Pres., 1967, Pres. 1972, Chm., Defence and Armaments Cttee, 1970–72, WEU); N Atlantic Assembly, 1959–74 (Leader, 1970–74; Pres., N Atlantic Assembly, Nov. 1972); Mem., British Delegn to European Parlt, Strasbourg, 1973–74; Hon. Dir, Cons. Party Internat. Office, 1975–76. Member Council: Victoria League for Commonwealth Friendship, 1974–83 (Dep. Chm., 1976–81; Chm., 1982–83; Dep. Pres. and Mem., Chairman's Adv. Cttee, 1983–); British Atlantic Cttee; Mem. Central Council, Royal Over-Seas League, 1980–86; Chairman: Hospitality and Branches Cttee of Victoria League, 1974–78, Hospitality Cttee, 1978–81; Overseas Students Adv. Cttee, 1980–81; Jt Standing Cttee of Victoria League and Royal Commonwealth Soc., 1975–83; Westminster for Europe Branch, European Movement, 1974–77. Mem. Ct of Assistants, Framework Knitters' Co. (Master, 1983). Dato Seri Laila Jasa Brunei 1969; Dato Setia Negara Brunei 1971. *Recreations:* varied. *Address:* 51 Cambridge Street, SW1V 4PR. *T:* (020) 7834 8762. *Clubs:* Carlton, Hurlingham; Hawks (Cambridge).

PEERS, Most Rev. Michael Geoffrey; Primate of the Anglican Church of Canada, since 1986; *b* 31 July 1934; *s* of Geoffrey Hugh Peers and Dorothy Enid Mantle; *m* 1963, Dorothy Elizabeth Bradley; two *s* one *d*. *Educ:* University of British Columbia (BA Hons); Universität Heidelberg (Zert. Dolm.-Interpreter's Certificate); Trinity Coll., Toronto (LTh). Deacon 1959, priest 1960; Curate: St Thomas', Ottawa, 1959–61; Trinity, Ottawa, 1961–65; University Chaplain, Diocese of Ottawa, 1961–66; Rector: St Bede's, Winnipeg, 1966–72; St Martin's, Winnipeg, with St Paul's Middlechurch, 1972–74; Archdeacon of Winnipeg, 1969–74; Rector, St Paul's Cathedral, Regina, 1974–77; Dean of Qu'Appelle, 1974–77; Bishop of Qu'Appelle, 1977–82; Archbishop of Qu'Appelle and Metropolitan of Rupert's Land, 1982–86. Hon. DD: Trinity Coll., Toronto, 1977; St John's Coll., Winnipeg, 1981; Wycliffe Coll., Toronto, 1987; Univ. of Kent, 1988; Montreal Dio. Coll., 1989; Coll. of Emmanuel and St Chad, Saskatoon, 1990; Vancouver Sch. of Theol., 1991; Thorneloe Univ., 1991; Bishop's Univ., Lennoxville, 1993. *Address:* 600 Jarvis Street, Toronto, ON M4Y 2J6, Canada. *T:* (416) 9249192.

PEET, Ronald Hugh, CBE 1974; Chief Executive, Legal & General Group plc, 1980–84; *b* 12 July 1925; *s* of Henry Leonard and Stella Peet; *m* 1st, 1949, Winifred Joy Adamson (*d* 1979); two *s* two *d*; 2nd, 1981, Lynette Judy Burgess Kinsella. *Educ:* Doncaster Grammar Sch.; Queen's Coll., Oxford (MA). Served in HM Forces, Captain RA, 1944–47. Legal and General Assurance Society Limited: joined 1952; emigrated to Australia, 1955; Sec., Australian Branch, 1955–59; Asst Life Manager, 1959–65; Manager and Actuary for Australia, 1965–69; returned to UK as General Manager (Ops), 1969; Dir, 1969–84; Chief Exec., 1972–84; Chm., 1980–84. Chairman: Aviation & General Insurance Co. Ltd, 1978–80; Stockley Plc, 1984–87; PWS Holdings plc, 1987–88; Director: AMEC Plc, 1984–96; Howard Gp plc, 1985–86; Independent Insurance Group plc, 1988–99. Director: City Arts Trust Ltd, 1976–90 (Chm., 1980–87); Royal Philharmonic Orchestra Ltd, 1977–88; English National Opera, 1978–84, 1985–95. Chm., British Insurance Assoc., 1978–79. FIA. *Recreations:* music, opera. *Address:* 9 Marlowe Court, Petyward, SW3 3PD. *Clubs:* Hurlingham, City of London.

PEGDEN, Jeffrey Vincent; QC 1996; a Recorder, since 1996; *b* 24 June 1950; *s* of George Vincent Pegden and Stella Blanche Katherine Pegden; *m* 1981, Delia Mary Coonan; one *s* one *d*. *Educ:* Univ. of Hull (LLB Hons 1972). Called to the Bar, Inner Temple, 1973. *Recreations:* reading, music, walking. *Address:* 3 Temple Gardens, Temple, EC4Y 9AU. *T:* (020) 7353 3102.

PEGG, Michael Anstice, PhD; University Librarian and Director, John Rylands University Library, University of Manchester, 1981–90; *b* 3 Sept. 1931; *s* of Benjamin and Rose Pegg; *m* 1st, 1955, Jean Williams; three *s*; 2nd, 1986, Margaret Rae. *Educ:* Burton-on-Trent Grammar Sch.; Univ. of Southampton. BA (London); PhD (Southampton); MA (Manchester) 1985. Captain, Royal Army Education Corps, Educn Officer, SHAPE, Paris, 1958–61; Asst Keeper, Nat. Library of Scotland, Edinburgh, 1961–67; Sec. and Estabt Officer, Nat. Library of Scotland, Edinburgh, 1967–76; Librarian, Univ. of Birmingham, 1976–80. Vis Fellow, Beinecke Library, Yale Univ., 1989. Member: British Library Bd, 1981–84; Standing Conference of Nat. and Univ. Libraries' Council, 1981–83. *Publications:* Les Divers Rapports d'Eustorg de Beaulieu (édn critique), 1964 (Geneva); Catalogue of German Reformation Pamphlets in Libraries of Great Britain and Ireland, 1973 (Baden Baden); Catalogue of Sixteenth-century German Pamphlets in Collections in France and England, 1977 (Baden Baden); Catalogue of Reformation Pamphlets in Swiss Libraries, 1983; Catalogue of Sixteenth-century German and Dutch books in the Royal Library Copenhagen, 1989; Catalogue of German Reformation Pamphlets in Swedish Libraries, 1994; Catalogue of German Reformation pamphlets in libraries of Belgium and the Netherlands, 1999; Catalogue of German Reformation Pamphlets in Libraries of Alsace, Pt 1: Colmar, 2000; occasional papers to learned jls. *Recreations:* travel, reading, railways. *Address:* c/o John Rylands University Library, University of Manchester, Oxford Road, Manchester M13 9PP.

PEGGIE, Robert Galloway Emslie, CBE 1986; Commissioner for Local Administration (Ombudsman) in Scotland, 1986–94; Chairman, Scottish Local Government Staff Commission, 1994–97; *b* 5 Jan. 1929; *s* of John and Euphemia Peggie; *m* 1955, Christine Jeanette Simpson (*d* 2000); one *s* one *d*; *m* 2001, Janice Helen Renton. *Educ:* Lasswade High Sch. Certified accountant; Accountancy apprenticeship, 1946–52; Accountant in industry, 1952–57; Public Service, Edinburgh City, 1957–74; Chief Exec., Lothian Regl Council, 1974–86. Trustee, Lloyds TSB Foundn, 1995–98. Mem., Gen. Convocation and Court, Heriot-Watt Univ., 1988–97 (Convener, Finance Cttee, 1989–97); Governor, Edinburgh Coll. of Art, 1989–99 (Vice-Chm., 1995–97; Chm., 1998–99). DUniv Heriot-Watt, 1998. *Recreation:* golf. *Address:* 9A Napier Road, Edinburgh EH10 5AZ. *T:* (0131) 229 6775. *Club:* New (Edinburgh).

PEI, Ieoh Ming, FAIA, RIBA; architect; Founding Partner, Pei Cobb Freed & Partners (formerly I. M. Pei & Partners), Architects, New York, 1955–96; *b* Canton, China, 26 April 1917; naturalized citizen of USA, 1954; *m* 1942, Eileen Loo; three *s* one *d*. *Educ:* St John's Middle Sch., Shanghai; MIT (BArch 1940); Harvard Grad. Sch. of Design (MArch 1946). FAIA 1964. Nat. Defense Res. Cttee, 1943–45; Asst Prof., Harvard Grad. Sch. of Design, 1945–48; Dir Architecture, Webb & Knapp Inc., 1948–55; Wheelwright Travelling Fellow, Harvard, 1951. Designed Nat. Center for Atmospheric Res., Boulder, Colo, 1961–67; other projects include: John F. Kennedy Library, Boston, 1965–79; E Building, Nat. Gall. of Art, Washington, 1968–78; Morton H. Myerson Symphony Center, Dallas, 1982–89; Four Seasons Hotel, NY, 1989–93; Rock and Roll Hall of Fame and Mus., Cleveland, 1990–95; also church, hosp., municipal and corporate bldgs, schs, libraries and museums in US; numerous projects worldwide include: Fragrant Hill Hotel, Beijing, 1979–82; Bank of China, Hong Kong, 1982–89; expansion and renovation, The Louvre, Paris, 1983–93. Member: Nat. Council on Humanities, 1966–70; Urban Design Council, NYC, 1967–72; AIA Nat. Urban Policy Task Force, 1970–74; Nat. Council on Arts, 1981–84. Member: Nat. Acad. Design, 1965; Amer. Acad. Arts and Scis, 1967; AAIL, 1975 (Chancellor, 1978–80); Institut de France, 1983. Hon. Degrees include: Pennsylvania, Columbia, NY, Brown, Colorado, Chinese Univ. of Hong Kong, Amer. Univ. of Paris. Numerous awards including: Arnold Brunner Award, Nat. Inst. Arts and Letters, 1961; Medal of Honour, NY Chapter, AIA, 1963; Thomas Jefferson Meml Medal for Architecture, 1976; Gold Medal, AAAL, 1979; Gold Medal, AIA, 1979; La Grande Médaille d'Or L'Académie d'Architecture, France, 1981; Architectural Firm Award, AIA, 1968; Praemium Imperiale, US, 1989; Ambassador for the Arts Award, 1994; Gold Medal, Architectural Soc. of China, Beijing, 1994; Jerusalem Prize for Arts and Letters, 1994; Jacqueline Kennedy Onassis Medal, Municipal Arts Soc., NY, 1996. Medal of Liberty, US, 1986; Officier de La Légion d'Honneur, 1993; US Medal of Freedom, 1993. *Address:* (office) 600 Madison Avenue, New York, NY 10022, USA. *T:* (212) 7513122.

PEIRCE, Rev. Canon (John) Martin; Canon Residentiary of Christ Church, Oxford, 1987–2001, now Canon Emeritus, and Oxford Diocesan Director of Ordinands, 1985–2001; *b* 9 July 1936; *s* of Martin Westley and Winifred Mary Peirce; *m* 1968, Rosemary Susan Milne; two *s*. *Educ:* Brentwood Sch.; Jesus Coll., Cambridge (MA); Westcott House, Cambridge. Served Royal Air Force, 1954–56. Teacher, St Stephen's Coll., Hong Kong, 1960–64; Curate, St John Baptist, Croydon, 1966–70; Team Vicar, St Columba, Fareham, 1970–76; Team Rector, Langley, Slough, 1976–85. *Recreations:* walking, gardening. *Address:* 8 Burwell Meadow, Witney, Oxon OX28 5JQ. *T:* (01993) 200103.

PEIRCE, Robert Nigel; HM Diplomatic Service; Counsellor, British Embassy, Washington, since 1999; *b* 18 March 1955; *s* of Kenneth Frank Peirce and Margaret Peirce; *m* 1st, 1978, Christina Anne Skipworth Davis (marr. diss. 1999); one *s* one *d*; 2nd,

2000, Robin Lynn Raphel; two step *d*. *Educ:* Taunton Sch.; St Catherine's Coll., Oxford (MA); Faculty of Oriental Studies, Univ. of Cambridge. Joined FCO, 1977; Hong Kong, 1979–80; Peking, 1980–83; FCO, 1983–85; Cabinet Office, 1985–86; Dep. Political Advr, Hong Kong, 1986–88; Private Sec. to Sec. of State for Foreign and Commonwealth Affairs, 1988–90; UK Mission to UN, 1990–93; Political Advr to Governor, Hong Kong, 1993–97; RCDS, 1998; Sec., Ind. Commn on Policing for NI, 1998–99. *Recreations:* family, friends, speculation. *Address:* c/o Foreign and Commonwealth Office, King Charles Street, SW1A 2AH. *Club:* Hong Kong (Hong Kong).

PEIRSE, Sir Henry Grant de la Poer B.; *see* Beresford-Peirse.

PEIRSE, Air Vice-Marshal Sir Richard (Charles Fairfax), KCVO 1988; CB 1984; Gentleman Usher of the Scarlet Rod, Order of the Bath, 1990–2001; *b* 16 March 1931; *s* of late Air Chief Marshal Sir Richard Peirse, KCB, DSO, AFC and late Lady Peirse; *m* 1st, 1955, Karalie Grace Cox (marr. diss. 1963); two *d*; 2nd, 1963, Deirdre Mary O'Donovan (*d* 1976); (one *s* decd); 3rd, 1977, Anna Jill Margaret Long (*née* Latey). *Educ:* Bradfield Coll.; RAF Coll., Cranwell. Commnd 1952; 2nd TAF No 266 Sqdn and HQ 2 Gp, 1952; Flying Instructor, Cranwell, 1956; Air Staff No 23 Gp, 1960; Staff Coll., 1962; Flt Comdr No 39 Sqdn and OC Ops Wg, Luqa, Malta, 1963; Air Sec.'s Dept, 1965; jssc 1968; OC No 51 Sqdn, 1968; Dep. Captain, The Queen's Flight, 1969; RCDS 1972; OC RAF Waddington, 1973; Dep. Dir, Op Requirements, 1976; Dir of Personnel (Air), 1977; Dir of Op Requirements, 1980; AOC and Comdt, RAF Coll. Cranwell, 1982; Defence Services Sec., 1985–88, retd. *Recreations:* theatre, archaeology. *Address:* The Old Mill House, Adderbury, near Banbury, Oxon OX17 3LW. *T:* (01295) 810196. *Club:* Royal Air Force.

PELHAM, family name of **Earls of Chichester** and **Yarborough**.

PELHAM, Hugh Reginald Brentnall, PhD; FRS 1988; Head, Cell Biology Division, and Deputy Director, Medical Research Council Laboratory of Molecular Biology, Cambridge, since 1996; *b* 26 Aug. 1954; *s* of late Reginald A. and of Pauline M. Pelham. *Educ:* Marlborough Coll., Wiltshire; Christ's Coll., Cambridge (MA, PhD). Research Fellow, Christ's Coll., 1978–84; Dept of Embryology, Carnegie Instn of Washington Baltimore, Md, 1979–81; Mem., Scientific Staff, MRC Lab. of Molecular Biol., Cambridge, 1981–. Visitor, Univ. of Zürich, 1987–88. Founder FMedSci 1998. Colworth Medal, Biochemical Soc., 1988; EMBO medal, 1989; Louis Jeantet Prize for Medicine, 1991; King Faisal Internat. Prize for Sci., 1996. *Publications:* papers in sci. jls on molecular and cell biology. *Address:* MRC Laboratory of Molecular Biology, Hills Road, Cambridge CB2 2QH. *T:* (01223) 248011.

PELHAM BURN, Angus Maitland; JP; DL; farmer; Vice Lord-Lieutenant for Kincardineshire, 1978–2000; Director, Bank of Scotland, 1977–2000 (Director, 1973–2001, Chairman, 1977–2001, North Local Board); Chairman: Scottish Provident Institution, 1995–98 (Director, 1975–98; Deputy Chairman, 1991–95); Aberdeen Asset Management (formerly Aberdeen Trust) plc, 1993–2000; *b* 13 Dec. 1931; *s* of late Brig. Gen. H. Pelham Burn, CMG, DSO, and late Mrs K. E. S. Pelham Burn; *m* 1959, Anne R. Pelham Burn (*née* Forbes-Leith); four *d*. *Educ:* Harrow; N of Scotland Coll. of Agriculture. Hudson's Bay Co., 1951–58. Director: Aberdeen and Northern Marts Ltd, 1970–86 (Chm., 1974–86); Jessfield Ltd, 1970–00, Aberdeen Meat Marketing Co. Ltd, 1973–86 (Chm., 1971–00), Prime Space Design (Scotland) Ltd, 1981–87; Status Timber Systems, 1986–90; Skeendale Ltd, 1987–88; Abtrust Scotland Investment Co., 1989–96; Dana Petroleum plc, 1999–; Chairman and Director: MacRobert Farms (Douneside) Ltd, 1970–87; Pelett Administration Ltd, 1973–94; Taw Meat Co., 1984–86. Chm., Aberdeen Airport Consultative Cttee, 1986–; Mem., Accounts Commn, 1980–94 (Dep. Chm., 1992–94). Mem. Council, Winston Churchill Meml Trust, 1984–93; Dir., Aberdeen Assoc. for Prevention of Cruelty to Animals, 1975–95 (Chm., 1984–89). Pres., Aberdeen Br., Inst. of Marketing, 1987–90. Member: Kincardine CC, 1967–75 (Vice Convener, 1973–75); Grampian Regional Council, 1974–94. Member, Queen's Body Guard for Scotland (Royal Co. of Archers), 1968–. Hon. FInstM. JP Kincardine and Deeside, 1984; DL Kincardineshire 1978. LlD Robert Gordon Univ., 1996. CStJ 1995 (OStJ 1978). *Recreations:* photography esp. wildlife, hill walking, vegetable gardening. *Address:* Kennels Cottage, Dess, Aboyne, Aberdeenshire AB34 5AY. *T:* (013398) 84445, *Fax:* (013398) 84430. *Club:* Royal Northern (Aberdeen).

PELIZA, Sir Robert (John), KBE 1998 (OBE 1989); ED 1955; company director, since 1962; Speaker, House of Assembly, Gibraltar, 1989–96; *b* 16 Nov. 1920; *s* of late Robert Peliza; *m* 1950, Irma Risso; three *s* four *d*. *Educ:* Christian Brothers' Coll., Gibraltar. Served in Gibraltar Defence Force (now Gibraltar Regt), 1939–61. Founder Mem., Integration with Britain Party (first leader), 1967; Chief Minister, 1969–72, apptd following Gen. Elections, 1969; elected MHA, 1969–84; Leader of the Opposition, 1972–73. Pres., Gibraltar Br, CPA, 1989–. Hon. Col, Gibraltar Regt, 1993–98. *Recreations:* walking, painting, reading, jogging, cycling, rowing. *Address:* 125 Beverley Drive, Edgware, Middlesex HA8 5NH. *T:* and *Fax:* (020) 8952 1712; *e-mail:* rjpeliza@pelizar.freeserve.co.uk.

PELL, Most Rev. George; *see* Sydney, Archbishop of, (RC).

PELL, Gordon Francis; Chairman, Retail Banking and Wealth Management, Royal Bank of Scotland Group, since 2001 (Executive Director and Chief Executive, Retail Banking, 2000–01); *b* 23 Feb. 1950; *s* of Denis and Anne Pell; *m* 1971, Marian Leak; two *s* one *d*. *Educ:* Wellington Coll.; Southampton Univ. (BA). FCIB. AIB. With Lloyds Bank, then Lloyds TSB, 1971–2000: Dir, Distribution, 1996–98; Gp Dir, Retail Banking, 1998–2000. Dir, Race for Opportunity, 1998–. FRSA 1999. *Recreations:* riding, clay shooting. *Address:* Retail Banking, Royal Bank of Scotland, Drapers Gardens, 12 Throgmorton Avenue, EC2N 2DL.

PELLEREAU, Maj.-Gen. Peter John Mitchell, MA, CEng, FIMechE, FIMgt; Secretary, Association of Consulting Engineers, 1977–87; *b* Quetta, British India, 24 April 1921; *s* of late Col J. C. E. Pellereau, OBE and Mrs A. N. V. Pellereau (*née* Betham); *m* 1949, Rosemary, *e d* of late S. R. Garnar; two *s*. *Educ:* Wellington Coll.; Trinity Coll., Cambridge. BA 1942, MA 1957. Commnd into Royal Engrs, 1942; War Service in NW Europe, 1944–45; OC 26 Armd Engr Sqdn, RE, 1946; ptsc, psc, 1950–51; Sec., Defence Research Policy Cttee, 1960; Asst Mil. Sec., WO, 1961; CO 131 Parachute Engr Regt RE TA, 1963; Mil. Dir of Studies, RMCS, 1965; Asst Dir RE Equipment Develt, 1967; Sen. Mil. Officer, Royal Armament R&D Estabt, 1970; Vice-Pres., 1973–75, Pres., 1975–76, Ordnance Board; retired 1976. Hon. Col, RE (Vol.) (Explosive Ordnance Disposal), 1980–86. Liveryman: Worshipful Co. of Plumbers, 1977–92; Worshipful Co. of Engineers, 1984–92. Mem., Smeatonian Soc. of Civil Engineers, 1981– (Pres., 2002). Vice-Pres., Surrey Hockey Umpires' Assoc., 1979–85; Pres., Oxted Hockey Club, 1975–84. Mem., Wolfe Soc. Cttee, 1978–; Chm., Westerham Motorway Action Gp, 1993–. *Recreations:* lawn tennis, golf. *Address:* Woodmans Folly, Crockham Hill, Edenbridge, Kent TN8 6RJ. *T:* (01732) 866309.

PELLEW, family name of **Viscount Exmouth**.

PELLEW, Dr Jill Hosford; Vice-President and Managing Director, GrenzebachGlier Europe, since 2000; *b* 29 April 1942; *d* of Prof. Frank Thistlethwaite, *qv* and of late Jane (*née* Hosford); *m* 1965, Mark Edward Pellew, *qv*; two *s*. *Educ:* Cambs High Sch. for Girls; St Hilda's Coll., Oxford (BA 1964; MA 1968); Queen Mary Coll., London (MA 1970); PhD London 1976. MoD, 1964–66; part-time univ. teaching, Univ. of Saigon, Univ. of Sussex, Hollins Coll., Va, American Univ., Washington, 1967–89; Exec. Sec., Chatham Hse Foundn, Washington, 1984–89; Develt Officer, St Hilda's Coll., Oxford, 1989–90; Dir of Develt, Imperial Coll. of Science, Technology and Medicine, London, 1991–94; Dir, Develt Office, Univ. of Oxford, 1994–99; Fellow, Trinity Coll., Oxford, 1995–99. Trustee: Council for Advancement and Support of Educn (Europe), 1996–99; Estorick Foundn, 1999–. *Publications:* The Home Office 1848–1914: from clerks to bureaucrats, 1982; (ed with S. Cassese) The Comparative History of Public Administration: the merit system, 1987; various articles in learned jls on admin. hist. *Recreations:* reading, listening to music, entertaining friends. *Address:* c/o Foreign and Commonwealth Office (Holy See), King Charles Street, SW1A 2AH. *Club:* Reform.

PELLEW, Mark Edward, CVO 2000 (LVO 1980); HM Diplomatic Service; Ambassador to the Holy See, since 1998; *b* 28 Aug. 1942; *e s* of late Comdr Anthony Pownoll Pellew, RN retd, and of Margaret Julia Critchley (*née* Cookson); *m* 1965, Jill Hosford Thistlethwaite (*see* J. H. Pellew); two *s*. *Educ:* Winchester; Trinity Coll., Oxford (BA). Entered HM Diplomatic Service, 1965; FO, 1965–67; Third Sec., Singapore, 1967–69; Second Sec., Saigon, 1969–70; FCO, 1970–76; First Sec., Rome, 1976–80; Asst Head of Personnel Ops Dept, FCO, 1981–83; Counsellor: Washington, 1983–89; on secondment to Hambros Bank, 1989–91; Head of N America Dept, FCO, 1991–96. *Recreations:* singing, playing the horn. *Address:* c/o Foreign and Commonwealth Office, King Charles Street, SW1A 2AH. *Club:* Hurlingham.

See also R. A. Pellew.

PELLEW, Robin Anthony, PhD; Chief Executive, Animal Health Trust, since 1999; *b* 27 Sept. 1945; *s* of late Comdr Anthony Pownoll Pellew, RN and Margaret Julia Critchley (*née* Cookson); *m* 1974, Pamela Daphne Gibson MacLellan; one *s* one *d*. *Educ:* Marlborough Coll.; Edinburgh Univ. (BSc 1968); University College London (MSc 1972; PhD 1981). Sen. Res. Scientist, Serengeti Res. Inst., Tanzania, 1973–78; BBC Natural History Unit, 1978–79; Res. Fellow, Physiology Lab., Cambridge, 1979–82; Cambridge University Press: Sen. Editor, 1982–86; Editorial Manager, 1986–87; Dir, Conservation Monitoring Centre, IUCN, 1987–88; Dir, World Conservation Monitoring Centre, Cambridge, 1988–93; Dir and Chief Exec., WWF-World Wide Fund for Nature, 1994–99. Member: Envt Cttee, RSA, 1993–98; UK Round Table on Sustainable Develt, 1995–99; Conservation and Science Cttee, 1997–, Inst. of Zool. Cttee, 1997–, Zool. Soc. of London. *Publications:* numerous scientific papers on wild life management and conservation in professional jls. *Recreations:* travelling to exotic places, watching wild life. *Address:* 26 Selwyn Gardens, Cambridge CB3 9AY.

See also M. E. Pellew.

PELLING, Andrew John; Member (C) Croydon and Sutton, London Assembly, Greater London Authority, since 2000; *b* 20 Aug. 1959; *s* of Anthony Adair Pelling, *qv*; *m* Sanae; one *s* two *d*. *Educ:* New Coll., Oxford (MA PPE). Croydon Borough Council: Mem. (C), 1982–; Chm., Educn, 1988–94; Dep. Leader, Cons. Gp, 1996–. Mem., London Develt Authy, 2000–. Mem., CATE, 1990–94. *Recreations:* Crystal Palace FC, sumo, sushi eating. *Address:* Greater London Authority, Romney House, 43 Marsham Street, SW1P 3PY. *T:* (020) 7983 4353; *e-mail:* andrew.pelling@london.gov.uk. *Club:* Reform.

PELLING, Anthony Adair; trade policy adviser; *b* 3 May 1934; *s* of Brian and Alice Pelling; *m* 1st, 1958, Margaret Lightfoot (*d* 1986); one *s* one *d*; 2nd, 1989, Virginia Glen-Calvert. *Educ:* Purley Grammar Sch.; London Sch. of Economics. BSc (Econ); MIPM. National Coal Board, 1957–67; entered MPBW as Principal, 1967; Asst Sec., 1970, Under Sec., 1981, DoE; seconded as Dep. Dir, Business in the Community, 1981–83; Dept of Transport, 1983–85; London Regional Dir, DoE, 1987–91; Dir, Construction Policy, DoE, 1991–93. Dir, GJW Government Relations Ltd, London and Washington, 1993–95. Pres., ESU, Richmond, 1998–2000; Chm., Region IV, and Mem. Nat. Bd, US ESU, 2000–. *Recreations:* music, theatre. *Address:* 70 West Square Drive, Richmond, VA 23233–6158, USA. *Club:* Reform.

See also A. J. Pelling.

PELLY, Derek Roland, (Derk); Deputy Chairman, Barclays Bank PLC, 1986–88 (Vice Chairman, 1984–85); *b* 12 June 1929; *s* of late Arthur Roland Pelly and late Elsie Pelly; *m* 1953, Susan Roberts; one *s* two *d*. *Educ:* Marlborough; Trinity Coll., Cambridge. Served RA, 1947–49 (2nd Lieut). Entered Barclays Bank, 1952; Local Director: Chelmsford, 1959; Luton, 1969; Vice Chm., 1977–85, Chm., 1986–87, Barclays Internat. Ltd. Dir, The Private Bank & Trust Co., 1989–94. Member: Milton Keynes Develt Corp., 1976–85; Council, ODI, 1984–89. Mem. Cttee, Family Assce Soc., 1988–91. Dir, Chelmsford Dio. Bd of Finance, 1989–96. Governor: London House for Overseas Graduates, 1985–91; Chelmsford Coll., 1994–95. *Recreation:* painting. *Address:* Kenbank, St John's Town of Dalry, Kirkcudbrightshire DG7 3TX. *T:* (01644) 430424.

PELLY, Sir Richard (John), 7th Bt *cr* 1840, of Upton, Essex; farmer, since 1991; *b* 10 April 1951; *s* of Richard Heywood Pelly, 2nd *s* of Sir Alwyne Pelly, 5th Bt, MC and of Mary Elizabeth Pelly (*née* Luscombe); *S* uncle, 1993; *m* 1983, Clare Gemma Dove; three *s*. *Educ:* Wellington Coll., Berks; Wadham Coll., Oxford (BA Agriculture and Forestry Science). ACA 1978–82. Price Waterhouse, London, 1974–78; Birds Eye Foods Ltd, 1978–81; New Century Software Ltd, 1981–99. *Recreations:* walking, cycling, windsurfing, shooting. *Heir:* *s* Anthony Alwyne Pelly, *b* 30 Oct. 1984. *Address:* The Manor House, Preshaw, Upham, Southampton SO32 1HP. *T:* (01962) 771757.

PEMBERTON; *see* Leigh-Pemberton, family name of Baron Kingsdown.

PEMBERTON, Col Alan Brooke, CVO 1988; MBE 1960; *b* 11 Sept. 1923; *s* of Eric Harry Pemberton (Canadian by birth) and Phyllis Edith Pemberton (*née* Brooke-Alder); *m* 1952, Pamela Kirkland Smith, of Winnipeg, Canada; two *s*. *Educ:* Uppingham School; Trinity College, Cambridge. Commissioned Coldstream Guards, 1942; war service in Italy and NW Europe; ADC to Earl Alexander of Tunis, Governor-General of Canada, 1951–52; ADC to Gen. Sir Gerald Templer, High Comr to Malaya, 1952–53; Commanded 1st Bn Coldstream Guards, 1963–66; Regtl Lt-Col, 1966–67; retired 1967 (Hon. Col). Queen's Body Guard, Yeomen of the Guard: Exon, 1967; Ensign; Clerk of the Cheque; Lieutenant, 1985–93. Chm. and Man. Dir, Diversified Corporate Services Ltd, 1970–85. Special Constable, A Div., Metropolitan Police, 1975–76. *Recreations:* painting, reading, travel. *Address:* Eastfields Farm, Stoke-by-Nayland, Colchester, Essex CO6 4TB. *Clubs:* Boodle's, Pratt's.

PEMBERTON, Sir Francis (Wingate William), Kt 1976; CBE 1970; DL; FRICS; company director; *b* 1 Oct. 1916; *s* of late Dr William Warburton Wingate (assumed Arms of Pemberton, by Royal Licence, 1921) and Viola Patience Campbell Pemberton; *m* 1941, Diana Patricia (*d* 1999), *e d* of late Reginald Salisbury Woods, MD, and Irene Woods, CBE, TD; two *s*. *Educ:* Eton; Trinity Coll., Cambridge (MA). Senior Consultant, Bidwells, Chartered Surveyors, 1980–89. Director: Agricultural Mortgage Corp. Ltd, 1969–91; Barclays Bank UK Ltd, 1977–81; Severn Trent Property Ltd, 1990–95. Chm. Adv. Cttee, Inst. of Animal Physiology and Genetics Res. (Cambridge and Edinburgh), 1983–90; Hon. Dir, Royal Show, 1963–68; Royal Agricultural Society of England: Mem. Council, 1951– (Pres., 1974–75, Dep. Pres., 1975–76); Chm. Exec. Bd, 1969–71; Trustee, 1969–; Gold Medal for distinguished services to agric., 1989. Trustee, Robinson Coll., Cambridge, 1973–85. Member: Water Resources Board, 1964–74; Winston Churchill Meml Trust, 1965–80; Economic Planning Council for East Anglia, 1965–74; National Water Council, 1974–81; Water Authorities Superannuation Pension Fund (Dep. Chm, Fund Management and Policy Cttee), 1983–89. High Sheriff, Cambridgeshire and Isle of Ely, 1965–66; DL Cambs, 1979. *Address:* The Flat, Trumpington Hall, Cambridge CB2 2LH. *T:* (01223) 841941. *Club:* Farmers'.

PEMBERTON, Gary Milton, AC 1999; Chairman TAB Ltd, since 1997; Qantas Airways Ltd, 1993–2000; *s* of Eric Pemberton; *m* Margaret Whitford; four *c*. *Educ:* Fort Street High Sch. Australian Wool Bd, 1961–72; joined Brambles Industries Ltd, 1972: Chief Exec., 1982–93; Dep. Chm., 1994–96; Director: Commonwealth Bank, 1989–93; John Fairfax Hldgs Ltd, 1992–93; CSR Ltd, 1993–94. Chief Exec. Officer, 1994–95, Pres., 1995–96, Sydney Organising Cttee of the Olympic Games.

PEMBERTON, Prof. John, MD London; FRCP, FFPHM; DPH Leeds; Professor of Social and Preventive Medicine, The Queen's University, Belfast, 1958–76; *b* 18 Nov. 1912; British; *m* 1937, Winifred Ethel Gray; three *s*. *Educ:* Christ's Hospital; University College and UCH, London. House Physician and House Surgeon, University College Hospital, 1936–37; Rowett Research Institute under the late Lord Boyd Orr, 1937–39; Rockefeller Travelling Fellow in Medicine, Harvard, Mass., USA, 1954–55; Director of MRC Group for research on Respiratory Disease and Air Pollution, and Reader in Social Medicine, University of Sheffield, 1955–58. Mem., Health Educn Council, DHSS, 1973–76. Milroy Lectr, RCP, 1976. *Publications:* (with W. Hobson) The Health of the Elderly at Home, 1954; (ed) Recent Studies in Epidemiology, 1958; (ed) Epidemiology: Reports on Research and Teaching, 1963; Will Pickles of Wensleydale, 1970; articles in Lancet, BMJ, etc. *Recreations:* reading, TV, walking, painting. *Address:* Iona, Cannon Fields, Hathersage, Hope Valley S32 1AG.

PEMBROKE, 17th Earl of, *cr* 1551, **AND MONTGOMERY**. 14th Earl of, *cr* 1605; **Henry George Charles Alexander Herbert,** Baron Herbert of Caerdiff, 1551; Baron Herbert of Shurland, 1605; Baron Herbert of Lea (UK), 1861; DL; Hereditary Grand Visitor of Jesus College, Oxford; *b* 19 May 1939; *s* of 16th Earl of Pembroke and Montgomery, CVO, and Mary Countess of Pembroke, CVO (*d* 1995); *S* father, 1969; *m* 1st, 1966, Claire Rose (marr. diss. 1981), *o d* of Douglas Pelly, Swaynes Hall, Widdington, Essex; one *s* three *d*; 2nd, 1988, Miranda Juliet, *d* of Comdr John Oram, Bulbridge House, Wilton; three *d*. *Educ:* Eton Coll.; Oxford Univ. Royal Horse Guards, 1958–60 (National Service); Oxford University, 1960–63. DL Wilts 1995. *Recreations:* photography, gardening, horse racing. *Heir:* *s* Lord Herbert, *qv*. *Address:* Wilton House, Salisbury, Wilts SP2 0BJ. *T:* (01722) 746700.

PEÑA, Paco; musician; flamenco guitar player, since 1954; Professor of Flamenco, Rotterdam Conservatory, since 1985; *b* 1 June 1942; *s* of Antonio Peña and Rosario Perez; *m* 1982, Karin Vaessen; two *d*. *Educ:* Córdoba, Spain. London début, 1968; New York début, 1983; founded: Paco Peña Flamenco Co., 1970; Centro Flamenco Paco Peña, Córdoba, 1981; composed Misa Flamenca, 1991. Ramón Montoya Prize, 1983. Officer, Order of Merit (Spain), 1997. *Address:* c/o Wim Visser, Staalstraat 10–12, 1011JL Amsterdam, Netherlands. *T:* (20) 6233700, (20) 6208212; c/o Karin Vaessen, 4 Boscastle Road, NW5 1EG. *Fax:* (020) 7485 2320.

PENDER, 3rd Baron *cr* 1937; **John Willoughby Denison-Pender;** Joint Chairman, Bremar Trust Ltd, 1977–83; Chairman, J. J. L. D. Frost plc, 1983–84; *b* 6 May 1933; *s* of 2nd Baron Pender, CBE and Camilla Lethbridge (*d* 1988), *o d* of late Willoughby Arthur Pemberton; *S* father, 1965; *m* 1962, Julia, *yr d* of Richard Nevill Cannon; one *s* two *d*. *Educ:* Eton. Formerly Lieut, 10th Royal Hussars and Captain, City of London Yeomanry (TA). Dir, Globe Investment Trust Ltd, 1969–70. Vice Pres., Royal Sch. for Deaf Children, 1992–99 (Treas., 1999–). Steward: Folkestone Racecourse, 1985–; Lingfield Park, 1989–. *Heir:* *s* Hon. Henry John Richard Denison-Pender [*b* 19 March 1968; *m* 1994, Vanessa, *d* of John Eley, NSW, Australia; one *s* one *d*]. *Address:* North Court, Tilmanstone, Kent CT14 0JP. *T:* (01304) 611726. *Clubs:* White's, Pratt's.

PENDER, David James; Sheriff of North Strathclyde, since 1995; *b* 7 Sept. 1949; *s* of James and Isa Pender; *m* 1974, Elizabeth Jean McKillop; two *s* two *d*. *Educ:* Queen's Park Sen. Secondary Sch., Glasgow; Edinburgh Univ. (LLB Hons). Qualified as Solicitor, 1973; Partner, MacArthur Stewart, Solicitors, Oban, 1977–95. Sec., Oban Faculty of Solicitors, 1977–95. *Recreations:* travel, bridge, reading. *Address:* Sheriff's Chambers, Paisley Sheriff Court, St James Street, Paisley PA3 2HW. *T:* (0141) 887 5291.

PENDER, Comr Dinsdale Leslie; Territorial Commander in United Kingdom and Republic of Ireland, Salvation Army, 1993–97; *b* 22 March 1932; *s* of William Leslie Pender and Florence Lilian Pender (*née* Widdowson); *m* 1954, Winifred Violet Dale; one *s* two *d*. *Educ:* Colfe's Grammar Sch., Lewisham; Bradford Grammar Sch.; William Booth Meml Trng Coll. Served RAF, 1949–51. Commnd and ordained as Salvation Army Officer, 1952; CO, Manchester, Bath, Coventry and London, 1953–73; Divl Comdr, Northern Div., 1973–77; Asst Field Sec., Nat. HQ, 1977–80; Chief Sec., NZ and Fiji, 1980–84; Territorial Commander: Southern Africa, 1984–86; Scotland, 1986–90; Australia Southern, 1990–93. Chm., Bd, Salvation Army Housing Assoc.; Res. Consultant, Salvation Army Internat. Heritage Centre. *Recreations:* music, swimming. *Address:* 4 Old School Court, Wraysbury, Berks TW19 5BP.

PENDERECKI, Krzysztof; Rector, State Academy of Music, Kraków, since 1972; Professor of Composition, School of Music, Yale University, New Haven, Conn, 1973–78; *b* Debica, Poland, 23 Nov. 1933; *s* of Tadeusz Penderecki and Zofia Penderecki; *m* 1965, Elzbieta Solecka; one *s* one *d*. *Educ:* State Acad. of Music, Kraków, Poland (Graduate 1958). Compositions include: Threnody to the Victims of Hiroshima, 1960 (52 strings); Passion According to St Luke, 1965–66 (oratorio); Dies irae, 1967; Utrenja, 1969–71 (oratorio); Devils of Loudun, 1969 (opera); Cello Concerto No 1, 1971–72; First Symphony, 1972; Magnificat, 1974 (oratorio); Awakening of Jacob, 1974 (orchestra); Paradise Lost, 1976–78 (rappresentazione for Chicago Lyric Opera; Milton libretto, Christopher Fry); Violin Concerto, 1977; Te Deum, 1979–80; (Christmas) Symphony No 2, 1980; Lacrimosa, 1980; Agnus Dei (for chorus a cappella), 1981; Cello Concerto No 2, 1982 (Grammy Award, Nat. Acad. of Recording Arts and Scis, 1988); Viola Concerto, 1983; Polish Requiem, 1983–84; Die schwarze Maske, 1986 (opera); Veni creator and Song of Cherubin (for chorus a cappella), 1987; Das unterbrochene Gedanke (for string quartet), 1988; Symphony No 3, 1988–95; Symphony No 4, 1989; Ubu Rex, 1991 (opera); Symphony No 5, 1991–92; Sinfonietta per archi, 1992; Flute Concerto, 1992–93; Quartet for clarinet and string trio, 1993; Violin Concerto No 2, 1995 (Grammy Award, 1999); Seven Gates of Jerusalem (oratorio), 1997; Credo (oratorio), 1998. Hon. Professor: Moscow Tchaikovsky Conservatory, 1997; Beijing Conservatory. Hon. Dr: Univ. of Rochester, NY; St Olaf Coll., Northfield, Minn; Katholieke Univ., Leuven; Univ. of Bordeaux; Georgetown Univ., Washington; Univ. of Belgrade; Universidad Autónoma, Madrid; Adam Mickiewicz Univ.; Warsaw Univ.; Acad. of Music, Cracow and Warsaw; Univ. of Glasgow; Duquesne Univ., Pittsburgh. Member: RAM (Hon.); Akad. der Künste, Berlin (Extraordinary); Akad. der Künste der DDR, Berlin (Corresp.); Kungl. Musikaliska Akad., Stockholm; Accad. Nazionale di Santa Cecilia, Rome (Hon.); Acad. Nacional de Bellas Artes, Buenos Aires (Corresp.); Royal Acad. of Music, Dublin; Akad. der schönen Künste, Munich (Corresp.); Hon. Foreign Mem., Amer. Acad. Arts and Letters. Grosser Kunstpreis des Landes Nordrhein-Westfalen, 1966; Prix Italia, 1967/68; Gottfried von Herder Preis der Stiftung FvS zu Hamburg, 1977; Prix Arthur Honegger, 1977; Sibelius Prize, Wihouri Foundn, 1983; Premio Lorenzo Magnifico, 1985; Wolf Prize, 1987; Manuel de Falla Gold Medal, Accademia de Bellas Artes, Granada, 1989; Grawemeyer Award, Univ. of Louisville, 1992; Internat. Music Council/UNESCO Prize for Music, 1993; Prime Time Emmy Award, Acad. of Television Arts and Scis, 1995 and 1996; Crystall Award, Econ. Forum, Davos, 1997; Music Award, City of Duisburg, 1999; Cannes Classical Award, 2000. Das Grosse Verdienstkreuz des Verdienstordens (Germany), 1990. *Publications:* all works published. *Recreations:* dendrology, gardening. *Address:* Am Daubhaus 6, 55276 Oppenheim, Germany. *Fax:* (6133) 926356; Schott Musik International, Concert Opera Media Division, Weihergarten 5, 55116 Mainz, Germany. *T:* (6131) 2460, *Fax:* (6131) 246250.

PENDERED, Richard Geoffrey; Chairman, Bunge & Co., 1987–90; *b* 26 Sept. 1921; *s* of Richard Dudley Pendered and Adèle Pendered (*née* Hall); *m* 1953, Jennifer Preston Mead; two *s* two *d*. *Educ:* Winchester College (Scholar); Magdalene College (Scholar). GCCS Bletchley, 1940–52 (renamed GCHQ); Bunge & Co., 1952–90, Dir, 1957, Man. Dir, 1963–86. *Recreations:* fishing, shooting, golf. *Address:* 41 Sandy Lodge Lane, Northwood, Middx HA6 2HX. *Club:* Moor Park Golf.

PENDLEBURY, Edward; Assistant Under Secretary of State (Sales Administration), Ministry of Defence, 1983–85, retired; *b* 5 March 1925; *s* of Thomas Cecil Pendlebury and Alice (*née* Sumner); *m* 1957, Joan Elizabeth Bell; one *s*. *Educ:* King George V Sch., Southport; Magdalen Coll., Oxford (MA). Served War, RNVR, 1943–46. Asst Principal, Min. of Food, 1949–53; Principal: MAFF, 1953–56; MoD (British Defence Staff, Washington), 1956–60; MAFF, 1960–66; Asst Secretary: DEA, 1966–70; MoD, 1970–80; Exec. Dir (Civilian Management), MoD, 1980–83. *Recreations:* gramophone, gardening, gazing. *Address:* Bosworth House, Draycott, near Moreton-in-Marsh, Glos GL56 9LF. *T:* (01386) 701059.

PENDOWER, John Edward Hicks, FRCS; Dean, Charing Cross and Westminster Medical School, 1989–93; *b* 6 Aug. 1927; *s* of Thomas Curtis Hicks Pendower and Muriel May Pendower (*née* Newbury); *m* 1st, 1960, Kate Tuohy (*d* 1987); one *s* two *d*; 2nd, 1989, Mrs Paulette Gleave. *Educ:* Dulwich College; King's College London; Charing Cross Hosp. Med. Sch. (MB BS (Hons Med.) 1950). FRCS 1955. Called to the Bar, Inner Temple, 1972. Served RAMC. Charing Cross Hosp. and St Mark's Hosp., 1950–62; Harvey Cushing Fellow, Harvard Med. Sch., 1959–60; Consultant Surgeon: Mayday Hosp., Croydon, 1964–89; Charing Cross Hosp., 1965–87 (Vice Dean, 1979–84; Sub Dean, Charing Cross and Westminster Med. Sch., 1984–87); former examr in surgery, London Univ. Mem., Hammersmith and Fulham, subseq. Riverside, HA, 1983–90. Special Trustee, Charing Cross Hosp.; Chm. Trustees, Sargent Cancer Care for Children (formerly Malcolm Sargent Cancer Fund for Children). *Recreations:* formerly squash rackets, now walking; collecting campaign medals. *Address:* Rosemary, Promenade de Verdun, Purley, Surrey CR8 3LN. *T:* (020) 8660 8949.

PENDRED, Piers Loughnan; Director General, International Psychoanalytical Association, since 2000; *b* 24 Aug. 1943; *s* of Loughnan Wildig Pendred and Dulcie Treen Hall; *m* 1973, Carol Ann Haslam; one *s* one *d*. *Educ:* Ardingly College; Trinity Hall, Cambridge (MA Fine Arts and Architecture). VSO teacher, S India, 1965–67; British Council, 1967–99: Television Officer, Sudan, 1967–69, Ethiopia, 1969–71; TV Training Officer, London, 1972–76; Head of Production, 1976–81; Dir, Design, Production and Publishing, 1981–84; Dir, Press and Inf., 1984–87; Controller, later Dir of Finance, 1987–94; Special Asst to Dir-Gen., 1994–95; Asst Dir-Gen., 1996–99. Sen. Exec. Programme, London Business Sch., 1987. Trustee, Centre for Internat. Briefing, 1996–99.

PENDRY, family name of **Baron Pendry.**

PENDRY, Baron *cr* 2001 (Life Peer), of Stalybridge in the County of Greater Manchester; **Thomas Pendry;** PC 2000; *b* 10 June 1934; *m* 1966, Moira Anne Smith (separated 1983); one *s* one *d*. *Educ:* St Augustine's, Ramsgate; Oxford Univ. RAF, 1955–57. Full time official, Nat. Union of Public Employees, 1960–70; Mem., Paddington Borough Council, 1962–65; Chm., Derby Labour Party, 1966. MP (Lab) Stalybridge and Hyde, 1970–2001. An Opposition Whip, 1971–74; a Lord Comr of the Treasury and Govt Whip, 1974, resigned 1977; Parly Under-Sec. of State, NI Office, 1978–79; Opposition spokesman on NI, 1979–81, on overseas development, 1981–82, on regional affairs and devolution, 1982–84, on sport and tourism, 1992–97. Member: Select Cttee on Envmt, 1987–92; Select Cttee on Members' Interests, 1987–92. Chairman: All Party Football Cttee, 1980–92; PLP Sports Cttee, 1984–92; All Party Tourism Gp; All Party Sports Cttee. Member: Speaker's Conf., 1973; UK delegn to WEU and Council of Europe, 1973–75; Industrial Law Soc. Chm., Football Trust. Steward, British Boxing Bd of Control, 1987–. President: Stalybridge Public Band; Music Users Council, 1997–; Patron, Nat. Fedn of Football Supporters, 1998–. Freeman, Bor. of Tameside and Lordship of Mottram in Longendale, 1995. *Recreations:* sport; football, cricket, boxing (sometime Middleweight Champion, Hong Kong; boxed for Oxford Univ.). *Address:* House of Lords, SW1A 0PW. *Clubs:* Wig and Pen, Lord's Taverners; Vincent's (Oxford).

PENDRY, Prof. John Brian, PhD; FRS 1984; Professor of Theoretical Solid State Physics, Department of Physics, since 1981, and Head, Department of Physics, since 1998, Imperial College of Science, Technology and Medicine, University of London; Dean, Royal College of Science, 1993–96; *b* 4 July 1943; *s* of Frank Johnson Pendry and Kathleen (*née* Shaw); *m* 1977, Patricia Gard. *Educ:* Downing Coll., Cambridge (MA; PhD 1969). Res. Fellow in Physics, Downing Coll., Cambridge, 1969–72; Mem. of Technical Staff, Bell Labs, USA, 1972–73; Sen. Asst in Res., Cavendish Lab., Cambridge Univ., and Fellow in Physics and Praelector, Downing Coll., 1973–75; SPSO and Head of Theory Gp, Daresbury Lab., 1975–81. Mem., PPARC, 1998–. *Publications:* Low Energy Electron Diffraction, 1974; Surface Crystallographic Information Service, 1987; scientific papers. *Recreations:* music, gardening, photography. *Address:* The Blackett Laboratory, Imperial College of Science, Technology and Medicine, SW7 2BZ. *T:* (020) 7594 7500. *Club:* Athenæum.

PENFOLD, Peter Alfred, CMG 1995; OBE 1986; HM Diplomatic Service; *b* 27 Feb. 1944; *s* of Alfred Penfold and Florence (*née* Green); *m* 1st, 1972, Margaret Quigley (marr. diss. 1983); 2nd, 1992, Celia Dolores Koenig. *Educ:* Sutton Co. Grammar Sch. Joined Foreign Service, 1963; Bonn, 1965–68; Kaduna, 1968–70; Latin American Floater, 1970–72; Canberra, 1972; FCO, 1972–75; Second Secretary: Addis Ababa, 1975–78; Port of Spain, 1978–81; First Sec., FCO, 1981–84; Dep. High Comr, Kampala, 1984–87; First Sec., FCO, 1987–91; Gov., BVI, 1991–95; Special Advr on Drugs in the Caribbean, 1995–96; High Comr, Sierra Leone, 1997–2000. *Recreations:* travel, flying, mountaineering, reading. *Address:* c/o Foreign and Commonwealth Office, King Charles Street, SW1A 2AH.

PENFOLD, Maj.-Gen. Robert Bernard, CB 1969; LVO 1957; *b* 19 Dec. 1916; *s* of late Bernard Hugh Penfold, Selsey, and late Ethel Ives Arnold; *m* 1940, Ursula, *d* of late Lt-Col E. H. Gray; two *d*. *Educ:* Wellington; RMC, Sandhurst. 2nd Lieut, Royal Leics Regt, 1936; commnd into 11th Sikh Regt, Indian Army, 1937; served in NWFP and during War of 1939–45 in Middle East, Central Mediterranean Forces; Instructor, Staff Coll., Quetta, 1946–47; transf. to British Army, RA, 1947; RN Staff Coll., 1953; Secretary, British Joint Services Mission, Washington, 1957–59; comdg 6 King's African Rifles, Tanganyika, 1959–61; Comdr 127 Inf. Bde (TA), 1962–64; Security Ops Adviser to High Commissioner, Aden, 1964–65; Imperial Defence Coll., 1966; Chief of Defence Staff, Kenya, 1966–69; GOC South East District, 1969–72. Gen. Manager and Chief Exec., Royal Hong Kong Jockey Club, 1972–80. Chm., Horseracing Adv. Council, 1980–86. *Recreations:* shooting, golf, gardening. *Address:* Park House, Amport, Andover, Hants SP11 8BW. *Club:* Army and Navy.

PENGELLY, Richard Anthony; Under Secretary, Welsh Office, 1977–85; *b* 18 Aug. 1925; *s* of Richard Francis Pengelly and Ivy Mildred Pengelly; *m* 1st, 1952, Phyllis Mary Rippon; one *s*; 2nd, 1972, Margaret Ruth Crossley; two *s* one *d*. *Educ:* Plymouth Coll.; School of Oriental and African Studies; London Sch. of Economics and Political Science (BScEcon). Served War: Monmouthshire Regt and Intell. Corps, 1943–47. Joined Min. of Supply as Asst Principal, 1950, Principal, 1954; NATO Defence Coll., 1960–61; Asst Sec., Min. of Aviation, 1964; RCDS 1971; Min. of Defence, 1972. *Recreations:* skiing, golf. *Address:* Byways, Wern Goch Road, Cyncoed, Cardiff, S Wales CF23 6SD. *T:* (029) 2076 4418.

PENHALIGON, Dame Annette, DBE 1993; Member, Carrick District Council, Cornwall, 1987–94; *b* 9 Feb. 1946; *d* of late Owen Bennett Lidgey and Mabel Lidgey; *m* 1968, David Charles Penhaligon, MP (*d* 1986); one *s* one *d*; *m* 1994, Robert William Egerton. *Educ:* Truro Girls' Grammar Sch. Subpostmistress, Chacewater PO, 1967–79; Sec. to husband, David Penhaligon, MP (L) Truro, 1974–86. Non-exec. Dir, Cornwall Independent Radio, 1992. *Publication:* Penhaligon, 1989. *Recreation:* supporting charities helping people with learning disabilities. *Address:* Trevillick House, Fore Street, Grampound, Truro, Cornwall TR2 4RS. *T:* (01726) 884451.

PENINGTON, Prof. David Geoffrey, AC 1988; Chairman, Cochlear Ltd, since 1995; *b* 4 Feb. 1930; *s* of Geoffrey Alfred Penington and Marjorie Doris (*née* Fricke); *m* 1st, 1956, Audrey Mary Grummitt (marr. diss.); two *s* two *d*; 2nd, 1984, Sonay Hussein. *Educ:* Magdalen Coll., Oxford (BA 1953; BM BCh 1955; MA 1957; DM 1969). MRCP 1957; MRACP 1968; FRCPA 1971; FRCP 1972; FRACP 1972. Consultant physician, London Hosp., 1963–67; Melbourne University: 1st Assistant in Medicine, 1968–70; Prof. and Chm. of Dept of Medicine, 1970–87; Dean, Faculty of Medicine, 1978–85; Vice-Chancellor, 1988–95. Vis. Res. Fellow, Wolfson Coll., Oxford, 1975–76; Sims Commonwealth Travelling Prof., RCS, 1981. Mem., Bd of Dirs, Pacific Dunlop, 1991–; Mem. Adv. Bd, Ernst & Young, 1996–. Chief Advr, Health Policy & Progs, Health Dept, Victoria, 1986–87; Chairman: Cttee of Inquiry into Rights of Private Practice in Public Hosps, 1984; AIDS Task Force, 1984–87; Nat. Blood Transfusion Cttee of Australian Red Cross Soc., 1976–87. Member of Board: Walter and Eliza Hall Inst. for Med. Res.; Ludwig Inst., Royal Melbourne Hosp. Pres., Museum of Victoria, 1994–. *Publications:* (ed) De Gruchy's Clinical Haematology in Medical Practice, 5th edn, 1989; res. pubns on clin. and exptl haematology. *Recreations:* music, painting, fishing. *Address:* 131/461 St Kilda Road, Melbourne, Vic 3004, Australia. *T:* (3) 98673889, *Fax:* (3) 98673989. *Club:* Melbourne (Melbourne).

PENLEY, William Henry, CB 1967; CBE 1961; PhD; FREng; engineering consultant, since 1985; *b* 22 March 1917; *s* of late William Edward Penley and late Clara (*née* Dodgson), Wallasey, Cheshire; *m* 1st, 1943, Raymonde Evelyn (*d* 1975), *d* of late Frederick Richard Gough, Swanage, Dorset; two *s* one *d*; 2nd, 1977, Marion Claytor, *d* of late Joseph Enoch Airey, Swanage, Dorset. *Educ:* Wallasey Grammar Sch.; Liverpool Univ.; BEng, 1937; PhD, 1940. FIEE (MIEE 1964); FRAeS 1967; FRSA 1975; FREng (FEng 1978). Head of Guided Weapons Department, Royal Radar Establishment, 1953–61; Director, Royal Radar Establishment, 1961–62; Director-General of Electronics Research and Development, Ministry of Aviation, 1962–64; Deputy Controller of Electronics, Ministry of Aviation, then Ministry of Technology, 1964–67; Dir, Royal Armament R&D Establishment, 1967–70; Chief Scientist (Army), 1970–75, Dep. Controller, Establishments and Res. B, 1971–75, MoD; Controller, R&D Establishments, and Research, MoD, and Professional Head of Science Gp of the Civil Service, 1976–77; Chm., Appleton Lab. Establishment Cttee, 1977–79; Dep. Dir, Under Water Weapons, Marconi Space and Defence Systems Ltd, Stanmore, 1979–82; Engrg Dir, Marconi Underwater Systems Ltd, 1982–85. Vis. Res. Fellow, Bournemouth Univ., 1996. Sec., Swanage Choral and Operatic Soc., 1986–2000. Silver Jubilee Medal, 1977. *Address:* 28 Walrond Road, Swanage, Dorset BH19 1PD. *T:* (01929) 425042. *Club:* Royal Commonwealth Society.

PENMAN, Ian Dalgleish, CB 1987; Deputy Secretary, Central Services, Scottish Office, 1984–91; *b* 1 Aug. 1931; *s* of late John B. Penman and Dorothy Dalgleish; *m* 1963, Elisabeth Stewart Strachan; three *s*. *Educ:* Glasgow Univ. (MA Classics); Balliol Coll., Oxford (MA Lit. Hum.; Snell Exhibnr and Ferguson Scholar). National Service, RAF, 1955–57 (Educn Br.). Asst Principal, HM Treasury, 1957–58; Scottish Office, 1958–91; Private Sec. to Parly Under-Sec. of State, 1960–62; Principal, Scottish Develt Dept, 1962–69; Asst Sec., Estab. Div., 1970–72; Asst Sec., Scottish Home and Health Dept, 1972–78; Under-Sec., Scottish Develt Dept, 1978–84. Member: Chm.'s Panel, CSSB, 1991–95; Sec. of State's Panel of Inquiry Reporters, 1992–94; Council on Tribunals, 1994–2001 (Mem., Scottish Cttee, 1994–2001); Church of Scotland Cttee on Probationers, 1994–98; C of S Bd of Ministry, 1998–. Chm., Viewpoint Housing Assoc., 1991–95; Chief Exec., Scottish Homes, April–Oct. 1991. *Recreations:* walking, music, travel. *Address:* 1/3 Fettes Rise, Edinburgh EH4 1QH. *T:* (0131) 552 2180. *Club:* New (Edinburgh).

PENN, Richard; consultant in public sector management; Chair, South Wales Probation Board, since 2001; *b* 4 Oct. 1945; *s* of George Stanley; *m* 1968, Jillian Mary Elias; three *s* one *d*. *Educ:* Canton High Sch., Cardiff; University Coll., Cardiff (BSc Econs Jt Hons); University Coll., Swansea (DipEd). MBPS. Lectr, University Coll., Cardiff, 1968–70; Glamorgan, then W Glamorgan, CC, 1970–76; Asst Chief Exec., Cleveland CC, 1976–78; Dep. Chief Exec., W Midlands CC, 1978–81; Chief Executive: Knowsley Metropolitan Council, 1981–89; City of Bradford Metropolitan Council, 1989–98. Member: EOC, 1997–; Legal Services Commn, 2000–; Advr, Nat. Assembly for Wales, 2000–. FIMgt; FRSA. *Recreations:* family, Rugby Union, theatre, good food. *Address:* c/o South Wales Probation Board, 33 Westgate Street, Cardiff CF10 1JE. *Club:* Royal Over-Seas League.

PENNANT; *see* Douglas-Pennant.

PENNANT-REA, Rupert Lascelles; Chairman: The Stationery Office, since 1996; Plantation & General Investments, since 1997; Key Asset Management, since 1997; Security Printing and Systems, since 1999; *b* 23 Jan. 1948; *s* of Peter Athelwold Pennant-Rea and Pauline Elizabeth Pennant-Rea; *m* 1986, Helen Jay; one *s*, and one *s* one *d* by previous marriage, and two step *d*. *Educ:* Peterhouse, Zimbabwe; Trinity Coll., Dublin (BA); Manchester Univ. (MA). Confedn of Irish Industry, 1970–71; Gen. and Municipal Workers Union, 1972–73; Bank of England, 1973–77; The Economist, 1977–93, Editor, 1986–93; Dep. Gov., Bank of England, 1993–95. Non-executive Director: British American Tobacco, 1995–; Gordon House Asset Management, 1995–; Sherritt Internat. Inc., 1995–; First Quantum Minerals, 2001–. Member Council: ODI, 1987–; Trinity Foundn, 1995–; Trustee, Action Res., 2000–. Gov., Peterhouse, Zimbabwe, 1994–. *Publications:* Gold Foil, 1979; (jtly) Who Runs the Economy?, 1980; (jtly) The Pocket Economist, 1983; (jtly) The Economist Economics, 1986. *Recreations:* music, tennis, fishing, family. *Address:* The Stationery Office, 51 Nine Elms Lane, SW8 5DR. *Clubs:* MCC, Reform; Harare (Zimbabwe).

PENNEFATHER, Maj.-Gen. David Anthony Somerset, CB 1996; OBE 1991; Commandant General Royal Marines, 1996–98; *b* 17 May 1945; *s* of late Capt. R. R. S. Pennefather, RN and Rachael Ann Pennefather (*née* Fawcitt); *m* 1972, Sheila Elizabeth Blacklee; one *s* one *d*. *Educ:* Wellington Coll. Entered RM, 1963; commando service incl. US Marine Corps exchange, 1965–76; Army Staff Coll., 1977 (psc(m)); commando service and MoD, 1978–85; DS, Army Staff Coll., 1986–88; CO, 42 Commando, 1988–90; rcds 1991; hcsc 1992; Comdr, 3rd Commando Bde, 1992–94; Dir of Operations for Bosnia, JHQ Wilton, 1994; COS to CGRM, 1995; Comdr, Rapid Reaction Force Ops Staff, Bosnia, 1995. Liveryman: Co. of Clockmakers, 1973– (Mem., Ct of Assts, 1998–); Co. of Plaisterers. Comdr, Legion of Merit (USA), 1997. *Recreations:* fell-walking, forestry, fishing. *Club:* Army and Navy.

PENNEY, Most Rev. Alphonsus Liguori; Archbishop (RC) of St John's (Newfoundland), 1979–91, now Emeritus; *b* 17 Sept. 1924; *s* of Alphonsus Penney and Catherine Penney (*née* Mullaly). *Educ:* St Bonaventure's Coll., St John's, Newfoundland; University Seminary, Ottawa (LPh, LTh). Assistant Priest: St Joseph's Parish, St John's, 1950–56; St Patrick's Parish, St John's, 1956; Parish Priest: Marystown, Placentia Bay, Newfoundland, 1957; Basilica Parish, St John's, 1969. Prelate of Honour, 1971. Bishop of Grand Falls, Newfoundland, 1972. Hon. LLD, Memorial Univ. of Newfoundland, 1980. Confederation Medal, 1967. *Recreations:* walking, golf. *Address:* 23 Mayor Avenue, St John's, NF A1C 4N4, Canada.

PENNEY, Jennifer Beverly; Senior Principal, Royal Ballet, retired 1988; *b* 5 April 1946; *d* of Beverley Guy Penney and Gwen Penney. *Educ:* in Canada (grades 1–12). Entered Royal Ballet Sch., 1962; joined Royal Ballet, 1963; became soloist during 1967, principal dancer during 1970, and senior principal dancer during 1974. Evening Standard Award, 1980. *Recreation:* painting (water-colours). *Address:* 2.258 Lower Ganges Road, Saltspring Island, BC V8K 1S7, Canada.

PENNEY, John Anthony, CMG 2000; political/business consultant and interpreter/translator, since 2000; *b* 30 Oct. 1940; *s* of late William Welch Penney and of Lily Penney; *m* 1st, 1968, Mary Hurley; 2nd, 1995, Miriam Franchini. *Educ:* Madrid Univ. (Dip. of Hispanic Studies 1960); St Catharine's Coll., Cambridge (BA (Hons) Mod. Langs, 1963; MA 1966); Nat. Autonomous Univ. of Mexico; Univ. of Paris IX, Ecole Supérieure d'Interpretation et de Traducteurs. HM Diplomatic Service, 1966–99: Jt Res. Dept, FCO, 1966–68; Lima, 1968–72; Hd, Americas Unit, FCO Res. Analysis Dept, 1973–95; 1st Sec., Political Cttee, CSCE, UKMIS to UN, Geneva, 1974–75; Central Amer. and Caribbean Dept, FCO, 1977–78; Mexico and Central Amer. Dept, FCO, 1981–82; Paris, 1984–86; Chief FCO Interpreter (Spanish), 1986–99; Antarctic Treaty UK Inspection Team, 1989; Minister-Counsellor, Consul-Gen., Dep. Hd of Mission and Commercial Manager, Brasilia, 1995–99. *Recreation:* music. *Address:* SMDB, Conj 4, Lote 3, Casa A, Lago Sul, Brasilia 71540-010, Brazil. *T:* (61) 3665344; *e-mail:* johnpenney@uol.com. br. *Club:* Brasilia Yacht.

PENNEY, Penelope Anne; Headmistress, Haberdashers' Aske's School for Girls, Elstree, since 1991; *b* 30 Sept. 1942; *d* of Richard Chamberlain, *qv* and late (Lydia) Joan (*née* Kay); *m* 1963, Rev. William Affleck Penney; one *s* two *d*. *Educ:* Chatelard Sch., Switzerland; Bristol Univ. (BA Hons 1964). Head of Langs and Communications, Astor of Hever Sch., Maidstone, 1974–79; Headmistress: Prendergast Sch., Catford, 1980–86; Putney High Sch. (GPDST), 1987–91. Pres., GSA, 1994–95 (Chm., Inspections Cttee, 2001–); Mem., Teacher Induction Panel, ISC, 1999–. Freeman, City of London, 1993. FIMgt 1995; MInstD 1995. FRSA. *Recreation:* fast cars. *Address:* Haberdashers' Aske's School for Girls, Aldenham Road, Elstree, Herts WD6 3BT. *T:* (020) 8266 2300.

PENNEY, Reginald John; Assistant Under-Secretary of State, Ministry of Defence, 1964–73, retired; *b* 22 May 1919; *s* of Herbert Penney and Charlotte Penney (*née* Affleck); *m* 1941, Eileen Gardiner; one *s* two *d*. *Educ:* Westminster School. War Service, Royal West Kent Regt, 1939–46. Civil Servant, Air Ministry, until 1964, including service with Far East Air Force, Singapore, 1960–63. Chm., Sherborne Soc., CPRE, 1976. *Recreation:* golf. *Address:* Rumbow Cottage, Acreman Street, Sherborne, Dorset DT9 3NX.

PENNICOTT, Maj.-Gen. Brian Thomas, CVO 1994; Gentleman Usher to the Queen, since 1995; management consultant, since 1998; *b* 15 Feb. 1938; *s* of Thomas Edward Pennicott and Vera Ethel (*née* Gale); *m* 1962, Patricia Anne Chilcott; two *s* three *d*. *Educ:* Portsmouth Northern Grammar Sch.; RMA, Sandhurst. Commnd, RA, 1957; RMCS, Shrivenham, 1969–70; Staff Coll., Camberley, 1971, GSO2 (W), Project Management Team 155mm Systems, 1972–73; NDC, Latimer, 1976–77; CO 29 Commando Regt, RA, 1977–80; SO1 Mil. Sec.'s Br. 6, MoD, 1980–82; Comdr Artillery, Falkland Is, 1982; Asst Mil. Attaché, Washington, 1982–83; Comdr Artillery, 1 Armd Div., 1983–86; NDC, Canada, 1986–87; Dep. Mil. Sec. (A), 1987–89; Dir, RA, 1989–91; Defence Services Sec., 1991–94 and ACDS (Personnel and Reserves), 1992–94. Gp Security Advr, 1994–95, Gp Personnel Manager, later Gp Human Resources Manager, 1995–96, Sun Alliance Gp; Gp Human Resources Manager, Royal & Sun Alliance Insurance Gp, 1996–98. Chm., Inksane (formerly BrandGuardian) Ltd (Hong Kong), 1999–. Chm., Hospital Saving Assoc., 1999–. Col Comdt, RA, 1991–96; Hon. Col, 289 Commando Battery, RA(V), 1991–99. Chm., Army FA, 1991–94. *Recreations:* golf, bridge. *Address:* c/o Lloyds TSB, Cox's & King's Branch, PO Box 1190, 7 Pall Mall, SW1Y 5NA. *Club:* Army and Navy.

PENNING-ROWSELL, Edmund Lionel; wine writer; Wine Correspondent: Country Life, 1954–87; Financial Times, 1964; *b* 16 March 1913; *s* of Edmund Penning-Rowsell and Marguerite Marie-Louise Penning-Rowsell (*née* Egan); *m* 1937, Margaret Wintringham; one *s* two *d*. *Educ:* Marlborough College. Journalist, Morning Post, 1930–35; Book Publisher, Frederick Muller Ltd, 1935–50; Sales Manager, B. T. Batsford, 1952–57; Dir, book publisher, Edward Hulton & Co./Studio-Vista, 1957–63; Manager, World Book Fair, Earl's Court, 1964. Mem. Cttee of Management, Internat. Exhibition Co-op. Wine Soc., 1959–87 (Chm., 1964–87); Chm., Internat. Co-operative Wine Soc., 1964–87; Founder Mem., William Morris Soc., 1953–54 (Vice-Pres.). Chevalier de l'Ordre du Mérite Agricole (France), 1971; Chevalier de l'Ordre du Mérite National (France), 1981. *Publications:* Red, White and Rosé, 1967; The Wines of Bordeaux, 1969, 6th edn 1989; (ed, trans. and updated) Higounet *et al*, Château Latour: the history of a great vineyard 1331–1992, 1993. *Recreation:* drinking wine, particularly claret. *Address:* Yew Trees House, Wootton, Woodstock, Oxford OX20 1EG. *T:* (01993) 811281. *Club:* Travellers.

PENNINGTON, Hugh; *see* Pennington, T. H.

PENNINGTON, Michael Vivian Fyfe; freelance actor and writer; *b* 7 June 1943; *s* of late Vivian Maynard Cecil Pennington and Euphemia Willock (*née* Fyfe); *m* Katharine Ann Letitia Barker (marr. diss.); one *s*. *Educ:* Marlborough Coll.; Trinity Coll., Cambridge (BA English). RSC, 1964–65; BBC, ITV, Woodfall Films Ltd, West End Theatre, Royal Court Theatre, etc, 1966–74; RSC, 1974–81: roles included Berowne, Angelo and Hamlet; Crime and Punishment, Lyric Hammersmith, 1983; National Theatre: Strider, 1984; Venice Preserv'd, 1984; Anton Chekhov, 1984; The Real Thing, Strand, 1985; Jt Artistic Dir, English Shakespeare Co., 1986–93: three world tours playing Henry V, Richard II, Coriolanus, Leontes, Macbeth, and Dir, Twelfth Night; Playing with Trains, RSC, 1989; Vershinin, The Three Sisters, Gate, Dublin, 1990; The Gift of the Gorgon, Barbican, 1992, Wyndhams, 1993; Dir, Twelfth Night, Tokyo, 1993; Hamlet, Gielgud, 1994; Taking Sides, Chichester, transf. Criterion, 1995; Dir, Twelfth Night, Chicago, 1996; The Entertainer, Hampstead, 1996; Waste, The Seagull, The Provok'd Wife, Anton Chekhov, Old Vic, 1997; The Misanthrope, Filumena, Major Barbara, Piccadilly, 1998; Gross Indecency, Gielgud, 1999; Timon of Athens, RSC, 1999; The Guardsman, Albery, 2000; *television* includes: Oedipus the King, 1985; Return of Sherlock Holmes, 1986; Dr Terrible's House of Horrible, 2001. *Publications:* Rossya—A Journey Through Siberia, 1977; The English Shakespeare Company, 1990; Hamlet: a user's guide, 1995; Twelfth Night: a user's guide, 1999; Are You There, Crocodile: inventing Anton Chekhov, 2002. *Recreations:* music, literature. *Address:* c/o Jonathan Altaras Associates, 13 Shorts Gardens, WC2H 9AT.

PENNINGTON, Prof. Robert Roland; Professor of Commercial Law, Birmingham University, 1968–94, subseq. Professor Emeritus; *b* 22 April 1927; *s* of R. A. Pennington; *m* 1965, Patricia Irene; one *d*. *Educ:* Birmingham Univ. (LLB, LLD). Solicitor. Reader, Law Soc.'s Sch. of Law, 1951–62; Mem. Bd of Management, Coll. of Law, 1962; Sen. Lectr in Commercial Law, 1962–68 and Dean, Faculty of Law, Birmingham Univ., 1979–82. Vis. Prof., QMW, 1995–96 and 1999–. Govt Adviser on Company Legislation, Trinidad, 1967 and Seychelles, 1970; UN Adviser on Commercial Law, 1970–; Special Legal Adviser to EEC, 1972–79. Editor, European Commercial Law Library, 1974–. *Publications:* Company Law, 1959, 8th edn 2001; Companies in the Common Market, 1962, 3rd edn as Companies in the European Communities, 1982; The Investor and the Law, 1967; Stannary Law: A History of the Mining Law of Cornwall and Devon, 1973; Commercial Banking Law, 1978; Gesellschaftsrecht des Vereinigten Königreichs, 1981 (in Jura Europae: Gesellschaftsrecht); The Companies Acts 1980 and 1981: a practitioners' manual, 1983; Stock Exchange Listing: the new regulations, 1985; Directors' Personal Liability, 1987; Company Liquidations: the substantive law: the procedure (2 vols), 1987; The Law of the Investment Markets, 1990; Pennington's Corporate Insolvency Law, 1991, 2nd edn 1997; Small Private Companies, 1998; The Reorganisation of Public and Private Companies' Share Capital, 1999. *Recreations:* travel, walking, history, archaeology. *Address:* Gryphon House, Langley Road, Claverdon, Warwicks CV35 8QA.

PENNINGTON, Prof. (Thomas) Hugh, PhD; FRCPath, FRCPE, FMedSci; FRSE; Professor of Bacteriology, University of Aberdeen, since 1979 (Dean, Faculty of Medicine, 1987–92); *b* 19 April 1938; *s* of Thomas Wearing Pennington and Dorothy Pennington; *m* 1965, Carolyn Ingram Beattie; two *d*. *Educ:* Lancaster Royal Grammar Sch.; St Thomas's Hosp. Med. Sch. (MB BS (Hons), Clutton Medal, Bristowe Medal, Beaney Scholarship; PhD). FRCPath 1990. House appts, St Thomas's Hosp., 1962–63; Asst Lectr, 1963–66, Lectr, 1966–67, Dept of Med. Microbiology, St Thomas's Hosp. Med. Sch.; Postdoctoral Fellow, Univ. of Wisconsin, 1967–69; Mem. Scientific Staff, 1969–70, Lectr, 1970–75, Sen. Lectr, 1975–79, MRC Virology Unit and Dept of Virology, Univ. of Glasgow. Chm., Expert Gp on 1996 E.coli O157 outbreak in Central Scotland, 1996–97; Member: Scottish Food Adv. Cttee, Food Standards Agency, Scotland, 2000–; Broadcasting Council for Scotland, 2000–; BBC Rural Affairs Adv. Cttee, 2000–. Gov., Rowett Res. Inst., 1980–88, 1995–. Lectures: Pumphandle, John Snow Soc., 1997; Appleyard, BVA, 1997; Col Stock, APHA, 1999; Frank May, Leicester Univ., 2001. Founder FMedSci 1998; FRES 1957; FRSA 1997; FRSE 1997; FRCPE 1998. Hon. DSc: Lancaster; Strathclyde. Caroline Walker Award, 1997; John Kershaw Meml Prize, RIPH&H, 1998; Silver Medal, Royal Scottish Soc. of Arts, 1999. *Publications:* (with D. A. Ritchie) Molecular Virology, 1975; papers on molecular virology, molecular epidemiology and systematics of pathogenic bacteria. *Recreations:* collecting books, dipterology. *Address:* Department of Medical Microbiology, University of Aberdeen, Medical School Buildings, Aberdeen AB25 2ZD. *T:* (01224) 681818.

PENNY, family name of **Viscount Marchwood**.

PENNY, (Francis) David, CBE 1982; FRSE; FREng; consulting engineer; *b* 20 May 1918; *s* of late David Penny and Esther Colley; *m* 1949, Betty E. Smith, *d* of late Oswald C. Smith. *Educ:* Bromsgrove County High School; University Coll., London (BSc; Fellow 1973). Engineering Apprenticeship, Cadbury Bros Ltd, 1934–39; Armament Design Establishment, Ministry of Supply, 1939–53; Chief Development Engineer, Fuel Research Station, 1954–58; Dep. Dir, Nat. Engineering Laboratory, 1959–66, Dir, 1967–69; Managing Director: YARD Ltd, 1969–79; Yarrow Public Ltd Co., 1979–83. Chairman: Control Systems Ltd, 1979–83; Automatic Revenue Controls Ltd, 1979–83. Mem. Bd, BSI, 1982–91. FIMarE; FIMechE (Mem. Council, 1964–85; a Vice-Pres., 1977–81; Pres., 1981–82); FREng (FEng 1980); Pres., Smeatonian Soc. of Civil Engrs, 1991–92. *Publications:* various technical papers. *Recreations:* gardening, walking. *Address:* The Park, Dundrennan, Kirkcudbright DG6 4QH. *T:* (01557) 500244.

PENNY, Nicholas Beaver, MA, PhD; Clore Curator of Renaissance Painting, since 1990, and Keeper, since 1998, National Gallery; *b* 21 Dec. 1949; *s* of Joseph Noel Bailey Penny, QC; *m* 1st, 1971, Anne Philomel Udy (marr. diss.); two *d*; 2nd, 1994, Mary Agnes Wall. *Educ:* Shrewsbury Sch.; St Catharine's Coll., Cambridge (BA, MA); Courtauld Inst., Univ. of London (MA, PhD). Leverhulme Fellow in the History of Western Art, Clare Hall, Cambridge, 1973–75; Lectr, History of Art Dept, Univ. of Manchester, 1975–82; Sen. Res. Fellow, History of Western Art, King's Coll., Cambridge, 1982–84; Keeper of Western Art, Ashmolean Mus., Oxford, and Professorial Fellow, Balliol Coll., Oxford, 1984–89. Slade Prof. of Fine Art, Univ. of Oxford, 1980–81; Mellon Prof. at Center for Advanced Study in the Visual Arts, Nat. Gall. of Art, Washington, 2000–Sept. 2002. Cavaliere nell'Ordine al merito della Repubblica Italiana, 1990. *Publications:* Church Monuments in Romantic England, 1977; Piranesi, 1978; (with Francis Haskell) Taste and the Antique, 1981; Mourning, 1981; (ed jtly) The Arrogant Connoisseur, 1982; (with Roger Jones) Raphael, 1983; (ed) Reynolds, 1986; Alfred and Winifred Turner, 1988; (with Robert Flynn Johnson) Lucian Freud, Works on Paper, 1988; Ruskin's Drawings, 1988; (jtly) From Giotto to Dürer, 1991; Catalogue of European Sculpture in the Ashmolean Museum: 1540 to the present day, 3 vols, 1992; The Materials of Sculpture, 1993; Picture Frames, 1997; (jtly) From Dürer to Veronese, 1999; reviews for London Review of Books; articles in Apollo, Burlington Magazine, Connoisseur, Jl of Warburg and Courtauld Insts, Past and Present, and elsewhere. *Address:* The National Gallery, Trafalgar Square, WC2N 5DN.

PENNYCUICK, Prof. Colin James, FRS 1990; Senior Research Fellow, University of Bristol, since 1997 (Research Professor in Zoology, 1993); *b* 11 June 1933; *s* of Brig. James Alexander Charles Pennycuick, DSO and Marjorie Pennycuick; *m* Sandy; one *s*. *Educ:* Wellington College; Merton College, Oxford (MA); Peterhouse, Cambridge (PhD). Lectr in Zoology, 1964–75, Reader, 1975–83, Bristol Univ.; seconded as Lectr in Zoology, Univ. of Nairobi, 1968–71, as Dep. Dir, Serengeti Res. Inst., 1971–73; Maytag Prof. of Ornithology, Univ. of Miami, 1983–92. *Publications:* Animal Flight, 1972; Bird Flight Performance, 1989; Newton Rules Biology, 1992. *Recreation:* gliding. *Address:* School of Biological Sciences, University of Bristol, Woodland Road, Bristol BS8 1UG.

PENRHYN, 6th Baron *cr* 1866; **Malcolm Frank Douglas-Pennant,** DSO 1945; MBE 1943; *b* 11 July 1908; 2nd *s* of 5th Baron Penrhyn and Alice Nellie (*d* 1965), *o d* of Sir William Charles Cooper, 3rd Bt; *S* father, 1967; *m* 1954, Elisabeth Rosemary, *d* of late Brig. Sir Percy Laurie, KCVO, CBE, DSO, JP; two *d*. *Educ:* Eton; RMC, Sandhurst. Colonel (retd), KRRC. *Heir:* *nephew* Simon Douglas-Pennant [*b* 28 June 1938; *m* 1963, Josephine Maxwell, *yr d* of Robert Upcott; two *s* two *d*]. *Address:* Edgedell Cottage, Chilland Lane, Martyr Worthy, Hants SO21 1EB. *Club:* Flyfishers'.

See also Sir T. R. Troubridge, Bt.

PENRITH, Bishop Suffragan of; *no new appointment at time of going to press.*

PENROSE, Rt Hon. Lord; George William Penrose; PC 2001; a Senator of the College of Justice in Scotland, since 1990; *b* 2 June 1938; *s* of late George W. Penrose and Janet L. Penrose; *m* 1964, Wendy Margaret Cooper; one *s* two *d*. *Educ:* Glasgow Univ. (MA, LLB). CA. Advocate, 1964; QC 1978; Advocate Depute, 1986; Home Advocate Depute, 1988. Procurator to Gen. Assembly of Ch. of Scotland, 1984–90. Pres., Scottish procs of Aircraft and Shipbuilding Industries Arbitration Tribunal, 1977–83; Mem., panel of Chairmen, Financial Services Tribunal, 1988–90. Hon. LLD Glasgow, 2000; DUniv Stirling, 2001. *Recreation:* walking. *Address:* Court of Session, Parliament House, Edinburgh EH1 1RQ.

PENROSE, Anne Josephine, (Mrs J. Penrose); *see* Robinson, A. J.

PENROSE, George William; *see* Penrose, Rt Hon. Lord.

PENROSE, Prof. Oliver, FRS 1987; FRSE; Professor of Mathematics, Heriot-Watt University, 1986–94, now Professor Emeritus; *b* 6 June 1929; *s* of Lionel S. Penrose, FRS, and Margaret Penrose (*née* Leathes); *m* 1953, Joan Lomas Dilley; two *s* one *d* (and one *s* decd). *Educ:* Central Collegiate Inst., London, Ont; University Coll. London (BSc); Cambridge Univ. (PhD). FRSE 1989. Mathematical Physicist, English Electric Co., Luton, 1952–55; Res. Asst, Yale Univ., 1955–56; Lectr, then Reader, in Mathematics, Imperial Coll., London 1956–69; Prof. of Mathematics, Open Univ., 1969–86. *Publications:* Foundations of Statistical Mechanics, 1970; about 75 papers in physics and maths jls; a few book reviews. *Recreations:* making music, chess. *Address:* 29 Frederick Street, Edinburgh EH2 2ND. *T:* (0131) 225 5879.

See also R. Penrose.

PENROSE, Sir Roger, OM 2000; Kt 1994; FRS 1972; Rouse Ball Professor of Mathematics, University of Oxford, 1973–98, now Emeritus; Fellow of Wadham College, Oxford, 1973–98, now Emeritus; *b* Colchester, Essex, 8 Aug. 1931; *s* of Lionel Sharples Penrose, FRS; *m* 1959, Joan Isabel Wedge (marr. diss. 1981); three *s*; *m* 1988, Vanessa Dee Thomas; one *s*. *Educ:* University Coll. Sch.; University Coll., Univ. of London (BSc spec. 1st cl. Mathematics), Fellow 1975; St John's Coll., Cambridge (PhD; Hon. Fellow, 1987). NRDC (temp. post, Feb.–Aug. 1956); Asst Lectr (Pure Mathematics), Bedford Coll., London, 1956–57; Research Fellow, St John's Coll., Cambridge, 1957–60; NATO Research Fellow, Princeton Univ. and Syracuse Univ., 1959–61; Research Associate King's Coll., London, 1961–63; Visiting Associate Prof., Univ. of Texas, Austin, Texas, 1963–64; Reader, 1964–66, Prof. of Applied Mathematics, 1966–73, Birkbeck Coll., London. Visiting Prof., Yeshiva, Princeton, Cornell, 1966–67 and 1969; Lovett Prof., Rice Univ., Houston, 1983–87; Distinguished Prof. of Physics and Maths, Syracuse Univ., NY, 1987–. Member: London Mathematical Soc.; Cambridge Philosophical Soc.; Inst. for Mathematics and its Applications; International Soc. for General Relativity and Gravitation. Adams Prize (Cambridge Univ.), 1966–67; Dannie Heineman Prize (Amer. Phys. Soc. and Amer. Inst. Physics), 1971; Eddington Medal (with S. W. Hawking), RAS, 1975; Royal Medal, Royal Soc., 1985; Wolf Foundn Prize for Physics (with S. W. Hawking), 1988; Dirac Medal and Prize, Inst. of Physics, 1989; Einstein Medal, 1990. *Publications:* Techniques of Differential Topology in Relativity, 1973; (with W. Rindler) Spinors and Space-time, Vol. 1, 1984, Vol. 2, 1986; The Emperor's New Mind, 1989 (Science Book Prize, 1990); Shadows of the Mind, 1994; (jtly) The Large, the Small and the Human Mind, 1997; many articles in scientific jls. *Recreations:* 3 dimensional puzzles, doodling at the piano. *Address:* Mathematical Institute, 24–29 St Giles, Oxford OX1 3LB. *T:* (01865) 273538.

PENRY-DAVEY, Hon. Sir David (Herbert), Kt 1997; **Hon. Mr Justice Penry-Davey;** a Judge of the High Court of Justice, Queen's Bench Division, since 1997; Presiding Judge, Northern Circuit, since 2000; *b* 16 May 1942; *s* of late Watson and Lorna Penry-Davey; *m* 1970, Judy Walter; two *s* one *d*. *Educ:* Hastings Grammar Sch.; King's Coll., London (LLB Hons; FKC 1998). British Univs debating tour of Canada, 1964. Called to the Bar, Inner Temple, 1965, Bencher, 1993; a Recorder, 1986–97; QC 1988; Leader, S Eastern Circuit, 1992–95; a Dep. High Court Judge, 1994–97. Chm., Gen. Council of the Bar, 1996 (Vice-Chm., 1995). *Recreations:* music, golf, cycling, hill-walking. *Address:* Royal Courts of Justice, Strand, WC2A 2LL.

PENTECOST, Prof. Brian Leonard, OBE 2000; MD; FRCP; Medical Director, British Heart Foundation, 1993–99; *b* 12 March 1934; *s* of Leonard Austin Pentecost and Florence Pentecost; *m* 1958, Janice Morgan Jones; one *s* two *d* (and one *d* decd). *Educ:* Erith Grammar Sch.; St Mary's Med. Sch., Univ. of London (MB BS 1957; MD 1965).

FRCP 1972. Jun. appts, St Mary's, Brompton and Hammersmith Hosps; Jun. Med. Specialist, RAMC, 1959–61; Consultant Physician and Cardiologist, United Birmingham Hosps, 1965–93; Dean of Postgraduate Med. and Dental Educn, 1987–91, Hon. Prof. of Medicine, 1991–96, now Emeritus, Univ. of Birmingham. Consultant Advr in Cardiology to CMO, 1986–93. Member: Med. Subcttee, UGC, 1985–89; Cttee on Safety of Medicines, 1984–89, 1996–98. Royal College of Physicians: Examnr, 1977–92; Mem. Council, 1979–82; Censor, 1982–84; Linacre Fellow, 1991–94; Med. Co-ordinator, Jt Cttee on Higher Med. Educn, 1991–94. Mem. Council, 1973–77, Sec., 1976–80, British Cardiac Soc. Chm. Trustees, Royal Medical Benevolent Fund. Gov., PPP Medical Healthcare Trust. Hon. DSc Aston, 1998. *Publications:* contribs on cardiovascular medicine to books and scientific jls. *Recreations:* gardening, theatre, golf. *Address:* 37 Farquhar Road, Edgbaston, Birmingham B15 3RA. *Club:* Army and Navy.

PENTREATH, Prof. Richard John, (Jan), DSc, PhD; CBiol, FIBiol; FSRP; Research Professor, Environmental Systems Science Centre, University of Reading, since 2000; *b* 28 Dec. 1943; *s* of John Alistair Dudley Pentreath and Mary Lena (*née* Gendall); *m* 1965, Elisabeth Amanda Leach; two *d*. *Educ:* Humphry Davy Grammar Sch.; QMC, London (BSc (Special)); DSc London; Univ. of Auckland (PhD). FIBiol 1980; CBiol 1984; FSRP 1989. Commonwealth Schol., 1966–68; SRC Fellow, 1969; Fisheries Radiobiol Lab., MAFF, 1969–89: Hd, Aquatic Envmtl Protection Div. and Dep. Dir, Fisheries Res., 1988–89; Chief Scientist, and Dir Water Quality, NRA, 1989–95; Chief Scientist, and Dir, Envmtl Strategy, EA, 1995–2000. Member: NERC, 1992–98; Adv. Bd, Centre for Social and Econ. Res. on Global Envt, 1994–; Res. Assessment Panel, HEFC, 1995–96, 1999–; Council, Marine Biol Assoc. of UK, 1998–2000; Council, Assoc. for Schs Science Engrg and Technol., 1998–2000; Council, SAHFOS, 2001–; Indep. Mem., JNCC, 2000–. Hon. Prof., UEA, 1996–; Vis. Prof., ICSTM, 1997–. Hon. DSc: Hertfordshire, 1998; UWE, 1999. *Publications:* Nuclear Power, Man and the Environment, 1980; contrib. numerous scientific papers. *Recreations:* Cornish history, crewing tall ships, visual arts. *Address:* 6 Court Gardens, Batheaston, Bath BA1 7PH. *T:* (01225) 859737.

PENZER, Dr Geoffrey Ronald, CChem, FRSC; Partner, Penzer Allen, since 1992; *b* 15 Nov. 1943; *s* of Ronald and Dora Penzer; *m* 1966, Sylvia Elaine (*née* Smith); one *s* one *d*. *Educ:* Merchant Taylors' Sch.; St John's Coll., Oxford (MA; DPhil 1969). CChem, FRSC 1979. Jun. Res. Fellow, Merton Coll., Oxford, 1967–69; Res. Chemist, Univ. of Calif, 1969–70; Lectr in Biol Chem., Univ. of York, 1970–75; British Council: Science Officer, Cairo, 1975–80; Science Officer, Mexico, 1980–84; Dir, Technical Co-operation Training Dept, 1984–87; Dir, Management Div., and Manager, HQ Location Project, 1987–91. Dir, Open Book Inspections, 1993–. Trustee, Outset, 1994–. FIMgt 1993. *Publications:* contrib. scientific books and jls. *Recreations:* music, landscapes, walking. *Address:* c/o Penzer Allen, 6 East Point, High Street, Seal, Sevenoaks, Kent TN15 0EG.

PENZIAS, Dr Arno Allan; Senior Technology Adviser, Lucent Technologies, Bell Labs Innovations, since 1998; Venture Partner, New Enterprise Associates, since 1998; *b* 26 April 1933; *s* of Karl and Justine Penzias; *m*; one *s* two *d*; *m* 1996, Sherry Levit Penzias. *Educ:* City Coll. of New York (BS Physics, 1954); Columbia Univ. (MA Physics, 1958; PhD Physics, 1962). Bell Laboratories: Mem., Technical Staff, 1961–72; Head, Radio Physics Res., 1972–76; Dir, Radio Res. Lab., 1976–79; Exec. Dir, Research, Communications Sciences, 1979–81; Vice-Pres., Research, 1981–95; Vice-Pres. and Chief Scientist, AT&T Bell Laboratories, 1995–96, Vice-Pres. and Chief Scientist, Lucent Technologies, Bell Labs Innovations, 1996–98. Lectr, Princeton Univ., 1967–72, Vis. Prof., Astrophysical Scis Dept, 1972–85; Res. Associate, Harvard Univ., 1968–80; Adjunct Prof., State Univ. of NY, Stony Brook, 1974–84; Lee Kuan Yew Dist. Vis., Nat. Univ. of Singapore, 1991. Lectures: Kompfner, Stanford Univ., 1979; Gamow, Colorado Univ., 1980; Jansky, NRAO, 1983; Michelson Meml, Dept US Navy, 1985; Tanner, Southern Utah State Coll., 1987; Klopsteg, Northwestern Univ., 1987; NSF Distinguished, 1987; Regent's, Univ. of Calif., Berkeley, 1990; Einstein, Princeton, 1996. Member: Sch. of Engrg and Applied Science (Bd Overseers), Univ. Pennsylvania, 1983–86; Union Councils for Soviet Jews Adv. Bd, 1983–; NSF Industrial Panel on Science and Technology, 1982–92; CIT Vis. Cttee, 1977–79; NSF Astronomy Adv. Panel, 1978–79; MNAS, 1975–; Wissenschaftliche Fachbeirat, Max-Planck Inst., Bonn, 1978–85 (Chm., 1981–83); Technology Adv. Council, EarthLink Network Inc., 1996–; Board of Directors: IMNET, 1986–92; A. D. Little, 1992–; Duracell, 1995–96; LCC, 1996–; Warpspeed, 1996–. Vice-Chm., Cttee of Concerned Scientists, 1976– (Mem., 1975–). Mem., National Acad. of Engrg, 1990. Hon. MIEEE, 1990. Trustee, Trenton State Coll., 1977–79. Dir, Grad. Faculties Alumni, Columbia Univ., 1987–. Hon. degrees: Paris Observatory, 1976; Wilkes Coll., City Coll. of NY, Yeshiva Univ., and Rutgers Univ., 1979; Bar Ilan Univ., 1983; Monmouth Coll., 1984; Technion-Israel Inst. of Technology, Pittsburgh Univ., Ball State Univ., Kean Coll., 1986; Ohio State Univ., Iona Coll., 1988; Drew Univ., 1989; Lafayette Coll., 1990; Columbia Univ., 1990; George Washington Univ., 1992; Rensselaer Polytechnic Inst., 1992; Pennsylvania Univ., 1992; Bloomfield Coll., 1994; Ranken Tech. Coll., 1997; Hebrew Union Coll., 1997. Henry Draper Medal, National Acad. of Sciences, 1977; Herschel Medal, RAS, 1977; (jtly) Nobel Prize for Physics, 1978; Townsend Harris Medal, City Coll. NY, 1979; Newman Award, City Coll. NY, 1983; Joseph Handleman Prize in the Scis, 1983; Grad. Faculties Alumni Award, 1984; Big Brothers Inc. of NY, City Achievement in Science Award, 1985; Priestly Award, Dickinson Coll., 1989; Pake Prize, APS, 1990; NJ Literary Hall of Fame, 1991; Pender Award, Pennsylvania Univ., 1992; NJ Science/Technology Medal, R&D Council of NJ, 1996; Industrial Res. Inst. Medalist, 1998. Mem. Editorial Bd, Annual Revs of Astronomy and Astrophysics, 1974–78; Associate Editor, Astrophysical Jl Letters, 1978–82. *Publications:* Ideas and Information: managing in a high-tech world, 1989; Digital Harmony: business, technology & life after paperwork, 1995; 100 published articles, principally in Astrophysical Jl. *Address:* 2490 Sand Hill Road, Menlo Park, CA 94025, USA. *T:* (650) 8549499, *Fax:* (415) 5440833; *e-mail:* apenzias@nea.com.

PEPPARD, Nadine Sheila, CBE 1970; race relations consultant; *b* 16 Jan. 1922; *d* of late Joseph Anthony Peppard and May Peppard (*née* Barber). *Educ:* Macclesfield High Sch.; Manchester Univ. (BA, Teacher's Dip.). French teacher, Maldon Grammar Sch., 1943–46; Spanish Editor, George G. Harrap & Co. Ltd, 1946–55; Trg Dept, Marks and Spencer, 1955–57; Dep. Gen.-Sec., London Council of Social Service, 1957–64; Nat. Advisory Officer for Commonwealth Immigrants, 1964–65; Gen. Sec., Nat. Cttee for Commonwealth Immigrants, 1965–68; Chief Officer, Community Relations Commn, 1968–72; Adviser on Race Relations, Home Office, 1972–83, retd. *Publications:* (trans.) Primitive India, 1954; (trans.) Toledo, 1955; various professional articles. *Recreations:* cookery, writing. *Address:* 321 The Cedars, Abbey Foregate, Shrewsbury SY2 6BY. *T:* (01743) 235124.

PEPPER, Prof. Gordon Terry, CBE 1990; Hon. Visiting Professor, City University Business School, 1987–90 and since 1998 (Director, Centre for Financial Markets, 1988–97 and Professor, 1991–97); Chairman, Lombard Street Research Ltd, since 2000 (Director, since 1998); *b* 2 June 1934; *s* of Harold Terry Pepper and Jean Margaret Gordon Pepper (*née* Furness); *m* 1958, Gillian Clare Huelin; three *s* one *d*. *Educ:* Repton; Trinity College, Cambridge (MA); FIA, FIIMR. Equity & Law Life Assurance Soc., 1957–60; W. Greenwell & Co.: Partner, 1962; Joint Senior Partner, 1980–86; Chairman, Greenwell Montagu & Co., 1986–87; Dir and Sen. Advr, Midland Montagu, 1985–90; Chm., Payton Pepper & Sons Ltd, 1987–97. Member: Cttee on Industry and Finance, NEDC, 1988–90; ESRC, 1989–93; Adv. Cttee, Dept of Applied Econs, Cambridge Univ., 1992–97; Shadow Monetary Policy Cttee, 1997–; Council of Econ. Advrs to Opposition front bench, 1999–. *Publications:* Money, Credit and Inflation, 1990; Money, Credit and Asset Prices, 1994; Inside Thatcher's Monetarist Revolution, 1998; (with M. Oliver) Monetarism under Thatcher - Lessons for the Future, 2001; papers to Jl of Inst. of Actuaries. *Recreations:* sailing, family. *Address:* Staddleden, Sissinghurst, Cranbrook, Kent TN17 2AN. *T:* (01580) 712852, *Fax:* (01580) 714853; *e-mail:* gordonpepper@compuserve.com. *Clubs:* Reform, Royal Ocean Racing.

PEPPER, Kenneth Bruce, CB 1965; Commissioner of HM Customs and Excise, 1957–73; *b* 11 March 1913; *s* of late E. E. Pepper; *m* 1945, Irene Evelyn Watts; two *s*. *Educ:* County High Sch., Ilford; London Sch. of Economics. Joined HM Customs and Excise, 1932; Asst Sec., 1949; Commissioner, 1957. Lieutenant, Intelligence Corps, 1944. *Address:* Fairfield, Cae Mair, Beaumaris, Gwynedd LL58 8YN.

PEPPER, Prof. Michael, FRS 1983; Professor of Physics, University of Cambridge, since 1987; Professorial Fellow of Trinity College, Cambridge, since 1987 (Senior Research Fellow, 1982–87); Joint Managing Director, Toshiba Research Europe Ltd (formerly Toshiba Cambridge Research Centre Ltd), since 1991; *b* 10 Aug. 1942; *s* of Morris and Ruby Pepper; *m* 1973, Jeannette Denise Josse, MB, BS, FRCPsych; two *d*. *Educ:* St Marylebone Grammar Sch.; Reading Univ. (BSc Physics, 1963; PhD Physics, 1967); MA 1987, ScD 1989, Cantab. FInstP 1991. Res. Physicist, Mullard Ltd, 1967–69; res. in solid state physics, The Plessey Co., Allen Clark Res. Centre, 1969–73; Cavendish Lab., 1973– (in association with The Plessey Co., 1973–82); Warren Res. Fellow of Royal Soc., Cavendish Lab., 1978–86; Principal Res. Fellow, GEC plc, Hirst Res. Centre, 1982–87. Mem., Univ. Council, 1993–97, Gen. Bd of Faculties, 1995–99, and various cttees of Council and Bd, 1993–99, Cambridge. Vis. Prof., Bar-Ilan Univ., Israel, 1984; Lectures: Inaugural Mott, Inst. of Physics, 1985; Royal Soc. Review, 1987; Rankin, Liverpool Univ., 1987; G. I. Taylor, Cambridge Philosophical Soc., 1988; Resnick, Bar-Ilan Univ., 1995. Past and present mem. of various cttees and panels of Inst. of Physics (Editl Bd, Jl of Physics, Condensed Matter, 1991–96), Royal Soc. (Associate Editor, 1983–89; Mem. Council, 1999–), Rutherford Meml Cttee, 1987–91, DTI and SERC (Cttees on Solid State Devices, Semiconductors, 1984–89). Fellow, Amer. Physical Soc., 1992. Hon. DSc: Bar-Ilan, 1993; Linköping, 1997. Guthrie Prize and Medal, Inst. of Physics, 1985; Hewlett-Packard Prize, European Physical Soc., 1985; Hughes Medal, Royal Soc., 1987; Mott Prize and Medal, Inst. of Physics, 2000. *Publications:* papers on semiconductors and solid state physics in jls. *Recreations:* whisky tasting, reading, travel, homework with two *d*. *Address:* Cavendish Laboratory, Madingley Road, Cambridge CB3 0HE. *T:* (01223) 337330; Toshiba Research Europe Ltd, 260 Cambridge Science Park, Milton Road, Cambridge CB4 4WE. *T:* (01223) 424666. *Clubs:* Athenæum; Arsenal Football.

PEPPER, Michael Peter Gregory, PhD; Head of Price and Business Statistics Group, Office for National Statistics (formerly Central Statistical Office), since 1993; *b* 2 June 1945; *s* of Arthur Pepper and Annie (*née* Panian); *m* 1991, Alice Fox; two *s* one *d*. *Educ:* Dr Challoner's Grammar Sch., Amersham; London Univ. (BSc Maths (Ext.)); Essex Univ. (MSc); PhD Bath. Res. Fellow, Univ. of Bath, 1970–74; Statistician, Dept of Energy, 1974–79; Sen. Statistician, Govt of Botswana, 1979–81; Statistician, Dept of Energy, 1981–86; Chief Statistician and Dir of Stats, Welsh Office, 1986–93. *Recreations:* squash, running, gardening, choral music. *Address:* Office for National Statistics, Government Buildings, Cardiff Road, Newport NP9 1XG. *T:* (01633) 812352.

PEPPIATT, Hugh Stephen Kenneth; Chairman, Moorfields Eye Hospital, 1991–98 (Special Trustee, 1991–2000); *b* 18 Aug. 1930; *s* of late Sir Leslie Peppiatt, MC and Lady (Cicely) Peppiatt; *m* 1960, Claire, *e d* of late Ian Douglas Davidson, CBE and Claire Davidson; three *s* two *d*. *Educ:* Winchester College; Trinity College, Oxford; Univ. of Wisconsin. Partner, Freshfields, Solicitors, 1960–90: Resident Partner, New York, 1977–81; Sen. Partner, 1982–90. Director: Greig Fester Gp, 1990–97; Hardy Oil & Gas, 1992–98; Benfield Greig Gp plc, 1997–99. Dir, St John Eye Hosp., Jerusalem, 1998–. Trustee, Help the Aged, 1991–97. *Recreations:* hillwalking, fly fishing, birdwatching. *Address:* 28 Bathgate Road, Wimbledon, SW19 5PN. *T:* (020) 8947 2709. *Clubs:* City of London; Royal Wimbledon Golf; Larchmont Yacht (New York).

PEPPITT, His Honour John Raymond; QC 1976; a Circuit Judge, 1991–2000; *b* 22 Sept. 1931; *s* of late Reginald Peppitt and Phyllis Claire Peppitt; *m* 1960, Judith Penelope James; three *s*. *Educ:* St Paul's Sch.; Jesus Coll., Cambridge (BA Classical Tripos). Called to the Bar, Gray's Inn, 1958, Bencher, 1982–2000; a Recorder, 1976–91. *Recreation:* collecting water-colours. *Address:* The Old Rectory, Snargate, Romney Marsh, Kent TN29 0EW.

PEPYS, family name of **Earl of Cottenham**.

PEPYS, Prof. Mark Brian, MD, PhD; FRCP, FRCPath, FMedSci; FRS 1998; Professor of Medicine, Head of Department of Medicine, and Hon. Consultant Physician, Royal Free and University College Medical School, London, since 1999; Head of National Health Service National Amyloidosis Centre, since 1999; *b* 18 Sept. 1944; *s* of Prof. Jack Pepys, MD, FRCP, FRCPE, FRCPath, and Rhoda Gertrude Pepys (*née* Kussel); *m* 1971, Dr Elizabeth Olga Winternitz; one *s* one *d*. *Educ:* Trinity Coll., Cambridge (BA, MA; MD 1982; PhD 1973); UCH Med. Sch., London. FRCP 1981; FRCPath 1991. Sen. Schol., 1964–65, Res. Schol., 1970–73, Fellow, 1973–79, Trinity Coll., Cambridge; MRC Trng Fellow, Dept of Pathology, Univ. of Cambridge, 1970–73; Registrar, then Sen. Registrar and Asst Lectr in Medicine, Hammersmith Hosp., 1973–75; Sen. Lectr, Hd of Immunology and Hon. Consultant Physician, Royal Free Hosp. Sch. of Medicine, 1975–77; Sen. Lectr in Medicine, 1977–80, Hon. Consultant Physician, 1977–99, Reader, 1980–84, Prof. of Immunol Medicine, 1984–99, RPMS, then ICSM, Hammersmith Hosp. Goulstonian Lectr, 1982, Lumleian Lectr, 1998, RCP; Sir Arthur Sims Travelling Prof., RCS, 1991; Kohn Lectr, RCPath, 1991; Chandos Lectr, Renal Assoc., 2000; Heberden Orator, British Soc. for Rheumatology, 2002. Founder FMedSci 1998. Moxon Trust Medal, RCP, 1999. *Publications:* contrib. articles on immunology, acute phase proteins and amyloidosis in learned jls. *Recreations:* ski-ing, tennis, surfing, wine. *Address:* 22 Wildwood Road, NW11 6TE. *T:* (020) 8455 9387. *Club:* Hurlingham.

PERAHIA, Murray, FRCM; pianist; co-artistic director, Aldeburgh Festival, 1981–89; *b* New York, 19 April 1947; *s* of David and Flora Perahia; *m* 1980, Naomi Shohet (Ninette); two *s*. *Educ:* High Sch. of Performing Arts; Mannes College (MS); studied piano with Jeanette Haien, M. Horszowski, Arthur Balsam. FRCM 1987; FRAM 1994. Hon. Dir, Britten-Pears Sch. for Advanced Musical Studies, 1981–. Won Kosciusko Chopin Prize, 1965; début Carnegie Recital Hall, 1966; won Leeds Internat. Piano Festival, 1972; Avery Fisher Award, 1975; regular tours of Europe, Asia, USA; numerous recordings include complete Mozart Piano Concertos (as dir and soloist with English Chamber Orch.), complete Beethoven Piano Concertos (with Bernard Haitink and Royal

Concertgebouw), Bartók Sonata for Two Pianos and Percussion (Grammy Award, 1989); Gramophone award for Handel and Scarlatti recording, 1997; Gramophone award for Bach English Suites recording, 1999. *Address:* c/o Askonas Holt Ltd, 27 Chancery Lane, WC2A 1PF.

PERCEVAL, family name of **Earl of Egmont**.

PERCEVAL, Viscount; Thomas Frederick Gerald Perceval; *b* 17 Aug. 1934; *e s* of 11th Earl of Egmont, *qv*.

PERCEVAL, Michael; HM Diplomatic Service, retired; Consul-General, Barcelona, 1992–96; *b* 27 April 1936; *o s* of late Hugh Perceval and Guida Brind; *m* 1968, Alessandra Grandis; one *s* one *d*. *Educ:* Downside Sch.; Christ Church, Oxford (Schol.; 2nd Cl. Hons English Lit.). Served Royal Air Force, Nicosia, 1956–60; film production asst, Athens, 1960; freelance correspondent, Madrid, 1961–69; joined FCO, 1970; First Sec. (Press), UK Rep. to EC, Brussels, 1972–74; First Sec. and subseq. Head of Chancery, British High Commission, Nicosia, 1974–78; Asst Head of Mexico and Caribbean Dept, FCO, 1978–79; Counsellor, Havana, 1980–82; Counsellor (Political and Economic) and Consul-Gen., Brasilia, 1982–85; Counsellor (Commercial), Rome, 1985–89; Consul-General, São Paulo, 1990–92. *Publication:* The Spaniards, 1969, 2nd edn 1972. *Recreations:* music, walking, the Mediterranean.

PERCEVAL, Robert Westby, TD 1968; Clerk Assistant, House of Lords, 1964–74; retired; *b* 28 Aug. 1914; *m* 1948, Hon. J. I. L. Littleton, *er d* of 5th Baron Hatherton; two *s* two *d*. *Educ:* Ampleforth; Balliol College, Oxford. Joined Parliament Office, House of Lords, 1938. Royal Artillery, 1939–44; General Staff, War Office, 1944–45. *Address:* Pillaton Old Hall, Penkridge, Staffs ST19 5RZ. *Clubs:* Beefsteak, Turf.

PERCHARD, Colin William, CVO 1997; OBE 1984; Minister (Cultural Affairs), India, British Council, 1993–2000; *b* 19 Oct. 1940; *m* 1970, Elisabeth Penelope Glynis, *d* of Sir Glyn Jones, GCMG, MBE; three *s*. *Educ:* Victoria Coll., Jersey; Liverpool Univ. (BA Hons History); Internat. Inst. for Educnl Planning, UNESCO, Paris (DipEd Planning and Admin). British Council: Asst Rep., Blantyre, Malawi, 1964–68; Regional Officer, Africa S of the Sahara, 1968–71: Asst Rep., Calcutta, 1971–72; Officer i/c Dhaka, 1972; Rep., Seoul, 1973–76; Dir, Technical Co-operation Trng Dept, 1976–79; Internat. Inst. for Educnl Planning, Paris, 1979–80; Rep., Harare, 1980–86; Controller, Africa Div., 1986–90; Dir and Cultural Counsellor, Turkey, 1990–93. *Recreations:* theatre, music, cooking. *Address:* Spring Farm, Rue de la Vignette, St Martin, Jersey JE3 6NY.

PERCIVAL, Prof. Ian Colin, PhD; FRS 1985; Research Professor in Physics, Queen Mary and Westfield (formerly Queen Mary) College, University of London, 1996–97 (Professor of Applied Mathematics, 1974–92); *b* 27 July 1931; *m* 1955, Jill Cuff (*née* Herbert) (*d* 1999); two *s* one *d*. *Educ:* Ealing County Grammar Sch.; UCL (BSc, PhD; Fellow, 1986). FRAS. Lectr in Physics, UCL, 1957–61; Reader in Applied Maths, QMC, 1961–67; Prof. of Theoret. Physics, Univ. of Stirling, 1967–74. Naylor Prize, London Mathematical Soc., 1985; Alexander von Humboldt Foundn Award, 1993; Dirac Medal and Prize, Inst. of Physics, 1999. *Publications:* (with Derek Richards) Introduction to Dynamics, 1983; (with Owen Greene and Irene Ridge) Nuclear Winter, 1985; Quantum State Diffusion, 1998; papers in learned jls on scattering theory, atomic and molecular theory, statistical mechanics, classical dynamics and theory of chaos and foundations of quantum theory. *Address:* Queen Mary and Westfield College, Mile End Road, E1 4NS. *T:* (020) 7882 5555; *e-mail:* i.c.percival@qmw.ac.uk.

PERCIVAL, Prof. John, FSA; Professor and Head of School of History and Archaeology, University of Wales College of Cardiff, 1988–96; Pro Vice-Chancellor, Cardiff University, since 1996; *b* 11 July 1937; *s* of Walter William Percival and Eva Percival (*née* Bowers); *m* 1st, 1962, Carole Ann Labrum (*d* 1977); two *d*; 2nd, 1988, Jacqueline Anne Gibson (*née* Donovan). *Educ:* Colchester Royal Grammar Sch.; Hertford Coll., Oxford (Lucy Schol.; 1st Cl. Lit. Hum.; MA; DPhil). FSA 1977. Harmsworth Sen. Schol., Merton Coll., Oxford, 1961; University College, Cardiff: Asst Lectr in Ancient History, 1962; Lectr, 1964; Sen. Lectr, 1972; Reader, 1979–88; Dean of Faculty of Arts, 1977–79; Dep. Principal, UWCC, 1987–90. Vice-Pres., 1989–, Chm. Council, 1990–95, Classical Assoc. (Jt Sec., 1979–89). Mem. Ct of Govs, Nat. Library of Wales, 1991–. *Publications:* The Reign of Charlemagne (with H. R. Loyn), 1975; The Roman Villa, 1976, 2nd edn 1988; articles in historical and archaeol jls. *Recreations:* music, gardening. *Address:* 26 Church Road, Whitchurch, Cardiff CF14 2EA. *T:* (029) 2061 7869.

PERCIVAL, John; freelance dance critic, since 1950; Editor, Dance & Dancers, since 1981; Joint Dance Critic, The Independent, since 1996; *b* 16 March 1927; *s* of Cecil Ernest Percival and Mua Phoebe Margaret Mary Percival (*née* Milchard); *m* 1954, Freda Betty Margaret Thorne-Large (marr. diss. 1972); *m* 1972, Judith Alymer Cruickshank. *Educ:* Sir George Monoux Grammar Sch., Walthamstow; St Catherine's Coll., Oxford (MA). On admin. staff, LCC, then GLC and ILEA, 1951–90. Archivist, Ballet Annual, 1960–64; ballet critic, New Daily, 1960–65; Associate Editor, Dance & Dancers, 1964–81; Chief Dance Critic, The Times, 1965–94; London correspondent: Dance Mag. (NY), 1965–89; German annual, Ballett, 1966–87; London dance critic, NY Times; Chm. and Dir, Dance & Dancers Ltd, 1991–; Eur. correspondent, Ballet Review (NY), 1996–. Advr, Nureyev Foundn, 1993–. Mem. Cttee, Gulbenkian Foundn. Has broadcast on radio and TV in Britain, Europe, America and Australia. *Publications:* Antony Tudor, 1963; Modern Ballet, 1970, rev. edn 1980; The World of Diaghilev, 1971, rev. edn 1979; Experimental Dance, 1971; Nureyev: aspects of the dancer, 1975, rev. edn 1979 (trans. Italian 1981, Japanese 1983); The Facts about a Ballet Company, 1979; Theatre in My Blood: a biography of John Cranko, 1983 (trans. German 1985); (with Alexander Bland) Men Dancing, 1984; contributed to: Enciclopedia dello Spettacolo, 1966; Marcia Haydee, Ballerina, 1975; Encyclopaedia of Dance and Ballet, 1977; Das Ballett und die Künste, 1981; John Neumeier und das Hamburger Ballett, 1983, 2nd edn 1993. *Recreations:* watching dance and writing and talking about it, reading thrillers, eating with friends. *Address:* 36 Great James Street, WC1N 3HB. *T:* (020) 7405 0267. *Club:* Critics' Circle (Past Pres.).

PERCIVAL-PRESCOTT, Westby William, FIIC; practising conservator and painter; *b* 22 Jan. 1923; *s* of William Percival-Prescott and Edith Percival; *m* 1948, Silvia Haswell Miller; one *s*. *Educ:* Edinburgh Coll. of Art (DA Hons). FIIC 1957. Andrew Grant Scholar, National Gall., 1945; restoration of Rubens Whitehall ceiling, 1947–51; Restorer i/c House of Lords frescos, 1953; worked in National Gall. Conservation Dept, 1954–56; directed restoration of Painted Hall, Greenwich, 1957–60; National Maritime Museum: estabd Picture Conservation Dept, 1961; Keeper and Head of Picture Dept, 1977–83; organised first internat. conf. on Comparative Lining Techniques, 1973 (Ottawa, 1974); produced and designed historical exhibitions: Idea and Illusion, 1960; Four Steps to Longitude, 1963; The Siege of Malta, 1970; Captain Cook and Mr Hodges, 1979; The Art of the Van de Veldes, 1982. Vis. Sen. Lectr, Dept of Fine Art, Univ. of Leeds, 1980; Leverhulme Trust Res. Award, 1996–97. Internat. Council of Museums: Co-ordinator, Conservation Cttee, 1975–84; Mem., Directory Bd, Conservation Cttee, 1981–84. *Publications:* The Coronation Chair, 1957; The Lining Cycle, 1974, Swedish edn 1975; Handbook of Lining Terms, 1974; Thornhill at Greenwich, 1978; Micro X-Ray Techniques, 1978; Techniques of Suction Lining, 1981; The Art of the Van de Veldes, 1982; technical papers. *Recreations:* listening to music, travel. *Address:* 34 Compayne Gardens, NW6 3DP. *T:* (020) 7624 4577.

PERCIVAL SMITH, Ven. (Anthony) Michael; Archdeacon of Maidstone, 1979–89; *b* 5 Sept. 1924; *s* of Kenneth and Audrey Smith; *m* 1950, Mildred Elizabeth; two *d*. *Educ:* Shrewsbury; Gonville and Caius Coll., Cambridge (MA); Westcott House Theological Coll. Served Army, Rifle Brigade, 1942–46. Cambridge, 1946–48; Westcott House, 1948–50. Deacon 1950, priest 1951; Curate, Holy Trinity, Leamington, 1950–53; Domestic Chaplain to Archbishop of Canterbury, 1953–57; Vicar of All Saints, Upper Norwood, 1957–66; Vicar of Yeovil, 1966–72; Prebendary of Wells Cathedral, 1968–72; RD of Murston, 1968–72; Vicar of St Mildred's, Addiscombe, Croydon, 1972–80; Hon. Canon of Canterbury Cathedral, 1980–; Diocesan Dir of Ordinands, 1980–89; RD of Rye, 1991–93. *Recreations:* reading, walking. *Address:* The Garden House, Horseshoe Lane, Beckley, East Sussex TN31 6RZ. *T:* (01797) 260514.

PERCY, family name of **Duke of Northumberland**.

PERCY, Earl; George Dominic Percy; *b* 5 May 1984; *e s* and *heir* of Duke of Northumberland, *qv*. A Page of Honour to the Queen, 1996–98.

PERCY, Algernon Eustace Hugh H.; *see* Heber-Percy.

PERCY, John Pitkeathly, (Ian), CBE 1997; CA; Chairman, Accounts Commission for Scotland, since 1992; Deputy Chairman, Scottish Provident, since 1993; *b* 16 Jan. 1942; *s* of John Percy and Helen Glass Percy (*née* Pitkeathly); *m* 1965, Sheila Isobel Horn; two *d*. *Educ:* Edinburgh Acad. Qualified as a Chartered Accountant with Graham Smart & Annan, Edinburgh, 1968; Grant Thornton: Partner, Edinburgh, 1970–78; London, 1978–91; Managing Partner, 1981–88; Sen. Partner, 1988–95. Chairman: Edinburgh Acad., 1995–; Director: Deutsche Scotland, 1992–; William Wilson (Holdings), 1993–; Weir Gp plc, 1996–; Kiln plc, 1998–; Ricardo plc, 2000–; Cala Gp Ltd, 2000–. Vice-Chm., UK Auditing Practices Bd, 1991–; Director: Companies House Steering Bd, 1995–; Scottish Legal Aid Bd, 2000–; Mem., Internat. Auditing Practices Cttee, 1995–2000. Hon. Prof. of Accounting and Auditing, Aberdeen Univ., 1988–. Mem., Convocation, Heriot-Watt Univ., 1992–. Pres., Inst. of Chartered Accountants of Scotland, 1990–91 (Sen. Vice-Pres., 1989–91). Freeman, City of London, 1983; Liveryman, Painter Stainers' Co., 1983. FRSA 1989. Hon. LLD Aberdeen, 1999. *Recreations:* golf, fishing. *Address:* 1–3 St Colme Street, Edinburgh EH3 6AA. *T:* (0131) 220 8214; 30 Midmar Drive, Edinburgh EH10 6BU. *T:* (0131) 452 8641, *Fax:* (0131) 447 6233. *Clubs:* Royal Automobile, Institute of Directors, Caledonian; New (Edinburgh); Denham Golf; Royal & Ancient (St Andrews), Hon. Company of Edinburgh Golfers.

PERCY, His Honour Rodney Algernon; a Circuit Judge, 1979–93; caravan site operator, 1993–99; *b* 15 May 1924; 3rd *s* of late Hugh James Percy, Solicitor, Alnwick; *m* 1948, Mary Allen, *d* of late J. E. Benbow, Aberystwyth; one *s* three *d*. *Educ:* Uppingham; Brasenose Coll., Oxford (MA). Lieut, Royal Corps of Signals, 1942–46, served in Burma, India, Malaya, Java. Called to Bar: Middle Temple, 1950; Lincoln's Inn, 1987 (*ad eund*). Dep. Coroner, N Northumberland, 1957; Asst Recorder, Sheffield QS, 1964; Dep. Chm., Co. Durham QS, 1966–71; a Recorder of the Crown Court, 1972–79. Pres., Tyneside Marriage Guidance Council, 1983–87; Founder Mem., Family Conciliation Service for Northumberland and Tyneside, 1982–93 (Pres., 1988–93). *Publications:* (ed) Charlesworth on Negligence, 4th edn 1962 to 6th edn 1977, 7th edn (Charlesworth & Percy on Negligence) 1983 to 10th edn 2001; (contrib.) Atkin's Court Forms, 2nd edn, Vol. 20, 1982, rev. edn 1987, 1993 (title Health and Safety at Work), and Vol. 29, 1983, rev. edn 1991 (title Negligence). *Recreations:* golf, gardening, hill walking, King Charles Cavalier spaniels, beach-combing. *Address:* Brookside, Lesbury, Alnwick, Northumberland NE66 3AT. *T:* (01665) 830326/830000.

PEREIRA, Sir (Herbert) Charles, Kt 1977; DSc; FRS 1969; Consultant, tropical agriculture research; *b* 12 May 1913; *s* of H. J. Pereira and Maud Edith (*née* Machin), both of London; *m* 1941, Irene Beatrice, *d* of David and May Sloan, Belfast; three *s* one *d*. *Educ:* Prince Albert Coll., Saskatchewan; St Albans Sch.; London Univ. Attached Rothamsted Expl Stn for PhD (London) 1941. Royal Engineers, 1941–46 (despatches). Colonial Agric. Service, Coffee Research Stn, Kenya, 1946–52; Colonial Research Service, established Physics Div. at East African Agriculture and Forestry Research Org., Kenya, 1952–61; DSc London 1961; Dir, ARC of Rhodesia and Nyasaland, 1961–63; Dir, ARC of Central Africa (Rhodesia, Zambia and Malawi), 1963–67; Dir, East Malling Research Station, 1969–72; Chief Scientist (Dep. Sec.), MAFF, 1972–77. Member: Natural Environment Res. Council, 1971–77; ARC, 1973–77; ABRC, 1973–77; Chm., Sci. Panel, Commonwealth Develt Corp., 1978–91; Pres., Tropical Agric. Assoc., 1990–. Mem. Bd of Trustees, Royal Botanic Gdns, Kew, 1983–86; Trustee, Marie Stopes Internat., 1991–. FInstBiol; FRASE 1977. Hon. DSc Cranfield, 1977. Haile Selassie Prize for Research in Africa, 1966. *Publications:* (jtly) Hydrological Effects of Land Use Changes in East Africa, 1962; Land Use and Water Resources, 1973; Policy and Practice in the Management of Tropical Watersheds, 1989; Simama (biog.), 2000; papers in research jls. *Recreations:* swimming, sailing. *Address:* Peartrees, Nestor Court, Teston, Maidstone, Kent ME18 5AD. *T:* (01622) 813333. *Clubs:* Athenæum; Harare (Zimbabwe).

PEREIRA, Margaret, CBE 1985; BSc; FIBiol; Controller, Home Office Forensic Science Service, 1982–88; *b* 22 April 1928. *Educ:* La Sainte Union Convent, Bexley Heath; Dartford County Grammar School for Girls; Chelsea Coll. of Science and Technol. BSc 1953. Joined Metropolitan Police Forensic Science Lab., New Scotland Yard, 1947; Dep. Dir, Home Office Forensic Science Central Res. Estab., 1976; Director, Home Office Forensic Science Laboratory: Aldermaston, 1977; Chepstow, 1979. *Address:* 24 Kingswood Close, Englefield Green, Egham, Surrey TW20 0NQ.

PEREIRA, Most Rev. Simeon Anthony; *see* Karachi, Archbishop of, (RC).

PEREIRA GRAY, Denis John; *see* Gray.

PEREIRA-MENDOZA, Vivian, MScTech, CEng, FIEE; Director, Polytechnic of the South Bank, 1970–80; *b* 8 April 1917; *o s* of Rev. Joseph Pereira-Mendoza, Manchester; *m* 1942, Marjorie, *y d* of Edward Lichtenstein; two *d*. *Educ:* Manchester Central High Sch.; Univ. of Manchester. Asst Lectr, Univ. of Manchester, 1939. Served War, 1940–45, in Royal Corps of Signals; Major, and GSO II (War Office). Sen. Lectr, Woolwich Polytechnic, 1948; Head of Dept: of Electrical Engrg, NW Kent Coll. of Technology, 1954; of Electrical Engrg and Physics, Borough Polytechnic, 1957; Vice-Principal, Borough Polytechnic, 1964; Principal, Borough Polytechnic, 1966–70. Mem. Council, Chelsea Coll., Univ. of London, 1972–85.

PERES, Shimon; Prime Minister of Israel, 1995–96; Member of Knesset, since 1959; *b* 1923; *s* of Yitzhak and Sarah Persky; *m* 1945, Sonia Gelman; two *s* one *d*. *Educ:* New York Univ.; Harvard Univ. Head of Naval Services, 1948–49; Head of Israel Defense Min.

delegn to US, 1949–52; Dir-Gen., Defense Min., 1953–59; Dep. Defense Minister, 1959–65; Sec. Gen., Rafi Party, 1965–68; Minister: of Immigrant Absorption, 1969–70; of Transport and Communications, 1970–74; of Information, 1974; of Defense, 1974–77; Acting Prime Minister, 1977; Prime Minister, 1984–86; Vice Premier, 1986–90; Minister of Foreign Affairs, 1986–88 and 1992–95; Minister of Finance, 1988–90. Chm, Israel Labour Party, 1977–92 and 1995–97; Vice-Pres., Socialist Internat., 1978. (Jtly) Nobel Peace Prize, 1994. *Publications:* The Next Phase, 1965; David's Sling, 1970; Tomorrow is Now, 1978; From These Men, 1980; Entebbe Diary, 1991; The New Middle East, 1993; Battling for Peace: memoirs, 1995. *Recreation:* reading. *Address:* The Knesset, Jerusalem, Israel.

PERETZ, David Lindsay Corbett, CB 1996; Senior Adviser, World Bank, since 1999; *b* 29 May 1943; *s* of Michael and April Peretz; *m* 1966, Jane Wildman; one *s* one *d*. *Educ:* The Leys Sch., Cambridge; Exeter Coll., Oxford (MA). Asst Principal, Min. of Technol., 1965–69; Head of Public Policy and Institutional Studies, IBRO, 1969–76; HM Treasury: Principal, 1976–80; Asst Sec., External Finance, 1980–84; Principal Pvte Sec. to Chancellor of Exchequer, 1984–85; Under-Secretary: Home Finance, 1985–86; Monetary Gp, Public Finance, 1986–90; UK Exec. Dir, IMF and World Bank, and Economic Minister, Washington, 1990–94; Dep. Dir, Internat. Finance, HM Treasury, 1994–99. *Recreations:* walking, sailing, listening to music. *Address:* World Bank, 1818 H Street NW, Washington, DC 20433, USA; *e-mail:* dperetz@worldbank.org.

PÉREZ DE CUÉLLAR, Javier, Hon. GCMG 1992; Ambassador of Peru to France, since 2001; *b* 19 Jan. 1920; *m* Marcela (*née* Temple); one *s* one *d*. *Educ:* Law Faculty, Catholic Univ., Lima, Perú. Joined Peruvian Foreign Ministry, 1940; Diplomatic Service, 1944; Sec., Peruvian Embassies in France, UK, Bolivia and Brazil and Counsellor, Embassy, Brazil, 1944–60; Mem., Peruvian Delegn to First Session of Gen. Assembly, UN, 1946; Dir, Legal, Personnel, Admin, Protocol and Political Affairs Depts, Min. of Foreign Affairs, Perú, 1961–63; Peruvian Ambassador to Switzerland, 1964–66; Perm. Under-Sec. and Sec.-Gen. of Foreign Office, 1966–69; Ambassador of Perú to USSR and to Poland, 1969–71; Perm. Rep. of Perú to UN, 1971–75 (Rep. to UN Security Council, 1973–74); Special Rep. of UN Sec.-Gen. in Cyprus, 1975–77; Ambassador of Perú to Venezuela, 1978; UN Under-Sec.-Gen. for Special Political Affairs, 1979–81; Sec.-Gen., UN, 1982–91. Prime Minister and Foreign Minister, Peru, 2000–01. Pres., World Commn on Culture and Develt, UN/UNESCO, 1992–; Chm. Emeritus, Inter-Amer. Dialogue, 1992–. Former Professor: of Diplomatic Law, Academia Diplomática del Perú; of Internat. Relations, Academia de Guerra Aérea del Perú. LLD *hc:* Univ. of Nice, France, 1983; Carleton Univ., Ottawa, 1985; Osnabruck Univ., 1986; Coimbra Univ., 1986; Oxford, 1993; other hon. degrees include: Jagiellonian Univ., Poland, 1984; Charles Univ. Czechoslovakia, 1984; Sofia Univ., Bulgaria, 1984; Universidad Nacional Mayor de San Marcos, Perú, 1984; Vrije Universiteit Brussel, Belgium, 1984; Sorbonne Univ., Paris, 1985; Cambridge Univ., 1989; Univ. of Salamanca, 1991; Oxford Univ., 1993. Various internat. awards including: Prince of Asturias Prize, 1987; Olof Palme Prize, 1989; Jawaharlal Nehru Award, 1989. Grand Cross, Order of El Sol (Perú); foreign decorations include: US Medal of Freedom; Grand Cross, Legion of Honour (France). *Publications:* Manual de Derecho Diplomático, 1964; Anarchy or Order, 1992; Pilgrimage for Peace, 1997. *Address:* Embassy of Peru, 50 avenue Kléber, 75116 Paris, France; Avenida Aurelio Miró Quesada 1071, Lima 27, Perú. *Clubs:* Travellers (Paris); Nacional, Ecuestre Huachipa, Jockey (Lima, Perú).

PÉREZ ESQUIVEL, Adolfo; sculptor; Hon. President: Servicio Paz y Justicia en América Latina, since 1986; Servicio Paz y Justicia Argentina, since 1973; President, International League for the Rights and Liberation of Peoples, since 1987; *b* 26 Nov. 1931; *m* 1956, Amanda Guerreño; three *s*. *Educ:* Nat. Sch. of Fine Arts, Buenos Aires. Prof. of Art, Manuel Belgrano Nat. Sch. of Fine Arts, Buenos Aires, 1956–76; Prof., Faculty of Architecture and Urban Studies, Univ. Nacional de la Plata, 1969–73; Gen. Co-ordinator, Servicio Paz y Justicia en América Latina, 1974–86. Work in permanent collections: Buenos Aires Mus. of Modern Art; Mus. of Fine Arts, Córdoba; Fine Arts Mus., Rosario. Joined group dedicated to principles of militant non-violence, and engaged in projects to promote self-sufficiency in urban areas, 1971; founded Paz y Justicia magazine, 1973. Co-founder, Ecumenical Movement for Human Rights, Argentina; Pres., Permanent Assembly for Human Rights. Premio la Nación de Escultura; Pope John XXIII prize, Pax Christi Orgn, 1977; Nobel Peace Prize, 1980. *Address:* Servicio Paz y Justicia, Piedras 730, CP 1070, Buenos Aires, Argentina.

PERFECT, Henry George, FICE, FCIWEM; Chairman, Babtie Group Ltd, since 1996; *b* 31 March 1944; *s* of George Hunter Perfect and Constance Mary Perfect (*née* Holland); *m* 1971, Kathleen Margaret Lilian Bain; two *s* one *d*. *Educ:* West Bridgford Grammar Sch., Nottingham; Birmingham Univ. (BSc Civil Engrg); Glasgow Univ. (MEng Foundn Engrg). FICE 1987; FCIWEM (FIWEM 1992). Asst Engr (working on coastal defence projects), C. H. Dobbie & Partners, 1965–69; Babtie Shaw & Morton, subseq. Babtie Group: Engr (projects incl. Kielder Water Scheme, and numerous reservoir, water and sewerage projects), 1969–83; Associate, 1983–86; Partner (responsible for water business in North of England), 1987–93; Man. Dir, Water Business, 1994–95. *Publications:* several papers on civil and water engrg. *Recreations:* hill walking, cycling. *Address:* Babtie Group Ltd, 95 Bothwell Street, Glasgow G2 7HX. *Clubs:* Western, Royal Scottish Automobile (Glasgow).

PERHAM, Linda; JP; MP (Lab) Ilford North, since 1997; *b* 29 June 1947; *d* of George Sidney Conroy and Edith Louisa Conroy (*née* Overton); *m* 1972, Raymond John Perham; two *d*. *Educ:* Mary Datchelor Girls' Sch.; Univ. of Leicester (BA Special Hons Classics); Ealing Tech. Coll. Postgrad. Dip. Liby Assoc.; ALA 1972. Library Asst, London Borough of Southwark, 1966; Inf. Officer, GLC Research Liby, 1970–72; City of London Polytechnic: Archives and Publications Librarian, 1972–76; Staff Develt Librarian, 1976–78; Cataloguer, Fawcett Liby, 1981–92; Bibliographical Librarian, Epping Forest Coll., 1992–97. Mem., Select Cttee on Trade and Industry, 1998–; Chm., All Party Gp on Libraries, 1998–; Vice Chairman: All Party Gp on Male Cancers; All Party Gp on Men's Health; Labour Friends of Israel; Hon. Secretary: All Party Gp on Ageing and Older People, 1998–; British-Israel Parly Gp, 1998–. JP Redbridge, 1990. *Publications:* Directory of GLC Library Resources, 1970, 2nd edn 1971; Greater London Council Publications 1965–71, 1972; Libraries of London, 1973; How to Find Out in French, 1977. *Recreations:* organising quizzes, arts, cinema, theatre (especially Shakespeare). *Address:* House of Commons, SW1A 0AA

PERHAM, Very Rev. Michael Francis; Dean (formerly Provost) of Derby, since 1998; *b* 8 Nov. 1947; *s* of Raymond Maxwell Perham and Marcelle Winifred Perham; *m* 1982, Alison Jane Grove; four *d*. *Educ:* Hardye's Sch., Dorchester; Keble Coll., Oxford (BA 1974; MA 1978); Cuddesdon Theol Coll. Curate, St Mary, Addington, 1976–81; Sec., C of E Doctrine Commn, 1979–84; Chaplain to Bp of Winchester, 1981–84; Team Rector, Oakdale Team Ministry, Poole, 1984–92; Canon Residentiary and Precentor, 1992–98, Vice Dean, 1995–98, Norwich Cathedral. Member: Liturgical Commn of C of E, 1986–; Archbishops' Commn on Church Music, 1988–92; Gen. Synod of C of E, 1989–92 and 1993–(Chm., Business Cttee, 2001–); Cathedrals' Fabric Commn for England, 1996–2001; Archbishops' Council, 1999–; Chairman: Praxis, 1990–97; Cathedrals' Liturgy Gp, 1994–2001. Mem., Church Heritage Forum, 1999–2001. Fellow, Woodard Corp., 2000–. *Publications:* The Eucharist, 1978, 2nd edn 1981; The Communion of Saints, 1980; Liturgy Pastoral and Parochial, 1984; (with Kenneth Stevenson) Waiting for the Risen Christ, 1986; (ed) Towards Liturgy 2000, 1989; (ed) Liturgy for a New Century, 1991; (with Kenneth Stevenson) Welcoming the Light of Christ, 1991; Lively Sacrifice, 1992; (ed) The Renewal of Common Prayer, 1993; (ed) Model and Inspiration, 1993; (compiled) Enriching the Christian Year, 1993; Celebrate the Christian Story, 1997; The Sorrowful Way, 1998; A New Handbook of Pastoral Liturgy, 2000. *Recreations:* reading, writing, creating liturgical texts, walking in the Yorkshire dales. *Address:* The Deanery, 9 Highfield Road, Derby DE22 1GX. *T:* (01332) 342971, 341201.

PERHAM, Nancy Jane; *see* Lane, N. J.

PERHAM, Prof. Richard Nelson, ScD, FRS 1984; Professor of Structural Biochemistry, Cambridge University, since 1989; Fellow, St John's College, Cambridge, since 1964; *b* 27 April 1937; *s* of Cyril Richard William Perham and Helen Harrow Perham (*née* Thornton); *m* 1969, Nancy Jane Lane, *qv*; one *s* one *d*. *Educ:* Latymer Upper School; St John's College, Cambridge; BA 1961, MA 1965, PhD 1965, ScD 1976; Scholar; Slater Studentship, 1961–64; Henry Humphreys Prize, 1963. Nat. Service RN, 1956–58. Cambridge University: MRC Scholar, Lab. of Molecular Biol., 1961–64; Univ. Demonstrator in Biochem., 1964–69, Lectr, 1969–77; Reader in Biochemistry of Macromolecular Structures, 1977–89; Head, Dept of Biochem., 1985–96; Res. Fellow, St John's Coll., 1964–67, Tutor, 1967–77, Pres., 1983–87. Helen Hay Whitney Fellow, Dept of Molecular Biophysics, Yale Univ., 1966–67; EMBO Fellow, Max-Planck-Institut für Medizinische Forschung, Heidelberg, 1971; Drapers' Vis. Prof., Univ. of New South Wales, 1972; Biochem. Soc. Visitor, Aust. and NZ, 1979; Fogarty Internat. Scholar, NIH, USA, 1990–93. Member: EMBO, 1983; SRC Enzyme Chem. and Tech. Cttee, 1973–75; Enzyme Panel, Biol. Scis Cttee, 1975–76; SERC Science Bd, 1985–90; Biochem. Soc. Cttee, 1980–84; British Nat. Cttee for Biochem., 1982–87; Dir's Adv. Gp, AFRC Inst. of Animal Physiology, 1983–86; Exec. Council, Novartis (CIBA) Foundn, 1989–; Chm., Biol Scis Cttee, SERC, 1987–90 (Mem., 1983–85); Pres., Section D (Biological Scis), BAAS, 1987–88. Chm., Scientific Adv. Cttee, Lister Inst. of Preventive Medicine, 2000– (Mem., 1992–98). Mem., Marshall Aid Commemoration Commn, FCO, 1999–. Mem., Academia Europaea, 1992. Syndic, CUP, 1988–. FRSA 1988. Max Planck Res. Prize, 1993; Novartis Medal and Prize, 1998; Silver Medal, Italian Biochem. Soc., 2000. *Publications:* (ed) Instrumentation in Amino Acid Sequence Analysis, 1975; papers in sci. jls. *Recreations:* gardening, rowing (Lady Margaret BC), theatre, nosing around in antique shops. *Address:* Department of Biochemistry, 80 Tennis Court Road, Cambridge CB2 1GA. *T:* (01223) 333663; St John's College, Cambridge CB2 1TP. *T:* (01223) 338600; 107 Barton Road, Cambridge CB3 9LL. *T:* (01223) 363752. *Clubs:* Oxford and Cambridge; Hawks (Cambridge).

PERKINS, Alice Elizabeth; Head of Civil Service Corporate Management, since 2000; *b* 24 May 1949; *d* of Derrick Leslie John Perkins and Elsa Rose Perkins, CBE (*née* Rink); *m* 1978, John Whitaker Straw, *qv*; one *s* one *d*. *Educ:* North London Collegiate Sch. for Girls; St Anne's Coll., Oxford (BA Hons Modern Hist. 1971). Joined CS, DHSS, 1971; Principal, 1976–84; Asst Sec., DHSS, then DSS, 1984–90; Dir of Personnel, DSS, 1990–93; Under Sec, Defence Policy and Materiel Gp, HM Treasury, 1993–95; Dep. Dir, Public Spending, HM Treasury, 1995–98; Dir, Corporate Mgt, DoH, 1998–2000. Trustee, Whitehall and Industry Gp, 1993–. Non-exec. Dir, Littlewoods Orgn, 1997–2000. *Recreations:* gardening, riding, looking at paintings. *Address:* Cabinet Office, Admiralty Arch, The Mall, SW1A 2WH.

PERKINS, Crispian G. S.; *see* Steele-Perkins.

PERKINS, Prof. Donald Hill, CBE 1991; FRS 1966; Professor of Elementary Particle Physics, 1965–93, and Fellow of St Catherine's College, since 1965, Oxford University; *b* 15 Oct. 1925; *s* of George W. and Gertrude Perkins; *m* 1955, Dorothy Mary (*née* Maloney); two *d*. *Educ:* Malet Lambert High School, Hull. BSc London 1945; PhD London 1948; 1851 Senior Scholar, 1948–51. G. A. Wills Research Associate in Physics, Univ. of Bristol, 1951–55; Lawrence Radiation Lab., Univ. of California, 1955–56; Lectr in Physics, 1956–60, Reader in Physics, 1960–65, Univ. of Bristol. Mem., SERC, 1985–89. Hon. DSc: Sheffield, 1982; Bristol, 1995. Guthrie Medal, Inst. of Physics, 1979; Holweck Medal and Prize, Société Française de Physique, 1992; Royal Medal, Royal Soc., 1997. *Publications:* The Study of Elementary Particles by the Photographic Method (with C. F. Powell and P. H. Fowler), 1959; Introduction to High Energy Physics, 1972, 4th edn 2000; about 50 papers and review articles in Nature, Physical Review, Philosophical Magazine, Physics Letters, Proc. Royal Soc., Nuovo Cimento, etc. *Recreations:* squash, tennis. *Address:* 2A Blenheim Drive, Oxford OX1 8DG. *T:* (01865) 311717.

PERKINS, John Vernon; District Judge (Magistrates' Courts) (formerly Metropolitan Stipendiary Magistrate), since 1999; *b* 13 June 1950; *s* of late Sidney and Lilian Florence Perkins; *m* 1975, Margaret Craig; one *s* one *d*. *Educ:* Tottenham Grammar Sch. Admitted Solicitor, 1975; Articled Clerk, 1970–75, Asst Solicitor, 1975–80, Partner, 1980–99 (Sen. Partner, 1988–99), J. B. Wheatley & Co. Mem., London Criminal Courts Solicitors' Assoc., 1975–99 (Hon. Mem. 1999). *Recreations:* walking, swimming, gardening. *Address:* c/o Principal Chief Clerk's Office, Secretariat Department, 65 Romney Street, SW1P 3RD.

PERKINS, Maj.-Gen. Kenneth, CB 1977; MBE 1955; DFC 1953; Commander, Sultan's Armed Forces, Oman, 1975–77 (successfully concluded Dhofar War); *b* 15 Aug. 1926; *s* of George Samuel Perkins and Arabella Sarah Perkins (*née* Wise); *m* 1st, 1949, Anne Theresa Barry (marr. diss. 1984); three *d*; 2nd, 1985, Hon. Celia Sandys, *d* of Rt Hon. Lord Duncan-Sandys, CH, PC and Diana, *d* of Rt Hon. Sir Winston Churchill, KG, OM, CH, FRS; one *s* one *d*. *Educ:* Lewes County Sch. for Boys; New Coll., Oxford. Enlisted 1944; commnd RA 1946; various appts in Middle and Far East, BAOR and UK until 1965, incl. air OP pilot in Korean War, Malayan Emergency, and Staff Coll. Quetta 1958; Instructor, Staff Coll. Camberley, 1965–66; CO 1st Regt Royal Horse Artillery, 1967–69; GSO 1 Singapore, 1970; Comdr 24 Bde, 1971–72; RCDS 1973; Central Staff, MoD, 1974; Maj.-Gen., 1975; Asst Chief of Defence Staff (Ops), 1977–80; Dir, Military Assistance Office, MoD, 1980–82. Defence Advr, BAe, 1982–86. Col Comdt, RA, 1980–85. Vice Pres., Sultan of Oman's Armed Forces Assoc., 1994– (Chm., 1987–94). Mem. Council, Res. Inst. for Study of Conflict, 1992–2000. Mil. Advr, The Sun newspaper, 1991–. Chm., Politicians' Complaints Commn, 1992–93. Trustee, Battlefield Trust, 1998–2001. Selangor Distinguished Conduct Medal (Malaya), 1955; Hashemite Order of Independence, first class, 1975; Order of Oman, 1977. *Publications:* Weapons and Warfare, 1987; A Fortunate Soldier (autobiog.), 1988; Khalida (novel), 1991; articles in press and professional jls. *Recreations:* writing, painting (exhibited RA), cycling, family pursuits. *Address:* 4 Bedwyn Common, Marlborough, Wilts SN8 3HZ. *Club:* Army and Navy.

PERL, Alfredo; pianist; *b* Chile, 25 June 1965. *Educ:* German Sch., Santiago; Cologne Conservatoire; with Maria Curcio in London. First performance at age of 9; début in Internat. Piano Series, Queen Elizabeth Hall, 1992; first recital at Wigmore Hall, 1994, and performed complete Beethoven Sonata cycle, 1996–97; UK recital appearances include: BBC Manchester and Scotland; Bridgewater Hall; St John's Smith Sq. Concert Series; has performed worldwide, including: Vienna Musikverein; London Barbican; Rudolfinum, Prague; Munich Herkulessaal; Izumi Hall, Osaka; Teatro Cólon, Buenos Aires; Sydney Town Hall; Nat. Arts Centre, Ottawa; Great Hall, Moscow Conservatoire; orchestral appearances include: LSO; BBC SO; RPO; Hague Residentie; Florida Philharmonic; Leipzig Radio; Adelaide SO; Melbourne SO; Mozarteum Orch.; Orch. de la Suisse Romande; MDR Leipzig; début at BBC Prom. Concerts, with BBC Philharmonic Orch., 1997. Has made numerous recordings, incl. complete Beethoven Sonatas. *Address:* c/o Askonas Holt Ltd, Lonsdale Chambers, 27 Chancery Lane, WC2A 1PF.

PERL, Prof. Martin Lewis, PhD; FInstP; Professor of Physics, Stanford Linear Accelerator Center, Stanford University, California, since 1963; *b* 24 June 1927; *s* of Oscar Perl and Fay Rosenthal Perl; *m*; three *s* one *d*. *Educ:* Polytechnic Univ., NY (BE Chem. 1948); Columbia Univ., NY (PhD Physics 1955). FInstP 1998. Chemical Engr, General Electric Co., 1948–50; Research Asst, Columbia Univ., 1950–55; Instructor, Asst Prof. and Associate Prof., Univ. of Michigan, 1955–63; Chm. of Faculty, Stanford Univ., 1991–. Mem., US Nat. Acad. of Scis, 1980–. Hon. DSc Chicago, 1990. Wolf Prize in Physics, Wolf Foundn, Israel, 1982; Nobel Prize in Physics, 1995. *Publications:* High Energy Hadron Physics, 1974; Physics Careers, Employment and Education, 1977; The Search for New Elementary Particles, 1992; The Tau-Charm Factory, 1994; Reflections on Experimental Science, 1996; numerous in physics and in science education. *Recreations:* collecting mechanical antiques, swimming, gardening. *Address:* Stanford Linear Accelerator Center, Stanford University, Stanford, CA 94309, USA. *T:* (650) 9262652.

PERLMAN, Itzhak; violinist and conductor; *b* Tel Aviv, 31 Aug. 1945; *s* of Chaim and Shoshana Perlman; *m* 1967, Toby Lynn Friedlander; two *s* three *d*. Studied at Tel Aviv Acad. of Music with Ryvka Goldgart, and at Juilliard Sch., NY, under Dorothy Delay and Ivan Galamian. First solo recital at age of 10 in Israel; New York début, 1958. Leventritt Meml Award, NY, 1964. Tours extensively in USA and plays with all major American symphony orchestras; recital tours of Canada, South America, Europe, Israel, Far East and Australia; Principal Guest Conductor, Detroit SO, 2001–. Has recorded numerous works for violin. Has received many Grammy Awards. Hon. degrees: Harvard; Yale; Brandeis. *Recreation:* cooking. *Address:* c/o Askonas Holt Ltd, Lonsdale Chambers, 27 Chancery Lane, WC2A 1PF.

PERMAN, Raymond John; Chief Executive, Scottish Financial Enterprise, since 1999; *b* 22 Aug. 1947; *s* of late Leonard Perman and Gladys Perman (*née* Rockingham); *m* 1974, Fay Young, writer and editor; three *s*. *Educ:* Univ. of St Andrews; BA Hons Open Univ.; Univ. of Edinburgh (MBA 1987). Journalist: Westminster Press, 1969–71; The Times, 1971–75; Financial Times, 1976–81; Dep. Editor, Sunday Standard, 1981–83; Man. Dir, Insider Publications Ltd, 1983–94; Director: Caledonian Publishing plc, 1994–96; GJWS, 1997–98. *Publications:* numerous newspaper and magazine articles. *Recreations:* forestry, painting, playing bass with the Blues Condition. *Address:* (office) 91 George Street, Edinburgh EH2 3ES. *T:* (0131) 247 7700; *e-mail:* rperman@sfe.org.uk.

PERMANAND, Rabindranath; High Commissioner in London for Trinidad and Tobago, 1993–96; *b* 17 July 1935; *s* of late Ram Narais Permanand and of Kalawatee Permanand (*née* Capildeo); *m* 1969, Ursel Edda Schmid; one *s* one *d*. *Educ:* Queen's Royal Coll., Trinidad; Univ. of Calcutta (BA Hons); Univ. of Delhi (MA); Univ. of West Indies (Dip. Internat. Relations). History Teacher, Queen's Royal Coll., 1959–66; joined Min. of Foreign Affairs, 1966; Dep. High Comr, Georgetown, Guyana, 1966–69; First Sec., Ottawa, 1969–72; Chief of Protocol, 1973–77; Counsellor and Minister Counsellor, Brussels, 1977–81; Consul-Gen., Toronto, 1981–84; Head, Political Div., 1984–88; Ambassador and Perm. Rep. to UN, Geneva, 1988–93. *Recreations:* reading, music, walking, cricket. *Address:* 1607 Scott Crescent, Kelowna, BC V1Z 2Y2, Canada.

PEROWNE, Rear-Adm. (Benjamin) Brian, CB 2001; Chief Executive, Naval Bases and Supply Agency, since 1999, and Chief of Fleet Support, since 2000; *b* 24 July 1947; *s* of Rear-Adm. Benjamin Cubitt Perowne, CB and of Phyllis Marjorie Perowne (*née* Peel); *m* 1975, Honora Rose Mary Wykes-Sneyd; two *s*. *Educ:* Gresham's Sch., Holt; BRNC, Dartmouth. Joined RN, 1965; served Far East, Mediterranean and N Atlantic, 1970–80; RN Staff Coll., 1977; HM Yacht Britannia, 1980–82; CO, HMS Alacrity, 1982–83; Staff, CBNS Washington, 1986–88; CO, HMS Brazen, 1988–89; Asst Dir (Strategic Systems), MoD, 1989–90; Chief Naval Signals Officer, MoD, 1990–92; rcds 1993; Commodore Clyde and Naval Base Comdr, 1994–96; Dir Gen., Fleet Support (Ops and Plans), 1996–99. ADC to the Queen, 1994–96. *Recreations:* family, country, cooking, most sports. *Address:* Management Suite, Spur 8, C Block, Ensleigh, Bath BA1 5AB. *Club:* Army and Navy.

PEROWNE, Adm. Sir James (Francis), KBE 2000 (OBE 1983); Deputy Supreme Allied Commander Atlantic, 1998–2002; *b* 29 July 1947; *s* of late Lt Comdr John Herbert Francis Perowne and of Mary Joy Perowne (*née* Dibb), Saundersfoot, Dyfed; *m* 1st, 1971, Susan Anne Holloway (marr. diss. 1990); four *s*; 2nd, 1992, Caroline Nicola Grimson. *Educ:* Sherborne Sch.; BRNC Dartmouth. CO, HMS Opportune, 1976–77; CO, HMS Superb, 1981–83; Staff of CBNS Washington, 1983–86; CO, HMS Boxer, 1986–88; Asst Dir, Naval Warfare, 1988–90; Captain, Second Submarine Sqdn, 1990–92; Captain, Sixth Frigate Sqdn and CO, HMS Norfolk, 1992–94; Sen. Naval Member, RCDS, 1995–96; Flag Officer Submarines, 1996–98; Comdr Submarines (NATO), Eastern Atlantic and Northwest Europe, 1996–98; COS (Ops) to C-in-C Fleet, 1996–98. Pres., Submarines Assoc. *Recreations:* golf, canal boating. *Address:* c/o Naval Secretary, Victory Building, HM Naval Base, Portsmouth PO1 3LS. *Clubs:* Army and Navy, Royal Navy of 1765 and 1785.

PERRETT, Desmond Seymour, QC 1980; **His Honour Judge Perrett;** a Circuit Judge, since 1992; *b* 22 April 1937; *s* of His Honour John Perrett and of Elizabeth Mary Perrett (*née* Seymour); *m* 1961, Pauline Merriel, *yr d* of late Paul Robert Buchan May, ICS, and of Esme May; one *s* one *d*. *Educ:* Westminster Sch. National Service, RN, 1955–57: midshipman RNVR, 1955; Suez, 1956, and Cyprus, 1957. Called to the Bar, Gray's Inn, 1962, Bencher, 1989; Oxford Circuit, 1963–72; Midland and Oxford Circuit, 1972–; a Recorder, 1978–92; Mem., Senate of the Inns of Court and of the Bar, 1983–87. Chm. Disciplinary Appeals Cttee, Cricket Council, 1986–97. *Recreations:* cricket, fishing, shooting. *Address:* The Old Bakehouse, Cartway, Bridgnorth, Salop WV16 4BG. *Club:* MCC.

PERRIN, Charles John; Vice Chairman, Royal Brompton & Harefield NHS Trust, since 1998; Deputy Chairman, Hambros Bank Ltd, 1986–98 (Chief Executive, 1995–98); *b* 1 May 1940; *s* of late Sir Michael Perrin, CBE, and Nancy May, *d* of late Rt Rev. C. E. Curzon; *m* 1966, Gillian Margaret, *d* of late Rev. M. Hughes-Thomas; two *d*. *Educ:* Winchester; New Coll., Oxford (Schol.; MA; Hon. Fellow, 1999). British Council Travelling Scholarship, 1962–63; called to the Bar, Inner Temple, 1965. Joined Hambros Bank, 1963, Dir, 1973–98; Chm., Hambro Pacific, Hong Kong, 1983–94; Dir, Hambros PLC, 1985–98. Non-executive Director: Harland and Wolff, 1984–89; Retroscreen Ltd, 1993–. Hon. Treas., UK Assoc. for International Year of the Child, 1979; Vice-Chm., UK Cttee for UNICEF, 1972–91. Mem., Royal Brompton Nat. Heart and Lung Hosps SHA, 1993–94; non-exec. Dir, Royal Brompton Hosp. NHS Trust, 1994–98. Member Council: Zoological Soc. of London, 1981–88 and 1991–; Univ. of London, 1994–; QMW, 1997– (Treas., 1999–). Governor: Queen Anne's Sch., Caversham, 1981–; London Hosp. Med. Coll., 1991–95. Hon. MRCP 1999. *Publication:* Darwinism Today (Endeavour Prize Essay, 1958). *Recreation:* sailing. *Address:* 4 Holford Road, Hampstead, NW3 1AD. *T:* (020) 7435 8103. *Club:* Athenæum.

PERRIN, Air Vice-Marshal Norman Arthur; Secretary General, ECTEL (European Conference of Telecommunications Industry Associations), 1991–97; *b* 30 Sept. 1930; *s* of late Albert Arthur and Mona Victoria (*née* Stacey); *m* 1956, Marie (*née* Bannon), *d* of late Peter and Lucy Bannon; one *s*. *Educ:* Liverpool Collegiate School; Hertford College, Oxford; RAF Technical College. BA; CEng, FRAeS. Nat. Service commn, Airfield Construction Branch, RAF, Suez Canal Zone, 1951–53; perm. commn, Tech. Branch, 1953; Advanced GW course, 1956–57; Air Ministry, 1958–61; HQ 11 Group, 1961–62; Staff Coll., 1963; FEAF, 1964–65; OC Eng Wing, RAF Seletar, 1966–67; JSSC 1967; Op. Requirements, SAGW, 1967–70; Chief Instructor, Systems Engineering, RAF Coll., 1970–72; Group Captain Plans, HQ Maintenance Comd, 1972–75; C. Mech. Eng., HQ Strike Comd, 1975–78; RCDS 1979; Dir Air GW MoD (PE), 1980–83; Vice-Pres. (Air), Ordnance Board, 1983: Pres., Ordnance Board, 1984–86. Dir, TEMA, 1987–91. *Recreations:* bridge, crosswords, Liverpool FC watching, choral singing. *Address:* c/o Barclays Bank, 10 High Street, Marlow, Bucks SL7 1AR. *Club:* Royal Air Force.

PERRING, Franklyn Hugh, OBE 1988; writer, lecturer, botanist, and traveller; *b* 1 Aug. 1927; *s* of Frank Arthur and Avelyn Millicent Perring; *m* 1st, 1951, Yvonne Frances Maud Matthews (marr. diss. 1972); one *s*; 2nd, 1972, Margaret Dorothy Barrow; one *d*. *Educ:* Earls Colne Grammar Sch.; Queens' Coll., Cambridge (MA, PhD). FLS; FIBiol 1979. Botanical Society of British Isles Distribution Maps Scheme: Hd, 1954–59; Dir, 1959–64; Hd, Biological Records Centre, Monks Wood Experimental Station, 1964–79; Botanical Sec., Linnean Soc. of London, 1973–78; Gen. Sec., RSNC, 1979–87. Chm., Wildlife Travel Ltd, 1988–. Pres., Botanical Soc. of the British Isles, 1993–95. Hon. Fellow, UC, Northampton, 2000. Hon. DSc Leicester, 1989. *Publications:* (jtly) Atlas of the British Flora, 1962; (jtly) A Flora of Cambridgeshire, 1964; Critical Supplement to the Atlas of the British Flora, 1968; (ed) The Flora of a Changing Britain, 1970; (ed jtly) The British Oak, 1974; (jtly) English Names of Wild Flowers, 1974, 2nd edn 1986; (jtly) British Red Data Book of Vascular Plants, 1977, 2nd edn 1983; (ed jtly) Ecological Effects of Pesticides, 1977; RSNC Guide to British Wild Flowers, 1984; (jtly) Ecological Flora of the Shropshire Region, 1985; (ed jtly) Changing Attitudes to Nature Conservation, 1988; (jtly) The Macmillan Guide to British Wildflowers, 1989; (ed jtly) The Nature of Northamptonshire, 1989; (ed jtly) Tomorrow is Too Late, 1990; Britain's Conservation Heritage, 1991; (ed jtly) Insects, Plants and Set-aside, 1995; (jtly) Scottish Plants for Scottish Gardens, 1996; sci. papers in Jl of Ecology, Watsonia, etc. *Recreations:* opera-going, poetry reading, gardening. *Address:* Green Acre, Wood Lane, Oundle, Peterborough PE8 5TP. *T:* (01832) 273388, *Fax:* (01832) 274568.

PERRING, Sir John (Raymond), 2nd Bt *cr* 1963, of Frensham Manor, Surrey; TD 1965; Chairman, Perrings Finance Ltd, since 1987; *b* 7 July 1931; *e s* of Sir Ralph Perring, 1st Bt and Ethel Mary (*d* 1991); *S* father, 1998; *m* 1961, Ella Christine, *e d* of late Tony and Ann Pelham; two *s* two *d*. *Educ:* Stowe School. Nat. Service, then TA, RA, 1949–60; Royal Fusiliers (City of London), 1960–65. Joined family business, Perring Furnishings, 1951, Dir 1957, Jt Man. Dir 1964, Vice-Chm., 1972, Chm., 1981–88. Nat. Pres., Nat. Assoc. of Retail Furnishers, 1971–73; Mem. Council, Retail Consortium, 1972–91 (Chm., non-food policy cttee, 1987–91); Mem. EDC (Distributive Trades), 1974–78. City of London: Sheriff, 1991–92; One of HM Lieutenants, 1963–; Assistant, Merchant Taylors' Co., 1980, Master, 1988, 1994; Master, Furniture Makers' Co., 1978. Trustee, Ranyard Meml Charitable Trust, 1983– (Chm., 1990–2001); Chm., Wimbledon DFAS, 1998–. Gov., Bishopsgate Foundn, 1993–. Pres., Bishopsgate Ward Club, 1997–98. FRSA. OStJ 1992. *Recreations:* outdoor pursuits. *Heir:* *s* John Simon Pelham Perring, *b* 20 July 1962. *Address:* 21 Somerset Road, Wimbledon, SW19 5JZ. *T:* (020) 8946 8971. *Clubs:* City Livery, Royal Automobile; Royal Wimbledon Golf; Bembridge Sailing.

PERRINS, Prof. Christopher Miles, LVO 1987; DPhil; FRS 1997; Director, Edward Grey Institute of Field Ornithology, 1974–Sept. 2002, and Professor of Ornithology, 1992–Sept. 2002, Oxford University; Fellow, 1970–74, Professorial Fellow, 1974–Sept. 2002, Wolfson College, Oxford; *b* 11 May 1935; *s* of Leslie Howard Perrins and Violet Amy (*née* Moore); *m* 1963, Mary Ceresole Carslake; two *s*. *Educ:* Charterhouse; QMC (BSc Hons Zool.; Hon. Fellow, QMW, 1996); Oxford Univ. (DPhil). Edward Grey Institute of Field Ornithology, University of Oxford: Research Officer, 1963–66; Sen. Res. Officer, 1966–84; Reader, 1984–92. Mem., General Bd of Faculties, Oxford Univ., 1983–91, 1995–99 (Chm., Bldgs Cttee, 1995–99); Delegate, OUP, 1994–Sept. 2002. The Queen's Swan Warden, 1993–. President: Internat. Ornithol Congress, 1990–94; European Ornithologists' Union, 1997–99; Hon. Corresp. Mem. 1976–83, Hon. Fellow 1983, Amer. Ornithologists Union; Hon. Fellow: German Ornithologists Union, 1991; Netherlands Ornithologists Union, 1992. Godman-Salvin Medal, British Ornithologists Union, 1988; Conservation Medal, RSPB, 1992. *Publications:* (ed with B. Stonehouse) Evolutionary Ecology, 1977; British Tits, 1979; (with T. R. Birkhead) Avian Ecology, 1983; (ed with A. L. A. Middleton) The Encyclopaedia of Birds, 1985; (with M. E. Birkhead) The Mute Swan, 1986; New Generation Guide: Birds, 1987; (ed with J. D. Lebreton and G. J. M. Hirons) Bird Population Studies, 1991; (Senior Ed.) Birds of the Western Palearctic, vol. VII, 1993, vols VIII and IX, 1994; (ed with D. W. Snow) The Birds of the Western Palearctic, concise edn, 2 vols, 1998. *Recreations:* photography, walking. *Address:* Edward Grey Institute of Field Ornithology, Department of Zoology, University of Oxford, South Parks Road, Oxford OX1 3PS. *T:* (01865) 271169.

PERRIS, Sir David (Arthur), Kt 1977; MBE 1970; JP; Secretary, Trades Union Congress West Midlands Regional Council, 1974–94; Vice President, Birmingham Hospital Saturday Fund, since 2000 (Vice-Chairman, 1975–85; Chairman, 1985–2000); *b* 25 May 1929; *s* of Arthur Perris; *m* 1955, Constance Parkes, BPharm, FRPharmS; one *s* one *d*. *Educ:* Sparkhill Commercial Sch., Birmingham. Film distribution industry, 1944–61; Reed Paper Group, 1961–65; Vice-Chm., ATV Midlands Ltd, 1980–81; Dir, Central Independent Television plc, 1982–83 (Vice Chm., W Midlands Bd). Sec., Birmingham Trades Council, 1966–83; a Chm., Greater Birmingham Supplementary Benefits Appeal Tribunal, 1982–89. Chairman: Birmingham Regional Hosp. Bd, 1970–74; West Midlands RHA, 1974–82; NHS National Trng Council, 1975–82; Mem. Bd of Governors, United Birmingham Hosps, 1965–74; Mem., Birmingham Children's Hosp. House Cttee, 1958–71 (Chm. 1967–71). Member: W Mids Econ. Planning Council, 1968–70; W Midlands Rent Assessment Panel, 1969–99; Midlands Postal Bd, 1974–81. Chairman: Central Telethon Trust, 1987–96; W Midlands Charitable Trust Gp,

1991–93; Pres., W Midlands Charity Trustees' Forum, 1999– (Chm., 1995–99). Life Governor, Univ. of Birmingham, 1972; Elective Gov. Birmingham & Midland Inst., 1989–. Mem. Council, Magistrates' Assoc., 1995–98 (Chm., 1975–86, Pres., 1986–98, Birmingham Br.); Pres., Public Service Announcements Assoc., subseq. Community Media Assoc., 1983–98; Pres., British Health Care Assoc., 1995–98 (Vice-Pres., 1994). Patron, Birmingham Rathbone Soc., 1998–. Life Fellow, British Fluoridation Soc., 1987. Hon. LLD Birmingham, 1981. JP Birmingham, 1961. *Recreation:* reading. *Address:* Broadway, 21 Highfield Road, Moseley, Birmingham B13 9HL. *T:* (0121) 449 3652.

PERRIS, John Douglas; HM Diplomatic Service, retired; *b* 28 March 1928; *s* of Frank William Perris and Alice Perris; *m* 1954, Kathleen Mary Lewington; one *s* two *d. Educ:* St Paul's, Knightsbridge; Westminster City Sch. Entered FO, 1945; Bahrain, 1951; Bucharest, 1953; Hamburg, 1955; FO, 1957; Tehran, 1960; Second Sec. (Admin), Caracas, 1963; Second Sec. (Econ.), Berlin, 1966; First Sec. (Admin), Baghdad, 1969; FCO (Inspectorate), 1972; First Sec./Head of Chancery/Consul, Tegucigalpa, 1974; First Sec. (Consular and Immigration), New Delhi, 1976; FCO, 1979; Counsellor (Admin), Bonn, 1982–86. *Recreations:* sport (non-active), reading (thrillers). *Address:* 128 Wakehurst Road, SW11 6BS. *T:* (020) 7228 0521.

PERROTT, John Gayford; HM Diplomatic Service; British High Commissioner, Gambia, since 2000; *b* 5 July 1943; *s* of Dr Charles Hardy Perrott and Dr Phylis Perrott (*née* Dearns); *m* 1964, (Joan) Wendy Lewis; one *s* one *d. Educ:* Newport High Sch. Joined CRO, later FCO, 1962; Karachi, 1966–69; Ankara, 1970–72; Calcultta, 1973–76; Kathmandu, 1979–84; Istanbul, 1984–88; St Helena, 1993–97. *Recreations:* swimming, golf. *Address:* c/o Foreign and Commonwealth Office, King Charles Street, SW1A 2AH.

PERROW, (Joseph) Howard; Chairman, Co-operative Union Ltd, 1975–83; Chief Executive Officer and Secretary, Greater Lancastria Co-operative Society Ltd, 1976–83; *b* 18 Nov. 1923; *s* of Joseph and Mary Elizabeth Perrow; *m* 1947, Lorraine Strick; two *s. Educ:* St Just, Penzance, Cornwall; Co-operative Coll., Stanford Hall, Leics (CSD). Joined Penzance Co-operative Soc., 1940. Served RAF, 1943–47. Various managerial positions in Co-operative Movement: in W Cornwall, with CRS N Devon, Carmarthen Soc., Silverdale (Staffs) and Burslem Socs; Mem., Co-operative Union Central Exec., 1966–83, Vice-Chm., 1973–75; Vice-Chm., NW Sectional Bd, 1970–75; Director: CWS, 1970–83; Nat. Co-operative Chemists, 1973–83; Greater Manchester Independent Radio, 1973–83; Mem., Central Cttee, Internat. Co-operative Alliance, 1975–83; Mem. Council (rep. Co-operative Union), Retail Consortium, 1976–83. President, Co-operative Congress, 1979. *Recreations:* football, cricket. *Address:* Blue Seas, Cliff Road, Mousehole, Penzance, Cornwall TR19 6QT. *T:* (01736) 731330. *Club:* Bolitho's (St Just).

PERRY, family name of **Baroness Perry of Southwark** and **Baron Perry of Walton**.

PERRY OF SOUTHWARK, Baroness *cr* 1991 (Life Peer), of Charlbury in the County of Oxfordshire; **Pauline Perry;** President, Lucy Cavendish College, Cambridge University, 1994–2001; *b* 15 Oct. 1931; *d* of John George Embleton Welch and Elizabeth Welch; *m* 1952, George Walter Perry; three *s* one *d. Educ:* Girton Coll., Cambridge (MA; Hon. Fellow 1995). Teacher in English Secondary Sch., Canadian and American High Schs, 1953–54 and 1959–61; High School Evaluator, New England, USA, 1959–61; Research Fellow, Univ. of Manitoba, 1956–57; Lecturer in Philosophy: Univ. of Manitoba, 1957–59; Univ. of Massachusetts at Salem, 1960–62; Lectr in Education (part-time), Univ. of Exeter, 1962–66; Tutor for In-Service Trng, Berks, 1966–70; Part-time Lectr in Educn, Dept of Educational Studies, Oxford Univ., 1966–70; HM Inspector of Schools, 1970–86; Staff Inspector, 1975; Chief Inspector, 1981. Dir, S Bank Poly., 1987–92; Vice-Chancellor, S Bank Univ., 1992–93. Alexander Stone Lectr in Rhetoric, Glasgow, 1999. Member: Cttee on Internat. Co-operation in Higher Educn, British Council, 1987–97; ESRC, 1988–91; Governing Body, Institute of Develt Studies, Sussex Univ., 1987–94; Bd, South Bank Centre, 1992–94; NI Higher Educn Council, 1992–94; Nat. Adv. Council on Educn and Training Targets, 1993–95; Prime Minister's Adv. Panel on Citizen's Charter, 1993–97; Overseas Project Bd, 1993–98; H of L Select Cttee on Science and Technol., 1992–95; H of L Select Cttee on relationships between local and central govt, 1995–96; H of L Select Cttee on Scrutiny of Delegated Powers, 1995–98; Royal Soc. Project Science Bd of Patrons, 1995–; Jt Select Cttee of Commons and Lords on Human Rights; H of L Select Cttee on Stem Cell Research; Chairman: DTI Export Gp for Educn and Trng Sector, 1993–98; Judges Panel on Citizen's Charter, 1997–; Advr on Police Trng to Home Office, 1991–93. Rector's Warden, Southwark Cath., 1990–94. MInstD; CIMgt 1994. Mem. Court, Univ. of Bath, 1991–99; Mem., Cambridge Univ. Foundn, 1997–; Pro-Chancellor, Univ. of Surrey, 2001–; Vice-Pres., C & G, 1994–99. Freeman, City of London, 1992. Liveryman, Bakers' Co., 1992. Hon. FCollP, 1987; Hon. FRSA, 1988. Hon. Fellow, Sunderland Polytechnic, 1990. Hon. LLD: Bath, 1991; Aberdeen, 1994; Hon. DLitt: Sussex, 1992; South Bank, 1994; City, 2000; DUniv Surrey, 1995; Hon. DEd Wolverhampton, 1994. Mem., Pedagogical Acad., Swedish Acad. of Sci., 1992. *Publications:* Case Studies in Teaching, 1969; Case Studies in Adolescence, 1970; Your Guide to the Opposite Sex, 1970; *contributions to:* Advances in Teacher Education, 1989; Women in Education Management, 1992; Public Accountability and Quality Control in Higher Education, 1990; The Future of Higher Education, 1991; Technology: the challenge to education, 1992; What is Quality in Higher Education?, 1993; Education in the Age of Information, 1993; School Inspection, 1995; Women and Higher Education, 1996; Against the Tide: women leaders in American and British higher education, 1996; Higher Education Reform, 2000; articles in various educnl jls; freelance journalism for radio and TV (incl. appearances on Question Time, Any Questions, Woman's Hour, Newsnight). *Recreations:* music, walking, cooking. *Address:* House of Lords, SW1A 0PW.

PERRY OF WALTON, Baron *cr* 1979 (Life Peer), of Walton, Bucks; **Walter Laing Macdonald Perry,** Kt 1974; OBE 1957; FRS 1985; FRSE 1960; Vice-Chancellor, The Open University, 1969–80, Fellow, since 1981; *b* 16 June 1921; *s* of Fletcher S. Perry and Flora M. Macdonald; *m* 1st, 1946, Anne Elizabeth Grant (marr. diss. 1971); three *s*; 2nd, 1971, Catherine Hilda Crawley; two *s* one *d. Educ:* Ayr Acad.; Dundee High Sch. MB, ChB 1943, MD 1948, DSc 1958 (University of St Andrews); MRCP (Edinburgh), 1963; FRCPE 1967; FRCP 1978; Fellow, UCL, 1981–. Medical Officer, Colonial Medical Service (Nigeria), 1944–46; Medical Officer, RAF, 1946–47; Member of Staff, Medical Research Council, 1947–52; Director, Department of Biological Standards, National Institute for Medical Research, 1952–58. Prof. of Pharmacology, University of Edinburgh, 1958–68, Vice-Principal, 1967–68. Member, British Pharmacopœia Commission, 1952–68; Secretary, British Pharmacological Society, 1957–61. Chairman: Community Radio Milton Keynes, 1979–82; Living Tapes Ltd, 1980–; Videotel Marine Internat., 1985–98 (Pres., 1998–). Chairman: Research Defence Soc., 1979–82 (Pres., 1993–); Delegacy of Goldsmiths' Coll., 1981–84; Standing Cttee on Continuing Educn, UGC and Nat. Adv. Body for Public Sector Higher Educn, 1985–89. Dep. Leader, SDP peers in House of Lords, 1981–83, 1988–89. Hon. DSc Bradford, 1974; Hon. LLD Dundee, 1975; Hon. DHL: Maryland, 1978; State Univ. of NY, 1982; DUniv: Athabasca, 1979; Stirling, 1980; Open, 1981; Hon. DLitt: Deakin Univ., Australia, 1981; Andhra Pradesh Open Univ., 1987; Hon. DEd Univ. of Victoria, 1992. Wellcome Gold Medal, 1994; Royal Medal, RSE, 2000. *Publications:* Open University, 1976; papers in Journal of Physiology, British Journal of Pharmacology and Chemo-therapy, etc. *Recreations:* making music and playing games. *Address:* The Open University, 10 Drumsheugh Gardens, Edinburgh EH3 7QJ. *Club:* Scottish Arts (Edinburgh).

PERRY, Alan Joseph; Director, Whitehall Strategic Management Consultants Ltd, 1992–95; *b* 17 Jan. 1930; *s* of late Joseph and Elsie Perry; *m* 1961, Vivien Anne Ball; two *s. Educ:* John Bright Grammar Sch., Llandudno; Dartford Grammar Sch. Served RE, 1948–50. HM Treasury, 1951–68 and 1970–78; CSD, 1968–70; Principal 1968, Asst Sec. 1976; Counsellor (Economic), Washington, 1978–80; Asst Sec., HM Treasury, 1980–86; Advr on Govt Affairs, Ernst & Whinney, 1986–88; Dir, Public Sector Services, Ernst & Young, 1989–92. Chm., Review of BBC External Services, 1984.

PERRY, David Gordon; Chairman: Anglian Group, 1996–2001; John Waddington, later Waddington, plc, 1993–97; *b* 26 Dec. 1937; *s* of late Elliott Gordon Perry and Lois Evelyn Perry; *m* 1961, Dorne Mary Busby; four *d. Educ:* Clifton Coll.; Christ's Coll., Cambridge. Management Trainee and Sales Exec., ES&A Robinson Ltd, 1960–66; Sales Dir 1966–69, Man. Dir 1969–78, Fell & Briant Ltd (subsid. of British Printing Corp.); British Printing Corporation: Chm. and Chief Exec., Packaging Div., 1978–80; Dir, 1980–81; John Waddington plc: Dep. Man. Dir, 1981–82; Man. Dir, 1982–88; Chief Exec., 1988–92. Non-executive Director: Whitecroft plc, 1991–95; Dewhirst Gp plc, 1992–; National & Provincial Building Soc., 1993–96; Kelda Gp plc (formerly Yorkshire Water plc), 1996–2000; Minorplanet Systems plc, 1997–; Euler Holdings UK plc, 1998–; Bellway plc, 1999–. CIMgt (CBIM 1985). FRSA 1990. *Recreation:* Rugby football (Cambridge Blue 1958, England XV 1963–66, Captain 1965). *Address:* Deighton House, Deighton, near Escrick, York YO19 6HQ. *Club:* Oxford and Cambridge.

PERRY, Sir David (Howard), KCB 1986; Chief of Defence Equipment Collaboration, Ministry of Defence, 1985–87, retired; *b* 13 April 1931; *s* of Howard Dace Perry and Annie Evelyn Perry; *m* 1961, Rosemary Grigg; one *s* two *d. Educ:* Berkhamsted Sch.; Pembroke Coll., Cambridge (MA). CEng, FRAeS. Joined Aero Dept, RAE, 1954; Aero Flt Div., 1954–66; Aero Projs Div., 1966–71; Head of Dynamics Div., 1971–73; RCDS, 1974; Head of Systems Assessment Dept, RAE, 1975–77; Ministry of Defence (Procurement Executive): Dir-Gen. Future Projects, 1978–80; Dir-Gen. Aircraft 1, 1980–81; Dep. Controller of Aircraft, 1981–82, Controller of Aircraft 1982; Chief of Defence Procurement, 1983–85. *Recreations:* gardening, painting. *Address:* 23 Rectory Road, Farnborough, Hants GU14 7BU.

PERRY, Sir David Norman; *see* Perry, Sir Norman.

PERRY, George Henry; *b* 24 Aug. 1920; *s* of Arthur and Elizabeth Perry; *m* 1944, Ida Garner; two *d. Educ:* elementary sch. and technical college. Engineering Apprentice, 1934–41. Naval Artificer, 1941–46 (Atlantic and Italy Stars; 1939–45 Star). Railway Fitter, 1946–66. Derby Town Councillor, 1955–66. Chairman: Derby Water Cttee, 1957–61; S Derbys Water Board, 1961–66; Derby Labour Party, 1961–62; Secretary, Derby Trades Council, 1961–66. Contested (Lab) Harborough, 1964; MP (Lab) Nottingham South, 1966–70. *Recreation:* walking. *Address:* 123 Hawthorn Street, Derby DE2 8BB. *T:* (01332) 44687.

PERRY, John; *see* Perry, R. J.

PERRY, Rt Rev. John Freeman; *see* Chelmsford, Bishop of.

PERRY, Rev. John Neville; *b* 29 March 1920; *s* of Robert and Enid Perry; *m* 1946, Rita Dyson Rooke; four *s* four *d. Educ:* The Crypt Gram. Sch., Gloucester; Univ. of Leeds (BA 1941), College of the Resurrection, Mirfield. Asst Curate, All Saints', Poplar, 1943–50; Vicar, St Peter De Beauvoir Town, Hackney, 1950–63; Vicar, St Dunstan with St Catherine, Feltham, Mddx, 1963–75; Rural Dean of Hounslow, 1967–75; Archdeacon of Middlesex, 1975–82; Rector of Orlestone with Ruckinge and Warehorne, Kent, 1982–86. Mem. Latey Cttee on the Age of Majority, 1966–67. *Recreation:* relief wood carving. *Address:* 73 Elizabeth Crescent, East Grinstead, West Sussex RH19 3JG.

PERRY, John William; Chairman, Trace Computers, 1996–2001 (non-executive Director, 1994–96 and since 2001); *b* 23 Sept. 1938; *s* of John and Cecilia Perry; *m* 1961, Gillian Margaret; two *d. Educ:* Wallington Grammar Sch.; Brasenose Coll., Oxford (MA). Burroughs: Dir of Marketing, UK, 1967–71, Europe Africa Div., 1977–78; Group Dir, Internat. Marketing, 1978–80; Vice-President: Strategic Planning, 1981; Financial Systems Gp., 1983; Central USA, 1985–86; Man. Dir, Burroughs UK, 1986; Chm. and Man. Dir, Unisys, 1987–94; Corporate Officer, 1990, Pres., Financial Services, 1993–94, Unisys Corp.; Director, 1987–94: Sperry; Burroughs Machines; BMX Information Systems; BMX Holdings; Unisys Holdings; Convergent Technologies (UK). Trustee, Information Age Project, 1989. Mem., Bd of Governors, Polytechnic of East London, 1989. *Recreations:* gardening, reading, music. *Address:* The Great Barn, Sandpit Lane, Bledlow, Bucks HP27 9QQ.

PERRY, Jonathan Peter Langman; Executive Chairman, Paragon Group of Companies PLC (formerly National Home Loans Holdings), since 1992; *b* 6 Sept. 1939; *s* of Thomas Charles Perry and Kathleen Mary Perry; *m* 1965, Sheila Johnson; two *s* one *d. Educ:* Peter Symonds Sch., Winchester. FCA. Butler Viney Childs, 1956–62; Cooper Brothers, 1962–66; Morgan Grenfell & Co., 1966–88 (Dir, 1973–88); Principal, Perry Associates, 1988–90; Chm. and Chief Exec., Ogilvie Adams & Rinehart, 1990–92; Vice-Chm., HSBC Investment Banking, 1997–99. *Recreations:* sailboat racing, golf, tennis, music. *Address:* Paragon Group of Companies PLC, 6 Greencoat Place, SW1P 1PL. *T:* (020) 7957 9700. *Clubs:* Brooks's; Royal Yacht Squadron, Itchenor Sailing; West Sussex Golf.

PERRY, Rev. Canon Michael Charles, MA; Canon Residentiary, 1970–98, now Canon Emeritus, and Sub-Dean, 1985–98, Durham Cathedral; Senior Chaplain to the Bishop of Durham, 1993–98; *b* 5 June 1933; *o s* of late Charlie Perry; *m* 1963, Margaret, *o d* of late John Middleton Adshead; two *s* one *d. Educ:* Ashby-de-la-Zouch Boys' Grammar Sch.; Trinity Coll., Cambridge (Sen. Schol.); Westcott House, Cambridge. Asst Curate of Berkswich, Stafford, 1958–60; Chaplain, Ripon Hall, Oxford, 1961–63; Chief Asst for Home Publishing, SPCK, 1963–70; Archdeacon of Durham, 1970–93. Examining Chaplain to Bishop of Lichfield, 1965–74. Sec., Archbishops' Commn on Christian Doctrine, 1967–70. Diocesan Chm., 1970–81, Mem. Council, 1975–81, USPG; Mem., 1981–88, Vice-Chm., 1982–88, Hosp. Chaplaincies Council, Gen. Synod; Mem. Council for the Deaf, Gen. Synod, 1986–90. Mem., Durham HA, 1982–88. Trustee, 1970–96, Chm., 1982–96, Lord Crewe's Charity; Chm., Churches' Fellowship for Psychical and Spiritual Studies, 1986–95 (Pres., 1998–). Lectures: Selwyn, NZ, 1976; Marshall Meml, Melbourne, 1976; Beard Meml, London, 1977; Maurice Elliott Meml, London, 1986; Shepherd Meml, Worcester, 1988. Editor, Church Quarterly, 1968–71; Editor, Christian Parapsychologist, 1978–. *Publications:* The Easter Enigma, 1959; The Pattern of Matins and Evensong, 1961; (co-author) The Churchman's Companion, 1963;

Meet the Prayer Book, 1963; (contrib.) The Miracles and the Resurrection, 1964; (ed) Crisis for Confirmation, 1967; (co-author) Declaring The Faith: The Printed Word, 1969; Sharing in One Bread, 1973; The Resurrection of Man, 1975; The Paradox of Worship, 1977; A Handbook of Parish Worship, 1977, 2nd edn 1989; (contrib.) Yes to Women Priests, 1978; (co-author) A Handbook of Parish Finance, 1981, 3rd edn 1992; Psychic Studies: a Christian's view, 1984; Miracles Then and Now, 1986; (ed) Deliverance, 1987, 2nd edn 1996; Gods Within: a critical guide to the New Age, 1992. *Address:* 15 Ferens Park, The Sands, Durham DH1 1NU. *T:* (0191) 386 1891.

PERRY, Sir Michael (Sydney), Kt 1994; CBE 1990 (OBE 1978); Chairman, Centrica plc, since 1997; *b* 26 Feb. 1934; *s* of Sydney Albert Perry and Jessie Kate (*née* Brooker); *m* 1958, Joan Mary Stallard; one *s* two *d*. *Educ:* King William's Coll., IoM; St John's Coll., Oxford (MA). Unilever, 1957–96: Chm., Lever Brothers (Thailand) Ltd, 1973–77; Pres., Lever y Asociados SACIF, Argentina, 1977–81; Chm., Nippon Lever KK, 1981–83; Jt Man. Dir, UAC Internat., 1983–85, Chm., 1985–87; Dir, Unilever plc and Unilever NV, 1985–96; Personal Products Co-ordinator, 1987–91; Vice-Chm., 1991–92, Chm., 1992–96, Unilever plc; Vice Chm., Unilever NV, 1992–96. Non-executive Director: Bass plc, 1991–2001 (Dep. Chm., 1996–2001); British Gas plc, 1994–97; Marks and Spencer plc, 1996–2001; Royal Ahold BV, 1997–; non-exec. Chm., Dunlop Slazenger Gp Ltd, 1996–. Mem., BOTB, 1986–92; Jt Chm., Netherlands British Chamber of Commerce, 1989–93; Chairman: Japan Trade Gp, 1991–99; Sen. Salaries Rev. Body, 1995–; Marketing Council, 1996–99. Pres., Advertising Assoc., 1993–96. Pres., Liverpool Sch. of Trop. Med., 1997– (Vice-Pres., 1991–97); Member Council: Cheltenham Coll., 1995–2000; Alice Ottley Sch., Worcester, 2001–. Chm., Shakespeare Globe Trust, 1993–; Trustee: Leverhulme Trust, 1991–; Glyndebourne Arts Trust, 1996–; Dyson Perrins Mus. Trust, 2000–. CIMgt (CBIM 1992). FRSA 1992. Hon. LLD South Bank, 1995; DUniv Brunel, 1995; Hon. DSc Cranfield, 1995. *Recreations:* music (choral), walking. *Clubs:* Oriental; Worcestershire Golf.

PERRY, Sir Norman, Kt 1977; MBE 1962; *b* 25 July 1914; *s* of Frederick and Letitia Perry; *m* 1939, Phyllis Ruth Conway; two *s* three *d*. Served War, 1942–44, 2nd NZEF, 28th (Maori) Bn. Engaged in tribal affairs, 1938–50; former Maori Welfare Dist Officer; Advr, 1961–62, then Sec., and Consultant, NZ Maori Council; Chm., Mahi Tahi Charitable Trust, reformative prog. Maori prison inmates, 1990–; advr to rural industries and tribal trusts. Lay Moderator, Presbyterian Church, 1965. Knighthood awarded for services to the community and the Maori people, New Zealand. *Address:* PO Box 12017, Chartwell Square, Hamilton, New Zealand.

PERRY, Norman Henry, PhD; Chief Executive, Housing Corporation, since 2000; *b* 5 March 1944; *s* of late Charles and Josephine Perry; *m* 1970, Barbara Ann Marsden; two *s*. *Educ:* Quintin Sch., NW8; University Coll. London (BA 1965; PhD 1969). Lectr in Geography, UCL, 1965–69; Sen. Res. Officer, GLC, 1969–73; Sen. Res. Fellow, SSRC Survey Unit, 1973–75; joined DoE, 1975; Principal, London and Birmingham, 1975–80; Asst Sec., W Midlands Regl Office, 1980–86; Head of Inner Cities Unit (G4), Dept of Employment, then DTI, 1986–88; Under Sec., and Dir W Midlands, DTI, 1988–90; Chief Exec. and Policy Co-ordinator, Wolverhampton MBC, 1990–95; Chief Exec., Solihull MBC, 1995–2000. Dir, Wolverhampton TEC, 1990–95; Gov., Univ. of Wolverhampton, 1993–95. Company Sec., Solihull Business Partnership Ltd, 1996–; Dir, Central Careers Ltd, 1996–99. Sec., Soc. of Metropolitan Chief Execs, 1998–; Chm., Assoc. of Local Authority Chief Execs, 1999–. FIMgt 1983; FRSA 1996. *Publications:* (contrib.) European Glossary of Legal and Administrative Terminology, 1974, 1979, 1988; contribs to books and learned jls in fields of geography, planning, organisational sociology and urban policy. *Address:* Housing Corporation, 149 Tottenham Court Road, W1P 0BN. *T:* (020) 7393 2104; *e-mail:* norman.perry@housingcorp.gsx.gov.uk.

PERRY, Roy James; Member (C) South East Region, England, European Parliament, since 1999 (Wight and Hampshire South, 1994–99); *b* 12 Feb. 1943; *s* of George and Dora Perry; *m* 1968, Veronica Haswell; two *d*. *Educ:* Tottenham County Grammar Sch.; Exeter Univ. Marks & Spencer, 1964–66; Lectr in Govt and Politics, 1966–75, Sen. Lectr, 1975–94, Southampton Tech. Coll. Leader, Test Valley Borough Council, 1985–94. Cons. spokesman on educn, culture and media, EP, 1994–; EPP co-ordinator, Petitions Cttee, 1999–. Mem., Trident Trust, 1996–; Trustee, Milestones Hampshire Museums Trust, 1998–. Mem. Court, Univ. of Surrey, 1999–. *Recreations:* bridge, French travel and food. *Address:* (office) Tarrants Farm House, Maurys Lane, Wellow, Romsey, Hants SO51 6DA. *Club:* Royal Naval and Royal Albert Yacht.

PERRY, (Rudolph) John; QC 1989; *b* 20 Feb. 1936; *s* of Rudolph Perry and late Beatrice (*née* Tingling, subseq. Robertson); *m* (marr. diss.); one *d*. *Educ:* Ruseas High Sch., Lucea, Jamaica; Southgate Technical Coll.; London Sch. of Economics (LLB (Hons), LLM); Univ. of Warwick (MA (Industrial Relations)). Lectr (part-time), LSE, 1970–78; Lectr, 1971, Sen. Lectr, 1974–78, City of London Poly. Called to the Bar, Middle Temple, 1975; in practice, 1976–; an Asst Recorder, 1988, Recorder, 1992. Mem. Panel of Chairmen, Public Disciplinary Appeals Tribunals, 1997–. *Recreations:* watching cricket, travel, cinema. *Address:* 3 Gray's Inn Square, Gray's Inn, WC1R 5AH. *T:* (020) 7520 5600, (020) 7831 2311.

PERRY, Prof. Samuel Victor, BSc (Liverpool), PhD, ScD (Cantab); FRS 1974; Professor of Biochemistry, 1959–85, now Emeritus, and Head of Department of Biochemistry, 1968–85, University of Birmingham; *b* 16 July 1918; *s* of late Samuel and Margaret Perry; *m* 1948, Maureen Tregent Shaw; one *s* two *d*. *Educ:* King George V Sch., Southport; Liverpool Univ.; Trinity Coll., Cambridge. Served in War of 1939–45, home and N. Africa; Royal Artillery, 1940–46, Captain; POW 1942–45. Research Fellow, Trinity Coll., Cambridge, 1947–51; Commonwealth Fund Fellow, University of Rochester, USA, 1948–49; University Lecturer, Dept of Biochemistry, Cambridge, 1950–59. Member: Standing Cttee for Research on Animals, ARC, 1965–72; Biol Scis and Enzyme Cttees, SRC, 1968–71; Medical Res. Cttee, Muscular Dystrophy Gp of GB, 1970–90; Systems Bd, MRC, 1974–77; Research Funds Cttee, British Heart Foundn, 1974–82; British Nat. Cttee for Biochemistry, 1978–87 (Chm., 1982–87); Council, Royal Soc., 1986–88; Chairman: Cttee of Biochemical Soc., 1980–83; Adv. Bd, Meat Res. Inst., 1980–85. Croonian Lectr, Royal Soc., 1984. FAAAS 1987. Hon. Mem., Amer. Soc. of Biol Chemists, 1978; Corresponding Mem., Société Royale des Sciences, Liège, 1978; Mem., Accad. Virgiliana, Mantova, 1979; Foreign Mem., Accademia Nazionale dei Lincei, 1989. CIBA Medal, Biochemical Soc., 1977. *Publications:* scientific papers in Biochemical Journal, Nature, Biochemica Biophysica Acta, etc. *Recreations:* gardening, building stone walls, Rugby football (Cambridge, 1946, 1947, England, 1947, 1948). *Address:* 41 Selly Wick Drive, Selly Park, Birmingham B29 7JQ. *T:* (0121) 472 2100.

PERRY, William Arthur; Command Secretary (Adjutant General, Personnel and Training Command), Ministry of Defence, 1994–97; *b* 5 Aug. 1937; *s* of Arthur Perry and Elizabeth Grace (*née* Geller); *m* 1962, Anne Rosemary Dight; two *d*. *Educ:* St Dunstan's Coll. Min. of Aviation, 1960–61; Second Sec. (Defence Supply), Bonn, 1964–66; Min. of Technology, then MoD, 1966–74; First Sec., UK Delegn to NATO, 1974–77; Head, Defence Secretariat 8, MoD, 1978–80; Counsellor (Defence Supply), Bonn, 1980–84; Regl Marketing Dir, Defence Exports Services Orgn, 1984–88; Asst Sec., MoD (PE), 1988–92; Dir (Finance and Secretariat), Air 1, MoD (PE), 1992–94. Mem., Royal Patriotic Fund Corp., 1994–97. *Recreations:* opera, gardening, genealogy.

PERRY, Dr William James; Professor, School of Engineering, Stanford University, since 1997; Secretary of Defense, United States of America, 1994–97; *b* Pa, 11 Oct. 1927; *m* Lee; three *s* two *d*. *Educ:* Butler High Sch., Butler, Pa; Carnegie Tech.; Stanford Univ. (BS Maths, MS); Penn State Univ. (PhD Maths). Served US Army: Fort Belvoir, Japan and Okinawa, 1946–47; Army Reserves, 1950–55. Dir, Electronic Defense Labs, Sylvania/General Telephone; Exec. Vice Pres., Hambrecht and Quist Inc.; Founder, ESL Inc., 1964, Pres., 1964–77; Under-Sec. of Defense for Res. and Engrg, 1977–81; Stanford University: Co-Dir, Center for Internat. Security and Arms Control, 1988–93; Chm., Technol. Strategies & Alliances, 1985–93; Dep. Sec. of Defense, 1993–94. Mem., Nat. Acad. Engrg; Fellow, Amer. Acad. Arts and Scis. Distinguished Public Service Medal, Dept of Defense, 1980 and 1981; Distinguished Service Medal, NASA, 1981; Medal of Achievement, Amer. Electronics Assoc., 1980; US Presidential Medal of Freedom, 1997. *Address:* Stanford University, CA 94305, USA.

PERRYMAN, (Francis) Douglas; Corporate Director for Finance (formerly Board Member), British Telecommunications, 1981–86; *b* 23 April 1930; *s* of Frank Smyth Perryman and Caroline Mary Anderson; *m* 1955, Margaret Mary Lamb; two *d*. *Educ:* West Hartlepool Grammar School; Durham Univ. BCom (Hons); FCA. Articled Clerk, 1951–55; Nat. Service, commnd RAPC, 1955–57; National Coal Board: Area Chief Accountant, Fife and Scottish South Areas, 1963–72; Finance Dir, Opencast Exec., 1972; Dir Gen. of Finance, 1978–81; Board Mem. for Finance, PO, 1981; Corporate Commercial Dir, BT, 1986–88. Mem. Council, CBI, 1987–88; Dir, Homes Assured Corp., 1989–90. *Recreations:* golf, Rugby football, music, Francophile. *Address:* 8 Henrietta Villas, Bath BA2 6LX. *T:* (01225) 460952.

PERSEY, Lionel Edward; QC 1997; *b* 19 Jan. 1958; *s* of Dr Paul Ronald Persey and Irene Persey; *m* 1984, Lynn Mear; one *s*. *Educ:* Haberdashers' Aske's Sch., Elstree; Birmingham Univ. (LLB Hons 1980). Called to the Bar, Gray's Inn, 1981; in practice as commercial and maritime barrister, 1982–; Mem., Supplementary Panel, Jun. Treasury Counsel, 1992–97. *Recreations:* classical music, opera, reading, gardening. *Address:* 4 Field Court, Gray's Inn, WC1R 5EA. *T:* (020) 7440 6900, *Fax:* (020) 7242 0197; *e-mail:* chambers@4fieldcourt.co.uk. *Club:* Reform.

PERSSON, Göran; Prime Minister of Sweden, since 1996; Chairman, Swedish Social Democratic Party, since 1996; *b* 20 Jan. 1949; *m* Annika Persson; two *d* from previous marriage. *Educ:* Orebro Univ. Organising Sec., 1971, Mem. of Bd, 1972–75, Swedish Social Democratic Youth League; mil. service, 1973–74; Sec., Workers' Educn Assoc., Sörmland, 1974–76; Chairman: Katrineholm Educn Authy, 1977–79; Bd of Educn, Södermanland Co., 1982–89. Mem., Riksdag (MP), 1979–84, 1991–94; Municipal Comr, Katrineholm, 1985–89; Minister for Schs and Educn, 1989–91; Minister of Finance, 1994–96. Vice-Chm., Oppunda Savings Bank, 1976–89; Chm., Södermanland Co-op. Soc., 1976–89; Nat. Auditor, Swedish Co-op. Wholesale Soc., 1988–89. Vice-Chm., Nordic Mus., 1983–89. *Address:* Office of the Prime Minister, Cabinet Office, 103 33 Stockholm, Sweden.

PERSSON, Rt Rev. William Michael Dermot; Suffragan Bishop of Doncaster, 1982–92; an Assistant Bishop, diocese of Bath and Wells, since 1994; *b* 27 Sept. 1927; *s* of Leslie Charles Grenville Alan and Elizabeth Mercer Persson; *m* 1957, Ann Davey; two *s* one *d*. *Educ:* Monkton Combe School; Oriel Coll., Oxford (MA); Wycliffe Hall Theological Coll. National service, Army, 1945–48; commissioned, Royal Signals. Deacon 1953, priest 1954; Curate: Emmanuel, South Croydon, 1953–55; St John, Tunbridge Wells, 1955–58; Vicar, Christ Church, Barnet, 1958–67; Rector, Bebington, Cheshire, 1967–79; Vicar, Knutsford with Toft, 1979–82. General Synod: Mem., House of Clergy, 1975–82, House of Bishops, 1985–92; Chm., Council for Christian Unity, 1991–92. *Recreations:* gardening, writing poetry. *Address:* Ryall's Cottage, Burton Street, Marnhull, Sturminster Newton, Dorset DT10 1PS.

PERT, Prof. Geoffrey James, PhD; FRS 1995; FInstP; Professor of Computational Physics, University of York, since 1987; *b* 15 Aug. 1941; *s* of Norman James Pert and Grace Winifred Pert (*née* Barnes); *m* 1967, Janice Ann Alexander; one *d*. *Educ:* Norwich Sch.; Imperial Coll., Univ. of London (BSc; PhD 1966). FInstP 1979. University of Alberta: Fellow, 1967–68; Asst Prof., 1968–69; Associate Prof., 1969–70; University of Hull: Lectr, 1970–74; Sen. Lectr, 1974–78; Reader, 1978–82; Prof., 1982–87. *Publications:* papers in learned scientific jls. *Recreations:* hill-walking, gardening. *Address:* Department of Physics, University of York, Heslington, York YO1 5DD. *T:* (01904) 432250.

PERT, Michael; QC 1992; a Recorder, since 1988; *b* 17 May 1947; *s* of Lieut Henry McKay Pert (RN, retd) and Noreen (*née* Murphy); *m* 1971, Vivien Victoria Braithwaite (marr. diss. 1993); one *s* two *d*. *Educ:* St Boniface's Coll., Plymouth; Manchester Univ. (LLB Hons). Called to the Bar, Gray's Inn, 1970. *Recreations:* beekeeping, sailing. *Address:* 36 Bedford Row, WC1R 4JH.

PERTH, 17th Earl of, *cr* 1605; **John David Drummond,** PC 1957; Baron Drummond of Cargill, 1488; Baron Maderty, 1609; Baron Drummond, 1686; Lord Drummond of Gilston, 1685; Lord Drummond of Rickertoun and Castlemaine, 1686; Viscount Strathallan, 1686; Hereditary Thane of Lennox, and Hereditary Steward of Menteith and Strathearn; Representative Peer for Scotland, 1952–63; First Crown Estate Commissioner, 1962–77; Chairman, Ditchley Foundation, 1963–66; *b* 13 May 1907; *o s* of 16th Earl of Perth, PC, GCMG, CB, and Hon. Angela Constable-Maxwell (*d* 1965), *y d* of 11th Baron Herries; *S* father, 1951; *m* 1934, Nancy Seymour (*d* 1996), *d* of Reginald Fincke, New York City; two *s*. *Educ:* Downside; Cambridge Univ. Lieut, Intelligence Corps, 1940; seconded to War Cabinet Offices, 1942–43, Ministry of Production, 1944–45. Partner, Schroder's, 1945–56; Minister of State for Colonial Affairs, 1957–62 (resigned). Chm., Reviewing Cttee on Export of Works of Art, 1972–76. Member: Court of St Andrews Univ., 1967–86; Adv. Council, V&A Museum, 1971–72; Trustee, Nat. Library of Scotland, 1968–95. Hon. FRIBA 1978; Hon. FRIAS 1988; Hon. FSA 1994. Hon. LLD St Andrews, 1986. *Heir: s* Viscount Strathallan, *qv*. *Address:* Stobhall, by Perth PH2 6DR.

PERTH (Australia), Archbishop of, and Metropolitan of Western Australia, since 1981; **Most Rev. Dr Peter Frederick Carnley,** AO 1998; Primate of Australia, since 2000; *b* 17 Oct. 1937; *s* of Frederick Carnley and Gweyennetth Lilian Carnley (*née* Read); *m* 1966, Carol Ann Dunstan; one *s* one *d*. *Educ:* St John's Coll., Morpeth, NSW; Australian Coll. of Theol. (ThL 1st Cl., 1962); Univ. of Melbourne (BA, 1st Cl. Hons, 1966); Univ. of Cambridge (PhD 1970). Deacon 1962, priest 1964, Bath; Licence to Officiate, dio. Melbourne, 1963–65; Asst Curate of Parkes, 1966; Licence to Officiate, dio. Ely, 1966–69; Chaplain, Mitchell Coll. of Advanced Education, Bath, 1970–72; Research Fellow, St John's Coll., Cambridge, 1971–72 (Hon. Fellow, 2000); Warden, St John's College, St Lucia, Queensland, 1973–81; Residentiary Canon, St John's Cathedral, Brisbane, 1975–81; Examining Chaplain to Archbishop of Brisbane, 1975–81. Fellow,

Trinity Coll., Univ. of Melbourne, 2000. DD *hc* Gen. Theological Seminary, NY, 1984; Hon. DLitt: Newcastle, 2000; W Australia, 2000; DUniv Charles Sturt, 2001. ChStJ 1982 (Sub Prelate, 1991). *Publications:* The Poverty of Historical Scepticism, in Christ, Faith and History (ed S. W. Sykes and J. P. Clayton), 1972; The Structure of Resurrection Belief, 1987; The Yellow Wallpaper and Other Sermons, 2001; Through the Eye of a Needle, 2001. *Recreations:* gardening, swimming. *Address:* GPO Box W2067, Perth, WA 6846, Australia. *T:* (office) (8) 9325 7455, *Fax:* (8) 9325 6741; *e-mail:* abcsuite@perth.anglican.org. *Clubs:* Western Australian, Weld (Perth); St John's (Brisbane).

PERTH (Australia) Archbishop of, (RC), since 1991; **Most Rev. Barry James Hickey;** *b* 16 April 1936; *s* of G. Hickey. *Educ:* Christian Brothers Coll., WA; St Charles Seminary, WA; Propaganda Fide Coll., Rome; Univ. of WA. Dir, Centacare, Perth (Catholic Family Welfare), 1972–82; Episcopal Vicar for Social Welfare, 1982–84; Parish Priest of Highgate, WA, 1983–84; Bishop of Geraldton, WA, 1984–91. Mem., Bd of Inst. of Family Studies, Melbourne, 1980–83; Chm., Nat. Liturgical Commn, 1995–2000. Mem., Australian Citizenship Council, 1998–2000. *Recreations:* tennis, walking. *Address:* Archbishop's House, Victoria Square, Perth, WA 6000, Australia.

PERTH (Australia), Assistant Bishops of; *see* Beaumont, Rt Rev. G. E.; Farran, Rt Rev. B. G.; Murray, Rt Rev. D. O.

PERTH, (St Ninian's Cathedral), Provost of; *see* Farquharson, Very Rev. H. B.

PERU, Bishop of, since 1998; **Rt Rev. (Harold) William Godfrey;** *b* 21 April 1948; *s* of Charles Robert Godfrey and Irene Eva Godfrey (*née* Kirk); *m* 1968, Judith Moya (*née* Fenton); one *s* two *d*. *Educ:* Chesterfield School; King's Coll., Univ. of London (AKC); St Augustine's Coll., Canterbury. VSO, Isfahan, Iran, 1966–67; Asst Curate, Warsop with Sookholme, Diocese of Southwell, 1972–75; Team Vicar of St Peter and St Paul, Hucknall Torkard, 1975–86; Bishop of Southwell's Ecumenical Officer, 1981–82; Rector of Montevideo, 1986–87, Archdeacon of Montevideo, 1986–87; Asst Bishop of Argentina and Uruguay, 1987–88; Bishop of Uruguay, 1988–98; Asst Presiding Bishop, Prov. of Southern Cone of America, 1989–95. Founder Mem., Jesus Caritas Fraternity (Anglican Communion), 1974. *Recreations:* walking, music. *Address:* Apartado 18–1032, Miraflores, Lima 18, Peru. *T:* and *Fax:* (1) 4229160; *e-mail:* wgodfrey@amauta.rcp.net.pe.

PERUTZ, Max Ferdinand, OM 1988; CH 1975; CBE 1963; PhD; FRS 1954; Member, scientific staff, Medical Research Council Laboratory of Molecular Biology, 1979– (Chairman, 1962–79); *b* 19 May 1914; *s* of Hugo and Adèle Perutz; *m* 1942, Gisela Peiser; one *s* one *d*. *Educ:* Theresianum, Vienna; Univ. of Vienna; Univ. of Cambridge (PhD 1940). Hon. Fellow: Peterhouse, Cambridge, 1962; Darwin Coll., Cambridge, 1984. Dir, MRC Unit for Molecular Biology, 1947–62; Chm., European Molecular Biology Orgn, 1963–69. Reader, Davy Faraday Res. Lab., 1954–68, and Fullerian Prof. of Physiology, 1973–79, Royal Instn. Hon. FRSE, 1976; Hon. FRCP 1993; Hon. Member American Academy of Arts and Sciences, 1963; Corresp. Member, Austrian Acad. of Sciences, 1963; Mem., Akademie Leopoldina, Halle, 1964; Foreign Member: American Philosophical Society, 1968; Royal Netherlands Acad., 1972; French Acad. of Sciences, 1976; Bavarian Acad. of Sciences, 1983; National Acad. of Sciences, Rome, 1983; Accademia dei Lincei, Rome, 1984; Acad. of Science of DDR, 1985; For. Associate, Nat. Acad. of Sciences, USA, 1970; Mem., Pontifical Acad. of Sciences, Rome, 1981. Hon. degrees: in philosophy: Vienna, 1965; Salzburg, 1972, Wales, 1995; in science: Edinburgh, 1965; East Anglia, 1967; Cambridge, 1981; York, 1990; Oxford, 1993; Paris, 1993; in medicine, Rome, 1988. Nobel Prize for Chemistry (jointly), 1962; Ehrenzeichen für Wissenschaft und Kunst (Austria), 1966; Royal Medal, 1971, Copley Medal, 1979, Royal Soc. Actonian Prize, Royal Instn, 1984; Lewis Thomas Prize, Rockefeller Univ., NY, 1997. Pour le Mérite, FRG, 1988. *Publications:* Proteins and Nucleic Acids, Structure and Function, 1962; (jtly) Atlas of Haemoglobin and Myoglobin, 1981; Is Science Necessary?, 1988; Mechanisms of Co-operativity and Allosteric Control in Proteins, 1990; Protein Structures: new approaches to disease and therapy, 1992; Science Is No Quiet Life, 1997; I Wish I'd Made You Angry Earlier, 1998. *Address:* 42 Sedley Taylor Road, Cambridge CB2 2PN; Laboratory of Molecular Biology, Hills Road, Cambridge CB2 2QH.

PERVEZ, Sir Mohammed (Anwar), Kt 1999; OBE 1992; Managing Director, Bestway Cash & Carry (Group) Ltd; *b* 15 March 1935. *Educ:* Jhelum, Pakistan. Board Member: Fedn of Wholesale Distributors; Nat. Grocers Benevolent Fund. Founder, Bestway Foundn Charitable Trust. *Address:* Bestway Cash & Carry (Group) Ltd, Abbey Road, Park Royal, NW10 7BW. *T:* (020) 8453 1234.

PERY, family name of **Earl of Limerick**.

PESARAN, Prof. (Mohammad) Hashem, FBA 1998; PhD; Professor of Economics, Cambridge University, and Fellow of Trinity College, Cambridge, since 1988; *b* 30 March 1946; *s* of Jamal and Effat Pesaran; *m* 1969, Marion Fay Swainston; three *s* two *d*. *Educ:* Salford Univ. (BSc 1968); Cambridge Univ. (PhD 1972). Jun. Res. Officer, Dept of Applied Econs, Cambridge Univ., and Lektor, Trinity Coll., Cambridge, 1971–73; Asst to Vice-Governor, 1973–74, and Head of Econ. Res. Dept, 1974–76, Central Bank of Iran; Under-Sec., Min. of Educn, Iran, 1977–78; Teaching Fellow, and Dir of Studies in Econs, Trinity Coll., Cambridge, 1979–88; Lectr in Econs, 1979–85, and Reader in Econs, 1985–88, Cambridge Univ. Prof. of Econs, and Dir, Program in Applied Econometrics, UCLA, 1989–93; Research Fellow: Inst. for Study of Labour, Bonn, 1999–; CESifo (Center for Economic Studies and Ifo Institute for Econ. Res.) Res. Network, Munich, 2000–. Visiting Lecturer: Harvard Univ., 1982; Dutch Network for Quantitative Econs, Groningen, 1985; Vis. Fellow, ANU, 1984 and 1988; Visiting Professor: Univ. of Rome, 1986; Univ. of Calif, LA, 1987–88; Univ. of Pennsylvania, 1993; Univ. of S Calif, 1995, 1997 and 1999. Director: Camfit Data Ltd, 1986–; Acorn Investment Trust, 1987–89 and 1991–93; Cambridge Econometrics, 1985, 1988–89 and 1992–96 (Hon. Pres., 1996–); (non-exec.), Chiltern Gp plc, 1999–. Member: HM Treasury Academic Panel, 1993–; Academic Econometric Panel, ONS, 1997–; Outside Mem., Meteorol Office, 1994–97. Member: Bd of Trustees, Econ. Res. Forum of Arab Countries, Iran and Turkey, 1996– (Mem. Adv. Bd and Res. Fellow, 1993–96); World Bank Council for the Middle East and N Africa region, 1996–; Bd of Trustees, British Iranian Trust, 1997–; Charter Mem., Oliver Wyman Inst., 1997–2000. Fellow, Econometric Soc., 1990. Founding Ed., Jl of Applied Econometrics, 1985–. Hon. DLitt Salford, 1993. *Publications:* World Economic Prospects and the Iranian Economy—a short term view, 1974 (also Persian); (with L. J. Slater) Dynamic Regression: theory and algorithms, 1980 (trans. Russian, 1984); (ed with T. Lawson) Keynes' Economics: methodological issues, 1985; The Limits to Rational Expectations, 1987; (with B. Pesaran) Data-FIT: an interactive software econometric package, 1987 (paperback edn, as Microfit, 1989); (ed with T. Barker) Disaggregation in Economic Modelling, 1990; (with B. Pesaran) Microfit 3.0, 1991, Microfit 4.0, 1996; (ed with S. Potter) Non-Linear Dynamics, Chaos and Econometrics, 1993; Handbook of Applied Econometrics, Vol. I (ed with M. Wickens), 1995, Vol. II (ed with P. Schmidt), 1997; (jtly) Energy Demand in Asian Developing Economies, 1998; (ed jtly) Analysis of Panels and Limited Dependent Variables, 1999; scientific papers in econ. and econometric jls. *Recreations:* basketball (half-blue, Cambridge University), squash, swimming. *Address:* Trinity College, Cambridge CB2 1TQ; 283 Hills Road, Cambridge CB2 2RP. *T:* (01223) 335216; *e-mail:* hashem.pesaran@econ.cam.ac.uk.

PESCOD, Prof. Mainwaring Bainbridge, OBE 1977; CEng, FICE, FCIWEM; Chairman and Managing Director, Environmental Technology Consultants Ltd, since 1988; Tyne and Wear Professor of Environmental Control Engineering, 1976–98, now Emeritus, and Head of Department of Civil Engineering, 1983–98, University of Newcastle upon Tyne; *b* 6 Jan. 1933; *s* of Bainbridge and Elizabeth Pescod; *m* 1957, Mary Lorenza (*née* Coyle); two *s*. *Educ:* Stanley Grammar Sch., Co. Durham; King's Coll., Univ. of Durham (BSc); MIT (SM). CEng 1973, FICE 1980; FCIWEM (FIPHE 1971; FIWES 1983; FIWEM 1987; MIWPC 1967); FInstWM 1997 (MInstWM 1985). Lectr in Engrg, Fourah Bay Coll, Freetown, Sierra Leone, 1957–61; Asst Engr, Babtie, Shaw & Morton, CCE, Glasgow, 1961–64; Asst and Associate Prof. of Environmental Engrg, 1964–72, Prof. and Head of Div. of Environmental Engrg, 1972–76, Asian Inst. of Technol., Bangkok, Thailand. Mem., Northumbrian Water Authority, 1986–89; Director: Northumbrian Water Group, 1989–97; Motherwell Bridge Envirotec, 1991–95; Chm., MB Technology (Malaysia) Sdn Bhd, 1996–. *Publications:* (ed with D. A. Okun) Water Supply and Wastewater Disposal in Developing Countries, 1971; (ed. with A. Arar) Treatment and Use of Sewage Effluent for Irrigation, 1988; (ed) Urban Solid Waste Management, 1991; pubns on water supply, wastewater treatment, environmental pollution control and management in learned jls and conf. proc. *Recreations:* golf, reading, advisory assignments in developing countries. *Address:* Tall Trees, High Horse Close Wood, Rowlands Gill, Tyne and Wear NE39 1AN. *T:* (01207) 542104. *Clubs:* British, Royal Bangkok Sports (Bangkok, Thailand).

PEŠEK, Libor, Hon. KBE 1996; Music Director, 1987–97, Conductor Laureate, since 1997, Royal Liverpool Philharmonic Society and Orchestra; *b* 22 June 1933. *Educ:* Academy of Musical Arts, Prague (studied conducting, piano, 'cello, trombone). Worked at Pilsen and Prague Opera Houses; Founder Director, Prague Chamber Harmony, 1958–64; Chief Conductor, Slovak Philharmonic, 1980–81; Conductor in residence, Czech Philharmonic, 1982– (tours and fests, Europe, Russia, Far East); guest conductor: Los Angeles Philharmonic, St Louis Symphony and other US orchestras; The Philharmonia, LSO, Orchestre Nat. de France, and other European orchestras; numerous recordings incl. much Czech repertoire. Pres., Prague Spring Fest. Hon. DMus Liverpool Polytechnic, 1989. *Recreations:* physics, Eastern philosophy and literature, particularly Kafka, Dostoyevsky and Tolstoy. *Address:* c/o IMG Artists (Europe), 616 Chiswick High Road, W4 5RX.

PESKETT, Stanley Victor, MA; Principal, Royal Belfast Academical Institution, 1959–78; *b* 9 May 1918; *o s* of Sydney Timber and Mary Havard Peskett; *m* 1948, Prudence Eileen, OBE 1974, *o d* of C. R. A. and M. A. Goatly; two *s* one *d* (and one *d* decd). *Educ:* Whitgift Sch.; St Edmund Hall, Oxford. Served War, 1939–46 (despatches) in Royal Marines, Norway, Shetland, Normandy, India and Java; Lt-Col, 1944; two Admiralty awards for inventions. Senior English Master, 1946–59, Housemaster 1954–59, The Leys School. Mem. Cttee, Headmasters' Conf., 1976; Mem. Council, Headmasters' Assoc., and Pres., Ulster Headmasters' Assoc., 1973–75, Chm., Northern Ireland Cttee, Voluntary Service Overseas, 1969–78; Founder Pres., Irish Schools Swimming Assoc., 1968–69 (Chm., Ulster Branch, 1968–78); Chm., NI Branch, School Library Assoc., 1964–73; Governor, Belfast Sch. of Music, 1974–77; Mem. Adv. Council, UDR, 1975–78. *Publications:* The Metfield Clock, 1980; (contrib.) People, Poverty and Protest in Hoxne Hundred 1780–1880, 1982; Only For a Day, 1984; Our Names, 1985; Wheelock 'Founder of Medfield', 1992; Monumental Inscriptions, Metfield, Suffolk, 1992; Clark's Kin, 1995; articles in educational jls. *Address:* Huntsman and Hounds Cottage, Metfield, Harleston, Norfolk IP20 0LB. *T:* (01379) 586425.

See also R. W. Seymour.

PESKIN, Richard Martin; Chairman, Great Portland Estates PLC, since 1986; *b* 21 May 1944; *s* of Leslie and Hazel Peskin; *m* 1979, Penelope Howard Triebner; one *s* two *d*. *Educ:* Charterhouse; Queens' Coll., Cambridge (MA, LLM). Great Portland Estates, 1967–: Dir, 1968; Asst Man. Dir, 1972–78; Jt Man. Dir, 1978–84; Man. Dir, 1984–2000. FRSA 1989. CIMgt (CBIM 1989). *Recreations:* crosswords, composing limericks, fine wine, racing, golf. *Address:* 41 Circus Road, NW8 9JH. *T:* (020) 7289 0492. *Clubs:* MCC, Royal Automobile; Wentworth Golf.

PESTELL, Catherine Eva; *see* Hughes, C. E.

PESTELL, John Edmund; Partnership Secretary, Linklaters & Paines, 1990–94; *b* 8 Dec. 1930; *s* of late Edmund Pestell and Isabella (*née* Sangster); *m* 1958, Muriel Ada (*née* Whitby); three *s*. *Educ:* Roundhay Sch.; New Coll., Oxford (State Scholar; MA). National Service, 1949–50. Jt Intell. Bureau, 1953–57; Asst Principal, WO, 1957–60; Private Sec. to Parly Under Sec. of State for War, 1958–60; Principal, WO and MoD, 1960–70; Admin. Staff Coll., Henley, 1963; Private Sec. to Minister of Defence (Equipment), 1969–70; Asst Sec., MoD, 1970–72; Press Sec. (Co-ordination), Prime Minister's Office, 1972–74; Asst Sec., CSD, 1974–76, Under Sec., 1976–81; Under Sec., HM Treasury, 1981–84; Asst Under-Sec. of State, MoD, 1984–88; Resident Chm., CSSB, 1988–90. Mem., CS Pay Res. Unit Bd, 1978–80. Governor, Cranleigh Sch., 1975–95. *Address:* New House, Bridge Road, Cranleigh, Surrey GU6 7HH. *T:* (01483) 273489. *Club:* Athenæum.

See also C. E. Hughes.

PESTELL, Sir John Richard, KCVO 1969; an Adjudicator, Immigration Appeals, Harmondsworth, 1970–87; *b* 21 Nov. 1916; *s* of late Lt-Comdr Frank Lionel Pestell, RN, and Winifred Alice Pestell; *m* 1951, Betty Pestell (*née* Parish); three *d*. *Educ:* Portsmouth Northern Secondary Sch. Joined British South Africa Police, Southern Rhodesia, 1939; retired, 1965, with rank of Asst Commissioner. Served, 1944–47, Gen. List, MELF, in Cyrenaica Defence Force. Secretary/Controller to Governor of S Rhodesia, Rt Hon. Sir H. V. Gibbs, 1965–69. *Recreation:* walking. *Address:* Batch Cottage, North Road, Charlton Horethorne, near Sherborne, Som DT9 4NS.

PESTON, family name of **Baron Peston**.

PESTON, Baron *cr* 1987 (Life Peer), of Mile End in Greater London; **Maurice Harry Peston;** Professor of Economics at Queen Mary College, University of London, 1965–88, now Emeritus; *b* 19 March 1931; *s* of Abraham and Yetta Peston; *m* 1958, Helen Conroy; two *s* one *d*. *Educ:* Belle Vue School, Bradford; Hackney Downs School; London School of Economics (BSc Econ; Hon. Fellow, 1995); Princeton Univ., NJ, USA. Scientific Officer, then Sen. Scientific Officer, Army Operational Research Group, 1954–57; Asst Lecturer, Lectr, Reader in Economics, LSE, 1957–65. Economic Adviser: HM Treasury, 1962–64; Min. of Defence, 1964–66; H of C Select Cttee on Nationalised Industries, 1966–70, 1972–73; Special Adviser to Sec. of State for Education, 1974–75, to Sec. of State for Prices 1976–79. Chairman: Pools Panel, 1991–95; NFER, 1991–97; Office of Health Econs, 1991–; Member: CNAA (and Chm. of Economics Bd), 1967–73;

SSRC (Chm. of Economics Bd), 1976–79; Council of Royal Pharmaceutical Soc. of GB, 1986–96; Hon. Mem., RPSGB, 1996. Fellow: Portsmouth Poly., 1987; QMW, 1992. Hon. FInstAM 1998. Hon. DEd E London, 1994. *Publications:* Elementary Matrices for Economics, 1969; Public Goods and the Public Sector, 1972; Theory of Macroeconomic Policy, 1974, 2nd edn 1982; Whatever Happened to Macroeconomics?, 1980; The British Economy, 1982, 2nd edn 1984; ed and contrib. to many other books; articles in economic jls. *Address:* House of Lords, SW1A 0PW. *T:* (020) 7219 3000.

PETCH, Barry Irvine, FCA; General Manager, IBM Financing International Ltd, 1989–93; *b* 12 Oct. 1933; *s* of Charles Reginald Petch and Anne (*née* Fryer); *m* 1966, Anne Elisabeth (*née* Johannessen); two *s* one *d. Educ:* Doncaster Grammar Sch.; Kingston Univ. (MA Distinction, Business and Public Sector Strategy, 1998). FCA 1967. IBM United Kingdom Ltd, 1959–80; Controller, IBM Europe, 1981–83; Vice-Pres., Finance, IBM Europe, 1983–89. Part-time Mem., Price Commn, 1973–77. Director: Pathfinder NHS Trust, 1995–99; IBM UK Pensions Trust Ltd, 1997–2000. Hon. Treas., RNID, 1998–. *Recreations:* tennis, golf, sailing. *Club:* Reform.

PETERBOROUGH, Bishop of, since 1996; **Rt Rev. Ian Patrick Martyn Cundy;** *b* 23 April 1945; *s* of Henry Martyn Cundy and Kathleen Ethel Cundy; *m* 1969, Josephine Katherine Boyd; two *s* one *d. Educ:* Monkton Combe Sch., 1958–63; Trinity Coll., Cambridge, 1964–67 (BA 1967; MA 1971); Tyndale Hall, Bristol, 1967–69. Ordained: deacon, 1969; priest, 1970; Asst Curate, Christ Church, New Malden, 1969–73; Tutor and Lectr in Church History, Oak Hill Coll., London, 1973–77; Team Rector, Mortlake with East Sheen, 1978–83; Warden, Cranmer Hall, St John's Coll., Durham, 1983–92; Suffragan Bishop of Lewes, 1992–96. Chm., Council for Christian Unity, 1998–. Pres., St John's Coll., Durham, 1999–. Trustee, Uppingham and Oakham Schs, 1996–. *Publication:* Ephesians—2 Thessalonians, 1981. *Recreations:* walking, music, photography, vintage cars. *Address:* The Palace, Peterborough, Cambs PE1 1YA. *T:* (01733) 562492, *Fax:* (01733) 890077.

PETERBOROUGH, Dean of; *see* Bunker, Very Rev. M.

PETERKEN, Laurence Edwin, CBE 1990; consultant, since 1996; Special Projects Director, NHS in Scotland, 1993–96; *b* 2 Oct. 1931; *s* of Edwin James Peterken and Constance Fanny (*née* Giffin); *m* 1st, 1955, Hanne Birgithe Von Der Recke (decd); one *s* one *d*; 2nd, 1970, Margaret Raynal Blair; one *s* one *d. Educ:* Harrow Sch. (Scholar); Peterhouse, Cambridge (Scholar); MA. Pilot Officer, RAF Regt, Adjt No 20 LAA Sqdn, 1950–52. Service Div. Manager, Hotpoint Ltd, 1961–63, Commercial Dir, 1963–66; Man. Dir, British Domestic Appliances Ltd, 1966–68; Dir, British Printing Corporation Ltd, 1969–73; Debenhams Ltd: Man. Dir, Fashion Multiple Div., 1974–76; Management Auditor, 1976–77; Controller, Operational Services, GLC, 1977–85; Acting Dir, Royal Festival Hall, 1983–85, to implement open foyer policy; Gen. Man., 1986–93, Dir, 1989–93, Gtr Glasgow Health Bd. Chairman: Working Party on Disposal of Clinical Waste in London, 1982–83; GLC Chief Officers' Guild, 1983–85; Member: Scottish Health Management Efficiency Gp, 1986–95; Scottish Health Clinical Resources and Audit Gp, 1989–93; Scottish Health Service Adv. Council, 1989–93; Criminal Injuries Compensation Appeal Panel, 1997–; Scottish Cttee, Council for Music in Hosps, 1997–. Vice Chm., RIPA, W of Scotland, 1991–93; Chm., Glasgow and W of Scotland Inst. of Public Admin, 1993–. Trustee, Rodolfus Choir, 1998–. Churchwarden, Haslemere Parish Church, 1985–86. *Recreations:* music, golf. *Address:* Carlston, Kilbarchan Road, Bridge of Weir, Renfrewshire PA11 3EG. *Clubs:* Athenæum; Western (Glasgow).

PETERKIEWICZ, Prof. Jerzy; novelist and poet; Professor of Polish Language and Literature, University of London, 1972–79; *b* 29 Sept. 1916; *s* of late Jan Pietrkiewicz and Antonina (*née* Politowska). *Educ:* Dlugosz Sch., Włocławek; Univ. of Warsaw; Univ. of St Andrews (MA 1944); King's Coll., London (PhD 1947). Freelance writer until 1950; Reader (previously Lectr) in Polish Language and Literature, Sch. of Slavonic and East European Studies, Univ. of London, 1952–72, Head of Dept of E European Lang. and Lit., 1972–77. *Publications:* Prowincja, 1936; Wiersze i poematy, 1938; Pogrzeb Europy, 1946; The Knotted Cord, 1953; Loot and Loyalty, 1955; Polish Prose and Verse, 1956; Antologia liryki angielskiej, 1958; Future to Let, 1958; Isolation, 1959; (with Burns Singer) Five Centuries of Polish Poetry, 1960 (enlarged edn 1970); The Quick and the Dead, 1961; That Angel Burning at my Left Side, 1963; Poematy londynskie, 1965; Inner Circle, 1966; Green Flows the Bile, 1969; The Other Side of Silence (The Poet at the Limits of Language), 1970; The Third Adam, 1975; (ed and trans.) Easter Vigil and other Poems, by Karol Wojtyla (Pope John Paul II), 1979; Kula magiczna (Poems 1934–52), 1980; (ed and trans.) Collected Poems, by Karol Wojtyla (Pope John Paul II), 1982; Poezje wybrane (Selected Poems), 1986; Literatura polska w perspektywie europejskiej (Polish Literature in its European context; essays trans. from English), 1986; Messianic Prophecy: a case for reappraisal, 1991; In the Scales of Fate (autobiog.), 1993; Wiersze dobrzynskie (early poems), 1994; (ed and trans.) The Place Within: the poetry of Pope John Paul II, 1994; Metropolitan Idyll (bilingual edn), 1998; Slowa sa bez poreczy (Selected Poems), 1998; (trans.) Poezje—poems by Karol Wojtyla (Pope John Paul II) (bilingual edn), 1998; (ed and trans.) Cyprian Norwid: poems, letters, drawings, 2000; essays, poems and articles in various periodicals; radio plays, BBC Radio 3. *Recreation:* travels, outward and inward. *Address:* 7 Lyndhurst Terrace, NW3 5QA.

PETERKIN, Maj. Gen. (Anthony) Peter G.; *see* Grant Peterkin.

PETERKIN, Sir Neville (Allan Mercer), Kt 1981; Chief Justice, West Indies Associated States, 1980–84; *b* 27 Oct. 1915; *s* of Joseph Allan Peterkin and Evelyn Peterkin; *m* 1942, Beryl Thompson; two *s* one *d. Educ:* Wellington Sch., Somerset, England. Called to Bar, Middle Temple, 1939. Registrar, St Lucia, 1943; Magistrate, Trinidad and Tobago, 1944; Resident Magistrate, Jamaica, 1954; High Court Judge: Trinidad, 1957; Associated States, 1967; Justice of Appeal, Associated States, 1975. *Recreations:* golf, bridge. *Address:* c/o Court of Appeal, PO Box 1093, Castries, St Lucia, West Indies.

PETERS, Prof. Adrien Michael, MD; FRCR, FRCP, FRCPath; Professor of Nuclear Medicine, University of Cambridge, since 1999; *b* 17 May 1945; *s* of Adrien John Peters and Barbara Muriel Peters; *m* 1980, Rosemary Cox; three *s* one *d. Educ:* St Mary's Hosp. Med. Sch., Univ. of London (BSc, MSc); Univ. of Liverpool (MB ChB, MD 1970). FRCR 1995; FRCPath 1996; FRCP 1997. GP, NSW, Australia, 1974–78, Liverpool, 1978–79; Res. Fellow, RPMS, 1979–82; Res. Physician, Glaxo Gp Res. Ltd, 1982–84; Sen. Lectr in Diagnostic Radiol., 1984–89, Reader in Nuclear Medicine, 1989–95, RPMS; Prof. of Diagnostic Radiol., RPMS, then ICSM, 1995–99. Consultant in Paediatric Radiol., 1984–88, Hon. Consultant, 1988–93 and 1996–, Hosp. for Sick Children, Gt Ormond St; Hon. Consultant: Hammersmith Hosp., 1984–99; Addenbrooke's Hosp., 1999–. *Publications:* Physiological Measurement with Radionuclides in Clinical Practice, 1998; (ed) Nuclear Medicine in Radiological Diagnosis, 2001; numerous contribs to learned jls. *Recreations:* football, jazz. *Address:* Department of Nuclear Medicine, Box 170, Addenbrooke's Hospital, Cambridge CB2 2QQ. *T:* (01223) 217147.

PETERS, Alan George, OBE 1990; furniture maker, since 1962; *b* 17 Jan. 1933; *s* of George Peters, BEM and Evelyn Gladys Amy Peters (*née* Weeks); *m* 1962, Laura Robinson; one *s* one *d. Educ:* Petersfield and Cowplain schools; Shoreditch Teacher Trng Coll., Egham (Dip. with distinction); Central Sch. of Arts and Crafts, London. Apprenticed to Edward Barnsley, CBE, 1949–56. Crafts Council Bursary, Japan, 1975; Winston Churchill Fellow, S Korea and Taiwan, 1980; Guest Advr, NZ Crafts Council, 1984. Vice-Pres., Devon Guild of Craftsmen, 1987–. Trustee, Crafts Study Centre, Bath, 1990–99. Exhibitions: Alan Peters Furniture, Cheltenham and touring, 1985–86; 30 Pieces for 30 Years (retrospective), Bedales Gall., Petersfield, 1992; Crafts Council nat. and touring exhibns, 1973–; work exhibited in: museums, incl. V&A, Cheltenham, Bristol, Leicester, Plymouth, Portsmouth and Bath; Crafts Council Collection; seating for Earth Gall., Gall. of Modern Art, Glasgow, 1996. Fellow, Soc. of Designer-Craftsmen, 1968 (Centennial Medal, 1988). *Publications:* Cabinetmaking: the professional approach, 1984; (ed) The Technique of Furniture Making, by Ernest Joyce, 1987, 4th edn 1997. *Recreations:* cycling, walking, real ale. *Address:* Maddocks Farm, Kentisbeare, Cullompton, Devon EX15 2BU. *T:* (01884) 266251.

PETERS, Most Rev. Arthur Gordon; *see* Nova Scotia, Archbishop of.

PETERS, Sir (David) Keith, Kt 1993; FRCP; FRS 1995; Regius Professor of Physic, University of Cambridge, and Fellow, Christ's College, Cambridge, since 1987; *b* 26 July 1938; *s* of Herbert Lionel and Olive Peters; *m* 1st, 1961, Jean Mair Garfield (marr. diss. 1978); one *s* one *d*; 2nd, 1979, Pamela Wilson Ewan; two *s* one *d. Educ:* Welsh National Sch. of Medicine (MB BCh 1961). MRCP 1964, FRCP 1975; FRCPath 1991; FRCPE 1995. Junior posts in United Cardiff Hosps, 1961–65; Med. Research Council, Clinical Res. Fellowship, 1965–68; Lectr in Med., Welsh Nat. Sch. of Med., 1968–69; Royal Postgraduate Medical School: Lectr, 1969; Sen. Lectr, 1974; Reader in Med., 1975; Prof. of Medicine and Dir, Dept of Medicine, 1977–87; Consultant Physician, Hammersmith Hosp., 1969–87. Member: MRC, 1984–88 (Chm., MRC Physiological Systems Bd, 1986–88); ACOST, 1987–90; Chairman: NRPB, 1994–98; Council of Hds of Med. Schs and Deans of UK Faculties of Medicine, 1996–97; BHF, 1998–. Trustee, Nat. Kidney Res. Fund (Chm., 1980–86). Chm., PPP Healthcare Med. Trust, 2002–; Member: Bd, Amersham Plc, 2000– (Mem., Sci. Adv. Bd (Chm., 2001–)); Council, Royal Soc., 1999–. Foreign Mem., Amer. Philos. Soc., 1999. Founder FMedSci 1998. Hon. Fellow: Univ. of Wales Coll. of Medicine, 1997; ICSM, 1999; Cardiff Univ., 2001; Univ. of Wales, Swansea, 2001. Hon. MD: Wales, 1987; Nottingham, 1996; Paris, 1996; Hon. DSc: Aberdeen, 1994; Leicester, 1999; Glasgow, 2001. *Publications:* (ed jtly) Clinical Aspects of Immunology, 4th edn 1982, 5th edn 1993; in various jls on immunology of renal and vascular disease. *Recreations:* tennis, chess. *Address:* 7 Chaucer Road, Cambridge CB2 2EB. *T:* (01223) 356117. *Club:* Garrick.

PETERS, Prof. George Henry; Research Professor in Agricultural Economics, International Development Centre, Queen Elizabeth House, University of Oxford, 1986–2001; Fellow, Wolfson College, Oxford, 1980–2001, now Emeritus (Vicegerent, 1991–93); *b* 2 Sept. 1934; *s* of William and Mary Peters; *m* 1959, Judith Mary Griffiths; two *d. Educ:* Mold Grammar Sch., Flintshire; University Coll. of Wales, Aberystwyth (BSc, MSc); King's Coll., Cambridge. National Service, Educn Br., RAF, 1957–59. Inst. for Res. in Agricl Econs, Univ. of Oxford, 1959–67; University of Liverpool: Lectr in Econs, 1967–69; Sen. Lectr, 1969–70; Brunner Prof. of Economic Science, 1970–79; Hd of Dept of Econs and Commerce, 1976–79; Dir, Inst. of Agricl Econs, Univ. of Oxford, 1980–86. Pres., Agricl Econs Soc., 1991–92. Ed., Procs of Internat. Assoc. of Agricl Economists, 1991–. *Publications:* Cost Benefit Analysis and Public Expenditure (IEA Eaton Paper 8), 1966, 3rd edn 1973; Private and Public Finance, 1971, 2nd edn 1975; ESRC/RSS Reviews of UK Statistical Sources, vol. 23, Agriculture, 1988; (ed with B. F. Stanton) Sustainable Agricultural Development: the role of international co-operation, 1992; (ed) Agricultural Economics, 1995; (ed with D. D. Hedley) Agricultural Competitiveness: market forces and policy choice, 1995; (ed jtly) Economics of Agro-Chemicals, 1996; (ed with J. von Braun) Food Security, Diversification and Resource Management: refocusing the rôle of agriculture, 1999; (ed with P. Pingali) Tomorrow's Agriculture: incentives, institutions, infrastructure and innovations, 2001; articles in Jl of Agricl Econs, Oxford Agrarian Studies, etc. *Recreations:* all sport, increasingly as a spectator. *Address:* Gable End Cottage, 33 The Moors, Kidlington, Oxford OX5 2AH. *T:* (01865) 372232.

PETERS, Sir Keith; *see* Peters, Sir D. K.

PETERS, Martin Trevor, CB 1991; CEng, FRAeS; Technical Planning Director, British Aerospace plc, 1992–94; *b* 23 Dec. 1936; *s* of Reginald Thomas Peters and Catherine Mary Peters (*née* Ings); *m* 1958, Vera Joan Horton; one *s. Educ:* Aylesbury Grammar Sch.; Watford Tech. Coll.; High Wycombe Coll. of Further Educn. MIMechE, CEng 1968; FRAeS 1988. Airtech, 1953–55; RAF, 1955–57; Airtech, 1957–59; RPE Westcott, 1959–64; NGTE Pyestock, 1964–71; MoD, 1971–77; Supt of Engineering, A&AEE Boscombe Down, 1977–79; NAMMA, Munich, 1979–81; Dir, Aircraft Post Design Services, MoD (PE), 1981–83; RCDS, 1984; Dir-Gen. Aircraft, 1984–87; Dep. Controller Aircraft, 1987–89; Dir, RAE, 1989–91; Tech. Dir, BAe Commercial Aircraft Ltd, 1991–92. *Recreations:* walking, music, 18th century ship modelling. *Address:* 96 East Avenue, Talbot Woods, Bournemouth BH3 7DD.

PETERS, Dame Mary (Elizabeth), DBE 2000 (CBE 1990; MBE 1973); self employed; Managing Director, Mary Peters Sports Ltd, since 1977; *b* 6 July 1939; *d* of Arthur Henry Peters and Hilda Mary Peters. *Educ:* Portadown Coll., Co. Armagh; Belfast Coll. of Domestic Science (DipDomSc). Represented Great Britain: Olympic Games: 4th place, Pentathlon, 1964; 1st, Pentathlon (world record), 1972; Commonwealth Games: 2nd, Shot, 1966; 1st, Shot, 1st Pentathlon, 1970; 1st, Pentathlon, 1974. Member: Sports Council, 1974–80, 1987–94; NI Sports Council, 1974–93 (Vice-Chm., 1977–81); Ulster Games Foundn, 1984–93; NI BBC Broadcasting Council, 1981–84; NI Tourist Bd, 1993–. Dir, Churchill Foundn Fellowship Scholarship, Calif, 1972. Asst Sec., Multiple Sclerosis Soc., 1974–78. President: NI WAAA, 1985–87; British Athletic Fedn, 1996–; Ulster Sports and Recreation Trust, 1996– (Trustee, 1972); Mem., Women's Cttee, IAAF, 1995–. Hon. Senior Athletic Coach, 1975–; BAAB Pentathlon Coach, 1976; Team Manager: GB women's athletic team, European Cup, 1979; GB women's athletic team, Moscow, 1980 and Los Angeles, 1984. President: OAPs' Coal and Grocery Fund; Lady Taverners, NI; Vice-President: Assoc. of Youth Clubs; NI Assoc. of Youth Clubs; Riding for the Disabled; Driving for the Disabled; Action Cancer; Patron: NIAAA, 1981–; Friends of Royal Victoria Hosp., Belfast, 1988–96. Freeman of Lisburn, 1998. Awards: BBC Sports personality, 1972; Athletic Writers', 1972; Sports Writers', 1972; Elizabeth Arden Visible Difference, 1976; Athletics, Dublin (Texaco), 1970 and 1972; British Airways Tourist Endeavour, 1981; Living Action, 1985; Evian Health, 1985. Hon. DSc New Univ. of Ulster, 1974; DUniv QUB, 1998; Hon. DLitt Loughborough, 1999. *Publication:* Mary P., an autobiography, 1974. *Address:* Willowtree Cottage, River Road, Dunmurry, Belfast, N Ireland BT17 9DP.

PETERS, Nigel Melvin; QC 1997; a Recorder of the Crown Court, since 1998; *b* 14 Nov. 1952; *s* of Sidney Peters and Maisie Peters (*née* Pepper). *Educ:* Hasmonean GS;

Leicester Univ. (LLB 1975). Called to the Bar, Lincoln's Inn, 1976 (Mansfield Schol.); Asst Recorder, 1994–98. *Recreations:* cricket, Real tennis, travel, food, wine. *Address:* 18 Red Lion Court, EC4A 3EB. *T:* (020) 7520 6000. *Club:* MCC (Mem. Cttee, 1999–).

PETERS, Prof. Richard Stanley, BA (Oxon), BA (London), PhD (London); Professor of the Philosophy of Education, University of London Institute of Education, 1962–82, now Emeritus Professor; Dean, Faculty of Education, London University, 1971–74; *b* 31 Oct. 1919; *s* of late Charles Robert and Mabel Georgina Peters; *m* 1943, Margaret Lee Duncan; one *s* two *d*. *Educ:* Clifton Coll., Bristol; Queen's Coll., Oxford; Birkbeck Coll., University of London. War service with Friends' Ambulance Unit and Friends' Relief Service in E. London, 1940–44. Classics Master, Sidcot School, Somerset, 1944–46; Birkbeck Coll., University of London: Studentship and part-time Lecturer in Philos. and Psychol., 1946–49; full-time Lecturer in Philos. and Psychol., 1949–58; Reader in Philosophy, 1958–62. Visiting Prof. of Education: Grad. School of Education, Harvard Univ., 1961; Univ. of Auckland, 1975; Visiting Fellow, Australian National Univ., 1969. Part-time lectureships, Bedford Coll., LSE; Tutor for University of London Tutorial Classes Cttee and Extension Cttee. Member, American National Academy of Education, 1966. *Publications:* (revised) Brett's History of Psychology, 1953; Hobbes, 1956; The Concept of Motivation, 1958; (with S. I. Benn) Social Principles and the Democratic State, 1959; Authority, Responsibility and Education, 1960; Ethics and Education, 1966; (ed) The Concept of Education, 1967; (ed) Perspectives on Plowden, 1969; (with P. H. Hirst) The Logic of Education, 1970; (ed with M. Cranston) Hobbes and Rousseau, 1971; (ed with R. F. Dearden and P. H. Hirst) Education and the Development of Reason, 1972; Reason and Compassion (Lindsay Meml Lectures), 1973; (ed) The Philosophy of Education, 1973; Psychology and Ethical Development, 1974; (ed) Nature and Conduct, 1975; (ed) The Role of the Head, 1976; Education and the Education of Teachers, 1977; (ed) John Dewey Reconsidered, 1977; Essays on Educators, 1981; Moral Development and Moral Education, 1981. *Address:* 16 Shepherd's Hill, N6 5AQ.

PETERS, Air Vice-Marshal Robert Geoffrey, CB 1992; Clerk to the Guild of Air Pilots and Air Navigators, 1998–2000; *b* 22 Aug. 1940; *s* of Geoffrey Ridgway Peters and Henriette Catharine Peters; *m* 1966, Mary Elizabeth (*née* Fletcher); one *d* three *s*. *Educ:* St Paul's Sch., London; RAF Coll., Cranwell (Gen. Duties/Pilot). Beverley C Mk1 Pilot Nos 34 and 47 Sqdns, Singapore and UK, 1961–66; Flt Comdr, No 46 Sqdn (Andovers), RAF Abingdon, 1967–68; MoD Central Staffs (Asst MA to Chief Adviser Personnel and Logistics), 1968–69; OC Flying Trng Sqdn, Air Electronics and Air Engr Trng Sch., RAF Topcliffe, 1970–72; RAF Staff Coll., Bracknell, 1973; Air Sec.'s Dept, MoD, 1974–76; OC 10 Sqdn (VC10), RAF Brize Norton, 1977–78; Directorate of Forward Policy (RAF), MoD, 1979–81; PSO to Dep. SACEUR(UK), SHAPE, Belgium, 1981–83; OC RAF St Mawgan, 1984–85; RCDS 1986; Comdr, RAF Staff and Air Attaché, Washington, 1987–90; Comdt, RAF Staff Coll., Bracknell, 1990–93; Dir of Welfare, RAF Benevolent Fund, 1993–97. President: RAF Fencing Union, 1986–93; Combined Services Fencing Assoc., 1988–97. Freeman, City of London, 1977; Liveryman, Co. of Coachmakers and Coach Harness Makers, 1977; Upper Freeman, GAPAN, 1997–2000. QCVSA 1973. *Recreations:* golf, sailing. *Clubs:* Royal Air Force; Weston Turville Golf.

PETERS, Theophilus, CMG 1967; HM Diplomatic Service, retired; freelance lecturer on Chinese Art and History; *b* 7 Aug. 1921; *er s* of late Mark Peters and Dorothy Knapman; *m* 1953, Lucy Bailey Summers, *d* of late Lionel Morgan Summers, Winter Park, Fla; two *s* three *d*. *Educ:* Exeter Sch., Exeter; St John's Coll., Cambridge (MA). Served War of 1939–45: 2nd Lieut, Intelligence Corps, 1942; Captain, 8 Corps HQ, 1944; Normandy, 1944; Holland, 1944–45 (despatches); Germany; Major. Entered HM Foreign (subseq. Diplomatic) Service; Vice-Consul/2nd Secretary, Peking, 1948; FO, 1951–52; Tripoli and Benghazi (Libya), 1953; FO, 1956; Dep. Secretary-General, Cento, 1960; Head of Chancery, Manila, 1962; Counsellor (Commercial), Peking, 1965; Dir, Diplomatic Service Language Centre, 1968–71, and Head of Training Dept, FCO, 1969–71; Counsellor and Consul-Gen., Buenos Aires, 1971–73; Consul-Gen., Antwerp, 1973–78. Dir, Theophilus Knapman & Co., 1979–87. *Address:* King's Mill, St Peter's Vale, Stamford, Lincs PE9 2QT.

PETERS, Prof. Timothy John, PhD, DSc; Professor and Head of Department of Clinical Biochemistry, King's College, London, since 1988; Hon. Consultant Physician and Pathologist, King's College Hospital, since 1988; *b* 10 May 1939; *s* of Stanley and Paula Peters; *m* 1965, Judith Mary Bacon; one *s* two *d*. *Educ:* King Edward VI Sch., Macclesfield; Univ. of St Andrews (MB ChB (Hons) 1964; MSc 1966; DSc 1986); RPMS, Univ. of London (PhD 1970). MRCPE 1969, FRCPE 1986; MRCP 1970, FRCP 1976; MRCPath 1983, FRCPath 1988. MRC Trng Fellow, RPMS, 1967–70; MRC Travelling Fellow, Rockefeller Univ., NY, 1970–72; Lectr, Sen. Lectr, then Reader, RPMS, and Hon. Cons. Physician, Hammersmith Hosp., 1972–79; Head, Div. of Clin. Cell Biology, MRC Clin. Res. Centre, 1979–88; Sub-Dean for Postgrads and Higher Degree, Sch. of Medicine, KCL, 1988–2000, Associate Dean (Flexible Trng), London and SE Region, London Univ., 2000–. FRSA 1998. *Publications:* (ed) Alcohol Misuse: a European perspective, 1996; (ed jtly) International Handbook of Alcohol Dependence and Problems, 2001; over 500 articles on subcellular fractionation, alcohol misuse and toxicology and iron metabolism, absorption and toxicology. *Recreations:* Baroque recorders, narrow boats and canals. *Address:* Department of Clinical Biochemistry, King's College Hospital, Denmark Hill, SE5 9PJ. *T:* (020) 7346 3008.

PETERS, Prof. Wallace, MD, DSc; FRCP; Director, Tropical Parasitic Diseases Unit, Northwick Park Institute for Medical Research, since 1999; Professor of Medical Protozoology, London School of Hygiene and Tropical Medicine, University of London, 1979–89, now Emeritus; *b* 1 April 1924; *s* of Henry and Fanny Peters; *m* 1954, Ruth (*née* Scheidegger). *Educ:* Haberdashers' Aske's Sch.; St Bartholomew's Hosp., London. MB BS, 1947; MRCS, DTM&H. Served in RAMC, 1947–49; practised tropical medicine in West and East Africa, 1950–52; Staff Mem., WHO, Liberia and Nepal, 1952–55; Asst Dir (Malariology), Health Dept, Territory of Papua and New Guinea, 1956–61; Research Associate, CIBA, Basle, Switzerland, 1961–66; Walter Myers Prof. of Parasitology, Univ. of Liverpool, 1966–79; Dean, Liverpool Sch. of Tropical Medicine, 1975–78; Jt Dir, Malaria Reference Lab., PHLS, 1979–89; Hon. Res. Fellow, Internat. Inst. of Parasitology, then CABI Bioscience, 1992–99. Vice-Pres. and Pres., Brit. Soc. Parasit., 1972–76; President: Brit. Sect., Soc. Protozool., 1972–75; Royal Soc. of Trop. Medicine and Hygiene, 1987–89 (Vice-Pres., 1982–83, 1985–87). Chm., WHO Steering Cttee on Chemotherapy of Malaria, 1975–83; Member: Expert Adv. Panel, WHO, 1967–; WHO Steering Cttees on Leishmaniasis, 1979; Editorial Bd, Ann. Trop. Med. Parasit., 1966–79; Trop. Med. Research Bd, MRC, 1973–77; Scientific Council, Inst. of Cellular and Molecular Path., 1981–84; Parasitol. Bd, Institut Pasteur, 1979–87; Sec., European Fedn Parasit., 1979–84 (Vice-Pres., 1975–79). Hon. Consultant on malariology to the Army, 1986–89. Hon. Fellow, Amer. Soc. of Tropical Medicine and Hygiene, 1995. Dr *hc*, Univ. Réne Descartes, Paris, 1992. Rudolf Leuckart Medal, German Soc. of Parasitol., 1980; King Faisal Internat. Prize in Medicine, 1983; Le Prince Medal, Amer. Soc. of Tropical Medicine and Hygiene, 1994; Emile Brumpt Medal and Prize, Soc. de Pathologie Exotique, Paris, 1999. *Publications:* A Provisional Checklist of Butterflies of the Ethiopian Region, 1952; Chemotherapy and Drug Resistance in Malaria, 1970, 2nd edn 1987; (with H. M. Gilles) A Colour Atlas of Tropical Medicine and Parasitology, 1976, 5th edn (with G. Pasvol), as Tropical Medicine and Parasitology, 2001; (ed with R. Killick-Kendrick) Rodent Malaria, 1978; (ed with W. H. G. Richards) Antimalarial Drugs, 2 vols, 1984; (ed with R. Killick-Kendrick) The Leishmaniases in Biology and Medicine, 1987; A Colour Atlas of Arthropods in Clinical Medicine, 1992; numerous papers in jls, on trop. med. and parasitology. *Recreation:* photography. *Address:* Northwick Park Institute for Medical Research, Watford Road, Harrow HA1 3UJ; Department of Infectious and Tropical Disease, London School of Hygiene and Tropical Medicine, Keppel Street, WC1E 7HT; *e-mail:* wallacepeters2@cs.com.

PETERS, William, CMG 1981; LVO 1961; MBE 1959; HM Diplomatic Service, retired; Vice-Chairman, Jubilee 2000 Coalition, since 1997 (Vice President, since 1997, and Board Member, since 1998); *b* 28 Sept. 1923; *o s* of John William Peters and Louise (*née* Woodhouse), Morpeth, Northumberland; *m* 1944, Catherine B. Bailey (*d* 1997); no *c*. *Educ:* King Edward VI Grammar Sch., Morpeth; Balliol Coll., Oxford (MA Lit. Hum. 1948); LSE and SOAS. War Service, Queen's Royal Rifles, KOSB, and 9th Gurkha Rifles, 1942–46. Joined HMOCS as Asst District Comr, Gold Coast, 1950; served in Cape Coast, Bawku and Tamale; Dep. Sec., Regional Comr, Northern Region, 1958–59; apptd to CRO as Asst Prin., 1959; Prin., 1959; 1st Sec., Dacca, 1960–63; 1st Sec., Cyprus, 1963–67; Head of Zambia and Malawi Dept, CRO, 1967–68; Head of Central African Dept, FCO, 1968–69; Dir, Internat. Affairs Div., Commonwealth Secretariat, 1969–71; Counsellor and Head of Chancery, Canberra, 1971–73; Dep. High Comr, Bombay, 1974–77; Ambassador to Uruguay, 1977–80; High Comr in Malaŵi, 1980–83. Member: Royal African Soc., 1980–85 (Hon. Treas., 1983–85); RSAA, 1987– (Mem., Editl Bd, 1990–); Exec., S Atlantic Council, 1985– (Vice Chm., 1997–); Chairman: Exec. Cttee, Lepra, 1984–92; Ethnic Minorities Sub-Cttee, Abbeyfield Soc., 1991–95; Council and Exec. Cttee, USPG, 1991–94 (Vice-Pres., 1994–; Governor, 1996–); Tibet Soc. of UK, 1986–94; Inter-Agency Safety Gp, Dover Dist, 1999–; Mem., Local Responsible Authorities, 1999–; Co-Chm., Jubilee 2000, 1994–97; Trustee, Tibet Relief Fund of UK, 1985–93 (Vice-Pres., 1994–); President: Downs Br., Royal British Legion, 1986–; Rotary Club of Deal, 1989–90; Dover Dist Assoc., Neighbourhood Watch, 2000–. Chm. of Govs, Walmer Sch., 1996–. FIMgt (FBIM 1984); FRSA 2000. MLitt Lambeth, 2001. Alchemist Award, Common Purpose, 2000. *Publications:* Diplomatic Service: Formation and Operation, 1971; (with M. Dent) Confronting a Global Crisis, 1998; (with M. Dent) The Crisis of Poverty and Debt in the Third World, 1999; contribs to Jls of Asian Affairs and of African Administration; Illustrated Weekly of India; Noticias (Uruguay); Army Qly and Defence Review; Bull. of Assoc. of Christian Economists, USA; Christian Aid; Oxford; Round Table. *Recreations:* music, carpentry. *Address:* 12 Crown Court, Middle Street, Deal, Kent CT14 7AG. *T:* (01304) 362822. *Clubs:* Oxford and Cambridge, Royal Commonwealth Society.

PETERS, Rt Hon. Winston (Raymond); PC 1998; MP Tauranga, since 1984 (Nat., 1984–93, NZ First, since 1993); Leader, New Zealand First Party, since 1993; *b* 11 April 1946; *s* of Len Peters and Joan (*née* McInnes); *m* 1973; one *s* one *d*. *Educ:* Auckland Univ. (BA 1969; LLB 1973); DipEd. With Russell, McVeagh, lawyers, 1974–78; estabd own legal practice, Howick, 1982. MP (Nat.) Hunua, 1979–81; Minister of Maori Affairs and i/c of Iwi Transition Agency, 1990–93; Dep. Prime Minister and Treasurer, NZ, 1996–98. *Address:* Parliament Building, Wellington, New Zealand.

PETERSEN, Sir Jeffrey (Charles), KCMG 1978 (CMG 1968); HM Diplomatic Service, retired; *b* 20 July 1920; *s* of Charles Petersen and Ruby Petersen (*née* Waple); *m* 1st, 1944, Catherine Judith Bayly (marr. diss. 1959); one *s* one *d*; 2nd, 1962, Karin Kristina Hayward; one *s* three *d*. *Educ:* Westcliff High Sch.; London School of Economics. Served RN (Lieut, RNVR), 1939–46. Joined Foreign Office, 1948; 2nd Secretary, Madrid, 1949–50; 2nd Secretary, Ankara, 1951–52; 1st Secretary, Brussels, 1953–56; NATO Defence College, 1956–57; FO, 1957–62; 1st Secretary, Djakarta, 1962–64; Counsellor, Athens, 1964–68; Minister (Commercial), Rio de Janeiro, 1968–71; Ambassador to: Republic of Korea, 1971–74; Romania, 1975–77; Sweden, 1977–80. Chairman: Barclays Bank SAE (Spain), 1981–87; GVA Internat. Ltd, 1983–89; North Sea Assets PLC, 1989–94; Ake Larson Ltd, 1990–93. Chm., British Materials Handling Bd, 1981–95. Pres., Anglo-Korean Soc.; Vice President: Anglo Swedish Soc.; Swedish Chamber of Commerce for UK. Knight Grand Cross, Order of Polar Star (Sweden), 1984; Order of Diplomatic Merit (Republic of Korea), 1985. *Recreations:* painting, making things, totting. *Address:* 32 Longmoore Street, SW1V 1JF. *T:* (020) 7834 8262; Crofts Wood, Petham, Kent CT4 5RX. *T:* (01227) 700537. *Clubs:* Travellers; Kent and Canterbury.

PETERSEN, Hon. Sir Johannes B.; *see* Bjelke-Petersen.

PETERSEN, Niels Helveg; MP (Social Liberal) Denmark, 1966–74, and since 1977; *b* 17 Jan. 1939; *s* of Lilly and Kresten Helveg Petersen; *m* 1984, Kirsten Lee, MD; two *s*. *Educ:* Univ. of Copenhagen (LLB 1965); Univ. of Stanford, Calif. Chief of Cabinet, Danish EU Comr, 1974–77; Chm., Parly Group, 1978–88; Minister for Economic Affairs, 1988–90; Minister for Foreign Affairs, 1993–2000. *Recreations:* chess, tennis, soccer football. *Address:* Folketinget, Christiansborg, 1240 Copenhagen, Denmark. *T:* (45) 33375500.

PETERSEN, Prof. Ole Holger, MD; FRCP; FRS 2000; George Holt Professor of Physiology, since 1981, and MRC Research Professor, since 1998, University of Liverpool; *b* 3 March 1943; *s* of Rear Adm. Joergen Petersen, Royal Danish Navy, and Elisabeth Klein, pianist; *m* 1st, 1968, Nina Bratting Jensen (marr. diss. 1995); two *s*; 2nd, 1995, Nina Burdakova. *Educ:* Univ. of Copenhagen Med. Sch. (MB ChB 1969; MD 1972). FRCP 2001. Lectr, 1969–73, Sen. Lectr, 1973–75, Inst. of Med. Physiology, Univ. of Copenhagen; Wellcome-Carlsberg Travelling Res. Fellow, Dept of Pharmacology, Univ. of Cambridge, 1971–72; Symers Prof. of Physiology, Univ. of Dundee, 1975–81. Vis. Prof., Stellenbosch Univ., 2000. Morton Grossman Meml Lectr, UCLA, 1985; Halliburton Lectr, KCL, 1986; Jacobaeus Prize Lectr, Nordic Insulin Foundn, 1994. Pres., FEPS, 2001–. MAE 1988; Foreign Mem., Royal Danish Acad. of Scis and Letters, 1988; Hon. Mem., Polish Physiological Soc., 1993 (Czubalski Medal, 1993). FMedSci 1998. Jubilee Medal, Charles Univ., Prague, 1998. *Publications:* The Electrophysiology of Gland Cells, 1980; (jtly) Landmarks in Intracellular Signalling, 1997; Measuring Calcium and Calmodulin Inside and Outside Cells, 2000; more than 200 articles in scientific jls on intracellular signalling mechanisms. *Recreation:* classical music. *Address:* MRC Secretory Control Research Group, Physiological Laboratory, University of Liverpool, Crown Street, PO Box 147, Liverpool L69 3BX. *T:* (0151) 794 5342, *Fax:* (0151) 794 5323, 794 5327; *e-mail:* o.h.petersen@liverpool.ac.uk; 5 Mount Park Court, Woolton Park, Liverpool L25 6JP. *T:* (0151) 428 8085.

PETERSHAM, Viscount; Charles Henry Leicester Stanhope; *b* 20 July 1945; *s* and *heir* of 11th Earl of Harrington, *qv*; *m* 1966, Virginia Alleyne Freeman Jackson, Mallow (marr. diss. 1983); one *s* one *d*; *m* 1984, Anita Countess of Suffolk and Berkshire. *Educ:* Eton. *Heir:* *s* Hon. William Henry Leicester Stanhope [*b* 14 Oct. 1967; *m* 2001, Candida,

e d of Ian Bond].
See also Viscount Linley.

PETERSON, Cathryn Mary; *see* Pope, C. M.

PETERSON, Col Sir Christopher (Matthew), Kt 1994; CBE 1983; TD 1952; Chairman, Cardiff Health Foods Ltd, since 1988; *b* 22 Feb. 1918; *s* of Oscar Peterson and Minnie Dee; *m* 1945, Grace Winifred McNeil (*d* 2000); one *s* one *d* (and one *s* decd). *Educ:* St Illtyd's Coll., Cardiff; Cardiff Tech. Coll. Shipbroker Office, Cardiff Docks, 1936–39; served RASC, 1940–46 (Capt.). Joined S Wales India Rubber Co., subseq. SWIRCO-Newton Gp, 1952, Chm., 1968–79; Dir, Dorada Hlgs plc, 1979–83; Chairman: Wales Local Bd, Commercial Union Assce Co., 1972–77; J. McNeil (Cameras), 1983–92; Randall Cox (Photographic), 1984–92; Cox & Tarry Ltd, 1984–89; Stanton-King Orgn, 1985–89; Taff Ely Enterprise Partnership, 1989–91; SWIRCO-Hall, 1990–92. Member: Cardiff City Council, 1968–71; S Glam CC, 1973–85. JP City of Cardiff, 1973; DL 1977, High Sheriff 1981–82, S Glam. Served TA, 1946–65; CO, 1961–65 (Lt-Col), Hon. Col, 1972–77, 157 Regt RCT. CStJ 1997. *Recreation:* walking. *Address:* 51 Rannoch Drive, Cyncoed, Cardiff CF2 6LP. *T:* (029) 2075 4062; 15 Castle Pill Crescent, Steyton, Milford Haven, Dyfed SA73 1HD. *Clubs:* Army and Navy; Cardiff and County.

PETERSON, Colin Vyvyan, CVO 1982; Lay Assistant to Bishop of Winchester, 1985–94; *b* 24 Oct. 1932; *s* of late Sir Maurice Drummond Peterson, GCMG; *m* 1966, Pamela Rosemary Barry; two *s* two *d*. *Educ:* Winchester Coll.; Magdalen Coll., Oxford. Joined HM Treasury, 1959; Sec. for Appointments to PM and Ecclesiastical Sec. to the Lord Chancellor, 1974–82; Under Sec., Cabinet Office (MPO), 1982–85. *Recreation:* fishing. *Address:* Balldown Farmhouse, Sparsholt, Hants SO21 2LZ. *T:* (01962) 776368.

PETERSON, Rev. David Gilbert, PhD; Principal, Oak Hill Theological College, since 1996; *b* 29 Oct. 1944; *s* of Gilbert Samuel and Marie Jean Peterson; *m* 1970, Lesley Victoria (*née* Stock); three *s*. *Educ:* Univ. of Sydney (MA); Moore Theol Coll., Sydney (BD (Lond.)); Univ. of Manchester (PhD 1978). Ordained deacon, 1968, priest, 1969; St Matthew's, Manly, dio. of Sydney, 1968–71; Lectr, Moore Theol Coll., 1971–75, 1978–79, 1984–96; Post-grad. study, Univ. of Manchester and Sunday Asst, St Mary's, Cheadle, dio. of Chester, 1975–78; Rector and Sen. Canon, St Michael's, Provisional Cathedral, Wollongong, dio. of Sydney, 1980–83. *Publications:* Hebrews and Perfection, 1982; Engaging with God, 1992; Possessed by God, 1995; The Book of Acts and its Theology, 1996; Where Wrath and Mercy Meet: proclaiming the atonement today, 2001. *Recreations:* golf, swimming, music. *Address:* Oak Hill Theological College, Chase Side, Southgate, N14 4PS.

PETERSON, Hon. David Robert; PC (Can.) 1992; QC (Can.) 1980; Senior Partner, since 1991, and Chairman, since 1998, Cassels Brock & Blackwell LLP; *b* 28 Dec. 1943; *s* of Clarence Marwin Peterson and Laura Marie (*née* Scott); *m* 1974, Shelley Christine Matthews; two *s* one *d*. *Educ:* Univ. of Western Ontario (BA Phil./PolSci); Univ. of Toronto (LLB). Called to Bar, Ontario, 1969. Chm. and Pres., C. M. Peterson Co. Ltd, 1969–75; MLA for London Centre, Ontario, 1975–90; Leader, Liberal Party of Ontario, 1982–90; Leader of the Opposition, 1982–85; Premier of Ontario, 1985–90. Chm. and Dir of public cos. CStJ 1987. Chevalier, Légion d'Honneur (France), 1994. *Recreations:* theatre, riding, jogging, ski-ing, tennis, scuba diving, golf, reading, gardening. *Address:* Cassels Brock & Blackwell LLP, 40 King Street W, Suite 2100, Scotia Plaza, Toronto, ON M5H 3C2, Canada. *Club:* London (Ontario) Hunt.

PETERSON, Rev. Canon John Louis, ThD; Secretary General, Anglican Consultative Council, since 1995; *b* 17 Dec. 1942; *s* of J. Harold Peterson and Edythe V. Peterson; *m* 1966, Kirsten Ruth Bratlie; two *d*. *Educ:* Concordia Coll. (BA 1965); Harvard Divinity Sch. (STB 1968); Chicago Inst. for Advanced Theol Studies (ThD 1976). Instr, OT and Syro-Palestinian Archaeol., Seabury-Western Theol Seminary, Evanston, 1968–76; Canon Theologian and Admin. Asst to Bishop, dio. of Western Michigan, 1976–82; Vicar, St Stephen's Plainwell, Mich, 1976–82; Dean of St George's Coll., and Canon Residentiary, St George's Cathedral, Jerusalem, 1982–94, Hon. Canon, 1995–. Hon. Canon: Cathedral Ch. of Christ the King, Kalamazoo, Mich, 1982–; Canterbury Cathedral, 1995; St Michael's Cathedral, Kaduna, Nigeria, 1999–; St Paul's Cathedral, 2000–. Hon. DD: Virginia Theol Seminary, 1993; Univ. of South (Sewanee), 1996; Seabury-Western Theol Seminary, 1997. *Publications:* A Walk in Jerusalem, 1998; contrib. Anchor Bible Dictionary, 1992. *Address:* Anglican Consultative Council, 157 Waterloo Road, SE1 8UT. *T:* (020) 7620 1110.

PETERSON, Rt Rev. Leslie Ernest; Bishop of Algoma, 1983–94; *b* 4 Nov. 1928; *s* of late Ernest Victor Peterson and of Dorothy Blanche Peterson (*née* Marsh); *m* 1953, Yvonne Hazel Lawton; two *s* three *d*. *Educ:* Univ. of Western Ontario (BA 1952); Huron College (LTh 1954; DD (*jd*) 1984); Teachers' Coll., North Bay, Ont., 1970. Deacon 1954, priest 1955; Incumbent of All Saints', Coniston, Ont., 1954–59; St Peter's Elliot Lake, 1959–63; Rector, Christ Church, North Bay, 1963–78; Teacher, Marshall Park Elem. School, 1970–78; Rector, Trinity Church, Parry Sound, 1978–83; Coadjutor Bishop, June-Sept. 1983. STD (*hc*) Thorneloe, 1992. *Recreations:* gardening, woodworking. *Address:* 615 Santa Monica Road, London, ON N6H 3W2, Canada.

PETERSON, Oscar Emmanuel, CC (Canada) 1984 (OC 1972); OOnt 1992; concert jazz pianist; *b* 15 Aug. 1925; *s* of Daniel Peterson and Olivia Peterson; *m* 1st, 1947, Lillian Alice Ann; two *s* three *d*; 2nd, 1966, Sandra Cythia, *d* of H. A. King; 3rd, Charlotte; one *s*; 4th, 1990, Kelly Ann Green; one *d*. *Educ:* (academic) Montreal High Sch.; (music) private tutors. 1st prize, amateur show, 1940; Carnegie Hall debut, 1950; 1950–: numerous jazz awards; TV shows; composer and arranger; yearly concert tours in N America, Europe, GB and Japan; has performed also in S America, Mexico, WI, Australia, NZ and Russia. *Television series:* (Canada): Oscar Peterson Presents, 1974; Oscar Peterson and Friends, 1980; (BBC) Oscar Peterson's Piano Party, 1974. Chancellor, York Univ., Ontario, 1991–94. Mem., Bd of Govs, Credit Valley Hosp., Mississauga, Ont., 1984–. Oscar Peterson scholarship established, Berklee Coll. of Mus., 1982. Grammy award, 1974, 1975, 1977, 1978, 1979, 1990, 1991; Grammy lifetime achievement award, 1997. Hon. LLD: Carleton Univ., 1973; Queen's Univ., Kingston, 1976; Concordia, 1979; MacMaster, 1981; Victoria, 1981; York, 1982; Toronto, 1985; Hon. DMus: Sackville, 1980; Laval, 1985; Hon. DFA: Northwestern, Ill, 1983; Niagara Univ., NY, 1996. Civic Award of Merit, Toronto, 1972, second mention, 1983; Diplôme d'Honneur, Canadian Conf. of the Arts, 1974; Toronto Arts Awards, Lifetime Achievement, 1991; Gov. General's Award, Lifetime Achievement, 1992; Glenn Gould Prize, 1993. Officer, Order of Arts and Letters (France), 1989; Chevalier, Order of Quebec, 1991. *Publications:* Oscar Peterson New Piano Solos, 1965; Jazz Exercises and Pieces, 1965; Jazz Playbook, vol. 1A, 1991, vol. 1B, 1993. *Recreations:* audio, photography, boating, fishing. *Address:* Regal Recordings Ltd, 2421 Hammond Road, Mississauga, ON L5K 1T3, Canada. *T:* (905) 8552370, *Fax:* (905) 8551773.

PETHERBRIDGE, Edward; actor and director; *b* 3 Aug. 1936; *s* of late William and Hannah Petherbridge; *m* 1st, 1957, Louise Harris (marr. diss. 1980); one *s*; 2nd, 1981, Emily Richard, actress; one *s* one *d*. *Educ:* Grange Grammar Sch., Bradford; Northern Theatre Sch. Early experience in repertory and on tour; London début, Dumain in Love's Labours Lost and Demetrius in A Midsummer Night's Dream, Regent's Park Open Air Theatre, 1962; All in Good Time, Mermaid, and Phoenix, 1963; with Nat. Theatre Co. at Old Vic, 1964–70, chief appearances in: Trelawny of the Wells, Rosencrantz and Guildenstern are Dead, A Flea in her Ear, Love for Love, Volpone, The Advertisement, The Way of the World, The White Devil; Alceste in The Misanthrope, Nottingham, Lulu, Royal Court, and Apollo, 1970; John Bull's Other Island, Mermaid, Swansong, opening of Crucible, Sheffield, 1971; Founder Mem., Actors' Co., 1972; chief appearances at Edinburgh Fests, NY, and on tour, 1972–75: 'Tis Pity she's a Whore, Rooling the Roost, The Way of the World, Tartuffe, King Lear; also devised, dir. and appeared in Knots (from R. D. Laing's book), The Beanstalk, a wordless pantomime, and dir. The Bacchae; RSC tour of Australia and NZ, 1976; dir. Uncle Vanya, Cambridge Theatre Co., 1977; Chasuble in The Importance of Being Earnest, and dir., devised and appeared in Do You Love Me (from R. D. Laing's book), Actors' Co. tour and Round House, 1977; Crucifer of Blood, Haymarket, 1979; Royal Shakespeare Company: tour, 1978, Twelfth Night; Three Sisters, 1979; Suicide, Newman Noggs in Nicholas Nickleby (Best Supporting Actor, London Drama Critics' Award, 1981), No Limits to Love, 1980; Nicholas Nickleby, Broadway, 1981; Twelfth Night, British Council tour (Philippines, Singapore, Malaysia, China and Japan), followed by season at Warehouse, London, 1982; Peter Pan, Barbican, 1983; The Rivals, NT, 1983; Strange Interlude, Duke of York's, 1984, Broadway, 1985 (Olivier Award, 1984); Love's Labours Lost, Stratford, 1984; Co-Dir, McKellen Petherbridge Co. at NT, 1984–86, acting in Duchess of Malfi, The Cherry Orchard, The Real Inspector Hound, and The Critic, 1985, company appeared at Internat. Theatre Fests, Paris and Chicago, 1986; Busman's Honeymoon, Lyric, Hammersmith, 1988; The Eight O'Clock Muse, one-man show, Riverside Studios, 1989; Alceste in The Misanthrope, co-prodn with Bristol Old Vic, 1989; The Power and the Glory, Chichester, 1990; Cyrano de Bergerac (title rôle), Greenwich, 1990; Point Valaine, and Valentine's Day (musical, from Shaw's You Never Can Tell), Chichester, 1991; Noël & Gertie, Duke of York's, 1991; The Seagull, RNT, 1994; Twelfth Night, Barbican, 1996; The Merry Wives of Windsor, Stratford, 1996; Cymbeline, Hamlet, Krapp's Last Tape, Stratford, 1997, transf. Barbican, NY, Washington and Edinburgh, 1997–98, Arts Th., 1999; The Accused, Haymarket Theatre Royal, 2000; The Relapse, RNT, 2001. Numerous television appearances include: Vershinin in Three Sisters (from RSC prod.); Lytton Strachey in No Need to Lie; Newman Noggs in Nicholas Nickleby (from RSC prod.); Gower in Pericles; Lord Peter Wimsey; Marsden in Strange Interlude; Uncle in Journey's End; No Strings. Hon. DLitt Bradford, 1989. *Recreations:* listening to music, photography, theatre history. *Address:* c/o Jonathan Altaras Associates, 13 Shorts Gardens, WC2H 9AT.

PETHICA, Prof. John Bernard, PhD; FRS 1999; Professor of Materials Science, University of Oxford, since 1996; Fellow of St Cross College, Oxford. *Educ:* Trinity Hall, Cambridge (BA 1974; PhD 1979); MA Oxon. Formerly, Lectr, Dept of Materials, Univ. of Oxford; Sony Corp. R&D Prof. (on leave of absence), Japan, 1993–94. Dir, Nano Instruments Inc., Knoxville, Tenn, 1985–98. Rosenhain Medal and Prize, Inst. of Materials, 1997. *Publications:* contribs to jls. *Address:* Department of Materials, Parks Road, Oxford OX1 3PH.

PETHICK, Brig. Geoffrey Loveston, CBE 1960; DSO 1944; *b* 25 Nov. 1907; *s* of late Captain E. E. Pethick, RN and May (*née* Brook); *m* 1st, 1939, Nancy Veronica Ferrand (*d* 1980); one *d*; 2nd, 1981, Mrs Paula Usborne (*d* 1996); 3rd, 1997, Mrs Neville Carr Selway. Commissioned, Royal Artillery, 1927; RHA 1934; served War of 1939–45: Staff Coll., Camberley, 1940; CO, Field Regt, 1942; Far East, 1945; jssc 1946; Dep. Dir, WO, 1948; idc, 1950; Comdr RA 3 Div. 1953; Army Council Staff, 1957; retired, 1960. Dir, British Paper Makers' Association, 1960–74. *Address:* Little Croft, Fireball Hill, Sunningdale, Berks SL5 9PJ. *T:* (01344) 622018.

PETIT, Sir Dinshaw Manockjee, 5th Bt *cr* 1890, of Petit Hall, Bombay; *b* 21 Jan. 1965; *er s* of Sir Dinshaw Manockjee Petit, 4th Bt and of his 1st wife, Nirmala Nanavatty; *S* father, 1998; *m* 1994, Laila, *d* of Homi Commissariat; one *s* one *d*. President: N. M. Petit Charities, 1998–; Sir D. M. Petit Charities, 1998–; F. D. Petit Sanatorium, 1998–; Persian Zoroastrian Amelioration Fund, 1998–; Petit Girls' Orphanage, 1998–; D. M. Petit Gymnasium, 1998–; J. N. Petit Institute, 1998–; Native Gen. Dispensary, 1998–. Trustee, Soc. for Prevention of Cruelty to Animals; Mem., Managing Cttee, B. D. Petit Parsi Gen. Hospital. *Heir:* *s* Rehan Jehangir Petit, *b* 4 May 1995. *Address:* Petit Hall, 66 Nepean Sea Road, Bombay 400006, India.

PETIT, Roland; Officier de la Légion d'honneur; Chevalier des Arts et des Lettres; Chevalier de l'Ordre National du Mérite; French choreographer and dancer; Artistic Director and Choreographer, Ballet National de Marseille, 1972–97; *b* Villemomble, 13 Jan. 1924; *m* 1954, Renée (Zizi) Jeanmaire; one *d*. *Educ:* Ecole de Ballet de l'Opéra de Paris. L'Opéra de Paris, 1940–44; founded Les Vendredis de la Danse, 1944, Les Ballets des Champs-Elysées, 1945, Les Ballets de Paris de Roland Petit, 1948; Artistic Dir and Choreographer, Ballets de Marseille. Choreographic works include: Les Forains, Le Jeune Homme et la Mort, Les Demoiselles de la nuit, Carmen, Deuil en 24 heures, Le Loup, L'éloge de la Folie, Les Chants de Maldoror, Notre Dame de Paris, Paradise Lost, Les Intermittences du coeur, La Symphonie fantastique, La Dame de Pique, Die Fledermaus, L'Arlésienne, Le Chat Botté, Coppelia, The Blue Angel, Pink Floyd Ballet, Ma Pavlova, Charlot Danse Avec Nous, etc; choreographer and dancer: La Belle au Bois Dormant; Cyrano de Bergerac. Appeared in films Hans Christian Andersen; Un, Deux, Trois, Quatre (arr. ballets, for film, and danced in 3); 4 ballets, Black Tights. *Address:* c/o Ballet National de Marseille, 20 Boulevard Gabès, 13008 Marseille, France.

PETO, Sir Henry (George Morton), 4th Bt *cr* 1855; *b* 29 April 1920; *s* of Comdr Sir Henry Francis Morton Peto, 3rd Bt, RN, and Edith (*d* 1945), *d* of late George Berners Ruck Keene; *S* father, 1978; *m* 1947, Frances Jacqueline, JP, *d* of late Ralph Haldane Evers; two *s*. *Educ:* Sherborne; Corpus Christi College, Cambridge. Served War with Royal Artillery, 1939–46. Manufacturing industry, 1946–80. *Heir:* *s* Francis Michael Morton Peto [*b* 11 Jan. 1949; *m* 1974, Felicity Margaret, *d* of late Lt-Col John Alan Burns; two *s*]. *Address:* Stream House, Selborne, Alton, Hants GU34 3LE.

PETO, Sir Michael (Henry Basil), 4th Bt *cr* 1927; *b* 6 April 1938; *s* of Brig. Sir Christopher Henry Maxwell Peto, 3rd Bt, DSO, and Barbara (*d* 1992), *yr d* of Edwyn Thomas Close; *S* father, 1980; *m* 1st, 1963, Sarah Susan (marr. diss. 1970), *y d* of Major Sir Dennis Stucley, 5th Bt; one *s* two *d*; 2nd, 1971, Lucinda Mary, *yr d* of Major Sir Charles Douglas Blackett, 9th Bt; two *s*. *Educ:* Eton; Christ Church, Oxford (MA). Called to the Bar, Inner Temple, 1960. Financial Consultant, Canada Life, Newcastle, 1998–. *Heir:* *s* Henry Christopher Morton Bampfylde Peto [*b* 8 April 1967; *m* 1998, Louise Imogen (marr. diss. 1999), *y d* of Christopher Balck-Foote]. *Address:* 12 St Helen's Terrace, Spittal, Berwick upon Tweed TD15 1RJ. *Club:* Pratt's.

PETO, Sir Richard, Kt 1999; FRS 1989; Professor of Medical Statistics and Epidemiology, University of Oxford, since 1992; Fellow of Green College, Oxford, since

1979; *b* 14 May 1943; *s* of Leonard Huntley Peto and Carrie Clarinda Peto; *m* 1970, Sallie Messum (marr. diss.); two *s*, and two *s* by Gale Mead. *Educ:* Trinity Coll., Cambridge (MA Natural Sci.); Imperial Coll., London (MSc Statistics). Research Officer: MRC, 1967–69; Univ. of Oxford, 1969–72; Lectr, Dept of Regius Prof. of Medicine, 1972–75, Reader in Cancer Studies, 1975–92, Univ. of Oxford. Founder FMedSci 1998. *Publications:* Natural History of Chronic Bronchitis and Emphysema, 1976; Quantification of Occupational Cancer, 1981; The Causes of Cancer, 1983; Diet, Lifestyle and Mortality in China, 1990; (jtly) Mortality from Smoking in Developed Countries 1950–2000, 1994. *Recreations:* science, children. *Address:* Radcliffe Infirmary, Oxford OX2 6HE. *T:* (01865) 552830/404801.

PETRE, family name of **Baron Petre**.

PETRE, 18th Baron *cr* 1603; **John Patrick Lionel Petre;** DL; *b* 4 Aug. 1942; *s* of 17th Baron Petre and of Marguerite Eileen, *d* of late Ion Wentworth Hamilton; *S* father, 1989; *m* 1965, Marcia Gwendolyn, *d* of Alfred Plumpton; two *s* one *d*. *Educ:* Eton; Trinity College, Oxford (MA). DL Essex, 1991. OStJ 1994. *Heir:* *s* Hon. Dominic William Petre [*b* 9 Aug. 1966; *m* 1998, Marisa Verna, *o d* of Anthony J. Perry; one *s* one *d*]. *Address:* Writtle Park, Highwood, Chelmsford, Essex CM1 3QF.

PETRE, His Honour Francis Herbert Loraine; a Circuit Judge, 1972–97; Chairman, Police Complaints Authority, 1989–92; *b* 9 March 1927; *s* of late Maj.-Gen. R. L. Petre, CB, DSO, MC and Mrs Katherine Sophia Petre; *m* 1958, Mary Jane, *d* of late Everard C. X. White and Sydney Mary Carleton White (*née* Holmes); three *s* one *d*. *Educ:* Downside; Clare Coll., Cambridge. Called to Bar, Lincoln's Inn, 1952; Dep. Chm., E Suffolk QS, 1970; Dep. Chm., Agricultural Lands Tribunal (Eastern Area), 1972; a Recorder, 1972; Regular Judge, Central Criminal Court, 1982–93. Mem., Parole Bd, 1997–2000. *Address:* The Ferriers, Bures, Suffolk CO8 5DL.

PETRIE, Sir Peter (Charles), 5th Bt *cr* 1918, of Carrowcarden; CMG 1980; Adviser on European and Parliamentary Affairs to Governor of Bank of England, since 1989; HM Diplomatic Service, retired; *b* 7 March 1932; *s* of Sir Charles Petrie, 3rd Bt, CBE, FRHistS and Jessie Cecilia (*d* 1987), *d* of Frederick James George Mason; *S* half-brother, 1988; *m* 1958, Countess Lydwine Maria Fortunata v. Oberndorff, *d* of Count v. Oberndorff, The Hague and Paris; two *s* one *d*. *Educ:* Westminster; Christ Church, Oxford. BA Lit. Hum., MA. 2nd Lieut Grenadier Guards, 1954–56. Entered HM Foreign Service, 1956; served in UK Delegn to NATO, Paris 1958–61; UK High Commn, New Delhi (seconded CRO), 1961–64; Chargé d'Affaires, Katmandu, 1963; Cabinet Office, 1965–67; UK Mission to UN, NY, 1969–73; Counsellor (Head of Chancery), Bonn, 1973–76; Head of European Integration Dept (Internal), FCO, 1976–79; Minister, Paris, 1979–85; Ambassador to Belgium, 1985–89. Member: Franco-British Council, 1994– (Chm., British section, 1997–); Inst de l'Euro, Lyon, 1995–99; Acad. de Comptabilité, 1997–. Mem. Council, City Univ., 1997–. *Recreations:* country pursuits. *Heir:* *s* Charles James Petrie [*b* 16 Sept. 1959; *m* 1981, France de Hauteclocque; three *s* (one *d* decd)]. *Address:* 16A Cambridge Street, SW1V 4QH; 40 rue Lauriston, 75116 Paris, France; Le Hameau du Jardin, Lestre, 50310 Montebourg, France. *Clubs:* Brooks's, Beefsteak; Jockey (Paris).

PETROW, Judith Caroline; *see* Bingham, J. C.

PETT, Maj.-Gen. Raymond Austin, CB 1995; MBE 1976; Director, Healthcare Projects Ltd, since 2001; *b* 23 Sept. 1941; *s* of late Richard John Austin Pett and Jessie Lyle Pett (*née* Adamson); *m* 1965, (Joan) Marie McGrath Price, *d* of FO Bernard Christopher McGrath, RAF (killed in action 1943) and of Mrs Robert Henry Benbow Price; one *s* one *d*. *Educ:* Christ's Coll.; RMA Sandhurst; rcds, psc. Commnd Lancashire Regt (Prince of Wales's Vols), 1961; regtl service in GB, BAOR, Swaziland and Cyprus; seconded 2nd Bn 6th QEO Gurkha Rifles, Malaysia and Hong Kong, 1967–69; Instr, RMA Sandhurst, 1969–72; Staff Coll., 1972–73; DAA&QMG, HQ 48 Gurkha Inf. Bde, 1974–75; 1st Bn, Queen's Lancashire Regt, 1976–78; GSO2 ASD 3, MoD, 1978–80; CO, 1st Bn King's Own Royal Border Regt, 1980–82; Staff Coll. (HQ and Directing Staff), 1983–84; Col ASD 2, MoD, 1984; Col Army Plans, MoD, 1985; Comd Gurkha Field Force, 1985–86, and Comd 48 Gurkha Inf. Bde, 1986–87, Hong Kong; RCDS 1988; Dir, Army Staff Duties, MoD, 1989–91; DCS and Sen. British Officer, HQ AFNORTH, 1991–94; Dir of Infantry, 1994–96. Dir of Capital Projects, Royal Hosps NHS Trust, 1996–97; Chief Exec., Bart's and the London NHS Trust, 1997–2000. Col, 6th QEO Gurkha Rifles, 1988–94; Col Comdt, King's Div., 1994–97. Trustee, Gurkha Welfare Trust, 1988–. Chm., Army Mountaineering Assoc., 1994–96. Vice-Pres., Mid-Somerset Agricl Soc., 1996–. FIMgt; FRSA 1997. Freeman, City of London, 2000; Liveryman, Painter Stainers' Co., 2000–. *Recreations:* the arts, house restoration, ski-ing. *Clubs:* Army and Navy, Ronnie Scott's.

PETTIFER, Julian; freelance writer and broadcaster; *b* 21 July 1935; *s* of Stephen Henry Pettifer and Diana Mary (*née* Burton); unmarried. *Educ:* Marlborough; St John's Coll., Cambridge. Television reporter, writer and presenter: Southern TV, 1958–62; Tonight, BBC, 1962–64; 24 Hours, BBC, 1964–69; Panorama, BBC, 1969–75; Presenter, Cuba—25 years of revolution (series), ITV, 1984; Host, Busman's Holiday, ITV, 1985–86. Numerous television documentaries, including: Vietnam, War without End, 1970; The World About Us, 1976; The Spirit of '76, 1976; Diamonds in the Sky, 1979; Nature Watch, 1981–82, 1985–86, 1988, 1990, 1992; Automania, 1984; The Living Isles, 1986; Missionaries, 1990; See for Yourself, 1991; Assignment, 1991; Nature, 1992; The Culling Fields, 1999; Warnings from the Wild, 2000, 2001; radio broadcasts include: Asia File, and Crossing Continents, BBC Radio 4; The Sixties, BBC Radio 2, 2000. Trustee, Royal Botanic Gdns, Kew, 1993–96. President: Berks, Bucks and Oxfordshire Naturalists Trust, 1990–; RSPB, 1995–2001; Vice-Pres., RSNC, 1992–. Reporter of the Year Award, Guild of Television Directors and Producers, 1968; Cherry Kearton Award for Contribution to Wildlife Films, RGS, 1990; Mungo Park Medal, RSGS, 1998. *Publications:* (jtly) Diamonds in the Sky: a social history of air travel, 1979; (jtly) Nature Watch, 1981; (jtly) Automania, 1984; (jtly) Missionaries, 1990; (jtly) Nature Watch, 1994. *Recreations:* travel, sport, cinema. *Address:* c/o Curtis Brown, 28–29 Haymarket, SW1Y 4SP. *T:* (020) 7396 6600. *Club:* Queen's.

PETTIFOR, Prof. David Godfrey, PhD; FRS 1994; Isaac Wolfson Professor of Metallurgy, Oxford University, since 1992; Fellow, St Edmund Hall, Oxford, since 1992; *b* 9 March 1945; *s* of late Percy Hayward Pettifor and Margaret Cotterill; *m* 1969, Lynda Ann Potgieter (marr. diss. 1989); two *s*. *Educ:* Univ. of Witwatersrand (BSc Hons 1967); PhD Cantab 1970. Lectr, Dept of Physics, Univ. of Dar es Salaam, 1971; Res. Asst, Cavendish Lab., Cambridge, 1974; Vis. Res. Scientist, Bell Labs, USA, 1978; Imperial College, London: Lectr and Reader, Dept of Mathematics, 1978–88; Prof. of Theoretical Solid State Physics, 1988–92. Lectures: Mott, Inst. of Physics, 1993; Maddin, Univ. of Pa, 1995. Hume-Rothery Award, Minerals, Metals and Materials Soc., USA, 1995; Armourers' and Brasiers' Award, Royal Soc., 1999. *Publications:* Bonding and Structure of Molecules and Solids, 1995; papers incl. Structures maps for pseudo-binary and ternary phases (Inst. of Metals Prize, 1989). *Recreation:* walking. *Address:* Department of Materials, University of Oxford, Parks Road, Oxford OX1 3PH. *T:* (01865) 273751.

PETTIGREW, Prof. John Douglas, FRS 1987; FAA 1987; Professor of Physiology, since 1983, Director, Vision, Touch and Hearing Research Centre, since 1988, University of Queensland; *b* 2 Oct. 1943; *s* of John James Pettigrew and Enid Dellmere Holt; *m* 1968, Rona Butler (marr. diss. 1996); one *s* two *d*. *Educ:* Katoomba High Sch.; Univ. of Sydney (BSc Med., MSc, MB BS). Jun. Resident MO, Royal Prince Alfred Hosp., 1969; Miller Fellow 1970–72, Res. Associate 1973, Univ. of California, Berkeley; Asst Prof. of Biology 1974, Associate Prof. of Biology 1978, CIT; Actg Dir, National Vision Res. Inst. of Aust., 1981. *Publications:* Visual Neuroscience, 1986; numerous pubns in Nature, Science, Jl of Physiol., Jl of Comp. Neurol., Exp. Brain Res., etc. *Recreations:* bird watching, mountaineering. *Address:* 207/180 Swann Road, Taringa, Qld 4068, Australia. *T:* (7) 38711062.

PETTIGREW, Sir Russell (Hilton), Kt 1983; FInstD; FCIT; Chairman, Chep Handling Systems NZ Ltd, 1980–93; *b* 10 Sept. 1920; *s* of Albert and Bertha Pettigrew; *m* 1965, Glennis Olive Nicol; one *s* one *d*. *Educ:* Hangatiki Sch., King Country; Te Kuiti Dist High Sch. Served War, Naval Service, 1941–44 (Service Medals). Hawkes Bay Motor Co., 1935–40; Pettigrews Transport, 1946–63; formed Allied Freightways (now Freightways Holdings Ltd), 1964. Chairman: NZ Maritime Holdings Ltd, 1981–89; AGC NZ, 1984–88; Dep. Chm., NZ Forest Products, 1980–88 (Dir, 1975–90). FCIT 1972 (Life Mem. 1995); Fellow, NZ Inst. of Dirs, 1972; Life Mem., NZ Road Transport Assoc., 1981. Knighthood for services to the Transport Industry. *Publication:* article in The Modern Freight Forwarder and the Road Carrier, 1971. *Recreations:* farming, Rugby, horse racing. *Address:* PO Box 16, Bay View, Napier 4151, New Zealand. *T:* (6) 8366426. *Clubs:* Auckland, Hawkes Bay (New Zealand).

PETTIT, Sir Daniel (Eric Arthur), Kt 1974; Chairman, PosTel Investment Management (formerly Post Office Staff Superannuation Fund), 1979–83; *b* Liverpool, 19 Feb. 1915; *s* of Thomas Edgar Pettit and Pauline Elizabeth Pettit (*née* Kerr); *m* 1940, Winifred, *d* of William and Sarah Bibby; two *s*. *Educ:* Quarry Bank High Sch., Liverpool; Fitzwilliam Coll., Cambridge (MA; Hon. Fellow, 1985). School Master, 1938–40 and 1946–47; War Service, Africa, India, Burma, 1940–46 (Major, RA); Unilever: Management, 1948–57; Associated Company Dir and Chm., 1958–70. Chm., Nat. Freight Corp., 1971–78 (part-time Mem. Bd, 1968–70); Member: Freight Integration Council, 1971–78; National Ports Council, 1971–80; Bd, Foundn of Management Educn, 1973–84; Waste Management Adv. Council, 1971–78; Chm., EDC for Distributive Trades, 1974–78. Chairman: Incpen, 1979–90; RDC Properties, 1987–; Director: Lloyds Bank Ltd, 1977–78 (Chm., Birmingham & W Midlands Bd, 1978–85); Lloyds Bank (UK) Ltd, 1979–85; Bransford Partnership, 1979–; Black Horse Life Assurance Co. Ltd, 1983–85; Lloyds Bank Unit Trust Managers Ltd, 1981–85; Bransford Farmers Ltd. Mem. Council, British Road Fedn Ltd. Hon. Col, 162 Regt RCT (V). Freeman, City of London, 1971; Liveryman, Worshipful Co. of Carmen, 1971. CMgt; FCIT (Pres. 1971–72); FRSA; FIM; MIPD. *Publications:* various papers on transport and management matters. *Recreations:* cricket, Association football (Olympic Games, 1936; Corinthian FC, 1935–); fly-fishing. *Address:* Bransford Court Farm, Worcester WR6 5JL. *Clubs:* Farmers', MCC; Hawks (Cambridge).

PETTITT, Sir Dennis, Kt 1998; Leader, Nottinghamshire County Council, since 1981; *b* 21 Aug. 1925; *m* 1949, Dorothy Mary. Served War of 1939–45. Electrician; trade unionist; Kenya, 1950–60; Vice Chm., Kenya League, 1952–53. Member (Lab): Birmingham CC, 1962–68; Broxtowe BC, 1974– (Leader, Lab Gp, 1974–77); Notts CC, 1977– (Leader, Lab Gp, 1979–). Chm., ACC, 1988–89, 1991–92. Mem., Cttee of the Regions, EU, 1993–. Contested (Lab) Carlton, Oct. 1974. Commander's Cross, Order of Merit (Poland), 1993. *Address:* 32 Scalby Close, Eastwood, Notts NG16 3QQ.

PETTITT, Gordon Charles, OBE 1991; transport management consultant; Managing Director, Regional Railways, British Rail, 1991–92; *b* 12 April 1934; *s* of Charles and Annie Pettitt; *m* 1956, Ursula Margareta Agnes Hokamp; three *d*. *Educ:* St Columba's Coll., St Albans; Pitman's Coll., London. FCIT. British Rail, 1950–92: Freight Sales Manager, Eastern Reg., 1976; Chief Passenger Manager, Western Reg., 1978; Divl Manager, Liverpool Street, Eastern Reg., 1979; Dep. Gen. Manager, 1983, Gen. Manager, 1985, Southern Reg.; Dir, Provincial, 1990–91. Director: Connex Rail Ltd, 1997–98; Heathrow Express Operating Co. Ltd, 1997–99. Pres., Instn of Railway Operators, 2000–. Governor, Middlesex Univ. (formerly Polytechnic), 1989–95. *Recreations:* walking, foreign travel, Victorian art. *Address:* Beeches Green, Woodham Lane, Woking, Surrey GU21 5SP.

PETTY, Very Rev. John Fitzmaurice; Chaplain, Mount House Residential Home for the Elderly, Shrewsbury, since 2001; *b* 1935; *m* 1963, Susan Shakerley; three *s* one *d*. *Educ:* RMA Sandhurst; Trinity Hall, Cambridge (BA 1959, MA 1965); Cuddesdon College. Commnd RE, 1955; seconded Gurkha Engineers, 1959–62; resigned commission as Captain, 1964. Deacon 1966, priest 1967; Curate: St Cuthbert, Sheffield, 1966–69; St Helier, Southwark Dio., 1969–75; Vicar of St John's, Hurst, Ashton-under-Lyne, 1975–87; Area Dean of Ashton-under-Lyne, 1983–87; Provost, then Dean, Coventry Cathedral, 1988–2000. Hon. Canon of Manchester Cathedral, 1986. Hon. DLitt Coventry, 1996. *Recreations:* cycling, ski-ing. *Address:* 4 Granville Street, Copthorne, Shrewsbury SY3 8NE. *T:* (01743) 231513.

PETTY, Prof. Michael Charles, PhD, DSc; Professor of Engineering, University of Durham, since 1994; Co-Director, Durham Centre for Molecular Electronics, since 1987; *b* 30 Dec. 1950; *s* of John Leonard Petty and Doreen Rosemary Petty (*née* Bellarby); *m* 1998, Anne Mathers Brawley; one step *d*. *Educ:* Sussex Univ. (BSc 1st Cl. Hons Electronics 1972; DSc 1994); Imperial Coll., London (PhD 1976). University of Durham: Lectr in Applied Physics, 1976–88; Sen. Lectr, Sch. of Engrg, 1988–94; Chm., Sch. of Engrg, 1997–2000. Sir James Knott Res. Fellow, 2000–01. *Publications:* Langmuir-Blodgett Films, 1995; Introduction to Molecular Electronics, 1995; numerous contribs on molecular electronics and nanoelectronics to scientific jls. *Recreations:* Yorkshire Dales, horse riding, supporter of Crystal Palace FC. *Address:* School of Engineering, University of Durham, South Road, Durham DH1 3LE. *T:* (0191) 374 2389.

PETTY, William Henry, CBE 1981; County Education Officer, Kent, 1973–84; *b* 7 Sept. 1921; *s* of Henry and Eveline Ann Petty, Bradford; *m* 1948, Margaret Elaine, *o d* of Edward and Lorna Bastow, Baildon, Yorks; one *s* two *d*. *Educ:* Bradford Grammar Sch.; Peterhouse, Cambridge; London Univ. MA 1950, BSc 1953. Served RA, India and Burma, 1941–45. Admin, teaching and lectrg in London, Doncaster and N R Yorks, 1946–57; Sen. Asst Educn Officer, W R Yorks CC 1957–64; Dep. County Educn Officer, Kent CC, 1964–73. Member: Council and Court, Univ. of Kent at Canterbury, 1974–84, 1992–; Local Govt Trng Bd, Careers Service Trng Cttee, 1975–84; Careers Service Adv. Council, 1976–84; Trng and Further Educn Cons. Gp, 1977–83; Vital Skills Task Gp, 1977–78; Manpower Services Commn, SE Counties Area Bd, 1978–83; Bd of Dirs, Industrial Trng Service, 1978–97; Exec. Mem. and Sec. for SE Reg., Soc. of Educn Officers, 1978–82; Pres., Soc. of Educn Officers, 1980–81; Chm., Assoc. of Educn Officers, 1979–80 (Vice-Chm., 1978–79); Member: JNC for Chief Officers, Officers' side, 1974–84 (Chm., 1981–84); C of E Bd of Educn, Schs Cttee, 1981–86; County

Educn Officers' Soc., 1974–84 (Chm., 1982–83); Youth Trng Task Gp, 1982; National Youth Trng Bd, 1983–84; Kent Area Manpower Bd, 1983–84; Canterbury Diocesan Bd of Educn, 1984–92 (Vice-Chm., 1989–92); Consultant, Further Educn Unit, 1984–90. Dir, Sennocke Services Ltd, 1989–97. Governor: Christ Church Coll., Canterbury, 1974–94 (Chm., 1992–94; Vice-Chm., 1988–92); Sevenoaks Sch., 1974–97; YMCA Nat. Coll., 1992–94. Hon. DLitt Kent, 1983. Prizewinner: Cheltenham Fest. of Lit., 1968; Camden Fest. of Music and Arts, 1969; Swanage Fest. of the Arts, 1995; Greenwood Prize, 1978; Lake Aske Meml Award, 1980; Kent Fedn of Writers Prize, 1995; White Cliffs Prize, 2000. *Publications:* No Bold Comfort, 1957; Conquest, 1967; (jtly) Educational Administration, 1980; Executive Summaries (booklets), 1984–90; Springfield, 1994; (with Robert Roberts) Genius Loci, 1995; The Louvre Imperial, 1997; Interpretations of History, 2000; contrib. educnl and lit. jls and anthologies. *Recreations:* literature, travel. *Address:* Willow Bank, Moat Road, Headcorn, Kent TN27 9NT. *T:* (01622) 890087. *Club:* Oxford and Cambridge.

PETTY-FITZMAURICE, family name of **Marquess of Lansdowne**.

PEYTON, family name of **Baron Peyton of Yeovil**.

PEYTON OF YEOVIL, Baron *cr* 1983 (Life Peer), of Yeovil in the County of Somerset; **John Wynne William Peyton;** PC 1970; Chairman, British Alcan Aluminium, 1987–91; *b* 13 Feb. 1919; *s* of late Ivor Eliot Peyton and Dorothy Helen Peyton; *m* 1947, Diana Clinch (marr. diss., 1966); one *s* one *d* (and one *s* decd); *m* 1966, Mrs Mary Cobbold. *Educ:* Eton; Trinity College, Oxford. Commissioned 15/19 Hussars, 1939; Prisoner of War, Germany, 1940–45. Called to the Bar, Inner Temple, 1945. MP (C) Yeovil, 1951–83; Parly Secretary, Ministry of Power, 1962–64; Minister of Transport, June-Oct. 1970; Minister for Transport Industries, DoE, 1970–74. Chm., Texas Instruments Ltd, 1974–90. Treas., Zoological Society of London, 1984–91. *Publications:* Without Benefit of Laundry, 1997; Solly Zuckerman: a scientist out of the ordinary, 2001. *Address:* The Old Malt House, Hinton St George, Somerset TA17 8SE. *T:* (01460) 73618; 6 Temple West Mews, West Square, SE11 4TJ. *T:* (020) 7582 3611. *Clubs:* Boodle's, Pratt's, Beefsteak.

PEYTON, Kathleen Wendy; writer (as K. M. Peyton); *b* 2 Aug. 1929; *d* of William Joseph Herald and Ivy Kathleen Herald; *m* 1950, Michael Peyton; two *d*. *Educ:* Wimbledon High Sch.; Manchester Sch. of Art (ATD). Taught art at Northampton High Sch., 1953–55; started writing seriously after birth of first child, although had already had 4 books published. *Publications: as Kathleen Herald:* Sabre, the Horse from the Sea, 1947, USA 1963; The Mandrake, 1949; Crab the Roan, 1953; *as K. M. Peyton:* North to Adventure, 1959, USA 1965; Stormcock Meets Trouble, 1961; The Hard Way Home, 1962; Windfall, 1963, USA (as Sea Fever), 1963; Brownsea Silver, 1964; The Maplin Bird, 1964, USA 1965 (New York Herald Tribune Award, 1965); The Plan for Birdsmarsh, 1965, USA 1966; Thunder in the Sky, 1966, USA 1967; Flambards Trilogy (Guardian Award, 1970): Flambards, 1967, USA 1968; The Edge of the Cloud, 1969, USA 1969 (Carnegie Medal, 1969); Flambards in Summer, 1969, USA 1970; Fly-by-Night, 1968, USA 1969; Pennington's Seventeenth Summer, 1970, USA (as Pennington's Last Term), 1971; The Beethoven Medal, 1971, USA 1972; The Pattern of Roses, 1972, USA 1973; Pennington's Heir, 1973, USA 1974; The Team, 1975; The Right-Hand Man, 1977; Prove Yourself a Hero, 1977, USA 1978; A Midsummer Night's Death, 1978, USA 1979; Marion's Angels, 1979, USA 1979; Flambards Divided, 1981; Dear Fred, 1981, USA 1981; Going Home, 1983, USA 1983; Who, Sir? Me, Sir?, 1983; The Last Ditch, 1984, USA (as Free Rein), 1983; Froggett's Revenge, 1985; The Sound of Distant Cheering, 1986; Downhill All the Way, 1988; Darkling, 1989, USA 1990; Skylark, 1989; No Roses Round the Door, 1990; Poor Badger, 1991, USA 1991; Late to Smile, 1992; The Boy Who Wasn't There, 1992, USA 1992; The Wild Boy, 1993; Snowfall, 1994, USA 1998; The Swallow Tale, 1995; Swallow Summer, 1996; Swallow the Star, 1997; Unquiet Spirits, 1997; Firehead, 1998; Blind Beauty, 1999. *Recreations:* riding, walking, gardening, sailing. *Address:* Rookery Cottage, North Fambridge, Chelmsford, Essex CM3 6LP.

PEYTON, Ven. Nigel; JP; Archdeacon of Newark, since 1999; *b* 5 Feb. 1951; *s* of Hubert Peyton and Irene Louise Peyton (*née* Ellis); *m* 1981, Anne Marie Thérèse (*née* McQuillan), *widow* of Colin Campbell; one *s* one *d* (and one *d* decd). *Educ:* Latymer Upper Sch.; Univ. of Edinburgh (MA 1973; BD 1976); Edinburgh Theol Coll.; Union Theol Seminary, NY (Scottish Fellow, 1976; STM 1977). Deacon 1976, priest 1977; Chaplain, St Paul's Cathedral, Dundee, 1976–82; Dio. Youth Chaplain, Brechin, 1976–85; Priest-in-charge, All Souls, Invergowrie, 1979–85; Vicar, All Saints, Nottingham, 1985–91; Priest-in-charge, Lambley, 1991–99; Dio. Ministry Develt Advr, Southwell, 1991–99. Chaplain: University Hosp., Dundee, 1982–85; Nottingham Bluecoat Sch., 1990–92. Bishops' Selector, 1992–2000, Sen. Selector, 2001–. Proctor in Convocation, 1995–. JP Nottingham, 1987. *Publication:* Dual Role Ministry, 1998. *Recreations:* music, reading, gardening, hill-walking. *Address:* (office) Dunham House, Westgate, Southwell, Notts NG25 0JL. *T:* (01636) 814490, *Fax:* (01636) 815882; *e-mail:* archdeacon-newark@southwell.anglican.org; (home) 4 The Woodwards, Newark, Notts NG24 3GG. *T:* (01636) 612249, *Fax:* (01636) 611952.

PEYTON, Oliver; Owner, Gruppo Ltd, since 1993; *b* 26 Sept. 1961; *s* of Patrick Peyton; *m* 1999, Charlotte Polizzi; one *s*. *Educ:* Leicester Poly. (Textiles course 1979). Founder, The Can night club, Brighton, 1981; owner, import business, 1985–92; proprietor of restaurants: Atlantic Bar and Grill, Regent Palace Hotel, London, 1994–; Coast, Mayfair, 1995–2000 (Best Restaurant, The Times; Restaurant of Year, Time Out, 1998); Mash, Oxford Circus, 1998–; Isola, Knightsbridge, 1999–; The Admiralty, Somerset House, 2000– (Best New Restaurant, Time Out). *Address:* Gruppo Ltd, 19–21 Great Portland Street, W1W 8QB. *T:* (020) 7637 7300.

PEYTON-JONES, Julia; Director, Serpentine Gallery, since 1991; *b* 18 Feb. 1952; *d* of Jeremy Peyton-Jones and Rhona (*née* Wood); *m* 1975, Prosper Riley-Smith (marr. diss. 1985). *Educ:* Tudor Hall; Byam Shaw Sch. of Art (Dip BS; LCAD); Royal Coll. of Art (MA). Started 20th century Picture Dept, Phillips, auctioneers, 1974–75; Lectr, Painting and Humanities Depts, Edinburgh Sch. of Art, 1978–79; Organiser: Atlantis Gall., London, 1980–81; Wapping Artists' Open Studios Exhibn, 1981–82; Tolly Cobbold Eastern Arts 4th Nat. Exhibn, Cambridge and tour, 1982–84; Raoul Dufy 1877–1953 exhibn, Hayward Gall., 1983–84; Linbury Prize for Stage Design (selection and exhibn), 1986–87 (Mem., Exec. Cttee, 1988–96); Sponsorship Officer, Arts Council and S Bank Bd, 1984–87; Curator, Hayward Gall., 1988–91. Arts Council: Collection Purchaser, 1989–90; Mem., Visual Arts Projects Cttee, 1991–93; Mem., Visual Arts, Photography and Architecture Panel, 1994–96. Trustee: Public Art Develt Trust, 1987–88; Chisenhale Trust, 1987–89; New Contemporaries Exhibn, 1988–90. Painter, 1974–87; exhibitions include: Riverside Studios (individual), 1978; ICA, 1973; John Moores, Liverpool, 1978; Royal Scottish Acad., 1979. Mem. Ct of Govs, London Inst., 1989–. *Recreations:* contemporary arts in general, visual arts in particular. *Address:* 25 Sudeley Street, N1 8HW.

PFIRTER, Rogelio (Francisco Emilio); Ambassador of the Argentine Republic to the Court of St James's, 1995–2000; *b* 25 Aug. 1948; *s* of Rogelio and Amanda Pfirter von Mayenfisch; *m* 1980, Isabel Serantes Braun. *Educ:* Colegio Inmaculada SJ, Argentina; Universidad de Litoral (grad as lawyer); Inst. of Foreign Service, Argentina. Third Sec., S America Dept, 1974; Second, then First Sec., Perm. Mission to UN, 1975–80; Counsellor: Undersecretariat of Foreign Affairs, 1980–81; London, 1982; Minister Counsellor, then Minister Plenipotentiary, Perm. Mission to UN, 1982–90; Alternate Perm. Rep. to UN, 1989; Dep. Hd, Foreign Minister's Cabinet, 1990–91; Dir, Internat. Security, Nuclear and Space Affairs, 1991; Under-Sec., Foreign Policy, 1992; Mem., Posting and Promotion Bd, 1993–95. Mem., Bd of Dirs, Argentine Nat. Commn for Space Activities, 1994–95. Pres., General Assembly, IMO, 1993–97; Mem., UN Adv. Bd on Disarmament Matters, 1993–96. Order of Merit, Cavaliere di Gran Croce (Italy), 1992; Order of Merit (Chile), 1992; Order of Isabel la Católica (Spain), 1994. *Publications:* (jtly) Cuentos Originales, 1965; articles on policy. *Address:* c/o The Argentine Embassy, 65 Brook Street, W1Y 1YE. *T:* (020) 7318 1300, *Fax:* (020) 7318 1301. *Clubs:* White's, Brooks's; Circulo de Armas, Los Pingüinos (Buenos Aires).

PFLEGER, Martin Charles; Deputy Auditor General, National Audit Office, since 2000; *b* 5 May 1948; *m*; two *s* one *d*; *m* 1995, Amanda Jane Dolphin. *Educ:* CIPFA. National Audit Office: Dir, IT Audit, 1986; Dir, Corporate Policy and Finance, 1988; Asst Auditor Gen., 1993. MInstD 1991. Editor, IntoIT. *Publications:* articles on IT and business management in the public sector. *Recreations:* golf, hill walking, bridge. *Address:* National Audit Office, 157–197 Buckingham Palace Road, SW1W 9SP. *T:* (020) 7798 7314.

PHAROAH, Prof. Peter Oswald Derrick, MD; FRCP, FRCPCH, FFPHM; Professor of Public Health (formerly of Community Health), University of Liverpool, 1979–97, now Professor Emeritus; *b* 19 May 1934; *s* of Oswald Higgins Pharoah and Phyllis Christine Gahan; *m* 1960, Margaret Rose McMinn; three *s* one *d*. *Educ:* Lawrence Memorial Royal Military School, Lovedale, India; Palmers School, Grays, Essex; St Mary's Hospital Medical School. MD, MSc. Graduated, 1958; Med. House Officer and Med. Registrar appointments at various London Hosps, 1958–63; MO and Research MO, Dept of Public Health, Papua New Guinea, 1963–74; Sen. Lectr in Community Health, London School of Hygiene and Tropical Medicine, 1974–79. *Publication:* Endemic Cretinism, 1971. *Recreations:* walking, philately. *Address:* 11 Fawley Road, Liverpool L18 9TE. *T:* (0151) 724 4896.

PHELAN, His Honour Andrew James; a Circuit Judge, 1974–95; *b* 25 July 1923; *e s* of Cornelius Phelan, Kilganey House, Clonmel, Eire; *m* 1950, Joan Robertson McLagan; one *s* two *d*. *Educ:* Clongoweswood, Co. Kildare; National Univ. of Ireland (MA); Trinity Coll., Cambridge. Called to: Irish Bar, King's Inn, 1945; English Bar, Gray's Inn, 1949. Jun. Fellow, Univ. of Bristol, 1948–50; in practice at English Bar, 1950–74. *Publications:* The Law for Small Boats, 2nd edn, 1970; Ireland from the Sea, 1998. *Recreations:* sailing, mountain walking. *Address:* 17 Hartington Road, Chiswick, W4 3TL. *T:* (020) 8994 6109. *Clubs:* Royal Cruising, Bar Yacht.

PHELPS, Anthony John, CB 1976; Deputy Chairman, Board of Customs and Excise, 1973–82; *b* 14 Oct. 1922; *s* of John Francis and Dorothy Phelps, Oxford; *m* 1st, 1949, Sheila Nan Rait (*d* 1967), *d* of late Colin Benton Rait, Edinburgh; one *s* two *d*; 2nd, 1971, Janet M. T., *d* of late Charles R. Dawson, Edinburgh. *Educ:* City of Oxford High Sch.; University Coll., Oxford. HM Treasury, 1946; Jun. Private Sec. to Chancellor of the Exchequer, 1949–50; Principal, 1950; Treasury Rep. in Far East, 1953–55; Private Sec. to the Prime Minister, 1958–61; Asst Sec., 1961; Under-Sec., 1968. Freeman, City of Oxford, 1971. *Publication:* (with Sir Richard Hayward) A History of Civil Service Cricket, 1993. *Recreations:* music, watching sport. *Address:* 1 Woodsyre, Sydenham Hill, SE26 6SS. *T:* (020) 8670 0735. *Clubs:* City Livery, MCC.

PHELPS, Howard Thomas Henry Middleton; Chairman, Brewery Court Ltd, 1990–94; *b* 20 Oct. 1926; *s* of Ernest Henry Phelps, Gloucester, and Harriet (*née* Middleton); *m* 1st, 1949, Audrey (*née* Ellis); one *d*; 2nd, 2000, Sybil Anne, *widow* of Lt-Col G. L. Ritchie, RAMC. *Educ:* Crypt Grammar Sch., Gloucester; Hatfield Coll.; Durham Univ. (BA Hons Politics and Econs 1951). National Coal Board, Lancs, Durham and London, 1951–72, finally Dep. Dir-Gen. of Industrial Relations; Personnel Dir, BOAC, 1972; British Airways: Gp Personnel Dir, 1972; Bd Mem., 1973–83; Dir of Operations, 1979–86. Chairman: Sutcliffe Catering Gp, 1986–88; Sterling Guards Ltd, 1986–89; Earls Court and Olympia Ltd, 1986–89; Niccol Centre Ltd, 1989–90. Non-exec. Chm., QA Training Ltd, Cirencester, 1989–94; Dir, P&OSN Co., 1986–89; Non-exec. Dir, Alden Press Ltd, Oxford, 1990–97. FRAeS; FCIT; FILT. Chm., Alice Ruston Housing Assoc., 1973–84; President: Durham Univ. Soc., 1988–99 (Chm., 1975–88); Hatfield Assoc., 1983–90. Chm. Council, Durham Univ., 1992–97 (Mem., 1985–88); Dep. Chm., Governing Body, Middlesex Polytechnic, 1987–89 (Vis. Prof., 1987–); Chairman: Cirencester Tertiary Coll., 1990–99; Rendcomb Coll., Cirencester, 1986–; Assoc. of Colleges, 1996–98. Hon. DCL Durham, 1995. *Recreations:* gardening, musical appreciation. *Address:* Tall Trees, Chedworth, near Cheltenham, Glos GL54 4AB. *T:* (01285) 720324. *Club:* Royal Over-Seas League.

PHELPS, Maj.-Gen. Leonard Thomas Herbert, CB 1973; OBE 1963; *b* 9 Sept. 1917; *s* of Abijah and Jane Phelps; *m* 1st, 1945, Jean Irene Dixon (*d* 1996); one *s* one *d*; 2nd, 2000, Sybil Anne, *widow* of Lt-Col G. L. Ritchie, RAMC. CIMgt (CBIM 1980; FBIM 1973). Served War, Hong Kong, 1940–41; India/Burma, 1941–47. Student, Staff Coll., Quetta, 1946; SO2, WO, 1948–51; DAQMG, HQ Land Forces Hong Kong, 1951–53; Second in Command, 4th Trng Bn, RAOC, 1955–57; War Office: DAAG, 1957–59; ADOS, 1961–63; AA & QMG Singapore Mil. Forces, 1963; Chief of Staff and Dep Comdr, 4th Malaysian Inf. Bde, 1964; ADOS, WO, 1965–67; Chief Inspector, Land Service Ammunition, 1967–70; Comdr, Base Organisation, RAOC, 1970; Dir, Ordnance Services, MoD (Army), 1971–73; retired 1973; Col Comdt, RAOC, 1976–78. Man. Dir, The Warrior Gp, 1975–78; Director: Leon Davis & Co., 1975–82; Debenhams Business Systems Ltd, 1982–84. Parchment Award for life saving, Royal Humane Soc., 1936. *Publication:* A History of the Royal Army Ordnance Corps 1945–1982, 1991.

PHELPS, Maurice Arthur; human resource consultant, since 1989; Managing Partner, Emslie Phelps Consultancy Group, since 1990; *b* 17 May 1935; *s* of H. T. Phelps; *m* 1960, Elizabeth Anne Hurley; two *s* one *d*. *Educ:* Wandsworth School; Corpus Christi College, Oxford Univ. BA Hons Modern History. Shell Chemical Co. Ltd, 1959–68; Group Personnel Planning Adviser, Pilkington Bros Ltd, 1968–70; Group Personnel Dir, Unicorn Industries Ltd, 1970–72; Dir of Labour and Staff Relations, W Midland Passenger Transport Exec., 1973–77; Dir of Personnel, Heavy Vehicle Div., Leyland Vehicles Ltd, 1977–80; Bd Mem. for Personnel and Industrial Relations, 1980–87, non-exec. Bd Mem., 1987–, British Shipbuilders; Dir of Personnel and Employee Relations, Sealink UK Ltd, 1987–89. Human Resource Consultant: Maurice Phelps Associates, 1989–; Emslie Phelps Associates, 1989–; Value Through People Ltd, 1991–; Saratoga (Europe), 1993–. Freeman: City of London, 1995; Co. of Watermen and Lightermen, 1995. *Publications:* The People Policies Audit, 1999; People Benchmarking, 2000. *Address:* Abbotsfield, Goring Heath, S Oxon RG8 7SA.

PHELPS, Richard Wintour, CBE 1986; General Manager, Central Lancashire New Town Development Corporation, 1971–86; *b* 26 July 1925; *s* of Rev. H. Phelps; *m* 1955, Pamela Marie Lawson; two *d*. *Educ:* Kingswood Sch.; Merton Coll., Oxford (MA). 14th Punjab Regt, IA, 1944–46. Colonial Admin. Service, Northern Region and Fed. Govt. of Nigeria, 1948–57 and 1959–61; Prin., HM Treasury, 1957–59 and 1961–65; Sen. Administrator, Hants CC, 1965–67; Gen. Manager, Skelmersdale New Town Develt Corp., 1967–71. Advr (part-time) on housing to Govt of Vanuatu, 1986–89; Consultant: in mgt of urban develt and housing, 1986–98; on housing policy to Falkland Is Govt, 1988–89; Chm., Examn in Public Replacement Structure Plan, Derbys CC, 1989, Notts CC and Northants CC, 1990, West Sussex CC, 1991, Leics CC, 1992, Cambs CC, 1994, Hants CC, 1996. Conducted indep. inquiry into possible abuses of planning system, Bassetlaw DC, 1996; Chm., Countryside movement inquiry into hunting with hounds, 1996–97. Contested (SDP) Barrow and Furness, 1987. Winston Churchill Trust Travelling Fellowship, 1971. *Recreations:* reading, living in Spain. *Address:* 38 Wharncliffe Road, Christchurch, Dorset BH23 5DE. *T:* (01425) 272242. *Club:* Royal Commonwealth Society.

PHILIP, Hon. Lord; Alexander Morrison Philip; a Senator of the College of Justice in Scotland, since 1996; *b* 3 Aug. 1942; *s* of late Alexander Philip, OBE and of Isobel Thomson Morrison; *m* 1971, Shona Mary Macrae; three *s*. *Educ:* High School of Glasgow; St Andrews University (MA 1963); Glasgow University (LLB 1965). Solicitor, 1967–72; Advocate 1973; Advocate-Depute, 1982–85; QC (Scotland), 1984; Chm., Scottish Land Court, 1993–96; Pres., Lands Tribunal for Scotland, 1993–96. Chm., Medical Appeal Tribunals, 1988–92. *Recreations:* golf, piping. *Address:* Parliament House, Parliament Square, Edinburgh EH1 1RQ. *Club:* Royal Scottish Pipers' Society (Edinburgh).

PHILIP, Alexander Morrison; *see* Philip, Hon. Lord.

PHILIPPE, André J., Hon. GCVO 1972; Luxembourg Ambassador to the United States of America, 1987–91; *b* Luxembourg City, 28 June 1926. Dr-en-Droit. Barrister-at-Law, Luxembourg, 1951–52. Joined Luxembourg Diplomatic Service, 1952; Dep. to Dir of Polit. Affairs, Min. of Foreign Affairs, 1952–54; Dep. Perm. Rep. to NATO, 1954–61 and to OECD, 1959–61; Dir of Protocol and Legal Adviser, Min. of For. Affairs, 1961–68; Ambassador and Perm. Rep. to UN and Consul-Gen., New York, 1968–72 (Vice-Pres., 24th Session of Gen. Assembly of UN, 1969); Ambassador to UK, Perm. Rep. to Council of WEU, and concurrently Ambassador to Ireland and Iceland, 1972–78; Ambassador to France, 1978–84; Ambassador to UN, NY, 1984–87. Commander: Order of Adolphe Nassau (Luxembourg); Légion d'Honneur (France); Grand Officer: Order of Merit (Luxembourg), 1983; Order of Oaken Crown (Luxembourg), 1988. *Address:* 25 rue Adolphe, 1116 Luxembourg.

PHILIPPS, family name of **Viscount St Davids** and **Baron Milford**.

PHILIPS, Prof. Sir Cyril (Henry), Kt 1974; Professor of Oriental History, University of London, 1946–80; Director, School of Oriental and African Studies, London, 1957–76; Vice-Chancellor, University of London, 1972–76 (Deputy Vice-Chancellor, 1969–70); *b* Worcester, 27 Dec. 1912; *s* of William Henry Philips; *m* 1st, 1939, Dorcas (*d* 1974), *d* of John Rose, Wallasey; one *d* (one *s* decd); 2nd, 1975, Joan Rosemary, *d* of William George Marshall. *Educ:* Rock Ferry High School; Univs of Liverpool (MA) and London (PhD). Bishop Chavasse Prizeman; Gladstone Memorial Fellow. Frewen Lord Prizeman (Royal Empire Soc.), 1935; Alexander Prizeman (Royal Hist. Soc.), 1938; Sir Percy Sykes Meml Medal (RSAA), 1976; Asst Lectr, Sch. of Oriental Studies, 1936. Served in Suffolk Infantry, Army Education Corps, 1940–43; Col Commandant, Army School of Education, 1945. Chief Instructor, Dept of Training, HM Treasury, 1945–46. Colonial Office Mission on Community Development, Africa, 1947. Lectures: Montague Burton, Univ. of Leeds, 1966; Creighton, Univ. of London, 1972; James Smart, on Police, 1979; Home Office Bicentenary, 1982; Police, Univ. of Bristol, 1982; Dawtry Meml, Univ. of Leeds, 1983. Chairman: UGC Cttee on Oriental, African and Slavonic Studies, 1965–70; UGC Cttee on Latin American Studies, 1966–70; India Cttee of Inter-University Council and British Council, 1972–; Royal Commn on Criminal Procedure, 1978–80; Police Complaints Bd, 1980–85; Council on Tribunals, 1986–89; Inst. of Archaeology, 1979–85, Inst. of Latin American Studies, 1978–87 (Univ. of London); Member: Social Development Cttee, Colonial Office, 1947–55; Colonial Office Research Council, 1955–57; University Grants Cttee, 1960–69; Commonwealth Education Commn, 1961–70; Postgraduate Awards Cttee (Min. of Education), 1962–64; Modern Languages Cttee (Min. of Education), 1964–67; Inter-Univ. Council, 1967–77; Court, London Univ., 1970–76; Governor: Chinese Univ. of Hong Kong, 1965–75; Mill Hill Sch., 1980–91 (Chm., 1982); Governor and Trustee, Richmond Coll., 1979–84. Pres., Royal Asiatic Soc., 1979–82, 1985–88. Hon. Fellow, Asiatic Soc., Bengal, 1995. Hon. DLitt: Warwick, 1967; Bristol, 1983; Sri Lanka, 1986; Hon. LLD Hong Kong, 1971. India Tagore Medal, 1968; Bombay Freedom Medal, 1977. *Publications:* The East India Company, 1940 (2nd edn 1961); India, 1949; Handbook of Oriental History, 1951 (2nd edn 1962); Correspondence of David Scott, 1951; Historians of India, Pakistan and Ceylon, 1961; The Evolution of India and Pakistan, 1962; Politics and Society in India, 1963; Fort William-India House Correspondence, 1964; History of the School of Oriental and African Studies, 1917–67, 1967; The Partition of India, 1970; The Correspondence of Lord William Bentinck, Governor General of India 1828–35, 1977; Beyond the Ivory Tower, 1995. *Address:* School of Oriental and African Studies, Malet Street, WC1E 7HP. *T:* (020) 7637 2388. *Club:* Athenæum.

PHILIPS, Justin Robin Drew; District Judge (Magistrates' Courts) (formerly Metropolitan Stipendiary Magistrate), since 1989; a Recorder, since 1999; *b* 18 July 1948; *s* of late Albert Lewis Philips, Solicitor and of Henrietta Philips (*née* Woolfson). *Educ:* John Lyon School, Harrow; College of Law, London. Called to the Bar, Gray's Inn, 1969; practised criminal bar, 1970–89; Chm., Youth Court, 1993–; an Asst Recorder, 1994–99. Hon. Sec., Hendon Reform Synagogue, 1990–94 (Mem. Council, 1979–90). Trustee, Tzedek Charity, 1993–. *Recreations:* music, reading, attempting to keep fit. *Address:* c/o West London Magistrates' Court, 181 Talgarth Road, W6 8DN. *T:* (0845) 600 8889.

PHILIPSON, Garry, DFC 1944; Managing Director, Aycliffe and Peterlee Development Corporation, 1974–85; *b* 27 Nov. 1921; *s* of George and Marian Philipson; *m* 1949, June Mary Miller Somerville (*d* 1997), one *d*. *Educ:* Stockton Grammar Sch.; Durham Univ. (BA(Hons)). Jubilee Prize, 1947. Served War, RAFVR (2 Gp Bomber Comd), 1940–46. Colonial Service and Overseas Civil Service, 1949–60. Various Dist and Secretariat posts, incl. Clerk, Exec. Council and Cabinet Sec., Sierra Leone; Principal, Scottish Develt Dept, 1961–66; Under Sec., RICS, 1966–67; Dir, Smith and Ritchie Ltd, 1967–70; Sec., New Towns Assoc., 1970–74; Vice-Chm. (NE), North Housing Assoc., 1985–92. Trustee, Dales-Care, 1988–91. *Publications:* Aycliffe and Peterlee New Towns 1946–88, 1988; Press articles and contribs to various jls. *Recreations:* country pursuits, history. *Address:* Little Lodge Farm, Lane End Common, North Chailey, East Sussex BN8 4JH. *T:* (01825) 723027. *Club:* Royal Air Force.

PHILIPSON-STOW, Sir Christopher, 5th Bt *cr* 1907; DFC 1944; retired; *b* 13 Sept. 1920; *s* of Henry Matthew Philipson-Stow (*d* 1953) (3rd *s* of 1st Bt) and Elizabeth Willes (*d* 1979), *d* of Sir Thomas Willes Chitty, 1st Bt; *S* cousin, 1982; *m* 1952, Elizabeth Nairn (*d* 1999), *d* of late James Dixon Trees and *widow* of Major F. G. McLaren, 48th Highlanders of Canada; two *s*. *Educ:* Winchester. *Heir: er s* Robert Matthew Philipson-Stow, *b* 29 Aug. 1953. *Address:* 26 Cambridge Street, Penetanguishene, ON L9M 1E6, Canada.

PHILLIMORE, family name of **Baron Phillimore**.

PHILLIMORE, 5th Baron *cr* 1918, of Shiplake, Oxfordshire; **Francis Stephen Phillimore;** Bt 1881; barrister; *b* 25 Nov. 1944; *o s* of 4th Baron Phillimore and Anne Elizabeth Phillimore (*d* 1995), *e d* of Major Arthur Algernon Dorrien-Smith, DSO; *S* father, 1994; *m* 1971, Nathalie Berthe Louisa Pequin; two *s* one *d*. *Educ:* Eton Coll.; Trinity Coll., Cambridge (BA). Called to the Bar, Middle Temple, 1972. Mem., Shiplake Parish Council. Mem., Ct of Assistants, Fishmongers' Co. Trustee, Venice in Peril Fund. Steward, Hurlingham Polo Assoc. *Recreations:* polo, sailing, the arts, shooting, Venetian rowing. *Heir: er s* Tristan Anthony Stephen Phillimore, *b* 18 Aug. 1977. *Address:* Coppid Hall, Binfield Heath, Henley-on-Thames, Oxon RG9 4JR. *T:* (01491) 573174. *Clubs:* Brooks's, Pratt's, City Barge; Royal Yacht Squadron.

PHILLIPS, family name of **Barons Phillips of Sudbury** and **Phillips of Worth Matravers**.

PHILLIPS OF SUDBURY, Baron *cr* 1998 (Life Peer), of Sudbury in the co. of Suffolk; **Andrew Wyndham Phillips,** OBE 1996; founding Partner, Bates, Wells & Braithwaite, solicitors, London, 1970; *b* 15 March 1939; *s* of Alan Clifford Phillips and late Dorothy Alice Phillips (*née* Wyndham); *m* 1968, Penelope Ann Bennett; one *s* two *d*. *Educ:* Uppingham; Trinity Hall, Cambridge (BA 1962). Qualified solicitor, 1964. Co-founder, 1971 and first Chm., Legal Action Gp; founder and first Chm., 1989–2000, first Pres., 2000–, Citizenship Foundn; Initiator and First Pres., Solicitors' Pro Bono Gp, 1997–; Mem., Nat. Lottery Charities Bd, 1994–96. Trustee, Scott Trust (Guardian/Observer), 1992–. Chm., Gough Hotels, 1975–; Dir, Dalehead Food Hldgs, 1975–. Regular broadcaster, as Legal Eagle, Jimmy Young Show, BBC Radio Two, 1966–. Contested: (Lab) Harwich, 1970; (L) Saffron Walden, July 1977 and 1979; (L/Alliance) Gainsborough and Horncastle, 1983; (L) NE Essex, European Parlt, 1979. *Publications:* The Living Law; Charitable Status: a practical handbook, 1980, 4th edn 1994; (jtly) Charity Investment: law and practice. *Recreations:* the arts, local history, architecture, golf, cricket, walking. *Address:* River House, The Croft, Sudbury, Suffolk CO10 1HW. *T:* (01787) 882151.

PHILLIPS OF WORTH MATRAVERS, Baron *cr* 1999 (Life Peer), of Belsize Park in the London Borough of Camden; **Nicholas Addison Phillips,** Kt 1987; PC 1995; Master of the Rolls, since 2000; Head of Civil Justice, since 2000; *b* 21 Jan. 1938; *m* 1972, Christylle Marie-Thérèse Rouffiac (*née* Doreau); two *d*, and one step *s* one step *d*. *Educ:* Bryanston Sch.; King's Coll., Cambridge (MA). Nat. Service with RN; commnd RNVR, 1956–58. Called to Bar, Middle Temple (Harmsworth Schol.), 1962, Bencher, 1984. In practice at Bar, 1962–87; Jun. Counsel to Minister of Defence and to Treasury in Admiralty matters, 1973–78; QC 1978; a Recorder, 1982–87; a Judge of High Court of Justice, QBD, 1987–95; a Lord Justice of Appeal, 1995–98; a Lord of Appeal in Ordinary, 1999–2000. Mem., Panel of Wreck Comrs, 1979. Chm., Law Adv. Cttee, British Council, 1991–97; Chm., Council of Legal Educn, 1992–97; Vice Pres., British Maritime Law Assoc., 1993–. Governor, Bryanston Sch., 1975– (Chm. of Governors, 1981–). Hon. LLD Exeter, 1998. *Recreations:* sea, mountains, Mauzac. *Address:* Royal Courts of Justice, Strand, WC2A 2LL. *Club:* Brooks's.

PHILLIPS, Adrian Alexander Christian, CBE 1998; freelance environmental consultant; Professor of Countryside and Environmental Planning, City and Regional Planning Department, University of Wales College of Cardiff, since 1992; *b* 11 Jan. 1940; *s* of Eric Lawrance Phillips, *qv*; *m* 1963, Cassandra Frances Elaïs Hubback, MA Oxon, *d* of D. F. Hubback, CB; two *s*. *Educ:* The Hall, Hampstead; Westminster Sch.; Christ Church, Oxford (1st Cl. Hons MA Geography). MRTPI 1966; FRGS 1984. Planning Services, Min. of Housing and Local Govt, 1962–68; Sen. Research Officer and Asst Director, Countryside Commission, 1968–74; Special Asst, Executive Director, United Nations Environment Programme (UNEP), Nairobi, Kenya, 1974–75; Head, Programme Coordination Unit, UNEP, Nairobi, 1975–78; Director of Programmes, IUCN, Switzerland, 1978–81; Dir, then Dir Gen., Countryside Commn, 1981–92. Chairman: Commn on Nat. Parks and Protected Areas, IUCN, 1994–96 (Dep. Chm., 1988–94); World Commn on Protected Areas, IUCN, 1996–2000; Sen. Advr on World Heritage, IUCN, 2000–; Chm., Policy Cttee, CPRE, 2001–. Chm., Cttee for Wales, RSPB, 1992–98. Trustee, WWF UK, 1997–. FRSA 1983. Hon. FLI. *Publications:* articles and chapters on envmtl and conservation topics. *Recreations:* walking, stroking the cat. *Address:* 2 The Old Rectory, Dumbleton, near Evesham, Worcs WR11 6TG. *T:* (01386) 882094; *e-mail:* adrianp@wcpa.demon.co.uk. *Club:* Royal Over-Seas League.

PHILLIPS, Alan; *see* Phillips, D. A.

PHILLIPS, Alan David John, CMG 1999; adviser on human and minority rights; Executive Director, Minority Rights Group, 1989–2000; *b* 4 April 1947; *s* of Reginald and Irene Phillips; *m* 1970, Hilary Siddell; one *s* two *d*. *Educ:* Brighton Coll.; Warwick Univ. (BSc Hons 1st class Physics; Pres., Students' Union, 1968–69). Systems Auditor, Rank Xerox, 1970–73; Gen. Sec., World Univ. Service (UK), 1973–81; Dep. Dir, British Refugee Council, 1982–89. NGO Expert to UK and EC delegns at intergovtl Human Rights fora, 1991–; UK nominated indep. expert, 1998–, Vice Pres., 1999–, Council of Europe Adv. Cttee, Framework Convention on Nat. Minorities. Member: Cttee, Council for Assisting Refugee Academics, 1998–; Bd, Greek Helsinki Monitor, 2001. Gov., Blatchington Mill Sch., 1997–. Chm., Brighton and Hove Organic Gardening, 2001–. *Publications:* British Aid for Overseas Students, 1980; UN Minority Rights Declaration, 1993; Universal Minority Rights, 1995; (contrib.) World Directory of Minorities, 1997. *Recreations:* family, organic gardening, swimming, education. *Address:* 67 Carlisle Road, Hove, Sussex BN3 4FQ; *e-mail:* alan@adjphillips.freeserve.co.uk. *Club:* Brighton and Hove Allotment Soc.

PHILLIPS, Andrew Bassett; Head, Legal Deposit Review, British Library, 1996–99; *b* 26 Sept. 1945; *s* of William Phillips and Doreen (*née* Harris); *m* 1976, Valerie Cuthbert; two *s* one *d*. *Educ:* Newport High Sch.; Reading Univ. (BA). ALA. British Nat. Bibliography Ltd, 1969–70; Research Officer, Nat. Libraries ADP Study, 1970–71; Admin. Officer, Nat. Council for Educnl Technol., 1971–73; British Library: various posts in Bibliographic Servs and Ref. (subseq. Humanities and Social Scis) Divs, 1973–86; Dir, Public Services and Planning and Admin, 1987–90; Dir, Humanities and Social Scis, 1990–96. Part-time Lectr, West London Coll, 1972–75. Director: Cedar Audio Ltd, 1992–94; Saga Continuation Ltd, 1993–99. Advr, British Univs Film and Video Council, 2000–. Mem. Governing Body, City Lit. Inst., 1982–87. Trustee, Shakespeare's Birthplace, 1991–. *Publications:* (ed) The People's Heritage, 2000; (contrib.) Inventing the

20th Century, 2000; various reviews, articles. *Address:* 23 Meynell Road, E9 7AP. *T:* (020) 8985 7413.

PHILLIPS, Anne, (Mrs Basil Phillips); *see* Dickinson, V. A.

PHILLIPS, Anne Fyfe; *see* Pringle, A. F.

PHILLIPS, Rev. Canon Anthony Charles Julian; Canon Theologian, Diocese of Truro, since 1986; Chapter Canon, Truro Cathedral, since 2001; *b* 2 June 1936; *s* of Arthur Reginald Phillips and Esmée Mary Phillips; *m* 1970, Victoria Ann Stainton; two *s* one *d.* *Educ:* Kelly Coll., Tavistock (schol.); King's Coll., London (BD, 1st cl.; AKC, 1st cl.; Archibald Robertson Prize, 1962; Jun. McCaul Hebrew Prize, 1963); Gonville and Caius Coll., Cambridge (PhD 1967); College of the Resurrection, Mirfield. Solicitor, 1958; ordained priest, 1967; Curate, Good Shepherd, Cambridge, 1966–69; Dean, Chaplain and Fellow, Trinity Hall, Cambridge, 1969–74; Chaplain and Fellow, 1975–86, Domestic Bursar, 1982–84, St John's Coll., Oxford; Lecturer in Theology: Jesus Coll., Oxford, 1975–86; Hertford Coll., Oxford, 1984–86; S. A. Cook Bye Fellow, Gonville and Caius Coll., 1984; Headmaster, King's Sch., Canterbury, 1986–96. Hon. Chaplain to Bishop of Norwich, 1970–71; Examining Chaplain to: Bp of Oxford, 1979–86; Bp of Manchester, 1980–86; Bp of Wakefield, 1984–86; Hon. Canon, Canterbury Cathedral, 1987–96. Archbps of Canterbury and York Interfaith Cons. for Judaism, 1984–86. Governor: Sherborne Sch., 1997–2001; Sherborne Sch. for Girls, 1997–; Cornwall Coll., 1997–2001; SPCK, 1998–2001 (Chair of Publishing, 2000–). *Publications:* Ancient Israel's Criminal Law, 1970; Deuteronomy (Cambridge Bible Commentary), 1973; God BC, 1977; (ed) Israel's Prophetic Tradition, 1982; Lower Than the Angels, 1983; Preaching from the Psalter, 1987; The Passion of God, 1995; contrib. to: Words and Meanings (ed P. R. Ackroyd and B. Lindars), 1968; Witness to the Spirit (ed W. Harrington), 1979; The Ministry of the Word (ed G. Cuming), 1979; Heaven and Earth (ed A. Linzey and P. Wexler), 1986; Tradition and Unity (ed Dan Cohn-Sherbok), 1991; Glimpses of God (ed Dan Cohn-Sherbok), 1993; Splashes of God Light (ed T. Copley and others), 1997; articles in theol jls, The Times, Expository Times, etc. *Recreations:* gardening, beachcombing. *Address:* The Old Vicarage, 10 St Peter's Road, Flushing, Falmouth, Cornwall TR11 5TP.

PHILLIPS, Prof. Calbert Inglis, FRCS, FRCSE; Professor of Ophthalmology, University of Edinburgh and Ophthalmic Surgeon, Royal Infirmary, Edinburgh, 1972–90, now Professor Emeritus; *b* 20 March 1925; *o s* of Rev. David Horner Phillips and Margaret Calbert Phillips; *m* 1962, Christina Anne Fulton, MB, FRCSE; one *s.* *Educ:* Glasgow High Sch.; Robert Gordon's Coll., Aberdeen; Aberdeen Univ. MB, ChB Aberdeen 1946; DPH Edinburgh 1950; FRCS 1955; MD Aberdeen 1957; PhD Bristol 1961; MSc Manchester 1969; FRCSE 1973. Lieut and Captain, RAMC, 1947–49. House Surgeon: Aberdeen Royal Infirmary, 1946–47 (House Phys., 1951); Aberdeen Maternity Hosp., 1949; Glasgow Eye Infirmary, 1950–51; Asst, Anatomy Dept, Glasgow Univ., 1951–52; Resident Registrar, Moorfields Eye Hosp., 1953–54; Sen. Registrar, St Thomas' Hosp. and Moorfields Eye Hosp., and Res. Asst, Inst. of Ophthalmology, 1954–58; Consultant Surg., Bristol Eye Hosp., 1958–63; Alexander Piggott Wernher Trav. Fellow, Dept of Ophthal., Harvard Univ., 1960–61; Consultant Ophthalmic Surg., St George's Hosp., 1963–65; Prof. of Ophthal., Manchester Univ., and Hon. Consultant Ophthalmic Surg. to United Manchester Hosps, 1965–72. Hon. FBOA 1975. *Publications:* (ed jtly) Clinical Practice and Economics, 1977; Basic Clinical Ophthalmology, 1984; Logic in Medicine, 1988, 2nd edn 1995; (jtly) Ophthalmology: a Primer for medical students and practitioners, 1994; papers in Eur., Amer., and Japanese Jls of Ophthal., Nature, Brain, BMJ, etc, mainly on intra-ocular pressure and glaucoma, retinal detachments, ocular surgery and hereditary diseases. *Address:* 5 Braid Mount Crest, Edinburgh EH10 6JN.

PHILLIPS, Caryl, FRSL; writer; Professor of English and Henry R. Luce Professor of Migration and Social Order, Barnard College, Columbia University, since 1998; *b* 13 March 1958. *Educ:* Queen's Coll., Oxford (BA English 1979). Writer in Residence: Literary Criterion Centre, Mysore, India, 1987; Univ. of Stockholm, Sweden, 1989; Nat. Inst. of Educn, Singapore, 1994; Amherst College, Massachusetts: Vis. Writer, 1990–92; Writer in Residence, 1992–94; Prof. of English and Writer in Residence, 1994–98; Visiting Professor: NY Univ., 1993; Univ. of WI, Barbados, 1999–2000. British Council Fiftieth Anniversary Fellow, 1984; Guggenheim Fellow, 1992; Rockefeller Foundn (Bellagio) Residency, 1993. Ed., Faber Caribbean series, 1998–2001. FRSL 2000. Hon. AM Amherst, 1995; DUniv Leeds Metropolitan, 1997. Giles Cooper Award, BBC, 1984; Bursary in Drama, Arts Council of GB, 1984; Martin Luther King Meml Prize, 1987; James Tait Black Meml Prize, 1994; Lannan Foundn Literary Award, 1994. *Publications: plays:* Strange Fruit, 1981; Where There is Darkness, 1982; The Shelter, 1984; *novels:* The Final Passage, 1985; A State of Independence, 1986; Higher Ground, 1989; Cambridge, 1991; Crossing the River, 1993; The Nature of Blood, 1997; *screenplay:* Playing Away, 1987; *non-fiction:* The European Tribe, 1987; The Atlantic Sound, 2000; A New World Order, 2001; *anthology:* (ed) Extravagant Strangers, 1997; (ed) The Right Set: the Faber Book of Tennis, 1999. *Recreations:* running, golf. *Address:* c/o Georgia Garrett, A. P. Watt Ltd, 20 John Street, WC1N 2DR.

PHILLIPS, Sir David; *see* Phillips, Sir J. D.

PHILLIPS, Prof. David, OBE 1999; Professor of Physical Chemistry, since 1989, Hofmann Professor of Chemistry, since 1999, and Head of Department of Chemistry, since 1992, Imperial College of Science, Technology and Medicine; *b* 3 Dec. 1939; *s* of Stanley and Daphne Ivy Phillips; *m* 1970, Caroline Lucy Scoble; one *d.* *Educ:* South Shields Grammar-Technical Sch.; Univ. of Birmingham (BSc, PhD). Post doctoral Fellow, Univ. of Texas, 1964–66; Vis. Scientist, Inst. of Chemical Physics, Acad. of Scis of USSR, Moscow, 1966–67; Lectr 1967–73, Sen. Lectr 1973–76, Reader 1976–80, in Phys. Chem., Univ. of Southampton; Royal Institution of Great Britain: Wolfson Prof. of Natural Philosophy, 1980–89; Actg Dir, Jan.–Oct. 1986; Dep. Dir, 1986–89. Vice-Pres. and Gen. Officer, BAAS, 1988–89. Mem., Faraday Council, RSC, 1990–93. Nyholm Lectr, RSC, 1994. Michael Faraday Award, Royal Soc., 1997. *Publications:* (jtly) Time-Correlated Single-Photon Counting, 1984; Polymer Photophysics, 1985; (jtly) Jet Spectroscopy and Dynamics, 1995; over 485 res. papers and revs in sci. lit. on photochem., photophys. and lasers. *Recreations:* music, travel. *Address:* 195 Barnett Wood Lane, Ashtead, Surrey KT21 2LP. *T:* (01372) 274385. *Club:* Athenæum.

PHILLIPS, His Honour (David) Alan; a Circuit Judge, 1983–95; Chancellor, diocese of Bangor, 1988–95; *b* 21 July 1926; *s* of Stephen Thomas Phillips, MC and Elizabeth Mary Phillips; *m* 1960, Jean Louise (*née* Godsell); two *s.* *Educ:* Llanelli Grammar Sch.; University Coll., Oxford (MA). Left school, 1944. Served War, Army, 1944; commnd, 1946, RWF; Captain (GS), 1947; demobilised, 1948. Oxford, 1948–51. Lectr, 1952–59. Called to Bar, Gray's Inn, 1960. Stipendiary Magistrate for Mid-Glamorgan, 1975–83; a Recorder of the Crown Court, 1974–83. *Recreations:* music, chess, swimming.

PHILLIPS, Prof. David George, DPhil; Professor of Comparative Education, University of Oxford, since 2000; Fellow of St Edmund Hall, Oxford, since 1984; *b* 15 Dec. 1944; *s* of George Phillips and Doris Anne Phillips (*née* Hales); *m* 1968, Valerie Mary Bache; two *d.* *Educ:* Sir Walter St John's Sch., Battersea; BA (ext.) London 1966; St Edmund Hall, Oxford (DipEd 1967; MA; DPhil 1984). Assistant teacher: Huntingdon Grammar Sch., 1967–69; Chipping Norton Sch., 1969–75; University of Oxford: Tutor, then Univ. Lectr, Dept of Educnl Studies, 1975–96; Reader in Comparative Educn, 1996–2000. Member: Teacher Educn Commn of Wissenschaftsrat, 1990–91; Council, 1992–98, Scientific Cttee, 1992–98, German Inst. for Internat. Educnl Res., Frankfurt-am-Main; Chm., British Assoc. for Internat. and Comparative Educn, 1998–2000. Editor, Oxford Review of Education, 1984–; Series Editor, Oxford Studies in Comparative Educn, 1991–. *Publications include:* Zur Universitätsreform in der Britischen Besatzungszone 1945–48, 1983; (ed) German Universities After the Surrender, 1983; (with Veronica Stencel) The Second Foreign Language, 1983; (ed) Which Language?, 1989; (with Caroline Filmer-Sankey) Diversification in Modern Language Teaching, 1993; Pragmatismus und Idealismus: das Blaue Gutachten und die Britische Hochschulpolitik in Deutschland 1948, 1995; (ed) Education in Germany: tradition and reform in historical context, 1995; (ed jtly) Learning from Comparing, vol. 1, 1999, vol. 2, 2000; (ed) Education in Eastern Germany since Unification, 2000; numerous articles in jls. *Recreations:* art history, antiquarian books. *Address:* Department of Educational Studies, 15 Norham Gardens, Oxford OX2 6PY; St Edmund Hall, Oxford OX1 4AR.

PHILLIPS, David John; QC 1997; a Recorder, since 1998; *b* 4 May 1953; *s* of Hon. Sir (John) Raymond Phillips MC, and of Hazel Bradbury Phillips; *m* 1981, Ann Nicola Beckett, *d* of late Ronald Beckett; one *s* one *d.* *Educ:* Rugby Sch.; Balliol Coll., Oxford (BA (Jurisprudence) 1977; MA 1996). Called to the Bar, Gray's Inn, 1976 (Arden, Atkin, Mould & Reid Prize, 1977); Mem., Wales and Chester Circuit; Asst Recorder, 1994–98. Mem. Cttee, Barristers' Benevolent Assoc., 1993– (Jt Hon. Treas., 1999–). *Recreations:* hill walking, cinema. *Address:* 199 Strand, WC2R 1DR. *T:* (020) 7379 9779, *Fax:* (020) 7379 9481; *e-mail:* davidphillips@199strand.co.uk.

PHILLIPS, Prof. Dewi Zephaniah; Rush Rhees Research Professor, University of Wales, Swansea, since 1996; Danforth Professor of the Philosophy of Religion, Claremont Graduate School, California, since 1992; *b* 24 Nov. 1934; *s* of David Oakley Phillips and Alice Frances Phillips; *m* 1959, Margaret Monica Hanford; three *s.* *Educ:* Swansea Grammar Sch.; UC Swansea (MA); St Catherine's Society, Oxford (BLitt). Asst Lectr, Queen's Coll., Dundee, Univ. of St Andrews, 1961–62; Lectr: at Queen's Coll., Dundee, 1962–63; UC Bangor, 1963–65; University College, Swansea, later University of Wales, Swansea: Lectr, 1965–67; Sen. Lectr, 1967–71; Prof. of Philosophy, 1971–96; Dean of the Faculty of Arts, 1982–85; Vice-Principal, 1989–92. Visiting Professor: Yale Univ., 1985; Claremont Graduate Sch., 1986. Hintz Meml Lectr, Univ. of Arizona, Tucson, 1975; Vis. Prof. and McMartin Lectr, Univ. of Carleton, 1976; Agnes Cuming Visitor, Univ. Coll. Dublin, 1982; Lectures: William James, Lousiana State Univ., 1982; Marett, Oxford, 1983; Riddell Meml, Newcastle, 1986; Aquinas, Oxford, 1987; Cardinal Mercier, Leuven, 1988; R. I. Aaron, Aberystwyth, 1993; Leibniz, Calif State Univ., 1995; McManis, Wheaton Coll., 1996. Pres., British Soc. for the Philosophy of Religion, 2001–. Editor, Philosophical Investigations, 1982–. Hon. PhD Åbo Akademi, Finland, 1998. *Publications:* The Concept of Prayer, 1965; (ed) Religion and Understanding, 1967; (ed) Saith Ysgrif Ar Grefydd, 1967; (with H. O. Mounce) Moral Practices, 1970; Death and Immortality, 1970; Faith and Philosophical Enquiry, 1970; (with Ilham Dilman) Sense and Delusion, 1971; Athronyddu Am Grefydd, 1974; Religion Without Explanation, 1976; Through A Darkening Glass: Philosophy, Literature and Cultural Change, 1981; Dramau Gwenlyn Parry, 1981; Belief, Change and Forms of Life, 1986; R. S. Thomas: poet of the hidden God, 1986; Faith after Foundationalism, 1988; (ed jtly) Wittgenstein: attention to particulars, 1989; From Fantasy to Faith, 1991; Interventions in Ethics, 1992; Wittgenstein and Religion, 1993; Writers of Wales: J. R. Jones, 1995; Introducing Philosophy, 1996; (ed) Religion and Morality, 1996; (ed) Can Religion Be Explained Away?, 1996; (ed jtly) Religion Without Transcendence, 1997; (ed) On Religion and Philosophy, by Rush Rhees, 1997; (ed) Wittgenstein and the Possibility of Discourse, by Rush Rhees, 1998; Religion and Hume's Legacy, 1999; Philosophy's Cool Place, 1999; (ed) Moral Questions, by Rush Rhees, 1999; (ed) Discussions of Simone Weil, by Rush Rhees, 1999; Recovering Religious Concepts, 2000; (ed jtly) Kant and Kierkegaard on Religion, 2000; (ed jtly) Philosophy of Religion and the 21st Century, 2001; (ed jtly) Religion and Wittgenstein's Legacy, 2001; Religion and the Hermeneutics of Contemplation, 2001; General Editor: Studies in Ethics and the Philosophy of Religion, 1968–74; Values and Philosophical Enquiry, 1976–86; Swansea Studies in Philosophy, 1989–; Claremont Studies in the Philosophy of Religion, 1993–; papers in philosophical jls. *Recreations:* lawn tennis and supporting Swansea City AFC. *Address:* Department of Philosophy, University of Wales Swansea, Singleton Park, Swansea SA2 8PP. *T:* (01792) 295189.

PHILLIPS, Diane Susan, CB 2000; Director, Transport Strategy, Department for Transport, Local Government and the Regions (formerly of the Environment, Transport and the Regions), since 2000; *b* 29 Aug. 1942; *d* of Michael Keogh and Jessie (*née* Tite); *m* 1967, John Phillips; two *d.* *Educ:* Univ. of Wales. NEDO, 1967–72; Civil Service, 1972–: Principal, DoE, 1972–77, Cabinet Office, 1977–78; Asst Sec., Dept of Transport, 1978–80; Department of the Environment, then Department of the Environment, Transport and the Regions, now Department for Transport, Local Government and the Regions, 1981–: Grade 4, Local Govt Finance, 1988–90; Under Sec. (Grade 3) and Principal Finance Officer, Property Hldgs, 1990–94; Dir, Social Housing Policy and Resources, 1994–98; Dir, Roads and Traffic, 1998–2000; Dep. Hd, Integrated Transport Taskforce, 2000. Mem. Bd, London & Quadrant Housing Trust, 1998–. Gov., St George's Coll., Weybridge, 1995–. *Address:* Department for Transport, Local Government and the Regions, 76 Marsham Street, SW1P 4DR.

PHILLIPS, Rt Rev. Donald David; *see* Rupert's Land, Bishop of.

PHILLIPS, Edward Thomas John, (Jack), CBE 1985; Controller, English Language and Literature Division, British Council, 1985–89; Consultant, British Executive Service Overseas, 1990–2000; *b* 5 Feb. 1930; *s* of late Edward Emery Kent Phillips and of Margaret Elsie Phillips; *m* 1952, Sheila May (*née* Abbott); two *s* two *d.* *Educ:* Exmouth Grammar Sch., University Coll. London; Inst. of Education, London; School of Oriental and African Studies London (BA Hons; postgraduate Cert. of Educn; Dip. in linguistics). RAF, 1948–49. HMOCS, Educn Officer, Nigeria, 1953–62; British Council: Head, Cultural and Educn Unit, Overseas Students' Dept, 1962–65; English Lang. Officer, Enugu, Nigeria, 1966–67; Sen. Lectr, Coll. of Educn, Lagos Univ., Nigeria, 1967–70; English Lang. Teaching Advr, Min. of Educn, Cyprus, 1970–72; Chief Inspector, English Teaching Div., London, 1972–75; Rep., Bangladesh, Dacca, 1975–77; Dir, Personnel Dept and Dep. Controller Personnel Staff Recruitment Div., 1977–80; Rep, Malaysia, 1980–85. Dir, Project Mala (India), 1992–. Member: British-Malaysia Soc.; Britain-Nigeria Assoc. *Publications:* (ed jtly) Organised English, Books I and II, 1973; contribs to English Language Teaching Jl. *Recreations:* music, theatre, tennis, golf, swimming. *Address:* 1 Bredune, off Church Road, Kenley, Surrey CR8 5DU. *T:* (020) 8660 1929.

PHILLIPS, Eric Lawrance, CMG 1963; retired; *b* 23 July 1909; *s* of L. Stanley Phillips and Maudie Phillips (*née* Elkan), London, NW1; *m* 1938, Phyllis Bray (*d* 1991), artist; two *s* one step *d. Educ:* Haileybury Coll.; Balliol Coll., Oxford (Scholar, BA). With Erlangers Ltd, 1932–39. Served War of 1939–45, Captain, RA. Principal, Bd of Trade, 1945, Monopolies Commn, 1949; Asst Secretary, Monopolies Commn, 1951, Bd of Trade, 1952; Under-Sec., Bd of Trade, 1964–69; Sec., Monopolies Commn, 1969–74; consultant to Monopolies and Mergers Commn, 1974–75. Hon. Chm., Abbeyfield West London Soc., 1980–86. *Recreations:* looking at pictures, places and buildings. *Address:* 46 Platts Lane, NW3 7NT. *T:* (020) 7435 7873. *Club:* Royal Automobile.
See also A. A. C. Phillips.

PHILLIPS, Sir Fred (Albert), Kt 1967; CVO 1966; QC (Barbados) 1991; *b* 14 May 1918; *s* of Wilbert A. Phillips, Brighton, St Vincent. *Educ:* London Univ. (LLB); Toronto Univ.; McGill Univ. (MCL); Hague Acad. of International Law. Called to the Bar, Middle Temple. Legal Clerk to Attorney-General of St Vincent, 1942–45; Sen. Officer, Secretariat, 1945–47; Windward Island: Chief Clerk, Governor's Office, 1948–49; District Officer/Magistrate of District III, 1949–53; Magistrate, Grenada, and Comr of Carriacou, 1953–56; Asst Administrator and MEC, Grenada, 1957–58 (Officer Administrating the Govt, April 1958); Senior Asst Sec., Secretariat, Fedn of W Indies (dealing with constitutional development), 1958–60; Permanent Sec. (Sec. to Cabinet), 1960–62 (when Fedn dissolved); actg Administrator of Montserrat, 1961–62; Sen. Lectr, Univ. of W Indies and Sen. Resident Tutor, Dept of Extra-mural Studies, Barbados, 1962–63; Registrar, Coll. of Arts and Science, Univ. of W Indies, 1963–64; Sen. Res. Fellow, Faculty of Law and Centre for Developing Area Studies, McGill Univ., 1964–65; Guggenheim Fellow, 1965; Administrator of St Kitts, 1966–67; Governor, St Kitts/Nevis/Anguilla, 1967–69. Chairman, Constitutional Review Commission: Grenada, 1984; St Kitts and Nevis, 1998; Antigua and Barbuda, 1999, 2000 and 2001. Has attended numerous conferences as a Legal or Constitutional Adviser. KStJ 1968. Hon. LLD West Indies, 1989. *Publications:* Freedom in the Caribbean: a study in constitutional change, 1977; The Evolving Legal Profession in the Commonwealth, 1978; West Indian Constitutions: post-Independence reforms, 1985; Caribbean Life and Culture: a citizen reflects, 1991; papers in various jls. *Recreations:* reading, bridge. *Address:* PO Box 206, Bridgetown, Barbados; PO Box 3298, St John's, Antigua.

PHILLIPS, Sir (Gerald) Hayden, KCB 1998 (CB 1989); Permanent Secretary, Lord Chancellor's Department, and Clerk of the Crown in Chancery, since 1998; *b* 9 Feb. 1943; *s* of Gerald Phillips and Dorothy Phillips; *m* 1st, 1967, Dr Ann Watkins (marr. diss.); one *s* one *d*; 2nd, 1980, Hon. Laura Grenfell; one *s* two *d. Educ:* Cambridgeshire High Sch.; Clare Coll., Cambridge (MA); Yale Univ., USA (MA). Home Office: Asst Principal, 1967; Economic Adviser, 1970–72; Principal, 1972–74; Asst Sec., and Principal Private Sec. to Sec. of State for Home Dept, 1974–76; Dep. Chef de Cabinet to Pres., Commn of European Communities, 1977–79; Asst Sec., Home Office, 1979–81, Asst Under-Sec. of State, 1981–86; Dep. Sec., Cabinet Office (MPO, subseq. Office of the Minister for the Civil Service), 1986–88; Dep. Sec., HM Treasury, 1988–92; Perm. Sec., DNH, later Dept for Culture, Media and Sport, 1992–98. Dir, St Just Farms Ltd, 1997–. Member: Council, KCL, 1993–99; Ct of Govs, Henley Mgt Coll., 1993–; Council, Marlborough Coll., 1997–; Bd, Inst. of Advanced Legal Studies, 1998–; Fitzwilliam Mus. Trust, 1999–. Hon. Bencher, Inner Temple, 1998. *Recreations:* fishing, other arts and sports, India. *Address:* Lord Chancellor's Department, House of Lords, SW1A 0PW. *Clubs:* Brooks's, Pratt's.

PHILLIPS, Sir Hayden; *see* Phillips, Sir G. H.

PHILLIPS, Sir Henry (Ellis Isidore), Kt 1964; CMG 1960; MBE 1946; Founder Member, 1970, and Hon. Vice-Chairman, SIFIDA Investment Co. (SA); director of other companies; *b* 30 Aug. 1914; *s* of late Harry J. Phillips, MBE; *m* 1st, 1941, Vivien Hyamson (marr. diss., 1965); two *s* one *d*; 2nd, 1966, Philippa Cohen. *Educ:* Haberdashers' Sch., Hampstead; University College London (BA 1936; MA 1939; Fellow 1991). FRHistS 1965. Inst. of Historical Research, 1936–39. Commissioned in Beds and Herts Regt, 1939; served War of 1939–45, with 5th Bn, becoming Adjutant; POW, Singapore, 1942. Joined Colonial Administrative Service and appointed to Nyasaland, 1946 (until retirement in 1965); Development Secretary, 1952; seconded to Federal Treasury of Rhodesia and Nyasaland, 1953–57, Dep. Sec., 1956; Financial Sec., Nyasaland Govt, 1957–64, and Minister of Finance, 1961–64. Man. Dir, Standard Bank Finance and Development Corp., 1966–72. Dir, Nat. Bank of Malawi, 1983–88; Chm., Ashley Industrial Trust plc, 1986–88. Mem., Civil Aviation Authority, 1975–80; Hon. Consultant, Air Transport Users Council, 1980–. Hon. Pres., Stonham Housing Assoc., 1995– (Founder Mem.; Hon. Treas., 1984; Vice Chm., 1984–92); Hon. Treasurer: Stonham Meml Trust, 1977– (Vice-Chm., then Chm., 1995–99); SOS Sahel Internat. (UK), 1987–. Mem. Finance Cttee, UCL, 1985–98; Hon. Vice-Pres., Friends of University Coll., 1992–. *Publication:* From Obscurity to Bright Dawn: how Nyasaland became Malawi—an insider's account, 1998. *Address:* 34 Ross Court, Putney Hill, SW15 3NZ. *T:* (020) 8789 1404. *Club:* MCC.

PHILLIPS, Sir Horace (Hyman), KCMG 1973 (CMG 1963); HM Diplomatic Service, retired; *b* 31 May 1917; *s* of Samuel Phillips and Polly Yaffie; *m* 1944, Idina Doreen Morgan; one *s* one *d. Educ:* Hillhead High Sch., Glasgow. Joined Board of Inland Revenue, 1935. Served War of 1939–45, Dorsetshire and 1st Punjab Regts, 1940–47. Transf. to FO, Oct. 1947; Acting Vice-Consul, Shiraz, Nov. 1947; Vice-Consul, Bushire, 1948; Consul, Shiraz, 1949; 1st Secretary, Kabul, Oct. 1949; Foreign Office, 1951; 1st Secretary, and Consul, Jedda, 1953; Counsellor, 1956; seconded to Colonial Office, Dec. 1956, as Protectorate Secretary, Aden, until Aug. 1960; Counsellor, British Embassy, Tehran, Oct. 1960; Deputy Political Resident in the Persian Gulf, at Bahrain, 1964–66; Ambassador to Indonesia, 1966–68; High Comr in Tanzania, 1968–72; Ambassador to Turkey, 1973–77. Resident Rep., Taylor Woodrow Internat. Ltd: Iran, 1978–79, Hong Kong, 1979–84, Bahrain, 1984–85, China (at Peking), 1985–87. Lecturer in International Relations: Bilkent Univ., Ankara, 1988–92, 1996–97; Erciyes Univ., Kayseri, Turkey, 1993–94. Vice-Pres., Anglo-Turkish Soc., London, 1985–. Hon. LLD Glasgow, 1977. Order of the Taj (Iran), 1961. *Publications:* Envoy Extraordinary, 1995; Ihsan Doğramacı, a remarkable Turk, 1997; articles of topical political and diplomatic interest in Asian Wall Street Jl, 1980–86. *Recreations:* languages, long-distance car driving. *Address:* 34a Sheridan Road, Merton Park, SW19 3HP. *T:* (020) 8542 3836. *Club:* Travellers.

PHILLIPS, Ian, FCA; Director: Schroder UK Growth Fund, since 1994; M&G Equity Investment Trust, since 2000; Chairman: Severn Trent Pension Fund, since 1998; Oxford University Press Pension Fund, since 1995; *b* 16 July 1938; *s* of Wilfrid and Dorothy Phillips; *m* 1961, Fay Rosemary Stoner; two *s. Educ:* Whitgift Sch., South Croydon. Articled clerk, Hatfield Dixon Roberts Wright & Co., Accountants, 1955–61; Robert J. Ward & Co., Accountants, 1961–65; John Lewis' Partnership, 1965–69; London Transport Executive: Director of Corporate Planning, 1969–75; Chief Business Planning Officer, 1975–78; Group Planning Director, 1978–80; Mem. Board, LTE, later LRT, 1980–84; Dir, Finance and Planning, BRB, 1985–88; Finance Dir, BBC, 1988–93; Chief Exec., BBC Pension Services Ltd, 1990–96; Chm., BBC Enterprises Ltd, 1991–93. Bd Mem., PanEuropean Property Unit Trust, 1996–. *Recreations:* playing golf, watching sport, the country, family. *Address:* Glebe Cottage, Duntisbourne Abbots, Cirencester, Glos GL7 7JN.

PHILLIPS, Prof. Ian, MD; FRCP, FRCPath, FFPHM; Professor of Medical Microbiology, 1974–96 (at St Thomas' Hospital, 1974–82), and Clinical Dean, 1992–96, United Medical and Dental Schools of Guy's and St Thomas's Hospitals, now Emeritus Professor; *b* 10 April 1936; *s* of late Stanley Phillips and Emma (*née* Price). *Educ:* St John's Coll., Cambridge (MA, MD); St Thomas's Hosp. Med. Sch. (MB BCh). FRCPath 1981; FRCP 1983; FFPHM 1996. House Officer, St Thomas' Hosp., 1961–62; Lecturer in Microbiology: St Thomas's Hosp. Med. Sch., 1962–66; Makere UC, 1966–69; Sen. Lectr, 1969–72, Reader, 1972–74, St Thomas's Hosp. Med. Sch.; Chm., Dist Mgt Team, St Thomas' Hosp., 1978–79; Hon. Cons. Microbiologist, St Thomas' Hosp., subseq. Guy's and St Thomas's Hosp. NHS Trust, 1969–96, now Emeritus Consultant; Chm., Pathology, Guy's and St Thomas's Hosp. NHS Trust, 1990–96. Civilian Consultant, RAF, 1979–2000. Mem., Veterinary Products Cttee, 1981–85. Editor, Clinical Microbiology and Infection, 1997–2000. Mem. Council, RCPath, 1974–76 and 1987–90; Chairman: Brit. Soc. for Antimicrobial Chemotherapy, 1979–82; Assoc. of Med. Microbiologists, 1989–93; Pres., European Soc. for Clinical Microbiol. and Infectious Diseases, 1995–96. Member: S London Botanical Inst.; BSBI. Mem., Victorian Soc. Hon. Mem., Croatian Acad. of Med. Sci., 1997. Freeman, City of London, 1975; Liveryman, Soc. of Apothecaries, 1975. *Publications:* (ed jtly) Laboratory Methods in Antimicrobial Chemotherapy, 1978; (jtly) Microbial Disease, 1979; contrib. chapters and papers. *Recreations:* botany, music. *Clubs:* Athenæum, Royal Society of Medicine.

PHILLIPS, Ian Peter; JP; Director, Kroll Buchler Phillips Ltd, since 1999; Chairman, Kroll (formerly Buchler Phillips) Lindquist Avey, since 1997; *b* 13 Oct. 1944; *s* of Bernard Phillips and Constance Mary Clayton; *m* 1970, Wendy Berne; one *s* one *d. Educ:* Highgate Sch.; Sorbonne, Paris. FCA, FCCA, FIPA, MICM. Partner, Bernard Phillips & Co., 1968; UK Head of Corporate Recovery Services, Arthur Andersen & Co., 1982; Chm., Buchler Phillips Gp, 1988–99. Jt Administrator, British and Commonwealth Holdings, 1990; Court Receiver, Estate of Robert Maxwell, 1991. Dir, Jt Insolvency Monitoring Unit, 1997–98. Pres., Insolvency Practitioners Assoc., 1988–89. Mem., Lord Chancellor's Adv. Cttee on JPs for Inner London. Chm., Hampstead Theatre, 1997– (Dir, 1991–). Mem., British Acad. of Experts. JP Inner London, 1979. *Recreations:* theatre, baroque and modern jazz music, horse riding, coastal path walking, close-up magic. *Address:* The Fourth House, 5 Turner Drive, NW11 6TX. *T:* (020) 8458 0758.

PHILLIPS, Jack; *see* Phillips, E. T. J.

PHILLIPS, Jeremy Patrick Manfred; QC 1980; *b* 27 Feb. 1941; *s* of late Manfred Henry Phillips, CA, and late Irene Margaret (*née* Symondson); *m* 1968, Virginia Gwendoline (*née* Dwyer) (marr. diss. 1974); one *s* (and one *s* decd); *m* 1976, Judith Gaskell (*née* Hetherington); two *s* two *d. Educ:* St Edmund's Sch., Hindhead, Surrey; Charterhouse. Apprentice Accountant, Thomson McLintock & Co., 1957–61. Called to Bar, Gray's Inn, 1964; in practice, 1964–; Hd of Chambers, 2 Temple Gdns, 1990–98; DTI Inspector, affairs of Queens Moat Houses plc, 1993–. Owner of Kentwell Hall, Long Melford, Suffolk, 1971–; organizer of Kentwell's Annual Historical Re-Creations of Tudor Domestic Life. Dir, CARE Britain. *Publications:* contrib. early edns of Cooper's Students' Manual of Auditing, Cooper's Manual of Auditing and various pamphlets, papers, guides, etc, on Kentwell Hall and Tudor period. *Recreations:* Kentwell Hall, historic buildings, Tudor history and Tudor domestic life. *Address:* Kentwell Hall, Long Melford, Suffolk CO10 9BA.

PHILLIPS, John, RIBA; architect in private practice, since 1955; *b* 25 Nov. 1926; *s* of John Tudor Phillips and Bessie Maud Phillips; *m* 1955, Eileen Margaret Fryer. *Educ:* Christ's Coll., Finchley; Northern Polytechnic, Holloway. ARIBA 1954. Studied under Romilly B. Craze, Architect, 1948–52. Surveyor to the Fabric: Truro Cathedral, 1961 (Consultant Architect, 1979–); Westminster Cathedral, 1976–97; RIBA 1979–96; Consultant Architect to Brisbane Cathedral, 1988–. Pres., Ecclesiastical Architects' and Surveyors' Assoc., 1982. KSS 1997. *Recreations:* looking at churches, choral singing. *Address:* 8 Friary Way, North Finchley, N12 9PH. *T:* (020) 8445 3414.

PHILLIPS, John Andrew; His Honour Judge Phillips; a Circuit Judge, since 1998; *b* 26 May 1950; *s* of Jack and Mary Nolan Phillips; *m* 1993, Moira Margaret Kynnersley; two *d. Educ:* Fitzwilliam Coll., Cambridge (MA). Mem., Fitzwilliam String Quartet, Quartet in Residence, York Univ., 1971–74; called to the Bar, Gray's Inn, 1976; in practice at the Bar, 1977–98. *Recreation:* playing the violin. *Address:* Courts of Justice, Earl Street, Carlisle, Cumbria CA1 1DJ. *T:* (01228) 520619.

PHILLIPS, Sir (John) David, Kt 2000; QPM 1994; Chief Constable of Kent, since 1993; *b* 22 April 1944; *s* of late Percy Phillips and of Alfreda Phillips; *m* 1970, Nancy Wynn Rothwell; one *s. Educ:* Leigh Grammar Sch.; Manchester Univ. (BA 1st Cl. Hons Econs). Served: Lancs Constabulary, 1963–84; Gtr Manchester Constabulary, 1984–89; Dep. Chief Constable, Devon and Cornwall, 1989–93. Chm., Nat. Crime Faculty; Pres., ACPO, 2001–. *Recreations:* history, golf. *Address:* Police Headquarters, Sutton Road, Maidstone, Kent ME15 9BZ.

PHILLIPS, Hon. John Harber, AC 1998; **Hon. Mr Justice Phillips;** Chief Justice of Victoria, since 1991; *b* 18 Oct. 1933; *s* of Anthony and I. Muriel Phillips; *m* 1962, Helen Isobel Rogers; two *s* one *d. Educ:* De La Salle Coll., Malvern; Univ. of Melbourne (LLB). Called to the Bar: Victoria, 1959; Middle Temple, 1979; practised at Victorian Bar, 1959–84; Justice: Supreme Court of Victoria, 1984–90; Federal Court of Australia, 1990–91. Mem., Victorian Bar Council, 1974–84; Chairman: Criminal Bar Assoc., 1982, 1983; Nat. Crime Authy, 1990–91; Attorney-Gen.'s Law Reform Council, 1994–; Victorian Council of Legal Educn, 1991–; Victoria Law Foundn, 1991–; Law Reform Council of Australia and NZ, 1997–. Chairman: Victorian Inst. of Forensic Medicine (formerly of Forensic Pathol.), 1985–; Nat. Inst. of Forensic Sci., 1991; Co-Convenor, Commonwealth Assoc. of Law Reform Agencies, 2000–. President: Lanchid Soc., 1990–; French Australian Lawyers Soc., 2000–. Vis. Prof. of Advocacy, Monash Univ., 1988–89. Hellenic Dist. for Service to Greek community of Victoria, 1992, 2000. *Publications:* (jtly) Forensic Science and the Expert Witness, 1985; Advocacy with Honour, 1986; The Trial of Ned Kelly, 1987; Poet of the Colours: the life of John Shaw Neilson, 1988; *plays:* By a Simple Majority: the trial of Socrates, 1990; Conference with Counsel, 1991; The Cab Rank Rule, 1995. *Address:* Chief Justice's Chambers, Supreme Court of Victoria, 210 William Street, Melbourne, Vic 3000, Australia. *T:* (3) 96036139, *Fax:* (3) 96036200.

PHILLIPS, John Randall; Member, 1995–99, Chairman, 1995–96, then Lord Mayor, 1996–97, Cardiff City and County Council; *b* 22 April 1940; *s* of James Phillips and Charlotte Phillips (*née* Phelps); *m* 1967, Margaret Ray Davies; one *s* one *d. Educ:* Cardiff High Sch.; University Coll., Cardiff (BA Econ. 1961). Dip. Soc. Studies 1967. Cardiff City Council, 1963–66; Glam CC, 1967–74; Mid Glam CC, 1974–96: Principal Trng Officer, 1974–82; Principal Asst (Child Abuse), 1982–89; Dist Social Services Officer,

Cynon Valley, 1989–94; Principal Officer, 1994–96. Cardiff City Council: Member, 1972–96; Chm. of Personnel, 1974–76 and 1979–83; Dep. Leader, Labour Gp, 1986, Ldr, 1990–94; Vice Chm., 1987, Chm., 1990, Policy; Leader, 1990–94; Dep. Lord Mayor, 1994–95. Mem., Cardiff Bay Develt Corp., 1990–99. First Pres., UWIC, 1996–97. *Recreations:* politics, listening to music. *Address:* 15 Kyle Crescent, Whitchurch, Cardiff CF14 1ST. *T:* (029) 2062 4878.

PHILLIPS, Jonathan, PhD; Director General, Resources and Services, Department of Trade and Industry, since 2000; *b* 21 May 1952; *s* of Gilbert Reginald Phillips and Ruby May Phillips (*née* Hughes); *m* 1974, Amanda Rosemary Broomhead; two *s*. *Educ:* Queen Mary's Grammar Sch., Walsall; St John's Coll., Cambridge (BA 1973; PhD 1978); London Univ. Inst. of Educn (PGCE 1974). Department of Trade, later Department of Trade and Industry, 1977–93: seconded: to CBI econs directorate, 1982–83; as Sec., Cttee of Inquiry into regulatory arrangements at Lloyd's, 1986–87; Asst Sec., 1987–93; Under-Sec., 1993; Dir, Exec. Agencies, Dept of Transport, 1993–96; Dir, Investigations and Enforcement, 1996–98, Finance and Resource Mgt, 1998–2000, DTI. *Recreations:* music, walking. *Address:* Department of Trade and Industry, 1 Victoria Street, SW1H 0ET. *T:* (020) 7215 6911; *e-mail:* jonathan.phillips@dti.gsi.gov.uk.

PHILLIPS, Leslie Samuel, OBE 1998; actor, director, producer; *b* 20 April 1924; *s* of late Frederick and Cecelia Phillips; *m* 1st, 1948, Penelope Bartley (marr. diss. 1965; she *d* 1981); two *s* two *d*; 2nd, 1982, Angela Scoular; one step *s*. *Educ:* Chingford Sch.; Italia Conti Stage Sch. Army, 1942–45 (Lieut, DLI; invalided out). *Theatre* includes: début, Peter Pan, London Palladium, 1937; Zeal of Thy House, Garrick, 1938; Otello, and Turandot, Covent Garden, 1939; Dear Octopus, Queen's, 1939–40; Nutmeg Tree, Lyric, 1941–42; The Doctor's Dilemma, Haymarket, 1942; Daddy Long-Legs, Comedy, 1947–48; Charley's Aunt, Saville, 1948; On Monday Next, Comedy, 1949; For Better, For Worse, Comedy, 1952–54; Diary of a Nobody, Arts, 1954; Lost Generation, Garrick, 1955; The Whole Truth, Aldwych, 1955–56; The Big Killing, Shaftesbury, 1961–62; Boeing-Boeing, Apollo, 1963–65; The Deadly Game (also dir), Savoy, 1967; The Man Most Likely To … (also dir), Vaudeville, 1968–69, tour, S Africa, 1970–71, Duke of York's, 1972, tour of Australia, 1974; Sextet, Criterion, 1977–78; Canaries Sometimes Sing, tour, 1978; Not Now Darling, Savoy, 1979, world tour, 1980; Pygmalion, tour, 1980; The Cherry Orchard, Haymarket, 1983; Chapter 17, tour, 1983; Passion Play, Wyndham's, 1984–85; Pride and Prejudice, tour, 1988; Taking Steps, world tour, 1989; Painting Churches, Playhouse, 1992; August, tour of Wales, 1994; Love for Love, Chichester, 1996; Merry Wives of Windsor, RSC, 1997; Camino Real, 1998; On The Whole It's Been Jolly Good, Edin. Fest., 1999, Hampstead, 2000; Naked Justice, W Yorks Playhouse, 2001; more than 100 *films*, including: A Lassie from Lancashire, 1938; The Citadel, 1938; Four Feathers, 1938; Mikado, 1938; Climbing High, 1939; Proud Valley, 1939; Thief of Baghdad, 1939; Train of Events, 1949; Sound Barrier, 1949; Pool of London, 1950; Gamma People, 1955; The Smallest Show on Earth, 1956; Brothers in Law, 1956; High Flight, 1957; Les Girls, 1957; Carry on Nurse, 1958; I Was Monty's Double, 1958; Carry on Constable, 1959; This Other Eden, 1959; Ferdinando, 1959; Doctor in Love, 1960; Very Important Person, 1961; In the Doghouse, 1961; Raising the Wind, 1961; Crooks Anonymous, 1962; Fast Lady, 1962; The Longest Day, 1963; Doctor in Clover, 1965; You Must Be Joking, 1965; Maroc 7 (also prod.), 1966; Some Will Some Won't, 1969; Doctor in Trouble, 1970; Magnificent Seven Deadly Sins, 1971; Don't Just Lie There, 1973; Spanish Fly, 1975; Out of Africa, 1986; Empire of the Sun, 1987; Scandal, 1988; Mountains of the Moon, 1989; King Ralph, 1990; August, 1995; Day of the Jackal, 1997; Cinderella, 1999; Saving Grace, 2000; Lara Croft: Tomb Raider, 2001; Thunderpants, 2001; Harry Potter and the Philosopher's Stone, 2001; *television* includes: Morning Departure (first TV from Alexandra Palace), 1948; My Wife Jacqueline, 1952; Our Man at St Mark's, 1963; Impasse, 1963; The Reluctant Debutante, 1965; The Gong Game, 1965; Foreign Affairs, 1966; Blandings Castle, 1967; Very Fine Line, 1968; The Suit, 1969; Casanova, 1973; Redundant and the Wife's Revenge, 1983; You'll Never See Me Again, 1983; Mr Palfrey of Westminster, 1985; Monte Carlo, 1986; Rumpole, 1988; Summer's Lease, 1989; Comic Strip, 1989, 1990, 1991; Chancer, 1989–90; Who Bombed Birmingham, 1990; Life After Life, 1990; Thacker, 1991; The Trials of Oz, 1991; Boon, 1992; Lovejoy, 1992; Bermuda Grace, 1993; The Changeling, 1993; Vanity Dies Hard, 1993; Love on a Branch Line, 1993; House of Windsor, 1994; Two Golden Balls, 1994; Honey for Tea, 1994; The Canterville Ghost, 1995; L for Liverpool, 1998; Dalziel & Pasco, 1998; The Best of British, 2000; Sword of Honour, 2000; Take a Girl Like You, 2000; Edgar Wallace series: The Pale Horse, 1996; Tales from the Crypt, 1996; *radio* includes: The Navy Lark, 1959–76; Three Men in a Boat, 1962; Vera Lynn Story, 1973; Would the Last Businessman to Leave England Please Turn out the Light, 1977–78; Round the World in 80 Days, 1991–92; Red Riding Hood and the Wolf's Story, 1994; England Their England, 1994; Wind in the Willows, 1994; Tuth in Dark Places, 1994–95; Falling Heads, 1995; Philip and Rowena, 1995; Envious Casca, 1996; Half a Sixpence, 1996; Me and Little Boots, 2000; Maclean the Memorex Years, 2000; Cousin Bette, 2000; Tales from the Backbench, 2001. Vice Pres., Royal Theatrical Fund; Founder Mem., Theatre of Comedy. Award for lifetime achievement in films, Evening Standard, 1997. *Recreations:* cats, restoration, racing, collecting, gardening, classical music, weaving, chess, all sport. *Address:* c/o Storm Artists, 47 Brewer Street, 1st Floor, W1R 3FD. *T:* (020) 7437 4313, *Fax:* (020) 7437 4314.

PHILLIPS, Malcolm Edward, MD; FRCP; Director of Renal Services, Hammersmith Hospitals NHS Trust, since 1994; *b* 24 March 1940; *s* of Albert H. Phillips and Kathleen M. Phillips; *m* 1967, Rona Lendon; one *s* one *d*. *Educ:* Charing Cross Hosp. Med. Sch., London (MB BS 1964; MD 1979). MRCS 1964; FRCP 1986. Jun. hosp. med. posts, Fulham Hosp. and Charing Cross Hosp., 1964–81; Wellcome Trust Fellow, Univ. of Naples, 1970–72; Consultant Physician and Nephrologist, Charing Cross Hosp., now Hammersmith Hosps NHS Trust, 1981–; Gen. Manager, 1989, Med. Dir, 1995–97, Charing Cross Hosp.; Hon. Consultant Nephrologist: West Middlesex Univ. Hosp., 1985–; Chelsea and Westminster Hosp., 1995–. Canterbury Trustbank Vis. Prof., Christchurch, NZ, 1997. *Publications:* articles in jls. *Recreations:* cricket, philately, keyboard. *Address:* The Ridings, 26 Pelhams Walk, Esher, Surrey KT10 8QD. *T:* (01372) 461098.

PHILLIPS, Margaret Corinna, (Mrs D. R. Hunt), FRCO; Professor in Charge of Organ, Royal College of Music, since 1998; Visiting Tutor in Organ Studies, Royal Northern College of Music, Manchester, since 1997; concert organist; *b* 16 Nov. 1950; *d* of John George Phillips and Cora Frances (*née* Hurford); *m* 1983, Dr David Richard Hunt, MA, ARCO. *Educ:* Sittingbourne Grammar Sch. for Girls; Maidstone Grammar Sch. for Girls; Royal Coll. of Music (ARCM). GRSM 1971; FRCO 1971. Director of Music, St Lawrence Jewry next Guildhall, London, 1976–85; Prof. of Organ and Harpsichord, London Coll. of Music, 1985–91; Tutor in Organ Studies, RNCM, 1993–97. Co-founder with Dr D. R. Hunt, and Chm., English Organ Sch. and Museum, Milborne Port, Som, 1996–. Pres., IAO, 1997–99; Mem. Council, RCO, 1982–. Recitals throughout Europe, USA, Mexico and Australia; radio broadcasts, UK, Scandinavia, Netherlands, Australia; numerous recordings of solo organ music and with The Sixteen, BBC Singers, etc. *Publications:* articles on style and performance of organ music. *Recreations:* reading, walking, playing the violin. *Address:* The Manse, Chapel Lane, Milborne Port, Sherborne DT9 5DL. *T:* (01963) 250899.

PHILLIPS, Marisa, DLitt; President, Mental Health Review Tribunal, since 1990; *b* 14 April 1932; *d* of Dr and Mrs J. Fargion; *m* 1956, Philip Harold Phillips; one *s* one *d*. *Educ:* Henrietta Barnet Sch., London; Univ. of Redlands, California (Fulbright Schol.; BA Hons); Rome Univ. (DLitt). Called to Bar, Lincoln's Inn, 1963. On return from Redlands Univ., worked for US Inf. Service, Rome, 1954–56; spent one year in Berlin, as husband then in Army; period of work with Penguin Books; read for the Bar, joining DPP as Legal Asst, 1964; Legal Adviser, Police Complaints Bd, 1977; returned to DPP, 1979; Asst Dir, DPP, 1981; Principal Asst DPP, 1985; Asst Hd of Legal Services, 1986–87, Dir of Legal Casework, 1987–90, Crown Prosecution Service. Sen. Legal Advr, Banking Ombudsman, 1990–. Comr, Mental Health Act Commn, 1991–96; Chm., Rent Assessment Panel, 1992–. *Recreations:* music, theatre, foreign travel.

PHILLIPS, Captain Mark Anthony Peter, CVO 1974; ADC(P); Chef d'Equipe and Coach, US Three Day Event Team, since 1993; Consultant, Gleneagles Mark Phillips Equestrian Centre, 1992–97; *b* 22 Sept. 1948; *s* of late P. W. G. Phillips, MC, and Anne Patricia (*née* Tiarks); *m* 1st, 1973, HRH The Princess Anne (marr. diss. 1992); one *s* one *d*; 2nd, 1997, Sandy Pflueger; one *d*. *Educ:* Marlborough Coll.; RMA Sandhurst. Joined 1st The Queen's Dragoon Guards, July 1969; Regimental duty, 1969–74; Company Instructor, RMA Sandhurst, 1974–77; Army Trng Directorate, MoD, 1977–78, retired. Personal ADC to HM the Queen, 1974–. Student, RAC Cirencester, 1978. Chm., British Olympic Equestrian Fund, subseq. British Equestrian Fedn Fund, 1989–. In Three Day Equestrian Event, GB winning teams: Team Championships: World, 1970; European, 1971; Olympic Gold Medallists (Team), Olympic Games, Munich, 1972; Olympic Silver Medallists (Team), Olympic Games, Seoul, 1988; Mem., Equestrian Team (Reserve), Olympic Games, Mexico, 1968 and Montreal, 1976. Winner, Badminton Three Day Event, 1971, 1972, 1974, 1981. Dir, Glos TEC, 1991–98; Liveryman: Farriers' Co.; Farmers' Co; Carmen's Co.; Loriners' Co.; Freeman: Loriners Co.; City of London; Yeoman, Saddlers' Co. *Recreations:* riding, Rugby football, athletics. *Address:* Aston Farm, Cherington, Tetbury, Glos GL8 8SW. *Club:* (Hon. Mem.) Buck's.

See also under Royal Family.

PHILLIPS, Mark Paul; QC 1999; a Recorder, since 2000; *b* 28 Dec. 1959; *s* of Norman John Phillips and Wendy Sharron Phillips; *m* 1984, Deborah Elizabeth Fisher; one *s* two *d*. *Educ:* John Hampden Sch., High Wycombe; Univ. of Bristol (LLB 1982; LLM 1983). Called to the Bar, Inner Temple, 1984; in practice, 1986–; Asst Recorder, 1998–2000. *Publications:* (ed jtly) Butterworth's Insolvency Law Handbook, 1987, 5th edn 1999; contrib. chapter on Insolvency in: Byles on Bills of Exchange, 26th edn 1983; Paget's Law of Banking, 10th edn 1989, 11th edn 1996; chap. on insolvency procedures in Insolvency of Banks: managing the risks, 1996. *Recreations:* motor sport, ski-ing, theatre. *Address:* 3–4 South Square, Gray's Inn, WC1R 5HP. *T:* (020) 7696 9900, *Fax:* (020) 7696 9911; *e-mail:* markphillips@southsquare.com.

PHILLIPS, (Mark) Trevor, OBE 1999; broadcaster and journalist; Member (Lab), since 2000 and Deputy Chairman, 2001–May 2002, London Assembly, Greater London Authority (Chairman, 2000–01); *b* 31 Dec. 1953; *s* of George Milton Phillips and Marjorie Eileen Phillips (*née* Canzius); *m* 1981, Asha Bhownagary; two *d*. *Educ:* Queen's Coll., Georgetown, Guyana; Imperial Coll., London (BSc; ARCS). Pres., NUS, 1978–80; London Weekend Television: researcher, 1980–81; producer, Black on Black, The Making of Britain, 1981–86; reporter, This Week, Thames TV, 1986–87; London Weekend Television: Editor, London Prog., 1987–92; Hd, Current Affairs, 1992–94; Presenter: London Prog., 1987–2000; Crosstalk, 1994–2000; The Material World, 1998–2000. Man. Dir, Pepper Prodns, 1994–. Chairman: Runnymede Trust, 1993–98; Hampstead Theatre, 1993–97; London Arts Bd, 1997–2000. FRSA 1995. Hon. MA N London, 1995; Hon. DLitt Westminster, 1999. Journalism Award, RTS, 1988 and 1993; Best Documentary Series (for Windrush), RTS, 1998. *Publications:* Windrush: the irresistible rise of multi-racial Britain, 1998; Britain's Slave Trade, 1999. *Recreations:* music, running, crosswords. *Address:* Greater London Authority, Romney House, 43 Marsham Street, SW1P 3PY. *T:* (020) 7983 4384; Pepper Productions, 47–49 Borough High Street, SE1 1NB. *Clubs:* Groucho, Home House.

PHILLIPS, Max; Assistant Under Secretary of State, Ministry of Defence, 1977–84; *b* 31 March 1924; *m* 1953, Patricia Moore; two *s* two *d*. *Educ:* Colston's Sch., Bristol; Christ's Hospital; Magdalene Coll., Cambridge (Schol.; 1st cl. Hist. Tripos, pts I and II; MA). Served War, RA, 1943–46. Appointed to Home Civil Service, 1949; Colonial Office, 1949–59; Sec., Nigeria Fiscal Commn, 1957–58; UKAEA, 1959–73; Procurement Exec., MoD, 1973–74; HM Treasury, 1974–77; retired 1984, re-employed as Asst Sec., MoD, 1984–87. Gov., Christ's Hospital, 1979– (Almoner, 1981–92). *Recreations:* modern myths, exploring the imagination and the countryside. *Address:* 2 Wilderness Farmhouse, Onslow Village, Guildford, Surrey GU2 7QP. *T:* (01483) 561308.

PHILLIPS, Mervyn John, AM 1987; FCPA, FAIB; Chairman, I.B.J. Australia Bank Ltd, since 1992; *b* 1 April 1930; *m* 1956, Moya, *d* of A. C. Bleazard; one *s* one *d*. *Educ:* De La Salle Coll., Ashfield; Univ. of Sydney (BEc). FAIB 1990; FCPA 1996. Commonwealth Bank of Australia, 1946–60; Reserve Bank of Australia, 1960–92: Manager for PNG, 1962–64; Chief Manager, Internat. Dept, 1976–79, Securities Markets Dept, 1980–82, Financial Markets Group, 1983–85; Adviser, 1982; Chief Admin. Officer, 1985–87; Dep. Gov. and Dep. Chm., 1987–92. Dir, CBOA Credit Union, 1964–73 (Chm., 1967–72); Chm., Note Printing Australia, 1990–93; Director: QBE Insurance Gp, 1992–; Alcoa of Australia, 1992–96; Aust. Gas Light Co., 1992– (Chm., 1996–); O'Connell Street Associates Pty, 1992–; Woolworths Ltd, 1993–2001; GRW Property Ltd, 1994–98; WMC Ltd, 1996–. Chm., For. Investment Review Bd, 1997–. Member: PNG Currency Conversion Commn, 1965–66; NSW Credit Union Adv. Cttee, 1968–72; Govt Cttees on PNG Banking, 1971–73; Off-shore Banking in Australia, 1984. Nat. Treas., Australian Catholic Relief, subseq. Caritas Australia, 1993–2001. Chancellor, Univ. of Western Sydney, 2001–; Member: Senate, Australian Catholic Univ., 1991–98; Adv. Council, Australian Grad. Sch. of Management, 1991–2001. Mem., Pontifical Council, Cor Unum, 1994–2000. *Address:* O'Connell Street Associates Pty Ltd, 2 O'Connell Street, Sydney, NSW 2000, Australia. *T:* (2) 92231822.

PHILLIPS, Prof. Owen Martin, FRS 1968; Decker Professor of Science and Engineering, Johns Hopkins University, 1975–98, now Emeritus; *b* 30 Dec. 1930; *s* of Richard Keith Phillips and Madeline Lofts; *m* 1953, Merle Winifred Simons; two *s* two *d*. *Educ:* University of Sydney; Trinity Coll., Cambridge (Hon. Fellow, 1997). ICI Fellow, Cambridge, 1955–57; Fellow, St John's Coll., Cambridge, 1957–60; Asst Prof., 1957–60, Assoc. Prof., 1960–63, Johns Hopkins Univ.; Asst Director of Research, Cambridge, 1961–64; Prof. of Geophysical Mechanics, Johns Hopkins Univ., 1963–68, of Geophysics, 1968–75. Mem. Council, Nat. Center of Atmospheric Research, Boulder, Colorado, 1964–68; Member: US Nat. Cttee Global Atmospheric Research Project, 1968; Res. Co-ord. Panel, Gas Research Inst., 1981–85; Principal Staff, Applied Phys. Lab., 1982–. Associate Ed., Jl of Fluid Mechanics, 1964–95; Regl Ed., Proc. of Royal Soc. series A,

1992–98; Mem. Adv. Cttee, Annual Review of Fluid Dynamics, 1995–98. Mem.-at-large, Amer. Meteorol. Soc. Publications Commn, 1971–75; Pres., Maryland Acad. of Scis, 1979–85. Sec., Bd of Trustees, Chesapeake Res. Consortium, 1973–74 (Trustee, 1972–75); Vis. Cttees, Univ. of Michigan Res. Initiatives, 1990–93, 1994–97. Mem., US NAE, 1996. Adams Prize, Univ. of Cambridge, 1965; Sverdrup Gold Medal, Amer. Metereol. Soc., 1975. *Publications:* The Dynamics of the Upper Ocean, 1966, 3rd edn 1976, Russian edn 1968; The Heart of the Earth, 1968, Italian edns 1970, 1975; The Last Chance Energy Book, 1979; (ed) Wave Dynamics and Radio Probing of the Ocean Surface, 1985; Flow and Reactions in Permeable Rocks, 1990; various scientific papers in Jl Fluid Mechanics, Proc. Cambridge Philos. Soc., Jl Marine Research, Proc. Royal Society, Deep Sea Research, Journal Geophys. Research. *Address:* 23 Merrymount Road, Baltimore, MD 21210, USA. *T:* (410) 4337195. *Clubs:* Johns Hopkins (Baltimore), Hamilton Street (Baltimore); Quissett Yacht (Mass).

PHILLIPS, Prof. Paddy Andrew, FRACP, FACP; Professor of Medicine, Flinders University of South Australia, since 1997; Head of Medicine, Flinders Medical Centre and Repatriation Hospitals, Adelaide, since 1997; *b* 26 Oct. 1956; *s* of Walter Alfred Peter Phillips and Lilian Phillips (*née* Watt); *m* 1995, Lynda Jane Dandie; one *s* one *d*. *Educ:* Univ. of Adelaide (MB, BS); Univ. of Oxford (DPhil; MA 1997). Intern, Royal Adelaide Hosp., 1980; Hon. Sen. House Officer, John Radcliffe Hosp., Oxford, 1981–83; Resident MO and Registrar, Prince Henry's Hosp., Melbourne, 1984–86; Fellow in Clinical Pharmacology, 1987, Res. Fellow, 1988–90, Consultant, 1988–96, Austin Hosp., Melbourne; Sen. Lectr, 1990–94, Associate Prof., 1994–96, Dept of Medicine, Melbourne Univ.; May Reader in Medicine, Nuffield Dept of Clinical Medicine, Univ. of Oxford, and Professorial Fellow, New Coll., Oxford, 1996–97; Consultant, Oxford Radcliffe NHS Trust, 1996–97. *Publications:* scientific papers in physiol., pharmacol., and cardiovascular disease. *Recreations:* fly fishing, ski-ing, collecting, music. *Address:* Department of Medicine, Flinders Medical Centre, Bedford Park, SA 5042, Australia. *T:* (8) 82045137.

PHILLIPS, Sir Peter (John), Kt 1990; OBE 1983; Chairman, Principality Building Society, 1991–2000 (Deputy Chairman, 1988–91); *b* 18 June 1930; *s* of Walter Alfred Phillips and Victoria Mary Phillips; *m* 1956, Jean Gwendoline Williams; one *s* one *d*. *Educ:* Radley College; Pembroke College, Oxford (MA). Joined Aberthaw and Bristol Channel Portland Cement Co., 1956, Jt Man. Dir, 1964–83; Western Area Dir, Blue Circle Industries, 1983–84; Dep. Chm., 1985, Chm., 1987–93, A. B. Electronic Products Gp. Dep. Chm. Bd of Governors, Univ. of Glam., 1996–98; Chm. Council, Univ. of Wales, Cardiff, 1998– (Vice-Chm., 1997–98). *Recreations:* walking, fishing, reading. *Address:* Great House, Llanblethian, near Cowbridge, South Glam CF7 7JG. *T:* (01446) 775163. *Club:* Cardiff and County.

PHILLIPS, Peter Sayer; Founder and Musical Director, The Tallis Scholars, since 1973; Music Critic, The Spectator, since 1983; *b* 15 Oct. 1953; *s* of Nigel Sayer Phillips and Patricia Ann Witchell (*née* Wyatt); *m* 1st, 1987, Clio (marr. diss. 1993), *d* of D. O. Lloyd-Jacob, *qv*; 2nd, 1997, Caroline Trevor; one *s*. *Educ:* Winchester Coll.; St John's Coll., Oxford (Organ Scholar). Teacher: Oxford Univ., 1976–81; Trinity Coll. of Music, 1980–84; RCM, 1981–88. Co-founder and Artistic Dir, Gimell Records, 1981–. Artistic Dir, Stamford Internat. Fest., 1998. Mem., Early Music Cttee, Arts Council 1987–90; Ed., Early Music Gazette, 1980–82; cricket correspondent, Spectator, 1989; Prop. and Adv. Ed., Musical Times, 1995–. Many awards for recordings made by Tallis Scholars, incl. Gramophone Record of the Year, 1987, and Early Music Record of the Year, 1987, 1991 and 1994, Gramophone magazine. *Publications:* English Sacred Music 1549–1649, 1991; (contrib.) Companion to Medieval and Renaissance Music, 1992; contrib. Spectator, Guardian, Musical Times, New Republic, Listener, Early Music, Music and Letters, Music and Musicians, 24 Hours, Royal Acad. magazine, Evening Standard. *Recreations:* black and white photography, cricket, cooking, Arabia. *Address:* 22 Gibson Square, N1 0RD. *T:* (020) 7354 0627, (020) 7226 8047, *Fax:* (020) 7704 1007; 48 rue des Francs Bourgeois, 75003 Paris, France. *T:* 42724461. *Clubs:* Chelsea Arts, MCC.

PHILLIPS, (Rachel) Sarah; Chairman, Multiple Sclerosis Society of Great Britain and Northern Ireland, since 1998; *b* 8 Feb. 1943; *d* of late Air Cdre John Kirby and Rachel Kirby; *m* 1966, Peter, *s* of Maj.-Gen. Sir Farndale Phillips, KBE, CB, DSO, and Lady (Lovering Catherine) Phillips; one *s* one *d*. *Educ:* Benenden Sch.; Heidelberg. Qualified as: LTA coach, 1978; remedial tutor, Kingsbury Centre, Washington, 1983; diagnosed with MS, 1981. Multiple Sclerosis Society of GB and NI: Chm., Colchester Br., 1989–98; Trustee, 1992–; Chm., Homes Cttee, 1993–98; Mem. Bd, Internat. Fedn of MS Socs, now MS Internat. Fedn, 1997–. Non-executive Director: Mid Essex Community and Mental Health Trust, 2000–01; N Essex Mental Health Partnership NHS Trust, 2001–. Trustee, Leonard Cheshire, 1999–. *Recreations:* bridge, choral singing, gardening. *Address:* Wistaria House, Coggeshall, Essex CO6 1UF. *Club:* Royal Commonwealth Society.

PHILLIPS, Raymond Mark; Adviser to Central and East European Governments, since 1998; Director of Policy and Process Design, Employment Service, Department for Education and Employment, 1995–97; *b* 15 April 1944; *s* of Vernon Phillips and Claudia Phillips; *m* 1968, Janet Harris; four *s*. *Educ:* Cowbridge Grammar Sch.; UC Cardiff. Department of Employment: Operational Planning and Res., 1976–78; Pay Policy Advr, 1978–79; Asst Sec., Standing Commn on Pay Comparability, 1979–80; Regl Gen. Manager, Trng Services Agency, 1980–82; Exec. Dir, Employment Service, 1982–83; Regional Director: MSC, 1983–86; Employment and Enterprise Gp, 1986–87; Regl Dir, 1987–93, Dir of Inf. and Systems, 1993–95, Employment Service, Dept. of Employment. *Recreations:* gardening, cosmology, running, tennis. *Address:* Stockport, Cheshire.

PHILLIPS, Richard Charles Jonathan; QC 1990; *b* 8 Aug. 1947; *yr s* of Air Commodore M. N. Phillips, MD, ChB, DMRD and Dorothy E. Phillips; *m* 1978, Alison Jane Francis (OBE 1991); one *d*. *Educ:* King's School, Ely; Sidney Sussex College, Cambridge (Exhibnr). Called to the Bar, Inner Temple, 1970. Asst Parly Boundary Comr, 1992–. *Recreations:* travel, natural history, photography, walking. *Address:* 2 Harcourt Buildings, Temple, EC4Y 9DB. *T:* (020) 7353 8415.

PHILLIPS, Rear Adm. Richard Thomas Ryder, CB 1998; FNI; Director, BAE SYSTEMS, since 2000; *b* 1 Feb. 1947; *s* of Thomas Hall Phillips and Arabella Phillips; *m* 1st, 1969, Susan Elizabeth Groves (*d* 1996); one *d*; 2nd, 1999, Belinda Susan Kelway Round Turner; one step *s* one step *d*. *Educ:* Kingsland Grange, Shrewsbury; Wrekin Coll. BRNC Dartmouth, 1965; Commanding Officer: HMS Scimitar, 1974; HMS Hubberston, 1978; ndc Canberra, 1981; Directorate of Naval Plans, 1982; Commanding Officer: HMS Charybdis, 1985; HMS Scylla, 1986; Asst Dir, Defence Op. Requirements (Maritime), 1987; CO, HMS Cornwall, and Capt., 8 Frigate Sqn, 1988; Capt., RN Presentation Team, 1991; Cabinet Office Top Mgt Prog., 1992; COS, Flag Officer Surface Flotilla, 1992; CO, HMS Illustrious, 1993; ACDS Op. Requirements (Sea Systems), 1996–99. Dir, Marconi Naval Systems, 1999–2000. ADC to the Queen, 1993. FNI 1999. *Publication:* contrib. Royal Naval Review. *Recreations:* shooting, gardening, sailing. *Address:* BAE SYSTEMS, The Grove, Warren Lane, Stanmore, Middx HA7 4LY. *T:* (020) 8420 3940. *Clubs:* Lansdowne; Royal Yacht Squadron, Royal Western Yacht, Cargreen Sailing.

PHILLIPS, Robin; actor and director; *b* 28 Feb. 1940; *s* of James William Phillips and Ellen Anne (*née* Barfoot). *Educ:* Midhurst Grammar School, Sussex. Trained as director, actor and designer, Bristol Old Vic Co.; first appearance, Bristol, as Mr Puff in The Critic, 1959; Associate Dir, Bristol Old Vic, 1960–61; played at Lyric, Hammersmith, 1961, Chichester Fest., 1962, and with Oxford Playhouse Co., 1964. Asst Dir, Timon of Athens and Hamlet, Royal Shakespeare Co., Stratford upon Avon, 1965; Dir or Associate Dir, Hampstead, Exeter, (Thorndike) Leatherhead, 1966–69; Artistic Dir, Stratford Festival, Canada, 1974–80; Artistic Dir, Grand Theatre Co., London, Ontario, 1982; Dir, Young Company, Stratford Festival Theatre, 1986; Dir Gen., The Citadel Theatre, Edmonton, Canada, 1990–95. Hon. Dr Univ. of Western Ontario, 1982. Guild Shield, Conestoga Coll., 1982. *London prodns include:* Tiny Alice, RSC, Aldwych, 1970; Abelard and Heloise, Wyndhams and Broadway; The Two Gentlemen of Verona, Stratford and Aldwych, 1970; Miss Julie, for RSC (also directed film); Virginia, Haymarket, 1981; Long Day's Journey Into Night, Lyric, 2000; Ghosts, Comedy, 2001; *Chichester:* Caesar and Cleopatra and Dear Antoine, 1971; played Dubedat in The Doctor's Dilemma and directed The Lady's Not for Burning and The Beggar's Opera, 1972; The Jeweller's Shop, 1982; Antony and Cleopatra, 1985; *Greenwich:* formed Company Theatre and apptd Artistic Dir, 1973: plays directed include: The Three Sisters, Rosmerholm, Zorba; *Stratford Festival prodns include:* 1975: The Two Gentlemen of Verona and The Comedy of Errors (both also Nat. tour), Measure for Measure, Trumpets and Drums and The Importance of Being Earnest; 1976–78: Hamlet, The Tempest, Antony and Cleopatra, A Midsummer Night's Dream, The Way of the World, Richard III, The Guardsman, As You Like It, Macbeth, The Winter's Tale, Uncle Vanya, The Devils, Private Lives, Hay Fever, Judgement; 1979: Love's Labours Lost, The Importance of Being Earnest, King Lear; 1980: Virginia, Long Day's Journey into Night; 1986: Cymbeline; 1987: The School for Scandal, As You Like It, Romeo and Juliet, Journey's End; 1988: Twelfth Night, King Lear, Oedipus, The Critic; 1993: King John; *Edmonton prodns include:* A Midsummer Night's Dream, The Crucible, 1989; The Philadelphia Story, 1990; Never the Sinner, The Mousetrap, Romeo and Juliet, Democracy, 1991; Lend Me A Tenor, Fallen Angels, Oedipus, Man of La Mancha (also Toronto, 1993), Black Comedy, Invisible Friends, The Royal Hunt of the Sun, Hamlet, As You Like It, 1992; La Bête, The Two of Us, She Stoops to Conquer, Saint Joan, Oliver!, Aspects of Love (also Toronto, US tour), 1993; Cyrano de Bergerac, Macbeth, Hay Fever (also Winnipeg), Caesar and Cleopatra, A Man for All Seasons, The Music Man, 1994; Richard III, The Cherry Orchard, The Beggar's Opera, The Alberta Quilt, 1995; *other prodns include:* The Marriage of Figaro, 1993, Beatrice and Benedict, 1996, Canadian Opera Co., Toronto; Owen Wingrave, Glyndebourne Touring Opera, 1995; Jekyll and Hyde, NY, 1997; Don Carlos, The Misanthrope, Soulpepper Th. Co., 1998. *Films:* as actor: Decline and Fall, David Copperfield (title part), Tales from the Crypt; as director: The Wars, Miss Julie, Waiting for the Parade. *TV:* Wilfred Desert in The Forsyte Saga; Constantin in The Seagull. *Address:* Wildwood House, RR3, Lakeside, ON N0M 2G0, Canada.

PHILLIPS, Sir Robin Francis, 3rd Bt *cr* 1912; Owner and Principal, Ravenscourt Theatre School, London, since 1989; *b* 29 July 1940; *s* of Sir Lionel Francis Phillips, 2nd Bt, and Camilla Mary, *er d* of late Hugh Parker, 22 Chapel Street, Belgrave Square, SW1; *S* father, 1944. *Educ:* Aiglon Coll., Switzerland. Chief Air Traffic Control Officer, Biggin Hill, 1970–78; Hazel Malaone Management, 1978–81; Devonair Radio, 1981–83; Radio Luxembourg, 1984; Hd of Casting, Corona Stage School, 1985–89. *Heir:* none. *Address:* 12 Manson Mews, Queens Gate, SW7 5AF.

PHILLIPS, (Ronald) William; Director: NB Selection Ltd, since 1991; Norman Broadbent International, since 1998; *b* 21 April 1949; *s* of Ronald Phillips and late Phoebe Nora Haynes; *m* 1979, Dorothy Parsons. *Educ:* Steyning Grammar Sch.; University College of Wales, Aberystwyth (BScEcon). Joined CS, 1971; served in Dept of Transport, PSA, DoE, Develt Commn (Private Sec. to Lord Northfield); Asst County Sec., Kent CC, 1979–80; UK Expert to EC Council of Ministers Wkg Party on Environmental Impact Assessment, 1980–83; Greater London Reg. Office, DoE (Local Govt Reorganisation), 1983–86; Head of Policy Unit, 1986–87, Man. Dir, 1987–91, Westminster CC. FRSA 1990; FIMgt (FBIM 1990). JP Maidstone, 1992–96. *Recreation:* travel. *Address:* Livesey Cottage, Livesey Street, Teston, Kent ME18 5AY.

PHILLIPS, Sarah; *see* Phillips, R. S.

PHILLIPS, Siân, CBE 2000; actress; *d* of D. Phillips and Sally Phillips; *m* 1960, Peter O'Toole, *qv* (marr. diss. 1979); two *d*; *m* 1979, Robin Sachs (marr. diss. 1992). *Educ:* Pontardawe Grammar Sch.; Univ. of Wales (Cardiff Coll.) (BA Hons English; Fellow, 1982); RADA (Maggie Albanesi Scholarship, 1956; Bancroft Gold Medal, 1958). BBC Radio Wales, mid 1940s–, and BBC TV Wales, early 1950s–; Newsreader and Announcer, and Mem. Rep. Co., BBC, 1953–55; toured for Welsh Arts Council with National Theatre Co., 1953–55; Arts Council Bursary to study drama outside Wales, 1955. Mem., Arts Council Drama Cttee, 1970–75. Governor: St David's Trust, 1970–73; Welsh Coll. of Music and Drama, 1992–. *Theatre:* London: Hedda Gabler, 1959; Ondine, and the Duchess of Malfi, 1960–61 (1st RSC season at Aldwych); The Lizard on the Rock, 1961; Gentle Jack, Maxibules, and The Night of the Iguana, 1964; Ride a Cock Horse, 1965; Man and Superman, and Man of Destiny, 1966; The Burglar, 1967; Epitaph for George Dillon, 1972; A Nightingale in Bloomsbury Square, 1973; The Gay Lord Quex, 1975; Spinechiller, 1978; You Never Can Tell, Lyric, Hammersmith, 1979; Pal Joey, Half Moon, 1980 and Albery, 1981; Dear Liar, Mermaid, 1982; Major Barbara, NT, 1982; Peg, Phoenix, 1984; Gigi, Lyric, Shaftesbury Ave., 1985; Thursday's Ladies, Apollo, 1987; Brel, Donmar, 1987; Paris Match, Garrick, 1989; Vanilla, Lyric, 1990; The Manchurian Candidate, Lyric, Hammersmith, and nat. tour, 1991; Painting Churches, Playhouse, 1992; The Glass Menagerie, Cambridge Theatre Co. nat. tour, 1989; Ghosts, Welsh Arts Council tour, and Sherman Theatre, Wales, 1993; The Lion in Winter, UK nat. tour, 1994; An Inspector Calls, NY, 1995; A Little Night Music, RNT, 1995; Marlene, nat. tour, 1996, Lyric, 1997, S Africa, Paris, 1998, NY, 1999; concert tour, UK and US, 2000; cabaret, NY, 2000, RNT and tour, 2001; Lettice and Lovage, tour, 2001. *TV drama series* include: Shoulder to Shoulder, 1974; How Green was my Valley, 1975; I, Claudius, 1976; Boudicca, and Off to Philadelphia in the Morning, 1977; The Oresteia of Aeschylus, 1978; Crime and Punishment, 1979; Sean O'Casey (RTE), 1980; Winston Churchill, The Wilderness Years, 1981; Language and Landscape (6 bilingual films, Welsh and English), 1985; The Snow Spider, 1988; Shadow of the Noose, 1989; Emlyn's Moon, 1990; Perfect Scoundrels, 1990; Tonight at 8.30: Hands Across the Sea; The Astonished Heart; Ways and Means, 1991; The Borrowers, 1992, 1993; The Aristocrats, 1999; Nikita, The Magician's House, 2000; *TV films* include: A Painful Case (RTE), 1985; While Reason Sleeps; Return to Endor, 1986 (USA); Siân (biographical), 1987; Heidi, 1993; Mind to Kill (also in Welsh), 1995; Summer Silence (musical, also in Welsh), 1995. *Films* include: Becket, 1963; Goodbye Mr Chips, and Laughter in the Dark, 1968; Murphy's War, 1970; Under Milk Wood, 1971; The Clash of the Titans, 1979; Dune, 1984; Ewocks Again, and The Doctor and the Devils, 1985; Valmont, 1989; Age of Innocence, 1994; House of

America, 1996; Alice Through the Looking Glass, 1999; Coming and Going, 2000. Has made recordings, incl. Peg, Gigi, I remember Mama, Pal Joey, Bewitched, Bothered and Bewildered, A Little Night Music, Marlene. RTS Annual Lecture (Eng. and Welsh transmissions), 1993. FWNCMD, 1991; Fellow, Cardiff Coll., Univ. of Wales, 1983; Hon. Fellow: Polytechnic of Wales, 1988; Trinity Coll., Carms, 1998; Univ. of Wales Swansea, 1998. Hon. DLitt Wales, 1984. Critics Circle Award, New York Critics Award, and Famous 7 Critics Award, for Goodbye Mr Chips, 1969; BAFTA Award for How Green was my Valley and I, Claudius, 1978; Royal Television Soc. Award for I, Claudius (Best Performer), 1978. Mem., Gorsedd of Bards, 1960 (for services to drama in Wales). *Publications:* Siân Phillips' Needlepoint, 1987; autobiography: Private Faces, 1999; Public Places, 2001; gen. journalism (Vogue, Cosmopolitan, Daily Mail, 3 years for Radio Times, Country Living, Options). *Recreations:* gardening, needlepoint, drawing. *Address:* c/o Lindy King, Peters, Fraser & Dunlop, 34–43 Russell Street, WC2B 5HA.

PHILLIPS, Stephen James; freelance writer, producer and broadcaster; *b* 28 May 1947; *s* of James Ronald Phillips and Diana Betty Phillips (*née* Bradshaw); *m* 1988, Simone Lila Lopez; two *d*. *Educ:* Univ. of London (ext. BA Ancient Hist.); St John's Coll., Cambridge (Dip. Classical Archaeol.). Reporter and critic, Yorks Evening Post, 1965–69; critic and feature writer, Daily Express, 1969–72; Manager, Holiday Village, Thasos, Greece, 1973; BBC reporter and presenter, 1973–76; Gen. Administrator, Prospect Theatre Co., Old Vic, 1976–78; presenter, Kaleidoscope and other BBC programmes, 1978–81; Arts Corresp., ITN and Channel Four, 1982–89; Series Ed., Signals, 1989–91; arts consultant, Meridian Broadcasting, 1996–2000; exec. producer, Antelope Films, 1992–2000. Vis. Res. Fellow, Sussex Univ., 1999–. Member: Arts Council of England, 1994–98 (Chm., Touring Adv. Panel, 1994–98); SE Arts Bd, 1999–; SE England Regl Assembly and Exec. Cttee, 2000–; Vice Chm., SE Regl Cultural Consortium, 2000–. Dir, Isaac Newton Arts Trust, 2000–. Board Member: Tricycle Theatre, Kilburn, 1998– (Chm., 1984–94); English Nat. Ballet, 1999–; Chichester Fest. Theatre Productions, 1999–; Chm., Arts for Everyone Lottery Panel, 1996–98. Chm., Friends of Herstmonceux Castle, 1995–; Trustee, Brighton's West Pier, 1997–; Patron, Brighton Dome Appeal, 1999–. *Recreations:* theatre, history, travel, my family. *Address:* West Wing, Carters Corner Place, Hailsham, East Sussex BN27 4HX.

PHILLIPS, Tom, RA 1989 (ARA 1984); RE 1987; painter, writer and composer; *b* 25 May 1937; *s* of David John Phillips and Margaret Agnes (*née* Arnold); *m* 1961, Jill Purdy (marr. diss. 1988); one *s* one *d*; *m* 1995, Fiona Maddocks, *qv*. *Educ:* St Catherine's College, Oxford (MA; Hon. Fellow, 1992); Camberwell School of Art. NDD. One man shows: AIA Galleries, 1965; Angela Flowers Gall., 1970–71; Marlborough Fine Art, 1973–75; Dante Works, Waddington Galleries, 1983; retrospective exhibitions: Gemeente Museum, The Hague, 1975; Kunsthalle, Basel, 1975; Serpentine, 1975; 50 years of Tom Phillips, Angela Flowers Gall., 1987; Mappin Art Gall., Sheffield, 1987; Nat. Gall., Jamaica, 1987; Bass Mus., Miami, 1988; Nat. Gall., Australia, 1988; City Art Inst., Sydney, 1988; Nat. Portrait Gall., 1989; N Carolina Mus., 1990; Royal Acad., 1992; V&A, 1992; Ulster Mus., 1993; Yale Center, USA, 1993; S London Art Gall., 1998; Dulwich Picture Gall., 1998; work in collections: British Museum, Tate Gall., V&A, Nat. Portrait Gall., Imperial War Mus., Ashmolean Mus., Oxford, Mus. Fine Arts, Budapest, MOMA NY, Philadelphia Museum, Bibliothèque Nationale, Paris, Gemeente Museum, Boymans Museum, Rotterdam, Nat. Museum, Stockholm, Nat. Gall. of Australia; designed tapestries for St Catherine's, Oxford; music: first perf. opera Irma, 1973; York, 1974; ICA, 1983; recordings incl. Irma, 1980 (new version, 1988); Intervalles/Music of Tom Phillips 1982; Six of Hearts, 1997; television: co-dir, Dante series, 1984–89 (1st prize Montreal Fest., 1990; Prix Italia, 1991); film scripts: Tom Phillips (Grierson Award, BFI, 1976; Golden Palm Award, Chicago, 1976); The Artist's Eye (TV film), 1988; Twenty Sites (TV film), 1989; designer, The Winter's Tale, Globe Theatre, 1997; designer and translator, Otello, ENO, 1998. Curator, Africa: the art of a continent, RA, 1995, Berlin and NY, 1996. Chairman: RA Library, 1987–95; RA Exhibns Cttee, 1995; Vice-Chm., British Copyright Council, 1984–88. Chm., Frua Foundn, NY, 1997–; Trustee: Ruskin House, 1996–; Nat. Portrait Gall., 1998–; BM, 1999–. Hon. Pres., S London Artists, 1987–. Hon. RP 1999. Hon. Fellow, London Inst., 1999. Francis Williams Prize, V&A 1983; First Prize, Hunting Gp of Cos, 1988. *Publications:* Trailer, 1971; A Humument, 1980, 2nd rev. edn 1998; illustr. trans. Dante's Inferno, 1982; Works/Texts to 1974, 1975; Heart of a Humument, 1985; The Class of Forty-Seven, 1990; Works/Texts vol. II, 1992; Humument Supplement, 1992; Plato's Symposium, 1992; (with Salman Rushdie) Merely Connect, 1994; (ed) Africa: the art of a continent, 1995; Music in Art, 1997; Aspects of Art, 1997; The Postcard Century, 2000. *Recreations:* ping pong, cricket, postcards. *Address:* 57 Talfourd Road, SE15 5NN. *T:* (020) 7701 3978, *Fax:* (020) 7703 2800. *Clubs:* Chelsea Arts, Groucho; Surrey County Cricket.

PHILLIPS, Tom Richard Vaughan, CMG 1998; HM Diplomatic Service; High Commissioner to Uganda, since 2000; *b* 21 June 1950; *s* of late Comdr Tom Vaughan Gerald Phillips, DSC, OBE, RN and of Margaret Sproull (*née* Gameson); *m* 1986, Anne de la Motte; two *s*. *Educ:* Harlow Technical Coll.; Exeter Univ.; Jesus Coll., Oxford; Wolfson Coll., Oxford (MLitt). Journalist, West Herts and Watford Observer, 1969–72; DHSS, 1977–83; FCO, 1983–85; First Sec., Harare, 1985–88; FCO, 1988–90; Dep. Head of Mission and Consul-Gen., Tel Aviv, 1990–93; Counsellor, Washington, 1993–97; Hd, Eastern Adriatic Dept, FCO, 1997–99. *Publication:* (as Tom Vaughan) No Second Prize, 1993. *Address:* c/o Foreign and Commonwealth Office, SW1A 2AH.

PHILLIPS, Trevor; *see* Phillips, M. T.

PHILLIPS, Trevor Thomas; *see* Phillips, Tom.

PHILLIPS, Vernon Francis, CPFA; FCA; Chief Executive, Bedfordshire County Council, 1989–92, retired; *b* 7 July 1930; *s* of Charles and May Phillips; *m* 1955, Valerie P. Jones; two *s* one *d*. *Educ:* Wilson Sch., Reading. CIPFA (Hons) 1954; ASAA 1958; FCA 1970. Berkshire CC, 1946–53; Swindon BC, 1953–55; Bristol City Council, 1955–58; Coventry City Council, 1958–61; Dep. Borough Treas., Luton CB, 1962–73; County Treas., Bedfordshire CC, 1973–89. Adviser to ACC, 1985–92. Member: Soc. of County Treas, 1973–; Assoc. of County Chief Execs, 1989–95; SOLACE, 1989–95. Chm., Bedford Citizens Housing Assoc., 1999–. Mem., Bedford Rotary Club. *Recreations:* reading, music (listening), dancing, walking, paperweights, stained glass windows, photography. *Address:* 5 Troon Close, Bedford MK41 8AY. *T:* (01234) 345628.

PHILLIPS, William; *see* Phillips, R. W.

PHILLIPS, Dr William Daniel; physicist; National Institute of Standards and Technology Fellow, since 1995; Professor of Physics, University of Maryland, 2001 (Adjunct Professor, 1992–2001); *b* 5 Nov. 1948; *s* of William Cornelius Phillips and Mary Catherine Savine Phillips; *m* 1970, Jane Van Wynen; two *d*. *Educ:* Juniata Coll. (BS Physics 1970); Massachusetts Inst. of Technol. (PhD Physics 1976). Chaim Weizmann Fellow, MIT, 1976–78; physicist, Nat. Bureau of Standards, later Nat. Inst. of Standards and Technol., 1978–95. Fellow: Amer. Physical Soc., 1986; Optical Soc. of America, 1994; Amer. Acad. of Arts and Scis, 1995. Mem., NAS, 1997. Gold Medal, Dept of Commerce, 1993; Michelson Medal, Franklin Inst., 1996; Nobel Prize in Physics, 1997; Schawlow Prize, Amer. Physical Soc., 1998. *Publications:* contrib. numerous articles in Physical Rev. Letters and other professional jls, and in proc. nat. and internat. confs. *Recreations:* photography, tennis, gospel music, Bible study. *Address:* 100 Bureau Drive, Stop 8424, PHY A155, National Institute of Standards and Technology, Gaithersburg, MD 20899–8424, USA.

PHILLIPS GRIFFITHS, Allen; *see* Griffiths.

PHILLIS, Robert Weston; Chief Executive, Guardian Media Group, since 1997; *b* 3 Dec. 1945; *s* of Francis William Phillis and Gertrude Grace Phillis; *m* 1966, Jean (*née* Derham); three *s*. *Educ:* John Ruskin Grammar Sch.; Nottingham Univ. (BA Industrial Econs 1968). Apprentice, printing industry, 1961–65; Thomson Regional Newspapers Ltd, 1968–69; British Printing Corp. Ltd, 1969–71; Lectr in Industrial Relations, Edinburgh Univ. and Scottish Business Sch., 1971–75; Vis. Fellow, Univ. of Nairobi, 1974; Personnel Dir, later Man. Dir, Sun Printers Ltd, 1976–79; Managing Director: Independent Television Publications Ltd, 1979–82 (Dir, 1979–87); Central Independent Television plc, 1981–87 (non-exec. Dir, 1987–91); Gp Man. Dir, Carlton Communications, 1987–91; Chief Exec., ITN, 1991–93; Man. Dir, BBC World Service, 1993–94; Chm., BBC Enterprises Ltd, 1993–94; Dep. Dir-Gen., BBC, 1993–97; Chm., later Chief Exec., BBC Worldwide, 1994–97. Chairman: ITV Network Programming Cttee, 1984–86; ITV Film Purchase Gp, 1985–87; Zenith Productions Ltd, 1984–91. Director: ITN Ltd, 1982–87 and 1991–93; Periodical Publishers Assoc., 1979–82; ITCA, 1982–87; Internat. Council, Nat. Acad. of Television Arts and Scis, 1985– (Vice Chm. (Internat.), 1994–97; Life Fellow, 1997); Worldwide Television News Corp., 1991–93. Vice-Pres., EBU, 1996–97. Dir and Trustee, Television Trust for the Environment, 1985–. Hon. Prof., Stirling Univ., 1997. FRSA 1984; FRTS 1988 (Chm., 1989–92; Vice Pres., 1994–). Hon. DLitt: Salford, 1999; City, 2000. *Recreations:* ski-ing, golf, military and political history. *Address:* Guardian Media Group plc, 75 Farringdon Road, EC1M 3JY. *Clubs:* Garrick, Reform, Groucho.

PHILO, Gordon Charles George, CMG 1970; MC 1944; HM Diplomatic Service, retired; *b* 8 Jan. 1920; *s* of Charles Gilbert Philo and Nellie Philo (*née* Pinnock); *m* 1952, Mavis (Vicky) Ella (*d* 1986), *d* of John Ford Galsworthy and Sybel Victoria Galsworthy (*née* Strachan). *Educ:* Haberdashers' Aske's Hampstead Sch.; Wadham Coll., Oxford. Methuen Scholar in Modern History, Wadham Coll., 1938. Served War, HM Forces, 1940–46: Royal West African Frontier Force, 1942–43; Airborne Forces, Normandy and Europe, 1944–45; India 1945–46. Alexander Korda Scholar, The Sorbonne, 1948–49; Lectr in Modern History, Wadham Coll., 1949–50; Foundn Mem., St Antony's Coll., Oxford, 1950–51. Foreign Office, 1951; Russian course, Christ's Coll., Cambridge, 1952–53; Istanbul, Third Sec., 1954–57; Ankara, Second Sec., 1957–58; FO, 1958–63; Kuala Lumpur, First Sec., 1963–67; FO, 1968; Consul-Gen., Hanoi, 1968–69; FCO, 1969–78. Extended Interview Assessor, Home Office Unit, CSSB, 1978–90. Chm. Council, Kipling Soc., 1986–88, 1997–99. Kesatria Mangku Negara (Hon.), Order of Malaysia, 1968. *Publications:* (jtly with wife, as Charles Forsyte): Diplomatic Death, 1960; Diving Death, 1962; Double Death, 1965; Murder with Minarets, 1968; The Decoding of Edwin Drood, 1980; articles in various jls. *Recreations:* travel, writing. *Address:* 10 Abercorn Close, NW8 9XS. *Club:* Athenæum.

PHILPOT, Nicholas Anthony John; His Honour Judge Philpot; a Circuit Judge, since 1992; *b* 19 Dec. 1944; *s* of late Oliver Lawrence Spurling Philpot, MC, DFC, and Margaret Nathalie Forsyth (*née* Owen); two *s*. *Educ:* Winchester Coll.; New Coll., Oxford (BA PPE 1966). VSO, Bolivia, 1966–67. Called to the Bar, Lincoln's Inn, 1970; Asst Recorder, 1987–90; Recorder, 1990–92. *Address:* c/o Inner London Crown Court, Newington Causeway, SE1 6AZ.

PHIPPARD, Sonia Clare; Head, Central Secretariat, Cabinet Office, since 2000; *b* 8 Jan. 1960; *d* of Brig. Roy Phippard and Gillian Phippard (*née* Menzies). *Educ:* Wadhurst Coll.; Somerville Coll., Oxford (BA Physics 1981). Joined Civil Service Department, later Cabinet Office (MPO), 1981: on secondment to DES, 1987–89; Private Sec. to Sec. of Cabinet, 1989–92; Asst Sec., Next Steps Project Dir, 1992–94; on secondment to Coopers and Lybrand, 1995–97; Dep. Dir, Central Secretariat, Cabinet Office, 1997–99. *Recreations:* amateur dramatics, food, time with friends. *Address:* Cabinet Office, 70 Whitehall, SW1A 2AS.

PHIPPS, family name of **Marquess of Normanby**.

PHIPPS, Belinda Clare; Chief Executive, National Childbirth Trust, since 1999; *b* 11 April 1958; *d* of Leonie May Kerslake; partner, Nigel John Simmons; three *d*. *Educ:* Crammer Sch., Wokingham; Bath Univ. (BSc Hons Microbiol. 1980); Ashridge Management Coll. (MBA 1992). Glaxo Pharmaceuticals, 1980–90; Man. Dir, NHS Blood Transfusion Service, 1991–94; co-ordinating Wells report on London Ambulance Service, 1995; CEO, East Berks Community Trust, 1996–99. *Recreation:* ballroom dancing. *Address:* National Childbirth Trust, Alexandra House, Oldham Terrace, W3 6NH. *T:* (020) 8992 2616.

PHIPPS, Colin Barry, PhD; Chairman: Greenwich Resources plc, since 1989; Recycling Services Group plc, since 1996; Desire Petroleum plc, since 1996; *b* 23 July 1934; *s* of Edgar Reeves Phipps and Winifred Elsie Phipps (*née* Carroll); *m* 1956, Marion May Phipps (*née* Lawrey); two *s* two *d*. *Educ:* Townfield Elem. Sch., Hayes, Mddx; Acton County; Swansea Grammar; University Coll. London; Birmingham Univ. BSc, 1st cl. Hons Geol. London 1955; PhD, Geol. Birm. 1957. Royal Dutch/Shell Geologist: Holland, Venezuela, USA, 1957–64; Consultant Petroleum Geologist, 1964–79; Dep. Chm. and Chief Exec., 1979–83, Chm., 1983–95, Clyde Petroleum; Dir, Gaelic Resources plc, 1997–. Chm., Brindex (Assoc. of British Independent Oil Exploration Cos), 1983–86. MP (Lab) Dudley W, Feb. 1974–1979. Mem., Council of Europe/WEU, 1976–79. Contested: (Lab) Walthamstow E, 1969; (SDP/L Alliance) Worcester, 1983; (SDP/L Alliance) Stafford, 1987. Founder mem., SDP; Mem. SDP Nat. Cttee, 1984–89; Chm., W Midland Regional council, SDP, 1986–89. FGS 1956; FInstPet 1972; CGeol 1991; Mem. Instn of Geologists, 1978. Chairman: Twentieth Century British Art Fair, 1988–93; Falklands Conservation (formerly Falkland Islands Foundn), 1990–92 (Trustee, 1983–99); English String Orch., 1990–92 (Dir, 1985–92). *Publications:* (co-ed) Energy and the Environment: democratic decision-making, 1978; What Future for the Falklands?, 1977 (Fabian tract 450); contrib.: Qly Jl Geol Sci., Geol. Mag., Geol. Jl, etc. *Recreation:* playing with my grandchildren. *Address:* Mathon Court, Mathon, Malvern WR13 5NZ. *T:* (01684) 892267; 24 Old Burlington Street, W1X 1RL. *T:* (020) 7287 1417. *Clubs:* Reform, Chelsea Arts.

PHIPPS, Maj. Gen. Jeremy Julian Joseph, CB 1997; Director of Special Accounts, Control Risks Group, since 2000; *b* 30 June 1942; *s* of Lt Alan Phipps, RN (killed in action, 1943), 2nd *s* of Rt Hon. Sir Eric Phipps, GCB, GCMG, GCVO, and of Hon. Veronica Phipps, 2nd *d* of 16th Lord Lovat, KT, GCVO, KCMG, CB, DSO; *m* 1974, Susan Louise, *d* of late Comdr Wilfrid and Patricia Crawford; one *s* one *d*. *Educ:*

Ampleforth Coll.; RMA, Sandhurst. Commnd Queen's Own Hussars, 1962; served in Germany, Middle East, Far East; student, US Armed Forces Staff Coll., Norfolk, Va, 1980; commanded Queen's Own Hussars, 1981–83; COS, RMA, Sandhurst, 1983–85; Comdr 11th Armoured Bde, 1985–89; Dir Special Forces, 1989–93; Sen. British Loan Service Officer, Sultanate of Oman, 1993–96; retd 1997. Man. Dir, Network Internat., 1997–2000. Order of Achievement (1st cl.), (Sultanate of Oman), 1995. *Recreations:* shooting, trout fishing, sailing, ski-ing. *Address:* Drummonds Branch, Royal Bank of Scotland, 49 Charing Cross, SW1A 2DX. *Clubs:* White's; Houghton.

See also Sir C. E. Maclean of Dunconnel, Bt.

PHIPPS, John Christopher; His Honour Judge Phipps; a Circuit Judge, since 1996; *b* 29 Aug. 1946; *s* of Thomas Phipps and Jane Bridget Phipps; *m* 1969, Elizabeth Bower; one *s* three *d. Educ:* Liskeard GS, Cornwall; Univ. of Liverpool (LLB Hons 1967). Called to the Bar, Middle Temple, 1970; practised on Northern Circuit, 1971–96; Asst Recorder, 1989–93; Recorder, 1993–96. *Recreations:* amateur Savoyard, theatre, Opera. *Address:* Crown Court, Crown Square, Manchester M3 3FL. *T:* (0161) 954 1800.

PHIPPS, Air Vice-Marshal Leslie William, CB 1983; AFC 1959; *b* 17 April 1930; *s* of late Frank Walter Phipps and Beatrice Kate (*née* Bearman). *Educ:* SS Philip and James Sch., Oxford. Commnd RAF, 1950; served, 1951–69: Fighter Sqdns; Stn Comdr, RAF Aqaba, Jordan; OC No 19 (F) Sqdn; Central Fighter Estab.; RN Staff Coll.; HQ 1 (British) Corps; Stn Comdr, RAF Labuan, Borneo; OC No 29 (F) Sqdn; Jt Services Staff Coll.; Dir, RAF Staff Coll., 1970–72; Comdr, Sultan of Oman's Air Force, 1973–74; RCDS, 1975; Comdr, UK Team to Kingdom of Saudi Arabia, 1976–78; Dir of Air Def. and Overseas Ops, 1978–79; Air Sec., (RAF), 1980–82; Sen. Directing Staff, RCDS, 1983; retired. BAe (Mil. Aircraft Div.), 1984–91. Service with nat. and local charities, 1991–. *Recreations:* sailing, squash, music. *Address:* 33 Knole Wood, Devenish Road, Sunningdale, Berks SL5 9QR. *Clubs:* Royal Air Force; Royal Air Force Yacht, Royal Southern Yacht (Hamble).

PHIZACKERLEY, Ven. Gerald Robert; Archdeacon of Chesterfield, 1978–96, now Emeritus; *b* 3 Oct. 1929; *s* of John Dawson and Lilian Mabel Ruthven Phizackerley; *m* 1959, Annette Catherine, *d* of Cecil Frank and Inez Florence Margaret Baker; one *s* one *d. Educ:* Queen Elizabeth Grammar School, Penrith; University Coll., Oxford (Open Exhibnr; MA); Wells Theological Coll. Curate of St Barnabas Church, Carlisle, 1954–57; Chaplain of Abingdon School, 1957–64; Rector of Gaywood, Norfolk, 1964–78; Rural Dean of Lynn, 1968–78; Hon. Canon of Norwich Cathedral, 1975, of Derby Cathedral, 1978; Priest-in-charge, Ashford-in-the-Water with Sheldon, 1978–90. Fellow, Woodard Corporation, 1981. JP Norfolk, 1972. *Publication:* (ed) The Diaries of Maria Gyte of Sheldon, Derbyshire, 1913–1920, 1999. *Recreations:* books, theatre, Border collies. *Address:* Archway Cottage, Hall Road, Leamington Spa, Warwickshire CV32 5RA. *T:* (01926) 332740.

PHYSICK, John Frederick, CBE 1984; DrRCA; FSA; Deputy Director, Victoria and Albert Museum, 1983; *b* 31 Dec. 1923; *s* of Nino William Physick and Gladys (*née* Elliott); *m* 1954, Eileen Mary Walsh; two *s* one *d. Educ:* Battersea Grammar Sch. Royal Navy, 1942–46 (Petty Officer Airman). Joined Victoria and Albert Museum, as Museum Asst, Dept of Engraving, Illustration and Design, 1948; Research Asst, 1949; Sen. Research Asst, 1965; Asst Keeper, Dept of Public Relations and Educn, 1967; Keeper, Dept of Museum Services, 1975–83; Sec. to Adv. Council, 1973–83; Asst to Dir, 1974–83, Leverhulme Trust Emeritus Fellow, 1984–86. Pres., Church Monument Soc., 1984–86, 1996–2001; Vice-Pres., Public Monuments and Sculpture Assoc., 1999– (Mem. Adv. Cttee, 1991–98); Chm., Monuments Sub-Cttee, 1984–2001 (Mem., 1978–2001), Conservation Cttees, 1993–2001 (Mem., 1984–93), Council for Care of Churches; Member: Rochester DAC for the Care of Churches, 1964–91 (Vice-Chm., 1987–91); RIBA Drawings Cttee, 1975; Cathedrals Adv. Cttee, 1977–81; Council, British Archaeol Assoc., 1985–88; Westminster Abbey Architectural Adv. Panel, 1985–98; Rochester Cathedral Fabric Cttee, 1987– (Vice-Chm., 1992–); Guildford Cath. Fabric Adv. Cttee, 1999–. Mem. Council, Soc. of Antiquaries, 1991–93. Trustee: London Scottish Regt, 1977–87. Freeman, City of London, 1997. DLitt Lambeth, 1996. Silver Jubilee Medal, 1977. *Publications:* Catalogue of the Engravings of Eric Gill, 1963; (ed) Handbook to the Departments Prints and Drawings and Paintings, 1964; The Duke of Wellington in caricature, 1965; Designs for English Sculpture 1680–1860, 1969; The Wellington Monument, 1970; (jtly) Victorian Church Art, 1971; Five Monuments from Eastwell, 1973; (with M. D. Darby) Marble Halls, 1973; Photography and the South Kensington Museum, 1975; (with Sir Roy Strong) V&A Souvenir Guide, 1977; The Victoria and Albert Museum—the history of its building, 1982; (ed) V&A Album II, 1983; (ed) Sculpture in Britain 1530–1830, 2nd edn 1988; (contrib.) Change and Decay, the Future of our Churches, 1977; (contrib.) Westminster Abbey, 1986; (contrib.) The Royal College of Art, 1987; (introd.) Westminster Abbey: the monuments, 1989; (contrib.) Design of the Times, 1996; (contrib.) The Dictionary of Art, 1996; (contrib.) The Albert Memorial, 2000; (contrib.) Kensal Green Cemetery, 2001. *Recreations:* photography, looking at church monuments. *Address:* 49 New Road, Meopham, Kent DA13 0LS. *T:* (01474) 812301; 14 Park Street, Deal, Kent CT14 6AG. *T:* (01304) 381621.

PIACHAUD, Prof. David François James; Professor of Social Policy (formerly Social Administration), London School of Economics, since 1987; *b* 2 Oct. 1945; *s* of Rev. Preb. François A. Piachaud and late Mary R. Piachaud; *m* 1988, Louise K. Carpenter, *d* of late Rev. Dr E. F. Carpenter, KCVO; one *s* one *d. Educ:* Westminster Sch.; Christ Church, Oxford (MA); Univ. of Michigan (MPA). Economic Asst, DHSS, 1968–70; Lectr, 1970–83, Reader, 1983–87, LSE. Policy Advr, Prime Minister's Policy Unit, 1974–79. *Publications:* The Causes of Poverty (jtly), 1978; The Cost of a Child, 1979; (jtly) Child Support in the European Community, 1980; The Distribution and Redistribution of Incomes, 1982; (jtly) The Fields and Methods of Social Planning, 1984; (jtly) The Goals of Social Policy, 1989; (jtly) The Price of Food, 1997; contribs to learned jls and periodicals. *Recreations:* carpentry, lighting, travelling. *Address:* London School of Economics, Houghton Street, WC2A 2AE. *T:* (020) 7405 7686.

PIANO, Renzo; architect; *b* 14 Sept. 1937; *m* 1st, 1962, Magda Ardnino; two *s* one *d*; 2nd, Milly Rossato. *Educ:* Milan Poly. Sch. of Architecture. Works include: Pompidou Centre, Paris (with Sir Richard Rogers), and IRCAM, 1977; Schlumberger research labs, Paris, 1984; Menil Collection Mus., Houston, 1986; S Nicola Football Stadium, Bari, Italy, 1990; Kansai Internat. Airport, Osaka, 1994; Concert Hall, hotel and shopping mall, Lingotto, Turin, 1994–96; Contemp. Art Mus. and Congress Centre, Lyon, 1996; Mus. of Sci. and Technol., Amsterdam, and Beyeler Foundn Mus., Basle, 1997; Daimler Benz projects for redevelopment of Potsdamer Platz, Berlin, 1997–98; KPN Telecom office tower, Rotterdam, 2000; Aurora Place high rise office block, Sydney, 2000; numerous exhibitions worldwide. Hon. FAIA, 1981; Hon. FRIBA, 1985; Hon. Fellow: Amer. Acad. of Arts and Scis, 1993; Amer. Acad. of Arts and Letters, 1994. RIBA Gold Medal, 1989; Kyoto Prize, Inamori Foundn, 1990; Erasmus Prize, Amsterdam, 1995; Pritzker Architect Prize, USA, 1998. Cavaliere di Gran Croce (Italy), 1989; Officier, Ordre Nat. du Mérite (France), 1994; Officier, Légion d'Honneur (France), 2000. *Publications:* (jtly) Antico é bello, il recupero della città, 1980; Chantier ouvert au public, 1985; Progetti e Architetture 1984–1986, 1986; Renzo Piano, 1987; (with R. Rogers) Du Plateau Beaubourg au Centre G. Pompidou, 1987; (jtly) Le Isole del tesoro, 1989; Renzo Piano Building Workshop 1964–1988, 1989; Renzo Piano Building and Projects 1971–1989, 1989; Renzo Piano Building Workshop 1964–1991: in search of a balance, 1992; The Making of Kansai International Airport Terminal, 1994; Giornale di Bordo, 1997; Fondation Beyeler: une maison de l'art, 1998. *Address:* Via Rubens 29, 16158 Genoa, Italy; 34 rue des Archives, 75004 Paris, France.

PICARDA, Hubert Alistair Paul; QC 1992; *b* 4 March 1936; *s* of late Pierre Adrien Picarda, Docteur en Droit (Paris), Avocat à la Cour d'Appel de Paris, Barrister, Middle Temple, and Winifred Laura (*née* Kemp); *m* 1976, Ann Hulse (marr. diss. 1995); one *s* one *d*; *m* 2000, Sarah Elizabeth Goss. *Educ:* Westminster Sch.; Magdalen Coll., Oxford (Open Exhibnr in Classics; BA Jurisprudence 1961; MA; BCL 1963); University Coll. London (Bunnell Lewis Prize for Latin Verse, 1962). Called to the Bar, Inner Temple, 1962, *ad eundem* Lincoln's Inn and Gray's Inn, 1965; in practice at Chancery Bar, 1964–; Night Lawyer, Daily Express, 1964–72; Lectr, Holborn Coll. Law, Langs and Commerce, 1965–68. Visiting Lecturer: Malaysian Bar Council, 1994, 1995, 1996; Law Soc. of Singapore, 1994, 1996; Hong Kong, 1994; Sarawak, 1995. Mem., Senate and Bar Council, 1978–81. Pres., Charity Law Assoc., 1992–; Mem., Trust Law Cttee, 1995–. Pres., Inst. Conveyancers, 2000. Pres., Hardwicke Soc., 1968–72; Member: Classical Assoc.; Horatian Soc. Managing Editor: Charity Law and Practice Rev., 1992–; Receivers, Administrators and Liquidators Qly, 1994–99 (Consulting Editor, 1999–); Member, Editorial Board: Butterworths Jl of Internat. Banking and Financial Law, 1995–; Trust Law Internat, 1992–. *Publications:* Study Guide to Law of Evidence, 1965; Law and Practice Relating to Charities, 1977, 3rd edn 1999; Law Relating to Receivers, Managers and Administrators, 1984, 2nd edn 1990; (ed) Receivers, in Halsbury's Laws of England, 4th edn, reissue, 1998; contrib. legal periodicals and The Spectator. *Recreations:* Spain in World War II, Andalusian baroque churches, Latin, music, conversation. *Address:* 3 New Square, Lincoln's Inn, WC2A 3RS. *T:* (020) 7405 5577. *Clubs:* Beefsteak, Pratt's, Turf.

PICCARD, Dr Jacques; scientist; President, Foundation for the Study and Preservation of Seas and Lakes; *b* Belgium, 1922; Swiss Citizen; *s* of late Prof. Auguste Piccard (explorer of the stratosphere, in lighter-than-air craft, and of the ocean depths, in vehicles of his own design); *m* 1953, Marie Claude (*née* Maillard); two *s* one *d. Educ:* Brussels; Switzerland. Grad., Univ. of Geneva, 1946; Dip. from Grad. Inst. of Internat. Studies. Asst Prof., Univ. of Geneva, 1946–48. With his father, he participated in design and operation of the first deep diving vessels, which they named the bathyscaph (deep ship); this vessel, like its successor, operated independently of a mother ship; they first constructed the FNRS-2 (later turned over to the French Navy) then the Trieste (ultimately purchased by US Navy); Dr J. Piccard piloted the Trieste on 65 successive dives (the last, 23 Jan. 1960, was the record-breaking descent to 35,800 feet in the Marianas Trench, off Guam in the Pacific Ocean). He built in 1963, the mesoscaph Auguste Piccard, the first civilian submarine, which made, in 1964–65, over 1,100 dives carrying 33,000 people into the depths of Lake Geneva; built (with Grumman) 2nd mesoscaph, Ben Franklin, and in 1969 made 1.500 miles/30 days drift dive in Gulf Stream. Founded: Fondation pour l'Etude et la Protection de la Mer et des Lacs, 1966 (built research submersible, F. A.-FOREL, 1978); Institut International d'Ecologie, 1972. Hon. doctorate in Science, Amer. Internat. Coll., Springfield, Mass, 1962; Hon. DSc Hofstra Univ., 1970. Holds Distinguished Public Service Award, etc. *Publications:* The Sun beneath the Sea, 1971; technical papers and a popularized account (trans. many langs) of the Trieste, Seven Miles Down (with Robert S. Dietz). *Address:* (office) Fondation pour l'Etude et la Protection de la Mer et des Lacs, 1096 Cully, Switzerland. *T:* (21) 7992565.

PICK, Hella Henrietta, CBE 2000; writer and journalist; *b* 24 April 1929; *d* of Ernst Pick and Johanna Marie Pick (*née* Spitz). *Educ:* Fairfield PNEU Sch., Ambleside; London Sch. of Econs (BSc Econ). Commercial Ed., West Africa mag., 1958–60; The Guardian: UN Corresp., 1960–67; Europe Corresp., 1967–72; Washington Corresp., 1972–75; East-West Affairs Corresp., 1975–82; Diplomatic Ed., 1983–94; Associate Foreign Affairs Ed., 1994–96. Goldenes Ehrenzeichen (Austria), 1980. *Publications:* Simon Wiesenthal: a life in search of justice, 1996, 2nd edn 2000; Guilty Victim: Austria from the Holocaust to Haider, 2000. *Recreations:* walking, swimming, travel, opera. *Address:* Flat 11, 115 Haverstock Hill, NW3 4RY. *T:* (020) 7586 3072. *Clubs:* University Women's, PEN (also Austria).

PICKARD, Prof. Huia Masters, FDSRCS; Professor of Conservative Dentistry, University of London, 1963–74, now Emeritus; *b* 25 March 1909; *o s* of late Ernest Pickard and Sophie Elizabeth Robins; *m* 1945, Daphne Evelyn (*d* 1995), *d* of Hugh F. Marriott; two *d. Educ:* Latymer Sch.; Royal Dental Hosp. of London Sch. of Dental Surgery; Charing Cross Hosp. MRCS, LRCP, FDSRCS. Private dental practice, pre-1940; EMS, East Grinstead, 1939. Served War, in RAMC, 8th Army (despatches), 1940–45. Dental practice and teaching, 1945; Dir, Dept of Conservative Dentistry, Royal Dental Hosp., and Consultant, 1955; Reader, London Univ., 1957–63; Dir of Dept of Restorative Dentistry, Royal Dental Hosp., 1965–74. Mem. Bd of Governors, St George's Hosp., 1969; First Pres., British Soc. for Restorative Dentistry, 1969; Pres., Odontological Section of Royal Soc. Med., 1971; Examr for Univs of London, Newcastle, Glasgow, Birmingham, Wales; also RCS. Governor, Latymer Sch., Edmonton, 1968–84 (Chm., 1980–83). Tomes Medal, BDA, 1983. *Publications:* Manual of Operative Dentistry, 1961, 8th edn 1996; contribs: Dental Record, Brit. Dental Jl, Internat. Dental Jl. *Address:* 14 Kingsdown, 115A Ridgway, Wimbledon, SW19 4RL. *T:* (020) 8879 1790.

PICKARD, John Anthony, (Tony); professional tennis coach; *b* 13 Sept. 1934; *s* of John William Pickard and Harriet Haywood Pickard; *m* 1958, Janet Sisson; one *s* twin *d. Educ:* Ripley Sch.; Diocesan Sch., Derby; Derby Tech. Coll. Worked under Harry Hopman, Australia (LTA), 1953–54; Sherwood Foresters, 1954–56; Mem., British Davis Cup team, 1958–63; Dir, Chellaston Brick Co., Derby, 1965; Dir, 1967, Man. Dir, 1971, F. Sisson & Sons and subsidiaries, Langley Mill; Captain, under-21 tennis team, winning Galea Cup, 1972; non-playing Captain, British Davis Cup team, 1973–76, 1991–94. Professional tennis coach to Stefan Edberg, 1985–94, to Greg Rusedski, 1997–98. GB Coach of the Year, 1988. *Recreations:* golf, walking, cars, spending time at home, football. *Address:* Whitemoor House, Blyth Road, Perlethorpe, Notts NG22 9ED. *T:* (01623) 822369. *Clubs:* All England Lawn Tennis; International Tennis Clubs of GB, America, Germany, Sweden; Ripley Tennis; Lindrick Golf.

PICKARD, Prof. John Douglas, FRCS, FRCSE, FMedSci; Bayer Professor of Neurosurgery, University of Cambridge, since 1991; Consultant Neurosurgeon, Addenbrooke's Hospital, Cambridge, since 1991; Chairman, Wolfson Brain Imaging Centre, since 1995; Professorial Fellow, St Catharine's College, Cambridge, since 1991; *b* 21 March 1946; *s* of late Reginald James Pickard and Eileen Muriel Pickard (*née* Alexander); *m* 1971, Charlotte Mary, *d* of late Robert Stuart Townshend and Maureen Charlotte Townshend (*née* Moran); one *s* two *d* (and one *s* decd). *Educ:* King George V Grammar Sch., Southport; St Catharine's Coll., Cambridge (BA 1st Class 1967; MA); King's Coll. Hosp. Med. Sch., London (MB BChir 1970; MChir 1981 (distinction)).

KCH, 1970–72; Inst. of Neurol Sci., Glasgow, 1972–73; Falkirk Hosp., 1973–74; Univ. of Pennsylvania Hosp., 1974–75; Registrar, Sen. Registrar, Lectr in Neurosurgery, Inst. of Neurol Sci., Glasgow, 1976–79; Consultant Neurosurgeon, Wessex Neurol Centre, Southampton, 1979–91; Sen. Lectr, 1979, Reader, 1984, Prof. of Clin. Neurol Scis, 1987–91, Univ. of Southampton. Mem. Council, Soc. of British Neurol Surgeons. Founder Trustee, British Brain and Spine Foundn. Founder FMedSci 1998. *Publications:* numerous articles in med. and sci. jls. *Recreation:* family life. *Address:* Academic Neurosurgical Unit, Addenbrooke's Hospital, Cambridge CB2 2QQ. *T:* (01223) 336946. *Club:* Athenæum.

PICKARD, Sir (John) Michael, Kt 1997; FCA; Chairman: National House-Building Council, since 1998; London Docklands Development Corporation, 1992–98 (Deputy Chairman, 1991–92); *b* 29 July 1932; *s* of John Stanley Pickard and Winifred Joan Pickard; *m* 1959, Penelope Jane (*née* Catterall); three *s* one *d*. *Educ:* Oundle School. Finance Dir, British Printing Corp., 1965–68; Man. Dir, Trust Houses Ltd/Trusthouse Forte Ltd, 1968–71; Founder Chm., Happy Eater Ltd, 1972–86; Dep. Chief Exec., 1986–88, Chief Exec., 1988–92, Sears plc; Chairman: Grattan plc, 1978–84; Courage Ltd and Imperial Brewing & Leisure Ltd, 1981–86; Dep. Chief Exec., Imperial Gp plc, 1985–86; Chm., Freemans, 1988–92. Director: Brown Shipley Hlgs, 1986–93; Electra Investment Trust plc, 1989–; Nationwide Building Soc., 1991–94; Pinnacle Leisure Gp Ltd (formerly Wates Leisure), 1992–99; Bentalls plc, 1993–; Racecourse Leisure Corp., 1993–96; United Racecourses (Holdings) Ltd, 1995–; Chairman: Bullough plc, 1996–; Servus (formerly Opus) Hldgs, 1997–; London First Centre, 1998–2001; The Housing Forum, 1999–; Freeport, 2001–. Chm. Council, Roedean Sch., 1980–91; Gov., Oundle Sch., 1988–2000. Member: Bd, BTA, 1968–71; Cttee, AA, 1994–99. Mem., Court of Assistants, Co. of Grocers, 1990– (Master, 1996). *Recreations:* cricket, golf. *Address:* 16 Grosvenor Hill Court, Bourdon Street, W1X 9HT. *Clubs:* Pilgrims, MCC; Walton Heath Golf; Headley Cricket.

PICKARD, Hon. Neil Edward William; Agent General for New South Wales, 1991–92; *b* 13 Feb. 1929; *s* of Edward Henry Pickard and Ruby (*née* McGilvray); *m* 1983, Sally Anne Egan. *Educ:* Sydney Univ. (BA, MEd, DipEd); Leigh Coll. (LTh). Mem., World Student Conf., Strasbourg, 1960. Minister, Methodist Ch., 1952–65; High Sch. teacher, 1966–69; Chm., Far W Ambulance Service, 1969–70; Sydney University: Lectr in Educn, 1970–73; Member: House Cttee, Wesley Coll.; Univ. Educn Res. Cttee. Alderman: Peak Hill Council, 1964–65; Dubbo CC, 1968–70. Liberal Party: Western Regl Chm., 1966–72; Mem., Central Exec., NSW, 1966–72; Chm., Educn and Agenda Cttees, 1966–72. New South Wales Parliament: MP (Lib) Hornsby, 1973–91; Chm., Parly Educn Cttee; Mem., Select Cttee on NSW Sch. Cert. Assessment Procedures, 1979–81; Minister for Educn, 1976; Shadow Minister for Educn, Develt, Mineral Resources and Energy, 1976–88; Minister for Minerals and Energy, 1988–91. Freeman, City of London, 1992. *Recreations:* music, international relations, travel, tennis, cricket, bowls, soccer. *Address:* 11 Woolcott Avenue, Wahroonga, NSW 2076, Australia. *Clubs:* Royal Automobile, East India; Australian (Sydney).

PICKARD, Tony; *see* Pickard, J. A.

PICKEN, Dr Laurence Ernest Rowland, FBA 1973; Fellow of Jesus College, Cambridge, 1944–76, now Emeritus (Hon. Fellow, 1989); *b* 1909. *Educ:* Oldknow Road and Waverley Road, Birmingham; Trinity Coll., Cambridge (Hon. Fellow, 1991). BA 1931; PhD 1935; ScD 1952. Asst Dir of Research (Zoology), Cambridge Univ., 1946–66; Asst Dir of Research (Oriental Music), Cambridge Univ., 1966–76. Editor: Musica Asiatica, 1977–84; Music from the Tang Court, 1981–. FIBiol. Hon. Fellow, SOAS, 1991. DUP *hc* 1988. Trail Award, Linnean Soc., 1960; Curt Sachs Award, Amer. Musical Instrument Soc., 1995. *Publications:* The Organization of Cells and Other Organisms, 1960; Folk Musical Instruments of Turkey, 1975; contribs to many learned jls. *Address:* Jesus College, Cambridge CB5 8BL.

PICKERING, Prof. Alan Durward, PhD, DSc; CBiol, FIBiol; Director, CEH Windermere (formerly Institute of Freshwater Ecology), 1995–2001 (acting Director, 1993–95); *b* 7 Sept. 1944; *s* of Frank Hadfield Pickering and Olive Pickering (*née* Page); *m* 1969, Christine Mary Pott; two *s* one *d*. *Educ:* Ecclesfield Grammar Sch.; Univ. of Nottingham (BSc 1st cl. Zoology 1966; PhD 1970; DSc 1986). CBiol, FIBiol 1995. Res. Physiologist, Freshwater Biological Assoc., 1969–89; Head, Windermere Lab., 1989–93. Associate Prof., Dept of Biology and Biochemistry, Brunel Univ., 1991–. *Publications:* (ed) Stress and Fish, 1981; numerous articles in scientific jls. *Recreations:* gardening, woodwork, golf, sailing, travel.

PICKERING, Prof. Brian Thomas; Deputy Vice-Chancellor, University of Bristol, 1992–2001; *b* 24 May 1936; *s* of Thomas Pickering and Dorothy May Pickering; *m* 1965, Joan Perry; two *d*. *Educ:* Haberdashers' Aske's Hatcham Boys' Sch.; Univ. of Bristol (BSc 1958; PhD 1961; DSc 1974). Research Biochemist, Hormone Res. Lab., Univ. of California, 1961–62; Scientific Staff, NIMR, MRC, 1963–65; University of Bristol: Lectr in Biochem. and Pharmacol., 1965–70 (Mem., MRC Gp for Res. in Neurosecretion); Lectr in Anatomy and Biochem., 1970–72; Reader in Anatomy and Biochem., 1972–78; Prof. of Anatomy and Head of Dept, 1978–92; Dean, Faculty of Medicine, 1985–87. Vis. Prof., Univ. of Geneva, 1977; Anatomical Soc. Review Lectr, 1984. Mem., Bristol & Weston HA, 1988–90; Non-exec. Dir, United Bristol Healthcare NHS Trust, 1990–98. Mem., Animal Grants Bd, AFRC, 1988–94 (Chm., 1991–94). Associate Editor, Jl of Endocrinology, 1972–77. European Society for Comparative Endocrinology: Sec. and Treasurer, 1971–77; Vice-Pres., 1986–90; Pres., 1990–94; Sec., British Neuroendocrine Gp, 1986–92; mem., other learned bodies. Hon. Fellow, Romanian Acad. of Med. Sci., 1991. Hon. MD Carol Davila, Bucharest, 1994; Hon. LLD Bristol, 2001. Medal, Soc. for Endocrinology, 1977. *Publications:* contribs to professional jls. *Address:* 51 Eastfield Road, Bristol BS9 4AE.

PICKERING, Sir Edward (Davies), Kt 1977; Executive Vice-Chairman, Times Newspapers Ltd, since 1982; Chairman, The Times Supplements Ltd, 1989–2000; *b* 4 May 1912; 3rd *s* of George and Louie Pickering; *m* 1st, 1936, Margaret Soutter (marr. diss., 1947); one *d*; 2nd, 1955, Rosemary Whitton; two *s* one *d*. *Educ:* Middlesbrough High Sch. Chief Sub-Editor Daily Mail, 1939. Served Royal Artillery 1940–44; Staff of Supreme Headquarters Allied Expeditionary Force, 1944–45. Managing Editor: Daily Mail, 1947–49; Daily Express, 1951–57; Editor, Daily Express, 1957–62; Dir, Beaverbrook Newspapers, 1956–64; Editorial Dir, The Daily Mirror Newspapers Ltd, 1964–68, Chm., 1968–70; Director: Scottish Daily Record and Sunday Mail Ltd, 1966–69; IPC, 1966–75; Chairman: International Publishing Corporation Newspaper Div., 1968–70; IPC Magazines, 1970–74; Mirror Group Newspapers, 1975–77; Director: Times Newspapers Holdings Ltd, 1981–; William Collins Sons & Co. Ltd, 1981–89; Harper Collins Publishers Ltd, 1989–. Member: Press Council, 1964–69, 1970–82 (Vice-Chm., 1976–82); Press Complaints Commn, 1991–94 (Consultant, 1994–). Treasurer, Fédération Internationale de la Presse Periodique, 1971–75; Chm. Council, Commonwealth Press Union, 1977–86. Chm., William Tyndale Quincentenary Appeal, 1991–94; Patron, William Tyndale Soc., 1999–. Hon. Freeman, Stationers' and Newspaper Makers' Co., 1985. Master, Guild of St Bride, 1981–97. Astor Award for distinguished service to Commonwealth Press, 1986. Hon. DLitt City, 1986. *Club:* Garrick.

PICKERING, Errol Neil, PhD; Director General, International Hospital Federation, 1987–98; *b* 5 May 1938; *s* of Russell Gordon and Sylvia Mary Pickering. *Educ:* York Univ., Canada (BA Hons); Univ. of Toronto (DipHA); Univ. of New South Wales (PhD). Asst Administrator, St Michael's Hosp., Toronto, 1971–73; Executive Director: Aust. Council on Hosp. Standards, 1973–80; Aust. Hosp. Assoc., 1980–87. Dir, Health Care Risk Solutions Ltd, 1994–98. Pres., UNICEF Australia, 1984–86. Chm., Internat. Assoc. Forum, 1990–92. Bd Mem., European Soc. of Assoc. Execs, 1995–98. *Publications:* many articles on hosp. and health policy issues. *Recreations:* classical music, bridge. *Address:* 13 Firestone Court, Robina Woods, Qld 4226, Australia. *Club:* University (Sydney).

PICKERING, Ven. Fred; Archdeacon of Hampstead, 1974–84; Archdeacon Emeritus since 1984; *b* 18 Nov. 1919; *s* of Arthur and Elizabeth Pickering; *m* 1948, Mabel Constance Threlfall; one *s* one *d*. *Educ:* Preston Grammar Sch.; St Peter's Coll., Oxford; St Aidan's Theol Coll., Birkenhead. BA 1941 (PPE), MA 1945. Curate: St Andrew's, Leyland, 1943–46; St Mary's, Islington, 1946–48; Organising Sec. for Church Pastoral Aid Soc. in NE England, 1948–51; Vicar: All Saints, Burton-on-Trent, 1951–56; St John's, Carlisle, 1956–63; St Cuthbert's, Wood Green, 1963–74; Rural Dean of East Haringey, 1968–73; Exam. Chaplain to Bp of Edmonton, 1973–84. *Address:* 16 The Close, Easton on the Hill, Stamford, Lincs PE9 3NA. *T:* (01780) 481318.

PICKERING, Janet Dolton; Headmistress, Withington Girls' School, since 2000; *b* 21 June 1949; *d* of George Browning and Marjorie Dolton Haywood; *m* 1971, William Ronald Pickering; two *s*. *Educ:* Bridlington High Sch.; Malton Grammar Sch.; Univ. of Sheffield (BSc 1st Cl. Biochem.). SRC res. student, Univ. of Sheffield, 1970–73; Scientific Officer, Hallamshire Hosp. Med. Sch., 1973–75; Teaching Fellow, Univ. of Leeds, 1975–79; freelance proof-reader, editor, indexer (sch. sci. texts and scientific jls), 1980–88; part-time teacher and tutor, Gordonstoun Sch., 1983–85; King's School, Canterbury, 1986–97: teacher, tutor, housemistress, 1990–94; Dep. Hd, 1994–97; Hd, St Bee's Sch., Cumbria, 1998–2000. HMC/ISI Inspector, 1994–. Chm., Sen. Mistresses Gp, HMC, 1995–96. Governor: Copthorne Prep. Sch., 1995–97; Windlesham House Sch., 1996–98. *Publications:* (jtly) Nucleic Acid Biochemistry, 1982; (contrib.) Children's Britannica, 4th edn 1988; contrib. articles to Jl Gen. Micro., Inserm, Hum. Hered. *Recreations:* reading, theatre, cinema, natural history, travel, being walked by the dog. *Address:* 119 Dane Road, Sale, Cheshire M33 2BY. *T:* (0161) 962 0764. *Club:* University Women's.

PICKERING, Prof. John Frederick; business management and economic consultant; Professor of Business Strategy, Bath University, 1997–2000; *b* 26 Dec. 1939; *er s* of William Frederick and Jean Mary Pickering; *m* 1967, Jane Rosamund Day; two *d*. *Educ:* Slough Grammar Sch.; University Coll. London (BSc Econ; PhD; DSc Econ); MSc Manchester. In indust. market res., 1961–62; Lectr, Univ. of Durham, 1964–66, Univ. of Sussex, 1966–73; Sen. Directing Staff, Admin. Staff Coll., Henley, 1974–75; UMIST: Prof. of Industrial Economics, 1975–88; Vice-Principal, 1983–85; Dep. Principal, 1984–85; Dean, 1985–87; Vice-Pres. (Business and Finance), 1988–90, actg Pres., 1990–91, Dep. Pres., 1991–92, Portsmouth Poly.; Dep. Vice Chancellor, Portsmouth Univ., 1992–94. Vis. Prof., Durham Univ. Business Sch., 1995–98. Mem., UGC Business and Management Studies sub-cttee, 1985–88. Dir, Staniland Hall Ltd, 1988–94; Dir and Chm., Univ. of Portsmouth (formerly Portsmouth Polytechnic) Enterprise Ltd, 1989–94. Consultant, NIESR, 1994–97. Mem., Gen. Synod of Church of England, 1980–90; Church Comr for England, 1983–90; Mem., Archbishop's Commn on Urban Priority Areas, 1983–85; Pres., BCMS-Crosslink (formerly BCMS), 1986–92. Member: Council of Management, Consumers' Assoc., 1969–73, 1980–83; Retail Prices Index Adv. Cttee, 1974–95; Monopolies and Mergers Commn, 1990–99; Appeals Panel, Competition Commn, 2000–. *Publications:* Resale Price Maintenance in Practice, 1966; (jtly) The Small Firm in the Hotel and Catering Industry, 1971; Industrial Structure and Market Conduct, 1974; The Acquisition of Consumer Durables, 1977; (jtly) The Economic Management of the Firm, 1984; papers and articles in learned jls in economics and management. *Recreations:* music, cricket, theatre. *Address:* 1 The Fairway, Rowlands Castle, Hants PO9 6AQ. *T:* (023) 9241 2007, *Fax:* (023) 9241 3385. *Club:* Royal Commonwealth Society.

PICKERING, His Honour Richard Edward Ingram; a Circuit Judge, 1981–98; *b* 16 Aug. 1929; *s* of late Richard and Dorothy Pickering; *m* 1962, Jean Margaret Eley; two *s*. *Educ:* Birkenhead Sch.; Magdalene Coll., Cambridge (MA), Called to the Bar, Lincoln's Inn, 1953; has practised on Northern Circuit, 1955–81; a Recorder of the Crown Court, 1977–81. Admitted as advocate in Manx Courts (Summerland Fire Inquiry), 1973–74. Councillor, Hoylake UDC, 1961–64; Legal Chm., Min. of Pensions and Nat. Insurance Tribunal, Liverpool, 1967–77; pt-time Chm., Liverpool Industrial Tribunal, 1977–79; Nominated Judge, NW Reg. (formerly Judicial Mem., Merseyside), Mental Health Rev. Tribunal, 1984–2001 (Legal Mem., 1967–79; Regional Chm., 1979–81); Northern Circuit Rep., Cttee, Council of Circuit Judges, 1984–89. *Recreations:* walking, gardening, study of military history. *Address:* Trelyon, Croft Drive, Caldy, Wirral CH48 2JN. *Clubs:* Oxford and Cambridge; Athenæum (Liverpool); Union (Cambridge).

PICKERING, Thomas Reeve; Senior Vice President, International Affairs, The Boeing Company, since 2001; *b* Orange, NJ, 5 Nov. 1931; *s* of Hamilton R. Pickering and Sarah C. (*née* Chasteney); *m* 1955, Alice J. Stover; one *s* one *d*. *Educ:* Bowdoin Coll. (AB); Fletcher Sch. of Law and Diplomacy (MA); Univ. of Melbourne (MA). Served to Lt-Comdr, USNR, 1956–59. Joined US For. Service, 1959; For. Affairs Officer, Arms Control and Disarmament Agency, 1961; Political Advr, US Delegn to 18 Nation Disarmament Conf., Geneva, 1962–64; Consul, Zanzibar, 1965–67; Counselor, Dep. Chief of Mission, Amer. Embassy, Dar-es-Salaam, 1967–69; Dep. Dir Bureau, Politico-Mil. Affairs, State Dept, 1969–73; Special Asst to Sec. of State and Exec. Sec., Dept of State, 1973–74; Amb. to Jordan, 1974–78; Asst Sec. for Bureau of Oceans, Internat. Environmental and Sci. Affairs, Washington, 1978–81; Ambassador: to Nigeria, 1981–83; to El Salvador, 1983–85; to Israel, 1986–88; Ambassador and US Perm. Rep. to UN, 1989–92; Ambassador: to India, 1992–93; to Russia, 1993–96; Under Sec. for Political Affairs, US Dept of State, 1997–2000. Mem. Council, For. Relns, IISS, 1973–. Phi Beta Kappa. Hon. LLD: Bowdoin Coll., 1984; Atlantic Union Coll., 1990; Tufts Univ., 1990; Hebrew Union Coll., 1991; Willamette Univ., 1991; Drew Univ., 1991; Franklin Pierce Coll., 1991; Hofstra, 1992; Lafayette Coll., 1992. *Address:* The Boeing Company, 1200 Wilson Boulevard, Arlington, VA 22209, USA. *Club:* Cosmos (Washington).

PICKETT, Prof. George Richard, DPhil; FRS 1997; Professor of Low Temperature Physics, University of Lancaster, since 1988. *Educ:* Magdalen Coll., Oxford (BA 1962; DPhil). Lectr, then Sen. Lectr, later Reader, Dept of Physics, Univ. of Lancaster. *Address:* Department of Physics, University of Lancaster, LA1 4YB; Thornber, Bentham, Lancaster LA2 7AQ. *T:* (01524) 261288.

PICKETT, Prof. John Anthony, PhD, DSc; FRS 1996; Head of Biological Chemistry Division (formerly Department of Insecticides and Fungicides, then Biological and

Ecological Chemistry Department), IACR-Rothamsted, since 1984; *b* 21 April 1945; *s* of Samuel Victor Pickett and Lilian Frances Pickett (*née* Hoar); *m* 1970, Ulla Birgitta Skålèn; one *s* one *d*. *Educ:* King Edward VII Grammar Sch., Coalville; Univ. of Surrey (BSc Hons Chem 1967; PhD Organic Chem 1971); DSc Nottingham 1993. CChem 1975. Postdoctoral Fellow, UMIST, 1970–72; Chem. Dept, Brewing Res. Foundn (flavour active components of hops and malt), 1972–76; Dept of Insecticides and Fungicides, Rothamsted Exptl Stn (semiochem. aspects of insect chem. ecology), 1976–83. Lectures: Boyce Thompson Inst. for Plant Res, Cornell Univ., 1991; Alfred M. Boyce, Univ. of California, Riverside, 1993; Woolhouse, Soc. for Experimental Biology, York Univ., 1998. Mem. Council, Royal Soc., 2000–Nov. 2002. Rank Prize for Nutrition and Crop Husbandry, 1995; Silver Medal, Internat. Soc. of Chem. Ecology, 2002. *Publications:* numerous papers and patents. *Recreation:* jazz trumpet playing. *Address:* Biological Chemistry Division, IACR-Rothamsted, Harpenden, Herts AL5 2JQ. *T:* (01582) 763133.

PICKETT, Philip; Director, New London Consort, since 1978. *Educ:* Guildhall Sch. of Music and Drama (Maisie Lewis Foundn Award; Wedgewood Award; FGSM 1985). Prof. of Recorder and Historical Performance Practice, GSMD, 1972–97. Began career as trumpet player; subseq. took up recorder, crumhorn, shawm, rackett, etc; as soloist, has performed with many leading ensembles, incl. Acad. of St Martin-in-the-Fields, London Chamber Orch., Polish Chamber Orch., English Chamber Orch., London Mozart Players; with New London Consort, performs a wide repertoire of medieval, Renaissance and Baroque music; resident early music ensemble, S Bank Centre; nat. and internat. concerts and recitals, incl. BBC Proms, and regular performances at art fests. Dir of Early Music, Globe Theatre, 1993–; Artistic Director: Purcell Room Early Music Series, 1993–; Aldeburgh Early Music Fest., 1994–97 (also Founder); Early Music Fest., S Bank Centre, 1996–. Appearances on radio and television; film soundtracks. Solo recordings incl. Handel recorder concertos and trio concertos, and Vivaldi and Telemann concertos. *Publications:* articles in books and jls. *Address:* New London Consort, 12 Vathouse, Regents Bridge Gardens, SW8 1HD.

PICKETT-HEAPS, Prof. Jeremy David, PhD; FRS 1995; FAA; Professor, School of Botany, University of Melbourne, since 1988; *b* 5 June 1940; *s* of Harold Arthur Pickett-Heaps and Edna Azura (*née* May); *m* 1st, 1965, Daphne Charmian Scott (*d* 1970); one *s* one *d*; 2nd, 1977, Julianne Francis Jack; two *s*. *Educ:* Clare Coll., Cambridge (BA; PhD 1965). Fellow, Research Sch. of Biol Sci., ANU, 1965–70; Prof., Dept of Molecular, Cellular and Developmental Biol., Univ. of Colorado, 1970–88. FAA 1992. *Publications:* Green Algae, 1972; numerous scientific res. papers. *Recreations:* various. *Address:* 47 St Leonards Road, Ascot Vale, Vic 3032, Australia. *T:* (3) 93444519.

PICKFORD, David Michael, FRICS; Chairman, Committee of Management: Lionbrook (formerly Lilliput) Property Unit Trust, since 1984; Gulliver Developments Property Unit Trust, since 1987; *b* 25 Aug. 1926; *s* of Aston Charles Corpe Pickford and Gladys Ethel Pickford; *m* 1956, Elizabeth Gwendoline Hooson; one *s* two *d*. *Educ:* Emanuel Sch., London; Coll. of Estate Management. FRICS 1953. Hillier Parker May & Rowden, 1943–46; LCC, 1946–48; London Investment & Mortgage Co., 1948–57; Haslemere Estates plc, 1957–86: Man. Dir, 1968–83; Chm., 1983–86; Dir, City & Metropolitan Building Soc., 1986–90; Chairman: Exeter Park Estates, 1986–91; Luis Palau Europe Ltd, 1980–; Dabet Ltd, 1986–; Compco Hldgs PLC, 1987–; Louth Estates (No 2) Ltd, 1989–2000; [illegible] Properties Ltd, 1990–2000; Stonechange Ltd, 1990–97; Wigmore Property Investment Trust Plc, 1993–96; Chm., Cttee of Mgt, Swift Balanced Property Unit Trust, 1993–97. President: London Dist, The Boys' Bde, 1967–86 (Hon. Life Pres., 1986); Christians in Property, 1990– (Chm., 1978–90); Chm., Drug and Alcohol Foundn, 1987–90 (Vice-Pres., 1990–92); Director: Mission to London, 1980–2000; London and Nationwide Missions, 1982–; Billy Graham Evangelistic Assoc., 1986–; CARE Campaigns Ltd (also Trustee), 1987–; Youth with a Mission, 1986–95; Trustee: David Pickford Charitable Foundn, 1968–; Pickford Trust, 1972–; Prison Fellowship, 1989–2001 (Chm. Trustees, 1990–93); London Prison Creative and Counselling Trust, 1991–93; Genesis Arts Trust, 1994–96. *Recreations:* sheep farming, youth work, gardening. *Address:* 33 Grosvenor Square, Mayfair, W1X 9LL. *T:* (020) 7493 1156; Elm Tree Farm, Mersham, near Ashford, Kent TN25 7HS. *T:* (01233) 720200, *Fax:* (01233) 720522.

PICKFORD, Prof. (Lillian) Mary, DSc; FRS 1966; Professor, Department of Physiology, University of Edinburgh, 1966–72 (Reader in Physiology, 1952–66); retired 1972, now Emeritus Professor; *b* 14 Aug. 1902; *d* of Herbert Arthur Pickford and Lillian Alice Minnie Wintle. *Educ:* Wycombe Abbey Sch.; Bedford and University Colls, Univ. of London. BSc (1st cl., Gen.) 1924; BSc (2nd cl., Physiology Special) 1925; MSc (Physiology) 1926; MRCS, LRCP 1933; DSc London 1951. FRSE 1954; FRCPE 1977. House Physician and Casualty Officer, Stafford Gen. Infirmary, 1935; Jun. Beit Memorial Research Fellow, 1936–39; Lectr, Dept of Physiology, Univ. of Edinburgh, 1939; Personal Chair, Dept of Physiology, Univ. of Edinburgh, 1966. Special Prof. of Endocrinology, Nottingham Univ., 1973–83. Fellow, University Coll., London, 1968–. Hon. DSc Heriot-Watt, 1991. *Publications:* The Central Role of Hormones, 1969; papers in Jl Physiology, British Jl Pharmacology, Jl Endocrinology. *Recreations:* walking, travel, painting. *Address:* Winton House, Nether Wallop, Stockbridge, Hants SO20 8HE.

PICKFORD, Prof. Mary; *see* Pickford, Prof. L. M.

PICKFORD, Michael Alan, CB 1994; FIA; Directing Actuary, Supervision of Insurance Companies and Friendly Societies, Government Actuary's Department, 1989–95; *b* 22 Aug. 1937. *Educ:* City of Oxford Sch. Govt Actuary's Dept, 1958–95.

PICKFORD, Stephen John; Director, International Finance, HM Treasury, since 2001; *b* 26 Aug. 1950; *s* of Frank and May Pickford; *m* 1978, Carolyn M. Ruffle; two *s*. *Educ:* St John's Coll., Cambridge (BA Hons 1971; MA 1974); Univ. of British Columbia (MA 1984). Economist, Dept of Employment, 1971–79; HM Treasury: Economist, 1979–85; Dep. Press Sec., 1985–87; Sen. Economic Advr, 1987–89, 1993–98; Manager, Macroeconomics, New Zealand Treasury, 1989–93; UK Exec. Dir, IMF and World Bank, 1998–2001; Minister (Econ.), British Embassy, Washington, 1998–2001. *Publication:* (contrib.) Government Economic Statistics, 1989. *Recreations:* running, ski-ing. *Address:* HM Treasury, Parliament Street, SW1P 3AG.

PICKING, Anne; MP (Lab) East Lothian, since 2001; *b* 30 March 1958; *m* 1984, David Adair Harold Picking; one *s*. *Educ:* Woodmill High Comprehensive Sch. Nurse: Fife Health Bd, 1975–80; NI Eastern Health and Social Service, 1980–83 (staff nurse, 1982–83); staff nurse, then nursing sister, E Kent Community Health Care NHS Trust, 1984–2001. Mem., NEC, COHSE, 1990; Mem., NEC, 1993–2001, Nat. Pres., 1999–2000, UNISON. Mem. (Lab), Ashford BC, 1994–98. *Address:* (office) 65 High Street, Tranent, East Lothian EH33 1LN; c/o House of Commons, SW1A 0AA.

PICKLES, Eric Jack; MP (C) Brentwood and Ongar, since 1992; *b* 20 April 1952; *m* 1976, Irene. *Educ:* Greenhead Grammar Sch.; Leeds Polytechnic. Joined Conservative Party, 1968; Young Conservatives: Area Chm., 1976–78; Nat. Vice-Chm., 1978–80; Nat. Chm., 1980–81; Conservative Party: Member: Nat. Union Exec. Cttee, 1975–91; One Nation Forum, 1987–91; Nat. Local Govt Adv. Cttee, 1985– (Chm., 1992–93); Lectr, Cons. Agents Examination Courses, 1988–; Local Govt Editor, Newsline, 1990–92; a Vice-Chm., 1993–97. Bradford Council: Councillor, 1979–91; Chm., Social Services, 1982–84; Chm., Educn, 1984–86; Leader, Cons. Gp, 1987–91; Leader of Council, 1988–90. Dep. Leader, Cons. Gp, AMA, 1989–91. PPS to Minister for Industry, 1993; Opposition frontbench spokesman on social security, 1998–2001; Shadow Transport Minister, 2001–. Chm., All Party Film Gp, 1997–; Vice-Chm., Cons. Envmt, Transport and Regions Cttee, 1997–98. Mem., Council of Europe, 1997–. Mem., Yorks Area RHA, 1982–90. *Recreations:* film buff, opera, serious walking. *Address:* House of Commons, SW1A 0AA.

PICKLES, His Honour James; a Circuit Judge, 1976–91; *b* 18 March 1925. Practised at Bradford, 1949–76; a Recorder of the Crown Court, 1972–76. *Publications:* Straight from the Bench, 1987; Judge for Yourself, 1992; Off the Record (novel), 1993. *Address:* Hazelwood, Heath Road, Halifax, West Yorks HX3 0BA.

PICKTHALL, Colin; MP (Lab) Lancashire West, since 1992; *b* 13 Sept. 1944; *s* of Frank Pickthall and Edith (*née* Bonser), Dalton-in-Furness; *m* 1973, Judith Ann Tranter; two *d*. *Educ:* Univ. of Wales (BA); Univ. of Lancaster (MA). Teacher, Ruffwood Comprehensive Sch., Kirkby, 1967–70; Edge Hill College of Higher Education: Sen. Lectr in English Lit., 1970–83; Head, European Studies, 1983–92. County Councillor, Ormskirk, Lancs CC, 1989–93. Contested (Lab) Lancashire West, 1987. *Recreations:* fell-walking, gardening, cricket, theatre. *Address:* 127 Burscough Street, Ormskirk, Lancs L39 2EP. *T:* (office) (01695) 570094.

PICKTHORN, Sir James (Francis Mann), 3rd Bt *cr* 1959, of Orford, Suffolk; Partner, Pickthorn, estate agents and chartered surveyors, since 1994; *b* 18 Feb. 1955; *o s* of Sir Charles William Richards Pickthorn, 2nd Bt and of Helen Antonia, *o d* of Sir James Gow Mann, KCVO; *S* father, 1995; *m* 1998, Clare, *yr d* of Brian Craig-McFeely; two *s*. *Educ:* Eton; Reading Univ. (BSc Estate Management). With Healey & Baker, 1977–82; Debenham Tewson & Chinnocks, 1982–86; Kinney & Green, 1986–94 (Partner, 1991–94); founded Pickthorn, 1994. TA (HAC), 1978–. *Recreation:* sailing. *Heir: s* William Edward Craig Pickthorn, *b* 2 Dec. 1998. *Address:* 45 Ringmer Avenue, SW6 5LP; (office) Pickthorn, 24 Lime Street, EC3M 7HS. *T:* (020) 7621 1380.

PICKUP, David Cunliffe; Chief Executive, Sports Council Trust Company, 1993–94; Director General, Sports Council, 1988–93; *b* 17 Sept. 1936; *s* of Robert and Florence Pickup; *m* 1960, Patricia Moira Aileen (*née* Neill); three *s*. *Educ:* Bacup and Rawtenstall Grammar Sch. Min. of Education, 1955–63; MPBW, 1964–71 (incl. periods as Pvte Sec. to four Ministers); Department of the Environment: Prin. Pvte Sec. to Minister for Housing and Construction, 1971–72; Asst Sec., 1972; Housing, 1972–75; Personnel, 1975–77; Under Sec., 1977; Regl Dir, Northern Reg., 1977–80; Housing, 1980–84; Local Govt, 1984–85; Dep. Sec., Assoc. of Dist Councils, 1986–88. FRSA 1992. *Publication:* Not Another Messiah, 1996. *Recreations:* reading, music, sport, walking. *Address:* 15 Sandford Road, Bromley, Kent BR2 9AL. *T:* (020) 8402 2354.

PICKUP, David Francis William; Solicitor (Grade 2), HM Customs and Excise, since 1995; *b* 20 May 1955; *s* of Joseph and Muriel Pickup; *m* 1975, Anne Elizabeth Round. *Educ:* Poole Grammar Sch.; Polytechnic of Central London (Univ. of London External LLB Hons). Called to the Bar, Lincoln's Inn, 1976, Gibraltar, 1988. Joined Treasury Solicitor's Dept as Legal Asst, 1978, Sen. Legal Asst, 1981; Grade 5 1987; Estabt Finance and Security Officer, 1988–90; Grade 3, Chancery Litigation Div., 1990; Legal Advr, MoD, 1991–95. *Recreations:* playing and watching cricket, ski-ing, listening to music, food and wine, travel. *Address:* (office) New King's Beam House, 22 Upper Ground, SE1 9PJ. *T:* (020) 7865 5121, *Fax:* (020) 7865 4820; *e-mail:* david.pickup@hmce.gsi.gov.uk. *Clubs:* Pyrford Cricket; Leominster Golf.

PICKUP, Ronald Alfred; actor; *b* 7 June 1940; *s* of Eric and Daisy Pickup; *m* 1964, Lans Traverse, USA; one *s* one *d*. *Educ:* King's Sch., Chester; Leeds Univ. (BA); Royal Academy of Dramatic Art. Repertory, Leicester, 1964; Royal Court, 1964 and 1965–66; National Theatre, 1965, 1966–73, 1977: appearances include: Rosalind, in all-male As You Like It, 1967; Richard II, 1972; Edmund, in Long Day's Journey into Night, 1971; Cassius, in Julius Caesar, 1977; Philip Madras, in The Madras House, 1977; Norman, in Norman Conquests, Globe, 1974; Play, Royal Court, 1976; Hobson's Choice, Lyric, Hammersmith, 1981; Astrov, in Uncle Vanya, Haymarket, 1982; Allmers in Little Eyolf, Lyric, Hammersmith, 1985; Gayev, in The Cherry Orchard, Aldwych, 1989; Amy's View, RNT, 1997, NY, 1999; Peer Gynt, Romeo and Juliet, RNT, 2000; *films:* Three Sisters, 1969; Day of the Jackal, 1972; Joseph Andrews, 1976; 39 Steps, Zulu Dawn, 1978; Nijinsky, 1979; Never Say Never Again, John Paul II, 1983; Eleni, Camille (remake), 1984; The Mission, 1985; The Fourth Protocol, 1986; Bring Me the Head of Mavis Davis, 1996; Breathtaking, 1999; *television:* series and serials: Dragon's Opponent, 1973; Jennie, Fight Against Slavery, 1974; Tropic, 1979; Life of Giuseppe Verdi, 1982; Wagner, 1982; Life of Einstein, 1983; Moving, 1984; The Fortunes of War, 1987; Behaving Badly, 1988; A Time to Dance, 1992; My Friend Walter, 1992; The Riff Raff Element, 1993, 1994; Ivanhoe, 1996; Hornblower, 1998; Dalziel and Pascoe, 1999; other: The Philanthropist, Ghost Trio, The Discretion of Dominic Ayres, 1977; Memories, Henry VIII, 1978; England's Green and Pleasant Land, Christ Hero, 1979; The Letter, Ivanhoe, 1981; Orwell on Jura, 1983; The Rivals, 1986; The Attic, Chekov in Yalta, 1988; A Murder of Quality, 1990; Absolute Hell, 1991; The War that Never Ends, 1991; The Golden Years, 1992; In the Cold Light of Day, 1994; Milner, 1994; A Case of Coincidence, 1994; A Very Open Prison, 1995; The Dying Day, Henry IV (title rôle), 1995. *Recreations:* listening to music, walking, reading.

PICTET, François-Charles; Ambassador of Switzerland to Austria, 1990–94, and Ambassador on Special Mission to the Holy See, 1993–97; *b* Geneva, 21 July 1929; *e s* of Charles Pictet, Geneva, and Elisabeth (*née* Decazes), France; *m* 1st, 1954, Elisabeth Choisy (*d* 1980), Geneva; three *s*; 2nd, 1983, Countess Marie-Thérèse Althann, Austria. *Educ:* College Calvin, Geneva; Univ. of Geneva (Faculty of Law). Called to the Swiss Bar, 1954. Joined Swiss Federal Dept of Foreign Affairs, 1956; Attaché, Vienna, 1957; Sec., Moscow, 1958–60; 1st Sec., Ankara, 1961–66; Dep. Dir, Internat. Orgns, Dept of For. Affairs, Berne, 1966–75; Minister Plenipotentiary, 1975; Ambassador to Canada and (non resident) to the Bahamas, 1975–79; Ambassador, Perm. Rep. to Internat. Orgns in Geneva, 1980–84; Ambassador to UK, 1984–89, to the Netherlands, 1989–90; Hd of Swiss Delgn to CSCE, Vienna, 1991–93. *Address:* 6 rue Robert-de-Traz, 1206 Geneva, Switzerland. *T:* (22) 7890086.

PIDDINGTON, Philip Michael, CBE 1988; HM Diplomatic Service, retired; Counsellor, Foreign and Commonwealth Office, 1987–90; *b* 27 March 1931; *s* of Percy Howard Piddington and Florence Emma (*née* Pearson); *m* 1955, Sylvia Mary Price; one *s* one *d*. *Educ:* Waverley Grammar Sch., Birmingham. Served HM Forces, 1949–51. Entered Min. of Works, 1947; FO, 1952; Jedda, 1956; Tokyo, 1962–66; First Sec., Lagos,

1969–71; Consul: NY, 1971–73; Istanbul, 1973–77; First Sec., FCO, 1978–83; Counsellor and Consul-Gen., Brussels, 1983–87. *Recreations:* riding, walking, photography. *Address:* The Pump House, St Mary's Road, East Claydon, Bucks MK18 2NA. *T:* (01296) 712302.

PIDGEON, Sir John (Allan Stewart), Kt 1989; Chairman, since 1980, and Managing Director, since 1960, F. A. Pidgeon & Son and associated companies; *b* 15 July 1926; *s* of Frederick Allan Pidgeon and Margaret Ellen Pidgeon, MBE; *m* 1st, 1952, Sylvia Dawn (*d* 1991); one *s* four *d*; 2nd, 1993, Mrs Pamela Barbara Howell. *Educ:* Church of England Grammar Sch., Brisbane. Fellow, Aust. Inst. of Building; FIDA. Served 2nd AIF, 1944–45. Joined F. A. Pidgeon & Son Pty, 1946. Director: Suncorp Building Soc., 1976–91; Folkestone Ltd, 1985–95. Chm., Builders' Registration Bd of Qld, 1985–93. Pres., Qld Master Builders' Assoc., 1970–72 (Trustee, 1978–). Chm., Salvation Army Adv. Bd., 1988–93. FAICD. *Recreations:* ski-ing, tennis, swimming. *Address:* 14 Otway Street, Holland Park, Brisbane, Qld 4121, Australia. *T:* (7) 38971137; Great Brampton House, Madley, Hereford HR2 9NA. *Clubs:* Brisbane, Queensland, Tattersalls, Polo, Brisbane Amateur Turf (Brisbane); Brisbane Yacht.

PIËCH, Ferdinand; Chairman, Board of Management, 1993–April 2002 (Member, 1992–April 2002), Chairman, Supervisory Board, from April 2002, Volkswagen AG; *b* Vienna, 17 April 1937; *s* of Dr jur Anton Piëch and Louise (*née* Porsche). *Educ:* in Switzerland; Tech. Univ. of Zurich. Mem., Management Bd i/c R and D, Audi NSU Auto Union AG/Audi AG, 1975–88; Chm., Bd of Management, Audi AG, 1988–92. Dr *hc* Vienna Technical Univ., 1984. *Address:* c/o Volkswagen AG, Brieffach 1880, 38436 Wolfsburg, Germany. *T:* (5361) 923596.

PIEŃKOWSKI, Jan Michał; author and illustrator, since 1958; Founder Director, Gallery Five Ltd, 1961; *b* 8 Aug. 1936; *s* of late Jerzy Dominik Pieńkowski and Wanda Maria Pieńkowska. *Educ:* Cardinal Vaughan Sch., London; King's Coll., Cambridge (MA Classics and English). Art Dir, J. Walter Thompson, William Collins, and Time and Tide, London, 1958–61. Work includes graphics and murals, posters and greeting cards, children's TV, and book illustration. *Stage designs:* Meg and Mog Show, 1981–88; Beauty and the Beast, Royal Opera House, 1986; Théâtre de Complicité, 1988; Sleeping Beauty, Euro Disney, 1992. Kate Greenaway Medal, Library Assoc., 1972 and 1979. *Publications:* illustrator: The Kingdom under the Sea, 1971; Meg and Mog series, 1973–90; Tale of a One Way Street, 1978; Past Eight O'Clock, 1986; A Foot in the Grave, 1989; M.O.L.E., 1993, etc; illustrator/author: Nursery series, 1973–91; Haunted House, 1979; Robot, 1981; Dinner Time, 1981; Christmas, 1984; Little Monsters, 1986; Small Talk, 1988; Easter, 1989; Fancy That, 1990; Phone Book, 1991; Door Bell, 1992; Road Hog, 1993; ABC Dinosaurs, 1993; Toilet Book, 1994; 1001 Words, 1994; Furrytails series, 1994; Nursery Cloth Books series, 1994; Botticelli's Bed and Breakfast, 1996; Nursery Pop-Up series, 1996–97; Tickle-me Books, 1997; Good Night, 1998; Bel and Bub and the Black Hole, 2000; Bel and Bub and the Big Brown Box, 2000; Bel and Bub and the Snow Angel, 2000; Bel and Bub and the Baby Bird, 2000; The Monster Pet, 2000; Pizza!, 2001; The Cat with Nine Lives, 2001; The Animals went in Two by Two, 2001. *Recreations:* movies, ski-ing, gardening, painting. *Address:* Oakgates, Barnes. *Clubs:* Chelsea Arts, Polish Hearth.

PIERCE, Rt Rev. Anthony Edward; *see* Swansea and Brecon, Bishop of.

PIERCY, family name of **Baron Piercy**.

PIERCY, 3rd Baron *cr* 1945, of Burford; **James William Piercy;** *b* 19 Jan. 1946; *s* of 2nd Baron Piercy and Oonagh Lavinia (*d* 1990), *d* of late Major Edward John Lake Baylay, DSO; *S* father, 1981. *Educ:* Shrewsbury; Edinburgh Univ. (BSc 1968). AMIEE; FCCA. *Heir: b* Hon. Mark Edward Pelham Piercy [*b* 30 June 1953; *m* 1979, Vivien Angela, *d* of His Honour Judge Evelyn Faithfull Monier-Williams, *qv*; one *s* three *d*]. *Address:* 36 Richford Street, W6 7HP.

PIERRE, Abbé; (Henri Antoine Grouès); Officier de la Légion d'Honneur, 1980; French priest; Founder of the Companions of Emmaüs; *b* Lyon, 5 Aug. 1912; 5th *c* of Antoine Grouès, Soyeux. *Educ:* Collège des Jésuites, Lyon. Entered Capuchin Monastery, 1930; studied at Capuchin seminary, Crest, Drôme, and Faculté de Théologie, Lyon. Secular priest, St Joseph Basilica, Grenoble. Served war of 1939–45 (Officier de la Légion d'Honneur, Croix de Guerre, Médaille de la Résistance); Alsatian and Alpine fronts; Vicar of the Cathedral, Grenoble; assumed name of Abbé Pierre and joined resistance movement, 1942; Chaplain of French Navy at Casablanca, 1944; of whole Free French Navy, 1945. Elected (Indep.) to 1st Constituent Assembly of 4th French Republic, 1945; elected as candidate of Mouvement Républicain Populaire to 2nd Constituent Assembly; re-elected 1946; contested (Indep.), 1951. Président de l'Exécutif du Mouvement Universel pour une Confédération Mondiale, 1949. Founded the Companions of Emmaüs, a movement to provide a roof for the "sanslogis" of Paris, 1949. *Publications* include: 23 Mois de Vie Clandestine; L'Abbé Pierre vous Parle; Vers l'Homme; Feuilles Eparses; Emmaüs ou Venger l'homme; Dieu merci; Dieu et les hommes; Testament...; Fraternité; Mémoire d'un croyant. *Address:* 183 bis rue Vaillant Couturier BP91, 94143 Alfortville Cedex, Val de Marne, France. *T:* (1) 48932950.

PIERS, Rear-Adm. Desmond William, DSC 1943; CM 1982; CD; RCN, retd; Agent General of Nova Scotia in the United Kingdom and Europe, 1977–79; *b* 12 June 1913; *s* of William Harrington Piers and Florence Maud Piers (*née* O'Donnell), MD; *m* 1941, Janet, *d* of Dr and Mrs Murray Macneill, Halifax, NS; one step *d*. *Educ:* Halifax County Acad.; RMC of Canada; RN Staff Coll.; Nat. Defence Coll. of Canada. Joined RCN as cadet, 1932; CO, HMC Destroyer Restigouche, and Sen. Officer, Fourth Canadian Escort Gp on N Atlantic convoy routes, 1941–43 (DSC); CO, HMC Destroyer Algonquin with Brit. Home Fleet, Scapa Flow, and participated in invasion of Normandy and convoys to N Russia, 1944–45, Comdr 1945; Exec. Officer, HMC Aircraft Carrier Magnificent (Comdr), 1947–48; Dir, Naval Plans and Ops, Naval Headquarters, Ottawa (Captain), 1949–50; Asst COS (Personnel and Admin.) to SACLANT, 1952–53; CO, HMC Cruiser Quebec, 1955–56; Sen. Canadian Offr Afloat (Atlantic), 1956–57; Comdt, RMC Canada, and Hon. ADC to the Governor General (Cdre), 1957–60; Asst Chief of Naval Staff (Plans), Naval HQ, 1960–62; Chm., Can. Def. Liaison Staff, Washington DC, and Can. Rep. on NATO Mil. Cttee (Rear-Adm.), 1962–66; retd 1967. Chm., NS Div. Can. Corps of Commissionaires, 1988–91. Hon. Life Mem., Nat. Trust for Scotland, 1984. Hon. DScMil, RMC of Canada, 1978. Freeman of City of London, 1978; KCLJ 1989. *Recreations:* golf, tennis, figure skating, photography. *Address:* The Quarter Deck, Chester, NS B0J 1J0, Canada. *T:* (902) 2754462. *Clubs:* Halifax (Halifax); Halifax Golf and Country, Chester Golf, Chester Tennis, Chester Curling (Nova Scotia).

PIERS, Sir James (Desmond), 11th Bt *cr* 1661, of Tristernagh Abbey, Westmeath; Partner, Russell & DuMoulin, lawyers, since 1982; *b* 24 July 1947; *s* of Sir Charles Robert Fitzmaurice Piers, 10th Bt and Ann Blanche Scott (*d* 1975); *S* father, 1996; *m* 1975, Sandra Mae Dixon; one *s* one *d*. *Educ:* Univ. of Victoria (BA 1969); Univ. of British Columbia (LLB 1973). Called to the Bar, British Columbia, 1974, Yukon Territory, 1975. *Heir: s* Stephen James Piers, *b* 14 Sept. 1979. *Address:* Russell & DuMoulin, 2100–1075 West Georgia Street, Vancouver, BC V6E 3G2, Canada.

PIETRONI, Prof. Patrick Claude, FRCP, FRCGP; Director, Educational Support Unit, London Region, NHS Executive; *b* 8 Nov. 1942; *s* of Michael and Jeannette Pietroni; *m* 1st, 1963, Theresa Wilkinson (marr. diss.); two *s* one *d*; 2nd, 1977, Marilyn Miller. *Educ:* Guy's Hosp. Med. Sch. (MB BS 1966). MRCP 1973, FRCP 2000; FRCGP 1985; MFPHM 2000. MO, RAMC, 1967–69; Principal, Gen. Practice, 1971–; Associate Prof., Family Medicine, Univ. of Cincinatti, 1978–80; Sen. Lectr in Gen. Practice, St Mary's Hosp. Med. Sch., 1981–93; Prof. and Dir, Centre for Community Care and Primary Health, 1993–97, Prof. Emeritus, 1998, Univ. of Westminster; Dean, Postgrad. Gen. Practice, N Thames (West) Dept of Postgrad. Med. and Dental Educn, London Univ., 1996. *Publications:* Holistic Living, 1986; The Greening of Medicine, 1990; Innovation in Community Care and Primary Health, 1995. *Recreations:* tennis, riding, bridge, opera. *Address:* 57 Fitzroy Road, NW1 8TP. *T:* (020) 7586 4430. *Clubs:* Savile; Globe Tennis.

PIGGOTT, Donald James; Director-General, British Red Cross Society, 1980–85; *b* 1 Sept. 1920; *s* of late James Piggott and Edith Piggott (*née* Tempest); *m* 1974, Kathryn Courtenay-Evans, *e d* of late William and Gwendoline Eckford. *Educ:* Bradford Grammar School; Christ's College, Cambridge (MA); London School of Economics. Served Army in NW Europe and India, 1941–46. PA to Finance and Supply Director, London Transport, 1947–50; Shell-Mex and BP Ltd, 1951–58; Manager Development Div., Marketing Dept, British Petroleum Co. Ltd, 1958–73; BRCS: Dir, Internat. Affairs, 1973; Head of Internat. Div., 1975; Asst Dir-Gen. International, 1980. Member: Central Appeals Adv. Cttee, BBC and IBA, 1980–83; Jt Cttee, St John and Red Cross, 1980–91; Dep. Pres., Suffolk Br., BRCS, 1987–93. Liveryman, Co. of Carmen, 1988–. FRSocMed 1993. OStJ 1983. *Recreations:* music, theatre. *Address:* Beech Tree House, The Green, Tostock, Bury St Edmunds, Suffolk IP30 9NY. *T:* (01359) 270589; 6 Pier House, Cheyne Walk, SW3 5HG. *T:* (020) 7352 1520. *Clubs:* Hawks (Cambridge); Achilles.

PIGGOTT, Lester Keith; jockey, 1948–85 and 1990–95; trainer, 1985–87; *b* 5 Nov. 1935; *s* of late Keith Piggott and Iris Rickaby; *m* 1960, Susan Armstrong; two *d*. Selection of races won: the Derby (9 times): 1954 (on Never Say Die); 1957 (on Crepello); 1960 (on St Paddy); 1968 (on Sir Ivor); 1970 (on Nijinsky); 1972 (on Roberto); 1976 (on Empery); 1977 (on The Minstrel); 1983 (on Teenoso); St Leger (8 times); The Oaks (6 times); 2,000 guineas (5 times); 1,000 guineas (twice). In many seasons 1955–85 he rode well over 100 winners a year, in this country alone; rode 4,000th winner in Britain, 14 Aug. 1982; record 30th classic win, 1 May 1992; Champion Jockey 11 times, 1960, 1964–71, 1981, 1982; rode frequently in France; won Prix de l'Arc de Triomphe on Rheingold, 1973, on Alleged, 1977 and 1978; won Washington, DC, International on Sir Ivor, 1968 (first time since 1922 an English Derby winner raced in USA), on Karabas, 1969, on Argument, 1980. *Relevant publication:* Lester, the Official Biography, by Dick Francis, 1986. *Recreations:* swimming, water skiing, golf. *Address:* Florizel, Newmarket, Suffolk CB8 0NY. *T:* (01638) 662584.

PIGNATELLI, Frank; Chief Executive, University for Industry, Scotland, since 1999; *b* 22 Dec. 1946; *s* of Frank and Elizabeth Pignatelli; *m* 1969, Rosetta Anne McFadyen; one *s* one *d*. *Educ:* Univ. of Glasgow (MA; DipEd, MEd); Jordanhill Coll. of Educn (Secondary Teachers Cert.). Teacher, St Mungo's Acad., Glasgow, 1970; Hd of Dept, St Gregory's Secondary Sch., Glasgow, 1974; Asst Headteacher, St Margaret Mary's Secondary Sch, Glasgow, 1977; Strathclyde Region: Educn Officer, Renfrew Div., 1978; Asst Dir of Educn, 1983; Depute Dir of Educn, 1985; Dir of Educn, 1988–96; Gp Dir, Human Resources, Associated Newspapers, London, 1996–97; Chm. and Man. Dir, Exec. Support and Develt Consultancy, 1997–2000; Chief Exec., ScotBIC, 1998–99. Hon. Lectr in Educn, 1988–90, Vis. Prof., 1990–, Univ. of Glasgow Sch. of Educn; Vis. Prof. of Mgt Educn, Univ. of Glasgow Business Sch., 1997–. Chairman: RIPA (West of Scotland), 1990–93; Scottish Mgt and Enterprise Council, 1999–; Scottish Skills and Employability Network, 1999–; Member: Adv. Scottish Council for Educn and Trng Targets, 1993–96; Bd, SCOTVEC, 1993–96 (Fellow, 1996); UK Nuffield Langs Inquiry, 1998–2000; Ministerial Trade Union Wkg Pty on Lifelong Learning, 2000–. Chairman: Technol. Review Gp, 1993–; Nat. Cttee for Review of Post 16 educn and trng, 1993–; Assoc. for Mgt Educn and Trng in Scotland, 1998–. Pres., Glasgow and West of Scotland Inst. of Mgt, 2001–; Hon. Pres., Scottish Assoc. for Language Teaching, 1998–2000. CIMgt 2000 (FBIM 1989; Pres., Renfrewshire, 1991–93). FRSA 1992; FSQA 1997; FICPD 1999. DUniv Paisley, 1993. *Publications:* Basic Knowledge 'O' French, 1974; Higher French Past Papers, 1975; Scottish Education Policy Review, 1994; contributor, World Year Book in Education, TES. *Recreations:* swimming, genealogy, do-it-yourself, reading. *Address:* 10 Whittingehame Drive, Glasgow G12 0XX. *T:* (0141) 334 3458, *Fax:* (0141) 579 5044.

PIGOT, Sir George (Hugh), 8th Bt *cr* 1764, of Patshull, Staffs; Secretary-General, Residential Sprinkler Association, since 1998; Managing Director, Custom Metalcraft Ltd, since 1998; *b* 28 Nov. 1946; *s* of Maj.-Gen. Sir Robert Pigot, 7th Bt, CB, OBE, DL, and Honor (*d* 1966), *d* of Captain Wilfred St Martin Gibbon; *S* father, 1986; *m* 1st, 1967, Judith Sandeman-Allen (marr. diss. 1973); one *d*; 2nd, 1980, Lucinda Jane (marr. diss. 1993), *d* of D. C. Spandler; two *s*. *Educ:* Stowe. Man. Dir, Padworth Fisheries Ltd, 1981–95; Dir, Southern Trout Ltd, 1993–95 (Man. Dir, 1994–95); business consultant, Positive Response, 1995–. Member: Council, British Trout Assoc., 1986–93 (Hon. Treas., 1990–92); Fish Farming Exec. Cttee, NFU, 1987–90 (Chm. Health and Technical Sub-Cttee, 1989–90). *Recreations:* classic cars, golf. *Heir:* s George Douglas Hugh Pigot, *b* 17 Sept. 1982. *Address:* Mill House, Mill Lane, Padworth, near Reading, Berks RG7 4JX.

PIGOTT, Sir (Berkeley) Henry (Sebastian), 5th Bt *cr* 1808; farmer; *b* 24 June 1925; *s* of Sir Berkeley Pigott, 4th Bt, and Christabel (*d* 1974), *d* of late Rev. F. H. Bowden-Smith; *S* father, 1982; *m* 1954, (Olive) Jean, *d* of John William Balls; two *s* one *d*. *Educ:* Ampleforth College. Served War with Royal Marines, 1944–45. *Recreation:* sailing (blue water). *Heir: er s* David John Berkeley Pigott [*b* 16 Aug. 1955; *m* 1st, 1981 (marr. diss.); 2nd, 1986, Julie Wiffen; one *d*]. *Address:* Brook Farm, Shobley, Ringwood, Hants BH24 3HT. *T:* (01425) 474423.

PIGOTT, Prof. Christopher Donald, PhD; Director, University Botanic Garden, Cambridge, 1984–95; *b* 7 April 1928; *s* of John Richards Pigott and Helen Constance Pigott (*née* Lee); *m* 1st, 1954, Margaret Elsie Beatson (*d* 1981); one *d*; 2nd, 1986, Sheila Lloyd (*née* Megaw). *Educ:* Mill Hill School; University of Cambridge. MA, PhD. Asst Lectr, and Lectr, Univ. of Sheffield, 1951–60; Univ. Lectr, Cambridge, 1960–64; Fellow of Emmanuel Coll., Cambridge, 1962–64; Prof. of Biology, Univ. of Lancaster, 1964–84, Prof. Emeritus, 1995–; Professorial Fellow, Emmanuel Coll., Cambridge, 1984–95; Member: Nature Conservancy, 1971–73; Nature Conservancy Council, 1979–82; Council, 1980–92, Properties Cttee, 1990–, Nat. Trust; Home Grown Timber Adv. Cttee, 1987–94, Res. Users Adv. Gp, 1993–96, Forestry Commn; Foreign Correspondent, Acad. d'Agriculture de France (Silviculture), 1982–. *Publications:* contribs

i. jls (ecology and physiology of plants). *Recreations:* walking, travelling. *Address:* enbank, Cartmel, Grange-over-Sands LA11 7SQ.

OTT, Ronald Wellesley, FRCS, FRCSI; Consultant Plastic Surgeon, Frenchay ospital, Bristol, 1969–93, Hon. Consultant, since 1993; *b* 16 Sept. 1932; *s* of Thomas Ian Vellesley Pigott and Kathleen Muriel (*née* Parsons); *m* 1958, Sheila King; four *s. Educ:* Dakham Sch., Rutland; Univ. of Dublin (BA, MB, BCh, BAO). FRCSI 1960; FRCS 1962. Short service commn, Parachute Field Ambulance, 1960–62. Sen. Registrar, Plastic Surgery, Stoke Mandeville Hosp., 1962–68; Robert Johnson Fellow, Univ. of Miami, 1967. Pioneered endoscopy of velopharyngeal isthmus in the condition of velopharyngeal incompetence; developed split screen recording of endoscopic and radiological examn of velopharyngeal isthmus with A. P. W. Makepeace; pioneered computer-based assessment of symmetry for application to cleft lip and nose deformity with B. Coghlan and D. Matthews. President: Eur. Assoc. of Plastic Surgeons, 1992–93; British Assoc. of Aesthetic Plastic Surgeons, 1993. James Halloran Bennet Medal in Surgery, 1956; James Berry Prize 1979, Jacksonian Prize 1979, RCS; Mowlem Award, Brit. Assoc. Plastic Surgeons, 1982. *Publications:* chapters regarding investigation and treatment of cleft lip and palate in: Advances in the Management of Cleft Lip and Palate, 1980; Clinics in Plastic Surgery, 1985; Scott Brown's Paediatric Otolaryngology, 5th edn 1987; Current Therapy in Plastic and Reconstructive Surgery, 1989; article on develt of endoscopy of palatopharyngeal isthmus, Proc. Royal Soc., 1977; articles in Lancet, Brit. Jl Plastic Surgery, Plastic Reconstructive Surgery, Annals Plastic Surgery, Scandinavian Jl Plastic Reconstructive Surgery. *Recreations:* formerly hockey (represented Ireland, University of Dublin and Army and Combined Services), tennis (represented Univ. of Dublin), painting, sculpture, gardening.

PIGOTT-BROWN, Sir William Brian, 3rd Bt *cr* 1902; *b* 20 Jan. 1941; *s* of Sir John Pigott-Brown, 2nd Bt (killed in action, 1942) and Helen (who *m* 1948, Capt. Charles Raymond Radclyffe), *o d* of Major Gilbert Egerton Cotton, Priestland, Tarporley, Cheshire; *S* father, 1942. *Heir:* none. *Address:* 47 Eaton Mews North, SW1X 8LL.

PIGOTT-SMITH, Timothy Peter; actor and director; *b* 13 May 1946; *s* of Harry Thomas Pigott-Smith and Margaret Muriel (*née* Goodman); *m* 1972, Pamela Miles; one *s. Educ:* Bristol Univ. (BA Hons 1967); Bristol Old Vic Theatre Sch. Bristol Old Vic, 1967–69; Prospect Th. Co., 1970–71; RSC, 1972–75; Birmingham, Cambridge, Nottingham and Royal Court Th., 1975–77; Benefactors, Vaudeville, 1984; Bengal Lancer (one-man show), Leicester, transf. Lyric, Hammersmith, 1985; Coming in to Land, Antony and Cleopatra, Entertaining Strangers, Winter's Tale, Cymbeline, and Tempest, NT, 1986–88; dir, Samuel Beckett's Company, Donmar Warehouse (Edinburgh Fest. Fringe award), 1987; Artistic Dir, Compass Th., 1989–92; Brutus in Julius Caesar, 1990; Salieri in Amadeus, 1991; Saki—an anthology, 1991; Mr Rochester in Jane Eyre, Playhouse, 1993; The Picture of Dorian Gray, Lyric, 1994; Retreat, Orange Tree, Richmond, 1995; The Letter, Lyric, 1995; Mary Stuart, The Alchemist, RNT, 1996; Heritage, Hampstead, 1997; The Iceman Cometh, Almeida, 1998, transf. Old Vic, then NY, 1999; Five Kinds of Silence, Lyric, 2000; Julius Caesar, RSC, 2001; director: Royal Hunt of the Sun, 1989; Playing the Wife, 1992; Hamlet, Regent's Park, 1994. *Films:* Aces High, 1975; Joseph Andrews, 1977; Sweet William, 1978; The Day Christ Died, 1979; Richard's Things, 1981; Clash of the Titans, 1981; Escape to Victory, 1981; Hunchback of Notre Dame, 1982; State of Emergency, 1986; Life Story (Best TV Film, BAFTA), 1987; The True Adventures of Christopher Columbus, 1992; The Remains of the Day, 1993; The Bullion Boys, 1993; The Shadowy Third, 1994; Four Feathers, Laissez Passer, Bloody Sunday, Gangs of New York, 2001; *television: series and serials:* Dr Who, 1970; Glittering Prizes, 1975; North and South, 1975; Wings, 1976; Eustace and Hilda, 1977; The Lost Boys, 1978; The Wilderness Years, 1982; Fame is the Spur, 1982; The Jewel in the Crown (Best TV Actor, BAFTA; TV Times Best Actor; BPG Best Actor), 1984; The Chief, 1989–91; The Vice, 2001; Kavanagh QC, 2001; *plays:* No Mama No, 1976; Measure for Measure, 1978; School Play, 1979; Henry IV part 1, 1980; *documentaries:* Calcutta Chronicles (presenter and writer), 1996; Innocents, 2000. *Publication:* Out of India, 1987. *Recreations:* music, sport. *Address:* c/o Peters, Fraser & Dunlop, Drury House, 34–43 Russell Street, WC2B 5HA.

PIHL, Brig. Hon. Dame Mary Mackenzie, DBE 1970 (MBE 1958); Director, Women's Royal Army Corps, 1967–70, retired; *b* 3 Feb. 1916; *d* of Sir John Anderson, later 1st Viscount Waverley, PC, GCB, OM, GCSI, GCIE, FRS, and Christina Mackenzie Anderson; *m* 1973, Frithjof Pihl (*d* 1988). *Educ:* Sutton High Sch.; Villa Brillantmont, Lausanne. Joined Auxiliary Territorial Service, 1941; transferred to Women's Royal Army Corps, 1949. Hon. ADC to the Queen, 1967–70.

PIKE, Baroness *cr* 1974 (Life Peer), of Melton, Leics; **Irene Mervyn Parnicott Pike,** DBE 1981; Chairman, Broadcasting Complaints Commission, 1981–85; *b* 16 Sept. 1918; *d* of I. S. Pike, Company Director, Okehampton, Devonshire. *Educ:* Hunmanby Hall; Reading University. BA Hons Economics and Psychology, 1941. Served WAAF, 1941–46. Mem., WRCC, 1955–57. Contested (C): Pontefract, 1951; Leek, Staffordshire, 1955. MP (C) Melton, Leics, Dec. 1956–Feb. 1974; Assistant Postmaster-General, 1959–63; Joint Parliamentary Under-Secretary of State, Home Office, 1963–64. Mem., Robens Cttee on Safety and Health of People at their Place of Work, 1970–72. Director: Watts, Blake, Bearne & Co. Ltd; Dunderdale Investments. Chairman: IBA Gen. Adv. Council, 1974–79; WRVS, 1974–81. *Recreations:* gardening, walking. *Address:* Hownam, near Kelso, Roxburgh TD5 8AL.

PIKE, Prof. (Edward) Roy, PhD; FRS 1981; Clerk Maxwell Professor of Theoretical Physics, University of London at King's College, since 1986 (Head of School of Physical Sciences and Engineering, 1991–94); *b* 4 Dec. 1929; *s* of Anthony Pike and Rosalind Irene Pike (*née* Davies); *m* 1955, Pamela Sawtell; one *s* two *d. Educ:* Southfield Grammar Sch., Oxford; University Coll., Cardiff (BSc, PhD; Fellow, 1981). CPhys, FInstP, CMath, FIMA. Served Royal Corps of Signals, 1948–50. Fulbright Schol., Physics Dept, MIT, 1958–60; Royal Signals and Radar Estabt Physics Group, 1960: theoretical and experimental research condensed matter physics and optics; Individual Merit: SPSO 1967; DCSO 1973; CSO, 1984–90. Vis. Prof. of Maths, Imperial Coll., London, 1985–86. Chairman: Oval (114) Ltd, 1984–85; Stilo Technology Ltd, 1995–; Stilo Internat. plc, 2000–; non-exec. Dir, Richard Clay plc, 1985–86. Govt assessor, SRC Physics Cttee, 1973–76. Mem. Council: Inst. of Physics, 1976–85; European Physical Soc., 1981–83; Vice-Pres. for Publications and Chm., Adam Hilger Ltd, 1981–85; Director: NATO Advanced Study Insts, 1973, 1976; NATO Advanced Res. Workshops, 1987–88, 1991 and 1996. Hon. Editor: Journal of Physics A, 1973–78; Optica Acta, 1978–83; Quantum Optics, 1989–94. Nat. Science Foundn Vis. Lectr, USA, 1959; Lectures: Univ. of Rome, 1976; Univ. of Bordeaux, 1977; Simon Fraser Univ., 1978; Univ. of Genoa, 1980. FKC 1993. Charles Parsons medal and lecture, Royal Society, 1975; MacRobert award (jtly) and lecture, Council of Engrg Instns, 1977; Worshipful Co. of Scientific Instrument Makers Annual Achievement award (jtly), 1978; Committee on Awards to Inventors award, 1980; Guthrie Medal and Prize, Inst. of Physics, 1996. Confrérie St-Etienne, 1980–. *Publications:* (jtly) The Quantum Theory of Radiation, 1995; (ed) High Power Gas Lasers, 1975; edited jointly: Photon Correlation and Light Beating Spectroscopy, 1974; Photon Correlation Spectroscopy and Velocimetry, 1977; Frontiers in Quantum Optics, 1986; Fractals, Noise and Chaos, 1987; Quantum Measurement and Chaos, 1987; Squeezed and Non-classical Light, 1988; Photons and Quantum Fluctuations, 1988; Inverse Problems in Scattering and Imaging, 1991; Photon Correlation and Light Scattering Spectroscopy, 1997; Scattering, 2001; numerous papers in scientific jls. *Recreations:* music, languages, woodwork. *Address:* 3a Golborne Mews, North Kensington, W10 5SB; 8 Bredon Grove, Malvern WR14 3JR.

PIKE, Rt Rev. Eric; *see* Port Elizabeth, Bishop of.

PIKE, Lt-Gen. Sir Hew (William Royston), KCB 1997; DSO 1982; MBE 1977; Director, Gap International Projects for Youth Exchange, since 2001; *b* 24 April 1943; *s* of Lt-Gen. Sir William Pike, KCB, CBE, DSO; *m* 1966, Jean, *d* of Col Donald Matheson, RAMC; one *s* two *d. Educ:* Winchester Coll.; RMA Sandhurst. Commissioned Parachute Regt, 1962; 3 Para, Middle East, Africa, Guyana, 1963–66; ADC, UK and Norway, 1966–67; 1 Para, Middle East, UK, 1967–70; Sch. of Infantry, 44 Para Bde (V), 1970–74; Staff College, 1975; Brigade Major, 16 Para Bde, 1976–77; Co. Comdr, 3 Para Germany and UK, 1978–79; CO, 3 Para, UK and Falkland Is Campaign, 1980–83 (despatches 1981); Comd 22 Armd Bde, Bergen-Hohne, 1987–90; RCDS 1990; GOC 3rd (UK) Div., 1992–94; Comdt, RMA, Sandhurst, 1994–95; Dep. C-in-C, and Inspector Gen. TA, HQ Land Comd, 1995–97; Dep. Comdr, SFOR, Bosnia, 1997–98; GOC and Dir of Mil. Ops, NI, 1998–2000. Freeman, City of London, 1982. *Recreations:* country pursuits, gardening. *Address:* c/o Lloyds TSB, Castle Street, Farnham, Surrey.

PIKE, Sir Michael (Edmund), KCVO 1989; CMG 1984; HM Diplomatic Service, retired; *b* 4 Oct. 1931; *s* of Henry Pike and Eleanor Pike; *m* 1962, Catherine (*née* Lim); one *s* two *d. Educ:* Wimbledon Coll.; London Sch. of Econs and Polit. Science; Brasenose Coll., Oxford (MA 1956). Service in HM Armed Forces, 1950–52. Editor, Cherwell, Oxford Univ., 1954; part-time News Reporter, Sunday Express, 1954–55; Feature Writer and Film Critic, Surrey Comet, 1955–56; joined HM Foreign (now Diplomatic) Service, 1956; Third Secretary: FO, 1956–57; Seoul, 1957–59; Second Secretary: Office of Comr Gen. for Singapore and SE Asia, 1960–62; Seoul, 1962–64; FO, 1964–68; First Sec., Warsaw, 1968–70; FCO, 1970–73; First Sec., Washington, 1973–75; Counsellor: Washington, 1975–78; Tel Aviv, 1978–82; RCDS, 1982; Ambassador to Vietnam, 1982–85; Minister and Dep. UK Perm. Rep. to NATO, Brussels, 1985–87; High Comr, Singapore, 1987–90. Political Affairs Advr, Sun Internat. Exploration and Production Co., 1991–93; Dir, Govett Asian Smaller Cos Investment Trust Ltd. Member: Bid Cttee, British Olympic Bid: Manchester 2000, 1991–93; Bid Cttee, English Commonwealth Games Bid, Manchester 2002, 1994–95; Sensitivity Review Unit, FCO, 1992–. Special Rep. of Sec. of State for Foreign and Commonwealth Affairs, 1992–99; HM Govt Co-ordinator, Conf., Britain in the World, 1995. Dir, Greenwich Millennium Trust, 1995–2000; Co-Chm., Greenwich Town Centre Management Agency, 1993–; Vice-Chm., Greenwich Develt Agency, 1998– (Mem., 1997–); Mem., Greenwich Tourism Partnership, 1998–2001. Pres., Union of Catholic Students of GB, 1955–56; Director: Catholic Housing Aid Soc., 1995–; Nat. New Infant and Parent Network, 1995–99. *Recreations:* reading, running, contemplating London. *Address:* c/o Records and Historical Department, Foreign and Commonwealth Office, SW1A 2AH.

PIKE, Peter Leslie; MP (Lab) Burnley, since 1983; *b* 26 June 1937; *s* of Leslie Henry Pike and Gladys (*née* Cunliffe); *m* 1962, Sheila Lillian Bull; two *d. Educ:* Hinchley Wood County Secondary Sch. (Commercial Dept); Kingston Technical Coll. Pt 1 Exam., Inst. of Bankers. National Service, RM, 1956–58. Midland Bank, 1954–62; Twinings Tea, 1962–63; Organiser/Agent, Labour Party, 1963–73; Mullard (Simonstone) Ltd, 1973–83. Mem., GMBATU (Shop Steward, 1976–83). Member (Lab): Merton and Morden UDC, 1962–63; Burnley BC, 1976–84 (Leader, Labour Gp, 1980–83; Gp Sec., 1976–80). Opposition front bench spokesperson: on Rural Affairs, 1990–92; on Housing, 1992–94. Member: Envmt Select Cttee, 1984–90; Procedural Select Cttee, 1995–97; Deregulation Select Cttee, 1995– (Chm., 1997–); Modernisation Select Cttee, 1997–. All-Party Groups: Chairman: Romania Gp, 1994–; Southern Africa Gp; Mongolia Gp; Joint Chairman: Road Passenger Transport Gp, 1995–; Associate Parly Transport Forum; Vice Chairman: Paper Industry Gp; Homelessness Gp; (Jt), Manufacturing Gp; Secretary: Pakistan Gp, 1997–; Building Socs Gp, 1997–; Jt Sec., Overseas Develt Gp; Treas., Road Transport Study Gp, 1997–2000. Chm., PLP Envmt Cttee, 1987–90. Member: Nat. Trust, 1974–; CND; Anti-Apartheid. *Recreation:* Burnley Football Club supporter. *Address:* 73 Ormerod Road, Burnley, Lancs BB11 2RU. *T:* (01282) 434719. *Clubs:* Byerden House Socialist; Philips Sports and Social.

PIKE, Sir Philip Ernest Housden, Kt 1969; Chief Justice of Swaziland, 1970–72, retired; *b* 6 March 1914; *s* of Rev. Ernest Benjamin Pike and Dora Case Pike (*née* Lillie); *m* 2nd, 1959, Millicent Locke Staples; one *s* one *d* of 1st marriage. *Educ:* De Carteret School, and Munro Coll., Jamaica; Middle Temple, London. Barrister at Law, 1938. Crown Counsel, Jamaica, 1947–49; Legal Draftsman, Kenya, 1949–52; Solicitor General, Uganda, 1952–58; QC (Uganda) 1953; Attorney General, Sarawak, 1958–65; QC (Sarawak) 1958; Chief Justice, High Court in Borneo, 1965–68; Judge, High Court of Malawi, 1969–70, Actg Chief Justice, 1970. Coronation Medal, 1953. PNBS-Sarawak, 1965; Malaysia Commemorative Medal, 1967; PMN Malaysia 1968. *Recreations:* golf, gardening. *Address:* 3 Earlewood Court, 180/184 Ron Penhaligon Way, Robina, Qld 4226, Australia.

PIKE, Dr Richard Andrew, CEng, FIMechE; FIChemE; FIEE; Managing Director, Heliochron Ltd, since 1998; *b* 2 April 1950; *s* of Tudor Morgan Pike and Eileen Mary (*née* Oxley); *m* 1986, Fiona Elizabeth Henry; one *s* two *d. Educ:* Gosport Co. Grammar Sch.; Downing Coll., Cambridge (BA 1st Cl. Engrg; MA; PhD 1977). CEng 1987; FIMechE 1988; FIChemE 1991; FIEE 1996. Joined British Petroleum as univ. apprentice, 1968; Maintenance Engr, BP Llandarcy, 1971–72; res. student, Cambridge, 1972–75; Develt Engr, BP Engrg, London, 1975–80; Area Commissioning Engr, Sullom Voe Terminal, Shetland, 1980–82; Business Develt Co-ordinator, Jt Ventures, London, 1982–83; Develt Supt, Pipelines and Facilities, Aberdeen, 1984–85; Offshore Prodn Engr, Forties, North Sea, 1985–86; Manager Technical, Sullom Voe Terminal, 1986–88; Manager, Jt Venture, Japan, 1988–89; Gen. Manager, Chems, BP Far East, Tokyo, 1989–93; Pres., BP Chems, Japan, 1991–93; Dir, Samsung-BP Chems, S Korea, 1989–91; Dir Gen., IMechE, 1993–98. *Recreations:* reading, swimming, languages, travel. *Address:* (office) 22 Shortheath Road, Farnham, Surrey GU9 8SR. *T:* (01252) 723287.

PIKE, Roy; *see* Pike, E. R.

PILBROW, Richard Hugh; Chairman, Theatre Projects Consultants, since 1957; *b* 28 April 1933; *s* of Arthur Gordon Pilbrow and Marjorie Pilbrow; *m* 1st, 1958, Viki Brinton; one *s* one *d*; 2nd, 1974, Molly Friedel; one *d. Educ:* Cranbrook Sch.; Central Sch. of Speech and Drama. Stage Manager, Teahouse of the August Moon, 1954; founded Theatre Projects, 1957. Lighting Designer for over 200 prodns in London, New York, Paris and Moscow, incl.: Brand, 1959; Blitz, 1962; Zorba, 1968; Annie, 1978; Oklahoma!, 1980; The Little Foxes, Windy City, 1982; Singin' In the Rain, 1983; Heliotrope

Bouquet, 1991; Four Baboons Adoring the Sun, 1992; The Magic Flute, LA, 1993; Showboat, 1993; The Life, 1997; for Nat. Theatre Co., 1963–, incl. Hamlet, 1963, Rosencrantz and Guildenstern are Dead, 1966; Heartbreak House, 1975; Love for Love, 1985. Theatrical Producer in London of prodns incl.: A Funny Thing Happened on the Way to the Forum, 1963, 1986; Cabaret, 1968; Company, 1972; A Little Night Music, 1975; West Side Story, 1984; The Mysteries, Lyceum, 1985; I'm Not Rappaport, 1986. Film Prod., Swallows and Amazons, 1973; TV Productions: All You Need is Love—the story of popular music, 1975; Swallows and Amazons for Ever, 1984; Dir, Mister, 1971. Theatre Projects Consultants have been consultants on over 600 theatres and arts centres, incl. Disney Concert Hall, LA, Philadelphia Kimmel Performing Arts Centre, New Amsterdam Theatre, Lincoln Center redevelt, NYC, Nat. Theatre of GB, Barbican Theatre, and theatres and arts centres in Canada, Iran, Hong Kong, Saudi Arabia, Mexico, Iceland, Nigeria, Singapore, USA, etc. Vice Pres., Assoc. of British Theatre Technicians; Co-founder, Soc. of Brit. Theatre Designers, 1975; Mem., Assoc. of Lighting Designers (Chm., 1982–85); Member: Drama Panel, Arts Council of GB, 1968–70; Soc. of West End Theatre; Council, London Acad. of Music and Drama. FRSA. *Publications:* Stage Lighting, 1970, 3rd edn 1991; Stage Lighting Design, 1997. *Recreations:* The Hebrides, cooking, dogs. *Address:* Theatre Projects Consultants Inc., 25 Elizabeth Street, South Norwalk, CT 06854–3025, USA. *Club:* Garrick.

PILCHER, Rosamunde; writing and publishing short stories and novels, since 1944; *b* 22 Sept. 1924; *d* of Charles Montagu Lawrence Scott and Helen Scott; *m* 1946, Graham Pilcher; two *s* two *d. Educ:* St Clare's, Polwithen, Penzance; Howell's Sch., Llandaff, Cardiff. Author of Year, Bertelsmann Book Club, Germany, 1991; Berliner Zeitung Kulturpreis, 1993; Deutscher Videopreis, 1996; Bambi Award, Bunte magazine, 1997; Goldene Kamera Award, Hörzu, 1998. *Publications:* Sleeping Tiger; Another View; End of Summer; Snow in April; Empty House; Day of the Storm; Under Gemini; Wild Mountain Thyme; Carousel; Blue Bedroom; The Shell Seekers (Amer. Booksellers' Assoc. award, 1991; televised); September, 1990; Voices in Summer; Flowers in Rain; Coming Home, 1995 (Romantic Novelist of the Year, RNA, 1996; televised, 1998); The World of Rosamunde Pilcher; Winter Solstice, 2000. *Recreations:* walking, gardening, reading, travel. *Address:* Penrowan, Longforgan, Dundee DD2 5ET.

PILDITCH, Sir Richard (Edward), 4th Bt *cr* 1929; *b* 8 Sept. 1926; *s* of Sir Philip Harold Pilditch, 2nd Bt, and Frances Isabella, *d* of J. G. Weeks, JP, Bedlington, Northumberland; *S* brother, Sir Philip John Frederick Pilditch, 3rd Bt, 1954; *m* 1950, Pauline Elizabeth Smith; one *s* one *d. Educ:* Charterhouse. Served War of 1939–45, with Royal Navy; in India and Ceylon, 1945–46. *Recreations:* shooting, fishing. *Heir: s* John Richard Pilditch, *b* 24 Sept. 1955. *Address:* 4 Fishermans Bank, Mudeford, Christchurch, Dorset BH23 3NP.

PILE, Colonel Sir Frederick (Devereux), 3rd Bt *cr* 1900; MC 1945; *b* 10 Dec. 1915; *s* of Gen. Sir Frederick Alfred Pile, 2nd Bt, GCB, DSO, MC; *S* father, 1976; *m* 1st, 1940, Pamela (*d* 1983), *d* of late Philip Henstock; two *d*; 2nd, 1984, Mrs Josephine Culverwell. *Educ:* Weymouth; RMC, Sandhurst. Joined Royal Tank Regt, 1935; served War of 1939–45, Egypt and NW Europe; commanded Leeds Rifles, 1955–56; Colonel GS, BJSM, Washington, DC, 1957–60; Commander, RAC Driving and Maintenance School, 1960–62. Secretary, Royal Soldiers' Daughters' School, 1965–71. *Publication:* Better than Riches, 1993. *Recreations:* fishing, cricket, travelling. *Heir: nephew* Anthony John Devereux Pile [*b* 7 June 1947; *m* 1977, Jennifer Clare Youngman; two *s* one *d*]. *Club:* MCC.

PILGER, John Richard; journalist, author and film-maker; *s* of Claude Pilger and Elsie (*née* Marheine); *m* Scarth Flett; one *s*; one *d* by Yvonne Roberts. *Educ:* Sydney High Sch. Cadet journalist, Sydney Daily Telegraph, Australia, qualified, 1961; freelance journalist, Italy, 1962; Reuter, London, 1962; feature writer, chief foreign correspondent, Daily Mirror, London, 1962–86 (reporter, Vietnam War, 1966–75, Cambodia, 1979–91, etc); columnist, New Statesman, 1991–; contributor: The Guardian, The Independent, NY Times, Sydney Morning Herald, The Age, Melbourne, S China Morning Post, The Nation, NY and Bangkok, Aftonbladet, Sweden. Campaigns incl. Thalidomide 'X list' victims, and Australian Aboriginal land rights. Documentary film-maker, 1970–, films include: The Quiet Mutiny, 1970; A Faraway Country (Czechoslovakia), 1977; Year Zero: the silent death of Cambodia, 1979; Nicaragua, 1983; Japan Behind the Mask, 1986; The Last Dream, 1988; Death of a Nation: the Timor conspiracy, 1994; Vietnam: the last battle, 1995; Inside Burma: land of fear, 1996; Breaking the Mirror: the Murdoch Effect, 1997; Apartheid Did Not Die, 1998; Paying the Price: killing the children of Iraq, 2000; The New Rulers of the World, 2001. Edward Wilson Fellow, Deakin Univ., Aust., 1995. Hon. DLitt: Staffordshire, 1994; Kingston, 1999; DPhil *hc* Dublin City, 1995; Hon. DArts Oxford Brookes, 1997; Hon. LLD St Andrews, 1999; DUniv Open, 2001. Awards include: Descriptive Writer of the Year, 1966; Reporter of the Year, 1967; Journalist of the Year, 1967, 1979; Internat. Reporter of the Year, 1970; News Reporter of the Year, 1974; Campaigning Journalist of the Year, 1977; UN Media Peace Prize and Gold Medal, 1979–80; George Foster Peabody Award, USA, 1990; Reporters Sans Frontiers Award, France, 1990; Richard Dimbleby Award, 1991; US TV Academy Award (Emmy), 1991; Premis Actual Award, Spain, 1996. *Publications:* The Last Day, 1975; Aftermath: the struggle of Cambodia and Vietnam, 1981; The Outsiders, 1984; Heroes, 1986; A Secret Country, 1989; Distant Voices, 1992; Hidden Agendas, 1998. *Recreations:* swimming, sunning, mulling. *Address:* 57 Hambalt Road, SW4 9EQ. *T:* (020) 8673 2848.

PILGRIM, Cecil Stanley, CCH 1986; High Commissioner for Guyana in London, 1986–92, and concurrently Ambassador (non-resident) to France, the Netherlands and Yugoslavia; *b* 1 Feb. 1932; *s* of Errol Pilgrim and Edith Pilgrim; *m* 1979, Cita I. Pilgrim; one *d. Educ:* Queen's Coll., Guyana; Univ. of Guyana (BSc; post graduate course in Internat. Relations). Diplomatic Cadet, Guyana, 1967; Second Sec., Jamaica, 1969; First Sec., China, 1974; Counsellor, USSR, 1978; Ambassador, Cuba, 1979. *Recreations:* reading, music, badminton, walking, cricket, enjoys sports of all types.

PILKINGTON, family name of **Baron Pilkington of Oxenford**.

PILKINGTON OF OXENFORD, Baron *cr* 1995 (Life Peer), of West Dowlish in the county of Somerset; **Rev. Canon Peter Pilkington;** Chairman, Broadcasting Complaints Commission, 1992–96; Hon. Canon of Canterbury Cathedral, 1975–90, now Canon Emeritus; *b* 5 Sept. 1933; *s* of Frank and Doris Pilkington; *m* 1966, Helen (*d* 1997), *d* of Charles and Maria Wilson; two *d. Educ:* Dame Allans Sch., Newcastle upon Tyne; Jesus Coll., Cambridge (BA 1955; MA 1958). Schoolmaster, St Joseph's Coll., Chidya, Tanganyika, 1955–57; ordained 1959; Curate in Bakewell, Derbys, 1959–62; Schoolmaster, Eton College, 1962–75, Master in College, 1965–75; Headmaster, King's Sch., Canterbury, 1975–86; High Master, St Paul's Sch., 1986–92. Mem., Parole Bd, 1990–95. *Address:* Oxenford House, near Ilminster, Somerset TA19 0PP. *T:* (01460) 52813. *Clubs:* Beefsteak, Garrick.

PILKINGTON, Godfrey; *see* Pilkington, R. G.

PILKINGTON, Air Vice-Marshal Michael John, CB 1991; CBE 1982; Air Officer Commanding Training Units, Royal Air Force Support Command, 1989–92, retired; *b* 9 Oct. 1937; *s* of David and Mary Pilkington; *m* 1960, Janet Ray[...] Grammar Sch. psc rcds. Commnd Royal Air Force, 1956; Bomb[...] No 27, 1959–70; RAF sc 1971; HQ Near East Air Force, 1972–[...] OCU, 1974–75; Defence Policy Staff, 1977–78; CO RAF Wadding[...] 1982; Branch Chief Policy, SHAPE, 1982–85; DG of Trng, RAF, [...] golf, gardening, theatre, wine. *Club:* Royal Air Force.

PILKINGTON, Muriel Norma, MA; Headteacher, Wycombe High S[...] *b* 1 Jan. 1941; *d* of Norman Herbert Fosbury and Lilian Alice Fosbury[...] Anthony Leonard Andrews; one *s*; 2nd, 1983, Derek Brogden Pilkington; [...] step *d. Educ:* Woking County Grammar Sch.; Helene Lange Hochschule, Han[...] Margaret Hall, Oxford (BA 1962; MA 1970). Asst Teacher, Shephalbury Sch., [...] 1962–64; 2nd in Dept, Hatfield Girls' Grammar Sch., 1964–66; Head of Dept/Fa[...] James Altham Sch., Watford, 1970–81; Dep. Head, Francis Bacon Sch., St [...] 1981–86. Chairman: Area 6 SHA, 1993–95; Wycombe Pupil Referral Unit Mgt [...] 1997–. Consultant, Centre for Educnl Mgt, 1999–. Trustee: Whitmore Vale Hou[...] Assoc., 1970–; London Arts Schs, 1994– (Mem. Council, 2000–). Governor: Bu[...] Chilterns UC (formerly Bucks Coll., Brunel Univ.), 1993– (consultant/guest lectr, 199[...] Vice Chm., Council, 2001–); John Hampden GS, 1998–; Disraeli Combined Sch., 1998–. FRSA 1990. *Recreations:* music, jogging, gastronomy, travel. *Address:* 18 Woodside Drive, Bradwell Grove, Burford, Oxon OX18 4XB.

PILKINGTON, (Richard) Godfrey; Partner and Director, Piccadilly Gallery, since 1953; *b* 8 Nov. 1918; *e s* of Col Guy R. Pilkington, DSO and Margery (*née* Frost); *m* 1950, Evelyn Edith (Eve) Vincent; two *s* two *d. Educ:* Clifton; Trinity Coll., Cambridge (MA). Lieut, RA, N Africa and Central Mediterranean, 1940–46. Joined Frost & Reed, art dealers, 1947; edited Pictures and Prints, 1951–60; founded Piccadilly Gallery, 1953. Master, Fine Art Trade Guild, 1964–66; Chm., Soc. of London Art Dealers, 1974–77. Governor, Wimbledon Sch. of Art, 1990–2000. *Publications:* numerous exhibn catalogues and magazine articles. *Recreations:* walking, boating, tennis, golf. *Address:* 45 Barons Court Road, W14 9DZ. *Clubs:* Athenæum, Garrick, Hurlingham.

PILKINGTON, Dr Roger Windle; author; *b* 17 Jan. 1915; 3rd *s* of Richard Austin Pilkington and Hon. Hope (*née* Cozens-Hardy); *m* 1st, 1937, Theodora Miriam Jaboor; one *d* (and one *s* decd); 2nd, 1973, Fru Ingrid Geijer, Stockholm. *Educ:* Rugby; Freiburg, Germany; Magdalene Coll., Cambridge (MA, PhD). Research, genetics, 1937; Chm., London Missionary Soc., 1962; Chm. of Trustees, Homerton Coll., Cambridge, 1962; Chm. of Govs, Hall Sch., 1962; jt author, Sex and Morality Report, Brit. Council of Churches, 1966; Vice-Pres., River Thames Soc., 1967; Master, Glass Sellers' Co., 1967. *Publications:* Males and Females, 1948; Stringer's Folly, Biology, Man and God, Sons and Daughters, 1951; How Your Life Began, 1953; Revelation Through Science, 1954; Jan's Treasure, In the Beginning, 1955; Thames Waters, The Facts of Life, 1956; Small Boat Through Belgium, The Chesterfield Gold, The Great South Sea, The Ways of the Sea, 1957; The Missing Panel, 1958; Small Boat Through Holland, Robert Boyle: Father of Chemistry, How Boats Go Uphill, 1959; Small Boat to the Skagerrak, World Without End, The Dahlia's Cargo, Don John's Ducats, 1960; Small Boat to Sweden, Small Boat to Alsace, The Ways of the Air, Who's Who and Why, 1961; Small Boat to Bavaria, Nepomuk of the River, Boats Overland, How Boats are Navigated, 1962; The River, (with Noel Streatfeild) Confirmation and After, Facts of Life for Parents, Small Boat to Germany, The Eisenbart Mystery, 1963; Heavens Alive, Small Boat Through France, 1964; Small Boat in Southern France, Glass, 1965; Small Boat on the Thames, The Boy from Stink Alley, 1966; Small Boat on the Meuse, Small Boat to Luxembourg, 1967; Small Boat on the Moselle, 1968; Small Boat to Elsinore, 1968; Small Boat in Northern Germany, 1969; Small Boat on the Lower Rhine, 1970; Small Boat on the Upper Rhine, 1971; Waterways in Europe, 1972; The Ormering Tide, 1974; The Face in the River, 1976; Geijer in England, 1983; Small Boat Down the Years, 1987; Small Boat in the Midi, 1989; I Sailed on the Mayflower, 1990; One Foot in France, 1992; View from the Shore, 1995; History and Legends of the European Waterways, 1998; The Day of the Sheriffs, 2000; contribs to Guardian, Daily Telegraph, Times, Family Doctor, Yachting World, etc. *Recreations:* inland waterways, walking. *Address:* Les Cactus, 34310 Montouliers, France.

PILKINGTON, Stephen Charles, QPM 1998; PhD; Chief Constable, Avon and Somerset Constabulary, since 1998; *b* 4 June 1948; *s* of Charles Leonard Pilkington and Joan Pilkington; *m* 1974, Anne Bernadette Brett; three *s. Educ:* Queen Elizabeth Coll., Univ. of London (BSc 1st cl. Hons Biology, 1969; PhD Plant Physiology, 1973). Joined Metropolitan Police, 1972; Constable, Battersea; seconded to American Police Force, 1984; Dep. Asst Comr, Central London, 1996–97. *Recreations:* walking, ornithology, Rugby (spectator), squash, kayaking and camping (holidays). *Address:* PO Box 37, Valley Road, Portishead, Bristol BS20 8QJ. *T:* (01275) 816007.

PILKINGTON, Sir Thomas Henry Milborne-Swinnerton-, 14th Bt *cr* 1635; Chairman, Charente Steamship Co. Ltd, since 1977; Deputy Chairman, Cluff Mining Ltd, since 1998; *b* 10 March 1934; *s* of Sir Arthur W. Milborne-Swinnerton-Pilkington, 13th Bt and Elizabeth Mary (she *m* 1950, A. Burke), *d* of late Major J. F. Harrison, King's Walden Bury, Hitchin; *S* father, 1952; *m* 1961, Susan, *e d* of N. S. R. Adamson, Durban, South Africa; one *s* two *d. Educ:* Eton College. Dir, 1963–99, Chm., 1980–99, Thos & James Harrison Ltd. Sen. Steward, Jockey Club, 1994–98. *Recreations:* golf, racing. *Heir: s* Richard Arthur Milborne-Swinnerton-Pilkington [*b* 4 Sept. 1964; *m* 1994, Katya (marr. diss. 2000), *d* of T. J. Clemence; one *d*]. *Address:* King's Walden Bury, Hitchin, Herts SG4 8JU. *Club:* White's.

PILL, Rt Hon. Sir Malcolm (Thomas), Kt 1988; PC 1995; **Rt Hon. Lord Justice Pill;** a Lord Justice of Appeal, since 1995; *b* 11 March 1938; *s* of late Reginald Thomas Pill, MBE and Anne Pill (*née* Wright); *m* 1966, Roisin Pill (*née* Riordan), DL; two *s* one *d. Educ:* Whitchurch Grammar Sch.; Trinity Coll., Cambridge. MA, LLM, Dip. Hague Acad. of Internat. Law. Served RA, 1956–58; Glamorgan Yeomanry (TA), 1958–67. Called to Bar, Gray's Inn, 1962, Bencher, 1987; Wales and Chester Circuit, 1963 (Treas., 1985–87; Presiding Judge, 1989–93); a Recorder, 1976–87; QC 1978; a Judge of the High Court, QBD, 1988–95; a Judge, Employment Appeal Tribunal, 1992–95. 3rd Sec., Foreign Office, 1963–64 (delegns to UN Gen. Assembly, ECOSOC, Human Rights Commn). Dep. Chm., Parly Boundary Commn for Wales, 1993–95. Chairman: UNA (Welsh Centre) Trust, 1969–77, 1980–87; Welsh Centre for Internat. Affairs, 1973–76; Eur. Parly Boundary Cttee for Wales, 1993. Chm., UK Cttee, Freedom from Hunger Campaign, 1978–87. Trustee, Dominic Barker Trust, 1997–. Hon. Fellow, Univ. of Wales Cardiff, 1998. Hon. LLD Glamorgan, 1998. *Publication:* A Cardiff Family in the Forties, 1999. *Address:* Royal Courts of Justice, Strand, WC2A 2LL. *Clubs:* Army and Navy; Cardiff and County.

PILLAR, Rt Rev. Kenneth Harold; Bishop Suffragan of Hertford, 1982–89; an Assistant Bishop, diocese of Sheffield, since 1990; *b* 10 Oct. 1924; *s* of Harold and Mary Pillar; *m* 1955, Margaret Elizabeth Davies; one *s* three *d. Educ:* Devonport High School; Queens' Coll., Cambridge (MA); Ridley Hall, Cambridge. Asst Curate, Childwall, Liverpool, 1950–53; Chaplain, Lee Abbey, Lynton, N Devon, 1953–57; Vicar: St Paul's,

Beckenham, 1957–62; St Mary Bredin, Canterbury, 1962–65; Warden of Lee Abbey, Lynton, N Devon, 1965–70; Vicar of Waltham Abbey, Essex, 1970–82; RD of Epping Forest, 1976–82. *Recreations:* walking, music, reading. *Address:* 75 Dobcroft Road, Millhouses, Sheffield S7 2LS. *T:* (0114) 236 7902.

PILLING, Sir Joseph Grant, KCB 2001 (CB 1995); Permanent Under-Secretary of State, Northern Ireland Office, since 1997; *b* 8 July 1945; *s* of late Fred and Eva Pilling; *m* 1968, Ann Cheetham; two *s*. *Educ:* Rochdale Grammar Sch.; King's Coll., London; Harvard. Asst Principal, 1966, Pvte Sec. to Minister of State, 1970, Home Office; Asst. Pvte Sec. to Home Sec., 1970–71; NI Office, 1972; Harkness Fellow, Harvard Univ. and Univ. of Calif at Berkeley, 1972–74; Home Office, 1974–78; Pvte Sec. to Sec. of State for NI, 1978–79; Home Office, 1979–84; Under Sec., DHSS, 1984–87; Dir of Personnel and Finance, HM Prison Service, Home Office, 1987–90; Dep. Under Sec. of State, NI Office, 1990–91; Dir-Gen., HM Prison Service, Home Office, 1991–92; Prin. Estabt and Finance Officer, DoH, 1993–97. *Address:* c/o Northern Ireland Office, 11 Millbank, SW1P 4QE. *Club:* Athenæum.

PILLING, Prof. Michael John, PhD; CChem, FRSC; Professor of Physical Chemistry, since 1989, and Dean for Research, Faculty of Mathematics and Physical Sciences, since 2000, University of Leeds; *b* 25 Sept. 1942; *s* of John and Joan Pilling; *m* 1966, Gwenda Madeline Harrison; one *s* one *d*. *Educ:* Bacup and Rawtenstall Grammar Sch.; Churchill Coll., Cambridge (MA, PhD). CChem, FRSC 1991. Cambridge University: SRC Fellow, 1967–68; Jun. Res. Fellow, Churchill Coll., 1967–70; ICI Fellow, 1969–70; Vis. Scientist, Nat. Bureau of Standards, USA, 1968–69; Lectr in Physical Chemistry, and Fellow and Tutor of Jesus Coll., Oxford Univ., 1970–89; Pro-Vice-Chancellor, 1992–94, Hd of Sch. of Chem., 1995–98, Univ. of Leeds. Visiting Professor: Univ. of Oregon, 1975; Univ. of Maryland, 1980; Univ. of Rome, 1984; Stanford Univ., 1987; John Jeyes Lectr, RSC, 2001. Vice Pres., 1991–98, Sec., 1992–98, Faraday Div., RSC; Mem. Council, NERC, 1995–2000 (Chm., Atmospheric Science and Tech. Bd, 1995–2000). Award in Reaction Kinetics, 1991, Michael Polanyi Medal, Gas Kinetics Gp, 1994, Award for Combustion and Hydrocarbon Oxidation Chem., 2001, RSC; Sugden Award, Combustion Inst., 1993. *Publications:* Reaction Kinetics, 1975; (ed jtly) Modern Gas Kinetics, 1985; (jtly) Reaction Kinetics, 1995; (jtly) Unimolecular Reactions, 1996; (ed) Low Temperature Combustion and Autoignition, 1997; res. papers in learned jls. *Recreation:* walking. *Address:* School of Chemistry, University of Leeds, Leeds LS2 9JT. *T:* (0113) 233 6451; *e-mail:* m.j.pilling@chem.leeds.ac.uk.

PILLINGER, Prof. Colin Trevor, PhD; FRS 1993; Professor of Planetary Science, Open University, since 1990; *b* 9 May 1943; *s* of Alfred Pillinger and Florence (*née* Honour); *m* 1975, Judith Mary Hay; one *s* one *d*. *Educ:* Kingswood Grammar Sch.; University Coll. Swansea, Univ. of Wales (BSc Hons Chem. 1965; PhD 1968). Department of Chemistry, University of Bristol: Post Doctoral Fellow, 1968–72; BSC Fellow, 1972–74; Res. Associate, 1974–76; Res. Associate and Sen. Res. Associate, Dept of Earth Sci., Cambridge, 1976–84; Sen. Res. Fellow, Dept of Earth Sci., Open Univ., 1984–90. Gresham Prof. of Astronomy, 1996–2000. Lead Scientist, British-led Beagle 2 mission to land on Mars in 2003, 1997–. FRAS 1981 (Mem. Council, 1989–91); Fellow, Meteoritical Soc., 1986; FRGS 1993; Mem., British Mass Spectrometry Soc. Hon. DSc Bristol, 1985. *Publications:* numerous papers in learned jls and contribs to radio and TV, UK and abroad. *Recreations:* farming, animals, soccer. *Address:* Planetary Sciences Research Institute, Open University, Milton Keynes MK7 6AA. *T:* (01908) 652119, *Fax:* (01908) 655910.

PIMENTA, His Eminence Simon Ignatius Cardinal; Archbishop of Bombay (RC), 1978–97; *b* 1 March 1920; *s* of late Joseph Anthony Pimenta and Rosie E. Pimenta. *Educ:* St Xavier's Coll., Bombay (BA with Maths); Propaganda Univ., Rome (Degree in Canon Law). Secretary at Archbishop's House, and Vice-Chancellor and Defensor Vinculi, Bombay, 1954; Vice Rector of Cathedral, 1960; Visiting Prof. of Liturgy, Bombay Seminary, 1960; Episcopal Vicar for Liturgy and Pastoral Formation of Junior Clergy, 1968; Rector of the Cathedral, 1967, Rector of Seminary, 1971; Auxiliary Bishop, 1971; Coadjutor Archbishop with right of succession, 1977. President: Catholic Bishops' Conf. of India, 1982–88; (Latin Rite), Conf. of Catholic Bishops of India, 1994–96. Cardinal, 1988. *Publications:* (edited) The Catholic Directory of Bombay, 1960 and 1964 edns; Circulars and Officials of the Archdiocese of Bombay, vols I and II, 1964, vol. III, 1971; booklet on the Cathedral of the Holy Name, 1964; Priest for Ever (homilies), 1999; Memoirs and Milestones (autobiog.), 2000. *Address:* Archbishop's House, 21 Nathalal Parekh Marg, Bombay 400 001, India. *T:* 2021093, 2021193, 2021293.

PIMLOTT, Prof. Benjamin John, FBA 1996; Warden, Goldsmiths College, University of London, since 1998; *b* 4 July 1945; *s* of late John Alfred Ralph Pimlott, CB, and Ellen Dench Howes Pimlott; *m* 1977, Jean Ann Seaton; three *s*. *Educ:* Rokeby Sch., Wimbledon; Marlborough Coll., Wilts; Worcester Coll., Oxford (Open Schol.; MA, BPhil); PhD Newcastle. FRHistS 1993. Lectr, Newcastle Univ., 1970–79; Res. Associate, LSE, 1979–81; Lectr 1981–86, Reader 1986–87, Prof. of Politics and Contemp. Hist., 1987–98, Hon. Fellow, 1999, Birkbeck Coll., London Univ. British Acad. Thank Offering to Britain Fellow, 1972–73; Nuffield Foundn Res. Fellow, 1977–78. Mem., Lord Plant Commn on Electoral Systems, 1991–93; Chm., ESRC Whitehall Prog. Commng Panel, 1993–94, Steering Cttee, 1994–99. Contested (Lab): Arundel, Feb. 1974; Cleveland and Whitby, Oct. 1974, and 1979. Mem. Exec., Fabian Soc., 1987– (Chm., 1993–94). Political columnist: Today, 1986–87; The Times, 1987–88; New Statesman (political editor), 1987–88; Sunday Times, 1988–89. Editor, Samizdat, 1988–90. FRSA 1996. Hon. Fellow, St Cross Coll., Oxford, 2001. *Publications:* Labour and the Left in the 1930s, 1977, 2nd edn 1986; (ed with Chris Cook) Trade Unions in British Politics, 1982, 2nd edn 1991; (ed) Fabian Essays in Socialist Thought, 1984; Hugh Dalton (Whitbread Biography Prize), 1985, 3rd edn 1995; (ed) The Second World War Diary of Hugh Dalton 1940–45, 1986; (ed) The Political Diary of Hugh Dalton 1918–40, 1945–60, 1987; (ed with Jean Seaton) The Media in British Politics, 1987; (ed with T. Wright and T. Flower) The Alternative, 1990; (ed with S. MacGregor) Tackling the Inner Cities, 1990; Harold Wilson, 1992, 2nd edn 1993; Frustrate Their Knavish Tricks, 1994; The Queen, 1996, 2nd edn 2001; articles in learned jls and articles and reviews in Guardian, Independent, Independent on Sunday, Observer, TLS, etc. *Address:* Goldsmiths College, New Cross, SE14 6NW. *T:* (020) 7919 7901.

PIMLOTT, Steven Charles; stage director; Associate Director, Royal Shakespeare Company, since 1996; Artistic Director, The Other Place, since 1998; *b* 18 April 1953; *m* 1991, Daniela Bechly; two *s* one *d*. *Educ:* Manchester Grammar Sch.; Sidney Sussex Coll., Cambridge (MA). Staff Producer, ENO, 1976–78; Associate Dir, Sheffield Crucible, 1987–88; Company Dir, RSC, Stratford, 1996. *Productions* include: *operas:* Opera North, 1978–80: La Bohème; Tosca; Nabucco; Werther; The Pearl Fishers, Scottish Opera; Don Giovanni, Victoria State Opera; Manon Lescaut, Australian Opera; La Traviata, Jerusalem Fest.; Samson et Dalila, Bregenz Fest., 1988; Carmen, 1989; Un Ballo in Maschera, Flanders Opera; Eugene Onegin, New Israeli Opera, 1991; La Bohème, ENO, 1993; Macbeth, Hamburg, 1997; L'Incoronazione di Poppea, ENO, 2000; *theatre:* Royal Exchange, Manchester: Ring Round the Moon, 1983; Carousel; Leeds Playhouse: On the Razzle; A Patriot for Me; York Mystery Plays, 1988; Sheffield Crucible: Carmen Jones; Twelfth Night, A Winter's Tale, 1987; The Park, 1988; Royal National Theatre: Sunday in the Park with George, 1990; The Miser, 1991; Joseph and the Amazing Technicolor Dreamcoat, Palladium, 1991, and tour of UK, Canada, Australia, USA; Never Land, Royal Court, 1998; Doctor Doolittle, Apollo Hammersmith, 1998; Ion, Almeida, 2000; Royal Shakespeare Company: Julius Caesar, 1991; Murder in the Cathedral, 1993; Unfinished Business, Measure for Measure, 1994; Richard III, 1995; As You Like It, The Learned Ladies, 1996; Camino Real, 1997; Bad Weather, 1998; Antony and Cleopatra, 1999; Richard II, 2000; Hamlet, 2001; *film:* Joseph and the Amazing Technicolor Dreamcoat, 1999. *Recreation:* playing the oboe. *Address:* c/o Cruickshank Cazenove Ltd, 97 Old South Lambeth Road, SW8 1XU. *T:* (020) 7735 2933.

PINA-CABRAL, Rt Rev. Daniel (Pereira dos Santos) de; an Assistant Bishop, Diocese of Europe (formerly Auxiliary Bishop, Diocese of Gibraltar in Europe), since 1976; Archdeacon of Gibraltar, 1986–94; *b* 27 Jan. 1924; *m* 1951, Ana Avelina Pina-Cabral; two *s* two *d*. *Educ:* University of Lisbon (Licentiate in Law). Archdeacon of the North in the Lusitanian Church, 1965; Suffragan Bishop of Lebombo (Mozambique), Church of the Province of Southern Africa, 1967; Diocesan Bishop of Lebombo, 1968; Canon of Gibraltar, 1976–. *Address:* Rua Henrique Lopes de Mendonça 253-4 °Dto-Hab. 42, 4150 Porto, Portugal. *T:* (2) 6177772.

PINCHAM, Roger James, CBE 1982; Chairman, Venture Consultants Ltd, since 1980; Consultant, Gerrard, since 2000; *b* 19 Oct. 1935; *y s* of late Sam and of Bessie Pincham; *m* 1965, Gisela von Ulardt (*d* 1974); one *s* two *d*. *Educ:* Kingston Grammar School. National Service, RAF, 1954–56. With Phillips & Drew, 1956–88, Partner, 1967–76, consultant, 1976–88. Mem., London Stock Exchange, 1963–91; MSI, 1992–. Director: Market Access Internat., then Europ. Political Consultancy Gp., 1985–94; Gerrard Vivian Gray, subseq. Greig Middleton, 1988–2000; Cornwall Independent Radio Ltd, 1991–99; ICOR(LPG) Internat. Ltd, 1992–; UK Radio Holdings Ltd, 1992–; Em Seven Communications Ltd (formerly Eventability), 1997–; County Sound Radio Network Ltd, 1998–; Star FM, 1999–. Contested (L) Leominster, 1970, Feb. and Oct. 1974, 1979, 1983. Liberal Party: Nat. Exec., 1974–75 and 1978–87; Assembly Cttee, 1974–87; Standing Cttee, 1975–83; Chm. of Liberal Party, 1979–82; Jt Negotiating Cttee with SDP, and signatory to A Fresh Start for Britain, 1981. Pres., St John Ambulance, St Pancras Div., 1996–2000. Founder Chm., Gladstone Club, 1973–; First Chairman: Indep. Educnl Assoc., 1974–; St James and St Vedast Schools, 1974–; Mem. Council, City Appeal for Eng. Coll. in Prague, 1991–; Gov., Sidney Perry Foundn, 1993–; Founder Trustee, John Stuart Mill Inst., 1992–; Trustee, Princess Margarita of Romania Trust, 1994–; Pres., Lloyd George Soc., 1996–. Pres., Kington Eisteddfod, 1978. FRSA 1994. Fellow, Churchill Meml, Fulton, Mo, 1997–. Freeman, City of London. Liveryman: Barbers' Co. (Master, 1993–94); Founders' Co.; Freeman, Co. of Watermen and Lightermen. *Publications:* (jtly) New Deal for Rural Britain, 1977; (ed) New Deal for British Farmers, 1978. *Recreations:* gardening, cricket, theatre, music. *Address:* 7 The Postern, Wood Street, Barbican, EC2Y 8BJ. *T:* (020) 7638 8154. *Clubs:* Beefsteak, Reform, National Liberal, City of London, Royal Automobile; Surrey County Cricket, Woolhope Naturalists' Field.

PINCHER, (Henry) Chapman; freelance journalist, novelist and business consultant; Assistant Editor, Daily Express, and Chief Defence Correspondent, Beaverbrook Newspapers, 1972–79; *b* Ambala, India, 29 March 1914; *s* of Major Richard Chapman Pincher, E Surrey Regt, and Helen (*née* Foster), Pontefract; *m* 1965, Constance, (Billee), Wolstenholme; one *s* one *d* (by previous *m*). *Educ:* Darlington Gram. Sch.; King's Coll., London (FKC 1979); Inst. Educn; Mil. Coll. of Science. Carter Medallist, London, 1934; BSc (hons Botany, Zoology), 1935. Staff Liverpool Inst., 1936–40. Joined Royal Armoured Corps, 1940; Techn SO, Rocket Div., Min. of Supply, 1943–46; Defence, Science and Medical Editor, Daily Express, 1946–73. Hon. DLitt Newcastle upon Tyne, 1979. Granada Award, Journalist of the Year, 1964; Reporter of the Decade, 1966. *Publications:* Breeding of Farm Animals, 1946; A Study of Fishes, 1947; Into the Atomic Age, 1947; Spotlight on Animals, 1950; Evolution, 1950; (with Bernard Wicksteed) It's Fun Finding Out, 1950; Sleep, and how to get more of it, 1954; Sex in Our Time, 1973; Inside Story, 1978; (jtly) Their Trade is Treachery, 1981; Too Secret Too Long, 1984; The Secret Offensive, 1985; Traitors—the Labyrinths of Treason, 1987; A Web of Deception, 1987; The Truth about Dirty Tricks, 1991; One Dog and Her Man, 1991; Pastoral Symphony (autobiog.), 1993; A Box of Chocolates, 1993; Life's a Bitch!, 1996; Tight Lines!, 1997; God's Dog, 1999; *novels:* Not with a Bang, 1965; The Giantkiller, 1967; The Penthouse Conspirators, 1970; The Skeleton at the Villa Wolkonsky, 1975; The Eye of the Tornado, 1976; The Four Horses, 1978; Dirty Tricks, 1980; The Private World of St John Terrapin, 1982; Contamination, 1989; original researches in genetics, numerous articles in scientific, agricultural and sporting jls. *Recreations:* fishing, natural history, country life; spy-hunting, ferreting in Whitehall and bolting politicians. *Address:* The Church House, 16 Church Street, Kintbury, near Hungerford, Berks RG17 9TR. *T:* (01488) 658855.

PINCHERA, Albert Anthony; Chief Executive, National Kidney Research Fund, since 1998; *b* 2 Sept. 1947; *s* of Albert Storre Pinchera and Edith Pinchera (*née* DeLuca); *m* 1971, Linda Avril Garrad; one *d*. *Educ:* Upton House Sch.; University Coll. London (BSc Hons Geol.). Exploration Geologist, 1969–72; Boots Company plc: Buyer, 1972–74; Sen. Buyer, 1974–77; Asst Merchandise Controller, 1977–81; Mktg Controller, 1981–86; Business Gen. Manager, 1986–90; Man. Dir, Boots Opticians, 1990–95; Hd, Internat. Retail Develt, 1995–97. *Recreations:* military history, art restoration, golf. *Address:* (office) King's Chambers, Priestgate, Peterborough PE1 1FG.

PINCHIN, Malcolm Cyril, CVO 1998; County Education Officer, Surrey, 1982–93; *b* 4 May 1933; *s* of Cyril Pinchin and Catherine Pinchin; *m* 1957, Diana Elizabeth Dawson; three *s*. *Educ:* Cheltenham Grammar Sch.; Univ. of Bristol (BSc). Education Officer, HMOCS, Malawi, 1958–67; Asst Educn Officer, Northampton, 1967–70; Asst Dir of Educn, 1970–74, Asst Dep. Dir of Educn, 1974–76, Leicestershire; Dep. Chief Educn Officer, Devon, 1976–82. Mem., Dio. of Westminster Educn Bd, 1993–97; RC Diocesan rep., Plymouth Educn Cttee, 1997–. Mem. Council, Outward Bound Trust, 1995–97; Trustee: Duke of Edinburgh Award, 1989–97; Children's Trust, Tadworth, 1993–97. FRSA 1986. *Recreations:* gardening, fly fishing, bee keeping, opera. *Address:* Maple Tree House, East Terrace, Budleigh Salterton, Devon EX9 6PG.

PINCHING, Prof. Anthony John, DPhil; FRCP; Louis Freedman Professor of Immunology, since 1992, and Head of Division of Molecular Pathology Infection and Immunity, since 1998, St Bartholomew's and Royal London School of Medicine and Dentistry, Queen Mary and Westfield College, London; *b* 10 March 1947; *s* of John Pinching and Wilhelmina Hermina Pinching (*née* Jonkers); *m* 1971, Katherine Susan Sloper; two *s* two *d*. *Educ:* Sherborne Sch., Dorset; St John's Coll., Oxford (BA 1968); St Edmund Hall, Oxford; Oxford Univ. Med. Sch. (DPhil 1972; BM BCh, MA 1973). MRCP 1976; FRCP 1986. Royal Postgraduate Medical School, London: Registrar and Sen. Registrar, Medicine and Immunology, 1976–79; Res. Fellow (Immunology),

1979–82; St Mary's Hospital Medical School, London: Sen. Lectr in Clinical Immunology, 1982–89; Reader, 1989–92; Clinical Dir, Infection and Immunity, St Bartholomew's Hosp. and Royal Hosps NHS Trust, 1992–99. Vis. Prof., Univ. of Malta, 1986. Terrence Higgins Trust Award, 1986; Evian Health Award, 1990. *Publications:* (ed) AIDS and HIV Infection, 1986; (ed jtly) AIDS and HIV Infection: the wider perspective, 1988; (ed jtly) New Dictionary of Medical Ethics, 1997; res. papers on neuroanatomy, autoimmune disease, HIV and AIDS and other immuno-deficiency. *Recreations:* music, especially opera, playing clarinet, literature, especially 20th Century, writing poetry, hill-walking. *Address:* Department of Immunology, St Bartholomew's Hospital, West Smithfield, EC1A 7BE. *T:* (020) 7601 8428.

PINCOTT, Leslie Rundell, CBE 1978; Managing Director, Esso Petroleum Co. Ltd, 1970–78; *b* 27 March 1923; *s* of Hubert George Pincott and Gertrude Elizabeth Rundell; *m* 1st, 1944, Mary Mae Tuffin (*d* 1996); two *s* one *d*; 2nd, 1997, Elaine Sunderland. *Educ:* Mercers' Sch., Holborn. FCA. Served War, Royal Navy, 1942–46 (Lieut, RNVR). Broads Paterson & Co. (Chartered Accountants), 1946–50; joined Esso Petroleum Co. Ltd, 1950; Comptroller, 1958–61; Asst Gen. Manager (Marketing), 1961–65; Dir and Gen. Manager, Cleveland Petroleum Co. Ltd, 1966–68; Standard Oil Co. (NJ): Exec. Asst to Pres., and later, to Chm., 1968–70; Vice-Chm., Remploy Ltd, 1979–87 (Dir, 1975–87); Chairman: Canada Permanent Trust Co. (UK) Ltd, 1978–80; Stone-Platt Industries PLC, 1980–82; Edman Communications Gp PLC, 1982–87; BR Southern Bd, 1986–89 (Dir, 1977–89). Director: George Wimpey PLC, 1978–85; Highlands Fabricators Ltd, 1984–91. A Dep. Chm., 1978–79, Chm., 1979–80, Price Commn; Chairman: Hundred Gp of Chartered Accountants, 1978–79; Oxford Univ. Business Summer Sch., 1975–78; Printing Industries EDC, NEDO, 1982–88; Mem., Investment Cttee, London Develt Capital Fund (formerly part of Guinness Mahon), 1985–99. Chm., Wandle Housing Assoc., 1996–2000. Pres., District Heating Assoc., 1977–79. Vice-Pres., English Schs Athletics Assoc., 1977–2000; Mem. Council, ISCO, 1982–97. Mem., The Pilgrims, 1971–. CIMgt; CIM. *Recreations:* tennis, travel. *Address:* 53 Hurlingham Court, Ranelagh Gardens, SW6 3UP. *Club:* Hurlingham (Chm., 1988–92; Trustee, 1996–98).

PINDER, Andrew; *see* Pinder, J. A.

PINDER, (John) Andrew; e-envoy, Cabinet Office, since 2000; *b* 5 May 1947; *s* of Norah Joan Pinder and William Gordon Pinder; *m* 1st, 1970, Patricia Munyard (marr. diss. 1980); one *d*; 2nd, 1981, Susan Ellen Tyrrell; one *d* and one step *s*. *Educ:* De La Salle Coll., Sheffield; Coleshill Grammar Sch., Warwicks; Univ. of Liverpool (BA Hons Social Studies). Inspector of Taxes, 1972–76; Board of Inland Revenue: Policy Div., 1976–79; Management Div., 1979–90, Under Sec., Dir of IT, 1989; Prudential Corporation: Dir of Systems, 1990–92; Dir, Gp Management Services, 1991–92; Dir, Systems and Business Ops, 1992–94; Citibank, 1995–99: Hd of Eur. Ops and Technol., 1995; Hd of Ops and Technol., Global Transaction Services, 1995–97; Hd of Eur. Br. Ops, Global Corp. Bank, 1998–99; indep. consultant on corporate and info. technol. strategy, 1999–2000. Chairman: Dovetail Sabrina Ltd, 1998–; Dovetail of Shrewsbury Ltd, 1999; Will Network Ltd, 2000–; Indep. Nat. Will Register, 2000–. Chm., Shropshire Learning & Skills Council, 2000–. FRSA 1995. Freeman, City of London, 1994; Liveryman, Co. of Information Technologists, 1995. *Recreations:* music, walking, gardening, reading, fly-fishing. *Address:* 6 Lambert Jones Mews, Barbican, EC2Y 8DP. *Clubs:* Reform, Institute of Directors.

PINDER, John Humphrey Murray, OBE 1973; Professor, 1970–99, Hon. Professor, since 1999, College of Europe; Chairman, Federal Trust, since 1985; *b* 20 June 1924; *s* of Harold Pinder and Lilian Pinder (*née* Murray); *m* 1964, Pauline Hawtayne Lewin. *Educ:* Marlborough Coll.; King's Coll., Cambridge (MA). Served RA, W African Artillery, 1943–47. Press Officer, Federal Union, 1950–52; EIU, 1952–64, Internat. Dir, 1957–64; Dir, PEP, then PSI, 1964–85. Member, Editorial Board: Government and Opposition, 1975–2001; Jl Common Mkt Studies, 1979–92. Pres., Union of Eur. Federalists, 1984–90 (Hon. Pres., 1990–); Vice-Pres., Eur. Movement (Internat.), 1990–2000; Member, Board: Eur. Movement (UK), 1998–2001 (Vice Chm., 1975–90; Dep. Chm., 1990–98); Inst. Eur. Envmtl Policy, 1990–2001; Trans Eur. Policy Studies Assoc., 1995–98; Member, Council: ODI, 1972–99; Hansard Soc., 1973–99; RIIA, 1985–91. Trustee: One World Trust, 1993–2000; James Madison Trust, 2001–. *Publications:* Britain and the Common Market, 1961; Europe against de Gaulle, 1963; (jtly) Europe after de Gaulle, 1969; (ed) The Economics of Europe, 1971; (ed) Fifty Years of PEP: looking forward 1931–1981, 1981; (jtly) Policies for a Constrained Economy, 1982; (ed) National Industrial Strategies and the World Economy, 1982; (ed jtly) One European Market?: a critical analysis of the Commission's internal market strategy, 1988; (ed jtly) Pacifism is not Enough: collected lectures and speeches of Lord Lothian, 1990; (jtly) Federal Union: the pioneers, 1990; The European Community and Eastern Europe, 1991; The Building of the European Union, 1991, 3rd edn 1998; (ed jtly) Maastricht and Beyond: building the European Union, 1994; (ed) Altiero Spinelli and the British Federalists, 1999; (ed) Foundations of Democracy in the European Union, 1999; The European Union: a very short introduction, 2001. *Recreations:* music, walking, foreign languages and literature. *Address:* 26 Bloomfield Terrace, SW1W 8PQ. *Club:* Brooks's.

PINE, Courtney, OBE 2000; jazz saxophonist; *b* 18 March 1964; *m* 1997, June Guishard; one *s* three *d*. *Albums* include: Journey to the Urge Within, 1987; Destiny's Song, 1988; The Vision's Tale, 1989; Closer to Home, 1990; Within the Realms of Our Dreams; To the Eyes of Creation; Modern Day Jazz Stories, 1995; Underground, 1997; Back in the Day, 2000; has also produced and arranged albums; contrib. to albums by other artists, incl. Mick Jagger, and to Larry Adler tribute album; has toured internationally. *Address:* Collaboration, 23 Avenue Crescent, W3 8ET.

PINHEIRO, Prof. João de Deus, PhD, DSc; Professor of Engineering Sciences, University of Minho, since 1981; Member, European Commission (formerly Commission of European Communities), 1993–99; *b* Lisbon, 11 July 1945; *s* of Agostinho de Matos Salvador Pinheiro and Maria de Lurdes Rogado Pereira Salvador Pinheiro; *m* 1970, Maria Manuela Vieira Paisana; three *s* one *d*. *Educ:* Technol High Inst., Portugal (Licentiate in Chem. Engrg); Univ. of Birmingham (MSc Chem. Engrg, PhD Engrg Scis, DSc Engrg). University of Minho, Portugal: Dir, Dept of Planning, 1978–81; Dir, Sch. of Engrg, 1979–80; Associate Vice-Chancellor, 1981–82; Vice-Chancellor, 1984–85; Sec. of State for Educn and Schs Admin, 1982–83; Minister of Educn, then Minister of Educn and Culture, then Minister for Foreign Affairs, 1985–92; Mem., Nat. Parliament, for Viana do Castelo, 1985–87, for Porto, 1987–95; Mem., Nat. Council, Social Democratic Party, 1987; Pres., Cttee of Ministers, Council of Europe, 1991; Hon. Pres., Council of Ministers, NATO, 1990–91; Pres., Council of Ministers, EC, 1992. Mem. 1979–83, Vice-Pres., 1983–84, Nat. Council for Scientific and Technol Res. For. Mem., Royal Acad. of Engrg, 1997. Grã-Cruz, Ordem Militar de Cristo (Portugal), 1993; numerous foreign decorations. *Recreations:* golf, tennis, reading, cinema, music, etc. *Address:* Rua Tomas d'Anunciacao, No 73-2 Esq, 1350-324 Lisboa, Portugal. *Clubs:* Aroeira Golf, Quinta da Marinha Golf and Tennis, VilaSol, Quinta do Lago, S Lourenço, Pinheiros Altos, Vilamoura (Portugal); Brabantse Golf (Brussels).

PINI, Yvonne Anne; *see* Coen, Y. A.

PININFARINA, Sergio; Cavaliere del Lavoro, 1976; engineer; Member, European Parliament (Liberal and Democratic Group), 1979–88; President, Pininfarina SpA; *b* 8 Sept. 1926; *s* of Battista Pininfarina and Rosa Copasso; *m* 1951, Giorgia Gianolio; two *s* one *d*. *Educ:* Polytechnic of Turin; graduated in Mech. Eng., 1950. President: Federpiemonte, 1983–88; OICA, 1987–89; Confindustria, 1988–92; Comitato Promotore Alta Velocità, 1991–; Vice-Pres., UNICE, 1990–94. Board Member: Ferrari; Banca Passadore; Banca Brignone; Toro Assicurazioni; Indep. Internat. Univ. of Social Studies, Rome. Foreign Mem., Royal Swedish Acad. of Engrg Scis, 1988. Hon. Dr Econs, Indep. Internat. Univ. of Social Studies, Rome, 1993. Légion d'Honneur, 1979. Hon. RDI 1983. Compasso d'Oro, Assoc. for Industrial Design, 1995. *Recreation:* golf. *Address:* PO Box 295, 10100 Turin, Italy. *T:* (11) 70911; Pininfarina SpA, corso Stati Uniti 61, 10129 Turin, Italy. *Clubs:* Società Whist Accademia Filarmonica, Rotary, Subalpino, Artisti (Turin); Golf Torino, Golf Garlenda, Associazione Sportiva I Roveri.

PINKER, Sir George (Douglas), KCVO 1990 (CVO 1983); FRCS, FRCSEd, FRCOG; Surgeon-Gynaecologist to the Queen, 1973–90; Consulting Gynaecological Surgeon and Obstetrician, St Mary's Hospital, Paddington and Samaritan Hospital, 1958–89; Consulting Gynaecological Surgeon, Middlesex and Soho Hospitals, 1969–80; Consultant Gynæcologist, King Edward VII Hospital for Officers, 1974–89; *b* 6 Dec. 1924; *s* of late Ronald Douglas Pinker and of Queenie Elizabeth Pinker (*née* Dix); *m* Dorothy Emma (*née* Russell); three *s* one *d* (incl. twin *s* and *d*). *Educ:* Reading Sch.; St Mary's Hosp., London Univ. MB BS London 1947; DObst 1949; MRCOG 1954; FRCS(Ed) 1957; FRCOG 1964; FRCS 1989. Late Cons. Gyn. Surg., Bolingbroke Hosp., and Res. Off., Nuffield Dept of Obst., Radcliffe Infirmary, Oxford; late Cons. Gyn. Surg., Queen Charlotte's Hosp. Arthur Wilson Orator, 1972 and 1989, Turnbull Scholar, and Hon. Consultant Obstetrician and Gynaecologist, 1972, Royal Women's Hosp., Melbourne. Examiner in Obst. and Gynae.: Univs of Cambridge, Dundee, London, and FRCS Edinburgh; formerly also in RCOG, and Univs of Birmingham, Glasgow and Dublin. Sims Black Travelling Prof., RCOG, 1979; Vis. Prof., SA Regional Council, RCOG, 1980. Pres., RCOG, 1987–90 (Hon. Treas., 1970–77; Vice-Pres., 1980–83). Pres., British Fertility Soc., 1987; Mem. Council, Winston Churchill Trust, 1979–95; Mem., Blair Bell Res. Soc.; FRSocMed (Pres., 1992–95); Hon. Mem., British Paediatric Assoc., 1988. Hon. FRCSI 1987; Hon. FRACOG 1989; Hon. FACOG 1990; Hon. Fellow, S African Soc. of Obstetricians and Gynaecologists, 1990; Hon. FCMSA 1991. Chm., Editorial Bd, Modern Medicine (Obs. and Gynae.), 1989–91 (Mem., 1980–91). *Publications:* (all jtly) Ten Teachers Diseases of Women, 1964; Ten Teachers Obstetrics, 1966; A Short Textbook of Obstetrics and Gynaecology, 1967. *Recreations:* music, gardening, sailing, ski-ing, fell walking. *Address:* Sycamore House, Willersey, Broadway, Worcs WR12 7PJ. *Club:* Garrick.

PINKER, Prof. Robert Arthur; Professor of Social Administration, London School of Economics and Political Science, 1993–96, now Emeritus; Member, since 1991, and Privacy Commissioner, since 1994, Press Complaints Commission; *b* 27 May 1931; *s* of Dora Elizabeth and Joseph Pinker; *m* 1955, Jennifer Farrington Boulton (*d* 1994); two *d*. *Educ:* Holloway County Sch.; LSE (Cert. in Social Sci. and Admin. 1959; BSc Sociology 1962; MSc Econ 1965). University of London: Head of Sociology Dept, Goldsmiths' Coll., 1964–72; Lewisham Prof. of Social Admin, Goldsmiths' Coll. and Bedford Coll., 1972–74; Prof. of Social Studies, Chelsea Coll., 1974–78; Prof. of Social Work Studies, LSE, 1978–93; Pro-Director, LSE, 1985–88; Pro-Vice-Chancellor for Social Scis, London Univ., 1989–90. Chm., British Library Project on Family and Social Research, 1983–86; Mem., Council, Advertising Standards Authority, 1988–95; Chm., Central Westminster Police/Community Consultative Gp, 1997–99. Chm. Governors, Centre for Policy on Ageing, 1988–94; Governor: BPMF, 1990–94; Goldsmiths Coll., Univ. of London, 2001 (Hon. Fellow, 1999). Chm., Editl Bd, Jl of Social Policy, 1981–86. *Publications:* English Hospital Statistics 1861–1938, 1964; Social Theory and Social Policy, 1971; The Idea of Welfare, 1979; Social Work in an Enterprise Society, 1990. *Recreations:* reading, writing, travel, unskilled gardening. *Address:* 76 Coleraine Road, Blackheath, SE3 7PE. *T:* (020) 8858 5320.

PINKER, Prof. Steven (Arthur), PhD; Professor, Department of Brain and Cognitive Sciences, Massachusetts Institute of Technology, since 1989; *b* Montreal, 18 Sept. 1954; *s* of Harry and Roslyn Pinker; US citizen; *m* 1st, 1980, Nancy Etcoff (marr. diss. 1992); 2nd, 1995, Ilavenil Subbiah. *Educ:* McGill Univ. (BA Psychol. 1976); Harvard Univ. (PhD Exptl Psychol. 1979). Postdoctoral Fellow, Center for Cognitive Sci., MIT, 1979–80; Assistant Professor, Department of Psychology: Harvard Univ., 1980–81; Stanford Univ., 1981–82; Massachusetts Institute of Technology: Asst Prof., Dept of Psychol., 1982–85; Associate Prof., Dept of Brain and Cognitive Scis, 1985–89; Co-Dir, Center for Cognitive Scis, 1985–94; Dir, McDonnell-Pew Center for Cognitive Neurosci., 1994–99; Margaret MacVicar Faculty Fellow, 2000. Hon. DSc McGill, 1999. Dist. Scientific Award, 1984, Boyd R. McCandless Young Scientist Award, 1986, Amer. Psychol Assoc.; Troland Res. Award, NAS, 1993; Golden Plate Award, Amer. Acad. Achievement, 1999. *Publications:* Language Learnability and Language Development, 1984; (ed) Visual Cognition, 1985; (ed with J. Mehler) Connections and Symbols, 1988; Learnability and Cognition: the acquisition of argument structure, 1989; (ed with B. Levin) Lexical and Conceptual Semantics, 1992; The Language Instinct, 1994 (Wm James Bk Prize, Amer. Psychol Assoc., 1995); How the Mind Works, 1997 (LA Times Bk Prize, 1998; Wm James Bk Prize, Amer. Psychol Assoc., 1999); Words and Rules: the ingredients of language, 1999; contrib. articles to Science, Cognition, Cognitive Sci. and other jls. *Recreations:* bicycling, photography. *Address:* Department of Brain and Cognitive Sciences, Massachusetts Institute of Technology, Cambridge, MA 02139, USA. *T:* (617) 2538946, *Fax:* (617) 2588654; *e-mail:* steve@psyche.mit.edu.

PINKERTON, Prof. (Charles) Ross, MD; Professor of Paediatric Oncology, Institute of Cancer Research, London, since 1995; Consultant Paediatric Oncologist and Head, Children's Unit, Royal Marsden Hospital, since 1989 (Senior Research Fellow, 1986–89); *b* 6 Oct. 1950; *s* of Prof. John Henry McKnight Pinkerton, *qv*; *m* 1989, Janet Hardy; three *d*. *Educ:* Campbell Coll.; Queen's Univ., Belfast (MD 1981). Postgrad. trng in paediatrics, Dublin and London, 1976–80; trng in children's cancer, London and France, 1980–86. Chm., UK Children's Cancer Study Gp, 2000–. *Publications:* editor: Paediatric Oncology: clinical practice and controversies, 1991, 2nd edn 1997; Childhood Cancer Management, 1995; Clinical Challenges in Paediatric Oncology, 1998; over 200 papers on children's cancer management. *Recreation:* tennis. *Address:* 3 Woodmansterne Lane, Banstead, Surrey SM7 3EX.

PINKERTON, Prof. John Henry McKnight, CBE 1983; Professor of Midwifery and Gynæcology, Queen's University, Belfast, 1963–85, now Emeritus; Gynæcologist: Royal Victoria and City Hospitals, Belfast, 1963–85; Ulster Hospital for Women and Children, 1963–85; Surgeon, Royal Maternity Hospital, Belfast, 1963–85; *b* 5 June 1920; *s* of late William Ross Pinkerton and Eva Pinkerton; *m* 1947, Florence McKinstry, MB, BCh, BAO; four *s*. *Educ:* Royal Belfast Academical Institution; Queen's Univ., Belfast.

Hyndman Univ. Entrance Scholar, 1939; MB, BCh, BAO Hons; Magrath Scholar in Obstetrics and Gynæcology, 1943. Active service in HM Ships as Surg.-Lt, RNVR, 1945–47. MD 1948; MRCOG 1949; FRCOG 1960; FZS 1960; FRCPI 1977. Sen. Lectr in Obstetrics and Gynæcology, University Coll. of the West Indies, and Consultant Obstetrician and Gynæcologist to University Coll. Hosp. of the West Indies, 1953–59; Rockefeller Research Fellow at Harvard Medical Sch., 1956–57; Prof. of Obstetrics and Gynæcology, Univ. of London, at Queen Charlotte's and Chelsea Hosps and the Inst. of Obstetrics and Gynæcology, 1959–63; Obstetric Surgeon to Queen Charlotte's Hosp.; Surgeon to Chelsea Hosp. for Women. Vice-Pres., RCOG, 1977–80; Chm., Inst. of Obstetrics and Gynæcol., RCPI, 1984–87. Hon. DSc NUI, 1986. *Publications:* various papers on obstetrical and gynæcological subjects. *Address:* 41c Sans Souci Park, Belfast BT9 5BZ. *T:* (028) 9068 2956.

See also C. R. Pinkerton, W. R. Pinkerton.

PINKERTON, Ross; *see* Pinkerton, C. R.

PINKERTON, William Ross, CBE 1977; JP; HM Nominee for Northern Ireland on General Medical Council, 1979–83, retired; a director of companies; *b* 10 April 1913; *s* of William Ross Pinkerton and Eva Pinkerton; *m* 1943, Anna Isobel Lyness; two *d*. Managing Director, H. Stevenson & Co. Ltd, Londonderry, 1941–76. Mem., Baking Wages Council (NI), 1957–74. Mem. later Chm, Londonderry/Gransha Psychiatric HMC, 1951–69; Vice-Chm., then Chm., North West HMC, 1969–72; Chm., Western Health and Social Services Board, 1972–79; Member: Central Services Agency (NI), 1972–79; NI Health and Social Services Council, 1975–79; Lay Mem., Health and Personal Social Services Tribunal, NI, 1978–. Member, New Ulster Univ. Court, 1973–85, Council, 1979–85. Hon. Life Governor: Altnagelvin, Gransha, Waterside, St Columb's, Roe Valley, Strabane, Foyle and Stradreagh Hosps. JP Co. Londonderry, 1965–84, Div. of Ards, 1984–91, Div. of Craigavon, 1991. *Recreations:* yachting, fishing. *Address:* 9 Harwich Mews, Culcavey Road, Hillsborough, Co. Down, Northern Ireland BT26 6RH. *T:* (028) 9268 2421. *Club:* Royal Highland Yacht (Oban).

See also J. H. McK. Pinkerton.

PINNER, Hayim, OBE 1989; consultant, administrator, linguist, educator, lecturer, journalist, broadcaster; Director, Sternberg Charitable Trust, 1991–96; *b* London, 25 May 1925; *s* of late Simon Pinner and Annie Pinner (*née* Wagner); *m* 1956, Rita Reuben, Cape Town (marr. diss. 1980); one *s* one *d*. *Educ:* Davenant Foundation School; London University; Yeshivah Etz Hayim; Bet Berl College, Israel. Served RAOC, 1944–48; Editor, Jewish Vanguard, 1950–74; Exec. Dir, B'nai B'rith, 1957–77; Sec. Gen., Board of Deputies of British Jews, 1977–91. Hon. Vice-Pres., Zionist Fedn of GB and Ireland, 1975– (Hon. Treasurer, 1971–75); Vice-Pres., Labour Zionist Movement (former Nat. Chm.); Hon. Sec., CCJ; Member: Jewish Agency and World Zionist Orgn; Adv. Council, World Congress of Faiths; Trades Adv. Council; Hillel Foundn; Jt Israel Appeal; Lab. Party Middle East Cttee; 'B' List of Lab. Parly Candidates; UNA; Founder Mem. Exec., Inter-Faith. FRSA. Freeman, City of London. Contribs to Radio 4, Radio London, London Broadcasting, BBC TV. Encomienda de la Orden del Mérito Civil (Spain), 1993. *Publications:* contribs to UK and foreign periodicals, Isra-Kit. *Recreations:* travelling, swimming, reading, talking. *Address:* 62 Grosvenor Street, W1X 9DA.

PINNER, Ruth Margaret, (Mrs M. J. Pinner); *see* Kempson, R. M.

PINNINGTON, Roger Adrian, TD 1967; Chairman, Armour Trust plc, since 1996; *b* 27 Aug. 1932; *s* of William Austin Pinnington and Elsie Amy Pinnington; *m* 1974, Marjorie Ann Pearson; one *s* three *d*. *Educ:* Rydal Sch., Colwyn Bay; Lincoln Coll., Oxford (MA). Marketing Dir, Jonas Woodhead & Sons, 1963–74; 1975–82: Vice Pres., TRW Europe Inc.; Man. Dir, CAM Gears Ltd; Pres., TRW Italia SpA; Dir Gen., Gemmer France; Pres., Torfinasa; Dep. Chm. and Chief Exec., UBM Group, 1982–85; Dir, Norcros, 1985–86; Dir and Chief Exec., Royal Ordnance PLC, 1986–87; Dir and Gp Chief Exec., RHP, subseq. Pilgrim House Gp, 1987–89. Chairman: Telfos Hldgs, subseq. Jenbacher Hldgs (UK), 1991–95; Lynx Holdings PLC, 1992–98; Cortworth PLC, 1994–97; British World Aviation Ltd, later BWA Gp plc, 1994–2000; Montanaro Hldgs Ltd, 1995–; Dep. Chm., Huntingdon Internat. Hldgs plc, 1998–99 (Chm., 1994–98). *Recreations:* gardening, arguing with Sally, collecting sauce bottle labels. *Address:* 15 Lennox Gardens Mews, SW1X 0DP. *T:* (020) 7581 9684. *Clubs:* Royal Automobile; Vincent's (Oxford).

PINNOCK, Comdr Harry James, RN retd; Director, Cement Makers' Federation, 1979–87; *b* 6 April 1927; *s* of Frederick Walter Pinnock and Kate Ada (*née* Shepherd); *m* 1962, Fru Inger Connie Åhgren (*d* 1978); one *d*. *Educ:* Sutton Valence Sch. Joined RN, 1945; Midshipman, HMS Nelson, 1945–47; Sub-Lieut/Lieut, HMS Belfast, Far East, 1948–50; RN Rhine Flotilla, 1951–52; Staff of First Sea Lord, 1952–55; Lt-Comdr, Mediterranean Minesweepers, 1955–57; HMS Ceylon, E of Suez, 1957–59; Staff of C-in-C Plymouth, 1960–61; HQ Allied Naval Forces, Northern Europe, Oslo, 1961–63; Comdr, MoD, 1964–67, retd. Cement Makers' Fedn, 1970–87. *Recreations:* walking, gardening, travel. *Address:* The Stables, Haining House, Selkirk TD7 5LR.

PINNOCK, Trevor, CBE 1992; ARCM; harpsichordist; conductor; Director, The English Concert, since 1973; Artistic Adviser, National Arts Centre Orchestra, Ottawa, since 1996 (Artistic Director and Principal Conductor, 1991–96); *b* Canterbury, 16 Dec. 1946. *Educ:* Canterbury Cathedral Choir Sch.; Simon Langton Grammar Sch., Canterbury; Royal Coll. of Music, London (Foundn Scholar; Harpischord and Organ Prizes). ARCM Hons (organ) 1965. London début with Galliard Harpsichord Trio (Jt Founder with Stephen Preston, flute and Anthony Pleeth, 'cello), 1966; solo début, Purcell Room, London, 1968. Formed The English Concert for purpose of performing music of baroque period on instruments in original condition or good modern copies, 1972, making its London début in English Bach Festival, Purcell Room, 1973. NY début at Metropolitan Opera, conducting Handel Giulio Cesare, 1988. Recordings of complete keyboard works of Rameau; Bach Toccatas, Partitas, Goldberg Variations, Concerti, Handel Messiah and Suites, Purcell Dido and Aeneas, orchestral and choral works of Bach, Handel, Vivaldi, complete symphonies of Mozart, etc. Hon. DMus: Ottawa, 1993; Kent, 1995. *Address:* c/o Ms Jan Burnett, Askonas Holt, Lonsdale Chambers, 27 Chancery Lane, WC2A 1PF. *T:* (020) 7400 1700.

PINSENT, Sir Christopher (Roy), 3rd Bt *cr* 1938; Lecturer and Tutor, Camberwell School of Art, 1962–86, retired; *b* 2 Aug. 1922; *s* of Sir Roy Pinsent, 2nd Bt, and Mary Tirzah Pinsent (*d* 1951), *d* of Dr Edward Geoffrey Walls, Spilsby, Lincs; *S* father, 1978; *m* 1951, Susan Mary, *d* of John Norton Scorer, Fotheringhay; one *s* two *d*. *Educ:* Winchester College. *Heir: s* Thomas Benjamin Roy Pinsent, *b* 21 July 1967. *Address:* Ramblers, The Cricket Green, Woodside Road, Chiddingfold, Surrey GU8 4UG.

PINSENT, Matthew Clive, CBE 2001 (MBE 1992); oarsman; *b* 10 Oct. 1970; *s* of Rev. Ewen and Jean Pinsent. *Educ:* Eton College; St Catherine's College, Oxford (BA Hons Geography 1993). Winner, coxless pairs: (with Tim Foster) Junior World Championship, 1988; (with Steven Redgrave): World Championship, 1991, 1993, 1994 and 1995; Olympic Gold Medal, 1992 and 1996; (with James Cracknell) coxed and coxless pairs, World Championship, 2001; Winner, coxless fours: World Championship, 1997, 1998, 1999; Olympic Gold Medal, 2000; Mem., Oxford Boat Race winning crew, 1990, 1991. *Recreations:* golf, flying. *Club:* Leander (Henley-on-Thames).

PINSON, Barry; QC 1973; *b* 18 Dec. 1925; *s* of Thomas Alfred Pinson and Alice Cicily Pinson; *m* 1950, Miriam Mary; one *s* one *d*; *m* 1977, Anne Kathleen Golby. *Educ:* King Edward's Sch., Birmingham; Univ. of Birmingham. LLB Hons 1945. Fellow Inst. Taxation. Mil. Service, 1944–47. Called to Bar, Gray's Inn, 1949, Bencher 1981. Trustee, RAF Museum, 1980–98; Chm., Addington Soc., 1987–90. *Publications:* Revenue Law, 17 edns. *Recreations:* music, photography. *T:* (020) 7798 8450. *Clubs:* Arts, Sloane.

PINTER, Lady Antonia; *see* Fraser, Antonia.

PINTER, Harold, CBE 1966; CLit 1998; FRSL; actor, playwright and director; Associate Director, National Theatre, 1973–83; *b* 10 Oct. 1930; *s* of J. Pinter; *m* 1st, 1956, Vivien Merchant (marr. diss. 1980; she *d* 1982); one *s*; 2nd, 1980, Lady Antonia Fraser, *qv*. *Educ:* Hackney Downs Grammar Sch. Actor (mainly repertory), 1949–57. *Directed:* The Collection (co-dir with Peter Hall), Aldwych, 1962; The Birthday Party, Aldwych, 1964; The Lover, The Dwarfs, Arts, 1966; Exiles, Mermaid, 1970; Butley, Criterion, 1971; Butley (film), 1973; Next of Kin, Nat. Theatre, 1974; Otherwise Engaged, Queen's, 1975, NY 1977; Blithe Spirit, Nat. Theatre, 1977; The Rear Column, Globe, 1978; Close of Play, Nat. Theatre, 1979; The Hothouse, Hampstead, 1980 (for TV, 1982); Quartermaine's Terms, Queen's, 1981; Incident at Tulse Hill, Hampstead, 1982; The Trojan War Will Not Take Place, Nat. Theatre, 1983; The Common Pursuit, Lyric Hammersmith, 1984; Sweet Bird of Youth, Haymarket, 1985; Circe and Bravo, Wyndham's, 1986; Vanilla, Lyric, 1990; The New World Order, Royal Court, 1991; Party Time, Almeida, 1991 (for TV, 1992); Oleanna, Royal Court, 1993; Taking Sides, Criterion, 1995; Twelve Angry Men, Comedy, 1996; The Late Middle Classes, Watford, 1999. Hon. DLitt: Reading, 1970; Birmingham, 1971; Glasgow, 1974; East Anglia, 1974; Stirling, 1979; Brown, 1982; Hull, 1986; Sussex, 1990; E London, 1994; Sofia, 1995. Shakespeare Prize, Hamburg, 1970; Austrian State Prize for European Literature, 1973; Pirandello Prize, 1980; Donatello Prize, 1982; Elmer Holmes Bobst Award, 1984; David Cohen British Literary Prize, 1995; Laurence Olivier Special Award, 1996. *Plays:* The Room (stage 1957, television 1965); The Birthday Party, 1957 (stage 1958, television 1960 and 1987, film 1968); The Dumb Waiter, 1957 (stage 1960, television 1964 and 1987); The Hothouse, 1958 (stage 1980, television 1981); A Slight Ache, 1958 (radio 1959, stage 1961, television 1966); A Night Out, 1959 (radio and television, 1960); The Caretaker, 1959 (stage 1960 and 1991, film 1963, television 1966 and 1982); Night School, 1960 (television 1960 and 1982, radio 1966); The Dwarfs (radio 1960, stage 1963); The Collection (television 1961 and 1979, stage 1962); The Lover (television 1962 (Italia Prize) and 1977, stage 1963); Tea Party, 1964 (television 1965, stage 1970); The Homecoming, 1964 (stage 1965, film 1973); The Basement, 1966 (television 1967, stage 1970); Landscape, 1967 (radio 1968, stage 1969); Silence, 1968 (stage 1968); Night, 1969; Old Times, 1970 (stage 1971, television 1975); Monologue, 1972 (television 1973); No Man's Land, 1974 (stage 1975 and 1992, television 1978); Betrayal (stage 1978 (SWET Award, 1979) and 1991, film 1983); Family Voices, 1980 (radio 1981 (Giles Cooper Award, 1982), stage 1981); A Kind of Alaska, 1982 (stage and television 1984); Victoria Station (stage 1982); One for the Road (stage and television 1984); Mountain Language (stage 1988); The New World Order (stage 1991); Party Time (stage 1991, television 1992); Moonlight (stage 1993); Ashes to Ashes (stage 1996); Celebration (stage 2000). *Screenplays:* The Caretaker, The Servant, 1962; The Pumpkin Eater, 1963; The Quiller Memorandum, 1966; Accident, 1967; The Birthday Party, The Homecoming, 1968; The Go-Between, 1969; Langrishe, Go Down, 1970 (adapted for television, 1978); A la Recherche du Temps Perdu, 1972; The Last Tycoon, 1974; The French Lieutenant's Woman, 1981; Betrayal, 1981; Victory, 1982; Turtle Diary, 1985; The Handmaid's Tale, 1987; The Heat of the Day, 1988; Reunion, 1989; The Trial, 1989; The Comfort of Strangers, 1990. *Publications:* The Caretaker, 1960; The Birthday Party, and other plays, 1960; A Slight Ache, 1961; The Collection, 1963; The Lover, 1963; The Homecoming, 1965; Tea Party, and, The Basement, 1967; (co-ed) PEN Anthology of New Poems, 1967; Mac, 1968; Landscape, and, Silence, 1969; Five Screenplays, 1971; Old Times, 1971; Poems, 1971; No Man's Land, 1975; The Proust Screenplay: A la Recherche du Temps Perdu, 1978; Betrayal, 1978; Poems and Prose 1949–1977, 1978; I Know the Place, 1979; Family Voices, 1981; Other Places, 1982; French Lieutenant's Woman and other screenplays, 1982; One For The Road, 1984; Collected Poems and Prose, 1986; (co-ed) 100 Poems by 100 Poets, 1986; Mountain Language, 1988; The Heat of the Day, 1989; The Dwarfs (novel), 1990; Party Time, 1991; Moonlight, 1993; (ed jtly) 99 Poems in Translation, 1994; Ashes to Ashes, 1996; Various Voices: prose, poetry, politics 1948–1998, 1998. *Recreation:* cricket. *Address:* c/o Judy Daish Associates Ltd, 2 St Charles Place, W10 6EG.

PIPE, Martin Charles, CBE 2000; racehorse trainer, National Hunt and flat racing; *b* 29 May 1945; *m* 1971, Mary Caroline; one *s*. First trainer's licence, 1977; jt founder, Pipe-Scudamore Racing Club PLC, 1989; only British trainer to saddle 200 winners in a season, 1989; eleven times champion trainer, National Hunt, to 2001; set new British record for Flat and jump winners with 2,989 winners, 2000. *Publication:* (with Richard Pitman) Martin Pipe: the champion trainer's story, 1992. *Address:* Pond House, Nicholashayne, near Wellington, Somerset TA21 9QY.

PIPER, Rt Rev. Dr Reginald John; Bishop of Wollongong, and an Assistant Bishop, Diocese of Sydney, since 1993; *b* 25 Feb. 1942; *s* of Leslie and Myra Elaine Piper; *m* 1967, Dorothy Patricia Lock; one *s* two *d*. *Educ:* Australian Nat. Univ. (BSc 1963); Moore Coll., Sydney (Theol. Schol. 1970); Melbourne Coll. of Divinity (BD 1975); Fuller Theol Seminary, LA (DMin 1992). Ordained deacon, 1966, priest, 1967; Curate: St Stephen's, Willougby, 1966–69; St Clement's, Lalor Park, 1970–71; Rector: St Aidan's, Hurstville Grove, 1972–75; Christ Church, Kiama, 1975–79; Holy Trinity, Adelaide, 1980–93. *Publication:* The Ephesus Plan, 1998. *Address:* Anglican Church Centre, 74 Church Street, Wollongong, NSW 2500, Australia.

PIPPARD, Prof. Sir (Alfred) Brian, Kt 1975; FRS 1956; Cavendish Professor of Physics, University of Cambridge, 1971–82, now Emeritus; *b* 7 Sept. 1920; *s* of late Prof. A. J. S. Pippard; *m* 1955, Charlotte Frances Dyer; three *d*. *Educ:* Clifton Coll.; Clare Coll., Cambridge (BA 1941; MA 1945; PhD 1949; ScD 1966; Hon. Fellow 1973). Scientific Officer, Radar Research and Development Establishment, Great Malvern, 1941–45; Stokes Student, Pembroke Coll., Cambridge, 1945–46; Demonstrator in Physics, University of Cambridge, 1946; Lecturer in Physics, 1950; Reader in Physics, 1959–60; John Humphrey Plummer Prof. of Physics, 1960–71; Pres., Clare Hall, Cambridge, 1966–73 (Hon. Fellow, 1993). Visiting Prof., Institute for the Study of Metals, University of Chicago, 1955–56. Fellow of Clare Coll., Cambridge, 1947–66. Cherwell-Simon Memorial Lectr, Oxford, 1968–69; Eddington Meml Lectr, Cambridge, 1988. Pres., Inst. of Physics, 1974–76 (FInstP 1970, Hon. FInstP 1995). Hughes Medal of the Royal Soc., 1959; Holweck Medal, 1961; Dannie-Heineman Prize, 1969; Guthrie Prize, 1970. *Publications:* Elements of Classical Thermodynamics, 1957; Dynamics of Conduction

Electrons, 1962; Forces and Particles, 1972; The Physics of Vibration, vol. 1, 1978, vol. 2, 1983; Response and Stability, 1985; Magnetoresistance, 1989; (ed and contrib.) 20th Century Physics, 1995; papers in Proc. Royal Soc., etc. *Recreation:* music. *Address:* 30 Porson Road, Cambridge CB2 2EU. *T:* (01223) 358713.

PIRELLI, Leopoldo; Knight, Order of Labour Merit, 1977; engineer; Hon. President, Pirelli & Co., since 1999 (Partner, 1957–99, and Chairman, 1995–99); *b* 27 Aug. 1925; *s* of Alberto Pirelli and Ludovica Zambeletti; *m* 1947, Giulia Ferlito; one *s* one *d*. *Educ:* Milan University (Politecnico); graduated in Mech. Eng. 1950. Mem., Bd of Dirs, 1954, Vice-Chm., 1956, Chm., 1965–96, Pirelli SpA; Mem., Bd of Dirs, 1956–65, Vice-Chm., 1979–99, Soc. Internat. Pirelli. Mem., Exec. Council, Confedn of Italian Industries, 1957– (Dep. Chm., 1974–80; Mem. Bd, 1974–82). *Address:* Via Gaetano Negri 10, 20123 Milan, Italy. *Clubs:* Clubino, Rotary, Unione (Milan); Yacht Club Italiano (Genoa).

PIRIE, Group Captain Sir Gordon (Hamish Martin), Kt 1984; CVO 1987; CBE 1946; JP; DL; Deputy High Bailiff of Westminster, 1978–87; Member, Westminster City Council, 1949–82 (Mayor, 1959–60; Leader of Council, 1961–69; Alderman, 1963–78; Lord Mayor, 1974–75); Director, Parker Gallery; *b* 10 Feb. 1918; *s* of Harold Victor Campbell Pirie and Irene Gordon Hogarth; *m* 1st, 1953, Margaret Joan Bomford (*d* 1972); no *c*; 2nd, 1982, Joanna, *widow* of John C. Hugill. *Educ:* Eton (King's scholar); RAF Coll., Cranwell. Permanent Commission, RAF, 1938. Served War of 1939–45: Dir of Ops, RNZAF, Atlantic and Pacific (despatches, CBE); retired as Group Captain, 1946. Comr No 1 (POW) Dist SJAB, 1960–69; Comdr St John Ambulance, London, 1969–75; Chm., St John Council for London, 1975–85. Vice-Pres., Services Sound and Vision Corp., 1990– (Chm., 1979–90). A Governor of Westminster Sch., 1962–94 (Hon. Fellow, 1995); Mem., Bd of Green Cloth Verge of Palaces, 1962–87; Vice-Pres., Engineering Industries Assoc., 1966–69; Mem., Council of Royal Albert Hall, 1965–92 (a Vice-Pres., 1985–92); a Trustee: RAF Museum, 1965–98; Dolphin Square Trust Ltd, 1971–97; Vice-Chm., London Boroughs Assoc., 1968–71; Pres., Conf. of Local and Regional Authorities of Europe, 1978–80 (Vice-Pres., 1974–75, 1977–78, 1980–82); a Vice-Pres., British Sect., IULA/CEM, 1980–88; Mem. Solicitors' Disciplinary Tribunal, 1975–93. Contested (LNat&U) Dundee West, 1955. DL, JP Co. of London, 1962; Mem., Inner London Adv. Cttee on appointment of Magistrates, 1969–87; Chm., S Westminster PSD, 1974–77. Liveryman, Worshipful Company of Girdlers (Master, 1996–97). FRSA. KStJ 1969. Pro Merito Medal, Council of Europe, 1982. Comdr, Legion of Honour, 1960; Comdr, Cross of Merit, SMO Malta, 1971; JSM Malaysia, 1974. *Recreations:* motoring, bird-watching. *Address:* Cottage Row, Tarrant Gunville, Blandford, Dorset DT11 8JJ. *T:* (01258) 830212. *Club:* Royal Air Force.

PIRIE, Iain Gordon; Sheriff of Glasgow and Strathkelvin, 1982–99; *b* 15 Jan. 1933; *s* of Charles Fox Pirie and Mary Ann Gordon; *m* 1960, Sheila Brown Forbes, MB, ChB; two *s* one *d*. *Educ:* Harris Acad., Dundee; St Andrews Univ. (MA, LLB). Legal Asst, Stirling, Eunson & Belford, Solicitors, Dunfermline, 1958–60; Depute Procurator Fiscal, Paisley, 1960–67; Sen. Depute Procurator Fiscal, Glasgow, 1967–71; Procurator Fiscal: Dumfries, 1971–76; Ayr, 1976–79; Sheriff of S Strathclyde, Dumfries and Galloway, 1979–82. *Recreations:* golf, tennis, reading, gardening, playing the violin.

PIRIE, Madsen (Duncan), PhD; President, Adam Smith Institute, since 1978; *b* 24 Aug. 1940; *s* of Douglas Gordon Pirie and Eva (*née* Madsen). *Educ:* Univ. of Edinburgh (MA Hons 1970); Univ. of St Andrews (PhD 1974); MPhil Cantab 1997. Distinguished Vis. Prof. of Philosophy, Hillsdale Coll., Michigan, 1975–78. Mem., Adv. Panel on Citizen's Charter, 1991–95. *Publications:* Trial and Error and the Idea of Progress, 1978; The Book of the Fallacy, 1985; Privatization, 1988; Micropolitics, 1988; (with Eamonn Butler) The Sherlock Holmes IQ Book, 1995. *Recreation:* calligraphy. *Address:* PO Box 316, London SW1P 3DJ.

PIRNIE, Graham John Campbell; HM Diplomatic Service; Counsellor and Deputy Head of Mission, Abu Dhabi, since 1998; *b* 9 Aug. 1941; *s* of late Ian Campbell Pirnie and of Emily Elizabeth Pirnie; *m* 1967, Kathleen Gunstone; two *s* one *d*. *Educ:* Surbiton Grammar Sch.; Birmingham Univ. (BSocSc). Graduate VSO, 1963–64; joined Foreign and Commonwealth Office, 1965: Information Res. Dept, 1965; FCO, 1966–68; Third Sec. and Vice Consul, Phnom Penh, 1968–70; Commercial Officer, Paris, 1970–74; Second Sec. (Commercial), The Hague, 1974–77; FCO, 1977–82; First Sec. and Consul, Geneva, 1982–86; JSDC 1986; FCO, 1986–89; Dep. Head of Mission and Consul, Quito, 1989–93; FCO, 1993–95; Ambassador to Paraguay, 1995–98. *Recreations:* fell-walking, natural history, antiques restoration, reading (political autobiographies), cross country skiing. *Address:* c/o Foreign and Commonwealth Office, King Charles Street, SW1A 2AH.

PIRNIE, Rear Adm. Ian Hugh, CB 1992; DL; FIEE; Chairman, Morecambe Bay Health Authority, since 1994; *b* 17 June 1935; *s* of late Hugh and Linda Pirnie; *m* 1958, Sally Patricia (*née* Duckworth); three *d*. *Educ:* Christ's Hosp., Horsham; Pembroke Coll., Cambridge (MA). FIEE 1986. Qualified in submarines, 1964; post-graduate educn, RMCS, Shrivenham, 1964–65; sea service in aircraft carriers, destroyers and submarines; commanded RNEC, Manadon, 1986–88; Chief, Strategic Systems Exec., MoD, 1988–92, RN retd, 1993. Chairman: Furness Enterprise Ltd, 1993–2000; Ashworth Hosp. Authority, 1999; non-exec. Dir, Cumbria Ambulance Service, 1992–94. DL Cumbria, 2000. *Recreations:* fell walking, bird watching, opera, classical music, topiary. *Club:* Army and Navy.

PIRRIE, David Blair, FCIB; Director of International and Private Banking, Lloyds Bank Plc, 1992–97; *b* 15 Dec. 1938; *s* of John and Sylvia Pirrie; *m* 1966, Angela Sellos; three *s* one *d*. *Educ:* Strathallen Sch., Perthshire; Harvard Univ. (Management Develt). FCIB 1987. Lloyds Bank: Gen. Man., Brazil, 1975–81; Dir, Lloyds Bank International, 1981–83; Gen. Man., Gp HQ, 1983–85; Sen. Dir, Internat. Banking, 1985–87; Sen. Gen. Man., UK Retail Banking, 1987–89; Dir, UK Retail Banking, 1989–92. *Recreations:* golf, theatre, music. *Address:* 29 Burton Court, Franklins Row, SW3 4SZ.

PIRZADA, Syed Sharif Uddin, SPk 1964; Hon. Senior Adviser to Chief Executive on Foreign Affairs, Law, Justice and Human Rights, Pakistan, since 2000; Member, National Security Council, since 1999; Ambassador-at-Large, since 1999; Attorney-General of Pakistan, 1965–66, 1968–71 and 1977–89; *b* 12 June 1923; *s* of Syed Vilayat Ali Pirzada; *m* 1960; two *s* two *d*. *Educ:* University of Bombay. LLB 1945; barrister-at-law. Secretary, Provincial Muslim League, 1945–47; Managing Editor, Morning Herald, 1947; Prof., Sind Muslim Law Coll., 1947–55; Advocate: Bombay High Court, 1946; Sind Chief Court, 1947; West Pakistan High Court, 1955; Supreme Court of Pakistan, 1961; Senior Advocate Supreme Court of Pakistan; Foreign Minister of Pakistan, 1966–68; Minister for Law and Parly Affairs, 1979–85; Advr to Chief Martial Law Administrator and Federal Minister, 1978. Ambassador-at-Large with status of Federal Minister, 1989–93; Chm., Heritage Council, 1989–93. Sec.-Gen., Orgn of the Islamic Conf., 1984–88 (Chm. Cttee of Experts for drafting statute of Islamic Internat. Ct of Justice, 1980). Represented Pakistan: before International Tribunal on Rann of Kutch, 1965; before Internat. Ct of Justice regarding Namibia, SW Africa, 1971; Pakistan Chief Counsel before ICAO Montreal in complaint concerning overflights over Indian territory; Leader of Pakistan delegations to Commonwealth Conf. and General Assembly of UN, 1966; former Mem., UN Sub-Commn on Prevention of Discrimination and Protection of Minorities (Chm., 1968). Hon. Advisor, Constitutional Commn, 1961; Chm., Pakistan Company Law Commn, 1962; Mem., Internat. River Cttee, 1961–68; President: Pakistan Br., Internat. Law Assoc., 1964–67; Karachi Bar Assoc., 1964; Pakistan Bar Council, 1966; Inst. of Internat. Affairs. Led Pakistan Delegn to Law of the Sea Conferences, NY, 1978 and 1979, and Geneva, 1980. Member: Pakistan Nat. Gp, Panel of the Permanent Ct of Arbitration; Panel of Arbitrators and Umpires, Council of Internat. Civil Aviation Organisation; Panel of Arbitrators, Internat. Centre for Settlement of Investment Disputes, Washington; Internat. Law Commn, 1981–86. Chm., Nat. Cttee for Quaid-I-Azam Year 2001. *Publications:* Pakistan at a Glance, 1941; Jinnah on Pakistan, 1943; Leaders Correspondence with Jinnah, 1944, 3rd edn 1978; Evolution of Pakistan, 1962 (also published in Urdu and Arabic); Fundamental Rights and Constitutional Remedies in Pakistan, 1966; The Pakistan Resolution and the Historic Lahore Session, 1970; Foundations of Pakistan, vol. I, 1969, vol. II, 1970; Some Aspects of Quaid-i-Azam's Life, 1978; Collected Works of Quaid-i-Azam Mohammad Ali Jinnah, vol. I, 1985, vol. II, 1986. *Recreation:* bridge. *Address:* Chief Executive Secretariat No 11, 5th Floor, Islamabad, Pakistan. *Clubs:* Sind (Karachi); Karachi Boat, Karachi Gymkhana.

PISANI, Edgard (Edouard Marie Victor); Chevalier de la Légion d'honneur; *b* Tunis, 9 Oct. 1918; *s* of François and Zoë Pisani. *Educ:* Lycée Carnot, Tunis; Lycée Louis-le-Grand, Paris. LèsL. War of 1939–45 (Croix de Guerre; Médaille de la Résistance). Chef du Cabinet, later Dir, Office of Prefect of Police, Paris, 1944; Dir, Office of Minister of Interior, 1946; Prefect: of Haute-Loire, 1946; of Haute-Marne, 1947; Senator (democratic left) from Haute-Marne, 1954; Minister of Agriculture, 1961; (first) Minister of Equipment, 1966; Deputy, Maine et Loire, 1967–68; Minister of Equipment and Housing, 1967; Conseiller Général, Maine et Loire, 1964–73; Mayor of Montreuil Bellay, 1965–75; Senator (socialist) from Haute-Marne, 1974–81; Mem., European Parlt, 1978–79 (Pres., Econ. and Monetary Affairs Cttee); Mem. for France, EEC, 1981–84; High Comr and Special Envoy to New Caledonia, 1984–85; Minister for New Caledonia, 1985–86. Member: Commn on Develt Issues (Brandt Commn), 1978–80; Economic and Social Cttee. Mem., Club of Rome, 1975. President: Inst. du Monde Arabe, 1988–95; Centre Internat. des Hautes Etudes Agronomiques Mediterranees, 1991–95. Dir, L'Evénement Européen, 1988–94. *Publications:* La région: pourquoi faire?, 1969; Le général indivis, 1974; Utopie foncière, 1977; Socialiste de raison, 1978; Défi du monde, campagne d'Europe, 1979; (contrib.) Pour la science, 1980; La main et l'outil, 1984; Pour l'Afrique, 1988; Persiste et Signe, 1992; Pour l'agriculture marchaude et ménagère, 1994; La passion de l'Etat, 1997.

PISCHETSRIEDER, Bernd; Chairman, Board of Management, Volkswagen AG, since 2001 (Member, since 2000); *b* 15 Feb. 1948. *Educ:* Munich Technical Univ. (Diplom-Ingenieur). BMW, 1973–99: Production Planning Engineer, Munich, 1973–75; Head, Ops Control Dept, Munich factory, 1975–77; Head, Work Preparation Div., Dingolfing factory, 1978–81; Dir of Production, Develt, Purchasing and Logistics, S Africa, 1982–85; Head, Quality Assurance, 1985–87; Head, Technical Planning, 1987–90; Dep. Mem., Exec. Bd, 1990 (Production); Mem., Exec. Bd, 1991 (Production); Chm., Bd of Mgt, BMW AG, 1993–99. *Address:* Volkswagen AG, 38436 Wolfsburg, Germany.

PITAKAKA, Sir (Puibangara) Moses, GCMG 1995; Governor-General, Solomon Islands, 1994–99; *b* 24 Jan. 1945; *s* of Isaiah Puibangara and Lilian Tanaquana; *m* 1967, Lois Qilariava; three *s* four *d*. *Educ:* Goldie Coll., Western Prov., Solomon Is; Solomon Is Teachers' Coll.; Univ. of Birmingham; Univ. of S Pacific, Fiji; Univ. of Manchester; Queen Elizabeth House, Oxford Univ. School teacher, Solomon Is, 1964–66; Educn Officer, 1969–71; Dist Officer, Lands Officer and Magistrate, 1972–75; Honiara Town Clerk, Jan.–May 1976; Hd of Foreign Affairs, Prime Minister's Office, 1977–79; managed family business, 1980–81; Chm., N New Georgia Timber Co-op. Commn of Inquiry, 1982; Human Resources Develt Manager, Unilever Gp in Solomon Is, 1983–85; Leadership Code Commission: Comr, 1987–88; Chm., 1989–94. Chairman: Solomon Is Citizenship Commn, 1978–88; Nat. Educn Bd, 1980–86; Comr to Judicial and Legal Services Commn, 1981–83. Deacon, World Wide Church of God, 1993–. *Recreations:* reading, canoeing, swimming, jogging, table tennis. *Address:* c/o Government House, PO Box 252, Honiara, Solomon Islands.

PITCHER, Sir Desmond (Henry), Kt 1992; CEng, FIEE, FBCS; Chairman, United Utilities (formerly North West Water Group), 1993–98 (Director, 1990–98; Deputy Chairman, 1991–93); *b* 23 March 1935; *s* of George Charles and Alice Marion Pitcher; *m* 1st, 1961 (marr. diss.); twin *d*; 2nd, 1978 (marr. diss.); two *s*; 3rd, 1991, Norma Barbara Niven. *Educ:* Liverpool Coll. of Technology. MIEEE (USA). A. V. Roe & Co., Develt Engr, 1955; Automatic Telephone and Elec. Co. (now Plessey), Systems Engr, 1958; Univac Remington Rand (now Sperry Rand Ltd), Systems Engr, 1961; Sperry Univac: Dir, Systems, 1966; Managing Dir, 1971; Vice-Pres., 1974; Dir, Sperry Rand, 1971–76, Dep. Chm., 1974–76; Man. Dir, Leyland Vehicles Ltd, 1976–78; Dir, British Leyland, 1976–78; Man. Dir, Plessey Telecommunications and Office Systems, 1978–83; Dir, Plessey Co., 1979–83; Director: The Littlewoods Orgn, 1983–95 (Gp Chief Exec., 1983–93; Vice-Chm., 1993–95); National Westminster Bank, 1994–98; Chairman: Mersey Barrage Co., 1986–96; Merseyside Develt Corp., 1991–98. Mem., Northern Adv. Bd, Nat. Westminster Bank, 1989–92. Pres., NW Chambers of Commerce, 1994–98. Vis. Prof. of Business Policy, Univ. of Manchester, 1993–98. Dir, CEI, 1979; Pres., TEMA, 1981–83. Dep. Chm., Everton Football Club, 1990–98 (Dir, 1987–98); Chm., Royal Liverpool Philharmonic Soc. Develt Trust, 1992–. DL Merseyside, 1992–99. Freeman, City of London, 1987; Liveryman, Co. of Information Technologists, 1992–. CIMgt; FRIAS; FRSA 1987; Hon. FIDE; Hon. Fellow, Liverpool John Moores Univ., 1993. Knight, Order of St Hubert (Austria), 1991. *Publications:* Institution of Electrical Engineers Faraday Lectures, 1974–75; various lectures on social implications of computers and micro-electronics. *Recreations:* golf, music. *Address:* Folly Farm, Sulhamstead, Berks RG7 4DF. *T:* (0118) 930 2326. *Clubs:* Brooks's, Royal Automobile; Royal Birkdale Golf; Delamere Golf; Lancs CC.

PITCHER, Prof. Wallace Spencer, PhD, DSc, DIC; George Herdman Professor of Geology, 1962–81, now Emeritus, and Leverhulme Emeritus Research Fellow, 1981–83, University of Liverpool; *b* 3 March 1919; *s* of Harry George and Irene Bertha Pitcher; *m* 1947, Stella Ann (*née* Scutt); two *s* two *d*. *Educ:* Acton Tech. Coll., Chelsea Coll. Asst Analytical Chemist, Geo. T. Holloway & Co., 1937–39. Served War, RAMC, 1939–44. Chelsea Coll., 1944–47; Imperial College: Demonstrator, 1947–48; Asst Lectr, 1948–50; Lectr, 1950–55; Reader in Geology, King's Coll., London, 1955–62. Geological Society London: Hon. Sec., 1970–73; Foreign Sec., 1974–75; Pres., 1976–77; Pres., Section C, British Assoc., 1979. FGS; FIMM. Hon. MRIA 1977; Hon. FRSE 1993. Hon. Member: GA, 1972; Geol Soc. America, 1982; Geol Soc. Peru, 2001. Hon. ScD Dublin, 1983; Hon. DSc Paris-Sud, 1993. Lyell Fund, 1956, Bigsby Medal, 1963, Murchison Medal, 1979, Geol Soc. of London; Liverpool Geol Soc. Silver Medal, 1969; Aberconway Medal, Instn of Geologists, 1983; Univ. Helsinki Medal, 1986. *Publications:* ed (with G. W. Flinn) Controls of Metamorphism, 1965; (with A. R. Berger) Geology of Donegal: a study of granite emplacement and unroofing, 1972; (with E. J. Cobbing) Geology of Western Cordillera of Northern Peru, 1981; (jtly) Magmatism at a Plate Edge: the Peruvian Andes, 1985; Nature and Origin of Granite, 1993, 2nd edn 1997; many papers on late Precambrian stratigraphy, tillites, Caledonian and Andean granites, structure of the Andes. *Address:* 8 Fletcher Close, Upton, Wirral, Merseyside CH49 5PH. *T:* (0151) 677 6896.

PITCHERS, Christopher John; His Honour Judge Pitchers; a Circuit Judge, since 1986; *b* 2 Oct. 1942; *s* of Thomas and Melissa Pitchers; *m* 1965, Judith Stevenson; two *s*. *Educ:* Uppingham Sch.; Worcester Coll., Oxford. MA. Called to the Bar, Inner Temple, 1965, Bencher, 1996; a Recorder, 1981–86. Dir of Studies, Judicial Studies Bd, 1996–97 (Mem., Criminal Cttee, 1991–95; Jt Dir, 1995–96). Hon. Sec., Council of HM Circuit Judges, 1992–95. (Pres., 1999). Vice-Pres., NACRO, 1994–. *Address:* The Crown Court, 60 Canal Street, Nottingham NG1 7EJ.

PITCHFORD, His Honour Charles Neville; a Circuit Judge, Wales and Chester Circuit, 1972–87. Called to the Bar, Middle Temple, 1948. *Address:* Llanynant, Kennel Lane, Coed Morgan, Abergavenny, Gwent NP7 9UR.

See also C. J. Pitchford.

PITCHFORD, Hon. Sir Christopher (John), Kt 2000; **Hon. Mr Justice Pitchford;** a Judge of the High Court, Queen's Bench Division, since 2000; *b* 28 March 1947; *s* of Charles Neville Pitchford, *qv*; *m* 1st, 1970, Rosalind (*née* Eaton) (marr. diss. 1991); two *d*; 2nd, 1991, Denise (*née* James); two *s*. *Educ:* Duffryn Comprehensive Sch., Newport, Gwent; Queen's Coll., Taunton, Somerset; Queen Mary Coll., London (LLB). Called to the Bar, Middle Temple, 1969, Bencher, 1996; QC 1987; a Recorder, 1987–2000; a Dep. High Ct Judge, 1996–2000; Leader, Wales & Chester Circuit, 1999–2000. Arbitrator, Motor Insurers Bureau, 1994–2000. *Recreation:* fishing. *Address:* Royal Courts of Justice, Strand, WC2A 2LL. *Clubs:* Cardiff and County (Cardiff); Bedlinog Racing.

PITFIELD, Hon. (Peter) Michael, CVO 1982; PC (Can.) 1984; QC (Can.) 1972; Senator, Canada, since Dec. 1982; *b* Montreal, 18 June 1937; *s* of Ward Chipman Pitfield and Grace Edith (*née* MacDougall); *m* 1971, Nancy Snow; one *s* two *d*. *Educ:* Lower Canada Coll., Montreal; Sedbergh Sch., Montebello; St Lawrence Univ. (BASc; Hon. DLitt 1979); McGill Univ. (BCL); Univ. of Ottawa (DESD). Lieut, RCNR. Read Law with Mathewson Lafleur & Brown, Montreal (associated with firm, 1958–59); called to Quebec Bar, 1962; QC (Fed.) 1972; Admin. Asst to Minister of Justice and Attorney-Gen. of Canada, 1959–61; Sec. and Exec. Dir, Royal Commn on Pubns, Ottawa, 1961–62; Attaché to Gov.-Gen. of Canada, 1962–65; Sec. and Res. Supervisor of Royal Commn on Taxation, 1963–66; entered Privy Council Office and Cabinet Secretariat of Govt of Canada, 1965; Asst Sec. to Cabinet, 1966; Dep. Sec. to Cabinet (Plans), and Dep. Clerk to Council, 1969; Dep. Minister, Consumer and Corporate Affairs, 1973; Clerk of Privy Council and Sec. to Cabinet, 1975–79 and 1980–Nov. 1982; Sen. Adviser to Privy Council Office, Nov.-Dec. 1982. Rep., UN Gen. Assembly, 1983; Chm., Senate Cttee on Security and Intelligence, 1983. Director: Power Corp., Montreal; Trust Co., LaPresse; Great West Life Assurance Co.; Investor's Gp Ltd, Winnipeg; Fellow, Harvard Univ., 1974; Mackenzie King Vis. Prof., Kennedy Sch. of Govt, Harvard, 1979–80. Member: Canadian, Quebec and Montreal Bar Assocs; Can. Inst. of Public Admin; Can. Hist. Assoc.; Can. Polit. Sci. Assoc.; Amer. Soc. Polit. and Social Sci.; Internat. Commn of Jurists; Beta Theta Pi. Trustee, Twentieth Century Fund, NY; Member Council, Canadian Inst. for Advanced Res., Toronto; IISS. *Recreations:* squash, ski-ing, reading. *Address:* (office) The Senate, 111 Wellington Street, Ottawa, ON K1A 0A4, Canada. *Clubs:* University, Mount Royal, Racket (Montreal).

PITKEATHLEY, family name of **Baroness Pitkeathley**.

PITKEATHLEY, Baroness *cr* 1997 (Life Peer), of Caversham in the Royal co. of Berkshire; **Jill Elizabeth Pitkeathley,** OBE 1993; Chairman, New Opportunities Fund, since 1998; *b* 4 Jan. 1940; *d* of Roland Wilfred Bisson and Edith May Bisson (*née* Muston); *m* 1961, W. Pitkeathley (marr. diss. 1978); one *s* one *d*. *Educ:* Ladies' Coll., Guernsey; Bristol Univ. (BA Econ). Social worker, 1961–64; Voluntary Service Co-ordinator, Manchester and Essex, 1970–83; Nat. Consumer Council, 1983–86; Dir, Nat. Council for Carers, 1986 until merger with Assoc. of Carers, 1988; Chief Exec., Carers Nat. Assoc., 1988–98. Advr to Griffith's Rev. of Community Care, 1986–88; Mem., Health Adv. Service, 1993–97; Chm. Adv. Gp, Gen. Social Care Council, 1999–2000. Pres., Community Council for Berks, 1998– (Vice-Pres., 1990–98); Patron, Bracknell CVS. Mem., RSA, 1992–. Mem. Bd of Governors, Nat. Inst. of Social Work, 1995–98. *Publications:* When I Went Home, 1978; Mobilising Voluntary Resources, 1982; Volunteers in Hospitals, 1984; Supporting Volunteers, 1985; It's my duty, isn't it?, 1989; Only Child, 1994; (with David Emerson) Age Gap Relationships, 1996. *Recreations:* gardening, grand-children, writing. *T:* (office) (020) 7211 1760.

PITMAN, Sir Brian (Ivor), Kt 1994; Chief Executive, 1983–97, Chairman, 1997–2001, Lloyds TSB Group plc (formerly Lloyds Bank Plc); Chairman, Next plc, 1998–May 2002; *b* 13 Dec. 1931; *s* of late Ronald Ivor Pitman and of Doris Ivy Pitman (*née* Short); *m* 1954, Barbara Mildred Ann (*née* Darby); two *s* one *d*. *Educ:* Cheltenham Grammar School. FCIB. Entered Lloyds Bank, 1952, Jt Gen. Manager, 1975; Exec. Dir, Lloyds Bank International, 1976, Dep. Chief Exec., 1978; Dep. Group Chief Exec., 1982, Dir, 1983–2001, Lloyds Bank Plc, subseq. Lloyds TSB Gp plc. Chm., Lloyds First Western Corp., 1983–94; Director: Lloyds Bank California, 1982–86; Nat. Bank of New Zealand Ltd, 1982–97; Lloyds and Scottish Plc, 1983; Lloyds Bank International Ltd, 1985–87; Lloyds Merchant Bank Holdings Ltd, 1985–88; NBNZ Holdings Ltd, 1990–97; Carlton Communications Plc, 1998–; Tomkins PLC, 2000–; Carphone Warehouse Gp, 2001–. Mem., Internat. Adv. Panel, Monetary Authy of Singapore, 1999–2001. President: BBA, 1996–97; CIB, 1997–98. Gov., Ashridge Mgt Coll., 1997–. Hon. DSc: City, 1996; UMIST, 2000. *Recreations:* golf, cricket, music. *Address:* c/o Lloyds TSB Group plc, 71 Lombard Street, EC3P 3BS. *Clubs:* MCC; Yorkshire CC; Gloucestershire CC; St George's Hill Golf.

PITMAN, David Christian; His Honour Judge Pitman; a Circuit Judge, since 1986; *b* 1 Dec. 1936; 3rd *s* of Sir (Isaac) James Pitman, KBE, and Hon. Margaret Beaufort Pitman (*née* Lawson-Johnston); *m* 1971, Christina Mary Malone-Lee; one *s* two *d*. *Educ:* Eton Coll.; Christ Church, Oxford (BA (PPE) 1961, MA 1964). Editorial role in publishing books in Initial Teaching Alphabet, 1960–63; called to Bar, Middle Temple,1963; commenced practice, 1964; a Recorder, 1986. National Service: 2nd Lieut, 60th Rifles, 1955–57; Territorial Army: Lieut Queen's Westminsters, KRRC, 1957–61; Captain, then Major, Queen's Royal Rifles (TA), 1961–67; Major, 5th (T) Bn RGJ, 1967–69. *Recreations:* music, the open air. *Address:* c/o The Crown Court, Snaresbrook, Hollybush Hill, E11 1QW.

PITMAN, Jennifer Susan, OBE 1998; professional racehorse trainer (National Hunt), 1975–99; Director, Jenny Pitman Racing Ltd, 1975–99; *b* 11 June 1946; *d* of George and Mary Harvey; *m* 1st, 1965, Richard Pitman (marr. diss.); two *s*; 2nd, 1997, David Stait. *Educ:* Sarson Secondary Girls' School. Training of major race winners includes: Midlands National, 1977 (Watafella); Massey Ferguson Gold Cup, Cheltenham, 1980 (Bueche Giorod); Welsh National, 1982 (Corbiere), 1983 (Burrough Hill Lad), 1986 (Stearsby); Grand National, 1983 (Corbiere), 1995 (Royal Athlete); Cheltenham Gold Cup, 1984 (Burrough Hill Lad), 1991 (Garrison Savannah); Welsh Champion Hurdle, 1991 (Wonderman), 1992 (Don Valentino); King George VI Gold Cup, 1984 (Burrough Hill Lad); Hennessey Gold Cup, Newbury, 1984 (Burrough Hill Lad); Whitbread Trophy, 1985 (Smith's Man); Ritz Club National Hunt Handicap, Cheltenham, 1987 (Gainsay), 1989 (Golden Freeze), 1991 (Smith's Cracker); Sporting Life Weekend Chase, Liverpool, 1987 (Gainsay); Philip Cornes Saddle of Gold Final, Newbury, 1988 (Crumpet Delite); Scottish National, 1995 (Willsford); Mildmay/Cazlet Memorial, 1996 (Superior Finish). Trainer of the Year, 1983/84, 1990. *Publications:* Glorious Uncertainty (autobiog.), 1984; Jenny Pitman: the autobiography, 1998. *Address:* Owl's Barn, Kintbury, Hungerford, Berks RG17 9SX. *Club:* International Sporting.

PITOI, Sir Sere, Kt 1977; CBE 1975; MACE; Chairman, Public Services Commission of Papua New Guinea, 1971; *b* Kapa Kapa Village, SE of Port Moresby, 11 Nov. 1935; *s* of Pitoi Sere and Laka Orira; *m* 1957, Daga Leva; two *s* three *d*. *Educ:* Sogeri (Teachers' Cert.); Queensland Univ. (Cert. in Diagnostic Testing and Remedial Teaching); Univ. of Birmingham, UK (Cert. for Headmasters and Administrators). Held a number of posts as teacher, 1955–57, and headmaster, 1958–68, in Port Moresby, the Gulf district of Papua, Eastern Highlands, New Britain. Apptd a District Inspector of Schools, 1968. Chm., Public Service Bd, Papua New Guinea, 1969–76. Fellow, PNG Inst. of Management. *Recreation:* fishing. *Clubs:* Rotary (Port Moresby); Cheshire Home (PNG).

PITT, Barrie (William Edward); author and editor of military histories; *b* Galway, 7 July 1918; *y s* of John Pitt and Ethel May Pitt (*née* Pennell); *m* 1st, 1943, Phyllis Kate (*née* Edwards); one *s* (decd); 2nd, 1953, Sonia Deirdre (*née* Hoskins) (marr. diss., 1971); 3rd, 1983, Frances Mary (*née* Moore). *Educ:* Portsmouth Southern Grammar Sch. Bank Clerk, 1935. Served War of 1939–45, in Army. Surveyor, 1946. Began writing, 1954. Information Officer, Atomic Energy Authority, 1961; Historical Consultant to BBC Series, The Great War, 1963; Editor, Purnell's History of the Second World War, 1964; Editor-in-Chief: Ballantine's Illustrated History of World War 2, 1967 (US Book Series); Ballantine's Illustrated History of the Violent Century, 1971; Editor: Purnell's History of the First World War, 1969; British History Illustrated, 1974–78; Consultant Editor, The Military History of World War II, 1986. *Publications:* The Edge of Battle, 1958; Zeebrugge, St George's Day, 1918, 1958; Coronel and Falkland, 1960; 1918 The Last Act, 1962; The Battle of the Atlantic, 1977; The Crucible of War: Western Desert 1941, 1980; Churchill and the Generals, 1981; The Crucible of War: Year of Alamein 1942, 1982; Special Boat Squadron, 1983; (with Frances Pitt) The Chronological Atlas of World War II, 1989; contrib. to: Encyclopaedia Britannica; The Sunday Times. *Recreations:* reading, listening to classical music. *Address:* 10 Wellington Road, Taunton, Somerset TA1 4EG. *T:* (01823) 337188. *Club:* Savage.

PITT, Desmond Gordon; Commissioner of HM Customs and Excise, 1979–83; *b* 27 Dec. 1922; *s* of Archibald and Amy Pitt; *m* 1946, Barbara Irene; one *s* two *d*. *Educ:* Bournemouth Sch. FCCA, ACIS, AIB. Officer, HM Customs and Excise, 1947; Inspector, 1958; Asst Sec., 1973; Under Sec., 1979. *Recreations:* history, exploring Wessex. *Address:* 1 [illegible] Road, Southbourne, Bournemouth, Dorset BH6 3ET.

PITT, Rt Rev. Mgr George Edward, CBE 1965; *b* 10 Oct. 1916; *s* of Francis Pitt and Anna Christina Oviedo. *Educ:* St Brendan's Coll., Bristol; Ven. English College, Rome. Priest, 1939; worked in Diocese of Clifton, 1940–43; joined Royal Navy as Chaplain, 1943; Principal Roman Catholic Chaplain, RN, 1963–69; Parish Priest, St Joseph's, Wroughton, Wilts, 1969–86. Nominated a Domestic Prelate, 1963. *Recreation:* music. *Address:* The Convent, 5 Litfield Place, Bristol BS8 3LU. *T:* (0117) 973 3235.

PITT, Sir Harry (Raymond), Kt 1978; BA, PhD; FRS 1957; Vice-Chancellor, Reading University, 1964–79; *b* 3 June 1914; *s* of H. Pitt; *m* 1940, Clemency Catherine, *d* of H. C. E. Jacoby, MIEE; four *s*. *Educ:* King Edward's Sch., Stourbridge; Peterhouse, Cambridge. Bye-Fellow, Peterhouse, Cambridge, 1936–39; Choate Memorial Fellow, Harvard Univ., 1937–38; Univ. of Aberdeen, 1939–42. Air Min. and Min. of Aircraft Production, 1942–45. Prof. of Mathematics, Queen's Univ., Belfast, 1945–50; Deputy Vice-Chancellor, Univ. of Nottingham, 1959–62; Prof. of Pure Mathematics, Univ. of Nottingham, 1950–64. Visiting Prof., Yale Univ., 1962–63. Chm., Universities Central Council on Admissions, 1975–78. Pres., IMA, 1984–85. Hon. LLD: Aberdeen 1970; Nottingham 1970; Hon. DSc: Reading, 1978; Belfast, 1981. *Publications:* Tauberian Theorems, 1957; Measure, Integration and Probability, 1963; Measure and Integration for Use, 1986; mathematical papers in scientific journals. *Address:* 105 Manor Green Road, Epsom, Surrey KT19 8LW.

PITT, Michael Edward, CEng, FICE; Chief Executive, Kent County Council, since 1997; *b* 2 Feb. 1949; *s* of Albert and Doris Joan Pitt; *m* 1969, Anna Maria Di Claudio; two *d*. *Educ:* University College London (first class Hons BSc Engrg). CEng 1974; FICE 1989. Civil Servant, 1970–72; motorway design and construction, 1972–75; transportation planner in private sector and local govt, 1975–80; Asst County Surveyor, Northumberland CC, 1980–84; Dir of Property Services and Dir of Tech. Services, Humberside CC, 1984–90; Chief Exec., Cheshire CC, 1990–97. *Publications:* papers in technical jls. *Recreations:* family life, walking, the voluntary sector. *Address:* Sessions House, County Hall, Maidstone, Kent ME14 1XQ. *T:* (01622) 694000.

PITT, William F.; *see* Fox-Pitt.

PITT, William Henry; Consultant Apprentice Co-ordinator, Canary Wharf Group plc, since 1999; *b* 17 July 1937; *m* 1961, Janet Pitt (*née* Wearn); one *d*. *Educ:* Heath Clark Sch., Croydon; London Nautical Sch.; Polytechnic of South Bank; Polytechnic of N London (BA Philos./Classics). Lighting Engineer, 1955–75; Housing Officer, Lambeth Borough Council, 1975–81. Chm., Lambeth Br., NALGO, 1979–81. Joined Liberal Party, 1959; contested: (L) Croydon NW, Feb. and Oct. 1974, 1979, 1983; Thanet South (L/Alliance), 1987, (Lib. Dem.), 1992. MP (L) Croydon NW, Oct. 1981–1983; joined Labour Party, 1996. *Recreations:* photography, choral singing, listening to music, reading, walking, going to France. *Address:* 10 Inverness Terrace, Broadstairs, Kent CT10 1QZ.

PITT-BROOKE, John Stephen; Director General, Corporate Communications, Ministry of Defence, since 1999; *b* 9 Sept. 1950; *s* of late Reginald Pitt-Brooke and of Hilda (*née* Wright); *m* 1st, 1986, Rosalind (*d* 1996), *d* of Prof. William Mulligan, *qv*; two *s*; 2nd, 1999, Frances Way, *d* of B. T. McDade. *Educ:* Salford Grammar Sch.; Queens' Coll., Cambridge (MA). MoD, 1971–74; NI Office, 1974–77; Private Sec. to Minister of State for NI, 1975–77; MoD, 1978; NATO Defence Coll., 1980; Private Sec. to Permanent Under Sec., MoD, 1984–87; Cabinet Office, 1988–89; Head of Industrial Relns Div., MoD, 1989–92; Private Sec. to Sec. of State for Defence, 1992–94; Comd Sec., Land Comd, MoD, 1995–98; Fellow, Center for Internat. Affairs, Harvard Univ., 1998–99. *Recreations:* family life, literature, cricket, Venice, supporting Manchester City

Football Club. *Address:* c/o Ministry of Defence, Horseguards Avenue, SW1A 2HB. *Club:* London Salfordians Amateur Rugby League.

PITT-RIVERS, Valerie; Vice Lord-Lieutenant of Dorset, since 1999; *b* 23 Jan. 1939; *d* of Derek Walter Milnes Scott and Eva Scott (*née* Kiaer); *m* 1964, George Anthony Lane-Fox Pitt-Rivers. *Educ:* Prior's Field, Godalming. Advertising and public relns, 1957–63; worked for NHS, charitable and arts orgns in Dorset, 1970–. Non-exec. Dir and Vice Chm., W Dorset Gen. Hosps NHS Trust, 1991–98. Founder, Arts in Hospital Project for NHS, Dorchester, 1987. Trustee and Mem. Council, Royal Sch. of Needlework, 2000–. DL Dorset, 1995. *Recreations:* gardens, opera. *Address:* Manor House, Hinton St Mary, Sturminster Newton, Dorset DT10 1NA.

PITTAM, Jonathan Charles; County Treasurer, Hampshire County Council, since 1997; *b* 9 June 1950; *s* of Brian and Sheila Pittam; *m* 1972, Mary Catherine Davey; two *s* one *d. Educ:* Tavistock Sch.; King's Coll., Univ. of London (BSc Hons). CPFA 1975. London Borough of Croydon: grad. trainee, 1971–73; Sen. Audit Asst, 1973; Accountant, 1973–75; Gp Accountant, 1975–76; Asst Prin. Accountant, 1976–78; Chief Accountant, 1979–80, Asst Dir, Finance and Admin, 1980–83, Cambs CC; Dep. Co. Treas., Hants CC, 1983–97. *Address:* Hampshire County Council, The Castle, Winchester, Hants SO23 8UB. *T:* (01962) 847400; *e-mail:* jon.pittam@hants.gov.uk.

PITTAWAY, David Michael; QC 2000; a Recorder, since 2000; *b* 29 June 1955; *s* of Michael Pittaway, JP, MRCVS, and Heather Yvette Pittaway (*née* Scott); *m* 1983, Jill Suzanne Newsam, *d* of Dr Ian Douglas Newsam, MRCVS; two *s. Educ:* Uppingham Sch.; Sidney Sussex Coll., Cambridge (Exhibnr; MA). Called to the Bar, Inner Temple, 1977 (Bencher, 1998); Asst Recorder, 1998; Midland and Oxford Circuit. Mem., Bar Council, 1999–. FCIArb 1992. *Publications:* (contrib.) Atkins Court Forms, vol. 8, Carriers, 1990, rev. edn 1999, vol. 29(2), Personal Injury and Professional Negligence, 1996, rev. edn 1999; (Gen. Ed.) Pittaway & Hammerton, Professional Negligence Cases, 1998. *Recreations:* gardening, travel, music. *Address:* 1 Serjeant's Inn, EC4Y 1LH. *T:* (020) 7415 6666. *Club:* Royal Automobile.

PITTS, Sir Cyril (Alfred), Kt 1968; Governor, University of Westminster (formerly Polytechnic of Central London), 1984–95 (Chairman of Governors, 1985–93); *b* 21 March 1916; *m* 1942, Barbara; two *s* one *d. Educ:* St Olave's; Jesus Coll., Cambridge. Chairman of ICI Companies in India, 1964–68; Chm., ICI (Export) Ltd and Gen. Manager, Internat. Coordination, ICI Ltd, 1968–78; Dir, ICI Americas Ltd, 1974–77; Dep. Chm., Ozalid Gp Holdings Ltd, 1975–77. Chairman: Process Plant EDC, 1979–83; Peter Brotherhood, 1980–83. President: Bengal Chamber of Commerce and Industry, and Associated Chambers of Commerce and Industry of India, 1967–68; British and S Asian Trade Assoc., 1978–83. Councillor, RIIA, 1968–77. Hon. DLitt Westminster, 1993. *Address:* 11 Middle Avenue, Farnham, Surrey GU9 8JL. *T:* (01252) 715864. *Clubs:* Oriental; Bengal (Calcutta).

PITTS, John Kennedy; Chairman, Legal Aid Board, 1988–95; *b* 6 Oct. 1925; *s* of Thomas Alwyn Pitts and Kathleen Margaret Pitts (*née* Kennedy); *m* 1st, 1957, Joan Iris Light (*d* 1986); 2nd, 1990, Julia Bentall. *Educ:* Bristol Univ. (BSc). Res. Officer, British Cotton Industry Res. Assoc., 1948–53; ICI, 1953–78; Dir, ICI Mond Div., 1969–71; Dep. Chm., ICI Agricl Div., 1972–77; Chairman: Richardsons Fertilizers, 1972–76; Hargreaves Fertilizers, 1975–77; Vice-Pres., Cie Neerlandaise de l'Azote, 1975–77. Chm. and Chief Exec., Tioxide Group, 1978–87. Mem., Tees and Hartlepool Port Authy, 1976–78; Chm., SASDA (formerly Shildon & Sedgefield Develt Agency), 1991–94. Pres., Chem. Industries Assoc., 1984–86. *Address:* Hall Garth House, Carthorpe, Bedale, N Yorks DL8 2LD. *Club:* Royal Automobile.

PITTS CRICK, Ronald; *see* Crick.

PIX WESTON, John; *see* Weston.

PIZZEY, Erin Patria Margaret; Founder of first Shelter for Battered Wives and their children, 1971; therapeutic consultant and fund-raiser, Women's Aid Ltd; *b* 19 Feb. 1939; *d* of late Cyril Edward Antony Carney, MBE and of Ruth Patricia Balfour-Last; *m* 1961, John Leo Pizzey (marr. diss. 1979); one *s* one *d. Educ:* St Antony's; Leweston Manor, Sherborne, Dorset. Somewhat chequered career as pioneering attracts frequent clashes with the law; appearances at such places as Acton Magistrates Court and the House of Lords could be considered milestones in the fulfilment of a career dedicated to defending women and children. Member: Soc. of Authors; AFI; Smithsonian Instn; Royal Soc. of Literature. Patron, Care and Comfort Romania, 1998–. Diploma of Honour, Internat. order of volunteers for peace, 1981; Distinguished Leadership Award, World Congress of Victimology, 1987; San Valentino d'Oro prize for lit., 1994. *Publications:* (as Erin Pizzey) Scream Quietly or the Neighbours Will Hear, 1974, 2nd edn 1978; Infernal Child (autobiog.), 1978; The Slut's Cookbook, 1981; Prone to Violence, 1982; Erin Pizzey Collects, 1983; Wild Child (autobiog.), 1996; *novels:* The Watershed, 1983; In the Shadow of the Castle, 1984; The Pleasure Palace, 1986; First Lady, 1987; The Consul General's Daughter, 1988; The Snow Leopard of Shanghai, 1989; Other Lovers, 1991; Morning Star, 1991; Swimming with Dolphins, 1992; For the Love of a Stranger, 1993; Kisses, 1995; The Wicked World of Women, 1996; The Fame Game, 1999; poems and short stories. *Recreations:* wine, books, travel. *Address:* Flat 5, 29 Lebanon Park, Twickenham TW1 3DH. *T:* (020) 8241 6541; *e-mail:* pizzey@cableinet.co.uk.

PLAISTOWE, (William) Ian (David), FCA; Director of Audit and Business Advisory Practice for Europe, Arthur Andersen, since 1993; *b* 18 Nov. 1942; *s* of late David William Plaistowe and Julia (*née* Ross Smith); *m* 1968, Carolyn Anne Noble Wilson; two *s* one *d. Educ:* Marlborough Coll., Queens' Coll., Cambridge. Joined Arthur Andersen & Co., 1964; Partner, 1976; Head of Accounting and Audit practice, London, 1984–87; Dir of Acctg and Audit for UK and Ireland, 1987–93. Chm., Auditing Practices Bd of UK and Ireland, 1994–. Institute of Chartered Accountants in England and Wales: Chairman: London Soc. of Chartered Accountants, 1981–82; Post Qualification Cttee, 1985–86; Practice Regulation Directorate, 1987–90; Mem. Council, 1985–; Vice-Pres., 1990–91; Dep. Pres., 1991–92; Pres., 1992–93. *Publications:* articles in learned jls. *Recreations:* golf, tennis, squash, ski-ing, gardening. *Address:* Heybote, Ellesborough, Aylesbury, Bucks HP17 0XF. *T:* (01296) 622758. *Clubs:* Carlton; Moor Park Golf.

PLANT, family name of **Baron Plant of Highfield**.

PLANT OF HIGHFIELD, Baron *cr* 1992 (Life Peer), of Weelsby in the County of Humberside; **Raymond Plant,** PhD; DLitt; Research Professor, Southampton University, since 1999; *b* 19 March 1945; *s* of Stanley and Marjorie Plant; *m* 1967, Katherine Sylvia Dixon; three *s. Educ:* Havelock Sch., Grimsby; King's Coll. London (BA); Hull Univ. (PhD 1971). Lectr, then Sen. Lectr in Philosophy, Univ. of Manchester, 1967–79; Prof. of Politics, 1979–94, Pro-Chancellor, 1996–99, Univ. of Southampton; Master, St Catherine's Coll., Oxford, 1994–99. Lectures: Stevenson, Univ. of Glasgow, 1981; Agnes Cumming, UC Dublin, 1987; Stanton, Univ. of Cambridge, 1989–90 and 1990–91; Sarum, Univ. of Oxford, 1991; Ferguson, Manchester Univ., 1994; Scott Holland, Manchester Cathedral, 1995; Charles Gore, Westminster Abbey, 1995; J. P. MacIntosh Meml, Edinburgh Univ., 1995; Eleanor Rathbone, Bristol Univ., 1997. Chair: Labour Party Commn on Electoral Systems, 1991–93; Fabian Soc. Commn on Taxation and Citizenship, 1999–2000. President: Acad. of Learned Socs in Social Scis, 2000–01; NCVO, 1999–. Times columnist, 1988–92. Hon. Fellow: Cardiff Univ., 2000; St Catherine's Coll., Oxford, 2000; Harris Manchester Coll., Oxford, 2000. Hon. DLitt: London Guildhall Univ., 1993; Hull, 1994. *Publications:* Hegel, 1974, 2nd edn 1984; Community and Ideology, 1974; Political Philosophy and Social Welfare, 1981; Philosophy, Politics and Citizenship, 1984; Conservative Capitalism in Britain and the United States: a critical appraisal, 1988; Modern Political Thought, 1991; Politics, Theology and History, 2000. *Recreations:* music, opera, thinking about the garden, listening to my wife playing the piano, reading. *Address:* 6 Woodview Close, Bassett, Southampton SO16 3PZ. *T:* (01703) 769529.

PLANT, Prof. Jane Ann, (Mrs P. R. Simpson), CBE 1997; PhD; CEng, CGeol; Chief Scientist and a Director, British Geological Survey, since 2000; *b* 1 Feb. 1945; *d* of Ralph Lunn and Marjorie Lunn (*née* Langton); *m* 1st, 1967, Dr I. D. Plant (marr. diss. 1974); one *s*; 2nd, 1974, Prof. P. R. Simpson; one *s* one *d. Educ:* Liverpool Univ. (BSc 1966 with Dist.; BSc Hons 1967); Leicester Univ. (PhD 1977). CEng 1986; CGeol 1990. British Geological Survey: SO to Atomic Energy Div. (subseq. Geochem. Div.), 1967–71; SO, 1971; PSO, 1977; sabbatical year to work in N America, 1988; Hd, Applied Geochem. Gp, 1989–91; Asst Dir and Chief Geochemist, 1991–97. Visiting Professor: Liverpool Univ., 1992; Imperial Coll., London, 2001; Special Prof., Nottingham Univ., 1996. Mem., Royal Commn on Envmtl Pollution, 2001–; Chm., Adv. Cttee on Hazardous Substances, 2001–. Freeman, City of London, 1999. FRSA 2000. DUniv Open, 1997; Hon. DSc Exeter, 2001. Lord Lloyd of Kilgerran Award, 1999. *Publications:* Your Life in Your Hands, 2000; (with G. Tidey) The Plant Programme, 2001; numerous peer-reviewed papers and contrib. books on econ. and envmtl geochem. *Recreations:* gardening, theatre. *Address:* British Geological Survey, Keyworth, Nottingham NG12 5GG.

PLANTIN, Marcus; Director of Programmes, United and LWT Productions, since 2000; *b* 23 Oct. 1945; *s* of Charles P. Plantin and Vera H. Plantin; *m*; two *s. Educ:* Surbiton County Grammar Sch.; Guildford Sch. of Acting. Producer, BBC TV, 1970–84; London Weekend Television: Head of Light Entertainment, 1985–87; Controller of Entertainment, 1987–90; Dir of Progs, 1990–92; Dir, London Weekend Productions and LWT Holdings, 1990–92; ITV Network Dir, 1992–97; Dir of Progs, LWT, 1997–2000. *Recreations:* travel, swimming, reading. *Address:* LWT, London Television Centre, Upper Ground, SE1 9LT.

PLASKETT, Maj.-Gen. Frederick Joseph, CB 1980; MBE 1966; FCIT; Director General and Chief Executive, Road Haulage Association, 1981–88; *b* 23 Oct. 1926; *s* of Frederick Joseph Plaskett and Grace Mary Plaskett; *m* 1st, 1950, Heather (*née* Kington) (*d* 1982); four *d*; 2nd, 1984, Mrs Patricia Joan Healy. RN (FAA), 1944–45; transf. to Army, 1945; commnd infantry, 1946; RASC, 1951; RCT, 1965; regimental and staff appts, India, Korea, Nigeria, Malaya, Germany and UK; Student, Staff Coll., Camberley, 1958; Jt Services Staff Coll., 1964; Instr, Staff Coll., Camberley, 1966–68; Management Coll., Henley, 1969; RCDS, 1975; Dir of Movements (Army), 1975–78; Dir Gen., Transport and Movements (Army), 1978–81, retired. Col Comdt, RCT, 1981–91 (Rep. Col Comdt, 1989). Chm., British Railways Bd, London Midland Region, 1989–92 (Mem., 1986–88). Director: Foden Trucks (Paccar UK) (formerly Sandbach Engrg Co.), 1981–97; RHA Insce Services Ltd, 1982–88; British Road Federation, 1982–88. Comr, Royal Hosp., Chelsea, 1985–88. Freeman, City of London, 1979; Liveryman, Co. of Carmen, 1979–. *Recreations:* fishing, sailing, gardening. *Address:* c/o National Westminster Bank, The Commons, Shaftesbury, Dorset SP7 8JY. *Club:* Army and Navy.

See also J. F. G. Logan.

PLASKITT, James Andrew; MP (Lab) Warwick and Leamington, since 1997; *b* 23 June 1954; *s* of late Ronald Plaskitt and of Phyllis Irene Plaskitt. *Educ:* Pilgrim Sch., Bedford; University Coll., Oxford (MPhil 1979; MA 1980). Lecturer in Politics: University Coll., Oxford, 1977–79; Christ Church, Oxford, 1984–86; Lectr in Govt, Brunel Univ., 1979–84; Oxford Analytica Ltd: Western European Editor, 1986–90; Dir of Consultancy, 1993–96. Mem. (Lab) Oxfordshire CC, 1985–97 (Leader, Labour Gp, 1990–96). Contested (Lab) Witney, 1992. *Address:* House of Commons, SW1A 0AA.

PLASTOW, Sir David (Arnold Stuart), Kt 1986; Chairman, Medical Research Council, 1990–98; *b* Grimsby, 9 May 1932; *s* of late James Stuart Plastow and Marie Plastow; *m* 1954, Barbara Ann May; one *s* one *d. Educ:* Culford Sch., Bury St Edmunds. Apprentice, Vauxhall Motors Ltd, 1950; joined Rolls-Royce Ltd, Motor Car Div., Crewe, Sept. 1958; apptd Marketing Dir, Motor Car Div., 1967; Managing Director: Motor Car Div., 1971; Rolls-Royce Motors Ltd, 1972 (Gp Man. Dir, 1974–80); Vickers Plc: Dir, 1975–92; Man. Dir, 1980–86; Chief Exec., 1980–92; Chm., 1987–92. Dep. Chm., 1987–89, Jt Dep. Chm., 1989–94, Guinness PLC; Dep. Chm., TSB Gp, 1991–95; Chm., Inchcape plc, 1992–95; Regional Dir, Lloyds Bank, 1974–76; non-executive Director: GKN, 1978–84; Legal & General Gp Plc, 1985–87; Cable & Wireless, 1991–93; F. T. Everard & Sons, 1991–; Lloyds TSB, 1996–99. Trustee, Royal Opera House Trust, 1992–93 (Chm., 1992–93). Mem., European Adv. Council, Tenneco, 1984–86 and 1992–96; Bd Mem., Tenneco Inc., 1985–92, 1996–. Vice-Pres., Inst. of Motor Industry, 1974–82; Pres., SMMT, 1976–77, 1977–78 (Dep. Pres., 1978–79, 1979–80); Pres., Motor Industry Res. Assoc., 1978–81; Chm., Grand Council, Motor and Cycle Trades Benevolent Fund, 1976–82. Chm., Industrial Soc., 1983–87 (Mem., 1981); Dep. Chm., Listed Cos Adv. Cttee, 1987–90; Member: Council, CBI, 1983–92; BOTB, 1980–83; Engineering Council, 1980–83; Offshore Energy Technology Bd, 1985–86; Bd of Companions, BIM; Council, Regular Forces Employment Assoc. Patron, The Samaritans, 1987–99; Chm., 40th Anniversary Appeal Cttee, Mental Health Foundn, 1988–91; Gov., BUPA, 1990–95 (Dep. Chm., 1992–95). Chancellor, Univ. of Luton, 1993– (Hon. Fellow, 1991). Chm. Governors, Culford Sch., 1979–. Pres., Crewe Alexandra FC, 1975–82. Liveryman, Worshipful Co. of Coachmakers & Coach Harness Makers. FRSA. Young Business Man of the Year Award, The Guardian, 1976. Hon. DSc Cranfield, 1978. *Recreations:* golf, music. *Clubs:* Boodle's; Royal and Ancient (St Andrews); Royal St George's (Sandwich); Pine Valley Golf, Merion Golf.

PLATELL, Amanda Jane; Head of Media, Conservative Party, 1999–2001; *b* 12 Nov. 1957; *d* of Francis Ernest Platell and Norma June Platell (*née* Malland). *Educ:* Univ. of Western Australia (BA Hons Philosophy and Politics). Dep. Ed., Today newspaper, 1987–92; Man. Ed., Mirror Gp, 1993; Mktg Dir, 1993–95, Man. Dir, 1995–96, The Independent; Acting Ed., Sunday Mirror, 1996–97; Ed., Sunday Express, 1998–99. *Publication:* Scandal, 1999. *Recreations:* travelling, cooking, cars, writing.

PLATER, Alan Frederick, FRSL 1985; freelance writer, since 1960; *b* 15 April 1935; *s* of Herbert Richard Plater and Isabella Scott Plater; *m* 1st, 1958, Shirley Johnson (marr. diss. 1985); two *s* one *d*; 2nd, 1986, Shirley Rubinstein; three step *s. Educ:* Pickering Road Jun. Sch., Hull; Kingston High Sch., Hull; King's Coll., Newcastle upon Tyne. ARIBA (now lapsed). Trained as architect and worked for short time in the profession before becoming full-time writer in 1960; has written extensively for radio, television, films and theatre, also for The Guardian, Listener, New Statesman, etc. Pres., Writers' Guild of GB, 1991–95 (Co-chair, 1986–87). FRSA 1991. Works include: *theatre:* A Smashing Day (also televised); Close the Coalhouse Door (Writers' Guild Radio Award, 1972); And a Little Love Besides; Swallows on the Water; Trinity Tales; The Fosdyke Saga; Fosdyke Two; On Your Way, Riley!; Skyhooks; A Foot on the Earth; Prez; Rent Party (musical); Sweet Sorrow; Going Home; I Thought I Heard a Rustling; Shooting the Legend; All Credit to the Lads; Peggy for You; *films:* The Virgin and the Gypsy; It Shouldn't Happen to a Vet; Priest of Love; Keep the Aspidistra Flying; *television:* plays: So Long Charlie; See the Pretty Lights; To See How Far It Is (trilogy); Land of Green Ginger; Willow Cabins; The Party of the First Part; The Blacktoft Diaries; Thank You, Mrs Clinkscales; Doggin' Around; The Last of the Blonde Bombshells; biographies: The Crystal Spirit; Pride of our Alley; Edward Lear—at the edge of the sand; Coming Through; series and serials: Z Cars; Softly Softly; Shoulder to Shoulder; Trinity Tales; The Good Companions; The Consultant; Barchester Chronicles (adaptation of The Warden, and Barchester Towers, by Trollope); The Beiderbecke Affair; The Fortunes of War (adaptation of Balkan and Levant trilogies by Olivia Manning); A Very British Coup (International Emmy; Golden Fleece of Georgia (USSR); Best Series BAFTA Award; Best Series RTS Award; Best Series Broadcasting Press Guild Award; Best Series and Grand Prix, Banff Internat. TV Fest., Canada); The Beiderbecke Connection; Campion (adapted from Margery Allingham); A Day in Summer (adaptation of J. L. Carr novel); Misterioso; A Few Selected Exits (adapted from Gwyn Thomas; Cymru Writing Award, BAFTA, Regl Programme Award, RTS, 1993); Oliver's Travels; Dalziel & Pascoe (from Reginald Hill); *radio:* The Journal of Vasilije Bogdanovic (Sony Radio Award, 1983); All Things betray Thee (from Gwyn Thomas); The Lower Depths (from Gorky); Only a Matter of Time. Hon. Fellow, Humberside Coll. of Higher Educn, 1983; Hon. DLitt Hull, 1985; Hon. DCL Northumbria, 1997. RTS Writer's Award, 1984/85; Broadcasting Press Guild Award, 1987; Writer's Award, BAFTA, 1988; Northern Personality Award, Variety Club of GB, 1989. *Publications:* The Beiderbecke Affair, 1985; The Beiderbecke Tapes, 1986; Misterioso, 1987; The Beiderbecke Connection, 1992; Oliver's Travels, 1994; plays and shorter pieces in various anthologies. *Recreations:* reading, theatre, snooker, jazz, grandchildren, talking and listening. *Address:* c/o Alexandra Cann Representation, 12 Abingdon Road, W8 6AF. *T:* (020) 7938 4002. *Clubs:* Dramatists', Ronnie Scott's.

PLATT, family name of **Baroness Platt of Writtle**.

PLATT OF WRITTLE, Baroness *cr* 1981 (Life Peer), of Writtle in the County of Essex; **Beryl Catherine Platt,** CBE 1978; FREng; DL; Chairman, Equal Opportunities Commission, 1983–88; *b* 18 April 1923; *d* of Ernest and Dorothy Myatt; *m* 1949, Stewart Sydney Platt; one *s* one *d*. *Educ:* Westcliff High School; Girton Coll., Cambridge (MA; Fellow, 1988). CEng, FREng (FEng 1987); FRAeS (Hon. FRAeS 1994). Technical Assistant, Hawker Aircraft, 1943–46; BEA, 1946–49. Mem. Bd, British Gas, 1988–94. Member: Engineering Council, 1981–90; Engrg Training Authy, 1990–92; Meteorological Office Adv. Cttee (UK), 1992–99 (Chm., 1995–99). Member, Chelmsford RDC, 1958–74. Member, Essex CC, 1965–85: Alderman, 1969–74; Vice-Chm., 1980–83; Chm., Education Cttee, 1971–80. Mem., H of L Select Cttee for Science and Technology, 1982–85, 1990–94 and 1996–2001, on Relationships between Central and Local Govt, 1995–96, on Stem Cell Res., 2001–; Vice Pres., Parly Scientific Cttee, 1996–2000. Mem., Adv. Cttee on Women's Employment, 1981–90. Vice-Chairman: Technician Education Council, 1979–81; London Regional Adv. Council for Technology Education, 1975–81. President: Chelmsford Engrg Soc., 1979–80; Cambridge Univ. Engrs Assoc., 1987–2001; Assoc. for Sci. Educn, 1988; Pipeline Industries Guild, 1994–96; Vice-President: UMIST, 1985–92; Engrg Section, BAAS (Pres., 1988); ACC, 1992–97 (Mem. Educn Cttee, 1974–80); Member: CNAA, 1973–79; Council, CGLI, 1974–94; Cambridge Univ. Appointments Bd, 1975–79; Council, Careers Research and Adv. Centre, 1983–93; Council, RSA, 1983–88; COPUS, 1990–93; Council, Foundn for Sci. and Technology, 1991–97. Patron, Women into Sci. and Engrg, 1995–. Member of Court: Essex Univ., 1964–99; City Univ., 1969–78; Brunel Univ., 1985–92; Cranfield Inst. of Technology, 1989–; Chancellor, Middlesex Univ., 1993–2000. Trustee, Homerton Coll., 1970–81. Liveryman, Engineers' Co., 1988– (Mem., Ct of Assistants, 1995–). DL Essex 1983. Freeman, City of London, 1988. Fellow, 1987, Dir, 1989–94, Smallpeice Trust; Fellow, Manchester Polytechnic, 1989. FIGasE 1990; CInstE 1993; CIPD 1995; FRSA. Hon. FIMechE 1984; Hon. FITD 1994; Hon. FCP 1987; Hon. FIStructE 1991; Hon. FICE 1991; Hon. Fellow: Polytechnic of Wales, 1985; Women's Engrg Soc., 1988; UMIST, 1992. Hon. DSc: City, 1984; Salford, 1984; Cranfield, 1985; Nottingham Trent, 1993; Westminster, 1997; DUniv: Open Univ., 1985; Essex, 1985; Middlesex, 1993; Hon. DEng Bradford, 1985; Hon. DTech: Brunel, 1986; Loughborough, 1993; Hon. LLD Cantab, 1988. European Engr, FEANI, 1987; Insignia Award *hc*, CGLI, 1988. *Recreations:* cooking, reading. *Address:* House of Lords, SW1A 0PW. *Club:* Oxford and Cambridge.

PLATT, Anthony Michael Westlake, CBE 1991; Chief Executive, London Chamber of Commerce and Industry, 1984–91; *b* 28 Sept. 1928; *s* of late James Westlake Platt, CBE and Veronica Norma Hope Platt (*née* Arnold); *m* 1st, 1952, Jennifer Susan Scott-Fox; three *s*; 2nd, 1984, Heather Mary Stubbs; one step *s* one step *d*; 3rd, 1987, Sarah Elizabeth Russell. *Educ:* Stowe School; Balliol College, Oxford (PPE 1951). Foreign Office, 1951, served Prague, 1953–54, NY, 1955–56; Shell Group of Cos: Switzerland, 1957; Guatemala, 1959; S Africa, 1961; Venezuela, 1963; London, 1969; The Hague, 1972; London, 1975–77 (Billiton UK); The Hague, 1977–78 (Billiton Internat.); London, 1979–84. Advr, Council of British Chambers in Europe, 1992–95. *Publication:* (ed) Parallel 40 North to Eureka, 2000. *Recreations:* gliding, opera, languages. *Address:* 17 Westgate Street, Bury St Edmunds, Suffolk IP33 1QG.

See also C. P. S. Platt.

PLATT, Prof. Colin Peter Sherard; Professor of History, Southampton University, 1983–99, now Emeritus; *b* 11 Nov. 1934; twin *s* of late James Westlake Platt and Veronica Norma Hope Arnold; *m* 1st, 1963, Valerie Ashforth (marr. diss. 1996); two *s* two *d*; 2nd, 1996, Claire Donovan. *Educ:* Collyers Grammar School, Horsham; Balliol College, Oxford (BA 1st cl., MA); Leeds University (PhD). Research Assistant in Medieval Archaeology, Leeds Univ., 1960–62, Lectr, 1962–64; Lectr, Sen. Lectr and Reader in History, Southampton Univ., 1964–83. *Publications:* The Monastic Grange in Medieval England, 1969; Medieval Southampton: the port and trading community AD 1000–1600, 1973; (with Richard Coleman-Smith) Excavations in Medieval Southampton 1953–1969, 2 vols, 1975; The English Medieval Town, 1976; Medieval England: a social history and archaeology from the Conquest to 1600 AD, 1978; The Atlas of Medieval Man, 1979; The Parish Churches of Medieval England, 1981; The Castle in Medieval England and Wales, 1982; The Abbeys and Priories of Medieval England, 1984; Medieval Britain from the Air, 1984; The Traveller's Guide to Medieval England, 1985; The National Trust Guide to late Medieval and Renaissance Britain, 1986; The Architecture of Medieval Britain: a social history (Wolfson Prize for History), 1990; The Great Rebuildings of Tudor and Stuart England: revolutions in architectural taste, 1994; King Death: the Black Death and its aftermath in late medieval England, 1996. *Recreations:* reading novels, visiting medieval antiquities. *Address:* Farley Semaphore, Farley Chamberlayne, Braishfield, Romsey, Hants SO51 0QR. *T:* (01794) 368726.

See also A. M. W. Platt.

PLATT, Denise, CBE 1996; Chief Inspector, Social Services Inspectorate, and Joint Head, Social Care Group, Department of Health, since 1998; *b* 21 Feb. 1945; *d* of Victor Platt and May Platt (*née* Keeling). *Educ:* UCW, Cardiff (BSc Econ 1967); AIMSW 1968. Social Worker, then Sen. Social Worker, Middx Hosp., 1968–73; Sen. Social Worker, Guy's Hosp., 1973–76; Gp Leader, Southwark Social Services, 1976–78; Prin. Social Worker, Hammersmith Hosp., 1978–83; London Borough of Hammersmith and Fulham: Asst Dir, Social Services, 1983–86; Dir, 1986–95 (on leave of absence, 1994–95); Under Sec., Social Services, AMA, 1994–97; Hd of Social Services, LGA, 1997–98. Pres., Assoc. Dirs of Social Services, 1993–94. Vice Chm., Nat. AIDS Trust, 1994– (Trustee, 1987–). Member: Central Council Educn and Trng in Social Work, 1994–; Youth Justice Task Force, 1997–; Disability Rights Task Force, 1997–; Ind. Reference Gp on Mental Health, 1997–; Review Team, Strategic Review of London's Health Services, 1997–98. Gov., Nat. Inst. for Social Work, 1995– (Chm., 1997–99). Hon. DSocSc Brunel, 1998. *Publications:* various articles in social services press. *Recreations:* music, watercolours, walking, travel. *Address:* 13 Hillmore Court, 32 Belmont Hill, SE13 5AZ. *T:* (020) 8852 9556. *Club:* Royal Over-Seas League.

PLATT, Eleanor Frances; QC 1982; a Recorder of the Crown Court, since 1982; a Deputy High Court Judge, Family Division, since 1987; *b* 6 May 1938; *er d* of late Dr Maurice Leon Platt and Sara Platt (*née* Stein), Hove, Sussex; *m* 1963; two *c*. *Educ:* Hove County School for Girls; University College London. LLB 1959. Called to the Bar, Gray's Inn, 1960; Jt Head of Specialist Family Law Chambers, 1990–. Mem., Matrimonial Causes Rule Cttee, 1986–90. Dep. Chm., NHS Tribunal, 1995–; Legal Assessor, GMC and GDC, 1995–; Mem., Gene Therapy Adv. Cttee, 1993–98. Treas., Family Law Bar Assoc., 1990–95 (Acting Chm., 1995); Pres., Jewish Family Mediation Register, 1998–. Chm., Law, Parly and Gen. Purposes Cttee, 1988–94, Dep. Chm. Defence Bd, 1997–, Bd of Deputies of British Jews; Chm., New London Synagogue, 1994–99. Mem. Council, Medico-Legal Soc., 1995–. *Recreations:* the arts, travel, ski-ing. *Address:* One Garden Court, Temple EC4Y 9BJ. *T:* (020) 7797 7900; *e-mail:* e.plattqc@onegardencourt.co.uk.

PLATT, Sir Harold (Grant), Kt 1995; Chairman, Uganda Law Reform Commission, 1995–2000; *b* 11 March 1925; *s* of Rev. Harold George Platt and Francis Eaton Platt; *m* 1971, Eleonore Magdolna Graffin Meran; one *d*. *Educ:* Ootacamund, S India; St Peter's Coll., Oxford. Called to the Bar, Middle Temple, 1952; joined Colonial Legal Service, 1954: Puisne Judge: Tanzania, 1965–73; Kenya, 1973–84; Judge of Court of Appeal, Kenya, 1984–89; Judge of Supreme Court, Uganda, 1989–95. *Recreations:* golf, tennis, gardening. *Address:* Johann Fuxgasse 8, 8010 Graz, Austria. *T:* (316) 323462. *Clubs:* Muthaiga Country (Kenya); Jockey (Vienna).

PLATT, John Richard; His Honour Judge Platt; a Circuit Judge, since 1992; *b* 21 Nov. 1942; *s* of Arthur James Platt and Joan Platt; *m* 1986, Jayne Mary Webb; two *d*. *Educ:* Sherborne Sch.; Trinity Hall, Cambridge. Partner, Lee Davies & Co., Solicitors, 1969–82; Registrar and District Judge, Bow County Court, 1982–92. *Publications:* A Guide to Judicial Pensions for Circuit Judges, 1995; A Guide to Judicial Pensions for District Judges, 1996; A Guide to Judicial Pensions for Stipendiary Magistrates, 1996; A Guide to the Judicial Pensions and Retirement Act, 1997; contribs to Jordans Civil Court Service, New Law Jl, Liverpool Law Review, Family Law. *Recreations:* wine and food, music, travel.

PLATT, Margaret; *see* Wright, M.

PLATT, Sir Martin Philip, 3rd Bt *cr* 1959, of Grindleford, co. Derby; *b* 9 March 1952; *o s* of Hon. Sir Peter Platt, 2nd Bt, AM and of Jean Halliday Platt (*née* Brentnall); *S* father, 2000; *m* 1971, Francis Corinne Moana, *d* of Trevor Samuel Conley; two *s* two *d*. *Heir: s* Philip Stephen Platt; *b* 17 Oct. 1972.

PLATT, Michael Edward Horsfall; Pensions Ombudsman, 1991–94; *b* 24 Aug. 1934; *s* of Fred Horsfall Platt and Alice Martha Taylor Platt (*née* Wilde). *Educ:* Taunton Sch.; The Queen's Coll., Oxford. Nat. Service, RAF, 1952–54. Min. of Labour, 1959; Min. of Pensions and Nat. Insurance, 1960; Min. of Social Security, 1966; Private Sec. to Minister of State, DHSS, 1968–70; Cabinet Office, 1970–71; DHSS, 1971–86; Chief Adjudication Officer, 1986–90. *Recreations:* theatre, music. *Address:* c/o Office of the Pensions Ombudsman, 11 Belgrave Road, SW1V 1RB. *T:* (020) 7834 9144.

PLATT, Norman, OBE 1985; opera director and writer; Artistic Director, Kent Opera, 1969–89 and 1991–96; *b* 29 Aug. 1920; *s* of Edward Turner Platt and Emily Jane Platt; *m* 1st, 1942, Diana Franklin Clay; one *s* one *d*; 2nd, 1963, Johanna Sigrid Bishop; one *s* two *d*. *Educ:* Bury Grammar Sch.; King's Coll., Cambridge (BA). Principal: Sadler's Wells Opera, 1946–48; English Opera Group, 1948; Mem. Deller Consort, and freelance singer, actor, teacher and producer in Britain and Western Europe; founded Kent Opera, 1969; co-founded Canterbury Theatre and Festival Trust, 1983; re-founded Kent Opera, 1991. His many prodns for Kent Opera include: The Return of Ulysses; Agrippina; The Seraglio; Dido and Aeneas; Peter Grimes. Hon. DCL Kent, 1981; Hon. DMus Greenwich, 1996. *Publications:* Making Music (autobiog.), 2001; translations of numerous songs and operas, incl. L'Incoronazione di Poppea, Don Giovanni and Fidelio; articles on musical subjects. *Recreations:* listening to music, being read to by my wife. *Address:* Pembles Cross, Egerton, Ashford, Kent TN27 9BN. *T:* (01233) 756237.

PLATT, Stephen; writer and journalist; *b* 29 Sept. 1954; *s* of Kenneth Norman Platt and Joyce (*née* Pritchard); one *d* by Diane Louise Paice; partner, Anna Elizabeth Sutton. *Educ:* Longton High Sch., Stoke-on-Trent; Wade Deacon Sch., Widnes; LSE (BSc (Econ)). Teacher, Moss Brook Special Sch., Widnes, 1972–73; Dir, Self Help Housing Resource Library, Poly. of N London, 1977–80; Co-ordinator, Islington Community Housing, 1980–83; News Editor, subseq. Acting Editor, New Society, 1985–88; Editor, Midweek, 1988–89; columnist and writer, 1988–91; Editor, New Statesman and Society, 1991–96; freelance writer, 1996–. Editor, Enjoying the Countryside, 1988–; Editl Consultant, Channel 4, 1996–; Website and Contributing Ed., Time Team, 1999–; Dispatches Website Ed., 1999–. *Publications:* various. *Recreations:* archaeology, amphibians, bears (real and fictional), countryside, football, growing things, mountains, music. *Address:* 46 Tufnell Park Road, N7 0DT. *T:* (020) 7263 4185, *Fax:* (0870) 124 5850; *e-mail:* plattsteve@aol.com. *Clubs:* Red Rose; Port Vale.

PLATT, Terence Charles, CB 1996; Deputy Under-Secretary of State and Principal Establishment Officer, Home Office, 1992–96; *b* 22 Sept. 1936; *yr s* of Bertram Reginald Platt, QPM and Nina Platt; *m* 1959, Margaret Anne Cotmore; two *s*. *Educ:* St Olave's and St Saviour's Grammar School; Joint Services School for Linguists; Russian Interpreter. HM Immigration Officer, 1957; Asst Principal, Home Office, 1962; Principal, 1966; Cabinet Office, 1970; Principal Private Sec. to Sec. of State for NI (Rt Hon. William Whitelaw), 1972–73; Asst Sec., Home Office, 1973–81; Asst Under-Sec. of State and Princ. Estabt and Finance Officer, NI Office, 1981–82; Asst Under-Sec. of State and Dir of Regimes and Services, Prison Dept, Home Office, 1982–86; Asst Under-Sec. of State (Ops and Resources), Immigration and Nationality Dept, Home Office, 1986–92; Chief Inspector, Immigration Service, 1991–92. Mem., Civil Service Appeal Bd, 1997–. *Publication:* New Directions in Prison Design (Wkg Party Report), 1985. *Recreations:* growing roses, photography, butterflies.

PLATT, Prof. Trevor, PhD; FRS 1998; FRSC 1990; Head of Biological Oceanography, Bedford Institute of Oceanography, Nova Scotia, since 1972; *b* 12 Aug. 1942; *s* of John Platt and Lily Platt (*née* Hibbert); *m* 1988, Shuba Sathyendranath. *Educ:* Univ. of Nottingham (BSc); Univ. of Toronto (MA); Dalhousie Univ. (PhD 1970). Res. Scientist in Marine Ecology, Bedford Inst. of Oceanography, Nova Scotia, 1965–72. Chairman: Jt Global Ocean Flux Study, 1991–93; Internat. Ocean-colour Co-ordinating Gp, 1996–. Pres., Amer. Soc. Limnology and Oceanography, 1990–92. *Publications:* numerous res. papers in scholarly jls. *Recreations:* cycling, fly-fishing, languages, music. *Address:* Bedford Institute of Oceanography, Dartmouth, NS B2Y 4A2, Canada. *T:* (902) 4263793.

PLATTEN, Very Rev. Stephen George; Dean of Norwich, since 1995; *b* 17 May 1947; *s* of George Henry and Marjory Platten; *m* 1972, Rosslie Thompson; two *s*. *Educ:* Stationers' Company's Sch.; Univ. of London (BEd Hons 1972); Trinity Coll., Oxford (Dip. Theol. 1974); Cuddesdon Theol Coll. Deacon 1975, Priest 1976; Asst Curate, St Andrew, Headington, Oxford, 1975–78; Chaplain and Tutor, Lincoln Theol Coll., 1978–82; Diocesan Dir of Ordinands and Canon Residentiary, Portsmouth Cathedral, 1983–89; Dir, post-ordination trng and continuing ministerial educn, Dio. Portsmouth, 1984–89; Archbishop of Canterbury's Sec. for Ecumenical Affairs, 1990–95. Hon. Canon of Canterbury Cathedral, 1990–95. Anglican Sec., ARCIC (II), 1990–95. Chm., Soc. for Study of Christian Ethics, 1983–88. Minister Provincial, European Province, Third Order, SSF, 1991–96. Dir, SCM Press, 1990– (Chm., 2001–); Mem. Council, Hymns Ancient and Modern, 1997–. Guestmaster, Nikaean Club, 1990–95. *Publications:* (contrib.) Deacons in the Ministry of the Church, 1987; (series editor) Ethics and Our Choices, 1990–; (contrib.) Spirituality and Psychology, 1990; (contrib.) Say One for Me, 1991; (jtly) Spirit and Tradition: an essay on Change, 1996; Pilgrims, 1996; (ed jtly) New Soundings, 1997; Augustine's Legacy: authority and leadership in the Anglican Communion, 1997; (ed jtly) Flagships of the Spirit: cathedrals in society, 1998; (ed and contrib.) Seeing Ourselves: who are the interpreters of contemporary society?, 1998; Pilgrim Guide to Norwich, 1998; Cathedrals and Abbeys of England, 1999; (ed and contrib.) The Retreat of the State, 1999; Ink and Spirit, 2000; Open Government, 2001; contribs to theol and educnl jls. *Recreations:* walking, music, literature, Northumberland. *Address:* The Deanery, Norwich, Norfolk NR1 4EG. *T:* (01603) 218308, *Fax:* (01603) 613309. *Clubs:* Athenæum; Norfolk (Norwich).

PLATTS-MILLS, John Faithful Fortescue; QC 1964; Barrister; *b* 4 Oct. 1906; *s* of John F. W. Mills and Dr Daisy Platts-Mills, Karori, Wellington, NZ; *m* 1936, Janet Katherine Cree (*d* 1992); six *s*. *Educ:* Nelson College, NZ; Victoria University, NZ (LLB 1st Cl. 1927, LLM 1st Cl. 1928); Balliol College, Oxford (Rhodes Scholar; BA 1st Cl. 1930, BCL 1931, MA 1948). MP (Lab) Finsbury, 1945–48, (Lab Ind) 1948–50. Pilot Officer, RAF, 1940; "Bevin Boy", 1944; collier, 1945. Bencher, Inner Temple, 1970. President: Haldane Soc.; Soc. for Cultural Relations with the USSR; Vice-Pres., Internat. Assoc. of Democratic Lawyers. Common Councilman, City of London, 1995–. *Address:* Cloisters, Temple, EC4Y 7AA. *T:* (020) 7827 4000. *Clubs:* Athenæum; Vincent's (Oxford); Leander (Henley-on-Thames).

See also M. F. Platts-Mills.

PLATTS-MILLS, Mark Fortescue; QC 1995; *b* 17 Jan. 1951; *s* of John Faithful Fortescue Platts-Mills, *qv*; *m* 1982, Dr Juliet Anne Britton; one *s*. *Educ:* Bryanston Sch.; Balliol Coll., Oxford (BA Eng. Sci. and Econ.). Called to the Bar, Inner Temple, 1974. *Recreations:* gardening, hockey, cricket. *Address:* 8 New Square, Lincoln's Inn, WC2A 3QP.

PLAYER, Dr David Arnott, FRCPE, FRCPsych, FFCM; District Medical Officer, South Birmingham Health Authority, 1987–91; *b* 2 April 1927; *s* of John Player and Agnes Gray; *m* 1955, Anne Darragh; two *s*. *Educ:* Calder Street Sch.; Bellahouston Acad., Glasgow; Glasgow Univ. (MB, ChB, DPH); DPM RCSI; St Andrews Univ. (MA Hons 1995). House Surgeon, Dumfries and Galloway Royal Infirmary, 1950; Consultant in Dermatology and VD, RAMC (Far East), 1950–52; House Surgeon, Western Infirmary, Glasgow, 1952; House Physician, Bridge of Earn Hosp., 1952–53; House Surgeon (Obst., Gyn. and Paed.), Halifax Royal Infirmary, 1953–54; GP, W Cumberland and Dumfriesshire, 1954–59; Registrar (Infectious Diseases), Paisley Infectious Diseases Hosp., 1959–60; Asst MOH, Dumfriesshire, 1960–62; Registrar (Psychiatry), Crighton Royal Hosp., Dumfries, 1962–64; MOH, Dumfries Burgh, 1964–70; MO (Mental Health Div.), SHHD and Med. and Psych. Adviser to Sec. of State for Scotland on Scottish Prison and Borstal Service, 1970–73; Dir, Scottish Health Educn Group, 1973–82; Dir Gen., Health Educn Council, 1982–87. Hon. Vis. Prof., Dept of Clinical Epidemiology and Gen. Practice, Royal Free Hosp. Sch. of Medicine, 1983–. *Publications:* articles in Health Bulletin, Internat. Jl of Health Educn, Scottish Trade Union Review. *Recreations:* golf, cycling. *Address:* 7 Ann Street, Edinburgh EH4 1PL.

PLAYER, Gary James; professional golfer, since 1953; *b* Johannesburg, 1 Nov. 1935; *s* of Francis Harry Audley Player and late Muriel Marie Ferguson; *m* 1957, Vivienne, *d* of Jacob Wynand Verwey; two *s* four *d*. *Educ:* King Edward Sch., Johannesburg. Won first, Dunlop tournament, 1956; major championship wins include: British Open, 1959, 1968, 1974; US Masters, 1961, 1974, 1978; US PGA, 1962, 1972; US Open, 1965; S African Open, thirteen times, 1956–81; S African PGA, 1959, 1960, 1969, 1979, 1982; Australian Open, seven times, 1958–74; Johnnie Walker Trophy, Spain, 1984; World Match Play Tournament, 1965, 1966, 1968, 1971, 1973. *Publications:* Golf Begins at 50 (with Desmond Tolhurst), 1988; To Be the Best, 1991. *Address:* c/o Gary Player Group, 3930 Rca Boulevard, Suite 3001, West Palm Beach, FL 33140–4291, USA.

PLAYFORD, Jonathan Richard; QC 1982; **His Honour Judge Playford;** a Circuit Judge, since 1998; *b* 6 Aug. 1940; *s* of late Cecil R. B. Playford and Euphrasia J. Playford; *m* 1978, Jill Margaret Dunlop; one *s* one *d*. *Educ:* Eton Coll.; London Univ. (LLB). Called to the Bar, Inner Temple, 1962, Bencher, 1991; a Recorder, 1985–98. Mem., CICB, 1995–98. *Recreations:* music, horology. *Address:* Reading Crown Court, Old Shire Hall, Forbury, Reading RG1 3EH. *Clubs:* Garrick, Royal Automobile; Huntercombe Golf (Henley).

PLAYLE, Colin; Managing Director, Cicero, The Talking Company, since 1995; *b* 13 May 1933; *s* of James and Florence Playle; *m* 1st, 1957, Reena Mary Cuppleditch (marr. diss. 1975); two *d*; 2nd, 1976, Patricia Margaret Golds (*d* 1998). *Educ:* University College London (BA Hons). CompIGasE. British Gas: Marketing and Customer Service, E Midlands Gas Bd, 1957–75; Regl Marketing Manager, E Midlands, 1975–78; Dir of Marketing, British Gas NE, 1978–86; Sen. Mem., British Gas Privatisation Team, 1986; HQ Dir, Industrial and Commercial Gas, London, 1988–91; Regl Chm., British Gas Scotland, 1991–94; Project Dir, Retail, 1994–95. Chm., Combined Heat and Power Assoc., 1991–93. Vis. Prof. in Business Studies, Liverpool Business Sch., 1997–. Co-ordinator, Azerbaijan, TAM programme, EBRD, 1999–2000. *Recreations:* ski-ing, ornithology, modern literature. *Address:* Upton Barn, Main Street, Upton, Newark, Notts NG23 5SY.

PLEDGER, Air Marshal Sir Malcolm (David), KCB 2001; OBE 1988; AFC 1981; Deputy Chief of Defence Staff (Personnel), since 1999; *b* 24 July 1948; *m* 1969, Betty Barker Kershaw; two *s*. *Educ:* Newcastle Univ. (BSc 1st Cl. Chemistry 1970). Commnd RAF, 1970; served RAF Stations at Akrotiri, Shawbury, Sek Kong, Upavon, RAF Staff Coll., and MoD, 1972–85; OC 240 Operational Conversion Unit, RAF Odiham, 1985–88, incl. tour as OC 78 Sqdn, RAF Mount Pleasant and Falkland Is; Air Sec.'s Dept, 1988–90; Station Comdr, RAF Shawbury, 1990–92; rcds 1993; Air Officer Plans, HQ RAF Strike Command, 1993–97; COS, Dep. C-in-C and AOC, Directly Administered Units, HQ RAF Logistics Comd, 1997–99; Air Mem. for Logistics and AOC-in-C, RAF Logistics Comd, 1999. *Recreation:* golf. *Address:* Ministry of Defence, St Giles Court, 1–13 St Giles High Street, WC2H 8LD. *Club:* Royal Air Force.

PLEMING, Nigel Peter; QC 1992; *b* 13 March 1946; *s* of late Rev. Percy Francis Pleming and of Cynthia Myra Pleming (now Mrs Leslie Tuxworth); *m* 1979, Evelyn Carol Joan Hoffmann; one *s* two *d*. *Educ:* King Edward VI Grammar Sch., Spilsby; Kingston Polytechnic (LLB); University Coll. London (LLM). Lectr, Kingston Poly, 1969–73; called to the Bar, Inner Temple, 1971; in practice at the Bar, 1974–; Junior Counsel to the Crown (Common Law), 1987–92. Vice-Chm., Mental Health Act Commn, 1994–97; Mem., Govt working party on mental health reform, 1998–99. Hon. LLD Kingston, 1999. *Recreations:* cricket, tennis, painting, blues guitar. *Address:* 39 Essex Street, WC2R 3AT. *T:* (020) 7832 1111. *Club:* Royal Automobile.

PLENDER, Richard Owen; QC 1989; barrister; a Recorder, since 1998; *b* 9 Oct. 1945; *s* of George Plender and Louise Mary (*née* Savage); *m* 1978, Patricia Clare (*née* Ward); two *d*. *Educ:* Dulwich Coll.; Queens' Coll., Cambridge (MA, LLB; Rebecca Squire Prize; LLD 1993); Univ. of Illinois (LLM; JSD 1972; College of Law Prize); Univ. of Sheffield (PhD 1973). Called to the Bar, Inner Temple, 1972 (Berridale-Keith Prize), Bencher, 1996; in practice at the Bar, 1974–. Consultant, UN Law and Population Programme, 1972–74; Legal Adviser, UN High Comr for Refugees, 1974–78; Legal Sec., Court of Justice of European Communities, 1980–83; Dir of Studies, 1987, Dir of Res., 1988, and Lectr, 1998, Hague Acad. of Internat. Law; Dir, Centre of European Law, KCL, 1988–91; Special Legal Advr to States of Jersey, 1988–. Leverhulme Fellow, Yale Law Sch., 1980; British Acad. Fellow, Soviet Acad. of Sciences, 1985; Sen. Mem., Robinson Coll., Cambridge, 1983–; Associate Prof., Univ. de Paris II (Univ. de Droit, d'Economie et des Sciences Sociales), 1989–90; Hon. Vis. Prof., City Univ., 1991–. *Publications:* International Migration Law, 1972, 2nd edn 1988; (ed and contrib.) Fundamental Rights, 1973; Cases and Materials on the Law of the European Communities, 1980 (with J. Usher), 3rd edn 1993; A Practical Introduction to European Community Law, 1980; (with J. Peres Santos) Introducción al Derecho Comunitario Europeo, 1984; Basic Documents on International Migration Law, 1988, 2nd edn 1996; (ed and contrib.) Legal History and Comparative Law: essays in honour of Albert Kiralfy, 1990; The European Contracts Convention: the Rome Convention on the Choice of Law for Contracts, 1991, 2nd edn 2001; (ed and contrib.) The European Courts Practice and Precedents, 1996, supplement 1997, as European Courts Procedure, 2000–; contribs in English, French, German and Spanish to jls and encyclopedias. *Recreations:* writing light verse, classical music (especially late nineteenth century orchestral). *Address:* 20 Essex Street, WC2R 3AL. *T:* (020) 7583 9294.

PLENDERLEITH, Ian; Executive Director, since 1994, Member, Monetary Policy Committee, since 1997, Bank of England; Senior Broker to Commissioners for Reduction of National Debt, since 1989; *b* 27 Sept. 1943; *s* of Raymond William Plenderleith and Louise Helen Plenderleith (*née* Martin); *m* 1967, Kristina Mary Bentley; one *s* two *d*. *Educ:* King Edward's Sch., Birmingham; Christ Church, Oxford (MA); Columbia Business Sch., NY (MBA; Beta Gamma Sigma Medal, 1971). Joined Bank of England, 1965; seconded to IMF, Washington DC, 1972–74; Private Sec. to Governor, 1976–79; Alternate Dir, EIB, 1980–86; Hd of Gilt-Edged Div., 1982–90; Asst Dir, 1986–90; Associate Dir, 1990–94. Dir, Bank of England Nominees Ltd, 1994–; Alternate Dir, BIS, 1994–. Dir, London Stock Exchange (formerly Mem., Stock Exchange Council), 1989–2001 (Dep. Chm., 1996). Chairman: Stock Borrowing and Lending Cttee, 1990–95; G-10 Gold and Foreign Exchange Cttee, 1995–; Co-Chm., Govt Borrowers Forum, 1991–94; Member: Editl Cttee, OECD Study on Debt Management, 1990–93; Legal Risk Rev. Cttee, 1991–92; Financial Law Panel, 1992–94. Member: Adv. Bd, Inst. of Archaeology Develt Trust, UCL, 1987–96; Bd of Overseers, Columbia Business Sch., 1991–; Fund-raising Planning Gp, St Bartholomew's Hosp., 1992–94; Fund-raising Planning Cttee, St Bartholomew's and The London Hosps, 1998–; Council, British Mus. Soc., subseq. British Mus. Friends, 1993–99 and 2000–. Dir, City Arts Trust, 1997–. MSI 1991. Fellow, ACT, 1989. Liveryman, Innholders' Co., 1977. *Recreations:* archaeology, theatre, cricket, ski-ing. *Address:* Bank of England, EC2R 8AH. *T:* (020) 7601 4444. *Clubs:* Bankers'; Tillington Cricket (Hon. Sec, 1983–).

PLEYDELL-BOUVERIE, family name of **Earl of Radnor**.

PLOMIN, Judith Frances; *see* Dunn, J. F.

PLOMIN, Prof. Robert, PhD; Research Professor in Behavioural Genetics, and Deputy Director, MRC Research Centre on Social, Genetic, and Developmental Psychiatry, Institute of Psychiatry, King's College, London, since 1994; *b* 20 Feb. 1948; *m* 1987, Judith Frances Dunn, *qv*. *Educ:* DePaul Univ., Chicago (BA Psychology 1970); Univ. of Texas, Austin (PhD Psychology 1974). University of Colorado: Faculty Fellow, Inst. for Behavioral Genetics, 1974–86; Asst Prof., 1974–78; Associate Prof., 1978–82; Prof., 1982–86; Dist. Prof. and Dir, Center for Develtl and Health Genetics, Pennsylvania State Univ., 1986–94. Pres., Behavior Genetics Assoc., 1989–90. Ed., Sage Series on Individual Differences and Development, 1990–. *Publications:* (with A. H. Buss) Temperament: early developing personality traits, 1984; (with J. C. DeFries) Origins of Individual Differences in Infancy: the Colorado Adoption Project, 1985; Development, Genetics and Psychology, 1986; (ed with J. Dunn) The Study of Temperament: changes, continuities, and challenges, 1986; (jtly) Nature and Nurture in Infancy and Early Childhood, 1988; (with J. Dunn) Separate Lives: why siblings are so different, 1990; (jtly) Behavioral Genetics: a primer, 2nd edn 1990 to 4th edn 2001; (ed jtly) Nature and Nurture during Middle Childhood, 1994; (ed jtly) Separate Social Worlds of Siblings: impact of nonshared environment on development, 1994; Genetics and Experience: the interplay between nature and nurture, 1994; (jtly) The Relationship Code, 2000; numerous articles in learned jls. *Address:* MRC Centre for Social, Genetic and Developmental Psychiatry, Institute of Psychiatry, De Crespigny Park, Denmark Hill, SE5 8AF.

PLOTKIN, Prof. Gordon David, PhD; FRS 1992; FRSE; Professor of Computation Theory, Edinburgh University, since 1986; *b* 9 Sept. 1946; *s* of Manuel Plotkin and Mary (*née* Levin); *m* 1st, 1984, Lynda (*née* Stephenson) (marr. diss.); one *s*; 2nd, 1994, Hephzibah (*née* Kolban). *Educ:* Univ. of Glasgow (BSc 1967); Univ. of Edinburgh (PhD 1972).

University of Edinburgh: Res. Associate and Res. Fellow, 1971–72; Lectr, 1975; Reader, 1982–86. BP Venture Res. Fellow, 1981–87; SERC Sen. Res. Fellow, 1992–97. MAE 1989. *Publications:* (ed with G. Kahn) Semantics of Data Types, 1984; (ed with G. Huet) Logical Frameworks, 1991; (ed with J.-L. Lassez) Computational Logic: essays in honour of Alan Robinson, 1991; (ed jtly) Situation Theory and its Applications, 1991; (ed with G. Huet) Logical Environments, 1993; (ed with M. Dezani-Ciancaglini) Typed Lambda Calculi and Applications, 1995; (ed jtly) Proof, Language and Interaction: essays in honour of Robin Milner, 2000; contribs to jls of computer science and logic. *Recreations:* hill-walking, chess. *Address:* Division of Informatics, University of Edinburgh, The King's Buildings, Edinburgh EH9 3JZ. *T:* (0131) 650 5158.

PLOTKIN, Prof. Henry Charles, PhD; Professor of Psychobiology, University College London, since 1993; *b* Johannesburg, 11 Dec. 1940; *s* of Bernard Solomon Plotkin and Edythe Plotkin (*née* Poplak); *m*, 1st, 1965, Patricia Ruehl (marr. diss. 1970); 2nd, 1975, Victoria Mary Welch; one *s* one *d. Educ:* Univ. of Witwatersrand (BSc 1st cl. Hons 1964); University College London (PhD 1968). Res. Asst, Univ. of Witwatersrand, 1964; Res. Scientist, MRC Unit on Neural Mechanisms of Behaviour, 1965–72; MRC Travelling Fellowship, Stanford Univ., Calif, 1970–71; Department of Psychology, University College London: Lectr, 1972–88; Reader, 1988–93; Head of Dept, 1993–98. *Publications:* Darwin Machines and the Nature of Knowledge, 1994; Evolution in Mind, 1997; *edited:* (with D. A. Oakley) Brain, Behaviour and Evolution, 1979; Essays in Evolutionary Epistemology, 1982; The Role of Behaviour in Evolution, 1988; articles in learned jls. *Recreations:* family, football, growing old gracefully with music. *Address:* Department of Psychology, University College London, WC1E 6BT. *T:* (020) 7679 7573.

PLOURDE, Most Rev. Joseph Aurèle; Archbishop of Ottawa (RC), 1967–89, now Emeritus; *b* 12 Jan. 1915; *s* of Antoine Plourde and Suzanne Albert. *Educ:* Bathurst Coll.; Bourget Coll., Rigaud; Major Seminary of Halifax; Inst. Catholique, Paris; Gregorian Univ., Rome. Auxiliary Bishop of Alexandria, Ont., 1964. Hon. DEducn, Moncton Univ., 1969. *Address:* Jean-Paul II Residence, 1243 Kilborn Place, Ottawa, ON K1H 6K9, Canada.

PLOUVIEZ, Peter William; Chairman, Equity Trust Fund, since 1992; *b* 30 July 1931; *s* of C. A. W. and E. A. Plouviez; *m* 1978, Alison Dorothy Macrae; two *d* by previous marr. Gen. Sec., British Actors' Equity Assoc., 1974–91. FRSA 1992. *Address:* c/o Equity Trust Fund, 222 Africa House, 64 Kingsway, WC2B 6BD.

PLOWDEN, William Julius Lowthian, PhD; independent consultant; *b* 7 Feb. 1935; *s* of Lord Plowden, GBE, KCB, and Lady Plowden, DBE; *m* 1960, Veronica Gascoigne; two *s* two *d. Educ:* Eton; King's Coll., Cambridge (BA, PhD); Univ. of Calif, Berkeley. Staff Writer, Economist, 1959–60; BoT, 1960–65; Lectr in Govt, LSE, 1965–71; Central Policy Review Staff, Cabinet Office, 1971–77; Under Sec., Dept of Industry, 1977–78; Dir-Gen., RIPA, 1978–88; Exec. Dir, UK Harkness Fellowships, NY, 1988–91; Sen. Advr, Harkness Fellowships, London, 1991–98; UK Dir, Atlantic Fellowships, 1995–98. Hon. Prof., Dept of Politics, Univ. of Warwick, 1977–82; Vis. Prof. in Govt, LSE, 1982–88; Vis. Prof., Univ. of Bath, 1992–; Sen. Res. Associate, IPPR, 1992–94; Vis. Sen. Res. Fellow, London Business Sch., 1993–94; Vis. Res. Fellow, Constitution Unit, UCL, 1999–. Member: W Lambeth DHA, 1982–87; QCA, 1999–. Trustee: CSV, 1984–; Southern Africa Advanced Educn Project, 1986–95; Public Mgt Foundn, 1992–98. Mem. Ct of Govs, LSE, 1987–, Council, 2000–. *Publications:* The Motor Car and Politics in Britain, 1971; (with Tessa Blackstone) Inside the Think Tank: advising the Cabinet 1971–1983, 1988; Mandarins and Ministers, 1994. *Address:* 49 Stockwell Park Road, SW9 0DD. *T:* (020) 7274 4535.

PLOWDEN ROBERTS, Hugh Martin; Director, Argyll Group plc, 1983–95; *b* 6 Aug. 1932; *s* of Stanley and Joan Plowden Roberts; *m* 1st, 1956, Susan Jane Patrick (*d* 1996); two *d*; 2nd, 2000, Mrs Jane Hall. *Educ:* St Edward's School, Oxford; St Edmund Hall, Oxford. BA 1954, MA 1956. FIGD 1980. Payne & Son Meat Group, 1954–60 (Dir, 1958); Asst Gen. Manager (Meat Group), Co-operative Wholesale Society, 1960–67; Allied Suppliers Ltd, 1967–82: Dir, 1971; Dep. Man. Dir, 1974; Man. Dir, 1978; Chm., 1980–82; Dir, Cavenham Ltd, 1979, Chm., 1981–82; Dep. Chm., Argyll Stores Ltd, 1983–85; Chm., Dairy Crest Foods, subseq. Dairy Crest Ltd, 1985–88; Dir, Lawson Mardon Group Ltd, 1987–91. Comr, Meat and Livestock Commn, 1975–79; Mem., MMB, 1983–89. *Recreations:* country pursuits. *Address:* Barn Cottage, Fulking, Henfield, W Sussex BN5 9NB. *T:* (01273) 857622. *Club:* Farmers'.

PLOWMAN, John Patrick; Chairman, Driver and Vehicle Operator Group, Department for Transport, Local Government and the Regions (formerly Department of the Environment, Transport and the Regions), since 2001; *b* 20 March 1944; *s* of late Robert and of Ruth Plowman, Lane End, Bucks; *m* 1973, Daphne Margaret Brock Kennett; two *s* one *d. Educ:* St Edward's Sch., Oxford; Grenoble Univ.; University Coll., Univ. of Durham (BA). MoD, 1967–75: Private Office, Minister of State for Defence, 1969–71; Resident Observer, CSSB, 1975; Cabinet Office, 1976–78; MoD and UK Delegn to UN Law of Sea Conf., 1979–81; Asst Sec., DoE, 1982–86; Counsellor, UK Repn to EC, 1986–90; Head, Envmtl Protection (Europe), 1990–93; Regl Dir for NW, DoE and Dept of Transport, 1993–94; Dir, Envmt and Transport, Govt Office for NW, DoE, 1994; Dir, Wildlife and Countryside, DoE, then DETR, 1994–98; Dir, Road Safety and Envmt, DETR, 1998–2001. Served Royal Marines Reserve, 1968–71. *Recreations:* music, fishing, tennis. *Address:* (office) Great Minster House, 76 Marsham Street, SW1P 4DR. *T:* (020) 7676 2050. *Club:* Royal Over-Seas League.

PLOWMAN, Hon. Sir John (Robin), Kt 1979; CBE 1970 (OBE 1949); Member of the Legislative Council, later Senator, Bermuda, 1966–82, Government Leader in the Senate, 1968–82; Minister of Government and Commercial Services, Bermuda, 1980–82; *b* Bermuda, 18 Sept. 1908; *s* of Owen and Elizabeth Plowman; *m* 1936, Marjorie Hardwick (*d* 1990); two *s. Educ:* Bermuda and England. Member, Ealing Borough Council, 1931–35; returned to Bermuda, 1935; Bermuda Volunteer Engineers, 1939–42; Dep. Dir, Dir and later Chm. of Bermuda Supplies Commission, 1942–47; Man. Director of Holmes, Williams & Purvey Ltd, 1947–78, Chairman of Board, 1961–97. Chm. or Mem. of various govt commns and bds, including Training and Employment, Ports Facilities, Transport Control and Civil Service; Minister of Organisation, 1968–77; Minister of Marine and Air Services, 1977–80. Attached to UK negotiating team for Bermuda II Civil Aviation agreement, 1977. Chm. Bd of Governors, Warwick Academy, 1946–73; Life Vice-Pres. Bermuda Olympic Assoc. and Bermuda Football Assoc. *Recreations:* golf, sports administration. *Address:* Chiswick, Paget, Bermuda. *Club:* Royal Hamilton Dinghy and Mid-Ocean (Bermuda).

PLOWRIGHT, David Ernest, CBE 1996; international television production and broadcasting consultant; Chairman, Granada Television Ltd, 1987–92; Deputy Chairman, Channel Four Television, 1992–97; Visiting Professor in Media Studies, Salford University, since 1992; *b* 11 Dec. 1930; *s* of late William Ernest Plowright and of Daisy Margaret Plowright; *m* 1953, Brenda Mary (*née* Key); one *s* two *d. Educ:* Scunthorpe Grammar Sch.; on local weekly newspaper and during National Service, Germany. Reporter, Scunthorpe Star, 1950; freelance corresp. and sports writer, 1952; Reporter, Feature Writer and briefly Equestrian Corresp., Yorkshire Post, 1954; Granada Television: News Editor, 1957; Producer, Current Affairs, 1960; Editor, World in Action, 1966; Head of Current Affairs, 1968; Controller of Programmes, 1969–79; Jt Man. Dir, 1975–81; Man. Dir, 1981–87; Director: Granada Internat., 1975–92; Granada Gp, 1981–92. Chm., Network Programme Cttee, ITV, 1980–82. Chm., ITCA, 1984–86. Director: Superchannel, 1986–89; Merseyside Tourism Board, 1986–88; British Satellite Broadcasting, 1987–90; British Screen, 1988–92; Tate Gall., Liverpool, 1988–91. Vice Pres., RTS, 1982–94; Member: Steering Cttee, European Film and TV Forum, 1988–91; Internat. Council, Nat. Acad. for TV Arts and Scis, 1988–92; Manchester Olympic Bid Cttee, 1988; Chm. Develt Cttee, Manchester City of Drama 1994, 1992–94. Trustee, BAFTA (Fellow, 1992). Gov., Manchester Polytechnic, 1988–90. Hon. DLitt Salford, 1989; Hon. DArt Liverpool Poly., 1991. *Recreations:* television, watching sport, messing about in a boat. *Address:* Westways, Wilmslow Road, Mottram St Andrew, Cheshire SK10 4QT. *T:* (01625) 820948.

See also J. A. Plowright.

PLOWRIGHT, Joan Ann, (The Lady Olivier), CBE 1970; leading actress with the National Theatre, 1963–74; Member of the RADA Council; *b* 28 Oct. 1929; *d* of late William Ernest Plowright and of Daisy Margaret (*née* Burton); *m* 1st, 1953, Roger Gage (marr. diss.); 2nd, 1961, (as Sir Laurence Olivier) Baron Olivier, OM (*d* 1989); one *s* two *d. Educ:* Scunthorpe Grammar School; Laban Art of Movement Studio; Old Vic Theatre School. First stage appearance in If Four Walls Told, Croydon Rep. Theatre, 1948; Bristol Old Vic and Mem. Old Vic Co., S Africa tour, 1952; first London appearance in The Duenna, Westminster, 1954; Moby Dick, Duke of York's, 1955; season of leading parts, Nottingham Playhouse, 1955–56; English Stage Co., Royal Court, 1956; The Crucible, Don Juan, The Death of Satan, Cards of Identity, The Good Woman of Setzuan, The Country Wife (transferred to Adelphi, 1957); The Chairs, The Making of Moo, Royal Court, 1957; The Entertainer, Palace, 1957; The Chairs, The Lesson, Phoenix, NY, 1958; The Entertainer, Royale, NY, 1958; The Chairs, The Lesson, Major Barbara, Royal Court, 1958; Hook, Line and Sinker, Piccadilly, 1958; Roots, Royal Court, Duke of York's, 1959; Rhinoceros, Royal Court, 1960; A Taste of Honey, Lyceum, NY, 1960 (Best Actress Tony Award); Rosmersholm, Greenwich, 1973; Saturday, Sunday, Monday, Queen's, 1974–75; The Sea Gull, Lyric, 1975; The Bed Before Yesterday, Lyric, 1975 (Variety Club of GB Award, 1977); Filumena, Lyric, 1977 (Soc. of West End Theatre Award, 1978); Enjoy, Vaudeville, 1980; The Cherry Orchard, Haymarket, 1983; The House of Bernada Alba, Globe, 1986; Time and the Conways, Old Vic, 1990; If We are Women, Greenwich, 1995; Chichester Festival: Uncle Vanya, The Chances, 1962; St Joan (Best Actress Evening Standard Award), Uncle Vanya, 1963; The Doctor's Dilemma, The Taming of the Shrew, 1972; Cavell, 1982; The Way of the World, 1984; National Theatre: St Joan, Uncle Vanya, Hobson's Choice, opening season, 1963; The Master Builder, 1964; Much Ado About Nothing, 1967, 1968; Three Sisters, 1967, 1968; Tartuffe, 1967, 1968; The Advertisement, 1968; Love's Labour's Lost, 1968; The Merchant of Venice, 1970; A Woman Killed With Kindness, 1971; The Rules of the Game, 1971; Eden End, 1974; Mrs Warren's Profession, 1985. Produced, The Travails of Sancho Panza, 1969; directed: Rites, 1969; A Prayer for Wings, 1985; Married Love, 1988. *Films include:* The Entertainer, 1960; Three Sisters, 1970; Equus; Britannia Hospital, 1982; Wagner, Revolution, 1985; Drowning by Numbers, The Dressmaker, 1988; I Love You to Death, Avalon, 1989; Stalin, 1992 (Golden Globe Award, 1993); Enchanted April, 1993 (Golden Globe Award, 1993); Denis the Menace, A Place for Annie, A Pin for the Butterfly, Widow's Peak, Last Action Hero, 1993; On Promised Land, Hotel Sorrento, A Pyromaniac's Love Story, The Scarlett Letter, 1994; Mr Wrong, 1995; Jane Eyre, 101 Dalmatians, Surviving Picasso, 1996; The Assistant, 1996; Dance with Me, 1998; America Betrayed, 1998; Tea with Mussolini, 1999; Return to the Secret Garden, Frankie and Hazel, 2000; *films for TV:* The Merchant of Venice; Brimstone and Treacle, 1982; A Dedicated Man; Return of the Natives, 1994; Tom's Midnight Garden, 1998; This Could Be the Last Time, 1998; other *television* appearances include: Daphne Laureola, 1976; The Birthday Party, 1987; The Importance of Being Earnest, 1988; And a Nightingale Sang, 1989; House of Bernada Alba, 1991; Clothes in the Wardrobe, 1992. 18th annual Crystal Award, Women in Film, USA, 1994. *Publication:* And That's Not All (memoirs), 2001. *Recreations:* reading, music, entertaining. *Address:* c/o ICM, 76 Oxford Street, W1N 0AX.

See also D. E. Plowright.

PLOWRIGHT, Rosalind Anne, (Mrs J. A. Kaye); mezzo-soprano; *b* 21 May 1949; *d* of Robert Arthur Plowright and Celia Adelaide Plowright; *m* 1984, James Anthony Kaye; one *s* one *d. Educ:* Notre Dame High Sch., Wigan; Royal Northern Coll. of Music, Manchester. LRAM. London Opera Centre, 1974–75; Glyndebourne Chorus and Touring Co., début as soprano, Agathe in Der Freischutz, 1975; WNO, ENO, Kent Opera, 1975–78; Miss Jessel in Turn of the Screw, ENO, 1979 (SWET award); début at Covent Garden as Ortlinde in Die Walküre, 1980; with Bern Opera, 1980–81, Frankfurt Opera and Munich Opera, 1981; débuts: in USA (Philadelphia and San Diego), Paris, Madrid and Hamburg, 1982; at La Scala, Milan, Edinburgh Fest., San Francisco and New York (Carnegie Hall), 1983; at Deutsche Oper, Berlin, 1984; in Houston, Pittsburgh, Verona, Montpellier and Venice, 1985; in Rome, Florence and Holland, 1986; in Tulsa, Buenos Aires, Santiago di Chile, Israel and Bonn, 1987; with NY Phil. and Paris Opera, 1987; in Lausanne, Geneva, Oviedo and Bilbao, 1988; in Zurich, Copenhagen, Lisbon and Torre del Lago, 1989; with Vienna State Opera, 1990; in Nice, 1991; in Wiesbaden, 1992; in Leeds, 1993; in Athens and Bregenz, 1994; BBC Prom. Concerts; with Berlin Deutsche Staatsoper, 1995. Principal rôles as soprano include: Ariadne; Aida; Amelia in Un Ballo in Maschera; Leonora in Il Trovatore; Leonora in La Forza del Destino; Desdemona in Otello; Violetta in La Traviata; Elena in I Vespri Siciliani; Abigaille in Nabucco; Elisabetta in Don Carlos; Lady Macbeth; Manon Lescaut; Giorgetta in Il Tabarro; Suor Angelica; Norma; Alceste; Médée; Maddalena in Andrea Chénier; La Gioconda; Tatyana in Eugene Onegin; Tosca; principal rôles as mezzo-soprano include: Amneris in Aida; Cassandra in Les Troyens; Kundry in Parsifal; Kostelnicka in Jenufa. Has given recitals and concerts in UK, USA and Europe, made opera and concert recordings, and opera telecasts; acting début, House of Elliott, TV serial, 1993. First prize, 7th Internat. Comp. for Opera Singers, Sofia, 1979; Prix Fondation Fanny Heldy, Acad. Nat. du Disque Lyrique, 1985. *Recreation:* fell walking. *Address:* c/o AOR Management Ltd, Westwood, Lorraine Park, Harrow Weald, Middx HA3 6BX. *T:* (020) 8954 7646, *Fax:* (020) 8420 7499.

PLOWRIGHT, Walter, CMG 1974; DVSc, FRS 1981, FRCVS; Head, Department of Microbiology, ARC Institute for Research on Animal Diseases, Compton, Berks, 1978–83; *b* 20 July 1923; 2nd *s* of Jonathan and Mahala Plowright, Holbeach, Lincs; *m* 1959, Dorothy Joy (*née* Bell). *Educ:* Moulton and Spalding Grammar Schs; Royal Veterinary Coll., London. DVSc (Pret.) 1964; MRCVS 1944; FRCVS 1977; FRVC 1987. Commissioned, RAVC, 1944–48; Colonial Service, 1950–64; Animal Virus Research Inst., Pirbright, 1964–71 (seconded E Africa, 1966–71); Prof. of Vet. Microbiology, RVC, 1971–78. Hon. Mem., Acad. Royale des Sciences d'Outre-Mer, Brussels, 1986. Hon. DSc: Univ. of Nairobi, 1984; Reading, 1986. J. T. Edwards Memorial Prize, 1964; R. B. Bennett Commonwealth Prize of RSA, 1972; Bledisloe Vet.

Award, RASE, 1979; King Baudouin Internat. Develt Prize, 1984; Dalrymple-Champneys Cup, BVA, 1984; Gold Award, Office Internat. des Epizooties, Paris, 1988; Outstanding Scientific Achievement Award, Animal Health Trust, 1991; Theiler Meml Trust Award, South Africa, 1994; World Food Prize, World Food Prize Foundn, Iowa, 1999. *Publications:* numerous contribs to scientific jls relating to virus diseases of animals. *Recreations:* gardening, reading on wine and investment, African history. *Address:* Whitehill Lodge, Goring-on-Thames, Reading RG8 0LL. *T:* (01491) 872891.

PLUMB, family name of **Baron Plumb**.

PLUMB, Baron *cr* 1987 (Life Peer), of Coleshill in the County of Warwickshire; **Charles Henry Plumb,** Kt 1973; DL; Member (C) The Cotswolds, European Parliament, 1979–99; *b* 27 March 1925; *s* of Charles and Louise Plumb; *m* 1947, Marjorie Dorothy Dunn; one *s* two *d*. *Educ:* King Edward VI School, Nuneaton. National Farmers Union: Member Council, 1959; Vice-President, 1964, 1965; Deputy-President, 1966, 1967, 1968, 1969; President, 1970–79. European Parliament: Chm., Agricl Cttee, 1979–82; Leader, EDG, 1982–87; Pres., 1987–89; Co-Chm., EU/ACP Jt Assembly, 1994; Vice-Pres., EPP, 1994–97; Leader, British Conservatives, 1994–97. Chm., British Agricl Council, 1975–79. Chm., Agricultural Mortgage Corp., 1994–95. Mem., Duke of Northumberland's Cttee of Enquiry on Foot and Mouth Disease, 1967–68; Member Council: CBI; Animal Health Trust. Chm., Internat. Agricl Trng Programme, 1987–. Pres., Royal Agric. Soc. of England, 1977, Dep. Pres. 1978; President: Internat. Fedn of Agricl Producers, 1979–82; Comité des Organisations Professionels Agricoles de la CEE (COPA), 1975–77. Pres., Nat. Fedn of Young Farmers' Clubs, 1976–; Patron, Warwicks Co. Fedn of YFC, 1974–; Hon. Pres., Ayrshire Cattle Soc. Chancellor, Coventry Univ., 1995–; Gov., RAC, Cirencester, 1995–. Liveryman, Farmers' Co. FRSA 1970; FRAgS 1974. DL Warwick 1977. Hon. Fellow, Wye Coll., London Univ., 1988. Hon. DSc: Cranfield, 1983; Silsoe Coll. of Technol., 1987; De Montfort, 1995; Hon. LLD Warwick, 1990; Hon. Dr Cheltenham & Gloucester Coll. of HE, 1999. Gold Medal, RASE, 1983; Robert Schuman Gold Medal, France, 1989. Ordén de Merito (Portugal), 1987; Order of Merit (Luxembourg), 1988; Grand Cross, Order of Civil Merit (Spain), 1989; Knight Comdr's Cross, Order of Merit (FRG), 1990 (Order of Merit, 1979); Grand Order of the Phoenix (Greece), 1997. *Recreations:* country pursuits, fishing. *Address:* The Dairy Farm, Maxstoke, Coleshill, Warwicks B46 2QJ. *T:* (01675) 463133, *Fax:* (01675) 464156; House of Lords, SW1A 0PW. *T:* (020) 7219 1233, *Fax:* (020) 7219 1649; *e-mail:* plumbh@parliament.uk. *Clubs:* St Stephen's Constitutional, Farmers', Coleshill Rotary (Hon. Member).

PLUMB, Sir John (Harold), Kt 1982; FBA 1968; historian; Master of Christ's College, Cambridge, 1978–82; Professor of Modern English History, University of Cambridge, 1966–74, now Emeritus; *b* 20 Aug. 1911; 3rd *s* of late James Plumb, Leicester. *Educ:* Alderman Newton's Sch., Leicester; University Coll., Leicester; Christ's Coll., Cambridge. BA London, 1st Class Hons History, 1933; PhD Cambridge, 1936; LittD Cambridge, 1957. Ehrman Research Fellow, King's Coll., Cambridge, 1939–46; FO, 1940–45; Fellow of Christ's Coll., 1946–, Steward, 1948–50, Tutor, 1950–59. Vice-Master, 1964–68. Univ. Lectr in History, 1946–62; Reader in Modern English History, 1962–65; Chm. of History Faculty, 1966–68, Univ. of Cambridge. Trustee: National Portrait Gallery, 1961–82; Fitzwilliam Museum, 1985–92 (Syndic, 1960–77); Member: Wine Standards Bd, 1973–75; Council, British Acad., 1977–80; Chm., Centre of E Anglian Studies, 1979–82. FRHistS; FSA; FRSL 1969. Visiting Prof., Columbia Univ., 1960; Distinguished Vis. Prof., NYC Univ., 1971–72, 1976; Cecil and Ida Green Honors Chair, Texas Christian Univ., 1974; Dist. Vis. Prof., Washington Univ., 1977; Lectures: Ford's, Oxford Univ., 1965–66; Saposnekov, City College, NY, 1968; Guy Stanton Ford, Univ. of Minnesota, 1969; Stenton, Reading, 1972; George Rogers Clark, Soc. of the Cincinnati, 1977. Chm., British Inst. of America, 1982–90; Hon. For. Mem., Amer. Acad. for Arts and Sciences, 1970; Hon. Member: Soc. of Amer. Historians, 1976; Amer. Historical Assoc., 1981. Hon. DLitt: Leicester, 1968; East Anglia, 1973; Bowdoin Coll., 1974; S California, 1978; Westminster Coll., 1983; Washington Univ., St Louis, 1983; Bard Coll., NY, 1988. Editor, History of Human Society, 1959–; Sen. Editor to American Heritage Co. Historical Adviser, Penguin Books, 1960–92; Editor, Pelican Social History of Britain, 1982–. *Publications:* England in the Eighteenth Century, 1950; (with C. Howard) West African Explorers, 1952; Chatham, 1953; (ed) Studies in Social History, 1955; Sir Robert Walpole, Vol. I, 1956, Vol. II, 1960, both vols repr. 1972; The First Four Georges, 1956; The Renaissance, 1961; Men and Places, 1962; Crisis in the Humanities, 1964; The Growth of Political Stability in England, 1675–1725, 1967; Death of the Past, 1969; In the Light of History, 1972; The Commercialisation of Leisure, 1974; Royal Heritage, 1977; New Light on the Tyrant, George III, 1978; Georgian Delights, 1980; Royal Heritage: The Reign of Elizabeth II, 1980; (with Neil McKendrick and John Brewer) The Birth of a Consumer Society, 1982; Collected Essays: Vol. I, The Making of a Historian, 1988; Vol. II, The American Experience, 1989; *contrib. to:* Man versus Society in Eighteenth Century Britain, 1968; Churchill Revised, 1969 (Churchill, the historian); *festschrift:* Historical Perspectives: Essays in Honour of J. H. Plumb, 1974. *Address:* Christ's College, Cambridge CB2 3BU. *T:* (01223) 334900. *Club:* Brooks's.

PLUMB, Paula Maria H.; *see* Hay-Plumb.

PLUMB, Prof. Raymond Alan, PhD; FRS 1998; Professor of Meteorology, Massachusetts Institute of Technology, since 1988; *b* 30 March 1948; *s* of Tom and Dorothy Plumb; *m* 1981, Janet Gormly; one *s* one *d*. *Educ:* Manchester Univ. (BSc Physics 1969; PhD Astronomy 1972). SO, then SSO, Met. Office, Bracknell, 1972–76; Res. Scientist, then Principal Res. Scientist, CSIRO Div. of Atmospheric Res., Aspendale, Vic, 1976–88. *Publications:* (ed with R. A. Vincent) Middle Atmosphere, 1989; numerous papers in refereed scientific jls, incl. Jl Atmospheric Scis, Jl Geophysical Res. *Recreations:* angling, hiking. *Address:* 76 Westford Street, Chelmsford, MA 01824, USA. *T:* (978) 2561402.

PLUMBLY, Sir Derek (John), KCMG 2001 (CMG 1991); HM Diplomatic Service; Ambassador to Saudi Arabia, since 2000; *b* 15 May 1948; *s* of late John C. Plumbly and Jean Elizabeth (*née* Baker); *m* 1979, Nadia Gohar; two *s* one *d*. *Educ:* Brockenhurst Grammar Sch.; Magdalen Coll., Oxford (BA PPE). VSO, Pakistan, 1970; Third Sec., FCO, 1972; MECAS, 1973; Second Sec., Jedda, 1975; First Sec., Cairo, 1977; FCO, 1980; First Sec., Washington, 1984; Dep. Head of Mission, Riyadh, 1988; Head of Chancery, UK Mission to UN, NY, 1992–96; Internat. Drugs Co-ordinator, and Dir, Drugs and Internat. Crime, FCO, 1996–97; Dir, Middle East and N Africa, FCO, 1997–2000. *Address:* c/o Foreign and Commonwealth Office, King Charles Street, SW1A 2AL.

PLUME, John Trevor; Regional Chairman, Industrial Tribunals (London North), 1984–87; *b* 5 Oct. 1914; *s* of William Thomas and Gertrude Plume; *m* 1948, Christine Mary Wells; one *d*. *Educ:* City of London School; Inns of Court School of Law. Called to the Bar, Gray's Inn, 1936, Bencher, 1969. Legal Associate Mem., Town Planning Inst., 1939; served Royal Artillery, 1940–46 (Captain). Practiced at Bar, specialising in property law, 1936–76; Chm., Industrial Tribunals, 1976–87. Liveryman, Clockmakers' Co. *Recreations:* beekeeping, carpentry, gardening, fishing. *Address:* Mulberry Cottage, Forest Side, Epping, Essex CM16 4ED. *T:* (01992) 572389.

PLUMMER, family name of **Baron Plummer of St Marylebone**.

PLUMMER OF ST MARYLEBONE, Baron *cr* 1981 (Life Peer), of the City of Westminster; **(Arthur) Desmond (Herne) Plummer,** Kt 1971; TD 1950; JP; DL; President, Portman Building Society, since 1990 (Chairman, 1983–90); *b* 25 May 1914; *s* of late Arthur Herne Plummer and Janet (*née* McCormick); *m* 1941, Pat Holloway (Pres., Cons. Women's Adv. Cttee, Greater London Area, 1967–71) (*d* 1998); one *d*. *Educ:* Hurstpierpoint Coll.; Coll. of Estate Management. Served 1939–46, Royal Engineers, Field and Staff. Member: TA Sports Bd, 1953–79; London Electricity Consultative Council, 1955–66; St Marylebone Borough Council, 1952–65 (Mayor, 1958–59); LCC, for St Marylebone, 1960–65; Inner London Educn Authority, 1964–76. Greater London Council: Mem. for Cities of London and Westminster, 1964–73, for St Marylebone, 1973–76; Leader of Opposition, 1966–67 and 1973–74; Leader of Council, 1967–73. Member: South Bank Theatre Board, 1967–74; Standing Conf. on SE Planning, 1967–74; Transport Co-ordinating Council for London, 1967–69; Local Authorities Conditions of Service Adv. Bd, 1967–71; Exec. Cttee, British Section of Internat. Union of Local Authorities, 1967–74; St John Council for London, 1971–94; Exec. Cttee, Nat. Union Cons. and Unionist Assocs, 1967–76; Chm., St Marylebone Conservative Assoc., 1965–66. Chm., Horserace Betting Levy Bd, 1974–82; Dep. Chm., Nat. Employers' Mutual Gen. Insurance Assoc., 1973–86; Chm., Nat. Employers' Life Assce, 1983–89; Pres., Met. Assoc. of Bldg Socs, 1983–89. Mem. Court, Univ. of London, 1967–77. Chairman: Epsom and Walton Downs Trng Grounds Man. Bd, 1974–82; National Stud, 1975–82; President: London Anglers' Assoc., 1976–; Thames Angling Preservation Soc., 1970–99. Liveryman, Worshipful Co. of Tin Plateworkers. FAI 1948; FRICS 1970; FRSA 1974; Hon. FASI (Hon. FFAS 1966). JP, Co. London, 1958; DL Greater London, 1970. KStJ 1986. *Publications:* Time for Change in Greater London, 1966; Report to London, 1970; Planning and Participation, 1973. *Recreations:* swimming (Capt. Otter Swimming Club, 1952–53); growing things, horse racing. *Address:* 4 The Lane, St Johns Wood, NW8 0PN. *Clubs:* Carlton (Chm., Political Cttee, 1979–84; Pres., 1984–98), Royal Automobile, MCC.

PLUMMER, (Arthur) Christopher (Orme), CC (Canada) 1968; actor; *b* Toronto, 13 Dec. 1929; *m* 1st, 1956, Tammy Lee Grimes; one *d*; 2nd, 1962, Patricia Audrey Lewis (marr. diss. 1966); 3rd, 1970, Elaine Regina Taylor. *Educ:* public and private schs, Montreal. French and English radio, Canada, 1949–52; Ottawa Rep. Theatre; Broadway: Starcross Story, 1951–52; Home is the Hero, 1953; The Dark is Light Enough, 1954 (Theatre World Award); The Lark, 1955; J. B., 1958 (Tony nomination); Arturo Ui, 1963; Royal Hunt of the Sun, 1965–66; Stratford, Conn, 1955: Mark Antony, Ferdinand; leading actor, Stratford Festival, Canada, 1956–67: Henry V, The Bastard, Hamlet, Leontes, Mercutio, Macbeth, Cyrano de Bergerac, Benedick, Aguecheek, Antony; Royal Shakespeare Co., Stratford-on-Avon, 1961–62: Benedick, Richard III; London debut as Henry II in Becket, Aldwych and Globe, 1961 (Evening Standard Best Actor Award, 1961); National Theatre, 1971–72: Amphytrion 38, Danton's Death; Broadway musical, Cyrano, 1973 (Outer Critics Circle Award and Tony Award for Best Actor in a Musical, NY Drama Desk Award); The Good Doctor, NY, 1974; Iago in Othello, NY, 1982 (Drama Desk Award); Macbeth, NY, 1988; No Man's Land, NY, 1994; Barrymore (one-man show), 1997 (Tony Award for Best Actor). *Films:* Stage-Struck, 1956; Across the Everglades, 1957; The Fall of the Roman Empire, 1963; The Sound of Music, 1964 (Golden Badge of Honour, Austria); Daisy Clover, 1964; Triple Cross, 1966; Oedipus Rex, 1967; The Battle of Britain, 1968; Royal Hunt of the Sun, 1969; The Pyx, 1973; The Man Who Would Be King, 1975; Aces High, 1976; The Moneychangers, 1976 (Emmy Award); International Velvet, 1978; The Silent Partner, 1978; Hanover Street, 1979; Murder by Decree, 1980 (Genie Award, Canada); The Disappearance, 1981; The Janitor, 1981; The Amateur, 1982; Dreamscape, 1984; Playing for Keeps, 1985; Lily in Love, 1985; Souvenir, 1989; Where The Heart Is, 1990; Twelve Monkeys, 1996; The Insider, 2000; Dracula 2001, 2001; Lucky Break, 2001, and others. TV appearances, Britain, Denmark, and major N American networks, incl. Hamlet at Elsinore, BBC and Danish TV, 1964 (4 Emmy Award nominations). First entertainer to win Maple Leaf Award (Arts and Letters), 1982. *Recreations:* tennis, ski-ing, piano. *Clubs:* Players, River (New York).

PLUMMER, Maj.-Gen. Brian Peter; Director General Training Support, Headquarters Land Command, since 1999; *b* 30 Aug. 1948. *Educ:* Univ. of Durham (BA). Commnd RWF, 1970; Regt and Staff Duty, 1974–85; jsdc, 1986; ASC, 1986–88; CO 1 RWF, 1989–91; HCSC, 1995; Comd, 1st Mechanised Bde, 1995–96; rcds, 1997; Comd, Combined Arms Trng Centre, 1998–99. Col, RWF, 2001–. *Address:* c/o RHQ RWF, Hightown Barracks, Wrexham, Clwyd LL13 8RD.

PLUMMER, Christopher; *see* Plummer, A. C. O.

PLUMMER, Maj.-Gen. Leo Heathcote, CBE 1974; retired 1979; *b* 11 June 1923; *s* of Lt-Col Edmund Waller Plummer and Mary Dorothy Brookesmith; *m* 1955, Judyth Ann Dolby; three *d*. *Educ:* Canford Sch.; Queens' Coll., Cambridge. Commnd RA, 1943; War Service, N Africa, Sicily, Italy, 1943–45 (mentioned in despatches, 1945); Adjt, TA, 1947–49; Staff Coll., Camberley, 1952, Directing Staff, 1961–63; Comdt, Sudan Staff Coll., 1963–65; CO, 20 Heavy Regt, 1965–67; Col, Gen. Staff, MoD, 1967; Brig., 1967; Comdr, 1st Artillery Bde, 1967–70; Dep. Dir Manning (Army), 1971–74; Asst Chief of Staff Ops, HQ Northern Army Gp, 1974–76; Maj.-Gen., 1976; Chief, Jt Service Liaison Orgn, Bonn, 1976–78. ADC to HM The Queen, 1974–76; Col Comdt, RA, 1981–86. Chm., Civil Service Commn Selection Bd, 1983–91. Hon. Sec., Old Meeting House Trust, Helmsley, 1993–97; Pres., 78 Div., Battleaxe Club, 1996–. *Recreation:* gardening. *Address:* Vivers Lodge, Old Road, Kirkbymoorside, York YO62 6BD. *Club:* Army and Navy.

PLUMMER, Peter Edward; Deputy Director, Department for National Savings, 1972–79; *b* 4 Nov. 1919; *s* of Arthur William John and Ethel May Plummer; *m* 1949, Pauline Wheelwright; one *s* one *d*. *Educ:* Watford Grammar Sch. Served War, REME, 1941–46. Customs and Excise, 1936–38; Dept for National Savings, 1938–79; Principal, 1956; Assistant Sec., 1964; seconded to Nat. Giro, 1970–71; Under-Sec., 1972. *Recreations:* gardening, photography. *Address:* Old Timbers, Farm Lane, Nutbourne, Chichester, W Sussex P018 8SA. *T:* (01243) 377450.

PLUMPTON, Alan, CBE 1980; BSc; FREng, FIEE; Chairman, Schlumberger plc, 1992–2001; Chairman, 1992–99, Director, 1999–2001, Beaufort Group PLC (formerly Beaufort Management Consultants); *b* 24 Nov. 1926; *s* of late John Plumpton and Doris Plumpton; *m* 1950, Audrey Smith; one *s* one *d*. *Educ:* Sunderland Technical Sch.; Durham Univ. (BSc Elec. Eng). FREng (FEng 1991). Pupil Engr, Sunderland Corp. Elec. Undertaking, 1942; various engrg and commercial appts, NEEB, 1948–61; Dist Manager, E Monmouthshire Dist, S Wales Electricity Bd, 1961–64. Admin. Staff Coll., Henley, 1963; Dep. Chief Commercial Engr, S Wales Elec. Bd, 1964–67; Chief Commercial Engr,

S Wales Elec. Bd, 1967–72; Dep. Chm., London Elec. Bd, 1972–76, Chm., 1976–81; Dep. Chm., Electricity Council, 1981–86. Chairman: Ewbank Preece Group, 1986–92; Manx Electricity Authority, 1986–97; Schlumberger Measurement and Systems, 1988–92; Dir, Eleco Holdings, 1993–97. MInstD 1986; CIMgt. Liveryman, Gardeners' Co. JP Mon, 1971–72. *Recreations:* golf, gardening. *Address:* Lockhill, Stubbs Wood, Amersham, Bucks HP6 6EX. *T:* (01494) 433791. *Club:* Harewood Downs Golf (Chm., 1996–98).

PLUMPTRE, family name of **Baron Fitzwalter**.

PLUMPTRE, Hon. (Wyndham) George; Founder and Editorial Director, greenfingers.com, since 1999; *b* 24 April 1956; 3rd *s* of 21st Baron Fitzwalter, *qv*; *m* 1984, Alexandra Elizabeth Cantacuzene-Speransky; two *s* one *d*. *Educ:* Radley Coll.; Jesus Coll., Cambridge (BA Mod. Hist.). Author, journalist, lecturer and broadcaster, 1978–; Gardens Correspondent, 1993–95, columnist, 1995–97, The Times; Ed., Sotheby's Preview Mag., 1995–97; Dir, S Africa, Sotheby's, 1997–99. Trustee, Kent Gardens Trust, 1992–; Mem., SE Regl Cttee, Nat. Trust, 1993–96. *Publications:* Royal Gardens, 1981; Collins Book of British Gardens, 1985; The Fast Set, 1985; The Latest Country Gardens, 1988; Homes of Cricket, 1988; Garden Ornament, 1989; Cricket Cartoons and Caricatures, 1989; Back Page Racing, 1989; The Golden Age of Cricket, 1990; The Water Garden, 1993; The Garden Makers, 1993; Great Gardens, Great Designers, 1994; Edward VII, 1995; The Country House Guide, 1996; Classic Planting, 1998. *Address:* The Old Laundry, Tudeley, Tonbridge, Kent TN11 0NW. *T:* (01732) 352314. *Clubs:* Pratt's, MCC (Mem., Arts and Liby Cttee, 1999–).

PLUMSTEAD, Isobel Mary, (Mrs N. J. Coleman); Her Honour Judge Plumstead; a Circuit Judge, since 2001; *b* 19 July 1947; *d* of John Archibald Plumstead, DFM, MA and Nancy Plumstead (*née* Drummond); *m* 1971, Nicholas John Coleman, *qv*; one *s* two *d*. *Educ:* Norwich High Sch. for Girls (GPDST); St Hugh's College, Oxford (BA 1969; MA 1985); Inns of Court Sch. of Law, Blackstone Entrance Scholar, 1967, Colombos Prize for Internat. Law, 1970, Harmsworth Scholar, 1970–73, Middle Temple. Called to the Bar, Middle Temple, 1970; Registrar, Principal Registry, Family Div. of High Court, 1990; District Judge, Principal Registry, Family Div. of the High Ct, 1990–2001; Asst Recorder, 1994–98; a Recorder, 1998–2001. Member: Independent Schs Tribunal, 1992–2000; Family Cttee (formerly Civil and Family Cttee), 1993–99, Main Bd, 1997–99, Judicial Studies Bd. Trustee: New Parents' Infant Network (Newpin), 1989–96; Hackney and E London Family Mediation Service, 1993–96; Vice Pres., Family Mediators Assoc., 1999–. Gov., St Margaret's Sch., Hampstead, 1993–98. *Publications:* (contrib.) Emergency Remedies in the Family Courts, 1997; (contrib.) Rayden and Jackson on Divorce and Family Matters, 1997. *Recreations:* gardening, gargling, gastronomy, snoozing. *Address:* Norwich Combined Court Centre, Bishopgate, Norwich, Norfolk NR3 1UR; Francis Taylor Building, Temple, EC4Y 7BY. *Club:* Aldeburgh Yacht.

PLUNKET, family name of **Baron Plunket**.

PLUNKET, 8th Baron *cr* 1827; **Robin Rathmore Plunket;** *b* 3 Dec. 1925; *s* of 6th Baron Plunket (*d* 1938) and Dorothé Mabel (*d* 1938), *d* of late Joseph Lewis and *widow* of Captain Jack Barnato, RAF; *S* brother, 1975; *m* 1951, Jennifer, *d* of late Bailey Southwell, Olivenhoutpoort, S Africa. *Educ:* Eton. Formerly Captain, Rifle Brigade. *Heir:* *b* Hon. Shaun Albert Frederick Sheridan Plunket [*b* 5 April 1931; *m* 1961, Judith Ann, *e d* of late G. P. Power; one *s* one *d*; *m* 1980, Mrs Elizabeth de Sancha (*d* 1986); *m* 1989, Mrs Andrea Reynolds]. *Address:* Rathmore, Chimanimani, Zimbabwe; 39 Lansdowne Gardens, SW8 2EL. *Club:* Boodle's.

PLUNKET GREENE, Mary, (Mrs Alexander Plunket Greene); *see* Quant, M.

PLUNKETT, family name of **Baron Dunsany,** and of **Baron Louth**.

PLUNKETT, William Joseph; Valuer and Estates Surveyor, Greater London Council, 1977–81; *b* 8 Nov. 1921; *s* of John Joseph Archer and Marjorie Martin Plunkett; *m* 1949, Gwendoline Innes Barron; two *s* five *d*. *Educ:* Finchley Catholic Grammar Sch.; Coll. of Estate Management. BSc(Est. Man.). FRICS. RN, 1941–46; commnd, 1942; Lt RNVR. Dep. County Valuer, Middlesex CC, 1962–65; Asst Valuer, Valuation and Estates Dept, GLC, 1965–73; Dep. Valuer and Estates Surveyor, GLC, 1973–74; Dir of Valuation and Estates Dept, GLC, 1974–77. Mem., South Bank Polytechnic Adv. Cttee on Estate Management, 1973–76; Chm., Covent Garden Officers' Steering Gp, 1977–81. Mem. General Council, RICS, 1978–80 (Pres. Planning and Develt Div., 1978–79; Chm., S London Br. Cttee, 1976–77); Pres., Assoc. of Local Authority Valuers and Estate Surveyors, 1980–81. *Publications:* articles on Compensation, Valuation and Development. *Address:* 63 Radnor Cliff, Folkestone, Kent CT20 2JL. *T:* (01303) 248868.

PLUTHERO, John; Chief Executive Officer, Freeserve plc, since 1998; *b* 10 Feb. 1964; one *d*. *Educ:* Colchester Royal Grammar Sch.; London Sch. of Econs (BSc 1st Cl. Hons Econs). Dir, Chelsea Harbour, P&O Develts, 1990–94; Strategy and Planning, Bass plc, 1994–95; Man. Dir, Mastercare DSG, 1998–99; Founder, Freeserve plc. MInstD. *Recreations:* modern art, golf, cricket, music. *Address:* Freeserve plc, Spring Way, Maylands Avenue, Hemel Hempstead, Herts HP2 7TG. *T:* (0870) 9090666. *Club:* Woburn Golf and Country.

PLYMOUTH, 3rd Earl of, *cr* 1905; **Other Robert Ivor Windsor-Clive;** Viscount Windsor (UK 1905); 15th Baron Windsor (England, *cr* 1529); DL. FRSA 1953; *b* 9 October 1923; *e s* of 2nd Earl of Plymouth, PC and Lady Irene Charteris (*d* 1989), *d* of 11th Earl of Wemyss; *S* father, 1943; *m* 1950, Caroline Helen, *o d* of Edward Rice, Dane Court, Eastry, Kent; three *s* one *d*. *Educ:* Eton. Mem., Museums and Galls Commn (formerly Standing Commn on Museums and Galls), 1972–82; Chm., Reviewing Cttee on Export of Works of Art, 1982–85. DL County of Salop, 1961. *Heir:* *s* Viscount Windsor, *qv*. *Address:* The Stables, Oakly Park, Ludlow, Shropshire SY8 2JW.

PLYMOUTH, Bishop Suffragan of, since 1996; **Rt Rev. John Henry Garton;** *b* 3 Oct. 1941; *s* of Henry and Dorothy Garton; *m* 1969, Pauline (*née* George); two *s*. *Educ:* RMA Sandhurst; Worcester Coll., Oxford (MA); Cuddesdon Coll., Oxford. Commissioned in Royal Tank Regt, 1962. Ordained, 1969; CF, 1969–73; Lectr, Lincoln Theol Coll., 1973–78; Rector of Coventry East Team Ministry, 1978–86; Principal, Ripon Coll., Cuddesdon, 1986–96. Hon. Canon of Worcester Cathedral, 1988–96. *Address:* 31 Riverside Walk, Tamerton Foliot, Plymouth PL5 4AQ. *T:* (01752) 769836.

PLYMOUTH, Bishop of, (RC), since 1986; **Rt Rev. Mgr Hugh Christopher Budd;** *b* 27 May 1937; *s* of John Alfred and Phyllis Mary Budd. *Educ:* St Mary's Primary School, Hornchurch, Essex; Salesian Coll., Chertsey, Surrey; Cotton Coll., North Staffs; English Coll., Rome. PhL; STD. Ordained Priest, 1962; post-ordination studies, 1963–65; Tutor, English Coll., Rome, 1965–71; Lectr at Newman Coll., Birmingham and part-time Asst Priest, Northfield, Birmingham, 1971–76; Head of Training, Catholic Marriage Advisory Council, National HQ, London, 1976–79; Rector, St John's Seminary, Wonersh, Surrey, 1979–85; Administrator, Brentwood Cathedral, Essex, Nov. 1985–Jan. 1986. *Recreations:* walking, cricket (watching), music (listening). *Address:* Bishop's House, 31 Wyndham Street West, Plymouth, Devon PL1 5RZ.

PLYMOUTH, Archdeacon of; *see* Wilds, Ven. A. R.

POCOCK, Dr Andrew John; HM Diplomatic Service; Head of African Department (Southern), Foreign and Commonwealth Office, since 2001; *b* 23 Aug. 1955; *s* of John Francis Pocock and Vida Erica Pocock (*née* Duruty); *m* 1st, 1976, Dayalini Pathmanathan (marr. diss. 1993); 2nd, 1995, Julie Mason. *Educ:* St Mary's Coll., Trinidad; Queen Mary Coll., London (BA, MA); Peterhouse, Cambridge (PhD 1987). Joined HM Diplomatic Service, 1981; Second, later First Sec., Lagos, 1983–86; First Secretary: Southern African Dept, FCO, 1986–87; Washington, 1988–92; Personnel Mgt Dept, FCO, 1992–94; Asst, S Asia Dept, FCO, 1994–95; Counsellor, on loan to RCDS, 1996; Dep. High Comr, Canberra, 1997–2001. Liveryman, Cutlers' Co., 1979–. *Recreations:* tennis, cricket, walking. *Address:* c/o Foreign and Commonwealth Office, King Charles Street, SW1A 2AH. *Club:* Commonwealth (Canberra).

POCOCK, Air Vice-Marshal Donald Arthur, CBE 1975 (OBE 1957); Director, British Metallurgical Plant Constructors Association, 1980–85; *b* 5 July 1920; *s* of late A. Pocock and of E. Broad; *m* 1947, Dorothy Monica Griffiths; two *s* three *d*. *Educ:* Crouch End. Served War of 1939–45: commissioned, 1941; Middle East, 1941–48. Transport Command, 1948–50; commanded RAF Regt Sqdn, 1950–52; Staff Coll., 1953; Staff Officer, HQ 2nd Allied TAF, 1954–57; comd RAF Regt Wing, 1957–58; MoD, 1958–59; HQ Allied Air Forces Central Europe, 1959–62; Sen. Ground Defence SO, NEAF, 1962–63; MoD, 1963–66; Sen. Ground Defence SO, FEAF, 1966–68; ADC to the Queen, 1967; Commandant, RAF Catterick, 1968–69; Dir of Ground Defence, 1970–73; Comdt-Gen. RAF Regt, 1973–75. Gen. Man., Iran, British Aerospace Dynamics Gp, 1976–79. *Address:* 16 Dence Park, Herne Bay, Kent CT6 6BQ. *T:* (01227) 374773. *Club:* Royal Air Force.

POCOCK, Gordon James; Director, Communications Educational Services Ltd, 1983–87; *b* 27 March 1933; *s* of late Leslie and Elizabeth Maud Pocock; *m* 1959, Audrey Singleton (*d* 1990). *Educ:* Royal Liberty Sch., Romford; Keble Coll., Oxford. Joined PO, 1954; Private Sec. to Dir Gen., 1958–59; Principal, 1960–68; Asst Sec., 1968–72; Dep. Dir, 1972–76; Dir, Ext. Telecomms, 1976–79; Dir, Telecommns Marketing, 1979, Sen. Dir, 1979–81; Chief Exec., Merlin Business Systems, BT, 1981–84. Fellow, Nolan Norton & Co., 1985–87. *Publications:* Corneille and Racine, 1973; Boileau and the Nature of Neo-Classicism, 1980; article on Nation, Community, Devolution and Sovereignty. *Recreations:* travel, theatre, local history. *Address:* 131 Lichfield Court, Sheen Road, Richmond, Surrey TW9 1AY. *T:* (020) 8940 7118.

POCOCK, Leslie Frederick, CBE 1985; Chairman, Liverpool Health Authority, 1982–86; *b* 22 June 1918; *s* of Frederick Pocock and Alice Helena Pocock; *m* 1946, Eileen Horton; two *s*. *Educ:* Emanuel School. FCCA. Chief Accountant: London & Lancashire Insurance Co. Ltd, 1959; Royal Insurance Co. Ltd, 1966; Chief Accountant and Taxation Manager, 1971, Dep. Gp Comptroller, 1974, Royal Insurance Gp; retired 1981. Gen. Comr of Income Tax, 1982–93. Dir, Federated Pension Services (Guarantee) Ltd, 1995–98. Pres., Assoc. of Certified Accountants, 1977–78. Mem., UK Central Council for Nursing, Midwifery and Health Visiting, 1983–87; Chm., Merseyside Residuary Body, 1985; Hon. Treas., 1986–96, Vice Chm., 1996–98, Merseyside Improved Houses, subseq. Riverside Housing Assoc. Chm. Governors, Sandown Coll., Liverpool, 1989–91. *Recreations:* countryside, golf. *Address:* Barn Lee, Tithebarn Close, Lower Heswall, Wirral, Merseyside CH60 0EY. *T:* (0151) 342 2917.

PODDAR, Prof. Ramendra Kumar, PhD; Professor of Biophysics, Calcutta University, 1973–95 (Vice-Chancellor, 1979–83); Member of Parliament (Rajya Sabha), 1985–93 (Vice-Chairman, 1987–89); *b* 9 Nov. 1930; *m* 1955, Srimati Jharna Poddar (decd); two *s* one *d*. *Educ:* Univ. of Calcutta (BSc Hons Physics, MSc Physics; PhD Biophysics); Associateship Dip., Saha Inst. of Nuclear Physics. Progressively, Research Asst, Lecturer, Reader, Associate Prof., Biophysics Div., Saha Inst. of Nuclear Physics, 1953–73. IAEA Advr to Govt of Mali, 1962. Study visits to Univ. of California, Berkeley, 1958–60, Cold Spring Harbor Biological Lab., 1960, Purdue Univ., 1960–61, California Inst. of Technology, 1970, CNRS, Paris, 1978. Advr, West Bengal Pollution Control Bd. Life Member: West Bengal Acad. of Science and Technol.; Indian Biophysical Soc.; Chm., Inst. of Wetland Management and Ecological Design, 1986–93. *Publications:* more than 50 research papers in the fields of biophysics, molecular biology and photobiology. *Address:* Department of Biophysics, Molecular Biology and Genetics, University College of Science, Calcutta 700009, India. *T:* (office) (33) 3508386; CF62 Salt Lake City, Calcutta 700064, India. *T:* (33) 3375646.

PODGER, Geoffrey John Freeman; Chief Executive, Food Standards Agency, since 2000; *b* 3 Aug. 1952; *s* of late Leonard Podger and of Beryl Podger (*née* Freeman). *Educ:* Worthing High Sch. for Boys; Pembroke Coll., Oxford (Open Scholar; BA Medieval and Modern Langs 1974; MA 1977). MoD, 1974–82; Internat. Staff, NATO HQ, Brussels, 1977–79; Department of Health and Social Security, subseq. Department of Health, 1982–96; loaned to Falkland Islands Govt as Sec. to Port Stanley Hosp. Fire Inquiry, 1985; Private Sec. to Chm. (subseq. Chief Exec.), NHS Management Bd and Sec. to Bd, 1985–87; Principal Private Sec. to Sec. of State for Social Services, 1987–88; Head, Internat. Relations Unit, 1992–93; Under Sec. for Health Promotion, 1993–96; Hd of Food Safety and Sci. Gp, MAFF, 1996–97; Hd, Jt Food Safety and Standards Gp, MAFF and DoH, 1997–2000. *Address:* Food Standards Agency, Aviation House, 125 Kingsway, WC2B 6NH. *T:* (020) 7276 8100.

PODMORE, Ian Laing; Chief Executive, Sheffield City Council, 1974–89; *b* 6 Oct. 1933; *s* of Harry Samuel Podmore and Annie Marion (*née* Laing); *m* 1961, Kathleen Margaret (*née* Langton); one *s* one *d*. *Educ:* Birkenhead School. Admitted Solicitor 1960. Asst Solicitor, Wallasey County Borough, 1960–63; Sen. Asst Solicitor, Southport Co. Borough, 1963–66; Deputy Town Clerk: Southport, 1966–70; Sheffield, 1970–74. *Recreations:* golf, gardening, watching football. *Club:* Abbeydale Golf.

PODRO, Prof. Michael Isaac, CBE 2001; PhD; FBA 1992; Professor, Department of Art History and Theory, University of Essex, 1973–97, now Emeritus; *b* 13 March 1931; *s* of Joshua Podro and Fanny Podro; *m* 1961, Charlotte Booth; two *d*. *Educ:* Berkhamsted Sch.; Jesus Coll., Cambridge (MA); University Coll. London (PhD). Hd of Dept of Art History, Camberwell Sch. of Art and Crafts, 1961–67; Lectr in the Philosophy of Art, Warburg Inst., Univ. of London, 1967–69; Reader, Dept of Art History and Theory, Univ. of Essex, 1969–73. Trustee, V&A Mus., 1987–96. DU Essex. *Publications:* Manifold in Perception: theories of art from Kant to Hildebrand, 1972; Critical Historians of Art, 1982; Depiction, 1998. *Address:* 1 Provost Road, NW3 4ST. *T:* (020) 7722 7435.

POGO, Most Rev. Ellison Leslie; *see* Melanesia, Archbishop of.

PÖHL, Karl Otto; Grosskreuz des Verdienstordens der Bundesrepublik Deutschland; Member, Shareholder Committee, Sal. Oppenheim Jr & Cie, since 1998 (Partner,

1992–98); Governor, Deutsche Bundesbank and German Governor, International Monetary Fund and Bank for International Settlements, 1980–91; *b* 1 Dec. 1929; *m* 1974; two *s* two *d*. *Educ:* Göttingen Univ. (Econs; Diplom.-Volkswirt). Div. Chief for Econ. Res., IFO-Institut, Munich, 1955–60; econ. journalist, Bonn, 1961–67; Mem. Exec., Fed. Assoc. of German Bank, Cologne, 1968–69; Div. Chief in Fed. Min. of Econs, Bonn, 1970–71; Dept Chief in Fed. Chancellery (Head, Dept for Econ. and Fiscal Policy), Bonn, 1971–72; Sec. of State in Fed. Min. of Finance, 1972–77; Dep. Governor, Deutsche Bundesbank, 1977–79; Chairman: EEC Monetary Cttee, 1976–77; Deputies of Gp of Ten, 1978–80; Gp of Ten, 1983–89; Cttee of Governors, Central Banks of EC Member States, 1990–91. Hon. DHL Georgetown Univ., 1983; Hon. DEconSc Ruhr Univ., 1985; Hon. DPhil Tel Aviv, 1986; Hon. Dr of Laws Univ. of Md, 1987; Hon. DSc: Buckingham, 1992; London, 1992. *Publications:* miscellaneous. *Address:* Sal. Oppenheim Jr & Cie, Königsberger Strasse 29, 60487 Frankfurt am Main, Germany.

POINTER, Martin John; QC 1996; barrister; *b* 17 July 1953; *s* of late Michael Edward Pointer and of Mary Isabel Pointer (*née* Simms); *m* 1st, 1985 (marr. diss. 1997); two *s* one *d*; 2nd, 2001, Janet Bridal. *Educ:* King's Sch., Grantham; Univ. of Leicester (LLB Hons). Called to the Bar, Gray's Inn, 1976 (Reid Schol., 1977). Fellow, Internat. Acad. of Matrimonial Lawyers, 1994. *Address:* 1 Mitre Court Buildings, Temple, EC4Y 7BS. *T:* (020) 7797 7070. *Club:* Travellers.

POITIER, Sidney, KBE (Hon.) 1974; actor, film and stage; director; Board Member, Walt Disney Company, since 1994; Ambassador of the Bahamas to Japan, since 1997; *b* Miami, Florida, 20 Feb. 1927; *s* of Reginald Poitier and Evelyn (*née* Outten); *m* 1950, Juanita Hardy (marr. diss.); four *d*; *m* 1975, Joanna Shimkus; two *d*. *Educ:* private tutors; Western Senior High Sch., Nassau; Governor's High Sch., Nassau. Served War of 1941–45 with 1267th Medical Detachment, United States Army. Started acting with American Negro Theatre, 1946. *Plays include:* Anna Lucasta, Broadway, 1948; A Raisin in the Sun, Broadway, 1959; *films include:* Cry, the Beloved Country, 1952; Red Ball Express, 1952; Go, Man, Go, 1954; Blackboard Jungle, 1955; Goodbye, My Lady, 1956; Edge of the City, 1957; Band of Angels, 1957; Something of Value, 1957; The Mark of the Hawk, 1958; The Defiant Ones, 1958 (Silver Bear Award, Berlin Film Festival, and New York Critics Award, 1958); Porgy and Bess, 1959; A Raisin in the Sun, 1960; Paris Blues, 1960; Lilies of the Field, 1963 (award for Best Actor of 1963, Motion Picture Academy of Arts and Sciences); The Bedford Incident, 1965; The Slender Thread, 1966; A Patch of Blue, 1966; Duel at Diablo, 1966; To Sir With Love, 1967; In the Heat of the Night, 1967; Guess Who's Coming to Dinner, 1968; For Love of Ivy, 1968; They Call Me Mister Tibbs, 1971; The Organization, 1971; The Wilby Conspiracy, 1975; Deadly Pursuit, 1988; Sneakers, 1991; Separate But Equal, 1990; Children of the Dust, 1995; To Sir With Love II, 1996; Mandela and De Klerk, 1996; One Man, One Vote, 1997; The Jackal, 1998; David and Lisa, 1998; Free of Eden, 1999; The Simple Life of Noah Dearborn, 1999; True Crime, 1999; director and actor: Buck and the Preacher, 1972; A Warm December, 1973; Uptown Saturday Night, 1974; Let's Do It Again, 1975; A Piece of the Action, 1977; *director:* Stir Crazy, 1981; Hanky Panky, 1982. *Publications:* This Life (autobiography), 1980; The Measure of a Man: a spiritual autobiography, 2000. *Address:* c/o CAA, Wilshire Boulevard, Beverley Hills, CA 90212, USA; c/o Ministry of Foreign Affairs, East Hill Street, PO Box N3746, Nassau, Bahamas.

POLAK, Cornelia Julia, OBE 1964 (MBE 1956); HM Diplomatic Service, retired; *b* 2 Dec. 1908; *d* of late Solomon Polak and late Georgina Polak (*née* Pozner). Foreign Office, 1925–38; Asst Archivist, British Embassy, Paris, 1938–40; Foreign Office, 1940–47; Vice-Consul, Bergen, 1947–49; Consul, Washington, 1949–51; Foreign Office, 1951–55; Consul, Paris, 1955–57; Consul, Brussels, 1957–60; Foreign Office, 1960–63; Head of Treaty and Nationality Department, Foreign Office, 1963–67; Consul General, Geneva, 1967–69, retired; re-employed at FCO, 1969–70. *Address:* Sunridge Court, 76 The Ridgeway, NW11 8PT.

POLAK, Prof. Julia Margaret, (Mrs Daniel Catovsky), FRCPath, FMedSci; Professor of Endocrine Pathology, London University, at Imperial College School of Medicine, since 1984; Head, Imperial College Interdisciplinary Group on Tissue Engineering, since 1997; Director, Centre for Tissue Engineering, Chelsea and Westminster Hospital, since 1999; *b* 26 June 1939; *d* of Carlos and Rebeca Polak; *m* 1961, Daniel Catovsky, *qv*; two *s* one *d*. *Educ:* Univ. of Buenos Aires (MD 1964; Dip Histopath. 1966); DSc London, 1980. Hospital appts, Buenos Aires, 1961–67; Royal Postgraduate Medical School, London: Research Assistant in Histochemistry, 1968–69; Asst Lectr, Lectr, and Sen. Lectr, 1970–82; Reader, 1982–84; Dep. Dir, Dept of Histopathol., Hammersmith Hosp., 1988–99; Member: Exec. Cttee, Acad. Bd, RPMS, 1990–97; Med. Exec. Unit, Hammersmith Hosp., 1990–; Sub-Cttee in Biotech., London Univ., 1988–. Chm., British Endocrine Pathologists Gp, 1988–; Mem., Exec. Cttee of Council, Amer. Heart Assoc., 1989–. Mem., editl bds of med. jls. FMedSci 1999. Benito de Udaondo Cardiology Prize, 1967; Medal, Soc. of Endocrinology, 1984; Sir Eric Sharpe Prize for Oncology, Cable and Wireless, 1986–87. *Publications:* contribs to Nature and numerous professional jls. *Address:* Tissue Engineering Centre, Imperial College, Chelsea and Westminster Hospital, 369 Fulham Road, SW10. *T:* (020) 8237 2670, *Fax:* (020) 8746 5619; *e-mail:* julia.polak@ic.ac.uk.

POLAND, Rear-Adm. Edmund Nicholas, CB 1967; CBE 1962; *b* 19 Feb. 1917; 2nd *s* of late Major Raymond A. Poland, RMLI and Mrs F. O. Bayly Jones; *m* 1941, Pauline Ruth Margaret Pechell; three *s* one *d* (and one *d* decd). *Educ:* Royal Naval Coll., Dartmouth. Served at sea during Abyssinian and Palestine crises, Spanish Civil War; War of 1939–45: convoy duties, Norwegian waters; Motor Torpedo Boats, Channel and Mediterranean; Torpedo Specialist, 1943; Staff Officer Ops to Naval Force Comdr, Burma; Sqdn T. Officer, HMS Royalist; HMS Hornet, 1946; Flotilla Torpedo and Anti-Submarine Officer of Third Submarine Flotilla, HMS Montclare; Air Warfare Div., Admiralty, 1950; British Naval Staff, Washington, 1953; jssc 1955; Directorate of Tactics and Ship Requirements, Admiralty; comd RN Air Station, Abbotsinch, 1956; Nato Standing Gp, Washington; Director of Under Sea Warfare (Naval), Ministry of Defence, 1962; Chief of Staff to C-in-C Home Fleet, 1965–68; retired. Commander, 1950; Capt., 1956; Rear-Adm., 1965. Vice-Pres., Internat. Prisoners' Aid Assoc., 1978, Chm. (UK), 1979; Vice-Pres., Scottish Assoc. for Care and Resettlement of Offenders, 1979 (Dir, 1974–79). *Publications:* The Torpedomen, 1992; Majumba's Survival Trail, 1992. *Recreation:* gardening. *Address:* 39 Limmer Lane, Felpham, Bognor Regis, West Sussex PO22 7HD.

See also R. D. Poland.

POLAND, Richard Domville, CB 1973; *b* 22 Oct. 1914; *er s* of late Major R. A. Poland, RMLI, and late Mrs F. O. Bayly-Jones; *m* 1948, Rosalind Frances, *y d* of late Surgeon-Captain H. C. Devas; one *s* one *d*. *Educ:* RN Coll., Dartmouth. Traffic Trainee, Imperial Airways, 1932; Traffic Clerk, British Continental Airways and North Eastern Airways, 1934–39. Ops Officer, Air Ministry, Civil Aviation Dept, 1939; Civil Aviation Dept Rep., W Africa, 1942–44; Private Secretary to Minister of Civil Aviation, 1944–48; Principal, 1946; Asst Secretary, 1953; Shipping Attaché, British Embassy, Washington, DC, 1957–60; Under-Secretary: Min. of Transport, 1964–70; DoE, 1970–74. Sec., Internat. Maritime Industry Forum, 1976–78. Chm., Kent Branch, CPRE, 1980. *Address:* 63 Alexandra Road, Kew, Surrey TW9 2BT. *T:* (020) 8948 5039.

See also Rear-Admiral E. N. Poland.

POLANI, Prof. Paul Emanuel, MD, DCH; FRCP, FRCOG; FRCPCH; FRS 1973; Prince Philip Professor of Pædiatric Research in the University of London, 1960–80, now Professor Emeritus; Geneticist, Pædiatric Research Unit, Guy's Hospital, London, since 1983 (in Division of Medical and Molecular Genetics of Guy's, King's and St Thomas' Hospitals' Medical School); Children's Physician, and Consultant Emeritus, Guy's Hospital; Geneticist, Italian Hospital; Director, SE Thames Regional Genetics Centre, 1976–82; *b* 1 Jan. 1914; first *s* of Enrico Polani and Elsa Zennaro; *m* 1944, Nina Ester Sullam (*d* 1999); no *c*. *Educ:* Trieste, Siena and Pisa (Scuola Normale Superiore, Italy). CM; MD (Pisa) 1938; DCH 1945; MRCP 1948; FRCP 1961; FRCOG *ad eund* 1979; FRCPCH 1997. Surg. Lieut, MN (aux.), 1939–40. National Birthday Trust Fund Fellow in Pædiatric Research, 1948; Assistant to Director, Dept of Child Health, Guy's Hospital Medical School, 1950–55; Research Physician on Cerebral Palsy and Director, Medical Research Unit, National Spastic Society, 1955–60; Dir, Paediatric Res. Unit, Guy's Hosp. Med. Sch., 1960–83. Consultant to WHO (Regional Office for Europe) on Pregnancy Wastage, 1959; Consultant, Nat. Inst. Neurol. Disease and Blindness, Nat. Insts of Health, USA, 1959–61. Chm., Mutagenesis Cttee, UK, 1975–86. Vis. Prof. of Human Genetics and Develt, Columbia Univ., 1977–86. Harveian Orator, 1988. FKC 1998. Hon. FRCPath 1985; Hon. FRCPI 1989; Hon. Fellow, UMDS of Guy's and St Thomas' Hospital, 1994. Sanremo Internat. Award and Prize for Genetic Res., 1984; Baly Medal, RCP, 1985; Gold Medal, International Cerebral Palsy Society, 1988. Commendatore, Order of Merit of the Republic, Italy, 1981. *Publications:* The Impact of Genetics on Medicine, 1990; chapters in books on human genetics, mental deficiency, psychiatry and pædiatrics; papers on human genetics, cytogenetics, experimental meiosis, congenital malformations and neurological disorders of children; historical reviews. *Recreations:* reading, riding, ski-ing. *Address:* Little Meadow, West Clandon, Surrey GU4 7TL. *T:* (01483) 222436. *Club:* Athenæum.

POLANYI, Prof. Hon. John Charles; PC (Can.) 1992; CC (Canada) 1979 (OC 1974); FRS 1971; FRSC 1966 (Hon. FRSC 1991); University Professor, since 1974 and Professor of Chemistry, University of Toronto, since 1962; *b* 23 Jan. 1929; *m* 1958, Anne Ferrar Davidson; one *s* one *d*. *Educ:* Manchester Grammar Sch.; Victoria Univ., Manchester (BSc, PhD, DSc). Research Fellow: Nat. Research Council, Ottawa, 1952–54; Princeton Univ., 1954–56; Univ. of Toronto: Lectr, 1956; Asst Prof., 1957–60; Assoc. Prof., 1960–62. Mem., Scientific Adv. Bd, Max Planck Inst. for Quantum Optics, Garching, Germany, 1982–92. Sloan Foundn Fellow, 1959–63; Guggenheim Meml Fellow, 1970–71, 1979–80; Sherman Fairchild Distinguished Scholar, CIT, 1982; Vis. Prof. of Chem., Texas A & M Univ., 1986; John W. Cowper Dist. Vis. Lectr, SUNY at Buffalo, 1986; Consolidated Bathurst Vis. Lectr, Concordia Univ., 1988; Beam Dist. Vis. Prof., Iowa Univ., 1992; Hitchcock Prof., Calif Univ., Berkeley, 1994; Lectures include: Centennial, Chem. Soc., 1965; Ohio State Univ., 1969 (and Mack Award); Reilly, Univ. of Notre Dame, 1970; Harkins Meml, Univ. of Chicago, 1971; Killam Meml Schol., 1974, 1975; F. J. Toole, Univ. of New Brunswick, 1974; Kistiakowsky, Harvard Univ., 1975; Camille and Henry Dreyfus, Kansas, 1975; Jacob Bronowski Meml, Toronto Univ., 1978; Hutchison, Rochester Univ., 1979; Priestley, Penn State Univ., 1980; Barré, Univ. of Montreal, 1982; Wiegand, Toronto Univ., 1984; Walker-Ames, Univ. of Washington, 1986; Morino, Japan, J. T. Wilson, Ont Sci. Centre, and Spiers Meml, Faraday Div., RSChem., 1987; Polanyi, IUPAC, W. B. Lewis, Atomic Energy of Canada Ltd, Killam, Univ. of Windsor, and Herzberg, Carleton Univ., 1988; C. R. Mueller, Purdue Univ., 1989; Phillips, Pittsburgh, 1991; Dove Meml, Toronto, 1992; Fritz London, Duke Univ., 1993; Linus Pauling, CIT, 1994; Hagey, Waterloo Univ., 1995. Hon. FRSE 1988; Hon. For. Mem., Amer. Acad. of Arts and Sciences, 1976; For. Associate, Nat. Acad. of Sciences, USA, 1978; Mem., Pontifical Acad. of Scis, 1986. Hon. DSc: Waterloo, 1970; Memorial, 1976; McMaster, 1977; Carleton, 1981; Harvard, 1982; Rensselaer, Brock, 1984; Lethbridge, Victoria, Ottawa, Sherbrooke, Laval, 1987; Manchester, York, 1988; Acadia, Univ. de Montréal, and Weizmann Inst. of Science, Israel, 1989; Univ. of Bari, Italy, Univ. of BC, and McGill Univ., 1990; Queen's, 1992; Free Univ., Berlin, 1993; Laurentian, Toronto, Liverpool, 1995; Hon. LLD: Trent, 1977; Dalhousie, 1983; St Francis Xavier, 1984; Concordia Univ., 1990; Calgary, 1994. Marlow Medal, Faraday Soc., 1963; Steacie Prize for Natural Scis, 1965; Chem. Inst. Canada Medal, 1976 (Noranda Award, 1967); Chem. Soc. Award, 1970; Henry Marshall Tory Medal, 1977, Michael Polanyi Medal, 1989, RSC; Remsen Award, Amer. Chem. Soc., 1978; (jtly) Wolf Prize in Chemistry, Wolf Foundn, Israel, 1982; (jtly) Nobel Prize for Chemistry, 1986; Killam Meml Prize, Canada Council, 1988; Royal Medal, 1989, Bakerian Prize, 1994, Royal Soc.; eponymous award, Canadian Soc. for Chem., 1992. KStJ 1987. *Film:* Concept in Reaction Dynamics, 1970. *Publications:* (with F. G. Griffiths) The Dangers of Nuclear War, 1979; papers in scientific jls, articles on science policy and on control of armaments. *Address:* Department of Chemistry, University of Toronto, 80 St George Street, Toronto, ON M5S 3H6, Canada; 142 Collier Street, Toronto, ON M4W 1M3, Canada.

POLE, Prof. Jack Richon, PhD; FBA 1985; FRHistS; Rhodes Professor of American History and Institutions, Oxford University, 1979–89; Fellow of St Catherine's College, since 1979; *b* 14 March 1922; *s* of Joseph Pole and Phœbe (*née* Rickards); *m* 1952, Marilyn Louise Mitchell (marr. diss. 1988); one *s* two *d*. *Educ:* Oxford Univ. (BA 1949); Princeton Univ. (PhD 1953). MA Cantab 1963. FRHistS 1970. Instr in History, Princeton Univ., 1952–53; Asst Lectr/Lectr in Amer. History, UCL, 1953–63; Cambridge University: Reader in Amer. History and Govt, 1963–79; Fellow, Churchill Coll., 1963–79 (Vice-Master, 1975–78); Mem., Council of Senate, 1970–74. Vis. Professor: Berkeley, 1960–61; Ghana, 1966; Chicago, 1969; Peking, 1984. Commonwealth Fund Amer. Studies Fellowship, 1956; Fellow, Center for Advanced Study in Behavioral Sciences, 1969–70; Guest Schol., Wilson Internat. Center, Washington, 1978–79; Goleib Fellow, NY Univ. Law Sch., 1990; Sen. Res. Fellow, Coll. of William & Mary, Va, 1991; Leverhulme Trust Emeritus Fellow, 1991–93. Jefferson Meml Lectr, Berkeley, 1971; Richard B. Russell Lectr, Ga, 1981. Vice-Pres., Internat. Commn for History of Representative and Parly Instns, 1990–; Member: Council, Inst. for Early Amer. History and Culture, 1973–76; Acad. Européenne d'Histoire, 1981. Hon. Vice-Pres., British Amer. Nineteenth Century Historians, 2000–. Hon. Fellow, Hist. Soc. of Ghana. *Publications:* Abraham Lincoln and the Working Classes of Britain, 1959; Abraham Lincoln, 1964; Political Representation in England and the Origins of the American Republic, 1966 (also USA); (ed) The Advance of Democracy, USA 1967; The Seventeenth Century: the origins of legislative power, USA 1969; (ed) The Revolution in America: documents of the internal development of America in the revolutionary era, 1971 (also USA); (co-ed) The Meanings of American History, USA 1971; Foundations of American Independence, 1763–1815, 1973 (USA 1972); (Gen. Editor) American Historical Documents (ed, Slavery, Secession and Civil War), 1975; The Decision for American Independence, USA 1975; The Idea of Union, USA 1977; The Pursuit of Equality in American History, USA 1978, 2nd edn 1993; Paths to the American Past, 1979 (also USA); The Gift of Government: political responsibility from the English Restoration to American Independence, USA 1983; (co-ed) Colonial British America: essays in the new history of the early modern era, USA 1983; (ed) The American Constitution: For and Against: the Federalist and Anti-Federalist papers, USA 1987; (co-ed) The Blackwell Encyclopedia of the American Revolution, 1991 (also USA), rev. edn as A Companion to the American Revolution, 2000; Freedom of Speech: right or privilege?, 1998; articles in Amer. Hist. Rev., William and Mary Qly, Jl of Southern Hist., Enc. Brit., Enc. of Amer. Congress. *Recreations:* cricket, painting, writing. *Address:* 20 Divinity Road, Oxford OX4 1LJ; St Catherine's College, Oxford OX1 3UJ. *Clubs:* MCC; Trojan Wanderers Cricket (Co-founder, 1957).

POLE, Sir Peter Van Notten, 5th Bt *cr* 1791; FASA; ACIS; accountant, retired; *b* 6 Nov. 1921; *s* of late Arthur Chandos Pole and late Marjorie, *d* of late Charles Hargrave, Glen Forrest, W Australia; *S* kinsman, 1948; *m* 1949, Jean Emily, *d* of late Charles Douglas Stone, Borden, WA; one *s* one *d*. *Educ:* Guildford Grammar Sch. *Recreations:* reading, travel. *Heir: s* Peter John Chandos Pole [*b* 27 April 1952; *m* 1973, Suzanne Norah, BAppSc(MT), *d* of Harold Raymond Hughes; two *s* one *d*]. *Address:* 249 Dartnell Parade, Cambrai Village, 85 Hester Avenue, Merriwa, WA 6030, Australia.

POLGE, Prof. (Ernest John) Christopher, CBE 1992; FRS 1983; Director, Mastercalf Ltd, since 1994; Hon. Professor of Animal Reproductive Biotechnology, University of Cambridge, since 1989; Fellow, Wolfson College, Cambridge, since 1984; *b* 16 Aug. 1926; *s* of late Ernest Thomas Ella Polge and Joan Gillet Polge (*née* Thorne); *m* 1954, Olive Sylvia Kitson; two *s* two *d*. *Educ:* Bootham Sch., York; Reading Univ. (BSc Agric.); PhD London 1955. Dept of Agricl Econs, Bristol Univ., 1947–48; Nat. Inst. for Med. Res., London, 1948–54; ARC Unit of Reproductive Physiology and Biochem., later Animal Res. Station, 1954–86, Officer-in-Charge, 1979–86; Scientific Dir, Animal Biotechnology Cambridge Ltd, Animal Res. Stn, Cambridge, 1986–93. Lalor Foundn Fellow, Worcester Foundn for Exptl Biol., Shrewsbury, Mass and Univ. of Illinois, 1967–68. Consultant: WHO, Geneva, 1965; FAO, Rome, 1983 and 1987. Member Committee: Soc. for Study of Fertility, 1955–64, 1976–83 (Sec., 1960–63; Chm., 1978–81); Soc. for Low Temp. Biol., 1974–79 (Chm., 1976–79). Chm., Journals of Reproduction and Fertility Ltd, 1982–87 (Mem., Council of Management and Exec. Cttee, 1972–79). Lectures: Sir John Hammond Meml, Soc. for Study of Fertility, 1974; Blackman, Oxford, 1979; Cameron-Gifford, Newcastle, 1984; E. H. W. Wilmott, Bristol, 1986; Clive Behrens, Leeds, 1988; Sir John Hammond Meml, British Soc. of Animal Production, 1989. Foreign Associate, US Nat. Acad. of Sci., 1997. FRAgS 1991; Hon. FRASE 1984; Hon. ARCVS 1986. Prof. *hc* and Dr *hc*, Ecological Univ. of Romania, 1991. Hon. DSc: Univ. of Illinois, 1990; Guelph, 1994. (Jtly) John Scott Award, City of Philadelphia, 1969; Sir John Hammond Meml Prize, British Soc. of Animal Prodn, 1971; Pioneer Award, Internat. Embryo Transfer Soc., 1986; Marshall Medal, Soc. for Study of Fertility, 1988; Internat. Prize for Agriculture, Wolf Foundn, 1988; Japan Prize for Science and Technology for Biological Prodn, 1992; first Lazzaro Spallanzani Internat. Award for Animal Reprodn, Italy, 1995; Bertebos Prize, Royal Swedish Acad. of Agric. and Forestry, 1997. *Publications:* papers on reproduction in domestic animals and low temp. biol., in biological jls. *Recreations:* gardening, fishing. *Address:* The Willows, 137 Waterbeach Road, Landbeach, Cambridge CB4 8EA. *T:* (01223) 860075, *Fax:* (01223) 861248.

POLIAKOFF, Stephen; playwright and film director; *b* 1 Dec. 1952; *s* of late Alexander Poliakoff, OBE and Ina Montagu; *m* 1983, Sandy Welch; one *s* one *d*. *Educ:* Westminster Sch.; King's Coll., Cambridge. *Plays:* Clever Soldiers, 1974; The Carnation Gang, 1974; Hitting Town, 1975; City Sugar (Evening Standard Most Promising Playwright Award), 1976; Strawberry Fields, NT, Shout Across the River, RSC, 1978; The Summer Party, 1980; Favourite Nights, 1981; Breaking the Silence, RSC, 1984; Coming in to Land, NT, 1987; Playing With Trains, RSC, 1989; Sienna Red, nat. tour, 1992; Sweet Panic, Hampstead, 1996; Blinded by the Sun, RNT (Critics' Circle Best Play Award), 1996; Talk of the City, RSC, 1998; Remember This, RNT, 1999; *films:* Hidden City; Close My Eyes (Evening Standard Best British Film Award), 1992; Century, 1995; The Tribe, 1998; Food of Love, 1998; *TV plays include:* Caught on a Train (BAFTA Award), 1980; She's Been Away (Venice Film Festival Prize); Shooting the Past (serial), 1999; Perfect Strangers (serial), 2001. *Publications:* all plays; Plays One, 1989; Plays Two, 1994; Plays Three, 1998. *Recreations:* watching cricket, going to the cinema. *Address:* 33 Devonia Road, N1 8JQ. *T:* (020) 7354 2695.

POLIZZI, Hon. Olga, (Hon. Mrs William Shawcross), CBE 1990; Director: RF Hotels, since 1996; Tresanton Hotel Ltd, since 1996; Millers Bespoke Bakery Ltd, since 1996; Forte plc, 1983–96 (Managing Director, Building and Design Department, 1980–96); *d* of Baron Forte, *qv*; *m* 1st, 1966, Alessandro Polizzi di Sorrentino (*d* 1980); two *d*; 2nd, 1993, Hon. William Hartley Hume Shawcross, *qv*. *Educ:* St Mary's Sch., Ascot. Westminster City Councillor, 1989–94. Trustee: Design Mus.; KCL; Italian Hosp. Fund; Nat. Maritime Mus., Cornwall. Gov., St Mary's Sch., Ascot, 1988–. *Recreations:* walking, opera. *Address:* (office) Savannah House, 11 Charles II Street, SW1Y 4QU.

See also Hon. Sir R. J. V. Forte.

POLKINGHORNE, Rev. Canon John Charlton, KBE 1997; PhD, ScD; FRS 1974; President, Queens' College, Cambridge, 1989–96 (Hon. Fellow, 1996); *b* 16 Oct. 1930; *s* of George Baulkwill Polkinghorne and Dorothy Evelyn Polkinghorne (*née* Charlton); *m* 1955, Ruth Isobel Martin; two *s* one *d*. *Educ:* Elmhurst Grammar Sch.; Perse Sch.; Trinity Coll., Cambridge (MA 1956; PhD 1955; ScD 1974); Westcott House, Cambridge, 1979–81. Commonwealth Fund Fellow, California Institute of Technology, 1955–56; Lecturer in Mathematical Physics, Univ. of Edinburgh, 1956–58; Cambridge University: Fellow, Trinity Coll., 1954–86; Lecturer in Applied Mathematics, 1958–65; Reader in Theoretical Physics, 1965–68; Prof. of Mathematical Physics, 1968–79; Fellow, Dean and Chaplain of Trinity Hall, Cambridge, 1986–89 (Hon. Fellow, 1989). Hon. Prof. of Theoretical Physics, Univ. of Kent at Canterbury, 1985. Ordained deacon 1981, priest 1982; Curate: St Andrew's, Chesterton, 1981–82; St Michael's, Bedminster, 1982–84; Vicar of St Cosmus and St Damian in the Blean, 1984–86; Canon Theologian, Liverpool Cathedral, 1994–; Six Preacher, Canterbury Cathedral, 1996–. Member: SRC, 1975–79; Human Genetics Adv. Commn, 1996–99; Human Genetics Commn, 2000–; Chairman: Nuclear Phys Bd, 1978–79; Cttee to Review the Research Use of Fetuses and Fetal Material, 1988–89; Task Force to Review Services for Drugs Misusers, 1994–96; Adv. Cttee on Genetic Testing, 1996–99. Member: C of E Doctrine Commn, 1989–95; Gen. Synod of C of E, 1990–2000. Chm. of Governors, Perse Sch., 1972–81; Governor, SPCK, 1984–. Licensed Reader, Diocese of Ely, 1975. Hon. DD: Kent, 1994; Durham, 1999; Hon. DSc: Exeter, 1994; Leicester, 1995. *Publications:* (jtly) The Analytic S-Matrix, 1966; The Particle Play, 1979; Models of High Energy Processes, 1980; The Way the World Is, 1983; The Quantum World, 1984; One World, 1986; Science and Creation, 1988; Science and Providence, 1989; Rochester Roundabout, 1989; Reason and Reality, 1991; Science and Christian Belief, 1994; Quarks, Chaos and Christianity, 1994; Serious Talk, 1995; Scientists as Theologians, 1996; Beyond Science, 1996; Searching for Truth, 1996; Belief in God in an Age of Science, 1998; Science and Theology, 1998; Faith, Science and Understanding, 2000; (jtly) The End of the World and the Ends of Gods, 2000; (jtly) Faith in the Living God, 2001; many articles on elementary particle physics in learned journals. *Recreation:* gardening. *Address:* Queens' College, Cambridge CB3 9ET.

POLL, Prof. (David) Ian (Alistair), PhD; FREng, FRAeS; Professor of Aerospace Engineering (formerly of Aerodynamics), and Director, Cranfield College of Aeronautics (formerly Head, College of Aeronautics), Cranfield University, since 1995; Technical Director, Cranfield Aerospace Ltd, since 1999 (Managing Director, 1995–99); *b* 1 Oct. 1950; *s* of Ralph Angus Poll and Mary Poll (*née* Hall); *m* 1975, Elizabeth Mary Read; two *s* one *d*. *Educ:* Heckmondwike Grammar Sch.; Imperial Coll. London (BSc Hons); Cranfield Inst. of Tech. (PhD). ACGI; FRAeS 1987; FREng (FEng 1996). Engineer, Future Projects, Hawker Siddeley Aviation, 1972–75; Res. Asst, 1975–78, Lectr, 1978–85, Sen. Lectr, 1985–87, Cranfield Inst. of Tech.; University of Manchester: Prof. of Aeronautical Engineering, and Dir of Goldstein Aeronaut. Engrg Lab., 1987–95; Man. Dir, Flow Science Ltd, 1990–95; Head, Dept. of Engineering, 1991–94. Royal Aeronautical Society: Mem. Council, 1996–; Vice Pres., 1998–2000; Pres., 2001–; Chairman: Learned Soc. Bd, 1996–2000; Strategic Review Bd, 2000–01; Cranfield Univ. Br., 1997–. Member: Fluid Dynamics Panel, AGARD, 1990–97; Council, Air League, 1997–; Gen. Assembly, Internat. Council of the Aeronautical Scis, 1997–; Foresight Action Steering Cttee, SBAC, 1997–; Aerospace Cttee, DTI, 1999–. FAIAA 2000. Freeman, City of London, 2001; Liveryman, Co. of Coachmakers and Coach Harness Makers, 2001. Hodgson Prize, RAeS, 2001. *Publications:* more than 100 papers on fluid mechanics in learned jls and for tech. conferences. *Recreations:* golf, aviation, home improvements. *Address:* College of Aeronautics, Cranfield University, Cranfield, Beds MK43 0AL. *T:* (01234) 754743; *e-mail:* d.i.a.poll@cranfield.ac.uk.

POLLACK, Anita Jean; Head of European Liaison, English Heritage, since 2000; *b* NSW, Australia, 3 June 1946; *d* of John and Kathleen Pollack; *m* 1986, Philip Bradbury; one *d*. *Educ:* City of London Polytechnic (BA 1979); Birkbeck Coll., Univ. of London (MSc Polit. Sociology 1981). Advertising copy writer, Australia, 1963–69; book editor, 1970–75; student, 1976–79; Research Asst to Rt Hon. Barbara Castle, MEP, 1981–89. MEP (Lab) London SW, 1989–99; contested (Lab) SE Region, 1999. *Recreation:* family. *Address:* 139 Windsor Road, E7 0RA.

POLLARD, Prof. Andrew John, PhD; Professor of Primary Education, University of Cambridge, since 2000; *b* 13 Nov. 1949; *s* of Michael and Anne Pollard; *m* 1971, Rosalind Croft; one *s* one *d*. *Educ:* Univ. of Leeds (BA); Univ. of Lancaster (PGCE 1972); Univ. of Sheffield (PhD 1981; MEd 1996). Teaching in primary schools, 1972–81; Sen. Lectr, 1981–84, Principal Lectr, 1984–85, Oxford Poly.; Reader, 1985–90, Associate Dean, 1990–95, UWE; Prof. of Educn, Univ. of Bristol, 1996–2000. *Publications:* The Social World of the Primary School, 1985; Reflective Teaching in the Primary School, 1987, 4th edn 2002; (jtly) Changing English Primary Schools, 1994; The Social World of Children's Learning, 1996; (with A. Filer) The Social World of Pupil Career, 1999; (with P. Triggs) What Pupils Say: changing policy and practice in primary education, 2000; (with A. Filer) The Social World of Pupil Assessment, 2000. *Recreations:* sailing, gardening, bird watching. *Address:* Faculty of Education, University of Cambridge, Shaftesbury Road, Cambridge CB2 2BX. *T:* (01223) 369631.

POLLARD, Maj.-Gen. Anthony John Griffin, CB 1992; CBE 1985; DL; General Officer Commanding, South West District, 1990–92, retired; *b* 8 April 1937; *s* of William Pollard and Anne Irene Griffin; *m* Marie-Luise; four *s*. *Educ:* Oakham Sch.; Jesus Coll., Cambridge. Commnd Royal Leics Regt, 1956; served Cyprus, Germany, Hong Kong, Borneo, Malta; Staff Coll., 1969; Staff 7 Armd Bde, 1970–72; Instr, Staff Coll., 1975–77; CO 1st Bn Royal Anglian Regt, 1977–79; (Norway, NI, Germany); QMG's Secretariat, 1980; Col, Tactical Doctrine, BAOR, 1981; Col, Ops and Tactical Doctrine, 1(BR) Corps, 1982; Comdr, British Forces, Belize, 1983–84; Comdt, Sch. of Infantry, 1984–87; Comdr, British Mil. Mission to Uganda, 1985–86; Dir Gen., Trng and Doctrine (Army), 1987–90. Dep. Col, Royal Anglian Regt, 1986–92; Colonel Commandant: Small Arms Sch. Corps, 1987–92; Queen's Div., 1990–92; Hon. Col Suffolk ACF, 1992–. DL Suffolk, 1999. *Recreations:* family, fishing, gardening, archaeology, ancient buildings. *Club:* Army and Navy.

POLLARD, Bernard, CB 1988; Deputy Secretary and Director General (Technical), Board of Inland Revenue, 1985–88; *b* 24 Oct. 1927; *m* 1961, Regina (*née* Stone); one *s* one *d*. *Educ:* Tottenham Grammar Sch.; London Univ. (BSc Econ; Gladstone Meml Prize (Econs), 1949). Called to the Bar, Middle Temple, 1968. Served RAF (Flying Officer), 1949–53. Entered Tax Inspectorate, Inland Revenue, 1953; Principal Inspector of Taxes, 1969; Asst Sec., 1973; Under Sec., 1979; Dir of Counter Avoidance and Evasion Div., 1981–85. *Recreations:* reading biographies, watching cricket and National Hunt racing. *Address:* 1 Albany House, 3 Balcombe Road, Poole, Dorset BH13 6DX. *T:* (01202) 763488.

POLLARD, Sir Charles, Kt 2001; QPM 1990; Chief Constable of Thames Valley Police, since 1991; *b* 4 Feb. 1945; *s* of Humphrey Charles Pollard and Margaret Isobel Pollard (*née* Philpott); *m* 1972, Erica Jane Allison Jack; two *s* one *d*. *Educ:* Oundle Sch.; Bristol Univ. (LLB). Metropolitan Police, 1964; Sussex Police, 1980; Asst Chief Constable, Thames Valley Police, 1985–88; Dep. Asst Comr, i/c No 5 (SW) Area of London, Metropolitan Police, 1988–91. Chm., Quality of Service Cttee, ACPO, 1993–94; Vice-Chm., Thames Valley Partnership (working for safer communities), 1992–. Mem., Youth Justice Bd for England and Wales, 1998–. Mem. Bd, Centre for Mgt and Policy Studies, 2000–. Chm., Oxford Common Purpose, 1996–98. Vis. Fellow, Nuffield Coll., Oxford, 1993–2001. Hon. LLD Buckingham, 2001. *Publications:* contribs to nat. media and learned jls on policing, criminal justice and restorative justice. *Recreations:* tennis, walking, family pursuits. *Address:* Thames Valley Police HQ, Kidlington, Oxon OX5 2NX. *T:* (01865) 846000.

POLLARD, Christopher Charles; Director: John Griffiths Motorsport, since 1999; Newgate Finance, since 2000; *b* 30 April 1957; *s* of Anthony Cecil and Margaret Noelle Pollard; *m* 1984, Margaret Ann Langlois; three *d*. *Educ:* Merchant Taylors' Sch., Northwood; Newland Park Coll. Gramophone, 1981–99: Editor, 1986–90; Man. Editor, 1990–93; Editl Dir, 1993–99. Dir, Jethou, 1995–. *Recreations:* Rugby football, cricket, cars, music. *Address:* Beechcroft, Hotley Bottom, Great Missenden, Bucks HP16 9PL.

POLLARD, Eve, (Lady Lloyd); *d* of late Ivor and Mimi Pollard; *m* 1st, 1968, Barry Winkleman (marr. diss. 1979); one *d*; 2nd, 1979, Sir Nicholas Lloyd, *qv*; one *s*. Fashion Editor: Honey, 1967–68; Daily Mirror Magazine, 1968–69; Women's Editor: Observer Magazine, 1970–71; Sunday Mirror, 1971–81; Asst Ed., Sunday People, 1981–83; Features Ed. and presenter, TV-am, 1983–85; Editor: Elle USA (launched magazine in NY), 1985–86; Sunday magazine, News of the World, 1986; You magazine, Mail on Sunday, 1986–88; Sunday Mirror and Sunday Mirror Magazine, 1988–91; Sunday Express and Sunday Express Magazine, 1991–94. Founder, Wedding magazine, 1999. Formerly contributor to Sunday Times. Member: English Tourism Council (formerly English Tourist Bd), 1993–2000; Competition Commn, 1999–. Chair and Founder Mem., Women in Journalism, 1995–. *Publications:* Jackie: biography of Mrs J. K. Onassis, 1971;

(jtly) Splash, 1995; (jtly) Best of Enemies, 1996; (jtly) Double Trouble, 1997; Unfinished Business, 1998. *Address:* c/o Simpson-Fox Associates, 52 Shaftesbury Avenue, W1V 7DE. *T:* (020) 7434 9167.

POLLARD, George Neil; Master of Costs Office (formerly Taxing Master) of the Supreme Court, since 1994; *b* 25 Nov. 1935; *s* of late Rev. George Pollard and of Elizabeth Beatrice Pollard (*née* Briggs). *Educ:* Queen's Coll., Taunton; Law Society Sch. of Law. Admitted Solicitor, 1958; Solicitor, E. W. Nickerson & Son, 1958–59, J. Clayton & Co., 1959–61; Partner, Duthie Hart & Duthie, 1962–94. President: W Essex Law Soc., 1984–85; London Criminal Court Solicitors' Assoc., 1988–89; Mem. Cttee, No 1 Legal Aid Area, 1978–94. *Recreations:* reading, sailing, music. *Club:* Royal Corinthian Yacht.

POLLARD, Kerry Patrick; JP; MP (Lab) St Albans, since 1997; *b* 27 April 1944; *s* of late Patrick Joseph Pollard and of Iris Betty Pollard; *m* 1966, Maralyn Murphy; five *s* two *d*. *Educ:* St Joseph's Primary Sch., Heywood, Lancs; Thornleigh Coll., Bolton. Engr, British Gas, 1960–92; Co-ordinator, Homes for Homeless People, 1992; Dir and Co. Sec., Cherry Tree Housing Assoc., 1992–97. Member (Lab): St Albans DC, 1982–98; Herts CC, 1989–97. Contested (Lab) St Albans, 1992. JP St Albans, 1984. *Recreations:* swimming, theatre, country walking. *Address:* (office) 28 Alma Road, St Albans, Herts AL1 3BW. *T:* (01727) 761031.

POLLARD, Richard Frederick David; His Honour Judge Pollard; a Circuit Judge, since 1990; *b* 26 April 1941; *s* of William Pollard and Anne Irene Pollard (*née* Griffin), CBE; *m* 1964, Angela Susan Hardy; one *s* two *d*. *Educ:* Oakham School; Trinity College Dublin (BA); Univ. of Cambridge (Dip. Crim.). Called to the Bar, Gray's Inn, 1967. *Recreations:* walking, art nouveau, looking out of the window. *Address:* c/o Midland and Oxford Circuit, The Priory Courts, 33 Bull Street, Birmingham B4 6DW.

POLLEN, Sir John Michael Hungerford, 7th Bt *cr* 1795 of Redenham, Hampshire; *b* 6 April 1919; *s* of late Lieut-Commander John Francis Hungerford Pollen, RN; *S* kinsman, Sir John Lancelot Hungerford Pollen, 6th Bt, 1959; *m* 1st, 1941, Angela Mary Oriana Russi (marr. diss. 1956); one *s* one *d*; 2nd, 1957, Mrs Diana Jubb (*d* 1995). *Educ:* Downside; Merton Coll., Oxford. Served War of 1939–45 (despatches). *Heir: s* Richard John Hungerford Pollen [*b* 3 Nov. 1946; *m* 1971, Christianne, *d* of Sir Godfrey Agnew, KCVO, CB; four *s* three *d*]. *Address:* Manor House, Rodbourne, Malmesbury, Wiltshire SN16 0EX.

POLLEN, Peregrine Michael Hungerford; Executive Deputy Chairman, 1975–77, Deputy Chairman, 1977–82, Sotheby Parke Bernet and Co.; *b* 24 Jan. 1931; *s* of late Sir Walter Michael Hungerford Pollen, MC, JP, and Lady Pollen; *m* 1958, Patricia Helen Barry; one *s* two *d*. *Educ:* Eton Coll.; Christ Church, Oxford. National Service, 1949–51. ADC to Sir Evelyn Baring, Governor of Kenya, 1955–57; Sotheby's, 1957–82: Dir, 1961; Pres., Sotheby Parke Bernet, New York, 1965–72. *Address:* Norton Hall Farmhouse, Mickleton, Glos GL55 6PU. *T:* (01386) 438218. *Clubs:* Brooks's, Beefsteak.

POLLINGTON, Viscount; John Andrew Bruce Savile; *b* 30 Nov. 1959; *s* and *heir* of 8th Earl of Mexborough, *qv*.

POLLINI, Maurizio; pianist; *b* Milan, 5 Jan. 1942; *s* of Gino Pollini and Renata Melotti; *m* 1968, Maria Elisabetta Marzotto; one *s*. Has performed with all major orchestras, including: Chicago Symphony; Cleveland; Berlin Philharmonic; Boston Symphony; LPO; LSO; New York Philharmonic; Vienna Philharmonic; has played at Berlin, Prague, Salzburg and Vienna Fests. First Prize, Internat. Chopin Competition, Warsaw, 1960; Ernst von Siemens Music Prize, Munich, 1996. Has made numerous recordings. *Address:* c/o Harrison Parrott Ltd, 12 Penzance Place, W11 4PA.

POLLOCK, family name of **Viscount Hanworth**.

POLLOCK, Alexander; Sheriff of Grampian, Highland and Islands at Aberdeen and Stonehaven, since 1993; *b* 21 July 1944; *s* of late Robert Faulds Pollock, OBE, and Margaret Findlay Pollock; *m* 1975, Verena Francesca Gertraud Alice Ursula Critchley; one *s* one *d*. *Educ:* Rutherglen Academy; Glasgow Academy; Brasenose Coll., Oxford (Domus Exhibnr; MA); Edinburgh Univ. (LLB); Univ. for Foreigners, Perugia. Solicitor, Bonar Mackenzie & Kermack, WS, 1970–73; passed advocate, 1973; Advocate Depute, 1990–91; Sheriff (floating) of Tayside, Central and Fife at Stirling, 1991–93. Contested (C) Moray, 1987. MP (C): Moray and Nairn, 1979–83; Moray, 1983–87. PPS to Sec. of State for Scotland, 1982–86, to Sec. of State for Defence, 1986–87. Mem., Commons Select Cttee on Scottish Affairs, 1979–82, 1986–87. Sec., British-Austrian Parly Gp, 1979–87. Mem., Queen's Body Guard for Scotland, Royal Co. of Archers, 1984–. *Publication:* (contrib.) Stair Memorial Encyclopaedia of Scots Law. *Recreations:* music, cycling, dogs. *Address:* Drumdarrach, Forres, Moray, Scotland IV36 0DW. *Clubs:* New (Edinburgh); Highland (Inverness).

POLLOCK, Brian; *see* Pollock, P. B.

POLLOCK, Prof. Christopher John, PhD, DSc; FIBiol; Director, Institute of Grassland and Environmental Research, since 1993; *b* 28 March 1947; *s* of Neil Cunningham Pollock and Margaret Pollock (*née* Charlton); *m* 1970, Elizabeth Anne Bates; one *s* one *d*. *Educ:* Trinity Hall, Cambridge (MA); Birmingham Univ. (PhD, DSc). FIBiol 1997. Post-Doctoral Fellow, Botany Sch., Cambridge, 1971–74; joined Welsh Plant Breeding Station, now Inst. of Grassland and Envmtl Res., 1974; Head, Res. Gp, 1985; Head, Envmtl Biology Dept, 1989. Fulbright Fellow, Univ. of California, Davis, 1978–79; NATO Sen. Res. Fellow, Purdue Univ., 1987–92; Hon. Professor: Univ. of Wales, Aberystwyth, 1993; Nottingham Univ., 1994. Chm., Scientific Steering Cttee for Farm-scale trials of GM crops, 1999–. FRAgS 2000. *Publications:* (jtly) Carbon Partitioning Within and Between Organisms, 1992; (with J. F. Farrar) The Biology of Fructans, 1993; approx. 100 reviews; papers in sci. jls. *Recreations:* golf, walking, woodwork. *Address:* Institute of Grassland and Environmental Research, Plas Gogerddan, Aberystwyth SY23 3EB. *T:* (01970) 823001. *Club:* St David's (Aberystwyth).

POLLOCK, David John Frederick; Director, The Continence Foundation, 1996–2001; *b* 3 Feb. 1942; *s* of Leslie William Pollock and late Dorothy Emily (*née* Holt); *m* 1976, Lois Jaques (marr. diss. 1991); one *s*. *Educ:* Beckenham and Penge Grammar Sch.; Keble Coll., Oxford (BA Lit. Hum. 1964); London Business Sch. British Coal Corporation, 1964–90: Head of Central Secretariat, 1972–78; Head of Staff Planning and Orgn, 1980–90; Dir, ASH, 1991–94. Mem., Hackney BC, 1974–78. Sec., Charity Law Reform Cttee, 1972–77. Member: Exec. Cttee, British Humanist Assoc. (Chm., 1970–72); Bd, Rationalist Press Assoc. (Chm., 1989–97). Treasurer, Hackney North Labour Party, 1989–92. *Publications:* Denial & Delay: the political history of smoking and health 1950–64, 1999; articles in humanist, health and other jls. *Recreations:* theatre, gardening. *Address:* 13 Dunsmure Road, N16 5PU. *T:* (020) 8800 3542, *Fax:* (020) 8880 2118; *e-mail:* david.pollock@virgin.net.

POLLOCK, Sir George F(rederick), 5th Bt *cr* 1866; artist-photographer, since 1963; *b* 13 Aug. 1928; *s* of Sir (Frederick) John Pollock, 4th Bt and Alix l'Estom (*née* Soubiran); *S* father, 1963; *m* 1951, Doreen Mumford, *o d* of N. E. K. Nash, CMG; one *s* two *d*. *Educ:* Eton; Trinity Coll., Cambridge. BA 1953, MA 1957. 2nd Lieut, 17/21 Lancers, 1948–49. Admitted Solicitor, 1956, retd. Hon. FRPS (Past Pres.). FRSA. Past Chm., London Salon of Photography. *Heir: s* David Frederick Pollock [*b* 13 April 1959; *m* 1985, Helena, *o d* of late L. J. Tompsett, OBE; one *d*]. *Address:* 83 Minster Way, Bath BA2 6RL. *T:* (01225) 464692; *e-mail:* sirpollock@aol.com. *Club:* Downhill Only (Wengen).

POLLOCK, Sir Giles (Hampden) Montagu-, 5th Bt *cr* 1872; management consultant, since 1974; Associate of Korn/Ferry International; *b* 19 Oct. 1928; *s* of Sir George Seymour Montagu-Pollock, 4th Bt, and Karen-Sofie (*d* 1991), *d* of Hans Ludwig Dedekam, Oslo; *S* father, 1985; *m* 1963, Caroline Veronica, *d* of Richard F. Russell; one *s* one *d*. *Educ:* Eton; de Havilland Aeronautical Technical School. de Havilland Enterprise, 1949–56; Bristol Aeroplane Co. Ltd, 1956–59; Bristol Siddeley Engines Ltd, 1959–61; Associate Dir, J. Walter Thompson Co. Ltd, 1961–69; Director: C. Vernon & Sons Ltd, 1969–71; Acumen Marketing Group Ltd, 1971–74; 119 Pall Mall Ltd, 1972–78; Associate, John Stork & Partners, subseq. John Stork Internat., then Korn/Ferry Internat., 1980–. *Recreations:* bicycling, water-skiing, walking. *Heir: s* Guy Maximilian Montagu-Pollock, *b* 27 Aug. 1966. *Address:* The White House, 7 Washington Road, SW13 9BG. *T:* (020) 8748 8491. *Club:* Institute of Directors.

POLLOCK, Adm. of the Fleet Sir Michael (Patrick), GCB 1971 (KCB 1969; CB 1966); LVO 1952; DSC 1944; *b* 19 Oct. 1916; *s* of late C. A. Pollock and Mrs G. Pollock; *m* 1st, 1940, Margaret Steacy (*d* 1951), Bermuda; two *s* one *d*; 2nd, 1954, Marjory Helen Reece (*née* Bisset); one step *d*. *Educ:* RNC Dartmouth. Entered Navy, 1930; specialised in Gunnery, 1941. Served War of 1939–45 in Warspite, Vanessa, Arethusa and Norfolk, N Atlantic, Mediterranean, Arctic and Indian Ocean (despatches thrice). Captain, Plans Div. of Admiralty and Director of Surface Weapons; comd HMS Vigo and Portsmouth Sqdn, 1958–59; comd HMS Ark Royal, 1963–64; Asst Chief of Naval Staff, 1964–66; Flag Officer Second in Command, Home Fleet, 1966–67; Flag Officer Submarines and Nato Commander Submarines, Eastern Atlantic, 1967–69; Controller of the Navy, 1970–71; Chief of Naval Staff and First Sea Lord, 1971–74; First and Principal Naval Aide-de-Camp to the Queen, 1972–74. Comdr, 1950; Capt., 1955; Rear-Adm., 1964; Vice-Adm., 1968; Adm., 1970. Bath King of Arms, 1976–85. Chm., Naval Insurance Trust, 1976–81; Liddle Hart Trustee, 1976–81. Councillor, Churchstoke Community Council, 1983–. *Recreations:* sailing, shooting, travel. *Address:* The Ivy House, Churchstoke, Montgomery, Powys SY15 6DU.

POLLOCK, (Peter) Brian; His Honour Judge Pollock; a Circuit Judge, since 1987; *b* 27 April 1936; *s* of late Brian Treherne Pollock and Helen Evelyn Pollock (*née* Holt-Wilson); *m* 1st, 1966, Joan Maryon Leggett (marr. diss. 1981); two *s* (and one *s* decd); 2nd, 1988, Jeannette Mary Nightingale; two step *s* one step *d*. *Educ:* St Lawrence College. Called to the Bar, Middle Temple, 1958. A Recorder of the Crown Court, 1986–87. *Recreations:* playing tennis, watching cricket, travel, walking, cooking, gardening. *Address:* Croydon Crown Court, Altyre Road, Croydon CR9 5AB. *T:* (020) 8681 2533. *Clubs:* MCC, Roehampton.

POLTIMORE, 7th Baron *cr* 1831; **Mark Coplestone Bampfylde;** Bt 1641; Managing Director, Eauctionroom.com, since 2000; *b* 8 June 1957; *s* of Captain the Hon. Anthony Gerard Hugh Bampfylde (*d* 1969) (*er s* of 6th Baron) and of Brita Yvonne (who *m* 2nd, 1975, Guy Elmes), *o d* of late Baron Rudolph Cederström; *S* grandfather, 1978; *m* 1982, Sally Anne, *d* of Dr Norman Miles; two *s* one *d*. Christie's: Associate Dir, 1984–87; Dir, 1987–2000; Dep. Chm., 1998–2000. Chm., UK Friends of Bundanon, 1999–. *Publication:* (with Philip Hook) Popular Nineteenth Century Painting: a dictionary of European genre painters, 1986. *Heir: s* Hon. Henry Anthony Warwick Bampfylde, *b* 3 June 1985. *Address:* North Hidden Farm, Hungerford, Berks RG17 0PY. *Club:* White's.

POLWARTH, 10th Lord *cr* 1690 (Scot.); **Henry Alexander Hepburne-Scott,** TD; Vice-Lord-Lieutenant, Borders Region (Roxburgh, Ettrick and Lauderdale), 1975–91; Member, Royal Company of Archers; a Scots Representative Peer, 1945–63; Chartered Accountant; *b* 17 Nov. 1916; *s* of late Hon. Walter Thomas Hepburne-Scott (*d* 1942); *S* grandfather, 1944; *m* 1st, 1943, Caroline Margaret (marr. diss. 1969; she *d* 1982), 2nd *d* of late Captain R. A. Hay, Marlefield, Roxburghshire, and Helmsley, Yorks; one *s* three *d*; 2nd, 1969, Jean, *d* of late Adm. Sir Angus Cunninghame Graham of Gartmore, KBE, CB, and formerly wife of C. E. Jauncey, QC (now Rt Hon. Lord Jauncey); two step *s* one step *d*. *Educ:* Eton Coll.; King's Coll., Cambridge. Served War of 1939–45, Captain, Lothians and Border Yeomanry. Former Partner, firm of Chiene and Tait, CA, Edinburgh; Governor, Bank of Scotland, 1966–72, Director, 1950–72 and 1974–87; Chm., General Accident, Fire & Life Assurance Corp., 1968–72; Director: ICI Ltd, 1969–72, 1974–81; Halliburton Co., 1974–87; Canadian Pacific Ltd, 1975–86; Sun Life Assurance Co. of Canada, 1975–84. Minister of State, Scottish Office, 1972–74. Chm., later Pres., Scottish Council (Develt and Industry), 1955–72. Member: Franco-British Council, 1981–90; H of L Select Cttee on Trade, 1984–85. Chairman: Scottish Nat. Orchestra Soc., 1975–79; Scottish Forestry Trust, 1987–90. Murrayfield Hosp., 1982–90. Chancellor, Aberdeen Univ., 1966–86. Hon. LLD: St Andrews; Aberdeen; Hon. DLitt Heriot-Watt; DUniv Stirling. FRSE; FRSA; Hon. FRIAS. DL Roxburgh, 1962. *Heir: s* Master of Polwarth, *qv*. *Address:* Wellfield Parva, Hawkchurch, Axminster, Devon EX13 5UT. *T:* (01297) 678735. *Club:* New (Edinburgh).

See also Baron Moran.

POLWARTH, Master of; Hon. Andrew Walter Hepburne-Scott; JP; *b* 30 Nov. 1947; *s* and *heir* of 10th Lord Polwarth, *qv*; *m* 1971, Anna, *e d* of late Maj. J. F. H. Surtees, OBE, MC; two *s* two *d*. *Educ:* Eton; Trinity Hall, Cambridge. JP Roxburgh Div., Scottish Borders, 1997. *Address:* Harden, Hawick, Roxburghshire TD9 7LP. *Clubs:* New (Edinburgh); Knickerbocker (New York).

POLYNESIA, Bishop in, since 1975; **Rt Rev. Jabez Leslie Bryce;** *b* 25 Jan. 1935. *Educ:* St John's College, Auckland, NZ (LTh); St Andrew's Seminary, Manila, Phillipines (BTh). Deacon 1960, priest 1962, Polynesia; Curate of Suva, 1960–63; Priest-in-charge: Tonga, 1964; St Peter's Chinese Congregation, Manila, 1965–67; Archdeacon of Suva, 1967–69; Deputy Vicar-General, Holy Trinity Cathedral, Suva, 1967–72; Lectr, St John Baptist Theological Coll., Suva, 1967–69; Vicar of Viti Levu W, 1969–75; Archdeacon in Polynesia, 1969–75; Vicar-General of Polynesia, 1972–75. Chm., Pacific Conf. of Churches, 1976–86; Sec., S Pacific Anglican Council, 1970– (Chm., 1995–); Pres., WCC for Oceania, 1998–. *Recreations:* tennis, golf. *Address:* Bishop's House, PO Box 35, Suva, Fiji Islands. *T:* (office) 304716, (home) 302553, *Fax:* 302687.

POMEROY, family name of **Viscount Harberton**.

POMEROY, Anthony Michael John, FCIT; Director of Education Training and Membership, Chartered Institute of Transport, 1989–95; *b* 11 Oct. 1930; *s* of Jack Pomeroy and Margaret (*née* Tyler); *m* 1957, Joan Olive Beard (*d* 1993); one *s* one *d*. *Educ:*

Univ. of Nottingham (BA Hist. 1954). FCIT 1967. Traffic Manager, Grey Green Coaches, 1954–57; Claims Manager, N. Francis & Co., 1957–59; Distribn Controller then Trng Exec., Advance Linen Services, 1959–63; Dir of Transport, Louis Reece (Kent) Ltd, 1963–85; freelance lectr in transport studies and transport consultant, 1985–89. Dir, Transport Tutorial Assoc., 1985–89. Chm., Somerset and Dorset Family History Soc., 1998–. FRSA 1991. *Publications:* contrib. various distance learning courses in transport hist., operations and policy. *Recreations:* family genealogy, music and theatre, transport, local history. *Address:* The Keep, 3 Stokehouse Street, Poundbury, Dorchester DT1 3GP. *T:* (01305) 257570, *Fax:* (01305) 257912; *e-mail:* pomerology@cs.com.

POMEROY, Brian Walter; Chairman, Centrepoint, since 1993; *b* 26 June 1944; *s* of Oscar Pomeroy and Eileen Pomeroy (*née* Rutter); *m* 1974, Hilary Susan Price; two *d*. *Educ:* King's Sch., Canterbury; Magdalene Coll., Cambridge (MA). FCA (ACA 1968). Partner, Touche Ross Mgt Consultants, subseq. Deloitte Consulting, 1975–99: on secondment as Under Sec., DTI, 1981–83; Man. Dir, 1987–95; Sen. Partner, 1995–99. Advr to govts on public policy, esp. regulation and public-private partnership. Non-exec. Dir, Rover Gp plc, 1985–88. Mem., Nat. Lottery Commn, 1999– (Chm., 1999–2000). Mem., Cttee of Enquiry into Regulatory Arrangements at Lloyd's, 1986; Ind. Mem. Council, Lloyd's, 1996–; Dep. Chm., Lloyd's Regulatory Bd, 1996–. Chm., Telecommunications Interconnection Cttee, 1988–91. Member: Disability Rights Task Force, 1997–99; Pensions, Protection and Investments Accreditation Bd, 2000–; Bd, Social Market Foundn, 2000–. Mem., Commn on Taxation and Citizenship, Fabian Soc., 1998–2000. Mem. Council, Mgt Consultants Assoc., 1996–99. Chairman: AIDS Awareness Trust, 1993–96; Eur. Public Health Foundn, 1997–; Homeless Link, 2001–. Trustee, Money Advice Trust, 1999–; Chm., The King's Consort, 2000–. Master, Mgt Consultants' Co., 2000–01. FRSA 1994. *Publications:* contrib. articles on public finance, regulation and public-private partnership. *Recreations:* photography and digital imaging, listening to music, theatre, cycling. *Address:* 7 Ferncroft Avenue, NW3 7PG. *T:* (020) 7435 2584; *e-mail:* pomeroybw@cs.com.

PONCE-VIVANCO, (José) Eduardo; Ambassador of Peru to Brazil, since 1999; *b* 8 March 1943; *s* of José Eduardo Ponce-Mendoza and Laura Vivanco de Ponce-Mendoza; *m* 1969, Clemencia Hilbck; one *d*. *Educ:* Colegio Jesuita de San José de Arequipa, Peru; Univ. Nacional de San Agustín de Arequipa; Pontificia Univ. Católica del Perú; Peruvian Diplomatic Acad.; Univ. des Hautes Etudes Internat., Geneva. Third Secretary: to Internat. Orgns Under-Secretariat, 1967–68; Tokyo, 1968–70; Second Sec., Quito, 1971–75; Prof. of Peruvian Diplomatic Hist., Diplomatic Acad., Peru, 1976; Asst to Advr for Legal and Maritime Affairs of Minister's Office, 1976–77; Hd, Dept for Equador, Columbia and Venezuela, Under-Secretariat for Political Affairs, 1977; Asst Dir for Planning, Min. of Foreign Affairs, 1978–79; Perm. Rep. to UN and Internat. Orgns, Geneva, 1979–83; Minister, London, 1984; Perm. Rep. to Internat. Commodities Orgns, London, 1984; Ministry of Foreign Affairs: Dir, Territorial Sovereignty, 1985; Dir, America Dept, 1986; Asst Under-Sec., Bilateral Policy for American Affairs, 1987–88; Perm. Rep. to Latin American Integration Assoc. (ALADI), Montevideo, 1988–89; Ambassador to Ecuador, 1990–94; Vice-Minister, Internat. Policy and Sec. Gen. of Foreign Affairs, 1994–95; Ambassador to UK, 1995–99. Pres., Peruvian Delegn to UN World Water Conf., 1977; Mem., numerous Peruvian delegns to UN, Geneva and other internat. orgns. Grand Cross: Orden El Sol del Perú (Peru), 1995; Orden al Mérito Naval (Peru), 1996; Commander: Orden por Servicios Distinguidos (Peru), 1979; Defensor Calificado de la Patria (Peru), 1995; also decorations from Japan, Brazil and Bolivia. *Publications:* The Resolutions of the United Nations General Assembly, 1969; seminar documents; contrib. to Rev. Peruvian Diplomatic Acad. *Recreations:* tennis, music, ballet. *Address:* Embassy of Peru, SES, Avenida das Nações, Lote 43, 70428-900 Brasília DF, Brazil. *Clubs:* Queen's, Travellers, Naval and Military; Nacional, Terrazas (Lima); Arequipa (Arequipa).

PONCET, Jean André F.; *see* François-Poncet.

POND, Christopher; MP (Lab) Gravesham, since 1997; *b* 25 Sept. 1952; *s* of Charles Richard Pond and Doris Violet Pond; *m* 1990, Carole Tongue, *qv* (marr. diss. 1999); one *d*. *Educ:* Univ. of Sussex (BA Hons Econs). Research Asst in Econs, Birkbeck Coll., Univ. of London, 1974–75; Res. Officer, Low Pay Unit, 1975–78; Lectr in Econs, CS Coll., 1978–79; Dir, Low Pay Unit, 1980–97. Vis. Lectr in Econs, Univ. of Kent, 1983–84; Hon. Vis. Prof. and Res. Fellow, Univ. of Surrey, 1984–86; Hon. Vis. Prof., Univ. of Middlesex, 1995–. Consultant, Open Univ., 1987–88 and 1991–92. Contested (Lab) Welwyn Hatfield, 1987. FRSA 1992. *Publications:* (jtly) To Him Who Hath, 1977; (jtly) Taxation and Social Policy, 1981; (contrib.) Old and New Poverty, 1995; Out of Poverty: towards prosperity, 1996; (contrib.) Working for Full Employment, 1997; (contrib.) Beyond 2002, 1999. *Recreations:* running, reading, amusing my daughter. *Address:* House of Commons, SW1A 0AA. *T:* (020) 7219 3000.

PONDER, Prof. Bruce Anthony John, PhD; FRCP, FMedSci; FRS 2001; Cancer Research Campaign Professor of Clinical Oncology, University of Cambridge, since 1996; Fellow, Jesus College, Cambridge, since 1993; *b* 25 April 1944; *s* of late Anthony West Ponder and of Dorothy Mary Ponder (*née* Peachey); *m* 1969, Margaret Ann Hickinbotham; one *s* three *d*. *Educ:* Charterhouse Sch.; Cambridge Univ.; St Thomas's Hosp. Med. Sch. MA, MB BChir (Cambridge); PhD (London); FRCP 1987; NHS hosp. appts, 1968–73; Clinical Research Fellow, ICRF, 1973–76; first Hamilton Fairley Fellow, CRC at Harvard Med. Sch., 1977–78; Clinical Scientific Officer, ICRF, St Bartholomew's Hosp., 1978–80; Institute of Cancer Research: CRC Fellow and Sen. Lectr in Med., Royal Marsden Hosp., 1980–87; Reader in Human Cancer Genetics and Head, Section of Cancer Genetics, 1987–89; Dir, CRC Human Cancer Genetics Gp, Univ. of Cambridge, 1989–; CRC Prof. of Human Cancer Genetics, Univ. of Cambridge, 1992–96. Hon. Consultant Physician: Royal Marsden Hosp., 1980–; Addenbrooke's Hosp., Cambridge, 1989–. Croonian Lectr, RCP, 1998. Gibb Fellow, CRC, 1990. Founder FMedSci 1998. Internat. Public Service Award, Nat. Neurofibromatosis Foundn, USA, 1992; Merck Prize, European Thyroid Assoc., 1996. *Publications:* papers on genetics, cancer, developmental biology. *Recreations:* gardening, travel, golf, sailboarding, wine. *Address:* CRC Department of Oncology, Hutchison/MRC Research Centre, Hills Road, Cambridge CB2 2XZ. *T:* (01223) 336900, *Fax:* (01223) 336902; 43 High Street, Cottenham, Cambridge CB4 8SA. *Clubs:* Royal Ashdown Forest Golf (Forest Row); Royal West Norfolk Golf (Brancaster).

PONSOLLE, Patrick Henry Jean; Managing Director and Vice Chairman, Morgan Stanley International, and President, Morgan Stanley Dean Witter, France, since 2001; *b* 20 July 1944; *s* of Jean Ponsolle and Marie-Rose Ponsolle (*née* Courthaliac); *m* 2nd, 1983, Nathalie Elie-Lefebvre; two *d*, and two step *s* two step *d*. *Educ:* Lycée Janson-de-Sailly, Paris; Lycée Henri IV, Paris; Ecole Normale Supérieure; Institut d'Etudes Politiques, Paris; Ecole Nationale d'Administration. Adminr, Min. of Econ. and Finance, 1973–77; Financial Attaché, French Embassy, Washington, 1977–79; Ministry of Economy and Finance: Chargé de Mission to Dir of Forecasting, 1980; Dep. Chief of Staff of Laurent Fabius, Minister responsible for the budget, 1981–83; Gen. Sec., Nat. Accounts and Budget Commn, France, 1980–81; Compagnie de Suez: Asst Dir Gen., 1983–87; Dir Gen., 1988–93; Adminr, 1991–93; Jt Chm., 1994–96, Exec. Chm., 1996–2001, Eurotunnel Gp; Chm., Eurotunnel SA, 1994–2001. Bd Mem., Alliance Unichem. *Address:* Morgan Stanley, 25 rue Balzac, 75008 Paris, France.

PONSONBY, family name of **Earl of Bessborough** and of **Barons de Mauley, Ponsonby of Shulbrede** and **Sysonby**.

PONSONBY OF SHULBREDE, 4th Baron *cr* 1930, of Shulbrede; **Frederick Matthew Thomas Ponsonby;** Baron Ponsonby of Roehampton (Life Peer), 2000; *b* 27 Oct. 1958; *o s* of 3rd Baron and of Ursula Mary, *yr d* of Comdr Thomas Stanley Lane Fox-Pitt, OBE, RN; *S* father, 1990. *Educ:* Holland Park Comprehensive Sch.; University Coll., Cardiff; Imperial Coll., London. FIMM 1996; CEng 1997. Councillor (Lab), London Borough of Wandsworth, 1990–94. Opposition frontbench spokesman on educn, H of L, 1992–97. Member: Sub-cttee C, European Select Cttee, H of L, 1997–98; Select Cttee on Sci. and Technol., H of L, 1998–99; Select Cttee on Constitution, 2001–. Deleg., Council of Europe and WEU, 1997–99. *Heir:* none. *Address:* House of Lords, SW1A 0PW.

PONSONBY, Sir Ashley (Charles Gibbs), 2nd Bt *cr* 1956; KCVO 1993; MC 1945; Director, J. Henry Schroder, Wagg & Co. Ltd, 1962–80; Lord-Lieutenant of Oxfordshire, 1980–96; *b* 21 Feb. 1921; *o s* of Col Sir Charles Edward Ponsonby, 1st Bt, TD, and Hon. Winifred (*d* 1984), *d* of 1st Baron Hunsdon; *S* father, 1976; *m* 1950, Lady Martha Butler, *yr d* of 6th Marquess of Ormonde, CVO, MC; four *s*. *Educ:* Eton; Balliol College, Oxford. 2nd Lieut Coldstream Guards, 1941; served war 1942–45 (North Africa and Italy, wounded); Captain 1943; on staff Bermuda Garrison, 1945–46. A Church Commissioner, 1963–80; Mem., Council of Duchy of Lancaster, 1977–92. DL Oxon, 1974–80. Hon. DArts Oxford Brookes, 1995; Hon. MA Oxon, 1996. *Heir: e s* Charles Ashley Ponsonby [*b* 10 June 1951; *m* 1983, Mary P., *yr d* of late A. R. Bromley Davenport and of Mrs A. R. Bromley Davenport, Over Peover, Knutsford, Cheshire; two *s* one *d*]. *Address:* Grim's Dyke Farm, Woodleys, Woodstock, Oxon OX20 1HJ. *T:* (01993) 811422. *Club:* Pratt's.

PONSONBY, Robert Noel, CBE 1985; Controller of Music, BBC, 1972–85; *b* 19 Dec. 1926; *o s* of late Noel Ponsonby, BMus, Organist Christ Church Cathedral, Oxford, and Mary White-Thomson; *m* 1st, 1957, Una Mary (marr. diss.), *er d* of late W. J. Kenny; 2nd, 1977, Lesley Margaret Black (marr. diss.), *o d* of late G. T. Black. *Educ:* Eton; Trinity Coll., Oxford. MA Oxon, Eng. Litt. Commissioned Scots Guards, 1945–47. Organ Scholar, Trinity Coll., Oxford, 1948–50; staff of Glyndebourne Opera, 1951–55; Artistic Director of the Edinburgh International Festival, 1955–60; with Independent Television Authority, 1962–64; Gen. Administrator, Scottish Nat. Orchestra, 1964–72. Adminr, Friends of the Musicians Benevolent Fund, 1987–93. Director: Commonwealth Arts Festival, Glasgow, 1965; Henry Wood Promenade Concerts, 1974–86; Artistic Dir, Canterbury Fest., 1987–88. Artistic Adviser to Internat. Arts Guild of Bahamas, 1960–72. Chm., London Choral Soc., 1990–94; Programme Consultant, RPO, 1993–96. Mem., Music Adv. Panel, Arts Council of GB, 1986–89; Music Advr, Wingate Scholarships, 1988–. Trustee: Young Concert Artists Trust, 1984–89; Nash Concert Soc., 1988–; Michael Tippett Musical Foundn, 1989–. Governor, Purcell Sch., 1985–88. Hon. RAM 1975; Hon. Mem., ISM, 1992. FRSA 1979. *Publication:* Short History of Oxford University Opera Club 1950. *Recreations:* fell-walking, bird-watching, English and Scottish painting, music. *Address:* 11 St Cuthbert's Road, NW2 3QJ.

PONTEFRACT, Bishop Suffragan of, since 1998; **Rt Rev. David Charles James,** PhD; *b* 6 March 1945; *s* of Charles George Frederick James and Cecilia Lily James; *m* 1971, Gillian Patricia Harrop; four *d*. *Educ:* Nottingham High Sch.; Exeter Univ. (BSc 1966; PhD 1971); Nottingham Univ. (BA 1973); St John's Theol Coll., Nottingham. Asst Lectr in Chemistry, Southampton Univ., 1969–70. Ordained deacon, 1973, priest, 1974; Curate: Highfield Church, Southampton, 1973–76; Goring by Sea, Worthing, 1976–78; Anglican Chaplain, UEA, 1978–82; Vicar of Ecclesfield, Sheffield, 1982–90; RD, Ecclesfield, 1987–90; Vicar of Highfield, Southampton, 1990–98. Hon. Canon of Winchester, 1998. Gov., King Alfred's UC, Winchester, 1992–97. *Address:* Pontefract House, 181a Manygates Lane, Sandal, Wakefield, W Yorks WF2 7DR. *T:* (01924) 250781.

PONTEFRACT, Archdeacon of; *see* Robinson, Ven. A. W.

PONTI, Signora Carlo; *see* Loren, Sophia.

PONTIFEX, Brig. David More, CBE 1977 (OBE 1965; MBE 1956); General Secretary, Army Cadet Force Association and Secretary, Combined Cadet Force Association, 1977–87; *b* 16 Sept. 1922; *s* of Comdr John Weddall Pontifex, RN, and Monica Pontifex; *m* 1968, Kathleen Betsy (*née* Matheson); one *s* four *d*. *Educ:* Worth Preparatory Sch.; Downside Sch. Commnd The Rifle Brigade, 1942; served War, Italy (despatches); Staff Coll., Camberley, 1951; HQ Parachute Brigade, 1952–54; Kenya, 1954–56; War Office, 1956–58; Armed Forces Staff Coll., USA, 1958–59; Brigade Major, 63 Gurkha Brigade, 1961–62; CO 1st Bn Federal Regular Army, Aden, 1963–64; GSO1 2nd Div., BAOR, 1965–66; Col GS, Staff Coll., Camberley, 1967–69; Divisional Brig., The Light Div., 1969–73; Dep. Dir, Army Staff Duties, MoD, 1973–75; Dep. Comdr and COS, SE District, 1975–77, retired 1977. ADC to the Queen, 1975–77. *Address:* 68 Shortheath Road, Farnham, Surrey GU9 8SQ. *T:* (01252) 723284. *Club:* Naval and Military.

PONTIN, John Graham; Chairman, JT Group Ltd, since 1961; *b* 2 June 1937; *s* of Charles Cyril Pontin and Phyllis (*née* Frieze); *m* 1st, 1966, Gillian Margaret Harris (marr. diss. 1971); one *s* one *d*; 2nd, 1977, Sylviane Marie-Louise Aubel (*d* 1998). *Educ:* Bristol Tech. Sch. (Building). Founder, JT Group, 1961. Chm., Dartington Hall Trust, 1984–97 (Trustee, 1980–97); Trustee, Gtr Bristol Foundn (formerly Gtr Bristol Community Trust), 1987–. *Recreations:* gardening, walking. *Address:* 8 High Street, Chew Magna, Bristol BS40 8PW. *T:* (01275) 373393. *Club:* Reform.

PONTIUS, Timothy Gordon; His Honour Judge Pontius; a Circuit Judge, since 1995; *b* 5 Sept. 1948; *s* of Gordon Stuart Malzard Pontius and Elizabeth Mary (*née* Donaldson). *Educ:* Boroughmuir Sen. Secondary Sch., Edinburgh; London Univ. (external, LLB Hons). Called to the Bar, Middle Temple, 1972; in practice at the Bar, 1972–88; Dep. Judge-Advocate, 1988–91; AJAG, 1991–95; a Recorder, 1993–95. *Recreations:* music, travel, bridge, swimming. *Address:* Blackfriars Crown Court, Pocock Street, SE1 0BT. *T:* (020) 7922 5800. *Club:* Naval and Military.

POOLE, family name of **Baron Poole**.

POOLE, 2nd Baron *cr* 1958, of Aldgate; **David Charles Poole;** Group Chief Executive, Ockham (formerly Sturge) Holdings PLC, since 1994; *b* 6 Jan. 1945; *s* of 1st Baron Poole, PC, CBE, TD and Betty Margaret Gilkison (*d* 1988); *S* father, 1993; *m* 1967; one *s*; *m* 1995, Mrs Lucinda Edsell. *Educ:* Dragon Sch., Oxford; Gordonstoun; Christ Church, Oxford (MA); INSEAD, Fontainebleau (MBA). Samuel Montagu & Co. Ltd, 1967–74; Bland Payne & Co. Ltd, 1974–78; Capel-Cure Myers, 1978–87; Bonomi Group, 1987–90; James Capel, 1990–94; Mem., Prime Minister's Policy Unit (on secondment),

1992–94. *Recreations:* cruising, ballet. *Heir: s* Hon. Oliver John Poole, *b* 30 May 1972. *Address:* 53 The Chase, SW4 0NP. *Clubs:* Brooks's, City of London; Royal Yacht Squadron, Island Sailing.

POOLE, Dame Anne; *see* Poole, Dame Avril A. B.

POOLE, Anthony Cecil James; Head of Administration Department, House of Commons, 1985–88, retired; *b* 9 Oct. 1927; *s* of Walter James Poole and Daisy Poole (*née* Voyle); *m* 1951, Amelia Keziah (*née* Pracy); one *d. Educ:* Headlands Grammar School, Swindon. Served RN, 1945–47; Department of Employment, 1947–76; Principal Establishments Officer, Manpower Services Commn, 1976–80; House of Commons, 1980, Head of Establishments Office, 1981. *Recreations:* golf, gardening.

POOLE, Dame (Avril) Anne (Barker), DBE 1992; Chief Nursing Officer, Department of Health (formerly of Health and Social Security), 1982–92; *b* 11 April 1934; *d* of Arthur George and Norah Heritage; *m* 1959, John Percy Poole. *Educ:* High Sch., Southampton. SRN 1955, SCM 1957, Health Visitors Cert., 1958. Asst Chief Nursing Officer, City of Westminster, 1967–69; Chief Nursing Officer, London Borough of Merton, 1969–73; Area Nursing Officer, Surrey AHA, 1974–81; Dep. Chief Nursing Officer, DHSS, 1981–82. Non-exec. Dir, SW Surrey HA, 1993–96; Mem., Criminal Injuries Compensation Panel, 1996–. Trustee, Marie Curie Cancer Care (formerly Marie Curie Meml Foundn), 1992–. FRSocMed 1993; CIMgt (CBIM 1984). *Address:* Ancaster House, Church Hill, Merstham, Surrey RH1 3BL.

POOLE, Christopher William Oldfield; Racing Correspondent: BBC World Service, 1968–98; London Evening Standard, 1971–98; *b* 30 Sept. 1937; *yr s* of William Percival Poole and Ellen Elizabeth Poole (*née* Oldfield); *m* 1959, Diana Faith Bennett; one *s* one *d. Educ:* Downs Sch. Bexhill-on-Sea Observer, 1957–59; Sussex Express, 1959–62; Manchester Evening News, 1962–66; Sheffield Telegraph, 1966–68; Daily Telegraph, 1968–71. Vice-Pres., Horserace Writers' Assoc., 1994–97 (Hon. Life Mem., 1998); Member: Press Cttee, Racecourse Assoc., 1976–98; Bd, Independent Betting Arbitration Service, 1999–. Clive Graham Award, 1979. *Publications:* (ed) William Hill Annuals, 1978–82; Classic Treble, 1982; (ed) Playfair Racing Annuals, 1983–88; A Lifetime in Racing, 1984; Guinness Book of Flat Racing, 1990; contrib. to overseas racing jls in France, Italy, USA. *Recreations:* cricket, opera, cooking (and eating), travel. *Address:* Flat 1, Glyne Hall, De La Warr Parade, Bexhill-on-Sea, E Sussex TN40 1BQ. *T:* (01424) 214225. *Clubs:* Carbine; Cricketers', Sussex CC.

POOLE, Hon. Sir David (Anthony), Kt 1995; **Hon. Mr Justice Poole;** a Judge of the High Court of Justice, Queen's Bench Division, since 1995; *b* 8 June 1938; *s* of William Joseph Poole and Lena (*née* Thomas); *m* 1974, Pauline Ann O'Flaherty; four *s. Educ:* Ampleforth; Jesus Coll., Oxford (Meyricke Exhibnr in Classics; MA; Hon. Fellow, 1997); Univ. of Manchester Inst. of Science and Technology (DipTechSc). Called to the Bar, Middle Temple, 1968 (Bencher, 1992); QC 1984; a Recorder, 1983–95. Chm., Assoc. of Lawyers for the Defence of the Unborn, 1985–92. *Address:* Royal Courts of Justice, Strand, WC2A 2LL. *Clubs:* London Irish Rugby Football, Vincent's.

POOLE, David Arthur Ramsay; Managing Director, Blue Circle Industries, 1987–89; *b* 30 Sept. 1935; *s* of late Arthur Poole and Viola Isbol (*née* Ramsay); *m* 1961, Jean Mary Male; three *d. Educ:* King's Sch., Canterbury; St Edmund Hall, Oxford (MA Jurisprudence). Nat. service, 2nd Lieut, RA, 1955–57. Baring Bros & Co., 1960–65; APCM Ltd (now BCI), 1965–70; Wm Brandts & Co., 1970–73; British Caledonian Gp, 1973–75; Blue Circle Industries, 1976–89. *Recreations:* shooting, ski-ing, travel. *Address:* Fairhaven, 23 Fairmile Avenue, Cobham, Surrey KT11 2JA. *T:* and *Fax:* (01932) 864830. *Clubs:* East India, Royal Automobile.

POOLE, David James, PPRP (RP 1969); ARCA; artist; *b* 5 June 1931; *s* of Thomas Herbert Poole and Catherine Poole; *m* 1958, Iris Mary Toomer; three *s. Educ:* Stoneleigh Secondary Sch.; Wimbledon Sch. of Art; Royal Coll. of Art. National Service, RE, 1949–51. Sen. Lectr in Painting and Drawing, Wimbledon Sch. of Art, 1962–77. Pres., Royal Soc. of Portrait Painters, 1983–91. One-man exhibns, Zurich and London. Portraits include: The Queen, The Duke of Edinburgh, The Queen Mother, Prince Charles, Princess Anne, Princess Margaret, Earl Mountbatten of Burma and The Duke of Kent; also distinguished members of govt, industry, commerce, medicine, the academic and legal professions. Work in private collections of the Queen and the Duke of Edinburgh, and in Australia, S Africa, Bermuda, France, W Germany, Switzerland, Saudi Arabia and USA. *Recreations:* French travel, food and drink. *Address:* Trinity Flint Barn, Weston Lane, Weston, Petersfield, Hants GU32 3NN. *T:* (01730) 265075.

POOLE, Isobel Anne; Sheriff of the Lothian and Borders, since 1979, at Edinburgh, since 1986; *b* 9 Dec. 1941; *d* of late John Cecil Findlay Poole, DM Oxon, and Constance Mary (*née* Gilkes), SRN. *Educ:* Oxford High Sch. for Girls; Edinburgh Univ. (LLB). Admitted to Faculty of Advocates, 1964. Formerly Standing Jun. Counsel to Registrar Gen. for Scotland. Member: Sheriffs' Council, 1980–85; Scottish Lawyers European Gp, 1977–. *Recreations:* country, arts, houses, gardens, friends. *Address:* Sheriff's Chambers, Sheriff Court House, Chambers Street, Edinburgh EH1 1LB. *Clubs:* New, Scottish Arts (Edinburgh).

POOLE, Col Peter Michael, CBE 1992; TD 1964; Vice Lord-Lieutenant, County of Merseyside, since 1994; Consultant, Denton Clark & Co., since 1995; *b* 29 Sept. 1929; *s* of Reginald and Madeline Isobel Poole; *m* 1956, Diana Rosemary Hiam Wilson; three *s* one *d. Educ:* Sedbergh Sch.; Gonville and Caius Coll., Cambridge. FRICS (Ryde Meml Prizewinner, 1955); Fellow, CAAV. Univ. Officer, Cambridge, 1954–60; Chartered Surveyor and Land Agent; Principal, Poole & Partners, Liverpool, 1960–91; Partner, Denton Clark & Co., 1991–95. Mem., Lord Chancellor's Panel of Arbitrators, 1977–95; Chm., Merseyside Adv. Cttee on Gen. Comrs of Income Tax, 1993–. Dir, Merseyside Youth Assoc., 1973–. Liveryman and Mem., Chartered Surveyors' Co., 1980–. JP Liverpool 1976–96; DL Merseyside 1975. CO, 107 Corps Engr Regt, RE (TA), 1965–67; Brevet Col, 1967; Hon. Col, 75 Engr Regt, RE (V), 1972–80; Chm., North West TA&VRA, 1990–92. *Publication:* The Valuation of Pipeline Easements and Wayleaves, 1962. *Recreations:* ornithology, golf, travel, photography. *Address:* Shelford, 3 Heron Court, Parkgate, Neston, Cheshire CH64 6TB. *T:* (0151) 336 2529. *Club:* Athenæum (Liverpool).

POOLE, Richard John; Director, Defence Operational Analysis Establishment, Ministry of Defence, 1986–89, retired; *b* 20 Feb. 1929; *s* of Leonard Richard Poole and Merrie Wyn Poole; *m* 1st, 1953, Jean Doreena Poole (*née* Welch) (*d* 1991); two *d*; 2nd, 1993, Jane Amelia (*née* Allen). *Educ:* Univ. of Adelaide, SA (BEng 1st Cl. Hons). Long Range Weapons Estabt, Aust. Dept of Defence, 1951; Ministry of Defence, UK: Admiralty Signals and Radar Estabt, 1957; Head of Div., 1971; Scientific Adviser, 1980, Dir Gen. (Estabts), 1984. *Recreations:* radio, cars, photography, computing.

POOLE-WILSON, Prof. Philip Alexander, MD, FRCP; Simon Marks British Heart Foundation Professor of Cardiology, National Heart and Lung Institute (formerly Cardiothoracic Institute), Imperial College School of Medicine, University of London, since 1988; *b* 26 April 1943; *s* of late Denis Smith Poole-Wilson, CBE, MCh, FRCS and Monique Michelle Poole-Wilson; *m* 1969, Mary Elizabeth, *d* of late William Horrocks Tattersall, MD and Joan Tattersall; two *s* one *d. Educ:* Marlborough Coll.; Trinity Coll., Cambridge (Major Scholar; MA, MD); St Thomas's Hosp. Med. Sch. FRCP 1983; FACC 1992. House appts, St Thomas' Hosp., Brompton Hosp., Hammersmith Hosp.; Lectr, St Thomas' Hosp.; British-American Travelling Fellowship from British Heart Foundn at UCLA, 1973–74; Cardiothoracic Institute, London University: Senior Lectr and Reader, 1976–83; Vice-Dean, 1981–84; apptd Prof. of Cardiology, 1983; Hon. Consultant Physician, Royal Brompton Nat. Heart and Lung Hosp. (formerly at Nat. Heart Hosp.), 1976–. Chm., Cardiac Muscle Research Group, 1984–87; Mem. Council, British Heart Foundn, 1985–97; Founding Chm., British Soc. for Heart Failure, 1999–2001; Pres.-elect, World Heart Fedn, 2001–. European Society of Cardiology: Fellow, 1988; Mem. Bd, 1988–98; Sec., 1990–92; Pres.-elect, 1992–94; Pres., 1994–96. Strickland-Goodall Lectr, 1983, Bradshaw Lectr, 1993, Paul Wood Lectr, 1999, British Cardiac Soc. Founder FMedSci 1998. *Publications:* articles and contribs to books on physiology and biochemistry of normal and diseased heart. *Recreations:* sailing, gardening, opera. *Address:* 174 Burbage Road, SE21 7AG. *T:* (020) 7274 6742. *Clubs:* Athenæum; Parkstone Yacht.

POOLES, Michael Philip Holmes; QC 1999; a Recorder, since 2000; *b* 14 Dec. 1955; *s* of late Dennis John Pooles and of Joan Ellen Pooles; *m* 1982, Fiona Grant Chalmers; two *s. Educ:* Perse Sch., Cambridge; Queen Mary Coll., Univ. of London (LLB). Called to the Bar, Inner Temple, 1978; in practice at the Bar, 1980–; Asst Recorder, 2000. *Publication:* (contrib.) Professional Negligence and Liability. *Recreations:* reading, gardening. *Address:* 4 Paper Buildings, Temple, EC4Y 7EX. *T:* (020) 7353 3366. *Club:* Royal Automobile.

POOLEY, Dr Derek, CBE 1995; consultant, Derek Pooley Associates, since 1998; *b* 28 Oct. 1937; *s* of Richard Pike Pooley and Evelyn Pooley; *m* 1961, Jennifer Mary Davey; two *s* one *d. Educ:* Sir James Smith's Sch., Camelford, Cornwall; Birmingham Univ. (BSc 1958; PhD 1961). FInstP 1979. A. A. Noyes Res. Fellow, Calif Inst. of Technol., Pasadena, 1961–62; UKAEA, Harwell: Res. Scientist, 1962–68; Leader of Defects Gp, later of Physics Applications Gp, 1968–76; Head of Materials Develt Div., 1976–81; Dir of Non-nuclear Energy Res., 1981–83; Chief Scientist, Dept of Energy, 1983–86; Dep. Dir, 1986–89, Dir, 1989–90, Atomic Energy Estabt, Winfrith, later AEA Technol.; Dir, AEA Thermal Reactor Services, 1990–91; Man. Dir, Nuclear Business Gp, AEA Technol., 1991–94; Chief Executive: UKAEA Govt Div., 1994–96; UKAEA, 1996–97. Non-exec. Dir, UK Nirex Ltd, 1995–97; Dir, BNES Ltd, 1997–2000. Pres., British Nuclear Energy Soc., 1992–94; Chm., Scientific and Technical Cttee, Euratom, 1994–99. *Publications:* Real Solids and Radiation, 1975; (contrib.) Radiation Damage Processes in Materials, 1975; (contrib.) Energy and Feedstocks in the Chemical Industry, 1983; (contrib.) A Radical Approach to Nuclear Decommissioning, 1995. *Recreations:* history, astronomy, gardening, walking. *Address:* 11 Halls Close, Drayton, Abingdon, Oxon OX14 4LU. *T:* (01235) 537507.

POOLEY, Peter, CMG 1996; Hon. Director General and Special Adviser, European Commission, since 1995; consultant on aid, trade and agricultural issues in European Union, since 1996; *b* 19 June 1936; *er* (twin) *s* of late W. M. Pooley, OBE, Truro, and of Grace Lidbury; *m* 1966, Janet Mary, *er d* of Jack Pearson, Banbury; one *s* one *d. Educ:* Brentwood Sch.; Clare Coll., Cambridge (BA). Joined MAFF as Asst Principal, 1959; seconded to: Diplomatic Service, 1961–63 (served in Brussels) and 1979–82 (Minister (Agric.), Office of UK Perm. Rep. to EEC, Brussels); CSD, 1977–79; Under-Sec., 1979, Fisheries Sec., 1982, MAFF; Dep. Dir Gen., Agric., EC, 1983–89; Dep. Dir Gen., 1989–92, Actg Dir Gen., 1993–94, Develt, EC. Sec.-Gen., COPA/COGECA, 1996. Chm., British African Business Assoc., 1996–2001; Exec. Vice-Pres., Business Council Europe–Africa, 1999–2001 (Pres., 1998). Mem. Bd, CARE Internat. UK, 2001–. Chm., Bd of Management, British Sch. of Brussels, 1991–94. *Address:* The Lodge, 25 Rosebery Road, Alresford, Hampshire SO24 9HQ. *T:* and *Fax:* (01962) 732779; *e-mail:* peter.pooley@lineone.net. *Club:* Oxford and Cambridge.
See also R. Pooley.

POOLEY, Robin, OBE 1997; Chairman, Abbey Group Ltd, since 1997; *b* 19 June 1936; *yr* (twin) *s* of late W. Melville Pooley, OBE and of Grace M. Pooley (*née* Lidbury); *m* 1972, Margaret Anne, *yr d* of Jack Pearson, Banbury; one *d. Educ:* Brentwood School. Various posts, Towers & Co. Ltd, 1954–71; Gen. Manager, CWS Gp, 1971–76; Man. Dir, Buxted Poultry Ltd, 1976–81; Chief Exec., Potato Marketing Bd, 1981–88; Managing Director: Anglian Produce Ltd, 1988–97; Anglian Potato Services Ltd, 1988–97; Chairman: Pseedco Ltd, 1995–98; United Pig Marketing Ltd, 1999–; English Apples & Pears Ltd, 2000–. Director: North Country Primestock Ltd, 1996–; Garden Isle (formerly Smith and Holbourne) Ltd, 1997–. Chm., NFU Corporate, 1998–; Mem. Council, NFU, 1996–. Chm., MAFF Enquiry into meat hygiene, 1999; Mem., Scientific and Economic Co-ordinating Cttee, Min. of Agriculture for Italy, 1998–. Special Lectr in Mgt, Univ. of Nottingham, 1996–. Pres., Cambridge Univ. Postgrad. Res. Assoc., 1999–. Master, Co. of Butchers, 1987. *Recreations:* country pursuits, freemasonry. *Address:* Barn Hill, Strumpshaw, Norfolk NR13 4NS. *T:* (01603) 715992. *Club:* Farmers'.
See also P. Pooley.

POORE, Duncan; *see* Poore, M. E. D.

POORE, Sir Herbert Edward, 6th Bt *cr* 1795; *b* April 1930; *s* of Sir Edward Poore, 5th Bt, and Amelia Guliemone; *S* father, 1938. *Heir: uncle* Nasionceno Poore [*b* 1900; *m* Juana Borda (*d* 1943); three *s* three *d*].

POORE, Dr (Martin Edward) Duncan, MA, PhD; FIBiol, FRGS; Senior Consultant (formerly Director), Forestry and Land Use Programme, International Institute for Environment and Development, and consultant in conservation and land use, since 1983; *b* 25 May 1925; *s* of T. E. D. Poore and Elizabeth McMartin; *m* 1948, Judith Ursula, *d* of Lt-Gen. Sir Treffry Thompson, KCSI, CB, CBE, and late Mary Emily, *d* of Rev. Canon Medd; two *s. Educ:* Trinity Coll., Glenalmond; Edinburgh Univ.; Clare Coll., Cambridge. MA, PhD Cantab.; MA Oxon. MICFor; MIEEM. GCCS, Bletchley Park and HMS Anderson, Colombo, 1943–45. Nature Conservancy, 1953–56; Consultant Ecologist, Hunting Technical Services, 1956–59; Prof. of Botany, Univ. of Malaya, Kuala Lumpur, 1959–65; Dean of Science, Univ. of Malaya, 1964–65; Lectr, Forestry Dept, Oxford, 1965–66; Dir, Nature Conservancy, 1966–73; Scientific Dir, Internat. Union for Conservation of Nature and Natural Resources, Switzerland, 1974–78; Prof. of Forest Science and Dir, Commonwealth Forestry Inst., Oxford Univ., 1980–83; Fellow of St John's Coll., Oxford, 1980–83. Member: Thames Water Authority, 1981–83; Nature Conservancy Council, 1981–84. Pres., British Assoc. of Nature Conservationists, 1984–92 (Vice Pres., 1993–); Vice-Pres., Commonwealth Forestry Assoc., 1989–; Hon. Member: Botanical Soc. of Scotland, 1992; IUCN (World Conservation Union), 1978 (Hon. Mem., and Fred M. Packard Award, 1990, Commn for Nat. Parks and Protected Areas). FRSA. *Publications:* The Vanishing Forest, 1986; No Timber without Trees, 1990; (with Jeffrey Sayer) The Management of Tropical Moist Forest Lands, 1991; Guidelines for Mountain Protected Areas, 1992; (with Judy Poore) Protected Landscapes in the United

Kingdom, 1992; Where Next?: reflections on the human future, 2000; papers on ecology and land use in various jls and scientific periodicals. *Recreations:* hill walking, natural history, music, gardening, photography. *Address:* Balnacarn, Glenmoriston, Inverness-shire IV63 7YJ. *T:* (01320) 340261. *Club:* Royal Over-Seas League.

POOT, Anton, Hon. CBE 1989; Officer, Order of Oranje-Nassau (Netherlands), 1989; Managing Director, 1983–88, Chairman, 1983–89, Philips Electronics & Associated Industries Ltd; Chairman, Philips UK Ltd, 1985–89; *b* 23 Nov. 1929; *m* 1983, Jesmond Masters; one *s* one *d* by a former marriage. *Educ:* High School in Holland; electronics and economics, Holland and Johannesburg. NV Philips' Gloeilampenfabrieken, Hilversum, Utrecht, Eindhoven, 1946–51; Philips S Africa, Fedn of Rhodesia and Nyasaland, 1951–63; NV Philips' Gloeilampenfabrieken, Eindhoven, 1963–66; Chairman and Man. Dir, Philips East Africa, 1967–71; Man. Dir, Ada (Halifax) Ltd and Philips Electrical Ltd UK, 1971–76; Man. Dir, NV Philips' Gloeilampenfabrieken, Eindhoven, 1976–78; Chm. and Man. Dir, Philips Appliances Div., 1978–83. Hon. Freeman, Co. of Information Technologists, 1988. FInstD; FRSA. *Recreations:* music, golf. *Address:* Priors Corner, Priorsfield Road, Godalming, Surrey GU7 2RQ.

POPAT, (Surendra) Andrew, CBE 1997; a Recorder, since 1998; *b* 31 Dec. 1943; *s* of late Dhirajlal Kurji Popat and Kashiben Popat (*née* Chitalia); *m* 1995, Suzanne Joy, *d* of Edward James Wayman and Beatrice Joyce Wayman; one *s*. *Educ:* Univ. of London (LLB); Univ. of Calif, Berkeley (LLM). Called to the Bar, Lincoln's Inn, 1969; Mem., Inner Temple, 1985; Associate Attorney, Willkie Farr & Gallaghar (NY), 1970–74; practising Barrister, specialising in criminal law, 1975–; Asst Recorder, 1992–98. Legal Mem., Criminal Injuries Compensation Appeals Panel, 2000–; Mem., Professional Conduct Cttee, GMC, 2000–. Contested (C): Durham NE, 1983; Bradford S, 1992; London Reg., EP, 1999. Dir, John Patten's election campaign, 1987. Treas., Surbiton Cons. Assoc., 1985. Chm., Disraeli Club, 1993–. Trustee, Brooke Hosp. for Animals, 1998–2000. Freeman, City of London, 1987; Liveryman, Plaisterers' Co., 1987– (Mem. Ct of Assts, 2001–). *Recreations:* travel, theatre, cricket, tennis. *Address:* 9 King's Bench Walk, Temple, EC4Y 7DX. *T:* (020) 7353 3909. *Clubs:* Carlton, MCC.

POPE, His Holiness the; *see* John Paul II.

POPE, Cathryn Mary; soprano; *b* 6 July 1957; *m* 1982, Stuart Petersen. *Educ:* Royal College of Music (ARCM); National Opera Studio. Début, ENO: Sophie, in Werther, 1983; Anna, in Moses, 1986; Susanna, in Marriage of Figaro, 1987; Gretel, in Hansel and Gretel, 1987; Oksana, in Christmas Eve, 1988; Despina, in Così fan tutte, 1988; Pamina, in Die Zauberflöte, 1989; Micaëla, in Carmen, 1993; Tatyana, in Eugene Onegin, 1994; Amsterdam: début, Gretel, 1990; Mélisande, in Pelléas et Mélisande, 1991; Elvira, in Don Giovanni, and Susanna, 1991; Opera Europa: Nedda, in Pagliacci, 1995; Giorgetta, in Il Tabarro; Nantes: Le Prostitué, in La Ronde. Numerous recordings.

POPE, Geoffrey George, CB 1986; PhD; FREng, FRAeS; aerospace technology consultant; *b* 17 April 1934; *s* of Sir George Reginald Pope and of Susie (*née* Hendy); *m* 1st, 1961, Rosemary Frances Harnden (*d* 1989); two *s*; 2nd, 1991, Helen Vernon Brewis. *Educ:* Epsom Coll.; Imperial Coll., London. MSc (Eng) 1959, DIC 1959, PhD 1963. FRAeS 1970; FCGI 1982; FREng (FEng 1988). Junior Technical Asst, Hawker Aircraft Ltd, 1952–53; Student, Imperial Coll., 1953–58; Royal Aircraft Establishment: Structures Dept, 1958–73 (Head, Research Div., 1969–73); Aerodynamics Dept, 1973–77 (Head, 1974–77); Gp Head, Aerodynamics, Structures and Materials Depts, 1978–79; Dep. Dir (Weapons), 1979–81; Asst Chief Scientific Advr (Projects), MoD, 1981–82; Dep. Controller and Adviser (Res. and Technol.), MoD, 1982–84; Dir, RAE, 1984–89; Dep. Chief Scientific Advr, MoD, 1989–94. Pres., RAeS, 1993–94. Mem. Council, 1995–, Pro Chancellor and Chair of Council, 1999–, Univ. of Exeter. Mem. Associé Etranger, Acad. Nat. de l'Air et de l'Espace, 1994. FRSA 1994. US Sec. of Defense Medal for Outstanding Public Service, 1994. *Publications:* papers on aeronautical technology in various technical jls. *Recreations:* music, photography, walking. *Address:* 3 Silver Street, Thorverton, Exeter EX5 5LT. *T:* (01392) 860159.

POPE, George Maurice, FRICS; independent surveyor, since 1999; *b* 12 Jan. 1943; *s* of Maj. John Pope; *m* 1968, Tessa Roselle Norman; one *s* two *d*. *Educ:* Eton. Capt., Coldstream Guards, 1962–69. With John D. Wood & Co., 1970–99, Chm., 1982–99. *Recreations:* racing, hunting, shooting, golf. *Address:* (office) 4 Pont Street, SW1X 9EL. *T:* (020) 7795 0646; Grounds Farm House, Fernham Road, Uffington, near Faringdon, Oxon SN7 7RD. *T:* (01367) 820234. *Clubs:* White's; Royal St George's Golf, Sunningdale Golf.

POPE, Gregory James; MP (Lab) Hyndburn, since 1992; *b* 29 Aug. 1960; *s* of Samuel J. Pope and Sheila M. (*née* Day); *m* 1985, Catherine M. Fallon; two *s* one *d*. *Educ:* St Mary's Coll., Blackburn; Univ. of Hull (BA Hons). Local govt officer, 1987–92. An Asst Govt Whip, 1997–99; a Lord Comr of HM Treasury (Govt Whip), 1999–2001. *Recreations:* walking, football, chess, music. *Address:* House of Commons, SW1A 0AA. *T:* (020) 7219 5842. *Club:* Old Band (Accrington).

POPE, Jeremy James Richard, OBE 1985; Deputy Chairman, South West of England Regional Development Agency, since 1999 (Board Member, since 1998); *b* 15 July 1943; *s* of late Philip William Rolph Pope and of Joyce Winifred Harcourt Pope (*née* Slade); *m* 1969, Hon. Jacqueline Best; three *s*. *Educ:* Charterhouse; Trinity Coll., Cambridge. Law tripos, MA. Solicitor. Eldridge, Pope & Co., 1969–99: Finance and Planning Dir, 1972–82; Jt Man. Dir, 1982–88; Man. Dir, 1988–99; Chairman: Eldridge, Pope Fine Wines Ltd, 1999–2000; Milk Link Ltd, 2000–. Non-executive Director: Exeter Investment Gp plc, 1999–; Chilworth Science Park Ltd, 2001–. Chm., Smaller Firms Council, CBI, 1981–83; Member: NEDC, 1981–85; Top Salaries Review Body, 1986–93; Exec. Cttee, Food and Drinks Fedn, 1986–89 (Dep. Pres., 1987–89). Member: Royal Commn on Environmental Pollution, 1984–92; Wessex Regl Rivers Adv. Cttee, NRA, 1994–95. Chairman: Winterbourne Hosp. plc, 1981–89; Trustees, Wessex Medical Trust, 1993–97 (Trustee, 1991–97); Dorset Private Sector Forum, 1997–2000; Bournemouth, Dorset & Poole Economic Partnership, 1997–99. Gov., Forres Sch., Swanage, 1984–92; Mem. Council, Southampton Univ., 1999–. Trustee: Devonshire and Dorset Regtl Charity, 1994–2000; Tank Mus., 2000–; Chm. Mgt Cttee, Mus. of Regts of Devon and Dorset, 1994–2000. FRSA. Hon. DLitt Bournemouth, 1999. *Recreations:* shooting, fishing, gardening, cooking the resultant produce. *Address:* Field Cottage, West Compton, Dorchester, Dorset DT2 0EY. *T:* (01300) 20469.

POPE, Air Vice-Marshal John Clifford, CB 1963; CBE 1959; CEng, FIMechE; FRAeS; RAF (retired); *b* 27 April 1911; *s* of George Newcombe-Pope; *m* 1950, Christine Agnes (*d* 1982), *d* of Alfred Hames, Chichester; one *s* two *d*. *Educ:* Tiverton Boys' Middle Sch.; RAF Technical Training Sch., Halton (aircraft apprentice); RAF Coll., Cranwell (cadet; Sir Charles Wakefield Scholar). Graduated as pilot and commnd, 1932; served with No 3 Sqdn, 1933, Nos 27 and 39, on NW Frontier, 1933–36. War of 1939–45; Comd RAF Station, Cleave, 1940–42; served in Egypt and Palestine, 1943–46; Asst Dir Research and Develt, Min. of Supply, 1947–50; Dir of Engineering, RNZAF, 1951–53; Comd RAF Station, Stoke Heath, 1954–57; Sen. Tech. Staff Officer, No 3 Gp Bomber Comd, 1957–59 and Flying Trng Comd, 1960–61; AOC and Comdt, RAF Technical College, 1961–63; Senior Technical Staff Officer, Transport Command, 1963–66. Life Vice-Pres., RAF Boxing Assoc. *Recreations:* scale model steam engineering, clock making. *Address:* Dilston, 47 Oxford Road, Stone, near Aylesbury, Bucks HP17 8PD. *T:* (01296) 748467. *Club:* Royal Air Force.

POPE, Sir Joseph (Albert), Kt 1980; DSc, PhD (Belfast), WhSc; Director, since 1960, Consultant, since 1988, TQ International (formerly TecQuipment Group), Nottingham (Chairman, 1974–88); *b* 18 October 1914; *s* of Albert Henry and Mary Pope; *m* 1940, Evelyn Alice Gallagher; one *s* two *d*. *Educ:* School of Arts and Crafts, Cambridge; King's College, London. Apprentice, Boulton & Pauls, Norwich, 1930–35. Whitworth Scholarship, 1935. Assistant Lecturer in Engineering, Queen's Univ., Belfast, 1938–44; Assistant Lecturer in Engineering, Univ. of Manchester, 1944–45; Lecturer, then Senior Lecturer, Univ. of Sheffield, 1945–49; Professor of Mechanical Engineering, Nottingham University, 1949–60; Research Dir, Mirrlees Nat. Research Div., Stockport, and Dir, Mirrlees National Ltd 1960–69; Vice-Chancellor, Univ. of Aston in Birmingham, 1969–79. Director: John Brown & Co. Ltd, 1970–82; Midlands Electricity Bd, 1975–80; Royal Worcester Ltd, 1979–83; Chm., W Midlands Econ. Planning Council, 1977–79. Gen. Treasurer, British Assoc., 1975–82; Pres., Whitworth Soc., 1978–79; Chm., Birmingham Civic Soc., 1978–79. Hon. LLD Birmingham, 1979; Hon. DUniv Heriot-Watt, 1979; Hon. DSc: Aston, 1979; Belfast, 1980; Salford, 1980; Nottingham, 1987. *Publications:* papers on the impact of metals and metal fatigue published in Proc. of Inst. of Mech. Engineers and Jl of Iron and Steel Inst. *Address:* 3 Mapperley Hall Drive, Nottingham NG3 5EP. *T:* (0115) 962 1146.

POPE, Rear-Adm. Michael Donald K.; *see* Kyrle Pope.

POPE, Very Rev. Robert William, OBE 1971; Dean of Gibraltar, 1977–82; *b* 20 May 1916; *s* of late Rev. Jonas George Pope and Marjorie Mary Pope (*née* Coates); *m* 1940, Elizabeth Beatrice Matilda (*née* Bressey); two *s* one *d*. *Educ:* English College, Temuco, Chile; Harvey Grammar Sch., Folkestone; Maidstone Grammar Sch.; St Augustine's Coll., Canterbury; Durham Univ. (LTh). Deacon 1939, priest, 1940, Rochester; Curate: Holy Trinity, Gravesend, 1939–41; St Nicholas, Guildford, 1942–43; Priest in charge, Peaslake, 1943–44; Chaplain, Royal Navy, 1944–71; Vicar of Whitchurch with Tufton and Litchfield, Dio. Winchester, 1971–77. Member of Sion College. Minister Provincial of European Province, 1985–91, and Minister Gen., 1987–90, Third Order of Soc. of St Francis. *Address:* The Manor House, St Hilary, Vale of Glamorgan CF71 7DP.

POPHAM, Maj.-Gen. Christopher John, CB 1982; Director, British Atlantic Committee, 1982–92; *b* 2 April 1927; *s* of late Gordon F. B. Popham and Dorothy A. L. Popham (*née* Yull); *m* 1950, Heather Margaret, *y d* of late Lt-Col and Mrs H. R. W. Dawson; two *s*. *Educ:* Merchant Taylors' School. Commnd Royal Engineers, 1946; served with King George V's Own Bengal Sappers and Miners, RIE and Royal Pakistan Engineers, 1946–48; UK and Germany, 1948–57; Staff Coll., 1958; Cyprus, 1959–62; OC 4 Field Sqdn, 1963–65; JSSC 1965; Mil. Asst to QMG, 1966–68, CO 36 Engineer Regt, 1968–70; CRE 4 Div., 1971–73, Comd 12 Engineer Bde, 1973–75; BGS Intelligence and Security, HQ BAOR and ACOS G-2 HQ Northern Army Group, 1976–79; Asst Chief of Staff (Intell.), SHAPE, 1979–82. Col Comdt, RE, 1982–87. FIMgt. *Recreations:* music, photography, railways. *Address:* c/o Barclays Bank, High Street, Andover, Hants SP10 1LN.

POPLE, John Anthony, FRS 1961; Trustees' Professor of Chemistry, Northwestern University, Evanston, since 1993; *b* 31 Oct. 1925; *e s* of Herbert Keith Pople and Mary Frances Jones, Burnham-on-Sea, Som.; *m* 1952, Joy Cynthia Bowers; three *s* one *d*. *Educ:* Bristol Grammar School; Cambridge University, MA, PhD. Mayhew Prize, 1948, Smith Prize, 1950, Cambridge; Fellow, Trinity College, 1951–58, Lecturer in Mathematics, 1954–58, Cambridge; Superintendent of Basic Physics Division, National Physical Laboratory, 1958–64; Prof. of Chem. Physics, subseq. John Christian Warner Univ. Prof. of Natural Scis, Carnegie-Mellon Univ., Pittsburgh, 1964–93; Adjunct Prof. of Chemistry, Northwestern Univ., 1986–93. Ford Visiting Professor, Carnegie Inst. of Technology, Pittsburgh, 1961–62. Fellow: Amer. Physical Soc., 1970; Amer. Acad. of Arts and Scis, 1971; AAAS, 1980. For. Associate, Nat. Acad. of Sci., 1977. Marlow Medal, Faraday Soc., 1958; ACS Pauling Award, 1977; Awards from American Chemical Society: Langmuir, 1970; Harrison Howe, 1971; Gilbert Newton Lewis, 1973; Pittsburgh, 1975; Computers in Chemistry, 1991. Sen. US Scientist Award, Alexander von Humboldt Foundn, 1981; G. Willard Wheland Award, Univ. of Chicago, 1981; Evans Award, Ohio State Univ., 1982; Oesper Award, Univ. of Cincinnati, 1984; Davy Medal, Royal Soc., 1988; Wolf Prize in Chemistry, Israel, 1991; (jtly) Nobel Prize for Chemistry, 1998. *Publications:* High Resolution nuclear magnetic resonance, 1959; Approximate Molecular Orbital Theory, 1970; Ab initio Molecular Orbital Theory, 1986; scientific papers on molecular physics and theoretical chemistry. *Recreations:* music, travel. *Address:* Northwestern University, 2145 Sheridan Road, Evanston, IL 60208–3113, USA; #7K, 1500 Sheridan Road, Wilmette, IL 60091, USA.

POPPLEWELL, Andrew John; QC 1997; *b* 14 Jan. 1959; *s* of Sir Oliver Popplewell, *qv* and late (Catharine) Margaret Popplewell; *m* 1984, Debra Ellen Lomas; one *s* two *d*. *Educ:* Radley Coll.; Downing Coll., Cambridge (MA 1st cl. Law). Called to the Bar, Inner Temple, 1981. *Address:* Brick Court Chambers, 7–8 Essex Street, WC2R 3LD. *T:* (020) 7379 3550. *Club:* Hawks (Cambridge).

POPPLEWELL, Sir Oliver (Bury), Kt 1983; Judge of the High Court of Justice, Queen's Bench Division, 1983–99; *b* 15 Aug. 1927; *s* of late Frank and Nina Popplewell; *m* 1954, Catharine Margaret Storey (*d* 2001); four *s* (and one *s* decd). *Educ:* Charterhouse (Schol.); Queens' Coll., Cambridge (Class. exhibnr; BA 1950; LLB 1951; MA). FCIArb 1996. CUCC, 1949–51. Called to the Bar, Inner Temple, 1951, Bencher, 1978; QC 1969; Chartered Arbitrator; Accredited Mediator, 2000. Recorder, Burton-on-Trent, 1970–71; Dep. Chm., Oxon QS, 1970–71; a Recorder of the Crown Court, 1972–82. Indep. Mem., Wages Councils, 1962–82, Chm. 1973–82; Mem., Home Office Adv. Bd on Restricted Patients, 1981–82; Vice-Chm., Parole Bd, 1986–87 (Mem., 1985–87); Mem., Parole Review Cttee, 1987–88; Pres., Employment Appeal Tribunal, 1986–88 (Mem., 1984–85); Mem., London Court of Internat. Arbitration, 2000–. Chairman: Inquiry into Crowd Safety and Control at sports grounds, 1985–86; Sports Dispute Panel, 2000–; English Rep., ICC Commn into Corruption, 1999; Mem., Ct of Arbitration for Sport, 2000–. MCC: Mem. Cttee, 1971–74, 1976–79, 1980–97; Trustee, 1983–94; Pres., 1994–96. Gov., Sutton's Hosp. in Charterhouse, 1986–88. Trustee, Bletchley Park Trust, 1999–. *Recreations:* sailing, cricket, tennis. *Address:* Lime Tree Farm, Chartridge, Chesham, Bucks HP5 2TT. *Clubs:* Garrick, MCC; Hawks (Cambridge); Blakeney Sailing.

See also A. J. Popplewell.

PORCHESTER, Lord; George Kenneth Oliver Molyneux Herbert; *b* 13 Oct. 1992; *s* and *heir* of Earl of Carnarvon, *qv*.

PORRITT, Hon. Sir Jonathon (Espie), 2nd Bt *cr* 1963, of Hampstead, co. London; CBE 2000; freelance writer and broadcaster; Chairman, Sustainable Development Commission, since 2000; Director, Forum for the Future, since 1996; *b* 6 July 1950; *s* of Baron Porritt, GCMG, GCVO, CBE and Kathleen Mary (*d* 1998), 2nd *d* of A. S. Peck; *S* to Btcy of father, 1994; *m* 1986, Sarah Staniforth, *qv*; two *d*. *Educ:* Eton; Magdalen Coll., Oxford (BA (First Cl.) Modern Languages). ILEA Teacher, 1975–84: Head of English and Drama, Burlington Danes School, W12, 1980–84; Dir, Friends of The Earth, 1984–90. Presenter, Where on earth are we going?, BBC TV, 1990. Ecology Party: candidate: General Elections, 79 and 1983; European Elections, 1979 and 1984; Local Elections, 1977, 1978, 1982; Party Council Member, 1978–80, 1982–84; Chairman, 1979–80, 1982–84. *Publications:* Seeing Green—the Politics of Ecology, 1984; Friends of the Earth Handbook, 1987; The Coming of the Greens, 1988; Where on Earth are We Going?, 1991; (ed) Save the Earth, 1991; Captain Eco (for children), 1991. *Recreation:* walking. *Heir: b* Hon. Jeremy Charles Porritt [*b* 19 Jan. 1953; m 1980, Penny, *d* of J. H. Moore; two *s*]. *Address:* 9 Lypiatt Terrace, Cheltenham, Glos GL50 2SX.

PORRITT, Sarah Elizabeth, (Hon. Lady Porritt); *see* Staniforth, S. E.

PORT ELIZABETH, Bishop of, since 1993; **Rt Rev. Eric Pike;** *b* 11 Nov. 1936; *s* of Eric and Elizabeth Pike; *m* 1st, 1963, Wendy Anne Walker; one *s* one *d*; 2nd, 1977, Joyce Davidson; two step *s* three step *d*. *Educ:* Graaff Reinet Teachers' Training Coll. (Primary Teachers Cert. 1957); St Paul's Theol Coll., Grahamstown (DipTh 1968). Worked in Govt Service, Transkei, SA, 1955; taught at Queen's Coll. Boys' High Sch., 1958–65; ordained deacon, 1968, priest, 1969; Asst Priest, St John's, E London, 1969–71; Rector: St Paul's, Komga, 1971–72; St Mark's, E London, 1972–77; Archdeacon of E London and Operation Outreach, 1978–87; Rector, St Alban's, E London, 1987–89; Suffragan Bishop of Grahamstown, 1989–93. *Recreations:* jogging, walking, gardening, bird watching. *Address:* PO Box 7109, Newton Park, Port Elizabeth 6055, South Africa. *T:* (41) 3651387, *Fax:* (41) 3652049; *e-mail:* epike@iafrica.com.

PORTAL, Sir Jonathan (Francis), 6th Bt *cr* 1901; FCA; freelance accountant, since 1993; *b* 13 Jan. 1953; *s* of Sir Francis Spencer Portal, 5th Bt, and of Jane Mary, *d* of late Albert Henry Williams, OBE; *S* father, 1984; *m* 1982, Louisa Caroline, *er d* of Sir John Hervey-Bathurst, Bt, *qv*; three *s*. *Educ:* Marlborough; Univ. of Edinburgh (BCom). FCA (ACA 1977). Gp Financial Controller, Henderson Admin, 1989–91; Finance Dir, Grosvenor Ventures Ltd, 1992–93. Mem., Clothworkers' Co. *Heir: s* William Jonathan Francis Portal, *b* 1 Jan. 1987. *Address:* Burley Wood, Ashe, Basingstoke, Hants RG25 3AG.

PORTARLINGTON, 7th Earl of, *cr* 1785; **George Lionel Yuill Seymour Dawson-Damer;** Baron Dawson 1770; Viscount Carlow 1776; *b* 10 Aug. 1938; *er s* of Air Commodore Viscount Carlow (killed on active service, 1944) and Peggy (who *m* 2nd, 1945, Peter Nugent; she *d* 1963), *yr d* of late Charles Cambie; *S* grandfather, 1959; *m* 1961, Davina, *e d* of Sir Edward Windley, KCMG, KCVO; three *s* one *d*. *Educ:* Eton. Page of Honour to the Queen, 1953–55. Director: G. S. Yuill & Co. Ltd, Sydney, 1964; Australian Stock Breeders Co. Ltd, Brisbane, 1966; Clyde Agriculture Ltd, Sydney, 1994–; Scottish Mortgage and Trust plc, Edinburgh, 1997–. *Heir: s* Viscount Carlow, *qv*. *Recreations:* fishing, ski-ing, books. *Address:* Gledswood, Melrose, Roxburghshire TD6 9DN. *T:* (01896) 822558, *Fax:* (01896) 823324; 118 Wolseley Road, Point Piper, NSW 2027, Australia, *T:* (2) 93639725, *Fax:* (2) 93274691. *Clubs:* Union, Australian (Sydney); Royal Sydney Golf.

PORTEN, Anthony Ralph; QC 1988; a Recorder, since 1993; *b* 1 March 1947; *s* of late Ralph Charles Porten and of Joan Porten (*née* Edden); *m* 1970, Kathryn Mary (*née* Edwards); two *d*. *Educ:* Epsom Coll.; Emmanuel Coll., Cambridge (BA; Athletics Blue, 1967). Called to the Bar, Inner Temple, 1969; joined Lincoln's Inn (*ad eund.*), 1973. Practising mainly in town and country planning and local government work. Fellow, Soc. for Advanced Legal Studies, 1999. *Address:* Clive Cottage, Claremont Drive, Esher, Surrey KT10 9LU. *T:* (01372) 467513; 2–3 Gray's Inn Square, WC1R 5JH. *T:* (020) 7242 4986. *Clubs:* Royal Automobile; Hawks (Cambridge).

PORTEOUS, Christopher, MA; Headmaster of Eltham College, 1959–83; *b* 2 April 1921; *e s* of late Rev. Gilbert Porteous; *m* 1944, Amy Clunis, *d* of Theodore J. Biggs; one *s* three *d*. *Educ:* Nottingham High Sch. (Foundation Scholar); Emmanuel Coll., Cambridge (Senior Scholar). First Classes, with distinction, in Classical Tripos. Master of Classical Sixth, Mill Hill Sch., 1947–55; Asst Director, HM Civil Service Commission, 1955–59. Mem., Admiralty Interview Bd, 1975–94. *Publication:* Eltham College, Past and Present, 1992. *Recreations:* grandchildren, growing unusual trees, travel. *Address:* Little Thatch, Edwardstone, Sudbury, Suffolk CO10 5PR.

PORTEOUS, Christopher Selwyn, CBE 1993; Solicitor to Commissioner of Police for the Metropolis, 1987–95; *b* 8 Nov. 1935; *s* of Selwyn Berkeley Porteous (*né* Potous) and Marjorie Irene Porteous; *m* 1960, Brenda Jacqueline Wallis; four *d*. *Educ:* Dulwich Coll.; Law Society Sch. of Law. Articled to Clerk to Malling RDC, 1954–60; qual. as solicitor, 1960; LCC, 1960–62; Legal Asst with Scotland Yard, 1962–68; Sen. Legal Asst, 1968–76; Asst Solicitor, 1976–87. Pres., Assoc. of Police Lawyers, 1995–98; Mem., Solicitors European Gp, 1991–96. Anglican Reader, 1958–; Mem., Pastoral Cttee, Rochester Dio., 1984–88. Hon. Mem., ACPO, 1995. *Recreations:* reading, poetry, hymn writing, walking, local history. *Address:* c/o Winckworth Sherwood, 35 Great Peter Street, SW1P 3LR. *T:* (020) 7593 5000.

PORTEOUS, James; DL; FREng, FIEE; Chairman and Chief Executive, Yorkshire Electricity Group plc, 1990–92; *b* 29 Dec. 1926; *e s* of James and Isabella Porteous; *m* 1960, Sheila Beatrice (*née* Klotz); two *d*. *Educ:* Jarrow Grammar School; King's College, Durham University (BSc Hons). FREng (FEng 1986). NESCo Ltd, NE Electricity Bd, NE Div., BEA, 1945–62; Central Electricity Generating Board: Operations Dept, HQ, 1962–66; System Op. Eng., Midlands Region, 1966–70; Dir, Operational Planning, SE Region, 1970–72; NE Region, 1972–75; Dir-Gen., Midlands Region, 1975–84; Chm., Yorks Electricity Bd, 1984–90. Mem., Electricity Council, 1984–90; Director: Electricity Association Ltd, 1990–92; National Grid Company (Holdings) plc, 1990–92. Chm., BR (Eastern) Board, 1990–92 (Mem., 1986–90); Mem., E Midlands Economic Planning Council, 1976–79. Director: Peter Peregrinus Ltd, 1981–92, 1993–96; Merz and McLellan Ltd, 1992–96; Parsons Brinckerhoff Ltd, 1995–98; Nuclear Generation Decommissioning Fund Ltd, 1996–; PB Power Ltd, 1998–. Vice-Pres., IEE, 1992–93 (Hon. FIEE 1997). National Vice-President: Opportunities for People with Disabilities, 1990–92; Neighbourhood Energy Action, 1992–. Hon. DSc Aston, 1990; Hon. DEng Bradford, 1991. DL N Yorks, 1991. *Recreations:* highland life, railways. *Club:* Caledonian.

PORTEOUS, Rev. Prof. Norman Walker, MA Edinburgh et Oxon, BD Edinburgh, DD St Andrews; Professor Emeritus, University of Edinburgh, since 1968; *b* Haddington, 9 Sept. 1898; *yr s* of late John Dow Porteous, MA, formerly Rector of Knox Memorial Inst, Haddington, and Agnes Paton Walker; *m* 1929, May Hadwen (*d* 1981), *y d* of late John Cook Robertson, Kirkcaldy; three *s* three *d*. *Educ:* Knox Memorial Institute, Haddington; Universities of Edinburgh, Oxford (Trinity College), Berlin, Tübingen and Münster; New Coll., Edinburgh. MA Edinburgh with 1st Class Honours in Classics; MA Oxon with 1st Class in Literæ Humaniores; BD Edinburgh with distinction in Old Testament; 1st Bursar at Edinburgh University, 1916; C. B. Black Scholar in New Testament Greek, 1920; John Edward Baxter Scholar in Classics, 1923; Ferguson Scholar in Classics, 1923; Senior Cunningham Fellow at New College and Kerr Travelling Scholar, 1927; served in army, 1917–19, commissioned 2nd Lieut, March 1918, served overseas with 13th Royal Scots; Ordained to Ministry of United Free Church of Scotland, 1929; Minister of Crossgates Church, Church of Scotland, 1929–31; Regius Professor of Hebrew and Oriental Languages in the University of St Andrews, 1931–35; University of Edinburgh: Professor of Old Testament Language, Literature and Theology, 1935–37; Prof. of Hebrew and Semitic Languages, 1937–68; Principal of New Coll., and Dean of Faculty of Divinity, 1964–68; retd, 1968. Hon. DD St Andrews, 1944; Lectures: Stone, Princeton Theological Seminary, 1953; Montague Burton, Leeds, 1974. President, Soc. for Old Testament Study, 1954. *Publications:* Das Alte Testament Deutsch 23: Das Danielbuch, 1962, 4th edn 1985 (English edition, 1965, 2nd, 1979); Living the Mystery: Collected Essays, 1967; Old Testament and History, 5 lectures in Annual of Swedish Theological Inst., vol. VIII, 1970–71; contributions to: Theologische Aufsätze Karl Barth zum 50 Geburtstag, 1936; Record and Revelation, 1938; The Old Testament and Modern Study, 1951; Peake's Commentary on the Bible, 1962. *Address:* 3 Hermitage Gardens, Edinburgh EH10 6DL. *T:* (0131) 447 4632.

PORTER, family name of **Baron Porter of Luddenham.**

PORTER OF LUDDENHAM, Baron *cr* 1990 (Life Peer), of Luddenham in the County of Kent; **George Porter,** OM 1989; Kt 1972; BSc (Leeds); MA, PhD, ScD (Cambridge); FRS 1960; Professor, since 1987, and Chairman of the Centre for Photomolecular Sciences, Imperial College of Science, Technology and Medicine, London, since 1990; Emeritus Professor, Royal Institution, since 1988; *b* 6 Dec. 1920; *m* 1949, Stella Jean Brooke; two *s*. *Educ:* Thorne Grammar Sch.; Leeds Univ.; Emmanuel Coll., Cambridge. Ackroyd Scholar, Leeds Univ., 1938–41. Served RNVR, Radar Officer, in Western Approaches and Mediterranean, 1941–45. Cambridge: Demonstrator in Physical Chemistry, 1949–52, Fellow of Emmanuel Coll., 1952–54; Hon. Fellow, 1967; Asst Director of Research in Physical Chemistry, 1952–54; Asst Director of British Rayon Research Assoc., 1954–55; Prof. of Physical Chemistry, 1955–63, Firth Prof. of Chemistry, 1963–66, Univ. of Sheffield; Resident Prof. and Dir, Royal Institution of Great Britain, 1966–85, Hon. Mem., 1988–. Member: ARC, 1964–66; Adv. Scientific Cttee, Nat. Gall., 1966–68; BBC Sci. Consultative Gp, 1967–75; Open Univ. Council, 1969–75; Science Mus. Adv. Council, 1970–73; Council and Science Bd, SRC, 1976–80; ACOST, 1987–91. Chancellor, Leicester Univ., 1986–95. Trustee, BM, 1972–74. President: Chemical Soc., 1970–72 (Pres. Faraday Div., 1973–74); Comité Internat. de photobiologie, 1968–72; Nat. Assoc. for Gifted Children, 1975–80; R&D Soc., 1977–82; Assoc. for Science Educn, 1985; BAAS, 1985–86; Royal Soc., 1985–90; Internat. Youth Sci. Fortnight, 1987–89; Nat. Energy Foundn, 1990–2000. Counsellor, Inst. for Molecular Sci., Okasaki, Japan, 1980–83. Master, Salters' Co., 1993–94 (Hon. Liveryman, 1981–). Fairchild Scholar, CIT, 1974; Hitchcock Prof., Univ. of Calif at Berkeley, 1978; Gresham Prof. of Astronomy, Gresham Coll., 1990–94. Lectures: Bakerian, 1977, Humphry Davy, 1985, Royal Soc.; Romanes, Oxford, 1978; Robertson Meml, Nat. Acad. of Scis, USA, 1978; Dimbleby, 1988; many other named lectures. Mem., Academia Europaea, 1987; Foreign Associate: Nat. Acad. of Scis; Amer. Acad. of Arts and Scis; Amer. Philos. Soc.; Pontifical Acad.; Japan Acad.; Accad. dei Lincei; Indian Nat. Science Acad.; Indian Acad. of Scis; acads of Madrid, Lisbon, Göttingen, Leopoldina, Hungary and NY; Foreign Mem., USSR Acad. of Sciences, 1988; Hon. Foreign Mem., Korean Acad. of Sci. and Technol., 1995; Hon. Mem., Acad. of Creative Endeavours, Moscow, 1995. Hon. Professor: Univ. of Kent; Beijing Tech. Univ.; Chinese Acad. of Scis; Hon. Fellow: Emmanuel Coll., Cambridge; QMC; Imperial Coll., London; Hon. FKC; Hon. FRSE 1983; Hon. FRSC 1991. Hon. doctorates: Utah, Sheffield, East Anglia, Durham, Leeds, Leicester, Heriot-Watt, City, Manchester, St Andrews, London, Kent, Oxon, Hull, Instituto Quimica de Sarria, Barcelona, Pennsylvania, Coimbra, Lille, Open, Surrey, Bristol, Notre Dame, Reading, Loughborough, Brunel, Bologna, Rio de Janeiro, Philippines, Córdoba, Liverpool, Cambridge (LLD), Central Lancashire, Mangalore, Buckingham, Bath. Royal Society of Chemistry: Corday-Morgan Medal, 1955; Tilden Medal, 1958; Liversidge Medal, 1970; Faraday Medal, 1980; Longstaff Medal, 1981; (jtly) Nobel Prize for Chemistry, 1967; Silvanus Thompson Medal, 1969; Royal Society: Davy Medal, 1971; Rumford Medal, 1978; Michael Faraday Award, 1991; Copley Medal, 1992; Kalinga Prize, UNESCO, 1977; first Porter Medal for photochemistry, Eur., Japanese and Inter-Amer. Photochemical Socs, 1988. *Publications:* Chemistry for the Modern World, 1962; Chemistry in Microtime, 1996; scientific papers in Proc. Royal Society, Trans. Faraday Society, etc. TV Series: Laws of Disorder, 1965–66; Young Scientist of the Year, 1966–81; Time Machines, 1969–70; Controversy, 1971–75; Natural History of a Sunbeam, 1976–77. *Recreation:* sailing. *Address:* Departments of Chemistry and Biochemistry, Imperial College, SW7 2AY.

PORTER, Alastair Robert Wilson, CBE 1985; Secretary and Registrar, Royal College of Veterinary Surgeons, 1966–91, retired; barrister; *b* 28 Sept. 1928; *s* of late James and Olivia Porter (*née* Duncan); *m* 1954, Jennifer Mary Priaulx Forman; two *s* one *d*. *Educ:* Irvine Royal Academy; Glasgow Academy; Merton Coll., Oxford (MA). Called to Bar, Gray's Inn, 1952. Resident Magistrate, N Rhodesia, 1954; Registrar of High Court of N Rhodesia, 1961; Permanent Secretary: Min. of Justice, N Rhodesia, 1964; Min. of Justice, Govt of Republic of Zambia, Oct. 1964. Mem., Fedn (formerly Liaison Cttee) of Veterinarians of the EEC, 1966–86, Sec.-Gen., 1973–79; Chm., EEC's Adv. Cttee on Veterinary Trng, 1986–87 (Vice-Chm., 1981–86). Lectures: Wooldridge Meml, BVA Congress, 1976; MacKellar Meml, Western Counties Veterinary Assoc., Tavistock, 1978; Weipers, Glasgow Univ., 1985; Keith Entwhistle Meml, Cambridge Univ., 1987. Vice-Chm., Haywards Heath Community Forum, 2000–. Hon. Member: BVA, 1978; British Small Animals Vet. Assoc., 1991; Australian Vet. Assoc., 1991; Latvian Vet. Assoc., 1997; Hon. Associate, RCVS, 1979. Pres., Blue Cross, 2000– (Gov., 1991–2000; Chm., Bd of Govs, 1995–98). Hon. DVMS Glasgow, 1994. Centenary Prize, 1981, and Victory Medal, 1991, Central Vet. Soc.; Akademische Ehrenbürger, Hannover Veterinary Sch., 1988. *Publication:* (jtly) An Anatomy of Veterinary Europe, 1972. *Address:* 4 Savill Road, Lindfield, Haywards Heath, West Sussex RH16 2NX. *T:* (01444) 482001.

PORTER, Andrew Brian; Music Critic, Times Literary Supplement, since 1997; *b* 26 Aug. 1928; *s* of Andrew Ferdinand Porter and Vera Sybil (*née* Bloxham). *Educ:* University Coll., Oxford (MA). Music Critic, Financial Times, 1952–72; Editor, Musical Times, 1960–67; Music Critic: New Yorker, 1972–92; The Observer, 1992–97. Vis. Fellow, All Souls Coll., Oxford, 1972–73; Bloch Prof., Univ. of Calif, Berkeley, 1980–81. Corresp. Mem., Amer. Musicol Soc., 1994. *Publications:* A Musical Season, 1974; The Ring of the Nibelung, 1976; Music of Three Seasons, 1978; Music of Three More Seasons, 1981; (ed with D. Rosen) Verdi's Macbeth: a sourcebook, 1984; The Tempest (opera libretto), 1985; Musical Events 1980–1983, 1987; Musical Events 1983–1986, 1989; The Song of Majnun (opera libretto), 1991; A Music Critic Remembers, 2000; many opera translations; contrib. Music & Letters, Musical Qly, etc. *Address:* 9 Pembroke Walk, W8 6PQ.

PORTER, Prof. Andrew Neil, PhD; Rhodes Professor of Imperial History, King's College, London, since 1993; *b* 12 Oct. 1945; *s* of Peter Tozer Porter and Muriel Betty Porter (*née* Luer); *m* 1972, Mary Faulkner; two *s*. *Educ:* Chester Cathedral Choir Sch.; Christ's Hosp., Horsham; St John's Coll., Cambridge (MA, PhD). LRAM. Lectr in History, Univ. of Manchester, 1970–71; King's College, London: Lectr in History, 1971–85; Reader, 1985–90; Head of History Dept, 1988–94 and 2000–01; Prof. of History, 1990–93. Hon. Sec., RHistS, 1986–90 (FRHistS 1980); Convenor, History at Univs Defence Gp, 1992–96 (Mem., Steering Cttee, 1990–99); Chm., Adv. Council (formerly Bd of Mgt), Inst. of Commonwealth Studies, 1994–. Mem. Council, Friends of PRO, 1991–99. FRSA 1998. Editor, Jl of Imperial and Commonwealth History, 1979–90. *Publications:* The Origins of the South African War, 1980; Victorian Shipping, Business and Imperial Policy, 1986; (jtly) British Imperial Policy and Decolonization 1938–64, vol. 1, 1987, vol. 2, 1989; (ed jtly) Money, Finance and Empire 1790–1860, 1985; (ed jtly) Theory and Practice in the History of European Expansion Overseas, 1988; (ed) Atlas of British Overseas Expansion, 1991 (Japanese edn, 1996); European Imperialism 1860–1914, 1994; (ed and contrib.) The Oxford History of the British Empire, Vol. III, The Nineteenth Century, 1999. *Recreations:* playing chamber music, mountain walking, travel. *Address:* 125 South Croxted Road, West Dulwich, SE21 8AX; Department of History, King's College London, Strand, WC2R 2LS. *T:* (020) 7848 1078.

PORTER, Prof. Arthur, OC 1983; MSc, PhD (Manchester); FIEE; FCAE; FRSC 1970; Professor of Industrial Engineering, and Chairman of Department, University of Toronto, Toronto, 1961–76, now Emeritus Professor; President, Arthur Porter Associates Ltd, since 1973; Associate, Institute for Environmental Studies, University of Toronto, since 1981; *b* 8 Dec. 1910; *s* of late John William Porter and Mary Anne Harris; *m* 1941, Phyllis Patricia Dixon; one *s*. *Educ:* The Grammar Sch., Ulverston; University of Manchester. Asst Lecturer, University of Manchester, 1936–37; Commonwealth Fund Fellow, Massachusetts Inst. of Technology, USA, 1937–39; Scientific Officer, Admiralty, 1939–45; Principal Scientific Officer, National Physical Laboratory, 1946; Prof. of Instrument Technology, Royal Military Coll. of Science, 1946–49; Head, Research Division, Ferranti Electric Ltd, Toronto, Canada, 1949–55; Professor of Light Electrical Engineering, Imperial College of Science and Technology, University of London, 1955–58; Dean of the College of Engineering, Saskatchewan Univ., Saskatoon, 1958; Acting Dir, Centre for Culture and Technology, Toronto Univ., 1967–68; Academic Comr, Univ. of W Ontario, 1969–71. Dir and Founding Chm., Scientists and Engineers for Energy and Environment Inc., 1981–84. Chairman: Canadian Environmental Adv. Council, 1972–75; Ontario Royal Commn on Electric Power Planning, 1975–80. *Publications:* An Introduction to Servomechanisms, 1950; Cybernetics Simplified, 1969; Towards a Community University, 1971; articles in Trans. Royal Society, Proc. Royal Society, Phil. Mag., Proc. Inst. Mech. Eng, Proc. IEE, Nature, etc. *Recreations:* tennis, travel, energy conservation. *Address:* 3314 Bermuda Village, Advance, NC 27006–9479, USA. *Club:* Bermuda Run Country (Advance, NC).

PORTER, Arthur Thomas, MRSL 1979; MA, PhD; Pro-Chancellor and Chairman of Court, University of Sierra Leone, Freetown, Sierra Leone, 1992–99 (Vice Chancellor, 1974–84); *b* 26 Jan. 1924; *m* 1953, Dagmar Sondergaard (*née* Rasmussen); one *s* one *d*. *Educ:* Fourah Bay Coll. (BA Dunelm); Cambridge Univ. (BA (Hist Tripos), MA); Boston Univ. (PhD). Asst, Dept of Social Anthropology, Edinburgh Univ., UK, 1951–52. Prof. of History and Head of Dept of Hist., also Dir of Inst. of African Studies, Fourah Bay Coll., 1963–64; Principal, University Coll., Nairobi, Univ. of E Africa, 1964–70; UNESCO Field Staff Officer; Educl Planning Adviser, Min. of Educn, Kenya, 1970–74. Mem. Exec. Bd, UNESCO, 1976–80. Africanus Horton Meml Lectr, Edinburgh Univ., 1983; Fulbright Schol.-in-Residence, Bethany Coll., Kansas, 1986–87. Chm., Bd of Dirs, Sierra Leone Nat. Diamond Mining Co., 1976–85. Hon. LHD Boston 1969; Hon. LLD Royal Univ. of Malta, 1969; Hon. DLitt: Sierra Leone, 1988; Nairobi, 1994. Phi Beta Kappa 1972. Symonds Medal, ACU, 1985. *Publications:* Creoledom, a Study of the Development of Freetown Society, 1963; contribs to The Times, Africa, African Affairs. *Recreation:* photography. *Address:* 85 Marlborough Avenue, Ottawa, ON K1N 8E8, Canada; 81 Fitzjohn Avenue, Barnet, Herts EN5 2HN; 26b Spur Road, Wilberforce, PO Box 1363, Freetown, Sierra Leone, West Africa. *T:* (22) 231736.

PORTER, David John; Director, David Porter Freelance Communications, since 1997; Head of Drama, Kirkley High School, Lowestoft, since 1998; *b* 16 April 1948; *s* of late George Porter and of Margaret Porter; *m* 1978, Sarah Jane Shaw; two *s* two *d*. *Educ:* Lowestoft Grammar School; New College of Speech and Drama, London. Teacher, London, 1970–72; Dir and Co-Founder, Vivid Children's Theatre, 1972–78; Head of Drama, Benjamin Britten High School, Lowestoft, 1978–81; Conservative Party Agent: Eltham, 1982–83; Norwich North, 1983–84; Waveney, 1985–87. MP (C) Waveney, 1987–97; contested (C) same seat, 1997. Member, Select Committee: on Social Security, 1991–92; for Educn, 1992–96; for Educn and Employment, 1996–97. *Recreations:* family, Waveney area—past, present and future. *Address:* 11 Irex Road, Pakefield, Lowestoft, Suffolk NR33 7BU.

PORTER, Henry Christopher Mansel; writer and journalist; London Editor, Vanity Fair, since 1992; *b* 23 March 1953; *s* of Major H. R. M. Porter, MBE and Anne Victoria Porter (*née* Seymour); *m* 1990, Elizabeth Mary Elliot; two *d*. *Educ:* Wellington Coll.; Manchester Univ. (BA Hons). Columnist, Sunday Times, 1982–87; Editor: Illustrated London News, 1987–89; Correspondent Mag., 1989–90; Exec. Ed., Independent on Sunday, 1990–91; contributor, 1991–, to London Evening Standard, Guardian, Observer, Daily Telegraph, Independent on Sunday. *Publications:* Lies, Damned Lies, 1984; *novels:* Remembrance Day, 1999; A Spy's Life, 2001. *Recreations:* painting, fishing, gardening, reading. *Address:* Lloyds Bank, Pershore, Worcs WR10 1BD.

PORTER, Ivor Forsyth, CMG 1963; OBE 1944; HM Diplomatic Service, retired; *b* 12 Nov. 1913; *s* of Herbert and Evelyn Porter; *m* 1951, Ann, *o d* of late Dr John Speares (marr. diss., 1961); *m* 1961, Katerina, *o c* of A. T. Cholerton; one *s* one *d*. *Educ:* Barrow Grammar Sch.; Leeds Univ. (BA, PhD). Lecturer at Bucharest Univ., 1939–40; Temp. Secretary, at Bucharest Legation, 1940–41; Raiding Forces, 1941–45 (Major). Joined Foreign (subseq. Diplomatic) Service, May 1946, as 2nd Secretary in Sen. Branch; 1st Secretary 1948; transferred to Washington, 1951; Foreign Office, 1953; UK Delegation to NATO Paris as Counsellor and Head of Chancery, 1956; Nicosia, 1959 (Deputy Head UK Mission), Deputy High Commissioner, 1961–62, Cyprus; Permanent Rep. to Council of Europe, Strasbourg, 1962–65 (with personal rank of Minister); Dep. High Commissioner, Eastern India, 1965–66; Ambassador, UK Delegn to Geneva Disarmament Conf., 1968–71 (Minister, 1967–68); Ambassador to Senegal, Guinea, Mali and Mauritania, 1971–73; later Dir, Atlantic Region, Research Dept, FCO, retired. *Publications:* (as Ivor Crane) The Think Trap (novel), 1972; Operation Autonomous: with SOE in wartime Roumania, 1989. *Recreations:* writing, walking. *Address:* 17 Redcliffe Road, SW10 9NP. *Clubs:* Travellers, PEN.

PORTER, James Forrest, CBE 1991; Director General (formerly Director) of the Commonwealth Institute, 1978–91; Leverhulme Research Fellow, and Visiting Fellow, London University Institute of Education, since 1991; *b* Frodsham, Cheshire, 2 Oct. 1928; *s* of Ernest Porter and Mary Violetta Porter; *m* 1952, Dymphna, *d* of Leo Francis Powell, London; two *d*. *Educ:* Salford Grammar Sch.; LSE (BSc Sociol.); Univ. of London Inst. of Educn (MA). Asst Master, St George in the East Sec. Sch., Stepney, 1948–50; Leverhulme Scholar, Univ. of London, 1950–55; Lectr in Sociol. and Educn, Worcester Coll., 1955–60; Head of Educn Dept, Chorley Coll., 1960–62; Dep. Principal, Coventry Coll., 1962–67; Principal, Bulmershe Coll. of Higher Educn, Reading, 1967–78. Director: bi-annual internat. courses on teacher educn, Brit. Council, 1975, 1977, 1979, on Museum Educn, 1982; Adult Literacy Support Services Fund, 1977–81. Consultant: Finland, 1976; Unesco, Paris, 1979–; Commonwealth Fellow, Australia, 1977. Chm., Newsconcern Foundn, 1984–91; Member: Nat. Cttee of Inquiry into Teacher Educn and Trng (James Cttee), 1971; Educn Cttee, UGC, 1970–78; Educnl Adv. Council, IBA, 1970–80; Nat. Council for Dance Educn, 1978; Exec. Cttee, Internat. Council of Museums, 1981–87; Educn Council, BBC, 1987–92; President: British Comparative Educn Soc., 1983–84; World Educn Fellowship, 1989– (Chm., 1979–82). Member: UK Delegn to Unesco, Geneva, 1975 (Vice-Pres., Commn on Changing Role of Teacher); Unesco Missions to Morocco and Senegal, 1982, to Jordan, 1983. Mem., Educn Council, Royal Opera House, Covent Garden, 1985–91. Mem., Editorial Bd, Higher Education Review, 1974–; Chm., Editorial Bd, Commonwealth Today, 1985–89 (Mem., 1982). FRSA 1978; Hon. FCP 1978; FRGS 1984. *Publications:* (ed) Rural Development and the Changing Countries of the World, 1969; (with N. Goble) The Changing Role of the Teacher, Paris 1977; Reschooling and the Global Future: politics, economics and the English experience, 1999. *Recreations:* writing, river watching. *Address:* House by the Water, Bolney Avenue, Shiplake, Oxon RG9 3NS; Institute of Education, University of London, 20 Bedford Way, WC1H 0AL.

PORTER, Janet S.; *see* Street-Porter.

PORTER, Air Vice-Marshal John Alan, OBE 1973; CEng, FRAeS, FIEE; Deputy Vice-Chancellor and Professor, University of Glamorgan, 1994–99, now Professor Emeritus; *b* 29 Sept. 1934; *s* of late Alan and Etta Porter; *m* 1961, Sandra Rose (marr. diss.); two *s*. *Educ:* Lawrence Sheriff School, Rugby; Bristol Univ. (BSc); Southampton Univ. (Dip Soton). Commissioned in Engineer Branch, RAF, 1953; appts in UK, USA and Cyprus, 1953–79; Royal College of Defence Studies, 1980; Dep. Gen. Manager, NATO MRCA Develt and Production Agency (NAMMA), Munich, 1981–84; Dir-Gen. Aircraft 2, MoD(PE), 1984–88; Dir-Gen., Communications, Inf. Systems and Orgn (RAF), 1988–89; RAF retd, 1989. Dir, Communications-Electronics Security Gp, 1989–91; Dir, Sci. and Technol., GCHQ, 1991–94. Vis. Fellow, Cranfield Univ., 1994–97. *Recreations:* music, horology. *Address:* University of Glamorgan, Pontypridd, Mid Glam CF37 1DC. *Club:* Royal Air Force.

PORTER, John Andrew, TD; JP; DL; Partner, Porter and Cobb, as Chartered Surveyor, 1940–81; *b* 18 May 1916; *s* of late Horace Augustus Porter, DFC, JP, and Vera Marion Porter; *m* 1941, Margaret Isobel Wisnom; two *d*. *Educ:* Radley Coll.; Sidney Sussex Coll., Cambridge (MA). Commissioned RA, TA, 1938; served War, 1939–46, Lt-Col. Director: Kent County Building Soc., 1947 (Chm., 1965–68); Hastings and Thanet Building Soc., 1968–78 (Chm., 1972–78); Anglia, Hastings and Thanet, later Anglia, Building Soc., 1978–87 (Chm., 1978–81). JP Gravesham PSD, 1952, Chm., Gravesham Div., 1976–83, Dep. Chm., 1983–85. Pres., Gravesend Cons. Assoc., 1965–77. Chm., Bd of Govs, Cobham Hall Sch., 1987–91. General Commissioner of Taxes, 1970–90. DL Kent, 1984. *Recreations:* cricket, reading, golf. *Address:* Leaders, Hodsoll Street, near Wrotham, Kent TN15 7LH. *T:* (01732) 822260. *Clubs:* Royal Automobile, MCC; Hawks (Cambridge); Kent CC (Pres., 1985–86).

PORTER, Sir John Simon H.; *see* Horsbrugh-Porter.

PORTER, Prof. Rev. Canon (Joshua) Roy; Professor of Theology, University of Exeter, 1962–86 (Head of Department, 1962–85), now Professor Emeritus; *b* 7 May 1921; *s* of Joshua Porter and Bessie Evelyn (*née* Earlam). *Educ:* King's Sch., Macclesfield; Merton Coll., Oxford (Exhibnr); S Stephen's House, Oxford. BA: Mod. Hist. (Cl. I), Theology (Cl. I), MA Oxon. Liddon Student, 1942; Deacon 1945, Priest 1946; Curate of S Mary, Portsea, 1945–47; Resident Chaplain to Bp of Chichester, 1947–49; Hon. Chaplain, 1949–50; Examining Chaplain from 1950; Fellow, Chaplain and Lectr, Oriel Coll., Oxford, 1949–62; Tutor, 1950–62; Kennicott Hebrew Fellow, 1955; Sen. Denyer and Johnson Schol., 1958; Select Preacher: Univs of Oxford, 1953–55, Cambridge, 1957, TCD, 1958; Canon and Preb. of Wightring and Theol Lectr in Chichester Cath., 1965–88; Wiccamical Canon and Preb. of Exceit, 1988–; Vis. Prof., Southeastern Seminary, Wake Forest, N Carolina, 1967; Dean of Arts, Univ. of Exeter, 1968–71; Proctor in Convocation of Canterbury for dio. of Exeter, 1964–75; for Other Univs (Canterbury), 1975–90; Examining Chaplain to Bps of Peterborough, 1973–86, of Truro, 1973–81, of London, 1981–91, and of Gibraltar in Europe, 1989–93. Ethel M. Wood Lectr, Univ. of London 1979; Michael Harrah Wood Lectr, Univ. of the South, Sewanee, Tenn, 1984; Lectr in Old Testament Studies, Holyrood Seminary, NY, 1987–95. Member: Gen. Synod, 1970–90 (Panel of Chairmen, 1984–86); ACCM, 1975–86; Council of Management, Coll. of St Mark and St John, 1980–85; Vice-Pres., Folklore Soc., 1979–83 (Pres., 1976–79; Hon. Mem., 1983); President: SOTS, 1983; Anglican Assoc., 1986–2001; Vice-Chm., Prayer Book Soc., 1987–96. FAMS. *Publications:* World in the Heart, 1944; Moses and Monarchy, 1963; The Extended Family in the Old Testament, 1967; Proclamation and Presence, 1970, 2nd rev. edn, 1983; The Non-Juring Bishops, 1973; Leviticus, 1976, Japanese edn 1984; Animals in Folklore, 1978; The Crown and the Church, 1978; Folklore and the Old Testament, 1981; trans. C. Westermann, The Living Psalms, 1989; Synodical Government in the Church of England, 1990; The Illustrated Guide to the Bible, 1995; Jesus Christ: the Jesus of history, the Christ of faith, 1999; The Lost Bible: forgotten scriptures revealed, 2001; *contributor to:* Promise and Fulfilment, 1963; A Source Book of the Bible for Teachers, 1970; The Journey to the Other World, 1975; Tradition and Interpretation, 1979; A Basic Introduction to the Old Testament, 1980; Divination and Oracles, 1981; Folklore Studies in the Twentieth Century, 1981; The Folklore of Ghosts, 1981; Israel's Prophetic Tradition, 1982; Tracts for Our Times, 1983; The Hero in Tradition and Folklore, 1984; Harper's Bible Dictionary, 1985, 2nd edn 1996; Arabia and the Gulf: from traditional society to modern states, 1986; The Seer in Celtic and Other Traditions, 1989; Schöpfung und Befreiung, 1989; A Dictionary of Biblical Interpretation, 1990; Christianity and Conservatism, 1990; The Oil of Gladness, 1993; Boundaries and Thresholds, 1993; The Oxford Companion to the Bible, 1993; World Mythology, 1993; The First and Second Prayer Books of Edward VI, 1999; Dictionary of Biblical Interpretation, 1999; Reconsidering Israel and Judah, 2000; Supernatural Enemies, 2001; numerous articles in learned jls and dictionaries. *Recreations:* theatre and opera, book-collecting, travel. *Address:* 36 Theberton Street, Barnsbury, N1 0QX. *T:* (020) 7354 5861; 68 Sand Street, Longbridge Deverill, near Warminster, Wilts BA12 7DS. *T:* (01985) 840311.

PORTER, Air Marshal Sir Kenneth; *see* Porter, Air Marshal Sir M. K. D.

PORTER, Sir Leslie, Kt 1983; President, Tesco PLC, 1985–90 (Chairman, 1973–85; Deputy Chairman and Managing Director, 1972–73); *b* 10 July 1920; *s* of late Henry Alfred and Jane Porter; *m* 1949, Shirley Cohen (*see* Dame Shirley Porter); one *s* one *d*. *Educ:* Holloway County Sch. Joined family textile business (J. Porter & Co), 1938. Served War: Techn. Quartermaster Sergt, 1st Bn The Rangers, KRRC, in Egypt, Greece, Crete, Libya, Tunisia, Algeria, Italy, 1939–46. Re-joined J. Porter & Co, 1946; became Managing Dir, 1955. Joined Tesco Stores (Holdings) Ltd: Dir, 1959; Asst Managing Dir, 1964; Dep. Chm., 1970. Member of Lloyd's, 1964–. Pres., Inst. of Grocery Distribution, 1977–80. Vice-Pres., NPFA; Chm., Sports Aid Foundn, 1985–88 (Hon. Vice Pres., 1988–). Internat. Vice-Pres., Mus. of the Diaspora, 1984–. Hon. Chm., Bd of Governors, 1989–, Chancellor, 1993–, Tel Aviv Univ.; Hon. PhD (Business Management), Tel Aviv Univ., 1973. OStJ 1992. *Recreations:* golf, yachting, bridge. *Clubs:* City Livery, Rugby; Dyrham Park Country (Barnet, Herts); Tamarisk Country, Mission Hills Country (Calif).

PORTER, Marguerite Ann, (Mrs Nicky Henson); Guest Artist, Royal Ballet Co., since 1986 (Senior Principal Dancer, 1976–85); *b* 30 Nov. 1948; *d* of William Albert and Mary Porter; *m* (marr. diss.); *m* 1986, Nicky Henson, *qv*; one *s*. *Educ:* Doncaster. Joined Royal Ballet School, 1964; graduated to Royal Ballet Co., 1966; soloist, 1972; Principal, 1976; favourite roles include: Juliet in Romeo and Juliet, Manon, Natalia in A Month in the Country; The Queen in Matthew Bourne's Swan Lake, NY, 1999. *Film:* Comrade Lady. *Publication:* Ballerina: a dancer's life, 1989. *Recreations:* my family, friends. *Address:* c/o Richard Stone Partnership, 2 Henrietta Street, WC2E 8PS.

PORTER, Air Marshal Sir (Melvin) Kenneth (Drowley), KCB 1967 (CB 1959); CBE 1945 (OBE 1942); Royal Air Force, retired; *b* 19 Nov. 1912; *s* of late Flt Lieut Edward Ernest Porter, MBE, DCM and late Helen Porter; *m* 1940, Elena (*d* 1993), *d* of F. W. Sinclair; two *s* one *d*. *Educ:* No. 1 School of Technical Training, Halton; RAF Coll., Cranwell. Commissioned, 1932; Army Co-operation Sqdn, Fleet Air Arm, 1933–36, as PO and FO; specialised on Signals, 1936–37, Flt-Lieut; Sqdn Leader, 1939. Served War of 1939–45 (despatches thrice, OBE, CBE, Legion of Merit, USA); Chief Signals Officer, Balloon Command, 1939, Actg Wing Commander; DCSO and CSO, HQ No 11 Group, 1940–42; Temp. Wing Comdr, 1941; CSO HQ No 83 Gp, Temp Gp Captain, 1943; CSO, HQ 2nd TAF, 1943–45; Actg Air Commodore, 1944–45; CSO, HQ Bomber Command, 1945; Air Min. Tech. Plans, 1946–47, Gp Captain, 1946; Member Directing Staff, RAF Staff Coll., Andover, 1947–49; Senior Tech. Staff Officer, HQ No. 205 Group, 1950–52; Comdg Nos 1 and 2 Air Signallers Schools, 1952–54; CSO HQ 2nd ATAF, 1954–55; CSO, HQ Fighter Command, Actg Air Commodore, 1955–58, Air Cdr, 1958; Student Imperial Defence Coll., 1959; Commandant of No 4 School of Technical Training, RAF St Athan, Glamorgan, and Air Officer Wales, 1960–61; Actg Air Vice-Marshal, 1961; Air Vice-Marshal, 1962; Director-General: Ground Training, 1961–63; of Signals (Air), Ministry of Defence, 1964–66; AOC-in-C, Maintenance Command, 1966–70; Hd of RAF Engineer Branch, 1968–70; Actg Air Marshal, 1966; Air Marshal, 1967. Dir of Tech. Educn Projects, UC Cardiff, 1970–74. CEng 1966; FIEE; FRAeS; CIMgt. *Recreations:* reading, writing. *Address:* c/o Lloyds TSB, 163 Whiteladies Road, Clifton, Bristol BS8 2RW.

PORTER, Peter Neville Frederick, FRSL; freelance writer, poet; *b* Brisbane, 16 Feb. 1929; *s* of William Ronald Porter and Marion Main; *m* 1st, 1961, Jannice Henry (*d* 1974); two *d*; 2nd, 1991, Christine Berg. *Educ:* Church of England Grammar Sch., Brisbane; Toowoomba Grammar Sch. Worked as journalist in Brisbane before coming to England in 1951; clerk, bookseller and advertising writer, before becoming full-time poet, journalist, reviewer and broadcaster in 1968. Chief work done in poetry and English literature. Hon. DLitt: Melbourne, 1985; Loughborough, 1987. *Publications:* Once Bitten, Twice Bitten, 1961; Penguin Modern Poets No 2, 1962; Poems, Ancient and Modern, 1964; A Porter Folio, 1969; The Last of England, 1970; Preaching to the Converted, 1972; (trans.) After Martial, 1972; (with Arthur Boyd) Jonah, 1973; (with Arthur Boyd) The Lady and the Unicorn, 1975; Living in a Calm Country, 1975; (jt ed) New Poetry 1, 1975; The Cost of Seriousness, 1978; English Subtitles, 1981; Collected Poems, 1983 (Duff Cooper Prize); Fast Forward, 1984; (with Arthur Boyd) Narcissus, 1985; The Automatic Oracle, 1987 (Whitbread Poetry Award, 1988); (with Arthur Boyd) Mars, 1988; A Porter Selected, 1989; Possible Worlds, 1989; The Chair of Babel, 1992; Millennial Fables, 1995; (ed) Oxford Book of Modern Australian Verse, 1996; (ed jtly) New Writing 5, 1996, 6, 1997; Dragons in their Pleasant Palaces, 1997; Collected Poems 1961–1999, 2 vols, 1999; Saving from the Wreck: essays on poetry, 2001. *Recreations:* buying records and listening to music; travelling in Italy. *Address:* 42 Cleveland Square, W2 6DA. *T:* (020) 7262 4289.

PORTER, Richard Bruce; Executive Director, Sight Savers International, since 1994; *b* 20 Jan. 1942; *s* of Maynard Eustace Prettyman Porter and Irene Marjorie Porter; *m* 1965, Susan Mary Early; two *d*. *Educ:* St Joseph's Coll., Ipswich; City of London Coll. (BSc Econ). Account Supervisor, A. C. Nielsen Co., 1965–70; Divl Manager, Brooke Bond Oxo Ltd, 1970–74; Market Develt Manager, Mackenzie Hill Hldgs, 1974–75; Management Consultant, 1975–79, Sen. Manager and Partner, 1984–94, KPMG Management Consulting; Project Economist, Engineering Science Inc, 1979–84. *Publication:* (jtly) Science Parks and the Growth of High Technology, 1988. *Recreations:* tennis, hockey, reading, bridge, gardening. *Address:* 15 Park Road, Burgess Hill, W Sussex RH15 8EU. *T:* (01444) 232602. *Club:* Royal Over-Seas League.

PORTER, Prof. Robert, AC 2001; DM, FRACMA, FRACP, FAA; Director, Research Development, Faculty of Medicine, Health and Molecular Sciences, James Cook University, Queensland, since 1999 (Planning Dean (Medicine), 1998–99); *b* 10 Sept. 1932; *s* of late William John Porter and Amy Porter (*née* Tottman); *m* 1961, Anne Dorothy Steell; two *s* two *d*. *Educ:* Univ. of Adelaide (BMedSc, DSc); Univ. of Oxford (MA, BCh, DM). Rhodes Scholarship, South Australia, 1954; Radcliffe Travelling Fellowship in Med. Sci., University Coll., Oxford, 1962; Lectr, Univ. Lab. of Physiology, Oxford, 1960–67; Fellow, St Catherine's Coll., and Medical Tutor, Oxford, 1963–67; Prof. of Physiology and Chm., Dept of Physiology, Monash Univ., 1967–79; Howard Florey Prof. of Med. Res., and Dir, John Curtin Sch. of Med. Res., ANU, 1980–89; Dean, Faculty of Medicine, 1989–98, Dep. Vice Chancellor (Res.), 1992–93, Monash Univ. Sen. Fulbright Travelling Fellow and Vis. Prof., Washington Univ. Sch. of Medicine, St Louis, Mo, 1973; Fogarty Scholar-in-Residence, NIH, 1986–87. Member: Bd of Dirs, Alfred Gp of Hosps and Monash Med. Centre, 1989–99; Bd of Govs, Menzies Sch. of Health Res., Darwin, 1985–92; Bd of Management, Baker Med. Res. Inst., 1980–99. Hon. DSc Sydney. *Publications:* (with C. G. Phillips) Corticospinal Neurones: their role in movement, 1977; (with R. N. Lemon) Corticospinal function and voluntary movement, 1993; articles on neurophysiology and control of movement by the brain. *Recreations:* outdoor sports. *Address:* 2 Denison Court, Toomulla Beach, Qld 4816, Australia. *T:* (office) (7) 47816266.

PORTER, Rt Rev. Robert George, OBE 1952; Bishop of The Murray, 1970–89; *b* 7 Jan. 1924; *s* of Herbert James and Eileen Kathleen Porter; *m* 1954, Elizabeth Mary Williams; two *d*. *Educ:* Canterbury Boys' High School; St John's Theological Coll., Morpeth, NSW; Moore College, Sydney (ThL Hons). Served with AIF, 1942–44. Deacon 1947, priest 1948; Assistant Curate, Christ Church Cathedral, Ballarat, Victoria, 1947–49; Assistant Curate, St Paul's, Burwood, Sydney, 1949–50; Priest in charge of Isivita and Agenehambo, Diocese of New Guinea, 1950–57; Archdeacon of Ballarat, 1957–70; Assistant Bishop of Ballarat, 1967–70. KSJ 1992. *Recreations:* gardening, reading.

PORTER, Robert Stanley, CB 1972; OBE 1959; Deputy Secretary (Chief Economist), Overseas Development Administration, Foreign and Commonwealth Office (formerly Ministry of Overseas Development), 1980–84; retired; *b* 17 Sept. 1924; *s* of S. R. Porter; *m* 1st, 1953, Dorothea Naomi (marr. diss. 1967), *d* of Rev. Morris Seale; one *d*; 2nd, 1967, Julia Karen (*d* 1992), *d* of late Edmund A. Davies; 3rd, 1993, Mary Napiorkowska (*née* Woolley). *Educ:* St Clement Danes, Holborn Estate, Grammar Sch.; New Coll., Oxford. Research Economist, US Economic Cooperation Administration Special Mission to the UK, 1949; British Middle East Development Division: Asst Statistical Adviser, Cairo, 1951; Statistical Adviser and Economist, Beirut, 1955; Min. of Overseas Development: Dir, Geographical Div., Economic Planning Staff, 1965; Dep. Dir-Gen. of Economic Planning, 1967; Dir-Gen. of Economic Planning, 1969. Vis. Prof., David Livingstone Inst. for Overseas Develt Studies, 1984–87. *Publications:* articles in Oxford Economic Papers, Kyklos, Review of Income and Wealth, ODI Development Policy Review. *Recreations:* music, theatre. *Address:* Lower Saunders, Cheriton Fitzpaine, Crediton, Devon EX17 4JA. *T:* (01363) 866645. *Club:* Athenæum.

PORTER, Rt Hon. Sir Robert (Wilson), Kt 1971; PC (NI) 1969; QC (NI) 1965; County Court Judge, Northern Ireland, 1978–95; *b* 23 Dec. 1923; *s* of late Joseph Wilson Porter and late Letitia Mary (*née* Wasson); *m* 1953, Margaret Adelaide, *y d* of late F. W. Lynas; one *s* one *d* (and one *d* decd). *Educ:* Model Sch. and Foyle Coll., Londonderry; Queen's Univ., Belfast. RAFVR, 1943–46; Royal Artillery (TA), 1950–56. Foundation Schol., Queen's Univ., 1947 and 1948; LLB 1949. Called to Bar: N Ireland, 1950; Ireland, 1975; Middle Temple, 1988. Lecturer in Contract and Sale of Goods, Queen's Univ., 1950–51; Jun. Crown Counsel, Co. Londonderry, 1960–63, Co. Down, 1964–65; Counsel to Attorney-General for N Ireland, 1963–64 and 1965; Recorder: of Londonderry, 1979–81; of Belfast, 1993–95. Vice-Chairman, 1959–61, Chairman, 1961–66, War Pensions Appeal Tribunal for N Ireland. MP (U) Queen's Univ. of Belfast, 1966–69, Lagan Valley, 1969–73, Parlt of N Ireland; Minister of Health and Social Services, N Ireland, 1969; Parly Sec., Min. of Home Affairs, 1969; Minister of Home Affairs, Govt of NI, 1969–70. Hon. Col, OTC, QUB, 1988–93. *Recreations:* gardening, golf. *Address:* Larch Hill, Church Close, Ballylesson, Belfast, N Ireland BT8 8JX. *Club:* Royal Air Force.

PORTER, Rev. Canon Roy; *see* Porter, Rev. Canon J. R.

PORTER, Prof. Roy Sydney, PhD; FBA 1994; Professor in the Social History of Medicine, Wellcome Institute for the History of Medicine, since 1993; *b* 31 Dec. 1946; *m* 1st, 1970, Susan Limb (marr. diss.); 2nd, 1983, J. Rainfray (marr. diss.); 3rd, 1987, Dorothy Watkins (marr. diss.). *Educ:* Christ's Coll., Cambridge (BA 1968; PhD 1974). Cambridge University: Res. Fellow, Christ's Coll.,1970–72; Fellow and Dir of Studies in History, 1972–79, Dean, 1977–79, Churchill Coll.; Asst Lectr, 1974–77, Lectr, 1977–79, in European Hist.; Sen. Lectr, 1979–91, Reader, 1991–93, Wellcome Inst. Vis. Prof., UCLA, 1988–89; Visiting Fellow: Princeton Univ., 1989; Stanford Univ., 1989. *Publications:* The Making of Geology, 1977; William Hobbs's The Earth Generated and Anatomized, 1981; English Society in the Eighteenth Century, 1982, 2nd edn 1990; (jtly) Documents of the Early Industrial Revolution, 1983; The Earth Sciences: an annotated bibliography, 1983; Mind Forg'd Manacles: madness and psychiatry in England from Restoration to Regency, 1987; Disease, Medicine and Society in England 1550–1860, 1987; A Social History of Madness, 1987; Edward Gibbon: making history, 1988; (jtly) In Sickness and in Health: the British Experience 1650–1850, 1988; Health for Sale: quackery in England 1650–1850, 1989; (jtly) Patient's Progress: doctors and doctoring in eighteenth century England, 1989; (jtly) Exoticism in the Enlightenment, 1990; Doctor of Society: Thomas Beddoes and the sick trade in late Enlightenment England, 1991; (jtly) Consumption and Culture in the Seventeenth and Eighteenth Centuries: a bibliography, 1991; Hysteria Beyond Fraud, 1993; London: a social history, 1994; (jtly) The Facts of Life: the creation of sexual knowledge in Britain 1650–1950, 1995; (ed) The Cambridge Illustrated History of Medicine, 1996; The Greatest Benefit to Mankind: a medical history, 1997; Gout: the patrician malady, 1998; Enlightenment: Britain and the creation of the modern world, 2000 (Wolfson Prize for History, 2001); Bodies Politic: disease, death and doctors in Britain 1650–1900, 2001; also edited and contrib. to many other books. *Address:* The Wellcome Institute for the History of Medicine, 183 Euston Road, NW1 2BE.

PORTER, Sally Curtis; *see* Keeble, S. C.

PORTER, Dame Shirley, (Lady Porter), DBE 1991; Councillor, Hyde Park Ward, 1974–93, Leader, 1983–91, Westminster City Council; Lord Mayor of Westminster, 1991–92; *b* 29 Nov. 1930; *d* of late Sir John (Edward) Cohen and Lady (Sarah) Cohen; *m* 1949, Sir Leslie Porter, *qv*; one *s* one *d*. *Educ:* Warren Sch., Worthing, Sussex; La Ramée, Lausanne, Switzerland. Founded Designers' Guild, 1970; Chairman: Neurotech Medical Systems, 1992–94; LBC, 1992–93; Dir, Capital Radio, 1982–88. Westminster City Council: Conservative Whip, 1974–77; Road Safety Cttee, 1974–82; Member: Co-ordinating Cttee, 1981–82; Chairman: Highways and Works Cttee, 1978–82 (Vice-Chm., 1977–78); Gen. Purposes Cttee, 1982–83; Policy Review Cttee, 1982–83; Policy and Resources Cttee, 1983–91. Chairman: (also Founder), WARS Campaign (Westminster Against Reckless Spending), 1981–84; Cleaner City Campaign, 1979–81; Pres., Eur. Conf. on Tourism and the Envmt, 1992–; Vice-Pres., Cleaner London Campaign, 1979–81; Mem. Exec., Keep Britain Tidy Gp, 1977–81. Pres., British Inst. of Cleaning Science, 1991–; Mem. Ct, Guild of Cleaners, 1976–. Former Dep. Chm., Bd, London Festival Ballet. Trustee, London Philharmonic Trust, 1991–93. Hon. Mem., London Community Cricket Assoc., 1989–. Governor, Tel Aviv Univ., 1982; Internat. Fellow, Porter Sch. of Envmtl Studies, Tel Aviv Univ. JP Inner London, 1972–84; DL Greater London, 1988. FRSA 1989. Hon. PhD Tel Aviv, 1991. *Recreations:* golf, tennis, ballet. *Clubs:* Queen's; Coombe Hill Golf, Dyrham Park Golf.

PORTERFIELD, Dr James Stuart; retired; Reader in Bacteriology, Sir William Dunn School of Pathology, Oxford University, and Senior Research Fellow, Wadham College, Oxford, 1977–89; now Emeritus Fellow; *b* 17 Jan. 1924; *yr s* of late Dr Samuel Porterfield and Mrs Lilian Porterfield, Widnes, Lancs, and Portstewart, Co. Londonderry, NI; *m* 1950, Betty Mary Burch; one *d* (one *s* decd). *Educ:* Wade Deacon Grammar Sch., Widnes; King's Sch., Chester; Liverpool Univ. MB, ChB 1947, MD 1949. Asst Lectr in Bacteriology, Univ. of Liverpool, 1947–49; Bacteriologist and Virologist, Common Cold Res. Unit, Salisbury, Wilts, 1949–51; Pathologist, RAF Inst. of Pathology and Tropical Med., Halton, Aylesbury, Bucks, 1952–53; seconded to W African Council for Med. Res. Labs, Lagos, Nigeria, 1953–57; Mem. Scientific Staff, Nat. Inst. for Med. Res., Mill Hill, 1949–77; WHO Regional Ref. Centre for Arthropod-borne Viruses, 1961–65; WHO Collaborating Lab., 1965–89; Ref. Expert on Arboviruses, Public Health Lab. Service, 1967–76. Chm., Arbovirus Study Gp, Internat. Cttee for Nomenclature of Viruses,

1968–78; Meetings Sec., Soc. for General Microbiology, 1972–77; Vice-Pres., Royal Soc. for Tropical Med. and Hygiene, 1980–81 (Councillor, 1973–76); Secretary and Vice-Pres., Royal Institution, 1973–78. *Publications:* (ed) Andrewes' Viruses of Vertebrates, 5th edn, 1989; (ed) Exotic Viral Infections, 1995; contribs to New DNB, medical and scientific jls. *Recreations:* fell-walking, gardening. *Address:* Green Valleys, Goodleigh, Barnstaple, Devon EX32 7NH.

PORTES, Prof. Richard David, DPhil; Professor of Economics, London Business School, since 1995; President (formerly Director), Centre for Economic Policy Research, since 1983; *b* 10 Dec. 1941; *s* of Herbert Portes and Abra Halperin Portes; *m* 1963, Bobbi Frank; one *s* one *d. Educ:* Yale Univ. (BA 1962 *summa cum laude* maths and philosophy); Balliol and Nuffield Colls, Oxford (Rhodes Schol., Woodrow Wilson Fellow, Danforth Fellow; MA 1965; DPhil 1969). Official Fellow and Tutor in Econs, Balliol Coll., Oxford, 1965–69; Asst Prof. of Econs and Internat. Affairs, Princeton Univ., 1969–72; Prof. of Econs, Birkbeck Coll., Univ. of London, 1972–94 (Head, Dept of Econs, 1975–77 and 1980–83). Dir d'Etudes, Ecole des Hautes Etudes en Sciences Sociales, Paris, 1978–. Guggenheim Fellow, 1977–78; British Acad. Overseas Vis. Fellow, 1977–78; Res. Associate, Nat. Bureau of Econ. Res., Cambridge, Mass, 1980–; Vis. Prof., Harvard Univ., 1977–78; Dist. Global Vis. Prof., Haas Business Sch., Univ. of Calif at Berkeley, 1999–2000. Vice-Chm., Econs Cttee, SSRC, 1981–84. Member: Bd of Dirs, Soc. for Econ. Analysis (Rev. of Econ. Studies), 1967–69, 1972–80 (Sec. 1974–77); RIIA, 1973– (Res. Cttee, 1982–92); Council on Foreign Relations, 1978–; Hon. Degrees Cttee, Univ. of London, 1984–89; Franco-British Council, 1997–; Commn Economique de la Nation, France, 1999–; ALSSS Commn on Social Scis, 2000–. Fellow, Econometric Soc., 1983–; Sec.-Gen., Royal Econ. Soc., 1992– (Mem. Council, 1986–92; Exec. Cttee, 1987–); Council, European Econ. Assoc., 1992–96. Co-Chm., Bd of Governors, and Sen. Editor, Economic Policy, 1985–. Hon. DSc Libre de Bruxelles, 2000; Hon. PhD London Guildhall, 2000. *Publications:* (ed) Planning and Market Relations, 1971; The Polish Crisis, 1981; Deficits and Détente, 1983; (ed) Threats to International Financial Stability, 1987; (ed) Global Macroeconomics: policy conflict and cooperation, 1987; (ed) Blueprints for Exchange Rate Management, 1989; (ed) Macroeconomic Policies in an Interdependent World, 1989; (ed) Economic Transformation in Hungary and Poland, 1990; (ed) External Constraints on Macroeconomic Policy: the experience of Europe, 1991; (ed) The Path of Reform in Central and Eastern Europe, 1991; (ed) Economic Transformation in Central Europe, 1993; (ed) European Union Trade with Eastern Europe, 1995; Crisis? What Crisis? Orderly Workouts for Sovereign Debtors, 1995; contribs to many learned jls. *Recreation:* living beyond my means. *Address:* London Business School, Regent's Park, NW1 4SA. *T:* (020) 7706 6886; *e-mail:* rportes@london.edu. *Club:* Groucho.

PORTILLO, Rt Hon. Michael (Denzil Xavier); PC 1992; MP (C) Kensington and Chelsea, since Nov. 1999; *b* 26 May 1953; *s* of late Luis Gabriel Portillo and of Cora Waldegrave Blyth; *m* 1982, Carolyn Claire Eadie. *Educ:* Harrow County Boys' School; Peterhouse, Cambridge (1st cl. Hons MA History). Ocean Transport & Trading Co., 1975–76; Conservative Res. Dept., 1976–79; Special Advr, Sec. of State for Energy, 1979–81; Kerr McGee Oil (UK) Ltd, 1981–83; Special Adviser: to Sec. of State for Trade and Industry, 1983; to Chancellor of the Exchequer, 1983–84. MP (C) Enfield, Southgate, Dec. 1984–1997; contested (C) same seat, 1997. An Asst Govt Whip, 1986–87; Parly Under Sec. of State, DHSS, 1987–88; Minister of State, Dept of Transport, 1988–90; Minister of State for Local Govt, DoE, 1990–92; Chief Sec. to HM Treasury, 1992–94; Sec. of State for Employment, 1994–95, for Defence, 1995–97; Shadow Chancellor, 2000–01. *Address:* House of Commons, SW1A 0AA. *Club:* Carlton.

PORTLAND, 12th Earl of, *cr* 1689; **Timothy Charles Robert Noel Bentinck;** Viscount Woodstock, Baron Cirencester, 1689; Count of the Holy Roman Empire; actor; *b* 1 June 1953; *s* of 11th Earl of Portland and Pauline (*d* 1967), *y d* of late Frederick William Mellowes; *S* father, 1997; *m* 1979, Judith Ann, *d* of John Robert Emerson; two *s. Educ:* Harrow; Univ. of East Anglia (BA Hons). Trained Bristol Old Vic Theatre Sch. Winner BBC Drama Schs Radio Competition, 1978. London theatre appearances include: Pirates of Penzance, Theatre Royal, Drury Lane, 1982; Reluctant Heroes, Theatre of Comedy, 1984; Hedda Gabler, King's Head Theatre, 1990; A Doll's House, Bridge Lane Theatre, London, 1992; Arcadia, Haymarket, 1994; Night Must Fall, Haymarket, 1996; *radio:* David Archer in The Archers; over 75 plays; *films:* North Sea Hijack, 1979; Pirates of Penzance, 1981; Winter Flight, 1985; Year of the Comet, 1992; Twelfth Night, 1995; Enigma, 2000; *television* includes: By the Sword Divided, 1983; Square Deal, 1989; Made in Heaven, 1990; Sharpe, 1993; Grange Hill, 1994; Strike Force, 1995; Prince Among Men, 1997; composer of theme music for Easy Money, BBC TV, 1984. Inventor of The Hippo (child-carrying device). HGV licence. *Recreations:* songwriting, ski-ing, swimming, house renovation, computer programming. *Heir: s* Viscount Woodstock, *qv.*

PORTMAN, family name of **Viscount Portman.**

PORTMAN, 10th Viscount *cr* 1873; **Christopher Edward Berkeley Portman;** Baron 1837; Chairman, Portman Settled Estates Ltd, since 1998; *b* 30 July 1958; *s* of 9th Viscount Portman and of Rosemary Joy Portman (*née* Farris); *S* father, 1999; *m* 1st, 1983, Caroline Steenson (marr. diss.); one *s*; 2nd, 1987, Patricia Martins Pim; two *s. Educ:* Marlborough Coll. *Recreations:* molecular nanotechnology, computer science, psychology, scuba diving, reading. *Heir: e s* Hon. Luke Oliver Berkeley Portman, *b* 31 Aug. 1984. *Address:* 38 Seymour Street, W1H 7BP. *T:* (020) 7563 1400. *Clubs:* Whites, Home House.

PORTSDOWN, Archdeacon of; *see* Lowson, Ven. C.

PORTSMOUTH, 10th Earl of, *cr* 1743; **Quentin Gerard Carew Wallop;** Viscount Lymington, Baron Wallop, 1720; Hereditary Bailiff of Burley, New Forest; *b* 25 July 1954; *s* of Oliver Kintzing Wallop (Viscount Lymington) (*d* 1984) and Ruth Violet (*d* 1978), *yr d* of Brig.-Gen. G. C. Sladen, CB, CMG, DSO, MC; *S* grandfather, 1984; *m* 1st, 1981, Candia (*née* McWilliam) (marr. diss. 1984); one *s* one *d*; 2nd, 1990, Annabel, *d* of Dr and Mrs Ian Fergusson; one *d. Educ:* Eton; Millfield. Dir, Grainger Trust plc, 1987–. Pres., Basingstoke Cons. Assoc., 1992–. Patron, Hampshire Br., BRCS, 1995–. Gov., Hatch Warren Jun. Sch., Basingstoke, 1997–. Mem., Fishmongers' Co., 1997–. *Heir: s* Viscount Lymington, *qv. Address:* Farleigh House, Farleigh Wallop, Basingstoke, Hants RG25 2HT.

PORTSMOUTH, Bishop of, since 1995; **Rt Rev. Kenneth William Stevenson,** PhD, DD, FRHistS; *b* 9 Nov. 1949; *s* of Frederik Robert and Margrete Stevenson; *m* 1970, Sarah Julia Mary (*née* Glover), one *s* three *d. Educ:* Edinburgh Acad.; Edinburgh Univ. (MA 1970); Southampton Univ. (PhD 1975); Manchester Univ. (DD 1987). FRHistS 1990. Ordained deacon, 1973, priest, 1974; Asst Curate, Grantham with Manthorpe, 1973–76; Lectr, Boston, 1976–80; part-time Lectr, Lincoln Theol Coll., 1975–80; Chaplain and Lectr, Manchester Univ., 1980–86; Team Vicar, 1980–82, Team Rector, 1982–86, Whitworth, Manchester; Rector, Holy Trinity and St Mary's, Guildford, 1986–95. Member: C of E Liturgical Commn, 1986–96; Faith and Order Advisory Gp, 1991–96; C of E Doctrine Commn, 1996–; Chm., Anglo-Nordic-Baltic Theol Conf., 1997– (Sec., 1985–97); Vice-Chm., Porvoo Panel, 1999. Vis. Prof., Univ. of Notre Dame, Indiana, 1983. Entered H of L, 1999. *Publications:* Nuptial Blessing, 1982; Eucharist and Offering, 1986; Jerusalem Revisited, 1988; The First Rites, 1989; Covenant of Grace Renewed, 1994; (with H. R. McAdoo) The Mystery of the Eucharist in the Anglican Tradition, 1995; Handing On, 1996; The Mystery of Baptism in the Anglican Tradition, 1998; All the Company of Heaven, 1998; Abba Father: understanding and using the Lord's Prayer, 2000; (ed jtly) Love's Redeeming Work: The Anglican quest for holiness, 2001; contribs to Scottish Jl of Theology, Ephemerides Liturgicae, Theology, etc. *Recreations:* historical biographies, thrillers, walking, piano, Denmark. *Address:* Bishopsgrove, 26 Osborn Road, Fareham, Hants PO16 7DQ. *T:* (01329) 280247, *Fax:* (01329) 231538; *e-mail:* bishports@clara.co.uk. *Clubs:* Farmers, Nikaean, Nobody's Friends.

PORTSMOUTH, Bishop of, (RC), since 1988; **Rt Rev. (Roger Francis) Crispian Hollis;** *b* 17 Nov. 1936; *s* of Christopher and Madeleine Hollis. *Educ:* Stonyhurst College; Balliol Coll., Oxford (MA); Venerable English College, Rome (STL). National Service as 2nd Lt, Somerset Light Infantry, 1954–56. Ordained priest, 1965; Assistant in Amesbury, 1966–67; RC Chaplain, Oxford Univ., 1967–77; RC Assistant to Head of Religious Broadcasting, BBC, 1977–81; Administrator, Clifton Cathedral, Bristol, 1981–87; Auxiliary Bishop of Birmingham (Bishop in Oxfordshire), 1987–88. *Recreations:* occasional golf, walking, cricket watching. *Address:* Bishop's House, Edinburgh Road, Portsmouth PO1 3HG.

PORTSMOUTH, Dean of; *see* Taylor, Very Rev. W. H.

POSKITT, Prof. Trevor John, DSc, PhD; consultant engineer, retired; Professor of Civil Engineering, Queen Mary and Westfield College (formerly Queen Mary College), University of London, 1972–94; *b* 26 May 1934; *s* of late William Albert Poskitt, Worthing, and Mrs D. M. Poskitt, Lincoln; *m* 1968, Gillian Mary, *d* of L. S. Martin, MBE, Romiley, Cheshire; one *s* one *d. Educ:* Corby Technical Sch.; Huddersfield Technical Coll.; Univ. of Leeds; Univ. of Cambridge. HND (Mech. Eng.); BSc Leeds, PhD Cambridge, DSc Manchester; CEng, FICE, FIStructE. Apprentice Engineer to Thos. Broadbent & Sons, Huddersfield, 1949–53; Graduate Assistant, English Electric Co. Ltd, 1958–60; Whitworth Fellow, 1960–63; Lectr, 1963–71, Senior Lectr, 1971–72, in Civil Engineering, Univ. of Manchester. *Publications:* numerous on civil engineering topics. *Recreations:* golf, music. *Address:* Tanglewood, Lunghurst Road, Woldingham, Surrey CR3 7EJ. *T:* (01883) 653101.

POSNANSKY, Jeremy Ross Leon; QC 1994; a Recorder, since 1998; *b* 8 March 1951; *s* of Anthony Posnansky and late Evelyn Davis (formerly Posnansky), JP; *m* 1974, Julia Sadler, *d* of late Richard Sadler, MBE; two *d. Educ:* St Paul's Sch.; Coll. of Law. Called to the Bar, Gray's Inn, 1972, Antigua and Barbuda, 1995; Asst Recorder, 1993–98; a Dep. High Court Judge, 1997–. Mem., Family Courts Business and Service Cttees, Inner London, 1991–94. Fellow, Internat. Acad. of Matrimonial Lawyers, 1996. *Publications:* contrib. Internat. Family Law, Family Law. *Recreations:* scuba diving, travel, computers. *Address:* 1 Mitre Court Buildings, Temple, EC4Y 7BS. *T:* (020) 7797 7070; *e-mail:* jeremy@posnansky.net.

POSNER, Michael Vivian, CBE 1983; Secretary-General, European Science Foundation, 1986–93; *b* 25 Aug. 1931; *s* of Jack Posner; *m* 1953, Rebecca Posner, *qv*; one *s* one *d. Educ:* Whitgift Sch.; Balliol Coll., Oxford. Research Officer, Oxford Inst. of Statistics, 1953–57; University of Cambridge: Asst Lecturer, Lecturer, then Reader in Economics, 1958–79; Fellow, Pembroke Coll., 1960–83; Chm., Faculty Bd of Economics, 1974–75. Visiting Professor: Brookings Instn, Washington, 1971–72; Bristol Univ. Grad. Sch. of Internat. Business, 1996–. Director of Economics, Ministry of Power, 1966–67; Economic Adviser to Treasury, 1967–69; Economic Consultant to Treasury, 1969–71; Consultant to IMF, 1971–72; Energy Adviser, NEDO, 1973–74; Econ. Adviser, Dept of Energy, 1974–75; Dep. Chief Econ. Adviser, HM Treasury, 1975–76. Chm., SSRC, 1979–83; Econ. Dir, NEDO, 1984–86. Member: BRB, 1976–84; Post Office Bd, 1978–79; Member: Adv. Council for Energy Conservation, 1974–82; Standing Commn on Energy and the Environment, 1978–81; a Dir, British Rail, later Railways, Pension Trustee Co., 1986–98. Mem. Council, PSI, 1978–83 (Senior Res. Fellow, 1983–84). DEd (*hc*) CNAA, 1989; Hon. LLD Bristol, 1992. *Publications:* (co-author) Italian Public Enterprise, 1966; Fuel Policy: a study in applied economics, 1973; (ed) Resource Allocation in the Public Sector, 1977; (ed) Demand Management, 1978; (co-author) Energy Economics, 1981; (ed) Problems of International Money 1972–1985, 1986; books and articles on economics. *Recreation:* country life. *Address:* Rushwood, Jack Straw's Lane, Oxford OX3 0DN. *T:* (01865) 763578. *Club:* Oxford and Cambridge.

POSNER, Prof. Rebecca; Professor of the Romance Languages, University of Oxford, 1978–96, now Emeritus; Fellow, St Hugh's College, Oxford, 1978–96, Hon. Fellow, 1996; Research Associate, Oxford University Centre for Linguistics and Philology, since 1996; *b* 17 Aug. 1929; *d* of William and Rebecca Reynolds; *m* 1953, Michael Vivian Posner, *qv*; one *s* one *d. Educ:* Somerville Coll., Oxford. MA, DPhil (Oxon); PhD (Cantab). Fellow, Girton Coll., Cambridge, 1960–63; Prof. of French Studies, Univ. of Ghana, 1963–65; Reader in Language, Univ. of York, 1965–78. Vis. Prof. of Romance Philology, Columbia Univ., NY, 1971–72; Vis. Senior Fellow, Princeton Univ., 1983; Emeritus Leverhulme Fellow, 1997. Vice-Pres., Philological Soc., 2000– (Pres., 1996–2000). *Publications:* Consonantal Dissimilation in the Romance Languages, 1961; The Romance Languages, 1966; (with J. Orr and I. Iordan) Introduction to Romance Linguistics, 1970; (ed with J. N. Green) Trends in Romance Linguistics and Philology: vol. 1, Romance Comparative and Historical Linguistics, 1980; vol. 2, Synchronic Romance Linguistics, 1981; vol. 3, Language and Philology in Romance, 1982; vol. 4, National and Regional Trends in Romance Linguistics and Philology, 1982; vol. 5, Bilingualism and Conflict in Romance, 1993; (contrib.) Legacy of Latin, ed R. Jenkyns, 1992; The Romance Languages, 1996 (trans. Spanish 1998); Linguistic Change in French, 1997; numerous articles. *Recreations:* walking, gardening, theatre, music. *Address:* St Hugh's College, Oxford OX2 6LE; Rushwood, Jack Straw's Lane, Oxford OX3 0DN. *T:* (01865) 763578.

POSNETT, Sir Richard (Neil), KBE 1980 (OBE 1963); CMG 1976; HM Diplomatic Service, retired; *b* 19 July 1919; *s* of Rev. Charles Walker Posnett, K-i-H, Medak, S India, and Phyllis (*née* Barker); *m* 1st; two *s* one *d*; 2nd, 1959, Shirley Margaret Hudson; two *s* one *d. Educ:* Kingswood; St John's Coll., Cambridge (won 120 yards hurdles for Cambridge *v* Oxford, 1940). BA 1940, MA 1947. Called to the Bar, Gray's Inn, 1951. HM Colonial Administrative Service in Uganda, 1941; Chm., Uganda Olympic Cttee, 1956; Colonial Office, London, 1958; Judicial Adviser, Buganda, 1960; Perm. Sec. for External Affairs, Uganda, 1962; Perm. Sec. for Trade and Industry, 1963; joined Foreign (subseq. Diplomatic) Service, 1964; FO, 1964; served on UK Mission to UN, NY, 1966–70; briefly HM Comr in Anguilla, 1969; Head of W Indian Dept, FCO, 1970–71; Governor and C-in-C of Belize, 1972–76; Special Mission to Ocean Island, 1977; Dependent Territories Adviser, FCO, 1977–79; British High Comr, Kampala, 1979. UK Comr, British Phosphate Comrs, 1978–81. Governor and C-in-C, Bermuda, 1981–83. Mem., Lord Chancellor's Panel of Ind. Inspectors, 1983–89. First ascent of South Portal Peak on Ruwenzori, 1942. Member: RIIA; Royal Forestry Soc.; Royal African Soc.

President: Kingswood Assoc., 1980; Godalming Joigny Friendship Assoc., 1987– (Chm., 1984–87). Gov., Kingswood Sch., 1985–93. KStJ 1972. *Publications:* (contrib.) Looking Back at the Uganda Protectorate, 1996; The Scent of Eucalyptus (autobiog.), 2001; articles in Uganda Journal, World Today. *Recreations:* ski-ing, golf, trees. *Address:* Bahati, Old Kiln Close, Churt, Surrey GU10 2JH. *Clubs:* Royal Commonwealth Society, Achilles; Hankley Common Golf; Privateers Hockey.

POSNETTE, Prof. Adrian Frank, CBE 1976; FRS 1971; VMH 1982; Director, East Malling Research Station, Kent, 1972–79 (Deputy Director, 1969–72, and Head of Plant Pathology Section, 1957–72); *b* 11 Jan. 1914; *e s* of late Frank William Posnette and Edith (*née* Webber), Cheltenham; *m* 1937, Isabelle, *d* of Dr Montgomery La Roche, New York; one *s* two *d*. *Educ:* Cheltenham Grammar Sch.; Christ's Coll., Cambridge. MA, ScD Cantab; PhD London; AICTA Trinidad; FIBiol. Research at Imperial Coll. of Tropical Agriculture, Trinidad, 1936–37; Colonial Agric. Service, Gold Coast, 1937; Head of Botany and Plant Pathology Dept, W African Cacao Research Inst., 1944; research at East Malling Research Stn, 1949–. Vis. Prof. in Plant Sciences, Wye Coll., Univ. of London, 1971–78. *Publications:* Virus Diseases of Apples and Pears, 1963; numerous research papers in Annals of Applied Biology, Jl of Horticultural Science, Nature, Tropical Agriculture. *Recreations:* ornithology, sailing, gardening. *Address:* Gwyn, Sutton Valence, Maidstone, Kent ME17 3AD. *T:* (01622) 843234. *Club:* Hawks (Cambridge).

POST, Herschel; International Managing Director, Business Development, Christie's International plc, since 2000; *b* 9 Oct. 1939; *s* of Herschel E. and Marie C. Post; *m* 1963, Peggy Mayne; one *s* three *d*. *Educ:* Yale Univ. (AB); Oxford Univ. (BA, MA); Harvard Law Sch. (LLB). Associate, Davis Polk & Wardwell, attorneys, 1966–69; Exec. Dir, Parks Council of NY, 1969–72; Dep. Adminr and Comr, Parks, Recreation and Cultural Affairs Admin, NYC, 1973; Vice-Pres., Morgan Guaranty Trust Co., 1974–83; Mem., Bd of Dirs, 1988–95, Dep. Chm., 1989–95, Internat. Stock Exchange, subseq. London Stock Exchange; Chief Operating Officer, Lehman Brothers Internat. (Europe) and Lehman Brothers Securities Ltd, 1990–94; Chief Operating Officer, 1994–95, Chief Exec. and Dep. Chm., 1995–2000, Coutts & Co. President: Shearson Lehman Global Asset Management, 1984–90; Posthorn Global Asset Management, 1984–90; Director: Euroclear Clearance Systems plc, 1992–; Investors Capital Trust plc, 1999–. Chm., Woodcock Foundn (US), 2000–; Trustee: Earthwatch Europe, 1988– (Chm., 1997–); Monteverdi Trust, 1997–. *Address:* Christie's International plc, 8 King Street, St James's, SW1Y 6QT. *Clubs:* Athenæum, Vanderbilt Racquet.

POST, Martin Richard, MA; Headmaster, Watford Grammar School for Boys, since 2000; *b* 3 Sept. 1958; *s* of Kenneth and Barbara Post; *m* 1999, Kate Watts. *Educ:* Univ. of York (BA Eng. and Related Lit.); MA Educnl Mgt Open Univ. King's Sch., Rochester, 1982–84; Darwin Coll., Cambridge, 1984–85; Mill Hill Co. High Sch., 1985–89; Richard Hale Sch., 1989–95; Dep. Head (Pastoral and Finance), Watford GS for Boys, 1995–2000. *Recreations:* sports, reading, theatre. *Address:* Watford Grammar School for Boys, Rickmansworth Road, Watford, Herts WD18 7JF. *T:* (01923) 208900.

POSTE, Dr George (Henry), CBE 1999; FRCPath, FMedSci; FRS 1997; FRCVS; Chief Executive Officer, Health Technology Networks, since 2000; *b* 30 April 1944; *s* of late John H. Poste and of Kathleen B. Poste; *m* 1992, Linda Suhler; one *s* two *d*. *Educ:* Bristol Univ. (BVSc 1st. cl. hons 1966; PhD Virology 1969). FRCVS 1987; FRCPath 1989; FIBiol 1998. Lectr, RPMS, Univ. of London, 1969–72; Prof. of Experimental Pathology, SUNY, 1972–80; SmithKline Beckman, then SmithKline Beecham: Vice Pres., R&D, 1980–88; Pres., R&D Technologies, 1989–90; Vice Chm. and Exec. Vice Pres., R&D, 1990–91; Dir, 1992–99; Pres., R&D, 1992–97; Chief Sci. and Technol. Officer, 1997–99. Partner, Care Capital, Princeton, 2000–; Non-executive Chairman: diaDexus, 1997–; Structural Genomi X, 2000–; Illumina Maxygen and Orchid Bioscis. Pitt Fellow, Pembroke Coll., Cambridge, 1995–; Fellow, Hoover Inst., Stanford Univ., 2000–. Member: Human Genetics Adv. Cttee, 1996–99; US Defense Sci. Bd, 2000–. Governor, Center for Molecular Medicine and Genetics, Stanford Univ., 1992–. Founder FMedSci 1998. Hon. FRCP 1993; Hon. FRVC 2000. Hon. Fellow, UCL, 1999. Hon DSc 1987, Hon. LLD 1995, Bristol; Hon. LLD Dundee, 1998; Hon. DSc Sussex, 1999. *Publications:* joint ed. of fifteen books; numerous reviews and papers in learned jls; column in FT. *Recreations:* automobile racing, military history, photography, helicopter piloting, exploring the deserts of American Southwest. *Address:* Health Technology Networks, 2338 Casmar Way, Gilbertsville, PA 19525, USA. *T:* (610) 7050828, *Fax:* (610) 7050810; *e-mail:* gposte@healthtechnetwork.com. *Clubs:* Athenæum; Union League (Philadelphia).

POSTGATE, Prof. (John) Nicholas, FBA 1993; Professor of Assyriology, University of Cambridge, since 1994; Fellow, Trinity College, Cambridge, since 1982; *b* 5 Nov. 1945; *s* of Ormond Oliver Postgate and Patricia Mary Postgate (*née* Peet); *m* 1st, 1968, Carolyn June Prater (marr. diss. 1999); one *s* one *d*; 2nd, 1999, Sarah Helen Blakeney; one *s*. *Educ:* Winchester Coll.; Trinity Coll., Cambridge (BA Oriental Studies 1967; MA 1970). Lectr in Akkadian, SOAS, 1967–71; Fellow, Trinity Coll., Cambridge, 1970–74; Asst Dir, British Sch. of Archaeology, Iraq, 1971–75; Dir, British Archaeol. Expedn to Iraq, 1975–81; Lectr in Hist. and Archaeol. of Ancient Near East, 1981–85, Reader in Mesopotamian Studies, 1985–94, Univ. of Cambridge. Director of excavations: Abu Salabikh, S Iraq, 1975–89; Kilise Tepe, S Turkey, 1994–99. *Publications:* Neo-Assyrian Royal Grants and Decrees, 1969; The Governor's Palace Archive, 1973; Taxation and Conscription in the Assyrian Empire, 1974; Fifty Neo-Assyrian Legal Documents, 1976; The First Empires, 1977; (ed) Abu Salabikh Excavations, vols 1–4, 1983–93; (with S. M. Dalley) Tablets from Fort Shalmaneser, 1984; The archive of Urad-Šerua and his family, 1988; Early Mesopotamia: society and economy at the dawn of history, 1992; (with F. M. Fales) Imperial administrative records, pt I 1992, pt II 1995; (with B. K. Ismail) Texts from Niniveh, 1993; (ed jtly) Concise Dictionary of Akkadian, 1999; articles in Iraq and other learned jls. *Address:* Trinity College, Cambridge CB2 1TQ. *T:* (01223) 338443.

POSTGATE, Prof. John Raymond, FRS 1977; FIBiol; Director, AFRC Unit of Nitrogen Fixation, 1980–87 (Assistant Director, 1963–80), and Professor of Microbiology, University of Sussex, 1965–87, now Emeritus; *b* 24 June 1922; *s* of Raymond William Postgate and Daisy Postgate (*née* Lansbury); *m* 1948, Mary Stewart; three *d*. *Educ:* principally Woodstock Sch., Golders Green; Kingsbury County Sch., Mddx; Balliol Coll., Oxford. BA, MA, DPhil, DSc. Research in chemical microbiology: with D. D. Woods on action of sulfonamide drugs, 1946–48, with K. R. Butlin on sulphate-reducing bacteria, 1948–59. Research on bacterial death, 1959–63, incl. Visiting Professor: Univ. of Illinois, 1962–63, working on sulphate-reducing bacteria; Oregon State Univ., 1977–78. President: Inst. of Biology, 1982–84; Soc. for Gen. Microbiology, 1984–87. Hon. DSc Bath, 1990; Hon. LLD Dundee, 1997. *Publications:* Microbes and Man, 1969, 4th edn 2000; Biological Nitrogen Fixation, 1972; A Plain Man's Guide to Jazz, 1973; Nitrogen Fixation, 1978, 3rd edn 1998; The Sulphate-Reducing Bacteria, 1979, 2nd edn 1984; The Fundamentals of Nitrogen Fixation, 1982; The Outer Reaches of Life, 1994; (with Mary Postgate) A Stomach for Dissent: the life of Raymond Postgate, 1994; Lethal Lozenges and Tainted Tea: a biography of John Postgate (1820–1881), 2001; ed, 4 scientific symposia; regular columnist in Jazz Monthly, 1952–72; numerous scientific papers in microbiol/biochem. jls; many jazz record reviews in specialist magazines; articles on jazz. *Recreations:* listening to jazz and attempting to play it. *Address:* 1 Houndean Rise, Lewes, Sussex BN7 1EG. *T:* (01273) 472675.

POSTGATE, Nicholas; *see* Postgate, J. N.

POSTLETHWAITE, Peter; actor; *b* 16 Feb. 1945; partner, Jacqueline Morrish; one *s* one *d*. *Educ:* Bristol Old Vic Theatre Sch. *Stage* includes: Troilus and Cressida, Bristol Old Vic; Royal Shakespeare Company: Richard III; Cyrano de Bergerac; King Lear; Fair Maid of the West; a Midsummer Night's Dream; Macbeth, Bristol Old Vic and tour, 1997; *television* includes: The Muscle Market; Coast to Coast, 1987; The Bill; Martin Chuzzlewit, 1994; Between the Lines; Lost for Words, 1999; Alice in Wonderland, 2000; The Sins, 2000; *films* include: A Private Function, 1985; Distant Voices, Still Lives, 1988; The Dressmaker, 1989; Usual Suspects; The Last of the Mohicans, 1991; Alien 3, 1992; In the Name of the Father, 1993; Dragonheart, 1996; Brassed Off, 1996; Romeo and Juliet, 1997; The Lost World: Jurassic Park, 1997; Amistad, 1997; Serpent's Kiss, 1997; Among Giants, 1998. *Address:* c/o Markham & Froggatt Ltd, 4 Windmill Street, W1P 1HF.

POSWILLO, Prof. David Ernest, CBE 1989; DDS, DSc; FRCPath, FDSRCS, FRACDS, FIBiol; Emeritus Professor of Oral and Maxillofacial Surgery, University of London, since 1992 (Professor of Oral and Maxillofacial Surgery, United Medical and Dental Schools of Guy's and St Thomas' Hospitals, 1983–92); *b* 1 Jan. 1927; *s* of Ernest and Amelia Poswillo, Gisborne, NZ; *m* 1956, Elizabeth Alison, *d* of Whitworth and Alice Russell, Nelson, NZ; two *s* two *d*. *Educ:* Gisborne Boys' High, NZ; Univ. of Otago. BDS 1948, DDS 1962, DSc 1975, Westminster Hosp.; FDSRCS 1952, FRACDS 1966, FIBiol 1974, FRCPath 1981. OC S District Hosp., RNZDC, 1949–51; Hill End Hosp., St Albans, 1952; Dir of Oral Surgery, Christchurch Hosp., NZ, 1953–68; Prof. of Teratology, RCS, 1969–77; Consultant Oral Surgeon, Queen Victoria Hosp., East Grinstead, 1969–77; Prof. of Oral Path. and Oral Surgery, Univ. of Adelaide, and Sen. Oral and Maxillofacial Surgeon, Royal Adelaide and Childrens' Hosps, 1977–79; Prof. of Oral Surgery, and Mem. Council, Royal Dental Hosp., London, 1977–83. Consultant Adviser to Chief MO, DHSS, 1979–86; Chairman: Wkg Pty on Anaesthesia, Sedation and Resuscitation in Dentistry (Poswillo Report), DoH, 1990; Cttee on Dental and Surgical Materials, DoH, 1993–95; Scientific Cttee on Tobacco and Health, DoH, 1994–98. Mem., Bd of Faculty of Dental Surgery, RCS, 1981–89. Medical Defence Union: Council Mem., 1983–; Chm., Dental Cttee, 1983–88; Mem., Bd of Management, 1992–97. Sec. Gen., Internat. Assoc. of Oral and Maxillofacial Surgeons, 1983–89 (Hon. Fellow, 1992); President: BAOMS, 1990–91; Section of Odontology, RSM, 1989–90 (Hon. Treas., 1994–). Trustee, Tobacco Products Research Trust, 1980–95; Human Task Force, WHO, 1976–78. Mem. Council of Govs, UMDS of Guy's and St Thomas' Hosps, 1983–92. Hunterian Trustee, RCS, 1994–. Hunterian Prof., RCS, 1968, 1976; Adjunct Prof. of Maxillofacial Surgery, Case Western Reserve Univ., 1984–93; Regents' Prof., Univ. of California, 1987. Lectures: Arnott Demonstrator, 1972; Erasmus Wilson, 1973; Darwin-Lincoln, Johns Hopkins, 1975; Waldron, Harvard, 1976; Richardson, Harvard, 1981; Tomes, RCS, 1982; President's, BAOMS, 1985; Friel Meml, European Orthodontic Soc., 1987; Sarnat, UCLA, 1989; William Guy, RCSE, 1990; Chalmers Lyons Meml, American Assoc. of Oral and Maxillofacial Surgeons, 1996. Fellow, German Acad. of Nat. Scis (Leopoldina), 1988; Foreign Associate, Inst. of Medicine, Nat. Acad. of Scis, USA, 1989. Hon. FFDRCSI, 1984; Hon. FIMFT, 1985; Hon. FRSocMed 1995. Hon. MD Zürich, 1983. RNZADC Prize, 1948; Tomes Prize, 1966; Down Medal, 1973; Kay-Kilner Prize, 1975; ASOMS Research Award, 1976; Hunter Medal and Triennial Prize, 1976; 2nd Orthog. Surg. Award, Univ. of Texas, 1982; Edison Award, Univ. of Michigan, 1987; Colyer Gold Medal, RCS, 1990; Goldman Medal and Lecture, BPMF, 1992. Por Cristo Medal (Ecuador), 1989. *Publications:* (with C. L. Berry) Teratology, 1975; (with B. Cohen and D. K. Mason) Oral Surgery and Pathology, 1978; (with B. Cohen and D. K. Mason) Oral Medicine and Diagnosis, 1978; (with D. J. Simpson and D. David) The Craniosynostoses, 1982; (with D. Henderson) Atlas of Orthognathic Surgery, 1984; (jtly) Dental, Oral and Maxillofacial Surgery, 1986; (jtly) The Effects of Smoking on the Foetus, Neonate and Child, 1992; Report of the Scientific Cttee on Tobacco and Health, 1998; papers on surgery, pathology and teratology in dental, medical and sci jls. *Recreations:* art, reading, gardening. *Address:* Whitegates, 5 Oldfield Road, Bickley, Kent BR1 2LE. *T:* (020) 8467 1578; *e-mail:* david@poswillo.freeserve.co.uk.

POTTER, Prof. Allen Meyers, PhD; James Bryce Professor of Politics, University of Glasgow, 1970–84, retired; *b* 7 March 1924; *s* of Maurice A. and Irene M. Potter; *m* 1949, Joan Elizabeth Yeo; two *d*. *Educ:* Wesleyan Univ., Conn (BA 1947, MA 1948); Columbia Univ., NY (PhD 1955). FSS 1967. Instructor, College of William and Mary, 1949–51; Lectr/Sen. Lectr, Univ. of Manchester, 1951–62; Vis. Professor, Univ. of Texas, 1960; Professor: Univ. of Strathclyde, 1963–65; Univ. of Essex, 1965–70; Pro-Vice-Chancellor, Univ. of Essex, 1969–70; Vice-Principal, Univ. of Glasgow, 1979–82. Dir, SSRC Data Bank, 1967–70. Member, US-UK Educational Commn, 1979–84. Governor, Glasgow Sch. of Art, 1979–82. *Publications:* American Government and Politics, 1955, 2nd edn 1978; Organised Groups in British National Politics, 1961; articles in American and British social science jls. *Recreation:* inventing table games.

POTTER, Christopher Frank Rendall, OBE 2001; MA; Headmaster, Old Swinford Hospital, Stourbridge, 1978–2001; *b* 9 Sept. 1939; *s* of late Cedric Hardcastle Potter and Phyllis Potter (*née* Rendall); *m* 1971, Charlotte Ann Millis, San Francisco; two *s* three *d*. *Educ:* March Grammar Sch.; Trinity Coll., Cambridge (MA Classics). Ardingly College, Sussex: Asst Master, 1961–78; Head of Classics, 1964–78; Housemaster, 1966–78. Chief Examr in Archaeol., London Exam Bd, 1976–80. Chm., State Boarding Inf. Service, 1996–98. Schoolmaster Studentship, Christ Church, Oxford, 1989. Pres., Stourbridge Archaeol and Historical Soc., 1988. Chm. Trustees, Knoll Sch., Kidderminster, 1989–; Vice Chm. Govs, The Elms Sch., Colwall, 1985–. *Publications:* (with T. W. Potter) Romano-British Village at Grandford, Cambridgeshire, 1980; (ed) Parish Register Transcripts: Romsley, Worcs, 1988; Stone, Worcs, 1989. *Recreations:* golf, Italian opera, genealogy, red wine, the poetry of Horace. *Address:* St Leonard's House, Upper Linney, Ludlow SY8 1EF. *T:* (01584) 878770.

POTTER, Very Rev. Christopher Nicholas Lynden; Dean of St Asaph, since 2001; *b* 4 Oct. 1949; *s* of Sir (Joseph) Raymond (Lynden) Potter and of (Daphne) Marguerite Potter; *m* 1993, Jenny Lees; three *s* one *d*. *Educ:* Haileybury Coll.; Univ. of Leeds (BA (Hons) English/Fine Art 1971); St Asaph Diocesan Ordination Trng Course. Lectr, Tutor and Librarian, Bradford Art Coll., 1971–73; self-employed furniture designer and cabinet maker, 1975–90; ordained deacon, 1993, priest, 1994; Curate, Flint, 1993–96; Vicar of grouped parishes of Llanfair DC, Llanelidan, Efenechtyd and Derwen, 1996–2001. *Recreations:* hill walking, reading, playing melodeon in ceilidh band, mending things. *Address:* The Deanery, St Asaph, Denbighshire LL17 0RL. *T:* (01745) 583597.

POTTER, Dr David Edwin, CBE 1997; FREng; Founder, and Chairman, Psion plc, since 1980 (Chief Executive, 1980–98); *b* 4 July 1943; *s* of Paul James Potter and Mary Agnes (*née* Snape); *m* 1969, Elaine Goldberg; three *s*. *Educ:* Trinity Coll., Cambridge

(Exhibnr; MA); Imperial Coll., London (PhD 1970). Lectr, Blackett Lab., Imperial Coll., London, 1970–80. Commonwealth Schol., 1966–69; Asst Prof., UCLA, 1974. Director: Charterhouse Venture Fund Management Ltd, 1985–94; Press Assoc. Ltd, 1994–97 (Vice-Chm., 1995–97); London First Centre, 1994–; Finsbury Technology Trust, 1995–; Chairman: Symbian Ltd, 1998–; Knowledge=Power, 2000. Member: Nat. Cttee of Inquiry into Higher Educn (Dearing Cttee), 1996–97; HEFCE, 1997–; Council for Sci. and Technol., Cabinet Office, 1998–. Mem., London Regl Council, CBI, 1993–99. Vis. Fellow, Nuffield Coll., Oxford, 1998–. Gov., London Business Sch., 2000–. Hon. Fellow: Imperial Coll., 1998; London Business Sch., 1998. FRSA 1989; FREng 2001. Hon. DTech: Kingston, 1998; Oxford Brookes, 1999; Hon. DSc: Brunel, 1998; Westminster, 1998; Warwick, 1999; Sheffield, 1999. Lectures: Stockton, London Business Sch., 1998; Millennium, 1999. Mountbatten Medal for Outstanding Services to Electronics Industry, Nat. Electronics Council, 1994. *Publications:* Computational Physics, 1972; contribs to various physics jls. *Recreations:* tennis, flute, bridge, reading, gardening. *Address:* Psion plc, 1 Red Place, W1Y 3RE. *Club:* Portland.

POTTER, David Roger William; Director, Noble Group, since 2000; Chairman, Infocanay, since 2000; *b* 27 July 1944; *s* of late William Edward Potter and of Joan Louise (*née* Frost); *m* 1966, Joanna Trollope, *qv* (marr. diss. 1983); two *d*; *m* 1991, Teresa Jill Benson; one *d*. *Educ:* Bryanston Sch.; University Coll., Oxford (MA). Nat. Discount Co., 1965–69; Managing Director: Credit Suisse First Boston and Credit Suisse White Weld, 1969–81; Samuel Montagu & Co. Ltd, 1981–89; Midland Montagu Corporate Banking, 1986–89; Gp Chief Exec., Guinness Mahon Holdings, 1990–98; Chm. and Chief Exec., Guinness Mahon & Co. Ltd, Merchant Bankers, 1990–98; Dep. Chm., Investec Bank (UK) Ltd, 1998–99. Director: Maybox plc, 1987–90; Thomas Cook, 1989–91; Tyndal plc, 1989–91; Rose Partnership, 2000. Chm., London Film Commn, 1996–2000. Governor: Bryanston Sch., 1982–; Mem. Council, KCL, 1997– (Treas., 1998–). Trustee: Worldwide Volunteering for Young People (formerly Youth for Britain), 1994–; Nat. Film and Television Sch. Foundn, 1997–; Nelson Mandela Children Foundn, 1998–. Mem., Adv. Bd, London Capital Club, 1995–. *Recreations:* shooting, gardening, golf. *Address:* (office) 6 Norland Square, W11 4PX; *e-mail:* david@pdjh.demon.co.uk. *Clubs:* Oxford and Cambridge, City; Vincent's (Oxford).

POTTER, Donald Charles; QC 1972; *b* 24 May 1922; *s* of late Charles Potter, Shortlands, Kent. *Educ:* St Dunstan's Coll.; London Sch. of Economics. RAC (Westminster Dragoons), 1942–46 (Lieut); served England, NW Europe (D-day), Germany; mentioned in despatches; Croix de Guerre (France). LLB London 1947; called to Bar, Middle Temple, 1948; Bencher, Lincoln's Inn, 1979. Asst Lectr in Law, LSE, 1947–49; practised at Bar, 1950–95. Chm., Revenue Bar Assoc., 1978–88. Special Comr of Income Tax (part-time), 1986–95; Chm. (part-time), VAT Tribunal, 1986–95. *Publications:* (with H. H. Monroe) Tax Planning with Precedents, 1954; (with K. J. Prosser) Tax Appeals, 1991. *Recreations:* music, theatre, reading. *Address:* 3 The Grove, Highgate, N6 6JU; Compass Cottage, East Portlemouth, Devon TQ8 8PE. *Club:* Garrick.

POTTER, Ernest Frank; Director, Finance, Cable & Wireless plc, 1979–87 (Director of Finance and Corporate Planning, 1977–79); *b* 29 April 1923; *s* of Frank William and Edith Mary Potter; *m* 1st, 1945, Madge (*née* Arrowsmith) (*d* 1990); one *s*; 2nd, 1992, Barbara (*née* Brewis-Levie). *Educ:* Dr Challoner's Grammar Sch., Amersham. FCMA, FCIS, MIMC. Commissioned Pilot and Navigator, RAF, 1941–49. Chief Accountant, Bulmer & Lumb Ltd, 1950–58; Director, Management Consulting, Coopers & Lybrand, 1959–71; British Steel Corporation, Cammell Laird Shipbuilders Ltd, 1972–77; Director (non-executive): Cable & Wireless (West Indies) Ltd, 1977–87; Bahrain Telecommunications Corp., 1982–89; Cable & Wireless North America Inc, 1980–87; Cable & Wireless Hongkong Ltd, 1982–87; Cable & Wireless (Leasing) Ltd, 1982–87; Bahrain Telecommunications Corp., 1982–89; Cable & Wireless Marine Ltd, 1984–87; Mercury Communications Ltd, 1985–87; Cable & Wireless (Bermuda) Ltd, 1986–87; General Hybrid Ltd, 1987–91; Cable Corp. Ltd, 1988–97; Windsor Cable Ltd, 1988–97; Telephone Corp. Ltd, 1988–92; Micrelec Gp, 1989–92; Chairman: Clebern Internat. Ltd, 1988–89; Holmes Protection Inc., 1990–91; Themes Internat., 1991–92. Mem., Accounting Standards Cttee, 1985–90. *Recreations:* golf, sailing. *Address:* Long Meadow, Gorse Hill Road, Virginia Water, Surrey GU25 4AS. *T:* (01344) 842178. *Clubs:* Royal Air Force; Foxhills (Surrey); St Mawes Sailing.

POTTER, His Honour (Francis) Malcolm; a Circuit Judge, 1978–97; *b* 28 July 1932; *s* of Francis Martin Potter and Zilpah Jane Potter; *m* 1970, Bertha Villamil; one *s* one *d*. *Educ:* Rugby Sch.; Jesus Coll., Oxford. Called to the Bar, Lincoln's Inn, 1956. A Recorder of the Crown Court, 1974–78. *Recreation:* painting. *Address:* 36 Greening Drive, Ampton Road, Edgbaston, Birmingham B15 2XA. *Club:* Army and Navy.

POTTER, Jeremy Patrick L.; *see* Lee-Potter.

POTTER, Maj.-Gen. Sir John, KBE 1968 (CBE 1963; OBE 1951); CB 1966; Chairman, Traffic Commissioners and Licensing Authority, Western Traffic Area, 1973–83; *b* 18 April 1913; *s* of late Major Benjamin Henry Potter, OBE, MC; *m* 1st, 1943, Vivienne Madge (*d* 1973), *d* of late Captain Henry D'Arcy Medlicott Cooke; one *s* one *d*; 2nd, 1974, Mrs D. Ella Purkis (*d* 2001); one step *s* one step *d*. Served War of 1939–45. Major-General, 1962; Colonel Comdt: RAOC, 1965–69; RCT, 1968–73. Director of Supplies and Transport, 1963–65; Transport Officer in Chief (Army), 1965–66; Dir of Movements (Army), MoD, 1966–68; retired. *Address:* Orchard Cottage, The Orchard, Freshford, Bath BA2 7WX.

POTTER, John Herbert, MBE 1974; HM Diplomatic Service, retired; *b* 11 Jan. 1928; *s* of Herbert George and Winifred Eva Potter; *m* 1953, Winifred Susan Florence Hall (*d* 2000); one *d*. *Educ:* elementary education at various state schools. Electrical Engineering jobs, 1942–45; served HM Forces, 1945–48; GPO, 1948–53; Foreign Office, 1953–55; Commercial Attaché, Bangkok, 1955–57; FO, 1957–60; Istanbul, 1960; Ankara, 1960–64; Second Secretary, Information, 1962; Second Sec., Information, Addis Ababa, 1964; Vice-Consul, Information, Johannesburg, 1964–66; DSAO, later FCO, 1966–70; First Sec. (Administration): Brussels, 1970–74; Warsaw, 1974–76; FCO (Inspectorate), 1976–80; Counsellor (Admin.) and Consul-Gen., Moscow, 1980–81; Counsellor (Administration), Bonn, 1981–82. *Recreations:* reading, languages, walking, gardening. *Address:* 6 Salvington Crescent, Bexhill-on-Sea, E Sussex TN39 3NP.

POTTER, John McEwen, DM, FRCS; Emeritus Fellow, Wadham College, Oxford; Director of Postgraduate Medical Education and Training, University of Oxford, 1972–87; *b* 28 Feb. 1920; *er s* of Alistair Richardson Potter and Mairi Chalmers Potter (*née* Dick); *m* 1943, Kathleen Gerrard; three *s*. *Educ:* Clifton Coll.; Emmanuel Coll., Cambridge; St Bartholomew's Hosp. BA, MB, BChir Cantab, 1943; MA 1945; FRCS 1951; MA, BM, BCh Oxon, 1963, DM 1964. Active service (Captain, RAMC), Europe, India and Burma, 1944–47. Lectr in Physiol. and Jun. Chief Asst, Surg. Professorial Unit, St Bart's Hosp., 1948–51; Graduate Asst to Nuffield Prof. of Surgery, Oxford, 1951–56; E. G. Fearnsides Scholar, Cambridge, 1954–56; Hunterian Prof., 1955; Cons. Neurosurgeon: Manchester Royal Infirmary, 1956–61; Radcliffe Infirm., Oxford, 1961–72; Hon. Cons. Neurosurgeon, Oxford RHA and Oxfordshire HA, 1972–87. Vis. Prof., UCLA, 1967; University of Oxford: Clin. Lectr in Neurosurgery, 1962–68; Univ. Lectr, 1968–87; Mem., Gen. Bd of Faculties, 1975–83; Hebdomadal Council, 1983–89; Fellow: Linacre Coll., 1967–69; Wadham Coll., 1969–87 (Professorial Fellow, 1974–87; Sub-Warden, 1978–81; Dean of Degrees, 1984–97). Governor, United Oxford Hosps, 1973. Cairns Lectr, Adelaide, 1974. Examr for Final BM, BCh Oxon; Ext. Examr, Med. Sciences Tripos Pt II, Cambridge Univ. FRSocMed (Pres., Sect. of Neurol., 1975–76); Member: GMC, 1973–89 (Chm., Registration Cttee, 1979–89); Oxfordshire HA, 1982–89; Medical Appeal Tribunal, 1987–92; Soc. of British Neurol Surgeons (formerly Hon. Sec. and Archivist); Vice-Pres., 4th Internat. Congress of Neurol Surgery. Corres. Member: Amer. Assoc. of Neurol Surgeons; Deutsche Gesellschaft für Neurochirurgie; Sociedad Luso-Espanhola de Neurocirurgia; Hon. Mem., Egyptian Soc. of Neurol Surgeons. *Publications:* The Practical Management of Head Injuries, 1961, 4th edn 1984; contrib. to books and jls on subjects relating mostly to neurology and med. educn. *Recreation:* fishing. *Address:* 47 Park Town, Oxford OX2 6SL. *T:* (01865) 557875.

POTTER, Malcolm; *see* Potter, F. M.

POTTER, Rt Hon. Sir Mark Howard, Kt 1988; PC 1996; **Rt Hon. Lord Justice Potter;** a Lord Justice of Appeal, since 1996; *b* 27 Aug. 1937; *s* of Prof. Harold Potter, LLD, PhD, and Beatrice Spencer Potter (*née* Crowder); *m* 1962, Undine Amanda Fay, *d* of Major James Miller, 5/6th Rajputana Rifles, and Bunty Miller, painter; two *s*. *Educ:* Perse Sch., Cambridge; Gonville and Caius Coll., Cambridge (Schol.; BA (Law Tripos) 1960; MA 1963; Hon. Fellow 1998). National Service, 15 Med. Regt RA, 1955–57 (commnd 1956); 289 Lt Parachute Regt RHA(TA), 1958–64. Asst Supervisor, Legal Studies, Girton, Gonville and Caius, Queens' and Sidney Sussex Colls, 1961–68; called to Bar, Gray's Inn, 1961, Bencher, 1987; in practice, 1962–88; QC 1980; a Recorder, 1986–88; a Judge of the High Court of Justice, QBD (Commercial Court), 1988–96; a Presiding Judge, Northern Circuit, 1991–94. Member: Supreme Ct Rule Cttee, 1980–84; Lord Chancellor's Civil Justice Review Cttee, 1985–88; Chm., Bar Public Affairs Cttee, 1987; Vice-Chm., Council of Legal Educn, 1989–91; Chairman: Lord Chancellor's Adv. Cttee on Legal Educn and Conduct, 1998–99; Legal Services Adv. Panel, 2000–. Mem. Council, Nottingham Univ., 1996–99. Trustee, Somerset House Trust, 1997–. Hon. LLD London Guildhall, 2000. *Recreations:* family and sporting. *Address:* Royal Courts of Justice, Strand, WC2A 2LL. *Clubs:* Garrick, Saintsbury; St Enedoc Golf.

POTTER, Rev. Philip Alford; General Secretary, World Council of Churches, 1972–84; *b* 19 Aug. 1921; *s* of Clement Potter and Violet Peters, Roseau, Dominica, Windward Is, WI; *m* 1st, 1956, Ethel Olive Doreen Cousins (*d* 1980), Jamaica, WI; 2nd, 1984, Rev. Barbel von Wartenberg (now Bishop of Holstein-Lübeck). *Educ:* Dominica Grammar Sch.; United Theological Coll., Jamaica; London Univ. BD, MTh. Methodist Minister. Overseas Sec., British SCM, 1948–50; Superintendent, Cap Haitien Circuit, Methodist Church, Haiti, 1950–54; Sec., later Dir, Youth Dept, WCC, 1954–60; Sec. for WI and W Africa, Methodist Missionary Society, London, 1961–66; Dir, Commn on World Mission and Evangelism, and Associate Gen. Sec., WCC, 1967–72. Chaplain, Univ. of WI and Lectr, United Theol Coll. of WI, 1985–90. Mem., then Chm., Youth Dept Cttee, WCC, 1948–54; Chm., World Student Christian Fedn, 1960–68. Editor: Internat. Review of Mission, 1967–72; Ecumenical Rev., 1972–84. Hon. Doctor of Theology: Hamburg Univ., Germany, 1971; Geneva, 1976; Theol Inst. of Rumanian Orthodox Church, 1977; Humboldt Univ., Berlin, 1982; Uppsala, 1984; Hon. LLD W Indies, 1974; Hon. DD Birmingham, 1985. Niwano Peace Prize, Japan, 1986. *Publications:* (with Prof. Hendrik Berkhof) Key Words of the Gospel, 1964; The Love of Power or the Power of Love, 1974; Life in all its Fullness, 1981; (with Barbel von Wartenberg) Freedom is for Freeing, 1990; (jtly) Seeking and Serving the Truth: first hundred years of the World Student Christian Federation, 1997; chapter in Explosives Lateinamerika (ed by T. Tschuy), 1969; essays in various symposia; contrib. various jls, incl. Ecumenical Rev., Internat. Rev. of Mission, Student World. *Recreations:* swimming, hiking, music, geology. *Address:* Plönniesstrasse 6, 23560 Lübeck, Germany.

POTTER, Raymond, CB 1990; Deputy Secretary, 1986–93 (Courts and Legal Services, 1986–91), Head of the Court Service and Deputy Clerk of the Crown in Chancery, 1989–93, Lord Chancellor's Department; *b* 26 March 1933; *s* of William Thomas Potter and Elsie May Potter; *m* 1959, Jennifer Mary Quicke; one *s*. *Educ:* Henry Thornton Grammar School. Called to the Bar, Inner Temple, 1971, Bencher, 1989. Central Office, Royal Courts of Justice, 1950; Western Circuit, 1963; Chief Clerk, Bristol Crown Court, 1972; Dep. Circuit Administrator, Western Circuit, 1976; Circuit Administrator, Northern Circuit, 1982–86. Pres., S Western Rent Assessment Panel, 1995–. *Recreation:* painting. *Address:* 8 Robinson Way, Backwell, Bristol BS48 3BP. *Club:* Athenæum.

POTTER, Ronald Stanley James; Director of Social Services, Surrey County Council, 1970–81; *b* 29 April 1921; *e s* of late Stanley Potter and Gertrude Mary Keable, Chelmsford; *m* 1954, Ann (Louisa Eleanor) Burnett; one *s* one *d*. *Educ:* King Edward VI Grammar Sch., Chelmsford. MISW. Territorial Army, 1939, War Service, 1939–47; commnd RA, 1942; Captain 1946. Area Welfare Officer, Essex CC, 1953–61; Dep. Co. Welfare Officer, Lindsey CC, 1962; County Welfare Officer: Lindsey CC, 1962–64; Herts CC, 1964–70. Dir, Watford Sheltered Workshop Ltd, 1964–70; Mem. Cttee of Enquiry into Voluntary Workers in Social Services, 1966–69; Dir, Industrial Advisers to Blind Ltd, 1969–74; Vice Pres., SE Regional Assoc. for Deaf, 1984–88 (Vice-Chm., 1968–76; Chm., 1976–84); Member: Council of Management, RNID, 1968–71, 1976–84; Nat. Jt Council for Workshops for the Blind, 1970–81; Adv. Council, Nat. Corp. for Care of Old People, 1974–77; Local Authorities Adv. Cttee on Conditions of Service of Blind Workers, 1974–81; Exec. Council, RNIB, 1975–81; Nat. Adv. Council on Employment of Disabled People, 1978–81; Dir, Remploy Ltd, 1974–86. *Recreations:* walking, swimming, caravanning, bowls. *Address:* Ridge Cottage, 16 Howard Ridge, Burpham Lane, Guildford, Surrey GU4 7LY. *T:* (01483) 504272.

POTTER, Maj.-Gen. Sir Wilfrid John; *see* Potter, Maj.-Gen. Sir John.

POTTERTON, Homan, FSA; art historian and writer; Editor, since 1993, and publisher, since 2000, Irish Arts Review; Director, National Gallery of Ireland, 1980–88; *b* 9 May 1946; sixth *s* of late Thomas Edward Potterton and Eileen Potterton (*née* Tong). *Educ:* Kilkenny Coll.; Trinity Coll., Dublin (BA 1968, MA 1973); Edinburgh Univ. (Dip. Hist. Art 1971). FSA 1981. Cataloguer, National Gall. of Ireland, 1971–73; Asst Keeper, National Gall., London, 1974–80. Mem. Bd, GPA Dublin Internat. Piano Competition, 1987–92. HRHA 1982. *Publications:* Irish Church Monuments 1570–1880, 1975; A Guide to the National Gallery, 1976, rev. edn 1980 (German, French, Italian and Japanese edns 1977); The National Gallery, London, 1977; Reynolds and Gainsborough: themes and painters in the National Gallery, 1976; Pageant and Panorama: the elegant world of Canaletto, 1978; (jtly) Irish Art and Architecture, 1978; Venetian Seventeenth Century Painting (National Gallery Exhibn Catalogue), 1979; introd. to National Gallery of Ireland Illustrated Summary Catalogue of Paintings, 1981; (jtly) National Gallery of Ireland, 50 Pictures, 1981; Dutch 17th and 18th Century Paintings in the National Gallery of Ireland: a complete catalogue, 1986; Rathcormick: a childhood recalled, 2001; contrib. Burlington

Mag., Apollo, Connoisseur, FT and Country Life. *Recreation:* France. *Address:* 22 Greycoat Gardens, SW1P 2QA; Mauriac, 81600 Gaillac, France. *T:* and *Fax:* (5) 63415146; *e-mail:* hpotterton@free.fr. *Clubs:* Royal Over-Seas League; St Stephen's Green (Dublin).

POTTINGER, Frank Vernon Hunter, RSA 1991; sculptor; *b* 1 Oct. 1932; *s* of William Pottinger and Veronica (*née* Irvine); *m* 1991, Evelyn Norah Smith; one step *s* two step *d.* *Educ:* Boroughmuir Secondary Sch.; Edinburgh Coll. of Art (DA 1963). Apprentice fitter engineer, 1948–53; nat. service, 1953–55; teacher: Portobello Secondary Sch., 1965–73; Aberdeen Coll. of Educn, 1973–85; vis. lectr, colls of art in Scotland, 1980–91; full-time artist, 1985–. *Address:* 30/5 Elbe Street, Edinburgh EH6 7HW. *T:* (0131) 225 2990.

POTTINGER, Graham Robert; Chief Executive, Scottish Mutual Assurance plc, since 1997 (Finance Director, 1992–96); Managing Director, Abbey National Financial Investment Services plc, since 1997; *b* 14 June 1949; *s* of Arthur and Mary Pottinger; *m* 1970, Dorothy McLean; one *s* one *d.* *Educ:* Jordanhill Coll. Sch., Glasgow; Glasgow Univ. (LLB). CA 1992; ACMA 1993. Peat Marwick Mitchell & Co., 1966–72; Partner, Deloitte Haskins & Sells, 1972–79; Controller, UK and Africa, Cargill Plc, 1980–92. Mem. Council, ICAS, 1995–. *Recreations:* performance cars, beach holidays. *Address:* Scottish Mutual Assurance plc, 287–301 St Vincent Street, Glasgow G2 5HN. *T:* (0141) 275 8654.

POTTINGER, Piers Julian Dominic; Joint Chief Executive and Deputy Chairman (formerly Group Managing Director), Chime Communications plc, since 1993; *b* 3 March 1954; *s* of late W. G. Pottinger; *m* 1979, Carolyn Ann Rhodes; one *s* three *d.* *Educ:* Edinburgh Acad.; Winchester Coll. Trainee, J. Henry Schroder Wagg, 1972–74; Res. Analyst, Laurence Prust and Co., 1974–78; Exec., Charles Barker, 1978–80; Dir, Media Relations Manufacturers, Hanover, NY, 1980–82; Man. Dir, Sterling Financial Public Relations, 1982–85; Man. Dir, then Chm., Bell Pottinger (formerly Lowe Bell) Financial, 1985–. Formerly Member: Bd, Scottish Ballet; Gen. Council, Poetry Soc. Trustee, Liver Res. Trust, 2001–. *Recreations:* horse racing, golf, Real tennis. *Address:* The Old Rectory, Wixoe, Sudbury, Suffolk CO10 8UG. *T:* (01440) 785241. *Clubs:* Garrick; Wentworth; Jockey Club Rooms (Newmarket); Newmarket Real Tennis.

POTTS, Archibold; Director, Bewick Press, since 1989; *b* 27 Jan. 1932; *s* of late Ernest W. Potts and Ellen Potts; *m* 1957, Marguerite Elsie (*née* Elliott) (*d* 1983); one *s* one *d.* *Educ:* Monkwearmouth Central Sch., Sunderland; Ruskin and Oriel Colls, Oxford (Dip. Econ. and Pol. Sci., 1958; BA PPE 2nd cl. hons, 1960); ext. postgrad. student, London Univ. (Postgrad. CertEd 1964) and Durham Univ. (MEd 1969). Nat. Service, RAF, 1950–53. Railway Clerk, 1947–50 and 1953–56. Lecturer: N Oxfordshire Tech. Coll., 1961; York Tech. Coll., 1962–65; Rutherford Coll. of Technology and Newcastle upon Tyne Polytechnic, 1965–80; Head of Sch. of Business Admin, 1980–87, Associate Dean, Faculty of Business and Professional Studies, 1988, Newcastle upon Tyne Polytechnic. Moderator, history courses, Tyneside Open Coll. Network, 1992–. Tyne and Wear County Council: Councillor, 1979–86; Vice-Chm., Planning Cttee, 1981–86; Vice-Chm., Council, 1983–84; Chm., Council, 1984–85. Contested (Lab) Westmorland, 1979. Chm., NE Labour History Soc., 1990–96 (Vice Pres., 1997–); Mem., Exec. Cttee, Soc. for Study of Labour History, 1987–96. *Publications:* Stand True, 1976; Bibliography of Northern Labour History, 1982–; (ed) Shipbuilders and Engineers, 1987; Jack Casey, the Sunderland Assassin, 1991; The Wearside Champions, 1993; Jack London, the forgotten champion, 1997; contribs to Dictionary of Labour Biography, vol. 2 1974, vol. 4 1977, vol. 5 1979, vol. 9 1993; articles on economics and history. *Recreations:* local history, watching old films. *Address:* 47 Graham Park Road, Gosforth, Newcastle upon Tyne NE3 4BJ. *T:* (0191) 284 5132. *Club:* Victory Service.

POTTS, Sir (Francis) Humphrey, Kt 1986; a Judge of the High Court of Justice, Queen's Bench Division, 1986–2001; *b* 18 Aug. 1931; *er s* of late Francis William Potts and Elizabeth Hannah (*née* Humphrey), Penshaw, Co. Durham; *m* 1971, Philippa Margaret Campbell, *d* of the late J. C. H. Le B. Croke and Mrs J. F. G. Downes; two *s* and two step *s.* *Educ:* Royal Grammar Sch., Newcastle upon Tyne; St Catherine's Society, Oxford. BCL 1954, MA 1957. Barrister-at-Law, Lincoln's Inn, 1955 (Tancred Student, 1953; Cholmeley Scholar, 1954), Bencher, 1979; North Eastern Circuit, 1955; practised in Newcastle upon Tyne, 1955–71; QC 1971; a Recorder, 1972–86; admitted to Hong Kong Bar, 1984; Presiding Judge, NE Circuit, 1988–91. Member: Mental Health Review Tribunal, 1984–86; Criminal Injuries Compensation Bd, 1985–86; Parole Bd, 1992–96 (Vice-Chm., 1995–96); Chm., Special Immigration Appeals Commn, 1997–. Trustee, Mental Health Foundn, 1990–96. Pres., Norcare, 1997–99. *Address:* c/o Royal Courts of Justice, Strand, WC2A 2LL.

POTTS, Paul John; Chief Executive, since 2000, Editor-in-Chief, since 1996, and a Director, since 1995, The Press Association; Editor, PA News, since 1995; *b* 21 Jan. 1950; *s* of late Michael Henry Potts and of Sylvia Brenda Potts; *m* 1st, 1976, Gabrielle Jane Fagan (marr. diss. 1994); one *s* two *d*; 2nd, 1994, Judith Anne Fielding. *Educ:* Worksop Coll. Gen. Reporter, Sheffield Star, 1968–74; Lobby Corresp., Yorkshire Post, 1974–78; General Reporter: Daily Telegraph, 1978–81; Mail on Sunday, 1981–82; Political Ed., News of the World, 1982–86; Political Ed., then Asst Ed., later Dep. Ed., Daily Express, 1986–95. Dir, Canada News Wire, 2000–. Mem., Code of Practice Cttee, 1996–. Patron, Sheffield Wednesday Supporters Trust, 2001. *Recreations:* military history, walking. *Address:* Press Association Ltd, PA NewsCentre, 292 Vauxhall Bridge Road, SW1V 1AE. *T:* (020) 7963 7000.

POTTS, Robin; QC 1982; barrister; *b* 2 July 1944; *s* of William and Elaine Potts; *m*; one *s*; *m* Helen Elizabeth Sharp; two *s* one *d.* *Educ:* Wolstanton Grammar Sch.; Magdalen Coll., Oxford (BA, BCL). Called to the Bar, Gray's Inn, 1968, Bencher, 1993. Consulting Ed., Gore-Browne on Companies, 43rd and 44th edns. *Address:* The Grange, Church Lane, Pinner, Middx HA5 3AB. *T:* (020) 8866 9013.

POULSEN, Ole Lønsmann, Hon. GCVO 2000; Ambassador of Denmark to Beijing, since 2001; *b* 14 May 1945; *s* of Aage Lønsmann Poulsen, head teacher, and Tove Alice (*née* Gyldenstein); *m* 1973, Zareen Mehta; two *s.* *Educ:* Copenhagen Univ. (LLM 1971). Hd of Dept, Danchurchaid, 1969–73; joined Danish Diplomatic Service, 1973; Hd of Section, Min. of Foreign Affairs, Denmark, 1973–76; Advr, Asian Develt Bank, Manila, 1976–77; First Sec., New Delhi and Trade Comr, Bombay, 1977–80; Alternate Exec. Dir, World Bank, Washington, 1980–83; Dep. Head, 1983–85, Head, 1985–88, Dept of Internat. Develt Co-operation, then Under-Sec. for Multilateral Affairs (Ambassador), 1988–92, Min. of Foreign Affairs; Ambassador to Austria and Perm. Rep. to IAEA, UNIDO and UN, Vienna, also accredited to Slovenia and Bosnia Hercegovina, 1992–93; State Sec., Min. of Foreign Affairs, 1993–96; Ambassador to UK, 1996–2001. Chm., Industrial Develt Bd, UNIDO, 1990–91. Alternate Gov., World Bank and Gov. for Asian, African and Interamerican Develt Banks, 1989–92 and 1993–96. Chairman: Scandinavian Seminar Coll., 1975–76; Nordic Develt Fund, 1990–91. Comdr, Order of Dannebrog (Denmark), 1999; Grand Cross (Austria), 1993. *Recreations:* music, literature, sport. *Address:* Royal Danish Embassy, San Li Tun, Dong Wu Jie 1, Beijing 100600, China.

POULTER, Brian Henry; Secretary, Northern Ireland Audit Office, 1989–2000; *b* 1 Sept. 1941; *s* of William Henry Poulter, PhC, MPS, and Marjorie Elizabeth Everett McBride; *m* 1968, Margaret Ann Dodds; one *s* twin *d.* *Educ:* Regent House Grammar Sch., Newtownards. Qual. as certified accountant, 1966. Hill, Vellacott and Bailey, Chartered Accountants, 1959–62; entered NICS, 1962; Min. of Health and Local Govt, 1962–65; Min. of Health and Social Services, 1965–71; Deputy Principal: Local Enterprise Develt Unit, 1971–74; Dept of Commerce, 1974–75; Chief Auditor 1975–81, Dep. Dir 1981–82, Dir 1982–87, Exchequer and Audit Dept; Dir, NI Audit Office, 1987–88. *Recreations:* reading, walking, cricket. *Address:* 20 Manse Road, Newtownards, Co. Down BT23 4TP.

POULTER, Jane Anne Marie; *see* Bonvin, J. A. M.

POULTON, Richard Christopher, MA; Clerk, All Saints Educational Trust, since 2001; *b* 21 June 1938; *e s* of Rev. Christopher Poulton and Aileen (*née* Sparrow); *m* 1965, Zara, *o d* of Prof. P. and Mrs J. Crossley-Holland; two *s* one *d.* *Educ:* King's Coll., Taunton; Wesleyan Univ., Middletown, Conn, USA; Pembroke Coll., Cambridge (BA 1961, CertEd 1962, MA 1965). Asst Master: Bedford Sch., 1962–63; Beckenham and Penge Grammar Sch., 1963–66; Bryanston School: Asst Master, 1966–80; Head of History Dept, 1971–76; Housemaster, 1972–80; Headmaster, Wycliffe Coll., 1980–86; Head Master, Christ's Hospital, Horsham, 1987–96; Founder Head Master, Internat. Sch. of the Regents, Pattaya, Thailand, 1996–97; Develt Officer, Inner Cities Young People's Project, 1998–2000. Governor: Oxford and Cambridge Examinations Bd, 1987–90; Aiglon Coll., Switzerland, 1998–; Royal Bridewell Hosp., 1999–; Presentation Gov., Christ's Hosp., 1999–. JP S Glos, 1985–86. Freeman, City of London, 1987; Yeoman, 1990, Liveryman, 1993, Mem. Court, 1999, Co. of Ironmongers. FRSA 1994. *Publications:* Victoria, Queen of a Changing Land, 1975; Kings and Commoners, 1977; A History of the Modern World, 1980. *Recreations:* writing, hill walking, choral music. *Address:* Red House, Lower Street, Fittleworth RH20 1EJ.

POULTON, William Dacres Campbell; His Honour Judge Poulton; a Circuit Judge, since 1994; *b* 15 Dec. 1937; *o s* of late Arthur Stanley Poulton and Winifred Evelyn Poulton (*née* Montgomery Campbell); *m* 1970, Carolyn Frances Macken; two *s* one *d.* *Educ:* Dover Coll.; New Coll., Oxford (BA 1961; MA 1964). Called to the Bar, Middle Temple, 1965; Recorder 1992–94. *Publications:* contribs to Law Quarterly Review and Halsbury's Laws of England (Landlord and Tenant). *Recreations:* ski-ing, gardening, walking.

POUND, Sir John David, 5th Bt *cr* 1905; *b* 1 Nov. 1946; *s* of Sir Derek Allen Pound, 4th Bt; *S* father, 1980; *m* 1st, 1968 (marr. diss.); one *s*; 2nd, 1978, Penelope Ann, *er d* of late Grahame Arthur Rayden, Bramhall, Cheshire; two *s.* Liveryman, Leathersellers' Co. *Heir:* *s* Robert John Pound, *b* 12 Feb. 1973.

POUND, Rev. Canon Keith Salisbury; a Chaplain to the Queen since 1988; *b* 3 April 1933; *s* of Percy Salisbury Pound and Annie Florence Pound. *Educ:* Roan School, Blackheath; St Catharine's Coll., Cambridge (BA 1954, MA 1958); Cuddesdon Coll., Oxford. Curate, St Peter, St Helier, Dio. Southwark, 1957–61; Training Officer, Hollowford Training and Conference Centre, Sheffield, 1961–64, Warden 1964–67; Rector of Holy Trinity, Southwark, with St Matthew, Newington, 1968–78; RD, Southwark and Newington, 1973–78; Rector of Thamesmead, 1978–86; Sub-Dean of Woolwich, 1984–86; Dean of Greenwich, 1985–86; Chaplain-Gen. and Archdeacon to Prison Service, 1986–93; Chaplain to HM Prison, Grendon and Spring Hill, 1993–98. Hon. Canon of Southwark Cathedral, 1985–. *Publication:* Creeds and Controversies, 1976. *Recreations:* theatre, music, books, crosswords. *Address:* Adeleine, Pett Road, Pett, East Sussex TN35 4HB. *T:* (01424) 813873. *Club:* Civil Service.

POUND, Stephen Pelham; MP (Lab) Ealing North, since 1997; *b* 3 July 1948; *s* of Pelham Pound and Dominica James; *m* 1976, Marilyn Anne Griffiths; one *s* one *d.* *Educ:* London Sch. of Economics (BSc Econ., Dip. Indust. Relations). Seaman, 1967–69; Bus Conductor, 1969–70; Hosp. Porter, 1970–79; student, 1980–84; Housing Officer, Camden Council, 1984–88; Homeless Persons Officer, Hammersmith and Fulham Council, 1988–90; Housing Officer, Paddington Churches HA, 1990–97. Councillor, London Borough of Ealing, 1982–98. *Recreations:* Fulham FC, cricket, walking, collecting comics. *Address:* House of Commons, SW1A 0AA. *T:* (020) 7219 6238; 115 Milton Road, Hanwell, W7 1LG. *Club:* St Joseph's Catholic Social; Fulham Football Club Supporters'.

POUNDER, Prof. Robert Edward, (Roy), MD, DSc; FRCP; Professor of Medicine, Royal Free and University College Medical School, since 1992; Hon. Consultant Physician and Gastroenterologist, Royal Free Hospital, since 1980; Vice President, Royal College of Physicians, from April 2002; *b* 31 May 1944; *s* of Edward Pounder and Annie Pounder (*née* Langdale); *m* 1972, Christine Lee; two *s.* *Educ:* Eltham Coll.; Peterhouse, Cambridge (BA 1st Cl. Hons Nat. Sci. 1966; BChir 1969; MB, MA 1970; MD 1977); Guy's Hosp. Med. Sch.; DSc (Med.) London 1992. MRCP 1971, FRCP 1984. Registrar, Central Middlesex Hosp., 1972–76; Sen. Registrar, St Thomas' Hosp., 1976–80; Royal Free Hospital School of Medicine: Sen. Lectr, 1980–85, Reader, 1985–91, in Medicine; Clin. Sub-Dean, 1986–88; Admissions Sub-Dean, 1992–95; Chm., Collegiate Cttee of Examrs, 1996–. Non-exec. Dir, Camden and Islington HA, 1996– (Vice-Chm., 2001–). Member Council: RCP, 1987–89, 1997–2000; British Digestive Foundn, 1987–98; British Soc. of Gastroenterology, 1996–2000 (Sec., 1982–86); Trustee, Alimentary Pharmacology and Therapeutics Trust, 1988–99. Chm., Friends of Peterhouse, 1999– (Mem. Council, 1982–). Gov., St Paul's Sch., London, 2001–. Founding Co-Editor, Alimentary Pharmacology and Therapeutics, 1987–; Ed.-in-Chief, GastroHep.com, 2000–. *Publications:* (ed) Long Cases in General Medicine, 1983, 2nd edn 1988; (ed) Doctor, There's Something Wrong with my Guts, 1983; (ed) Recent Advances in Gastroenterology, 6th edn 1986 to 10th edn 1994; (ed jtly) Diseases of the Gut and Pancreas, 1987, 2nd edn 1994 (trans. Italian and Greek); (ed jtly) Advanced Medicine, 1987; (ed jtly) A Colour Atlas of the Digestive System, 1989 (trans. Japanese); (ed) Landmark Papers: the histamine H_2-receptor antagonists, 1990; (ed jtly) Current Diagnosis and Treatment, 1996; (ed jtly) Inflammatory Bowel Disease, 1998; papers on pharmacological control of acid secretion, and inflammatory bowel disease. *Recreations:* gardening, family life, travelling. *Address:* Centre for Gastroenterology, Royal Free and University College Medical School, Rowland Hill Street, NW3 2PF. *T:* (020) 7830 2243. *Club:* Garrick.

POUNDS, Maj.-Gen. Edgar George Derek, CB 1975; retired; *b* 13 Oct. 1922; *s* of Edgar Henry Pounds, MBE, MSM, and Caroline Beatrice Pounds; *m* 1944, Barbara Winifred May Evans; one *s* one *d.* *Educ:* Reading Sch. War of 1939–45: enlisted, RM, 1940 (King's Badge, trng); HMS Kent, 1941–42 (Atlantic); commissioned as Reg. Off., Sept. 1942 (sword for dist., trng); HMS Berwick, 1943–44 (Atlantic and Russia). Co. Comdr, RM, 1945–51: Far East, Palestine, Malta, UK (Sniping Wing), Korea (US Bronze Star, 1950); Captain 1952. Instr, RM Officers' Trng Wing, UK, 1952–54; Adjt, 45 Commando, RM, 1954–57, Malta, Cyprus (despatches), Suez; RAF Staff Coll., Bracknell, 1958; Staff Captain, Dept of CGRM, London, 1959–60; Major 1960; Amphibious Ops

Officer, HMS Bulwark, 1961–62, Kuwait, Aden, E Africa, Borneo; Corps Drafting Off., UK, 1962–64; 40 Commando RM: 2nd in Comd, 1964–65, Borneo, and CO, 1966–67, Borneo and Far East; CO, 43 Commando, RM, 1967–68, UK based; GSO1 Dept CGRM, 1969–70; Col 1970; Naval Staff, MoD, 1970–72; Comdt Commando Trng Centre, RM, 1972–73; Actg Maj.-Gen. 1973; Maj.-Gen., RM, 1974; Commanding Commando Forces, RM, 1973–76, retired. Chief Exec., British Friesian Cattle Soc., 1976–87; Chm., RM Officers' Widows Pension Funds, 1987–92. Agricl Cons. (Europe), 1987. Mem. Council, Devon Co. Agricl Assoc., 1993–. *Publications:* articles on strategy, amphibious warfare, and tactics in professional jls, on cattle breeding and dairying in farming jls, and on computing in computer jls. *Recreations:* target rifle shooting, gardening, computer usages, reading. *Club:* Army and Navy.

POUNDS, Prof. Kenneth Alwyne, CBE 1984; FRS 1981; Professor of Space Physics, since 1973, and Head of Department of Physics and Astronomy, since 1986, University of Leicester; *b* 17 Nov. 1934; *s* of Harry and Dorothy Pounds; *m* 1st, 1961, Margaret Mary (*née* Connell); two *s* one *d*; 2nd, 1982, Joan Mary (*née* Millit); one *s* one *d*. *Educ:* Salt Sch., Shipley, Yorkshire; University Coll. London (BSc, PhD; Fellow, 1993). Department of Physics, University of Leicester: Asst Lectr, 1960; Lecturer, 1961; Sen. Lectr, 1969; Chief Exec., PPARC (on leave of absence from Univ. of Leicester), 1994–98. Member: SERC, 1980–84 (Chm., Astronomy, Space and Radio Bd); Management Bd, British Nat. Space Centre, 1986–88; Pres., RAS, 1990–92. DUniv York, 1984; Hon. DSc: Loughborough, 1992; Sheffield Hallam, 1997; Warwick, 2001. Gold Medal, RAS, 1989. *Publications:* many, in Monthly Notices, Nature, Astrophysical Jl, etc. *Recreations:* sport, music. *Address:* 12 Swale Close, Oadby, Leicester LE2 4GF. *T:* (0116) 271 9370.

POUNTAIN, Sir Eric (John), Kt 1985; DL; Chairman: James Beattie PLC, since 1987 (Deputy Chairman, 1985–87; Director, since 1984); Tarmac PLC, 1983–94 (Group Chief Executive, 1979–92); IMI PLC, 1989–2001 (Director, since 1988); *b* 5 Aug. 1933; *s* of Horace Pountain and Elsie Pountain; *m* 1960, Joan Patricia Sutton; one *s* one *d*. *Educ:* Queen Mary Grammar Sch., Walsall. CIMgt; FFB, FIHE, FCIB; FRSA. Joined F. Maitland Selwyn & Co., auctioneers and estate agents, 1956, joint principal, 1959; founded Midland & General Develts, 1964, acquired by John McLean & Sons Ltd, 1969; Chief Exec., John McLean & Sons, 1969, acquired by Tarmac PLC, 1974; Chief Exec., newly formed Tarmac Housing Div., until 1979. Director: Tarmac PLC, 1977–94; Midland Bank, 1986–92; United Newspapers, 1992–98; Lloyds Chemists plc, 1993–97; John Maunders Gp, 1994–98; Tay Homes plc, 1999–. Member: Adv. Council, Prince's Youth Business Trust, 1988–; President's Appeal Cttee, Age Concern, 1991–93; Trustee: Lichfield Cathedral Trust, 1995–; Crimestoppers Trust, 1995–. Pres., Midlands Industrial Council, 1988–; Patron, Staffs Agricl Soc. DL Stafford, 1985. *Recreations:* golf, shooting, tennis. *Address:* James Beattie PLC, 71/78 Victoria Street, Wolverhampton WV1 3PQ.

POUNTNEY, David Willoughby, CBE 1994; freelance director; *b* 10 Sept. 1947; *s* of late Dorothy and Willoughby Pountney; *m* 1980, Jane Henderson; one *s* one *d*. *Educ:* St John's College Choir School, Cambridge; Radley College; St John's College, Cambridge (MA). Joined Scottish Opera, 1970; 1st major production Katya Kabanova (Janacek), Wexford Fest., 1972; Dir of Productions, Scottish Opera, 1976–80; individual guest productions for all British Opera companies, also USA (Metropolitan Opera début, world première of The Voyage by Philip Glass, 1992), Aust., Italy, Germany, The Netherlands; Dir of Prodns, ENO, 1982–93; productions for ENO include: Rusalka (Dvorak); Osud (Janacek); Dr Faust (Busoni); Lady Macbeth of Mtsensk (Shostakovich); Wozzeck (Berg); Pelléas and Mélisande (Debussy); Don Carlos (Verdi); Falstaff (Verdi); The Adventures of Mr Broucek (Janacek); The Fairy Queen (Purcell); Nabucco (Verdi), 2000; other major productions include: The Doctor of Myddfai (and libretto) (Peter Maxwell Davies), WNO, 1996; Julietta (Martinu), Opera North, 1997; Dalibor (Smetana), Scottish Opera, 1998; Guillaume Tell (Rossini), Vienna State Opera, 1998; Greek Passion, Bregenz, 1999, Royal Opera House, 2000; Faust (Gounod), Munich, 2000; Mr Emmet Takes a Walk (Peter Maxwell Davies), première, Orkney Fest., 2000; Genoveva (and trans.) (Schumann), Opera North, 2000; Paradise Moscow, Opera North, 2001. Martinu Medal, Prague, 2000. Chevalier de l'Ordre des Arts et des Lettres (France), 1993. *Publications:* (with Mark Elder and Peter Jonas) Power House, 1992; numerous trans. of opera, esp. Czech and Russian repertoire. *Recreations:* croquet, food and wine. *Address:* Suite 130, 78 Marylebone High Street, W1M 4AP. *T:* (07003) 937373. *Club:* Garrick.

POUT, Harry Wilfrid, CB 1978; OBE 1959; CEng, FIEE; Marconi Underwater Systems Ltd, 1982–86, Defence Consultant, since 1986; *b* 11 April 1920; British; *m* 1949, Margaret Elizabeth (*née* Nelson); three *d*. *Educ:* East Ham Grammar Sch.; Imperial Coll., London. BSc (Eng); ACGI 1940. RN Scientific Service, 1940; Admty Signal Estab. (later Admty Signal and Radar Estab.), 1940–54; Dept of Operational Research, Admty, 1954–59; idc 1959; Head of Guided Weapon Projects, Admty, 1960–65; Asst Chief Scientific Adviser (Projects), MoD, 1965–69; Dir, Admiralty Surface Weapons Estabt, 1969–72; Dep. Controller, Guided Weapons, 1973, Guided Weapons and Electronics, 1973–75, Air Systems, 1975–79, Aircraft Weapons and Electronics, 1979–80, MoD. Defence consultant, 1980–82. FCGI 1972; FIMgt. *Publications:* (jtly) The New Scientists, 1971; (contrib.) Radar at Sea—the Royal Navy in World War 2, 1993; (contrib.) The Applications of Radar in the Royal Navy in World War 2, 1995; classified books; contribs to jls of IEE, RAeS, RUSI, Jl of Naval Sci., etc. *Recreations:* mountaineering, gardening and do-it-yourself activities, amateur geology. *Address:* Oakmead, Fox Corner, Worplesdon, near Guildford, Surrey GU3 3PP. *T:* (01483) 232223.

POVER, Alan John, CMG 1990; HM Diplomatic Service, retired; High Commissioner to the Republic of Gambia, 1990–93; *b* 16 Dec. 1933; *s* of John Pover and Anne (*née* Hession); *m* 1964, Doreen Elizabeth Dawson; one *s* two *d*. *Educ:* Salesian College, Thornleigh, Bolton. Served HM Forces, 1953–55; Min. of Pensions and Nat. Insce, 1955–61; Commonwealth Relations Office, 1961; Second Secretary: Lagos, 1962–66; Tel Aviv, 1966–69; Second, later First, Sec., Karachi/Islamabad, 1969–73; First Sec., FCO, 1973–76; Consul, Cape Town, 1976–80; Counsellor, Diplomatic Service Inspector, 1983–86; Counsellor and Consul-Gen., Washington, 1986–90. *Recreations:* cricket, golf, gardening. *Address:* 6 Farriers Lane, East Ilsley, Berks RG20 7JB. *Clubs:* Royal Commonwealth Society; West Berkshire Golf.

POVEY, Sir Keith, Kt 2001; QPM 1991; HM Inspector of Constabulary, since 1997; *b* 30 April 1943; *s* of late Trevor Roberts Povey and Dorothy (*née* Parsonnage); *m* 1964, Carol Ann Harvey; two *d*. *Educ:* Abbeydale Grammar Sch., Sheffield; Sheffield Univ. (BA Law). Joined Sheffield City Police, 1962; Chief Superintendent, S Yorks, seconded as Staff Officer to Sir Lawrence Byford, HMCIC, 1984–86; Asst Chief Constable, Humberside, 1986–90; Dep. Chief Constable, Northants, 1990–93; Chief Constable, Leics, 1993–97. Hon. Secretary: ACPO General Purposes Cttee, 1994–96 (Chm., 1996–97); ACPO Crime Prevention Sub-cttee, 1994–96 (Chm., 1996–97). *Recreations:* jogging, flying (private pilot's licence). *Address:* HM Inspectorate of Constabulary, Block 6, Westbrook Centre, Milton Road, Cambridge CB4 1YG. *T:* (01223) 467115.

POWELL; *see* Baden-Powell.

POWELL, family name of **Baron Powell of Bayswater**.

POWELL OF BAYSWATER, Baron *cr* 2000 (Life Peer), of Canterbury in the County of Kent; **Charles David Powell,** KCMG 1990; Chairman: Sagitta Asset Management Ltd; Phillips de Pury Luxembourg LVMH (UK); *b* 6 July 1941; *s* of Air Vice Marshal John Frederick Powell, *qv*; *m* 1964, Carla Bonardi; two *s*. *Educ:* King's Sch., Canterbury; New Coll., Oxford (BA). Diplomatic Service, 1963–83: served Helsinki, Washington, Bonn; Counsellor, 1979; Special Counsellor for Rhodesia negotiations, 1979–80; Private Sec. to the Prime Minister, 1983–91. Director: National Westminster Bank, 1991–2000; Jardine Matheson Hldgs, 1991–2000; Matheson & Co., 1991–; Mandarin Oriental Hotel Gp, 1992; J. Rothschild Name Co., 1993–; Said Holdings, 1994–2000; LVMH Moet-Hennessy-Louis Vuitton, 1995–; British-Mediterranean Airways, 1998– (Dep. Chm.); Caterpillar Inc., 2001–; Textron Inc., 2001–. Member, European Advisory Board: Rolls Royce, 2000–; Hicks Muse Tate & Furst; Mem. Internat. Adv. Bd, Barrick Gold, 2000–; HCL Technologies, 1999–; Mem., Internat. Adv. Council, Textron Corp., 1995–. Chm., Singapore British Business Council, 1994–; Pres., China-Britain Business Council, 1998–. Trustee, Aspen Inst., 1995–; Chm., Trustees, Oxford Business Sch. Foundn, 1998–. *Recreation:* walking. *Address:* House of Lords, SW1A 0PW. *Club:* Turf.

See also J. C. Powell, J. N. Powell.

POWELL, Albert Edward; JP; General President of Society of Graphical and Allied Trades, 1973–82, of SOGAT '82 1982–83; *b* 20 May 1927; *s* of Albert and Mary Powell; *m* 1947, Margaret Neville; one *s* two *d*. *Educ:* Holy Family Elementary Sch., Morden. FIWSP. London Organiser, SOGAT, 1957, Organising Secretary, 1967. Has served on various Committees and Boards, including: past Chairman, Croydon College of Art, past Governor, London College of Printing. Chairman, Paper & Paper Products Industry Trng Bd, 1975 (Mem. Central Arbitration Cttee, 1976); Member: TUC Printing Industries Cttee, 1971; NEDO Printing Industries Sector Working Party, 1980; Methods-Time Measurement Assoc., 1966. Member: Industrial Tribunal, 1983; Social Security Appeal Tribunal, 1984; Parole Bd, 1986. JP: Wimbledon, 1961–75; Southend-on-Sea, 1975–80; Bexley, 1980. Silver Jubilee Medal, 1977. *Recreations:* gardening reading (science fiction), music. *Address:* 31 Red House Lane, Bexleyheath, Kent DA6 8JF. *T:* (020) 8304 7480.

POWELL, Sir Arnold Joseph Philip; *see* Powell, Sir Philip.

POWELL, Christopher; *see* Powell, J. C.

POWELL, Gen. Colin Luther, Hon. KCB 1993; Legion of Merit, Bronze Star, Air Medal, Purple Heart; Secretary of State, USA, since 2001; *b* 5 April 1937; *s* of late Luther Powell and Maud Ariel Powell (*née* McKoy); *m* 1962, Alma V. Johnson; one *s* two *d*. *Educ:* City Univ. of New York (BS Geology); George Washington Univ. (MBA). Commissioned 2nd Lieut, US Army, 1958; White House Fellow, 1972–73; Comdr, 2nd Brigade, 101st Airborne Div., 1976–77; exec. asst to Sec. of Energy, 1979; sen. mil. asst to Dep. Sec. of Defense, 1979–81; Asst Div. Comdr, 4th Inf. Div., Fort Carson, 1981–83; sen. mil. asst to Sec. of Defense, 1983–86; US V Corps, Europe, 1986–87; dep. asst to President 1987, asst 1987–89, for Nat. Security Affairs; General 1989; C-in-C, US Forces Command, Fort McPherson, April–Sept. 1989; Chm., Jt Chiefs of Staff, 1989–93. *Publication:* My American Journey (autobiog.), 1995 (UK title, A Soldier's Way). *Recreations:* racquetball, restoring old Volvos. *Address:* Department of State, 2201 C Street NW, Washington, DC 20520, USA; 1317 Ballantrae Farm Drive, McLean, VA 22101, USA.

POWELL, His Honour (Dewi) Watkin; JP. a Circuit Judge, and Official Referee for Wales, 1972–92; *b* Aberdare, 29 July 1920; *o s* of W. H. Powell, AMICE and of M. A. Powell, Radyr, Glam; *m* 1951, Alice, *e d* of William and Mary Williams, Nantmor, Caerns; one *d*. *Educ:* Penarth Grammar Sch.; Jesus Coll., Oxford (MA). Called to Bar, Inner Temple, 1949. Dep. Chm., Merioneth and Cardigan QS, 1966–71; Dep. Recorder of Cardiff, Birkenhead, Merthyr Tydfil and Swansea, 1965–71; Junior, Wales and Chester Circuit, 1968; Liaison Judge for Dyfed, 1974–84, for Mid Glamorgan, 1984–91. Vice-Pres., South and Mid Glamorgan and Gwynedd branches of Magistrates' Assoc. Mem. Exec. Cttee, Plaid Cymru, 1943–55. Chairman: Constitutional Cttee, 1967–70; Govt of Wales Bill Drafting Gp, 1994–97; Constitutional Wkg Party, Parlt for Wales Campaign, 1994–; Member Council: Hon. Soc. of Cymmrodorion, 1965–93 (Chm., 1978–84; Vice Pres., 1984–); Cytun, 1993–98. Member, Court and Council: Univ. of Wales; Univ. of Wales Coll. of Cardiff (Vice Pres. and Vice Chm. of Council, 1987–98; Hon. Fellow). Hon. Mem., Gorsedd of Bards. President: Cymdeithas Theatr Cymru, 1984–89; Baptist Union of Wales, 1993–94; Pres., Free Church Council of Wales, 1994–98 (Vice-Pres., 1993–94). JP Mid Glamorgan. Hon. LLD Wales, 1997. *Publications:* Ymadroddion Llys Barn (Forensic Phraseology), 1974; (contrib.) Y Gair a'r Genedl, 1986; (contrib.) Lawyers and Laymen, 1986; (contrib.) Challenges to a Challenging Faith, 1995; (with John Osmond) Power to the People of Wales (Grym i Bobl Cymru), 1997; Cynulliad i Genedl, 1999. *Recreations:* gardening, reading theology, Welsh history and literature. *Address:* Nanmor, Morannedd, Cricieth, Gwynedd LL52 0PP.

POWELL, Earl Alexander, III, PhD; Director, National Gallery of Art, Washington, since 1992; *b* 24 Oct. 1943; *s* of Earl Alexander Powell and Elizabeth Powell; *m* 1971, Nancy Landry; three *d*. *Educ:* A. B. Williams Coll.; Harvard Univ. (PhD 1974); A. M. Fogg Art Mus. Teaching Fellow in Fine Arts, Harvard Univ., 1970–74 (Travelling Fellowship, 1973–74); Curator, Michener Collection and Asst Prof. of Art History, Univ. of Texas at Austin, 1974–76; National Gallery of Art, Washington: Mus. Curator, Sen. Staff Asst to Asst Director and Chief Curator, 1976–78; Exec. Curator, 1979–80; Dir, LA County Mus. of Art, 1980–92. Hon. DFA: Otis Parsons, 1987; Williams, 1993. King Olav Medal (Norway), 1978; Chevalier of Arts and Letters (France), 1985; Grand Official, Order of Infante D. Henrique (Portugal), 1995; Commendatore, Ordine al Merito (Italy), 1998; Chevalier, Legion of Honour (France), 2000. *Publication:* Thomas Cole, 1990. *Address:* National Gallery of Art, 6th and Constitution Avenue NW, Washington, DC 20565, USA. *T:* (202) 8426001. *Clubs:* Metropolitan (Washington); Knickerbocker (New York).

POWELL, Francis Turner, MBE 1945; Chairman, Laing & Cruickshank, Stockbrokers, 1978–80; *b* 15 April 1914; *s* of Francis Arthur and Dorothy May Powell; *m* 1940, Joan Audrey Bartlett; one *s* one *d*. *Educ:* Lancing College. Served War, Queen's Royal Regt (TA), 1939–45 (Major). Joined L. Powell Sons & Co. (Stockbrokers), 1932, Partner, 1939; merged with Laing & Cruickshank, 1976. Mem. Council, Stock Exchange, 1963–78 (Dep. Chm., 1976–78). *Recreations:* golf, gardening. *Address:* 2 Horsley Court, East Horsley, Leatherhead, Surrey KT24 6QS.

POWELL, Geoffrey; *see* Powell, J. G.

POWELL, Prof. James Alfred, OBE 1996; DSc; CEng; Eur Ing; FIOA; Professor of Academic Enterprise, and Pro Vice Chancellor for Enterprise and Regional Affairs, Salford University, since 2001; *b* Sutton, 30 Oct. 1945; *s* of James Herbert Powell and Eileen Powell (*née* Newell); *m* 1969, Jennifer Elizabeth Morton; one *s*. *Educ:* De Burgh Sch.,

Tadworth; UMIST (BSc, MSc; AUMIST); Salford Univ. (PhD; DSc 2000). FIOA 1984; CEng 1996. ICI Schol., Salford Univ., 1970–71; Lectr, then Sen. Res. Associate, Sch. of Architecture, Dundee Univ., 1971–74; School of Architecture, Portsmouth Polytechnic: Reader in Building Utilisation, 1975–84; Prof. of Design Studies, 1984–91; Hd of Dept, 1990–91; Dep. Dean of Technol., Hd of Dept of Engrg and Mfg Systems and Lucas Prof. of Design Systems, Brunel Univ., 1991–94; Lucas Prof. of Informing Design Technol., 1994–2001, Dir of Acad. Enterprise, 1999–2001, Salford Univ. Science and Engineering Research Council: IT Applications Co-ordinator, 1988–93; Mem., Engrg Bd, 1988–93; Chm., Educn and Trng Cttee, 1988–93; IT Awareness in Engrg Co-ordinator, EPSRC, 1994. Mem., Learning Foresight Panel, OST, 1996–. Internat. Speaker, Nat. IT Council of Malaysia, 1998–. Designer, Menuhin Auditorium for Portsmouth String Quartet Fest., 1980. Award for Interactive Audio in Multi Media, European Multi Media Assoc., 1992. *Publications:* Design: Science: Methods, 1981; Changing Design, 1982; Designing for Building Utilisation, 1984; Noise at Work Regulations, 1990, 2nd edn 1994; Intelligent Command and Control Acquisition and Review using Simulation, 1992; The Powell Report: review of SERC engineering education and training, 1993; Informing Technologies for Construction, Civil Engineering and Transport, 1993; Neural Computing, 1994; Engineering Decision Support, 1995; Virtual Reality and Rapid Prototyping, 1995. *Recreations:* meditation, cycling, squash, yoga, boating, painting. *Address:* Academic Enterprise, Faraday House, University of Salford, Salford M5 4WT. *T:* (0161) 745 5464.

POWELL, (John) Christopher; Chairman: BMP DDB Ltd, since 1999; Ealing, Hammersmith & Hounslow Health Authority, since 2000; *b* 4 Oct 1943; *s* of Air Vice-Marshal John Frederick Powell, *qv*; *m* 1973, Rosemary Jeanne Symmons; two *s* one *d*. *Educ:* St Peter's Sch., York; London Sch. of Econs (BSc Econ.). Worked in advertising agencies, in London, 1965–69; BMP, subseq. BMP DDB: Partner, 1969–82; Jt Man. Dir, 1975–85; Chief Exec., 1986–98. Non-executive Director: Riverside Studios, 1989–; United News & Media plc, 1995–. Dep. Chm., Riverside Community NHS Trust, 1994–2000. Hon. Advr, Bd of Internat. Family Health, 1997–. Pres., Inst. Practitioners in Advertising, 1993–95. Trustee: IPPR, 1999– (Chm., 2001–); Divert, 2000–. *Recreations:* riding, tennis, gardening, theatre. *Address:* BMP DDB Ltd, 12 Bishop's Bridge Road, W2 6AA. *T:* (020) 7258 3979. *Club:* Groucho.

See also Baron Powell of Bayswater, J. N. Powell.

POWELL, Air Vice-Marshal John Frederick, OBE 1956; Warden and Director of Studies, Moor Park College, 1972–77; *b* 12 June 1915; *y s* of Rev. Morgan Powell, Limpley Stoke, Bath; *m* 1939, Geraldine Ysolda, *e d* of late Sir John Fitzgerald Moylan, CB, CBE; four *s*. *Educ:* Lancing; King's Coll., Cambridge (MA). Joined RAF Educnl Service, 1937; Lectr, RAF College, 1938–39; RAFVR (Admin. and Special Duties) ops room duties, Coastal Comd, 1939–45 (despatches); RAF Educn Br., 1946; Sen. Instructor in History, RAF Coll., 1946–49; RAF Staff Coll., 1950; Air Min., 1951–53; Sen. Tutor, RAF Coll., 1953–59; Educn Staff, HQ FEAF, 1959–62; MoD, 1962–64; Comd Educn Officer, HQ Bomber Comd, 1964–66; OC, RAF Sch. of Educn, 1966–67; Dir of Educational Services, RAF, 1967–72; Air Commodore, 1967; Air Vice-Marshal, 1968. *Recreations:* choral music, gardening. *Address:* Barker's Hill Cottage, Donhead St Andrew, Shaftesbury, Dorset SP7 9EB. *T:* (01747) 828505. *Club:* Royal Air Force.

See also Baron Powell of Bayswater, J. C. Powell, J. N. Powell.

POWELL, (John) Geoffrey, CBE 1987; Deputy Chairman, Local Government Boundary Commission for England, 1984–90; *b* 13 Jan. 1928; *s* of H. W. J. and W. A. S. Powell. *Educ:* Shrewsbury. FRICS; FSVA; ACIArb. Lieut, Welsh Guards, 1945–48. Chm., Property Adv. Gp, DoE, 1982–86 (Chm., New Towns Sub-Gp, 1982–86); Member: Skelmersdale New Town Corp., 1978–85; Review Cttee of Govt Valuation Services, 1982; British Rail Property Board, 1985–91; NCB Pension Fund Adv. Panel, 1985–90. Sec.-Gen., European Group of Valuers of Fixed Assets, 1982–87; European Rep., Internat. Assets Valuation Standards Cttee, 1984–87. Chm., RICS Cttees, 1960–83, incl. Assets Valuation Standards Cttee, 1981–83. External Examr, Reading Univ., 1986–88; Member: Liverpool Univ. Dept. of Civic Design Adv. Cttee, 1986–90; Adv. Panel, Law Center, USC, 1987–. Mem. Editl Bd, Rent Review and Lease Renewal, 1985–89. *Address:* Whites Farmhouse, Mickleton, near Chipping Campden, Glos GL55 6PU. *T:* (01386) 438146.

POWELL, John Lewis; QC 1990; a Recorder, since 2000; *b* 14 Sept. 1950; *s* of Gwyn Powell and Lilian Mary Powell (*née* Griffiths); *m* 1973, Eva Zofia Lomnicka; one *s* two *d*. *Educ:* Christ Coll., Brecon; Amman Valley Grammar Sch.; Trinity Hall, Cambridge (MA, LLB). Called to the Bar, Middle Temple, 1974 (Harmsworth Schol.), Bencher 1998. In practice, 1974–. Pres., Soc. of Construction Law, 1991–93; Chm., Law Reform Cttee, Bar Council, 1997–98. Contested (Lab) Cardigan, 1979. *Publications:* (with R. Jackson, QC) Professional Negligence, 1982, 5th edn; (with Eva Lomnicka) Encyclopedia of Financial Services Law, 1987; Palmer's Company Law, 24th edn 1987, 25th edn 1992; Issues and Offers of Company Securities: the new regimes, 1988; various articles. *Recreations:* travel, walking, sheep farming. *Address:* 4 New Square, Lincoln's Inn, WC2A 3RJ. *T:* (020) 7822 2000.

POWELL, Jonathan Leslie; Director of Drama and Co-production, Carlton Television, since 1993; *b* 25 April 1947; *s* of James Dawson Powell and Phyllis Nora Sylvester (*née* Doubleday); *m* 1990, Sally Jane Brampton, *qv*; one *d*. *Educ:* Sherborne; University of East Anglia. BA Hons (English and American Studies). Script editor and producer of drama, Granada TV, 1970–77; BBC TV: Producer, drama serials, 1977–83; Hd of Drama Series and Serials, 1983–87; Hd of Drama, 1987; Controller, BBC1, 1988–92. *TV serials include:* Testament of Youth, 1979 (BAFTA award); Tinker Tailor Soldier Spy, 1979; Pride and Prejudice, 1980; Thérèse Raquin, 1980; The Bell, 1982; Smiley's People, 1982 (Peabody Medal, USA); The Old Men at the Zoo, 1983; Bleak House, 1985; Tender is the Night, 1985; A Perfect Spy, 1987. Royal Television Soc. Silver Award for outstanding achievement, 1979–80. *Address:* c/o Carlton Television, 35–38 Portman Square, W1H 9FU. *T:* (020) 7486 6688.

POWELL, Jonathan Nicholas; Chief of Staff to the Prime Minister, since 1997 (to the Leader of Opposition, 1995–97); *b* 14 Aug. 1956; *s* of Air Vice-Marshal John Frederick Powell, *qv* and Geraldine Ysolda Powell (*née* Moylan); *m* 1980, Karen Elizabeth Drayne (marr. diss. 1997); two *s*; partner, Sarah Helm; two *d*. *Educ:* University Coll., Oxford (MA Hist.); Univ. of Pennsylvania (MA Hist.). With BBC, 1978; Granada TV, 1978–79; joined FCO, 1979; Lisbon, 1980–83; FCO, 1983–85; Member, British Delegation to: CDE, Stockholm, 1985; CSCE, Vienna, 1985–89; FCO, 1989–91; Washington, 1991–95. *Recreations:* hyphenated sports. *Address:* 10 Downing Street, SW1A 2AA.

See also Baron Powell of Bayswater, J. C. Powell.

POWELL, Kenneth George; architectural critic and journalist; Consultant Director, Twentieth Century Society, since 1995; *b* 17 March 1947; *s* of Alan Powell and Winifred Alice Powell (*née* Hill); *m* 1969, Susan Harris-Smith. *Educ:* Canton High Sch. for Boys, Cardiff; London Sch. of Econs (BA 1968); Univ. of Manchester (MA Arch 1979). Research Assistant: Inst. of Historical Res., London, 1971–74; History of Univ. of Oxford, 1974–77; Temp. Lectr in Hist., UCL, 1977–78; worked in museums and as freelance researcher, 1978–84; Sec., SAVE Britain's Heritage, 1984–87; Architectural Corresp., Daily Telegraph, 1987–94; freelance writer. Member: Art and Architecture Cttee, Westminster Cathedral, 1994–; London DAC, 1996–. Hon. FRIBA 2000. *Publications:* Stansted: Norman Foster and the architecture of flight, 1991; Vauxhall Cross, 1992; (with R. Moore) Structures, Space and Skin, 1993; World Cities: London, 1993; Richard Rogers, 1994; Edward Cullinan Architects, 1995; Grand Central Terminal, 1996; Richard Rogers: complete works (I), 1999; Architecture Transformed, 1999; Jubilee Line Architecture, 2000; The City Transformed, 2000; (jtly) The National Portrait Gallery: an architectural history, 2000; contrib. many articles in Country Life, Architects Jl, etc. *Recreations:* looking at buildings, painting, Christian Liturgy, places (especially Yorkshire and Italy). *Address:* Flat 1, 78 Nightingale Lane, SW12 8NR. *T:* (020) 8673 3383; 7 Woodbine Terrace, Headingley, Leeds LS6 4AF. *T:* (0113) 275 6538.

POWELL, Prof. Kenneth Leslie, PhD; Professor, University College London, since 1995; *b* 23 July 1949; *s* of Alec and Ada Powell; *m* 1st, 1968, Anne (marr. diss. 1974); 2nd, 1975, Dorothy J. M. Purifoy; two *d*, and one step *s* one step *d*. *Educ:* Apsley Grammar Sch.; Univ. of Reading (BSc Microbiology 1970); Univ. of Birmingham (PhD 1973). Post-doctoral Fellow, 1973–75, Asst Prof., 1975–77, Baylor Coll. of Medicine, Houston; Lectr, 1978–85, Sen. Lectr, 1985–86, Univ. of Leeds; Wellcome Foundation: Head of: Biochemical Virology, 1986–88; Antiviral Res., 1988–90; Cell Biology, 1990–93; Biology, 1993–95; Dep. Dir, Cruciform Project, subseq. Wolfson Inst. for Biomed. Res., 1995–2000. Vis. Prof., Univ. of Michigan, 1985. Chief Executive Officer: Inpharmatica Ltd, 1998–2000; Arrow Therapeutics, 1998–. *Publications:* more than 50 articles in learned jls. *Recreations:* farming, bowling. *Address:* Wolfson Institute for Biochemical Research, University College London, WC1E 6BT. *T:* (020) 7504 4175. *Club:* West Beckenham Bowling.

POWELL, Prof. Lawrie William, AC 1990; MD, PhD; FRACP, FRCP; FTSE; Professor of Medicine, University of Queensland, since 1975; Director, Queensland Institute of Medical Research, 1990–2000; *b* 4 Dec. 1934; *s* of Victor Alexander Powell and Ellen Evelyn (*née* Davidson); *m* 1958, Margaret Emily Ingram; two *s* three *d*. *Educ:* Univ. of Queensland (MB BS 1958; MD 1965; PhD 1973); Univ. of London; Harvard Medical Sch. FRACP 1975; FRCP 1991; Hon. FRCP Thailand, 1997. Hon. Lectr, Royal Free Hosp. and Univ. of London, 1963–65; Vis. Prof., Harvard Medical Sch., 1972–73. FTSE 1995. DUniv Griffith, 1996. *Publications:* Metals and the Liver, 1978; Fundamentals of Gastroenterology, 1975, 6th edn 1995. *Recreations:* music, chess, bushwalking. *Address:* 22 Paten Road, The Gap, Brisbane, Qld 4061, Australia.

POWELL, Prof. Michael James David, FRS 1983; John Humphrey Plummer Professor of Applied Numerical Analysis, University of Cambridge, 1976–2001, now Emeritus; Fellow of Pembroke College, Cambridge, since 1978; *b* 29 July 1936; *s* of William James David Powell and Beatrice Margaret (*née* Page); *m* 1959, Caroline Mary Henderson; two *d* (one *s* decd). *Educ:* Eastbourne Coll.; Peterhouse, Cambridge (Schol.; BA 1959; ScD 1979). Mathematician at Atomic Energy Research Estabt, Harwell, 1959–76; special merit research appt to banded level, 1969, and to senior level, 1975. For. Associate, NAS, US, 2001. Hon. DSc UEA, 2001. George B. Dantzig prize in Mathematical Programming, 1982; Naylor Prize, 1983, Sen. Whitehead Prize, 1999, London Math. Soc.; Gold Medal, IMA, 1996. *Publications:* Approximation Theory and Methods, 1981; papers on numerical mathematics, especially approximation and optimization calculations. *Recreations:* canals, golf, walking. *Address:* 134 Milton Road, Cambridge CB4 1LE.

POWELL, Sir Nicholas (Folliott Douglas), 4th Bt *cr* 1897; Company Director; *b* 17 July 1935; *s* of Sir Richard George Douglas Powell, 3rd Bt, MC, and Elizabeth Josephine (*d* 1979), *d* of late Lt-Col O. R. McMullen, CMG; *S* father, 1980; *m* 1st, 1960, Daphne Jean (marr. diss. 1987), 2nd *d* of G. H. Errington, MC; one *s* one *d*; 2nd, 1987, Davina Allsopp; two *s* one *d*. *Educ:* Gordonstoun. Lieut Welsh Guards, 1953–57. *Heir: s* James Richard Douglas Powell [*b* 17 Oct. 1962; *m* 1991, Susanna, *e d* of David Murray Threipland; two *s* one *d*]. *Address:* Hillside Estate, Bromley, Zimbabwe.

POWELL, Prof. Percival Hugh, MA, DLitt, Dr Phil.; Professor of German, Indiana University, 1970–83, now Emeritus; *b* 4 Sept. 1912; 3rd *s* of late Thomas Powell and late Marie Sophia Roeser; *m* 1944, Dorothy Mavis Pattison (*née* Donald) (marr. diss. 1964); two *s* one adopted *d*; *m* 1966, Mary Kathleen (*née* Wilson); one *s*. *Educ:* University College, Cardiff (Fellow 1981); Univs of Rostock, Zürich, Bonn. 1st Class Hons German (Wales), 1933; Univ. Teachers' Diploma in Education, 1934; MA (Wales) Dist. 1936; Research Fellow of Univ. of Wales, 1936–38; Modern Languages Master, Towyn School, 1934–36; Dr Phil. (Rostock) 1938; Lektor in English, Univ. of Bonn, 1938–39; Asst Lectr, Univ. Coll., Cardiff, 1939–40; War Service, 1940–46 (Capt. Intelligence Corps); Lecturer in German, Univ. Coll., Leicester, 1946, Head of Department of German, 1954; Prof. of German, Univ. of Leicester, 1958–69. Barclay Acheson Prof. of Internat. Studies at Macalester Coll., Minn., USA, 1965–66. DLitt (Wales) 1962. British Academy award, 1963; Fritz Thyssen Foundation Award, 1964; Leverhulme Trust Award, 1968. *Publications:* Pierre Corneilles Dramen in Deutschen Bearbeitungen, 1939; critical editions of dramas of Andreas Gryphius, 1955–72; critical edn of J. G. Schoch's Comœdia vom Studentenleben, 1976; Trammels of Tradition, 1988; Louise von Gall, 1993; Fervor and Fiction, 1996; Heinrich Burkart, 1997; Berliner Don Quixote, facsimile of 1832–33 edn, 2001; articles and reviews in English and foreign literary jls. *Recreation:* music. *Address:* c/o Department of Germanic Studies, Ballantine Hall, Indiana University, Bloomington, IN 47405, USA.

POWELL, Sir Philip, CH 1984; Kt 1975; OBE 1957; RA 1977 (ARA 1972); FRIBA; Partner of Powell and Moya, Architects, since 1946, and Powell, Moya and Partners, 1976–91; *b* 15 March 1921; *yr s* of late Canon A. C. Powell and late Mary Winnifred (*née* Walker), Epsom and Chichester; *m* 1953, Philippa, *d* of Lt-Col C. C. Eccles, Tunbridge Wells; one *s* one *d*. *Educ:* Epsom Coll.; AA Sch. of Architecture (Hons Diploma). *Works include:* Churchill Gdns flats, Westminster, 1948–62 (won in open competition; Civic Trust Special Award for most outstanding winner 1960–99); houses and flats at Gospel Oak, St Pancras, 1954, Vauxhall Park, Lambeth, 1972, Covent Garden, 1983; houses at: Chichester, 1950; Toys Hill, 1954; Oxshott, 1954; Baughurst, Hants, 1954; Skylon for Fest. of Britain, 1951 (won in open competition); British Pavilion, Expo 70, Osaka, Japan, 1970; Mayfield Sch., Putney, 1955; Plumstead Manor Sch., Woolwich, 1970; Dining Rooms at Bath Acad. of Art, Corsham, 1970, and Eton Coll., 1974; extensions, Brasenose Coll., Oxford, 1961, and Corpus Christi Coll., Oxford, 1969; picture gall. and undergrad. rooms, Christ Church, Oxford, 1967; Wolfson Coll., Oxford, 1974; Cripps Building, St John's Coll., Cambridge, 1967; Cripps Court, Queens' Coll., Cambridge, 1976; Chichester Fest. Theatre, 1962; Swimming Baths, Putney, 1967; Hosps at Swindon, Slough, High Wycombe, Wythenshawe, Woolwich, Maidstone, Hastings, Ashington, Great Ormond Street, 1959–93; Museum of London, 1976; London and Manchester Assurance HQ, near Exeter, 1978; Sch. for Advanced Urban Studies, Bristol Univ., 1981; NatWest Bank, Shaftesbury Ave, London, 1982; labs etc, and Queen's Building, RHBNC, Egham, 1986–90; Queen Elizabeth II Conf. Centre, Westminster, 1986. Mem.

Justices' Clerks' Soc., 1983–90 (Chm., Parly Cttee, Chm., Conf. and Social Cttee); Mem., Inner London Probation Cttee, 1996–2001. *Recreations:* conjuring (Sec., The Magic Circle), cartophily. *Address:* Bow Street Magistrates' Court, 28 Bow Street, WC2E 7AS. *Club:* Magic Circle.

PRATT, Michael John; QC 1976; a Recorder of the Crown Court, 1974–94; *b* 23 May 1933; *o s* of W. Brownlow Pratt; *m* 1960, Elizabeth Jean Hendry; two *s* three *d*. *Educ:* West House Sch., Edgbaston; Malvern Coll. LLB (Birmingham). Army service, 2nd Lieut, 3rd Carabiniers (Prince of Wales's Dragoon Guards); Staff Captain. Called to the Bar, Middle Temple, 1954, Bencher, 1986; a Dep. High Court Judge, 1982–94. Chm. Govs, West House Sch., Edgbaston, 1975–2000; Gov., Malvern Coll., 1976–. *Recreations:* music, theatre, sport generally. *Address:* 9 Moorland Road, Edgbaston, Birmingham B16 9JP. *T:* (0121) 454 1071. *Clubs:* Cavalry and Guards; Edgbaston Golf.

PRATT, (Richard) Camden; QC 1992; a Recorder, since 1993; a Deputy High Court Judge (Family Division), since 1995; *b* 14 Dec. 1947; *s* of late Richard Sheldon Pratt, MA Oxon, and Irene Gladys Pratt; *m* 1973, (Dorothy Jane) Marchia Allsebrook. *Educ:* Boston Grammar Sch.; Westcliff High Sch.; Lincoln Coll., Oxford (MA Jurisp). Called to the Bar, Gray's Inn, 1970. Chairman: Sussex Courts Liaison Cttee, 1993–; Sussex Sessions Bar Mess, 1994–; Mem., Area Criminal Justice Liaison Cttee, 1994–. *Recreations:* walking, sailing, travel, people. *Address:* 1 King's Bench Walk, Temple, EC4Y 7DB. *T:* (020) 7936 1500, *Fax:* (020) 7936 1590.

PRATT, Richard Charles; Director General, Jersey Financial Services Commission, since 1999; *b* 3 Nov. 1949; *s* of Charles Pratt and Rosemary Pratt (*née* Robson); *m* 1974, Christine Whiteman; one *s*. *Educ:* Eltham Coll.; Bristol Univ. (BSc Politics and Econs 1972); Sch. of Oriental and African Studies, London Univ. (MA 1973). Joined Civil Service, 1973; Press Officer, Prime Minister's Office, 1975–76; Asst Private Sec., Lord Privy Seal's Office, 1976; Head of Pay Negotiations Br., CSD, 1977–80; Head of Special Employment Measures Br., Dept of Employment, 1980–82; HM Treasury: Head of NI Public Expenditure Br., 1982–84; Mem., Central Unit for UK Budget, 1984–86; Head of Gen. Expenditure Div., 1986–87; Economic Counsellor, Washington, 1987–90 (on secondment); Head, EC Div. (EMU and Trade Policy), 1990–93; Advr to Sec. of State for Social Services on Expenditure Review, DSS, 1993; Head of Securities and Mkts Div., HM Treasury, 1993–95; Dir of External Affairs, LIFFE, 1995–98. *Recreations:* tennis, flying, travelling, net surfing. *Address:* Jersey Financial Services Commission, PO Box 267, Nelson House, David Place, St Helier, Jersey JE4 8TP. *T:* (01534) 822000. *Clubs:* Dulwich Lawn Tennis, Caesarean Croquet and Lawn Tennis; Jersey Aero.

PRATT, Roger Allan, CBE 1996; Boundary Review Project Director, Conservative Central Office, since 2000; *b* 28 Dec. 1950; *s* of Allan Pratt and Joyce Isobel Pratt (*née* Dodds); *m* 1st, 1975, Ann Heaton (marr. diss. 1993); one *s* one *d*; 2nd, 1993, Lynn Mary Tomlinson; one step *s* one step *d*. *Educ:* King Edward's Fiveways Sch., Birmingham. Organiser, E Midlands Area YC, 1971–72; NW Area Youth Develt Officer, 1972–74; Agent, Liverpool Wavertree Cons. Assoc., 1975–76; Nat. YC Organiser, 1976–79; Agent, Pendle, Burnley and Hyndburn Cons. Assocs, 1980–84; North West Area, then NW Region: Dep. Central Office Agent, 1984–89; Central Office Agent, 1989–93; Regl Dir, 1993; Dir, Cons. Pty in Scotland, 1993–97; Conservative Central Office: Dep. Dir, Campaigning Dept, 1997–98; Area Campaign Dir, London Western, and Regl Eur. Campaign Dir for London, 1998–2000. *Recreation:* cricket. *Address:* Conservative Central Office, 32 Smith Square, Westminster, SW1P 3HH. *T:* (020) 7222 9000.

PRATT, Simon; His Honour Judge Pratt; a Circuit Judge, since 1995; *b* 23 June 1949; *s* of Harry James Roffey Pratt and Ann Loveday Pratt (*née* Peter); *m* 1974, Sheena Maynard; one *s* one *d*. Called to the Bar, Inner Temple, 1971; a Recorder, SE Circuit, 1989–95. Freeman, City of London, 1984. *Recreations:* music, walking, gardening, cookery, travel. *Address:* 3 Temple Gardens, Temple, EC4Y 9AU. *T:* (020) 7353 3102.

PRATT, Timothy Jean Geoffrey, CB 1993; Senior Fellow, Cambridge University Centre for European Legal Studies, 1999–2001 (Visiting Fellow, 1998); *b* 25 Nov. 1934; *s* of Geoffrey Cheeseborough Pratt and Elinor Jean (*née* Thomson); *m* 1963, Pamela Ann Blake; two *d*. *Educ:* Brighton College; Trinity Hall, Cambridge (MA). Called to the Bar, Middle Temple, 1959; in practice, 1959–61; joined Treasury Solicitor's Dept, 1961; Law Officers' Dept, 1972; DTI, 1974; Legal Advisor: Dir-Gen. of Fair Trading, 1979; Cabinet Office (European Secretariat), 1985; Dep. Treasury Solicitor, 1990–93; Counsel to Speaker (Eur. Legislation), H of C, 1993–97. Advr on EU Law to BSE Inquiry, 1998–2000. *Address:* The Old Vicarage, Radwinter, Saffron Walden, Essex CB10 2SN. *T:* and *Fax:* (01799) 599507. *Club:* Oxford and Cambridge.

PRAWER, Prof. Siegbert Salomon, FBA 1981; Taylor Professor of German Language and Literature, University of Oxford, 1969–86, now Professor Emeritus; Professorial Fellow, 1969–86, Supernumerary Fellow, 1986–90, Hon. Fellow, 1990, The Queen's College, Oxford (Dean of Degrees, 1978–93); *b* 15 Feb. 1925; *s* of Marcus and Eleonora Prawer; *m* 1949, Helga Alice (*née* Schaefer); one *s* two *d* (and one *s* decd). *Educ:* King Henry VIII Sch., Coventry; Jesus Coll., Cambridge (Charles Oldham Shakespeare Scholar, 1945, MA 1950; Hon. Fellow, 1996); PhD Birmingham, 1953; LittD Cantab 1962; MA 1969, DLitt 1969, Oxon. Adelaide Stoll Res. Student, Christ's Coll., Cambridge, 1947–48; Asst Lecturer, Lecturer, Sen. Lecturer, University of Birmingham, 1948–63; Prof. of German, Westfield Coll., London Univ., 1964–69. Fulbright Exchange Schol., 1956; Visiting Professor: City Coll., NY, 1956–57; University of Chicago, 1963–64; Harvard Univ., 1968; Hamburg Univ., 1969; Univ. of Calif, Irvine, 1975; Otago Univ., 1976; Pittsburgh Univ., 1977; Visiting Fellow: Knox Coll., Dunedin, 1976; Humanities Research Centre, ANU, 1980; Tauber Inst., Brandeis Univ., 1981–82; Russell Sage Foundn, NY, 1988. Hon. Director, London Univ. Inst. of Germanic Studies, 1966–68. President: British Comp. Lit. Assoc., 1984–87 (Hon. Fellow, 1989); English Goethe Soc., 1990–94 (Vice-Pres., 1994–). Hon. Fellow, London Univ. Inst. Germanic Studies, 1987; Corresp. Fellow, Deutsche Akademie für Sprache und Dichtung, 1989. Hon. Mem., Modern Language Assoc. of America, 1986. Hon. Dr. phil. Cologne, 1984; Hon. DLitt Birmingham, 1988. Goethe Medal, 1973; Friedrich Gundolf Prize, 1986; Gold Medal, German Goethe Soc., 1995. Co-editor: Oxford German Studies, 1971–75; Anglica Germanica, 1973–79. *Publications:* German Lyric Poetry, 1952; Mörike und seine Leser, 1960; Heine's Buch der Lieder: A Critical Study, 1960; Heine: The Tragic Satirist, 1962; The Penguin Book of Lieder, 1964; The Uncanny in Literature (inaug. lect.), 1965; (ed, with R. H. Thomas and L. W. Forster) Essays in German Language, Culture and Society, 1969; (ed) The Romantic Period in Germany, 1970; Heine's Shakespeare, a Study in Contexts (inaug. lect.), 1970; (ed) Seventeen Modern German Poets, 1971; Comparative Literary Studies: an Introduction, 1973; Karl Marx and World Literature, 1976 (Isaac Deutscher Meml Prize, 1977); Caligari's Children: the film as tale of terror, 1980; Heine's Jewish Comedy: a study of his portraits of Jews and Judaism, 1983; A. N. Stencl: poet of Whitechapel (Stencl Meml Lect.), 1984; Coalsmoke and Englishmen (Bithell Meml Lecture), 1984; Frankenstein's Island: England and the English in the writings of Heinrich Heine, 1986; Israel at Vanity Fair: Jews and Judaism in the writings of W. M. Thackeray, 1992; (introd) Das Kabinett des Dr Caligari (first printing of original screenplay), 1996; Breeches and Metaphysics: Thackeray's German discourse, 1997; W. M. Thackeray's European Sketch Books: a study of literary and graphic portraiture, 2000; articles on German, English and comparative literature in many specialist periodicals and symposia. *Recreation:* portrait drawing. *Address:* 9 Hawkswell Gardens, Oxford OX2 7EX.

See also Mrs R. P. Jhabvala.

PRAWER JHABVALA, Ruth; *see* Jhabvala.

PREBBLE, David Lawrence; Master, Queen's Bench Division, Supreme Court of Justice, since 1981; *b* 21 Aug. 1932; *s* of late George Wilson Prebble and Margaret Jessie Prebble (*née* Cuthbertson); *m* 1959, Fiona W. Melville; three *d*. *Educ:* Cranleigh; Christ Church, Oxford. MA. National Service, 1950–52; commissioned in 3rd Carabiniers (Prince of Wales's Dragoon Guards); served TA, 1952–61, City of London Yeomanry (Rough Riders) TA (Captain). Called to the Bar, Middle Temple, 1957; practised at Bar, 1957–81. *Recreations:* reading; operetta; hounds and dogs; friends' horses; own wife and family; (not necessarily in foregoing order as to precedence). *Address:* 16 Wool Road, Wimbledon, SW20 0HW. *T:* (020) 8946 1804. *Club:* Royal Wimbledon Golf.

PREBBLE, Stuart Colin; Chief Executive: ITV Network, since 2001; ITV Digital (formerly ONdigital), since 1999; *b* 15 April 1951; *s* of Dennis Stanley Prebble and Jean Margaret Prebble; *m* 1978, Marilyn Anne Charlton; one *d* (and one *d* decd). *Educ:* Univ. of Newcastle upon Tyne (BA Hons English Lang. and Lit.). Reporter, BBC TV News, 1975–80; Presenter, Granada TV, 1981; Producer, 1983–88, Editor, 1988–89, World in Action; Head of Regl Progs, Granada, 1989–90; Man. Dir, North East TV, 1990–91; Head of Factual Progs, Granada, 1992; Controller, ITV Network Factual Progs, 1993–96; Chief Exec., Granada Sky Broadcasting, 1996–98; Man. Dir, Channels and Interactive Media, Granada Media Gp, 1999. *Publications:* A Power in the Land, 1988; The Lazarus File, 1989. *Recreations:* walking, cinema, music. *Address:* ITV Network Ltd, 200 Gray's Inn Road, WC1X 8HF.

PRENDERGAST, Prof. Christopher Alan Joseph, PhD; FBA 1996; Fellow, King's College, Cambridge, since 1970; Professor of Modern French Literature, Cambridge University, since 1997 (Reader, 1992–97); *b* 27 Sept. 1942; *s* of James Prendergast and Celia (*née* Sevitt); *m* 1st, 1965, Shirley Busbridge (marr. diss. 1979); two *d*; 2nd, 1997, Inge Birgitte Siegumfeldt; one *d*. *Educ:* Keble Coll., Oxford (BA 1965; BPhil 1967); MA 1968, PhD 1989, Cantab. Lectr, Pembroke Coll., Oxford, 1967–68; Fellow, Downing Coll., Cambridge, 1968–70; Univ. Lectr, Cambridge Univ., 1968–89; Distinguished Prof. in French and Comparative Literature, Grad. Sch., City Univ. of NY, 1989–92. Vis. Prof., Univ. of Copenhagen, Denmark, 1998–2000. *Publications:* Balzac: fiction and melodrama, 1978; The Order of Mimesis, 1986; (ed) Nineteenth-Century French Poetry, 1990; Paris and the Nineteenth Century, 1992; (ed jtly) Anthology of World Literature, 1994; (ed) Cultural Materialism, 1996; Napoleon and History Painting, 1997; The Triangle of Representation, 2000. *Recreations:* piano, poker. *Address:* King's College, Cambridge CB2 1ST. *T:* (01223) 331338.

PRENDERGAST, Sir Kieran; *see* Prendergast, Sir W. K.

PRENDERGAST, Robert James Christie Vereker; His Honour Judge Prendergast; a Circuit Judge, since 1989; *b* 21 Oct. 1941; *s* of Richard Henry Prendergast and Jean (*née* Christie); *m* 1971, Berit, (Bibi), Thauland; one *d*. *Educ:* Downside; Trinity Coll., Cambridge (BA (Hons) Law; MA). Called to the Bar, Middle Temple, 1964; Harmsworth Law Schol.; S Eastern Circuit, 1964–89; an Asst Recorder, 1984–87; a Recorder, 1987–89. Chm., NE London Crown Court Liaison Cttee, 1984–89. Mem., S Eastern Circuit Wine Cttee, 1987–89. Pres., St Gregory's Soc., 1999–. *Recreations:* most gentle pursuits. *Address:* 5 King's Bench Walk, Temple, EC4Y 7DN. *T:* (020) 7353 5638, *Fax:* (020) 7353 6166.

PRENDERGAST, Dame Simone (Ruth), DBE 1986 (OBE 1981); JP, DL; *b* 2 July 1930; *d* of late Mrs Neville Blond, OBE and late Norman Laski; *m* 1st, 1953, Albert Kaplan (marr. diss. 1957); 2nd, 1959, Christopher Anthony Prendergast, CBE (*d* 1998); one *s*. *Educ:* Queen's College; Cheltenham Ladies' College. Lady Mayoress of Westminster, 1968–69; Member: Lord Chancellor's Adv. Cttee for Inner London, 1981–91; Solicitors' Disciplinary Tribunal, 1986–; E London and Bethnal Green Housing Assoc., 1988–90; Exec. Cttee, Westminster Children's Soc., 1970–97 (Chm., 1980–90); Chairman: Greater London Area Nat. Union of Conservative Assocs, 1984–87; Blond McIndoe Centre for Med. Research, 1986–; Jewish Refugees Cttee, 1980–96; Vice-Chm., Age Concern, Westminster, 1989–; Comr (part-time), CRE, 1996–98. Jt Treas., 1991–, Vice Pres., 1997–, Central British Fund for World Jewish Relief (Mem. Council, 1969–97); Life Patron, British Fedn of Women Zionists, 1994. Comdt, Jewish Lads' and Girls' Bde, 1996–2000. Court of Patrons, RCS, 1987. FRSA 1988. JP Inner London 1971; DL Greater London 1982. Associate CStJ 1982. *Recreations:* reading, walking. *Address:* 52 Warwick Square, SW1V 2AJ.

PRENDERGAST, Sir (Walter) Kieran, KCVO 1991; CMG 1990; Under Secretary-General for Political Affairs, United Nations, New York, since 1997; HM Diplomatic Service, retired; *b* 2 July 1942; *s* of late Lt-Comdr J. H. Prendergast and Mai Hennessy; *m* 1967, Joan Reynolds; two *s* two *d*. *Educ:* St Patrick's College, Strathfield, Sydney, NSW; Salesian College, Chertsey; St Edmund Hall, Oxford. Turkish language student Istanbul, 1964; Ankara, 1965; FO (later FCO), 1967; 2nd Sec. Nicosia, 1969; Civil Service Coll., 1972; 1st Sec. FCO, 1972; The Hague, 1973; Asst Private Sec. to Foreign and Commonwealth Sec. (Rt Hon. Anthony Crosland, Rt Hon. Dr David Owen), 1976; UK Mission to UN, NY, 1979 (detached for duty Jan.-March 1980 at Govt House, Salisbury); Counsellor, Tel Aviv, 1982; Head of Southern African Dept, FCO, 1986–89; High Comr to Zimbabwe, 1989–92; High Comr to Kenya, 1992–95; Ambassador to Turkey, 1995–97. Rhodesia Medal, 1980; Zimbabwe Independence Medal, 1980. *Recreations:* family, walking, reading, rough shooting. *Address:* Room S 3770-A, UN Secretariat Building, New York, NY 10017, USA. *T:* (212) 9635055, *Fax:* (212) 9635065. *Clubs:* Beefsteak, Garrick; Muthaiga (Nairobi); Lotos (New York).

PRENTICE, Dr Ann; Director, MRC Resource Centre for Human Nutrition Research, since 1998; *b* 8 April 1952; *d* of Alexander Rubach and Beryl Ann Rubach; *m* 1976, Andrew Major Prentice; two *d*. *Educ:* Somerville Coll., Oxford (BA Hons Chemistry; MA 1977); Univ. of Surrey (MSc Med. Physics); Darwin Coll., Cambridge (PhD Natural Scis, 1978). Scientist, MRC Dunn Nutrition Gp, Keneba, Gambia, 1978–83; Scientist, 1984–91, Sen. Scientist, 1991–98, MRC Dunn Nutrition Unit, Cambridge. Hon. Prof., Shenyang Med. Coll., People's Republic of China, 1995–. *Publications:* book chapters and reviews; numerous contribs to peer-reviewed scientific jls. *Recreations:* music, theatre, literature, foreign travel. *Address:* MRC Resource Centre for Human Nutrition Research, Elsie Widdowson Laboratory, Fulbourn Road, Cambridge CB1 9NL. *T:* (01223) 426356.

PRENTICE, Bridget Theresa; JP; MP (Lab) Lewisham East, since 1992; *b* 28 Dec. 1952; *d* of James and Bridget Corr; *m* 1975, Gordon Prentice, *qv* (marr. diss. 2000). *Educ:* Glasgow Univ. (MA English Lit. and Mod. Hist.); London University: Avery Hill Coll.

PRAG, Derek; Member (C) Hertfordshire, European Parliament, 1979–94; *b* 6 Aug. 1923; *s* of late Abraham J. Prag and Edith Prag; *m* 1948, Dora Weiner; three *s*. *Educ:* Bolton Sch.; Emmanuel Coll., Univ. of Cambridge (Scholar; MA; Cert. of Competent Knowledge in Russian). Served War, Intelligence Corps, England, Egypt, Italy, Austria, 1942–47. Economic journalist with Reuters News Agency in London, Brussels and Madrid, 1950–55; Information Service of High Authority, European Coal and Steel Community, 1955–59; Head of Division, Jt Information Service of European Communities, 1959–65; Director, London Information Office of European Communities, 1965–73; ran own consultancy company on relations with EEC, 1973–79. Mem., 1982–94, Dep. Chm., 1989–94, Institutional Cttee (EDG spokesman, 1982–84 and 1987–92; EPP dep. spokesman, and British Cons. spokesman, 1992–94); Political spokesman for European Democratic (Cons.) Group, 1984–87; Chm., European Parlt All-Party Disablement Gp, 1980–94; Vice-Pres., Eur. Parlt-Israel Intergroup, 1990–94; Founder Mem., Cons. Gp for Europe (Dep. Chm., 1974–77, 1991–93). Member: Anglo-Spanish Soc.; Luxembourg Soc.; RIIA. Hon. Dir, EEC Commn, 1974; Hon. Mem., EP, 1994. Hon. DLitt Hertfordshire, 1993. Silver Medal of European Merit, Fondation du Mérite Européen, 1974. Comdr, Order of Leopold II (Belgium), 1996. *Publications:* (with E. D. Nicholson) Businessman's Guide to the Common Market, 1973; various reports on Europe's internat. role, and booklets and articles on European integration. *Recreations:* reading, theatre, music, walking, swimming, gardening; speaks seven languages. *Address:* 47 New Road, Digswell, Welwyn, Herts AL6 0AQ. *Clubs:* Royal Over-Seas League, Anglo-Belgian; Royal Automobile (Brussels).

PRAG, John; *see* Prag, A. J. N. W.

PRAGNELL, Anthony William, CBE 1982 (OBE 1960); DFC 1944; Deputy Director-General, Independent Broadcasting Authority (formerly Independent Television Authority), 1961–83; Director, Channel Four Television, 1983–88; *b* 15 Feb. 1921; *s* of William Hendley Pragnell and Silvia Pragnell; *m* 1st, 1955, Teresa Mary (*d* 1988), *d* of Leo and Anne Monaghan, Maidstone; one *s* one *d*; 2nd, Fiona Carter, *d* of James Thomson, CMG, MM, and Ivy Thomson, Edinburgh. *Educ:* Cardinal Vaughan Sch., London. Asst Examiner, Estate Duty Office, 1939. Served RAF, 1942–46. Examiner, Estate Duty Office, 1946. LLB London Univ., 1949. Asst Principal, General Post Office, 1950; Asst Secretary, ITA, 1954; Secretary, ITA, 1955. Vis. Fellow, European Inst. for the Media, Univ. of Manchester, 1983–92, Düsseldorf, 1992–97. Fellow, Royal Television Soc., 1980. Emile Noël European Prize, 1987. *Publications:* Television in Europe: quality and values in a time of change, 1985; (ed) Opening up the Media, 1993. *Recreations:* reading, music. *Address:* 10 Courtwood Drive, Sevenoaks, Kent TN13 2LR. *T:* (01732) 453240. *Club:* Royal Air Force.

PRAIS, Prof. Sigbert Jon, FBA 1985; Senior Research Fellow, National Institute of Economic and Social Research, London, since 1970; *b* Frankfurt am Main, Germany, 19 Dec. 1928; *s* of Samuel and Bertha Prais; came to England as refugee, 1934; UK citizen, 1946; *m* 1971, Vivien Hennessy, LLM, solicitor; one *s* three *d*. *Educ:* King Edward's School, Birmingham; Univ. of Birmingham (MCom); Fitzwilliam Coll., Cambridge (PhD 1953; DSc 1974). Dept of Applied Economics, Cambridge, 1950–57; post-doctoral Fellow, Univ. of Chicago, 1953–54; research officer, NIESR, 1953–59; UN Tech. Assistance Orgn, 1959–60; IMF Washington, 1960–61; Finance Dir, Elbief Co., 1961–70. Vis. Prof. of Econs, City Univ., 1975–84. Mem. Council, Royal Economic Soc., 1979–83. Mem. Council, City Univ., 1990–94. Hon. DLitt City Univ., 1989. *Publications:* Analysis of Family Budgets (jtly), 1955, 2nd edn 1971; Evolution of Giant Firms in Britain, 1976, 2nd edn 1981; Productivity and Industrial Structure, 1981; Productivity, Education and Training, 1995; (jtly) From School to Productive Work in Britain and Switzerland, 1997; articles in economic and statistical jls, esp. on influence of educn on economic progress. *Address:* 83 West Heath Road, NW3 7TN. *T:* (020) 8458 4428; (office) (020) 7222 7665.

PRANCE, Sir Ghillean (Tolmie), Kt 1995; DPhil; FRS 1993; FLS, FIBiol; FRGS; Scientific Director, Eden Project, Cornwall, since 1999; McBryde Professor, National Tropical Botanical Garden, Kalaheo, Hawaii, since 2000; *b* 13 July 1937; *s* of Basil Camden Prance, CIE, OBE and Margaret Hope Prance (*née* Tolmie); *m* 1961, Anne Elizabeth Hay; two *d*. *Educ:* Malvern Coll.; Keble Coll., Oxford (BA, MA, DPhil). FLS 1961; FIBiol 1988. New York Botanical Garden: Res. Asst, 1963–66; Associate Curator, 1966–68; B. A. Krukoff Curator of Amazonian Botany, 1968–75; Dir of Research, 1975–81; Vice-Pres., 1977–81; Senior Vice-Pres., 1981–88; Dir, Royal Botanic Gdns, Kew, 1988–99. Adjunct Prof., City Univ. of NY, 1968–; Vis. Prof. in Tropical Studies, Yale, 1983–89; Vis. Prof., Reading Univ., 1988–; Dir of Graduate Studies, Instituto Nacional de Pesquisas da Amazônia, Manaus, Brazil, 1973–75; 14 botanical expedns to Amazonia. President: Assoc. of Tropical Biol., 1979–80; Amer. Assoc. of Plant Taxonomists, 1984–85; Systematics Assoc., 1989–91; Econ. Botany Soc., 1996–97; Linnean Soc., 1997–2000; Inst. of Biology, 2000–Apr. 2002; Mem. Council, RHS, 1990–2000. FRGS 1989; Fellow, AAAS, 1990; Corresponding Member: Brazilian Acad. of Scis, 1976; Botanical Soc. of America, 1994; Foreign Member: Royal Danish Acad. of Scis and Letters, 1988; Royal Swedish Acad. of Scis, 1989; Associate Mem., Third World Acad. of Scis, 1993; Hon. Mem., British Ecol Soc., 1996. Hon. Freeman, Gardeners' Co., 1997. Fil Dr *hc* Univ. Göteborgs, Sweden, 1983; Hon. DSc: Kent, Portsmouth, Kingston, 1994; St Andrews, 1995; Bergen Univ., Norway, 1996; Florida Internat. Univ., Herbert H. Lehman Coll., NY, and Sheffield Univ., 1997; Liverpool, 1998; Glasgow, Plymouth, 1999; Keele, Exeter, 2000. Henry Shaw Medal, Missouri Botanical Garden, St Louis, 1988; Linnean Medal, 1990; Patron's Medal, RGS, 1994; Janaki Ammal Medal, Soc. of Ethnobotany, 1996; Internat. Award of Excellence, Botanical Res. Inst., Texas, 1998; VMH 1999; Lifetime of Discovery Award, Discovery Channel and RGS, 1999; Fairchild Medal for Plant Exploration, Nat. Tropical Botanical Gdn, 2000. *Publications:* Arvores de Manaus, 1975; Algumas Flores da Amazonia, 1976; Extinction is Forever, 1977; Biological Diversification in the Tropics, 1981; Amazonia: key environments, 1985; Leaves, 1986; Manual de Botânica Econômica do Maranhão, 1988; Flowers for all Seasons, 1989; Out of the Amazon, 1992; Bark, 1993; The Earth Under Threat: a Christian perspective, 1996; Rainforests: water, fire, earth and air, 1997. *Recreations:* flower stamp collecting, bird watching. *Address:* The Old Vicarage, Silver Street, Lyme Regis, Dorset DT7 3HS. *T:* (01297) 444991, *Fax:* (01297) 444955; *e-mail:* gtolmiep@aol.com. *Club:* Explorers (New York) (Fellow).

PRANKERD, Thomas Arthur John, FRCP; Professor of Clinical Haematology, 1965–79 and Dean, 1972–77, University College Hospital Medical School; Hon. Consultant Physician: University College Hospital; Whittington Hospital; *b* 11 Sept. 1924; *s* of late H. A. Prankerd, Barrister-at-Law, and J. D. Shorthose; *m* 1950, Margaret Vera Harrison Cripps; two *s* (and one *s* one *d* decd). *Educ:* Charterhouse Sch.; St Bartholomew's Hospital Med. Sch. MD (London) Gold Medal 1949; FRCP 1962. Jnr med. appts, St Bart's and University Coll. Hosp., 1947–60. Major, RAMC, 1948–50. Univ. Travelling Fellow, USA, 1953–54; Consultant Physician, University Coll. Hosp., 1960–65. Goulstonian Lectr, RCP, 1963; Assoc. of Physicians, 1965; Examr, RCP, and various univs. Visiting Professor: Univ. of Perth, WA, 1972; Univ. of Cape Town, 1973. Mem., NE Thames RHA, 1976–79. Mem. Bd of Governors, UCH, 1972–74. *Publications:* The Red Cell, 1961; Haematology in Medical Practice, 1968; articles in med. jls. *Recreations:* fishing, gardening, music. *Address:* 6 Stinsford House, Stinsford, Dorchester DT2 8PT. *T:* (01305) 751521.

PRASHAR, Baroness *cr* 1999 (Life Peer), of Runnymede in the county of Surrey; **Usha Kumari Prashar,** CBE 1995; First Civil Service Commissioner, since 2000; Chairman, National Literacy Trust, since 2001 (Deputy Chairman, 1992–2000); *b* 29 June 1948; *d* of Nauhria Lal Prashar and Durga Devi Prashar; *m* 1973, Vijay Kumar Sharma. *Educ:* Duchess of Gloucester Sch., Nairobi; Wakefield Girls' High Sch. (Head Girl, 1966–67); Univ. of Leeds (BA Hons Pol. Studies); Univ. of Glasgow (postgrad. Dip. Social Admin). Race Relations Bd, 1971–75; Asst Dir, Runnymede Trust, 1976–77, Dir, 1977–84; Res. Fellow, PSI, 1984–86; Dir, NCVO, 1986–91. CS Comr (part-time), 1990–96. Chm., Parole Bd, 1997–2000. Non-executive Director: Channel 4, 1992–99; Unite plc, 2001–. Vice-Chm., British Refugee Council, 1987–89. Member: Arts Council of GB, 1979–81, Arts Council of England, 1994–97; Study Commn on the Family, 1980–83; Social Security Adv. Cttee, 1980–83; Exec. Cttee, Child Poverty Action Gp, 1984–85; GLAA, 1984–86; London Food Commn, 1984–90; BBC Educnl Broadcasting Council, 1987–89; Adv. Council, Open College, 1987–89; Solicitors' Complaints Bureau, 1989–90; Royal Commn on Criminal Justice, 1991–93; Lord Chancellor's Adv. Cttee on Legal Educn and Conduct, 1991–97; Council, PSI, 1992–97; Bd, Energy Saving Trust, 1992–98; King's Fund, 2000–. Hon. Vice-Pres., Council for Overseas Student Affairs, 1986–. Trustee: Thames Help Trust, 1984–86; Charities Aid Foundn, 1986–91; Independent Broadcasting Telethon Trust, 1987–92; Acad. of Indian Dance, 1987–91; Camelot Foundn, 1996–; Ethnic Minority Foundn, 2000–; Chm., English Adv. Cttee, Nat. AIDS Trust, 1988–89; Patron: Sickle Cell Soc., 1986–; Elfrida Rathbone Soc., 1988–. Chancellor, De Montfort Univ., 2000– (Gov., 1996–). FRSA. Hon. Fellow, Goldsmiths' Coll., Univ. of London, 1992. Hon. LLD: De Montfort, 1994; South Bank Univ., 1994; Greenwich, 1999; Leeds Metropolitan, 1999; Ulster, 2000; Oxford Brookes, 2000. *Publications: contributed to:* Britain's Black Population, 1980; The System: a study of Lambeth Borough Council's race relations unit, 1981; Scarman and After, 1984; Sickle Cell Anaemia, Who Cares? a survey of screening, counselling, training and educational facilities in England, 1985; Routes or Road Blocks, a study of consultation arrangements between local authorities and local communities, 1985; Acheson and After: primary health care in the inner city, 1986. *Recreations:* reading, country walks, music, golf. *Address:* House of Lords, SW1A 0PW. *Clubs:* Reform, Royal Commonwealth Society.

PRATCHETT, Terence David John, OBE 1998; author; *b* 28 April 1948; *s* of David and Eileen Pratchett; *m* 1968, Lyn Purves; one *d*. *Educ:* High Wycombe Tech. High Sch.; Beaconsfield Public Library. Assorted journalism, 1965–80; Press Officer, CEGB, 1980–87. Chm., Soc. of Authors, 1994–95. Hon. DLitt Warwick, 1999. *Publications:* The Carpet People, 1971; The Dark Side of the Sun, 1976; Strata, 1981; The Colour of Magic, 1983; The Light Fantastic, 1986; Equal Rites, 1987; Mort, 1987; Sourcery, 1988; Wyrd Sisters, 1988; Pyramids, 1989; Truckers, 1989; Guards! Guards!, 1989; The Unadulterated Cat, 1989; Eric, 1989; (with N. Gaiman) Good Omens, 1990; Moving Pictures, 1990; Diggers, 1990; Wings, 1990; Reaper Man, 1991; Witches Abroad, 1991; Small Gods, 1992; Only You Can Save Mankind, 1992; Lords and Ladies, 1992; Johnny and the Dead, 1993; Men At Arms, 1993; Soul Music, 1994; Interesting Times, 1994; Maskerade, 1995; Johnny and the Bomb, 1996; Feet of Clay, 1996; Hogfather, 1996; Jingo, 1997; The Last Continent, 1998; Carpe Jugulum, 1998; The Fifth Elephant, 1999; (jtly) The Science of Discworld, 1999; (jtly) Nanny Ogg's Cookbook, 1999; The Truth, 2000; Thief of Time, 2001. *Recreation:* letting the mind wander. *Address:* c/o Colin Smythe, PO Box 6, Gerrards Cross, Bucks SL9 8XA. *T:* (01753) 886000.

PRATLEY, Alan Sawyer; Deputy Financial Controller, Commission of the European Communities, 1990–98 (Director, Financial Control, 1986–90); *b* 25 Nov. 1933; *s* of Frederick Pratley and Hannah Pratley (*née* Sawyer); *m* 1st, 1960, Dorothea Rohland (marr. diss. 1979); two *d*; 2nd, 1979, Josette Kairis (marr. diss. 1994); one *d*; 3rd, 1996, Marie-Hélène Ledivelec. *Educ:* Latymer Upper School; Sidney Sussex Coll., Cambridge (BA Modern Languages (German, Russian)). Head, German Dept, Stratford Grammar Sch., West Ham, 1958–60; Asst Dir, Examinations, Civil Service Commn, 1960–68; Home Office, 1968–73; Commission of the European Communities: Head, Individual Rights Div., 1973–79; Dep. Chef de cabinet to Christopher Tugendhat, 1979–80; Adviser to Michael O'Kennedy, 1980–81; Dir of Admin, 1981–86. *Recreations:* tennis, gardening. *Address:* 18 Avenue de l'Armée, 1040 Brussels, Belgium. *T:* (2) 7352483, *Fax:* (2) 7325549.

PRATLEY, David Illingworth; Principal, David Pratley Associates, since 1996; *b* 24 Dec. 1948; *s* of Arthur George Pratley and Olive Constance Illingworth; *m* 1996, Caryn Faure Walker (*née* Becker). *Educ:* Westminster Abbey Choir Sch.; Westminster Sch.; Univ. of Bristol (LLB). PRO, Thorndike Theatre, Leatherhead, 1970–71; Gen. Asst, Queen's Univ. Festival, Belfast, 1971–73; Dep. Dir, Merseyside Arts Assoc., 1973–76; Dir, Greater London Arts Assoc., 1976–81; Regl Dir, Arts Council of GB, 1981–86; Chief Exec., Royal Liverpool Philharmonic Soc., 1987–88; Man. Dir, Trinity Coll. of Music, 1988–91; Dir of Leisure, Tourism and Econ. Develt, Bath CC, 1992–96. Chm., Alliance Arts Panel, 1987–88; Council Mem., Nat. Campaign for the Arts, 1986–92 (Chm., 1988–92); Dir, Dance Umbrella Ltd, 1986– (Chm., 1990–92). Lottery Policy Advr, Arts Council of England, 1996–. FRSA. *Publications:* (co-ed) Culture for All, 1981; reports: The Pursuit of Competence—the Arts and the European Community, 1987; Musicians Go To School, 1993. *Recreations:* music, theatre, art, countryside, travel. *Address:* 54 Walnut Tree Walk, SE11 6DN. *Club:* Athenæum.

PRATT, family name of **Marquess Camden**.

PRATT, (Arthur) Geoffrey, CBE 1981; Hon. Secretary, Institution of Gas Engineers, 1982–87; *b* 19 Aug. 1922; *s* of William Pratt, Willington, Co. Durham; *m* 1st, 1946, Ethel (Effie), Luck (*d* 1997); two *s* twin *d*; 2nd, 1998, Mrs Mavis Scargill. *Educ:* King James I Grammar Sch., Bishop Auckland. CEng, FIGasE. Joined E Mids Gas Bd, 1951: Chief Engr, 1964; Dir of Engrg, 1967; Dep. Chm., S Eastern Gas Bd, 1970–72; Chm., SE Gas Region, 1972–81; part-time Mem., British Gas Corp., 1981–82. Chm., Metrogas Building Soc., 1977–85. Pres., IGasE, 1974–75; Hon. FIGasE 1987. *Recreations:* keep-fit, swimming. *Address:* 3 Hither Chantlers, Langton Green, Tunbridge Wells, Kent TN3 0BJ.

PRATT, Camden; *see* Pratt, R. C.

PRATT, Christopher Leslie; a District Judge (Magistrates' Courts) (formerly Metropolitan Stipendiary Magistrate), since 1990; *b* 15 Dec. 1947; *s* of late Leslie Arthur Cottrell Pratt and Phyllis Elizabeth Eleanor Pratt; *m* 1973, Jill Rosemary Hodges; two *s*. *Educ:* Highgate Sch. Admitted Solicitor, 1972. Court Clerk, Hendon, Harrow and Uxbridge Courts, 1967–72; Dep. Clerk to the Justices, Wimbledon and Uxbridge, 1972–76; Clerk to the Justices, Highgate, Barnet and S Mimms, 1976–90; Clerk to Barnet Magistrates' Courts Cttee and Trng Officer, Justices and staff, 1986–90. Mem. Council,

Cancer, 1991; scientific papers on diagnosis, prevention and treatment of breast cancer. *Recreations:* horse riding, ski-ing, reading. *Address:* Green Hedges, Coulsdon Lane, Chipstead, Surrey CR5 3QL; Royal Marsden Hospital, London and Sutton, Downs Road, Sutton, Surrey SM2 5PT. *T:* (020) 8661 3361, *Fax:* (020) 8770 7313; *e-mail:* trevor.powles@rmh.nthames.nhs.uk. *Club:* Royal Automobile.
See also R. L. Powles.

POWLETT; *see* Orde-Powlett.

POWLEY, John Albert; Enquiry Officer, Post Office, 1991–96; *b* 3 Aug. 1936; *s* of Albert and Evelyn Powley; *m* 1957, Jill (*née* Palmer); two *s* one *d*. *Educ:* Cambridge Grammar Sch.; Cambridgeshire Coll. of Arts and Technology. Apprenticeship, Pye Ltd, 1952–57; RAF, 1957–59; retail shop selling and servicing radio, television and electrical goods, 1960–84. Member (C): Cambs CC, 1967–77, 1997– (Chm., Social Services Cttee, 1998–); Cambridge City Council, 1967–79 (Leader, Cons. Group, 1973–79; Chm., Housing Cttee, 1972–74, 1976–79; Leader of Council, 1976–79). Contested (C): Harlow, 1979; Norwich S, 1987. MP (C) Norwich S, 1983–87. Chm., Soham Cons. Assoc., 1991–. Sec./Manager, Wensum Valley Golf Club, Taverham, Norfolk, 1989–90. *Recreations:* golf, cricket, football. *Address:* Kyte End, 70A Brook Street, Soham, Ely, Cambs CB7 5AE. *T:* (01353) 624552; *e-mail:* john.powley@cambridgeshire.gov.uk.

POWNALL, David; novelist and playwright, since 1970; *b* 19 May 1938; *s* of John Charles Pownall and Elsie Pownall (*née* Russell); *m* 1962, Glenys Elsie Jones (marr. diss. 1973; she *d* 1995); one *s*; partner 1972–89, Mary Ellen Ray; one *s*; *m* 1993, Jean Alexander Sutton; one *s*. *Educ:* Greasby Primary Sch., Wirral; Lord Wandsworth Coll., Long Sutton; Keele Univ. (BA Hons 1960). Grad. Trainee, then Personnel Officer, Ford Motor Co., 1960–63; Personnel Manager, Anglo-American Corp., Zambian Copperbelt, 1963–69. FRSL 1976. Hon. DLitt Keele, 2000. John Whiting Award, 1981; Giles Cooper Award, 1981, 1985; Sony Silver Award, 1993, 1994, Sony Gold Award, 1995. *Publications: novels:* The Raining Tree War, 1974; African Horse, 1975; God Perkins, 1977; Light on a Honeycomb, 1978; Beloved Latitudes, 1981; The White Cutter, 1987; The Gardener, 1988; Stagg and his Mother, 1990; The Sphinx and the Sybarites, 1993; The Catalogue of Men, 1999; *plays:* The Dream of Chief Crazy Horse (for children), 1975; Music to Murder By, 1976; Motocar/Richard III Part Two, 1979; An Audience Called Edouard, 1979; Master Class, 1983; The Composer Plays, 1993; Death of a Faun, 1996; Radio Plays, 1998; Getting the Picture, 1998; Collected Plays, 2000; *short stories:* My Organic Uncle and other stories, 1976; The Bunch from Bananas (for children), 1980; *poetry:* Another Country, 1978; *non-fiction:* Between Ribble and Lune, 1980. *Recreations:* fishing, fell-walking, gardening, music. *Address:* c/o John Johnson, Clerkenwell House, 45/47 Clerkenwell Green, EC1R 0HT. *T:* (020) 7251 0125.

POWNALL, His Honour Henry Charles; QC 1979; a Circuit Judge, 1984–99; *b* 25 Feb. 1927; *er s* of late John Cecil Glossop Pownall, CB, and Margaret Nina Pownall (*née* Jesson); *m* 1955, Sarah Bettine, *d* of late Major John Deverell; one *s* one *d* (and one *d* decd). *Educ:* Rugby Sch.; Trinity Coll., Cambridge; BA 1950, MA 1963; LLB 1951. Served War, Royal Navy, 1945–48. Called to Bar, Inner Temple, 1954, Bencher, 1976; joined South-Eastern Circuit, 1954. Junior Prosecuting Counsel to the Crown at the Central Criminal Court, 1964–71; a Sen., subseq. 2nd, Prosecuting Counsel, 1971–79; a Recorder of the Crown Court, 1972–84; Resident Judge, Knightsbridge Crown Court, 1984–88; Permanent Judge, Central Criminal Court, 1997–99 (a Resident Judge, 1988–97); a Judge, Courts of Appeal of Jersey and Guernsey, 1980–86. Mem., Jt Service Review of Honours and Awards, MoD, 1992–2000. Orders and Medals Research Society: Mem. Cttee, 1961–82; Pres., 1971–75, 1977–81; Trustee, 1994–. Mem. Cttee, Nat. Benevolent Instn, 1964–2001. Freeman, City of London, 1989; Fruiterers' Co., 2001. OStJ 1996. *Publications:* Korean Campaign Medals, 1950–53, 1957; (jtly) Royal Service, Vol. I, 1996, Vols II and III, 2001. *Recreations:* travel, medals and medal ribbons. *Address:* c/o Coutts & Co., 440 Strand, WC2R 0QS. *Clubs:* Pratt's, Hurlingham; Ebury Court.
See also J. L. Pownall, Sir D. M. Mountain.

POWNALL, John Harvey; Director, DTI-North West, 1988–93; *b* 24 Oct. 1933; *s* of Eric Pownall and Gladys M. Pownall (*née* Baily); *m* 1958, Pauline M. Marsden, *o d* of William Denton Marsden; one *s* two *d*. *Educ:* Tonbridge School; Imperial College, London (BSc Eng Met). ARSM; MIMM; CEng. Scientific Officer, Atomic Energy Research Estab., Harwell, 1955–59; Warren Spring Lab., DSIR, 1959–64; Dept of Economic Affairs, 1964–66; Board of Trade/Dept of Trade and Industry, 1966–83; Dir-Gen., Council of Mechanical and Metal Trade Assocs, 1983–85; Hd of Electricity Div., Dept of Energy, 1985–87; Under Sec., DTI, 1987, on secondment to CEGB, 1987–88. Mem. Council, 1989–, Pro-Chancellor, 2001–, Salford Univ. (Chm., Estates Cttee, 1993–). *Publications:* papers in professional jls. *Address:* The West House, Arley Hall, Northwich, Cheshire CW9 6LZ. *T:* (01565) 777448. *Club:* St James's (Manchester).

POWNALL, Brig. John Lionel, OBE 1972; Deputy Chairman, Police Complaints Authority, 1986–93 (Member, 1985–86); *b* 10 May 1929; *yr s* of late John Cecil Glossop Pownall, CB and Margaret Nina Pownall (*née* Jesson); *m* 1962, Sylvia Joan Cameron Conn, *d* of late J. Cameron Conn, WS and Florence Conn (*née* Lennox); two *s*. *Educ:* Rugby School; RMA Sandhurst. Commissioned 16th/5th Lancers, 1949; served Egypt, Cyrenaica, Tripolitania, BAOR, Hong Kong, Cyprus; psc, jssc; Comd 16th/5th The Queen's Royal Lancers, 1969–71; Adjutant-Gen.'s Secretariat, 1971–72; Officer i/c RAC Manning and Records, 1973–75; Col, GS Near East Land Forces/Land Forces Cyprus, 1975–78; Asst Dir, Defence Policy Staff, MoD, 1978–79; Brig. RAC, UKLF, 1979–82; Brig. GS, MoD, 1982–84; retired 1984. Col, 16th/5th The Queen's Royal Lancers, 1985–90. *Recreations:* country pursuits, arts. *Address:* Sweatmans, Milland, Liphook, Hampshire GU30 7JT. *Clubs:* Cavalry and Guards, Army and Navy.
See also H. C. Pownall.

POWNALL, Leslie Leigh, MA, PhD; Chairman, NSW Planning and Environment Commission, 1974–77, retired; *b* 1 Nov. 1921; *y s* of A. de S. Pownall, Wanganui, New Zealand; *m* 1943, Judith, *d* of late Harold Whittaker, Palmerston North. *Educ:* Palmerston North Boys' High Sch.; Victoria University College, University of Canterbury, University of Wisconsin. Asst Master, Christchurch Boys' High Sch., 1941–46; Lecturer in Geography: Christchurch Teachers' Coll., 1946–47; Ardmore Teachers' Coll., 1948–49; Auckland University College, 1949–51; Senior Lecturer in Geography, 1951–60, Prof. of Geography, 1960–61, Vice-Chancellor and Rector, 1961–66, University of Canterbury; Clerk of the University Senate, Univ. of London, 1966–74. Consultant, Inter-University Council for Higher Educn Overseas, London, 1963; Consultant to Chm. of Working Party on Higher Educn in E Africa, 1968–69. Member Meeting, Council on World Tensions on Social and Economic Development (S Asia and Pacific), Kuala Lumpur, Malaysia, 1964; Governor, Internat. Students Trust, London, 1967–74; Member: Central Governing Body, City Parochial Foundation, London, 1967–74 (Mem., Grants Sub-Cttee; Chm., Finance and Gen. Purposes Cttee); UK Commonwealth Scholarship Commn, 1979–80. *Publications:* New Zealand, 1951 (New York); geographic contrib. in academic journals of America, Netherlands and New Zealand. *Recreations:* music, literature. *Club:* University (Christchurch, NZ).

POWNALL, Michael Graham; Reading Clerk, House of Lords, since 1997; *b* 11 Oct. 1949; *s* of Raymond Pownall and Elisabeth Mary Pownall (*née* Robinson); *m* 1974, Deborah Ann, *e d* of T. H. McQueen; two *d*. *Educ:* Repton Sch.; Exeter Univ. Joined Parliament Office, House of Lords, 1971: seconded to CSD as Private Sec. to Leader of House and Govt Chief Whip, 1980–83; Estabt Officer and Sec. to Chm. of Cttees, 1983–88; Principal Clerk of Private Bills, 1988–90; Principal Clerk, Overseas Office, 1988–95; Clerk of Cttees, 1991–95; Clerk of the Journals, 1995–97. *Recreations:* bird-watching, squash. *Address:* 13 Flanders Road, Chiswick, W4 1NQ. *T:* (020) 8994 0797. *Club:* Riverside.

POWNALL, (Stephen) Orlando (Fletcher); Senior Treasury Counsel, Central Criminal Court, since 1995; *b* 13 Nov. 1952; *s* of Alan Pownall and Carola Pownall (*née* Thielker); *m* 1978, Katherine Higgins; one *s* two *d*. *Educ:* Oundle Sch.; Faculté de Droit, Paris. Called to the Bar, Inner Temple, 1975; Jun. Treasury Counsel, 1991–95. *Recreations:* Rugby, golf, painting, gardening. *Address:* 1 Hare Court, Temple, EC4Y 7BE.

POWYS, family name of **Baron Lilford**.

POYNTER, Kieran Charles, FCA; Senior Partner, PricewaterhouseCoopers (formerly Price Waterhouse), since 2000; *b* 20 Aug. 1950; *s* of Kenneth and Betty Poynter; *m* 1977, Marylyn Melvin; three *s* one *d*. *Educ:* Salesian Coll.; Imperial Coll., London (BSc, ARCS). FCA 1977. Price Waterhouse, 1971–98, PricewaterhouseCoopers, 1998–: articled clerk, 1971; Partner, 1982; Dir, Insce Services, 1982–95; Member: Supervisory Bd, 1993–95; Mgt Bd, 1995–; Man. Partner, 1996–2000. Member: Insce Cttee, ICAEW, 1982–95; Life Accounting Cttee, ABI, 1992; Govt Task Force on Deregulation of Financial Services, 1993. Lloyd's Committees: Member: Accounting and Auditing Standards, 1988–90; Solvency and Reporting, 1994–95; Disputes Resolution Panel, 1996–97; Chm., Gooda Walker Loss Review, 1991–92. Member: Council for Industry and Higher Educn, 1997–; President's Cttee, CBI, 2001–; Council, Prince of Wales' Internat. Business Leaders Forum, 2001–. Trustee, Industry in Educn, 1999–. FRSA 1997. KHS 1999. *Publications:* contrib. various insurance articles to professional jls. *Recreations:* golf, watching sport. *Address:* (office) 1 Embankment Place, WC2N 6RH. *T:* (020) 7804 3188; Cranbrook, The South Border, Purley, Surrey CR8 3LL. *T:* (020) 8660 4723. *Club:* Royal Automobile.

POYNTON, (John) Orde, AO 2000; CMG 1961; MD; Consulting Bibliographer, University of Melbourne, 1962–74; Fellow of Graduate House, University of Melbourne, 1971–84; *b* 9 April 1906; *o s* of Frederick John Poynton, MD, FRCP, and Alice Constance, *d* of Sir John William Powlett Campbell-Orde, 3rd Bt, of Kilmory; *m* 1965, Lola, *widow* of Group Captain T. S. Horry, DFC, AFC. *Educ:* Marlborough Coll.; Gonville and Caius Coll., Cambridge; Charing Cross Hospital (Univ. Schol. 1927–30). MA, MD (Cambridge); MD (Adelaide) 1948; MRCS, LRCP; Horton-Smith prize, University of Cambridge, 1940. Sen. Resident MO, Charing Cross Hosp., 1932–33; Health Officer, Fed. Malay States, 1936–37; Res. Officer Inst. for Med. Research, FMS, 1937–38, Pathologist, 1938–46; Lectr in Pathology, Univ. of Adelaide, 1947–50; Pathologist, Inst. of Med. and Veterinary Science, S Australia, 1948–50, Director, 1950–61. Dir, Commercial Finance Co., 1960–70. Life Gov., Nat. Gallery of Australia, 1990. Hon. LLD Melbourne, 1977. *Publications:* monographs and papers relating to medicine and bibliography. *Recreation:* bibliognostics. *Address:* The Terraces, 2 Mount Eliza Way, Mount Eliza, Victoria 3930, Australia. *T:* (3) 97873660. *Club:* MCC.

POYNTZ, Rt Rev. Samuel Greenfield; Bishop of Connor, 1987–95; *b* 4 March 1926; *s* of James and Katharine Jane Poyntz; *m* 1952, Noreen Henrietta Armstrong; one *s* two *d*. *Educ:* Portora Royal School, Enniskillen; Univ. of Dublin. Mod., Mental and Moral Sci. and Oriental Langs, 1948; 1st cl. Div. Test., 1950; MA 1951; BD 1953; PhD 1960. Deacon 1950, priest 1951; Curate Assistant: St George's, Dublin, 1950–52; Bray, 1952–55; St Michan and St Paul, Dublin, 1955–59; Rector of St Stephen's, Dublin, 1959–67; Vicar of St Ann's, Dublin, 1967–78; Archdeacon of Dublin, 1974–78; Exam. Chaplain to Archbishop of Dublin, 1974–78; Bishop of Cork, Cloyne and Ross, 1978–87. Chairman: Youth Dept, British Council of Churches, 1965–69; Irish Council of Churches, 1986–88; Vice-Pres., BCC, 1987–90. Hon. DLitt Ulster, 1995. *Publications:* The Exaltation of the Blessed Virgin Mary, 1953; St Stephen's—One Hundred and Fifty Years of Worship and Witness, 1974; Journey towards Unity, 1975; St Ann's—the Church in the heart of the City, 1976; (ed) Church the Way, the Truth, and Your Life, 1955; Our Church—Praying with our Church Family, 1983. *Recreations:* interest in Rugby football, travel, stamp collecting. *Address:* 10 Harmony Hill, Lisburn, Co. Antrim, N Ireland BT27 4EP. *T:* (028) 9267 9013.

POZNANSKY, Dulcie Vivien; *see* Coleman, D. V.

PRACY, Robert, FRCS; Dean of the Institute of Laryngology and Otology, University of London, 1981–85, retired; a Medical Chairman, Pensions Appeal Tribunals, since 1984 (Medical Member, since 1982); *b* 19 Sept. 1921; *s* of Douglas Sherrin Pracy and Gwendoline Blanche Power; *m* 1946, Elizabeth Patricia Spicer; one *s* two *d* (and one *s* decd). *Educ:* Berkhamsted Sch.; St Bartholomew's Hosp. Med. Coll. (MB BS 1945); MPhil (Lond.) 1984. LRCP 1944; MRCS, FRCS 1953. Former Captain, RAMC. House Surgeon appts, St Bartholomew's Hosp.; formerly: Registrar, Royal Nat. Throat, Nose and Ear Hosp.; Consultant Surgeon: Liverpool Regional Board, 1954; United Liverpool Hosps, 1959; Alder Hey Childrens' Hosp., 1960; Royal Nat. Throat, Nose and Ear Hosp.; Hosp. for Sick Children, Gt Ormond St; Dir, Dept of Otolaryngology, Liverpool Univ. Mem. Ct of Examnrs, RCS and RCSI. Lectures: Yearsley, 1976; Joshi, 1978; Wilde, 1979; Semon, London Univ., 1980. Pres., British Assoc. of Otolaryngologists; FRSocMed (Pres., Sect. of Laryngology, 1982–83). Hon. FRCSI 1982; Hon. Fellow: Irish Otolaryngol Assoc.; Assoc. of Otolaryngologists of India; Polish Otolaryngological Assoc. *Publications:* (jtly) Short Textbook: Ear, Nose and Throat, 1970, 2nd edn 1974 (trans. Italian, Portuguese, Spanish); (jtly) Ear, Nose and Throat Surgery and Nursing, 1977; contribs to learned jls. *Recreations:* painting, engraving, theatre. *Address:* Ginkgo House, New Road, Moreton-in-Marsh, Glos GL56 0AS. *T:* (01608) 650740.

PRAG, (Andrew) John (Nicholas Warburg), MA, DPhil; FSA; Keeper of Archaeology, Manchester Museum, University of Manchester, since 1969; *b* 28 Aug. 1941; *s* of Adolf Prag and Frede Charlotte (*née* Warburg); *m* 1969, Kay (*née* Wright); one *s* one *d*. *Educ:* Westminster Sch. (Queen's Scholar); Brasenose Coll., Oxford (Domus Exhibnr 1960; Hon. Scholar 1962; BA 1964; Dip. Classical Archaeol. 1966; Sen. Hulme Scholar, 1967; MA 1967; DPhil 1975). FSA 1977. Temp. Asst Keeper, Ashmolean Museum, Oxford, 1966–67; Hon. Lectr, Dept of History, 1977–83, Dept of Archaeology, 1984–, Univ. of Manchester. Vis. Prof. of Classics, McMaster Univ., 1978; Vis. Fellow, British Sch. at Athens, 1994. Editor, Archaeological Reports, 1975–87. *Publications:* The Oresteia: iconographic and narrative tradition, 1985; (with Richard Neave) Making Faces Using the Forensic and Archaeological Evidence, 1997; (ed jtly) Periplous: papers on classical art and archaeology, 2000; articles on Greek art and archaeology in learned jls. *Recreations:* travel, walking, cooking, music. *Address:* Manchester Museum, The University, Manchester M13 9PL. *T:* (0161) 275 2665; *e-mail:* john.prag@man.ac.uk.

Royal Fine Art Commn, 1969–94; Treas. RA, 1985–95. Trustee, Sir John Soane's Museum, 1978–. Has won numerous medals and awards for architectural work, inc. Royal Gold Medal for Architecture, RIBA, 1974. *Recreations:* travel, listening to music. *Address:* 16 The Little Boltons, SW10 9LP. *T:* (020) 7373 8620.

POWELL, Sir Raymond, Kt 1996; MP (Lab) Ogmore, since 1979; *b* 19 June 1928; *s* of Albert and Lucy Powell; *m* 1950, Marion Grace Evans; one *s* one *d. Educ:* Pentre Grammar Sch.; National Council of Labour Colls; London School of Economics. British Rail, 1945–50; Shop Manager, 1950–66; Secretary/Agent to Walter Padley, MP, 1967–69, voluntarily, 1969–79; Sen. Administrative Officer, Welsh Water Authority, 1969–79. Welsh Regl Opposition Whip, 1983–95, Opposition Pairing Whip, 1987–95. Member: Select Cttee, Employment, 1979–82; Welsh Select Cttee, 1982–85; Select Cttee, H of C Services, 1983–87; Cttee of Selection, 1983–95; Liaison Select Cttee, 1987–96; Chm., Parly New Building Cttee, 1987–; Chm., All-Party Parly Showman's Guild, 1987–96. Chairman: Labour Party Wales, 1977–78; S Wales Euro-Constituency Labour Party, 1979–. Secretary: Welsh PLP, 1984–90; Welsh Parly Party; Anglo-Bulgarian All Party Gp, 1984–; Treas., Anglo-Romanian All Party Gp, 1984–; Vice-Chm., Parly Agric. Cttee, 1987. *Recreations:* gardening, sport, music. *Address:* 8 Brynteg Gardens, Bridgend, Mid-Glam CF31 3EW. *T:* (01656) 652159. *Club:* Ogmore Constituency Labour Party Social.

POWELL, Sir Richard (Royle), GCB 1967 (KCB 1961; CB 1951); KBE 1954; CMG 1946; Deputy Chairman, Permanent Committee on Invisible Exports, 1968–76; Chairman, Alusuisse (UK) Ltd and subsidiary companies, 1969–84; *b* 30 July 1909; *er s* of Ernest Hartley and Florence Powell; unmarried. *Educ:* Queen Mary's Grammar Sch., Walsall; Sidney Sussex Coll., Cambridge (Hon. Fellow, 1972). Entered Civil Service, 1931 and apptd to Admiralty; Private Sec. to First Lord, 1934–37; Member of British Admiralty Technical Mission, Canada, and of British Merchant Shipbuilding Mission, and later of British Merchant Shipping Mission in USA, 1940–44; Civil Adviser to Commander-in-Chief, British Pacific Fleet, 1944–45; Under-Secretary, Ministry of Defence, 1946–48. Dep. Sec., Admiralty, 1948–50; Dep. Sec., Min. of Defence, 1950–56; Permanent Secretary, Board of Trade, 1960–68 (Min. of Defence, 1956–59). Dir, Philip Hill Investment Trust, 1968–81; Director: GEC, 1968–79; Albright & Wilson, 1968–73 (Chm., 1969–73); Whessoe Ltd, 1968–88; Hill Samuel Group, 1970–79; Sandoz Gp of Cos, 1972–87 (Chm.); Clerical, Medical and General Life Assurance Soc., 1972–85; Wilkinson Match, 1973–80 (Chm., 1976–80); BPB Industries PLC, 1973–83; Ladbroke Gp, 1980–86; Bridgewater Paper Co. Ltd, 1984–90. Pres., Inst. for Fiscal Studies, 1970–78. *Address:* 5 Westwood Court, 174 Norwich Road, Ipswich IP1 2QX. *T:* (01473) 226076. *Club:* Athenæum.

POWELL, Dame Sally (Ann Vickers), (Dame Sally Coleman), DBE 2001; *b* 2 Oct. 1955; *d* of Alan Vickers Powell and Ena Esther Power; *m* 1996, Iain Coleman, *qv*; one *s. Educ:* Royal Ballet Sch.; Univ. of Southampton (LLB 1984); Coll. of Law (Law Soc. Finals). Sadler's Wells Royal Ballet, 1974–80; joined Lewis Silkin, Solicitors, 1985; with Glazer Delmar, Solicitors, until 1997. Mem. (Lab) Hammersmith and Fulham London BC, 1986– (Dep. for Regeneration). Dep. Leader, Assoc. of London Govt; Chm., Gtr London Enterprise; Dep. Chm., Business Link for London; Mem. Bd, London Develt Agency; Dep. Leader, Labour Gp, LGA. *Recreations:* theatre, football. *Address:* 30 Coverdale Road, W12 8JL. *T:* (020) 8749 1043.

POWELL, Sally Jane, (Mrs Jonathan Powell); *see* Brampton, S. J.

POWELL, William Rhys; barrister, arbitrator; *b* 3 Aug. 1948; *s* of late Rev. Canon Edward Powell and Anne Powell; *m* 1973, Elizabeth Vaudin; three *d. Educ:* Lancing College; Emmanuel College, Cambridge (BA 1970; MA 1973); DipArb Reading Univ. 2000. FCIArb 2001. Called to the Bar, Lincoln's Inn, 1971. MP (C) Corby, 1983–97; contested (C) same seat, 1997. PPS to Minister for Overseas Develt, 1985–86, to Sec. of State for the Envmt, 1990–92. Member, Select Committee: on Procedure, 1987–90; on Foreign Affairs, 1990–91; on Sci. and Technol., 1992–95; on Agriculture, 1995–97; Mem., Jt Parly Ecclesiastical Cttee, 1987–97; Joint Secretary: Cons. Back-bench For. Affairs Cttee, 1985 and 1987–90; Cons. Back-bench Defence Cttee, 1988–90; Chairman: All-Party Parly Gp for the Gulf, 1993–97; British-Italian Parly Gp, 1992–96; British-Taiwan Parly Gp, 1992–97; British-Mongolia Parly Gp, 1993–97; British-Tunisia Parly Gp, 1995–97. Jt Chm., CAABU, 1992–95; Mem. Council, British Atlantic Cttee, 1985–90. Fellow, Industry and Parlt Trust, 1991. As Private Mem. piloted Copyright (Computer Software) Amendment Act, 1985. Vis. Scholar, Academia Sinaca, Taiwan, 1999; Vis. Prof., Univ. of Kansai, Japan, 1999. *Address:* Lynch House, Lynch Lane, Fowlmere, Cambs SG8 7SX; Regency Chambers, Market Square, Peterborough PE1 1XW. *Club:* Corby Conservative.

POWELL-COTTON, Christopher, CMG 1961; MBE 1951; MC 1945; JP; Uganda CS, retired; *b* 23 Feb. 1918; *s* of Major P. H. G. Powell-Cotton and Mrs H. B. Powell-Cotton (*née* Slater); unmarried. *Educ:* Harrow School; Trinity College, Cambridge. Army Service, 1939–45: commissioned Buffs, 1940; seconded KAR, Oct. 1940; T/Major, 1943. Apptd to Uganda Administration, 1940, and released for Mil. Service. District Commissioner, 1950; Provincial Commissioner, 1955; Minister of Security and External Relations, 1961. Landowner in SE Kent. Chm. of Govs, Powell-Cotton Museum. *Address:* Quex Park, Birchington, Kent CT7 0BH. *T:* (01843) 841836. *Club:* MCC.

POWELL-JONES, John Ernest, CMG 1974; HM Diplomatic Service, retired; Ambassador to Switzerland, 1982–85; *b* 14 April 1925; *s* of late Walter James Powell-Jones and Gladys Margaret (*née* Taylor); *m* 1st, 1949, Ann Murray (marr. diss. 1967); one *s* one *d* (and one *s* decd); 2nd, 1968, Pamela Sale. *Educ:* Charterhouse; University Coll., Oxford (1st cl. Modern Hist.). Served with Rifle Bde, 1943–46. HM Foreign (now Diplomatic) Service, 1949; 3rd Sec. and Vice-Consul, Bogota, 1950–52; Eastern and later Levant Dept, FO, 1952–55; 2nd, later 1st Sec., Athens, 1955–59; News Dept, FO, 1959–60; 1st Sec., Leopoldville, 1961–62; UN Dept, FO, 1963–67; ndc Canada 1967–68; Counsellor, Political Adviser's Office, Singapore, 1968–69; Counsellor and Consul-General, Athens, 1970–73; Ambassador at Phnom Penh, 1973–75; RCDS 1975; Ambassador to Senegal, Guinea, Mali, Mauritania and Guinea-Bissau, 1976–79, to Cape Verde, 1977–79; Ambassador and Perm. Rep., UN Conf. on Law of the Sea, 1979–82. Chm., Inter Counsel UK Ltd, 1986–93. Member: Waverley BC, 1987–95; Wonersh Parish Council, 1987–99 (Vice-Chm., 1990–99). Chm., Wonersh United Charities, 1999–. Member: Bd, Surrey Historic Bldgs Trust, 1989–92; Council, SE England Agricl Soc., 1991–95. *Recreations:* gardening, walking. *Address:* Gascons, Gaston Gate, Cranleigh, Surrey GU6 8QY. *T:* (01483) 274313. *Club:* Travellers.
See also M. E. P. Jones.

POWELL-SMITH, Christopher Brian, TD 1985; company director; *b* 3 Oct. 1936; *s* of Edgar and Theodora Powell-Smith; *m* 1964, Jennifer Goslett; two *s* two *d. Educ:* City of London Sch. Asst Solicitor, McKenna & Co., 1959; Nat. Service, 4th Regt, RHA, 1959–61; McKenna & Co.: Partner, 1964–97; Finance Partner, 1975–84; Managing Partner, 1984–87; Head, Corporate Dept, 1987–92; Sen. Partner, 1992–97; Partner, Cameron McKenna, 1997. Non-executive Director: Black and Decker Gp Inc., 1980–; KBC Advanced Technology plc, 1997–; MPG Gp Ltd, 1998–. CO and Regimental Col, HAC, 1975–79. *Recreations:* golf, choral singing. *Address:* 32 The Avenue, Kew, Surrey TW9 2AJ. *T:* (020) 8395 0333; *e-mail:* cpowell_smith@compuserve.com. *Club:* Royal Mid-Surrey Golf.

POWER, Sir Alastair John Cecil, 4th Bt *cr* 1924, of Newlands Manor; *b* 15 Aug. 1958; *s* of Sir John Patrick McLannahan Power, 3rd Bt and of Melanie, *d* of Hon. Alastair Erskine; *S* father, 1984; *m* 1981, Virginia Newton; one *s* two *d. Heir: s* Mark Alastair John Power, *b* 15 Oct. 1989.

POWER, Mrs Brian St Quentin; *see* Stack, (Ann) Prunella.

POWER, Sir Noel (Plunkett), GBS 1999; Kt 1999; a Non-Permanent Judge, Hong Kong Court of Final Appeal, since 1997; *b* 4 Dec. 1929; *s* of John Joseph Power and Hilda Power; *m* 1965, Irma Maroya; two *s* one *d. Educ:* Downlands Coll.; Univ. of Queensland (BA, LLB). Called to the Bar, Supreme Court of Queensland and High Court of Australia, 1955; Magistrate, Hong Kong, 1965–76; Pres., Lands Tribunal, Hong Kong, 1976–79; a Judge of the Supreme Court of Hong Kong, 1979–87; a Judge of Appeal, 1987–93; a Vice-Pres. of the Court of Appeal of the Supreme Court, then a Justice of Appeal, Appeal Court of the High Court, Hong Kong, 1993–99; Acting Chief Justice, Hong Kong, 1996–97. Chm., Hong Kong Island, 1984–99, Asia-Pacific Zone, 1994–99, Gold Coast, 1999–, Internat. Wine and Food Soc. Chm. Editl Bd, Hong Kong Law Reports, 1994–97. *Publications:* (ed) Lands Tribunal Law Reports, 1976–79. *Recreations:* travel, cooking, reading. *Address:* 44 The Quay, Surfers Waters, 40 Cotlew Street, Southport, Qld 4215, Australia. *Clubs:* Hong Kong (Hong Kong); Queensland (Brisbane).

POWERS, Dr Michael John; QC 1995; *b* 9 Feb. 1947; *os* of late Reginald Frederick and of Kathleen Powers; *m* 1968, Meryl Hall (marr. diss.); one *s* one *d*; *m* 2001, Pamela Barnes. *Educ:* Poole Grammar Sch.; Middlesex Hosp. Med. Sch., London Univ. (BSc, MB BS, DA). House Surgeon, Middlesex Hosp., 1972; House Physician, Royal S Hants Hosp., 1973; Sen. House Officer, Anaesthetics, Royal United Hosp., Bath, 1974; GP, Parson Drove, Cambs, 1975; Registrar in Anaesthetics, Northwick Park Hosp., Harrow, 1975–77; called to the Bar, Lincoln's Inn, 1979, Bencher, 1998; HM Asst Dep. Coroner, Westminster, 1981–87. Pres., S of England Coroners' Soc., 1987–88. *Publications:* Thurston's Coronership: the law and practice on coroners, 1985; Medical Negligence, 1990, 3rd edn (ed jtly), as Clinical Negligence, 2000; chapters in medical and legal texts on medico-legal subjects. *Recreations:* music, hill-walking, sailing, painting. *Address:* 4 Paper Buildings, Temple, EC4Y 7EX. *T:* (020) 7353 3366; *e-mail:* powersqc@medneg.co.uk. *Clubs:* Savage, Royal Society of Medicine.

POWERSCOURT, 10th Viscount *cr* 1743; **Mervyn Niall Wingfield;** Baron Wingfield, 1743; Baron Powerscourt (UK), 1885; *b* 3 Sept. 1935; *s* of 9th Viscount Powerscourt and Sheila Claude (*d* 1992), *d* of late Lt-Col Claude Beddington; *S* father, 1973; *m* 1st, 1962, Wendy Ann Pauline (marr. diss. 1974), *d* of R. C. G. Slazenger; one *s* one *d*; 2nd, 1979, Pauline (marr. diss. 1995), *d* of W. P. Van, San Francisco. *Educ:* Stowe; Trinity Coll., Cambridge. Formerly Irish Guards. *Heir: s* Hon. Mervyn Anthony Wingfield, *b* 21 Aug. 1963.
See also Sir J. H. Langrishe, Bt.

POWIS, 8th Earl of, *cr* 1804; **John George Herbert;** Baron Clive (Ire.), 1762; Baron Clive (GB), 1794; Viscount Clive, Baron Herbert of Chirbury, Baron Powis, 1804; Assistant Professor, Redeemer College, Ontario, Canada, 1990–92; *b* 19 May 1952; *s* of 7th Earl of Powis and of Hon. Katharine Odeyne de Grey, *d* of 8th Baron Walsingham, DSO, OBE; *S* father, 1993; *m* 1977, Marijke Sophia, *d* of Maarten Nanne Guther, Ancaster, Canada; two *s* two *d. Educ:* Wellington; McMaster Univ., Ontario, Canada (MA; PhD 1994). Formerly Lectr, McMaster Univ. *Heir: s* Viscount Clive, *qv. Address:* Powis Castle Estate Office, Welshpool, Powys SY21 8RG.

POWLES, Prof. Raymond Leonard, MD; FRCP; FRCPath; Physician in Charge, since 1974, and Group Head, Haemato-Oncology, since 1993, Leukaemia and Myeloma Units, Royal Marsden Hospital; Professor of Haemato-Oncology, University of London, at Institute of Cancer Research, since 1997; *b* 9 March 1938; *s* of late Leonard William David Powles and Florence Irene Powles (*née* Conolly); *m* 1980, Louise Jane Richmond; three *s* one *d. Educ:* Eltham Coll.; St Bartholomew's Hosp. Med. Coll. (BSc 1961; MB BS 1964; MD 1976). MRCP 1968, FRCP 1980; FRCPath 1993. House Physician and Surgeon, St Bartholomew's Hosp., 1965–66; RMO, Royal Marsden Hosp., 1967–68; Leukaemia Res. Fund Fellow, Ville Juif, Paris, 1968; Tata Meml Fund Fellow, Royal Marsden Hosp. and Inst. of Cancer Res., Sutton, 1969–72; SSO, ICRF, St Bartholomew's Hosp. and Royal Marsden Hosp., 1972–74. Clin. Tutor, RCP, 1990; internat. lectures on leukaemia, myeloma and bone marrow transplantation. Member: MRC Wkg Party on Leukaemia, 1974–; Royal Marsden SHA, 1989–92; Standing Med. Adv. Sub-Cttee on Cancer, DoH, 1991–93; WHO Cttee on Internat. Programme Chernobyl Accident, 1990–92; Bd, European Soc. Med. Oncology, 1985–90. Scientific Advr, Internat. Myeloma Foundn, 1995–. Member: Bd, Bone Marrow Transplantation, 1986–; Bd, Experimental Haematology, 1992–. Lifetime Achievement Award, Cancer Patients Aid Assoc., India, 1999. *Publications:* more than 600 sci. papers, articles, and chapters in books on leukaemia, myeloma and bone marrow transplantation. *Recreations:* sport, travel, cinema. *Address:* Little Garratts, 19 Garratts Lane, Banstead, Surrey SM7 2EA. *T:* (01737) 353632, *Fax:* (office) (020) 8770 7313; *e-mail:* myeloma@clara.net.
See also T. J. Powles.

POWLES, Stephen Robert; QC 1995; a Recorder, since 1997; *b* 7 June 1948; *s* of Andrew Frederick Arthur Powles and Nora (*née* Bristol); *m* 1975, Geraldine Patricia Hilda Adamson; one *s* one *d. Educ:* Westminster Sch.; University Coll., Oxford (MA). Called to the Bar: Middle Temple, 1972 (Harmsworth Maj. Exhibnr, 1971; Astbury Law Schol., 1972); Lincoln's Inn (*ad eundem*), 1977. CEDR accredited mediator; CIMechE. *Recreations:* hill-walking, sailing, my border terrier. *Address:* 2 Harcourt Buildings, Temple, EC4Y 9DB. *T:* (020) 7583 9020. *Club:* Royal Solent Yacht.

POWLES, Prof. Trevor James, PhD; FRCP; Consultant Physician in Breast Cancer, since 1978, Head of Breast Cancer Unit, since 1993, and Medical Director, Common Tumours Division, since 2000, Royal Marsden Hospital; Professor of Breast Oncology, Institute of Cancer Research, London University, since 1998; *b* 8 March 1938; *s* of late Leonard William David Powles and Florence Irene Powles (*née* Conolly); *m* 1968, Penelope Margaret Meyers; two *s* one *d. Educ:* Eltham Coll.; St Bartholomew's Hosp. Med. Coll. (PhD). FRCP 1983. House Physician and Registrar, Hammersmith Hosp., 1967–68; Med. Registrar, St Bartholomew's Hosp., 1965–70; MRC Clin. Res. Fellow, Inst. of Cancer Res., 1971–73; Sen. Registrar and Sen. Lectr, Royal Marsden Hosp., 1974–78. Visiting Professor: M. D. Anderson Cancer Center, Houston, 1993; Dana Farber Cancer Center, Harvard, Boston, 1996; Tom Baker Cancer Centre, Calgary, 1998. Director: Oncotech Inc., Calif, 1996–; Neothermia Inc., Ohio, 2000–. Vice Pres., Internat. Soc. for Prevention of Cancer, 1996–. MInstD 2001. *Publications:* Breast Cancer Management, 1981; Prostaglandins and Cancer, 1982; Medical Management of Breast

PGCE); Southlands Coll. (Adv. Dip. in Careers Educn and Guidance); South Bank Univ. (LLB 1992). Teacher, ILEA, 1974–88. Councillor, Hammersmith and Fulham London BC, 1986–92. An Asst Govt Whip, 1997–98. JP Inner London, 1985. *Recreations:* music, reading, crosswords, knitting, my two cats, football. *Address:* House of Commons, SW1A 0AA.

PRENTICE, Prof. Daniel David; Allen & Overy Professor of Corporate Law, Oxford University, since 1991; Fellow of Pembroke College, Oxford; *b* 7 Aug. 1941; *s* of Thomas James Prentice and Agnes Prentice (*née* Fox); *m* 1965, Judith Mary Keane; one *s* one *d.* *Educ:* St Malachy's Coll., Belfast; Queen's Univ., Belfast (LLB); Univ. of Chicago (JD); MA Oxford (by special resolution). Called to the Bar, Lincoln's Inn, 1982; Mem., Erskine Chambers. Associate Prof., Univ. of Ontario, 1966–68; Lectr, UCL, 1968–73; Lectr, 1973–90, Reader, 1991, Univ. of Oxford. Vis. Prof., various univs. Asst. Editor, Law Qly Rev., 1988–. *Publication:* (ed) Chitty, Law of Contracts, 25th edn 1983, 26th edn 1989. *Recreation:* squash. *Address:* Pembroke College, Oxford OX1 1DW. *T:* (01865) 276438.

PRENTICE, Gordon; MP (Lab) Pendle, since 1992; *b* 28 Jan. 1951; *s* of Esther and William Prentice; *m* 1975, Bridget Theresa Corr (*see* B. T. Prentice) (marr. diss. 2000). *Educ:* Univ. of Glasgow (MA; Pres., Glasgow Univ. Union, 1972–73). Mercury House Publications, 1974–78; Local Govt Officer, 1978–81; Labour Party Policy Directorate, 1982–92. Mem. Council, London Borough of Hammersmith and Fulham, 1982–90 (Leader of Council, 1986–88). *Recreations:* cooking, hill walking, gardening. *Address:* House of Commons, SW1A 0AA. *T:* (020) 7219 3000.

PRENTICE, (Hubert Archibald) John, CEng; FInstP; consultant on manufacturing and management strategies to several UK and USA companies; *b* 5 Feb. 1920; *s* of Charles Herbert Prentice and Rose Prentice; *m* 1947, Sylvia Doreen Elias; one *s.* *Educ:* Woolwich Polytechnic, London; Salford Univ. (BSc, MSc). CEng; MRAeS 1962; FInstP 1967. Min. of Supply, 1939–56; R&D posts, res. estabts and prodn, MoD, 1956–60; Space Dept, RAE, Min. of Aviation, 1960–67; Head, Road User Characteristics Res., 1967–70, and Head, Driver Aids and Abilities Res., 1970–72, MoT; Head, Road User Dynamics Res., DoE, 1972–75; Counsellor (Sci. and Technol.), British Embassy, Tokyo, 1975–80. *Recreations:* walking, climbing. *Address:* 5 Foxhill Crescent, Camberley, Surrey GU15 1PR. *T:* (01276) 66373.

PRENTICE, Thomas, MC 1945; Life President, Harrisons & Crosfield plc, now Elementis plc, since 1988 (Chairman, 1977–88); *b* 14 Oct. 1919; *s* of Alexander and Jean Young Prentice; *m* 1949, Peggy Ann Lloyd; two *s* two *d.* *Educ:* McLaren High Sch., Callander, Perthshire. Served Army, 1939–46. Harrisons & Crosfield (Sabah) Sdn. Bhd., Malaysia, 1947–67; Harrisons & Crosfield plc, now Elementis plc, 1967–. *Recreations:* golf, gardening. *Club:* East India, Devonshire, Sports and Public Schools.

PRENTICE, Hon. Sir William (Thomas), Kt 1977; MBE 1945; Senior Member, Administrative Appeals Tribunal, Australia, 1981–87; *b* 1 June 1919; *s* of Claud Stanley and Pauline Prentice; *m* 1946, Mary Elizabeth, *d* of F. B. Dignam; three *s* one *d.* *Educ:* St Joseph's College, Hunters Hill; Sydney Univ. (BA, LLB). AIF, Middle East and New Guinea, 2–33 Inf. Bn and Staff Captain 25 Aust. Inf. Bde, Owen Stanleys and Lae Ramu campaigns; Staff Course, Duntroon, 1944; Staff Captain, 7 Aust. Inf. Bde, Bougainville campaign, 1944–45. Resumed law studies, 1946; admitted Bar, NSW, 1947; Judge, Supreme Court, PNG, 1970; Senior Puisne Judge, 1975; Deputy Chief Justice on independence, PNG, 1975, Chief Justice 1978–80. *Recreations:* bush walking, swimming, reading. *Address:* 16 Olympia Road, Naremburn, NSW 2065, Australia. *Clubs:* Tattersall's, Cricketers' (Sydney).

PRENTICE, Dame Winifred (Eva), DBE 1977 (OBE 1972); SRN; President, Royal College of Nursing, 1972–76; *b* 2 Dec. 1910; *d* of Percy John Prentice and Anna Eva Prentice. *Educ:* Northgate Sch. for Girls, Ipswich; E Suffolk and Ipswich Hosp. (SRN); W Mddx Hosp. (SCM Pt I); Queen Elizabeth Coll., London Univ. (RNT); Dip. in Nursing, London Univ. Ward Sister: E Suffolk and Ipswich Hosp., 1936–39; Essex County Hosp., 1941–43; Nurse Tutor, King's Lynn Hosp., 1944–46; Principal Tutor, Stracathro Hosp., Brechin, Angus, 1947–61, Matron, 1961–72. *Publications:* articles in Nursing Times and Nursing Mirror. *Recreations:* music, amateur dramatics, gardening. *Address:* Marleish, 4 Duke Street, Brechin, Angus DD9 6JY. *T:* (01356) 622606.

PRESCOTT, John Barry, AC 1996; Chairman, Horizon Private Equity Pty Ltd, since 1998; Managing Director and Chief Executive Officer, The Broken Hill Pty Co. Ltd, 1991–98 (Director, 1988–98); *b* 22 Oct. 1940; *s* of late John Norman Prescott and Margaret Ellen (*née* Brownie); *m* 1985, Jennifer Cahill; one *s* three *d.* *Educ:* N Sydney Boys' High Sch.; Univ. of NSW (BComm Industrial Relns). Joined The Broken Hill Pty Co. Ltd as Industrial Relns Trainee, 1958: various industrial relns positions, 1958–69; Superintendent, Industrial Relns, Shipping and Stevedoring, Newcastle and Sydney, 1969–74; Asst Fleet Manager, Ops, Newcastle, 1974–79; Exec. Asst to Gen. Manager, Transport, 1979–80; Manager Ops, Transport, 1980–82; Gen. Manager, Transport, 1982–87; Exec. Gen. Manager and Chief Exec. Officer, BHP Steel, 1987–91. Director: Tubemakers of Aust. Ltd, 1988–92; (non-exec.), Normandy Mining Ltd, 1999–; Member: Adv. Bd, Booz, Allen & Hamilton Inc., 1991–; Internat. Council, J. P. Morgan, 1994–; Asia Pacific Adv. Cttee, New York Stock Exchange Inc., 1995–. Member Board: Business Council of Aust., 1995–97; Walter and Eliza Hall Inst. of Med. Res., 1994–98; Bd of Trustees, Conf. Bd, 1995–. Mem. Internat. Council, Asia Soc., 1991–. Hon. LLD Monash, 1994; Hon. DSc NSW, 1995. *Recreations:* tennis, golf. *Address:* (office) Level 28, 140 William Street, Melbourne, Vic 3000, Australia. *Clubs:* Australian, Melbourne (Melbourne); Newcastle (Newcastle); Huntingdale Golf, National Golf (Vic).

PRESCOTT, Prof. John Herbert Dudley, PhD; FIBiol; FRAgS; Principal, Wye College, and Professor of Animal Production, University of London, 1988–2000, now Professor Emeritus; *b* 21 Feb. 1937; *s* of Herbert Prescott and Edith Vera Prescott; *m* 1960, Diana Margaret Mullock; two *s* two *d.* *Educ:* Haileybury; Univ. of Nottingham (BSc (Agric), PhD). FIBiol 1983; FRAgS 1986. Lectr in Animal Prodn, Univ. of Newcastle upon Tyne, 1963–72; Animal Prodn Officer in Argentina, FAO, UN, 1972–74; Head of Animal Prodn Advisory and Develt, E of Scotland Coll. of Agric., 1974–78; Prof. of Animal Prodn, Univ. of Edinburgh, 1978–84, and Head of Animal Div., Edinburgh Sch. of Agric., 1978–84; Dir, Grassland, later Animal and Grassland, Res. Inst., 1984–86; Dir, Grassland and Animal Prodn Res., AFRC, 1986–88. Visiting Professor: Univ. of Reading, 1985–88; UCW, Aberystwyth, 1988. Non-exec. Dir, Natural Resources Internat. Ltd, 1997–2000 (Actg Chm., 1996). Chm., Tech. Cttee on Response to Nutrients, AFRC, 1988–94. British Council: Member: Cttee for Internat. Co-operation in Higher Educn, 1989–2000; Agric. and Vet. Adv. Cttee, 1988–96; Vice-Chm., Sci., Engrg and Envmt Adv. Cttee, 1997–2001. Member: Adv. Bd, Centre for Tropical Medicine, 1978–84; Board of Directors: Hill Farming Res. Orgn, 1980–84; Hannah Res. Inst., 1981–84; Scientific Adv. Cttee, 1990–92, Governing Body, 1992–97, Macaulay Land Use Res. Inst.; various cttees on cattle and beef, MLC, 1969–90. President: British Soc. of Animal Prodn, 1988; Agricl and Forestry Sect., BAAS, 1994–95; Mem. Council, British Grassland Soc., 1984–87. Chairman: Stapledon Meml Trust, 1992–; Natural Resources Internat. Foundn, 1997–; Trustee, E Malling Trust for Horticl Res., 1998–. Member: Gov. Body and Corp., Hadlow Coll., 1988–98; Council: RVC, 1988–98; Univ. of Kent, 1988–2000. Liveryman, Farmers' Co., 2000–. FRSA 2000. Hon. Fellow: Inst. for Grassland and Envmtl Res., 1989; Wye Coll., 2000; ICSTM, 2001. *Publications:* scientific papers in Animal Prodn and Agricultural Science; technical articles. *Recreations:* farming, walking, wildlife, the countryside. *Address:* 38 Oxenturn Road, Wye, Ashford, Kent TN25 5BE. *Club:* Farmers.

PRESCOTT, Rt Hon. John (Leslie); PC 1994; MP (Lab) Kingston upon Hull East, since 1997 (Kingston upon Hull (East), 1970–83; Hull East, 1983–97); Deputy Prime Minister, since 1997, and First Secretary of State, since 2001; Deputy Leader of the Labour Party, since 1994; *b* 31 May 1938; *s* of late John Herbert Prescott, JP and of Phyllis Prescott; *m* 1961, Pauline Tilston; two *s.* *Educ:* Ellesmere Port Secondary Modern Sch.; WEA; correspondence courses; Ruskin Coll., Oxford (DipEcon/Pol Oxon); Hull Univ. (BSc Econ). Trainee Chef, 1953–55; Steward, Passenger Lines, Merchant Navy, 1955–63; Ruskin Coll., Oxford, 1963–65; Recruitment Officer, General and Municipal Workers Union (temp.), 1965; Hull Univ., 1965–68. Full-time Official, National Union of Seamen, 1968–70. Contested (Lab) Southport, 1966. PPS to Sec. of State for Trade, 1974–76; opposition spokesman on Transport, 1979–81; opposition front bench spokesman on Regional Affairs and Devolution, 1981–83, on Transport, 1983–84 and 1988–93, on Employment, 1984–87 and 1993–94, on Energy, 1987–88; Mem., Shadow Cabinet, 1983–97; Sec. of State for the Envmt, Transport and the Regions, 1997–2001. Member: Select Cttee Nationalized Industries, 1973–79; Council of Europe, 1972–75; European Parlt, 1975–79 (Leader, Labour Party Delegn, 1976–79). Mem., NEC, Labour Party, 1989–. *Publication:* Not Wanted on Voyage, 1966. *Address:* House of Commons, SW1A 0AA.

PRESCOTT, Sir Mark, 3rd Bt *cr* 1938, of Godmanchester; racehorse trainer, in Newmarket; *b* 3 March 1948; *s* of late Major W. R. Stanley Prescott (MP for Darwen Div., 1943–51; 2nd *s* of Colonel Sir William Prescott, 1st Bt) and Gwendolen (who *m* 2nd, 1952, Daniel Orme (*d* 1972); she *d* 1992), *o c* of late Leonard Aldridge, CBE; *S* uncle, Sir Richard Stanley Prescott, 2nd Bt, 1965. *Educ:* Harrow. *Address:* Heath House, Moulton Road, Newmarket, Suffolk CB8 8DU. *T:* (01638) 662117.

PRESCOTT, Brig. Peter George Addington, MC 1944; Secretary, National Rifle Association, 1980–88; *b* 22 Sept. 1924; *s* of Col and Mrs John Prescott; *m* 1953, June Marian Louise Wendell; one *s* one *d.* *Educ:* Eton Coll.; Staff Coll. (psc 1957); Royal Coll. of Defence Studies (rcds 1973). Commnd Grenadier Guards, 1943; 2nd Armoured Bn Gren. Gds, 1944–45; comd 2nd Bn Gren. Gds, 1966–69; Comdr 51st Inf. Bde, 1970–72; Dep. Comdr NE Dist, 1974–77; Dep. Dir of Army Trng, 1977–79, retd. Chevalier, Royal Order of the Sword, Sweden, 1954. *Recreations:* sailing, painting, gardening. *Address:* West House, 66 High Street, Rolvenden, Kent TN17 4LW.

PRESCOTT, Peter John; Director, Arts Division, British Council, 1990–93, retired; *b* 6 April 1936; *s* of Wentworth James Prescott and Ellen Marie (*née* Burrows); *m* 1971, Gillian Eileen Lowe. *Educ:* Windsor Grammar School; Pembroke College, Oxford (MA). Joined British Council, 1963; Asst Cultural Attaché, Egypt, 1964–67; London, 1967–70; Sussex Univ., 1970–71; France, 1971–75; London, 1975–79; on secondment to Dept of Education and Science, 1979–81; Australia, 1981–84; Rep., France, and Cultural Counsellor, British Embassy, Paris, 1984–90. *Recreations:* reading, music, painting, theatre, walking, swimming, travel. *Address:* 6/22 Greville Place, NW6 5JG. *T:* (020) 7624 6269.

PRESCOTT, Peter Richard Kyle; QC 1990; *b* 23 Jan. 1943; *s* of Richard Stanley Prescott and Sarah Aitchison Shand; *m* 1967, Frances Rosemary Bland; two *s* one *d.* *Educ:* St George's Coll., Argentina; Dulwich Coll.; University Coll. London (BSc); Queen Mary Coll., London (MSc). Called to the Bar, Lincoln's Inn, 1970, Bencher, 2001. *Publication:* The Modern Law of Copyright (with Hugh Laddie, QC, and Mary Vitoria), 1980, 3rd edn 2000. *Recreations:* music, flying, reading, cooking. *Address:* 8 New Square, Lincoln's Inn, WC2A 3QP. *T:* (020) 7405 4321.

PRESCOTT, Westby William P.; *see* Percival-Prescott.

PRESLAND, Frank George; Chief Executive, William A. Bong Ltd, and other companies in Elton John Group, since 1999; *b* 27 Feb. 1944; *s* of Reginald Charles Presland and Elsie Presland; *m*; one *s* one *d.* *Educ:* London Sch. of Economics (BSc Econ); University Coll. of Rhodesia and Nyasaland (Fairbridge Schol.). Admitted solicitor, 1973; Partner, Frere Cholmeley, 1976–92; Chm., Frere Cholmeley Bischoff, 1992–98, when co. merged with Eversheds; Jt Chm., Eversheds, 1998–99. Dir, Elton John AIDS Foundn, UK and USA. *Recreation:* yachting. *Address:* (office) 1 Blythe Road, W14 0HG. *Club:* Little Ship.

PRESS, Dr Frank; Principal, Washington Advisory Group, since 1996; *b* 4 Dec. 1924; *m* 1946, Billie Kallick; one *s* one *d.* *Educ:* City Coll., NY (BS 1944); Columbia Univ. (MA 1946; PhD 1949). Columbia University: Res. Associate, 1946–49; Instr in Geology, 1949–51; Asst Prof. of Geology, 1951–52; Associate Prof., 1952–55; Prof. of Geophysics, 1955–65 and Dir, Seismol. Lab., 1957–65, CIT; Prof. of Geophysics and Chm., Dept of Earth and Planetary Scis, MIT, 1965–77; Sci. Advisor to Pres. and Dir, Office of Sci. and Tech. Policy, 1977–80; Prof., MIT, 1981; Pres., NAS, 1981–93; Cecil and Ida Green Sen. Fellow, Carnegie Instn of Washington, 1993–97. Member: President's Sci. Adv. Commn, 1961–64; Nat. Sci. Bd, 1970–; Lunar and Planetary Missions Bd, NASA; participant, bilateral scis agreement with Peoples Republic of China and USSR; US Deleg. to Nuclear Test Ban Negotiations, Geneva and Moscow. Mem., Acad. of Arts and Scis, and other US and internat. bodies. Numerous awards, incl. Japan Prize, Sci. and Technol. Foundn of Japan, 1993, US Nat. Medal of Science, 1994, and hon. degrees. Officer, Legion of Honour, 1989. *Publications:* (jtly) Propagation of Elastic Waves in Layered Media, 1957; (ed jtly) Physics and Chemistry of the Earth, 1957; (jtly) Earth, 1986; Understanding Earth, 1994; numerous papers. *Address:* Suite 616 South, 2500 Virginia Avenue NW, Washington, DC 20037–1901, USA.

PRESS, John Bryant, FRSL; author and poet; *b* 11 Jan. 1920; *s* of late Edward Kenneth Press and late Gladys (*née* Cooper); *m* 1947, Janet Crompton; one *s* one *d.* *Educ:* King Edward VI Sch., Norwich; Corpus Christi Coll., Cambridge, 1938–40 and 1945–46. Served War of 1939–45: RA, 1940–45. British Council, 1946–79: Athens, 1946–47; Salonika, 1947–50; Madras, 1950–51; Colombo, 1951–52; Birmingham, 1952–54; Cambridge, 1955–62; London, 1962–65; Paris, 1966–71 (also Cultural Attaché, British Embassy); Regional Dir, Oxford, 1972–78; Literature Advr, London, 1978–79. Mem. Council, RSL, 1961–88. Gave George Elliston Poetry Foundation Lectures at Univ. of Cincinnati, 1962; Vis. Prof., Univ. of Paris, 1981–82. *Publications:* The Fire and the Fountain, 1955; Uncertainties, 1956; (ed) Poetic Heritage, 1957; The Chequer'd Shade, 1958 (RSL Heinemann Award); Andrew Marvell, 1958; Guy Fawkes Night, 1959; Herrick, 1961; Rule and Energy, 1963; Louis MacNeice, 1964; (ed) Palgrave's Golden Treasury, Book V, 1964, Book VI, 1994; A Map of Modern English Verse, 1969; The Lengthening Shadows, 1971; John Betjeman, 1974; Spring at St Clair, 1974; Aspects of

Paris, (with illus by Gordon Bradshaw), 1975; (with Edward Lowbury and Michael Riviere) Troika, 1977; Poets of World War I, 1983; Poets of World War II, 1984; A Girl with Beehive Hair, 1986. Libretto, new version of Bluebeard's Castle, for Michael Powell's colour television film of Bartok's opera, 1963. *Recreations:* travel (especially in France), theatre, opera, concerts, cinema; architecture and visual arts. *Address:* 5 South Parade, Frome BA11 1EJ. *T:* (01373) 302166.

PRESTON, family name of **Viscount Gormanston**.

PRESTON, Dame Frances Olivia C.; *see* Campbell-Preston.

PRESTON, Geoffrey Averill; Assistant Counsel to Chairman of Committees, House of Lords, 1982–89; *b* 19 May 1924; *s* of George and Winifred Preston; *m* 1953, Catherine Wright. *Educ:* St Marylebone Grammar Sch. Barrister-at-Law. Served, RNVR, 1942–46. Called to Bar, Gray's Inn, 1950. Treasury Solicitor's Dept, 1952–71; Solicitor's Department: Dept of Environment, 1971–74; Dept of Trade, 1974–75; Under-Sec. (Legal), Dept of Trade, 1975–82. *Recreations:* gardening, carpentry, chess. *Address:* Ledsham, Glaziers Lane, Normandy, Surrey GU3 2DQ. *T:* (01483) 811250.

PRESTON, Dr Ian Mathieson Hamilton, CBE 1993; FREng, FIEE; Chairman, Motherwell Bridge Holdings, 1996–2001; *b* 18 July 1932; *s* of John Hamilton Preston and Edna Irene Paul; *m* 1958, Sheila Hope Pringle; two *s*. *Educ:* Univ. of Glasgow (BSc 1st cl. Hons; PhD). MInstP 1959; FIEE 1974; FREng (FEng 1982). Asst Lectr, Univ. of Glasgow, 1954–59; joined SSEB, 1959, Chief Engineer, Generation Design and Construction, 1972–77; Dir Gen., Generation Develt and Construction Div., CEGB, 1977–83; Dep. Chm., SSEB, 1983–90; Chief Exec., Scottish Power, 1990–95. Director: Deutsche (Scotland) (formerly Morgan Grenfell (Scotland)), 1994–; Clydeport plc, 1994–2000. Chairman: Mining Scotland, 1995–98; East of Scotland Water Authy, 1995–98. Pres., Scottish Council Develt and Industry, 1997–99 (Chm., 1992–97). Hon. FCIWEM 1995. *Recreations:* fishing, gardening. *Address:* 10 Cameron Crescent, Carmunnock, Glasgow G76 9DX.

PRESTON, Jeffrey William, CB 1989; Director General, Energy, Department of Trade and Industry, 1996–98; *b* 28 Jan. 1940; *s* of William and Sybil Grace Preston (*née* Lawson). *Educ:* Liverpool Collegiate Sch.; Hertford Coll., Oxford (MA Lit. Hum. 1966). Asst Principal, Min. of Aviation, 1963; Private Sec. to Permanent Sec., BoT, 1966; Principal: BoT, 1967; HM Treasury, 1970; DTI, 1973; Asst Sec., Dept of Trade, 1975–82; Under Sec. and Regional Dir, Yorks and Humberside Region, DTI, 1982–85; Dep. Sec., Industrial and Economic Affairs, Welsh Office, 1985–90; Dep. Dir Gen., OFT, 1990–96 (Acting Dir Gen., 1995). Chm., Hertford Soc., 1987–95. FRSA. *Recreations:* motoring, opera, swimming. *T:* (020) 8940 7166. *Club:* Oxford and Cambridge (Chm., 1999–2001).

PRESTON, Kieran Thomas, FCIT; Director General, West Yorkshire Passenger Transport Executive, since 1993; *b* 30 Nov. 1950; *s* of Charles Edward Preston and Mary Kate Preston; *m* 1974, Denise Marie Gregory; two *s*. *Educ:* Leeds Poly. (BA Hons Mgt and Admin). FCIT 1994. Local Govt Officer, various appts, 1972–89; Leeds City Council: Projects Dir, 1989–91; Actg Dir of Admin, 1991–92; Chief Services Officer, 1992–93. Chm., PTE Gp, 2001–. FIPD (FIPM 1992). *Recreations:* keeping fit, horse riding, football, cricket, judo. *Address:* West Yorkshire Passenger Transport Executive, Wellington House, 40–50 Wellington Street, Leeds LS1 2DE; 15 Morritt Avenue, Leeds LS15 7EP. *T:* (0113) 260 9093.

PRESTON, Michael Richard, ATD; FCSD; consultant designer; *b* 15 Oct. 1927; *s* of Major Frederick Allan Preston, MC and Winifred Gertrude (*née* Archer); *m* 1st, 1955, Anne Gillespie Smith; 2nd, 1980, Judith Gaye James. *Educ:* Whitgift Sch.; Guildford Sch. of Art; Goldsmiths' Coll., London Univ. (NDD 1953; ATD 1954); Dip. in Humanities (London) 1964. FCSD (FSIAD 1972; MSIAD 1953). Served HM Forces, Queen's Royal Regt, 1944–48, Queen's Royal Regt, TA & HAC, 1948–61. Asst Art Master, Whitgift Sch., 1954–55; Drawing Master, Dulwich Coll., 1955–64; Science Mus., 1964–87; Head of Design, 1964–86; Keeper, Dept of Museum Services, 1987; designed exhibitions, including: Centenary of Charles Babbage, 1971; A Word to the Mermaids, 1973; Tower Bridge Observed, 1974; The Breath of Life, 1974; Nat. Rly Mus., York, 1975; Sci. and Technol. of Islam, 1976; Nat. Mus. of Photography, Bradford, 1977–83; Stanley Spencer in the Shipyard, 1979; Wellcome Mus. of Hist. of Medicine, 1980; Sci. and Technol. of India, 1982; The Great Cover-up Show, 1982; Beads of Glass, 1983; Louis Pasteur and Rabies, 1985. Advisory Assignments on Museum Projects: Iran, 1976–79; Spain, 1977–80; Germany, 1978–79; Canada, 1979–82, 1984–86; Trinidad, 1982–83; Turkey, 1984–94; Hong Kong, 1985; consultant to: Dean and Chapter of Canterbury, 1987–96; Wellcome Foundn, 1987–95; TAVRA Greater London, 1988–94; Mus. of East Asian Art, Bath, 1988–93; Design Expo '89, Nagoya; Bank of England Museum, 1989; Norwich Tourism Agency, 1989–91; Tricycle Theatre, 1989–90; Nat. Theatre, 1989–90; Scottish Office, 1990; English Heritage, 1990; Richmond Theatre, 1990; Accademia Italiana, 1990–94; Société Générale, 1992–95; Castrol Internat., 1994–95; Dean and Chapter of Westminster Abbey, 1997–98; Westminster CC, 1997–99. Mem., BTEC Validation Panel, 1986–92. Chm., Greenwich Soc., 1961–64. Society of Industrial Artists and Designers (now Chartered Society of Designers): Mem., 1953–; Vice-Pres., 1976, 1979–81; Chm., Membership Bd, 1976–79; Chm., Design Management Panel, 1976–80. Mem., ICOM, 1964–. Trustee, Vivat Trust, 1989–92. Hon. Keeper of Pictures, Arts Club, 1992–. Vis. Prof., NID, Ahmedabad, 1989–2000. Guild of Glass Engravers: Hon. FGGE 1980; Pres., 1986–92. FRSA 1955–68. *Recreations:* travel, food, conversation, jazz. *Club:* Arts.

PRESTON, Myles Park; HM Diplomatic Service, retired; *b* 4 April 1927; *s* of Robert and Marie Preston; *m* 1st, 1951, Ann Betten (marr. diss.); one *s* one *d*; 2nd, 1981, Joy Moore (*née* Fisher). *Educ:* Sudley Road Council Sch.; Liverpool Inst. High Sch.; Clare Coll., Cambridge. Instructor Lieut, RN, 1948–51; Asst Principal, Admty, 1951–53; CRO, 1953–54; 2nd Sec., British High Commn, New Delhi, 1954–56; 1st Sec., CRO, 1956–59; 1st Sec., Governor-General's Office and British High Commn, Lagos, 1959–62; CRO, 1962–64; 1st Sec., British High Commn, Kampala, 1964–67; Commonwealth Office and FCO, 1967–69; Counsellor and Consul-Gen., Djakarta, 1969–72; Canadian Nat. Defence Coll., 1972–73; FCO, 1973–77; Dep. Governor, Solomon Islands, 1977–78; Consul-Gen., Vancouver, 1978–79. *Address:* 20 Prince Edwards Road, Lewes, East Sussex BN7 1BE. *T:* (01273) 475809.

PRESTON, Prof. Paul, CBE 2000; FRHistS; FBA 1994; Professor of International History, London School of Economics, since 1991; *b* 21 July 1946; *s* of Charles Ronald Preston and Alice Hoskisson; *m* 1983, Gabrielle Patricia Ashford-Hodges; two *s*. *Educ:* St Edward's Coll., Liverpool; Oriel Coll., Oxford. Lectr in Modern History, Univ. of Reading, 1974–75; Queen Mary College, University of London: Lectr and Reader in Modern History, 1975–85; Prof. of History, 1985–91. Comendador de la Orden de Mérito Civil (Spain), 1986. *Publications:* (ed) Spain in Crisis, 1976; The Coming of the Spanish Civil War, 1978, 2nd edn 1994; (ed) Revolution and War in Spain 1931–1939, 1984; (with Denis Smyth) Spain, the EEC and NATO, 1984; The Triumph of Democracy in Spain, 1986; The Spanish Civil War 1936–1939, 1986; The Politics of Revenge, 1990; Franco, 1993 (Yorkshire Post Book of the Year, 1993); Las tres Es[illegible] fue, 1998); Comrades! Portraits from the Spanish Civil War, 199[illegible] music, opera, modern fiction, wine, supporting Everton Footba[illegible] Department of International History, London School of Economics, H[illegible] WC2A 2AE. *T:* (020) 7955 7107.

PRESTON, Peter John; journalist and writer; Co-Director, Guardian Foundation, [illegible] 1997; *b* 23 May 1938; *s* of John Whittle Preston and Kathlyn (*née* Chell); *m* 1962, J[illegible] Mary Burrell; two *s* two *d*. *Educ:* Loughborough Grammar Sch.; St John's Coll., Oxfor[illegible] (MA EngLit). Editorial trainee, Liverpool Daily Post, 1960–63; Guardian: Political Reporter, 1963–64; Education Correspondent, 1965–66; Diary Editor, 1966–68; Features Editor, 1968–72; Production Editor, 1972–75; Editor, 1975–95; Ed.-in-chief and Chm., Guardian and Observer, 1995–96; Editl Dir, Guardian Media Gp, 1996–98. Mem., Scott Trust, 1976–. British Exec. Chm., IPI, 1988– (World Chm., 1995–97); Chm., Assoc. of British Editors, 1996–99. Mem., UNESCO Adv. Gp on Press Freedom, 2000–. Gov., British Assoc. for Central and Eastern Europe, 2000–. Hon. DLitt: Loughborough, 1982; City, 1997; DU Essex, 1994. *Publications:* Dunblane: reflecting tragedy, 1996; The Fifty-First State (novel), 1998; Bess (novel), 1999. *Recreations:* football, films; four children. *Address:* The Guardian, 119 Farringdon Road, EC1R 3ER.

PRESTON, Sir Philip (Charles Henry Hulton), 8th Bt *cr* 1815, of Beeston St Lawrence, Norfolk; *b* 31 Aug. 1946; *s* of Lt-Col Philip Henry Herbert Hulton Preston, OBE, MC and Katherine Janet Preston (*née* Broomhall); *S* cousin, 1999; *m* 1980, Kirsi Sylvi Annikk, *d* of Eino Yrjö Pullinen; one *s* two *d*. *Educ:* Nautical Coll., Pangbourne. *Heir:* *s* Philip Thomas Henry Hulton Preston, *b* 1990. *Address:* 3 Place Gilbert Gaffet, Crécy-en-Ponthieu, 80150 Somme, Picardie, France.

PRESTON, Rev. Prof. Ronald Haydn, DD; Professor of Social and Pastoral Theology in the University of Manchester, 1970–80, now Emeritus; *b* 12 March 1913; *o s* of Haydn and Eleanor Jane Preston; *m* 1st, 1948, Edith Mary Lindley (*d* 1994); one *s* two *d*; 2nd, 1997, Mary Elizabeth Smith. *Educ:* London School of Economics, University of London; St Catherine's Coll., Oxford. BSc (Econ.) 1935, Cl. II, Div. I; Industrial Secretary of Student Christian Movement, 1935–38; BA Cl. I Theology, 1940; MA 1944; MA Manchester 1974; BD, DD Oxon 1983. Curate, St John, Park, Sheffield, 1940–43; Study Secretary, Student Christian Movement, 1943–48; Warden of St Anselm Hall, University of Manchester, 1948–63; Lectr in Christian Ethics, Univ. of Manchester, 1948–70; Examining Chaplain: to Bishop of Manchester, 1948–2000; to Bishop of Sheffield, 1971–80; Canon Residentiary of Manchester Cathedral, 1957–71, Sub-Dean 1970–71, Hon. Canon 1971, Canon Emeritus, 1980. Editor, The Student Movement, 1943–48. *Publications:* (jointly) Christians in Society, 1939; (jointly) The Revelation of St John the Divine, 1949; Technology and Social Justice, 1971; (ed) Industrial Conflicts and their Place in Modern Society, 1974; (ed) Perspectives on Strikes, 1975; (ed) Theology and Change, 1975; Religion and the Persistence of Capitalism, 1979; (ed jtly) The Crisis in British Penology, 1980; Explorations in Theology, No 9, 1981; Church and Society in the late Twentieth Century, 1983; The Future of Christian Ethics, 1987; Religion and the Ambiguities of Capitalism, 1991; (jtly) Christian Capitalism or Christian Socialism?, 1994; Confusions in Christian Social Ethics, 1994; The Middle Way: theology, politics and economics in the later thought of R. H. Preston, 2000; contrib. Theology, etc. *Address:* 161 Old Hall Lane, Manchester M14 6HJ. *T:* (0161) 225 3291.

PRESTON, Rosalind, OBE 1993; Vice President, Board of Deputies of British Jews, 1991–94; *b* 29 Dec. 1935; *d* of Benjamin and Marie Morris; *m* 1958, Ronald Preston; one *s* one *d*. *Educ:* Talbot Heath Sch., Bournemouth. Voluntary sector activity, 1960–; Nat. Pres., Nat. Council of Women, 1988–90; Vice Pres., British Section, Women's Internat. Zionist Orgn, 1993–99, now Hon. Vice Pres.; Co-Vice-Chm., Inter Faith Network for UK, 1994–; Jt Hon. Sec., CCJ, 1996–. Dir (non-exec.), Harrow and Hillingdon Healthcare NHS Trust, 1994–96. Chm., Nightingale Home, 2001–. Trustee, Jewish Chronicle, 2000–. FRSA 1990. Paul Harris Fellow, Rotary Internat., 1992. *Recreations:* walking, reading newspapers, family and friends. *Address:* c/o National Council of Women, 36 Danbury Street, N1 8JU.

PRESTON, Simon John, OBE 2000; Organist and Master of the Choristers, Westminster Abbey, 1981–87; *b* 4 Aug. 1938. *Educ:* Canford Sch.; King's Coll., Cambridge (Dr Mann Organ Student; BA 1961; MusB 1962; MA 1964). ARCM, FRAM. Sub Organist, Westminster Abbey, 1962–67; Acting Organist, St Albans Abbey, 1968–69; Organist and Lecturer in Music, Christ Church, Oxford, 1970–81. Conductor, Oxford Bach Choir, 1971–74. FRSA. Hon. FRCO 1975; Hon. FRCCO 1986; Hon. FRCM 1986. Edison Award, 1971; Grand Prix du Disque, 1979; Performer of the Year Award, NY Chapter, Amer. Guild of Organists, 1987. *Recreations:* croquet, theatre. *Address:* Little Hardwick, Langton Green, Tunbridge Wells, Kent TN3 0EY. *T:* (01892) 862042.

PRESTON, Timothy William; QC 1982; a Recorder of the Crown Court, since 1979; *b* 3 Nov. 1935; *s* of Charles Frank Preston, LDS, RCS and Frances Mary, *o d* of Captain W. Peters, 5th Lancers; *m* 1965, Barbara Mary Haygarth. *Educ:* Haileybury; Jesus Coll., Oxford (BA 1960). 2/Lieut 16/5 Lancers, 1955; Captain, Staffs Yeomanry, retd. Called to the Bar, Inner Temple, 1964; Bencher, 1991. Mem., Criminal Injuries Compensation Bd, 1989–2000. *Recreations:* hunting, golf. *Address:* 2 Temple Gardens, EC4Y 9AY. *T:* (020) 7583 6041. *Club:* Cavalry and Guards.

PRESTON, Walter James, FRICS; Partner, Jones Lang Wootton, 1957–87, Consultant, 1987–99; *b* 20 March 1925; *s* of Walter Ronald and Agnes Ann McNeil Preston; *m* 1956, Joy Dorothea Ashton; two *s* one *d*. *Educ:* Dollar Academy, Perthshire. Served Royal Engineers, 1943–47. Jones Lang Wootton, 1948–, Staff, 1948–57. Dir (non-exec.), Lynton Property and Reversionary plc, 1985–88. Liveryman: Chartered Surveyors' Co., 1977–; Vintners' Co., 1990–. *Recreation:* golf. *Address:* Barry Lodge, Pond Road, Hook Heath, Woking, Surrey GU22 0JY. *T:* (01483) 763420. *Clubs:* Carlton; Phyllis Court (Henley); Woking Golf; Trevose Golf and Country, St Enodoc Golf (North Cornwall).

PRESTT, His Honour Arthur Miller; QC 1970; a Circuit Judge (formerly Judge of County Courts), 1971–90; Hon. Recorder of Manchester and Senior Circuit Judge, Manchester, 1982–90; *b* 23 April 1925; *s* of Arthur Prestt and Jessie (*née* Miller), Wigan; *m* 1949, Jill Mary, *d* of late Graham Dawbarn, CBE, FRIBA, FRAeS, and of Olive Dawbarn (*née* Topham); one *s* one *d*. *Educ:* Bootham Sch., York; Trinity Hall, Cambridge (MA). Served 13th Bn Parachute Regt, France, Belgium, India, Malaya, Java, 1944–46; Major Legal Staff and War Crimes Prosecutor, 1946–47. Called to Bar, Middle Temple, 1949. Chm., Mental Health Review Tribunal, 1963–70; Dep. Chm., Cumberland QS, 1966–69, Chm., 1970–71. Has held various appts in Scout Assoc. (Silver Acorn, 1970). Pres., SW Lancs Parachute Regt Assoc., 1980–91. JP Cumberland, 1966. 5 years Medal, Ampleforth Lourdes Hospitalite, 1976. *Recreations:* gardening, golf. *Address:* 10 Heigham Grove, Norwich NR2 3DQ. *Club:* Norfolk (Norwich).

PRESTWICH, Prof. Michael Charles, FRHistS; FSA; Professor of History, University of Durham, since 1986 (Pro-Vice-Chancellor, 1992–99 and Sub-Warden, 1997–99); *b* 30 Jan. 1943; *s* of John Oswald Prestwich and late Menna Prestwich; *m* 1973, Margaret Joan Daniel; two *s* one *d*. *Educ:* Charterhouse; Magdalen Coll., Oxford (MA, DPhil). FSA 1980. Res. Lectr, Christ Church, Oxford, 1965–69; Lectr in Mediaeval History, Univ. of St Andrews, 1969–79; Reader in Medieval History, Univ. of Durham, 1979–86. *Publications:* War, Politics and Finance under Edward I, 1972; The Three Edwards: war and state in England 1272–1377, 1980; Documents illustrating the Crisis of 1297–98 in England, 1980; Edward I, 1988; English Politics in the Thirteenth Century, 1990; Armies and Warfare in the Middle Ages, 1996; articles in learned jls. *Recreation:* ski-ing. *Address:* 46 Albert Street, Western Hill, Durham DH1 4RJ. *T:* (0191) 386 2539.

PRETORIA, Bishop of, since 1998; **Rt Rev. Dr Johannes Thomas Seoka;** *b* 29 Aug. 1948; *s* of Isaac and Margaret Seoka; *m* 1980, Sybil Elizabeth Nomathonya; two *s*. *Educ:* school in Stanger; Eshowe Coll. of Educn, Zululand (grad. as teacher, 1971); St Bede's Coll., Umtata; Chicago Theol Seminary, Ill, USA (MTh); Univ. of Chicago (DMin); studies in industrial mgt, W Germany and USA. Deacon 1974, priest 1975, Natal; Curate, St Augustine, Umlazi, Natal, 1976–78; Rector, St Peter's, Greytown, 1978–80; Rector, St Hilda's, Senaoane, Soweto, 1980; seconded as Dir of Industrial Mission, 1981; Priest-in-Charge: Trinity Episcopal Church, Chicago, Ill, 1986; St James's, Diepkloof, Soweto, 1993–95; Church of the Good Shepherd, Tladi, Soweto, 1995–96; Dean of Pretoria and Rector, St Alban's Cathedral, 1996–98. Continuing urban and industrial work, including: Dir, Agency for Industrial Mission; Dir, Urban and Industrial Mission, 1994. CPSA Rep., Faith and Order Commn, WCC; Mem., WCC Adv. Gp on Urban and Rural Mission, 1983–. *Publications:* contribs to books and magazines. *Address:* PO Box 1032, Pretoria 0001, S Africa. *T:* (12) 3222218; 237 Schoeman Street, Pretoria 0002.

PRETTEJOHN, Nicholas Edward Tucker; Chief Executive, Lloyd's of London, since 1999; *b* 22 July 1960; *s* of Dr Edward Joseph Tucker Prettejohn and Diana Sally Prettejohn; *m* 1st, 1986, Elizabeth Esch (marr. diss. 1997); 2nd, 1997, Claire Helen McKenna. *Educ:* Balliol Coll., Oxford (BA 1st Cl. Hons PPE 1981; Pres., Oxford Union, 1980). Mgt Consultant, Bain & Co., 1982–91; Dir, Apax Partners, 1991–94; Dir of Corporate Strategy, NFC plc, 1994–95; Lloyd's: Head of Strategy, 1995–97; Man. Dir, Business Develt Unit, 1997–99, and N America Business Unit, 1998–99. Non-exec. Dir, Anglo & Overseas Trust plc, 1998–. Chm., English Pocket Opera, 2001–. *Recreations:* opera, music, theatre, horse racing, golf, cricket, Rugby. *Address:* (office) One Lime Street, EC3M 7HA. *T:* (020) 7327 6920. *Clubs:* Lloyd's Golf, Taunton and Pickeridge Golf.

PRETTY, Dr Katharine Bridget, FSA; Principal, Homerton College, Cambridge, since 1991; *b* 18 Oct. 1945; *d* of M. W. and B. E. W. Hughes; *m* 1988, Prof. Tjeerd Hendrik van Andel. *Educ:* King Edward VI High Sch. for Girls, Birmingham; New Hall, Cambridge (MA, PhD). New Hall, Cambridge: College Lectr and Fellow in Archaeology, 1972–91; Admissions Tutor, 1979–85; Sen. Tutor, 1985–91; Emeritus Fellow, 1995–; University of Cambridge: Member: Council of Senate, 1981–89; Financial Bd, 1986–96; Gen. Bd, 1997–; Chm. Council, Sch. of Humanities and Social Scis, 1997–. Chairman: Rescue, 1978–83; OCR Examng Bd, 1998–. Governor: Bancroft's Sch., 1985–90; Felsted Sch., 1990–91; Leys Sch., 1993–98. Vice-Pres., RSA, 1998–. FSA 2000. *Recreations:* archaeology, botany, Arctic travel. *Address:* Homerton College, Cambridge CB2 2PH. *T:* (01223) 507131.

PREVEZER, Susan Rachel; QC 2000; a Recorder, since 2000; *b* 25 March 1959; *d* of late Prof. Sydney Prevezer and of Enid Margaret Prevezer (*née* Austin); *m* 1994, Benjamin Freedman; two *d*. *Educ:* St Paul's Girls' Sch.; Girton Coll., Cambridge (MA). Called to the Bar, Inner Temple, 1983. *Address:* Essex Court Chambers, 24 Lincoln's Inn Fields, WC2A 3ED.

PREVIN, André (George), Hon. KBE 1996; conductor, pianist and composer; Conductor Laureate, London Symphony Orchestra, since 1992; Music Director, Oslo Philharmonic, from summer 2002; *b* Berlin, Germany, 6 April 1929; *s* of Jack Previn and Charlotte Epstein; *m* 1970; three *s* (inc. twin *s*), three *d*; *m* 1982, Heather, *d* of Robert Sneddon; one *s*. *Educ:* Berlin and Paris Conservatoires; private study with Pierre Monteux, Castelnuovo-Tedesco. Composer of film scores, 1950–62 (four Academy Awards). Music Dir, Houston Symphony Orchestra, 1967–69; Principal Conductor, London Symphony Orchestra, 1968–79, Conductor Emeritus, 1979; Music Director: Pittsburgh Symphony Orchestra, 1976–84; Los Angeles Phil. Orch., 1986–89; Music Dir, 1985–86, Prin. Conductor, 1987–91, RPO; Guest Conductor, most major orchestras, US and Europe, Covent Garden Opera, Salzburg Festival, Edinburgh Festival, Osaka Festival; Music Dir, London South Bank Summer Festival, 1972–74. Formed André Previn Jazz Trio, 1990. Member: Composers Guild of GB; Amer. Composers League; Dramatists League. Recording artist. Principal compositions: Cello Sonata; Violin Sonata, 1994; Bassoon Sonata; Guitar Concerto; Wind Quintet; Serenades for Violin; piano preludes; Piano Concerto, 1984; Trio for piano, oboe and bassoon, 1994; Principals, Reflections (for orchestra); Every Good Boy Deserves Favour (text by Tom Stoppard); Six Songs Mezzo-Soprano (text by Philip Larkin); Honey and Rue (text by Toni Morrison); Sally Chisum Remembers Billy the Kid (text by Michael Ondaatje); Four Songs for soprano, cello and piano (text by Toni Morrison), 1994; The Magic Number (for soprano and orch.), 1997; A Streetcar Named Desire (opera), 1998. Annual TV series: specials for BBC; PBS (USA). *Publications:* Music Face to Face, 1971; (ed) Orchestra, 1979; André Previn's Guide to Music, 1983; No Minor Chords (autobiog.), 1992; *relevant publications:* André Previn, by Edward Greenfield, 1973; Previn, by H. Ruttencutter, 1985. *Address:* c/o Columbia Artists Management, 165 W 57th Street, New York, NY 10019, USA.

PREVITE, His Honour John Edward; QC 1989; a Circuit Judge, 1992–2001; *b* 11 May 1934; *s* of late Lt Col K. E. Previte, OBE and Edith Frances (*née* Capper); *m* 1959, Hon. Phyllida Browne, *d* of 6th Baron Kilmaine, CBE; two *s*. *Educ:* Wellington Coll.; Christ Church, Oxford (MA). Called to the Bar, Inner Temple, 1959, Bencher, 1986; a Recorder, Western Circuit, 1987–92. *Recreation:* sailing. *Address:* c/o Inner Temple, EC4Y 7HL.

PREVOST, Sir Christopher (Gerald), 6th Bt *cr* 1805; *b* 25 July 1935; *s* of Sir George James Augustine Prevost, 5th Bt and Muriel Emily (*d* 1939), *d* of late Lewis William Oram; *S* father, 1985; *m* 1964, Dolores Nelly, *o d* of Dezo Hoffmann; one *s* one *d*. *Educ:* Cranleigh School. Served 60th Regt (formed by Prevost family) and Rifle Bde; Kenya Service Medal, 1955. IBM, 1955–61; Pitney-Bowes, 1963–76; founder of Mailtronic Ltd, manufacturers and suppliers of mailroom equipment, 1977, Chm. and Man. Dir, 1977–91. Member: Huguenot Soc.; Soc. of Genealogists. Lord of the Manor, Stinchcombe, Glos. *Recreation:* ski-ing. *Heir:* *s* Nicholas Marc Prevost, *b* 13 March 1971. *Address:* 1 Crispian Close, Neasden Lane, NW10 1PW.

PRICE, Adam; MP (Plaid Cymru) Carmarthen East and Dinefwr, since 2001; *b* 23 Sept. 1968. *Educ:* Amman Valley Comprehensive Sch.; Saarland Univ.; Univ. of Wales Coll. of Cardiff (BA 1991). Res. Associate, Dept of City and Regl Planning, UWCC, 1991–93; Project Manager, 1993–95, Exec. Manager, 1995–96, Exec. Dir, 1996–98, Menter an Busnes; Man. Dir, Newidiem Econ. Develt Consultancy, 1998–2001. Mem., Welsh Affairs Select Cttee, 2001–. Contested (Plaid Cymru) Gower, 1992. *Publications:* The Collective Entrepreneur; (jtly) The Welsh Renaissance: innovation and inward investment in Wales, 1992; Rebuilding Our Communities: a new agenda for the valleys, 1993; Quiet Revolution? language, culture and economy in the nineties, 1994; The Diversity Dividend, 1996; (jtly) The Other Wales: the case for objective 1 funding post 1999, 1998. *Recreations:* contemporary culture, good friends, good food, travel. *Address:* (office) 37 Wind Street, Ammanford, Carmarthenshire SA18 3DN. *T:* (01269) 597677, *Fax:* (01269) 591334; c/o House of Commons, SW1A 0AA. *T:* (020) 7219 8486.

PRICE, (Alan) Anthony; author and journalist; Editor, The Oxford Times, 1972–88; *b* 16 Aug. 1928; *s* of Walter Longsdon Price and Kathleen Price (*née* Lawrence); *m* 1953, Yvonne Ann Stone; two *s* one *d*. *Educ:* King's Sch., Canterbury; Merton Coll., Oxford (Exbnr; MA). Oxford & County Newspapers, 1952–88. *Publications:* The Labyrinth Makers, 1970 (CWA Silver Dagger); The Alamut Ambush, 1971; Colonel Butler's Wolf, 1972; October Men, 1973; Other Paths to Glory, 1974 (CWA Gold Dagger, 1974; Swedish Acad. of Detection Prize, 1978); Our Man in Camelot, 1975; War Game, 1976; The '44 Vintage, 1978; Tomorrow's Ghost, 1979; The Hour of the Donkey, 1980; Soldier No More, 1981; The Old Vengeful, 1982; Gunner Kelly, 1983; Sion Crossing, 1984; Here Be Monsters, 1985; For the Good of the State, 1986; A New Kind of War, 1987; A Prospect of Vengeance, 1988; The Memory Trap, 1989; Eyes of the Fleet, 1990. *Recreations:* military history, travelling, gardening, cooking. *Address:* Wayside Cottage, Horton-cum-Studley, Oxford OX33 1AW. *T:* (01865) 351326.

PRICE, (Arthur) Leolin, CBE 1996; QC 1968; *b* 11 May 1924; 3rd *s* of late Evan Price and Ceridwen Price (*née* Price), Hawkhurst, Kent; *m* 1963, Hon. Rosalind Helen Penrose Lewis, CBE (*d* 1999), *er d* of 1st Baron Brecon, PC, and of Mabel, Baroness Brecon, CBE, JP; two *s* two *d*. *Educ:* Judd Sch., Tonbridge; Keble Coll., Oxford (Schol.; MA). War service, 1943–46 with Army: Capt., RA; Adjt, Indian Mountain Artillery Trng Centre and Depot, Ambala, Punjab, 1946. Treas., Oxford Union, 1948; Pres., Oxford Univ. Conserv. Assoc., 1948. Tutor, Keble Coll., Oxford, 1951–59. Called to Bar, Middle Temple, 1949, Bencher, 1970–, Treas. 1990; Barrister of Lincoln's Inn, 1959. QC (Bahamas) 1969; QC (NSW) 1987; Barrister: BVI, 1994; Gibraltar, 1996. Member: Editorial Cttee, Modern Law Review, 1954–65; Bar Council Law Reform Cttee, 1969–75; Cttee, Soc. of Cons. Lawyers, 1971– (Vice-Chm., 1987–90). Director: SR (formerly Thornton) Pan-European Investment Trust (formerly Child Health Res. Investment Trust), 1980– (Chm., 1987–99; Pres., 1999–); Marine Adventure Sailing Trust plc, 1981–89; Thornton Asian Emerging Markets Investment Trust plc, 1989–95. Institute of Child Health: Chairman, 1976–; Mem., Cttee of Mgt, 1972–; Fellow, 1996. Chm., Child Health Res. Appeal Trust, 1976–. Governor, Gt Ormond St Hosp. for Sick Children, 1972–92 (Trustee, 1992–); Mem., Falkland Islands Cttee, 1972–. Governor, Christ Coll., Brecon, 1977–. Chancellor, Diocese of Swansea and Brecon, 1982–99. *Publications:* articles and notes in legal jls. *Address:* 32 Hampstead Grove, NW3 6SR. *T:* (020) 7435 9843; 10 Old Square, Lincoln's Inn, WC2A 3SU. *T:* (020) 7405 0758, *Fax:* (020) 7831 8237; Moor Park, Llanbedr, near Crickhowell, Powys NP8 1SS. *T:* (01873) 810443, *Fax:* (01873) 810659; Selborne Chambers, 174 Phillip Street, Sydney, NSW 2000, Australia. *T:* (2) 92335188. *Club:* Carlton.

See also V. W. C. Price.

PRICE, Barry; *see* Price, W. F. B.

PRICE, Barry David Keith, CBE 1991; QPM 1981; intelligence consultant, since 1993; Co-ordinator, National Drugs Intelligence Unit, 1987–92; *b* 28 June 1933; *s* of John Leslie Price and Lena Price; *m* 1953, Evelyne Jean Horlick; three *d*. *Educ:* Southall Grammar Sch. FBIM 1975. Metropolitan Police, 1954–75: Constable, uniform and CID, then through ranks to Det. Chief Supt; Asst Chief Constable, Northumbria Police, 1975–78; Dep. Chief Constable, Essex Police, 1978–80; Chief Constable, Cumbria Constabulary, 1980–87. Member: Adv. Council on the Misuse of Drugs, 1982–87; Drugs Intelligence Steering Gp, 1987–; Advr to ACPO Crime Cttee on drugs matters, 1985–88 (past Chm. and Sec.). President: English Police Golf Assoc., 1981–92; Northern Police Cricket League, 1983–87; Patron, NW Counties Schoolboys ABA, 1980–87. SBStJ 1982 (County Dir, St John Amb. Assoc., 1981–87). Police Long Service and Good Conduct Medal, 1976. *Publications:* various articles in law enforcement and med. pubns. *Recreations:* golf, painting, gardening.

PRICE, (Benjamin) Terence; Secretary-General, Uranium Institute, 1974–86; *b* 7 January 1921; *er s* of Benjamin and Nellie Price; *m* 1947, Jean Stella Vidal; one *s* one *d*. *Educ:* Crypt School, Gloucester; Queens' College, Cambridge (Scholar). Naval electronics res., 1942–46; Lieut RNVR, 1945–46; Atomic Energy Research Establishment, Harwell (Nuclear Physics Division), 1947–59; Head of Reactor Development Division, Atomic Energy Estabt, Winfrith, 1959–60; Chief Scientific Officer, Ministry of Defence, 1960–63; Assistant Chief Scientific Adviser (Studies), Ministry of Defence, 1963–65; Director, Defence Operational Analysis Establishment, MoD, 1965–68; Chief Scientific Adviser, Min. of Transport, 1968–71; Dir of Planning and Development, Vickers Ltd, 1971–73. Chairman: OECD Transport Res. Gp, 1969–71; NEDO Mechanical Handling Sector Working Party, 1976–80. Mem., MRC Review Cttee on Industrial Psychology Res., 1964–66. Reviewer, CET, 1984–85. *Publications:* Radiation Shielding, 1957; Political Electricity, 1990. *Recreations:* making music, writing, ski-ing. *Address:* Seers Bough, Wilton Lane, Jordans, Beaconsfield, Bucks HP9 2RG. *T:* (01494) 874589. *Club:* Athenæum.

PRICE, Bernard Albert, CBE 1997; County Clerk and Chief Executive, Staffordshire County Council, and Clerk to the Lieutenancy, since 1983; Clerk to the Staffordshire Police Authority, since 1995; *b* 6 Jan. 1944; *s* of Albert and Doris Price; *m* 1966, Christine Mary, *d* of Roy William Henry Combes; two *s* one *d*. *Educ:* Whitchurch Grammar Sch., Salop; King's Sch., Rochester, Kent; Merton Coll., Oxford (BA 1965, MA 1970). DMS, Wolverhampton Polytechnic, 1972. Articled, later Asst Solicitor, Worcs CC, 1966–70; Asst Solicitor, subseq. Dep. Dir of Admin, Staffs CC, 1970–80; Sen. Dep. Clerk, Staffs CC, 1980–83. *Recreations:* sailing, walking. *Address:* The Cottage, Yeatsall Lane, Abbots Bromley, Rugeley, Staffs WS15 3DY. *T:* (01283) 840269.

PRICE, Cedric John, RIBA; Sole Principal, Cedric Price Architects, since 1960; *b* 11 Sept. 1934; *s* of Arthur John Price and Doreen Price. *Educ:* St John's Coll., Cambridge (BA 1955; MA); Architectural Assoc., London (Dip. 1959). ARIBA 1959. Major projects include: (jtly) Snowdon Aviary, London Zoo; Interaction Centre, Kentish Town. Hon. DDes East London, 1994. *Publication:* Works, vol. 2, 1984. *Address:* (office) 38 Alfred Place, WC1E 7DP. *T:* (020) 7636 5220. *Club:* Hot Stuff (Life Pres.).

PRICE, Hon. Charles H., II; Director, Mercantile Bancorporation, St Louis; *b* 1 April 1931; *s* of Charles Harry Price and Virginia (*née* Ogden); *m* 1969, Carol Ann Swanson; two *s* three *d*. *Educ:* University of Missouri. Chairman: Price Candy Co., 1969–81; American Bancorpn, 1973–81; American Bank & Trust Co., 1973–81; American Mortgage Co., 1973–81; Ambassador: to Belgium, 1981–83; to UK, 1983–89; Chm. Bd,

Mercantile Bank, Kansas City, 1990–96. Non-executive Director, 1989–: Hanson PLC; New York Times Co.; Texaco Inc.; non-exec. Chm., Midwest Res. Inst., 1990–99 (Vice-Chm. and Mem. Exec. Cttee, 1978–81); Mem. Bd of Dirs, Civic Council, Greater Kansas City, 1979–80. Member: Young Presidents Orgn; IISS; World Business Council. Hon. Fellow, Regent's Coll., London, 1986. Hon. Dr Westminster Coll., Missouri, 1984; Hon. Dr of Laws Missouri, 1988. Salvation Army's William Booth Award, 1985; Kansas City Mayor's World Citizen of the Year, 1985, Trustee Citation Award, Midwest Res. Inst., 1987; Distinguished Service Award, Internat. Relations Council, 1989; Mankind Award, Cystic Fibrosis Foundn, 1990; Gold Good Citizen Award, Sons of the American Revolution, 1991; William F. Yates Medallion for Distinguished Service, 1996. *Recreations:* golf, shooting. *Address:* 1 West Armour Boulevard, Ste 300, Kansas City, Mo 64111, USA. *Clubs:* White's, Mark's; Swinley Forest Golf; Metropolitan (Washington); Eldorado Country (Palm Springs); Castle Pines Country (Denver); Kansas City Country, River (Kansas City).

PRICE, Christopher; Director, Statesman & Nation Publishing Co. Ltd, since 1991 (Chairman, 1994–95); freelance journalist and broadcaster; *b* 26 Jan. 1932; *s* of Stanley Price; *m* 1956, Annie Grierson Ross; two *s* one *d. Educ:* Leeds Grammar School; Queen's College, Oxford. Sec., Oxford Univ. Labour Club, 1953; Chm., Nat. Assoc. of Labour Student Organisations, 1955–56. Sheffield City Councillor, 1962–66; Dep. Chm., Sheffield Educn Cttee, 1963–66. Contested (Lab): Shipley, 1964; Birmingham, Perry Barr, 1970; Lewisham W, 1983. MP (Lab): Perry Barr Division of Birmingham, 1966–70; Lewisham W, Feb. 1974–1983; PPS to Secretary of State for Education and Science, 1966–67 and 1975–76; Chm., H of C Select Cttee on Educn, Science and the Arts, 1980–83. Mem., European Parlt, 1977–78. Dir, London Internat. Festival of Theatre Ltd, 1982–86; Pro-Asst Dir, The Polytechnic of the South Bank, 1983–86; Dir, Leeds Poly., 1986–92, Principal, Leeds Metropolitan Univ., 1992–94. Chm., Council, Nat. Youth Bureau, 1977–80; Member: Council, Inst. for Study of Drug Dependence, 1984–86; Bd, Phoenix House Ltd (Britain's largest gp of drug rehabilitation houses), 1986–87 (Chm., 1980–86); Council, Public Concern at Work, 1994–; Arts Council of England, 1997–98. Co-Chm., Campaign for Freedom of Information, 1990–94; Chair: Yorks and Humberside, then Yorks, Arts, 1997–2000 (Mem. Bd, 1994; Chm., Audit Cttee, 1995–97); LGA Commn on Organisation of Sch. Year, 2000–. Pres., BEMAS, 1992–94; Member: Delegacy, Univ. of London Goldsmiths' Coll., 1981–86; Court, Polytechnic of Central London, 1982–86; London Centre for Biotechnology Trust, 1984–86; Council, Open Univ., 1996–; Fellow, Internat. Inst. of Biotechnology, 1984. Vis. Sen. Fellow, Office of Public Management, 1994–96; Vis. Fellow, Centre for Policy Studies in Educn, Univ. of Leeds, 1994–97; Vis. Prof., UCE, 1996–. Vice Chm., Cttee for the Restitution of the Parthenon Marbles, 1997–. FRSA 1988. Editor, New Education, 1967–68; Founding Editor, The Stakeholder (Editor, 1997–2000); Educn corresp., New Statesman, 1969–74; Columnist: TES, 1983–85; THES, 1990–92. DUniv Leeds Metropolitan, 1994. *Publications:* (contrib.) A Radical Future, 1967; Crisis in the Classroom, 1968; (ed) Your Child and School, 1968; Which Way?, 1969; (contrib.) Life and Death of the Schools Council, 1985; (contrib.) Police, the Constitution and the Community, 1985. *Address:* 9 Pickwick Road, SE21 7JN.

See also H. M. Jackson.

PRICE, Curtis Alexander, PhD; Principal, Royal Academy of Music, since 1995; *b* 7 Sept. 1945; *s* of Dalias Price and Lillian Price (*née* Alexander); *m* 1981, Rhian Samuel; one step *s. Educ:* Southern Illinois Univ. (BA 1967); Harvard Univ. (AM 1970; PhD 1974). Washington University, St Louis: Asst Prof., 1974–79; Associate Prof., 1979–82; King's College London: Lectr, 1982–85; Reader in Historical Musicology, 1985–88; King Edward Prof. and Head of Dept of Music, 1988–95; FKC 1994. Guggenheim Fellow, 1982–83. Pres., Royal Musical Assoc., 1999–. Hon. RAM, 1993. Einstein Award, Amer. Musicol. Soc., 1979; Dent Medal, Royal Musical Assoc., 1985. *Publications:* Music in the Restoration Theatre, 1979; Henry Purcell and the London Stage, 1984; Dido and Aeneas: a critical score, 1986; The Impresario's Ten Commandments, 1992. *Address:* Royal Academy of Music, Marylebone Road, NW1 5HT. *T:* (020) 7873 7377, *Fax:* (020) 7873 7314.

PRICE, Maj.-Gen. David; *see* Price, Maj.-Gen. M. D.

PRICE, Sir David (Ernest Campbell), Kt 1980; DL; *b* 20 Nov. 1924; *o s* of Major Villiers Price; *m* 1960, Rosemary Eugénie Evelyn, *o d* of late Cyril F. Johnston, OBE; one *d. Educ:* Eton; Trinity College, Cambridge; Yale University, USA; Rosebery Schol., Eton; Open History Schol., Trinity College, Cambridge. Served with 1st Battalion Scots Guards, CMF; subsequently Staff Captain (Intelligence) HQ, 56 London Div., Trieste, 1942–46. Trin. Coll., Cambridge, BA Hons, MA. Pres. Cambridge Union; Vice-Pres. Fedn of Univ. Conservative and Unionist Assocs, 1946–48; Henry Fellow of Yale Univ., USA, 1948–49. Industrial Consultant. Held various appts in Imperial Chemical Industries Ltd, 1949–62. MP (C) Eastleigh Div. of Hampshire, 1955–92; Parly Sec., Board of Trade, 1962–64; Opposition Front-Bench spokesman on Science and Technology, 1964–70; Parly Sec., Min. of Technology, June-Oct. 1970; Parly Sec., Min. of Aviation Supply, 1970–71; Parly Under-Sec. of State, Aerospace, DTI, 1971–72. Member: Public Accounts Cttee, 1974–75; Select Cttee on Transport, 1979–83; Select Cttee on Social Services, 1983–90; Select Cttee on Health, 1990–92; Vice-Pres., Parly and Scientific Cttee, 1975–79 and 1982–86 (Vice-Chm., 1965–70, Chm., 1973–75 and 1979–82). Vice-Chm., Cons. Arts and Heritage Cttee, 1979–81 and 1983–87; Chm., Cons. Shipping and Ship-Building Cttee, 1985–91; President: Wessex Area Cons. and Unionist Party, 1986–89 (Life Vice-Pres., 1991); Romsey and Waterside Cons. Assoc., 1993–99; Itchen Test and Avon Cons. Euro-Forum, 1994–99. British Representative to Consultative Assembly of the Council of Europe, 1958–61. Dir, Assoc. British Maltsters, 1966–70. Gen. Cons. to IIM (formerly IWM), 1973–90; Cons. to Union International Ltd, 1974–92; Non-exec. Dir, Southampton Univ. Hosps Trust, 1993–97. Vice-Pres., IIM, 1980–92. President: Wessex Glyndebourne Assoc., 1990–2001; Wessex Rehabilitation Assoc., 1990–2000; Chm., Hants CC Community Care Forum, 1993–96; Trustee: Wessex Medical Trust, 1988–96; Nuffield Theatre, 1990–; Mayflower Theatre, 1990–. Governor, Middlesex Hospital, 1956–60. DL Hants, 1982. *Recreations:* swimming, arts and heritage, wine, cooking, gardening. *Address:* Forest Lodge, Moonhills Lane, Beaulieu, Hampshire SO42 7YW. *T:* (01590) 612537. *Clubs:* Beefsteak, Sloane.

PRICE, David William James; farmer; Chairman, Foreign and Colonial Management Ltd, since 1999; *b* 11 June 1947; *s* of Richard James Emlyn Price and Miriam Joan Dunsford; *m* 1971, Shervie Ann Lander Whitaker, *d* of Sir James Whitaker, 3rd Bt, OBE; one *s* one *d. Educ:* Ampleforth Coll.; Corpus Christi Coll., Oxford (MA). Director: Mercury Asset Management Gp, 1978–97 (Dep. Chm., 1985–97); S. G. Warburg and Co. Ltd, 1982–86; London Bd, Halifax Building Soc., 1993–96; Mercury European Investment Trust; Equitable Life Assurance Soc., 1996–2001; Govett Oriental Investment Trust, 1997–98; Scottish American Investment Co., 1997–; Booker plc, 1998–2000; Chairman: Govett Asian Recovery Trust, 1998–; Gartmore Absolute Growth & Income Trust, 2000–; Iceland Group, 2001. Dir, Heritage Trust of Lincs, 1997–. Councillor (C), London Borough of Lambeth, 1979–82. *Recreations:* history, gardening, shooting. *Address:* Harrington Hall, Spilsby, Lincs PE23 4NH. *T:* (01790) 753764. *Clubs:* Brooks's; Lincolnshire.

PRICE, Eric Hardiman Mockford; Proprietor, Energy Economics Consultancy, since 1995; Director, Robinson Brothers (Ryders Green) Ltd, since 1985; *b* 14 Nov. 1931; *s* of Frederick H. Price and Florence N. H. Price (*née* Mockford); *m* 1963, Diana M. S. Robinson; one *s* three *d. Educ:* St Marylebone Grammar Sch.; Christ's Coll., Cambridge. Econs Tripos, 1955; MA 1958. FREconS, 1956; FSS 1958; MInstPet 1992. Army service, 1950–52; HAC, 1952–57. Supply Dept, Esso Petroleum Co. Ltd, 1955–56; Economist: Central Electricity Authority, 1956–57; Electricity Council, 1957–58; British Iron & Steel Fedn, 1958–62; Chief Economist, Port of London Authority, 1962–67; Sen. Econ. Adviser, Min. of Transport, 1966–69; Chief Econ. Adviser, Min. of Transport, 1969–71; Dir of Econs, 1971–75, Under Sec., 1972–76, Dir of Econs and Stats, 1975–76, DoE; Under Sec., Econs and Stats Div., Depts of Industry, Trade and Consumer Protection, 1977–80; Head of Econs and Stats Div., Dept of Energy, 1980–92; Chief Econ. Advr, Dept of Energy, later DTI, 1980–93. Special Consultant, Nat. Econ. Res. Associates, 1993–. Member: Soc. of Business Economists, 1961; Expert Adv. Gp on Entry into Freight Transport Market, EEC, 1973–75; Northern Regional Strategy Steering Gp, 1976–77; Expert Gp on Venture Capital for Industrial Innovation, EEC, 1978–79; Soc. of Strategic and Long-range Planning, 1980–; Council, Internat. Assoc. of Energy Economists, 1981–85; Energy Panel, SSRC, 1980–83; Council, British Inst. of Energy Economics, 1986 (Mem., 1980–; Vice-Chm., 1981–82 and 1988–89; Chm., 1982–85); Steering Cttee, Jt Energy Programme, RIIA, 1981–89, Steering Cttee, Energy and Envmtl Prog., 1989–; Adv. Council, Energy Econs Centre, Univ. of Surrey, 1989–. UK rep., Econ. Res. Cttee, European Council of Ministers of Transport, 1968–76; UK rep. on Six Nations' Prog. on Govt Policies towards Technological Innovation in Industry, 1977–80; Mem., World Bank's Groupe des Sages on Econs of Global Warming, 1990–. Member, Advisory Board: Transport Studies Unit, Oxford Univ., 1973–75; Centre for Res. in Industrial, Business and Admin Studies, Univ. of Warwick, 1977–80. FInstD 1990. *Publications:* various articles in learned jls on transport and industrial economics, energy and energy efficiency, investment, public sector industries, technological innovation in industry, regional planning, environmental abatement policies, and East European energy issues. *Recreations:* tennis, squash, local history, horse racing. *Address:* Batchworth Heath Farm, London Road, Rickmansworth, Herts WD3 1QB. *Clubs:* Moor Park Golf, Batchworth Park Golf; Riverside Health and Leisure (Northwood, Middx).

PRICE, Sir Francis (Caradoc Rose), 7th Bt *cr* 1815; QC (Can.) 1992; barrister and solicitor; *b* 9 Sept. 1950; *s* of Sir Rose Francis Price, 6th Bt and of Kathleen June, *d* of late Norman W. Hutchinson, Melbourne; *S* father, 1979; *m* 1975, Marguerite Jean Trussler, Justice, Court of Queen's Bench, Alberta, *d* of Roy S. Trussler, Victoria, BC; three *d. Educ:* Eton; Trinity College, Melbourne Univ. (Sen. Student 1971–72, LLB Hons 1973); Univ. of Alberta (LLM 1975); Canadian Petroleum Law Foundn Fellow, 1974–75. Admitted barrister and solicitor, Province of Alberta 1976, Northwest Territories 1978, Canada; Bencher, Law Soc. of Alberta, 1990–94. Lectr, 1979–89, and Course Head, 1983–89, Alberta Bar Admission Course. Chartered Arbitrator, Arbitration and Mediation Inst. of Canada, 1994. CLJ 2000. *Publications:* Pipelines in Western Canada, 1975; Mortgage Actions in Alberta, 1985; Conducting a Foreclosure Action, 1996; contribs to Alberta and Melbourne Univ. Law Revs, etc. *Recreations:* cricket, opera, running, theatre. *Heir: b* Norman William Rose Price, [*b* 17 March 1953; *m* 1987, Charlotte Louise, *yr d* of R. R. B. Baker]. *Address:* 9626 95th Avenue, Edmonton, AB T6C 2A4, Canada. *Club:* Faculty (Edmonton).

PRICE, Sir Frank (Leslie), Kt 1966; Chairman, Price-Brown Associates (formerly Sir Frank Price Associates), since 1985; *b* 26 July 1922; *s* of G. F. Price; marr. diss.; one *s*; *m* Daphne Ling. *Educ:* St Matthias Church Sch., Birmingham; Vittoria Street Arts Sch. FRICS (FSVA 1960); FCIT 1969. Dir, 1958–68, Man. Dir, 1965–68, Murrayfield Real Estate Co.; Chairman: Birmingham Midland Investments, 1967–74; Alexander Stevens Real Estate, 1968–80; Wharf Holdings, 1968–72; Beagle Shipping, 1968–72; Butlers & Colonial Wharfs, 1971–76. Elected to Birmingham City Council, 1949; Alderman, 1958–74; Lord Mayor, 1964–65. Member: Council, Town and Country Planning Assoc., 1958–74; W Midlands Economic Planning Council, 1965–72; Nat. Water Council, 1975–79; Chm., British Waterways Bd, 1968–84. Founder/Chm., Midlands Art Centre for Young People, 1960–71; Chairman: W Midlands Sports Council, 1965–69; Telford Development Corporation, 1968–71; Comprehensive Develt Assoc., 1968–80; Dir, National Exhibn Centre, 1968–74. Member: Minister of Transport's Cttee of Inquiry into Major Ports, 1961; English Tourist Board, 1976–83; President: BAIE, 1979–83; Mojacar Assoc. of Commerce, 1994–. Mem., Fédn Internat. des Professions Immobilières. FRSA. DL: Warwicks, 1970–77; West Midlands, 1974–77; Herefordshire and Worcestershire, 1977–84. Freeman, City of London; Liveryman, Basketmakers' Co., 1966–. *Publications:* Being There, 2001; various pamphlets and articles on town planning, transport and public affairs. *Recreations:* painting, cruising. *Address:* Casa Non Such, Apartado 534, Mojacar, Almeria 04638, Spain. *Club:* Reform.

PRICE, Gareth; Director, Thomson Foundation, since 1993; *b* 30 Aug. 1939; *s* of Rowena and Morgan Price; *m* 1962, Mari Griffiths; two *s* one *d. Educ:* Aberaeron Grammar School and Ardwyn Grammar School, Aberystwyth; University College of Wales, Aberystwyth (BA Econ). Asst Lectr in Economics, Queen's Univ., Belfast, 1962–64; BBC Wales: Radio Producer, Current Affairs, 1964–66; Television Producer, Features and Documentaries, 1966–74; Dep. Head of Programmes, 1974–81; Head of Programmes, 1981–85; Controller, 1986–90. Controller of Broadcasting, Thomson Foundn, 1990–93. Hon. Prof. of Communication, Univ. of Wales, Cardiff, 1994–99; Hon. Fellow, Univ. of Wales, Aberystwyth, 2000–. Consultant to UNESCO and broadcasting corps of India, Bulgaria, Namibia, South Africa. *Publication:* David Lloyd George (with Emyr Price and Bryn Parry), 1981. *Recreation:* travel. *Address:* The Thomson Foundation, 37 Park Place, Cardiff CF10 3BB. *Club:* Cardiff and County (Cardiff).

PRICE, Geoffrey Alan; DL; IPFA; Chairman, Herefordshire Community Health Trust, 1997–2000. Local Govt. finance posts in Glos CC, Cheshire CC, Southend-on-Sea and W Sussex CC, 1954–70; Dep. Co. Treas., 1970–76, Co. Treas., 1976–83, Hants CC; Chief Exec., 1983–93, Co. Treas., 1988–93, Hereford and Worcester CC; Clerk: to Lord Lieutenant, Hereford and Worcester, 1983–93; to West Mercia Police Authority, 1983–93; non-exec. Dir, Herefordshire HA, 1993–97. DL Hereford and Worcester, 1993.

PRICE, Rt Hon. George (Cadle); PC 1982; Prime Minister of Belize, 1981–84, and 1989–93 (Premier from 1964 until Independence, 1981); *b* 15 Jan. 1919; *s* of William Cadle Price and Irene Cecilia Escalante de Price. *Educ:* Holy Redeemer Primary Sch., Belize City; St John's Coll., Belize City. Private Sec. to late Robert S. Turton; entered politics, 1944; City Councillor, 1947–65 (Mayor of Belize City several times); founding Mem., People's United Party, 1950; Party Sec., 1950–56; became Leader, 1956; elected to National Assembly, 1954; under 1961 Ministerial System, led People's United Party to 100victory at polls and became First Minister; under 1964 Self-Govt Constitution, title changed to Premier; has led delegns to Central American and Caribbean countries;

spearheaded internationalization of Belize problem at internat. forums; addressed UN's Fourth Cttee, 1975, paving way for overwhelming victory at UN when majority of nations voted in favour of Belize's right to self-determination and territorial integrity. *Address:* c/o House of Representatives, Belmopan, Belize.

PRICE, Geraint; *see* Price, W. G.

PRICE, Gerald Alexander Lewin; QC 1992; **His Honour Judge Gerald Price;** a Circuit Judge, since 2000; *b* 13 Sept. 1948; *s* of Denis Lewin Price and Patricia Rosemary (*née* Metcalfe); *m* 1974, Theresa Elisabeth Iremonger-Watts; two *s*. *Educ:* Haileybury Coll.; College of Law; Inns of Court Law Sch. Called to the Bar, Middle Temple, 1969; in private practice, Cardiff, 1970–77; Bermuda: Resident Stipendiary Magistrate, 1977–81; Chief Stipendiary Magistrate and Sen. Coroner, 1981–84; in private practice, Cardiff, 1984–2000; a Recorder, 1990–2000. Chairman: Liquor Licence Authority, Land Valuation Appeals Tribunal, Price Control Commn and Jury Revising Tribunal, 1981–84. Mem., Commonwealth Magistrates and Judges Assoc., 1984–. Mem., RYA. *Recreations:* travel, classical music, sunshine, tennis. *Clubs:* Royal Commonwealth Society; Glamorgan Lawn Tennis and Croquet (Merthyr Mawr).

PRICE, Isobel Clare M.; *see* McKenzie-Price.

PRICE, Sir James Keith Peter Rugge-, 10th Bt *cr* 1804, of Spring Grove, Richmond, Surrey; *b* 8 April 1967; *er s* of Sir Keith Rugge-Price, 9th Bt and of Jacqueline Mary Rugge-Price (*née* Loranger); *S* father, 2000. *Heir: b* Andrew Philip Richard Rugge-Price, *b* 6 Jan. 1970.

PRICE, James Richard Kenrick; QC 1995; *b* 14 Sept. 1948; *s* of Lt-Col Kenrick Jack Price, DSO, MC, 9th Lancers and Juliet Hermione, *d* of Marshal of the Royal Air Force Sir John Cotesworth Slessor, GCB, DSO, MC; *m* 1983, Hon. Virginia Yvonne, *d* of Baron Mostyn, MC. *Educ:* Eton College; St Edmund Hall, Oxford. Called to the Bar, Inner Temple, 1974. Dir, Mostyn Estates Ltd. *Recreations:* fine and decorative arts, gardening, mountains, ski-ing. *Address:* 5 Raymond Buildings, Gray's Inn, WC1R 5BP. *T:* (020) 7242 2902. *Clubs:* Brooks's, Beefsteak.

PRICE, John Alan; QC 1980; a Recorder of the Crown Court, since 1980; a Deputy Circuit Judge, since 1975; *b* 11 Sept. 1938; *s* of Frederick Leslie Price and Gertrude Davilda Alice Price; *m* 1964, Elizabeth Myra (*née* Priest) (marr. diss. 1982); one *s* one *d*; *m* 1984, Alison Elizabeth Curran (*née* Ward); two step *d*. *Educ:* Stretford Grammar Sch.; Manchester Univ. (LLB Hons 1959). Called to the Bar, Gray's Inn, 1961; in practice on Northern Circuit; Head of 60 King St Chambers, Manchester, 1978–80. *Recreations:* tennis, squash, football, golf. *Address:* 25 Byrom Street, Manchester M3 4PF. *Club:* Wilmslow Rugby Union Football.

PRICE, Prof. John Frederick, MD; FRCP, FRCPCH; Consultant Paediatrician, King's College Hospital, since 1978; Professor of Paediatric Respiratory Medicine, University of London, since 1992; Clinical Director of Paediatrics, King's NHS Healthcare Trust, 1993–96 and since 1999; *b* 26 April 1944; *s* of Drs Cyril Frederick Price and Dora Elizabeth Price; *m* 1971, Dr Valerie Pickup; two *d*. *Educ:* Dulwich Coll.; St John's Coll., Cambridge (MB BCh; MA; MD 1986); Guy's Hosp., London. DCH 1973; FRCP 1985; FRCPCH 1997. MRC Trng Fellowship, Inst. of Child Health and Gt Ormond St Hosp., 1975–78; Hd, Acad. Dept of Child Health, 1995–98, and Chm., Div. of Child Health and Reproductive Medicine, 1995–98, GKT Med. and Dental Sch., KCL (formerly King's Coll. Sch. of Medicine and Dentistry), Univ. of London. Vis. Prof. and Ext. Examr, Hong Kong Univ. and Univ. of Malaya, 1997. Altounyan Address, Brit. Thoracic Soc., 1989; C. Elaine Field Lecture, Hong Kong Paediatric Soc., 1997, 2000. Sec., Paediatric Section, Royal Soc. Medicine, 1988–90; Chm., Brit. Paediatric Respiratory Soc., 1992–94; Council Member: Brit. Thoracic Soc., 1990–; European Respiratory Soc., 1990–95. Trustee: Nat. Asthma Campaign, 1990–; Brit. Lung Foundn, 1990–95. Member: Med. Adv. Panel, Nat. Eczema Soc., 1987–91; Res. and Med. Adv. Cttee, Cystic Fibrosis Trust, 1993–. Associate Editor: Respiratory Medicine, 1987–93; European Respiratory Jl, 1990–93. *Publications:* (with J. Rees) ABC of Asthma, 1984, 3rd edn 1995; contrib. chapters in books; numerous articles in learned jls related to respiratory disease in childhood. *Recreations:* theatre, music, Austen, Trollope, conversations with family and friends. *Address:* Department of Child Health, Guy's, King's and St Thomas' School of Medicine, Bessemer Road, SE5 9PJ. *T:* (020) 7346 3215/3562. *Club:* Hawks (Cambridge).

PRICE, Air Vice-Marshal John Walter, CBE 1979 (OBE 1973); DL; UK Manager, Courage Energy Corporation (UK Manager, Altaquest Energy Corporation, 1997); *b* Birmingham, 26 Jan. 1930; *s* of late Henry Walter Price and Myrza Price (*née* Griffiths); *m* 1956, Margaret Sinclair McIntyre (*d* 1989), Sydney, Aust. *Educ:* Solihull Sch.; RAF Coll., Cranwell. MRAeS 1971; MInstPet; CIMgt 1997 (FBIM 1979). Joined RAF, 1948; Adjutant, No 11 (Vampire) Sqn, 1950–52; No 77 (Meteor) Sqn, RAAF, Korea, 1952–53 (mentioned in despatches, 1953); No 98 Sqn (Venoms and Vampires), 1953–54; No 2 (F) Op. Trng Unit (Vampires) and No 75 (F) Sqn (Meteors), RAAF, 1954–56; Cadet Wing Adjutant, RAF Tech. Coll., Henlow, 1956–60; RAF Staff Coll., 1960; Air Ministry (Ops Overseas), 1961–64; Comd No 110 Sqn (Sycamore and Whirlwind), 1964–66; Directing Staff, RAF Staff Coll., 1966–68; PSO to Chief of Air Staff, 1968–70; Comd No 72 (Wessex) Sqn, 1970–72; Dep. Dir Ops (Offensive Support and Jt Warfare), MoD (Air), 1973–75; sowc 1975–76; Comd RAF Laarbruch, 1976–78; Gp Capt. Ops, HQ Strike Comd, 1979; Dir of Ops (Strike), MoD (Air), 1980–82; ACAS (Ops), 1982–84, retd. Clyde Petroleum plc, 1984–95 (Manager, External Affairs and Exploration Admin, 1986–95). Mem. Council, Inst. of Management, 1994–2000. Governor: Solihull Sch., 1979– (Chm., 1983–); Royal Nat. Coll. for Blind, 1999–. DL Hereford and Worcester, 1995. *Recreations:* motorcycling, golf, cabinet making. *Address:* 2 Palace Yard, Hereford HR4 9BJ. *Clubs:* Army and Navy, Royal Air Force.

PRICE, Leolin; *see* Price, A. L.

PRICE, Leonard Sidney, OBE 1974; HM Diplomatic Service, retired 1981; *b* 19 Oct. 1922; *s* of late William Price and late Dorothy Price; *m* 1958, Adrienne Mary (*née* Wilkinson); two *s* one *d*. *Educ:* Central Foundation Sch., EC1. Served War, 1942–45: Inns of Court Regt; D-Day assault to Danish border. Foreign Office, 1939–42 and 1945–48; Chungking, later Vice-Consul, 1948; Mexico City, 1950; Rome, 1953; Vice-Consul, later Second Sec., Katmandu, 1954; FO, 1957; Consul, Split, 1960; Consul and First Sec., Copenhagen, 1963; FO, later FCO, 1967; First Sec. i/c, Kuching, 1970; Suva, 1972; Parly Clerk, FCO, 1975; Counsellor (Admin), Canberra, 1977–81. Dep. Dir, St John Ambulance Assoc., Somerset, 1982–84; Hon. Treas., Council of Order of St John, Somerset, 1983–88. *Recreation:* reading ancient, medieval and military history. *Address:* 5 Staplegrove Manor, Staplegrove, Taunton, Somerset TA2 6EG. *T:* (01823) 337093. *Club:* Civil Service.

PRICE, Leontyne; Opera Prima Donna (Soprano), United States; *b* 10 Feb. 1927. *Educ:* Public Schools, Laurel, Mississippi; Central State College, Wilberforce, Ohio (BA); Juilliard Sch. of Music, NY. Four Saints, 1952; Porgy and Bess, 1952–54. Operatic Debut on TV, 1955, as Tosca; Concerts in America, England, Australia, Europe. Operatic debut as Madame Lidouine in Dialogues of Carmelites, San Francisco, 1957; Covent Garden, Verona Arena, Vienna Staatsoper, 1958; five roles, inc. Leonora in Il Trovatore, Madame Butterfly, Donna Anna in Don Giovanni, Metropolitan, 1960–61; Salzburg debut singing soprano lead in Missa Solemnis, 1959; Aida in Aida, Liu in Turandot, La Scala, 1960; opened season at Metropolitan in 1961 as Minnie in Fanciulla del West; opened new Metropolitan Opera House, 1966, as Cleopatra in world premiere of Samuel Barber's Antony and Cleopatra; debut Teatre Dell'Opera, Rome, in Aida, 1967; debut Paris Opera, in Aida, 1968; debut Teatro Colon, Buenos Aires, as Leonora in Il Trovatore, 1969; opened season at Metropolitan Opera, in Aida, 1969. Numerous recordings. Vice-Chm., Nat. Inst. for Music Theatre. Member: Metropolitan Opera Assoc.; Bd of Dirs, Dance Theatre of Harlem; Bd of Trustees, NY Univ. Life Mem., NAACP. Fellow, Amer. Acad. of Arts and Sciences. Hon. Dr of Music: Howard Univ., Washington, DC, 1962; Central State Coll., Wilberforce, Ohio, 1968; Hon. DHL, Dartmouth Univ., 1962; Hon. Dr of Humanities, Rust Coll., Holly Springs, Miss, 1968; Hon. Dr of Humane Letters, Fordham Univ., New York, 1969. Hon. Mem. Bd of Dirs, Campfire Girls, 1966. Presidential Medal of Freedom, 1965; Spingarn Medal, NAACP, 1965; Nat. Medal of Arts, 1985; 18 Grammy Awards, Nat. Acad. Recording Arts and Scis. Order of Merit (Italy), 1966; Commandeur, Ordre des Arts et des Lettres (France), 1986. *Recreations:* cooking, dancing, shopping for clothes, etc, antiques for homes in Rome and New York. *Address:* c/o Columbia Artists Management Inc., 165 W 57th Street, New York, NY 10019, USA.

PRICE, (Llewelyn) Ralph, CBE 1972; Director, Honeywell, since 1971 (Chairman, 1971–81); *b* 23 Oct. 1912; *s* of late L. D. Price, schoolmaster, and late Lena Elizabeth (*née* Dixon); *m* 1939, Vera Patricia Harrison; one *s* two *d*. *Educ:* Quarry Bank Sch., Liverpool. Chartered Accountant, 1935; Sec. to Honeywell Ltd, 1936; Cost Investigator, Min. of Supply, 1943–46; Dir of Manufacturing (Scotland), Honeywell Ltd, 1947; Financial Dir, Honeywell Europe, 1957; Dir, Computer Div., Honeywell, 1960; Managing Dir, Honeywell Ltd, 1965; Chm., Honeywell UK Adv. Council, 1981–. Chm., ML Hldgs Ltd, 1976–87. Pres., British Industrial, Measuring & Control Apparatus Manufrs Assoc., 1971–76. CIMgt. *Recreations:* golf, bridge, music. *Address:* Nascot, Pinkneys Drive, Pinkneys Green, Maidenhead, Berks SL6 6QD. *T:* (01628) 628270. *Clubs:* Royal Automobile; Temple Golf (Maidenhead).

PRICE, Dame Margaret (Berenice), DBE 1993 (CBE 1982); opera singer; with Bayerische Staatsoper München; *b* Tredegar, Wales, 13 April 1941; *d* of late Thomas Glyn Price and of Lilian Myfanwy Richards. *Educ:* Pontllanfraith Secondary Sch.; Trinity Coll. of Music, London. Debut as Cherubino in Marriage of Figaro, Welsh Nat. Opera Co., 1962; debut, in same rôle, at Royal Opera House, Covent Garden, 1963; has subseq. sung many principal rôles at Glyndebourne, San Francisco Opera Co., Cologne Opera House, Munich State Opera, Hamburg State Opera, Vienna State Opera, Lyric Opera, Chicago, Paris Opera; La Scala, Milan; Metropolitan Opera House, NY. Major rôles include: Countess in Marriage of Figaro; Pamina in The Magic Flute; Fiordiligi in Così Fan Tutte; Donna Anna in Don Giovanni; Konstanze in Die Entführung; Amelia in Simone Boccanegra; Agathe in Freischütz; Desdemona in Otello; Elisabetta in Don Carlo; Amelia in Un Ballo In Maschera; title rôles in Aida, Norma and Ariadne auf Naxos. BBC recitals and concerts, also TV appearances. Has made recordings. Hon. FTCL; Hon. DMus Wales, 1983. Elisabeth Schumann Prize for Lieder; Ricordi Prize for Opera; Silver Medal, Worshipful Co. of Musicians; Bayerische Kammersängerin. *Recreations:* cooking, driving, reading, walking, swimming. *Address:* c/o Stefan Hahn, Artist Management HRA, Sebastiansplatz 3, 80331 München, Germany.

PRICE, Maj.-Gen. (Maurice) David, CB 1970; OBE 1956; *b* 13 Feb. 1915; *s* of Edward Allan Price and Edna Marion Price (*née* Turner); *m* 1st, 1938, Ella Lacy (*d* 1971), *d* of late H. L. Day; two *s* two *d*; 2nd, 1972, Mrs Olga Marion Oclee (*d* 1989). *Educ:* Marlborough; RMA, Woolwich. 2nd Lt R Signals, 1935; Vice-Quartermaster-Gen., MoD (Army), 1967–70, retired. Col Comdt, Royal Corps of Signals, 1967–74. *Address:* The Cross, Chilmark, Salisbury, Wiltshire SP3 5AR. *T:* (01722) 716212.

PRICE, Michael Anthony, LVO 1991; HM Diplomatic Service; High Commissioner, Fiji, since 2000, also (non-resident) to Kiribati, Tuvalu and Nauru; *b* 13 Aug. 1944; *s* of Francis George and Lena Beatrice Price; *m* 1968, Elizabeth Anne Cook; one *s* one *d*. *Educ:* Forest Grammar Sch. Bd of Trade, 1964; Diplomatic Service, 1966–; served New Delhi, Freetown, Paris, Montreal; JSDC, 1983–84; Dep. Head of News Dept, FCO, 1984; First Sec. (Press and Public Affairs), Washington, 1988; Counsellor and HM Consul-Gen., Tokyo, 1992; on loan to No 10 Downing St, 1994–95; Counsellor, Paris, 1995–2000. *Recreations:* cricket, Gilbert and Sullivan, cooking. *Address:* c/o Foreign and Commonwealth Office, SW1A 2AH.

PRICE, Nicholas Peter Lees; QC 1992; a Recorder of the Crown Court, since 1987; *b* 29 Sept. 1944; *s* of Frank Henry Edmund Price, MBE (mil.) and Agnes Lees Price; *m* 1969, Wilma Ann Alison (*née* Steel); one *s* one *d*. *Educ:* Prince of Wales Sch., Nairobi; Edinburgh Univ. (LLB). Called to the Bar, Gray's Inn, 1968; Bencher, 2000. Member: Gen. Council of the Bar, 1993–95 (Jt Vice Chm., Legal Services Cttee, 1994; Vice Chm., Public Affairs Cttee, 1995); Gray's Inn Continuing Educn Cttee, 1998– (Vice Chm., 1999–2000; Chm., 2001–); Associate Mem., Criminal Bar Assoc., 1993–95. *Recreations:* watching Rugby, crosswords, destructive gardening, cinema. *Address:* 3 Raymond Buildings, Gray's Inn, WC1R 5BH. *T:* (020) 7400 6400.

PRICE, Nick; golfer; *b* Durban, 28 Jan. 1957; *m* Sue Price; one *s* one *d*. Wins include: US PGA, 1992, 1994; Open, Turnberry, 1994; Vardon Trophy, 1993; record for PGA Tournament lowest score (269), 1994. *Address:* c/o Professional Golfers' Association Tour, 100 Avenue of the Champions, Palm Beach Gardens, FL 33410–9601, USA.

PRICE, Sir Norman (Charles), KCB 1975 (CB 1969); Member, European Court of Auditors, 1977–83; Chairman, Board of Inland Revenue, 1973–76 (Deputy Chairman, 1968–73); *b* 5 Jan. 1915; *s* of Charles William and Ethel Mary Price; *m* 1940, Kathleen Beatrice (*née* Elston); two *d*. *Educ:* Plaistow Grammar School. Entered Civil Service as Executive Officer, Customs and Excise, 1933; Inspector of Taxes, Inland Revenue, 1939; Secretaries' Office, Inland Revenue, 1951; Board of Inland Revenue, 1965. *Recreations:* music, history. *Address:* 73 Linkswood, Compton Place Road, Eastbourne BN21 1EF. *T:* (01323) 7225941.

PRICE, Pamela Joan V.; *see* Vandyke Price.

PRICE, Rt Rev. Peter Bryan; *see* Kingston-upon-Thames, Area Bishop of.

PRICE, Peter Nicholas; European Strategy Counsel, since 1994; *b* 19 Feb. 1942; *s* of Rev. Dewi Emlyn Price and Kate Mary Price; *m* 1988, Joy Bhola; one *d*. *Educ:* Worcester Royal Grammar Sch.; Aberdare Boys' Grammar Sch.; Univ. of Southampton (BA (Law)); Coll. of Law, Guildford; KCL (Postgrad. Dip. in EC Law). Solicitor. Interviewer and current affairs freelance broadcaster, 1962–67; Asst Solicitor, Glamorgan CC, 1967–68; solicitor in private practice, 1966–67 and 1968–85; part-time EC consultant: Payne Hicks Beach, 1990–93; Howard Kennedy, 1993–2001; Standing Orders Comr, Nat. Assembly for Wales, 1998–99; pt-time Chm., Employment Tribunal, Cardiff, 2000–. Contested (C) Gen. Elecs: Aberdare 1964, 1966; Caerphilly 1970; Nat. Vice-Chm., Young Conservatives, 1971–72; Mem., Nat. Union Exec. Cttee, 1969–72 and 1978–79; Vice-Chm., Cons. Pol. Centre Nat. Cttee, 1978–79; Hon. Sec., For. Affairs Forum, 1977–79; Vice-Chm., Cons. Gp for Europe, 1979–81; Mem. Council, Europ. Movement, 1971–81. MEP (C): Lancashire W, 1979–84; London SE, 1984–94; Hon. MEP, 1994; European Parliament: Chm., Budgetary Control Cttee, 1989–92 (Vice-Chm., 1979–84, and its Rapporteur for series of 4 major reports on Community finances, 1985–86); spokesman for EDG, Legal Affairs Cttee, 1984–87, Budgets Cttee, 1986–89; Member: ACP/EEC Jt Assembly, 1981–94; Ext. Econ. Relns Cttee, 1992–94; delgns for relns with Japan, 1989–92, US Congress, 1992–94. Member: Lib Dem Federal Policy Cttee, 1998–; ELDR Council, 1999–; Lib Dem Federal Finance Cttee, 2001–. Contested (Lib Dem) Wales, EP elecn, 1999. Non-executive Director: Bureau Veritas Quality Internat. Ltd, 1991–; Ravensbourne NHS Trust, 1998–. Mem., NEC, FPA, 1973–77 (Mem., then Chm., Long-term Planning Gp, 1973–76). Fellow, Industry and Parlt Trust, 1981–82; Vice-Pres., UK Cttee, Europ. Year of Small and Med.-sized Enterprises, 1983. Mem., RIIA. Vice-Pres., Llangollen Internat. Eisteddfod, 1981–. Governor, Thames Valley Univ., 1996–. *Publications:* misc. pol. pamplets and newspaper articles. *Recreations:* theatre, music, photography. *Address:* 37 Heol St Denys, Lisvane, Cardiff CF14 0RU. *T:* (029) 2076 1792; 60 Marlings Park Avenue, Chislehurst, Kent BR7 6RD. *T:* (01689) 820681, *Fax:* (01689) 890622; *e-mail:* peterprice@btinternet.com.

PRICE, Rev. Peter Owen, CBE 1983; BA; FPhS; RN retired; Minister of Blantyre Old Parish Church, Glasgow, 1985–96; *b* Swansea, 18 April 1930; *e s* of late Idwal Price and Florence Price; *m* 1957, Margaret Trevan (*d* 1977); three *d*; *m* 1996, Mary Hamill Robertson. *Educ:* Wyggeston Sch., Leicester; Didsbury Theol Coll., Bristol. BA Open Univ. Ordained, 1960, Methodist Minister, Birmingham; commnd RN as Chaplain, 1960; served: HMS Collingwood, 1960; RM, 1963–64; Staff of C-in-C Med., 1964–68; RNAS Brawdy, 1968–69; RM, 1970–73; HMS Raleigh, 1973; HMS Drake, 1974–78; BRNC Dartmouth, 1978–80; Principal Chaplain, Church of Scotland and Free Churches (Naval), MoD, 1981–84. Hon. Chaplain to the Queen, 1981–84. *Recreations:* warm water sailing, music, golf. *Address:* Duncraigan, 22 Old Bothwell Road, Bothwell, Glasgow G71 8AW.

PRICE, Philip John; His Honour Judge Price; QC 1989; a Circuit Judge, since 1993; *b* 16 May 1943; *s* of Ernest Price and Eunice Price (*née* Morgan); *m* 1967, Mari Josephine Davies; one *s* two *d*. *Educ:* Cardiff High Sch.; Pembroke Coll., Oxford (MA). Lectr in Law, Univ. of Leeds, 1966–70; called to the Bar, Gray's Inn, 1969; in practice on Wales and Chester Circuit and Temple, 1971–93; a Recorder, 1985–93. Chancellor, Dio. Monmouth, 1992–; Pres., Disciplinary Tribunal, Church in Wales, 2001–. Mem., Mental Health Rev. Tribunal, 1995–. Mem., Governing Body, Church in Wales, 1993–. *Recreations:* architecture, books, cricket. *Address:* Civil Justice Centre, 2 Park Street, Cardiff CF10 1ET. *T:* (029) 2037 6402. *Club:* Cardiff and County.

PRICE, Ralph; *see* Price, L. R.

PRICE, Richard Mervyn, OBE 1995; QC 1996; *b* 15 May 1948; *s* of late William James Price and Josephine May Price; *m* 1971, Caroline Sarah, *d* of Geoffrey and Mary Ball; one *s* two *d*. *Educ:* King Edward VII Sch., Sheffield; King's Coll., London (LLB Hons). Called to the Bar, Gray's Inn, 1969. Standing Counsel on Election Law to Conservative Central Office, 1986–. *Recreations:* politics, theatre, films, music, walking, cycling. *Address:* Littleton Chambers, 3 King's Bench Walk North, Temple, EC4Y 7HR. *T:* (020) 7797 8600. *Clubs:* Royal Automobile, St Stephen's Constitutional.

PRICE, Richard Neville Meredith; His Honour Judge Richard Price; a Circuit Judge, since 1996; *b* 30 May 1945; *s* of Christopher Llewelyn Price and Valerie Ruby Price (*née* Greenham); *m* 1971, Avril Judith Lancaster; three *s*. *Educ:* Marsh Court, Stockbridge, Hants; Sutton Valence, Kent. Admitted solicitor, 1970; Asst Recorder, 1985–90; called to the Bar, Middle Temple, 1990; Recorder, 1990–96. *Recreations:* choral singing, sailing, reading, listening to music. *Address:* Portsmouth Combined Court Centre, Courts of Justice, Winston Churchill Avenue, Portsmouth, Hants PO1 2DL. *Clubs:* Royal Victoria Yacht, Seaview Yacht (IoW).

PRICE, Air Vice-Marshal Robert George, CB 1983; *b* 18 July 1928; *s* of Charles and Agnes Price, Hale, Cheshire; *m* 1st, 1958, Celia Anne Mary Talamo (*d* 1987); one *s* four *d*; 2nd, 1989, Edith Barbara Dye. *Educ:* Oundle Sch.; RAF Coll., Cranwell. 74 Sqn, 1950; Central Flying Sch., 1952; 60 Sqn, 1956; Guided Weapons Trials Sqn, 1958; Staff Coll., 1960; Bomber Comd, 1961; JSSC 1964; CO 31 Sqn, 1965; PSO to Dep. SACEUR, 1968; CO RAF Linton-on-Ouse, 1970; RCDS 1973; Dep. Dir Operations, 1974; Group Captain Flying Trng, Support Comd, 1978; Dep. Chief of Staff, Support HQ, 2nd Allied Tactical Air Force, 1979; AOA, RAF Germany, 1980; AOA, HQ Strike Comd, 1981–83. *Recreations:* golf, ski-ing, bridge. *Club:* Royal Air Force.

PRICE, Sir Robert (John) G.; *see* Green-Price.

PRICE, Roy Kenneth, CB 1980; Under-Secretary (Legal), in office of HM Treasury Solicitor, 1972–81; *b* 16 May 1916; *s* of Ernest Price and Margaret Chapman Price (*née* Scott); *m* 1948, Martha (*née* Dannhauser); one *s* one *d*. *Educ:* Eltham Coll. Qualified as Solicitor, 1937. Town Clerk, Borough of Pembroke, and Clerk to Castlemartin Justices, 1939–40. Served War, Army, 1940–46. Officer in Charge, Legal Aid (Welfare), Northern Command, 1946 (Lt-Col). Joined HM Treasury Solicitor, as Legal Asst, 1946; Sen. Legal Asst, 1950; Asst Solicitor, 1962. Mem. Exec. Council, RNIB, 1981–99; Pres., Richmond Assoc., Nat. Trust, 1985–; Trustee, Richmond Almshouse Charities, 1987–99; Chm., Portcullis Trust, 1980–90. *Recreations:* theatre, travel, local history. *Address:* 16 Queensberry House, Friars Lane, Richmond, Surrey TW9 1NT. *T:* (020) 8940 6685. *Club:* Law Society.

PRICE, Sarah Helena; HM Diplomatic Service; Deputy Head of Mission, Belgrade, since 2000; *b* 4 June 1966; *d* of John Michael Anthony Price and Mary Price. *Educ:* Holy Child Sch., Edgbaston; Somerville Coll., Oxford (BA Hons Classics and Mod. Langs 1989). Joined FCO, 1990: Third Sec., FCO, 1990–92; Second Secretary: UK Delegn to CSCE, Helsinki, 1992–93; Prague, 1993–96; First Sec., FCO, 1996–99; on secondment to Finnish Foreign Ministry, 1999–2000. *Address:* c/o Foreign and Commonwealth Office, King Charles Street, SW1A 2AH.

PRICE, Terence; *see* Price, B. T.

PRICE, Vivian William Cecil; QC 1972; *b* 14 April 1926; 4th *s* of late Evan Price, Hawkhurst, Kent; *m* 1961, Elizabeth Anne, *o c* of late Arthur Rawlins and Georgina (*née* Guinness); three *s* two *d*. *Educ:* Judd Sch., Tonbridge, Kent; Trinity Coll., Cambridge (BA); Balliol Coll., Oxford (BA). Royal Navy, 1946–49, Instructor Lieut. Called to the Bar: Middle Temple, 1954 (Bencher, 1979); Hong Kong, 1975; Singapore, 1979. Dep. High Court Judge (Chancery Div.), 1975–85; a Recorder of the Crown Court, 1984. Sec., Lord Denning's Cttee on Legal Educn for Students from Africa, 1960; Junior Counsel (Patents) to the Board of Trade, 1967–72; Mem., Patents Procedure Cttee, 1973. Mem., Incorporated Council of Law Reporting for England and Wales, 1980–85. *Address:* Redwall Farmhouse, Linton, Kent ME17 4AX. *T:* (01622) 743682. *Club:* Travellers.
See also A. L. Price.

PRICE, (William Frederick) Barry, OBE 1977; HM Diplomatic Service, retired; Consul-General, Amsterdam, 1983–85; *b* 12 Feb. 1925; *s* of William Thomas and Vera Price; *m* 1948, Lorraine Elisabeth Suzanne Hoather; three *s* two *d*. *Educ:* Worcester Royal Grammar Sch.; St Paul's Training Coll., Cheltenham; Open Univ. (BA Hons 1994). Served War: Armed Forces, 1944–47: commissioned Royal Warwicks, 1945; demobilised, 1947. Primary Sch. Teacher, 1948. Joined Bd of Trade, 1950; Asst Trade Comr: in Delhi, 1954; in Nairobi, 1957; Trade Commissioner, Accra, 1963; transferred to HM Diplomatic Service, 1966; 1st Sec., Sofia, 1967; seconded to East European Trade Council, 1971; Consul-Gen., Rotterdam, 1973–77; Consul, Houston, 1978–81; Counsellor (Commercial and Economic), Bangkok, 1981–82; Kuala Lumpur, 1982. Chm., Anglo-Netherlands Soc., 1989–94. Comdr, Order of Orange-Nassau (Netherlands), 1989. *Recreation:* Dutch literary translation. *Address:* 46 Finchley Park, N12 9JL. *T:* (020) 8445 4642. *Club:* Oriental.

PRICE, Prof. (William) Geraint, FRS 1988; FREng, FIMechE, FRINA; Professor of Ship Science, since 1990, and Head of School of Engineering Sciences, since 1998, University of Southampton; *b* 1 Aug. 1943; *s* of Thomas Price and Ursula Maude Price (*née* Roberts); *m* 1967, Jennifer Mary Whitten; two *d*. *Educ:* Merthyr Tydfil County Grammar Sch.; University Coll. Cardiff (Univ. of Wales) (G. H. Latham Open Sci. Scholar; BSc, PhD); Univ. of London (DSc(Eng)). FRINA 1980; FREng (FEng 1986); FIMechE 1989. Res. Asst, later Lectr, UCL, 1969–81; Reader in Applied Mechanics, Univ. of London, 1981–82; Prof. of Applied Mechanics, Brunel Univ., 1982–90. Fellow, Japan Soc. for Promotion of Science, 1987; Foreign Mem., Chinese Acad. of Engrg, 2000. *Publications:* Probabilistic Theory of Ship Dynamics, 1974; Hydroelasticity of Ships, 1979. *Recreations:* walking, Rugby, golf, barbecueing. *Address:* Tŷ Gwyn, 45 Palmerston Way, Alverstoke, Gosport, Hants PO12 2LY. *T:* (023) 9235 1719.

PRICE, William John R.; *see* Rea Price.

PRICE, Winford Hugh Protheroe, OBE 1983; FCA; City Treasurer, Cardiff City Council, 1975–83; *b* 5 Feb. 1926; *s* of Martin Price and Doris Blanche Price. *Educ:* Cardiff High Sch. IPFA 1952; FCA 1954. Served War, RAFVR, 1944–48. City Treasurer's and Controller's Dept, Cardiff, 1942; Dep. City Treasurer, Cardiff, 1973–75. Public Works Loan Comr, 1979–83. Treasurer and Financial Adviser, Council for the Principality, 1975–83; Financial Adviser, Assoc. of Dist Councils Cttee for Wales, 1975–83; Treasurer: The Queen's Silver Jubilee Trust (S Glam), 1976–83; Royal National Eisteddfod of Wales (Cardiff), 1978. Occasional lectr on local govt topics. *Publications:* contrib. to jls. *Recreation:* chess.

PRICE EVANS, David Alan; *see* Evans.

PRICHARD, David Colville Mostyn; Headmaster, Wycliffe College, 1994–98; *b* 26 May 1934; *s* of Rev. George Mostyn Prichard and Joan Mary Mostyn Prichard; *m* 1992, Catherine Elizabeth Major (formerly Headmistress, Warwick Prep. Sch.). *Educ:* Radley Coll.; Pembroke Coll., Oxford (Captain of Boats; MA; Mem., Society Cttee, 1956–). FCollP. Asst Master, Monkton Combe Sch., 1955–68 (Dir, Centenary Appeal, 1962; Founder, GB 1st Vol. Police Cadets, 1964; CO, CCF, 1964–68); Headmaster, Port Regis, Motcombe Park, 1969–93. Founder, Nat. Conf. for Govs, Bursars and Heads, 1981–93; Chm., IAPS, 1989–90. Mem. Develt Cttee, SW Arts, 1998–. Trustee, Smallpeice Trust, 1980–; Chm., Smallpeice Enterprises, 1986–95; Co-Chm., Operation New World, 1992–99; Vice President: Glos Pied Piper Appeal, 1995; Wycliffe Watermen, 1998–. Governor: Swanbourne House Sch., 1985–2000; Holmewood House Sch., 1987–98; Orwell Park Sch., 1995–98; St John's Sch., Chepstow, 1995–99; West Hill Park Sch., 1998–; Sherborne Prep. Sch., 1999–; Trustee, Sherborne House Trust, 1998–. Cttee, Friends of Yeatman Hosp., 2000–. Church Warden, Castleton Church, 1999–. Freeman, City of London, 1990; Liveryman, Lorimers' Co., 1990–. FRSA. *Publication:* Training for Service, 1967. *Recreations:* education, travel, gardening, rowing (OUBC Isis VIII). *Address:* Castleton House, Sherborne, Dorset DT9 3SA. *T:* (01935) 816539. *Clubs:* National, Carlton; Leander.

PRICHARD, Mathew Caradoc Thomas, CBE 1992; DL; Chairman, Agatha Christie Ltd, since 1971; *b* 21 Sept. 1943; *s* of late Major H. de B. Prichard and of Rosalind Hicks; *m* 1967, Angela Caroline Maples; one *s* two *d*. *Educ:* Eton College; New College, Oxford. BA (PPE). Penguin Books, 1965–69. Pres., Nat. Mus. of Wales, 1996– (Mem. Court of Governors and Council, 1975–); Member: Welsh Arts Council, 1980–94 (Chm., 1988–94); Arts Council of GB, 1983–94. High Sheriff, Glamorgan, 1972–73; DL S Glam, 1994. *Recreations:* golf, cricket, bridge. *Address:* Pwllywrach, Colwinston, Cowbridge, Vale of Glamorgan CF71 7NJ. *T:* (01446) 772256. *Clubs:* Boodle's, MCC; Cardiff and County; Royal & Ancient Golf (St Andrews); Royal Porthcawl Golf, Loch Lomond Golf.

PRICHARD, Air Vice-Marshal Richard Augustin R.; *see* Riseley-Prichard.

PRICHARD-JONES, Sir John, 2nd Bt *cr* 1910; barrister; farmer and bloodstock breeder; *b* 20 Jan. 1913; *s* of Sir John Prichard-Jones, 1st Bt and Marie, *y d* of late Charles Read, solicitor; *S* father, 1917; *m* 1937, Heather, (from whom he obtained a divorce, 1950), *er d* of late Sir Walter Nugent, 4th Bt; one *s*; *m* 1959, Helen Marie Thérèse, *e d* of J. F. Liddy, dental surgeon, 20 Laurence Street, Drogheda; one *d*. *Educ:* Eton; Christ Church, Oxford (BA Hons; MA). Called to Bar, Gray's Inn, 1936. Commnd, Queen's Bays, 1939, and served throughout War. *Heir: s* David John Walter Prichard-Jones, BA (Hons) Oxon, *b* 14 March 1943. *Address:* Allenswood House, Lucan, Co. Dublin.

PRICKETT, Prof. (Alexander Thomas) Stephen, PhD; Professor of English, Duke University, USA, since 2001; *b* 4 June 1939; *s* of Rev. William Ewart Prickett and Barbara Browning (*née* Lyne); *m* 1st, 1967, Diana Joan Mabbutt; one *s* one *d*; 2nd, 1983, Mària Angelica Alvarez (marr. diss. 2001). *Educ:* Kent Coll., Canterbury; Trinity Hall, Cambridge (BA 1961; PhD 1968); University Coll., Oxford (DipEd). FAHA 1986. English teacher, Uzuakoli, E Nigeria, 1962–64; Asst Lectr, Lectr, and Reader, Univ. of Sussex, 1967–82; Prof. of English, ANU, Canberra, 1983–89; Regius Prof. of English Lang. and Lit., Univ. of Glasgow, 1990–2001. Vis. Lectr, Smith Coll., Mass, USA, 1970–71; Vis. Fulbright Prof., Univ. of Minnesota, 1979–80. Trustee, Higher Educn Foundn, 1976–. President: Soc. for Study of Literature and Theology, 1991–; George MacDonald Soc., 1994–. Fellow, Soc. for Values in Higher Educn, USA, 1992; FRSA 1993. *Publications:* Do It Yourself Doom, 1962; Coleridge and Wordsworth: the poetry of growth, 1970, 2nd edn 1980; Romanticism and Religion, 1976; Victorian Fantasy, 1979, 2nd edn 1982; Words and the Word: language poetics and biblical interpretation, 1986,

2nd edn 1988; England and the French Revolution, 1988; Reading the Text: biblical criticism and literary theory, 1991; (jtly) The Bible, 1991; Origins of Narrative: the romantic appropriation of the Bible, 1996; (ed) World's Classics Bible, 1997; The Bible and Literature: a reader, 1999; Narrative, Science and Religion, 2002. *Recreations:* walking, ski-ing, drama. *Address:* Faculty of Arts and Sciences, Duke University, Durham, NC 27708, USA.

PRICKETT, Air Chief Marshal Sir Thomas (Other), KCB 1965 (CB 1957); DSO 1943; DFC 1942; RAF retired; *b* 31 July 1913; *s* of late E. G. Prickett; *m* 1st, 1942, Elizabeth Gratian, (*d* 1984), *d* of late William Galbally, Laguna Beach, Calif, USA; one *s* one *d*; 2nd, 1985, Shirley Westerman. *Educ:* Stubbington House Sch.; Haileybury Coll. Assistant, later Manager, sugar estates, India with Begg Sutherland Ltd, 1932–37. Served Bihar Light Horse, Indian Army (Auxiliary). Joined RAF, 1937; Desert Air Force, Bomber Comd, 1939–44; RAF Delegn, Washington; Dep. Dir Trng, 1944–45; commanded RAF Tangmere, 1949–51; Group Captain operations, HQ Middle East Air Force, 1951–54; commanded RAF Jever, 1954–55; attended Imperial Defence Coll., 1956; Chief of Staff Air Task Force, 1956; Director of Policy, Air Ministry, 1957–58; SASO, HQ No 1 Group, 1958–60; ACAS (Ops) Air Ministry, 1960–63; ACAS (Policy and Planning) Air Ministry, 1963–64; AOC-in-C, NEAF, Comdr British Forces Near East, and Administrator, Sovereign Base Area, 1964–66; AOC-in-C, RAF Air Support Command, 1967–68; Air Mem. for Supply and Organisation, MoD, 1968–70; Dir, Goodwood Estate, 1970–78; Man. Dir, Goodwood Terrena, 1970–78. *Recreations:* polo, sailing, golf. *Address:* 46 Kingston Hill Place, Kingston upon Thames KT2 7QY. *Club:* Royal Air Force.

PRIDDIS, Rt Rev. Anthony Martin; *see* Warwick, Bishop Suffragan of.

PRIDDLE, Robert John, CB 1994; Executive Director, International Energy Agency, since 1994; *b* 9 Sept. 1938; *s* of late Albert Leslie Priddle and Alberta Edith Priddle; *m* 1962, Janice Elizabeth Gorham; two *s*. *Educ:* King's Coll. Sch., Wimbledon; Peterhouse, Cambridge (MA). Asst Principal, Min. of Aviation, 1960, Principal 1965; Private Sec. to Minister for Aerospace, 1971–73; Asst Sec., DTI, 1973, and Dept of Energy, 1974; Under Sec., Dept of Energy, 1977–85; Under Sec., DTI, 1985–89; Dep. Sec. and Dir Gen. of Energy Resources, Dept of Energy, subseq. DTI, 1989–92; Dep. Sec., Corporate and Consumer Affairs, DTI, 1992–94. Pres., Conf. of European Posts and Telecommunications Administrations, 1987–89; Chm. Governing Bd, Internat. Energy Agency, 1991–92. Mem., Financial Reporting Council, 1992–94. *Publication:* Victoriana, 1959, 2nd edn 1963. *Address:* International Energy Agency, 9 rue de la Fédération, 75739 Paris, France.

PRIDEAUX, Sir Humphrey (Povah Treverbian), Kt 1971; OBE 1945; DL; Chairman, Morland & Co., 1983–93 (Director, 1981–93; Vice Chairman, 1982); Chairman, Lord Wandsworth Foundation, 1966–92; *b* 13 Dec. 1915; 3rd *s* of Walter Treverbian Prideaux and Marion Fenn (*née* Arbuthnot); *m* 1939, Cynthia, *er d* of late Lt-Col H. Birch Reynardson, CMG; four *s*. *Educ:* St Aubyns, Rottingdean; Eton; Trinity Coll., Oxford (MA). Commissioned 3rd Carabiniers (Prince of Wales's Dragoon Guards) 1936; DAQMG Guards Armd Div., 1941; Instructor, Staff Coll., 1942; AQMG 21 Army Gp, 1943; AA QMG Guards Armd Div., 1944; Joint Planning Staff, War Office, 1945; Naval Staff Coll., 1948; Commandant School of Administration, 1948; Chiefs of Staff Secretariat, 1950; retired, 1953. Director, NAAFI, 1956–73 (Man. Dir, 1961–65; Chm., 1963–73); Dir, London Life Association Ltd, 1964–88 (Vice-Pres., 1965–72; Pres., 1973–84); Chm., Brooke Bond Liebig Ltd, 1972–80 (Dir, 1968; Dep. Chm., 1969–71); Vice-Chm., W. H. Smith & Son Ltd, 1977–81 (Dir, 1969–77); Dir, Grindlays, 1982–85. DL Hants 1983. *Recreations:* country pursuits. *Address:* Kings Cottage, Buryfields, Odiham, Hants RG29 1NE. *T:* (01256) 703658. *Club:* Cavalry and Guards.

See also J. H. Prideaux.

PRIDEAUX, John Denys Charles Anstice, CBE 1994; PhD; Chairman, Altram (Manchester) Ltd, since 1999; Director, Angel Train Contracts, since 1996; *b* 8 Aug. 1944; *s* of Denys Robert Anstice-Prideaux and Frances Hester Dorothy Anstice-Prideaux (*née* Glaze); *m* 1972, Philippa Mary (*née* Morgan); one *s* one *d*. *Educ:* St Paul's; Univ. of Nottingham (BSc, PhD). British Railways: Operational Research, 1965; Area Manager, Newton Abbot, 1972; Strategic Planning Officer, 1974; Divl Manager, Birmingham, 1980; Dir, Policy Unit, 1983–86; Dir, 1986–91, Man. Dir, 1991, InterCity; Man. Dir, New Ventures, 1992–94; Chm., Union Railways, 1992–93; Director: Green Arrow, 1994–95; Docklands Light Railway, 1994–98; Chairman: Prideaux and Associates, 1994–99; Image Scan Hldgs Plc, 1998–2000. Member: Adv. Cttee on Trunk Road Assessment, 1977; Transport Cttee, SERC and ESRC, 1982; Planning and Envmt Cttee, ESRC, 1985. Mem, Council, Manchester Business School, 1987. *Publications:* railway histories, papers on management and transport. *Recreations:* riding, hunting, shooting, sailing, ski-ing, design. *Address:* 17 Highgate West Hill, N6 6NP.

PRIDEAUX, Julian Humphrey, OBE 1995; Deputy Director-General and Secretary, National Trust, since 1997; *b* 19 June 1942; 2nd *s* of Sir Humphrey Povah Treverbian Prideaux, *qv*; *m* 1967, Jill, 3rd *d* of R. P. Roney-Dougal; two *s*. *Educ:* St Aubyns, Rottingdean; Eton; Royal Agricultural Coll. (Dip. Estate Management). ARICS 1966, FRICS 1974. Land Agent with Burd & Evans, Shrewsbury, 1964–67; Agent to Col Hon. C. G. Cubitt and others, 1967–69; National Trust: Land Agent, Cornwall Region, 1969–77; Dir, Thames and Chilterns Region, 1978–86; Chief Agent, 1987–96. FRSA 1995. *Recreations:* walking, fishing. *Address:* Bellbrook, Donhead St Mary, Shaftesbury, Dorset SP7 9DL. *Club:* Farmers'.

PRIDHAM, Brian Robert; HM Diplomatic Service, retired; Hon. Research Fellow, Centre for Arab Gulf Studies, University of Exeter, 1995–2000 (Research Fellow, 1983–95; Director, 1985–86, 1987–95); *b* 22 Feb. 1934; *s* of Reginald Buller Pridham and Emily Pridham (*née* Winser); *m* 1954, Fay Coles (marr. diss. 1996); three *s*. *Educ:* Hele's Sch., Exeter. MA Exon, 1984. RWAFF (Nigeria Regt), 1952–54; Foreign Office, 1954–57; MECAS, 1957–59; Bahrain, 1959; Vice-Consul, Muscat, 1959–62; Foreign Office, 1962–64; 2nd Sec., Algiers, 1964–66, 1st Sec., 1966–67; Foreign Office, 1967–70; Head of Chancery: La Paz, 1970–73; Abu Dhabi, 1973–75; Dir of MECAS, Shemlan, Lebanon, 1975–76; Counsellor, Khartoum, 1976–79; Head of Communications Ops Dept, FCO, 1979–81. University of Exeter: Lectr in Arabic, Dept of Arabic and Islamic Studies, 1984–87; Dep. Dir, Centre for Arab Gulf Studies, 1984–85. Dep. Hd, EU Observer Mission to Palestinian Elections, 1995–96; Hd, OSCE Observer Mission to Albanian Elections, 1997; Hd, EU Observer Mission to Tanzanian Elections, 2000. Jt Ed., New Arabian Studies series, 1994–. *Publications:* (ed) Contemporary Yemen: politics and historical background, 1984; (ed) Economy, Society and Culture in Contemporary Yemen, 1984; (ed) The Arab Gulf and the West, 1985; (ed) Oman: economic, social and strategic developments, 1986; The Arab Gulf and the Arab World, 1987; (trans.) Omani-French Relations 1715–1905, 1996. *Recreations:* shrubs, photography.

PRIDHAM, Kenneth Robert Comyn, CMG 1976; HM Diplomatic Service, retired; *b* 28 July 1922; *s* of late Colonel G. R. Pridham, CBE, DSO, and Mignonne, *d* of late Charles Cumming, ICS; *m* 1965, Ann Rosalind, *d* of late E. Gilbert Woodward, Metropolitan Magistrate, and of Mrs Woodward. *Educ:* Winchester; Oriel Coll., Oxford. Lieut, 60th Rifles, 1942–46; served North Africa, Italy, Middle East (despatches). Entered Foreign (subseq. Diplomatic) Service, 1946; served at Berlin, Washington, Belgrade and Khartoum, and at the Foreign Office; Counsellor: Copenhagen, 1968–72; FCO, 1972–74; Asst Under Sec. of State, FCO, 1974–78; Ambassador to Poland, 1978–81. Vis. Res. Fellow, RIIA, 1981–82. *Address:* c/o Lloyds TSB, 8/10 Waterloo Place, SW1Y 4BE. *Club:* Travellers.

PRIEST, Rear-Adm. Colin Herbert Dickinson C.; *see* Cooke-Priest.

PRIEST, Prof. Eric Ronald, PhD; FRSE; Gregory Professor of Mathematics, University of St Andrews, since 1997; *b* 7 Nov. 1943; *s* of Ronald Priest and Olive Vera Priest (*née* Dolan); *m* 1970, Clare Margaret Wilson; three *s* one *d*. *Educ:* Nottingham Univ. (BSc 1965); Leeds Univ. (MSc 1966; PhD 1969). FRSE 1985. St Andrew's University: Lectr, 1968–77; Reader, 1977–83; Prof. of Theoretical Solar Physics, 1983–97. Marlar Lectr, Rice Univ., 1991; Lindsay Meml Lectr, Washington, 1998. Mem., Norwegian Acad. Scis and Letters, 1994. *Publications:* Solar Magnetohydrodynamics, 1982 (trans Russian 1985); (jtly) Plasma Astrophysics, 1994; (jtly) Magnetic Reconnection: MHD Theory and Applications, 2000; *edited:* Solar Flare Magnetohydrodynamics, 1981; Solar System Magnetic Fields, 1985; Dynamics and Structure of Quiescent Solar Prominences, 1989; (jtly) Magnetic Flux Ropes, 1990; (jtly) Mechanisms of Chromospheric and Coronal Heating, 1991; (jtly) Advances in Solar System Magnetohydrodynamics, 1991 (trans Russian 1995); (jtly) Reconnection in the Solar Corona and Magnetospheric Substorms, 1997; (jtly) A Crossroads for European Solar and Helospheric Physics, 1998; over 350 res. papers and articles. *Recreations:* bridge, hill walking, aerobics, singing, having fun with my family. *Address:* Mathematical and Computational Science Department, St Andrews University, St Andrews, Fife KY16 9SS. *T:* (01334) 463709.

PRIEST, Prof. Robert George, MD, FRCPsych; Professor of Psychiatry, University of London and Head of Department of Psychiatry at St Mary's Hospital Medical School, Imperial College of Science, Technology and Medicine, 1973–96, now Emeritus Professor; Hon. Consultant Psychiatrist, St Mary's Hospital, London, since 1973; *b* 28 Sept. 1933; *er s* of late James Priest and of Phoebe Priest; *m* 1955, Marilyn, *er d* of late Baden Roberts Baker and of Evelyn Baker; two *s*. *Educ:* University Coll., London and University Coll. Hosp. Med. Sch. MB, BS 1956; DPM 1963; MRCPE 1964; MD 1970; MRCPsych 1971 (Foundn Mem.); FRCPE 1974; FRCPsych 1974. Lectr in Psychiatry, Univ. of Edinburgh, 1964–67; Exchange Lectr, Univ. of Chicago, 1966; Consultant, Illinois State Psychiatric Inst., Chicago, 1966; Sen. Lectr, St George's Hosp. Med. Sch., London, 1967–73; Hon. Consultant: St George's Hosp., London, 1967–73; Springfield Hosp., London, 1967–73. University of London: Mem., Bd of Studies in Medicine, 1968–93 (Chm., 1987–89); Mem., Academic Adv. Bd in Medicine, 1987–90; Mem. Senate, 1989–93; Mem., Academic Council, 1989–93. Examiner in Psychiatry, NUI, 1975–78, 1980–83. Chm., Psychiatric Adv. Sub-Cttee, NW Thames RHA, 1976–79 (Vice-Chm., Reg. Manpower Cttee, 1980–83). Member: Council (Chm. Membership Cttee), British Assoc. for Psychopharmacology, 1977–81; World Psychiatric Assoc., 1980–93 (Mem. Cttee, 1985–93, Mem. Council, 1989–93); Central Cttee for Hosp. Med. Services, 1983–89 (Chm., Psych. Sub-Cttee, 1983–87); Pres., Soc. for Psychosomatic Res., 1980–81 (Vice-Pres., 1978–80); Chm., Mental Health Gp Cttee, BMA, 1982–85 (Mem. 1978–85, 1990–); Internat. Coll. of Psychosomatic Medicine: Fellow, 1977; Mem. Gov. Body and UK Delegate, 1978–81; Treasurer, 1981–83; Secretary, 1981–85; Vice-Pres., 1985–87; Royal College of Psychiatrists: Mem., Public Policy Cttee, 1972–80, 1983–89 (Chm., 1983–88); Mem. Council, 1982–88; Registrar, 1983–88; Chm., Gen. Psych. Cttee, 1985–89; Mem., Court of Electors, 1983–88 (Chm., Fellowship Sub-Cttee, 1984–88). A. E. Bennett Award, Soc. for Biol Psychiatry, USA (jtly), 1965; Doris Odlum Prize (BMA), 1968; Gutheil Von Domarus Award, Assoc. for Advancement of Psychotherapy and Amer. Jl of Psychotherapy, NY, 1970. *Publications:* Insanity: A Study of Major Psychiatric Disorders, 1977; (ed jtly) Sleep Research, 1979; (ed jtly) Benzodiazepines Today and Tomorrow, 1980; (ed) Psychiatry in Medical Practice, 1982; Anxiety and Depression, 1983, 3rd edn 1996; (ed) Sleep, 1984; (ed) Psychological Disorders in Obstetrics and Gynaecology, 1985 (Spanish edn 1987); (jtly) Minski's Handbook of Psychiatry, 7th edn, 1978, 8th edn as Handbook of Psychiatry, 1986; (jtly) Sleepless Nights, 1990; (jtly) Depression and Anxiety, 1992 (Spanish edn 1992); (jtly) Depression in General Practice, 1996; chapters in: Current Themes in Psychiatry, 1978; Mental Illness in Pregnancy and the Puerperium, 1978; Psychiatry in General Practice, 1981; Modern Emergency Department Practice, 1983; The Scientific Basis of Psychiatry, 1983, 2nd edn 1992; The Psychosomatic Approach: contemporary practice of wholeperson care, 1986; articles in BMJ, Brit. Jl of Psychiatry, Amer. Jl of Psychotherapy and other learned jls. *Recreations:* squash, tennis, foreign languages, nature study. *Address:* Woodeaves, 29 Old Slade Lane, Richings Park, Iver, Bucks SL0 9DY. *T:* (01753) 653178.

PRIESTLEY, Clive, CB 1983; Chairman, St Bartholomew's Hospital Medical College Trust, since 1997 (Member, 1996–97); *b* 12 July 1935; *s* of late Albert Ernest and Annie May Priestley; *m* 1st, 1961, Barbara Anne Wells (marr. diss. 1984); two *d*; 2nd, 1985, Daphne June Challis Loasby, OBE, JP, DL, *o d* of late W. Challis and Dorothy Franks. *Educ:* Loughborough Grammar Sch.; Nottingham Univ. BA 1956; MA 1958. Nat. Service, RA, RAEC, 1958–60. Joined HM Home Civil Service, 1960; Min. of Educn, later DES, 1960–65; Schools Council, 1965–67; Harkness Commonwealth Fund Fellow, Harvard Univ., 1967–68; CSD, 1969–79; Prime Minister's Office, 1979–83 (Chief of Staff to Sir Derek Rayner); Under Sec., 1979–83; MPO, 1982–83; Div. Dir, British Telecom plc, 1983–88. Consultant: Corp. of London, 1988–90; Metropolitan Police Comr, 1989–91; LDDC, 1990–91; NEDC, 1992–93. Chm., Review of structure of arts funding in NI for govt, 1992, of responsibilities and gradings of chief officers of nat. museums, galleries and libraries, 1994; Assessor, Review of museums policy in NI, 1995. Member: Council, Univ. of Reading, 1984–86; Develt Trust, Univ. of Nottingham, 1994–97; Council, QMW, 1995–; Philharmonia Trust, 1985–87; Univ. of Cambridge Careers Service Syndicate, 1986–90; Adv. Council, Buxton Festival, 1987–97; Arts Council, of GB, 1991–94, of England, 1994–95 and 1996–97; British Soc. of Gastroenterology, 2000–; Thiepval Proj., 2000–; Chairman: London Arts Bd, 1991–97; Trafalgar Square 2000, 1996–98; Council for Dance Educn and Trng, 1997–2000. Vice-Pres., St Bartholomew's Hosp. Med. Coll., 1993–95 (Mem. Council, 1990–95). Governor: Royal Shakespeare Co., 1984–; City Lit. Inst., 1995–96; Trinity Coll. of Music, 1997–. Wandsman, St Paul's Cathedral, 1983–97; jt planner, Millennial Service for London, St Paul's Cathedral, 1998–2000. Hon. Perpetual Student, St Bartholomew's Hosp. Medical Coll., 1995; Hon. FTCL 1996. Freeman, City of London, 1989; Liveryman, Worshipful Co. of Glaziers and Painters of Glass, 1989. *Publications:* financial scrutinies of the Royal Opera House, Covent Garden Ltd, and of the Royal Shakespeare Co., 1984. *Address:* Field House, Ham, Wilts SN8 3QR. *T:* and *Fax:* (01488) 669094. *Club:* Army and Navy.

PRIESTLEY, Rev. Canon John Christopher; Vicar of Christ Church, Colne, since 1975; Chaplain to the Queen, since 1990; *b* 23 May 1939; *s* of Ronald Edmund Priestley and Winifred Mary Priestley (*née* Hughes); *m* 1964, Margaret Ida Machan; one *s* one *d*.

Educ: William Hulme Grammar Sch.; Trinity Coll., Oxford (MA); Wells Theol Coll.; MMin Sheffield, 1993; MTh Oxon, 1998. Asst Master, St James Sch., Clitheroe, 1961–64; Dep. Headmaster, Green Sch., Padiham, 1964–70; ordained, Blackburn Cathedral, 1968; Asst Curate: All Saints, Habergham, Burnley, 1968–70; St Leonard's, Padiham, 1970–75. Convenor, Pastoral Auxiliaries, dio. Blackburn, 1987–91; Rural Dean of Pendle, 1991–96; Dir, Post Ordination Trng, dio. Blackburn, 1996–2000; Hon. Canon of Blackburn Cathedral, 2000–. *Publications:* contribs to Church Times, Church of England Newspaper. *Recreation:* music, reading, long-distance walking, ornithology, flying light aircraft (private pilot's licence). *Address:* Christ Church Vicarage, Colne, Lancs BB8 7HF. *T:* (01282) 863511.

PRIESTLEY, Julian Gordon; Secretary-General, European Parliament, since 1997; *b* 26 May 1950; *s* of Arthur David Noel Priestley and Patricia (*née* Maynard). *Educ:* St Boniface's Coll., Plymouth; Balliol Coll., Oxford (BA Hons PPE). European Parliament, 1973–: Head of Div., Secretariat of Cttee on Energy, Res. and Technology, 1983–87; Dir, Parly Cttees, 1987–89; Sec.-Gen., Socialist Gp, 1989–94; Head, Private Office of the Pres., 1994–97. *Recreations:* golf, cinema, reading. *Address:* 5 Avenue de la Sauvagine, Brussels 1170, Belgium.

PRIESTLEY, Kathleen, (Kate), (Mrs Alan Humphreys); Chief Executive, NHS Estates, Department of Health, since 1998; *b* 25 Aug. 1949; *d* of late John Fletcher Taylor and Joan Taylor (*née* Hannon); *m* 1st, 1967 (marr. diss. 1983); one *s*; 2nd, 1985, Alan Humphreys. *Educ:* Notre Dame, Manchester; Manchester Univ. (CQSW); Edinburgh Univ. (MBA). Psychiatric social worker and Sen. Social Worker, Oldham, 1972–79; Manager, Mental Health Service, Salford, 1979–84; Chief Exec., Family Care, Edinburgh, 1984–89; Asst Dir, Social Services, Newcastle upon Tyne, 1989–92; Exec. Dir, Northern RHA, 1992–94; Dir, Purchase Performance Mgt, Northern and Yorkshire Reg., NHS Exec., DoH, 1994–97. Non-exec. Dir, Scarborough Bldg Soc., 2001–. Mem. Editl Bd, Building magazine, 2000–. FRSA 1999. Hon. Fellow: Univ. of Manchester, 1993; Univ. of York, 1995; Inst. Healthcare Engrg and Estate Mgt, 2000. MInstD. *Publications:* Best Practice in Health Care Commissioning, 1995; Truth and the Child, 1998. *Recreations:* graphology, cooking and entertaining, opera. *Address:* Kitty Frisk House, Corbridge Road, Hexham, Northumberland NE46 1UN. *T:* (01434) 601533.

PRIESTLEY, Leslie William, TD 1974; FCIB; CIMgt; FCIM; Chairman: CAA Pension Scheme Trustees, since 1993; Caviapen Investments Ltd, since 1993; *b* 22 Sept. 1933; *s* of Winifred and George Priestley; *m* 1960, Audrey Elizabeth (*née* Humber); one *s* one *d*. *Educ:* Shooters Hill Grammar School. Head of Marketing, Barclaycard, 1966–73; Asst Gen. Manager, Barclays Bank, 1974–77, Local Dir, 1978–79; Sec. Gen., Cttee of London Clearing Bankers, 1979–83; Dir, Bankers' Automated Clearing Services, 1979–83; Man. Dir, Barclays Insurance Services Co., 1983–84; Regional Gen. Manager, Barclays Bank, 1984–85; Dir and Chief Exec., TSB England & Wales plc (formerly TSB England and Wales and Central Trustee Savings Bank), 1985–89; Director: TSB Gp plc, 1986–89; Hill Samuel Bank, 1988–89; Pearce Signs Gp (formerly Pearce Gp Hldgs), 1989–. Director: London Electricity plc (formerly London Electricity Board), 1984–97; Pinnacle Insurance, 1990–; Omnia/ICL, 1991–94; London Chamber of Commerce and Industry, 1993–96; Expatriate Management Ltd, 1994–99; Prudential Banking plc, 1996–; Egg plc, 2000–. Banking Advr, Touche Ross & Co., 1990–96; Financial Services Advr, ICL, 1991–97. Member: Monopolies and Mergers Commn, 1990–96; Bd, CAA, 1990–96; Guernsey Financial Services Commn, 1999–. Member of Council: Chartered Inst. of Bankers, 1988–89; Assoc. for Payment Clearing Services, 1988–89. Vis. Fellow, UCNW, 1989–95. Consultant Editor, Bankers' Magazine, 1972–81. FCIM (FInstM 1987). FRSA. *Publication:* (ed) Bank Lending with Management Accounts, 1981. *Recreations:* reading, gardening, swimming, golf. *Address:* Civil Aviation Authority Pension Scheme, 1 Kemble Street, WC2B 4AP. *Clubs:* Royal Automobile; Sundridge Park Golf; Alderney Golf.

PRIESTLEY, Prof. Maurice Bertram, MA, PhD; Professor of Statistics, University of Manchester Institute of Science and Technology, 1970–96, now Emeritus (Head of Department of Mathematics, 1973–75, 1977–78, 1980–85 and 1987–89); *b* 15 March 1933; *s* of Jack and Rose Priestley; *m* 1959, Nancy, *d* of late Ralph and Hilda Nelson; one *s* one *d*. *Educ:* Manchester Grammar Sch.; Jesus Coll., Cambridge. BA (Wrangler, 1954), MA, DipMathStat (Cambridge); PhD (Manchester). Scientific Officer, RAE, 1955–56; Asst Lectr, Univ. of Manchester, 1957–60, Lectr, 1960–65; Vis. Professor, Princeton and Stanford Univs, USA, 1961–62; Sen. Lectr, UMIST, 1965–70; Dir, Manchester-Sheffield Sch. of Probability and Stats, and Hon. Prof. of Probability and Stats, Sheffield Univ., 1976–79, 1988–89, 1991–92. Mem. Court and Council, UMIST, 1971–74 and 1989–96. FIMS; FSS; Member Council: Royal Statistical Soc., 1971–75; Manchester Statistical Soc., 1986–96; Mem., ISI. Editor-in-chief, Jl of Time Series Analysis, 1980–. *Publications:* Spectral Analysis and Time Series, Vols I and II, 1981; Non-linear and non-stationary time series analysis, 1988; papers and articles in Jl RSS, Biometrika, Technom., Automatica, Jl of Sound and Vibration. *Recreations:* music, hi-fi and audio, golf. *Address:* Department of Mathematics, University of Manchester Institute of Science and Technology, PO Box 88, Manchester M60 1QD. *T:* (0161) 236 3311.

PRIESTLEY, Philip John, CBE 1996; HM Diplomatic Service; High Commissioner to Belize, since 2001; *b* 29 Aug. 1946; *s* of late Frederick Priestley and Caroline (*née* Rolfe); *m* 1972, Christine Rainforth; one *s* one *d*. *Educ:* Boston Grammar Sch.; Univ. of East Anglia (BA Hons). FCO 1969; served Sofia and Kinshasa; First Sec., FCO, 1976; Wellington, 1979–83; FCO, 1984–87; Commercial Counsellor and Dep. Head of Mission, Manila, 1987–90; Ambassador to Gabon, 1990–91; Fellow, Center for Internat. Affairs, Harvard Univ., 1991–92; Consul-Gen., Geneva, 1992–95; Hd, N America Dept, FCO, 1996–2000. FRSA 1999. *Recreations:* golf, tennis, bridge, Rotary, theatre. *Address:* c/o Foreign and Commonwealth Office, King Charles Street, SW1A 2AH.

PRIESTLEY, Dr Robert Henry; management consultant, since 1997; *b* 19 March 1946; *s* of Henry Benjamin Priestley, MA, BSc and Margaret Alice (*née* Lambert); *m* 1970, Penelope Ann Fox, BSc; two *d*. *Educ:* Brunts Grammar Sch., Mansfield; Univ. of Southampton (BSc 1967); Univ. of Exeter (PhD 1972). FIBiol 1988. Plant Pathologist, Lord Rank Res. Centre, Rank Hovis McDougall, 1970–73; National Institute of Agricultural Botany: Cereal Pathologist, 1973–78; Head of Cereal Path. Section, 1978–82; Head of Plant Path. Dept, 1982–88; Gen. Sec., Inst. of Biol., 1989–97. Mgt consultant, HQ Strike Comd, RAF High Wycombe, 1998–. Sec., UK Cereal Pathogen Virulence Survey, 1974–82; Member: Council Fedn of British Plant Pathologists, 1980–81; Internat. Soc. for Plant Path., 1988–92; Treasurer, British Soc. for Plant Path., 1981–87; Member: British Nat. Cttee for Microbiology, 1982–89; Cttee of Management, Biol. Council, 1989–91; Bd, CSTI, 1989–97; Parly and Sci. Cttee, 1989–97; Chairman: European Communities Biol. Assoc., 1992–96; Eur. Biologist Registration Cttee, 1994–97. FIMgt 1997; FRSA 1997. *Publications:* papers on diseases of crops; popular articles; consultancy reports. *Recreations:* music, art, architecture, football. *Address:* 17 Wallingford Gardens, High Wycombe, Bucks HP11 1QS. *T:* (01494) 446660; *e-mail:* rhpriestley@hotmail.com.

PRIESTMAN, Jane, OBE 1991; FCSD; design management consultant; *b* 7 April 1930; *d* of late Reuben Stanley Herbert and Mary Elizabeth Herbert (*née* Ramply); *m* 1954, Arthur Martin Priestman (marr. diss. 1986); two *s*. *Educ:* Northwood College; Liverpool Coll. of Art (NDD, ATD). Design practice, 1954–75; Design Manager, Gen. Manager, Architecture and Design, BAA, 1975–86; Dir, Architecture and Design, BRB, 1986–91. Member: LRT Design Panel, 1985–88; Jaguar Styling Panel, 1988–91; Percentage for Art Steering Gp, Arts Council, 1989–91; Council, Design Council, 1996–99. Vis. Prof. of Internat. Design, De Montfort Univ., 1997–2001. Governor: Commonwealth Inst., 1987–99; Kingston Univ. (formerly Kingston Polytechnic), 1988–96. Hon. FRIBA; FRSA. Hon. DDes: De Montfort, 1994; Sheffield Hallam, 1998. *Recreations:* textiles, city architecture, opera, travel. *Address:* 30 Duncan Terrace, N1 8BS. *T:* (020) 7837 4525. *Club:* Architecture.

PRIESTMAN, John David; Clerk of the Parliamentary Assembly of the Council of Europe, 1971–86; *b* 29 March 1926; *s* of Bernard Priestman and Hermine Bréal; *m* 1951, Nada Valić (*d* 1999); two *s* two *d*. *Educ:* private sch. in Paris; Westminster Sch.; Merton Coll. and Christ Church, Oxford (Hon. Mods, Lit. Hum.). Served Coldstream Guards, 1944–47, Temp. Captain. Third, subseq. Second, Sec., Belgrade, 1949–53; Asst Private Sec. to Rt Hon. Anthony Eden, 1953–55; joined Secretariat, Council of Europe, 1955; Head of Sec. Gen's Private Office, 1961; Sec., Cttee of Ministers, 1966; Dep. Clerk of Parly Assembly, 1968–71. Hon. Life Mem., Assoc. of Secretaries General of Parlt, 1986. Rep. in Alpes Maritimes, French Nat. Assoc. of Prison Visitors, 1987–99. *Recreations:* off-piste Alpine ski-ing, music, competition bridge, gastronomic research. *Address:* 13 chemin de la Colle, 06160 Antibes, France. *T:* 493617724; 6 rue Adolphe Wurtz, 67000 Strasbourg, France. *T:* 388354049.

PRIGOGINE, Vicomte Ilya; Grand-Croix de l'Ordre de Léopold II, Belgium, 1977 (Commandeur, 1968); Professor, Université Libre de Bruxelles, 1951–87, now Emeritus; Director, Instituts Internationaux de Physique et de Chimie, since 1959; Director, Ilya Prigogine Center of Statistical Mechanics, Thermodynamics and Complex Systems, since 1967 and Ashbel Smith Regental Professor, since 1984, University of Texas at Austin; *b* Moscow, 25 Jan. 1917; created Viscount, 1989; *m* 1961, Marina Prokopowicz; two *s*. *Educ:* Univ. of Brussels (Lic. Sc. Physiques, 1939; Dr en Sciences Chimiques, 1941). Prof., Dept of Chemistry, Enrico Fermi Inst. for Nuclear Studies, and Inst. for Study of Metals, Univ. of Chicago, 1961–66. Associate Dir of Studies, l'Ecole des Hautes Etudes en Sciences Sociales, France, 1987; Hon. Prof., Banaras Hindu Univ., Varanasi, 1988; RGK Foundn Centennial Fellow, Univ. of Texas, 1989–90; Dist. Visitor, Inst. for Advanced Study, Princeton, 1993. Special Advr, EEC, 1993. Member: Sci. Adv. Bd, Internat. Acad. for Biomedical Drug Res., 1990; Eur. Assembly of Scis and Technols, EC, 1994. Pres., Séminaire Ilya Prigogine, Penser la Science, Univ. Libre de Bruxelles, 1997. Hon. Pres., Université Philosophique Européenne, Paris, 1985; Member: Académie Royale de Belgique, 1960; Royal Soc. of Sciences, Uppsala, Sweden, 1967; German Acad. Naturforscher Leopoldina, GDR, 1970; Acad. Internat. de Philosophie des Sciences, 1973; Acad. Européenne des Scis, des Arts et des Lettres, Paris, 1980 (Vice-Pres., 1980); Accademia Mediterranea delle Scienze, Catania, 1982; Acad. Internat. de Prospective Sociale, Geneva, 1983; Haut Conseil de la Francophonie, Paris, 1984–88; Max-Planck Foundn, Fed. Republic of Germany, 1984; World Inst. of Sci., 1992; Assoc. Descartes, 1992; Academia Scientiarium et Artium Europaea, Salzburg, 1993; MAE 1989; Hon. Member: Amer. Acad. of Arts and Sciences, 1960; Chem. Soc., Warsaw, 1971; Soc. for Studies on Entropy, Japan, 1983; Biophys. Soc., China, 1986; Royal Soc. of Chemistry, Belgium, 1987. Fellow: Acad. of Sciences, New York, 1962; World Acad. of Art and Science, 1986; Centennial Foreign Fellow, Amer. Chem. Soc., 1976; Foreign Fellow: Indian Nat. Sci. Acad., 1979; Acad. das Ciencias de Lisbôa, 1988; Foreign Associate, Nat. Acad. of Sciences, USA, 1967; Hon. Fellow, Nat. Acad. of Scis of India, 1992; Foreign Member: Akad. der Wissenschaften der DDR, Berlin, 1980; USSR Acad. of Scis, 1982; Corresponding Member: Acad. of Romania, 1965; Soc. Royale des Sciences, Liège, 1967; Section of Phys. and Math., Akad. der Wissenschaften, Göttingen, 1970; Akad. der Wissenschaften, Vienna, 1971; Rheinish-Westfählische Akad. der Wissenschaften, Düsseldorf, 1980; Archives de Psychologie, Univ. of Geneva, 1982; Accad. Nazionale di Scienze, Lettere e Arti, Modena, 1992. Dr (*hc*): Newcastle upon Tyne, Poitiers, 1966; Chicago, 1969; Bordeaux, 1972; Uppsala, Liège, 1977; Aix-Marseille, 1979; Georgetown, 1980; Rio de Janeiro, Cracow, Stevens Inst. of Technology, Hoboken, 1981; Heriot-Watt, Universidad Nacional de Educación a Distancia, Madrid, 1985; Tours, France, Nanking, Peking, 1986; Buenos Aires, 1989; Facolta di Magistero, Cagliari Univ., Univ. of Siena, 1990; Nice, France, Philippines, Santiago, Tucumán, Argentina, 1991; Moscow Lomonosov, 1993; 'Al.I. Cuza' Iaşi, Romania, San Luis and Palermo Univs, Argentina, Institut Nat. Polytechnique de Lorraine, 1994; Vrije Univ. Brussel, SUNY, Valladolid, St Petersburg and Kerala Univs, 1995; Salvador Univ., Buenos Aires, Xanthi Univ., Greece, 1996; Univ. Nacional Autónoma, Mexico, Wroclaw Univ. of Technol., 1998. Prizes: Van Laar, Société Chimique de Belgique, 1947; A. Wetrems 1950, and Annual (jtly) 1952, Acad. Royale de Belgique; Francqui, 1955; E. J. Solvay, 1965; Nobel Prize for Chemistry, 1977; Southwest Science Forum, New York Acad. of Science, 1976; Honda, Honda Foundn, Tokyo, 1983; Umberto Biancamano, Pavia, Italy, 1987; (jtly) Gravity Res. Foundn Award, 1988. Gold Medals: Swante Arrhenius, Royal Acad. of Sciences, Sweden, 1969; Cothenius, German Acad. Naturforscher Leopoldina, 1975; Rumford, Royal Soc., 1976; Bourke Medal, Chem. Soc., 1972; Medal, Assoc. for the Advancement of Sciences, Paris, 1975; Karcher Medal, Amer. Crystallographic Assoc., 1978; Descartes Medal, Univ. Descartes, Paris, 1979; Médaille d'Or de la Ville de Pavie, 1987; Médaille d'Or de la Ville d'Ostende, 1987; Médaille d'Or de l'Université de Padoue, 1988; Distinguished Service Medal, Austin, Texas, 1989. Hon. Citizen: Dallas, USA, 1983; Montpellier, France, 1983; Uccle, Belgium, 1984. Commandeur, l'Ordre du Mérite, France, 1977; Commandeur, l'Ordre des Arts et des Lettres, France, 1984; Commandeur de la Légion d'Honneur, France, 1989; Order of the Rising Sun, Japan, 1990. *Publications:* (with R. Defay) Traité de Thermodynamique, conformément aux méthodes de Gibbs et de Donder: Vol. I, Thermodynamique Chimique, 1944 (Eng. trans. 1954); Vol. II, Tension Superficielle et Adsorption, 1951 (Eng. trans. 1965); Etude Thermodynamique des Phénomènes Irreversibles, 1947; Introduction to Thermodynamics of Irreversible Processes, 1954 (3rd edn 1967); (with A. Bellemans and V. Mathot) The Molecular Theory of Solutions, 1957; Non. Equilibrium Statistical Mechanics, 1962; (with R. Herman) Kinetic Theory of Vehicular Traffic, 1971; (with P. Glansdorff) Thermodynamic Theory of Structure, Stability and Fluctuations, 1971 (also French edn); (with G. Nicolis) Self-Organization in Non Equilibrium Systems, 1977; (with I. Stengers) La Nouvelle Alliance: les métamorphoses de la science, 1979 (Prix du Haut Comité de la langue française, Paris, 1981) (also English, German, Italian, Yugoslavian, Spanish, Rumanian, Swedish, Dutch, Danish, Portuguese, Russian, Japanese, Chinese, Bulgarian, Korean, Polish, Turkish, Greek and Hungarian edns); From Being to Becoming: time and complexity in the physical sciences, 1980 (also French, German, Japanese, Russian, Italian, Chinese, Rumanian and Portuguese edns); (with I. Stengers) Entre le temps et l'éternité, 1988 (also Dutch, Italian, Portuguese and Spanish edns); (with G. Nicolis) Exploring Complexity, 1989 (also German, Chinese, Russian, Italian, French, Spanish and Japanese edns); (with I. Stengers) Das Paradox der Zeit, 1993; Les Lois du Chaos, 1994; La Fin des Certitudes, 1996 (also Spanish, Portuguese, Dutch, English, Italian, Korean, Japanese and Greek edns); (with Dilip Kondepudi) Modern Thermodynamics: from heat engines to dissipative structures, 1998 (also French edn). *Recreations:* art, music. *Address:* avenue Fond'Roy 67, 1180 Bruxelles, Belgium. *T:* (2)3742952.

PRIMAROLO, Dawn; MP (Lab) Bristol South, since 1987; HM Paymaster General, since 1999; *b* 2 May 1954; *m* 1972 (marr. diss.); one *s*; *m* 1990, Thomas Ian Ducat. *Educ:* Thomas Bennett Comprehensive Sch., Crawley; Bristol Poly.; Bristol Univ. Mem., Avon CC, 1985–87. Opposition front bench spokesman on health, 1992–94, on Treasury affairs, 1994–97; Financial Sec., HM Treasury, 1997–99. Mem., Select Cttee on Members' Interests, 1988–92. *Address:* House of Commons, SW1A 0AA; (office) PO Box 1002, Bristol BS99 1WH. *T:* (0117) 909 0063.

PRIMROSE, family name of **Earl of Rosebery**.

PRIMROSE, Sir John Ure, 5th Bt *cr* 1903, of Redholme, Dumbreck, Govan; *b* 28 May 1960; *s* of Sir Alasdair Neil Primrose, 4th Bt and of Elaine Noreen, *d* of Edmund Cecil Lowndes, Buenos Aires; *S* father, 1986; *m* 1983, Marion Cecilia (marr. diss. 1987), *d* of Hans Otto Altgelt; two *d*. *Heir: b* Andrew Richard Primrose; *b* 19 Jan. 1966. *Educ:* St Peter's School and Military Acad. BA.

PRIMUS, The; *see* Cameron, Most Rev. A. B., Bishop of Aberdeen and Orkney.

PRINCE, David; Director of Operations, Audit Commission for Local Authorities and NHS in England and Wales, since 2000; *b* 31 May 1948; *s* of late Charles and Phyllis Grace Prince; *m* 1973, Davina Ann Pugh. *Educ:* Exeter Univ. (BA Hons English). CPFA. Hants CC Grad. Trainee, 1969–71; finance posts, Berks CC, 1971–76; Chief Accountant, Cambs CC, 1976–81, and Asst Co. Treasurer; Dep. Co. Treasurer, Herts CC, 1981–86; Dir, Finance and Admin, Cambs CC, 1986–91; Chief Exec., Leics CC, 1991–94; Chief Exec., Dist Audit Service, then Dist Audit, Audit Commn, 1994–2000. FRSA. *Recreations:* theatre, music, gardening. *Address:* Audit Commission, 1 Vincent Square, SW1P 2PN. *T:* (020) 7396 1328, *Fax:* (020) 7396 1302; *e-mail:* d_prince@audit_commission. gov.uk.

PRINCE, Prof. Frank Templeton, MA (Oxon); *b* Kimberley, South Africa, 13 Sept. 1912; 2nd *s* of late H. Prince and Margaret Templeton (*née* Hetherington); *m* 1943, Pauline Elizabeth, *d* of late H. F. Bush; two *d*. *Educ:* Christian Brothers' Coll., Kimberley, South Africa; Balliol Coll., Oxford. Visiting Fellow, Graduate Coll., Princeton, NJ, 1935–36. Study Groups Department, Chatham House, 1937–40. Served Army, Intelligence Corps, 1940–46. Department of English, 1946–57, Prof. of English, 1957–74, Southampton Univ.; Prof. of English, Univ. of WI, Jamaica, 1975–78. Hurst Vis. Prof., Brandeis Univ., 1978–80; Vis. Prof., Washington Univ., St Louis, 1980–81, Sana'a Univ., N Yemen, 1981–83; Visiting Fellow, All Souls Coll., 1968–69. Clark Lectr, Cambridge, 1972–73. Pres., English Assoc., 1985–86. Hon. DLitt Southampton, 1981; DUniv York, 1982. *Publications:* Poems, 1938; Soldiers Bathing (poems), 1954; The Italian Element in Milton's Verse, 1954; The Doors of Stone (poems), 1963; Memoirs in Oxford (verse), 1970; Drypoints of the Hasidim (verse), 1975; Collected Poems, 1979; Later On (poems), 1983; Walks in Rome (verse), 1987; Collected Poems, 1993. *Recreations:* music, etc. *Address:* 32 Brookvale Road, Southampton SO17 1QR. *T:* (023) 8055 5457.

PRINCE, Harold; theatrical director/producer; *b* NYC, 30 Jan. 1928; *s* of Milton A. Prince and Blanche (*née* Stern); *m* 1962, Judith Chaplin; two *d*. *Educ:* Univ. of Pennsylvania (AB 1948). Co-Producer: The Pajama Game, 1954–56 (co-prod film, 1957); Damn Yankees, 1955–57 (co-prod film, 1958); New Girl in Town, 1957–58; West Side Story, 1957–59; Fiorello!, 1959–61 (Pulitzer Prize); Tenderloin, 1960–61; A Call on Kuprin, 1961; They Might Be Giants, London 1961; Side By Side By Sondheim, 1977–78. Producer: Take Her She's Mine, 1961–62; A Funny Thing Happened on the Way to the Forum, 1962–64; Fiddler on the Roof, 1964–72; Poor Bitos, 1964; Flora the Red Menace, 1965. Director-Producer: She Loves Me, 1963–64, London 1964; Superman, 1966; Cabaret, 1966–69, London 1968, tour and NY, 1987; Zorba, 1968–69; Company, 1970–72, London 1972; A Little Night Music, 1973–74, London 1975 (dir. film, 1977); Pacific Overtures, 1976. Director: A Family Affair, 1962; Baker Street, 1965; Something For Everyone (film), 1970; New Phoenix Rep. prodns of Great God Brown, 1972–73, The Visit, 1973–74, and Love for Love, 1974–75; Some of my Best Friends, 1977; On the Twentieth Century, 1978; Evita, London 1978, USA 1979–83, Australia, Vienna, 1980, Mexico City, 1981; Sweeney Todd, 1979, London 1980; Girl of the Golden West, San Francisco Op., 1979; world première, Willie Stark, Houston Grand Opera, 1981; Merrily We Roll Along (musical) 1981; A Doll's Life (musical), 1982; Madama Butterfly, Chicago Lyric Op., 1982; Turandot, Vienna State Op., 1983; Play Memory, 1984; End of the World, 1984; Diamonds, 1985; The Phantom of the Opera, London, 1986, NY, 1988, Los Angeles, 1989, Canada, 1989; Roza, USA, 1987; Cabaret (20th anniversary revival), tour and Broadway, 1987; Kiss of the Spider Woman, 1990, Toronto, London, Broadway, 1993; (also adapted) Grandchild of Kings, 1992; Showboat, Toronto, 1993, NY, 1994; Parade (musical), NY, 1999; 3HREE, Philadelphia and LA. Directed for NY City Opera: Ashmedai, 1976; Kurt Weill's Silverlake, 1980; Candide, 1982, 1997; Don Giovanni, 1989; Faust, Metropolitan Opera, 1990; co-Director-Producer, Follies, 1971–72; co-Producer-Director: Candide, 1974–75; Merrily We Roll Along, 1981; A Doll's Life, 1982; Grind (musical), 1985. Antoinette Perry Awards for: The Pajama Game; Damn Yankees; Fiorello!; A Funny Thing Happened on the Way to the Forum; Fiddler on the Roof; Cabaret; Company; A Little Night Music; Candide; Sweeney Todd; Evita; The Phantom of the Opera; Show Boat, etc (total of 20); SWET award: Evita, 1977–78. Member: League of New York Theatres (Pres., 1964–65); Council for National Endowment for the Arts. Hon. DLit, Emerson College, 1971; Hon. Dr of Fine Arts, Univ. of Pennsylvania, 1971. Drama Critics' Circle Awards; Best Musical Award, London Evening Standard, 1955–58, 1972 and 1992. Kennedy Center Honoree, 1994. *Publication:* Contradictions: notes on twenty-six years in the theatre, 1974. *Recreation:* tennis. *Address:* Suite 1009, 10 Rockefeller Plaza, New York, NY 10020, USA. *T:* (212) 3990960.

PRINCE, Maj.-Gen. Hugh Anthony, CBE 1960; retired as Chief, Military Planning Office, SEATO, Bangkok; *b* 11 Aug. 1911; *s* of H. T. Prince, FRCS, LRCP; *m* 1st, 1938, Elizabeth (*d* 1959), *d* of Dr Walter Bapty, Victoria, BC; two *s*; 2nd, 1959, Claude-Andrée, *d* of André Romanet, Château-de-Tholot, Beaujeu, Rhône; one *s*. *Educ:* Eastbourne Coll.; RMC, Sandhurst. Commissioned, 1931; served in 6th Gurkha Rifles until 1947; The King's Regt (Liverpool), 1947. *Recreations:* golf, gardening, antiques. *Address:* 36 Route de la Crau, 13280 Raphèle-les-Arles, France. *T:* 490984693.

PRINCE-SMITH, Sir (William) Richard, 4th Bt *cr* 1911; *b* 27 Dec. 1928; *s* of Sir William Prince-Smith, 3rd Bt, OBE, MC, and Marjorie, Lady Prince-Smith (*d* 1970); *S* father, 1964; *m* 1st, 1955, Margaret Ann Carter; one *d* (one *s* decd); 2nd, 1975, Ann Christina Faulds. *Educ:* Charterhouse; Clare Coll., Cambridge (MA). BA (Agric.) 1951. *Recreations:* music, photography, travel. *Heir:* none. *Address:* 40–735 Paxton Drive, Rancho Mirage, CA 92270–3516, USA. *T:* (760) 3211975. *Club:* Springs Country (Rancho Mirage).

PRINDL, Dr Andreas Robert, Hon. CBE 2001; Chairman, CapCLEAR Ltd, since 2000; *b* 25 Nov. 1939; *s* of Frank Joseph Prindl and Vivian Prindl (*née* Mitchell); *m* 1963, Veronica Maria Koerber; one *s* one *d*. *Educ:* Princeton Univ. (BA); Univ. of Kentucky (MA, PhD). Morgan Guaranty Trust Company: NY and Frankfurt, 1964–70; Vice-Pres., IMM, London, 1970–76; Gen. Manager, Tokyo, 1976–80; CEO Saudi Internat. Bank, London, 1980–82; Vice-Pres., Mergers and Acquisitions, Morgan Guaranty, 1982–84; Man. Dir, Nomura Internat., 1984–86; Man. Dir, 1986–90, Chm., 1990–97, Nomura Bank Internat. Chm., Banking Industry Trng and Develt Council, 1994–96; Provost, Gresham Coll., 1996–99. President: Chartered Inst. of Bankers, 1994–95; Assoc. of Corporate Treasurers, 1996. Vis. Prof., People's Univ. of China, Beijing, 2000–. Freeman, City of London, 1999; Liveryman: Musicians' Co., 1999–; World Traders' Co., 2000–. Hon. Treas., C&G, 1998. Hon. Fellow, Acad. of Moral Sci., Beijing, 1998. Hon. DSc City, 1996. *Publications:* (jtly) International Money Management, 1972; Foreign Exchange Risk, 1976; Japanese Finance, 1981; Money in the Far East, 1986; (ed) Banking and Finance in Eastern Europe, 1992; (ed jtly) Ethical Conflicts in Finance, 1994; The First XV, 1995; A Companion to Lucca, 2000. *Recreation:* classical music (member, Brighton Festival Chorus). *Address:* Wings Place, Ditchling, Sussex BN6 8TS. *Club:* Reform.

PRING, Prof. Richard Anthony; Professor and Director of Department of Educational Studies, University of Oxford, since 1989; Fellow of Green College, Oxford, since 1989; *b* 20 April 1938; *s* of Joseph Edwin and Anne-Marie Pring; *m* 1970, Helen Faye Evans; three *d*. *Educ:* Gregorian Univ. and English College, Rome (PhL); University Coll. London (BA Hons Philosophy); Univ. of London Inst. of Education (PhD); College of St Mark and St John (PGCE). Asst Principal, Dept of Educn and Science, 1962–64; teacher in London comprehensive schools, 1965–67, 1973–78; Lectr in Education: Goldsmiths' Coll., 1967–70; Univ. of London Inst. of Educn, 1972–78; Prof. of Educn, Univ. of Exeter, 1978–89. Hon. DLitt Kent, 1995. Editor, British Jl of Educational Studies, 1986–. Bene Merenti Medal (Pius XII), 1958. *Publications:* Knowledge and Schooling, 1976; Personal and Social Education, 1984; The New Curriculum, 1989; Closing the Gap: liberal education and vocational preparation, 1995; (ed with Geoffrey Walford) Affirming the Comprehensive Ideal, 1997; Philosophy of Educational Research, 2000. *Recreations:* running marathons, cycling, writing, campaigning for comprehensive schools. *Address:* Department of Educational Studies, 15 Norham Gardens, Oxford OX2 6PY; Green College, Oxford, OX2 6HG.

PRING-MILL, Robert Duguid Forrest, DLitt; FBA 1988; Fellow of St Catherine's College, Oxford, since 1965; *b* 11 Sept. 1924; *o s* of late Major Richard Pring-Mill, RA and Nellie (*née* Duguid); *m* 1950, Maria Brigitte Heinsheimer; one *s* one *d*. *Educ:* Colegio de Montesión, Palma de Mallorca; New Coll., Oxford (BA 1st cl. Mod. Langs, 1949; DLitt 1986). Enlisted, 1941; commnd The Black Watch, RHR, 1942; temp. Capt., 1945; despatches, 1947. Oxford University: Sen. Demy, Magdalen Coll., 1950–52; Univ. Lectr in Spanish, 1952–88; Lectr, New Coll., 1956–88, Exeter Coll., 1963–81; Tutor, St Catherine's Coll., 1965–88. English Editor: Romanistisches Jahrbuch, 1953–; Estudios Lulianos, 1957–; Commissió Editora Lul·liana, 1960–. Magister, Maioricensis Schola Lullistica, 1957; Corresp. Mem., Inst. d'Estudis Catalans, 1966. Pres., Asociación Internacional de Nerudistas, 1995–. Premi Pompeu Fabra, 1956; Premi Ciutat de Palma, 1979; Premi Catalònia, 1991. Cross of St George (Generalitat de Catalunya), 1990; Commander, Order of Isabel la Católica (Spain), 1990; Officer, Order of Bernardo O'Higgins (Chile), 1992. *Publications:* Chinese Triad Societies, 1946; (ed) Lope de Vega: Five Plays, 1961; El Microcosmos Lul·lià, 1961; Ramón Llull y el Número Primitivo de las Dignidades, 1963; (with N. Tarn) The Heights of Macchu Picchu, 1966; (with Katya Kohn) Neruda Poems, 1969; (ed) Raymundus Lullus, Quattuor Libri Principiorum, 1969; Neruda: A Basic Anthology, 1975; Cardenal: Marilyn Monroe & Other Poems, 1975; The Scope of Spanish-American Committed Poetry, 1977; (with Donald Walsh) Cardenal: Apocalypse and Other Poems, 1977; Spanish American Committed Poetry: canciones de lucha y esperanza, 1978; (ed jtly) Studies in Honour of P. E. Russell, 1981; (ed jtly) Hacia Calderón, 1982; Cantas-Canto-Cantemos, 1983; Gracias a la vida: the power and poetry of song, 1990; Estudis sobre Ramón Llull, 1991 (Premi Crítica Serra d'Or, 1992); A Poet for all Seasons, 1993; Der Mikrokosmos Ramón Llulls: eine Einführung in das mittelalterliche Weltbild, 2000; Calderón: estructura y ejemplaridad, 2001; articles in learned jls, Encyc. Britannica, etc, on Ramón Llull, Calderón, modern poetry and Spanish-American protest song. *Recreations:* travel and photography in Latin America. *Address:* 11 North Hills, Brill, Bucks HP18 9TH. *T:* (01844) 237481.

PRINGLE, Maj. Gen. Andrew Robert Douglas, CB 2000; CBE 1992 (MBE 1980); Chief of Staff, Permanent Joint Headquarters, 1998–2001; *b* 9 Oct. 1946; *s* of Douglas Alexander Pringle and Wendy Pringle (*née* Gordon); *m* 1975, Jane Carolyn Mitchison; one *s* two *d*. *Educ:* Wellington Coll.; RMA, Sandhurst; RMCS, Shrivenham (BSc Hons). Commnd RGJ, 1967: served in UK, Cyprus, NI, Germany, 1967–77; Staff Coll., Camberley, 1977–78; Staff and Regtl appts, NI, 1979–82; Directing Staff, Staff Coll., Camberley, 1983–85; CO, 3rd Bn, RGJ, 1985–88; MoD, 1988–91; Higher Comd and Staff Course, 1990; rcds, 1991; Cabinet Office, 1992–94; Commander: 20 Armoured Bde, 1994–96; UN Sector SW, Bosnia , 1995; Dir, Land Warfare, 1996–97; Comdr, Multi-Nat. Div. (SW), Bosnia, 1997–98. Regtl (formerly Rep.) Col Comdt, Royal Green Jackets, 1999–; Col Comdt, 2nd Bn Royal Green Jackets, 1999–. QCVS 1996 and 1998. *Recreations:* reading, ski-ing, Cresta Run, a little light farming. *Clubs:* Army and Navy; St Moritz Tobogganing.

PRINGLE, Anne Fyfe; HM Diplomatic service; Ambassador to the Czech Republic, since 2001; *b* 13 Jan. 1955; *d* of George Grant Pringle and Margaret Fyfe Pringle (*née* Cameron); *m* 1987, Bleddyn Glynne Leyshon Phillips. *Educ:* Glasgow High Sch. for Girls; St Andrews Univ. (MA Hons French and German). Joined FCO, 1977: Third Sec., Moscow, 1980-82; Vice Consul, San Francisco, 1983-85; Second Sec., UK Rep., Brussels, 1986-87; FCO, 1988–91; First Sec., Eur. Political Co-operation Secretariat, Brussels, 1991–93; Dep. Hd, Security Co-ordination Dept, then African Dept (Equatorial), FCO, 1994–96; Head, Common Foreign and Security Policy Dept, FCO, 1996–98 and European Correspondent; Head, Eastern Dept, FCO, 1998–2001. FRSA 2001. *Recreations:* sport, gardening, walking. *Address:* c/o Foreign and Commonwealth Office, King Charles Street, SW1A 2AH. *T:* (020) 7270 2131.

PRINGLE, Air Marshal Sir Charles (Norman Seton), KBE 1973 (CBE 1967); MA; FREng; *b* 6 June 1919; *s* of late Seton Pringle, OBE, FRCSI, Dublin; *m* 1946, Margaret, *d* of late B. Sharp, Baildon, Yorkshire; one *s*. *Educ:* Repton; St John's Coll., Cambridge. Commissioned, RAF, 1941; served India and Ceylon, 1942–46. Air Ministry, 1946–48; RAE, Farnborough, 1949–50; attached to USAF, 1950–52; appts in UK, 1952–60; STSO No 3 Group, Bomber Comd, 1960–62, and Air Forces Middle East, 1962–64; Comdt RAF St Athan and Air Officer Wales, 1964–66; MoD, 1967; IDC, 1968. Dir-Gen. of Engineering (RAF) MoD, 1969–70; Air Officer Engineering, Strike Command, 1970–73; Dir-Gen. Engineering (RAF), 1973; Controller, Engrg and Supply (RAF), 1973–76; Sen. Exec., Rolls Royce Ltd, 1976–78; Dir, Hunting Engineering Ltd, 1976–78; Dir and Chief Exec., SBAC, 1979–84. Director: FR Group plc, 1985–89; Aeronautical Trusts Ltd, 1987–97. President: RAeS, 1975–76; IMGTechE, 1979–82; Vice-Chm., 1976–77, Chm.,

1977–78, CEI. Mem., Defence Industries Council, 1978–84. Member Council: Air League, 1976–92; CBI, 1979–84; RSA, 1978–83 and 1986–92. Chm. Governors, Repton Sch., 1985–92. Liveryman, Coachmakers' and Coach Harness Makers' Co. FREng (FEng 1977). Hon. FRAeS 1989. CIMgt. *Recreations:* photography, ornithology, motor sport. *Address:* Appleyards, Fordingbridge, Hants SP6 3BP; K9 Sloane Avenue Mansions, SW3 3JP. *T:* (020) 7584 3432. *Club:* Royal Air Force.

PRINGLE, Derek Raymond; Cricket Correspondent, The Independent, since 1995; *b* Nairobi, 18 Sept. 1958; *s* of late Donald James Pringle and of Doris May Pringle (*née* Newton). *Educ:* St Mary's Sch., Nairobi; Felsted Sch., Essex; Fitzwilliam Coll., Cambridge (MA). Professional cricketer, Essex and England, 1978–93; Cricket Corresp., Independent on Sunday, 1993–95. *Recreations:* photography, music, conchology. *Address:* c/o The Independent, 191 Marsh Wall, E14 9RC. *T:* (020) 7005 2000.

PRINGLE, Sir John (Kenneth), Kt 1993; Justice of the High Court of Northern Ireland, 1993–99; *b* 23 June 1929; *s* of late Kenneth Pringle and Katie (*née* Batchen); *m* 1960, Ruth Henry; two *s* one *d.* *Educ:* Campbell Coll., Belfast; Queen's Univ., Belfast (BSc 1st Cl. Hons 1950; LLB 1st Cl. Hons 1953). Called to the Bar, NI, 1953, Bencher, 1973; QC (NI), 1970; Recorder of Belfast, 1984–93. Chm., Bar Council of NI, 1975–80. *Recreations:* gardening, being outdoors.

PRINGLE, Margaret Ann; Associate Director, Centre for the Study of Comprehensive Schools, since 1995; *b* 28 Sept. 1946. *Educ:* Holton Park Girls' Grammar Sch.; Somerville College, Oxford (MA, BLitt English Lang. and Lit.). English Teacher, Selhurst High School, Croydon, 1972–76; Head of English, Thomas Calton School, Peckham, 1976–81; Dep. Head, George Green's School, Isle of Dogs, 1981–86; Head, Holland Park Sch., 1986–95. *Recreations:* all food, all music, most dancing, and occasionally not thinking about education. *Address:* Flat 3, 64 Pembridge Villas, W11 3ET.

PRINGLE, Prof. Michael Alexander Leary, CBE 2001; FRCP, FRCGP; Professor of General Practice, University of Nottingham, since 1993; *b* 14 May 1950; *s* of Alexander and Yvonne Pringle; *m* 1974, Nicola Mary Wood; three *d.* *Educ:* St Edward's Sch., Oxford; Guy's Hosp. Med. Sch. (MB BS 1973). FRCGP 1989; FRCP 2000. Vocational Trng Scheme for Gen. Practice, Reading, 1975-78. Principal in gen. practice, Collingham, Notts, 1979-; Lectr and Sen. Lectr, Dept of Gen. Practice, Univ. of Nottingham, 1983-93. Chm. Council, RCGP, 1998-2001. Co-Chm., Expert Ref. Gp for Diabetes Nat. Service Framework, 1999-2001. FMedSci 1999. *Publications:* (jtly) Managing Change in Primary Care, 1991; (ed) Change and Teamwork in Primary Care, 1993; (ed) Fellowship by Assessment, 1995; (jtly) A Guide for New Principals, 1996; (ed) Primary Care: core values, 1998; contrib. numerous chapters in books, res. articles and editorials in jls. *Recreations:* chess, reading, Italy, walking. *Address:* Slacks Farmhouse, Low Street, Besthorpe, Newark, Notts NG23 7HJ. *T:* (01636) 892298; *e-mail:* mike.pringle@nottingham.ac.uk.

PRINGLE, Lt Gen. Sir Steuart (Robert), 10th Bt *cr* 1683, of Stichill, Roxburghshire; KCB 1982; Commandant General Royal Marines 1981–84; Chairman and Chief Executive, Chatham Historic Dockyard Trust, 1984–91; *b* 21 July 1928; *s* of Sir Norman H. Pringle, 9th Bt and Lady (Oonagh) Pringle (*née* Curran) (*d* 1975); *S* father, 1961; *m* 1953, Jacqueline Marie Gladwell; two *s* two *d.* *Educ:* Sherborne. Royal Marines: 2nd Lieut, 1946; 42 Commando, 1950–52; 40 Commando, 1957–59; Chief Instructor, Signal Trng Wing, RM, 1959–61; Bde Signal Officer, 3 Commando Bde, RM, 1961–63; Defence Planning Staff, 1964–67; Chief Signal Officer, RM, 1967–69; 40 Commando, Far East, 1969–71; CO 45 Commando Group, 1971–74; HQ Commando Forces, 1974–76; RCDS, 1977; Maj.-Gen. RM Commando Forces, 1978–79; Chief of Staff to Comdt Gen., RM, 1979–81. Col Comdt, RM, 1989–90, Representative Col Comdt, 1991–92. President: St Loye's Coll., 1984–2000; City of London Br., RM Assoc., 1984–; Vice-Pres., Officers Pensions Soc., 1984–99; Mem. Council, Union Jack Club, 1982–85; Vice-Patron, Royal Naval Benevolent Trust, 1984–. CIMgt. Liveryman, Plaisterers' Co., 1984. Hon. DSc City, 1982; Hon. LLD Exeter, 1994. Hon. Admiral, Texas Navy; Hon. Mem., Co. of Bear Tamers. *Publications:* (contrib) Peace and the Bomb, 1982; The Future of British Seapower, 1984; contribs to RUSI Jl, Navy International, etc. *Heir: s* Simon Robert Pringle [*b* 6 Jan. 1959; *m* 1992, Pamela Margaret, *d* of George Hunter; one *d*]. *Address:* 76 South Croxted Road, Dulwich, SE21 8BD. *Clubs:* Army and Navy; Royal Thames Yacht, MCC.

PRIOR, family name of **Baron Prior**.

PRIOR, Baron *cr* 1987 (Life Peer), of Brampton in the County of Suffolk; **James Michael Leathes Prior;** PC 1970; Chairman, The General Electric Company plc, 1984–98; *b* 11 Oct. 1927; 2nd *s* of late C. B. L. and A. S. M. Prior, Norwich; *m* 1954, Jane Primrose Gifford, 2nd *d* of late Air Vice-Marshal O. G. Lywood, CB, CBE; three *s* one *d.* *Educ:* Charterhouse; Pembroke College, Cambridge (1st class degree in Estate Management, 1950; Hon. Fellow, 1992). Commissioned in Royal Norfolk Regt, 1946; served in India and Germany; farmer and land agent in Norfolk and Suffolk. MP (C): Lowestoft, Suffolk, 1959–83; Waveney, 1983–87. PPS to Pres. of Bd of Trade, 1963, to Minister of Power, 1963–64, to Mr Edward Heath, Leader of the Opposition, 1965–70; Minister of Agriculture, Fisheries and Food, 1970–72; Lord Pres. of Council and Leader of House of Commons, 1972–74; Opposition front bench spokesman on Employment, 1974–79; Sec. of State for Employment, 1979–81; Sec. of State for NI, 1981–84. A Dep. Chm., Cons. Party, 1972–74 (Vice-Chm., 1965). Chairman: Allders, 1989–94; East Anglian Radio PLC, 1992–96; African Cargo Handling Ltd, 1998–; Ispat Energy Hldgs Ltd, 1998–2000; Dep. Chm., MSI Cellular Investments BV, 2000–; Director: United Biscuits (Holdings), 1984–94; Barclays Bank, 1984–89; Barclays International, 1984–89; J. Sainsbury, 1984–92; Member: Tenneco European Adv. Bd, 1986–97; Internat. Adv. Bd, Amer. Internat. Gp, 1988–. Chancellor, Anglia Poly. Univ., 1992–99 (Hon. PhD 1992). Chairman: Council for Industry and Higher Educn, 1986–91; Archibishops' Commn on Rural Areas, 1988–91; Great Ormond Street Wishing Well Appeal, 1985–89; Special Trustees, Great Ormond Street, 1989–94; Industry and Parliament Trust, 1990–94; Rural Housing Trust, 1990–99; Royal Veterinary Coll., 1990–99; Arab-British Chamber of Commerce, 1996. *Publications:* (jtly) The Right Approach to the Economy, 1977; A Balance of Power, 1986. *Recreations:* cricket, tennis, golf, gardening. *Address:* House of Lords, SW1A 0PW. *Clubs:* Garrick, MCC; Butterflies Cricket.
See also Hon. D. G. L. Prior.

PRIOR, Anthony Basil, FRICS; Consultant Valuer, Institute of Revenues Rating & Valuation, since 2001; *b* 23 March 1941; *s* of Rev. Christopher Prior and May Prior (*née* Theobald); *m* 1967, Susan Margaret Parry; two *s.* *Educ:* Commonweal Grammar Sch., Swindon. FRICS 1977; IRRV 1988. Joined Valuation Office, 1967: Dist Valuer, Southampton, 1979–84; Superintending Valuer, Chief Valuer's Office, 1984–91; Regl Dir, Western Reg., later London Reg., 1991–98; Dir, Professional and Customer Services, and Mem., Mgt Bd, Valuation Office Agency, 1999–2001. Member: Rating Valuers' Assoc., 1984; Council, IRRV, 1988–. *Publication:* (jtly) Encyclopedia on Contractors Basis of Valuation, 1990. *Recreations:* bee-keeping, fly fishing, Greek and Roman history. *Address:* c/o Institute of Revenues Rating & Valuation, 41 Doughty Street, WC1N 2LF.

PRIOR, Ven. Christopher, CB 1968; Archdeacon of Portsmouth, 1969–77, Archdeacon Emeritus since 1977; *b* 2 July 1912; *s* of late Ven. W. H. Prior; *m* 1945, Althea Stafford (*née* Coode) (*d* 1999); two *d.* *Educ:* King's Coll., Taunton; Keble Coll., Oxford; Cuddesdon Coll. Curate of Hornsea, 1938–41; Chaplain RN from 1941, Chaplain of the Fleet, 1966–69. Served in: HMS Royal Arthur, 1941; HMHS Maine, 1941–43; HMS Scylla, 1943–44; HMS Owl, 1944–46; various ships, 1946–58; Britannia RNC, Dartmouth, 1958–61; HMS Blake, 1961–62; HM Dockyard, Portsmouth, 1963–66; QHC, 1966–69. *Recreation:* walking. *Address:* Ponies End, West Melbury, Shaftesbury, Dorset SP7 0LY. *T:* (01747) 811239.

PRIOR, Hon. David (Gifford Leathes); Deputy Chairman and Chief Executive, Conservative Party, 1999–2001 (Vice Chairman, 1998–99); *b* 3 Dec. 1954; *s* of Lord Prior, *qv*; *m* 1987, Caroline Henrietta Holmes; twin *s* and *d.* *Educ:* Charterhouse; Pembroke Coll., Cambridge (Exhibnr; MA Law 1976). Called to the Bar, Gray's Inn, 1977; Commercial Dir, British Steel, 1980–87; Chm., various private manufg cos. MP (C) N Norfolk, 1997–2001; contested (C) same seat, 2001. *Recreations:* gardening, farming, most sports. *Address:* Swannington Manor, Swannington, Norwich NR9 5NR. *T:* (01603) 861560. *Club:* Royal Automobile.

PRIOR, Peter James, CBE 1980; DL; Chairman, H. P. Bulmer Holdings PLC, 1977–82 (Director, 1977–85; Managing Director, H. P. Bulmer Ltd, 1966–77); *b* 1 Sept. 1919; *s* of Percy Prior; *m* 1957, Prinia Mary (*d* 2001), *d* of late R. E. Moreau, Berrick Prior, Oxon; two *s.* *Educ:* Royal Grammar Sch., High Wycombe; London Univ. BSc(Econ). FCA, FIMC, FIMgt, FRSA. Royal Berks Regt, 1939; Intell. Corps, 1944–46 (Captain) (Croix-de-Guerre 1944). Company Sec., Saunders-Roe (Anglesey) Ltd, 1948; Consultant, Urwick, Orr & Partners, 1951; Financial Dir, International Chemical Co., 1956; Financial Dir, British Aluminium Co., 1961; Dep. Chm., Holden Hydroman, 1984–88; Dir, Trebor, 1982–86. Member: English Tourist Bd, 1969–75; Midlands Electricity Bd, 1973–83; Chairman: Inquiry into Potato Processing Industry, 1971; Motorway Service Area Inquiry, 1977–78; Home Office Deptl Inquiry into Prison Discipline, 1984–85. Pres., Incorp. Soc. of British Advertisers' Council, 1980–83; Mem. Council, BIM, 1974–82. Chm. Trustees, Leadership Trust, 1975–79; Member: Council, Regular Forces Employment Assoc., 1981–86; Council, Operation Raleigh, 1984–89. DL Hereford and Worcester, 1983. Communicator of the Year Award, British Assoc. of Industrial Editors, 1982. *Publications:* Leadership is not a Bowler Hat, 1977; articles on management and leadership. *Recreations:* flying, motor-cycling, swimming, mountain walking, formerly parachuting (UK record for longest delayed drop (civilian), 1981). *Address:* Highland, Holbach Lane, Sutton St Nicholas, Hereford HR1 3DF. *T:* (01568) 797222. *Clubs:* Army and Navy, Special Forces.

PRIOR, William Johnson, CBE 1979; CEng, FIEE; Chairman, Manx Electricity Authority, 1984–85; retired; *b* 28 Jan. 1924; *s* of Ernest Stanley and Lilian Prior; *m* 1945, Mariel (*née* Irving); two *s* one *d.* *Educ:* Goole and Barnsley Grammar Schs. Barugh, Mexborough, Stuart Street (Manchester) and Stockport Power Stations, 1944–52; Keadby, 1952–56, Supt, 1954–56; Supt, Berkeley, 1957–58; Supt, Hinkley Point Generating Station, 1959–66; CEGB and predecessors: Asst Reg. Dir (Generation), NW Region, 1967–70; Dir (Generation), SW Region, 1970–72; Dir-Gen., SE Region, 1972–76; Mem., Electricity Council, 1976–79; Chm., Yorks Electricity Bd, 1979–84. Member: NCB, 1977–83; Adv. Cttee on Safety of Nuclear Installations, 1980–87. *Recreation:* country walking. *Address:* Highfield House, Lime Kiln Lane, Kirk Deighton, Wetherby, W Yorks LS22 4EA. *T:* (01937) 584434.

PRISK, Mark Michael; MP (C) Hertford and Stortford, since 2001; *b* 12 June 1962; *s* of Michael Raymond Prisk and June Irene Prisk; *m* 1989, Lesley Titcomb. *Educ:* Truro Sch., Cornwall; Univ. of Reading (BSc (Hons) Land Mgt). Knight Frank & Rutley, 1983–85; Chartered Surveyor, 1985–; Dir, Derrick, Wade & Waters, 1989–91; Principal: Mark Prisk Connection, 1991–97; mp2, 1997–2001. Contested (C): Newham NW, 1992; Wansdyke, 1997. Nat. Vice Chm., FCS, 1981–82; Chm., Youth for Peace through NATO, 1983–85. Chm. Governors, Stratford GM Sch., 1992–93. *Recreations:* piano, choral music, Rugby and cricket supporter. *Address:* House of Commons, SW1A 0AA. *T:* (020) 7219 3000. *Clubs:* Middlesex CC; Saracens RF.

PRITCHARD, Arthur Alan, CB 1979; JP; formerly Deputy Under Secretary of State, Ministry of Defence; *b* 3 March 1922; *s* of Arthur Henry Standfast Pritchard and Sarah Bessie Myra Pritchard (*née* Mundy); *m* 1949, Betty Rona Nevard (*née* Little); two *s* one *d.* *Educ:* Wanstead High Sch., Essex. Board of Trade, 1939. RAFVR Pilot, 1941–52; CFS Instr, 1946. Joined Admiralty, 1952; Asst Sec., 1964; Royal College of Defence Studies, 1972; Asst Under-Sec. of State, Naval Personnel and Op. Requirements, MoD, 1972–76; seconded as Dep. Sec., NI Office, 1976–78; Secretary to the Admiralty Bd, 1978–81. Management consultant, 1984–89. Pres., Fordingbridge and Dist Community Assoc., 1996– (Chm., 1990–95); Chm., Sandleheath Parish Council, 2001–. JP Ringwood, 1986 (Totton and New Forest, 1981–86; Chm., Ringwood Bench, 1991–92). *Recreation:* walking. *Address:* Courtlands, Manor Farm Road, Fordingbridge, Hants SP6 1DY. *Club:* Royal Air Force.

PRITCHARD, David Alan; Group Director, Economic Development Department, National Assembly for Wales, since 2000; *b* 23 March 1946; *s* of John Merfyn Pritchard and Anne Louise Pritchard; *m* 1970, Kathryn Henton; two *s.* *Educ:* UCNW, Bangor (BA Hons Econs). Welsh Office: Head: Industry Policy Div., 1989; Health Strategy and Rev. Div., 1990–97; Local Govt Policy and Finance Div., 1997–99; Nat. Assembly Corporate Planning Unit, 1999–2000. Non-exec. Dir, Carbon Trust. *Recreations:* walking, golf, reading, gardening. *Address:* National Assembly for Wales, Cathays Park, Cardiff CF10 3NQ. *T:* (029) 2082 6646; (home) Ty'r Ardd, Cardiff Road, Creigiau CF15 9NL. *T:* (029) 2089 0932.

PRITCHARD, David Peter; Group Director, Wholesale and International Banking, Lloyds TSB Group plc, since 1998; *b* 20 July 1944; *s* of Norman and Peggy Pritchard; *m* 1993, Elizabeth Cresswell; one *s* one *d.* *Educ:* Read Sch., Drax, Yorks; Southampton Univ. (BScEng 1966). Hawker Siddeley Aviation, 1966–71; Wm Brandt's Sons & Co., 1971–73; Edward Bates & Sons Ltd, 1973–78; Man. Dir, Citicorp Investment Bank, 1978–87; Vice Chm., Orion Royal Bank, 1987–88; Gen. Manager, Europe, Royal Bank of Canada, 1988–95; Treas., TSB Gp plc, 1995–96; on secondment to FSA, 1996–98. *Recreations:* cycling, Nordic ski-ing, photography. *Address:* 17 Thorney Crescent, SW11 3TT. *T:* (020) 7585 2253. *Club:* London Capital.

PRITCHARD, Rear-Adm. Gwynedd Idris, CB 1981; *b* 18 June 1924; *s* of Cyril Idris Pritchard and Lily Pritchard; *m* 1975, Mary Thérèsa (*née* Curtin); three *s* (by previous marriage). *Educ:* Wyggeston Sch., Leicester. FBIM, MNI. Joined Royal Navy, 1942; Sub-Lieut 1944; Lieut 1946; Lt-Comdr 1954; Comdr 1959; Captain 1967; Rear-Adm. 1976; Flag Officer Sea Training, 1976–78; Flag Officer Gibraltar, 1979–81; retired list, 1981.

Chm., SW Regl Planning Conf., 1990–93. Mem., Dorset CC, 1985–2001. *Recreations:* gardening, golf. *Address:* Hoofprints, Beach Road, Burton Bradstock, Dorset DT6 4RF.

PRITCHARD, Gwynn; *see* Pritchard, I. G.

PRITCHARD, (Iorwerth) Gwynn; Secretary General, International Public Television Screening Conference, since 2001; *b* 1 Feb. 1946; *s* of Rev. Islwyn Pritchard and Megan Mair Pritchard; *m* 1st, 1970, Marilyn Bartholomew (*d* 1994); two *s* one *d*; 2nd, 1998, Althea Sharp. *Educ:* King's Coll., Cambridge (MA). Producer and Director: BBC Television, London, 1969–78; BBC Wales, 1979–81; HTV Wales, 1982–85; Commissioning Editor, 1985–88, Sen. Commissioning Editor for Educn, 1989–92, Channel 4; Hd of Welsh Progs, then of Welsh Broadcasting, BBC Cymru/Wales, 1992–2001. Pres., INPUT Internat. Bd, 1988–93. Trustee: Welsh Writers Trust, 1990–; Broadcasting Support Services, 1990–92; Nat. Inst. for Adult and Contg Educn, 1990–92. Member Board: Sheffield Internat. Documentary Fest., 1993–96; Welsh (formerly Aberystwyth) Internat. Film Fest., 1993–98. Mem. Council, Coleg Harlech, 1992–2000; Gov., Ysgol Gynradd Pencae, 1992–. Winston Churchill Fellow, Winston Churchill Meml Trust, 1973; Huw Weldon Fellow, UCNW, Bangor, 1990–91. Chevalier de l'Ordre des Arts et des Lettres (France), 1990. *Recreations:* swimming, walking, cinema, reading. *Address:* 25 Westbourne Road, Penarth, Vale of Glamorgan CF64 3HA. *T:* (029) 2070 3608.

PRITCHARD, Rt Rev. John Lawrence; *see* Jarrow, Bishop Suffragan of.

PRITCHARD, John Michael; Founder and Chairman, Legalease Ltd, Publishers, since 1988; *b* 18 June 1949; *s* of Arthur Glyn Pritchard and Sybil Roderick Pritchard; *m* 1976, Mary Margaret Freeman (marr. diss. 1998); two *s* one *d*; *m* 1999, Hilary Baker. *Educ:* Penarth Grammar Sch.; Bristol Univ. Admitted solicitor, 1974; articled with Thompsons, solicitors, London; in practice with Powell Spencer, Kilburn, 1974–89. Chm., Internat. Centre for Commercial Law, 1997–. Editor-in-Chief of periodicals: Legal Business, 1990–; Practical Lawyer, 1991–; In House Lawyer, 1993–; European Legal Business, 1995–; Lawyer Internat., 1997–; Property Law Jl, 1997–; IT & Communications Law Report & Newsletter, 1997–. *Publications:* (ed) Penguin Guide to the Law, 1982, 4th edn, as New Penguin Guide to the Law: your rights and the law explained, 1993; (ed) Legal 500, annually 1988–; Young Solicitors' Handbook, 1990, rev. edn 1991; (ed) Who's Who in the Law: eminent practising lawyers in the UK, 1991; (ed) European Legal 500, annually 1991–; Which Firm of Solicitors?, 1993; Legal Experts, annually 1994–; (ed) Commercial Client Directory: guide to legal service buyers at the UK's top 15,000 companies, 1996; (ed) Asia Pacific Legal 500, annually 1996–; Kanzleien in Deutschland, annually 1997–; (ed) Cabinet's d'Avocats en France, annually, 1999–. *Recreation:* anything that does not involve lawyers. *Address:* c/o 28–33 Cato Street, W1H 5HS. *T:* (020) 7396 9292, *Fax:* (020) 7396 9300.

PRITCHARD, Kenneth John, CB 1982; Director, Greenwich Hospital, 1987–92; *b* 18 March 1926; *s* of William Edward Pritchard and Ethel Mary Pritchard (*née* Cornfield); *m* 1st, 1949, Elizabeth Margaret Bradshaw (*d* 1978); two *d*; 2nd, 1979, Angela Madeleine Palmer; one *s* two *d*. *Educ:* Newport High Sch.; St Catherine's Coll., Oxford (MA 1951). Served Army, 1944–48; Indian Mil. Acad., Dehra Dun, 1945; served with 8th/12th Frontier Force Regt and 2nd Royal W Kent Regt. Asst Principal, Admiralty, 1951; Private Sec. to Sec. of State for Wales, 1964; Asst Sec., Min. of Aviation, 1966; RCDS, 1972; Principal Supply and Transport Officer (Naval), Portsmouth, 1978, Exec. Dir 1980; Dir Gen. of Supplies and Transport (Naval), MoD, 1981–86, retd. Vice Patron, Royal Naval Benevolent Trust, 1992–. Chm., Frome Tourist Information Ltd, 1996–. Freeman, City of London, 1988; Liveryman, Coopers' Co., 1988. Mem., Cousinerie de Bourgogne, 1997. FCIPS (FInstPS 1986). *Recreations:* tennis, music hall, good wine. *Address:* Pickford House, Beckington, Som BA11 6SJ. *T:* (01373) 830329.

PRITCHARD, Kenneth William, OBE 1992; WS; part-time Sheriff, since 2000 (Temporary Sheriff, 1995–99); Secretary of the Law Society of Scotland, 1976–97; *b* 14 Nov. 1933; *s* of Dr Kenneth Pritchard, MB, BS, DPH, and Isobel Pritchard, LDS (*née* Broom); *m* 1962, Gretta (*née* Murray), BL, MBA, WS; two *s* one *d*. *Educ:* Dundee High Sch.; Fettes Coll.; St Andrews Univ. (BL). National Service, Argyll and Sutherland Highlanders, 1955–57; commnd 2nd Lieut, 1956; TA 1957–62 (Captain). Joined J. & J. Scrimgeour, Solicitors, Dundee, 1957, Sen. Partner, 1970–76; WS 1984. Hon. Sheriff, Dundee, 1978. Member: Sheriff Court Rules Council, 1973–76; Lord Dunpark's Cttee Considering Reparation upon Criminal Conviction, 1973–77; Secretary, Scottish Council of Law Reporting, 1976–97. Governor, Moray House Coll. of Educn, 1982–84; Mem. Ct, Univ. of Dundee, 1990–93. Mem., National Trust for Scotland Jubilee Appeal Cttee, 1980–82. Pres., Dundee High Sch. Old Boys Club, 1975–76; Captain of the Former Pupil RFC, Dundee High Sch., 1959–62. Hon. Prof. of Law, Strathclyde Univ., 1986–94. *Recreation:* golf. *Address:* 22/4 Kinellan Road, Edinburgh EH12 6ES. *T:* (0131) 337 4294. *Clubs:* New, Bruntsfield Links Golfing Society (Edinburgh); Hon. Company of Edinburgh Golfers (Muirfield).

PRITCHARD, Sir Neil, KCMG 1962 (CMG 1952); HM Diplomatic Service, retired; Ambassador in Bangkok, 1967–70; *b* 14 January 1911; *s* of late Joseph and Lillian Pritchard; *m* 1943, Mary Burroughes (*d* 1988), Pretoria, S Africa; one *s*. *Educ:* Liverpool Coll.; Worcester Coll., Oxford. Dominions Office, 1933; Private Secretary to Permanent Under-Sec., 1936–38; Assistant Secretary, Rhodesia-Nyasaland Royal Commission, 1938; Secretary, Office of UK High Commissioner, Pretoria, 1941–45; Principal Secretary, Office of UK Representative, Dublin, 1948–49; Assistant Under-Secretary of State, Commonwealth Relations Office, 1951–54; Dep. UK High Commissioner: Canada, 1954–57; Australia, 1957–60; Actg Dep. Under-Sec. of State, CRO, 1961; British High Comr in Tanganyika, 1961–63; Deputy Under-Secretary of State, Commonwealth Office (formerly CRO), 1963–67. *Recreation:* golf. *Address:* Little Garth, Daglingworth, Cirencester, Glos GL7 7AQ.

PRITCHARD, Prof. Thomas Owen; JP; Chairman, Cynefin Environmental Ltd, consultants in sustainable development, since 1991; Deputy Chairman, National Heritage Memorial Fund, since 1999; Professorial Fellow, University of Wales; *b* 13 May 1932; *s* of late Owen and Mary Pritchard; *m* 1957, Enyd Ashton; one *s* one *d*. *Educ:* Botwnnog Grammar Sch.; Univ. of Wales (BSc Hons Botany and Agric. Botany); Univ. of Leeds (PhD Genetics). Midlands Regl Officer and Head of Educn, Nature Conservancy, 1957–67; Dep. Dir for Wales, Nature Conservancy—NERC 1967–73; Dir for Wales, NCC, 1973–91. Consultant, Council of Europe, 1968. Vis. Prof., Dept of Forestry and Resource Management, Univ. of California, Berkeley, 1981–. Dir, CTF Training Ltd, 1982–91; Chairman: Coed Cymru Ltd, 1983–92; Slate Ecology Co. Ltd, 1995–. Chairman: Bardsey Island Trust, 1987–93; Welsh Historic Gdns Trust, 1994–98 (Pres., 2001); Exec., POW Cttee, 1971–73; Country Cttee for Wales, Heritage Lottery Fund, 1999–; Vice Chm. (Educn), IUCN, 1966–73; former Chm. and Mem., conservation and envtl bodies, nat. and internat. Member: Genetical Soc.; British Ecological Soc. Member: Ct of Govs and Council: Univ. of Wales, Bangor (formerly UC, Bangor), 1981–; Nat. Museum of Wales, 1981–91. Member: Gorsedd of Bards, Royal Nat. Eisteddfod; Hon. Soc. of Cymmrodorion. FRSA. JP Bangor, 1978. *Publications:* Cynefin y Cymro, 1989; numerous contribs to sci. and educn jls. *Recreation:* sailing. *Address:* Graig Lwyd, 134 Ffordd Penrhos, Bangor, Gwynedd LL57 2BX. *T:* (01248) 370401.

PRITCHETT, Matthew, (Matt); front page cartoonist for Daily Telegraph, since 1988; *b* 14 July 1964; *s* of Oliver Pritchett and Joan Pritchett (*née* Hill); *m* 1992, Pascale Charlotte Marie Smets; one *s* two *d*. *Educ:* Addey and Stanhope Sch.; St Martin's Sch. of Art. Freelance cartoonist for New Statesman, Punch and Spectator, 1986–88. Awards from: What the Papers Say, 1992; Cartoon Arts Trust, 1995, 1996, 1999; UK Press Gazette, 1996, 1998; British Press Awards, 2000. *Publications:* Best of Matt, annually, 1991–; 10 Years of Matt, 2001. *Address:* c/o The Daily Telegraph, 1 Canada Square, Canary Wharf, E14 5DT.

PRITTIE, family name of **Baron Dunalley**.

PROBERT, David Henry, CBE 1996; FCIS, FCMA, FCCA; *b* 11 April 1938; *s* of William David Thomas Probert and Doris Mabel Probert; *m* 1968, Sandra Mary Prince; one *s* one *d*. *Educ:* Bromsgrove High School. Dir, 1976, Chief Exec., 1979–86, and Chm., 1986–98, W. Canning plc. A Crown Agent for Oversea Govts and Admins, 1981–98 (Dep. Chm., 1985–90; Chm., 1990–98); Crown Agent for Holdings and Realisation Bd, 1981–98. Dir, Private Patients Plan Ltd, 1988–96; Chm., PPP Healthcare Group plc, 1996–98; Gov., PPP Medical Trust, 1998–99. Chairman: Leigh Interests plc, 1996–98 (Dir, 1995–98); Saville Gordon Estates plc, 1999–2001 (Dir, 1998–2001); Ash & Lacy plc, 1998–2000; Director: BSA Ltd, 1971–73; Mills and Allen International Ltd, 1974–76; HB Electronics plc, 1977–86; British Hallmarking Council, 1983–91; Linread Public Limited Company, 1983–90; ASD plc, 1985–90; Sandvik Ltd, 1985–90; Rockwool Ltd, 1988–90, 1992–94; Richard Burbridge Ltd, 1990–91; William Sinclair plc, 1994–2001; Hampson Industries plc, 1994–. Pres., Birmingham Chamber of Commerce and Industry, 1994–95 (Vice Pres., 1992–94). Gov., UCE, 1998–2001. Liveryman: Chartered Secretaries and Administrators' Co., 1984; Founders' Co., 1997. CIMgt. *Recreations:* theatre, music, sport. *Address:* 4 Blakes Field Drive, Barnt Green, Worcs B45 8JT. *Club:* Lord's Taverners (Regl Chm., 1996–99).

PROBERT, (William) Ronald; Managing Director, Business Development, 1992–93, Member of the Board, 1985–93, Group Executive Member, 1989–93, British Gas plc (formerly British Gas Corporation), retired; *b* 11 Aug. 1934; *s* of William and Florence Probert; *m* 1957, Jean (*née* Howard); three *s*. *Educ:* Grammar Sch., Ashton-under-Lyne; Univ. of Leeds (BA). FIGasE; CIMgt. Entered gas industry, 1957; various marketing appts in E Midlands Gas Bd, 1957–67; Conversion Manager, 1967, Service Manager, 1971, Marketing Dir, 1973, E Midlands Gas Bd; Asst Dir of Marketing, 1975, Dir of Sales, 1977, British Gas Corp.; Man. Dir Marketing, British Gas, 1982–89; Man. Dir, Gas Supply and Strategy, 1989–92. Dir, E Berks NHS Trust, 1991–. *Recreations:* narrowboats, music, winemaking. *Address:* 32 Austen Way, Gerrards Cross, Bucks SL9 8NW. *T:* (01753) 888527.

PROBINE, Dr Mervyn Charles, CB 1986; FRSNZ; FInstD; FNZIM; company director and consultant, since 1986; *b* 30 April 1924; *s* of Frederick Charles and Ann Kathleen Probine; *m* 1949, Marjorie Walker; one *s* one *d*. *Educ:* Univ. of Auckland (BSc); Victoria Univ. of Wellington (MSc); Univ. of Leeds (PhD). Physicist, DSIR, 1946–67; Dir, Physics and Engineering Lab., 1967–77; Asst Dir-Gen., DSIR, 1977–79; State Services Commission: Comr, 1979–80; Dep. Chm., 1980–81; Chm., 1981–86, retired. Chm., GEC (NZ), 1986–95; Dir, Fujitsu (NZ), 1986–2000. Chairman: Legislation Adv. Cttee, 1991–96; Insurance and Savings Ombudsman Commn, 1994–98. Trustee, Nat. Library of NZ, 1992–98. FRSNZ 1964; FNZIM 1985; FInstD 1993. *Publications:* numerous scientific research papers and papers on application of science in industry. *Recreations:* bridge, sailing, angling. *Address:* 24 Bloomfield Terrace, Lower Hutt, New Zealand. *T:* (4) 9730425. *Club:* Wellington (Wellington, NZ).

PROBY, Sir Peter, 2nd Bt *cr* 1952; FRICS; Lord-Lieutenant of Cambridgeshire, 1981–85; *b* 4 Dec. 1911; *s* of Sir Richard George Proby, 1st Bt, MC, and Betty Monica (*d* 1967), *d* of A. H. Hallam Murray; *S* father, 1979; *m* 1944, Blanche Harrison, *o d* of Col Henry Harrison Cripps, DSO; one *s* three *d* (and one *s* decd). *Educ:* Eton; Trinity College, Oxford. BA 1934. Served War of 1939–45, Captain, Irish Guards. Bursar of Eton College, 1953–71. *Heir: s* William Henry Proby, MA, FCA [*b* 13 June 1949; *m* 1974, Meredyth Anne Brentnall; four *d*. *Educ:* Eton; Lincoln Coll., Oxford (MA)]. *Address:* Pottle Green, Elton, Peterborough PE8 6SG. *T:* (01832) 280434.

PROCHASKA, Dr Alice Marjorie Sheila, FRHistS; University Librarian, Yale University, since 2001; *b* 12 July 1947; *d* of John Harold Barwell and Hon. Sheila McNair; *m* 1971, Dr Franklyn Kimmel Prochaska; one *s* one *d*. *Educ:* Perse Sch. for Girls, Cambridge; Somerville Coll., Oxford (BA 1968; MA 1973; DPhil 1975). Assistant Keeper: London Museum, 1971–73; Public Record Office, 1975–84; Sec. and Librarian, Inst. of Historical Res., 1984–92; Dir of Special Collections, BL, 1992–2001. Chm., Nat. Council on Archives, 1991–95; Mem., Royal Commn on Historical MSS, 1998–2001. Member: History Working Gp on Nat. Curriculum, DES, 1989–90; Council, RHistS, 1991–95 (Vice Pres., 1995–99); Heritage Educn Trust, 1992–2001; Hereford Mappa Mundi Trust, 1992–95; Adv. Council, Inst. of Historical Res., 1992–2001; Library Panel, Wellcome Inst., 1993–97; Adv. Panel, Qualidata, Univ. of Essex, 1995–98; Sir Winston Churchill Archive Trust, 1995–2001. Gov., London Guildhall Univ., 1995–2001. *Publications:* London in the Thirties, 1973; History of the General Federation of Trade Unions 1899–1980, 1982; Irish History from 1700: a guide to sources in the Public Record Office, 1986; (ed jtly with F. K. Prochaska), Margaretta Acworth's Georgian Cookery Book, 1987; contribs to learned jls. *Recreations:* family life, collecting watercolours. *Address:* Sterling Memorial Library, Yale University, PO Box 208240, New Haven, CT 06520-8240, USA.

PROCKTOR, Patrick, RA 1996; RWS 1981; RE 1991; painter since 1962; *b* 12 March 1936; 2nd *s* of late Eric Christopher Procktor and Barbara Winifred (*née* Hopkins); *m* 1973, Kirsten Bo (*née* Andersen) (*d* 1984); one *s*. *Educ:* Highgate; Slade Sch. (Diploma). Many one-man exhibns, Redfern Gallery, from 1963; retrospective tour, England and Wales, 1990; Paintings in Hospitals (exhibn of paintings distributed to hosps), 1999; exhibn in favour of St Marylebone Fire Brigade, 1999. Designed windows for AIDS Recreation Centre, St Stephen's Hosp., Fulham, 1988. *Publications:* One Window in Venice, 1974; Coleridge's Rime of the Ancient Mariner (new illustrated edn), 1976; A Chinese Journey (aquatint landscapes), 1980; (illustrated) Sailing through China, by Paul Theroux, 1983; Patrick Procktor Prints 1959–85 (catalogue raisonné), 1985; A Shropshire Lad, by A. E. Housman (new illustrated edn), 1986; Self-Portrait (autobiog.), 1991; *relevant publications:* Patrick Procktor (monograph by Patrick Kinmonth), 1985; Patrick P, by John McEwen, 1997. *Recreation:* Russian ballet. *Address:* c/o Redfern Gallery, 20 Cork Street, W1X 2HL. *Club:* Garrick.

PROCTER, Jane Hilary; Editorial Director, PeopleNews Network, since 1999; *m* 1985, Thomas Charles Goldstaub; one *s* one *d*. *Educ:* Queen's Coll., Harley St. Fashion Asst,

Vogue, 1974–75; Asst Fashion Editor, Good Housekeeping, 1975–77; Actg Fashion Editor, Woman's Jl, 1977–78; Fashion Writer, Country Life, 1978–80; Freelance Fashion Editor, The Times, Sunday Times and Daily Express, 1980–87; Editor: British W, 1987–88; Tatler, 1990–99. *Publication:* Dress Your Best, 1983. *Recreations:* sailing, ski-ing. *Address:* PeopleNews Network, 77 Dean Street, W1D 3SH. *T:* (020) 7025 1818.

PROCTER, (Mary) Norma; contralto; international concert singer; *b* Cleethorpes, Lincolnshire, 15 Feb. 1928. *Educ:* Wintringham Secondary Sch. Vocal studies with Roy Henderson, musicianship with Alec Redshaw, lieder with Hans Oppenheim and Paul Hamburger. London début, Southwark Cathedral, 1948; operatic début, Lucretia, in Britten's Rape of Lucretia, Aldeburgh Festival, 1954; Covent Garden début, Gluck's Orpheus, 1960. Specialist in concert works, oratorios and recitals; appeared with all major conductors and orchestras, and in all major festivals, UK and Europe; performed in Germany, France, Spain, Italy, Portugal, Holland, Belgium, Norway, Denmark, Sweden, Finland, Austria, Luxembourg, Israel, S America; BBC Last Night of the Proms, 1974. Many recordings. Hon. RAM 1974. *Address:* 194 Clee Road, Grimsby, NE Lincs DN32 8NG.

PROCTER, Robert John Dudley; Chief Executive, Lincolnshire County Council, 1983–95; *b* 19 Oct. 1935; *s* of Luther Donald Procter and Edith Muriel Procter; *m* 1962, Adrienne Allen; one *s* one *d*. *Educ:* Cheltenham Grammar School. Admitted Solicitor, 1961. Articled Clerk, Glos CC, 1956–61; Assistant Solicitor: Bath City, 1961–63; Cumberland CC, 1963–65; Lindsey County Council: Sen. Asst Solicitor, 1965–69; Asst Clerk, 1969–71; Dep. Clerk, Kesteven CC, 1971–73; Dir of Personnel, 1973–77, Dir of Admin, 1977–83, Lincolnshire CC. Chm., Assoc. of County Chief Execs, 1994–95. Mem., Warner Cttee of Inquiry into recruitment and selection of staff in children's homes, 1992. Vice Chm., Linkage Community Trust, 2001; Treas., Lincoln Cathedral Community Assoc., 2001. Chm. Govs, Lincoln Christ's Hosp. Sch. and Foundn, 2001. *Recreations:* horse racing, swimming, keyboard playing, freemasonry. *Address:* Flat 3, The Lodge, 38B Nettleham Road, Lincoln LN2 1RE. *T:* (01522) 532105.

PROCTER, Sidney, CBE 1986; Commissioner, Building Societies Commission, 1986–93; company director; *b* 10 March 1925; *s* of Robert and Georgina Margaret Procter; *m* 1952, Isabel (*née* Simmons); one *d*. *Educ:* Ormskirk Grammar School. Served RAF, 1943–47. Entered former Williams Deacon's Bank, 1941; Asst General Manager, 1969; Dep. Dir, Williams & Glyn's Bank, 1970; Divl Dir, 1975; Exec. Dir, 1976–85; Asst Chief Executive, 1976; Dep. Chief Executive, 1977; Chief Exec., 1978–82; Dep. Gp Man. Dir, Royal Bank of Scotland Gp, 1979–82; Gp Chief Exec., 1982–85; Vice Chm., 1986; Director: Royal Bank of Scotland, 1978–86 (Vice Chm., 1986); Provincial Insurance Co., 1985–86; Dep. Chm., Provincial Group, 1991–94 (Dir, 1986–94); Chairman: Exeter Bank, 1991–97; Provincial Group Holdings, 1994–96. Adviser to Governor, Bank of England, 1985–87. Chm., Exeter Trust, 1986–97 (Dir, 1985–97).

PROCTOR, His Honour Anthony James; a Circuit Judge, 1988–2001; *b* 18 Sept. 1931; *s* of James Proctor and Savina Maud (*née* Horsfield); *m* 1964, Patricia Mary Bryan; one *d*. *Educ:* Mexborough Grammar Sch., Yorkshire; St Catharine's Coll., Cambridge (MA, LLM). Flying Officer, RAF, 1953–55. Articled to Sir Bernard Kenyon, County Hall, Wakefield, 1955–58; admitted Solicitor 1958. Sen. Prosecuting Solicitor, Sheffield Corp., 1959–64; Partner, Broomhead & Neals, Solicitors, Sheffield, 1964–74; Dist Registrar and County Court Registrar, Barrow in Furness, Lancaster, Preston, 1974–88; a Recorder, 1985–88; Hon. Recorder of Lancaster, 2000–. Pres., Assoc. of Dist and Court Registrars, 1985–86. *Recreations:* fell walking, travel, genealogy. *Address:* The Sessions House, Lancaster Road, Preston PR1 2PD. *T:* (01772) 821451.

PROCTOR, Harvey; *see* Proctor, K. H.

PROCTOR, (Keith) Harvey; Director, Proctor's Shirts and Ties, since 1992; *b* 16 Jan. 1947; *s* of late Albert Proctor and Hilda Tegerdine. *Educ:* High School for Boys, Scarborough; Univ. of York. BA History Hons, 1969. Asst Director, Monday Club, 1969–71; Research Officer, Conservative 1970s Parliamentary Gp, 1971–72; Exec. Director, Parliamentary Digest Ltd, 1972–74; British Paper & Board Industry Federation: Asst Sec., 1974–78; Secretary, 1978–79; Consultant, 1979–87. MP (C): Basildon, 1979–83; Billericay, 1983–87. Mem., Exec. Council, Monday Club, 1983–87. Chief Exec., Richmond Bor. Chamber of Commerce, 1996–98 (Vice-Pres., 1990–92; Pres., 1992–94). Trustee, SW London Community Foundn, 1993–94; Chairman: Richmond Town Centre Cttee, 1995–97; Parkview Court Residents' Assoc., 1996–97 (Sec., 1994–96); Co-Chm., Richmond Victorian Evening Cttee, 1999–. Editor, News and Views, 1991–98. *Publication:* Billericay in Old Picture Postcards, 1985. *Recreations:* tennis, collecting British contemporary art. *Address:* 11 Brewers Lane, Richmond Upon Thames, Surrey TW9 1HH. *T:* and *Fax:* (020) 8332 7722.

PROCTOR, William Angus; Clerk of Delegated Legislation, House of Commons, since 1999; *b* 1 May 1945; 3rd *s* of late George Longmate Proctor and Anne Ines Louis Proctor (*née* Angus); *m* 1969, Susan Irene Mottram; two *s* one *d*. *Educ:* Bristol Cathedral Sch. (chorister); Keele Univ. (BA Hons English and Political Instns). A Clerk, H of C, 1968–70 and 1972–; Res. Associate, Manchester Univ., 1970–72; Delegn Sec., H of C Overseas Office, 1972–74; Clerk, Select Committees on: Sci. and Technol., 1974–77; Procedure, 1977–79; Transport, 1979–82; Foreign Affairs, 1982–87; Sec., H of C Commn, 1987–92; Principal Clerk: of Financial Cttees and Clerk, Treasury and CS Cttee, 1992–95; of Standing Cttees, 1995–97; of Bills, 1997–99. Procedure Advr to Pres., Council of Europe Assembly, 1989–92. *Publications:* (jtly) The European Parliament, 1973; (ed with J. Sweetman) The Parliamentary Assembly: procedure and practice, 9th edn 1990; contrib. articles and reviews to parly jls. *Recreations:* music, theatre, nocturnal reading as escape from dysfunctional family. *Address:* House of Commons, SW1A 0AA. *T:* (020) 7219 0447.

PROCTOR-BEAUCHAMP, Sir Christopher Radstock; *see* Beauchamp.

PRODI, Romano; President, European Commission, since 1999; *b* Scandiano, Italy, 9 Aug. 1939; *m* Flavia Franzoni; two *s*. *Educ:* Catholic Univ. of Milan (degree in law); LSE (post-grad. studies; Hon. Fellow). Asst in Political Econs, 1963–71, Prof. of Industrial Organisation and Industrial Policy, 1971–99, Univ. of Bologna; Researcher: Lombard Inst. of Economic and Social Studies, 1963–64; Stanford Res. Inst., 1968. Prof. of Econs and Indust. Politics, Free Univ. of Trento, 1973–74; Vis. Prof., Harvard Univ., 1974. Minister of Industry, 1978–79; Chm., Inst. for Industrial Reconstruction, 1982–89, 1993–94. Chm., Ulivo (centre-left coalition gp), 1995. MP, 1996–99; Prime Minister of Italy, 1996–98. Hon. Mem., Real Academia de Ciencias Morales y Politicas, Madrid. Hon. Dr: Madras; Sofia; Brown. Premio Schumpeter, 1999. *Address:* European Commission, 200 rue de la Loi, 1000 Brussels, Belgium.

PROFIT, (George) Richard, OBE 1980; AFC 1974; FRAeS; Board Member, and Group Director, Safety Regulation, Civil Aviation Authority, since 1997; *b* 31 Oct. 1940; *s* of Richard George Profit and Lilian Cotterill Profit; *m* 1965, Pamela Shepherd; one *d*. *Educ:* Oldershaw Grammar Sch.; Army Staff Coll., Camberley; RCDS. FRAeS 1989. Commissioned Royal Air Force, 1961: operational pilot, UK, Singapore, Germany, 1963–77; Officer Commanding: No 3 (F) Sqdn, 1977–80; RAF Coltishall, 1982–85; Inspector of Flight Safety, 1987–90; retd in rank of Air Cdre, 1990; Dir, Safety, Security and Quality Assurance, NATS Ltd, 1990–97; Hd, Aerodrome and Air Traffic Services, Safety Regulation Gp, CAA, 1997. Non-exec. Dir, Railway Safety, 2001–. FIMgt 1988. *Publication:* Systematic Safety Management in the Air Traffic Services, 1995. *Recreations:* trout fishing, painting. *Address:* Civil Aviation Authority, Safety Regulation Group, Aviation House, Gatwick Airport South, W Sussex RH6 0YR. *T:* (01293) 573083. *Club:* Royal Air Force.

PROFUMO, John Dennis, CBE 1975 (OBE (mil.) 1944); 5th Baron of Italy (*cr* 1903); *b* 30 Jan. 1915; *e s* of late Baron Albert Profumo, KC; *m* 1954, Valerie Hobson, actress (*d* 1998); one *s*. *Educ:* Harrow; Brasenose College, Oxford. 1st Northamptonshire Yeomanry, 1939 (despatches); Brigadier, Chief of Staff UK Mission in Japan, 1945. MP (C) Kettering Division, Northamptonshire, 1940–45; MP (C) Stratford-on-Avon Division of Warwickshire, 1950–63; Parliamentary Secretary, Ministry of Transport and Civil Aviation, Nov. 1952–Jan. 1957; Parliamentary Under-Secretary of State for the Colonies, 1957–58; Parliamentary Under-Sec. of State, Foreign Affairs, Nov. 1958–Jan. 1959; Minister of State for Foreign Affairs, 1959–60; Secretary of State for War, July 1960–June 1963. Dir, Provident Life Assoc. of London, 1975– (Dep. Chm., 1978–82). Mem., Bd of Visitors, HM Prison, Grendon, 1968–75. Chm., Toynbee Hall, 1982–85, Pres. 1985– (Hon. Life Mem., 2001). Hon. Fellow, Queen Mary, Univ. of London, 2001. *Recreations:* fishing, gardening, DIY. *Heir:* *s* David Profumo [*b* 30 Oct. 1955; *m* 1980, Helen, *o d* of Alasdair Fraser; two *s* one *d*]. *Club:* Boodle's.

See also A. M. D. Havelock-Allan.

PROKHOROV, Prof. Alexander Mikhailovich; Hero of Socialist Labour, 1969, 1986; Order of Lenin (five-fold); Physicist; Director, Centre for Natural Science Research, General Physics Institute, Russian Academy of Sciences, Moscow, since 1998; Editor-in-Chief, Bolshaya Rossiyskaya (formerly Bolshaya Sovetskaya) Encyclopedia Publishing House, since 1970; *b* Atherton, Australia, 11 July 1916; *s* of Mikhail Prokhorov; *m* 1941, Galina Alexeyevna (*née* Shelepina); one *s*. *Educ:* Leningrad State University; Lebedev Inst. of Physics. Academy of Sciences of the USSR, now Russian Academy of Sciences (Department of General Physics and Astronomy): Corresp. Mem., 1960–66; Full Mem., 1966–; Mem. Presidial Body, 1970; Academician-Secretary, 1973–87; Dir, 1983–98, Hon. Dir, 1998–, Gen. Physics Inst. Chm., Nat. Commn of Soviet Physicists, 1973–. Professor, Moscow University, 1958–. Hon. Professor: Delhi Univ.; Bucharest Univ., 1971; Cluz Univ., 1977; Praha Politechnical Inst., 1980. Member: European Phys. Soc., 1977; European Acad. of Scis, Art and Literature, 1986; Hon. Member: Amer. Acad. of Arts and Sciences, 1972; Acad. of Sciences of Hungary, 1976; Acad. of Sciences, German Democratic Republic, 1977; Acad. of Scis of Czechoslavakia, 1982; Acad. of Scis Leopoldina, 1984. Joined Communist Party of the Soviet Union, 1950. Awarded Lenin Prize, 1959; Nobel Prize for Physics (jointly with Prof. N. G. Basov and Prof. C. H. Townes), 1964. *Publications:* contributions on non-linear oscillations, radiospectroscopy and quantum radio-physics. *Address:* General Physics Institute, Russian Academy of Sciences, Vavilova Street 38, Moscow 117942, Russia.

PROKHOROVA, Violetta; *see* Elvin, V.

PROPHET, Prof. Arthur Shelley, CBE 1980; DDS; DpBact; FDSRCS; FFDRCSI; Professor of Dental Surgery, University of London, 1956–83, now Emeritus; *b* 11 Jan. 1918; *s* of Eric Prophet and Mabel Wightman; *m* 1942, Vivienne Mary Bell; two *s*. *Educ:* Sedbergh School; University of Manchester. BDS Hons (Preston Prize and Medal), 1940; Diploma in Bacteriology (Manchester), 1948; DDS (Manchester) 1950; FDSRCS 1958; FFDRCS Ireland, 1964. RNVR (Dental Branch), 1941–46; Nuffield Dental Fellow, 1946–48; Lecturer in Dental Bacteriology, University of Manchester, 1948–54; Lecturer in Dental Surgery, QUB, 1954–56; Dir of Dental Studies, 1956–74, Dean of Dental Studies, 1974–77, UCH Dental Sch.; Dean, UCH Medical Sch., 1977–80; Dean, 1980–82, Vice-Dean, 1982–83, Faculty of Clinical Scis, UCL. Lectures: Charles Tomes, RCS, 1977; Wilkinson, Univ. of Manchester, 1978; Elwood, QUB, 1979; Shefford, UCL, 1983. Rep. of University of London on Gen. Dental Council, 1964–84. Elected Mem. Bd, Faculty of Dental Surgery, RCS, 1964–80 (Vice-Dean, 1972–73); Member: Cttee of Management, Inst. of Dental Surgery, 1963–83; Dental Sub-Cttee, UGC, 1968–78; Bd of Governors, UCH, 1957–74; Camden and Islington AHA(T), 1974–82; Bloomsbury HA, 1982–83. WHO Consultant, 1966; Consultant Dental Advr, DHSS, 1977–83. DSc *hc* Malta, 1987. *Publications:* contrib. to medical and dental journals. *Recreations:* golf, gardening. *Address:* Morton Rough, Morton Green, Wellan, Malvern WR13 6LR. *T:* (01684) 311965.

PROPHET, John; His Honour Judge Prophet; a Circuit Judge, since 1997; President of Employment (formerly Industrial) Tribunals for England and Wales, since 1997; *b* 19 Nov. 1931; *s* of Benjamin and Elsie Prophet; *m* 1961, Pauline Newby; three *d*. *Educ:* Trinity Coll., Cambridge (MA). Called to the Bar, Lincoln's Inn, 1956; Shell International, 1956–60; private practice at the Bar, 1960–; Sen. Lectr, Law Faculty, Leeds Univ., 1968–76; full-time Chm. of Industrial Tribunals, 1976–88; Regl Chm. of Industrial Tribunals, Yorkshire and Humberside, 1988–97. Consultant, Nat. Assoc. of Local Councils, 1968–89. *Publications:* The Structure of Government, 1968; The Parish Councillor's Guide, 1974, 17th edn 2000; Fair Rents, 1976; The Councillor, 1979, 11th edn 1997. *Recreations:* tennis, chess, gardening.

PROPHIT, Prof. Penny Pauline; Professor of Nursing Studies, University of Edinburgh, 1983–92 (Head of Department, 1983–88); *b* 7 Feb. 1939; *d* of C. Alston Prophit and Hortense Callahan. *Educ:* Marillac Coll., St Louis Univ., USA (BSN); Catholic Univ. of America (MSN, BNSc, PhD). Asst Prof., Catholic Univ. of America, 1975; Associate Professor: Univ. of Southern Mississippi, 1975; Louisiana State Univ. Med. Center, 1975; Cons., WHO, Europ. Office, Copenhagen, 1977–; Prof., Katholieke Univ., Leuven, Belgium, 1977. Mental Welfare Comr for Scotland, 1985; Mem., UK Central Council for Nursing, Midwifery and Health Visiting, 1988. Delta Epsilon Sigma, Nat. Catholic Scholastic Honor Soc., 1966; Sigma Theta Tau, Internat. Nursing Scholastic Honor Soc., 1970; Sigma Epsilon Phi, Catholic Univ. of Amer. Honor Soc., 1975. *Publications:* Understanding/Responding, 1982; res. articles on nursing care of the elderly, stress in nursing, interdisciplinary collaboration, etc. *Recreations:* jogging, reading and writing poetry and short stories, playing piano and listening to music of all kinds.

PROSSER, Rt Hon. Lord; William David Prosser; PC 2000; a Senator of the College of Justice in Scotland and Lord of Session, 1986–2001; *b* 23 Nov. 1934; *yr s* of David G. Prosser, MC, WS, Edinburgh; *m* 1964, Vanessa, *er d* of Sir William O'Brien Lindsay, KBE, Nairobi; two *s* two *d*. *Educ:* Edinburgh Academy; Corpus Christi Coll., Oxford (MA); Edinburgh Univ. (LLB). Advocate, 1962; QC (Scotland) 1974; Standing Junior Counsel in Scotland, Board of Inland Revenue, 1969–74; Advocate-Depute, 1978–79; Vice-Dean, Faculty of Advocates, 1979–83; Dean of Faculty, 1983–86. Mem., Scottish Cttee, Council on Tribunals, 1977–84. Chm., Royal Fine Art Commn for Scotland, 1990–95. Chairman: Royal Lyceum Theatre Co., 1987–92; Scottish Historic Buildings Trust, 1988–98;

Chamber Gp of Scotland, 1993–98; Edinburgh Sir Walter Scott Club, 1993–96; Scottish Architectural Educn Trust, 1994–; Mem., Franco-British Council, 1997–; Pres., Franco-British Lawyers' Soc., 1999–. Hon. FRIAS 1995. *Address:* 7 Randolph Crescent, Edinburgh EH3 7TH. *T:* (0131) 225 2709; 6 cité Pigalle, 75009 Paris, France. *T:* 40230433. *Clubs:* New, Scottish Arts (Edinburgh).

PROSSER, Charles; *see* Prosser, L. C.

PROSSER, David John, FIA; Chief Executive, Legal & General Group, since 1991; *b* 26 March 1944; *s* of Ronald and Dorothy Prosser; *m* 1971, Rosemary Margaret Snuggs; two *d. Educ:* Univ. of Wales (BSc). Sun Alliance Group, 1965–69; Hoare Govett, 1969–73; CIN Management, 1973–88; Legal & General, 1988–. Dir, SWALEC, 1991–96. Mem. of Bd, ABI, 1994–97, 1999–. *Recreation:* family life. *Address:* Legal & General Group, Temple Court, 11 Queen Victoria Street, EC4N 4TP. *Club:* Royal Automobile.

PROSSER, His Honour (Elvet) John; QC 1978; a Circuit Judge, 1988–2001; Resident Judge, Newport (Gwent) Crown Court, 1993–2001; *b* 10 July 1932; *s* of David and Hannah Prosser; *m* 1957, Mary Louise Cowdry; two *d. Educ:* Pontypridd Grammar Sch.; King's Coll., London Univ. LLB. Flt Lt, RAF, 1957–59. Called to the Bar, Gray's Inn, 1956, Bencher, 1986; Mem., Senate of Inns of Court and the Bar, 1980–87; a Recorder, 1972–88; Leader, Wales and Chester Circuit, 1984–87. Part-time Chm. of Industrial Tribunals, 1975–81. An Asst Boundary Comr for Wales, 1977–. *Recreations:* watching cricket and television. *Address:* 60 Mill Road, Lisvane, Cardiff CF14 0XS. *Clubs:* East India, Devonshire, Sports and Public Schools; Cardiff and County (Cardiff).

PROSSER, Gwynfor Mathews, (Gwyn); MP (Lab) Dover, since 1997; *b* 27 April 1943; *s* of late Glyndwr Jenkin Prosser and of Edith Doreen Prosser; *m* 1972, Rodina Beaton MacLeod; one *s* two *d. Educ:* Dunvant Sch., Swansea; Swansea Secondary Tech. Sch. Nat. Dip. Mech. Engrg; First Cl. Cert. Steam and Motor Engrg; CEng, MIMarE. Merchant Navy Engr Cadet, 1960–65; sea-going Marine Engr, 1965–72; shore-based Marine Engr, Greenock and Saudi Arabia, 1972–79; Chief Engr, Sealink, 1979–92; OPCS, 1992–96. Mem. (Lab), Kent CC, 1989–97 (Chm., Economic Develt Cttee, 1993–97). *Recreations:* hill walking, family outings, awaiting the revival of Welsh Rugby. *Address:* 26 Coombe Valley Road, Dover, Kent CT17 0EP. *T:* (01304) 201199. *Club:* Marine Officers' (Dover).

PROSSER, Sir Ian (Maurice Gray), Kt 1995; FCA; Executive Chairman, Bass PLC, since 2000 (Chairman and Chief Executive, 1987–2000); *b* 5 July 1943; *s* of late Maurice and of Freda Prosser; *m* 1964, Elizabeth Herman (separated); two *d. Educ:* King Edward's School, Bath; Watford Grammar School; Birmingham Univ. (BComm). Coopers & Lybrand, 1964–69; Bass Charrington Ltd, later Bass PLC, 1969–: Financial Dir, 1978–84; Vice Chm., 1982–87; Gp Man. Dir, 1984–87. Director: Boots Co., 1984–96; Lloyds TSB Gp (formerly Lloyds Bank), 1988–99; BP, 1997– (Dep. Chm., 1999–); Glaxo Smithkline plc (formerly Smithkline Beecham PLC), 1999–. Chm., Stock Exchange Listed Cos Adv. Cttee, 1992–98 (Mem., 1990–98). Chm., Brewers and Licensed Retailers Assoc. (formerly Brewers' Soc.), 1992–94 (Dir, 1983–2000). *Recreations:* bridge, theatre, music. *Address:* Bass PLC, 20 North Audley Street, W1K 6WN. *T:* (020) 7409 1919. *Club:* Royal Automobile.

PROSSER, Jeffrey; Chairman, Kings Lynn and Wisbech NHS Trust, since 2000; *b* 13 June 1942; *s* of Trevor and Beryl Prosser; *m* 1st, 1968, Margaret Sumpter (marr. diss. 1988); three *s*; 2nd, 1989, Sandra Walmsley. *Educ:* University Coll., Cardiff (Dip. Social Services); Leicester Univ. (Dip. Social Work). Social worker, Herts CC, 1968–72; Principal Social Worker, Northwick Park Hosp., 1972–74; Divl Manager, Cambs CC, 1974–79; Asst Dir, Haringey LBC, 1979–82; Area Dir, Devon CC, 1982–84; Dep. Dir of Social Services, Enfield LBC, 1984–86; Gen. Manager, Tower Hamlets HA, 1986–89; Dir of Community Care, Court Cavendish plc, 1989–92; Controller of Community Services, 1993–95, Dir of Community Services, 1995–99, Dir of Social Affairs, 1999, London Bor. of Barnet. Chm., Flagship Hsg Gp, 1999–; Vice Chm., Peddars Way Housing Assoc., 1998–99. Chm., Weeting Parish Council, 1999–2000. *Recreations:* gardening, horse riding, cycling, photography. *Address:* The Old Rectory, Rectory Lane, Weeting, Brandon, Suffolk IP27 0PX. *T:* (01842) 812672. *Club:* Ariel Motor Cycle Owners.

PROSSER, Kevin John; QC 1996; tax barrister; a Recorder, since 2000; *b* 26 Aug. 1957; *s* of Sidney Ronald Prosser and Rita Lillian Prosser; *m* 1994, Mary Elizabeth Stokes; one *s* one *d. Educ:* Broxbourne Sch.; UCL (LLB); St Edmund Hall, Oxford (BCL). Called to the Bar, Lincoln's Inn, 1982; Asst Recorder, 2000. *Publication:* (with D. C. Potter) Tax Appeals, 1990. *Recreations:* opera, squash, reading. *Address:* 16 Bedford Row, WC1R 4EB. *T:* (020) 7414 8080. *Club:* Garrick.

PROSSER, (Leslie) Charles, DFA; Secretary to Royal Fine Art Commission for Scotland, since 1976; *b* 27 Oct. 1939; *s* of Dr Leslie John Prosser and Eleanor Alice May (*née* Chapman); *m* 1960, Coral Williams; one *s* two *d. Educ:* Sedbergh Sch.; Bath Acad. of Art, Corsham; Slade Sch. of Fine Art (DFA); Kungl. Akademien Konsthögskolan, Stockholm; Inst. of Educn, Leeds Univ. (DAEd). Asst Lectr in Fine Art, Blackpool Sch. of Art, 1962–64; Leverhulme European Arts Research Award, Stockholm, 1964–65; Lectr in Fine Art, Leeds Coll. of Art, later Jacob Kramer Coll. of Art, 1965–76; research in art educn, 1974–75. Ed., Royal Fine Art Commn for Scotland pubns, 1976–. Mem. UK Cttee, Hong Kong Architecture Exhibn, Edinburgh, 1996–97. Mem., Scotch Malt Whisky Soc., Leith, 1991–. FRSA 1997; Hon. FRIAS 1997. *Publications:* contrib. to environmental design jls. *Recreation:* pondering about structures. *Address:* 28 Mayfield Terrace, Edinburgh EH9 1RZ. *T:* (0131) 668 1141.

PROSSER, Margaret Theresa, OBE 1997; Deputy General Secretary, Transport and General Workers' Union, since 1999; Treasurer, Labour Party, since 1996; *b* 22 Aug. 1937; *d* of Frederick James and Lillian (*née* Barry); *m* (marr. diss.); one *s* two *d. Educ:* St Philomena's Convent, Carshalton; North East London Polytechnic (Post Grad. Dip. in Advice and Inf. Studies, 1977). Associate Mem., Inst. of Legal Execs, 1982. Advice Centre Organiser, Southwark Community Develt Project, 1974–76; Advr, Southwark Law Project, 1976–83; Transport and General Workers' Union: official, 1983–; Nat. Sec., 1984–92; Nat. Organiser, 1992–99. Pres., TUC, 1995–96. Member: Equal Opportunities Commn, 1987–93; Employment Appeal Tribunal, 1995–; Central Arbitration Cttee, 2000–; Low Pay Commn, 2000–. *Recreations:* walking, gardening, reading. *Address:* 24 Shannon Way, Beckenham, Kent BR3 1WG. *T:* (020) 8658 3281.

PROSSER, Raymond Frederick, CB 1973; MC 1942; *b* 12 Sept. 1919; *s* of Frederick Charles Prosser and Jane Prosser (*née* Lawless); *m* 1949, Fay Newmarch Holmes; two *s* three *d. Educ:* Wimbledon Coll.; The Queen's Coll., Oxford (1938–39 and 1946). Served Royal Artillery (Field), 1939–45 (MC, despatches): service in Egypt, Libya, India and Burma; Temp. Major. Asst Principal, Min. of Civil Aviation, 1947; Sec., Air Transport Advisory Council, 1952–57; Private Sec. to Minister of Transport and Civil Aviation, 1959, and to Minister of Aviation, 1959–61; Counsellor (Civil Aviation), HM Embassy, Washington, DC, 1965–68; Under-Sec., Marine Div., BoT, later DTI, 1968–72; Deputy Sec., Regional Industrial Organisation and Policy, DTI, later DoI, 1972–77; Principal Estabt and Finance Officer, Depts of Industry, Trade, and Prices and Consumer Protection, 1977–79, retired. Dir, European Investment Bank, 1973–77. Mem. (part-time), CAA, 1980–85. *Address:* Juniper House, Shalford Common, Shalford, Guildford, Surrey GU4 8DF. *T:* (01483) 566498.

PROSSER, William David; *see* Prosser, Hon. Lord.

PROTHEROE, Alan Hackford, CBE (mil.) 1991 (MBE (mil.) 1980); TD 1981; DL; journalist and media consultant; Director, Europac Group Ltd, since 1989 (Chairman, 1990–2000); *b* 10 Jan. 1934; *s* of Rev. B. P. Protheroe and R. C. M. Protheroe; *m* 1956, Anne Miller (*d* 1999); two *s. Educ:* Maesteg Grammar Sch., Glamorgan. FBIM; MIPR. Nat. Service, 2nd Lieut The Welch Regt, 1954–56; Lt-Col, Royal Regt of Wales (TA), 1979–84; Col, 1984–90. Reporter, Glamorgan Gazette, 1951–53; BBC Wales: Reporter, 1957–59; Industrial Correspondent, 1959–64; Editor, News and Current Affairs, 1964–70; BBC TV News: Asst Editor, 1970–72; Dep. Editor, 1972–77; Editor, 1977–80; Asst Dir, BBC News and Current Affairs, 1980–82; Asst Dir Gen., BBC, 1982–87. During BBC career wrote, produced, directed and presented films and radio programmes, reported wars, and travelled widely; seconded to Greek Govt to assist in reorganisation of Greek TV, 1973. Man. Dir, Services Sound and Vision Corp., 1988–94; Director: Visnews Ltd, 1982–87; Defence Public Affairs Consultants Ltd, 1987–. Mem., Steering Cttee, EBU News Gp, 1977–87. Mem. Council, RUSI, 1984–87; Association of British Editors: Founder Mem., 1984–; Dep. Chm., 1984–87; Chm., 1987. Chm., Eastern Wessex Reserve Forces Assoc., 1991–99 (Dep. Chm., 1990–91). St James's Vice Pres., 1990–, and Mem. Bd of Mgt, 1992–, RBL; Dir, RBL Training, 1992–99. Hon. Col, TA Information Officers, 1991–96. DL Bucks, 1993. *Publications:* contribs to newspapers and specialist jls on industrial, media and defence affairs. *Recreations:* wine, travel, photography. *Address:* Amberleigh House, 60 Chapman Lane, Flackwell Heath, Bucks HP10 9BD. *T:* and *Fax:* (01628) 528492. *Club:* Army and Navy.

PROUDFOOT, Bruce; *see* Proudfoot, V. B.

PROUDFOOT, (George) Wilfred; owner, self-service stores; consultant in distribution; professsional hypnotist and hypnotherapist, Master Practitioner of Neuro-Linguistic Programming; owner, Proudfoot School of Hypnosis and Hypnotherapy; *b* 19 December 1921; *m* 1950, Margaret Mary, *d* of Percy Clifford Jackson, Pontefract, Yorks; two *s* one *d. Educ:* Crook Council Sch.; Scarborough Coll. Served War of 1939–45, NCO Fitter in RAF, 1940–46. Served Scarborough Town Council, 1950–58 (Chm. Health Cttee, 1952–58). MP (C) Cleveland Division of Yorkshire, Oct. 1959–Sept. 1964; PPS to Minister of State, Board of Trade, Apr.-July 1962, to Minister of Housing and Local Govt and Minister for Welsh Affairs (Rt Hon. Sir Keith Joseph, Bt, MP), 1962–64; MP (C) Brighouse and Spenborough, 1970–Feb. 1974; Minister of State, Dept of Employment, 1970; contested (C) Brighouse and Spenborough, Oct. 1974. Man. Dir, Radio 270, 1965–. Chm., Scarborough Cons. Assoc., 1978–80; Chm., Cleveland European Constituency Cons. Assoc., 1979–. Professional hypnotist; face lifted by Dr John Williams, USA, 1978. Chm., UK Guild of Hypnotist Examiners, 1983–; Mem., Virginia Satir Internat. Avanta Network, 1987–. *Publications:* The Two Factor Nation, or How to make the people rich, 1977; The Consumer Guide to Hypnosis, 1990. *Recreations:* reading, photography, caravanning, travel, walking, jogging. *Address:* 278 Scalby Road, Scarborough, North Yorkshire YO12 6EA. *T:* (01723) 367027.

PROUDFOOT, Prof. (Vincent) Bruce, OBE 1997; FSA 1963; FRSE 1979; FRSGS; Professor of Geography, University of St Andrews, 1974–93, Emeritus 1993; *b* 24 Sept. 1930; *s* of late Bruce Falconer Proudfoot; *m* 1961, Edwina Valmai Windram Field; two *s. Educ:* Royal Belfast Academical Instn; Queen's Univ., Belfast (BA, PhD). Research Officer, Nuffield Quaternary Research Unit, QUB, 1954–58; Lectr in Geography, QUB, 1958–59, Durham Univ., 1959–67; Tutor, 1960–63, Librarian, 1963–65, Hatfield Coll., Durham; Visiting Fellow, Univ. of Auckland, NZ, and Commonwealth Vis. Fellow, Australia, 1966; Associate Prof., 1967–70, Prof., 1970–74, Univ. of Alberta, Edmonton, Canada; Acting Chm., Dept of Geography, Univ. of Alberta, 1970–71; Co-ordinator, Socio-Economic Opportunity Studies, and Staff Consultant, Alberta Human Resources Research Council, 1971–72. Trustee, Nat. Mus. of Antiquities of Scotland, 1982–85. Chairman: Rural Geog. Study Gp, Inst. of British Geographers, 1980–84; Soc. for Landscape Studies, 1979–83. Royal Society of Edinburgh: Mem. Council, 1982–85 and 1990–91; Vice-Pres., 1985–88; Gen. Sec., 1991–96; Bicentenary Medal, 1997. Vice-Pres., Soc. of Antiquaries of Scotland, 1982–85; Pres., Section H (Anthrop. and Archaeol.), BAAS, 1985; Hon. Pres., Scottish Assoc. of Geography Teachers, 1982–84; Royal Scottish Geographical Society: Mem. Council, 1975–78, 1992–93; Chm. Council, 1993–99; Vice-Pres., 1993–; Hon. Editor, 1978–92; Fellow, 1991; Chm., Dundee Centre, 1993–99 (Mem., Cttee, 1976–93, 1999–). Lectures: Lister, BAAS, 1964; Annual, Soc. for Landscape Studies, 1983; Estyn Evans, QUB, 1985. *Publications:* The Downpatrick Gold Find, 1955; (with R. G. Ironside *et al*) Frontier Settlement Studies, 1974; (ed) Site, Environment and Economy, 1983; numerous papers in geographical, archaeological and soils jls. *Recreation:* gardening. *Address:* Westgate, Wardlaw Gardens, St Andrews, Scotland KY16 9DW. *T:* (01334) 473293. *Club:* New (Edinburgh).

PROUDFOOT, Wilfred; *see* Proudfoot, G. W.

PROUDMAN, Sonia Rosemary Susan, (Mrs C. Cartwright); QC 1994; a Recorder, since 2000; *b* 30 July 1949; *d* of Kenneth Oliphant Proudman and Sati Proudman (*née* Hekimian); *m* 1987, Crispian Cartwright; one *d. Educ:* St Paul's Girls' Sch. (Foundn Schol.); Lady Margaret Hall, Oxford (Open Schol.; BA 1st Cl. Hons Jurisprudence 1971; MA 1973). Called to the Bar, Lincoln's Inn, 1972 (Kennedy Schol., Buchanan Prize), Bencher, 1996; Oxford Univ. Eldon Law Schol., 1973; in practice at Chancery Bar, 1974–. Mem., Oxford Law Faculty Adv. Bd, 2000–. *Recreation:* taking enormous notice of hats and backchat. *Address:* 11 New Square, Lincoln's Inn, WC2A 3QB. *Clubs:* Hurlingham, CWIL.

PROUT, family name of **Baron Kingsland**.

PROVAN, James Lyal Clark; Member (C) South East Region, England, European Parliament, since 1999 (South Downs West, 1994–99); Member Board, Rowett Research Institute, since 1990 (Chairman, 1992–98); farmer, businessman; *b* 19 Dec. 1936; *s* of John Provan and Jean (*née* Clark); *m* 1960, Roweena Adele Lewis; twin *s* one *d. Educ:* Ardvreck Sch., Crieff; Oundle Sch., Northants; Royal Agricultural Coll., Cirencester. Member: Tayside Regional Council, 1978–82; Tay River Purification Bd, 1978–82. Chairman: McIntosh Donald Ltd, 1989–94; James McIntosh & Co., 1990–94. MEP (C) NE Scotland, 1979–89; European Parliament: Quaestor, 1987–89; Cons. Chief Whip, 1994–96; Vice Pres., 1999–; Member: Agriculture and Fisheries Cttee, 1979–89 (EDG spokesman on agricl and fisheries affairs, 1982–87); Environment, Consumer Affairs and Public Health Cttee, 1979–89; Vice Pres. and Chief Whip, EPP, 1996–99. Exec. Dir, Scottish Financial Enterprise, 1990–91; non-exec. Dir, CNH Global NV, 1999– (Director: New Holland Holdings NV, 1995–99; New Holland NV, 1996–99). Mem.,

AFRC, 1990–94. Area President, Scottish NFU, 1965 and 1971; Treasurer, Perth and E Perthshire Conservative Assoc., 1975–77; Member, Lord Lieutenant's Queen's Jubilee Appeal Cttee, 1977. ARAgS 1996. FRSA 1987. *Publications:* The European Community: an ever closer union?, 1989; Europe's Freedom to Farm, 1996; Europe's Fishing Blues, 1997. *Recreations:* country pursuits, sailing, flying, musical appreciation, travel. *Address:* Middle Lodge, Barns Green, Horsham, West Sussex RH13 7NL. *T:* (01403) 733700, *Fax:* (01403) 733588. *Clubs:* Farmers', East India; Royal Perth Golfing Society.

PROVAN, Marie; *see* Staunton, M.

PROVERA, Marco T.; *see* Tronchetti Provera.

PROWSE, Florence Irene, (Mrs W. A. Prowse); *see* Calvert, F. I.

PROWSE, Philip (John); theatre director and designer; Co-director, Glasgow Citizens' Theatre, since 1970; Head of Theatre Design Department, since 1995 and Professor of Art, since 1999, Slade School of Fine Art, University College London; *b* 29 Dec. 1937; *s* of late Alan William Auger Prowse and Violet Beatrice (*née* Williamson). *Educ:* King's Sch., Worcester; Malvern Coll. of Art; Slade Sch. of Fine Art. Professional début: Diversions for Royal Ballet, Royal Opera House, 1961; subsequent prodns and designs for opera, ballet and drama including: Glasgow Citizens' Theatre; rep. theatres; West End theatres; Royal Nat. Theatre; RSC, Barbican; Old Vic Theatre; Royal Opera; Royal Ballet; ENO; Sadler's Wells Royal Ballet; Birmingham Royal Ballet; WNO; Scottish Opera; Opera North; English Nat. Ballet (Festival Ballet); Scottish Ballet; prodns in Europe and US; festival appearances: Rome, Wiesbaden, Holland, Warsaw, Zurich, Belgrade, Edinburgh, Cologne, Hamburg, Venice, Parma, E Berlin, Halle, Caracas. *Recreation:* work. *Address:* Citizens' Theatre, 119 Gorbals Street, Glasgow G5 9DS. *T:* (0141) 429 5561.

PRUSINER, Prof. Stanley Ben, MD; Professor of Virology, University of California at Berkeley, since 1984; Professor of Neurology, since 1984, and Professor of Biochemistry, since 1988, University of California at San Francisco; *b* 28 May 1942; *s* of Lawrence Albert Prusiner and Miriam Prusiner (*née* Spigel); *m* 1970, Sandra Lee Turk; two *d. Educ:* Univ. of Pennsylvania (AB 1964; MD 1968). University of California at San Francisco: Med. Intern, 1968–69; Resident in Neurology, 1972–74; Asst Prof. of Neurology, 1974–80; Associate Prof., 1980–84; Prof., 1984–. FAAAS 1998. Foreign Mem., Royal Soc., 1997. Max Planck Res. Award, Alexander von Humboldt Foundn and Max Planck Soc., 1992; Gairdner Foundn Award, 1994; Wolf Prize for Medicine, 1996; Nobel Prize for Physiology or Medicine, 1997. *Publications:* (ed) The Enzymes of Glutamine Metabolism, 1973; Slow Transmissible Diseases of the Nervous System, 2 vols, 1979; Prions, 1987; Prion Diseases of Humans and Animals, 1992; Molecular and Genetic Basis of Neurologic Disease, 1993, 2nd edn 1997; Prions, Prions, Prions, 1996; more than 270 articles in learned jls. *Address:* University of California, 513 Parnassus Avenue, San Francisco, CA 94143, USA.

PRYCE, (George) Terry, CBE 1994; Chairman, G. T. Pryce (Farms) Ltd, since 1996; *b* 26 March 1934; *s* of Edwin Pryce and Hilda Florence (*née* Price); *m* 1957, Thurza Elizabeth Tatham, JP; two *s* one *d. Educ:* Welshpool Grammar Sch.; National Coll. of Food Technol. MFC, FIFST, CIMgt. Dir, various food cos in THF Gp, 1965–70; Asst Man. Dir, Dalgety (UK) Ltd, 1970–72; Man. Dir, Dalgety (UK) and Dir, DPLC, 1972–78; Man. Dir, 1978–81, Chief Exec., 1981–89, Dalgety PLC. Chairman: Solway Foods Ltd, 1990–94; York House Group Ltd, 1996–; Jas Bowman and Sons Ltd, 1999– (Dir, 1991–); Dir, H. P. Bulmer Holdings PLC, 1984–94. Chm., British Soc. for Horticultural Res., later Horticulture Res. Internat., 1990–97; Council Member: AFRC, 1986–94; UK Food and Drink Fedn, 1987–89; Mem. Adv. Bd, Inst. of Food Res., 1988–94. Chm., UK Food Assoc., 1986–88. *Recreation:* sport. *Address:* 89 Brookmans Avenue, Brookmans Park, Hatfield, Herts AL9 7QG. *T:* (01707) 642039. *Clubs:* Athenæum, MCC.

PRYCE, Rt Rev. James Taylor; a Suffragan Bishop of Toronto (Area Bishop of York-Simcoe), 1985–2000; *b* 3 May 1936; *s* of James Pryce and Florence Jane (*née* Taylor); *m* 1962, Marie Louise Connor; two *s* one *d* (and one *s* decd). *Educ:* Bishop's Univ., Lennoxville, Quebec (BA, LST). Ordained deacon, 1962, priest, 1963; Asst Curate, Church of the Ascension, Don Mills, 1962–65; Incumbent: St Thomas' Church, Brooklin, Ont, 1965–70; St Paul's, Lorne Park, 1970–75; Christ Church, Scarborough, 1975–81; St Leonard's, North Toronto, 1981–85. Hon. DD Wycliffe Coll., 1986. *Address:* 8 Pinehurst Court, Aurora, ON L4G 6B2, Canada. *T:* (905) 7277863.

PRYCE, Jonathan; actor; *b* 1 June 1947; lives with partner, Kate Fahy; two *s* one *d. Educ:* RADA. FWCMD 1995. Patron, Friends United Network, 1992–. *Theatre includes:* The Comedians, Nottingham Old Vic, 1975, NY 1976 (Tony Award); title rôle, Hamlet, Royal Court, 1980 (Olivier Award); The Caretaker, Nat. Th., 1981; Accidental Death of an Anarchist, Broadway, 1984; The Seagull, Queen's, 1985; title rôle, Macbeth, RSC, 1986; Uncle Vanya, Vaudeville, 1988; Miss Saigon, Drury Lane, 1989 (Olivier Award and Variety Club Award), NY, 1991 (Tony Award for Best Actor in Musical, 1991); Oliver!, Palladium, 1994; My Fair Lady, RNT, transf. Theatre Royal, Drury Lane, 2001; *television includes:* Roger Doesn't Live Here Anymore (series), 1981; Timon of Athens, 1981; Martin Luther, 1983; Praying Mantis, 1983; Whose Line Is It Anyway?, 1988–; The Man from the Pru, 1990; Selling Hitler, 1991; Mr Wroe's Virgins, 1993; Thicker Than Water, 1993; David, 1997; *films include:* Something wicked this way comes, 1982; The Ploughman's Lunch, 1983; Brazil, 1985; The Doctor and the Devils, 1986; Haunted Honeymoon, 1986; Jumpin' Jack Flash, 1987; Consuming Passions, 1988; The Adventures of Baron Munchausen, 1988; The Rachel Papers, 1989; Glengarry Glen Ross, 1992; The Age of Innocence, 1992; Barbarians at the Gate, 1992; Great Moments in Aviation, 1993; A Business Affair, 1993; Shopping, 1994; Carrington, 1995 (Best Actor Award: Cannes, 1995; Evening Standard, 1996); Evita, 1996; Regeneration, 1997; Tomorrow Never Dies, 1997; Ronin, 1998; Stigmata, 1999; Very Annie Mary, 2001; Bride of the Wind, 2001; *recordings include:* Miss Saigon; Nine—the Concert; Under Milk Wood; Cabaret; Oliver!; Evita; Hey Mr Producer; My Fair Lady. *Address:* c/o Julian Belfrage Associates, 46 Albemarle Street, W1X 4PP.

PRYCE, Maurice Henry Lecorney, FRS 1951; Professor of Physics, University of British Columbia, 1968–78, now Emeritus Professor; *b* 24 Jan. 1913; *e s* of William John Pryce and Hortense Lecorney; *m* 1939, Susanne Margarete Born (marr. diss., 1959); one *s* three *d*; *m* 1961, Freda Mary Kinsey. *Educ:* Royal Grammar Sch., Guildford; Trinity Coll., Cambridge. Commonwealth Fund Fellow at Princeton, NJ, USA, 1935–37; Fellow of Trinity Coll., Cambridge, and Faculty Asst Lecturer, University of Cambridge, 1937–39; Reader in Theoretical Physics, University of Liverpool, 1939–45. Engaged on Radar research with Admiralty Signal Establishment, 1941–44, and on Atomic Energy Research with National Research Council of Canada, Montreal, 1944–45. University Lecturer in Mathematics and Fellow of Trinity Coll., Cambridge, 1945–46; Wykeham Professor of Physics, University of Oxford, 1946–54; Henry Overton Wills Professor of Physics, University of Bristol, 1954–64; Prof. of Physics, University of Southern California, 1964–68. Visiting Professor: Princeton Univ., NJ, USA, 1950–51; Duke Univ., NC, USA, 1958; Univ. of Sussex, 1976–77. Mem., Technical Adv. Cttee to Atomic Energy of Canada Ltd on Nuclear Fuel Waste Management Program, 1979–96. *Publications:* various on Theoretical Physics, in learned journals. *Recreations:* theoretical scientific research, reading, music. *Address:* 4754 West 6th Avenue, Vancouver, BC V6T 1C5, Canada; Physics Department, University of British Columbia, 6224 Agriculture Road, Vancouver, BC V6T 1Z1, Canada. *Club:* Athenæum.

PRYCE, Prof. Roy; Director, 1983–90, Senior Research Fellow, 1990–99, Federal Trust for Education and Research; *b* 4 Oct. 1928; *s* of Thomas and Madeleine Pryce; *m* 1954, Sheila Rose, *d* of Rt Hon. James Griffiths, CH; three *d. Educ:* Grammar Sch., Burton-on-Trent; Emmanuel Coll., Cambridge (MA, PhD). MA Oxon. Research Fellow: Emmanuel Coll., Cambridge, 1953–55; St Antony's Coll., Oxford, 1955–57; Head of London Information Office of High Authority of European Coal and Steel Community, 1957–60; Head of London Inf. Office, Jt Inf. Service of European Communities, 1960–64; Rockefeller Foundn Res. Fellow, 1964–65; Dir, Centre for Contemp. European Studies, Univ. of Sussex, 1965–73; Directorate General for Information, Commission of the European Communities: Dir, 1973–78; Sen. Advr for Direct Elections, 1978–79; Chief Advr for Programming, 1979–81. Vis. Professorial Fellow, Centre for Contemporary European Studies, Univ. of Sussex, 1973–81; Vis. Professor: Coll. of Europe, Bruges, 1965–72; Eur. Univ. Inst., Florence, 1981–83; Eur. Inst. for Public Admin, Maastricht, 1983–88. *Publications:* The Italian Local Elections 1956, 1957; The Political Future of the European Community, 1962; (with John Pinder) Europe After de Gaulle, 1969, German and Ital. edns 1970; The Politics of the European Community, 1973; (ed) The Dynamics of European Union, 1987; (ed jtly) Maastricht and Beyond, 1994; Heathfield Park: a private estate and a Wealden town, 1996; Heathfield and Waldron: an illustrated history, 2000; Rotherfield Hall, 2001. *Recreations:* gardening, collecting paintings and prints.

PRYCE, Terry; *see* Pryce, G. T.

PRYDE, Roderick Stokes, OBE 1999; Director, Educational Enterprises, British Council, since 2000; *b* 26 Jan. 1953; *s* of William Gerard Pryde and Patricia Mary Pryde; *m* 1989, Susanne Mona Graham Hamilton; one *s* three *d. Educ:* George Watson's Coll., Edinburgh; Univ. of Sussex (BA Hons); UCNW, Bangor (PGCE, TESL). Lectr, Univ. of Dijon, 1975–76; English Teaching Co-ordinator, Cie Française des Pneumatiques, Michelin, 1979–81; British Council, 1981–: Asst Regl Lang. Officer, London, 1981–83; Dir of Studies, Milan, 1983–87; Regional Director: Andalucia, 1987–88; Bilbao, 1988–89; Director: Kyoto and Western Japan, 1990–94; English Lang. Centre, Hong Kong, 1994–98; Portugal, 1998–2000. FRSA. *Recreations:* walking, family, reading. *Address:* c/o British Council, 10 Spring Gardens, SW1A 2BN. *T:* (020) 7930 8466. *Clubs:* Royal Commonwealth Society; Watsonian (Edinburgh); Grémio Literário (Lisbon).

PRYER, (Eric) John, CB 1986; Chief Land Registrar, 1983–90; Assistant Secretary, Council for Licensed Conveyancers, 1991–92; *b* 5 Sept. 1929; *s* of late Edward John and Edith Blanche Pryer; *m* 1962, Moyra Helena Cross; one *s* one *d. Educ:* Beckenham and Penge County Grammar Sch.; Birkbeck Coll., London Univ. (BA Hons). Called to the Bar, Gray's Inn, 1957. Exec. Officer, Treasury Solicitor's Dept, 1948; Legal Asst, HM Land Registry, 1959; Asst Land Registrar, 1965; Dist Land Registrar, Durham, 1976; Dep. Chief Land Registrar, 1981–83. Hon. Associate Mem., RICS, 1986. *Publications:* (ed) Ruoff and Roper, The Law and Practice of Registered Conveyancing, 5th edn 1986, 6th edn 1991; Land Registration Handbook, 1990; official pubns; articles in jls. *Recreation:* reading.

PRYKE, Sir Christopher Dudley, 4th Bt *cr* 1926, of Wanstead, co. Essex; *b* 17 April 1946; *s* of William Dudley Pryke and Lucy Irene Pryke (*née* Madgett); *S* uncle, 1998; *m* 1973, Angela Gay Meek (marr. diss. 1986); one *s. Educ:* Hurstpierpoint. ARICS. *Heir: s* James Dudley Pryke, *b* 29 Dec. 1977. *Address:* 69 Wendell Road, Stamford Brook, W12 9SB.

PRYKE, Roy Thomas; Director of the Virtual Staff College, University of Exeter, since 2000; *b* 30 Nov. 1940; *s* of Thomas George and Nellie Matilda Pryke; *m* 1962, Susan Pauline Andrew; one *s* three *d. Educ:* Univ. of Wales (BA Hons); Univ. of Manchester (PGCE). Teacher, Manchester, 1963–71; Education Officer, Devon, 1971–79; Deputy Chief Education Officer: Somerset, 1980–82; Devon, 1983–87; Dep. Chief Educn Officer and Head of Operations, Cambridgeshire, 1987–89; Dir, Educn Services, Kent CC, 1989–98. Adviser to: Council of Local Educn Authorities, 1992–98; ACC, 1994–97; LGA, 1997–98; Chm., Assoc. of Chief Educn Officers, 1996–97. Chm., DFEE Adv. Gp, Schs Improvement Internat., 1999–; Mem., President of Zimbabwe's Commn on Educn and Trng, 1998–99. Vis. Prof. of Educn, Univ. of Exeter, 1998–. FRSA 1988; Hon. FCP 1991. Chevalier, Ordre des Palmes Académiques (France), 1994. *Publications:* contributor to: Open Plan Schools, 1978; The Head's Legal Guide, 1984; The Revolution in Education and Training, 1986; articles in Education Jl on curriculum and on education management. *Recreations:* foreign travel and languages, photography, tennis, running. *Address:* Marinhay, Douglas Avenue, Exmouth, Devon EX8 2EY. *T:* (01395) 277173.

PRYN, Maj.-Gen. William John, OBE 1973; MB, BS; FRCS, FRCSEd; Director of Army Surgery, and Consulting Surgeon to the Army, 1982–86, retired; *b* 25 Jan. 1928; *s* of late Col Richard Harold Cotter Pryn, FRCS, late RAMC and Una St George Ormsby (*née* Roe); *m* 1st, 1952, Alison Lynette (marr. diss.), 2nd *d* of Captain Norman Arthur Cyril Hardy, RN; two *s* one *d*; 2nd, 1982, June de Medina, *d* of Surg. Comdr Norman Bernard de Medina Greenstreet, RN; one step *s* one step *d. Educ:* Malvern Coll.; Guy's Hosp. Med. Sch., London Univ. (MB, BS 1951). MRCS, LRCP 1951; FRCS 1958; FRCSEd 1984. Trooper, 21st SAS Regt (Artists Rifles), TA, 1948–50. House appts, Gen. Hosp., Ramsgate and Royal Berks Hosp., Reading, 1951–52; commnd into RAMC, 1952; Regtl MO to No 9 Training Regt RE, 1952–53; surg. appts in mil. hosps in UK, Cyprus and N Africa, 1953–58; seconded as Surg. Registrar, Royal Postgrad. Med. Sch., Hammersmith Hosp., 1958–59; Officer i/c Surg. Div. and Consultant Surgeon to mil. hosps, Malaya, Singapore, N Borneo and UK, 1959–69; CO BMH Dhekelia, 1969–72; Sen. Consultant Surgeon in mil. hosps, UK and NI, 1972–77; Consulting Surgeon to BAOR, 1977–82; Consultant in Surgery to Royal Hosp., Chelsea, 1982–86; Hon. Consultant to S Dist, Kensington and Chelsea and Westminster AHA (T), 1981. Member: EUROMED Gp on Emergency Medicine, 1980–86; Specialty Bd in Surgery, and Reg. Trng Cttee in Gen. Surgery, Defence Medical Services, 1982–86; Med. Cttee, Defence Scientific Adv. Council, 1982–86; BMA, 1950–; Wessex Surgeons Club, 1976–. Member Council: RAMC, 1982–86; Mil. Surgical Soc., 1982–. Fellow, Assoc. of Surgeons of GB and Ireland, 1960 (Mem., Educn Adv. Cttee, 1982–86). QHS 1981–86. OStJ 1984. Mem., Editorial Bd, Injury, 1982–86. *Publications:* (contrib.) Field Surgery Pocket Book, 1981; original articles in the Lancet and British Jl of Surgery. *Recreations:* fishing, shooting and other country pursuits, golf, tennis, sailing, gardening, joinery, house maintenance.

PRYNNE, Andrew Geoffrey Lockyer; QC 1995; *b* 28 May 1953; *s* of late Maj.-Gen. Michael Whitworth Prynne, CB, CBE and Jean Violet Prynne; *m* 1977, Catriona Mary Brougham; three *d. Educ:* Marlborough Coll.; Univ. of Southampton (LLB Hons). Called to the Bar, Middle Temple, 1975. Mem., Lord Chancellor's Multi-Party Actions Wkg Gp,

1997–. Asst Boundary Comr, 2000–. CEDR Accreditated Mediator, 2000. *Recreations:* sailing, shooting, ski-ing. *Address:* 2 Harcourt Buildings, Temple, EC4Y 9DB. *T:* (020) 7583 9020. *Clubs:* Royal Yacht Squadron, Royal Solent Yacht, Island Sailing (IoW); Bar Yacht.

PRYOR, Arthur John, CB 1997; PhD; competition consultant, since 1996; Head, Competition Policy Division, Department of Trade and Industry, 1993–96; *b* 7 March 1939; *s* of late Quinton Arthur Pryor, FRICS and Elsie Margaret (*née* Luscombe); *m* 1964, Marilyn Kay Petley; one *s* one *d. Educ:* Harrow County Grammar Sch.; Downing Coll., Cambridge (MA; PhD). Asst Lectr, then Lectr, in Spanish and Portuguese, UC Cardiff, 1963–66; Asst Principal, BoT and ECGD, 1966–69; Principal, DTI, 1970–73; First Sec., British Embassy, Washington, 1973–75; Principal, Dept of Trade, 1975–77; Assistant Secretary: Shipping Policy Div., Dept of Trade, 1977–80; Air Div., DoI, 1980–83; Department of Trade and Industry: Asst Sec., Internat. Trade Policy Div., 1984–85; Under Sec. and Regional Dir, W Midlands Region, 1985–88; Dir Gen., BNSC, 1988–93. Mem., Competition (formerly Monopolies and Mergers) Commn, 1998– (Mem., Appeal Panel, 2000–). *Publications:* contribs to modern lang., space and competition jls. *Recreations:* tennis, golf, book collecting. *Address:* c/o Competition Commission, New Court, 48 Carey Street, WC2A 2JT. *T:* (020) 7271 0100.

PRYOR, His Honour Brian Hugh; QC 1982; a Circuit Judge, 1986–2001; *b* 11 March 1931; *s* of Lt-Col Ronald Ernest Pryor, Royal Sussex Regt, and Violet Kathleen Pryor (*née* Steele); *m* 1955, Jane Mary Smith; one *s* two *d. Educ:* Chichester High Sch.; University Coll., Oxford (Open Exhibnr Mod. History; BA Jurisprudence). Called to the Bar, Lincoln's Inn, 1956; Sir Thomas More Bursary, Lincoln's Inn, 1958. Member: SE Circuit Bar Mess, 1957; Kent County Bar Mess, 1957; Chm., Kent Bar Mess, 1979–82; Mem., SE Circuit Bar Mess Wine Cttee, 1979–82. A Recorder, 1981–86; Resident Judge, Woolwich Crown Court, 1993–99. Mem., Res. Ethics Cttee, Camberwell HA and King's Healthcare NHS Trust, 1990–95. *Recreation:* gardening.

PRYOR, John Pembro, MS; FRCS; Reader, Institute of Urology, University College, London, since 1996; Hon. Consultant Urological Surgeon to St Peter's Hospital; *b* 25 Aug. 1937; *s* of William Benjamin Pryor and Kathleen Pryor; *m* 1959, Marion Hopkins; four *s. Educ:* Reading Sch.; King's Coll. and King's Coll. Hosp. Med. Sch. (MB, BS). AKC 1961; FRCS 1967; MS London 1971. Training appointments: Doncaster Royal Infirm., 1965–66; Univ. of Calif, San Francisco, 1968–69; KCH and St Paul's Hosp., 1971–72; Consultant Urol Surgeon to KCH and St Peter's Hosp., 1975–94; Dean, Inst. of Urology, London Univ., 1978–85. Hunterian Prof., RCS, 1971 and 1995. Chairman: (first), British Andrology Soc., 1979–84; European Assoc. of Genital Microsurgeons, 1992–95; Impotence Assoc., 1999–2001; Eur. Sexual Alliance, 1999–; Pres., Eur. Soc. for Impotence Research, 1999–2001. Treas., British Jl of Urology, 1991–99. St Peter's Medal, British Assoc. of Urol Surgeons, 1995. *Publications:* (ed jtly) Andrology, 1987; (ed) Urological prostheses, appliances and catheters, 1992; (jtly) Impotence: an integrated approach to clinical practice, 1992; articles on urology and andrology in scientific jls. *Address:* Andrology Unit, Lister Hospital, Chelsea Bridge Road, SW1W 8RH. *T:* (020) 7730 3417.

PRYOR, Robert Charles; QC 1983; **His Honour Judge Pryor;** a Circuit Judge, since 1991; *b* 10 Dec. 1938; *s* of Charles Selwyn Pryor and Olive Woodall Pryor; *m* 1969, Virginia Sykes; one *s* one *d. Educ:* Eton; Trinity Coll., Cambridge (BA). National Service, KRRC, 2nd Lieut 1958. Called to the Bar, Inner Temple, 1963; a Recorder, 1989–91. Director, Sun Life Corp. (formerly Sun Life Assurance) plc, 1977–91. *Address:* Falcon Chambers, Falcon Court, EC4Y 1AA.

PRYS-DAVIES, family name of **Baron Prys-Davies**.

PRYS-DAVIES, Baron *cr* 1982 (Life Peer), of Llanegryn in the County of Gwynedd; **Gwilym Prys Prys-Davies;** Partner, Morgan Bruce (formerly Morgan Bruce & Nicholas), Solicitors, Cardiff, Pontypridd, 1957–87, retired; *b* 8 Dec. 1923; *s* of William and Mary Matilda Davies; *m* 1951, Llinos Evans; three *d. Educ:* Towyn Sch., Towyn, Merioneth; University College of Wales, Aberystwyth. Served RN, 1942–46. Faculty of Law, UCW, Aberystwyth, 1946–52; President of Debates, Union UCW, 1949; President Students' Rep. Council, 1950; LLB 1949; LLM 1952. Admitted Solicitor, 1956. Contested (Lab) Carmarthen, 1966. Special Adviser to Sec. of State for Wales, 1974–78. Official opposition spokesman: on health, 1983–89; on N Ireland, 1982–93; on Welsh Office, 1987–95. Member, H of L Select Committee: on Parochial Charities Bill and Small Charities Bill, 1983–84; on murder and life imprisonment, 1988–89; on Central and Local Govt, 1995–96; Member: British-Irish Inter-Parly Body, 1990–; Jt Cttee on Statutory Instruments, 1990–98; Delegated Powers and Deregulation Cttee, 1998–. Chm., Welsh Hosps Bd, 1968–74; Member: Welsh Council, 1967–69; Welsh Adv. Cttee, ITA, 1966–69; Working Party on 4th TV Service in Wales, Home Office and Welsh Office, 1975–; Adv. Gp, Use of Fetuses and Fetal Material for Res., DHSS and Welsh Office, 1972; Econ. and Social Cttee, EEC, 1978–82. Chm., NPFA (Cymru), 1998–. Vice-Pres., Hon. Soc. of Cymmrodorion, 1993–. Pres., Univ. of Wales Swansea, 1997–; Vice-Pres., Coleg Harlech, 1989–. Hon. Fellow: UCW, Aberystwyth, 1992; Trinity Coll., Carmarthen, 1995; Univ. of Wales Inst., Cardiff, 1995. Hon. LLD Wales, 1996. OStJ 1968. *Publications:* A Central Welsh Council, 1963; Y Ffermwr a'r Gyfraith, 1967; Llafur y Blynyddaedd, 1993. *Address:* Lluest, 78 Church Road, Tonteg, Pontypridd, Mid Glam CF38 1EN. *T:* (01443) 202462.

PRYS-ROBERTS, Prof. Cedric, DM; FRCA; Professor of Anaesthesia, University of Bristol, 1976–99, Emeritus since 2000; President, Royal College of Anaesthetists, 1994–97; *b* 8 Aug. 1935; *s* of late William Prys Roberts and Winifred Prys Roberts (*née* Osborne Jones); *m* 1961, Linda Joyce Bickerstaff; two *s* two *d. Educ:* Dulwich Coll.; St Bartholomew's Hosp. Med. Sch. (MB BS London); MA, DM Oxon; PhD Leeds. FANZCA. Research Fellow, Univ. of Leeds, 1964–67; Clinical Reader in Anaesthetics, Oxford Univ., 1967–76; Fellow, Worcester Coll., Oxford, 1970–76; Hon Cons. Anaesthetist, Radcliffe Infirmary, 1967–76; Prof. of Anaesthesia, Univ. of California, San Diego, 1974; Hon. Consultant Anaesthetist, Bristol Royal Infirmary and Bristol Royal Hosp. for Sick Children, 1976–99. Hunterian Prof., RCS, 1978. *Publications:* (ed) The Circulation in Anaesthesia, 1980; (ed) Pharmacokinetics of Anaesthesia, 1984; (ed) Monitoring in Anaesthesia and Intensive Care, 1994; (ed) International Practice of Anaesthesia, 2 vols, 1996; contribs to learned jls. *Recreations:* mountaineering, ski-ing, philately, music (playing trumpet). *Address:* Foxes Mead, Cleeve Hill Road, Cleeve, Bristol BS49 4PG.

PUAPUA, Rt Hon. Sir Tomasi, KBE 1998; PC 1982; Governor General of Tuvalu, since 1998; *b* 10 Sept. 1938; *s* of Fitilau and Olive Puapua; *m* 1971, Riana Tabokai; two *s* two *d. Educ:* King George V Secondary Sch.; Fiji Sch. of Medicine; Otago Med. Sch., NZ (DPH). Gilbert and Ellice Islands Colony Government: gen. med. practitioner, 1964–70; MO, Public Health, 1971–76; Tuvalu: MP Vaitupu, 1977–98; Prime Minister, 1981–89; Speaker of Parliament, 1993–98. *Recreations:* cricket, fishing, gardening, reading. *Address:* Government House, Funafuti, Tuvalu.

PUDDEPHATT, Andrew Charles; Executive Director, Article 19, International Centre Against Censorship, since 1999; *b* 2 April 1950; *s* of Andrew Ross Puddephatt and Margaret McGuire; two *d. Educ:* Sidney Sussex College, Cambridge (BA 1971). Worked as teacher in 1970s; computer programmer, 1978–81. Councillor, Hackney Council, 1982–90 (Leader, 1986–89). Gen. Sec., NCCL, subseq. Liberty, 1989–95; Dir, Charter 88, 1995–99. *Recreations:* literature, music. *Address:* Article 19, Lancaster House, 33 Islington High Street, N1 9LH. *T:* (020) 7278 9292.

PUDDEPHATT, Prof. Richard John, PhD; FRS 1998; FRS (Can) 1991; Professor of Chemistry, University of Western Ontario, since 1978; *b* 12 Oct. 1943; *s* of Harry and Ena Puddephatt; *m* 1979, Alice Ruth Poulton; one *s* one *d. Educ:* University Coll. London (BSc 1965; PhD 1968). Teaching Fellow, Univ. of Western Ont, 1968–70; Lectr, 1970–77, Sen. Lectr, 1977–78, Univ. of Liverpool. Sen. Editor, Canadian Jl Chem., 1998–. Royal Society of Chemistry: Noble Metals Award, 1991; Nyholm Award, 1997; Chemical Society of Canada: Alcan Award, 1985; Steacie Award, 1996; CIC Medal, 1998; Hellmuth Prize, 2000. *Publications:* The Periodic Table of the Elements, 1972, 2nd edn 1986; The Chemistry of Gold, 1978; contrib. numerous papers to learned jls, mostly on organometallic chemistry. *Recreations:* gardening, golf. *Address:* Department of Chemistry, University of Western Ontario, London, ON N6A 5B7, Canada. *T:* (519) 6792111.

PUENTE, Most Rev. Pablo; Apostolic Nuncio to the Court of St James's, since 1997; *b* 16 June 1931. Ordained priest, Dio. Santander, 1956; entered Diplomatic Service of Holy See, 1962: served in: Paraguay, Santo Domingo, Kenya, Secretariat of State, 1969–73; Lebanon, 1973–75; Yugoslavia, 1976–80; Pro-Nuncio: Indonesia, 1980–86; Senegal, Mali, Capo-Verde Is, Mauritania and Guinea Bissau, 1986–89; Nuncio: Lebanon, 1989–97; Kuwait (and delegate to Arabian Peninsula), 1993–97. *Address:* Apostolic Nunciature, 54 Parkside, SW19 5NE. *T:* (020) 8946 1410, *Fax:* (020) 8947 2494.

PUGH, Alastair Tarrant, CBE 1986; Consultant, Goldman Sachs International Ltd, since 1988; Executive Vice Chairman/Director of Strategy, British Caledonian Group plc, 1985–88; *b* 16 Sept. 1928; *s* of Sqdn Leader Rev. Herbert Cecil Pugh, GC, MA, and Amy Lilian Pugh; *m* 1957, Sylvia Victoria Marlow; two *s* one *d. Educ:* Tettenhall Coll., Staffs; De Havilland Aeronautical Tech. Sch. FRAeS; FCIT; FIFF; CBIM. Design Dept, De Havilland Aircraft Co., 1949–52; Sen. Designer, H. M. Hobson, 1952–55; journalist, Flight, 1955–61; Channel Air Bridge, 1961–63; British United Airways, 1963–70: Planning Dir, 1968; British Caledonian Airways: Dir, R&D, 1970; Production Dir, 1973–74; Corporate Planning Dir, 1974–77; Dep. Chief Exec., 1977–78; Man. Dir, 1978–85. President: Inst. of Freight Forwarders, 1981–82; CIT, 1988–89. Trustee, Brooklands Mus. Trust, 1988–. *Recreation:* the chain-driven Frazer Nash. *Address:* England's Cottage, Sidlow Bridge, Reigate, Surrey RH2 8PN. *T:* (01737) 243456.

PUGH, Alun John; Member (Lab) Clwyd West, National Assembly for Wales, since 1999; Deputy Education Minister, since 2001; *b* 9 June 1955; *s* of Maurice Thomas Pugh, coal miner, and Violet Jane Pugh, nurse; *m* 1978, Janet Hughes; one *s* one *d. Educ:* Tonypandy Grammar Sch.; Poly. of Wales; UC, Cardiff. Lectr in Accounting, Bridgend Coll., 1983–87; Sen. Lectr, Newcastle Coll., 1987–92; Head of Sch., Llandrillo Coll., 1992–96; Asst Principal, W Cheshire Coll., 1996–99. Dep. Health and Social Services Sec., Nat. Assembly for Wales, 2000–01. *Recreation:* mountaineering. *Address:* National Assembly for Wales, Cardiff Bay, Cardiff CF99 1NA. *Club:* Oesterreichische Alpenverein (Innsbrück).

PUGH, Andrew Cartwright; QC 1988; a Recorder, since 1990; *b* 6 June 1937; *s* of late Lewis Gordon Pugh and Erica Pugh; *m* 1984, Chantal Hélène Langevin; two *d. Educ:* Tonbridge; New Coll. Oxford (MA). Served Royal Sussex Regt, 1956–57. Bigelow Teaching Fellow, Law Sch., Univ. of Chicago, 1960–61. Called to the Bar, Inner Temple, 1961, Bencher, 1989. Legal Assessor, GMC and GDC, 1991–. *Recreations:* gardening, reading, tennis. *Address:* Blackstone Chambers, Blackstone House, Temple, EC4Y 9BW. *T:* (020) 7583 1770. *Clubs:* Oxford and Cambridge; Waldron Cricket.

PUGH, Charles Edward, (Ted), CBE 1988; Managing Director, National Nuclear Corporation Ltd, 1984–87; *b* 17 Sept. 1922; *s* of Gwilym Arthur and Elsie Doris Pugh; *m* 1945, Edna Wilkinson; two *s* and *d. Educ:* Bolton and Salford Technical Colleges. CEng, MIMechE; FInstE 1987. Lancashire Electric Power Co., 1941–48; CEGB Project Manager responsible for construction of 6 power stations, 1951–71; Chief Electrical and Control and Instrumentation Engineer, CEGB, Barnwood, 1971–73; Special Services, CEGB, 1973–76; Dir of Projects, CEGB, 1976–82; PWR Project Dir, NNC, 1982–84. Pres., Inst. of Energy, 1988–89. Hon. FINucE 1984. *Recreations:* power stations, sculpture, painting, music, gardening, walking.

PUGH, Edward Clevely; Director, British Council, Poland, 1994–97; *b* 14 Sept. 1937; *s* of late Edgar Pallister Pugh and Dora Lois Pugh (*née* Clevely); *m* 1962, Thirza Carolyn Browning; one *s* one *d. Educ:* Exeter Univ. (BA Econs and Govt 1962); SOAS, Univ. of London. Nat. Service, RN, 1955–57. Robinson Waxed Paper Co. Ltd, 1955 and 1962; British Council, 1963–97: Lectr, Tehran, 1963–67; Asst Rep., Tripoli, 1967–71; Regl Dir, Ndola, Zambia, 1971–74; Dep. Rep., 1974–75, Rep., 1975–77, Ethiopia; seconded to ODM, 1977–79; Dir, FE and Pacific Dept, London, 1979–80; Rep., Tanzania, 1980–83; Dep. Rep., Delhi, 1983–86; Rep., Thailand, 1986–90; Americas, Pacific and Asia Division: Asst Dir, 1990–91; Dep. Dir, 1991–92; Dir, 1992–93; Regl Dir, S Asia and Oceania, 1993–94. *Recreations:* reading, music, theatre, art, walking, swimming. *Address:* 43 Offham Road, W Malling, Maidstone, Kent ME19 6RB. *T:* (01732) 843317.

PUGH, Dr Gillian Mary, OBE 1998; Chief Executive, Coram Family (formerly Thomas Coram Foundation for Children), since 1997; *b* 13 May 1944; *d* of Robert Quested Drayson, *qv*; *m* 1975, Gareth Nigel Pugh (*d* 1981); one *d*; *m* 1989, Martin Waldron; one step *s* two step *d. Educ:* Ashford Sch. for Girls; Univ. of Exeter (BA Hons). Editor: Careers Res. and Adv. Centre, Cambridge, 1966–67; Humanities Curriculum Project, Schs Council/Nuffield Foundn, 1967–70; Asst Dir of Information, Schs Council for Curriculum and Examinations, 1970–74; National Children's Bureau: Sen. Information Officer, 1974–77; Sen. Develt Officer, 1980–86; Dir, Early Childhood Unit, 1986–97; Develt Officer, Voluntary Council for Handicapped Children, 1978–80. Mem., Effective Preschool Educn Project Adv. Gp, DfEE, 1997–. Pres., Child Develt Soc., 1994–96; Chm., Parenting Educn and Support Forum, 1999–; Vice President: Preschool Learning Alliance, 1998 ; British Assoc. of Early Childhood Educn, 1998–; Chair of Govs, Thomas Coram Early Childhood Centre, 1998–. Trustee, Nat. Family and Parenting Inst., 1999–. Vis. Professorial Fellow, London Univ. Inst. of Educn, 2000–. FRSA 1993. Hon. DEd: Manchester Metropolitan, 1994; West of England, 1998; DUniv Open, 1995. Jt Editor, Children & Society, 1992–. *Publications* include: (jtly) The Needs of Parents, 1984; Contemporary Issues in the Early Years, 1992, 3rd edn 2001; Confident Parents, Confidential Children, 1994; (jtly) Learning to Be a Parent, 1996; (jtly) Training to Work in the Early Years, 1998. *Recreations:* gardening, choral singing, walking, tennis. *Address:* Weathervane, Old Shire Lane, Chorleywood, Herts WD3 5PW. *T:* (01923) 285505. *Club:* New Cavendish.

PUGH, Sir Idwal (Vaughan), KCB 1972 (CB 1967); Chairman, Chartered Trust Ltd, 1979–88; Director: Standard Chartered Bank, 1979–88; Halifax Building Society, 1979–88; *b* 10 Feb. 1918; *s* of late Rhys Pugh and Elizabeth Pugh; *m* 1946, Mair Lewis (*d* 1985); one *s* one *d*. *Educ:* Cowbridge Grammar Sch.; St John's Coll., Oxford (Hon. Fellow, 1979). Army Service, 1940–46. Entered Min. of Civil Aviation, 1946; Alternate UK Rep. at International Civil Aviation Organisation, Montreal, 1950–53; Asst Secretary, 1956; Civil Air Attaché, Washington, 1957–59; Under Secretary, Min. of Transport, 1959; Min. of Housing and Local Govt, 1961; Dep. Sec., Min. of Housing and Local Govt, 1966–69; Permanent Sec., Welsh Office, 1969–71; Second Permanent Sec., DoE, 1971–76. Parly Comr for Administration and Health Service Comr for England, Wales and Scotland, 1976–79. Chm., Develt Corp. of Wales, 1980–83. Chm., RNCM, 1988–92 (Hon. Mem., 1992); Vice-Pres, UC Swansea, 1988–94 (Hon. Fellow, 1995); President: Coleg Harlech, 1990–98; Cardiff Business Club, 1991–98. Hon. LLD Wales, 1988. *Address:* 5 Murray Court, 80 Banbury Road, Oxford OX2 6LQ. *Club:* Brooks's.

PUGH, John Arthur, OBE 1968; HM Diplomatic Service, retired; British High Commissioner to Seychelles, 1976–80; *b* 17 July 1920; *er s* of late Thomas Pugh and Dorothy Baker Pugh. *Educ:* Brecon Grammar Sch.; Bristol Univ. RN, 1941–45. Home CS, 1950–54; Gold Coast Admin. Service, 1955–58; Adviser to Ghana Govt, 1958–60; First Sec., British High Commn, Lagos, 1962–65; First Sec. (Economic), Bangkok, and British Perm. Rep. to Economic Commn for Asia and Far East, 1965–68; British Dep. High Comr, Ibadan, 1971–73; Diplomatic Service Inspector, 1973–76. *Publications:* The Friday Man, 1992; editorial and other contributions to jls etc on political affairs, travel and history. *Recreations:* Oriental ceramics, travel. *Address:* Pennybrin, Hay on Wye, Hereford HR3 5RS. *T:* (01497) 820695. *Club:* Royal Commonwealth Society.

PUGH, Dr John David; MP (Lib Dem) Southport, since 2001; *b* 28 June 1948; *s* of James and Patricia Pugh; *m* 1971, Annette; one *s* three *d*. *Educ:* Maidstone Grammar Sch.; Durham Univ.; PhD Manchester; MPhil Nottingham; MA Liverpool. Head: Social Studies, Salesian High Sch., Bootle, 1972–83; Philosophy and Religious Studies, Merchant Taylors' Sch., Crosby, 1983–2001. Mem. (Lib Dem) Sefton MBC, 1987– (Leader, Lib Dem Gp, 1992–; Leader of Council, 2000). *Publication:* The Christian Understanding of God, 1990. *Recreation:* cycling. *Address:* House of Commons, SW1A 0AA; 27 The Walk, Birkdale, Southport, Lancs PR8 4BS. *T:* (01704) 569025. *Club:* National Liberal.

PUGH, John Stanley; Corporate Affairs Executive, Wavertree Technology Park, Liverpool, 1982–99; *b* 9 Dec. 1927; *s* of John Albert and Winifred Lloyd Pugh; *m* 1953, Kathleen Mary; two *s* one *d*. *Educ:* Wallasey Grammar School. Editor: Liverpool Daily Post, 1969–78; Liverpool Echo, 1978–82. *Recreations:* golf, ornithology. *Address:* 21 Church Meadow Lane, Heswall, Wirral, Merseyside L60 4SB. *Club:* Royal Liverpool (Hoylake).

PUGH, Lionel Roger Price, CBE 1975; VRD 1953; Executive Member, British Steel Corporation, 1972–77; *b* 9 May 1916; *s* of late Henry George Pugh, Cardiff; *m* 1942, Joyce Norma Nash; one *s* one *d*. *Educ:* Clifton. FCA. Supply Officer, RNVR, 1938–60; war service mainly in Mediterranean, 1939–46; retired as Lt Comdr, RNR, 1960. With Deloitte & Co., 1933–47; joined Guest Keen Bladwins Iron & Steel Co. Ltd, 1947; Dir 1955; Man. Dir 1960; Chm. 1962; Jt Man. Dir, GKN Steel, 1964. Dir, Product Co-ordination, British Steel Corp., 1967; Dep. Commercial Man. Dir, 1969; Man. Dir, Ops and Supplies, 1970; Mem., Corporate Finance and Planning, 1972; Chairman: BSC (UK) Ltd, 1974–77; BSC Chemicals Ltd, 1974–77; Redpath Dorman Long Ltd, 1974–77. Dir, 1973, Dep. Chm., 1977–86, Bridon plc; Dir, Ryan Internat., 1979–85. Pres., Iron and Steel Inst., 1973; Hon. Member: American Iron and Steel Inst. 1973; Metals Soc., 1976; Inst. of Metals, 1985; Inst. of Materials, 1992. Mem., Civil Aviation Council for Wales, 1962–66; part-time Mem., S Wales Electricity Bd, 1963–67. DL S Glamorgan (formerly Glamorgan), 1963–78. Gold Cross of Merit (Poland), 1942. *Address:* Brook Cottage, Bournes Green, Oakridge, Glos GL6 7NL. *T:* (01452) 770554. *Club:* Cirencester Golf.

PUGH, Peter David S.; *see* Storie-Pugh.

PUGH, Ted; *see* Pugh, C. E.

PUGH, William David, CBE 1965; JP; FIM; CIMgt; retired; Deputy Chairman, English Steel Corporation Ltd, 1965–67 (Managing Director, 1955–65); Director of Personnel, British Steel Corporation (Midland Group), 1967–70; *b* 21 Nov. 1904; *s* of late Sir Arthur and Lady Pugh; *m* 1936, Mary Dorothea Barber; one *d*. *Educ:* Regent Street Polytechnic; Sheffield Univ. Joined Research Dept, Vickers Ltd, Sheffield, 1926, Director, Vickers Ltd, 1962–67; Chairman: The Darlington Forge Ltd, 1957–66; Taylor Bros & Co. Ltd, 1959–66; Director: (and alternate Chairman), Firth Vickers Stainless Steels Ltd, 1948–67; High Speed Steel Alloys Ltd, 1953–68; Industrial Training Council Service, 1960–67; British Iron and Steel Corp. Ltd, 1962–67; Sheffield Boy Scouts Holdings Ltd, 1965–85 (Scout Silver Wolf, 1983); Sheffield Centre for Environmental Research Ltd. Associate of Metallurgy (Sheffield University; Mappin Medallist). Hon. Fellow, Sheffield Hallam Univ. (formerly Sheffield Poly.), 1969. Hon. DMet Sheffield, 1966. *Recreations:* gardening, golf, reading, voluntary work, drystone-walling. *Address:* 8 Royal Croft Drive, Baslow, Bakewell, Derbys DE45 1SN. *T:* (01246) 582386.

PUGSLEY, David Philip; His Honour Judge Pugsley; a Circuit Judge, since 1992; *b* 11 Dec. 1944; *s* of Rev. Clement Pugsley and Edith (*née* Schofield); *m* 1966, Judith Mary Mappin; two *d*. *Educ:* Shebbear College; St Catharine's College, Cambridge (MA); MPhil Birmingham, 1995. Called to the Bar, Middle Temple, 1968; practised Midland and Oxford Circuit until 1985; Chm. of Industrial Tribunals, Birmingham Reg., 1985–92; a Recorder, 1991–92. Pres., Council of Industrial Tribunal Chairmen, 1991–92; Mem., Parole Bd, 1999–. Mem., Editl Bd, Civil Court Procedure, 1999–. *Publications:* (jtly) Industrial Tribunals Compensation for Loss of Pension Rights, 1990; (jtly) The Contract of Employment, 1997; (jtly) Butterworths Employment Compensation Calculator, 1999. *Recreations:* golf, fly fishing, theatre. *Address:* 3 Fountain Court, Steelhouse Lane, Birmingham B4 6DR.

PUIG de la BELLACASA, José Joaquín, Hon. GCVO 1986; Grand Cross of Isabel la Católica; Grand Cross of Merito Naval; Encomienda de Numero de Carlos III; Counsellor of State, Spain, since 1997 (Chairman, Council for Foreign Affairs, 1995–97); *b* 5 June 1931; *s* of José Maria Puig de la Bellacasa and Consuelo de Urdampilleta; *m* 1960, Paz de Aznar Ybarra; four *s* two *d*. *Educ:* Areneros Jesuit Coll., Madrid; Madrid Univ. Barrister-at-law. Entered Diplomatic Service, 1959; Dirección General Politica Exterior, 1961–62; Minister's Cabinet, 1962–69; Counsellor, Spanish Embassy, London, 1971–74; Private Sec. to Prince of Spain, 1974–75, to HM King Juan Carlos, 1975–76; Director-General: Co-op. Tecnica Internacional, 1976; Servicio Exterior, 1977–78; Under-Sec. of State for Foreign Affairs, 1978–80; Ambassador to Holy See, 1980–83; Ambassador to UK, 1983–90; Sec.-Gen., Spanish Royal Household, 1990–91; Ambassador to Portugal, 1991–95. Hon. Fellow, QMC, 1987. Holds several foreign decorations. *Address:* Felipe IV 7, Madrid 28014, Spain. *Clubs:* Beefsteak, White's; Nuevo, Golf de Puerta de Hierro (Madrid).

PULFORD, Richard Charles; Chief Executive, Society of London Theatre and Theatrical Management Association, since 2001; *b* 14 July 1944; *s* of late Charles Edgar Pulford and Grace Mary Pulford (*née* Vickors). *Educ:* Royal Grammar Sch., Newcastle upon Tyne; St Catherine's Coll., Oxford (BA Jurisprudence). Voluntary service in the Sudan, 1966–67; Home Civil Service, 1967–79: Department of Education and Science: Asst Principal, 1967–72, Principal, 1972–75; HM Treasury, 1975–77; Asst Secretary, DES, 1977–79. Arts Council of GB: Dep. Sec.-Gen., 1979–85; South Bank Planning Dir, 1985–86; Gen. Dir (Admin), South Bank Centre, 1986–92; consultant on cultural policy and admin, 1993–2001, including work with/for Min. of Culture, Bulgaria, Min. of Culture, Hungary, Arts Council of GB, Arts Council of England, British Council, Millennium Commn, London Arts Bd, Royal Opera House, Wales Millennium Centre, Birmingham Rep. Theatre. Bd Mem., Internat. Soc. of Performing Arts Administrators, 1988–92 (Pres., 1990–91); Member: South Bank Theatre Bd, 1985–92; Council, English Stage Co., 1989–; Vice Pres., Nat. Campaign for the Arts, 1996– (Chm., 1992–96). Trustee, Crusaid and STAR Foundn, 1993–. *Publications:* articles in various newspapers and specialist magazines. *Recreations:* entertaining at home, Brasiliana, primary smoking, contract bridge. *Address:* 905 Beatty House, Dolphin Square, SW1V 3PN. *T:* (020) 7798 8308, *Fax:* (020) 7387 6353.

PULLAN, Prof. Brian Sebastian, PhD; FBA 1985; Professor of Modern History, University of Manchester, 1973–98; *b* 10 Dec. 1935; *s* of late Horace William Virgo Pullan and Ella Lister Pullan; *m* 1962, Janet Elizabeth Maltby; two *s*. *Educ:* Epsom Coll.; Trinity Coll., Cambridge (MA, PhD); MA Manchester. Nat. Service, RA, 1954–56. Cambridge University: Res. Fellow, Trinity Coll., 1961–63; Official Fellow, Queens' Coll., 1963–72; Univ. Asst Lectr in History, 1964–67; Lectr, 1967–72; Dean, Faculty of Arts, Manchester Univ., 1982–84. Feoffee of Chetham's Hosp. and Library, Manchester, 1981–. Corresp. Fellow, Ateneo Veneto, 1986. Serena Medal, British Academy, 1991. *Publications:* (ed) Sources for the History of Medieval Europe, 1966; (ed) Crisis and Change in the Venetian Economy in the Sixteenth and Seventeenth Centuries, 1968; Rich and Poor in Renaissance Venice, 1971; A History of Early Renaissance Italy, 1973; The Jews of Europe and the Inquisition of Venice, 1983; (ed with Susan Reynolds) Towns and Townspeople in Medieval and Renaissance Europe: essays in memory of Kenneth Hyde, 1990; (ed with David Chambers) Venice: a documentary history 1450–1630, 1992; Poverty and Charity: Europe, Italy, Venice, 1400–1700, 1994; (with Michele Abendstern) A History of the University of Manchester 1951–73, 2000; articles and reviews in learned jls and collections. *Recreations:* dogs, theatre. *Address:* 33 Green Pastures, Heaton Mersey, Stockport SK4 3RB.

PULLÉE, Ernest Edward, CBE 1967; ARCA, ACSD, FSAE, NEAC; painter; Chief Officer, National Council for Diplomas in Art and Design, 1967–74; retired; *b* 19 Feb. 1907; *s* of Ernest and Caroline Elizabeth Pullée; *m* 1933, Margaret Fisher, ARCA, NEAC; one *s*. *Educ:* St Martin's Sch., Dover; Royal Coll. of Art, London. Principal: Gloucester Coll. of Art, 1934–39; Portsmouth Coll. of Art, 1939–45; Leeds Coll. of Art, 1945–56; Leicester Coll. of Art and Design, 1956–67. Regular exhibitor, RA summer exhibns and at London and provincial galls. Pres., Nat. Soc. for Art Educn, 1945, 1959; Chm., Assoc. of Art Instns, 1959; Mem., Nat. Adv. Coun. for Art Educn, 1959; Mem., Nat. Coun. for Diplomas in Art and Design, 1961. FRSA 1952. Hon. Life Mem., NEAC, 1986. Hon. Fellow: Portsmouth Polytechnic, 1976; Leicester Polytechnic, 1977. Hon. DA (Manchester), 1961. *Publications:* contribs to professional and academic jls. *Recreation:* travel. *Address:* c/o Michael Pullée, 48 Wray Common Road, Reigate, Surrey RH2 0NB. *Club:* Chelsea Arts.

PULLEIN-THOMPSON, Denis; *see* Cannan, D.

PULLEIN-THOMPSON, Josephine Mary Wedderburn, MBE 1984; writer; General Secretary, English Centre, International PEN, 1976–93; *b* 3 April 1924; *e d* of H. J. Pullein-Thompson, MC and Joanna Cannan, novelist. *Educ:* briefly at Wychwood Sch., Oxford. Horsewoman and writer; Vis. Comr, 1960–68, Dist Comr, 1970–76, Pony Club; Member: Cttee, Crime Writers' Assoc., 1971–73; Cttee, Children's Writers' Gp, Soc. of Authors, 1973–79 (Dep. Chm., 1978–79); English Centre of International PEN: Cttee, 1974–76; Pres., 1993–97; Vice Pres., 1997–. *Publications:* How Horses are Trained, 1961; (jtly) Ponies in Colour, 1962; Learn to Ride Well, 1966; Horses and Their Owners (anthology), 1970; Ride Better and Better, 1974; (with sisters) Fair Girls and Grey Horses: memories of a country childhood, 1996; *fiction:* It Began with Picotee (with sisters), 1946; Six Ponies, 1946; I had Two Ponies, 1947; Plenty of Ponies, 1949; Pony Club Team, 1950; The Radney Riding Club, 1951; Prince Among Ponies, 1952; One Day Event, 1954; Show Jumping Secret, 1955; Patrick's Pony, 1956; Pony Club Camp, 1957; The Trickjumpers, 1958; All Change, 1961; Race Horse Holiday, 1971; Proud Riders, 1973; Black Ebony, 1975; Star Riders of the Moor, 1976; Fear Treks the Moor, 1978; Black Nightshade, 1978; Ride to the Rescue, 1979; Ghost Horse on the Moor, 1980; The No Good Pony, 1981; Treasure on the Moor, 1982; The Prize Pony, 1982; Black Raven, 1982; Pony Club Cup, 1982; Save the Ponies, 1984; Mystery on the Moor, 1984; Pony Club Challenge, 1984; Pony Club Trek, 1985; Suspicion Stalks the Moor, 1986; Black Swift, 1991; A Job with Horses, 1994; *crime:* Gin and Murder, 1959; They Died in the Spring, 1960; Murder Strikes Pink, 1963; (as J Mann) A Place with Two Faces, 1972. *Recreations:* travelling, gardening, reading, theatre going. *Address:* 16 Knivet Road, SW6 1JH.

See also D. Cannan, D. L. A. Farr.

PULLEN, Dr Roderick Allen; HM Diplomatic Service; High Commissioner to Ghana, since 2000; *b* 11 April 1949; *s* of Derrick Brian Pullen and late Celia Ada Pullen (*née* Wood); *m* 1971, Karen Lesley Sketchley; four *s* one *d*. *Educ:* Maidstone Grammar Sch.; Mansfield Coll., Oxford (BA); Sussex Univ. (DPhil). MoD, 1975–78; Second Sec., UK Delegn to NATO, 1978–80; MoD, 1980–81; First Sec., UK Delegn to CSCE, 1981–82; FCO, 1982–84; Dep. High Comr, Suva, 1984–88; FCO, 1988–90; Counsellor, Paris, 1990–94; Dep. High Comr, Nairobi, 1994–97; Dep. High Comr, Lagos, 1997–2000. *Address:* c/o Foreign and Commonwealth Office, King Charles Street, SW1A 2AH.

PULLEYBLANK, Prof. Edwin George, PhD; FRSC; Professor of Chinese, University of British Columbia, 1966–87, now Emeritus; *b* Calgary, Alberta, 7 Aug. 1922; *s* of W. G. E. Pulleyblank, Calgary; *m* 1945, Winona Ruth Relyea (decd), Arnprior, Ont; one *s* two *d*. *Educ:* Central High School, Calgary; University of Alberta; University of London. BA Hons Classics, Univ. of Alberta, 1942; Nat. Research Council of Canada, 1943–46. School of Oriental and African Studies, Univ. of London: Chinese Govt Schol., 1946; Lectr in Classical Chinese, 1948; PhD in Classical Chinese, 1951; Lectr in Far Eastern History, 1952; Professor of Chinese, University of Cambridge, 1953; Head, Dept of Asian Studies, Univ. of British Columbia, 1968–75. Fellow of Downing Coll., Cambridge, 1955–66. Corresp. Fellow, Italian Inst. for the Middle and Far East, 1993. *Publications:* The Background of the Rebellion of An Lu-Shan, 1955; Middle Chinese, 1984; Lexicon of Reconstructed Pronunciation in Early Middle Chinese, Late Middle Chinese and Early

Mandarin, 1991; Outline of Classical Chinese Grammar, 1995; articles in Asia Major, Bulletin of School of Oriental and African Studies, etc. *Address:* c/o Department of Asian Studies, University of British Columbia, Vancouver, BC V6T 1Z2, Canada.

PULLINGER, Sir (Francis) Alan, Kt 1977; CBE 1970; DL; Chairman, Haden Carrier Ltd, 1961–79; *b* 22 May 1913; *s* of William Pullinger; *m* 1st, 1946, Felicity Charmian Gotch Hobson (decd); two *s* one *d*; 2nd, 1966, Jacqueline Louise Anne Durin (decd). *Educ:* Marlborough Coll.; Balliol Coll., Oxford (MA). Pres., IHVE, 1972–73. Chm., Hertfordshire Scouts, 1976–91. Vice Chm. Council, Benenden Sch., 1980–97. Hon. FCIBSE, 1977. DL Herts, 1982. *Recreations:* mountaineering, sailing, beagling. *Address:* Grange Farm Cottage, Bovingdon Green Lane, Bovingdon, Herts HP3 0LB. *T:* (01442) 831816. *Clubs:* Alpine, Travellers.

PULLMAN, Philip Nicholas Outram, FRSL; author and playwright; *b* 19 Oct. 1946; *s* of Alfred and Audrey Pullman (*née* Merrifield); *m* 1970, Judith Speller; two *s*. *Educ:* Ysgol Ardudwy, Harlech; Exeter Coll., Oxford (BA English Lang. and Lit. 1968). Teacher, Oxford Middle Schools, 1973–86; Lectr (part-time), Westminster Coll., Oxford, 1986–96. Patron, Centre for the Children's Book, 2000. Hon. Fellow, Westminster Inst. of Educn, 1999. Booksellers Assoc. Author of the Year, 2000. *Plays:* Sherlock Holmes and the Adventure of the Limehouse Horror, 1984; The Three Musketeers, 1985; Frankenstein, 1986; Puss in Boots, 1997. *Publications: novels and stories:* Galatea, 1978; Count Karlstein, 1982, illustrated edn 1991; The Ruby in the Smoke, 1985 (Children's Book Award, Internat. Reading Assoc., 1988); The Shadow in the North, 1987; How To Be Cool, 1987; Spring-Heeled Jack, 1989; The Broken Bridge, 1990; The Tiger in the Well, 1991; The White Mercedes, 1992, re-issued as The Butterfly Tattoo, 1998; The Wonderful Story of Aladdin and the Enchanted Lamp, 1993; The Tin Princess, 1994; Thunderbolt's Waxwork, 1994; The Gas-Fitters' Ball, 1995; The Firework-Maker's Daughter, 1995 (Smarties Gold Award, 1996); His Dark Materials: Book One: Northern Lights, 1995 (US title: The Golden Compass) (Guardian Children's Fiction Award, 1996; Carnegie Medal, 1996; British Book Award: Children's Book of the Year, 1996); Book Two: The Subtle Knife, 1997; Book Three: The Amber Spyglass, 2000 (British Book Award: Children's Book of the Year, 2001); Clockwork, or All Wound Up, 1996 (Smarties Silver Award, 1997); I Was a Rat!, 1999; Mossycoat, 1999; Puss in Boots, 2000; *plays:* Sherlock Holmes and the Adventure of the Limehouse Horror, 1993; Frankenstein, 1992. *Recreations:* drawing, music. *Address:* 24 Templar Road, Oxford OX2 8LT. *T:* (01865) 513536.

PULMAN, Prof. Stephen Guy, PhD; FBA 2001; Professor of General Linguistics, University of Oxford, since 2000; Fellow, Somerville College, Oxford, since 2000; *b* 1 Oct. 1949; *s* of Raymond Pulman and Celia Margaret Pulman; *m* 1989, Nicola Jane Verney; one *s* two *d*. *Educ:* Bedford Coll., London (BA Hons English 1972); Univ. of Essex (MA Theoretical Linguistics 1974; PhD Linguistics 1977). Lecturer: Dept of Lang. and Linguistics, Univ. of Essex, 1977–78; Sch. of English and American Studies, UEA, 1978–84; University of Cambridge Computer Laboratory: Lectr, 1984–97; Reader in Computational Linguistics, 1997–2000; Dep. Hd, 1999–2000; Dir, 1988–97, Principal Scientist, 1998–2001, SRI Internat. (formerly Stanford Res. Inst.) Cambridge Computer Sci. Res. Centre. *Publications:* Word Meaning and Belief, 1983; (jtly) Computational Morphology: practical mechanisms for the English lexicon, 1992; contrib. papers to Computational Linguistics, Artificial Intelligence, Linguistics and Philosophy, Philosophical Trans of Royal Soc., etc. *Recreations:* gardening, bird-watching, bell-ringing. *Address:* Somerville College, Oxford OX2 6HD.

PULVERTAFT, Rear-Adm. David Martin, CB 1990; Secretary, Defence, Press and Broadcasting Advisory Committee, 1992–99; *b* 26 March 1938; *s* of late Captain William Godfrey Pulvertaft, OBE, RN and Annie Joan Pulvertaft (*née* Martin); *m* 1961, Mary Rose Jeacock; one *s* two *d*. *Educ:* Canford Sch., Dorset; Britannia RN Coll., Dartmouth; RN Engineering Coll., Manadon. BSc (Eng) 1962. FIMechE 1989 (MIMechE 1974). HMS Ceylon, 1958–59; HMS Anchorite, Singapore, 1963–66; HMS Dreadnought, 1967–71; 10th Submarine Sqdn, 1971–72; HM Dockyard, Devonport, 1973–75; Nat. Defence Coll., Latimer, 1975–76; MoD 1976–78; HM Dockyard, Devonport, 1979–82; RCDS, 1983; MoD, 1984–87; Dir Gen. Aircraft (Navy), 1987–90; Dir Gen., Procurement and Support Orgn (Navy), 1990–92. Chm. of Trustees, Plymouth Naval Base Mus., 2001–; Chm., SW Maritime Hist. Soc., 2000–. *Recreations:* genealogy, printing, bookbinding, British warship figureheads. *Address:* Tucketts, Trusham, Newton Abbot, Devon TQ13 0NR. *Club:* Army and Navy.

PULZER, Prof. Peter George Julius, PhD; FRHistS; Professorial Fellow, Institute for German Studies, University of Birmingham, 1996–99; Gladstone Professor of Government and Public Administration, University of Oxford, 1985–96, now Emeritus; Fellow of All Souls College, 1985–96, now Emeritus; *b* 20 May 1929; *s* of Felix and Margaret Pulzer; *m* 1962, Gillian Mary Marshall; two *s*. *Educ:* Surbiton County Grammar Sch.; King's Coll., Cambridge (1st Cl. Hons Historical Tripos 1950; PhD 1960); London Univ. (1st Cl. Hons BSc Econ 1954). FRHistS 1971. Lectr in Politics, Magdalen Coll. and Christ Church, Oxford, 1957–62; University Lectr in Politics, Oxford, 1960–84; Official Student and Tutor in Politics, Christ Church 1962–84. Visiting Professor: Univ. of Wisconsin, 1965; Sch. of Advanced Internat. Studies, Johns Hopkins Univ., 1972; Univ. of Calif, LA, 1972; Eric Voegelin, Munich Univ., 1988; Potsdam Univ., 1993; Technical Univ., Dresden, 1997; Humboldt Univ., Berlin, 2000. Chairman: Academic Adv. Cttee, Centre for German-Jewish Studies, Univ. of Sussex, 1997–; Leo Baeck Inst., London, 1998–; Mem. Governing Body, Historisches Kolleg, Munich, 1993–97. *Publications:* The Rise of Political Anti-Semitism in Germany and Austria, 1964, 2nd edn 1988 (German edn 1966); Political Representation and Elections in Britain, 1967, 3rd edn 1975; Jews and the German State, 1992; German Politics 1945–1995, 1995; Germany 1870–1945: politics, state formation and war, 1997; (ed with K. R. Luther) Austria 1945–1995: fifty years of the Second Republic, 1998; (ed with Wolfgang Benz) Jews in the Weimer Republic, 1998; (contrib.) German-Jewish History in Modern Times, 1998; contrib. to jls, year books and symposia. *Recreations:* opera, walking. *Address:* All Souls College, Oxford OX1 4AL.

PUMFREY, Hon. Sir Nicholas (Richard), Kt 1997; **Hon. Mr Justice Pumfrey;** a Judge of the High Court of Justice, Chancery Division, since 1997; *b* 22 May 1951; *s* of Peter and Maureen Pumfrey. *Educ:* St Edward's Sch., Oxford; St Edmund Hall, Oxford (BA Physics, 1972, Law, 1974). Called to the Bar, Middle Temple, 1975, Bencher, 1998; QC 1990; Jun. Counsel to HM Treasury (Patents), 1987–90. *Address:* Royal Courts of Justice, Strand, WC2A 2LL.

PUMPHREY, Sir (John) Laurence, KCMG 1973 (CMG 1963); HM Diplomatic Service, retired; Ambassador to Pakistan (formerly High Commissioner), 1971–76; *b* 22 July 1916; *s* of late Charles Ernest Pumphrey and Iris Mary (*née* Moberly-Bell); *m* 1945, Jean, *e d* of Sir Walter Buchanan Riddell, 12th Bt; four *s* one *d*. *Educ:* Winchester; New College, Oxford. Served War of 1939–45 in Army. Foreign Service from 1945. Head of Establishment and Organisation Department, Foreign Office, 1955–60; Counsellor, Staff of British Commissioner-General for SE Asia, Singapore, 1960–63; Counsellor, HM Embassy, Belgrade, 1963–65; Deputy High Commissioner, Nairobi, 1965–67; British High Comr, Zambia, 1967–71. Military Cross, 3rd Class (Greece), 1941. *Address:* Caistron, Thropton, Morpeth, Northumberland NE65 7LG.

PURCELL, Philip James; Chairman and Chief Executive Officer, Morgan Stanley (formerly Morgan Stanley Dean Witter & Co.), since 1997; *b* 5 Sept. 1943; *m* 1964, Anne Marie McNamara. *Educ:* Univ. of Notre Dame (BBA 1964); LSE (MSc 1966); Univ. of Chicago (MBA 1967). Man. Dir, McKinsey & Co., 1967–78; Vice Pres. of Planning and Admin, Sears, Roebuck & Co., 1978–82; CEO, and Pres., subseq. Chm., Dean Witter Discover & Co., 1982–97. Dir, NY Stock Exchange, 1991–96. *Address:* Morgan Stanley, 1585 Broadway, Suite B2, New York, NY 10036-8293, USA.

PURCELL, (Robert) Michael, CMG 1983; HM Diplomatic Service, retired; Adviser and Secretary, East Africa Association, 1984–87; *b* 22 Oct. 1923; *s* of late Lt-Col Walter Purcell and Constance (*née* Fendick); *m* 1965, Julia Evelyn, *o d* of late Brig. Edward Marsh-Kellett; two *d*. *Educ:* Ampleforth Coll. Served 60th Rifles (Greenjackets), 1943–47 (Italian Campaign, 1944–45). Colonial Service, later HMOCS, Uganda, 1949–62, retd; 1st Sec., CRO, later FCO, 1964–68; 1st Sec. (Commercial/Economic), Colombo, 1968–69; FCO, 1969–71; 1st Sec. (Aid), Singapore, 1971–73; Head of Chancery, HM Legation to the Holy See, 1973–76; Counsellor and Dep. High Comr, Malta, 1977–80; Ambassador to Somali Democratic Republic, 1980–83. KCSG 1976. *Recreations:* country life, books, bridge. *Address:* French Mill Cottage, Shaftesbury, Dorset SP7 0LT. *T:* (01747) 53615.

PURCHAS, Christopher Patrick Brooks; QC 1990; a Recorder, since 1986; *b* 20 June 1943; *s* of Rt Hon. Sir Francis Purchas, *qv*; *m* 1st, 1974, Bronwen Mary Vaughan (marr. diss. 1995); two *d*; 2nd, 1998, Diana, *widow* of Dr Ian Hatrick. *Educ:* Summerfield Sch.; Marlborough Coll.; Trinity Coll., Cambridge (MA). Called to the Bar, Inner Temple, 1966, Bencher, 1995. *Recreations:* golf, tennis, shooting, ski-ing. *Address:* Crown Office Chambers, Temple, EC4Y 7EP. *T:* (020) 7797 8100.

See also R. M. Purchas.

PURCHAS, Rt Hon. Sir Francis (Brooks), Kt 1974; PC 1982; a Lord Justice of Appeal, 1982–93; *b* 19 June 1919; *s* of late Captain Francis Purchas, 5th Royal Irish Lancers and late Millicent Purchas (*née* Brooks); *m* 1942, Patricia Mona Kathleen, *d* of Lieut Milburn; two *s*. *Educ:* Summerfields Sch., Oxford; Marlborough Coll.; Trinity Coll., Cambridge. Served RE, 1940–46: North Africa, 1943 (despatches); Hon. Lt-Col retd (Africa Star, Italy Star, 1939–45 Medal; Defence Medal). Allied Mil. Commission, Vienna. Called to Bar, Inner Temple, 1948, QC 1965, Bencher, 1972; practised at Bar, 1948–74; Leader, SE Circuit, 1972–74; Dep. Chm., E Sussex QS, 1966–71; Recorder of Canterbury, 1969–71 (Hon. Recorder of Canterbury, 1972–74); Recorder of the Crown Court, 1972–74; a Judge of the High Court of Justice, Family Div., 1974–82; Presiding Judge, SE Circuit, 1977–82. Comr, Central Criminal Court, 1970–71. Mem., Bar Council, 1966–68, 1969–71, 1972–74. Judicial Mem., City Disputes Panel, 1994–99; Dep. Appeal Comr, PIA, 1994–. FCIArb 1995. Mem. of Livery, Worshipful Co. of Broderers, 1962. *Recreations:* shooting, golf, fishing. *Address:* Parkhurst House, near Haslemere, Surrey GU27 3BY. *T:* (01428) 707280. *Clubs:* Boodle's; Hawks (Cambridge); Royal St George's Golf, West Sussex Golf.

See also C. P. B. Purchas, R. M. Purchas.

PURCHAS, Robin Michael; QC 1987; a Recorder, since 1989; Deputy High Court Judge, since 1994; *b* 12 June 1946; *s* of Rt Hon. Sir Francis Brooks Purchas, *qv*; *m* 1970, Denise Anne Kerr Finlay; one *s* one *d*. *Educ:* Summerfields; Marlborough College; Trinity College, Cambridge (MA). Called to the Bar, Inner Temple, 1968, Bencher, 1996. Bar Council, 2000–. *Recreations:* opera, music, fishing, tennis, ski-ing, sailing, shooting, golf. *Address:* (chambers) 2 Harcourt Buildings, Temple, EC4Y 9DB. *T:* (020) 7353 8415. *Clubs:* Boodle's, Lansdowne, Queen's; Royal West Norfolk Golf; Royal Worlington and Newmarket Golf; Brancaster Staithe Sailing.

See also C. P. B. Purchas.

PURCHASE, Kenneth; MP (Lab and Co-op) Wolverhampton North East, since 1992; *b* 8 Jan. 1939; *m* 1960, Brenda Sanders; two *d*. *Educ:* Springfield Secondary Modern Sch.; Wolverhampton Polytechnic (BA). Toolmaker: Lucas, 1960–68; Ever Ready, 1968–76; with Telford Development Corp., 1977–80; with Walsall MBC, 1981–82; Business Development Advr and Company Sec., Black Country CDA Ltd, 1982–92. Mem., Wolverhampton HA, 1972–87. Mem. (Lab) Wolverhampton CBC, subseq. MBC, 1970–90. Contested (Lab) Wolverhampton North East, 1987. PPS to Sec. of State for Foreign Affairs, 1997–2001, to Pres. of the Council and Ldr of the H of C, 2001–. Mem., Select Cttee on Trade and Industry, 1993–97; Jt Chm., All Party Exports Gp, 1993; Chm., PLP Trade and Industry Cttee, 1992–97; Sec., All Party Jazz Appreciation Soc., 1996–98. *Address:* House of Commons, SW1A 0AA.

PURDEN, Roma Laurette, (Laurie), (Mrs J. K. Kotch), MBE 1973; journalist and writer; *b* 30 Sept. 1928; *d* of George Cecil Arnold Purden and Constance Mary Sheppard; *m* 1957, John Keith Kotch (*d* 1979); two *d*. *Educ:* Harecroft Sch., Tunbridge Wells. Fiction Editor, Home Notes, 1948–51; Asst Editor, Home Notes, 1951–52; Asst Editor, Woman's Own, 1952; Sen. Asst Editor, Girl, 1952–54; Editor of: Housewife, 1954–57; Home, 1957–62; House Beautiful, 1963–65; Good Housekeeping, 1965–73; Editor-in-Chief: Good Housekeeping, and Womancraft, 1973–77; Woman's Journal, 1978–88; Woman & Home, 1982–83. Dir, Brickfield Publications Ltd, 1978–80. Magazine Editor of the Year, 1979, British Soc. of Magazine Editors; Consumer Magazine of the Year awarded by Periodical Publishers Assoc. to Woman's Journal, 1985. *Address:* 174 Pavilion Road, SW1X 0AW. *T:* (020) 7730 4021.

PURDON, Maj.-Gen. Corran William Brooke, CBE 1970; MC 1945; CPM 1982; *b* 4 May 1921; *s* of Maj.-Gen. William Brooke Purdon, DSO, OBE, MC, KHS, and Dorothy Myrtle Coates; *m* 1945, Maureen Patricia, *d* of Major J. F. Petrie, Guides Infantry, IA; two *s* one *d*. *Educ:* Rokeby, Wimbledon; Campbell Coll., Belfast; RMC Sandhurst. MBIM. Commnd into Royal Ulster Rifles, 1939; service with Army Commandos, France and Germany, 1940–45 (wounded; MC); 1st Bn RU Rifles, Palestine, 1945–46; GHQ MELF, 1949–51; psc 1955; Staff, Malayan Emergency, 1956–58; Co. Comdr, 1 RU Rifles, Cyprus Emergency, 1958; CO, 1st Bn RU Rifles, BAOR and Borneo War, 1962–64; GSO1 and Chief Instructor, Sch. of Infantry, Warminster, 1965–67; Comdr, Sultan's Armed Forces, Oman, and Dir of Ops, Dhofar War, 1967–70 (Sultan's Bravery Medal, 1968 and Distinguished Service Medal for Gallantry, 1969, Oman; CBE); Commandant: Sch. of Infantry, Warminster, 1970–72; Small Arms Sch. Corps, 1970–72; GOC, NW Dist, 1972–74; GOC Near East Land Forces, 1974–76, retired. Dep. Comr, Royal Hong Kong Police Force, 1978–81; St John Ambulance: Comdr, Wilts, 1981–84; Mem. Council, 1981–86; Pres., Devizes Div., 1993–. Hon. Colonel: Queen's Univ. Belfast OTC, 1975–78; D (London Irish Rifles), 4th Bn Royal Irish Rangers, 1986–93. Pres. Army Gymnastic Union, 1973–76; Patron, Small Arms Sch. Corps Assoc., 1985–90; Governor, Royal Humane Soc., 1985–. KStJ 1983 (Service Medal, 1999). Commendation Medal (Oman), 1992; Médaille d'Honneur de St Nazaire, 2000. *Publications:* List the Bugle: reminiscences of an Irish soldier, 1993;

articles in military jls. *Recreations:* physical training, swimming, dogs (English bull terriers, German shepherds). *Address:* Old Park House, Devizes, Wilts SN10 5JR. *Clubs:* Army and Navy; Hong Kong.

PURDUE, Marie Theresa; *see* Conte-Helm, M. T.

PURDY, George; *see* Purdy, W. G.

PURDY, (William) George; Chief Scout, since 1996; *b* 16 April 1942; *s* of George Purdy and Amelia Jane Purdy (*née* McConnell); *m* 1969, Judith Sara Isabell Kerr; two *s*. *Educ:* Annadale Grammar Sch. NICS, 1960–91, 1993–96; Chief Exec., NI Software Industry Fedn, 1991–93. Scout Leader, 1962–94, Chief Comr, NI, 1994–96, Scout Assoc. *Recreations:* golf, tennis. *Address:* Scout Association, Gilwell Park, Chingford, E4 7QW. *T:* (020) 8433 7104, *Fax:* (020) 8433 7108; *e-mail:* chief.scout@scout.org.uk.

PURKIS, Dr Andrew James; Chief Executive, Diana, Princess of Wales Memorial Fund, since 1998; *b* 24 Jan. 1949; *s* of late Clifford Henry Purkis and Mildred Jeannie Purkis; *m* 1980, Jennifer Harwood Smith; one *s* one *d*. *Educ:* Highgate Sch.; Corpus Christi Coll., Oxford; St Antony's Coll., Oxford. 1st class Hons MA Mod. Hist. 1970; DPhil 1978. Home Civil Service, N Ireland Office, 1974; Private Sec. to Perm. Under-Sec. of State, NI Office, 1976–77; Head of Policy Unit, 1980, Asst Dir, 1986, NCVO; Dir, CPRE, 1987–91; Public Affairs Advr to the Archbishop of Canterbury, 1992–98. Member: Bd, Contact a Family (charity), 1986–93; Bd, Green Alliance, 1992–; Chair, Pedestrians' Assoc., 1999–. *Publications:* (with Paul Hodson) Housing and Community Care, 1982; (with Rosemary Allen) Health in the Round, 1983. *Recreations:* walking, surf-riding, bird-watching, music, theatre. *Address:* 38 Endlesham Road, Balham, SW12 8JL. *T:* (020) 8675 2439.

PURKISS, Robert Ivan, MBE 2000; independent consultant on diversity and change management; Chairman, European Monitoring Centre on Racism and Xenophobia, since 2001; *b* 11 Nov. 1945; *s* of Howard Flanagan and Betty Purkiss; *m* 1971, Monica Dell Richardson; two *d*. *Educ:* Toynbee Rd Boys' Sch.; Southampton Inst. of Higher Educn; Southampton Univ. (Dip. Industrial Relns). Chief Petty Officer, MN, 1961–72; Advr, Industrial Soc., 1972–74; Nat. Officer, Nat. Workers' Union of Jamaica, 1974–76; TGWU, 1976–2000 (Nat. Sec., 1989–2000); Principal Consultant, Focus Consultancy, 2000–. Mem., CRE, 1993–2001. *Publications:* contrib. numerous articles on anti-racism, industrial relns and diversity. *Recreations:* football referee (Mem., Southampton Referees Soc.), athletics (Vice-Chm., Team Solent Athletics Club). *Address:* 182 Rownhams Lane, N Baddesley, Southampton, Hants SO52 9LQ. *T:* (023) 8073 0294; 93 Comeraugh Road, W14 9HS.

PURLE, Charles Lambert; QC 1989; *b* 9 Feb. 1947; *s* of Robert Herbert Purle and Doreen Florence (*née* Button); *m* 1st, 1969, Lorna Barbara Brown (marr. diss. 1990); one *s* one *d*; 2nd, 1991, Virginia Dabney Hopkins Rylatt; two *s* two *d*. *Educ:* Nottingham Univ. (LLB 1969); Worcester Coll., Oxford (BCL 1971). Called to the Bar, Gray's Inn, 1970; in practice, 1972–. *Recreations:* opera, music, food and wine, my children. *Address:* 12 New Square, Lincoln's Inn, WC2A 3SW. *T:* (020) 7419 1212.

PURNELL, James; MP (Lab) Stalybridge and Hyde, since 2001; *b* 2 March 1970; *s* of John and Janet Purnell. *Educ:* Balliol Coll., Oxford (BA PPE). Researcher for Tony Blair, MP, 1989–92; Strategy Consultant, Hydra Associates, 1992–94; Res. Fellow, Media and Communications, IPPR, 1994–95; Hd, Corporate Planning, BBC, 1995–97; Special Advr to Prime Minister on culture, media, sport and the knowledge econ., 1997–2001. Mem. (Lab) Islington BC, 1994–95 (Chairman: Early Years Cttee; Housing Cttee). *Publications:* contrib. various publications for IPPR. *Recreations:* football, film, theatre, music. *Address:* House of Commons, SW1A 0AA. *Club:* Stalybridge Labour.

PURNELL, Nicholas Robert; QC 1985; a Recorder, since 1986; *b* 29 Jan. 1944; *s* of late Oliver Cuthbert Purnell and of Pauline Purnell; *m* 1970, Melanie Stanway; four *s*. *Educ:* Oratory Sch.; King's Coll. Cambridge (Open Exhibnr; MA). Called to the Bar, Middle Temple, 1968 (Astbury Schol.), Bencher 1990; Junior of Central Criminal Court Bar Mess, 1972–75; Prosecuting Counsel to Inland Revenue, 1977–79; Jun. Treasury Counsel, 1979–85. Mem., Bar Council and Senate, 1973–77, 1982–85, 1989–91 (Chm., Legal Aid Fees Cttee, 1989–90); Member: Lord Chancellor's and Home Secretary's Working Party on the Training of the Judiciary, 1975–78; Crown Court Rules Cttee, 1982–88; Lord Chancellor's Adv. Cttee on Educn and Conduct, 1991–97; Criminal Cttee, Judicial Studies Bd, 1991–96. Chm., Criminal Bar Assoc., 1990–91. Governor, The Oratory Sch., 1994–. *Recreations:* living in France as much as possible, watching Wimbledon FC. *Address:* 23 Essex Street, WC2R 3AS. *T:* (020) 7413 0353.
See also P. O. Purnell.

PURNELL, Paul Oliver; QC 1982; a Recorder, since 1985; *b* 13 July 1936; *s* of Oliver Cuthbert and Pauline Purnell; *m* 1966, Celia Consuelo Ocampo; one *s* two *d*. *Educ:* The Oratory Sch.; Jesus Coll., Oxford (MA). Served 4th/7th Royal Dragoon Guards, 1958–62. Called to the Bar, Inner Temple, 1962, Bencher, 1991. Jun. Treasury Counsel at Central Criminal Court, 1976–82. *Recreations:* tennis, windsurfing, motorcycling. *Address:* 1 Middle Temple Lane, EC4Y 9AA. *T:* (020) 7583 0659. *Club:* Hurlingham.
See also N. R. Purnell.

PURSE, Hugh Robert Leslie; barrister; part-time Chairman of Employment (formerly Industrial) Tribunals, since 1996; *b* 22 Oct. 1940; *s* of Robert Purse and Elsie Purse (*née* Kemp). *Educ:* St Peter's School, York; King's College London (LLB). Called to the Bar, Gray's Inn, 1964 (Atkin Scholar). Legal Asst, Dept of Employment, 1969; Legal Adviser to Price Commission, 1978–79; Govt legal service, 1979–96: Legal Advr, Dept of Employment, and Principal Asst Treasury Solicitor, 1988–96. *Address:* Regional Office of Employment Tribunals, 19–29 Woburn Place, WC1H 0LU.

PURSEY, Nigel Thomas; Chief Executive, Shropshire County Council, since 1997; *b* 4 Aug. 1949. *Educ:* Manchester Univ. (MusB). CPFA 1975. Trainee Accountant, Cheshire CC, 1971–75; Accountant, Mid Glamorgan CC, 1975–78; Wiltshire County Council: Group Accountant, 1978–81; Chief Admin. Assistant (Finance), 1981–83; Chief Accountant, 1983–86; Asst County Treasurer, 1986–92; County Treas., Shropshire CC, 1992–97. Clerk to Shropshire Lieutenancy. Dep. Chm., Shropshire Learning and Skills Council; Observer Mem., Shropshire HA. Asst Master of the Music, Shrewsbury Abbey. *Recreations:* music, sport, bridge, family activities. *Address:* The Shirehall, Abbey Foregate, Shrewsbury, Shropshire SY2 6ND. *T:* (01743) 252902.

PURSSELL, Anthony John Richard; Governor, National Society for Epilepsy, since 1993 (Chairman, 1995–98); *b* 5 July 1926; *m* 1952, Ann Margaret Batchelor; two *s* one *d*. *Educ:* Oriel Coll., Oxford (MA Hons Chemistry). Managing Director: Arthur Guinness Son & Co. (Park Royal) Ltd, 1968; Arthur Guinness Son & Co. (Dublin) Ltd, 1973; Arthur Guinness & Sons plc, 1975–81; Jt Dep. Chm., 1981–83. Regl Dir, 1982–91, Chm., 1989–91, Thames Valley and S Midlands Regl Bd, Lloyds Bank plc. Member: IBA, 1976–81; Bd, CAA, 1984–90. Trustee and Hon. Treas., Oxfam, 1985–92. *Recreations:* travel, golf, books. *Address:* Allendale, 53 Bulstrode Way, Gerrards Cross, Bucks SL9 7QT. *Club:* Leander (Henley).

PURVES, Dame Daphne (Helen), DBE 1979; Senior Lecturer in French, Dunedin Teachers College, 1967–73, retired (Lecturer, 1963–66); *b* 8 Nov. 1908; *d* of Irvine Watson Cowie and Helen Jean Cowie; *m* 1939, Herbert Dudley Purves; one *s* two *d*. *Educ:* Otago Girls' High Sch., Dunedin, NZ; Univ. of Otago, Dunedin (MA 1st Cl. Hons English and French). Secondary sch. teacher, 1931–40 and 1957–63. Pres., NZ Fedn of University Women, 1962–64; Internat. Fedn of University Women: Mem., Cultural Relations Cttee, 1965–68, Convener, 1968–71; 3rd Vice-Pres., 1971–74; 1st Vice-Pres., 1974–77; Pres., 1977–80. Chm., National Theme Cttee, The Child in the World, NZ Nat. Commn for Internat. Year of the Child, 1978–80; Mem., Internat. Year of the Child Telethon Trust, 1978–81; Exec. Mem., NZ Cttee for Children (IYC) Inc., 1980–82. Mem., NZ Nat. Commn, Unesco, 1964–68. Pres., Friends of Olveston Inc., 1986–88. Mem., Theomin Gall. Management Cttee, 1986–91. *Relevant publication:* Nothing Like a Dame: a biography of Dame Daphne Purves, by Molly Anderson, 1998. *Recreations:* reading, croquet, bridge, travel, heraldry. *Address:* 12 Grendon Court, 36 Drivers Road, Dunedin, New Zealand. *T:* (3) 4675105. *Clubs:* University (Dunedin); Punga Croquet (Pres., 1988–90); Dunedin Bridge, Otago Bridge.

PURVES, Elizabeth Mary, (Libby), (Mrs Paul Heiney), OBE 1999; writer and broadcaster; *b* 2 Feb. 1950; *d* of late James Grant Purves, CMG; *m* 1980, Paul Heiney; one *s* one *d*. *Educ:* Convent of the Sacred Heart, Tunbridge Wells; St Anne's Coll., Oxford (1st Cl. Hons Eng. Lang. and Lit.). BBC Local Radio (Oxford), 1972–76; Radio 4: Reporter, 1976–79, Presenter, 1979–81, Today; Presenter, Midweek, 1984–. Editor, Tatler, March–Oct. 1983, resigned; columnist, The Times, 1990–. Pres., Council for Nat. Parks, 2000–01. *Publications:* (ed) The Happy Unicorns, 1971; (ed) Adventures Under Sail, H. W. Tilman, 1982; Britain At Play, 1982; Sailing Weekend Book, 1985; How Not to be a Perfect Mother, 1986; Where Did You Leave the Admiral, 1987; (jtly) The English and their Horses, 1988; The Hurricane Tree, 1988; One Summer's Grace, 1989; How Not to Raise a Perfect Child, 1991; Getting the Story, 1993; Working Times, 1993; How Not to be a Perfect Family, 1994; Casting Off (novel), 1995; A Long Walk in Wintertime (novel), 1996; (with Paul Heiney) Grumpers' Farm, 1996; Home Leave (novel), 1997; Holy Smoke, 1998; More Lives Than One (novel), 1998; Regatta (novel), 1999; Nature's Masterpiece: a family survival book, 2000; Passing Go (novel), 2000; A Free Woman (novel), 2001. *Recreations:* sailing, walking, writing, radio. *Address:* c/o Lisa Eveleigh, 11/12 Dover Street, W1S 4LJ. *Club:* Royal Cruising.

PURVES, Sir William, Kt 1993; CBE 1988; DSO 1951; Chairman, 1990–98, Chief Executive, 1990–92, HSBC Holdings plc; *b* 27 Dec. 1931; *s* of Andrew and Ida Purves; *m* 1st, 1958, Diana Troutbeck Richardson (marr. diss. 1988); two *s* two *d*; 2nd, 1989, Rebecca Jane Lewellen. *Educ:* Kelso High School. FIBScot; FCIB. National Service, with Commonwealth Div. in Korea (Subaltern; DSO). National Bank of Scotland, 1948–54; Hongkong and Shanghai Banking Corporation: Germany, Hong Kong, Malaysia, Singapore, Sri Lanka, Japan, 1954–70; Chief Accountant, Hong Kong, 1970; Manager, Tokyo, 1974; Sen. Manager Overseas Operations, 1976; Asst General Manager, Overseas Operations, 1978; General Manager, 1979; Executive Director, 1982–98; Dep. Chm., 1984–86; Chm. and Chief Exec., 1986–92; Chm., Midland Bank Plc, 1994–97 (Dir, 1987–98); Dir, Marine Midland Banks Inc., 1982–98. Chairman: British Bank of ME, 1979–98; Hakluyt & Co., Ltd, 2000–; non-executive Director: Shell Transport and Trading, 1993–; Trident Safeguards Ltd, 1999–; Dep. Chm., Alstom, 1998–. Hon. Dr Stirling, 1987; Hon. LLD: Sheffield, 1993; Hong Kong, 1994; Hon. DBA: Hong Kong Poly., 1993; Napier, 1998; Hon. MBA Strathclyde, 1996; UMIST, 2001. GBM 1999. *Recreations:* golf, Rugby. *Address:* 100 Ebury Mews, SW1W 9NX. *Clubs:* Royal Automobile; New (Edinburgh); Hong Kong Jockey.

PURVIS, Bryan John; Head Master, William Hulme's Grammar School, Manchester, 1997–99; *b* 6 Aug. 1947; *s* of Robert Hunt Purvis and Eleanor Liddel Purvis; *m* 1969, Irene Anne Griffiths; one *s* two *d*. *Educ:* Tynemouth High Sch.; Bedford Coll., London (BSc); Durham Univ. (MSc). Biology Master, St Joseph's Grammar Tech. Sch., Hebburn on Tyne, 1969–74; Dep. Headmaster and Head of Biology, King's Sch., Tynemouth, 1974–93; Head Master, Altrincham GS for Boys, 1993–97. *Recreations:* gardening, hill-walking, watching football (Manchester City) and Rugby. *Address:* Grange End, 219 Hale Road, Hale, Cheshire WA15 8DL. *T:* (0161) 980 4506; *e-mail:* bpurvis@uk.packardbell.org. *Club:* East India, Devonshire Sports and Public Schools.

PURVIS, Air Vice-Marshal Henry R.; *see* Reed-Purvis.

PURVIS, John Robert, CBE 1990; Member (C) Scotland, European Parliament, since 1999; Partner, Purvis & Co., since 1986; *b* 6 July 1938; *s* of Lt-Col R. W. B. Purvis, MC, JP, and Mrs R. W. B. Purvis, JP; *m* 1962, Louise S. Durham; one *s* two *d*. *Educ:* Cargilfield, Barnton, Edinburgh; Trinity Coll., Glenalmond, Perthshire; St Salvator's Coll., Univ. of St Andrews (MA Hons). National Service, Lieut Scots Guards, 1956–58. First National City Bank, New York, 1962–69: London, 1962–63; New York, 1963–65; Milan, 1965–69; Treasurer, Noble Grossart Ltd, Edinburgh, 1969–73; Man. Dir, Gilmerton Management Services Ltd, 1973–92. Mem. (C) Mid-Scotland and Fife, European Parlt, 1979–84, contested same seat, 1984; European Democratic Group, European Parliament: whip, 1980–82; spokesman on energy, research and technology, 1982–84. Vice Pres., Scottish Cons. and Unionist Assoc., 1987–89 (Chm., Industry Cttee, 1986–97); Mem., IBA, 1985–89 (Chm., Scottish Adv. Cttee, 1985–89); Mem., Scottish Adv. Cttee on Telecommunications, 1990–98. Director: James River Fine Papers Ltd, 1984–95; Edgar Astaire & Co. Ltd, 1993–94; Jamont NV, 1994–95; Legg Mason (formerly Johnson Fry) European Utilities Trust plc, 1994–; Curtis Fine Papers Ltd, 1995–2001; Crown Vantage Ltd, 1995–2001; Chairman: Kingdom FM Radio Ltd, 1997–; Belgrave Capital Management Ltd, 1999–. *Publication:* (section 'Money') in Power and Manoeuvrability, 1978. *Address:* European Parliament, Rue Wiertz 43, 1047 Brussels, Belgium. *T:* (2) 2845684; *e-mail:* jpurvis@europarl.eu.int; Gilmerton, Dunino, St Andrews, Fife, Scotland KY16 8NB. *T:* (01334) 475830; *e-mail:* purvisco@compuserve.com. *Clubs:* Cavalry and Guards, Farmers'; New (Edinburgh); Royal and Ancient (St Andrews).

PURVIS, Sir Neville, KCB 1992; Vice Admiral, retired; Chairman: Reliance Secure Task Management, since 2001; Grays International of Cambridge, since 2001; *b* 8 May 1936; *s* of Charles Geoffrey and Sylvia Rose Purvis; *m* 1970, Alice Margaret (*née* Hill); two *s*. *Educ:* Charterhouse; Selwyn College, Cambridge (MA). BRNC Dartmouth, 1953; reading engineering at Cambridge, 1954–57; joined submarine service, 1959; served in HM Ships Turpin, 1960, Dreadnought, 1963, Repulse, 1967; Naval Staff, 1970; Sqdn Engineer Officer, 3rd Submarine Sqdn, 1973; Staff of Flag Officer, Submarines, 1975; RCDS 1980; in Command, HMS Collingwood, 1985–87; Dir Gen., Future Material Projects (Naval), 1987–88; Dir Gen., Naval Manpower and Trng, 1988–90; Mem., Admiralty Bd, and Chief of Fleet Support, 1991–94; Chief Exec., BSI, 1994–96; Dir Gen., British Safety Council, 1997–2001. FInstD 1993; CIMgt 1996; FRSA 1992. *Recreations:* gardening, chess. *Address:* Laundry Cottage, Selhurst Common, Bramley, Guildford, Surrey GU5 0LS.

URVIS, Stewart Peter, CBE 2000; Chief Executive, Independent Television News Ltd, since 1995; *b* 28 Oct. 1947; *s* of late Peter and Lydia Purvis; *m* 1972 (marr. diss. 1993); one *d*; partner, Jacqui Marson; two *s*. *Educ:* Dulwich Coll.; Univ. of Exeter (BA). Presenter, Harlech TV, 1968–69; BBC News trainee, 1969; ITN journalist, 1972; Programme Editor, News At Ten, 1980; Editor, Channel Four News, ITN, 1983; Dep. Editor, 1986, Editor, 1989, Editor-in-Chief, 1991, ITN. Director: ITN Ltd, 1989–; Travel News Ltd, 1995–; London News Radio, 1996–. Director: King's Cross Partnership, 1996–; Royal Marsden NHS Trust, 1999–. Mem. Council, European Journalism Centre, 1996–. FRTS 1991. BAFTA Award for Best News or Outside Broadcast, 1986, 1987; BPG Award for Best News or Current Affairs Prog., 1988. *Address:* ITN Ltd, 200 Gray's Inn Road, WC1X 8XZ. *T:* (020) 7833 3000.

PUSACK, George Williams, MS; Chief Executive, Mobil Oil Australia Ltd, 1980–85, retired; *b* 26 Sept. 1920; *s* of George F. Pusack and Winifred (*née* Williams); *m* 1942, Marian Preston; two *s* one *d*. *Educ:* Univ. of Michigan; Univ. of Pennsylvania. BSE (AeroEng), BSE (Eng.Math), MS (MechEng). Aero Engr, US Navy, 1942–45; Corporal, US Air Force, 1945–46; Mobil Oil Corp.: Tech. Service and Research Manager, USA, 1946–53; Product Engrg Manager, USA, 1953–59; International Supply Manager, USA, 1959–69; Vice-Pres., N Amer. Div., USA, 1969–73; Regional Exec., Mobil Europe, London, 1973–76; Chm. and Chief Exec, Mobil Oil Co. Ltd, 1976–80. Pres., County Hospice, York, SC, 1989–91. Trustee, Victorian State Opera Foundn, 1983–85. Teacher, layreader, vestryman and warden of Episcopal Church (Trustee, York, SC, 1992–). *Recreations:* golf, travel. *Address:* 400 Avinger Lane #431, Davidson, NC 28036, USA. *T:* (704) 8961431. *Clubs:* River Hills Country (Pres., 1991) (Clover, USA); Australian, Royal Melbourne Golf (Melbourne).

PUSEY, Nathan Marsh, PhD; President Emeritus, Harvard University; *b* Council Bluffs, Iowa, 4 April 1907; *s* of John Marsh Pusey and Rosa Pusey (*née* Drake); *m* 1936, Anne Woodward; two *s* one *d*. *Educ:* Harvard University, USA. AB 1928, AM 1932, PhD, 1937. Assistant, Harvard, 1933–34; Sophomore tutor, Lawrence Coll., 1935–38; Asst Prof., history and literature, Scripps Coll., Claremont, Calif., 1938–40; Wesleyan Univ.: Asst Prof., Classics, 1940–43, Assoc. Prof., 1943–44; President: Lawrence Coll., Appleton, Wisconsin, 1944–53; Harvard Univ., 1953–71; Andrew Mellon Foundn, 1971–75. Pres., United Bd for Christian Higher Educn in Asia, 1979–83. Holds many hon. degrees from Universities and colleges in USA and other countries. Officier de la Légion d'Honneur, 1958. *Publications:* The Age of the Scholar, 1963; American Higher Education 1945–1970, 1978. *Address:* 200 East 66th Street (A-501), New York, NY 10021, USA.

PUSEY, Prof. Peter Nicholas, PhD; FRS 1996; FRSE; FInstP; Professor of Physics, since 1991 and Head, Department of Physics and Astronomy, 1994–97 and since 2000, University of Edinburgh; *b* 30 Dec. 1942; *s* of Harold Kenneth Pusey and Edith Joan Pusey (*née* Sparks); *m* 1966, Elizabeth Ann Nind; two *d*. *Educ:* St Edward's Sch., Oxford; Clare Coll., Cambridge (MA); Univ. of Pittsburgh (PhD 1969). FInstP 1981; FRSE 1996. Postdoctoral Fellow, IBM T. J. Watson Res. Center, Yorktown Heights, NY, 1969–72; SPSO, later Grade 6, RSRE, Malvern, 1972–91. *Publications:* numerous contribs in scientific literature. *Address:* Department of Physics and Astronomy, University of Edinburgh, Mayfield Road, Edinburgh EH9 3JZ. *T:* (0131) 650 5255.

PUSINELLI, (Frederick) Nigel (Molière), CMG 1966; OBE 1963; MC 1940; HM Overseas Civil Service, retired; *b* 28 April 1919; second *s* of late S. Jacques and T. May Pusinelli, Frettenham, Norfolk and Fowey, Cornwall; *m* 1941, Joan Mary Chaloner (*d* 1999), *d* of late Cuthbert B. and Mildred H. Smith, Cromer, Norfolk and Bexhill-on-Sea, Sussex; one *s* one *d*. *Educ:* Aldenham School; Pembroke College, Cambridge (BA Hons in law). Commissioned RA 1939; served BEF, 1940; India/Burma, 1942–45; Major, 1942; Staff College, Quetta, 1945. Administrative officer, Gilbert and Ellice Islands Colony, 1946–57. Transferred to Aden, 1958; Dep. Financial Sec. and frequently Actg Financial Sec. till 1962; Director of Establishments, 1962–68, and Assistant High Commissioner, 1963–68, Aden and Federation of South Arabia. Member E African Currency Board, 1960–62. Salaries Commissioner various territories in West Indies, 1968–70. Chm., Overseas Service Pensioners' Assoc., 1978–99. Chairman: Chichester Harbour Conservancy, 1987–90 (Vice-Chm., 1985–87; Mem., Adv. Cttee, 1971–); RYA Southern Region, 1979–96; Chichester Harbour Fedn of sailing clubs and yachting orgns, 1980–87. RYA Yachtsman's Award, 1996. *Publication:* Report on Census of Population of Gilbert and Ellice Islands Colony, 1947. *Recreation:* dinghy racing. *Address:* Mile End House, Westbourne, Emsworth, Hants PO10 8RP. *T:* (01243) 372915. *Clubs:* Royal Commonwealth Society; Royal Yachting Assoc., Cambridge University Cruising, Emsworth Sailing.

PUTIN, Vladimir Vladimirovich; President of Russia, since 2000; *b* Leningrad, 7 Oct. 1952; *s* of late Vladimir Putin and Maria Putin; *m* 1983, Lyudmila; two *d*. *Educ:* Leningrad State Univ. (law degree, 1975). With KGB, in USSR and Germany, 1975–90; Adviser: to Rector, Leningrad State Univ., 1990; to Mayor of Leningrad, 1990–91; Chm., Cttee on Foreign Relations, Office of the Mayor, St Petersburg, 1991–94; first Dep. Mayor, and Chm. Cttee on Foreign Relations, St Petersburg, 1994–96; first Dep. Hd, Gen. Mgt Dept of Presidential Admin, 1996–97; Hd of Control Dept, 1997–98, first Dep. Hd of Admin, 1998, Kremlin; Dir, Fed. Security Service, Russia, 1998–99; Sec., Security Council, Russia, 1999; Prime Minister of Russia, 1999. *Publication:* First Person (autobiog.), 2000. *Address:* c/o The Kremlin, Moscow, Russia.

PUTTNAM, family name of **Baron Puttnam**.

PUTTNAM, Baron *cr* 1997 (Life Peer), of Queensgate in the Royal Borough of Kensington and Chelsea; **David Terence Puttnam,** Kt 1995; CBE 1983; Chairman: Enigma Productions Ltd, since 1978; General Teaching Council, since 2000; *b* 25 Feb. 1941; *s* of Leonard Arthur Puttnam and Marie Beatrix Puttnam; *m* 1961, Patricia Mary (*née* Jones); one *s* one *d*. *Educ:* Minchenden Grammar Sch., London. Advertising, 1958–66; photography, 1966–68; film prodn, 1968–2000. Producer of feature films including: Bugsy Malone, 1976 (four BAFTA awards); The Duellists, 1977 (Jury Prize, Cannes); Midnight Express, 1978 (two Acad. Awards, three BAFTA Awards); Chariots of Fire, 1981 (four Acad. Awards, three BAFTA Awards, incl. awards for best film); Local Hero, 1982 (two BAFTA Awards); Cal, 1984 (Acting Prize, Cannes); The Killing Fields, 1985 (three Acad. Awards, eight BAFTA Awards incl. Best Film); The Mission, 1986 (Palme d'Or, Cannes, 1986, one Acad. Award, three BAFTA awards, 1987); Memphis Belle, 1990; Meeting Venus, 1991; Being Human, 1993; War of the Buttons, 1994; Le Confessional, 1995; My Life So Far, 2000. Chm. and Chief Exec. Officer, Columbia Pictures, 1986–88. Producer of films and series for television. Vis. Industrial Prof., Drama Dept, Bristol Univ., 1986–98. Director: National Film Finance Corp., 1980–85; Anglia Television Gp, 1982–99; Village Roadshow Corp., 1989–99; Survival Anglia, 1989–99; Chrysalis Group, 1993–96; Chairman: Internat. Television Enterprises Ltd, 1988–99; Spectrum Strategy Consultants, 1999–; Governor: National Film and Television Sch., 1974– (Chm., 1988–96); LSE, 1997– (Vis. Prof.); London Inst., 1998–; Member: Governing Council, Nat. Coll. for Sch. Leadership; Academic Adv. Bd, Inst. for Advanced Studies, Univ. of Bristol. Vice President: BAFTA, 1993–; CPRE, 1995– (Pres., 1985–92). Member: Film and Television Adv. Gp, British Council, 1982 (Chm., 1993–99); British Screen Adv. Council, 1988–98; Arts Council Lottery Panel, 1995–98; Educn Standards Task Force, 1997–; British Educnl Communications and Technol. Agency; Arts and Humanities Res. Bd; Senate, Engrg Council. Chairman: NESTA, 1998–; Media and Culture Sector Adv. Gp, QCA; Forum for the Future; Nat. Meml Arboretum; Nat. Mus. of Photography, Film and Television, 1996. Trustee: Tate Gall., 1986–93; Science Museum, 1996–; Royal Acad. of Arts, 2000–; Chm. Trustees, Nat. Teaching Awards. Chancellor, Univ. of Sunderland, 1998–. FRGS; FRSA; FRPS; Fellow, BFI, 1997; FCGI 1999. Hon. Fellow, Manchester Polytechnic, 1990; Hon. FCSD 1990; Hon. FLI 1994. Hon. LLD Bristol, 1983; Hon. DLitt: Leicester, 1986; Sunderland, 1992; Bradford, 1993; Humberside, 1996; Westminster, 1997; Kent, 1998; London Guildhall, 1999; City, Nottingham, 2000; Heriot-Watt, 2001; Hon. LittD Leeds, 1992; Hon. DLit QUB, 2001; Hon. Dr of Drama RSAMD, 1998; Hon. DPhil Cheltenham and Gloucester Coll. of Higher Educn, 1998; Hon. DSc (Med.) Imperial Coll., London, 1999; Hon. DFA American Univ. in London, 2000. Hon. Dr Sheffield Hallam, 2000. Michael Balcon Award for outstanding contribn to British Film Industry, BAFTA, 1982; Benjamin Franklin Medal, RSA, 1996; Crystal Award, World Economic Forum, 1997. Officier de l'Ordre des Arts et des Lettres (France), 1992. *Publications:* (with Brian Wenham) The Third Age of Broadcasting, 1982; (jtly) Rural England, 1988; What Needs to Change?, 1996; Undeclared War, 1997. *Recreations:* reading, going to the cinema. *Clubs:* Athenæum, Chelsea Arts, MCC.

See also L. D. G. Grossman.

PUXON, (Christine) Margaret, (Mrs Margaret Williams); QC 1982; MD, FRCOG; medical/legal consultant; practising barrister, 1954–93; *b* 25 July 1915; *d* of Reginald Wood Hale and Clara Lilian Hale; *m* 1955, F. Morris Williams (*d* 1986), MBE; two *s* one *d*. *Educ:* Abbey Sch., Malvern Wells; Birmingham Univ. (MB, ChB; MD Obstetrics 1944). MRCS, LRCP 1942; FRCOG 1976. Gynaecological Registrar, Queen Elizabeth Hosp., Birmingham, and later Consultant Gynaecologist, Essex CC, 1942–49. Called to the Bar, Inner Temple, 1954. A Dep. Circuit Judge, 1970–86; a Recorder, 1986–88. Privy Council Member, Council of Royal Pharmaceutical Soc., 1975–90; Member: Genetic Manipulation Adv. Gp, 1979–84; Ethics Cttee, RCGP, 1981–93; Chm., Ethics Cttee, Lister Hosp. IVF Unit, 1983–. Consulting Editor, Medical Law Reports, 1993–99. Liveryman, Worshipful Soc. of Apothecaries, 1982–. *Publications:* The Family and the Law, 1963, 2nd edn 1971; contributed to: Progress in Obstetrics and Gynaecology, 1983; In Vitro Fertilisation: Past, Present and Future, 1986; Gynaecology (ed Shaw, Souter and Stanton), 1991; Safe Practice in Obstetrics and Gynaecology (ed Clements), 1994; contrib. med. and legal jls, incl. Proc. RSM, Practitioner, New Law Jl and Solicitors' Jl. *Recreations:* cooking, travel, opera. *Address:* 19 Clarence Gate Gardens, Glentworth Street, NW1 6AY. *T:* (020) 7723 7922, *Fax:* (020) 7258 1038.

PYBUS, William Michael; Chairman, AAH Holdings plc, 1968–92; *b* 7 May 1923; *s* of Sydney James Pybus and Evelyn Mary (*née* Wood); *m* 1959, Elizabeth Janet Whitley; two *s* two *d*. *Educ:* Bedford Sch.; New College, Oxford (1st cl. hons Jurisprudence). Served War, 1942–46: commissioned 1st King's Dragoon Guards; Lieut attached XIth Hussars in Normandy (wounded); King's Dragoon Guards, Egypt, Palestine, Syria, Lebanon; Prosecutor, Mil. Courts, Palestine, 1946 (Major). Admitted Solicitor, 1950 (Scott Scholar, and Grotius Prize, 1950); Partner, Herbert Oppenheimer, Nathan & Vandyk, Solicitors, 1953–88. Consultant, Denton Hall Burgin & Warrens, later Denton Hall, 1988–94. Chairman: British Fuel Co., 1968–87; Inter-Continental Fuels Ltd, 1975–88; Siebe (formerly Siebe Gorman Hldgs), 1980–90 (Dir, 1972–97); Leigh Interests, 1982–89; Homeowners Friendly Soc. Ltd, 1991–96 (Dir, 1980–96); Dep. Chm., R. Mansell Ltd, 1980–85; Director: National Westminster Bank (Outer London Region), 1977–88; Cornhill Insurance PLC, 1977–97; Overseas Coal Developments Ltd, 1979–88; Bradford & Bingley Building Soc., 1983–94; Vestric Ltd, 1985–91; Conservation Foundn, 1991–97; Conservation Foundn Enterprise Ltd, 1991–97. Part-time Member: British Railways (London Midland) Bd, 1974; British Railways (Midlands and West) Bd, 1975–77; Chm., BR (London Midland) Bd, 1977–89. Pres., Coal Trade Benevolent Assoc., 1998 (Dir, 1969–); Vice-Pres., Coal Industry Soc., 1981– (Pres., 1976–81); Pres., Chagford Agricl and Horticl Soc., 1992. Governor, Harpur Trust, 1979–87. Master: Pattenmakers' Co., 1972–73; Fuellers' Co., 1994–95. Chairman: Ashdown House School Trust Ltd, 1975–89; City Univ. Club, 1975–76; Devon Community Foundn, 1997–2000. CIMgt (CBIM 1974); FCIM (FInstM 1974); FRSA 1984. *Recreation:* fishing. *Clubs:* Cavalry and Guards, Royal Automobile, MCC; Yorkshire CC.

PYE, Prof. John David, FLS; Professor of Zoology, Queen Mary and Westfield College (formerly Queen Mary College), University of London, 1973–91, now Emeritus; *b* 14 May 1932; *s* of Wilfred Frank Pye and Gwenllian Pye (*née* Davies); *m* 1958, Dr Ade Pye (*née* Kuku), Sen. Lectr, UCL. *Educ:* Queen Elizabeth's Grammar School for Boys, Mansfield; University Coll. of Wales, Aberystwyth (BSc 1954, Hons 1955); Bedford Coll., London Univ. (PhD 1961). Research Asst, Inst. of Laryngology and Otology, London Univ., 1958–64; Lectr in Zoology, 1964–70, Reader, 1970–73, King's Coll. London; Head of Dept of Zoology and Comparative Physiology, Queen Mary Coll., 1977–82. A founder Dir, QMC Instruments Ltd, 1976–89. Linnean Society: Editor, Zoological Jl, 1981–85; Editl Sec. and Mem. Council, 1985–91; Vice-Pres., 1987–90; Mem., IEE Professional Gp Cttee E15, Radar, Sonar, Navigation and Avionics, 1983–86. Mem., RHS, 1988–. Member Editorial Boards: Zoolog. Soc., 1972–77, 1978–83, 1985–90; Jl of Exper. Biol., 1974–78; Jl of Comp. Physiol. A, 1978–96; Bioacoustics, 1987–. Royal Institution: Associate Mem., 1979–92; Mem., 1992–; delivered Friday discourses 1979, 1983, and televised Christmas Lects for Children, 1985–86; co-organizer, discussion evenings, 1994–; Mem. Council, 1999–. *Publications:* Bats, 1968; (with G. D. Sales) Ultrasonic Communication by Animals, 1974; (ed with R. J. Bench and A. Pye) Sound Reception in Mammals, 1975; Polarised Light in Science and Nature, 2001; articles and research papers. *Recreations:* baking and brewing, travel, arts. *Address:* Woodside, 24 St Mary's Avenue, Finchley, N3 1SN. *T:* (020) 8346 6869; (office) (020) 7882 3293.

PYE, Prof. Kenneth, ScD, PhD; CGeol, FGS; Professor of Environmental Geology, Royal Holloway, University of London, since 1999; *b* 24 Aug. 1956; *s* of Leonard Pye and Joyce Pye; *m* 1979, Diane Cadman; one *s* one *d*. *Educ:* Upholland Grammar Sch., Lancs; Hertford Coll., Oxford (Scholar; BA 1977; MA 1981); St John's Coll., Cambridge (PhD 1981; ScD 1992). CGeol 1995; FGS 1980. Cambridge University: NERC Postdoctoral Res. Fellow, 1980–82; Sarah Woodhead Res. Fellow, 1980–83, Non-stipendiary Fellow, 1983–89, Girton Coll.; Royal Society 1983 Univ. Res. Fellow, 1983–88; Reading University: Lectr in Quaternary Sedimentology, 1989–92; Reader in Sedimentology, 1992–94; Prof. of Envmtl Sedimentology, 1994–98. Founder Dir, Cambridge Envmtl Research Consultants Ltd, 1986–95. Expert Witness, forensic geology (criminal and civil investigations). Leverhulme Trust Fellowship, 1991; Leverhulme Trust Sen. Res. Fellowship, 1996. Sedgwick Prize, Univ. of Cambridge, 1984; British Geomorphological Research Group: Wiley Award, 1989; Gordon Warwick Award, 1991. *Publications:* Chemical Sediments and Geomorphology, 1983; Aeolian Dust and Dust Deposits, 1987; Aeolian Sand and Sand Dunes, 1990; Saltmarshes, 1992; The Dynamics and Environmental Context of Aeolian Sedimentary Systems, 1993; Aeolian Sediments

Ancient and Modern, 1993; Sediment Transport and Depositional Processes, 1994; Environmental Change in Drylands, 1994; Backscattered Scanning Electron Microscopy and Image Analysis of Sediments and Sedimentary Rocks, 1998; Coastal and Estuarine Environments: sedimentology, geomorphology and geoarchaeology, 2000; contribs to learned jls. *Recreations:* world travel, visiting historic sites and houses, collecting rocks and minerals, reading. *Address:* Department of Geology, Royal Holloway, University of London, Egham, Surrey TW20 0EX. *T:* (01784) 443613.

PYE, Prof. Norman; Professor of Geography, University of Leicester, 1954–79, now Emeritus; Pro-Vice-Chancellor, 1963–66; Dean, Faculty of Science, 1957–60; Chairman of Convocation, 1982–85; *b* 2 Nov. 1913; *s* of John Whittaker Pye and Hilda Constance (*née* Platt); *m* 1940, Isabella Jane (*née* Currie) (*d* 2000); two *s*. *Educ:* Wigan Grammar School; Manchester University. Manchester University: BA Hons Geography Class I, 1935, Diploma in Education Class I, 1936. Asst Lecturer in Geography, Manchester Univ., 1936–37 and 1938–46; Mem., Cambridge Univ. Spitsbergen Expedn, 1938. Seconded to Hydrographic Dept, Admiralty, for War Service, 1940–46; pt-time lectr, Univ. of Bristol Cttee on Educn in HM Forces, 1941–45. Lecturer in Geography, 1946–53, Sen. Lecturer, 1953–54, Manchester Univ; Mem. Expedn to US Sonora and Mojave Deserts, 1952. Chm., Conf. of Heads of Depts of Geography in British Univs, 1968–70. Vis. Professor: Univ. of Ghana, 1958, 1960; Univ. of BC, 1964, 1983; Univ. of Alberta, Edmonton, 1967, 1968, 1969, 1973, 1974, 1975, 1978; External Examnr: Univ. of E Africa, 1964–67; Univ. of Guyana, 1974–78. Editor, "Geography", 1965–80. Member Corby Development Corp., 1965–80. Governor, Up Holland Grammar Sch., 1953–74; Member: Northants CC Educn Cttee, 1956–74; Court, Nottingham Univ., 1964–79; Standing Conf. on Univ. Entrance, 1966–79; Schools Council, 1967–78. Member: Council, RMetS, 1953–56; Council, Inst. of Brit. Geographers, 1954, 1955; Council, RGS, 1967–70 (Hon. Fellow, 1991); Council for Urban Studies Centres, 1974–81; Brit. Nat. Cttee for Geography, 1970–75; Civic Trust Educn Gp (formerly Heritage Educn Gp), 1976–90; Young Enterprise Leics Area Bd, 1983–96; Hon. Mem., Geographical Assoc., 1983– (Mem. Council, 1965–83; Hon. Vice-Pres., 1979–83). *Publications:* The Land Utilisation Survey of Britain: Part 44, Isle of Man, 1941; Leicester and its Region (ed and contrib.), 1972; research papers, articles and revs in learned journals. *Recreations:* travel, oenology, music, gardening. *Address:* 2 Austen Avenue, Oliver's Battery, Winchester SO22 4HP. *T:* (01962) 869052. *Club:* Geographical.

PYE, William Burns, FRBS 1992; sculptor; *b* 16 July 1938; *m* 1963, Susan Marsh; one *s* two *d*. *Educ:* Charterhouse; Wimbledon Sch. of Art; Royal Coll. of Art (ARCA). Vis. Prof., Calif. State Univ., 1975–76. Directed film, Reflections, 1971. *Solo exhibitions:* Winchester Great Hall, 1979; Hong Kong (retrospective), 1987; *public sculpture:* Zemran, South Bank, London, 1971; Curlicue, Greenland Dock, London, 1989; Cader Idris, Cardiff, 1998; *public water sculpture:* Slipstream and Jetstream, Gatwick Airport, 1988; Chalice, Fountain Sq., London, 1990; Water Wall and Portico, Expo '92, Seville, 1992; Orchid, the Peacocks, Woking, 1992; Cristos, St Christopher's Place, London, 1993; Confluence, Hertford, 1994; Downpour, British Embassy, Oman, 1995; Derby Cascade, Derby, 1995; Antony House, Cornwall, 1996; Archimedes Screw feature, West India Quay, London, 1997; Cader Idris, Central Square, Cardiff, 1999; Aquarena, Millennium Square, Bristol, 2000; Scaladaqua Tonda, Nat. Botanical Gardens, Wales, 2000; tureen, St John's Coll., Cambridge, monolith, Sunderland Winter Garden, cornucopia, Millfield Sch., Scala Aquae Pembrochiana, Wilton House, Charybdis, Seaham Hall, Sunderland, 2001; *portrait bust of* Rt Hon. Douglas Hurd, Nat. Portrait Gall., 1996. Hon. FRIBA 1993. Prix de Sculpture, Vth Internat. Sculpture Exhibn, Budapest; Peace Sculpture Prize, W Midlands CC, 1984; ABSA Awards for Best Sculpture in UK (Gatwick Airport), 1988, and in Scotland (Glasgow), 1989; UENO Royal Museum Award, Japan, 1989. *Recreation:* playing the flute. *Address:* 43 Hambalt Road, Clapham, SW4 9EQ. *T:* (home) (020) 8673 2318, (studio) (020) 8682 2727.

PYLE, Derek Colin Wilson; Sheriff of Tayside, Central and Fife, since 2000; *b* 15 Oct. 1952; *s* of Colin Lawson Pyle and Mary Best Johnston Pyle; *m* 1980, Jean Blackwood Baillie May; five *s* one *d*. *Educ:* Royal High Sch., Edinburgh; Univ. of Edinburgh (LLB Hons). Law Apprentice, Lindsays, WS, Edinburgh, 1974–76; Partner, Dove Lockhart, WS, Solicitors, Edinburgh, 1977–80; Sole Partner, Wilson Pyle & Co., WS, Solicitors, Edinburgh, 1980–88; Partner, Henderson Boyd Jackson, WS, Solicitors, Edinburgh, 1989–99. *Recreations:* golf, writing unpublished best-sellers. *Address:* [illegible] Grange, Errol, Perthshire PH2 7SZ. *T:* (01821) 642198. *Club:* Luffness N[illegible]

PYM, family name of **Baron Pym**.

PYM, Baron *cr* 1987 (Life Peer), of Sandy in the County of Bedfordshire; **Franci[illegible] Pym;** PC 1970; MC 1945; DL; *b* 13 Feb. 1922; *s* of late Leslie Ruthven Pym, M[illegible] Iris, *d* of Charles Orde; *m* 1949, Valerie Fortune Daglish; two *s* two *d*. *Educ:* E[illegible] Magdalene Coll., Cambridge (Hon. Fellow 1979). Served War of 1939–45 (despatch[illegible] 1944 and 1945, MC): 9th Lancers, 1942–46; African and Italian campaigns. Contested (C) Rhondda West, 1959; MP (C): Cambridgeshire, 1961–83; Cambridgeshire South East, 1983–87. Asst Govt Whip (unpaid), Oct. 1962–64; Opposition Whip, 1964–67; Opposition Dep. Chief Whip, 1967–70; Parly Sec. to the Treasury and Govt Chief Whip, 1970–73; Sec. of State for NI, 1973–74; Opposition spokesman on: agriculture, 1974–76; H of C affairs and devolution, 1976–78; Foreign and Commonwealth affairs, 1978–79; Sec. of State for Defence, 1979–81; Chancellor of the Duchy of Lancaster and Paymaster Gen., and Leader of the House of Commons, 1981; Lord Pres. of the Council and Leader of the House of Commons, 1981–82; Sec. of State for Foreign and Commonwealth Affairs, 1982–83. Chairman: Diamond Cable Communications plc, 1995–99; Christie Brockbank Shipton Ltd, 1994–99. Pres., Atlantic Treaty Assoc., 1985–87. Chm., E-SU, 1987–92. Member: Council, BESO, 1988–98; Bd, The Landscape Foundn, 1993–98; Vice-Pres., Registered Engineers for Disaster Relief, 1986–98. Mem. Herefordshire County Council, 1958–61. DL Cambs, 1973. *Publications:* The Politics of Consent, 1984; Sentimental Journey: tracing an outline of family history, 1998. *Address:* Everton Park, Sandy, Beds SG19 2DE. *Club:* Buck's.

PYMAN, Avril; *see* Sokolov, A.

PYMONT, Christopher Howard; QC 1996; *b* 16 March 1956; *s* of John and Joan Pymont; *m* 1996, Meriel Rosalind, *d* of Roger and late Ann Lester; one *s* one *d*. *Educ:* Marlborough Coll.; Christ Church, Oxford (BA Hons 1977; MA 1979). Called to the Bar, Gray's Inn, 1979; in practice at the Bar, 1980–. *Address:* Maitland Chambers, 7 Stone Buildings, Lincoln's Inn, WC2A 3SZ. *T:* (020) 7406 1200.

PYPER, Mark Christopher Spring-Rice; Principal (formerly Headmaster), Gordonstoun School, since 1990; *b* 13 Aug. 1947; *s* of late Arthur Spring-Rice Pyper and of Rosemary Isabel Pyper; *m* 1979, Jennifer Lindsay Gilderson; one *s* two *d*. *Educ:* Winchester College; Balliol College, Oxford (BA Mod. Hist.). Asst Master, Stoke Brunswick Sch., East Grinstead, 1966–68; Asst Master, then Joint Headmaster, St Wilfrid's Sch., Seaford, 1969–79; Registrar, Housemaster, then Dep. Headmaster, Sevenoaks Sch., 1979–90. Dir, Sevenoaks Summer Festival, 1979–90. *Address:* Headmaster's House, Gordonstoun School, Elgin, Moray IV30 2RF. *T:* (01343) 837837. *Club:* MCC.

PYTCHES, Rt Rev. (George Edward) David; Vicar of St Andrew's, Chorleywood, Rickmansworth, 1977–96; *b* 9 Jan. 1931; 9th *c* and 6th *s* of late Rev. Thomas Arthur Pytches and late Eirene Mildred Pytches (*née* Welldon); *m* 1958, Mary Trevisick; four *d*. *Educ:* Old Buckenham Hall, Norfolk; Framlingham Coll., Suffolk; Univ. of Bristol (BA); Trinity Coll., Bristol; MPhil Nottingham, 1984. Deacon 1955, priest 1956; Asst Curate, St Ebbe's, Oxford, 1955–58; Asst Curate, Holy Trinity, Wallington, 1958–59; Missionary Priest in Chol Chol, Chile, 1959–62; in Valparaiso, Chile, 1962–68; Rural Dean, Valparaiso, 1966–70; Diocese of Chile, Bolivia and Peru: Asst Bishop, 1970–72; Vicar General, 1971–72; Bishop, 1972–77. Co-ordinator, Fellowship of Ind. Anglican Churches, 1992–; Co-ordinating Director: New Wine Family Conf., 1989–99; Soul Survivor Youth Confs, 1993; Lakeside Family Conf., 1994–99. Dir, Kingdom Power Trust, 1987–. *Publications:* (contrib.) Bishop's Move, 1977; Come Holy Spirit, 1985; (contrib.) Riding the Third Wave, 1987; Does God Speak Today?, 1989; Some Said It Thundered, 1990; (jtly) New Wineskins, 1991; Prophecy in the Local Church, 1993; (contrib.) Recovering the Ground, 1995; (contrib.) Meeting John Wimber, 1996; (ed) John Wimber: his influence and legacy, 1998; Leadership for New Life, 1998; (ed) Burying the Bishop, 1999; (ed) Four Funerals and a Wedding, 1999; (ed) Out of the Mouths of Babes, 1999. *Recreations:* reading, travelling, enjoying eleven grandchildren. *Address:* Red Tiles, Homefield Road, Chorleywood, Rickmansworth, Herts WD3 5QJ. *T:* (01923) 283763, *Fax:* (01923) 283762; *e-mail:* pytches@new-wine.org.

Q

QESKU, Pavli; Ambassador of the Republic of Albania to the Court of St James's, 1993–97; *b* 16 June 1943; *s* of Mihal and Vasilika Qesku; *m* 1973, Lidia Daka; one *s* one *d. Educ:* Tirana State Univ. (English Language). Translator at State publishing house, 1968; English teaching, 1975; translator and editor at publishing house, 1978; Ministry of Foreign Affairs, 1993. *Recreations:* reading, writing, music. *Address:* c/o Ministry of Foreign Affairs, Tirana, Albania.

QUAN, Sir Henry (Francis), KBE 1997; JP; Managing Director, family business, since 1972; *b* 19 Dec. 1936; *s* of Augustine Quan Hong and Mary Woo; *m* 1961, Margaret Wong; three *s* one *d. Educ:* Canton, China; Sydney, Australia. Founder, Pres. and Vice-Pres., Solomon Is Chinese Youth Orgn; Founder, Chm. and Vice-Chm., Solomon Is Chinese Assoc. JP Solomon Is. Independence Medal (Solomon Is), 1978; 10th Anniversary Medal (Solomon Is), 1988. *Recreation:* sport in general. *Address:* PO Box 209, Honiara, Solomon Islands. *T:* 22351. *Clubs:* Australian Jockey, Sydney Turf, South Sydney Junior Rugby League (Sydney).

QUANT, Mary, (Mrs A. Plunket Greene), OBE 1966; RDI 1969; Director, since 1955, Co-Chairman, since 1991, Mary Quant Group of companies; *b* 11 Feb. 1934; *d* of Jack and Mildred Quant; *m* 1957, Alexander Plunket Greene (*d* 1990); one *s. Educ:* Goldsmiths' College of Art (Hon. Fellow, 1993). Fashion designer. Mem., Design Council, 1971–74. Member: British/USA Bicentennial Liaison Cttee, 1973; Adv. Council, V&A Museum, 1976–78. Non-exec. Dir, House of Fraser, 1997–. Exhibition, Mary Quant's London, London Museum, 1973–74. FCSD (FSIA 1967); Sen. FRCA 1991; FRSA 1996. Maison Blanche Rex Award (US), 1964; Sunday Times Internat. Award, 1964; Piavola d'Oro Award (Italy), 1966; Annual Design Medal, Inst. of Industrial Artists and Designers, 1966; Hall of Fame Award, British Fashion Council, 1990. *Publications:* Quant by Quant, 1966; Colour by Quant, 1984; Quant on Make-up, 1986; Classic Make-up and Beauty Book, 1996. *Address:* 3 Ives Street, SW3 2NE. *T:* (020) 7584 8781.

QUANTRILL, Prof. Malcolm, RIBA; architect, author and critic; Distinguished Professor of Architecture, Texas A&M University, since 1986; *b* Norwich, Norfolk, 25 May 1931; *s* of Arthur William Quantrill and Alice May Newstead; *m* 1971, Esther Maeve, *d* of James Brignell Dand and Winifred Dand, Chester; two *s* two *d. Educ:* City of Norwich Sch.; Liverpool Univ. (BArch); Univ. of Pennsylvania (MArch); Univ. of Wroclaw (Doc. Ing Arch, now redesignated DScEng). RIBA 1961. Fulbright Scholar and Albert Kahn Meml Fellow, Univ. of Pennsylvania, 1954–55; Asst Prof., Louisiana State Univ., 1955–60; Lecturer: Univ. of Wales, Cardiff, 1962–65; UCL, 1965–66; Asst to Dir, Architectural Assoc., 1966–67, Dir, 1967–69; Lectr, Univ. of Liverpool, 1970–73; Dean, Sch. of Environmental Design, Polytechnic of N London, 1973–80; Prof. of Architecture and Urban Design, Univ. of Jordan, Amman-Jordan, 1980–83. Vis. Professor: Univ. of Illinois, Chicago, 1973–75; Carleton Univ., Ottawa, 1978; Gastprofessor, Technische Universität, Wien, 1975–77; Fellow, Graham Foundn for Advanced Studies in the Fine Arts, Chicago, 1984. Lectures: Sir William Dobell Meml in Modern Art, Sydney, NSW, 1978; Thomas Cubitt, London, 1993; Kivett Meml, Kansas City, 1994; Finland, Smithsonian Instn, Washington, 1997. Knight Commander, Order of Finnish Lion (Finland), 1988. *Plays performed:* Honeymoon, 1968; Life Class, 1968 (TV); Dust, 1990; radio plays include: The Fence, 1964; Let's Get This Straight, 1977; Immortal Bite, 1982. *Publications:* The Gotobed Trilogy (novels), 1962–64; Ritual and Response in Architecture, 1974; Monuments of Another Age, 1975; On the Home Front (novel), 1977; The Art of Government and the Government of Art, 1978; Alvar Aalto—a critical study, 1983; Reima Pietilä—architecture, context and modernism, 1985; The Environmental Memory, 1987; Reima Pietilä: one man's odyssey in search of Finnish architecture, 1988; (ed) Constancy and Change in Architecture, 1991; (ed) Urban Forms, Suburban Dreams, 1993; Finnish Architecture and the Modernist Tradition, 1995; The Culture of Silence, 1998; The Norman Foster Studio, 1999; Latin American Architecture: six voices, 2000; articles in RIBA Jl, Arch. Assoc. Qly, Arch. Design, Jl of Arch. Educn, and Art Internat. *Address:* College of Architecture, Texas A&M University, College Station, TX 77843–3137, USA. *Club:* Garrick.

QUANTRILL, William Ernest; HM Diplomatic Service, retired; Ambassador to the Republic of Cameroon, and concurrently to the Central African Republic, Equatorial Guinea and the Republic of Chad, 1991–95; *b* 4 May 1939; *s* of late Ronald Frederick Quantrill and Norah Elsie Quantrill (*née* Matthews); *m* 1964, Rowena Mary Collins; three *s* one *d. Educ:* Colston's Sch., Bristol; Hatfield Coll., Univ. of Durham (BA Hons French). Entered FO, 1962; served Brussels, Havana, Manila, Lagos, 1964–80; Head of Training Dept, FCO, 1980–81; Dep. Head of Personnel Ops Dept, FCO, 1981–84; Counsellor and Hd of Chancery, Caracas, 1984–88; Dep. Gov., Gibraltar, 1988–90. *Recreations:* wild life, travel. *Address:* Tor House, 36 Newtown, Bradford-on-Avon, Wilts BA15 1NF. *T:* (01225) 866245; *e-mail:* wquantrill@msn.com.

QUARMBY, David Anthony, MA, PhD; FCIT; FILT; Chairman: British Tourist Authority, since 1996; Docklands Light Railway Ltd, since 1999 (Member Board, since 1998); *b* 22 July 1941; *s* of Frank Reginald and Dorothy Margaret Quarmby; *m* 1968, Hilmary Hunter; four *d. Educ:* Shrewsbury Sch.; King's Coll., Cambridge (MA); Leeds Univ. (PhD, Dip. Industrial Management). Asst Lectr, then Lectr, Dept of Management Studies, Leeds Univ., 1963; Economic Adviser, Economic Planning Directorate, Min. of Transport, 1966; London Transport Executive: Dir of Operational Research, 1970; Chief Commercial and Planning Officer, 1974; Mem., 1975–84; Man. Dir (Buses), 1978–84; Mem., London Regional Transport, 1984; Director: Homebase Ltd, 1987–89; Shaw's Supermarkets Inc., 1987–92; Jt Man. Dir, J. Sainsbury plc, 1988–96 (Dir, 1984–96). Chairman: English Tourist Bd, 1996–99; S London Business Leadership Ltd, 1996–99; Dep. Chm., S London Econ. Develt Alliance, 1999–; Director: New Millennium Experience Co. Ltd, 1997– (Chm., May–Sept. 2000; Dep. Chm., 2000–); London First, 1998–; BRB (Shadow Strategic Rail Authy), 1999–2001; Strategic Rail Authy, 2001–; Mem., Panel 2000, 1999–. Chm., Retail Action Gp for Crime Prevention, Home Office, 1995–96; Mem., Crime Prevention Agency Bd, Home Office, 1995–97; non-exec. Dir, Dept of Transport Central Mgt Bd, 1996–97, DETR Bd, 1997–; Mem. Bd, Transport for London, 2000– (Ministerial Advr, 1999–2000). Vice-President: Bus and Coach Council, 1981–84; CIT, 1987–91; Mem., Nat. Council, Freight Transport Assoc., 1985–88. Member: London Educn Business Partnership, 1988–92; Sch. Curriculum and Assessment Authy, 1993–95; Southwark Diocesan Synod, 1982–85; London Adv. Bd, Salvation Army, 1982–87. Dir, and Chm. Develt Cttee, Blackheath Concert Halls, 1990–94. Gov., 1987– (Chm., 1995–98), Chm., Finance Cttee, 1991–95, James Allen's Girls' Sch., London; Mem. Ct, Greenwich Univ., 2000–. Pres., Inst. of Logistics, 1996–99. CompOR; CIMgt. Hon. DSc Huddersfield, 1999. *Publications:* Factors Affecting Commuter Travel Behaviour (PhD Thesis, Leeds), 1967; contribs to Jl of Transport Economics and Policy, Regional Studies, Enterprise Management, and to books on transport, distribution, economics and operational research. *Recreations:* music, singing, walking, family life. *Address:* British Tourist Authority, Thames Tower, Black's Road, W6 9EL. *T:* (020) 8846 9000.

QUARREN EVANS, His Honour (John) Kerry; a Circuit Judge, on South Eastern circuit, 1980–95; *b* 4 July 1926; *s* of late Hubert Royston Quarren Evans, MC and Violet Soule Quarren Evans (*née* George); *m* 1958, Janet Shaw Lawson; one *s* one *d. Educ:* King Henry VIII Sch., Coventry; Cardiff High Sch.; Trinity Hall, Cambridge, 1948–51 (MA, LLM). 21st Glam. (Cardiff) Bn Home Guard, 1943–44; enlisted, Grenadier Gds, 1944; commnd Royal Welch Fusiliers, 1946, from OTS Bangalore; att. 2nd Bn The Welch Regt, Burma, 1946–47; Captain 1947. Admitted solicitor, 1953; Partner: Lyndon Moore & Co., Newport, 1954–71; T. S. Edwards & Son, Newport, 1971–80; Recorder, Wales and Chester Circuit, 1974–80. Clerk to Gen. Comrs of Income Tax, Dinas Powis Div., 1960–80; Chm., Newport Nat. Insurance Local Tribunal, 1968–71. *Recreations:* golf, Rugby football, oenology, staurologosophy, old things. *Address:* 2 Mount Park Crescent, Ealing, W5 2RN. *Clubs:* Arkaves (Cardiff); Woodpeckers, Denham Golf, Royal Porthcawl Golf, Crawshay's Welsh Rugby Football.

QUARTA, Roberto; Chairman, BBA Group plc (Group Chief Executive, 1993–2000; Director, since 1993); Partner, Clayton, Dubilier & Rice, since 2001; *b* 10 May 1949; *m*; one *s* one *d. Educ:* Italy and USA; Coll. of the Holy Cross, Mass, USA (BA 1971). Management Trainee, David Gessner, 1971–73; Worcester Controls Corp., 1973–78: Manager, Purchasing and Production Control; Vice-Pres., Internat. Procurement; BTR plc, 1979–85: Manufacturing Dir, Worcester Controls Corp.; Man. Dir, Worcester Controls UK; Group Man. Dir, Valves Group; Chief Exec., Hitchiner Manufacturing Corp., 1985–89; a Chief Divl Exec., BTR, 1989–93 (Dir, Main Bd, 1993). Non-exec. Dir, PowerGen, 1996–. *Recreations:* tennis, golf, music. *Address:* BBA Group plc, 70 Fleet Street, EC4Y 1EU. *T:* (020) 7842 4900; Clayton, Dubilier & Rice, 55 Grosvenor Street, W1X 9DA.

QUARTANO, Ralph Nicholas, CBE 1987; Chairman, PosTel Investment Management Ltd, 1987–91 (Chief Executive, 1983–87); *b* 3 Aug. 1927; *s* of late Charles and Vivienne Mary Quartano; *m* 1954, Cornelia Johanna de Gunst (*d* 1996); two *d. Educ:* Sherborne Sch.; Pembroke Coll., Cambridge (MA). Bataafsche Petroleum Mij, 1952–58; The Lummus Co, 1958–59; Temple Press, 1959–65; Man. Director: Heywood Temple Industrial Publications, 1965–68; Engineering Chemical and Marine Press, 1968–70. The Post Office, 1971–74; Sen. Dir, Central Finance, 1973–74; Chief Exec., Post Office Staff Superannuation Fund, 1974–83. Dir, 1985–93, Dep. Chm., 1987–93, SIB. Director: London American Energy NV, 1981–88; Britoil plc, 1982–88; 3i Group plc (formerly Investors in Industry), 1986–97; John Lewis Partnership Pensions Trust, 1986–89; Clerical Medical Investment Group, 1987–98; Booker plc, 1988–98; British Maritime Technology Ltd, 1988–97 (Chm., 1995–97); Heitman Financial LLC, 1991–2000; Laird Group, 1991–98; Enterprise Oil, 1991–97; Lyonnaise Pension Trustees Ltd, 1994–; Chm., Murray Emerging Economies Trust plc, 1994–98. Member: Engrg Council, 1981–83; City Capital Markets Cttee, 1985–93; Investment Cttee, Pensioen Fonds PGGM, Netherlands, 1986–98; Investment Cttee, KPN (formerly PTT) Pensioen, Netherlands, 1988–98; Financial Reporting Council, 1990–93. City Advr to Dir-Gen., CBI, 1985–93. Sloan Fellow of London Business School. Gov., BUPA, 1987–98. Mem. Council, 1993–99, and Treas., 1994–99, RSA. Trustee, Monteverdi Trust, 1986–93. *Address:* 20 Oakcroft Road, SE13 7ED. *T:* (020) 8852 1607. *Club:* Athenæum.

QUAYLE, James Danforth, (Dan), JD; Vice Chairman, JD Ford & Co., since 2000; Vice-President of the United States of America, 1989–93; *b* 4 Feb. 1947; *m* 1972, Marilyn Tucker; two *s* one *d. Educ:* DePauw Univ. (BS 1969); Indiana Univ. (JD 1974). Admitted to Indiana Bar, 1974. Journalist, 1965–69, Associate Publisher and Gen. Manager, 1974–76, Huntington Herald Press; Investigator, Consumer Protection Div., Office of the Attorney General, Indiana, 1970–71; Admin. Assistant to Gov. of Indiana, 1971–73; Dir, Inheritance Tax Div., Indiana, 1973–74; professor of business law, Huntington Coll., 1975. Mem. of Congress, 1976–80; Mem. for Indiana, US Senate, 1981–88. Chairman: Circle Investors, Inc., 1993–; Competitiveness Center, Hudson Inst., 1993–. *Publications:* Standing Firm, 1994; The American Family, 1996; Worth Fighting For, 1999. *Address:* 2425 E Camelback Road, Suite 1080, Phoenix, AZ 85016, USA.

QUAYLE, Prof. John Rodney, PhD; FRS 1978; Vice-Chancellor, University of Bath, 1983–92; *b* 18 Nov. 1926; *s* of John Martin Quayle and Mary Doris Quayle (*née* Thorp); *m* 1951, Yvonne Mabel (*née* Sanderson); one *s* one *d. Educ:* Alun Grammar Sch., Mold; University Coll. of North Wales, Bangor (BSc, PhD; Hon. Fellow, 1996); Univ. of Cambridge (PhD); MA Oxon. Res. Fellow, Radiation Lab., Univ. of California,

1953–55; Sen. Scientific Officer, Tropical Products Institute, London, 1955–56; Mem. Scientific Staff, MRC Cell Metabolism Res. Unit, Univ. of Oxford, 1956–63; Lectr, Oriel Coll., Oxford, 1957–63; Sen. Lectr in Biochemistry, 1963–65, West Riding Prof. of Microbiol., 1965–83, Sheffield Univ. Vis. Res. Prof. of Gesellschaft für Strahlen und Umweltforschung, Institut für Mikrobiologie, Universität Göttingen, 1973–74; Walker-Ames Vis. Prof., Univ. of Washington, Seattle, 1981. Chm., British Nat. Cttee for Microbiol., 1985–90; Member: AFRC, 1982–84; Adv. Council, RMCS, 1983–92; Council, Royal Soc., 1982–84; Biol Sciences Cttee, SERC, 1981–84; Pres., Soc. for General Microbiology, 1990–93. Member: Council of Management, Bath Festival Soc., 1992–93 (Trustee, 1984–89); Bd, Bath Festivals Trust, 1993–98; Bd, Bristol Exploratory, 1995–. Korrespondierendes Mitglied, Akademie der Wissenschaften, Göttingen, 1976. Hon. Dr *rer. nat.*, Göttingen, 1989; Hon. DSc: Bath, 1992; Sheffield, 1992. Ciba Medal, Biochem. Soc., 1978. *Publications:* articles in scientific jls. *Recreations:* hill-walking, gardening, bread-making. *Address:* The Coach House, Vicarage Lane, Compton Dando, Bristol BS39 4LA. *T:* (01761) 490399.

QUAYLE, Quinton Mark; HM Diplomatic Service; International Director, British Trade International, since 1999; *b* 5 June 1955; *s* of Eric Stanley Quayle and late Elizabeth Jean (*née* Thorne); *m* 1979, Alison Marshall; two *s*. *Educ:* Humphry Davy GS; Bristol Univ. (BA). Entered HM Diplomatic Service, 1977; Third, later Second Sec., Bangkok, 1979–82; FCO, 1983–86; Ecole Nat. d'Admin, Paris, 1986–87; First Sec., Paris, 1987–91; FCO, 1991–93; on secondment to Price Waterhouse Management Consultants, 1993–94; Dir, Jt Export Promotion Directorate, FCO, 1994–96; Counsellor, Consul-Gen. and Dep. Hd of Mission, Jakarta, 1996–99. *Recreation:* book collecting. *Address:* British Trade International, 66–74 Victoria Street, SW1E 6SW.

QUAYLE, Maj.-Gen. Thomas David Graham, CB 1990; Non-executive Director, Salisbury Health Care NHS Trust, since 1999; *b* 7 April 1936; *s* of Thomas Quayle and Phyllis Gwendolen Johnson; *m* 1962, Susan Jean Bradford; three *d*. *Educ:* Repton; Trinity College, Oxford. Commissioned RA 1958; Student, Indian Staff Coll., 1968; Comdr, The Chestnut Troop, 1971–72; Instructor, Staff Coll., Camberley, 1974–76; Comdr, 40 Field Regt (The Lowland Gunners), 1976–79; Comdr Artillery, 4th Armoured Div., 1981–83; Defence Attaché, Bonn, 1983–86; Comdr Artillery, 1st British Corps, 1987–90, retd. Ombudsman for Estate Agents (formerly for Corporate Estate Agents, 1990–99. Mem., Mortgage Code Compliance Bd, 1999–. *Recreations:* shooting, fishing, bridge. *Address:* Oriole House, Figheldean, Salisbury, Wilts SP4 8JJ.

QUEBEC, Archbishop of, (RC), and Primate of Canada, since 1990; **Most Rev. Maurice Couture;** *b* 3 Nov. 1926. Perpetual vows with Vincentian Fathers, 1948; ordained priest, 1951; Patros de la Baie, Plessisville, Port Alfred and Bagotville, 1952–55; in charge of Minor Seminary of his Congregation, 1955–65; founder and Rector, Inter-Congregational Seminary, Cap-Rouge, 1965–70; Provincial Superior, 1970–76, Superior General of Congregation, 1976–82; Titular Bishop of Talattula and Auxiliary Bishop of Québec, 1982–88; Bishop of Baie-Comeau, 1988–90. *Address:* Office of the Archbishop of Québec, 1073 Boulevard René Levesque Ouest, Québec, QC G1S 4R5, Canada.

QUEBEC, Bishop of, since 1991; **Rt Rev. Alexander Bruce Stavert;** *b* 1 April 1940; *s* of Ewart and Kathleen Stavert; *m* 1982, Diana Greig; one *s* two *d*. *Educ:* Lower Canada Coll., Montreal; Bishop's Univ., Lennoxville, PQ (BA 1961): Trinity Coll., Univ. of Toronto (STB 1964; MTh, 1976). Incumbent of Schefferville, Quebec, 1964–69; Fellow, 1969–70, Chaplain, 1970–76, Trinity Coll., Univ. of Toronto; Incumbent, St Clement's Mission East, St Paul's River, PQ, 1976–81; Chaplain, Bishop's Univ., Lennoxville, 1981–84; Dean and Rector, St Alban's Cathedral, Prince Albert, Sask., 1984–91. Hon. DD Toronto, 1986. *Recreations:* swimming, ski-ing. *Address:* 31 rue des Jardins, Québec, QC G1R 4L6, Canada. *T:* (418) 6923858. *Club:* Garrison (Québec).

QUEENSBERRY, 12th Marquess of, *cr* 1682; **David Harrington Angus Douglas;** late Royal Horse Guards; Viscount Drumlanrig and Baron Douglas, 1628; Earl of Queensberry, 1633; Bt (Nova Scotia), 1668; Professor of Ceramics, Royal College of Art, 1959–83; Partner, Queensberry Hunt Levien design group; *b* 19 Dec. 1929; *s* of 11th Marquess of Queensberry and late Cathleen Mann; *S* father, 1954; *m* 1st, 1956, Mrs Ann Radford; two *d*; 2nd, 1969, Alexandra (marr. diss. 1986), *d* of Guy Wyndham Sich; three *s* one *d*. *Educ:* Eton. Mem. Council, Crafts Council; Pres., Design and Industries Assoc., 1976–78. FCSD; Sen. FRCA, 1990. Hon. DDes Staffordshire, 1993. *Heir: s* Viscount Drumlanrig, *qv*.

QUEENSLAND, NORTH, Bishop of, since 1996; **Rt Rev. Clyde Maurice Wood,** BA, ThL; *b* 7 Jan. 1936; *s* of Maurice O. Wood and Helen M. Wood; *m* 1957, Margaret Joan Burls; two *s* one *d*. *Educ:* Perry Hall, Melbourne (ThL 1964); Monash Univ. (BA 1974). Deacon 1965, priest 1965; Curate: St John's, Bentleigh, 1965–66; St Paul's, Ringwood, 1966–67; in Dept of Evangelism and Extension, 1967–70; Curate-in-Charge: St Philip's, Mount Waverley, 1967–70; Armadale/Hawksburn, 1970–73; Rector and Canon Res., Christ Church Cathedral, Darwin, 1974, Dean 1978–83; on leave, Rector St Timothy's Episcopal Church, Indianapolis, USA, 1981; Bishop of the Northern Territory, 1983–92; Bishop of the Western Region, and Asst Bishop, dio. of Brisbane, 1992–96. OStJ 1980; ChStJ 1985. *Recreations:* golf, sailing. *Address:* PO Box 1244, Townsville, Qld 4810, Australia. *T:* (7) 47714175, *Fax:* (7) 47211756.

QUÉGUINER, Jean; Légion d'Honneur, 1970; Administrateur Général des Affaires Maritimes, France; maritime consultant, since 1985; *b* 2 June 1921; *s* of Etienne Quéguiner and Anne Trehin; *m* 1952, Marguerite Gaillard; one *s* one *d*. *Educ:* Lycée Buffon, Collège Stanislas and Faculté de Droit, Paris; Coll. of Administration of Maritime Affairs, St Malo. Docteur en Droit (maritime), Bordeaux. Head of Maritime Dist of Caen, 1953; Dep. Head of Coll. of Admin. of Maritime Affairs, 1955; Head of Safety of Navigation Section, 1963; Vice-Chm. of Maritime Safety Cttee, 1965–68, Dep. Sec.-Gen., 1968–77, IMCO; Chm., Chantiers Navals de l'Esterel, 1981–85. Maritime expert to the Courts, 1986–. Mem. Cttee, Chambre d'Arbitrage de la Rochelle Centre Ouest-Atlantique (formerly de la Rochelle), 1992–. *Publications:* Législation et réglementation maritime, 1955; Le code de la mer, 1965; La croisière cotière, 1967; Le code fluvial à l'usage des plaisanciers, 1970. *Recreation:* sailing. *Address:* 13 rue de l'Horizon, 17480 Le Château d'Oléron, France.

QUELCH, Prof. John Anthony, DBA; Senior Associate Dean and Lincoln Filene Professor of Business Administration, Harvard Business School, since 2001; *b* 8 Aug. 1951; *s* of Norman Quelch and Laura Sally (*née* Jones); *m* 1978, Joyce Ann Huntley. *Educ:* Norwich Sch.; Exeter Coll., Oxford (BA 1972); Wharton Sch., Univ. of Pennsylvania (MBA 1974); Harvard Univ. (DBA 1977; MS 1978). Asst Prof. of Business Admin, Univ. of Western Ontario, 1977–79; Harvard Business School: Asst Prof. of Business Admin, 1979–84, Associate Prof., 1984–88, Prof., 1988–93; Sebastian S. Kresge Prof. of Marketing, 1993–98; Dean and Prof. of Mktg, London Business Sch., 1998–2001. Non-executive Director: Reebok Internat. Ltd, 1985–97; European Communication Mgt Ltd, 1988–97; WPP Gp plc, 1988–; US Office Products Co., 1995–97; Pentland Gp plc, 1997–99; Blue Circle Industries plc, 2000–01; easyJet plc, 2000–. Director: Council of Better Business Bureaux, 1995–97; Graduate Mgt Admissions Council, 1999–2001. CIMgt 1998. FRSA 1998. *Publications:* (jtly) Advertising and Promotion Management, 1983; (jtly) Cases in Advertising and Promotion Management, 1983, 4th edn 1996; (jtly) Marketing Management, 1985, 2nd edn 1993; (jtly) Global Marketing Management, 1988, 4th edn 1999; How to Market to Consumers, 1989; Sales Promotion Management, 1989; (jtly) The Marketing Challenge of Europe 1992, 1990, 2nd edn 1991; (jtly) Ethics in Marketing, 1992; (jtly) Cases in Product Management, 1995; (jtly) Cases in Marketing Management and Strategy, 1996; (jtly) Cases in European Marketing Management, 1997; contribs to learned and professional jls. *Recreations:* squash, tennis. *Address:* Harvard Business School, Morgan Hall 171, Soldiers Field, Boston, MA 02163, USA. *T:* (617) 4956325, *Fax:* (617) 4965637; *e-mail:* jquelch@hbs.edu. *Clubs:* Brook's, Harvard (Boston).

QUENNELL, Joan Mary, MBE 1958; *b* 23 Dec. 1923; *o c* of late Walter Quennell, Dangstein, Rogate. *Educ:* Dunhurst and Bedales Schools. War Service, WLA and BRCS. Vice-Chairman, Horsham Division Cons. Assoc., 1949 (Chairman, 1958–61); W Sussex CC, 1951–61. Served on Finance, Local Government, Selection and Education Cttees, etc; also as Governor various schools and colleges; Governor, Crawley Coll., Further Education, 1956–69; Member: Southern Reg. Council for Further Education, 1959–61; Reg. Adv. Council, Technological Education (London and Home Counties), 1959–61. MP (C) Petersfield, 1960–Sept. 1974; PPS to the Minister of Transport, 1962–64; Member: Select Cttee on Public Accounts, 1970–74; Speaker's Panel of Temporary Chairmen of House of Commons, 1970–74; Cttee of Selection, House of Commons, 1970–74; Select Cttee on European Secondary Legislation, 1973–74. Chm., EUW, Hampshire, 1978–80. JP W Sussex, 1959–80. *Recreations:* reading, gardening. *Address:* Dangstein, Rogate, near Petersfield, Hants GU31 5BZ.

QUENTIN, Caroline; actress; *b* 11 July 1960; *d* of Frederick and Katie Emily Jones; adopted stage name of Quentin; *m* 1991, Paul James Martin, *qv* (marr. diss. 1999); one *d* by Sam Farmer. *Educ:* Arts Educnl, Tring Park. *Theatre includes:* The Seagull, tour; Roots, RNT; Our Country's Good, Garrick; Low Level Panic, Sugar and Spice, Royal Court; Les Miserables, Barbican, transf. Palace; An Evening with Gary Lineker; A Game of Love and Chance, RNT; Les Enfants du Paradis, tour; Lysistrata; Mirandolina, Lyric, Hammersmith; The Live Bed Show, Garrick, 1994; The London Cuckolds, RNT, 1998; dir, Dead Funny, Palace, Watford, 1998. *Television includes:* series: Don't Tell Father, 1992; Men Behaving Badly, 1992–97; Jonathan Creek, 1997–; Kiss Me Kate, 1998–; The Innocent, 2001; *film:* An Evening with Gary Lineker, 1994. *Recreation:* bird-watching. *Address:* c/o Amanda Howard Associates, 21 Berwick Street, W1F 0PZ.

QUICK, Anthony Oliver Hebert; Headmaster of Bradfield College, 1971–85, retired; *b* 26 May 1924; *er s* of late Canon O. C. Quick, sometime Regius Prof. of Divinity at Oxford, and late Mrs F. W. Quick; *m* 1955, Eva Jean, *er d* of late W. C. Sellar and of Mrs Hope Sellar; three *s* one *d*. *Educ:* Shrewsbury Sch.; Corpus Christi Coll., Oxford; Sch. of Oriental and African Studies, Univ. of London (Govt Schol.). 2nd cl. hons Mod. History, Oxford. Lieut, RNVR, serving mainly on East Indies Stn, 1943–46. Asst Master, Charterhouse, 1949–61; Headmaster, Rendcomb Coll., Cirencester, 1961–71. *Publications:* (jtly) Britain 1714–1851, 1961; Britain 1851–1945, 1967; Twentieth Century Britain, 1968; Charterhouse: a history of the school, 1990; (contrib.) A History of Rendcomb College, vol. 2, 1995. *Recreations:* walking, gardening, sailing. *Address:* Corbin, Scorriton, Buckfastleigh, Devon TQ11 0HU.

QUICK, Dorothy, (Mrs Charles Denis Scanlan); a District Judge (Magistrates' Courts) (formerly Metropolitan Stipendiary Magistrate), since 1986; *b* 10 Dec. 1944; *d* of Frederick and Doris Quick; *m* 1971, Charles Denis Scanlan; two *s*. *Educ:* Glanafan Grammar Sch., Port Talbot; University Coll. London (LLB). Called to the Bar, Inner Temple, 1969; barrister-at-law, 1969–86. Mem., British Acad. of Forensic Sciences, 1987–. *Recreations:* gardening, theatre, books. *Address:* c/o Highbury Corner Magistrates' Court, 51 Holloway Road, N7 8JA.

QUICKE, Sir John (Godolphin), Kt 1988; CBE 1978; DL; *b* 20 April 1922; *s* of Captain Noel Arthur Godolphin Quicke and Constance May Quicke; *m* 1953, Prudence Tinné Berthon, *d* of Rear-Adm. (E) C. P. E. Berthon; three *s* three *d*. *Educ:* Eton; New Coll., Oxford. Vice-Chm., North Devon Meat, 1982–86; Mem., SW Reg. Bd, National Westminster Bank, 1974–92. Chairman: Minister of Agriculture's SW Regional Panel, 1972–75; Agricl EDC, NEDO, 1983–88, Agricl Sector Gp, 1988–90; RURAL, 1983–96; Estates Panel, NT, 1984–92; Member: Consultative Bd for R&D in Food and Agric., 1981–84; Severn Barrage Cttee, 1978–80; Countryside Commn, 1981–88 (Chm., Countryside Policy Review Panel, 1986–87); Properties Cttee, NT, 1984–97. President: CLA, 1975–77; Royal Bath & West of England Soc., 1989–90. Mem. Bd of Governors, Univ. of Plymouth (formerly Polytechnic SW), 1989–93. DL Devon, 1985. Hon. FRASE, 1989. Hon. DSc: Exeter, 1989; Polytechnic South West, 1991. Bledisloe Gold Medal for Landowners, RASE, 1985. *Recreations:* reading, music, gardening. *Address:* Sherwood, Newton St Cyres, near Exeter, Devon EX5 5BT. *T:* (01392) 851216. *Club:* Boodle's.

QUICKE, Rev. Michael John; C. W. Koller Professor of Preaching and Communication, Northern Baptist Theological Seminary, Chicago, since 2000; Interim Preacher, First Baptist Church, Wheaton, Illinois, since 2000; *b* 30 July 1945; *s* of George and Joan Quicke; *m* 1968, Carol Bentall; two *s*. *Educ:* Jesus Coll., Cambridge (MA); Regent's Park Coll., Oxford (MA). Nat. Sec. for Student Work, Baptist Union, 1967–69; Minister: Leamington Road Baptist Church, Blackburn, 1972–80; St Andrew's Street Baptist Church, Cambridge, 1980–93; Principal, Spurgeon's Coll., 1993–2000. Religious Advr, ITV, 1987–88. Mem. Council, Baptist Union of GB, 1976–2000; Vice Chm., Doctrine Commn, 1990–95, Worship Commn, 1995–, Baptist World Alliance. Member: Council of Mgt, Open Theol Coll., 1993–2000; Council, Evangelical Alliance, 1997–2000. Mem., Acad. of Homiletics, 1995–. Fellow, Coll. of Preachers, 1996 (Mem., Exec., 1996–2000). Hon. DD William Jewell Coll., Liberty, USA, 1994. *Publications:* Christian Apologetics, 1976; Something to Declare, 1996; On the Way of Trust, 1997. *Recreations:* listening to sermons, music, travel. *Address:* Northern Baptist Theological Seminary, 660 East Butterfield Road, Lombard, IL 60148, USA.

QUIGLEY, Anthony Leslie Coupland, CEng, FIEE; Tony Quigley Consulting, since 2001; *b* 14 July 1946; *s* of late Leslie Quigley and of Vera Barbara Rodaway (*née* Martin); *m* 1968, Monica Dean; one *s* two *d*. *Educ:* Apsley Grammar Sch.; Queen Mary Coll., Univ. of London (BSc Eng). Command Control and Computer Divs, ASWE, 1967–81 (Exchange Scientist, US Naval Surface Weapons Center, 1976–79); Supt, Command and Control Div., 1981–84, Hd, Command, Control and Assessment Gp, 1984–87, RARDE; Dep. Head, Science and Technology Assessment Office, Cabinet Office, 1987–90; Dir, SDI Participation Office, 1990–93, Asst Chief Scientific Advr (Nuclear), 1993–95, MoD; Under Sec., OST, 1995–99 (on secondment); Dir Gen., Scrutiny and Analysis, MoD, 1999–2001. Mem. Council, Foundn for Sci. and Technol. *Publications:* technical papers on radar tracking and command and control. *Recreation:* golf. *Address:* 21 Yew Tree Road, Tunbridge Wells, Kent TN4 0BD. *Club:* Chartham Park Golf.

QUIGLEY, Sir George; *see* Quigley, Sir W. G. H.

QUIGLEY, Sir (William) George (Henry), Kt 1993; CB 1982; PhD; Chairman: Short Brothers, since 1999 (Director, since 1989); Ulster Bank Ltd, 1989–2001 (Deputy Chairman, 1988–89); *b* 26 Nov. 1929; *s* of William George Cunningham Quigley and Sarah Hanson Martin; *m* 1971, Moyra Alice Munn, LLB. *Educ:* Ballymena Academy; Queen's Univ., Belfast (BA (1st Cl. Hons), 1951; PhD, 1955). Apptd Asst Principal, Northern Ireland Civil Service, 1955; Permanent Secretary: Dept of Manpower Services, NI, 1974–76; Dept of Commerce, NI, 1976–79; Dept of Finance, NI, 1979–82; Dept of Finance and Personnel, NI, 1982–88. Director: Irish-American Partnership, 1989–; Nat. Westminster Bank, 1990–99; Independent News and Media (UK), 2001–; Chm., Natwest Pension Trustees Ltd, 1998–. Chairman: Co-operation North, 1994–96; NI Economic Council, 1994–98. Chm., Royal Group of Hospitals Trust, NI, 1992–95. Chm., NI Div., Inst. of Dirs, 1990–94; Member: Fair Employment Commn for NI, 1989–93; Council, NI Chamber of Commerce and Industry, 1989–92; Council, NI Div., CBI, 1990–95. Chm., Scottish Fee Support Review, 1998–2000; Member: Nat. Cttee of Inquiry into Higher Educn, 1996–97; Qualifications and Curriculum Authority, 1997–99. President: Econ. and Social Res. Inst., 1999–; Inst. of Internat. Trade of Ireland, 1999–. Professorial Fellow, QUB, 1989–93. Fellow, Inst. of Bankers in Ireland, 1989. CIMgt. Hon. Fellow, IMgtI. Hon. LLD QUB, 1996; DUniv Ulster, 1998. Compaq Lifetime Achievement Award, 1997. *Publication:* (ed with E. F. D. Roberts) Registrum Iohannis Mey: The Register of John Mey, Archbishop of Armagh, 1443–1456, 1972. *Recreations:* historical research, reading, music, gardening. *Address:* Short Brothers Ltd, PO Box 241, Airport Road, Belfast BT3 9DX.

QUILLEY, Denis Clifford; actor; *b* 26 Dec. 1927; *s* of Clifford Charles Quilley and Ada Winifred (*née* Stanley); *m* 1949, Stella Chapman; one *s* two *d. Educ:* Bancroft's, Woodford, Essex. First appearance, Birmingham Rep. Theatre, 1945; The Lady's not for Burning, Globe, 1949; Old Vic and Young Vic Cos, 1950–51: parts included: Fabian in Twelfth Night (on tour, Italy), Gratiano in Merchant of Venice; Revue, Airs on a Shoe String (exceeded 700 perfs), Royal Court, 1953; first leading rôle in West End as Geoffrey Morris in Wild Thyme, Duke of York's, 1955; subseq. parts incl.: Tom Wilson in Grab Me a Gondola (over 600 perfs), Lyric; Captain Brassbound, and Orlando, Bristol Old Vic; Candide, Saville; Benedick in Much Ado about Nothing, Open Air Th.; Archie Rice in The Entertainer, Nottingham Playhouse; Krogstad in A Doll's House, Brighton; Nat. Theatre, 1971–76: Aufidius (Coriolanus); Macbeth; Bolingbroke (Richard II); Caliban (The Tempest); Lopakin (Cherry Orchard); Jamie (Long Day's Journey into Night); Claudius (Hamlet); Hector (Troilus and Cressida); Bajazeth (Tamburlaine); Privates on Parade, Aldwych, 1977, Piccadilly, 1978 (SWET award, 1977); Morell in Candida, Albery Theatre, 1977; Deathtrap, Garrick, 1978; title rôle in Sweeney Todd, Theatre Royal Drury Lane (SWET award), 1980; Molokov in Chess, Barbican, 1985; Antony, in Antony and Cleopatra, Chichester, 1985; Fatal Attraction, Haymarket, 1985; La Cage aux Folles, Palladium, 1986; Pizarro in Royal Hunt of the Sun, UK tour, 1989; The School for Scandal, NT, 1990; Brachiano in The White Devil, NT, 1991; Venus Observed, She Stoops to Conquer, Chichester, 1992; Sweeney Todd, RNT, 1993; The Merry Wives of Windsor, RNT, A Patriot for Me, RSC, 1995; Prospero in The Tempest, Regent's Park Open Air Th., 1996; Horsham in Waste, Pozzo in Waiting for Godot, Gloucester in King Lear, Old Vic, 1997; Racing Demon, Katherine Howard, Chichester, 1998; Troilus and Cressida, Candide, Money, RNT, 1999; Polonius in Hamlet, RNT, 2000; Humble Boy, RNT, 2001; has played in NY, Melbourne and Sydney. *Films:* Life at the Top, 1965; Anne of the Thousand Days, 1969; Murder on the Orient Express, 1974; The Black Windmill, 1974; The Antagonists, 1980; Evil Under the Sun, 1981; Privates on Parade, 1982; King David, 1985; Foreign Body, 1986; The Shell-seekers, 1989; Mr Johnson, 1990; A Dangerous Man, 1991. *TV plays and series* incl.: Merchant of Venice; The Father; Henry IV (Pirandello); Murder in the Cathedral; Time Slip; Contrabandits (Aust.); Clayhanger; The Serpent Son; The Crucible; Gladstone, in No 10; Masada; Anno Domini; Murder of a Moderate Man, 1988; Rich Tea and Sympathy, 1991. *Recreations:* playing the piano, flute and cello, walking. *Address:* c/o Bernard Hunter Associates, 13 Spencer Gardens, SW14 7AH.

QUILLIAM, Hon. Sir (James) Peter, Kt 1988; **Hon. Mr Justice Quilliam;** Judge of the High Court and Court of Appeal, Cook Islands, since 1988; Chief Justice of the Cook Islands, 1995–2000; *b* 23 March 1920; *s* of Ronald Henry Quilliam, CBE and Gwendoline Minnie Quilliam; *m* 1945, Ellison Jean Gill; two *s* one *d. Educ:* Wanganui Collegiate Sch.; Victoria Univ. of Wellington (LLB). Private practice as barrister and solicitor, 1945–69; Crown Prosecutor, New Plymouth, NZ, 1955–69; Judge, High Court of NZ, 1969–88, and Senior Puisne Judge, 1985–88; Judge of the Ct of Appeal, Fiji, 1992–95. NZ Police Complaints Authy, 1989–92. Pres., Taranaki Dist Law Soc., 1965–67. *Recreations:* golf, fishing, gardening, reading. *Address:* 9 Puketiro Avenue, Northland, Wellington 5, New Zealand. *T:* (4) 758166. *Clubs:* Wellington, Wellington Golf (NZ).

QUILLIAM, Prof. Juan Pete, (Peter), OBE 1986; DSc; FRCP; Professor of Pharmacology, University of London, at St Bartholomew's Hospital Medical College, 1962–83, now Emeritus; *b* 20 Nov. 1915; *e s* of late Thomas Quilliam, Peel, IoM and Maude (*née* Pavitt); *m* 1st, 1946, Melita Kelly (*d* 1957); one *s* one *d*; 2nd, 1958, Barbara Lucy Marion, *y d* of late Rev. William Kelly, Pelynt, Cornwall. *Educ:* University Coll. Sch.; UCL (exhibnr); UCH Med. Sch. MSc 1938, MB BS 1941; DSc 1969; FRCP 1975. Vice-Pres., London Univ. Athletic Union, 1938; Pres., London Univ. Boat Club, 1939–40 (rowing purple 1938). Sharpey Physiol Schol., UCL, 1939–41; House Phys. and House Surg., UCH, 1941; House Phys., Brompton Hosp. for Diseases of Chest, 1941–42; Asst TB Officer, Chelsea, 1941–42; Exptl Officer, Min. of Supply, 1942–43; served RAFVR Med. Br. (Central Fighter Estabt), 1943–46; Lectr in Pharmacol., KCL, 1945–55; London Univ. Travelling Fellow, 1949–50; Fellow, Johns Hopkins Hosp. Med. Sch., 1949–50; Sen. Lectr and Head of Pharmacol. Dept, 1956, Reader, 1958, St Bartholomew's Hosp. Med. Coll.; formerly Hon. Clinical Asst, St Bartholomew's Hosp. Gresham Prof. of Physic, 1967–68. University of London Convocation: Mem. Standing Cttee, 1966–73; Senator, Medicine, 1968–73; Chm., 1973–90; Mem. Mgt Cttee, 1973–90; Trustee, 1990–99; Chm., Univ. of London Convocation Trust, 1973–90; Mem. Ct and Senate, London Univ., 1973–90. Examiner in Pharmacol. and Clinical Pharmacol. to Univs of London, Edinburgh, Cambridge, Dundee, Liverpool, Manchester, TCD, NUI and Cardiff, also to Fac. of Anaesthetists and Apothecaries Soc. Mem., 1960–88, Dep. Chm., 1975–88, Gen. Optical Council; Gen. Sec., British Pharmacol Soc., 1968–71 (Hon. Mem., 1999); British Medical Association: Mem. Council, 1971–85; Chairman: Med. Academic Staff Cttee, 1978, 1980, 1982; Bd of Sci. and Educn, 1982–85; Fellow, 1981; Vice-Pres., 1988. Member: CMO's Academic Forum, 1980–81; Academic Medicine Gp, RCP, 1982–; Cttee CH/30, BSI, 1984–. Member: IBA Advertising Adv. Cttee, 1984–92; Joint BBC/IBA Central Appeals Adv. Cttee, 1987–92. Crouch Harbour Authority: Mem., 1987; Vice-Chm., 1988; Chm., 1989–94; Mem., 1974, Chm., 1987–, Crouch Area Yachting Fedn; Associate Mem., Burnham Week Regatta Jt Clubs Cttee, 1984–. Trustee: City Parochial Foundn, 1977–89; Trust for London, 1986–89; Nat. Heart Forum (formerly Nat. Forum for Coronary Heart Disease Prevention), 1989– (Hon. Treas., 1990–94; Hon. Mem.); Founder Trustee, 1984–94, Co-Chm., 1984–99, Help the Hospices Trust; Mem., Grants Council, Charities Aid Foundn, 1990–99. Vice-Pres., Totteridge Residents' Assoc., 1997–. Press Editor, British Jl of Pharmacol., 1957–60. *Publications: jointly:* Medical Effects of Nuclear War, 1983; Boxing, 1984; Young People and Alcohol, 1986; Long term environment effects of nuclear war, 1986; Alternative Therapy, 1986; The Torture Report, 1986; papers on visual purple, blood/acqueous humour barrier permability, intra-ocular fluid, DFP and synaptic transmission in heart and muscle, action drugs on the iris, the ocular critical flicker fusion frequency, the auditory flutter fusion frequency, the electro-pharmacology of sedatives, general anaesthetics on autonomic ganglia as a model of brain synapses, GABA-like actions on lobster muscle, effects of staphylococcal α-toxin on intestine, the ultrastructural effects in autonomic ganglia in the presence of chemical substances, World Medicine, University "Cuts" 1983. *Recreations:* work, sailing. *Address:* Hornbeams, 34 Totteridge Common, Totteridge, N20 8NE. *Club:* United Hospitals Sailing (Burnham-on-Crouch) (Cdre, 1974–).

QUILLIAM, Hon. Sir Peter; *see* Quilliam, Hon. Sir J. P.

QUILLIAM, Peter; *see* Quilliam, J. P.

QUILTER, Sir Anthony (Raymond Leopold Cuthbert), 4th Bt *cr* 1897; landowner since 1959; *b* 25 March 1937; *s* of Sir (John) Raymond (Cuthbert) Quilter, 3rd Bt and Margery Marianne (*née* Cooke); *S* father, 1959; *m* 1964, Mary Elise, *er d* of late Colonel Brian (Sherlock) Gooch, DSO, TD; one *s* one *d. Educ:* Harrow. Is engaged in farming. *Recreations:* shooting, golf. *Heir: s* Guy Raymond Cuthbert Quilter [*b* 13 April 1967; *m* 1992, Jenifer, *o d* of John Redvers-Cox; two *s*]. *Address:* Sutton Hall, Sutton, Woodbridge, Suffolk IP12 3EQ. *T:* (01394) 411246.

QUILTER, David (Cuthbert) Tudway; Vice Lord-Lieutenant of Somerset, 1978–96; Local Director, Barclays Bank, Bristol, 1962–84 (Director, Barclays Bank UK Ltd, 1971–81); *b* 26 March 1921; *o s* of Percy Cuthbert Quilter and Clare Tudway; *m* 1953, Elizabeth Mary, *er d* of Sir John Carew Pole, 12th Bt, DSO, TD; one *s* two *d. Educ:* Eton. Served War of 1939–45, Coldstream Guards, 1940–46. Dir, Bristol Evening Post, 1982–91. JP London Juvenile Courts, 1959–62. Mayor of Wells, 1974–75; Chm. of Trustees, Wells Cathedral Preservation Trust, 1976–; Chm., Somerset Gardens Trust, 1991–99; Treasurer, Bristol Univ., 1976–88; Governor, Wells Cathedral Sch., 1968–; Member: Council, Outward Bound Trust, 1959–92; Garden Soc., 1973–; Trustee, Carnegie UK Trust, 1981–2000. Master, Soc. of Merchant Venturers, 1984–85. DL 1970, High Sheriff 1974–75, Somerset. Hon. LLD Bristol, 1989. *Publications:* No Dishonourable Name, 1947; A History of Wells Cathedral School, 1985. *Recreations:* gardening, music. *Address:* Milton Lodge, Wells, Somerset BA5 3AQ. *T:* (01749) 672168. *Clubs:* Boodle's, Army and Navy, Pratt's.

QUIN; *see* Wyndham-Quin, family name of **Earl of Dunraven**.

QUIN, Rt Hon. Joyce (Gwendolen); PC 1998; MP (Lab) Gateshead East and Washington West, since 1997 (Gateshead East, 1987–97); *b* 26 Nov. 1944; *d* of Basil Godfrey Quin and Ida (*née* Ritson). *Educ:* Univ. of Newcastle upon Tyne (BA French, 1st Cl. Hons); Univ. of London (MSc Internat. Relns). Research Asst, Internat. Dept, Labour Party Headquarters, Transport House, 1969–72; Lecturer in French, Univ. of Bath, 1972–76; Resident Tutor, St Mary's Coll., and Lectr in French and Politics, Univ. of Durham, 1977–79. Mem. (Lab) European Parliament, S Tyne and Wear, 1979–84, Tyne and Wear, 1984–89. Opposition front bench spokesman on trade and industry, 1989–92, on employment, 1992–93, on European affairs, 1993–97; Minister of State: Home Office, 1997–98; (Minister for Europe), FCO, 1998–99, MAFF, 1999–2001. Mem., Select Cttee on Treasury and Civil Service, 1987–89. Hon. Fellow: Sunderland Polytechnic, subseq. Univ. of Sunderland, 1986; St Mary's Coll., Durham Univ., 1994. *Publications:* various articles in newspapers and journals. *Recreations:* North-East local history (Newcastle upon Tyne City Guide), music, theatre, walking, cycling. *Address:* House of Commons, SW1A 0AA; (office) Design Works, William Street, Felling, Gateshead, Tyne & Wear NE10 0JP.

QUINAN, Lloyd; Member (SNP) West Scotland, Scottish Parliament, since 1999; *b* 29 April 1957; *s* of Andrew and Ann Quinan. *Educ:* Queen Margaret Coll., Edinburgh. Actor, 1978–83; theatre dir, 1983–89; television presenter, producer and dir, 1989–99. *Recreations:* reading, travel, music, football. *Address:* c/o Scottish Parliament HQ, George IV Bridge, Edinburgh EH99 1SP. *T:* (0131) 348 5734.

QUINCE, Peter; *see* Thompson, John W. McW.

QUINLAN, Rt Rev. Alan Geoffrey; a Bishop Suffragan, Diocese of Cape Town, 1988–98; *b* 20 Aug. 1933; *s* of late Robert Quinlan and of Eileen Beatrice Quinlan; *m* 1963, Rosalind Arlen Sallie (*née* Reed); three *s* one *d. Educ:* Kelham Theological College. RAF, 1952–54. Deacon 1958, priest 1959; Asst Curate, St Thomas's, Leigh, Lancs, 1958–61; Rector: St Margaret's, Bloemfontein, 1962–68; St Michael and All Angels, Sasolburg, OFS, 1968–72; Warden, Community of Resurrection, Grahamstown and Chaplain, Grahamstown Training Coll., 1972–76; Priest-in-Charge of Training in Ministries and Discipleship, Cape Town Diocese, 1976–80; Rector, All Saints, Plumstead, Cape Town, 1980–88. Canon, St George's Cathedral, Cape Town, 1980–88. *Publications:* A Manual for Worship Leaders; Discipleship and the Alternative Society; Churchwardens' Handbook. *Recreations:* chess, reading, bird-watching, computers, music, painting. *Address:* 132 Woodley Road, Plumstead, Cape Town, 7800, South Africa.

QUINLAN, Sir Michael (Edward), GCB 1991 (KCB 1985; CB 1980); Director, Ditchley Foundation, 1992–99; *b* 11 Aug. 1930; *s* of late Gerald and Roseanne Quinlan; *m* 1965, (Margaret) Mary Finlay; two *s* two *d. Educ:* Wimbledon Coll.; Merton Coll., Oxford. (1st Cl. Hon. Mods, 1st Cl. LitHum; MA; Hon. Fellow, 1989). RAF, 1952–54. Asst Principal, Air Ministry, 1954; Private Sec. to Parly Under-Sec. of State for Air, 1956–58; Principal, Air Min., 1958; Private Sec. to Chief of Air Staff, 1962–65; Asst Sec., MoD, 1968; Defence Counsellor, UK Delegn to NATO, 1970–73; Under-Sec., Constitution Unit, Cabinet Office, 1974–77; Dep. Under-Sec. of State (Policy), MoD, 1977–81; Dep. Sec. (Industry), HM Treasury, 1981–82; Perm. Sec., Dept of Employment, 1983–88; Perm. Under-Sec. of State, MoD, 1988–92. Chm., Civil Service Sports Council, 1985–89; Pres., CS Cricket Assoc., 1992–98. Vis. Prof., KCL, 1992–95; Public Policy Scholar, Woodrow Wilson Center, Washington, 2000. Director: Lloyds Bank, 1992–95; Lloyds TSB Gp, 1996–98; Pilkington, 1992–99. Trustee, Science Mus., 1992–2001. Governor, Henley Management Coll., 1983–88. Pres., Merton Soc., 1992–95. CIMgt (CBIM 1983). *Publications:* Thinking About Nuclear Weapons, 1997; many articles on defence and public admin and ethics. *Recreations:* golf, watching cricket, listening to music. *Address:* 3 Adderbury Park, West Adderbury, Oxon OX17 3EN. *Clubs:* Royal Air Force, MCC; Chipping Norton Golf.

QUINN, Aiden O'Brien; *see* Quinn, J. A. O'B.

QUINN, Andrea Helen, (Mrs R. Champ); conductor; Music Director, New York City Ballet, since 2001; *b* 22 Dec. 1964; *d* of Desmond Bone and Theresa Bone (who *m* 1971, John Quinn); *m* 1991, Dr Roderick Champ; one *s* two *d. Educ:* Nottingham Univ. (BA

Hons); Royal Acad. of Music (Adv. Cert. in Conducting; ARAM 1999). Music Director: London Philharmonic Youth Orch., 1993–96; Royal Ballet, 1998–2001. Hon. FTCL 2000. *Recreations:* horse riding, literature, Italian, art galleries. *Address:* c/o Clarion/Seven Muses, 47 Whitehall Park, Highgate, N19 3TW. *T:* (020) 7272 4413.

QUINN, Andrew; Chief Executive, ITV, 1992–95; *b* 29 March 1937. Granada TV, 1964–92: Gen. Manager, 1977; Man. Dir, Granada Cable and Satellite, 1983; Man. Dir, 1987; Chief Exec., 1992. Dir, Border TV, 1996.

QUINN, Brian, CBE 1996; Managing Director, Brian Quinn Consultancy plc, since 1996; *b* 18 Nov. 1936; *s* of Thomas Quinn and Margaret (*née* Cairns); *m* 1961, Mary Bradley; two *s* one *d*. *Educ:* Glasgow Univ. (MA Hons); Manchester Univ. (MA Econs); Cornell Univ. (PhD). FCIBS 1995. Economist, African Dept, IMF, 1964–70, Rep., Sierra Leone, 1966–68; joined Bank of England, 1970; Economic Div., 1970–74; Chief Cashier's Dept, 1974–77; Head of Information Div., 1977–82; Asst Dir, 1982–88; Head of Banking Supervision, 1986–88; Exec. Dir, 1988–96. Chairman: Nomura Bank Internat., 1996–99; Celtic plc, 2000–; non-executive Director: Bankgesellschaft Berlin UK plc, 1996–; Britannic (formerly Britannia) Asset Mgt, 1998–. Chm., Financial Markets Gp, LSE, 1996–2000. Advr, Singapore Govt, 1997–; Consultant: World Bank, 1997–; McKinsey and Co., 1998–; Mem. Adv. Bd, Toronto Centre, 1998–. *Publications:* (contrib.) Surveys of African Economies, vol. 4, 1971; (contrib.) The New Inflation, 1976; articles in learned jls. *Recreations:* fishing, golf, cycling, football. *Address:* 14 Homewood Road, St Albans, Herts AL1 4BH. *Clubs:* Bankers', Reform; New York Anglers'.

QUINN, Brian; *see* Quinn, J. S. B.

QUINN, Prof. David Beers, DLit (QUB), PhD (London), MRIA, FRHistS; Andrew Geddes and John Rankin Professor of Modern History, University of Liverpool, 1957–76; *b* 24 April 1909; *o s* of late David Quinn, Omagh and Belfast, and Albertina Devine, Cork; *m* 1937, Alison Moffat Robertson, MA (*d* 1993), *d* of late John Ireland Robertson, Edinburgh; two *s* one *d*. *Educ:* Clara (Offaly) No 2 National Sch.; Royal Belfast Academical Institution; Queen's Univ., Belfast; King's Coll., University of London. University Schol., QUB, 1928–31 (1st Class Hons in Medieval and Modern History, 1931); PhD London, 1934. Asst Lecturer, 1934, and Lecturer, 1937, University College, Southampton; Lecturer in History, QUB, 1939–44; seconded to BBC European Service, 1943; Prof. of History, University College, Swansea, 1944–57; DLit (QUB), 1958. Secretary, Ulster Society for Irish Historical Studies, 1939–44; Member: Council of Hakluyt Society, 1950–54, 1957–60 (Vice-Pres., 1960–82, 1987–, Pres., 1982–87); Council of Royal Historical Society, 1951–55, 1956–60 (Vice-Pres., 1964–68, Hon. Vice-Pres., 1983); Fellow, Folger Shakespeare Lib. (Washington, DC), 1957, 1959, 1963–64; Fellow, John Carter Brown Lib., 1970, 1982; Leverhulme Res. Fellow, 1963; British Council Visiting Scholar, NZ, 1967; Hungary, 1972; Fellow, Huntington Library, 1980; Fellow, Nat. Inst. for the Humanities, 1983; Fulbright Fortieth Anniversary Dist. Fellow, 1986–87; Harrison Vis. Prof., Coll. of William and Mary, Williamsburg, Va, 1969–70; Visiting Professor: St Mary's Coll., St Mary's City, Md, 1976–78, 1980–82, 1984; Michigan Univ., 1979. Mem., President's Council, Coll. of William and Mary, Va, 1998–. Founding Mem., Bermuda Maritime Mus. Hon. Mem. American Historical Assoc., 1986. Hon. FBA 1984. Hon. DLitt: Newfoundland, 1964; New Univ. of Ulster, 1975; NUI, 1981; Hon. DHL: St Mary's Coll., 1978; Coll. of William and Mary, 1995; Hon. LLD Univ. of N Carolina, 1980. Hon. Phi Beta Kappa, 1984. Medallist, John Carter Brown Library, 1996. *Publications:* The Port Books or Petty Customs Accounts of Southampton for the Reign of Edward IV, 2 vols, 1937–38; The Voyages and Colonising Enterprises of Sir Humphrey Gilbert, 2 vols, 1940; Raleigh and the British Empire, 1947; The Roanoke Voyages, 1584–90, 2 vols, 1955; (with Paul Hulton) The American Drawings of John White, 1577–1590, 1964; (with R. A. Skelton) R. Hakluyt's Principall Navigations (1589), 1965; The Elizabethans and the Irish, 1966; Richard Hakluyt, Editor, 1967; North American Discovery, 1971; (with W. P. Cumming and R. A. Skelton) The Discovery of North America, 1972; (with N. M. Cheshire) The New Found Land of Stephen Parmenius, 1972; (with A. M. Quinn) Virginia Voyages from Hakluyt, 1973; England and the Discovery of America 1481–1620, 1974; The Hakluyt Handbook, 2 vols, 1974; (with W. P. Cumming, S. E. Hillier and G. Williams) The Exploration of North America, 1630–1776, 1974; The Last Voyage of Thomas Cavendish, 1975; North America from First Discovery to Early Settlements, 1977; (with A. M. Quinn and S. Hillier) New American World, 5 vols, 1979; Early Maryland and a Wider World, 1982; (with A. M. Quinn) The First Settlers, 1982; (with A. M. Quinn) English New England Voyages 1602–1608, 1983; (with A. N. Ryan) England's Sea Empire, 1550–1642, 1983; Set Fair for Roanoke, 1985; (ed) John Derricke, The Image of Ireland, 1986; contrib. to A New History of Ireland, vol. 2, ed A. Cosgrove, 1987; Raleigh and Quinn: the explorer and his Boswell, ed H. G. Jones, 1988; Explorers and Colonies: America 1500–1625, 1990; Ireland and America 1500–1640, 1991; Thomas Harriot and the Problem of America, 1992; (ed with A. M. Quinn) Richard Hakluyt, Discourse of Western Planting, 1994; Sir Francis Drake as seen by his contemporaries, 1996; European Approaches to North America 1450–1640, 1998; contribs on Irish history and the discovery and settlement of N America in historical journals. *Address:* 9 Knowsley Road, Cressington Park, Liverpool L19 0PF. *T:* (0151) 427 2041.

QUINN, (James) Aiden O'Brien; QC (Seychelles) 1973; Vice-President, Immigration Appeal Tribunal, since 1996 (Adjudicator, since 1990, and Special Adjudicator, since 1993); *b* 3 Jan. 1932; *s* of late William Patrick Quinn (Comr, Gárda Siochána) and Helen Mary (*née* Walshe); *m* 1960, Christel Tyner; two *s* one *d*. *Educ:* Presentation Coll., Bray, Co. Wicklow, Ireland; University Coll., Dublin, NUI (BA, LLB Hons). Called to the Bar: Kings' Inns, Dublin, 1957; Inner Temple, 1967. National City Bank, Dublin, 1949–53; in practice at the Bar, under Colonial Office Scheme, 1958–60; Crown Counsel and Actg Sen. Crown Counsel, Nyasaland, 1960–64; Asst Attorney Gen. and Actg Attorney Gen., West Cameroon, 1964–66; Procureur Général, West Cameroon, and Avocat Général, Fed. Republic of Cameroon, 1966–68; Fed. Republic of Cameroon, 1968–72: Conseiller, Cour Fédérale de Justice; Judge, W Cameroon Supreme Court; Conseiller Technique (Harmonisation des Lois), Ministère de la Justice, Yaoundé; Président, Tribunal Administratif, Cameroun Occidental; Chargé de Cours, Ecole Nationale de l'Administration et de la Magistrature, Yaoundé; Republic of Seychelles: Attorney Gen., also of British Indian Ocean Territory, 1972–76; MLC, MEC and Mem. Parlt, 1972–76; Chief Justice, 1976–77; Actg Dep. Governor, 1974; Mem., Official Delegn on Self-Govt, 1975, and on Independence Constitutions, 1976; collab. with Prof. A. G. Chloros on translation and up-dating of Code Napoleon, 1975–76; Chm., Judicial Service Commn, 1976–77; Gilbert Islands (Kiribati): Chief Justice, 1977–81; Chm., Judicial Service Commn, 1977–81; set up new Courts' system, 1978; Mem., Council of State, 1979–81; Judge, High Court of Solomon Is, 1977–79; Special Prosecutor, Falkland Is, 1981; Botswana: Chief Justice, 1981–87; Chm., Judicial Service Commn, 1981–87; retired, 1987–89; Investment Advr, 1989–90. Mem., Panel of Experts of UN on Prevention of Crime and Treatment of Offenders, 1985–87. Chevalier, Ordre de la Valeur, Republic of Cameroon, 1967; Kiribati Independence Medal, 1979. *Publications:* Magistrates' Courts Handbook: West Cameroon, 1968; Kiribati, 1979; edited: West Cameroon Law Reports, 1961–68; Gilbert Islands Law Reports, 1977–79; Kiribati Law Reports, 1977–80; articles in Commonwealth Law Jl, The Magistrate, etc. *Recreations:* languages, travel, reading, swimming. *Address:* (office) Field House, 15-25 Bream's Buildings, EC4A 1DZ. *Clubs:* Royal Commonwealth Society, Royal Over-Seas League.

QUINN, James Charles Frederick; film producer and exhibitor; Chairman, The Minema, 1984–94; *b* 23 Aug. 1919; *y s* of Rev. Chancellor James Quinn and Muriel Alice May (*née* MaGuire); *m* 1942, Hannah, 2nd *d* of Rev. R. M. Gwynn, BD (Sen. Fellow and Vice-Provost, TCD), and Dr Eileen Gwynn; one *s* one *d*. *Educ:* Shrewsbury Sch.; TCD (Classical Exhibnr); Christ Church, Oxford (MA; Dip. in Econ. and Polit. Sci.). Served War, Irish Guards, Italy, NW Europe; British Army Staff, France, and Town Major, Paris, 1945–46. Courtaulds Ltd, 1949–55. Dir, BFI, 1955–64: National Film Theatre built; London Film Festival inaugurated; 1st Univ. Lectureship in Film Studies in UK estabd at Slade Sch. of Fine Art, University Coll., London; BFI's terms of ref. enld to incl. television; 1st world TV Fest., NFT, 1964. UK Mem. Jury, Cannes and Venice Internat. Film Fests, 1956; Chm. Jury, Berlin Film Fest., 1961. Council of Europe Fellowship, 1966. Chairman: Internat. Short Film Conf., 1971–78 (Life Pres., 1979); National Panel for Film Festivals, 1974–83. Member: Gen. Adv. Council, BBC, 1960–64; Bd, Gardner Arts Centre, Sussex Univ., 1968–71; British Council Film Television and Video Adv. Cttee, 1983–90. Trustee: Imperial War Museum, 1968–78; Grierson Meml Trust, 1975–2001; Nat. Life Story Collection, 1986–91. Invited to stand by New Ulster Movement as Indep. Unionist Parly candidate, S Down, 1968. Foreign Leader Award, US State Dept, 1962. Films: co-producer, Herostratus, 1966; Producer, Overlord, 1975. Silver Bear Award, Berlin Internat. Film Festival, 1975; Special Award, London Evening News British Film Awards, 1976. Chevalier de l'Ordre des Arts et des Lettres, France, 1979. *Publications:* Outside London, 1965; The Film and Television as an Aspect of European Culture, 1968; contrib. Chambers's Encyclopaedia (cinema), 1956–59. *Recreations:* lawn tennis; formerly Eton Fives. *Address:* Crescent Cottage, 108 Marine Parade, Brighton, E Sussex BN2 1AT. *Clubs:* Cavalry and Guards; Vincent's (Oxford).

QUINN, (James Steven) Brian; Director, Digital Computer Services, 1985–96 (Chief Executive, 1989–92; Chairman, 1992–96); *b* 16 June 1936; *s* of James and Elizabeth Quinn; *m* 1962, Blanche Cecilia James (marr. diss. 1987); two *s* one *d*. *Educ:* St Mary's Coll., Crosby; Waterpark Coll., Ireland; University Coll., Dublin (BCL, LLB). Kings Inn, Dublin. Director: Johnson Radley, 1966–68; United Glass Containers, 1968–69; Head of Industrial Activities, Prices and Incomes Board, 1969–71; Dir, M. L. H. Consultants, 1971–79; Corporate Develt Advr, Midland Bank Internat., 1977–80; Chief Industrial Advr, Price Commn, 1977–78. Chairman: BrightStar Communications, 1983–85; BAJ Holdings, 1985–87; Harmer Holbrook, 1987–88; Signet Online, 1996–99; Loan Line Ltd, 1997–2000; Man. Dir, Visnews, 1980–86; Dir, Telematique Services, 1985–90. Legal res., TCD, 1995–97. Institute of Management (formerly British Institute of Management): CIMgt (CBIM 1985; FBIM 1978); Mem. Council, 1981–87, 1990–98; Mem. Finance Cttee, 1981–84; Chm., City of London Branch, 1981–83; Vice Pres., 1983–90; Chm., Gtr London Regl Council, 1990–94. International Institute of Communications: Trustee, 1982–88, 1992–97; Chm., Exec. Cttee, 1984–88; Pres., 1988–91. Mem., Exec. Cttee, Inst. of European Trade and Technology, 1983–96. Trustee: Internat. Center of Communications, San Diego State Univ., 1990–. Chm., Finance Cttee, Great Japan Exhbn, 1979–82. Chm., Editl Bd, Professional Manager, 1993–98. *Recreations:* golf, reading, veteran vehicles. *Address:* 29 Bliss Mill, Chipping Norton, Oxon OX7 5JR. *Club:* Athenæum.

QUINN, Lawrence William; MP (Lab) Scarborough and Whitby, since 1997; *b* 25 Dec. 1956; *s* of late Jimmy Quinn and Sheila Quinn; *m* 1982, Ann Eames. *Educ:* Pennine Way Schs, Carlisle; Harraby Sch., Carlisle; Hatfield Poly. (BSc). CEng. Formerly Planning Develt Engr, London NE, Railtrack. Chm., All Party Railways (formerly Rail Freight) Gp, 1997–; Sec., Labour backbench Agriculture Cttee, 1997–. Sec., PLP Yorks and Humber Gp; PLP Rep., Nat. Policy Forum. *Address:* 53 Westborough, Scarborough, N Yorks YO11 1TU.

QUINN, Ruairi; TD (Lab) Dublin South-East, 1977–81, and since 1982; *b* 2 April 1946; *s* of Malachi Quinn and Julia Quinn; *m* 1st, 1969, Nicola Underwood; one *s* one *d*; 2nd, 1990, Liz Allman; one *s*. *Educ:* University Coll., Dublin (BArch, Higher Dip. in Ekistics). Dublin City Council: Mem., 1974–77; Leader, Lab Gp and Civic Alliance, 1991–93. Mem., Seanad Eireann, 1976–77 and 1981–82; Minister of State, Envmt, 1982–83; Minister: for Labour, 1984–87, and for Public Service, 1986–87; for Enterprise and Employment, 1993–94; for Finance, 1995–97. Leader, Irish Labour Party, 1997–. *Publications:* contrib. to Architects Jl, Irish Architect, Ekistics, Tilt. *Recreations:* reading, cooking, walking, music, gardening, cycling. *Address:* Dáil Eireann, Kildare Street, Dublin 2, Republic of Ireland.

QUINN, Dame Sheila (Margaret Imelda), DBE 1987 (CBE 1978); FRCN; President, Royal College of Nursing, 1982–86, now Life Vice President; *b* 16 Sept. 1920; *d* of late Wilfred Amos Quinn and Ada Mazella (*née* Bottomley). *Educ:* Convent of Holy Child, Blackpool; London Univ. (BScEcon Hons); Royal Lancaster Infirmary (SRN 1947); Birmingham (SCM); Royal Coll. of Nursing, London (RNT). FRCN 1978. Admin. Sister, then Principal Sister Tutor, Prince of Wales' Gen. Hosp., London, 1950–61; Internat. Council of Nurses, Geneva: Dir, Social and Econ. Welfare Div., 1961–66; Exec. Dir, 1967–70; Chief Nursing Officer, Southampton Univ. Hosps, 1970–74; Area Nursing Officer, Hampshire AHA (Teaching), 1974–78; Regional Nursing Officer, Wessex RHA, 1978–83. Member: E Dorset DHA, 1987–90; Dorset FHSA, 1990–96. Nursing Advr, BRCS, 1983–88. Pres., Standing Cttee of Nurses of EEC, 1983–91; Member: Council, Royal Coll. of Nursing, 1971–79 (Chm. Council, 1974–79; Dep. Pres., 1980–82); Bd of Dirs, Internat. Council of Nurses, 1977–85 (first Vice-Pres., 1981–85); Mem., EEC Adv. Cttee on Trng in Nursing, 1978–90. Hon. DSc (Social Sciences) Southampton, 1986. *Publications:* Nursing in The European Community, 1980; Caring for the Carers, 1981; ICN Past and Present, 1989; Nursing, the EC Dimension, 1993; articles, mainly on internat. nursing and EEC, in national and internat. jls. *Recreations:* travel, gardening. *Address:* 31 Albany Park Court, Winn Road, Southampton SO17 1EN. *T:* (023) 8067 6592. *Clubs:* St John's House, Royal Society of Medicine.

QUINN, Stephen; Permanent Secretary, Department of the Environment, Northern Ireland Assembly, since 1999; *b* 22 Aug. 1950; *s* of Thomas Charles Quinn and Jane Quinn (*née* Kirkpatrick); *m* 1983, Deirdre Mary Brady. *Educ:* Portora Royal Sch., Enniskillen; Trinity Coll., Dublin (BA Hons Hist. and Pol Sci.). Northern Ireland Civil Service: Dept of Finance, 1974–86 (Sec., Kincora Inquiry, 1984–85); Assistant Secretary: Dept of Health and Social Services, 1986–87; Dept of Finance and Personnel, 1987–90; Dept of Educn, 1990–92; Central Secretariat, 1992–94; Under Secretary: Dept of Finance and Personnel, 1994–98; DoE, 1998–99. *Address:* c/o Department of the Environment, Clarence Court, Adelaide Street, Belfast BT2 8GB.

QUINN, Terence James; President, Reader inc. (US), since 2000; *b* 17 Nov. 1951; *s* of Thomas Quinn and Shirley (*née* Anderson); *m* 1973, Patricia Anna-Maria Gillespie; one *s* one *d* (and one *s* decd). *Educ:* St Aloysius Coll., Glasgow. Editor: Telegraph & Argus,

Bradford, 1984–89; Evening News, Edinburgh, 1989–92; Dep. Editl Dir, 1992–94, Editl Dir, 1994, Thomson Regl Newspapers; Editor, Daily Record, 1994–98; Sen. Vice Pres., Readership, Thomson Newspapers (US), 1998–2000. *Recreations:* tennis, sailing, ski-ing. *Address:* Reader inc., PO Box 2218, Darien, CT 06820, USA. *T:* (203) 6628990; *e-mail:* terryjquinn@aol.com.

QUINN, Dr Terence John; Director, Bureau International des Poids et Mesures, Sèvres, France, since 1988 (Deputy Director, 1977–88); *b* 19 March 1938; *s* of John Henry and Olive Hilda Quinn; *m* 1962, Renée Marie Goujard; two *s*. *Educ:* Univ. of Southampton (BSc 1959); Univ. of Oxford (DPhil 1963). National Physical Laboratory, Teddington: Jun. Res. Fellow, 1962–64; Staff Mem., 1964–77. Vis. Scientist, Nat. Bureau of Standards, Washington, DC, 1967–68; Royal Soc. Vis. Fellow, Cavendish Lab., and Dist. Vis. Fellow, Christ's Coll., Cambridge, 1984–85. FInstP 1975; Fellow, APS, 1995; FAAAS 2001. Hon. Prof., Birmingham Univ., 2000. Hon. Dr Conservatoire Nat. des Arts et Métiers, Paris, 2000. *Publications:* Temperature, 1983, 2nd edn 1990; papers in sci. press on thermometry, radiometry, mass standards, lab. gravitational experiments, fundamental phys. constants and gen. metrology. *Recreations:* photography, violin playing. *Address:* Bureau International des Poids et Mesures, Pavillon de Breteuil, 92312 Sèvres, France. *T:* (1) 45077070, *Fax:* (1) 45342021; *e-mail:* tquinn@bipm.org. *Club:* Athenæum.

QUINNEN, Peter John; Chairman, Frew Macmaster, 1990–99; *b* 4 April 1945; *s* of John Norman Quinnen and Elisabeth Clark; *m* 1972, Pammy Urquhart; two *s*. *Educ:* St Benedict's School, Ealing; Christ Church, Oxford (MA Jurisp). FCA. Peat, Marwick, Mitchell & Co., 1966–72; James Capel & Co., 1972–90, Dir, 1982, Chm., and Chief Exec., 1986–90. Dir, Gold Greenlees Trott, 1994–98. *Recreations:* golf, opera, music, ballet, sport. *Clubs:* Pie and Pints Society; Royal Mid-Surrey Golf, Woebegones Golf, St George's Hill, Wednesday Golf.

QUINTON, family name of **Baron Quinton**.

QUINTON, Baron *cr* 1982 (Life Peer), of Holywell in the City of Oxford and County of Oxfordshire; **Anthony Meredith Quinton,** FBA 1977; Chairman of the Board, British Library, 1985–90; *b* 25 March 1925; *s* of late Richard Frith Quinton, Surgeon Captain, RN, and late Gwenllyan Letitia Quinton; *m* 1952, Marcelle Wegier; one *s* one *d*. *Educ:* Stowe Sch.; Christ Church, Oxford (St Cyres Scholar; BA 1st Cl. Hons PPE 1948). Served War, RAF, 1943–46: flying officer and navigator. Fellow: All Souls Coll., Oxford, 1949–55; New Coll., Oxford, 1955–78 (Emeritus Fellow, 1980; Hon. Fellow, 1997); Pres., Trinity Coll., Oxford, 1978–87 (Hon. Fellow, 1987). Delegate, OUP, 1970–76. Mem., Arts Council, 1979–81; Vice Pres., British Acad., 1985–86. Visiting Professor: Swarthmore Coll., Pa, 1960; Stanford Univ., Calif, 1964; New Sch. for Social Res., New York, 1976–77; Brown Univ., 1994. Lecturer: Dawes Hicks, British Acad., 1971; Gregynog, Univ. of Wales, Aberystwyth, 1973; T. S. Eliot, Univ. of Kent, Canterbury, 1976; Robbins, Univ. of Stirling, 1987; Hobhouse, LSE, 1988; Tanner, Warsaw, 1988; R. M. Jones, QUB, 1988; Carter, Lancaster, 1989. President: Aristotelian Soc., 1975–76; Soc. for Applied Philosophy, 1988–91; Royal Inst. of Philosophy, 1990–; Assoc. of Indep. Libraries, 1991–97; Friends of Wellcome Inst., 1992–97. Chm., Kennedy Meml Trust, 1990–95. Governor, Stowe Sch., 1963–84 (Chm. Governors, 1969–75); Fellow, Winchester Coll., 1970–85. DHumLit NY Univ., 1987; DHum Ball State Univ., 1990. Order of Leopold II, Belgium, 1984. *Publications:* Political Philosophy (ed), 1967; The Nature of Things, 1973; Utilitarian Ethics, 1973; (trans.) K. Ajdukiewicz (with H. Skolimowski) Problems and Theories of Philosophy, 1973; The Politics of Imperfection, 1978; Francis Bacon, 1980; Thoughts and Thinkers, 1982; From Wodehouse to Wittgenstein, 1998; Hume, 1998. *Recreations:* sedentary pursuits. *Address:* A11 Albany, Piccadilly, W1J 0AL. *Clubs:* Garrick, Beefsteak, Brooks's.

QUINTON, Sir John (Grand), Kt 1990; Chairman: Barclays Bank PLC, 1987–92 (Deputy Chairman, 1985–87); Metropolitan Police Committee, since 1995; *b* 21 Dec. 1929; *s* of William Grand Quinton and Norah May (*née* Nunn); *m* 1954, Jean Margaret Chastney; one *s* one *d*. *Educ:* Norwich Sch.; St John's Coll., Cambridge (MA 1954); FCIB (FIB 1964). Joined Barclays Bank, 1953: Manager, King's Cross, 1965; seconded to Min. of Health as Principal, Internat. Div. and UK Deleg., World Health Assembly, 1966; Asst Gen. Manager, 1968; Local Dir, Nottingham, 1969; Reg. Gen. Manager, 1971; Gen. Manager, 1975; Dir and Sen. Gen. Man., 1982–84; Vice-Chm., 1985. Dep. Chm., Mercantile Credit Co. Ltd, 1975–79; non-executive Chairman: FA Premier League, 1992–99; Wimpey PLC, 1993–95; non-exec. Dir, Norwich and Peterborough BS, 1993–99 (Dep. Chm., 1996–99). Chairman: Chief Exec. Officers, Cttee of London Clearing Bankers, 1982–83; Adv. Council, London Enterprise Agency, 1986–90; Office of the Banking Ombudsman, 1987–92; Cttee of London and Scottish Bankers, 1989–91. Member: City Capital Markets Cttee, 1981–86; NE Thames RHA, 1974–87; Accounting Standards Cttee, 1982–85; Econ. and Financial Policy Cttee, CBI, 1985–88 (Chm., 1987–88). Treasurer, Chartered Inst. of Bankers, 1980–86 (Pres., 1989–90); Hon. Treas. and Bd Mem., Business in the Community, 1986–91. Chairman: British Olympic Appeal, 1988; Royal Anniversary Trust Appeal, 1992. Trustee: Royal Acad. Trust, 1987–93; Westminster Abbey Trust, 1991–98; Thrombosis Res. Inst., 1993–2001; Chm. Bd of Trustees, Botanic Gdns Conservation Internat, 1991–99. Pres., East of England Show, 1992. Chm., Motability Finance Ltd, 1978–85; Gov., Motability, 1985– (Hon. Treas., 1998–); Vice-Chm., Motability Tenth Anniversary Trust Ltd, 1995–. Gov., Ditchley Foundn, 1987–92; Member: Court of Governors, Royal Shakespeare Theatre, 1986–2000; Court, Henley Coll., 1987–92. FRSA 1988. Freeman: Norwich, 1952; City of London, 1989. *Recreations:* gardening, music, golf. *Address:* Chenies Place, Chenies, Bucks WD3 6EU. *Club:* Reform.

QUIRK, family name of **Baron Quirk**.

QUIRK, Baron *cr* 1994 (Life Peer), of Bloomsbury in the London Borough of Camden; **Charles Randolph Quirk,** Kt 1985; CBE 1976; FBA 1975; President, British Academy, 1985–89; Fellow of University College London; *b* 12 July 1920; *s* of late Thomas and Amy Randolph Quirk, Lambfell, Isle of Man; *m* 1st, 1946, Jean (marr. diss. 1979; she *d* 1995), *d* of Ellis Gauntlett Williams; two *s*; 2nd, 1984, Gabriele, *d* of Judge Helmut Stein. *Educ:* Cronk y Voddy Sch.; Douglas High Sch., IOM; University College London. MA, PhD, DLit London. Served RAF, 1940–45. Lecturer in English, University College London, 1947–54; Commonwealth Fund Fellow, Yale Univ. and University of Michigan, 1951–52; Reader in English Language and Literature, University of Durham, 1954–58; Professor of English Language in the University of Durham, 1958–60, in the University of London, 1960–68; Quain Prof. of English Language and Literature, University Coll. London, 1968–81; Vice-Chancellor, Univ. of London, 1981–85. Dir, Survey of English Usage, 1959–83. Member: Senate, Univ. of London, 1970–85 (Chm., Acad. Council, 1972–75); Ct, Univ. of London, 1972–85; Bd, British Council, 1983–91; BBC Archives Cttee, 1975–81; RADA Council, 1985–; Select Cttee on Sci., H of L, 1998–. President: Inst. of Linguists, 1982–85; Coll. of Speech Therapists, 1987–91; North of England Educn Conf., 1989; Vice-Pres., Foundn for Science and Technology, 1986–90; Governor: British Inst. of Recorded Sound, 1975–80; E-SU, 1980–85; Richmond Coll., London, 1981–; City Technology Colls, 1986–. Chairman: Cttee of Enquiry into Speech Therapy Services, 1969–72; Hornby Educnl Trust, 1979–93; Anglo-Spanish Foundn, 1983–85; British Library Adv. Cttee, 1984–97; Vice-Chm., English Language Cttee, E-SU, 1985–. Trustee: Wolfson Foundn, 1987–; American Sch. in London, 1987–89; Royal Comr, 1851 Exhibn, 1987–95. Mem., Academia Europaea, 1988. Foreign Fellow: Royal Belgian Acad. of Scis, 1975; Royal Swedish Acad., 1987; Finnish Acad. of Scis, 1991; American Acad. of Arts and Scis, 1994. Hon. FCST; Hon. FIL; Hon. Fellow: Imperial Coll., 1985; QMC, 1986; Goldsmiths' Coll., 1987; King's Coll., 1990; RHBNC, 1990. Hon. Bencher, Gray's Inn, 1982. Hon. Fil. Dr: Lund; Uppsala; Helsinki; Copenhagen; Hon. DU: Essex; Bar Ilan; Brunel; DUniv Open; Hon. DHC: Liège; Paris; Prague; Hon. DLitt: Reading; Newcastle upon Tyne; Durham; Bath; Salford; California; Sheffield; Glasgow; Poznan; Nijmegen; Richmond Coll.; Hon. DCL Westminster; Hon. LLD: Leicester; London; Hon. DSc Aston. Jubilee Medal, Inst. of Linguists, 1973. *Publications:* The Concessive Relation in Old English Poetry, 1954; Studies in Communication (with A. J. Ayer and others), 1955; An Old English Grammar (with C. L. Wrenn), 1955, enlarged edn (with S. E. Deskis), 1994; Charles Dickens and Appropriate Language, 1959; The Teaching of English (with A. H. Smith), 1959, revised edn, 1964; The Study of the Mother-Tongue, 1961; The Use of English (with Supplements by A. C. Gimson and J. Warburg), 1962, enlarged edn, 1968; Prosodic and Paralinguistic Features in English (with D. Crystal), 1964; A Common Language (with A. H. Marckwardt), 1964; Investigating Linguistic Acceptability (with J. Svartvik), 1966; Essays on the English Language—Mediaeval and Modern, 1968; (with S. Greenbaum) Elicitation Experiments in English, 1970; (with S. Greenbaum, G. Leech, J. Svartvik) A Grammar of Contemporary English, 1972; The English Language and Images of Matter, 1972; (with S. Greenbaum) A University Grammar of English, 1973; The Linguist and the English Language, 1974; (with V. Adams, D. Davy) Old English Literature: a practical introduction, 1975; (with J. Svartvik) A Corpus of English Conversation, 1980; Style and Communication in the English Language, 1982; (with S. Greenbaum, G. Leech, J. Svartvik) A Comprehensive Grammar of the English Language, 1985; (with H. Widdowson) English in the World, 1985; Words at Work: lectures on textual structure, 1986; (with G. Stein) English in Use, 1990; (with S. Greenbaum) A Student's Grammar of the English Language, 1990; (with G. Stein) An Introduction to Standard English, 1993; Grammatical and Lexical Variance in English, 1995; contrib. to: conf. proceedings and volumes of studies; papers in linguistic and literary journals. *Address:* University College London, Gower Street, WC1E 6BT. *T:* (020) 7679 2000. *Club:* Athenæum.

QUIRK, Barry John, CBE 2001; PhD; Chief Executive, London Borough of Lewisham, since 1994; *b* 20 Nov. 1953; *s* of John Quirk and Iris (*née* Cope; now Aldridge); *m* 2nd, 1996, Zerena Khan; three *s* one *d* by previous *m*. *Educ:* London Univ. (ext. BSc Hons 1975); Portsmouth Poly. (PhD 1984). Head of Corporate Policy, London Borough of Newham, 1987; Asst Chief Exec., London Borough of Lewisham, 1987–94. Vis. Fellow of Social Policy and Politics, Goldsmiths Coll., Univ. of London. *Address:* 54 Meadowcourt Road, Blackheath, SE3 9DY.

QUIRK, John Stanton S.; *see* Shirley-Quirk.

QUIRKE, Pauline; actress; *b* 8 July 1959; *m* Steve; one *s* one *d*. *Educ:* Anna Scher Theatre Sch., London. Appeared in Dixon of Dock Green, BBC TV, 1968; A Tale of Two Cities, Royal Court Theatre, 1979; *television series include:* Angels, 1976; Shine on Harvey Moon, 1982; Rockliffe's Babies, 1987; Birds of a Feather (8 series), 1989–98; Jobs for the Girls, 1993; First Sign of Madness, 1996; Double Nougat, 1996; Real Women, 1997-99; Maisie Raine, 1998-99; Down to Earth, 2000–; Office Gossip, 2001; *television drama includes:* The Sculptress, 1996; Our Boy, 1997; Deadly Summer, 1997; David Copperfield, 1999; The Flint Street Nativity, 1999. *Films include:* Little Dorrit, 1986; Getting it Right, 1988; The Return of the Soldiers, 1988; Still Lives – Distant Voices, 1989; The Canterville Ghost, 1997; Check-out Girl, 1998. *Address:* c/o DB Management, Pinewood Studios, Iver, Bucks SL10 0NH.

R

RA JONG-YIL, Dr; Ambassador of the Republic of Korea to the Court of St James's, since 2001; *b* 5 Dec. 1940; *s* of Ra Iong-Gwyn and Ra Gwi-Nye; *m* 1968, Ra Jae-Ja; one *s* three *d. Educ:* Seoul Nat. Univ. (BA Pol Sci, MA Pol Sci.); Trinity Coll., Cambridge (PhD Internat. Relns, 1972). Kyung Hee University, Korea: Prof. of Pol Sci., 1972–; Dean: Coll. of Econs and Pol Sci., 1980–81; Grad. Sch., 1988–92. Fellow Commoner, Churchill Coll., Cambridge, 1981; Fulbright Sen. Fellow, Univ. of Southern Calif, 1985. Vice-Chm., Forum of Democratic Leaders in Asia-Pacific, 1994; Mem., Exec. Cttee and Special Asst to Pres., Nat. Congress for New Politics, 1996–97; Hd, Admin. Office, Presidential Transition Cttee, 1997; 2nd and 1st Dir, Nat. Security Planning Bd, 1998; 1st Dir, Nat. Intelligence Service, 1998–99; Director-General: Res. Inst. of Peace Studies, 1999–2000; Circle Millennium Korea, 1999–2000; Special Assistant: to Pres., Foreign and Security Affairs, Millennium Democratic Party, 1999–2000; to Dir-Gen., Foreign Affairs, Nat. Intelligence Service, 2000–01. *Publications:* Co-operation and Conflict, 1986; Points of Departure, 1992; Human Beings and Politics, 1995; Preparing for the New Millennium, 1998. *Recreations:* tennis, golf, Kendo, Aikido. *Address:* Embassy of the Republic of Korea, 60 Buckingham Gate, SW1E 6AJ. *T:* (020) 7227 5512. *Clubs:* Travellers, Athenæum; Wentworth Golf, Coombe Hill Golf, London Golf.

RABAN, Antony John; Director, Cambridge University Careers Service, since 1992; *b* 10 Dec. 1941; *s* of Rev. Harry Priaulx Raban and Freda Mary Raban (*née* Probert); *m* 1965, Sandra Gilham Brown. *Educ:* St John's Sch., Leatherhead; Corpus Christi Coll., Cambridge (MA Hist.). Asst Master, Doncaster GS, 1964–67; Careers Officer, 1967–69, Professional Asst, 1969–71, Cambs & Isle of Ely CC; Asst Sec. (Careers Advr), Oxford Univ. Careers Service, 1971–74; Careers Advr, Cambridge Univ. Careers Service, 1974–92. Chm., Assoc. of Grad. Careers Adv. Services, 1979–81; Pres., Eur. Forum on Student Guidance, 1988–92; Mem. Council, CRAC, 1998–. Mem. Cttee, Assoc. Bernard Gregory, 1996–. *Publications:* Working in the European Union: a guide for graduate recruiters and job-seekers, 1985, 4th edn 1995; The Entry of New Graduates into the European Labour Market, 1991; numerous reports and contribs to professional jls. *Recreations:* art history, France. *Address:* Cambridge University Careers Service, Stuart House, Mill Lane, Cambridge CB2 1XE. *T:* (01223) 338282.

RABAN, Jonathan, FRSL; author; *b* 14 June 1942; *s* of late Rev. Canon J. Peter C. P. Raban and of Monica (*née* Sandison); *m* 1992, Jean Lenihan; one *d. Educ:* Univ. of Hull (BA Hons English). FRSL 1975. Lecturer in English and American Literature: UCW, Aberystwyth, 1965–67; Univ. of E Anglia, 1967–69; professional writer, 1969–. *Publications:* The Technique of Modern Fiction, 1969; Mark Twain: Huckleberry Finn, 1969; The Society of the Poem, 1971; Soft City, 1973; Arabia Through the Looking Glass, 1979; Old Glory, 1981 (Heinemann Award, RSL, 1982; Thomas Cook Award, 1982); Foreign Land, 1985; Coasting, 1986; For Love and Money, 1987; God, Man & Mrs Thatcher, 1989; Hunting Mister Heartbreak, 1990 (Thomas Cook Award, 1991); (ed) The Oxford Book of the Sea, 1992; Bad Land, 1996 (National Book Critics Circle Award, 1997); Passage to Juneau, 1999. *Recreation:* sailing. *Address:* c/o Gillon Aitken Associates Ltd, 29 Fernshaw Road, SW10 0TG. *Clubs:* Groucho, Cruising Association.

RABBATTS, Heather Victoria, CBE 2000; Chief Executive Officer, iMPower, since 2000; a Governor of the BBC, since 1999; *b* 6 Dec. 1955; *d* of Thomas Rabbatts and Hyacinth Rabbatts; one *s* by Edmund Gerard O'Sullivan. *Educ:* London Sch. of Econs (BA Hons Hist.; MSc). Called to the Bar, Lincoln's Inn, 1981. Equalities Officer, then Parly Liaison Officer, Local Govt Inf. Unit, 1983–86; London Borough of Hammersmith and Fulham: Hd, Women's Dept, 1987–89; Dir of Personnel, 1989–91; Dep. Chief Exec. and Dir, Strategic Services, 1991–93; Chief Executive: Merton LBC, 1993–95; Lambeth LBC, 1995–2000. Member: Bd, Qualifications and Curriculum Authority, 1997–99; Bd, British Council, 1998–; ESRC, 1998–2000. Trustee, Runnymede Trust, 1997–99. Gov., LSE, 1997–. *Recreations:* opera, literature, shopping, champagne. *Address:* iMPower, 40A Dover Street, W1X 3RB.

RABBI, The Chief; *see* Sacks, Rabbi Dr J. H.

RABBITT, Prof. Patrick Michael Anthony, PhD; Research Professor in Gerontology and Cognitive Psychology, University of Manchester, since 1983; *b* 23 Sept. 1934; *s* of Joseph Bernard Rabbitt and Edna Maude Smith; *m* 1st, 1955, Adriana Habers (marr. diss. 1976); one *s* two *d*; 2nd, 1976, Dorothy Vera Bishop, *qv*. *Educ:* Queens' Coll., Cambridge (MA, PhD); MA Oxon; Manchester Univ. (MSc). Scientific Staff, MRC Applied Psychology Unit, Cambridge, 1962–68; Univ. Lectr in Psychology, and Official Fellow, Queen's Coll., Univ. of Oxford, 1968–82; Prof. of Psychology, Univ. of Durham, 1982–83. Adjunct Prof. of Psychology, Univ. of Western Australia, 1991–. FRSA 1997. Hon. Mem., Experimental Psychol. Soc., 1999; Hon. FBPsS 1995. Hon. DSc Western Australia, 2001. *Publications:* (ed jtly) Cognitive Gerontology, 1990; Methodology of Frontal and Executive Function, 1997; 274 papers in learned jls. *Recreations:* whisky, nostalgia. *Address:* Age and Cognitive Performance Research Centre, University of Manchester, Manchester M13 9PL. *T:* (0161) 275 2873.

RABBITTS, Dr Terence Howard, FRS 1987; Member, Scientific Staff, since 1973, Joint Head of Protein and Nucleic Acid Division, since 1988, MRC Laboratory of Molecular Biology, Cambridge; *b* 17 June 1946; *s* of Joan and Frederick Rabbitts; *m* 1984, Pamela Gage; one *d. Educ:* John Ruskin Grammar School; Univ. of East Anglia (BSc); Nat. Inst. for Medical Research (PhD). Research Fellow, Dept of Genetics, Univ. of Edinburgh, 1971–73. Founder FMedSci 1998. Colworth Medal, 1981, Ciba Medal and Prize, 1993, Biochemical Soc. *Publications:* papers in scientific jls. *Address:* MRC Laboratory of Molecular Biology, Hills Road, Cambridge CB2 2QH. *T:* (01223) 248011.

RABENIRINA, Most Rev. Remi Joseph; *see* Indian Ocean, Archbishop of the.

RABIN, Prof. Brian Robert; Professor of Biochemistry, 1988–93, now Emeritus, Fellow since 1984, University College, London; *b* 4 Nov. 1927; *s* of Emanuel and Sophia Rabin, both British; *m* 1954; one *s* one *d. Educ:* Latymer Sch., Edmonton; University Coll., London. BSc 1951, MSc 1952, PhD 1956. University College, London: Asst Lectr, 1954–57; Lectr, 1957–63; Reader, 1963–67; Prof. of Enzymology, 1967–70; Hd of Dept of Biochemistry, 1970–88. Rockefeller Fellow, Univ. of California, 1956–57. Founder Dir, London Biotechnology Ltd, 1985–. *Publications:* numerous in Biochem. Jl, European Jl of Biochem., Nature, Proc. Nat. Acad. Sciences US, etc. *Recreations:* travel, listening to music, carpentry. *Address:* 34 Grangewood, Potters Bar, Herts EN6 1SL. *T:* (01707) 654576. *Club:* Athenæum.

RABINOVITCH, Prof. Benton Seymour, FRS 1987; Professor of Chemistry, University of Washington, Seattle, 1957–86, now Emeritus; *b* 19 Feb. 1919; *s* of Samuel Rabinovitch and Rachel Schachter; *m* 1st, 1949, Marilyn Werby; two *s* two *d*; 2nd, 1980, Flora Reitman. *Educ:* McGill Univ. (BSc, PhD). Served Canadian Army overseas, Captain, 1942–46. Milton Fellow, Harvard Univ., 1946–48; University of Washington: Asst Prof., 1948–53; Associate Prof., 1953–57. Guggenheim Fellow, 1961–62. Fellow, Amer. Acad. of Arts and Scis, 1979. Hon. Liveryman, Goldsmiths' Co., 2000. Hon. DSc Technion, Haifa, 1991. Sigma Xi Dist. Res. Award, 1981; Peter Debye Award, ACS, 1984; Michael Polanyi Medal, RSC, 1984. *Publications:* Physical Chemistry, 1964; Antique Silver Servers, 1990; Contemporary Silver, 2000; (ed) annual reviews Phys. Chem., 1975–85; over 200 contribs to jls. *Recreation:* silversmithing. *Address:* Department of Chemistry Box 351700, University of Washington, Seattle, WA 98195, USA. *T:* (206) 5431636.

RABINOWITZ, Harry, MBE 1977; freelance conductor and composer; *b* 26 March 1916; *s* of Israel and Eva Rabinowitz; *m* 1944, Lorna Thurlow Anderson (marr. diss. 2000); one *s* two *d*; *m* 2001, Mitzi Scott. *Educ:* Athlone High Sch., S Africa; Witwatersrand Univ.; Guildhall Sch. of Music. Conductor, BBC Radio, 1953–60; Musical Dir, BBC TV Light Entertainment, 1960–68; Head of Music, LWT, 1968–77; freelance film, TV, radio and disc activities, 1977–. Conductor: Cats, New London Th., 1981; Song and Dance, Palace Th., 1982; Hollywood Bowl Concerts, 1983 and 1984; Boston "Pops" concerts, 1985, 1986, 1988–92; concerts with RPO, LSO and London Concert Orch.; *films:* conductor: La Dentellière, 1977; Mon Oncle d'Amérique, 1980; The Time Bandits, 1980; Chariots of Fire, 1981; Heat and Dust, 1982; The Missionary, 1983; Electric Dreams (actor/conductor), 1984; The Bostonians, 1984; Return to Oz, Lady Jane Grey, and Revolution—1776, 1985; F/X, and Manhattan Project, 1986; Masters of the Universe, Maurice, 1987; Simon Wiesenthal, Camille Claudet, 1988; Shirley Valentine (jt composer/conductor), Queen of Hearts, 1989; Music Box, Lord of the Flies, La Fille des Collines, 1990; Jalousie, La Tribu, Jesuit Joe, Iran Day of Crisis, Ballad of the Sad Café, J'embrasse pas, Pour Sascha, 1991; Howards End, The Ark and the Flood, 1992; The Remains of the Day, Taxi de Nuit, Moonfish, Petite Apocalypse, 1993; Grosse Fatigue, The Flemish Board, Mantegna & Sons, 1994; Jefferson in Paris, Jenny et Mr Arnaud, The Stupids, 1995; The Proprietor, Secret Agent, Star Command, Surviving Picasso, The English Patient, 1996; Tonka, Wings of the Dove, My Story So Far, 1997; City of Angels, Soldiers' Daughters Don't Cry, Place Vendôme, 1998; Message in a Bottle, Cotton Mary, The Talented Mr Ripley, 1999; The Golden Bowl, 2000; *television:* composer-conductor: Agatha Christie Hour, 1982; Reilly Ace of Spies, 1983; Glorious Day, 1985; Land of the Eagle, 1990; D. W. Griffiths Father of Film, Memento Mori, 1993; Project Ayrton Senna, 1995; Alien Empire, 1996; Battle of the Sexes, Impossible Journeys, 1998. Freeman, City of London, 1995. Gold Badge of Merit, British Acad. of Songwriters, Composers and Authors, 1985; award for lifetime contribution to Wavendon Allmusic, 1990. *Recreations:* listening to others making music, gathering edible fungi, wine tasting. *Address:* 11 Mead Road, Cranleigh, Surrey GU6 7BG. *T:* and *Fax:* (01483) 278676; *e-mail:* mitziscott@aol.com.

RACE, (Denys Alan) Reg; management and policy consultant; *b* 23 June 1947; *s* of Denys and Elsie Race. *Educ:* Sale Grammar School; Univ. of Kent. BA (Politics and Sociology), PhD (Politics). Senior Research Officer, National Union of Public Employees, 1972. MP (Lab) Haringey, Wood Green, 1979–83. Contested (Lab) Chesterfield, 2001. Head of Programme Office, GLC, 1983–86; Special Res. Officer, ACTT, 1986; County Dir, Derbys County Council, 1988. Advr, Health Policy Adv. Unit, 1989–93; Partner, Quality Health management consultants, 1993–; Advr on NHS to IMPAC Ltd, 1997–. *Publications:* The Challenge Now (report on management and organisation of ACTT), 1986; numerous pamphlets and articles in Labour Movement press.

RACE, Steve, (Stephen Russell Race), OBE 1992; broadcaster, musician and author; *b* Lincoln, 1 April 1921; *s* of Russell Tinniswood Race and Robina Race (*née* Hurley); *m* 1st, Marjorie Clair Leng (*d* 1969); one *d*; 2nd, Léonie Rebecca Govier Mather. *Educ:* Lincoln Sch. (now Christ's Hospital Sch.); Royal Academy of Music. FRAM 1978. Served War, RAF, 1941–46; free-lance pianist, arranger and composer, 1946–55; Light Music Adviser to Associated-Rediffusion Ltd, 1955–60; conductor for many TV series incl. Tony Hancock and Peter Sellers Shows. Appearances in radio and TV shows include: My Music, A Good Read, Jazz in Perspective, Any Questions?, Music Now, Music Weekly, Kaleidoscope, Musician at Large, Captain Pepper's Autograph Album, Jazz Revisited, With Great Pleasure, Desert Island Discs, Steve Race Presents the Radio Orchestra Show, Gershwin Among Friends, Irving Berlin Among Friends, The Two Worlds of Joseph Race; radio reviews in The Listener, 1975–80; long-playing records and commentary for Nat. Gall., London, Glasgow Art Gall. and Nat. Mus. of Wales, 1977–80. Dep. Chm., PRS, 1973–76. Member: Council, Royal Albert Hall of Arts and Scis, 1976–95; Exec. Council, Musicians' Benevolent Fund, 1985–95. FRSA 1975. Freeman,

City of London, 1982. Governor of Tokyo Metropolis Prize for Radio, 1979; Wavendon Allmusic Media Personality of the Year, 1987; Radio Prog. of the Year, TV and Radio Industries Club Awards, 1988; Gold Badge of Merit for services to British music, BASCA, 1991. *Principal compositions:* Nicola (Ivor Novello Award); Faraway Music; The Pied Piper; incidental music for Richard The Third, Cyrano de Bergerac, Twelfth Night (BBC); Cantatas: Song of King David; The Day of the Donkey; Song of Praise; My Music—My Songs; misc. works incl. ITV advertising sound-tracks (Venice Award, 1962; Cannes Award, 1963); film scores include: Calling Paul Temple, Three Roads to Rome, Against The Tide, Land of Three Rivers. *Publications:* Musician at Large: an autobiography, 1979; My Music, 1979; Dear Music Lover, 1981; Steve Race's Music Quiz, 1983; You Can't be Serious, 1985; The Penguin Masterquiz, 1985; With Great Pleasure, 1986; The Two Worlds of Joseph Race, 1988; (contrib.) The Illustrated Counties of England, 1984; contribs to DNB, Punch, Literary Review, Times, Daily Telegraph (crossword compiler, 1998–), Daily Mail, Independent, Listener, Country Living. *Recreations:* recording books for the blind, avoiding smokers, quietly reminiscing. *Address:* Martins End Lane, Great Missenden, Bucks HP16 9HS.

RACEY, Prof. Paul Adrian, FRSE; FIBiol; Regius Professor of Natural History, University of Aberdeen, since 1993; *b* 7 May 1944; *s* of Albert and Esme Racey; *m* 1968, Anna Priscilla Notcutt; three *s*. *Educ:* Ratcliffe Coll.; Downing Coll. Cambridge (MA); London Univ. (PhD); Univ. of Aberdeen (DSc). FIBiol 1987; FRSE 1992. Rothamsted Experimental Station, 1965–66; Zoological Soc. of London, 1966–71; Res. Fellow, Univ. of Liverpool, 1971–73; University of Aberdeen: Lectr and Sen. Lectr in Zoology, 1973–85; Prof. of Zoology, 1985–. Chairman: Chiroptera Specialist Gp, IUCN Species Survival Commn, 1986–; Bat Conservation Trust, 1990–96; Member: Scottish Exam. Bd, 1985–90; Management Cttee, Scottish Univs Res. and Reactor Centre, 1991–95 (Mem. Sci. Adv. Bd, 1986–90); Council, Fauna & Flora International (formerly Fauna & Flora Preservation Soc.), 1990– (Chm., Conservation Cttee, 1993–); Bd of Govs, Macaulay Land Use Res. Inst., 1990–2001; NCC for Scotland, 1991–92; Terrestrial and Freshwater Sci. Cttee, NERC, 1991–94; Exec. Cttee, Mammal Soc., 1991–98; Res. Bd, 1992–94, Scientific Adv. Cttee, 1994–2001 (Chm., 1996), SE Regl Bd, 1996–97, Scottish Natural Heritage; Council, Zool Soc. of London, 1999– (Mem. Adv. Cttee for Sci. and Conservation, 1996–2000); Council for Scotland, WWF, 1997–2000. *Publications:* numerous res. papers in professional jls. *Recreations:* riding, sailing, walking, farming. *Address:* Chapelhouses, Oldmeldrum, AB51 OAW. *T:* (01651) 872769.

RADCLIFFE, Andrew Allen; QC 2000; a Recorder, since 2000; *b* 21 Jan. 1952; *s* of Reginald Allen Radcliffe and Sheila Radcliffe (*née* McNeil); *m* 1977, Nicola Stanhope (marr. diss. 1990); two *s* one *d*. *Educ:* Birkenhead Sch.; St Edmund Hall, Oxford (BA Hons 1974). Called to the Bar, Middle Temple, 1975; Asst Recorder, 1998–2000. Mem. Cttee, Criminal Bar Assoc., 1998–2001. *Recreation:* sport. *Address:* 2 Hare Court, Temple, EC4Y 7BH. *T:* (020) 7353 5324. *Club:* Radlett Cricket.

RADCLIFFE, Anthony Frank, FSA; Hon. Keeper of Renaissance and Baroque Sculpture, Fitzwilliam Museum, since 1996; *b* Wivenhoe, Essex, 23 Feb. 1933; *s* of late Dr Walter Radcliffe and of Muriel Laure Radcliffe (*née* Brée); *m* 1960, Enid Clair Cawkwell; two *s*. *Educ:* Oundle Sch.; Gonville and Caius Coll., Cambridge (MA). Victoria and Albert Museum: joined Dept of Circulation, 1958; transferred to Dept of Architecture and Sculpture, 1960; Res. Asst, Dept of Circulation, 1961–67; Asst to Dir, 1967–74; Asst Keeper, Dept of Architecture and Sculpture, 1974–79; Keeper of Sculpture, 1979–89; Head of Res., 1989–90; Keeper Emeritus, 1990–96. Mellon Sen. Vis. Curator, Nat. Gall. of Art, Washington, 1990; Guest Scholar, J. Paul Getty Mus., 1991, 1995; Samuel H. Kress Prof., CASVA, Nat. Gall. of Art, Washington, 1993–94. Member: Adv. Council, NACF, 1993–; Consultative Cttee, Burlington Magazine, 1990–. Medal, Accademia delle Arti del Disegno, Florence, 1986. *Publications:* European Bronze Statuettes, 1966; Jean-Baptiste Carpeaux, 1968; (with J. Pope-Hennessy and T. Hodgkinson) The Frick Collection: an illustrated catalogue, III, IV, 1970; (with C. Avery) Giambologna, sculptor to the Medici, 1978; (with M. Baker and M. Maek Gérard) The Thyssen-Bornemisza Collection: Renaissance and later sculpture, 1992; The Robert H. Smith Collection: Bronzes 1500–1650, 1994; contribs to Burlington Mag., Apollo, Connoisseur, etc. *Address:* Shirley Cottage, 5 Kennylands Road, Sonning Common, Reading RG4 9JR. *T:* (0118) 972 2182.

RADCLIFFE, Francis Charles Joseph; *b* 23 Oct. 1939; *s* of Charles Joseph Basil Nicholas Radcliffe and Norah Radcliffe (*née* Percy); *m* 1968, Nicolette, *e d* of Eugene Randag; one *s* two *d*. *Educ:* Ampleforth Coll.; Gonville and Caius Coll., Cambridge (MA). Called to the Bar, Gray's Inn, 1962; a Recorder of the Crown Court, 1979. Mem., Assoc. of Lawyers for the Defence of the Unborn. Contested (Christian: stop abortion candidate) York, 1979; founded York Christian Party, 1981. Chm., Life, York. *Recreations:* shooting, beagling, gardening, etc. *Address:* 11 King's Bench Walk, Temple, EC4Y 7EQ.

RADCLIFFE, Nora; Member (Lib Dem) Gordon, Scottish Parliament, since 1999; *b* 4 March 1946; *d* of James Stuart MacPherson and Doreen MacPherson (*née* McRobb); *m* 1972, Michael Anthony Radcliffe; one *s* one *d*. *Educ:* Bowmore Primary Sch.; Peterculter Primary Sch.; High Sch. for Girls, Aberdeen; Aberdeen Univ. Hotel mgt, 1968–72; Community Liaison Team, 1993–96, Primary Care Develt Team, 1996–99, Grampian Health Bd. Mem. (Lib Dem), Gordon DC, 1988–92. *Recreations:* reading, walking, good food. *Address:* 3 King Street, Inverurie, Aberdeenshire AB51 4SY. *T:* (01467) 622575.

RADCLIFFE, Sir Sebastian Everard, 7th Bt *cr* 1813; *b* 8 June 1972; *s* of Sir Joseph Benedict Everard Henry Radcliffe, 6th Bt, MC and of Marcia Anne Helen (who *m* 1988, H. M. S. Tanner), *y d* of Major David Turville Constable Maxwell, Bosworth Hall, Husbands Bosworth, Rugby; *S* father, 1975. *Heir: cousin* Mark Hugh Joseph Radcliffe [*b* 22 April 1938; *m* 1963, Anne, twin *d* of Maj.-Gen. Arthur Evers Brocklehurst, CB, DSO; three *d*]. *Address:* Le Château de Cheseaux, 1033 Cheseaux, Vaud, Switzerland.

RADCLIFFE, Most Rev. Timothy Peter Joseph, OP; Master of the Order of Preachers (Dominicans), 1992–2001; *b* 22 Aug. 1945; 3rd *s* of late Hugh John Reginald Joseph Radcliffe, MBE. *Educ:* Downside; St John's College, Oxford (MA; Hon. Fellow, 1993). Entered Dominican Order, 1965; Chaplain to Imperial Coll., 1976–78; taught theology at Blackfriars, Oxford, 1978–88; Prior of Blackfriars, 1982–88; Faculty of Theology, Oxford Univ., 1985–88; Provincial of the English Province, OP, 1988–92. John Toohey Schol. in Residence, Sydney Univ., 1984. Grand Chancellor: Pontifical Univ. of St Thomas (Angelicum), Rome, 1992–2001; Univ. of Santo Tomas, Manila, 1992–2001; Theol. Faculty, Fribourg, 1992–2001; Ecole Biblique, Jerusalem, 1992–2001. Pres., Conf. of Major Religious Superiors, 1991–. Chm. Editl Bd, New Blackfriars, 1983–88. Hon. STD Providence Coll., RI, 1993; Hon. LLD Barry Univ., Florida, 1996; Hon. DHumLit Ohio Dominican Coll., 1996. Prix de littérature religieuse, 2001. *Publications:* El Manantial de la Esperanza Salamanca, 1998; Sing a New Song: the Christian vocation, 2000; I Call You Friends, 2001; articles in books and periodicals. *Recreations:* walking and talking with friends, reading Dickens. *Address:* St Dominic's Priory, Southampton Road, NW5 4LB. *T:* (020) 7482 9210.

See also Sir S. E. Radcliffe, Bt.

RADCLYFFE, Sarah; Managing Director, Sarah Radclyffe Productions Ltd, since 1993; *b* 14 Nov. 1950; *d* of Charles Raymond Radclyffe and Helen Egerton Radclyffe; one *s* by Graham Bradstreet; *m* 1996, William Godfrey; one *s*. *Educ:* Heathfield Sch., Ascot. Jt Founder, 1984, Jt Man. Dir, 1984–93, Working Title; *films* produced include: My Beautiful Laundrette, 1984; Caravaggio, 1985; Wish You Were Here, 1985; Paperhouse, 1987; Sammy and Rosie Get Laid, 1988; A World Apart, 1988; Fools of Fortune, 1989; Robin Hood, 1990; Edward II, 1991; Sirens, 1993; Second Best, 1993; Bent, 1997; Cousin Bette, 1997; Les Misérables, 1997; The War Zone, 1998; There's Only One Jimmy Grimble, 1999. Non-exec. Dir, Channel Four TV, 1995–99; Gov., BFI, 1996–99; Dir, Film Council, 2000–. Simon Olswang Business Woman of the Year Award, 1993. *Recreations:* travel, ski-ing. *Address:* Sarah Radclyffe Productions Ltd, 5th Floor, 83/84 Berwick Street, W1V 3PJ; 15 Shirlock Road, Hampstead, NW3 2HR.

RADDA, Prof. Sir George (Karoly), Kt 2000; CBE 1993; MA, DPhil; FRS 1980; Chief Executive, Medical Research Council, since 1996; British Heart Foundation Professor of Molecular Cardiology, University of Oxford, since 1984 (on leave of absence); Professiorial Fellow, Merton College, Oxford, since 1984; *b* 9 June 1936; *s* of Dr Gyula Radda and Dr Anna Bernolak; *m* 1st, 1961, Mary O'Brien (marr. diss. 1995); two *s* one *d*; 2nd, 1995, Sue Bailey. *Educ:* Pannonhalma, Hungary; Eötvös Univ., Budapest, Hungary; Merton Coll., Oxford (BA Cl. 1, Chem., 1960; DPhil 1962). Res. Associate, Univ. of California, 1962–63; Lectr in Organic Chemistry, St John's Coll., Oxford, 1963–64; Fellow and Tutor in Organic Chem., Merton Coll., Oxford, 1964–84; University Lectr in Biochem., 1966–84, Hd of Dept of Biochem., 1991–96, Oxford Univ. Vis. Prof., Cleveland Clinic, 1987. Medical Research Council: Mem. Council, 1988–92; Chm., Cell Biology and Disorders Bd, 1988–92; Chm., Human Genome Directed Programme Cttee, 1992–96; Hon. Dir, Unit of Biochemical and Clin. Magnetic Resonance, 1988–96; Member of Council: Royal Soc., 1990–92; ICRF, 1991–96 (Chm., Scientific Adv. Cttee, 1994–96). Non-exec. Dir, BTG plc, 1999–. Mem., various Editorial Bds of scientific jls including: Editor, Biochemical and Biophysical Research Communications, 1977–85; Man. Editor, Biochimica et Biophysica Acta, 1977–94 (Chm. Editl Bd, 1989–94). Founder Mem., Oxford Enzyme Gp, 1970–86; Pres., Soc. for Magnetic Resonance in Medicine, 1985–86. Mem., Fachbeirat, Max Planck Inst. für Systemphysiologie, Dortmund, 1987–93. Mem., EMBO, 1997; MAE 1999; Fellow, Soc. of Magnetic Resonance, 1994. Founder FMedSci 1998. Hon. FRCR 1985; Hon. MRCP 1987, Hon. FRCP 1997; Hon. Fellow, Amer. Heart Assoc., 1988. Hon. DM Bern, 1985; Hon. DSc (Med) London, 1991; Hon. DSc: Stirling, 1998; Sheffield, 1999; Debrecen, Hungary. Colworth Medal, Biochem. Soc., 1969; Feldberg Prize, Feldberg Foundn, 1982; British Heart Foundn Prize and Gold Medal for cardiovascular research, 1982; CIBA Medal and Prize, Biochem. Soc., 1983; Gold Medal, Soc. for Magnetic Resonance in Medicine, 1984; Buchanan Medal, Royal Soc., 1987; Internat. Lectr and Citation, Amer. Heart Assoc., 1987; Skinner Lecture and Medal, RCR, 1989; Rank Prize in Nutrition, 1991. *Publications:* articles in books and in jls of biochemistry and medicine. *Recreations:* opera, swimming, jazz. *Address:* Medical Research Council, 20 Park Crescent, W1N 4AL.

RADEGONDE, Sylvestre Louis; High Commissioner of The Seychelles to Malaysia, India, Australia and New Zealand, and Ambassador to Japan, Republic of Korea, China and Indonesia, since 1998; *b* 16 March 1956. *Educ:* Seychelles Coll.; Polytechnic of Central London (MA Diplomatic Studies). Seychelles Police Force, 1974–85; Dir, Nat. Council for Children, 1985–86; Personnel Manager, Seychelles Hotels, 1986–87; Chief of Protocol and Desk Officer for Americas, Min. Planning and Ext. Relns, 1987–89; Counsellor and Actg High Comr, 1989–92, High Comr, 1992–93, London; Ambassador to EC and Belgium, 1993–97, concurrently to Germany, Netherlands and Luxembourg. *Recreations:* cooking, swimming. *Address:* Seychelles High Commission, 50 Jalan SS 19/1D, 47500 Subang Jaya, Selangor, Malaysia.

RADER, Gen. Paul Alexander; General of the Salvation Army, 1994–99; *b* 14 March 1934; *s* of Lt-Col Lyell Rader and Gladys (*née* Damon); *m* 1956, (Frances) Kay Fuller; one *s* two *d*. *Educ:* Asbury Coll. and Seminary, USA (BA, BD); Southern Baptist Seminary (MTh); Fuller Theol Seminary (DMiss). Salvation Army: trng work in Korea, 1962–73; Trng Principal, 1973; Educn Sec., 1974–76; Asst Chief Sec., 1976, Chief Sec., 1977–84, Korea; Trng Principal, USA Eastern Territory, 1984–87; Divl Comdr, 1987–89; Chief Sec., 1989; Territorial Comdr, USA Western, 1989–94. Hon. LLD Asbury Coll., USA, 1984; Hon. DD: Asbury Theol Seminary, USA, 1995; Roberts Wesleyan Coll., USA, 1998; Hon. LHD Greenville Coll., USA, 1997. *Recreations:* jogging, reading, music. *Address:* 3953 Rock Lodge Lane, Lexington, KY 40513, USA.

RADFORD, Rt Rev. Andrew John; *see* Taunton, Bishop Suffragan of.

RADFORD, Dr David; Chief Executive, Somerset County Council, since 1997; *b* 22 April 1949; *s* of Ken and Dorothy Radford; *m* 1st, 1970, Josephine Mogridge; one *d*; 2nd, 1976, Madeleine Margaret Simms; two *d*. *Educ:* RN Sch., Malta; St John's Sch., Singapore; Manchester Univ. (BSc Hons Chem., MSc Organisation of Technology, PhD). Consumer Services Manager, CWS, 1974–75; Res. Dir, Welsh Consumer Council, 1975–77; Head of Res., Inst. of Housing, 1977–81; Asst Dir of Housing, Wolverhampton MBC, 1981–86; Asst Chief Exec., Wolverhampton MBC, 1986–90; Asst Chief Exec., Northants CC, 1990–97. *Recreations:* hill and coast walking, concert-going, sailing. *Address:* Somerset County Council, Taunton, Somerset TA1 4DY. *T:* (01823) 355000; Hawksworth House, 1 Holway Avenue, Taunton, Somerset TA1 3AP.

RADFORD, David Wyn; His Honour Judge Radford; a Circuit Judge, since 1996; *b* 3 Jan. 1947; *s* of Robert Edwin Radford, *qv*; *m* 1972, Nadine Radford, *qv*; two *s* two *d*. *Educ:* Cranleigh Sch.; Selwyn Coll., Cambridge (MA, LLM). Called to the Bar, Gray's Inn, 1969; Asst Recorder, 1988; Recorder, 1993. *Recreations:* supporting Manchester City FC, theatre, walking, spending time with family. *Address:* c/o South Eastern Circuit Office, New Cavendish House, 18 Maltravers Street, WC2R 3EU.

RADFORD, Joseph; Public Trustee, 1978–80; *b* 7 April 1918; *s* of Thomas Radford and Elizabeth Ann Radford (*née* Sanders); *m* 1976, Rosemary Ellen Murphy. *Educ:* Herbert Strutt, Belper; Nottingham Univ. Admitted solicitor, 1940. First Cl. Hons, Law Soc. Intermediate, 1937; Dist., Law Soc. Final, 1940. Served War, 1940–47, RA; 41st (5th North Staffordshire) RA; 1st Maritime Regt, RA; Staff, MELF (Major). Joined Public Trustee Office, 1949; Chief Admin. Officer, 1973–75; Asst Public Trustee, 1975–78. Mem., Law Soc., 1945– (Hon. Auditor, 1963–65). Freeman, City of London, 1983. Silver Jubilee Medal, 1977. *Address:* 80 Cunningham Park, Harrow, Mddx HA1 4QJ.

RADFORD, Nadine Poggioli, BA; QC 1995; a Recorder of the Crown Court, since 1995; *m* 1972, David Wyn Radford, *qv*; two *s* two *d*. Called to the Bar, Lincoln's Inn, 1974, Bencher, 1999; formerly an Assistant Recorder. *Address:* 2 Dyers Buildings, Holborn, EC1N 2JT. *T:* (020) 7404 1881.

RADFORD, Prof. Peter Frank, PhD; Professor and Head of Department of Sport Sciences, Brunel University, since 1997; *b* 20 Sept. 1939; *s* of Frank Radford and Lillian E. Radford (*née* Marks); *m* 1961, Margaret M. (*née* Beard); one *d*. *Educ:* Tettenhall Coll.;

Cardiff Coll. of Educn (Dip. of Physical Educn); Purdue Univ., USA (MSc); Univ. of Glasgow (PhD 1978). Mem., GB Athletics Teams, 1958–64: held British 100m record, 1958–78; World Records: Jun. 100m and Jun. 200m, 1958; Indoor 50m, 1959; 200m and 220 yards, 1960; 4 × 110 yards Relay, 1963; Bronze Medals, 100m and 4 × 100m Relay, Olympic Games, Rome, 1960. Lectr and Asst Prof., Sch. of Physical Educn and Athletics, McMaster Univ., 1967–75; University of Glasgow: Professor and Head of Departments of: Physical Educn and Recreation, 1976–87; Physical Educn and Sports Sci., 1987–94. Vice-Chm., 1992–93, Chm., 1993–94, Exec. Chm., 1994–97, British Athletic Fedn. Scottish Sports Council: Mem., 1983–90; Mem., 1988–91, Chm., 1991–96, Drug Adv. Gp; Chm., Rev. of Coaching in Sport, 1991–93. Mem., Internat. Wkg Gp on Anti-Doping in Sport, 1991–93; Vice-Chm., 1992–94, Chm., 1994–98, Internat. Doping Convention, Council of Europe; Member: Saudi/British Memorandum of Understanding for Sport and Youth Welfare, 1990–; Compliance with Commitments Project, Council of Europe, 1998–99. *Publications:* The Celebrated Captain Barclay, 2001; contrib. to various jls, conf. proc. and books on topics of sport, educn, sports science, sports history and doping control. *Recreations:* sports history 1650–1850, 18th and 19th century sporting art, gardening. *Address:* Brunel University, Department of Sport Sciences, Osterley Campus, Borough Road, Isleworth, Middx TW7 5DU. *T:* (020) 8891 8309.

RADFORD, Robert Edwin, CB 1979; Assistant Director General, St John Ambulance Association, 1981–84; Deputy Secretary and Principal Finance Officer, Department of Health and Social Security, 1977–81; *b* 1 April 1921; *s* of late Richard James Radford and late May Eleanor Radford (*née* Briant); *m* 1945, Eleanor Margaret, *d* of late John Idwal Jones; one *s* one *d*. *Educ:* Royal Grammar Sch., Guildford. Board of Educn, 1938. Served War, Lieut, RNVR, 1940–46. Colonial Office: Asst Principal, 1947; Private Sec. to Permanent Under-Sec. of State for the Colonies, 1950–51; Principal, 1951; First Sec., UK Commn, Singapore, 1961–63; Asst Sec., Dept of Techn. Co-op., 1963; transferred to ODM, 1964; Counsellor, British Embassy, Washington, and UK Alternate Exec. Dir, IBRD, 1965–67; Under Secretary: FCO (ODA), 1973; DHSS, 1974–76. Mem., SW Surrey HA, 1982–89. *Recreations:* walking, reading. *Address:* 10 Edgeborough Court, Upper Edgeborough Road, Guildford, Surrey GU1 2BL. *T:* (01483) 561822.
See also D. W. Radford.

RADFORD, Timothy Robin; Science Editor, The Guardian, since 1992; *b* NZ, 9 Oct. 1940; *s* of Keith Ballantyn Radford and Agnes Radford (*née* Hunt); *m* 1964, Maureen Grace Coveney; one *s* one *d*. *Educ:* Sacred Heart Coll., Auckland. Reporter, NZ Herald, 1957–60; sub-ed., Fishing News, London, 1961–62; reporter, Hull Daily Mail, 1963–65; sub-ed., Dover Express, 1965-68; COI, 1968–73; joined The Guardian, 1973: Letters Ed., 1975–77; Arts Ed., 1977–80; Dep. Features Ed., 1980–88; Literary Ed., 1989–91. FRGS 1990. *Publication:* The Crisis of Life on Earth, 1990. *Recreations:* reading, walking, travel. *Address:* The Guardian, 119 Farringdon Road, EC1R 3ER. *T:* (020) 7239 9604.

RADICE, Baron *cr* 2001 (Life Peer), of Chester-le-Street in the County of Durham; **Giles Heneage Radice;** PC 1999; *b* 4 Oct. 1936. *Educ:* Winchester; Magdalen Coll., Oxford. Head of Research Dept, General and Municipal Workers' Union (GMWU), 1966–73. MP (Lab) Chester-le-Street, March 1973–1983, Durham North, 1983–2001. Front bench spokesman on foreign affairs, 1981, on employment, 1981–83, on education, 1983–87; Mem., Treasury and Civil Service Select Cttee, 1987–96; Chairman: Public Service Select Cttee, 1996–97; Treasury Select Cttee, 1997–2001. Mem., Council, Policy Studies Inst., 1978–83. Chairman: European Movt, 1995–2001; British Assoc. for Central and Eastern Europe, 1997– (Vice Chm., 1991–97). Parly Fellow, St Antony's Coll., Oxford, 1994–95. *Publications:* Democratic Socialism, 1965; (ed jointly) More Power to People, 1968; (co-author) Will Thorne, 1974; The Industrial Democrats, 1978; (co-author) Socialists in Recession, 1986; Labour's Path to Power: the new revisionism, 1989; Offshore: Britain and the European idea, 1992; The New Germans, 1995; (ed) What Needs to Change, 1996. *Recreations:* reading, tennis. *Address:* 58A Dartmouth Park Road, NW5 1SN.

RADJI, Parviz Camran; diplomat; Ambassador of Iran to the Court of St James's, 1976–79; *b* 1936; *m* 1986, Golgoun Partovi. *Educ:* Trinity Hall, Cambridge (MA Econs). National Iranian Oil Co., 1959–62; Private Sec. to Minister of Foreign Affairs, 1962–65; Private Sec. to Prime Minister, subseq. Personal Asst, 1965–72; Special Adviser to Prime Minister, 1972–76. *Publication:* In the Service of the Peacock Throne: the diaries of the Shah's last Ambassador to London, 1983. *Address:* 20 Embankmemt Gardens, SW3 4LW.

RADLEY-SMITH, Eric John, MS; FRCS; Surgeon Emeritus: Royal Free Hospital, London; Brentford Hospital; Epsom Hospital; Neurosurgeon, Royal National Throat, Nose and Ear Hospital. *Educ:* Paston; King's College, London; King's College Hospital. MB, BS (Hons, Distinction in Medicine, Surgery, Forensic Medicine and Hygiene), 1933; MS London, 1936; LRCP 1933; FRCS 1935 (MRCS 1933). Served War of 1939–45, Wing Comdr i/c Surgical Div. RAFVR. Formerly: Surgical Registrar, King's Coll. Hosp.; House Surgeon, National Hosp. for Nervous Diseases, Queen Square. Examnr in Surgery, Univs of London and West Indies. Mem. Court, RCS. Mem. Assoc. of British Neurosurgeons; Fellow, Assoc. of Surgeons of Great Britain. *Publications:* papers in medical journals. *Recreations:* football and farming.

RADNOR, 8th Earl of, *cr* 1765; **Jacob Pleydell-Bouverie;** Bt 1713–14; Viscount Folkestone, Baron Longford, 1747; Baron Pleydell-Bouverie, 1765; *b* 10 Nov. 1927; *e s* of 7th Earl of Radnor, KG, KCVO, and Helen Olivia, *d* of late Charles R. W. Adeane, CB; *S* father, 1968; *m* 1st, 1953, Anne (marr. diss. 1962), *d* of Donald Seth-Smith, Njoro, Kenya and Whitsbury Cross, near Fordingbridge, Hants; two *s*; 2nd, 1963, Margaret Robin (marr. diss. 1985), *d* of late Robin Fleming, Catter House, Drymen; four *d*; 3rd, 1986, Mary Jillean Gwenellan Pettit. *Educ:* Harrow; Trinity Coll., Cambridge (BA Agriculture). *Heir: s* Viscount Folkestone, *qv*.

RAE, Barbara Davis, CBE 1999; RA 1996, RSA 1992 (ARSA 1980); RSW 1975; RGI; artist; *b* 10 Dec. 1943; *d* of James Rae and Mary (*née* Young); *m* twice; one *s*. *Educ:* Morrison's Acad., Crieff; Edinburgh Coll. of Art (Dip.; Postgrad. Travelling Schol.); Moray House Coll. of Education. Art Teacher: Ainsley Park Comprehensive, Edinburgh, 1968–69; Portobello Secondary Sch., Edinburgh, 1969–72; Lectr in Drawing, Painting and Printmaking, Aberdeen Coll. of Educn, 1972–75; Lectr in Drawing and Painting, Glasgow Sch. of Art, 1975–96; exchange teacher, Fine Art Dept, Univ. of Md, 1984. Member: Art Panel, CNAA, 1986–93; Bd of Friends, Royal Scottish Acad.; Royal Fine Art Commn for Scotland, 1995–; Trustee, Arts Educnl Trust, 1986–90. Mem., SSA (Pres., 1983); Mem. Council, RSW, 1986–90, Vice-Pres. (E), 1991–. Member, Board of Trustees: British Sch. at Rome, 1997–; Hospitalfield House, Arbroath, 1997–99. Solo exhibitions include: New '57 Gall., Edinburgh, 1967, 1971; Univ. of York, 1969; Univ. of Aberdeen and Aberdeen Art Gall., 1974; Peterloo Gall., Manchester, 1975; Stirling Gall. and Greenock Arts Guild, 1976; Univ. of Edinburgh, 1978, 1979; Gilbert Parr Gall., London, 1977; Scottish Gall., Edinburgh, 1979, 1983, 1987, 1988, 1990, 1995, 1998, 2000; Wright Gall., Dallas, 1988; Leinster Fine Art, London, 1986; Glasgow Print Studio, 1987, 1992, 1997; Scottish Gall., London, 1989, 1990; Wm Jackson Gall., London, 1990, 1992; Perth Mus. and Art Gall., 1991; Clive Jennings Gall., London, 1992; Jorgensen Fine Art, Dublin, 1993, 1995; Waxlander Gall., Santa Fe, 1996; Bohun Gall., Henley on Thames, 1996; Art First, London, 1996, 1997, 1999; Graphic Studio, Dublin, 1997; Printmakers Workshop, Edinburgh, 1997; Gall. Galtung, Oslo, 1998; touring exhibn, Scotland and Leeds, 1993–94; numerous gp exhibitions in Britain, Europe, USA, S America and Australia; works in public and private collections in Britain, Europe and America; commissions include: tapestry for Festival Theatre, Edinburgh, 1994; rug for Royal Mus. of Scotland, 1999; portraits. Awards: Arts Council, 1968; Major Arts Council, 1975–81; Guthrie Medal, RSA, 1977; May Marshall Brown, RSW Centenary Exhibn, 1979; RSA Sir Wm Gillies Travel, 1983; Calouste Gulbenkian Printmaking, 1983; Alexander Graham Munro, RSW, 1989; Hunting Gp Prizewinner, 1990; Scottish PO Bd, RSA, 1990; Scottish Amicable, RGI, 1990; W. J. Burness, Royal Scottish Acad., 1990. Hon. DA Napier, 1999. *Recreations:* gardening, travelling. *Address:* c/o Art First, 9 Cork Street, W1X 1PD. *Club:* Glasgow Art.

RAE, Gordon Hamilton; Director General, Royal Horticultural Society, 1993–99; *b* 12 Sept. 1938; *s* of Peter and Gwendoline Elizabeth Rae; *m* 1965, Judith Elizabeth Pickup; one *s* two *d*. *Educ:* Bablake Sch., Coventry; Wye Coll., Univ. of London (BSc Agric. Hons); Clare Coll., Cambridge (Dip. Agric.); Imperial Coll. of Tropical Agric., Trinidad (DTA). Agricl and Dist Agricl Officer, HM Colonial Service, Kenya, 1962–65; ICI, 1965–93: Gen. Manager, Agricl Chemicals Div., ICI do Brasil, São Paulo, 1980–84; Gen. Manager, ICI Garden and Professional Products, 1989–92. Non-exec. Dir, D. J. Squire & Co. Ltd, 1999–. FIHort 1996. VMH 1999. *Recreations:* gardening, fly fishing, photography. *Address:* New House, Church Lane, Grayshott, Hindhead, Surrey GU26 6LY. *T:* (01428) 606025. *Club:* Farmers'.

RAE, Dr John; Chief Executive, AWE plc, since 2000; *b* 29 Sept. 1942; *s* of late John Rae and of Marion Rae (*née* Dow); *m* 1968, Irene (*née* Cassells); one *s* one *d*. *Educ:* Rutherglen Academy; University of Glasgow (BSc 1964, PhD 1967). FInstE 1987; FInstP 1996. Lecturing and research in physics: Univ. of Glasgow, 1967–68; Univ. of Texas, 1968–70; Univ. Libre, Brussels, 1970–72; Queen Mary College London, 1972–74; Theoretical Physics Div., Harwell: Industrial Fellow, 1974–76; Leader, Theory of Fluids Group, 1976–85; Acting Div. Head, 1985; Chief Scientist, Dept of Energy, 1986–89; Chief Exec., AEA Envmt & Energy, 1990–93; Business Develt Dir, 1993–95, Dir, Nat. Envmtl Technology Centre, 1994–95, AEA Technology; Man. Dir, NPL Mgt Ltd, 1995–2000. Member: SERC, 1986–89; NERC, 1986–89. Pres., NPL Sports Club, 1996–2000. Freeman, City of London, 1997; Liveryman, Scientific Instrument Makers' Co., 1997–. *Publications:* scientific papers in professional jls. *Recreations:* music, especially singing; gardening, astronomy. *Address:* AWE Aldermaston, Reading, Berks RG7 4PR. *T:* (0118) 981 4111.

RAE, Dr John (Malcolm); author; Headmaster, Westminster School, 1970–1986; *b* 20 March 1931; *s* of late Dr L. John Rae, radiologist, London Hospital, and Blodwen Rae; *m* 1955, Daphné Ray Simpson, JP, *d* of John Phimester Simpson; two *s* four *d*. *Educ:* Bishop's Stortford Coll.; Sidney Sussex Coll., Cambridge. MA Cantab 1958; PhD 1965. 2nd Lieut Royal Fusiliers, 1950–51. Asst Master, Harrow School, 1955–66; Dept of War Studies, King's Coll., London, 1962–65; Headmaster, Taunton School, 1966–70; Dir, Laura Ashley Foundn, 1986–89. Director: The Observer Ltd, 1986–93; Portman Gp, 1989–96. Gresham Prof. of Rhetoric, 1988–90. Robert Birley Meml Lectr, Charterhouse Sch., 1997. Chairman: HMC, 1977; Council for Educn in World Citizenship, 1983–87. Member: Nat. Bd for Crime Prevention, 1993–95; Council, Nat. Cttee for Electoral Reform; Council, King's Coll. London, 1981–84. Trustee: Children's Film Unit, 1979–; Imperial War Mus., 1980–85. Gov. Highgate Sch., 1989–. Judge, Whitbread Prize, 1980. Freeman, City of London, 1985. JP Middlesex, 1961–66. Hon. FCP 1982. *Publications:* The Custard Boys, 1960 (filmed 1979); (jtly, film) Reach for Glory (UN Award); Conscience and Politics, 1970; The Golden Crucifix, 1974; The Treasure of Westminster Abbey, 1975; Christmas is Coming, 1976; Return to the Winter Palace, 1978; The Third Twin: a ghost story, 1980; The Public School Revolution: Britain's independent schools, 1964–1979, 1981; Letters from School, 1987; Too Little, Too Late?, 1989; Delusions of Grandeur: a headmaster's life 1966–1986, 1993; Letters to Parents: how to get the best available education for your child, 1998; Sister Genevieve, 2001; articles in The Times, Encounter; columnist in Times Ed. Supp. *Recreations:* writing, swimming, cinema. *Address:* 2s Cedar Lodge, Lythe Hill Park, Haslemere, Surrey GU27 3TD. *T:* (01428) 652616. *Clubs:* East India, Devonshire, Sports and Public Schools; Hawks (Cambridge).

RAE, Rita Emilia Anna; QC (Scot.) 1992; Sheriff of Glasgow and Strathkelvin, since 1997; *b* 20 June 1950; *d* of Alexander Smith Cowie Rae and Bianca Bruno. *Educ:* Univ. of Edinburgh (LLB Hons). Apprentice, 1972–74, Asst Solicitor, 1974–76, Biggart Baillie & Gifford, Glasgow; Asst Solicitor and Partner, Ross Harper & Murphy, Glasgow, 1976–81; Advocate, 1982–; Temporary Sheriff, 1988–97. Tutor in Advocacy and Pleading, Strathclyde Univ., 1979–82. *Recreations:* classical music, opera, theatre, walking, gardening. *Address:* Sheriff's Chambers, 1 Carlton Place, Glasgow G5 9DA. *T:* (0141) 429 8888.

RAE, Hon. Robert Keith; PC (Can.) 1998; QC (Can.) 1984; Partner, Goodmans LLP (formerly Goodman Phillips & Vineberg), since 1996; Premier of Ontario, 1990–95; *b* 2 Aug. 1948; *s* of Saul Rae and Lois (*née* George); *m* 1980, Arlene Perly; three *d*. *Educ:* Ecole Internationale, Geneva; Univ. of Toronto (BA Hons 1969; LLB 1977); Balliol Coll., Oxford (BPhil 1971). MP for Broadview-Greenwood, Ontario, 1978–82; Finance Critic, New Democratic Party, 1979–82; MPP (NDP) York South, Ontario, 1982–95; Leader, Ontario New Democrats, 1982–96; Leader, Official Opposition, Ontario legislature, 1987–90. Dir, Tembec Ltd, 1997–. Adjunct Prof., Univ. of Toronto, 1997–; Sen. Associate, Massey Coll., 1997–. Dir, Canadian Ditchley Foundn, 1997–. Chairman: Forum of Fedns, 1999–; Royal Conservatory of Music, 2000–. Trustee, University Health Network, 1999–. Gov., Univ. of Toronto, 1999–. Nat. spokesperson, Leukemia Res. Fund of Canada, 1996–. Hon. LLD: Law Soc. of Upper Canada, 1998; Toronto, 1999. *Publications:* From Protest to Power, 1996; The Three Questions, 1998. *Recreations:* tennis, golf, ski-ing, fishing, reading. *Address:* Goodmans, 250 Yonge Street, Suite 2400, Toronto, ON M5B 2M6, Canada. *T:* (416) 9792211, ext. 655.

RAE, Hon. Sir Wallace (Alexander Ramsay), Kt 1976; Agent-General for Queensland, in London, 1974–80; formerly grazier, Ramsay Park, Blackall, Queensland; *b* 31 March 1914; *s* of George Ramsay Rae and Alice Ramsay Rae. *Educ:* Sydney, Australia. Served War: RAAF Coastal Command, 1939; Pilot, Flt Lt, UK, then OC Test Flight, Amberley, Qld. Mem., Legislative Assembly (Nat. Party of Australia) for Gregory, Qld, 1957–74; Minister for: Local Govt and Electricity, 1969–74; Lands and Forestry, Qld, 1974. Founder Pres., Pony Club Assoc. of Queensland. *Recreations:* music, bowls. *Address:* 94 Garden Village, Findlay Avenue, Port Macquarie, NSW 2444, Australia. *Clubs:* United Service, Tattersall's (Brisbane); Longreach (Longreach).

RAE, Air Vice-Marshal William McCulloch, CB 1993; dealer in early English barometers, since 1997; Director, United Services Trustee, since 1996; *b* 22 June 1940; *s* of William Brewster Rae and Margaret Rae; *m* 1964, Helen, *d* of Thomas and Eileen Reading; two *d*. *Educ:* Aberdeen Grammar School; psc, ndc, rcds. RAF 1958; Nos 213, 10, 55 Sqns, 1960–64; CFS (helicopter element), 1965–67; Radar Res. Flying Unit,

Pershore, 1968–70; Sqn Comdr, 6 FTS, 1970–72; Inspectorate of Recruiting, 1973; RAF Staff Coll., 1974; Air Sec's Dept, 1975–77; NDC, 1978; OC 360 Sqn, 1979–81; CDS Staff, 1981–82; Central Policy Staff, MoD, 1982–85; Station Comdr, RAF Finningley, 1985–87; RCDS, 1988; Branch Chief, Policy, SHAPE, 1989–91; Sen. DS (Air), RCDS, 1992–95; Sen. Assessor, Charter Mark, Cabinet Office, 1996–97. *Recreations:* antiques, wine, golf. *Club:* Royal Air Force.

RAE SMITH, David Douglas, CBE 1976; MC 1946; MA; FCA; Senior Partner, Deloitte Haskins & Sells, Chartered Accountants, 1973–82 (Partner, 1954); *b* 15 Nov. 1919; *s* of Sir Alan Rae Smith, KBE, and Lady (Mabel Grace) Rae Smith; *m* 1947, Margaret Alison Watson, *d* of James Watson; three *s* one *d. Educ:* Radley Coll.; Christ Church, Oxford (MA). FCA 1959. Served War, RA, 1939–46: ME, N Africa and NW Europe; Captain; MC and mentioned in despatches. Chartered accountant, 1950. Hon. Treasurer, RIIA, 1961–81. Director: Thomas Tilling Ltd, 1982–83; Sandoz Products Ltd, 1983–92; Dep. Chm., Bankers Trustee Co., 1984–91. Member: Licensed Dealers Tribunal, 1974–88; Council, Radley Coll., 1966–92 (Chm., 1976–92). *Recreations:* horse racing, golf. *Address:* Oakdale, Crockham Hill, Edenbridge, Kent TN8 6RL. *T:* (01732) 866220.

RAEBURN, David Antony; Grammatikos (tutor in Ancient Greek Language), Faculty of Literae Humaniores, 1991–96, Grocyn Lecturer, 1992–96, University of Oxford; *b* 22 May 1927; *e s* of late Walter Augustus Leopold Raeburn, QC; *m* 1961, Mary Faith, *d* of Arthur Hubbard, Salisbury, Rhodesia; two *s* one *d. Educ:* Charterhouse; Christ Church, Oxford (Schol., MA). 1st cl. hons Hon. Mods, 2nd in Greats. Nat. Service, 1949–51: Temp. Captain, RAEC. Asst Master: Bristol Grammar Sch., 1951–54; Bradfield Coll., 1955–58 (prod. Greek Play, 1955 and 1958); Senior Classics Master, Alleyn's Sch., Dulwich, 1958–62; Headmaster: Beckenham and Penge Grammar Sch., 1963–70 (school's name changed to Langley Park School for Boys, Beckenham in 1969); Whitgift Sch., Croydon, 1970–91. Schoolteacher Fellow-Commoner, Jesus Coll., Cambridge, 1980. Vis. Fellow, New Coll., Oxford, 1997. Chm. Classics Cttee, Schs Council, 1974–80; Pres., Jt Assoc. of Classical Teachers, 1983–85; Treas., HMC, 1984–89. FRSA 1969. *Publications:* essays on education; articles on Greek tragedy and Greek play production. *Recreation:* play production (produced Cambridge Greek Play, 1980, 1983). *Address:* 13A St Anne's Road, Eastbourne, Sussex BN21 2AJ. *T:* (01323) 724696; 122 Southfield Park, Oxford OX4 2BA. *T:* (01865) 245179.

RAEBURN, Maj.-Gen. Sir Digby; *see* Raeburn, Maj.-Gen. Sir W. D. M.

RAEBURN, Prof. John Ross, CBE 1972; BSc (Agric.), PhD, MS; FRSE; FIBiol; Strathcona-Fordyce Professor of Agriculture, Aberdeen University, 1959–78; Principal, North of Scotland College of Agriculture, 1963–78; *b* 20 Nov. 1912; *s* of late Charles Raeburn and Margaret (*née* Ross); *m* 1941, Mary, *o d* of Alfred and Cathrine Roberts; one *s* three *d. Educ:* Manchester Grammar School; Edinburgh and Cornell Universities. Professor of Agricultural Economics, Nanking University, 1936–37; Research Officer, Oxford University, 1938–39; Ministry of Food Divisional statistician, 1939–41, Head Agricultural Plans Branch, 1941–46; Senior research officer, Oxford University, 1946–49; Reader in Agricultural Economics, London University, 1949–59. Visiting Professor: Cornell, 1950; Wuhan, 1983. Consultant to UN. Member: Agricultural Mission to Yugoslavia, 1951; Mission of Enquiry into Rubber Industry, Malaya, 1954; Colonial Economic Research Committee, 1949–61; Scottish Agricultural Improvement Council, 1960–71; Scottish Agricultural Develt Council, 1971–76; Verdon-Smith Committee, 1962–64; Council, Scottish Agricultural Colls, 1974–78. Hon. MA Oxford, 1946. FRSE 1961; FIBiol 1968. Vice-President, International Association of Agricultural Economists, 1964–70 (Hon. Life Mem., 1976–); President, Agric. Econ. Society, 1966–67 (Hon. Life Mem., 1981–). *Publications:* Preliminary economic survey of the Northern Territories of the Gold Coast, 1950; (jtly) Problems in the mechanisation of native agriculture in tropical African Territories, 1950; Agriculture: foundations, principles and development, 1984; (jtly) History of the IAAE, 1990; research bulletins and contributions to agricultural economic journals. *Recreation:* gardening. *Address:* Kilravock, Flat 15, 5 Oswald Road, Edinburgh EH9 2HE.

RAEBURN, Michael Edward Norman; (4th Bt, *cr* 1923, but does not use the title); *b* 12 Nov. 1954; *s* of Sir Edward Alfred Raeburn, 3rd Bt, and of Joan, *d* of Frederick Hill; *S* father, 1977; *m* 1979, Penelope Henrietta Theodora, *d* of Alfred Louis Penn; two *s* three *d. Heir: s* Christopher Edward Alfred Raeburn, *b* 4 Dec. 1981. *Address:* Fourways, Turners Green, Wadhurst, East Sussex TN5 6TU.

RAEBURN, Susan Adiel Ogilvie; QC (Scot.) 1991; Sheriff of Glasgow and Strathkelvin, since 1993; *b* 23 April 1954; *d* of George Ferguson Raeburn and Rose Anne Bainbridge (*née* Morison). *Educ:* St Margaret's Sch. for Girls, Aberdeen; Edinburgh Univ. (LLB). Admitted to Faculty of Advocates, 1977; temp. Sheriff, 1988–93. Part-time Chairman: Social Security Appeal Tribunals, 1986–92; Med. Appeal Tribunals, 1992–93. *Recreations:* travel, the arts. *Address:* Sheriff's Chambers, Sheriff Court House, 1 Carlton Place, Glasgow G5 9OA. *T:* (0141) 429 8888. *Club:* Scottish Arts.

RAEBURN, Maj.-Gen. Sir (William) Digby (Manifold), KCVO 1979; CB 1966; DSO 1945; MBE 1941; Major and Resident Governor, HM Tower of London, and Keeper of the Jewel House, 1971–79; *b* 6 Aug. 1915; *s* of late Sir Ernest Manifold Raeburn, KBE, and Lady Raeburn; *m* 1960, Adeline Margaret (*née* Pryor). *Educ:* Winchester; Magdalene College, Cambridge (MA). Commnd into Scots Guards, 1936; despatches, 1942; comd 2nd Bn Scots Guards, 1953; Lieut-Col Comdg Scots Guards, 1958; Comdr, 1st Guards Bde Group, 1959; Comdr, 51st Infty Bde Group, 1960; Director of Combat Development (Army), 1963–65; Chief of Staff to C-in-C, Allied Forces, N Europe, 1965–68; Chief Instructor (Army), Imperial Defence College, 1968–70. Freeman of City of London, 1972. *Recreation:* shooting. *Address:* 25 St Ann's Terrace, NW8 6PH. *Clubs:* Pratt's, Cavalry and Guards; Royal Yacht Squadron.

RAFF, Prof. Martin Charles, FRS 1985; Professor of Biology, University College London, since 1979; *b* 15 Jan. 1938; *s* of David and Reba Raff; *m* 1979, Carol Winter; two *s* one *d. Educ:* McGill Univ. (BSc; MD; CM). House Officer, Royal Victoria Hosp., Montreal, 1963–65; Resident in Neurology, Massachusetts General Hosp., 1965–68; Postdoctoral Fellow, Nat. Inst. for Med. Res., 1968–71; Dir, MRC Develtl Neurobiology Programme, 1971. Pres., British Soc. of Cell Biology, 1991–95. Founder FMedSci 1998. *Publications:* (jtly) T and B Lymphocytes, 1973; (jtly) Molecular Biology of the Cell, 1983, 3rd edn 1994; (jtly) Essential Cell Biology, 1997. *Address:* 67 Upper Park Road, NW3 2UL. *T:* (020) 7722 5610.

RAFFAN, Keith William Twort; Member (Lib Dem) Scotland Mid and Fife, Scottish Parliament, since 1999; *b* 21 June 1949; *s* of A. W. Raffan, TD, MB, ChB, FFARCS and late Jean Crampton Raffan (*née* Twort), MB, ChB. *Educ:* Robert Gordon's Coll., Aberdeen; Trinity Coll., Glenalmond; Corpus Christi Coll., Cambridge (BA 1971; MA 1977). Parly Correspondent and sketch writer, Daily Express, 1981–83; internat. public relns consultant, NY, 1992–94; presenter, Welsh Agenda, HTV, 1994–98. Contested (C) Dulwich, Feb. 1974, and East Aberdeenshire, Oct. 1974; MP (C) Delyn, 1983–92. Mem., Select Cttee on Welsh Affairs, 1983–92. Introduced: Controlled Drugs (Penalties) Act (Private Member's Bill, 1985); Tourism (Overseas Promotion) (Wales) Act, 1991. Chief spokesman on home affairs, Scottish Lib Dem Party, 1998. Nat. Chm., PEST, 1970–74. *Address:* c/o Scottish Parliament, Edinburgh EH99 1SP. *Clubs:* Chelsea Arts, Royal Automobile.

RAFFERTY, Hon. Dame Anne (Judith), (Dame Anne Barker), DBE 2000; **Hon. Mrs Justice Rafferty;** a Judge of the High Court of Justice, Queen's Bench Division, since 2000; *m* 1977, Brian John Barker, *qv;* three *d* (and one *d* decd). *Educ:* Univ. of Sheffield (LLB). Called to the Bar, Gray's Inn, 1973, Inner Temple *ad eundem*, 1996; Bencher, Gray's Inn, 1998; QC 1990; a Recorder, 1991–2000; Head of Chambers, 1994–2000; a Dep. High Court Judge, 1996–2000. Criminal Bar Association: Mem. Cttee, 1986–91; Sec., 1989–91; Vice-Chm., 1993–95; Chm., 1995–97; Chm., Bar Conf., 1992. Mem., Royal Commn on Criminal Justice, 1991–93. Member: SE Circuit Wine Cttee, 1987–90; Pigot Cttee, 1988–89; Circuit Cttee, SE Circuit, 1991–94; Criminal Cttee, Judicial Studies Bd, 1998–. Gov., Expert Witness Inst., 1997–99. Gov., St Andrew's Prep. Sch., Eastbourne, 1990–; Mem. Council, Eastbourne Coll., 1993–. FRSA 1993. *Address:* Royal Courts of Justice, Strand, WC2A 2LL.

RAFFERTY, Hon. Joseph Anstice, BA; FAIM, FID; JP; Agent General for Victoria in London, 1979–83; investor and primary producer, Australia, since 1983; *b* 10 Jan. 1911; *s* of late Col Rupert A. Rafferty, DSO, and Rose Sarah Anne Rafferty; *m* 1st, 1940, Miriam K. (decd), *d* of late Frank Richards, Devonport, Tas; two *s;* 2nd, 1973, Lyn, *d* of Grace Jones, Brisbane, Qld. *Educ:* Christ Coll., Univ. of Tas (BA); Univ. of Melbourne. FAIM 1954; FID 1960. Commonwealth Public Service, 1934–45; Personnel Manager, Australian National Airways, 1945–53; Personnel Management and Indust. Relations Consultant, 1953–70 (own practice; co. dir). MP (Lib) for: Caulfield, Vic, 1955–58; Ormond, Vic, 1958–67; Glenhuntly, Vic, 1967–79; Chm. Cttees and Dep. Speaker, Victorian Legislative Assembly, 1961–65; Parly Sec. for Cabinet, 1965–70; Minister for Labour and Industry, 1970–76; Asst Minister for Educn, 1970–72; Minister for Consumer Affairs, 1972–76; Minister for Fed. Affairs, 1974–76; Minister for Transport, 1976–78; Chief Sec. and Minister for Police and Emergency Services, 1978–79; Leader, Aust. Delegn to ILO Conf., Geneva, 1974. Pres., Melbourne Jun. Chamber of Commerce, 1950; Treasurer, Nat. Assoc. of Jun. Chambers of Commerce of Australia, 1951; Councillor: Melbourne Chamber of Commerce, 1950–76; Victorian Employers' Fedn, 1952–65. Dep. Leader, Aust. Delegn, 5th World Congress, Jun. Chamber of Commerce, Manila, 1950; Aust. Delegate, 6th World Congress, Jun. Chamber of Industry, Montreal, 1951; Delegate, 17th Triennial Congress, British Empire Chambers of Commerce, London, 1951. Mem. Council, La Trobe Univ., Vic, 1964–70; Trustee, Caulfield Racecourse Reserve, 1965–. Silver Jubilee Medal, 1977. Freeman, City of London, 1979. JP Victoria, 1970. *Recreations:* golf, swimming, walking, world travel, public speaking. *Address:* 8 Matlock Court, Caulfield North, Vic 3161, Australia. *T:* (3) 95000282. *Clubs:* Athenæum, Metropolitan Golf, MCC (Melbourne).

RAFFERTY, Kevin Robert; Managing Editor, International Media Partners, New York, 1989; *b* 5 Nov. 1944; *s* of Leo and Thérèse Rafferty; *m* 1985, Michelle Misquitta. *Educ:* Marist Coll., Kingston upon Hull; Queen's Coll., Oxford (MA). Journalistic training, The Guardian, Sun, 1966–69; Financial Times, 1970–76; Founder Editor, Business Times Malaysia, 1976–77; Consultant Editor, Indian Express Gp, 1978–79; Foreign Correspondent, Financial Times, 1980; Asia Pacific Editor, Institutional Investor, 1981–87; Ed., The Universe, 1987–88. Founder Editor, then Associate Editor, Asia and Pacific Review, Saffron Walden, 1980–. *Publications:* City on the Rocks: Hong Kong's uncertain future, 1989; Inside Japan's Power Houses, 1995. *Recreations:* travelling, meeting ordinary people, reading. *Clubs:* Oxford and Cambridge; Foreign Correspondents (Hong Kong).

RAGG, Rt Rev. Theodore David Butler, DD; Bishop of Huron, 1974–84; *b* 23 Nov. 1919; *s* of late Rt Rev. Harry Richard Ragg, sometime Bishop of Calgary and Winifred Mary Ragg (*née* Groves); *m* 1945, Dorothy Mary Lee; one *s* two *d. Educ:* Univ. of Manitoba; Trinity Coll., Univ. of Toronto (BA, LTh); General Synod (BD). Deacon, 1949; priest, 1950; Asst Curate, St Michael and All Angels, Toronto, 1949; Rector: Nokomis, 1951; Wolseley, 1953; St Clement's N Vancouver, 1955; St Luke's, Victoria, 1957; Bishop Cronyn Memorial, London, 1962; St George's, Owen Sound, 1967. Examining Chaplain to Bishop of Huron, 1964–67; Archdeacon of Saugeen, 1967; elected Suffragan Bishop of Huron, 1973. Hon. DD: Huron Coll., London, Ont., 1975; Trinity Coll., Toronto, Ont., 1975. *Recreations:* woodworking, golf. *Address:* 2314 Oak Bay Avenue, Victoria, BC V8R 1G6, Canada.

RAGGATT, Timothy Walter Harold; QC 1993; a Recorder, since 1994; *b* 13 April 1950; *s* of late Walter George and Norah Margaret Raggatt; *m* 1991, Carol Marion Allison; two *s* one *d. Educ:* Redditch County High Sch.; King's Coll. London (LLB 1971). Called to the Bar, Inner Temple, 1972, Bencher, 1999; Tutor, Inns of Court Sch. of Law, 1972–73; in practice on Midland and Oxford Circuit, 1974–; an Asst Recorder, 1991–94. Mem., Professional Assoc. of Diving Instructors, 1992–. *Recreations:* golf, scuba diving, bridge and snooker. *Address:* 4 King's Bench Walk, Temple, EC4Y 7DL; 3 Fountain Court, Steelhouse Lane, Birmingham B4 6DR. *Clubs:* Royal Automobile; Birmingham, Edgbaston Priory (Birmingham); Blackwell Golf.

RAGHUNATHAN, Prof. Madabusi Santanam, Padma Shri, 2001; PhD; FRS 2000; FIASc, FNA; Professor of Eminence, Tata Institute of Fundamental Research, Mumbai, since 1997; *b* 11 Aug. 1941; *s* of Madabusi Sudarsanam Iyengar Santanam and Ambuja Santanam; *m* 1968, Ramaa Rangarajan; one *s. Educ:* Vivekananda Coll., Univ. of Madras (BA Hons 1960); Bombay Univ. (PhD 1966). Tata Institute of Fundamental Research: Associate Prof., 1966–70; Prof., 1970–80; Sen. Prof., 1980–90; Distinguished Prof., 1990–97. FIASc 1974; FNA 1975; Fellow, Third World Acad. of Scis, 1994. Bhatnagar Award, Council of Scientific and Industrial Res., India, 1977; Third World Acad. Award, Trieste, 1991. *Publications:* Discrete Subgroups of Lie Groups, 1972; contrib. papers to Annals of Maths, Inventiones Mathematicae, etc. *Address:* Tata Institute of Fundamental Research, Homi Bhabha Road, Colaba, Mumbai 400 005, India. *T:* (office) (22) 2188654, (22) 2152971; (home) (22) 2152466.

RAGLAN, 5th Baron *cr* 1852; **FitzRoy John Somerset;** Chairman, Cwmbran New Town Development Corporation, 1970–83; *b* 8 Nov. 1927; *er s* of 4th Baron Raglan and Hon. Julia Hamilton, CStJ (*d* 1971), *d* of 11th Baron Belhaven and Stenton, CIE; *S* father, 1964; *m* 1973, Alice Baily (marr. diss. 1981), *yr d* of Peter Baily, Great Whittington, Northumberland. *Educ:* Westminster; Magdalen College, Oxford; Royal Agricultural College, Cirencester. Captain, Welsh Guards, RARO. Crown Estate Comr, 1970–74. Mem., Agriculture and Consumer Affairs sub-cttee, House of Lords Select Cttee on the European Community, 1974–83, 1985–90 (Chm., 1975–77). President: UK Housing Trust, 1983–89 (Chm., S Wales Region, 1976–89); United Welsh Housing Assoc., 1989–. Pres., Pre Retirement Assoc., 1970–77, Vice-Pres. 1977–, Hon. Treas., 1987–. Chairman: Bath Preservation Trust, 1975–77; The Bath Soc., 1977–; Bugatti Owners' Club, 1988–97

(Patron, 1999–). President: Usk Civic Soc.; Bath Centre of Nat. Trust; Usk Rural Life Mus.; Monmouthshire Brecon and Abergavenny Canals Trust; Gwent Beekeepers Assoc.; Caerleon Civic Soc.; S Wales Reg., RSMHCA, 1971–; Vice-President: Mansel Thomas Trust; Gwent Talking Newsaper for the Blind; Mem., Distinguished Members Panel, National Secular Soc.; Patron: Usk Farmers Club; The Raglan Baroque Players; Archimedes Concerts for All; Gwent County History Assoc.; Hospice of the Valleys; Parity; Mon Crossroads; Friends of Swanage Pier; Trustee: Bugatti Trust; Cwmbran Arts Trust; Dir, Green Park Station Ltd. JP 1958, DL 1971, Gwent (formerly Monmouthshire). *Recreation:* being mechanic to a Bugatti. *Heir: b* Hon. Geoffrey Somerset [*b* 29 Aug. 1932; *m* 1956, Caroline Rachel, *d* of late Col E. R. Hill, DSO; one *s* two *d*]. *Address:* Cefntilla, Usk, Monmouthshire NP15 1DG. *T:* (01291) 672050. *Clubs:* Beefsteak, Vintage Sports Car; Usk Farmers'.

RAHTZ, Prof. Philip Arthur; Professor of Archaeology, University of York, 1978–86, now Emeritus; *b* 11 March 1921; *s* of Frederick John Rahtz and Ethel May Rahtz; *m* 1st, 1940, Wendy Hewgill Smith (*d* 1977); three *s* two *d*; 2nd, 1978, Lorna Rosemary Jane Watts; one *s*. *Educ:* Bristol Grammar Sch. MA Bristol 1964. FSA. Served RAF, 1941–46. Articled to accountant, 1937–41; photographer (Studio Rahtz), 1946–49; schoolteacher, 1950–53; archaeological consultant, 1953–63; Univ. of Birmingham: Lectr, 1963–75; Sen. Lectr, later Reader, 1975–78. Pres., Council for British Archaeology, 1986–89. Hon. MIFA. *Publications:* Rescue Archaeology, 1973; Chew Valley Lake Excavations, 1978; Saxon and Medieval Palaces at Cheddar, 1979; Invitation to Archaeology, 1985, 2nd edn 1991; Tamworth Saxon Watermill, 1992; Glastonbury, 1993; Cannington Cemetery, 2000; Living Archaeology, 2001; contrib. nat. and regional jls in England, W Africa and Poland. *Recreations:* swimming, sunbathing, music, travel. *Address:* The Old School, Harome, Helmsley, North Yorkshire YO62 5JE. *T:* (01439) 770862.

RAIKES, Vice-Adm. Sir Iwan (Geoffrey), KCB 1976; CBE 1967; DSC 1943; DL; Flag Officer Submarines, and Commander Submarines, Eastern Atlantic Area, 1974–76; retired 1977; *b* 21 April 1921; *s* of late Adm. Sir Robert Henry Taunton Raikes, KCB, CVO, DSO and bar, and Lady (Ida Guinevere) Raikes; *m* 1947, Cecilla Primrose Hunt; one *s* one *d*. *Educ:* RNC Dartmouth. Entered Royal Navy, 1935; specialised in Submarines, 1941; comd HM Submarines: H43, 1943; Varne, 1944; Virtue, 1946; Talent, 1948–49; Aeneas, 1952; Logistics Div., Allied Forces Mediterranean, 1953–55; Comdr SM Third Submarine Sqn, 1958–60; comd HM Ships: Loch Insh, 1961; Kent, 1968; Exec. Officer, HMS Newcastle, 1955–57; Dep. Dir, Undersurface Warfare, 1962–64; Dir, Plans & Operations, Staff of C-in-C Far East, 1965–66; JSSC, 1957; IDC, 1967. Rear-Adm., 1970; Naval Sec., 1970–72; Vice-Adm., 1973; Flag Officer, First Flotilla, 1973–74. Chm., United Usk Fishermens' Assoc., 1978–93. Mem., Governing Body, 1979–93, Rep. Body, 1982–93, Church in Wales. DL Powys, 1983. *Recreations:* shooting, fishing, gardening. *Address:* Aberyscir Court, Brecon, Powys LD3 9NW. *Club:* Naval and Military.

RAILTON, David; QC 1996; a Recorder, since 2000; *b* 5 June 1957; *s* of late Andrew Scott Railton, MC and of Margaret Elizabeth Railton (*née* Armit); *m* 1996, Sinéad Major; one *s*. *Educ:* Balliol Coll., Oxford (BA). Called to the Bar, Gray's Inn, 1979. *Recreations:* cricket, golf. *Address:* Fountain Court, Temple, EC4Y 9DH.

RAINBOW, (James) Conrad (Douglas), CBE 1979; Chairman, Sovereign Country House Ltd, 1979–96; *b* 25 Sept. 1926; *s* of Jack Conrad Rainbow and Winifred Edna (*née* Mears); *m* 1974, Kathleen Margaret (*née* Holmes); one *s* one *d*. *Educ:* William Ellis Sch., Highgate; Selwyn Coll., Cambridge (MA). Asst Master, St Paul's Sch., London, 1951–60; HM Inspector of Schools, 1960–69; Dep. Chief Educn Officer, Lancashire, 1969–74, Chief Educn Officer, 1974–79. Vis. Prof., Univ. of Wisconsin, 1979. Education Consultant: ICI, 1980–85; Shell Petroleum Co. Ltd, 1980–; Advr to H of C Select Cttee on Educn, 1980–82. Mem., Exec. Cttee, Council of British Internat. Schs in EEC, 1975–91. Chairman of Governors: Northcliffe Sch., Hants, 1984–90; Elmslie Sch., Blackpool, 1994–98. *Publications:* various articles in educnl jls. *Recreations:* rowing (now as an observer), music, reading. *Address:* 70 Clifton Drive, Lytham St Annes, Lancs FY8 1AT. *T:* (01253) 737245. *Club:* Leander.

RAINBOW, Prof. Philip Stephen, DSc, PhD; CBiol, FIBiol; Keeper of Zoology, Natural History Museum, since 1997; *b* 21 Oct. 1950; *s* of Frank Evelyn Rainbow, OBE and Joyce May Victoria Rainbow (*née* Turner); *m* 1973, Mary Meaken; two *s*. *Educ:* Bedford Sch., Bedford; Clare Coll., Cambridge (MA); UCNW, Bangor (PhD 1975; DSc 1994). CBiol 1998, FIBiol 1998. Queen Mary College, later Queen Mary and Westfield College, University of London: Lectr, 1975–89; Reader in Marine Biology, 1989–94; Prof. of Marine Biology, 1994–97; Head, Sch. of Biol Scis, 1995–97; Vis. Prof., 1997. *Publications:* (ed jtly) Aspects of Decapod Crustacean Biology, 1988; (ed jtly) Heavy Metals in the Marine Environment, 1990; (ed jtly) Ecotoxicology of Metals in Invertebrates, 1993; (jtly) Biomonitoring of Trace Aquatic Contaminants, 1993, 2nd edn 1994; (ed jtly) Forecasting the Environmental Fate and Effects of Chemicals, 2001; numerous papers in scientific jls. *Recreations:* cricket, Rugby, natural history. *Address:* Department of Zoology, Natural History Museum, Cromwell Road, SW7 5BD. *T:* (020) 7942 5275. *Clubs:* Zoological; Hertford (Hertford).

RAINE, Craig Anthony; poet; Fellow of New College, Oxford, since 1991; Editor, Areté, since 1999; *b* 3 Dec. 1944; *s* of Norman Edward Raine and Olive Marie Raine; *m* 1972, Ann Pasternak Slater; one *d* three *s*. *Educ:* Barnard Castle Sch.; Exeter Coll., Oxford (BA Hons in English; BPhil). College Lecturer, Oxford University: Exeter Coll., 1971–72; Lincoln Coll., 1974–75; Exeter Coll., 1975–76; Christ Church, 1976–79. Books Editor, New Review, 1977–78; Editor, Quarto, 1979–80; Poetry Editor: New Statesman, 1981; Faber & Faber, 1981–91. Cholmondeley Poetry Award, 1983; Sunday Times Writer of the Year, 1998. *Publications:* The Onion, Memory, 1978, 5th edn 1986; A Martian Sends a Postcard Home, 1979, 8th edn 1990; A Free Translation, 1981, 2nd edn 1981; Rich, 1984, 3rd edn 1985; The Electrification of the Soviet Union, 1986; (ed) A Choice of Kipling's Prose, 1987; The Prophetic Book, 1988; '1953', 1990; Haydn and the Valve Trumpet (essays), 1990; (ed) Rudyard Kipling: Selected Poetry, 1992; History: The Home Movie, 1994; Clay. Whereabouts Unknown, 1996; (ed jtly) New Writing 7, 1998; A la recherche du temps perdu, 2000; In Defence of T. S. Eliot (essays), 2000; Collected Poems 1978–1999, 2000. *Recreation:* music. *Address:* c/o New College, Oxford OX1 3BN.

RAINE, John Stephen; County Director, then Chief Executive, Derbyshire County Council, 1989–97; *b* 13 April 1941; *s* of Alan and Ruby Raine; *m* 1961, Josephine Marlow; two *s*. *Educ:* Sir Joseph Williamson's Mathematical School, Rochester. MIPR. Journalist; Kent Messenger, Sheffield Morning Telegraph, Sheffield Star, Raymond's News Agency, 1957–70; Derbyshire County Council: County Public Relations Officer, 1973–79; Asst to Clerk and Chief Exec., 1979–81; Asst Chief Exec., 1981–88; Dep. County Dir, 1988–89. Chm., Derbys Probation Bd, 2001–. Chairman: Hearing Aid Council, 1997–; Derbys Assoc. for the Blind, 1997–. Non-exec. Dir, Chesterfield and N Derbys Royal Hosp. NHS Trust, 1998–. *Recreations:* walking, travel, smallholding. *Address:* Far Hill Farm, Far Hill, Ashover, Chesterfield, Derbyshire S45 0BB. *T:* (01246) 590501.

RAINE, June Munro, FRCPE; Director, Post-Licensing Division, Medicines Control Agency, Department of Health, since 1998; *b* 20 June 1952; *d* of David Harris and Isobel Harris (*née* Munro); *m* 1975, Prof. Anthony Evan Gerald Raine (*d* 1995); one *s* one *d*. *Educ:* Herts & Essex High Sch.; Somerville Coll., Oxford (BA Hons 1st Cl. 1974; MSc 1976; BM BCh 1978). MRCP 1980; MRCGP 1982; FRCPE 1995. Department of Health: SMO, Medicines Div., 1985–89; Gp Manager, Medicines Control Agency, 1989–98; Principal Assessor to Medicines Commn, 1992–. Member: wkg gps on aspects of pharmaceutical regulation, EC; Foresight Healthcare Task Force (Public and Patients), DTI, 1999–2000. FRSocMed 2000. *Publications:* papers on pharmacology, adverse drug effects and regulation of medicines. *Recreations:* music, opera, travel, ski-ing. *Address:* Medicines Control Agency, Department of Health, Market Towers, 1 Nine Elms Lane, SW8 5NQ. *T:* (020) 7273 0400, *Fax:* (020) 7273 0675.

RAINE, Kathleen Jessie, (Mrs K. J. Madge), CBE 2000; FRSL; poet; *b* 1908; *o d* of late George Raine, schoolmaster, and Jessie Raine; *m* Charles Madge (marr. diss.; he *d* 1996); one *s* one *d*. *Educ:* Girton College, Cambridge. Founder, Temenos Acad., 1990. Hon. DLitt: Leicester, 1974; Durham, 1979; Caen, 1987. Queen's Gold Medal for Poetry, 1992. Comdr, Ordre des Arts et des Lettres (France), 2000 (Officier, 1995). *Publications:* Stone and Flower, 1943; Living in Time, 1946; The Pythoness, 1949; The Year One, 1952; Collected Poems, 1956; The Hollow Hill (poems), 1965; Defending Ancient Springs (criticism), 1967, 1985; Blake and Tradition (Andrew Mellon Lectures, Washington, 1962), Princeton 1968, London 1969 (abridged version, Blake and Antiquity, Princeton 1978, London 1979, trans. Japanese, 1988); (with George Mills Harper) Selected Writings of Thomas Taylor the Platonist, Princeton and London, 1969; William Blake, 1970; The Lost Country (verse), 1971 (W. H. Smith & Son Award, 1972); On a Deserted Shore (verse), 1973; Yeats, the Tarot and The Golden Dawn (criticism), 1973; Faces of Day and Night, 1973; Farewell Happy Fields (autobiog.), 1973 (French trans. as Adieu prairies heureuses, 1978; Prix du meilleur livre étranger); Death in Life and Life in Death (criticism), 1974; The Land Unknown (autobiog.), 1975 (French trans. as Le royaume inconnu, 1978), The Oval Portrait (verse), 1977; The Lion's Mouth (autobiography), 1977 (French trans. as La Gueul du Lion, 1987); David Jones and the Actually Loved and Known (criticism), 1978; From Blake to a Vision (criticism), 1979; The Oracle in the Heart (verse), 1979; Blake and the New Age (criticism), 1979; Collected Poems, 1981; The Human Face of God, 1982; The Inner Journey of the Poet and other papers (criticism), 1982; L'Imagination Créatrice de William Blake; Yeats the Initiate, 1986; The Presence (verse), 1988; Selected Poems, 1988; Visages du Jour et de la Nuit, 1989; India Seen Afar, 1990; Golgonooza, City of the Imagination, 1991; Living with Mystery (verse), 1992; Le Monde Vivant de l'Imagination, 1998; W. B. Yeats and the Learning of the Imagination, 1999; Collected Poems, 2000; French trans. of verse: Isis errante, 1978; Sur un rivage désert, 1978; Le Premier Jour, 1980; Le Royaume Invisible, 1991; Spanish trans.: En una desierta orilla, 1980; Swedish trans.: Den Osedda Rosen (selected poetry), 1988; Editor, Temenos, a bi-annual Review devoted to the Arts of the Imagination, 1982–93 (Jt Editor, 1981–82) (10th issue 1989); contributions to literary journals. *Address:* 47 Paultons Square, SW3 5DT. *Club:* University Women's.

RAINE, Sandra Margaret; Company Secretary, Paddington Churches Housing Association, since 1999; *b* 7 March 1958; *d* of Charles Kitchener Lovell and Mary Rosalind Lovell (*née* O'Hare); *m* 1980, Ian Henry Raine. *Educ:* Univ. of Newcastle upon Tyne (BA Hons Sociol. and Social Admin). ACIS 1986. Pensions Asst, Dunlop Ltd, 1980; Admin Officer, NE Council on Alcoholism, 1980–82; Sen. Admin Asst, Newcastle upon Tyne Poly., 1982–85; Asst Co-ordinator, Urban Programmes, Gateshead MBC, 1985–86; Asst Divl Dir, Berks Social Services, 1986–90; Asst Co. Sec., AA, 1990–91; Ben Fund Sec., Chartered Inst Building, 1992–94; Sec. and Chief Exec., IGasE, 1994–99. *Recreations:* keep fit, cycling, reading. *Address:* Paddington Churches Housing Association, Canterbury House, Canterbury Road, NW6 5SQ. *Clubs:* Anglo-Belgian, New Cavendish; Nirvana (Berkshire).

RAINER, Luise; actress and painter; *b* Vienna, 12 Jan.; *d* of Heinz Rainer; *m* 1937, Clifford Odets (from whom she obtained a divorce, 1940; he *d* 1963); *m* 1945, Robert (*d* 1989), *s* of late John Knittel; one *d*. *Educ:* Austria, France, Switzerland and Italy. Started stage career at age of sixteen under Max Reinhardt in Vienna; later was discovered by Metro-Goldwyn-Mayer talent scout in Vienna; came to Hollywood; starred in: Escapade, 1935; The Great Ziegfeld, 1936; The Good Earth, Emperor's Candlesticks, Big City, 1937; Toy Wife (Frou Frou), The Great Waltz, Dramatic School, 1938; Hostages, 1942; The Gambler, 1998; received Motion Picture Academy of Arts and Sciences Award for the best feminine performance in 1936 and 1937. One-man exhibn of paintings at Patrick Seale Gallery, SW1, 1978. US tour in dramatised recitation of Tennyson's Enoch Arden with music by Richard Strauss, 1983–84. TV film (wrote and starred), By herself—a dancer, 1986. George Eastman Award, George Eastman Inst., Rochester, NY, 1982. Grand Cross 1st class, Order of Merit (Federal Republic of Germany), 1985. *Recreations:* formerly mountain climbing, now writing, painting. *Address:* 54 Eaton Square, Belgravia.

RAINEY, Simon Piers Nicholas; QC 2000; a Recorder, since 2001; *b* 14 Feb. 1958; *s* of Peter Michael Rainey and Theresa Cora Rainey (*née* Heffernan); *m* 1st, 1986, Pia Witlox (marr. diss. 1999); twin *s* one *d*; 2nd, 2000, Charlotte Rice. *Educ:* Cranbrook Sch.; Corpus Christi Coll., Cambridge (BA 1st Cl. Hons Law 1980; MA 1984); Univ. Libre de Bruxelles (Licence en Droit Européen (Dist) 1981). Called to the Bar, Lincoln's Inn, 1982; Western Circuit. *Publications:* Maritime Laws of West Africa, 1985; Ship Sale and Purchase, 1993; Law of Tug and Tow, 1996. *Recreations:* classical music, print-collecting. *Address:* 4 Essex Court, Temple, EC4Y 9AJ. *T:* (020) 7653 5653; *e-mail:* srainey@4sx.co.uk.

RAINGER, Peter, CBE 1978; FRS 1982; FREng; Deputy Director of Engineering, British Broadcasting Corporation, 1978–84, retired; *b* 17 May 1924; *s* of Cyril and Ethel Rainger; *m* 1st, 1953, Josephine Campbell (decd); two *s*; 2nd, 1972, Barbara Gibson. *Educ:* Northampton Engrg Coll.; London Univ. (BSc(Eng)). CEng, FIEE; FREng (FEng 1979). British Broadcasting Corporation: Head of Designs Dept, 1968–71; Head of Research Dept, 1971–76; Asst Dir of Engrg, 1976–78. Chairman: Professional Gp E14, IEE, 1973–76; various working parties, EBU, 1971–84. Fellow, Royal Television Soc., 1969. Geoffrey Parr Award, Royal TV Soc., 1964; J. J. Thompson Premium, IEE, 1966; TV Acad. Award, Nat. Acad. of Arts and Scis, 1968; David Sarnoff Gold Medal, SMPTE, 1972. *Publications:* Satellite Broadcasting, 1985; technical papers in IEE, Royal TV Soc. and SMPTE jls. *Recreations:* sculpture, model engineering. *Address:* 22 Mill Meadow, Milford on Sea, Hants SO41 0UG.

RAINS, Prof. Anthony John Harding, CBE 1986; MS, FRCS; Professor of Surgery, Charing Cross Hospital Medical School, University of London, and Hon. Consultant Surgeon, Charing Cross Hospital, 1959–81; *b* 5 Nov. 1920; *s* of late Dr Robert Harding Rains and Mrs Florence Harding Rains; *m* 1943, Mary Adelaide Lillywhite; three *d*. *Educ:* Christ's Hospital School, Horsham; St Mary's Hospital, London. MB, BS London 1943; MS London 1952; MRCS; LRCP 1943; FRCS 1948. Ho. Surg. and Ho. Phys. St Mary's, 1943. RAF, 1944–47. Ex-Service Registrar to Mr Handfield-Jones and Lord Porritt,

1947–48; Res. Surgical Officer, Bedford County Hosp., 1948–50; Lectr in Surgery, Univ. of Birmingham, 1950–54, Sen. Lectr, 1955–59; Asst Dir, BPMF, Univ. of London, and Postgraduate Dean, SW Thames RHA, 1981–85. Hon. Consulting Surgeon, United Birmingham Hospitals, 1954–59; Hon. Consultant Surgeon to the Army, 1972–82. Royal College of Surgeons of England: Mem. Court of Examiners, 1968–74; Mem. Council, 1972–84; Dean, Inst. of Basic Med. Scis, 1976–82; Hunterian Trustee, 1982–95; Vice-President, 1983–84; Hon. Librarian, 1984–95. Chm., Med. Commn on Accident Prevention, 1974–83. Pres., Nat. Assoc. of Theatre Nurses, 1979–81. Trustee, Smith and Nephew Foundn, 1972–95. Sir Arthur Keith medal, RCS. Editor: Annals of RCS; Jl of RSocMed, 1985–94. *Publications:* (ed with Dr P. B. Kunkler) The Treatment of Cancer in Clinical Practice, 1959; Gallstones: Causes and Treatment, 1964; (ed) Bailey and Love's Short Practice of Surgery, 13th edn (ed with W, M. Capper), 1965, 20th edn (ed with C. V. Mann), 1988; Edward Jenner and Vaccination, 1975; Emergency and Acute Care, 1976; Lister and Antisepsis, 1977; 1,001 Multiple Choice Questions and Answers in Surgery, 1978, 4th edn 1996; articles on the surgery of the gall bladder, on the formation of gall stones, inguinal hernia and arterial disease. *Recreations:* gardening, poetry. *Address:* 39A St Cross Road, Winchester, Hants SO23 9PR. *T:* (01962) 869419.

RAISER, Rev. Dr Konrad; General Secretary, World Council of Churches, since 1993; *b* Magdeburg, 25 Jan. 1938; *m* 1967, Elisabeth von Weizsäcker; four *s. Educ:* Univ. of Tübingen (DTheol 1970). Ordained into German Evangelical Ch., 1964; Asst Pastor, Württemberg, 1963–65; Lectr, Prostestant Theol. Faculty, Tübingen, 1967–69; World Council of Churches: Study Sec., Commn on Faith and Order, 1969–73; Dep. Gen. Sec., 1973–83; Prof. of Systematic Theol. and Ecumenics, and Dir, Ecumenical Inst., Protestant Theol. Faculty, Univ. of Ruhr, 1983–93. *Publications:* Identität und Sozialität, 1971; Ökumene im Ubergang, 1989 (Ecumenism in Transition, 1991); (contrib.) Dictionary of the Ecumenical Movement, 1991; Wir stehen noch am Anfang, 1994; To Be the Church, 1997; many essays and articles. *Address:* World Council of Churches, 150 Route de Ferney, PO Box 2100, 1211 Geneva 2, Switzerland.

RAISMAN, Geoffrey, DPhil, DM; FMedSci; FRS 2001; Head, Division of Neurobiology, National Institute for Medical Research, since 1974; *b* 28 June 1939; *s* of Harry Raisman and Celia Raisman (*née* Newton); *m* 1958, Vivien Margolin; one *d. Educ:* Roundhay Sch., Leeds; Pembroke Coll., Oxford (Theodore Williams Open Schol. in Medicine; BA 1st Cl. Hons Animal Physiol. 1960); Christ Church, Oxford (MA, DPhil 1964; BM BCh 1965); DM Oxon 1974. Demonstrator, 1965–66, Schorstein Res. Fellow, 1965–67, Univ. Lectr, 1966–74, Dept of Human Anatomy, Oxford Univ. Med. Sch.; Res. Fellow, Dept of Anatomy, Harvard Univ., 1968–69; Fellow, 1970–74, Med. Tutor, 1973–74, Oriel Coll., Oxford. Scientific Director: Norman and Sadie Lee Res. Centre, Mill Hill, 1987–; Teijin Biomed. Centre, MRC Collaborative Centre, Mill Hill, 1992–97. Visiting Professor: in Neuroscis, KCL, 1977–82; of Anatomy and Develtl Biol., UCL, 1989–; Royal Soc. Exchange Prog. with China at Shanghai Physiol. Inst., Chinese Acad. of Scis, 1982; Norman and Sadie Lee Vis. Scientist, City of Hope Med. Center, Duarte, Calif, 1983. Member: MRC Co-ordinating Gp on Rehabilitation after Acute Brain Damage, 1977–85; MRC Neurobiol. and Mental Health Bd, 1980–83; Scientific Cttee, Internat. Spinal Res. Trust, 1986–. Trustee: British Neurol Res. Trust, 1987–95; American Friends of BNRT, 1995–. Mem., Editl Bds, incl. Brain Res., Anatomy and Embryol., Exptl Brain Res., Exptl Neurol. FMedSci 1999. Wakeman Award for Res. in Neuroscis, Duke Univ., N Carolina, 1980. *Publications:* contrib. articles on brain structure and plasticity, sexual dimorphism in the brain and repair of spinal cord injury to scientific jls. *Recreations:* writing, travel, ancient civilisations, Chinese, Japanese. *Address:* Division of Neurobiology, National Institute for Medical Research, The Ridgeway, Mill Hill, NW7 1AA. *T:* (020) 8913 8555, *Fax:* (020) 8913 8587; *e-mail:* graisma@nimr.mrc.ac.uk. *Club:* Royal Society of Medicine.

RAISMAN, Jeremy Philip; Senior Partner, Eversheds, London (formerly Jaques & Lewis), 1992–99; *b* 6 March 1935; *s* of Sir (Abraham) Jeremy Raisman, GCMG, GCIE, KCSI, and Renee Mary (*née* Kelly); *m* 1963, Diana Rosamund Clifford, *d* of late Maj.-Gen. Cedric Rhys Price, CB, CBE; one *s* two *d. Educ:* Dragon Sch., Oxford; Rugby Sch. Articled, Norton Rose, 1953–59; admitted solicitor, 1959; Asst Solicitor, Clifford-Turner & Co., 1954–62; Asst Solicitor, then Partner, Nabarro Nathanson & Co., 1962–67; Partner, Jaques & Co., 1967, subseq. Jaques & Lewis, 1982, then Eversheds, London, 1995. *Recreations:* beagling (Jt Master, W Surrey & Horsell Beagles 1959–71), sailing, walking, trekking. *Address:* Furzefield, Hoe Lane, Peaslake, Guildford, Surrey GU5 9SL. *T:* (01306) 730406. *Clubs:* Bosham Sailing (Chichester); Rock Sailing (Wadebridge, Cornwall).

RAISMAN, John Michael, CBE 1983; Chairman, Council for Industry and Higher Education, 1991–98 (Member, 1988–98); *b* 12 Feb. 1929; *er s* of Sir Jeremy Raisman, GCMG, GCIE, KCSI, and late Renee Mary Raisman; *m* 1953, Evelyn Anne, *d* of Brig. J. I. Muirhead, CIE, MC; one *s* three *d. Educ:* Dragon Sch., Oxford; Rugby Sch.; The Queen's Coll., Oxford (Jodrell Schol., MA Lit Hum). CIMgt (CBIM 1980). Joined Royal Dutch/Shell Group, 1953; served in Brazil, 1954–60; General Manager, Shell Panama, 1961–62; Asst to Exploration and Production Coordinator, The Hague, 1963–65; Gen. Man., Shell Co. of Turkey, 1966–69; President, Shell Sekiyu K. K. Japan, 1970–73; Head, European Supply and Marketing, 1974–77; Man. Dir, Shell UK Oil, 1977–78; Regional Coordinator, UK and Eire, Shell Internat. Pet. Co. Ltd, 1978–85; Shell UK Ltd: Dep. Chm., 1978–79; Chief Exec., 1978–85; Chm., 1979–85; Govt Dir, 1984–87, Dep. Chm., 1987–91, British Telecom. Chm., British Biotech plc, 1995–98 (Dir, 1993–98); Director: Vickers PLC, 1981–90; Glaxo Hldgs PLC, 1982–90; Lloyds Bank Plc, 1985–95; Lloyds Merchant Bank Hldgs Ltd, 1985–87; Candover Investments PLC, 1990–98; Tandem Computers Ltd, 1991–97; Lloyds TSB plc, 1996–98. Chairman: Adv. Council, London Enterprise Agency, 1979–85; UK Oil Industry Emergency Cttee, 1980–85; Council of Industry for Management Educn, 1981–85; Investment Bd, Electra-Candover Partners, 1985–95. Member: Council, CBI, 1979–90 (Chm., CBI Europe Cttee, 1980–88; Mem., President's Cttee, 1980–88); Council, Inst. of Petroleum, 1979–81; Council, Inst. for Fiscal Studies, 1982–; Governing Council, Business in the Community, 1982–85; Council, UK Centre for Econ. and Environmental Develt, 1985–89; Royal Commn on Environmental Pollution, 1986–87; Chm., Electronics Industry EDC, 1986–87. Chm., Langs Lead Body, 1990–95; Dep. Chm., Nat. Commn on Educn, 1991–; Pres., Council for Educn in World Citizenship, 1992–. Mem., Council for Charitable Support, 1986–91; Chm., RA Trust, 1987–96, Trustee, RA, 1983–; Governor, NIESR, 1983–; Pro-Chancellor, Aston Univ., 1987–93. DUniv Stirling, 1983; Hon. LLD: Aberdeen, 1985; Manchester, 1986; Hon. DSc Aston, 1992. *Recreations:* golf, music, theatre, travel. *Address:* Netheravon House, Netheravon Road South, W4 2PY. *T:* (020) 8994 3731. *Clubs:* Brooks's; Royal Mid-Surrey; Sunningdale Golf.

RAISON, Dr John Charles Anthony, MA, MD; FFPHM; Consultant in Public Health Medicine, Wessex Regional Health Authority, 1982–91, retired; *b* 13 May 1926; *s* of late Cyril A. Raison, FRCS, Edgbaston, Birmingham, and of Ceres Raison; *m* 1st, 1951 (marr. diss. 1982); one *s* two *d*; 2nd, 1983, Ann Alexander, *d* of Captain Faulkner, MM and Mrs J. H. R. Faulkner, Southampton; three step *d. Educ:* Malvern Coll.; Trinity Hall, Cambridge; Birmingham Univ. Consultant Clinical Physiologist in Cardiac Surgery, Birmingham Reg. Hosp. Bd, 1962; Hon. Associate Consultant Clinical Physiologist, United Birmingham Hosps, 1963; Sen. Physiologist, Dir of Clinical Res. and Chief Planner, Heart Research Inst., Presbyterian-Pacific Medical Center, San Francisco, 1966; Chief Scientific Officer and Sen. Princ. Medical Officer, Scientific Services, DHSS, 1974–78; Dep. Dir, Nat. Radiological Protection Bd, 1978–81. Vis. Consultant, Civic Hosps, Lisbon (Gulbenkian Foundn), 1962; Arris and Gale Lectr, Royal College of Surgeons, 1965. Councillor, Southam RDC, 1955–59. *Publications:* chapters in books, and papers in medical jls on open-heart surgery, extracorporeal circulation, intensive care, scientific services in health care, and computers in medicine. *Recreations:* gardening, golf, singing. *Address:* 15 The Woodlands, Church Lane, Kings Worthy, near Winchester, Hants SO23 7QQ. *T:* (01962) 885722.

RAISON, Rt Hon. Sir Timothy (Hugh Francis), Kt 1991; PC 1982; Chairman: Advertising Standards Authority, 1991–94; Aylesbury Vale Community Healthcare NHS Trust, 1992–98; *b* 3 Nov. 1929; *s* of late Maxwell and Celia Raison; *m* 1956, Veldes Julia Charrington; one *s* three *d. Educ:* Dragon Sch., Oxford; Eton (King's Schol.); Christ Church, Oxford (Open History Schol.). Editorial Staff: Picture Post, 1953–56; New Scientist, 1956–61; Editor: Crossbow, 1958–60; New Society, 1962–68. Member: Youth Service Develt Council, 1960–63; Central Adv. Council for Educn, 1963–66; Adv. Cttee on Drug Dependence, 1966–70; Home Office Adv, Council on Penal System, 1970–74; (co-opted) Inner London Educn Authority Educn Cttee, 1967–70; Richmond upon Thames Council, 1967–71. MP (C) Aylesbury, 1970–92; PPS to Sec. of State for N Ireland, 1972–73; Parly Under-Sec. of State, DES, 1973–74; Opposition spokesman on the Environment, 1975–76; Minister of State, Home Office, 1979–83; Minister of State, FCO, and Minister for Overseas Develt, 1983–86. Chm., Select Cttee on Educn, Science and the Arts, 1987–89. Sen. Fellow, Centre for Studies in Soc. Policy, 1974–77; Mem. Council, PSI, 1978–79; Vice-Chm. Bd, British Council, 1987–92. Trustee, BM, 1991–99. Mem. Council, Nat. Trust, 1997–2000. Nansen Medal (for share in originating World Refugee Year), 1960. *Publications:* Why Conservative?, 1964; (ed) Youth in New Society, 1966; (ed) Founding Fathers of Social Science, 1969; Power and Parliament, 1979; Tories and the Welfare State, 1990; various political pamphlets. *Recreations:* golf, gardening, history of art. *Club:* Beefsteak.

RAITT, Prof. Alan William, DPhil; FBA 1992; FRSL; Professor of French Literature, Oxford University, 1992–97, now Professor Emeritus; Fellow, Magdalen College, Oxford, 1966–97, now Fellow Emeritus; *b* 21 Sept. 1930; *s* of William Raitt, MBE, BSc and May (*née* Davison); *m* 1st, 1959, Janet Taylor (marr. diss. 1971); two *d*; 2nd, 1974, Lia Noémia Rodrigues Correia. *Educ:* King Edward VI Grammar Sch. Morpeth; Magdalen Coll., Oxford (MA 1955; DPhil 1957). Oxford University: Fellow (by Examn), Magdalen Coll., 1953–55; Fellow and Lectr in French, Exeter Coll., 1955–66; Lectr in French, Magdalen Coll., 1966–97; Reader in French Lit., 1979–92. Vis. Lectr, Univ. of Georgia, 1986; Vis. Prof., Sorbonne, Paris, 1987–88. Gen. Editor, French Studies, 1987–97. FRSL 1971. Médaille d'Argent, Grand Prix du Rayonnement de la Langue Française, French Acad., 1987. Commandeur, Ordre des Palmes Académiques, 1995. *Publications:* Villiers de l'Isle-Adam et le Mouvement symboliste, 1965; Life and Letters in France: the nineteenth century, 1966; Prosper Mérimée, 1970; The Life of Villiers de l'Isle-Adam, 1981; (ed jtly) Villiers de l'Isle-Adam: Œuvres complètes, 1986; Villiers de l'Isle-Adam exorciste du réel, 1987; Flaubert: Trois Contes, 1991; (ed) Mallarmé, Villiers de l'Isle-Adam, 1993; (ed) Villiers de l'Isle-Adam, L'Eve future, 1993; (ed) Flaubert, Pour Louis Bouilhet, 1994; A. C. Friedel et 'Le Nouveau Théâtre allemand': un intermédiaire méconnu, 1996; Flaubert et le théâtre, 1998. *Recreation:* watching sport on television. *Address:* Magdalen College, Oxford OX1 4AU. *T:* (home) (01865) 515587.

RAITZ, Vladimir Gavrilovich; airline and travel consultant; Director, Scantours Ltd; *b* 23 May 1922; *s* of Dr Gavril Raitz and Cecilia Raitz; *m* 1954, Helen Antonia (*née* Corkrey); three *d. Educ:* Mill Hill Sch.; LSE (BSc(Econ.), Econ History, 1942). British United Press, 1942–43; Reuters, 1943–48; Chm., Horizon Holidays, 1949–74 (pioneered holidays by air). Member: NEDC for Hotels and Catering Industry, 1968–74; Cinematograph Films Council, 1969–74; Ct of Governors, LSE, 1971–95. Cavaliere Ufficiale, Order of Merit (Italy), 1971. *Publication:* (with Roger Bray) Flight to the Sun: the story of the holiday revolution. *Recreation:* watching grandchildren grow up. *Address:* 32 Dudley Court, Upper Berkeley Street, W1H 7PH. *T:* (020) 7262 2592. *Club:* Reform.

RAJ, Prof. Kakkadan Nandanath; Hon. Emeritus Fellow, Centre for Development Studies, Trivandrum, Kerala State, since 1983 (Fellow, 1973–84); National Professor, since 1992; *b* 13 May 1924; *s* of K. N. Gopalan and Karthiayani Gopalan; *m* 1957, Dr Sarasamma Narayanan; two *s. Educ:* Madras Christian Coll., Tambaram (BA (Hons), MA, in Economics); London Sch. of Economics (PhD (Econ); Hon. Fellow, 1982). Asst Editor, Associated Newspapers of Ceylon, Nov. 1947–July 1948; Research Officer, Dept of Research, Reserve Bank of India, Aug. 1948–Feb. 1950; Asst Chief, Economic Div., Planning Commn, Govt of India, 1950–53; University of Delhi: Prof. of Economics, Delhi Sch. of Economics, 1953–73; Vice-Chancellor, 1969–70; Nat. Fellow in Economics, 1971–73; Jawaharlal Nehru Fellow, 1987–88. Mem., Economic Adv. Council to Prime Minister of India, 1983–91. Visiting Prof., Johns Hopkins Univ., Jan.-June, 1958; Vis. Fellow, Nuffield Coll., Oxford, Jan.-June, 1960. Corresp. Fellow, British Academy, 1972. Hon. Fellow, Amer. Economic Assoc. *Publications:* The Monetary Policy of the Reserve Bank of India, 1948; Employment Aspects of Planning in Underdeveloped Economies, 1956; Some Economic Aspects of the Bhakra-Nangal Project, 1960; Indian Economic Growth-Performance and Prospects, 1964; India, Pakistan and China-Economic Growth and Outlook, 1966; Investment in Livestock in Agrarian Economies, 1969; (ed jtly) Essays on the Commercialization of Indian Agriculture, 1985; Organizational Issues in Indian Agriculture, 1990; also articles in Economic Weekly, Economic and Political Weekly, Indian Economic Review, Oxford Economic Papers. *Address:* Nandavan, Kumarapuram, Trivandrum 695011, Kerala State, India. *T:* (home) (471) 443309, (office) (471) 448881, 448412.

RAKE, Michael Derek Vaughan, FCA; Senior Partner, KPMG UK, since 1998; Chairman, KPMG Europe, since 2000; *b* 17 Jan. 1948; *s* of Derek Shannon Vaughan Rake and Rosamund Rake (*née* Barrett); *m* 1st, 1970, Julia (*née* Cook); three *s*; 2nd, 1986, Caroline (*née* Thomas); one *s. Educ:* Wellington Coll. FCA 1970. Turquands Barton Mayhew, London and Brussels, 1968–74, KPMG: Brussels, 1974; Partner, 1979–; Partner i/c of Audit, Belgium and Luxembourg, 1983–86; Sen. Resident Partner, ME, 1986–89; Partner, London office, 1989–; Mem., UK Bd, 1991–; Regl Man. Partner, SE Reg., 1992–94; Chief Exec., London and SE Reg., 1994–96; Chief Operating Officer, UK, 1996–98. Dep. Chm., BITC, 1998– (Chm., Corporate Community Investment Leadership Team, 1998–); Member: Bd, Prince of Wales Business Leaders Forum, 1999–; CBI President's Cttee, 2001–. Chm., Adv. Bd, RNIB, 2001–; Mem., Private Appeal Cttee, SCF, 2000–. Reviseur d'Entreprise, Luxembourg; Mem., Institut des Experts-Comptables, Belgium. *Recreations:* polo, ski-ing. *Address:* KPMG, 8 Salisbury Square, EC4Y 8BB. *T:* (020) 7311 1000, *Fax:* (020) 7311 3311.

RALEIGH, Dr Jean Margaret Macdonald C.; *see* Curtis-Raleigh.

RALLI, Sir Godfrey (Victor), 3rd Bt *cr* 1912; TD; *b* 9 Sept. 1915; *s* of Sir Strati Ralli, 2nd Bt, MC; *S* father, 1964; *m* 1st, 1937, Nora Margaret Forman (marr. diss. 1947; she *d* 1990); one *s* two *d*; 2nd, 1949, Jean (*d* 1998), *er d* of late Keith Barlow. *Educ:* Eton. Joined Ralli Bros Ltd, 1936. Served War of 1939–45 (despatches), Captain, Berkshire Yeomanry RA. Dir and Vice-Pres., Ralli Bros Ltd, 1946–62; Chm., Greater London Fund for the Blind, 1962–82. *Recreations:* fishing, golf. *Heir: s* David Charles Ralli [*b* 5 April 1946; *m* 1975, Jacqueline Cecilia, *d* of late David Smith; one *s* one *d*]. *Address:* Piers House, 52 New Street, Sandwich, Kent CT13 9BB. *T:* (01304) 611355. *Club:* Naval and Military.

RALLING, (Antony) Christopher, OBE 1992; FRGS; freelance writer/director; *b* 12 April 1929; *s* of Harold St George Ralling and Dorothy Blanche Ralling; *m* 1963, Angela Norma (*née* Gardner); one *d*. *Educ:* Charterhouse; Wadham Coll., Oxford (BA 2nd Cl. Hons English). Joined BBC External Services, Scriptwriter, 1955; British Meml Foundn Fellowship to Australia, 1959; Dep. Editor, Panorama, BBC TV, 1964; joined BBC TV Documentaries, 1966; directed The Search for the Nile, 1972 (Amer. Acad. Award, 1972; Peabody Award, 1972); Mem., British Everest Expedn, 1975; produced The Voyage of Charles Darwin, 1978 (British Acad. Award, 1978; Desmond Davies British Acad. Award, 1978; RTS Silver Medal, 1979); Hd of Documentaries, BBC TV, 1980; left BBC to start Dolphin Productions, 1982; directed: The History of Africa, 1984; Chasing a Rainbow (Josephine Baker), 1986 (Amer. Acad. Award, 1986); Prince Charles at Forty, LWT, 1988; The Kon-Tiki Man, BBC, 1989; The Buried Mirror, BBC, 1992. FRGS 1978. *Publications:* Muggeridge Through the Microphone, 1967; The Voyage of Charles Darwin, 1978; Shackleton, 1983; The Kon-Tiki Man, 1990; A Diplomat in Japan, 1992; Return to Everest, 1993. *Recreations:* tennis, ski-ing. *Address:* Tankerville Cottage, Kingston Hill, Surrey KT2 7JH. *Club:* Alpine.

RALLS, Peter John Henry; QC 1997; a Recorder, since 2000; *b* 18 July 1947; *s* of Ivan Jack Douglas Ralls and Sybil Gladys Child; *m* 1st, 1979, Anne Elizabeth Marriott (marr. diss. 1986); 2nd, 1997, Tonia Anne Clark; one *s* one *d*. *Educ:* Royal Russell Sch., Surrey; UCL (LLB Hons). Called to the Bar, Middle Temple, 1972; admitted Solicitor, 1981; returned to the Bar, 1982; an Asst Recorder, 1998–2000. *Recreations:* yacht racing, cricket. *Address:* 29 Bedford Row, WC1R 4HE. *T:* (020) 7831 2626. *Clubs:* MCC; Royal London Yacht.

RALPH, Richard Peter, CMG 1997; CVO 1991; HM Diplomatic Service; Ambassador to Romania and to Moldova, since 1999; *b* 27 April 1946; *s* of Peter and Marion Ralph; *m* 1970, Margaret Elisabeth Coulthurst (marr. diss. 2001); one *s* one *d*. *Educ:* King's Sch., Canterbury; Edinburgh Univ. (MSc). Third Sec., FCO, 1969–70; Third, later Second, Sec., Vientiane, Laos, 1970–73; Second, later First, Sec., Lisbon, 1974–77; FCO, 1977–81; Head of Chancery, Harare, Zimbabwe, 1981–85; Counsellor, FCO, 1985–89; Head of Chancery and Congressional Counsellor, Washington, 1989–93; Ambassador to Latvia, 1993–95; Gov., Falkland Is, and Comr for S Georgia and S Sandwich Is, 1996–99. *Recreation:* motorcycles. *Address:* c/o Foreign and Commonwealth Office, King Charles Street, SW1A 2AH.

RALPHS, Enid Mary, (Lady Ralphs), CBE 1984; JP; DL; Chairman of the Council, 1981–84, Vice-President, since 1984, Magistrates' Association; *b* 20 Jan. 1915; *d* of Percy William Cowlin and Annie Louise Cowlin (*née* Willoughby); *m* 1938, Sir (Frederick) Lincoln Ralphs, Kt 1973 (*d* 1978); one *s* two *d*. *Educ:* Camborne Grammar Sch.; University Coll., Exeter (BA); DipEd Cambridge. Pres., Guild of Undergrads, Exeter, 1936–37; Vice-Pres., NUS, 1937–38. Teacher, Penzance Grammar Sch., 1937–38; Staff Tutor, Oxford Univ. Tutorial Classes Cttee, 1942–44; pt-time Sen. Lectr, Keswick Hall Coll. of Educn, 1948–80. Member: Working Party on Children and Young Persons Act 1969, 1977–78; Steering Cttee on Community Alternatives for Young Offenders, NACRO, 1979–82; Consultative Cttee on Educn in Norwich Prison, 1982–87; Home Office Adv. Bd on Restricted Patients, 1985–91; Chairman: Working Party on the Victim in Court, 1988; Working Party on Sentencing, a way ahead, 1989. Member: Religious Adv. Council, BBC Midland Reg., 1963–66; Guide Council for GB, 1965–68. President: Norwich and Dist Br., UNA, 1973–; Norfolk Guides (formerly Girl Guides), 1987–. Governor: Norwich Sch.; Culford Sch.; Visitor, Wymondham Coll., 1991–. Trustee, Norfolk Children's Projects, 1982–. JP Norwich 1958; Chairman: Norwich Juvenile Panel, 1964–79; Norwich Bench, 1977–85; former Mem., Licensing Cttee; Mem., Domestic Panel, 1981–85; Vice-Pres., Norfolk Br., Magistrates' Assoc., 1986–; Dep. Chm., Norfolk Magistrates' Courts Cttee, 1978–85 (Chm., Trng Sub-Cttee); Mem., Central Council, Magistrates' Courts Cttees, 1974–81. DL Norfolk 1981. Hon. DCL East Anglia, 1989. *Publications:* (jtly) The Magistrate as Chairman, 1987; contribs to various jls. *Recreations:* gardening, travel. *Address:* Jesselton, 218 Unthank Road, Norwich NR2 2AH. *T:* (01603) 453382. *Clubs:* Royal Over-Seas League; Norfolk (Norwich).

RALSTON, Gen. Joseph W., DFC, DSM; Supreme Allied Commander, Europe, since 2000; Commander-in-Chief, United States European Command, since 2000; *b* 4 Nov. 1943; *m* 1989, Diana Dougherty; one *s* one *d*, and one step *s* one step *d*. *Educ:* Miami Univ. (BA Chemistry 1965); Central Michigan Univ. (MA Personnel Mgt 1976); John F. Kennedy Sch. of Govt, Harvard Univ. Commissioned USAF, Reserve Officer Trng Corps Program, 1965; F-105 Pilot, Laos and N Vietnam; US Army Comd and Gen. Staff Coll., 1976; Nat. War Coll., Washington, 1984; Asst Dep. COS (Ops), and Dep. COS (Requirements), HQ Tactical Air Comd, 1987–90; Dir, Tactical Progs, 1990–91, Opnl Requirements, 1991–92, HQ USAF; Comdr, Alaskan Comd, 11 Air Force, Alaskan N Amer. Aerospace Defense Comd Reg., and Jt Task Force Alaska, 1992–94; Dep. COS (Plans and Ops), HQ USAF, 1994–95; Comdr, Air Combat Comd, 1995–96; Vice Chm., Jt Chiefs of Staff, 1996–2000. US Legion of Merit, DDSM, MSM, Air Medal, Air Force Commendation Medal. Highest degree, Mil. Order of Merit (Morocco), 1996; Officer, Legion of Honour (France), 1997; Kt Comdr's Cross, Order of Merit (Germany), 1999; Grand Cross, Royal Norwegian Order of Merit (Norway), 2000. *Recreations:* hunting, fishing, gardening. *Address:* Château Gendebien, 32 Chaussée de Binche, 7000 Mons, Belgium.

RAMA RAU, Santha; free-lance writer since 1945; English teacher at Sarah Lawrence College, Bronxville, NY, since 1971; *b* Madras, India, 24 Jan. 1923; *d* of late Sir Benegal Rama Rau, CIE and Lady Dhanvanthi Rama Rau; *m* 1st, 1951, Faubion Bowers (marr. diss. 1966); one *s*; 2nd, Gurdon W. Wattles. *Educ:* St Paul's Girls' School, London, England; Wellesley College, Mass, USA. Feature writer for the Office of War Information, New York, USA, during vacations from college, 1942–45. Hon. doctorate: Bates College, USA, 1961; Russell Sage College, 1965; Phi Beta Kappa, Wellesley College, 1960; Roosevelt Coll., 1962; Brandeis Univ., 1963; Bard Coll., NY, 1964. *Publications:* Home to India, 1945; East of Home, 1950; This is India, 1953; Remember the House, 1955; View to the South-East, 1957; My Russian Journey, 1959; A Passage to India (dramatization), 1962; Gifts of Passage, 1962; The Adventuress, 1971; Cooking of India, 1971 (2 vols); A Princess Remembers (with Rajmata Gayatri Devi of Jaipur), 1976; An Inheritance (with Dhanvanthi Rama Rau), 1977; many articles and short stories in New Yorker, Art News, Horizon, Saturday Evening Post, Reader's Digest, National Geographic, etc. *Address:* 508 Leedsville Road, Amenia, NY 12501, USA.

RAMACHANDRAN, Prof. Gopalasamudram Narayana, FRS 1977; Indian National Science Academy Albert Einstein National Professor, 1984–89; retired; specialist in molecular biology, biophysics and mathematical logic; *b* 8 Oct. 1922; *s* of G. R. Narayana Iyer and Lakshmi Ammal; *m* 1945, Rajalakshmi Sankaran; two *s* one *d*. *Educ:* Maharaja's Coll., Ernakulam, Cochin; Indian Inst. of Science; Univ. of Madras (MA, MSc, DSc); Univ. of Cambridge (PhD). Lectr in Physics, Indian Inst. of Science, 1946–47, Asst Prof., 1949–52; 1851 Exhibn Scholar, Univ. of Cambridge, 1947–49; Prof., Univ. of Madras, 1952–70 (Dean, Faculty of Science, 1964–67); Indian Institute of Science: Prof. of Biophysics, 1970–78; Prof. of Mathematical Philosophy, 1978–81; Hon. Fellow, 1984; Dist. Scientist, Centre for Cellular and Molecular Biology, Hyderabad, 1981–83. Dir, Univ. Grants Commn Centre of Advanced Study in Biophysics, 1962–70; part-time Prof. of Biophysics, Univ. of Chicago, 1967–78. Member: Physical Res. Cttee, 1959–69; Nat. Cttee for Biophysics, 1961–; Bd of Sci. and Ind. Res., India, 1962–65; Council, Internat. Union of Pure and Applied Biophysics, 1969–72; Commn on Macromolecular Biophysics, 1969; Chm., Nat. Cttee for Crystallography, 1963–70; Senior Vis. Prof., Univ. of Michigan, 1965–66; Jawaharlal Nehru Fellow, 1968–70; Fogarty Internat. Schol., NIH, 1977–78. Fellow, Indian Acad. of Sciences, 1950 (Mem. Council, 1953–70; Sec., 1956–58; Vice-Pres., 1962–64); Fellow, Indian Nat. Sci. Acad., 1963; FRSA 1971. Hon. Mem., Amer. Soc. of Molecular Biology, 1965; Hon. Foreign Mem., Amer. Acad. of Arts and Scis; Founder Member: Indian Acad. of Yoga, 1980; Third World Acad., Rome, 1982. Hon. DSc: Roorkee, 1979; Indian Inst. Technology, Madras, 1985; Hyderabad, 1989; Banaras Hindu, 1991. Bhatnagar Meml Prize, 1961; Watumull Prize, 1964; John Arthur Wilson Award, 1967; Ramanujan Medal, 1971; Maghnad Saha Medal, 1971; J. C. Bose Gold Medal and Prize of Bose Inst., 1975; Fogarty Medal, 1978; Distinguished Alumni Award, Indian Inst. of Sci., 1978; C. V. Raman Award, 1982; Birla Award for Medical Science, 1984. Editor: Current Science, 1950–58; Jl Indian Inst. of Sci., 1973–77; Member Editorial Board: Jl Molecular Biol., 1959–66; Biochimica et Biophysica Acta, 1965–72; Indian Jl Pure and Applied Physics, 1963–80; Internat. Jl Peptide and Protein Res., 1969–82; Indian Jl Biochem. and Biophys., 1970–78; Connective Tissue Research 1972–84; Biopolymers, 1973–86; Jl Biomolecular Structure and Dynamics, 1984–. *Publications:* Crystal Optics, in Handbuch der Physik, vol. 25; Molecular Structure of Collagen, in Internat. Review of Connective Tissue Research, vol. 1; Conformation of Polypeptides and Proteins, in Advances in Protein Chemistry, vol. 23; Conformation Polypeptide Chains, in Annual Reviews in Biochemistry, vol. 39; Fourier Methods in Crystallography, 1970; (ed) Advanced Methods of Crystallography; (ed) Aspects of Protein Structure; (ed) Treatise on Collagen, 2 vols, 1967; (ed) Conformation of Biopolymers, vols 1 and 2, 1967; (ed) Crystallography and Crystal Perfection; (ed) Biochemistry of Collagen. *Recreations:* Indian and Western music; detective fiction. *Address:* 13–1 Navdeep Apartments, Navjyoth Complex, Near A-One School, Subash Chowk, Memnager, Ahmedabad 380052, India.

RAMADHANI, Rt Rev. John Acland; *see* Zanzibar, Bishop of.

RAMAGE, (James) Granville (William), CMG 1975; HM Diplomatic Service, retired; *b* 19 Nov. 1919; *s* of late Rev. George Granville Ramage and Helen Marion (*née* Middlemass); *m* 1947, Eileen Mary Smith; one *s* two *d*. *Educ:* Glasgow Acad.; Glasgow University. Served in HM Forces, 1940–46 (despatches). Entered HM Foreign Service, 1947; seconded for service at Bombay, 1947–49; transf. to Foreign Office, 1950; First Sec. and Consul at Manila, 1952–56; South-East Asia Dept, FO, 1956–58; Consul at Atlanta, Ga, 1958–62; Gen. Dept, FO, 1962–63; Consul-General, Tangier, 1963–67; High Comr in The Gambia, 1968–71; Ambassador, People's Democratic Republic of Yemen, 1972–75; Consul General at Boston, Massachusetts, 1975–77. *Recreations:* music, golf. *Address:* 4 Merton Hall Road, Wimbledon, SW19 3PP. *T:* (020) 8715 7939.

RAMAGE, Prof. Robert, DSc; FRS 1992; CChem, FRSC; FRSE; Forbes Professor of Organic Chemistry, University of Edinburgh, 1984–2001; *b* 4 Oct. 1935; *s* of Robert Bain Ramage and Jessie Boag Ramage; *m* 1961, Joan Fraser Paterson; three *d*. *Educ:* Whitehill Sen. Secondary Sch., Glasgow; Univ. of Glasgow (BSc Hons 1958; PhD 1961; DSc 1982). Fulbright Fellow and Fellow of Harvard Coll., 1961–63; Research at Woodward Res. Inst., 1963–64; Lectr then Sen. Lectr, Univ. of Liverpool, 1964–77; Prof., 1977–84, Head of Dept, 1979–84, UMIST; Head, Dept of Chem., Univ. of Edinburgh, 1987–90, 1997–2000; Dir, Edinburgh Centre for Protein Technology, 1996–2000. Man. Dir, Albachem Ltd. FRSE 1986; FRSA 1990. Dr (*hc*) Lille. *Recreations:* sport, gardening, current affairs. *Address:* c/o Department of Chemistry, University of Edinburgh, West Mains Road, Edinburgh EH9 3JJ. *T:* (0131) 650 4721.

RAMAKRISHNAN, Prof. Tiruppattur Venkatachalamurti, FRS 2000; Professor of Physics, 1981–84 and since 1986, and INSA Srinivasa Ramanujan Research Professor, since 1997, Indian Institute of Science, Bangalore; *b* 14 Aug. 1941; *s* of Tiruppattur Ramaseshayyar Venkatachala-Murti and Jayalakshmi Murti; *m* 1970, Meera Rao; one *s* one *d*. *Educ:* Banaras Hindu Univ., Varanasi (BSc 1959; MSc 1961); Columbia Univ., NY (PhD 1966). Lectr, 1966, Asst Prof., 1967, Indian Inst. of Technol., Kanpur; Asst Res. Physicist, UCSD, 1968–70; Asst Prof., 1970–77, Prof. of Physics, 1977–80, Indian Inst. of Technol., Kanpur; Prof. of Physics, Banaras Hindu Univ., 1984–86. Vis. Res. Physicist, 1978–81, Vis. Prof., 1990–91, Princeton Univ. Consultant, Bell Labs, 1979–81. Fellow: INSA, 1984; APS, 1984; Third World Acad. of Scis, 1990. *Publications:* (jtly) Physics, 1988, 2nd edn 1994; (with C. N. R. Rao) Superconductivity Today, 1990, 2nd edn 1997; about 100 research papers and 6 review articles. *Recreation:* trekking. *Address:* Department of Physics, Indian Institute of Science, Bangalore 560012, India. *T:* (80) 3092579, 3600591.

RAMAPHOSA, (Matamela) Cyril; Chairman, Rebhold Services (Pty) Ltd, since 2000; *b* 17 Nov. 1952; *s* of late Samuel Ramaphosa and of Erdmuth Ramaphosa; *m* 1996, Tshepo Motsepe; two *s* two *d*. *Educ:* Sekano-Ntoane High Sch., Soweto; Univ. of North, Turfloop (BProc 1981). Detained under Terrorism Act for 11 months, 1974, and 6 months, 1976; active in Black People's Convention, 1975; articled clerk, Attorney Henry Dolovitz, 1977; Legal Adv., Council of Unions of SA, 1981–82; First Gen. Sec., NUM, SA, 1982–91; arrested and detained under Riotous Assemblies Act, 1984; organised first legal one day strike by black mineworkers, 1984; African National Congress: Mem., Nat. Exec. Cttee, 1991–; Sec.-Gen., 1991–96; Leader, ANC Delegn to Multi-Party Negotiations, 1992–94; Chm., Constitutional Assembly, Govt of Nat. Unity, 1994–96. Exec. Dep. Chm., New Africa Investments Ltd, 1996–99; Chm. and Chief Exec., Molope Gp, 1999–2000. Vis. Prof. of Law, Stanford Univ., USA, 1991. Hon. Dr Massachusetts, 1992; Hon. PhD Port Elizabeth, 1995; Hon. LLD: Natal, 1997; Cape Town, 1997. *Recreation:* fly-fishing. *Address:* PO Box 782922, Sandton 2146, South Africa. *T:* (11) 4631744. *Club:* Rand (Johannesburg).

RAMBAHADUR LIMBU, Captain, VC 1966; MVO 1984; HM the Queen's Gurkha Orderly Officer, 1983–84; employed in Sultanate of Negara Brunei Darussalam, 1985–92; *b* Nov. 1939; *s* of late Tekbir Limbu; *m* 1st, 1960, Tikamaya Limbuni (*d* 1966); two *s*; 2nd,

67, Punimaya Limbuni; three *s.* Army Cert. of Educn 1st cl. Enlisted 10th Princess Mary's Own Gurkha Rifles, 1957; served on ops in Borneo (VC); promoted Sergeant, 1971; WOII, 1976; commissioned, 1977. Hon. Captain (Gurkha Commnd Officer), 1985. *Publication:* My Life Story, 1978. *Recreations:* football, volley-ball, badminton, basketball. *Address:* Ward No 13 Damak, Nagar Palika, PO Box Damak, District Jhapa, Mechi Zone, East Nepal. *Clubs:* VC and GC Association, Royal Society of St George (England).

RAMGOOLAM, Hon. Dr Navinchandra; MP Mauritius, since 1991; Prime Minister of Mauritius, 1995–2000; *b* 14 July 1947; *s* of Rt Hon. Sir Seewoosagur Ramgoolam, GCMG, PC (1st Prime Minister of Mauritius) and Lady Sushill Ramgoolam; *m* 1979, Veena Brizmohun. *Educ:* Royal Coll. of Surgeons, Dublin; London Sch. of Econs (LLB Hons; Hon. Fellow, 1998); Inns of Court Sch. of Law. LRCP, LRCSI 1975. Called to the Bar, Inner Temple, 1993. Mauritius Labour Party: Leader, 1991–; Pres., 1991–92. Leader of the Opposition, Mauritius, 1991–95. *Recreations:* reading, music, water ski-ing, chess. *Address:* River Walk, Vacoas, Mauritius. *Club:* Mauritius Turf.

RAMIN, Mme Manfred; *see* Cotrubas, I.

RAMM, Rev. Canon (Norwyn) MacDonald; Vicar of St Michael at the North Gate with St Martin and All Saints, Oxford, 1961–88 (Curate, 1957–61); City Rector, Oxford, 1961–89; Chaplain to the Queen, 1985–94; *b* 8 June 1924; *s* of Rev. Ezra Edward and Dorothy Mary Ramm; *m* 1962, Ruth Ellen, *d* of late Robert James Kirton, CBE, FIA; two *s* one *d. Educ:* Berkhamsted School; St Peter's Theological College, Jamaica; Lincoln College, Oxford. Jamaica appointments: Curate, St James, Montego Bay, 1951–53, deacon 1951, priest, 1952; Master, Cornwall College; Rector, St Jude's, Stony Hill with Mount James, 1953–57; Master, Wolmers Girls' School; Chaplain to Approved Sch., Stony Hill; Priest in charge, St Martin and All Saints, Oxford, 1961–71; Hon. Canon, Christ Church Cathedral, Oxford, 1985–88, now Emeritus. Chaplain to: HM Prison, Oxford, 1975–88; British Fire Services Assoc., 1980–96. Pres., Isis Dist Scout Assoc., 1984–99 (Chm., 1969–72); Patron, Headington Sch., 1994– (Mem. Council, 1981–84, Chm., 1984–93); Founder and Pres., Samaritans of Oxford, 1963–. Member: Oxford Rotary Club; Oxford Probus Club, 1996–. *Publication:* Graces Old and New from Oxford, 1990, 2nd edn 1995. *Recreations:* ski-ing, gardening, collecting Graces. *Address:* Fairlawn, Church Lane, Harwell, Abingdon, Oxon OX11 0EZ. *T:* (01235) 835454. *Clubs:* Clarendon, Frewen (Oxford).

RAMMELL, William Ernest; MP (Lab) Harlow, since 1997; *b* 10 Oct. 1959; *s* of William Ernest Rammell and Joan Elizabeth Rammell; *m* 1983, Beryl Jarhall; one *s* one *d. Educ:* University Coll., Cardiff (BA French). Pres., Cardiff Students' Union, 1982–83; mgt trainee, BR, 1983–84; NUS Regl Official, 1984–87; Hd of Youth Services, Basildon Council, 1987–89; Gen. Manager, Students' Union, KCL, 1989–94; Sen. Univ. Business Manager, Univ. of London, 1994–97. Chm., Lab Movt for Europe. *Recreations:* football, cricket, socialising. *Address:* House of Commons, SW1A 0AA. *T:* (020) 7219 1205; 9 Orchard Croft, Harlow, Essex CM20 3BA. *T:* (01279) 439706.

RAMOS, Gen. Fidel Valdez; President of the Philippines, 1992–98; *b* 18 March 1928; *s* of Narciso Ramos and Angela (*née* Valdez); *m* Amelita Martinez; five *d. Educ:* Nat. Univ. of Manila; USMA W Point; Univ. of Illinois. Active service in Korea and Vietnam; Dep. Chief of Staff, 1981, Chief of Staff, 1986, Philippines Armed Forces; Sec. of Nat. Defence, 1988. Leader, People's Power Party. Légion d'honneur (France), 1987. *Address:* 26/F Urban Bank Plaza, Urban Avenue, Makati City, Philippines; 120 Maria Cristina Street, Ayala Alabang Village, Muntinlupa City, Philippines; *e-mail:* rpdeu@skyinet.net.

RAMOS-HORTA, José; Founder Director and Lecturer, Diplomacy Training Programme, since 1990, and Visiting Professor, since 1996, Law Faculty, University of New South Wales, Sydney; *b* Dili, E Timor, 26 Dec. 1949; *s* of late Francisco Horta and of Natalina Ramos Filipe Horta; *m* 1978, Ana Pessoa (marr. diss.); one *s. Educ:* Hague Acad. of Internat. Law; Internat. Inst. of Human Rights, Strasbourg; Columbia Univ., NY; Antioch Univ. (MA 1984). Journalist, radio and TV correspondent, 1969–74; Minister for Ext. Affairs and Inf., E Timor, Dec. 1975; Perm. Rep. for Fretilin to UN, NY, 1976–89; Public Affairs and Media Dir, Embassy of Mozambique, Washington, 1987–88; Special Rep. of Nat. Council of Maubere Resistance, 1991–. Member: Peace Action Council, Unrepresented Nations and Peoples Orgn, The Hague (UNPO Award, 1996); Exec. Council, Internat. Service for Human Rights, Geneva; Bd, E Timor Human Rights Centre, Melbourne. Sen. Associate Mem., St Antony's Coll., Oxford, 1987–. Nobel Peace Prize (jtly), 1996. Order of Freedom (Portugal), 1996. *Publications:* Funu: the unfinished saga of East Timor, 1987; contrib. to newspapers and periodicals in Portugal, France, USA and Australia. *Recreation:* tennis. *Address:* (office) Rua São Lazaro 16, 1°, 1150 Lisbon, Portugal. *T:* (1) 8863727, *Fax:* (1) 8863791.

RAMPHAL, Sir Shridath Surendranath, OE 1983; GCMG 1990 (CMG 1966); OM (Jamaica) 1990; OCC 1991; Kt 1970; QC (Guyana) 1965, SC 1966; Co-Chairman, Commission on Global Governance, since 1992; Chief Negotiator on External Economic Relations in the Caribbean Region, since 1997; Secretary-General of the Commonwealth, 1975–90; *b* 3 Oct. 1928; *m. Educ:* King's Coll., London (LLM 1952). FKC 1975; Fellow, LSE, 1979. Called to the Bar, Gray's Inn, 1951 (Hon. Bencher 1981). Colonial Legal Probationer, 1951; Arden and Atkin Prize, 1952; John Simon Guggenheim Fellow, Harvard Law Sch., 1962. Crown Counsel, British Guiana, 1953–54; Asst to Attorney-Gen., 1954–56; Legal Draftsman, 1956–58; First Legal Draftsman, West Indies, 1958–59; Solicitor-Gen., British Guiana, 1959–61; Asst Attorney-Gen., West Indies, 1961–62, Attorney-Gen., Guyana, 1965–73; Minister of State for External Affairs, Guyana, 1967–72; Foreign Minister and Attorney General, Guyana, 1972–73; Minister, Foreign Affairs and Justice, 1973–75; Mem., National Assembly, Guyana, 1965–75. Member: Independent (Brandt) Commn on International Development Issues, 1977–83; Ind. (Palme) Commn on Disarmament and Security Issues, 1980–89; Ind. Commn on Internat. Humanitarian Issues, 1983–88; World (Brundtland) Commn on Environment and Develt, 1984–87; South Commn, 1987–90; Carnegie Commn on Preventing Deadly Conflict, 1994–98; Chm., W Indian Commn, 1990–92. Special Advr, Sec. Gen., UN Conf. on Envmt and Develt, 1992; Chm., UN Cttee on Develt Planning, 1984–87. Chairman: Internat. Adv. Cttee, Future Generations Alliance Foundn, Kyoto, 1994–97; Bd, Internat.Inst. for Democracy and Electoral Assistance, Stockholm, 1995–2001; Pres., Internat. Steering Cttee, Leadership in Envmt and Develt, 1991–98; Member: Bd, Internat. Develt Res. Centre, Ottawa, 1994–98; Council, Internat. Negotiating Network, Carter Centre, Atlanta 98, 1991–97. Mem., Internat. Commn of Jurists, 1970–. Chancellor: Univ. of Guyana, 1988–92; Univ. of Warwick, 1989–; Univ. of WI, 1989–. Visiting Professor: Exeter Univ., 1988; Faculty of Laws, KCL, 1988. Toronto Univ., 1995; Osgoode Hall Law Sch., Univ. of York, Toronto, 1995. FRSA 1981; CIMgt (CBIM 1986). Hon. Fellow, Magdalen Coll., Oxford, 1982; Companion, Leicester Poly., 1991. Hon. LLD: Panjab, 1975; Southampton, 1976; St Francis Xavier, NS, 1978; Univ. of WI, 1978; Aberdeen, 1979; Cape Coast, Ghana, 1980; London, 1981; Benin, Nigeria, 1982; Hull, 1983; Yale, 1985; Cambridge, 1985; Warwick, 1988; York, Ont, 1988; Malta, 1989; Otago, 1990; DUniv: Surrey, 1979; Essex, 1980; Hon. DHL: Simmons Coll., Boston, 1982; Duke Univ., 1985; Hon. DCL: Oxon, 1982; E Anglia, 1983; Durham, 1985; Hon. DLitt: Bradford, 1985; Indira Gandhi Nat. Open Univ., New Delhi, 1989; Hon. DSc Cranfield Inst. of Technology, 1987. Albert Medal, RSA, 1988; Internat. Educn Award, Richmond Coll., 1988; Rene Dubos Human Envmt Award, 1993. AC 1982; ONZ 1990; Comdr, Order of Golden Ark (Netherlands), 1994. *Publications:* One World to Share: selected speeches of the Commonwealth Secretary-General 1975–79, 1979; Nkrumah and the Eighties: Kwame Nkrumah Memorial Lectures, 1980; Sovereignty and Solidarity: Callander Memorial Lectures, 1981; Some in Light and Some in Darkness: the long shadow of slavery (Wilberforce Lecture), 1983; The Message not the Messenger (STC Communication Lecture), 1985; The Trampling of the Grass (Economic Commn for Africa Silver Jubilee Lecture), 1985; Inseparable Humanity: an anthology of reflections of Shridath Ramphal (ed Ron Sanders), 1988; An End to Otherness (eight speeches by the Commonwealth Secretary-General), 1990; Our Country, The Planet, 1992; contrib. various political, legal and other jls incl. International and Comparative Law Qly, Caribbean Qly, Public Law, Guyana Jl, Round Table, Foreign Policy, Third World Qly, RSA Jl Internat. Affairs. *Address:* 31 St Matthew's Lodge, 50 Oakley Square, NW1 1NB. *Clubs:* Athenæum, Royal Automobile, Travellers.

RAMPHUL, Sir Indurduth, Kt 1991; Governor, Bank of Mauritius, 1982–96; *b* 10 Oct. 1931; *m* 1962, Taramatee Seedoyal; one *s* one *d. Educ:* Univ. of Exeter (Dip. Public Admin). Asst Sec., Min. of Finance, 1966–67; Bank of Mauritius: Manager, 1967; Chief Manager, 1970; Man. Dir, 1973. Alternate Governor, IMF for Mauritius, 1982–96. *Recreations:* reading, swimming. *Address:* 9 Buswell Avenue, Quatre Bornes, Mauritius. *T:* 4541643, *Fax:* 4540559; *e-mail:* sirindur@internet.mu. *Clubs:* Mauritius Turf; Cadets.

RAMSAY, family name of **Earl of Dalhousie**.

RAMSAY OF CARTVALE, Baroness *cr* 1996 (Life Peer), of Langside in the City of Glasgow; **Meta Ramsay;** international affairs consultant; *b* 12 July 1936; *d* of Alexander Ramsay and Sheila Ramsay (*née* Jackson). *Educ:* Hutchesons' Girls' Grammar Sch.; Univ. of Glasgow (MA; MEd); Graduate Inst. of Internat. Studies, Geneva. President: Students' Rep. Council, Univ. of Glasgow, 1958–59; Scottish Union of Students, 1959–60; Associate Sec. for Europe, Co-ordinating Secretariat, Nat. Unions of Students, Leiden, Netherlands, 1960–63; Manager, Fund for Internat. Student Co-operation, 1963–67; HM Diplomatic Service, 1969–91: Stockholm, 1970–73; Helsinki, 1981–85; Counsellor, FCO, 1987–91. Foreign Policy Advr to Leader of Opposition, 1992–94; Special Advr to Shadow Sec. of State for Trade and Industry, 1994–95; a Baroness in Waiting (Govt Whip), 1997–2001. Mem., Labour Finance and Industry Gp, 1997–. Co-Chair, Scottish Constitutional Convention, 1997–. Hon. Vis. Res. Fellow in Peace Studies, Univ. of Bradford, 1996. Mem., Lewisham CHC, 1992–94. Chm., Bd of Governors, Fairlawn Primary Sch., Lewisham, 1991–97. Member: RIIA; Inst. of Jewish Policy Res.; Fabian Soc.; Labour Movement in Europe; Cooperative Party. FRSA 1995. Hon. DLitt Bradford, 1997. *Recreations:* theatre, opera, ballet. *Address:* House of Lords, SW1A 0PW. *T:* (020) 7219 5353. *Clubs:* Reform, University Women's; Royal Scottish Automobile (Glasgow).

RAMSAY, Lord; Simon David Ramsay; *b* 18 April 1981; *s* and *heir* of Earl of Dalhousie, *qv. Educ:* Harrow. *Recreations:* history of art and design, sculpture, country sports. *Address:* Brechin Castle, Brechin, Angus DD9 6SH.

RAMSAY, Sir Alexander William Burnett, 7th Bt *cr* 1806, of Balmain (also *heir-pres.* to Btcy of Burnett, *cr* 1626 (Nova Scotia), of Leys, Kincardineshire, which became dormant, 1959, on death of Sir Alexander Edwin Burnett of Leys, and was not claimed by Sir Alexander Burnett Ramsay, 6th Bt, of Balmain); *b* 4 Aug. 1938; *s* of Sir Alexander Burnett Ramsay, 6th Bt and Isabel Ellice, *e d* of late William Whitney, Woodstock, New South Wales; *S* father, 1965; *m* 1963, Neryl Eileen, *d* of J. C. Smith Thornton, Trangie, NSW; three *s. Heir: s* Alexander David Ramsay [*b* 20 Aug. 1966; *m* 1990, Annette Yvonne, *d* of H. M. Plummer; two *d*]. *Address:* Bulbah, Warren, NSW 2824, Australia.

RAMSAY, Sir Allan (John Heppel Ramsay), KBE 1992; CMG 1989; HM Diplomatic Service, retired; Ambassador to the Kingdom of Morocco, 1992–96; *b* 19 Oct. 1937; *s* of Norman Ramsay Ramsay and Evelyn Faith Sorel-Cameron; *m* 1966, Pauline Therèse Lescher; two *s* one *d. Educ:* Bedford Sch.; RMA Sandhurst; Durham Univ. Served Army, 1957–70: Somerset Light Infantry, 1957–64; Trucial Oman Scouts, 1964–66; DLI, 1966–68. MECAS, 1968–69; entered FCO, 1970; First Sec. (Commercial), Cairo, 1973–76; First Sec. and Hd of Chancery, Kabul, 1976–78; Counsellor and Head of Chancery: Baghdad, 1980–83; Mexico City, 1983–85; Ambassador: to Lebanon, 1988–90; to Sudan, 1990–91. *Address:* Le Genest, 53190 Landivy, France.

RAMSAY, Andrew Charles Bruce; Director, Creative Industries and Broadcasting Group, Department for Culture, Media and Sport, since 2000; *b* 30 May 1951; *s* of Norman Bruce Ramsay and Marysha Octavia Ramsay; *m* 1983, Katharine Celia Marsh; two *d. Educ:* Winchester Coll.; Bedford Coll., London Univ. (BA). Joined DoE, 1974; Private Sec. to Parly Sec., Dept of Transport, 1978–80; Principal, DoE and Dept of Transport, 1980–85; Asst Sec., DoE, 1986–93; Under Sec. and Head of Arts, Sport and Lottery Gp, DNH, 1993–96; Under Sec. and Hd of Finance, Lottery and Personnel, then Corporate Services, Gp, DNH then DCMS, 1996–2000. *Recreations:* gardening, opera, birds. *Address:* Department for Culture, Media and Sport, 2–4 Cockspur Street, SW1Y 5DH; West Hall, Sedgeford, Hunstanton, Norfolk PE36 5LY.

RAMSAY, Maj.-Gen. Charles Alexander, CB 1989; OBE 1979; landowner and farmer; *b* 12 Oct. 1936; *s* of Adm. Sir Bertram Home Ramsay, KCB, KBE, MVO, Allied Naval C-in-C, Invasion of Europe, 1944 (killed on active service, 1945), and Helen Margaret Menzies; *m* 1967, Hon. Mary MacAndrew, *d* of 1st Baron MacAndrew, PC, TD; two *s* two *d. Educ:* Eton; Sandhurst. Commissioned Royal Scots Greys, 1956; attended Canadian Army Staff Coll., 1967–68; served abroad in Germany, Middle East and Far East; Mil. Asst to VCDS, 1974–77; commanded Royal Scots Dragoon Guards, 1977–79; Colonel General Staff, MoD, 1979–80; Comdr 12th Armoured Bde, BAOR and Osnabrück Garrison, 1980–82; Dep. Dir of Mil. Ops, MoD, 1983–84; GOC Eastern District, 1984–87; Dir Gen., Army Orgn and TA, 1987–89; resigned from Army. Col, Royal Scots Dragoon Guards, 1992–98. Director: John Menzies plc, 1990–; Potomac Hldgs Inc., USA; Morningside Mgt LLC USA, and other cos; Chairman: Eagle Enterprises Ltd, Bermuda, 1991–95; Cockburns of Leith, 1992–. Member, Queen's Body Guard for Scotland, Royal Company of Archers. *Recreations:* field sports, equitation, travel, motoring, aviation. *Address:* Bughtrig, Coldstream, Berwickshire TD12 4JP. *T:* (01890) 840678; Chesthill, Glenlyon, Perthshire PH15 2NH. *T:* (01887) 877224. *Clubs:* Boodle's, Cavalry and Guards, Pratt's; New (Edinburgh).

RAMSAY, Donald Allan, CM 1997; ScD; FRS 1978; FRSC 1966; Principal Research Officer, National Research Council of Canada, 1968–87; *b* 11 July 1922; *s* of Norman Ramsay and Thirza Elizabeth Beckley; *m* 1946, Nancy Brayshaw (*d* 1998); four *d*; *m* 2000, Marjorie Craven Findlay. *Educ:* Latymer Upper Sch.; St Catharine's Coll., Cambridge. BA 1943, MA 1947, PhD 1947, ScD 1976 (all Cantab). Research Scientist, National Research

Council of Canada: Div. of Chemistry, 1947–49; Div. of Physics, 1949–75; Herzberg Inst. of Astrophysics, 1975–94; Steacie Inst. of Molecular Scis, 1994–. Fellow, Amer. Phys. Soc., 1964; FCIC 1970 (CIC Medal, 1992); Vice-Pres., Acad. of Science, 1975–76; Hon. Treas., RSC, 1976–79, 1988–91 (Centennial Medal, 1982). Alexander von Humboldt Res. Award, 1993–95. Dr *hc* Reims, 1969; Fil.Hed. Stockholm, 1982. Silver Jubilee Medal, 1977; Commemorative Medal for 125th anniversary of Canadian Confederation, 1992. *Publications:* numerous articles on molecular spectroscopy and molecular structure, espec. free radicals. *Recreations:* sailing, fishing, organ playing. *Address:* 4000 Laurier Avenue East, Apt 11, Ottawa, ON K1N 8Y2, Canada. *T:* (613) 2376667. *Club:* Leander (Henley).

RAMSAY, Gordon James; Chef and Patron, Gordon Ramsay Restaurant, since 1998; *b* 8 Nov. 1966; *s* of Gordon Scott Ramsay and Helen Ramsay (*née* Mitchell); *m* 1996, Cayetana Elizabeth Hutcheson; one *s* two *d* (of whom one *s* one *d* are twins). *Educ:* Stratford-upon-Avon High Sch.; North Oxon Tech. Coll., Banbury (HND Hotel Mgt 1987). Professional footballer, Glasgow Rangers FC, 1982–85; worked: with Marco Pierre White at Harvey's, 1989–91; with Albert Roux at La Gavroche, 1992–93; in Paris kitchens of Guy Savoy and Joël Robuchon, 1993–94; opened Aubergine restaurant, 1994 (Michelin Star, 1995, 1997); opened Gordon Ramsay Restaurant, Chelsea, 1998 (Michelin Star, 2001). *Publications:* Passion for Flavour, 1996; (with R. Denny) Passion for Seafood, 1999; A Chef for All Seasons, 2000; Just Desserts, 2001. *Recreations:* salmon fishing, scuba diving, long distance running. *Address:* Gordon Ramsay Restaurants Ltd, 68 Royal Hospital Road, SW3 4HP. *T:* (020) 7352 4441; (office) 208 Fulham Road, SW10 9PJ.

RAMSAY, Prof. John Graham, CBE 1992; FRS 1973; Professor of Geology, Eidgenössische Technische Hochschule and University of Zürich, 1977–92, now Professor Emeritus; *b* 17 June 1931; *s* of Robert William Ramsay and Kathleen May Ramsay; *m* 1st, 1952, Sylvia Hiorns (marr. diss. 1957); 2nd, 1960, Christine Marden (marr. diss. 1987); three *d* (and one *d* decd); 3rd, 1990, Dorothee Dietrich. *Educ:* Edmonton County Grammar Sch.; Imperial Coll., London. DSc, PhD, DIC, BSc, ARCS, FGS. Musician, Corps of Royal Engineers, 1955–57; academic staff Imperial Coll., London, 1957–73: Prof. of Geology, 1966–73; Prof. of Earth Sciences, Leeds Univ., 1973–76. Mem., NERC, 1989–92. Vice-Pres., Société Géologique de France, 1973. For. Associate, US Nat. Acad. of Scis, 1985. Dr *hc* Rennes, 1978. *Publications:* Folding and Fracturing of Rocks, 1967; The Techniques of Modern Structural Geology, vol. 1, 1983, vol. 2, 1987, vol. 3, 2000. *Recreations:* chamber music, ski-ing, writing poetry. *Address:* Cratoule, Issirac, 30760 St Julien de Peyrolas, France.

RAMSAY, Jonathan William Alexander, FRCS; Consultant Urologist: Charing Cross Hospital, since 1988; West Middlesex Hospital, since 1988; *b* 27 Oct. 1953; *s* of Raymond Ramsay, MBE, FRCS and Lillian Jane Ramsay (*née* Bateman); *m* 1983, Priscilla Jaqueline Russell Webster; two *s* one *d*. *Educ:* Bradfield Coll.; St Bartholomew's Hosp. Med. Coll. (MB BS, MS). FRCS 1981. Qualified, St Bartholomew's Hosp. (Brackenbury Schol.), 1977; Chief Asst (Urology), St Bartholomew's, 1985–88; Hon. Consultant Urologist: St Luke's Hosp. for Clergy, 1989–; King Edward VII Hosp., London, 1996–. Royal College of Surgeons: Regl Specialty Advr, 1995–; Mem., Court of Examrs, 1997–; Regl Advr, 1999–. President: W London Medico-Chirurgical Soc., 1999; Eur. Intrarenal Surgery Soc., 1999–. Fellow, Eur. Bd of Urology, 1991. *Publications:* contribs on treatment of stones by minimally invasive techniques. *Recreations:* fishing, sailing. *Address:* Yew Trees House, Southlea Road, Datchet SL3 9BY; 149 Harley Street, W1N 1HG. *Clubs:* Athenæum, Royal Society of Medicine.

RAMSAY, Patrick George Alexander; Controller, BBC Scotland, 1979–83; retired; *b* 14 April 1926; *yr s* of late Rt Rev. Ronald Erskine Ramsay, sometime Bishop of Malmesbury, and Winifred Constance Ramsay (*née* Partridge); *m* 1948, Hope Seymour Dorothy, *y d* of late Rt Rev. Algernon Markham, sometime Bishop of Grantham, and Winifred Edith Markham (*née* Barne); two *s*. *Educ:* Marlborough Coll.; Jesus Coll., Cambridge (MA). Served War, Royal Navy (Fleet Air Arm), 1944–46. Joined BBC as Report Writer, Eastern European Desk, Monitoring Service, 1949; Liaison Officer, US Foreign Broadcasts Information Service, Cyprus, 1951–52; Asst, Appts Dept, 1953–56; Sen. Admin. Asst, External Broadcasting, 1956–58; Admin. Officer News and Head of News Administration, 1958–64; Planning Manager, Television Programme Planning, 1964–66; Asst Controller: Programme Services, 1966–69; Programme Planning, 1969–72; Controller, Programme Services, 1972–79. General Managerial Advr, Oman Broadcasting Service, 1984–85. A Dir, Windsor Festival Soc., 1973–76. Councillor and Alderman, Royal Borough of New Windsor, 1962–67; Chm., Windsor and Eton Soc., 1971–76. FRSA. *Recreations:* fellwalking, gardening, foreign travel, history, looking in junk shops, thwarting bureaucrats. *Address:* Abcott Manor, Clungunford, Shropshire SY7 0PX.

RAMSAY, Richard Alexander McGregor; Managing Director for Regulation and Financial Affairs, Office of Gas and Electricity Supply (OFGEM), since 2001; *b* 27 Dec. 1949; *s* of Alexander John McGregor Ramsay and Beatrice Kent Lanauze; *m* 1975, Elizabeth Catherine Margaret Blackwood; one *s* one *d*. *Educ:* Dalhousie Sch.; Trinity Coll., Glenalmond; Aberdeen Univ. (MA Hons in Politics and Sociology). ACA 1975; FCA. Price Waterhouse & Co., 1972–75; Grindlay Brandts, 1976–78; Hill Samuel & Co. Ltd, 1979–87 (Dir, 1984–87); on secondment as Dir, Industrial Develt Unit, DTI, 1984–86; Dir, 1988–93, Man. Dir, Corporate Finance Div., 1991–93, Barclays De Zoete Wedd; Director: Ivory & Sime, 1993–94; Ivory & Sime Investment Mgt, 1994–96; Finance Dir, Aberdeen FC, 1997–2000. *Recreations:* hill walking, ski-ing, classic cars, gardening. *Address:* The Little Priory, Sandy Lane, South Nutfield, Surrey RH1 4EJ. *T:* (01737) 822329.

RAMSAY, Robert, CMG 2000; DPhil; Director General for Research, European Parliament, 1989–99; *b* 11 Sept. 1940; *s* of Robert and Mabel Hamilton Ramsay; *m* 1963, Patricia Buckley; four *s* (and one *s* decd). *Educ:* Royal Belfast Academical Instn; Queen's Univ., Belfast (BA Hons); Univ. of Ulster (DPhil 1979). Commonwealth Fellow, Victoria Univ. of Wellington, 1963–65; entered NICS, 1965; Principal Private Sec. to Prime Minister, 1971–72; European Dir, Inward Investment, Brussels, 1972–74; Sec. to Economic Council, 1974–76; Principal Private Sec. to Sec. of State for NI, 1976–78; Under Sec., DoE, 1978–83; Sec. Gen., EDG, EP, 1983–87; Dir, President's Office, EP, 1987–89. Leverhulme Fellow, 1978. *Publication:* The Corsican Time Bomb, 1983. *Recreations:* sailing, European literature. *e-mail:* ramsayrobert@hotmail.com. *Club:* Carlton.

RAMSAY-FAIRFAX-LUCY, Sir Edmund John William Hugh Cameron; *see* Fairfax-Lucy.

RAMSBOTHAM, family name of **Viscount Soulbury**.

RAMSBOTHAM, Gen. Sir David (John), GCB 1993 (KCB 1987); CBE 1980 (OBE 1974); HM Chief Inspector of Prisons for England and Wales, 1995–2001; *b* 6 Nov. 1934; *s* of Rt Rev. J. A. Ramsbotham; *m* 1958, Susan Caroline (*née* Dickinson); two *s*. *Educ:* Haileybury Coll.; Corpus Christi Coll., Cambridge (BA 1957, M 2001). Nat. Service, 1952–54; Rifle Bde, UK and BAOR, 1958–6 1962–63; Staff Coll., 1964; Rifle Bde, Far East, 1965; Staff, 7 Armou and 2 Green Jackets (BAOR), 1968–71; MA to CGS (Lt-Col), 197 1974–76; Staff, 4 Armd Div., BAOR, 1976–78; Comd, 39 Infantry RCDS, 1981; Dir of Public Relns (Army), 1982–84; Comdr, 3 Armd Comdr, UK Field Army and Inspector Gen., TA, 1987–90; Adjt Gen., 1 Gen. to the Queen, 1990–93. Dir of Internat. Affairs, DSL Ltd, 199 Hillingdon Hosp. NHS Trust, 1995. Mem. Council, IISS, 1996–. Col C Battalion, The Royal Green Jackets, 1987–92; Hon. Col, Cambridge Un 1987–93. FRSA 1999; FCGI 2000. Hon. DCL Huddersfield, 1999. *Recreations* shooting, gardening. *Clubs:* Athenæum, MCC.

RAMSBOTHAM, Hon. Sir Peter (Edward), GCMG 1978 (KCMG 1972; C 1964); GCVO 1976; DL; HM Diplomatic Service, retired; *b* 8 Oct. 1919; *yr s* of Viscount Soulbury, PC, GCMG, GCVO, OBE, MC; *b* and *heir pres.* to 2nd Viscou Soulbury, *qv*; *m* 1st, 1941, Frances Blomfield (*d* 1982); two *s* (one *d* decd); 2nd, 1985, D Zaida Hall, *widow* of Ruthven Hall. *Educ:* Eton College; Magdalen College, Oxford (Hon. Fellow, 1991). Intelligence Corps, Europe, 1943–46 (Lt-Col; despatches; Croix de Guerre, 1945). Control Office for Germany and Austria from 1947; Regional Political Officer in Hamburg; entered Foreign Service, Oct. 1948; Political Division of Allied Control Commission, Berlin, Nov. 1948; transferred to Foreign Office, 1950; 1st Secretary, 1950; Head of Chancery, UK Delegation, New York, 1953; Foreign Office, 1957; Counsellor, 1961, Head of Western Organisations and Planning Dept; Head of Chancery, British Embassy, Paris, 1963–67; Foreign Office, 1967–69 (Sabbatical year, Inst. of Strategic Studies, 1968); High Comr, Cyprus, 1969–71; Ambassador to Iran, 1971–74; Ambassador to the United States, 1974–77; Governor and C-in-C of Bermuda, 1977–80. Director: Lloyds Bank, 1981–90; Lloyds Bank Internat., 1981–83; Southern Regl Bd, Lloyds Bank, 1981–90 (Chm., 1983–90); Commercial Union Assurance Co., 1981–90. Trustee, Leonard Cheshire Foundn, 1981–94; Chairman: Ryder-Cheshire Foundn for the Relief of Suffering, 1982–99; World Meml Fund for Disaster Relief, 1992–96 (Trustee, 1989–); Gov., Ditchley Foundn, 1978–. Pres., British-American-Canadian Associates, 1994–97. Governor, King's Sch., Canterbury, 1981–90. DL Hants, 1992. Hon. LLD: Akron Univ., 1975; Coll. of William and Mary, 1975; Maryland Univ., 1976; Yale Univ., 1977. KStJ 1976. *Recreations:* gardening, fishing. *Address:* East Lane, Ovington, near Alresford, Hants SO24 0RA. *T:* (01962) 732515. *Clubs:* Garrick; Metropolitan (Washington).

RAMSBURY, Area Bishop of, since 1999; **Rt Rev. Peter Fearnley Hullah;** *b* 7 May 1949; *s* of Ralph and Mary Hullah; *m* 1971, Hilary Sargent Long; one *s* one *d*. *Educ:* Bradford Grammar Sch.; King's Coll., London (BD, AKC); Makerere Univ., Kampala; Cuddesdon Coll., Oxford. Curate, St Michael and All Angels, Summertown, Oxford, 1974–77; Asst Chaplain, St Edward's Sch., Oxford, 1974–77; Chaplain, 1977–82, Housemaster, 1982–87, Internat. Centre, Sevenoaks Sch.; Sen. Chaplain, King's Sch., Canterbury, 1987–92; Headmaster, Chetham's Sch. of Music, 1992–99. Chm., Chaplains' Conf., 1987–92. Canon, Manchester Cathedral, 1995–99. Chm., Salisbury Sudan Link, 2000–. Chm. Trustees, Bloxham Project, 1999– (Mem., 1979–99, Chm., 1996–99, Steering Cttee). Governor: Dauntsey's Sch., 1999–; De Montfort Univ., 1999–; Marlborough Coll., 2000–; Malvern Coll., 2000–. FRSA 1993. *Recreations:* pilgrimage, music, reaching the highest point in Africa. *Address:* Bishop's Croft, Winterbourne Earls, Salisbury SP4 6HJ. *T:* (01380) 840373, *Fax:* (01380) 848247; *e-mail:* hullahp@aol.com. *Club:* Athenæum.

RAMSDEN, Prof. Herbert, MA, Dr en Filosofía y Letras; Professor of Spanish Language and Literature, University of Manchester, 1961–82, now Emeritus; *b* 20 April 1927; *s* of Herbert and Ann Ramsden; *m* 1953, Joyce Robina Hall, SRN, ONC, CMB; three *s* (incl. twin *s*) twin *d*. *Educ:* Sale Grammar Sch.; Univs of Manchester, Strasbourg, Madrid and Sorbonne. National Service, Inf. and Intell. Corps, 1949–51 (commnd). Travel, study and research abroad (Kemsley Travelling Fellow, etc), 1951–54; University of Manchester: Asst Lectr in Spanish, 1954–57; Lectr in Spanish, 1957–61; Pres., Philological Club, 1966–68. British Hispanists' rep., Nat. Council for Modern Languages, 1972–73; British rep., Asociación Europea de Profesores de Español, 1975–80. *Publications:* An Essential Course in Modern Spanish, 1959; Weak-Pronoun Position in the Early Romance Languages, 1963; (ed with critical study) Azorín, La ruta de Don Quijote, 1966; Angel Ganivet's Idearium español: A Critical Study, 1967; The Spanish Generation of 1898, 1974; The 1898 Movement in Spain, 1974; (ed with critical study) Lorca, Bodas de sangre, 1980; Pío Baroja: La busca, 1982; Pío Baroja: La busca 1903 to La busca 1904, 1982; (ed with critical study) Lorca, La casa de Bernarda Alba, 1983; Lorca's Romancero gitano, 1988; (ed, with critical study) Lorca, Romancero gitano, 1988; articles in Bulletin of Hispanic Studies, Modern Language Review, Modern Languages, etc. *Recreations:* family, hill-walking, foreign travel. *Address:* 7 Burford Avenue, Bramhall, Stockport, Cheshire SK7 1BL. *T:* (0161) 439 4306.

RAMSDEN, Rt Hon. James Edward; PC 1963; President, Northern Horticultural Society, since 1996; *b* 1 Nov. 1923; *s* of late Capt. Edward Ramsden, MC, and Geraldine Ramsden, OBE, Breckamore Hall, Ripon; *m* 1949, Juliet Barbara Anna, *y d* of late Col Sir Charles Ponsonby, 1st Bt, TD, and Hon. Lady Ponsonby, *d* of 1st Baron Hunsdon; three *s* two *d*. *Educ:* Eton; Trinity College, Oxford (MA). Commnd KRRC, 1942; served North-West Europe with Rifle Brigade, 1944–45. MP (C) Harrogate, WR Yorks, March 1954–Feb. 1974; PPS to Home Secretary, Nov. 1959–Oct. 1960; Under-Sec. and Financial Sec., War Office, Oct. 1960–Oct. 1963; Sec. of State for War, 1963–64; Minister of Defence for the Army, April-Oct. 1964. Director: UK Board, Colonial Mutual Life Assurance Society, 1966–72; Standard Telephones and Cables, 1971–81; Prudential Assurance Co. Ltd, 1972–91 (Dep. Chm., 1976–82); Prudential Corp. Ltd, 1979–91 (Dep. Chm., 1979–82). Dir, London Clinic, 1973–96 (Chm., 1984–96). Mem., Historic Buildings Council for England, 1971–72. *Address:* Old Sleningford Hall, Ripon, North Yorks HG4 3JD. *T:* (01765) 635229, *Fax:* (01765) 635485. *Club:* Pratt's.

RAMSDEN, Sir John (Charles Josslyn), 9th Bt *cr* 1689, of Byram, Yorks; HM Diplomatic Service; Head, Central and North West Europe Department, Foreign and Commonwealth Office, since 1999; *b* 19 Aug. 1950; *s* of Sir Caryl Oliver Imbert Ramsden, 8th Bt, CMG, CVO, and of Anne, *d* of Sir Charles Wickham, KCMG, KBE, DSO; *S* father, 1987; *m* 1985, (Jennifer) Jane Bevan; two *d*. *Educ:* Eton; Trinity Coll., Cambridge (MA). With merchant bank, Dawnay, Day & Co. Ltd, 1972–74. Entered FCO, 1975; 2nd Sec., Dakar, 1976; 1st Sec., MBFR, Vienna, 1978; 1st Sec., Head of Chancery and Consul, Hanoi, 1980; FCO, 1982–90; Counsellor, E Berlin, 1990; Counsellor and Dep. Hd of Mission, Berlin, 1991–93; Hd, Information Dept, FCO, 1993–96; UK Dep. Perm. Rep. to UN, Geneva, 1996–99. *Heir: kinsman* Colin John Ramsden [*b* 22 Jan. 1949; *m* 1st, 1976, Kim O'Halloran (marr. diss); one *s* one *d*; 2nd, 1994, Sandra Robinson; one *d*]. *Address:* c/o Foreign and Commonwealth Office, King Charles Street, SW1A 2AH.

RAMSDEN, (John) Michael; Editor of Publications, Royal Aeronautical Society, 1989–93; *b* 2 Oct. 1928; *s* of John Leonard Ramsden and Edith Alexandra Ramsden; *m* 1953, Angela Mary Mortimer; one *s* one *d*. *Educ:* Bedford Sch.; de Havilland Aeronautical Tech. Sch. CEng, FRAeS. With de Havilland Aircraft Co. Ltd, 1946–55; Flight, 1955–89: Air Transport Editor, 1961–64; Editor, 1964–81; Editor-in-Chief, Flight International, 1981–89. Chm., Press and Broadcasting Side, Defence Press and Broadcasting Cttee, 1983–89. Dir, de Havilland Aircraft Mus., 1970–. Trustee, Geoffrey de Havilland Flying Foundn, 1992–. Cumberbatch Trophy, GAPAN, 1981; Wakefield Gold Medal, RAeS, 1987; Douglas Weightman Award, Flight Safety Cttee, 1988. Silver Jubilee Medal, 1977. *Publications:* The Safe Airline, 1976, 2nd edn 1978 (Publications Award, Flight Safety Foundn, 1976); Caring for the Mature Jet, 1981. *Recreations:* light-aircraft flying, water-colour painting. *Club:* London School of Flying (Elstree).

RAMSDEN, Michael; *see* Ramsden, J. M.

RAMSDEN, Prof. Richard Thomas, FRCS; Consultant Otolaryngologist, Manchester Royal Infirmary, since 1977; Professor of Otolaryngology, University of Manchester, since 1994; *b* 30 Dec. 1944; *s* of Thomas William Ramsden and Elaine Napier Ramsden (*née* Meikle); *m* 1st, 1968, Wendy Margaret Johnson (marr. diss.); one *s* two *d*; 2nd, 1987, Eileen Gillian Richardson (*née* Whitehurst); two step *s*. *Educ:* Madras Coll., St Andrews; St Andrews Univ. (MB ChB 1968). FRCS 1972. Registrar in Otolaryngol., 1972–74, Sen. Registrar, 1974–75, RNTNEH; Sen. Registrar, Otolaryngol., London Hosp., 1975–77. TWJ Travelling Fellow to N America, 1978. Lectures: Subramaniam, Indian Soc. of Otolaryngol., McBride, Univ. of Edinburgh, 1987; Dalby, Otology Section, RSocMed, 1992; Younis, Pakistan Soc. of Otolaryngol., 1993; Wilde, Irish Otolaryngol Soc., Graham Fraser, Otology Section, RSocMed, 1994; Goldman, Groote Schoor Hosp., Univ. of Cape Town, 1998; Yearsley, RCS, 2001. FRCSE (*ad hominem*) 2000. Hon. Mem., German, Irish and Danish ENT socs. Dalby Prize, W. J. Harrison Prize, RSocMed; Jobson Horne Prize, BMA. *Publications:* chapters on aspects of otology and neuro-otology; contrib. learned jls of otology and neuro-otology. *Recreation:* none (sadly). *Address:* Anson Medical Centre, 23 Anson Road, Manchester M14 5BZ. *T:* (0161) 224 2022. *Clubs:* Royal Society of Medicine; Wilmslow Golf; St Andrews New Golf; St Andrews Society of Manchester (Pres.).

RAMSEY, Basil Albert Rowland; Editor, Music & Vision, since 1999; *b* 26 April 1929; *s* of Florence Lily Ramsey (*née* Childs) and Alfred John Rowland Ramsey; *m* 1953, Violet Mary Simpson; one *s* two *d*. *Educ:* State schools. ARCO. Novello & Co.: Music Editor, 1949; Head of Publishing, 1963; established own publishing Co., 1976; Serious Music Publishing Consultant, Filmtrax plc, 1987–90. Editor: Organists' Review, 1972–84; Music & Musicians, 1989–90; The Musical Times, 1990–92; Choir & Organ, 1993–98. *Publications:* The Music of Charles Camilleri, 1996; articles and reviews in Musical Times, 1955–93; regular contributor to weekly and daily press on musical matters. *Recreations:* reading, calligraphy. *Address:* 604 Rayleigh Road, Eastwood, Leigh-on-Sea, Essex SS9 5HU. *T:* (01702) 524305.

RAMSEY, Brig. Gael Kathleen, CBE 1992 (MBE 1976); Chief Executive, British Executive Service Overseas, since 1997; *b* 8 June 1942; *d* of Lt Col William Hammond, MBE and Kathleen Hammond; *m* 1977 (marr. diss. 1996). *Educ:* Convent of Good Shepherd, Singapore; High Sch. for Girls, Worcester, Gloucester and Dover. Commissioned, WRAC, 1968; Dir, WRAC, 1989–92; ADC to the Queen, 1989–92; Dir Women (Army), 1992; Comdr, Aldershot Bde Area, 1992–95, retd. Dep. Col Comdt, AGC, 1998–. Mem., PRO-NED, 1995–. Freeman, City of London, 1991; Member: Guild of Freemen of City of London, 1992–; Council, WRAC Assoc., 1989– (Life Vice-Pres.). Mem., Wilton Park Acad. Council, 1998–. FInstD 1995. *Recreations:* golf, tennis, reading, needlework, travel, messing about with plants. *Address:* BESO, 164 Vauxhall Bridge Road, SW1V 2RB. *T:* (020) 7630 0644. *Clubs:* Army and Navy; Queen's.

RAMSEY, Prof. Norman Foster; Higgins Professor of Physics, Harvard University, since 1947; Senior Fellow, Harvard Society of Fellows, since 1971; *b* 27 Aug. 1915; *s* of Brig.-Gen. and Mrs Norman F. Ramsey; *m* 1940, Elinor Stedman Jameson (*d* 1983); four *d*; *m* 1985, Ellie A. Welch. *Educ:* Columbia Univ.; Cambridge Univ. (England). Carnegie Fellow, Carnegie Instn of Washington, 1939–40; Assoc., Univ. of Ill, 1940–42; Asst Prof., Columbia Univ., 1942–45; Research Assoc., MIT Radiation Laboratory, 1940–43; Cons. to Nat. Defense Research Cttee, 1940–45; Expert Consultant to Sec. of War, 1942–45; Grp Leader and Assoc. Div. Head, Los Alamos Lab. of Atomic Energy Project, 1943–45; Chief Scientist of Atomic Energy Lab. at Tinian, 1945; Assoc. Prof., Columbia Univ., 1945–47; Head of Physics Dept, Brookhaven Nat. Lab., 1946–47; Assoc. Prof., Harvard Univ., 1947–50; John Simon Guggenheim Fell., Oxford Univ., 1953–54; George Eastman Vis. Prof., Oxford Univ., 1973–74; Luce Prof. of Cosmology, Mt Holyoke, 1982–83; Prof., Univ. of Virginia, 1983–84. Dir Harvard Nuclear Lab., 1948–50, 1952; Chm., Harvard Nuclear Physics Cttee, 1948–60; Science Adviser, NATO, 1958–59; Fell. Amer. Phys. Soc. and Amer. Acad. of Arts and Sciences; Nat. Acad. of Sciences; Amer. Philos. Soc.; Foreign Associate, French Acad. of Science; Sigma Xi; Phi Beta Kappa; Amer. Assoc. for Advancement of Science, 1940– (Chm., Phys. Sect., 1976). Bd of Directors, Varian Associates, 1964–66; Bd of Trustees: Associated Univs; Brookhaven Nat. Lab., 1952–55; Carnegie Endowment for Internat. Peace; Univ. Research Assoc. (Pres., 1966–81, Pres. Emeritus 1981–); Rockefeller Univ., 1976–; Air Force Sci. Adv. Bd, 1948–54; Dept of Defense Panel on Atomic Energy, 1953–59; Bd of Editors of Review of Modern Physics, 1953–56; Chm. Exec. Cttee for Camb. Electron Accelerator, 1956–63; Coun. Amer. Phys. Soc., 1956–60 (Vice-Pres., 1977; Pres., 1978); Chm., Bd of Governors, Amer. Inst. of Physics, 1980–86. Gen. Adv. Cttee, Atomic Energy Commn, 1960–72. Chm., High Energy Accelerator Panel of President's Sci. Adv. Cttee and AEC, 1963. Chm. Bd, Physics and Astronomy Nat. Res. Council, 1986–89. Pres., Phi Beta Kappa, 1985 (Vice-Pres., 1982). Presidential Certificate of Merit, 1947; E. O. Lawrence Award, 1960; Davisson-Germer Prize, 1974; Award for Excellence, Columbia Univ. Graduate Alumni, 1980; Medal of Honor, IEEE, 1984; Rabi Prize, Frequency Control Symposium, IEEE, 1985; Monie Ferst Prize, Sigma Xi, 1985; Compton Award, Amer. Inst. of Physics, 1985; Rumford Premium, Amer. Acad. of Arts and Scis, 1985; Oersted Medal, Amer. Assoc. of Physics Teachers, 1988; Nat. Medal of Science, 1988; (jtly) Nobel Prize for Physics, 1989; Pupin Medal, Columbia Univ., 1992; Erice Science for Peace Prize, 1992; Einstein Medal, Optical and Quantum Electronics Soc., 1993; Vannevar Bush Award, US Nat. Sci. Bd, 1995; Alexander Hamilton Award, Columbia Univ., 1995. Hon. MA Harvard, 1947; Hon. ScD Cambridge, 1953; Hon. DSc: Case Western Reserve, 1968; Middlebury Coll., 1969; Oxford, 1973; Rockefeller Univ., 1986; Chicago, 1989; Houston, 1992; Michigan, 1993; Hon. DCL Oxford, 1990. *Publications:* Experimental Nuclear Physics, 1952; Nuclear Moments, 1953; Molecular Beams, 1956; Quick Calculus, 1965; Spectroscopy with Coherent Radiation, 1999; and numerous articles in Physical Review and other scientific jls. *Recreations:* tennis, ski-ing, walking, sailing, etc. *Address:* 24 Monmouth Court, Brookline, MA 02146, USA. *T:* (617) 2772313.

RAMSEY, Vivian Arthur; QC 1992; a Recorder, since 2000; *b* 24 May 1950; *s* of Rt Rev. Ian Thomas Ramsey and late Margretta Ramsey (*née* McKay); *m* 1974, Barbara Walker; two *s* two *d*. *Educ:* Harley Sch., Rochester, NY; Abingdon Sch., Oxon; Oriel Coll., Oxford (MA); City Univ. (Dip. Law). CEng, MICE 1977. Civil and Structural Engineer, Ove Arup & Partners, 1972–77, 1979–80; called to the Bar, Middle Temple, 1979; Barrister and Arbitrator, 1981–; Asst Recorder, 1998–2000. Special Prof., Dept of Civil Engineering, Nottingham Univ., 1990–. Chm., Swanley Action Gp, 1989–. Editor, Construction Law Jl, 1984–. *Publication:* (ed) Keating on Building Contracts, 7th edn, 2000. *Recreation:* building renovation. *Address:* Keating Chambers, 10 Essex Street, WC2R 3AA. *T:* (020) 7544 2600, *Fax:* (020) 7240 7722.

RAMSEY, Waldo Emerson W.; *see* Waldron-Ramsey.

RANASINGHE, (Kulatilaka Arthanayake) Parinda; Chief Justice of Sri Lanka, 1988–91; *b* 20 Aug. 1926; *s* of Solomon Ranasinghe and Somawathie Ranasinghe; *m* 1956, Chitra (*née* Mapaguneratne); one *s* three *d*. *Educ:* Royal Coll., Colombo. Advocate of the Supreme Court; appointed Magistrate, 1958; District Judge, 1966–74; High Court Judge, 1974–78; Judge, Court of Appeal, 1978–82, Pres. 1982; Judge, Supreme Court, 1982–88. *Recreation:* walking. *Address:* 18/48 Muhandiram E. D. Dabare Mawatha, Colombo 5, Sri Lanka. *T:* (1) 508310.

RANATUNGA, Gen. Sugathapala Cyril; High Commissioner for Sri Lanka in London, 1993–95; *b* 19 Feb. 1930; *m* 1957, Myrtle Sumanasekera; two *s*. *Educ:* St Sylvester's Coll., Kandy; RMA Sandhurst. Joined Sri Lanka Army, as Officer Cadet, 1950; commnd Ceylon LI, 1952; Staff Coll., 1962–63; RCDS, 1974–75; COS, Sri Lanka Army, 1982–85; Sen. Exec. Dir, Airport and Aviation Services Ltd, 1983–85; Lt-Gen. 1985; GOC, Jt Ops Comd, 1985–88; Gen. 1986; Security Advr to Pres. and Sec. to Minister of State for Defence, 1989–90; Sec. to Min. of Defence, 1990–93. Chancellor, Sir John Kotelawela Defence Acad., 1990–. *Recreations:* reading, bridge, golf. *Address:* Erabububela Estate, Mawanella, Sri Lanka. *Clubs:* Planters' Club (Kegalle); Nuwara Eliya Golf.

RANCHHODLAL, Sir Chinubhai Madhowlal, 3rd Bt *cr* 1913, of Shahpur, Ahmedabad, India; *b* 25 July 1929; *s* of 2nd Bt and Tanumati (*d* 1970), *d* of Javerilal Mehta; *S* father, 1990; grandfather, 1st Bt, was only member of Hindu Community to receive a baronetcy; *m* 1953, Muneera Khodad Fozdar; one *s* three *d*. Arjuna Award, 1972. *Heir: s* Prashant Ranchhodlal [*b* 15 Dec. 1955; *m* 1977, Swati Hrishikesh Mehta; three *d*]. *Clubs:* Willingdon, Cricket of India (Bombay).

RANDALL, family name of **Baron Randall of St Budeaux**.

RANDALL OF ST BUDEAUX, Baron *cr* 1997 (Life Peer), of St Budeaux in the co. of Devon; **Stuart Jeffrey Randall;** *b* 22 June 1938; *m* 1963, Gillian Michael; three *d*. *Educ:* University Coll., Cardiff (BSc Elect. Engrg). English Electric Computers and Radio Corp. of America, USA, 1963–66; Marconi Automation, 1966–68; Inter-Bank Res. Orgn, 1968–71; BSC, 1971–76; BL, 1976–80; Nexos Office Systems, 1980–81; Plessey Communications Systems, 1981–83. MP (Lab) Hull West, 1983–97. PPS to Shadow Chancellor of the Exchequer, 1984–85; Opposition front bench spokesman on Agricl, Food and Fisheries Affairs, 1985–87, on Home Affairs, 1987–92. *Recreations:* sailing, flying, jazz, opera. *Address:* House of Lords, SW1A 0PW.

RANDALL, (Alexander) John; MP (C) Uxbridge, since Aug. 1997; *b* 5 Aug. 1955; *s* of late Alec Albert Randall and of Joyce Margaret (*née* Gore); *m* 1986, Katherine Frances Gray; two *s* one *d*. *Educ:* Rutland House Sch., Hillingdon; Merchant Taylors' Sch., Herts; SSEES, Univ. of London (BA Hons Serbo-Croat Lang. and Lit. 1979). Dir, Randalls of Uxbridge Ltd, 1981– (Man. Dir, 1986–97). An Opposition Whip, 2000–01. *Recreations:* ornithology, theatre, opera, travel. *Address:* 36 Harefield Road, Uxbridge, Middx UB8 1PH. *T:* (01895) 239465. *Club:* Uxbridge Conservative.
See also P. A. Gore-Randall.

RANDALL, Col Charles Richard, OBE 1969; TD 1947; Vice Lord-Lieutenant for the County of Bedfordshire, 1978–91; *b* 21 Jan. 1920; *s* of Charles Randall and Elizabeth Brierley; *m* 1945, Peggy Dennis (*d* 1977); one *s* one *d*. *Educ:* Bedford Sch. Served War, 1939–45: commissioned Bedfordshire Yeomanry, 1939. High Sheriff, Bedfordshire, 1974–75. *Recreations:* shooting, fishing, gardening. *Club:* MCC.

RANDALL, Rev. Edmund Laurence, AM 1980; Warden, St Barnabas' Theological College, 1964–85, retired; Scholar in Residence, Diocese of Wangaratta, since 1986; *b* 2 June 1920; *s* of Robert Leonard Randall and Grace Annie Randall (*née* Young); unmarried. *Educ:* Dulwich College; Corpus Christi College, Cambridge. BA 1941. MA 1947. Served War, 1940–45, with Royal Artillery (AA). Corpus Christi Coll., 1938–40 and 1945–47. Wells Theological College, 1947–49. Deacon, 1949; Priest, 1950. Assistant Curate at St Luke's, Bournemouth, 1949–52; Fellow of Selwyn College, Cambridge, 1952–57; Chaplain, 1953–57; Residentiary Canon of Ely and Principal of Ely Theological Coll., 1957–59; Chaplain, St Francis Theological Coll., Brisbane, 1960–64; Hon. Canon of Adelaide, 1979–86, of Wangaratta, 1989–. Pres., Adelaide Coll. of Divinity, 1984–85. Vis. Lectr, St Barnabas' Theol Coll., and Lectr in Theology, Flinders Univ. of SA, Feb–July 1990. *Recreation:* swimming. *Address:* 44 Mackay Street, Wangaratta, Vic 3677, Australia. *T:* (3) 57219007.

RANDALL, Jeff William; Business Editor, BBC, since 2001; *b* 3 Oct. 1954; *s* of Jeffrey Charles Randall and Grace Annie (*née* Hawkridge); *m* 1986, Susan Diane Fidler; one *d*. *Educ:* Royal Liberty Grammar Sch., Romford; Nottingham Univ. (BA Hons Econs); Univ. of Florida. Hawkins Publishers, 1982–85; Asst Editor, Financial Weekly, 1985–86; City Corresp., Sunday Telegraph, 1986–88; The Sunday Times: Dep. City Editor, 1988–89; City Editor, 1989–94; City and Business Editor, 1994–95; Asst Editor and Sports Editor, 1996–97; Editor, Sunday Business, 1997–2001. Dir, Times Newspapers, 1994–95; Dep. Chm., Financial Dynamics Ltd, 1995–96. Freelance contributor: Daily Telegraph; EIU; Euromoney; Sporting Life; Golf World. Financial Journalist of the Year, FT-Analysis, 1991; Business Journalist of the Year, London Press Club, 2001. *Recreations:* golf, horseracing. *Address:* 4 Crossways, Shenfield, Essex CM15 8QX. *Club:* Wentworth.

RANDALL, John; *see* Randall, A. J.

RANDALL, John Norman; Registrar General for Scotland, since 1999; *b* 1 Aug. 1945; *s* of Frederick William Randall and Daphne Constance Randall (*née* Gawn); *m* 1st, 1967, Sandra Philpott (marr. diss. 1991); one *s* one *d*; 2nd, 1997, Eileen Wilson. *Educ:* Bromley Grammar Sch.; Bristol Univ. (BA Hons Geography); Glasgow Univ. (MPhil Town and Regl Planning 1968; MPhil Econs 1979). Economist: Dept of Economic Affairs, 1968–70; Scottish Office, 1970–85; Dep. Registrar Gen. for Scotland, 1985–89; Asst Sec., Scottish Office, 1989–99. *Recreations:* hill walking, natural history. *Address:* General Register Office for Scotland, New Register House, Edinburgh EH1 1YT. *T:* (0131) 314 4435.

RANDALL, John Paul; Chief Executive, Quality Assurance Agency for Higher Education, 1997–2001; *b* 23 Nov. 1947; *s* of late E. T. (Ted) Randall and of Mollie Randall (*née* Macrae); *m* (marr. diss.); one *s* one *d*; 2nd, 1993, Marie Catherine Hague. *Educ:* Wallington County Grammar Sch. for Boys; Univ. of York (BA Hons Biol and

Educn 1971). National Union of Students: Dep. Pres., 1971–73; Pres., 1973–75; Civil Service Union: Asst Sec., 1975–77; Asst Gen. Sec., 1977–81; Dep. Gen. Sec., 1981–87; Dir, Professional Standards and Develt, Law Soc., 1987–97. Mem. Council, NCVQ, 1992–97 (Chm., Accreditation Cttee, 1993–96; Chm., NVQ Policy Cttee, 1996–97; Mem. Jt Cttee, NCVQ and Schools Curriculum and Asssessment Authy, 1996–97); Mem. Bd, Internat. Network of QAAs, 1999–. Mem. Council, C&G, 1999–. Mem. Bd of Mgt, Focus Housing Assoc., 1996–99. FRSA 1998. Hon. LLD Nottingham Trent, 1998. *Publications:* articles in educnl and legal jls. *Recreations:* running, walking, music, wine, travel. *Address:* Orchard Cottage, The Rampings, Longdon, Worcs GL20 6AL. *Clubs:* South London Harriers, Orion Harriers.

RANDALL, John Yeoman; QC 1995; a Recorder, since 1999; a Deputy High Court Judge, since 2000; *b* 26 April 1956; *s* of Richard and Jean Randall; *m* 1982, Christine Robinson; one *s* one *d. Educ:* Rugby Sch.; Loomis Inst., USA; Jesus Coll., Cambridge (MA). Called to the Bar: Lincoln's Inn, 1978; NSW, 1979; in practice at English Bar, 1980–; an Asst Recorder, 1995–99. Mem., Legal Services Consultative Panel, 2000–. *Recreations:* travel, sports, music. *Address:* St Philip's Chambers, 55 Temple Row, Birmingham B2 5LS. *T:* (0121) 246 7000; *e-mail:* clerks@st-philips.co.uk.

RANDALL, Philip Allan G.; *see* Gore-Randall.

RANDELL, Peter Neil; Head of Finance and Administration, Institute of Metals, 1984–89; *b* 18 Nov. 1933; *s* of Donald Randell and Dorothy (*née* Anthonisz); *m* 1962, Anne Loraine Mudie; one *s* one *d. Educ:* Bradfield Coll.; Wye Coll., Univ. of London (BSc (Agric) Hons). FCIS. Farming and other employments, Rhodesia, 1955–61; Asst to Sec., British Insulated Callenders Cables Ltd, 1962–65; Asst Sec., NRDC, 1965–73, Sec. 1973–83, Board Member 1980–81; Sec. Admin and Personnel, British Technology Gp (NRDC and NEB), 1981–83. *Recreations:* the outdoors, reading. *Address:* Wood Dene, Golf Club Road, Hook Heath, Woking, Surrey GU22 0LS. *T:* (01483) 763824.

RANDERSON, Jennifer Elizabeth; JP; Member (Lib Dem) Cardiff Central, National Assembly for Wales, since 1999; Minister (formerly Secretary) for Culture, Sports and the Welsh Language, since 2000; *b* 26 May 1948; *m* 1970, Dr Peter Frederick Randerson; one *s* one *d. Educ:* Bedford Coll., London Univ. (BA Hons History); Inst. of Educn, London Univ. (PGCE 1970). Teacher: Sydenham High Sch., 1970–72; Spalding High Sch., 1972–74; Llanishen High Sch., 1974–76; Lectr, Coleg Glan Hafren, Cardiff, 1976–99. Member (L, then Lib Dem): Cardiff City Council, 1983–96; Cardiff County Council, 1995–2000 (Leader of Opposition, 1995–99). Chair of Exec., Welsh Lib Dems, 1988–90. Contested: (L) Cardiff S and Penarth, 1987; (Lib Dem) Cardiff Central, 1992, 1997. JP Cardiff 1982. *Recreations:* travel, theatre and concert going, gardening. *Address:* National Assembly for Wales, Cardiff Bay, Cardiff CF99 1NA. *T:* (029) 2089 8355.

RANDLE, James Neville, FREng; RDI 1994; Director, Automotive Engineering Centre, University of Birmingham, since 1993; Chairman, Randle Engineering and Design, since 1994; Director, since 1997, Chief Executive Officer, since 2000, Lea Francis Ltd; *b* Birmingham, 24 April 1938; *s* of James Randle and Florence (*née* Wilkins); *m* 1963, Jean Violet Allen; one *s* one *d. Educ:* Waverley Grammar Sch., Birmingham. MIMechE 1969, FIMechE 1980; FREng (FEng 1988). Rover Car Company: apprentice, 1954–59; design and develt engr, 1959–63; Project Manager, 1963–65; Jaguar: R&D Engr, 1965–72; Chief Res. Engr, 1972–78; Vehicle Engrg Dir, 1978–80; Product Engrg Dir, 1980–91. Hon. Prof., Univ. of Birmingham, 1992–. Dir, Volvo Aero Turbines, 1992–98. Institution of Mechanical Engineers: Mem. Bd, 1979–88, Chm., 1986–87, Automobile Div.; Mem. Council, 1986–93. Mem., Prince Philip Design Prize Cttee, 1992–95 and 1997–. Pres., Engrg Div., BAAS, 1995–96. FInstD 1986. FRAS 1989. James Clayton Prize, 1986, Crompton Lanchester Medal, 1986, IMechE. *Publications:* technical papers on automobile engrg design. *Recreations:* flying powered aircraft (private pilot's licence), sailing (yacht master's certificate), ski-ing, hill walking, designing automobiles. *Address:* Pear Tree House, High Street, Welford on Avon, Warwickshire CV37 8EF.

RANDLE, Prof. Sir Philip (John), Kt 1985; MD, FRCP; FRS 1983; Professor of Clinical Biochemistry, University of Oxford, 1975–93, now Emeritus; Fellow of Hertford College, Oxford, 1975–93, now Emeritus; *b* 16 July 1926; *s* of Alfred John and Nora Anne Randle; *m* 1952, Elizabeth Ann Harrison; three *d* (one *s* decd). *Educ:* King Edward VI Grammar Sch., Nuneaton; Sidney Sussex Coll., Cambridge (MA, PhD, MD); UCH, London (Fellow, UCL, 1990). Med. and Surg. Officer, UCH, 1951; Res. Fellow in Biochem., Cambridge, 1952–55; Univ. Lectr, Biochem., Cambridge, 1955–64; Fellow of Trinity Hall and Dir of Med. Studies, 1957–64 (Hon. Fellow, Trinity Hall, 1988); Prof. of Biochem., Univ. of Bristol, 1964–75. Member: Board of Governors, United Cambridge Hospitals, 1960–64; Clinical Endocrinology Cttee, MRC, 1957–64; Chm., Grants Cttee, MRC, 1975–77; Pres., European Assoc. for Study of Diabetes, 1977–80; Chairman, Research Committee: British Diabetic Assoc., 1971–78; British Heart Foundn, 1987–92. DHSS: Mem. Cttee on Med. Aspects Food Policy, 1981–89; Chm., COMA Panel on Diet and Cardiovascular Disease, 1981–84; Consultant Adviser in Biochemistry to CMO, 1981–89. Member: General Medical Council, 1967–75; Gen. Dental Council, 1971–75; Council, Royal Soc., 1987–89 (Vice Pres., 1988–89). Pres., Biochemical Soc., 1995–2000. Lectures: Banting, British Diabetic Assoc., 1965; Minkowski, European Assoc. for Study of Diabetes, 1966; Copp, La Jolla, 1972; Humphry Davy Rolleston, RCP, 1983; Ciba Medal and Lectr, Biochem. Soc., 1984; Kroc, San Diego, 1992. Founder FMedSci 1998. Corresp. Mem. of many foreign medical and scientific bodies. Hon. DSc Oxford Brookes, 1997. *Publications:* numerous contribs to books and med. sci. jls on diabetes mellitus, control of metabolism and related topics. *Recreations:* travel, swimming, bricklaying. *Address:* 11 Fitzherbert Close, Iffley, Oxford OX4 4EN; Department of Clinical Biochemistry, Radcliffe Infirmary, Oxford OX2 6HE.

RANDOLPH, Denys, BSc; CEng, MRAeS, FIProdE, FIEE, FInstD, CIMgt; Director, Partnership Wines Ltd, 1995–2000; *b* 6 Feb. 1926; *s* of late Harry Beckham Randolph and Margaret Isabel Randolph; *m* 1951, Marjorie Hales; two *d. Educ:* St Paul's School: Queen's Univ., Belfast (BSc). Served Royal Engineers, 1944–48 (Captain). Queen's Univ., Belfast, 1948–52; post-grad. apprenticeship, Short Bros & Harland, 1952–55; Wilkinson Sword Ltd: Prod. Engr/Prod. Dir, Graviner Div., 1955–66; Man. Dir, Hand Tools Div., 1966–69; Chm., Graviner Div., 1969–79; Chm., 1972–79; Pres., 1980–85; Wilkinson Match Ltd: Dir, 1974–80; Chm., 1976–79. Chairman: Woodrush Investments Ltd, 1980–93; Poitires Eyots Ltd, 1972–93; Dir, Henley Distance Learning Ltd, 1985–94. Proprietor, Clapcot Vineyards, 1986–98. Institute of Directors: Chm., 1976–79; Vice-Pres., 1979–96. Past Master: Worshipful Co. of Scientific Instrument Makers, 1977; Cutlers' Co., 1986. Mem. Council, Brunel Univ., 1986–91; Governor, Henley Admin. Staff Coll., 1979–91. FRSA (Manufactures and Commerce). *Publication:* From Rapiers to Razor Blades—The Development of the Light Metals Industry (paper, RSA). *Recreation:* viticulture. *Address:* Ickleton Fields, Wantage Road, Streatley, Reading, Berks RG8 9PY. *Clubs:* City Livery, Little Ship.

RANDS, Dr Michael Russell Wheldon; Director and Chief Executive, BirdLife International, since 1996; *b* 2 Aug. 1956; *s* of late Russell Fuller Rands and of Freda Millicent Rands; *m* 1984, Dr Gillian Frances Porter Goff; one *s* one *d. Educ:* Univ. of E Anglia (BSc Hons Envmtl Sci. 1978); Wolfson Coll., Oxford (DPhil 1982). Res. Biologist, Game Conservancy, 1982–86; Programme Dir, ICBP, 1986–94; Dir, Strategic Planning and Policy, BirdLife Internat., 1994–96. *Publications:* (with P. J. Hudson) Ecology and Management of Gamebirds, 1988; contrib. numerous papers to learned jls. *Recreations:* bird-watching, travelling with family, music. *Address:* 77 Thornton Road, Girton, Cambridge CB3 0NR.

RANELAGH, John O'B.; *see* O'Beirne Ranelagh.

RANFURLY, 7th Earl of, *cr* 1831 (Ire.); **Gerald François Needham Knox;** Baron Welles 1781; Viscount Northland 1791; Baron Ranfurly (UK) 1826; *b* 4 Jan. 1929; *s* of Captain John Needham Knox, RN (*d* 1967) (*g g g s* of 1st Earl) and Monica B. H. (*d* 1975), *d* of Maj.-Gen. Sir Gerald Kitson, KCVO, CB, CMG; *S* cousin, 1988; *m* 1955, Rosemary, *o d* of Air Vice-Marshal Felton Vesey Holt, CMG, DSO; two *s* two *d. Educ:* Wellington College. Served RN, 1947–60; retired as Lieut Comdr. Member of Stock Exchange, 1964; Partner in Brewin & Co., 1965; Senior Partner, 1982, Chm., 1987–95, Brewin Dolphin & Co. *Recreation:* foxhunting. *Heir: s* Edward John Knox [*b* 21 May 1957; *m* 1st, 1980, Rachel Sarah (marr. diss. 1984), *d* of F. H. Lee; 2nd, 1994, Johanna Humphrey, *d* of Sqdn Leader H. R. Walton, MBE; one *s*]. *Address:* Maltings Chase, Nayland, Colchester, Essex CO6 4LZ.

RANG, Prof. Humphrey Peter, DPhil; FRS 1980; Director, Sandoz, later Novartis, 1983–97, Institute for Medical Research, and Professor of Pharmacology, 1979–83 and since 1995, University College London; *b* 13 June 1936; *s* of Charles Rang and Sybil Rang; *m* 1992, Isobel Heyman. *Educ:* University Coll. Sch.; University Coll. London (MSc 1960); UCH Med. Sch. (MB, BS 1961); Balliol Coll., Oxford (DPhil 1965). J. H. Burn Res. Fellow, Dept of Pharmacol., Oxford, 1961–65; Vis. Res. Associate, Albert Einstein Coll. of Medicine, NY, 1966–67; Univ. Lectr in Pharmacol., Oxford, 1966–72; Fellow and Tutor in Physiol., Lincoln Coll., Oxford, 1967–72; Prof. of Pharmacology: Univ. of Southampton, 1972–74; St George's Hosp. Med. Sch., London, 1974–79; Fellow, 1983, and Vis. Prof., 1983–95, UCL. Founder FMedSci 1998. *Publications:* Drug Receptors, 1973; Pharmacology, 1987. *Recreations:* sailing, music. *Address:* 1 Willow Road, NW3 1TH.

RANGER, Prof. Terence Osborn, DPhil; FBA 1988; Rhodes Professor of Race Relations, and Fellow of St Antony's College, University of Oxford, 1987–97, now Emeritus Professor and Fellow; *b* 29 Nov. 1929; *s* of Leslie and Anna Ranger; *m* 1954, Shelagh Campbell Clark; three *d. Educ:* Highgate Sch.; Univ. of Oxford (BA, MA; DPhil 1960). Lecturer: RNC, Dartmouth, 1955–56; Coll. of Rhodesia and Nyasaland, 1957–63; Prof. of History, Univ. of Dar es Salaam, 1963–69; Prof. of African History, Univ. of Calif, LA, 1969–74; Prof. of Modern History, Univ. of Manchester, 1974–87; Chm., Oxford Univ. Cttee on African Studies, 1987–94. Vis. Prof., Univ. of Zimbabwe, 1998– 2000. Chm., Jl of Southern African Studies, 1976–92; Vice-Chm., Past and Present, 1987–. Hon. DLitt Zimbabwe, 1995. *Publications:* Revolt in Southern Rhodesia 1896–7, 1967; The African Voice in Southern Rhodesia 1898–1930, 1970; Dance and Society in Eastern Africa, 1975; Peasant Consciousness and Guerrilla War in Zimbabwe, 1985; Are We Not Also Men?, 1995; Voices From the Rocks: nature, culture and history in the Matepas mountains in Zimbabwe, 1999. *Recreations:* theatre, opera, walking. *Address:* 3 College Flats, St Kilda Road, Mount Pleasant, Harare, Zimbabwe. *Club:* Royal Commonwealth Society.

RANK, Sir Benjamin (Keith), Kt 1972; CMG 1955; MS, FRCS; FRACS; FACS; Consulting Plastic Surgeon, Royal Melbourne Hospital, Repatriation Department, Victoria Eye and Ear Hospital; *b* 14 Jan. 1911; *s* of Wreghitt Rank and Bessie Rank (*née* Smith); *m* 1938, Barbara Lyle Facy; one *s* three *d. Educ:* Scotch College, Melbourne; Ormond College, University of Melbourne. MB, BS Melbourne, 1934; Resident Medical Officer, Royal Melbourne Hospital, 1935–36; MS (Melb.), 1937; MRCS, LRCP 1938; Resident Surgical Officer, London County Council, 1938–39 (St James' Hospital, Balham); FRCS 1938; Assistant Plastic Surgeon (EMS) at Hill End (Bart's), 1939–40; AAMC, 1940–45; Officer i/c AIF Plastic Surgery Unit in Egypt, and later at Heidelberg Military Hospital, Victoria, Australia (Lt-Col); Hon. Plastic Surgeon, Royal Melbourne Hosp., 1946–66. Carnegie Fellow, 1947. Member: Dental Board of Victoria 1949–73, Joske Orator 1974; BMA State Council, 1950–60; Chm. Exec. Cttee, RACS (Pres., 1966–68); Chm., Cttee of Management, Victorian Plastic Surgery Unit (Preston Hosp.), 1966–85; Member: Bd of Management, Royal Melbourne Hosp., 1976–82 (Vice-Pres., 1979–82); Motor Accident Bd, Victoria, 1972–82. Chm., Consult. Council on Casualty Services, Victoria Health Council; Pres., St John's Ambulance Council, Victoria, 1983–88 (Chm. 1978–83). Sir Arthur Sims Commonwealth Travelling Prof., RCS, 1958; Moynihan Lectr, 1972; Vis. Prof., Harvard Med. Sch., 1976. Syme Orator, RACS, 1976; Stawell Orator, 1977. 87th Mem., James IV Assoc. of Surgeons; Pres., British Assoc. of Plastic Surgeons, 1965. Pres., 5th Internat. Congress of Plastic Surgery, Melbourne, 1971. FRACS 1943; Hon. FACST 1952; Hon. FRCS Canada; Hon. FRCSE 1973; Hon. FACS. Hon. DSc Punjabi Univ., 1970; Hon. Member: Société Française de Chirurgie Plastique; Indian Association of Surgeons. KStJ 1988 (CStJ 1982). *Publications:* (jointly) Surgery of Repair as applied to Hand Injuries, 1953; Jerry Moore, 1975; Head and Hands, 1987; The Family Story, 1992; papers in British, American and Australian Surgical Jls. *Recreations:* golf, gardening, painting. *Address:* 12 Jerula Avenue, Mount Eliza, Victoria 3930, Australia. *Clubs:* Melbourne (Melbourne); Peninsula Golf.

RANK-BROADLEY, Ian, FSNAD, FRBS; sculptor and medallist, since 1976; *b* 4 Sept. 1952; *s* of late John Kenneth Broadley and of Barbara Anne Broadley (*née* Barker); *m* 1980, Hazel G. Rank; one *s* one *d. Educ:* Epsom Sch. of Art; Slade Sch. of Fine Art; University Coll. London (Boise Travelling Schol., Italy). *T:* and *Fax:* FSNAD 1990; FRBS 1994. Effigy of: HM Queen Elizabeth II, for use on UK and Commonwealth coinage, 1998, and Golden Jubilee hallmark, 2002; HM Queen Elizabeth the Queen Mother, for Centenary Crown, 2000; the Queen for Golden Jubilee crown and Medal, 2002. *Works in public collections:* British Mus.; Nat. Portrait Gall.; Royal Mus. of Scotland; Fitzwilliam Mus.; Goldsmiths' Hall; London Library; Staatliche Mus., Berlin; Rijksmus., Leiden; Nat. Collection of Finland; Royal Swedish Coin Cabinet. Brother, Art Workers' Guild, 1995 (Mem. Cttee, 1999–2002); Freeman: City of London, 1996; Goldsmiths' Co., 1996. Prizewinner, XI Biennale Dantesca, Ravenna, Italy, 1996; first prize, Goldsmiths' Craft and Design Council Awards, 2000. *Recreations:* swimming, naturism, yoga. *Address:* Stanfields, Kingscourt Lane, Rodborough, Stroud, Glos GL5 3QR. *T:* (01453) 765985.

RANKEILLOUR, 4th Baron *cr* 1932, of Buxted; **Peter St Thomas More Henry Hope;** farmer and landowner; *b* 29 May 1935; *s* of 3rd Baron Rankeillour and Mary Sibyl, *d* of late Col Wilfrid Ricardo, DSO; *S* father, 1967; unmarried. *Educ:* Ampleforth. *Recreations:* architecture, grand-scale landscaping; agricultural equipment inventor. *Heir:* cousin Michael Richard Hope [*b* 21 Oct. 1940; *m* 1964, Elizabeth Rosemary, *e d* of Col F. H. Fuller; one *s* two *d*]. *Address:* Achaderry House, Roy Bridge, West Inverness-shire PH31 4AN. *T:* (01397) 712206.

RANKIN, Andrew; QC 1968; a Recorder of the Crown Court, 1972–97; *b* 3 Aug. 1924; *s* of William Locke Rankin and Mary Ann McArdle, Edinburgh; *m* 1st, 1944, Winifred (marr. diss. 1963), *d* of Frank McAdam, Edinburgh; two *s* two *d* (and one *s* decd); 2nd, 1964, Veronica (*d* 1990), *d* of George Aloysius Martin, Liverpool; 3rd, 1991, Jenifer Margaret, *d* of Alfred George Hodges Bebington, Wirral. *Educ:* Royal High Sch., Edinburgh; Univ. of Edinburgh; Downing Coll., Cambridge. Served War of 1939–45: Sub-Lt, RNVR, 1943. BL (Edin.) 1946; BA, 1st cl. hons Law Tripos (Cantab), 1948. Royal Commonwealth Soc. Medal, 1942; Cecil Peace Prize, 1946; Lord Justice Holker Exhibn, Gray's Inn, 1947–50; Lord Justice Holker Schol., Gray's Inn, 1950–53; Univ. Blue, Edin., 1943 and 1946 and Camb., 1948. Lectr in Law, Univ. of Liverpool, 1948–52. Called to Bar, Gray's Inn, 1950. *Publications:* (ed, 4th edn) Levie's Law of Bankruptcy in Scotland, 1950; various articles in UK and foreign legal jls. *Recreations:* swimming, travel by sea, racing (both codes), watching soccer (especially Liverpool FC). *Address:* Chelwood, Pine Walks, Prenton, Birkenhead, Merseyside CH42 8LQ. *T:* (0151) 608 2987; 69 Cliffords Inn, EC4 1BX. *T:* (020) 7405 2932. *Address:* 4 Field Court, Gray's Inn, WC1R 5EA. *T:* (020) 7440 6900, *Fax:* (020) 7242 0197.

RANKIN, Ian James; novelist; *b* 28 April 1960; *s* of James Hill Rankin and Isobel Rankin (*née* Vickers); *m* 1986, Anna Miranda Harvey; two *s*. *Educ:* Beath Sen. High Sch.; Univ. of Edinburgh (MA Hons). Tax Collector, then punk musician, then alcohol researcher, then swineherd, then music journalist, 1986–90. Fulbright/Chandler Fellow, USA, 1991–92. Chm., Crime Writers Assoc., 1999–2000 (Short Story Dagger, 1994, 1996); Mem., Detection Club, 1998–. Book and culture reviewer, radio and newspapers. Hon. DLitt: Abertay Dundee, 1999; St Andrews, 2000. *Publications:* The Flood, 1986; Watchman, 1988; Westwind, 1989; *Inspector Rebus series:* Knots and Crosses, 1987; Hide and Seek, 1990; Tooth and Nail, 1992; A Good Hanging and other stories, 1992; Strip Jack, 1992; The Black Book, 1993; Mortal Causes, 1994; Let it Bleed, 1995; Black and Blue (CWA Gold Dagger award), 1997; The Hanging Garden, 1998; Death is not the End (novella), 1998; Dead Souls, 1999; Set in Darkness, 2000; The Falls, 2001; *as Jack Harvey:* Witch Hunt, 1993; Bleeding Hearts, 1994; Blood Hunt, 1995. *Recreations:* couch potato, regular visitor to Edinburgh pubs, '70s rock music. *Address:* c/o Curtis Brown Ltd, 28/29 Haymarket, SW1Y 4SP. *T:* (020) 7396 6600.

RANKIN, Sir Ian (Niall), 4th Bt *cr* 1898, of Bryngwyn, Much Dewchurch, Co. Hereford; Chairman, I. N. Rankin Oil Ltd, since 1981; *b* 19 Dec. 1932; *s* of Lt-Col Arthur Niall Rankin (*d* 1965) (*yr s* of 2nd Bt) and Lady Jean Rankin, DCVO; *S* uncle, 1988; *m* 1st, 1959, Alexandra (marr. diss.), *d* of Adm. Sir Laurence Durlacher, KCB, OBE, DSC; one *s* one *d*; 2nd, 1980, Mrs June Norman (marr. diss. 1998), *d* of late Captain Thomas Marsham-Townshend; one *s*. *Educ:* Eton College; Christ Church, Oxford (MA). Lieut, Scots Guards. Chm., Slumberfleece Ltd, 1979–; Director: Lindsay and Williams Ltd, 1973; Bayfine Ltd and subsidiaries, 1974–85 (Jt Chm., 1974–81); Highgate Optical and Industrial Co. Ltd and subsidiary, 1976–84 (Jt Chm., 1976–81); New Arcadia Explorations Ltd, 1987–; Bristol Scotts, 1993–2001. Patron, Samaritans, 1991–; Mem. Council, Alexandra Rose Day, 1970–. *Recreations:* shooting, ski-ing, chess. *Heir: s* Gavin Niall Rankin, *b* 19 May 1962. *Address:* 97 Elgin Avenue, W9 2DA. *T:* (office) (020) 7286 0251, (home) (020) 7286 5117. *Clubs:* White's, Beefsteak, Pratt's; Royal Yacht Squadron.

RANKIN, James Deans, FREng, FIChemE; Senior Science and Technology Associate, ICI, 1995–2000; *b* 17 Feb. 1943; *s* of Dr James Deans Rankin and Florence Elizabeth (*née* Wight); *m* 1973, Susan Margaret Adams; one *s* one *d*. *Educ:* Merchiston Castle Sch., Edinburgh; Gonville and Caius Coll., Cambridge (MA). FREng (FEng 1987); FIChemE 1987. Joined ICI, 1965: Agricl Div., 1965–83; Process Technology Gp Manager, New Sci. Gp, 1983–88; Melinex R&D Manager, 1988–93; Technology, 1993–2000. Royal Acad. of Engrg Vis. Prof. of Engrg Design, Univ. of Oxford, 1997–2000; Vis. Prof., UMIST, 2000–. *Recreations:* steam boats, motoring. *Address:* Department of Chemical Engineering, UMIST, PO Box 88, Sackville Street, Manchester M60 1QD.

RANKIN, John James; HM Diplomatic Service; Counsellor and Deputy Head of Mission, Dublin, since 1999; *b* 12 March 1957; *s* of late James Rankin, CBE, and Agnes Rankin (*née* Stobie); *m* 1987, Lesley Marshall; one *s* two *d*. *Educ:* Hutcheson's Boys' Grammar Sch.; Univ. of Glasgow (LLB 1st Cl. Hons); McGill Univ., Montreal (LLM with distinction). Solicitor and Mem., Law Soc. of Scotland. Lectr in Public Law, Univ. of Aberdeen, 1984–88; Asst, then Sen. Asst Legal Advr, FCO, 1988–90; Legal Advr, UKMIS and UKDIS, Geneva, 1991–94; Legal Counsellor, FCO, 1995; Dep. Head, OSCE Dept, 1996–98. *Publications:* articles on Scots law and international law. *Recreations:* tennis, golf, gardening, food. *Address:* c/o Foreign and Commonwealth Office, SW1A 2AH. *T:* (Dublin) (1) 2053712.

RANKIN, Rear-Adm. Neil Erskine, CB 1995; CBE 1988; Chairman, Scottish Environment LINK, since 2000; *b* 24 Dec. 1940; *s* of late James Hall Rankin and of Jean Laura Rankin (*née* Honeyman); *m* 1969, Jillian Mary Cobb; one *s* one *d*. *Educ:* HMS Conway; BRNC Dartmouth. Joined RN 1958; pilot's wings, 1963; CO HMS Achilles, 1977; CO HMS Bacchante, 1978; Comdr (Air), RNAS Yeovilton, 1979, HMS Invincible, 1981; Naval Air Warfare, MoD, 1982; COS, Flag Officer Third Flotilla, 1984; CO, Captain F8, HMS Andromeda, 1985; Sen. Naval Officer, Middle East, 1985; Dep. Dir, Naval Warfare, MoD, 1987; CO HMS Ark Royal, 1990; Comdr, British Forces Falkland Is, 1992–93; FO, Portsmouth, 1993–96. Chm., Caledonian Macbrayne Ltd, 1996–99. Director: Portsmouth Naval Base Property Trust, 1997–; Former Royal Yacht Britannia Trust, 1999–. Chm., Scottish Seabird Centre, 1997–; Mem., Central Council, King George's Fund for Sailors, 1997–; Pres., MND Care and Res. Soc., 1994–. Mem., RNSA, 1995–. Comr, Queen Victoria Sch., Dunblane, 1999–. Liveryman, Shipwrights' Co., 1992–; Younger Brother, Trinity House, 1993–; Mem., Incorporation of Hammermen, Glasgow, 1998–. *Recreations:* Rugby (former Pres., Combined Services RFU, and RNRU, Pres., United Services Portsmouth RFC, 1994–96), sailing, golf. *Address:* c/o Lloyds TSB, Cox's & King's Branch, Pall Mall, SW1Y 5NA. *Clubs:* Royal Navy of 1765 and 1785, Naval; Royal Naval Golfing; North Berwick Golf; Royal Yacht Squadron; Royal Naval and Royal Albert Yacht; East Lothian Yacht.

RANKIN, Robert Craig McPherson, CompICE; Chairman, BKR Financial Ltd, since 1988; Director, British Shipbuilders, 1985–91; *b* 15 Aug. 1937; *s* of Robert Craig Rankin and Julia Rankin (*née* Duff); *m* 1963, Alison Barbara Black Douglas; one *s* one *d*. *Educ:* The Academy, Ayr; Royal College of Science and Technology, Glasgow. CompICE 1987; CIMgt (CBIM 1987). Dir, Balfour Beatty Construction (Scotland) Ltd, 1973–74; Dir 1974–83, Exec. Dir 1983–85, Balfour Beatty Construction Ltd; Balfour Beatty Ltd: Dir, 1983–88; Dep. Man. Dir, 1985–86; Man. Dir, 1986–87; Chief Exec., 1986–88; Dir, BICC PLC, 1987–88; Non-executive Director: London & Edinburgh Trust PLC, 1988–91; LDDC, 1989–93. *Recreations:* opera, music, golf, field sports.

RANKINE, Jean Morag, (Mrs N. A. Hall); Deputy Director of the British Museum, 1983–97; *b* 5 Sept. 1941; *d* of Alan Rankine and Margaret Mary Sloan Rankine (*née* Reid); *m* 1992, Norman Anthony Hall. *Educ:* Central Newcastle High Sch.; University College London (BA, MPhil; Fellow, 1990); Univ. of Copenhagen. Grad. Assistant, Durham Univ. Library, 1966–67; British Museum: Res. Assistant, Dept of Printed Books, 1967–73; Asst Keeper, Director's Office, 1973–78; Head of Public Services, 1978–83. *Recreations:* sculling, ski-ing, fell-walking, opera, motorcycling. *Address:* 49 Hartington Road, W4 3TS. *Clubs:* Thames Rowing; Clydesdale Amateur Rowing (Glasgow).

RANNIE, Prof. Ian, FRCPath 1964; FIBiol 1964; Professor of Pathology (Dental School), University of Newcastle upon Tyne, 1960–81, Professor Emeritus 1981; *b* 29 Oct. 1915; *o s* of James Rannie, MA, and Nicholas Denniston McMeekan; *m* 1943, Flora Welch; two *s*. *Educ:* Ayr Academy; Glasgow University. BSc (Glas), 1935; MB, ChB (Glas), 1938; BSc Hons Pathology and Bacteriology (Glas), 1939; Hutcheson Research Schol. (Pathology), 1940. Assistant to Professor of Bacteriology, Glasgow, 1940–42; Lecturer in Pathology, 1942–60, King's College, Univ. of Durham. Consultant Pathologist, United Newcastle upon Tyne Hospitals, 1948–81, Hon. Consultant 1981–. Pres., International Soc. of Geographical Pathology, 1969–72; Vice-President: Assoc. of Clinical Pathologists, 1978–80; Internat. Union of Angiology. Hon. Mem., Hungarian Arteriosclerosis Res. Soc. *Publications:* papers on various subjects in medical journals. *Recreation:* golf. *Address:* Apartment G, 8 Osborne Villas, Newcastle upon Tyne NE2 1JU. *T:* (0191) 281 3163. *Clubs:* East India, Royal Over-Seas League.

RANSFORD, John Anthony, CBE 1997; Head of Social Affairs, Health and Housing, Local Government Association, since 1999; *b* 19 Sept. 1948; *s* of Sydney George Ransford and Ethel Alice Ransford (*née* Peters); *m* 1971, Liz Hainsworth; one *s* one *d*. *Educ:* Letchworth Grammar Sch.; Univ. of Sussex (BA Hons Sociol.; MSocWork). CQSW 1972. Probation Officer, SE London Probation and After-Care Service, 1972–74; Kirklees Metropolitan Council: Trng Officer, Social Services Dept, 1974–77; Health Liaison Officer, 1977–79; Asst Dir, Social Services, 1979–82, Dir, 1982–87; Actg Chief Exec., 1987; Dir, Social Services, 1988–94, Chief Exec., 1994–99, N Yorks CC. Hon. Sec., Assoc. of Dirs of Social Services, 1993–96. *Recreations:* theatre, foreign travel, current affairs. *Address:* Local Government Association, LGA House, Smith Square, SW1P 3HZ. *T:* (020) 7664 3236.

RANT, James William, CB 1995; QC 1980; **His Honour Judge Rant;** a Circuit Judge, since 1984, at Central Criminal Court, since 1986; Judge Advocate General of the Army and Royal Air Force, since 1991; *b* 16 April 1936; *s* of late Harry George Rant, FZS and Barbara Rant; *m* 1963, Helen Rant (*née* Adnams), BA; one *s* two *d* (and one *s* decd). *Educ:* Stowe Sch.; Selwyn Coll., Cambridge (MA, LLM). Called to the Bar, Gray's Inn, 1961, Bencher, 1996; pupillage with late James N. Dunlop, 1962–63; a Dep. Circuit Judge, 1975–79; a Recorder, 1979–84; an occasional judge, Court of Appeal (Criminal Div.), 1997–. FRSA 1996. Freeman: City of London, 1986; Clockmakers' Co., 1989. *Publication:* Courts-Martial Handbook: practice and procedure, 1998. *Recreations:* cookery, music. *Address:* 3 Temple Gardens, Middle Temple Lane, EC4Y 9AA.

RANTZEN, Esther Louise, (Mrs Desmond Wilcox), OBE 1991; Television Producer/Presenter, since 1968; *b* 22 June 1940; *d* of late Harry Rantzen and of Katherine Rantzen; *m* 1977, Desmond John Wilcox (*d* 2000); one *s* two *d*. *Educ:* North London Collegiate Sch.; Somerville Coll., Oxford (MA). Studio manager making dramatic sound effects, BBC Radio, 1963; BBC TV: Researcher, 1965; Dir, 1967; Reporter, Braden's Week, 1968–72; Producer/Presenter, That's Life, 1973–94, scriptwriter, 1976–94; Producer, documentary series, The Big Time, 1976; Presenter: Esther Interviews …, 1988; Hearts of Gold, 1988; Esther, 1994–; That's Esther, 1999–; Producer/Presenter, Drugwatch, Childwatch, The Lost Babies and other progs on social issues; reporter/producer, various documentaries, religious and current affairs TV progs. Member: Nat. Consumer Council, 1981–90; Health Educn Authority, 1989–95; Task Force to review services for drug misusers, DoH, 1994. Chm., ChildLine; President: Meet-a-Mum Assoc.; Community Meeting Point, Harpenden; Hon. Pres., ME Assoc. Young People's Gp, 1995–; a Vice-President: ASBAH; Health Visitors' Assoc.; Nat. Deaf Children's Soc.; Iain Rennie Hospice at Home; Vice-Patron, Rose Road Appeal (people with disabilities in S Hants); Patron: Addenbrookes Kidney Patients Assoc.; Contact-a-Family (families of disabled children); DEMAND (furniture for the disabled); Downs Children's Assoc.; Children with Aids; Headway; Children Head Injuries Trust; Hesley Foundn; Komso Children's Hosp.; S Wessex Addiction Centre; ADFAM (Nat. Charity for Families and Friends of Drug Users); SIMR (Seriously Ill for Medical Research); John Grooms Assoc.; Hillingdon Manor Sch. for Autistic Children, 1999–; The New Sch. at West Heath (The Princess Diana Sch.), 2000–. Champion, Community Legal Service, 2000. Trustee, Ben Hardwick Meml Fund. Hon. Mem., NSPCC, 1989. FRTVS 1995. Hon. DLitt, Southampton Inst. for FE, 1994. Personality of 1974, RTS award; BBC TV Personality of 1975, Variety Club of GB; European Soc. for Organ Transplant Award, 1985; Special Judges' Award for Journalism, RTS, 1986; Richard Dimbleby Award, BAFTA, 1988; Snowdon Award for Services to Disabled People, 1996; RTS Hall of Fame Award, 1998. SSStJ 1992. *Publications:* (with Desmond Wilcox) Kill the Chocolate Biscuit, 1981; Baby Love, 1985; (with Shaun Woodward) Ben: the story of Ben Hardwick, 1985; Esther (autobiog.), 2001. *Recreations:* family life, the countryside, appearing in pantomime. *Address:* BBC TV, White City, 201 Wood Lane, W12 7RJ. *T:* (020) 8752 5252; Billy Marsh Associates, 174–178 North Gower Street, NW1 2NB. *T:* (020) 7388 6858.

RAO, Calyampudi Radhakrishna, Padma Vibhushan, 2001; FRS 1967; Eberly Professor of Statistics, and Director, Centre for Multivariate Analysis, Penn State University, since 1988; Adjunct Professor, University of Pittsburgh, since 1988 (University Professor, 1979–88); *b* 10 Sept. 1920; *s* of C. D. Naidu and A. Laksmikantamma; *m* 1948, C. Bhargavi Rao; one *s* one *d*. *Educ:* Andhra Univ. (MA, 1st Class Maths); Calcutta Univ. (MA, 1st Class Statistics; Gold Medal); PhD, ScD, Cambridge (Hon. Fellow, King's Coll., Cambridge, 1975). Indian Statistical Institute: Superintending Statistician, 1943–49; Professor and Head of Division of Theoretical Research and Training, 1949–64; Dir, Res. and Training Sch., 1964–76 (Sec., 1972–76); Jawaharlal Nehru Professor, 1976–84. Nat. Prof., India, 1987–92. Co-editor, Sankhya, Indian Jl of Statistics, 1964–72, Editor, 1972–. Member, Internat. Statistical Inst., 1951 (Mem. Statistical Educn Cttee, 1958–; Treasurer, 1962–65; Pres.-elect, 1975–77, Pres., 1977–79, Hon. Mem. 1982); Chm., Indian Nat. Cttee for Statistics, 1962–; President: Biometric Soc., 1973–75 (Hon. Life Mem., 1986); Indian Econometric Soc., 1971–76; Forum for Interdisciplinary Mathematics, 1982–84. Fellow: Indian Nat. Sci. Acad., 1953 (Vice-Pres., 1973, 1974); Inst. of Math. Statistics, USA, 1958 (Pres., 1976–77); Amer. Statistical Assoc., 1972; Econometric Soc., 1972; Indian Acad. of Scis, 1974; Founder Fellow: Third World Sci. Acad., 1983; Nat. Acad. of Scis, India, 1988; Nat. Acad. of Scis, USA, 1995; Foreign Mem., Lithuanian Acad. of Scis, 1997. Hon. Fellow: Royal Stat. Soc., 1969; Amer. Acad. of Arts and Scis, 1975; Calcutta Stat. Assoc., 1985; Biometric Soc., 1986; Finnish Statistical Soc., 1990; Inst. of Combinatorics and its Applications, 1995. Shanti Swarup Bhatnagar Memorial Award, 1963; Guy Medal in Silver, Royal Stat. Soc., 1965; Padma Bhushan, 1968; Meghnad Saha Medal, 1969; J. C. Bose Gold Medal, 1979; S. S. Wilke's Meml Medal, 1989; Mahalandois Birth Centenary Gold Medal, 1996; Dist. Achievement Medal, Sect. on Stats and Envmt, Amer. Stat. Assoc., 1997; Carol and Emanuel Parzen Prize for statistical innovation, Texas A&M Univ., 2000. Hon. DSc: Andhra; Leningrad; Athens; Osmania; Ohio State; Philippines; Tampere; Neuchatel; Poznan; Indian Statistical Inst.; Colorado State; Hyderabad; Barcelona; Slovak Acad. of Scis; Guelph; Munich; Venkateswara; Waterloo;

Brasilia; Athens; Kent; Cyprus; Hon. DLitt Delhi. Hon. Prof., Univ. of San Marcos, Lima. *Publications:* (with Mahalanobis and Majumdar) Anthropometric Survey of the United Provinces, 1941, a statistical study, 1949; Advanced Statistical Methods in Biometric Research, 1952; (with Mukherjee and Trevor) The Ancient Inhabitants of Jebal Moya, 1955; (with Majumdar) Bengal Anthropometric Survey, 1945, a statistical study, 1959; Linear Statistical Inference and its Applications, 1965; (with A. Matthai and S. K. Mitra) Formulae and Tables for Statistical Work, 1966; Computers and the Future of Human Society, 1968; (with S. K. Mitra) The Generalised Inverse of Matrices and its Applications, 1971; (with A. M. Kagan and Yu. V. Linnik) Characterization Problems of Mathematical Statistics, 1973; (with J. Kleffe) Estimation of Variance Components and its Applications, 1988; Statistics and Truth, 1989; (with H. Toutenburg) Linear Models, 1995; (with D. N. Shaubhag) Choquet-Deny Type Functional Equations with Applications to Stochastic Models, 1994; (with M. B. Rao) Matrix Algebra and its Applications to Statistics and Econometrics, 1998. *Address:* Department of Statistics, 326 Thomas Building, Penn State University, University Park, PA 16802–2111, USA.

RAO, Prof. Chintamani Nagesa Ramachandra, Padma Shri, 1974; Padma Vibhushan, 1985; FRS 1982; CChem, FRSC; Hon. President and Linus Pauling Research Professor, Jawaharlal Nehru Centre for Advanced Scientific Research, Bangalore, India, since 2000 (President, 1994–99); *b* 30 June 1934; *s* of H. Nagesa Rao; *m* 1960, Indumati; one *s* one *d.* *Educ:* Univ. of Mysore (DSc); Univ. of Purdue, USA (PhD). Research Chemist, Univ. of California, Berkeley, 1958–59; Lectr, Indian Inst. of Science, 1959–63; Prof., Indian Inst. of Technology, Kanpur, 1963–76, Head of Chemistry Dept, 1964–68, Dean of Research, 1969–72; Jawaharlal Nehru Fellow, 1973–75; Indian Institute of Science, Bangalore: Chm., Solid State and Structural Chemistry Unit and Materials Res. Laboratory, 1976–84; Dir, 1984–94. Commonwealth Vis. Prof., Univ. of Oxford, and Fellow, St Catherine's Coll., 1974–75; Jawaharlal Nehru Vis. Prof., Univ. of Cambridge, and Professorial Fellow, Kings' Coll., Cambridge, 1983–84; Linnett Vis. Prof., Univ. of Cambridge, 1998. Blackett Lectr, Royal Soc., 1991. US Nat. Acad. of Sci. Lect., 1993. President: INSA, 1985–87; IUPAC, 1985–87; Indian Sci. Congress, 1987–88; Indian Acad, of Scis, 1989–91; Materials Res. Soc. of India, 1989–91. Member: First Nat. Cttee of Science and Technology, Govt of India, 1971–74; Science Adv. Cttee to Union Cabinet of India, 1981–86 (Chm., 1997–98); Chm., Science Adv. Council to Prime Minister, 1986–90. Member: Gen. Council, ICSU; Internat. Sci. Adv. Bd, UNESCO, 1996–99. Foreign Member: Slovenian Acad. of Scis, 1983; Serbian Acad. of Scis, 1986; Amer. Acad. of Arts and Scis, 1986; USSR Acad. of Scis, 1988; Czechoslovak Acad. of Scis, 1988; Polish Acad. of Scis, 1988; US Nat. Acad. of Scis, 1990; Pontifical Acad. of Scis, 1990; Amer. Philosophical Soc., 1995; Academia Europaea, 1997; Brazilian Acad. of Scis, 1997; European Acad. of Arts, Scis and Humanities, 1997; Japan Acad., 1998; Royal Spanish Acad. of Scis, 1999; French Acad of Scis, 2000; Hon. Fellow, UWCC, 1997; Founder Mem., Third World Acad. of Scis (Pres., 2000–). Hon. DSc: Purdue, 1982; Bordeaux, 1983; Sri Venkateswara, 1984; Roorkee, 1985; Banaras, Osmania, Mangalore and Manipur, 1987; Anna, Mysore, Burdwan, 1988; Wroclaw, 1989; Andhra, Karnatak, 1990; Bangalore, Hyderabad, Indian Inst. of Technology, Kharagpur, 1991. Many awards and medals, incl.: Marlow Medal of Faraday Soc. (London), 1967; Royal Soc. of Chemistry (London) Medal, 1981; Centennial For. Fellowship of Amer. Chemical Soc., 1976; Hevrovsky Gold Medal, Czech. Acad. of Scis, 1989; Golden Jubilee Prize, CSIR, 1992; P. C. Ray Meml Award, 1994; Sahabdeen Award for Sci., Sri Lanka, 1994; Medal for Chemistry, Third World Acad. of Scis, 1995; Albert Einstein Gold Medal, UNESCO, 1996; Shatabdi Puraskar prize, Indian Sci. Congress Assoc., 1999; Centenary Medal, RSC, 2000; Hughes Medal, Royal Soc., 2000; Millennium Plaque of Honour, Indian Sci. Cong., 2000. *Publications:* 35 books including: Ultraviolet and Visible Spectroscopy, 1960, 3rd edn 1975; Chemical Applications of Infrared Spectroscopy, 1964; Spectroscopy in Inorganic Chemistry, 1970; Modern Aspects of Solid State Chemistry, 1970; University General Chemistry, 1973; Solid State Chemistry, 1974; Phase Transitions in Solids, 1978; Preparation and Characterization of Materials, 1981; The Metallic and the Non-metallic States of Matter, 1985; New Directions in Solid State Chemistry, 1986; Chemistry of Oxide Superconductors, 1988; Chemical and Structural Aspects of High Temperature Oxide Superconductors, 1988; Bismuth and Thallium Superconductors, 1989; Advances in Catalyst Design, 1991; Chemistry of High Temperature Superconductivity, 1991; Superconductivity Today, 1992; Chemistry of Advanced Materials, 1992; Chemical Approaches to the Synthesis of Inorganic Materials, 1994; Transition Metal Oxides, 1995; Metal-Insulator Transition Revisited, 1996; Understanding Chemistry, 2000; 1000 research papers. *Recreations:* gourmet cooking, gardening. *Address:* Jawaharlal Nehru Centre for Advanced Scientific Research, Jakkur Post, Bangalore 560064, India. *T:* (office) (80) 8563075, (home) (80) 3601410.

RAO, P. V. Narasimha; Prime Minister of India, and Leader of the Congress (I) Party, 1991–96; *b* Karimnagar, Andhra Pradesh, 28 June 1921; widower; three *s* five *d.* *Educ:* Osmania Univ., Hyderabad; Bombay Univ.; Nagpur Univ. (BSc, LLB). Career as leader, writer, poet, agriculturalist, advocate and administrator. Member, Andhra Pradesh Legislative Assembly, 1957–77; Minister in Andhra Pradesh Govt, 1962–71; Chief Minister of the State, 1971–73. Chm., Telugu Academy, Andhra Pradesh, 1968–74; Vice-Pres., Dakshin Bharat Hindi Prachar Sabha, Madras, 1972; Gen. Sec., All India Congress Cttee, 1975–76. Elected to Lok Sabha (from Hanamkonda, Andhra Pradesh) 1972, 1977 and 1980, (from Ramtek) 1984, 1991, 1996; Minister: for External Affairs, 1980–84; for Home Affairs, 1984; of Defence, 1985; of Human Resources Develt, 1985–88; of Health and Family Welfare, 1986–88; of External Affairs, 1988–89. Chairman: Public Accounts Cttee, 1978–79; Bharatiya Vidya Bhavan's Andhra Centre. Has lectured on political matters in univs in USA and Federal Republic of Germany, and has visited many countries. *Publications:* many, including Sahasra Phan (Hindi trans.). *Recreations:* music, cinema, theatre. *Address:* Vangara Post, Karimnagar District, Andhra Pradesh, India.

RAPER, (Alfred) Graham, CBE 1988; PhD; FREng; Chairman, Projecta, consulting engineers, 1987–99; Chief Executive and Deputy Chairman, Davy Corporation, 1985–87; *b* 15 May 1932; *s* of Hilda and Alfred William Raper; *m* 1st, Elizabeth Williams (marr. diss. 1975); two *s* one *d*; 2nd, Valerie Benson; one *s.* *Educ:* Lady Manners School, Bakewell; Univ. of Sheffield (BScTech Hons, PhD). FREng (FEng 1986); FIChemE, FIM. Asst Lectr, Univ. of Sheffield, 1955–57; Research Engineer, Head Wrightson Co., 1957–59; Technical Manager, Davy United Engineering, 1959–65; Steel Plant Manager, Highveld Steel & Vanadium, S Africa, 1965–69; joined Davy Corp., 1969; Vice-Chm., Kvaerner Davy, 1995–97. Non-exec. Dir, Vosper Thornycroft (UK) Ltd, 1995–. *Publications:* articles in jls of Iron & Steel Institute and British Association. *Recreations:* golf, gardening. *Address:* 54 Golf Links Road, Ferndown, Wimborne, Dorset BH22 8BZ. *T:* (01202) 873512.

RAPER, Maj.-Gen. Anthony John, CBE 1996 (MBE 1987); Chief Executive, Defence Communications Services Agency, since 1998; *b* 14 April 1950. *Educ:* RMA Sandhurst; Selwyn Coll., Cambridge (BA 1974). Commnd Royal Signals, 1970; posts in UK, Germany, Cyprus, Bosnia and NATO; Commander: 4th Armoured Div. and Signal Regt, 1988–91; 1st Signal Bde, Allied Comd Europe, 1994–95; Defence Intelligence Staff; Directorate of Land Warfare; directing staff, RMA Sandhurst and Staff Coll.; Dir, Operational Requirements for Inf. and Communication Services. *Address:* Defence Communications Services Agency, Basil Hill Site, Park Lane, Corsham, Wilts SN13 9NR.

RAPHAEL, Adam Eliot Geoffrey; political correspondent, The Economist; *b* 22 April 1938; *s* of Geoffrey George Raphael and Nancy Raphael (*née* Rose); *m* 1970, Caroline Rayner Ellis; one *s* one *d.* *Educ:* Arnold House, Charterhouse; Oriel Coll., Oxford (BA Hons History). 2nd Lieut Royal Artillery, 1956–58. Copy Boy, Washington Post, USA, 1961; Swindon Evening Advertiser, 1962–63; Film Critic, Bath Evening Chronicle, 1963–64; The Guardian: Reporter, 1965; Motoring Correspondent, 1967–68; Foreign Correspondent, Washington and S Africa, 1969–73; Consumer Affairs Columnist, 1974–76; Political Correspondent, The Observer, 1976–81, Political Editor, 1981–86; Presenter, Newsnight, BBC TV, 1987–88; an Asst Editor, 1988, Exec. Editor, 1988–93, The Observer; writer on Home Affairs, The Economist, 1994. Awards include: Granada Investigative Journalist of the Year, 1973; British Press Awards, Journalist of the Year, 1973. *Publications:* My Learned Friends, 1989; Ultimate Risk: the inside story of the Lloyd's catastrophe, 1994. *Recreations:* tennis, ski-ing. *Address:* 50 Addison Avenue, W11 4QP. *T:* (020) 7603 9133. *Clubs:* Garrick, Hurlingham, Royal Automobile, Ski Club of Great Britain.

RAPHAEL, Caroline Sarah; Commissioning Editor, BBC Radio Four, since 1997; *b* 15 Jan. 1958; *d* of Arnold Raphael and Lily Suzanne (*née* Shaffer); *m* 1982, Michael Eaves (marr. diss. 2001); one *s.* *Educ:* Putney High Sch.; Manchester Univ. (BA Hons Drama). Theatre director: Nuffield Theatre, 1980–81; Bristol Old Vic, 1981–83; Gate Theatre, London, 1983; Literary Agent and Publisher, Chappels Music, 1983; joined BBC Radio, 1984: Script Reader, Producer, Editor Drama, 1984–90; Editor Drama, Features, Youth Programmes, Radio 5, 1990–94; Hd of Drama, BBC Radio, 1994–97. Mem. Bd, Paines Plough Theatre Co., 1996–. *Recreations:* listening to radio, theatre, cinema, reading. *Address:* Broadcasting House, W1A 1AA. *T:* (020) 7580 4465.

RAPHAEL, Prof. David Daiches, DPhil, MA; Emeritus Professor of Philosophy, University of London, since 1983; *b* 25 Jan. 1916; 2nd *s* of late Jacob Raphael and Sarah Warshawsky, Liverpool; *m* 1942, Sylvia (*d* 1996), *er d* of late Rabbi Dr Salis Daiches and Flora Levin, Edinburgh; two *d.* *Educ:* Liverpool Collegiate School; University College, Oxford (scholar). 1st Class, Classical Moderations, 1936; Hall-Houghton Junior Septuagint Prizeman, 1937; 1st Class, Literae Humaniores, 1938; Robinson Senior Scholar of Oriel College, Oxford, 1938–40; Passmore Edwards Scholar, 1939. Served in Army, 1940–41. Temporary Assistant Principal, Ministry of Labour and National Service, 1941–44; temp. Principal, 1944–46. Professor of Philosophy, University of Otago, Dunedin, NZ, 1946–49; Lecturer in Moral Philosophy, Univ. of Glasgow, 1949–51; Senior Lecturer, 1951–60; Edward Caird Prof. of Political and Social Philosophy, Univ. of Glasgow, 1960–70; Prof. of Philosophy, Univ. of Reading, 1970–73; Prof. of Philosophy, Imperial Coll., Univ. of London, 1973–83 (Acad. Dir of Associated Studies, 1973–80; Head of Dept of Humanities, 1980–83; Hon. Fellow 1987). Visiting Professor of Philosophy, Hamilton Coll., Clinton, NY (under Chauncey S. Truax Foundation), and Univ. of Southern California, 1959; Mahlon Powell Lectr, Indiana Univ., 1959; Vis. Fellow, All Souls Coll., Oxford, 1967–68; John Hinkley Vis. Prof. of Political Sci., Johns Hopkins Univ., 1984. Independent Member: Cttee on Teaching Profession in Scotland (Wheatley Cttee), 1961–63; Scottish Agricultural Wages Board, 1962–84; Agricultural Wages Bd for England and Wales, 1972–78. Mem. Academic Adv. Cttee, Heriot-Watt Univ., Edinburgh, 1964–71; Mem. Cttee on Distribution of Teachers in Scotland (Roberts Cttee), 1965–66; Independent Member Police Advisory Board for Scotland, 1965–70; Member Social Sciences Adv. Cttee, UK Nat. Commission, UNESCO, 1966–74; Vice-Pres., Internat. Assoc. Philosophy of Law and Social Philosophy, 1971–87; Pres., Aristotelian Soc., 1974–75. Academic Mem., Bd of Governors, Hebrew Univ. of Jerusalem, 1969–81, Hon. Governor 1981–. Chm., Westminster Synagogue, 1987–89. *Publications:* The Moral Sense, 1947; Edition of Richard Price's Review of Morals, 1948; Moral Judgement, 1955; The Paradox of Tragedy, 1960; Political Theory and the Rights of Man, 1967; British Moralists 1650–1800, 1969; Problems of Political Philosophy, 1970, 2nd edn 1990; (ed jtly) Adam Smith's Theory of Moral Sentiments, 1976; Hobbes: Morals and Politics, 1977; (ed jtly) Adam Smith's Lectures on Jurisprudence, 1978; (ed jtly) Adam Smith's Essays on Philosophical Subjects, 1980; Justice and Liberty, 1980; Moral Philosophy, 1981, 2nd edn 1994; (trans. jtly with Sylvia Raphael) Richard Price as Moral Philosopher and Political Theorist, by Henri Laboucheix, 1982; Adam Smith, 1985; Concepts of Justice, 2001; articles in jls of philosophy and of political studies. *Address:* 54 Sandy Lane, Petersham, Richmond, Surrey TW10 7EL.

RAPHAEL, Frederic Michael; author; *b* 14 Aug. 1931; *s* of late Cedric Michael Raphael and of Irene Rose (*née* Mauser); *m* 1955, Sylvia Betty Glatt; two *s* (one *d* decd). *Educ:* Charterhouse; St John's Coll., Cambridge (MA (Hons)). FRSL 1964. *Publications: novels:* Obbligato, 1956; The Earlsdon Way, 1958; The Limits of Love, 1960; A Wild Surmise, 1961; The Graduate Wife, 1962; The Trouble with England, 1962; Lindmann, 1963; Orchestra and Beginners, 1967; Like Men Betrayed, 1970; Who Were You With Last Night?, 1971; April, June and November, 1972; Richard's Things, 1973; California Time, 1975; The Glittering Prizes, 1976; Heaven and Earth, 1985; After the War, 1988 (adapted for television, 1989); The Hidden I, 1990; A Double Life, 1993; Old Scores, 1995; Coast to Coast, 1998; *short stories:* Sleeps Six, 1979; Oxbridge Blues, 1980 (also pubd as scripts of TV plays, 1984); Think of England, 1986; The Latin Lover, 1994; All His Sons, 1999; *biography:* Somerset Maugham and his World, 1977; Byron, 1982; *memoir:* Eyes Wide Open: a memoir of Stanley Kubrick and Eyes Wide Shut, 1999; Personal Terms (notebooks 1951–1969), 2001; *essays*: Bookmarks (ed), 1975; Cracks in the Ice, 1979; Of Gods and Men, 1992; France, the Four Seasons, 1994; The Necessity of Anti-Semitism, 1997; Karl Popper, 1998; (ed jtly and contrib.) The Great Philosophers from Socrates to Turing, 2000; The Benefits of Doubts, 2002; *screenplays:* Nothing but the Best, 1964; Darling, 1965 (Academy Award); Two For The Road, 1967; Far From the Madding Crowd, 1967; A Severed Head, 1972; Daisy Miller, 1974; The Glittering Prizes, 1976 (sequence of TV plays) (Writer of the Year 1976, Royal TV Soc.); Rogue Male, 1976; (and directed) Something's Wrong (TV), 1978; School Play (TV), 1979; The Best of Friends (TV), 1979; Richard's Things, 1981; After the War (TV series), 1989; (and directed) The Man In The Brooks Brothers Shirt, 1991 (ACE Award); Eyes Wide Shut, 1999; For God's Sake (TV documentary series), 1998; *plays:* From The Greek, Arts, Cambridge, 1979; The Daedalus Dimension (radio), 1982; The Thought of Lydia (radio), 1988; The Empty Jew (radio), 1993; *translations:* Petronius: Satyrica, 2001; (with Kenneth McLeish): Poems of Catullus, 1976; The Oresteia, 1978 (televised as The Serpent Son, BBC, 1979); The Complete Plays of Aeschylus, 1991; Medea, 1994; Hippolytus, 1997; Aias, 1998; Bacchae, 1999. *Recreations:* tennis, having gardened. *Address:* c/o Deborah Rogers, 20 Powis Mews, W11 1JN. *Clubs:* Savile, The Queen's.

RAPHAEL, Ven. Timothy John; Archdeacon of Middlesex, 1983–96; *b* 26 Sept. 1929; *s* of Hector and Alix Raphael; *m* 1957, Anne Elizabeth Shepherd; one *s* two *d.* *Educ:* Christ's College, Christchurch, NZ; Leeds Univ. (BA). Asst Curate, St Stephen, Westminster, 1955–60; Vicar of St Mary, Welling, Kent, 1960–63; Vicar of St Michael, Christchurch, NZ, 1963–65; Dean of Dunedin, 1965–73; Vicar, St John's Wood,

London, 1973–83. *Recreations:* contemporary poetry, theatre, beach-combing. *Address:* 121 Hales Road, Cheltenham, Glos GL52 6ST. *T:* (01242) 256075.

RAPHOE, Bishop of, (RC), since 1995; **Most Rev. Philip Boyce,** DD; *b* 25 Jan. 1940; *s* of Joseph Boyce and Brigid Gallagher. *Educ:* Downings, Co. Donegal; Castlemartyr Coll., Co. Cork; Carmelite House of Studies, Dublin; Pontifical Theol Faculty (Teresianum), Rome (DD). Entered Discalced Carmelites, 1959; studied philosophy in Dublin and theology in Rome; ordained priest, 1966; on teaching staff of Pontifical Theol Faculty (Teresianum), Rome, 1972–95. Mem., Congregation for Divine Worship and Discipline of Sacraments, 1999–. *Publications:* The Challenge of Sanctity: a study of Christian perfection in the writings of John Henry Newman, 1974; Spiritual Exodus of John Henry Newman and Thérèse of Lisieux, 1979; articles on themes of spiritual theology. *Address:* Ard Adhamhnáin, Letterkenny, Co. Donegal, Ireland. *T:* (74) 21208.

RAPINET, Michael William; a Vice-President, Immigration Appeal Tribunal, since 1997; *b* 13 April 1935; *s* of Charles Herbert Rapinet and Eleanor Adelaide Rapinet (*née* Hunt); *m* 1962, Christina Mary, *d* of Captain William Eric Brockman, CBE, RN; one *s* one *d*. *Educ:* St Edward's Coll., Malta; St Joseph's Coll., London. Admitted Solicitor, 1957; Sen. Partner, Kidd Rapinet, 1958–85. Pt-time Chm., Industrial Tribunals, 1987–91; pt-time Chm., 1989–92, Chm., 1992–97, Immigration Tribunal. Pres., Council of Immigration Judges, 2000–01. Member (C): Wandsworth LBC, 1958–62; Berks CC, 1968–75 (Chm., Schs Cttee; Member: Finance Cttee; Personnel and Mgt Cttee). Liveryman, Tallow Chandlers' Co. Founder, Order of Malta Homes Trust, and Order of St John Trust, 1975. CStJ 1988; Kt of Magistral Grace, 1973, Kt Grand Cross, 1996, SMO (Malta). *Recreations:* fishing, gardening, walking, reading, theatre, music. *Address:* Stayes, Northend, Henley-on-Thames, Oxon RG9 6LH. *T:* (01491) 638382. *Clubs:* Carlton; Leander.

RAPLEY, Prof. Christopher Graham, PhD; Director, British Antarctic Survey, NERC, since 1998; Fellow, St Edmund's College, Cambridge, since 1999; *b* 8 April 1947; *s* of Ronald Rapley and Barbara Helen Rapley (*née* Stubbs); *m* 1970, Norma Khan; twin *d*. *Educ:* Jesus Coll., Oxford (BA Hons Physics 1969; MA 1974; four shooting half blues; Captain, OU Rifle Club); Manchester Univ. (MSc Radio Astronomy 1970); UCL (PhD X-ray Astronomy 1976). Associate Dir, Mullard Space Sci. Lab., 1990–97, and Prof. of Remote Sensing, 1991–97, UCL. Vis. Scientist and Mem., Cassini Titan Radar Sci. Team, NASA Jet Propulsion Lab., 1994–; Exec. Dir, Internat. Geosphere-Biosphere Prog., Royal Swedish Acad. of Scis, 1994–97. Vice Pres., Internat. Scientific Cttee on Antarctic Res., 2000–; Member: Exec., Eur. Polar Bd, 1999–; Earth Sci. Adv. Council, ESA, 2000–; UK Deleg., Governing Council, ESF, 2000–. Hon. Professor: UCL, 1998–; UEA, 1999–. *Publications:* more than 140 res. papers on space astronomy, remote sensing, global change, earth system sci. *Recreations:* jogging, photography. *Address:* Flat 3, 51 Bateman Street, Cambridge CB2 1LR. *T:* (01223) 523336.

RAPSON, Sydney Norman John, BEM 1984; MP (Lab) Portsmouth North, since 1997; *b* 17 April 1942; *s* of late Sidney Rapson and of Doris Rapson (*née* Fisher); *m* 1967, Phyllis Edna, *d* of Frank and Beatrice Williams; one *s* one *d*. *Educ:* Southsea and Paulsgrove Secondary Modern Sch.; Portsmouth Dockyard Coll. Apprentice aircraft fitter, 1958–63, Aircraft Engr, 1963–97, MoD. Member (Lab): Portsmouth CC, 1971–97 (Lord Mayor, 1990–91; Hon. Alderman, 1999); Hants CC, 1973–76. Non-exec. Dir, Portsmouth Healthcare NHS Trust, 1993–97. Freeman, City of London, 1990. Imperial Service Medal, 1998. *Address:* House of Commons, SW1A 0AA.

RASCH, Sir Simon (Anthony Carne), 4th Bt *cr* 1903, of Woodhill, Danbury, Essex; *b* 26 Feb. 1948; *s* of Sir Richard Guy Carne Rasch, 3rd Bt and Anne Mary (*d* 1989), *e d* of Maj. John Henry Dent-Brocklehurst, OBE; *S* father, 1996; *m* 1987, Julia, *er d* of Maj. Michael Godwin Plantagenet Stourton; one *s* one *d*. *Educ:* Eton; RAC Cirencester. ARICS 1973. A Page of Honour to HM The Queen, 1962–64. *Heir:* *s* Toby Richard Carne Rasch, *b* 28 Sept. 1994. *Address:* The White House, Manningford Bruce, near Pewsey, Wilts SN9 6JW.

RASHBASS, Dr Barbara, FRCP; barrister-at-law; Director and Secretary: Wolfson Foundation, 1990–97; Wolfson Family Charitable Trust, 1989–97; *d* of late Leonard Cramer and Sarina (*née* Klinger); *m* 1956, Cyril Rashbass (*d* 1982); two *s* one *d*. *Educ:* Godolphin Sch., Salisbury; University Coll. London (MB, BS; Fellow 1999). DCH 1961; DPH 1968; FRCP 1995. Called to the Bar, Middle Temple, 1969. PMO, MRC, 1983–87. Dep. Chm., Harrow HA, 1982–84; non-exec. Dir, Harrow and Hillingdon Healthcare NHS Trust, 1998–. Mem., Med. Legal Soc., 1970–. FRSocMed 1989. Trustee, Ronald Raven Cancer Res. Trust, 2000–. *Recreations:* tennis, 'cello, gardening.

RASHLEIGH, Sir Richard (Harry), 6th Bt *cr* 1831; management accountant; self-employed, since 1990; *b* 8 July 1958; *s* of Sir Harry Evelyn Battie Rashleigh, 5th Bt and Honora Elizabeth (*d* 1987), *d* of George Stuart Sneyd; *S* father, 1984; *m* 1996, Emma, *o d* of John McGougan and Jennifer (*née* Dyke; she *m* 1987, Sir Antony Acland, *qv*); one *s* one *d*. *Educ:* Allhallows School, Dorset. Management Accountant with Arthur Guinness Son & Co., 1980–82; Dexion-Comino International Ltd, 1982–84; United Biscuits, 1985–88; Wessex Housing, 1988–90. *Recreations:* sailing, tennis, shooting. *Heir:* *s* David William Augustine Rashleigh, *b* 1 April 1997. *Address:* Menabilly, Par, Cornwall PL24 2TN. *T:* (01726) 815432. *Club:* Royal Fowey Yacht.

RASHLEIGH BELCHER, John; *see* Belcher.

RASMUSSEN, Poul Nyrup; MP (SDP) Herning-Kredsen, Denmark, since 1988; Prime Minister of Denmark, since 1993; *b* 15 June 1943; *s* of Oluf Nyrup Rasmussen and Vera Nyrup Rasmussen; *m* 1st (marr. diss.); (one *c* decd); 2nd (marr. diss.); 3rd, 1994, Lone Dybkjær, MEP. *Educ:* Esbjerg Statsskole; Univ. of Copenhagen (MA Econs). With Danish Trade Union Council, 1980–86: in Brussels, 1980–81; Chief Economist, 1981–86; Man. Dir, Employees' Capital Pension Fund, 1986–88. Dep. Chm., SDP, 1987–92, Chm., 1992–. *Address:* Office of the Prime Minister, Christiansborg, Prins Jørgens Gaard 11, 1218 Copenhagen K, Denmark. *T:* 33923300.

RASSOOL, Bertrand Louis Maurice; High Commissioner of Seychelles to the United Kingdom, since 1999; *b* 10 April 1957; *m* 1978, Estelle Guntier; one *s* two *d*. *Educ:* London Sch. of Econs (BSc Econs (Mathematical Econs and Econometrics)). Central Bank of Seychelles: economist, 1980; Asst Dir of Res., 1981–86; Dir of Res., 1986–88; Dir Gen., Planning and Econ. Co-operation Div., Min. of Planning and Ext. Relns, 1988–93; Principal Secretary: Min. of Foreign Affairs, Planning and Envmt, 1993–94; Min. of Industry, 1994–98; Min. of Tourism and Civil Aviation, 1998–99. *Recreations:* fishing, chess, horse-racing. *Address:* Seychelles High Commission, 2nd Floor, Eros House, Baker Street, W1M 1FE. *T:* (020) 7224 1660.

RATCLIFF, Antony Robin Napier; Director, Eagle Star Investment Managers (formerly Eagle Star Asset Management) Ltd, since 1995; Deputy Chairman and Chief Executive, Eagle Star Insurance, 1985–87; Visiting Professor, City University Business School, since 1987; *b* 26 Sept. 1925; *m* 1956, Helga Belohlawek, Vienna; one *s*. FIA 1953; Aktuar, DAV, 1994; ASA. Nat. Correspondent for England, Internat. Actuarial Assoc., 1965–70; Mem. Council, Assoc. of British Insurers (formerly British Insurance Assoc.), 1969–87. Pres., Inst. of Actuaries, 1980–82; Vice-President: London Insce Inst., 1964–; Chartered Insce Inst., 1983–84. Hon. Mem., Assoc. internat. pour l'Etude de l'Economie de l'Assurance, 1991– (Vice-Pres., 1986–90). Trustee, Soc. for the Protection of Life from Fire, 1989–(Chm., 1998–2000). Mem., Evangelische Forschungs-akad., Berlin. Corresponding Member: Deutsche Gesellschaft für Versicherungsmathematik; Verein zur Förderung der Versicherungswirtschaft. FRSA. Hon. Treasurer, German Christ Church, London; Trustee, St Paul's German Evangelical Reformed Ch Trust. Messenger and Brown Prize-Winner, Inst. of Actuaries, 1963. Hon. DLitt City, 1986. *Publications:* (jtly) Lessons from Central Forecasting, 1965; (jtly) Strategic Planning for Financial Institutions, 1974; (jtly) A House in Town, 1984; contribs to Jl of Inst. of Actuaries, Trans of Internat. Congress of Actuaries, Jl London Insce Inst., Jl Chartered Insce Inst., Blätter der Deutschen Gesellschaft für Versicherungsmathematik. *Address:* 8 Evelyn Terrace, TW9 2TQ. *Clubs:* Actuaries, Anglo-Austrian Society.

RATCLIFFE, Frederick William, CBE 1994; MA, PhD; JP; University Librarian, University of Cambridge, 1980–94, now Emeritus; Life Fellow, since 1994 (Fellow, 1980–94), and Parker Librarian, 1995–2000, Corpus Christi College, Cambridge; *b* 28 May 1927; *y s* of late Sydney and Dora Ratcliffe, Leek, Staffs; *m* 1952, Joyce Brierley; two *s* one *d*. *Educ:* Leek High Sch., Staffs; Manchester Univ. (MA, PhD); MA Cantab. Served in N Staffs Regt, 1945–48. Manchester University: Graduate Res. Scholarship, 1951; Res. Studentship in Arts, 1952; Asst Cataloguer and Cataloguer, 1954–62; Sub-Librarian, Glasgow Univ., 1962–63; Dep. Librarian, Univ. of Newcastle upon Tyne, 1963–65; University Librarian, 1965–80, Dir, John Rylands University Library, 1972–80, Manchester University. Trustee, St Deiniol's Library, Hawarden, 1975–98. Hon. Lectr in Historical Bibliography, Manchester Univ., 1970–80; External Prof., Dept of Library and Inf. Studies, Loughborough Univ., 1981–86; Hon. Res. Fellow, Dept of Library, Archive and Inf. Studies, UCL, 1987–; Sandars Reader in Bibliography, Cambridge Univ., 1988–89. Founder, later Pres., Consortium of Univ. Res. Libraries, 1984–94; Chm., Library Panel, The Wellcome Trust, 1988–94. Fellow, Chapter of Woodard Schools (Eastern Div.), 1981–97, now Emeritus (Vice-Provost, 1994–97). Chm., Adv. Cttee, Nat. Preservation Office, 1984–94. Trustee: Cambridge Foundn, 1989–94; Malaysian Commonwealth Studies Centre, 1994–98. Hon. FLA 1986. JP Stockport, 1972–80, Cambridge, 1981–97. Encomienda de la Orden del Merito Civil (Spain), 1988. *Publications:* Preservation Policies and Conservation in British Libraries, 1984; many articles in learned journals. *Recreations:* book collecting, hand printing, cricket. *Address:* Ridge House, The Street, Rickinghall Superior, Diss, Norfolk IP22 1DY. *T:* (01379) 898232.

RATCLIFFE, (John) Michael; writer; *b* 15 June 1935; *s* of Donald Ratcliffe and Joyce Lilian Dilks. *Educ:* Cheadle Hulme Sch.; Christ's Coll., Cambridge (MA). Trainee journalist, Sheffield Telegraph, 1959–61; Asst Literary and Arts Editor, Sunday Times, 1962–67; Literary Editor, 1967–72, chief book reviewer, 1972–82, The Times; freelance writer, 1982–83; theatre critic, 1984–89, Literary Ed., 1990–95, Contributing Ed., 1995–96, Observer. Commended Critic of the Year, British Press Awards, 1989. *Publications:* The Novel Today, 1968; The Bodley Head 1887–1987 (completed for J. W. Lambert), 1987. *Recreations:* music, travel, architecture, walking, gardening, cycling. *Address:* 4 Elia Street, N1 8DE. *T:* (020) 7837 1687, *Fax:* (020) 7713 6286.

RATFORD, Sir David (John Edward), KCMG 1994 (CMG 1984); CVO 1979; HM Diplomatic Service, retired; *b* 22 April 1934; *s* of George Ratford and Lilian (*née* Jones); *m* 1960, Ulla Monica, *d* of Oskar and Gurli Jerneck, Stockholm; two *d*. *Educ:* Whitgift Middle Sch.; Selwyn Coll., Cambridge (1st Cl. Hons Mod. and Med. Langs). National Service (Intell. Corps), 1953–55. Exchequer and Audit Dept, 1952; FO, 1955; 3rd Sec., Prague, 1959–61; 2nd Sec., Mogadishu, 1961–63; 2nd, later 1st Sec., FO, 1963–68; 1st Sec. (Commercial), Moscow, 1968–71; FCO, 1971–74; Counsellor (Agric. and Econ.), Paris, 1974–78; Counsellor, Copenhagen, 1978–82; Minister, Moscow, 1983–85; Asst Under-Sec., of State (Europe), 1986–90, and Dep. Political Dir, 1987–90, FCO; UK Rep., Permanent Council of WEU, 1986–90; Ambassador to Norway, 1990–94. Comdr, Order of the Dannebrog, Denmark, 1979. *Recreations:* music, tennis, walking. *Address:* Wisborough Cottage, Wisborough Green, West Sussex RH14 0DZ; Käringön, Bohuslän, Sweden. *Club:* Travellers.

RATHBONE, John Rankin, (Tim); Chairman, Sponsorship Consulting Ltd, since 1997; *b* 17 March 1933; *s* of J. R. Rathbone, MP (killed in action 1940) and Lady Wright (*see* Beatrice Wright); *m* 1st, 1960, Margarita Sanchez y Sanchez (marr. diss. 1981); two *s* one *d*; 2nd, 1982, Mrs Susan Jenkin Stopford Sackville. *Educ:* Eton; Christ Church, Oxford; Harvard Business School. 2nd Lieut KRRC, 1951–53. Robert Benson Lonsdale & Co., Merchant Bankers, 1956–58; Trainee to Vice-Pres., Ogilvy & Mather Inc., NY, 1958–66; Chief Publicity and Public Relations Officer, Conservative Central Office, 1966–68; Director: Charles Barker Group, 1968–87; Ayer Barker Ltd, 1971–87 (Man. Dir 1971–73; Dep. Chm., 1973–79); Charles Barker City, 1981–87; Charles Barker Manchester, 1983–87 (Chm., 1983–86). MP (C) Lewes, Feb. 1974–1997; contested (C) same seat, 1997. PPS to Minister of Health, 1979–82, to Minister for Trade (Consumer Affairs), 1982–83, to Minister for the Arts, 1985. Member, Select Committee: on Sound Broadcasting of H of C, 1983–87; on Nat. Heritage, 1996–97; Founder Member: All Party Parly Drugs Misuse Gp, 1984 (Chm., 1987–97); Parly Engrg Develt Gp, 1987 (Chm., 1992–97); formerly Member, All-Party Groups: Human Rights; Energy; Envmt; Consumers; Vol Orgns; British-Amer.; British-Latin Amer.; British-Cuban; British-Southern Africa (Chm.); British-Japanese; British-China; British-Jordan; British-Spanish; British-Lebanon (Chm.); British-UAE; British-Iraqi Shias; Sane Planning. Mem., European Movt. Deleg. to Council of Europe and WEU, 1987–96; formerly Mem., Cons. ME Council. Formerly Mem. Council, Nat. Cttee for Electoral Reform. Mem., Steering Gp on Drugs, the Business Agenda, BITC, 1998–99; Dir, Phoenix House, 1999–; Mem., London Drug Policy Forum, 2000–. Vice-Pres., Tree Council, 1992–. Trustee, Mentor Foundn UK, 1999–. Gov., Bancroft's Sch., 1998–; Mem., Council, Arab-British Centre, 2000–. FRSA 1979 (Mem. Council, 1985–88). *Publications:* It's my problem as well: drugs prevention and education, 1992; pamphlet on nursery schooling. *Recreation:* family. *Address:* 10 Ursula Street, SW11 3DW. *T:* (020) 7738 1078. *Clubs:* Brooks's, Pratt's; Sussex.

RATHBONE, Tim; *see* Rathbone, J. R.

RATHBONE, William; Director and Chief Executive, Royal United Kingdom Beneficent Association and Universal Beneficent Association, 1988–2001; *b* 5 June 1936; *s* of William Rathbone and Margaret Hester (*née* Lubbock); *m* 1960, Sarah Kynaston Mainwaring; one *s* one *d*. *Educ:* Radley Coll.; Christ Church, Oxford (MA 2nd Cl. Hons PPE 1959); IMEDE, Lausanne (Dip. Business Studies 1972). Nat. Service, RA, 1954–56. Ocean Group PLC, 1959–88: Elder Dempster Lines, 1959–69; tanker and bulk carrier div., 1969–71; Dir, Wm Cory & Sons Ltd, 1973–74; Gen. Manager, Ocean Inchcape Ltd, 1974–79; Exec, Dir, Gastransco Ltd, 1979–88. Dir, Rathbone Bros plc, 1994–. Trustee,

Queen's Nursing Inst., 1974–(Vice-Chm., 1974–99); Pres., Community and Dist Nursing Assoc., 1984–99; Vice Pres., Christ Church (Oxford) United Clubs, 1991–. Trustee: Eleanor Rathbone Charitable Trust, 1958–; New England Co., 1974–; St Peter's Convent, Woking, 1992–; Southwark Cathedral Millenium Trust, 2000–; Gov., Centre for Policy on Ageing, 2000–. Liveryman, Skinners' Co., 1969–. *Recreations:* fishing, the arts, friends. *Address:* 7 Brynmaer Road, SW11 4EN. *T:* (020) 7978 1935. *Clubs:* Brooks's; Leander (Henley-on-Thames).

RATHCAVAN, 3rd Baron *cr* 1953, of The Braid, Co. Antrim; **Hugh Detmar Torrens O'Neill;** Bt 1929; Deputy Chairman, Lamont Holdings, since 1996 (Director, since 1973); *b* 14 June 1939; *o s* of 2nd Baron Rathcavan, PC (NI) and his 1st wife, Clare Désirée (*d* 1956), *d* of late Detmar Blow; *S* father, 1994; *m* 1983, Sylvie Marie-Thérèse Wichard; one *s*. *Educ:* Eton. Captain, Irish Guards. Financial journalism, Observer, Irish Times, FT; Dep. Chm., IPEC Europe, 1978–82; Chairman: Northern Ireland Airports, 1986–92; NI Tourist Board, 1988–96; Director: St Quentin, 1980–94; The Spectator, 1982–84; Old Bushmills Distillery Co., 1989–99; Savoy Management, 1989–94; Northern Bank Ltd, 1990–97; Berkeley Hotel Co. Ltd, 1995–97. Mem., BTA, 1988–96. Member: H of L European Select Cttee D, 1997–99; British-Irish Interparly Body, 1997–99. *Recreations:* food, travel. *Heir: s* Hon. François Hugh Nial O'Neill, *b* 26 June 1984. *Address:* Cleggan Lodge, Ballymena, Co. Antrim BT43 7JW. *T:* (028) 2586 2222, *Fax:* (028) 2586 2000; 14 Thurloe Place, SW7 2RZ. *T:* (020) 7584 5293. *Clubs:* Beefsteak, Pratt's.

RATHCREEDAN, 3rd Baron *cr* 1916; **Christopher John Norton;** Partner, Norton & Brooksbank, Pedigree Livestock Auctioneers, since 1983; *b* 3 June 1949; *er s* of 2nd Baron Rathcreedan, TD and of Ann Pauline, *d* of late Surg.-Capt. William Bastian, RN; *S* father, 1990; *m* 1978, Lavinia Anne Ross, *d* of late A. G. R. Ormiston; two *d*. *Educ:* Wellington Coll.; RAC Cirencester. Partner, Hobsons, Pedigree Livestock Auctioneers; founded Norton & Brooksbank, 1983. *Recreations:* horse racing, gardening. *Heir: b* Hon. Adam Gregory Norton [*b* 2 April 1952; *m* 1980, Hilary Shelton, *d* of Edmond Ryan; two *d*.]. *Address:* Stoke Common House, Purton Stoke, Swindon, Wilts SN5 4LL. *T:* (01793) 772492. *Club:* Turf.

RATHDONNELL, 5th Baron *cr* 1868; **Thomas Benjamin McClintock Bunbury;** *b* 17 Sept. 1938; *o s* of William, 4th Baron Rathdonnell and Pamela (*d* 1989), *e d* of late John Malcolm Drew; *S* father, 1959; *m* 1965, Jessica Harriet, *d* of George Gilbert Butler, Scatorish, Bennettsbridge, Co. Kilkenny; three *s* one *d*. *Educ:* Charterhouse; Royal Naval College, Dartmouth. Lieutenant RN. *Heir: s* Hon. William Leopold McClintock Bunbury, *b* 6 July 1966. *Address:* Lisnavagh, Rathvilly, County Carlow, Ireland. *T:* (503) 61104.

RATLEDGE, Prof. Colin, PhD; CChem, FRSC; CBiol, FIBiol; Professor of Microbial Biochemistry, University of Hull, since 1983; *b* 9 Oct. 1936; *s* of Fred Ratledge and Freda Smith Ratledge (*née* Proudlock); *m* 1961, Janet Vivien Bottomley; one *s* two *d*. *Educ:* Bury High Sch.; Manchester Univ. (BSc Tech, PhD). AMCST; CChem, FRSC 1970; CBiol, FIBiol 1982. Res. Fellowship, MRC Ireland, 1960–64; Res. Scientist, Unilever plc, 1964–67; Hull University, 1967–: Lectr, 1967–73; Sen. Lectr, 1973–77; Reader, 1977–83; Head of Dept of Biochemistry, 1986–88. Visiting Lecturer: Australian Soc. of Microbiol., 1986; NZ Soc. of Microbiol., 1986; Kathleen Barton Wright Meml Lectr (Inst. of Biol./Soc. Gen. Microbiol.), 1995; Visiting Professor: Univ. of Malaya, 1993; Hong Kong Poly., 1994; Univ. of OFS, Bloemfontein, 1994. Mem., AFRC Food Res. Cttee, 1989–92; Chairman: AFRC Food Res. Grants Bd, 1989–92; AFRC Food-borne Pathogens Co-ord. Prog., 1992–95; Brit. Co-ordinating Cttee for Biotechnology, 1989–91; Inst. of Biol. Industrial Biol. Cttee, 1992–; Vice-Pres., SCI, 1993–96 (Chm. Biotechnol. Gp, 1990–91; Mem. Council, 1991–93); Sec., Internat. Cttee of Envmtl and Applied Microbiology, 1991–94; Mem., Biotechnology Cttee, Internat. Union of Biochemistry, 1984–97. Fellow, Internat. Inst. of Biotechnology, 1993. Editor: World Jl of Microbiol. and Biotechnol., 1987–; Biotechnology Techniques, 1988–99; Biotechnology Letters, 1996–. *Publications:* The Mycobacteria, 1977; Co-Editor: Microbial Technology: current state, future prospects, 1979; The Biology of the Mycobacteria, vol. 1 1982, vol. 2 1983, vol. 3 1989; Biotechnology for the Oils and Fats Industry, 1984; Microbial Technology in the Developing World, 1987; Microbial Lipids, vol. 1 1988, vol. 2 1989; Microbial Physiology and Manufacturing Industry, 1988; Biotechnology: Social and Economic Impact, 1992; Industrial Application of Single Cell Oils, 1992; Biochemistry of Microbial Degradation, 1993; Mycobacteria: molecular biology and virulence, 1999; Basic Biotechnology, 2nd edn 2001; numerous scientific papers in biol science jls. *Recreations:* hill walking, bonsai gardening. *Address:* Department of Biological Sciences, University of Hull, Hull HU6 7RX; *e-mail:* c.ratledge@biosci.hull.ac.uk; (home) 49 Church Drive, Leven, Beverley, E Yorks HU17 5LH. *T:* (01964) 542690.

RATNER, Gerald Irving; Chief Executive, Ratners Group, 1986–92; Director, The Workshop Health & Fitness Club, Henley, since 1997; *b* 1 Nov. 1949; *s* of Leslie and Rachelle Ratner; *m* 1st (marr. diss. 1989); two *d*; 2nd, 1989, Moira Day; one *s* one *d*. *Educ:* Hendon Co. Grammar Sch. Ratners (Jewellers), subseq. Ratners Group: Jt Man. Dir, 1978–84, Man. Dir, 1984–92; Chm., 1986–92. Dir, Norweb, 1989–91. *Recreations:* keeping fit, art, chess.

RATTEE, Sir Donald (Keith), Kt 1989; a Judge of the High Court of Justice, Chancery Division, 1993–2000 (Family Division, 1989–93); *b* 9 March 1937; *s* of Charles Ronald and Dorothy Rattee; *m* 1964, Diana Mary, *d* of John Leslie and Florence Elizabeth Howl; four *d*. *Educ:* Clacton County High School; Trinity Hall, Cambridge (MA, LLB). Called to the Bar, Lincoln's Inn, 1962, Bencher, 1985; Second Junior Counsel to the Inland Revenue (Chancery), 1972–77; QC 1977; Attorney Gen. of the Duchy of Lancaster, 1986–89; a Recorder, 1989. Liaison Judge, Family Div. (NE Circuit), 1990–93; Mem., Gen. Council of the Bar, 1970–74. Chm., Inns of Court and Bar Educnl Trust, 1997–. *Recreations:* golf, walking, music, gardening. *Address:* 29 Shirley Avenue, Cheam, Surrey SM2 7QS. *Clubs:* Royal Automobile; Banstead Downs Golf (Banstead).

RATTLE, Sir Simon, Kt 1994; CBE 1987; Chief Conductor and Artistic Director, Berlin Philharmonic Orchestra, from Sept. 2002; Principal Guest Conductor, Orchestra of the Age of Enlightenment, since 1992; *b* Liverpool, 19 Jan. 1955; *m* 1st, 1980, Elise Ross (marr. diss. 1995), American soprano; two *s*; 2nd, 1996, Candace Allen. Won Bournemouth John Player Internat. Conducting Comp., when aged 19. Has conducted: Bournemouth Sinfonietta; Philharmonia; Northern Sinfonia; London Philharmonic; London Sinfonietta; Berlin Philharmonic; Boston Symphony; Chicago Symphony; Cleveland; Concertgebouw; Stockholm Philharmonic; Toronto Symphony, etc. Débuts: Festival Hall, 1976; Glyndebourne, 1977; ENO, 1985; Royal Opera, 1990; Vienna Philharmonic, 1993; Philadelphia, 1993; Royal Albert Hall (Proms etc), 1976–; Asst Conductor, BBC Scottish Symphony Orch., 1977–80; Principal Conductor and Artistic Advr, 1980–90, Music Dir, 1990–98, CSBO. Associate Conductor, Royal Liverpool Philharmonic Soc., 1977–80; Principal Conductor, London Choral Soc., 1979–84; Artistic Dir, South Bank Summer Music, 1981–83; Principal Guest Conductor: Rotterdam Philharmonic, 1981–84; Los Angeles Philharmonic, 1981–92. Exclusive contract with EMI Records. Hon. Fellow, St Anne's Coll., Oxford, 1991. Hon. DMus: Birmingham, 1985; Birmingham Poly., 1985; Oxford, 1999. Shakespeare Prize, Toepfer Foundn, Hamburg, 1996; Albert Medal, RSA, 1997. Chevalier des Arts et des Lettres (France), 1995. *Address:* c/o Askonas Holt Ltd, Lonsdale Chambers, 27 Chancery Lane, WC2A 1PF. *T:* (020) 7400 1700.

RATTRAY, (Raphael) Carl, OJ 1994; President, Court of Appeal, Jamaica, 1993–99; *b* 18 Sept. 1929; *s* of late Benjamin Bruce Rattray and Agnes Agatha Rattray (*née* Wright); *m* 1951, Audrey Elaine Da Costa; two *s* two *d*. *Educ:* Beckford Smith's High Sch., Jamaica; Univ. of London (ext. LLB). Called to the Bar, Lincoln's Inn, 1956; Stipendiary Magistrate, Cayman Is, 1957–58; in private practice at Jamaican Bar, 1958–75; QC (Jamaica) 1969; Senator, Jamaican Parlt, 1975–83; Attorney Gen. and Minister of Justice, 1976–80; Leader: Govt Business in Senate, 1975–80; Opposition Business in Senate, 1980–83; Founding Mem., Rattray, Patterson, Rattray, 1981; in practice at Bar, 1981–89; MP (PNP), 1989–93; Attorney Gen. and Minister of Legal Affairs, 1989–92. Vice-Pres., Jamaican Bar Council, 1988–89. Hon. LLD Capital, Columbus, Ohio, 1990. *Publications:* Firstlings: a collection of poems, 1951; contrib. to Caribbean Law Rev., Jamaican Law Jl. *Recreations:* reading, writing, walking. *Address:* 4 Rockhampton Drive, Kingston 8, Jamaica. *T:* 9252723.

RAU, Johannes; President, Federal Republic of Germany, since 1999; *b* Wuppertal, 16 Jan. 1931; *s* of Ewald and Helene Rau; *m* 1982, Christina Delius; one *s* two *d*. Served apprenticeship as publisher and bookseller; publishing director, 1954–67. North Rhine-Westphalia Landtag: Mem. (SPD), 1958–99; Chm., SPD Parly Gp, 1967–70; Minister for Sci. and Res., 1970–78; Premier, 1978–98. Mem., Wuppertal City Council, 1964–78 (Lord Mayor, 1969–70). Joined SPD, 1957; Dep. Chm., 1982–99. Mem., Rhineland, Synod of Evangelical Church, 1965–99. *Address:* Office of the President, Spreeweg 1, 10557 Berlin, Germany.

RAU, Santha Rama; *see* Rama Rau, S.

RAUSING, Dr Hans A.; Hon. Chairman, Tetra Laval Group, 1993–95; *b* 25 March 1926; *s* of Ruben and Elisabeth Rausing; *m* 1958, Märit Norrby; one *s* two *d*. *Educ:* Univ. of Lund, Sweden. Tetra Pak: Man. Dir, 1954–83; Exec. Chm. and Chief Exec. Officer, 1983–91; Chm., Gp Bd, 1985–91; Chm. and Chief Exec. Officer, Tetra Laval Gp, 1991–93. Member, Board: Stockholms Enskilda Bank, Sweden, 1970–72; Skandinaviska Enskilda Banken, Sweden, 1973–82; South-Swedish Univs, Sweden, 1975–80; Business Internat., NY, 1975–79. Mem., Co-ordination Council for Foreign Investments, Russia, 1995. Hon. Prof., Univ. of Dubna, 1996; Vis. Prof., Mälardalens Högskola, Sweden, 2001. Member: Royal Swedish Acad. of Engrg Scis, 1984 (Hon. Mem., 1994); Russian Acad. of Inventors; Foreign Mem., Russian Acad. of Agriculture. Hon. Mem., Acad. of Natural Scis, Russia, 1994. Hon. doctorates: Econs, Lund, 1979; DTech Royal Inst. of Technol., Stockholm, 1985; Econs, Stockholm Sch. of Econs, 1987; American Univ. in London. *Address:* PO Box 216, Wadhurst, E Sussex TN5 6LW. *T:* (01892) 783693.

RAVEN, Prof. John Albert, FRS 1990; FRSE; CBiol, FIBiol; Boyd Baxter Professor of Biology, University of Dundee, since 1995; *b* 25 June 1941; *s* of John Harold Edward Raven and Evelyn Raven; *m* 1985, Linda Lea Handley. *Educ:* Wimbish County Primary Sch.; Friends' Sch., Saffron Walden; St John's College, Cambridge (MA, PhD). FRSE 1981; CBiol, FIBiol 1998. University of Cambridge: Research Fellow, and Official Fellow, St John's Coll., 1966–71; Univ. Demonstrator in Botany, 1968–71; Lectr, and Reader, 1971–80, Prof. (personal chair), 1980–95, Dept of Biol Scis, Univ. of Dundee. Hon. PhD Umeå, Sweden, 1995. *Publications:* Energetics and Transport in Aquatic Plants, 1984; (with Paul Falkowski) Aquatic Photosynthesis, 1997; numerous papers in learned jls and chapters in multi-author vols. *Recreations:* aviation, walking, literature. *Address:* Spital Beag, Waterside, Invergowrie, Dundee DD2 5DQ.

RAVEN, John Armstrong, CBE 1982; Director-General, International Express Carriers' Conference, 1991–93 and 1995–99 (Director (Facilitation), 1993–94); Consultant, World Bank, since 1983; Adviser, International Air Cargo Association; *b* 23 April 1920; *s* of late John Colbeck Raven; *m* 1st, 1945, Megan Humphreys (*d* 1963); one *s* one *d*; 2nd, 1965, Joy Nesbitt (*d* 1983); one step *d*. *Educ:* High Sch., Cardiff; Downing Coll., Cambridge (MA). Called to Bar, Gray's Inn, 1955. Dir, British Coal Exporters' Fedn, 1947–68; Section Head, Nat. Economic Develt Office, 1968–70. Dir-Gen., Assoc. of British Chambers of Commerce, 1972–74; Vice-Chm., SITPRO, 1974–82. *Recreation:* wondering. *Address:* 215 Avenue de Messidor, 1180 Brussels, Belgium. *T:* (2) 3457620. *Club:* Oxford and Cambridge.

RAVEN, Martin Clark; HM Diplomatic Service; Counsellor, Deputy Head of Mission and Consul General, Stockholm, since 1998; *b* 10 March 1954; *s* of Basil Raven and Betty Raven (*née* Gilbert); *m* 1978, Philippa Michale Morrice Ruddick; two *s*. *Educ:* Bury Grammar Sch., Lancs; Univ. of Sussex (BA Intellectual Hist.). Joined HM Diplomatic Service, 1976: Korea/Mongolia Desk, then Yugoslavia/Albania Desk, FCO, 1976–78; Third Sec., Lagos, 1978; Hindi lang. trng, SOAS, 1979; Third, later Second Sec., Delhi, 1979–83; First Secretary: N America, then Non-Proliferation Depts, FCO, 1983–88; Human Rights and Social Issues, UK Mission to UN, NY and Alternate Rep. to Commn on Human Rights, 1988–92; Dep. Hd, S Atlantic and Antarctic Dept, FCO and Dep. Comr, British Antarctic Territory, 1993–96; Hd, Drugs and Internat. Crime Dept, FCO, 1996–98. *Recreations:* cycling, cinema, food, theatre, reading novels, listening to music, watching football and cricket, eating olives. *Address:* c/o Foreign and Commonwealth Office, King Charles Street, SW1A 2AH. *Clubs:* Lancashire County Cricket; Sallskapet (Stockholm).

RAVENSCROFT, John Robert Parker, (John Peel), OBE 1998; broadcaster/journalist, since 1961; *b* 30 Aug. 1939; *s* of Robert Leslie and Joan Mary Ravenscroft; *m* 1974, Sheila Mary Gilhooly; two *s* two *d*. *Educ:* Woodlands Sch., Deganwy, N Wales; Shrewsbury. National Service, Royal Artillery (B2 Radar Operator), 1957–59. Mill operative, Rochdale, 1959–60; office boy, Dallas, Texas, 1960–65; part-time disc-jockey, 1961–; computer programmer, 1965; Pirate Radio, London, 1967; BBC Radio 1, 1967–; Home Truths, BBC Radio 4, 1998–. Hon. MA East Anglia, 1989; Hon. DMus Anglia Poly., 1999. *Recreations:* making plans to go and live in France, staring out of the window. *Address:* c/o BBC Radio 1, W1A 4DJ. *T:* (020) 7580 4468.

RAVENSCROFT, Ven. Raymond Lockwood; Archdeacon of Cornwall and Canon Librarian of Truro Cathedral, 1988–96; *b* 15 Sept. 1931; *s* of Cecil and Amy Ravenscroft; *m* 1957, Ann (*née* Stockwell); one *s* one *d*. *Educ:* Sea Point Boys' High School, Cape Town, SA; Leeds Univ. (BA Gen. 1953); College of the Resurrection, Mirfield. Assistant Curate: St Alban's, Goodwood, Cape, SA, 1955–58; St John's Pro-Cathedral, Bulawayo, S Rhodesia, 1958–59; Rector of Francistown, Bechuanaland, 1959–62; Asst Curate, St Ives, Cornwall, 1962–64; Vicar: All Saints, Falmouth, 1964–68; St Stephen by Launceston with St Thomas, 1968–74; Team Rector of Probus Team Ministry, 1974–88; RD of Powder, 1977–81; Hon. Canon of Truro Cathedral, 1982–88. *Recreations:* walking, reading, local history. *Address:* 19 Montpelier Court, St David's Hill, Exeter EX4 4DP. *T:* (01392) 430607.

RAVENSDALE, 3rd Baron *cr* 1911; **Nicholas Mosley,** MC 1944; Bt 1781; *b* 25 June 1923; *e s* of Sir Oswald Mosley, 6th Bt (*d* 1980) and Lady Cynthia (*d* 1933), *d* of 1st Marquess Curzon of Kedleston; *S* to barony of aunt, who was also Baroness Ravensdale of Kedleston (Life Peer), 1966, and to baronetcy of father, 1980; *m* 1st, 1947, Rosemary Laura Salmond (marr. diss. 1974; she *d* 1991); three *s* one *d*; 2nd, 1974, Mrs Verity Bailey; one *s*. *Educ:* Eton; Balliol College, Oxford. Served in the Rifle Brigade, Captain, 1942–46. *Publications:* (as Nicholas Mosley): Spaces of the Dark, 1951; The Rainbearers, 1955; Corruption, 1957; African Switchback, 1958; The Life of Raymond Raynes, 1961; Meeting Place, 1962; Accident, 1964; Experience and Religion, 1964; Assassins, 1966; Impossible Object, 1968; Natalie Natalia, 1971; The Assassination of Trotsky, 1972; Julian Grenfell: His Life and the Times of his Death, 1888–1915, 1976; The Rules of the Game: Sir Oswald and Lady Cynthia Mosley 1896–1933, 1982; Beyond the Pale: Sir Oswald Mosley 1933–1980, 1983; Efforts at Truth (autobiog.), 1995; Rules of the Game and Beyond the Pale, 1998; *novels* (series): Catastrophe Practice, 1979; Imago Bird, 1980; Serpent, 1981; Judith, 1986; Hopeful Monsters (Whitbread Prize), 1990; Children of Darkness and Light, 1996; The Hesperides Tree, 2001. *Heir: s* Hon. Shaun Nicholas Mosley [*b* 5 August 1949; *m* 1978, Theresa Clifford; five *s* one *d*]. *Address:* 2 Gloucester Crescent, NW1 7DS. *T:* (020) 7485 4514.

RAVENSWORTH, 8th Baron *cr* 1821; **Arthur Waller Liddell;** Bt 1642; JP; *b* 25 July 1924; *s* of late Hon. Cyril Arthur Liddell (2nd *s* of 5th Baron) and Dorothy L., *d* of William Brown, Slinfold, Sussex; *S* cousin 1950; *m* 1950, Wendy, *d* of J. S. Bell, Cookham, Berks; one *s* one *d*. *Educ:* Harrow. Radio Engineer, BBC, 1944–50. JP Northumberland, 1959. *Heir: s* Hon. Thomas Arthur Hamish Liddell [*b* 27 Oct. 1954; *m* 1983, Linda, *d* of H. Thompson; one *s* one *d*]. *Address:* Eslington Park, Whittingham, Alnwick, Northumberland NE66 4UR. *T:* (01665) 574239.

RAVIV, Moshe; Ambassador of Israel to the Court of St James's, 1993–97; *b* Romania, 23 April 1935; *s* of David and Elka Raviv; *m* 1955, Hanna Kaspi; two *s* one *d*. *Educ:* Hebrew Univ., Jerusalem; Univ. of London (grad. Internat. Relations). Israel Ministry of Foreign Affairs: 2nd Sec., London, 1961–63; Office of Foreign Minister, Mrs Golda Meir, 1964–65; Political Sec. to Foreign Minister, Abba Eban, 1966–68; Counsellor, Washington, 1968–74; Dir, E European Div., 1974–76; Dir, N American Div., 1976–78; Ambassador to the Phillipines, 1978–81; Dir, Economic Div., 1981–83; Minister, London, 1983–88; Dep. Dir Gen., i/c Information, 1988–93. *Publication:* Israel At Fifty: five decades of struggle for peace, 1998. *Recreations:* reading, chess, jogging.

RAWBONE, Rear-Adm. Alfred Raymond, CB 1976; AFC 1951; *b* 19 April 1923; *s* of A. Rawbone and Mrs E. D. Rawbone (*née* Wall); *m* 1943, Iris Alicia (*née* Willshaw); one *s* one *d*. *Educ:* Saltley Grammar Sch., Birmingham. Joined RN, 1942; 809 Sqdn War Service, 1943; CO 736 Sqdn, 1953; CO 897 Sqdn, 1955; CO Loch Killisport, 1959–60; Comdr (Air) Lossiemouth and HMS Ark Royal, 1961–63; Chief Staff Officer to Flag Officer Naval Air Comd, 1965–67; CO HMS Dido, 1968–69; CO RNAS Yeovilton, 1970–72; CO HMS Kent, 1972–73; Dep. ACOS (Operations), SHAPE, 1974–76. Comdr 1958; Captain 1964; Rear-Adm. 1974. Director: Vincents of Yeovil, 1983–86; Vindata, 1984–86; Vincents (Bridgewater) Ltd, 1984–86. *Address:* Halstock Leigh, Halstock, near Yeovil, Somerset BA22 9QU.

RAWCLIFFE, Rt Rev. Derek Alec, OBE 1971; Bishop of Glasgow and Galloway, 1981–91; *b* 8 July 1921; *s* of James Alec and Gwendoline Rawcliffe; *m* 1977, Susan Speight (*d* 1987). *Educ:* Sir Thomas Rich's School, Gloucester; Univ. of Leeds (BA, 1st cl. Hons English); College of the Resurrection, Mirfield. Deacon 1944, priest 1945, Worcester; Assistant Priest, Claines St George, Worcester, 1944–47; Asst master, All Hallows School, Pawa, Solomon Islands, 1947–53; Headmaster, 1953–56; Headmaster, S Mary's School, Maravovo, Solomon Is, 1956–58; Archdeacon of Southern Melanesia, New Hebrides, 1959–74; Assistant Bishop, Diocese of Melanesia, 1974–75; First Bishop of the New Hebrides, 1975–80; Asst Bishop, dio. of Ripon, 1991–96. New Hebrides Medal, 1980; Vanuatu Independence Medal, 1980. *Publications:* The Meaning of it All is Love (articles and essays), 2000; The Stone and the Hazel Nut (poems), 2000. *Recreations:* music, poetry. *Address:* 7 Dorset Avenue, Leeds LS8 3RA. *T:* (0113) 249 2670.

RAWES, Francis Roderick, MBE 1944; MA; *b* 28 Jan. 1916; *e s* of late Prescott Rawes and Susanna May Dockery; *m* 1940, Dorothy Joyce, *d* of E. M. Hundley, Oswestry; two *s* one *d*. *Educ:* Charterhouse; St Edmund Hall, Oxford. Served in Intelligence Corps, 1940–46; GSO3(I) 13 Corps; GSO1 (I) HQ 15 Army Group and MI14 WO. Asst Master at Westminster School, 1938–40 and 1946–64; Housemaster, 1947–64; Headmaster, St Edmund's School, Canterbury, 1964–78; Adminr, ISIS Assoc., 1979–83. C of E Lay Reader, 1979–96. Chm. Governing Body, Westonbirt Sch., 1983–91 (Governor, 1979–95). *Address:* Peyton House, Chipping Campden, Glos GL55 6AL.

RAWLEY, Alan David; QC 1977; a Recorder of the Crown Court, 1972–99; Fellow Commoner, Magdalene College, Cambridge, since 1991; *b* 28 Sept. 1934; *er s* of late Cecil David Rawley and of Theresa Rawley (*née* Pack); *m* 1964, Ione Jane Ellis; two *s* one *d*. *Educ:* Wimbledon Coll.; Brasenose Coll., Oxford. Nat. Service, 1956–58; commnd Royal Tank Regt. Called to the Bar, Middle Temple, 1958; Bencher, 1985. Dep. Chairman, Cornwall Quarter Sessions, 1971. Member: CICB, 1999–; CICAP, 2000–. *Address:* 35 Essex Street, Temple, WC2R 3AR. *T:* (020) 7353 6381. *Clubs:* Garrick, Pilgrims, MCC.

RAWLINGS, Baroness *cr* 1994 (Life Peer), of Burnham Westgate in the County of Norfolk; **Patricia Elizabeth Rawlings;** *b* 27 Jan. 1939; *d* of Louis Rawlings and Mary (*née* Boas de Winter); *m* 1962, David Wolfson (*see* Baron Wolfson of Sunningdale) (marr. diss. 1967). *Educ:* Oak Hall, Haslemere, Surrey; Le Manoir, Lausanne; Florence Univ.; University Coll. London (BA Hons); London School of Economics (post grad. diploma course, Internat. Relns). Children's Care Cttee, LCC, 1959–61; WNHR Nursing, Westminster Hosp., until 1968. Contested (C): Sheffield Central, 1983; Doncaster Central, 1987. MEP (C) Essex SW, 1989–94; contested (C) Essex West and Hertfordshire East, Eur. parly elecns, 1994. European Parliament, 1989–94: EPP British Section Rep. on Conservative Nat. Union; Vice Pres., Albanian, Bulgarian and Romanian Delegn; EDG spokesman on Culture Cttee, substitute on Foreign Affairs Cttee; Dep. Whip, 1989–92. Opposition Whip, H of L, 1997–98; opposition spokesman on internat. develt, H of L, 1998–. British Red Cross Society: Mem., 1964–; Chm., Appeals, London Br., until 1988; Nat. Badge of Honour, 1981, Hon. Vice Pres., 1988; Patron, London Br., 1997–. Member Council: British Bd of Video Classification, 1986–89; Peace through NATO; British Assoc. for Central and Eastern Europe, 1994–; Mem. Adv. Council, PYBT, 1998–; Special Advr to Ministry on Inner Cities, DoE, 1987–88. Chm. Council, KCL, 1998–. Member: IISS; RIIA; EUW. Dir, English Chamber Orch. and Music Soc. Hon. LittD Buckingham, 1998. Order of the Rose, Silver Class (Bulgaria), 1991; Grand Official, Order of the Southern Cross (Brazil), 1997. *Recreations:* music, art, golf, ski-ing, travel. *Address:* House of Lords, SW1A 0PW. *Clubs:* Queen's, Grillions (Hon. Sec.); Royal West Norfolk Golf.

RAWLINGS, Flt Lieut Jerry John; President, Republic of Ghana, 1992–2001; *b* 22 June 1947; *s* of John Rawlings and Victoria Agbotui; *m* 1977, Nana Konadu Agyeman; one *s* three *d*. *Educ:* Achimota Sch., Accra; Ghana Military Acad. Enlisted in Ghana Air Force, 1967; commnd Pilot Officer, 1969; tried for mutiny, May 1979; forcibly released from cell, June 1979, by popular uprising; became Chm., Armed Forces Revolutionary Council; handed over to democratically elected Govt, Sept. 1979; overthrew Govt, Dec. 1981; Chm., Provisional Nat. Defence Council, 1982–92. *Recreations:* flying, swimming, riding, reading. *Address:* c/o Office of the President, PO Box 1627, Accra, Ghana. *T:* (21) 665415.

RAWLINGS, Prof. Rees David, PhD; CEng; Professor of Materials Science, since 1993, and Pro Rector (Educational Quality), since 2000, Imperial College of Science, Technology and Medicine; *b* 30 Sept. 1942; *s* of Aubrey Rhys Islwyn Rawlings and Daphne Irene Rawlings (*née* Sangster); *m* 1964, Ann Margaret Halliday; two *d*. *Educ:* Sir Thomas Rich High Sch., Gloucester; Imperial Coll. (BSc Engrg 1st cl. Hons 1964; PhD Metallurgy 1967); ARSM 1964; DIC 1967; DSc London 1989. CEng 1980; FIM 1985; MILT 2000. Imperial College: Lectr, 1966–81; Reader, 1981–93; acting Hd, Earth Resources Engrg, 1996–98; Dean, Royal Sch. of Mines, 1995–98; Mem. Governing Body, 1995–98; Mem. Court, 1998–; Partner, Matcon (Materials Consultants), 1974–90. Subject Specialist Assessor: HEFCE, 1996–98; HEFCW, 1997–98. Deputy Editor: Jl Materials Science, 1993–; Jl Materials Science Letters, 1993–. Hon. FRCA, 2001. L. B. Pfeil Medal and Prize, Inst. of Materials, 1990. *Publications:* (jtly) Materials Science, 1974, 4th edn 1990; (jtly) Composite Materials: engineering and science, 1994; articles in learned jls, conf. proceedings and books on materials science. *Recreations:* sport (but no longer active), gardening, photography, theatre. *Address:* Imperial College of Science, Technology and Medicine, Prince Consort Road, SW7 2BP. *T:* (020) 7594 7400. *Club:* Kingston Athletic and Polytechnic Harriers.

RAWLINS, Colin Guy Champion, OBE 1965; DFC 1941; Director of Zoos and Chief Executive, Zoological Society of London, 1966–84; *b* 5 June 1919; *s* of R. S. C. Rawlins and Yvonne Blanche Andrews; *m* 1946, Rosemary Jensen; two *s* one *d*. *Educ:* Prince of Wales Sch., Nairobi; Charterhouse; Queen's Coll., Oxford (MA). Served with RAF, 1939–46: Bomber Comd, NW Europe; POW, 1941–45; Sqdn-Leader. HM Overseas Civil Service, 1946–66: Administrative Officer, Northern Rhodesia (later Zambia); appointments at Headquarters and in field; Provincial Commissioner, Resident Secretary. Mem., Pearce Commn on Rhodesian Opinion, 1972. Past Pres., Internat. Union of Dirs of Zool. Gardens. Chm. of Trustees, Zimbabwe Trust, 1993–. FCIS 1967. *Recreations:* aviation, gardening. *Address:* Riverain, Gossmore Lane, Marlow, Bucks SL7 1QF. *T:* (01628) 472796.

RAWLINS, Brig. Gordon John, OBE 1986; Director, Members Services, Institution of Electrical Engineers, since 2000 (Deputy Secretary, 1991–2000); *b* 22 April 1944; *s* of Arthur and Joyce Rawlins; *m* 1st, 1965, Ann Beard (*d* 1986); one *s*; 2nd, 1986, Margaret Anne Ravenscroft; one step *s* one step *d*. *Educ:* Peter Symond's, Winchester; Welbeck College; RMA Sandhurst; RMCS Shrivenham (BSc Eng). CEng, FIEE, psc. Commissioned REME, 1964; served Aden, Oman, Jordan, Hong Kong, BAOR, UK, 1964–77; Staff Coll., 1978; MoD 1978–80; 2 i/c 5 Armd Wksp, REME, BAOR, 1981–82; CO 7 Armd Wksp, REME, BAOR, 1982–84; MoD, 1984–87 (Sec. to COS Cttee, 1987); Comd Maint., 1 (BR) Corps, BAOR, 1988. Sec., Instn of Production, subseq. Manufacturing, Engrs, 1988–91. Liveryman, Turners' Co., 1991. *Recreations:* opera, blues music, Rugby, cricket, compiling general knowledge quizzes. *Address:* Institution of Electrical Engineers, Savoy Place, WC2R 0BL. *T:* (020) 7240 1871. *Club:* Army and Navy.

RAWLINS, Surg. Vice-Adm. Sir John (Stuart Pepys), KBE 1978 (OBE 1960; MBE 1956); *b* 12 May 1922; *s* of Col S. W. H. Rawlins, CB, CMG, DSO and Dorothy Pepys Cockerell; *m* 1944, Diana Colbeck (*d* 1992); one *s* three *d*. *Educ:* Wellington Coll.; University Coll., Oxford (Hon. Fellow, 1991); St Bartholomew's Hospital. BM, BCh 1945; MA, FRCP, FFCM, FRAeS. Surg. Lieut RNVR, HMS Triumph, 1947; Surg. Lieut RN, RAF Inst. Aviation Med., 1951; RN Physiol Lab., 1957; Surg. Comdr RAF Inst., Aviation Med., 1961; HMS Ark Royal, 1964; US Navy Medical Research Inst., 1967; Surg. Captain 1969; Surg. Cdre, Dir of Health and Research (Naval), 1973; Surg. Rear-Adm. 1975; Dean of Naval Medicine and MO i/c, Inst. of Naval Medicine, 1975–77; Actg Surg. Vice-Adm. 1977; Medical Dir-Gen. (Navy), 1977–80. QHP 1975. Chairman: Deep Ocean Engineering Inc., 1983–89; Medical Express Ltd, 1984–; Trident Underwater Engrg (Systems) Ltd, 1985–; General Offshore Corp. (UK) Ltd, 1988–91; Director: Diving Unlimited International Ltd, 1980–; Deep Ocean Technology Inc., 1989– (Chm., 1983–89); Deep Ocean Engrg, 1989–91. Pres., Soc. for Underwater Technology, 1980–84 (Hon. Fellow, 1986); Vice-Pres., Underseas Med. Soc.; Hon. Life Mem., British Sub-Aqua Club, 1983; Founder-Mem. European Underseas Biomed. Soc.; Fellow Aerospace Med. Soc. (Armstrong Lectr, 1980); FRAeS 1973; FRSocMed. Hon. Fellow, Lancaster Univ., 1986. Hon. DTech Robert Gordon's Inst. of Technology, 1991. Erroll-Eldridge Prize 1967; Sec. of US Navy's Commendation 1971; Gilbert Blane Medal 1971; Tuttle Meml Award 1973; Chadwick Medal and Prize 1975; Nobel Award, Inst. of Explosives Engrs, 1987; NOGI Award, US Acad. of Underwater Arts and Scis, 1998; Colin McLeod Award, British Sub-Aqua Club, 2000; Lowell Thomas Award, Explorers' Club, 2000; Man of the Year, British Council for Rehabilitation of the Disabled, 1964. *Publications:* papers in fields of aviation and diving medicine. *Recreations:* diving, fishing, stalking, riding. *Address:* Little Cross, Holne, Newton Abbot, S Devon TQ13 7RS. *T:* (01364) 631249, *Fax:* (01364) 631400. *Club:* Vincent's (Oxford).

RAWLINS, Sir Michael (David), Kt 1999; DL; MD; FRCP, FRCPE, FFPM, FMedSci; Ruth and Lionel Jacobson Professor of Clinical Pharmacology, University of Newcastle upon Tyne, since 1973; *b* 28 March 1941; *s* of Rev. Jack and Evelyn Daphne Rawlins; *m* 1963, Elizabeth Cadbury Hambly; three *d*. *Educ:* St Thomas's Hosp. Med. Sch., London (BSc 1962; MB BS 1965); MD London 1973. FRCP 1977; FRCPE 1987; FFPM 1989. Lectr in Medicine, St Thomas's Hosp., London, 1967–71; Sen. Registrar, Hammersmith Hosp., London, 1971–72; Vis. Res. Fellow, Karolinska Inst., Stockholm, Sweden, 1972–73; Public Orator, Univ. of Newcastle upon Tyne, 1990–93. Ruiting van Swieten Vis. Prof., Academic Med. Centre, Amsterdam, 1998. Pres., NE Council on Addictions, 1991–; Chm., Adv. Council on Misuse of Drugs, 1998–; Vice-Chm., Northern RHA, 1990–94; Member: Nat. Cttee on Pharmacology, 1977–83; Cttee on the Safety of Medicines, 1980–98 (Chm., 1993–98); Cttee on Toxicity, 1989–92; Standing Gp on Health Technology Assessment, 1993–95; Chm., Nat. Inst. for Clinical Excellence, 1999–. Chm., Newcastle SDP, 1981–84. Bradshaw Lectr, RCP, 1986; Welcome Lectr, Soc. of Apothecaries, 1996. DL Tyne and Wear, 1999. FRSocMed 1972; Founder FMedSci 1998. Hon. FRCA 2000. Univ. Medal, Helsinki, 1978; William Withering Medal, RCP, 1994; Dixon Medal, Ulster Med. Soc., 1995; Lilly Medal, British Pharmacol Soc., 1997. *Publications:* Variability in Human Drug Response, 1973; (ed) Textbook of Pharmaceutical Medicine, 1994; articles on clinical pharmacology in med. and scientific jls. *Recreations:* music, golf. *Address:* 29 The Grove, Gosforth, Newcastle upon Tyne NE3 1NE. *T:* (0191) 285 5581; Shoreston House, Shoreston, near Seahouses, Northumberland

NE68 7SX. *T:* (01665) 720203. *Clubs:* Northern Counties (Newcastle); Bamburgh Castle Golf.

RAWLINS, Brig. Peregrine Peter, MBE 1983; Clerk to the Grocers' Company, since 1998; *b* 3 March 1946; *s* of Lt-Col John Walter Rawlins, Northamptonshire Regt, and Elizabeth Joan Rawlins (*née* Delmé-Radcliffe); *m* 1976, Marlis Müller; one *s* one *d. Educ:* Malvern Coll.; RMA, Sandhurst; Lincoln Coll., Oxford (BA Hons Geography 1970). Royal Anglian Regiment: commnd 2nd Bn, 1966; Comd, 2nd Bn, 1985–87; Dep. Col, 1996–98. Staff Coll., 1978; Directing Staff, RMCS, 1988–90; COS, Directorate of Infantry, 1990–92; NATO Defence Coll., Rome, 1992; Defence Attaché, Bonn, 1992–96; Dep. Comdt, RMCS, 1996–98, retd. Hon. Sec., British-German Officers Assoc., 1998–. *Recreations:* bird watching, fishing, gardening, golf. *Address:* The Grey House, Low Road, Little Cheverell, Devizes, Wilts SN10 4JS; Grocers' Hall, Princes Street, EC2R 8AD. *Club:* Army and Navy.

RAWLINS, Peter Jonathan, FCA; business strategy consultant, since 1994; *b* 30 April 1951; *e s* of late Kenneth Raymond Ivan Rawlins and of Constance Amande Rawlins (*née* Malzy); *m* 1st, 1973, Louise Langton (marr. diss. 1999); one *s* one *d*; 2nd, 2000, Christina Conway; one *d. Educ:* Arnold House Sch.; St Edward's Sch., Oxford; Keble Coll., Oxford (Hons English Lang. and Lit.; MA). Arthur Andersen & Co., 1972–85: Manager, 1977; Partner, 1983; UK Practice Devel Partner, 1984; full-time secondment to Lloyd's of London as PA to Chief Exec. and Dep, Chm., 1983–84; Dir, Sturge Holdings, and Man. Dir, R. W. Sturge & Co., 1985–89; Chief Exec., Internat., subseq. London, Stock Exchange, 1989–93; Director: Sturge Lloyd's Agencies, 1986–89; Wise Speke Holdings, 1987–89; non-exec. Dir, Lloyd-Roberts & Gilkes, 1989–94; Man. Dir (Europe, ME and Africa), Siegel & Gale Ltd, 1996–97; Director: Scala Business Solutions, NV, 1998–2000; Logistics Resources Ltd, 1999–; Oyster Partners Ltd, 2001–. Mem., Cttee, Lloyd's Underwriting Agents Assoc., 1986–89 (Treasurer, 1986–87; Dep. Chm., 1988); Mem., standing cttees, Council of Lloyd's, 1985–89. Director: London Sinfonietta Trust, 1985–88; Half Moon Theatre, 1986–88; Mem. Council and Dir, ABSA, 1982–96; Dir and Trustee, London City Ballet Trust, 1986–93; Mem., Develt Council, RNT, 1991–95; Vice-Chm., Spitalfields Fest., 2000–. Chairman: London First Neighbourhood Approach, 1993–95; Assoc. for Res. into Stammering in Children, 1993–. FRSA 1990. *Recreations:* performing arts, tennis, squash, shooting, travelling. *Address:* 70A Redcliffe Gardens, SW10 9HE. *Clubs:* City of London, MCC.

RAWLINSON, family name of **Baron Rawlinson of Ewell**.

RAWLINSON OF EWELL, Baron *cr* 1978 (Life Peer), of Ewell in the County of Surrey; **Peter Anthony Grayson Rawlinson;** PC 1964; Kt 1962; QC 1959; QC (NI) 1972; *b* 26 June 1919; *o* surv. *s* of late Lt-Col A. R. Rawlinson, OBE, and Ailsa, *e d* of Sir Henry Mulleneux Grayson, Bt, KBE; *m* 1st, 1940, Haidee Kavanagh; two *d* (and one *d* decd); 2nd, 1954, Elaine Dominguez, Newport, Rhode Island, USA; two *s* one *d. Educ:* Downside; Christ's Coll., Cambridge (Exhibitioner 1938, Hon. Fellow 1980). Officer Cadet Sandhurst, 1939; served in Irish Guards, 1940–46; N Africa, 1943 (despatches); demobilized with rank of Major, 1946. Called to Bar, Inner Temple, 1946, Bencher, 1962, Reader, 1983, Treas., 1984; Recorder of Salisbury, 1961–62; called to Bar, Northern Ireland, 1972; Recorder of Kingston upon Thames, 1975–; Leader, Western Circuit, 1975–82; retired from practice at the Bar, 1985. Contested (C) Hackney South, 1951; MP(C) Surrey, Epsom, 1955–74, Epsom and Ewell, 1974–78. Solicitor-General, July 1962–Oct. 1964; Opposition Spokesman: for Law, 1964–65, 1968–70; for Broadcasting, 1965; Attorney-General, 1970–74; Attorney-General for NI, 1972–74. Chm., Parly Legal Cttee, 1967–70. Member of Council, Justice, 1960–62, 1964; Trustee of Amnesty, 1960–62; Member, Bar Council, 1966–68; Mem. Senate, Inns of Court, 1968, Vice-Chm., 1974; Vice-Chm., Bar, 1974–75; Chairman of the Bar and Senate, 1975–76; Pres., Senate of Inns of Court and Bar, 1986–87; Chm., Enquiry into Constitution of the Senate, 1985–86. Chm. of Stewards, RAC, 1985–2000. Director: Pioneer International (formerly Pioneer Concrete Services) Ltd, Sydney, 1985–91 (Chm., UK subsidiary); Daily Telegraph plc, 1985–; STC plc, 1986–91; Mem., London Adv. Cttee, Hongkong and Shanghai Banking Corp., 1984–90. Chm., London Oratory Appeal, 1983–94; Gov., London Oratory Sch., 1985–95. Hon. Fellow, Amer. Coll. of Trial Lawyers, 1973; Hon. Mem., Amer. Bar Assoc., 1976. SMO Malta. *Publications:* War Poems and Poetry today, 1943; Public Duty and Personal Faith—the example of Thomas More, 1978; A Price Too High (autobiog.), 1989; The Jesuit Factor, 1990; *novels:* The Colombia Syndicate, 1991; Hatred and Contempt (Rumpole Award, CWA), 1992; His Brother's Keeper, 1993; Indictment for Murder, 1994; The Caverel Claim, 1998; The Richmond Diary, 2001; articles and essays in law jls. *Recreations:* the theatre and painting. *Address:* Wardour Castle, Tisbury, Wilts SP3 6RH. *Clubs:* White's, Royal Automobile, MCC.

See also Baron Swaythling.

RAWLINSON, Sir Anthony Henry John, 5th Bt *cr* 1891; photographer and inventor; *b* 1 May 1936; *s* of Sir Alfred Frederick Rawlinson, 4th Bt and Bessie Ford Taylor (*d* 1996), *d* of Frank Raymond Emmatt, Harrogate; *S* father, 1969; *m* 1st, 1960, Penelope Byng Noel (marr. diss. 1967), 2nd *d* of Rear-Adm. G. J. B. Noel, RN; one *s* one *d*; 2nd, 1967, Pauline Strickland (marr. diss. 1976), *d* of J. H. Hardy, Sydney; one *s*; 3rd, 1977, Helen Leone (marr. diss. 1997), *d* of T. M. Kennedy, Scotland; one *s. Educ:* Millfield School. Coldstream Guards, 1954–56. *Recreations:* tennis, sailing. *Heir: s* Alexander Noel Rawlinson, *b* 15 July 1964. *Address:* Heath Farm, Guist, Dereham, Norfolk NR20 5PG.

RAWLINSON, Charles Frederick Melville; Chairman, Boxford Suffolk Group, 1992–2000; *b* 18 March 1934; *s* of Rowland Henry Rawlinson and Olivia Melville Rawlinson; *m* 1962, Jill Rosalind Wesley; three *d. Educ:* Canford Sch.; Jesus Coll., Cambridge (MA). FCA, FCT. With A. E. Limehouse & Co., Chartered Accts, 1955–58; Peat Marwick Mitchell & Co., 1958–62; Morgan Grenfell & Co. Ltd, Bankers, 1962–87: Dir, 1970–87; Jt Chm., 1985–87; Morgan Grenfell Group PLC: Dir, 1985–88; Vice-Chm., 1987–88; Sen. Advr, 1988–93; Chm., Morgan Grenfell (Asia), Singapore, 1976–88, Hon. Pres., 1988–93; seconded as Man. Dir, Investment Bank of Ireland Ltd, Dublin, 1966–68; Director: Associated Paper Industries plc, 1972–91 (Chm., 1979–91); Willis Faber plc, 1981–89; Hedley Wright & Co. Ltd, 1994–99. Sen. Advr, West Merchant Bank, 1993–97. Chairman: The Hundred Gp of Finance Dirs, 1984–86; Industrial Mems Adv. Cttee on Ethics, ICAEW, 1991–99; Member: Chartered Accountants' Jt Ethics Cttee, 1994–; Council, ICAEW, 1995–97; Exec. Cttee, Jt Disciplinary Scheme, 1995–. Dir, Britten Sinfonia, 1988– (Dep. Chm., 1997–); Mem., Council, Order of St Etheldreda, Ely Cathedral, 1999–. Chm., Peache Trustees, 1980–; Hon. Vice Pres., NABC—Clubs for Young People, 1995– (Jt Hon. Treas., 1983–91; Dep. Chm., 1989–92; Chm., 1992–94). *Recreations:* music, sailing, shooting. *Address:* The Old Forge, Arkesden, Saffron Walden, Essex CB11 4EX. *Club:* Brooks's.

See also under Royal Family.

RAWLINSON, Dennis George Fielding, OBE 1978; JP; FCIT; company director; *b* 3 Sept. 1919; *s* of George and Mary Jane Rawlinson; *m* 1943, Lilian Mary; one *s* one *d. Educ:* Grocers' Co.'s Sch. Army, 1939–46. Various progressive positions in omnibus industry. Mem., Transport Tribunal, 1986–91. JP Darlington, 1971. *Recreations:* theatre, music, golf and various lesser sports. *Address:* 62 Cleveland Avenue, Darlington, Co. Durham DL3 7HG. *T:* (01325) 461254. *Club:* Army and Navy.

RAWLINSON, Ivor Jon, OBE 1988; HM Diplomatic Service, retired; Ambassador to Tunisia, 1999–2002; *b* 24 Jan. 1942; *s* of Vivian Hugh Rawlinson and Hermione (*née* Curry); *m* 1976, Catherine Paule Caudal; one *s* two *d. Educ:* Christ Church, Oxford (MA). Joined FO, 1964; Polish lang. student, 1965–66; Warsaw, 1966–69; Bridgetown, 1969–71 (course at Univ. of W Indies); Second Sec., News Dept, FCO, 1971–73; Asst Private Sec. to Minister of State, FCO, 1973–74; Second Sec. (Econ.), Paris, 1974–78; First Secretary: FCO, 1978–80; (Commercial), Mexico City, 1980–84; Consul, Florence and Consul-Gen., San Marino, 1984–88; First Sec., later Counsellor (Inspectorate), FCO, 1988–93; RCDS, 1993; Consul-Gen., Montreal, 1993–98. *Recreations:* painting, tennis, winter sports, collecting books, restoring farmhouse in France. *Address:* 17 Malwood Road, SW12 8EN. *Club:* Hurlingham.

RAWLINSON, Richard Anthony; Managing Partner (formerly Director), Monitor Company Group, since 1993; Member, Competition (formerly Monopolies and Mergers) Commission, since 1998; *b* 11 Feb. 1957; *s* of Sir Anthony Rawlinson, KCB and Lady (Mary) Rawlinson; *m* 1991, Sharon Sofer; two *s. Educ:* Eton Coll. (King's Schol.); Christ Church, Oxford (BA Politics and Econs 1978; MA); Harvard Business Sch. (Baker Schol.; MBA 1983). J. Henry Schroder Wagg & Co. Ltd, 1978–81; Associates Fellow, Harvard Business Sch., 1983–84; Monitor Company: Cambridge, Mass, 1984–85; London, 1985–89; Tokyo, 1989–93; Hong Kong, 1994–96; London, 1996–. *Publications:* (contrib.) Competition in Global Industries, 1986; articles in Harvard Business Review. *Recreations:* mountain walking, reading. *Address:* (office) Michelin House, 81 Fulham Road, SW3 6RD. *Clubs:* Oxford and Cambridge, Hurlingham.

RAWNSLEY, Andrew Nicholas James; author, broadcaster and journalist; Chief Political Columnist and Associate Editor, The Observer, since 1993; *b* 5 Jan. 1962; *s* of Eric Rawnsley and Barbara Rawnsley (*née* Butler); *m* 1990, Jane Leslie Hall; three *d. Educ:* Lawrence Sheriff Grammar Sch., Rugby; Rugby Sch.; Sidney Sussex Coll., Cambridge (1st Cl. Hons Hist.; MA). BBC, 1983–85; The Guardian: reporter, 1985–87; sketchwriter, 1987–93. TV presenter: A Week in Politics, 1989–97; series: The Agenda, 1996; Bye Bye Blues, 1997; Blair's Year, 1998; radio presenter, The Westminster Hour, 1998–; The Unauthorised Biography of the United Kingdom, 1999. Student Journalist of Year, Guardian/NUS Student Media Awards, 1982; Young Journalist of Year, British Press Awards, 1987; Columnist of Year, What the Papers Say awards, 2000. *Publication:* Servants of the People: the inside story of New Labour, 2000 (Channel 4/Politico Book of the Year, 2001). *Recreations:* books, movies, mah-jong, scuba-diving, ski-ing. *Address:* The Observer, 119 Farringdon Road, EC1R 3ER; Press Gallery, House of Commons, SW1A 1AA.

RAWSON, Christopher Selwyn Priestley; JP; *b* 25 March 1928; *e s* of late Comdr Selwyn Gerald Caygill Rawson, OBE, RN (retd) and late Dr Doris Rawson, MB, ChB (*née* Brown); *m* 1959, Rosemary Ann Focke; two *d. Educ:* The Elms Sch., Colwall, near Malvern, Worcs; The Nautical College, Pangbourne, Berks. Navigating Apprentice, Merchant Service, T. & J. Brocklebank Ltd, 1945–48. Sheriff of the City of London, 1961–62; Member of Court of Common Council (Ward of Bread Street), 1963–72; Alderman, City of London, (Ward of Lime Street), 1972–83; one of HM Lieutenants of City of London, 1980–83. A Younger Brother of Trinity House, 1988–. Chairman: Governors, The Elms Sch., Colwall, near Malvern, Worcs, 1965–84; Port and City of London Health Cttee, 1967–70; Billingsgate and Leadenhall Mkt Cttee, 1972–75. Silver Medal for Woollen and Worsted Raw Materials, City and Guilds of London Institute, 1951; Livery of Clothworkers' Company, 1952 (Mem. Court of Assistants, 1977; Master, 1988–89); Freeman, Company of Watermen and Lightermen, 1966 (Mem. Ct of Assts, 1974, Master, 1982–84). Hon. Mem., London Metal Exchange, 1979. ATI 1953; AIMarE 1962. CStJ 1985. JP City of London, 1967. Commander: National Order of Senegal, 1961; Order of the Ivory Coast, 1962; Star of Africa, Liberia, 1962. *Recreations:* shooting, sailing. *Address:* 23 Cristowe Road, SW6 3QF. *Clubs:* Garrick, Royal London Yacht (Cdre, 1990–91), City Livery Yacht (Cdre, 1987–90).

RAWSON, Prof. Jessica Mary, CBE 1994; LittD; FBA 1990; Warden, Merton College, Oxford, since 1994; Professor of Chinese Art and Archaeology, University of Oxford, since 2000; *b* 20 Jan. 1943; *d* of Roger Nathaniel Quirk and Paula Quirk; *m* 1968, John Rawson; one *d. Educ:* New Hall, Cambridge (BA Hons History; LittD 1991; Hon. Fellow, 1997); London Univ. (BA Hons Chinese Lang. and Lit.). Asst Principal, Min. of Health, 1965–67; Department of Oriental Antiquities, British Museum: Asst Keeper II, 1967–71; Asst Keeper I, 1971–76; Dep. Keeper, 1976–87; Keeper, 1987–94. Visiting Professor: Kunsthistorisches Inst., Heidelberg, 1989; Dept of Art, Univ. of Chicago, 1994. Lectures: Barlow, Sussex Univ., 1979; Levintvitt Meml., Harvard, 1989; A. J. Pope, Smithsonian Instn, 1991; Harvey Buchanan, Cleveland Mus. of Art, 1993; Pratt Inst., 1998; Beatrice Blackwood, Oxford, 1999; Millennium, Oxford, 2000; Creighton, Univ. of London, 2000. Member: Nuffield Langs Inquiry, 1998–99; British Library Bd, 1999–. Chm., Oriental Ceramic Soc., 1993–96; Vice-Chm., Exec. Cttee, GB-China Centre, 1985–87. Gov., SOAS, Univ. of London, 1998–. Hon. DSc St Andrews, 1997; Hon. DLitt: London, 1998; Sussex, 1998; Newcastle, 1999. *Publications:* Chinese Jade Throughout the Ages (with John Ayers), 1975; Animals in Art, 1977; Ancient China, Art and Archaeology, 1980; Chinese Ornament: the lotus and the dragon, 1984; Chinese Bronzes: art and ritual, 1987; The Bella and P. P. Chiu Collection of Ancient Chinese Bronzes, 1988; Western Zhou Ritual Bronzes from the Arthur M. Sackler Collections, 1990; (with Emma Bunker) Ancient Chinese and Ordos Bronzes, 1990; (ed) The British Museum Book of Chinese Art, 1992; Chinese Jade from the Neolithic to the Qing, 1995; Mysteries of Ancient China, 1996. *Address:* Merton College, Oxford OX1 4JD. *T:* (01865) 276352, 276368, *Fax:* (01865) 276282; 3 Downshire Hill, NW3 1NR. *T:* (020) 7794 4002.

RAWSON, Prof. Kenneth John, MSc; FREng; RCNC; consultant; Professor and Head of Department of Design and Technology, 1983–89, Dean of Education and Design, 1983–89, Brunel University; *b* 27 Oct. 1926; *s* of late Arthur William Rawson and Beatrice Anne Rawson; *m* 1950, Rhona Florence Gill; two *s* one *d. Educ:* Northern Grammar Sch., Portsmouth; HM Dockyard Technical Coll., Portsmouth; RN Colls, Keyham and Greenwich. RCNC; FREng (FEng 1984); FRINA; FCSD. WhSch. At sea, 1950–51; Naval Construction Res. Estabt, Dunfermline, 1951–53; Ship Design, Admiralty, 1953–57; Lloyd's Register of Shipping, 1957–59; Ship and Weapons Design, MoD, Bath, 1959–69; Naval Staff, London, 1969–72; Prof. of Naval Architecture, University Coll., Univ. of London, 1972–77; Ministry of Defence, Bath: Head of Forward Design, Ship Dept, 1977–79; Dep. Dir, Ship Design and Chief Naval Architect (Under Sec.), 1979–83. FRSA. Hon. DEng Portsmouth, 1995. *Publications:* Photoelasticity and the Engineer, 1953; (with E. C. Tupper) Basic Ship Theory, 1968, 5th edn 2001; contrib. numerous technical publications. *Recreations:* cabinet making, wine making, gardening, walking. *Address:* Moorlands, The Street, Chilcompton, Radstock BA3 4HB. *T:* (01761) 232793.

RAWSTHORNE, Anthony Robert; a Senior Clerk, House of Lords, since 2000; *b* 25 Jan. 1943; *s* of Frederic Leslie and Nora Rawsthorne; *m* 1967, Beverley Jean Osborne; one *s* two *d*. *Educ:* Ampleforth College; Wadham College, Oxford (MA). Home Office, 1966–97: Asst Sec., 1977; Crime Policy Planning Unit, 1977–79; Establishment Dept, 1979–82; Sec., Falkland Islands Review Cttee, 1982; Principal Private Sec., 1983; Immigration and Nationality Dept, 1983–86; Assistant Under-Secretary: Establishment Dept, 1986–91; Equal Opportunities and Gen. Dept, 1991; Asst Under-Sec., then Dep. Dir-Gen., Policy, Immigration and Nationality Directorate, 1991–97; Dir, Customs Policy, and a Comr, HM Customs and Excise, 1997–2000. Mem., Professional Conduct Cttee, GMC. *Recreations:* bridge, squash, holidays in France and Italy. *Address:* Committee Office, House of Lords, SW1A 0PW.

RAWSTHORNE, Rt Rev. John; *see* Hallam, Bishop of, (RC).

RAY, Hon. Ajit Nath; Chief Justice of India, Supreme Court of India, 1973–77; *b* Calcutta, 29 Jan. 1912; *s* of Sati Nath Ray and Kali Kumari Debi; *m* 1944, Himani Mukherjee; one *s*. *Educ:* Presidency Coll., Calcutta; Calcutta Univ. (Hindu Coll. Foundn Schol., MA); Oriel College, Oxford (MA; Hon. Fellow, 1975). Called to Bar, Gray's Inn, 1939; practised at Calcutta High Court, 1940–57; Judge, Calcutta High Court, 1957–69; Judge, Supreme Court of India, 1969–73. Pres., Governing Body, Presidency Coll., Calcutta, 1959–70; Vice-President: Asiatic Soc., 1963–65 (Hon. Treas. 1960–63); Internat. Law Assoc., 1977– (Pres., 1974–76; Pres., Indian Br., 1973–77); Indian Law Inst., New Delhi, 1973–77; Mem., Internat. Court of Arbitration, 1976–. Vice-Pres., Ramakrishna Mission Inst. of Culture, 1981–; Chm., Guru Saday Folk Art Soc., Calcutta, 1986–; Pres., Soc. for Welfare of Blind, Narendrapur, 1959–80. Mem., Karma Samiti (Exec. Council), 1963–67 and 1969–72, and Samsad (Court), 1967–71, Visva-Bharati Univ., Santiniketan. *Address:* 15 Panditia Place, Calcutta 700029, India. *T:* (33) 4541452. *Club:* Calcutta (Calcutta).

RAY, Edward Ernest, CBE 1988; Chairman, C T Baker Ltd, since 1986; Senior Partner, Spicer and Pegler, Chartered Accountants, 1984–88 (Partner, 1957); *b* 6 Nov. 1924; *s* of Walter James Ray and Cecilia May Ray; *m* 1949, Margaret Elizabeth, *d* of George Bull; two *s*. *Educ:* Holloway Co. Sch.; London Univ. (External) (BCom). Served RN, 1943–46. Inst. of Chartered Accountants: Mem., 1950; FCA 1955; Council Mem., 1973; Vice Pres., 1980; Dep. Pres., 1981; Pres., 1982, 1983. Chm., London Chartered Accountants, 1972–73. Dir, SIB, 1985–90; Chm., Investors' Compensation Scheme Ltd, 1988–91; Member: City Capital Markets Cttee, 1984–88; Marketing of Investments Bd Organising Cttee, 1984–88. *Publications:* Partnership Taxation, 1972, 3rd edn 1987; (jtly) VAT for Accountants and Businessmen, 1972; contrib. accountancy magazines. *Recreations:* walking, birdwatching, golf.

RAY, Kenneth Richard, OBE 1996; FDSRCS, FRCS; Dean, Faculty of Dental Surgery, Royal College of Surgeons of England, 1992–95; Chairman, Joint Committee for Specialist Training in Dentistry, 1996–98; *b* 25 Jan. 1930; *s* of late John Thomas Ray and Edith Rose (*née* Hobbs); *m* 1958, Pamela Ann Thomas; one *s* two *d*. *Educ:* City of Oxford High Sch.; Univ. of Birmingham (LDS, BDS). FDSRCS 1959; FRCS 1995; FRACDS 1995. Hse Surgeon, Gen. Hosp., Birmingham, 1955; Sen. Hse Officer, Midlands Regl Plastic and Jaw Surgery Centre, 1956; Registrar, then Sen. Registrar, Royal Dental Hosp. of London and St George's Hosp., 1957–60; Sen. Lectr and Hon. Cons. in Oral Surgery, Univ. of London at Royal Dental Hosp. Sch. of Dental Surgery, 1960–73; Cons. in Oral Surgery, Royal Berks Hosp., Reading and Oxford RHA, 1963–92. Mem., GDC, 1993–95. Chm., Central Cttee for Hosp. Dental Services, 1979–86; Mem., Jt Consultants Cttee, 1979–86 and 1992–95. Royal College of Surgeons: Mem. Bd, Fac. of Dental Surgery, 1981–95; Vice-Dean, 1989; Colyer Gold Medal, 1999; British Dental Association: Mem. Council, 1979–87; Pres., Berks, Bucks and Oxon Br., 1978; Pres., Hosp. Gp, 1979; Pres., BAOMS, 1985. UK Rep., EC Dental Liaison Cttee, 1981–89; UK Rep., EC Adv. Cttee on Trng of Dental Practitioners, 1981–92. Hon. Fellow, BDA, 1990; Hon. FDSRCSE 1997; Hon. FDSRCPSGlas 1998. *Publications:* articles in learned jls and contrib. to textbooks on oral and maxillofacial surgery, local analgesia and health service planning. *Recreations:* fell-walking, natural history, English inns. *Address:* Jacobs Spinney, Rag Hill, Aldermaston, Berks RG7 4NS. *T:* (0118) 971 2550. *Clubs:* Savage, Royal Society of Medicine.

RAY, Philip Bicknell, CMG 1969; Ministry of Defence 1947–76, retired; *b* 10 July 1917; *s* of late Basil Ray and Clare (*née* Everett); *m* 1946, Bridget Mary Robertson (decd); two *s* one *d*. *Educ:* Felsted Sch.; Selwyn Coll., Cambridge (MA). Indian Police, 1939–47. *Address:* 3 South Green Road, Newnham, Cambridge CB3 9JP.

RAY, Hon. Robert (Francis); Senator for Victoria, since 1981; Minister for Defence, Australia, 1990–96, and Deputy Leader of Government in the Senate, 1993–96; *b* Melbourne, 8 April 1947; *m* (Victoria) Jane Petheram. *Educ:* Monash Univ.; Rusden State Coll. Former technical sch. teacher. Australian Labor Party: Mem., 1966–; Deleg., Vic. State Conf., 1970–96; Mem., Nat. Exec., 1983–98; Minister for Home Affairs and Dep. Manager of Govt Business in the Senate, 1987; Minister assisting the Minister for Transport and Communications, 1988; Minister for Immigration, Local Govt and Ethnic Affairs, 1988–90; Manager of Govt Business in the Senate, 1988–91. *Address:* Level 2, Suite 3, Illoura Plaza, 424 St Kilda Road, Melbourne, Vic 3004, Australia.

RAYANANONDA, Vidhya; Ambassador for Thailand to the Court of St James's and concurrently to the Republic of Ireland, since 1994; *b* 2 March 1942; *s* of Adm. Thavil Rayananonda and M. L. Penari Rayananonda; *m* 1971, Nantana; two *d*. *Educ:* Thammasat Univ., Thailand (BA Internat. Relns); USA (MA Pol Sci.); Nat. Defence Coll., Thailand. Joined Thai Diplomatic Service; Third Sec., Washington; Second Sec., SE Asian Div., Pol Affairs Dept; First Sec., Manila; Ministry of Foreign Affairs: Dir, FE Div., Pol Affairs Dept; Dep. Dir-Gen., Inf. Dept; Consul-Gen., LA, USA; Ambassador attached to Min. of Foreign Affairs; Dep. Sec.-Gen., then Sec.-Gen., to Prime Minister; Dir-Gen., Protocol Dept; Ambassador to Switzerland and Holy See. Kt Grand Cordon, Most Noble Order of Crown (Thailand), 1992; Kt Grand Cross (1st Cl.), Most Exalted Order of White Elephant (Thailand); Order of Sacred Treasure (Gold and Silver Star) (Japan). *Recreation:* playing golf. *Address:* Royal Thai Embassy, 30 Queen's Gate, SW7 5JB.

RAYCHAUDHURI, Prof. Tapan Kumar, DPhil, DLitt; Professor of Indian History and Civilisation, University of Oxford, 1992–93; Fellow, St Antony's College, Oxford, 1973–93, now Emeritus; *b* 8 May 1926; *s* of Amiya Kumar and Prativa Raychaudhuri; *m* 1960, Pratima Sen-Roy; one *d*. *Educ:* Presidency Coll., Calcutta; Balliol Coll., Oxford. MA, DPhil Calcutta; MA, DPhil, DLitt Oxon. Lectr, Calcutta Univ., 1948–55; Dep. Dir, Nat. Archives of India, 1957–59 (Acting Dir, 1957–58); Delhi School of Economics: Reader in Econ. History, 1959–64; Prof., 1964–70; Dir, 1965–67; Prof. of History, Delhi Univ., 1971–72; Reader in Mod. S Asian History, Univ. of Oxford, 1973–92. Visiting Professor: Duke Univ., 1964; Univ. of Calif., Berkeley, 1964; Univ. of Penn., 1969; Harvard, 1969–70; El Colegio de Mexico, 1981; Univ. of Sydney, 1986. Fellow: Woodrow Wilson Center, 1993–94; Wissenschaftskolleg zu Berlin, 1997–98. Gen. Ed (with D. Kumar), Cambridge Economic History of India, 1982–83. *Publications:* Bengal under Akbar and Jahangir: an introductory study in social history, 1953, 2nd edn 1969; Jan Company in Coromandel 1605–1690: European trade and Asia's traditional economies, 1962; (ed with I. Habib) Cambridge Economic History of India, vol. I, 1982, vol. II, 1983; Europe Reconsidered: perceptions of the West in Nineteenth Century Bengal, 1986; Perceptions, Sensibilities, Emotions: essays on India's Colonial and post-Colonial experiences, 1999; (with G. Forbes) Memoirs of Dr Haimavati Sen: from child widow to lady doctor, 2000. *Recreations:* travel, cinema, reading. *Address:* 1 Hawkswell Gardens, Oxford OX2 7EX. *T:* (01865) 559421.

RAYLEIGH, 6th Baron *cr* 1821; **John Gerald Strutt;** Company Chairman, since 1988; *b* 4 June 1960; *s* of Hon. Charles Richard Strutt (*d* 1981) (2nd *s* of 4th Baron) and of Hon. Jean Elizabeth, *d* of 1st Viscount Davidson, PC, GCVO, CH, CB; *S* uncle, 1988; *m* 1991, Annabel Kate, *d* of W. G. Patterson; four *s*. *Educ:* Eton College; Royal Agricultural College, Cirencester. Lieut, Welsh Guards, 1980–84. Chm., Lord Rayleigh's Farms Ltd, 1988–. MRI. *Recreations:* cricket, gardening, shooting, silviculture. *Heir: s* Hon. John Frederick Strutt, *b* 29 March 1993. *Clubs:* Brooks's, MCC.

See also Hon. B. C. Jenkin.

RAYMER, Michael Robert, OBE 1951; Assistant Secretary, Royal Hospital, Chelsea, 1975–82; *b* 22 July 1917; surv. *s* of late Rev. W. H. Raymer, MA; *m* 1948, Joyce Marion Scott; two *s* one *d*. *Educ:* Marlborough College (Foundation Scholar); Jesus College, Cambridge (Rustat Schol.). BA (Hons) 1939. Administrative Officer, Nigeria, 1940–49 and 1952–55. Served in Royal W African Frontier Force, 1940–43. Colonial Sec. to Govt of the Falkland Islands, 1949–52; Prin. Estab. Officer, N Nigeria, 1954; Controller of Organisation and Establishments, to Government of Fiji, 1955–62; retired, 1962; Principal, MoD, 1962–75. *Recreation:* gardening. *Address:* The Stable House, Manor Farm, Apethorpe, Northants PE8 5DG.

RAYMOND, Robert Jacques; Permanent Representative of European Central Bank to International Monetary Fund, Washington, since 1999; *b* 30 June 1933; *s* of Henri Raymond and Andrée (*née* Aubrière); *m* 1970, Monique Brémond, MD. *Educ:* Sorbonne (Masters Econs 1955). With Bank of France, 1951–94: Audit Dept, 1958–66; Rep. in NY, 1966–67; Hd, Balance of Payments Div., 1969–73; Director: Internat. Affairs, 1973–75; Monetary Stats and Analysis, 1975–76; Dep. Sec. Gen., Conseil Nat. du Crédit, 1975–81; Dep. Hd, 1976–82, Dir Gen., 1982–90, Res. Dept; Dir Gen., Credit Dept, 1990–94; Dir Gen., European Monetary Inst., 1994–98. Mem. Bd, various public financial instns in Paris, 1981–94. Chm., monetary experts, Cttee of Govs of EEC, 1981–91. Officier de la Légion d'Honneur (France), 1996 (Chevalier, 1984); Officier, Ordre national du Mérite (France), 1988. *Publications:* La Monnaie, 1976; (jtly) Les relations économiques et monétaires internationales, 1982, 3rd edn 1986; Les institutions monétaires en France, 1991, 2nd edn 1996; L'unification monétaire en Europe, 1993, 2nd edn 1996. *Address:* European Central Bank, Kaiserstrasse 29, 60311 Frankfurt am Main, Germany. *T:* (69) 13440.

RAYMOND, William Francis, CBE 1978; FRSC; agricultural science consultant; *b* 25 Feb. 1922; *m* 1949, Amy Elizabeth Kelk; three *s* one *d*. *Educ:* Bristol Grammar Sch.; The Queen's Coll., Oxford (MA). Research Officer, MRC, 1943–45; Head of Animal Science Div. and later Asst Dir, Grassland Research Inst., Hurley, 1945–72; Dep. Chief Scientist, 1972–81, Chief Scientist (Agriculture and Horticulture), 1981–82, MAFF. Mem., ARC, 1981–82. Sec., 8th Internat. Grassland Congress, 1960; President: Brit. Grassland Soc., 1974–75; Brit. Soc. Animal Production, 1981–82. Vis. Prof. in Agriculture, Wye Coll., 1978–83. Chm., Stapledon Meml Trust, 1983–93; Member: Policy Cttee, CPRE, 1993–96; Cttee, Family Farmers' Assoc., 1996– (Vice-Chm., 1998–); Hon. Treas., RURAL, 1984–; Chm., Internat. Agricl Res. Review, Council for Res. Policy, Denmark, 1992; Mem., Internat. Agricl Res. Review, Min. of Agric. and Forestry, Finland, 1996. Chm., Henley and Mapledurham Dist, CPRE, 2001–. *Publications:* (with Shepperson and Waltham) Forage Conservation and Feeding, 1972, 5th edn 1996; EEC Agricultural Research Framework Programme, 1983; Research in Support of Agricultural Policies in Europe, FAO Regional Conf., Reykjavik, 1984; over 250 papers in scientific jls. *Recreation:* gardening. *Address:* Periwinkle Cottage, Christmas Common, Watlington OX49 5HR. *T:* (01491) 612942.

RAYNE, family name of **Baron Rayne.**

RAYNE, Baron *cr* 1976 (Life Peer), of Prince's Meadow in Greater London; **Max Rayne,** Kt 1969; Chairman, London Merchant Securities plc, 1960–2000, Life President, since 2000; *b* 8 Feb. 1918; *er s* of Phillip and Deborah Rayne; *m* 1st, 1941, Margaret Marco (marr. diss. 1960); one *s* two *d*; 2nd, 1965, Lady Jane Antonia Frances Vane-Tempest-Stewart, *er d* of 8th Marquess of Londonderry; two *s* two *d*. *Educ:* Central Foundation Sch. and University Coll., London. Served RAF 1940–45. Dir, First Leisure Corp. plc, 1984–99 (Dep. Chm., 1984–92; Chm., 1992–95); Dep. Chm., British Lion Films, 1967–72; Dir, Housing Corp. (1974) Ltd, 1974–78; Dir, other companies. Gov., 1962–74, Special Trustee, 1974–92, St Thomas' Hosp.; Governor: Royal Ballet Sch., 1966–79; Malvern Coll., 1966–; Centre for Environmental Studies, 1967–73; Member: Gen. Council, King Edward VII's Hosp. Fund for London, 1966–96; RADA Council, 1973–; South Bank Bd, 1986–92; Council, St Thomas's Hospital Medical School, 1965–82; Council of Governors, UMDS of Guy's and St Thomas's Hosps, 1982–89. Vice-Pres., Yehudi Menuhin Sch., 1987– (Gov., 1966–87); Hon. Vice-Pres., Jewish Care, 1966–; Chairman: London Festival Ballet Trust, 1967–75; Nat. Theatre Board, 1971–88; Founder Patron, The Rayne Foundation, 1962–; Founder Mem., Motability, 1979–96 (Life Vice-Pres., 1996). Hon. Fellow: Darwin Coll., Cambridge, 1966; UCL, 1966; LSE 1974; RCPsych, 1977; King's Coll. Hosp. Med. Sch., 1980; UC, Oxford, 1982; King's Coll. London, 1983; Westminster Sch., 1989; RCP, 1992; UMDS, 1992. Hon. LLD London, 1968. Officier, Légion d'Honneur, 1987 (Chevalier 1973). *Address:* 33 Robert Adam Street, W1U 3HR. *T:* (020) 7935 3555.

RAYNER, Bryan Roy, CB 1987; Deputy Secretary, Department of Health (formerly of Health and Social Security), 1984–91; *b* 29 Jan. 1932; *s* of Harold and Florence Rayner; *m* 1957, Eleanora Whittaker; one *d*. *Educ:* Stationers' Company's School, N8. Clerical Officer, Customs and Excise, 1948; Asst Private Sec. to Minister of Health, 1960–62; Principal, 1965, Asst Sec., 1970, Under Sec., 1975, DHSS. *Recreation:* listening to music. *Address:* 18 Trevelyan Place, Heath Road, Haywards Heath, W Sussex RH16 3AZ.

RAYNER, Claire Berenice, OBE 1996; writer and broadcaster; *b* 22 Jan. 1931; *m* 1957, Desmond Rayner; two *s* one *d*. *Educ:* City of London Sch. for Girls; Royal Northern Hosp. Sch. of Nursing, London (Gold Medal; SRN 1954); Guy's Hosp. (midwifery). Formerly: Nurse, Royal Free Hosp.; Sister, Paediatric Dept, Whittington Hosp. Woman's Own: Med. Correspondent, as Ruth Martin, 1966–75, as Claire Rayner, 1975–87; advice column: The Sun, 1973–80; The Sunday Mirror, 1980–88; Today, 1988–91; columnist, Woman, 1988–92. Radio and television broadcasts include: family advice, Pebble Mill at One, BBC, 1972–74; (co-presenter) Kitchen Garden, ITV, 1974–77; Contact, BBC Radio, Wales, 1974–77; Claire Rayner's Casebook (series), BBC, 1980, 1983, 1984; TV-am Advice Spot, 1985–92; A Problem Shared, Sky TV Series, 1989; Good Morning with

Anne and Nick, BBC, 1992–93. Associate non-exec. Dir, Royal Hosps NHS Trust, 1995–. Mem., Royal Commn on Long Term Care of the Elderly, 1997–98; Founder Mem., Forum on Children and Violence. FRSocMed; FRSA. President: Gingerbread; Patients' Assoc.; Nat. Assoc. of Bereavement Counsellors; British Humanist Assoc., 1999–; Patron: Terrence Higgins Trust; Turning Point; Royal Philanthropic Soc., and others. Hon. Fellow, Polytechnic of N London, 1988. Freeman, City of London, 1981. Med. Journalist of the Year, 1987; Best Specialist Consumer Columnist Award, 1988. *Publications:* Mothers and Midwives, 1962; What Happens in Hospital, 1963; The Calendar of Childhood, 1964; Your Baby, 1965; Careers with Children, 1966; Essentials of Out-Patient Nursing, 1967; For Children, 1967; Shall I be a Nurse, 1967; 101 Facts an Expectant Mother should know, 1967; 101 Key Facts of Practical Baby Care, 1967; Housework - The Easy Way, 1967; Home Nursing and Family Health, 1967; A Parent's Guide to Sex Education, 1968; People in Love, 1968 (subseq. publd as About Sex, 1972); Protecting Your Baby, 1971; Woman's Medical Dictionary, 1971; When to Call the Doctor - What to Do Whilst Waiting, 1972; The Shy Person's Book, 1973; Childcare Made Simple, 1973; Where Do I Come From?, 1975; (ed and contrib.) Atlas of the Body and Mind, 1976; (with Keith Fordyce) Kitchen Garden, 1976; (with Keith Fordyce) More Kitchen Garden, 1977; Family Feelings, 1977; Claire Rayner answers your 100 Questions on Pregnancy, 1977; (with Keith Fordyce) Claire and Keith's Kitchen Garden, 1978; The Body Book, 1978; Related to Sex, 1979; (with Keith Fordyce) Greenhouse Gardening, 1979; Everything your Doctor would Tell You if He Had the Time, 1980; Claire Rayner's Lifeguide, 1980; Baby and Young Child Care, 1981; Growing Pains, 1984; Claire Rayner's Marriage Guide, 1984; The Getting Better Book, 1985; Woman, 1986; When I Grow Up, 1986; Safe Sex, 1987; The Don't Spoil Your Body Book, 1989; Life and Love and Everything: children's questions, 1993; *fiction:* Shilling a Pound Pears, 1964; The House on the Fen, 1967; Starch of Aprons, 1967 (subseq. publd as The Hive, 1968); Lady Mislaid, 1968; Death on the Table, 1969; The Meddlers, 1970; A Time to Heal, 1972; The Burning Summer, 1972; Sisters, 1978; Reprise, 1980; The Running Years, 1981; Family Chorus, 1984; The Virus Man, 1985; Lunching at Laura's, 1986; Maddie, 1988; Clinical Judgements, 1989; Postscripts, 1991; Dangerous Things, 1993; First Blood, 1993; Second Opinion, 1994; Third Degree, 1995; Fourth Attempt, 1996; Fifth Member, 1997; The Performers: Book 1, Gower Street, 1973; Book 2, The Haymarket, 1974; Book 3, Paddington Green, 1975; Book 4, Soho Square, 1976; Book 5, Bedford Row, 1977; Book 6, Long Acre, 1978; Book 7, Charing Cross, 1979; Book 8, The Strand, 1980; Book 9, Chelsea Reach, 1982; Book 10, Shaftesbury Avenue, 1983; Book 11, Piccadilly, 1985; Book 12, Seven Dials, 1986; Poppy Chronicle: Book 1, Jubilee, 1987; Book 2, Flanders, 1988; Book 3, Flapper, 1989; Book 4, Blitz, 1990; Book 5, Festival, 1992; Book 6, Sixties, 1992; Quentin Quartet: Book 1, London Lodgings, 1994; Book 2, Paying Guests, 1995; *as Sheila Brandon: fiction:* The Final Year, 1962; Cottage Hospital, 1963; Children's Ward, 1964; The Lonely One, 1965; The Doctors of Downlands, 1968; The Private Wing, 1971; Nurse in the Sun, 1972; *as Ann Lynton:* Mothercraft, 1967; contrib. Lancet, Med. World, Nursing Times, Nursing Mirror, and national newspapers and magazines, incl. Design. *Recreations:* talking, cooking, party-giving, theatre-going. *Address:* PO Box 125, Harrow, Middx HA1 3XE.

RAYNER, David Edward, CBE 1992; FCIT; Chairman: Catalis Rail Training (formerly College of Railway Technology) Ltd, since 1998; Oakburn Properties plc, since 1998; *b* 26 Jan. 1940; *s* of Marjory and Gilbert Rayner; *m* 1966, Enid Cutty; two *d*. *Educ:* St Peter's School, York; Durham University (BSc Hons). Joined British Railways, 1963; Passenger Marketing Manager, BR Board, 1982; Dep. Gen. Manager, BR, London Midland Region, 1984–86; Gen. Manager, BR, Eastern Region, 1986–87; British Railways Board: Mem., 1987–94; Jt Man. Dir, 1987–89; Man. Dir, Engrg and Operations, 1989–92; Man. Dir, Safety and Operations, 1992–94; Bd Mem., Railtrack Gp, 1994–97; Dir Safety and Standards, Railtrack, 1994–97. Chm., Rail Investments Ltd, 1998–99; non-exec. Dir, Connex Transport UK (formerly Connex Rail) Ltd, 1998–. Chm., Rail Industry Training Council, 1992–95. Vis. Prof., UCL, 1998–. Trustee: Science Mus., 1997–; York and N Yorks Community Foundn, 2000–. Hon. Col, Railway Sqn, RLC (TA), 1992–99. *Recreation:* collector.

RAYNER, Edward John, CBE 1990; Controller, Europe (formerly Europe and North Asia) Division, British Council, 1986–89; *b* 27 Feb. 1936; *s* of Edward Harold Rayner and Edith Rayner; *m* 1960, Valerie Anne Billon; one *s* one *d*. *Educ:* Slough Grammar Sch.; London Univ. (BSc Econs). British Council: Asst Regional Rep., Lahore, Pakistan, 1959–62; Asst Rep., Lagos, Nigeria, 1962–65; Inspector, Complements Unit, 1965–67; Head, Overseas Careers, Personnel Dept, 1967–70; Dep. Rep., Pakistan, 1970–71; Regional Dir, Sao Paulo, Brazil, 1972–75; Controller, Estabts Div., 1975–78; Secretary, 1978–82; Rep., Brazil, 1983–86. *Recreations:* theatre, music.

RAYNER, Rabbi John Desmond, CBE 1993; Minister, Liberal Jewish Synagogue, 1957–89, now Rabbi Emeritus; *b* 30 May 1924; *s* of Ferdinand and Charlotte Rahmer; *m* 1955, Jane Priscilla Heilbronn; two *s* one *d*. *Educ:* Durham Sch.; Emmanuel Coll., Cambridge (MA); Hebrew Union Coll.-Jewish Inst. of Religion, Cincinnati (Hon. DD). Minister, S London Liberal Synagogue, 1953–57; Sen. Minister, Liberal Jewish Synagogue, 1961–89; Leo Baeck College: Lectr in Rabbinic Literature, 1966– (Vice-Pres., 1969–). Hon. Life Pres., Union of Liberal and Progressive Synagogues, 1994; Pres., London Soc. of Jews and Christians, 1990; Chm., Council of Reform and Liberal Rabbis, 1969–71, 1982–84, 1989–92. *Publications:* The Practices of Liberal Judaism, 1958; Towards Mutual Understanding between Jews and Christians, 1960; (ed jtly) Service of the Heart, 1967; Guide to Jewish Marriage, 1975; (ed jtly) Gate of Repentance, 1977; (jtly) Judaism for Today, 1978; (jtly) The Jewish People: their history and their religion, 1987; (ed jtly) Siddur Lev Chadash, 1995; An Understanding of Judaism, 1997; A Jewish Understanding of the World, 1998; Jewish Religious Law, 1998; Principles of Jewish Ethics, 1999. *Recreations:* reading, walking. *Address:* 37 Walmington Fold, N12 7LD. *T:* (020) 8446 6196.

RAYNER, Most Rev. Keith, AO 1987; Archbishop of Melbourne and Metropolitan of the Province of Victoria, 1990–99; Primate of Australia, 1991–99 (Acting Primate, 1989–91); *b* 22 Nov. 1929; *s* of Sidney and Gladys Rayner, Brisbane; *m* 1963, Audrey Fletcher; one *s* two *d*. *Educ:* C of E Grammar Sch., Brisbane; Univ. of Queensland (BA 1951; PhD 1964). Deacon, 1953; Priest, 1953. Chaplain, St Francis' Theol Coll., Brisbane, 1954; Mem., Brotherhood of St John, Dalby, 1955–58; Vice-Warden, St John's Coll., Brisbane, 1958; Rotary Foundn Fellow, Harvard Univ., 1958–59; Vicar, St Barnabas', Sunnybank, 1959–63; Rector, St Peter's, Wynnum, 1963–69; Bishop of Wangaratta, 1969–75; Archbishop of Adelaide and Metropolitan of South Australia, 1975–90. Pres., Christian Conference of Asia, 1977–81; Chm., International Anglican Theological and Doctrinal Commission, 1980–88. Hon. ThD Aust. Coll. of Theology, 1987; DUniv Griffith, 2001. *Address:* 36 Highfield Avenue, St Georges, SA 5064, Australia.

RAYNER, Prof. Peter John Wynn, PhD; Professor of Signal Processing, University of Cambridge, since 1998; Fellow, Christ's College, Cambridge, since 1969; *b* 22 July 1941; *s* of John Austin Rayner and Amelia Victoria Rayner; *m* 1960, Patricia Ann Gray; two *d*. *Educ:* Univ. of Aston (PhD 1968); MA Cantab 1969. Student apprentice, Pye TVT Ltd, 1957–62; Sen. Engr, Cambridge Consultants, 1962–65; Res. Student, Univ. of Aston, 1965–68; Cambridge University: Lectr, Dept of Engrg, 1968–90; Dir, Studies in Engrg, Christ's Coll., 1971–99; Reader in Inf. Engrg, 1990–98. *Publications:* (with S. J. Godsill) Digital Audio Restoration, 1998; book chapters; numerous contribs to learned jls. *Recreations:* scuba-diving, flamenco and blues guitar, gardening, cycling. *Address:* Department of Engineering, Cambridge University, Trumpington Street, Cambridge CB2 1PZ. *T:* (01223) 332646.

RAYNER JAMES, Jonathan Elwyn; *see* James.

RAYNES, Prof. Edward Peter, FRS 1987; Professor of Optoelectronic Engineering, University of Oxford, since 1998; Fellow of St Cross College, Oxford, since 1998; *b* 4 July 1945; *s* of Edward Gordon and Ethel Mary Raynes; *m* 1970, Madeline Ord; two *s*. *Educ:* St Peter's School, York; Gonville and Caius College, Cambridge (MA, PhD). CPhys, FInstP. Royal Signals and Radar Establishment, 1971–92: SPSO, 1981; DCSO, 1988–92; Chief Scientist, 1992–95, Dir of Res., 1995–98, Sharp Labs of Europe Ltd, Oxford. Rank Prize for Opto-electronics, 1980; Paterson Medal, Inst. of Physics, 1986; Special Recognition Award, Soc. for Information Display, 1987. *Publications:* (ed jtly) Liquid Crystals: their physics, chemistry and applications, 1983; numerous scientific papers and patents. *Recreation:* choral and solo singing. *Address:* Department of Engineering Science, University of Oxford, Parks Road, Oxford OX1 3PJ. *T:* (01865) 273024, *Fax:* (01865) 273905.

RAYNHAM, Viscount; Charles George Townshend; *b* 26 Sept. 1945; *s* and *heir* of 7th Marquess Townshend, *qv*; *m* 1st, 1975, Hermione (*d* 1985), *d* of Lt-Cdr R. M. D. Ponsonby and Mrs Dorothy Ponsonby; one *s* one *d*; 2nd, 1990, Mrs Alison Marshall, *yr d* of Sir Willis Combs, KCVO, CMG. *Educ:* Eton; Royal Agricultural College, Cirencester. Chm. and Dir, AIMS Ltd, 1977–87; Man. Dir, Raynham Workshops Ltd, 1986–94; Chm., Pera International, 1988–96. Gen. Comr, Income Tax, Norwich, 1989–. Member Council: Design Gp Great Britain Ltd, 1984–90 (Chm., 1988); Norfolk Br., RASE, 1982–94. *Heir: s* Hon. Thomas Charles Townshend, *b* 2 Nov. 1977. *Address:* Pattesley House, Fakenham, Norfolk NR21 7HT. *T:* (01328) 701818. *Club:* White's.

RAYNOR, Philip Ronald; QC 1994; **His Honour Judge Raynor**; a Circuit Judge, since 2001; *b* 20 Jan. 1950; *s* of Wilfred Raynor and Sheila (*née* Zermansky); *m* 1974, Judith Braunsberg; one *s* one *d*. *Educ:* Roundhay Sch., Leeds; Christ's Coll., Cambridge (Schol., MA). Lectr in Law, Univ. of Manchester, 1971–74; called to the Bar, Inner Temple, 1973; in practice, 1973–2001; a Recorder, 1993–2001; Head of Chambers, 40 King Street, Manchester, 1996–2001. *Recreations:* travel, opera, dining out. *Address:* Law Courts, Crown Square, Manchester, M3 3FL.

RAYNSFORD, Rt Hon. Nick; *see* Raynsford, Rt Hon. W. R. N.

RAYNSFORD, Rt Hon. Wyvill Richard Nicolls, (Rt Hon. Nick); PC 2001; MP (Lab) Greenwich and Woolwich, since 1997 (Greenwich, 1992–97); Minister of State, Department for Transport, Local Government and the Regions, since 2001; *b* 28 Jan. 1945; *s* of Wyvill Raynsford and Patricia Raynsford (*née* Dunn); *m* 1968, Anne Raynsford (*née* Jelley); three *d*. *Educ:* Repton Sch.; Sidney Sussex Coll., Cambridge (MA); Chelsea Sch. of Art (DipAD). Market research, A. C. Nielsen Co. Ltd, 1966–68; Gen. Sec., Soc. for Co-operative Dwellings, 1972–73; SHAC: Emergency Officer, 1973–74; Research Officer, 1974–76; Dir, 1976–86; Partner, 1987–90, Dir, 1990–92, Raynsford and Morris, housing consultants; Dir, Raynsford Dallison Associates, housing consultants, 1992–93; Consultant, HACAS, 1993–97. Councillor (Lab) London Borough of Hammersmith & Fulham, 1971–75 (Chm., Leisure and Recreation Cttee, 1972–74). Contested (Lab) Fulham, 1987. MP (Lab) Fulham, April 1986–1987. Opposition front bench spokesman on London, 1993–97, on housing, 1994–97; Parly Under-Sec. of State, DoE and Dept of Transport, subseq. DETR, 1997–99; Minister of State, DETR, 1999–2001. Mem., Envmt Select Cttee, 1992–93. *Publication:* A Guide to Housing Benefit, 1982, 7th edn 1986. *Recreation:* photography. *Address:* House of Commons, SW1A 0AA; 10 Charlton Road, Blackheath, SE3 7HG.

RAZ, Prof. Joseph, FBA 1987; Professor of the Philosophy of Law, Oxford, since 1985, and Fellow of Balliol College, Oxford; *b* 21 March 1939. *Educ:* Hebrew University, Jerusalem (MJur 1963); University Coll., Oxford (DPhil 1967). Lectr, Hebrew Univ., Jerusalem, 1967–70; Research Fellow, Nuffield Coll., Oxford, 1970–72; Tutorial Fellow, Balliol Coll., Oxford, 1972–85. Vis. Prof., Columbia Law Sch., NY, 1995–. For. Hon. Mem., Amer. Acad. of Arts and Scis, 1992. Hon. Dr Catholic Univ., Brussels, 1993. *Publications:* The Concept of a Legal System, 1970, 2nd edn 1980; Practical Reason and Norms, 1975, 2nd edn 1990; The Authority of Law, 1979; The Morality of Freedom, 1986; Ethics in the Public Domain, 1994, rev. edn 1995; Engaging Reason, 2000. *Address:* Balliol College, Oxford OX1 3BJ. *T:* (01865) 277721.

RAZZALL, family name of **Baron Razzall**.

RAZZALL, Baron *cr* 1997 (Life Peer), of Mortlake in the London Borough of Richmond; **Edward Timothy Razzall,** CBE 1993; Partner, Argonaut Associates, since 1996; *b* 12 June 1943; *s* of late Leonard Humphrey Razzall; *m* 1st, 1965, Elizabeth Christina Wilkinson (marr. diss. 1974); one *s* one *d*; 2nd, 1982, Deirdre Bourke Martineau (*née* Taylor Smith). *Educ:* St Paul's Sch.; Worcester Coll., Oxford (BA). Teaching Associate, Northwestern Univ., Chicago, 1965–66; with Frere Cholmeley Bischoff, solicitors, 1966–96 (Partner, 1973–96). Councillor (L), Mortlake Ward, London Borough of Richmond, 1974–98; Dep. Leader, Richmond Council, 1983–97. Treasurer: Liberal Party, 1986–87; Liberal Democrats, 1987–2000; Chm., Lib Dem Campaign Cttee, 2000–. Pres., Assoc. of Lib Dem Councillors, 1990–95. European Lawyer of Year, Inst. of Lawyers in Europe, 1992. *Recreation:* all sports. *Address:* (office) 14/16 Regent Street, SW1Y 4PH. *T:* (020) 7976 1233. *Clubs:* National Liberal, Soho House, MCC.

REA, family name of **Baron Rea**.

REA, 3rd Baron *cr* 1937, of Eskdale; **John Nicolas Rea,** MD; Bt 1935; General Medical Practitioner, Kentish Town, NW5, 1957–62 and 1968–93; *b* 6 June 1928; *s* of Hon. James Russell Rea (*d* 1954) (2nd *s* of 1st Baron) and Betty Marion (*d* 1965), *d* of Arthur Bevan, MD; *S* uncle, 1981; *m* 1st, 1951, Elizabeth Anne (marr. diss. 1991), *d* of late William Hensman Robinson; four *s* two *d*; 2nd, 1991, Judith Mary, *d* of late Norman Powell. *Educ:* Dartington Hall School; Belmont Hill School, Mass, USA; Dauntsey's School; Christ's Coll., Cambridge Univ.; UCH Medical School. MA, MD (Cantab); FRCGP; DPH, DCH, DObstRCOG. Research Fellow in Paediatrics, Lagos, Nigeria, 1962–65; Lecturer in Social Medicine, St Thomas's Hosp. Medical School, 1966–68. Vice-Chm., Nat. Forum for Prevention of Coronary Heart Disease, 1985–95; Chairman: Appropriate Health Resources and Technology Action Gp, 1992–97; Parly Food & Health Forum, 1992–. Opposition spokesman on health, devolt and co-operation, H of L, 1992–97; elected Mem., H of L, 1999. FRSocMed (Pres., Section of Gen. Practice, 1985–86). *Publications:* Interactions of Infection and Nutrition (MD Thesis, Cambridge Univ.), 1969; (jtly) Learning Teaching—an evaluation of a course for GP Teachers, 1980; articles on epidemiology and medical education in various journals. *Recreations:* music (bassoon), foreign travel, outdoor activities. *Heir: s* Hon. Matthew James Rea, *b* 28 March 1956. *Address:* 1 Littledene Cottages, Glynde, E Sussex BN8 6LA. *T:* (weekdays) (020) 7607 0546, *Fax:* (020) 7687 1219.

REA, Christopher William Wallace; Communications Manager, International Rugby Board, since 2000; *b* 22 Oct. 1943; *s* of Col William Wallace Rea and Helen Rea; *m* 1974, Daphne Theresa Manning; one *d. Educ:* High Sch. of Dundee; Univ. of St Andrews (MA). With BBC Radio Sports Dept, 1972–81; Rugby and Golf Corresp., Scotsman, 1981–84; Publisher and Ed., Rugby News Mag., 1984–88; Presenter, BBV TV Rugby Special, 1988–94; Asst Sec., then Head, Marketing and Public Affairs, MCC, 1995–2000. Rugby Corresp., Independent on Sunday, 1990–2000. Played Rugby Union for Scotland, 1968–71 (13 Caps); Mem., British Lions tour to NZ, 1971; played for Barbarians, 1971. *Publications:* Illustrated History of Rugby Union, 1977; Injured Pride, 1980; Scotland's Grand Slam, 1984. *Recreations:* golf, hill walking. *Address:* 75 Seamount, St Helen's, Stillorgan Road, Co. Dublin, Eire.

REA, Rev. Ernest; Head of Religious Broadcasting, BBC, 1989–2001; *b* 6 Sept. 1945; *s* of Ernest Rea and Mary Wylie (*née* Blue). *Educ:* Methodist Coll., Belfast; Queen's Univ., Belfast; Union Theological Coll., Belfast. Asst Minister, Woodvale Park Presb. Ch., Belfast, 1971–74; Minister, Bannside Presb. Ch., Banbridge, Co. Down, 1974–79; Religious Broadcasting Producer, BBC Belfast, 1979–84; Sen. Religious Broadcasting Producer, BBC S and W, 1984–88; Editor, Network Radio, BBC S and W, 1988–89; Hd of Religious Progs, BBC Radio, 1989–93. Vis. Lectr, Manchester Univ., 1999–. *Recreations:* reading, watching cricket, playing tennis and golf, theatre, music. *Address:* Clifden, Oatlands, Macclesfield Road, Alderley Edge, Cheshire SK9 7BL.

REA, Dr John Rowland, FBA 1981; Lecturer in Documentary Papyrology, University of Oxford, 1965–96; Senior Research Fellow, Balliol College, Oxford, 1969–96, now Emeritus Fellow; *b* 28 Oct. 1933; *s* of Thomas Arthur Rea and Elsie Rea (*née* Ward); *m* 1959, Mary Ogden. *Educ:* Methodist Coll., Belfast; Queen's Univ., Belfast (BA); University Coll. London (PhD). Asst Keeper, Public Record Office, 1957–61; Res. Lectr, Christ Church, Oxford, 1961–65. *Publications:* The Oxyrhynchus Papyri, Vol. XL, 1972, Vol. XLVI, 1978, Vol. LI, 1984, Vol LV, 1988, Vol. LVIII, 1991, LXIII, 1996, also contribs to Vols XXVII, XXXI, XXXIII, XXXIV, XXXVI, XLI, XLIII, XLIX, L, LXII, LXIV; (with P. J. Sijpesteijn) Corpus Papyrorum Raineri V, 1976; articles in classical jls. *Address:* Aurolaine, 1 Shirley Drive, St Leonards-on-Sea, East Sussex TN37 7JW.

REA, Rupert Lascelles P.; *see* Pennant-Rea.

REA PRICE, (William) John, OBE 1991; Director, National Children's Bureau, 1991–98; *b* 15 March 1937; *s* of late John Caxton Rea Price and of Mary Hilda Rea Price. *Educ:* University College Sch.; Corpus Christi Coll., Cambridge (MA); LSE (DSA; Cert. Applied Social Studies). London Probation Service, 1962–65; London Borough of Islington Children's Dept, 1965–68; Nat. Inst. for Social Work, 1968–69; Home Office, Community Develt Project, 1969–72; Dir of Social Services, London Borough of Islington, 1972–90. Pres., Assoc. of Dirs of Social Services, 1989–90. *Recreations:* cycling, archaeology, history of landscape. *Address:* 15 Farriers House, 4 Errol Street, EC1Y 8TB. *T:* (020) 7638 0578; *e-mail:* John.Reaprice@btinternet.com. *Club:* Reform.

READ, Miss; *see* Saint, D. J.

READ, Rt Rev. Allan Alexander; Bishop of Ontario, 1981–92; *b* 19 Sept. 1923; *s* of Alex P. Read and Lillice M. Matthews; *m* 1949, Mary Beverly Roberts; two *s* two *d. Educ:* Trinity Coll., Univ. of Toronto (BA, LTh). Incumbent, Mono East and Mono West, 1947–54; Rector, Trinity Church, Barrie, 1954–71; Canon of St James Cathedral, Toronto, 1957; Archdeacon of Simcoe, 1961–72; Bishop Suffragan of Toronto, 1972–81; priest-in-charge: St Patrick's Cathedral, Meath and Kildare, 1992; Dunster, dio. of Bath and Wells, 1993; St Ippolyts, dio. of St Albans, 1994; St Mary, Westerham, dio. of Rochester, 1995; Cathedral of St John the Baptist, dio. of Cashel, Church of Ireland, 1996; All Saints, Goodmayes, Chelmsford, 1997; Associate Priest, Merrickville and Burritts Rapids, Ont. Chaplain, Simcoe County Gaol, Kingston, Ont, 1954–82. Hon. Asst, St George's Cathedral, Kingston, Ont, 1992–; licensed as a Bishop, dio. of Albany, USA, 1995–. Member: Gen. Synod, Anglican Church of Canada, 1959–89; Provincial Synod of Ontario, 1955–91; Hon. Pres., Rural Workers Fellowship, Episcopal Church, with members from USA and Anglican Church of Canada, 1981–; Hon. Mem., Toronto and Metropolitan Region Conservation Authy, 1977–. Hon. DD: Trinity Coll., Toronto, 1972; Wycliffe Coll., Toronto, 1972; Hon. STD Thornloe Coll., Sudbury, 1982. Citizen of the Year, Barrie, 1966; Honorary Reeve, Black Creek, Toronto, 1980; Govt of Ontario citizenship awards. *Publications:* Shepherds in Green Pastures, 1952; Unto the Hills, 1954. *Recreations:* organ music, reading, Canadian history, 1837 Rebellion Upper Canada. *Address:* 39 Riverside Drive, RR1, Kingston, ON K7L 4V1, Canada.

READ, Air Marshal Sir Charles (Frederick), KBE 1976 (CBE 1964); CB 1972; DFC 1942; AFC 1958; Chief of the Air Staff, RAAF, 1972–75, retired; *b* Sydney, NSW, 9 Oct. 1918; *s* of J. F. Read, Bristol, England; *m* 1946, Betty E., *d* of A. V. Bradshaw; three *s. Educ:* Sydney Grammar Sch. Former posts include: OC, RAAF Base, Point Cook, Vic., 1965–68; OC, RAAF, Richmond, NSW, 1968–70; Dep. Chief of Air Staff, 1969–72. *Recreation:* yachting. *Address:* 18 Ocean Drive, Safety Beach, Woolgoolga, NSW 2456, Australia. *T:* (2) 66540883.

READ, Prof. David John, PhD; FRS 1990; Professor of Plant Science, Sheffield University, since 1990; *b* 20 Jan. 1939; *s* of O. Read; *m* (marr. diss.); one *s. Educ:* Sexey's Sch., Bruton, Som; Hull Univ. (BSc 1960; PhD 1963). Sheffield University: Jun. Res. Fellow, 1963–66; Asst Lectr, 1966–69; Lectr, 1969–79; Sen. Lectr, 1979–81; Reader in Plant Sci., 1981–90. *Publications:* editor of numerous books and author of papers in learned jls mostly on subject of symbiosis, specifically the mycorrhizal symbiosis between plant roots and fungi. *Recreations:* walking, botany. *Address:* Minestone Cottage, Youlgrave, Bakewell, Derbys DE4 1WD. *T:* (01629) 636360.

READ, Prof. Frank Henry, FRS 1984; Langworthy Professor of Physics, Victoria University of Manchester, since 1998 (Professor of Physics, 1975–98); *b* 6 Oct. 1934; *s* of late Frank Charles Read and Florence Louise (*née* Wright); *m* 1961, Anne Stuart (*née* Wallace); two *s* two *d. Educ:* Haberdashers' Aske's Hampstead Sch. (Foundn Scholar, 1946); Royal Coll. of Science, Univ. of London (Royal Scholar, 1952; ARCS 1955; BSc 1955). PhD 1959, DSc 1975, Victoria Univ. of Manchester. FInstP 1968; MIEE 1982, FIEE 1998; CEng; CPhys. University of Manchester: Lectr, 1959; Sen. Lectr, 1969; Reader, 1974; Res. Dean, Faculty of Sci., 1993–95. Vis. Scientist: Univ. of Paris, 1974; Univ. of Colorado, 1974–75; Inst. for Atomic and Molecular Physics, Amsterdam, 1979–80. Consultant to industry, 1976–. Vice Pres., Inst. of Physics, 1985–89 (Chm., IOP Publishing Ltd, 1985–89); Member: Science Bd, SERC, 1987–90; Council, Royal Soc., 1987–89. Hon. Editor, Jl of Physics B, Atomic and Molecular Physics, 1980–84. *Publications:* (with E. Harting) Electrostatic Lenses, 1976; Electromagnetic Radiation, 1980; papers in physics and instrumentation jls. *Recreations:* stone-masonry, farming. *Address:* Hardingland Farm, Macclesfield Forest, Cheshire SK11 0ND. *T:* (01625) 425759.

READ, Brig. Gregory, CBE 1984; Clerk to Vintners' Company, 1984–96; *b* 11 Oct. 1934; *s* of Edward Charles Read and Margaret Florence Maud Holdsworth; *m* 1957, Rosemary Patricia Frost; three *s. Educ:* Sherborne Sch.; RMA Sandhurst; RMCS Shrivenham (BSc Eng). Commnd RTR, 1955; Comd 3 RTR, 1973–76; Comd RAC 1 (BR) Corps, 1979–81; Dir, Combat Develt, 1981; Dir, Battlefield Doctrine, 1982–84. Mem., Wine Standards Board, 1984–96; Trustee, Wine and Spirit Educn Trust, 1989–92. Vice-Chm., Riverpoint Charity, 1996– (Trustee, 1994–). Pres., S Wilts MENCAP, 2000–. *Recreations:* marathons, European history, travel. *Address:* The Girnel, Broad Chalke, Salisbury, Wilts SP5 5EN. *T:* (01722) 780276.

READ, Harry; British Commissioner, Salvation Army, 1987–90; Editor, Words of Life, 1990–2000; *b* 17 May 1924; *s* of Robert and Florence Read; *m* 1950, Winifred Humphries; one *s* one *d. Educ:* Sir William Worsley Sch., Grange Town, Middlesbrough. Served RCS, 1942–47 (6th Airborne Div., 1943–45). Commnd Salvation Army Officer, 1948; pastoral work, 1948–54; Lectr, Internat. Training Coll., 1954–62; pastoral work, 1962–64; Divl Youth Sec., 1964–66; Lectr, Internat. Training Coll., 1966–72; Dir, Information Services, 1972–75; Divl Comdr, 1975–78; Principal, Internat. Training Coll., 1978–81; Chief Sec., Canada Territory, 1981–84; Territorial Comdr, Australia Eastern Territory, 1984–87. *Recreations:* writing, hymns, poetry. *Address:* 4 Kingswood, 29 West Cliff Road, Bournemouth, Dorset BH4 8AY. *T:* (01202) 766457.

See also J. L. Read.

READ, Imelda Mary, (Mel); Member (Lab) East Midlands Region, European Parliament, since 1999 (Leicester, 1989–94; Nottingham and Leicestershire North West, 1994–99); *b* Hillingdon, 8 Jan. 1939; *d* of Robert Alan Hocking and Teresa Mary Hocking; *m*; one *s* one *d*, and one step *s. Educ:* Bishopshalt Sch., Hillingdon, Mddx; Nottingham Univ. (BA Hons 1977). Laboratory technician, Plessey, 1963–74; researcher, Trent Polytechnic, 1977–80; Lectr, Trent Polytechnic and other instns, 1980–84; Employment Officer, Nottingham Community Relations Council, 1984–89. European Parliament: Chair, British Labour Gp, 1990–92; Quastor, 1992–94. Contested (Lab): Melton, 1979; Leicestershire NW, 1983. Member: Nat Exec. Council, ASTMS, 1975; NEC, MSF; TUC Women's Adv. Cttee; Chair, Regl TUC Women's Cttee. *Publication:* (jtly) Against a Rising Tide, 1992. *Recreations:* beekeeping, gardening. *Address:* Marlene Reid Centre, 85 Belvoir Road, Coalville, Leics LE67 3PH.

READ, Sir John (Emms), Kt 1976; FCA 1947; President, Charities Aid Foundation, 1994–98 (Trustee, 1985–98; Chairman of Trustees, 1990–94); *b* 29 March 1918; *s* of late William Emms Read and of Daysie Elizabeth (*née* Cooper); *m* 1942, Dorothy Millicent Berry; two *s. Educ:* Brighton, Hove and Sussex Grammar Sch. Served Royal Navy, 1939–46 (rank of Comdr (S) RNVR); Admiral's Secretary: to Asst Chief of Naval Staff, Admty, 1942–45; to Brit. Admty Technical Mission, Ottawa, Canada, 1945–46. Ford Motor Co. Ltd, 1946–64 (Admin. Staff Coll., Henley, 1952), Dir of Sales, 1961–64; Dir, Electric and Musical Industries Ltd, 1965–87; EMI Group: Jt Man. Dir, 1967; Chief Exec., 1969–79; Dep. Chm., 1973–74; Chm., 1974–79; Thorn EMI: Dep. Chm., 1979–81, Dir, 1981–87. Director: Capitol Industries-EMI Inc., 1970–83; Dunlop Holdings Ltd, 1971–84; Thames Television, 1973–88 (Dep. Chm., 1981–88); Wonderworld plc, 1984–97; Hill Samuel Gp, 1987–88; Caflash (formerly Cafman) Ltd, 1990–; Chairman: TSB Holdings Ltd, 1980–86; Trustee Savings Banks Central Bd, 1980–88; Central TSB Ltd, 1983–86; TSB England and Wales, 1983–86; TSB Gp plc, 1986–88; UDT, 1981–85; Target Gp plc, 1987–88; FI Group plc, 1989–93. Chm., EDC for Electronics Industry, 1977–80. Member: (part time), PO Bd, 1975–77; Engineering Industries Council, 1975–80; BOTB, 1976–79; Armed Forces Pay Review Body, 1976–83; Nat. Electronics Council, 1977–80; Groupe des Présidents des Grandes Enterprises Européennes, 1977–80. Vice-Pres., Inst. of Bankers, 1982–89. Gen. Partner, Midland Enterprise Bd for SE, 1991–98; Member: RN Film Corp., 1975–83; Brighton Festival Soc. Council of Management, 1977–82; CBI Council, 1977–90 (Mem., Presidents' Cttee, 1977–84; Chm., F&GP Cttee, 1978–84); White Ensign Assoc. Council of Management, 1979–95; Council, The Prince's Youth Business Trust, 1987–89; Nat. Theatre Develt Council, 1987–90; Court, Surrey Univ., 1986–96; Governing Body and F&GP Cttee, BPMF, London Univ., 1982–96 (Dep. Chm., 1987–96); Governing Council, Business in the Community, 1985–89; Council, British Heart Foundn, 1986–89; Chm., Inst. of Neurology Council of Management, 1980–97; Trustee: Westminster Abbey Trust, 1978–85; Brain Res. Trust, 1982– (Chm., 1986–); Crimestoppers Trust (formerly Community Action Trust), 1987–; Eyeless Trust, 1991–; Dir and Trustee, Brighton Fest. Trust, 1977–92; Dir, NCVO Ltd, 1990–94. President: SABC Clubs for Young People (formerly Sussex Assoc. of Boys' Clubs), 1982–97; Cheshire Homes, Seven Rivers, Essex, 1979–85; Governor, Admin. Staff Coll., Henley, 1974–92 (Hon. Fellow 1993). CIMgt (FBIM 1974); CompIERE 1974; FIB 1982. Hon. Fellow, UCL, 1999. DUniv. Surrey, 1989; Hon. DBA Internat. Management Centre, Buckingham, 1990. *Recreations:* music, arts, sports. *Address:* Flat 68, 15 Portman Square, W1H 9HE. *T:* (020) 7935 7888. *Clubs:* Royal Over-Seas League, MCC.

READ, John Leslie, FCA; Chairman, Carvest Inc., since 1988; *b* 21 March 1935; *s* of Robert and Florence Read; *m* 1958, Eugenie Ida (*née* Knight); one *s* one *d. Educ:* Sir William Turner's School. Partner, Price Waterhouse & Co., 1966–75; Finance Dir, then Jt Chief Exec., Unigate plc, 1975–80; Chairman: Macarthy plc, 1989–92 (Dir, 1986–92); LEP Gp, 1982–91; Director: MB-Caradon Group (formerly Metal Box) plc, 1979–92; Equity Law Life Assurance Soc. plc, 1980–87; Border and Southern Stockholders Investment Trust, later Govett Strategic Investment Trust, 1985–92. Chm., Audit Commn for Local Authorities in England and Wales, 1983–86. *Recreations:* music, sport, reading, photography. *Address:* 2 Milbrook, Esher, Surrey KT10 9EJ. *Club:* Royal Automobile.

See also H. Read.

READ, Keith Frank, CBE 1997; CEng, FIMarE; FIEE; Director General, Institute of Marine Engineers, since 1999; *b* 25 April 1944; *s* of Alan George Read, OBE and Dorothy Maud Read (*née* Richardson); *m* 1966, Sheila Roberts; one *s* two *d. Educ:* King's Sch., Bruton; Britannia Royal Naval Coll., Dartmouth; Royal Naval Engrg Coll., Manadon. CEng 1972; FIEE 1988; FIMarE 1998. Joined Royal Navy, 1962: trng appts, 1963–67; HM Submarine Ocelot, 1968–69; Nuclear Reactor Course, RNC, Greenwich, 1969; HM Submarine Sovereign, 1970–73; Sen. Engr, HM Submarine Repulse, 1974–76; Staff of Capt. Submarine Sea Trng, 1976–79; Comdr 1980; Sch. Comdr, HMS Collingwood, 1980; Ops (E), MoD, 1981–84; jsdc 1984; Exec. Officer, Clyde Submarine Base, 1984–88; Capt. 1988; Dep. Dir, Naval Logistic Plans, 1989; rcds 1990; Capt. Surface Ship Acceptance, 1991–92; Naval Attaché, Rome and Albania, 1992–96; retd RN, 1996; Manager, Southern Europe, Ganley Gp, 1997–98. Mem., Adv. Bd, GMI, 1999. FRSA 2000. Freeman, City of London, 2000. *Recreations:* Italy, music, theatre, sailing. *Address:* Institute of Marine Engineers, 80 Coleman Street, EC2R 5BJ. *T:* (020) 7382 2660. *Club:* Naval and Military.

READ, Leonard Ernest, (Nipper), QPM 1976; National Security Adviser to the Museums and Galleries Commission, 1978–86; *b* 31 March 1925; *m* 1st, 1951, Marion Alexandra Millar (marr. diss. 1979); one *d*; 2nd, 1980, Patricia Margaret Allen. *Educ:* elementary schools. Worked at Players Tobacco factory, Nottingham, 1939–43; Petty Officer, RN, 1943–46; joined Metropolitan Police, 1947; served in all ranks of CID; Det. Chief Supt on Murder Squad, 1967; Asst Chief Constable, Notts Combined Constabulary, 1970; National Co-ordinator of Regional Crime Squads for England and Wales, 1972–76. British Boxing Board of Control: Mem. Council, 1976–82; Admin. Steward, 1982–88; Vice Chm., 1988–96, Chm., 1996–2000; Vice Pres., 1991–97, Pres., 1997–; Vice Pres., 1989–, Sen. Vice Pres., 1997–, World Boxing Council. Freeman, City of London, 1983. *Publication:* Nipper (autobiog.), 1991. *Recreations:* home computing, playing the keyboard. *Address:* 23 North Barn, Broxbourne, Herts EN10 6RR.

READ, Lionel Frank; QC 1973; a Recorder of the Crown Court, 1974–98; a Deputy High Court Judge, 1989–98; *b* 7 Sept. 1929; *s* of late F. W. C. Read and Lilian (*née* Chatwin); *m* 1956, Shirley Greenhalgh; two *s* one *d*. *Educ:* Oundle Sch.; St John's Coll., Cambridge (MA). Mons OCS Stick of Honour; commnd 4 RHA, 1949. Called to Bar, Gray's Inn, 1954 (Bencher, 1981; Treas., 2001); Mem., Senate of the Inns of Court and the Bar, 1974–77. A Gen. Comr of Income Tax, Gray's Inn Div., 1986–90. Chm., Local Government and Planning Bar Assoc., 1990–94 (Vice-Chm., 1986–90); Member: Bar Council, 1990–94; Council on Tribunals, 1990–96. *Recreations:* golf, gardening. *Address:* Cedarwood, Church Road, Ham Common, Surrey TW10 5HG. *T:* (020) 8940 5247. *Clubs:* Garrick; Hawks (Cambridge).

READ, Malcolm James; District Judge (Magistrates' Courts) (formerly Metropolitan Stipendiary Magistrate), since 1993; *b* 4 May 1948; *s* of Frank James Cruickshank Read and Anne Elizabeth (*née* Oldershaw); *m*; one *s* by previous marriage. *Educ:* Wallington Independent Grammar Sch.; Council of Legal Educn. Called to the Bar, Gray's Inn, 1979; Clerk to Justices, Lewes Magistrates' Court, 1980–81; Clerk to: Hastings, Bexhill, Battle and Rye Justices, 1981–91; E Sussex Magistrates' Courts Cttee, 1981–91; in private practice, Brighton, 1991–93. *Recreations:* motor-cycling, golf (occasionally), dog walking. *Address:* Thames Magistrates' Court, 58 Bow Road, E3 4DJ. *T:* (020) 8271 1201.

READ, Dr Martin Peter; Managing Director and Chief Executive, Logica plc, since 1993; *b* 16 Feb. 1950; *s* of Peter Denis Read and Dorothy Ruby Read; *m* 1974, Marian Eleanor Gilbart; one *s* one *d*. *Educ:* Queen Mary's Grammar Sch., Basingstoke; Peterhouse, Cambridge (BA Nat. Scis 1971); Merton Coll., Oxford (DPhil Physics 1974). CDipAF 1976. Posts in sales and marketing, finance, ops, and systems develt, UK and overseas, Overseas Containers Ltd, 1974–81; Corp. Commercial Dir, Marine Coatings, 1981–84, Gen. Manager, Europe, 1984–85, International Paint, part of Courtaulds; joined GEC Marconi, 1985; Gen. Manager, Marconi Secure Radio, 1986–87; Dir, Marconi Defence Systems Ltd, 1987–89; Man. Dir, Marconi Command and Control Systems Ltd, 1989–91; Gp Man. Dir, Marconi Radar and Control Systems Gp, 1991–93. Non-executive Director: ASDA Gp plc, 1996–99; Southampton Innovations Ltd, 1999–; Boots Co. plc, 1999–; British Airways, 2000–. Trustee: Hampshire Technology Centre, 1990–; Southern Focus (formerly Portsmouth Housing) Trust, 1992–2000; Dir, Portsmouth Housing Assoc., 1993–. Gov., Highbury Coll., Portsmouth, 1989–99; Mem. Council, Southampton Univ., 1999–. Hon. DTech Loughborough, 2000. *Publication:* article in Jl of Applied Physics. *Recreations:* French and German novels, drama, military history, travel, gardening. *Address:* Logica plc, Stephenson House, 75 Hampstead Road, NW1 2PL. *T:* (020) 7344 3666. *Club:* Swanmore Lawn Tennis.

READ, Mel; *see* Read, I. M.

READ, Piers Paul, FRSL; author; *b* 7 March 1941; 3rd *s* of Sir Herbert Read, DSO, MC and late Margaret Read, Stonegrave, York; *m* 1967, Emily Albertine, *o d* of Evelyn Basil Boothby, CMG and of Susan Asquith; two *s* two *d*. *Educ:* Ampleforth Coll.; St John's Coll., Cambridge (MA). Artist-in-residence, Ford Foundn, Berlin, 1963–64; Sub-Editor, Times Literary Supplement, 1965; Harkness Fellow, Commonwealth Fund, NY, 1967–68. Member: Council, Inst. of Contemporary Arts, 1971–75; Cttee of Management, Soc. of Authors, 1973–76; Literature Panel, Arts Council, 1975–77. Adjunct Prof. of Writing, Columbia Univ., NY, 1980. Bd Mem., Aid to the Church in Need, 1988–. Governor: Cardinal Manning Boys' Sch., 1985–91; More House Sch., 1996–2000. Chm., Catholic Writers' Guild (the Keys), 1992–97. TV plays: Coincidence, 1968; The House on Highbury Hill, 1972; The Childhood Friend, 1974; radio play: The Family Firm, 1970. *Publications: novels:* Game in Heaven with Tussy Marx, 1966; The Junkers, 1968 (Sir Geoffrey Faber Meml Prize); Monk Dawson, 1969 (Hawthornden Prize and Somerset Maugham Award; filmed 1997); The Professor's Daughter, 1971; The Upstart, 1973; Polonaise, 1976; A Married Man, 1979 (televised 1983); The Villa Golitsyn, 1981; The Free Frenchman, 1986 (televised 1989); A Season in the West, 1988 (James Tait Black Meml Prize); On the Third Day, 1990; A Patriot in Berlin, 1995; Knights of the Cross, 1997; Alice in Exile, 2001; *non-fiction:* Alive, 1974 (filmed 1992); The Train Robbers, 1978; Quo Vadis? the subversion of the Catholic Church, 1991; Ablaze: the story of Chernobyl, 1993; The Templars, 1999. *Address:* 50 Portland Road, W11 4LG.

READE, Brian Anthony; HM Diplomatic Service, retired; *b* 5 Feb. 1940; *s* of Stanley Robert Reade and Emily Doris (*née* Lee); *m* 1964, Averille van Eugen; one *s* one *d*. *Educ:* King Henry VIII Sch., Coventry; Univ. of Leeds (BA Hons 1963). Interlang Ltd, 1963–64; Lectr, City of Westminster Coll., 1964–65; 2nd Sec., FCO, 1965–69; 2nd Sec., Bangkok, 1970–71, 1st Sec., 1971–74; FCO, 1974–77; Consul (Econ.), Consulate-General, Düsseldorf, 1977–81; FCO, 1981–82; 1st Sec., Bangkok, 1982–84; Counsellor (ESCAP), Bangkok, 1984–86; Counsellor, FCO, 1986–93. *Recreations:* watching sport, conversation, reading. *Clubs:* Coventry Rugby Football; Royal Bangkok Sports (Thailand).

READE, Sir Kenneth Roy, 13th Bt *cr* 1661, of Barton, Berkshire; *b* 23 March 1926; *s* of Leverne Elton Reade (*d* 1943; 5th *s* of Sir George Compton Reade, 9th Bt), and Norma B. Ward; *S* cousin, 1982; *m* 1944, Doreen D. Vinsant; three *d*. *Heir:* none.

READE, Ven. Nicholas Stewart; Archdeacon of Lewes and Hastings, since 1997; *b* 9 Dec. 1946; *s* of late Sqdn Ldr Charles Sturrock Reade and Eileen Vandermere (*née* Fleming); *m* 1971, Christine Jasper, *d* of late Very Rev. R. C. D. Jasper, CBE, DD and of Ethel Jasper; one *d*. *Educ:* Elizabeth Coll., Guernsey; Univ. of Leeds (BA, DipTh); Coll. of the Resurrection, Mirfield. Ordained deacon, 1973, priest, 1974; Assistant Curate: St Chad's, Coseley, 1973–75; St Nicholas, Codsall, and Priest-in-charge of Holy Cross, Bilbrook, 1975–78; Vicar, St Peter's, Upper Gornal and Chaplain, Burton Road Hosp., Dudley, 1978–82; Vicar: St Dunstan's, Mayfield, 1982–88; St Mary's, Eastbourne, 1988–97. Rural Dean: Dallington, 1982–88; Eastbourne, 1988–97; Canon of Chichester Cathedral, 1990– (Prebendary, 1990–97). Mem., Gen. Synod of C of E, 1995–2000. *Recreations:* cycling, steam trains, modern ecclesiastical and political biographies. *Address:* The Archdeaconry, 27 The Avenue, Lewes BN71 1QT. *T:* (01273) 479530, *Fax:* (01273) 476529; *e-mail:* archlewes@pavilion.co.uk.

READING, 4th Marquess of, *cr* 1926; **Simon Charles Henry Rufus Isaacs;** Baron 1914; Viscount 1916; Earl 1917; Viscount Erleigh 1917; international management consultant; *b* 18 May 1942; *e s* of 3rd Marquess of Reading, MBE, MC, and of Margot Irene, *yr d* of late Percy Duke, OBE; *S* father, 1980; *m* 1979, Melinda Victoria, *yr d* of late Richard Dewar, Hay Hedge, Bisley, Glos; one *s* two *d*. *Educ:* Eton. Served 1st Queen's Dragoon Guards, 1961–64. Member of Stock Exchange, 1970–74. Director: Nelson Recovery Trust; Nat. Biblical Heritage Trust; Cheltenham and Gloucester Coll. Trust; Flying Hosp. Inc. Pres., Dean Close Sch., 1990–2001. Hon. Dr Soka, Tokyo, 1989. *Heir: s* Viscount Erleigh, *qv*. *Address:* Jaynes Court, Bisley, Glos GL6 7BE. *Clubs:* Cavalry and Guards, White's, MCC, All England Lawn Tennis and Croquet.

READING, Area Bishop of, since 1997; **Rt Rev. Dominic Edward William Murray Walker,** OGS; *b* 28 June 1948; *s* of Horace John and Mary Louise Walker. *Educ:* Plymouth Coll.; King's Coll. London (AKC); Heythrop Coll., London (MA). Ordained priest, 1972; Asst Curate, St Faith, Wandsworth, 1972–73; Domestic Chaplain to the Bishop of Southwark, 1973–76; Rector, Newington, 1976–85; Rural Dean, Southwark and Newington, 1980–85; Vicar, Team Rector, and Rural Dean of Brighton, 1985–97; Canon and Prebendary, Chichester Cathedral, 1985–97. Mem., CGA, 1967–83; Mem., OGS, 1983– (Superior, 1990–96). Hon. DLitt Brighton, 1998. *Publication:* The Ministry of Deliverance, 1997. *Address:* Bishop's House, Tidmarsh Lane, Tidmarsh, Reading RG8 8HA. *T:* (0118) 984 1216, *Fax:* (0118) 984 1218; *e-mail:* bishopreading@oxford.anglican.org.

READING, Peter Gray, FRSL; writer, since 1970; *b* 27 July 1946; *s* of Wilfred Gray Reading and Ethel Mary Reading; *m* 1968, Diana Joy Gilbert (marr. diss. 1996); one *d*; *m* 1996, Deborah Joyce Jackson. *Educ:* Liverpool Coll. of Art (BA Fine Art and Painting). Art Teacher, Ruffwood Sch., 1967–68; Lectr, Liverpool Coll. of Art, 1968–70; animal feedmill worker, 1970–92. FRSL 1988. *Publications: poetry:* Water and Waste, 1970; For the Municipality's Elderly, 1974; The Prison Cell and Barrel Mystery, 1976; Nothing for Anyone, 1977; Fiction, 1979; Tom o'Bedlam's Beauties, 1981; Diplopic, 1983; 5x5x5x5x5, 1983; C, 1984; Ukulele Music, 1985; Going On, 1985; Stet, 1986; Final Demands, 1988; Perduta Gente, 1989; Shitheads, 1989; Evagatory, 1992; Last Poems, 1994; Escatalogical, 1996; Collected Poems, vol. 1, 1995, vol. 2, 1996; Work in Regress, 1997; Chinoiserie, 1997; Ob, 1998; Apopthegmatic, 1999; Marfan, 2000; untitled, 2001; Faunal, 2002. *Recreations:* ornithology, natural sciences. *Address:* c/o Bloodaxe Books, Highgreen, Tarset, Northumberland NE48 1RP.

READING, Dr Peter Richard; Chief Executive, University Hospitals of Leicester NHS Trust, since 2000; *b* 1 May 1956; *s* of Dr Harold Garnar Reading and Barbara Mary Reading (*née* Hancock); two *d*. *Educ:* St Edward's Sch., Oxford; Gonville and Caius Coll., Cambridge (MA); Birmingham Univ. (PhD); Moscow State Univ. Health service mgt posts in London, 1984–94; Chief Executive: Lewisham and Guy's Mental Health NHS Trust, 1994–98; UCL Hosps NHS Trust, 1998–2000. *Recreations:* children, cats, dog, Oxford United, Russian history. *Address:* University Hospitals of Leicester NHS Trust, Glenfield Hospital, Groby Road, Leicester LE3 9QP. *T:* (0116) 258 3188, *Fax:* (0116) 256 3187; *e-mail:* peter.reading@uhl-tr.nhs.uk.

REAGAN, Ronald, Hon. GCB 1989; President of the United States of America, 1981–89; *b* Tampico, Ill, 6 Feb. 1911; *m* 1st, 1940, Jane Wyman (marr. diss. 1948); one *s* (one *d* decd); 2nd, 1952, Nancy Davis; one *s* one *d*. *Educ:* public schools in Tampico, Monmouth, Galesburg, and Dixon, Ill; Eureka Coll., Ill (AB). Sports Announcer, WHO, Des Moines, 1932–37; actor, films and television, 1937–66; Host and Program Superviser, Gen. Electric Theater (TV), 1954–62; Host, Death Valley Days (TV), 1962–65. Pres., Screen Actors' Guild, 1947–52, 1959–60; Chm., Motion Picture Industry Council, 1949. Served with USAAF, 1942–45. Governor, State of California, 1967–74; Chairman, State Governors' Assoc., 1969. Republican Candidate for nomination for the Presidency, 1976. Operates horsebreeding and cattle ranch. Hon. Fellow, Keble Coll., Oxford, 1994. Presidential Medal of Freedom, USA, 1992. *Publications:* Where's the Rest of Me? (autobiog.), 1965 (repr. 1981 as My Early Life); Abortion and the Conscience of the Nation, 1984; An American Life (autobiog.), 1990.

REAMSBOTTOM, Barry Arthur; General Secretary, Public and Commercial Services Union, 1998–May 2002; *b* 4 April 1949; *s* of Agnes Reamsbottom. *Educ:* St Peter's RC Secondary Sch., Aberdeen; Aberdeen Academy. Scientific Asst, Isaac Spencer & Co., Aberdeen, 1966–69; Social Security Officer, DHSS, Aberdeen, 1969–76; Area Officer, NUPE, Edinburgh, 1976–79; Civil and Public Services Association: Head of Educn Dept, 1979–87; Editor, Press Officer, 1987–92; Gen. Sec., 1992–98. Vice-Pres., Trade Union Cttee for European and Transatlantic Understanding, 1996–. Mem., Amnesty Internat., 1978–. *Recreations:* reading, golf, politics, music, taking photographs, watching Coronation Street. *Address:* Public and Commercial Services Union, 160 Falcon Road, SW11 2LN. *T:* (020) 7924 2727.

REARDON, Rev. John Patrick, OBE 1999; General Secretary, Council of Churches for Britain and Ireland, 1990–99; Moderator, General Assembly of the United Reformed Church, 1995–96; *b* 15 June 1933; *s* of John Samuel Reardon and Ivy Hilda Reardon; *m* 1957, Molly Pamela Young; four *s* one *d*. *Educ:* Gravesend Grammar Sch. for Boys; University College London (BA Hons English); King's College London (postgraduate Cert. in Educn). Teacher, London and Gravesend, 1958–61; Minister, Horsham Congregational Church, 1961–68 (Chm., Sussex Congregational Union, 1967); Minister, Trinity Congregational Church, St Albans, 1968–72 (Chm., Herts Congregational Union, 1971–72); Sec., Church and Society Dept, 1972–90, and Dep. Gen. Sec., 1983–90, URC. *Publications:* More Everyday Prayers (contrib.), 1982; (ed) Leaves from the Tree of Peace, 1986; (ed) Threads of Creation, 1989. *Recreations:* modern literature, photography, philately, travel. *Address:* 1 Newbolt Close, Newport Pagnell, Bucks MK16 8ND. *T:* (01908) 217559.

REARDON, Rev. Canon Martin Alan, OBE 1997; General Secretary, Churches Together in England, 1990–97; *b* 3 Oct. 1932; *s* of Ernest William Reardon, CBE and Gertrude Mary; *m* 1964, Ruth Maxim Slade; one *s* one *d*. *Educ:* Cumnor House Sch.; St Edward's Sch., Oxford; Selwyn Coll., Cambridge (MA); Cuddesdon Coll., Oxford; Univ. of Geneva; Univ. of Louvain. Asst Curate, Rugby Parish Church, 1958–61; Sec., Sheffield Council of Churches, 1962–71; Sub-Warden, Lincoln Theol Coll., 1971–78; Sec., Bd for Mission and Unity, Gen. Synod of C of E, 1978–89; Rector, Plumpton with East Chiltington, 1989–90. Hon. Canon, Lincoln Cathedral, 1979–. *Publications:* Christian Unity in Sheffield, 1967; (with Kenneth Greet) Social Questions, 1964; What on Earth is the Church For?, 1985; Christian Initiation, 1991; contribs to One in Christ, Theology, Clergy Review, etc. *Recreations:* walking, sketching. *Address:* The Little School House, 3 Turvey Court, High Street, Turvey, Beds MK43 8DB.

REARDON SMITH, Sir William (Antony John), 4th Bt *cr* 1920, of Appledore, Devon; management and charities consultant; Trustee and Chairman, Joseph Strong Frazer Trust, since 1980; Chairman, North Eastern Rubber Company Ltd, since 1980; *b* 20 June 1937; *e s* of Sir William Reardon Reardon-Smith, 3rd Bt and his 1st wife, Nesta

Florence Phillips (*d* 1959); *S* father, 1995; *m* 1962, Susan Wight, *d* of Henry Wight Gibson; three *s* one *d*. *Educ:* Wycliffe Coll. Nat. Service, RN, Suez, 1956. Sir William Reardon Smith & Sons Ltd and Reardon Smith Line plc, 1957–85 (Dir, 1959–85); Director: London World Trade Centre, 1986–87; Milford Haven Port Authority, 1988–99; Marine and Port Services Ltd, Milford Docks, 1990–99. Member: Baltic Exchange, 1959–87 (Dir, 1982–87; Assoc. Mem., 1990–92); Chamber of Shipping Documentary Cttee, 1963–72 (Chm., 1968–72); Documentary Council, Baltic and Internat. Conf., 1964–82. Dir, UK Protection and Indemnity Club and Freight, Demurrage and Defence Assoc., 1968–80. Trustee: Royal Merchant Navy Sch. Foundn, 1966– (Vice-Pres., 1992–); Bearwood Coll., 1966–; Member: Council, King George's Fund for Sailors, 1981–95; City of London Cttee, RNLI, 1976–. Liveryman: Poulters' Co, 1991–; Shipwrights' Co, 1994–. KLJ 1997. *Recreations:* golf, shooting. *Heir: s* William Nicolas Henry Reardon Smith [*b* 10 June 1963; *m* 2001, Julia, *er d* of D. Martin Slade]. *Address:* 26 Merrick Square, SE1 4JB. *T:* (020) 7403 5723. *Clubs:* Cardiff and County; Royal Porthcawl Golf.

REASON, Prof. James Tootle, FBA 1999; FRAeS; FBPsS; Professor of Psychology, University of Manchester, since 1977; *b* 1 May 1938; *s* of late George Stanley Tootle and Hilda Alice Reason; *m* 1964, Rea Jaari; two *d*. *Educ:* Royal Masonic Sch.; Univ. of Manchester (BSc 1962); Univ. of Leicester (PhD 1967). FBPsS 1988; FRAeS 1998. RAF Inst. of Aviation Medicine, 1962–64; Lectr and Reader, Dept of Psychology, Univ. of Leicester, 1964–76. Dist. Foreign Colleague Award, US Human Factors and Ergonomics Soc., 1995. *Publications:* Man in Motion, 1974; Motion Sickness, 1975; Human Error, 1990; Beyond Aviation Human Factors, 1995; Managing the Risks of Organizational Accidents, 1997. *Recreations:* reading, gardening, walking, sailing. *Address:* Woodburn, Red Lane, Disley, Cheshire SK12 2NP. *T:* (01663) 762406; *e-mail:* reason@redlane.demon.co.uk.

REASON, John; journalist and author; Rugby Union correspondent, Daily Telegraph and Sunday Telegraph, 1964–94; Director, Rugby Football Books Ltd, since 1971; *s* of C. L. Reason and G. M. Reason; *m* Joan Wordsworth; two *s* (and one *s* decd). *Educ:* Dunstable Grammar Sch.; London Univ. Res. at ICI; local journalist, Watford and Dunstable; Sports Ed., West Herts Post, Watford, 1952; sports journalist: News Chronicle, Manchester, 1953; The Recorder, London, 1953–54; News of the World, Manchester, 1954; sports and feature writer: News of the World, London, 1955–63; Daily Telegraph, 1964–80; Sunday Telegraph, 1980–94; Asst Ed. and feature writer, The Cricketer, 1965–79. *Publications:* The 1968 Lions, 1968; The 1971 Lions, 1971, 5th edn 1973; The Lions Speak, 1972, 2nd edn 1973; The Unbeaten Lions, 1974, 2nd edn 1975; Lions Down Under, 1977; The World of Rugby, 1978 (TV series); Backs to the Wall, 1980. *Recreation:* trying to work out how the Conservative Party could possibly miss every single one of the boats in the harbour of the 2001 General Election. *Address:* c/o D. A. Hurrell, 69 Kensington Church Street, W8. *Clubs:* MCC; Dunstablians Rugby Football (Life Pres.); Royal Mid-Surrey Golf.

REAY, 14th Lord *cr* 1628, of Reay, Caithness; **Hugh William Mackay;** Bt of Nova Scotia, 1627; Baron Mackay of Ophemert and Zennewijnen, Holland; Chief of Clan Mackay; *b* 19 July 1937; *s* of 13th Lord Reay and Charlotte Mary Younger; *S* father, 1963; *m* 1st, 1964, Hon. Annabel Thérèse Fraser (*see* A. T. Keswick) (marr. diss. 1978); two *s* one *d*; 2nd, 1980, Hon. Victoria Isabella Warrender, *d* of 1st Baron Bruntisfield, MC; two *d*. *Educ:* Eton; Christ Church. Mem., European Parlt, 1973–79 (Vice-Chm., Cons. Gp); Delegate, Council of Europe and WEU, 1979–86. Lord in Waiting (Govt Whip), 1989–91; Parly Under-Sec. of State, DTI, 1991–92; Mem., Select Cttee on European Communities, H of L, 1993–99 (Chm., Sub-Cttee on Food and Agric., 1996–99); elected Mem., H of L, 1999. *Heir: s* The Master of Reay, *qv*. *Address:* House of Lords, SW1A 0PW.

REAY, Master of; Aeneas Simon Mackay; *b* 20 March 1965; *s* and *heir* of 14th Lord Reay, *qv*. *Educ:* Westminster School; Brown Univ., USA. *Recreations:* most sports, especially football, cricket and shooting.

REAY, Lt-Gen. Sir Alan; *see* Reay, Lt-Gen. Sir H. A. J.

REAY, David William, CEng, FIEE; CPhys, FInstP; Chairman, Northumberland Mental Health NHS Trust, 1992–2001; *b* 28 May 1940; *s* of late Stanley Reay and Madge Reay (*née* Hall); *m* 1964, Constance Susan Gibney; two *d*. *Educ:* Monkwearmouth Grammar School, Sunderland; Newcastle upon Tyne Polytechnic. Independent Television Authority, 1960–62; Alpha Television (ATV and ABC) Services Ltd, 1962–64; Tyne Tees Television Ltd, 1964–72; HTV Ltd: Engineering Manager, 1972–75; Chief Engineer, 1975–79; Dir of Engineering, 1979–84; Man. Dir, 1984–91, Chief Exec., 1991, Tyne Tees Television Hldgs. Chairman: Hadrian Television Ltd, 1988–91; Legend Television Ltd, 1989–91; Man. Dir, Tyne Tees Television Ltd, 1984–91; Director: Tyne Tees Music, 1984–91; Tyne Tees Enterprises, 1984–91; ITCA, now ITVA, 1984–91; Independent Television Publications, 1984–89; Tube Productions, 1986–91; ITN, 1990–91; Tyne and Wear Develt Corp., 1986–88; The Wearside Opportunity Ltd, 1988–91. Mem. Council, Univ. of Newcastle upon Tyne, 1989–94. CIMgt (CBIM 1987); FRTS 1984; FRSA 1992. *Recreations:* walking, reading, music, watching soccer (particularly Sunderland AFC). *Address:* Warreners House, Northgate, Morpeth, Northumberland NE61 3BX.

REAY, Lt-Gen. Sir (Hubert) Alan (John), KBE 1981; FRCP, FRCP(Edin); Chairman, Lambeth Health Care (formerly West Lambeth Community Care) NHS Trust, 1992–97; Director General, Army Medical Services, 1981–85; *b* 19 March 1925; *s* of Rev. John Reay; *m* 1960, Ferelith Haslewood Deane, artist and printmaker; two *s* two *d* (and one *s* decd). *Educ:* Lancing College; Edinburgh Univ. MB, DTM&H, DCH. Field Medical Services, Malaya, 1949–52 (despatches); Exchange Physician, Brooke Hosp., San Antonio, Texas, 1957; Command Paediatrician: Far East, 1962; BAOR, 1965; Adviser in Paediatrics, MoD (Army), 1968; Hon. Out-patient Consultant, Great Ormond Street Hosp., 1975–79, 1985–87; QHP 1976–85; Postgraduate Dean and Comdt, Royal Army Med. Coll., 1977–79; DMS, HQ BAOR, 1979–81. Hon. Col, 217 (London) General Hosp. RAMC (Volunteers) TA, 1986–90. Chm., Med. Cttee, Royal Star and Garter Home, 1986–92. Member Council: SSAFA, 1986–93; RSocMed, 1987–91 (Pres., Paediatric Section, 1984–85). Pres., Friends of St Thomas' Hosp., 1993–. Vice-Chm., Thames Reach Homelessness Project, 1992–94; Chm., Mosaic Clubhouse for people with mental illness, 1997–2001; Trustee: Children's Hospice for Eastern Reg., Cambridge, 1988–97; Burtle Trust, 1991–. Chief Hon. Steward, Westminster Abbey, 1985–97. Inaugural Lectr, Soc. of Armed Forces Med. Consultants, Univ. of Health Scis, Bethesda, 1984. FRCPCH 1997 (Hon. Mem., BPA, 1988); Hon. FRCGP 1985. CStJ 1981 (OStJ 1979). *Publications:* paediatric articles in med. jls. *Address:* 63 Madrid Road, Barnes, SW13 9PQ.

REAY, Dr John Sinclair Shewan; Director, Warren Spring Laboratory, Department of Trade and Industry, 1985–92; *b* Aberdeen, 8 June 1932; *s* of late George Reay, CBE and Tina (*née* Shewan); *m* 1958, Rhoda Donald Robertson; two *s* one *d*. *Educ:* Robert Gordon's College, Aberdeen; Univ. of Aberdeen; Imperial College, London (Beit Fellow). BSc, PhD, DIC. CChem, FRSC. Joined Scottish Agricultural Industries, 1958; Warren Spring Lab., Min of Technology, 1968; Head of Air Pollution Div., DoI, 1972–77; Head, Policy and Perspectives Unit, DTI, 1977–79; Head of Branch, Research Technology Div., DoI, 1979–81; Dep. Dir, Warren Spring Lab., 1981–85. *Publications:* papers on surface chemistry and air pollution. *Recreations:* playing violin, listening to music. *Address:* 13 Grange Hill, Welwyn, Herts AL6 9RH. *T:* (01438) 715587.

REAY-SMITH, Richard Philip Morley; Chairman: MEI Europe Ltd, since 1999; Director, Legal & General Bank Ltd, since 2001; *b* 24 Nov. 1941; *m* 1972, Susan Margaret Hill; two *s*. *Educ:* Stowe Sch.; Durham Univ. (LLB); Harvard Business Sch. (AMP). Barclays Bank 1963–98: Local Dir, Shrewsbury, 1984–87; Dep. Chief Exec., Central Retail Services Div., 1987–91; Chief Exec., Barclaycard, 1991–94; Man. Dir, Personal Banking, 1995–98; Chm., Barclays Life Assurance Co. Ltd, 1996–98; Chief Exec., UK Retail Banking, 1998. Dir, Visa Internat. Services Assoc., 1991–98. First Chm., 1980–85, Vice-Chm., 1985–, Painshill Park Trust. FRSA. *Recreations:* sailing, flying, music.

REBUCK, Gail Ruth, (Mrs Philip Gould), CBE 2000; Chairman and Chief Executive, Random House Group (formerly Random House UK) Ltd, since 1991; *b* 10 Feb. 1952; *d* of Gordon and Mavis Rebuck; *m* 1985, Philip Gould, *qv*; two *d*. *Educ:* Lycée Français de Londres; Univ. of Sussex (BA). Production Asst, Grisewood & Dempsey, 1975–76; Editor, then Publisher, Robert Nicholson Publications, 1976–78; Publisher, Hamlyn Paperbacks, 1978–82; Publishing Dir, Century Publishing, 1982–85; Publisher, Century Hutchinson, 1985–89; Chm., Random House Div., Random Century, 1989–91. Member: COPUS, 1995–97; Creative Industries Taskforce, 1997–. Trustee, IPPR, 1993–. Member: Court, Univ. of Sussex, 1997–; Council, RCA, 1999–. FRSA 1989. *Recreations:* reading, travel. *Address:* Random House Group Ltd, 20 Vauxhall Bridge Road, SW1V 2SA. *T:* (020) 7840 8886. *Club:* Groucho.

RECKERT, Prof. (Frederick) Stephen, FBA 1994; Camoens Professor of Portuguese, University of London, 1967–82, now Emeritus; Founder Member, Institute for Study of Symbology, New University of Lisbon, since 1980; Hon. Senior Research Fellow, Institute of Romance Studies, University of London, since 1995; *b* 31 May 1923; *o c* of Frederick Carl Reckert and Aileen Templeton Adams Reckert; *m* 1st, 1946, Olwen Roberts (*d* 1963); two *s* one *d*; 2nd, 1965, Dídia Mateus Marques. *Educ:* Phillips Exeter Acad., USA; Saybrook Coll., Yale (BA *summa cum laude* 1945, ranked first in class); Trinity Coll., Cambridge (MLitt 1948); Berkeley Coll., Yale (PhD 1950). Japanese translator with RAF, Bletchley, 1943–45; Fellow, Berkeley Coll. and Asst Prof. of Spanish, Yale, 1948–58; Prof. and Head of Hispanic Studies, Univ. of Wales, 1958–66; Head, Portuguese and Brazilian Studies, Univ. of London, 1967–82. Visiting Professor: Univ. of Madrid, 1971; New Univ., Lisbon, 1974–78; Univ. of Rome, 1985; Kate Elder Lectr, London Univ., 1996; Guest Lectr, Univs of Lisbon, Oporto, Évora, Seville, Warsaw, Jagiellonian Univ. of Cracow. Corresp. Fellow: Hispanic Soc. of America; Portuguese Acad. of Scis.; Royal Spanish Acad. Hon. Fellow, Asociación Hispánica de Literatura Medieval. Mem., Phi Beta Kappa. Nobiling Medal for Medieval Studies, Brazil, 1978. Comendador, Order of Southern Cross (Brazil), 1979; Grand Cross, Order of Henry the Navigator (Portugal), 1990. *Publications:* (with Dámaso Alonso) Vida y Obra de Medrano, 1958; (with Helder Macedo) Do Cancioneiro de Amigo, 1976, 3rd edn 1996; Gil Vicente, 1977; (with Y. K. Centeno) Fernando Pessoa, 1978; Espírito e Letra de Gil Vicente, 1986; Um Ramalhete para Cesário, 1987; Beyond Chrysanthemums, 1993; Play it Again, Sam, 1997; From the Resende Songbook, 1998; Más allá de las neblinas de noviembre, 2001; as Frederick Carlson: A Perfeição, Musée de l'Homme, Contos da Palma da Mão, 1994; Brasil e Alguns Poemas, 1999; contribs to jls and collective vols. *Recreations:* poetry, music, travel, conviviality, ailurophilia. *Address:* Rua das Janelas Verdes 17-4°, 1200–690 Lisbon, Portugal. *T:* 213962292; Ayot Weir, Weybridge, Surrey KT13 8HR. *T:* (01932) 843589. *Clubs:* Oxford and Cambridge; PEN (Portuguese centre).

RECKITT, Lt-Col Basil Norman, TD 1946; Director, Reckitt and Colman Ltd, retired 1972 (Chairman, 1966–70); *b* 12 Aug. 1905; *s* of Frank Norman Reckitt, Architect, and Beatrice Margaret Hewett; *m* 1st, 1928, Virginia Carre-Smith (*d* 1961); three *d*; 2nd, 1966, Mary Holmes (*née* Peirce), *widow* of Paul Holmes, Malham Tarn, near Settle. *Educ:* Uppingham; King's Coll., Cambridge (MA). Joined Reckitt & Sons Ltd, 1927; Dir, Reckitt & Colman Ltd, 1938. 2nd Lieut, 62nd HAA Regt (TA), 1939; Bde Major, 39th AA Brigade, 1940; CO 141 HAA (M) Regt, 1942; Military Government, Germany, 1944–45. Hull University: Chm. Council, 1971–80; Pro-Chancellor, 1971–93, now Emeritus. Sheriff of Hull, 1970–71. Chm., Friends of Abbot Hall Art Gall. and Museums, Kendal, 1982–87; Vice-Chm., YMCA Nat. Centre, Lakeside, Windermere, 1982–87. Hon. LLD, Hull University, 1967. *Publications:* History of Reckitt & Sons Ltd, 1951; Charles I and Hull, 1952; The Lindley Affair, 1972; Diary of Military Government in Germany, 1989; The Journeys of William Reckitt, 1989; Diary of Anti-Aircraft Defence, 1990; Brothers at War, 1991; Petronella, 1994; The Death Hole, 1994; Sibella, 1996; Roos-in-Holderness Occasional Papers. *Address:* Haverbrack, Milnthorpe, Cumbria LA7 7AH. *T:* (01539) 563142.

REDDAWAY, Brian; *see* Reddaway, W. B.

REDDAWAY, David Norman, CMG 1993; MBE 1980; HM Diplomatic Service; Director, Public Services, Foreign and Commonwealth Office, since 1999; *b* 26 April 1953; *s* of late George Frank Norman Reddaway, CBE and of Jean Reddaway, OBE (*née* Brett); *m* 1981, Roshan Taliyeh Firouz; two *s* one *d*. *Educ:* Oundle Sch. (Schol.); Fitzwilliam Coll., Cambridge (Exhibnr; MA Hist.). Volunteer teacher, Ethiopia, 1972. Joined FCO, 1975; language student, SOAS, 1976 and Iran, 1977; Tehran: Third Sec. later Second Sec. (Commercial), 1977–78; Second Sec. later First Sec. (Chancery), 1978–80; First Secretary: (Chancery), Madrid, 1980–84; FCO, 1985–86; Private Sec. to Minister of State, 1986–88; (Chancery), New Delhi, 1988–90; Chargé d'Affaires, Tehran, 1990–93 (Counsellor, 1991); Minister, Buenos Aires, 1993–97; Hd, Southern European Dept, FCO, 1997–99. Hon. Vice-Pres., Raleigh Internat., 1998–. *Recreations:* ski-ing, tennis, Persian carpets and art. *Address:* c/o Foreign and Commonwealth Office, King Charles Street, SW1A 2AH. *Clubs:* Hawks (Cambridge); Leander (Henley-on-Thames).

REDDAWAY, Prof. (William) Brian, CBE 1971; FBA 1967; Professor of Political Economy, University of Cambridge, 1969–80, now Emeritus; Fellow of Clare College, Cambridge, since 1938; Economic Consultant to the World Bank, since 1966; *b* 8 Jan. 1913; *s* of late William Fiddian Reddaway and late Kate Waterland Reddaway (*née* Sills); *m* 1938, Barbara Augusta Bennett (*d* 1996); three *s* one *d*. *Educ:* Oundle Sch.; King's Coll., Cambridge; Maj. schol. natural science; 1st cl. Maths tripos, part I, 1st cl. 1st div. Economics tripos, part II; Adam Smith Prize; MA. Assistant, Bank of England, 1934–35; Research Fellow in Economics, University of Melbourne, 1936–37; Statistics Division, Board of Trade (final rank Chief Statistician), 1940–47; University Lectr in Economics, 1939–55, Reader in Applied Economics, 1957–65, Dir of Dept of Applied Economics, 1955–69, Univ. of Cambridge. Economic Adviser to OEEC, 1951–52; Visiting Economist, Center for International Studies, New Delhi, 1959–60; Vis. Lectr, Economic Develt Inst. (Washington), 1966–67; Consultant, Harvard Develt Adv. Service (in Ghana), 1967; Vis. Prof., Bangladesh Inst. of Develt Studies, 1974–75. Economic Consultant to

CBI, 1972–83. Regional Adviser, Economic Commn for Western Asia, 1979–80; Consultant to World Bank on Nigerian economy, 1983–87. Member: Royal Commn on the Press, 1961–62; NBPI, 1967–71; Chm., Inquiry into Consulting Engineering Firms' Costs and Earnings, 1971–72. Editor, Economic Jl, 1971–76. *Publications:* Russian Financial System, 1935; Economics of a Declining Population, 1939; (with C. F. Carter, Richard Stone) Measurement of Production Movements, 1948; The Development of the Indian Economy, 1962; Effects of UK Direct Investment Overseas, Interim Report, 1967, Final Report, 1968; Effects of the Selective Employment Tax, First Report, 1970, Final Report, 1973; (with G. C. Fiegehen) Companies, Incentives and Senior Managers, 1981; Some Key Issues for the Development of the Economy of Papua New Guinea, 1986; articles in numerous economic journals. *Recreations:* skating, walking. *Address:* 12 Manor Court, Grange Road, Cambridge CB3 9BE. *T:* (01223) 350041.

REDDICLIFFE, Paul, OBE 1998; HM Diplomatic Service; Research Analyst for Cambodia, Laos, Thailand, and Vietnam, Foreign and Commonwealth Office; *b* 17 March 1945; *s* of Donald Reddicliffe and Vera Irene (*née* Elleby); *m* 1974, Wee Siok Boi; two *s.* *Educ:* Bedford Mod. Sch.; Jesus Coll., Oxford (MA Lit. Hum. 1967); Sch. of Oriental and African Studies, Univ. of London (MA SE Asian Studies 1973); Univ. of Kent. VSO, Vientiane, Laos, 1968–70 and 1971–72; joined HM Diplomatic Service, 1977; Indochina Analyst, Res. Dept, FCO, 1977–85; First Sec., Canberra, 1985–89; Indochina Analyst, 1989–92, Hd, S and SE Asia Section, 1992–94, Res. later Res. and Analysis, Dept, FCO; Ambassador to Kingdom of Cambodia, 1994–97. *Recreations:* bird-watching, books, collecting foreign bank-notes. *Address:* c/o Foreign and Commonwealth Office, King Charles Street, SW1A 2AH.

REDDIHOUGH, John Hargreaves; His Honour Judge Reddihough; a Circuit Judge, since 2000; *b* 6 Dec. 1947; *s* of Frank Hargreaves Reddihough and Mabel Grace Reddihough (*née* Warner); *m* 1981, Sally Margaret Fryer; one *s* one *d.* *Educ:* Manchester Grammar Sch.; Univ. of Birmingham (LLB Hons). Called to the Bar, Gray's Inn, 1969; barrister, 1971–2000; Asst Recorder, 1991–94; Recorder, 1994–2000. *Recreations:* ski-ing, gardening, running, music, travel, reading, sport. *Address:* Grimsby Combined Court, Town Hall Square, Grimsby, S Humberside DN31 1HX. *T:* (01472) 311811.

REDDINGTON, (Clifford) Michael; Chief Executive, Liverpool City Council, 1986–88; *b* 14 Sept. 1932; *s* of Thomas Reddington and Gertrude (*née* Kenny); *m* 1968 Ursula Moor. *Educ:* St Michael's Coll., Leeds; St Edward's Coll., Liverpool; Liverpool Univ. BCom 1953; CPFA (IPFA 1958); MBCS 1964. Served RAF, 1958–60. City Treasury, Liverpool, 1953–58 and 1960–86; Dep. City Treasurer, 1974, City Treasurer, 1982–86. Mem., Indep. Inquiry into Capital Market Activities of London Borough of Hammersmith and Fulham, 1990. Chairman: Liverpool Welsh Choral Union, 1990–93; Convocation, Univ. of Liverpool, 1993–96; Trust Fund Manager, Hillsborough Disaster Appeal Fund, 1989–98; Chm., James Bulger Meml Trust, 1993–98. Mem. Governing Body, and Chm. Finance Cttee, Nugent Care Soc., 1992–. *Recreations:* fell-walking, cooking. *Address:* Entwood, Westwood Road, Noctorum, Birkenhead CH43 9RQ. *T:* (0151) 652 6081. *Club:* Athenæum (Liverpool).

REDDISH, Prof. Vincent Cartledge, OBE 1974; PhD, DSc; FRSE; Professor Emeritus, Edinburgh University, 1980; *b* 28 April 1926; *s* of William H. M. Reddish and Evelyn Reddish; *m* 1951, Elizabeth Waltho; two *s.* *Educ:* Wigan Techn. Coll.; London Univ. (BSc Hons, PhD, DSc). FRSE 1965. Lectr in Astronomy, Edinburgh Univ., 1954; Lectr in Radio Astronomy, Manchester Univ., 1959; Royal Observatory, Edinburgh: Principal Scientific Officer, 1962; Sen. Principal Sci. Off., 1966; Dep. Chief Sci. Off., 1974; Regius Prof. of Astronomy, Edinburgh Univ., Dir, Royal Observatory, Edinburgh, and Astronomer Royal for Scotland, 1975–80. Governor, Rannoch Sch., 1981–97. *Publications:* Evolution of the Galaxies, 1967; The Physics of Stellar Interiors, 1974; Stellar Formation, 1978; The D-Force, 1993; numerous sci. papers in Monthly Notices RAS, Trans RSE, Nature and other jls. *Recreations:* walking, sailing, ornithology, do-it-yourself. *Address:* 11 Rothes Drive, Murieston, Livingston, West Lothian EH54 9HR. *T:* and *Fax:* (01506) 414393.

REDESDALE, 6th Baron *cr* 1902; **Rupert Bertram Mitford;** Baron Mitford (Life Peer), 2000; *b* 18 July 1967; *s* of 5th Baron and of Sarah Georgina Cranstoun, *d* of Brig. Alston Cranstoun Todd, OBE; *S* father, 1991; *m* 1998, Helen, *e d* of David Shipsey; one *s.* *Educ:* Highgate Sch.; Newcastle Univ. (BA Hons Archaeology). Outdoor instructor, Fernwood Adventure Centre, South Africa, 1990–91. Lib Dem spokesman on overseas development, H of L, 1993–; Member: H of L Select Cttee on Sci. and Technology, 1994–97; EU (D) Agric. Select Cttee, 1998–2000. Mem. Council, IAM, 1995–; Pres., Natural Gas Vehicle Assoc., 1997–. Hon. Vice Pres., Raleigh Internat., 2000–. *Recreations:* caving, climbing, ski-ing. *Heir:* *s* Hon. Bertram David Mitford, *b* 29 May 2000. *Address:* 2 St Mark's Square, NW1 7TP. *T:* (020) 7722 1965. *Club:* Newcastle University Caving.

REDFERN, Rt Rev. Alastair Llewellyn John; *see* Grantham, Bishop Suffragan of.

REDFERN, Michael Howard; QC 1993; a Recorder, since 1999; *b* 30 Nov. 1943; *s* of Lionel William Redfern and Kathleen Roylance Redfern (*née* Brownston); *m* 1st, 1966, Sylvia Newlands (marr. diss. 1989); one *d*; 2nd, 1991, Diana Barbara Eaglestone (Her Honour Judge Eaglestone); one *d*, and two step *d.* *Educ:* Stretford Grammar Sch. for Boys; Leeds Univ. (LLB Hons). Teacher, 1967–68; Lectr in Law, 1968–69; called to the Bar, Inner Temple, 1970. *Recreations:* music, sport (preferably participating), travel, history. *Address:* 28 St John Street, Manchester M3 4DJ. *T:* (0161) 834 8418.

REDFERN, Philip, CB 1983; Deputy Director, Office of Population Censuses and Surveys, 1970–82; *b* 14 Dec. 1922; *m* 1951, Gwendoline Mary Phillips; three *d.* *Educ:* Bemrose Sch., Derby; St John's Coll., Cambridge. Wrangler, Mathematical Tripos, Cambridge, 1942. Asst Statistician, Central Statistical Office, 1947; Chief Statistician, Min. of Education, 1960; Dir of Statistics and Jt Head of Planning Branch, Dept of Educn and Science, 1967. *Recreation:* walking from Yorkshire to Wester Ross.

REDFORD, (Charles) Robert; American actor and director; *b* 18 Aug. 1937; *s* of Charles Redford and Martha (*née* Hart); *m* 1958, Lola Jean Van Wagenen (marr. diss. 1985); one *s* two *d.* *Educ:* Van Nuys High Sch.; Univ. of Colorado; Pratt Inst., Brooklyn; Amer. Acad. of Dramatic Arts. *Theatre:* appearances include: Tall Story, Broadway, 1959; Sunday in New York, Broadway, 1961–62; Barefoot in the Park, Biltmore, NY, 1963–64; *television:* appearances include, The Iceman Cometh, 1960; *films* include: as actor: War Hunt, 1962; Inside Daisy Clover, 1965; Barefoot in the Park, 1967; Butch Cassidy and the Sundance Kid, 1969; The Candidate, 1972; The Way We Were, 1973; The Sting, 1973; The Great Gatsby, 1974; All the President's Men, 1976; The Electric Horseman, 1979; The Natural, 1984; Out of Africa, 1985; Legal Eagles, 1986; Havana, 1990; Sneakers, 1992; as director: Ordinary People, 1980 (Acad. Award for Best Dir, 1981); Milagro Beanfield War (also prod.), 1988; A River Runs Through It, 1992; Indecent Proposal (also actor), 1993; The River Wild, 1995; Up Close and Personal, 1996; The Horse Whisperer (also actor), 1998; The Legend of Bagger Vance, 2001. *Publication:* The Outlaw Trail, 1978. *Address:* c/o Wildwood Enterprises, 1101 Montana Avenue #E, Santa Monica, CA 90403, USA.

REDFORD, Donald Kirkman, CBE 1980; DL; President, The Manchester Ship Canal Company, since 1986 (Managing Director, 1970–80; Chairman, 1972–86); *b* 18 Feb. 1919; *er s* of T. J. and S. A. Redford; *m* 1942, Mabel (*née* Wilkinson), Humberstone, Lincs; one *s* one *d.* *Educ:* Culford Sch.; King's Coll., Univ. of London (LLB). Served, 1937–39, and War until 1945, in RAFVR (retd as Wing Comdr). Practice at the Bar until end of 1946, when joined The Manchester Ship Canal Company, with which Company has since remained. Chairman, Nat. Assoc. of Port Employers, 1972–74; Dep. Chm., British Ports Assoc., 1973–74, Chm. 1974–78. Member: Cttee of Management, RNLI, 1977– (Chm., Search and Research Cttee, 1984–89); Court, Manchester Univ., 1977– (Dep. Treas., 1980–82, Treas., 1982–83, Mem. of Council, 1977–92, Chm. of Council, 1983–87). DL Lancs 1983. Hon. LLD Manchester, 1988. *Recreations:* reading, history, golf. *Address:* North Cotes, 8 Harrod Drive, Birkdale, Southport PR8 2HA. *T:* (01704) 67406. *Clubs:* Oriental; Union (Southport).

REDFORD, Robert; *see* Redford, C. R.

REDGRAVE, Adrian Robert Frank; QC 1992; a Recorder of the Crown Court, since 1985; *b* 1 Sept. 1944; *s* of Cecil Frank Redgrave and Doris Edith Redgrave (*née* Goss); *m* 1967, Ann Cooper; two *s* one *d.* *Educ:* Abingdon Sch.; Univ. of Exeter (LLB 1966). Called to the Bar, Inner Temple, 1968. *Recreations:* tennis, wine, garden, France, Bangalore Phall. *Address:* 1 Serjeants' Inn, Fleet Street, EC4Y 1LL. *T:* (020) 7415 6666.

REDGRAVE, Lynn; actress; *b* 8 March 1943; *d* of late Sir Michael Redgrave, CBE, and of Rachel Kempson, *qv*; *m* 1967, John Clark; one *s* two *d.* *Educ:* Queensgate Sch.; Central Sch. of Speech and Drama. Nat. Theatre of GB, 1963–66 (Tulip Tree, Mother Courage, Andorra, Hay Fever, etc); Black Comedy, Broadway 1966; The Two of Us, Slag, Zoo Zoo Widdershins Zoo, Born Yesterday, London 1968–71; A Better Place, Dublin 1972; My Fat Friend, Knock Knock, Mrs Warren's Profession, Broadway 1973–76; The Two of Us, California Suite, Hellzapoppin, US tours 1976–77; Saint Joan, Chicago and NY 1977; Twelfth Night, Amer. Shakespeare Festival, Conn, 1978; Les Dames du Jeudi, LA, 1981; Sister Mary Ignatius Explains It All For You, LA, 1983; The King and I, N American Tour, 1983; Aren't We All, 1985, Sweet Sue, 1987, Love Letters, 1989, Broadway; Les Liaisons Dangereuses, Don Juan in Hell, LA, 1989–91; Three Sisters, Queen's, 1990; A Little Hotel on the Side, The Master Builder, Broadway, 1991–92; The Notebook of Trigorin, Ohio, 1996; The Mandrake Root, Conn, 2001; Noises Off, Piccadilly, 2001. One-woman show, Shakespeare for my Father, NY and US tour, 1993. *Films include:* Tom Jones, Girl with Green Eyes, Georgy Girl (NY Film Critics, Golden Globe and IFIDA awards, Academy nomination Best Actress), Deadly Affair, Smashing Time, Virgin Soldiers, Last of the Mobile Hotshots, Every Little Crook and Nanny, National Health, Happy Hooker, Everything You Always Wanted to Know about Sex, The Big Bus, Sunday Lovers, Morgan Stewart's Coming Home, Getting it Right, Midnight, Shine, Gods and Monsters (Best Supporting Actress, Golden Globe award, 1999), Strike, The Simian Line, Touched, The Annihilation of Fish, The Next Best Thing, How to Kill Your Neighbor's Dog, My Kingdom, Unconditional Love. *Television includes:* USA: Co-host of nationally televised talk-show, Not For Women Only, appearances in documentaries, plays, The Muppets, Centennial, Beggarman Thief, The Seduction of Miss Leona, Rehearsal for Murder, The Old Reliable, Jury Duty, Whatever Happened to Baby Jane?, Calling the Shots, Toothless, Indefensible: the truth about Edward Brannigan, White Lies, Different, and series: Housecalls (CBS); Teachers Only (NBC); Chicken Soup (ABC); Rude Awakening; BBC: A Woman Alone, 1988; Death of a Son, 1989; Calling the Shots, 1994. *Publication:* Diet for Life (autobiog.) (US as This is Living), 1991. *Recreations:* cooking, gardening, horse riding.

REDGRAVE, Rachel, (Lady Redgrave); *see* Kempson, R.

REDGRAVE, Maj.-Gen. Sir Roy Michael Frederick, KBE 1979; MC 1945; FRGS; *b* 16 Sept. 1925; *s* of late Robin Roy Redgrave and Michelene Jean Capsa; *m* 1953, Caroline Margaret Valerie, *d* of Major Arthur Wellesley and Margaret Baker-Kirby; two *s.* *Educ:* Sherborne Sch. Served War of 1939–45: enlisted Trooper, Royal Horse Guards, 1943; Lieut, 1st Household Cavalry Regt, NW Europe, 1944–45. GSO III Intell., HQ Rhine Army, 1950; Canadian Army Staff Coll., 1955; GSO II Ops HQ, London Dist, 1956; Recce, Sqn Ldr, Cyprus, 1959 (despatches); Mil. Assistant to Dep. SACEUR, Paris, 1960–62; JSSC 1962; Comd Household Cavalry Regt (Mounted), 1963–64; Comd Royal Horse Guards (The Blues), 1965–67; AAG PS12, MoD, 1967–68; Chief of Staff, HQ 2nd Div., 1968–70; Comdr, Royal Armoured Corps, 3rd Div., 1970–72; Nat. Defence Coll., Canada, 1973; Comdt Royal Armoured Corps Centre, 1974–75; British Comdt, Berlin, 1975–78; Comdr, British Forces, Hong Kong, and Maj.-Gen. Brigade of Gurkhas, 1978–80. Hon. Col 31st Signal Regt (V), 1983–88. Dir Gen., Winston Churchill Meml Trust, 1980–82. Member: Council, Charing Cross and Westminster Med. Sch., 1981–85; Hammersmith SHA, 1981–85; Council, Victoria League for Commonwealth Friendship; Britain Nepal Soc., 1982–. Chairman: Hammersmith and Fulham HA, 1981–85; Lambrook Appeal, 1984–85; Charing Cross and West London Hosps, 1988–97 (Special Trustee, 1981–99); Trustee: Westminster and Roehampton Hosps, 1988–93; Governor General's Horse Guards, Canada, 1987–; Chelsea and Westminster Hosp., 1993–97; Governor, Commonwealth Trust, 1989–97. Guest Lectr, tours to N Cyprus, Mexico, NZ, Albania, High Arctic, N Africa, 1982–. Grand Master, OSMTH, Order of Knights Templar, 1998–. *Publication:* Balkan Blue, 2000. *Recreations:* walking, archaeology, philately. *Address:* 44 Slaidburn Street, Chelsea, SW10 0JW. *Club:* Cavalry and Guards.

REDGRAVE, Sir Steven (Geoffrey), Kt 2001; CBE 1997 (MBE 1987); DL; oarsman; sports consultant; *b* 23 March 1962; *m* 1988, Elizabeth Ann Callaway; one *s* two *d.* *Educ:* Great Marlow Sch. Represented: Marlow Rowing Club, 1976–2000; Leander, 1987–2000. Rowed coxless pairs with Andrew Holmes, until 1989, then with Matthew Pinsent; subseq. rowed coxless fours with Matthew Pinsent, James Cracknell and Tim Foster; winner: Commonwealth Games, 1986 (single sculls, coxed fours, coxless pairs); World Championships, coxed pairs, 1986, coxless pairs, 1987, 1991, 1993, 1994 and 1995; Gold Medal, Olympic Games, 1984 (coxed fours), 1988, 1992 and 1996 (coxless pairs), 2000 (coxless fours); Gold Medal, World Championships, coxless fours, 1997, 1998 and 1999. Hon. DCL. DL Bucks, 2001. *Publications:* Steven Redgrave's Complete Book of Rowing, 1992; (with Nick Townsend) A Golden Age (autobiog.), 2000. *Address:* c/o Athole Still International Management Ltd, Foresters Hall, 25–27 Westow Street, SE19 3RY. *T:* (020) 8771 5271. *Club:* Leander (Henley-on-Thames).

REDGRAVE, Vanessa, CBE 1967; actress since 1957; *b* 30 Jan. 1937; *d* of late Sir Michael Redgrave, CBE, and of Rachel Kempson, *qv*; *m* 1962, Tony Richardson (marr. diss. 1967; he *d* 1991); two *d.* *Educ:* Queensgate School; Central School of Speech and Drama. Frinton Summer Repertory, 1957; Touch of the Sun, Saville, 1958; Midsummer Night's Dream, Stratford, 1959; Look on Tempests, 1960; The Tiger and the Horse, 1960; Lady from the Sea, 1960; Royal Shakespeare Theatre Company: As You Like It, 1961, Taming of the Shrew, 1961, Cymbeline, 1962; The Seagull, 1964; The Prime of Miss Jean Brodie, Wyndham's, 1966; Daniel Deronda, 1969; Cato Street, 1971; The Threepenny Opera, Prince of Wales, 1972; Twelfth Night, Shaw Theatre, 1972; Antony and Cleopatra, Bankside Globe, 1973; Design for Living, Phoenix, 1973; Macbeth, LA, 1974; Lady from the Sea, NY, 1976, Roundhouse, 1979; The Aspern Papers, Haymarket, 1984; The Seagull, Queen's, 1985; Chekhov's Women, Lyric, 1985; The Taming of the Shrew and Antony and Cleopatra, Haymarket, 1986; Ghosts, Young Vic, transf. Wyndham's, 1986; Touch of the Poet, Young Vic, transf. Comedy, 1988; Orpheus Descending, Haymarket, 1988, NY, 1989; A Madhouse in Goa, Lyric, Hammersmith, 1989; Three Sisters, Queen's, 1990; When She Danced, Globe, 1991; Heartbreak House, Haymarket, 1992; The Liberation of Skopje, Antony and Cleopatra, Riverside, 1995; John Gabriel Borkman, NT, 1996; The Tempest, Globe, 2000; The Cherry Orchard, RNT, 2000. *Films:* Morgan—A Suitable Case for Treatment, 1966 (Cannes Fest. Award, Best Actress 1966); The Sailor from Gibraltar, 1967; Blow-Up, 1967; Camelot, 1967; Red White and Zero, 1967; Charge of the Light Brigade, 1968; Isadora, 1968; A Quiet Place in the Country, 1968; The Seagull, 1969; Drop-Out, 1970; La Vacanza, 1970; The Trojan Women, 1971; The Devils, 1971; Mary, Queen of Scots, 1972; Murder on the Orient Express, 1974; Out of Season, 1975; Seven Per Cent Solution, 1975; Julia, 1976 (Academy Award, 1977; Golden Globe Award); Agatha, 1978; Yanks, 1978; Bear Island, 1978; Playing for Time, 1980; My Body, My Child, 1981; Wagner, 1983; The Bostonians, 1984; Wetherby, 1985; Steaming, 1985; Comrades, 1987; Prick Up Your Ears, 1987; Consuming Passions, 1988; A Man For All Seasons, 1988; Orpheus Descending, 1990; Young Catherine, 1990; Whatever Happened to Baby Jane, 1990; The Ballad of the Sad Café, 1991; Howards End, 1992; The House of the Spirits, 1994; Mother's Boys, 1994; Little Odessa, 1995; A Month by the Lake, 1996; Mission: Impossible, 1996; Looking for Richard, 1997; Wilde, 1997; Smilla's Feeling for Snow, 1997; Mrs Dalloway, 1998; Deep Impact, 1998; Cradle Will Rock, 2000. Has appeared on TV. *Publications:* Pussies and Tigers (anthology of writings of school children), 1963; Vanessa Redgrave: an autobiography, 1991. *Address:* c/o Gavin Barker Associates, 2d Wimpole Street, W1M 7AA.

See also N. J. Richardson.

REDGROVE, Peter William, FRSL; poet, analytical psychologist; Resident Author, Falmouth School of Art, 1966–83; *b* 2 Jan. 1932; *s* of late Gordon James Redgrove and Nancy Lena Cestrilli-Bell; *m* Penelope Shuttle, *qv*; one *d*; (two *s* one *d* by former marr.). *Educ:* Taunton Sch.; Queens' Coll., Cambridge. Scientific journalist and copywriter, 1954–61; Visiting Poet, Buffalo Univ., NY, 1961–62; Gregory Fellow in Poetry, Leeds Univ., 1962–65; study with John Layard, 1968–69. O'Connor Prof. of Literature, Colgate Univ., NY, 1974–75; Leverhulme Emeritus Fellow, 1985–87; Writer at large, N Cornwall Arts, 1988. FRSL 1982. Hon. DLitt Sheffield. George Rylands' Verse-speaking Prize, 1954; Fulbright Award, 1961; Poetry Book Society Choices, 1961, 1966, 1979, 1981; Arts Council Awards, 1969, 1970, 1973, 1975, 1977, 1982; Guardian Fiction Prize, 1973; Prudence Farmer Poetry Award, 1977; Cholmondeley Award, 1985; Queen's Gold Medal for Poetry, 1996; Authors' Foundn Grant, 1998. *Publications: poetry:* The Collector, 1960; The Nature of Cold Weather, 1961; At the White Monument, 1963; The Force, 1966; Penguin Modern Poets 11, 1968; Work in Progress, 1969; Dr Faust's Sea-Spiral Spirit, 1972; Three Pieces for Voices, 1972; The Hermaphrodite Album (with Penelope Shuttle), 1973; Sons of My Skin: Selected Poems, 1975; From Every Chink of the Ark, 1977; Ten Poems, 1977; The Weddings at Nether Powers, 1979; The Apple-Broadcast, 1981; The Working of Water, 1984; The Man Named East, 1985; The Mudlark Poems and Grand Buveur, 1986; In the Hall of the Saurians, 1987; The Moon Disposes, 1987; Poems 1954–1987, 1989; The First Earthquake, 1989; Dressed as for a Tarot Pack, 1990; Under the Reservoir, 1992; The Laborators, 1993; My Father's Trapdoors, 1994; Abyssophone, 1995; Assembling a Ghost, 1996; Orchard End, 1997; What the Black Mirror Saw, 1997; Selected Poems, 1999; *prose fiction:* In the Country of the Skin, 1973; The Terrors of Dr Treviles (with Penelope Shuttle), 1974; The Glass Cottage, 1976; The Sleep of the Great Hypnotist, 1979; The God of Glass, 1979; The Beekeepers, 1980; The Facilitators, 1982; The One Who Set out to Study Fear, 1989; The Cyclopean Mistress, 1993; From the Virgil Caverns, 2002; *plays:* Miss Carstairs Dressed for Blooding (play-book containing several dramatic pieces), 1976; (for radio): In the Country of the Skin, 1973; The Holy Sinner, 1975; Dance the Putrefact, 1975; The God of Glass, 1977 (Imperial Tobacco Award 1978); Martyr of the Hives, 1980 (Giles Cooper Award 1981); Florent and the Tuxedo Millions, 1982 (Prix Italia); The Sin-Doctor, 1983; Dracula in White, 1984; The Scientists of the Strange, 1984; Time for the Cat-Scene, 1985; Trelamia, 1986; Six Tales from Grimm, 1987; Six Views to a Haunt, 1992; An Inspector Named Horse, 1995; (for television): The Sermon, 1963; Jack Be Nimble, 1980; *non-fiction:* The Wise Wound (with Penelope Shuttle), 1978, rev. edn 1986; The Black Goddess and the Sixth Sense, 1987; Alchemy for Women, 1995. *Recreations:* work, photography, judo (1st Kyu Judo: Otani and Brit. Judo Assoc.), yoga. *Address:* c/o David Higham Associates, 5–8 Lower John Street, Golden Square, W1R 4HA.

REDHEAD, Prof. Michael Logan Gonne, FBA 1991; Professor of History and Philosophy of Science, Cambridge University, 1987–97; Fellow, Wolfson College, Cambridge, 1988–97, now Emeritus Fellow (Vice-President, 1992–96); Centennial Professor of Philosophy, London School of Economics, since 1999; *b* 30 Dec. 1929; *s* of Robert Arthur Redhead and Christabel Lucy Gonne Browning; *m* 1964, Jennifer Anne Hill; three *s*. *Educ:* Westminster Sch.; University College London (BSc 1st Cl. Hons Physics 1950; PhD Mathematical Phys. 1970). FInstP 1982. Dir, Redhead Properties Ltd, 1962; Partner, Galveston Estates, 1970; Lectr, Sen. Lectr in Philosophy of Science, 1981–84, Prof., Philosophy of Physics, 1984–85, Chelsea Coll., Univ. of London; Prof. of Philosophy of Physics, King's College London, 1985–87; Hd, 1987–93, Chm., 1993–95, Dept of Hist. and Philosophy of Sci., Cambridge Univ. Actg Dir, Centre for Philosophy of Natural and Social Sci., LSE, 1998 and 1999. Tarner Lectr, Trinity Coll., Cambridge, 1991–94; Visiting Fellow: Pittsburgh Univ., 1985; Princeton Univ., 1991; LSE, 1994; All Souls Coll., Oxford, 1995. Pres., British Soc. for Philos. of Sci., 1989–91. Mem., Acad. Internat. de Philosphie des Sciences, 1995. FKC 2000. Lakatos Award in Philosophy of Science, 1988. Editor, Studies in History and Philosophy of Modern Physics, 1993–2001. *Publications:* Incompleteness, Nonlocality and Realism, 1987; From Physics to Metaphysics, 1995; papers in learned jls. *Recreations:* tennis, poetry, music. *Address:* 34 Coniger Road, SW6 3TA. *T:* (020) 7736 6767. *Clubs:* Athenæum, Hurlingham, Queen's.

REDIKER, Dennis L.; Chief Executive, ECC International Inc., since 1999 (Group Chief Executive, English China Clays plc, 1996–99); Executive Vice President, Imetal Group (Pigment and Additives), since 1999; *b* USA, 1 Jan. 1944; *m* 1st, 1965, Carolyn M. Hoehn; two *s*; 2nd, 1983, Sharon A.; one *d*. *Educ:* Del Mar High, Campbell, Calif; Univ. of Calif, Santa Barbara (BS Electrical Engrg 1966). MIEEE. Various rôles in Engrg, Sales, Product and Mkt Planning, IBM, 1966–83; Mead Corporation, 1983–93: Vice-Pres., Strategy and Mkt Develt, 1983–85 and Systems and Technol., 1985–86, Mead Data Central; Vice-Pres., Corporate Planning, Strategy and Planning, 1986–89; Pres., Mead Coated Board Div., 1989–93; English China Clays plc, subseq. ECC International Inc., 1993–: Pres. and CEO, ECCI Ampac; Exec. Dir, 1995–. *Address:* ECC International, Inc., 100 Mansell Court East, Suite 300, Roswell, GA 30076, USA. *T:* (770) 594 0660, *Fax:* (770) 645 3384.

REDING, Dr Viviane; Member, European Commission, since 1999; *b* 27 April 1951; *m* 1980, Zois Dimitris; three *s*. *Educ:* Sorbonne, Paris (PhD). Journalist, Luxemburger Wort, 1978–99; Pres., Luxembourg Union of Journalists, 1986–98. MP (PCS) Luxembourg, 1979–89; MEP (EPP) Luxembourg, 1989–99. Nat. Pres., Christian-Social Women, 1988–93; Vice Pres., Parti Chrétien-Social, Luxembourg, 1995–99. *Address:* European Commission, 200 rue de la Loi, 1049 Brussels, Belgium.

REDMAN, Anthony James, FRICS; Managing Partner, Whitworth Co. Partnership, Architects and Surveyors, since 1985; *b* 1 May 1951; *s* of Alan Redman and Diana Redman (*née* Cooke); *m* 1974, Caroline Blackwood Ford; two *d*. *Educ:* Walton-on-Thames Secondary Modern Sch.; Surbiton Grammar Sch.; Univ. of Reading (BSc Hons Estate Mgt). FRICS 1998; IHBC 1998. Surveyor: Lister Drew and Associates, 1972–74; Suffolk CC, 1974–79; Asst Surveyor, Whitworth & Hall, 1979–85. Surveyor of Fabric, St Edmundsbury Cathedral, 1992–. Chm., RICS Bldg Conservation Gp, 1997–2000. Member: Gen. Synod of C of E, 1989–; Council for Care of Churches, 1990–2001 (Jt Vice Chm., 1996–2001); Westminster Abbey Fabric Adv. Commn, 1998–; St Albans DAC, 1998–; Cathedrals Fabric Commn for England, 1999–. Mem., Baptist Union Listed Bldg Adv. Panel, 1997–. *Publication:* (ed jtly) A Guide to Church Inspection and Repair, 1996. *Recreations:* gardening, apiculture, contemporary art, water-colour painting, avoiding household maintenance. *Address:* (office) 18 Hatter Street, Bury St Edmunds, Suffolk IP33 1NE. *T:* (01284) 760421; *e-mail:* whitcp@globalnet.co.uk; tony@tandcredman.fsnet.co.uk.

REDMAN, Prof. Christopher Willard George, FRCP, FRCOG; Consultant and Clinical Professor of Obstetric Medicine, Nuffield Department of Obstetrics and Gynaecology, Oxford University, since 1992; Fellow of Lady Magaret Hall, Oxford, since 1988; *b* 30 Nov. 1941; *s* of late Roderick Oliver Redman and Annie Kathleen Redman (*née* Bancroft); *m* 1964, Corinna Susan Page; four *s* one *d*. *Educ:* St John's Coll., Cambridge (MA; MB, BChir). FRCP 1981; FRCOG (*ad eund*) 1993. Oxford University: Clinical Lectr, Dept of Regius Prof. of Medicine, 1970–76; Univ. Lectr and Consultant, Nuffield Dept of Obstetrics and Gynaecol., 1976–89; Clinical Reader and Cons., 1989–92. *Publications:* scientific articles about pre-eclampsia in med. jls. *Recreation:* hill-walking. *Address:* Nuffield Department of Obstetrics and Gynaecology, John Radcliffe Maternity Hospital, Headington, Oxford OX3 9DU. *T:* (01865) 221009.

REDMAN, Maj.-Gen. Denis Arthur Kay, CB 1963; OBE 1942; retired; Colonel Commandant, REME, 1963–68; Director, Electrical and Mechanical Engineering, War Office, 1960–63; *b* 8 April 1910; *s* of late Brig. A. S. Redman, CB; *m* 1943, Penelope, *d* of A. S. Kay; one *s* one *d*. *Educ:* Wellington Coll.; London Univ. BSc (Eng) 1st class Hons (London); FCGI, MIMechE, AMIEE. Commissioned in RAOC, 1934; served in Middle East, 1936–43; transferred to REME, 1942; Temp. Brig., 1944; DDME 1st Corps, 1951; Comdt REME Training Centre 1957–59. Graduate of Staff Coll., Joint Services Staff Coll. and Imperial Defence Coll. Pres., Ramsbury RBL, 1985–96. *Recreations:* normal. *Club:* Army and Navy.

REDMAN, Maurice; Chairman, Scottish Region, British Gas Corporation, 1974–82 (Deputy Chairman, 1970–74); *b* 30 Aug. 1922; *s* of Herbert Redman and Olive (*née* Dyson); *m* 1960, Dorothy (*née* Appleton); two *d*. *Educ:* Hulme Grammar Sch., Oldham; Manchester Univ. BSc(Tech), 1st cl. Hons. Joined staff of Co. Borough of Oldham Gas Dept, 1943; Asst, later Dep. Production Engr, North Western Gas Bd, 1951; Chief Develt Engr, NW Gas Bd, 1957; Chief Engr, Southern Gas Bd, 1966; Dir of Engrg, Southern Gas Bd, 1970. Mem., Internat. Gas Union Cttee on Manufactured Gases, 1961–82. *Publications:* papers to Instn of Gas Engrs, Inst. of Fuel, various overseas conferences, etc. *Recreations:* gardening, music, photography. *Address:* Avington, 3 Cramond Regis, Edinburgh EH4 6LW. *T:* (0131) 312 6178. *Club:* New (Edinburgh).

REDMAN, Sydney, CB 1961; *b* 12 Feb. 1914; *s* of John Barritt Redman and Annie Meech; *m* 1939, Barbara Mary Grey; one *s* two *d*. *Educ:* Manchester Gram. Sch.; Corpus Christi Coll., Oxford. Asst Principal, WO, 1936; Principal Private Sec. to Secretary of State for War, 1942–44; Asst Under-Sec. of State: War Office, 1957–63; Ministry of Defence, 1963–64; Dep. Under-Sec. of State (Navy), MoD, 1964–73. Dir-Gen., Timber Trade Fedn, 1973–82. *Address:* Littlehurst, Birch Avenue, Haywards Heath, West Sussex RH17 7SL. *T:* (01444) 413738.

REDMAYNE, Clive; retired aeronautical engineer; *b* 27 July 1927; *s* of late Procter Hubert Redmayne and Emma (*née* Torkington); *m* 1952, Vera Muriel, *d* of late Wilfred Toplis and Elsie Maud Toplis; one *s* one *d*. *Educ:* Stockport Sch. BSc (Hons Maths) London External. CEng, MIMechE; FRAeS. Fairey Aviation Co.: apprentice, 1944–48; Stress Office, 1948–50; English Electric Co., Warton: Stress Office, 1950–51; A. V. Roe & Co., Chadderton: Stress Office, 1951–55; A. V. Roe & Co., Weapons Research Div., Woodford: Head of Structural Analysis, 1955–62; Structures Dept, RAE, 1962–67; Asst Director, Project Time and Cost Analysis, Min. of Technology, 1967–70; Sen. Officers' War Course, RNC, Greenwich, 1970; Asst Dir, MRCA, MoD(PE), 1970–74; Division Leader, Systems Engrg, NATO MRCA Management Agency (NAMMA), Munich, 1974–76; Chief Supt, A&AEE, Boscombe Down, 1976–78; Dir, Harrier Projects, MoD(PE), 1978–80; Director General, Future Projects, MoD(PE), 1980–81; Dir Gen. Aircraft 3, Procurement Exec., MoD, 1981–84. *Recreations:* reading, chess, ski-ing, sailing, caravanning. *Address:* Bowstones, 5 Westbrook View, Stottingway Street, Upwey, Weymouth, Dorset DT3 5QA. *T:* (01305) 814691.

REDMAYNE, Hon. Sir Nicholas (John), 2nd Bt *cr* 1964; *b* 1 Feb. 1938; *s* of Baron Redmayne, DSO, PC (Life Peer) and Anne (*d* 1982), *d* of John Griffiths; *S* to baronetcy of father, 1983; *m* 1st, 1963, Ann Saunders (marr. diss. 1976; she *d* 1985); one *s* one *d*; 2nd, 1978, Christine Diane Wood Hewitt (*née* Fazakerley); two step *s*. *Educ:* Radley College; RMA Sandhurst. Grenadier Guards, 1957–62. Joined Grieveson, Grant, later Kleinwort Benson Securities, 1963; Dir, 1987, Chief Exec., 1994–96, Kleinwort Benson Ltd; Dir, 1989–96, Dep. Chm., 1996, Kleinwort Benson Gp; Chairman: Kleinwort Benson Securities, 1990–96; Kleinwort Benson Investment Mgt, 1995–96. *Recreations:* shooting, ski-ing. *Heir:* *s* Giles Martin Redmayne [*b* 1 Dec. 1968; *m* 1994, Claire Ann O'Halloran; one *s*]. *Address:* Walcote Lodge, Walcote, Lutterworth, Leics LE17 4JR.

REDMOND, Phil; writer and television producer; Chairman, The Mersey Television Co. Ltd; *m* Alexis Jane Redmond. *Educ:* Univ. of Liverpool (BA Hons). Writer, Grange Hill, 1978–81; Executive Producer: Brookside, 1982–; Hollyoaks, 1996–. Hon. Prof. of Media, 1989, Fellow, 1989, Liverpool John Moores Univ. FRSA 1996. *Recreations:* photography, boating, digital media. *Address:* (office) Campus Manor, Childwall Abbey Road, Liverpool L16 0JP. *T:* (0151) 722 9122. *Clubs:* Groucho, Teatro.

REDMOND, Robert Spencer, TD 1953; Director and Chief Executive, National Federation of Clay Industries, 1976–84; *b* 10 Sept. 1919; *m* 1949, Marjorie Helen Heyes; one *s*. *Educ:* Liverpool Coll. Commissioned The Liverpool Scottish (TA), 1938; served War, Army and Special Ops Exec.; released, rank of Major, 1946. Conservative Agent, 1947–56 (Wigan, 1947–49, Knutsford, 1949–56). Managing Dir, Heyes & Co. Ltd, Wigan, 1956–66; Ashley Associates Ltd: Commercial Manager, 1966–69; Managing Dir, 1969–70; Dir, 1970–72. Dir, Manchester Chamber of Commerce, 1969–74. MP (C)

Bolton West, 1970–Sept. 1974; Vice-Chm., Cons. Parly Employment Cttee, 1972–74 (Sec., 1971–72). President: Alderley Edge RBL, 1968–76; Knutsford and Dist RBL, 2000– (Chm., 1990–99); Chm. (and Founder), NW Export Club, 1958–60. *Publications:* How to Recruit Good Managers, 1989; The Atrocities of the Pirates, 1997. *Address:* 194 Grove Park, Knutsford, Cheshire WA16 8QE. *T:* (01565) 632657. *Club:* Army and Navy.

REDPATH, John Thomas, CB 1969; MBE 1944; FRIBA; Director General of Research and Development, Department of the Environment, 1967–71; architect in private practice, 1977–87; *b* 24 Jan. 1915; *m* 1st, 1939, Kate (*née* Francis) (*d* 1949); one *d*; 2nd, 1949, Claesina (*née* van der Vlerk); three *s* one *d*. *Educ:* Price's Sch.; Southern Coll. of Art. Served with RE, 1940–47. Asst Architect: Kent CC, 1936–38; Oxford City Coun., 1938–40; Princ. Asst Architect, Herts, CC, 1948–55; Dep. County Architect, Somerset CC, 1955–59; Chief Architect (Abroad), War Office, 1959–63; MPBW later DoE: Dir of Development, 1963–67; Dir Gen. of Develt, 1971–72; Dep. Chief Executive, PSA, 1972–75; Man. Dir, Millbank Technical Services Educn Ltd, 1975–77. *Publications:* various articles in architectural jls. *Recreation:* golf. *Address:* Pines Edge, Sandy Lane, Cobham, Surrey KT11 2EU. *Club:* Arts.

REDSHAW, Peter Robert Gransden; HM Diplomatic Service, retired; Group Security Adviser, Gallaher Ltd; *b* 16 April 1942; *s* of late Robert Henry Gransden Redshaw and of Audrey Nita Redshaw (*née* Ward); *m* 1970, Margaret Shaun (*née* Mizon); one *s* two *d*. *Educ:* Boxgrove School; Charterhouse; Trinity College, Cambridge (MA). ACA. Price Waterhouse, 1964–67; FCO, 1968; Kampala, 1970–73; 1st Sec., 1971; FCO, 1973; Lagos, 1982–85; Counsellor, 1985; FCO, 1985–88; Kuala Lumpur, 1988–91; FCO, 1992–96. *Recreations:* books, sailing, models, travel. *Clubs:* Wey Kyak; Kampala.

REDWOOD, Rt Hon. John (Alan); PC 1993; DPhil; MP (C) Wokingham, since 1987; *b* 15 June 1951; *s* of William Charles Redwood and Amy Emma Redwood (*née* Champion); *m* 1974, Gail Felicity Chippington; one *s* one *d*. *Educ:* Kent Coll., Canterbury; Magdalen and St Antony's Colls, Oxford. MA, DPhil Oxon. Fellow, All Souls Coll., 1972–87. Investment Adviser, Robert Fleming & Co., 1973–77; Investment Manager and Dir, N. M. Rothschild & Sons, 1977–87; Norcros plc: Dir, 1985–89; Jt Dep. Chm., 1986–87; non-exec. Chm., 1987–89. Non-exec. Chm., Mabey Securities, 1999–; non-exec. Dir, BNB, 2001–. Adviser, Treasury and Civil Service Select Cttee, 1981; Head of PM's Policy Unit, 1983–85. Councillor, Oxfordshire CC, 1973–77. Parly Under Sec. of State, DTI, 1989–90; Minister of State: DTI, 1990–92; DoE, 1992–93; Sec. of State for Wales, 1993–95; Opposition front bench spokesman on trade and industry, 1997–99, on the envmt, 1999–2000. Head, Cons. Parly Campaigns Unit, 2000–01. Vis. Prof., Middx Business Sch., 2000–. Governor of various schools, 1974–83. *Publications:* Reason, Ridicule and Religion, 1976; Public Enterprise in Crisis, 1980; (with John Hatch) Value for Money Audits, 1981; (with John Hatch) Controlling Public Industries, 1982; Going for Broke, 1984; Equity for Everyman, 1986; Popular Capitalism, 1988; The Global Marketplace, 1994; The Single Currency, 1995; Action Not Words, 1996; Our Currency, Our Country, 1997; The Death of Britain?, 1999; Stars and Strife, 2001; Just Say No, 2001; pamphlets on Cons. matters. *Recreations:* water sports, village cricket. *Address:* House of Commons, SW1A 0AA. *T:* (office) (020) 7219 4205; (home) (020) 7976 6603.

REDWOOD, Sir Peter (Boverton), 3rd Bt *cr* 1911; consultant, since 1996; Colonel, late King's Own Scottish Borderers, retired 1987; *b* 1 Dec. 1937; *o s* of Sir Thomas Boverton Redwood, 2nd Bt, TD, and Ruth Mary Redwood (*née* Creighton, then Blair); *S* father, 1974; *m* 1964, Gilian, *o d* of John Lee Waddington Wood, Limuru, Kenya; three *d*. *Educ:* Gordonstoun. National Service, 1956–58, 2nd Lieut, Seaforth Highlanders; regular commn, KOSB, 1959; served in UK (despatches 1972), BAOR, Netherlands, ME, Africa and Far East; Staff Coll., Camberley, 1970; Nat. Defence Coll., Latimer, 1978–79. Dir, SERCO-IAL Ltd, 1992–95. Mem., Queen's Body Guard for Scotland (Royal Co. of Archers). Liveryman, Goldsmiths' Co. *Recreations:* shooting, silver and silversmithing. *Heir: half-b* Robert Boverton Redwood [*b* 24 June 1953; *m* 1978, Mary Elizabeth Wright; one *s* one *d*]. *Address:* c/o Royal Bank of Scotland, 8–9 Quiet Street, Bath, BA1 2JN. *Club:* New (Edinburgh).

REECE, Sir Charles (Hugh), Kt 1988; Research and Technology Director, Imperial Chemical Industries, 1979–89; *b* 2 Jan. 1927; *s* of Charles Hugh Reece and Helen Youlle; *m* 1951, Betty Linford; two *d*. *Educ:* Pocklington Sch., E Riding; Huddersfield Coll.; Leeds Univ. (PhD, BSc Hons). FRSC 1981. ICI: joined Dyestuffs Div., 1949; Head of Medicinal Process Develt Dept, Dyestuffs Div., 1959; Manager, Works R&D Dept, 1965; Jt Research Manager, Mond Div., 1967; Dir, R&D, Mond Div., 1969; Dep. Chm., Mond Div., 1972; Chm., Plant Protection Div., 1975. Dir, Finnish Chemicals, 1971–75; Chm., Teijin Agricultural Chemicals, 1975–78; non-executive Director: APV plc (formerly APV Holdings), 1984–96; British Biotechnology Gp, 1989–95. Chm., Univ. of Surrey Robens Inst. of Indust. and Envtl Health and Safety Cttee, 1985–92; Member: ACARD, 1983–87, ACOST, 1987–89; Adv. Cttee on Industry, Cttee of Vice-Chancellors and Principals, 1983–; Council, RSC, 1985–86; SERC, 1985–89; ABRC, 1989–91; UFC, 1989–93; Royal Instn of GB, 1979–92 (Mem. Council, 1985–88); SCI; Parly and Sci. Cttee, 1979– (Vice-Chm., 1986). Hon. DSc: St Andrews, 1986; Queen's, 1988; Bristol, 1989; South West Poly., 1991; DUniv Surrey, 1989. FRSA 1988. *Publications:* reports and papers in learned jls. *Recreations:* sailing, gardening. *Address:* Heath Ridge, Graffham, Petworth, W Sussex GU28 0PT.

REECE, (Edward Vans) Paynter; His Honour Judge Paynter Reece; a Circuit Judge, since 1982; *b* 17 May 1936; *s* of Clifford Mansel Reece and Catherine Barbara Reece (*née* Hathorn); *m* 1967, Rosamund Mary Reece (*née* Roberts); three *s* one *d*. *Educ:* Blundell's Sch.; Magdalene Coll., Cambridge (MA). Called to the Bar, Inner Temple, 1960; a Recorder of the Crown Court, 1980–82. *Recreations:* fishing, golf. *Clubs:* Garrick; New Zealand Golf.

REECE, Dr Henry Michael; Secretary to Delegates, and Chief Executive, Oxford University Press, since 1998; Fellow of Jesus College, Oxford, since 1998; *b* 10 Aug. 1953; *s* of David Reece and Persis Rebecca Reece; *m* 1993, Allison Jane King. *Educ:* Univ. of Bristol (BA 1st Cl. Hons); St John's Coll., Oxford (DPhil Modern Hist. 1981). Tutor in Hist., Univ. of Exeter, 1977–78; Prentice Hall International: Field Sales Editor, 1979–82; Academic Sales Manager, 1982–84; UK Sales Manager, 1984–85; Asst Vice-Pres., Simon & Schuster Internat., 1985–88; Exec. Ed., Allyn & Bacon (US), 1988–91; Man. Dir, Pitman Publishing, 1991–94; Executive Director: Longman Gp Ltd, 1994–95; Pearson Professional, 1995–97; Man. Dir, Financial Times Professional, 1997–98. Non-exec. Dir, Knowledge Pool Trng Ltd, 2000–. Mem. Council, Publishers Assoc., 1999–. *Recreations:* reading crime novels, watching Wales win occasionally at Rugby. *Address:* Oxford University Press, Great Clarendon Street, Oxford OX2 6DP. *T:* (01865) 267600.

REECE, Paynter; *see* Reece, E. V. P.

REECE, Richard Marsden, DPhil; FSA; Reader in Late Roman Archaeology and Numismatics, Institute of Archaeology, University College London, 1994–99; *b* 25 March 1939; *o s* of Richard Marsden Reece and Alice Reece (*née* Wedel). *Educ:* Cirencester Grammar Sch.; UCL (BSc Biochem. 1961); Wadham Coll., Oxford (DipEd 1962; DPhil 1972). FSA 1968. Asst Master, St John's Sch., Leatherhead, 1962–65; Head of Chem. Dept, St George's Sch., Harpenden, 1966–68; London Institute of Archaeology, subseq Institute of Archaeology, University College London: Lectr, 1970–81; Sen. Lectr, 1981–93; Tutor to Arts students, 1988–91. Membre d'Honneur, Romanian Numismatic Soc. *Publications:* Roman Coins, 1970; Excavations on Iona 1964–74, 1981; Coinage in Roman Britain, 1987; My Roman Britain, 1988; Later Roman Empire, 1999; articles in learned jls. *Recreations:* reading novels, music. *Address:* The Apple Loft, The Waterloo, Cirencester, Glos GL7 2PU.

REED, Hon. Lord; Robert John Reed; a Senator of the College of Justice in Scotland, since 1998; *b* 7 Sept. 1956; *s* of George Thomas Reed and Elizabeth Irving Reed; *m* 1988, Jane Elizabeth Mylne; two *d*. *Educ:* George Watson's Coll.; Univ. of Edinburgh (LLB); Balliol Coll., Oxford (DPhil). Admitted to Faculty of Advocates, 1983; called to the Bar, Inner Temple, 1991; Standing Junior Counsel: Scottish Educn Dept, 1988–89; Scottish Office Home and Health Dept, 1989–95; QC (Scot.) 1995; Advocate Depute, 1996–98; *ad hoc* Judge, European Court of Human Rights, 1999. *Publications:* Scottish Ed., European Law Reports, 1997–; (contrib.) Scottish Planning Encyclopaedia, 1996; (contrib.) Devolution to Scotland: the legal aspects, 1997; (contrib.) Constitutional Reform in the United Kingdom: practice and principles, 1998; (contrib.) Human Rights Law and Practice, 1999; articles in legal jls. *Recreation:* music. *Address:* Parliament House, Parliament Square, Edinburgh EH1 1RQ.

REED, Adrian Harbottle, CMG 1981; HM Diplomatic Service, retired; Consul-General, Munich, 1973–80; *b* 5 Jan. 1921; *s* of Harbottle Reed, MBE, FRIBA, and Winifred Reed (*née* Rowland); *m* 1st, 1947, Doris Davidson Duthie (marr. diss. 1975); one *s* one *d*; 2nd, 1975, Maria-Louise, *d* of Dr and Mrs A. J. Boekelman, Zeist, Netherlands. *Educ:* Hele's Sch., Exeter; Emmanuel Coll., Cambridge. Royal Artillery, 1941–47. India Office, 1947; Commonwealth Relations Office, 1947; served in UK High Commission: Pakistan, 1948–50; Fedn of Rhodesia and Nyasaland, 1953–56; British Embassy, Dublin, 1960–62; Hd Econ. Relns, 1962–65, Far East and Pacific Depts, 1966–68, CO; Counsellor (Commercial), and Consul-Gen., Helsinki, 1968–70; Economic Counsellor, Pretoria, 1971–73. Chairman: Cold Harbour Working Wool Mus., 1983–86; Devon and Exeter Instn, 1989–2001; SW Maritime Hist. Soc., 1994–97; Devon Hist. Soc., 1994–. Bavarian Order of Merit, 1980. *Publications:* articles and reviews on historical (mainly maritime) subjects. *Recreations:* maritime history, the English countryside. *Address:* Old Bridge House, Uffculme, Cullompton, Devon EX15 3AX. *T:* (01884) 840595.

REED, Alec Edward, CBE 1994; Founder, 1960, and Chairman, Reed Executive PLC; *b* 16 Feb. 1934; *s* of Leonard Reed and Anne Underwood; *m* 1961, Adrianne Mary Eyre; two *s* one *d*. *Educ:* Grammar School. FCMA, FCIM, FIPD. Founded: Reed Executive; Medicare; ICC PLC; Reed College of Accountancy; Womankind Worldwide; Ethiopiaid; Women @ Risk; Acad. of Enterprise. President: Inst. of Employment Consultants, 1974–78; Internat. Confedn of Private Employment Agency Assocs, 1978–81; Economics and Business Educn Assoc., 2001–; Hon. Chm. and Chief Exec., Andrews & Partners, 1985–89 (charity-owned); Mem. Exec. Cttee and Council, CIMA, 1991–95; Mem. Bd, Enterprise Insight, 2001–. Hon. Prof., Enterprise and Innovation, Royal Holloway, Univ. of London, 1993– (Fellow, RHBNC, 1988); Vis. Prof., London Guildhall Univ., 1999–. Mem. Council, RHC, 1979–85. Hon. PhD London Guildhall, 1999. *Recreations:* family, cinema, tennis, riding, portrait painting. *Address:* Reed Executive plc, 6 Sloane Street, SW1X 9LE.

REED, Andrew John; MP (Lab and Co-op) Loughborough, since 1997; *b* 17 Sept. 1964; *s* of James Donald Reed and Margaret Anne Reed; *m* 1992, Sarah Elizabeth Chester. *Educ:* Riverside Jun. Sch.; Stonehill High Sch.; Longslade Community Coll.; Leicester Poly. (BA Hons Public Admin 1987). Parly Asst to Keith Vaz, MP, 1987–88; Urban Regeneration Officer, Leicester CC, 1988–90; Sen. Economic Develt Officer, 1990–94, European Officer, 1994–97, Leics CC. *Recreations:* Rugby, volleyball, tennis, running. *Address:* House of Commons, SW1A 0AA. *Clubs:* Loughborough Labour; Birstall Rugby Football, Leicester Rugby Football.

REED, Air Cdre April Anne, RRC 1981; Director of RAF Nursing Services, 1984–85, retired; *b* 25 Jan. 1930; *d* of Captain Basil Duck Reed, RN, and Nancy Mignon Ethel Reed. *Educ:* Channing Sch., Highgate. SRN, SCM. SRN training, Middlesex Hosp., 1948–52; midwifery training, Royal Maternity Hosp., Belfast, 1953; joined Royal Air Force, 1954; Dep. Matron, 1970; Sen. Matron, 1976; Principal Matron, 1981; Matron in Chief (Director), 1984. *Recreations:* sailing, ornithology, antiques, gardening, interest in oriental carpets. *Address:* 1 Garners Row, Burnham Thorpe, Kings Lynn, Norfolk PE31 8HN. *Club:* Royal Air Force.

REED, Barry St George Austin, CBE 1988; MC 1951; Chairman, Austin Reed Group PLC, 1973–96; *b* 5 May 1931; *s* of late Douglas Austin Reed and Mary Ellen (*née* Philpott); *m* 1956, Patricia (*née* Bristow); one *s* one *d*. *Educ:* Rugby Sch. Commnd Middlesex Regt (DCO), 1950; served Korea, 1950–51; TA, 1951–60. Joined Austin Reed Group, 1953; Dir, 1958–99; Man. Dir, 1966–85. National Westminster Bank: Dir, City and West End Regions, 1980–87; Dir, 1987–90; Chm., Eastern Regl Adv. Bd, 1987–92; Dir, UK Adv. Bd, 1990–92. Pres., Menswear Assoc. of Britain, 1966–67; Chairman: Retail Alliance, 1967–70; British Knitting and Clothing Export Council, 1985–89; Dir, British Apparel and Textile Confedn, 1992–99; Member: Bd, Retail Trading-Standards Assoc., 1964–78; Consumer Protection Adv. Cttee, 1973–79; European Trade Cttee, 1975–84; Cttee, Fleming American Exempt Fund, 1979–94; Council, Royal Warrant Holders Assoc., 1980– (Pres., 1990). Dir, Independent Broadcasting Telethon Trust Ltd, 1991–94. Pres., Vale of York Cons. Assoc., 1995–2000. Dir, Hambleton and Richmondshire Partnership Against Crime, 1997–99. Chm., Queen Elizabeth Scholarship Trust, 1990–95; Trustee, Third Age Challenge Trust, 1994–96. Member: Ripon and Leeds Dio. Synod, 1997–; Ripon and Leeds Dio. Bd of Finance, 1997–; Vice-Chm., 1997–2000, Chm., 2000–, Ripon and Leeds Dio. Parsonages Bd. Freeman, City of London, 1963; Liveryman, Glovers' Co., 1963– (Master 1980–81). DL Greater London, 1977–99; Rep. DL, London Borough of Hackney, 1980–86. FRSA. *Publications:* papers in clothing, textile and banking jls. *Recreations:* travel, gardens, reading. *Address:* Crakehall House, Crakehall, Bedale, North Yorks DL8 1HS. *T:* (01677) 422743. *Clubs:* Naval and Military, Pilgrims, MCC.

See also L. D. Reed.

REED, David; Director of Corporate Communications, Whitbread plc, since 1990; *b* 24 April 1945; *s* of Wilfred Reed and Elsie Swindon; *m* 1973, Susan Garrett, MA Oxon, MScEcon. *Educ:* West Hartlepool Grammar Sch. Former journalist and public relations adviser to Investors in Industry, Rank Xerox, Ernst & Whinney, Hewlett-Packard. Dir and Hd of Corporate and Financial PR, Ogilvy and Mather. MP (Lab) Sedgefield, Co. Durham, 1970–Feb. 1974. *Publications:* many articles in national newspapers and other jls. *Recreations:* theatre, music, walking the dog. *Address:* St Luke's Cottage, Stonor, Oxon RG9 6HE.

1987–96; Chairman: LASMO, 1988–94; General Cable Ltd, 1990–95; CLM plc, 1994–99. Chm., Duty Free Confedn, 1987–99. Member: Council and Court of Governors, Museum of Wales, 1987–96; Museums and Galleries Commn, 1988–96. *Address:* 39 Headfort Place, SW1X 7DE; Goytre Hall, Abergavenny, Gwent NP7 9DL. *Clubs:* Boodle's, Beefsteak, White's, Pratt's.

REES, Allen Brynmor; Regional Chairman, Employment (formerly Industrial) Tribunals, Birmingham, since 1995; *b* 11 May 1936; *s* of late Allen Brynmor Rees and Elsie Louise Rees (*née* Hitchcock); *m* 1961, Nerys Eleanor Evans; two *d*. *Educ:* Monmouth Sch.; UCW, Aberystwyth (LLB 1958). Admitted Solicitor, 1961. Partner, Francis Ryan and Co., 1961–62; Solicitor, SW Div., NCB, 1962; Rexall Drug and Chemical Co., 1962–65; Rees Page (incorp. Page Son and Elias, Skidmore Hares and Co., and Darbey-Scott-Rees), 1965–93, Sen. Partner, 1974–93; Chm., Employment (formerly Industrial) Tribunals, 1993–. Prin. Solicitor, Birmingham Midshires Building Soc., 1976–93. Chairman: W Midlands Rent Assessment Panel, 1968–93; Social Security Tribunals, 1980–93; Mem. Cttee, Legal Aid Bd, 1975–93. Columnist (Solicitors' Notebook), Solicitors' Jl, 1968–92; Ed., Employment Tribunals Chairman's Handbook, 1999–. *Recreations:* canoeing, ski-ing, gardening, walking, watching Rugby. *Address:* (office) Phoenix House, 1–3 Newhall Street, Birmingham B3 3NH; Rossleigh, Shaw Lane, Albrighton, Wolverhampton WV7 3DS; Yr Hen Ystabl, Meifod, Powys SY22 6BP. *Club:* Old Monmothians (Monmouth).

REES, Prof. Andrew Jackson; Regius Professor of Medicine, University of Aberdeen, since 1994; *b* 11 June 1946; *s* of late Gordon Jackson Rees and of Elisabeth Rees; *m* 1st, 1972, Ann Duncan (marr. diss. 1974); 2nd, 1979, Daphne Elizabeth Wood (marr. diss. 1985); two *d*; 3rd, 1999, Renate Kain; two *c*. *Educ:* King William's Coll., Isle of Man; Liverpool Univ. (MB ChB 1969); London Univ. (MSc). Trained in gen. medicine and nephrology, at Liverpool, Guy's, and Hammersmith Hosps, 1969–79; Consultant Physician, Hammersmith Hosp., 1979–90; Prof. of Nephrology, RPMS, 1990–94. Vis. Prof., Nat. Jewish Hosp., Denver, 1983–84; Goulstonian Lectr, RCP, 1984. Pres., Nephrology Section, RSocMed, 1994–95. Chm., 1995–2000, Vice-Pres., 2000–, Nat. Kidney Res. Fund; Pres., Renal Assoc. of GB and Ireland, 2001; Mem. Council, Internat. Soc. of Nephrology, 1998–. *Publications:* (ed with C. D. Pusey) Rapidly Progressive Glomerulonephritis, 1998; papers on pathogenesis and treatment of glomerulonephritis. *Recreations:* contemporary theatre and music, ski-ing. *Address:* The Old Rectory, Catterline, Stonehaven, Kincardineshire AB39 2UN.

REES, (Anthony) John (David); school master, Cheltenham College; *b* 20 July 1943; *s* of Richard Frederick and Betty Rees; *m* 1967, Carol Stubbens; one *s* one *d* (and one *d* decd). *Educ:* Newcastle Royal Grammar Sch.; Clare Coll., Cambridge (Exhibr; BA 2nd Cl. Hons Geog.); PGCE 1966. Head of Economics, Harrow Sch., 1966–80; Head Master, Blundell's Sch., Tiverton, Devon, 1980–92; Rector, Edinburgh Acad., 1992–95; Director: Harrow Sch. Develt Trust, 1995–97; The Bradfield Foundn, 1998–2000. Established Notting Dale Urban Study Centre, 1972; Vis. Tutor, London Inst. of Education, 1973–. Member Executive Committee: Queen's Silver Jubilee Appeal, 1976–82; and Admin. Council, Royal Jubilee Trusts, 1978–82; Chairman: Prince's Trust for Devon, 1981–83; Youth Clubs UK, 1987–89; Founder Dir, Mid Devon Enterprise Agency, 1984–91; Chm., Crested, 1996–97. Member: CoSIRA Cttee for Devon, 1981–83; Council, Drake Fellowship, 1981–; Cttee, HMC, 1986–91; Prince of Wales Community Venture, 1985–; Board: Devon and Cornwall Prince's Youth Business Trust, 1987–92; Fairbridge in Scotland, 1992–95. *Publications:* articles on economics and community service in many jls incl. Economics, Youth in Society, etc. *Recreations:* hill walking, family and friends. *Address:* Cheltenham College, Bath Road, Cheltenham, Glos GL53 7LD. *T:* (01242) 265642.

REES, Brian, MA Cantab; Headmaster, Rugby School, 1981–84; *b* 20 Aug. 1929; *s* of late Frederick T. Rees; *m* 1st, 1959, Julia (*d* 1978), *d* of Sir Robert Birley, KCMG; two *s* three *d*; 2nd, 1987, Juliet Akehurst (*née* Gowan). *Educ:* Bede Grammar Sch., Sunderland; Trinity Coll., Cambridge (Scholar). 1st cl. Historical Tripos, Part I, 1951; Part II, 1952. Eton College: Asst Master, 1952–65; Housemaster, 1963–65; Headmaster: Merchant Taylors' Sch., 1965–73; Charterhouse, 1973–81. Pres., Conference for Independent Further Education, 1973–82; Chm., ISIS, 1982–84. Res. Fellow, City Univ., 1989–90. Patron, UC of Buckingham, 1973–91. Liveryman, Merchant Taylors' Co., 1981. *Publications:* A Musical Peacemaker: biography of Sir Edward German, 1987; (ed) History and Idealism: essays, addresses and letters, by Sir Robert Birley, 1990; Camille Saint-Saëns: a life, 1999. *Recreations:* music, gardening. *Address:* 52 Spring Lane, Flore, Northampton NN7 4LS. *T:* (01327) 340621.

REES, Prof. Brinley Roderick, MA Oxon; PhD, Hon. LLD Wales; Principal, Saint David's University College, Lampeter, 1975–80; *b* 27 Dec. 1919; *s* of John David Rees and Mary Ann (*née* Roderick); *m* 1951, Zena Muriel Stella Mayall; two *s*. *Educ:* Christ Coll., Brecon; Merton Coll., Oxford (Postmaster). 1st Cl., Class. Hons Mods and Hon. Mention, Craven and Ireland Schols, 1946. Welch Regt, 1940–45. Asst Classics Master, Christ Coll., Brecon, 1947; Cardiff High Sch., 1947–48; Asst Lectr in Classics, University Coll. of Wales Aberystwyth, 1948–49; Lectr 1949–56; Sen. Lectr in Greek, Univ. of Manchester, 1956–58; UC Cardiff: Prof. of Greek, 1958–70; Dean of Faculty of Arts, 1963–65; Dean of Students, 1967–68; Hon. Lectr, 1980–88; Prof. Emeritus, 1981; Vice-Pres., 1986–88; University of Birmingham: Prof. of Greek, 1970–75; Dean of Faculty of Arts, 1973–75; Hon. Life Mem. of Court, 1983. Welsh Supernumerary Fellow, Jesus Coll., Oxford, 1975–76; Leverhulme Emeritus Fellow, 1984–86. Hon. Secretary, Classical Association, 1963–69, Vice-Pres., 1969–78, 1979–, Pres., 1978–79. Hon. LLD Wales, 1981. *Publications:* The Merton Papyri, Vol. II (with H. I. Bell and J. W. B. Barns), 1959; The Use of Greek, 1961; Papyri from Hermopolis and other Byzantine Documents, 1964; (with M. E. Jervis) Lampas: a new approach to Greek, 1970; Classics: an outline for intending students, 1970; Aristotle's Theory and Milton's Practice, 1972; Strength in What Remains, 1980; Pelagius: a reluctant heretic, 1988; Letters of Pelagius and his Followers, 1991; Pelagius: life and letters, 1998; articles and reviews in various classical and other jls. *Address:* 31 Stephenson Court, Wordsworth Avenue, Cardiff CF24 3FX. *T:* (029) 2047 2058.

REES, Caroline, (Lady Rees); *see* Humphrey, C.

REES, Prof. Charles Wayne, CBE 1995; DSc; FRS 1974; FRSC; Hofmann Professor of Organic Chemistry, Imperial College, London, 1978–93, now Emeritus Professor; *b* 15 Oct. 1927; *s* of Percival Charles Rees and Daisy Alice Beck; *m* 1953, Patricia Mary Francis; three *s*. *Educ:* Farnham Grammar Sch.; University Coll., Southampton (BSc, PhD). Lectr in Organic Chem.: Birkbeck Coll., Univ. of London, 1955–57; King's Coll., Univ. of London, 1957–63, Reader, 1963–65; Prof. of Organic Chem., Univ. of Leicester, 1965–69; Prof. of Organic Chem., 1969–77, Heath Harrison Prof. of Organic Chem., 1977–78, Univ. of Liverpool. Visiting Prof., Univ. of Würzburg, 1968. Royal Society of Chemistry (formerly Chemical Society): Tilden Lectr, 1973–74; Award in Heterocyclic Chem., 1980; Pres., Perkin Div., 1981–83; Pedler Lectr, 1984–85; Pres., 1992–94; Internat. Award in Heterocyclic Chem., 1995; Pres., Chemistry Sect., BAAS, 1984. FKC 1999. Hon. DSc: Leicester, 1994; Sunderland, 2000. *Publications:* Organic Reaction Mechanism (8 annual vols), 1965–72; Carbenes, Nitrenes, Arynes, 1969; (ed jtly) Comprehensive Heterocyclic Chemistry (8 vols), 1984, 2nd edn (10 vols), 1996; (ed jtly) Organic Functional Group Transformations (7 vols), 1995; about 400 research papers and reviews, mostly in jls of Chemical Soc. *Recreations:* music, theatre, London. *Address:* Department of Chemistry, Imperial College of Science, Technology and Medicine, South Kensington, SW7 2AY. *T:* (020) 7594 5768, *Fax:* (020) 7594 5800.

REES, Christina Henking Muller; media and public relations consultant, since 1985; writer, since 1986; broadcaster, since 1990; *b* 6 July 1953; *d* of John Muller, Jr and Carol Benton Muller; *m* 1978, Christopher Rees; two *d*. *Educ:* Pomona Coll., Calif (BA English 1975); King's Coll., London (MA Theology 1998). Asst PR Officer, Children's Soc., 1985–87. Member: Gen. Synod of C of E, 1990–; Archbishops' Council, 1999–2000; Chair, Women and the Church, 1996–; spokesperson, Movt for Ordination of Women, 1992–94. Consultant: IBA, 1979; BBC Children in Need Appeal, 1997–. Contribs to radio and TV progs, 1990–, incl. Thought for the Day, Radio 4, 1991–. *Publications:* Sea Urchin, 1990; The Divine Embrace, 2000; contrib. to The Times, Guardian, Independent, Church of England Newspaper, etc. *Recreations:* rare breeds, beachcombing, improving Anglo-American relations. *Address:* Churchfield, Pudding Lane, Barley, Royston, Herts SG8 8JX. *T:* (01763) 848822, 848472.

REES, Sir Dai; *see* Rees, Sir David A.

REES, Prof. David, FRS 1968; Emeritus Professor of Pure Mathematics, University of Exeter (Professor, 1958–83); *b* 29 May 1918; *s* of David and Florence Gertrude Rees; *m* 1952, Joan Sybil Cushen; four *d*. *Educ:* King Henry VIII Grammar School, Abergavenny; Sidney Sussex College, Cambridge. Manchester University: Assistant Lecturer, 1945–46, Lecturer, 1946–49; Cambridge University: Lecturer, 1949–58; Fellow of Downing College, Cambridge, 1950–58, Hon. Fellow, 1970–. Mem. Council, Royal Soc., 1979–81. Hon. DSc Exeter, 1993. Polya Prize, London Mathematical Soc., 1993. *Publications:* papers on Algebraic topics in British and foreign mathematical journals. *Recreations:* reading and listening to music. *Address:* 6 Hillcrest Park, Exeter EX4 4SH. *T:* (01392) 259398.

REES, Sir David Allan, (Sir Dai Rees), Kt 1993; BSc, PhD, DSc; FRCPE, FMedSci; FRS 1981; FRSC, FIBiol; Medical Research Council scientist, 1996–2001; *b* 28 April 1936; *s* of James Allan Rees and Elsie Bolam; *m* 1959, Myfanwy Margaret Parry Owen; two *s* one *d*. *Educ:* Hawarden Grammar Sch., Clwyd; University Coll. of N Wales, Bangor, Gwynedd (BSc 1956; PhD 1959; Hon. Fellow, 1988); DSc Edinburgh, 1970. FRCPE 1999. DSIR Res. Fellow, University Coll., Bangor, 1959, and Univ. of Edinburgh, 1960; Asst Lectr in Chem., 1961, Lectr, 1962–70, Univ. of Edinburgh; Section Manager, 1970–72, Principal Scientist, 1972–82, and Sci. Policy Exec., 1978–82, Unilever Res., Colworth Lab.; Chm., Science Policy Gp for Unilever Res., 1979–82. Associate Dir (pt-time), MRC Unit for Cell Biophysics, KCL, 1980–82; Dir, Nat. Inst. for Med. Res., Mill Hill, 1982–87; Sec., subseq. Chief Exec., MRC, 1987–96. Vis. Professorial Fellow, University Coll., Cardiff, 1972–77. Philips Lecture, Royal Soc., 1984. Member: MRC, 1984–96; Council, Royal Soc., 1985–87. Pres., ESF, 1994–99. FKC 1989. Founder FMedSci 1998. Hon. FRCP 1986. Hon. DSc: Edinburgh, 1989; Wales, 1991; Stirling, 1995; Leicester, 1997. Colworth Medal, Biochemical Soc., 1970; Carbohydrate Award, Chemical Soc., 1970. *Publications:* various, on carbohydrate chem. and biochem. and cell biology. *Recreations:* river boats, reading, listening to music. *Address:* Ford Cottage, 1 High Street, Denford, Kettering, Northants NN14 4EQ. *T:* (01832) 733502, *Fax:* (01832) 732013; *e-mail:* drees@nimr.mrc.ac.uk.

REES, Edward Parry; QC 1998; *b* 18 June 1949; *s* of Edward Howell Rees and Margaret Rees Parry; *m* 1983, Kathleen Wiltshire; one *s* one *d*. *Educ:* University Coll. of Wales, Aberystwyth (LLB Hons). Called to the Bar, Gray's Inn, 1973. Hon. Fellow in Criminal Process, Univ. of Kent, 1992. *Publications:* contrib. to legal jls. *Recreations:* two gardens, two children and one wife! *Address:* 11 Doughty Street, WC1N 2PG. *T:* (020) 7404 1313.

REES, Eleri Mair; District Judge (Magistrates' Courts) (formerly Metropolitan Stipendiary Magistrate), since 1994; a Recorder, since 1997; *b* 7 July 1953; *d* of late Ieuan Morgan and Sarah Alice Morgan (*née* James); *m* 1975, Alan Rees. *Educ:* Ardwyn Grammar Sch., Aberystwyth; Univ. of Liverpool (LLB Hons). Called to the Bar, Gray's Inn, 1975. Clerk to Justices, Bexley Magistrates' Court, 1983–94. Editor, Family Court Reporter, 1992–94. Mem., Magisterial Cttee, Judicial Studies Bd, 1989–94. *Publications:* contrib. various jls on subject of family law. *Recreations:* travel, cookery, ski-ing. *Address:* Inner London Magistrates' Courts Service, 65 Romney Street, SW1P 3RD.

REES, Harland, MA, MCh, FRCS; Hon. Consultant Urological Surgeon, King's College Hospital; Hon. Consultant Surgeon and Urological Surgeon, Royal Free Hospital; *b* 21 Sept. 1909; *yr s* of Dr David Charles Rees, MRCS, LRCP, and Myrtle May (*née* Dolley); *m* 1950, Helen Marie Tarver; two *s* (one *d* decd). *Educ:* St Andrew's Coll., Grahamstown, S Africa; University Coll., Oxford; Charing Cross Hospital. Rhodes Scholar, Oxford University. Served RAMC, 1942–46; OC Surgical Div. 53, Indian General Hospital. Adviser in Surgery, Siam (Thailand). Examiner in Surgery, University of Cambridge, 1963–73. Councillor (C), S Beds DC, 1978–95 (Chm., 1986–87). *Publications:* articles and chapters in various books and journals, 1952–63. *Recreations:* walking, cultivation of trees; Rugby football, Oxford *v* Cambridge, 1932–33. *Address:* Kensworth Gorse, Clayhall Road, Kensworth, near Dunstable, Beds LU6 3RF. *T:* (01582) 872411. *Club:* Vincent's (Oxford).

REES, Dr Helen Blodwen; freelance curator and consultant; Lecturer in Art Gallery and Museum Studies, School of Art History and Archaeology, University of Manchester; *b* 23 Aug. 1960; *d* of late Edward Elgar Rees and of Dorothy Rees (*née* Banham); *m* 1997, Dr Michael Gordon Leahy. *Educ:* Gaisford High Sch. for Girls, Worthing; New Hall, Cambridge (MA); City Univ.; Univ. of Manchester (PhD 1999). Information Officer, Conran Foundn, 1984–86; Curator, 1986–89, Dir, 1989–92, Design Mus.; Communications Dir, Eureka!, The Mus. for Children, 1992; Asst Dir and Head of Public Affairs, NACF, 1992–95. Member: Adv. Panel, Arts Council of England, 1992–95; Design Adv. Cttee, RSA, 1990–94; Visual Arts Advr, NW Arts Bd, 1996–. Gov., Design Dimension Educnl Trust, 1990–. Trustee: Cardiff Old Library Trust, 1995–2000; Cornerhouse, Manchester, 1996–. Editor (and contrib.) Design Museum Publications, 1989–92. *Publications:* 14:24 British Youth Culture, 1986; (contrib.) The Authority of the Consumer, ed Nigel Whiteley, 1993; (contrib.) The Culture of Craft, ed Peter Dormer, 1997. *Recreations:* friends, films, books. *Address:* 37 Merchants House, North Street, Leeds LS2 7PN. *T:* (0113) 245 0873.

REES, Prof. Hubert, DFC 1945; PhD, DSc; FRS 1976; Professor of Agricultural Botany, University College of Wales, Aberystwyth, 1968–91, now Emeritus; *b* 2 Oct. 1923; *s* of Owen Rees and Tugela Rees, Llangennech, Carmarthenshire; *m* 1946, Mavis Hill; two *s* two *d*. *Educ:* Llandovery and Llanelli Grammar Schs; University Coll. of Wales, Aberystwyth (BSc). PhD, DSc Birmingham. Served RAF, 1942–46. Student,

REED, David; Regional Chairman of Employment Tribunals, Newcastle upon Tyne, since 1998; *b* 11 Oct. 1946; *s* of Thomas and Olive Reed; *m* 1976, Sylvia Mary Thompson. *Educ:* London Univ. (LLB ext.). Admitted Solicitor (William Hutton Prize), 1972, in practice, 1972–91; full-time Chm., Industrial Tribunals, 1991–. *Address:* Quayside House, 110 Quayside, Newcastle upon Tyne NE1 3DX. *T:* (0191) 260 6900.

REED, Edward John; Clerk to the Clothworkers' Company of the City of London, 1963–78; *b* 2 Sept. 1913; *o c* of late Edward Reed; *m* 1939, Rita Isabel Venus Cheston-Porter; one *s* one *d.* *Educ:* St Paul's School. Admitted Solicitor, 1938. Territorial Service with HAC; commnd 1940; served BEF and BAOR with 63 (WR) Medium Regt RA; Capt. 1942. Clerk to Governors of Mary Datchelor Girls' Sch., 1963–78. Vice Pres., Metropolitan Soc. for the Blind, 1979– (Chm., 1965–79); Chm., Indigent Blind Visiting Society, 1965–79; Vice-Pres., N London District, St John Ambulance, 1969–81. Cttee, St John Ophthalmic Hosp., Jerusalem, 1964–85. Chm., City Side, Joint Grand Gresham Cttee, 1984. Member: Court of Common Council, City of London, for Tower Ward, 1978–86; Lloyds, 1979–97. Clothworkers' Co.: Liveryman, 1964; Sen. Warden, 1981; Mem., Ct of Assistants, 1982–96, Assistant Emeritus, 1998. Governor: Christ's Hosp., 1981–86; City of London Freemen's Sch., 1982–86. Hon. MA Leeds, 1979. CStJ 1968. Chevalier, Order of Leopold with Palm, and Croix de Guerre with Palm, Belgium, 1944. *Recreations:* sailing, photography. *Address:* 54 Hillcrest Gardens, Hinchley Wood, Esher, Surrey KT10 0BX. *T:* (020) 8398 3904. *Club:* City Livery.

REED, Gavin Barras; Chairman, John Menzies plc, since 1997 (Director, since 1992); *b* 13 Nov. 1934; *s* of late Lt-Col Edward Reed and Greta Milburn (*née* Pybus); *m* 1957, Muriel Joyce, *d* of late Humphrey Vaughan Rowlands; one *s* three *d.* *Educ:* Eton; Trinity Coll., Cambridge (BA). National Service, Fleet Air Arm Pilot, 1953–55. Joined Newcastle Breweries Ltd, 1958; Dir, Scottish & Newcastle Breweries Ltd, 1970–94; Gp Man. Dir, 1988–91, Gp Vice-Chm., 1991–94, Scottish & Newcastle plc; Chm., Hamilton & Inches Ltd, 1998–; Dir, Burtonwood Brewery plc, 1996–. Chm., N Region, CBI, 1987–88. Liveryman, Brewers' Co., 1992–. *Recreations:* shooting, tennis. *Address:* Whitehill, Aberdour, Burntisland, Fife KY3 0RW; Broadgate, West Woodburn, Northumberland NE48 2RN. *Clubs:* Naval; New (Edinburgh).

REED, Jane Barbara, CBE 2000; Director of Corporate Affairs, News International plc, 1989–2000; 2nd *d* of late William and Gwendoline Reed, Letchworth, Herts. *Educ:* Royal Masonic Sch.; sundry further educational establishments. Worked on numerous magazines; returned to Woman's Own, 1965; Editor, 1970–79; Publisher, IPC Women's Monthly Group, 1979–81; Editor-in-Chief, Woman magazine, 1981–82; IPC Magazines: Asst Man. Dir, Specialist Educn and Leisure Gp, 1983; Man. Dir, Holborn Publishing Gp, 1983–85; Man. Editor (Features), Today, News (UK) Ltd, 1985–86; Man. Editor, Today, 1986–89. Pres., Media Soc., 1995. Member: Royal Soc. COPUS, 1986–96; Council, Nat. Literacy Trust, 1992–97; CSV Media. Hon. Lectr, Film and Media Studies, Stirling Univ. Trustee, St Katharine and Shadwell Trust. *Publications:* Girl About Town, 1964; (jtly) Kitchen Sink—or Swim?, 1982. *Address:* 1 Virginia Street, E1 9XY.

REED, Dr John Langdale, CB 1993; FRCP, FRCPsych; Medical Inspector, HM Inspectorate of Prisons, since 1996; *b* 16 Sept. 1931; *s* of John Thompson Reed and Elsie May Abbott; *m* 1959, Hilary Allin; one *s* one *d.* *Educ:* Oundle Sch.; Cambridge Univ.; Guy's Hosp. Med. Sch. FRCP 1974; FRCPsych 1974. Maudsley Hosp., 1960–67; Consultant Psychiatrist and Sen. Lectr in Psychol Medicine, St Bartholomew's Hosp., 1967–96. SPMO, Health Care Div. (Medical), DHSS, subseq. DoH, 1986–93. Special Advr in Forensic Psychiatry, DoH, 1993–96. Chairman: DoH/Home Office Rev. of Services for Mentally Disordered Offenders, 1991–92; DoH Wkg Gp on High Security Psychiatric Care, 1992–93; DoH Wkg Gp on Psychopathic Disorder, 1992–93; Adv. Cttee on Mentally Disordered Offenders, 1993–96. QHP 1990–93. *Publications:* (with G. Lomas) Psychiatric Services in the Community, 1984; papers on psychiatric services, on drug abuse, and on health care in prisons. *Recreations:* genealogy, opera, bridge, walking (preferably in the Lake District). *Address:* HM Inspectorate of Prisons, Home Office, 50 Queen Anne's Gate, SW1H 9AT.

REED, Ven. John Peter Cyril; Archdeacon of Taunton, since 1999; *b* 21 May 1951; *s* of C. Gordon Reed and M. Joan Reed (*née* Stenning); *m* 1979, Gillian Mary Coles; one *s* one *d.* *Educ:* Monkton Combe Sch., Bath; King's Coll. London (BD, AKC 1978); Ripon Coll., Cuddesdon. With Imperial Group, 1969–73; Research and Marketing, Wales & the West Ltd, Cardiff, 1973–75. Deacon 1979, priest 1980; Curate, Croydon Parish Church, 1979–82; Precentor, St Albans Abbey, 1982–86; Rector, Timsbury and Priston and Chaplain for Rural Affairs, Archdeaconry of Bath, 1986–93; Team Rector, Ilminster and Dist Team Ministry, 1993–99. *Recreations:* family, cricket, tennis, fishing, countryside. *Address:* 4 Westerkirk Gate, Staplegrove, Taunton TA2 6BQ. *T:* (01823) 323838; *e-mail:* adtaunton@compuserve.com.

REED, John Shepard; Joint Chairman and Co-Chief Executive Officer, Citigroup, 1998–2000; *b* 7 Feb. 1939; *m* 1st, 1964, Sally Foreman (marr. diss.); four *c*; 2nd, 1994, Cindy McCarthy. *Educ:* Washington and Jefferson Coll. (BA Amer. Lit. 1961); MIT (BS Physical Metallurgy 1961; MS Mgt 1965). Served Corps of Engrs, US Army, Korea, 1962–64. Joined Citibank, later Citicorp, 1965; Planning Dept, Internat. Div., 1965–67; NY HQ, 1967; Asst Vice-Pres., 1968–69; Exec. Vice-Pres. and Hd of Operating Gp, 1970–74; Hd of Consumer Service Gp, 1974–79; Sen. Exec. Vice-Pres., 1979–82; Vice-Chm. i/c Individual Bank, 1982–84; Dir, 1982; Chm. and CEO, 1984–98; Citicorp merged with Travelers Gp to form Citigroup, 1998. *Address:* c/o Citigroup, 153 East 53rd Street, New York, NY 10043, USA.

REED, Julie Therese; *see* Mellor, J. T.

REED, Laurance Douglas; *b* 4 Dec. 1937; *s* of late Douglas Austin Reed and Mary Ellen Reed (*née* Philpott). *Educ:* Gresham's Sch., Holt; University Coll., Oxford (MA). Nat. Service, RN, 1956–58; worked and studied on Continent (Brussels, Bruges, Leyden, Luxembourg, Strasbourg, Paris, Rome, Bologna, Geneva), 1963–66; Public Sector Research Unit, 1967–69. MP (C) Bolton East, 1970–Feb. 1974; PPS to Chancellor of Duchy of Lancaster, 1973–74. Jt Sec., Parly and Scientific Cttee, 1971–74; Member: Soc. for Underwater Technology; Select Cttee on Science and Technology, 1971–74. *Publications:* Europe in a Shrinking World, 1967; An Ocean of Waste, 1972; Political Consequences of North Sea Oil, 1973; The Soay of Our Forefathers, 1986; Philpott of Fordingbridge, 1994. *Recreations:* gardening, historical research. *Address:* 1 Disraeli Park, Beaconsfield, Bucks HP9 2QE. *T:* (01494) 673153. *Club:* Carlton.
See also B. St G. A. Reed.

REED, Leslie Edwin, PhD; Chief Industrial Air Pollution Inspector, Health and Safety Executive, 1981–85; *b* 6 Feb. 1925; *s* of Edwin George and Maud Gladys Reed; *m* 1947, Ruby; two *s.* *Educ:* Sir George Monoux Grammar Sch., Walthamstow; University Coll. London (BScEng, MScEng, PhD). Engineering Officer, RNVR, 1945–47; Fuel Research Station, 1950–58; Warren Spring Laboratory, 1958–70; Central Unit on Environmental Pollution, DoE, 1970–79; Head, Air and Noise Div., DoE, 1979–81. *Address:* 20 Deards Wood, Knebworth, Herts SG3 6PG. *T:* (01438) 813272.

REED, Robert John; *see* Reed, Hon. Lord.

REED, Roger William Hampson, FCIS; Chairman, South East Arts Board, 1995–2001; Member, Arts Council of England, 1996–98; *b* 23 Oct. 1938; *s* of late Thomas Henry Walter Reed and Lily Reed (*née* Hampson); *m* 1961, Jane Noelle Madeline Bowring Gabriel; one *s* one *d.* *Educ:* Trinity Sch. of John Whitgift; City of London Coll. FCIS 1968; CompIEE 1990. Mgt trainee, Albright and Wilson Gp, 1957–61; Asst Co. Sec., Powell Duffryn Gp, 1961–62; Jt Chief Accountant, John Mowlem Gp, 1962–68; Ewbank Preece Group: Dir and Co. Sec., 1968–91; Chm., 1991–93; Chm., Old Ship Hotel (Brighton) Ltd, 1979–93; Dir, Regency Bldg Soc., 1984–88. Partner, Gratwicke Farm, 1982–. Founder Dir, Sussex Enterprise (formerly Sussex TEC), 1991–95. Chm., Sussex Br., Inst. Dirs, 1986–89. Trustee, Brighton Fest. Trust and Dir, Brighton Fest. Soc., 1980–95. Chm., Royal Alexandra Hosp. for Sick Children Centenary Fund and Rockinghorse Appeal, 1991–. Fellow, Woodard Foundn, 1993–2001. FCIM 1982; FRSA 1982. Gov., Hurstpierpoint Coll., 1989–2001. *Recreations:* farming, the arts, cooking and entertaining, sport. *Address:* Gratwicke, Cowfold, W Sussex RH13 8EA. *T:* (01403) 864284. *Clubs:* Savile, MCC; W Sussex Golf (Pulborough).

REED, Prof. Terence James, (Jim), FBA 1987; Taylor Professor of the German Language and Literature, and Fellow, Queen's College, Oxford, since 1989; *b* 16 April 1937; s of William Reed and Ellen (*née* Silcox); *m* 1960, Ann Macpherson; one *s* one *d.* *Educ:* Shooters' Hill Grammar Sch., Woolwich; Brasenose Coll., Oxford (MA). Sen. Scholar, Christ Church, Oxford, 1960–61; Jun. Res. Fellow, Brasenose Coll., Oxford, 1961–63; Fellow and Tutor in Mod. Langs, St John's Coll., Oxford, 1963–88 (Hon. Fellow, 1997). Schiller Prof., Univ. of Jena, 1999. Pres., English Goethe Soc., 1995–. Corresp. Mem., Göttingen Acad. of Scis, 1997. Gold Medal, Goethe Soc., Weimar, 1999. Co-founder and Editor, Oxford German Studies, 1965–; Editor, Oxford Magazine, 1985–. *Publications:* (ed) Death in Venice, 1972, German edn 1983; Thomas Mann, The Uses of Tradition, 1974, 2nd edn 1997; The Classical Centre: Goethe and Weimar 1775–1832, 1980, German edn 1982; Goethe, 1984; (trans.) Heinrich Heine: Deutschland, a not so sentimental journey, 1986; Schiller, 1991; Death in Venice: making and unmaking a master, 1994; (trans. with D. Cram) Heinrich Heine, Poems, 1997; (trans.) Goethe: The Flight to Italy: diaries and letters 1786, 1999; (ed) Goethe: poems, 1999; (ed and trans. jtly) Goethe: poems, 2000; Humanpraxis Literatur (essays), 2001. *Recreation:* hill walking. *Address:* 14 Crick Road, Oxford OX2 6QL. *T:* (01865) 558511.

REED-PURVIS, Air Vice-Marshal Henry, CB 1982; OBE 1972; Sales Director, British Aerospace Dynamics Group, 1983–89; *b* 1 July 1928; *s* of late Henry Reed and of Nancy Reed-Purvis; *m* 1951, Isabel Price; three *d.* *Educ:* King James I School, Durham; Durham Univ. BSc Hons 1950. Entered RAF, 1950; various Op. Sqdns, 1951–58; Instr, Jt Nuclear Biological and Chemical Sch., 1958–60; RMCS Shrivenham (Nuclear Sci. and Tech.), 1961; MoD Staff, 1962–64; OC No 63 Sqdn, RAF Regt, Malaya, 1964–66; Exchange Duties, USAF, 1966–69; USAF War Coll., 1969–70; OC No 5 Wing RAF Regt, 1970–72; Gp Capt. Regt, HQ Strike Comd, 1972–74, HQ RAF Germany, 1974–76; ADC to the Queen, 1974–76; Dir, RAF Regt, 1976–79; Comdt Gen. RAF Regt and Dir Gen. of Security (RAF) 1979–83. Dir, Forces Help Soc. and Lord Roberts Workshops, 1986–97; Council Mem., Trustee and Dir, SSAFA/Forces Help, 1997–99. Vice Pres., Council for Cadet Rifle Shooting, 1985–. Pres., 2120 Sqdn ATC Welfare Cttee, 1995–. *Recreations:* golf, bridge and music. *Address:* Waterford House, Sherborne, Cheltenham, Glos GL54 3DR. *T:* (01451) 844199.

REEDER, John; QC 1989; *b* 18 Jan. 1949; *s* of Frederick and Barbara Reeder; *m* 1st, 1971, Barbara Kotlarz (marr. diss. 1994); 2nd, 1995, Pauline Madden. *Educ:* Catholic Coll., Preston; University Coll. London (LLM); PhD Birmingham 1976. Called to the Bar, Gray's Inn, 1971, NSW 1986. Lectr in Law, Univ. of Birmingham, 1971–76; commenced practice, 1976; Junior Counsel to the Treasury (Admiralty), 1981–89; a Recorder, 1991–97; Lloyd's salvage arbitrator, 1991–. Lawyer, PNG, 1984. *Recreations:* sailing, travel. *Address:* 4 Field Court, Gray's Inn, WC1R 5EA. *T:* (020) 7440 6900; 72 Bracondale Road, Norwich NR1 2BE. *Club:* Royal Corinthian Yacht.

REEDIE, Craig Collins, CBE 1999; Chairman, British Olympic Association, since 1992; Member: International Olympic Committee, since 1994; Board, World Anti-Doping Agency, since 2000; *b* 6 May 1941; *s* of late Robert Lindsay Reedie and Anne Reedie; *m* 1967, Rosemary Jane Biggart; one *s* one *d.* *Educ:* High Sch., Stirling; Univ. of Glasgow (MA, LLB). Partner, D. L. Bloomer & Partners, Glasgow. Sec. and Pres., Scottish Badminton Union, 1966–81; Council Mem., Chm. and Pres., Internat. Badminton Fedn, 1970–84; Mem. Council and Treas., Gen. Assoc. of Internat. Sports Fedns, 1984–92. Mem., NHS Resource Allocation Steering Gp, 1998–99. FRSA 1995. *Recreations:* reading, golf, sport, sport and more sport. *Address:* 53 Bothwell Street, Glasgow G2 6TS. *T:* (0141) 248 7268. *Clubs:* East India; Royal & Ancient Golf (St Andrews), Western Gailes Golf, Ranfurly Castle Golf.

REEDY, Norris John, (Jack); media consultant, since 1994; Managing Director, The Speaking Business Ltd; *b* 1934; *s* of John Reedy; *m* 1964, Sheila Campbell McGregor; one *d.* *Educ:* Chorlton High Sch., Manchester; Univ. of Sheffield. Newspaper journalist, 1956–; Sunday Times, 1961; Guardian, 1964; Birmingham Post, 1964–82 (Editor, 1974–82); Regl Officer, Midlands, IBA, 1983–88; Sen. Nat. and Regl Officer, ITC, 1988–94; PRO, Inst. of Dirs (Midland Br.), 1994–99. Tutor in media skills and public speaking, RCN, 1985–. Mem. Coventry and Warwickshire Area Bd, The Prince's Trust (Business). Former Chm. W Midlands Region, and Nat. Vice-Pres., Guild of British Newspaper Editors; Sec., Midlands Centre, Royal Television Soc.; Council Mem., Rotary Club of Birmingham. Chairman: House Committee: Birmingham Press Club; Merton House Holiday Hotel Ltd, Ross-on-Wye. Mem., W Midlands Employer Liaison Cttee, TA & VRA. *Recreations:* astronomy, riding, natural history, painting, photography. *Address:* The Old Manor, Rowington, near Warwick CV35 7DJ. *T:* (01564) 783129.

REES; *see* Merlyn-Rees.

REES, family name of **Baron Rees**.

REES, Baron *cr* 1987 (Life Peer), of Goytre in the County of Gwent; **Peter Wynford Innes Rees;** PC 1983; QC 1969; chairman and director of companies; *b* 9 Dec. 1926; *s* of late Maj.-Gen. T. W. Rees, Indian Army, Goytre Hall, Abergavenny; *m* 1969, Mrs Anthea Wendell, *d* of late Major H. J. M. Hyslop, Argyll and Sutherland Highlanders. *Educ:* Stowe; Christ Church, Oxford. Served Scots Guards, 1945–48. Called to the Bar, 1953, Bencher, Inner Temple, 1976; Oxford Circuit. Contested (C): Abertillery, 1964 and 1965; Liverpool, West Derby, 1966. MP (C): Dover, 1970–74 and 1983–87; Dover and Deal, 1974–83; PPS to Solicitor General, 1972; Minister of State, HM Treasury, 1979–81; Minister for Trade, 1981–83; Chief Sec. to HM Treasury, 1983–85. Dep. Chm., Leopold Joseph Holdings Plc, 1985–97; Dir, Fleming Mercantile Investment Trust,

Aberystwyth, 1946–50; Lectr in Cytology, Univ. of Birmingham, 1950–58; Sen. Lectr in Agric. Botany, University Coll. of Wales, Aberystwyth, 1958, Reader 1966. *Publications:* Chromosome Genetics, 1977; B Chromosomes, 1982; articles on genetic control of chromosomes and on evolutionary changes in chromosome organisation. *Recreation:* fishing. *Address:* Irfon, Llanbadarn Road, Aberystwyth, Dyfed SY23 1EY. *T:* (01970) 623668.

REES, Hugh; *see* Rees, J. E. H.

REES, Hugh Francis E.; *see* Ellis-Rees.

REES, Rt Rev. Ivor; *see* Rees, Rt Rev. J. I.

REES, John; *see* Rees, A. J. D., and Rees, P. J.

REES, Rev. John; *see* Rees, Rev. V. J. H.

REES, John Charles; QC 1991; *b* 22 May 1949; *s* of Ronald Leslie Rees and Martha Therese Rees; *m* 1970, Dianne Elizabeth Kirby; three *s* one *d*. *Educ:* St Illtyd's College, Cardiff; Jesus College, Cambridge (double first class Hons; BA (Law), LLB (Internat. Law), MA, LLM; repr. Univ. in boxing and Association Football; boxing Blue). Called to the Bar, Lincoln's Inn, 1972. Trustee and Governor, St John's College, Cardiff, 1987–. Representative Steward, and Chm., Welsh Area Council, BBB of C. *Recreations:* all sport, esp. boxing and Association Football; theatre. *Address:* Marleigh Lodge, Druidstone Road, Old St Mellons, Cardiff CF3 9XD. *T:* (029) 2079 4918; 33 Park Place, Cardiff CF1 3BA. *Club:* Hawks (Cambridge).

REES, (John Edward) Hugh; Chartered Surveyor; *b* 8 Jan. 1928; *s* of David Emlyn Rees, Swansea; *m* 1961, Gillian Dian Milo-Jones (decd); two *s*. MP (C) Swansea, West Division, Oct. 1959–64; Assistant Government Whip, 1962–64. UK Rep., Econ. and Soc. Cttee, EEC, 1972–78. Dir, Abbey National plc (formerly Abbey National Building Soc.), 1976–91; Chairman: Cambrian Housing Soc., 1968–; Abbey Housing Association Ltd, 1980–92. Mem., Welsh Develt Agency, 1980–86. Trustee, Ffynone House Sch. Trust, 1973– (Chm. 1977–85). Member Council: Nat. Mus. of Wales, 1968–94; Univ. of Wales Swansea, 1970–. FRICS. *Address:* Sherwood, 35 Caswell Road, Newton, Mumbles, Swansea, W Glamorgan SA3 4SD.

REES, Rt Rev. (John) Ivor; Bishop of St Davids, 1991–95; *b* 19 Feb. 1926; *o s* of David Morgan Rees and Cecilia Perrott Rees; *m* 1954, Beverley Richards; three *s*. *Educ:* Llanelli Gram. Sch.; University Coll. of Wales (BA 1950); Westcott House, Cambridge. Served RN, Coastal Forces and British Pacific Fleet, 1943–47. Deacon 1952, priest 1953, Dio. St David's; Curate: Fishguard, 1952–55; Llangathen, 1955–57; Priest-in-Charge, Uzmaston, 1957–59; Vicar: Slebech and Uzmaston, 1959–65; Llangollen, 1965–74; Rural Dean of Llangollen, 1970–74; Rector of Wrexham, 1974–76; Dean of Bangor, 1976–88; Vicar of Cathedral Parish of Bangor, 1979–88; Archdeacon of St Davids and Asst Bp, Dio. of St Davids, 1988–91. Canon of St Asaph, 1975–76; Chaplain, Order of St John for County of Clwyd, 1974–76, County of Gwynedd, 1976–88. Hon. Fellow, Trinity Coll., Carmarthen, 1996. SBStJ 1975, OStJ 1981, Sub-Prelate, 1993. *Publications:* Monograph—The Parish of Llangollen and its Churches, 1971; Keeping 40 Days—Sermons for Lent, 1989. *Recreations:* music and good light reading. *Address:* Llys Dewi, 45 Clover Park, Uzmaston Road, Haverfordwest, Pembs SA61 1UE. *T:* (01437) 764846.

REES, John Samuel; Editor, Western Mail, 1981–87; *b* 23 Oct. 1931; *s* of John Richard Rees and Mary Jane Rees; *m* 1957, Ruth Jewell; one *s* one *d*. *Educ:* Cyfarthfa Castle Grammar Sch., Merthyr Tydfil. Nat. Service, Welch Regt and RAEC, 1950–52. Reporter, 1948–50, Sports Editor, 1952–54, Merthyr Express; The Star, Sheffield: Reporter, 1954–56; Sub Editor, 1956–58; Dep. Chief Sub Editor, 1958–59; Dep. Sports Editor, 1959–61; Asst Editor, 1961–66; Dep. Editor, Evening Echo, Hemel Hempstead, 1966–69; Editor: Evening Mail, Slough and Hounslow, 1969–72; The Journal, Newcastle upon Tyne, 1972–76; Evening Post-Echo, Hemel Hempstead, 1976–79, Asst Man. Dir, Evening Post-Echo Ltd, 1979–81. Lectr, Centre for Journalism Studies, Univ. of Wales Coll. of Cardiff, 1988–92. *Recreations:* marquetry, watching cricket and rugby, walking, gardening. *Address:* 2 Alton Close, Whirlowdale Park, Sheffield S11 9QQ. *T:* (0114) 235 1028.

REES, Jonathan Nigel; Director, Consumer Affairs, Department of Trade and Industry, since 2000; *b* 29 Sept. 1955; *s* of late Arthur Ernest Rees and of Thelma Maureen Rees; *m* 1996, Kathryn Jayne Taylor; one *d*. *Educ:* Jesus Coll., Oxford (MA Hons Modern History). Joined DTI, 1977; Private Sec. to Minister for Trade, 1981–84; EC, 1984–86 (on secondment); DTI, 1986–89; Industry Counsellor, UK Rep. to EU, 1989–94; Prime Minister's Policy Unit, 1994–97; Dir, Citizen's Charter Unit, then Modernising Public Services Gp, Cabinet Office, 1997–2000. *Recreations:* sport, travel, theatre. *Address:* Department of Trade and Industry, 1 Victoria Street, SW1H 0ET. *T:* (020) 7215 0310. *Club:* MCC.

REES, Prof. Judith Anne, PhD; Professor of Environmental and Resources Management, since 1995, and Pro-Director, since 1998, London School of Economics; *b* 26 Aug. 1944; *d* of Douglas S. Hart and Eva M. Hart (*née* Haynes); *m* 1st, 1968, Prof. Raymond Rees, *qv* (marr. diss. 1972); 2nd, 1981, Prof. David Keith Crozier Jones. *Educ:* Bilborough Grammar Sch., Nottingham; London Sch. of Economics (BSc Econ 1965; MPhil 1967; PhD 1978). Lectr, Agricl Econs, Wye Coll., London Univ., 1967–69; Lectr, 1969–85, Sen. Lectr, 1985–89, in Geography, LSE; University of Hull: Prof. of Geography, 1989–95; Dean of Sch. of Geography and Earth Resources, 1991–93; Pro-Vice Chancellor, 1993–95. Nat. Water and Sewerage Policy Advr, Australian Dept of Urban and Regl Develt, 1974–75; Member: Exec. Panel on Pollution Res., SSRC, 1977–80; Adv. Cttee, Centre for Regulated Industries, 1990–; ESRC Trng Bd, 1994–98; ESRC Global Envmtl Change Cttee, 1995–98; Technical Adv. Cttee, Global Water Partnership, 1996–; Competition (formerly Monopolies and Mergers) Commn, 1996–; Link/Teaching Co. Scheme Bd, OST, 1997–; Chm., Ofwat Southern Customer Service Cttee, 1990–96. Member: Council, RGS, 1979–82 (Vice Pres., 1995–97); Council, Inst. of British Geographers, 1981–83. *Publications:* Industrial Demands for Water, 1969; Natural Resources Allocation, Economics and Policy, 1985, 2nd edn 1990; (jtly) The International Oil Industry: an interdisciplinary perspective, 1987; (jtly) Troubled Water, 1987; Water for Life, 1993; articles on water resources and envmtl mgt in books and learned jls. *Address:* London School of Economics, Houghton Street, WC2A 2AE. *T:* (020) 7955 6228. *Club:* Geographical.

REES, Laurence Mark; Creative Director, BBC TV History Programmes, since 2000 (Head, History Programmes Unit, BBC TV, 1999–2000, and Editor, History Zone, BBC 2, 2000); *b* 19 Jan. 1957; *s* of late Alan Rees and Margaret Julia Rees (*née* Mark); *m* 1987, Helena Brewer; two *s* one *d*. *Educ:* Solihull Sch.; Worcester Coll., Oxford (BA). Joined BBC TV, 1978: prodn trainee, 1978–79; writer/producer/dir, 1982–; *productions* include: Crisis (drama documentary), 1987; A British Betrayal, 1991; We Have Ways of Making You Think (History of Propaganda series), 1992; Nazis: a warning from history (series; awards include: BAFTA, IDA, Peabody, BPG), 1997; War of the Century (series), 1999; Horror in the East (series), 2000; as Executive Producer, awards include: Emmy Awards, 1994 (2) and 1996; Amnesty Press Award, 1994; Internat. Documentary Assoc. Award, 1997; Western Heritage Award, 2000. *Publications:* Electric Beach (novel), 1990; Selling Politics, 1992; Nazis: a warning from history, 1997; War of the Century, 1999; Horror in the East, 2001. *Recreation:* my three children. *Address:* BBC, White City, 201 Wood Lane, W12 7TS. *T:* (020) 8752 6255.

REES, Dame Lesley Howard, DBE 2001; MD, DSc; FRCP; FRCPath; Professor of Chemical Endocrinology, St Bartholomew's and the Royal London School of Medicine and Dentistry, Queen Mary and Westfield College (formerly St Bartholomew's Hospital Medical College), London University, since 1978; *b* 17 Nov. 1942; *d* of Howard Leslie Davis and Charlotte Patricia Siegrid Young; *m* 1969, Gareth Mervyn Rees. *Educ:* Pates Girls' Grammar Sch., Cheltenham; Malvern Girls' Coll.; London Univ. (MB BS 1965; MD 1972; MSc 1974; DSc 1989). MRCP 1967, FRCP 1979; MRCPath 1976, FRCPath 1988. Editor, Clinical Endocrinology, 1979–84; Subdean, 1983–88, Dean, 1989–95, St Bartholomew's Hosp. Med. Coll.; Public Orator, London Univ., 1984–86. Chm., Soc. for Endocrinology, 1984–87; Sec.-Gen., Internat. Soc. of Endocrinology, 1984–. Mem., Press Complaints Commn, 1991–94. Royal College of Physicians: Dir, Internat. Office, 1997–99; Dir, Educn Dept, 1997–2001. Founder FMedSci 1998. *Recreations:* music, poetry, reading, ski-ing, administrative gardening. *Address:* 23 Church Row, Hampstead, NW3 6UP. *T:* and *Fax:* (020) 7794 4936. *Club:* Mosimann's.

REES, Rt Rev. Leslie Lloyd; Assistant Bishop, Diocese of Winchester, since 1987; *b* 14 April 1919; *s* of Rees Thomas and Elizabeth Rees; *m* 1944, Rosamond Smith (*d* 1989); one *s* (and one *s* decd). *Educ:* Pontardawe Grammar Sch.; Kelham Theological College. Asst Curate, St Saviour, Roath, 1942; Asst Chaplain, HM Prison, Cardiff, 1942; Chaplain, HM Prison; Durham, 1945; Dartmoor, 1948; Vicar of Princetown, 1948; Chaplain, HM Prison, Winchester, 1955; Chaplain General of Prisons, Home Office Prison Dept, 1962–80; Bishop Suffragan of Shrewsbury, 1980–86. Chaplain to the Queen, 1971–80. Mem., Parole Bd, 1987–90. Hon. Canon of Canterbury, 1966–80, of Lichfield, 1980–. Freeman, City of London. ChStJ 1985. *Recreation:* music. *Address:* Kingfisher Lodge, Arle Gardens, Alresford, Hants SO24 9BA.

REES, Linford; *see* Rees, W. L. L.

REES, Sir Martin (John), Kt 1992; FRS 1979; Royal Society Research Professor, Cambridge University, since 1992; Fellow, King's College, Cambridge, since 1973 (and 1969–72); Astronomer Royal, since 1995; *b* 23 June 1942; *s* of late Reginald J. and Joan Rees; *m* 1986, Prof. Caroline Humphrey, *qv*. *Educ:* Shrewsbury Sch.; Trinity Coll., Cambridge (Hon. Fellow, 1995); MA, PhD (Cantab). Fellow, Jesus Coll., Cambridge, 1967–69 (Hon. Fellow, 1996); Research Associate, California Inst. of Technology, 1967–68 and 1971; Mem., Inst. for Advanced Study, Princeton, 1969–70; Prof., Univ. of Sussex, 1972–73; Cambridge University: Plumian Prof. of Astronomy and Experimental Philosophy, 1973–91; Dir, Inst. of Astronomy, 1977–82 and 1987–91. Visiting Professor: Harvard Univ., 1972, 1986–88; Inst. for Advanced Studies, Princeton, 1982, 1995; Imperial Coll., London, 2001–; Hitchcock Vis. Prof., UC Berkeley, 1994; Regents Fellow of Smithsonian Instn, Washington, 1984–88; Oort Prof., Leiden, 1999; Hon. Prof., Univ. of Leicester, 2001. Lectures: H. P. Robertson Meml, US Nat. Acad. Sci, 1975; George Darwin, Royal Astron. Soc., 1976; Halley, Oxford, 1978; Milne, Oxford, 1980; Bakerian, Royal Soc., 1982; Danz, Univ. of Washington, 1984; Lauritsen, CIT, 1987; UK–Canada Rutherford, Royal Soc./RSC, 1998; Mautner, UCLA, 1998; Pauli, Zurich, 1999; Leverhulme, 1999; Scribner, Princeton, 2000. Trustee: BM, 1996–; NESTA, 1998–2001; Inst. for Adv. Study, Princeton, 1998–; Kennedy Meml Trust, 1999–. President: RAS, 1992–94; BAAS, 1994–95; Chm., Science Adv. Cttee, ESA, 1976–78; Member: Council, Royal Soc., 1983–85 and 1993–95; PPARC, 1994–97. Member: Academia Europaea, 1989; Pontifical Acad. of Sci., 1990; For. Hon. Mem., Amer. Acad. of Arts and Sciences, 1975; Foreign Associate, Nat. Acad. of Sciences, USA, 1982; Foreign Member: Amer. Phil. Soc., 1993; Royal Swedish Acad. Sci., 1993; Russian Acad. of Sci., 1994; Norwegian Acad. of Arts and Letters, 1996; Accademia Lincei, Rome, 1996; Royal Netherlands Acad. of Arts and Sciences, 1998. Hon. FIASc 1990; Hon. FInstP 2001. Hon. Fellow, Cardiff Univ., 1998. Hon. DSc: Sussex, 1990; Leicester, 1993; Copenhagen, 1994; Keele, Newcastle and Uppsala, 1995; Toronto, 1997; Durham, 1999; Oxford, 2000. Hopkins Prize, Cambridge Phil. Soc., 1982; Heinemann Prize, Amer. Inst. Physics, 1984; Bappu Award, Indian Nat. Science Acad., 1986; Gold Medal, RAS, 1987; Guthrie Medal and Prize, Inst. of Physics, 1989; Balzan Prize, Balzan Foundn, 1989; Schwarzschild Medal, Astron. ges., 1989; Robinson Prize for Cosmology, Univ. of Newcastle upon Tyne, 1990; Bruce Gold Medal, Astron. Soc. of Pacific, 1993; Science writing award, Amer. Inst. of Physics, 1996; Bower Award for Science, Franklin Inst., 1998; Rossi Prize, American Astron. Soc., 2000; Cosmology Prize, Gruber Foundn, 2001. Officier, Ordre des Arts et des Lettres (France), 1991. *Publications:* Perspectives in Astrophysical Cosmology, 1995; (with M. Begelman) Gravity's Fatal Attraction: black holes in the universe, 1996; Before the Beginning: our universe and others, 1997; Just Six Numbers, 1999; Our Cosmic Habitat, 2001; mainly scientific papers; numerous general articles. *Address:* c/o King's College, Cambridge CB2 1ST. *T:* (01223) 331100; (office) (01223) 337548.

REES, Meuric; *see* Rees, R. E. M.

REES, Rev. Canon Michael; *see* Rees, Rev. Canon R. M.

REES, Owen, CB 1991; Deputy Chairman, Qualifications, Curriculum and Assessment Authority for Wales, since 1997; *b* 26 Dec. 1934; *s* of late John Trevor and Esther Rees, Trimsaran, Dyfed; *m* 1958, Elizabeth Gosby (*d* 1991); one *s* two *d*. *Educ:* Llanelli Grammar Sch.; Univ. of Manchester. BA(Econ). Bank of London and South America, 1957; regional development work in Cardiff, Birmingham and London, BoT, 1959–69; Cabinet Office, 1969–71; Welsh Office, 1971–94: Asst Sec. (European Div.), 1972; Under Sec., 1977–94; Sec. for Welsh Educn, 1977–78; Head, Educn Dept, 1978–80; Dir, Industry Dept, 1980–85; Head, Economic and Regl Policy Gp, 1985–90; Head, Agriculture Dept, 1990–94. *Address:* 4 Llandennis Green, Cyncoed, Cardiff CF23 6JX. *T:* (029) 2075 9712.

REES, Dr (Peter) John, FRCP; Consultant Physician, and Senior Lecturer in Medicine, Guy's, King's and St Thomas' Hospitals Medical and Dental School of King's College London (formerly United Medical and Dental Schools of Guy's and St Thomas' Hospitals), since 1983; *b* 2 March 1949; *s* of Joseph Thomas Rees and Doris Mary Williams; *m* 1973, Helen Mary Heath; one *s* one *d*. *Educ:* Whitchurch Grammar Sch., Cardiff; Christ's Coll., Cambridge (MB BChir; MA; MD); Guy's Hosp., London. FRCP 1988. Guy's Hospital, later UMDS of Guy's and St Thomas' Hospitals, then Guy's, King's and St Thomas' Hospitals Medical and Dental School of King's College London: Lectr, 1979–83; Asst Clin. Dean, 1993–2000; Gp Clin. Dir for Acute Med. Services, 1995–2000; Dep. Chm., Academic Bd, 1996–98; Site Dean, Guy's Hosp., 2000–. Non-exec. Mem., Lewisham and N Southwark HA, 1990–92; non-executive Director: Mildmay Mission Hosp., 1992–; Lewisham Hosp. Trust Bd, 1995–; Mem. Exec. Cttee, British Lung

Foundn, 1988–95. *Publications:* (jtly) ABC of Asthma, 1984, 4th edn 1999; (jtly) Practical Management of Asthma, 1985, 2nd edn 1996; A Medical Catechism, 1986; (jtly) A New Short Textbook of Medicine, 1988; Diagnostic Tests in Respiratory Medicine, 1988; Asthma: family doctor guide, 1988; (jtly) A Colour Atlas of Asthma, 1989; (jtly) Aids to Clinical Pharmacology and Therapeutics, 1993; (jtly) Principles of Clinical Medicine, 1995; (jtly) Asthma: current perspectives, 1996; (jtly) 100 Cases in Clinical Medicine, 2000. *Recreations:* theatre, opera, cricket, squash, walking. *Address:* Guy's Hospital, London Bridge, SE1 9RT. *T:* (020) 7955 4479.

REES, Peter Magnall; a Senior Clerk, House of Lords, 1981–84; *b* 17 March 1921; *s* of late Edward Saunders Rees and Gertrude Rees (*née* Magnall); *m* 1949, Moya Mildred Carroll. *Educ:* Manchester Grammar Sch.; Jesus Coll., Oxford. Served War, RA, 1941–46 (SE Asia, 1942–45). HM Overseas Service, Nigeria, 1948; Dep. Govt Statistician, Kenya, 1956; Dir of Economics and Statistics, Kenya, 1961; HM Treasury, 1964; Chief Statistician, 1966; Under-Sec., DTI later Dept of Industry, 1973–81. Consultant, OECD, 1981. *Publications:* articles in statistical jls. *Recreations:* choral singing, music, studying architecture. *Address:* The Old Orchard, Sandford Orcas, Sherborne, Dorset DT9 4RP. *T:* (01963) 220244. *Club:* Royal Commonwealth Society.

REES, Peter Wynne, RIBA; FRTPI; City Planning Officer, Corporation of London, since 1987; *b* 26 Sept. 1948; *s* of Gwynne Rees, MM, CEng, MIMechE, FMES, and late Elizabeth Rodda Rees (*née* Hynam). *Educ:* Pontardawe Grammar Sch.; Whitchurch Grammar Sch., Cardiff; Bartlett Sch. of Architecture, UCL (BSc Hons); Welsh Sch. of Architecture, Univ. of Wales (BArch); Polytechnic of the South Bank (BTP). Architectural Asst, Historic Bldgs Div., GLC, 1971–72; Asst to Gordon Cullen, CBE, RDI, FSIA, 1973–75; Architect, Historic Areas Conservation, DoE, 1975–79; UK Rep., Council of Europe Wkg Parties studying New Uses for Historic Buildings and The Economics of Building Conservation, 1977–78; Asst Chief Planning Officer, London Bor. of Lambeth, 1979–85; Controller of Planning, Corp. of London, 1985–87. Trustee, Building Conservation Trust, 1985–91. Founder Mem. and Dir, British Council for Offices, 1989–. London Rep., EC (formerly European) Working Party on Technological Impact on Future Urban Change, 1989–92; Member: Steering Gp, London World City Study, 1990–91; Officers' Gp, London Pride Partnership, 1994–98; London Office Review Panel, 1996–. FRSA 1988. *Publications:* City of London Local Plan, 1989; City of London Unitary Development Plan, 1994; contribs to professional studies and jls. *Recreations:* swimming, Nordic ski-ing, playing the viola, music, tidying. *Address:* City Planning Officer, Guildhall, EC2P 2EJ. *T:* (020) 7332 1700. *Club:* Guildhall.

REES, Philip; a Recorder of the Crown Court, since 1983; *b* 1 Dec. 1941; *s* of John Trevor Rees and Olwen Muriel Rees; *m* 1969, Catherine Good; one *s* one *d*. *Educ:* Monmouth Sch.; Bristol Univ. (LLB Hons). Called to the Bar, Middle Temple, 1965. An Asst Boundary Comr, 1996–. *Recreations:* music, sport. *Address:* 9 Park Place, Cardiff CF1 3DP. *T:* (029) 2038 2731. *Club:* Cardiff and County (Cardiff).

REES, Prof. Philip Howell, PhD; FBA 1998; Professor of Population Geography, University of Leeds, since 1990; *b* 17 Sept. 1944; *s* of Foster and Mona Rees; *m* 1968, Laura Campbell; one *s* one *d*. *Educ:* King Edward's Sch., Birmingham; St Catharine's Coll., Cambridge (BA Geog. 1966; MA 1970); Univ. of Chicago (MA Geog. 1968; PhD 1973). University of Leeds: Lectr, 1970–80; Reader, 1980–90. Hofstee Vis. Fellow, Netherlands Interdisciplinary Demographic Inst., The Hague, 1995; Dist. Vis. Fellow, Univ. of Adelaide, 1996. Gill Meml Award, RGS, 1996. *Publications:* Spatial Population Analysis, 1977; Residential Patterns in American Cities, 1979; (ed jtly) Population Structures and Models, 1985; (ed) Migration Processes and Patterns, Vol. 2, 1992; (ed jtly) Population Migration in the European Union, 1996; The Determinants of Migration Flows in England, 1998. *Recreation:* walking. *Address:* School of Geography, University of Leeds, Leeds LS2 9JT. *T:* (0113) 233 3341; (home) 8 Moseley Wood Gardens, Cookridge, Leeds LS16 7HR. *T:* (0113) 267 6968.

REES, Prof. Ray; Professor of Economics, University of Munich, since 1993 (Dean of Economics Faculty, 1999–2000); *b* 19 Sept. 1943; *s* of Gwyn Rees and Violet May (*née* Powell); *m* 1976, Denise Sylvia (*née* Stinson); two *s*. *Educ:* Dyffryn Grammar Sch., Port Talbot; London School of Economics and Political Science (MScEcon). Lectr 1966–76, Reader 1976–78, Queen Mary Coll., Univ. of London; Economic Advr, HM Treasury (on secondment), 1968–72; Prof. of Econs, UC, Cardiff, 1978–87; Prof. of Econs, Univ. of Guelph, Ont, 1987–93. Member (part-time), Monopolies and Mergers Commn, 1985–87. *Publications:* A Dictionary of Economics, 1968, 3rd edn 1984; Public Enterprise Economics, 1975, 3rd edn 1992; Microeconomics, 1981, 2nd edn 1992; Economics: a mathematical introduction, 1991; Introduction to Game Theory, 1992; The Theory of Principal and Agent, 1992; Mathematics for Economics, 1996; articles in Economic Jl, Amer. Econ. Rev., Jl of Political Econ., Jl of Public Econs, Economica, and others. *Recreations:* playing the guitar, losing chess games. *Address:* Ungererstrasse 34, 80802 Munich, Germany. *T:* (89) 33036706.

REES, (Richard Ellis) Meuric, CBE 1982; JP; FRAgS; Lord-Lieutenant for Gwynedd, 1990–99; Vice Chairman, Hill Farming Advisory Committee (Chairman, Committee for Wales); *b* Pantydwr, Radnorshire, 1924; *m*; three *d*. President: YFC in Wales, 1961; Merioneth Agricl Soc., 1972; Royal Welsh Agricl Show, 1978; former Chm., Welsh Council of NFU; Mem., CLA. Member: Agricl Trng Bd, 1974 (Chm., Cttee for Wales); Countryside Commn, 1981 (Chm., Cttee for Wales). Governor: Welsh Agricl Coll., Aberystwyth; Coleg Meirionnydd, Dolgellau. Mem., Tywyn UDC, 1967–73. Chm., N Wales Police Authority, 1982–84. JP Tywyn, 1957 (Chm. of Bench, 1974–94); High Sheriff of Gwynedd, 1982–83; DL Gwynedd, 1988. FRAgS 1973. *Address:* Escuan Hall, Tywyn, Gwynedd LL36 9HR.

REES, Rev. Canon (Richard) Michael; Canon Emeritus, Chester Cathedral, since 2000; *b* 31 July 1935; *s* of Richard and Margaret Rees; *m* 1958, Yoma Patricia; one *s* one *d*. *Educ:* Brighton College; St Peter's College, Oxford (MA Theol); Tyndale Hall, Bristol. Curate: Crowborough, 1959–62; Christ Church, Clifton, Bristol, 1962–64; Vicar: Christ Church, Clevedon, 1964–72; Holy Trinity, Cambridge, 1972–84; Proctor, General Synod for Ely Diocese, 1975–85; Chief Sec., Church Army, 1984–90; Residentiary Canon, Chester Cathedral and Canon Missioner, Dio. of Chester, 1990–2000; Vice-Dean, Chester Cathedral, 1993–2000; Cheshire County Ecumenical Officer, 1991–99. C of E Rep., BCC, 1983–90 (Moderator, Evangelism Cttee, 1986–90). Editor, Missionary Mandate, 1955–68. *Publication:* Celebrating the Millennium in the Local Church, 1997. *Recreations:* photography, filling waste paper baskets. *Address:* 65 Tennyson Avenue, King's Lynn, Norfolk PE30 2QJ. *T:* (01553) 691982.

REES, Prof. Teresa Lesley, PhD; Professor of Social Sciences, Cardiff University, since 2000; *b* 11 June 1949; *d* of Gordon Leslie Baggs and Vera Geddes-Ruffle; *m* 1974, Gareth Meredydd Rees; two *s*. *Educ:* Univ. of Exeter (BA Hons Sociology and Politics); PhD Wales 1993. Res. Officer, Univ. of Exeter, 1970–73; Res. Fellow, UWIST, 1973–76; Sen. Res. Asst, Mid Glamorgan CC, 1977–78; University College, Cardiff: Res. Fellow, 1976–77, 1978–88; Dir, Social Res. Unit, and Lectr in Sociology, 1988–92; Bristol University: Sen. Res. Fellow, 1993–94; Reader, 1994–95; Prof. of Labour Mkt Studies, 1995–2000. Mem., EOC, 1996–. Hon. Pres., S Wales Br., WEA, 1996–. *Publications:* (ed jtly) Youth Unemployment and State Intervention, 1982; (ed jtly) Our Sisters' Land: the changing identities of women in Wales, 1994; Women and the Labour Market, 1992; Mainstreaming Equality in the European Union, 1998; Women and Work, 1999; (jtly) Adult Guidance and the Learning Society, 2000. *Recreations:* campaigning for gender equality, watching Oscar ceremonies. *Address:* School of Social Sciences, Cardiff University, Glamorgan Building, King Edward VII Avenue, Cardiff CF10 3WT. *T:* (029) 2087 4803.

REES, Victoria Kirstyn; *see* Williams, V. K.

REES, Rev. (Vivian) John (Howard); Principal Registrar, Province of Canterbury, since 2000; *b* 21 April 1951; *s* of Herbert John Rees and Beryl Rees; *m* 1980, Dianne Elizabeth Hamilton; two *d*. *Educ:* Skinners' Sch., Tunbridge Wells; Southampton Univ. (LLB 1972); Wycliffe Hall, Oxford (MA); MPhil Leeds 1984. Admitted Solicitor, 1975; Ecclesiastical Notary; Asst Solicitor, Cooke Matheson & Co., 1975–76; Hosp. Administrator, Multan, Pakistan, 1976; ordained deacon 1979, priest 1980; Asst Curate, Moor Allerton Team Ministry, Leeds, 1979–86; Chaplain and Tutor, Sierra Leone Theol Hall, Freetown, 1982–85; with Winckworth Sherwood, 1986– (Partner, 1988–). Proctor in Convocation for Oxford, 1995–2000; Legal Advr, ACC, 1996–; Diocesan Registrar, Dio. Oxford, 1998–. Mem., Legal Adv. Commn, General Synod, 2000–. Treas., Ecclesiastical Law Soc., 1995–. *Recreations:* photography, walking, cycling, second-hand bookshops. *Address:* (office) 16 Beaumont Street, Oxford OX1 2LZ. *T:* (01865) 297200, *Fax:* (01865) 726274; (home) 36 Cumnor Hill, Oxford OX2 9HB, *T:* and *Fax:* (01865) 865875.

REES, William Howard Guest, CB 1988; Chief Veterinary Officer, State Veterinary Service, 1980–88; *b* 21 May 1928; *s* of Walter Guest Rees and Margaret Elizabeth Rees; *m* 1952, Charlotte Mollie (*née* Collins); three *s* one *d*. *Educ:* Llanelli Grammar Sch.; Royal Veterinary Coll., London (BSc). MRCVS; DVSM. Private practice, Deal, Kent, 1952–53; joined MAFF as Veterinary Officer, 1953; stationed Stafford, 1953–66; Divl Vet. Officer, Vet. Service HQ, Tolworth, 1966–69; Divl Vet. Officer, Berks, 1969–71; Dep. Regional Vet. Officer, SE Reg., 1971–73; Regional Vet. Officer, Tolworth, 1973–76, Asst Chief Vet. Officer, 1976–80. Mem., AFRC, 1980–88. FRASE 1988. Hon. FRCVS 2000. Bledisloe Award, RASE, 1988; Gold Medal, Office Internat. des Epizooties, 1994. *Recreations:* Rugby and cricket follower, golf.

REES, William Hurst; Member of Lands Tribunal, 1973–89; *b* 12 April 1917; *s* of Richard and Florence A. Rees; *m* 1941, Elizabeth Mary Wight; two *s* one *d*. *Educ:* College of Estate Management, Univ. of London (BSc (Est. Man.)). Served War, RA and RE (SO2), 1940–46; Liaison Officer, Belgian Army Engrs. Head of Valuation Dept, Coll. of Estate Management, 1948–51. Principal in Private Practice as Chartered Surveyor: City of London, Richard Ellis & Son, 1951–61; East Grinstead, Sx, Turner, Rudge & Turner, 1961–73. Gov., Coll. of Estate Management, 1965–72; Mem. Council, RICS, 1967–70; Chm. Bd of Studies in Estate Management, Univ. of London, 1970–74; Chm., Surveying Bd, CNAA, 1976–77; Hon. Mem., Rating Surveyors Assoc. Pres., BSc (Estate Management) Club, 1961–62; Chm., Exams Bd, RICS (formerly Incorporated Soc. of Valuers and Auctioneers), 1984–. Hon. RICS (Hon. FSVA 1987; FRICS). Hon. DTech Nottingham Trent, 2000. *Publications:* Modern Methods of Valuation, 1943, (jointly) 6th edn 1971; (ed) Valuations: Principles into Practice, 1980, 5th edn 2001. *Recreation:* music, mainly opera. *Address:* Brendon, Carlton Road, South Godstone, Godstone, Surrey RH9 8LD. *T:* and *Fax:* (01342) 892109.

REES, (William) Linford (Llewelyn), CBE 1978; FRCP; FRCPsych; Emeritus Professor of Psychiatry, University of London, 1980; Consulting Physician, St Bartholomew's Hospital, since 1981; *b* 24 Oct. 1914; *e s* of late Edward Parry Rees and Mary Rees, Llanelli, Carmathenshire; *m* 1940, Catherine (*d* 1993), *y d* of late David Thomas, and of Angharad Thomas, Alltwen, Glam; two *s* two *d*. *Educ:* Llanelli Grammar School; University Coll., Cardiff; Welsh Nat. Sch. of Medicine; The Maudsley Hosp.; Univ. of London. BSc 1935; MB, BCh 1938; DPM 1940; DSc London, 1978; MRCP 1942; MD 1943; FRCP 1950; FRCPsych 1971 (Pres., 1975–78); Hon. FRCPsych 1978. David Hepburn Medal and Alfred Hughes Medal in Anatomy, 1935; John Maclean Medal and Prize in Obstetrics and Gynaecology, 1937, etc. Specialist, EMS, 1942; Dep. Med. Supt, Mill Hill Emergency Hosp., 1945; Asst Physician and Postgrad. Teacher in Clinical Psychiatry, The Maudsley Hosp., 1946; Dep. Physician Supt, Whitchurch Hosp., 1947; Regional Psychiatrist for Wales and Mon, 1948; Consultant Physician, The Bethlem Royal Hosp. and The Maudsley Hosp., 1954–66; Recognised Clin. Teacher in Mental Diseases, Inst. of Psychiatry, Univ. of London, 1956–78; Lecturer in Psychol Med., St Bartholomew's Med. Coll., 1958–78; Med. Dir, Charter Clinic, London, 1980–89; Chief Psychiatrist and Exec. Med. Dir, Charter Medical, 1984–89; Dir and Med. Advr, Huntercombe Manor Hosp., and Rehabilitation Gp Ltd, 1989– (Pres., 1992–); Consultant, and Chm. Med. Adv. Cttee, Ultramind, 1996. Chm., Armed Services Consultant Adv. Bd in Psych., 1979–90; Consultant Advisor in Psychiatry to RAF; WHO Consultant to Sri Lanka, 1973; Hon. Consultant, Royal Sch. for Deaf Children. Lectures to Univs and Learned Socs in Europe, USA, Asia, Australia and S America. Examiner: Diploma Psychological Medicine, RCP, 1964–69; MRCP, RCP, RCPE and RCPGlas, 1969–; MB and DPM, Univ. of Leeds, 1969–. President: Soc. for Psychosomatic Research, 1957–58; Royal Coll. of Psychiatrists, 1975–78 (Vice-Pres., 1972–75; Chm., E Anglian Region); Section of Psychiatry, RSM, 1971–72 (Vice-Pres., 1968; Hon. Mem., 1982); BMA, 1978–79 (Fellow, 1981); Psychiatric Rehabilitation Assoc., 1995; Welsh Psychiatric Soc., 1996; Chm., Medico-Pharmaceutical Forum, 1982 (Vice-Chm., 1981). Treasurer, World Psychiatric Assoc., 1966– (Hon. Mem., 1982). Member: Clinical Psychiatry Cttee, MRC, 1959; Council, Royal Medico-Psychological Assoc. (Chm., Research and Clinical Section, 1957–63); Soc. for Study of Human Biology; Asthma Research Council; Cttee on Safety of Medicines (also Toxicity and Clinical Trials Sub-Cttee), 1971; Cttee on Review of Medicines (Chm., Psychotropic Drugs Sub-Cttee); Psychological Medicine Group, BMA, 1967. Formerly Chm., Univ. of London Teachers of Psych. Cttee; Member: Bd of Advanced Med. Studies, Univ. of London, 1966–69; Higher Degrees Cttee, Univ. of London; Acad. Council Standing Sub-Cttee in Medicine, Univ. of London; Cttee of Management, Inst. of Psychiatry, Maudsley Hosp., 1968; Council and Exec. Cttee, St Bartholomew's Hosp. Med. Coll., 1972; Jt Policy Cttee, QMC, St Bartholomew's Hosp. and London Hosp., 1973; Central Health Services Council; Standing Medical Adv. Cttee; Jt Consultants Cttee; Conference of Presidents of Royal Colls; GMC, 1980–84 (Mem., Educn Cttee, Preliminary Health Cttee and Prof. Conduct Cttee). Founder Mem., Internat. Coll. of Neuro-psychopharmacology. Hon. Mem. Learned Socs in USA, Sweden, Venezuela, East Germany, Spain and Greece. FRSocMed; Fellow: Eugenics Soc.; and Vice-Pres., Internat. Coll. of Psychosomatic Medicine, 1973; University Coll., Cardiff, 1980 (Governor, 1984–); Distinguished Fellow, Amer. Psychiatric Assoc., 1968; Hon. Fellow: Amer. Soc. of Physician Analysts; Amer. Coll. Psychiatrists; Biological Psychiatry Assoc., USA; Hong Kong Psychiatric Soc., 1982. Chm. Bd of Trustees, 1981–, Vice-Pres., 1984–, Stress Syndrome Foundn (Chm., Scientific Adv. Council). Governor: The Bethlem Royal Hosp. and The Maudsley Hosp.;

Med. Coll. of St Bartholomew's Hosp., 1980–96. President: Extend, 1976; Golden Jubilee Appeal, Welsh Nat. Sch. of Med., 1980. Co-Editor, Jl of Psychosomatic Research. Liveryman: Barber Surgeons; Apothecaries. Hon. LLD Wales, 1981. Bard of Welsh Gorsedd. *Publications:* (with Eysenck and Himmelweit) Dimensions of Personality, 1947; Short Textbook of Psychiatry, 1967; (jtly) Textbook of Psychiatry, 1997; *chapters in:* Modern Treatment in General Practice, 1947; Recent Progress in Psychiatry, 1950; Schizophrenia: Somatic Aspects, 1957; Psychoendocrinology, 1958; Recent Progress in Psychosomatic Research, 1960; Stress and Psychiatric Disorders, 1960. Papers in: Nature, BMJ, Jl of Mental Sci., Jl of Psychosomatic Research, Eugenics Review, etc. Contribs to Med. Annual, 1958–68. *Recreations:* swimming, photography, amusing grandchildren. *Address:* Penbryn, 62 Oakwood Avenue, Purley, Surrey CR8 1AQ. *Club:* Athenæum.

REES-JONES, Geoffrey Rippon, MA Oxon; Principal, King William's College, Isle of Man, 1958–79; *b* 8 July 1914; *er s* of W. Rees-Jones, BA, Ipswich; *m* 1950, Unity Margaret McConnell (*d* 1982), *d* of Major P. M. Sanders, Hampstead; one *s* one *d*. *Educ:* Ipswich School (scholar); University College, Oxford (open scholar). Assistant Master, Eastbourne College, 1936–38, Marlborough College, 1938–54 (Housemaster, C2, 1946–54); Headmaster, Bembridge School, 1954–58. Served War mainly in Commandos, 1940–45; Commandant, Commando Mountain Warfare School, 1943; Staff College, Camberley, 1944 (sc); Brigade Major, 4 Commando Bde, 1944–45 (despatches). *Recreations:* sailing, cricket, golf, fives; Oxford Rugby blue, 1933–35, Wales XV, 1934–36. *Address:* Red Lion Cottage, Braaid, Isle of Man IM4 2AJ. *T:* (01624) 851360.

REES-MOGG, family name of **Baron Rees-Mogg**.

REES-MOGG, Baron *cr* 1988 (Life Peer), of Hinton Blewitt in the County of Avon; **William Rees-Mogg,** Kt 1981; Chairman, Pickering & Chatto (Publishers) Ltd, since 1983; Director, E. F. G. Private Bank, since 1993; *b* 14 July 1928; *s* of late Edmund Fletcher Rees-Mogg and late Beatrice Rees-Mogg (*née* Warren), Temple Cloud, Somerset; *m* 1962, Gillian Shakespeare Morris, *d* of T. R. Morris; two *s* three *d*. *Educ:* Charterhouse; Balliol Coll., Oxford (Brackenbury Scholar). President, Oxford Union, 1951. Financial Times, 1952–60, Chief Leader Writer, 1955–60; Asst Editor, 1957–60; Sunday Times, City Editor, 1960–61; Political and Economic Editor, 1961–63; Deputy Editor, 1964–67; Editor, The Times, 1967–81; columnist, 1992–; Mem., Exec. Bd, Times Newspapers Ltd, 1968–81; Director: The Times Ltd, 1968–81; Times Newspapers Ltd, 1978–81. Chm., Sidgwick & Jackson, 1985–89; Dir, GEC, 1981–97. Vice-Chm., Bd of Governors, BBC, 1981–86; Chairman: Arts Council of GB, 1982–89; Broadcasting Standards Council, 1988–93; IBC plc, 1994–98. Contested (C) Chester-le-Street, Co. Durham, By-election 1956; General Election, 1959. Treasurer, Institute of Journalists, 1960–63, 1966–68, Pres., 1963–64; Vice-Chm. Cons. Party's Nat. Advisory Cttee on Political Education, 1961–63. Pres., English Assoc., 1983–84. Mem., Internat. Cttee, Pontifical Council for Culture, 1983–87. Vis. Fellow, Nuffield Coll., Oxford, 1968–72. High Sheriff, Somerset, 1978. Hon. LLD Bath, 1977. *Publications:* The Reigning Error: the crisis of world inflation, 1974; An Humbler Heaven, 1977; How to Buy Rare Books, 1985; Picnics on Vesuvius: steps toward the millenium, 1992; (with James Dale Davidson): Blood in the Streets, 1988; The Great Reckoning, 1991; The Sovereign Individual, 1997. *Recreation:* collecting. *Address:* 17 Pall Mall, SW1Y 5NB. *Club:* Garrick.

REES-WILLIAMS, family name of **Baron Ogmore**.

REES-WILLIAMS, Jonathan, FRCO; Organist and Master of the Choristers, St George's Chapel, Windsor Castle, since 1991; *b* 10 Feb. 1949; *s* of Ivor and Barbara Rees-Williams; *m* 1985, Helen Patricia Harling; one *s* two *d*. *Educ:* Kilburn Grammar Sch.; Royal Academy of Music; New Coll., Oxford (Organ Scholar; MA 1972). LRAM, DipRAM 1969; ARAM 1984; FRCO 1968. Organist: St Edmund, Yeading, 1967; Church of the Ascension, Wembley, 1968; Actg Organist, New Coll., Oxford, 1972; Assistant Organist: Hampstead Parish Church and St Clement Danes, 1972–74; Salisbury Cathedral, 1974–78; Dir of Music, Salisbury Cathedral Sch., 1974–78; Organist and Master of Choristers, Lichfield Cathedral, 1978–91; Conductor, Lichfield Cathedral Special Choir, 1978–91. Chorusmaster, Portsmouth Festival Choir, 1974–78; Accompanist and Asst Dir, Salisbury Musical Soc., 1974–78. *Recreations:* cycling, wine, railways, vintage model railways. *Address:* 25 The Cloisters, Windsor Castle, Windsor, Berks SL4 1NJ. *T:* (01753) 848797; *e-mail:* Jonathan.Reeswilliams@stgeorges-windsor.org.

REESE, Prof. Colin Bernard, PhD, ScD; FRS 1981; FRSC; Professor of Organic Chemistry, King's College, University of London, since 1999 (Daniell Professor of Chemistry, 1973–98); *b* 29 July 1930; *s* of Joseph and Emily Reese; *m* 1968, Susanne Bird; one *s* one *d*. *Educ:* Dartington Hall Sch.; Clare Coll., Cambridge (BA 1953, PhD 1956, MA 1957, ScD 1972). 1851 Sen. Student, 1956–58; Research Fellow: Clare Coll., Cambridge, 1956–59; Harvard Univ., 1957–58; Official Fellow and Dir of Studies in Chem., Clare Coll., 1959–73; Cambridge University: Univ. Demonstrator in Chem., 1959–63; Asst Dir of Res., 1963–64; Univ. Lectr in Chem., 1964–73. FKC 1989. *Publications:* scientific papers, mainly in chemical jls. *Address:* Department of Chemistry, King's College London, Strand, WC2R 2LS. *T:* (020) 7848 2260.

REESE, Colin Edward; QC 1987; FCIArb; a Recorder, since 1994; Deputy Judge, Technology and Construction Court (formerly Deputy Official Referee), High Court, since 1994; *b* 28 March 1950; *s* of late Robert Edward Reese and Katharine Reese (*née* Moore); *m* 1978, Diana Janet Anderson; two *s* one *d*. *Educ:* Hawarden Grammar School; King Edward VI School, Southampton; Fitzwilliam College, Cambridge (BA 1972; MA 1976). Called to the Bar, Gray's Inn, 1973 (Mould Schol., 1974; Bencher, 1998); admitted, *ad eund.*, Lincoln's Inn, 1976; in practice, 1975–. An Asst Parly Boundary Comr, 1992–. Pres., Mental Health Review Tribunals, 2000–. Vice Chm., 1997–2000, Chm., 2000–, Technol. and Construction (formerly Official Referees) Bar Assoc. Pres., Cambridge Univ. Law Soc., 1971–72. Liveryman, Bakers' Co., 1991–. *Address:* 1 Atkin Building, Gray's Inn, WC1R 5AT. *T:* (020) 7404 0102.

REEVE, Sir Anthony, KCMG 1992 (CMG 1986); KCVO 1995; HM Diplomatic Service, retired; High Commissioner (formerly Ambassador) to South Africa, 1991–96; *b* 20 Oct. 1938; *s* of Sidney Reeve and Dorothy (*née* Mitchell); *m* 1st, 1964, Pamela Margaret Angus (marr. diss. 1988); one *s* two *d*; 2nd, 1997, Susan Doull (*née* Collins), Durban, S Africa. *Educ:* Queen Elizabeth Grammar Sch., Wakefield; Marling Sch., Stroud; Merton Coll., Oxford (MA). Lever Brothers & Associates, 1962–65; joined HM Diplomatic Service, 1965; Middle East Centre for Arab Studies, 1966–68; Asst Political Agent, Abu Dhabi, 1968–70; First Secretary, FCO, 1970–73; First Sec., later Counsellor, Washington, 1973–78; Head of Arms Control and Disarmament Dept, FCO, 1979–81; Counsellor, Cairo, 1981–84; Head of Southern Africa Dept, FCO, 1984–86; Asst Under Sec. of State (Africa), FCO, 1986–87; Ambassador to Jordan, 1988–91. Dir, Barclays Private Bank Ltd, 1997–2001; Dep. Chm., Union-Castle Travel, 1998–. *Recreations:* golf, music. *Address:* Box Cottage, Horsley, Stroud, Glos GL6 0QB. *Clubs:* Oxford and Cambridge; Leander (Henley-on-Thames); Minchinhampton Golf.

REEVE, Derek Charles; Director of Finance and Information Systems, Deputy Town Clerk and Deputy Chief Executive, Royal Borough of Kensington and Chelsea, since 1991; *b* 7 Dec. 1946; *s* of Charles Reeve and Sylvia Reeve (*née* Prynne); *m* 1968, Janice Rosina Williamson; one *s* one *d*. *Educ:* Dame Alice Owen's Grammar Sch. for Boys, Islington; Tottenham and E Ham Tech. Colls. Various posts, Islington LBC, 1965–74; Asst Borough Treas., Greenwich LBC, 1974–79; Dep. Dir of Finance, RBK&C, 1979–91. Pres., Soc. of London Treasurers, 2000–2001. *Recreations:* golf, painting (watercolours), reading, gardening, music, following Arsenal FC. *Address:* The Town Hall, Hornton Street, W8 7NX. *T:* (020) 7361 2384. *Clubs:* The Warren (Pres.); Birchwood Park Golf (Wilmington).

REEVE, James Ernest, CMG 1982; HM Diplomatic Service, retired; international management consultant, since 1992; *b* 8 June 1926; *s* of Ernest and Anthea Reeve; *m* 1947, Lillian Irene Watkins; one *s* one *d*. *Educ:* Bishop's Stortford Coll. Vice-Consul, Ahwaz and Khorramshahr, Iran, 1949–51; UN General Assembly, Paris, 1951; Asst Private Sec. to Rt Hon. Selwyn Lloyd, Foreign Office, 1951–53; 2nd Secretary: Brit. Embassy, Washington, 1953–57; Brit. Embassy, Bangkok, 1957–59; FO, 1959–61; HM Consul, Frankfurt, 1961–65; 1st Secretary: Brit. Embassy in Libya, 1965–69; Brit. Embassy, Budapest, 1970–72; Chargé d'Affaires, Budapest, 1972; Counsellor (Commercial), East Berlin, 1973–75; Consul-Gen., Zurich and Principality of Liechtenstein, 1975–80; HM Minister and Consul-Gen., Milan, 1980–83. Secretariat, Internat. Primary Aluminium Inst., London, 1985–93. Dir, Sprester Investments Ltd, 1986–91. *Publication:* Cocktails, Crises and Cockroaches: a diplomatic trail. *Recreations:* theatre, tennis, travel. *Address:* 46c Montpellier Spa Road, Cheltenham, Glos GL50 1UL. *T:* and *Fax:* (01242) 578033; 5 Andalucia Garden Club, Calle Las Azaleas, Nueva Andalucia, Marbella, Spain. *T:* and *Fax:* (952) 818026. *Clubs:* New (1874), East Gloucestershire (Cheltenham).

REEVE, John; Executive Chairman, Willis (formerly Willis Corroon) Group Ltd, 1995–2000; *b* 13 July 1944; *s* of Clifford Alfred Reeve and Irene Mary Turnidge Reeve; *m* 1974, Sally Diane Welton; one *d*. *Educ:* Westcliff High School (Grammar). FCA; CIMgt. Selbey Smith & Earle, 1962–67; Peat Marwick McLintock, 1967–68; Vickers, Roneo Vickers Group, 1968–76; Wilkinson Match, 1976–77; Amalgamated Metal Corp., 1977–80; Group Finance Director: British Aluminium Co., 1980–83; Mercantile House Holdings, 1983–87; Dep. Man. Dir, 1988, Man. Dir, 1989, Sun Life Assurance Society plc; Gp Man. Dir, 1990–95, non-exec. Dir, 1995–96, Sun Life Corp. plc. Director: The English Concert, 1987– (Chm., 1993–); HMC Group plc, 1988–94; Temple Bar Investment Trust PLC, 1992–; London First, 1998–. Pres., Inst. of Business Ethics, 1997–2000 (Mem. Adv. Council, 1986–91; Dep. Pres., 1991–96). Chm., E London Business Alliance, 2000–; Member: E London Partnership Bd, 1991–2000 (Chm., 1996–2000); Council, BITC, 1995–2000; Life Insce Council, 1991–94; Bd, ABI, 1993–95; Bd, 1993–, Exec. Cttee, 1996–, Internat. Insurance Soc. Inc. Governor: Res. into Ageing, 1991–96; NIESR, 1995–2000. FRSA 1999. *Recreations:* yachting, music, theatre. *Address:* Cliff Dene, 24 Cliff Parade, Leigh-on-Sea, Essex SS9 1BB. *T:* (01702) 477563, *Fax:* (01702) 479092; *e-mail:* reevej@compuserve.com. *Clubs:* Athenæum; Essex Yacht.

REEVE, Rear Adm. Jonathon, CEng; Deputy Chief Executive, Warship Support Agency, and Member, Navy Board, since 2001; *b* 1 Oct. 1949; *e s* of late Lawrence Alick Reeve and of Joan Reeve; *m* 1980, Jennifer Anne, *d* of Guy and Betty Wickman; one *s* one *d*. *Educ:* Marlborough Coll.; St Catharine's Coll., Cambridge (MA 1972). CEng, MIEE 1978, FIEE 2000. Joined Royal Navy, 1967: qualified submarines, 1974; HMS Renown, 1974–76; HMS Dreadnought, 1979–82; RNSC, 1982; Naval Sec.'s Dept, MoD, 1982–84; Strategic Systems Exec., 1985–88; Naval Manpower Trng, 1989–91; Capt. 1991; Asst Dir, MoD Defence Systems, 1991–93; Head of Integrated Logistics Support (Navy), Ship Support Agency, MoD, 1994–96; rcds 1997; Cdre 1998; Naval Base Comdr, Devonport, 1998–2000; COS (Corporate Develt) to C-in-C Fleet, 2000. *Recreations:* golf, tennis, gardening. *Address:* c/o Naval Secretary, Victory Building, HM Naval Base, Portsmouth, Hants PO1 3LS. *Club:* Army and Navy.

REEVE, Prof. Michael David, FBA 1984; Kennedy Professor of Latin, and Fellow of Pembroke College, University of Cambridge, since 1984; *b* 11 Jan. 1943; *s* of Arthur Reeve and Edith Mary Barrett; *m* 1970, Elizabeth Klingaman (marr. diss. 1999); two *s* one *d*. *Educ:* King Edward's Sch., Birmingham; Balliol Coll., Oxford (MA). Harmsworth Senior Scholar, Merton Coll., Oxford, 1964–65; Woodhouse Research Fellow, St John's Coll., Oxford, 1965–66; Tutorial Fellow, Exeter Coll., Oxford, 1966–84, now Emeritus Fellow. Visiting Professor: Univ. of Hamburg, 1976; McMaster Univ., 1979; Univ. of Toronto, 1982–83. Fellow, Società Internazionale per lo Studio del Medioevo Latino, 1996; Corresp. Mem., Akademie der Wissenschaften, Göttingen, 1990; For. Mem., Istituto Lombardo, Milan, 1993. Editor, Classical Quarterly, 1981–86. *Publications:* Longus, Daphnis and Chloe, 1982; contribs to Texts and Transmission, ed L. D. Reynolds, 1983; Cicero, Pro Quinctio, 1992; articles in European and transatlantic jls. *Recreations:* chess, music, gardening, mountain walking. *Address:* Pembroke College, Cambridge CB2 1RF.

REEVE, Robin Martin, MA; Head Master, King's College School, Wimbledon, 1980–97; *b* 22 Nov. 1934; *s* of Percy Martin Reeve and Cicely Nora Parker; *m* 1959, Brianne Ruth Hall; one *s* two *d*. *Educ:* Hampton Sch.; Gonville and Caius Coll., Cambridge (Foundation Schol.; BA cl. 1 Hist. Tripos, 1957; MA). Asst Master, King's Coll. Sch., Wimbledon, 1958–62; Head of History Dept, 1962–80, and Dir of Studies, 1975–80, Lancing Coll. Member: CATE, 1993–94; ISC (formerly ISJC), 1991–99; Council, Brighton Coll., 1997–99; Council, Lancing Coll., 1997– (Chm., 1999–). *Publication:* The Industrial Revolution 1750–1850, 1971. *Recreations:* English history and architecture, gardening. *Address:* The Old Rectory, Coombes, Lancing, W Sussex BN15 0RS. *Club:* Athenæum.

REEVE, Roy Stephen, CMG 1998; HM Diplomatic Service, retired; Ambassador of the Organisation for Security and Co-operation in Europe to Armenia, since 1999; *b* 20 Aug. 1941; *s* of Ernest Arthur Reeve and Joan Elizabeth (*née* Thomas); *m* 1964, Gill Lee; two *d*. *Educ:* Dulwich Coll.; LSE (BSc Econs 1965; MSc 1966). Joined FCO, 1966; Moscow, 1968–71; First Secretary: FCO, 1973–78; (Commercial) Moscow, 1978–80; Counsellor on loan to Home Civil Service, 1983–85; Dep. Consul-General, Johannesburg, 1985–88; Hd, Commercial Management and Export Dept, FCO, 1988–91; Consul-Gen., Sydney, 1991–95; Ambassador to Ukraine, 1995–99. Hon. Sen. Res. Fellow, Centre for Russian and E European Studies, Univ. of Birmingham. *Recreations:* Rugby Union, scuba diving.

REEVES, Christopher Reginald; Senior Adviser, Merrill Lynch Holdings Ltd, since 2000; *b* 14 Jan. 1936; *s* of Reginald and Dora Reeves; *m* 1965, Stella, *d* of Patrick and Maria Whinney; three *s*. *Educ:* Malvern College. National Service, Rifle Bde, 1955–57. Bank of England, 1958–63; Hill Samuel & Co. Ltd, 1963–67; joined Morgan Grenfell & Co. Ltd, 1968; Dir, 1970; Gp Chief Exec., 1980–87, and Dep. Chm., 1984–87, Morgan Grenfell Gp; Jt Chm., Morgan Grenfell & Co., 1984–87; Sen. Advr to Pres., Merrill Lynch, 1988–89; Vice Chm., Merrill Lynch Internat., 1989–93; Chm., Merrill Lynch Europe and Merrill Lynch International, 1993–98; Senior Adviser: Office of Dep. Chm.,

1998–99, Office of Chm., 1999–2000, Merrill Lynch Inc.; Merrill Lynch Internat., 1999–2000. Director: London Board, Westpac Banking Corp. (formerly Commercial Bank of Australia Ltd) 1972–90 (Chm., 1976–82, Dep. Chm., 1982–89); Midland and International Banks Ltd, 1976–83; Balfour Beatty (formerly BICC), 1982–; Andrew Weir & Co., 1982–92; Cornhill Insurance PLC (formerly Allianz Internat. Insurance Co. Ltd), 1983–; Oman Internat. Bank, 1984–2001; International Freehold Properties SARL, 1988–96; Smith Borkum Hare Pty Ltd, 1996–99; DSP Financial Consultants Ltd, 1995–; MGM Assurance, 1999– (Chm., 2000–). Chm., Mercury Energy Fund, 1998–. Dir, Exec. Cttee, Amer. Chamber of Commerce (UK), 1992–. Member: BESO, 1994–; Adv. Panel, City University Business Sch., 1972–81 (Chm., 1979–81); Council, City Univ. Business Sch., 1986–93; Council, Inst. for Fiscal Studies, 1982–87; Council, CBI, 1998–; Treas., Council, City Univ., 1992–; Governor: Stowe Sch., 1976–81; Dulwich College Prep. Sch., 1977–96; Mermaid Theatre Trust, 1981–85; Trustee, Chichester Fest. Theatre Trust, 1992–. Hon. DSc City, 2000. *Recreations:* sailing, shooting, ski-ing. *Address:* (office) Ropemaker Place, 25 Ropemaker Street, EC2Y 9LY. *Clubs:* Boodle's; Royal Southern Yacht (Southampton).

REEVES, Dr Colin Leslie, CBE 1999; Director, Accountancy Foundation Review Board, since 2001; *b* 4 April 1949; *s* of Leslie and Isabelle Reeves; *m* 1978, Christine Lloyd; two *d*. *Educ:* Birkenhead Sch.; Clare Coll., Cambridge (BA 1970; MA); UCNW, Bangor (MSc 1971; PhD 1973); DBA Cornell Univ. 1990. CPFA (IPFA 1976). Lectr, UCNW, Bangor, 1971–73; Accountancy and Audit Assistant, Warrington County Borough, 1973–75; Asst Treas., Ellesmere Port and Neston BC, 1975–80; Deputy Director of Finance: Stratford-on-Avon DC, 1980–84; NW Thames RHA, 1984–85; Director of Finance: Paddington and N Kensington DHA, 1985–86; NW Thames RHA, 1986–94; Dir of Finance and Performance, NHS Exec., 1994–2001. Member: Adv. Cttee on Mentally Disordered Offenders, 1993–94; Culyer Cttee on R&D, 1993–94; NHS Steering Gps on Capitation and on Capital, 1993–94; Chancellor of Exchequer's Pvte Finance Panel, 1994–95; CMO's Nat. Screening Cttee, 1996–2001. Mem. Bd, Accountancy NTO, 1999–. *Publications:* The Applicability of the Monetary Base Hypothesis to the UK, the USA, France and West Germany, 1974; contrib. professional jls. *Recreations:* sport, especially cricket and golf, history of Test Match cricket, hockey (former regl internat. and county player). *Address:* Hillcrest, 82 Wallingford Road, Goring-on-Thames, Oxon RG8 0HN. *T:* (01491) 872166. *Clubs:* Royal Automobile, MCC; Goring and Streatley Golf; Henley-on-Thames Rugby Football.

REEVES, Rev. Donald St John; Rector, St James's Church, Piccadilly, 1980–98; *b* 18 May 1934; *s* of Henry and Barbara Reeves. *Educ:* Sherborne; Queens' Coll., Cambridge (BA Hons 1957); Cuddesdon Theol Coll. 2nd Lieut, Royal Sussex Regt, 1952–54. Lectr, British Council, Beirut, 1957–60; Tutor, Brasted Theol Coll., 1960–61; Cuddesdon Theol Coll., 1961–63; deacon, 1963, priest, 1964; Curate, All Saints, Maidstone, 1963–65; Chaplain to Bishop of Southwark, 1965–68; Vicar of St Peter's, Morden, 1969–80. Mem., Gen. Synod of C of E, 1990–94. Dir, The Soul of Europe Project, 1999–. *Publications:* (ed) Church and State, 1984; For God's Sake, 1988; Making Sense of Religion, 1989; Down to Earth: a new vision, 1995. *Recreations:* playing the organ, bee-keeping, watching TV soap operas. *Address:* The Coach House, Church Street, Crediton EX17 2AQ. *T:* (01363) 775100, *Fax:* (01363) 773911.

REEVES, Gordon; *see* Reeves, W. G.

REEVES, Dame Helen May, DBE 1999 (OBE 1986); Chief Executive (formerly Director), National Association of Victim Support Schemes, since 1980; *b* 22 Aug. 1945; *d* of Leslie Percival William Reeves and Helen Edith Reeves (*née* Brown). *Educ:* Dartford Grammar School for Girls; Nottingham University (BA Hons Social Admin. 1966). Probation Officer, Inner London Probation Service, 1967–79 (Senior Probation Officer, 1975–79). Member: Nat. Bd for Crime Prevention, 1993–95; Govt Working Gp on Vulnerable and Intimidated Witnesses, 1998–99; Home Office Steering Gp on Review of Sexual Offences, 1999; EC Cttee of Experts on Victims of Crime, 1998–99. Vice Pres., World Soc. of Victimology, 1994–; Sec., Eur. Forum for Victim Services, 1994–. Trustee, Kidscape, 1993–97. Hon. MA Nottingham, 1998. *Recreations:* social and local history and architecture, food, gardens. *Address:* Cranmer House, 39 Brixton Road, SW9 6DZ. *T:* (020) 7735 9166.

REEVES, Marjorie Ethel, CBE 1996; MA (Oxon), PhD (London), DLitt (Oxon); FRHistS; FBA 1974; Vice-Principal, St Anne's College, Oxford, 1951–62, 1964–67; *b* 17 July 1905; *d* of Robert J. W. Reeves and Edith Saffery Whitaker. *Educ:* The High School for Girls, Trowbridge, Wilts; St Hugh's Coll., Oxford; Westfield Coll., London. Asst Mistress, Roan School, Greenwich, 1927–29; Research Fellow, Westfield Coll., London, 1929–31; Lecturer, St Gabriel's Trng Coll., London, 1931–38; Tutor, later Fellow of St Anne's College, 1938–72, Hon. Fellow, 1973. Member: Central Advisory Council, Min. of Educn, 1947–61; Academic Planning Bd, Univ. of Kent; Academic Advisory Cttee, University of Surrey; formerly Member: Educn Council, ITA; British Council of Churches; School Broadcasting Council. Corresp. Fellow, Medieval Acad. of America, 1979. Hon. DLitt: Bath, 1992; London, 1998. Medlicott Medal, Historical Assoc., 1993. Hon. citizenship, Commune of S. Giovanni, Fiore, 1994. *Publications:* Growing Up in a Modern Society, 1946; (ed, with L. Tondelli, B. Hirsch-Reich) Il Libro delle Figure dell'Abate Gioachino da Fiore, 1953; Three Questions in Higher Education (Hazen Foundation, USA), 1955; Moral Education in a Changing Society (ed W. Niblett), 1963; ed, Eighteen Plus: Unity and Diversity in Higher Education, 1965; The Influence of Prophecy in the later Middle Ages: a study in Joachimism, 1969; Higher Education: demand and response (ed W. R. Niblett), 1969; (with B. Hirsch-Reich) The Figurae of Joachim of Fiore, 1972; Joachim of Fiore and the Prophetic Future, 1976; Sheep Bell and Ploughshare, 1978; Why History, 1980; (with W. Gould) Joachim of Fiore and the Myth of the Eternal Evangel in the Nineteenth Century, 1987; Competence, Delight and the Common Good: reflections on the crisis in higher education, 1988; (with J. Morrison) The Diaries of Jeffery Whitaker, 1989; (ed) Prophetic Rome in the High Renaissance Period, 1992; Pursuing the Muses, 1998; (ed) Christian Thinking and Social Order, 1999; (with Jenyth Worsley) Favourite Hymns: 2000 years of Magnificat, 2000; Then and There Series: The Medieval Town, 1954, The Medieval Village, 1954, Elizabethan Court, 1956, The Medieval Monastery, 1957, The Norman Conquest, 1958, Alfred and the Danes, 1959; The Medieval Castle, 1960, Elizabethan Citizen, 1961; A Medieval King Governs, 1971; Explorers of the Elizabethan Age, 1977; Elizabethan Country House, 1984; The Spanish Armada, 1988; contributions on history in Speculum, Medieval and Renaissance Studies, Traditio, Sophia, Recherches de Théologie, etc, and on education in Times Educational Supplement, New Era, etc. *Recreations:* music, gardening, bird-watching. *Address:* 38 Norham Road, Oxford OX2 6SQ. *T:* (01865) 557039. *Club:* University Women's.

REEVES, Prof. Nigel Barrie Reginald, OBE 1987; DPhil; FIL; Pro-Vice-Chancellor for External Relations, Aston University, since 1996; *b* 9 Nov. 1939; *s* of Reginald Arthur Reeves and Marjorie Joyce Reeves; *m* 1982, Minou (*née* Samimi); one *s* one *d*. *Educ:* Merchant Taylors' Sch.; Worcester Coll., Oxford (MA); St John's Coll., Oxford (DPhil 1970). FIL 1981. Lectr in English, Univ. of Lund, Sweden, 1964–66; Lectr in German, Univ. of Reading, 1968–74; Alexander von Humboldt Fellow, Univ. of Tübingen, 1974–75; University of Surrey: Prof. of German, 1975–90; Hd of Dept of Linguistic and Internat. Studies, 1979–90; Dean, Faculty of Human Studies, 1986–90; Prof. of German and Head of Dept of Modern Langs, Aston Univ., 1990–96. Guest Prof. of German, Royal Holloway Coll., London Univ., 1976; Vis. Prof., European Business Sch., 1981–88; Sen. Alexander von Humboldt Fellow, Univ. of Hamburg, 1986; UK Short-term Visitor to Japan, Japan Foundn, 1997. Chm., Nat. Congress on Langs in Educn, 1986–90; President: Nat. Assoc. of Language Advisers, 1986–91; Assoc. of Teachers of German, 1988–89; Vice-President: Conf. of University Teachers of German, 1995–97 (Vice-Chm., 1988–91); Inst. of Linguists, 1990– (Chm. Council, 1985–88); Convenor, British Inst. of Traffic Educn Res., 2001–; Member: Academic Adv. Council, Linguaphone Inst., 1991–; Modern Langs Steering Cttee, Open Univ., 1991–96; Academic Adv. Council, Univ. of Buckingham, 1994–; Bd, British Trng Internat., 1998–2001; SHEFC, 2000–; Irish Res. Council for Humanities and Social Scis, 2001–. Gov., Germanic Inst., Univ. of London, 1989–94; Chm. Governors, Matthew Boulton Further and Higher Educn Corp., Birmingham, 1999–. FRSA 1986; CIEx 1987. Goethe Medal, Goethe Inst., Munich, 1989; Medal, European Foundn for Quality Management, 1996. Officer's Cross, Order of Merit (Germany), 1999. *Publications:* Merkantil-Tekniska Stilar, 2 Vols, 1965–66; Heinrich Heine: poetry and politics, 1974; (with K. Dewhurst) Friedrich Schiller: medicine, psychology and literature, 1978; (with D. Liston) Business Studies, Languages and Overseas Trade, 1985; (jtly) Making Your Mark: effective business communication in Germany, 1988; (with D. Liston) The Invisible Economy: a profile of Britain's invisible exports, 1988; (jtly) Franc Exchange, effective business communication in France, 1991; (jtly) Spanish Venture, basic business communication in Spain, 1992; (with C. Wright) Linguistic Auditing, 1996; (ed) The German Business Environment, 1997; over 80 articles in learned jls on language, language educn, literature and overseas trade. *Recreations:* gardening, walking. *Address:* Aston University, Aston Triangle, Birmingham B4 7ET.

REEVES, Rt Rev. Sir Paul Alfred, GCMG 1985; GCVO 1986; QSO 1990; Kt 1985; Chair, Fijian Constitutional Review Commission, 1995–96; Visiting Professor, Auckland University of Technology, since 2000; *b* 6 Dec. 1932; 2nd *s* of D'Arcy Lionel and Hilda Mary Reeves; *m* 1959, Beverley Gwendolen Watkins; three *d*. *Educ:* Wellington Coll., New Zealand; Victoria Univ. of Wellington (MA); St John's Theol. Coll., Auckland (LTh); St Peter's Coll., Univ. of Oxford (MA; Hon. Fellow, 1980). Deacon, 1958; Priest, 1960; Curate: Tokoroa, NZ, 1958–59; St Mary the Virgin, Oxford, 1959–61; Kirkley St Peter, Lowestoft, 1961–63; Vicar, St Paul, Okato, NZ, 1964–66; Lectr in Church History, St John's Coll., Auckland, NZ, 1966–69; Dir of Christian Educn, Dio. Auckland, 1969–71; Bishop of Waiapu, 1971–79; Bishop of Auckland, 1979–85; Primate and Archbishop of New Zealand, 1980–85; Governor-General, NZ, 1985–90; Anglican Observer at UN, and Assisting Bishop, Episcopal Dio. of NY, 1991–93; Dean, Te Rau Kahikatea Theol Coll., Auckland, 1994–95. Chm., Environmental Council, 1974–76. Dep. Leader, Commonwealth Observers, S African elections, 1994; Leader, Commonwealth Observers, Ghanaian elections, 1996. Vis. Prof., Univ. of Auckland, 1997–2000. KStJ 1986. Hon. DCL Oxford, 1985; Hon LLD Wellington, 1989; Hon. DD: Gen. Theol Seminary, NY, 1992; Church Divinity Sch. of Pacific, San Francisco, 1994; Hon. Dr Edinburgh, 1994. Hon. CF (Fiji), 1999. *Recreations:* jogging, sailing, swimming. *Address:* 16E Cathedral Place, Parnell, Auckland, New Zealand.

REEVES, Philip Thomas Langford, RE 1964; RSA 1976 (ARSA 1971); artist in etching and other mediums; Senior Lecturer, Glasgow School of Art, 1973–91; President, Royal Scottish Society of Painters in Water Colours, since 1998; *b* 7 July 1931; *s* of Herbert Reeves and Lilian; *m* 1964, Christine MacLaren (*d* 1994); one *d*. *Educ:* Naunton Park Sch., Cheltenham. Student, Cheltenham Sch. of Art, 1947–49. Army service, 4th/7th Royal Dragoon Guards, Middle East, 1949–51. RCA, 1951–54 (ARCA 1st Cl.); Lectr, Glasgow Sch. of Art, 1954–73. Associate, Royal Soc. of Painter Etchers, 1954; RSW 1962; RGI 1981. Works in permanent collections: Arts Council; V&A; Gall. of Modern Art, Edinburgh; Glasgow Art Gall.; Glasgow Univ. Print Collection; Hunterian Art Gall., Glasgow; Manchester City Art Gall.; Royal Scottish Acad.; Aberdeen Art Gall.; Paisley Art Gall.; Inverness Art Gall.; Milngavie Art Gall.; Dept of the Environment; Dundee Art Gall.; Scottish Develt Agency; Stirling and Strathclyde Univs; Contemporary Art Soc. *Recreation:* walking. *Address:* 13 Hamilton Drive, Glasgow G12 8DN. *Club:* Traverse (Edinburgh).

REEVES, William Desmond, CB 1993; Secretary, UK Management Board, PricewaterhouseCoopers, since 1998; *b* 26 May 1937; *s* of late Thomas Norman and Anne Reeves; *m* 1967, Aase Birte Christensen; two *d*. *Educ:* Darwen Grammar Sch.; King's Coll., Cambridge (BA Hist.). National service, RAEC, 1959–61. Joined Admiralty as Asst Principal, 1961; MoD, 1964; Asst Sec., 1973; seconded to Pay Board, 1973–74; Asst Under Sec. of State, Air, MoD (PE), 1982–84, Resources and Progs, MoD, 1984, Systems, Office of Management and Budget, MoD, 1985–88; Under Sec., Cabinet Office, 1989–92; Asst Under Sec. of State (Commitments), MoD, 1992–94. Partnership Sec., Coopers & Lybrand, 1994–98. *Recreation:* horse racing. *Address:* PricewaterhouseCoopers, 1 Embankment Place, WC2N 6RH.

REEVES, Prof. (William) Gordon, FRCP, FRCPath; Professor and Head of Department of Microbiology and Immunology, College of Medicine, Sultan Qaboos University, Muscat, Oman, 1993–98; *b* 9 July 1938; *s* of Rev. W. H. and Mrs E. L. Reeves; *m* 1970, Elizabeth Susan, *d* of Surg.-Comdr L. A. and Mrs P. Moules; one *s* one *d*. *Educ:* Perse Sch., Cambridge; Guy's Hosp. Med. Sch. (BSc, MB BS). MRCS, LRCP 1964; MRCP 1966; FRCP 1978; FRCPath 1985. Editor, Guy's Hosp. Gazette, 1962–63. HO and Med. Registrar appts at Guy's, Central Middx, Brompton, National, Middx, and University Coll. Hosps, 1964–68; Lecturer: Clinical Pharmacology, Guy's Hosp. Med. Sch., 1968–71; Immunology and Medicine, Royal Postgrad. Med. Sch., 1971–73; Consultant Immunologist, Nottingham HA, 1973–88; Nottingham University: Sen. Lectr, 1975–85; Prof. of Immunology, 1985–88; Editor, The Lancet, 1989–90; Med. Editor and Consultant, Communicable Disease Surveillance Centre, PHLS, 1991–93. Vis. Prof. in Immunology of Infectious Disease, St Mary's Hosp. Med. Sch., 1992–97. *Publications:* (with E. J. Holborow) Immunology in Medicine: a comprehensive guide to clinical immunology, 1977, 2nd edn 1983; Lecture Notes on Immunology, 1987, 4th edn 2000; contribs to med. and scientific books and jls on medicine, immunology and infectious diseases. *Recreations:* the English countryside, la vie française.

REFFELL, Adm. Sir Derek (Roy), KCB 1984; Governor and Commander-in-Chief, Gibraltar, 1989–93; *b* 6 Oct. 1928; *s* of late Edward (Roy) and Murielle Reffell; *m* 1956, Janne Gronow Davis; one *s* one *d*. *Educ:* Culford Sch., Suffolk; Royal Naval Coll., Dartmouth. Various ships at Home, Mediterranean, West Indies and Far East, 1946–63; qualified Navigating Officer, 1954; Comdr 1963; Comd HMS Sirius, 1966–67; Comdr BRNC Dartmouth, 1968–69; Captain 1970; Naval Staff, 1971–74; Comd HMS Hermes, 1974–76; Director Naval Warfare, 1976–78; Commodore Amphibious Warfare, 1978–79; Asst Chief of Naval Staff (Policy), 1979–82; Flag Officer Third Flotilla and

Comdr Anti-Submarine Group Two, 1982–83; Flag Officer, Naval Air Comd, 1983–84; Controller of the Navy, 1984–89, retd. Governor, Royal Sch., Hindhead, 1995–98. Trustee, Special Olympics UK, 1998–. Chm., Friends of Gibraltar Heritage Soc., 1994–. Master, Coachmakers' Company, 1998–99. KStJ 1989. *Recreations:* golf, painting.

REFSHAUGE, Maj.-Gen. Sir William (Dudley), AC 1980; Kt 1966; CBE 1959 (OBE 1944); ED 1965; Secretary-General, World Medical Association, 1973–76; Hon. Consultant to Australian Foundation on Alcoholism and Drugs of Dependence, since 1979; *b* 3 April 1913; *s* of late F. C. Refshauge, Melbourne; *m* 1942, Helen Elizabeth, *d* of late R. E. Allwright, Tasmania; four *s* one *d*. *Educ:* Hampton High Sch.; Scotch Coll., Melbourne; Melbourne University. MB, BS (Melbourne) 1938; FRCOG 1961; FRACS 1962; FRACP 1963; Hon. FRSH 1967; FACMA 1967; FRACOG 1978. Served with AIF, 1939–46; Lt-Col, RAAMC (despatches four times). Medical Supt, Royal Women's Hosp., Melbourne, 1948–51; Col, and Dep. DGAMS, Aust., 1951–55; Maj.-Gen., and DGAMS, Aust., 1955–60; QHP, 1955–64. Commonwealth Dir-Gen. of Health, Australia, 1960–73. Chairman: Council, Aust. Coll. of Nursing, 1958–60 (Chm. Educn Cttee, 1951–58); Nat. Health and MRC, 1960–73; Nat. Fitness Council, 1960–73; Nat. Tuberculosis Adv. Council, 1960–73; Prog. and Budget Cttee, 15th World Health Assembly, 1962; Admin., Fin. and Legal Cttee 19th World Health Assembly (Pres., 24th Assembly, 1971); Exec. Bd, WHO, 1969–70 (Mem., 1967–70). Member: Council, Aust. Red Cross Soc., 1954–60; Mem. Nat. Blood Transfusion Cttee, ARCS 1955–60; Nat. Trustee, Returned Services League Aust., 1961–73, 1976–; Mem. Bd of Management, Canberra Grammar Sch., 1963–68; Mem. Bd of Trustees, Walter and Eliza Hall Inst. of Med. Res., Melbourne, 1977–86 (Chm., Ethics Cttee, 1983–88); Chm., Governing Bd, Menzies Sch. of Health Research, Darwin, 1983–87. Chm., ACT Cttee, Mem., Nat. Cttee and Mem. Nat. Exec., Sir Robert Menzies Foundn, 1979–84; Chm., Australian-Hellenic Meml Cttee, 1986–88. Hon. Life Mem., Australian Dental Assoc., 1966. Patron: Australian Sports Medicine Assoc., 1971–; ACT Br., Aust. Sports Medicine Fedn, 1980–; Totally and Permanently Incapacitated Assoc., ACT, 1982–; 2/2 (2nd AIF) Field Regtl Assoc., 1984–; Medical Assoc. for Prevention of War (MAPW), 1989–; ACT Hospice Soc., 1991–; 15 Field Ambulance Assoc., 1991–. Leader, Commemorative Tour of Europe for 60th anniversary, RSL. Nat. Pres., 1st Pan Pacific Conf. on alcohol and drugs, 1980. Hon MD Sydney, 1988. Anzac Peace Prize, 1990, Meritorious Medal, 1992, RSL. *Publications:* contribs to Australian Med. Jl, NZ Med. Jl, etc. *Recreations:* bowls, rug-making, gardening. *Address:* 26 Birdwood Street, Hughes, Canberra, ACT 2605, Australia. *Clubs:* Royal Society of Medicine (London); Naval and Military, Cricket (Melbourne); Commonwealth (Canberra); Bowling (Canberra); Royal Automobile (Victoria).

REGAN, Charles Maurice; Clerk to the Trustees, Hampstead Wells and Campden Trust, 1985–93; Under-Secretary, Department of Health and Social Security, 1972–79 and 1981–85; *b* 31 Oct. 1925; *m* 1961, Susan (*née* Littmann) (*d* 1972); one *s* one *d*. *Educ:* Taunton Sch.; London Sch. of Economics and Political Science (BSc(Econ)). Academic research, 1950–52. Asst Principal, Min. of National Insurance, 1952; Principal Private Sec. to Minister of Pensions and National Insurance, 1962–64; Asst Sec., 1964; Treasury/Civil Service Dept, 1967–70; Under-Sec., DES, 1979–81. *Recreations:* walking, travel. *Address:* 35 Crediton Hill, NW6 1HS. *T:* (020) 7794 6404. *Club:* Athenæum.

REGAN, Hon. Donald Thomas; financier, author; Chief of Staff to the President of the United States, 1985–87; *b* 21 Dec. 1918; *s* of late William F. Regan and Kathleen A. Regan; *m* 1942, Ann Gordon Buchanan; two *s* two *d*. *Educ:* Cambridge Latin Sch.; Harvard Univ. (BA). Served War, US Marine Corps, 1940–46; retd as Lt Col, Marine Corps Reserve. Merrill Lynch, Pierce, Fenner & Smith Inc., 1946–81: Vice Pres., 1959–64; Exec. Vice Pres., 1964–68; Pres., 1968–71; Chm. of Bd, 1971–80; Chm. of Bd, Merrill Lynch & Co., Inc., 1973–81; Sec. of the Treasury, US Treasury Dept, 1981–85. Pres., Regdon Associates, 1987–95. Hon. LLD: Hahnemann Med. Coll. and Hosp., 1968; Tri-State Coll., 1969; Univ. of Penn., 1972; Hon. Dr of Commercial Science, Pace Univ., 1973; Hon DHL Colgate Univ., 1984. Fortune magazine's Hall of Fame for business leadership, 1981. Legion of Honour, 1982. *Publications:* A View from the Street, 1972; For the Record: from Wall Street to Washington, 1988. *Recreations:* golf, reading, painting. *Address:* 240 McLaws Circle, Suite 142, Williamsburg, VA 23185–5650, USA. *Club:* Army-Navy (Washington, DC).

REGAN, Rt Rev. Edwin; *see* Wrexham, Bishop of, (RC).

REGAN, Hon. Gerald Augustine; PC (Can.) 1980; QC (Can.) 1970; President, Hawthorne Developments, since 1984; lawyer; *b* Windsor, NS, 13 Feb. 1929; *s* of Walter E. Regan and Rose M. Greene; *m* 1956, A. Carole, *d* of John H. Harrison; three *s* three *d*. *Educ:* Windsor Academy; St Mary's and Dalhousie Univs, Canada; Dalhousie Law Sch. (LLB). Called to Bar of Nova Scotia, 1954. Liberal candidate in Provincial gen. elecs, 1956 and 1960, and in Fed. gen. elec., 1962. MP for Halifax, NS, House of Commons of Canada, 1963–65; Leader, Liberal Party of Nova Scotia, 1965–80; MLA for Halifax-Needham, Provincial gen. elec., 1967, re-elected, 1970–74 and 1978; Premier of Nova Scotia, 1970–78, Leader of the Opposition 1978–80; Minister of Labour, Govt of Canada, 1980–81, Minister responsible for Fitness and Amateur Sport, 1980–82; Secretary of State for Canada, 1981–82; Minister for International Trade, 1982–84; Minister of Energy, Mines and Resources, June–Sept. 1984. Mem., NS Barristers Soc.; Chm. Exec. Cttee, Commonwealth Parly Assoc., 1973–76; Mem., Canadian Delegn, UN, 1965. Chm., Trenton Works Inc.; former Chm., Canadian Exporters Assoc.; Director: United Financial Management; Canadian Surety Co.; Air Atlantic; Sceptre Resources; Roman Corp.; Provigo Inc. Governor, Olympic Trust of Canada; Vice-Chm., Tennis Canada. *Recreations:* tennis, ski-ing. *Address:* PO Box 828 Station B, Ottawa, ON K1P 5P9, Canada; (home) 140 Shore Drive, Bedford, NS B4A 2E4, Canada. *Club:* Halifax (Halifax, NS).

REGAN, Prof. Lesley, (Mrs John Summerfield), MD; FRCOG; Professor and Head of Department of Obstetrics and Gynaecology, Imperial College School of Medicine at St Mary's Hospital, since 1996; *b* 8 March 1956; *d* of Jack Regan and Dorothy Hull (*née* Thorne); *m* 1990, Prof. John Summerfield; twin *d*, and two step *s* two step *d*. *Educ:* Royal Free Hosp. Sch. of Medicine (MB BS 1980; MD 1989). MRCOG 1985, FRCOG 1998. Sen. Registrar in Obstetrics and Gynaecology, Addenbrooke's Hosp., Cambridge, 1986–90; Teaching Fellow (Medicine), 1986–90, Dir of Medical Studies, 1987–90, Girton Coll., Cambridge; Sen. Res. Associate, MRC Embryo and Gamete Res. Gp, Univ. of Cambridge, 1987–89; Sen. Lectr, ICSM, and Hon. Consultant in Obstetrics and Gynaecology, St Mary's Hosp., London, 1990–96; Dir, Subspecialty Trng Prog. in Reproductive Medicine for ICSM at St Mary's and Hammersmith Hosps, 1995–. Rosenfelder Vis. Fellow, Boston, USA, 1999; Vis. Prof., Harvard Centre of Excellence for Women's Health, 2000–Sept. 2002. Member: Expert Adv. Panels in Reproductive Medicine and Contraception, FIGO, 1997; Gynaecol Vis. Soc.; Soc. for Gynaecol Investigation, USA. *Publications:* Miscarriage: what every woman needs to know, 1997; numerous chapters in reproductive medicine textbooks; scientific articles on sporadic and recurrent pregnancy loss in BMJ, Lancet, Human Reproduction, British Jl of Obstetrics and Gynaecol., Amer. Jls of Obstetrics and Gynaecol. *Recreations:* mother to my twin girls, opera, spending time in the South of France. *Address:* Department of Obstetrics and Gynaecology, Imperial College School of Medicine at St Mary's Hospital, South Wharf Road, Paddington, W2 1NY. *T:* (020) 7886 1731.

REGAN, Maj.-Gen. Michael Dalrymple, CB 1996; OBE 1985; Controller, The Army Benevolent Fund, since 1997; *b* 6 Jan. 1942; *s* of late M. L. R. Regan and G. I. Regan (*née* Dalrymple); *m* 1974, Victoria, *o d* of late Comdr V. C. Grenfell, DSO; two *d*. *Educ:* St Boniface's Coll.; RMA, Sandhurst. Commnd 1st KSLI, 1962; Instructor, Sch. of Infantry, 1968–70; Adjutant, 3rd LI, 1971–73; Staff Coll., Camberley, 1973–74; BM, 12th Mech. Bde, 1975–76; Company Comdr, 1st LI, 1977–78; MA to C-in-C, UKLF, 1979–82; CO, 3rd LI, 1982–84; Col MS 2, MoD, 1985; Comdr, 20th Armd Bde, 1986–87; RCDS, 1988; DCOS, HQ UKLF, 1989–91; GOC Wales and Western Dist (5 Div.), 1991–94; Dir Gen., AGC, 1994–95; COS, HQ Adjt Gen., 1995–96. Col, LI, 1992–96; Asst Col Comdt, AGC, 1995–96. *Recreations:* tennis, golf, ski-ing, sailing, gardening. *Club:* Army and Navy.

REGAN, Michael John; HM Diplomatic Service; Foreign and Commonwealth Office, since 1998; *b* 17 Aug. 1955; *s* of late Brig. John Joseph Regan, OBE and Edith Nancy Cunliffe; *m* 1986, Carolyn Gaye Black; two *s*. *Educ:* St George's Coll., Weybridge; Nottingham Univ. (BA Jt Hons Econs and Agricl Econs). SSC, 3rd RTR, 1977–82. Insurance Broker, Fenchurch Gp, 1982–83; joined Diplomatic Service, 1983; FCO, 1983–86; Kabul, 1986–88; FCO, 1988–89; First Sec. (Chancery/Economic), Dubai, 1989–91, FCO, 1991–95; Counsellor (ESCAP), Bangkok, 1995–98. *Recreations:* hockey, tennis, golf, sailing, walking. *Address:* c/o Foreign and Commonwealth Office, King Charles Street, SW1A 2AH. *Club:* Hankley Common Golf.

REGINA, Archbishop of (RC), since 1995; **Most Rev. Peter Joseph Mallon;** *b* 5 Dec. 1929; *s* of Joseph P. Mallon and Sheila (*née* Keenan). *Educ:* Christ the King Seminary, Mission, BC, Canada. Ordained priest, 1956; Asst Priest, Holy Rosary Cathedral, Vancouver, 1956–64; Chancellor, Archdio. of Vancouver, 1964–65; Administrator, Guardian Angels Parish, Vancouver, 1965–66; Rector of Holy Rosary Cathedral, 1966–82; Dir of Religious Educn, 1971–73; Pastor, St Anthony's Parish, W Vancouver, 1982–89; Bishop of Nelson, BC, 1989–95. *Address:* 445 Broad Street North, Regina, SK S4R 2X8, Canada. *T:* (306) 545 0510.

REGO, (Maria) Paula (Figueiroa), (Mrs Victor Willing); artist; *b* 26 Jan. 1935; *d* of José Fernandes Figueiroa Rego and Maria de S José Pavva Figueiroa Rego; *m* 1959, Victor Willing (*d* 1988); one *s* two *d*. *Educ:* St Julian's Sch., Carcavelos, Portugal; Slade School of Fine Art, UCL. First Associate Artist, Nat. Gall., Jan.–Dec. 1990. Selected solo exhibitions: (1st at) Soc. Nat. de Belas Artes, Lisbon, 1965; Gal. S Mamede, Lisbon, 1971; Gal. Modulo, Porto, 1977; Gal. III, Lisbon, 1978; Air Gall., London, 1981; Edward Totah Gall., 1982, 1985, 1987; Arnolfini, 1983; Art Palace, NY, 1985; Gulbenkian Foundn, 1988, 1999; Serpentine Gall. (retrospective), 1988; Marlborough Graphics (nursery rhymes), 1989; Nat. Gall., 1991–92; Marlborough Gall., 1992, 1994; Tate Gall., Liverpool (retrospective), 1997; Dulwich Picture Gall., 1998. Many collective shows include: ICA, 1965; S Paulo Biennale, 1969, 1985; British Art Show, 1985, 2000; Hayward Gall., 1994 and 1996; Saatchi Gall., 1994–95; also in Japan, Australia, all over Europe. Large painting, Crivelli's Garden, in restaurant of Sainsbury Wing, Nat. Gall., 1992. Sen. Fellow, RCA, 1989. Hon. DLitt: St Andrews, 1999; E Anglia, 1999; Hon. DFA Rhode Island Sch. of Design, 2000. *Relevant Publication:* Paula Rego, by John McEwen, 1992. *Recreations:* going to the movies, plays. *Address:* c/o Marlborough Fine Art, 6 Albemarle Street, W1X 4BY. *T:* (020) 7629 5161.

REHNQUIST, William H.; Chief Justice of the United States, since 1986; *b* 1 Oct. 1924; *s* of William Benjamin and Margery Peck Rehnquist; *m* 1953, Natalie Cornell (*d* 1991); one *s* two *d*. *Educ:* Stanford and Harvard Univs. BA, MA 1948, LLB 1952, Stanford; MA Harvard 1949. Law Clerk for Mr Justice Robert H. Jackson, 1952–53; Partner, Phoenix, Ariz: Evans, Kitchell & Jenckes, 1953–55; Ragan & Rehnquist, 1956–57; Cunningham, Carson & Messenger, 1957–60; Powers & Rehnquist, 1960–69; Asst Attorney-Gen., Office of Legal Counsel, Dept of Justice, 1969–72; Associate Justice, Supreme Court, 1972–86. Phi Beta Kappa; Order of the Coif. *Publications:* contrib. US News and World Report, Jl of Amer. Bar Assoc., Arizona Law Review. *Recreations:* swimming, tennis, reading, hiking. *Address:* Supreme Court of the United States, Washington, DC 20543, USA. *Club:* National Lawyers (Washington, DC).

REICH, Peter Gordon; Assistant Chief Scientist (G), Royal Air Force, 1984–85; *b* 16 Sept. 1926; *s* of Douglas Gordon Reich and Josephine Grace Reich; *m* 1948, Kathleen, *d* of Alan and Florence Lessiter, Banstead; three *d*. *Educ:* Sutton Grammar Sch.; London Univ. (BSc). FRIN 1967 (Bronze Medal, 1967). Served RN, 1944–47. Entered Civil Service as Scientific Officer, 1952; Armament Res. Estab., 1952–54; Opl Res. Br., Min. of Transport and Civil Aviation, 1955–60; RAE, 1960–68; Asst Dir of Electronics Res. and Develt (2), Min. of Technol., 1968–70; Asst Dir of Res. (Avionics, Space and Air Traffic), Min. of Aviation Supply, 1971–73; Supt, Def. Opl Analysis Estab., MoD, 1973–76; Mem., Reliability and Costing Study Gp, MoD, 1976–79; Counsellor (Defence Res.), Canberra, and Head of British Defence Res. and Supply Staffs, Australia, 1979–83. *Publications:* papers in Jl of Inst. of Nav., and Jl of Opl Res. Soc. *Recreations:* racquet games, walking, aural pleasures.

REICH, Steve; composer; *b* 3 Oct. 1936; *s* of Leonard Reich and June Carroll (*née* Sillman); *m* 1976, Beryl Korot; one *s*, and one *s* from previous *m*. *Educ:* Cornell Univ. (BA Hons Philos. 1957); Juilliard Sch. of Music; Mills Coll. (MA Music 1963); Inst. for African Studies, Univ. of Ghana. Guggenheim Fellow, 1978; Montgomery Fellow, Dartmouth Coll., 2000. Mem., AAAL, 1994. Founded ensemble, Steve Reich and Musicians, 1966, toured the world, 1971–. Music performed by major orchestras, including: NY Philharmonic; San Francisco Symphony; St Louis Symphony; Brooklyn Philharmonic; LA Philharmonic; BBC Symphony; London Symphony Orch.; commissions received include: Fest. d'Automne, Paris for 200th Anniv. of French Revolution, 1989; BBC Proms in honour of centennial, 1995. Member: Amer. Acad. of Arts and Letters, 1994; Bavarian Acad. of Fine Arts, 1995. Sauman Prize, Columbia Univ., 2000.Commandeur, Ordre des Arts et des Lettres (France), 1999. *Compositions include:* Drumming, 1971; Music for 18 Musicians, 1976; Eight Lines, 1979–83; Tehillim, 1981; The Desert Music, 1984; Sextet, 1985; Different Trains, 1988 (Grammy Award for Best Contemporary Composition, 1990); The Cave, 1993; Nagoyd Marimba, 1994; City Life, 1995; Proverb, 1995; Triple Quartet, 1999. *Publications:* Writings About Music, 1974; Writings on Music 1965–2000, 2001. *Address:* c/o Andrew Rosner Allieds Artists, 42 Montpelier Square, SW7 1JZ.

REID, Alan; MP (Lib Dem) Argyll and Bute, since 2001; *b* 7 Aug. 1954; *s* of James Smith Reid and Catherine Graham Reid (*née* Steele). *Educ:* Prestwick Acad.; Ayr Acad.; Strathclyde Univ. (BSc Hons Pure & Applied Maths). Strathclyde Regional Council: Maths Teacher, 1976–77; Computer Programmer, 1977–85; Computer Project Manager, Glasgow Univ., 1985–2001. *Recreations:* playing chess, walking, reading, watching TV.

Address: House of Commons, SW1A 0AA; 131 Fairhaven, Kirn, Dunoon, Argyll PA23 8NS. *T:* (01369) 703212.

REID, Dr Alexander Arthur Luttrell; Director-General, Royal Institute of British Architects, 1994–2000; *b* 11 Jan. 1941; *s* of late Capt. Philip Reid, RN and of Louisa (*née* Luttrell); *m* 1st, 1964, Sara Louise Coleridge (marr. diss. 1987); two *d*; 2nd, 1988, Sian Tudor Roberts; one *s* one *d*. *Educ:* Winchester Coll. (Schol.); Trinity Coll., Cambridge (MA); University Coll., London (MSc; PhD 1974). Served RN, Lieut (helicopter pilot), 1962–67. Post Office Telecommunications: Hd, Long Range Studies, 1972–77; Director: Prestel, 1977–80; Business Systems, 1980–83; Acorn Computer Gp PLC, 1984–85; Octagon Investment Mgt Ltd, 1984–; Chief Exec., DEGW Ltd, 1991–94. Royal College of Art: Council Mem., 1988–90; Chm., 1990–93. *Recreations:* carpentry, sailing. *Address:* 27 Millington Road, Cambridge CB3 9HW. *T:* (01223) 356100.

REID, Sir Alexander (James), 3rd Bt *cr* 1897; JP; DL; *b* 6 Dec. 1932; *s* of Sir Edward James Reid, 2nd Bt, KBE, and Tatiana (*d* 1992), *d* of Col Alexander Fenoult, formerly of Russian Imperial Guard; *S* father, 1972; *m* 1955, Michaela Ann, *d* of late Olaf Kier, CBE; one *s* three *d*. *Educ:* Eton; Magdalene Coll., Cambridge. Nat. Certificate Agriculture (NCA). 2nd Lieut, 1st Bn Gordon Highlanders, 1951; served Malaya; Captain, 3rd Bn Gordon Highlanders (TA), retired 1964. Director: Ellon Castle Estates Co. Ltd, 1965–96; Cristina Securities Ltd, 1970–. Chm., Clan Donnachaidh Soc., 1994–. Governor, Heath Mount Prep. Sch., Hertford, 1970, Chm., 1976–92. JP Cambridgeshire and Isle of Ely, 1971, DL 1973; High Sheriff, Cambridgeshire, 1987–88. *Recreations:* shooting, travel. *Heir: s* Charles Edward James Reid, *b* 24 June 1956. *Address:* Lanton Tower, Jedburgh, Roxburghshire TD8 6SU. *T:* (01835) 863443. *Clubs:* Caledonian; New (Edinburgh).

REID, Andrew Milton; Deputy Chairman, Imperial Group, 1986–89; *b* 21 July 1929; *s* of late Rev. A. R. R. Reid, DD and of Lilias Symington Tindal; *m* 1st, 1953, Norma Mackenzie Davidson (*d* 1993); two *s*; 2nd, 1995, Audrey Janet Wilson Bruell. *Educ:* Glasgow Academy; Jesus Coll., Oxford. Imperial Tobacco Management Pupil, 1952; Asst Managing Director, John Player & Sons, 1975; Dir, Imperial Group Ltd, 1978; Chm., Imperial Tobacco Ltd, 1979–86. Dep. Chm., Trade Indemnity plc, 1994–96 (Dir, 1982–96); Dir, Renold PLC, 1983–96. Member, Tobacco Adv. Council, 1977–86. Member: Council, RSCM, 1987–89; Court and Council, Bristol Univ., 1986–99; Board, Bristol Develt Corp., 1989–96 (Dep. Chm., 1993–). Chm. Governors, Colston's Collegiate Sch., 1986–94. Master, Soc. of Merchant Venturers of Bristol, 1991–92. High Sheriff of Avon, 1991. *Recreations:* sailing, golf, fishing. *Address:* Parsonage Farm, Publow, Pensford, near Bristol BS18 4JD.

REID, Andrew Stephen; Senior Partner, Reid Minty, Solicitors, since 1980; Deputy Supreme Court Taxing Master, since 1991; *b* 2 March 1954; *s* of Leon Ralph Reid and Fay Marion Reid. *Educ:* University College Sch., London (LLB Hons). ACIArb 1979. Admitted solicitor, 1979; founded Reid Minty, Solicitors, 1980. Mem., Radio Authy, 1994–99. Racehorse trainer, London, 1999–. *Recreations:* polo, hunting, gardening, shooting, sailing. *Address:* 14 Grosvenor Street, Mayfair, W1K 4PS. *T:* (020) 7318 4444. *Clubs:* Annabel's, MCC; Belmont Polo; Guards' Polo; Oakley Hunt.

REID, Anne Prudence; *see* Wakefield, A. P.

REID, Caroline Jean Vernon; Director General, Projects Directorate, European Investment Bank, since 1999; *b* 6 April 1948; *d* of late Colin Beever and of Dorothy Beever; *m* 1970, Michael Francis Reid; two *s*. *Educ:* Lycée Châteaubriand, Rome; Bedford High Sch. for Girls; Univ. of Bristol (BSc Hons Econs and Stats). Asst economist, British Gas Council, 1969–71; with NIESR, 1972–74; joined European Investment Bank, 1974: Energy Economist, 1974–85; loan officer, Energy/Envmt Div., Dept for Lending, Rome, 1985–88, Hd of Div., 1988–94; Dir, Italy Dept, 1994–99. *Address:* c/o European Investment Bank, 100 Boulevard K. Adenauer, Kirchberg, Luxembourg 2950. *T:* 43791.

REID, David James Glover; Member, Arts Council of England, 1995–98 (Acting Deputy Chairman, 1997–98; Chairman, Audit Committee, 1996–98); *b* 14 Aug. 1936; *s* of Alexander Robert Reid and Maisie Cullen Mowat; *m* 1963, Norma Scott Elder Chalmers; two *s*. *Educ:* Edinburgh Royal High Sch.; Univ. of Edinburgh (BSc Maths and Math. Physics). Joined IBM, 1962; USA, 1967–75; Manager, IBM Product 3250, 1977; Graphics Product Manager, 1979; lab. ops Manager, 1983; Resident Dir for Scotland, N England and NI, 1985, for England, Wales and NI, 1990; retired, 1993. Chairman: Scottish Cttee, ABSA, 1986; Scottish Enterprise Foundn, 1986; Southern Regl Arts Bd, 1991–98; Business in the Arts South, 1991–98; Member: Scottish Econ. Council, 1988; Exec., Scottish Business in the Community, 1988. Trustee, Arts Foundn, 1996–98. Gov., Univ. of Portsmouth, 1991–96. *Recreations:* bridge, computing, music, sailing, theatre, walking.

REID, Derek Donald; Board Member, Scottish Enterprise Tayside, since 1996; *b* 30 Nov. 1944; *s* of Robert Slorach Reid and Selina Mons Lewis Reid (*née* Donald); *m* 1977, Janice Anne Reid; one *s* one *d*. *Educ:* Inverurie Acad., Aberdeen; Aberdeen Univ. (MA); Robert Gordon Inst. of Technol. (Dip. Personnel Mgt). Cadbury Schweppes: mgt trainee, 1968; Divl Dir, 1982–86; Founder Mem., Premier Brands and Dir, Tea Business after mgt buy-out, 1986–89; Man. Dir, Tea Business, 1989–90; Chief Exec., Scottish Tourist Bd, 1994–96; Dep. Chm., Sea Fish Industry Authy, 1996–2000; Chm., Scotland's Hotels of Distinction, 1998–2001; Chm., Cherrybank Partnership, 1999–; dir, various small cos. Trustee, Lomond Shores, 1999–. Vis. Prof. of Tourism, Aberdeen Univ., 2000–. Hon. DBA Robert Gordon Univ., Aberdeen, 1995. *Recreations:* golf, cricket, fishing, art appreciation, classical music. *Address:* Bonhard House, by Scone, Perth PH2 7PQ. *T:* (01738) 552471. *Clubs:* Murrayshall Golf (Perth), Gleneagles.

REID, Dominic, RIBA; Pageantmaster, Lord Mayor's Show, since 1992; Principal, Reid and Reid, since 1992; Executive Director, Oxford and Cambridge Boat Race, since 2000; *b* 24 Sept. 1961; *s* of late John Reid, OBE, DL and of Sylvia Reid; *m* 1991, Suzanne Jessup (*née* Schultz). *Educ:* Oundle Sch.; Downing Coll., Cambridge (BA 1984; MA 1988); University College London (DipArch 1987). RIBA 1991. SSLC, 49 Field Regt, Royal Artillery, 1981. Architect: Doshi-Raje, Ahmedabad, India, 1984–85; Austin-Smith:Lord, 1986–89; Richard Horden Associates Ltd, 1989–90; John and Sylvia Reid, 1990–92; Dir, Designer's Collaborative, 1996–2000; Chief Exec., London Film Commission, 1999–2000. FRSA 1991. Liveryman, Grocers' Co., 1999–. OStJ 1999. *Recreations:* telemarking, coaching rowing, the 'cello. *Address:* 1 Queens Road, Hertford, Herts SG14 1EN. *T:* (01992) 505306, *Fax:* (01992) 505304; *e-mail:* dominic@reidreid.abel.co.uk. *Clubs:* HAC; Leander (Henley-on-Thames), Hawks (Cambridge).

REID, Dougal Gordon, CMG 1983; HM Diplomatic Service, retired; Director of Studies, Royal Institute of Public Administration International, 1985–92; *b* Hong Kong, 31 Dec. 1925; *e s* of late Douglas Reid and Catherine Jean (*née* Lowson), Forfar; *m* 1950, Georgina Elizabeth Johnston; one *s* (and one *s* decd). *Educ:* Sedbergh Sch.; Trinity Hall, Cambridge; LSE. Served in Royal Marines, 1944–46. Cadet, Colonial Admin. Service (later HMOCS), Sierra Leone, 1949; District Comr 1956; retd as Perm. Sec., Min. of Natural Resources, 1962. Arthur Guinness Son & Co. Ltd, 1962–63. Entered CRO, later FCO, 1963; served in: Accra, 1964–65; CO, 1966; Accra, 1966–68 (concurrently Lomé, 1967–68); Seoul, 1968–71; FCO, 1971–74; Kinshasa (and concurrently at Brazzaville, Bujumbura and Kigali), 1974–77; New Delhi, 1977–78; Singapore, 1979–80; Ambassador to Liberia, 1980–85. Mem., Internat. Cttee, Leonard Cheshire Foundn, 1985–92. *Recreations:* military history, jazz, watching sport. *Clubs:* Travellers, Royal Commonwealth Society, MCC; London Scottish Football; Sadan Pubin (Seoul).

REID, Elizabeth Margaret; Chief Executive, Technology Colleges Trust; *b* 16 April 1947; *d* of John A. McConachie, MB ChB, FRCPE and J. Margaret McConachie, MB ChB; *m* 1st, 1970, Robin Reid, MA (marr. diss. 1975); 2nd, 1982, Martin J. Monk, BA Hons Oxon (marr. diss. 2000). *Educ:* Aberdeen Univ. (MA Hons 1969); London Univ. (MA Educnl Admin 1980). Asst Principal, CS, 1969–70; Inner London Education Authority: schoolteacher, 1970–78; Advr for 16–19 educn, 1978–79; Professional Asst, London Borough of Ealing, 1979–80; Asst Educn Officer, London Borough of Haringey, 1980–83; Sen. Principal Officer (Educn), AMA, 1983–85; Inner London Education Authority: Admin. Head, Further and Higher Educn Br., 1985–88; Dep. Dir of Educn (Further and Higher Educn), 1988–89; Dep. Provost, London Guildhall Univ. (formerly City of London Poly.), 1989–93; Director of Education: Lothian Regional Council, 1993–96; City of Edinburgh Council, 1996–98; London Borough of Hackney, 1998–2000. Vice Chm., Scottish Qualifications Authy, 1996–98. Member Board: QAA; Nat. Children's Bureau; Understanding Industry. FRSA 1989; FSQA 1998. *Recreations:* theatre, opera, music, reading, gardening. *Address:* Technology Colleges Trust, 23rd Floor (West), Millbank Tower, 21–24 Millbank, SW1P 4QP.

REID, Rt Rev. Gavin Hunter, OBE 2000; Bishop Suffragan of Maidstone, 1992–2000; *b* 24 May 1934; *s* of Arthur William Reid and Jean Smith Reid (*née* Guthrie); *m* 1959, Mary Eleanor Smith; two *s* one *d*. *Educ:* Roan Sch., Greenwich; Queen Mary Coll. and King's Coll., London Univ. (BA 1956); Oak Hill Theol Coll. Ordained, Chelmsford Cathedral: deacon, 1960; priest, 1961; Assistant Curate: St Paul's, East Ham, 1960–63; Rainham Parish Church, 1963–66; Publications Sec., CPAS, 1966–71; Editorial Sec., United Soc. for Christian Lit., 1971–74; Sec. for Evangelism, 1974–90, Consultant Missioner, 1990–92, CPAS; Advr, Gen. Synod Bd of Mission, 1990–92. Seconded: Nat. Dir, Mission England, 1982–85; Project Dir, Mission 89, 1988–89. Chm., Archbishops' Adv. Gp for the Millennium, 1995–2000. *Publications:* The Gagging of God, 1969; The Elaborate Funeral, 1972; A New Happiness, 1974; To Be Confirmed, 1977; Good News to Share, 1979; Starting Out Together, 1981; To Reach a Nation, 1987; Beyond Aids, 1987; Lights that Shine, 1991; Brushing up on Believing, 1991; Our Place in his Story, 1994; various symposia. *Recreations:* golf, sailing, walking, birdwatching. *Address:* 17 Richard Crampton Road, Beccles, Suffolk NR34 9HN.

REID, George Newlands; journalist; Member (SNP) Mid Scotland & Fife, Scottish Parliament, since 1999; Deputy Presiding Officer, Scottish Parliament, 1999; *b* 4 June 1939; *s* of late George Reid, company director, and of Margaret Forsyth; *m* 1968, Daphne Ann MacColl; one *d*, and one *d* from previous marriage. *Educ:* Tullibody Sch.; Dollar Academy; Univ. of St Andrews (MA Hons). Pres., Students' Representative Council. Features Writer, Scottish Daily Express, 1962; Reporter, Scottish Television, 1964; Producer, Granada Television, 1965; Head of News and Current Affairs (Scottish Television), 1968; presenter, BBC, 1979. Head of Inf., 1984–86, Dir of Public Affairs, 1986–90, Dir of Internat. Promotion, 1990–92, League of Red Cross and Red Crescent Socs, Geneva. MP (SNP) Stirlingshire E and Clackmannan, Feb. 1974–1979; Mem., British Parly Delegn to Council of Europe and WEU, 1977–79. Vice-Convener, SNP, 1997–99. Contested (SNP) Ochil, 1997. Dir, Scottish Council Res. Inst., 1974–77. Chief Red Cross deleg. to Armenia, Dec. 1988–Jan. 1989. *Address:* Scottish Parliament, Edinburgh EH99 1SP. *T:* (0131) 348 5911, *Fax:* (0131) 348 5966; *e-mail:* george.reid.msp@scottish.parliament.uk.

REID, Gordon; *see* Reid, J. G.

REID, Ven. Gordon; *see* Reid, Ven. W. G.

REID, Graham Livingstone, CB 1991; Director General of Strategy, International and Analytical Services, Department for Education and Employment, 1995–97; *b* 30 June 1937; *s* of late William L. Reid and of Louise M. Reid; *m* 1st, 1973, Eileen M. Loudfoot (marr. diss. 1983); 2nd, 1985, Sheila Rothwell (*d* 1997). *Educ:* Univ. of St Andrews (MA); Queen's Univ., Kingston, Canada (MA). Dept of Social and Economic Res., Univ. of Glasgow: Asst Lectr in Applied Economics, 1960, Lectr 1963, Sen. Lectr 1968, Reader 1971; Sen. Econ. Adviser and Head of Econs and Statistics Unit, Scottish Office, 1973–75; Dir, Manpower Intelligence and Planning Div., MSC, 1975–84; Department of Employment: Chief Economic Adviser and Hd, Economic and Social Div., 1984–88 and Dir, Enterprise and Deregulation Unit, 1987; Dep. Sec., Manpower Policy, 1988–90, Resources and Strategy, 1991, Indust. Relns and Internat. Directorate, 1991–95. Vis. Associate Prof., Mich State Univ., 1967; Vis. Res. Fellow, Queen's Univ., Canada, 1969. FRSA 1996. *Publications:* Fringe Benefits, Labour Costs and Social Security (ed with D. J. Robertson), 1965; (with K. J. Allen) Nationalised Industries, 1970 (3rd edn 1975); (with L. C. Hunter and D. Boddy) Labour Problems of Technological Change, 1970; (with K. J. Allen and D. J. Harris) The Nationalised Fuel Industries, 1973; contrib. to Econ. Jl, Brit. Jl of Indust. Relations, Scot. Jl of Polit. Econ., Indust & Lab. Relns Rev. *Recreations:* golf, music, gardening. *Address:* 4 Chequers Lane, Fingest, Henley-on-Thames, Oxon RG9 6QF. *Club:* Royal Over Seas League.

REID, Sir (Harold) Martin (Smith), KBE 1987; CMG 1978; HM Diplomatic Service, retired; *b* 27 Aug. 1928; *s* of late Marcus Reid and late Winifred Mary Reid (*née* Stephens); *m* 1956, Jane Elizabeth Harwood; one *s* three *d*. *Educ:* Merchant Taylors' Sch.; Brasenose Coll., Oxford (Open Scholar). RN, 1947–49. Entered HM Foreign Service, 1953; served in: FO, 1953–54; Paris, 1954–57; Rangoon, 1958–61; FO, 1961–65; Georgetown, 1965–68; Bucharest, 1968–70; Dep. High Comr, Malaŵi, 1970–73; Private Sec. to successive Secs of State for NI, 1973–74; Head of Central and Southern Africa Dept, FCO, 1974–78; Minister, British Embassy, Pretoria/Cape Town, 1979–82; Resident Chm. (Dip. Service) CS Selection Bd, 1983–84; High Comr to Jamaica, and Ambassador (non-resident) to Haiti, 1984–87; Research Advr, FCO, 1987–88. Hon. Sec., Friends of Student Christian Movement, 1989–92. Paintings regularly exhibited, notably in one-man shows in Westminster, 1983, Kingston, 1987 and Dulwich, 1995; works in Jamaican nat. collection. *Publication:* Pissarro, 1993. *Recreation:* painting. *Address:* 43 Carson Road, SE21 8HT. *T:* (020) 8670 6151.

See also M. H. M. Reid.

REID, Henry William, (Harry); Editor, The Herald, Glasgow, 1997–2000; *b* 23 Sept. 1947; *s* of late William Reid and of Catherine Robertson Craighead Reid (*née* Maclean); *m* 1980, Julie Wilson Davidson; one *d*. *Educ:* Aberdeen Grammar Sch.; Fettes Coll.; Worcester Coll., Oxford (BA). The Scotsman: reporter, sports writer, leader writer, 1970–73; educn correspondent, 1973–77; Features Ed., 1977–81; Sport and Leisure Ed., Sunday Standard, 1981–82; Exec. Ed., 1982–83, Dep. Ed., 1983–97, The Herald,

Glasgow. Vis. Fellow, Faculty of Divinity, Univ. of Edinburgh, 2001–. DUniv Glasgow, 2001; Dr *hc* Edinburgh, 2001. *Publication:* Dear Country: a quest for England, 1992. *Recreations:* exploring Scotland and European cities, hill walking, supporting Aberdeen FC, reading novels, listening to Bob Dylan. *Address:* 12 Comely Bank, Edinburgh EH4 1AN. *T:* (0131) 332 6690.

REID, Sir Hugh, 3rd Bt *cr* 1922; farmer; *b* 27 Nov. 1933; *s* of Sir Douglas Neilson Reid, 2nd Bt, and Margaret Brighton Young (*d* 1992), *d* of Robert Young Maxtone, MBE, JP; *S* father, 1971. *Educ:* Loretto. Royal Air Force, 1952–56; RAFVR, 1956–78 (Flying Officer, Training Branch, 1965–78). *Recreations:* skiing, travel. *Heir:* none. *Address:* Caheronaun Park, Loughrea, Co. Galway.

REID, Iain; Dean, The Arts Educational Schools, London, since 1998; *b* 27 March 1942; *s* of Jean Reid (*née* Money) and George Aitken Reid; *m* 1st, 1968, Judith Coke; 2nd, 1982, Kay Barlow; one *s* one *d*. *Educ:* Uppingham; RADA; Lancaster Univ. (MA). Actor, 1963–73; theatre administrator, 1973–77; Drama Officer, Greater London Arts, 1977–82; Dir of Arts, Calouste Gulbenkian Foundn (UK), 1982–89; Dir, Arts Co-ordination, later Arts Develt, Arts Council of GB, 1989–94; Dir of Combined Arts, Arts Council of England, 1994–98. FRSA 1992. *Recreations:* skating, sailing. *Address:* (office) 14 Bath Road, Chiswick, W4 1LY.

REID, Ian George; Director, Centre for European Agricultural Studies, Wye College, University of London, 1974–86; *b* 12 May 1921; 2nd *s* of James John Reid and Margaret Jane Reid; *m* 1946, Peggy Eileen Bridgman. *Educ:* Merchant Taylors' Sch.; London Sch. of Econs (BScEcon); Christ's Coll., Cambridge (Dip. Agric.). Lectr, Reading Univ., 1945–53; Lectr, 1953–63, and Sen. Lectr, 1963–86, Wye Coll. Pres., Agricultural Econs Soc., 1981–82. *Recreations:* enjoying music, gardening, art. *Club:* Farmers'.

REID, (James) Gordon; QC (Scot) 1993; *b* 24 July 1952; *s* of James R. Reid and Constance M. Lawrie or Reid; *m* 1984, Hannah Hogg Hopkins; three *s* one *d*. *Educ:* Melville Coll., Edinburgh; Edinburgh Univ. (LLB Hons). Solicitor, 1976–80; Advocate, 1980–; called to the Bar, Inner Temple, 1991. Part-time Chm., VAT and Duties Tribunals, 1997–; Dep. Special Comr for Income Tax Purposes, 1997–. FCIArb 1994. *Recreations:* classical guitar, tennis, golf. *Address:* Blebo House, by St Andrews, Fife KY15 5TZ.

REID, James Robert; QC 1980; **His Honour Judge Reid;** a Circuit Judge, since 1999; *b* 23 Jan. 1943; *s* of late Judge J. A. Reid, MC and Jean Ethel Reid; *m* 1974, Anne Prudence Wakefield, *qv*; two *s* one *d*. *Educ:* Marlborough Coll.; New Coll., Oxford (MA). FCIArb. Called to the Bar, Lincoln's Inn, 1965, Bencher, 1988; a Recorder, 1985–99. Mem., Senate of Inns of Court and the Bar, 1977–80; Mem., Gen. Council of the Bar, 1990–96 (Chm., Professional Conduct Cttee, 1995–96). Chm., Barristers Benevolent Assoc., 1995–99 (Hon. Jt Treas., 1986–91; Dep. Chm., 1991–95). Mem., Court of Arbitration for Sport, 1999–; Chm., Football League Appeal Cttee, 2000–. *Recreations:* fencing, cricket.

REID, Rt Hon. John; PC 1998; PhD; MP (Lab) Hamilton North and Bellshill, since 1997 (Motherwell North, 1987–97); Secretary of State for Northern Ireland, since 2001; *b* 8 May 1947; *s* of late Thomas Reid and of Mary Reid; *m* 1969, Catherine (*née* McGowan) (*d* 1998); two *s*. *Educ:* St Patrick's Senior Secondary Sch., Coatbridge; Stirling Univ. (BA History, PhD Economic History). Scottish Research Officer, Labour Party, 1979–83; Political Adviser to Rt Hon. Neil Kinnock, 1983–85; Scottish Organiser, Trades Unionists for Labour, 1985–87. Opposition spokesman on children, 1989–90, on defence, 1990–97; Minister of State, MoD, 1997–98; Minister of Transport, 1998–99; Sec. of State for Scotland, 1999–2001. Member: Public Accounts Cttee, 1988–89; Armed Forces Cttee and Reserved Forces Cttee, 1996–97. *Recreations:* football, reading, crossword puzzles. *Address:* Parliamentary Office, Montrose House, 154 Montrose Crescent, Hamilton ML3 6LL. *T:* (01698) 454672, *Fax:* (01698) 424732.

REID, John Boyd, AO 1980; LLB; FAIM; former Chairman, James Hardie Industries Ltd (Director, 1964–96); *b* 27 Dec. 1929; *s* of Sir John Thyne Reid, CMG. *Educ:* Scotch College; Melbourne Univ. Chm., Comsteel Vickers Ltd, 1983–86; Vice-Chm., Qantas Airways, 1981–86 (Dir, 1977–86); Director: Broken Hill Pty Co., 1972–97; Barclays Internat. Australia, 1982–85; Bell Resources Ltd, 1987–88; Peregrine Capital Australia Ltd, 1991–95; Focus Publishing, 1991–. Chm., Australian Bicentennial Authy, 1979–85; Dir, World Expo 88, 1986–89; Member: Admin. Review Cttee, 1975–76; Indep. Inquiry into Commonwealth Serum Labs, 1978; Patron, Australia Indonesia Business Co-operation Cttee, 1979–88 (Pres., 1973–79); Dir, Thailand-Australia Foundn Ltd, 1993–; Mem., Internat. Adv. Bd, Swiss Banking Corp., 1986–; Chm., Review of Commonwealth Admin, 1981–82. Trustee and Internat. Counsellor, Conference Bd USA; Internat. Council, Stanford Res. Inst., USA. Chairman: NSW Educn and Trng Foundn, 1989–93; Cttee, Aust. Scout Educn and Trng Foundn, 1991; Museum of Contemp. Art, 1994–. Chm. Council, Pymble Ladies Coll., 1975–82 (Mem., 1965–75); Governor, Ian Clunies Ross Meml Foundn, 1975–; Chm., Sydney Adv. Cttee, 1995–, and Red Shield Appeal, 1993–, Salvation Army. Mem., Inst. of Company Dirs. Life Governor, AIM (Sydney Div.). Melbourne Univ. Graduate Sch. of Business Admin Award, 1983; John Storey Medal, AIM, 1985. *Clubs:* Australian (Sydney); Royal Sydney Yacht Squadron.

REID, Rev. Prof. John Kelman Sutherland, CBE 1970; TD 1961; Professor of Christian Dogmatics, 1961–70, of Systematic Theology 1970–76, University of Aberdeen; *b* 31 March 1910; *y s* of late Reverend Dr David Reid, Calcutta and Leith, and of late Mrs G. T. Reid (*née* Stuart); *m* 1950, Margaret Winifrid Brookes (*d* 1989). *Educ:* George Watson's Boys' College, Edinburgh; Universities of Edinburgh (MA and BD), Heidelberg, Marburg, Basel, and Strasbourg. MA 1st Cl. Hons Philosophy, 1933. Prof. of Philosophy in Scottish Church Coll., Univ. of Calcutta, 1935–37; BD (dist. in Theol.), 1938, and Cunningham Fellow. Ordained into Church of Scotland and inducted into Parish of Craigmillar Park, Edinburgh, 1939. CF, chiefly with Parachute Regt, 1942–46. Jt Ed. Scot. Jl Theol. since inception, 1947; Hon. Sec. Jt Cttee on New Translation of the Bible, 1949–82; Prof. of Theology and Head of Department of Theology, University of Leeds, 1952–61. Hon. DD (Edinburgh), 1957. *Publications:* The Authority of Scripture, 1957; Our Life in Christ, 1963; Christian Apologetics, 1969. Translation of: Oscar Cullmann's The Earliest Christian Confessions, 1949; Baptism in the New Testament, 1952; Calvin's Theological Treatises, ed and trans. 1954; Jean Bosc's The Kingly Office of the Lord Jesus Christ, 1959; Calvin's Concerning the Eternal Pre-destination of God, ed and trans., 1961, repr. 1982. *Address:* 8 Abbotsford Court, 18 Colinton Road, Edinburgh EH10 5EH. *Club:* Mortonhall Golf (Edinburgh).

REID, Prof. John Low, OBE 2001; DM; Regius Professor of Medicine and Therapeutics, University of Glasgow, since 1989; Chairman, Division of Medicine, North Glasgow University Hospitals NHS Trust, since 2000; *b* 1 Oct. 1943; *s* of Dr James Reid and Irene M. Dale; *m* 1964, Randa Pharaon; one *s* one *d*. *Educ:* Fettes Coll., Edinburgh; Magdalen Coll., Oxford. MA; DM; FRCP 1986; FRCPGlas 1979; FRCPI 1997; FRSE 1995. House Officer, Radcliffe Infirmary, Oxford, and Brompton Hosp., 1967–70; Res. Fellow, RPMS, 1970–73; Vis. Fellow, Nat. Inst. of Mental Health, USA, 1973–74; Royal Postgraduate Medical School: Sen. Lectr in Clin. Pharmacol., and Consultant Physician, 1975–77; Reader in Clin. Pharmacol., 1977–78; Regius Prof. of Materia Medica, Univ. of Glasgow, 1978–89; Clinical Dir, Acute Medicine, New Glasgow Hosps, 1993–2000. Founder FMedSci 1998. *Publications:* Central Action of Drugs in Regulation of Blood Pressure, 1975; Lecture Notes in Clinical Pharmacology, 1982; Handbook of Hypertension, 1983; papers on cardiovascular and neurological diseases in clinical and pharmacological journals. *Recreations:* books, gardening, the outdoors. *Address:* Department of Medicine, Western Infirmary, Glasgow G11 6NT. *T:* (0141) 211 2886.

REID, Rt Rev. John Robert; United Mission to Nepal, 1995–97; Bishop of South Sydney, 1983–93 (Assistant Bishop, Diocese of Sydney, 1972–93); *b* 15 July 1928; *s* of John and Edna Reid; *m* 1955, Alison Gertrude Dunn; two *s* four *d*. *Educ:* Melbourne Univ. (BA); Moore Coll., Sydney (ThL). Deacon 1955, Priest 1955; Curate, Manly, 1955–56; Rector, Christ Church, Gladesville, NSW, 1956–69; Archdeacon of Cumberland, NSW, 1969–72. *Recreation:* walking. *Address:* 35 Arden Avenue, Avoca Beach, NSW 2251, Australia.

REID, Prof. Kenneth Bannerman Milne, PhD; FMedSci; FRS 1997; Professor of Immunochemistry, University of Oxford, since 1993; Fellow, Green College, Oxford, since 1986; Director, MRC Immunochemistry Unit, Oxford University, since 1985; *b* 22 Sept. 1943; *s* of John McBean Reid and Maria Anderson (*née* Smith); *m* 1969, Margery Robertson Gilmour; one *s* two *d*. *Educ:* Univ. of Aberdeen (BSc 1965; PhD 1968). SO, Fisheries Res. Unit, Aberdeen Univ., 1968–69; ICI Res. Fellowship, Dept Biochem., Univ. of Oxford, 1969–70; Mem., Scientific Staff, 1970–84, Dep. Dir, 1984–85, MRC Immunochemistry Unit, Dept of Biochemistry, Univ of Oxford. Fellow, EMBO, 1991; Founder FMedSci 1998. Second Wellcome Trust Lecture Award, 1981. *Publications:* Complement, 1988, 2nd edn 1995; author or co-author of numerous papers in jls such as Nature, Biochem. Jl, Jl Immunology. *Recreations:* hill-walking, racket sports (squash, tennis). *Address:* MRC Immunochemistry Unit, Department of Biochemistry, University of Oxford, South Parks Road, Oxford OX1 3QU. *T:* (01865) 275353.

REID, Prof. Kenneth Gilbert Cameron; WS; FRSE; Professor of Property Law, University of Edinburgh, since 1994; Member, Scottish Law Commission, since 1995; *b* 25 March 1954; *s* of Gilbert Beith Reid and Mary Henry Reid (*née* Sinclair); *m* 1981, Elspeth Christie; two *s* one *d*. *Educ:* Loretto; St John's Coll., Cambridge (MA); Univ. of Edinburgh (LLB). Admitted solicitor, 1980; WS 1999. University of Edinburgh: Lectr in Law, 1980–91; Sen. Lectr, 1991–94. FRSE 2000. *Publications:* (jtly) The Laws of Scotland: Stair Memorial Encyclopaedia, Vol. 18, 1993, rev. edn as The Law of Property in Scotland, 1996; (with G. L. Gretton) Conveyancing, 1993, 2nd edn 1999; (ed jtly) A History of Private Law in Scotland, 2000; numerous papers in learned jls. *Recreation:* classical music, both listening and doing. *Address:* Faculty of Law, University of Edinburgh, Old College, South Bridge, Edinburgh EH8 9YL. *T:* (0131) 650 2015.

REID, Leslie, CBE 1978; HM Diplomatic Service, retired; Director General, The Association of British Mining Equipment Companies, 1980–83; *b* 24 May 1919; *s* of late Frederick Sharples and Mary Reid; *m* 1942, Norah Moorcroft; three *d*. *Educ:* King George V Sch., Southport, Lancs. Served War of 1939–45, W Europe and SEAC, Major, XX The Lancashire Fusiliers. Board of Trade, 1947–49; Asst Trade Commissioner: Salisbury, Rhodesia, 1949–55; Edmonton, Alberta, 1955–56; Trade Comr, Vancouver, 1956–60; Principal, BoT, 1960–62; Trade Comr and Economic Advisor, British High Commn, Cyprus, 1962–64; BoT, 1964–66; 1st Sec., FCO, 1966–68; Sen. Commercial Sec., British High Commn, Jamaica, and 1st Sec., British Embassy, Port-au-Prince, Haiti, 1968–70; Commercial and Economic Counsellor, Ghana, 1970–73; Consul Gen., Cleveland, Ohio, 1973–79. *Recreations:* golf, reading. *Address:* Kingsdowne, Albert Terrace, Norwich NR2 2JD.

REID, Prof. Lynne McArthur; Simeon Burt Wolbach Professor of Pathology, Harvard Medical School, since 1976; Pathologist-in-Chief, Children's Hospital, Boston, 1976–90, now Pathologist-in-Chief Emeritus; *b* Melbourne, 12 Nov. 1923; *er d* of Robert Muir Reid and Violet Annie Reid (*née* McArthur). *Educ:* Wimbledon Girls' Sch. (GPDST); Janet Clarke Hall, Trinity Coll., Melbourne Univ.; Royal Melbourne Hosp. MB, BS Melb. 1946; MRACP 1950; MRCP 1951; FRACP, MRCPath (Foundn Mem.) 1964; FRCPath 1966; FRCP 1969; MD Melb. 1969. House Staff, Royal Melb. Hosp., 1946–49; Res. Fellow, Nat. Health and MRC, Royal Melb. Hosp. and Eliza Hall, 1949–51; Res. Asst, Inst. Diseases of Chest, 1951–55; Sen. Lectr founding Res. Dept of Path., Inst. Diseases of Chest, 1955; Reader in Exper. Path., London Univ., 1964; Prof. of Exper. Path., Inst. of Diseases of Chest (later Cardiothoracic Inst.), 1967–76; Hon. Lectr, UC Med. Sch., 1971–76; Hon. Consultant in Exper. Path., Brompton Hosp., 1963–76; Dean, Cardiothoracic Inst. (British Postgrad. Med. Fedn), 1973–76. 1st Hastings Vis. Prof. in Path., Univ. of California, 1965; Holme Lectr, UC Med. Sch., 1969; Walker-Ames Prof., Univ. of Washington, 1971; Neuhauser Lectr, 1976; Fleischner Lectr, 1976; Waring Prof., Stanford and Denver, 1977; Amberson Lectr, Amer. Thoracic Soc., 1978. Mem. Fleischner Soc., 1971 (Pres., 1977); 1st Hon. Fellow, Canadian Thoracic Soc., 1973; Chm., Cystic Fibrosis Res. Trust, 1974 (Mem. Med. Adv. Cttee 1964); Royal Soc. Medicine (Sect. Pathology): Vice-Pres. 1974; Standing Liaison Cttee on Sci. Aspects of Smoking and Health, 1971; Commn of European Cttees (Industrial Safety and Medicine), 1972; Mem. Bd of Governors, Nat. Heart and Chest Hosps, 1974; Manager, Royal Instn of Gt Britain, 1973 (Vice-Pres. 1974); Mem. Gov. Body, British Postgrad. Med. Fedn, 1974. *Publications:* The Pathology of Emphysema, 1967; numerous papers in sci. jls. *Recreations:* music, travel, reading. *Address:* Department of Pathology, Children's Hospital, 300 Longwood Avenue, Boston, MA 02115, USA. *T:* (617) 3557440, *Fax:* (617) 7310954; 50 Longwood Avenue, #216, Brookline, MA 02446, USA. *Clubs:* University Women's; Harvard (Boston).

REID, Malcolm Herbert Marcus; Chief Executive, Life Assurance and Unit Trust Regulatory Organisation, 1986–89; *b* 2 March 1927; *s* of late Marcus Reid and Winifred Stephens; *m* 1st, 1956, Eleanor (*d* 1974), *d* of late H. G. Evans, MC; four *s*; 2nd, 1975, Daphne (*d* 2000), *e d* of Sir John Griffin, QC. *Educ:* Merchant Taylors' Sch.; St John's Coll., Oxford. Served in Navy, 1945–48 and in RNVR, 1949–53. Entered Board of Trade, 1951; Private Secretary to Permanent Secretary, 1954–57; Trade Comr in Ottawa, 1957–60; Board of Trade, 1960–63; Private Secretary to successive Prime Ministers, 1963–66; Commercial Counsellor, Madrid, 1967–71; Asst Sec., DTI, 1972–74; Under Sec., Dept of Industry, 1974–78, of Trade, 1978–83, DTI, 1983–84; Registrar, Registry of Life Assurance Commn, 1984–86. Dir, Mercury Life Assurance Co. Ltd, 1989–97. Mem., Appeal Cttee, ICA, 1990–96. *Recreations:* National Hunt racing, inland waterways. *Address:* 7 Church Street, St Ives, Cambs PE27 6DG. *T:* (01480) 469753. *Club:* Oxford and Cambridge.

See also Sir H. M. S. Reid.

REID, Sir Martin; *see* Reid, Sir H. M. S.

REID, Sir Norman (Robert), Kt 1970; DA (Edinburgh); FMA; FIIC; Director, the Tate Gallery, 1964–79; *b* 27 December 1915; *o s* of Edward Daniel Reid and Blanche, *d* of Richard Drouet; *m* 1941, Jean Lindsay Bertram; one *s* one *d*. *Educ:* Wilson's Grammar School; Edinburgh Coll. of Art; Edinburgh Univ. Served War of 1939–46, Major, Argyll and Sutherland Highlanders. Joined staff of Tate Gallery, 1946; Deputy Director, 1954; Keeper, 1959. Fellow, International Institute for Conservation (IIC) (Secretary General, 1963–65; Vice-Chm., 1966); British Rep. Internat. Committee on Museums and Galleries of Modern Art, 1963–79; President, Penwith Society of Arts; Member: Council, Friends of the Tate Gall., 1958–79 (Founder Mem.); Arts Council Art Panel, 1964–74; Inst. of Contemporary Arts Adv. Panel, 1965–; Contemporary Art Soc. Cttee, 1965–72, 1973–77; "Paintings in Hospitals" Adv. Cttee, 1965–69; British Council Fine Arts Cttee, 1965–77 (Chm. 1968–75); Culture Adv. Cttee of UK Nat. Commn for Unesco, 1966–70; Univ. of London, Bd of Studies in History of Art, 1968; Cttee, The Rome Centre, 1969–77 (Pres. 1975–77); Adv. Council, Paul Mellon Centre, 1971–78; Council of Management, Inst. of Contemp. Prints, 1972–78; Council, RCA, 1974–77. Mem. Bd, Burlington Magazine, 1971–75. Trustee, Graham and Kathleen Sutherland Foundn, 1980–85. Represented in collections: Scottish Nat. Gall. of Modern Art; Tate Gall. Hon. LittD East Anglia, 1970. Officer of the Mexican Order of the Aztec Eagle. *Club:* Arts.

REID, Paul Campbell; QC 2001; a Recorder of the Crown Court, since 1993; *b* 27 March 1949; *s* of Stuart Wemyss Reid and Elsie Reid; *m* 1978, Pauline Brown; two *s*. *Educ:* Merchant Taylors' Sch., Crosby; Christ's Coll., Cambridge (MA). Called to the Bar, Gray's Inn, 1973; an Assistant Recorder, 1989–93. *Recreations:* tennis, amateur dramatics, acoustic guitar. *Address:* Lincoln House Chambers, 1 Brazennose Street, Manchester M2 5EL. *T:* (0161) 832 5701. *Clubs:* Liverpool Ramblers Association Football; Alderley Edge Cricket.

REID, Maj.-Gen. Peter Daer, CB 1981; *b* 5 Aug. 1925; *s* of Col S. D. Reid and Dorothy Hungerford (*née* Jackson); *m* 1958, Catherine Fleetwood (*née* Boodle); two *s* two *d*. *Educ:* Cheltenham College; Wadham Coll., Oxford. Commissioned into Coldstream Guards, 1945; transferred Royal Dragoons, 1947; served: Germany, Egypt, Malaya, Gibraltar, Morocco; Staff Coll., 1959; Comdg Officer, The Royal Dragoons, 1965–68; student, Royal College of Defence Studies, 1973; Commander RAC, 3rd Div., 1974–76; Dir, RAC, 1976–78; Chief Exec., Main Battle Tank 80 Proj., 1979–80; Dir, Armoured Warfare Studies, 1981; Defence Advr, GKN, 1983–88; Mil. Advr, Howden Airdynamics, 1982–88; Associate Mem., Burdeshaw Associates Ltd (USA), 1982–94; Defence Consultant, Vickers Defence Systems Ltd, 1989–94. *Recreations:* sailing, ski-ing, fishing, bird watching. *Address:* The Border House, Cholderton, near Salisbury, Wilts SP4 0DU. *Clubs:* Army and Navy; Royal Western Yacht; Kandahar Ski.

REID, Philip; *see* under Ingrams, R. R.

REID, Sir Robert Paul, (Sir Bob), Kt 1990; Deputy Governor, Bank of Scotland, since 1997 (Director, since 1987); non-executive Director, Hbos, since 2001; *b* 1 May 1934; *m* 1958, Joan Mary; three *s*. *Educ:* St Andrews Univ. (MA Pol. Econ. and Mod. Hist.). Joined Shell, 1956; Sarawak Oilfields and Brunei, 1956–59; Nigeria 1959–67 (Head of Personnel); Africa and S Asia Regional Orgn, 1967–68; PA and Planning Adviser to Chairman, Shell & BP Services, Kenya, 1968–70; Man. Dir, Nigeria, 1970–74; Man. Dir, Thailand, 1974–78; Vice-Pres., Internat. Aviation and Products Trading, 1978–80; Exec. Dir, Downstream Oil, Shell Co. of Australia, 1980–83; Co-Ordinator for Supply and Marketing, London, 1983; Dir, Shell International Petroleum Co., 1984–90; Chm. and Chief Exec., Shell UK, 1985–90; Chairman: BRB, 1990–95; London Electricity plc, 1994–97; Sears plc, 1995–99; British-Borneo Oil & Gas plc, 1995–2000; Internat. Petroleum Exchange, 1999–; Sondex Ltd, 1999–. Director: British Borneo Petroleum, 1993–; AVIS Europe, 1997–; Sun Life Assurance Co. of Canada, 1997–; Siemens plc, 1998–. Chairman: Foundn for Management Educn, 1986–; BIM, 1988–90; Council, Industrial Soc., 1993–98; Foundn for Young Musicians, 1994–; Learning Through Landscapes, 2000–; Conservatoire for Dance and Drama, 2001. Dir, Merchants Trust, 1995–. Chancellor, Robert Gordon Univ., 1993–. Hon. LLD: St Andrews, 1987; Aberdeen, 1988; Sheffield Hallam, 1995; South Bank, 1995. *Recreations:* golf, sailing. *Address:* (office) 38 Threadneedle Street, EC2P 2EH. *T:* (020) 7601 6521. *Clubs:* MCC; Royal and Ancient Golf; Royal Melbourne (Melbourne); Frilford Heath Golf.

REID, Seona Elizabeth; Director, Glasgow School of Art, since 1999; *b* 21 Jan. 1950; *d* of George Robert Hall and Isobel Margaret Reid. *Educ:* Park Sch., Glasgow; Strathclyde Univ. (BA Hons Sociology); Liverpool Univ. (DBA). Business Manager, Lincoln Theatre Royal, 1972–73; Press and Publicity Officer, Northern Dance Theatre, 1973–76; Press and PRO, Ballet Rambert, 1976–79; freelance Arts consultant, 1979–80; Dir, Shape, 1980–87; Asst Dir, Strategy and Regl Develt, Greater London Arts, 1987–90; Dir, Scottish Arts Council, 1990–99. FRSA 1991. Hon. DArts Robert Gordon Univ., Aberdeen, 1995. *Recreations:* walking, travel, food, arts. *Address:* Glasgow School of Art, 167 Renfrew Street, Glasgow G3 6RQ. *T:* (0141) 353 4500, *Fax:* (0141) 353 4528; *e-mail:* s.reid@gsa.ac.uk.

REID, Whitelaw; President, Reid Enterprises; *b* 26 July 1913; *s* of late Ogden M. Reid and Mrs Ogden M. Reid; *m* 1st, 1948, Joan Brandon (marr. diss. 1959); two *s*; 2nd, 1959, Elizabeth Ann Brooks; one *s* one *d*. *Educ:* Lincoln Sch., NYC; St Paul's Sch., Concord, New Hampshire; Yale Univ. (BA). New York Herald Tribune: in various departments, 1938–40; foreign correspondent, England, 1940; Assistant to Editor, 1946; Editor, 1947–55; Pres., 1953–55; Chm. of Bd, 1955–58; Director, 1946–65; Dir, 1946–65, Pres., 1946–62, Herald Tribune Fresh Air Fund. Served War of 1939–45, 1st Lieut naval aviator, USNR. Formerly Director: Farfield Foundn; Freedom House; Golden's Bridge Hounds Inc., 1970–83; Dir, Yale Westchester Alumni Assoc. Chm., NY State Cttee on Public Employee Security Procedures, 1956–57. Ambassador to inauguration of President Ponce, Ecuador, 1956. Member: Nat. Commn for Unesco, 1955–60; President's Citizen Advisers on the Mutual Security Program, 1956–57; Yale Alumni Board (Vice-Chm., 1962–64), Yale Univ. Council (Chm., Publications Cttee, 1965–70; Sec., Class of Yale 1936, 1986–91); Nat. Inst. of Social Sciences, 1959–95; Mem., Council on Foreign Relations, 1941–94. District Comr, Purchase Pony Club, 1964–70; Pres., New York State Horse Council (formerly Empire State Horsemen's Assoc.), 1975–80. Fellow, Pierson Coll., Yale, 1949–. *Address:* (home and office) Reid Enterprises, Ophir Farm North, 73 West Patent Road, Bedford Hills, NY 10507, USA. *Clubs:* Century, Overseas Press, Silurians, Pilgrims, Yale, Amateur Ski (New York); Metropolitan (Washington); Bedford Golf and Tennis; St Regis Yacht.

REID, Flight Lt William, VC 1943; agricultural consultant; Agriculture Adviser, The MacRobert Trust, Douneside, Tarland, Aberdeenshire, 1950–59; *b* 21 Dec. 1921; *s* of late William Reid, Baillieston, Glasgow; *m* 1952, Violet Gallagher, 11 Dryburgh Gdns, Glasgow, NW1; one *s* one *d*. *Educ:* Coatbridge Secondary Sch.; Glasgow Univ.; West of Scotland Coll. of Agriculture. Student of Metallurgy, Sept. 1940; BSc (Agric.), 1949; Post-Graduate World Travelling Scholarship for 6 months, to study Agric. and Installations in India, Australia, NZ, USA and Canada, 1949–50. Joined RAF 1941; trained in Lancaster, Calif, USA. Won VC during a trip to Düsseldorf, 3 Nov. 1943, when member of 61 Squadron; pilot RAFVR, 617 Squadron (prisoner); demobilised, 1946; recalled to RAF for 3 months, Dec. 1951. Joined RAFVR, commissioned Jan. 1949, 103 Reserve Centre, Perth. Nat. Cattle and Sheep Advr, Spillers Ltd, 1959–81. Vice-Chm., VC and GC Assoc., 2000–. Freedom of City of London, 1988. *Recreations:* golf, shooting, fishing, etc. *Address:* Cranford, Ferntower Place, Crieff, Perthshire PH7 3DD. *T:* (01764) 652462. *Club:* Royal Air Force.

REID, William, CBE 1987; FSA; Director, National Army Museum, 1970–87; Consultative Director, The Heralds' Museum, 1988–92; *b* Glasgow, 8 Nov. 1926; *o s* of Colin Colquhoun Reid and Mary Evelyn Bingham; *m* 1958, Nina Frances Brigden. *Educ:* Glasgow and Oxford. Commnd RAF Regt, 1946–48. Joined staff of Armouries, Tower of London, 1956. Organising Sec., 3rd Internat. Congress of Museums of Arms and Military History, London, Glasgow and Edinburgh, 1963; Sec.-Gen., Internat. Assoc. of Museums of Arms and Military History, 1969–81, Pres., 1981–87, Hon. Life Pres., 1987; Member: British Nat. Cttee, ICOM, 1973–88; Council, Chelsea Soc., 1979–85; Founding Council, Army Records Soc., 1983–88. FSA 1965 (Mem. Council, 1975–76); FMA 1974–88, resigned. Trustee: The Tank Museum, 1970–87; RAEC Museum, 1985–99; Museum of Richmond, 1987–; Florence Nightingale Museum Trust, 1987–2000; Royal Hants Regt Mus., 1990–97; Lord Brock Meml Trust, 1994–; AGC Mus., 1999–. Mem., Conservative Adv. Cttee on the Arts and Heritage, 1988–. Vice Pres., Arms and Armour Soc., 2000–. Hon. Life Mem., Friends of the Nat. Army Mus., 1987; Hon. Member: Amer. Soc. of Arms Collectors, 1975; Indian Army Assoc., 1981. Freeman, Scriveners' Co., 1989–98 (Liveryman, 1990); Freeman, City of London, 1989. *Publications:* (with A. R. Dufty) European Armour in the Tower of London, 1968; The Lore of Arms, 1976 (Military Book Society choice) (also trans. Chinese, French, German, Danish, Italian, Spanish and Swedish); contribs to British and foreign jls. *Recreations:* the study of armour and arms, military history, music, bird-watching. *Address:* 66 Ennerdale Road, Richmond, Surrey TW9 2DL. *T:* (020) 8940 0904. *Club:* Athenæum.

REID, Ven. William Gordon; Archdeacon of Italy and Malta, and Chaplain of All Saints, Milan, since 2000; *b* 28 Jan. 1943; *s* of William Albert Reid and Elizabeth Jean Inglis. *Educ:* Galashiels Academy; Edinburgh Univ. (MA); Keble Coll., Oxford (MA); Cuddesdon College. Deacon 1967, priest 1968; Curate, St Salvador's, Edinburgh, 1967–69; Chaplain and Tutor, Salisbury Theological Coll., 1969–72; Rector, St Michael and All Saints, Edinburgh, 1972–84; Provost of St Andrew's Cathedral, Inverness, 1984–88; Chaplain of St Nicolas, Ankara, 1988–89, of St Peter and St Sigfrid's Church, Stockholm, 1989–92; Canon, Gibraltar Cathedral, 1992–98; Vicar-Gen., Dio. of Gibraltar in Europe, 1992–; Archdeacon in Europe, 1996–98; Dean of Gibraltar, 1998–2000. Councillor, Lothian Regional Council, 1974–84; Chm., Lothian and Borders Police Bd, 1982–84. *Publications:* (ed) The Wind from the Stars, 1992; Every Comfort at Golgotha, 1999. *Recreations:* travel and languages, Church and politics. *Address:* Via Solferino 17, 20121 Milan, Italy. *T:* (02) 655 2258. *Club:* New (Edinburgh).

REID, Sir William (Kennedy), KCB 1996 (CB 1981); Chairman: Advisory Committee on Distinction Awards, 1997–2000; Mental Welfare Commission for Scotland, 1997–2000; Parliamentary Commissioner for Administration, and Health Service Commissioner for England, Scotland and Wales, 1990–96; *b* 15 Feb. 1931; 3rd *s* of late James and Elspet Reid; *m* 1959, Ann, *d* of Rev. Donald Campbell; two *s* one *d*. *Educ:* Robert Gordon's Coll.; George Watson's Coll.; Univ. of Edinburgh; Trinity Coll., Cambridge. MA 1st cl. Classics Edinburgh and Cantab. Ferguson scholar 1952; Craven scholar 1956. Nat. service, 1952–54. Min. of Educn, 1956; Cabinet Office, 1964; Private Sec. to Sec. of Cabinet, 1965–67; Sec., Council for Scientific Policy, 1967–72; Under Sec., 1974–78, Accountant-General, 1976–78, DES; Dep. Sec. (Central Services), Scottish Office, 1978–84; Sec., SHHD, 1984–90. Chm. of Govs, Scottish Police Coll., 1984–90. Member: Council on Tribunals, 1990–96; Commns for Local Administration in England and in Wales, 1990–96. A Dir, Internat. Ombudsman Inst., 1992–96. Chm. Council, St George's Sch. for Girls, 1997–. Lectures: Crookshank, RCR, 1994; Sydenham, Soc. of Apothecaries, 1994; Hunt, RCGP, 1996. Queen Mother Fellow, Nuffield Trust, 1998. FRCPE 1997; FRSE 1999. Hon. LLD: Aberdeen, 1996; Reading, 1998; Hon. DLitt Napier, 1998. *Recreation:* hill walking. *Address:* 11 Inverleith Terrace, Edinburgh EH3 5NS. *Clubs:* Oxford and Cambridge; New (Edinburgh).

REID, William Macpherson; Sheriff of Tayside, Central and Fife, since 1983; *b* 6 April 1938; *s* of William Andrew Reid and Mabel McLeod; *m* 1971, Vivien Anne Eddy; three *d*. *Educ:* Elgin Academy; Aberdeen Univ.; Edinburgh Univ. MA; LLB. Admitted Advocate, 1963; Sheriff of: Lothian and Borders, 1978; Glasgow and Strathkelvin, 1978–83. *Address:* Sheriffs' Chambers, Sheriff Court House, Mar Street, Alloa FK10 1HR.

REID BANKS, Lynne; *see* Banks.

REIDHAVEN, Viscount, (Master of Seafield); James Andrew Ogilvie-Grant; *b* 30 Nov. 1963; *s* and *heir* of Earl of Seafield, *qv*. *Educ:* Harrow.

REIF, Prof. Stefan Clive, PhD; Professor of Medieval Hebrew Studies, Faculty of Oriental Studies, and Fellow of St John's College, University of Cambridge, since 1998; Director, Genizah Research Unit, since 1973, and Head, Oriental Division, University Library, since 1983, Cambridge University; *b* 21 Jan. 1944; *s* of late Peter Reif and of Annie Reif (*née* Rapstoff); *m* 1967, Shulamit, *d* of late Edmund and Ella Stekel; one *s* one *d*. *Educ:* Jews' Coll., Univ. of London (BA 1964); PhD London 1969; MA Cantab 1976. Lectr in Hebrew and Semitic Langs, Univ. of Glasgow, 1968–72; Asst Prof. of Hebrew Lang. and Lit., Dropsie Coll., Philadelphia, 1972–73. Visiting Professor: Hebrew Univ. of Jerusalem, 1989, 1996–97; Univ. of Pennsylvania, 2001. President: Jewish Historical Soc. of England, 1991–92; British Assoc. for Jewish Studies, 1992. *Publications:* Shabbethai Sofer and his Prayer-Book, 1979; (ed) Interpreting the Hebrew Bible, 1982; Published Material from the Cambridge Genizah Collections, 1988; (ed) Genizah Research After Ninety Years, 1992; Judaism and Hebrew Prayer, 1993; Hebrew Manuscripts at Cambridge University Library, 1997; A Jewish Archive from Old Cairo, 2000; Why Medieval Hebrew Studies?, 2001; over 200 articles. *Recreations:* squash, football, cooking matza-brei for his grandchildren. *Address:* Genizah Research Unit, Cambridge University Library, West Road, Cambridge CB3 9DR. *T:* (01223) 333000.

REIGATE, Archdeacon of; *see* Kajumba, Ven. D. S. K.

REIHER, Sir Frederick (Bernard Carl), KBE 1992; CMG 1982; Investment and finance consultant, 1992; Director, Harrisons & Crosfield (PNG) Ltd, 1982–91; Chairman, Harcos Trading (PNG) Ltd, 1982–91; *b* 7 Feb. 1945; *s* of William and Ruth Reiher; *m* 1974, Helen Perpetua; two *s* two *d*. *Educ:* Chanel Coll., Rabaul; Holy Spirit National Seminary, Port Moresby; Univ. of Papua New Guinea (BD). Private Sec. to Minister for Finance, PNG, 1973–76. Joined Diplomatic Service, 1976; established Diplomatic Mission for PNG in London, 1977; High Comr for PNG in London, 1978–80, concurrently accredited Ambassador to FRG, Belgium, EEC and Israel; Sec. of Dept of Prime Minister, PNG, 1980–82. Chairman: PNG Agriculture Bank, 1986–91;

PNG Nat. Airline Commn, 1992. *Address:* PO Box 7500, Boroko, Papua New Guinea. *Clubs:* Aviat Social & Sporting, South Pacific Motor Sports, Royal Yacht, PNG Pistol.

REILLY, David, FRCP, FFHom; Glasgow Homoeopathic Hospital: Lead Consultant Physician, since 1990; Hon. Senior Lecturer in Medicine, since 1991; Director, Academic Departments, since 1985; *b* 4 May 1955. *Educ:* Glasgow Univ. (MB ChB with commendation). MRCP 1981, FRCP 1993; MRCGP 1982; MFHom 1983, FFHom 1989. Various trng posts in conventional medicine, homoeopathy and complementary medicine; Hon. Sen. Registrar in Gen. Medicine and RCCM/MRC Res. Fellow, Univ. Dept of Medicine, Glasgow Royal Infirmary, 1987–90. Vis. Faculty Mem., Harvard Med. Sch., 1994–; Vis. Prof., Univ. of Maryland Sch. of Med., 1999–. Co-founding Ed., Interprofessional Care, 1992–96; Internat. Ed., Alternative Therapies in Health and Medicine, 1995–96. Co-Founder and Dir, AdHominem charity, 1998–. RAMC Meml Prize, 1978; Merit Award, Gtr Glasgow Health Council, 1998. *Publications:* (ed) The Foundations of Homoeopathy, 1984, 15th edn 1999; contrib. to numerous scientific pubns and book chapters exploring human healing and the meeting of orthodox and unorthodox care. *Recreations:* living, loving, lounging and laughing. *Address:* Glasgow Homoeopathic Hospital, 1053 Great Western Road, Glasgow G12 0XQ. *T:* (0141) 211 1621.

REILLY, David Nicholas, (Nick), CBE 2000; Vice-President, General Motors Corporation, since 1997; Vice-President of Sales, Marketing and Aftersales, General Motors Europe, since 2001; Chairman, IBC Vehicles, since 1996; *b* 17 Dec. 1949; *s* of late John Reilly and of Mona Reilly; *m* 1976, Susan Haig; one *s* two *d*. *Educ:* Harrow Sch.; St Catharine's Coll., Cambridge (MA). Investment Analyst, 1971–74; joined Gen. Motors, 1974; Finance Dir, Moto Diesel Mexicana, 1980–83; Supply Dir, Vauxhall Motors, 1984–87; Vice Pres., IBC, 1987–90; Manufg Dir, Vauxhall Ellesmere Port, 1990–94; Vice Pres., Quality, Gen. Motors Europe, 1994–96; Man. Dir, Vauxhall Motors Ltd, 1996–2001 (Chm., 1996–). Mem. Bd, Saab GB, 1996–. Chairman: Chester, Ellesmere, Wirral TEC, 1990–94; Trng Standards Council, 1997–2001; Adult Learning Inspectorate, 2001–. Mem., Commn for Integrated Transport, 1999–. Vice Pres., SMMT, 1996–. Chm., Econ. Affairs Cttee, CBI, 1999–2001. Chm., Oundle Sch. Foundn, 1997–2001. FIMI 1990 (Vice Pres., 1995). *Address:* General Motors Europe, Glattbrugg, Zürich, Switzerland.

REILLY, Lt-Gen. Sir Jeremy (Calcott), KCB 1987; DSO 1973; Commander Training and Arms Directors, 1986–89, retired; *b* 7 April 1934; *s* of late Lt-Col J. F. C. Reilly and E. N. Reilly (*née* Moreton); *m* 1960, Julia Elizabeth (*née* Forrester); two *d* (and one *d* decd). *Educ:* Uppingham; RMA Sandhurst. Commissioned Royal Warwickshire Regt, 1954; served Egypt, Cyprus (Despatches), Ireland, Hong Kong, Germany, Borneo, BJSM Washington DC; psc 1965; Brigade Major, BAOR, 1967–69; Chief Instructor, RMA, 1969–71; CO 2nd Bn Royal Regt of Fusiliers, 1971–73 (DSO); Instructor, Staff Coll., 1974–75; Col GS (Army Deployment), MoD, 1975–77; PSO to Field Marshal Lord Carver and attached FCO (Rhodesia), 1977–79; Comdr 6 Field Force and UK Mobile Force, 1979–81; Comdr 4th Armoured Div., BAOR, 1981–83; Dir Battle Develt, MoD, 1983–84; ACDS (Concepts), MoD, 1985–86. Dep. Col, RRF (Warwickshire), 1981–86; Col, RRF, 1986–96; Col Comdt, The Queen's Div., 1988–90. *Address:* RHQ RRF, HM Tower of London, EC3N 4AB.

REILLY, Michael David, PhD; HM Diplomatic Service; Head, Cultural Relations Department, Foreign and Commonwealth Office, since 2000; *b* 1 March 1955; *s* of Hugh Aidan Reilly and Mary Sheila Reilly; *m* 1981, Won-Kyong Kang; one *s* one *d*. *Educ:* Ulverston Grammar Sch.; Barnard Castle Sch.; Univ. of Liverpool (BA 1975; PhD 1986). Joined HM Diplomatic Service, 1978: Lang. Trng, Seoul, 1979–84; First Secretary: FCO, 1984–88; UK Delegn to OECD, Paris, 1988–91; (Political), Seoul, 1991–94; FCO, 1994–96; Dep. Hd of Mission, Manila, 1997–2000. *Publications:* articles in Urban History Yearbook and Jl Transport History. *Recreations:* ski-ing, scuba diving, steam engines. *Address:* c/o Foreign and Commonwealth Office, King Charles Street, SW1A 2AH. *T:* (020) 7270 3000.

REILLY, Nick; *see* Reilly, D. N.

REIMAN, Dr Donald Henry; Editor, Shelley and his Circle, Carl H. Pforzheimer Collection, New York Public Library, since 1986; Adjunct Professor of English, University of Delaware, since 1992; *b* 17 May 1934; *s* of Mildred A. (Pearce) Reiman and Henry Ward Reiman; *m* 1st, 1958, Mary A. Warner (marr. diss. 1974); one *d*; 2nd, 1975, Hélène Dworzan. *Educ:* Coll. of Wooster, Ohio (BA 1956; Hon. LittD 1981); Univ. of Illinois (MA 1957; PhD 1960). Instructor, 1960–62, Asst Prof. 1962–64, Duke Univ.; Associate Prof., Univ. of Wisconsin, Milwaukee, 1964–65; Editor, Shelley and his Circle, Carl H. Pforzheimer Liby, 1965–86. James P. R. Lyell Reader in Bibliography, Oxford Univ., 1988–89. Gen. Editor, Manuscripts of the Younger Romantics, 1984–98 (29 vols); Editor-in-Chief, Bodleian Shelley MSS, 1984–2000 (23 vols). *Publications:* Shelley's The Triumph of Life, 1965; Percy Bysshe Shelley, 1969, 2nd edn 1990; (ed) The Romantics Reviewed, 9 Vols, 1972; (ed) Shelley and his Circle, vols V–VI, 1973, Vols VII–VIII, 1986, Vols IX–X, 2001; (with D. D. Fischer) Byron on the Continent, 1974; (ed with S. B. Powers) Shelley's Poetry and Prose, 1977, 2nd edn (with N. Fraistat), 2001; (ed) The Romantic Context: Poetry, 128 vols, 1976–79; (ed jtly) The Evidence of the Imagination, 1978; English Romantic Poetry 1800–1835, 1979; Romantic Texts and Contexts, 1987; Intervals of Inspiration, 1988; The Study of Modern Manuscripts, 1993; (ed with N. Fraistat) The Complete Poetry of Percy Bysshe Shelley, vol. I, 2000; contribs to scholarly books, reviews and learned jls. *Address:* 907 Aster Avenue, Newark, DE 19711-2631, USA. *T:* (302) 3687199; *e-mail:* dhreiman@udel.edu.

REINERS, William Joseph; Director of Research Policy, Departments of the Environment and Transport, 1977–78, retired 1978; *b* 19 May 1923; *s* of late William and Hannah Reiners; *m* 1952, Catharine Anne Palmer; three *s* one *d*. *Educ:* Liverpool Collegiate Sch.; Liverpool Univ. RAE Farnborough, 1944–46; Min. of Works, 1946–50; Head, Building Operations and Economics Div., Building Research Station, 1950–63; Dir of Research and Information, MPBW, 1963–71; Dir of Research Requirements, DoE, 1971–77. Chm., Aldwyck Housing Assoc., 1993–95 (Mem. Bd, 1980–97). *Publications:* various on building operations and economics. *Address:* Valais, Berks Hill, Chorleywood, Herts WD3 5AQ. *T:* (01923) 448604.

REINHARDT, Max; Chairman: Reinhardt Books Ltd (formerly HFL (Publishers) Ltd), since 1947; The Nonesuch Press Ltd, since 1986; *b* 30 Nov. 1915; *s* of Ernest Reinhardt and Frieda Reinhardt (*née* Darr); *m* 1st, 1947, Margaret Leighton, CBE (marr. diss. 1955; she *d* 1976); 2nd, 1957, Joan, *d* of Carlisle and Dorothy MacDonald, New York City; two *d*. *Educ:* English High Sch. for Boys, Istanbul; Ecole des Hautes Etudes Commerciales, Paris; London School of Economics. Acquired HFL (Publishers) Ltd, 1947; founded Max Reinhardt Ltd, 1948, which bought: The Bodley Head Ltd, 1956 (Man. Dir, 1957–81; Chm., 1981–87); Putnam & Co., 1963; Jt Chm., Chatto, Bodley Head and Jonathan Cape Ltd, 1973–87. Mem. Council: Publishers' Assoc., 1963–69; Royal Academy of Dramatic Art, 1965–96; The Pilgrims, 1966–. *Recreations:* reading for pleasure, swimming, bridge. *Address:* Flat 2, 43 Onslow Square, SW7 3LR. *T:* (020) 7589 5527. *Clubs:* Beefsteak, Garrick, Royal Automobile.

REINTON, Sigurd Evang; Chairman, London Ambulance Service NHS Trust, since 1999; *b* 9 Nov. 1941; *s* of Dr Lars Reinton and Ingrid Evang Reinton (*née* Evang); *m* 1966, Arlette Jeanne Gisele Dufresne; two *d*. *Educ:* Lund Univ. (MBA 1964). Sales Dir, Audio-Nike AB, 1964–66; Account Supervisor, Young & Rubicam, 1966–68; Associate, 1968–76, Principal, 1976–81, Dir, 1981–88, McKinsey & Co., Inc.; Chm., Express Aviation Services, 1988–91; Dir, Aubin Hldgs Ltd, 1988–98; Chm., Mayday Healthcare NHS Trust, 1997–99. Dir, Freewheel Film Finance Ltd, 2000–. Mem., Nat. Council, NHS Confedn, 1998–. *Publications:* contrib. McKinsey Qly and Financial Times on corporate leadership. *Recreations:* flying (private pilot's licence/instrument rating), sailing, theatre. *Address:* c/o London Ambulance Service NHS Trust, 220 Waterloo Road, SE1 8SD. *T:* (020) 7921 5185. *Club:* Royal Automobile.

REISS, Charles Alexander; Political Editor, Evening Standard, since 1985; *b* 23 March 1942; *s* of Dr Joseph Charles Reiss and Jenny Francisca Reiss; *m* 1978, Sue Rosemary Newson-Smith; three *d*. *Educ:* Bryanston Sch., Dorset. Reporter: Hampstead & Highgate Express, 1964–66; London office, Glasgow Citizen, and Scottish Daily Express, 1966–68; Press Officer, Labour Party, 1968–71; Lobby Correspondent: E Anglia Daily Times, etc, 1971–73; Birmingham Post, 1973–75; Political Correspondent: and leader writer, Evening News, 1975–80; and chief leader writer, Evening Standard, 1980–85. Chm., Parly Lobby Journalists, 1995–96. *Recreations:* opera, walking, reading. *Address:* Press Gallery, House of Commons, SW1A 0AA. *Club:* Royal Automobile.

REISS, Ven. Robert Paul; Archdeacon of Surrey, since 1996; *b* 20 Jan. 1943; *s* of Paul Michael Reiss and Beryl Aileen Reiss (*née* Bryant); *m* 1985, Dixie Nichols; one *d*. *Educ:* Haberdashers' Aske's Sch., Hampstead; Trinity Coll., Cambridge (MA); Westcott House, Cambridge; Theol Inst., Bucharest, Rumania. Ordained deacon, 1969, priest, 1970; Asst Curate, St John's Wood Parish Church, London, 1969–73; Asst Missioner, Rujshahi, dio. of Dacca, Bangladesh, 1973; Chaplain, Trinity Coll., Cambridge, 1973–78; Selection Sec., ACCM, 1978–85 (Sen. Selection Sec., 1983–85); Team Rector of Grantham, dio. of Lincoln, 1986–96. Mem., General Synod of C of E, 1990–. *Publication:* (contrib.) Say One for Me, 1992. *Recreations:* cricket, golf. *Address:* Archdeacon's House, New Road, Wormley, near Godalming, Surrey GU8 5SU. *T:* (01428) 682563. *Clubs:* Oxford and Cambridge, MCC.

REISZ, Karel; film director; *b* 21 July 1926; *s* of Joseph Reisz and Frederika; *m* 1963, Betsy Blair; three *s*. *Educ:* Leighton Park Sch., Reading; Emmanuel Coll., Cambridge (BA). Formerly: co-ed with Lindsay Anderson, film magazine, Sequence; worked for BFI; first Programme Dir, National Film Theatre. Co-directed, with Tony Richardson, Momma Don't Allow, 1956; produced: Every Day Except Christmas, 1957; This Sporting Life, 1960; directed: We Are the Lambeth Boys, 1958; Saturday Night and Sunday Morning, 1959; Night Must Fall, 1963; Morgan, a Suitable Case for Treatment, 1965; Isadora, 1967; The Gambler, 1975; Dog Soldiers, 1978; The French Lieutenant's Woman, 1981; Sweet Dreams, 1986; Everybody Wins, 1991; Act Sans Paroles, 2000; *stage plays:* Gardenia, Manhattan Theatre Club, 1991; The Gigli Concert, The Deep Blue Sea, Almeida, 1992; Gate Theatre, Dublin: A Doll's House, 1993; Moonlight, 1994, transf. NY, 1995; Happy Days, transf. NY and Almeida, 1996; A Kind of Alaska, 1997; Long Day's Journey Into Night, 1998; The Yalta Game, 2001. *Publication:* The Technique of Film Editing (also ed), 1953.

REITH, Barony of (*cr* 1940); title disclaimed by 2nd Baron; *see under* Reith, Christopher John.

REITH, Christopher John; farmer; *b* 27 May 1928; *s* of 1st Baron Reith, KT, PC, GCVO, GBE, CB, TD, of Stonehaven, and Muriel Katharine, *y d* of late John Lynch Odhams; *S* father, 1971, as 2nd Baron Reith, but disclaimed his peerage for life, 1972; *m* 1969, Penelope Margaret Ann, *er d* of late H. R. Morris; one *s* one *d*. *Educ:* Eton; Worcester College, Oxford (MA Agriculture). Served in Royal Navy, 1946–48; farming thereafter. *Recreations:* fishing, gardening, forestry. *Heir (to disclaimed peerage): s* Hon. James Harry John Reith; *b* 2 June 1971. *Address:* Glendene, 13 Polinard, Comrie, Perthshire PH6 2HJ.

REITH, Douglas, CBE 1994; TD 1994; QC (Scotland) 1957; a Social Security (formerly National Insurance) Commissioner, 1960–92; *b* 29 June 1919; *s* of William Reith and Jessie McAllan; *m* 1949, Elizabeth Archer Stewart; one *s* one *d*. *Educ:* Aberdeen Grammar School; Aberdeen University (MA, LLB). Became Member of Faculty of Advocates in Scotland, 1946. Served in Royal Signals, 1939–46. Standing Junior Counsel in Scotland to Customs and Excise, 1949–51; Advocate-Depute, Crown Office, Scotland, 1953–57; Pres., Pensions Appeal Tribunal (Scotland), 1958–64; Chm., Nat. Health Service Tribunal (Scotland), 1963–65. *Address:* 2 Ravelston Court, Ravelston Dykes, Edinburgh EH12 6HQ. *T:* (0131) 337 0332. *Club:* New (Edinburgh).

REITH, Fiona Lennox; QC (Scot.) 1996; Sheriff of Glasgow and Strathkelvin, since 2000; *b* 17 July 1955; *d* of Patrick Donald Metcalfe Munro and late Francesca Diana Munro (*née* Fendall, later Sutherland); *m* 1979, David Stewart Reith, WS (marr. diss. 1990). *Educ:* Perth Acad.; Aberdeen Univ. (LLB). Solicitor, Edinburgh, 1979–82; WS 1981; admitted to Faculty of Advocates, 1983; Standing Jun. Counsel in Scotland to Home Office, 1989–92; Advocate-Depute, 1992–95; Standing Jun. Counsel to Scottish Office Envmt Dept, 1995–96; Sheriff of Tayside Central and Fife at Perth, 1999–2000. Mem., Sheriff Courts Rules Council, 1989–93. External Examr in Professional Conduct, Faculty of Advocates, 2000–. FSAScot. *Recreations:* walking, theatre, good food and wine, travel. *Address:* Sheriff's Chambers, Sheriff Court House, 1 Carlton Place, Glasgow GS 9DA. *T:* (0141) 429 8888.

REITH, Lt Gen. John George, CB 2000; CBE 1991 (OBE 1989); Chief of Joint Operations, Permanent Joint Headquarters, since 2001; *b* 17 Nov. 1948; *s* of John and Jean Reith; *m* 1st, 1971, Cherry Parker; one *s* one *d*; 2nd, 1987, June Nightingale; two *s*. *Educ:* Elliots Green; RMA Sandhurst. Commnd, 1969; CO 1st Bn Parachute Regt, 1986–88 (despatches 1987); COS 1 Armd Div., 1988–92; Comd, 4 Armd Bde, 1992–94; Dir, Internat. Orgns, 1994, Dir, Mil. Ops, 1995–97, MoD; Comdr, ACE Mobile Force (Land), 1997–99; Comdr, Albania Force, 1999; ACDS (Policy), MoD, 2000–01. QCVS 1994. *Recreations:* hill walking, gardening, good food. *Club:* Army and Navy.

REITH, Martin; HM Diplomatic Service, retired; *b* 6 Dec. 1935; *s* of late James Reith and of Christian (*née* Innes); *m* 1964, Ann Purves; four *s*. *Educ:* Royal High Sch. of Edinburgh. Served: India (Calcutta), 1957–59; Uganda, 1962–66; Scottish Office, Edinburgh, 1966–68; Australia (Canberra), 1969–72; Asst Head of Central and Southern Africa Dept, FCO, 1974–77; Commercial Sec., Beirut, 1977–78; UN Dept, FCO, 1979; Counsellor, NATO Def. Coll., Rome, 1980; Dep. High Comr, Malta, 1980–83; High Comr, Swaziland, 1983–87; Ambassador, Republic of Cameroon, 1987–91. *Recreations:* bridge, bowling, family history, Scottish country dancing, travel. *Address:* Ardnagaul House, Strathtay, by Pitlochry, Perthshire PH9 0PG.

REITH, Hon. Peter Keaston; Minister for Defence, Australia, 2000–01 and Leader of the House of Representatives, 1996–2001; *b* 15 July 1950; *s* of Dr A. C. Reith and E. V. Sambell; *m* 1973, Julie Treganowan; four *s*. *Educ:* Brighton Grammar Sch., Vic; Monash Univ. (BEc, LLB). Solicitor, 1974–82. MP (L) Flinders, Victoria, 1984–2001; Shadow Attorney-Gen., 1987–88; Shadow Industrial Relns, 1988–89; Shadow Minister of Educn, 1989–90; Shadow Treas., 1990–93; Dep. Leader of Opposition, 1990–93; Shadow Special Minister of State, 1993; Shadow Minister for Defence, 1994; responsibility for Native Title legislation, 1994; Shadow Minister: for Foreign Affairs, 1994–95; of Industrial Relns and Manager, Opposition Business in the House, 1995–96; Minister assisting Prime Minister for Public Service, 1996–97; Minister: for Industrial Relns, 1996–97; for Employment, Workplace Relns and Small Business, 1998–2000. Pres., Shire, Phillip Is. Council, 1980–81. Sec., Newhaven Coll., Phillip Is., 1977–82. *Recreations:* reading, sailing, golf. *Address:* c/o Sergeant's Office, House of Representatives, Parliament House, Canberra, ACT 2600, Australia.

REITZLE, Dr Wolfgang; President, Premier Automotive Group, Ford Motor Co., since 1999; *b* 7 March 1949. *Educ:* Munich Tech. Univ. (Dipl.Ing; Dipl. Wirtschafts Ing; Dr.Ing); Harvard Business Sch. (AMP). Joined BMW AG, Munich, 1976; Head: Pilot Plant and New Manufg Technologies, 1980–82; Powertrain Manufg, 1982–83; Asst to CEO, to co-ordinate Product Develt, 1983–84; Dir, Technical Planning, 1984–85; Dir Gen., Product Develt, 1985–86; Mem. Bd of Mgt, R & D, subseq. also Global Purchasing, and Sales and Marketing, 1986–99. Bundesverdienstkreuz (Germany), 1997. *Publication:* Roboter-Technik, 1981. *Recreations:* golf, ski-ing. *Address:* (office) 51 Berkeley Square, W1J 5BB. *T:* (020) 7529 7102.

RELLIE, Alastair James Carl Euan, CMG 1987; HM Diplomatic Service, retired; business consultant; *b* 5 April 1935; *s* of William and Lucy Rellie; *m* 1961, Annalisa (*née* Modin); one *s* two *d*. *Educ:* Michaelhouse, SA; Harvard Univ., USA (BA). Rifle Bde, 1958–60. Second Sec., FCO, 1963–64; Vice-Consul, Geneva, 1964–67; First Secretary: FCO, 1967–68; (Commercial), Cairo, 1968–70; Kinshasa, 1970–72; FCO, 1972–74; (and later Counsellor), UK Mission to UN, New York, 1974–79; FCO, 1979–92. Dir, Market Relations, BAe, 1993–2000. Mem. Bd, Eur. Defence Industries Gp, 1994–, and NATO Industrial Adv. Gp, 1994– (Head, UK delegn to both Gps, 1998–). Mem. Council, UK Defence Manufrs Assoc., 1994–. *Address:* 50 Smith Street, SW3 4EP. *T:* (020) 7352 5734. *Clubs:* Brooks's, Greenjackets.

RELPH, Michael Leighton George; film producer, director, designer, writer; *s* of late George Relph and Deborah Relph (later Harker); *m* 1st, 1939, Doris Gosden (marr. diss.); one *s*; 2nd, 1950, Maria Barry; one *d*. *Educ:* Bembridge Sch. Stage designer, 1940–50: West-end prodns include: Indoor Fireworks; The Doctor's Dilemma; Up and Doing; Watch on the Rhine; The Man Who Came to Dinner; Frieda; Saloon Bar; Old Acquaintance; Quiet Week-end; Heartbreak House; Relative Values; A Month in the Country; The Last of Summer; Love in Idleness; The White Carnation; The Petrified Forest; The Banbury Nose; They Came to a City. Began film career as apprentice, then Asst Art Dir, Gaumont British Studios; Art Dir, Warner Brothers Studios; Art Dir, Ealing Studios, 1942–45: prodns include: The Bells Go Down; Dead of Night; Champagne Charley; Nicholas Nickleby; Saraband for Dead Lovers (nominated Hollywood Oscar); Associate Producer to Michael Balcon, 1945; subseq. Producer with Basil Dearden as Dir until Dearden's death, 1972: prodns include: The Captive Heart; Kind Hearts and Coronets; The Blue Lamp (Best British Film Award, Brit. Film Acad.); Frieda; Saraband for Dead Lovers; I Believe in You (co-author); The Ship that Died of Shame; The Rainbow Jacket; The Square Ring; The Gentle Gunman; Cage of Gold; Pool of London. Director: Davy, 1957; Rockets Galore, 1958; Producer: Violent Playground; Sapphire (Best British Film Award, Brit. Film Acad.); All Night Long; The Smallest Show on Earth. Founder Dir, Allied Film Makers: produced: League of Gentlemen; Victim; Man in the Moon (co-author); Life for Ruth; The Mind Benders; Woman of Straw; Masquerade (co-author); The Assassination Bureau (also author and designer); The Man Who Haunted Himself (co-author); in charge of production, Boyd's Company, 1978–82: Scum (exec. producer), 1979; An Unsuitable Job for a Woman (co-producer), 1982; Treasure Houses of Britain (TV; exec. producer), 1985; Heavenly Pursuits, 1986; The Torrents of Spring, 1988 (production consultant); screenplays, 1995–96: Seven Against the West; (with Fay Weldon) My Mother's Profession; William Tell: the untold story. Chm., Film Prodn Assoc. of GB, 1971–76; Mem., Cinematograph Films Council, 1971–76; Governor, BFI, 1972–79 (Chm., Prodn Bd, 1972–79). Hon. DLitt De Montfort, 1999. *Recreations:* reading, theatre going, painting. *Address:* 71 The Maltings, Henty Gardens, Chichester, West Sussex PO19 3DN. *T:* (01243) 839811.

See also S. G. M. Relph.

RELPH, Simon George Michael; independent film producer; Director: Skreba Films, since 1980; Greenpoint Films, since 1980; *b* 13 April 1940; *s* of Michael Leighton George Relph, *qv*; *m* 1963, Amanda, *d* of Anthony Grinling, MC; one *s* one *d*. *Educ:* Bryanston School; King's College, Cambridge (MA Mech. Scis). Asst Dir, Feature Films, 1961–73; Production Administrator, Nat. Theatre, 1974–78; Chief Exec., British Screen Finance Ltd, 1985–90. Chm., BAFTA, 2000–01 (Vice Chm., 1994–98); Mem. Council, RCA, 1989–99 (Hon. Fellow, 1999). Gov., BFI, 1991–97. *Films* include: Production Supervisor, Yanks, 1978; Executive Producer: Reds, 1980; Laughterhouse, 1984; Enchanted April, 1991; Hideous Kinky, 1998; Producer/Co-Producer: The Return of the Soldier, 1981; Privates on Parade, 1982; Ploughman's Lunch, 1983; Secret Places, 1984; Wetherby, 1985; Comrades, 1986; Damage, 1992; The Secret Rapture, 1992; Camilla, 1993; Look Me in the Eye, 1994; Blue Juice, 1995; The Slab Boys, 1996; Land Girls, 1997. Chevalier, Ordre des Arts et des Lettres (France), 1992. *Recreations:* gardening, photography, golf. *Address:* The Old Malt House, Westwood, Bradford-on-Avon, Wilts BA15 2AG.

REMEDIOS, Alberto Telisforo, CBE 1981; opera and concert singer; *b* 27 Feb. 1935; *s* of Albert and Ida Remedios; *m* 1st, 1958, Shirley Swindells (marr. diss.); one *s*; 2nd, 1965, Judith Annette Hosken; one *s* one *d*. *Educ:* studied with Edwin Francis, Liverpool, and with Joseph Hislop. Début: Sadler's Wells Opera, 1956; Proms, 1960; Royal Opera, Covent Gdn, 1965; San Francisco, 1973; Los Angeles, 1974; WNO, 1975; NY Met., 1976; San Diego, 1978; Scottish Opera, 1977. Principal tenor, Frankfurt Opera, 1968–70; Member: Royal Opera Co., 1982–84; Australian Opera Co., 1984–86. Repertoire of over 80 principal roles; notable for Wagner interpretations, esp. Walther von Stolzing, Siegmund, Siegfried and Tristan, Sadler's Wells/ENO, under direction of Sir Reginald Goodall, 1968–81; first British tenor since 1935 to sing Siegfried at Covent Gdn, 1980–81 and 1981–82 seasons. Conductors worked with include: Richard Bonynge, Sir Colin Davis, Sir Edward Downes and Sir Charles Mackerras. Gives lectures, workshops, masterclasses. Recordings include Wagner's Ring; Tippett's A Midsummer Marriage; Stravinsky's Oedipus Rex. Mem., Wagner Soc. Queen's Prize, RCM, 1957; 1st prize for Tenor (Bulgarian Song), Union of Bulgarian Composers, and 1st prize, Bulgarian Internat. Opera Contest, 1963; Sir Reginald Goodall Award, Wagner Soc., 1995. *Recreations:* soccer (Hon. Mem., Liverpool FC), motoring, record collecting, old radios and record players.

REMNANT, family name of **Baron Remnant**.

REMNANT, 3rd Baron *cr* 1928, of Wenhaston; **James Wogan Remnant;** Bt 1917; CVO 1979; FCA; Director, Bank of Scotland, 1989–96 (Director 1973–96, and Chairman, 1979–92, London Board); Chairman, National Provident Institution, 1990–95 (Director, 1963–95); *b* 23 Oct. 1930; *s* of 2nd Baron Remnant, MBE and Dowager Lady Remnant (*d* 1990); *S* father, 1967; *m* 1953, Serena Jane Loehnis, *o d* of Sir Clive Loehnis, KCMG; three *s* one *d*. *Educ:* Eton. FCA 1955. Nat. Service, Coldstream Guards, 1948–50 (Lt). Partner, Touche Ross & Co., 1958–70; Man. Dir, 1970–80, Chm., 1981–89, Touche, Remnant & Co.; Chairman: TR City of London Trust, 1978–90 (Dir, 1973–90); TR Pacific Investment Trust, 1987–94. Dep. Chm., Ultramar, 1981–91 (Dir, 1970–91); Director: Australia and New Zealand Banking Group, 1968–81 (Mem., Internat. Bd of Advice, 1987–91); Union Discount Co. of London, 1968–92 (Dep. Chm., 1970–86); London Merchant Securities, 1994–, and other cos. Chm., Assoc. of Investment Trust Cos, 1977–79. A Church Comr, 1976–84. Chm., Institutional Shareholders Cttee 1977–78. Trustee, Royal Jubilee Trusts, 1990–2000 (Hon. Treasurer, 1972–80; Chm., 1980–89); President: Wokingham Constituency Cons. Assoc., 1981–96; Nat. Council of YMCAs, 1983–96; Florence Nightingale Foundn, 1987–; Chm., Learning Through Landscapes Trust, 1989–2000. Master, Salters' Co., 1995–96. GCStJ (Bailiff of Egle, 1993–99). *Heir:* *s* Hon. Philip John Remnant, *qv*. *Address:* Bear Ash, Hare Hatch, Reading RG10 9XR.

REMNANT, Hon. Philip John; Director General, Takeover Panel, since 2001; *b* 20 Dec. 1954; *s* and *heir* of Baron Remnant, *qv*; *m* 1977, Caroline Elizabeth Clare Cavendish; one *s* two *d*. *Educ:* Eton Coll.; New Coll., Oxford (MA Law). ACA 1979. Peat, Marwick, Mitchell & Co., 1976–82; Kleinwort Benson Ltd, 1982–90 (Dir, 1988–90); Barclays de Zoete Wedd, 1990–97: Man. Dir, 1992–97; Hd, UK Corporate Finance, 1993–94; Dep. Hd, Global Corporate Finance, 1995–96; Co-Hd, Global M&A, 1997; Man. Dir and Dep. Hd, UK Investment Banking, Credit Suisse First Boston, 1997–2001. *Address:* Ham Farm House, Baughurst, Basingstoke, Hants RG26 5SD.

REMNICK, David Jay; Editor, The New Yorker, since 1998; *b* 29 Oct. 1958; *m* 1987, Esther B. Fein; two *s* one *d*. *Educ:* Princeton Univ. (BA). Washington Post: staff writer, 1982–88; Moscow corresp., 1988–92; staff writer, The New Yorker, 1992–. Vis. Fellow, Council on Foreign Relns. *Publications:* Lenin's Tomb, 1993 (Pulitzer Prize, George Polk Award, 1994); Resurrection, 1997; The Devil Problem (and Other True Stories), 1997; King of the World, 1998; contribs to NY Rev. of Books, Vanity Fair, Esquire, New Republic. *Address:* The New Yorker, 4 Times Square, New York, NY 10036, USA.

RENALS, Sir Stanley, 4th Bt *cr* 1895; formerly in the Merchant Navy; *b* 20 May 1923; 2nd *s* of Sir James Herbert Renals, 2nd Bt; *S* brother, Sir Herbert Renals, 3rd Bt, 1961; *m* 1957, Maria Dolores Rodriguez Pinto, *d* of late José Rodriguez Ruiz; one *s*. *Educ:* City of London Freemen's School. *Heir:* *s* Stanley Michael Renals, BSc, CEng, MIMechE, MIProdE [*b* 14 Jan. 1958; *m* 1982, Jacqueline Riley; one *s* one *d*]. *Address:* 52 North Lane, Portslade, East Sussex BN4 2HG.

RENDEL, David Digby; MP (Lib Dem) Newbury, since May 1993; *b* 15 April 1949; *s* of Alexander Rendel and Elizabeth (*née* Williams); *m* 1974, Dr Susan Taylor; three *s*. *Educ:* Eton (schol.); Magdalen Coll., Oxford (BA); St Cross Coll., Oxford. Shell Internat., 1974–77; British Gas, 1977–78; Esso Petroleum, 1978–90. Mem., Newbury DC, 1987–95. Lib Dem spokesman: on Local Govt, 1993–97; on Higher Educn, 2001–. Member: Public Accounts Cttee, 1999–; Procedures Cttee, 2001–. Ldr, Lib Dem Parly Welfare Team, 1997–. *Address:* House of Commons, SW1A 0AA. *T:* (020) 7219 3000; Tudor Lodge, Stroud Green, Newbury, Berks RG14 7JA. *T:* (01635) 581048.

RENDELL, family name of **Baroness Rendell of Babergh**.

RENDELL OF BABERGH, Baroness *cr* 1997 (Life Peer), of Aldeburgh in the co. of Suffolk; **Ruth Barbara Rendell,** CBE 1996; crime novelist, since 1964; *b* 17 Feb. 1930; *d* of Arthur Grasemann and Ebba Kruse; *m* 1950, Donald Rendell; marr. diss. 1975; remarried Donald Rendell, 1977 (he *d* 1999); one *s*. *Educ:* Loughton County High School. FRSL. Arts Council National Book Award for Genre Fiction, 1981; Sunday Times Award for Literary Excellence, 1990. *Publications:* From Doon with Death, 1964; To Fear a Painted Devil, 1965; Vanity Dies Hard, 1966; A New Lease of Death, 1967; Wolf to the Slaughter, 1967 (televised 1987); The Secret House of Death, 1968; The Best Man to Die, 1969; A Guilty Thing Surprised, 1970; One Across Two Down, 1971; No More Dying Then, 1971; Murder Being Once Done, 1972; Some Lie and Some Die, 1973; The Face of Trespass, 1974 (televised, as An Affair in Mind, 1988); Shake Hands for Ever, 1975; A Demon in my View, 1976 (film 1991); A Judgement in Stone, 1977; A Sleeping Life, 1978; Make Death Love Me, 1979; The Lake of Darkness, 1980 (televised, as Dead Lucky, 1988); Put on by Cunning, 1981; Master of the Moor, 1982 (televised 1994); The Speaker of Mandarin, 1983; The Killing Doll, 1984; The Tree of Hands, 1984 (film 1989); An Unkindness of Ravens, 1985; Live Flesh, 1986; Heartstones, 1987; Talking to Strange Men, 1987; (ed) A Warning to the Curious—The Ghost Stories of M. R. James, 1987; The Veiled One, 1988 (televised 1989); The Bridesmaid, 1989; Ruth Rendell's Suffolk, 1989; (with Colin Ward) Undermining the Central Line, 1989; Going Wrong, 1990; Kissing the Gunner's Daughter, 1992; The Crocodile Bird, 1993; Simisola, 1994; (ed) The Reason Why, 1995; The Keys to the Street, 1996; Road Rage, 1997; A Sight for Sore Eyes, 1998; Harm Done, 1999; Adam and Eve and Pinch Me, 2001; *short stories:* The Fallen Curtain, 1976; Means of Evil, 1979; The Fever Tree, 1982; The New Girl Friend, 1985; Collected Short Stories, 1987; The Copper Peacock, 1991; Blood Linen, 1995; Piranha to Scurfy, 2000; (as Barbara Vine): A Dark-Adapted Eye, 1986 (televised 1994); A Fatal Inversion, 1987 (televised 1992); The House of Stairs, 1988; Gallowglass, 1990; King Solomon's Carpet, 1991; Asta's Book, 1993; No Night Is Too Long, 1994; The Brimstone Wedding, 1996; The Chimney Sweeper's Boy, 1998. *Recreations:* reading, walking, opera. *Address:* House of Lords, SW1A 0PW. *Clubs:* Groucho, Detection.

RENDLE, Michael Russel; Managing Director, British Petroleum plc, 1981–86; Deputy Chairman, British-Borneo Petroleum Syndicate plc, since 1986; Director, Medical Defence Union, since 1998; Chairman, Willis Pension Trustees, since 1998 (Director, since 1986); *b* 20 Feb. 1931; *s* of late H. C. R. Rendle and Valerie Patricia (*née* Gleeson); *m* 1957, Heather, *d* of J. W. J. Rinkel; two *s* two *d*. *Educ:* Marlborough; New College, Oxford. MA. Joined Anglo-Iranian Oil Co. (now BP), 1954; Man. Dir, BP Trinidad, 1967–70; Man. Dir, BP Australia, 1974–78; Dir, BP Trading Ltd, 1978–81; Chairman: BP Chemicals Int., 1981–83; BP Coal, 1983–86; BP Nutrition, 1981–86. Chm., Forestry Investment Management, 1992– (Dir, 1989–); Deputy Chairman: Imperial Continental Gas Assoc., 1986–87; Tace, 1991; Chairman: Markheath, later TBI, 1991–95; Campbell & Armstrong PLC, 1996–98 (Dir, 1992–); Director: London Adv. Bd, Westpac Banking Corp. (formerly Commercial Bank of Australia), 1978–89; Willis Faber, then Willis Corroon plc, 1985–98; Petrofina SA, 1986–87; OIS International Inspection plc, 1993–96

(Chm., 1995–96). Mem. BOTB, 1982–86; Chm., European Trade Cttee, 1982–86. Chm. Social Affairs Cttee, UNICE, 1984–87; Mem. Internat. Council and UK Adv. Bd, INSEAD, 1984–86. Mem. Council, Marlborough Coll., 1987–95. *Recreations:* golf, music, outdoor sports, gardening. *Address:* c/o Willis Corroon plc, 10 Trinity Square, EC3P 3AX. *T:* (020) 7481 7152. *Clubs:* Vincent's (Oxford); Australian (Melbourne).

RENDLE, Peter Critchfield; Under-Secretary (Principal Finance Officer), Scottish Office, 1978–80, retired; *b* Truro, 31 July 1919; *s* of late Martyn and Florence Rendle; *m* 1944, Helen Barbara Moyes; three *s*. *Educ:* Queen Elizabeth's Sch., Hartlebury. Clerical Officer, Min. of Transport, 1936–49. Served War, Royal Navy, 1940–46 (Lieut RNVR). Min. of Town and Country Planning, 1949; Dept of Health for Scotland, 1950–59 (Sec., Guest Cttee on Bldg Legislation in Scotland); Scottish Home and Health Dept, 1959–63 and 1972–73; Scottish Educn Dept, 1963–72; Under Sec., Housing, Scottish Development Dept, 1973–78. Member: Legal Aid Central Cttee for Scotland, 1980–87; Scottish Is Councils Cttee of Inquiry, 1982–84; Scottish Legal Aid Bd, 1987–89. *Publication:* Rayner Report, Scrutiny of HM Inspectors of Schools in Scotland, 1981. *Recreations:* theatre, taking photographs. *Address:* 3/6 Caithness Place, Clark Road, Edinburgh EH5 3AE. *T:* (0131) 552 8024. *Clubs:* Royal Over-Seas League; Scottish Arts (Edinburgh).

RENDLESHAM, 9th Baron *cr* 1806 (Ire.); **Charles William Brooke Thellusson;** *b* 10 Jan. 1954; *o s* of 8th Baron Rendlesham and his 2nd wife, Clare, *d* of Lt-Col D. H. G. McCririck; *S* father, 1999; *m* 1988, Lucille Clare, *d* of Rev. Henry Ian Gordon Cumming; one *d*. *Educ:* Eton. *Heir: unde* Hon. Peter Robert Thellusson [*b* 25 Jan. 1920; *m* 1st, 1947, Pamela Tufnell (*née* Parker) (marr. diss. 1950); 2nd, 1952, Celia Walsh; two *s*].

RENÉ, (France) Albert; barrister-at-law; President of the Republic of Seychelles, since 1977 (re-elected, 1979, 1984, 1989, 1993, 1998, 2001); *b* Mahé, Seychelles, 16 Nov. 1935; *s* of Price René and Louisa Morgan; *m* 1st, 1956, Karen Handlay; one *d*; 2nd, 1975, Geva Adam; one *s*; 3rd, 1993, Sarah Zarqani; one *s* two *d*. *Educ:* St Louis Coll., Seychelles; Collège du Sacré Cœur, St Maurice, Valais, Switzerland; St Mary's Coll., Southampton, England; King's Coll., Univ. of London; Council of Legal Educn, 1956; LSE, 1961. Called to Bar, 1957. Leader, Founder, Pres., 1964–78, Seychelles People's United Party (first effective political party and liberation movement in Seychelles); MP, 1965; Mem. in Governing Council, 1967; Mem., Legal Assembly, 1970 and 1974; Minister of Works and Land Development, 1975; Prime Minister, 1976–77; Minister: of Transport, 1984–86; of Admin, Finance and Industries, Planning and External Relns, 1984–89; of Defence, 1986–92. Founder, Leader and Sec.-Gen., Seychelles People's Progressive Front, 1978. Order of the Golden Ark (1st cl.), 1982. *Address:* President's Office, State House, Republic of Seychelles.

RENFREW, family name of **Baron Renfrew of Kaimsthorn**.

RENFREW OF KAIMSTHORN, Baron *cr* 1991 (Life Peer), of Hurlet in the District of Renfrew; **Andrew Colin Renfrew,** FBA 1980; Disney Professor of Archaeology, University of Cambridge, since 1981; Director, McDonald Institute for Archaeological Research, Cambridge, since 1991; *b* 25 July 1937; *s* of late Archibald Renfrew and Helena Douglas Renfrew (*née* Savage); *m* 1965, Jane Margaret, *d* of Ven. Walter F. Ewbank, *qv*; two *s* one *d*. *Educ:* St Albans Sch.; St John's Coll., Cambridge (Exhibr); British Sch. of Archaeology, Athens. Pt I Nat. Scis Tripos 1960; BA 1st cl. hons Archaeol. and Anthrop. Tripos 1962; MA 1964; PhD 1965; ScD 1976. Pres., Cambridge Union Soc., 1961; Sir Joseph Larmor Award 1961. Nat. Service, Flying Officer (Signals), RAF, 1956–58. Res. Fellow, St John's Coll., Cambridge, 1965; Bulgarian Govt Schol., 1966; University of Sheffield: Lectr in Prehistory and Archaeol., 1965–70; Sen. Lectr, 1970–72; Reader, 1972; Prof. of Archaeology, Southampton Univ., 1972–81; Professorial Fellow, St John's Coll., Cambridge, 1981–86; Master, 1986–97, Professorial Fellow, 1997–, Jesus Coll., Cambridge. Visiting Lecturer: Univ. of Calif at Los Angeles, 1967; Univ. of Minnesota, 1987. Contested (C) Sheffield Brightside, 1968; Chm., Sheffield Brightside Conserv. Assoc., 1968–72. Member: Ancient Monuments Bd for England, 1974–84; Royal Commn on Historical Monuments (England), 1977–87; Historic Buildings and Monuments Commn for England, 1984–86; Ancient Monuments Adv. Cttee, 1984–2001; UK Nat. Commn for UNESCO, 1984–86 (Mem. Culture Adv. Cttee, 1984–86); Exec. Cttee, NACF, 2001–; Trustee: Antiquity Trust, 1974–; British Mus., 1991–2001; Chm., Hants Archaeol Cttee, 1974–81; a Vice-Pres., RAI, 1982–85. Chm., Governors, The Leys, 1984–92. Lectures: Dalrymple in Archaeol., Univ. of Glasgow, 1975 and 2000; George Grant MacCurdy, Harvard, 1977; Patten, Indiana Univ., 1982; Harvey, New Mexico Univ., 1982; Hill, Univ. of Minnesota, 1987; Tanner, Stanford Univ., 1993; Neubergh, Univ. of Göteborg, 1997; Hitchcock, Univ. of Calif, Berkeley, 1997; Kroon, Amsterdam, 1999; McDonald, Cambridge Univ., 1999; Rhind, Edinburgh, 2001. Excavations: Saliagos near Antiparos, 1964–65; Sitagroi, Macedonia, 1968–70; Phylakopi in Melos, 1974–76; Quanterness, Orkney, 1972–74; Maes Howe, 1973–74; Ring of Brodgar, 1974; Liddle Farm, 1973–74. FSA 1968 (Vice-Pres., 1987–92); FSAScot 1970 (Hon. FSAScot 2001); Hon. FRSE 2001; Hon. Fellow, Archael. Soc. of Athens, 1990. For. Associate, Nat. Acad. of Scis, USA, 1997; Corresp. Mem., Österreichische Akad. der Wissenschaften, 2000. Freeman, City of London, 1987. Hon. LittD: Sheffield, 1987; Southampton, 1995; Dr *hc* Athens, 1991. Rivers Meml Medal, 1979, Huxley Meml Medal, 1991, RAI; Fyssen Prize, Fyssen Foundn, Paris, 1996. *Publications:* (with J. D. Evans) Excavations at Saliagos near Antiparos, 1968; The Emergence of Civilisation, 1972; (ed) The Explanation of Culture Change, 1973; Before Civilisation, 1973; (ed) British Prehistory, a New Outline, 1974; Investigations in Orkney, 1979; (ed) Transformations: Mathematical Approaches to Culture Change, 1979; Problems in European Prehistory, 1979; (with J. M. Wagstaff) An Island Polity, 1982; (ed) Theory and Explanation in Archaeology, 1982; Approaches to Social Archaeology, 1984; The Prehistory of Orkney, 1985; The Archaeology of Cult, 1985; Archaeology and Language, 1987; (with G. Daniel) The Idea of Prehistory, 1988; The Cycladic Spirit, 1991; (with P. Bahn) Archaeology, 1991; (ed) America Past, America Present, 2000; Loot, Legitimacy and Ownership, 2000; (ed) Archaeogenetics, 2000; articles in archaeol jls. *Recreations:* modern art, numismatics, travel. *Address:* McDonald Institute for Archaeological Research, Downing Street, Cambridge CB2 3ER. *T:* (01223) 333521. *Clubs:* Athenæum, Oxford and Cambridge.

RENFREW, Glen McGarvie; Managing Director and Chief Executive, Reuters Ltd, 1981–91; *b* 15 Sept. 1928; *s* of Robert Renfrew and Jane Grey Watson; *m* 1954, Daphne Ann Hailey; one *s* two *d* (and one *d* decd). *Educ:* Sydney Univ., NSW, Australia (BA). Joined Reuters, London, 1952; reporting and/or management assignments in Asia, Africa and Europe, 1956–64; London management posts in computer and economic information services, 1964–70; Manager, Reuters N America, 1971–80. *Recreation:* sailing. *Club:* Manhasset Bay Yacht (Long Island, NY).

RENFREY, Rt Rev. Lionel Edward William; Dean of Adelaide, 1966–97; Assistant Bishop of Adelaide, 1969–89; *b* Adelaide, SA, 26 March 1916; *s* of late Alfred Cyril Marinus Renfrey and Catherine Elizabeth Rose Frerichs (*née* Dickson); *m* 1948, Joan Anne, *d* of Donald Smith, Cooke's Plains, SA; one *s* five *d*. *Educ:* Unley High School; St Mark's Coll., Univ. of Adelaide; St Barnabas' Theological Coll., Adelaide. BA (First Cl. Hons English), ThL (ACT) (Second Cl. Hons). Deacon 1940, priest 1941, Dio. Adelaide; Curate, St Cuthbert's, Prospect, 1940–43; Mission Chaplain, Mid Yorke Peninsula, 1943–44; Warden, Brotherhood of St John Baptist, 1944–47; Priest-in-charge: Berri-Barmera, 1948–50; Kensington Gardens, 1950–57; Rector, St James', Mile End, 1957–63; Rural Dean, Western Suburbs, 1962–63; Organising Chaplain, Bishop's Home Mission Soc., 1963–66; Editor, Adelaide Church Guardian, 1961–66; Archdeacon of Adelaide, 1965–66; Examining Chaplain to Bishop of Adelaide, 1965–85; Administrator (*sede vacante*), Diocese of Adelaide, 1974–75; Rector, Mallala and Two Wells, 1981–88. Patron: Prayer Book Soc. in Australia, 1980–; Monarchist League, 1994–. OStJ 1981 (SBStJ 1969). *Publications:* Father Wise: a Memoir, 1951; Short History of St Barnabas' Theological College, 1965; What Mean Ye By This Service?, 1978; (ed) Catholic Prayers, 1980; (ed) SS Peter and Paul Prayer Book, 1982; Arthur Nutter Thomas, Bishop of Adelaide 1906–1940, 1988. *Recreation:* reading. *Address:* 13 Northcote Terrace, Medindie, SA 5081, Australia. *Club:* Adelaide (Adelaide).

RENNARD, Baron *cr* 1999 (Life Peer), of Wavertree in the county of Merseyside; **Christopher John Rennard,** MBE 1989; Director of Campaigns and Elections, Liberal Democrats, since 1989; *b* 8 July 1960; *s* of late Cecil Langton Rennard and Jean Winifred Rennard (*née* Watson); *m* 1989, Ann McTegart. *Educ:* Mosspits Lane County Primary Sch.; Liverpool Blue Coat Sch.; Univ. of Liverpool (BA Hons Politics and Economics). Liberal Party: Agent, Liverpool Mossley Hill constituency, 1982–84; Area Agent, East Midlands region, 1984–88; Election Co-ordinator, Social & Liberal Democrats, 1988–89. *Publications:* Winning Local Elections, 1988; The Campaign Manual, 1990, 2nd edn 1995. *Recreations:* cooking, wine, France. *Address:* 19 Stockwell Park Road, SW9 0AP.

RENNELL, 3rd Baron *cr* 1933, of Rodd, Herefordshire; **John Adrian Tremayne Rodd;** *b* 28 June 1935; *s* of Hon. Gustaf Guthrie Rennell Rodd (*d* 1974) (*yr s* of 1st Baron) and Yvonne Mary Rodd (*d* 1982), *d* of late Sir Charles Murray Marling, GCMG, CB; *S* uncle, 1978; *m* 1977, Phyllis, *d* of T. D. Neill; one *s* three *d*. *Educ:* Downside; RNC, Dartmouth. Served Royal Navy, 1952–62. With Morgan Grenfell & Co. Ltd, 1963–66; free-lance journalist, 1966–67; Marks of Distinction Ltd, 1968–79; Dir, Tremayne Ltd, 1980–91. Team Leader for Vladimir Kramnik, World Championship Chess Match, 2000. *Recreations:* Scotland Rugby XV, 1958–65; golf, Real tennis. *Heir:* *s* Hon. James Roderick David Tremayne Rodd, *b* 9 March 1978. *Clubs:* White's, Portland; Sunningdale (Ascot).

RENNET, Roderick James, CBE 2000; CEng; FICE; Chief Executive, East of Scotland Water, 1996–2000; *b* 25 March 1942; *s* of James Mowat Rennet and Rachel Rennet; *m* 1965, Lesley Margaret Irving Love; one *s* one *d*. *Educ:* Dundee Inst. of Technol. (BSc Hons). CEng 1969; FICE 1986; FCIWEM (FIWEM 1987); FIWO 1992. Civil engrg apprentice, Dundee Harbour Trust, 1960–62; asst engr, Chester CBC, 1966–68; asst engr, then sen. engr, Durham CC, 1969–70; sen. engr, then principal engr, Dundee Corp., 1970–75; Tayside Regional Council: Depute Dir of Water Services, 1975–87; Dir of Water Services, 1988–95. *Recreations:* hill-walking, photography, cycling. *Address:* 1A Polwarth Terrace, Edinburgh EH11 1NF.

RENNIE, Alexander Allan, CBE 1980; QPM 1971; Chief Constable, West Mercia Constabulary, 1975–81, retired; *b* 13 June 1917; *s* of late Charles Rennie and Susan Parsons Rennie; *m* 1941, Lucy Brunt; one *s* one *d*. *Educ:* Ellon Acad., Aberdeenshire. Armed Services, 1941–45: commnd 30 Corps Royal Northumberland Fusiliers; active service in Europe (mentioned in despatches, 1945). Joined Durham County Constab., 1937; Chief Supt, 1963; Dep. Chief Constable, Shropshire, 1963–67; Dir, Sen. Comd Course, Police Coll., Bramshill, 1967–69; Asst Chief Constable, West Mercia, 1969–72, Dep. Chief Constable, 1973–75. OStJ 1975. *Recreations:* golf, hill walking. *Address:* 14 Minter Avenue, Droitwich, Worcs WR9 8RP.

RENNIE, Archibald Louden, CB 1980; Secretary, Scottish Home and Health Department, 1977–84, retired; *b* 4 June 1924; *s* of John and Isabella Rennie; *m* 1950, Kathleen Harkess; four *s*. *Educ:* Madras Coll.; St Andrews University (BSc). Minesweeping Res. Div., Admty, 1944–47; Dept of Health for Scotland, 1947–62; Private Sec. to Sec. of State for Scotland, 1962–63; Asst Sec., SHHD, 1963–69; Registrar Gen. for Scotland, 1969–73; Under-Sec., Scottish Office, 1973–77. Member: Scottish Records Adv. Council, 1985–94; Council on Tribunals, 1987–88. Gen. Council Assessor, St Andrews Univ. Court, 1984–85; Chancellor's Assessor and Finance Convener, 1985–89; Vice-Chm., Adv. Cttee on Distinction Awards for Consultants, 1985–94; Chm., Disciplined Services Pay Review Cttee, Hong Kong, 1988. Trustee, Lockerbie Air Disaster Trust, 1988–91; Dir, Elie Harbour Trust, 1989– (Chm., 1994–98). Mem. Bd, Madras Coll., 1994–99. Cdre, Elie and Earlsferry Sailing Club, 1991–93. Hon. FDSRCS 1995. Hon. LLD St Andrews, 1990. *Recreations:* Scottish literature, sea-fishing, firth-watching. *Address:* Well Wynd House, South Street, Elie, Fife KY9 1DN. *T:* (01333) 330741. *Club:* Scottish Arts (Edinburgh).

RENNIE, James Douglas Milne, CB 1986; Parliamentary Counsel, 1976–92; *b* 2 Nov. 1931; *s* of Douglas Frederick Milne Rennie and Margaret Wilson Fleming Rennie (*née* Keanie); *m* 1962, Patricia Margaret Calhoun Watson; one *s* one *d*. *Educ:* Charterhouse; New Coll., Oxford (Schol.). 1st cl. Hon. Mods 1953; 2nd cl. Lit. Hum. 1955; 2nd cl. Jurisprudence 1957; MA. Called to Bar, Lincoln's Inn, 1958 (Cholmeley Schol.). Asst Lectr, UCW Aberystwyth, 1957; practised at Chancery Bar, 1958–65; Asst Parly Counsel, HM Treasury, 1965; Sen. Asst Parly Counsel, 1972; Dep. Parly Counsel, 1973–75. *Recreations:* opera, travel. *Address:* 8 Wellesley Road, W4 4BL. *T:* (020) 8994 6627.

RENNIE, John Chalmers; Town Clerk of Aberdeen, 1946–68; retired; *b* 16 April 1907; *s* of late John Chalmers Rennie, Pharmacist, Wishaw; *m* 1937, Georgina Stoddart, *d* of late Henry Bell, Engineer and Ironfounder, Wishaw; one *s*. *Educ:* University of Glasgow (BL). Admitted solicitor, 1929. Town Clerk Depute, Motherwell and Wishaw, 1929–43; Town Clerk Depute, Aberdeen, 1943–46. Dep. Controller, Civil Defence Servs, Motherwell and Wishaw, 1939–43; Secretary: Aberdeen Harbour Bd, 1946–60; NE Fire Area Jt Bd, 1948–68. Mem. Council, Law Soc. of Scotland, 1958–61. Hon. Solicitor (Scotland), NALGO, 1949–64. *Recreation:* surviving. *Address:* 77 Forest Road, Aberdeen AB2 4BJ. *T:* (01224) 638635.

RENNIE, Sir John Shaw, GCMG 1968 (KCMG 1962; CMG 1958); OBE 1955; Commissioner-General, United Nations Relief and Works Agency for Palestine Refugees, 1971–77 (Deputy Commissioner-General, 1968–71); *b* 12 Jan. 1917; *s* of late John Shaw Rennie, Saskatoon, Sask, Canada; *m* 1946, Mary Winifred Macalpine Robertson; one *s*. *Educ:* Hillhead High School; Glasgow University; Balliol College, Oxford. Cadet, Tanganyika, 1940; Asst District Officer, 1942; District Officer, 1949; Deputy Colonial Secretary, Mauritius, 1951; British Resident Comr, New Hebrides, 1955–62; Governor and C-in-C of Mauritius, 1962–March 1968, Governor-General, March-Aug. 1968. Hon. LLD Glasgow, 1972. *Address:* 26 College Cross, N1 1PR. *Club:* Royal Commonwealth Society.

RENO, Janet; Attorney General of the United States of America, 1993–2001; *b* 21 July 1938. *Educ:* Cornell Univ. (AB Chem. 1960); Harvard Law Sch. (LLB 1963). Started legal career in private practice; Staff Dir, Judiciary Cttee, Florida House of Reps, 1971–72; Asst State Attorney, Florida, 1973–76; Partner, Steel, Hector & Davis, Miami, 1976–78; State Attorney, Miami, 1978–93. Pres., Fla Prosecuting Attorneys Assoc., 1984–85; American Bar Association: Member: Special Cttee on Criminal Justice in a Free Soc., 1986–88; Task Force on Minorities and the Justice System, 1992. Herbert Harley Award, Amer. Judicature Soc., 1981; Medal of Honor, Fla Bar Assoc., 1990. *Address:* c/o Department of Justice, 10th & Constitution Avenue NW, Washington, DC 20530, USA.

RENOWDEN, Ven. Glyndwr Rhys, CB 1987; Chaplain in Chief, Royal Air Force, 1983–88; *b* 13 Aug. 1929; *s* of Charles and Mary Elizabeth Renowden; *m* 1956, Mary Kinsey-Jones; one *d*. *Educ:* Llanelli Grammar Sch.; St David's Coll., Lampeter (BA, LTh). Curate: St Mary's, Tenby, 1952–55; St Mary's, Chepstow, 1955–58; Chaplain, RAF, 1958–88; Asst Chaplain in Chief, 1975–83. QHC, 1980–88. *Recreations:* Rugby football, bridge. *Address:* Red Cedars, Kenystyle, Penally, near Tenby, Pembrokeshire SA70 7PJ.

RENSHAW, Sir (Charles) Maurice (Bine), 3rd Bt *cr* 1903; *b* 7 Oct. 1912; *s* of Sir (Charles) Stephen (Bine) Renshaw, 2nd Bt and of Edith Mary, *d* of Rear-Adm. Sir Edward Chichester, 9th Bt, CB, CMG; *S* father, 1976; *m* 1942, Isabel Bassett (marr. diss. 1947), *d* of late Rev. John L. T. Popkin; one *s* one *d* (and one *s* decd); *m* 2nd, Winifred May, *d* of H. F. Gliddon, Ashwater, Devon, and formerly wife of James H. T. Sheldon; three *s* three *d*. *Educ:* Eton. Served as Flying Officer, RAF (invalided). *Heir: s* John David Renshaw [*b* 9 Oct. 1945; *m* 1970, Jennifer (marr. diss. 1988), *d* of Group Captain F. Murray, RAF; one *s* two *d*]. *Address:* Tam-na-Marghaidh, Balquhidder, Perthshire FK19 8PB; Linwood, Instow, N Devon EX39 4HX.

RENTON, family name of **Barons Renton** and **Renton of Mount Harry**.

RENTON, Baron *cr* 1979 (Life Peer), of Huntingdon in the County of Cambridgeshire; **David Lockhart-Mure Renton,** KBE 1964; TD; PC 1962; QC 1954; MA; BCL; DL; a Deputy Speaker of the House of Lords, 1982–88; *b* 12 Aug. 1908; *s* of late Dr Maurice Waugh Renton, The Bridge House, Dartford, Kent, and Eszma Olivia, *d* of late Allen Walter Borman; *m* 1947, Claire Cicely Duncan (*d* 1986); three *d*. *Educ:* Stubbington; Oundle; University College, Oxford (BA Hons Jurisprudence, 1930; BCL, 1931; MA; Hon. Fellow, 1990). Called to Bar, Lincoln's Inn, 1933; South-Eastern Circuit; elected to General Council of the Bar, 1939; Bencher, Lincoln's Inn, 1962, Treasurer, 1979. Commnd RE (TA), 1938; transferred to RA 1940; served throughout War of 1939–45; Capt. 1941; Major, 1943; served in Egypt and Libya, 1942–45. MP (Nat L) 1945–50, (Nat L and C) 1950–68, (C) 1968–79, Huntingdonshire; Parly Sec., Min. of Fuel and Power, 1955–57, Ministry of Power, 1957–58; Joint Parly Under-Sec. of State, Home Office, 1958–61; Minister of State, Home Office, 1961–62; Chm., Select Cttee for Revision of Standing Orders, House of Commons, 1963 and 1970; Dep. Chm., Special Select Cttee on H of C Procedure, 1976–78; Mem., Cttee of Privileges, 1973–79. Recorder of Rochester, 1963–68, of Guildford, 1968–71; Vice-Chm., Council of Legal Educn, 1968–70, 1971–73. Member: Senate of Inns of Court, 1967–69, 1970–71, 1975–79; Royal Commn on the Constitution, 1971–73; Chm., Cttee on Preparation of Legislation, 1973–75. Pres., Statute Law Soc., 1980–2000. Pres., Mencap (Royal Soc. for Mentally Handicapped Children), 1982–88 (Hon. Treas., 1976–78; Chm., 1978–82). President: Conservation Soc., 1970–71; Nat. Council for Civil Protection (formerly Nat. Council for Civil Defence), 1980–91; Pres., All Party Arts and Heritage Gp, 1989–. Patron: Huntingdon Conservative Assoc., 1979–; Ravenswood Foundn, 1979–; Huntingdonshire RBL, 1984–; Gtr London Assoc. for the Disabled, 1986–; DEMAND (Design and Manufacture for Disablement), 1986–. DL Huntingdonshire, 1962, Huntingdon and Peterborough, 1964, Cambs, 1974. Coronation and Jubilee Medals. *Recreations:* outdoor sports and games, gardening. *Address:* Moat House, Abbots Ripton, Huntingdon, Cambs PE17 2PE. *T:* (01487) 773227; 16 Old Buildings, Lincoln's Inn, WC2A 3TL. *T:* (020) 7242 8986. *Clubs:* Carlton, Pratt's.

See also T. J. W. Scott.

RENTON OF MOUNT HARRY, Baron *cr* 1997 (Life Peer), of Offham in the co. of Sussex; **Ronald Timothy Renton;** PC 1989; *b* 28 May 1932; *yr s* of R. K. D. Renton, CBE, and Mrs Renton, MBE; *m* 1960, Alice Fergusson of Kilkerran, Ayrshire; two *s* three *d*. *Educ:* Eton Coll. (King's Schol.); Magdalen Coll., Oxford (Roberts Gawen Schol.). First cl. degree in History, MA Oxon. Joined C. Tennant Sons & Co. Ltd, London, 1954; with Tennants' subsidiaries in Canada, 1957–62; Dir, C. Tennant Sons & Co. Ltd and Managing Dir of Tennant Trading Ltd, 1964–73; Director: Silvermines Ltd, 1967–84; Australia & New Zealand Banking Group, 1967–76; Fleming Continental European Investment Trust, 1992–99 (Chm., 1999–), and other cos. Mem., BBC Gen. Adv. Council, 1982–84; Vice Chm., British Council, 1992–97; Mem., British Council Bd, 1997–99. Contested (C) Sheffield Park Div., 1970. MP (C) Mid-Sussex, Feb. 1974–1997. PPS to Rt Hon. John Biffen, MP, 1979–81, to Rt Hon. Geoffrey Howe, MP, 1983–84; Parly Under Sec. of State, FCO, 1984–85; Minister of State: FCO, 1985–87; Home Office, 1987–89; Parly Sec. to HM Treasury and Govt Chief Whip, 1989–90; Minister of State, Privy Council Office (Minister for the Arts), 1990–92. Member: Select Cttee on Nationalised Industries, 1974–79; Select Cttee on Nat. Heritage, 1995–97; Vice-Chm., Cons. Parly Trade Cttee, 1974–79; Chairman: Parly British–Hong Kong All-Party Gp, 1992–97; Cons. Foreign and Commonwealth Council, 1982–84; Mem. Sub-Cttee A, EC Cttee, H of L, 1997–; Vice-Pres., 1978–80, Pres., 1980–84, Cons. Trade Unionists; Fellow, Industry and Parlt Trust, 1977–79. Member: Adv. Bd, Know-How Fund for Central and Eastern Europe, 1992–; Develt Council, Parnham Trust, 1992–; Criterion Theatre Trust, 1992–97; APEX. Pres. Council, Roedean Sch., 1998– (Mem., 1982–97). Trustee: Mental Health Foundn, 1985–89; Brighton West Pier Trust, 1997–. Founding Pres. (with Mick Jagger), Nat. Music Day, 1992–97; Chairman: Outsider Art Archive, 1995–; Sussex Downs Conservation Bd, 1997–. Mem. Council, Univ. of Sussex, 2000–. *Publications:* The Dangerous Edge (novel), 1994; Hostage to Fortune (novel), 1997. *Recreations:* writing, messing about in boats, listening to opera, bicycling. *Address:* Mount Harry House, Offham, Lewes, East Sussex BN7 3QW. *Club:* Garrick.

RENTON, Air Cdre Helen Ferguson, CB 1982; Director, Women's Royal Air Force, 1980–86; *b* 13 March 1931; *d* of late John Paul Renton and Sarah Graham Renton (*née* Cook). *Educ:* Stirling High Sch.; Glasgow Univ. (MA). Joined WRAF, 1954; commnd, 1955; served in UK, 1955–60; Cyprus, 1960–62; HQ Staff, Germany, 1967; MoD Staff, 1968–71; NEAF, 1971–73; Training Comd, 1973–76; MoD Staff, 1976–78. Hon. LLD Glasgow, 1981. *Publication:* (jtly) Service Women, 1977. *Recreations:* needlework, gardening, reading. *Club:* Royal Air Force.

RENTON, Stuart, MBE 1973; RSA 1997 (ARSA 1983); Senior Partner, Reiach and Hall, architects, 1982–91; *b* 15 Sept. 1929; *s* of William Langlands Renton and Mary Renton (*née* Crighton); *m* 1953, Ethnie Sloan; one *s* one *d*. *Educ:* Royal High Sch., Edinburgh; Sch. of Architecture, Edinburgh Coll. of Art (DA 1952). ARIBA 1953, FRIBA 1971; ARIAS 1953, FRIAS 1985. Served RAF, 1953–55, RAFVR, 1955–65. Joined Alan Reiach's practice, 1955, Partner, 1959; Founding Partner: Reiach and Hall, 1965; Reiach Hall Blyth, 1973–83. Major projects include: New Club, Edinburgh (with Alan Reiach), 1969; Hugh Nisbet Building, Heriot-Watt Univ., 1973; Teesside Coll. of Educn, 1974; BSC Clydesdale and Airdrie, 1977 (British Steel and RIBA Awards, 1978); Life Association of Scotland: HQ, 1989 (Civic Trust Award, 1991), and 10 George Street, Edinburgh, 1992 (RIBA Award, 1994); Midlothian Council HQ, 1990 (Civic Trust Award, 1992); Strathclyde Grad. Business Sch., 1992 (RIBA Award, 1993). Vis. Prof., Strathclyde Univ., 1992–98. Gov., Edinburgh Coll. of Art, 1985–98 (Chm., 1992–98). Other architectural awards include: Construction Industry, 1990; Civic Trust, 1993. *Recreations:* ski-ing, gamefishing, Italian hill villages. *Address:* Grianan, Killichonan, Rannoch, Perthshire PH17 2QW. *T:* (01882) 633247. *Club:* New (Edinburgh).

RENWICK, family name of **Barons Renwick** and **Renwick of Clifton**.

RENWICK, 2nd Baron *cr* 1964, of Coombe; **Harry Andrew Renwick;** Bt 1927; *b* 10 Oct. 1935; *s* of 1st Baron Renwick, KBE, and Mrs John Ormiston, Miserden House, Stroud, *er d* of late Major Harold Parkes, Alveston, Stratford-on-Avon; *S* father, 1973; *m* 1st, 1965, Susan Jane (marr. diss. 1989), *d* of late Captain Kenneth S. B. Lucking and Mrs Moir P. Stormonth-Darling, Lednathie, Glen Prosen, Angus; two *s*; 2nd, 1989, Mrs Homayoun Mazandi, *d* of late Col Mahmoud Yazdanparst Pakzad. *Educ:* Eton. Grenadier Guards (National Service), 1955–56. Partner, W. Greenwell & Co., 1964–80; Dir, General Technology Systems Ltd, 1975–93; Chm., European Information Society Group, 1994–2000 (Pres., 2000–). Mem., H of L Select Cttee on the European Communities, 1988–92, on Science and Technology, 1992–95; Hon. Sec., Parly Information Technology Cttee, 1991–2000. Vice-Pres., British Dyslexia Assoc., 1982– (Chm., 1977–82); Chm., Dyslexia Educnl Trust, 1986–. *Heir: s* Hon. Robert James Renwick, *b* 19 Aug. 1966. *Address:* 38 Cadogan Square, SW1X 0JL. *Clubs:* White's, Turf, Carlton.

RENWICK OF CLIFTON, Baron *cr* 1997 (Life Peer), of Chelsea in the Royal Borough of Kensington and Chelsea; **Robin William Renwick,** KCMG 1989 (CMG 1980); Vice-Chairman, Investment Banking, JP Morgan plc, since 2001; Deputy Chairman, Fleming Family and Partners, since 2000; *b* 13 Dec. 1937; *s* of late Richard Renwick, Edinburgh, and Clarice (*née* Henderson); *m* 1965, Annie Colette Giudicelli; one *s* one *d*. *Educ:* St Paul's Sch.; Jesus Coll., Cambridge (Hon. Fellow, 1992); Univ. of Paris (Sorbonne). Army, 1956–58. Entered Foreign Service, 1963; Dakar, 1963–64; FO, 1964–66; New Delhi, 1966–69; Private Sec. to Minister of State, FCO, 1970–72; First Sec., Paris, 1972–76; Counsellor, Cabinet Office, 1976–78; Rhodesia Dept, FCO, 1978–80; Political Adviser to Governor of Rhodesia, 1980; Vis. Fellow, Center for Internat. Affairs, Harvard, 1980–81; Head of Chancery, Washington, 1981–84; Asst Under Sec. of State, FCO, 1984–87; Ambassador to S Africa, 1987–91; Ambassador to Washington, 1991–95. Dir, 1996–2000, Dep. Chm., 1999–2000, Robert Fleming Hldgs Ltd. Chairman: Save & Prosper Gp, 1996–98; Fluor Ltd, 1996–; Director: Compagnie Financière Richemont AG, 1995–; British Airways plc, 1996–; Liberty Internat., 1996–2000; Canal Plus, 1997–2000; Billiton plc, 1997–; Fluor Corp., 1997–; South African Breweries, 1999–; Harmony Gold, 1999–. Trustee, The Economist, 1996–. FRSA. Hon. LLD: Wits Univ., 1990; Amer. Univ. in London, 1993; Hon. DLitt: Coll. of William and Mary, 1993; Oglethorpe Univ., 1995. *Publications:* Economic Sanctions, 1981; Fighting with Allies, 1996; Unconventional Diplomacy, 1997. *Recreations:* tennis, trout fishing. *Address:* JP Morgan plc, 10 Aldermanbury, EC2V 7RF. *Clubs:* Brooks's, Hurlingham, Travellers.

RENWICK, Sir Richard Eustace, 4th Bt *cr* 1921; *b* 13 Jan. 1938; *er s* of Sir Eustace Deuchar Renwick, 3rd Bt, and of Diana Mary, *e d* of Colonel Bernard Cruddas, DSO; *S* father, 1973; *m* 1966, Caroline Anne, *er d* of Major Rupert Milburn; three *s*. *Educ:* Eton. *Heir: s* Charles Richard Renwick, [*b* 10 April 1967; *m* 1993, Jane Ann Lyles (*née* Bush); two *s*]. *Address:* Whalton House, Whalton, Morpeth, Northumberland NE61 3UZ. *T:* (01670) 775383. *Club:* Northern Counties (Newcastle).

REPORTER, Sir Shapoor (Ardeshirji), KBE 1973 (OBE 1969); Consultant on Economic and Political Matters concerning Iran, since 1962; *b* 26 Feb. 1921; *s* of Ardeshirji Reporter and Shirin Reporter; *m* 1952, Assia Alexandra; one *s* one *d*. *Educ:* Zoroastrian Public Sch., Teheran; matriculated in Bombay (specially designed course in Political Science under Cambridge Univ. Tutors, UK). PRO, British Legation, Teheran, 1941–43; in charge of Persian Unit of All India Radio, New Delhi, 1943–45; Teaching English, Imperial Staff Coll., Teheran, 1945–48; Political Adviser, US Embassy, Teheran, 1948–54; Free-lance Correspondent, 1954–62; Economic Consultant to major British interests in Iran, 1962–73. *Publications:* English-Persian Phrases, 1945 (Delhi); Dictionary of English-Persian Idioms, 1956 (Teheran); Dictionary of Persian-English Idioms, 1972 (Teheran Univ.). *Recreations:* tennis, walking, travelling.

REPP, Richard Cooper, DPhil; Master, St Cross College, Oxford, since 1987; *b* 1 April 1936; *s* of Robert Mathias Repp, Jun., and Martha Repp (*née* Cooper); *m* 1972, Catherine Ross MacLennan; one *s* one *d*. *Educ:* Shady Side Acad., Pittsburgh; Williams Coll., Mass (BA); Worcester Coll., Oxford (1st Cl. Hons Oriental Studies, MA, DPhil; Hon. Fellow 1989). Instr in Humanities, Robert Coll., Istanbul, 1959–62; Oxford University: Univ. Lectr in Turkish History, 1963–; Sen. Proctor, 1979–80; Vice-Chm., Staff Cttee, 1982–84; Member: Gen. Bd of the Faculties, 1982–84, 1985–89; Hebdomadal Council, 1991–2000; Pro-Vice-Chancellor, 1994–; Linacre College: Fellow, 1964–87, Hon. Fellow, 1987; Sen. Tutor, 1985–87. Chm., Visitors of the Ashmolean Mus., 1995–. *Publications:* The Müfti of Istanbul, 1986; various articles on Ottoman history. *Recreations:* gardening, music. *Address:* St Cross College, Oxford OX1 3LZ. *T:* (01865) 278493. *Club:* Williams (New York).

REPTON, Bishop Suffragan of, since 1999; **Rt Rev. David Christopher Hawtin;** *b* 7 June 1943; *m* 1968, Elizabeth Ann (*née* Uden); one *s* two *d*. *Educ:* King Edward VII Sch., Lytham St Annes; Keble Coll., Oxford (BA 1965; MA 1970); William Temple Coll., Rugby; Cuddesdon Coll., Oxford. Ordained deacon, 1967, priest 1968; Curate: St Thomas, Pennywell, Sunderland, 1967–71; St Peter's, Stockton, 1971–74; Priest in charge, St Andrew's, Leam Lane, Gateshead, 1974–79; Rector, Washington, 1979–88; Diocesan Ecumenical Officer, Durham, 1988–92; Archdeacon of Newark, 1992–99. Member: Gen. Synod, 1983–99 (Mem., Bd for Mission and Unity, 1986–91); BCC, 1987–90; Churches Together in England, 1990– (Enabling Gp, 1991–99; Dep. Moderator, CTE Forum, 1995–99); Council of Churches for Britain and Ireland, 1990–; Chairman: Diocesan Bd of Educn, Southwell, 1993–99; E Midlands Consortium for Educn and Trng for Ministry, 1996–2001; Derby Diocesan Council for Mission and Unity, 1999–2001; Derby Diocesan Pastoral Cttee, 1999–. Churches Project Co-ordinator, Nat. Garden Fest., Gateshead, 1988–91. Local Unity Advr, Durham Ecumenical Relations Gp, 1991–92; Consultant: Council for Christian Unity, 1991–96; CCU Local Unity Panel, 1999–. Member: N Notts and N Derbys Coalfield Alliance Bd, 1999–; Derbys Partnership, 2001. *Address:* Repton House, Lea, Matlock, Derbys DE4 5JP. *T:* (01629) 534644.

RESNAIS, Alain; French film director; *b* Vannes, 3 June 1922; *s* of Pierre Resnais and Jeanne (*née* Gachet); *m* 1969, Florence Mairaux. *Educ:* Collège St François-Xavier, Vannes; Institut des hautes études cinématographiques. Assistant to Nicole Védrée for film Paris 1900, 1947–48; has directed his own films (many of which have won prizes), since

48. Short films, 1948–59, include: Van Gogh, 1948; Guernica (jtly with Robert essens), 1950; Les statues meurent aussi (jtly with Chris Marker), 1952; Nuit et rouillard, 1955. Full length films include: Hiroshima mon amour, 1959; L'année dernière Marienbad, 1961; Muriel, 1963; La guerre est finie, 1966; Je t'aime, je t'aime, 1968; Stavisky, 1974; Providence, 1977; Mon Oncle d'Amérique, 1980; La vie est un roman, 1983; L'amour à Mort, 1984; Mélo, 1986; Je veux rentrer à la maison, 1989; Smoking, 1993; No Smoking, 1993; On connait la chanson, 1998.

RESTREPO-LONDOÑO, Andrés; Order of Boyacá, Colombia; private financial consultant, since 1993; President, Empresa Colombiana de Petróleos-ECOPETROL, 1988–92; *b* 20 Jan. 1942; *m* 1968, Ghislaine Ibiza; one *s* three *d*. *Educ:* Universidad de Antioquia; Université de Paris (postgraduate courses, 1966). Professor and Head of Economic Dept., Univ. de Antioquia, 1967–68; Gen. Man., La Primavera chain of stores, 1969–76; Finance Man., Empresas Públicas de Medellín, 1976–79; Gen. Man., Carbones de Colombia (Colombian Coal Bd), 1979–80; Minister for Economic Develt, 1980–81; Ambassador to UK, 1981–82. Chm., Proban SA (Banana Exporting Co.), 1983–84; Pres., Industrias e Inversiones Samper SA (Cement Co.), 1985–88. Order Sol of Perú; Order Cruzeiro do Sul, Brazil. *Publications:* Carbones Térmicos en Colombia, Bases para una Política Contractual, 1981; several articles in El Colombiano, daily newspaper of Medellín, Colombia. *Recreations:* fishing, tennis. *Address:* Calle 136A No 57B-17, Bogotá, DE, Colombia; (office) Calle 93B No 12–28 Of. 303, Santafé de Bogotá, DC, Colombia. *T:* (1) 6217905, 6217954. *Club:* Lagartos (Bogotá).

RETTIE, (James) Philip, CBE 1987; TD 1962; farmer, since 1964; Director: Edinburgh and Glasgow Investment Co., since 1989; Rettie & Co., since 1992; *b* 7 Dec. 1926; *s* of James Rettie and Rachel Buist; *m* 1st, 1955, Helen Grant; two *s* one *d*; 2nd, 1980, Mrs Diana Harvey (*née* Ballantyne). *Educ:* Trinity College, Glenalmond. Royal Engineers, 1945–48; RE (TA), 1949–65. Wm Low & Co. plc, 1948–85 (Chm., 1980–85); Mem., TSB Scotland Area Bd, 1983–88; Partner, Crossley & Rettie, 1989–95. Chm., Sea Fish Industry Authority, 1981–87. Director: Unicorn Preservation Soc., 1990–; Tayside Conservation Trust, 1992–. Chm., Scottish Soc. for Employment of ex-Regular Sailors, Soldiers and Airmen, 1995–. Trustee, Scottish Civic Trust, 1983–. Hon. Colonel: 117 (Highland) Field Support Squadron, RE, TAVR, 1982–87; 277 Airfield Damage Repair Sqdn, RE(T), 1984–89. FRSA. *Recreations:* shooting, gardening, hill-walking, fishing. *Address:* Hill House, Ballindean, Inchture, Perthshire PH14 9QS. *T:* (01828) 686337.

REUPKE, Michael; editor/publisher, since 1992; Director, Company Information Exchange Ltd, since 1992; *b* Potsdam, Germany, 20 Nov. 1936; *s* of Dr Willm Reupke and Dr Frances G. Reupke (*née* Kinnear); *m* 1963, (Helen) Elizabeth Restrick; one *s* two *d*. *Educ:* Latymer Upper Sch., London; Jesus Coll., Cambridge (MA Mod. Langs); Collège d'Europe, Bruges. Pilot Officer, RAF (Technical Training Comd), 1957–58. Joined Reuters, 1962; reporter, France, Switzerland, Guinea and West Germany, 1962–69; Asst European Manager, Gen. News Div., 1970–72; Chief Rep., West Germany, 1973–74; Manager, Latin America and the Caribbean, 1975–77; Editor-in-Chief, 1978–89; Gen. Manager, 1989. Director: Visnews, 1985–89; Internat. Business Information Services SA, 1991–93; Staria Ltd, 1993–94. Mem. Bd, Radio Authy, 1994–99. Member: IPI, 1978–97; Internat. Inst. of Communications, 1987–. Trustee, Reuter Foundn, 1982–89. *Recreations:* travel, cooking, wine. *Address:* Tippings, The Common, Stokenchurch, Bucks HP14 3UD. *T:* (01494) 482341; 60 rue St Georges, 75009 Paris, France. *T:* (1) 42805459. *Clubs:* Royal Automobile; Leander (Henley-on-Thames).

REUTER, Edzard; Chairman, Board of Management, Daimler-Benz, 1987–95. *Educ:* Univs of Berlin and Göttingen (maths and physics); Free Univ. of Berlin (law). Research Asst, Free Univ. of Berlin Law Faculty, 1954–56; Universum Film, 1957–62; Manager, TV prod. section, Bertelsmann Group, Munich, 1962–64; Daimler-Benz: exec., finance dept, 1964; responsible for management planning and organization, 1971; Dep. Mem., Bd, 1973; Full Mem., Exec. Bd, 1976. Chairman, Supervisory Board: Berliner Bank and Bankges. Berlin, 1978–99 (Hon. Chm., 1999–); Airbus Industrie, 1994–97; Mem., Conseil d'Admin, Air Liquide, Paris. Member: Bd of Trustees, Ernst Reuter Foundn, Berlin; Bd, German Nat. Foundn, Weimar; Bd of Trustees, Aspen Inst., Berlin. Hon. Citizen, Berlin, 1998. *Publications:* Vom Geist der Wirtschaft, 1986; Horizonte der Wirtschaft, 1993; Schein und Wirklichkeit, 1998. *Address:* Friedrichstrasse 90, 10117 Berlin, Germany.

REVANS, Prof. Reginald William, PhD; MIMinE; Founder, Action Learning Trust, 1977; Professorial Fellow in Action Learning, University of Manchester, since 1986; *b* 14 May 1907; *s* of Thomas William Revans, Principal Ship Surveyor, Board of Trade; *m* 1st, 1932, Annida Aquist, Gothenburg (marriage dissolved, 1947); three *d*; 2nd, 1955, Norah Mary Merritt, Chelmsford; one *s*. *Educ:* Battersea Grammar School; University Coll., London; Emmanuel Coll., Cambridge. BSc London, PhD Cantab. Commonwealth Fund Fellow, Univ. of Michigan, 1930–32; Research Fellow, Emmanuel Coll., Cambridge, 1932–35; Dep. Chief Education Officer, Essex CC, 1935–45; Dir of Education, Mining Assoc. of Gt Britain, 1945–47 and NCB, 1947–50; Research on management of coalmines, 1950–55; Prof., Industrial Admin., Univ. of Manchester, 1955–65; Res. Fellow, Guy's Hosp. Med. Sch., 1965–68; External Prof., Management Studies, Leeds Univ., 1976–78. Dist. Vis. Scholar, Southern Methodist Univ., USA, 1972. Pres., European Assoc. of Univ. Management Centres, 1962–64. Hon. DSc Bath, 1969. Chevalier, Order of Leopold, Belgium, 1971. *Publications:* Report on Education for Mining Industry, 1945; Education of the Young Worker, 1949; Standards for Morale, 1964; Science and the Manager, 1965; The Theory and Practice of Management, 1965; Developing Effective Managers, 1971; (ed) Hospitals, Communication, Choice and Change, 1972; Workers' Attitudes and Motivation (OECD Report), 1972; Childhood and Maturity, 1973; Action Learning in Hospitals, 1976; The ABC of Action Learning, 1978; Action Learning, 1979; The Origins and Growth of Action Learning, 1982; various in professional magazines upon application of analytical methods to understanding of industrial morale. *Recreations:* British Olympic Team, 1928; holder of Cambridge undergraduate long jump record, 1929–62. *Address:* 21 Tilstock, Whitchurch, Shropshire SY13 3NS.

REVELL, Surg. Vice-Adm. Anthony Leslie, CB 1997; FRCA; Surgeon General, Ministry of Defence, 1994–97; *b* 26 April 1935; *s* of Leslie Frederick Revell and Florence Mabel (*née* Styles). *Educ:* King's Coll. Sch., Wimbledon; Ashford and Eastbourne Grammar Schs; Univ. of Birmingham Med. Sch. (MB, ChB); DA 1968. FRCA (FFARCS 1969). Joined RN, 1960; HMS Troubridge, 1960–62; HMS Dampier, 1962; HMS Loch Fada and 5th Frigate Sqdn, 1963; Anæsthetist, RN Hosp., Plymouth, 1964–65; HMS Eagle, 1965–67; Clin. Assistant, Radcliffe Infy, Oxford, Alder Hey Children's Hosp., Liverpool, and various courses, 1967–69; Anæsthetist, RN Hosp., Plymouth, 1969–70; RAF Hosps Nocton Hall and Akrotiri, Cyprus, 1970–72; ANZUK Mil. Hosp., Singapore, 1972–74; Cons. Anæsthetist, RN Hosp., Haslar, 1974–79; *ndc*, Latimer, 1979–80; Recruiter, MoD, 1980; Dir of Studies, Inst. of Naval Medicine, 1980–82; on staff, Surg. Rear-Adm. (Naval Hosps), 1982–84; Dir, Med. Personnel, 1984–86; RCDS, 1986; MO i/c, RN Hosp., Plymouth, 1987–88; on staff., C-in-C Fleet, 1988–90; Dir, Clinical Services, Defence Med. Directorate, 1990–91; Surg. Rear-Adm., Operational Med. Services, 1991–92; CSO (Med. and Dental) to C-in-C Fleet, 1992–93; Med. Dir Gen. (Navy), 1993–94; QHS, 1989–97. Member Council: Epsom Coll., 1997–; Royal Med. Foundn, 1997– (Vice Chm., 1999); Pilgrims Sch., Winchester, 1997–. Trustee, John Ellerman Foundn, 1997–. FRSocMed 1970. Hon. MD Birmingham, 1996. CStJ 1993. *Publications:* Haslar: the Royal Hospital, 1979; (ed jtly) Proc. World Assoc. Anæsthetists, 1970. *Recreation:* choral music. *Address:* 29 Little Green, Alverstoke, Gosport, Hants PO12 2EX. *Club:* Naval and Military.

REVELSTOKE, 5th Baron *cr* 1885, of Membland, Devon; **John Baring;** *b* 2 Dec. 1934; *er s* of 4th Baron Revelstoke and Hon. Florence Fermor-Hesketh (*d* 1971), 2nd *d* of 1st Baron Hesketh; *S* father, 1994. *Educ:* Eton. *Heir: b* Hon. James Cecil Baring [*b* 16 Aug. 1938; *m* 1st, 1968, Aneta (marr. diss.), *yr d* of Erskine A. H. Fisher; two *s*; 2nd, 1983, Sarah, *d* of William Edward Stubbs, MBE; one *d*].

REVERDIN, Prof. Olivier, DrLitt; Professor of Greek, University of Geneva, 1958–83 (Hon. Professor, since 1983); Member, Consultative Assembly of Council of Europe, 1963–74 (President, 1969–72); Deputy (Liberal) for Geneva, Swiss National Council, 1955–71, Council of States (Senate), 1971–79; *b* 15 July 1913; *m* 1936, Renée Chaponnière; two *s* one *d*. *Educ:* Geneva, Paris and Athens. LicLitt 1935; DrLitt Geneva, 1945. Foreign Mem., French Sch. of Archaeology, Athens, 1936–38; Attaché Swiss Legation, Service of Foreign Interests, Rome, 1941–43; Privatdocent of Greek, Univ. of Geneva, 1945–57; Parly Redactor, 1945–54; Chief Editor 1954–59, Manager 1954–67, Pres., 1972–79, Journal de Genève. Mem. 1963–80, Pres. 1968–80, Swiss National Research Council; Mem., Swiss Science Council, 1958–80; Président: Fondation Hardt pour l'étude de l'antiquité classique, Geneva, 1959–96; Fondation Archives Jean Piaget, 1973–87; Vice-Pres., European Science Foundn, 1974–77, Mem. Exec. Council, 1977–80; Chm., Collections Baur, Geneva, 1984–. Hon. Mem., Soc. for Promotion of Hellenic Studies; Corresp. Mem., Acads of Athens and Vienna. Dr *hc*, Heidelberg, Strasbourg, Bucharest, Sorbonne, Zurich, Lausanne. *Publications:* La religion de la cité platonicienne, 1945; La guerre du Sonderbund, 1947, 2nd edn 1987; La Crète, berceau de la civilisation occidentale, 1960; Connaissance de la Suisse, 1966; Les premiers cours de Grec au Collège de France, 1984; Henri Estienne à Genève, 1988; Impressions grecques en Suisse au XVIe et XVIIe siècles, 1991. *Address:* 8 rue des Granges, 1204 Geneva, Switzerland. *T:* (22) 3115191.

REW, Paul Francis, FCA; Partner, PricewaterhouseCoopers (formerly Price Waterhouse), since 1987; *b* 20 May 1953; *s* of late Lt Col Peter Rew and of Diana Edith Rew (*née* Moore); *m* 1982, Mary Ellen Pleasant; two *d*. *Educ:* Churcher's Coll., Petersfield; Exeter Univ. (BSc Engrg Sci.). ACA 1977; FCA 1983. Price Waterhouse: articled, London, 1974; Johannesburg office, 1982–84; Partner, 1987; on secondment to DTI as Under Sec. and Dir, Industrial Develt Unit, 1992–94. Mem., Steering Bd, Insolvency Service, 1992–94. Mem., Bd of Mgt, St Bartholomew's and Queen Alexandra's Coll. of Nursing and Midwifery, 1990–95. *Recreations:* golf, humanistic psychology. *Address:* PricewaterhouseCoopers, 1 Embankment Place, WC2N 6NN. *T:* (020) 7804 4071; Clayton, Ruxley Crescent, Claygate, Surrey KT10 0TX

REX, Prof. John Arderne; Research Professor on Ethnic Relations, 1984–90, now Emeritus, and Associate Director, Centre for Research in Ethnic Relations, 1974–90, University of Warwick; *b* 5 March 1925; *s* of Frederick Edward George Rex and Winifred Natalie Rex; *m* 1st, 1949, Pamela Margaret Rutherford (marr. diss. 1963); two *d*; 2nd, 1965, Margaret Ellen Biggs; two *s*. *Educ:* Grey Institute High Sch. and Rhodes University Coll., S Africa. BA (S Africa), PhD (Leeds). Served War, Royal Navy (Able Seaman), 1943–45. Graduated, 1948; Lecturer: Univ. of Leeds, 1949–62; Birmingham, 1962–64; Prof. of Social Theory and Institutions, Durham, 1964–70; Prof. of Sociology, Univ. of Warwick, 1970–79; Dir, SSRC Research Unit on Ethnic Relations, Univ. of Aston in Birmingham, 1979–84. Visiting Professor: Univ. of Toronto, 1974–75; Univ. of Cape Town, 1991; NY Univ., 1996. *Publications:* Key Problems of Sociological Theory, 1961; (with Robert Moore) Race Community and Conflict, 1967, 2nd edn 1973; Race Relations in Sociological Theory, 1970; Discovering Sociology, 1973; Race, Colonialism and the City, 1974; (ed) Approaches to Sociology, 1974; Sociology and the Demystification of the Modern World, 1974; (with Sally Tomlinson) Colonial Immigrants in a British City, 1979; Social Conflict, 1980; (ed) Apartheid and Social Research, 1981; Race and Ethnicity, 1986; The Ghetto and the Underclass, 1988; Ethnic Identity and Ethnic Organisation in Britain, 1991; (with Beatrice Drury) Ethnic Mobilisation in a Multicultural Europe, 1994; Ethnic Minorities in the Modern Nation State, 1996; (with Montserrat Guibernau) The Ethnicity Reader, 1997. *Recreations:* politics, race relations work. *Address:* 33 Arlington Avenue, Leamington Spa, Warwicks CV32 5UD.

REYNOLD, Frederic; QC 1982; *b* 7 Jan. 1936; *s* of late Henry and Regina Reynold. *Educ:* Battersea Grammar School; Magdalen College, Oxford. BA Hons Jurisprudence. Called to the Bar, Gray's Inn, 1960, Bencher, 1991; commenced practice, 1963. *Publication:* The Judge as Lawmaker, 1967. *Recreations:* music, the arts, association croquet, dining out among friends. *Address:* 5 Hillcrest, 51 Ladbroke Grove, W11 3AX. *T:* (020) 7229 3848. *Club:* Sussex County Croquet.

REYNOLDS, Alan (Munro); painter, maker of reliefs, and printmaker; *b* 27 April 1926; *m* 1957, Vona Darby. *Educ:* Woolwich Polytechnic Art School; Royal College of Art (Scholarship and Medal). One man exhibitions: Redfern Gall., 1952, 1953, 1954, 1956, 1960, 1962, 1964, 1966, 1970, 1972, 1974; Durlacher Gall., New York, 1954, 1959; Leicester Galleries, 1958; Aldeburgh, Suffolk, 1965; Arnolfini Gall., Bristol, 1971 (graphics); Annely Juda Fine Art, 1978, 1991; Juda Rowan Gall., 1982, 1986; Thomas Agnew, Albemarle Street Gall., 1982; Gall. Wack, Kaiserslautern, 1986, 1990, 1995, 1999; Galerie Lalumière, Paris, 1990; Galerie Art, Nürnberg, 1992. Work in exhibitions: Carnegie (Pittsburgh) Internat., USA, 1952, 1955, 1958, 1961; Internat. Exhibn, Rome, (awarded one of the three equal prizes), subsequently Musée d'Art Moderne, Paris, and Brussels; British Council Exhibn, Oslo and Copenhagen, 1956; Redfern Gall., 1971; Spectrum, Arts Council of GB, 1971; British Painting 1952–77, Royal Academy, 1977; Galerie Loyse Oppenheim, Nyon, Switzerland, 1977; Galerie Renée Ziegler, Zürich, 1981; group exhibitions: Scottish Nat. Gall. of Modern Art, Edinburgh, 1984; Annely Juda Fine Art and Juda Rowan Gall., London, 1985; Galeries Renée Ziegler, Zürich, 1985–86; Annely Juda Fine Art, 1986 and 1996; Wilhelm-Hack Mus., Ludwigshafen am Rhein, 1987 and 1996 (retrospective); Stiftung für Konkrete Kunst, Reutlingen, 1992–93; Städtische Galerie, Wolfsburg, 1996 (retrospective). Works acquired by: Tate Gall.; V&A; National Galleries of: S Aust.; Felton Bequest, Vic., Aust.; NZ; Canada; City Art Galleries of: Birmingham; Bristol; Manchester; Wakefield; Mus. of Modern Art, NY; Contemporary Art Soc.; British Council; Arts Council of GB; Rothschild Foundn; The Graves Art Gall., Sheffield; Nottingham Castle Mus.; Fitzwilliam Mus., Cambridge; Mus. of Modern Art, São Paulo, Brazil; Leeds Art Gall.; Toledo Art Gall., Ohio, USA; Oriel Coll., Oxford; Warwick Univ.; Mus. and Art Galls, Brighton and Plymouth; Texas Univ., Austin, USA; Berlin Nat. Gall.; McCrory Corp., NY; Wilhelm-Hack Mus., Ludwigshafen am Rhein; Louisiana Mus., Denmark; Tel Aviv Mus., Israel; Musée des

Beaux Arts de Grenoble; Mus. Pfalzgalerie, Kaiserslautern, W Germany; Inst. für Kultur, Nordhein Westfalen. CoID Award, 1965; Arts Council of GB Purchase Award, 1967. *Relevant Publication:* The Painter, Alan Reynolds, by J. P. Hodin, 1962. *Address:* Briar Cottage, High Street, Cranbrook, Kent TN17 3EN.

REYNOLDS, Albert; Member of the Dáil (TD) (FF), since 1977; Taoiseach (Prime Minister of Ireland), 1992–94; President, Fianna Fáil, 1992–94 (Vice-President, 1983–92); *b* Rooskey, Co. Roscommon, 3 Nov. 1932; *m* Kathleen Coen; two *s* five *d*. *Educ:* Summerhill Coll., Sligo. Minister: for Posts and Telegraphs, and for Transport, 1979–81; for Industry and Energy, March–Dec. 1982; Opposition spokesperson: for Industry and Employment, 1983–85; for Energy, 1985–87; Minister for: Industry and Commerce, 1987–88; Finance, 1988–91. Mem., Oireachtas Jt Cttee on Commercial State-Sponsored Bodies, 1983–87. Mem., Longford CC, 1974–79. Pres., Longford Chamber of Commerce, 1974–78. *Address:* Government Buildings, Upper Merrion Street, Dublin 2, Ireland. *T:* (1) 6685333.

REYNOLDS, (Arthur) Graham, CVO 2000; OBE 1984; FBA 1993; Keeper of the Department of Prints and Drawings, 1961–74 (of Engraving, Illustration and Design, 1959–61), and of Paintings, Victoria and Albert Museum, 1959–74; *b* Highgate, 10 Jan. 1914; *o s* of late Arthur T. Reynolds and Eva Mullins; *m* 1943, Daphne, painter and engraver, *d* of late Thomas Dent and Florence Haskett, Huddersfield. *Educ:* Highgate School; Queens' College, Cambridge. Joined staff of Victoria and Albert Museum, 1937. Seconded to Ministry of Home Security, 1939–45. Hon. Keeper of Portrait Miniatures, Fitzwilliam Mus., Cambridge, 1994–. Member: Adv. Council, Paul Mellon Centre for Studies in British Art, 1977–84; Reviewing Cttee on the Export of Works of Art, 1984–90. Trustee, William Morris Gallery, Walthamstow, 1972–75; Chm., Gainsborough's House Soc., Sudbury, 1977–79. Leverhulme Emeritus Fellowship, 1980–81. *Publications:* Twentieth Century Drawings, 1946; Nicholas Hilliard and Isaac Oliver, 1947, 2nd edn 1971; Van Gogh, 1947; Nineteenth Century Drawings, 1949; Thomas Bewick, 1949; An Introduction to English Water-Colour Painting, 1950, rev. edn 1988; Gastronomic Pleasures, 1950; Elizabethan and Jacobean Costume, 1951; English Portrait Miniatures, 1952, rev. edn 1988; Painters of the Victorian Scene, 1953; Catalogue of the Constable Collection, Victoria and Albert Museum, 1960, rev. edn 1973; Constable, the Natural Painter, 1965; Victorian Painting, 1966, 2nd edn 1987; Turner, 1969; A Concise History of Water Colour Painting, 1972; Catalogue of Portrait Miniatures, Wallace Collection, 1980; Constable's England, 1983; The Later Paintings and Drawings of John Constable, 2 vols, 1984 (Mitchell Prize); The Earlier Paintings and Drawings of John Constable, 2 vols, 1996; Catalogue of Portrait Miniatures, Metropolitan Museum of Art, 1996; The Sixteenth and Seventeenth Century Miniatures in the Collection of Her Majesty the Queen, 1999; Editor of series English Masters of Black and White; contribs to Burlington Magazine, Apollo, etc. *Address:* The Old Manse, Bradfield St George, Bury St Edmunds, Suffolk IP30 0AZ. *T:* (01284) 386610. *Club:* Athenæum.

REYNOLDS, Barbara, MA Cantab; BA (Hons), PhD London; author, lexicographer; Reader in Italian Studies, University of Nottingham, 1966–78; *b* 13 June 1914; *d* of late Alfred Charles Reynolds; *m* 1st, 1939, Prof. Lewis Thorpe (*d* 1977); one *s* one *d*; 2nd, 1982, Kenneth Imeson(*d* 1994). *Educ:* St Paul's Girls' Sch.; UCL. Asst Lectr in Italian, LSE 1937–40. Chief Exec. and Gen. Editor, The Cambridge Italian Dictionary, 1948–81; Man. Editor, Seven, an Anglo-American Literary Review, 1980–. Mem. Coun. Senate, Cambridge Univ., 1961–62. University Lecturer in Italian Literature and Language, Cambridge, 1945–62 (Faculty Assistant Lecturer, 1940–45); Warden of Willoughby Hall, Univ. of Nottingham, 1963–69. Vis. Professor: Univ. of Calif., Berkeley, 1974–75; Wheaton Coll., Illinois, 1977–78, 1982; Trinity Coll., Dublin, 1980, 1981; Hope Coll., Mich., 1982. Hon. Reader in Italian, Univ. of Warwick, 1975–80. Pres., Dorothy L. Sayers Soc., 1995– (Chm., 1986–94). Hon. DLitt: Wheaton Coll., Illinois, 1979; Hope Coll., Mich., 1982; Durham Univ., 1995. Silver Medal for Services to Italian culture (Italian Govt), 1964; Edmund Gardner Prize, 1964; Silver Medal for services to Anglo-Veneto cultural relations, Prov. Admin of Vicenza, 1971; Cavaliere Ufficiale al Merito della Repubblica Italiana, 1978. *Publications:* (with K. T. Butler) Tredici Novelle Moderne, 1947; The Linguistic Writings of Alessandro Manzoni: a Textual and Chronological Reconstruction, 1950; rev. edn with introd., Dante and the Early Astronomers, by M. A. Orr, 1956; The Cambridge Italian Dictionary, Vol. I, Italian-English, 1962, Vol. II, English-Italian, 1981; (with Dorothy L. Sayers) Paradise: a translation into English triple rhyme, from the Italian of Dante Alighieri, 1962; (with Lewis Thorpe) Guido Farina, Painter of Verona, 1967; La Vita Nuova (Poems of Youth); trans. of Dante's Vita Nuova, 1969; Concise Cambridge Italian Dictionary, 1975; Orlando Furioso, trans. into rhymed octaves of Ariosto's epic, Vol. I, 1975 (Internat. Literary Prize, Monselice, Italy, 1976) Vol. II, 1977; (ed) Cambridge-Signorelli Dizionario Italiano-Inglese, Inglese-Italiano, 1986; (ed jtly) The Translator's Art, 1987; The Passionate Intellect: Dorothy L. Sayers' encounter with Dante, 1989; Dorothy L. Sayers: her life and soul, 1993; (ed) The Letters of Dorothy L. Sayers, Vol. I, 1995, Vol. II, 1997, Vol. III, 1998, Vol. IV, 2000; numerous articles on Italian literature in learned jls. *Address:* 220 Milton Road, Cambridge CB4 1LQ. *T:* (01223) 565380, *Fax:* (01223) 424894. *Clubs:* University Women's (Chm., 1988–90), Royal Air Force.
See also A. C. Thorpe.

REYNOLDS, Christopher Douglas; Managing Director, British Horseracing Board, since 2000; *b* 24 March 1957; *s* of Geoffrey Butler and Margaret Williams (*née* Reynolds); *m* 1993, Deborah Pegden; one *s* one *d*. *Educ:* Ellesmere Coll.; St John's Coll., Durham Univ. (BA 1978). Mktg trainee, Grants of St James's, 1978–80; Product Manager, Eden Vale, 1980–82; various mktg roles, incl. Mktg and Sales Dir, Europe, Dunlop Slazenger Internat. Ltd, 1982–90; Vice-Pres., Apparel, Internat. Div., Reebok Internat. Ltd, 1990–93; Brand Dir, Pringle of Scotland, 1994–95; Vice-Pres., Mktg, Sara Lee Champion Europe, Florence, 1995–97; Founder Partner, Pegden Reynolds Consultancy, 1997–2000. MInstD 2000. *Recreations:* golf, tennis, squash, lapsed Rugby/cricket - too slow/old, family, wines - passionate collector/imbiber. *T:* (01483) 417679. *Clubs:* MCC; Hankley Common Golf (Tilford, Surrey); Guildford and Godalming Rugby.

REYNOLDS, Prof. David; Professor of Leadership and School Effectiveness, University of Exeter, since 2000; *b* 3 May 1949; *s* of Colin Reynolds and Joyce Reynolds (*née* Jones); *m* 1994, Meriel Jones; two step *s*. *Educ:* Norwich Sch.; Univ. of Essex. Mem., Scientific Staff, MRC, 1971–75; Lectr in Social Admin, UC Cardiff, 1976–82; Lectr, then Sen. Lectr in Educn, UC Cardiff, subseq. UWCC, 1983–93; Professor: of Educn, Univ. of Newcastle upon Tyne, 1993–99; of Sch. Effectiveness and Sch. Improvement, Loughborough Univ., 1999–2000. Mem., Literacy Task Force, 1996–97; Chm., Numeracy Task Force, 1997–98; Member: Literacy and Numeracy Strategy Gp, DfEE, 1998–; Bd, British Educnl Communications and Technol. Agency, 1999–; Bd, TTA, 2000–. Advr, Teachers' Gp, DfEE, 1999–. Non-exec. Dir, Goal plc, 2000–. FRSA 1996. *Publications:* jointly: (ed) Studying School Effectiveness, 1985; The Comprehensive Experiment, 1987; Education Policies: controversies and critiques, 1989; (ed) School Effectiveness and School Improvement, 1989; International School Effects Research, 1992; (ed) School Effectiveness, 1992; Advances in School Effectiveness Research, 1994; (ed) Merging Traditions, 1996; Making Good Schools, 19… Decentralisation, 1996; Worlds Apart?, 1996; Improving Scho… potential, 1999; The International Handbook of School Effectiven… World Class Schools, 2001; contrib. articles to acad. jls, professional jls a… *Recreations:* working, walking, wine, travelling, opera. *Address:* Tondrug… Llantrisant CF72 8NZ. *T:* (01443) 223417. *Club:* St Davids.

REYNOLDS, Sir David James, 3rd Bt *cr* 1923; *b* 26 Jan. 1924; *er s* of Sir J… Roskell Reynolds, 2nd Bt, MBE, JP and Milicent (*d* 1931), *d* of late Major J… Ewing and late Lady Margaret Orr-Ewing, *d* of 7th Duke of Roxburghe; *S* fath… *m* 1966, Charlotte Baumgartner; one *s* two *d*. *Educ:* Downside. Active service in 1942–47, Italy, etc; on demobilisation, Captain 15/19 Hussars. *Recreation:* sport. *I*… James Francis Reynolds, *b* 10 July 1971.

REYNOLDS, David James, PhD; Reader in International History, University o… Cambridge, since 1997; Fellow of Christ's College, Cambridge, since 1983; *b* 17 Feb. 1952; *s* of late Leslie Reynolds and Marian Reynolds (*née* Kay); *m* 1977, Margaret Philpott Ray; one *s*. *Educ:* Dulwich Coll.; Gonville and Caius Coll., Cambridge (BA, MA, PhD 1980). Choate Fellow, 1973–74, Warren Fellow, 1980–81, Harvard Univ.; Res. Fellow, Gonville and Caius Coll., Cambridge, 1978–80, 1981–83; Asst Lectr in History, 1984–88, Lectr, 1988–97, Univ. of Cambridge. *Publications:* The Creation of the Anglo-American Alliance, 1937–41, 1981 (Bernath Prize, Soc. for Historians of Amer. For. Relns, 1982); (jtly) An Ocean Apart: the relationship between Britain and America in the 20th century, 1988; Britannia Overruled: British policy and world power in the 20th century, 1991; (ed jtly) Allies at War: the Soviet, American, and British experience 1939–45, 1994; (ed) The Origins of the Cold War in Europe, 1994; Rich Relations: the American occupation of Britain 1942–45, 1995 (Soc. for Mil. Hist. Distinguished Book Award, 1996); One World Divisible: a global history since 1945, 2000; From Munich to Pearl Harbor: Roosevelt's America and the origins of the Second World War, 2001. *Address:* Christ's College, Cambridge CB2 3BU. *T:* (01223) 334900.

REYNOLDS, Prof. (Edward) Osmund (Royle), CBE 1995; MD; FRCP, FRCOG, FMedSci; FRS 1993; Professor of Neonatal Paediatrics, University College London (formerly University College Hospital) Medical School, 1976–96, now Emeritus Professor, University of London; *b* 3 Feb. 1933; *s* of Edward Royle Reynolds and Edna Reynolds; *m* 1956, Margaret Lindsay Ballard; two *s*. *Educ:* St Paul's Sch.; St Thomas's Hosp. Med. Sch. (Henry Myers Exhbn, 1958). BSc, MD London; DCH; FRCP 1975; FRCOG (*ad eundem*) 1983. Posts at St Thomas' Hosp., 1959–63; Research Fellow in Pediatrics: Harvard Med. Sch., 1963–64; Yale Med. Sch., 1964; Res. Asst, then Lectr and Sen. Lectr, UCH Med. Sch., 1964–76; Hd, Dept of Paediatrics, UCMSM, 1987–93. Consultant Paediatrician, UCH, 1969–94. Hon. Prof. of Paediatrics, Inst. of Child Health, 1994; William Julius Mickle fellow, Univ. of London, 1976–77. Numerous visiting professorships, incl. RSocMed Foundn Vis. Prof. to Amer. Acad. of Pediatrics, 1989. Specialist Advr (perinatal medicine), H of C Social Services and Health Select Cttees, 1978–92; Member: Scientific Adv. Panel, Foundn for Study of Infant Deaths, 1994–98; Bd of Management, Inst. of Child Health, 1990–96 (Hon. Fellow, 1996). President: BLISS (Baby Life Support Systems), 1982–97; Neonatal Soc., 1991–94; Member: Hooke Cttee, Royal Soc., 1993–2000; Soirée Cttee, Royal Soc., 1995–2000. Founding Scientific Patron, Liggins Inst., Univ. of Auckland, 2001. Foundn Fellow, UCL Hosps, 1999. Founder FMedSci 1998. Hon. FRCPCH 1997; Hon. FRSocMed 2000. Hon. Member: Argentine Paediatric Assoc.; Italian Soc. for Perinatal Medicine; British Assoc. of Perinatal Medicine, 1992 (Founder's Lectr, 1992). Lectures: Charles West, RCP, 1989; George Frederic Still Meml, BPA, 1995; Perinatal, Belfast, 1997. Dawson Williams Meml Prize, BMA, 1992; James Spence Medal, BPA, 1994; Maternité Prize, Europ. Assoc. of Perinatal Medicine, 1994; Harding Award, Action Research, 1995. *Publications:* chapters and papers on neonatal physiology and medicine. *Recreations:* travel, music, photography, sport (particularly fencing, in the past; mem., British foil team, 3rd in World Championship, Rome, 1955). *Address:* 72 Barrowgate Road, Chiswick, W4 4QU. *T:* (020) 8994 3326; 4 Ginge, Oxon OX12 8QR. *T:* (01235) 861494; *e-mail:* reynolds@dircon.co.uk.

REYNOLDS, Eva Mary Barbara; *see* Reynolds, Barbara.

REYNOLDS, Fiona Claire, (Mrs R. W. T. Merrill), CBE 1998; Director-General, National Trust, since 2001; *b* 29 March 1958; *d* of Jeffrey Alan Reynolds and Margaret Mary (*née* Watson); *m* 1981, Robert William Tinsley Merrill; three *d*. *Educ:* Rugby High Sch. for Girls; Newnham Coll., Cambridge (MA, MPhil 1980). Sec., Council for Nat. Parks, 1980–87; Asst Dir, 1987–91, Dir, 1992–98, CPRE; Dir, Women's Unit, Cabinet Office, 1998–2000. Global 500 Award, UN Envmt Programme, 1990. *Recreations:* hillwalking, classical music and opera, reading. *Address:* National Trust, 36 Queen Anne's Gate, SW1H 9AS; 13 Ferntower Road, Highbury, N5 2JE.

REYNOLDS, Prof. Francis Martin Baillie, DCL; FBA 1988; Professor of Law, University of Oxford, 1992–2000, now Emeritus; Fellow of Worcester College, Oxford, 1960–2000, now Emeritus; *b* 11 Nov. 1932; *s* of Eustace Baillie Reynolds and Emma Margaret Hanby Reynolds (*née* Holmes); *m* 1965, Susan Claire Shillito; two *s* one *d*. *Educ:* Winchester Coll.; Worcester Coll., Oxford (BA 1956; BCL 1957; MA 1960; DCL 1986). Bigelow Teaching Fellow, Univ. of Chicago, 1957–58. Called to the Bar, Inner Temple, 1960, Hon. Bencher 1979. Reader in Law, Oxford Univ., 1977–92. Visiting Professor, Nat. Univ. of Singapore, UCL, Univ. of Melbourne, Monash Univ., Otago Univ., Univ. of Sydney, Univ. of Auckland; Hon. Prof. of Internat. Maritime Law, Internat. Maritime Law Inst., Malta. Hon. QC 1993. Gen. Editor, Lloyd's Maritime and Commercial Law Qly, 1983–87; Editor, Law Qly Review, 1987–. *Publications:* (ed jtly) Chitty on Contracts, 24th edn 1977, to 27th edn 1994; (ed jtly) Benjamin's Sale of Goods, 1st edn 1974, to 5th edn 1997; Bowstead on Agency, (ed jtly) 13th edn 1968, 14th edn 1976, (sole ed.) 15th edn, 1985, 16th edn as Bowstead and Reynolds on Agency, 1996; (ed jtly) English Private Law, 2000; published lectures and contribs to legal jls. *Recreations:* music, walking. *Address:* 61 Charlbury Road, Oxford OX2 6UX. *T:* (01865) 559323, *Fax:* (01865) 511894.

REYNOLDS, Gillian, MBE 1999; Radio Critic, The Daily Telegraph, since 1975; *b* 15 Nov. 1935; *d* of Charles Morton and Ada (*née* Kelly); *m* 1958, Stanley Reynolds (marr. diss. 1982); three *s*. *Educ:* St Anne's Coll., Oxford (MA; Hon. Fellow, 1996); Mount Holyoke Coll., South Hadley, Mass, USA. TV journalist, 1964–; Radio Critic, The Guardian, 1967–74; Programme Controller, Radio City, Liverpool, 1974–75. Fellow (first to be apptd), Radio Acad., 1990; FRTS 1996; FRSA. Media Soc. Award for distinguished contrib. to journalism, 1999. *Recreation:* listening to the radio. *Address:* Flat 3, 1 Linden Gardens, W2 4HA. *T:* (020) 7229 1893.

REYNOLDS, Graham; *see* Reynolds, A. G.

REYNOLDS, Guy Edwin K.; *see* King-Reynolds.

REYNOLDS, Maj.-Gen. Jack Raymond, CB 1971; OBE 1945; ERD 1948; DL; Director of Movements (Army), Ministry of Defence, 1968–71, retired; *b* 10 June 1916; *s* of Walter Reynolds and Evelyn Marion (*née* Burrows); *m* 1940, Joan Howe Taylor; one *s* one *d*. *Educ:* Haberdashers' Aske's. Student Apprentice, AEC Ltd, 1934. Commissioned RASC (SR), 1936. Served War of 1939–45, France, Middle East and Italy (despatches). CRASC 7th Armoured Div., 1955–57; GSO 1 War Office, 1958–60; Col GS; UK Delegn to NATO Standing Group, Washington, DC, 1960–62; DDST, Southern Command, 1962–64; Commandant, RASC Training Centre, 1964–65; Imperial Defence College, 1966; Dep. Quarter-Master-General, BAOR, 1967–68. Col Comdt, Royal Corps of Transport, 1972–78. Dir-Gen., BHS, 1971–75; Dir-Gen., 1975–85, Pres., 1985–88, BEF. FCIT. DL Northants, 1984. *Recreation:* fishing. *Address:* Old Mill House, Hellidon, near Daventry, Northants NN11 6LG.

REYNOLDS, (James) Kirk; QC 1993; *b* 24 March 1951; *s* of late James Reynolds, sometime Judge of the High Ct, Eastern Reg. of Nigeria, and of Alexandra Mary (*née* Strain). *Educ:* Campbell Coll., Belfast; Peterhouse, Cambridge (MA). Called to the Bar, Middle Temple, 1974; Bencher, 2000. Hon. Mem., RICS, 1997. *Publications:* The Handbook of Rent Review, 1981; The Renewal of Business Tenancies, 1985, 2nd edn 1997; Dilapidations: the modern law and practice, 1995; Essentials of Rent Review, 1995. *Address:* Falcon Chambers, Falcon Court, EC4Y 1AA. *T:* (020) 7353 2484.

REYNOLDS, Joyce Maire, FBA 1982; Fellow of Newnham College, 1951–84, now Hon. Fellow, and Reader in Roman Historical Epigraphy, 1983–84, University of Cambridge; *b* 18 Dec. 1918; *d* of late William Howe Reynolds and Nellie Farmer Reynolds. *Educ:* Walthamstow County High Sch. for Girls; St Paul's Girls' Sch., Hammersmith; Somerville Coll., Oxford (Hon. Fellow, 1988). Temp. Civil Servant, BoT, 1941–46; Rome Scholar, British Sch. at Rome, 1946–48; Lectr in Ancient History, King's Coll., Newcastle upon Tyne, 1948–51; Cambridge University: Asst Lectr in Classics, 1952–57; Univ. Lectr 1957–83; Dir of Studies in Classics, 1951–79 and Lectr in Classics, 1951–84, Newnham Coll. Woolley Travelling Fellow, Somerville Coll., Oxford, 1961; Mem., Inst. for Advanced Study, Princeton, USA, 1984–85; Vis. Prof., Univ. of Calif at Berkeley, 1987. President: Soc. for Libyan Studies, 1981–86; Soc. for the Promotion of Roman Studies, 1986–89. Corresponding Member: German Archaeol Inst., 1971–; Austrian Archaeol Inst., 1991–. Hon. DLitt Newcastle upon Tyne, 1984. *Publications:* (with J. B. Ward Perkins) The Inscriptions of Roman Tripolitania, 1952; Aphrodisias and Rome, 1982; (with R. Tannenbaum) Jews and Godfearers at Aphrodisias, 1987; articles on Roman history and epigraphy in jls, 1951–. *Recreation:* walking. *Address:* Newnham College, Cambridge CB3 9DF. *T:* (01223) 335700.

REYNOLDS, Kirk; *see* Reynolds, J. K.

REYNOLDS, Martin Paul; His Honour Judge Reynolds; a Circuit Judge, since 1995; *b* 25 Dec. 1936; *s* of Cedric Hinton Fleetwood Reynolds and Doris Margaret (*née* Bryan); *m* 1961, Gaynor Margaret Phillips; three *s*. *Educ:* University College Sch., Hampstead; St Edmund Hall, Oxford (MA). ACIArb 1982. Called to the Bar, Inner Temple, 1962. Councillor, London Borough of Islington, 1968–71 and 1972–82. Contested (Lab) Harrow West, Oct. 1994. *Recreations:* navigating European waterways in a Dutch barge, gastronomy, music. *Address:* Snaresbrook Crown Court, Hollybush Hill, Snaresbrook, E11 1QW. *T:* (020) 8982 5500. *Clubs:* Savage; Bar Yacht.

REYNOLDS, Dr Martin Richard Finch; Associate Director of Health Policy and Public Health, East Riding Health Authority, 1993–99; *b* 26 July 1943; 2nd *s* of Gerald Finch Reynolds and Frances Bertha (*née* Locke); *m* 1965, Shelagh (*née* Gray); two *d*. *Educ:* Newton Abbot Grammar Sch.; Univ. of Bristol. MB ChB, DPH; FFPHM; FRCP. House posts in medicine, surgery, infectious diseases and paediatrics, 1966–67; Dep. Med. Officer, Glos CC, 1967–70; Sen. Dep. Med. Officer, Bristol City and Asst Sen. Med. Officer, SW Regional Hosp. Bd, 1970–74; Dist Community Physician, Southmead Dist of Avon AHA (Teaching) and Med. Officer for Environmental Health, Northavon Dist Council, 1974–79; Area Med. Officer, Wilts AHA, 1979–80; Regional MO/Chief Med. Advr, South Western RHA, 1980–86; Specialist in Community Medicine, 1986–89, Consultant in Public Health Medicine, 1989–93, Hull HA. Registrar, FPHM, 1995–97. Voluntary work with Wycliffe Associates for Bible trans., 1999–. *Publications:* contrib. various articles in professional jls on subjects in community medicine. *Address:* Knights Cottage, Callas, Bishop Burton, Beverley, N Humberside HU17 8QL.

REYNOLDS, Michael Emanuel, CBE 1977; Founder/Owner, Susan Reynolds Books Ltd, 1977–84; *b* 22 April 1931; *s* of Isaac Mark and Henrietta Rosenberg; *m* 1964, Susan Geraldine Yates; two *d*. *Educ:* Haberdashers' Aske's (HSC). Marks & Spencer Ltd, 1951–61; Food Controller, British Home Stores Ltd, 1961–64; Spar (UK) Ltd, 1964–77: Trading Controller, 1964–67; Chm. and Managing Dir, 1967–77; BV Intergroup Trading (IGT), 1974–77: Founder Mem., Bd of Admin.; Dir, 1974–75; Chm. and Dir, 1975–77. *Recreations:* tennis, squash, bridge.

REYNOLDS, Maj.-Gen. Michael Frank, CB 1983; author (military history); *b* 3 June 1930; *s* of Frank Reynolds and Gwendolen Reynolds (*née* Griffiths); *m* 1955, Anne Bernice (*née* Truman); three *d*. *Educ:* Cranleigh; RMA Sandhurst (Infantry Prize). Commnd Queen's Royal Regt, 1950 (last Adjt, 1959); served Germany, Korea (severely wounded), Cyprus (EOKA emergency), Canada (exchange officer), Persian Gulf, Netherlands, Belgium; psc 1960; GSO 1 Ops, HQ AFCENT, 1970–71; CO 2 Queen's, BAOR and Ulster, 1971–73; GSO 1 Ops, N Ireland, 1973–74; Comdr 12 (Mech) Bde, BAOR, 1974–76; RCDS, 1977; Dep. Adjt Gen., BAOR, 1978–80; Comdr, Allied Command Europe Mobile Force (Land), 1980–83; Asst Dir, IMS (Plans and Policy), HQ NATO, 1983–86. Col Comdt, The Queen's Division, 1984–86; (Last) Col, The Queen's Regt, 1989–92. Pres., E Anglian Aviation Soc., 1996–98. Comdr First Cl., Order of the Dannebrog (Denmark), 1990; Grand Cross, Order of Orange-Nassau (Netherlands), 1992. *Publications:* The Devil's Adjutant, 1995; Steel Inferno, 1997; Men of Steel, 1999; Sons of the Reich, 2002. *Recreations:* military history (especially Normandy and Battle of the Ardennes, 1944), writing.

REYNOLDS, Osmund; *see* Reynolds, E. O. R.

REYNOLDS, Sir Peter (William John), Kt 1985; CBE 1975; Director: Boots Co. plc, since 1986; Avis Europe Ltd, since 1988; Cilva Holdings plc, since 1989; *b* 10 Sept. 1929; *s* of Harry and Gladys Victoria Reynolds; *m* 1955, Barbara Anne, *d* of Vincent Kenneth Johnson, OBE; two *s*. *Educ:* Haileybury Coll., Herts. National Service, 2nd Lieut, RA, 1948–50. Unilever Ltd, 1950–70: Trainee; Managing Dir, then Chm., Walls (Meat & Handy Foods) Ltd. Ranks Hovis McDougall: Asst Gp Managing Dir, 1971; Gp Man. Dir, 1972–81; Chm., 1981–89; Dep. Chm., 1989–93. Director: Guardian Royal Exchange Assurance plc, 1986–99; Pioneer International, until 1999; Nationwide Anglia Building Soc., 1990–92; Chm., Pioneer Concrete (Hldgs), 1990–99. Chairman: EDC Employment and Trng Cttee, 1982–87; Resources Cttee, Food and Drink Fedn (formerly Food and Drink Industries Council), 1983–86; Member: EDC for Food and Drink Manufg Industry, 1976–87; Consultative Bd for Resources Develt in Agriculture, 1982–84; Covent Garden Market Authority, 1989–97; Dir, Industrial Develt Bd for NI, 1982–89; Mem., Peacock Cttee on Financing the BBC, 1985–86. Dir, Freemantle Trust (formerly Bucks Comm. Housing Trust), 1992–. Gov., Berkhamsted Sch., 1985–; Life Gov., Haileybury, 1985. High Sheriff, Bucks, 1990–91. *Address:* Rignall Farm, Rignall Road, Great Missenden, Bucks HP16 9PE. *T:* (01240) 64714.

REYNOLDS, Prof. Philip Alan, CBE 1986; DL; Vice-Chancellor, University of Lancaster, 1980–85; *b* 15 May 1920; *s* of Harry Reynolds and Ethel (*née* Scott); *m* 1946, Mollie Patricia (*née* Horton); two *s* one *d*. *Educ:* Worthing High Sch.; Queen's Coll., Oxford (BA 1940, 1st Cl. Mod. Hist.; MA 1950). Served War, 1940–46: HAA and Staff, UK, ME and Greece; Major 1945. Asst Lectr, then Lectr in Internat. History, LSE, 1946–50; Woodrow Wilson Prof. of Internat. Politics, UCW Aberystwyth, 1950–64 (Vice-Principal, 1961–63); Prof. of Politics and Pro-Vice-Chancellor, Univ. of Lancaster, 1964–80. Vis. Professor: in Internat. Relations, Toronto, 1953; in Commonwealth History and Instns, Indian Sch. of Internat. Studies, New Delhi, 1958; Anspach Fellow, Univ. of Pa, 1971; Vis. Res. Fellow, ANU Canberra, 1977. Vice-Chm., Cttee of Vice-Chancellors and Principals, 1984–85; Chm., Brit. Internat. Studies Assoc., 1976, Hon. Pres., 1981–84; Mem. Council, RIIA, 1975–80. DL Lancs, 1982. Hon. DLitt Lancaster, 1985; DUniv Open, 1994. *Publications:* War in the Twentieth Century, 1951; Die Britische Aussenpolitik zwischen den beiden Weltkriegen, 1952 (rev. edn, 1954, as British Foreign Policy in the Inter-War Years); An Introduction to International Relations, 1971, 3rd edn 1994 (Japanese edn 1977, Spanish edn 1978, Chinese edn 1997); (with E. J. Hughes) The Historian as Diplomat: Charles Kingsley Webster and the United Nations 1939–46, 1976; contrib. New Cambridge Mod. Hist., History, Slavonic Rev., Pol. Qly, Pol. Studies, Internat. Jl, Internat. Studies, Brit. Jl of Internat. Studies, Educn Policy Bulletin, Higher Educn, Univs Qly, Minerva. *Recreations:* music, bridge, eating and drinking. *Address:* Lattice Cottage, Borwick, Carnforth, Lancs LA6 1JR. *T:* (01524) 732518.

REYNOLDS, Dr Roy Gregory, CMG 2000; Chief Executive, Commonwealth Development Corporation, 1994–99; *b* 4 May 1939; *s* of Henry Herbert Reynolds and Alice Emily Reynolds; *m* 1963, Monica Cecelia; one *s* one *d*. *Educ:* George Dixon Grammar Sch., Birmingham; Birmingham Univ. (BSc Chem. Eng 1960); Imperial Coll., London (PhD 1964). Shell Internat. Petroleum Co., 1964–92. Dir, Flemings Emerging Markets Trust, 1999–; non-executive Director: LASMO plc, 1997–2001; Merasis, 2000–. *Recreations:* keeping fit, golf, general reading. *Club:* Royal Automobile.

REYNOLDS, Susan Mary Grace, FRHistS; FBA 1993; Senior Research Fellow, Institute of Historical Research, since 1993; Hon. Research Fellow, History Department of University College London, since 1987, and of Birkbeck College, since 1995; *b* 27 Jan. 1929; *d* of Hugh Reynolds and Maisie Reynolds (*née* Morten). *Educ:* The Study, Montreal; Howell's Sch., Denbigh; Lady Margaret Hall, Oxford (History Cl. II, MA); Dip. Archive Admin, UCL. FRHistS 1968. Archive Asst, 1951–52; Victoria County Histories, 1952–59; school teacher, 1959–64; Fellow and Tutor in Modern History, LMH, Oxford, 1964–86, Emeritus Fellow, 1986; Lectr in Modern History, Oxford Univ., 1965–86. Visiting Professor: Dartmouth Coll., USA, 1986–87; Central European Univ., Budapest, 1994. *Publications:* (ed) Register of Roger Martival, Bishop of Salisbury, vol. 3, 1965; Introduction to the History of English Medieval Towns, 1977; Kingdoms and Communities in Western Europe 900–1300, 1984, 2nd edn 1997; Fiefs and Vassals, 1994; Ideas and Solidarities of the Medieval Laity, 1995; articles in historical jls. *Address:* Flat 3, 26 Lennox Gardens, SW1X 0DQ. *T:* (020) 7584 2505.

REYNOLDS, William Oliver, OBE 1973 (MBE 1944); *b* 2 Nov. 1915; General Manager, Eastern Region, British Rail, 1973–76; *s* of Edgar Ernest Reynolds and Elizabeth Wilson Biesterfield; *m* 1944, Eleanor Gill; two *s*. *Educ:* Royal Grammar Sch., Newcastle upon Tyne. LNER Traffic apprentice, 1936. Served War, with Royal Engineers, 1940–46: despatches, 1942 and 1944; Lt-Col, 1944. Lt-Col, Engineer and Railway Staff Corps, RE (T&AVR IV), 1971–97. Divisional Manager, London Midland, BR, 1960; Asst Gen. Manager, Scottish Region, 1964; Chief Operating Manager, BR Bd, 1968; Exec. Dir, BR Bd, 1969. Mem., Adv. Council, Science Mus. 1975–84; Chm., Friends of Nat. Railway Mus. 1984–93. FCIT. *Recreations:* fishing, golf, gardening. *Address:* Oak House, Follifoot, Harrogate, N Yorks HG3 1DR. *Club:* Oriental.

REYNTIENS, Nicholas Patrick, OBE 1976; Head of Fine Art, Central School of Art and Design, London, 1976–86; *b* 11 Dec. 1925; *s* of Nicholas Serge Reyntiens, OBE, and Janet MacRae; *m* 1953, Anne Bruce; two *s* two *d*. *Educ:* Ampleforth; Edinburgh Coll. of Art (DA). Served Scots Guards, 1943–47. St Marylebone Sch. of Art, 1947–50; Edinburgh Coll. of Art, 1950–51. Founder (with wife, Anne Bruce, the painter), Reyntiens Trust, which ran art sch., Burleighfield, where pupils from UK, Ireland, France, Germany, Japan, Canada, Australia, New Zealand, US and Iceland learned art of stained glass, and which had facilities for tapestry design and teaching, a printing house for editioning in lithography, etching and silkscreen, as well as workshops for stained glass, ceramics, drawing and painting. Has lectured in USA, Spain, Mexico, France and Switzerland; British Council lectr, India, 1995–96 and 1997–98; occasional Vis. Prof., Pilchuck Sch. of Glass, Washington State, USA. Many commissions, including glass for Liverpool RC Metropolitan Cathedral; for 35 years interpreted painters' designs into stained glass, as well as own commissions for stained glass, 1953–, including baptistery window, Coventry Cathedral, Eton Coll. Chapel, Robinson Coll., Cambridge, St Margaret's Westminster (all with John Piper), Derby Cathedral and Liverpool Metropolitan Cathedral (with Ceri Richards), All Saints Basingstoke (with Cecil Collins); completed glazing of Christ Church Hall, Oxford, 1980–84; designed and painted Great West Window, Southwell Minster, Notts, 1995. Retrospective exhibn of autonomous panels, Ontario, 1990. Member: Court, RCA; Adv. Cttee in Decoration, Brompton Oratory; Adv. Cttee in Decoration, Westminster Cathedral; Adv. Cttee, Westminster Abbey, 1981–95. Art Critic, Catholic Herald; art correspondent, The Oldie. *Publications:* Technique of Stained Glass, 1967, 2nd edn 1977; The Beauty of Stained Glass, 1990; has written for architectural, art, literary and political magazines and on cooking for Harpers & Queen. *Address:* Winterbourne Lodge, Ilford Bridges Farm, Close Stocklinch, Ilminster, Som TA19 9HZ. *T:* (01460) 52241, *Fax:* (01460) 57150.

RHIND, Prof. David William, CBE 2001; Vice-Chancellor and Principal, City University, since 1998; *b* 29 Nov. 1943; *s* of late William Rhind and of Christina Rhind; *m* 1966, Christine Young; one *s* two *d*. *Educ:* Berwick Grammar School; Bristol Univ. (BSc); Edinburgh Univ. (PhD); London Univ. (DSc). FRGS; FRICS 1991. Research Fellow, Royal College of Art, 1969–73; Lectr then Reader, Univ. of Durham, 1973–81; Birkbeck College, London University: Prof. of Geography, 1982–91; Dean, Faculty of Economics, 1984–86; Governor, 1986–90; Hon. Fellow, 2000; Dir Gen. and Chief Exec., Ordnance Survey, 1992–98. Visiting Fellow: Internat. Trng Centre, Netherlands, 1975; ANU, 1979. Vice-Pres., Internat. Cartographic Assoc., 1984–91; Mem., Govt Cttee on Enquiry into handling of geographic inf., 1985–87; Advisor, H of L Select Cttee on Sci. and Tech., 1983–84; Member: ESRC, 1996–2000; Statistics Commn, 2000–. Chairman: Bloomsbury Computing Consortium Management Cttee, 1988–91; Royal Soc. Ordnance Survey Scientific Cttee, 1989–91; Commn on Social Scis, Acad. of Learned Socs for Social Scis, 2000–. Governor: City of London Girls' Sch., 1999–2001; Ashridge

Mgt Coll., 2000–. Hon. Sec., RGS, 1988–91. CIMgt 1998. Hon. DSc: Bristol, 1993; Loughborough, 1996; Southampton, 1998; Kingston, 1999; Durham, 2001. Centenary Medal, RSGS, 1992; Patron's Medal, RGS, 1997; Decade Award for Achievement, Assoc. for Geographic Inf., 1997. *Publications:* (jtly) Land Use, 1980; The Census User's Handbook, 1983; (jtly) Atlas of EEC Affairs, 1984; (jtly) Geographical Information Systems, 1991, revised 1999; (jtly) Postcodes: the new geography, 1992; Framework for the World, 1997; (jtly) Geographical Information Systems and Science, 2001; numerous papers on map-making and computerised databases. *Recreations:* travelling, mowing the lawn. *Address:* City University, Northampton Square, EC1V 0HB. *T:* (020) 7477 8000.

RHODES, Col Sir Basil (Edward), Kt 1987; CBE 1981 (OBE (mil.) 1945; MBE (mil.) 1944); TD 1946; DL; Partner, Gichard & Co., solicitors, since 1946; *b* Rotherham, 8 Dec. 1915; *s* of late Col Harry Rhodes and of Astri Rhodes (*née* Natvig); *m* 1962, Joëlle, *er d* of Robert Vilgard, Paris; one *s*. *Educ:* St Edward's Sch., Oxford. Served War of 1939–45, Western Desert, Greece, Crete and Burma (wounded; mentioned in despatches). Admitted solicitor, 1946. Director: Carlton Main Brickworks; Wessex Fare; Yorkshire Merchant Securities. Mem. (C) Town Council, Rotherham, 1949–74, Mayor, 1970–71; Chm., 1949–75, Pres., 1975–, Rotherham Cons. Assoc.; Chm., S Yorks Cons. Fedn, 1964–76; Treas., Cons. Central Office Yorks Area, 1983–88. DL 1975, High Sheriff, 1982–83, S Yorks. *Recreations:* fieldsports, ski-ing, gardening. *Address:* Bubnell Hall, Baslow, Bakewell, Derbys DE4 1RL. *T:* (01246) 583266. *Club:* Cavalry and Guards.

RHODES, Gary; chef and restaurateur; *b* 22 April 1960; *s* of Jean Rhodes (*née* Ferris) and step *s* of John Smellie; *m* 1989, (Yolanda) Jennifer Adkins; two *s*. *Educ:* Thanet Technical Coll., Broadstairs (C&G qualifs; Student of the Year, Chef of the Year, 1979). Commis, then Chef de Partie, Amsterdam Hilton, 1979–81; Sous Chef: Reform Club, 1982–83; Capital Hotel, Knightsbridge, 1983–85; Head Chef: Whitehall, Broxted, 1985–86; Castle Hotel, Taunton, 1986–90 (Michelin Star, annually, 1986–90); The Greenhouse, London, 1990–96 (Michelin Star, 1996); Chef and Co-Proprietor: city rhodes, 1997– (Michelin Star, 1997, 1998, 1999); Rhodes in the Square, 1998– (Michelin Star, 2000); Rhodes & Co., Manchester, 1999–, Edinburgh, 1999– (Bib Gourmond Award). Consultant: Tate & Lyle Sugar, 1996–; Richardson Sheffield, 1999–. *Television series:* Hot Chefs, 1988; Rhodes Around Britain, 1994; More Rhodes Around Britain, 1995; Open Rhodes Around Britain, 1996; Gary Rhodes, 1997; Gary's Perfect Christmas, 1998; Gary Rhodes' New British Classics, 1999; Masterchef, 2001; At the Table, 2001. Rhodes on the Road (tour), 1997; columnist, BBC Good Food magazine, 1996–. *Publications:* Rhodes Around Britain, 1994; More Rhodes Around Britain, 1995; Open Rhodes Around Britain, 1996; Short-cut Rhodes, 1997; Fabulous Food, 1997; Sweet Dreams, 1998; New British Classics, 1999; At the Table, 2000. *Recreations:* driving, art, fashion. *Address:* city rhodes, 1 New Street Square, EC4A 3BF. *Clubs:* Les Ambassadeurs, St James's.

RHODES, George Harold Lancashire, TD 1946; Regional Chairman of Industrial Tribunals: Manchester, 1985–88; Liverpool, 1987–88; *b* 29 Feb. 1916; *er s* of Judge Harold and Ena Rhodes of Bowdon, Cheshire. *Educ:* Shrewsbury School; The Queen's College, Oxford (MA 1941). Commissioned 52nd Field Regt RA TA, 1938; war service, BEF, 1940, Middle East, 1942, Italy, 1943–46 (Major). Called to the Bar, Gray's Inn, 1947; practised on N Circuit; the Junior, 1948; Office of Judge Advocate General (Army and RAF), 1953; Asst Judge Advocate General, 1967; Chm., Industrial Tribunals (Manchester), 1974, Dep. Regional Chm., 1975. *Recreation:* walking. *Address:* 42 Custerson Court, Saffron Walden, Essex CB11 3HF.

RHODES, John Andrew, FCIT; independent public transport consultant, since 1999; *b* 22 May 1949; *s* of George and Elsie Rhodes; *m* 1985, Marie Catherine Carleton. *Educ:* Queen Elizabeth Sch., Barnet; Wadham Coll., Oxford (MA Mod. History). Civil Service: various posts in DoE, Cabinet Office, Dept of Transport, 1971–87; Dir Gen., W Yorks PTE, 1988–92; Strategy and Planning Advr, BRB, 1992–93; Dir, Passenger Services Gp, Office of Rail Regulator, 1993–99. Non-exec. Dir, E and N Herts NHS Trust, 2000–. Chm., Bishop's Stortford Civic Soc., 2000–. Hon. Sen. Res. Fellow, Constitution Unit, UCL. FRSA. *Recreations:* music, transport history, gardening. *Address:* 26 Warwick Road, Bishop's Stortford, Herts CM23 5NW. *T:* (01279) 656482.
See also P. J. Rhodes.

RHODES, Sir John (Christopher Douglas), 4th Bt *cr* 1919; *b* 24 May 1946; *s* of Sir Christopher Rhodes, 3rd Bt, and of Mary Florence, *d* of late Dr Douglas Wardleworth; *S* father, 1964. *Heir: b* Michael Philip James Rhodes [*b* 3 April 1948; *m* 1973, Susan, *d* of Patrick Roney-Dougal; one *d*].

RHODES, Prof. John David, CBE 2000 (OBE 1992); PhD, DSc; FRS 1993; FREng; Chairman and Chief Executive Officer, Filtronic Ltd, since 1977; Chairman, Filtronic plc, since 1994; Industrial Professor, Leeds University, since 1981; *b* 9 Oct. 1943; *s* of Jack and Florence Rhodes; *m* 1965, Barbara Margaret Pearce; one *s* one *d*. *Educ:* Univ. of Leeds (BSc, PhD, DSc). FIEEE 1980; FIEE 1984; FREng (FEng 1987). Leeds University: Res. Asst, 1964–66; Res. Fellow, 1966–67; Sen. Res. Engr, Microwave Develt Labs, USA, 1967–69; Leeds University: Lectr, 1969–72; Reader, 1972–75; Prof., 1975–81. Hon. DEng Bradford, 1988; Hon. DSc Napier, 1995. *Publication:* Theory of Electrical Filters, 1976. *Recreation:* golf. *Address:* Dabarda, West Winds, Moor Lane, Menston, Ilkley LS29 6QD. *T:* (office) (01274) 530622.

RHODES, John David McKinnon; Director, BNFL Partnership Team, Department of Trade and Industry, since 2000; *b* 20 Aug. 1950; *s* of John Ivor McKinnon Rhodes, *qv*; *m* 1984, Sarah Elizabeth Rickard; two *s* one *d*. *Educ:* Dulwich Coll.; Sussex Univ. (BA Hons); London Business Sch. (Sloan Fellow 1983). With Lithotype Inc., 1971–72; joined Department of Trade and Industry, 1972: Principal Private Sec. to Sec. of State for Trade, 1981–83; Asst Sec., Internat. Projects, 1984–86; Director: British Trade and Investment Office (USA), NY, 1987–90; EC Single Market Policy, 1991–94; Electricity and Nuclear Fuels, 1994–96; Nuclear Sponsorship, DTI, 1996–97; Sec., Low Pay Commn, 1997–98; Dir, Infrastructure and Energy Projects, DTI, 1998–2000. *Recreations:* family, cooking. *Address:* Department of Trade and Industry, 1 Victoria Street, SW1H 0ET.

RHODES, John Ivor McKinnon, CMG 1971; *b* 6 March 1914; *s* of late Joseph Thomas Rhodes and late Hilda (*née* McKinnon); *m* 1939, Eden Annetta Clark (*d* 1990); one *s* one *d*. *Educ:* Leeds Modern School. Exec. Officer, WO, 1933; Financial Adviser's Office, HQ British Forces in Palestine, 1938; Major 1940; Asst Comd Sec., Southern Comd, 1944; Financial Adviser, London District, 1946; Principal 1947, Asst Sec. 1959, HM Treasury; Minister, UK Mission to UN, 1966–74. Member: UN Pension Board, 1966–71; UN Cttee on Contributions, 1966–71, 1975–77; Chm., UN Adv. Cttee on Admin. and Budgetary Questions, 1971–74; Senior Adviser (Asst Sec.-Gen.) to Administrator, UNDP, 1979–80. *Recreations:* gardening, playing the electronic organ. *Address:* Quintins, Watersfield, Pulborough, W Sussex RH20 1NE. *T:* (01798) 831634.
See also J. D. McK. Rhodes.

RHODES, Prof. Jonathan Michael, MD; FRCP, FMedSci; Professor of Medicine, University of Liverpool, since 1995; Consultant Gastroenterologist, Royal Liverpool University Hospital, since 1991; *b* 21 April 1949; *s* of Wilfred Harry Rhodes and Ellen Linda Rhodes (*née* Wreford); *m* 1978, Elizabeth Geraldine Helen Morris; three *d*. *Educ:* Kingston Grammar Sch.; St John's Coll., Cambridge (MA); St Thomas's Hosp. Med. Sch. (MD 1982). FRCP 1989. House surgeon, St Thomas' Hosp., 1973; house physician and SHO, Kingston Hosp., 1974–75; SHO, Hammersmith Hosp., 1976; Registrar and Res. Fellow, Royal Free Hosp., 1976–81; Sen. Registrar, Queen Elizabeth and Selly Oak Hosps, Birmingham, 1981–85; Sen. Lectr, 1985–91, Reader, 1991–95, Univ. of Liverpool. Chairman: Educn Cttee, British Soc. Gastroenterology, 1996–2000; Gastroenterology Speciality Cttee, RCP, 1997–2001; Mem. Exec. Cttee, Assoc. Physicians, 1999–2001. FMedSci 1999. Avery Jones Res. Medal, British Soc. Gastroenterology, 1989. *Publications:* (ed jtly) Inflammatory Bowel Disease, 3rd edn 1997; contrib. papers on inflammatory bowel disease, colon cancer, lectins and glycobiology. *Recreations:* fell-walking, classical guitar, rowing coaching. *Address:* Department of Medicine, University of Liverpool, Liverpool L69 3GA. *T:* (0151) 706 4073. *Clubs:* Hawks (Cambridge); Leander (Henley); Bristol Owners.

RHODES, Sir Peregrine (Alexander), KCMG 1984 (CMG 1976); HM Diplomatic Service, retired; Director-General, British Property Federation, 1986–93; *b* 14 May 1925; *s* of Cyril Edmunds Rhodes and Elizabeth Jocelyn Rhodes; *m* 1st, 1951, Jane Marion Hassell (marr. diss.); two *s* one *d*; 2nd, 1969, Margaret Rosemary Page. *Educ:* Winchester Coll.; New Coll., Oxford (BA Lit. Hum. (1st cl)). Served with Coldstream Guards, 1944–47. Joined FO, 1950; 2nd Sec., Rangoon, 1953–56; Private Sec. to Minister of State, 1956–59; 1st Sec., Vienna, 1959–62; 1st Sec., Helsinki, 1962–65; FCO, 1965–68, Counsellor 1967; Inst. for Study of Internat. Organisation, Sussex Univ., 1968–69; Counsellor, Rome, 1970–73; Chargé d'Affaires, E Berlin, 1973–75; on secondment as Under Sec., Cabinet Office (Chief of Assessments Staff), 1975–78; High Comr, Cyprus, 1979–82; Ambassador, Greece, 1982–85. Chm., Anglo-Hellenic League, 1986–90; Vice-Pres. British Sch., Athens, 1982–. FRSA 1988. *Recreations:* photography, reading. *Address:* Pond House, Thorpe Morieux, Bury St Edmunds, Suffolk IP30 0NW. *Club:* Travellers (Chm., 1994–98).

RHODES, Prof. Peter John, FBA 1987; Professor of Ancient History, University of Durham, since 1983; *b* 10 Aug. 1940; *s* of George Thomas Rhodes and Elsie Leonora Rhodes (*née* Pugh); *m* 1971, Jan Teresa Adamson. *Educ:* Queen Elizabeth's Boys' Grammar Sch., Barnet; Wadham Coll., Oxford (minor schol.; BA (1st cl. Mods, 1st cl. Greats); MA; DPhil). Harmsworth Schol., Merton Coll., Oxford, 1963–65; Craven Fellow, Oxford Univ., 1963–65; Lectr in Classics and Ancient History, 1965, Sen. Lectr, 1977, Durham Univ. Jun. Fellow, Center for Hellenic Studies, Washington, DC, 1978–79; Visiting Fellow: Wolfson Coll., Oxford, 1984; Univ. of New England, Aust., 1988; Corpus Christi Coll., Oxford, 1993; All Souls Coll., Oxford, 1998; Leverhulme Res. Fellow, 1994–95; Langford Family Eminent Scholar, Florida State Univ., 2002. Mem., Inst. for Advanced Study, Princeton, USA, 1988–89. *Publications:* The Athenian Boule, 1972; Greek Historical Inscriptions 359–323 BC, 1972; Commentary on the Aristotelian Athenaion Politeia, 1981; (trans.) Aristotle: the Athenian Constitution, 1984; The Athenian Empire, 1985; The Greek City States: a source book, 1986; (ed) Thucydides Book II, 1988; (ed) Thucydides Book III, 1994; (with D. M. Lewis) The Decrees of the Greek States, 1997; (ed with L. G. Mitchell) The Development of the Polis in Archaic Greece, 1997; (ed) Thucydides Book IV.1–Book V.24, 1999; articles and reviews in jls. *Recreations:* music, typography, travel. *Address:* Department of Classics, University of Durham, 38 North Bailey, Durham, DH1 3EU. *T:* (0191) 374 2073.
See also J. A. Rhodes.

RHODES, Philip, FRCS, FRCOG, FRACMA, FFOM; Regional Postgraduate Dean of Medical Studies, and Professor of Postgraduate Medical Education, Southampton University, 1980–87, retired; *b* 2 May 1922; *s* of Sydney Rhodes, Dore, Sheffield; *m* 1946, Mary Elizabeth Worley, Barrowden, Rutland; three *s* two *d*. *Educ:* King Edward VII Sch., Sheffield; Clare Coll., Cambridge; St Thomas's Hospital Medical School. BA(Cantab) 1943, MB, BChir(Cantab) 1946; FRCS 1953; MRCOG 1956; FRCOG 1964; FRACMA 1976; FFOM 1990. Major RAMC, 1948–50. Medical appointments held in St Thomas' Hosp., Folkestone, Harrogate, Chelsea Hosp. for Women, Queen Charlotte's Hosp., 1946–58; Consultant Obstetric Physician, St Thomas' Hosp., 1958–63; Prof. of Obstetrics and Gynæcol., St Thomas's Hosp. Med. Sch., Univ. of London, 1964–74, Dean, 1968–74; Dean, Faculty of Medicine, Univ. of Adelaide, 1975–77; Postgrad. Dean and Dir, Regional Postgrad. Inst. for Med. and Dentistry, Newcastle Univ., 1977–80. Member: SW Metropolitan Regional Hosp. Board, 1967–74; SE Thames Reg. Health Authority, 1974; GMC, 1979–89 (Educn Cttee, 1984–89). Mem. Steering Cttee of DHSS on management of NHS, 1971–72. Mem., Adv. Cttee, Nat. Inst. of Medical Hist., Australia, 1976. Chm., Educn Cttee, King Edward's Hosp. Fund for London, 1981–87; Member: UGC Working Party on Continuing Educn, 1983; Council for Postgrad. Med. Educn in England and Wales, 1984–87. Governor: Dulwich Coll., 1966–74; St Thomas' Hosp., 1969–74; Pembroke Sch., Adelaide, 1976–77. FRSA 1989. *Publications:* Fluid Balance in Obstetrics, 1960; Introduction to Gynæcology and Obstetrics, 1967; Reproductive Physiology for Medical Students, 1969; Woman: A Biological Study, 1969; The Value of Medicine, 1976; Dr John Leake's Hospital, 1978; Letters to a Young Doctor, 1983; An Outline History of Medicine, 1985; Wakerley: a village in Northamptonshire, 1994; A Short History of Clinical Midwifery, 1995; Gynaecology for Everywoman, 1996; Barrowden: a village in Rutland, 1998; Associate Editor, The Oxford Companion to Medicine, 1986; contrib. Encyclopedia Britannica, New DNB; articles in Jl of Obstetrics and Gynæcology of the British Empire, Lancet, Brit. Med. Jl, Med. Jl of Australia. *Recreations:* reading, gardening, photography. *Address:* 1 Wakerley Court, Wakerley, Oakham, Leics LE15 8NZ.

RHODES, Richard David Walton; JP; Principal, Rossall Schools, 2000–01; *b* 20 April 1942; *er s* of Harry Walton Rhodes and Dorothy Rhodes (*née* Fairhurst); *m* 1966, Stephanie Heyes, 2nd *d* of Frederic William Heyes and Catherine Heyes; two *d*. *Educ:* Rossall Sch.; St John's Coll., Durham (BA 1963). Asst Master, St John's Sch., Leatherhead, 1964–75 (Founder Housemaster, Montgomery House, 1973–75); Deputy Headmaster, Arnold Sch., Blackpool, 1975–79, Headmaster, 1979–87; Headmaster, Rossall Sch., 1987–99. Member: Lancs CC Social Services Adv. Cttee, 1992–; Lancs Magistrates' Courts Cttee, 1993–96. Chairman: NW Div., HMC, 1987; Northern ISIS, 1993–95. Member Council: Univ. of Salford, 1987–93; Lawrence House Sch., Lytham St Annes, 1988–93; Trustee, Lawrence House Trust, 1994–97 (Chm., 2000–); Gov., Terra Nova Sch., Jodrell Bank, 1989– (Chm. Govs, 2000–). JP Fylde, 1978, Wyre, 1999. *Recreations:* photography, sports, motoring, gardening in the Lake District. *Address:* Fairview, Staveley in Cartmel, Newby Bridge, Ulverston, Cumbria LA12 8NS. *T:* (01539) 531634.

RHODES, Robert Elliott; QC 1989; a Recorder, since 1987; *b* 2 Aug. 1945; *s* of late Gilbert G. Rhodes, FCA and of Elly, who *m* 2nd, Leopold Brook, *qv*; *m* 1971, Georgina Caroline (marr. diss. 1996), *d* of J. G. Clarfelt, *qv*; two *s* one *d*. *Educ:* St Paul's School; Pembroke Coll., Oxford. MA. Called to the Bar, Inner Temple, 1968. Second Prosecuting Counsel to Inland Revenue at Central Criminal Court and Inner London Crown Courts, 1979, First Prosecuting Counsel, 1981–89. Hd of Chambers, 1998–.

Deputy Chairman: IMRO Membership Tribunal Panel, 1992–; ICAEW Appeal Cttee, 1998–. *Recreations:* opera, theatre, reading, art, cricket, real tennis. *Address:* 4 King's Bench Walk, Temple, EC4Y 7DL. *T:* (020) 7822 8822. *Clubs:* Garrick, Annabel's, MCC; Epee.

RHODES, Zandra Lindsey, CBE 1997; RDI 1976; DesRCA, FCSD; Managing Director, Zandra Rhodes (UK) Ltd and Zandra Rhodes (Shops) Ltd, since 1975; *b* 19 Sept. 1940; *d* of Albert James Rhodes and Beatrice Ellen (*née* Twigg). *Educ:* Medway Technical Sch. for Girls, Chatham; Medway Coll. of Art; Royal Coll. of Art (DesRCA 1964). FSIAD 1982. With Alexander MacIntyre, set up print factory and studio, 1965; sold designs (and converted them on to cloth) to Foale and Tuffin and Roger Nelson; formed partnership with Sylvia Ayton and began producing dresses using her own prints, 1966; opened Fulham Road Clothes Shop, designing dresses as well as prints, first in partnership, 1967–68, then (Fulham Road shop closed) alone, producing first clothes range in which she revolutionised use of prints in clothes by cutting round patterns to make shapes never before used; took collection to USA, 1969; sold to Fortnum and Mason, London, 1969, Piero de Monzi, 1971; began building up name and business in USA (known for her annual spectacular Fantasy Shows); also started designing in jersey and revolutionised its treatment with lettuce edges and seams on the outside; with Knight and Stirling founded Zandra Rhodes (UK) Ltd and Zandra Rhodes (Shops) Ltd, 1975–86; opening first shop in London, 1975; others opened in Bloomingdales NY, Marshall Field, Chicago, Seibu, Tokyo and Harrods, London, 1976; new factory premises opened in Hammersmith, London, 1984; closed Mayfair shop, 1991 to show on a more personal and individual scale in her Hammersmith showroom. Since 1976 Zandra Rhodes has tried to reach a wider public through licensing her name in UK, USA, Australia and Japan, making full use of the Zandra Rhodes textile design talent for: wallpapers and furnishing fabrics, bathmats, mens ties, sheets and bed linen, printed shawls and scarves, hosiery, teatowels, kitchen accessories and jewellery. Notable licences include: Eve Stillman Lingerie (USA), 1977, Wamsutta sheets and pillowcases (USA), 1976, CVP Designs interior fabrics and settings (UK), 1977, Philip Hockley Decorative Furs (UK), 1986 and Zandra Rhodes Saris (India), 1987 (which she launched with 'West meets East' shows of Saris and Shalwar Chamises in Bombay and Delhi—the first Western designer to do so), Littlewoods Catalogues (UK), 1988 for printed T-shirts and Intasia sweaters; Hilmet silk scarves and men's ties (UK), 1989; Bonnay perfume, Coats Patons needlepoint (UK), 1993; Pologeorgis Furs (USA), Zandra Rhodes II handpainted ready-to-wear collection (HK, China), 1995; Grattons Catalogue sheets and duvets (UK), 1996. One-man exhibitions: Oriel, Cardiff (Welsh Arts Council), 1978; Texas Gall., Houston, 1981; Otis Parsons, Los Angeles, 1981; La Jolla Museum of Contemporary Art, San Diego, 1982; ADITI Creative Power, Barbican Centre, 1982; Sch. of Art Inst., Chicago, 1982; Parsons Sch. of Design, NY, 1982; Art Museum of Santa Cruz Co., Calif, 1983; retrospective exhibition of 'Works of Art' with textiles, Museum of Art, El Paso, Texas, 1984; retrospective of Garments & Textiles (also Lead Speaker for Art to Wear exhibn), Columbus, Ohio, 1987; retrospectives for Seibu Seed Hall, Seibu, Tokyo, 1987 and 1991; Mint Mus., N Carolina, 1992; Athenæum Liby, La Jolla, 1996; water colour exhibition: Dyansen Galls, NY, LA and New Orleans, 1989; major group exhibitions: Nat. Gall. of Australia, 1993; V&A, 1994; RCA 1996. Work represented in major costume collections: UK: V&A; City Mus. and Art Gall., Stoke-on-Trent; Bath Mus.; Royal Pavilion Brighton Mus.; Platt Fields Costume Mus., Manchester; City Art Gall., Leeds; overseas: Metropolitan Mus., NY; Chicago Historical Soc.; Smithsonian Instn; Royal Ontario Mus.; Mus. of Applied Arts and Scis, Sydney; Nat. Mus. of Victoria, Melbourne, La Jolla Mus. of Contemp. Art, LA County Mus. of Art. Opening speaker, Famous Women of Fashion, Smithsonian Inst., Washington, 1978. Founded Zandra Rhodes Mus. of Fashion and Textiles, 1996. Hon. DFA Internat. Fine Arts Coll, Miami, Florida, 1986; Hon. Dr RCA, 1986; Hon. DD CNAA, 1987; Hon. DLitt Westminster, 2000. Designer of the Year, English Fashion Trade UK, 1972; Emmy Award for Best Costume Designs in Romeo and Juliet on Ice, CBS TV, 1984; Woman of Distinction award, Northwood Inst., Dallas, 1986; Top UK Textile Designer, Observer, 1990; Hall of Fame Award, British Fashion Council, 1995; citations and commendations from USA estabs. *Publications:* The Art of Zandra Rhodes, 1984, US edn 1985; The Zandra Rhodes Collection by Brother, 1988. *Recreations:* travelling, drawing, gardening, cooking. *Address:* (office) 79–85 Bermondsey Street, SE1 3XF. *T:* (020) 7403 5333.

RHYMES, Rupert John; Chief Executive: Society of London Theatre, 1987–2001; Theatrical Management Association, 1987–2001; *b* 24 June 1940; *s* of Elson John Rhymes and Phyllis Rhymes (*née* Rawlings); *m* 1970, Susan Mary Chennells; one *s* one *d. Educ:* King Edward's Sch., Bath; Magdalen Coll., Oxford (BA Mod. Hist. 1962; MA). Box Office Clerk, RSC, Aldwych Theatre, 1962; Asst Manager, Sadler's Wells Theatre, 1963; Theatre Manager, Nat. Theatre, Old Vic, 1963–69; Sadler's Wells Opera, then English National Opera, 1969–87: Asst to Admin. Dir, then Head of Press and Publicity, then Gen. Manager, 1969–72, Co. Sec., and Admin. Dir, 1972–87. Chm., Oxford Stage Co., 1987–97. Director: West End Theatre Managers, 1978–87 (Pres., 1979–82; Vice Pres., 1982–83); Nat. Campaign for the Arts, 1988– (Vice Chm., 1999–); Nat. Council for Drama Trng, 1997–. Dir, JFMG Ltd, 1997–. Founding Mem., later Mem., Exec. Council, Performing Arts Employers Assocs League, Europe, 1991– (Chm., 2000–). Trustee: Raymond Mander and Joe Mitchenson Theatre Collection, 1977–2001 (Chm., 1986–2001); Chichester Fest. Theatre, 1998–; Stephen Arlen Meml Fund, 1993–. Gov., Central Sch. of Speech and Drama, 1990– (Vice Chm., 1991–92). *Recreations:* finding time for theatre, protesting against further destruction in the city of Bath. *Address:* Honeysuckle Farm, Foxhill, Bath BA2 5AU. *T:* (01225) 832629, *Fax:* (01225) 834188.

RHYS, family name of **Baron Dynevor**.

RHYS, Prof. David Garel, OBE 1989; FIMI; SMMT Professor of Motor Industry Economics, and Director, Centre for Automotive Industry Research, Cardiff Business School, Cardiff University; *b* 28 Feb. 1940; *s* of Emyr Lewys Rhys and Edith Phyllis Rhys (*née* Williams); *m* 1965, Charlotte Mavis Walters; one *s* two *d. Educ:* Ystalyfera Grammar Sch.; University Coll., Swansea (BA); Univ. of Birmingham (MCom). IOTA 1972. Asst Lectr, then Lectr in Econs, Univ. of Hull, 1965–70; University College, Cardiff, subseq. University of Wales College of Cardiff, now Cardiff University: Lectr in Econs, 1971–77; Sen. Lectr, 1977–84; Prof. of Motor Industry Econs, 1984–; seconded to Cardiff Business Sch., UWIST, 1987–88, until merger with UC Cardiff to form UWCC; Head of Economics, 1987–99; Dir, Centre for Automotive Industry Res., 1991–. Member: RPI Adv. Cttee, 1992–96; Bd, WDA, 1994–99 (Special Advr, 1999–); UK Round Table on Sustainable Develt, 1996–2000. Chm., Welsh Automotive Forum, 2000–. Key Consultant, UNIDO, 1995–96. Advr to H of C and H of L select cttees, 1975–96. Vice Pres., Inst. of the Motor Industry, 1990–. FRSA 1991. Freeman, City of London, 2000; Liveryman, Carmen's Co., 2000–. *Publications:* The Motor Industry: an economic survey, 1972; The Motor Industry in the European Community, 1989; contrib. Jl Industrial Econs, Jl Transport Hist., Jl Transport Econs and Policy, Bulletin of Econ. Res., Scottish Jl of Political Economy, Industrial Relns Jl, Accounting and Business Res., Jl Econ. Studies. *Recreations:* walking, gardening, theatre and opera, sports' spectator. *Address:* 14 Maes Yr Awel, Radyr, Cardiff CF15 8AN. *T:* (029) 2084 2714. *Club:* Royal Automobile.

RHYS JONES, Griffith; actor, writer, director and producer; *b* 16 Nov. 1953; *s* of Elwyn Rhys Jones and Gwyneth Margaret Jones; *m* 1981, Joanna Frances Harris; one *s* one *d. Educ:* Brentwood Sch.; Emmanuel Coll., Cambridge. BBC Radio Producer, 1976–79; *television:* Not the Nine O'Clock News (also co-writer), 1979–81; Alas Smith and Jones (also co-writer), 1982–87; Porterhouse Blue (serial), 1987; The World according to Smith and Jones, 1987; Small Doses (series of short plays) (writer, Boat People), 1989; A View of Harry Clark, 1989; Smith and Jones, 1992, 1995, 1997, 1998; Demob (drama series), 1993; Bookworm (presenter), 1994–; *theatre:* Charley's Aunt, 1983; Trumpets and Raspberries, 1985; The Alchemist, 1985; Arturo Ui, 1987; Smith & Jones (also co-writer), 1989–; The Wind in the Willows, Royal Nat. Th., 1990; dir, Twelfth Night, RSC, 1991; The Revengers' Comedies, Strand, 1991; An Absolute Turkey, Globe, 1994; Plunder, Savoy, 1996; The Front Page, Donmar, 1997; *films:* Morons from Outer Space, 1985; Wilt, 1989; As You Like It, 1992; Staggered, 1994; Up and Under, 1998; *opera:* Die Fledermaus, Royal Opera Covent Garden, 1989; *radio* series: (also writer) Do Go On, 1997–; (also writer) Griff Rhys Jones, 2000. Director: TalkBack, Advertising and Production; Playback, 1987–; Smith Jones Campbell (formerly Smith Jones Brown & Cassie), 1988–99. Chm., Hackney Empire Appeal Cttee, 1998–. *Publications:* Janet lives with Mel and Griff, 1988; The Lavishly Tooled Smith and Jones; Smith and Jones Head to Head, 1992. *Address:* c/o TalkBack, 20–21 Newman Street, W1P 3HB. *T:* (020) 7861 8000.

RHYS WILLIAMS, Sir (Arthur) Gareth (Ludovic Emrys), 3rd Bt *cr* 1918, of Miskin, Parish of Llantrisant, Co. Glamorgan; Director, Central Europe, BPB plc, since 1996; *b* 9 Nov. 1961; *s* of Sir Brandon Rhys Williams, 2nd Bt, MP and of Caroline Susan, *e d* of L. A. Foster; *S* father, 1988; *m* 1996, Harriet, *d* of Maj. Tom Codner; one *s. Educ:* Eton; Durham Univ. (BSc Hons Eng); Insead (MBA). CEng; MIEE; MIMechE; MIOM; MIMgt. Materials Manager, Lucas CAV, 1987–88; Managing Director: NFI Electronics, 1990–93; Rexam Custom Europe, 1992–96. *Recreations:* shooting, travel, chess. *Heir: s* Ludo Dhanlagiri Rhys Williams, *b* 12 Oct. 2001. *Address:* 9 Matheson Road, W14 8SN. *Club:* Garrick.

RIBBANS, Prof. Geoffrey Wilfrid, MA; Kenan University Professor of Hispanic Studies, Brown University, USA, 1978–99, now Emeritus; *b* 15 April 1927; *o s* of late Wilfrid Henry Ribbans and Rose Matilda Burton; *m* 1956, Magdalena Cumming (*née* Willmann), Cologne; one *s* two *d. Educ:* Sir George Monoux Grammar Sch., Walthamstow; King's Coll., Univ. of London. BA Hons Spanish 1st cl., 1948; MA 1953. Asst Lectr, Queen's Univ., Belfast, 1951–52; Asst, St Salvator's Coll., Univ. of St Andrews, 1952–53; Univ. of Sheffield: Asst Lectr, 1953–55; Lectr, 1955–61; Sen. Lectr, 1961–63; Gilmour Prof. of Spanish, Univ. of Liverpool, 1963–78; First Director, Centre for Latin-American Studies, 1966–70; Dean, Faculty of Arts, 1977–78; Chm., Dept of Hispanic and Italian Studies, Brown Univ., USA, 1981–84. Andrew Mellon Vis. Prof., Univ. of Pittsburgh, 1970–71; Leverhulme Res. Fellow, 1975; NEH Univ. Fellowship, 1991; Hon. Prof., Univ. of Sheffield, 1994–; Vis. Prof., Univ. of Salamanca, 1995. Lectures: Fundación Juan March, Madrid, 1984; E. Allison Peers, Univ. of Liverpool, 1985, 1994; Norman Maccoll, Univ. of Cambridge, 1985; Fordham Cervantes, NY, 1988; Raimundo Lido Meml, Harvard, 1998. Vice-Pres., Internat. Assoc. of Hispanists, 1974–80 (Pres., Local Organising Cttee, 8th Congress, Brown Univ., 1983); Pres., Anglo-Catalan Soc., 1976–78. Dir, Liverpool Playhouse, 1974–78. Editor, Bulletin of Hispanic Studies, 1964–78. Hon. Fellow, Inst. of Linguists, 1972. Corresp. Member: Real Academia de Buenas Letras, Barcelona, 1978; Hispanic Soc. of Amer., 1981. Hon. Mem., N American Catalan Soc., 2001. MA *ad eund.* Brown Univ., 1979. Special Prize for excellence in Galdós Studies, Las Palmas, 1997. Encomienda de la Orden de Isabel la Católica (Spain), 1997; J. M. Batista i Roca Prize for contributions to Catalan studies, Barcelona, 2000. *Publications:* Catalunya i València vistes pels viatgers anglesos del segle XVIIIè, 1955, 2nd edn 1993; Niebla y Soledad: aspectos de Unamuno y Machado, 1971; ed, Soledades, Galerias, otros poemas, by Antonio Machado, 1975, 15th rev. edn 1998; Antonio Machado (1875–1939): poetry and integrity, 1975; B. Pérez Galdós: Fortunata y Jacinta, a critical guide, 1977 (trans. Spanish 1989); (ed) Campos de Castilla, by Antonio Machado, 1989, 9th rev. edn 1999; History and Fiction in Galdós's Narratives, 1993; Conflicts and Conciliations: the evolution of Galdós's Fortunata y Jacinta, 1997; numerous articles on Spanish and Catalan literature in specialised publications; *festschrift:* Hispanic Studies in Honour of Geoffrey Ribbans, 1992. *Recreations:* travel, fine art. *Address:* c/o Department of Hispanic Studies, Box 1961, Brown University, Providence, Rhode Island 02912, USA.

RIBBINS, Maureen Margaret; Headmistress, Woldingham School, 1997–2000; *b* 16 Aug. 1947; *d* of Guy and Eileen Shoebridge; *m* 1969, Peter Michael St John Ribbins, Prof. of Educn Mgt, Birmingham Univ. *Educ:* St Joseph's Convent GS, Abbey Wood; Lady Margaret Hall, Oxford (MA Hons Physics 1968; PGCE 1969); Thames Poly. (MSc Hons Solid State Physics, London, 1972); Birkbeck Coll., London Univ. (BSc Botany 1977). Teacher of Mathematics and Physics, Farringtons Sch., Chislehurst, 1969–73; Head of Science, Dartford Girls' GS, 1973–80; Headmistress: Walton Girls' High Sch., 1980–83; Wolverhampton Girls' High Sch., 1983–97. Assessor, Nat. Educn Assessment Centre, 1991–; accredited OFSTED Inspector, 1995–. *Publications:* reviews and articles in Jl of Educnl Admin, and Pastoral Care in Educn. *Recreations:* reading modern literature, Chinese brush painting, botanical illustration, walking dog, music.

RICE; *see* Spring Rice, family name of Baron Monteagle of Brandon.

RICE, Prof. C(harles) Duncan, PhD; FRSE; FRHistS; Principal and Vice-Chancellor, University of Aberdeen, since 1996; *b* 20 Oct. 1942; *s* of James Inglis Rice and Jane Meauras Findlay (*née* Scroggie); *m* 1967, Susan Wunsch (*see* S. Rice); two *s* one *d. Educ:* Univ. of Aberdeen (MA 1st Cl. Hons Hist. 1964); Univ. of Edinburgh (PhD 1969). FRHistS 1996; FRSE 1998. Lectr, Univ. of Aberdeen, 1966–69; Yale University: Asst Prof. of Hist., 1970–75; Associate Prof., 1975–79; Prof. of History, Hamilton Coll., Clinton, NY, 1979–85; New York University: Prof. of History, 1985–96; Dean, Faculty of Arts and Sci., 1985–94; Vice-Chancellor, 1994–96. Dir, BT Scotland, 1998–; Vice Chm., Grampian Enterprise Ltd, 1999–. Board Member: Univs and Colls Employers' Assoc., 1997–; Council, Nat. Trust for Scotland, 1998–; Rowett Res. Inst., 1998–; Scottish Opera, 1998–; Scottish Ballet, 1998–; Chm., UK Socrates-Erasmus Council, 1999–. FRSA 1996. *Publications:* The Rise and Fall of Black Slavery, 1975; The Scots Abolitionists 1831–1961, 1982. *Recreations:* hill-walking, contemporary Scottish literature, opera. *Address:* University of Aberdeen, Regent Walk, King's College, Aberdeen AB24 3FX. *T:* (01224) 272134, 272135.

RICE, Condoleezza, PhD; National Security Advisor, and Assistant to the President for National Security Affairs, USA, since 2001; *b* Birmingham, Ala, 14 Nov. 1954. *Educ:* Univ. of Denver (BA Internat. Relns 1974; PhD 1981); Univ. of Notre Dame, Indiana. Prof., Stanford Univ., Calif, 1981–88; Dir, Soviet and E Eur. Affairs, Nat. Security Council, Special Asst to Pres. for nat. security affairs and Sen. Dir for Soviet Affairs, 1988–91; Stanford University, California: Prof., 1991–93; Provost, 1993–99; on leave of absence as foreign policy advr to George W. Bush, 2000–01. Hon. Dr Notre Dame, 1995.

Publications: Uncertain Allegiance: the Soviet Union and the Czechoslovak Army, 1984; (with A. Dallin) The Gorbachev Era, 1986; (with P. Zelikow) Germany Unified and Europe Transformed, 1995; contrib. numerous articles on Soviet and E European foreign and defense policy. *Address:* The White House, Washington, DC 20504, USA.

RICE, Dennis George, PhD; Social Security (formerly National Insurance) Commissioner, 1979–98; a Child Support Commissioner, 1993–98; a Recorder, 1991–97; *b* 27 Nov. 1927; *s* of George Henry Rice and Ethel Emily Rice; *m* 1959, Jean Beryl Wakefield; one *s*. *Educ:* City of London Sch.; King's Coll., Cambridge (Scholar and Prizeman; 1st Cl. Classical Tripos Pt I, Law Tripos Pt II; BA 1950, LLB 1951, MA 1955); London Sch. of Econs (PhD 1956). Called to the Bar, Lincoln's Inn, 1952. Served RAF, 1946–48. Entered J. Thorn and Sons Ltd, 1952; Dir, 1955; Man. Dir, 1956; Chm. and Man. Dir, 1958–69; in practice at Chancery Bar, 1970–79. Member: Cttee of Timber Bldg Manufrs Assoc., 1967–69; Cttee of Joinery and Woodwork Employers Fedn, 1968–69. *Publications:* Rockingham Ornamental Porcelain, 1965; Illustrated Guide to Rockingham Pottery and Porcelain, 1971; Derby Porcelain: the golden years, 1750–1770, 1983; English Porcelain Animals of the Nineteenth Century, 1989; articles on company law in legal jls and on Rockingham porcelain in art magazines. *Recreations:* history of English porcelain, gardening. *Address:* 10 Peel Street, Kensington, W8 7PD. *Club:* Reform.

RICE, Maj.-Gen. Sir Desmond (Hind Garrett), KCVO 1989 (CVO 1985); CBE 1976 (OBE 1970); Vice Adjutant General, 1978–79; *b* 1 Dec. 1924; *s* of Arthur Garrett Rice and Alice Constance (*née* Henman); *m* 1954, Denise Ann (*née* Ravenscroft); one *d*. *Educ:* Marlborough College. Commissioned into The Queen's Bays, 1944; psc 1954; 1st The Queen's Dragoon Guards, 1958; jssc 1963; First Comdg Officer, The Royal Yeomanry, 1967–69; Col GS 4 Div., 1970–73; BGS (MO) MoD, 1973–75; rcds 1976; Director of Manning (Army), 1977–78. Col, 1st The Queen's Dragoon Guards, 1980–86. Sec., Central Chancery of Orders of Knighthood, 1980–89. An Extra Gentleman Usher to the Queen, 1989–. *Recreations:* field sports, gardening. *Address:* Fairway, Malacca Farm, West Clandon, Surrey GU4 7UQ. *T:* (01483) 222677. *Club:* Cavalry and Guards.

RICE, His Honour Gordon Kenneth; a Circuit Judge, 1980–2000; *b* 16 April 1927; *m* 1967. *Educ:* Brasenose Coll., Oxford (MA). Called to the Bar, Middle Temple, 1957. *Address:* 4 Kings Road, Westcliff-on-Sea, Essex SS0 8BH.

RICE, Maureen; *see* Rice-Knight, M.

RICE, Noel Stephen Cracroft, MD; FRCS, FRCOphth; Consulting Surgeon, Moorfields Eye Hospital, since 1996 (Consultant Surgeon, 1967–96); Hospitaller, St John of Jerusalem, since 1996; *b* 26 Dec. 1931; *s* of late Raymond Arthur Cracroft Rice and Doris Ivy Rice (*née* Slater); *m* 1st, 1957, Karin Elsa Brita Linell (*d* 1992); two *s* one *d*; 2nd, 1997, Countess Ulla Mörner. *Educ:* Haileybury and ISC; Clare Coll., Cambridge (MA, BChir, MD); St Bartholomew's Hosp. House appts, St Bartholomew's Hosp., 1956–57; Jun. Specialist, RAF, 1957–60 (Flt Lt); Registrar, Sen. Registrar, Moorfields Eye Hosp., 1962–65; Sen. Lectr, 1965–70, Clin. Teacher, 1970–91, Dean, 1991–96, Inst. of Ophthalmology. Vice-Pres., Ophthalmol Soc.; Member: Council, Coll. of Ophthalmologists; Internat. Council of Ophthalmol.; Acad. Ophth. Internat. Vis. Prof., Nat. Univ. of Singapore. St Eric's Medal, Karolinska Inst., Stockholm. KStJ 1996. Order of the Falcon (Iceland). *Publications:* contribs to sci. jls on subjects related to ophthalmology. *Recreation:* fly fishing. *Address:* The St John Eye Hospital, Priory House, 25 St John's Lane, EC1M 4PP. *T:* (020) 7253 2582, *Fax:* (020) 7253 2612. *Clubs:* Oriental; Piscatorial Society.

RICE, Olwen Mary; freelance journalist; Editor, Woman's Weekly, 1993–98; *b* 2 Aug. 1960; *d* of James Rice and Mary Rice (*née* Wood); *m* 1990, Andrew Tilley; one *d*. *Educ:* Hagley Park Comprehensive Sch.; London Coll. of Printing. News Reporter, Oxford Mail, 1980–84; News Editor, Fitness mag., 1984–85; Health and Beauty Editor, Chat mag., 1985–87; Asst Editor, then Dep. Editor, Best, 1987–88; Editor, Living, 1988–93. *Recreations:* swimming, reading, cycling, writing. *Address:* c/o King's Reach Tower, Stamford Street, SE1 9LS. *T:* (020) 7261 6131.

RICE, Peter Anthony Morrish; stage designer; *b* 13 Sept. 1928; *s* of Cecil Morrish Rice and Ethel (*née* Blacklaw); *m* 1954, Patricia Albeck; one *s*. *Educ:* St Dunstan's Coll., Surrey; Royal Coll. of Art (ARCA 1951). Designed first professional prodn, Sex and the Seraphim, Watergate Theatre, London, 1951, followed by The Seraglio, Sadler's Wells Opera, 1952, and Arlecchino, Glyndebourne, 1954; subsequently has designed over 100 plays, operas and ballets, including: *plays:* Time Remembered, 1954; The Winter's Tale, and Much Ado About Nothing, Old Vic, 1956; Living for Pleasure, 1956; A Day in the Life of …, 1958; The Lord Chamberlain Regrets, and Toad of Toad Hall, 1961; The Farmer's Wife, The Italian Straw Hat, and Heartbreak House, Chichester, 1966; Flint, and Arms and the Man, 1970; Happy Birthday, 1977; Private Lives, Greenwich and West End, 1980; Present Laughter, Greenwich and West End, 1981; Cavell, and Goodbye Mr Chips, Chichester, 1982; The Sleeping Prince, Chichester and West End, 1983; Forty Years On, Chichester and West End, 1984; Thursday's Ladies, Apollo, 1987; Hay Fever, Chichester, and Re: Joyce!, Fortune, 1988; Don't Dress for Dinner, Apollo, 1990; Night Must Fall, Haymarket, 1996; The Importance of Being Earnest, Chichester, transf. Haymarket, 1999; *operas:* Count Ory, Sadler's Wells, 1962; Arabella, Royal Opera, 1964, Paris Opera, 1981, Chicago, 1984, and Covent Garden, 1986; The Thieving Magpie, and The Violins of St Jacques, Sadler's Wells, 1967; La Bohème, Scottish Opera, 1970; The Magic Flute, Ottawa, 1974; Tosca, Scottish Opera, 1980; The Secret Marriage, Buxton Fest., 1981; The Count of Luxembourg, Sadler's Wells, 1982, 1987; Death in Venice, Antwerp, and Die Fledermaus, St Louis, USA, 1983; Manon, Covent Garden, 1987; Così Fan Tutte, Ottawa, 1990, Hong Kong, 1991; Carmen, Hong Kong, 1992; Ottone, Tokyo, 1992, QEH, 1993; Madama Butterfly, Holland, 1993; L'Infedelta Delusa, Garsington, 1993; L'Etoile, La Bohème, Carmen, 1995–97, Martha, 2000, Castleward Opera, NI; Un Ballo in Maschera, Iris, Eugene Onegin, 1996–97, Così fan tutte, The Yeomen of the Guard, 2000, Opera Holland Park; *ballets:* Romeo and Juliet, Royal Danish Ballet, 1955, new prodn 1995, and London Festival Ballet, 1985; Sinfonietta, Royal Ballet, 1966; The Four Seasons, Royal Ballet, 1974. Theatre interiors: Vaudeville Theatre, London; Grand Theatre, Blackpool; His Majesty's Theatre, Aberdeen; Minerva Studio Theatre, Chichester. *Publications:* The Clothes Children Wore, 1973; Farming, 1974; Narrow Boats, 1976. *Recreation:* ancient films. *Address:* 4 Western Terrace, W6 9TX. *T:* (020) 8748 3990. *Club:* Garrick.

RICE, Peter D.; *see* Davis-Rice.

RICE, Susan; Chief Executive, Lloyds TSB Scotland, since 2000; *b* 7 March 1946; *m* 1967, Prof. C(harles) Duncan Rice, *qv*; two *s* one *d*. *Educ:* Wellesley Coll., Mass (BA); Univ. of Aberdeen (MLitt); DBA Robert Gordon Univ. 2001. Chartered Banker; FCIB 2000. Dean, Saybrook Coll., Yale Univ., 1973–79; Staff Aide to Pres., Hamilton Coll., 1980–81; Dean of Students, Colgate Univ., 1981–86; Sen. Vice Pres. and Div. Hd, Nat West Bancorp., 1986–96; Dir, Business Projects, Hd, Branch Banking, then Man. Dir, Personal Banking, Bank of Scotland, 1997–2000. *Recreations:* opera, modern art, hill-walking, cycling. *Address:* 120 George Street, Edinburgh EH2 4LH.

RICE, Sir Timothy (Miles Bindon), Kt 1994; writer and broadcaster; *b* 10 Nov. 1944; *s* of late Hugh Gordon Rice and of Joan Odette Rice; *m* 1974, Jane Artereta McIntosh; one *s* one *d*; partner Nell Sully; one *d*. *Educ:* Lancing Coll. EMI Records, 1966–68; Norrie Paramor Org., 1968–69. Lyrics for stage musicals (with music by Andrew Lloyd Webber): Joseph and the Amazing Technicolor Dreamcoat, 1968 (rev. 1973); Jesus Christ Superstar, 1970; Evita, 1976 (rev. 1978); Cricket, 1986; (with music by Stephen Oliver) Blondel, 1983; (with music by Benny Andersson and Björn Ulvaeus) Chess, 1984 (rev. 1986); (with music by Michel Berger and book by Luc Plamondon) Tycoon, 1992; (with music by Alan Menken) Beauty and the Beast, 1994 (some songs only); (with music by John Farrar) Heathcliff, 1996; (with music by Alan Menken) King David, 1997; (with music by Elton John) Aida, 1998; lyrics for film musicals: (with music by Alan Menken) Aladdin, 1992; (with music by Elton John) The Lion King, 1994, expanded for theatre, 1997; (with music by Elton John) The Road to El Dorado, 2000. Producer, Anything Goes, Prince Edward Theatre, 1989. Lyrics for songs, 1975–, with other composers, incl. Marvin Hamlisch, Rick Wakeman, Vangelis, Paul McCartney, Mike Batt, Francis Lai, John Barry, Freddie Mercury, Richard Kerr, Burt Bacharach, Graham Gouldman and Lalo Schifrin. Awards include: Oscar and Golden Globe for Best Original Film Song, A Whole New World (music by Alan Menken), 1992, for Can You Feel the Love Tonight (music by Elton John), 1994 and for You Must Love Me (music by Andrew Lloyd Webber), 1996; gold and platinum records in over 20 countries, 12 Ivor Novello Awards, 3 Tony Awards and 6 Grammy Awards. Founder and Director: GRRR Books, 1978–; Pavilion Books, 1981–97. TV includes: Lyrics by Tim Rice; Three More Men in a Boat; Musical Triangles (series); Tim Rice (series); radio incls: numerous quiz shows from Just a Minute and Trivia Test Match downwards; script for 15-part series on hist. of Western popular music for BBC World Service Broadcasts to China. Film début as actor in insultingly small rôle, The Survivor, 1980. Chairman: Stars Organization for Spastics, 1983–85; Shaftesbury Avenue Centenary Cttee, 1984–86; Foundn for Sport and the Arts, 1991–; Pres., Lord's Taverners, 1988–90 and 2000. Pres., Richmond Pk Cons. Assoc., 1996–. *Publications:* Heartaches Cricketers' Almanack, yearly, 1975–; (ed) Lord's Taverners Sticky Wicket Book, 1979; Treasures of Lord's, 1989; Oh, What a Circus (autobiog.), 1999; (with Andrew Lloyd Webber): Evita, 1978; Joseph and the Amazing Technicolor Dreamcoat, 1982; (jtly) Guinness Books of British Hit Singles and Albums and associated pubns, 1977–96, 31 books in all; (jtly) The Complete Eurovision Song Contest Companion, 1998. *Recreations:* cricket, history of popular music, chickens. *Clubs:* Garrick, MCC, Groucho, Dramatists', Saints and Sinners (Chm., 1990); Cricket Writers; Cricketers' (NSW).

RICE, Victor Albert; Chief Executive, LucasVarity plc, 1996–99; *b* 7 March 1941; *o s* of late Albert Edward Rice and of Rosina Emmeline (*née* Pallant); *m* 1984, Corinne Sutcliffe. Left sch. at 16 to join Finance Dept, Ford UK, 1957; various finance posts with Ford, Cummins and Chrysler, 1957–70; Comptroller, Northern European Ops, Perkins Engines Gp, 1970–75; Corporate Comptroller, Massey Ferguson (Perkins' parent co.), 1975–78; Varity Corporation: Pres. and Chief Operating Officer, 1978–80; Chm. and CEO, 1980–96. Liveryman, Glaziers' Co., 1978–. *Recreations:* golf, gardening, opera, ballet, theatre. *Address:* Ravelin LLC, Suite 202, 374 Delaware Avenue, Buffalo, NY 14202-1611, USA.

RICE-KNIGHT, Maureen, (Maureen Rice); Editor, Options magazine, 1991–98; *b* 13 Dec. 1958; *d* of Patrick Rice and Anastasia Rice (*née* McGuire); *m* 1986, David Peter Knight; one *s* one *d*. *Educ:* Gumley House Convent Grammar Sch., Isleworth; Polytechnic of Central London (BA Hons Media Studies). Magazines: Features Editor, Mizz, 1985; Dep. Editor, No 1, 1985; Editor, Mizz, 1986; Editor, 19, 1988. *Recreations:* reading, cinema.

RICE-OXLEY, James Keith, CBE 1981; Chairman, Merchant Navy Training Board, 1981–97; *b* 15 Aug. 1920; *o s* of late Montague Keith Rice-Oxley and Margery Hyacinth Rice-Oxley (*née* Burrell), Kensington; *m* 1949, Barbara, *yr d* of late Frederick Parsons, Gerrards Cross; two *d*. *Educ:* Marlborough Coll.; Trinity Coll., Oxford. MA(Law). Served War of 1939–45: Wiltshire Regt, Royal West Kents (wounded El Alamein); GSO III, HQ 3 Corps; GSO II, HQ Land Forces, Greece (despatches). Joined Shipping Fedn, 1947, Dir, 1965–75; Dir, Internat. Shipping Fedn, 1970–80; Dir, Gen. Council of British Shipping, 1975–80. Chm., Nat. Sea Training Trust, 1965–80; Mem. Nat. Maritime Bd, 1965–80; Mem., Merchant Navy Welfare Bd, 1965–80; Internat. Shipowners' Chm. and British Shipowners' Rep. on Jt Maritime Commn of ILO, 1970–80; Chm., Shipowners' Gp at Internat. Labour (Maritime) Confs, 1969, 1970, 1975, 1976; a Vice-Pres., IMCO/ILO Maritime Conf., 1978. Chm., Maritime Studies Cttee, BTEC, 1980–87; Mem. Industrial Tribunals (England and Wales), 1981–88; General Comr of Income Tax, 1986–95. Barnardo's: Mem. Council and Exec. Cttee, 1981–95; Vice-Chm. Council, 1988–89 and 1993–94; Chm., Shaftesbury Civic Soc., 1982–85; Mem. Council, King George's Fund for Sailors, 1965–82; UK Mem., Bd of Governors, World Maritime Univ., Malmö, 1983–89. *Recreation:* ceramics. *Address:* Ox House, Bimport, Shaftesbury SP7 8AX. *T:* (01747) 852741.

RICH, Michael Anthony; Regional Chairman, Industrial Tribunals, Southampton, 1987–96; *b* 16 March 1931; *s* of Joseph and Kate Alexandra Rich; *m* 1959, Helen Kit Marston, MB, BS; one *s* one *d*. *Educ:* Kimbolton Sch., Hunts; Leicester Univ. (LLM). Admitted Solicitor, 1954. Army Legal Aid, 1954–56; Partner, Rich and Carr, Leicester, 1960–76; Part-time Chm., 1972 and 1996–99, Permanent Chm., 1976, Industrial Tribunals. President: Leicester Law Soc., 1976–77; Council of Industrial Tribunal Chairmen, 1993–94. Trustee, Ulverscroft Foundn, 1972–97. *Publications:* (with I. A. Edwards) Mead's Unfair Dismissal, 5th edn, 1994; Industrial Tribunal Chairmen's Handbook, 1997. *Recreations:* railway modelling, France. *Address:* 4 Hickory Drive, Harestock, Winchester, Hants SO22 6NJ.

RICH, Michael Samuel; QC 1980; **His Honour Judge Rich;** a Circuit Judge, since 1991; *b* 18 Aug. 1933; *s* of late Sidney Frank Rich, OBE and of Erna Babette; *m* 1963, Janice Sarita Benedictus; three *s* one *d*. *Educ:* Dulwich Coll.; Wadham Coll., Oxford (MA, 1st Class Hons PPE). Called to the Bar, Middle Temple, 1958, Bencher, 1985; a Recorder, 1986–91; authorized to undertake Official Referee's business, 1991; Deputy High Court Judge: Chancery Div., 1992–; QBD, 1993–. Mem., Lands Tribunal, 1993–. Hon. Pres., Dulwich Soc., 2001. Medal of Merit, Boy Scouts Assoc., 1970. *Publication:* (jtly) Hill's Law of Town and Country Planning, 5th edn, 1968. *Address:* 18 Dulwich Village, SE21 7AL. *T:* (020) 8693 1957. *Club:* Garrick.

RICH, Nigel Mervyn Sutherland, CBE 1995; Deputy Chairman, Exel plc, since 2000; Chairman, Hamptons Group Ltd, since 1997; *b* 30 Oct. 1945; *s* of Charles Albert Rich and Mina Mackintosh Rich; *m* 1970, Cynthia Elizabeth (*née* Davies); two *s* two *d*. *Educ:* Sedbergh Sch.; New Coll., Oxford (MA). FCA. Deloitte, Plender Griffiths, London, 1967–71; Deloitte, Haskins & Sells, New York, 1971–73; Jardine Matheson, Hong Kong, Johannesburg, Manila, 1974–94; Man. Dir, Jardine Matheson Holdings Ltd, 1989–94; Chief Exec., Trafalgar House, 1994–96; Chm., Ocean Gp, 1997–2000. Director:

Matheson & Co., 1994–; Harvey Nichols, 1996–; John Armit Wines, 1996–; Pacific Assets, 1997–; Granada, 1998–. Hon. Steward, Royal HK Jockey Club, 1994. Freeman, City of London, 1970; Liveryman, Tobacco Pipemakers and Tobacco Blenders Co., 1975– (Mem. Court of Assts, 1996–). *Recreations:* tennis, golf, windsurfing, horseracing. *Clubs:* Boodle's, Hurlingham, Turf, MCC; Royal and Ancient Golf; Wisley Golf.

RICHARD, family name of **Baron Richard.**

RICHARD, Baron *cr* 1990 (Life Peer), of Ammanford in the County of Dyfed; **Ivor Seward Richard;** PC 1993; QC 1971; *b* 30 May 1932; *s* of Seward Thomas Richard, mining and electrical engineer, and Isabella Irene Richard; *m* 1st, 1956, Geraldine Moore (marr. diss. 1962); one *s*; 2nd, 1962, Alison Imrie (marr. diss. 1983); 3rd, 1989, Janet Jones; one *s*. *Educ:* St Michael's Sch., Bryn, Llanelly; Cheltenham Coll.; Pembroke Coll., Oxford (Wightwick Scholar; Hon Fellow, 1981). BA Oxon (Jurisprudence) 1953; MA 1970; called to Bar, Inner Temple, 1955, Bencher, 1985. Practised in chambers, London, 1955–74. UK Perm. Representative to UN, 1974–79; Mem., Commn of EEC, 1981–84; Chm., Rhodesia Conf., Geneva, 1976. Parly Candidate, S Kensington, 1959; MP (Lab) Barons Court, 1964–Feb. 1974. Delegate: Assembly, Council of Europe, 1965–68; Western European Union, 1965–68; Vice-Chm., Legal Cttee, Council of Europe, 1966–67; PPS, Sec. of State for Defence, 1966–69; Parly Under-Sec. (Army), Min. of Defence, 1969–70; Opposition Spokesman, Broadcasting, Posts and Telecommunications, 1970–71; Dep. Spokesman, Foreign Affairs, 1971–74; Leader of the Opposition, H of L, 1992–97; Lord Privy Seal and Leader, H of L, 1997–98. Chm., World Trade Centre Wales Ltd (Cardiff), 1985–97. Member: Fabian Society; Society of Labour Lawyers; Inst. of Strategic Studies; Royal Inst. of Internat. Affairs. *Publications:* (jtly) Europe or the Open Sea, 1971; We, the British, 1983 (USA); (jtly) Unfinished Business, 1999; articles in various political jls. *Recreations:* playing piano, watching football matches, talking. *Address:* House of Lords, SW1A 0PW.

RICHARD, Alain; Minister of Defence, France, since 1997; *b* 29 Aug. 1945; *m* 1988, Elisabeth Couffignal; one *s* one *d*, and one *s* by a previous marriage. *Educ:* Lycée Henri IV, Paris; Univ. of Paris; Institut d'Etudes Politiques; Ecole Nationale d'Administration. Auditor, 1971, Maître des requêtes, 1978, Council d'Etat; teaching posts, Univs of Reims, Paris I, and Institut d'Etudes Politiques; Mem., Nat. Office, Parti Socialiste Unifié, 1972–74; Mayor, Saint-Ouen-l'Aumône, 1977–97; Deputy, 1978–93, Senator, 1995–97, for Val-d'Oise (Vice-Pres., Commission des Lois, 1981–86; Vice-Pres., Nat. Assembly, 1987–88); Mem., Conseil d'Etat, 1993. Mem. Cttee, 1979, Exec. Bd, 1988, Parti Socialiste. Founder and Vice-Pres., Forum for Mgt of Towns, 1985–97. *Address:* Ministry of Defence, 14 rue Saint Dominique, 00450 Armées, France; 28 rue René Clair, 95310 Saint Ouen l'Aumône, France.

RICHARD, Sir Cliff, Kt 1995; OBE 1980; singer, actor; *b* 14 Oct. 1940; *s* of late Rodger Webb and Dorothy Webb; *né* Harry Rodger Webb; changed name to Cliff Richard, 1958. *Educ:* Riversmead Sch., Cheshunt. Awarded 13 Gold Discs for records: Living Doll, 1959; The Young Ones, 1962; Bachelor Boy, 1962; Lucky Lips, 1963; Congratulations, 1968; Power to all Our Friends, 1973; Devil Woman, 1976; We Don't Talk Anymore, 1979; Wired for Sound, 1981; Daddy's Home, 1981; Living Doll (with The Young Ones), 1986; All I Ask of You (with Sarah Brightman), 1986; Mistletoe and Wine, 1988; also 37 Silver Discs and 3 Platinum Discs (Daddy's Home, 1981; All I Ask of You, 1986; The Millennium Prayer, 1999). Films: Serious Charge, 1959; Expresso Bongo, 1960; The Young Ones, 1962; Summer Holiday, 1963; Wonderful Life, 1964; Finders Keepers, 1966; Two a Penny, 1968; His Land, 1970; Take Me High, 1973. Own TV series, ATV and BBC. Stage: rep. and variety seasons; Time, Dominion, 1986–87; Heathcliff, Apollo, 1997. Top Box Office Star of GB, 1962–63 and 1963–64. *Publications:* Questions, 1970; The Way I See It, 1972; The Way I See It Now, 1975; Which One's Cliff, 1977; Happy Christmas from Cliff, 1980; You, Me and Jesus, 1983; Mine to Share, 1984; Jesus, Me and You, 1985; Single-minded, 1988; Mine Forever, 1989; Jesus Here and Now, 1996; My Story: a celebration of 40 years in show business, 1998. *Recreation:* tennis. *Address:* c/o PO Box 46C, Esher, Surrey KT10 0RB. *T:* (01372) 467752. *Club:* All England Lawn Tennis and Croquet.

RICHARDS, family name of **Baron Milverton.**

RICHARDS, Alun; *see* Richards, R. A.

RICHARDS, (Anthony) Charles, MVO 1997; Deputy Master of HM Household and Equerry to the Queen, since 1999; *b* 20 Feb. 1953; *s* of Dudley Raymond Richards and Eleonora Caroline Richards (*née* Otter); *m* 1978, Serena Anne Spencer; three *s*. *Educ:* Marlborough Coll.; RMA Sandhurst. Commissioned Welsh Guards, 1973; served with 1st Bn Welsh Guards, UK and BAOR, 1973–82; seconded 1st Bn 2nd Gurkha Rifles, Hong Kong, 1982–84; Staff Coll., 1985; BAOR, 1986–90; 2 i/c 1st Bn Welsh Guards, UK, 1990–92; Staff Officer, HQ London Dist, 1992–94; Equerry to the Duke of Edinburgh, 1994–97; Div. Lt Col, Foot Guards, 1997–99, retired 1999. *Recreations:* shooting, fishing, travel. *Address:* Rotherby Grange, Melton Mowbray, Leics LE14 2LP. *T:* (01664) 434206.

RICHARDS, Arthur Cyril, FIA; consultant; *b* 7 April 1921; *s* of Ernest Arthur Richards and Kate Richards; *m* 1st, 1944, Joyce Bertha Brooke (marr. diss. 1974); two *s* two *d*; 2nd, 1975, Els Stoyle; two step *s* one step *d*. *Educ:* Tollington Sch., London. FIA 1949; FSVA 1962. Insurance, 1937–41. Served RAF, 1941–46. Insurance, consulting actuary, steel manufacture, investment banking, internat. property develt, 1946–64; Advr, Samuel Montagu & Co. Ltd, 1965–67; Gp Finance Dir, Bovis Ltd, 1967–71; United Dominions Trust Ltd: Gp Finance Dir, 1971–76; Gp Man. Dir, 1976–80; Chief Exec., 1981–83; Dir, 1978–88, Chm., 1983–88, Blackwood Hodge plc. Chm., Federated Land, 1982; Director: MSL Gp Internat., 1970–81; TSB Trust Co., 1981–88; Combined Lease Finance PLC, 1985–89; Hermes Gp, 1990–. *Recreations:* sailing, antiques.

RICHARDS, Brian Henry, CEng, FIEE; Weapon Systems Director, Alenia-Marconi Systems (formerly GEC-Marconi Dynamics), Missile Systems (formerly Dynamics) Division, since 1995; *b* 19 July 1938; *s* of Alfred Edward Richards and Lilian Maud Richards (*née* Bennett); *m* 1961, Jane Wilkins; one *s* one *d*. *Educ:* Buckhurst Hill County Grammar Sch.; St John's College, Cambridge (Mech. Sci. Tripos, 1st Class Hons 1959, BA 1960; MA 1965). GEC Electronics, later Marconi Defence Systems, 1960–87: Guided Weapons Division: develt, systems, project management appts, 1960–76; Business Develt Manager, 1977; Manager, 1978; Asst Gen. Manager and Manager, 1982; Dir, Guided Weapons, 1985; RCDS, 1986; Asst Man. Dir, 1987; Technical Dir, Hunting Engineering, 1988–90; Chief Exec., Atomic Weapons Estabt, 1990–94. *Recreations:* golf, listening to music, water colour painting, DIY, gardening. *Address:* Alenia-Marconi Systems, Missile Systems Division, Borehamwood, Herts WD6 1RX.

RICHARDS, Sir Brian (Mansel), Kt 1997; CBE 1990; PhD; Chairman, Alizyme plc, since 1996; *b* 19 Sept. 1932; *s* of Cyril Mansel Richards and Gwendolyn Hyde Richards; *m* 1952, Joan Lambert Breese; one *s* one *d*. *Educ:* Lewis Sch., Pengam, Glam; University Coll. of Wales, Aberystwyth (BSc); King's College London (PhD). British Empire Cancer Fellowship, 1955–57; Nuffield Fellowship, 1957; MRC Biophysics Research Unit, 1957–64; Reader in Biology, Univ. of London, 1964–66; Research Div., G. D. Searle & Co., 1966–86; Vice-Pres., UK Preclinical R&D, 1980–86; Chairman: British Biotechnology Ltd, 1986–89; British Bio-technology Gp, 1989–94; Oxford BioMedica plc, 1996–98; CeNes Ltd, 1996–; LGC (Holdings) Ltd, 1996–; Peptide Therapeutics Group plc, 1997 (Exec. Chm., 1995–97; Dir, 1998–); Cozart Biosciences Ltd, 2001–; MAN Alternative Investments Ltd, 2001–. Director: Prelude Trust plc, 1997–; Innogenetics SA, 1997–; Drug Royalty Corp., 1998–. Hon. Prof. in Life Scis, UCW, Aberystwyth, 1991–. Chm., Biotechnology Working Party, CBI, 1988; Mem., Res. and Manufg Cttee, CBI, 1988; Mem., Sci. Bd, SERC, 1987; Chairman: Biotechnology Jt Adv. Bd, SERC/DTI, 1989; Science-based Cos Cttee, London Stock Exchange, 1994; Member: Adv. Cttee for Genetic Modification (previously Manipulation), HSE, 1984–96; Gene Therapy Adv. Cttee, DoH, 1994–98; BBSRC, 1994–97; Consultant on Biotechnology, OECD, 1987; Specialist Advr, H of L Select Cttee II on Biotechnol. Regulation, 1993. Chm., Roslin Inst., 1995–. Hon. DSc Abertay Dundee, 1997. *Publications:* papers in sci. jls. *Recreations:* collecting Jaguar cars, photography, deprecating ball games. *Address:* La Fosse, Rue Jacques Guille, Moulin Huet, St Martins, Guernsey GY4 6EH.

RICHARDS, Sir Brooks; *see* Richards, Sir F. B.

RICHARDS, Charles; *see* Richards, A. C.

RICHARDS, Clare Mary Joan; *see* Spottiswoode, C. M. J.

RICHARDS, David Anthony Stewart; QC 1992; *b* 9 June 1951; *s* of Kenneth Richards and Winifred Richards; *m* 1979, Gillian, *er d* of Lt-Col W. A. Taylor; one *s* twin *d*. *Educ:* Oundle; Trinity Coll., Cambridge (BA 1973; MA 1980). Called to the Bar, Inner Temple, 1974; Junior Counsel (Chancery), DTI, 1989–92. *Address:* Erskine Chambers, 30 Lincoln's Inn Fields, WC2A 3PF.

RICHARDS, David Gordon, CBE 1989; FCA; non-executive Chairman, Walker Greenbank plc, 1990–99 (Director, 1988–99); *b* 25 Aug. 1928; *s* of late Gordon Charles Richards and Vera Amy (*née* Barrow); *m* 1960, Stephanie, *er d* of late E. Gilbert Woodward, Metropolitan Magistrate and of Mrs Woodward; one *s* two *d*. *Educ:* Highgate Sch. FCA 1961. Articled to Harmood Banner & Co., 1945; served, 8th Royal Tank Regt, 1947–49; Partner: Harmood Banner & Co., 1955–74; Deloitte Haskins & Sells, 1974–84. Admitted Associate Mem. Inst. of Chartered Accountants in England and Wales, 1951 (Council, 1970–87; Vice-Pres., 1977–78; Dep. Pres., 1978–79; Centenary Pres., 1979–80; Mem., Gen. Purposes and Finance Cttee, 1977–83; Chm., Internat. Affairs Cttee, 1980–83); Mem., Cttee of London Soc. of Chartered Accountants, 1966–70, 1981–82 (Chm., 1969–70); Chm., Cons. Cttee of Accountancy Bodies, 1979–80; UK and Ireland rep. on Council, Internat. Fedn of Accountants, 1981–83. Dep. Chm., Monopolies and Mergers Commn, 1983 90; Member: Cttees of Investigation under Agricultural Marketing Act (1958), 1972–88; Council for Securities Industry, 1979–80; Panel on Take Overs and Mergers, 1979–80; Review Body on Doctors' and Dentists' Remuneration, 1984–90; Chm., Disciplinary Bd, BPsS, 1988–95 (Hon. Life Mem., 1996). Governor: Highgate Sch., 1982–98 (Chm. 1983–98); Associated Bd of Royal Schs of Music, 1987–; Trustee: The Bob Champion Cancer Trust, 1983–94; Royal Acad. of Music Foundn, 1985–2000; Prince's Youth Business Trust, 1986–93; Royal Acad. of Music, 2000–. Pres., Old Cholmeleian Soc., 1988–89. Hon. FRAM 1995. Master, Worshipful Co. of Chartered Accountants in England and Wales, 1986–87. *Publications:* numerous contribs to professional press and lectures on professional topics given internationally. *Recreations:* golf, lawn tennis, sailing, shooting, silviculture, music. *Address:* Eastleach House, Eastleach, Glos GL7 3NW. *T:* (01367) 850416.

RICHARDS, David Thomas; Principal Finance Officer, National Assembly for Wales, since 1999; *b* 30 Nov. 1954; *s* of Ralph Henry Richards and Brenda Mary Elizabeth Richards; *m* 1979, Veryan Cumming Black; one *s* two *d*. *Educ:* Whitchurch High Sch., Cardiff; New Univ. of Ulster, Coleraine (BA Philosophy). Exec. Officer, DTI, 1978–79; Welsh Office: fast stream trainee, 1979–83; Principal: Housing Div., 1983–86; Local Govt Finance Div., 1986–90; Assistant Secretary: Econ. Policy Div., 1990–92; Industrial Policy Div., 1992–94; Finance Programmes Div., 1994–97; Principal Finance Officer, 1997–99. Mem., Steering Bd, Patent Office. *Recreations:* wine, coffee, books. *Address:* National Assembly for Wales, Cathays Park, Cardiff CF10 3NQ. *T:* (029) 2082 5111.

RICHARDS, David Wyn; His Honour Judge Wyn Richards; a Circuit Judge, since 1998; *b* 22 Sept. 1943; *s* of late Evan Gwylfa Richards and Florence Margretta Richards (*née* Evans); *m* 1972, Thelma Frances Hall; five *s*. *Educ:* Gwendraeth GS; Llanelli GS; Trinity Hall, Cambridge. Called to the Bar, 1968; a Recorder, 1985–98. Asst Comr, Boundary Commn for Wales, 1982–86, 1992–96. *Address:* Civil Justice Centre, Caravella House, Quay West, Quay Parade, Swansea SA1 1SP. *T:* (01792) 510350, *Fax:* (01792) 473520.

RICHARDS, Denis Edward, CMG 1981; HM Diplomatic Service, retired; Ambassador to the United Republic of Cameroon and the Republic of Equatorial Guinea, 1979–81; *b* 25 May 1923; *m* 1947, Nancy Beryl Brown; one *d* (and one *d* decd). *Educ:* Wilson's Grammar Sch., London; St Peter's Coll., Oxford. Lieut RNVR, 1941–46; Colonial Service (HMOCS), 1948–60: District Admin. and Min. of Finance, Ghana (Gold Coast); HM Diplomatic Service, 1960–81: CRO, 1960; Karachi, 1961–63; FO (News Dept), 1964–68; Brussels (NATO), 1969; Brussels (UK Negotiating Delegn), 1970–72; Counsellor, Kinshasa, 1972–74; Consul-Gen., Philadelphia, 1974–79. *Recreations:* music, watching cricket. *Address:* Tresco House, Spencer Road, Birchington, Kent CT7 9EY. *T:* (01843) 845637.

RICHARDS, Denis George, OBE 1990; author; *b* 10 Sept. 1910; *s* of late George Richards and Frances Amelia Gosland; *m* 1940, Barbara, *d* of J. H. Smethurst, Heaton, Bolton; four *d*. *Educ:* Owen's Sch.; Trinity Hall, Cambridge (Scholar). BA 1931 (1st Cl. in both Parts of Historical Tripos); MA 1935; Asst Master, Manchester Grammar School, 1931–39; Senior History and English Master, Bradfield Coll., 1939–41; Narrator in Air Ministry Historical Branch, writing confidential studies on various aspects of the air war, 1942–43; Sen. Narrator, 1943–47; Hon. Sqdn Ldr RAFVR, 1943–47; engaged in writing, under Air Min. auspices, an official History of the Royal Air Force in the Second World War, 1947–49; was established in Admin. Civil Service, Principal, Department of Permanent Under Secretary of State for Air, 1949–50; Principal, Morley College, 1950–65; Longman Fellow in Univ. of Sussex, 1965–68. Chm., Women's League of Health and Beauty, 1966–88; Vice-Pres., Purcell Sch. for Young Musicians, 1984–. *Publications:* An Illustrated History of Modern Europe, 1938; Modern Europe (1919–39 section for revised edn of work by Sydney Herbert), 1940; (with J. W. Hunt) An Illustrated History of Modern Britain, 1950; (with late Hilary St G. Saunders) Royal Air Force 1939–45–an officially commissioned history in 3 volumes, 1953–54 (awarded C. P. Robertson Memorial Trophy, 1954); (with J. Evan Cruikshank) The Modern Age, 1955; Britain under the Tudors and Stuarts, 1958; Offspring of the Vic: a history of Morley College, 1958; (with Anthony Quick) Britain 1714–1851, 1961; (with J. A. Bolton)

Britain and the Ancient World, 1963; (with Anthony Quick) Britain, 1851–1945, 1967; (with Anthony Quick) Twentieth Century Britain, 1968; (with A. W. Ellis) Medieval Britain, 1973; Portal of Hungerford, 1978; (with Richard Hough) The Battle of Britain: the Jubilee history, 1989; (ed) The Few and the Many, 1990; The Hardest Victory: RAF Bomber Command in the Second World War, 1994; Just to Recall the Flavour: recollections 1910–41, 1999; It Might Have Been Worse: recollections 1941–96, 1999. *Recreations:* music, pictures, residual golf, the lightest tasks in the garden. *Address:* 4 Sussex Gate, Sussex Gardens, N6 4LS. *T:* (020) 8340 5259. *Clubs:* Arts, Garrick, Royal Air Force, PEN.

See also Dame H. Shovelton.

RICHARDS, Sir (Francis) Brooks, KCMG 1976 (CMG 1963); DSC and Bar, 1943; *b* 18 July 1918; *s* of Francis Bartlett Richards; *m* 1941, Hazel Myfanwy (*d* 2000), *d* of Lt-Col Stanley Price Williams, CIE; one *s* one *d.* *Educ:* Stowe School; Magdalene College, Cambridge. Served with RN, 1939–44 (Lieut-Comdr RNVR). HM Embassy: Paris, 1944–48; Athens, 1952–54; First Sec. and Head of Chancery, Political Residency, Persian Gulf, 1954–57; Assistant Private Secretary to Foreign Secretary, 1958–59; Counsellor (Information), HM Embassy, Paris, 1959–64; Head of Information Policy Dept, 1964, and of Jt Inf. Policy and Guidance Dept, FO/CRO, 1964–65; seconded to Cabinet Office, 1965–69; HM Minister, Bonn, 1969–71; HM Ambassador, Saigon, 1972–74; HM Ambassador, Greece, 1974–78; Dep. Sec., Cabinet Office, 1978–80; NI Office, 1980–81. Chm., CSM Parliamentary Consultants Ltd, 1984–96. Vice-Pres., Friends of Imperial War Museum, 1991–97 (Chm., 1989–91); Chairman: Paintings in Hosps, 1990–96; Anglo Hellenic League, 1990–93. Chevalier, Légion d'Honneur and Croix de Guerre (France), 1944. *Publication:* Secret Flotillas, 1996 (trans. French 2000). *Recreations:* collecting, gardening, travelling. *Club:* Special Forces.

See also F. N. Richards.

RICHARDS, Francis Neville, CMG 1994; CVO 1991; HM Diplomatic Service; Director, Government Communications Headquarters, since 1998; *b* 18 Nov. 1945; *s* of Sir Francis Brooks Richards, *qv*; *m* 1971, Gillian Bruce Nevill, *d* of late I. S. Nevill, MC and of Dr L. M. B. Dawson; one *s* one *d.* *Educ:* Eton; King's Coll., Cambridge (MA). Royal Green Jackets, 1967 (invalided, 1969). FCO, 1969; Moscow, 1971; UK Delegn to MBFR negotiations, Vienna, 1973; FCO, 1976–85 (Asst Private Sec. to Sec. of State, 1981–82); Economic and Commercial Counsellor, New Delhi, 1985–88; FCO, 1988–90 (Head, S Asian Dept); High Comr, Windhoek, 1990–92; Minister, Moscow, 1992–95; Dir (Europe), FCO, 1995–97; Dep. Under-Sec. of State, FCO, 1997–98. *Recreations:* walking, travelling, riding. *Address:* c/o GCHQ, Priors Road, Cheltenham, Glos GL52 5AJ. *Club:* Special Forces.

RICHARDS, Graham; *see* Richards, W. G.

RICHARDS, Sir (Isaac) Vivian (Alexander), KGN 1999; OBE 1994; cricketer; Captain, West Indies Cricket Team, 1985–91; *b* St Johns, Antigua, 7 March 1952; *s* of Malcolm Richards; *m* Miriam Lewis; one *s* one *d.* *Educ:* Antigua Grammar School. First class débuts, Leeward Islands, 1971, India (for WI), 1974; played for: Somerset, 1974–86; Queensland, 1976–77; Rishton, Lancs League, 1987; Glamorgan, 1990–93; played in 100th Test Match, 1988; scored 100th first class century, 1988; 100th Test Match catch, 1988; highest Test score, 291, *v* England, Oval, 1976; highest first class score, 322, *v* Warwicks, Taunton, 1985; fastest Test century *v* England, Antigua, 1986; highest number of Test runs by a West Indian batsman, 1991. WI team coach, tour of NZ, 1999. An ICC Ambassador. Hon. DLitt Exeter, 1986. *Publications:* (with David Foot) Viv Richards (autobiog.), 1982; (with Patrick Murphy) Cricket Masterclass, 1988; (with Michael Middles) Hitting across the Line (autobiog.), 1991; (with Bob Harris) Sir Vivian (autobiog.), 2000. *Recreations:* golf, tennis, music, football. *Address:* c/o Jane Morgan Management, Café Royal, 68 Regent Street, W1R 6EL. *T:* (020) 7287 6045.

RICHARDS, James Alan, OBE 1979; Agent-General for Western Australia in London, 1975–78, retired; *b* 8 Oct. 1913; *s* of James Percival Richards and Alice Pearl Richards (*née* Bullock) Adelaide; *m* 1939, Mabel Joyce, *d* of R. H. Cooper, Riverton, S Austr.; three *s* one *d.* *Educ:* Unley High Sch.; Coll. of Business Admin, Univ. of Hawaii. Served War of 1939–45, 2nd AIF. Ampol Petroleum Ltd, 1946–75: Sales Man., South Australia, 1952–53; State Man., Western Australia, 1954–75. *Recreation:* bowls. *Address:* 106/250 Baltimore Parade, Merriwa, WA 6030, Australia.

RICHARDS, John; *see* Richards, R. J. G.

RICHARDS, Rt Rev. John; Bishop Suffragan of Ebbsfleet, 1994–98; Episcopal Visitor for the Province of Canterbury, 1994–98; Hon. Assistant Bishop, diocese of Exeter, since 1998; *b* 4 Oct. 1933; *s* of William and Ethel Mary Richards; *m* 1958, Ruth Haynes; two *s* three *d.* *Educ:* Reading School; Wyggeston Grammar School, Leicester; Sidney Sussex Coll., Cambridge (MA); Ely Theological Coll. Asst Curate, St Thomas, Exeter, 1959–64; Rector of Holsworthy with Hollacombe and Cookbury, 1964–74; RD of Holsworthy, 1970–74; Rector of Heavitree with St Paul's, Exeter, 1974–81; RD of Exeter, 1978–81; Archdeacon of Exeter and Canon Res. of Exeter Cathedral, 1981–94; Assistant Bishop: dios of Lichfield and of Oxford, 1994–98; dio. of Bath and Wells, 1996–98. Chm. of House of Clergy, Exeter Diocesan Synod, 1979–82; Mem. Gen. Synod, 1985–94. Mem., C of E Pensions Bd, 1989–97. A Church Commissioner, 1988–94 (Mem. Bd of Govs, 1993–94). *Recreations:* gardening, fishing, walking. *Address:* Penberth, Stoney Road, Lewdown, Okehampton, Devon EX20 4DQ.

RICHARDS, Lt-Gen. Sir John (Charles Chisholm), KCB 1980; KCVO 1991; HM Marshal of the Diplomatic Corps, 1982–92; Extra Equerry to the Queen, since 1992; *b* 21 Feb. 1927; *s* of Charles C. Richards and Alice Milner; *m* 1953, Audrey Hidson; two *s* one *d.* *Educ:* Worksop Coll., Notts. Joined Royal Marines, 1945; 45 Commando, Malaya, 1950–52; Instructor, Officers' Sch., 1953–55; HMS Birmingham, 1955–56; Canadian Army Staff Coll., 1959–61; Adjt and Company Comdr, 43 Commando, 1962–63; Naval staff, 1963–64; Instructor, Staff Coll., Camberley, 1965–67; 45 Commando: 2nd in Comd, Aden, 1967; CO, 1968–69; GSO1 Plymouth Gp, 1969; CO 42 Commando, 1970–72; Chief of Staff, Brit. Def. Staff, Washington DC, UN Deleg., and Mem. Mil. Staff Cttee, 1972–74; Comdr 3rd Commando Bde, 1975–76; Commandant General, Royal Marines, 1977–81. Col Comdt, RM, 1987–88, Representative Col Comdt, 1989–90. Admiral, Texas Navy, 1983. Director: DSC Communications (Europe), 1986–92; Andrew Ltd, 1987–95. CIMgt (CBIM 1980). Freeman, City of London, 1982. *Recreations:* golf, swimming, gardening. *Address:* c/o National Westminster Bank, Market Place, Kingston-upon-Thames KT1 1JX. *Club:* Army and Navy.

RICHARDS, John Deacon, CBE 1978; RSA 1989 (ARSA 1974); RIBA; PPRIAS; architect; Principal, John Richards Associates, since 1986; *b* 7 May 1931; *s* of late William John Richards and Ethel Richards; *m* 1958, Margaret Brown, RIBA, ARIAS; one *s* three *d.* *Educ:* Geelong Grammar Sch., Vic.; Cranleigh Sch.; Architect. Assoc. Sch. of Arch., London (Dipl. 1954). RIBA 1955; FRIAS 1968 (PRIAS, 1983–85). RE, 1955–57. Partner, 1964–86, Chm., 1983–86, Senior Consultant, 1986–90, Robert Matthew, Johnson-Marshall and Partners. Buildings include: Stirling Univ., 1965–; Royal Commonwealth Pool, Edinburgh, 1970. Member: Royal Fine Art Commn for Scotland, 1975–89; Bd, Housing Corp., 1982–89 (Chm., Scottish Cttee, 1982–89); Bd, Scottish Homes, 1988–93 (Dep. Chm., 1989–93). Housing Assoc. Ombudsman for Scotland, 1994–2000. Mem., Agrément Bd, 1980–83. Trustee, Nat. Galleries of Scotland, 1986–90. DUniv: Stirling, 1976; Napier, 1996. Gold Medallist, RSA, 1972. *Recreation:* country life. *Address:* Lady's Field, Whitekirk, Dunbar, East Lothian EH42 1XS. *T:* (01620) 870206. *Club:* Athenæum.

RICHARDS, Prof. Keith Sheldon, PhD; Professor of Geography, University of Cambridge, since 1995; Director, Scott Polar Research Institute, since 1997; Fellow of Emmanuel College, Cambridge, since 1984 (Professorial Fellow, since 1995); *b* 25 May 1949; *s* of Maurice and Jean Richards; *m* 1973, Susan Mary Brooks. *Educ:* Falmouth Grammar Sch.; Jesus Coll., Cambridge (MA 1974; PhD 1975). Lectr, then Sen. Lectr, Lanchester Poly., 1973–78; Lectr, then Sen. Lectr, Univ. of Hull, 1978–84; Department of Geography, University of Cambridge: Lectr, 1984–95; Reader in Physical Geog., 1995; Head of Dept, 1994–99. Chairman: Brit. Geomorph. Res. Gp, 1994–95; Mem., various NERC Cttees, 1990–93, 1995–97. Cuthbert Peek Award, RGS, 1983. *Publications:* Stochastic Processes in One-dimensional Series: an introduction, 1979; (ed jtly) Geomorphological Techniques, 1982; Rivers: form and process in alluvial channels, 1982; (ed jtly) Geomorphology and Soils, 1985; (ed) River Channels: environment and process, 1987; (ed jtly) Slope Stability: geotechnical engineering and geomorphology, 1987; (ed jtly) Landform Monitoring, Modelling and Analysis, 1998; (ed jtly) Glacier Hydrology and Hydrochemistry, 1998; numerous papers on geomorphol., hydrology, river and slope processes in various jls. *Recreations:* reading, travel, opera. *Address:* Department of Geography, University of Cambridge, Cambridge CB2 3EN. *T:* (01223) 333393.

RICHARDS, Prof. Martin Paul Meredith; Professor of Family Research, since 1997, and Director of the Centre for Family Research, since 1969, Cambridge University; *b* 26 Jan. 1940; *s* of Paul Westmacott Richards and Sarah Anne Richards (*née* Hotham); *m* 1st, 1961, Evelyn Cowdy (marr. diss. 1966); 2nd, 1999, Sarah Smalley. *Educ:* Westminster Sch.; Trinity Coll., Cambridge (BA 1962; MA 1965; PhD 1965; ScD 1999). SRC Post-Doctoral Fellow, 1965–67; University of Cambridge: Res. Fellow, Trinity Coll., 1965–69; Mental Health Res. Fund Fellowship, 1970; Lectr in Social Psychology, 1970–89; Reader in Human Develt, 1989–97; Chm., Faculty of Soc. and Pol Scis, 1997, Head of Dept, 1996–99. Member: Medicine and Soc. Panel, Wellcome Trust, 1998–; Human Genetics Commn, 2000–. Vis. Fellow, Princeton Univ., 1966–67; Visitor, Centre for Cognitive Studies, Harvard Univ., 1967 and 1968; Winegard Vis. Prof., Univ. of Guelph, 1987; Hon. Vis. Prof., City Univ., 1992–94; de Lissa Fellow, Univ. of SA, 1993; William Evans Vis. Fellow, Univ. of Otago, 1997. Chm., Bardsey Is Trust, 1993–2000. *Publications:* (ed jtly) Race, Culture and Intelligence, 1972; (ed) The Integration of a Child into a Social World, 1974; (ed jtly) Benefits and Hazards of the New Obstetrics, 1977; (ed jtly) Separation and Special Care Baby Units, 1978; Infancy: the world of the newborn, 1980; (ed jtly) Parent-Baby Attachment in Premature Infants, 1983; Children in Social Worlds, 1986; (with J. Burgoyne and R. Ormrod) Divorce Matters, 1987; (ed jtly) The Politics of Maternity Care, 1990; (ed jtly) Obstetrics in the 1990s, 1992; (with J. Reibstein) Sexual Arrangements, 1992; (ed jtly) The Troubled Helix, 1996; (ed jtly) What is a Parent?, 1999. *Recreations:* bird-watching, listening to country music, alpine gardening. *Address:* Centre for Family Research, University of Cambridge, Free School Lane, Cambridge CB2 3RF. *T:* (01223) 334510.

RICHARDS, Menna; Controller, BBC Wales, since 2000; *b* 27 Feb. 1953; *d* of late Penri T. Richards and of Dilys M. Richards; *m* 1985, Patrick Hannan. *Educ:* Maesteg Grammar Sch.; UCW, Aberystwyth (BA). Journalist, BBC Wales, 1975–83; HTV Wales: journalist, 1983–91; Controller, Factual and Gen. Programmes, 1991–93; Dir of Programmes, 1993–97; Man. Dir, 1997–99. Hon. Fellow, Univ. of Wales, Aberystwyth, 1999. *Recreations:* music, gardening, family, friends. *Address:* c/o BBC, Broadcasting House, Llandaff, Cardiff CF5 2YQ. *T:* (029) 2032 2001. *Clubs:* Royal Over-Seas League; Newport Boat.

RICHARDS, Prof. Michael Adrian, CBE 2001; MD; FRCP; Sainsbury Professor of Palliative Medicine, Guy's, King's and St Thomas' School of Medicine, King's College London, since 1995; National Cancer Director, England, since 1999; *b* 14 July 1951; *s* of Donald Hibbert Richards and Peronelle Imogen (*née* Armitage-Smith). *Educ:* Dragon Sch., Oxford; Radley Coll.; Trinity Coll., Cambridge (MA); St Bartholomew's Hosp., London (MB BChir, MD 1988). FRCP 1993. ICRF Res. Fellow, St Bartholomew's Hosp., 1982–86; ICRF Sen. Lectr, 1986–91, Reader in Med. Oncology, 1991–95, Guy's Hosp., London; Clinical Dir of Cancer Services, Guy's and St Thomas' Hosps, 1993–99. *Publications:* papers on breast cancer, cancer service delivery, palliative care, quality of life. *Recreations:* hill-walking, classical music. *Address:* Department of Palliative Medicine, St Thomas' Hospital, SE1 7EH. *T:* (020) 7922 8009; 42 Liberia Road, N5 1JR.

RICHARDS, Maj.-Gen. Nigel William Fairbairn, CB 1998; OBE 1987; Chairman, Confederation of British Service and Ex-Service Organisations, since 1999; *b* 15 Aug. 1945; *s* of late Lt-Col William Fairbairn Richards RA and of Marjorie May Richards; *m* 1968, Christine Anne Helen Woods; two *s* one *d.* *Educ:* Eastbourne Coll.; RMA Sandhurst; Peterhouse, Cambridge (MA). Commissioned, RA, 1965; reglt duty, 1966–76, UK, Germany, NI, Cyprus, Malaya; RN Staff Coll., 1976–77; MoD, 1978–80; Comd J Anti-Tank Battery, RHA, 1980–81; Directing Staff, RMCS, 1982–83; CO 7 Para Regt, RHA, 1983–86; MoD, 1986–88; Higher Comd and Staff Course, 1988; Comdr 5 Airborne Brigade, 1989–90; RCDS 1991; Dir Army Staff Duties, MoD, 1991–93; Chief of Combat Support, HQ Allied Command Europe Rapid Reaction Corps, 1994–96; GOC 4th Div., 1996–98. President: British Scouts Western Europe, 1994–96; Army Boxing and Hockey, 1996–98. Hon. Col, 7 Para Regt RHA, 1999–; Col Comdt, RA, 2001–. *Recreations:* cricket, fishing, ski-ing, golf. *Address:* 14 Berkeley Place, Wimbledon, SW19 4NN. *Club:* Army and Navy.

RICHARDS, Prof. Peter, FMedSci; President, Hughes Hall, Cambridge, since 1998; *b* 25 May 1936; *s* of William and Barbara Richards; *m* 1st, 1959, Anne Marie Larsen (marr. diss. 1986); one *s* three *d*; 2nd, 1987, Dr Carol Anne Seymour. *Educ:* Monkton Combe Sch.; Emmanuel Coll., Cambridge (BA 1957; MB BChir 1960; MA 1961; MD 1971); St George's Hosp. Medical Sch.; Royal Postgraduate Medical Sch. (PhD 1966); FRCP 1976. Consultant Physician, St Peter's Hosp., Chertsey and Hon. Sen. Lectr in Medicine, St Mary's Hosp. Med. Sch., 1970–73; Sen. Lectr in Medicine, St George's Hosp. Med. Sch., 1973–79; Dean and Prof. of Medicine, 1979–95, Emeritus Prof., 1995, St Mary's Hosp. Med. Sch. (part of ICSTM, from 1988), Univ. of London; Pro-Rector (Medicine), Imperial Coll., 1988–95; Med. Dir, Northwick Park and St Mark's NHS Trust, 1995–98. Non-exec. Dir, W Suffolk Hosps NHS Trust, 2001–. Chm., Council of Deans of UK Med. Schs and Faculties, 1994–95. Mem., Septemviri, Univ. of Cambridge, 2000–. Med. Advr to Health Service Ombudsman, 1999–. Member: GMC, 1994–(Dep. Chm., Professional Conduct Cttee, 1999–); Council, RCP, 1994–97. Mem. Council, Anglo-Finnish Soc., 1984–. Freeman, City of London, 1985; Liveryman, Soc. of Apothecaries,

1984–. Founder FMedSci 1998. *Publications:* The Medieval Leper, 1977; (ed jtly) Clinical Medicine and Therapeutics, Vol. I, 1977, Vol. II, 1979; Understanding Water, Electrolyte and Acid/Base Metabolism, 1983; Learning Medicine, 1983, 15th edn 2000; Living Medicine, 1990; UCAS Guide to Entry to Medicine, 1996, 2nd edn 1997; (with S. Stockhill) The New Learning Medicine, 1997 (Soc. of Authors Prize for best gen. med. book, 1998); scientific papers esp. concerning kidney disease and criteria for selection of medical students in Lancet, BMJ, etc. *Recreations:* walking, listening to music, Finland, social history, cycling. *Address:* Hughes Hall, Cambridge CB1 2EW. *T:* (01223) 334890, *Fax:* (01223) 311179; *e-mail:* pr229@cam.ac.uk. *Club:* Garrick.

RICHARDS, Peter Graham Gordon; a District Judge (Magistrates' Courts) (formerly Stipendiary Magistrate), Staffordshire, since 1991; *b* 16 July 1939; *s* of David Gordon and Irene Florence Richards; *m* 1965, Jeanette Uncles (*d* 1997); two *d. Educ:* Univ. of London (LLM 1966). Schoolmaster, 1962–65; Lectr, 1965–68; called to the Bar, Middle Temple, 1968; Midland and Oxford Circuit, 1968–91. *Recreations:* sports broadcasting, travel, theatre, astronomy. *Address:* c/o Clerk to the Justices, Baker Street, Fenton, Stoke on Trent ST4 3BX. *T:* (01782) 845353.

RICHARDS, Philip Brian; His Honour Judge Philip Richards; a Circuit Judge, since 2001; *b* 3 Aug. 1946; *s* of late Glyn Bevan Richards and Nancy Gwenhwyfar Richards (*née* Evans); *m* 1st, 1971, Dorothy Louise George (marr. diss.); two *d*; 2nd, 1994, Julia Jones; one *d*, and one step *s. Educ:* Univ. of Bristol (LLB Hons). Called to the Bar, Inner Temple, 1969; Asst Recorder, 1995–2000; Recorder, 2000–01. *Publication:* (jtly) Government of Wales Bill, 1996. *Recreations:* music, sport, theatre, literature, the history, culture, languages and constitution of Wales. *Address:* Cardiff Crown Court, Cathays Park, Cardiff CF10 3PG. *T:* (029) 2041 4400. *Clubs:* Cardiff and County; Mountain Ash Rugby Football.

RICHARDS, Sir Rex (Edward), Kt 1977; DSc Oxon 1970; FRS 1959; FRSC; Chancellor, Exeter University, 1982–98; *b* 28 Oct. 1922; *s* of H. W. and E. N. Richards; *m* 1948, Eva Edith Vago; two *d. Educ:* Colyton Grammar School, Devon; St John's College, Oxford. Senior Demy, Magdalen College, Oxford, 1946; MA; DPhil; Fellow, Lincoln College, Oxford, 1947–64, Hon. Fellow, 1968; Research Fellow, Harvard University, 1955; Dr Lee's Prof. of Chemistry, Oxford, 1964–70; Fellow, Exeter College, 1964–69; Warden, Merton Coll., Oxford, 1969–84, Hon. Fellow, 1984; Vice-Chancellor, Oxford Univ., 1977–81; Hon. Fellow, St John's Coll., Oxford, 1968; Associate Fellow, Morse Coll., Yale, 1974–79. Director: IBM-UK Ltd, 1978–83; Oxford Instruments Group, 1982–91. Chm., BPMF, 1986–93; Dir, Leverhulme Trust, 1984–93; Chm., Task Force on Clinical Academic Careers, 1996–97. Member: Chemical Society Council, 1957, 1987–93; Faraday Society Council, 1963; Royal Soc. Council, 1973–75; Scientific Adv. Cttee, Nat. Gall., 1978–; ABRC, 1980–83; ACARD, 1984–87; Comr, Royal Commn for the Exhibition of 1851, 1984–97; Pres., Royal Soc. of Chemistry, 1990–92; Trustee: CIBA Foundn, 1978–97; Nat. Heritage Memorial Fund, 1980–84; Tate Gall., 1982–88, 1991–93; Nat. Gall., 1982–88, 1989–93; Henry Moore Foundn, 1989– (Vice-Chm., 1993–94; Chm., 1994–2001); Chm., Nat. Gall. Trust, 1995–99. Tilden Lectr, 1962. FRIC 1970. Hon. FRCP 1987; Hon. FBA 1990; Hon. FRAM 1991. Hon. DSc: East Anglia, 1971; Exeter, 1975; Leicester, 1978; Salford, 1979; Edinburgh, 1981; Leeds, 1984; Kent, 1987; Birmingham, 1993; London, 1994; Hon. LLD: Dundee, 1977; Oxford Brookes, 1998; Warwick, 1999; Hon. ScD Cambridge, 1987. Centenary Fellow, Thames Polytechnic (subseq. Univ. of Greenwich), 1990. For. Associate, Académie des Sciences, France, 1995. Corday-Morgan Medal of Chemical Soc., 1954; Davy Medal, Royal Soc., 1976; Award in Theoretical Chemistry and Spectroscopy, Chem. Soc., 1977; Educn in Partnership with Industry or Commerce Award, DTI, 1982; Medal of Honour, Rheinische Friedrich-Wilhelms Univ., Bonn, 1983; Royal Medal, Royal Soc., 1986; President's Medal, Soc. of Chemical Ind., 1991. *Publications:* various contributions to scientific journals. *Recreation:* enjoying painting and sculpture. *Address:* 13 Woodstock Close, Oxford OX2 8DB. *T:* (01865) 513621.

RICHARDS, (Richard) Alun; Welsh Secretary in charge of Welsh Office Agriculture Department, 1978–81, retired; *b* 2 Jan. 1920; *s* of Sylvanus and Gwladys Richards, Llanbrynmair, Powys; *m* 1944, Ann Elonwy Mary, (Nansi), Price (decd), Morriston, Swansea; two *s. Educ:* Machynlleth County Sch.; Liverpool Univ. (BVSc, MRCVS, 1942). Veterinary Officer with State Vet. Service, Caernarfon and Glamorgan, 1943–57; Divl Vet. Officer, HQ Tolworth and in Warwick, 1957–65; Dep. Reg. Vet. Officer (Wales), 1965–67; seconded to NZ Govt to advise on control of Foot and Mouth disease, 1967–68; Reg. Vet. Officer, HQ Tolworth, 1968–71; Asst Chief Vet. Officer, 1971–77; Asst Sec., Welsh Dept, MAFF, 1977–78; Under-Sec., 1978. *Publications:* contrib. to vet. jls. *Recreations:* beekeeping, fishing, playing bridge. *Address:* Isfryn, Llandre, Aberystwyth SY24 5BS. *T:* (01970) 828246.

See also S. P. Richards.

RICHARDS, (Robert) John (Godwin); Chief Executive, Hammerson plc, since 1999; *b* 11 Jan. 1956; *m* 1987, Amanda Joseph; two *s. Educ:* Poly. of Wales (BSc). FRICS. Joined Hammerson plc, 1981; Dir, 1990–; UK Develt Dir, 1990–93; UK Man. Dir, 1993–97; Internat. Man. Dir, 1997–99. *Address:* Hammerson plc, 100 Park Lane, W1K 7AR. *T:* (020) 7887 1000.

RICHARDS, Roderick; Member (C) Wales North, National Assembly for Wales, since 1999; *b* 12 March 1947; *s* of Ivor George Richards and Lizzie Jane Richards (*née* Evans); *m* 1975, Elizabeth Knight; two *s* one *d. Educ:* Llandovery College; Univ. of Wales (BSc Econ). Short service commn, RM, 1969–71. Ministry of Defence, 1977–83; broadcaster and journalist, 1983–89; Special Adviser to Sec. of State for Wales, 1990. Contested (C): Carmarthen, 1987; Vale of Glamorgan, May 1989. MP (C) Clwyd North West, 1992–97; contested (C) Clwyd West, 1997. PPS to Minister of State, FCO, 1993–94; Parly Under-Sec. of State, Welsh Office, 1994–96. Mem. Welsh Affairs Select Cttee, 1992–93. *Recreations:* Rugby, cricket, walking, games. *Address:* National Assembly for Wales, Cardiff Bay, Cardiff CF99 1NA. *Clubs:* Special Forces; Llanelli Rugby; Colwyn Bay Cricket.

RICHARDS, Hon. Sir Stephen (Price), Kt 1997; **Hon. Mr Justice Richards;** a Judge of the High Court of Justice, Queen's Bench Division, since 1997; *b* 8 Dec. 1950; *s* of Richard Alun Richards, *qv*; *m* 1976, Lucy Elizabeth Stubbings, MA; two *s* one *d. Educ:* King's Coll. Sch., Wimbledon; St John's Coll., Oxford (open schol.; BA Lit.Hum. 1972; BA Jurisprudence 1974; MA 1977). Called to the Bar, Gray's Inn, 1975 (Arden Schol. and Bacon Schol.; Bencher, 1992); Second Jun. Counsel, 1987–89, Standing Counsel, 1989–91, to Dir Gen. of Fair Trading; a Jun. Counsel to the Crown, 1990–91, First Jun. Treasury Counsel, 1992–97, Common Law; an Asst Recorder, 1992–96; a Recorder, 1996–97; a Presiding Judge, Wales and Chester Circuit, 2000–. Governor, King's Coll. Sch., Wimbledon, 1998–. *Publication:* (ed jtly) Chitty on Contracts, 25th edn 1983, 26th edn 1989. *Recreation:* the Welsh hills. *Address:* Royal Courts of Justice, Strand, WC2A 2LL.

RICHARDS, Sir Vivian; *see* Richards, Sir I. V. A.

RICHARDS, Prof. (William) Graham, CBE 2001; DPhil, DSc; Professor of Chemistry, since 1996, and Chairman of Chemistry, since 1997, Oxford University; Fellow of Brasenose College, Oxford, since 1966; *b* 1 Oct. 1939; *o s* of Percy Richards and Julia Richards (*née* Evans); *m* 1st, 1970, Jessamy Kershaw (*d* 1988); two *s*; 2nd, 1996, Mary Elizabeth Phillips. *Educ:* Birkenhead Sch.; Brasenose Coll., Oxford (MA; DPhil 1964; DSc 1985). ICI Res. Fellow, Balliol Coll., Oxford, 1964; Res. Fellow, CNRS, Paris, 1965; Lectr, 1966–94, Reader in Computational Chemistry, 1994–96, Dept of Physical Chemistry, Oxford Univ. Dir, Oxford Molecular Gp plc, 1989–99 (Founding Scientist, 1989, Chm., 1990–93). Res. Schol., Stanford Univ., 1975–76; Visiting Professor: Univ. of Calif at Berkeley, 1975–76; Stanford Univ., 1978–82. Mem., Bd of Dirs, Assoc. for Internat. Cancer Res., 1995–99. Editor, Jl of Molecular Graphics, 1984–96. Marlow Medal, 1972, Award for Theoretical Chem., 1989, RSC; Lloyd of Kilgerran Prize, Foundn for Sci. and Technol, 1996; Mullard Award, Royal Soc., 1998. *Publications:* Ab Initio Molecular Orbital Calculations for Chemists, 1970, 2nd edn 1983; Bibliography of Ab Initio Wave Functions, 1971, supplements, 1974, 1978, 1981; Entropy and Energy Levels, 1974; Structure and Spectra of Atoms, 1976; Quantum Pharmacology, 1977, 2nd edn 1983; Spin-Orbit Coupling in Molecules, 1981; Structure and Spectra of Molecules, 1985; The Problems of Chemistry, 1986; Computer-Aided Molecular Design, 1989; Energy Levels of Atoms and Molecules, 1994; Computational Chemistry, 1995; An Introduction to Statistical Thermodynamics, 1995. *Recreations:* sport, running, swimming. *Address:* Brasenose College, Oxford OX1 4AJ. *T:* (01865) 277830. *Club:* Vincent's (Oxford).

RICHARDSON, family name of **Barons Richardson** and **Richardson of Duntisbourne** and **Baroness Richardson of Calow**.

RICHARDSON, Baron *cr* 1979 (Life Peer), of Lee in the County of Devon; **John Samuel Richardson,** 1st Bt, *cr* 1963; Kt 1960; LVO 1943; MD, FRCP; retired; President, General Medical Council, 1973–80; Hon. Consulting Physician: St Thomas' Hospital; King Edward VII's Hospital for Officers; Consultant Emeritus to the Army; Consulting Physician: Metropolitan Police, 1957–80; London Transport Board, since 1964; *b* 16 June 1910; *s* of Major John Watson Richardson, solicitor, and Elizabeth Blakeney, *d* of Sir Samuel Roberts, 1st Bt, both of Sheffield; *m* 1933, Sybil Angela Stephanie (*d* 1991), *d* of A. Ronald Trist, Stanmore; two *d. Educ:* Charterhouse; Trinity Coll., Cambridge (Hon. Fellow, 1979); St Thomas' Hosp. (Bristowe Medal; Hadden Prize, 1936; Perkins Fellowship, 1938). MB BChir 1936, MD 1940; MRCP 1937, FRCP 1948; FRCPE 1975. Major, RAMC (temp.), 1939; Lt-Col, RAMC (temp.), 1942. 1st asst, Med. Professorial Unit, St Thomas' Hosp., 1946; Physician to St Thomas' Hosp., 1947–75. Examiner to Univs of Cambridge, London, Manchester, NUI, RCP London and Edinburgh Conjoint Bd. President: Internat. Soc. of Internal Medicine, 1966–70 (Hon. Pres. 1970); Royal Soc. of Medicine, 1969–71 (Hon. Librarian, 1957–63; Pres., Med. Educn Sect., 1967–68); BMA, 1970–71; 2nd Congress, Assoc. Européene de Médicine Interne d'Ensemble, Bad-Godesberg, 1973 (Hon. Mem. 1974); Assoc. for the Study of Med. Educn, 1978–80 (Vice-Pres., 1974–78, Hon. Mem., 1980); Vice-President: Med. Soc. of London, 1961–63 (Hon. Fellow, 1981); Royal Coll. of Nursing, 1972–; Chairman: Jt Consultants Cttee, 1967–72; Council for Postgrad. Med. Educn in England and Wales, 1972–80; Medico-Pharmaceutical Forum, 1973–76; Armed Forces Med. Adv. Bd, MoD, 1975–80. Mem., Bd of Governors, St Thomas's Hosp., 1953–59, 1964–74. Mem. Ct, Soc. of Apothecaries, 1960–85 (Master, 1971–72). Lectures: Lettsomian, Med. Soc. of London, 1963; Scott Heron, Royal Victoria Hosp., Belfast, 1969; Maudsley, RCPsych, 1971; Wilkinson Meml, Inst. of Dental Surgeons, London Univ., 1976; Harveian Oration, RCP, 1978; Orator, Med. Soc. of London, 1981. Hon. Fellow: Swedish Soc. Med. Scis, 1970; RSocMed 1973; Heberden Soc., 1973; Osler Club of London, 1973; Hon. Mem., Assoc. of Clinical Tutors of GB, 1980; Hon. FRPharms (Hon. FPS 1974); Hon. FRCPI 1975; Hon. FFCM 1977; Hon. FRCPsych 1979; Hon. FRCS 1980; Hon. FRCPSG 1980; Hon. FRCPE 1981; Hon. Fellow: KCL; UMDS. Hon. Bencher, Gray's Inn, 1974. Hon. DSc: NUI, 1975; Hull, 1981; Hon. DCL Newcastle, 1980; Hon. LLD: Nottingham, 1981, Liverpool, 1983. CStJ 1970. Baron de Lancey Law Prize, RSM, 1978; Gold Medal, BMA, 1982; Guthrie Medal, RAMC, 1982. Editor-in-Chief, British Encylopaedia of Medical Practice, 1970–74. *Publications:* The Practice of Medicine, 2nd edn 1960; Connective Tissue Disorders, 1963; Anticoagulant Prophylaxis and Treatment (jointly), 1965. *Heir* to baronetcy: none. *Address:* Windcutter, Lee, near Ilfracombe, North Devon EX34 8LW. *T:* (01271) 863198.

RICHARDSON OF CALOW, Baroness *cr* 1998 (Life Peer), of Calow in the co. Derbyshire; **Rev. Kathleen Margaret Richardson,** OBE 1996; Moderator, Free Churches' Council (formerly Free Church Federal Council), 1995–99; a President, Churches Together in England, 1995–99; *b* 24 Feb. 1938; *d* of Francis and Margaret Fountain; *m* 1964, Ian David Godfrey Richardson; three *d. Educ:* St Helena Sch., Chesterfield; Stockwell Coll. (Cert Ed); Deaconess Coll., Ilkley; Wesley House, Cambridge. School teacher, 1958–61. Wesley Deaconess, Champness Hall, Rochdale, 1961–64; Lay Worker, Team Ministry, Stevenage, 1973–77; Minister, Denby Dale and Clayton West Circuit, 1979–87; ordained presbyter, 1980; Chm., West Yorks Dist, 1987–95. Pres., Methodist Conf., 1992–93. Hon. DLitt Bradford, 1994; Hon. LLD Liverpool, 1999; Hon. DD Birmingham, 2000. *Recreations:* reading, needlework.

RICHARDSON OF DUNTISBOURNE, Baron *cr* 1983 (Life Peer), of Duntisbourne in the County of Gloucestershire; **Gordon William Humphreys Richardson,** KG 1983; MBE 1944; TD 1979; PC 1976; DL; Governor, Bank of England, 1973–83, Member, Court of the Bank of England, 1967–83; Senior International Adviser, Morgan Stanley & Co. Inc., since 1997; *b* 25 Nov. 1915; *er s* of John Robert and Nellie Richardson; *m* 1941, Margaret Alison, *er d* of Canon H. R. L. Sheppard; one *s* one *d. Educ:* Nottingham High School; Gonville and Caius College, Cambridge (MA, LLB). Commnd S Notts Hussars Yeomanry, 1939; Staff Coll., Camberley, 1941; served until 1946. Called to Bar, Gray's Inn, 1946 (Hon. Bencher, 1973); Mem. Bar Council, 1951–55; ceased practice at Bar, Aug. 1955. Industrial and Commercial Finance Corp. Ltd, 1955–57; Director: J. Henry Schroder & Co., 1957; Lloyds Bank Ltd, 1960–67 (Vice-Chm., 1962–66); Legal and General Assurance Soc., Ltd, 1956–70 (Vice-Chm. 1959–70); Rolls Royce (1971) Ltd, 1971–73; ICI Ltd, 1972–73; Chairman: J. Henry Schroder Wagg & Co. Ltd, 1962–72; Schroders Ltd, 1966–73; Schroders Inc. (NY), 1968–73; Morgan Stanley Internat. Inc., 1986–95. Member: Eur. Adv. Bd, Morgan Stanley Dean Witter; Internat. Adv. Bd, Chase Manhattan. Chm., Industrial Develt Adv. Bd, 1972–73. Mem. Company Law Amendment Committee (Jenkins Committee), 1959–62; Chm. Cttee on Turnover Taxation, 1963. Member: Court of London University, 1962–65; NEDC, 1971–73, 1980–83; Trustee, National Gallery, 1971–73, Chm., Pilgrim Trust, 1984–88. One of HM Lieutenants, City of London, 1974–; High Steward of Westminster, 1985–89; DL Glos, 1983. Deputy High Steward, Univ. of Cambridge, 1982–; Hon. Fellow: Gonville and Caius Coll., 1977; Wolfson Coll., Cambridge, 1977. Hon. LLD Cambridge, 1979; Hon. DSc: City Univ., 1976; Aston, 1979; Hon. DCL East Anglia, 1984. Benjamin Franklin Medal, RSA, 1984. *Address:* 25 St Anselm's Place, W1Y 1FG. *T:* (020) 7629 4448. *Clubs:* Athenæum, Brooks's, Pratt's.

See also Sir John Riddell, Bt.

RICHARDSON, Anthony; *see* Richardson, H. A.

RICHARDSON, Sir Anthony (Lewis), 3rd Bt *cr* 1924; *b* 5 Aug. 1950; *s* of Sir Leslie Lewis Richardson, 2nd Bt, and of Joy Patricia, Lady Richardson, *d* of P. J. Rillstone, Johannesburg; *S* father, 1985; *m* 1985, Honor Gillian Dauney; one *s* one *d*. *Educ:* Diocesan College, Cape Town, S Africa. Stockbroker with L. Messel & Co., London, 1973–75; Insurance Broker with C. T. Bowring, London and Johannesburg, 1975–76; Stockbroker with Fergusson Bros, Hall, Stewart & Co., Johannesburg and Cape Town, 1976–78; Stockbroker with W. Greenwell & Co., London, 1979–81; with Rowe & Pitman, subseq. S. G. Warburg Securities, then SBC Warburg, London, 1981–99 (Dir, 1986–99), seconded to Potter Partners, Melbourne and Sydney, 1986–89, seconded to SBC Warburg, Johannesburg, 1996–99; Dir, Barclays Private Bank, London, 1999–. *Recreations:* various sports, photography. *Heir: s* William Lewis Richardson, *b* 15 Oct. 1992. *Address:* Triggs, Crondall Road, Crondall, Hampshire GU10 5RU. *Clubs:* Boodle's, Hurlingham.

RICHARDSON, David; Director, London Office, International Labour Organisation, 1982–91; *b* 24 April 1928; *s* of Harold George Richardson and Madeleine Raphaële Richardson (*née* Lebret); *m* 1951, Frances Joan Pring; three *s* one *d*. *Educ:* Wimbledon Coll.; King's Coll., London (BA Hons). FIPM 1986. RAF, 1949. Unilever, 1951. Inland Revenue, 1953; Min. of Labour, 1956; Sec., Construction Industry Training Bd, 1964; Chm., Central Youth Employment Exec., 1969; Royal Coll. of Defence Studies, 1971; Under Sec., Dept of Employment, 1972; Dir, Safety and Gen. Gp, Health and Safety Exec., 1975; Dir and Sec., ACAS, 1977. Director: The Tablet, 1985–98; Industrial Training Service Ltd, 1987–93. *Recreations:* music, walking, landscape gardening, ceramics. *Address:* 183 Banstead Road, Carshalton, Surrey SM5 4DP. *T:* (020) 8241 4614.

RICHARDSON, Rev. David John; His Honour Judge Richardson; a Circuit Judge, since 2000; *b* 23 June 1950; *s* of Abraham Eric Richardson and Gwendoline Richardson (*née* Ballard); *m* 1980, Jennifer Margaret Richardson (*née* Cooke); one *s* one *d*. *Educ:* John Ruskin Grammar Sch., Croydon; Trinity Hall, Cambridge (BA 1971, MA; LLB 1972); Southwark Ordination Trng Course. Called to the Bar, Middle Temple, 1973; in practice, 1973–2000; an Asst Recorder, 1992–97; a Recorder, 1997–2000. Ordained deacon, 1985, priest, 1986; Hon. Curate, Emmanuel Church, S Croydon, 1985–. *Recreations:* walking, reading, supporter of Crystal Palace FC.

RICHARDSON, Sir Eric; *see* Richardson, Sir J. E.

RICHARDSON, Prof. Genevra Mercy; Professor of Public Law, Queen Mary, University of London, since 1994; *b* 1 Sept. 1948; *d* of John Lawrence Richardson and Josephine Juliet Richardson; *m* 1977, Oliver Thorold (*see* Sir A. O. Thorold); one *s* one *d*. *Educ:* King's Coll., London (LLB, LLM). Res. Officer, Centre for Socio-Legal Studies, Oxford, 1974–78; Lectr, UEA, 1979–87; Lectr, 1987–89, Reader, 1989–94, Dean, Faculty of Law, 1996–99, QMW. Chm., Expert Cttee Advising Ministers on Reform of Mental Health Legislation, 1998–99. Mem., Council on Tribunals, 2001–. Member: Mental Health Act Commn, 1987–92; Animal Procedures Cttee, 1998–; Chm., Prisoner's Advice Service, 1994–. Mem. Council, MRC, 2001–. *Recreations:* walking, travel. *Address:* Department of Law, Queen Mary, University of London, Mile End Road, E1 4NS. *T:* (020) 7882 5134; *e-mail:* g.richardson@qmw.ac.uk.

RICHARDSON, George Barclay, CBE 1978; Warden, Keble College, Oxford, 1989–94 (Hon. Fellow, 1994); Pro-Vice-Chancellor, Oxford University, 1988–94; *b* 19 Sept. 1924; *s* of George and Christina Richardson; *m* 1957, Isabel Alison Chalk (marr. diss. 1998); two *s*. *Educ:* Aberdeen Central Secondary Sch. and other schs in Scotland; Aberdeen Univ.; Corpus Christi Coll., Oxford (Hon. Fellow, 1987). BSc Physics and Maths, 1944 (Aberdeen); MA (Oxon) PPE 1949. Admty Scientific Res. Dept, 1944; Lieut, RNVR, 1945. Intell. Officer, HQ Intell. Div. BAOR, 1946–47; Third Sec., HM Foreign Service, 1949; Student, Nuffield Coll., Oxford, 1950; Fellow, St John's Coll., Oxford, 1951–89, Hon. Fellow, 1989; University Reader in Economics, Oxford, 1969–73; Sec. to Delegates and Chief Exec., OUP, 1974–88 (Deleg., 1971–74). Economic Advr, UKAEA, 1968–74. Member: Economic Develt Cttee for Electrical Engineering Industry, 1964–73; Monopolies Commn, 1969–74; Royal Commn on Environmental Pollution, 1973–74; Council, Publishers Assoc., 1981–87. Mem., UK Delegation, CSCE Cultural Forum, 1985. Visitor, Ashmolean Mus., 1992–96. Hon. DCL Oxon, 1988; Hon. LLD Aberdeen, 1996. *Publications:* Information and Investment, 1960, 2nd edn 1991; Economic Theory, 1964; The Economics of Imperfect Knowledge, 1998; articles in academic jls. *Address:* 33 Belsyre Court, Woodstock Road, Oxford OX2 6HU. *Club:* Oxford and Cambridge.

RICHARDSON, George Taylor; Hon. Chairman: James Richardson & Sons, Limited, Winnipeg, Canada, since 2000 (Chairman, 1993–2000; President 1966–93; Vice-President 1954); RBC Dominion Securities Inc., since 1996; *b* 22 Sept. 1924; *s* of late James Armstrong Richardson and Muriel (*née* Sprague); *m* 1948, Tannis Maree Thorlakson; two *s* one *d*. *Educ:* Grosvenor Sch. and Ravenscourt Sch. Winnipeg; Univ. of Manitoba (BComm). Joined family firm of James Richardson & Sons Ltd, 1946. Dir of cos owned by James Richardson & Sons Ltd. Mem., Winnipeg Commodity Exchange. Hon. Dir, Canada's Aviation Hall of Fame. Hon. LLD: Manitoba; Winnipeg. *Recreations:* hunting, helicopter flying. *Address:* c/o James Richardson & Sons, Limited, Richardson Building, One Lombard Place, Winnipeg, MB R3B 0Y1, Canada. *T:* (904) 9345811. *Clubs:* MB, St Charles (Winnipeg); Vancouver (Vancouver); Toronto (Toronto).

RICHARDSON, (Henry) Anthony; a Recorder of the Crown Court, 1978–96; a Deputy Traffic Commissioner and a Deputy Licensing Authority, North Eastern Traffic Area, 1989–93; barrister, retired; *b* 28 Dec. 1925; *er s* of late Thomas Ewan Richardson and Jessie (*née* Preston), Batley, W Yorks; *m* 1954, Georgina (*née* Lawford), *d* of late Rosamond Bedford and step *d* of Gp Captain G. R. Bedford, MB, ChB, RAF retd. *Educ:* Giggleswick Sch.; Leeds Univ. (LLB 1950, LLM 1956). Called to the Bar, Lincoln's Inn, 1951; North-Eastern Circuit; Dep. Circuit Judge, 1972–78. Chm., a Police Disciplinary Appeal Tribunal, 1983. *Publications:* articles in legal periodicals. *Recreations:* walking, gardening, listening to music. *Address:* Grey Thatch, Wetherby Road, Scarcroft, Leeds LS14 3BB.

RICHARDSON, Hugh; Deputy Director General, Joint Research Centre, European Commission, since 1996; *b* 12 May 1947; *s* of Robert Richardson and Pauline (*née* Broadhurst); *m* (marr. diss.); two *s* two *d*. *Educ:* Pembroke Coll., Oxford (BA 1969; BCL 1970). Commission of the European Communities: with Secretariat Gen., 1974–79; Directorate-Gen. for External Relns, 1979–84; Counsellor and Dep. Head, Tokyo Delegn, 1984–88; Asst to DG for External Relns, 1988–91; Dir, Rights and Obligations, Directorate-Gen. for Personnel and Admin, 1991–96. *Publication:* EC-Japan Relations: after adolescence, 1989. *Recreations:* sailing, ski-ing, running. *Address:* Commission of the European Communities, 200 rue de la Loi, 1049 Brussels, Belgium. *T:* (2) 2959096.

RICHARDSON, Ian William, CBE 1989; actor; *b* 7 April 1934; *s* of John Richardson and Margaret Drummond; *m* 1961, Maroussia Frank; two *s*. *Educ:* Tynecastle; Edinburgh; Univ. of Glasgow. Studied for stage at Coll. of Dramatic Art, Glasgow (James Bridie Gold Medal, 1957). FRSAMD 1971. Joined Birmingham Repertory Theatre Co. 1958 (leading parts incl. Hamlet); joined Shakespeare Meml Theatre Co. (later RSC), 1960; rôles, Stratford and Aldwych, 1960–: Arragon in Merchant of Venice; Sir Andrew Aguecheek, 1960; Malatesti in Duchess of Malfi, 1960; Oberon in A Midsummer Night's Dream, 1961; Tranio in Taming of the Shrew, 1961; the Doctor in The Representative, 1963; Edmund in King Lear, 1964; Antipholus of Ephesus in Comedy of Errors, 1964; Herald and Marat in Marat/Sade, 1964, 1965; Ithamore, The Jew of Malta, 1964; Ford, Merry Wives of Windsor, 1964, 1966, 1969; Antipholus of Syracuse in Comedy of Errors, 1965; Chorus, Henry V, 1965; Vindice, The Revengers Tragedy, 1965, 1969; Coriolanus, 1966; Bertram, All's Well That Ends Well, 1966; Malcolm, Macbeth, 1966; Cassius, Julius Caesar, 1968; Pericles, 1969; Angelo, Measure for Measure, 1970; Buckingham, Richard III, 1970; Proteus, Two Gentlemen of Verona, 1970; Prospero, The Tempest, 1970; Richard II/Bolingbroke, Richard II, 1973; Berowne, Love's Labour's Lost, 1973; Iachimo, Cymbeline, 1974; Shalimov, Summer Folk, 1974; Ford, Merry Wives of Windsor, 1975; Richard III, 1975; tours with RSC: Europe and USSR, NY, 1964; NY, 1965; USSR, 1966; Japan, 1970; NY, 1974, 1975; Tom Wrench in musical Trelawny, Sadler's Wells, 1971–72; Professor Higgins, My Fair Lady, Broadway, 1976 (Drama Desk Award, 1976); Jack Tanner, in Man and Superman, and Doctor in The Millionairess, Shaw Festival Theatre, Niagara, Ont; The Government Inspector, Old Vic, 1979; Romeo and Juliet, Old Vic, 1979; Lolita, Broadway, 1981; The Miser, Chichester, 1995; The Magistrate, Chichester, 1997, transf. Savoy, 1998; The Seven Ages of Man (one-man show), Guildford, 1999. *Films:* Captain Fitzroy in The Darwin Adventure, 1971; Priest in Man of la Mancha, 1972; Montgomery in Ike—the War Years, 1978; Charlie Muffin, 1979; The Sign of Four, 1982; Hound of the Baskervilles, 1982; Brazil, 1984; Whoops Apocalypse, 1987; The Fourth Protocol, 1987; Burning Secret, 1989; The Year of the Comet, 1992; M. Butterfly, 1994; Words upon the Window Pane, 1995; BAPS, 1997; From Hell, 2002. *Television: plays:* Danton's Death, 1978; Churchill and the Generals, 1979; A Cotswold Death, Passing Through, 1981; Russian Night, Kisch-Kisch, Beauty and the Beast, Salad Days, 1982; Slimming Down, 1984; Star Quality, 1985; The Devil's Disciple, 1987; The Winslow Boy, 1989; An Ungentlemanly Act, 1992; The Canterville Ghost, 1997; The Woman in White, 1997; *films:* Monsignor Quixote, 1985; Blunt, 1987; Rosencrantz and Guildenstern Are Dead, 1990; Baps, 1996; The Fifth Province, 1996; Dark City, 1996; *serials and series:* Eyeless in Gaza, 1971; Tinker, Tailor, Soldier, Spy, 1979; Private Schulz, 1981; The Woman in White, 1982; Ramsay Macdonald, in Number 10, 1982; The Master of Ballantrae, 1984; Six Centuries of Verse, 1984; Mistral's Daughter, 1985; Nehru, in Mountbatten—the last Viceroy, 1986; Porterhouse Blue, 1987; Troubles, 1988; Twist of Fate, 1989; Under a Dark Angel's Eye, 1989; Phantom of the Opera, 1990; The Plot to Kill Hitler, 1990; The Gravy Train, 1990; House of Cards, 1990 (BAFTA Best Actor Award, 1991); The Gravy Train Goes East, 1991; To Play the King, 1993; Remember, 1994; Catherine the Great, 1994; The Final Cut, 1995; The Magician's House, 1999; Gormenghast, 2000; Murder Rooms, 2000; Murder Rooms II, 2001. Hon. DDra RSAMD, 1999. RTS Award, 1982. *Publication:* Preface to Cymbeline (Folio Soc.), 1976. *Recreations:* music, exploring churches and castles. *Address:* c/o London Management, 2–4 Noel Street, W1V 3RB. *T:* (020) 7237 9000. *Club:* Garrick.

RICHARDSON, Rt Hon. Sir Ivor (Lloyd Morgan), Kt 1986; PC 1978; SJD; **Rt Hon. Justice Richardson;** President, Court of Appeal of New Zealand, since 1996 (Judge, 1977–96); *b* 24 May 1930; *s* of W. T. Richardson; *m* 1955, Jane, *d* of I. J. Krchma; three *d*. *Educ:* Canterbury Univ. (LLB); Univ. of Mich (LLM, SJD). Partner, Macalister Bros, Invercargill, 1957–63; Crown Counsel, Crown Law Office, Wellington, 1963–66; Prof. of Law, Victoria Univ. of Wellington, 1967–73 (Dean of Law Faculty, 1968–71; Pro-Chancellor, 1979–84; Chancellor, 1984–86); Partner, Watts & Patterson, Wellington, 1973–77. Chm., Cttees of Inquiry into Inflation Accounting, 1975–76, into Solicitors Nominee Cos, 1983. Chairman: Council of Legal Educn, 1983–92; Royal Commn on Social Policy, 1986–88; Orgnl Rev. of Inland Revenue Dept, 1993–94. Hon. LLD: Canterbury, 1987; Victoria, 1989. *Publications:* books and articles on legal subjects. *Address:* 29 Duthie Street, Wellington 5, New Zealand. *T:* (4) 4769310. *Club:* Wellington (Wellington, NZ).

RICHARDSON, Hon. James Armstrong; PC (Can.) 1968; President, Jarco Ltd; Chairman, Max Bell Foundation, 1972–97; *b* Winnipeg, Manitoba, 28 March 1922; *s* of James Armstrong Richardson and Muriel Sprague; *m* 1949, Shirley Anne, *d* of John Rooper, Shamley Green, Surrey, England; two *s* three *d*. *Educ:* St John's-Ravenscourt, Winnipeg; Queen's Univ., Kingston, Ont. (BA). Pilot with No 10 BR Sqdn, before entering family firm of James Richardson & Sons, Ltd, Winnipeg, Oct. 1945; he was Chm. and Chief Exec. Officer of this company, but resigned to enter public life, 1968. Dir Emeritus, Canadian Imperial Bank of Commerce; Past Director: Internat. Nickel Co.; Investors' Gp, Hudson's Bay Co.; Canadian Pacific Rly; Canada's America's Cup Challenge 1982–83. MP (L), June 1968 (re-elected Oct. 1972, July 1974); Minister, Canadian Federal Cabinet, July 1968; Minister of Supply and Services, May 1969; Minister of Nat. Defence, 1972–76; resigned from Federal Cabinet over constitutional language issue, Oct. 1976; crossed floor of House to sit as an Independent MP, 27 June 1978. Founding Dir, Canada West Foundn, 1970–97; Hon. Pres., Commonwealth Games Assoc. of Canada, Inc, 1983–97. Former Trustee, Queen's Univ., Kingston; Chm., 1952–65, Hon. Chm., 1965–78, St John's Ravenscourt Sch. *Address:* 407 Bower Boulevard, Winnipeg, MB R3P 0L6, Canada.

See also G. T. Richardson.

RICHARDSON, Rev. Canon James John; Team Rector, Bournemouth Town Centre Parish, since 1996 and Priest-in-Charge, St Augustine, Bournemouth, since 2001; *b* 28 March 1941; *s* of late James John Richardson and of Gladys May (*née* Evans); *m* 1966, Janet Rosemary Welstand; two *s* one *d*. *Educ:* Catford Central Sch.; Hull Univ. (BA); Sheffield Univ. (DipEd); Cuddesdon Coll., Oxford; MA Leicester 1995. Assistant Master, Westfield Comp. Sch., Sheffield, 1964–66; Curate, St Peter's Collegiate Church, Wolverhampton, 1969–72; Priest i/c, All Saints, Hanley, Stoke-on-Trent, 1972–75; Rector of Nantwich, 1975–82; Vicar of Leeds, 1982–88; Exec. Dir, CCJ, 1988–92; Priest-in-Charge: Gt Brington, Whilton and Norton (Northampton), dio. of Peterborough, 1993–96; E Haddon and Holdenby, Church and Chapel Brampton and Harlestone, 1994–96. Hon. Canon, 1982–88, Canon Emeritus, 1988–, Ripon Cathedral. Chaplain: to Earl Spencer, 1993–96; to High Sheriff of Northants, 1995–96. Chm., Racial Harrassment Commn, Leeds, 1986–87; N of England Vice-Pres., UN Year of Peace, 1986–87. Chairman: Bournemouth Town Centre Detached Youth Project, 1997–; Churches Together in Bournemouth, 1998–; Director: Bournemouth Millennium Co., 1998–99; Hope FM Radio, 1998–2001. Member: Council, Centre for the Study of Judaism and Jewish/Christian Relations, Selly Oak Coll., 1989–94; Internat. Council of Christians and Jews Adv. Cttee, 1992–96. Mem. Court, Leeds Univ., 1986–88; Chairman of Governors: Abbey Grange High Sch., Leeds, 1982–86; Leeds Grammar Sch., 1983–88; Governor: Leeds Girls' High Sch., 1982–88; Leeds Music Fest., 1982–88. FRSA 1991. *Publications:* (contrib.) Four Score Years, 1989; contrib. Yorkshire Post, 1982–90. *Recreations:* leading pilgrimages to Israel, biography—especially life and times of Rupert Brooke, deciphering

Elizabethan churchwardens' accounts. *Address:* The Rectory, 18 Wimborne Road, Bournemouth BH2 6NT. *T:* and *Fax:* (01202) 554058.

RICHARDSON, Prof. Jeremy John, PhD; Nuffield Professor of Comparative European Politics and Director, Centre for European Politics, Economics and Society, University of Oxford, since 1998; Fellow, Nuffield College, Oxford, since 1998; *b* 15 June 1942; *s* of Samuel Radcliffe Richardson and Sarah Doris Richardson; *m* 1966, Anne Philippsen (marr. diss. 1993); one *s* one *d*; *m* 1994, Sonia Pauline Mazey; two *d*. *Educ:* Univ. of Keele (BA Hons Politics and Econs); Univ. of Manchester (MA Econ; PhD 1970). Asst Lectr, Lectr, then Reader, Univ. of Keele, 1966–82; Professor: Dept of Politics, Univ. of Strathclyde, 1982–92; Univ. of Warwick, 1992–95; Univ. of Essex, 1995–98. Hon. Dr Pol Sci., Umeå, 1995. *Publications:* The Policy-Making Process, 1969; (ed with R. Kimber) Campaigning for the Environment, 1974; (ed with R. Kimber) Pressure Groups in Britain: a reader, 1974; (with A. Grant Jordan) Governing Under Pressure: the policy process in a post-parliamentary democracy, 1979; (ed with R. Henning) Policy Responses to Unemployment in Western Democracies, 1984; (with J. Moon) Unemployment in the UK: politics and policies, 1985; (with A Grant Jordan) Government & Pressure Groups in Britain, 1987; (ed jtly) The Politics of Economic Crisis: lessons from Western Europe, 1989; (jtly) Local Partnership and the Unemployment Crisis in Britain, 1989; (with G. Dudley) Politics and Steel in Britain 1967–1988, 1990; (ed) Privatisation and Deregulation in Canada and Britain, 1990; (with S. Mazey) Lobbying in the European Community, 1993; (ed) Pressure Groups, 1993; (jtly) True Blues: the politics of Conservative Party membership, 1994; (jtly) Networks for Water Policy: a comparative perspective, 1994; (with W. Maloney) Managing Policy Change in Britain: the politics of water policy, 1995; (ed) European Union: power and policy-making, 1996, 2nd edn 2001; (with G. Dudley) Why Does Policy Change?: lessons from British transport policy 1945–1999, 2000. *Recreations:* gardening, DIY, walking, playing with the children. *Address:* 88 Lonsdale Road, Oxford OX2 7ER. *T:* (01865) 510096.

RICHARDSON, Jeremy William; QC 2000; a Recorder, since 2000; *b* 3 April 1958; *s* of late Thomas William Sydney Raymond Richardson and of Jean Mary Richardson (*née* Revill). *Educ:* Forest Sch.; Queen Mary Coll., Univ. of London (LLB Hons 1979). Called to the Bar, Inner Temple, 1980; in practice at the Bar, NE Circuit, 1982–; Asst Recorder, 1998–2000. Mem., Gen. Council of the Bar, 1992–94. Sec., NE Circuit, 1991–96. *Address:* 11 King's Bench Walk, Temple, EC4Y 7EQ. *T:* (020) 7353 3337.

RICHARDSON, Joanna, MA Oxon; FRSL; author; *o d* of late Frederick Richardson and late Charlotte Elsa (*née* Benjamin). *Educ:* The Downs School, Seaford; St Anne's College, Oxford. Contributions to BBC include: translated plays; interviews; numerous features for Radios 3 and 4. Mem. Council, Royal Soc. of Literature, 1961–86. Chevalier de l'Ordre des Arts et des Lettres, 1987. *Publications include:* Fanny Brawne: a biography, 1952; Théophile Gautier: his Life and Times, 1958; Edward FitzGerald, 1960; (ed) FitzGerald: Selected Works, 1962; The Pre-Eminent Victorian: a study of Tennyson, 1962; The Everlasting Spell: a study of Keats and his Friends, 1963; (ed) Essays by Divers Hands (trans. Royal Soc. Lit.), 1963; introd. to Victor Hugo: Choses Vues (The Oxford Lib. of French Classics), 1964; Edward Lear, 1965; George IV: a Portrait, 1966; Creevey and Greville, 1967; Princess Mathilde, 1969; Verlaine, 1971; Enid Starkie, 1973; (ed and trans.) Verlaine, Poems, 1974; Stendhal: a critical biography, 1974; (ed and trans.) Baudelaire, Poems, 1975; Victor Hugo, 1976; Zola, 1978; Keats and his Circle: an album of portraits, 1980; (trans.) Gautier, Mademoiselle de Maupin, 1981; The Life and Letters of John Keats, 1981; Letters from Lambeth: the correspondence of the Reynolds family with John Freeman Milward Dovaston 1808–1815, 1981; Colette, 1983; Judith Gautier, 1987 (trans. French 1989; Prix Goncourt for Biography); Portrait of a Bonaparte: the life and times of Joseph-Napoleon Primoli 1851–1927, 1987; Baudelaire, 1994; has contributed to The Times, The Times Literary Supplement, French Studies, French Studies Bulletin, Modern Language Review, Keats-Shelley Memorial Bulletin, etc. *Recreation:* antique-collecting. *Address:* c/o Curtis Brown Group, Haymarket House, 28–29 Haymarket, SW1Y 4SP. *T:* (020) 7396 6600.

RICHARDSON, Joely; actress; *b* 9 Jan. 1965; *d* of late Tony Richardson and of Vanessa Redgrave, *qv*; *m* 1992, Tim Bevan, *qv* (marr. diss.); one *d*. *Educ:* Lycée Française de Londres; St Paul's Girls' Sch.; Pinellas Park High Sch., Florida; Thacher Sch., Calif; RADA. West End début, Steel Magnolias, Lyric, 1989. *Films include:* Wetherby, 1985; Drowning by Numbers, 1988; Shining Through, Rebecca's Daughters, 1992; Sister, My Sister, 1995; Loch Ness, Believe Me, 101 Dalmatians, Hollow Reed, 1996; Event Horizon, 1997; Wrestling with Alligators, Under Heaven, 1998; Maybe Baby, Return to Me, The Patriot, 2000. *television includes:* Body Contact, 1987; Behaving Badly, 1989; Heading Home, 1991; The Storyteller, Lady Chatterley's Lover, 1993; The Tribe, Echo, 1998. *Address:* c/o ICM, Oxford House, 76 Oxford Street, W1N 0AX.
See also N. J. Richardson.

RICHARDSON, John Burke; Ambassador and Head of European Commission Delegation to the United Nations, New York, since 2001; *b* 22 Dec. 1944; *s* of Alan and Mary Richardson; *m* 1969, Irmtraud Hübner; three *d*. *Educ:* Downing Coll., Cambridge (BA Chemistry; MA 1970); University Coll. London (MSc Econs 1969). Economist, Unilever, 1969–73; joined European Commn, 1973: Negotiator for Internat. Trade in Services, 1982–88; Head of Unit: for USA, 1988–92; for Japan, 1992–96; Dep. Hd of Delegn to USA, 1996–2001. Mem. Bd, Salzburg Seminar, 1998–. *Publications:* contrib. on trade in services to learned jls. *Recreations:* gardening, bird watching, Mediterranean life. *Address:* Delegation of the European Commission, 3 Dag Hammarskjöld Plaza, 305 East 47th Street, New York, NY 10017, USA. *Club:* International Château St Anne (Brussels).

RICHARDSON, John Charles; Managing Director, Historical Publications Ltd, since 1975; *b* 7 June 1935; *s* of Joseph and Vera Richardson; *m* 1st, 1957, Laura Caroline Bourne Webb (marr. diss. 1962); two *s*; 2nd, 1967, Elizabeth Noel Ballard (marr. diss. 1981); two *s*; 3rd, 1981, Helen Warnock English. *Educ:* Barking Abbey GS. J. Walter Thompson, 1965–72; KMP, 1974–84. Member: St Pancras BC, 1959–66; Camden BC, 1966–71. Joint Founder: GLAA, 1966; Camden Arts Centre, 1966; Chm., Bubble Theatre Co., 1968–74. Chm., Camden Hist. Soc., 1970–. *Publications:* The Local Historian's Encyclopedia, 1974; Covent Garden, 1979; Highgate: its history since the fifteenth century, 1983; Hampstead One Thousand, 1985; Islington Past, 1986; Highgate Past, 1989; Camden Town and Primrose Hill Past, 1991; London and its People, 1995; Covent Garden Past, 1995; Kentish Town Past, 1997; A History of Camden, 1999; The Annals of London, 2000. *Recreations:* visiting the London Library, architecture. *Address:* 32 Ellington Street, N7 8PL. *T:* (020) 7607 1628.

RICHARDSON, Sir (John) Eric, Kt 1967; CBE 1962; PhD, DSc, BEng, CEng, FIEE, MIMechE, FBHI, FBOA, FPS; FRSA; Director, The Polytechnic of Central London, 1969–70; *b* 30 June 1905; *e surv. s* of late William and Mary Elizabeth Richardson, Birkenhead; *m* 1941, Alice May, *d* of H. M. Wilson, Hull; one *s* two *d* (and one *d* decd). *Educ:* Birkenhead Higher Elementary Sch.; Liverpool Univ. BEng 1st Cl. Hons, 1931, PhD 1933, Liverpool. Chief Lectr in Electrical Engineering, 1933–37, Head of Engineering Dept, 1937–41, Hull Municipal Technical Coll.; Principal: Oldham Municipal Technical Coll., 1942–44; Royal Technical Coll., Salford, 1944–47; Northampton Polytechnic, London, EC1, 1947–56; Dir Nat. Coll. of Horology and Instrument Technology, 1947–56; Dir of Educn, Regent Street Polytechnic, W1, 1957–69. Hon. Sec., Assoc. of Technical Insts, 1957–67, Chm., 1967–68; Pres. Assoc. of Principals of Technical Instns, 1961–62; Dep. Chm., Council for Overseas Colls of Arts, Science and Technology, 1949–62; Member: Council for Tech. Educn and Trng in Overseas Countries, 1962–73 (Chm. Technical Educn Cttee, 1971–73); and Vice-Chm. Council and Cttees, London and Home Counties Regional Adv. Council for Technol Educn, 1972–84; Chm., Adv. Cttee on Educn for Management, 1961–66; Pres. and Chm., CICRIS, 1972–89; Member: Governing Council of Nigerian Coll. of Art, Science and Technology, 1953–61; Council, Univ. Coll., Nairobi, 1961–70; Provisional Council, Univ. of East Africa, 1961–63; Governing Body, College of Aeronautics, Cranfield, 1956–59; Council of British Horological Institute, 1951–56; Gen. Optical Council, 1959–78 (Chm., 1975–78); Assoc. of Optical Practitioners (Vice-Pres., 1983–84; Pres., 1984–95); Science and Technol Cttee of CNAA, 1965–71; Electrical Engrg Bd of CNAA (Chm.); Industrial Trg Bd for Electricity Supply Industry, 1965–71; Univ. and Polytechnic Grants Cttee, Hong Kong, 1972–77; Council, RSA, 1968–78 (Chm. Exams Cttee, 1969–78, Hon. Treasurer, 1974–78); Council and Exec. Cttee, Leprosy Mission, 1970–84 (Chm., 1974–84; Vice-Pres., 1984–98); Council and Exec. Cttee, City and Guilds of London Inst., 1969–80 (Chm. Policy and Overseas Cttees; Vice-Chm. Technical Educn Cttee; Jt Hon. Sec., 1970–80; Vice-Pres., 1979–82; Hon. FCGI 1981); Chm., Ealing Civic Soc., 1972–76. Chairman: Africa Evangelical Fellowship (SAGM), 1950–70; Nat. Young Life Campaign, 1949–64; Council, Inter-Varsity Fellowship of Evangelical Unions, 1966–69; Pres., Crusaders Union, 1972–86. Chm. Governors, Clarendon Sch., Abergele, 1971–75; Governor, London Bible Coll., 1968– (Chm., 1970–77; Pres., 1978–90). *Publications:* paper in IEE Jl (Instn Prize); various papers on higher technological education in UK and Nigeria. *Recreations:* gardening, photography. *Address:* 1 Westcombe Terrace, Plymstock, Plymouth PL9 9QQ. *T:* (01752) 406881.

RICHARDSON, John Francis; Director and Chief Executive, National & Provincial Building Society, 1985–86; *b* 16 June 1934; *s* of Francis and Stella Richardson; *m* 1960, Jacqueline Mary Crosby; two *d*. *Educ:* Wadham College, Oxford (PPE). FCBSI. Burnley Building Society, 1959–82; Chief General Manager, 1980–82; Dep. Chief Executive, National & Provincial Building Society, 1983–85. Pres., CBSI, 1985. *Recreations:* golf, gardening, military history. *Address:* Low Gables, Spofforth Hill, Wetherby, West Yorks LS22 4SF.

RICHARDSON, Rt Rev. John Henry; *see* Bedford, Bishop Suffragan of.

RICHARDSON, John Patrick; writer; *b* 6 Feb. 1924; *s* of Sir Wodehouse Richardson, KCB, DSO and Clara Pattie (*née* Crocker). *Educ:* Stowe; Slade Sch. of Art. US Rep., Christie's, 1964–72; Vice-Pres., M. Knoedler & Co., NYC, 1972–76; Man. Dir, Artemis Gp, London and New York, 1976–78; Editor-at-large, House and Garden (US), 1981–91; Contributing Ed., Vanity Fair, 1990–94. Slade Prof. of Art History, Oxford, 1995–96. Corresp. FBA 1993. Whitbread Book of Year Award, 1991; La Vanguardia Book of Year Award, Barcelona, 1997. *Publications:* Picasso: watercolors and gouaches, 1956; Manet, 1958; Braque, 1959; A Life of Picasso, Vol. I, 1991, Vol. II, 1996; The Sorcerer's Apprentice: Picasso, Provence, and Douglas Cooper, 1999; contrib. to TLS, Burlington Mag., New York Rev. of Books, New Yorker, etc. *Address:* 73 Fifth Avenue, New York City, NY 10003, USA; 263 West Meeting House Road, New Milford, CT 06776, USA.

RICHARDSON, Very Rev. John Stephen; Vicar of Wye and Brook with Hastingleigh, and Chaplain, Wye Agricultural College, since 2001; *b* 2 April 1950; *s* of James Geoffrey and Myra Richardson; *m* 1972, Elizabeth Susan Wiltshire; one *s* two *d* (and one *s* decd). *Educ:* Haslingden Grammar Sch.; Univ. of Southampton (BA Hons Theology); St John's Theological Coll., Nottingham. Deacon 1974, priest 1975; Asst Curate, St Michael's, Bramcote, 1974–77; Priest-in-Charge, Emmanuel Church, Radipole and Melcombe Regis, 1977–80; Asst Diocesan Missioner and Lay Trainer Adviser, dio. of Salisbury and Priest-in-Charge of Stinsford, Winterborne Monkton and Winterborne Came with Witcombe, 1980–83; Vicar of Christ Church, Nailsea, 1983–90; Adviser in Evangelism, dio. of Bath and Wells, 1985–90; Provost, subseq. Dean, of Bradford, 1990–2001. Dir, Spring Harvest, 1998–. Chaplain, W Yorks Police, 1995–2001. Bishop's Selector, ABM, 1993–97. Mem., General Synod, 1993–2001. Member: Exec. Bd, Common Purpose, 1992–2000; BBC North Adv. Panel, 1990–94; Bradford Breakthrough, 1992–2001; Council, Evangelical Alliance Management Gp, 1994–; Council, Scripture Union, 2000–. Mem. Council, Bradford Chamber of Commerce, 1992–2001. Trustee: Acorn Healing Trust, 1990– (Vice Chm.); Spennithorne Hall, 1990–98. Council Mem., St John's Theological Coll., Nottingham, 1988–94; Governor: Bradford Grammar Sch., 1990–2001; Giggleswick Sch., 1993–; Bradford Cathedral Community Coll. (formerly Fairfax Sch., then Bowling Community Coll.), 1994–2001. Chaplain to High Sheriff, W Yorks, 1994–95, 2000–2001. MInstD 1994. *Publication:* Ten Rural Churches, 1988. *Recreations:* football, cricket, North Western Municipal Bus Operators, walking, writing, broadcasting. *Address:* The Vicarage, Cherry Garden Crescent, Wye, Ashford, Kent TN25 5AS. *Clubs:* Athenæum; Bradford (Bradford).

RICHARDSON, Kenneth Augustus, CVO 1994; CBE 1989; JP; Secretary to the Cabinet, Bermuda, 1984–93; *b* 13 Feb. 1939; *s* of Augustus J. Richardson; *m* 1966, Brenda Joyce (*née* Smith); one *s* one *d*. *Educ:* Howard Univ., Washington DC (BSc); Manchester Polytechnic (Dip. Personnel Admin and Labour Relations). Teacher, Sandys Secondary School, Bermuda, 1964; Admin. Cadet, Colonial Sec.'s Office, 1967; Training and Recruitment Officer, Bermuda Govt, 1969; Perm. Sec., Labour and Home Affairs, 1974. MIPM 1973; MInstD 1988. JP 1984. *Recreations:* sport (soccer, tennis). *Address:* Mahogany, 19 Trimingham Hill, Paget, Bermuda; PO Box HM 1703, Hamilton HM GX, Bermuda. *T:* 236 1788.

RICHARDSON, Margaret Ann, FSA; Curator, Sir John Soane's Museum, since 1995 (Assistant Curator, 1985–95); *b* 11 Sept. 1937; *d* of late James Ballard and Edna (*née* Johnstone); *m* 1963, Anthony George Richardson; two *d*. *Educ:* Harrogate Coll.; University Coll. London (BA Hons; Fellow, 2001); Courtauld Inst. of Art (Acad. Dip.). FSA 1996. Asst Curator, 1963–68, Jt Dep. Curator, 1972–85, Drawings Collection, British Architectural Liby. Pres., Twentieth Century Soc., 1995– (Mem. Cttee, 1984–); Trustee: Save Britain's Heritage, 1975–; Lutyens Trust, 1984– (Chm., 1994–2001); Greenwich Foundn for RNC, 1997–. Hon. FRIBA 1994. *Publications:* (ed) RIBA Catalogue series, vols A, B, C–F, and S, 1969–76; Edwin Lutyens, 1973; Lutyens and the Sea Captain, 1981; (jtly) Great Drawings from the RIBA, 1983; Architects of the Arts and Crafts Movement, 1983; 66 Portland Place: the London headquarters of the RIBA, 1984; (jtly) The Art of the Architect, 1984; Sketches by Lutyens, 1994; (ed jtly) John Soane Architect: master of space and light, 1999. *Address:* Sir John Soane's Museum, 13 Lincoln's Inn Fields, WC2A 3BP. *T:* (020) 7405 2107.
See also J. G. Ballard.

RICHARDSON, Michael Elliot; Director of Continuing Education and Secretary, Board of Continuing Education, University of Cambridge, and Fellow of Wolfson

College, Cambridge, since 1990; *b* 29 Sept. 1938; *s* of late Rev. Emery Lonsdale Richardson and Margaret Ann Richardson (*née* Elliot); *m* 1968, Gillian Miles Jones; two *d*. *Educ:* Pocklington Sch., York; St John's Coll., Cambridge (MA 1967); Lincoln Theol Coll.; Univ. of Nottingham (DipAdEd 1970). FCIPD. Schoolmaster, Middlesborough Boys' High Sch., 1964–65; Adult Educn Tutor, Ibstock Community Coll., 1965–67; Principal, Alfreton Hall Adult Educn Centre, 1967–69; Open University, 1969–90: Dep. Regl Dir, Northern, 1969–76; Regl Dir, NW, 1976–79; Dir, Educnl Services for Cont. Educn, 1979–81; Pro-Dir, 1981–84, Dir, 1984–86, Centre for Cont. Educn; Pro-Vice Chancellor, Cont. Educn, 1985–90. Chm., Council for Educn and Training of Youth and Community Workers, 1985–90; Sec., UACE, 1998– (Mem. Council, 1990–); Mem. Council, CRAC, 1990–98; Mem., numerous cttees and boards, 1980–. Trustee, Nat. Extension Coll., 1988–. DUniv Open 1994. FRSA. *Publications:* Preparing to Study, 1979; Continuing Education for the Post Industrial Society, 1982; contribs to educn jls. *Recreations:* gardening, angling, walking. *Address:* University of Cambridge Board of Continuing Education, Madingley Hall, Madingley, Cambridge CB3 8AQ. *T:* (01954) 280204.

RICHARDSON, Michael John; Under Secretary, Director for Employment Policy, Department for Education and Skills (formerly Department for Education and Employment), since 1998; *b* 17 March 1946; *s* of Philip George Richardson and Susan Rowena (*née* Pearce); *m* 1967, Celia, *d* of Rev. Canon Peter and Daphne Bradshaw; one *s* one *d*. *Educ:* Eton Coll.; St Edmund Hall, Oxford (BA Lit.Hum. 1968). Joined HM Diplomatic Service, 1968; Hong Kong, 1969–71; 3rd, later 2nd Sec., Peking, 1972–74; 1st Secretary: FCO, 1974–75; EEC, 1976; Western European Dept, FCO, 1977–78; Private Secretary to: Minister of State, 1978–79; Lord Privy Seal, 1979–80; 1st Sec., Rome, 1980–85; Asst Head, EC Dept, 1985; Head, EC Presidency Unit, FCO, 1986–87; Dept for Educn, later DFEE, then DFES, 1987–, Under Sec., 1992–. Dep. Chm., London & Quadrant Housing Assoc., 2000–. *Recreations:* family, reading, gardening, theatre-going. *Address:* 12 Northumberland Place, W2 5BS.

RICHARDSON, Sir Michael (John de Rougemont), Kt 1990; Chairman, Invesco English & International Trust, since 1961; *b* 9 April 1925; *s* of Arthur Wray Richardson and Audrey de Rougemont; *m* 1949, Octavia Mayhew (*d* 1999); one *s* two *d*. *Educ:* Harrow; Kent Sch., Conn, USA. Captain, Irish Guards, 1943–49. Drayton Gp, 1949–52; Partner: Panmure Gordon & Co., 1952–71; Cazenove & Co., 1971–81; Man. Dir, 1981–90, Vice Chm., 1990–94, N. M. Rothschild & Sons Ltd; Chm., 1990–94, Consultant, 1995–96, Smith New Court plc; Vice-Chairman: J. O. Hambro Magan & Co., 1995–96; NatWest Market Corp. Advy, then Hawkpoint Partners, 1996–99. *Recreations:* fox hunting, sailing. *Clubs:* Cavalry and Guards; Island Sailing, Bembridge Sailing (IoW).

RICHARDSON, Miranda; actress; *b* 3 March 1958; *d* of William Alan Richardson and Marian Georgina Townsend. *Educ:* St Wyburn, Southport, Merseyside; Southport High Sch. for Girls; Bristol Old Vic Theatre Sch. Repertory: Manchester Library Theatre, 1979–80; Derby Playhouse, Duke's Playhouse, Lancaster, Bristol Old Vic and Leicester Haymarket, 1982–83; West End début, Moving, Queen's, 1980–81; Royal Court: Edmund, 1985; A Lie of the Mind, 1987; Etta Jenks, 1990; National Theatre: The Changeling, and Mountain Language, 1988; The Designated Mourner, 1996; Orlando, Edinburgh Fest., 1996; Aunt Dan and Lemon, Almeida, 1999. *Television:* series include: Agony; Sorrell and Son; Blackadder II and III; Die Kinder, 1990; The True Adventures of Christopher Columbus, 1992; A Dance to the Music of Time, 1998; plays include: The Master Builder; The Demon Lover; After Pilkington; Sweet as You Are (RTS Award, 1987–88); Ball-trap on the Côte Sauvage, 1989; Old Times, 1991; Merlin, 1998; Alice in Wonderland, 2000; *films:* Dance with a Stranger (role, Ruth Ellis) (City Limits Best Film Actress, 1985; Evening Standard Best Actress, 1985; Variety Club Most Promising Artiste, 1985); Underworld; Death of the Heart; Empire of the Sun; The Mad Monkey; Eat the Rich; Redemption, 1991; Enchanted April, 1992 (Golden Globe Award, Best Comedy Actress, 1993); Mr Wakefield's Crusade, The Bachelor, 1992; Damage (BAFTA Award, Best Supporting Actress, 1993; NY Critics Circle Award; Film Critics Circle, Best Actress 1994; Royal Variety Club of GB, Best Film Actress of 1994); The Crying Game, 1992; Century, 1993; Tom and Viv (Best Actress, Nat. Bd of Review of Motion Pictures), 1994; La Nuit et Le Moment, 1994; Kansas City, 1996; Evening Star, 1996; Swann, 1997; Designated Mourner, 1998; Apostle, 1998; All For Love, 1998; Jacob Two Two and the Hooded Fang, 1998; The Big Brass Ring, 1998; Sleepy Hollow, 2000; Chicken Run (voice), 2000; Snow White, 2000; The Hours, 2001; Spider, 2001. *Recreations:* reading, walking, softball, gardening, music, junkshops, occasional art, animals. *Address:* c/o ICM, 76 Oxford Street, W1N 0AX.

RICHARDSON, Natasha Jane; actress; *b* 11 May 1963; *d* of late Tony Richardson and of Vanessa Redgrave, *qv*; *m* 1st, 1990, Robert Fox, *qv* (marr. diss. 1994); 2nd, 1994, Liam Neeson; two *s*. *Educ:* Lycée Française de Londres; St Paul's Girls' Sch.; Central Sch. of Speech and Drama. Season at Leeds Playhouse; A Midsummer Night's Dream, New Shakespeare Co.; Ophelia in Hamlet, Young Vic; The Seagull, Lyric Hammersmith, tour and Queen's, 1985; China, Bush Th., 1986; High Society, Leicester Haymarket and Victoria Palace, 1986; Anna Christie, Young Vic, 1990, NY, 1992 (Outer Critics Circle Award, 1993); Cabaret, NY (Tony Award), 1998; Closer, NY, 1999. *Films:* Every Picture Tells a Story, 1985; Gothic, 1987; A Month in the Country, 1987; Patty Hearst, 1988; Fat Man and Little Boy, 1989; The Handmaid's Tale, 1990; The Comfort of Strangers, 1990; The Favour, the Watch and the Very Big Fish, 1992; Past Midnight; Widows Peak, 1994 (Best Actress, Prague Film Fest., 1994); Nell, 1994; The Parent Trap, 1998; Waking up in Reno, 2000; Blow Dry, 2001. *Television:* In a Secret State, 1985; Ghosts, 1986; Hostages, 1992; Suddenly Last Summer, 1993; Zelda, 1993; Tales from the Crypt, 1996; Haven (series), 2000. Most Promising Newcomer Award, Plays and Players, 1986; Best Actress: Evening Standard Film Awards, 1990; London Theatre Critics, 1990; Plays and Players, 1990.

RICHARDSON, Nigel Peter Vincent; Headmaster, The Perse School, Cambridge, since 1994; *b* 29 June 1948; *s* of Vincent Boys Richardson and Jean Frances (*née* Wrangles); *m* 1979, (Averon) Joy James; two *s*. *Educ:* Highgate Sch.; Trinity Hall, Cambridge (MA Hist.); Bristol Univ. (PGCE). Uppingham School: Hist. Dept, 1971–89; Sixth Form Tutor, 1977–83; Second Master, 1983–89; Headmaster, Dragon Sch., Oxford, 1989–92; Dep. Headmaster and Dir of Studies, King's Sch., Macclesfield, 1992–94. Course Dir, Summer Lang. Sch., Sweden and Bell Sch., Cambridge, 1972–82. BBC Radio 4: jt question compiler, Top of the Form, 1982–87; contrib., Thought for the Day, 1982–. Governor: Greycotes Sch., Oxford, 1989–92; King's Coll. Sch., Cambridge, 1998–. Ed., Conference and Common Room, 1999–. *Publications:* The Effective Use of Time, 1984, 2nd edn 1989; First Steps in Leadership, 1987; various histories and biographies for school use; contrib. TES, The Times, etc. *Recreations:* music, writing, sport, gardening, travel. *Address:* The Perse School, Hills Road, Cambridge CB2 2QF. *T:* (01223) 568300.

RICHARDSON, Rt Rev. Paul; Assistant Bishop of Newcastle, since 1998; *b* 16 Jan. 1947; *s* of William and Ilene Richardson. *Educ:* Keswick Sch.; The Queen's Coll., Oxford (BA (Mod. History) 1968, (Theol.) 1970; MA 1975); Harvard Divinity Sch.; Cuddesdon Theol Coll. Ordained deacon, 1972, priest, 1973; Asst Curate, St John's, Earlsfield, 1972–75; Asst Chaplain, Oslo, Norway, 1975–77; Mission Priest, Nambaiyufa, PNG, 1977–79; Lectr, 1979–81, Principal, 1981–85, Newton Theol Coll.; Dean, St John's Cathedral, Port Moresby, 1985–86; Bishop of Aipo Rongo, PNG, 1987–95; Bishop of Wangaratta, 1995–97. *Recreations:* reading, walking, travel. *Address:* Close House, St George's Close, Jesmond, Newcastle upon Tyne NE2 2TF. *T:* (0191) 281 2556. *Club:* Melbourne.

RICHARDSON, Prof. Peter Damian, FRS 1986; Professor of Engineering and Physiology, Brown University, USA, since 1984; *b* West Wickham, Kent, 22 Aug. 1935; *s* of late Reginald William Merrells Richardson and Marie Stuart Naomi (*née* Ouseley). *Educ:* Imperial College, Univ. of London (BSc (Eng) 1955; PhD 1958; DSc (Eng) 1974; ACGI 1955; DIC 1958; DSc 1983); MA Brown Univ. 1965. Demonstrator, Imperial Coll., 1955–58; Brown University: Vis. Lectr, 1958–59; Research Associate, 1959–60; Asst Prof. of Engrg, 1960–65; Associate Prof. of Engrg, 1965–68; Prof. of Engrg, 1968–84; Chair, University Faculty, 1987– (Vice-Chair, 1986–87). Sen. Vis. Fellow, Univ. of London, 1967; Prof. d'échange, Univ. of Paris, 1968; leave at Orta Doğu Teknik Univ., Ankara, 1969. FASME 1983. Humboldt-Preis, A. von Humboldt Sen. Scientist Award, 1976; Laureate in Medicine, Ernst Jung Foundn, 1987. *Publications:* (with M. Steiner) Principles of Cell Adhesion, 1995; numerous articles in learned jls. *Recreations:* photography, travel, country life. *Address:* Box D, Brown University, Providence, Rhode Island 02912, USA. *T:* (401) 8632687.

RICHARDSON, Prof. Robert Coleman, PhD; Professor of Physics, Cornell University, since 1975; *b* 26 June 1937; *s* of Robert Franklin Richardson and Lois Richardson (*née* Price); *m* 1962, Betty Marilyn McCarthy; two *d*. *Educ:* Virginia Poly. Inst. and State Univ.; Duke Univ. Served US Army, 1959–60. Cornell University: Res. Associate, 1966–67; Asst Prof., 1968–71; Associate Prof., 1972–74. Chm., C-5 Cttee, IUPAP, 1981–84; Mem., Bd of Assessment, Nat. Bureau of Standards, 1983–. FAAAS. (Jtly) Nobel Prize for Physics, 1996. *Publications:* (jtly) Discovering Complexity: decomposition and localization as strategies in scientific research, 1993; (jtly) Experimental Techniques in Condensed Matter Physics at Low Temperatures, 1998; articles in learned jls. *Address:* Department of Physics, Cornell University, Clark Hall, Ithaca, NY 14853, USA.

RICHARDSON, Lt-Gen. Sir Robert (Francis), KCB 1982; CVO 1978; CBE 1975 (OBE 1971; MBE 1965); Lieutenant of the Tower of London, 1992–95; Administrator, MacRobert Trusts, 1985–95; *b* 2 March 1929; *s* of late Robert Buchan Richardson and Anne (*née* Smith); *m* 1st, 1956, Maureen Anne Robinson (*d* 1986); three *s* one *d*; 2nd, 1988, Alexandra Inglis (*née* Bomford); two step *s*. *Educ:* George Heriot's Sch., Edinburgh; RMA Sandhurst. Commnd into The Royal Scots, 1949; served in BAOR, Korea, and Middle East with 1st Bn The Royal Scots until 1960; Defence Services Staff Coll., India, 1960–61; psc 1961; GSO II MO4, MoD, 1961–64; jssc 1964; Brigade Major Aden Bde, 1967 (Despatches); GSO II ACDS (Ops), MoD, 1968–69; CO 1st Bn The Royal Scots, 1969–71; Col Gen. Staff, Staff Coll. Camberley, 1971–74; Comdr 39 Infantry Bde, Northern Ireland, 1974–75; Deputy Adjutant General, HQ BAOR, 1975–78; GOC Berlin (British Sector), 1978–80; Vice Adjutant Gen. and Dir of Army Manning, 1980–82; GOC NI, 1982–85. Col, The Royal Scots (The Royal Regt), 1980–90. Chm., Greencastle Farming plc, 1995–. Man. Trustee, BLESMA, 1995–. *Recreations:* golf, shooting, gardening. *Address:* c/o Bank of Scotland, London Chief Office, 38 Threadneedle Street, EC2P 2EH. *Clubs:* Royal Scots (Trustee, 1995–) (Edinburgh); Hon. Co. of Edinburgh Golfers (Muirfield).

RICHARDSON, Hon. Ruth Margaret; consultant; Ruth Richardson (NZ) Ltd, strategic and economic policy advice, since 1994; *b* 13 Dec. 1950; *d* of Ross Pearce Richardson and Rita Joan Richardson; *m* 1975, Andrew Evan Wright; one *s* one *d*. *Educ:* Canterbury Univ., NZ (LLB Hons 1971). Admitted to the Bar, 1973; Legal Adviser: Law Reform Div., Dept of Justice, 1972–75; Federated Farmers of NZ, 1975–80. MP (Nat. Party) Selwyn, NZ, 1981–94; Opposition spokesman: on Education and on Youth Issues, 1984–87; on Finance, 1987–90; Minister of Finance, 1990–93. Dir, Reserve Bank of NZ, 1999–. *Recreations:* running, swimming, gardening. *Address:* RD5, Christchurch, New Zealand. *T:* (3) 3479146.

RICHARDSON, Prof. Sam Scruton, AO 1980; CBE 1965 (OBE 1960); Commissioner for Law Revision, Northern States of Nigeria, since 1987; Foundation Principal, Canberra College of Advanced Education (subsequently University of Canberra), 1969–84, Emeritus Fellow, 1984–90, Emeritus Professor, since 1990; *b* 31 Dec. 1919; *s* of Samuel and Gladys Richardson; Australian citizen, 1975; *m* 1949, Sylvia May McNeil (*d* 2000); two *s* one *d*. *Educ:* Magnus Sch., Newark-on-Trent; Trinity Coll., Oxford (State Scholar, 1937; BA PPE, 1940; MA 1946); Sch. of Oriental and African Studies, Univ. of London. Called to the Bar, Lincoln's Inn, 1958. Served War, 1940–46: commnd Royal Marines; Commando Bdes, Europe and Far East (despatches); demob., Major, 1946. Dist Comr, Sudan Polit. Service, 1946–54 (served in Kordofan and Darfur, 1946–53; Resident, Dar Masalit, 1953–54); HMOCS, Nigeria, 1954–67: Dist Comr, Bornu Prov., 1954–58; Comr for Local Courts in Attorney Gen.'s Chambers, N Nigeria, 1958–60; Dir, Inst. of Admin, Zaria, 1960–67; Dep. Vice-Chancellor, Ahmadu Bello Univ., Nigeria, 1962–67; Prof. of Public Admin, 1967–68, and Acting Vice-Chancellor, 1968, Univ. of Mauritius; occasional Lectr in Islamic Law, ANU, 1971–82; Vis. Prof., Ahmadu Bello Univ., Nigeria, 1986. Consultant: Aust. Law Reform Commn, 1980–; Museum of Australia, 1985–. Chm., Aust. Conf. of Principals, 1979–80; Pres., Internat. Assoc. of Schs and Insts of Admin, 1982–89; Member: Council, Inst. of Admin, Papua New Guinea, 1970–84; Immigration Adv. Council, 1971–74; Nat. Standing Control Cttee on Drugs of Dependence, 1974–84; Australian Council on Overseas Prof. Qualifications, 1975–; Adv. Council, Aust. Jt Services Staff Coll., 1977–84; Academic Adv. Council, RAN Coll., Jervis Bay, 1978–; Council, ANU, 1981–84; Exec. Cttee, Internat. Inst. of Admin. Scis, 1982–90. Mem., Bd of Management, Aust. Inst. of Sport, 1980–84. Governor, Portsmouth Polytechnic, 1989–92 (Hon. Fellow, 1984). Nat. Pres., Australia Britain Soc., 1980–84; Vice-Pres., Britain Australia Soc., 1984–. Freeman, City of London, 1989–. Hon. Fellow, Univ. of Portsmouth, 1993. Hon. LLD Ahmadu Bello, 1967; Hon. Dr Canberra, 1990. *Publications:* Notes on the Penal Code of N Nigeria, 1959, 4th edn 1987; (with T. H. Williams) The Criminal Procedure Code of N Nigeria, 1963; (with E. A. Keay) The Native and Customary Courts of Nigeria, 1965; Parity of Esteem—the Canberra College of Advanced Education 1968–78, 1979; A Saga 1961–1991: the history of International Association of Schools and Institutes of Administration, 1992; Royal Marines and Hong Kong 1840–1997, 1997; No Weariness: the personal memoir of a generalist administrator in public life, 2001; book revs in Canberra Times, 1970–; articles on public admin, customary law and higher educn in learned jls. *Recreations:* travel, reading, community service. *Address:* The Malt House, Wylye, Warminster, Wilts BA12 0QP. *T:* (01985) 248348. *Clubs:* Oxford and Cambridge; University House (ANU, Canberra).

RICHARDSON, Sir Simon Alaisdair S.; *see* Stewart-Richardson.

RICHARDSON, Stephen John; Chief Executive, Banking, Robert Fleming & Co., since 1999; *b* 18 Jan. 1953; *m* 1978, Heather Mary Boor; one *s* one *d*. *Educ:* Imperial Coll., London (BSc Mech. Engrg). FCIB 1990. Barclays Bank plc, 1974–96: Dir, UK Personal Sector, 1989–93; Man. Dir, Barclaycall, 1993–95; Man. Dir, Save & Prosper Gp, 1996–98. Non-executive Director: FOCUS Central London Ltd, 1998–; Proshare (UK) Ltd, 1999–. *Recreations:* sport, music. *Address:* (office) 25 Copthall Avenue, EC2R 7DR.

RICHARDSON, Maj.-Gen. Thomas Anthony, (Tony), CB 1976; MBE 1960; Secretary, Christmas Tree Growers Association of Western Europe, since 1989; *b* 9 Aug. 1922; *s* of late Maj.-Gen. T. W. Richardson, Eaton Cottage, Unthank Road, Norwich, and late Mrs J. H. Boothby, Camberley; *m* 1st, 1945, Katharine Joanna Ruxton Roberts (*d* 1988), Woodland Place, Bath; one *s* one *d*; 2nd, 1991, Anthea Rachel Fry, Wimbledon. *Educ:* Wellington Coll., Berks. Technical Staff Course, psc, Fixed Wing Pilot, Rotary Wing Pilot, Parachutist. War of 1939–45: enlisted, Feb. 1941; commissioned, RA, March 1942; Essex Yeomanry (France and Germany), 1942–45; Air Observation Post, 1945–46. Tech. Staff/G Staff, 1949–52, 1954–55, 1959–60, 1963–64; Regt duty, 1942–45, 1952–54, 1957–58, 1961–62. Instr, Mil. Coll. Science, 1955–56; CO, 7th Para, RHA, 1965–67; CRA, 2 Div., 1967–69; Dir, Operational Requirements (Army), 1969–71; Dir, Army Aviation, 1971–74; Defence and Military Advr, India, 1974–77. Col Comdt, RA, 1978–83. Asst Sec., 1978–80, Sec. 1980–84, Timber Growers England and Wales Ltd; Sec., British Christmas Tree Growers Assoc., 1980–98; Dep. Chm., 1984–86, Chm., 1986–88, Tree Council. Chm., Queen Mary's Roehampton Trust, 2001–. Pres., Essex Yeomanry Assoc., 1982–. *Recreations:* sailing, skiing, fishing, shooting. *Address:* 12 Lauriston Road, Wimbledon, SW19 4TQ. *Club:* Army and Navy.

RICHARDSON, Sir Thomas (Legh), KCMG 2000 (CMG 1991); HM Diplomatic Service; Ambassador to Italy, 1996–2000; *b* 6 Feb. 1941; *s* of Arthur Legh Turnour Richardson and Penelope Margaret Richardson; *m* 1979, Alexandra Frazier Wasiqullah (*née* Ratcliff). *Educ:* Westminster Sch.; Christ Church, Oxford. MA (Hist.). Joined Foreign Office, 1962; seconded to Univ. of Ghana, 1962–63; FO, 1963–65; Third Sec., Dar-Es-Salaam, 1965–66; Vice-Consul (Commercial), Milan, 1967–70; seconded to N. M. Rothschild & Sons, 1970; FCO, 1971–74; First Sec., UK Mission to UN, 1974–78; FCO, 1978–80; seconded to Central Policy Review Staff, Cabinet Office, 1980–81; Head of Chancery, Rome, 1982–86; Head of Economic Relns Dept, FCO, 1986–89; UK Dep. Perm. Rep. to UN, with personal rank of Ambassador, 1989–94; Asst Under-Sec. of State (Western Europe), FCO, 1994–96. *Recreations:* reading, walking, travel, music.

RICHARDSON, Maj.-Gen. Tony; *see* Richardson, Maj.-Gen. Thomas A.

RICHARDSON-BUNBURY, Sir (Richard David) Michael; *see* Bunbury.

RICHBOROUGH, Bishop Suffragan of, from March 2002; **Rt Rev. Keith Newton;** Provincial Episcopal Visitor, Canterbury, from March 2002; *b* 10 April 1952; *s* of James Henry and Eva Newton; *m* 1973, Gillian Irene Newton (*née* Donnison); two *s* one *d*. *Educ:* Alsop High Sch., Liverpool; KCL (BD, AKC 1973); Christchurch Coll., Canterbury (PGCE 1975); St Augustine's Coll., Canterbury. Ordained deacon, 1975, priest, 1976; Curate, St Mary's, Gt Ilford, 1975–78; Vicar, i/c St Matthews, Wimbledon Team Ministry, 1978–85; Rector, St Paul's, Blantyre, Dio. Southern Malaŵi, 1985–86; Dean of Blantyre, 1986–91; Priest i/c, 1991–93, Vicar, 1993–2002, Holy Nativity, Knowle; Priest i/c, All Hallows, Easton, 1997–2002. RD, Brislington, 1995–99; Area Dean, Bristol S, 1999–2001. Hon. Canon: Southern Malaŵi, 1986–; Bristol Cathedral, 2000–. *Recreation:* travel. *Address:* c/o Faith House, 7 Tufton Street, Westminster, SW1P 3QN.

RICHER, Julian; Founder and Chairman: Richer Sounds plc, since 1978; Richer Partnership, since 1997; *b* 9 March 1959; *s* of Percy Isaac Richer and Ursula Marion (*née* Haller); *m* 1982, Rosemary Louise Hamlet. *Educ:* Clifton Coll., Bristol. Salesman, Hi-Fi Markets Ltd, 1977; Founder and Chairman: JR Properties, 1989–; Audio Partnership plc, 1994–; Richer Sounds Internat. Ltd, 1995–; Richer Sounds Holland, 1997–; JR Publishing, 1998–; Lomo Ltd, 1998–; Richer Jet Ltd, 1999–; Marks Ltd, 2000–; Definitely Marketing Ltd, 2000–; Chairman: Home Ltd, 1999–; Grey Frog plc, 2000–; Director: Ducky Originals Ltd, 1998–. Urban Spaces Ltd, 1999–; Poptones plc, 2000–; WILink.com plc, 2000–; CANHELPNOW Ltd, 2000–. Dire and Mem. Exec. Cttee, League Against Cruel Sports, 2000–; Dir, Whizz-Kidz 10th Birthday Bd, 2000–. Founder and Chm., Persula Foundn, 1994–; Ambassador for Youth, 1998–; Chm., Gold Service Panel, Irwell Valley Housing Assoc., 1998–; Patron, Big Issue, 1999–; Ambassador, Centrepoint, 2000–. Special advr, Freedom Food, 1998–. *Publications:* The Richer Way, 1995, rev. edn 2001; Richer on Leadership, 1999. *Recreations:* radio controlled models, drumming, reading, walking, travel. *Address:* c/o Richer Sounds plc, Richer House, Hankey Place, SE1 4BB. *T:* (020) 7403 1310.

RICHES, Anne Clare, (Mrs T. C. Coltman), OBE 1999; FSA; free-lance architectural historian, since 1989; *b* 12 April 1943; *d* of late Rt Rev. Kenneth Riches and of Kathleen Mary Riches (*née* Dixon); *m* 1989, Timothy Charles Coltman. *Educ:* Headington Sch., Oxford; Edinburgh Univ. (MA 1965; Dip. Hist of Art 1966). FSA 1985. Historian, Historic Bldgs Div., GLC, 1966–78; Inspector, then Principal Inspector, Historic Bldgs and Monuments Directorate, Scottish Develt Dept, 1978–89. Society of Architectural Historians of Great Britain: Sec., 1978–83; Conf. Sec., 1978–85; Chm., 1985–88. Member: Adv. Panel, Railway Heritage Trust, 1985–; Nat. Cttee, Assoc. of Preservation Trusts, 1989–95; RCHME, 1991–99; Royal Commn on Ancient and Historical Monuments of Scotland, 1995–; Council for Care of Churches, 2001–. Trustee: Scottish Historic Bldgs Trust, 1989–; Theatres Trust, 1996–; Heritage Trust for Lincolnshire: Dir, 1990–; Chm., Archaeol. Adv. Cttee, 1991–94; Chm., Bldgs Adv. Cttee, 1992–. *Publications:* (with R. Barber) A Dictionary of Fabulous Beasts, 1972; Victorian Church Building and Restoration in Suffolk, 1982; (jtly) Building of Scotland: Glasgow, 1990; contrib. Architectl Hist. *Recreations:* gardening, hill-farming, visiting buildings. *Address:* Skellingthorpe Hall, Lincoln LN6 5UU. *T:* (01522) 694609.

RICHINGS, Lewis David George; *b* 22 April 1920; *s* of Lewis Vincent Richings and Jessie Helen (*née* Clements); *m* 1944, Margaret Alice Hume; three *d*. *Educ:* Battersea Grammar Sch.; Devonport High Sch.; Darlington Grammar Sch.; London Sch. of Econs and Polit. Science (part-time). Served War, Army, 1939–46: commnd 2 Lieut Inf., 1940; attached 8 DLI, 1940–41; seconded 11 KAR, 1941–45; Actg Major, 1945; various postings, UK, 1945–46. MAFF, 1937–58; attached MoD, 1958; Gen. Administrator, AWRE, 1958–65; Health and Safety Br., UKAEA, 1965–70; Sec., Nat. Radiol Protection Bd, 1970–79, Dep. Dir, 1978–80. Mem., Radiol Protection and Public Health Cttee, Nuclear Energy Agency, OECD, 1966–80 (Chm., 1972–74). FRSA. *Publications:* articles in press and jls on admin and technical matters relating to common land, rural electrification, earthquakes, and radiol protection. *Recreation:* boats. *Address:* 31 Kennedy Street, Blairgowrie, Vic 3942, Australia; 26 Three Acre Road, Newbury, Berks RG14 7AW.

RICHMAN, Stella; television producer; *b* 9 Nov. 1922; *d* of Jacob Richman and Leoni Richman; *m* 1st, Alec Clunes; 2nd, 1953, Victor Brusa (*d* 1965); one *s* one *d*. *Educ:* Clapton County Secondary Sch. for Girls. Started TV career at ATV, running Script Dept 1960; created and produced Love Story, 1963; joined Rediffusion, 1964; Exec. Head of Series (prod The Informer); Exec. Prod., award-winning Man of Our Times, Half Hour Story and Blackmail; prod first 6 plays, Company of Five, for newly formed London Weekend Television, 1968; Man. Dir, London Weekend Internat., 1969, and Controller of Programmes, London Weekend Television, 1970–71 (first woman to sit on bd of a television co.); in partnership with David Frost formed Stella Richman Productions (first independent TVco.), 1972–78: resp. for Miss Nightingale, Jennie, Clayhanger, Bill Brand, Just William. Chm. and owner, White Elephant Club, 1960–88. FRTS 1982. *Publications:* The White Elephant Cook Books, 1973, 1979. *Recreations:* travel, reading biographies, theatre. *Address:* Garden Flat, 5 Hill Road, NW8 9QE.

RICHMOND, 10th Duke of, *cr* 1675, **LENNOX,** 10th Duke of, *cr* 1675 (Scot.), **AND GORDON,** 5th Duke of, *cr* 1876; **Charles Henry Gordon-Lennox;** Baron Settrington, Earl of March, 1675; Lord of Torboulton, Earl of Darnley (Scot.), 1675; Earl of Kinrara, 1876; Duc d'Aubigny (France), 1684; Hereditary Constable of Inverness Castle; Lord-Lieutenant of West Sussex, 1990–94; *b* 19 Sept. 1929; *s* of 9th Duke of Richmond and Gordon, and Elizabeth Grace (*d* 1992), *y d* of late Rev. T. W. Hudson; *S* father, 1989; *m* 1951, Susan Monica, *o d* of late Colonel C. E. Grenville-Grey, CBE, Hall Barn, Blewbury, Berks; one *s* four *d*. *Educ:* Eton; William Temple Coll. 2nd Lieut, 60th Rifles, 1949–50. Chartered Accountant, 1956. Dir of Industrial Studies, William Temple Coll., 1964–68; Chancellor, Univ. of Sussex, 1985–98 (Treasurer, 1979–82). Church Commissioner, 1963–76; Mem. Gen. Synod of Church of England, formerly Church Assembly, 1960–80 (Chm., Bd for Mission and Unity, 1967–77); Mem., Central and Exec. Cttees, World Council of Churches, 1968–75; Chairman: Christian Orgn Res. and Adv. Trust, 1965–87; House of Laity, Chichester Diocesan Synod, 1976–79; Vice-Chm., Archbishop's Commn on Church and State, 1966–70; Member: W Midlands Regional Economic Planning Council, 1965–68; Steering Gp, W Sussex Economic Forum, 1997–; Chm., W Sussex Coastal Strip Enterprise Hub, 2000–. Chairman: Goodwood Group of Cos, 1969–; Dexam International Holdings Ltd, 1969–; Ajax Insurance (Holdings) Ltd, 1987–89; John Wiley and Sons Ltd, 1992–99 (Dir, 1984–92); Dir, Radio Victory Ltd, 1982–87. Historic Houses Association: Hon. Treas., 1975–82; Chm., SE Region, 1975–78; Dep. Pres., 1982–86; President: Sussex Rural Community Council, 1973– (Chm., Rural Housing Adv. Cttee, 1996–); British Horse Soc., 1976–78; South of England Agricultural Soc., 1981–82; SE England Tourist Bd, 1990– (Vice-Pres., 1974–90); Chm., Assoc. of Internat. Dressage Event Organisers, 1987–94; Chairman: Rugby Council of Social Service, 1961–68; Dunford Coll., (YMCA), 1969–82; Dir, Country Gentlemen's Assoc. Ltd, 1975–89. Chairman: of Trustees, Sussex Heritage Trust, 1978–2001; Planning for Economic Prosperity in Chichester and Arun, 1984–89 (Pres., 1989–); Chichester Cathedral Develt Trust, 1985–91; President: Chichester Festivities, 1975–; Sussex CCC, 1991–2001 (Patron, 2001–). DL W Sussex, 1975–90. CIMgt (CBIM 1982). Hon LLD Sussex, 1986. Medal of Honour, British Equestrian Fedn, 1983. *Heir: s* Earl of March and Kinrara, *qv*. *Address:* Molecomb, Goodwood, Chichester, W Sussex PO18 0PZ. *T:* (office) (01243) 755000, (home) (01243) 527861, *Fax:* (office) (01243) 755005.

See also Lord N. C. Gordon Lennox.

RICHMOND, Archdeacon of; *see* Good, Ven. K. R.

RICHMOND, Rear-Adm. Andrew John, CB 1987; Chief Executive (formerly Executive Director), Royal Society for the Prevention of Cruelty to Animals, 1987–91; *b* 5 Nov. 1931; *s* of Albert George Richmond and Emily Margaret (*née* Denbee); *m* 1957, Jane Annette (*née* Ley); one *s* two *d*. *Educ:* King's School, Bruton; Nautical College, Pangbourne. Joined RN 1950; staff of C-in-C East Indies, 1953; flying training, 1955; Cyprus 847 Sqdn, 1956; HMS Victorious 824 Sqdn, 1958; staff of FO Arabian Seas, 1960; BRNC Dartmouth, 1963; Sec., FO Carriers and Amphibious Ships, 1968; Supply School, HMS Pembroke, 1970; Fleet Supply Officer, 1974; Asst Dir Naval Manpower, 1976; Sec., C-in-C Naval Home Comd, 1977; Captain, HMS Cochrane, 1979; Dir, Naval Logistic Planning, 1982; ADC 1984; ACDS (Logistics), 1985, and Chief Naval Supply and Secretariat Officer, 1986. *Recreations:* home, gardening, golf. *Address:* c/o Royal Bank of Scotland, South Street, Chichester, West Sussex PO19 1DS. *Club:* Goodwood Golf.

RICHMOND, David Frank; HM Diplomatic Service; UK Representative to EU Political and Security Committee and UK Permanent Representative to the Council, Western European Union, Brussels, since 2000; *b* 9 July 1954; *s* of Frank George Richmond and Constance Lillian Richmond (*née* Hilling); *m* 1990, Caroline Matagne; one *s* one *d*. *Educ:* Merchant Taylors' Sch.; Trinity Hall, Cambridge (BA). FCO, 1976; MECAS, 1977–78; Baghdad, 1979–82; Second, later First Sec., FCO, 1982–87; UK Rep., Brussels, 1987–91; Dep. Head, Near East and N Africa Dept, FCO, 1991–94; Head, Economic Relations Dept, FCO, 1994–96; Head of Chancery, UK Mission to UN, NY, 1996–2000. *Address:* c/o Foreign and Commonwealth Office, SW1A 2AH.

RICHMOND, Rt Rev. (Francis) Henry (Arthur); Bishop Suffragan of Repton, 1986–98; Hon. Assistant Bishop, diocese of Oxford, since 1999; *b* 6 Jan. 1936; *s* of Frank and Lena Richmond; *m* 1966, Caroline Mary Berent; two *s* one *d*. *Educ:* Portora Royal School, Enniskillen; Trinity Coll., Dublin (MA); Univ. of Strasbourg (BTh); Linacre Coll., Oxford (MLitt); Wycliffe Hall, Oxford. Deacon, 1963, priest, 1964; Asst Curate, Woodlands, Doncaster, 1963–66; Sir Henry Stephenson Research Fellow, Sheffield Univ. and Chaplain, Sheffield Cathedral, 1966–69; Vicar, St George's, Sheffield, 1969–77; Anglican Chaplain to Sheffield Univ. and Mem. Sheffield Chaplaincy for Higher Education, 1974–77; Warden, Lincoln Theol Coll., and Canon and Prebendary of Lincoln Cathedral, 1977–85. Examng Chaplain to Bishop of Lincoln; Proctor in Convocation for Lincoln, 1980. *Recreations:* listening to classical music, reading, theatre, walking, gardening. *Address:* 39 Hodges Court, Marlborough Road, Oxford OX1 4NZ. *T:* (01865) 790466.

RICHMOND, Prof. John, CBE 1993; MD, FRCP, FRCPE; FRSE; President, Royal College of Physicians of Edinburgh, 1988–91; Emeritus Professor of Medicine, University of Sheffield, since 1989; *b* 30 May 1926; *m* 1951, Jenny Nicol; two *s* one *d*. *Educ:* Doncaster Grammar Sch.; Univ. of Edinburgh. MB, ChB 1948 (with Distinction in Medicine); MD 1963. FRCPE 1963; FRCP 1970; FRCPS 1988; FRCPI 1990; FCPS (Pak) 1990; FRCSE 1991; Hon. FACP 1990; Hon. FFPM 1990; Hon. FRACP 1991; Hon. FCP(SoAf) 1991; Hon. FFPHM 1991. RAMC, Military Mission to Ethiopia, Captain 1st Bn King's African Rifles, N Rhodesia, 1949–50; Rural Gen. Practice, Galloway, Scotland, 1950–52; Res. Fellow, Meml Sloan Kettering Cancer Center, New York, 1958–59; Sen. Lectr, later Reader in Medicine, Univ. of Edinburgh, 1963–73; University of Sheffield: Prof. of Medicine, 1973–89; Chm., Academic Div. of Medicine, 1978–85; Dean of Medicine and Dentistry, 1985–88. Censor, 1981–82, Sen. Vice-Pres. and Sen. Censor, 1984–85, RCP; Mem. Council, RCPE, 1987–88. Chm., MRCP (UK) Part 2 Examining Bd, 1985–89. Member: Clin. Standards Adv. Gp, Dept of Health, 1991–94; Bd of Advrs, London Univ., 1984–93; External Advr, Chinese Univ. of Hong

Kong, 1984–96. Member: Scottish Adv. Cttee, British Council, 1991–97; Scottish Cttee, Marie Curie Meml Foundn, 1992–2001. Hon. MD Sheffield, 1994. *Publications:* contribs to books and papers in med. jls, mainly on haematology and oncology. *Address:* 15 Church Hill, Edinburgh EH10 4BG.

RICHMOND, Sir Mark (Henry), Kt 1986; PhD, ScD; FRCPath; FRS 1980; Member, School of Public Policy, University College London, since 1996; *b* 1 Feb. 1931; *s* of Harold Sylvester Richmond and Dorothy Plaistowe Richmond; *m* 1958, Shirley Jean Townrow; one *s* one *d* (and one *d* decd). *Educ:* Epsom College; Clare Coll., Cambridge. BA, PhD, ScD. Scientific Staff, MRC, 1958–65; Reader in Molecular Biology, Univ. of Edinburgh, 1965–68; Prof. of Bacteriology, Univ. of Bristol, 1968–81; Vice-Chancellor, and Prof. of Molecular Microbiol., Victoria Univ. of Manchester, 1981–90; Chm., SERC, 1990–94 (Mem., 1981–85); Gp Hd of Res., Glaxo Hldgs, 1993–95. Director: Whittington Hosp. NHS Trust, 1996–98; Core Gp plc, 1997–99; Genentech Inc., 1999–; OSI Pharmaceuticals Inc., 1999–. Member: Bd, PHLS, 1976–85; Fulbright Cttee, 1980–84; Chairman: British Nat. Cttee for Microbiol., 1980–85; CVCP, 1987–89; Cttee on Microbiological Food Safety, 1989–91; Member: Genetic Manipulation Adv. Gp, 1976–84; Adv. Cttee on Genetic Manipulation, 1984–85; Internat. Scientific Adv. Bd, UNESCO, 1996–; Council, CRC, 1997– (Chm., CRC Technology, 1997–). Pres., Epsom Coll., 1992–. Member: IBM Academic Adv. Bd, 1984–90; Knox Fellowship Cttee, 1984–87; CIBA-Geigy Fellowship Trust, 1984–91; Jarrett Cttee for University Efficiency, 1985; Governing Body, Lister Inst., 1987–90; Council, ACU, 1988–90; Council, Royal Northern Coll. of Music, 1990–92; Educn Cttee, Royal Anniversary Trust, 1994–97; Trustee: Nat. Gall., 1994–2000; Tate Gall., 1995–99; Dyson Perrins Mus., Worcester, 1993–2001. *Publications:* several in microbiology and biochemistry jls. *Recreation:* hill-walking. *Address:* School of Public Policy, University College London, 29–30 Tavistock Square, WC1H 9EZ. *Club:* Athenæum.

RICHMOND, Prof. Peter, PhD, DSc; CPhys, FInstP; Director, EPM Associates Ltd, since 1998; *b* 4 March 1943; *s* of John Eric Richmond and Nellie (*née* Scholey); *m* 1967, Christine M. Jackson (*d* 1995); one *s* one *d*. *Educ:* Whitcliffe Mount Grammar Sch., Cleckheaton; Queen Mary Coll., London (BSc, PhD); London Univ. (DSc). MRSC. ICI Res. Fellow, Univ. of Kent, 1967–69; Univ. of NSW, 1969–71; Queen Elizabeth II Res. Fellow, Inst. of Advanced Studies, ANU, 1971–73; Unilever Res., 1973–82; Hd, Process Physics, AFRC Food Res. Inst., Norwich, 1982–86; Industrial Prof., Univ. of Loughborough, 1985–88; Dir, AFRC Inst. of Food Res., Norwich Lab., 1986–92; Gen. Man., CWS Quality and Consumer Care, 1992–94; Head of Regulatory Affairs, CWS, 1994–96; Head, Sci. and Regulatory Affairs, United Biscuits (UK) Ltd, 1996. Hon. Prof., Sch. of Inf. Systems, UEA, 1986–; EU Marie Curie Res. Fellow, Vis. Prof., 1998–, TCD. 1998–99. Member: MAFF/DoH Adv. Cttee on novel foods and processes, 1988–94; FDF Scientific and Technical Cttee, 1992–95; FDF Res. Strategy Gp, 1993–96; EC Training and Mobility of Researchers Grant Assessment Panel, 1996–98; FDF Sci. and Regulatory Affairs Cttee, 1997. Mem., Council, 1995–96, Gen. Merchandise Cttee, 1995–96, British Retail Consortium. *Publications:* (with R. D. Bee and J. Mingins) Food Colloids, 1989; (with P. J. Frazier and A. Donald) Starch Structure and Functionality, 1997; contribs to learned jls. *Recreations:* music, cooking, concepts of God. *Club:* Athenæum.

RICHTER, Prof. Burton; Paul Pigott Professor in the Physical Sciences, Stanford University, USA, since 1980 (Professor of Physics, since 1967); Director, Stanford Linear Accelerator Center, 1984–99, now Emeritus (Technical Director, 1982–84); *b* 22 March 1931; *s* of Abraham Richter and Fannie Pollack; *m* 1960, Laurose Becker; one *s* one *d*. *Educ:* Massachusetts Inst. of Technology. BS 1952, PhD (Physics) 1956. Stanford University: Research Associate, Physics, High Energy Physics Lab., 1956–60; Asst Prof., 1960–63; Associate Prof., 1963–67; full Prof., 1967. Loeb Lectr, Harvard, 1974; De Shalit Lectr, Weizmann Inst., 1975. Member, Board of Directors: Varian Corp., then Varian Associates,1989–99; Litel Instruments, 1990–; Varian Med. Systems, 1999–. Pres., IUPAP, 1999–Sept. 2002 (Pres. Designate, 1997–99). FAPS 1984 (Pres., 1994); Fellow, Amer. Acad. of Arts and Scis, 1990 (Mem., 1989); Mem., Nat. Acad. of Scis, 1977. E. O. Lawrence Award, 1975; Nobel Prize for Physics (jointly), 1976. *Publications:* over 300 articles in various scientific journals. *Address:* Stanford Linear Accelerator Center, PO Box 20450, Stanford University, Stanford, CA 94309-0450, USA.

RICKARD, Rear Adm. Hugh Wilson, CBE 1996; Chief Executive, Liberal Democrats, since 2000; *b* 1 Sept. 1948; *s* of Charles Thomas Rickard and Isobel Rickard; *m* 1982, Patricia Ann Seager; two *s* one *d*. *Educ:* Surbiton Co. Grammar Sch.; Northern Poly. (BSc London Hons). MIL 1994. Joined RN, 1972; qualified as Meteorological and Oceanographic Officer, 1974; Naval Staff Course, 1982; UK Defence and Naval Attaché, The Hague, 1992–95; CO, HMS Raleigh, 1995–98; Sen. Naval DS, RCDS, 1998–2000. *Recreations:* sailing, bridge, hill-walking. *Address:* High Burrows, The Drive, Sutton, Surrey SM2 7DP. *T:* (020) 8661 6258. *Club:* Naval.

RICKARD, Dr John Hellyar; independent consultant economist; *b* 27 Jan. 1940; *s* of Peter John Rickard and Irene Eleanor (*née* Hales); *m* 1963, Christine Dorothy Hudson; one *s* two *d*. *Educ:* Ilford County High Sch.; St John's Coll., Oxford (MA 1966; DPhil 1976); Univ. of Aston in Birmingham (MSc 1969). Lectr, Univ. of Aston, 1967–70; Economist, Programmes Analysis Unit, AEA, Harwell, 1970–72; Res. Associate, and Dep. Head, Health Services Evaluation Gp, Dept of Regius Prof. of Medicine, Univ. of Oxford, 1972–74; Econ. Adviser, Dept of Health, 1974–76; Sen. Econ. Adviser: Dept of Prices and Consumer Protection, 1976–78; Central Policy Review Staff, Cabinet Office, 1978–82; HM Treasury, 1982–84; Econ. Adviser, State of Bahrain, 1984–87; Chief Economic Advr, Dept of Transport, 1987–91; Under Sec. (Econs), HM Treasury, 1991–94; Chief Econ. Advr, Dept of Transport, 1994–95; IMF Fiscal Advr, Min. of Finance, Republic of Moldova, 1995. MCIT 1996. *Publications:* (with D. Aston) Macro-Economics: a critical introduction, 1970; Longer Term Issues in Transport, 1991; articles in books and learned jls. *Recreations:* sailing, music. *Address:* Bay House, Lanes End, Totland Bay, Isle of Wight PO39 0BE. *T:* (01983) 754669. *Club:* Royal Solent Yacht.

RICKARD, Prof. Peter, DPhil, PhD, LittD; Drapers Professor of French, University of Cambridge, 1980–82, Emeritus since 1983; Fellow of Emmanuel College, Cambridge, 1953, Professorial Fellow, 1980, Life Fellow, since 1983; *b* 20 Sept. 1922; *yr s* of Norman Ernest Rickard and Elizabeth Jane (*née* Hosking); unmarried. *Educ:* Redruth County Grammar Sch., Cornwall; Exeter Coll., Oxford (Final Hons Mod. Langs (French and German), Cl. I, 1948; MA 1948). DPhil Oxon 1952; PhD Cantab 1952; LittD Cambridge 1982. Served War, 1st Bn Seaforth Highlanders and Intell. Corps, India, 1942–46. Heath Harrison Travelling Scholar (French), 1948; Amelia Jackson Sen. Scholar, Exeter Coll., Oxford, 1948–49; Lectr in Mod. Langs, Trinity Coll., Oxford, 1949–52; Univ. of Cambridge: Asst Lectr in French, 1952–57, Lectr, 1957–74; Reader in French Lang., 1974–80; Mem., St John's Coll., 1952–; Tutor, Emmanuel Coll., 1954–65. *Publications:* Britain in Medieval French Literature, 1956; La langue française au XVIe siècle, 1968; (ed with T. G. S. Combe) The French Language: studies presented to Lewis Charles Harmer, 1970; (ed and trans.) Fernando Pessoa, Selected Poems, 1971; A History of the French Language, 1974; Chrestomathie de la langue française au XVe siècle, 1976; (ed with T. G. S. Combe) L. C. Harmer, Uncertainties in French Grammar, 1979; The Embarrassments of Irregularity, 1981; The French Language in the 17th Century: contemporary opinion in France, 1992; The Transferred Epithet in Modern English Prose, 1996; articles in Romania, Trans Phil Soc., Neuphilologische Mitteilungen, Cahiers de Lexicologie, and Zeitschrift für Romanische Philologie. *Recreations:* travel, music. *Address:* Emmanuel College, Cambridge CB2 3AP. *T:* (01223) 334223; Upper Rosevine, Portscatho, Cornwall TR2 5EW. *T:* (01872) 580582.

RICKARDS, Prof. (Richard) Barrie, CGeol, FGS; Professor of Palaeontology and Biostratigraphy, University of Cambridge, since 2000; Curator, Sedgwick Museum of Geology, since 1969; Fellow, Emmanuel College, Cambridge, since 1977; Hon. Curator, Emmanuel College Museum, 1994–99; *b* 12 June 1938; *s* of Robert Rickards and Eva (*née* Sudborough); *m* 1960, Christine Townsley (marr. diss. 1991); one *s*. *Educ:* Goole Grammar Sch.; Univ. of Hull (BSc; PhD 1963; DSc 1990); MA Cantab, 1969; ScD Cantab, 1976. *Educ:* FGS 1960; Founder MIFM 1969; CGeol 1990. Reckitt Scholar, Univ. of Hull, 1960–63; Curator, Garwood Library, UCL, 1963; Asst in Research, Univ. of Cambridge, 1964–66; SSO, BM (Natural History), 1967; Lectr, TCD, 1967–69; University of Cambridge: Lectr, 1969–90; Reader, 1990–2000; Official Lectr, Emmanuel Coll., 1977–2000. Founder and first Sec., Pike Anglers' Club; Founding Mem., Nat. Anglers' Council; Deleg, E Reg., 1987–, Mem., Gen. Purposes Cttee, 1989–, Nat. Fedn of Anglers; Mem. Council, Waterbeach Angling Club, 1980–84; first Fishery Manager, Leland Water, 1982–83. Consultant, Shakespeare Co. (UK) Ltd, 1988–. President: Lure Fishing Soc. of GB, 1992–; Nat. Assoc. of Specialist Anglers, 1993–; Trustee, Specialist Anglers' Conservation Gp, 1995–. Gov., Caldecote Co. Primary Sch., Cambs, 1994–95. Murchison Fund, 1982, Lyell Medal, 1997, Geol Soc.; John Phillips Medal, Yorks Geol Soc., 1988. *Publications: angling:* (with R. Webb) Fishing for Big Pike, 1971, (sole author) 3rd edn, as Big Pike, 1986; Perch, 1974; (with R. Webb) Fishing for Big Tench, 1976, 2nd edn 1986; Pike, 1976; (with K. Whitehead) Plugs and Plug Fishing, 1976, and Spinners, Spoons and Wobbled Baits, 1977, rev. edn of both titles as A Textbook of Spinning, 1987; (with N. Fickling) Zander, 1979, 2nd edn 1990; (with K. Whitehead) Fishing Tackle, 1981; (with K. Whitehead) A Fishery of Your Own, 1984; Angling: fundamental principles, 1986; (with M. Gay) A Technical Manual of Pike Fishing, 1986; (ed) River Piking, 1987; (ed) Best of Pikelines, 1988; (with M. Gay) Pike, 1989; (with M. Bannister) The Ten Greatest Pike Anglers, 1991; (jtly) Encyclopaedia of Fishing, 1991; Success with Pike, 1992; Success with the Lure, 1993; over 500 articles on angling in newspapers and magazines; *geology:* Graptolites: writing in the rocks, 1991; (ed with D. C. Palmer) H. B. Whittington, Trilobites, 1992; (ed with S. Rigby) Graptolites in Colour: a teaching aid, 1998; upwards of 200 scientific articles and monographs in internat. jls, mostly on fossils (graptolites) and evolution. *Recreations:* angling, marathon running, angling administration (from local to national). *Address:* Emmanuel College, Cambridge CB2 3AP. *T:* (01223) 334282.

RICKETS, Brig. Reginald Anthony Scott, (Tony); Director, Nobel Exhibition Trust, (The Big Idea), since 1997; Depute Chairman, Irvine Housing Association, since 1997; *b* 13 Dec. 1929; *s* of Captain R. H. Rickets and Mrs V. C. Rickets (*née* Morgan); *m* 1952, Elizabeth Ann Serjeant; one *s* one *d*. *Educ:* St George's Coll., Weybridge; RMA Sandhurst. 2nd Lieut, RE, 1949; served with airborne, armoured and field engrs in UK, Cyrenaica, Egypt, Malaya, Borneo, Hong Kong and BAOR; special employment military forces Malaya, 1955–59; Staff Coll., Camberley, 1962; BM Engr Gp, BAOR, 1963–66; OC 67 Gurkha Indep. Field Sqn, 1966–68; DS Staff Coll., 1968–70; Comdt Gurkha Engrs/CRE Hong Kong, 1970–73; COS British Sector, Berlin, 1973–77; Col GS RSME, 1977–78; Chief Engr UKLF, 1978–81. Man. Dir, Irvine Develt Corp., 1981–95. Director: Enterprise Ayrshire, 1990–97; Kelvin Travel, 1995–98. President: Ayrshire Chamber of Industries, 1985–86; Ayrshire Chamber of Commerce and Industry, 1989–91; German–British Chamber of Industry and Commerce in Scotland, 1998–; Mem. Exec. Bd, Scottish Council (Develt and Industry), 1990–92. Chm., ASSET Enterprise Trust, 1996–97; Mem., Ex-Services Mental Welfare Soc., 1986–90. Mem. Exec. Bd, Scottish Maritime Mus., 1986–. *Recreation:* sailing. *Address:* Burnbrae Cottage, Montgreenan, Ayrshire KA13 7QZ. *Club:* Royal Engineer Yacht (Commodore, 1979–81).

RICKETT, William Francis Sebastian; Director-General, Transport Strategy, Roads and Local Transport, Department for Transport, Local Government and the Regions, since 2001; *b* 23 Feb. 1953; *s* of Sir Denis Rickett, KCMG, CB; *m* 1979, Lucy Caroline Clark; one *s* one *d*. *Educ:* Trinity Coll., Cambridge (BA 1974). Joined Department of Energy, 1975; Private Sec. to Perm. Under Sec. of State, 1977; Principal, 1978; Private Sec. to Prime Minister, 1981–83; seconded to Kleinwort Benson Ltd, 1983–85; Asst Sec., Oil Div., Dept of Energy, 1985; Asst Sec., Electricity Privatisation, 1987; Grade 4, Electricity Div., 1989; Under Sec., 1990; Dir Gen., Energy Efficiency Office, Dept of Energy, 1990–92, DoE, 1992–93; Dir of Finance (Central) and Principal Finance Officer, DoE, 1993–97; Dir of Town and Country Planning, DoE, then DETR, 1997–98; Dep. Sec. and Hd, Economic and Domestic Secretariat, Cabinet Office, 1998–2000; Hd, Integrated Transport Taskforce, subseq. Dir-Gen., Transport Strategy and Planning, DETR, 2000–01. *Recreations:* children, painting, sports. *Address:* Department for Transport, Local Government and the Regions, Great Minster House, 76 Marsham Street, SW1P 4DR.

RICKETTS, Prof. Martin John, DPhil; Professor of Economic Organisation, University of Buckingham, since 1987; *b* 10 May 1948; *s* of Leonard Alfred Ricketts and Gertrude Dorothy (*née* Elgar); *m* 1975, Diana Barbara Greenwood; one *s* one *d*. *Educ:* City of Bath Boys' Sch.; Univ. of Newcastle upon Tyne (BA Hons Econ.); Univ. of York (DPhil). Econ. Asst, Industrial Policy Gp, 1970–72; Res. Fellow, Inst. Econ. and Social Res., Univ. of York, 1975–77; University College at Buckingham, later University of Buckingham: Lectr in Econs, 1977–82; Sen. Lectr, 1982–85; Reader, 1985–87; Dean, Sch. of Business (formerly Sch. of Accountancy, Business and Econs), 1993–97; Pro-Vice-Chancellor, 1993. Economic Dir, NEDO, 1991–92. Vis. Prof., Virginia Poly. Inst. and State Univ., 1984. Hon. Prof., Heriot-Watt Univ., 1996. Trustee, Inst. of Econ. Affairs, 1992–. *Publications:* (with M. G. Webb) The Economics of Energy, 1980; The Economics of Business Enterprise: new approaches to the firm, 1987, 2nd edn 1994; papers on public finance, public choice, housing econs and econ. orgn. *Recreation:* music, student of piano and oboe. *Address:* 22 Bradfield Avenue, Buckingham MK18 1PR; School of Economics, University of Buckingham, Hunter Street, Buckingham MK18 1EG.

RICKETTS, Michael Rodney, MA; Headmaster, Sutton Valence School, 1967–80; *b* 29 Sept. 1923; *er s* of late Rt Rev. C. M. Ricketts, Bishop of Dunwich, and Dorothy Ricketts; *m* 1958, Judith Anne Caroline Corry; two *s* two *d*. *Educ:* Sherborne; Trinity Coll., Oxford. Served War of 1939–45: in 8th Army, Africa, Italy, with 60th Rifles, 1942–47. Trinity Coll., Oxford, 1947–50; Asst Master and Housemaster, Bradfield Coll., 1950–67. Dir, ISIS (Eastern England), 1980–93; Nat. ISIS Management Cttee, 1981–93. Member: HMC Cttee, 1976–79 (Chm., HMC/SHA Services Cttee, 1975–80); British Atlantic Cttee, 1974–93, Council, 1979–93; Chairman: British Atlantic Educn Cttee, 1984–87 (Mem., 1974–93); Atlantic Educn Cttee, 1986–93. Former Governor: Gresham's Sch.; Orwell Park; Vinehall. Fellow, Woodard Corp. *Recreations:* cricket, shooting, country activities. *Address:* Breakers, Atlantic Terrace, New Polzeath, Wadebridge, Cornwall PL27 6UG. *Clubs:* East India, Devonshire, Sports and Public Schools, Free Foresters, Harlequins, I Zingari, MCC; Vincent's (Oxford).

RICKETTS, Peter Forbes, CMG 1999; HM Diplomatic Service; Political Director, Foreign and Commonwealth Office, since 2001; *b* 30 Sept. 1952; *s* of Maurice and Dilys Ricketts; *m* 1980, Suzanne Julia Horlington; one *s* one *d.* *Educ:* Bishop Vesey's Grammar Sch.; Pembroke Coll., Oxford (MA). Joined FCO, 1974; Singapore, 1975–78; UK Delegn to NATO, 1978–81; FCO, 1981–86, Private Sec. to Sec. of State for Foreign and Commonwealth Affairs, 1983–86; Washington, 1986–89; FCO, 1989–94, Head, Hong Kong Dept, 1991–94; Economic and Financial Counsellor, Paris, 1994–97; Dep. Pol Dir, FCO, 1997–99; Dir, Internat. Security, FCO, 1999–2000; Chm., Jt Intelligence Cttee, Cabinet Office (on secondment), 2000–01. *Recreations:* restoring Normandy farmhouse, Victorian art and literature. *Address:* c/o Foreign and Commonwealth Office, King Charles Street, SW1A 2AH. *T:* (020) 7270 3000.

RICKETTS, Sir Robert (Cornwallis Gerald St Leger), 7th Bt *cr* 1828; retired Solicitor; *b* 8 Nov. 1917; *s* of Sir Claude Albert Frederick Ricketts, 6th Bt, and Lilian Helen Gwendoline (*d* 1955), *o d* of Arthur M. Hill, late 5th Fusiliers; *S* father, 1937; *m* 1945, Anne Theresa Cripps, CBE (*d* 1998); two *s* two *d.* *Educ:* Haileybury; Magdalene College, Cambridge (2nd Cl. Hons in History and Law, BA 1939, MA 1943). Served War of 1939–45 (Captain, Devon Regiment); Personal Assistant to Chief of Staff, Gibraltar, 1942–45; ADC to Lieutenant-Governor of Jersey, 1945–46. Formerly Partner in Wellington and Clifford. FRSA. Hon. Citizen, Mobile, USA, 1970. *Heir:* *s* Robert Tristram Ricketts, *qv.* *Address:* Forwood House, Minchinhampton, Stroud, Glos GL6 9AB. *T:* (01453) 882160.

See also J. A. Bird, G. F. P. Mason.

RICKETTS, (Robert) Tristram; Secretary General, British Horseracing Board, since 2000 (Chief Executive, 1993–2000); *b* 17 April 1946; *s* of Sir Robert Ricketts, Bt, *qv* and Anne Theresa Ricketts, CBE (*d* 1998); *m* 1969, Ann Lewis; one *s* one *d.* *Educ:* Winchester Coll.; Magdalene Coll., Cambridge (BA Hons 1968; MA 1972). Admin. Officer, GLC, 1968–72; Personal Asst to Leader of GLC, 1972–73; Horserace Betting Levy Board: Asst Principal Officer, 1974–76; Dep. Sec., 1976–79; Sec., 1980–84; Chief Exec., 1984–93; Mem., 1993–98, 2000–. *Recreations:* horseracing, theatre, cinema, making bonfires. *Address:* 47 Lancaster Avenue, SE27 9EL. *T:* (020) 8670 8422. *Club:* Athenæum.

RICKETTS, Simon Henry Martin, CB 2000; Ministry of Defence, 1975–2000; *b* 23 July 1941; *s* of Ralph Robert Ricketts and Margaret Adeliza Mary (*née* Royds); *m* 1973, Annabel Ophelia Clare Lea; one *s* one *d.* *Educ:* Ampleforth; Magdalen Coll., Oxford (BA Hons History). Senior Systems Analyst, George Wimpey & Co., 1963–71; Lectr in Liberal Studies, Hammersmith Coll. of Art and Building, 1967–68; Kulu Trekking Agency, 1971; Teacher, British Inst. of Florence, 1971–73; Royalties Clerk, Cape & Chatto Services, 1973–75. Mem., Friends of Georgian Soc. of Jamaica. *Recreation:* passing time congenially. *Address:* c/o Lloyds TSB, 8 Fore Street, Budleigh Salterton, Devon EX9 6NQ.

RICKETTS, Tristram; *see* Ricketts, R. T.

RICKFORD, Jonathan Braithwaite Keevil, CBE 2001; solicitor, regulatory consultant; Project Director, Department of Trade and Industry's Review of Company Law, 1998–2001; *b* 7 Dec. 1944; *s* of R. B. K. Rickford, MD, FRCS, FRCOG and of Dorothy Rickford (*née* Lathan); *m* 1968, Dora R. Sargant; one *s* two *d.* *Educ:* Sherborne School; Magdalen College, Oxford (MA (Jurisp.); BCL). Barrister, 1970–85; Solicitor, 1985–. Teaching Associate, Univ. of California Sch. of Law, 1968–69; Lectr in Law, LSE, 1969–72; Legal Asst, Dept of Trade, 1972–73; Senior Legal Assistant: Dept of Prices and Consumer Protection, 1974–76; Law Officers' Dept, Attorney General's Chambers, 1976–79; Dept of Trade and Industry (formerly Dept of Trade): Asst Solicitor (Company Law), 1979–82; Under Sec. (Legal), 1982–85; Solicitor, 1985–87; British Telecom: Solicitor and Chief Legal Advr, 1987–89; Dir of Govt Relns, 1989–93; Dir of Corporate Strategy, 1993–96. Mem., Competition (formerly Monopolies and Mergers) Commn, 1997–. Member: Europe Cttee, CBI, 1993–98; Council, European Policy Forum, 1993–. FRSA 1992. *Publications:* articles in learned jls. *Recreation:* sailing. *Clubs:* Reform; Bosham Sailing.

RICKINSON, Prof. Alan Bernard, PhD; FRS 1997; Professor and Head of Division of Cancer Studies, University of Birmingham, since 1983; *b* 12 Nov. 1943; *s* of Lawrence and Annie Rickinson; *m* 1968, Barbara; one *s* two *d.* *Educ:* Corpus Christi Coll., Cambridge (MA, PhD 1969). FRCP 1996. *Recreations:* walking, poetry. *Address:* CRC Institute for Cancer Studies, University of Birmingham, Edgbaston, Birmingham B15 2TT. *T:* (0121) 414 4492.

RICKMAN, Alan; actor. *Educ:* Latymer Upper Sch.; Chelsea Sch. of Art (DipAD); Royal Coll. of Art; RADA. *Theatre* includes: The Devil is an Ass, Measure for Measure, Birmingham, Edinburgh Fest., Nat. Theatre, European tour, 1976–77; The Tempest, Captain Swing, Love's Labour's Lost, Antony and Cleopatra, RSC, 1978–79; The Summer Party, Crucible, 1980; Commitments, Bush, 1980; The Devil Himself, Lyric Studio, 1980; Philadelphia Story, Oxford Playhouse, 1981; The Seagull, Royal Court, 1981; Brothers Karamazov, Edinburgh Fest. and USSR, 1981; The Last Elephant, Bush, 1981; Bad Language, Hampstead, 1983; The Grass Widow, 1983, The Lucky Chance, 1984, Royal Court; As You Like It, Troilus and Cressida, Les Liaisons Dangereuses, Mephisto, RSC, 1985–86; Les Liaisons Dangereuses, West End and Broadway, 1986–87; Tango at the End of Winter, Edinburgh and West End, 1991; Hamlet, Riverside Studios and Brit. Tour, 1992; Antony and Cleopatra, RNT, 1998; Private Lives, Albery, 2001; *director:* Desperately Yours, NY, 1980; (asst dir) Other Worlds, Royal Ct, 1983; Live Wax, Edin. Fest., 1986; Wax Acts, West End and tour, 1992; The Winter Guest, Almeida, 1995; *films:* Die Hard, 1988; The January Man, 1989; Quigley Down Under, 1990; Truly, Madly, Deeply, 1991; Closetland, 1991; Close My Eyes, 1991; Robin Hood, Prince of Thieves, 1991; Bob Roberts, 1992; Fallen Angels (TV, USA), 1993; Mesmer, 1993; An Awfully Big Adventure, 1995; Sense and Sensibility, 1996; Michael Collins, 1996; Rasputin, 1996; (dir) The Winter Guest (Best Film, Chicago Film Fest.; Premio Cinema Avvenire, OCIC Award, Venice Film Fest.), 1997; Dark Harbor, 1999; Judas Kiss, 1999; Dogma, 1999, Galaxy Quest, 2000; Blow Dry, 2001; Play, 2001; Harry Potter and the Philosopher's Stone, 2001; *television* includes: Thérèse Raquin, 1979; Barchester Chronicles, 1982; Pity in History, 1984; Revolutionary Witness, Spirit of Man, 1989; also radio performances. Bancroft Gold Medal, RADA, 1974; Seattle Film Fest. Best Actor, 1991; Time Out Award for Tango at the End of Winter, 1992; BAFTA Film Award for Best Supporting Actor, 1992; Evening Standard Film Award for Best Actor, 1992; Best Actor, Montreal Film Fest., 1994; Emmy Award for Best Actor, 1996; Golden Globe Award for Best Actor, 1997; Screen Actors Guild Award for Best Actor, 1997. *Publication:* (contrib.) Players of Shakespeare, Vol 2, 1989. *Address:* c/o ICM, Oxford House, 76 Oxford Street, W1N 0AX.

RICKMAN, Prof. Geoffrey Edwin, FBA 1989; Professor of Roman History, University of St Andrews, 1981–97, now Emeritus; *b* 9 Oct. 1932; *s* of Charles Edwin Rickman and Ethel Ruth Mary (*née* Hill); *m* 1959, Ann Rosemary Wilson; one *s* one *d.* *Educ:* Peter Symonds' Sch., Winchester; Brasenose Coll., Oxford (MA, DipClassArchaeol, DPhil). FSA 1966; FRSE 2001. Henry Francis Pelham Student, British Sch. at Rome, 1958–59; Jun. Res. Fellow, The Queen's Coll., Oxford, 1959–62; University of St Andrews: Lectr in Ancient History, 1962–68; Sen. Lectr, 1968–81; Master of the United Coll. of St Salvator and St Leonard, 1992–96; Pro-Vice-Chancellor, 1996–97. Vis. Fellow, Brasenose Coll., Oxford, 1981; Mem., IAS, Princeton, 1997–98. Mem., Faculty of Archaeol., History and Letters, 1979–87 (Chm., 1983–87), Chm. Council, 1997–, British Sch. at Rome; Mem., Humanities Res. Bd, British Acad., 1995–98. *Publications:* Roman Granaries and Storebuildings, 1971; The Corn Supply of Ancient Rome, 1980. *Recreations:* opera, swimming, walking beside the sea. *Address:* 56 Hepburn Gardens, St Andrews, Fife KY16 9DG. *T:* (01334) 472063.

RICKS, Prof. Christopher Bruce, FBA 1975; Warren Professor of the Humanities, since 1998, and Co-Director, Editorial Institute, since 1999, Boston University (Professor of English, 1986–97); *b* 18 Sept. 1933; *s* of James Bruce Ricks and Gabrielle Roszak; *m* 1st, 1956, Kirsten Jensen (marr. diss.); two *s* two *d*; 2nd, 1977, Judith Aronson; one *s* two *d.* *Educ:* King Alfred's Sch., Wantage; Balliol Coll., Oxford (BA 1956; BLitt 1958; MA 1960; Hon. Fellow, 1989). 2nd Lieut, Green Howards, 1952. Andrew Bradley Jun. Res. Fellow, Balliol Coll., Oxford, 1957; Fellow of Worcester Coll., Oxford, 1958–68 (Hon. Fellow, 1990); Prof. of English, Bristol Univ., 1968–75; University of Cambridge: Prof. of English, 1975–82; King Edward VII Prof. of English Lit., 1982–86; Fellow, Christ's Coll., 1975–86 (Hon. Fellow, 1993). Visiting Professor: Berkeley and Stanford, 1965; Smith Coll., 1967; Harvard, 1971; Wesleyan, 1974; Brandeis, 1977, 1981, 1984. Lectures: Lord Northcliffe, UCL, 1972; Alexander, Univ. of Toronto, 1987; T. S. Eliot, Univ. of Kent, 1988; Clarendon, Univ. of Oxford, 1990; Clark, Trinity Coll., Cambridge, 1991. A Vice-Pres., Tennyson Soc. Co-editor, Essays in Criticism. Fellow, American Acad. of Arts and Scis, 1991. Hon. DLitt Oxon, 1998. George Orwell Meml Prize, 1979; Beefeater Club Prize for Literature, 1980. *Publications:* Milton's Grand Style, 1963; (ed) The Poems of Tennyson, 1969, rev. edn 1987; Tennyson, 1972, rev. edn 1989; Keats and Embarrassment, 1974; (ed with Leonard Michaels) The State of the Language, 1980, new edn 1990; The Force of Poetry, 1984; (ed) The New Oxford Book of Victorian Verse, 1987; (ed) A. E. Housman: Collected Poems and Selected Prose, 1988; T. S. Eliot and Prejudice, 1988; (ed with William Vance) The Faber Book of America, 1992; Beckett's Dying Words, 1993; Essays in Appreciation, 1996; (ed) Inventions of the March Hare: poems 1909–1917 by T. S. Eliot, 1996; (ed) The Oxford Book of English Verse, 1999. *Address:* 39 Martin Street, Cambridge, MA 02138, USA. *T:* (617) 3547887; Lasborough Cottage, Lasborough Park, near Tetbury, Glos GL8 8UF. *T:* (01666) 890252.

RICKS, David Trulock, CMG 1997; OBE 1981; British Council Director, France, and Cultural Counsellor, British Embassy, Paris, 1990–96; *b* 28 June 1936; *s* of Percival Trulock Ricks and Annetta Helen (*née* Hood); *m* 1960, Nicole Estelle Aimée Chupeau; two *s.* *Educ:* Kilburn Grammar Sch.; Royal Acad. of Music; Merton Coll., Oxford (MA); Univ. of London Inst. of Educn; Univ. of Lille (LèsL). Teaching in Britain, 1960–67; joined British Council, 1967: Rabat, 1967–70; Univ. of Essex, 1970–71; Jaipur, 1971–74, New Delhi, 1974; Dar Es Salaam, 1974–76; Tehran, 1976–80; London, 1980–85; Rep., Italy, and Cultural Counsellor, British Embassy, Rome, 1985–90. Mem., Rome Cttee, Keats-Shelley Meml House, Rome, 1985–90; Founder Mem., Assoc. Bourses Entente Cordiale, 1996. Gov., British Inst., Florence, 1985–90. *Publications:* (jtly) Penguin French Reader, 1967; (jtly) New Penguin French Reader, 1992. *Recreations:* music, playing the piano, ski-ing. *Address:* Saint Jean, Boulevard Raoul Dufy, 04300 Forcalquier, France. *T:* 492752063. *Club:* Oxford and Cambridge.

RICKS, Robert Neville; Deputy Legal Adviser, Treasury Advisory Division, Treasury Solicitor's Department, since 1998; *b* 29 June 1942; *s* of Sir John Plowman Ricks. *Educ:* Highgate Sch.; Worcester Coll., Oxford (MA). Admitted Solicitor, 1967. Entered Treasury Solicitor's Dept as Legal Asst, 1969; Sen. Legal Asst, 1973; Asst Solicitor, 1981; Prin. Asst Solicitor, 1986; Legal Advr, DES, then DfEE, 1990–97; Special Projects Dir, Treasury Solicitor's Dept, 1997–98. *Recreations:* collecting original cartoons, wine. *Address:* 2 Eaton Terrace, Aberavon Road, E3 5AJ. *T:* (020) 8981 3722.

RICKSON, Ian; Artistic Director, Royal Court Theatre, since 1998; *b* 8 Nov. 1963; *s* of Richard and Eileen Rickson; one *s* by Kate Gould. *Educ:* Essex Univ. (BA Eng and Eur. Lit. Hons); Goldsmiths' Coll., London Univ. (PGTC). Freelance Dir, King's Head, The Gate, Chichester Fest. Theatre; Special Projects Dir, Young Peoples' Th., 1991–92, Associate Dir, 1993–98, Royal Court Theatre. Plays directed include: Me and my Friend, Chichester, 1992; The House of Yes, Gate Th., 1993; La Serva Padrona (opera), Broomhill, 1993; The Day I Stood Still, RNT, 1997; *Royal Court Theatre:* Wildfire, Sab, and Killers, 1992; Some Voices, and Ashes and Sand, 1994; Mojo, 1995, NY 1996; Pale Horse, 1995; The Lights, 1996; The Weir, 1997, transf. Duke of York's, then NY, 1998; Dublin Carol, 2000; Mouth to Mouth, transf. Albery, 2001. *Address:* c/o Royal Court Theatre, Sloane Square, SW1W 8AS.

RICKUS, Gwenneth Margaret, CBE 1981; Director of Education, London Borough of Brent, 1971–84; *b* 1925; *d* of Leonard William Ernest and Florence Rickus. *Educ:* Latymer Sch., Edmonton; King's Coll., Univ. of London. BA, PGCE. Teaching, 1948–53; Asst Sec., AAM, 1953–61; Education Administration: Mddx CC, 1961–65; London Borough of Brent, 1965–84. Cllr (Lib Dem), New Forest DC, 1991–99. Co-opted Mem. Educn Cttee, Hampshire CC, 1985–97. Comr for Racial Equality, 1977–80. *Recreations:* reading, crafts, gardening, music, politics.

RIDD, John William Gregory; HM Diplomatic Service, retired; Regional Director, British Executive Service Overseas, since 1994; *b* 4 June 1931; *s* of William John and Lilian Gregory Cooke; adoptive *s* of Philip and Elizabeth Anne Ridd; *m* 1956, Mary Elizabeth Choat; three *s* one *d.* *Educ:* Lewis' Sch., Pengam; Wallington County Grammar Sch.; St Edmund Hall, Oxford (BA Hons 1954). National Service, 1949–51 (Army). Foreign Office, 1954; Buenos Aires, 1957–61; First Sec., Cairo, 1963–66, Prague, 1968–70, Brasilia, 1974–77; First Sec., later Counsellor, FCO, 1978–91. *Recreations:* books, distance running, allotment gardening, travel, music, the South Downs.

RIDDELL, Alan Gordon; Regional Director, Government Office for the East of England, since 1998; *b* 8 Sept. 1948; *s* of George Riddell and Elizabeth (*née* Mellin); *m* 1976, Barbara Kelly; two *d.* *Educ:* Greenock Acad.; Glasgow Univ. (MA Hons Mod. Hist. and Pol Econ.). History teacher, Greenock Acad., 1971–74; Hd of History, Eyemouth High Sch., 1974–75; Department of the Environment, 1975–97: Asst Private Sec. to Minister of Housing, 1981–83; Inner Cities Div., 1983–86; Private Rented Sector Div., 1986–87; Private Sec. to Minister for Local Govt, 1987–90; Hd, Private Rented Sector Div., 1990–92; Principal Private Sec. to Sec. of State, 1992–94; Sec., Cttee on Standards in Public Life (Nolan Cttee), 1994–97; Hd, Regeneration Policy Div., DETR, 1997–98. *Recreations:* walking, boats. *Address:* GO-East, Westbrook, Milton Road, Cambridge CB4 1YG. *T:* (01223) 346766.

RIDDELL, (John) Alistair, OBE 1988; Treasurer, British Medical Association, 1987–96; *b* 11 Feb. 1930; *s* of Alexander Riddell and Mamie McFarlane MacKintosh; *m* 1st, 1956, Elizabeth Park McDonald Davidson (*d* 1999); one *s* three *d*; 2nd, 1999, Susan Anne Fraser, MD, FRCPGlas. *Educ:* Glasgow Acad.; Glasgow Univ. (MB ChB). FRCGP 1983; FRCPGlas 1996. GP E Glasgow, 1956–95; Clinical Asst, Geriatrics, Lightburn Hosp., 1968–78. Member: Glasgow Local Med. Cttee, 1964–95 (Med. Sec., 1978–91); Scottish GDC, 1975–82; Gen. Med. Services Cttee, 1972–96 (Negotiator, 1982–87; Vice-Chm., 1985–87); Chairman: Scottish Gen. Med. Services Cttee, 1983–86; Glasgow Area Med. Cttee, 1974–90. Mem. Council, BMA, 1983– (Chm., Community Care Cttee, 1991–94; Mem., Scottish Council, 1982–); Mem., GMC, 1994–99 (Chm., Assessment Referral Cttee, 1997–99); Treas., Commonwealth Med. Assoc., 1989–. Dir, GP Finance Corp., 1975–90 (Vice-Chm., 1989–90); Dir, BMA Services, 1987–97; Chm., BMA Prof. Services, 1994–96. Dir, Silver Birch (Scotland) Ltd, 1996– (Chm., 1997–). Mem., CAB Easter House, 1974–77. Mem., Bonnetmakers' Craft and Grand Antiquity Soc., Glasgow. *Publications:* contrib. BMJ and Scottish Med. Jl. *Recreations:* golf, ski-ing, sailing. *Address:* 27 Upper Glenburn Road, Bearsden, Glasgow G61 4BN. *T:* (0141) 942 0235. *Club:* Royal Society of Medicine.

RIDDELL, Sir John (Charles Buchanan), 13th Bt *cr* 1628; CVO 1990; CA; Extra Equerry to HRH the Prince of Wales, since 1990; Lord-Lieutenant of Northumberland, since 2000; Chairman, Northern Rock plc, since 2000 (Director, 1981–1985, and since 1990; Deputy Chairman, 1992–99); *b* 3 Jan. 1934; *o s* of Sir Walter Buchanan Riddell, 12th Bt, and Hon. Rachel Beatrice Lyttelton (*d* 1965), *y d* of 8th Viscount Cobham; *S* father, 1934; *m* 1969, Hon. Sarah (LVO 1993), *o d* of Baron Richardson of Duntisbourne, *qv*; three *s*. *Educ:* Eton; Christ Church, Oxford. 2nd Lieut Rifle Bde, 1952–54. With IBRD, Washington DC, 1969–71; Associate, First Boston Corp., 1972–75; Director: First Boston (Europe) Ltd, 1975–78; UK Provident Instn, 1975–85; Northumbrian Water Gp, 1992–97; Alpha Bank London Ltd, 1995–; Chm., Govett Strategic Investment Trust, 1995–; Dep. Chm., Credit Suisse First Boston Ltd, 1990–95 (Dir, 1978–85). Dep Chm., IBA, 1981–85; Private Sec., 1985–90, and Treasurer, 1986–90, to TRH the Prince and Princess of Wales; Member, Prince's Council, 1985–90. Contested (C): Durham NW, Feb. 1974; Sunderland S, Oct. 1974. Mem., Bloomsbury DHA, 1982–85; Dir, Poplar Housing and Regeneration Community Assoc., 1998–2000. Trustee, Guinness Trust, 1998–2001. Chm., Northumbria Regl Cttee, NT, 1995–. FRSA 1990. DL Northumberland, 1990. *Heir: s* Walter John Buchanan Riddell, *b* 10 June 1974. *Address:* Hepple, Morpeth, Northumberland NE65 7LN. *TA:* Hepple; 49 Campden Hill Square, W8 7JR. *Clubs:* Garrick; Northern Counties (Newcastle upon Tyne).

See also R. L. Ollard, Sir J. L. Pumphrey.

RIDDELL, Nicholas Peter; His Honour Judge Riddell; a Circuit Judge, since 1995; *b* 24 April 1941; *s* of late Peter John Archibald Riddell and Cynthia Mary Riddell (later Douglas); *m* 1976, Barbara Helen Glucksmann; three *d*. *Educ:* Harrow; Magdalene Coll., Cambridge (BA Cantab). Called to the Bar, Inner Temple, 1964; practised at the Bar, 1964–95. Mem. Bd, Circle 33 Housing Trust Ltd, 1998–. *Address:* 18 Myddelton Square, EC1R 1YE. *T:* (020) 7837 4034.

RIDDELL, Norman Malcolm Marshall; Chairman, Norman Riddell and Associates Ltd, since 1997; *b* 30 June 1947; *s* of Malcolm Riddell and Euphemia Richardson Riddell (*née* Wight); *m* 1969, Leila Jean White; three *s*. *Educ:* George Heriot's Sch., Edinburgh. MCIBS, AIIMR. National Commercial Bank and Royal Bank of Scotland, 1965–78; Man. Dir, Britannia Investment Services, 1978–86; Chief Executive: Capital House Investment Management, 1986–93; INVESCO plc, 1993–96; Chairman: United Overseas Gp plc, 1997–99; Savoy Asset Mgt plc, 1997–2000. Director: Charterhouse Gp, 1986–89; Life Assce Hldg Corp., 1995–; Asset Management Investment Co., 1997–; Clubhaus, 1999–; Improvement Pathway, 1999–; Progressive Value Mgt, 1999–. *Recreations:* plate collecting, gardening, most sports (spectator), travel, music, wine. *Address:* Norman Riddell and Associates Ltd, The Pavilion, 3 Broadgate, EC2M 2QS. *Club:* Capital.

RIDDELL, Peter John Robert; Political Columnist, since 1991 and Assistant Editor (Politics), since 1993, The Times; *b* 14 Oct. 1948; *s* of late Kenneth Robert Riddell and of Freda Riddell (*née* Young); *m* 1994, Avril Walker; one *d*. *Educ:* Dulwich Coll.; Sidney Sussex Coll., Cambridge (BA Hist. and Econs 1970, MA). Joined Financial Times, 1970: Property Corresp., 1972–74; Lex Column, 1975–76; Economics Corresp., 1976–81; Political Editor, 1981–88; US Editor and Washington Bureau Chief, 1989–91; joined The Times, 1991, Political Editor, 1992–93. Regular broadcaster, Week in Westminster, Talking Politics, Radio 4, and on TV. Vis. Prof. of Political History, QMW, 2000–. Chm., Parly Press Gall., 1997; Member: Council, Hansard Soc., 1995–; Bd, Inst. of Contemp. British Hist., 1996–. FRHistS 1998. Hon. DLitt Greenwich, 2001. Wincott Award for Economic and Financial Journalism, 1981; House Magazine Political Journalist of the Year, 1986. *Publications:* The Thatcher Government, 1983, rev. edn 1985; The Thatcher Decade, 1989, rev. edn as The Thatcher Era, 1991; Honest Opportunism, the rise of the career politician, 1993, rev. edn 1996; Parliament under Pressure, 1998, rev. edn as Parliament under Blair, 2000; contrib. chaps in books, incl. A Conservative Revolution?, 1994, The Major Effect, 1994, and The Blair Effect, 2001; contrib. to Spectator, New Statesman, Political Qly, British Journalism Rev., TLS, Jl of Lesgislative Studies. *Recreations:* watching cricket, opera, theatre. *Address:* 22 Falkland Road, NW5 2PX. *Clubs:* Garrick, MCC.

RIDDELL, Richard Rodford; Director of Education, Bristol City Council, since 1995; *b* 28 Jan. 1953; *m* 1975, Millie Mitchell; one *s* one *d*. *Educ:* Manchester Grammar Sch.; Magdalen Coll., Oxford (MA); Madeley Coll. of Educn (PGCE); Bulmershe Coll. of Higher Educn (MPhil). Teacher: John Mason Sch., Abingdon, 1975–77; Waingel's Copse Sch., Reading, 1977–81; Asst Educn Officer, Wilts CC, 1981–86; Educn Officer, Notts CC, 1986–90; Asst Dir of Educn, Avon CC, 1990–95. FRSA 1999. *Address:* PO Box 57, The Council House, College Green, Bristol BS99 7EB. *T:* (0117) 903 7961.

RIDDELSDELL, Dame Mildred, DCB 1972; CBE 1958; Second Permanent Secretary, Department of Health and Social Security, 1971–73; (Deputy Secretary, 1966–71); *b* 1 Dec. 1913; 2nd *d* of Rev. H. J. Riddelsdell. *Educ:* St Mary's Hall, Brighton; Bedford Coll., London. Entered Min. of Labour, 1936; Asst Sec., Min. of National Insurance, 1945; Under Secretary, 1950; On loan to United Nations, 1953–56; Secretary, National Incomes Commission, 1962–65; Ministry of Pensions and National Insurance, 1965, Social Security, 1966. Chm., CS Retirement Fellowship, 1974–77. *Recreation:* gardening. *Address:* 6 Prebendal Court, Shipton-under-Wychwood, Oxon OX7 6BB.

RIDDICK, Graham Edward Galloway; Business Development Director, De Havilland Information Services plc, since 2000; *b* 26 Aug. 1955; *s* of late John Julian Riddick and Cecilia Margaret Riddick (*née* Ruggles-Brise); *m* 1988, Sarah Northcroft; one *s* two *d*. *Educ:* Stowe Sch., Buckingham; Univ. of Warwick (Chm., Warwick Univ. Cons. Assoc.). Sales management with Procter & Gamble, 1977–82; Coca-Cola, 1982–87. MP (C) Colne Valley, 1987–97 (first Cons. MP in Colne Valley for 102 years); contested (C) same seat, 1997. Gp Mktg Dir, subseq. Gp Mktg and Communications Dir, Onyx Evironmental Gp plc, 1997–2000. PPS to Financial Sec. to HM Treasury, 1990–92, to Sec. of State for Transport, 1992–94. Mem., Educn Select Cttee, 1994–96; Vice Chm., Cons. Trade and Industry Cttee, 1990; Secretary: Cons. Employment Cttee, 1988–90; All Party Textiles Gp, 1988–97. Chm., Angola Study Gp, 1988; Pres., Yorks CPC, 1993–97. *Recreations:* fishing, shooting, sports, photography, bridge. *Club:* Royal Automobile.

RIDDLE, Howard Charles Fraser; a District Judge (Magistrates' Courts) (formerly Metropolitan Stipendiary Magistrate), since 1995; *b* 13 Aug. 1947; *s* of Cecil Riddle and Eithne Riddle (*née* McKenna); *m* 1974, Susan Hilary Hurst; two *d*. *Educ:* Judd Sch., Tonbridge; London School of Economics (LLB); Coll. of Law. Admitted Solicitor, 1978. Sub-Editor, Penguin Books, 1969–70; Editor, McGill-Queens University Press, 1970–71; Publications Officer, Humanities and Social Science Res. Council, Canada, 1971–76; Solicitor, Edward Fail, Bradshaw and Waterson, 1976–95 (Sen. Partner, 1985–95). Vice-Chm., London Area Cttee, Legal Aid Bd, 1993–95. *Recreations:* village activities, Rugby football, tennis, visiting France. *Address:* c/o Greenwich Magistrates' Court, 9 Blackheath Road, SE10 8PF. *T:* (020) 8276 1302. *Clubs:* Druidstone (Dyfed); Tonbridge Juddians Rugby Football.

RIDDLE, Hugh Joseph, (Huseph), RP 1960; artist; portrait painter; *b* 24 May 1912; *s* of late Hugh Howard Riddle and late Christine Simons Brown; *m* 1936, Joan Claudia Johnson (*d* 1994); one *s* two *d*. *Educ:* Harrow; Magdalen Coll., Oxford; Slade School of Art; Byam Shaw School of Art and others. Specialises in portraits of children and adults; work includes HRH Prince Edward, aged 9, and HM the Queen. *Recreations:* sailing, swimming, gardening. *Address:* 18 Boulevard Verdi, Domaine du château de Tournon, Montauroux 83440, France.

RIDEOUT, Prof. Roger William; Professor of Labour Law, University College, London, 1973–2000; *b* 9 Jan. 1935; *s* of Sidney and Hilda Rideout; *m* 1st, 1959, Marjorie Roberts (marr. diss. 1976); one *d*; 2nd, 1977, Gillian Margaret Lynch. *Educ:* Bedford School; University Coll., London (LLB, PhD). Called to the Bar, Gray's Inn, 1964. National Service, 1958–60; 2nd Lt RAEC, Educn Officer, 1st Bn Coldstream Guards. Lecturer: Univ. of Sheffield, 1960–63; Univ. of Bristol, 1963–64. University Coll., London: Sen. Lectr, 1964–65; Reader, 1965–73; Dean of Faculty of Laws, 1975–77; Fellow, 1997. ILO missions to The Gambia, 1982–83, Somalia, 1989–90, Egypt, 1992–94. Deputy Chairman: Central Arbitration Cttee; Employment Tribunals. ACAS panel arbitrator, 1981–; Vice-Pres., Industrial Law Society. Mem., Zool Soc. of London. Jt Editor, Current Legal Problems, 1975–92; Gen. Editor, Federation News, 1989–2001. *Publications:* The Right to Membership of a Trade Union, 1962; The Practice and Procedure of the NIRC, 1973; Trade Unions and the Law, 1973; Principles of Labour Law, 1972, 5th edn 1989. *Address:* 255 Chipstead Way, Woodmansterne, Surrey SM7 3JW. *T:* (01737) 213489. *Club:* MCC.

RIDER, Prof. Barry Alexander Kenneth, PhD; Director, Institute of Advanced Legal Studies, University of London, since 1995; Fellow Commoner, Jesus College, Cambridge, since 2001; *b* 30 May 1952; *s* of Kenneth Leopold Rider and Alexina Elsie Rider (*née* Bremner); *m* 1976, Normalita Antonina Furto Rosales; one *d*. *Educ:* Bexleyheath Boys' Secondary Modern Sch.; Poly. of N London (Intermediate Ext. LLB 1970); Queen Mary Coll., London (LLB Hons 1973; PhD 1976); Jesus Coll., Cambridge (MA 1976; PhD 1978). Called to the Bar, Inner Temple, 1977. Univ. teaching officer, Univ. of Cambridge, 1980–95; Fellow, 1976–2001, Dean, 1989–96, Jesus Coll., Cambridge. Vis. Sen. Fellow, Centre for Commercial Law Studies, QMC, 1979–90; University of London: Chm., Acad. Policy and Standards Cttee, Sch. of Advanced Study, 1997–; Mem., Bd of Mgt, Inst. of US Studies, 1997–. Hon. Prof., Dept of Mercantile Law, Univ. of OFS, RSA, 1998. General Editor: Company Lawyer, 1980–; European Business Law Rev., 1996–; Jl Financial Crime, 1994–; European Financial Services Law, 1996–98; Jl Money Laundering Control, 1996–; Amicus Curiae, 1997–; Internat. and Comparative Corporate Law Jl, 1998–; Financial Crime Rev., 2000–; European Financial Law Rev., 2000–; Editor: CUP series on Corporate Law, 1996–; Kluwer series on Company and Financial Law, 1997–. Exec. Dir, Centre for Internat. Documentation on Organised and Econ. Crime, 1989–. Special Advr to H of C Select Cttee on Trade and Industry, 1989–93. Chairman: Exec. Cttee, Soc. for Advanced Legal Studies, 1997–; Hamlyn Trust for Legal Educn, 2001–. Former Consultant to internat. bodies, incl. UNDP, IMF, Commonwealth Fund for Tech. Co-operation, and Commonwealth Secretariat. Mem. Court, City Univ., 2001–. Freeman, City of London, 1984; Mem., Court of Assts, Co. of Pattenmakers, 1998–. Hon. LLD: Dickinson Law Sch., USA, 1996; Free State, RSA, 2001. *Publications:* (jtly) The Regulation of Insider Trading, 1979; Insider Trading, 1983; (jtly) Guide to the Financial Services Act, 1987, 2nd edn 1989; (jtly) Insider Crime, 1993; (jtly) Guide to Financial Services Regulation, 1997; (jtly) Anti-Money Laundering Guide, 1999; *edited:* The Regulation of the British Securities Industry, 1979, CCH Financial Services Reporter, 3 vols, 1987; The Fiduciary, the Insider and the Conflict, 1995; Money Laundering Control, 1996; Corruption: the enemy within, 1997; Developments in European Company Law, vol. I 1997, vol. II 1998; International Tracing of Assets, 2 vols, 1997; Commercial Law in a Global Context, 1998; The Corporate Dimension, 1998; The Realm of Company Law, 1998; contrib. to numerous books and legal periodicals on company law, financial law and control of economic crime. *Recreations:* riding, judo, parasailing. *Address:* Institute of Advanced Legal Studies, Charles Clore House, 17 Russell Square, WC1B 5DR. *T:* (020) 7862 5838; Jesus College, Cambridge CB5 8BL. *Clubs:* Athenæum, Oxford and Cambridge, Civil Service.

RIDER, Stephen Henry; Main Presenter, BBC Grandstand, since 1992; *b* 28 April 1950; *s* of Alfred Charles Rider and Shirley Jeanette (*née* Walls); *m* 1985, Jane Eydmann; one *s* one *d*. *Educ:* Roan Grammar Sch., Blackheath. Local sports journalist, S London and sports presenter for London Broadcasting, 1969–76; Sports Presenter: Anglia TV, 1976–80; ITV Network, incl., World of Sport, 1980 Olympics, Midweek Sports Special, Network Golf, 1980–85; Network Presenter for BBC Sport: Main Presenter, Sportsnight, 1985–92; network golf coverage; Olympic Games, Seoul, 1988, Barcelona, 1992, Atlanta, 1996; Commonwealth Games, 1986, 1990, 1994 and 1998; main network golf presenter, 1991–; motor sport specialist; Presenter, Grandstand, 1985–. Sports Presenter of Year, TRIC, 1994, RTS, 1995. *Recreations:* golf, family. *Address:* c/o Blackburn Sachs Associates, Eastgate House, 16–19 Eastcastle Street, W1N 7PA.

RIDGE, Anthony Hubert; Director-General, International Bureau, Universal Postal Union, Bern, 1973–74 (Deputy Director-General, 1964–73); *b* 5 Oct. 1913; *s* of Timothy Leopold Ridge and Magdalen (*née* Hernig); *m* 1938, Marjory Joan Sage; three *s* one *d*. *Educ:* Christ's Hospital; Jesus College, Cambridge. Entered GPO, 1937; seconded to Min. Home Security, 1940; GPO Personnel Dept, 1944; PPS to Postmaster General, 1947; Dep. Dir, London Postal Region, 1949; Asst Sec., Overseas Mails, 1951, Personnel, 1954, Overseas Mails, 1956; Director of Clerical Mechanization and Buildings, and Member of Post Office Board, GPO, 1960–63. Mem., Postling Parish Council, 1979–87. Governor, Christ's Hosp. *Recreations:* music, languages, transport, gardening. *Address:* Staple, Postling, Hythe, Kent CT21 4HA. *T:* (01303) 862315. *Clubs:* Christ's Hospital, Oxford and Cambridge, Cambridge Society.

RIDGE, Rupert Leander Pattle; Director, Leonard Cheshire International (formerly International Director, Leonard Cheshire Foundation), since 1994; *b* 18 May 1947; *y s* of late Major Robert Vaughan Ridge and Marian Ivy Edith Ridge (*née* Pattle); *m* 1971, Mary Blanche Gibbs; two *s* two *d*. *Educ:* King's Coll., Taunton. Officer, LI, 1969–73. BAC, then British Aerospace Defence Ltd, 1973–94. Trustee: Action around Bethlehem Children with Disability, 1994– (Chm., 1998–); CHAD, 1998–. *Recreations:* gardening, being in the country. *Address:* (office) 30 Millbank, SW1P 4QD. *Club:* Army and Navy.

RIDGWAY, Maj. Gen. Andrew Peter, CB 2001; CBE 1995; Head, Defence Training Review Implementation Team, since 2001; *b* 20 March 1950; *s* of late Robert Hamilton Ridgway and of Betty Patricia Ridgway (*née* Crane); *m* 1974, Valerie Elizabeth Shawe; three *s* one *d*. *Educ:* Hele's Sch., Exeter; RMA, Sandhurst; St John's Coll., Cambridge (MPhil). Commnd RTR, 1970: served Germany, NI, Belize, Bosnia, Kuwait, Macedonia, Kosovo and UK; CO, 3 RTR, 1991–92; Col, Army Prog., MoD, 1992–93; Comdr, 7 Armd Bde, 1993–95 (Comdr, UN Sector SW Bosnia Herzegovina, Feb.–Nov. 1994); Dir, Operational Capability, MoD, 1995–97; Chief, Jt Rapid Deployment Force, 1997–98; COS, ACE RRC, 1998–2001 (COS, Kosovo Force, 1999). Col Comdt, RTR, 1999–. Chm., Army Bobsleigh, 1998–; Dir, Army Ice Sports, 1999–. *Recreations:* ski-ing, fishing, walking, paying school fees. *Address:* RHQ Royal Tank Regiment, Bovington, Dorset BH20 6JA. *T:* (01929) 403360. *Club:* Army and Navy.

RIDGWAY, David Frederick Charles, CMG 2000; OBE 1988; HM Diplomatic Service; retired; *b* 9 June 1941; *m* 1966, Dora Beatriz Siles; one *s* one *d*. Entered FO, 1960; served La Paz, Colombo and Durban, 1963–77; First Sec. (Commercial), Buenos Aires, 1980–82; FCO, 1982–84; Chargé d'Affaires *ai*, San Salvador, 1984–87; FCO, 1988–91; Dir of Trade Promotion, Madrid, 1991–95; Ambassador to: Bolivia, 1995–98; Cuba, 1998–2001. *Address:* 84 Chesilton Road, SW6 5AB.

RIDLER, Anne (Barbara), OBE 2001; FRSL; author; *b* 30 July 1912; *o d* of late H. C. Bradby, housemaster of Rugby School, and Violet Milford; *m* 1938, Vivian Ridler, *qv*; two *s* two *d*. *Educ:* Downe House School; King's College, London; and in Florence and Rome. FRSL 1998. Cholmondely Award for Poetry, 1998. *Publications: poems:* Poems, 1939; A Dream Observed, 1941; The Nine Bright Shiners, 1943; The Golden Bird, 1951; A Matter of Life and Death, 1959; Selected Poems (New York), 1961; Some Time After, 1972; (contrib.) Ten Oxford Poets, 1978; New and Selected Poems, 1988; Collected Poems, 1994; *plays:* Cain, 1943; The Shadow Factory, 1946; Henry Bly and other plays, 1950; The Trial of Thomas Cranmer, 1956; Who is my Neighbour?, 1963; The Jesse Tree (libretto), 1972; The King of the Golden River (libretto), 1975; The Lambton Worm (libretto), 1978; Crucifixion Cantata (libretto), 1993; *translations:* Italian opera libretti: Rosinda, 1973; Orfeo, 1975; Eritrea, 1975; Return of Ulysses, 1978; Orontea, 1979; Agrippina, 1981; Calisto, 1984; Così fan Tutte, 1986; Don Giovanni, 1990; Marriage of Figaro, 1991; Coronation of Poppea, 1992; Gluck's Orfeo, 1996; Magic Flute, 1996; *biography:* Olive Willis and Downe House, 1967; *criticism:* (jtly) Profitable Wonders: aspects of Traherne, 1989; A Measure of English Poetry, 1991; Working for T. S. Eliot, 2000; *edited:* Shakespeare Criticism, 1919–35; A Little Book of Modern Verse, 1941; Best Ghost Stories, 1945; Supplement to Faber Book of Modern Verse, 1951; The Image of the City and other essays by Charles Williams, 1958; Shakespeare Criticism 1935–60, 1963; Poems of James Thomson, 1963; Thomas Traherne, 1966; (with Christopher Bradby) Best Stories of Church and Clergy, 1966; Selected Poems of George Darley, 1979; Poems of William Austin, 1983; A Victorian Family Postbag, 1988. *Recreations:* music; the theatre; the cinema. *Address:* 14 Stanley Road, Oxford OX4 1QZ. *T:* (01865) 247595.

RIDLER, Vivian Hughes, CBE 1971; MA Oxon 1958 (by decree; Corpus Christi College); Printer to the University of Oxford, 1958–78; *b* 2 Oct. 1913; *s* of Bertram Hughes Ridler and Elizabeth Emmeline (*née* Best); *m* 1938, Anne Barbara Bradby (*see* A. B. Ridler); two *s* two *d*. *Educ:* Bristol Gram. Sch. Appren. E. S. & A. Robinson, Ltd, 1931–36. Works Manager University Press, Oxford, 1948; Assistant Printer, 1949–58. Pres., British Federation of Master Printers, 1968–69. Professorial Fellow, St Edmund Hall, 1966, Emeritus Fellow, 1978. *Recreations:* printing, theatre, cinema, cinematography. *Address:* 14 Stanley Road, Oxford OX4 1QZ. *T:* (01865) 247595.

RIDLEY, family name of **Viscount Ridley**.

RIDLEY, 4th Viscount *cr* 1900; **Matthew White Ridley,** KG 1992; GCVO 1994; TD 1960; JP; DL; Baron Wensleydale, 1900; Bt 1756; Lord-Lieutenant and Custos Rotulorum of Northumberland, 1984–2000; Lord Steward of HM Household, 1989–2001; *b* 29 July 1925; *e s* of 3rd Viscount Ridley; *S* father, 1964; *m* 1953, Lady Anne Lumley, 3rd *d* of 11th Earl of Scarbrough, KG, GCSI, GCIE, GCVO, PC; one *s* three *d*. *Educ:* Eton; Balliol College, Oxford. ARICS 1951. Coldstream Guards (NW Europe), 1943–46, Captain, 1946; Northumberland Hussars, 1947–64 (Lt-Col 1961, Bt Col 1964); Hon. Colonel: Northumberland Hussars Sqdn, Queen's Own Yeomanry, 1979–86; Queen's Own Yeomanry RAC TA, 1984–86; Northumbrian Univs OTC, 1986–90; Col Comdt, Yeomanry RAC TA, 1982–86. Director: Northern Rock Building Soc., 1962– (Chm., 1987–92); Tyne Tees Television, 1964–90; Barclays Bank (NE) Ltd, 1964–90; Municipal Mutual Insurance, 1982–93. Pres., British Deer Soc., 1970–73. Member: Layfield Cttee of Enquiry into Local Govt Finance, 1974–; Commonwealth War Graves Commn, 1991–99. Chm., Internat. Dendrology Soc., 1988–93; Pres., Natural Hist. Soc. of Northumbria, 1997–. Chm., N of England TA Assoc., 1980–84; Pres., TA & VRA Council, 1984–95 (Patron, 1995–). Chm., Newcastle Univ. Develt. Trust, 1981–84; Chancellor, 1978–80, Hon. Fellow, 1980, Newcastle upon Tyne Polytechnic; Chancellor, Newcastle Univ., 1989–99. Hon. FRHS 1986; Hon. FRICS 1986. JP 1957, CC 1958, CA 1963, DL 1968, Northumberland; Chm., Northumberland CC, 1967–74, Chm., new Northumberland CC, 1974–79; Pres., ACC, 1979–84. Pres., Blyth Spartans FC, 2000. KStJ 1984; Hon. DCL Newcastle, 1989. Order of Merit, West Germany, 1974. *Heir: s* Hon. Matthew White Ridley [*b* 7 Feb. 1958; *m* 1989, Dr Anya Hurlbert, *d* of Dr Robert Hurlbert, Houston, Texas; one *s*]. *Address:* Boston House, Blagdon, Seaton Burn, Newcastle upon Tyne NE13 6DB. *T:* (01670) 789236, *Fax:* (01670) 789560. *Clubs:* Boodle's, Pratt's; Northern Counties (Newcastle upon Tyne).

RIDLEY, Sir Adam (Nicholas), Kt 1985; Director General, London Investment Banking Association, since 2000; Chairman of Trustees, Equitas Group of Companies, since 1996; *b* 14 May 1942; *s* of late Jasper Maurice Alexander Ridley and Helen Cressida Ridley (*née* Bonham Carter); *m* 1981, Margaret Anne Passmore; three *s* (inc. twin *s*). *Educ:* Eton Coll.; Balliol Coll., Oxford (1st cl. hons PPE 1965); Univ. of California, Berkeley. Foreign Office, 1965, seconded to DEA, 1965–68; Harkness Fellow, Univ. of California, Berkeley, 1968–69; HM Treasury, 1970–71, seconded to CPRS, 1971–74; Economic Advr to shadow cabinet and Asst Dir, Cons. Res. Dept, 1974–79; Special Advr to Chancellor of the Exchequer, 1979–84, to Chancellor of the Duchy of Lancaster, 1985. Director: Hambros Bank, 1985–97; Hambros PLC, 1985–97; non-executive Director: Leopold Joseph Holdings, 1997–; IFSL, 2000–. Chm., Names Adv. Cttee, 1995–96, Mem. Council, 1997–99, Mem., Regulatory Bd, 1997–99, Lloyds of London. Mem., National Lottery Charities Bd, 1994–2000 (Dep. Chm., 1995–2000). *Publications:* articles on regional policy, public spending, international and Eastern European economics. *Recreations:* music, pictures, travel. *Address:* c/o London Investment Banking Association, 6 Frederick's Place, EC2R 8BT. *Club:* Garrick.

RIDLEY, Dame Betty; *see* Ridley, Dame M. B.

RIDLEY, Prof. Brian Kidd, FRS 1994; Research Professor of Physics, University of Essex, since 1991; *b* 2 March 1931; *s* of Oliver Archbold Ridley and Lillian Beatrice Ridley; *m* 1959, Sylvia Jean Nicholls; one *s* one *d*. *Educ:* Univ. of Durham (BSc 1st Cl. Hons Physics, PhD). CPhys, FInstP. Research Physicist, Mullard Research Lab., Redhill, 1956–64; Essex University: Lectr in Physics, 1964–67; Sen. Lectr, 1967–71; Reader, 1971–84; Prof., 1984–91. Dist. Vis. Prof., Cornell Univ., 1967; Vis. Prof. at univs in USA, Denmark, Sweden and Holland. Paul Dirac Medal and Prize, Inst. of Physics, 2001. *Publications:* Time, Space and Things, 1976, 3rd edn 1995; The Physical Environment, 1979; Quantum Processes in Semiconductors, 1982, 4th edn 1999; Electrons and Phonons in Semiconductor Multilayers, 1997; On Science, 2001. *Recreations:* tennis, piano. *Address:* Department of Electronic Systems Engineering, University of Essex, Colchester CO4 3SQ. *T:* (01206) 872873.

RIDLEY, Prof. Frederick Fernand, OBE 1978; PhD; Senior Fellow, Institute of Public Administration and Management, and Professor Emeritus, University of Liverpool, since 1995 (Professor of Political Theory and Institutions, 1965–95); *b* 11 Aug. 1928; *s* of late J. and G. A. Ridley; *m* 1967, Paula Frances Cooper Ridley, *qv*; two *s* one *d*. *Educ:* The Hall, Hampstead; Highgate Sch.; LSE (BScEcon, PhD); Univs of Paris and Berlin. Lectr, Univ. of Liverpool, 1958–65. Vis. Professor: Graduate Sch. of Public Affairs, Univ. of Pittsburgh, 1968; Coll. of Europe, Bruges, 1975–83. Manpower Services Commission, Merseyside: Chm., Job Creation Prog., 1975–77; Vice-Chm., 1978–87, Chm., 1987–88, Area Manpower Bd. Member: Jt Univ. Council for Social and Public Admin, 1964–95 (Chm., 1972–74); Exec., Polit. Studies Assoc., 1967–75 (Hon. Vice-Pres., 1995–); Council, Hansard Soc., 1970–94; Polit. Science Cttee, SSRC, 1972–76; Cttee, European Gp on Public Admin, 1973–92; Public and Social Admin Bd, CNAA, 1975–82; Social Studies Res. Cttee, CNAA, 1980–83 (Chm.); Academic Cttee, Assoc. Internat. de la Fonction Publique, 1988–93; Vice-Pres., Rencontres Européennes des Fonctions Publiques/Entretiens Universitaires pour l'Admin en Europe, 1990–2001. Member: Exec., Merseyside Arts (RAA), 1979–84; Adv. Council, Granada Foundn, 1984–98; Council, Forschungsinst. für Verwaltungswissenschaft, Speyer, 1993–; Trustee, Friends of Merseyside Museums and Galleries, 1977–85. Pres., Politics Assoc., 1976–81 (Hon. Fellow, 1995). Editor: Political Studies, 1969–75; Parliamentary Affairs, 1975–. *Publications:* Public Administration in France, 1964; Revolutionary Syndicalism in France, 1970; The Study of Government, 1975; numerous articles and edited vols on political sci. and public admin. *Address:* Riversdale House, Grassendale Park, Liverpool L19 0LR. *T:* (0151) 427 1630.

RIDLEY, Gordon, OBE 1980; MA; FICE, FIHT; retired; Director of Planning and Transportation, Greater London Council, 1978–80; *b* 1 Nov. 1921; *s* of Timothy Ridley and Lallah Sarah Ridley; *m* 1952, Doreen May Browning; one *s* one *d*. *Educ:* Selwyn Coll., Cambridge (MA). FICE 1965; FIMunE 1964; FInstHE 1966. Served War, Admiralty Signals Estab., 1941–46. Engrg appts, various local authorities, 1946–55; Bridges Br., MoT, 1955–58; AEA, 1958–63; LCC, 1963–65; engrg appts, GLC, 1965–78. *Publications:* papers on engrg topics presented to learned instns. *Recreation:* words. *Address:* 26 Greenacres, Preston Park Avenue, Brighton BN1 6HR. *T:* (01273) 559951.

RIDLEY, Jasper Godwin; author; *b* 25 May 1920; *s* of Geoffrey Ridley and Ursula (*née* King); *m* 1949, Vera, *d* of Emil Pollak of Prague; two *s* one *d*. *Educ:* Felcourt Sch.; Sorbonne, Paris; Magdalen Coll., Oxford. Certif. of Honour, Bar Finals. Called to Bar, Inner Temple, 1945. St Pancras Borough Council, 1945–49. Pres., Hardwicke Soc., 1954–55. Contested (Lab): Winchester, 1955; Westbury, 1959. Vice-Pres. for life, English Centre of Internat. PEN, 1985; Pres., Tunbridge Wells Writers, 1994–. Mem. Ct of Assts, Carpenters' Co. (Master, 1988–89, 1990–91). Has written many radio scripts on historical subjects. FRSL 1963. *Publications:* Nicholas Ridley, 1957; The Law of Carriage of Goods, 1957; Thomas Cranmer, 1962; John Knox, 1968; Lord Palmerston, 1970 (James Tait Black Meml Prize, 1970); Mary Tudor, 1973; Garibaldi, 1974; The Roundheads, 1976; Napoleon III and Eugénie, 1979; History of England, 1981; The Statesman and the Fanatic: Thomas Wolsey and Thomas More, 1982; Henry VIII, 1984; Elizabeth I, 1987; The Tudor Age, 1988; The Love Letters of Henry VIII, 1988; Maximillian and Juárez, 1992; Tito, 1994; History of the Carpenters' Company, 1995; Mussolini, 1997; The Freemasons, 1999; Bloody Mary's Martyrs, 2001. *Recreations:* walking, opera, chess. *Address:* 6 Oakdale Road, Tunbridge Wells, Kent TN4 8DS. *T:* (01892) 522460.

RIDLEY, Michael; *see* Ridley, R. M.

RIDLEY, Sir Michael (Kershaw), KCVO 2000 (CVO 1992); Clerk of the Council, Duchy of Lancaster, 1981–2000; *b* 7 Dec. 1937; *s* of late George K. and of Mary Ridley; *m* 1968, Diana Loraine McLernon; two *s*. *Educ:* Stowe; Magdalene College, Cambridge. MA. FRICS. Grosvenor Estate, Canada and USA, 1965–69, London, 1969–72; Property Manager, British & Commonwealth Shipping Co., 1972–81. A Gen. Comr of Income Tax, 1984–98. Mem., Adv. Panel, Greenwich Hosp., 1978–. Mem. Court, Lancaster Univ., 1981–2000. Trustee, St Martin's-in-the-Fields Almshouse Assoc.; Dir, Feathers Clubs Assoc.; Hon. Treas., Chartered Surveyors' Co. *Recreation:* golf. *Address:* 37 Chester Row, SW1W 9JE. *Clubs:* Brooks's, Garrick; Royal Mid-Surrey Golf.

RIDLEY, Dame (Mildred) Betty, DBE 1975; MA (Lambeth) 1958; Third Church Estates Commissioner, 1972–81; a Church Commissioner, 1959–81; *b* 10 Sept. 1909; *d* of late Rt Rev. Henry Mosley, sometime Bishop of Southwell; *m* 1929, Rev. Michael Ridley (*d* 1953), Rector of Finchley; three *s* one *d*. *Educ:* North London Collegiate School; Cheltenham Ladies' College. Member: General Synod of Church of England, 1970–81, and its Standing Cttee, 1971–81; Central Board of Finance, 1955–79; Mem., Faculty Jurisdiction Commn, 1980–83; Vice-Pres. British Council of Churches, 1954–56. Hon. DSc (SocSc) Southampton, 1993. *Recreation:* listening to music. *Address:* Brendon House, Park Road, Winchester SO23 7BE. *T:* (01962) 855758. *Club:* Reform.

RIDLEY, Paula Frances Cooper, OBE 1996; JP; DL; MA; Chair, Liverpool Housing Action Trust, since 1992; Chairman, Board of Trustees, Victoria and Albert Museum, since 1998; Director, Gulbenkian Foundation (UK), since 1999; *b* 27 Sept. 1944; *d* of Ondrej Clyne and Ellen (*née* Cooper); *m* 1967, Frederick Fernand Ridley, *qv*; two *s* one *d*. *Educ:* Kendal High Sch., Westmorland; Univ. of Liverpool (BA, MA). Lectr in Politics and Public Admin., Liverpool Polytechnic, 1966–71; Proj. Co-ordinator, Regeneration Projects Ltd, 1981–84; Dir, Community Initiatives Res. Trust, 1983–90; Consultant, BAT Industries Small Businesses Ltd, 1983–95; Bd Mem., Brunswick Small Business Centre Ltd, 1984–95; Associate, CEI Consultants, 1984–88. Dir, Merseyside Develt Corp., 1991–98. Mem., Royal Commn on Long Term Care for the Elderly, 1997–99. Presenter and Assoc. Editor, Granada Action, 1989–92; Mem., IBA, 1982–88. Chm., Stocktonwood County Primary Sch., 1976–79; Member: Liverpool Heritage Bureau, 1971–88; Management Cttee, Liverpool Victoria Settlement, 1971–86 (Vice-Chm.,

1977–86); Granada Telethon Trust, 1988–94. Trustee: Tate Gall., 1988–98; Nat. Gall., 1995–98; Chm., Tate Gall., Liverpool, 1988–98. Liverpool University: Lady Pres., Guild of Undergraduates, Clerk of Convocation, 1972–74; Member: Court, 1972–; Council, 1998–; Life Governor, Liverpool and Huyton Colls, 1979–94. Merseyside Civic Society: Hon. Sec., 1971–82; Vice-Chm., 1982–86; Chm., 1986–91. JP Liverpool, 1977. DL Merseyside, 1989. FRSA. *Address:* Riversdale House, Grassendale Park, Liverpool L19 0LR. *T:* (0151) 427 1630; 69 Thomas More House, Barbican, EC2Y 8BT. *T:* (020) 7628 8573.

RIDLEY, (Robert) Michael; Principal, Royal Belfast Academical Institution, since 1990; *b* 8 Jan. 1947; *s* of Maurice Roy Ridley and Jean Evelyn Lawther (*née* Carlisle); *m* 1985, Jennifer Mary Pearson; two *d. Educ:* Clifton Coll.; St Edmund Hall, Oxford (MA, Cert Ed). Wellington Coll., Berks, 1970–82 (Housemaster, 1975–82); Hd of English, Merchiston Castle Sch., Edinburgh, 1982–86; Headmaster, Denstone Coll., 1986–90. Mem., Rotary Club, Belfast, 1990–. *Recreations:* cricket (Oxford Blue, 1968–70), golf, reading, travel. *Address:* The Royal Belfast Academical Institution College Square East, Belfast BT1 6DL. *T:* (028) 9024 0461. *Clubs:* East India; Vincent's (Oxford); Boat of Garten Golf (Inverness-shire); Malone Golf.

RIDLEY, Prof. Tony Melville, CBE 1986; PhD; FREng, FICE, FCIT; Professor of Transport Engineering (formerly Rees Jeffreys Professor), 1991–99, now Professor Emeritus, and Head of Department of Civil and Environmental Engineering (formerly Department of Civil Engineering), 1997–99, Imperial College of Science, Technology and Medicine; *b* 10 Nov. 1933; *s* of late John Edward and Olive Ridley; *m* 1959, Jane (*née* Dickinson); two *s* one *d. Educ:* Durham Sch.; King's Coll. Newcastle, Univ. of Durham (BSc); Northwestern Univ., Ill (MS); Univ. of California, Berkeley (PhD); Stanford Univ., Calif (Sen. Exec. Prog.). Nuclear Power Group, 1957–62; Univ. of California, 1962–65; Chief Research Officer, Highways and Transportation, GLC, 1965–69; Director General, Tyne and Wear Passenger Transport Exec., 1969–75; Man. Dir, Hong Kong Mass Transit Rly Corp., 1975–80; Bd Mem., 1980–88, Man. Dir (Rlys), 1980–85, LTE, then LRT; Chm., 1985–88, Man. Dir, 1985–88, Chief Exec., 1988, London Underground Ltd; Man. Dir-Project, Eurotunnel, 1989–90 (Dir, 1987–90). Chm., Docklands Light Railway Ltd, 1987–88; Director: Halcrow Fox and Associates, 1980–; London Transport Internat., 1982–88. President: Light Rail Transit Assoc., 1974–92; Assoc. for Project Mgt, 1999–; Commonwealth Engineers Council, 2000–; Internat. Pres, CIT, 1999– (Vice-Pres., 1987–90); Mem. Council, ICE, 1990–97 (Chm., Transport Bd, 1990–93; Vice Pres., 1992–95; Pres., 1995–96); Mem., Senate, Engrg Council, 1997– (Chm., Bd for the Engrg Profession, 1997–99). Freeman, City of London, 1982. FREng (FEng 1992); FHKIE, FITE, FIHT 1992 (Highways Award, 1988). FCGI 1996. Hon. FAPM 1996; Hon. FIA 1999. Hon. DTech Napier, 1996; Hon. DEng Newcastle upon Tyne, 1997. *Publications:* articles in transport, engrg and other jls. *Recreations:* theatre, music, international affairs, rejuvenation of Britain. *Address:* Department of Civil and Environmental Engineering, Imperial College, SW7 2BU. *T:* (020) 7594 6086, *Fax:* (020) 7594 6102. *Clubs:* Royal Automobile (Mem., Public Policy Cttee, 1997–); Hong Kong, Jockey (Hong Kong).

RIDLEY, Rear-Adm. William Terence Colborne, CB 1968; OBE 1954; Admiral Superintendent/Port Admiral, Rosyth, 1966–72; Chairman, Ex-Services Mental Welfare Society, 1973–83; *b* 9 March 1915; *s* of late Capt. W. H. W. Ridley, RN and late Vera Constance (*née* Walker); *m* 1st, 1938, Barbara Allen (*d* 1989); one *s*; 2nd, 1993, Joan Elaine Norman. *Educ:* Emsworth House; RNC, Dartmouth (Robert Roxburgh Prize); RNEC, Keyham. HMS Exeter, 1936; HMS Valiant, 1939; HMS Firedrake, 1940 (despatches twice); E-in-C Dept Admty, 1941; HMS Indefatigable, 1944; Admty Fuel Experimental Stn, 1947; Seaslug Project Officer, RAE Farnborough, 1950; HMS Ark Royal, 1956; E-in-C Dept Admty, Dreadnought Project Team, 1958; CO, RNEC, 1962; Staff of C-in-C Portsmouth, 1964. Lt-Comdr 1944; Comdr 1947; Capt. 1957; Rear-Adm. 1966. *Recreations:* gardening, do-it-yourself. *Address:* Flat 18, Fitzroy House, 55–59 Great Pulteney Street, Bath BA2 4DW.

RIDLEY-THOMAS, Roger; Managing Director, Thomson Regional Newspapers Ltd, 1989–94; *b* 14 July 1939; *s* of late John Montague Ridley-Thomas, MB, ChB, FRCSE, Norwich, and Christina Anne (*née* Seex); *m* 1962, Sandra Grace McBeth Young; two *s* two *d. Educ:* Gresham's Sch. Served Royal Norfolk Regt, 1958–60. Newspaper Publisher: Eastern Counties Newspapers, 1960–65; Thomson Regional Newspapers, 1965–94 (Dir, 1985–94); Managing Director: Aberdeen Journals, 1980–84; Scotsman Publications, 1984–89; Director: Caledonian Offset, 1979–94; Radio Forth, 1978–81; TRN Viewdata, 1978–89; Thomson Scottish Organisation, 1984–89; Northfield Newspapers, 1984–89; The Scotsman Communications, 1984–94; The Scotsman Publications, 1984–94; Central Publications, 1984–94; Aberdeen Journals, 1980–84, 1990–94; Belfast Telegraph Newspapers, 1990–94; Chester Chronicle, 1990–94; Newcastle Chronicle & Journal, 1990–94; Western Mail & Echo, 1990–94; Cardrona Ltd, 1995–; Milex Ltd, 1996–; Adscene Gp plc, 1996–99; Roys (Wroxham) Ltd, 1997–; Norfolk Christmas Trees Ltd, 2000–; Chairman: Anglia FM, 1996–98; NorCor Hldgs plc, 1996–2000. Director: Aberdeen Chamber of Commerce, 1981–84; Scottish Business in the Community, 1984–89; Scottish Business Achievement Award Trust, 1985–; Edinburgh Ch. of Commerce and Manufrs, 1985–88. Pres., Scottish Daily Newspaper Soc., 1983–85; Mem. Council, CBI, 1983–86; Mem., Scottish Wildlife Appeal Cttee, 1985–88. *Recreations:* vegetable growing, shooting, fishing, golf, tennis, travel. *Address:* Booton Manor, Booton, Reepham, Norfolk NR10 4NZ. *Club:* New (Edinburgh).

RIDSDALE, Sir Julian (Errington), Kt 1981; CBE 1977; *b* 8 June 1915; *m* 1942, Victoire Evelyn Patricia Bennett (*see* V. E. P. Ridsdale); one *d. Educ:* Tonbridge; Sandhurst. 2nd Lieutenant, Royal Norfolk Regiment, 1935; attached British Embassy, Tokyo, 1938–39; served War of 1939–45: Royal Norfolk Regt, Royal Scots, and Somerset Light Infantry; Asst Mil. Attaché, Japan, 1940; GSO3, Far Eastern Sect., War Office, 1941; GSO2, Joint Staff Mission, Washington, 1944–45; retired from Army with rank of Major, 1946. Contested SW Islington (C), LCC, 1949, N Paddington (C), Gen. Elec., 1951; MP (C) Harwich Div. of Essex, Feb. 1954–1992. PPS to Parly Under-Sec. of State for Colonies, 1957–58; PPS to Minister of State for Foreign Affairs, 1958–60; Parly Under-Sec. of State: for Air and Vice-President of the Air Council, 1962–64; for Defence for the Royal Air Force, Ministry of Defence, April–Oct. 1964. Chairman: British Japanese Parly Group, 1964–92; Parly Gp for Engrg Develt, 1985–92; Vice-Chm., UN Parly Assoc., 1966–82; Mem., Select Cttee of Public Accounts, 1970–74. Leader, Parly Delegns to Japan, 1973, 1975, annually 1977–82, 1988. Member: Trilateral Commn, EEC, USA and Japan, 1973–92; North Atlantic Assembly, 1979–92 (Vice-Pres., Political Cttee, 1983–87). Dep. Chm., Internat. Triangle, USA, Japan and Europe, 1981–85. Chm., Japan Soc., London, 1976–79. British Comr Gen., British Garden Expo 90, Osaka, Japan, 1990. Master, Skinners' Co., 1970–71. Hon. Fellow UCL, 1992. Ordre du Commanderie du Bon Temps de Médoc et de Graves, 1996. Order of the Sacred Treasure (Japan), 1967, Grand Cordon, 1990. *Recreations:* tennis, chess, gardening, travelling, sailing. *Address:* 12 The Boltons, SW10 9TD. *T:* (020) 7373 6159.

See also Sir P. H. Newall.

RIDSDALE, Victoire Evelyn Patricia, (Paddy), (Lady Ridsdale), DBE 1991; *b* 11 Oct. 1921; *d* of Col J. and Edith Marion Bennett; *m* 1942, Sir Julian Ridsdale, *qv*; one *d. Educ:* Sorbonne. Sec., DNI, 1939–42; Sec. to her husband, 1953–. Chm., Conservative MP's Wives, 1978–91. British Gold Hero Award, ARP/050, 1998. *Address:* 12 The Boltons, SW10 9TD. *T:* (020) 7373 6159.

See also Sir P. H. Newall.

RIESCO ZAÑARTU, Germán; commercial entrepreneur; Chilean Ambassador to the Court of St James's, 1990–93, and non-resident Ambassador to Ireland, 1992–93; *b* 17 Aug. 1941; *s* of Ignacio Riesco and Eliana Zañartu de Riesco; *m* 1974, Jacqueline Cassel; four *s* two *d. Educ:* Colegio San Ignacio, Santiago; Univ. of California, Davis (agric. degree; Special Award); Univ. of California, Berkeley (Economics). MP Nuble (National Party), 1969–73; Pres., Cttee on Economy, Chamber of Deputies; Dir, Agric. Planning Office, 1976–78. Vice-Pres., Nat. Party, 1983–88; Pres., Nat. Party for No Vote, 1988; Pres., PAC-Centre Alliance Party, 1988–90. Board Mem., Fundación Chile, 1983–90. Pres., Nat. Agric. Soc., Chile, 1979–81, 1981–83. Negotiator at FAO, World Bank and other internat. orgns. *Publications:* papers on Chilean agric. and econs. *Recreations:* music, theatre, tennis, ski-ing. *Address:* 5308 Agustín Denegri, Vitacura, Santiago, Chile. *T:* (562) 2182799, 2184049. *Clubs:* Chile, De La Union, Los Leones Country (Santiago, Chile).

RIFKIN, Joshua; Founder, and Director, The Bach Ensemble, since 1978; *b* 22 April 1944; *s* of Harry H. Rifkin and Dorothy (*née* Helsh); *m* 1st, 1970, Louise Litterick (marr. diss. 1984); 2nd, 1995, Helen Palmer; one *d. Educ:* Juilliard Sch. of Music (BS 1964); Princeton Univ. (MFA 1969). Musical Consultant, later Musical Dir, Nonesuch Records, NY, 1963–75; Brandeis University: Instructor, 1970–71; Asst Prof., 1971–77; Associate Prof., 1977–82. Visiting Professor, 1973–2000: NY Univ.; Harvard Univ.; Yale Univ.; Rutgers Univ.; Bard Coll.; Princeton Univ.; Stanford Univ.; King's Coll. London; Basel Univ.; Ohio State Univ.; Dortmund Univ. (Gambrinus Prof.); Munich Univ. Numerous concerts with Bach Ensemble in UK, Europe, US and Canada; Guest Conductor: English Chamber Orch., 1983, 1984; Scottish Chamber Orch., 1984, 1994; St Louis SO, 1985; Schola Cantorum Basiliensis, 1986, 1990, 1993, 1997; Victoria State SO, 1989; San Francisco SO, 1989; St Paul Chamber Orch., 1989; LA Chamber Orch., 1990; City of Glasgow SO, 1992; Cappella Coloniensis, Germany, 1993, 1994; Orch. Haydn/Bolzano, 1995; Solistas de México, BBC Concert Orch., and City of London Sinfonia, 1996; Jerusalem SO, Prague Chamber Orch., 1997; Nat. Arts Centre Orch., Houston SO, Camerata de las Américas, 1999. Numerous recordings. Fellow, Wissenschaftskolleg, Berlin, 1984–86. Hon. PhD Dortmund, 1999. *Publications:* contrib. New Grove Dictionary of Music and Musicians, 1980; numerous articles in scholarly jls. *Recreations:* food, wine, cinema, theatre, computers, fiction. *e-mail:* jrifkin@compuserve.com.

RIFKIND, Rt Hon. Sir Malcolm (Leslie), KCMG 1997; PC 1986; QC (Scot.) 1985; *b* 21 June 1946; *yr s* of late E. Rifkind, Edinburgh; *m* 1970, Edith Amalia Rifkind (*née* Steinberg); one *s* one *d. Educ:* George Watson's Coll.; Edinburgh Univ. LLB, MSc. Lectured at Univ. of Rhodesia, 1967–68. Vis. Prof., Inst. for Advanced Studies in the Humanities, Edinburgh Univ., 1998. Called to Scottish Bar, 1970. Non-executive Director: Ramco Energy plc; Foreign & Colonial Emerging Markets Investment Trust; British Assets Investment Trust; Authoriszor Inc.; Consultant: BHP; PricewaterhouseCoopers; Petrofac. Contested (C) Edinburgh, Central, 1970. MP (C) Edinburgh, Pentlands, Feb. 1974–1997; contested (C) same seat, 1997, 2001. Opposition front bench spokesman on Scottish Affairs, 1975–76; Parly Under Sec. of State, Scottish Office, 1979–82, FCO, 1982–83; Minister of State, FCO, 1983–86; Secretary of State: for Scotland, 1986–90; for Transport, 1990–92; for Defence, 1992–95; for Foreign and Commonwealth Affairs, 1995–97. Jt Sec., Cons. Foreign and Commonwealth Affairs Cttee, 1978; Member: Select Cttee on Europ. Secondary Legislation, 1975–76; Select Cttee on Overseas Develt, 1978–79. Hon. Pres., Scottish Young Conservatives, 1975–76; Pres., Scottish Cons.-Unionist Party, 1998–. Mem., Royal Co. of Archers, Queen's Body Guard for Scotland, 1992. Hon. Col, 162 Movt Control Regt (V), RLC, 1996–. Hon. Dep. Col, City of Edinburgh Univs OTC, 1999–. Hon. LLD Napier, 1998. Comdr, Order of Merit (Poland), 1998. *Recreations:* walking, reading, field sports. *Address:* c/o Pentlands Conservatives, 20 Spylaw Street, Collinton, Edinburgh EH13 0JX. *Clubs:* Pratt's; New (Edinburgh).

RIGBY, Sir Anthony (John), 3rd Bt *cr* 1929, of Long Durford, Rogate. co. Sussex; *b* 3 Oct. 1946; *e s* of Lt-Col Sir (Hugh) John (Macbeth) Rigby, 2nd Bt and Mary Patricia Erskine Rigby (*née* Leacock); *S* father, 1999; *m* 1978, Mary Oliver; three *s* one *d. Educ:* Rugby. *Heir: e s* Oliver Hugh Rigby, *b* 20 Aug. 1979.

RIGBY, Brian; Deputy Chief Executive, Office of Government Commerce, since 2000; *b* 30 Aug. 1944; *s* of Donald Rigby and Margaret Rigby (*née* Dorrity); *m* 1986, Ann Passmore; one *s. Educ:* Birkenhead Sch.; Hertford Coll., Oxford (MA 1970); LSE (MSc 1972). Principal, DoE, 1971–77; British Telecommunications: joined, 1977; Dir, London, 1984–88; Dep. Man. Dir, Enterprises, 1988–92; Dir, Supply Mgt, 1992–97; Dir, Procurement Gp, HM Treasury, 1997–2000. *Recreations:* people, places. *Address:* Office of Government Commerce, Fleetbank House, 2–6 Salisbury Square, EC4Y 8AE. *Club:* Naval and Military.

RIGBY, Bryan; Chairman, Elliott Ross Associates Ltd, since 1998; *b* 9 Jan. 1933; *s* of William George Rigby and Lily Rigby; *m* 1978, Marian Rosamund; one *s* one *d* of a former marriage, and one step *s* one step *d. Educ:* Wigan Grammar Sch.; King's Coll., London (BSc Special Chemistry, Dip. Chem. Engrg). UKAEA Industrial Gp, Capenhurst, 1955–60; Beecham Gp, London and Amsterdam, 1960–64; Laporte Industries (Holdings) Ltd, 1964–78; Dep. Dir-Gen., CBI, 1978–83; Man. Dir, UK Ops, 1984–87, UK, Ireland and Scandinavia, 1987–93, BASF Group. Chm., Streamline Hldgs, 1994–98; Dir, MEDEVA plc, 1993–99. Chm., Nurses' Pay Review Body, 1995–98. Mem., Social Security Adv. Cttee, 1994–99. Vice-Pres., BAAS, 1992–96. Trustee, Anglo-German Foundn, 1992– (Chm., 1998–); Gov., Henley Management Coll., 1993–. *Recreations:* music, golf, gardening. *Address:* Cluny, 61 Penn Road, Beaconsfield, Bucks HP9 2LW. *T:* (01494) 673206. *Club:* Reform.

RIGBY, Jean Prescott, (Mrs Jamie Hayes); mezzo-soprano; Principal, English National Opera, 1982–90; *d* of late Thomas Boulton Rigby and of Margaret Annie Rigby; *m* 1987, Jamie Hayes; three *s. Educ:* Birmingham and Midland Inst. Sch. of Music (ABSM 1976); Royal Acad. of Music (Dip.RAM; Hon. ARAM 1984; Hon. FRAM 1989). ARCM 1979; ABC 1996. Début: Royal Opera House, Covent Garden, 1983; Glyndebourne Festival Opera, 1984; rôles, 1990–, include: Nicklaus, in The Tales of Hoffmann, Olga in Eugene Onegin, Royal Opera; Isabella, in The Italian Girl in Algiers, Buxton; title rôle, La Cenerentola, and Idamante in Idomeneo, Garsington; Charlotte, in Werther, San Diego and Seattle; Irene, in Theodora, Geneviève, in Pelléas and Mélisande, Eduige, in Rodelinda, Hippolyta, in A Midsummer Night's Dream, and Emilia, in Otello, Glyndebourne; *English National Opera:* Penelope, in The Return of Ulysses; title rôle, in The Rape of Lucretia; Amastris, in Xerxes; Rosina, in The Barber of Seville; Helen, in King Priam; Maddalena, in Rigoletto. Several TV performances. *Recreations:* British heritage, sport, cooking. *Address:* c/o Askonas Holt Ltd, Lonsdale Chambers, 27 Chancery Lane, WC2A 1PF.

RIGBY, Peter William Jack, PhD; Chief Executive, Institute of Cancer Research, University of London, since 1999; *b* 7 July 1947; *s* of Jack and Lorna Rigby; *m* 1st, 1971, Paula Webb (marr. diss. 1983); 2nd, 1985, Julia Maidment; one *s*. *Educ:* Lower Sch., John Lyon, Harrow; Jesus Coll., Cambridge (BA, PhD). MRC Lab. of Molecular Biol., Cambridge, 1971–73; Helen Hay Whitney Foundn Fellow, Stanford Univ. Med. Sch., 1973–76; Imperial College London: Lectr, then Sen. Lectr in Biochem., 1976–83; Reader in Tumour Virology, 1983–86; Vis. Prof., 1986–94; Head, Div. of Eukaryotic Molecular Genetics, NIMR, MRC, 1986–99 (Head, Genes and Cellular Controls Gp, 1986–96). Chm., MRC Gene Therapy Co-ordinating Cttee, 1992–96; Member: MRC Cell Bd, 1988–92; EMBO, 1979; Science Council, Celltech, 1982–; Scientific Adv. Bd, Somatix Therapy Corp., 1989–97; Scientific Cttee, Cancer Res. Campaign, 1983–88, 1996–99. Chairman, Scientific Advisory Board: Prolifix Ltd, 1996–; Hexagen Technology Ltd, 1996–99; Scientific Advisory Board: deVGen NV, 1998–; KuDOS Pharmaceuticals, 1999–. European Editor, Cell, 1984–97. *Publications:* papers on molecular biology in sci. jls. *Recreations:* narrow boats, listening to music, sport. *Address:* Chester Beatty Laboratories: Institute of Cancer Research, 237 Fulham Road, SW3 6JB. *T:* (020) 7878 3824.

RIGG, Dame Diana, DBE 1994 (CBE 1988); actress; Director, United British Artists, since 1982; *b* Doncaster, Yorks, 20 July 1938; *d* of Louis Rigg and Beryl Helliwell; *m* 1982, Archibald Stirling; one *d*. *Educ:* Fulneck Girls' Sch., Pudsey. Trained for the stage at Royal Academy of Dramatic Art. First appearance on stage in RADA prod. in York Festival, at Theatre Royal, York, summer, 1957 (Natella Abashwili in The Caucasian Chalk Circle); after appearing in repertory in Chesterfield and in York she joined the Royal Shakespeare Company, Stratford-upon-Avon, 1959; first appearance in London, Aldwych Theatre, 1961 (2nd Ondine, Violanta and Princess Berthe in Ondine); at same theatre, in repertory (The Devils, Becket, The Taming of the Shrew), 1961; (Madame de Tourvel, The Art of Seduction), 1962; Royal Shakespeare, Stratford-upon-Avon, Apr. 1962 (Helena in A Midsummer Night's Dream, Bianca in The Taming of the Shrew, Lady Macduff in Macbeth, Adriana in The Comedy of Errors, Cordelia in King Lear); subseq. appeared in the last production at the Aldwych, Dec. 1962, followed by Adriana in The Comedy of Errors and Monica Stettler in The Physicists, 1963. Toured the provinces, spring, 1963, in A Midsummer Night's Dream; subseq. appeared at the Royal Shakespeare, Stratford, and at the Aldwych, in Comedy of Errors, Dec. 1963; again played Cordelia in King Lear, 1964, prior to touring with both plays for the British Council, in Europe, the USSR, and the US; during this tour she first appeared in New York (State Theatre), 1964, in same plays; Viola in Twelfth Night, Stratford, June 1966; Heloise in Abelard and Heloise, Wyndham's, 1970, also at the Atkinson, New York, 1971; joined The National Theatre, 1972: in Jumpers, 'Tis Pity She's a Whore and Lady Macbeth in Macbeth, 1972; The Misanthrope, 1973, Washington and NY, 1975; Phaedra Britannica, 1975 (Plays and Players Award for Best Actress); The Guardsman, 1978; Pygmalion, Albery, 1974; Night and Day, Phoenix, 1978 (Plays and Players award, 1979); Colette, USA, 1982; Heartbreak House, Haymarket, 1983; Little Eyolf, Lyric, Hammersmith, 1985; Antony and Cleopatra, Chichester, 1985; Wildfire, Phoenix, 1986; Follies, Shaftesbury, 1987; Love Letters, San Francisco, 1990; All for Love, Almeida, 1991; Berlin Bertie, Royal Court, 1992; Medea, Almeida, 1992, transf. Wyndhams, 1993–94 (Evening Standard Drama Award), then NY, 1994 (Tony Award); Mother Courage, RNT, 1995; Who's Afraid of Virginia Woolf?, Almeida, 1996; Phèdre, and Britannicus, Albery, 1998; Humble Boy, RNT, 2001; *films include:* A Midsummer Night's Dream, Assassination Bureau, On Her Majesty's Secret Service, Julius Caesar, The Hospital, Theatre of Blood, A Little Night Music, The Great Muppet Caper, Evil Under the Sun (Film Actress of the Year Award, Variety Club, 1983), A Good Man in Africa; *TV appearances include:* Sentimental Agent, The Comedy of Errors, The Avengers (Special Award, BAFTA, 2000), Married Alive, Diana (US series), In This House of Brede (US), Three Piece Suite, The Serpent Son, Hedda Gabler, The Marquise, Little Eyolf, King Lear, Witness of the Prosecution, Bleak House, Mother Love (BAFTA award), Unexplained Laughter, Moll Flanders (serial), Rebecca (Emmy Award for Best Supporting Actress, 1997), The Mrs Bradley Mysteries, Victoria and Albert, and others. Chair: Islington Fest.; MacRoberts Arts Centre; Member: Council, ABSA; BM Develt Fund. A Vice-Pres., Baby Life Support Systems (BLISS), 1984–. Cameron Mackintosh Vis. Prof. of Contemporary Theatre, Oxford Univ., 1999. *Publications:* No Turn Unstoned, 1982; So to the Land, 1994. *Recreations:* reading and trying to get organized. *Address:* c/o ARG, 4 Great Portland Street, W1W 8PA.

RIGGE, Marianne, (Mrs Trevor Goodchild), OBE 2000; Director, College of Health, since 1983; *b* 10 May 1948; *d* of late Dr Patrick Noel O'Mahony and of Elizabeth Nora O'Mahony (*née* Daly); *m* 1st, 1968, John Simon Rigge; two *d* (one *s* decd); 2nd, 1990, Trevor Goodchild. *Educ:* St Angela's Ursuline Convent, London; University College London (BA Hons French). PA, Consumers' Assoc., 1971–76; Res. Asst to Chm., Nat. Consumer Council, 1976–77; founder Dir, Mutual Aid Centre, 1977–83. Member: Clinical Outcomes Gp, 1993–97; Clinical Systems Gp, 1997–2000; NICE Partners Council, 1999–.; Nat. Access Taskforce, 2000–. Editor, Self Health, 1985–87; columnist, Health Service Jl, 1999–. *Publications:* (with Michael Young) Mutual Aid in a Selfish Society, 1979; Building Societies and the Consumer, 1981; Hello, Can I Help You, 1981; Prospects for Worker Co-operatives in Europe, 1981; (with Michael Young) Revolution from Within, 1983; Annual Guide to Hospital Waiting Lists, 1984–92. *Recreations:* gardening, cooking, music. *Address:* 157 Whipps Cross Road, E11 1NP. *T:* (020) 8530 4420.

RIGGS, David George; Chief Financial Officer, Australian Government Solicitor, since 1998; *b* 6 May 1942. *Educ:* Bury GS; Manchester Univ. (BA Econ.). CPFA (IPFA 1963). With Bury CBC, 1958–68; Greater London Council, 1968–82: Finance Officer, 1968–74; Hd of Public Services Finance, 1974–76; Asst Comptroller of Finance, 1976–82; Dir of Finance, ILEA, 1982–90; Dir of Finance, Benefits Agency, 1991–98. *Address:* 48 Jacka Crescent, Campbell, ACT 2612, Australia.

RIGNEY, Howard Ernest; HM Diplomatic Service, retired; Consul-General, Lyons, 1977–82; *b* 22 June 1922; *o s* of late Wilbert Ernest and Minnie Rigney; *m* 1950, Margaret Grayling Benn; one *s*. *Educ:* Univs of Western Ontario, Toronto and Paris. BA Western Ont. 1945, MA Toronto 1947. Lectr, Univ. of British Columbia, 1946–48; grad. studies, Paris Univ., 1948–50; COI, 1953–56; CRO, 1956; Regional Information Officer, Dacca, 1957–60, Montreal, 1960–63; CRO, 1963–65; FO/CO, 1965–67; Consul (Information), Chicago, 1967–69; Dep. Consul-Gen., Chicago, 1969–71; Head of Chancery and Consul, Rangoon, 1971–73; Head of Migration and Visa Dept, FCO, 1973–77. Hon DLitt, Winston Churchill Coll., Ill, 1971. *Recreations:* opera, book-collecting, gardening, golf. *Address:* The Old Forge, Frinstead, Sittingbourne, Kent ME9 0TF.

RILEY, Bridget Louise, CH 1999; CBE 1972; Artist; *b* 24 April 1931; *d* of late John Riley and Louise (*née* Gladstone). *Educ:* Cheltenham Ladies' College; Goldsmiths' School of Art; Royal College of Art. ARCA 1955. AICA critics Prize, 1963; Stuyvesant Bursary, 1964; Ohara Mus. Prize, Tokyo, 1972; Gold Medal, Grafik Biennale, Norway, 1980. Mem., RSA. One-man shows: London, 1962, 1963, 1969, 1971 (retrospective, at Hayward Gall.), 1976, 1981, 1983, 1987, 1989, 1992 (retrospective, at Hayward Gall.), 1994 (retrospective, at Tate Gall.), 1996, 1999 (retrospective at Serpentine Gall.), 2000; New York, Los Angeles, 1965; New York, 1967, 1975, 1978, 1986, 1990, 2000 (retrospectives at PaceWildenstein and DIA Center for the Arts); Hanover, 1970; Turin, Düsseldorf, Berne, Prague, 1971; Basle, 1975; Sydney, 1976; Tokyo, 1977, 1983, 1990; Stockholm and Zurich, 1987; Rome, 1996; Kendal, 1998–99 (retrospective at Abbot Hall Art Gall.); Düsseldorf, 1999 (retrospective at Kunstverein fur die Rheinlande und Westfalen); touring retrospective, USA, Aust. and Japan, 1978–80. Exhibited in group shows: England, France, Israel, America, Germany, Italy. Represented Britain: Paris Biennale, 1965; Venice Biennale, 1968 (awarded Chief internat. painting prize). Public collections include: Tate Gallery; Victoria and Albert Museum; Arts Council; British Council; Museum of Modern Art, New York; Australian Nat. Gallery, Canberra; Museum of Modern Art, Pasadena; Ferens Art Gallery, Hull; Allbright Knox, Buffalo, USA; Museum of Contemporary Art, Chicago; Ulster Museum, Ireland; Stedelijk Museum, Amsterdam; Berne Kunsthalle; Mus. of Modern Art, Tokyo. Designed Colour Moves, for Ballet Rambert, 1983. Trustee, Nat. Gallery, 1981–88. Hon. DLitt: Manchester, 1976; Ulster, 1986; Oxford, 1993; Cambridge, 1995; De Montfort, 1996; Exeter, 1997. *Address:* c/o Karsten Schubert, 47 Lexington Street, W1R 3LG.

RILEY, Christopher John; Chief Economist, Department for Transport, Local Government and the Regions (formerly Department of the Environment, then Department of the Environment, Transport and the Regions), since 1995; *b* 20 Jan. 1947; *s* of Bernard Francis Riley and Phyllis (*née* Wigley); *m* 1982, Helen Marion Mynett; two *s*. *Educ:* Ratcliffe Coll., Leicester; Wadham Coll., Oxford (MA Maths); Univ. of East Anglia (MA Econs). Economist, HM Treasury, 1969–77; Res. Fellow, Nuffield Coll., Oxford, 1977–78; Sen. Economic Advr, 1978–88, Under Sec., 1988–95, HM Treasury. *Publications:* various articles in books and learned jls. *Recreation:* music, especially choral singing. *Address:* Department for Transport, Local Government and the Regions, Great Minster House, 76 Marsham Street, SW1P 4DR. *T:* (020) 7944 3640, *Fax:* (020) 7944 2177; *e-mail:* chris_riley@dtlr.gsi.gov.uk.

RILEY, Very Rev. Kenneth Joseph; Dean of Manchester, since 1993; *b* 25 June 1940; *s* of Arthur and Mary Josephine Riley; *m* 1968, Margaret; two *d*. *Educ:* Holywell GS; UCW, Aberystwyth (BA 1961); Linacre Coll., Oxford (BA 1964; MA); Wycliffe Hall., Oxford. Ordained deacon, 1964, priest, 1965; Asst Curate, Emmanuel Ch., Fazakerley, Liverpool, 1964–66; Chaplain: Brasted Place Coll., 1966–69; Oundle Sch., 1969–74; Liverpool Univ., 1974–83; Vicar, Mossley Hill, Liverpool, 1975–83; RD, Childwall, 1982–83; Canon Treas., 1983–87, Canon Precentor, 1987–93, Liverpool Cathedral. *Publication:* Liverpool Cathedral, 1987. *Recreations:* music, drama, films. *Address:* Manchester Cathedral, Manchester M3 1SX. *T:* (0161) 833 2220.

RILEY, Victor; Lord Mayor of Cardiff, 1993–94; *b* 4 Oct. 1916; *s* of William Riley and Constance Evelyn Riley (*née* Cator); *m* 1944, Zoë Marion Elsie Sowden (*d* 1997); four *d*. *Educ:* Hull Grammar Sch. FIHospE 1970. Electrical Apprenticeship, Hull Corp. Engineers Dept, 1932–37; Electrical Engineer: Hull Elect. Dept, 1937–40; HM Ships in Dockyards, NE Coast, 1940–44; Engr in Group of Hosps and subseq. in NHS, 1944–56; Elect. Engr, Crown Agents, Nairobi, 1956–60; Principal Asst Engr, Welsh Health Tech. Services, 1960–81, retired. Councillor, Cardiff City Council, 1976–96. Mem., Whitchurch Royal British Legion, 1967–; Founder Mem., Welsh Chapter, Ordre des Chevaliers Bretvin, 1993–. Hon. FIHEEM. *Recreations:* gardening, Rugby, cricket. *Address:* 12 Coed Arian, Whitchurch, Cardiff CF14 2ND. *T:* (029) 2052 2342. *Club:* Cardiff Athletic.

RILEY-SMITH, Prof. Jonathan Simon Christopher, FRHistS; Dixie Professor of Ecclesiastical History, Cambridge University, and Fellow, Emmanuel College, Cambridge, since 1994; *b* 27 June 1938; *s* of late William Henry Douglas Riley-Smith and Elspeth Agnes Mary Riley-Smith (*née* Craik Henderson); *m* 1968, Marie-Louise Jeannetta, *d* of Wilfred John Sutcliffe Field; one *s* two *d*. *Educ:* Eton College; Trinity College, Cambridge (MA, PhD, LittD). Dept of Mediaeval History, University of St Andrews: Asst Lectr, 1964–65; Lectr, 1966–72; Faculty of History, Cambridge: Asst Lectr, 1972–75; Lectr, 1975–78; Chm., Bd, 1997–99; Queens' College, Cambridge: Fellow and Dir of Studies in History, 1972–78; Praelector, 1973–75; Librarian, 1973, 1977–78; Prof. of History, Univ. of London, 1978–94 (at RHC, 1978–85, at RHBNC, 1985–94); Head of Dept of History, RHC, then RHBNC, 1984–90. Chairman: Bd of Management, Inst. of Historical Res., 1988–94 (Hon. Fellow, 1997); Victoria County Hist. Cttee, 1989–97; Pres., Soc. for the Study of the Crusades and the Latin East, 1990–95. KStJ 1969 (Librarian of Priory of Scotland, 1966–78, of Grand Priory, 1982–); KM 1971 (Officer of Merit, 1985). Prix Schlumberger, Acad. des Inscriptions et Belles-Lettres, Paris, 1988. *Publications:* The Knights of St John in Jerusalem and Cyprus, 1967; (with U. and M. C. Lyons) Ayyubids, Mamlukes and Crusaders, 1971; The Feudal Nobility and the Kingdom of Jerusalem, 1973; What were the Crusades?, 1977, 2nd edn 1992; (with L. Riley-Smith) The Crusades: idea and reality, 1981; The First Crusade and the Idea of Crusading, 1986; The Crusades: a short history, 1987 (trans. French, 1990, Italian, 1994); (ed) The Atlas of the Crusades, 1991 (trans. German 1992, French 1996); The Oxford Illustrated History of the Crusades, 1995; (with N. Coureas) Cyprus and the Crusades, 1995; (jtly) Montjoie, 1997; The First Crusaders, 1997; Hospitallers: the history of the Order of St John, 1999; Al seguito delle Crociate, 2000; (jtly) Dei gesta per Francos, 2001; articles in learned jls. *Recreation:* the past and present of own family. *Address:* Emmanuel College, Cambridge CB2 3AP. *T:* (01223) 334200.

RIMER, Hon. Sir Colin (Percy Farquharson), Kt 1994; **Hon. Mr Justice Rimer;** a Judge of the High Court of Justice, Chancery Division, since 1994; *b* 30 Jan. 1944; *s* of Kenneth Rowland Rimer and Maria Eugenia Rimer (*née* Farquharson); *m* 1970, Penelope Ann Gibbs; two *s* one *d*. *Educ:* Dulwich Coll.; Trinity Hall, Cambridge (MA, LLB). Legal Assistant, Inst. of Comparative Law, Paris, 1967–68; called to the Bar, Lincoln's Inn, 1968, Bencher, 1994; QC 1988; in practice, 1969–94. *Recreations:* music, photography, novels, walking. *Address:* Royal Courts of Justice, Strand, WC2A 2LL.

RIMINGTON, John David, CB 1987; Director-General, Health and Safety Executive, 1984–95; *b* 27 June 1935; *s* of late John William Rimington, MBE, and of Mabel Dorrington; *m* 1963, Dame Stella Rimington, *qv*; two *d*. *Educ:* Nottingham High Sch.; Jesus Coll., Cambridge (Cl. I Hons History, MA). Nat. Service Commn, RA, 1954–56. Joined BoT, 1959; seconded HM Treasury (work on decimal currency), 1961; Principal, Tariff Div., BoT, 1963; 1st Sec. (Economic), New Delhi, 1965; Mergers Div., DTI, 1969; Dept of Employment, 1970; Asst Sec. 1972 (Employment Policy and Manpower); Counsellor, Social and Regional Policy, UK perm. representation to EEC, Brussels, 1974; MSC, 1977–81; Under Sec. 1978; Dir, Safety Policy Div., HSE, 1981–83; Dep. Sec., 1984; Permanent Sec., 1992. Non-executive Director: Magnox Electric, 1996–98; BNFL, 1998–; Angel Train Contracts Ltd, 1999–. Mem. Nat. Council, 1995–, Vice Chm., 2001–, Consumers' Assoc. Visiting Professor: Univ. of Strathclyde, 1997–99; Salford Univ., 1999–. CIMgt 1993. Hon. DSc Sheffield, 1995. *Publications:* articles on risk;

contrib. to RIPA Jl, New Asia Review, Trans IChemE, etc. *Recreations:* walking, gardening, watching cricket. *Address:* 9 Highbury Hill, N5 1SU.

RIMINGTON, Dame Stella, DCB 1996; Director General, Security Service, 1992–96; *b* 1935; *m* 1963, John David Rimington, *qv*; two *d.* *Educ:* Nottingham High Sch. for Girls; Edinburgh Univ. (MA). Security Service, 1969. Non-executive Director: Marks & Spencer plc, 1997–; Whitehead Mann GKR (formerly GKR), 1997–; BG plc, 1997–2000; BG Gp, 2000–; Royal Marsden NHS Trust, 1998–. Chm., Inst. of Cancer Res., 1997–. Trustee, RAF Mus., 1998–. Hon. Air Cdre, No 7006 (VR) Intelligence Sqn, RAuxAF, 1997–2001. Hon. LLD: Nottingham, 1995; Exeter, 1996. *Publication:* Open Secret (autobiog.), 2001. *Address:* PO Box 1604, SW1P 1XB.

RIMMER, Henry, (Harry), CBE 1994; DL; Member (Lab) Liverpool City Council, 1952–53 and 1987–96; Leader, Liverpool City Council, 1990–96; *b* 19 May 1928; *s* of Thomas and Sarah Ellen Rimmer; *m* 1st, 1951, Doreen Taylor (marr. diss. 1978); three *s* one *d*; 2nd, 1978, Joan Conder. *Educ:* Oulton High Sch.; Liverpool Collegiate Sch. Mem., Merseyside CC, 1981–86 (Dep. Leader, 1982–86). Member: Merseyside Police Authy, 1987–96 (Vice-Chm., 1990–92); Bd, Merseyside Develt Corp., 1991–98. Director: Wavertree Technology Park Co., 1987–96; Liverpool Airport PLC, 1989–96. DL Merseyside, 1997. *Recreations:* country walking, supporting Liverpool Football Club. *Address:* 21 Ash Grange, Brookside Avenue, Knotty Ash, Liverpool L14 7NE. *T:* (0151) 220 6022.

RIMMER, Air Vice-Marshal Thomas William, CB 2001; OBE 1987; FRAeS; Commander, British Forces Cyprus, since 2000; *b* 16 Dec. 1948; *s* of William Thompson Rimmer and Elizabeth Comrie Rimmer (*née* Baird); *m* 1976, Sarah Caroline Hale; one *s* one *d.* *Educ:* Morrison's Academy, Crieff; Edinburgh Univ. (MA Hons 1970). FRAeS 1997. Graduated RAF Cranwell, 1972; served Central Flying Sch., RAF Linton-on-Ouse, RAF Bruggen, RAF Coltishall, to 1983; French Air Force Staff Coll., 1983–84; Chief Instructor, RAF Cottesmore, 1984–87; HQ RAF Germany, 1987–89; Head, RAF Presentation Team, 1989–90; Station Comdr, RAF Cottesmore, 1990–92; Senior UK Mil. Officer, WEU, 1992–94; rcds 1995; MoD, 1996–98; AOC and Comdt, RAF Coll., Cranwell, 1999–2000. Liveryman, Tallow Chandlers' Co., 1992–. QCVSA 1983. *Recreations:* offshore sailing, golf, gardening. *Club:* Royal Air Force.

RING, Prof. James, CBE 1983; Emeritus Professor of Physics, Imperial College of Science, Technology and Medicine, since 1984; *b* 22 Aug. 1927; *s* of James and Florence Ring; *m* 1949, Patricia, *d* of Major H. J. Smith, MBE; two *s.* *Educ:* Univ. of Manchester (BSc, PhD). FInstP, FRAS. Reader in Spectrometry, Univ. of Manchester, 1957; Prof. of Applied Physics, Hull Univ., 1962; Prof. of Physics, 1967, and Associate Hd of Physics Dept, 1979, Imperial Coll. of Sci. and Technol. Director: Queensgate Instruments, 1979–97; Infrared Engrg, 1970–91; IC Optical Systems, 1970–97. Member: IBA, 1974–81; ITC, 1991–94; Inquiry into Cable Expansion and Broadcasting Policy, 1982; Dep. Chm., Cable Authority, 1984–90. *Publications:* numerous papers and articles in learned jls. *Recreations:* stargazing, dinghy sailing. *Address:* 1 Mude Gardens, Mudeford, Dorset BH23 4AR.

RINGADOO, Sir Veerasamy, GCMG 1986; Kt 1975; QC 1983; Officier de l'Ordre National Malgache 1969; President, Republic of Mauritius, 1992 (Governor-General and Commander-in-Chief of Mauritius, 1986–92); *b* 1920; *s* of Nagaya Ringadoo; *m* 1954, Lydie Vadamootoo; one *s* one *d.* *Educ:* Port Louis Grammar Sch.; LSE Eng. (LLB; Hon. Fellow, 1976). Called to Bar, 1949. Municipal Councillor, Port Louis, 1956; MLC for Moka-Flacq, 1951–67; Minister: Labour and Social Security, 1959–63; Education, 1964–67; Agriculture and Natural Resources, 1967–68; Finance, 1968–82; attended London Constitutional Conf., 1965; first MLA (Lab) for Quartier Militaire and Moka, 1967, re-elected 1976. Governor, IMF and African Develt Bank, 1970–82; Chm., Bd of Governors, African Development Bank and African Development Fund, 1977–78. Hon. DCL Mauritius, 1976; Hon. DLit Andhra, 1978; Dr *hc* Bordeaux Univ., 1988; Bharatidasan Univ., Tiruchirapalli, 1988. Médaille de l'Assemblée Nat. Française, 1971. *Address:* Cnr Antelme and Farquhar Streets, Quatre Bornes, Mauritius.

RINGEN, Prof. Stein; Professor of Sociology and Social Policy, and Fellow of Green College, University of Oxford, since 1990; *b* 5 July 1945; *s* of John Ringen and Anna Ringen (*née* Simengard). *Educ:* Univ. of Oslo (MA, dr. philos.). Broadcasting reporter, Norwegian Broadcasting Corp., 1970–71; Fellow, Internat. Peace Res. Inst., Oslo, 1971–72; Head of Secretariat, Norwegian Level of Living Study, 1972–76; Fellow, Inst. for Social Res., Oslo, 1976–78; Head of Res., Min. of Consumer Affairs and Govt Admin, Oslo, 1978–83; Prof. of Welfare Studies, Univ. of Stockholm, 1983–86; Sen. Res. Scientist, Central Bureau of Statistics, Oslo, 1986–88; Asst Dir Gen., Min. of Justice, Oslo, 1988–90. Mem., Royal Commn on Human Values, Norway, 1998–2001. *Publications:* The Possibility of Politics, 1987; Citizens, Families and Reform, 1997; Reformdemokratiet, 1997; The Family in Question, 1998. *Address:* University of Oxford, St Cross Building, Manor Road, Oxford OX1 3UL. *T:* (01865) 271564.

RINGROSE, Ven. Hedley Sidney; Archdeacon of Cheltenham, since 1998; *b* 29 June 1942; *s* of Sidney and Clara Ringrose; *m* 1969, Rosemary Anne Palmer; one *s* two *d.* *Educ:* West Oxfordshire Coll.; Salisbury Theol Coll.; BA Open Univ. 1979. Deacon 1968, priest 1969; Curate: Bishopston, Bristol, 1968–71; Easthampstead, Berks, 1971–75; Vicar, St George, Gloucester with Whaddon, 1975–88; RD Gloucester City, 1983–88; Vicar of Cirencester, 1988–98; RD Cirencester, 1989–97; Hon. Canon, 1986–98, Reserved Canonry, 1998–, Gloucester Cathedral. Chairman: Dio. Bd of Patronage, 1990–98; Dio. House of Clergy, 1994–98; Dio. Bd of Education, 1998–. Mem., Gen. Synod of C of E, 1990–. Trustee: Glenfall House, 1998–; Foundation of St Matthias, 1998–. *Recreations:* travel, gardening, cycling, driving. *Address:* The Sanderlings, Thorncliffe Drive, Cheltenham, Glos GL51 6PY. *T:* (01242) 522923, *Fax:* (01242) 235925; *e-mail:* archdchelt@star.co.uk.

RINGROSE, Prof. John Robert, FRS 1977; FRSE; Professor of Pure Mathematics, 1964–93, now Emeritus, and a Pro-Vice-Chancellor, 1983–88, University of Newcastle upon Tyne; *b* 21 Dec. 1932; *s* of Albert Frederick Ringrose and Elsie Lilian Ringrose (*née* Roberts); *m* 1956, Jean Margaret Bates; three *s.* *Educ:* Buckhurst Hill County High School, Chigwell, Essex; St John's Coll., Cambridge (MA, PhD). Lecturer in Mathematics: King's Coll., Newcastle upon Tyne, 1957–61; Univ. of Cambridge (also Fellow of St John's Coll.), 1961–63; Sen. Lectr in Mathematics, Univ. of Newcastle upon Tyne, 1963–64. Pres., London Mathematical Soc., 1992–94. *Publications:* Compact Non-self-adjoint Operators, 1971; (with R. V. Kadison) Fundamentals of the Theory of Operator Algebras, 1983; mathematical papers in various research jls. *Address:* 6 Polwarth Road, Brunton Park, Newcastle upon Tyne NE3 5ND. *T:* (0191) 236 3035.

RINK, John Stuart; Managing Partner, Allen & Overy, since 1994; *b* 25 Oct. 1946; *s* of Paul Lothar Max Rink and Mary Ida McCall Rink (*née* Moore); *m* 1971, Elizabeth Mary Pitkethly; one *s* one *d.* *Educ:* Sedbergh Sch.; London Univ. (LLB ext.). Allen & Overy: Trainee Solicitor, 1970–72; Asst Solicitor, 1972–77; Partner, 1977–; Man. Partner, Litigation Dept, 1989–94; Legal Dir, British Aerospace, 1994–95 (on secondment). *Recreations:* golf, Rugby, walking, opera. *Address:* 2 Camp View, Wimbledon, SW19 4UL. *T:* (020) 8947 4800. *Clubs:* MCC, City Law; Royal Wimbledon Golf, Royal West Norfolk Golf; Windermere Motor Boat Racing.

RIORDAN, Stephen Vaughan; QC 1992; a Recorder, since 1990; *b* 18 Feb. 1950; *s* of Charles Maurice Riordan and Betty Morfydd Riordan; *m* 1983, Jane Elizabeth Thomas; two *d.* *Educ:* Wimbledon Coll.; Univ. of Liverpool (LLB Hons). Called to the Bar, Inner Temple, 1972; Asst Recorder, 1986–90. *Recreation:* singing. *Address:* 25–27 Castle Street, Liverpool L2 4TA. *T:* (0151) 236 5072.

RIPA di MEANA, Carlo; Member for Italy, European Parliament, 1979–84 and 1994–99; *b* 15 Aug. 1929; *m* 1982, Marina Punturieri. Editor, Il Lavoro (Ital. Gen. Conf. of Labour weekly newspaper), and Editor, foreign dept, Unita (Ital. Communist Party daily paper), 1950–53; rep. of Italy on UIE, Prague, 1953–56; founded jointly Nuova Generazione, 1956; left Ital. Communist Party, 1957; founded jointly Passato e Presente, 1957 (chief editor); joined Italian Socialist Party (PSI), 1958; worked in publishing until 1966; Councillor for Lombardy (PSI), 1970–74 (Chm., Constitutional Cttee); leader, PSI Group, regional council; head, international relations PSI, 1979–80; left PSI 1993; Leader, Green Party, Italy, 1993–98; joined South Tyrol People's Party. Mem. for Italy, EEC, 1985–92; Minister for Environment, Italy, 1992–93. Pres., Inst. for Internat. Economic Cooperation and Develt Problems, 1983; Sec.-Gen., Club Turati, Milan, 1967–76; Mem. Board, Scala Theatre, Milan, 1970–74; Mem. Council, Venice Biennale 1974–82 (Chm., 1974–79); founder Mem., Crocodile Club; Pres., Fernando Santi Inst.; Pres., Unitary Fedn, Italian Press abroad; Vice-Chm., Internat. Cttee for Solidarity with Afghan People. *Publications:* Un viaggio in Viet-Nam (A Voyage to Vietnam), 1956; A tribute to Raymond Roussel and his Impressions of Africa, 1965; Il governo audiovisivo (Audiovisual Government), 1973. *Recreations:* horse riding, sailing.

RIPLEY, Prof. Brian David, PhD; FRSE; Professor of Applied Statistics, and Fellow of St Peter's College, University of Oxford, since 1990; *b* 29 April 1952; *s* of Eric Lewis Ripley and Sylvia May (*née* Gould); *m* 1973, Ruth Mary Appleton. *Educ:* Farnborough Grammar Sch.; Churchill Coll., Cambridge (MA, PhD). FIMS 1987; FRSE 1990. Lectr in Statistics, Imperial Coll., London, 1976–80; Reader, Univ. of London, 1980–83; Prof. of Statistics, Univ. of Strathclyde, 1983–90. Mem., Internat. Statistical Inst., 1982. Adams Prize, Univ. of Cambridge, 1987. *Publications:* Spatial Statistics, 1981; Stochastic Simulation, 1987; Statistical Inference for Spatial Processes, 1988; Modern Applied Statistics with S-Plus, 1994, 3rd edn 1999; Pattern Recognition and Neural Networks, 1996; S Programming, 2000; numerous papers on statistics and applications in astronomy, biology, chemistry and earth sciences. *Recreation:* natural history. *Address:* 1 South Parks Road, Oxford OX1 3TG. *T:* (01865) 272861.

RIPLEY, Sir Hugh, 4th Bt *cr* 1880; former Director, John Walker & Sons Ltd, Scotch Whisky Distillers, retired 1981; *b* 26 May 1916; *s* of Sir Henry William Alfred Ripley, 3rd Bt, and Dorothy (*d* 1964), *e d* of late Robert William Daker Harley; *S* father, 1956; *m* 1st, 1946, Dorothy Mary Dunlop Bruce-Jones (marr. diss. 1971); one *s* one *d*; 2nd, 1972, Susan, *d* of W. Parker, Leics; one *d.* *Educ:* Eton. Served in Africa and Italy with 1st Bn KSLI (despatches twice, American Silver Star); retired regular Major. *Publication:* Whisky for Tea, 1991. *Recreations:* golf, fishing, shooting. *Heir:* *s* William Hugh Ripley, *b* 13 April 1950. *Address:* 20 Abingdon Villas, W8 6BX; The Oak, Bedstone, Bucknell, Salop SY7 0BJ. *Club:* Boodle's.

RIPON, Dean of; *see* Methuen, Very Rev. J. A. R.

RIPON AND LEEDS, Bishop of, since 2000; **Rt Rev. John Richard Packer;** *b* 10 Oct. 1946; *s* of John and Muriel Packer; *m* 1971, Barbara Jack; two *s* one *d.* *Educ:* Manchester Grammar Sch.; Keble Coll., Oxford (MA); Ripon Hall, Oxford; York Univ. (DSA). Ordained deacon, 1970, priest, 1971; Curate, St Peter, St Helier, 1970–73; Director of Pastoral Studies: Ripon Hall, 1973–75; Ripon Coll., Cuddesdon, 1975–77; Chaplain, St Nicolas, Abingdon, 1973–77; Vicar, Wath Upon Dearne with Adwick Upon Dearne, 1977–86; Rural Dean of Wath, 1983–86; Rector, Sheffield Manor, 1986–91; Rural Dean of Attercliffe, 1990–91; Archdeacon of W Cumberland, 1991–96; Priest i/c of Bridekirk, 1995–96; Bp Suffragan of Warrington, 1996–2000. Mem., Gen. Synod of C of E, 1985–91, 1992–96 and 2000–. *Recreations:* history, walking. *Address:* Bishop Mount, Ripon, N Yorks HG4 5DP. *T:* (01765) 602045, *Fax:* (01765) 600758.

RIPPENGAL, Derek, CB 1982; QC 1980; Counsel to Chairman of Committees, House of Lords, 1977–99; *b* 8 Sept. 1928; *s* of William Thomas Rippengal and Margaret Mary Rippengal (*née* Parry); *m* 1963, Elizabeth Melrose (*d* 1973); one *s* one *d.* *Educ:* Hampton Grammar Sch.; St Catharine's Coll., Cambridge (Scholar; MA). Called to Bar, Middle Temple, 1953 (Harmsworth schol.). Entered Treasury Solicitor's Office, 1958, after Chancery Bar and univ. posts; Sen. Legal Asst, 1961; Asst Treasury Solicitor, 1967; Principal Asst Treasury Solicitor, 1971; Solicitor to DTI, 1972–73; Dep. Parly Counsel, 1973–74, Parly Counsel, 1974–76, Law Commn. *Recreations:* music, fishing. *Address:* 62 Gwydir Street, Cambridge CB1 2LL. *Club:* Athenæum.

RIPPON, Angela; broadcaster; Chairman, English National Ballet, since 2000; *b* 12 Oct. 1944; *d* of John and Edna Rippon; *m* 1967, Christopher Dare (marr. diss.). *Educ:* Plymouth Grammar Sch. Journalist, The Independent, Plymouth; presenter and reporter, BBC TV, Plymouth, 1966–69; editor, producer and presenter, Westward TV, 1967–73; reporter, nat. news, 1973–75, newsreader, 1975–81, BBC TV; co-founder, and presenter, TV-am, 1983; arts and entertainment correspondent, WNEV-TV, Boston, USA, 1984–85; presenter, LBC, 1990–94. *Television series include:* presenter: Angela Rippon Reporting, 1980–81; Antiques Roadshow, 1980–83; In the Country, 1980–83; Masterteam, 1985–87; Come Dancing, 1988–91; What's My Line, 1988–90; compère, Eurovision Song Contest, 1976; also presenter, radio progs. Vice-Pres., British Red Cross, 1999–. TRIC Newsreader of the Year, 1975, 1976, 1977. Hon. DHum Amer. Coll. in London, 1994. *Publications:* Riding, 1980; In the Country, 1980; Victoria Plum (children's stories), 1981; Mark Phillips: the man and his horses, 1982; Angela Rippon's West Country, 1983; Badminton: a celebration, 1987. *Address:* c/o Knight Ayton, 114 St Martin's Lane, WC2N 4AZ.

RISCHARD, Jean-François; Vice-President for Europe, World Bank, since 1998; *b* 2 Oct. 1948; *s* of Dr Charles-Edouard Rischard and Huguette (*née* Navereau); *m* 1979, Jacqueline Salvo; three *s.* *Educ:* Univ. of Aix-en-Provence (LèsScEcons 1971; DèsScEcon 1973); Univ. of Luxembourg (Dr Law 1971); Harvard Business Sch. (MBA 1975). World Bank: Project Officer, Industrial Projects, 1975–82; Chief, Financial Mgt Div., 1982–86; Sen. Vice Pres., Internat. Fixed Income Mkts, Drexel Burnham Lambert, NY, 1986–90; World Bank: Dir, Investment Dept, 1990–93; Vice Pres., Finance and Private Sector Develt, 1993–98. Founding Comr, Global Inf. Infrastructure Commn, 1995–. Pres., Professional Bankers' Assoc., Washington, 1993–98. Mem., Governing Bd, Inst. of Develt Studies, Sussex. Officier, Couronne de Chêne (Luxembourg), 1995. *Publications:* contrib. numerous articles on internat. finance, global issues and global governance problems.

Recreations: ski-ing, golf, history, music. *Address:* World Bank, 66 avenue d'Iéna, 75116 Paris, France. *T:* (1) 40693010.

RISELEY-PRICHARD, Air Vice-Marshal Richard Augustin; Principal Medical Officer, Royal Air Force Support Command, 1980–85, retired; Member, Swindon District Health Authority, 1988–90 (Associate Member, 1990–93); *b* 19 Feb. 1925; *s* of late Dr J. A. Prichard and Elizabeth (*née* Riseley); *m* 1953, Alannah *d* of late Air Cdre C. W. Busk, CB, MC, AFC; four *d. Educ:* Beaudesert Park; Radley Coll.; Trinity Coll., Oxford (MA, BM, BCh); St Bartholomew's Hosp., London. FFCM. Commnd RAF Med. Br., 1951; pilot trng, 1951–52; served at RAF Coll., Cranwell, 1953–56; Dep. Principal Med. Officer (Flying), HQ Transport Comd and HQ RAF Germany, 1956–63; RAF Staff Coll., 1964; SMO, British Forces, Aden, 1967; Dep. Principal Med. Officer, HQ Strike Comd, 1970–73; Commanding Officer: RAF Hosp. Wegberg, Germany, 1973–76; Princess Alexandra Hosp., Wroughton, 1977–80. QHS 1980–85. Hon. Air Cdre, No 4626, RAuxAF Sqn, 1986–. Gen. Comr of Income Tax, 1987–. Dir (non-exec.) and Vice Chm., Wiltshire Ambulance Service NHS Trust, 1993–. Mem., Armed Forces Cttee, BMA, 1989–. Governor: Dauntsey's Sch., 1982– (Vice-Chm., 1985–86, Chm., 1986–); BUPA Medical Foundn, 1990–96. CStJ. *Recreations:* tennis, squash, bridge, gardening. *Address:* The Little House, Allington, Devizes, Wilts SN10 3NN. *T:* (01380) 860662. *Clubs:* Royal Air Force; All England Lawn Tennis.

RISIUS, Maj. Gen. Gordon, CB 2000; Director of Army Legal Services and the Army Prosecuting Authority, since 1997; *b* 10 July 1945; *s* of late Rudolf Risius and Irene Risius (*née* Spier); *m* 1980, Lucinda Mary, *d* of Marshal of the Royal Air Force Sir Michael Beetham, *qv*; one *s* two *d. Educ:* University College Sch.; Coll. of Law. Admitted Solicitor, 1972; commnd as Capt., Army Legal Services, 1973; served HQ Land Forces Hong Kong, HQ BAOR, HQ NI, MoD, HQ 4th Armd Div., HQ Land Forces Cyprus; Col, Army Legal Services 2, MoD, 1992–94; Brig., Legal, HQ BAOR/UKSC (Germany), 1994–95; Brig., Legal HQ Land Command, 1995–96; Brig., Prosecutions, 1997. Asst Recorder, 1991–95; a Recorder, 1995–. Vice-Pres., Internat. Soc. for Military Law and the Law of War, 1997–; Mem., Internat. Inst. of Humanitarian Law, 1994–. *Publications:* articles on the law of war. *Recreations:* music, reading, computers, travel. *Address:* Directorate of Army Legal Services, Trenchard Lines, Upavon, Pewsey, Wilts SN9 6BE.

RISK, Douglas James; QC (Scot.) 1992; Sheriff Principal of Grampian, Highland and Islands, 1993–2001; *b* 23 Jan. 1941; *s* of James Risk and Isobel Katherine Taylor Risk (*née* Dow); *m* 1967, Jennifer Hood Davidson; three *s* one *d. Educ:* Glasgow Academy; Gonville and Caius Coll., Cambridge (BA 1963, MA 1967); Glasgow Univ. (LLB 1965). Admitted to Faculty of Advocates, 1966; Standing Junior Counsel, Scottish Education Dept, 1975; Sheriff of Lothian and Borders at Edinburgh, 1977–79; Sheriff of Grampian, Highland and Islands at Aberdeen and Stonehaven, 1979–93. Hon. Prof., Faculty of Law, Univ. of Aberdeen, 1994– (Hon. Lectr, 1981–94). *Club:* Royal Northern and University (Aberdeen).

RISK, Sir Thomas (Neilson), Kt 1984; FRSE; Governor of the Bank of Scotland, 1981–91 (Director, 1971; Deputy Governor, 1977–81); *b* 13 Sept. 1922; *s* of late Ralph Risk, CBE, MC, and Margaret Nelson Robertson; *m* 1949, Suzanne Eiloart; three *s* (and one *s* decd). *Educ:* Kelvinside Academy; Glasgow Univ. (BL). Flight Lieut, RAF, 1941–46; RAFVR, 1946–53. Partner, Maclay Murray & Spens, Solicitors, 1950–81; Director: Standard Life Assurance Co., 1965–88 (Chm., 1969–77); British Linen Bank, 1968–91 (Governor, 1977–86); Howden Group, 1971–87; Merchants Trust, 1973–94; MSA (Britain) Ltd, 1958–98; Shell UK Ltd, 1982–92; Barclays Bank, 1983–85; Bank of Wales, 1986–91; Chm., Scottish Financial Enterprise, 1986–89. Member: Scottish Industrial Develt Bd, 1972–75; Scottish Econ. Council, 1983–91; NEDC, 1987–91. Chm., Univ. of Glasgow Trust, 1992–2001; Trustee, Hamilton Bequest. FRSE 1988. Hon. LLD Glasgow, 1985; Dr *hc* Edinburgh, 1990. *Address:* 10 Belford Place, Edinburgh EH4 3DH. *T:* (0131) 332 9425. *Clubs:* Royal Air Force; New (Edinburgh).

RIST, Prof. John Michael, FRSC; Professor of Classics and Philosophy, University of Toronto, 1983–96, Emeritus Professor, since 1997; *b* 6 July 1936; *s* of Robert Ward Rist and Phoebe May (*née* Mansfield); *m* 1960, Anna Thérèse (*née* Vogler); two *s* two *d. Educ:* Trinity Coll., Cambridge (BA 1959, MA 1963). FRSC 1976. Univ. of Toronto: firstly Lectr, finally Prof. of Classics, 1959–80; Chm., Grad. Dept of Classics, 1971–75; Regius Prof. of Classics, Aberdeen Univ., 1980–83. Vis. Prof., Augustinianum, Rome, 1998–. *Publications:* Eros and Psyche, Canada 1964; Plotinus: the road to reality, 1967; Stoic Philosophy, 1969; Epicurus: an introduction, 1972; (ed) The Stoics, USA 1978; On the Independence of Matthew and Mark, 1978; Human Value, 1982; Platonism and its Christian Heritage, 1985; The Mind of Aristotle, 1989; Augustine, 1994; Man, Soul and Body, 1996; On Inoculating Moral Philosophy Against God, 2000; contrib. classical and phil jls. *Recreations:* travel, swimming, hill-walking. *Address:* 50 Roseford Road, Cambridge CB4 2HD.

RITBLAT, John Henry, FRICS; Chairman and Managing Director, The British Land Company PLC, since 1970; *b* 3 Oct. 1935; *m* 1st, 1960, Isabel Paja (*d* 1979); two *s* one *d*; 2nd, 1986, Jill Zilkha (*née* Slotover). *Educ:* Dulwich Coll.; London Univ. College of Estate Management. FRICS 2000. Articles with West End firm of Surveyors and Valuers, 1952–58. Founder Partner, Conrad Ritblat & Co., Consultant Surveyors and Valuers, 1958; Chairman: Conrad Ritblat Gp plc, 1993–97; Milner Estates plc, 1997; Colliers Conrad Ritblat Erdman, 2000–; Man. Dir, Union Property Holdings (London) Ltd, 1969–. Comr, Crown Estate Paving Commn, 1969–. Hon. Surveyor, King George's Fund for Sailors, 1979. Member: Council, Business in the Community, 1987–; Prince of Wales' Royal Parks Tree Appeal Cttee, 1987–; British Olympic Assoc., 1979; Olympic Appeal Cttee, 1984, 1988, 1996 and 2000; Patrons of British Art, Tate Gall.; English Heritage; Royal Horticultural Soc.; Architecture Club; SPAB; Nat. Art-Collections Fund; British Library Bd, 1995–; Life Member: Nat. Trust; Zool Soc. of London; Georgian Gp; RGS; Trollope Soc.; and Patron, Investment Property Forum, 1999–. Trustee, Zool Soc. of London Develt Trust, 1986–89. Patron, London Fedn of Boys' Clubs Centenary Appeal; Founder Sponsor, Young Explorers Trust; Sponsor: RGS, 1982–85; (sole), British Nat. Ski Championships, 1978–; Pres., British Ski and Snowboard Fedn (formerly British Ski Fedn)1994– (Vice-Pres., 1984–89). Dep. Chm. Governors, Hall Sch.; Member, Board of Governors: London Business Sch., 1990– (Hon. Fellow, 2000); The Weizmann Inst., 1991–; Dir and Gov., RAM, 1998– (Dep. Chm., 1999–; Hon. Fellow, 2000). FRGS 1982; CIMgt; Life FRSA. *Recreations:* antiquarian books and libraries, bees, Real tennis, golf, ski-ing. *Address:* (office) 10 Cornwall Terrace, Regent's Park, NW1 4QP. *T:* (020) 7486 4466. *Clubs:* Carlton, Royal Automobile, MCC, The Pilgrims, Queen's; Cresta (St Moritz).

RITCHESON, Prof. Charles Ray; University Professor of History and University Librarian Emeritus, University of Southern California, since 1991; *b* 26 Feb. 1925; *s* of Charles Frederick and Jewell Vaughn Ritcheson; *m* 1st, 1953, Shirley Spackman (marr. diss. 1964); two *s*; 2nd, 1965, Alice Luethi; four *s. Educ:* Univs of Harvard, Zürich, Oklahoma and Oxford. DPhil (Oxon). FRHistS. Prof. and Chm. of History, Kenyon Coll., 1953–65; Chm. and Dir, Graduate Studies, Southern Methodist Univ., 1966–70; Lovell Prof. of History, Univ. of Southern Calif., 1971–74; Cultural Attaché, US Embassy, 1974–77; University of Southern California: Lovell Distinguished Prof. of History, 1977–84; Univ. Prof., Univ. Librarian, Dean and Special Asst. to Pres., 1984–91; Dist. Emeritus Prof., 2000. Vis. Prof., Univs of Edinburgh and Cambridge, 1965–66. Chm., British Inst. of the US, 1979–81. Vice-Pres., Board of Dirs, Amer. Friends of Covent Garden, 1978–84; Exec. Vice Pres., Fund for Arts and Culture in Central and Eastern Europe, 1992–96; Member: National Council for the Humanities, 1983–87 and 1988–91; US Bd of Foreign Scholarships, 1987–88; Adv. Council, Amer. Ditchley Foundn, 1977–; Adv. Council, Univ. of Buckingham (formerly UC Buckingham), 1977–90; Examination Jury, Ecole Nat. de l'Admin, 1998–. Member: Assoc. pour le Rayonnement d'Opéra à Paris, 1993–; French Archaeol Soc., 1998–. Hon. DLitt Leicester, 1976. *Publications:* British Politics and the American Revolution, 1954; Aftermath of Revolution: British policy toward the United States 1783–1795, 1969 (paperback, 1971); The American Revolution: the Anglo-American relation, 1969; (with E. Wright) A Tug of Loyalties, 1971. *Recreations:* horseback riding, swimming, opera. *Address:* 85 Boulevard Haussmann, 75008 Paris, France. *T:* 47424484. *Clubs:* Beefsteak, Brooks's.

RITCHIE, family name of **Baron Ritchie of Dundee.**

RITCHIE OF DUNDEE, 5th Baron *cr* 1905; **Harold Malcolm Ritchie;** English and Drama Teacher, Bedgebury School, Kent, retired 1984; Social and Liberal Democrat (formerly Liberal) spokesman on education, House of Lords, 1985–92; *b* 29 Aug. 1919; 4th *s* of 2nd Baron Ritchie of Dundee and Sarah Ruth (*d* 1950), *d* of J. L. Jennings, MP; *S* brother, 1978; *m* 1948, Anne, *d* of late Col C. G. Johnstone, MC; one *s* one *d. Educ:* Stowe School; Trinity College, Oxford. MA 1940. Served in Middle East, Italy and Greece, Captain KRRC, 1940–46. Assistant Headmaster, Brickwall House School, Northiam, Sussex, 1952–65; Headmaster, 1965–72. President: Rye Meml Care Centre, 1990–; Arts Dyslexia Trust, 1998–. *Recreations:* gardening, drama, music. *Heir: s* Hon. Charles Rupert Rendall Ritchie [*b* 15 March 1958; *m* 1984, Tara Van Tuyl Koch (marr. diss. 1992)]. *Address:* The Roundel, Spring Steps, Winchelsea, Sussex TN36 4EG.

RITCHIE, Albert Edgar, CC 1975; Canadian Diplomat, retired Nov. 1981; *b* 20 Dec. 1916; *m*; two *s* two *d. Educ:* Mount Allison Univ., New Brunswick (BA 1938); Queen's College, Oxford (Rhodes Scholar, 1940; BA). Officer, Econ. Affairs Dept, UN, and Secretariat of Gen. Agreement on Tariffs and Trade, 1946–48; Counsellor, Office of Canadian High Comr, London, UK, 1948–52; Deputy Under-Secretary of State for External Affairs, Canada, 1964–66; Canadian Ambassador to USA, 1966–70; Under-Sec. of State for External Affairs, Canada, 1970–74; Special Advisor to Privy Council Office, Canada, 1974–76; Canadian Ambassador to Republic of Ireland, 1976–81. Hon. LLD: Mount Allison Univ., 1966; St Thomas Univ., 1968; Carleton Univ., 1985. *Address:* 1335–1695 Playfair Drive, Ottawa, ON K1H 8J6, Canada. *Club:* Rideau (Ottawa).

RITCHIE, David Robert, CB 2001; Regional Director, Government Office for the West Midlands, 1994–2001 (Regional Director, West Midlands Regional Office, Departments of the Environment and Transport, 1989–94); *b* 10 March 1948; *s* of late James Ritchie and of Edith Ritchie (*née* Watts); *m* 1989, Joan Gibbons. *Educ:* Manchester Grammar School; St John's College, Cambridge (BA, MA). *Address:* Min. of Transport, 1970; DoE, 1970. Mem., Bishop's Council, Dio. Birmingham, 1992–. *Recreations:* fell-walking, cooking. *Address:* 14 Ashfield Road, Birmingham B14 7AS.

RITCHIE, Prof. Donald Andrew, FRSE; Professor of Genetics, University of Liverpool, since 1978; Deputy Chairman, Environment Agency, since 2000; *b* 9 July 1938; *s* of Andrew Ritchie and Winifred Laura (*née* Parkinson); *m* 1962, Margaret Jeanne (*née* Collister); one *s* one *d. Educ:* Latymer's Sch., London; Univ. of Leicester (BSc 1959); RPMS, London (PhD 1964). FIBiol 1978; CBiol 1985; FRSE 1979. MRC Microbial Genetics Res. Unit, London, 1959–64; Res. Associate, Biophysics Dept, Johns Hopkins Univ., Baltimore, USA, 1964–66; Lectr, 1966–72, Sen. Lectr, 1972–78, Virology Dept, Univ. of Glasgow; Pro-Vice-Chancellor, Liverpool Univ., 1992–95. Royal Soc. Leverhulme Trust Sen. Res. Fellow, 1991–92. Mem., Biotechnol. Jt Adv. Bd, DTI, 1990–95. Member: NERC, 1990–95 (Chm., Terrestrial and Freshwater Life Scis Cttee, 1991–95); Science Bd, SERC, 1989–92; Food Res. Cttee, AFRC, 1991–94; Bd, Envmt Agency, 1998– (Chm., Water and Flood Risk Mgt Adv. Gp, 2000–). Member Council: Marine Biol Assoc., 1991–94; Soc. for Gen. Microbiol., 1981–86 (Professional Affairs Officer, 1998–2001); Mem., Finance Cttee, 1996–, and Environment Cttee, 1996–99, Inst. of Biol. Member: Mil. Educn Cttee, Liverpool Univ., 1981– (Chm., 1995–); Council, Liverpool Sch. of Tropical Medicine, 1993–99; Exec. Cttee, Council of Mil. Educn Cttees, 1994–; RFCA (formerly TAVRA), NW England & IOM, 1995–; Liverpool Scottish Regtl Council, 1999–. Chairman: Merseyside Reg., NACF, 1996–2000; Liverpool Scottish Mus. Trust, 1999–. Governor: Merseyside Open Coll. Network, 1995–99; IOM Internat. Business Sch., 2000–. Chm., Inst. of Popular Music, 1995–2000. FRSA 1983. *Publications:* (with T. H. Pennington) Molecular Virology, 1971; (with K. M. Smith) Introduction to Virology, 1980; pubns on microbial molecular genetics and environmental microbiology in learned jls. *Recreations:* painting, gardening, walking, photography. *Address:* School of Biological Sciences, University of Liverpool, Liverpool CH69 7ZD. *T:* (0151) 794 3624; *e-mail:* d.a.ritchie@liverpool.ac.uk. *Club:* Athenæum (Liverpool).

RITCHIE, Rear-Adm. George Stephen, CB 1967; DSC 1942; writer; retired hydrographer; *b* 30 Oct. 1914; *s* of Sir (John) Douglas Ritchie, MC and late Margaret Stephen, OBE 1946, JP, Officer of the Order of Orange-Nassau, *d* of James Allan, Methlick, Aberdeenshire; *m* 1942, Mrs Disa Elizabeth Smith (*née* Beveridge) (*d* 2000); three *s* one *d. Educ:* RNC, Dartmouth. Joined RN Surveying Service, 1936; attached Eighth Army, 1942–43; served in HM Survey Ship Scott for invasion of Europe, 1944; comd HMS Challenger on scientific voyage round world, 1950–51; comd HM New Zealand Survey Ship Lachlan and NZ Surveying Service, 1953–56; comd HM Surveying Ship Dalrymple, Persian Gulf, 1959; comd HM Surveying Ship Vidal, West Indies and Western Europe, 1963–65; ADC to the Queen, 1965; Hydrographer of the Navy, 1966–71; Vis. Research Fellow, Southampton Univ., 1971–72; Pres., Directing Cttee, Internat. Hydrographic Bureau, Monaco, 1972–82; Founder Pres., 1972–73, Emeritus Mem., 1988–, Hydrographic Soc. Hon. Member: Canadian Hydrographic Assoc., 1981; Hydrographic Soc. of SA, 1985; Challenger Soc., 1992 (Hon. Life Mem., 1993). Chm., Collieston Harbour Trustees, 1991–96. Columnist, Hydro Internat. jl, 1997–. Founder's Medal, RGS, 1972; Prix Manley-Bendall, Académie de Marine, Paris, 1977; Gold Medal, Royal Inst. of Navigation, 1978. *Publications:* Challenger, 1957; The Admiralty Chart, 1967, new edn 1995; No Day Too Long, 1992; papers on navigation and oceanography in various jls, including Developments in British Hydrography since days of Captain Cook (RSA Silver Medal, 1970). *Recreations:* conserving Collieston, boules, sea-fishing. *Address:* Sea View, Collieston, Ellon, Aberdeenshire AB41 8RS. *Clubs:* Reform; Royal Northern and University (Aberdeen) (Hon. Mem.); Collieston Boules; Monte Carlo (Emeritus Mem.).

RITCHIE, Hamish Martin Johnston; Chairman, Marsh & McLennan Companies UK Ltd, since 2000; *b* 22 Feb. 1942; *s* of James Martin Ritchie and Noreen Mary Louise

Ritchie; *m* 1967, Judith Carol Young; one *s* one *d*. *Educ:* Loretto Sch.; Christ Church, Oxford (MA). Man. Dir, Hogg Robinson UK Ltd, 1980–81 (Dir, 1974–80); Chairman: Bowring London Ltd, 1981–93; Marsh Mercer Holdings Ltd (formerly Bowring Gp), 1983–; and Chief Exec., Bowring Marsh & McLennan Ltd, 1985–96; Marsh Europe SA, 1992–; Dir, Marsh Ltd, 1997–. Director: RAC, 1990–99; Halma plc, 1997–. Dep. Chm., BIBA, 1987–91; Pres., Insurance Inst. of London, 1995–96. CIMgt 1985. Trustee, Princess Royal Trust for Carers, 2000–. Gov., English Nat. Ballet, 2001–. *Recreations:* music, golf. *Address:* Oldhurst, Bulstrode Way, Gerrards Cross, Bucks SL9 7QT. *T:* (01753) 883262. *Clubs:* MCC, Royal Automobile; Royal & Ancient Golf (St Andrews), Denham Golf, Rye Golf.

RITCHIE, Ian Carl, CBE 2000; RA 1998; RIBA; Principal, Ian Ritchie Architects, since 1981; Consultant, Rice Francis Ritchie, since 1987; *b* 24 June 1947; *s* of Christopher Charles Ritchie and Mabel Berenice (*née* Long); *m* 1972, Jocelyne van den Bossche; one *s*. *Educ:* Varndean, Brighton; Liverpool Sch. of Architecture; Polytechnic of Central London Sch. of Architecture (Dip. Arch. distinction). MCSD. With Foster Associates, 1972–76; in private practice in France, 1976–78; Partner, Chrysalis Architects, 1979–81; Co-founder and Dir, RFR (Rice Francis Ritchie), 1981–87. Major works include: Ecology Gall., Nat. Hist. Mus.; B8, Stockley Park, London; Roy Square housing, Limehouse, London; Eagle Rock House, E Sussex; Culture Centre, Albert, France; roofs, Louvre Sculpture Courts, Paris; roof and glass facades, Mus. Nat. de Science, Techniques et de l'Industrie, La Villette, Paris; pharmacy, Boves, France; Fluy House, Picardy, France; Terrasson Cultural Greenhouse, France; HV Pylons for EDF, France (Millennium Product award, Design Council, 1999); glass towers, Centro de Arte Reina Sofia, Madrid; Leipzig Glashalle; Bermondsey Underground Stn, and Crystal Palace Concert Platform (Millennium Product award, Design Council, 1999), London; Scotland's Home of the Future, Glasgow; White City, London; Nat. Monument, Dublin; Nat. Rowing Centre, Royal Albert Dock, London; Light Monument, Milan. Mem., Royal Fine Art Commn, now Commn for Architecture and the Built Envmt, 1995–2001. Architectural Adviser: Natural Hist. Mus., 1991–95; to the Lord Chancellor, 1999–. External examiner, RIBA, 1986–96. Vis. Prof., Vienna Technical Univ., 1994–95. Mem., Technology Foresight Construction Panel Chairman: EUROPAN UK, 1997–; Collections and Library Cttee, RA, 2000–. Council Mem., Steel Construction Inst., 1994–97. FRSA. Tableau de l'Ordre des Architectes Français, 1982; Architectural Design Silver Medal, 1982; IRITECNA (Italian state construction industry) European Prize, 1992; Eric Lyons Meml Award, for European housing, 1992; Robert Matthew Award, Commonwealth Assoc. of Architects, 1994; AIA Award, 1997; Civic Trust Award, 1998; RFAC Arts Bldg of the Year Award, 1998; Stephen Lawrence Prize, 1998; RIBA Award, 1998, 2000; Acad. d'Architecture VII Silver Medal, 2000; RFAC Sports Bldg of the Year Award, 2000; Internat. Outstanding Structure Award, IABSE, 2000. *Publications:* (Well) Connected Architecture, 1994; The Biggest Glass Palace in the World, 1997; Ian Ritchie Technoecology, 1999. *Recreations:* art, swimming, reading, writing, film making. *Address:* (office) 110 Three Colt Street, E14 8AZ. *T:* (020) 7338 1100; *e-mail:* iritchie@ianritchiearchitects.co.uk.

RITCHIE, Ian Charles Stewart; arts management consultant, since 1994; *b* 19 June 1953; *s* of Kenneth John Stewart Ritchie and Wanda Margaret Angela Ritchie; *m* 1st, 1977, Angela Mary (marr. diss. 1993); two *d*; 2nd, 1997, Kathryn Alexandra McDowell, *qv*. *Educ:* Stowe Sch.; Royal Coll. of Music; Trinity Coll., Cambridge (MA); Guildhall Sch. of Music and Drama. General Manager, City of London Sinfonia, 1979–84; Artistic Dir, City of London Fest., 1983–84; Man. Dir, Scottish Chamber Orchestra, 1984–93; Gen. Dir, Opera North, 1993–94. Artistic Co-Dir, St Magnus Fest., Orkney, 1988–93; Dir, Highland Fest., 1994–96. *Recreations:* wine, cricket, golf, tennis, ski-ing, song. *Address:* 7 Waldemar Avenue, SW6 5LB. *T:* (020) 7731 0591. *Club:* MCC.

RITCHIE, Ian Cleland, CEng, FREng, FBCS; Chairman: Voxar Ltd, since 1994; Orbital Software Group Ltd, since 1995; Active Navigation (formerly Multicosm) Ltd, since 1997; Digital Bridges Ltd, since 2000; Deputy Chairman, Vis Interactive PLC, since 1995; *b* 29 June 1950; *s* of late Alexander Ritchie and Jean Russell Ritchie (*née* Fowler); *m* 1974, Barbara Allan Cowie (*d* 2001); one *s* one *d*. *Educ:* Heriot-Watt Univ. (BSc Hons Computer Sci. 1973). CEng 1991; FBCS 1992. Develt Engr/Manager, ICL, 1974–83; CEO and Man. Dir, Office Workstations Ltd (OWL), Edinburgh and Seattle, 1984–92 (OWL pioneered develt of hypertext (web-browsing) technol.; sold to Panasonic, 1989); special project, Heriot-Watt Univ., 1992–94. Director: Northern Venture Trust PLC, 1996–2001; Scran, 1996–; Indigo Active Vision Systems Ltd, 1997–2000; Epic Gp PLC, 1998–; Scottish Enterprise, 1999–; Channel 4 TV, 2000–; Bletchley Park Trust, 2000–; Scottish Science Trust, 2001–; Mindwarp Pavilion Ltd, 2001–. Mem., PPARC, 1999–. Pres., BCS, 1998–99. Hon. Prof., Heriot-Watt Univ., 1993–. FREng 2001. DUniv Heriot-Watt, 2000; Hon. DSc Robert Gordon, 2001. *Publications:* New Media Publishing: opportunities from the digital revolution, 1996; contrib. various technol. papers and articles. *Recreations:* travel, theatre and arts, web-browsing. *Address:* Coppertop, Green Lane, Lasswade EH18 1HE. *T:* (0131) 663 9486. *Club:* Royal Over-Seas League.

RITCHIE, Ian Russell; Chief Executive Officer, Associated Press Television News, since 2000; *b* 27 Nov. 1953; *s* of Hugh Russell Ritchie and Sheelah Ritchie; *m* 1982, Jill Evelyn Middleton-Walker; two *s*. *Educ:* Leeds Grammar Sch.; Trinity Coll., Oxford (MA Jurisprudence). Called to the Bar, Middle Temple, 1976. Practised at the Bar, 1976–78; Industrial Relations Advr, EEF, 1978–80; Granada TV, 1980–88 (Head of Prodn Services, 1987–88); Dir of Resources, 1988–91, Man. Dir, 1991–93, Tyne Tees TV; Gp Dep. Chief Exec., Yorkshire Tyne Tees TV, 1992–93; Managing Director: Nottingham Studios, Central Television, 1993–94; London News Network, 1994–96; Chief Exec., 1996, Chief Operating Officer, 1996–97, Channel 5 Broadcasting; Partner and Man. Dir, Russell Reynolds Associates, 1997–98; CEO, Middle East Broadcasting, 1998–2000. Dir, West Ham United plc, 1999–. FRSA. *Recreations:* golf, tennis, theatre, music. *Address:* Virginia Water, Surrey. *Club:* Vincent's (Oxford).

RITCHIE, Jean Harris, (Mrs G. T. K. Boney); QC 1992; a Recorder, since 1993; *b* 6 April 1947; *d* of late Walter Weir Ritchie and of Lily (*née* Goodwin); *m* 1976, Guy Thomas Knowles Boney, *qv*; two *s*. *Educ:* King's Coll., London (LLB); McGill Univ., Montreal (LLM). Called to the Bar, Gray's Inn, 1970 (Churchill Schol., 1968; Bencher, 2000); on Western Circuit; Head of Chambers, 2000–. Chairman: Clunis Inquiry (care in the community for patients suffering from schizophrenia), 1993–94; Inquiry into Clinical Governance (arising from actions of Rodney Ledward), 1999–2000. Member: Supreme Ct Rule Cttee, 1993–97; Judicial Studies Bd, 1998– (Mem., Civil Cttee, 1997–). Chm. Govs, Norman Court Prep. Sch., W Tytherley, 1996–2000. *Publication:* (contrib.) Safe Practice in Obstetrics and Gynaecology, ed R. V. Clements, 1994. *Recreation:* family. *Address:* 4 Paper Buildings, Temple, EC4Y 7EX. *T:* (020) 7353 3366.

RITCHIE, Dr John Hindle, MBE 1985; architect; development management consultant; *b* 4 June 1937; *s* of Charles A. Ritchie; *m* 1963, Anne B. M. Leyland; two *d*. *Educ:* Royal Grammar School, Newcastle upon Tyne; Univ. of Liverpool (BArch Hons); Univ. of Sheffield (PhD Building Science). Science Research Council, 1963–66; Town Planner, Liverpool City Council, 1966–69; Rowntree Housing Trust, Univ. of Liverpool, 1969–72; R&D Architect, Cheshire County Council, 1972–74; Asst County Planner (Envmt), Merseyside CC, 1974–80; Dir of Develt, 1980–85, Chief Exec. and Mem., 1985–91, Merseyside Develt Corp. Chm., Merseyside Educn Training Enterprise Ltd, 1986–91; Member: Merseyside Tourism Bd, 1986–88; Internat. Organising Cttee, Grand Regatta Columbus '92, 1986–92; Board: Gardners Row Business Centre, 1987–90; Merseyside Enterprise Trust, 1988–91; Instant Muscle Ltd, 1993–95; Merseyside Sculptors Guild, 1993–97; Wirral Community Healthcare Trust, 1993–95; Landscape Trust, 1996–. Mem., Lord Chancellor's Panel of Ind. Inspectors, 1994–. Gov., Liverpool Community Coll., 1995–. Major projects include: natural resource management, pollution control, land reclamation and urban conservation progs and projects, Merseyside Strategic Plan; Liverpool South Docks and Riverside reclamation and develt, Liverpool Internat. Garden Fest., 1984 (Civic Trust Award); Albert Dock Conservation (European Gold Medal, 1986; Civic Trust Jubilee Award, 1987). CIMgt. *Publications:* scientific and planning papers on urban environment obsolescence and regeneration. *Address:* Cartref, 8 The Mount, Heswall, Wirral CH60 4RD.

RITCHIE, Prof. J(oseph) Murdoch, PhD, DSc; FRS 1976; Eugene Higgins Professor of Pharmacology, Yale University, since 1968; *b* 10 June 1925; *s* of Alexander Farquharson Ritchie and Agnes Jane (*née* Bremner); *m* 1951, Brenda Rachel (*née* Bigland); one *s* one *d*. *Educ:* Aberdeen Central Secondary Sch.; Aberdeen Univ. (BSc Maths); UCL (BSc Physiol., PhD, DSc; Fellow 1978). CPhys, FInstP, 1997. Res. in Radar, Telecommunications Res. Estabt, Malvern, 1944–46; University Coll. London: Hon. Res. Asst, Biophysics Res. Unit, 1946–49; Lectr in Physiol., 1949–51; Mem. staff, Nat. Inst. for Med. Res., Mill Hill, 1951–55; Asst Prof. of Pharmacology, 1956–57, Associate Prof., 1958–63 and Prof., 1963–68, Albert Einstein Coll. of Medicine, NY; Overseas Fellow, Churchill Coll., Cambridge, 1964–65; Chm., Dept of Pharmacol., 1968–74, Dir, Div. of Biol Scis, 1975–78, Yale Univ. Hon. MA Yale, 1968; Hon. DSc Aberdeen, 1987. *Publications:* papers on nerve and muscle physiol. and biophysics in Jl of Physiol. *Recreations:* skiing, chess. *Address:* 47 Deepwood Drive, Hamden, CT 06517, USA. *T:* (home) (203) 7770420 (office) (203) 7854567. *Club:* Yale (NYC).

RITCHIE, Kathryn Alexandra; *see* McDowell, K. A.

RITCHIE, Dr Kenneth George Hutchison; Chief Executive, Electoral Reform Society, since 1997; *b* 8 Dec. 1946; *s* of William Ritchie and late Margaret Morton Ritchie (*née* Hutchison); *m* 1985, Elizabeth Anne Black; one *s* one *d*. *Educ:* George Heriot's Sch., Edinburgh; Edinburgh Univ. (BSc); Aston Univ. (PhD 1981). Maths teacher, VSO, Tanzania, 1968–69; systems analyst, ICI, 1970–73; Hd, Internat. Service, UNA, 1976–83; Exec. Dir, Appropriate Health Resources and Technologies Action Gp, 1983–88; Dep. Dir, British Refugee Council, 1988–94; UK Dir, Intermediate Technol., 1994–96. Hon. Treas., War on Want, 1980–85; Treas., Western Sahara Campaign, 1984–. Mem., Council for Advancement of Arab-British Understanding, 1989–94. Dir, Make Votes Count, 1998–. Contested (Lab): Beckenham, 1987 and 1992; Daventry, 1997. *Recreations:* golf, music, walking the dog. *Address:* 37 Ware Road, Barby, Rugby CV23 8UE. *T:* (01788) 890942.

RITCHIE, Kenneth Gordon, CMG 1968; HM Diplomatic Service, retired; *b* 19 Aug. 1921; *s* of Walter Ritchie, Arbroath; *m* 1951, Esme Stronsa Nash (*d* 1995). *Educ:* Arbroath High Sch.; St Andrews Univ. (MA). Joined FO, 1944; Embassy, Ankara, 1944–47; Foreign Office, 1947–49; Khorramshahr, 1949–50; Tehran, 1950–52; Djakarta, 1952–55; Foreign Office, 1955–57; Peking, 1957–62; Santiago, 1962–64; Elisabethville, 1965–66; Dep. High Commissioner, Lusaka, 1966–67; High Commissioner, Guyana, 1967–70; Head of Perm. Under-Sec.'s Dept, FCO, 1970–73; High Comr, Malaŵi, 1973–77. *Address:* Dalforbie, North Esk Road, Edzell, Angus DD9 7TW.

RITCHIE, Margaret Claire; JP; Headmistress of Queen Mary School, Lytham, 1981–98; *b* 18 Sept. 1937; *d* of Roderick M. Ritchie, Edinburgh. *Educ:* Leeds Girls' High Sch.; Univ. of Leeds (BSc). Postgraduate Certificate in Education, Univ. of London. Asst Mistress, St Leonards Sch., St Andrews, 1960–64; Head of Science Dept, Wycombe Abbey Sch., High Wycombe, 1964–71; Headmistress, Queenswood Sch., 1972–81. JP Fylde, 1991–99, Preston PSD, 1999. *Address:* 29 Walmer Road, Lytham St Annes, Lancs FY8 3HL.

RITCHIE, Peter, FCCA; Head of Finance, Fife Council, since 1995; *b* 16 March 1951. *Educ:* Kirkland High Sch.; Buckhaven High Sch. FCCA 1975. Fife CC, 1969–75; Fife Regional Council, 1975–: Chief Accountant, 1980–84; Sen. Asst Dir of Finance, 1984–88; Dep. Dir of Finance, 1988–95. *Recreations:* hill-walking, gardening, theatre, cinema, photography. *Address:* 40 Demarco Drive, Glenrothes, Fife KY7 6FD. *T:* (01592) 741412.

RITCHIE, Robert Blackwood, (Robin); grazier running family sheep and cattle property, Western Victoria, 1958–2001; *b* 6 April 1937; *s* of Alan Blackwood Ritchie and Margaret Louise (*née* Whitcomb); *m* 1965, Eda Natalie Sandford Beggs; two *s* one *d*. *Educ:* Geelong Grammar Sch.; Corpus Christi Coll., Cambridge (MA; Rowing Blue, 1958). Dir, Agricl Investments Australia, 1968–89 (Chm., 1968–85). Exec. Mem., Graziers Assoc. of Vic, 1968–72; Mem., National Rural Adv. Council, 1974–75; Chairman: Exotic Animal Disease Preparedness Consultative Council, 1990–95; Renewable Energy Authority, Vic, 1993–98. Dir-Gen., Min. for Economic Develt, Vic, 1981–83. Geelong Grammar School: Mem. Council, 1966–78 (Chm., 1973–78); Chief Exec., 1979–80 (during period between Head Masters). *Recreation:* sailing. *Address:* 42 Griffith Street, Port Fairy, Vic 3284, Australia. *T:* (55) 681447. *Club:* Melbourne (Melbourne).

RITCHIE, Shirley Anne; *see* Anwyl, S. A.

RITCHIE, Prof. William, OBE 1994; PhD; FRSGS; FRICS; FRSE; Vice Chancellor, Lancaster University, since 1995; *b* 22 March 1940; *s* of Alexander Ritchie and Rebecca Smith Ritchie; *m* 1965, Elizabeth A. Bell; two *s* one *d*. *Educ:* Glasgow Univ. (BSc, PhD 1966). FRSGS 1980; FRSE 1982; FRICS 1989. Research Asst, Glasgow Univ., 1963; Aberdeen University: Lectr, 1964–72; Sen. Lectr, 1972–79; Prof., 1979–95; Dean, 1988–89; Vice Principal, 1989–95. Post-doctoral Vis. Prof. and Hon. Prof. appts in geog. and coastal geog., Louisiana State Univ., USA, at various times, 1971–95. *Publications:* Mapping for Field Scientists, 1977; Surveying and Mapping for Field Scientists, 1988, 4th edn 1996; The Environmental Impact of the Wreck of the Braer, 1994; numerous papers mainly in jls of physical and coastal geog. and envmtl mgt. *Address:* Lancaster University, Lancaster LA1 4YW. *T:* (01524) 592000.

RITTERMAN, Janet Elizabeth, PhD; Director, Royal College of Music, since 1993; *b* 1 Dec. 1941; *d* of Charles Eric Palmer and Laurie Helen Palmer; *m* 1970, Gerrard Peter Ritterman. *Educ:* North Sydney Girls' High Sch.; NSW State Conservatorium of Music; Univ. of Durham (BMus 1971); King's Coll. London (MMus 1977; PhD 1985). Pianist, accompanist, chamber music player; Senior Lecturer in Music: Middlesex Poly., 1975–79; Goldsmiths' Coll., Univ. of London, 1980–87; Dartington College of Arts: Head of Music, 1987–90; Dean, Academic Affairs, 1988–90; Acting Principal, 1990–91; Principal,

1991–93; Hon. Vis. Prof. of Music Educn, Univ. of Plymouth, 1993–. Chm., Assoc. Bd of Royal Schs of Music (Publishing) Ltd, 1993–. Former Mem., music educn and arts orgns; Member: Arts Council, 2000– (Mem., Music Panel, 1992–98); Council, Royal Musical Assoc., 1994– (Vice-Pres., 1998–); Bd, ENO, 1996–; Postgrad. Panel, AHRB, 1999–; Vice-Pres., Nat. Assoc. of Youth Orchestras, 1993–. Chairman: Adv. Council, Arts Res. Ltd, 1997–; Fedn of British Conservatoires, 1998–. Governor: Assoc. Bd, Royal Schs of Music, 1993–; Purcell Sch., 1996–2000. Trustee, Countess of Munster Musical Trust, 1993–. FRNCM 1996; Fellow: Nene Coll., 1997; Dartington Coll. of Arts, 1997. Hon. RAM 1995; Hon. GSMD 2000. DUniv Central England, 1996. *Publications:* articles in learned jls, France and UK. *Recreations:* reading, theatre-going. *Address:* Royal College of Music, Prince Consort Road, SW7 2BS. *T:* (020) 7589 3643; *e-mail:* jritterman@rcm.ac.uk.

RITTNER, Luke Philip Hardwick; Chief Executive, Royal Academy of Dancing, since 1999; *b* 24 May 1947; *s* of late George Stephen Hardwick Rittner and of Joane (*née* Thunder); *m* 1974, Corinna Frances Edholm; one *d. Educ:* Blackfriars School, Laxton; City of Bath Technical Coll.; Dartington Coll. of Arts; London Acad. of Music and Dramatic Art. Asst Administrator, Bath Festival, 1968–71, Jt Administrator, 1971–74, Administrative Director, 1974–76; Founder, and Dir, Assoc. for Business Sponsorship of the Arts, 1976–83; Sec. Gen., Arts Council of GB, 1983–90; Dir, Marketing and Communications, then Corporate Affairs, Sotheby's Europe, 1992–99. Chm., English Shakespeare Co., 1990–94. UK Cultural Dir, Expo '92, Seville; Corporate Advr on cultural sponsorship to: Eurotunnel; J. Sainsbury plc. Non-exec. Bd Mem., Carlton Television, 1991–93. Member: Adv. Council, V&A Museum, 1980–83; Music Panel, British Council, 1979–83; Drama Panel, Olivier Awards, 1992–94; Council, and Chm., Exec. Bd, LAMDA, 1994–; Council, Almeida Th., 1997–. Chm., London Choral Soc., 1994–. Trustee: Bath Preservation Trust, 1968–73; Theatre Royal, Bath, 1979–82; City Ballet of London, 1997–2000; Foundn Trustee, Holburne Museum, Bath, 1981–83; Governor, Urchfont Manor, Wiltshire Adult Educn Centre, 1982–83. *Recreations:* the arts, people, travel. *Address:* Royal Academy of Dancing, 36 Battersea Square, SW11 3RA. *Club:* Garrick.

RIVERDALE, 3rd Baron *cr* 1935, of Sheffield, co. York; **Anthony Robert Balfour;** Bt 1929; *b* 23 Feb. 1960; *s* of Hon. Mark Robin Balfour (*d* 1995) and Susan Ann Phillips (*d* 1996); *S* grandfather, 1998. *Heir: uncle* Hon. David Rowland Balfour, *b* 15 May 1938.

RIVERINA, Bishop of, since 1993; **Rt Rev. Bruce Quinton Clark;** *b* Brisbane, Qld, 22 May 1939; *s* of Quinton Clark; *m* 1965, Elizabeth Shufflebotham. *Educ:* Brisbane Boys Coll.; St Francis Theol Coll., Brisbane (ThL). Ordained deacon and priest, 1963; Assistant Curate: All Saints, Chermside, 1963–65; St Matthew's, Groveley, 1965–67; Vicar, St Luke's, Miles, 1967–70; Rector: St Matthew's, Gayndah, 1970–76; St Peter's, Gympie, 1976–83; St Paul's, Maryborough, 1983–89; Surfers Paradise Parish, 1989–93. Archdeacon: Wide Bay, Burnett, 1985–89; Moreton, 1989–91; Gold Coast and Hinterland, 1991–93. *Recreations:* restoring furniture, music, photography. *Address:* Bishop's Lodge, PO Box 10, 127 Audley Street, Narrandera, NSW 2700, Australia. *T:* (2) 69591177.

RIVERS, Valerie Lane-Fox P.; *see* Pitt-Rivers.

RIVETT, Dr Geoffrey Christopher; Senior Principal Medical Officer, Department of Health (formerly of Health and Social Security), 1985–92; *b* 11 Aug. 1932; *s* of Frank Andrew James Rivett and Catherine Mary Rivett; *m* 1976, Elizabeth Barbara Hartman; two *s* by previous marr. *Educ:* Manchester Grammar Sch.; Brasenose Coll., Oxford (MA 1st Cl. Hons Animal Physiol.); University Coll. Hosp. (BM, BCh); FRCGP, DObst RCOG. House Officer, Radcliffe Inf., Oxford, 1957; House Phys., London Chest Hosp., 1958; RAMC, 1958–60; GP, Milton Keynes, 1960–72; DHSS, subseq. DoH, 1972–92. Liveryman: Soc. of Apothecaries, 1981–; Co. of Barbers, 1993–. ARPS 1971. *Publications:* The Development of the London Hospital System 1823–1982, 1986; From Cradle to Grave: fifty years of the NHS, 1998. *Recreations:* photography, house conversion. *Address:* 173 Shakespeare Tower, Barbican, EC2Y 8DR. *T:* (020) 7786 9617; *e-mail:* geoffrey@rivett.net. *Club:* Royal Society of Medicine.

RIVETT-CARNAC, Miles James; DL; Chairman, Tribune Investment Trust, since 1985; Vice Lord-Lieutenant of Hampshire, since 1999; *b* 7 Feb. 1933; *s* of Vice-Adm. James William Rivett-Carnac, CB, CBE, DSC (2nd *s* of 6th Bt) (*d* 1970), and Isla Nesta Rivett-Carnac (*d* 1974), *d* of Harry Officer Blackwood; *heir-pres.* to brother, Rev. Canon Sir Nicholas Rivett-Carnac, Bt, *qv*; *m* 1958, April Sally Villar; two *s* one *d. Educ:* Royal Naval College, Dartmouth, RN, 1950–70 (despatches 1965); Commander, 1965; US Staff Coll., 1966; Commanded HMS Dainty, 1967–68; MoD, 1968–70. Joined Barings, 1971; Dir, Baring Bros & Co., 1976; Pres., Baring Bros Inc., 1978; Managing Dir, Baring Bros & Co., 1981; Dep. Chm., Barings plc, 1988–93; Chairman: Baring Asset Management, 1989–93; Baring Securities, 1993–94. Director: London Stock Exchange, 1991–94; Allied Domecq (formerly Allied Lyons) plc, 1992–97. Chm., Hampshire Boys' Clubs, 1982–90. Mem. Council, King George V Fund for Sailors, 1989. Elder Brother, Trinity House, 1992–. High Sheriff, Hants, 1995, DL Hants, 1996. *Recreations:* tennis, golf, shooting, philately (FRPS). *Address:* Martyr Worthy Manor, Winchester, Hants SO21 1DY. *T:* (01962) 779311. *Clubs:* White's, Naval and Military; Links, Racquet (NY).

RIVETT-CARNAC, Rev. Canon Sir (Thomas) Nicholas, 8th Bt *cr* 1836; Pastor, Ashburnham Place, Battle, 1993–96; Hon. Canon of Southwark Cathedral, 1980–96, now Canon Emeritus; *b* 3 June 1927; *s* of Vice-Admiral James William Rivett-Carnac, CB, CBE, DSC (2nd *s* of 6th Bt) (*d* 1970), and of Isla Nesta Rivett-Carnac (*d* 1974), *d* of Harry Officer Blackwood; *S* uncle, 1972; *m* 1977, Susan Marigold MacTier Copeland, *d* of late Harold and Adeline Copeland. *Educ:* Marlborough College. Scots Guards, 1945–55. Probation Service, 1957–59. Ordained, 1963; Curate: Holy Trinity, Rotherhithe, 1963–68; Holy Trinity, Brompton, 1968–72; Vicar, St Mark's, Kennington, 1972–89; Rural Dean of Lambeth, 1978–82; Pastor, Kingdom Faith Ministries, Roffey Place, Horsham, 1989–93. *Heir: b* Miles James Rivett-Carnac, *qv*. *Address:* The Haven, Sandhurst Lane, Little Common, Bexhill-on-Sea, East Sussex TN39 4RH.

RIVLIN, Geoffrey; QC 1979; **His Honour Judge Rivlin;** a Circuit Judge, since 1989; *b* 28 Nov. 1940; *s* of late M. Allenby Rivlin and late May Rivlin; *m* 1974, Maureen Smith, Hon. ARAM, Prof. of violin, RCM; two *d. Educ:* Bootham Sch.; Leeds Univ. (LLB). Called to the Bar, Middle Temple, 1963 (Colombos Prize, Internat. Law); Bencher, 1987. NE Circuit Junior 1967; a Recorder, 1978–89. Mem., Senate of Inns of Court and the Bar, 1976–79. Chm. Adv. Bd, Computer Crime Centre, QMW, 1996–. Governor: St Christopher's Sch., Hampstead, 1990–99; NLCS, Edgware, 1993–. *Publication:* First Steps in the Law, 1999. *Address:* South Eastern Circuit Office, 18 Maltravers Street, WC2R 3EU.

RIX, family name of **Baron Rix**.

RIX, Baron *cr* 1992 (Life Peer), of Whitehall in the City of Westminster and of Hornsea in Yorkshire; **Brian Norman Roger Rix,** Kt 1986; CBE 1977; DL; actor-manager, 1948–77; President, Mencap (Royal Society for Mentally Handicapped Children and Adults), since 1998 (Secretary-General, 1980–87; Chairman, 1988–98); Chairman, Mencap City Foundation, since 1988 (Founder and Governor, since 1984); *b* 27 Jan. 1924; *s* of late Herbert and Fanny Rix; *m* 1949, Elspet Jeans Macgregor-Gray; two *s* two *d. Educ:* Bootham Sch., York. Stage career: joined Donald Wolfit, 1942; first West End appearance, Sebastian in Twelfth Night, St James's, 1943; White Rose Players, Harrogate, 1943–44. Served War of 1939–45, RAF and Bevin Boy. Became actor-manager, 1948; ran repertory cos at Ilkley, Bridlington and Margate, 1950; toured Reluctant Heroes and brought to Whitehall Theatre, 1950–54; Dry Rot, 1954–58; Simple Spymen, 1958–61; One For the Pot, 1961–64; Chase Me Comrade, 1964–66; went to Garrick Theatre, 1967, with repertoire of farce: Stand By Your Bedouin; Uproar in the House; Let Sleeping Wives Lie; after 6 months went over to latter, only, which ran till 1969; then followed: She's Done It Again, 1969–70; Don't Just Lie There, Say Something!, 1971–73 (filmed 1973); New Theatre, Cardiff, Robinson Crusoe, 1973; Cambridge Theatre, A Bit Between The Teeth, 1974; Fringe Benefits, Whitehall Theatre, 1976; returned to theatre 1988; Dry Rot, Lyric Theatre, 1989; dir., You'll Do For Me!, tour, 1989. Entered films, 1951: subsequently made eleven, including Reluctant Heroes, 1951, Dry Rot, 1956. BBC TV contract to present farces on TV, 1956–72; first ITV series Men of Affairs, 1973; A Roof Over My Head, BBC TV series, 1977. Presenter, Let's Go …, BBC TV series (first ever for people with a learning disability), 1978–83; BBC Radio 2 series, 1978–80. Dir and Theatre Controller, Cooney-Marsh Group, 1977–80; Trustee, Theatre of Comedy, 1983–93; Arts Council: Mem., 1986–93; Chairman: Drama Panel, 1986–93; Monitoring Cttee, Arts and Disabled People, 1988–93; Indep. Devel Council for People with Mental Handicap, 1981–86; Friends of Normansfield, 1975–; Libertas, 1987–. Chancellor, Univ. of E London, 1997–. DL Greater London, 1987; Vice Lord-Lieut of Greater London, 1988–97. Hon. MA: Hull, 1981; Open, 1983; DUniv: Essex, 1984; Bradford, 2000; Hon. LLD: Manchester, 1986; Dundee, 1994; Exeter, 1997; Hon. DSc Nottingham, 1987. Hon. Fellow, Humberside Coll. of Higher Educn, 1984; Hon. FRSocMed 1998; Hon. FRCPsych 1999. Evian Health Award, 1988; Communicator of the Year, RNID, 1990; Campaigner of the Year, Spectator, 1999. *Publications:* My Farce from My Elbow: an autobiography, 1975; Farce about Face (autobiog.), 1989; Tour de Farce, 1992; Life in the Farce Lane, 1995; (ed and contrib.) Gullible's Travails, 1996. *Recreations:* cricket, amateur radio (G2DQU; Hon. Vice-Pres., Radio Soc. of GB, 1979). *Address:* House of Lords, SW1A 0PW. *Clubs:* Garrick, MCC; Yorkshire County Cricket.

RIX, Rt Hon. Sir Bernard (Anthony), Kt 1993; PC 2000; **Rt Hon. Lord Justice Rix;** a Lord Justice of Appeal, since 2000; *b* 8 Dec. 1944; *s* of late Otto Rix and Sadie Silverberg; *m* 1983, Hon. Karen Debra, *er d* of Baron Young of Graffham, *qv*; three *s* two *d* (inc. twin *s*). *Educ:* St Paul's School, London; New College, Oxford (BA: Lit.Hum. 1966, Jur. 1968; MA); Harvard Law School (Kennedy Scholar 1968; LLM 1969). Called to Bar, Inner Temple, 1970, Bencher, 1990; QC 1981; a Recorder, 1990–93; a Judge of the High Court, QBD, 1993–2000; Judge in charge of Commercial List, 1998–99. Member: Senate, Inns of Court and Bar, 1981–83; Bar Council, 1981–83. Chm., Commercial Bar Assoc., 1992–93. Dir, London Philharmonic Orchestra, 1986–. Vice-Chm., Central Council for Jewish Community Services, 1994–96 (author, report on youth services and orgns, 1994). Dir, Spiro Inst., 1995–99. Chm., British Friends of Bar-Ilan Univ., 1987–99 (Hon. Vice-Pres., 1999–); Mem. Bd of Trustees, Bar-Ilan Univ., 1988–99. *Recreations:* music, opera, Italy, formerly fencing. *Address:* Royal Courts of Justice, Strand, WC2A 2LL.

RIX, Dr (Edward) Martyn; freelance writer and botanist, since 1978; *b* 15 Aug. 1943; *s* of Edward Lionel Reussner Rix and Elizabeth Joyce Rix; *m* 1983, Alison Jane Goatcher; two *d. Educ:* Sherborne Sch., Dorset; Trinity Coll., Dublin (MA); Corpus Christi Coll., Cambridge (PhD). Res. Fellow, Univ. of Zürich, 1971–73; botanist, RHS, Wisley, 1974–78. Gold Veitch Meml Medal, RHS, 1999. *Publications:* The Art of the Botanist, 1981; Growing Bulbs, 1983; The Redouté Album, 1990; with R. Phillips: Bulbs, 1981; Freshwater Fish, 1985; Roses, 1988; Shrubs, 1989; Perennials, 2 vols, 1991; Vegetables, 1993; The Quest for the Rose, 1993; Conservatory and Indoor Plants, 1997; Annuals, 1999. *Recreations:* fishing, sailing, travel. *Address:* c/o Macmillan Publishers Ltd, 25 Eccleston Place, SW1W 9NF.

RIX, Sir John, Kt 1977; MBE 1955; DL; FREng; Chairman, Seahorse International Ltd, 1986–89; Deputy Chairman, The Victorian Cruise Line Ltd, 1987–96; *b* 30 Jan. 1917; *s* of Reginald Arthur Rix; *m* 1953, Sylvia Gene Howe; two *s* one *d. Educ:* Southampton Univ. FRINA; FIMarE; FREng (FEng 1979). Chm. and Chief Exec., Vosper Thornycroft (UK) Ltd, 1970–78; Chm. and Dir, Vosper PLC, 1978–85; Chairman: Vosper Shiprepairers Ltd, 1977–78; David Brown Vosper (Offshore) Ltd, 1978–85; Vosper Hovermarine Ltd, 1980–85; David Brown Gear Industries Ltd, 1980–85; Mainwork Ltd, 1980–85; Director: Vosper Private Ltd, 1966–77 and 1978–85; Charismarine Ltd, 1976–88; Southampton Cable Ltd, 1986–88; Chilworth Centre Ltd, 1986–94. Liveryman, Shipwrights' Co., 1973–. DL Hants 1985. *Recreations:* sailing, tennis, golf, walking. *Address:* Lower Baybridge House, Owslebury, Winchester, Hants SO21 1JN. *T:* (01962) 777306. *Clubs:* Royal Thames Yacht; Hockley Golf.

RIX, Martyn; *see* Rix, E. M.

RIX, Michael David; General Secretary, Associated Society of Locomotive Engineers and Firemen, since 1998; *b* 11 April 1963; *s* of Roy Rix; *m* 1984, Ophelia Williams (separated); one *s* one *d. Educ:* Primrose Hill High Sch., Leeds; Bradford and Ilkley TUC Coll.; various TUC/ASLEF educn projects. Left sch. at 16 with no formal qualifications; work experience, Yorks copper works, 1979; trainee driver, BR, Leeds, 1979–86; qualified BR driver, 1986. Leeds ASLEF: Mem., Br. Cttee, 1980–84; Asst Br. Sec., 1984–98; Br. Sec., 1988–98; Negotiating Chair, 1992; Dist Council Chm., 1995; Dist Sec., No 3 Reg., 1998. Mem., Labour Party, 1980–97. *Recreations:* football, swimming, reading, very little time though to pursue. *Address:* ASLEF, 9 Arkwright Road, Hampstead, NW3 6AB. *T:* (020) 7317 8600.

RIX, Timothy John, CBE 1997; Chairman, Longman Group Ltd, 1984–90 (Chief Executive, 1976–89); *b* 4 Jan. 1934; *s* of late Howard Terrell Rix and Marguerite Selman Rix; *m* 1st, 1960, Wendy Elizabeth Wright (marr. diss. 1967); one *d*; 2nd, 1967, Gillian Diana Mary Greenwood; one *s* one *d. Educ:* Radley Coll.; Clare Coll., Cambridge (BA); Yale Univ., USA. Sub-Lieut, RNVR, 1952–54. Mellon Fellow, Yale, 1957–58; joined Longmans, Green & Co. Ltd, subseq. Longman Gp, 1958; Overseas Educnl Publisher, 1958–61; Publishing Manager, Far East and SE Asia, 1961–63; Head of English Language Teaching Publishing, 1964–68; Divl Man. Dir, 1968–72; Jt Man. Dir, 1972–76. Director: Pearson Longman Ltd, 1979–83; Goldcrest Television, 1981–83; Yale Univ. Press, London, 1984–; ECIC (Management) Ltd, 1990–92; Blackie and Son Ltd, 1990–93; B. H. Blackwell Ltd, 1990–95; Blackwell Ltd, 1993–95; HEA Publishing Adv. Bd, 1993–95; Geddes and Grosset Ltd, 1996–98; Jessica Kingsley Publishers Ltd, 1997–; Frances Lincoln Ltd, 1997–; Meditech Media Ltd, 1997–; Scottish Book Source, 1999–. Chm., Book

Marketing Ltd, 1990–; Senior Consultant: Pofcher Co., 1990–95; van Tulleken Co., 1996–. Chm., Pitman Examns Inst., 1987–90. Publishers Association: Chm., Trng Cttee, 1974–78; Chm., Book Develt Council, 1979–81; Vice-Pres., 1980–81 and 1983–84; Pres., 1981–83. Chairman: Book Trust, 1986–88; Book House Training Centre, 1986–89; British Library Centre for the Book, 1990–96; Society of Bookmen, 1990–92; British Library Publishing, 1992–; Book Aid International, 1994–March 2002; Nat. Book Cttee, 1997–March 2002. Member: Exec. Cttee, NBL, 1979–86 (Dep. Chm., 1984–86); Publishers Adv. Panel, British Council, 1978–98 (Chm., 1994–98); Arts Council Literature Panel, 1983–86; British Library Adv. Council, 1982–86; British Library Bd, 1986–96; British Council Bd, 1988–97; Finance Cttee, Delegacy of OUP, 1992–; Bd, HEA, 1996–99. Hon. Pres., Independent Publishers' Guild, 1993–. Governor: Bell Educnl Trust, 1990– (Chm. Govs, 1995–2001); ESU, 1999–2001. CIMgt (CBIM 1981); FRSA 1986. *Publications:* articles on publishing in trade jls. *Recreations:* reading, landscape, wine. *Address:* Top Flat, 27 Wolseley Road, N8 8RS. *T:* (020) 8341 4160. *Club:* Garrick.

RIZA, Alper Ali; QC 1991; a Recorder, since 2000; *b* 16 March 1948; *s* of Ali Riza and Elli Liasides; *m* 1981, Vanessa Hall-Smith; two *d*. *Educ:* American Academy, Larnaca, Cyprus; English Sch., Nicosia. Called to the Bar, Gray's Inn, 1973. Pupillage, 1974–75; Turnpike Lane Law and Advice, 1975–77; Appeals Lawyer, Jt Council for Welfare of Immigrants, 1977–82; private practice, 1982–. Founder Mem., Assoc. of Greek, Turkish and Cypriot Affairs, 1990–. Jt Editor, Butterworths's Immigration Law Service, 1991–95. *Recreations:* music, philosophy, drinking and smoking, sport, walking around London W2 and W11 esp. Hyde Park, Kensington Gardens and Holland Park. *Address:* 10 King's Bench Walk, EC4Y 7EB. *T:* (020) 7353 2501, *Fax:* (020) 7353 0658.

RIZK, Waheeb, CBE 1984 (OBE 1977); MA, PhD; FREng, FIMechE; Engineering Consultant, W R Associates, since 1986; *b* 11 Nov. 1921; *s* of Dr and Mrs I. Rizk; *m* 1952, Vivien Moyle, MA (Cantab); one *s* one *d* (and one *d* decd). *Educ:* Emmanuel College, Cambridge. MA, PhD. Joined English Electric Co., 1954, Chief Engineer, Gas Turbine Div., 1957, Gen. Manager, new div., combining gas turbines and industrial steam turbines, 1967; after merger with GEC became Man. Dir, GEC Gas Turbines Ltd, 1971; Chairman: GEC-Ruston Gas Turbines Ltd, 1983–86; GEC Diesels Ltd, 1983–86. Chm. of Bd, BSI, 1982–85. Pres., IMechE, 1984–85 (Mem. Council, 1978–89); Mem. Council, Fellowship of Engrg, 1982–85. Pres., Internat Council on Combustion Engines (CIMAC), 1973–77. Chm., Smallpeice Trust, 1991–98. Mem. Council, Cranfield Inst. of Technology, 1985–95; Member Court: Brunel Univ., 1986–; Cranfield Univ., 1986–. Liveryman, Worshipful Co. of Engineers. Gold Medal, CIMAC, 1983. *Publications:* technical papers to IMechE, Amer. Soc. of Mech. Engineers and CIMAC. *Recreations:* intelligent tinkering with any mechanism, photography, old motor cycles. *Address:* 231 Hillmorton Road, Rugby CV22 5BD. *T:* (01788) 565093. *Club:* Athenæum.

RIZZELLO, Michael Gaspard, OBE 1977; PPRBS; FCSD; sculptor and coin designer; *b* 2 April 1926; *s* of Arthur Rizzello and Maria Rizzello (*née* D'Angelo); *m* 1950, Sheila Semple Maguire; one *d*. *Educ:* Oratory Central Boys Sch., SW3; Royal College of Art. Military Service, 1944–48; served in India and Far East; commissioned 1945. Major Travelling Scholarship (Sculpture) and Drawing Prize, RCA, 1950. ARCA 1950; ARBS 1955, FRBS 1961, PRBS 1976–86; FCSD (FSIAD 1978). Pres., Soc. of Portrait Sculptors, 1968. Prix de Rome (Sculpture), 1951. Sir Otto Beit Medal for Sculpture, 1961. Sculptor: National Memorial to David Lloyd George, Cardiff; Official Medals for Investiture of HRH Prince of Wales, 1969, and 25th anniv., 1994; 900th Anniversary of Westminster Abbey, 1965; Churchill Centenary Trust, 1974; Sir Thomas Beecham bust, Royal Opera House, 1979, and Royal Festival Hall, 1986; sculptures at Nat. Postal Mus., 1972, London Docklands, 1988 and 1990 and Plaza, Oxford Street, London, 1997; bronze water feature and fountain, Hemel Hempstead, 1993; meml bronze of Nancy, Lady Astor, H of C, 1996; statues of Edward Jenner, St George's Hosp. Med. Sch., 1996 and Edward Jenner Inst. for Vaccine Res., 1997; bronze of Lord Taylor of Gosforth, Royal Cts of Justice, 1999; designer, Conspicuous Gallantry Cross, 1995. Designer and Sculptor of coinages for over 90 countries, incl. UK £2.00 coin, for 50th Anniversary of UN, 1995. *Recreation:* people. *Address:* Melrose Studio, 7 Melrose Road, SW18 1ND. *T:* (020) 8870 8561. *Club:* Reform.

RIZZI, Carlo; conductor; Musical Director, Welsh National Opera, since 1992; *b* 19 July 1960. *Educ:* Milan Conservatoire; Accademia Musicale Chigiana, Siena. *Débuts:* Australian Opera Co., 1989; Netherlands Opera, 1989; Royal Opera, 1990; WNO, 1991; Deutsche Oper, Berlin, 1992; Cologne Opera, 1992; Israel Philharmonic, 1993; Metropolitan Opera, NY, 1993; has made numerous recordings. *Address:* c/o Allied Artists Agency, 42 Montpelier Square, SW7 1JZ. *T:* (020) 7589 6243, *Fax:* (020) 7581 5269.

ROACH, Prof. Gary Francis, FRSE; Professor of Mathematics, University of Strathclyde, 1979–96, now Emeritus; *b* 8 Oct. 1933; *s* of John Francis Roach and Bertha Mary Ann Roach (*née* Walters); *m* 1960, Isabella Grace Willins Nicol. *Educ:* University Coll. of S Wales and Monmouthshire (BSc); Univ. of London (MSc); Univ. of Manchester (PhD, DSc). FRAS, FIMA, CMath. RAF (Educn Branch), Flying Officer, 1955–58; Research Mathematician, BP, 1958–61; Lectr, UMIST, 1961–66; Vis. Prof., Univ. of British Columbia, 1966–67; University of Strathclyde: Lectr, 1967; Sen Lectr, 1970; Reader, 1971; Prof., 1979; Dean, Faculty of Science, 1982–87. Mem., Edinburgh Mathematical Soc. (Past Pres.). Deacon, Incorp. of Bonnetmakers and Dyers of Glasgow, 1997–98. FRSA 1991. Hon. Fellow, Solvay Inst. Hon. ScD Lodz, 1993. OStJ 1992. *Publications:* Green's Functions, 1970, 2nd edn 1982; articles in learned jls. *Recreations:* mountaineering, photography, philately, gardening, music. *Address:* 11 Menzies Avenue, Fintry, Glasgow G63 0YE. *T:* (01360) 860335.

ROADS, Dr Christopher Herbert; Associate Director (Consultancy), Research & Development Department, British Library, 1992–94; consultant in museums and audio visual archives; *b* 3 Jan. 1934; *s* of late Herbert Clifford Roads and Vera Iris Roads; *m* 1976, Charlotte Alicia Dorothy Mary Lothian (marr. diss.); one *d*. *Educ:* Cambridge and County Sch.; Trinity Hall, Cambridge (MA; PhD 1961). Nat. Service, 2nd Lieut, RA, Egypt, 1952–54. Adviser to WO on Disposal of Amnesty Arms, 1961–62; Imperial War Museum: Keeper of Dept of Records, 1962–70; Dep. Dir-Gen. at Main Building, Southwark, 1964–79, at Duxford, Cambridge, 1976–79, HMS Belfast, Pool of London, 1978–79; Dir, Museums & Archives Develt Associates Ltd, 1977–85; Dir, Nat. Sound Archive, 1983–92. UNESCO consultant designing major audio visual archives or museums in Philippines, Panama, Bolivia, Kuwait, Jordan and Saudi Arabia, 1976–. Founder and Dir, Cambridge Coral/Starfish Res. Gp, 1968–; Director: Nat. Discography Ltd, 1986–92; Historic Cable Ship John W. Mackay, 1986–; AVT Communications Ltd, 1988–92; Cedar Audio Ltd, 1989–92. Chm., Coral Conservation Trust, 1972–; President: Historical Breechloading Small Arms Assoc., 1973–; Internat. Film and TV Council (UNESCO Category A), 1990–92 (Pres., Archives Commn, 1970–); Hon. Pres., World Expeditionary Assoc. (Vice Pres., 1971); Vice President: Duxford Aviation Soc., 1974–; English Eight Club, 1980–; Cambridge Univ. Rifle Assoc., 1987– (Mem. Council, 1955–87); Mem. Council, Scientific Exploration Soc., 1971–82; Sec., Nat. Archives Cttee, Internat. Assoc. of Sound Archives, 1988–92; Hon. Sec., Cambridge Univ. Long Range Rifle Club, 1979–; Mem., Home Office Reference Panel for Historic Firearms, 1997–. Trustee: HMS Belfast Trust, 1970–78; Nat. Life Stories Collection, 1986–92; NSA Wild Life Sound Trust, 1986–92. Adjt, English VIII, 1964–88. Churchill Fellowship, 1970; Vis. Fellow, Centre of Internat. Studies, Univ. of Cambridge, 1983–84. FRGS. Liveryman, Gunmakers' Co., 1996; Freeman, City of London, 1996. Silver Jubilee Medal, 1977. Order of Independence, 2nd cl. (Jordan), 1977. *Publications:* The British Soldier's Firearm, 1850–1864, 1964; (jtly) New Studies on the Crown of Thorns Starfish, 1970; The Story of the Gun, 1978. *Recreations:* rifle shooting, marine and submarine exploration, wind surfing, motorcycling, videography. *Address:* The White House, 90 High Street, Melbourn, near Royston, Herts SG8 6AL. *T:* (01763) 260866, *Fax:* (01763) 262521; DX 12 Urbanización Bahia Dorada, 29693 Estepona, Málaga, Spain. *T:* and *Fax:* (95) 2796407. *Clubs:* Oxford and Cambridge; Hawks (Cambridge).

ROADS, Peter George, MD; FFCM, FFPHM; Regional Medical Officer, South West Thames Regional Health Authority, 1973–82, retired; *b* 14 Nov. 1917; *s* of Frank George Roads and Mary Dee Hill Roads (*née* Bury); *m* 1949, Evelyn Clara (*née* Daniel); one *s* one *d*. *Educ:* Bedford Sch.; Univ. of London (St Mary's Hosp. Med. Sch.); Hon. Society of Inner Temple. MD (London); FFCM, Royal Colls of Physicians. Served War, in China, 1944–46. MRC, Pneumoconiosis Unit, 1949–50; Dep. MOH, etc, City and Co. of Bristol, 1956–59; MOH, Principal Sch. Med. Officer and Port Med. Officer for City and Port of Portsmouth, 1959–73; Med. Referee to Portchester Crematorium, 1959–73. Mem., Central Midwives Bd, 1964–76; Adviser on Health Services, Assoc. of Municipal Corporations, 1966–74. FRSocMed; Fellow, Soc. of Public Health (formerly of Community Medicine) (Pres., 1988–89). Chairman: Bucks Br., Historical Assoc., 1987–93; Bucks Family History Soc., 1990–93; Bucks Management Cttee, Oxford Diocesan Council for the Deaf, 1991–93. Mem. Deanery Synod, and Church Warden, Stone Dinton and Hartwell, 1988–91. *Publications:* Care of Elderly in Portsmouth, 1970; Medical Importance of Open Air Recreation (Proc. 1st Internat. Congress on Leisure and Touring), 1966. *Recreations:* open air, walking, forestry, history, touring. *Address:* Pasture Cottage, School Lane, Dinton, near Aylesbury, Bucks HP17 8UZ. *T:* (01296) 748504.

ROBARTS, (Anthony) Julian; Director and Chief Executive, Iveagh Trustees Ltd, 1993–98; Managing Director, Coutts & Co., 1986–91; *b* 6 May 1937; *s* of late Lt-Col Anthony V. C. Robarts, DL and of Grizel Mary Robarts (Grant); *m* 1961, Edwina Beryl Hobson; two *s* one *d*. *Educ:* Eton College. National Service, 11th Hussars (PAO), 1955–57; joined Coutts & Co., 1958, Dir, 1963, Dep. Man. Dir, 1976–86; Director: Coutts Finance Co., 1967–91; F. Bolton Group, 1970–; International Fund for Institutions Inc., USA, 1983–93; Chm., Hill Martin, 1993–; Regional Dir, Nat. Westminster Bank, 1971–92. Hon. Treasurer, Union Jack Club, 1969–. Trustee: Beit Med. Meml Fellowships, 1993–2001; Sargent Cancer Care for Children, 1997–2000. *Recreations:* shooting, gardening, opera. *Address:* Bromley Hall, Standon, Ware, Herts SG11 1NY. *Clubs:* Brooks's, Pratt's, MCC.

ROBATHAN, Andrew Robert George; MP (C) Blaby, since 1992; *b* 17 July 1951; *s* of late Robert Douglas Brice Robathan and of Sheena Mary Martin (*née* Gimson); *m* 1991, Rachael Maunder; one *s* one *d*. *Educ:* Merchant Taylors' Sch., Northwood; Oriel Coll., Oxford (MA). Served Coldstream Guards, 1974–89, resigned as Major; rejoined Army for Gulf War, Jan.–April 1991 (COS, POW Guard Force). Councillor, London Borough of Hammersmith and Fulham, 1990–92. PPS to Minister of State for Nat. Heritage, 1995–97. Mem., Internat. Develt Select Cttee, 1997–; Chm., All-Party Cycling Gp, 1994–97; Vice Chairman: Parly Renewable and Sustainable Energy Gp, 1992–94, 1997–; Cons. back bench Defence Cttee, 1993–94, 1997– (Chm., 1994–95); Cons. NI Cttee, 1994–95, 1997–. *Recreations:* hill-walking, ski-ing, running, shooting, architecture, history, conservation. *Address:* House of Commons, SW1A 0AA. *T:* (020) 7219 3000.

ROBB, Sir John (Weddell), Kt 1999; Chairman, British Energy, 1995–2001; *b* 27 April 1936; *s* of John and Isabella Robb; *m* 1965, Janet Teanby; two *s* one *d*. *Educ:* Daniel Stewart's College, Edinburgh. Beecham Group: Marketing Exec., Toiletry Div., Beecham Products, 1966; Man. Dir, Beecham (Far East), Kuala Lumpur, 1971; Vice-Pres., W. Hemisphere Div., Beecham Products, USA, 1974; Man. Dir, Food and Drink Div., Beecham Products, 1976; Group Board, 1980; Chm., Food and Drink Div., 1980; Chm., Beecham Products, 1984–85; Gp Man. Dir, 1985–88; Wellcome Plc: Dep. Chief Exec., 1989–90; Chief Exec., 1990–95; Chm., 1994–95. Non-executive Dir, Unigate, 1996–. Dep. Chm., Horserace Betting Levy Bd, 1993–; Trustee, Royal Botanic Gdn, Edinburgh, 1997–. *Recreations:* golf, gardening, racing. *Club:* Sunningdale.

ROBB, Prof. Michael Alfred, PhD, DSc; FRS 2000; Professor of Chemistry, since 1992, and Head of Department of Chemistry, King's College, London; *b* 19 Feb. 1944; *s* of Robert Fredrick Robb and Dorothy Estelle Robb; *m* 1967, Brenda Elizabeth Donald (*d* 2000); one *s*. *Educ:* Toronto Univ. (PhD 1970); DSc London 1987. Lectr, 1971–88, Reader, 1988–92, KCL. *Publications:* contrib. to chemistry jls. *Address:* Department of Chemistry, King's College London, Strand, WC2R 2LS. *T:* (020) 7848 2284.

ROBBE-GRILLET, Alain; literary consultant, writer and cinéaste; Editions de Minuit, Paris, since 1955; *b* 18 Aug. 1922; *s* of Gaston Robbe-Grillet and Yvonne Canu; *m* 1957, Catherine Rstakian. *Educ:* Lycée Buffon, Paris; Lycée St Louis, Paris; Institut National Agronomique, Paris. Engineer: Institut National de la Statistique, 1945–49; Institut des Fruits et Agrumes Coloniaux, 1949–51. *Films:* L'Immortelle, 1963; Trans-Europ-Express, 1966; L'Homme qui ment, 1968; L'Eden et après, 1970; Glissements progressifs du plaisir, 1974; Le jeu avec le feu, 1975; La belle captive, 1983; Un Bruit qui rend fou, 1995. *Publications:* Les Gommes, 1953 (The Erasers, 1966); Le Voyeur, 1955 (The Voyeur, 1959); La Jalousie, 1957 (Jealousy, 1960); Dans le labyrinthe, 1959 (In the Labyrinth, 1967); L'Année dernière à Marienbad, 1961 (Last Year in Marienbad, 1962); Instantanés, 1962 (Snapshots, and, Towards a New Novel, 1965); L'Immortelle, 1963 (The Immortal One, 1971); Pour un nouveau roman, 1964; La Maison de rendezvous, 1965 (The House of Assignation, 1968); Projet pour une révolution à New York, 1970 (Project for a Revolution in New York, 1972); Glissements progressifs du plaisir, 1974; Topologie d'une cité fantôme, 1976 (Topology of a Phantom City, 1978); La Belle captive, 1976; Souvenirs du Triangle d'or, 1978 (Recollections of the Golden Triangle, 1985); Un Régicide, 1978; Djinn, 1981; Le Miroir qui revient (autobiog.), 1985 (Ghosts in the Mirror, 1988); Angélique ou l'enchantement (autobiog.), 1988; Les Derniers jours de Corinthe, 1994; La Reprise, 2001. *Address:* 18 Boulevard Maillot, 92200 Neuilly-sur-Seine, France. *T:* 47223122.

ROBBINS, Christopher William; HM Diplomatic Service; Ambassador to Lithuania, 1998–2001; *b* 16 June 1946; *s* of William Henry Meech Robbins and Marion Elizabeth Millington Robbins (*née* Rees); *m* 1st, 1978 (marr. diss.); 2nd, 2000, Brigitte Anna Petronella van Dijke. *Educ:* Skinners' Sch., Tunbridge Wells; Univ. of Sussex (BA); Warburg Inst., Univ. of London (MPhil). Lectr in Philosophy, Univ. of York, 1969–75; Principal, Welsh Office, 1975–77; Adminr, Directorate of Economic and Social Affairs, Council of Europe, 1977–84; joined HM Diplomatic Service, 1984; EC Dept, FCO, 1984–87; First Sec., New Delhi, 1987–90; Asst Head, Central and Southern Africa Dept, 1990–91; Head, Projects and Export Policy Branch I, DTI (on secondment), 1991–94;

Commercial Counsellor, The Hague, 1994–98, and Consul-Gen., Amsterdam, 1996–98. *Publications:* (contrib.) La Santé Rationnée?, 1981; (contrib.) The End of an Illusion, 1984; articles in philosophical and social policy jls. *Recreation:* the enjoyment of beauty. *Address:* c/o Foreign and Commonwealth Office, SW1A 2AH.

ROBBINS, Prof. Frederick C., MD; Bronze Star (US Army), 1945; President, Institute of Medicine, National Academy of Sciences, Washington, DC, 1980–85; University Professor, Case Western Reserve University, 1985, Emeritus, since 1986 (Professor of Pediatrics, School of Medicine, 1952–80, Dean, 1966–80, now Emeritus); *b* 25 Aug. 1916; *s* of William J. Robbins and Christine Chapman Robbins; *m* 1948, Alice Havemeyer Northrop; two *d. Educ:* University of Missouri (AB); University of Missouri Medical School (BS); Harvard Medical School (MD). US Army, 1942–46; rank on discharge, Major. Various posts in the Children's Hospital, Boston, from 1940, finishing as Chief Resident in Medicine, 1948; Sen. Fellow in Virus Diseases, National Research Council, 1948–50; Research Fellow in Pediatrics, Harvard Med. Sch., 1948–50; Instr in Ped., 1950–51, Associate in Ped., 1951–52, at Harvard Medical School; Dir, Department of Pediatrics, Cleveland Metropolitan General Hospital, 1952–66. Associate, Research Div. of Infectious Diseases, the Children's Medical Center, Boston, 1950–52; Research Fellow in Ped., the Boston Lying-in Hospital, Boston, Mass, 1950–52; Asst to Children's Medical Service, Mass Gen. Hosp., Boston, 1950–52. Visiting Scientist, Donner Lab., Univ. of California, 1963–64. President: Soc. for Pediatric Research, 1961–62; Amer. Pediatric Soc., 1973–74. Member: Nat. Acad. of Sciences, 1972 (Co-Chm., Forum on Human Experimentation, 1974); Amer. Philosophical Soc., 1972; Adv. Cttee, Office of Technol. Assessment for Congress, 1973; Adv. Cttee on Med. Research, Pan American Health Organization, WHO, 1981–. First Mead Johnson Award, 1953; Nobel Prize in Physiology or Medicine, 1954; Award for Distinguished Achievement (Modern Medicine), 1963; Med. Mutual Honor Award for 1969; Abraham Flexner Award for Distinguished Service to Medical Educn, AAMC, 1987; Camille Cosby World of Children Award, Judge Baker Children's Center, 1988; NASA Public Service Award, 1989; Ohio Sci. and Technology Hall of Fame, 1992. Hon. Dr of Science: John Carroll University, 1955; Missouri, 1958; North Carolina, 1979; Tufts, 1983; Med. Coll. of Ohio, 1983; Albert Einstein Coll. of Medicine, 1984; Med. Coll. of Wisconsin, 1984; Hon. Dr of Laws, New Mexico, 1968; Hon. Dr Med. Sci., Med. Coll. of Pa, 1984. *Publications:* numerous in various jls, primarily on subject of viruses and infectious diseases. *Recreations:* music, tennis, sailing. *Address:* 2626 West Park Boulevard, Shaker Heights, OH 44120, USA; (office) CWRU School of Medicine, 10900 Euclid Avenue, Cleveland, OH 44106–4945, USA.

ROBBINS, Prof. Keith Gilbert; Vice-Chancellor (formerly Principal), University of Wales (formerly St David's University College), Lampeter, since 1992; Senior Vice-Chancellor, University of Wales, 1995–2001; *b* 9 April 1940; *s* of Gilbert Henry John and Edith Mary Robbins; *m* 1963, Janet Carey Thomson; three *s* one *d. Educ:* Bristol Grammar Sch.; Magdalen and St Antony's Colls, Oxford (MA, DPhil); DLitt Glasgow. FRSE 1991. University of York: Asst Lectr in History, 1963; Lectr in Hist., 1964; Prof. of History, 1971–79, Dean of Faculty of Arts, 1977–79, UCNW, Bangor; Prof. of Modern Hist., Glasgow Univ., 1980–91. Visiting Professor: British Columbia Univ., 1983; Univ. of Western Australia, 1995. Lectures: Enid Muir, Newcastle Univ., 1981; A. H. Dodd, UCNW, Bangor, 1984; Raleigh, British Acad., 1984; Ford, Oxford Univ., 1986–87. Winston Churchill Travelling Fellow, 1990. Pres., Historical Assoc., 1988–91; Chm. Cttee, Hds of Higher Educn, Wales, 1996–98. Mem., and Chm. Res. Cttee, Humanities Res. Bd, British Acad., 1994–97; Mem., Arts and Humanities Res. Bd, 1998–. Pres., Old Bristolians' Soc., 1995–96. Editor, History, 1977–86; Member: Editorial Bd, Jl of Ecclesiastical History, 1978–93. Hon. DLitt UWE, 1999. *Publications:* Munich 1938, 1968; Sir Edward Grey, 1971; The Abolition of War: The British Peace Movement 1914–1919, 1976; John Bright, 1979; The Eclipse of a Great Power: Modern Britain 1870–1975, 1983; The First World War, 1984; Nineteenth-Century Britain: integration and diversity, 1988; Appeasement, 1988; (ed) Blackwell Biographical Dictionary of British Political Life in the Twentieth Century, 1990; (ed) Protestant Evangelicalism, 1991; Churchill, 1992; History, Religion and Identity in Modern British History, 1993; Politicians, Diplomacy and War in Modern British History, 1994; A Bibliography of British History 1914–1989, 1996; Great Britain: identities, institutions and the idea of Britishness, 1997; The World since 1945: a concise history, 1998; articles in Historical Jl, Internat. Affairs, Jl of Contemporary Hist., Jl of Ecclesiastical Hist., Jl of Commonwealth and Imperial Hist., etc. *Recreations:* music, gardening, walking. *Address:* University of Wales, Lampeter, Ceredigion SA48 7ED. *T:* (01570) 424717, *Fax:* (01570) 421011; *e-mail:* k.robbins@admin.lampeter.ac.uk.

ROBBINS, Michael; *see* Robbins, Raymond F. M.

ROBBINS, Michael; *see* Robbins, Richard M.

ROBBINS, Dr (Raymond Frank) Michael, CBE 1987; Director, Polytechnic South West (formerly Plymouth Polytechnic), 1974–89, Hon. Fellow, 1989; *b* 15 Feb. 1928; *s* of Harold and Elsie Robbins; *m* 1955, Eirian Meredith Edwards; two *d. Educ:* Grove Park Grammar Sch., Wrexham; UCW Aberystwyth. PhD 1954; FRIC 1962. Research Chemist, Monsanto Chemicals Ltd, 1954–55; Research Fellow, Univ. of Exeter, 1955–56; Lectr, Nottingham Coll. of Technology, 1956–59; Sen. Lectr, Hatfield Coll. of Technology, 1960–61; Head of Dept of Chem. Sciences, Hatfield Polytechnic, 1961–70; Dep. Dir, Plymouth Polytechnic, 1970–74. Chm., Sci. Prog. Adv. Gp, PCFC, 1989–92; Mem., British Accreditation Council, 1984–93. *Publications:* papers on organic chemistry in chem. jls, various reviews and articles in sci. and educnl press. *Recreations:* hill walking, creative gardening.

ROBBINS, (Richard) Michael, CBE 1976; *b* 7 Sept. 1915; *er s* of late Alfred Gordon Robbins and Josephine, *d* of R. L. Capell, Northampton; *m* 1939, Rose Margaret Elspeth, *er d* of late Sir Robert Reid Bannatyne, CB (*d* 1993), Lindfield, Sussex; one *s* two *d. Educ:* Westminster Sch. (King's Schol.); Christ Church, Oxford (Westminster Schol.; MA); Univ. of Vienna. Joined London Passenger Transport Board, 1939. War service, RE (Transportation), 1939–46: Persia and Iraq, 1941–43; GHQ, MEF, 1943–44; Major, AML (Greece), 1944–45. Rejoined London Transport, 1946; Sec. to Chm., 1947–50; Sec., London Transp. Exec., 1950–55; Sec. and Chief Public Relations Off., 1955–60; Chief Commercial and Pub. Rel. Off., 1960–65; Mem., London Transport Exec., 1965–80 (Man. Dir, Rlys, 1971–78). Chm., Transport Adv. Cttee, Transport and Road Res. Lab., 1977–81. Pres., Inst. of Transport, 1975–76 (Mem. Council, 1957–60 and 1962–64; Chm., Metrop. Sect., 1962–63; Chm., Educn and Trg Cttee, 1969–72; Vice-Pres., 1972–75); Pres., Omnibus Soc., 1965; Chairman: Middx Victoria County History Council, 1963–76; Middx Local History Council, 1958–65; Internat. Metrop. Rlys Cttee, Internat. Union of Public Transport, 1976–81; Victorian Soc., 1978–81; President: London and Middx Archæol. Soc., 1965–71 (Mem. Council, 1951–56 and 1960–65); Greater London Industrial Archæol. Soc., 1969–; Rly Students Assoc., 1967–68; St Marylebone Soc., 1971–74; Mem., Ancient Monuments Adv. Cttee, English Heritage, 1986–91. Dunhill lectr on industrial design, Australia, 1974. FSA 1957; Pres., Soc. of Antiquaries, 1987–91 (Mem. Council, 1965–67, 1970–71; Treas., 1971–87); Chm., Museum of London, 1979–90 (Governor, 1968–); Vice Chm., Greater Manchester Museum of Science and Industry, 1987–90 (Trustee, 1982–90); Trustee, London Museum, 1970–75. Hon. DLitt City Univ., 1987. *Publications:* The North London Railway, 1937; 190 in Persia, 1951; The Isle of Wight Railways, 1953; Middlesex, 1953; (ed) Middlesex Parish Churches, 1955; The Railway Age, 1962, rev. edn 1998; (with T. C. Barker) History of London Transport, vol. 1, 1963, vol. 2, 1974; George and Robert Stephenson, 1966, rev. edn 1981; Points and Signals, 1967; A Public Transport Century, 1985; Joint Editor, Journal of Transport History, 1953–65; contribs to transport and historical jls. *Recreations:* exploring cities and suburbs; travelling abroad and in branch railway trains; concert-going. *Address:* 18 Fullerton Court, Udney Park Road, Teddington, Middx TW11 9BF. *T:* (020) 8977 6714. *Club:* Athenæum.

ROBBINS, Stephen Dennis; His Honour Judge Robbins; a Circuit Judge, since 1994; *b* 11 Jan. 1948; *s* of Lt-Col Dennis Robbins, OBE, TD and Joan Robbins (*née* Mason); *m* 1974, Amanda Smith, JP; three *d. Educ:* Orwell Park; Marlborough; Coll. d'Europe, Bruges (Churchill Award). Infantry, HAC, 1966–69. Called to the Bar, Gray's Inn, 1969; practised SE Circuit, 1972–94; Asst Recorder, 1983–87; Recorder, 1987–94. Former Mem., Overseas Cttee, Bar Council; Hon. Sec., London Common Law Bar Cttee; Hon. Legal Advr, Katharine Lowe Centre, Battersea, 1974–79. Pres., Mental Health Rev. Tribunals, 1994–. Chm., Disciplinary Cttee, Potato Marketing Bd. *Recreations:* collecting ephemera, shooting, swimming, walking, music. *Address:* Hillcrest Farm, Sevington, near Ashford, Kent TN24 0LJ. *T:* (01233) 502732; 1/2 The Studios, 17/19 Edge Street, Kensington Church Street, W8 7PN. *T:* (020) 7727 7216.

ROBBINS, Prof. Trevor William, PhD; FBPsS, FMedSci; Professor of Cognitive Neuroscience, University of Cambridge, since 1997; Fellow, Downing College, Cambridge, since 1990; *b* 26 Nov. 1949; *s* of William Walter Robbins and Eileen Hilda Robbins; *m* 1979, Barbara Jacquelyn Sahakian; two *d. Educ:* Battersea GS; Jesus Coll., Cambridge (Schol.; BA 1st cl. Hons; MA; PhD). FBPsS 1990. Univ. Demonstrator, 1973–78, Univ. Lectr, 1978–92, Reader in Cognitive Neuroscience, 1992–97, Dept. of Exptl Psychology, Univ. of Cambridge. Chm. and Council Mem., Neuroscience Bd, MRC, 1995–99 (Mem., 1989–93); Council Mem., European Neuroscience Assoc., 1996–98; President: European Behavioural Pharmacology Soc., 1992–94; British Assoc. for Psychopharmacology, 1996–98. Ed., Psychopharmacology, 1982–. Foreign Mem., American Coll. of Neuropsychopharmacology, 1994. FMedSci 1999. Spearman Medal, BPsS, 1982. *Publications:* (ed jtly) Psychology for Medicine, 1988; (ed) Seminars in the Neurosciences: milestones in dopamine research, 1992; (ed jtly) The Prefrontal Cortex, 1998; more than 380 articles in learned books and jls. *Recreations:* chess, cricket, cinema. *Address:* Department of Experimental Psychology, University of Cambridge, Downing Street, Cambridge CB2 3EB. *T:* (01223) 333558, *Fax:* (01223) 314547; *e-mail:* twr2@cus.cam.ac.uk.

ROBBS, John Edward; Head, Food Industry, Competitiveness and Flood Defence Group, Department for Environment, Food and Rural Affairs (formerly Ministry of Agriculture, Fisheries and Food), since 2000; *b* 26 June 1955; *s* of Eric and Christine Robbs; *m* 1989, Jacqueline Tozer; two *s. Educ:* King Edward VII Sch., King's Lynn; Queens' Coll., Cambridge (MA); London Sch. of Econs (MSc Econ). Joined Ministry of Agriculture, Fisheries and Food, 1977: Private Sec. to Perm. Sec., 1981–82; Private Sec. to Minister, 1982–83; on secondment to UK Perm. Repn to EU, Brussels, 1985–89; Head: of Envmt Task Force Div., 1991–94; of Conservation Policy Div., 1994–95; of Fisheries (Common Fisheries Policy) Div., 1995–99; of EU Internat. Div., 1999–2000. *Recreations:* family, friends, gardening. *Address:* Department for Environment, Food and Rural Affairs, Whitehall Place, SW1A 2HH.

ROBERG, Rabbi Meir; Hon. Consultant, since 1995, for Jewish schools and colleges established in the Ukraine following independence; Inspector of schools, UK, since 1997; *b* 25 June 1937; *s* of late Julius and Hannchen Roberg; *m* 1961, Mirjam Nager; three *s* two *d. Educ:* Manchester Grammar Sch. (Gratrix Scholar); Talmudical Coll., Israel (Rabbinical Diploma); Univ. of London (BA 1st Cl. Hons 1960; DipEd 1970; MPhil 1972). Asst Teacher, 1960–62, Dep. Head, 1962–65, Yavneh Grammar Sch., London; Hasmonean High School: Asst Teacher and Head of Classics, 1965–71; Dep. Head, 1971–80; Headmaster, 1980–93; Principal of Jewish Day Schs and Dean of Talmudical Coll., Kiev, 1993–95. Lectr, Colls of Further Educn, 1962–93; Headmaster, Mddx Regl Centre, 1965–73. Delegate, Internat. Religious Conf., Jerusalem, 1963 and 1980. Member: Keren Hatorah; Hendon Adass; Massoret Inst. (Chm., 1980–95); Assoc. of Headteachers of Jewish Day Schs (Pres., 1991–93; Life Pres., 1993–). *Publications:* (contrib.) Responsa Literature, 1996, 1998, 2000; reviews for Comparative Education, Jewish Tribune, and Parent-Teacher Monthly (NY). *Recreations:* Talmudic research, hiking. *Address:* 19 Sorotzkin Street, Jerusalem, Israel.

ROBERTS, family name of **Barons Clwyd** and **Roberts of Conwy**.

ROBERTS OF CONWY, Baron *cr* 1997 (Life Peer), of Talyfan in the co. of Gwynedd; **Ieuan Wyn Pritchard Roberts,** Kt 1990; PC 1991; *b* 10 July 1930; *s* of late Rev. E. P. Roberts and Margaret Ann Roberts; *m* 1956, Enid Grace Williams; three *s. Educ:* Harrow; University Coll., Oxford. Sub-editor, Liverpool Daily Post, 1952–54; News Asst, BBC, 1954–57; TWW Ltd: News, Special Events and Welsh Language Programmes Producer, 1957–59; Production Controller, 1959–60; Exec. Producer, 1960–68; Welsh Controller, 1964–68; Programme Exec., Harlech TV, 1969. MP (C) Conway, 1970–83, Conwy, 1983–97. PPS to Sec. of State for Wales, 1970–74; opposition front bench spokesman on Welsh Affairs, 1974–79; Parly Under-Sec. of State, 1979–87, Minister of State, 1987–94, Welsh Office. Vice-Pres., Assoc. of District Councils, 1975–79. Mem. of Gorsedd, Royal National Eisteddfod of Wales, 1966. Member, Court of Governors: Nat. Library of Wales, 1970–91; Nat. Museum of Wales, 1970–91; University Coll. of Wales, Aberystwyth, 1970–91. Pres., Univ. of Wales Coll. of Medicine, 1997. Hon. Fellow: Univ. of Wales, Bangor, 1995, Aberystwyth, 1997. *Recreation:* gardening. *Address:* Tan y Gwalia, Conwy, Gwynedd LL32 8TY. *T:* (01492) 650371. *Clubs:* Savile; Cardiff and County (Cardiff).

ROBERTS, Prof. Adam; *see* Roberts, E. A.

ROBERTS, Prof. Alan Clive, OBE 2001 (MBE 1982); TD 1969; PhD; JP; DL; Professor of Biomaterials in Surgery, University of Hull, since 1994; *b* 28 April 1934; *s* of Major William Roberts, MBE and Kathleen Roberts; *m* 1956, Margaret Mary Shaw; two *s. Educ:* MPhil CNAA 1975; PhD 1988 Bradford Univ. CBiol 1971; FIBiol 1987; CIMechE 1995. Nat. Service, 1950–54. Scientific Officer, Royal Victoria Infirmary, Newcastle, 1954–56; Sen. Scientific Officer, Leeds Hosps, 1956–60; Prin. Clin. Scientist, Dept of Plastic Surgery, 1960–67, Consultant Clin. Scientist, 1990–, St Luke's Hosp., Bradford; Vis. Sen. Res. Fellow, Biomedical Scis, 1961–, Dir, Biomaterials Res. Unit, 1990–, Hon. Prof., 2000, Univ. of Bradford; Dir of R&D, Bradford Hosps NHS Trust, 1992–. Council of Europe Res. Fellow, Sweden, 1968. Pres., British Inst. of Surgical Tech. (Vice-Pres., 1996). ADC to the Queen, 1980–83. Sec., Bradford Medico-Chirurgical Soc., 1995–; Chm., COMEC, 1990–96; Mem., NY Acad. of Scis, 1987. Chm., Court and Council, 1986–, Pro-Chancellor, 1986–2000, Univ. of Leeds; Dir, Univ. of Leeds Foundn, 1986–. Trustee: Edward Boyle Trust, 1986–97; Yorks Sculpture

Park, 1995. Mem. Council, BRCS, 1995– (Pres., W Yorks, 1983–; Badge of Honour, 1992); President: Leeds RBL; W Yorks SSAFA, 2000– (Chm., 1985); Leeds NSPCC. Col and Dep. Comdr, NE Dist TA, 1980–83; Hon. Col, 269 Batt., RA, 1983–; Col Comdt, RA, 1996–2001; Regtl Col, Leeds Univ. OTC, 2000–; Mem., HAC, 2000–. Patron, Age Concern, 1994–. Hon. Sub Dean, N Yorks, RSocMed, 2001. Hon. Freeman and Liveryman, Clothworkers' Co., 2000–. JP Leeds, 1977; DL W Yorks, 1982. CGIA, 1969, 1976, FCGI 1990 (Pres., City and Guilds Assoc., 1998–); FRSocMed 1993; FLS 1998. Hon. LLD Leeds, 2000. Prince Philip Medal for Science, C&G, 1970. Lead researcher and inventor of Indermil Tissue Adhesive, 1993. OStJ 1994. *Publications:* Obturators and Prosthesis for Cleft Palate, 1968; Facial Restoration by Prosthetic Means, 1975; Maxillo-Facial Prosthetics: a multi-disciplinary practice, 1975; numerous articles in med. and dental jls. *Recreations:* sculpture, silversmithing, avoiding holidays. *Address:* The Grange, Rein Road, Morley, Leeds, W Yorks LS27 0HZ. *T:* (0113) 253 4632. *Clubs:* Army and Navy; Leeds.

ROBERTS, Alfred, PhD; Chief Executive, Institution of Electrical Engineers, since 1999; *b* 24 June 1945; *s* of Oswald and Ellen Roberts; *m* 1978, Elizabeth Ann King; one *s* one *d. Educ:* University Coll. London (BSc 1st cl. Hons 1967); Univ. of Manchester (PhD 1970). Central Electricity Generating Board: Res. Officer, 1971–73; Section Manager, Applied Physics, 1973–75; Div. Head, Engrg Sci., 1975–81; Regl Financial Controller, 1981–85; Gp Financial Controller, 1985–88; Dir, Engrg Services, 1988–89; Commercial Dir, PowerGen plc, 1989–98. *Publications:* articles in Nuclear Physics; conf. proceedings on nucleon transfer reactions; conf. papers on privatisation and deregulation of the electricity industry. *Recreations:* science, technology, history, music, literature, football. *Address:* Institution of Electrical Engineers, Savoy Place, WC2R 0BL. *T:* (020) 7344 5484.

ROBERTS, Allan Deverell; Director, Legal (Legislation Unit), Department for Transport, Local Government and the Regions (formerly Department of the Environment, Transport and the Regions), since 1999; *b* 14 July 1950; *s* of Irfon Roberts and Patricia Mary (*née* Allan); *m* 1991, Irene Anne Graham Reilly; three *s. Educ:* Eton Coll.; Magdalen Coll., Oxford (MA). Solicitor in private practice, 1974–76; Solicitor's Office, DHSS, 1976–96, Under-Sec. (Legal), 1989–96; Dir, Legal (Envmt, Planning and Countryside), DoE, 1996–97; Dir, Legal (Envmt, Housing and Local Govt), DETR, 1997–99. *Recreations:* tegestology, football, listening to music. *Address:* (office) Eland House, Bressenden Place, SW1E 5DU.

ROBERTS, Alwyn; Pro Vice Chancellor, University of Wales, Bangor, 1994–97; *b* 26 Aug. 1933; *s* of late Rev. Howell Roberts and Buddug Roberts; *m* 1960, Mair Rowlands Williams; one *s. Educ:* Penygroes Grammar Sch.; Univ. of Wales, Aberystwyth and Bangor (BA, LLB); Univ. of Cambridge (MA). Tutor, Westminster Coll., Cambridge, 1959; Principal, Pachhunga Meml Govt Coll., Aijal, Assam, India, 1960–67; Lectr in Social Admin, University Coll., Swansea, 1967–70; University College of North Wales, later University of Wales, Bangor: Lectr, subseq. Sen. Lectr, Dept of Social Theory and Instns, 1970–79; Dir of Extra Mural Studies, 1979–95; Vice Principal, 1985–94. BBC National Governor for Wales, 1979–86; Chm., Broadcasting Council for Wales, 1979–86 (Mem., 1974–78); Member: Welsh Fourth TV Channel Auth., 1981–86; Gwynedd CC, 1973–81 (Chm., Social Services Cttee, 1977–81); Gwynedd AHA, 1973–80; Royal Commn on Legal Services, 1976–79; Parole Bd, 1987–90. Pres., Royal National Eisteddfod of Wales, 1994–96 (Vice-Chm., 1987–89; Chm., 1989–92; Mem. Council, 1979–); Chm., Acen (Cyf.), 1989–; Vice Chm., Arts Council of Wales, 1994–2000; Mem. Bd, Cwmni Theatr Cymru, 1982–86. Hon. Fellow, Univ. of Wales, Aberystwyth, 1999. Hon. LLD Wales, 2000. *Address:* Brithdir, 43 Talycae, Tregarth, Bangor, Gwynedd LL57 4AE. *T:* (01248) 600007.

ROBERTS, Andrew; writer; *b* 13 Jan. 1963; *s* of Simon and Katie Roberts; *m* 1995, Camilla Sophie, *e d* of Roger Anthony Henderson, *qv*; one *s* one *d. Educ:* Cranleigh Sch.; Gonville and Caius Coll., Cambridge (exhibnr, Hon. Sen. Schol.; BA 1st Cl. Hons Hist.; Chm., CU Cons. Assoc., 1984). Corporate broker, Robert Fleming Securities Ltd, 1985–87; freelance journalist and book reviewer, 1987–; regular contributor, Sunday Telegraph, 1999–. Trustee: Roberts Foundn, 1989–; Lady Colyton Prize for Political Thought, 2000–. Hon. DHL Westminster Coll., Fulton, Mo, 2000. *Publications:* The Holy Fox: a life of Lord Halifax, 1991; Eminent Churchillians, 1994; The Aachen Memorandum, 1995; Salisbury: Victorian Titan, 1999 (James Stern Silver Pen Award, Wolfson Award for Hist., 2000); Napoleon and Wellington, 2001. *Address:* 2 Tite Street, SW3 4HY. *Clubs:* Beefsteak, Brooks's, Annabel's; University Pitt (Cambridge).

ROBERTS, Air Vice-Marshal Andrew Lyle, CB 1992; CBE 1983; AFC 1969; FRAeS; defence consultant; Chairman of Public Inquiries, Lord Chancellor's Panel of Independent Inspectors, since 1994; *b* 19 May 1938; *s* of Ronald and Norah Roberts; *m* 1962; three *d. Educ:* Cranbrook Sch.; RAF Coll., Cranwell. Commnd RAF, 1958; ADC to AOC No 18 Gp, 1965–66; Flight Comdr, 201 Sqdn, 1967–68 (AFC); RNSC, 1969; Personal Air Sec. to Parly Under-Sec. of State (RAF), MoD, 1970–71; i/c 236 Operational Conversion Unit, 1972–74; US Armed Forces Staff Coll., 1974; staff, SACLANT, 1975–77; i/c RAF Kinloss, 1977–79; Gp Capt. Ops, HQ Strike Command, 1980–82 (CBE); RCDS, 1983; Dir, Air Plans, MoD, 1984–86; C of S, HQ No 18 Gp, 1987–89; ACDS (Concepts), 1987–92; Hd of RAF Manpower Structure Study Team, 1992–94. Chm., Coastal Comd and Maritime Air Assoc., 1995–. Trustee, Gwennili Trust (sailing for the disabled), 1995–. *Recreations:* cross-country and hill walking, natural history, classical music, church organ, choral singing, off-shore sailing. *Address:* c/o HSBC, 61 High Street, Staines, Middx TW18 4QW. *Club:* Royal Air Force.

ROBERTS, Angus Thomas; Director of Litigation and Prosecution, Post Office Solicitor's Office (formerly Principal Assistant Solicitor to General Post Office), 1965–74; *b* 28 March 1913; *s* of late Edward Roberts and late Margaret (*née* Murray); *m* 1940, Frances Monica, *d* of late Frederick and late Agnes Bertha Cane; two *s. Educ:* Felsted School. Admitted Solicitor, 1936. Entered Post Office Solicitor's Dept, 1939. Served in Royal Navy, 1941–46 (Lieut, RNVR). Asst Solicitor to GPO, 1951. *Recreations:* golf, fishing, gardening. *Address:* 8 Watermill Court, Bath Road, Woolhampton, Berks RG7 5RD. *T:* (0118) 971 3075.

ROBERTS, Ann; *see* Clwyd, Ann.

ROBERTS, (Anthony) John, CBE 1991; Board Member, since 1985 and Chief Executive, since 1995, Consignia plc (formerly The Post Office); Chairman, Post Office Ltd (formerly Post Office Counters Ltd), since 1993; *b* 26 Aug. 1944; *s* of Douglas and Margaret Roberts; *m* 1970, Diana June (*née* Lamdin); two *s. Educ:* Hampton Sch.; Exeter Univ. (BA Hons). Open Entrant, Administrative Class Civil Service, The Post Office, 1967; PA to Dep. Chairman and Chief Executive, 1969–71; Principal, Long Range Planning, 1971–74; Controller Personnel and Finance, North Western Postal Board, 1974–76; Principal Private Sec. to Chairman, 1976–77; Director, Chairman's Office, 1977–80; Secretary Designate, 1980–81, Sec., 1981–82; Dir, 1981–85, Man. Dir, 1985–93, Counter Services, subseq. Post Office Counters Ltd; Man. Dir, Gp Services, 1993–95; Chm., Subscription Services, 1993–95. Chm., South Thames TEC, 1989–92; Dir, Internat. Posts Corp., 1996–; Member: Govt New Deal Task Force, 1997–; CBI Educn and Trng Affairs Cttee, 1998–. Mem. Council, Inst. of Employment Studies, 1995– (Pres., 1998); Governor: Henley Mgt Coll., 1996–; Europ. Foundn for Quality Management, 1996–2001 (Pres., 1998). CIMgt; FRSA 1992. Freeman, City of London, 1983. *Recreations:* golf, gardening, music. *Address:* Consignia plc, 148 Old Street, EC1V 9HQ. *T:* (020) 7250 2888. *Club:* Betchworth Park Golf.

ROBERTS, Barbara Haig; *see* MacGibbon, B. H.

ROBERTS, Prof. Benjamin Charles, MA Oxon; Professor of Industrial Relations, London School of Economics, University of London, 1962–84, now Emeritus; *b* 1 Aug. 1917; *s* of Walter Whitfield Roberts and Mabel Frances Roberts; *m* 1945, Veronica Lilian (*d* 2001), *d* of George Frederick and Vera Lilian Vine-Lott; two *s. Educ:* LSE (Hon. Fellow, 1988); New Coll., Oxford. Research Student, Nuffield Coll., Oxford, 1948–49; Part-time Lectr, Ruskin Coll., Oxford, 1948–49; London Sch. of Economics: Lectr in Trade Union Studies, 1949–56; Reader in Industrial Relations, 1956–62; Mem. Ct of Govs, 1964–69, 1979–83. Vis. Prof: Princeton Univ., 1958; MIT 1959; Univ. of Calif., Berkeley, 1965. Assoc., Internat. Inst. of Labour Studies, Geneva, 1966; Member: Council, Inst. Manpower Studies; British-N American Cttee; Nat. Reference Tribunal of Coal Mining Industry, 1970–93; Council, ACAS, 1979–86; Bruges Gp, 1990–. Editor, British Jl of Industrial Relations, 1963–89, Hon. Editor, 1990–. Pres., British Univs Industrial Relations Assoc., 1965–68; Pres., Internat. Industrial Relations Assoc., 1967–73. Consultant to EEC, 1976–79. Chm., Economists' Bookshop, 1979–87. Wincott Lecture, IEA, 1987. *Publications:* Trade Unions in the New Era, 1947; Trade Union Government and Administration in Great Britain, 1956; National Wages Policy in War and Peace, 1958; The Trades Union Congress, 1868–1921, 1958; Trade Unions in a Free Society, 1959; (ed) Industrial Relations: Contemporary Problems and Perspectives, 1962; Labour in the Tropical Territories of the Commonwealth, 1964; (ed) Manpower Planning and Employment Trends 1966; (with L. Greyfié de Bellecombe) Collective Bargaining in African Countries, 1967; (ed) Industrial Relations: Contemporary Issues, 1968; (with John Lovell) A Short History of the TUC, 1968; (with R. O. Clarke and D. J. Fatchet) Workers' Participation in Management in Britain, 1972; (with R. Loveridge and J. Gennard) Reluctant Militants: a study of industrial technicians, 1972; (with H. Okomoto and G. Lodge) Collective Bargaining and Employee Participation in Western Europe, North America and Japan, 1979; also Evidence to Royal Commn on Trade Unions, 1966, and Report to ILO on Labour and Automation: Manpower Adjustment Programmes in the United Kingdom, 1967; Industrial Relations in Europe: the imperatives of change, 1985; (with T. Kochan and N. Meltz) New Departures in Industrial Relations: developments in USA, the UK and Canada, 1988; Europe—Uniformity or Freedom?: the real EC questions, 1991. *Address:* 28 Temple Fortune Lane, NW11 7UD. *T:* (020) 8458 1421. *Clubs:* Reform, Political Economy.

ROBERTS, Bernard, FRCM; concert pianist; Piano Professor, Royal College of Music, 1962–99; *b* 23 July 1933; *s* of William Wright Roberts and Elsie Alberta Roberts (*née* Ingham); *m* 1st, 1955, Patricia May Russell (marr. diss. 1988); two *s*; 2nd, 1992, Caroline Velleman Ireland. *Educ:* William Hulme's Grammar Sch., Manchester; Royal Coll. of Music (ARCM 1951; FRCM 1982). Début as concert pianist, Wigmore Hall, 1957; recital, concerto and chamber music pianist, 1957–; has appeared with major British orchestras as soloist, incl. Promenade Concerts, 1979; recitals in UK and abroad, incl. master classes in major centres; has broadcast on BBC Radio 3. Member: Parikian-Fleming-Roberts Trio, 1975–84; Piano Trio with sons, 1991–. DUniv Brunel, 1989. *Recreations:* philosophy, religion, model railways. *Address:* Uwchlaw'r Coed, Llanbedr, Gwynedd LL45 2NA. *T:* (01341) 241532; *e-mail:* bernard-roberts@classical-artists.com.

ROBERTS, Bertie; Director, Department of the Environment, 1971–79; *b* 4 June 1919; *y s* of late Thomas and Louisa Roberts, Blaengarw, S Wales; *m* 1st, 1946, Dr Peggy Clark; one *s*; 2nd, 1962, Catherine Matthew. *Educ:* Garw Grammar School. HM Forces, 1942–46, Captain RAOC (active service in France (Normandy), Belgium); leader of study on feasibility of using computers in Min. of Public Bldg and Works, 1958; formed and directed operational computer orgn, 1962; Comptroller of Accounts, 1963, also Dir of Computer Services, 1967; Head of Organisation and Methods, 1969; Dir of Estate Management Overseas, Dept of the Environment (with FCO), 1971; Reg. Dir (equiv. Maj.-Gen.), DoE, British Forces Germany, 1976–79. Mem., Community Health Council (Hastings Health Dist), 1982–90. *Recreations:* foreign travel, music. *Address:* Fairmount, 41 Hollington Park Road, St Leonards-on-Sea, E Sussex TN38 0SE. *T:* (01424) 714177. *Club:* Rotary of St Leonard's-on-Sea.

ROBERTS, Brian Stanley; HM Diplomatic Service, retired; independent adviser on education and English teaching; *b* 1 Feb. 1936; *s* of Stanley Victor Roberts and Flora May (*née* McInnes); *m* 1st, 1961, Phyllis Hazel Barber (marr. diss. 1976); two *s*; 2nd, 1985, Jane Catharine Chisholm; one *d. Educ:* Liverpool Collegiate Sch., Christ's Coll., Cambridge (MA); Courtauld Institute, London (MA). Served Royal Navy, 1955–57. Staff, Edinburgh Univ., 1960–62; Lecturer in Art History, Goldsmiths' Coll., London, 1962–69; entered FCO, 1970: First Secretary, Capetown/Pretoria, 1972; FCO, 1974; attached to Hong Kong Govt, 1977; FCO, 1980; Counsellor, Stockholm, 1983–87; Cabinet Office, 1987. Teacher, Art Hist., Cheltenham Ladies' Coll., 1988–89; Head of Art Hist., Putney High Sch., 1989–97. *Recreations:* walking, looking at pictures. *Address:* 21 Crieff Road, SW18 2EB. *Clubs:* Oxford and Cambridge, Lansdowne.

ROBERTS, Dr Brynley Francis, CBE 1993; Librarian, National Library of Wales, 1985–94; Moderator, General Assembly of the Presbyterian Church of Wales, 2001–July 2002; *b* 3 Feb. 1931; *s* of Robert F. Roberts and Laura Jane Roberts (*née* Williams); *m* 1957, Rhiannon Campbell; twin *s. Educ:* Grammar School, Aberdare; University College of Wales, Aberystwyth (BA Hons Welsh, MA, PhD). Fellow, Univ. of Wales, 1956–57; Lectr, Sen. Lectr, Reader, Dept of Welsh, University Coll. of Wales, Aberystwyth, 1957–78; Prof. of Welsh Language and Literature, University Coll. Swansea, 1978–85. Sir John Rhys Fellow, Jesus Coll., Oxford, 1973–74. Chairman: United Theological Coll., Aberystwyth, 1977–98; Gwasg Pantycelyn, Caernarfon, 1977–98. Pres., Welsh Library Assoc., 1985–94; Chm., Welsh Books Council, 1989–94 (Vice-Chm., 1986–89); Mem., HEFCW, 1993–2000. Editor: Dictionary of Welsh Biography, 1987–; Y Traethodydd, 1999–. Hon. Fellow, Univ. of Wales, Swansea, 1996, Aberystwyth, 2000; Hon. Prof., Cardiff, 2001. Hon. FLA 1994. Hon. DLitt Wales, 1996. *Publications:* Gwasanaeth Meir, 1961; Brut y Brenhinedd, 1971, 2nd edn 1984; Cyfranc Lludd a Llefelys, 1975; Brut Tysilio, 1980; Edward Lhuyd: the making of a scientist, 1980; Gerald of Wales, 1982; Itinerary through Wales, 1989; Studies on Middle Welsh Literature, 1992; (ed) Y Bywgraffiadur Cymreig 1951–1970, 1997; (ed) Dictionary of Welsh Biography 1941–1970, 2001; articles in learned jls. *Recreations:* walking, music. *Address:* Hengwrt, Llanbadarn Road, Aberystwyth SY23 1HB. *T:* (01970) 623577.

ROBERTS, Rear-Adm. Cedric Kenelm, CB 1970; DSO 1952; *b* 19 April 1918; *s* of F. A. Roberts; *m* 1940, Audrey, *d* of T. M. Elias; four *s. Educ:* King Edward's Sch., Birmingham. Joined RN as Naval Airman 2nd Cl., 1940; commnd Temp. Sub-Lt (A), RNVR, 1940; sunk in HMS Manchester, 1942, Malta Convoy; interned in Sahara;

released, Nov. 1942; Personal Pilot to Vice-Adm. Sir Lumley Lyster, 1943; HMS Trumpeter, Russian Convoys, 1944; perm. commn as Lt RN, HMS Vindex, Pacific, 1945; CO 813 Sqdn, 1948; Naval Staff Coll., 1949; CO 767 Sqdn, 1950–51; CO 825 Sqdn, 1951–52: served Korean War; shot down, rescued by US Forces; lent to RAN as Dep. Dir, Air Warfare, 1953–55; CO, RNAS Eglinton, 1958–59; Chief Staff Officer: FONFT, 1959–61; FOAC, 1961–62; Capt., HMS Osprey, 1962–64; Capt., RNAS Culdrose, 1964–65; Chief Staff Officer (Ops), Far East Fleet, 1966–67; Flag Officer, Naval Flying Training, 1968–71; retired 1971; farmed in Somerset, 1971–79; emigrated to Australia, 1979. Comdr 1952; Capt. 1958; Rear-Adm. 1968. *Recreations:* sitting in the sun, drinking plonk, and watching the sheilas go by. *Address:* 11 Collins Street, Merimbula, NSW 2548, Australia. *T:* (2) 64951754.

ROBERTS, Cedric P.; *see* Prys-Roberts.

ROBERTS, Christopher William, CB 1986; Deputy Secretary, 1983–97, and Director-General of Trade Policy, 1987–97, Department of Trade and Industry; Senior Trade Analyst, Covington and Burling, since 1998; *b* 4 Nov. 1937; *s* of Frank Roberts and Evelyn Dorothy Roberts. *Educ:* Rugby Sch.; Magdalen Coll., Oxford (MA). Lectr in Classics, Pembroke Coll., Oxford, 1959–60; Asst Principal, BoT, 1960; Second Sec. (Commercial), British High Commn, New Delhi, 1962–64; Asst Private Sec. to Pres. of BoT, 1964–65; Principal, 1965; Cabinet Office, 1966–68; Private Sec. to Prime Minister, 1970–73; Asst Sec., 1972; Dept of Trade, 1973–77; Under Secretary: Dept of Prices and Consumer Protection, 1977–79; Dept of Trade, 1979–82; Chief Exec., BOTB, 1983–87. Non-exec. Dir, NHBC, 1998–. Chairman: Wine Standards Bd, 1999–; Liberalisation of Trade in Services Cttee, Internat. Financial Services London, 2000–. *Recreations:* travel, cricket, opera. *Address:* 11 Sprimont Place, SW3 3HT. *Clubs:* Oxford and Cambridge, MCC.

ROBERTS, Prof. Colin, MD; FRCP, FRCPath; Consultant Medical Microbiologist, and Medical and Scientific Postgraduate Dean, Public Health Laboratory Service, 1993–99; locum consultant microbiologist, John Radcliffe Hospital, Oxford, since 2000; *b* 25 Jan. 1937; *s* of Theophilus and Daisy Roberts; *m* 1961, Marjorie Frances Conway; two *s*. *Educ:* Univ. of Liverpool (BSc 1960; MB ChB 1963; MD 1968); Univ. of Manchester (Dip. Bact. (Dist.) 1972). MRCPath 1973, FRCPath 1986; MRCP 1996, FRCP 1999; FRIPHH 1992; FFPHM 1997; FFPath, RCPI 2000. House physician/surgeon, 1963–64, Registrar in Pathology, 1964–66, Sefton Gen. Hosp., Liverpool; Hon. Sen. Registrar, United Liverpool Hosps, 1966–70, and Lectr in Pathology, 1966–69, in Med. Microbiol., 1969–70, Univ. of Liverpool; Asst Microbiologist (Sen. Registrar), Regl Public Health Lab., Fazakerley Hosp., Liverpool, 1970–73; Liverpool Public Health Laboratory: Sen. Microbiologist, 1973–75; Consultant Med. Microbiologist, 1975–87; Dep. Dir, 1977–87; Dep. Dir, PHLS, London, 1987–93. Visiting Professor: Envmtl Health Div., Univ. of Strathclyde, 1993–; LSHTM, 1997–. Mem. Editl Bd, Jl Clin. Pathol., 1992–97. Founder FMedSci 1998. Hon. FRCPCH 1996; Hon. Fellow, Liverpool John Moores Univ., 2001. Hon. Dip. HIC 1999. *Publications:* contrib. chapters and proceedings, including: (contrib.) Infectious and Communicable Diseases in England and Wales, 1990; (ed jtly) Quality Control: principles and practice in the microbiology laboratory, 1991, 2nd edn 1999; (jtly) A Supervisor's Handbook of Food Hygiene and Safety, 1995; contribs to academic jls. *Recreations:* theatre, music, art, literature, sport (represented Wales at schoolboy and youth level in soccer). *Address:* Level 6, Microbiology Department, John Radcliffe Hospital, Headington, Oxford OX3 9DU. *T:* (01865) 220886. *Clubs:* Athenæum, Savage, Naval and Military, Royal Society of Medicine.

ROBERTS, His Honour David Ewart; a Circuit Judge, 1982–93; *b* 18 Feb. 1921; *s* of John Hobson Roberts and Dorothy Roberts. *Educ:* Abingdon Sch.; St John's Coll., Cambridge. MA, LLB. Served War, 1941–46; commnd RA (Field); service in Middle East, North Africa, Italy, Yugoslavia and Germany. Called to Bar, Middle Temple, 1948. Asst Recorder, Coventry QS, 1966–71; a Recorder of the Crown Court, 1978–82. *Recreations:* travel, photography. *Address:* 4 Greville Drive, Birmingham B15 2UU. *T:* (0121) 440 3231.

ROBERTS, David Francis; Deputy Director General, responsible for trade issues, Directorate General for Agriculture, European Commission, since 1996; *b* 28 Aug. 1941; *s* of Arthur Roberts and Mary Roberts; *m* 1974, Astrid Suhr Henriksen; two *s* one *d*. *Educ:* Priory Grammar School, Shrewsbury; Worcester College, Oxford (MA). Joined MAFF, 1964; seconded to FCO as First Sec. (Agric.), Copenhagen, 1971–74; Principal Private Sec. to Minister of Agriculture, 1975–76; seconded to HM Treasury as Head of Agric. Div., 1979–80; Under Sec., 1985, seconded to FCO as Minister (Agric.), UK Repn to the European Communities, Brussels, 1985–90; Dep. Dir Gen., resp. for agricl support, DG VI, EC, 1990–96. *Recreations:* sailing, squash, rowing. *Address:* Directorate-General for Agriculture, Commission of the European Communities, 130 rue de la Loi, 1049 Brussels, Belgium.

ROBERTS, David George; HM Diplomatic Service; Deputy Head of Mission, Director of Trade and Investment and Consul General to Switzerland and Liechtenstein, Berne, since 2000; *b* 11 April 1955; *s* of David Ceredig Roberts and Margaret (*née* Burns), Dolgellau, Wales; *m* 1985, Rosmarie Rita Kunz, Winterthur, Switzerland; one *s* one *d*. *Educ:* Bishop Vesey's Grammar Sch., Sutton Coldfield; Pembroke Coll., Oxford (MA Hons Mod. Hist. 1976). Joined FCO, 1976: Desk Officer, E Germany and WEU, 1976–77; Third, later Second, Sec. (Chancery), Jakarta, 1977–81; Second Sec. (Chancery), Havana, 1981–83; Desk Officer for nuclear deterrence, strategic defence and test ban matters, Defence and Arms Control and Disarmament Depts, FCO, 1983–86; Section Head for N Africa, Near East and N Africa Dept, FCO, 1986–88; First Secretary: (Eur. and Econ. Affairs), Madrid, 1988–90; (EU and Financial Affairs), Paris, 1990–94; Deputy Head: Hong Kong Dept, FCO, 1994–96; of Mission, and Consul Gen., Santiago, 1996–2000. *Recreations:* enjoying languages (Spanish, French, German, Indonesian), attempting to keep fit, reading, gardening, listening to classical music, eating and drinking. *Address:* c/o Foreign and Commonwealth Office, King Charles Street, SW1A 2AH.

ROBERTS, (David) Gwilym (Morris), CBE 1987; FREng; Chairman: Acer Group Ltd, 1987–92; Acer-ICF Ltd, 1990–92; *b* 24 July 1925; *er s* of late Edward and Edith Roberts of Crosby; *m* 1st, 1960, Rosemary Elizabeth Emily (*d* 1973), *d* of late J. E. Giles of Tavistock; one *s* one *d*; 2nd, 1978, Wendy Ann, *d* of late Dr J. K. Moore of Beckenham and Alfriston. *Educ:* Merchant Taylors' School, Crosby; Sidney Sussex College, Cambridge (Minor Scholar, MA; Hon. Fellow, 1993). FICE, FIMechE; FREng (FEng 1986). Engineering Officer, RNVR, 1945–47; Lieut Comdr RNR, retired 1961. Asst Engineer, 1947–55, Partner, 1956–90 (Sen. Partner, 1981–90), John Taylor & Sons; principally development of water and wastewater projects, UK towns and regions, and Abu Dhabi, Bahrain, Egypt, Iraq, Kuwait, Mauritius, Qatar, Saudi Arabia and Thailand. Director: Acer Gp Ltd, 1987–92; various transportation projects in UK and abroad. Vis. Prof., Loughborough Univ., 1991–95. Chairman: BGS Programme Bd, 1989–93; Football Stadia Adv. Design Council, 1990–93; 2nd Severn Crossing Technical Adjudication Panel, 1991–97; Member: UK Cttee, IAWPRC, 1967–83; Bd of Control, AMBRIC (American British Consultants), 1978–92; (Construction Industry) Group of Eight, 1983–85, 1987–88; President: IPHE, 1968–69 (IPHE Silver Medal 1974; Gold Medal 1987); ICE, 1986–87 (Vice-Pres., 1983–86; Overseas Premium, 1978; Halcrow Premium, 1985; George Stephenson Medal, 1986). Council Member: Brighton Polytechnic, 1983–86; NERC, 1987–93; CIRIA, 1988–92. Member: Exec. Cttee, British Egyptian Soc., 1991–93; Nat. Cttee, British-Arab Univ. Assoc., 1991–93. Governor: Chailey Sch., 1988–92; Roedean Sch., 1989–93. Freeman, City of London, 1977; Liveryman: Engineers' Co., 1985; Constructors' Co., 1990; Water Conservators' Co., 2000. Hon. FCIWEM. *Publications:* (co-author) Civil Engineering Procedure, 3rd edn 1979; Built By Oil, 1995; From Kendal's Coffee House to Great George Street, 1995; papers to Royal Soc., Arab League, ICE, IPHE. *Recreations:* tennis, golf, family history. *Address:* North America Farm, Hundred Acre Lane, Westmeston, Hassocks, Sussex BN6 8SH. *T:* (01273) 890324. *Clubs:* St Stephen's Constitutional, Oxford and Cambridge, MCC; Piltdown Golf.

ROBERTS, Maj.-Gen. David Michael, MD; FRCP, FRCPE; equestrian centre proprietor, 1990–95; *b* 9 Sept. 1931; *s* of James Henry and Agnes Louise Roberts; *m* 1964, Angela Louise Squire; one *s* two *d*. *Educ:* Emanuel Sch., London; Royal Free Hospital School of Medicine (MB, BS). Qualified in medicine, 1954; commissioned RAMC, 1955; service in field units, BAOR, 1955–59; Hon. Registrar in Medicine, Radcliffe Infirmary, Oxford, 1960; various medical specialty appts in military hosps in UK, BAOR and Hong Kong, 1960–75; graded consultant physician, 1968; Joint Professor of Military Medicine, RAMC and RCP, London, 1975–81; Command Cons. Physician, BAOR, 1981–84; Dir of Army Medicine and Cons. Physician to the Army, 1984–88, retired. Consulting Physician, Royal Hosp., Chelsea, 1984–88; MO (Res.), MoD, 1988–90. Lectr in Tropical Medicine, Mddx Hosp. Medical Sch., 1976–81; Examiner in Tropical Medicine for RCP, 1981–88. Mem., British Soc. of Gastroenterology, 1973–90. QHP 1984–88. *Publications:* many articles on gastroenterological subjects. *Recreation:* horse trials follower.

ROBERTS, (David) Paul; Capita Strategic Education Services, since 2001; Director of Education, Haringey Council; *b* 6 Sept. 1947; *s* of Percival and Nancy Roberts; *m* 1969, Helen Margaret Shone; two *d*. *Educ:* Univ. of Bristol (BSc Hons 1969; CertEd 1970); Cambridge Inst. Educn (AdvDip 1982). Maths Teacher, then Dir of Studies, Ipswich Sch., 1970–74; Dep. Hd Teacher, Harlington Upper Sch., Beds, 1974–83; Chief Inspector, then Dep. Dir of Educn, Notts CC, 1983–97; Dir of Educn, Nottingham CC, 1997–2001. Dir, Guideline Careers Co. Ltd, 1997–2001. FRSA. *Publications:* articles in educnl and maths jls. *Recreations:* arts, hill-walking. *Address:* 55 Dunster Road, West Bridgford, Nottingham NG2 6JE. *T:* (0115) 923 1775.

ROBERTS, Denis Edwin, CBE 1974 (MBE (mil.) 1945); Managing Director, Posts, 1977–80; *b* 6 Jan. 1917; *s* of late Edwin and Alice G. Roberts; *m* 1940, Edith (*née* Whitehead); two *s*. *Educ:* Holgate Grammar Sch., Barnsley. Served War of 1939–45, Royal Signals, France, N Africa, Italy and Austria. Entered Post Office, Barnsley, 1933; various appts, 1933–71; Dir Postal Ops, 1971–75; Sen. Dir, Postal Services, 1975–77. Mem., Industrial Tribunal, 1982–86. Chm., British Philatelic Trust, 1981–85. Liveryman, Gardeners' Co. *Address:* 302 Gilbert House, Barbican, EC2Y 8BD. *T:* (020) 7638 0881. *Club:* City of London.

ROBERTS, Dennis Laurie Harold; Director, Road Transport Directorate, Department for Transport, Local Government and the Regions, since 2001; *b* 24 Jan. 1949; *s* of William Roberts and Vera Roberts; *m* 1980, Anne Mary Hillhouse; one *s*. *Educ:* Sheffield Univ. (BA, MSc). CSO, 1971–76; DoE, 1976–83; MoD, 1983–85; Department of the Environment: Head: Local Govt Finance Div., 1985–89; Water Envmt Div., 1989–92; Finance Div., 1992–94; OPCS, 1994–96; Dir, Socio-Economic Stats and Analysis Gp, 1996–98, Dir, Corp. Services Gp, 1998–99, ONS; Dir, Roads and Traffic Directorate, DETR, 2000–01. *Recreations:* walking, reading, watching football. *Address:* 19 Shawfield Park, Bickley, Bromley, Kent BR1 2NQ. *T:* (020) 8464 8325.

ROBERTS, Hon. Sir Denys (Tudor Emil), KBE 1975 (CBE 1970; OBE 1960); SPMB; Chief Justice of Negara Brunei Darussalam, 1979–2001; *b* 19 Jan. 1923; *s* of William David and Dorothy Elizabeth Roberts; *m* 1st, 1949, Brenda Marsh (marr. diss. 1973); one *s* one *d*; 2nd, 1985, Anna Fiona Dollar Alexander; one *s*. *Educ:* Aldenham; Wadham Coll., Oxford, 1942 and 1946–49 (MA 1948, BCL 1949; Hon. Fellow, 1984); served with Royal Artillery, 1943–46, France, Belgium, Holland, Germany, India (Captain). English Bar, 1950–53; Crown Counsel, Nyasaland, 1953–59; QC Gibraltar 1960; QC Hong Kong 1964; Attorney-General, Gibraltar, 1960–62; Solicitor-General, Hong Kong, 1962–66; Attorney-General, Hong Kong, 1966–73; Chief Secretary, Hong Kong, 1973–78; Chief Justice, Hong Kong, 1979–88; Pres., Court of Appeal, Bermuda, 1988–94. Hon. Bencher, Lincoln's Inn, 1978. SPMB (Negara Brunei Darussalam), 1984. *Publications:* Smuggler's Circuit, 1954; Beds and Roses, 1956; The Elwood Wager, 1958; The Bones of the Wajingas, 1960; How to Dispense with Lawyers, 1964; Doing them Justice, 1986; I'll Do Better Next Time, 1995; Yes Sir But, 2000. *Recreations:* cricket, walking, writing. *Address:* The Supreme Court, Bandar Seri Begawan, Brunei; Leithen Lodge, Innerleithen, Peeblesshire EH44 6NW. *Clubs:* Garrick, MCC (Pres., 1989–90).

ROBERTS, Derek Franklyn, FCII, FCIB; Chairman, Yorkshire Building Society, 1997–2001; *b* 16 Oct. 1942; *s* of Frank Roberts, MBE, and May Evelyn Roberts; *m* 1969, Jacqueline (*née* Velho); two *s* one *d*. *Educ:* Park High Grammar Sch., Birkenhead; Liverpool Coll. of Commerce; Harvard Business Sch. (AMP (Grad.)). Royal Insurance Co. Ltd, 1961–72; Huddersfield Building Society: Insce Services Man., 1972; apptd to Executive, as Business Develt Man., 1975; Develt Man., 1979; on formation of Yorkshire Building Soc., 1982, apptd Asst Gen. Man. (Marketing); Dir and Chief Exec., 1987–96. Director: Yorkshire Water Services (formerly Yorkshire Water), 1996–; Kelda Gp, 1999–. Dir, Bradford City Challenge Ltd, 1993–97; Mem., W Yorks Rural Develt Cttee, 1992–96. CIMgt. *Recreations:* golf, gardening, ski-ing, walking the dogs, keeping friendships in constant repair. *Address:* The Ark, 20 Arkenley Lane, Almondbury, Huddersfield HD4 6SQ. *T:* (01484) 426414. *Clubs:* Huddersfield Borough; Huddersfield Golf, Royal Liverpool Golf; Huddersfield Rugby Union FC.

ROBERTS, Sir Derek (Harry), Kt 1995; CBE 1983; FRS 1980; FREng, FInstP; Hon. Senior Research Fellow, School of Public Policy, University College London, since 1999; *b* 28 March 1932; *s* of Harry and Alice Roberts; *m* 1958, Winifred (*née* Short); one *s* one *d*. *Educ:* Manchester Central High Sch.; Manchester Univ. (BSc). MIEE. Joined Plessey Co.'s Caswell Res. Lab., 1953; Gen. Man., Plessey Semiconductors, 1967; Dir, Allen Clark Res. Centre, 1969; Man. Dir, Plessey Microelectronics Div., 1973; Technical Dir, 1983–85, Jt Dep. Man. Dir (Technical), 1985–88, GEC; Provost of UCL, 1989–99. Pres., BAAS, 1996–97. Hon. DSc: Bath, 1982; Loughborough, 1984; City, 1985; Lancaster, 1986; Manchester, 1987; Salford, Essex, London, 1988; DUniv Open, 1984. *Publications:* about 20 pubns in scientific and technical jls. *Recreations:* reading, gardening. *Address:* School of Public Policy, University College London, Gower Street, WC1E 6BT. *T:* (020) 7679 7234.

ROBERTS, Prof. (Edward) Adam, FBA 1990; Montague Burton Professor of International Relations and Fellow of Balliol College, Oxford, since 1986; *b* 29 Aug. 1940;

s of late Michael Roberts, poet and Janet Roberts, OBE, writer (as Janet Adam Smith); *m* 1966, Frances P. Dunn; one *s* one *d*. *Educ:* Westminster School; Magdalen College, Oxford (BA 1962, MA 1981). Asst Editor, Peace News Ltd, 1962–65; Noel Buxton Student in Internat. Relations, LSE, 1965–68; Lectr in Internat. Relations, LSE, 1968–81; Alastair Buchan Reader in Internat. Relations, Oxford, and Professorial Fellow, St Antony's Coll., Oxford, 1981–86; Leverhulme Res. Fellow, 2000–. Mem., Council, RIIA, 1985–91. Hon. Fellow, LSE, 1997. *Publications:* (ed) The Strategy of Civilian Defence, 1967; (jtly) Czechoslovakia 1968, 1969; Nations in Arms, 1976, 2nd edn, 1986; (ed jtly) Documents on the Laws of War, 1982, 3rd edn 2000; (ed jtly) United Nations, Divided World, 1988, 2nd edn 1993; (ed jtly) Hugo Grotius and International Relations, 1990; Humanitarian Action in War, 1996. *Recreations:* rock climbing, mountaineering. *Address:* Balliol College, Oxford OX1 3BJ. *T:* (01865) 277777. *Club:* Alpine.

ROBERTS, Sir (Edward Fergus) Sidney, Kt 1978; CBE 1972; former Federal President, Australian Country Party; grazier and manager of companies; *b* 19 April 1901; *s* of late E. J. Roberts. *Educ:* Scots Coll., Sydney. Gen. Manager, Ungra, Brisbane, 1957–70; owner, Boolaroo Downs, Clermont, Qld, 1928–63. United Graziers' Assoc., Qld: Mem. Council, 1948–76; Vice-Pres., 1950–52. Aust. Road Fedn: Mem., 1954–63; Nat. Pres., 1962–63. Mem. Bd, Queensland Country Life Newspaper, 1969–77; Pres., Aust. Country Party, Qld, 1967; Chm., Federal Council, ACP, 1969–74. Knighthood awarded for distinguished service to Primary Industry, Australia. *Address:* 53 Eldernell Avenue, Hamilton, Queensland 4007, Australia. *Club:* Queensland (Brisbane).

ROBERTS, Eifion; *see* Roberts, H. E. P.

ROBERTS, Eirlys Rhiwen Cadwaladr, CBE 1977 (OBE 1971); Deputy Director, Consumers' Association (Which?), 1973–77 (Head of Research and Editorial Division, 1958–73); *b* 3 Jan. 1911; *d* of Dr Ellis James Roberts and Jane Tennant Macaulay; *m* 1941, John Cullen (marr. diss.); no *c*. *Educ:* Clapham High School; Girton College, Cambridge. BA (Hons) Classics. Sub-editor in Amalgamated Press; Military, then Political Intelligence, 1943–44 and 1944–45; Public Relations in UNRRA, Albanian Mission, 1945–47; Information Division of the Treasury, 1947–57. Chief Exec., Bureau of European Consumer Orgns, 1973–78. Mem., Royal Commn on the Press, 1974–77. Mem., Economic and Social Cttee of EEC, 1973–82 (Chm., Environment and Consumer Protection section, 1978–82); Chm., European Res. into Consumer Affairs, 1978–97. *Publication:* Consumers, 1966. *Recreations:* walking, reading detective novels. *Address:* 8 Lloyd Square, WC1X 9BA. *T:* (020) 7837 2492.

ROBERTS, Sir Gareth (Gwyn), Kt 1997; FRS 1984; President, Wolfson College, Oxford, since 2001; *b* 16 May 1940; *s* of Edwin and Meri Roberts; *m* 1st, 1962; two *s* one *d*; 2nd, 1994, Carolyn Mary Butler; two step *d*. *Educ:* UCNW, Bangor (BSc, PhD, DSc; Hon. Fellow, 1989); MA Oxon 1987. Lectr in Physics, Univ. of Wales, 1963–66; Res. Physicist, Xerox Corp., USA, 1966–68; Sen. Lectr, Reader, and Professor of Physics, NUU, 1968–76; Prof. of Applied Physics and Head, Dept of Applied Physics and Electronics, Univ. of Durham, 1976–85; Chief Scientist, 1985, Dir of Research, 1986–90, Thorn EMI plc; Vice-Chancellor, Univ. of Sheffield, 1991–2000; Fellow of Brasenose Coll., 1985–95 (Hon. Fellow, 1995) and Vis. Prof. of Electronic Engrg, 1985–93, Oxford Univ. BBC/Royal Instn Christmas Lectures, 1988. Member: UFC, 1989–92; HEFCE, 1997–; Bd, Retained Organs Commn, 2001–; Bd, COPUS, 2001–; Chairman: Defence Scientific Adv. Council, 1993–97; CVCP, 1995–97; Res. Careers Initiative, 1997–; Genome Valley Steering Gp, DTI, 2000–01; HM Treasury Review on Supply of Scientists and Engrg in UK, 2001–. Chm., Medical Solutions plc, 2000–; Director: e-University Holding Co., 2001–; Isis Innovations Ltd, 2001–. Director: Sheffield Develt Corp., 1992–97; DERA, 1994–97; Sheffield HA, 1996–99; Univs Superannuation Scheme, 1997–2001; Yorkshire Forward, 1999–2000. President: Inst. of Physics, 1998–2000; Science Council, 2000–; Techniquest, 2002–. Mem. Council, Foundn for Sci. and Technol., 2000–. Gov., Wellington Coll., 1991–. Hon. Fellow: UCNW, 1990; Univ. of Wales Coll. of Medicine, 1996; NE Wales Inst., 1997. Hon. LLD Wales, 1990; Hon. DSc UWE, 1997. Holweck Gold Medal and Prize, Inst. of Physics, 1986. *Publications:* Insulating Films on Semiconductors, 1979; Langmuir-Blodgett Films, 1990; many publications and patents on physics of semiconductor devices and molecular electronics. *Recreations:* watching soccer and supporting Tottenham Hotspurs, listening to classical music, hosting town and gown functions. *Address:* Wolfson College, Oxford OX2 6UD. *Club:* Athenæum.

ROBERTS, Prof. Geoffrey Frank Ingleson, CBE 1978; FREng; Chairman, British Pipe Coaters Ltd, 1978–88; Professor of Gas Engineering, University of Salford, 1983–89, Professorial Fellow, 1989–91; *b* 9 May 1926; *s* of late Arthur and Laura Roberts; *m* 1st, 1949, Veronica (*d* 1993), *d* of late Captain J. Busby, Hartlepool; two *d*; 2nd, 1995, Patricia, *widow* of Neville H. H. Johnson, Ilkley. *Educ:* Cathedral Sch., and High Sch. for Boys, Hereford; Leeds Univ. (BSc hons). FIChemE; FInstE; FREng (FEng 1978). Pupil engr, Gas Light & Coke Co., and North Thames Gas Bd, 1947–50; North Thames Gas Board: Asst Engr, 1950–59; Stn Engr, Slough, 1959–61; Dept. Stn Engr, Southall Stn, 1961–66; Group Engr, Slough Group, 1966–68; Dep. Dir (Ops) Gas Council, 1968–71; Mem. for Production and Supply, Gas Council, later British Gas Corp., 1972–78; Mem. for External Affairs, British Gas Corp., 1979–81, retired. President: IGasE, 1980–81 (Hon. FIGasE); Inst. of Energy, 1983–84. *Recreations:* woodwork, travel. *Address:* 2 Birchwood Court, South Parade, Ilkley, West Yorks LS29 9AW. *T:* (01943) 601671.

ROBERTS, George Arnott; Head of Administration Department, House of Commons, 1988–91; *b* 16 April 1930; *s* of David Roberts and Doris (*née* Sykes); *m* 1956, Georgina (*née* Gower); two *s* one *d*. *Educ:* Rastrick Grammar Sch.; London Univ. (extra-mural). Min. of Labour, then Dept of Employment, 1947–74; Advisory, Conciliation and Arbitration Service, 1974–85: Sec., Central Arbitration Cttee, 1978–80; Dir of Administration, 1980–83; Dir, London Region, 1983–85; House of Commons, 1985–91: Hd of Establishment Office, 1985–88. *Recreations:* golf, gardening. *Club:* Sonning Golf.

ROBERTS, Sir Gilbert (Howland Rookehurst), 7th Bt *cr* 1809; *b* 31 May 1934; *s* of Sir Thomas Langdon Howland Roberts, 6th Bt, CBE, and of Evelyn Margaret, *o d* of late H. Fielding-Hall; *S* father, 1979; *m* 1958, Ines, *o d* of late A. Labunski; one *s* one *d*. *Educ:* Rugby; Gonville and Caius Coll., Cambridge (BA 1957). CEng, MIMechE. *Recreation:* hang gliding. *Heir:* *s* Howland Langdon Roberts, *b* 19 Aug. 1961. *Address:* 3340 Cliff Drive, Santa Barbara, CA 93109, USA; *e-mail:* ghrr3340@aol.com.

ROBERTS, Gillian Frances; Academic Registrar, University of London, since 1983; *b* 3 Nov. 1944; *d* of late Frank Murray and of Mabel Murray; *m* 1969, Andrew Clive Roberts. *Educ:* Sydenham High Sch.; Southampton Univ. (BA Hist., 1966). Academic Dept, London Univ., 1967–83. Chm., Bd, London Voluntary Sector Resource Centre, 1997–. Mem. Local Governing Body, Bromley High Sch., 1989–. Trustee, City Parochial Foundn, 1993–. *Address:* Senate House, University of London, Malet Street, WC1E 7HU. *T:* (020) 7862 8030.

ROBERTS, Prof. Gordon Carl Kenmure, PhD; Professor of Biochemistry, since 1986, Director, Leicester Biological NMR Centre, since 1986, and Head of Department of Biochemistry, since 2000, University of Leicester; *b* 28 May 1943; *s* of Rev. Douglas M. A. K. Roberts and Hilda (*née* Engelmann); *m* 1963, Hilary Margaret Lepper; two *s* one *d*. *Educ:* University Coll., London (BSc Hons Biochem. 1964); PhD Biochem. London 1967. Res. Chemist, Merck Sharp & Dohme Res. Labs, Rahway, NJ, 1967–69; Member scientific staff: MRC Molecular Pharmacol. Res. Unit, Dept of Pharmacol., Univ. of Cambridge, 1969–72; NIMR, 1972–86. *Publications:* NMR in Molecular Biology (with O. Jardetzky), 1981; (ed) NMR of Biological Macromolecules, 1993; numerous papers in scientific jls. *Recreation:* gardening. *Address:* Biological NMR Centre, Medical Sciences Building, University of Leicester, PO Box 138, Lancaster Road, Leicester LE1 9HN. *T:* (0116) 252 2978.

ROBERTS, Sir Gordon (James), Kt 1984; CBE 1975; JP; DL; Chairman, Oxford Regional Health Authority, 1978–90; Member, Commission for the New Towns, 1978–94 (Deputy Chairman, 1978–82); *b* 30 Jan. 1921; *s* of Archie and Lily Roberts; *m* 1944, Barbara Leach; one *s* one *d*. *Educ:* Deanshanger Sch., Northants. Chairman: Northants AHA, 1973–78; Supervisory Bd, NHS Management Adv. Service, 1982–85; NHS Computer Policy Cttee, 1981–85; RHA Chairmen, 1982–84; Member: Oxford Reg. Hosp. Bd, 1968–74; St Crispin Hosp. Management Cttee, 1965–74; Northants Exec. Council, NHS, 1954–74; E Midlands Econ. Planning Council, 1975–79; Bd, Northampton Develt Corp., 1976–85 (Dep. Chm., 1985). Contested (Lab) S Northants, 1970. Mem., Towcester RDC, 1953–56; Mem., Northants CC, 1954–77 (Leader, 1973–77). JP Northants, 1952; Chm., Towcester Bench, 1977–83. DL Northants, 1984, High Sheriff, 1989. FRSA 1985. *Publication:* (with Dr O. F. Brown) Passenham—the history of a forest village, 1975. *Recreations:* music, reading, walking, local history. *Address:* 114 Ridgmont, Deanshanger, Milton Keynes, Bucks MK19 6JG. *T:* (01908) 562605.

ROBERTS, Gwilym; *see* Roberts, D. G. M.

ROBERTS, Gwilym Edffrwd, PhD; FIS; Chairman, First Community NHS Trust, since 1998; *b* 7 Aug. 1928; *s* of William and Jane Ann Roberts; *m* 1954, Mair Griffiths; no *c*. *Educ:* Brynrefail Gram. Sch.; UCW (Bangor); City Univ. BSc. Industrial Management, 1952–57; Lecturer (Polytechnic and University), 1957–66, 1970–74. Mem., Cannock Chase DC, 1983– (Leader, 1992–99). MP (Lab): South Bedfordshire, 1966–70; Cannock, Feb. 1974–1983; PPS, DoI, 1976–79. Contested (Lab): Ormskirk, 1959; Conway, 1964; S Beds, 1970; Cannock and Burntwood, 1983, 1987. Business Analyst, Economic Forecasting, Market and Operational Research, 1957–. Institute of Statisticians: Vice-Pres., 1978–; Hon. Officer, 1983–84; Editor, Newsletter, 1967–78. FIMgt. Hon. Fellow, Royal Stat. Soc., 1993. *Publications:* many articles on technical, political, parliamentary and European matters. *Recreations:* cricket, table tennis. *Address:* 18 Church Street, Rugeley, Staffs WS15 2AB. *T:* (01889) 583601, (office) (01582) 573893.

ROBERTS, Sir Hugh Ashley, KCVO 2001 (CVO 1998; LVO 1995); FSA; Director of the Royal Collection and Surveyor of the Queen's Works of Art, since 1996; *b* 20 April 1948; *s* of Rt Rev. Edward James Keymer Roberts and late Dorothy Frances, *d* of Rev. Canon Edwin David Bowser; *m* 1975, Hon. Priscilla Jane Stephanie Low (*see* Hon. P. J. S. Roberts); two *d*. *Educ:* Winchester Coll.; Corpus Christi Coll., Cambridge (MA). FSA 1994. With Christie Manson and Woods, 1970–87 (Dir, 1978–87); Dep. Surveyor of the Queen's Works of Art, 1988–96. Mem., Sec. of State's Adv. Gp, Historic Royal Palaces Agency, 1990–98. Member: Exec. Cttee, NACF, 1988–2000; Arts Panel, NT, 1988– (Chm., 1997–); Council, Attingham Trust, 1988–; Trustee, Historic Royal Palaces Trust, 1998–. Mem., Soc. of Dilettanti, 1991–. *Publications:* For the King's Pleasure: the furnishing and decoration of George IV's apartments at Windsor Castle, 2001; contrib. to Furniture History, Burlington Mag., Apollo, etc. *Recreation:* gardening. *Address:* Adelaide Cottage, Home Park, Windsor, Berks SL4 2JQ. *T:* (01753) 855581.

ROBERTS, His Honour (Hugh) Eifion (Pritchard); QC 1971; DL; a Circuit Judge, 1977–98; *b* 22 Nov. 1927; *er s* of late Rev. and Mrs E. P. Roberts, Anglesey; *m* 1958, Buddug Williams; one *s* two *d*. *Educ:* Beaumaris Grammar Sch.; University Coll. of Wales, Aberystwyth (LLB); Exeter Coll., Oxford (BCL). Called to Bar, Gray's Inn, 1953; practised as a Junior Counsel on Wales and Chester Circuit, Sept. 1953–April 1971. Dep. Chairman: Anglesey QS, 1966–71; Denbighshire QS, 1970–71; a Recorder of the Crown Court, 1972–77. Formerly Asst Parly Boundary Comr for Wales; Mem. for Wales of the Crawford Cttee on Broadcasting Coverage. Chm. Council, Univ. of Wales, Bangor. DL Clwyd, 1988. *Recreation:* gardening. *Address:* Maes-y-Rhedyn, Gresford Road, Llay, Wrexham, Clwyd LL12 0NN. *T:* (01978) 852292.

ROBERTS, Hugh Martin P.; *see* Plowden Roberts.

ROBERTS, Prof. Ian Gareth, PhD; Professor and Head of Department of Linguistics, and Fellow of Downing College, University of Cambridge, since 2000; *b* 23 Oct. 1957; *s* of Idris Michael Roberts and Dorothy Sybil Roberts (*née* Moody); *m* 1993, Lucia Cavalli; one *s* one *d*. *Educ:* Stamford Sch.; Eirias High Sch., Colwyn Bay; UCNW (Bangor) (BA Hons Linguistics 1979); Univ. of Southern Calif (PhD 1985). Translator, Motor Ind. Res. Assoc., Nuneaton, 1980–81; University of Geneva: Asst de linguistique anglaise, 1985–86; Maître-asst de linguistique générale, 1986–91; Professor: of Linguistics, UCNW (Bangor), then Univ. of Wales, Bangor, 1991–96; of English Linguistics, Univ. of Stuttgart, 1996–2000. Ed., Jl Linguistics, 1994–2000. *Publications:* The Representation of Implicit and Rethematised Subjects, 1987; Verbs and Diachronic Syntax, 1993; Comparative Syntax, 1996; contrib. numerous articles to learned jls. *Recreations:* reading, walking, music. *Address:* Downing College, Cambridge CB2 1DQ. *T:* (01223) 331733.

ROBERTS, Ian White; HM Diplomatic Service, retired; Hon. Visiting Fellow, School of Slavonic and East European Studies, University of London, 1985–99; SSEES historian; *b* 29 March 1927; *s* of George Dodd Roberts and Jessie Dickson Roberts (*née* White); *m* 1956, Pamela Johnston; one *d*. *Educ:* Royal Masonic Sch., Bushey, Herts; Gonville and Caius Coll., Cambridge (MA 1st Cl. Hons Mod. Langs). Served Royal Air Force (Pilot Officer), 1948–50; postgrad. student, Cambridge (Scarbrough Award), 1950. Joined Foreign Office, 1951–: Klagenfurt, 1952; Munich, 1954; Berlin, 1955; FCO, 1957–61; Second (later First) Secretary, Budapest, 1961–63; FCO, 1963; Bujumbura, 1965; FCO, 1965–66; Buenos Aires, 1966; FCO, 1969–74; Oslo, 1974–76; FCO, 1976–84; Counsellor, 1976. *Publications:* Nicholas I and the Russian Intervention in Hungary, 1991; History of School of Slavonic and East European Studies, University of London, 1991; articles in philatelic jls. *Recreations:* music, reading, philately. *Address:* c/o Lloyds TSB, 1 Butler Place, SW1H 0PR. *Club:* Travellers.

ROBERTS, Sir Ivor (Anthony), KCMG 2000 (CMG 1995); HM Diplomatic Service; Ambassador to Ireland, since 1999; *b* 24 Sept. 1946; *s* of late Leonard Moore Roberts and of Rosa Maria Roberts (*née* Fusco); *m* 1974, Elizabeth Bray Bernard Smith; two *s* one *d*. *Educ:* St Mary's Coll., Crosby; Keble Coll., Oxford (Gomm schol.; MA); FIL 1991. Entered HM Diplomatic Service, 1968; MECAS, 1969; Third, later Second Sec., Paris, 1970–73; Second, later First Sec., FCO, 1973–78; First Sec., Canberra, 1978–82; First

Sec., later Counsellor, FCO, 1982–88; Minister and Dep. Head of Mission, Madrid, 1989–93; Chargé d'Affaires, Belgrade, 1994–96; Ambassador to Yugoslavia, 1996–97; Sen. Associate Mem., St Antony's Coll., Oxford, 1997–98. *Recreations:* opera, ski-ing, golf, photography. *Address:* c/o Foreign and Commonwealth Office, SW1A 2AH. *Clubs:* Oxford and Cambridge; Downhill Only (Wengen).

ROBERTS, Hon. Jane; *see* Roberts, Hon. P. J. S.

ROBERTS, Jeremy Michael Graham; QC 1982; **His Honour Judge Jeremy Roberts;** a Circuit Judge, at the Central Criminal Court, since 2000; *b* 26 April 1941; *s* of late Lt-Col J. M. H. Roberts and E. D. Roberts; *m* 1964, Sally Priscilla Johnson, *d* of late Col F. P. Johnson, OBE. *Educ:* Winchester; Brasenose Coll., Oxford. BA. Called to the Bar, Inner Temple, 1965, Bencher, 1992. A Recorder, 1981–2000. Head of Chambers, 1997–2000. *Recreations:* racing, reading, theatre, opera, canals. *Address:* Central Criminal Court, Old Bailey, EC4M 7EH.

ROBERTS, John; *see* Roberts, A. J.

ROBERTS, John Anthony; QC 1988; FCIArb; a Recorder of the Crown Court, 1987–98; *b* Sierra Leone, 17 May 1928; *s* of late John Anthony Roberts of Brazil and Regina Roberts of Sierra Leone; *m* 1961, Eulette Valerie; one *s*. *Educ:* St Edward's RC Secondary Sch., Sierra Leone; Inns of Court Sch. of Law. Costs Clerk, Taylor Woodrow W Africa Ltd; Civil Servant, Sierra Leone; RAF 1952–62 (GSM Malaya), served UK, Europe, Near East, Far East, S Pacific; qualified Air Traffic Control Officer, 1962–64; qualified pilot; Civil Service, UK, 1964–69, incl. Inland Revenue; part time law student; called to the Bar, Gray's Inn, 1969, Bencher, 1996; Mem., Lincoln's Inn, 1972; Head of Chambers, 1975; Asst Recorder, 1983–87. First person of African ancestry to be appointed QC at the English Bar; called to the Bar in: Jamaica, 1973; Sierra Leone, 1975; Trinidad and Tobago, 1978; Bahamas, 1984; St Kitts and Nevis, 1988. Judge, Supreme Cts of BVI and Anguilla, BWI, 1992–93. Bencher, Council of Legal Educn, Sierra Leone, 1990. Tutor, Inns of Ct Sch. of Law, London, 1990–92. Mem., UK Br., West Indian Ex-Servicemen's Assoc. Hon. Citizen, Atlanta, Ga, USA, 1991. Freeman, City of London, 1996; Mem. Guild of Freemen, 1997. Hon. DCL City, 1996. *Recreations:* music, singing in a choir (Latin Mass and Gregorian Chant), flying light aircraft, playing piano, organ and guitar, reading, dancing, athletics, boxing (former sprinter and boxer, RAF).

ROBERTS, John Arthur, CEng, FIEE; Under-Secretary, Department of Energy, 1974–77; *b* 21 Dec. 1917; *s* of late John Richard and Emily Roberts; *m* 1st, 1944, Winifred Wilks Scott (*d* 1976); two *s* one *d*; 2nd, 1977, Rosetta Mabel Price. *Educ:* Liverpool Institute; Liverpool Univ. (BEng). Apprentice, Metropolitan-Vickers Electrical Co Ltd, 1939. Served War, Royal Signals, 1940–46, Major. Sen. Lectr, Applied Science, RMA, Sandhurst, 1947–49; SSO and PSO, RAE, Farnborough, 1949–59; Head, Control and Computers Section, Applications Br., Central Electricity Generating Bd, 1959–62; Project Ldr, Automatic Control, CEGB, 1962–67; DCSO, Min. of Tech. and DTI, 1967–72; Under-Sec., DTI, 1972–74. *Address:* Damery, High Street, Wookey, Wells, Somerset BA5 1JZ. *T:* (01749) 678025.

ROBERTS, John Charles Quentin; Chairman, International Advisory Board of All-Russia State Library for Foreign Literature, Moscow, since 1994 (Member, 1991–93); Director, Britain-Russia Centre (formerly Great Britain-USSR Association), 1974–93; *b* 4 April 1933; *s* of Hubert and Emilie Roberts; *m* 1st, 1959, Dinah Webster-Williams (marr. diss.); one *s* one *d*; 2nd, 1982, Elizabeth Roberts (*née* Gough-Cooper); two step *d*. *Educ:* Quainton Hall; King's Coll., Taunton (open scholar); Merton Coll., Oxford (MA). MIL 1972. Royal Air Force CSC Interpreter, 1953; Russian Language Tutor, SSEES, Univ. of London, 1953; Shell International Petroleum Co. Ltd, 1956; Shell Co. of E Africa Ltd: Representative, Zanzibar and S Tanganyika, 1957, Kenya Highlands, 1958; PA to Man. Dir, Shell Austria AG Vienna, 1960; Pressed Steel Co. Ltd, Oxford, 1961; Asst Master, Marlborough Coll., 1963–74. Chairman: Organising Cttee for British Week in Siberia, 1978; Steering Cttee, British Month in USSR (Kiev), 1990. Mem. Council, Amer. Friends of the Russian Country Estate Inc., Washington, 1998–. Member Council: SSEES, Univ. of London, 1981–93; Academia Rossica, 2000–; Vice Pres., Assoc. of Teachers of Russian, 1984–89. Governor, Cobham Hall, 1984–88. *Publications:* Speak Clearly into the Chandelier: cultural politics between Britain and Russia 1973–2000 (memoir), 2000; translations from Russian literature; contribs to specialist jls; occasional journalism. *Recreations:* family, landscape gardening, forestry. *Address:* Crookedstane Rig, Elvanfoot, Biggar ML12 6TJ. *T:* (01864) 505233, *Fax:* (01864) 505258; 52 Paultons Square, SW3 5DT. *T:* (020) 7352 3882; *e-mail:* jcqr@crookedstane.demon.co.uk. *Club:* Athenæum.

ROBERTS, John Edward, CEng, FIEE, FCCA; Chief Executive, United Utilities, since 1999; *b* 2 March 1946; *s* of Arthur and Dora Roberts; *m* 1970, Pamela Baxter; one *s* one *d*. *Educ:* Liverpool Univ. (BEng). FCCA 1983; CEng, FIEE 1988; DMS; CIMgt. Merseyside and North Wales Electricity Board, subseq. Manweb: Chief Accountant, 1984–90; Finance Dir, 1990–91; Man. Dir, 1991–92; Chief Exec., 1992–95; Chief Exec., S Wales Electricity, then Hyder Utilities, 1996–99. Dir, Hyder Gp, 1996–99. Mem., Royal Commn on Envmtl Pollution, 1998–. CIMgt. *Recreations:* squash, walking, gardening. *Club:* West Cheshire Squash Rackets.

ROBERTS, John Herbert; former tax administrator; *b* 18 Aug. 1933; *s* of late John Emanuel Roberts and Hilda Mary Roberts; *m* 1965, Patricia Iris; one *s* three *d*. *Educ:* Canton High Sch.; London School of Economics (BScEcon Hons). Entered Civil Service by Open Competition as Inspector of Taxes, 1954; National Service, commnd RASC, 1955–57; returned to Inland Revenue, 1957; Principal Inspector, 1974; Sen. Principal Inspector, 1979; Under Secretary, 1981; Director of Operations, 1981–85; Dir, Technical Div. 2, 1985–88; Dir, Compliance and Collection Div., 1988–92; Dir of Ops (DO2), 1992–93; consultant, overseas tax admin, 1994–99. *Recreations:* music, walking.

ROBERTS, John Houghton; His Honour Judge John H. Roberts; a Circuit Judge, since 1993; Resident Judge, Bolton Crown Court, since 1997; *b* 14 Dec. 1947; *s* of John Noel Roberts and Ida Roberts, Irby, Wirral; *m* 1st, 1972, Anna Elizabeth (marr. diss. 1990), *e d* of Peter and Elizabeth Sheppard; three *s*; 2nd, 1991, Janice Mary, *er d* of Frederic and Patricia Wilkinson, Blundellsands. *Educ:* Calday Grange Grammar Sch., West Kirby; Trinity Hall, Cambridge (Schol; BA Double 1st Cl. Hons Law Tripos; MA). Lectr in Law, Liverpool Univ., 1969–71; called to the Bar, Middle Temple, 1970 (Harmsworth Major Entrance Exhibn 1968; Astbury Law Schol. 1970). Practised Northern Circuit, 1970–93. Asst Recorder, 1983; Recorder, 1988–93. *Recreations:* Rugby football, golf, cricket, music. *Address:* Bolton Crown Court, Bolton BL1 1SU. *T:* (01204) 392881. *Clubs:* Athenæum (Liverpool); Heswall Golf, Nefyn and District Golf, Wirral Ladies' Golf; Oxton Cricket; Waterloo Football.

ROBERTS, Dr John Laing; independent consultant in health policy, since 1997; adviser to Government of Malaŵi, since 1999, to Government of Mauritius, since 2000; *b* 26 Dec. 1939; *s* of Charles F. Roberts and May Roberts; *m* 1st, 1963, Meriel F. Dawes (marr. diss. 1980); three *d*; 2nd, 1981, Judith Mary Hare. *Educ:* Latymer Upper School; Univ. of Birmingham. PhD, BSocSc. FHA. NHS Nat. Administrative Trainee, 1962–63; Senior Administrative Asst, United Birmingham Hosps, 1964–66; Sen. Res. Associate, Dept of Social Medicine, Univ. of Birmingham, 1966–69; Dep. Dir, Res. Div., Health Education Council, 1969–74; Operational Services Gen. Administrator, S Glamorgan AHA (T), 1974–77; Regional Gen. Administrator, W Midlands RHA, 1977–82; Regional Administrator, 1983–85, Regl Prevention Manager, 1985–89, N Western RHA; Regl Advr in Health Services, WHO Office for Europe, Copenhagen, 1990–92; Consultant, WHO Office for Europe, 1992–94; Health Economist/Planner, Min. of Econ. Planning and Develt, Mauritius, 1994–97. Dir, Adhealth, 1989–96. Hon. Sen. Res. Fellow, Manchester Univ., 1990–2000. Mem. Editl Bd, Internat. Jl of Health Promotion, 1996–. *Publications:* papers on health education, health service administration, economics and health; PhD thesis, Studies of Information Systems for Health Service Resource Planning and Control. *Recreations:* swimming, hill walking, tennis. *Address:* Ty Ffynnon, Garth Obry, Pontfadog, Llangollen LL20 7AT; Habasha, Morcellement Mont Choisy, Mont Choisy, Mauritius. *T:* 7509849; *e-mail:* jlrobertsy@aol.com.

ROBERTS, John Lewis, CMG 1987; Assistant Under-Secretary of State (Equipment Collaboration), Ministry of Defence, 1985–88; *b* 21 April 1928; *s* of Thomas Hubert and Meudwen Roberts; *m* 1952, Maureen Jocelyn (*née* Moriarty); two *s*. *Educ:* Pontardawe Grammar Sch.; Trinity Hall, Cambridge. BA (Hons) History. Joined Min. of Civil Aviation, 1950; Private Sec. to the Parly Sec., 1953; Principal: in Railways, then in Sea Transport; branches of MoT and Civil Aviation, 1954–59; Civil Air Attaché, Bonn Embassy, 1959–62; Defence Supply Counsellor, Paris Embassy, 1966–69; Ministry of Defence: Asst Sec., Internat. Policy Div., 1971–74; Assistant Under-Secretary of State: Air MoD PE, 1974–76; Sales, 1976–77; Personnel, (Air), 1977–80; Supply and Organisation, (Air), 1980–82; Internat. and Industrial Policy, PE, 1982–85. FRSA 1988. *Recreations:* angling, sailing.

ROBERTS, John Mervyn; His Honour Judge Mervyn Roberts; a Circuit Judge, since 1999; *b* 19 Feb. 1941; *s* of Mervyn and Catherine Roberts; *m* 1972, Phillippa Ann Critien; one *d*. *Educ:* Hereford Cathedral Sch.; King's Coll., London (LLB Hons 1962). Called to the Bar, Inner Temple, 1963; in practice at the Bar, 1963–99; a Recorder, 1994–99. Mem., Criminal Injuries Compensation Bd, 1998–99. *Recreations:* music, golf, travel. *Address:* Wood Green Crown Court, Woodall House, Lordship Lane, N22 5LF.

ROBERTS, Dr John Morris, CBE 1996; Warden, Merton College, Oxford, 1984–94; a Governor of the BBC, 1988–93; *b* 14 April 1928; *s* of late Edward Henry Roberts and late Dorothy Julia Roberts, Bath, Som.; *m* 1964, Judith Cecilia Mary, *e d* of late Rev. James Armitage and Monica Armitage; one *s* two *d*. *Educ:* Taunton Sch.; Keble Coll., Oxford (Schol.; Hon. Fellow, 1981). National Service, 1949–50; Prize Fellow, Magdalen Coll., Oxford, 1951–53; Commonwealth Fund Fellow, Princeton and Yale, 1953–54; Merton College, Oxford: Fellow and Tutor, 1953–79 (Hon. Fellow, 1980–84, 1994–); acting Warden, 1969–70, 1977–79; Sen. Proctor, Oxford Univ., 1967–68; Vice-Chancellor and Prof., Southampton Univ., 1979–85. Mem., Inst. for Advanced Study, Princeton, 1960–61; Vis. Prof., Univ. of S Carolina, 1961; Sec. of Harmsworth Trust, 1962–68; Member: Council, European Univ. Inst., 1980–88; US/UK Educn Commn, 1981–88; Gen. Cttee, Royal Literary Fund, 1975–; Bd, British Council, 1991–98. Trustee, Nat. Portrait Gall., 1984–98; Rhodes Trustee, 1988–94. Editor, English Historical Review, 1967–77; General Editor: Purnell's History of the 20th Century, 1967–69; The Short Oxford History of the Modern World, 1969–; The New Oxford History of England, 1979–. Pres. Council, Taunton Sch., 1978–89. Presenter, TV series, The Triumph of the West, 1985. Hon. DLitt Southampton, 1987. Cavalier, Order of Merit (Italy), 1991. *Publications:* French Revolution Documents, 1966; Europe 1880–1945, 1967, 3rd edn 2001; The Mythology of the Secret Societies, 1972; The Paris Commune from the Right, 1973; Revolution and Improvement: the Western World 1775–1847, 1976; History of the World, 1976, 3rd edn 1997; The French Revolution, 1978, 2nd edn 1997; The Triumph of the West, 1985; A History of Europe, 1996; Twentieth Century, 1999; articles and reviews in learned jls. *Recreation:* music. *Address:* c/o Merton College, Oxford OX1 4JD. *Clubs:* Oxford and Cambridge, Groucho, Grillion's.

ROBERTS, Rear-Adm. John Oliver, CB 1976; MNI; Managing Director, Demak Ltd, International Consultants, since 1983; *b* 4 April 1924; *er s* of J. V. and M. C. Roberts; *m* 1st, 1950, Lady Hermione Mary Morton Stuart (marr. diss. 1960; she *d* 1969); one *d*; 2nd, 1963, Honor Marigold Gordon Gray (marr. diss 1987); one *s* one *d*; 3rd, 1987, Sheila Violet Mary Traub (*née* Barker). *Educ:* RN Coll., Dartmouth. Served War: Midshipman, HM Ships Renown and Tartar, 1941–43; Sub-Lt, HMS Serapis, 1943–44; Lieut, 1945; Pilot Trg, 1944–46. HMS Triumph, 1947–49; RNAS, Lossiemouth, 1949–51; Flag-Lt to FOGT, 1952; Lt-Comdr, 1953; HMAS Vengeance and Sydney, 1953–54; RNVR, Southern Air Div., 1954–56; CO, No 803 Sqdn, HMS Eagle, 1957–58; Comdr, 1958; RNAS, Brawdy, 1958–60; CO, HMS St Bride's Bay, 1960–61; Naval Staff, 1962–64; Captain, 1964; CSO, Flag Officer Aircraft Carriers, 1964–66; CO, HMS Galatea, 1966–68; Naval Staff, 1968–70; CO, HMS Ark Royal, 1971–72; Rear-Adm., 1972; Flag Officer Sea Training, 1972–74; COS to C-in-C Fleet, 1974–76; Flag Officer, Naval Air Command, 1976–78. Non-exec. Dir, Aeronautical & General Instruments Ltd, 1981–82 (Head of Marketing and Sales, Defence Systems Div., 1980–81); Dir Gen., British Printing Industries Fedn, 1981–82. FRSA. *Recreations:* Rugby football, cricket, athletics, sailing, skiing. *Address:* Priory House, Blakesley, Northants. *Club:* East India, Devonshire, Sports and Public Schools.

ROBERTS, Julian; *see* Roberts, R. J.

ROBERTS, Prof. Kevin William Stuart, DPhil; Sir John Hicks Professor of Economics, University of Oxford, since 1999; Fellow, Nuffield College, Oxford, since 1999; *b* 29 Feb. 1952; *s* of Basil Roberts and Dorothy Roberts (*née* Heaven); *m* 1981, Julia Clarke (marr. diss. 1996); two *d*. *Educ:* Cheltenham Grammar Sch.; Univ. of Essex (BA Math. Econ. 1973); Nuffield Coll., Oxford (BPhil Econ. 1975; DPhil Econ. 1977). Jun. Res. Fellow, St John's Coll., Oxford, 1975–77; Asst Prof., MIT, 1977–78; Univ. Lectr and Official Fellow, St Catherine's Coll., Oxford, 1978–82; Professor: of Econ. Theory, Univ. of Warwick, 1982–87; of Economics, LSE, 1987–99. Fellow, Econometric Soc., 1984. *Publications:* articles in internat. learned jls incl. Econometrica and Rev. Econ. Studies. *Recreations:* country walks, old buildings and their preservation. *Address:* 94 Southmoor Road, Oxford OX2 6RB. *T:* (01865) 558468.

ROBERTS, Prof. Lewis Edward John, CBE 1978; FRS 1982; Wolfson Professor of Environmental Risk Assessment, University of East Anglia, 1986–90; Emeritus Professor, since 1990; *b* 31 Jan. 1922; *s* of William Edward Roberts and Lilian Lewis Roberts; *m* 1948, Eleanor Mary Luscombe; one *s*. *Educ:* Swansea Grammar Sch.; Jesus Coll., Oxford (MA, DPhil). Clarendon Laboratory, Oxford, 1944; Scientific Officer, Chalk River Res. Estabt, Ont, Canada, 1946–47; AERE, Harwell, 1947, Principal Scientific Officer, 1952; Commonwealth Fund Fellow, Univ. of Calif, Berkeley, 1954–55; Dep. Head, Chemistry Div., 1966, Asst Dir, 1967, Dir, 1975–86, AERE. Mem., UKAEA, 1979–86. Pres., British Nuclear Energy Soc., 1985–87; Mem. Council and Vice Pres., Royal Instn, 1991–94.

R. M. Jones Lectr, QUB, 1981; Rutherford Meml Lectr, Royal Soc., 1992. Governor, Abingdon Sch., 1978–86. *Publications:* Nuclear Power and Public Responsibility, 1984; Power Generation and the Environment, 1990; papers in qly revs and in scientific journals and IAEA pubns. *Recreations:* reading, gardening. *Address:* Penfold Wick, Chilton, Didcot OX11 0SH. *T:* (01235) 834309.

ROBERTS, Martin Geoffrey; Director, Insurance and Friendly Societies, Financial Services Authority, since 1999; Chairman, Friendly Societies Commission, since 1998; *b* 3 July 1946; *s* of Arthur and Mary Roberts; *m* 1969, Christine Muriel George; two *s*. *Educ:* Priory Grammar Sch., Shrewsbury; Worcester Coll., Oxford (MA). Min. of Technology, 1970; Private Sec. to Minister without Portfolio, 1973–74; seconded: to FCO, 1979–82; to DoE as Controller, Yorks and Humberside Regl Office, 1984–85; Sec., BOTB, 1985–89; Hd of Investigations Div., 1992–96, Dir, Finance and Resource Mgt, 1996–98, DTI; Dir, Insurance, HM Treasury, 1998. Mem., Exec. Cttee, 1998–, Chm., Tech. Cttee, 2000–, Internat. Assoc. of Insce Supervisors. *Recreation:* sailing. *Address:* Financial Services Authority, 25 North Colonnade, Canary Wharf, E14 5HS. *T:* (020) 7676 1000.

ROBERTS, Rev. Michael Graham Vernon; Principal, Westcott House, Cambridge, since 1993; *b* 4 Aug. 1943; *s* of Walter Graham Southall Roberts and Pamela Middleton Roberts (*née* Abel, now Murray); *m* 1970, Susan Elizabeth (*née* Merry); one *s* two *d*. *Educ:* Eton Coll.; Keble Coll., Oxford (BA 1965; MA); Cuddesdon Coll.; Church Divinity Sch. of Pacific, Berkeley, Calif. (MDiv 1967). Curate, Exmouth, 1967–70; Chaplain, Clare Coll., Cambridge, 1970–74; Vicar, St Mark, Bromley, 1974–79; Tutor, Queen's Coll., Birmingham, 1979–85; Team Rector, High Wycombe, 1985–90; Vice-Principal, Westcott House, Cambridge, 1990–93. *Recreations:* gardening, walking, gites, reading, Devon, Israel and Palestine. *Address:* Westcott House, Jesus Lane, Cambridge CB5 8BP. *T:* (01223) 741000.

ROBERTS, Michèle Brigitte, (Mrs L. J. Latter); novelist and poet; *b* 20 May 1949; *d* of Reginald George Roberts and Monique Pauline Joseph (*née* Caulle); *m* 1991, Laurence James Latter. *Educ:* Somerville Coll., Oxford (MA); University Coll. London. ALA 1972; FRSL 1999. British Council Librarian, Bangkok, 1973–74; writer, 1974–; Poetry Editor: Spare Rib, 1974; City Limits, 1981–83. Vis. Fellow in Creative Writing, UEA, 1992; Research Fellow in Writing, 1995–96, Vis. Prof., 1996–, Nottingham Trent Univ. Chm., Lit. Cttee, British Council, 1998–. Mem., Soc. of Authors. *Publications: novels:* A Piece of the Night, 1978; The Visitation, 1983; The Wild Girl, 1984; The Book of Mrs Noah, 1987; In the Red Kitchen, 1990; Daughters of the House, 1992 (W. H. Smith Literary Award, 1993); Flesh and Blood, 1994; Impossible Saints, 1997; Fair Exchange, 1999; The Looking-Glass, 2000; *stories:* During Mother's Absence, 1993; The Yellow-Haired Boy, 2000; Playing Sardines, 2001; *poetry:* The Mirror of the Mother, 1986; Psyche and the Hurricane, 1991; All the Selves I Was, 1995; *plays:* The Journeywoman, 1988; Child-Lover, 1995; *film:* The Heavenly Twins, 1993; *essays:* Food, Sex and God: on inspiration and writing, 1998; *anthology:* (ed jtly) Mind Readings, 1996. *Recreations:* cooking, gardening. *Address:* c/o Gillon Aitken, Gillon Aitken Associates, 29 Fernshaw Road, SW10 0TG. *T:* (020) 7351 7561.

ROBERTS, Patrick John; Consultant, Abel Hadden and Co. Ltd, since 1999; *b* 21 Oct. 1942; *s* of Frank and Hilda Mary Roberts; *m* 1978, Alison Mary Taylor; one *s* one *d*. *Educ:* Rotherham Grammar Sch.; Lincoln Coll., Oxford (BA Hons Modern Langs). Foreign Office, 1965; Bangkok, 1966; FCO, 1970; First Sec., Lagos, 1971; FCO, 1974; UK Repn to EEC, Brussels, 1977; FCO, 1980; Counsellor (Inf.), Paris, 1984. Edelman Public Relations Worldwide: Dir of Eur. Affairs, 1989–90; Dir of Public, then Business and Corporate, Affairs, 1991–95; Dep. Man. Dir, 1995–99. *Recreation:* cooking. *Address:* Abel Hadden and Co. Ltd, 15 Berkeley Street, W1J 8DY. *T:* (020) 7629 8771. *Club:* Oxford and Cambridge.

ROBERTS, Paul; *see* Roberts, D. P.

ROBERTS, Prof. Paul Harry, PhD, ScD; FRS 1979; FRAS; Professor of Mathematics, University of California at Los Angeles, since 1986; *b* 13 Sept. 1929; *s* of Percy Harry Roberts and Ethel Frances (*née* Mann); *m* 1989, Mary Frances (*née* Tabrett). *Educ:* Ardwyn Grammar Sch., Aberystwyth; University Coll. of Wales, Aberystwyth; Gonville and Caius Coll., Cambridge (George Green Student; BA, MA, PhD, ScD). FRAS 1955. Res. Associate, Univ. of Chicago, 1954–55; Scientific Officer, AWRE, 1955–56; ICI Fellow in Physics, 1956–59, Lectr in Phys, 1959–61, Univ. of Durham; Associate Prof. of Astronomy, Univ. of Chicago, 1961–63; Prof. of Applied Maths, Univ. of Newcastle upon Tyne, 1963–85. Fellow: Amer. Geophysical Union; Amer. Acad. of Arts and Scis. Editor, Geophysical and Astrophysical Fluid Dynamics, 1976–91. John Adam Fleming Medal, Amer. Geophysical Union, 1999. *Publications:* An Introduction to Magnetohydrodynamics, 1967; contrib. to Geophys. and Astrophys. Fluid Dyn., Jl Low Temp. Phys., Astrophys. Jl, Jl Fluid Mech., Jl Phys. Soc. and Proc. and Trans Royal Soc. *Recreations:* playing bassoon, chess. *Address:* Department of Mathematics, UCLA, Los Angeles, CA 90095, USA. *T:* (310) 8257764; (310) 2062707.

ROBERTS, Percy Charles; Chairman and Chief Executive, Mirror Group Newspapers Ltd, 1977–80; *b* 30 July 1920; *s* of late Herbert Bramwell Roberts and Alice (*née* Lang); *m* 1st 1946, Constance Teresa Violet Butler (marr. diss. 1977); two *s*; 2nd, 1978, Pauline Moore. *Educ:* Brighton Hove and Sussex Grammar Sch. Reporter, Sussex Daily News, 1936–39. Served War of 1939–45: Sussex Yeomanry, in France and ME (Captain). Sub-Editor, Egyptian Mail, Cairo, 1946; Reporter, Mid-East Mail, Palestine, 1947; Sub-Editor: Sussex Daily News, 1948; Liverpool Daily Post, 1949; Editor, Nigerian Citizen, 1949–51; Editorial Adviser, Gen. Manager, Managing Dir, Nigerian Daily Times, 1951–60; Managing Dir, Mirror Gp Newspapers in Caribbean, 1960–62; Gen. Manager, Mirror Newspapers in Manchester, 1962–66; Dir, 1964–80, Managing Dir, 1966–80, Daily Mirror Newspapers Ltd; Vice-Chm., West of England Newspapers Ltd, 1965–69; Managing Dir, IPC Newspapers Ltd, 1968–75; Dir, Scottish Daily Record & Sunday Mail Ltd, 1969–74; Chm., Overseas Newspapers Ltd, 1969–75; Dep. Chm. and Chief Exec., Mirror Gp Newspapers Ltd, 1975–77. Dir, Reed Publishing Holdings Ltd, 1975–80; Mem., Reed Internat. UK Cttee, 1975–80. Mem., CBI Employment Policy Cttee, 1975–78. Mem. Council, CPU, 1979–83. Pres., Ross Rotary Club, 1992–93; Mem., Ross CAB. CIMgt. *Address:* Magnolia Cottage, Bromsash, Ross-on-Wye, Herefordshire HR9 7PR. *T:* (01989) 750706. *Club:* MCC.

ROBERTS, Philip Bedlington; a Recorder of the Crown Court, 1982–93; Consultant, Scholfield Roberts & Hill, 1990–97; *b* 15 Dec. 1921; *s* of late R. J. S. Roberts, solicitor and A. M. Roberts; *m* 1944, Olive Margaret, *d* of E. R. Payne, Mugswell, Chipstead, Surrey; one *s* one *d*. *Educ:* Dawson Court, Kensington; St Matthew's Sch., Bayswater. RAFVR, 1940–46. Admitted solicitor, 1949; in private practice with Scholfield Roberts & Hill, 1950–75; part-time Chm. of Industrial Tribunals, 1966–75, 1990–94, Chm., 1975–84, Regional Chm. (Bristol), 1984–90, retd. Chairman: Nat. Insce Tribunals, 1959–75; Compensation Appeals Tribunal, 1962. Solicitor, Somerset British Legion, 1960–75. *Publications:* contribs to professional jls. *Recreations:* illiterate computing, fair weather, gardening. *Address:* Charlynch House, Spaxton, Bridgwater, Somerset TA5 1BY. *T:* (01278) 671356. *Club:* Royal Air Force.

ROBERTS, Phyllida Katharine S.; *see* Stewart-Roberts.

ROBERTS, Hon. (Priscilla) Jane (Stephanie), (Hon. Lady Roberts), LVO 1995 (MVO 1985); Curator of the Print Room, Royal Library, Windsor Castle, since 1975; *b* 4 Sept. 1949; *d* of 1st Baron Aldington, KCMG, CBE, DSO, TD, PC; *m* 1975, Hugh Ashley Roberts (*see* Sir H. A. Roberts); two *d*. *Educ:* Cranborne Chase School; Westfield College, Univ. of London (BA Hons); Courtauld Inst., Univ. of London (MA). *Publications:* Holbein, 1979; Leonardo: Codex Hammer, 1981; Master Drawings in the Royal Collection, 1985; Royal Artists, 1987; A Dictionary of Michelangelo's Watermarks, 1988; (jtly) Leonardo da Vinci, 1989; A Souvenir Album of Sandby Views of Windsor, 1990; A King's Purchase: King George III and the Collection of Consul Smith, 1993; Holbein and the Court of Henry VIII, 1993; Views of Windsor: watercolours by Thomas and Paul Sandby, 1995; Royal Landscape: the gardens and parks of Windsor, 1997; Ten Religious Masterpieces: a Millennium Celebration, 2000; articles in Burlington Magazine, Report of Soc. of Friends of St George's. *Recreations:* singing, sewing. *Address:* Adelaide Cottage, Home Park, Windsor, Berks SL4 2JQ. *T:* (01753) 855581.

ROBERTS, Ven. Raymond Harcourt, CB 1984; Chairman, Customer Service Committee for Wales, Office of Water Services, 1990–2001; licensed to officiate, diocese of Llandaff, since 1995; *b* 14 April 1931; *s* of Thomas Roberts and Carrie Maud Roberts. *Educ:* St Edmund Hall, Oxford (MA English); St Michael's Theol Coll., Llandaff. Nat. Service, RN, 1949–51. Deacon 1956, priest 1957, dio. of Monmouth (Curate of Bassaleg); Chaplain RNVR, 1958, RN, 1959; Destroyers and Frigates, Far East, 1959; HMS Pembroke, 1962; Dartmouth Trng Sqdn, 1963; RM Commando Course, 1965; 45 Commando, S. Arabia, 1965; RN Engrg Coll., 1967; HMS Bulwark, 1968; BRNC Dartmouth, 1970; HMS Ark Royal, 1974; Commando Trng Centre, RM, 1975; HMS Drake and HM Naval Base, Plymouth, 1979; Chaplain of the Fleet and Archdeacon for RN, 1980–84, Archdeacon Emeritus, 1985–; QHC, 1980–84; Hon. Canon, Cathedral of Holy Trinity, Gibraltar, 1980–84; Gen. Sec., Jerusalem and ME Church Assoc., 1985–89; licensed, dio. of Guildford, 1986–91; Hon. Chaplain, Llandaff Cathedral, 1991–95. Mem., Nat. Customer Council, Ofwat, 1993–2001. Chaplain: Welsh Livery Guild, 1993–; to the High Sheriff of S Glam, 1993–94; Drapers' Co., 1996–97. Governor, Rougemont Sch., Gwent, 1993–. *Recreations:* cooking and listening to Mozart, not necessarily simultaneously. *Address:* 8 Baynton Close, Llandaff, Cardiff CF5 2NZ. *T:* (029) 2057 8044.

ROBERTS, Richard (David Hallam); occasional academic and writer, yachtmaster, bookbinder's mate, competent househusband, gardener, woodman, antiquarian cyclist; *b* 27 July 1931; *s* of Arthur Hallam Roberts, Barrister-at-law, sometime Attorney-General, Zanzibar, and Ruvé Constance Jessie Roberts; *m* 1960, Wendy Ewen Mount; three *s*. *Educ:* King's Sch., Canterbury; Jesus Coll., Cambridge. Commissioned into RA 6th Field Regt, 1952. Asst Master, King's Sch., Canterbury, 1956; Housemaster, 1957; Head of Modern Language Dept, 1961; Senior Housemaster, 1965; Headmaster: Wycliffe Coll., Stonehouse, 1967–80; King Edward's Sch., Witley, 1980–85. Chairman: Alde and Ore Assoc., 1991–94; Orford Town Trust, 1995–99. *Address:* Smithy Cottage, Orford, Suffolk IP12 2NW. *Club:* Orford Sailing.

ROBERTS, Dr Richard John, FRS 1995; Director of Research, New England Biolabs, since 1992; *b* 6 Sept. 1943; *s* of John Walter Roberts and Edna Wilhelmina Roberts; *m* 1st, 1965, Elizabeth Dyson; one *s* one *d*; 2nd, 1986, Jean (*née* Tagliabue); one *s* one *d*. *Educ:* Sheffield Univ. (BSc Chm. 1965; PhD 1968). Harvard University: Res. Fellow, 1969–70; Res. Associate in Biochem., 1971–72; Cold Spring Harbor Laboratory: Sen. Staff Investigator, 1972–86; Asst Dir for Research, 1986–92. Miller Prof., UC Berkeley, 1991. Mem., Editl Bd, Computer Applications in the Bioscis, 1985–; Exec. Editor, Nucleic Acids Res., 1987– (Mem. Editl Bd, 1977–); Panel Mem., NLM Study Section, Comp. Biol, 1993–. Hon. MD Uppsala, 1992; Hon. MD Bath, 1994; Hon. DSc Sheffield, 1994. (Jtly) Nobel Prize in Physiology or Medicine, 1993. *Publications:* numerous papers on restriction endonucleases, DNA methylases, computational molecular biology. *Recreations:* collecting games, croquet. *Address:* New England Biolabs, 32 Tozer Road, Beverly, MA 01915, USA. *T:* (508) 9273382.

ROBERTS, (Richard) Julian, FSA; Deputy Librarian, 1986–97, and Keeper of Printed Books, 1974–97, Bodleian Library, Oxford; Fellow of Wolfson College, Oxford, 1975–97, now Emeritus; *b* 18 May 1930; *s* of A. R. and K. M. Roberts; *m* 1957, Anne Ducé; one *s* one *d*. *Educ:* King Edward's Sch., Birmingham; Magdalen Coll., Oxford. ALA 1956; FSA 1983. Asst Keeper, BM, 1958–74. Vicegerent, Wolfson Coll., Oxford, 1983–85. Regents' Prof., UCLA, 1991. Pres., Bibliographical Soc., 1986–88. *Publications:* (ed) Bewty in Raggs: poems by Cardell Goodman, 1958; John Dee's Library Catalogue, 1990; contrib. to Library, Book Collector, Jl of Librarianship, etc. *Recreations:* walking, antiquarianism. *Address:* St John's Farm House, Tackley, Oxford OX5 3AT. *T:* (01869) 331249.

ROBERTS, Robert Evan, CBE 1976; National General Secretary, National Council of YMCAs, 1965–75; *b* 16 July 1912; *s* of late Robert Thomas Roberts, Llanilar, Denbighshire; *m* 1939, Rhoda, *d* of late William Driver, Burnley, Lancs; one *s* one *d*. *Educ:* Cilcain, Flintshire; Liverpool. YMCA: Asst Sec.: Central YMCA Liverpool, 1933; Hornsey (N London), 1935; Asst Div. Sec., Lancs/Cheshire, 1937; Div. Sec., NW Div. (Cumberland, Westmorland, N Lancs), 1939; Dep. Dir, YMCA Welfare Services, NW Europe, 1944–46; Mem. 21st Army Gp, Council of Voluntary Welfare Work, 1944–46 (mentioned in despatches). Nat. Sec., Ireland, 1946; Sec., Personnel Dept, Nat. Council of YMCAs, London, 1948; Nat. Sec., Nat. Council of YMCAs, Wales, 1956–65; Hon. Sec/Treasurer, Assoc. of Secs of YMCAs of Gt Brit. and Ireland, 1963–65; Dep. Chm., Welsh Standing Conf. of Nat. Vol. Youth Orgs. 1963–65. Past Member: Welsh Nat. Council of Social Service; Welsh Jt Educn Cttee; Nat. Inst. of Adult Educn. Member: Nat. Council of Social Service, 1965–75; Brit. Council of Churches (and its Exec.), 1965–74; Council of Voluntary Welfare Work, 1965–75; World Council of YMCAs (and its Finance Cttee), 1965–75; Vice-Pres., Welsh Nat. Council of YMCAs, 1975; Chm., Job Creation Programme, Barrow and S Lakeland, 1976–80; Exec. Member: SE Cumbria Community Health Council, 1977–82; S Lakeland Voluntary Action, 1978–85; S Cumbria Community Health Council, 1982–92 (Vice-Chm., 1986–89); S Cumbria DHA Ethics of Medical Research Cttee, 1983–92; Cumbria FHSA, 1990–92; CHC Observer, Cumbria FPC, 1984–90. Trustee, Framlington Trust, 1973–96. Age Concern: Mem., 1976–82, Vice Chm., 1981–82, Exec. Cttee, Cumbria; Chm., S Lakeland, 1977–82; Exec. Mem. and Trustee, Kendal and Ulveston. Meals on Wheels, 1975–86, Books on Wheels, 1986–97, S Cumbria Social Services Dept. Dist Judge, Cumbria Best Kept Village, 1977–85; Warden, Lakeland Horticultural Soc. Gardens, 1977–98. Fellow, Royal Commonwealth Soc., 1974. Silver Jubilee Medal, 1977. *Recreation:* househusband. *Address:* 19 Strand Court, The Esplanade, Grange over Sands, Cumbria LA11 7HH. *T:* (01539) 533277.

ROBERTS, Prof. Ronald John, PhD; FRCPath, FIBiol, FRCVS; FRSE; Professor of Aquatic Pathobiology and Director, Institute of Aquaculture, University of Stirling, 1971–96, now Professor Emeritus; *b* 28 March 1941; *s* of Ronald George Roberts and Marjorie Kneale; *m* 1964, Helen, *d* of Gordon Gregor Macgregor; two *s*. *Educ:* Campbeltown Grammar Sch., Argyll; Univ. of Glasgow Vet. Sch. (PhD, BVMS). FIBiol 1984; FRCPath 1988; FRCVS 1992; FRSE 1978. Univ. of Glasgow: Asst in Microbiology, 1964–66; Lectr in Vet. Pathology, 1966–71. Hagerman Dist. Vis. Prof., Univ. of Idaho, 1997–. Consultant in Fish Diseases: Dept Agric. and Fisheries for Scotland, 1968–71; ODA, now DFID, 1974–; FAO, Rome, 1978–83; World Bank, 1989. Dir, Machrihanish Marine Envmtl Res. Lab., 1991–96. Mem., Cabinet Office Science Panel, 1993–94; Res. Grants Panel, SHEFC, 2001–. Editor: Jl Fish Diseases, 1978–; Aquaculture Research (formerly Aquaculture and Fisheries Management), 1978–2000. Chm., Stirling Aquaculture, 1987–95; Director: Stirling Salmon, 1987–94; Tarbert Fyne Foods, 1987–90; Stirling Aquatic Technology, 1987–90; Campbeltown and Kintyre Enterprise, 1992– (Chm., 1996–); Landcatch Ltd, 1996–. Scientific Advr, Lithgow Gp, 1996–. Chm., Argyll and Bute Countryside Trust, 1994–; Sec., Lady Linda McCartney Meml Trust. Buckland Prof. and Medallist, 1985–86; C-Vet Award, BVA, 1989; Dalrymple-Champneys Cup and Medal, BVA, 1990. Commander, Most Noble Order of the Crown (Thailand), 1992. *Publications:* (with C. J. Shepherd) Handbook of Salmon and Trout Diseases, 1974, 3rd edn 1996; Fish Pathology, 1978, 3rd edn 2000; various scientific publications on histopathology of fishes. *Recreations:* arboriculture, rhododendron culture, golf, squash, admiring and conserving the Scottish natural environment. *Address:* 9 Alexander Drive, Bridge of Allan, Stirling FK9 4QB. *T:* (01786) 833078; Carrick Point Farm, Ardnacross Shorelands, by Campbeltown, Argyll PA28 5QR. *T:* (01586) 554417. *Clubs:* Farmers', Royal Commonwealth Society; Machrihanish Golf (Kintyre).

ROBERTS, Sir Samuel, 4th Bt *cr* 1919, of Ecclesall and Queen's Tower, City of Sheffield; Barrister; *b* 16 April 1948; *s* of Sir Peter Geoffrey Roberts, 3rd Bt, and Judith Randell (*d* 1998), *d* of late Randell G. Hempson; *S* father, 1985; *m* 1977, Georgina Ann, *yr d* of David Cory; one *s* three *d*. *Educ:* Harrow School; Sheffield Univ. (LLB); Manchester Business School. Called to the Bar, Inner Temple, 1972. Chairman: Cleyfield Properties Ltd, 1984–; Wiltshire and Co. Ltd, 1988–; Angermann, Goddard and Loyd Ltd, 1994. *Heir: s* Samuel Roberts, *b* 12 Aug. 1989. *Address:* 6 Caversham Street, SW3 4AH.

ROBERTS, Sir Sidney; *see* Roberts, Sir E. F. S.

ROBERTS, Stephen Cheveley; Headmaster, Felsted School, since 1993; *b* 23 Aug. 1956; *s* of David Roberts and Elizabeth Roberts (*née* Thornborough); *m* 1985, Joanna Meryl Cunnison; two *s*. *Educ:* Mill Hill Sch.; University Coll., Oxford (BA 1978; PGCE 1979; MA 1982). Credit Analyst, Orion Bank, 1979–80; Asst Master, Christ's Hosp., Horsham, 1980–86; Oundle School: Hd of Physics, 1986–90; Housemaster, 1990–93. *Recreations:* golf, hockey, music, reading. *Address:* Stephenson's, Stebbing Road, Felsted, Dunmow, Essex CM6 3JD. *T:* (01371) 820258. *Clubs:* East India; Vincent's (Oxford).

ROBERTS, Sir Stephen (James Leake), Kt 1981; Chairman, Milk Marketing Board, 1977–87; *b* 13 April 1915; *s* of Frank Roberts and Annie Leake; *m* 1940, Muriel Hobbins; two *s* two *d*. *Educ:* Wellington Grammar Sch. Farmer; founded Wrekin Farmers Ltd, 1960 (Chm., 1960–77); founded Dairy Crest, 1980, Chm., 1980–86. Shropshire delegate to NFU Council, 1962–70; Member: W Midland Region, MMB, 1966–87; Food from Britain Council, 1983–87. *Recreation:* football (now spectator). *Address:* Lydebrook House, Coalmoor Road, Little Wenlock, Telford, Shropshire TF6 5AS. *T:* (01952) 504569. *Club:* Farmers'.

ROBERTS, Stephen Pritchard; baritone; professional singer, since 1972; *b* 8 Feb. 1949; *s* of Edward Henry Roberts and Violet Pritchard. *Educ:* Royal College of Music (schol.). ARCM 1969; GRSM 1971. Professional Lay-Cleric, Westminster Cathedral Choir, 1972–76; now sings regularly in London, UK and Europe, with all major orchs and choral socs; has also sung in USA, Canada, Israel, Hong Kong, Singapore and S America. Mem., Vocal Faculty, RCM, 1993–. *Opera* rôles include: Count, in Marriage of Figaro; Falke, in Die Fledermaus; Ubalde, in Armide; Ramiro, in Ravel's L'Heure Espagnole; Aeneas, in Dido and Aeneas; Don Quixote, in Master Peter's Puppet Show; Mittenhofer, in Elegy for Young Lovers; *television* appearances include: Britten's War Requiem; Weill's Seven Deadly Sins; Delius' Sea Drift; Handel's Jeptha; Handel's Judas Maccabaeus; Penderecki's St Luke Passion, 1983 Proms; Walton's Belshazar's Feast, 1984 Proms; *recordings* include: Tippett's King Priam; Birtwistle's Punch and Judy; Gluck's Armide; Orff's Carmina Burana; Vaughan Williams' Five Mystical Songs, Epithalamion, Sea Symphony, Fantasia on Christmas Carols, Hodie, and Serenade; Elgar's Apostles, and Caractacus; Penderecki's St Luke Passion; Fauré's Requiem; Dyson's Canterbury Pilgrims; Stravinsky songs; works by J. S. Bach, C. P. E. Bach and Duruflé; records for co. which sends classical music through internet. *Address:* 144 Gleneagle Road, SW16 6BA. *T:* (020) 8516 8830, *Fax:* (020) 8516 8831.

ROBERTS, Stewart Brian, MA; Headmaster, Dauntsey's School, since 1997; *b* 21 March 1952; *s* of late Evan John and Joyce Roberts; *m* 1985, Anna Susan Norman; one *s* one *d*. *Educ:* Birkenhead Sch.; St Peter's Coll., Oxford (BA 1974; PGCE 1975; MA 1978). Asst Master, Birkenhead Sch., 1975–78; Asst Master, 1978–93, (Housemaster, 1984–93), Shrewsbury Sch.; Headmaster-des., Chand Bagh Sch., Lahore, 1994; Second Master, Dauntsey's Sch., 1995–97. Gov., St Francis Sch., Pewsey, 1997–. Freeman, City of London, 2000. *Address:* Headmaster's House, Dauntsey's School, West Lavington, near Devizes, Wilts SN10 4HE. *T:* (01380) 814500.

ROBERTS, Prof. Thomas Michael, PhD; CBiol, FIBiol; Chief Executive, Central Science Laboratory, Department of Environment, Food and Rural Affairs, since 2001; *b* 12 May 1948; *e s* of Robert Stanley Roberts and Mary Roberts (*née* Cliffe); *m* 1968, Ann Vaughan-Williams; one *s* two *d*. *Educ:* St Asaph Grammar Sch.; Univ. of Wales, Swansea (BSc 1969; PhD 1972). CBiol 1991; FIBiol 1991; MIEEM 1995. Asst Prof., Dept of Botany, Univ. of Toronto, 1972–74; Lectr, Dept of Botany, Univ. of Liverpool, 1974–78; Section Head, Terrestrial Ecology, Biology Section, CEGB, 1978–89; Dir, Inst. of Terrestrial Ecology, 1989–99, Dir, Centre for Ecology and Hydrology, 1999–2001, NERC; Hon. Prof., York Univ., 1993–. Ed., Jl of Applied Ecology, 1981–86. Member: DoE Adv. Cttee on Hazardous Substances, 1992–2000; HSE Adv. Cttee on Genetic Modification, 1994–99; MAFF Adv. Cttee on Pesticides, 1996–2001. Chm., UK Man and Biosphere Cttee, 1993–2001. Trustee, Nat. Biodiversity Network, 2000–01. *Publications:* Planning and Ecology, 1984; Ecological Aspects of Radionuclide Releases, 1985; numerous articles on applied ecology in learned jls. *Recreations:* village cricket, real ale, running, golf. *Address:* Central Science Laboratory, Department of Environment, Food and Rural Affairs, Sand Hutton, York YO41 1LZ.

ROBERTS, Thomas Somerville; JP; FCIT; Chairman, Milford Haven Conservancy Board, 1976–82; *b* Ruabon, N Wales, 10 Dec. 1911; *s* of Joseph Richard Roberts, Rhosllanerchrugog and Lily Agnes (*née* Caldwell); *m* 1st, 1938, Ruth Moira Teasdale; two *s*; 2nd, 1950, Margaret Peggy Anderson, Sunderland. *Educ:* Roath Park Elem. Sch., Cardiff; Cardiff High Sch.; Balliol Coll., Oxford (Domus Exhibnr). Traffic Apprentice, LNER, 1933; Docks Manager, Middlesbrough and Hartlepool, 1949; Chief Docks Manager: Hull, 1959; S Wales, 1962; Port Dir, S Wales Ports, 1970–75. Chm., S Wales Port Employers, 1962–75; Member: Nat. Jt Council for Port Transport Industry, 1962–75; Nat. Dock Labour Bd, 1970–75; Race Relations Bd, 1968–76. Dir, Develt Corp. for Wales, 1965–80, Vice-Pres. 1979–83; Dep. Chm., Welsh Develt Agency, 1976–80. Member: Court, Univ. of Wales; Pwyllgor Tywysog Cymru (Prince of Wales' Cttee), 1977–81; Exec. Cttee, Welsh Environment Foundn, 1977–. Hon. Fellow and Life Governor, Univ. of Wales Coll. Cardiff (formerly University Coll., Cardiff and UWIST). JP City of Cardiff, 1966. *Recreation:* TV. *Address:* Marcross Lodge, 9 Ely Road, Llandaff, Cardiff CF5 2JE. *T:* (029) 2056 1153.

ROBERTS, Sir William (James Denby), 3rd Bt *cr* 1909; *b* 10 Aug. 1936; *s* of Sir James Denby Roberts, 2nd Bt, OBE, and of Irene Charlotte D'Orsey, *yr d* of late William Dunn, MB, CM; *S* father, 1973. *Educ:* Rugby; Royal Agricultural Coll., Cirencester. MRAC, FRICS. Farms at Strathallan Castle. Founder, 1969, and owner 1969–81, Strathallan Aircraft Collection. *Recreations:* swimming and flying. *Heir: nephew* James Elton Denby Roberts-Buchanan, *b* 12 July 1966. *Address:* Strathallan Castle, Auchterarder, Perthshire PH3 1JZ. *T:* (01764) 662131.

ROBERTS CAIRNS, Patricia Rose Marie, (Mrs D. A. O. Cairns), OBE 2000; Consultant, National Magazine Co., since 1999; *b* 27 Nov. 1947; *d* of late Maj. William Roberts, MBE, RA and Catherine (*née* Slawson); *m* 1993, Dr David A. O. Cairns. *Educ:* St Barnabas Sch., Woodford Green. Reporter, Independent Newspapers, Essex, 1965–68; features writer, IPC mags, 1968–72; Founder Editor, Girl About Town (London's first free mag.), 1972–80; feature writer, Femail, Daily Mail, 1980–82; Associate Editor, Family Circle, 1982–84; Editor, Over 21, 1984–89; Founder Editor, House Beautiful, 1989–95; Editor-in-Chief, Good Housekeeping, 1995–99. Member: Editl Cttee, Periodical Trng Council, 1992–; Women of Year Cttee, 1993–; BSME Cttee, 1993–99; Editl Public Affairs Cttee, PPA, 1993–99; Press Complaints Commn, 1998–99. FRSA. Launch Editor of Year, BSME, 1990; Editor of Year, PPA, 1992. *Publications:* Living Images: styling yourself to success, 1990; House Beautiful Home Handbook, 1992. *Address:* 12 Clifton Terrace, Brighton BN1 3HA. *Club:* University Women's.

ROBERTS-WEST, Lt-Col George Arthur Alston-; *see* West.

ROBERTSHAW, Patrick Edward; His Honour Judge Robertshaw; a Circuit Judge, since 1994; *b* 7 July 1945; *s* of late George Edward Robertshaw and May (*née* Tallis); *m* 1972, Sally Christine Greenburgh (*née* Searle); two *s* two *d*. *Educ:* Hipperholme Grammar Sch.; Southampton Univ. (LLB). Called to the Bar, Inner Temple, 1968; a Recorder, 1989–94. *Publications:* contrib. to legal periodicals. *Recreations:* reading, listening to music, travel, photography. *Address:* Sheffield Combined Court Centre, 50 West Bar, Sheffield S3 8PH. *T:* (0114) 281 2400.

ROBERTSON, family name of **Barons Robertson of Oakridge, Robertson of Port Ellen** and **Wharton**.

ROBERTSON, Hon. Lord; Ian Macdonald Robertson, TD 1946; a Senator of the College of Justice in Scotland, 1966–87; *b* 30 Oct. 1912; *s* of late James Robertson and Margaret Eva Wilson, Broughty Ferry, Angus, and Edinburgh; *m* 1938, Anna Love Glen, *d* of late Judge James Fulton Glen, Tampa, Florida, USA; one *s* two *d*. *Educ:* Merchiston Castle School; Balliol College, Oxford; Edinburgh University. BA Oxford (Mod. Greats), 1934; LLB Edinburgh 1937; Vans Dunlop Schol. in Law, Edinburgh 1937. Member Faculty of Advocates, 1939; Advocate-Depute, 1949–51; QC (Scot.), 1954; Sheriff of Ayr and Bute, 1961–66; Sheriff of Perth and Angus, 1966. Chairman: Medical Appeals Tribunal, 1957–63; Scottish Jt Council for Teachers' Salaries, 1965–81; Scottish Valuation Adv. Council, 1977–86; Member Court of Session Rules Council; UK Rep., Central Council, Internat. Union of Judges, 1974–87. Formerly, External Examiner in law subjects, Aberdeen, Glasgow, Edinburgh and St Andrews Universities; Member Committee on Conflicts of Jurisdiction affecting Children, 1958; Governor of Merchiston Castle School, 1954, Chm., 1970–96; Assessor on Court of Edinburgh Univ., 1967–81. Chairman: Edinburgh Centre of Rural Economy, 1967–85; Edinburgh Centre for Tropical Veterinary Medicine. Served War of 1939–45, 8th Bn The Royal Scots (The Royal Regt); commd 1939; SO (Capt.), 44th Lowland Brigade (15th Scottish Division), Normandy and NW Europe (despatches). *Publication:* From Normandy to the Baltic, 1945. *Recreation:* golf. *Address:* 13 Moray Place, Edinburgh EH3 6DT. *T:* (0131) 225 6637. *Clubs:* New, Honourable Company of Edinburgh Golfers (Captain 1970–72).

ROBERTSON OF OAKRIDGE, 2nd Baron *cr* 1961; **William Ronald Robertson;** Bt 1919; Member of the London Stock Exchange, 1973–95; *b* 8 Dec. 1930; *s* of General Lord Robertson of Oakridge, GCB, GBE, KCMG, KCVO, DSO, MC, and Edith (*d* 1982), *d* of late J. B. Macindoe; *S* father, 1974; *m* 1972, Celia Jane, *d* of William R. Elworthy; one *s*. *Educ:* Hilton Coll., Natal; Charterhouse; Staff Coll., Camberley (psc). Served The Royal Scots Greys, 1949–69. Mem. Salters' Co (Master, 1985–86). *Heir: s* Hon. William Brian Elworthy Robertson, *b* 15 Nov. 1975.

ROBERTSON OF PORT ELLEN, Baron *cr* 1999 (Life Peer) of Islay in Argyll and Bute; **George Islay MacNeill Robertson;** PC 1997; Secretary-General, NATO, since 1999; *b* 12 April 1946; *s* of George Philip Robertson and Marion I. Robertson; *m* 1970, Sandra Wallace; two *s* one *d*. *Educ:* Dunoon Grammar Sch.; Univ. of Dundee (MA Hons 1968). Res. Asst, Tayside Study, 1968–69; Scottish Res. Officer, G&MWU, 1969–70, Scottish Organiser, 1970–78. MP (Lab) Hamilton, 1978–97, Hamilton South, 1997–99. PPS to Sec. of State for Social Services, 1979; opposition spokesman on Scottish Affairs, 1979–80, on Defence, 1980–81, on Foreign and Commonwealth Affairs, 1981–93; principal spokesman on European Affairs, 1984–93; principal opposition front bench spokesman on Scotland, 1993–97; Sec. of State for Defence, 1997–99. Chm., Scottish Labour Party, 1977–78; Mem., Scottish Exec. of Lab. Party, 1973–79, 1993–97; Sec., Manifesto Gp of PLP, 1979–84; Chm., British-German Parly Gp, 1992–93. Vice Chm. Bd, British Council, 1985–94; Vice-Pres., Raleigh Internat. (formerly Operation Raleigh), 1982–; Member: Bd, Scottish Develt Agency, 1975–78; Governing Body, GB/E Europe Centre, 1983–91 (Vice Chm., 1990–91); Council, RIIA, 1984–91; Steering Cttee, Atlantic Conf., 1987–; Council, GB/Russia Centre, 1986–97 (Vice-Chm., 1995–97); Council, BESO, 1991–97; Vice-Chm., Westminster Foundn for Democracy, 1992–94. Governor, Ditchley Foundn, 1989–. Hon. Regtl Col, London Scottish (Volunteers), 2000–. FRSA 1999. Hon. LLD: Dundee, Bradford, 2000; Baku State Univ., Azerbaijan, 2001; Hon. DSc RMCS Cranfield, 2000. Commander's Cross, Order of Merit (Germany), 1991; Grand Cross, Order of Star (Romania), 2000. *Recreations:* reading, family, photography, golf. *Address:* NATO, Boulevard Leopold III, 1110 Brussels, Belgium. *Clubs:* Army and Navy; Islay Golf.

ROBERTSON, Alastair, PhD; Director, Institute of Food Research, BBSRC, since 2000; *b* 18 July 1949; *s* of Robert Russell Robertson and Brenda Scott Robertson; *m* 1975, Wendy Kathleen Purchase; one *s* one *d*. *Educ:* Univ. of Bath (BSc Hons Applied Biology 1973; PhD Plant Biochemistry 1976). FRSC 1983; FIFST 1983. Postdoctoral Fellow,

Univ. of Cambridge, 1976–79; Process Biochemist, Sigma Chemical Co., 1979–81; Head of Chemistry and Biochemistry, 1981–86, Dir of Food Science, 1986–92, Campden and Chorley Wood Food Res. Assoc.; Head of Res. and Develt, 1992–95, Technical Dir, 1995–2000, Safeway Stores plc. Hon. Prof., UEA, 2000–. *Publications:* 50 articles in jls on biochemistry and food sci. areas. *Recreations:* gardening, music, angling, sports. *Address:* Institute of Food Research, Norwich Research Park, Colney, Norwich NR4 7HA.

ROBERTSON, Andrew James; QC 1996; a Recorder, since 1994; *b* 14 May 1953; *s* of Pearson Robertson and Zillah Robertson (*née* Robinson); *m* 1981, Gillian Amanda Frankel; two *s* one *d*. *Educ:* Bradford GS; Christ's Coll., Cambridge (MA Cantab). Called to the Bar, Middle Temple, 1975; North Eastern Circuit. *Recreations:* hockey, winter climbing, history. *Address:* 11 King's Bench Walk, Temple, EC4Y 7EQ.

ROBERTSON, Andrew Ogilvie, OBE 1994; Senior Partner, T. C. Young & Son, since 1994; *b* 30 June 1943; *s* of Alexander McArthur Ogilvie Robertson and Charlotte Rachel Robertson (*née* Cuthbert); *m* 1974, Sheila Sturton; two *s*. *Educ:* Sedbergh Sch.; Edinburgh Univ. (LLB 1964). Apprentice Solicitor, Maclay Murray & Spens, 1964–67; Asst Solicitor, 1967–68, Partner, 1968–, T. C. Young & Son. Secretary: Erskine Hosp., 1976–; Clydesdale Fedn of Community-based Housing Assocs, 1978–83 (also Treas.); Briggait Co. Ltd, 1983–88; Princess Royal Trust for Carers, 1990– (also legal Advr); Chairman: Post Office Users' Council for Scotland, 1988–99; Gtr Glasgow Community and Mental Health Services NHS Trust, 1994–97; Glasgow Royal Infirmary Univ. NHS Trust, 1997–99; Gtr Glasgow Primary Care NHS Trust, 1998–; Member: POUNC, 1988–99; Gtr Glasgow Health Bd, 1999–. Chm., Lintel Trust (formerly Scottish Housing Assocs Charitable Trust), 1990–; Trustee, Housing Assocs Charitable Trust (UK), 1990–97. Non exec. Dir, Scottish Building Soc., 1994–. Gov., Sedbergh Sch., 2000–. *Recreations:* climbing, sailing, swimming, reading, fishing. *Address:* 11 Kirklee Road, Glasgow G12 0RQ. *T:* (0141) 357 1555. *Club:* Western (Glasgow).

ROBERTSON, Angus; MP (SNP) Moray, since 2001; *b* 28 Sept. 1969. *Educ:* Broughton High Sch., Edinburgh; Univ. of Aberdeen (MA 1991). News Editor, Austrian Broadcasting Corp., 1991; reporter, BBC, Austria, etc, 1991–99; communications consultant and journalist, 1999–. SNP spokesman on foreign affairs, 2001–. Contested (SNP) Midlothian, Scottish Parlt, 1999. *Address:* (office) 17 South Street, Elgin, Moray IV30 1JZ; c/o House of Commons, SW1A 0AA.

ROBERTSON, Bryan Charles Francis, OBE 1961; author, broadcasting and television, etc; regular contributor to The Spectator; *b* 1 April 1925; *yr s* of A. F. Robertson and Ellen Dorothy Black; unmarried. *Educ:* Battersea Grammar School. Worked and studied in France and Germany, 1947–48; Director: Heffer Gallery, Cambridge, 1949–51; Whitechapel Art Gallery, London, 1952–68. Mem. Arts Council Art Panel, 1958–61, 1980–84; Mem. Contemporary Art Soc. Cttee, 1958–73. US Embassy Grant to visit United States, 1956; Lectr on art, Royal Ballet School, 1958; Ford Foundn Grant for research for writing, 1961; British Council Lecture Tour, SE Asia and Australian State Galleries, 1960. Dir, State Univ. of NY Museum, 1970–75. Since 1953 has organized major exhibitions at Whitechapel, including Turner, Hepworth, Moore, Stubbs, John Martin, Rowlandson and Gillray, Bellotto, Mondrian, de Stäel, Nolan, Davie, Smith, Malevich, Pollock, Richards, Australian Painting, Rothko, Tobey, Vaughan, Guston, Poliakof, Caro, Medley, etc. *Publications:* Jackson Pollock, a monograph, 1960; Sidney Nolan, a monograph, 1961; (jtly) Private View, 1965; (with H. Tatlock Miller) Loudon Sainthill, 1973; Edward Burra, 1978; contribs (art criticism) to London Magazine, Art News (US), Spectator, Harpers & Queen, Twentieth Century, Listener, Cambridge Review, Museums Jl, etc. *Address:* 73 Barnsbury Street, N1 1EJ. *Club:* Athenæum.

ROBERTSON, Rev. Charles; Parish Minister, Canongate (The Kirk of Holyroodhouse), since 1978; Chaplain: to the Queen in Scotland, since 1991; to the High Constables and Guard of Honour of Holyroodhouse, since 1993; *b* 22 Oct. 1940; *s* of late Thomas Robertson and Elizabeth Halley; *m* 1965, Alison Margaret Malloch; one *s* two *d*. *Educ:* Camphill School, Paisley; Edinburgh Univ. (MA); New College, Edinburgh. Asst Minister, North Morningside, Edinburgh, 1964–65; Parish Minister, Kiltearn, Ross-shire, 1965–78. Chaplain to Lord High Comr, 1990–91, 1996 (the Princess Royal). Convener, Gen. Assembly's Panel on Worship, 1995– (Sec., 1982–95); C of S rep. on Joint Liturgical Group, 1984– (Chm., 1994–99). Mem., Broadcasting Standards Council, 1988–91, 1992–93. Chaplain: Clan Donnachaidh Soc., 1981–96; New Club, Edinburgh, 1986–; Royal Scots Club, Edinburgh, 1998–; Moray House Coll. of Educn, then Edinburgh Univ. at Moray House, 1986–; No 2 (City of Edinburgh) Maritime HQ Unit, 1987–99, No 603 (City of Edinburgh) Sqn, 1999–, RAAF; Incorp. of Goldsmiths of City of Edinburgh, 2000–. Lectr, St Colm's Coll., 1980–94. Mem., Historic Buildings Council for Scotland, 1990–99. Chairman: Bd of Queensberry House Hosp., 1989–96 (Mem., 1978–); Queensberry Trust, 1996–; Gov., St Columba's Hospice, 1986–; Trustee: Edinburgh Old Town Trust, 1987–94; Edinburgh Old Town Charitable Trust, 1994–; Edinburgh World Heritage Trust, 1999–2000; Church Hymnary Trust, 1987–; Pres., Church Service Soc., 1988–91. JP Edinburgh, 1980–. Sec. of cttees which compiled Hymns for a Day, 1983, Songs of God's People, 1988, Worshipping Together, 1991, Clann ag Urnaigh, 1991, Common Order, 1994 and Ordinal and Service Book, 1997; Sec., Cttee to Revise Church Hymnary, 1995–. *Publications:* (ed) Singing the Faith, 1990; (ed) St Margaret Queen of Scotland and her Chapel, 1994; (jtly) By Lamplight, 2000. *Recreations:* Scottish and Edinburgh history and literature, hymnody, collecting Canongate miscellanea. *Address:* Manse of Canongate, Edinburgh EH8 8BR. *T:* (0131) 556 3515. *Clubs:* Athenæum; Puffins, New (Hon. Mem.), Royal Scots (Hon. Mem.) (Edinburgh).

ROBERTSON, Prof. (Charles) Martin, FBA 1967; Lincoln Professor of Classical Archæology and Art, University of Oxford, 1961–78; *b* 11 Sept. 1911; *s* of late Professor Donald Struan Robertson, FBA, FSA, and Petica Coursolles Jones; *m* 1st, 1942, Theodosia Cecil Spring Rice (*d* 1984); four *s* two *d*; 2nd, 1988, Louise Berge (*née* Holstein). *Educ:* Leys School, Cambridge; Trinity College, Cambridge (Hon. Fellow, 1987). BA Cambridge, 1934, MA 1947; student at British School of Archæology, Athens, 1934–36; Asst Keeper, Dept of Greek and Roman Antiquities, British Museum, 1936–48 (released for service, War of 1939–45, 1940–46); Yates Professor of Classical Art and Archæology in the Univ. of London (Univ. Coll.), 1948–61. Corresp. Mem., German Archæological Inst., 1953; Ordinary Mem., 1953; Chm., Man. Cttee, British School at Athens, 1958–68. Mem., Inst. for Advanced Study, Princeton, 1968–69. Guest Schol., J. Paul Getty Museum, Malibu, 1980 and 1988. Hon. Fellow: Lincoln Coll., Oxford, 1980; UCL, 1980. For. Hon. Mem., Archaeological Inst. of America, 1985. Hon. DLit QUB, 1978. Kenyon Medal, British Acad., 1987. *Publications:* Why Study Greek Art? (Inaugural Lecture), 1949; Greek Painting, 1959; Between Archæology and Art History (Inaugural Lecture), 1963; Crooked Connections (poems), 1970; indexes and editorial work in late Sir John Beazley's Paralipomena, 1971; For Rachel (poems), 1972; A History of Greek Art, 1975; (with Alison Frantz) The Parthenon Frieze, 1975; A Hot Bath at Bedtime (poems), 1977; The Sleeping Beauty's Prince (poem), 1977; (with John Boardman) Corpus Vasorum Antiquorum, Castle Ashby, 1978; A Shorter History of Greek Art, 1981; The Attic Black-figure and Red-figure Pottery, in Karageorghis, Excavations at Kition IV, 1981; Catalogue of Greek, Etruscan and Roman Vases in the Lady Lever Art Gallery, 1987; The Art of Vase-painting in Classical Athens, 1992; articles, notes and reviews since 1935, in British and foreign periodicals. *Address:* 7a Parker Street, Cambridge CB1 1JL. *T:* (01223) 311913.

ROBERTSON, Daphne Jean Black, WS; Sheriff of Lothian and Borders at Edinburgh, 1996–2000; *b* 31 March 1937; *d* of Rev. Robert Black Kincaid and Ann Parker Collins; *m* 1965, Donald Buchanan Robertson, *qv*. *Educ:* Hillhead High Sch.; Greenock Acad.; Edinburgh Univ. (MA); Glasgow Univ. (LLB). Admitted solicitor, 1961; WS 1977; Sheriff of Glasgow and Strathkelvin, 1979–96.

ROBERTSON, Donald Buchanan; QC (Scot.) 1973; Temporary Judge, Court of Session, Scotland, since 1991; *b* 29 March 1932; *s* of Donald Robertson, yachtbuilder, Sandbank, Argyll, and Jean Dunsmore Buchanan; *m* 1st, 1955, Louise Charlotte, *d* of Dr J. Linthorst-Homan; one *s* one *d*; 2nd, 1965, Daphne Jean Black Kincaid (*see* D. J. B. Robertson). *Educ:* Dunoon Grammar Sch.; Glasgow Univ. (LLB). Admitted Solicitor, 1954; Royal Air Force (National Service), 1954–56. Passed Advocate, 1960; Standing Junior to Registrar of Restrictive Practices, 1970–73. Member: Sheriff Court Rules Council, 1972–76; Royal Commn on Legal Services in Scotland, 1976–80; Legal Aid Central Cttee, 1982–85; Criminal Injuries Compensation Bd, 1986–; Chm., VAT Tribunal, 1978–85. Hon. Sheriff, Lothian and Peebles, 1982–. FSA (Scot.) 1982. *Recreations:* shooting, numismatics, genealogy. *Address:* 11 Grosvenor Crescent, Edinburgh EH12 5EL. *T:* (0131) 337 5544; Cranshaws Castle, By Duns, Berwickshire TD11 3SJ. *T:* (01361) 890268. *Club:* New (Edinburgh).

ROBERTSON, Geoffrey Ronald; QC 1988; a Recorder, since 1999; barrister; author; *b* 30 Sept. 1946; *s* of Francis Albert Robertson and Bernice Joy (*née* Beattie); *m* 1990, Kathy Lette; one *s* one *d*. *Educ:* Epping Boys' High Sch.; Univ. of Sydney (BA 1966; LLB Hons 1970); University Coll., Oxford (BCL 1972; Rhodes Schol.). Called to the Bar, Middle Temple, 1973, Bencher, 1997; Supreme Court of NSW, 1977, of Antigua, 1990, of Trinidad, 1992. An Asst Recorder, 1993–99. Head, Doughty Street Chambers, 1990–. Visiting Fellow: Univ. of NSW, 1977; Warwick Univ., 1980–81; Vis. Prof., Birkbeck Coll., London Univ., 1997–. Consultant on Human Rights to Attorney Gen. of Australia, 1983; Consultant (Commonwealth Secretariat) to Constitutional Convention, Seychelles, 1993. Chm., Inquiry into Press Council, 1982–83; Counsel: Royal Commn on Arms Trafficking, Antigua, 1990–91; Commn on Admin of Justice, Trinidad, 2000. Member: BFI Wkg Party on New Technologies, 1984; Exec. Council, ICA, 1987–97; Freedom of Inf. Campaign, 1987–; Charter 88, 1988–96; Justice, 1991–. Chm., BMA Cttee on Medical Inf. and Patient Privacy, 1994. Chm., Common Sense, 1998–. *Television:* Moderator, Hypotheticals, 1981–; writer and presenter, Tree of Liberty, 1982; Chm., The World This Week, 1987; writer and narrator, 44 Days (documentary), 1992. Editor, legal column, The Guardian, 1980–85. Freedom of Information Award, 1993. *Publications:* The Trials of Oz (play), 1973 (televised 1991); Whose Conspiracy?, 1974; Reluctant Judas, 1976; Obscenity, 1979; People Against the Press, 1983; (with A. Nicol) Media Law, 1984, 4th edn 2001; Hypotheticals, 1986; Does Dracula have Aids?, 1987; Freedom, the Individual and the Law, 6th edn 1989, 7th edn 1993; Geoffrey Robertson's Hypotheticals, 1991; The Justice Game, 1998; Crimes Against Humanity, 1999, rev. US edn, 2000; contribs to anthologies and learned jls. *Recreations:* tennis, opera, fishing. *Address:* Doughty Street Chambers, 11 Doughty Street, WC1N 2PG. *T:* (020) 7404 1313, *Fax:* (020) 7404 2283.

ROBERTSON, Air Marshal Graeme Alan, CBE 1988 (OBE 1985); Senior Military Adviser, BAE SYSTEMS (formerly Defence and Air Adviser, British Aerospace), since 1999; *b* 22 Feb. 1945; *s* of Ronald James Harold Robertson, DFC and Constance Rosemary (*née* Freeman); *m* 1972, Barbara Ellen (*née* Mardon); one *d*. *Educ:* Bancroft's Sch.; RAF Coll., Cranwell. BA Open Univ. Pilot: 8 Sqn, 1968–69; 6 Sqn, 1970–72; 228 OCU, 1972–73; Flight Commander: 550 TFTS, USAF, 1973–76; 56 Sqn, 1976–77; RAF Staff Coll., 1977–78; OR/Air Plans Staff, MoD, 1978–82; Commanding Officer: 92 Sqn, 1982–84; 23 Sqn, 1984–85; RAF Wattisham, 1985–87; Hon. ADC to the Queen, 1985–87; Dir of Air Staff Briefing and Co-ordination, MoD, 1987–88; RCDS, 1989; Dir of Defence Programmes, MoD, 1990–91; Dep. C-in-C, RAF Germany, 1991–93; AOC No 2 Gp, 1993–94; ACDS (Programmes), MoD, 1994–96; C of S and Dep. C-in-C, Strike Comd, 1996–98. Hon. Col, 77 Engr Regt (Vols), 1996–99. FRSA 1995; FRAeS 1997. Freeman, City of London, 1997. QCVSA 1973. *Recreations:* shooting, sailing, golf, winter sports. *Address:* c/o National Westminster Bank, Sleaford, Lincs NG34 7BJ. *Clubs:* Royal Air Force, MCC.

ROBERTSON, Hamish, CB 1992; MBE 1966; Under Secretary, Scottish Office Education Department (formerly Scottish Education Department), 1987–92; *b* 6 April 1931; *s* of James and Elizabeth Robertson, Huntly; *m* 1955, Barbara Suzanne Taylor, *d* of late Dr G. C. Taylor, Peterhead; two *s* two *d*. *Educ:* The Gordon Schs, Huntly; Aberdeen Univ. (MA). RA, 1952–54. Joined Colonial Admin. Service; Nyasaland, 1954–64; HMOCS, Malawi, 1964–67; Scottish Office: Principal, 1967; Asst Sec., 1973. *Recreations:* country pursuits. *Address:* 14 Harviestoun Road, Dollar FK14 7HG. *T:* (01259) 742374.

ROBERTSON, Hugh Michael, FRGS; MP (C) Faversham and Mid Kent, since 2001; *b* 9 Oct. 1962; *s* of George and June Robertson. *Educ:* King's Sch., Canterbury; RMA Sandhurst; Reading Univ. (BSc Hons Land Mgt (Property Investment)). Served Life Guards, 1985–95 (Armourers' and Brasiers' Prize, 1986): active service: NI, 1988; UN Cyprus, 1988; Gulf War, 1991; Bosnia, 1994; i/c Household Cavalry on Queen's Birthday Parade and State Opening of Parlt as Field Officer of the Escort, 1993; Silver Stick Adjutant, 1994–95; Schroder Investment Mgt, 1995–2001 (Asst Dir, 1999–2001). FRGS 1995. Sultan of Brunei's Personal Order of Merit, 1993. *Recreations:* cricket, ski-ing, country sports. *Address:* House of Commons, SW1A 0AA. *T:* (020) 7219 8230. *Clubs:* Cavalry and Guards, MCC (Playing Mem.).

ROBERTSON, Iain Samuel, CA; Chairman, Corporate Banking and Financial Markets, Royal Bank of Scotland, since 2001 (Chief Executive, 2000–01); *b* 27 Dec. 1945: *s* of Alfred and Kathleen Robertson; *m* 1972, Morag; two *s* two *d*. *Educ:* Jordanhill College Sch.; Glasgow Univ. (LLB). Industry and professional practice 1966–72; Civil Servant, 1972–83; Dir, Locate in Scotland, 1983–86; Chief Exec., SDA, 1987–90; Gp Finance Dir, County Natwest, 1990–92; Royal Bank of Scotland: Man. Dir, Corporate and Instnl Banking Div., 1992–98; Chief Exec., UK Bank, 1998–2000. Non-executive Director: Scottish Development Finance, 1983–90; Selective Assets Trust plc, 1989–96; British Empire Securities & Gen. Trust plc, 1995–. *Recreations:* golf, reading. *Address:* 135 Bishopsgate, EC2M 3UR.

ROBERTSON of Brackla, Maj.-Gen. Ian Argyll, CB 1968; MBE 1947; MA; DL; Vice-Lord-Lieutenant, Highland Region (Nairn), 1980–88; Representative in Scotland of Messrs Spink & Son, 1969–76; Chairman, Royal British Legion, Scotland, 1974–77 (Vice-Chairman, 1971–74); *b* 17 July 1913; 2nd *s* of John Argyll Robertson and Sarah Lilian Pitt Healing; *m* 1939, Marjorie Violet Isobel Duncan; two *d*. *Educ:* Winchester Coll.; Trinity Coll., Oxford. Commnd Seaforth Highlanders, 1934; Brigade Major: 152 Highland Bde,

1943; 231 Infantry Bde, 1944; GSO2, Staff College, Camberley, 1944–45; AAG, 15 Indian Corps, 1945–46; GSO1, 51 Highland Div., 1952–54; Comdg 1st Bn Seaforth Highlanders, 1954–57; Comdg Support Weapons Wing, 1957–59; Comdg 127 (East Lancs) Inf. Bde, TA, 1959–61; Nat. Defence College, Delhi, 1962–63; Comdg School of Infantry, 1963–64; Commanding 51st Highland Division, 1964–66; Director of Army Equipment Policy, Ministry of Defence, 1966–68; retd. Mem. Council, Nat. Trust for Scotland, 1972–75. DL Nairn 1973. *Recreations:* various in a minor way. *Address:* Gardeners Cottage, Brackla, Cawdor, Nairn IV12 5QY. *T:* (01667) 404220. *Clubs:* Army and Navy, MCC; Vincent's (Oxford).

ROBERTSON, Rear-Adm. Ian George William, CB 1974; DSC 1944; *b* 21 Oct. 1922; *s* of late W. H. Robertson, MC, and Mrs A. M. Robertson; *m* 1947, Barbara Irène Holdsworth; one *s* one *d*. *Educ:* Radley College. Joined RNVR, 1941; qual. Pilot; Sub-Lt 1943; air strike ops against enemy shipping and attacks against German battleship Tirpitz, 1944 (DSC); Lieut, RN, 1945; flying and instructional appts, 1944–53; Comdr (Air): RNAS Culdrose, 1956; HMS Albion, 1958; in command: HMS Keppel, 1960; HMS Mohawk, 1963; RNAS Culdrose, 1965; idc 1968; in comd, HMS Eagle, 1970; Admiral Comdg Reserves, 1972–74; retd 1974. Comdr 1954; Captain 1963; Rear-Adm. 1972. Dir-Gen., Navy League, 1975–76; Scoutreach Resources Organiser, Scout Assoc., 1976–79. Pres., Craft Club, 1992–99. *Recreations:* golf, sailing, fishing. *Address:* Moons Oast, Barcombe Road, Piltdown, Sussex TN22 3XG. *T:* (01825) 722279. *Clubs:* Naval; Piltdown Golf.

ROBERTSON, Ian Gordon, FMA; Director, National Army Museum, since 1988; *b* 4 April 1943; *s* of Major Gordon Pentelow Robertson and Florence (*née* Alder); *m* 1968, Barbara Burton; one *d*. *Educ:* Highgate Sch.; Queen's Coll., Oxford (MA). Asst Curator, Chelmsford and Essex Mus., 1965–67; Curator, Passmore Edwards Mus., London, 1967–88. Member: Exec. Council, Area Museums Service for S Eastern England; Exec. Council, ICOM (UK); Ancient Monuments Adv. Cttee, English Heritage, 1984–90. Museums Association: Mem. Council, 1977–88; Hon. Treasurer, 1981–84; Vice Pres., 1984–86; Pres., 1986–88. Founder Pres., London Fedn of Museums and Art Galleries; President: South Midlands Museums Fedn; Soc. for Post-Medieval Archaeology, 1982–85. Member: Bd, Nat. Postal Mus., 1990–98; PO Heritage Bd, 1999–. Trustee, RA Histl Trust, 1991–; Dir, RA Museums Ltd, 1992–. Served TA, 7th Bn Mddx Regt and 4th/5th Bn Essex Regt. *Publications:* papers on museological and allied topics. *Recreations:* gardening, Essex local history. *Address:* National Army Museum, Royal Hospital Road, Chelsea, SW3 4HT. *T:* (020) 7730 0717.

ROBERTSON, Ian Macdonald; *see* Robertson, Hon. Lord.

ROBERTSON, Maj.-Gen. James Alexander Rowland, CB 1958; CBE 1956 (OBE 1949; MBE 1942); DSO 1944 (Bar 1945); *b* 23 March 1910; *s* of Colonel James Currie Robertson, CIE, CMG, CBE, IMS, and Catherine Rowland Jones; *m* 1st, 1949, Ann Madeline Tosswill (*d* 1949); 2nd, Joan Wills (*née* Abercromby), *widow* of R. L. Wills, CBE, MC. *Educ:* Aysgarth School; Epsom College, RMC, Sandhurst. Commissioned 2 Lieutenant IA, 1930, attached 1st KOYLI; posted 6th Gurkha Rifles, 1931; Instructor Sch. of Physical Training, 1936–37; Staff Coll., Quetta, July-Dec. 1941; Bde Major 1 (Maymyo) Bde, Jan.-June, 1942; Bde Major, 106 I Inf. Bde, 1942–44; Comdr 1/7 Gurkha Rifles, 1944–45; Comdr 48 Ind. Inf. Bde, 1945–47; GSO 1, Instr Staff Coll., Quetta, June-Nov., 1947; Comdr 1/6th Gurkha Rifles, 1947–48; GSO 1 Gurkha Planning Staff, March-June, 1948; GSO 1 Malaya comd, June-Nov. 1948; BGS 1948–49. GSO 1, War Office, 1950–52; Col GS, 1 Corps, Germany, 1952–54; Comdr 51 Indep. Bde, 1955–57; Commander 17 Gurkha Division Overseas Commonwealth Land Forces, and Maj.-Gen. Brigade of Gurkhas, 1958–61; GOC Land Forces, Middle East Command, 1961–63; Gurkha Liaison Officer, War Office, 1963–64, retd. Personnel Dir, NAAFI, 1964–69. Colonel, 6th Queen Elizabeth's Own Gurkha Rifles, 1961–69; Chm., 1968–80, Pres., 1980–87, Life Vice-Pres., 1987–, Gurkha Brigade Assoc. DL Greater London, 1977. *Recreations:* fishing, sculpture.

ROBERTSON, James Andrew Stainton, PhD; Director, National Audit Office, since 1995; *b* 23 April 1949; *s* of James Robertson and Margaret Elodie Robertson (*née* Stainton); *m* 1979, Ann Leatherbarrow; one *s* one *d*. *Educ:* Highgate Sch.; Univ. Of Essex (BA Econs); LSE (MSc Econs, PhD). Sen. Econ. Asst and Econ. Advr, Dept of Employment, 1975–82; Econ. Advr, Dept of Energy, 1982–86; Senior Economic Adviser: DTI, 1986–89; Dept of Transport, 1989–90; Hd of Industrial and Regl Econs, DTI, 1990–93; Chief Econ. Advr, Dept of Employment, subseq. DFEE, 1993–95. *Publications:* contrib. various learned jls. *Recreations:* family, do-it-yourself, recreational computing. *Address:* National Audit Office, 157–197 Buckingham Palace Road, SW1W 9SP.

ROBERTSON, James Downie, RSA 1989 (ARSA 1974); RSW 1962; RGI 1979; Senior Lecturer in Fine Art (Drawing and Painting), 1975–96, Painter in Residence, 1996–98, Glasgow School of Art; *b* 2 Nov. 1931; *s* of Thomas Robertson and Mary Welsh; *m* 1970, Ursula Orr Crawford; two step *s* one step *d*. *Educ:* Hillhead High Sch., Glasgow; Glasgow Sch. of Art. DA Glasgow. RGI 1980. Taught at Keith Grammar Sch., 1957–58; Glasgow School of Art: part time Lectr, 1959; Lectr in Drawing and Painting, 1967. Vis. Lectr, Art Schools and Univs, Scotland, England and overseas; one-man exhibitions, 1961–, UK, Ireland, Spain, USA, including: Christopher Hull Gallery, London, 1984, 1987, 1989; Jorgenson Gall., Dublin, 1995; Roger Billcliffe Gall., Glasgow, 2000; retrospective: Glasgow Sch. of Art, 2000; numerous group exhibns; annual exhibns at RSA, RSW, RGI, RA; works in public collections of arts socs, art galleries (incl. RSA), corporations, banks, univs and in many private collections. Hon. Dr Glasgow, 2001. Awards: RGI, 1971, 1982, 1990; RSW, 1976, 1981, 1987, 1999; RSA, 1993 (Scottish Post Office Award); Shell Exploration and Production Award, 1985; Dunfermline Building Soc. Prize, RSA, 2001. *Recreations:* drawing, painting. *Address:* Carruthmuir, by Kilbarchan, Renfrewshire PA10 2QA. *T:* (01505) 613592. *Club:* Glasgow Art.

ROBERTSON, Rev. Canon James Smith, OBE 1984; Canon Emeritus, Zambia, 1965; Secretary, United Society for the Propagation of the Gospel, 1973–83; a Chaplain to the Queen, 1980–87; *b* 4 Sept. 1917; *s* of Stuart Robertson and Elizabeth Mann Smith, Forfar; *m* 1950, Margaret Isabel Mina Mounsey; one *d*. *Educ:* Glasgow Univ.; Edinburgh Theol Coll.; London Univ. MA Glasgow 1938; PCE London 1953. Curate, St Salvador's, Edinburgh, 1940–45; Mission Priest, UMCA, N Rhodesia, 1945–50; St Mark's Coll., Mapanza, 1950–55; Chalimbana Trng Coll., Lusaka, 1955–65, Principal 1958–65; Head, Educn Dept, Bede Coll., Durham, 1965–68; Sec., Church Colls of Educn, Gen. Synod Bd of Educn, 1968–73; Sec., USPG, 1973–83. British Council of Churches: Chm., Conf. for World Mission, 1977–81; Vice-Pres., 1984–87. Fellow, Selly Oak Colls, Birmingham, 1993. *Publications:* contributed to: Education in South Africa, 1970; The Training of Teachers, 1972; Values and Moral Development in Higher Education, 1974; Grow or Die, 1981; A Dictionary of Religious Education, 1984; Stepping Stones, 1987. *Recreations:* music, electronics, philosophy. *Address:* Flat 8, 26 Medway Street, SW1P 2BD. *T:* (020) 7222 1091.

ROBERTSON, John; MP (Lab) Glasgow and Anniesland, since Nov. 2000; *b* 17 April 1952; *s* of Charles Robertson and Agnes Millen Robertson (*née* Webster); *m* 1973, Eleanor Munro; three *d*. *Educ:* Shawlands Acad.; Langside and Stow Coll. (HNC Electrical Engrg). GPO, subseq. PO, then British Telecom, 1969–2000 (Customer Service Field Manager, BT, 1991–2000). *Recreations:* football, cricket, reading, music. *Address:* House of Commons, SW1A 0AA; (constituency office) 131 Dalsetter Avenue, Glasgow G15 8TE. *T:* (0141) 944 7298. *Clubs:* Garrowhill Cricket, Cambus Athletic Football (Glasgow).

ROBERTSON, John David H.; *see* Home Robertson.

ROBERTSON, John Davie Manson, CBE 1993 (OBE 1978); DL; FRSE; Chairman, S. & J. D. Robertson Group, since 1979; *b* 6 Nov. 1929; *s* of late John Robertson and Margaret Gibson (*née* Wright); *m* 1959, Elizabeth Amelia Macpherson; two *s* two *d*. *Educ:* Kirkwall Grammar Sch.; Univ. of Edinburgh (BL). Anglo Iranian Oil Co., later BP, UK and ME, 1953–58; S. & J. D. Robertson Gp, 1958–. Dir, Stanley Services, Falkland Is, 1987–; Chm., Lloyds TSB Foundn for Scotland, 1997–99 (Trustee, 1989–99). Chairman: Orkney Health Bd, 1983–91 (Mem., 1974–79, Vice-Chm., 1979–83); Highland Health Bd, 1991–97; N of Scotland Water Authy, 1995–98. Chm., Scottish Health Mgt Efficiency Gp, 1985–95; Chm. and Vice-Chm., Scottish Health Bds Chairmen's Gp, 1995–97; Member: NHS Tribunal, 1990–; Highlands and Is Enterprise, 1990–95. Mem., Bd of Mgt, Orkney Hosps, 1970–74; Chairman: Children's Panel, Orkney, 1971–76 (Chm., Adv. Cttee, 1977–82); Highlands and Is Savings Cttee, 1975–78; Mem., Highlands and Is Consultative Council, 1988–91. Hon. Sheriff, Grampian Highland and Islands, 1977–. Hon. Vice Consul for Denmark, 1972–; Hon. Consul for Germany, 1976–. FRSA 1993; FRSE 2000. DL Sutherland, 1999. Knight, Order of Dannebrog (Denmark), 1982; Officer's Cross, Order of Merit (Germany), 1999 (Cavalier's Cross, 1986). *Publications:* Uppies and Doonies, 1967; (ed) An Orkney Anthology, 1991. *Recreations:* shooting, fishing, history, art. *Address:* S. & J. D. Robertson Gp, Dunkirk, Shore Street, Kirkwall, Orkney KW15 1LG; Spinningdale House, Spinningdale, Sutherland IV24 3AD. *T:* (01862) 881240. *Club:* New (Edinburgh).

ROBERTSON, Sir John (Fraser), KCMG 1994; CBE 1982; consultant; Chief Ombudsman, New Zealand, 1984–94; *b* 3 Aug. 1925; *s* of Maurice Leigh Robertson and Violet Caroline Robertson (*née* Poultny); *m* 1947, Phyllis Irene Walter; two *s* one *d*. *Educ:* Univ. of Canterbury, NZ; Victoria Univ. of Wellington (DPA). FCA. Public Administration, 1946–82, incl. Sec. of Defence, 1969–79, Sec. for Justice, 1979–82; company dir and management consultant, 1982–84. Harkness Commonwealth Fund Fellow, 1961–62; RCDS 1968. Pres., Internat. Ombudsman Inst., 1992–94. *Publications:* numerous articles on public admin issues. *Recreations:* golf, bowls, bush and beach walking. *Address:* 5 Kabul Street, Khandallah, Wellington 6004, New Zealand. *T:* (4) 4791338.

ROBERTSON, Rear Adm. John Keith, CB 1983; FIEE; *b* 16 July 1926; *s* of G. M. and J. L. Robertson; *m* 1951, Kathleen (*née* Bayntun); one *s* three *d*. *Educ:* RNC Dartmouth; Clare Coll., Cambridge (BA 1949). FIEE 1981; FBIM 1980. RNC Dartmouth, 1940–43; served, 1943–83 (Clare Coll., Cambridge, 1946–49): HM Ships Queen Elizabeth, Zest, Gabbard, Aisne and Decoy; Staff, RNC Dartmouth; Grad. Recruiting; Weapon Engr Officer, HMS Centaur; Comdr, RNEC Manadon; RCDS; Captain Technical Intell. (Navy), 1974–76; Captain Fleet Maintenance, Portsmouth, 1976–78; Dir, Naval Recruiting, 1978–79; Dir, Management and Support of Intelligence, MoD, 1980–82; ACDS (Intelligence), 1982–83. *Recreations:* hockey, tennis, golf, wood carving. *Address:* Alpina, Kingsdown, Corsham, Wilts SN13 8BJ. *Clubs:* Corkscrew (Bath); Kingsdown Golf.

ROBERTSON, John Windeler; Senior Partner, Wedd Durlacher Mordaunt, 1979–86; *b* 9 May 1934; *s* of late John Bruce Robertson and Evelyn Windeler Robertson; *m* 1st 1959, Jennifer-Ann Gourdou (marr. diss.); one *s* one *d*; 2nd 1987, Rosemary Helen Jane Banks. *Educ:* Winchester Coll. National Service, RNVR, 1953–55. Joined Wedd Jefferson & Co. (Members of Stock Exchange), 1955; Partner, 1961. Dep. Chm., Barclays de Zoete Wedd Securities Ltd (BZW), 1986–88. Dep. Chm., Stock Exchange, 1976–79 (Mem. Council, 1966–86); Dir, Securities Assoc., 1986–88. Mem., City Capital Markets' Cttee, 1981–88. Trustee, Lloyds TSB (formerly TSB) Foundn, 1991–98. Mem. Council, GDBA, 1989–2000 (Chm., 1993–2000). *Recreations:* golf, deer stalking, 17th and 18th century marine art. *Address:* Eckensfield Barn, Compton, near Chichester, West Sussex PO18 9NT. *T:* (023) 9263 1239. *Club:* City of London.

ROBERTSON, Julia Ann; *see* Burdus, J. A.

ROBERTSON, Laurence Anthony; MP (C) Tewkesbury, since 1997; *b* 29 March 1958; *s* of James Robertson and Jean (*née* Larkin); *m* 1989, Susan (*née* Lees); two step *d*. *Educ:* St James C of E Sch., Farnworth; Farnworth Grammar Sch.; Bolton Inst. Higher Educn. Work study engr, 1976–82; industrial consultant, 1982–92; charity fundraising, 1992–97 (raised about £2 million for various charities). Contested (C): Makerfield, 1987; Ashfield, 1992. Member: Envmt Audit Select Cttee, 1997–99; Social Security Select Cttee, 1999–2001; European Scrutiny Select Cttee, 1999–; Educn and Skills Select Cttee, 2001–; Jt Cttee on Consolidation of Bills, 1997–; Secretary: Cons. Back Bench Constitutional Cttee, 1997–; 92 Gp, 2001–. *Recreations:* sport (ran 6 marathons), reading, writing, history, the Church. *Address:* House of Commons, SW1A 0AA. *T:* (020) 7219 3000; Tewkesbury Conservative Office, Lloyds TSB Chambers, Abbey Terrace, Winchcombe, Glos GL54 5LL. *T:* (01242) 602388.

ROBERTSON, Sir Lewis, Kt 1991; CBE 1969; FRSE; industrialist and administrator; Chairman, Carnegie Trust for Universities of Scotland, since 1990 (Trustee, Executive Committee, since 1963); *b* 28 Nov. 1922; *s* of John Farquharson Robertson and Margaret Arthur; *m* 1950, Elspeth Badenoch (*d* 2001); two *s* one *d* (and one *s* decd). *Educ:* Trinity Coll., Glenalmond. Accountancy training; RAF Intelligence. Chm., 1968–70, and Man. Dir, 1965–70, Scott & Robertson Ltd; Chief Executive, 1971–76, and Dep. Chm., 1973–76, Grampian Holdings plc; Director: Scottish and Newcastle Breweries plc, 1975–87; Whitman (International) SA (formerly IC Industries (International) SA), Geneva, 1987–90; Bank of Edinburgh Group (formerly Aristuein), 1990–94; EFM Income Trust plc, 1991–99; Scottish Financial Enterprise, 1991–93; Berkeley Hotel Co., 1995–97; Chairman: Girobank Scotland, 1984–90; Borthwicks (formerly Thomas Borthwick & Sons plc), 1985–89; F. J. C. Lilley, subseq. Lilley, 1986–93; Triplex Lloyd, 1987–90 (F. H. Lloyd Hldgs, 1982–87; Triplex, 1983–87); Havelock Europa plc, 1989–92; Stakis plc, 1991–95; Postern Exec. Gp Ltd, 1991–96. Mem, 1975–76, Dep. Chm. and Chief Exec., Scottish Devclt Agency, 1976–81. Chm., Eastern Regional Hosp. Bd (Scotland), 1960–70; Member: Provincial Synod, Episcopal Church of Scotland, 1963–83 (Chm. Policy Cttee, 1974–76); (Sainsbury) Cttee of Enquiry, Pharmaceutical Industry, 1965–67; Court (Finance Convener), Univ. of Dundee, 1967–70; Monopolies and Mergers Commn, 1969–76; Arts Council of GB (and Chm., Scottish Arts Council), 1970–71; Scottish Economic Council, 1977–83; Scottish Post Office Bd, 1984–90; British Council (Chm., Scottish Adv. Cttee), 1978–87; Council, BESO, 1995–98 (Chm., Scotland, 1995–98); Council, Scottish Business School, 1978–82; Restrictive Practices Court, 1983–96; Edinburgh Univ. Press Cttee, 1985–88; Bd, Friends of Royal Scottish

Acad., 1986–95; Chairman: Bd for Scotland, BIM, 1981–83; Scotland, Imperial Soc. of Kts Bachelor, 1994–99. Mem., Adv. Bd, Edinburgh edn of Waverley novels, 1984–. Trustee: Foundn for Study of Christianity and Society, 1980–88; RSE Scotland Foundn, 1996–2000 (Chm., 1999–2000); Foundn for Skin Res., 2000–; Scottish Cancer Foundn, 2000–; Trustee and Mem. Bd, Advanced Mgt Prog., Scotland, 1996–. FRSE 1978 (Mem. Council, 1992–; Treasurer, 1994–99; Bicentenary Medal, 2001); FRSA 1981; CIMgt (CBIM 1976). Hon. FRCSE 1999. Hon. LLD: Dundee, 1971; Aberdeen, 1999; Hon. DBA Napier, 1992; DUniv Stirling, 1993. *Recreations:* work, foreign travel, computer use, music, reading, listmaking, things Italian. *Address:* 32 Saxe Coburg Place, Edinburgh EH3 5BP. *T:* (0131) 332 5221; *e-mail:* lr32scp@talk21.com. *Clubs:* Athenæum; New (Edinburgh).

ROBERTSON, Martin; *see* Robertson, C. M.

ROBERTSON, Nelson; *see* Robertson, W. N.

ROBERTSON, Prof. Norman Robert Ean, CBE 1991; FDSRCPSGlas; Professor of Orthodontics, 1970–92, Dean of the Dental School, 1985–92, University of Wales College of Medicine; Hon. Consulting Orthodontist, South Glamorgan Health Authority, since 1992 (Hon. Consultant in Orthodontics, 1970–92); *b* 13 March 1931; *s* of late Robert Robertson and Jean Robertson (*née* Dunbar); *m* 1954, Morag Wyllie, *d* of George McNicol, MA; three *s* two *d*. *Educ:* Hamilton Acad.; Glasgow Univ. (BDS); Manchester Univ. (MDS 1962; DDS 1989). FDSRCPSGlas 1967. Registrar, then Sen. Registrar in Orthodontics, Glasgow Dental Hosp., 1957–59; Lectr in Orthodontics, 1960–62, Sen. Lectr in Orthodontics, 1962–70, Manchester Univ. Member: GDC, 1985–94; Standing Dental Adv. Cttee, 1989–92; S Glamorgan HA, 1976–92. *Publications:* Oral Orthopaedics and Orthodontics for Cleft Lip and Palate, 1983; articles in dental and med. jls. *Recreations:* leisure painting, sailing in summertime, walking in wintertime. *Address:* 26 Heol Tyn y Cae, Rhiwbina, Cardiff CF14 6DJ. *T:* (029) 2061 3439.

ROBERTSON, Patrick Allan Pearson, CMG 1956; *b* 11 Aug. 1913; *s* of A. N. McI. Robertson; *m* 1st, 1939, Penelope Margaret Gaskell (*d* 1966); one *s* two *d*; 2nd, 1975, Lady Stewart-Richardson. *Educ:* Sedbergh School; King's College, Cambridge. Cadet, Tanganyika, 1936; Asst Dist Officer, 1938; Clerk of Exec. and Legislative Councils, 1945–46; Dist Officer, 1948; Principal Asst Sec., 1949; Financial Sec., Aden, 1951; Asst Sec., Colonial Office, 1956–57; Chief Sec., Zanzibar, 1958; Civil Sec., Zanzibar, 1961–64; Deputy British Resident, Zanzibar, 1963–64; retired, 1964. Associate Member, Commonwealth Parliamentary Association. Freeman, City of London. *Recreations:* gardening, fishing. *Address:* Lynedale, Longcross, Chertsey, Surrey KT16 0DP. *T:* (01932) 872329. *Club:* Royal Commonwealth Society.
See also Sir Simon Stewart-Richardson, Bt.

ROBERTSON, Raymond Scott; Chairman, Scottish Conservative Party, since 1997 (Vice-Chairman, 1993–95); *b* 11 Dec. 1959; *s* of James and Marion Robertson. *Educ:* Glasgow Univ. (MA Hist. and Politics); Jordanhill Coll. Teacher, Hist. and Mod. Studies, Smithycroft Secondary Sch., Glasgow, 1982–83, Dumbarton Acad., 1983–89; NE Political Dir, Scottish Cons. Party, 1989–92. MP (C) Aberdeen South, 1992–97; contested (C) same seat, 1997. PPS to Min. of State, NI Office, 1994–95; Parly Under-Sec. of State, Scottish Office, 1995–97. *Address:* Scottish Conservative Party, 83 Princes Street, Edinburgh EH2 2EP.

ROBERTSON, (Richard) Ross, RSA, FRBS; DA; sculptor; *b* Aberdeen, 10 Sept. 1914; *s* of Rev. R. R. Robertson; *m* Kathleen May Matts; two *d*. *Educ:* Glasgow School of Art; Gray's School of Art, Aberdeen (DA). Lectr, Gray's Sch. of Art, 1946–79. FRBS 1963 (ARBS 1951); RSA 1977 (ARSA 1969). *Recreation:* study of art. *Address:* Creaguir, Woodlands Road, Rosemount, Blairgowrie, Perthshire PH10 7JX.

ROBERTSON, Robert Henry; Australian diplomat, retired; *b* 23 Dec. 1929; *s* of James Rowland Robertson and Hester Mary (*née* Kay); *m*; 2nd, 1958, Jill Bryant Uther (marr. diss. 1982); two *s* one *d*; 3rd, 1986, Isabelle Costa de Beauregard, *d* of Comte and Comtesse René Costa de Beauregard. *Educ:* Geelong Church of England Grammar Sch.; Trinity Coll., Univ. of Melbourne (LLB). Third Secretary, Australian High Commn, Karachi, 1954–56; Second Sec., Mission to UN, New York, 1958–61; First Sec., later Counsellor, Washington, 1964–67; Ambassador to Jugoslavia, Romania and Bulgaria, 1971–73; Asst Sec., Personnel Br., Dept of Foreign Affairs, Canberra, 1974–75; First Asst Sec., Western Div., 1975–76, Management and Foreign Service Div., 1976–77; Ambassador to Italy, 1977–81; Dep. High Comr in London, 1981–84; Perm. Rep. to UN in Geneva, 1984–88; Ambassador to Argentina, Uruguay and Paraguay, 1989–92. Chm., Exec. Cttee, UN High Comr for Refugees, 1987–88. *Address:* 53 Williams Road, Mount Eliza, Vic 3930, Australia. *T:* and *Fax:* (3) 97752078. *Club:* Melbourne.

ROBERTSON, Ross; *see* Robertson, R. R.

ROBERTSON, Brig. Sidney Park, MBE 1962; TD 1967; JP; Vice Lord-Lieutenant of Orkney, 1987–90; Director, S. & J. D. Robertson Group Ltd (Chairman, 1965–79); *b* 12 March 1914; *s* of John Davie Manson Robertson and Elizabeth Park Sinclair; *m* 1940, Elsa Miller Croy (*d* 1997); one *s* one *d*. *Educ:* Kirkwall Grammar Sch.; Edinburgh Univ. (BCom 1939; Hon. Fellow 1996). MIBS 1936. Served War; commnd RA, 1940 (despatches, NW Europe, 1945). Managerial posts, Anglo-Iranian Oil Co., ME, 1946–51; Manager, Operation/Sales, Southern Div., Shell Mex and BP, 1951–54; founded Robertson firm, 1954. Chm., Orkney Hosps Bd of Management/Orkney Health Bd, 1965–79. Maj. comdg 861 (Ind.) LAA Batt., RA (Orkney and Zetland) TA, 1956–61; Lt-Col comdg Lovat Scouts, TA, 1962–65; CRA 51st Highland Div., TA, 1966–67 (Brig.); Hon. Col, 102 (Ulster and Scottish) Light Air Defence Regt, RA (TA), 1975–80; Hon. Col Comdt, RA, 1977–80; Chm., RA Council of Scotland, 1980–84; Vice Pres., Nat. Artillery Assoc., 1977–; Pres., RBL Scotland, Kirkwall Br., 1957–97; Hon. Vice Pres., RBL Scotland, Highlands and Is Area, 1975–; Hon. President: Orkney Bn, Boys' Bde, 1972–; Friends of St Magnus Cathedral, 1994; Orkney Family History Soc., 1996; Orkney Norway Friendship Assoc., 1999; Vice-Pres., 1985, Life Vice Pres., 1989, RNLI (Chm., 1972–97, Pres., 1997–, Kirkwall Stn Cttee). Pres., Villars Curling Club, 1978–80, 1986–88. DL Orkney, 1968; Hon. Sheriff, Grampian, Highlands and Islands, 1969–. Freedom of Orkney, 1990. *Recreations:* travel, hill walking, angling. *Address:* Daisybank, Kirkwall, Orkney KW15 1LX. *T:* (01856) 872085. *Clubs:* Army and Navy, Caledonian; New (Edinburgh).

ROBERTSON, Simon Manwaring; Managing Director, Goldman Sachs & Co., and President, Goldman Sachs Europe, since 1997; *b* 4 March 1941; *s* of David Lars Manwaring Robertson, CVO; *m* 1965, Virginia Stewart Norman; one *s* two *d*. *Educ:* Eton. Joined Kleinwort Benson, 1963; Dir, 1977–97; Dep. Chm., 1992–96; Chm., 1996–97. Director: John Mowlem Gp, 1989–98; Inchcape, 1996–; BTR, 1997–99; London Stock Exchange, 1998–2001; Berry Bros & Rudd, 1998–; Invensys, 1999–. *Recreations:* ski-ing, walking in the Alps. *Clubs:* Boodle's, White's; Racquet (New York).

ROBERTSON, Stanley Stewart John, CBE 1998; CEng, FIEE, FCIT; safety engineering consultant; HM Chief Inspector of Railways, Health and Safety Executive, 1993–98; *b* 14 July 1938; *s* of Jock Stanley Robertson and Florence Kathleen Robertson (*née* Carpenter); *m* 1961, Valerie Housley; two *s* two *d*. *Educ:* Liverpool Poly. (Dip. EE 1961). FIEE 1987; FCIT 1998. Student engrg apprentice, UKAEA, 1956–62; Asst Electrical Engr, CEGB, 1961–67; Elec. Engrg Manager, Shell Chemicals UK, 1967–74; Health and Safety Executive: Sen. Electrical Inspector, 1974–77; Dep. Superintending Inspector, 1977–80; Superintending Inspector, 1980–91; Dep. Chief Inspector and Regl Dir, 1991–93. Chairman: Rly Industry Adv. Cttee, HSC, 1993–98; Nat. Inspection Council for Elec. Installation Contracting, 1993–95. Non-exec. Dir, NQA Ltd, 1993–95. *Publications:* tech. papers on electrical safety matters. *Recreations:* music, gardening. *Address:* Squirrel Dreys, Caldy Road, Caldy, Wirral CH48 1LW. *T:* (0151) 625 9520, *Fax:* (0151) 625 8680.

ROBERTSON, Tina; *see* Tietjen, T.

ROBERTSON, Toby, (Sholto David Maurice Robertson), OBE 1978; director and actor, theatre, opera and television; *s* of David Lambert Robertson and Felicity Douglas (*née* Tomlin); *m* 1963, Teresa Jane McCulloch (marr. diss. 1981); two *s* two *d*. *Educ:* Stowe; Trinity Coll., Cambridge (BA 1952, MA 1981). Formerly an actor. Dir. first prof. prodn, The Iceman Cometh, New Shakespeare, Liverpool, 1958. Dir. plays, London, Pitlochry and Richmond, Yorks, and for RSC, 1959–63. Member: Bd, Prospect Productions Ltd, 1964– (Artistic Dir, Prospect Theatre Co., 1964–79); Bd, Cambridge Theatre Co., 1970–74; Director: Old Vic Theatre, 1977–80, Old Vic Co., 1979–80; Acting Co., Kennedy Centre, Washington, 1983; Associate Dir, Circle Rep., New York, 1983–84; Dir, Theatr Clwyd, Mold, 1985–92. Drama Advr, Argo Records, 1979–; Prof. of Theatre, Brooklyn Coll., City Univ. NY, 1981–82; Hon. Prof. of Drama, 1987–90, Hon. Prof. of English, 1990–92, Fellow, 1996, UCNW. Lectures: Wilson Meml, Cambridge Univ., 1974; Hamlet, Athens Univ., 1978; Rikstheatre, Stockholm, 1980; Hamlet, Gulbenkian Foundn, Lisbon, 1987. Director of over 40 prodns for *Prospect Theatre Co.*, many staged in London and Edinburgh, 1964–79, including: The Soldier's Fortune; You Never Can Tell; The Confederacy; The Importance of Being Earnest; The Square; Howard's End; The Man of Mode; Macbeth; The Tempest; The Gamecock; A Murder of No Importance; A Room with a View; No Man's Land; The Beggar's Opera; The Servant of Two Masters; Edward II; Much Ado About Nothing; Boswell's Life of Johnson; Venice Preserved; King Lear and Love's Labour's Lost (Australian tour); Alice in Wonderland; Richard III; Ivanov; The Grand Tour; Twelfth Night, Pericles and The Royal Hunt of the Sun (internat. fests, Moscow, Leningrad and Hong Kong); The Pilgrim's Progress; A Month in the Country (Chichester Fest.); directed for *Old Vic Co.*: War Music; Antony and Cleopatra; Smith of Smiths; Buster; The Lunatic, The Lover and The Poet; Romeo and Juliet; The Government Inspector; The Padlock; Ivanov; Hamlet (Elsinore, and first visit by a British co., China, 1980); directed for *Theatr Clwyd*: Medea (also Young Vic), 1986; Barnaby and the Old Boys, 1987 (also Vaudeville, 1989); Edward III (jtly adapted, attrib. William Shakespeare) (also Cambridge and Taormina Fests), 1987; Captain Carvallo, 1988, transf. Greenwich; Revenger's Tragedy, 1988; The Old Devils, 1989; Othello, 1989; The Importance of Being Earnest, 1990; Enemy of the People, 1991, transf. Lyric Hammersmith; The Cherry Orchard, 1991 (also Brighton Festival); Marching Song, 1992; Hamlet (also Nat. Tour), 1991–92; The Seagull, 1992; Loot, 1995; directed *other productions*, including: Next Time I'll Sing to You, Greenwich, 1980; Beggar's Opera, Lyric, Hammersmith, 1980; Measure for Measure, People's Arts Theatre, Peking, 1981; Pericles, NY, 1981 (Obie award, 1982); Night and Day (opening prodn), 1982 and The Taming of the Shrew, 1983, Huntingdon Theatre Co., Boston; The Tempest (opening prodn), New Cleveland Playhouse, 1983; Love's Labour's Lost, Shakespeare Workshop, 1983, Circle Rep., 1984, NYC; York Cycle of Mystery Plays, York Fest., 1984; Midsummer Night's Dream, Open Air Theatre, Regent's Park, 1985; (jt dir) Antony and Cleopatra, The Taming of the Shrew, Haymarket, 1986; Coriolanus, festivals in Spain, 1986; You Never Can Tell, Haymarket, 1988; Richard II, Folger Theatre, Washington; Trelawny of the 'Wells', Comedy, 1992; The Old Devils, Philadelphia, 1993; The Taming of the Shrew, Regent's Park, 1993; Macbeth, Tel Aviv, 1994; Hamlet, Oberlin Coll., Ohio, 1997. *Opera:* for Scottish Opera, incl.: A Midsummer Night's Dream, 1972; Hermiston, 1975; Marriage of Figaro, 1977; for Opera Co. of Philadelphia: Elisir d'Amore (with Pavarotti and winners of Pavarotti competition), Dido and Aeneas, Oedipus Rex, 1982; Faust, 1984; Wiesbaden: A Midsummer Night's Dream, 1984; NY City Opera: Barber of Seville, 1984; Wexford Opera: The Kiss, 1984. Asst Dir, Lord of the Flies (film), 1961. Dir of more than 25 television prodns, incl.: The Beggar's Opera; Richard II; Edward II. *Recreation:* painting. *Address:* 192 Camberwell Grove, SE5 8RJ. *Club:* Garrick.

ROBERTSON, Vernon Colin, OBE 1977; self employed consultant, specialising in environmental issues in developing countries; *b* 19 July 1922; *s* of Colin John Trevelyan Robertson and Agnes Muriel Robertson (*née* Dolphin). *Educ:* Imperial Service College, Windsor; Univ. of Edinburgh (BSc Agr subs. Forestry); Univ. of Cambridge (Dip Agr 1950; MA). Joined Home Guard, 1940; enlisted RA, 1941, commissioned 1942; served 12th HAC Regt RHA, N Africa, Italy, Austria, 1942–45 (despatches 1945); with 1st Regt RHA, Italy, 1945–46 (Adjutant). Staff, Sch. of Agric., Cambridge, 1950; joined Hunting Aerosurveys Ltd, 1953, as ecologist heading new natural resources survey dept; developed this into overseas land and water resource consultancy, renamed Hunting Technical Services Ltd (Managing Director, 1959–77; after retirement continuing as Director and Consultant until 1987), development planning in Africa, Asia and Latin America. Director: Hunting Surveys and Consultants Ltd, 1962–77; Groundwater Development Consultants (International) Ltd, 1975–85; Vice-Chm. and acting Chm., Environmental Planning Commn, Internat. Union for Conservation of Nature, 1972–78; Chm., Trop. Agric. Assoc. (UK), 1981–85; Mem. Bd, Commonwealth Develt Corp., 1982–90. *Publications:* articles in learned jls. *Recreations:* natural history, esp. plants and birds, gardening, painting, photography, music, sailing. *Address:* Brickfields, Quay Lane, Kirby-le-Soken, Essex CO13 0DP. *T:* (01255) 674585. *Club:* Honourable Artillery Company.

ROBERTSON, Prof. William Bruce, MD, FRCPath; Professor of Histopathology, St George's Hospital Medical School, 1969–84, now Emeritus; Director of Studies, Royal College of Pathologists, 1984–92; *b* 17 Jan. 1923; *s* of late William Bruce Robertson and Jessie Robertson (*née* McLean); *m* 1948, Mary Patricia Burrows two *d*. *Educ:* The Academy, Forfar; Univ. of St Andrews. BSc 1944, MB ChB 1947, MD 1959; MRCPath 1963, FRCPath 1969. Junior appts, Cumberland Infirm., Carlisle, 1947–48; RAMC, E Africa, 1948–50; Registrar Pathology, Cumberland Infirm., 1950–53; Demonstr Pathology, Royal Victoria Infirm., Newcastle upon Tyne, 1953–56; Sen. Lectr Pathology, Univ. of the West Indies, Jamaica, 1956–64; Reader in Morbid Anatomy, St George's Hosp. Med. Sch., Univ. of London, 1964–69. Visiting Professor: Louisiana State Univ., New Orleans, USA, 1961–62; Katholieke Universiteit te Leuven, Belgium, 1972–73. *Publications:* scientific papers and book chapters in various med. jls and publns. *Address:* 3 Cambisgate, Church Road, Wimbledon, SW19 5AL. *T:* (020) 8947 6731.

ROBERTSON, Air Cdre William Duncan, CBE 1968; Royal Air Force, retired; Senior Air Staff Officer, HQ 38 Group, Royal Air Force, 1975–77; *b* 24 June 1922; *s* of

William and Helen Robertson, Aberdeen; *m* 1st, 1952, Doreen Mary (*d* 1963), *d* of late Comdr G. A. C. Sharp, DSC, RN (retd); one *s* one *d*; 2nd, 1968, Ute, *d* of late Dr R. Koenig, Wesel, West Germany; one *d*. *Educ:* Robert Gordon's Coll., Aberdeen. Sqdn Comdr, No 101 Sqdn, 1953–55, No 207 Sqdn, 1959–61. Gp Dir, RAF Staff Coll., 1962–65; Station Comdr, RAF Wildenrath, 1965–67; Dep. Dir, Administrative Plans, 1967; Dir of Ops (Plans), 1968; Dir of Ops Air Defence and Overseas, 1969–71; RCDS, 1971–72; SASO RAF Germany, 1972–74; SASO 46 Group, 1975. *Recreations:* golf, tennis. *Address:* Parkhouse Farm, Leigh, Surrey RH2 8QE. *Clubs:* Royal Air Force; Walton Heath Golf.

ROBERTSON, (William) Nelson, CBE 1996; FCII; Director, Alliance Trust, since 1996; *b* 14 Dec. 1933; *s* of James Bogue and Eleanor Robertson; *m* 1964, Sheila Catherine Spence; two *d*. *Educ:* Berwick Grammar Sch.; Edinburgh Univ. (MA). FCII 1963. Served RA, 1955–57. General Accident Fire & Life Assurance Corporation Ltd, later General Accident plc, 1958–95: Asst Gen. Man. (Overseas), 1972; Gen. Man., 1980; Dir, 1984; Dep. Chief Gen. Man., 1989; Gp Chief Exec., 1990–95. Director: Morrison Construction Gp, 1995–2001; Second Alliance Trust, 1996–; Edinburgh New Tiger Trust, 1996–2001; Edinburgh Leveraged Income Trust plc, 1996–; Edinburgh Zeros 2008 plc, 1996–; Scottish Community (formerly Caledonian) Foundn, 1996–99; Supervisory Bd, Scottish Amicable, 1997–. Bd Mem., ABI, 1991–95. Mem. Court, Univ. of Abertay, Dundee, 1996–99. *Recreations:* hill-walking, gardening. *Club:* Caledonian.

ROBIN, Dr Gordon de Quetteville; Director, 1958–82, Senior Associate, since 1982, Scott Polar Research Institute, University of Cambridge; Fellow since 1964 and Vice-Master, 1974–78, Darwin College, Cambridge; *b* Melbourne, 17 Jan. 1921; *s* of Reginald James Robin and Emily Mabel Robin; *m* 1953, Jean Margaret Fortt, Bath; two *d*. *Educ:* Wesley Coll., Melbourne; Melbourne Univ. ScD Cantab, MSc Melbourne, PhD Birmingham; FInstP. War service, RANVR: anti-submarine, 1942–44; submarine, RN, 1944–45 (Lieut). Physics Dept, Birmingham Univ.: research student, lectr, ICI Research Fellow, 1945–56; Sen. Fellow, Geophysics Dept, ANU, 1957–58. Meteorologist and Officer i/c Signy Is, South Orkneys, with Falkland Is Dependencies Survey, 1947–48; Physicist and Sen. British Mem. of Norwegian-British-Swedish Antarctic Expedn, 1949–52 (made first effective measurements of Antarctic ice thickness); further researches: in Antarctic in 1959 (ocean wave penetration into pack ice); in Arctic, 1964, 1966, 1973, and Antarctic, 1967, 1969, 1974 (testing and developing airborne radar type sounding technique; discovered largest known sub-ice lake); UK deleg., 1958–84, Sec., 1958–70, Pres., 1970–74, and Hon. Mem., Scientific Cttee on Antarctic Research of ICSU; Mem. Adv. Bd, Geophysical Inst., Univ. of Alaska, 1974–81. President: Antarctic Club, 1974; Arctic Club, 1986; Chm., Trans Antarctic Assoc., 1992–97. Hon. DPhil Stockholm, 1978. Kongens Fortjensmedalje, Norway, 1952; Back Grant, RGS, 1953; Bruce Medal, RSE, 1953; Polar Medal, 1956; Patrons Medal, RGS, 1974; Seligman Crystal, Internat. Glaciological Soc., 1986. *Publications:* scientific reports of Norwegian-British-Swedish Antarctic Expedition (Glaciology III, 1958; Upper Winds, 1972); (ed) Annals of the IGY, Vol. 41, Glaciology, 1967; (ed and contrib.) The Climatic Record in Polar Ice Sheets, 1983; papers and articles on polar glaciology in scientific jls, incl. (jtly) paper in Nature, 1996, on freshwater lake beneath ice of central East Antarctica. *Recreations:* Mallorca, walking. *Address:* 10 Melbourne Place, Cambridge CB1 1EQ. *T:* (01223) 358463.

ROBIN, Ian (Gibson), FRCS; retired; *b* 22 May 1909; *s* of Dr Arthur Robin, Edinburgh, and Elizabeth Parker; *m* 1st, 1939, Shelagh Marian (*d* 1978), *d* of late Colonel C. M. Croft; one *s* two *d*; 2nd, 1994, Patricia Lawrence. *Educ:* Merchiston Castle School; Clare College, Cambridge. MA, MB, BCh Cantab 1933; LRCP 1933; FRCS 1935. Guy's Hosp.; late House Phys.; Sen. Science Schol., 1930; Treasurer's Gold Medals in Clinical Surgery and Medicine, 1933; Arthur Durham Travelling Schol., 1933; Charles Oldham Prize in Ophthalmology, 1933; Registrar and Chief Clin. Asst, ENT Dept, 1935–36; late Consulting ENT Surgeon: Royal Chest Hosp., 1939–44; Royal Northern Hosp., 1937–74; St Mary's Hosp., Paddington, 1948–74; Princess Louise (Kensington) Hosp. for Children, 1948–69; Paddington Green Children's Hosp., 1969–74; Surgeon EMS, Sector III London Area, 1939–45. Late Vice-Chm., Royal Nat. Institute for the Deaf. Member Hunterian Soc.; Council of Nat. Deaf Children's Soc.; Past Pres., Brit. Assoc. of Otolaryngologists, 1971–72; Past Pres., Laryng. Section, RSM, 1967–68; Vice-Pres., Otolog. Section, RSM, 1967–68, 1969; late Examiner for DLO of RCS of England. Lectures: Yearsley, 1968; Jobson Horne, 1969. Mem., Royal Water-Colour Soc. *Publications:* (jt) Diseases of Ear, Nose and Throat (Synopsis Series), 1957; papers in various med. treatises, jls, etc. *Recreations:* golf, gardening, sketching; formerly athletics and Rugby. *Address:* Merchiston, 4 Lodge Gardens, Oakham, Rutland LE15 6EP. *Clubs:* Hawks (Cambridge); Achilles (Great Britain).

ROBINS, David Anthony; Chairman, Infoshare Europe Ltd, since 2001; *b* 2 Sept. 1949; *s* of John Anthony Robins and Ruth Wenefrede Robins (*née* Thomas); *m* 1981, Joanna Christina Botting; two *s* one *d*. *Educ:* University Coll. London (BSc Econ). Economic Analyst, Investment and Res. Dept, Commonwealth Bank, Sydney, Australia, 1973–74; Economist, Overseas Dept, Bank of England, 1976–78; Exec., Japanese Dept, James Capel, 1978–80; Chief Internat. Economist, Phillips & Drew, 1980–86; Hd of Res., UBS Phillips & Drew Ltd, Tokyo, 1986–88; Hd, Internat. Securities Dept, UBS Securities Inc., NY, 1988–90; Functional Advr, Securities and Res., Union Bank of Switzerland, Zurich, 1990–93; Chief Exec. Officer, UBS UK Ltd, 1994–98; Exec. Vice Pres. and Hd, Region Europe, Union Bank of Switzerland, 1997–98; Chm. and Chief Exec. Officer, ING Barings, 1998–2000; Mem., Exec. Bd, ING Gp, 2000. Non-executive Director: MPC Investors Ltd, 2001–; Hackney Empire Ltd, 2001–. Dep. Chm., E London Business Alliance, 2000– (Chm., Hackney Bd, 1999–). *Recreations:* tennis, swimming, walking. *Address:* East London Business Alliance, Superintendent's House, Abbey Mills Pumping Station, Abbey Lane, E15 2RW.

ROBINS, John Vernon Harry; Chairman: Lane, Clark and Peacock (Actuaries), since 2000; Xchanging Ltd, since 2000; Austin Reed Group PLC, since 2000; *b* 21 Feb. 1939; *s* of Col William Vernon Harry Robins, DSO and Charlotte Mary (*née* Grier); *m* 1962, Elizabeth Mary Banister; two *s* one *d*. *Educ:* Winchester Coll. Nat. Service, 2nd Lieut 2/10 Princess Mary's Own Gurkha Rifles, 1959–61. Man. Dir, SNS Communications Ltd, 1966–74; Chief Exec., Bally Gp (UK) Ltd, 1974–79; Group Financial Director: Fitch Lovell plc, 1979–84; Willis Faber, subseq. Willis Corroon Gp plc, 1984–94; Chief Exec., Guardian Royal Exchange plc, 1994–99; Chm., Hyder plc, 1998–2000. Director: Wellington Underwriting plc, 1999 2001; Axa Asia Pacific Hldgs Ltd, Melbourne, 1999–. Chm., Policyholders Protection Bd, 1998–2000. *Recreations:* clocks, Baroque music, grand-children. *Club:* Brooks's.

ROBINS, Group Captain Leonard Edward, CBE (mil.) 1979; AE 1958 (and 2 clasps); Inspector, Royal Auxiliary Air Force, 1973–83; *b* 2 Nov 1921; *yr s* of late Joseph Robins, Bandmaster RM, and late Louisa Josephine (*née* Kent); *m* 1949, Jean Ethelwynne (Headteacher) (*d* 1985), *d* of late Roy and Bessie Searle, Ryde, IoW. *Educ:* Singlegate, Mitcham, Surrey; City Day Continuation School, EC. Entered Civil Service, GPO, 1936; War service, Radar Br., RAF, UK, SEAC, Ceylon, India, 1941–46; resumed with GPO, 1946; Min. of Health, 1948; Min. of Housing and Local Govt, 1962; DoE, 1970–80, retired. Airman, No 3700 (Co. of London) Radar Reporting Unit RAuxAF, 1950; Commissioned 1953, radar branch; transf. to No 1 (Co. of Hertford) Maritime HQ Unit RAuxAF, intelligence duties, 1960; OC No 1 Maritime Headquarters Unit, RAuxAF, 1969–73; Gp Capt., Inspector RAuxAF, 1973–83. ADC to the Queen, 1974–83. Selected Air Force Mem., Greater London TAVRA, 1973–83 and City of London TAVRA, 1980–84; Mem., HAC, 1997–. Patron, World War II Air Forces Radar Reunion, 2001. Lord Mayor of London's personal staff, as researcher and speech writer, 1977–78, 1980–81, 1982–83 and 1986–94. Pres., Wandsworth Victim Support Scheme, 1980–87. Trustee, Royal Foundn of Greycoat Hosp., 1983–88. Freeman, City of London, 1976. Coronation Medal, 1953; Silver Jubilee Medal, 1977. Officer of Merit with Swords, SMO Malta, 1986. DL Greater London, 1978–97, Rep. DL, Bor. of Wandsworth, 1979–97. FIMgt. *Recreations:* naval, military and aviation history; book hunting; kipping; speech writing. *Address:* 5 Varley Terrace, Dean Street, Liskeard, Cornwall PL14 4AN. *T:* (01579) 348740. *Club:* Royal Air Force.

ROBINS, Malcolm Owen, CBE 1978; Learned Societies Officer, Royal Society/British Academy, 1979–81; a Director, Science Research Council, 1972–78; *b* 25 Feb. 1918; *s* of late Owen Wilfred Robins and Amelia Ada (*née* Wheelwright); *m* 1944, Frances Mary, *d* of late William and Frances Hand; one *s* one *d*. *Educ:* King Edward's Sch., Stourbridge; The Queen's Coll., Oxford (Open Scholar in Science). MA (Oxon) 1943. On scientific staff of Royal Aircraft Establishment, 1940–57; a Div. Supt in Guided Weapons Dept, RAE, 1955–57; Asst Dir, Guided Weapons, Min. of Supply, London, 1957–58; UK Project Manager for jt UK/USA Space Research programme, and hon. Research Associate, University Coll. London, 1958–62; a Dep. Chief Scientific Officer and Head of Space Research Management Unit, Office of Minister for Science (later Dept of Educn and Science), 1962–65; Head of Astronomy, Space and Radio Div., SRC, 1965–68; a Research Planning post in Min. of Technology (later Dept of Trade and Industry), 1968–72. Vis. Prof., University Coll., London, 1974–77. FInstP 1945; FRAS 1974. *Publications:* (with Sir Harrie Massey) History of British Space Science, 1986; (with K. Proust and S. C. B. Gascoigne) The Creation of the Anglo-Australian Observatory, 1990; papers on space research in scientific jls. *Recreations:* gardening, golf. *Address:* 4 The Lindens, Great Austins, Farnham, Surrey GU9 8LA. *T:* (01252) 723186.

ROBINS, Sir Ralph (Harry), Kt 1988; DL; FREng; FRAeS; Chairman, Rolls-Royce plc, since 1992; *b* 16 June 1932; *s* of Leonard Haddon and Maud Lillian Robins; *m* 1962, Patricia Maureen Grimes; two *d*. *Educ:* Imperial Coll., Univ. of London (BSc; ACGI; FIC 1993). MIMechE; FREng (FEng 1988); FRAeS 1990. Development Engr, Rolls-Royce, Derby, 1955–66; Exec. Vice-Pres., Rolls-Royce Inc., 1971; Man. Dir, RR Industrial & Marine Div., 1973; Commercial Dir, RR Ltd, 1978; Chm., International Aero Engines AG, 1983–84; Rolls-Royce plc: Man. Dir, 1984–89; Dep. Chm., 1989–92; Chief Exec., 1990–92. Non-executive Director: Standard Chartered plc, 1988–; Schroders plc, 1990–; Marks & Spencer plc, 1992–2001; Cable and Wireless plc, 1994– (non-exec. Chm., 1998–). Chm., Defence Industries Council, 1986–; Pres., SBAC, 1986–87. Mem., Council for Sci. and Technology, 1993–98. FCGI 1990. DL Derbys, 2000. Hon. FRAeS; Hon. FIMechE 1996. Hon. DSc Cranfield, 1990; DUniv Derby, 1992; Hon. DBA Strathclyde, 1996. Commander's Cross, Order of Merit (Germany), 1996. *Recreations:* tennis, golf, music, classic cars. *Address:* Rolls-Royce plc, 65 Buckingham Gate, SW1E 6AT. *Club:* Athenæum.

ROBINS, William Edward Charles; Metropolitan Stipendiary Magistrate, 1971–89; solicitor; *b* 13 March 1924; *s* of late E. T. and late L. R. Robins; *m* 1946, Jean Elizabeth, *yr d* of Bruce and Flora Forsyth, Carlyle, Saskatchewan, Canada; one *s* one *d*. *Educ:* St Alban's Sch. Served War: commissioned as Navigator, RAF, 1943–47. Admitted as a Solicitor, 1948; joined Metropolitan Magistrates' Courts' service, 1950; Dep. Chief Clerk, 1951–60; Chief Clerk, 1960–67; Sen. Chief Clerk, Thames Petty Sessional Div., 1968–71. Sec., London Magistrates' Clerks' Assoc., 1953–60 (Chm. 1965–71). Member, Home Office working parties, on: Magistrates' Courts' Rules; Legal Aid; Motor Vehicle Licences; Fines and Maintenance Orders Enforcement, 1968–71; Member: Lord Chancellor's Sub-Cttee on Magistrates' Courts' Rules, 1969–70; Adv. Council on Misuse of Drugs, 1973–86. Fellow Commoner, Corpus Christi Coll., Cambridge, Michaelmas 1975. *Recreations:* touring off the beaten track, music, theatre.

ROBINS, Maj.-Gen. William John Pherrick, CB 1998; OBE 1984 (MBE 1979); CEng, FIEE; FBCS; Director, C4ISTAR Development Avionics Group, BAE SYSTEMS, since 2001; *b* 28 July 1941; *s* of John Robins and Helen Hamilton (*née* Urry); *m* 1st, 1967, Anne Marie Cornu (marr. diss. 1985); one *s* one *d*; 2nd, 1993, Kathy Walsh. *Educ:* Henry Mellish Grammar Sch., Nottingham; Welbeck Coll.; RMA Sandhurst; RMCS Shrivenham (BSc (Eng) London, 1966); Staff Coll., Camberley; Cranfield Inst. of Technology (MPhil (Information Systems) 1993). CEng 1991, FIEE 1992; FBCS 1995. 16 Parachute Bde, 1966–70; Special Communications, 1970–72; Germany and UK, 1972–79; CO 14 Signal Regt (Electronic Warfare), 1979–82; Mil. Asst to MGO, 1982–84; Army ADP Co-ordinator, 1984–87; Project Dir, 1987–89; Dir, CIS (Army), 1989–92; ACDS (Command, Control, Communications and Information Systems), 1992–94; Dir Gen., Information and Communication Services, MoD, 1995–98. Director: Marconi Radar and Defence Systems, 1998–99; Alenia Marconi Systems, 1999–2000; Future Systems Dir, BAE Systems, 2000–01. Hon. Fellow, Sch. of Defence Management, Cranfield Univ., 1994. *Recreations:* cartoons, looking at pictures, making high quality compost, running, hill walking. *Address:* c/o RHQ Royal Signals, Blandford Camp, Dorset DT11 8RH. *Club:* Special Forces.

ROBINSON, family name of **Baron Martonmere**.

ROBINSON, Alastair; *see* Robinson, F. A. L.

ROBINSON, Sir Albert (Edward Phineas), Kt 1962; Director, E. Oppenheimer and Son (Pty) Ltd, 1963–2000; *b* 30 Dec. 1915; *s* of late Charles Phineas Robinson (formerly MP Durban, S Africa) and of late Mabel V. Robinson; *m* 1st, 1944, Mary Judith Bertram (*née* Bertish) (*d* 1973); four *d*; 2nd, 1975, Mrs M. L. Royston-Piggot (*née* Barrett). *Educ:* Durban High School; Universities of Stellenbosch, London (LSE), Cambridge (Trinity Coll.) and Leiden; MA (Cantab). Pres., Footlights Club, Cambridge, 1936–37. Barrister, Lincoln's Inn. Served War of 1939–45, in Imperial Light Horse, Western Desert, N Africa, 1940–43. Member Johannesburg City Council, 1945–48 (Leader United Party in Council, 1946–47); MP (United Party), S African Parlt, 1947–53; became permanent resident in Rhodesia, 1953. Dep. Chm., General Mining and Finance Corp. Ltd, 1963–71; Chairman: Johannesburg Consolidated Investment Co., 1971–80; Rustenburg Platinum Mines, 1971–80; Australian Anglo American Ltd, 1980–85; Director: Anglo American Corp., Zimbabwe Ltd, 1964–86; Founders Bldg Soc., 1954–86; Rand Mines Ltd, 1965–71; Anglo American Corp. of SA Ltd, 1965–88; Johannesburg Consolidated Investment Co., 1965–85; Standard Bank Investment Corp., 1972–86; Director, in Zimbabwe and South Africa, of various Mining, Financial and Industrial Companies. Chm. Central African Airways Corp., 1957–61. Member, Monckton Commission, 1960; High Commissioner in the UK for the Federation of Rhodesia and Nyasaland, 1961–63.

Chancellor, Univ. of Bophuthatswana, 1980–91. Hon. DComm Univ. of Bophuthatswana, 1990. *Recreations:* people, music and conversation. *Address:* 43 St Mary Abbots Court, Warwick Gardens, W14 8RB. *Clubs:* Carlton; Country (Johannesburg); Country (Durban).

ROBINSON, Alwyn Arnold; Managing Director, Daily Mail, 1975–89; *b* 15 Nov. 1929. Mem., Press Council, 1977–87 (Jt Vice-Chm., 1982–83).

ROBINSON, Ann; *see* Robinson, M. A.

ROBINSON, Dr Ann; Director General, National Association of Pension Funds Ltd, 1995–2000; *b* 28 Jan. 1937; *d* of Edwin Samuel James and Dora (*née* Thorne); *m* 1961, Michael Finlay Robinson; two *s*. *Educ:* St Anne's Coll., Oxford (MA); McGill Univ. (MA, PhD). Financial journalist, Beaverbrook Newspapers, 1959–61; University Lecturer: Durham, 1962–65; Bristol, 1970–72; Bath, 1972–75; Cardiff, 1972–89 (Sen. Lectr, 1987–89); Head of Policy Unit, Inst. of Dirs, 1989–95. Director: Great Western Hldgs, 1996–98; Almeida Capital, 2001–. ICSA Vis. Prof. of Corporate Governance, Bournemouth Univ., 2000–. Member: Equal Opportunities Commn, 1980–85; Econ. and Social Cttee, EEC, 1986–93 (Chm., Industry Section, 1990–92); Welsh Arts Council, 1991–93; HEFCW, 1993–97; Competition (formerly Monopolies and Mergers) Commn, 1993–99; Bd, Harwich Haven Authy, 1999–; Pensions Protection and Investments Accreditation Bd, 2001–. Dir, WNO, 1992–94. Member: Council, RIIA, 1991–97; Bd of Academic Govs, Richmond Coll., London, 1992–; Bd of Govs, Commonwealth Inst., 1992–97; Council, Clifton Coll. (Vice-Chm. Council, 1998–); Council, City Univ., 1998–. Trustee: Foundn for Business Responsibilities, 1997–; Dixons Retirement and Employee Security Scheme, 2000–. Contested (C) S E Wales, EP election, 1979. *Publications:* Parliament and Public Spending, 1978; (jtly) Tax Policy Making in the United Kingdom, 1984; articles in acad. jls and chapters on public expenditure control by Parliament. *Recreations:* Alpine sports (summer and winter), gardening. *Address:* Northridge House, Usk Road, Shirenewton, Monmouthshire NP16 6RZ. *Club:* Reform.

ROBINSON, Anne Josephine; journalist and broadcaster; *b* 26 Sept. 1944; *d* of late Bernard James Robinson and Anne Josephine Robinson (*née* Wilson); *m* 1st, 1968, Charles Martin Wilson, *qv* (marr. diss. 1973); one *d*; 2nd 1980, John Penrose. *Educ:* Farnborough Hill Convent; Les Ambassadrices, Paris. Reporter: Daily Mail, 1967–68; Sunday Times, 1968–77; Daily Mirror: Women's Editor, 1979–80; Asst Editor, 1980–93; columnist, 1983–93; columnist: Today, 1993–95; The Times, 1993–95; The Sun, 1995–97; The Express, 1997–98; The Times, 1998–. Presenter: Anne Robinson Show, Radio 2, 1988–93; Watchdog, 1993–2001; presenter and writer, BBC Television: Points of View, 1987–98; Weekend Watchdog, 1997–2001; Going for a Song, 2000; The Weakest Link, 2000– (also USA, 2001–). Hon. Fellow, Liverpool John Moores Univ., 1996. *Publication:* Memoirs of an Unfit Mother, 2001. *Recreations:* dogs, houses, gossip, decently cooked food, having opinions. *Address:* Penrose Media, 19 Victoria Grove, W8 5RW. *T:* (020) 7584 2969. *Clubs:* Bibury Cricket (Vice-Pres.), Bibury Tennis (Pres.).

ROBINSON, Ven. Anthony William; Archdeacon of Pontefract, since 1997; *b* 25 April 1956; *m* 1981, Susan Boddy; two *s* one *d*. *Educ:* Bedford Modern Sch.; Salisbury and Wells Theol Coll. Ordained deacon, 1982, priest, 1983; Asst Curate, St Paul, Tottenham, 1982–85; Team Vicar, 1985–89, Team Rector, 1989–97, Resurrection, Leicester. Rural Dean, Christianity North, Leicester, 1992–97; Hon. Canon, Leicester Cathedral, 1994–97. *Address:* 10 Arden Court, Horbury, Wakefield WF4 5AH. *T:* (01924) 276797, *Fax:* (01924) 261095.

ROBINSON, Ariadne Elizabeth; *see* Singares McAlman, A. E.

ROBINSON, Arthur Alexander; Director of Computing Centre, University of Wales College of Cardiff (formerly at University of Wales Institute of Science and Technology), 1976–91; *b* 5 Aug. 1924; *o s* of Arthur Robinson and Elizabeth (*née* Thompson); *m* 1956, Sylvia Joyce Wagstaff; two *s* one *d*. *Educ:* Epsom Coll.; Clare Coll., Cambridge (MA); Univ. of Manchester (PhD). English Electric Co. Ltd, 1944; Ferranti Ltd, 1950; Dir and Gen. Man., Univ. of London Atlas Computing Service, 1962; Dir, Univ. of London Computer Centre, 1968; Dir, National Computing Centre Ltd, 1969–74. *Publications:* papers in Proc. IEE. *Recreations:* travel, gardening. *Address:* 6 Portland Close, Penarth, Vale of Glamorgan CF64 3DY.

ROBINSON, (Arthur) Geoffrey, CBE 1978; Chairman, Medway Ports Authority, 1978–87; *b* 22 Aug. 1917; *s* of Arthur Robinson and Frances M. Robinson; *m* 1st, 1943, Patricia MacAllister (*d* 1971); three *s* one *d*; 2nd, 1973, Hon. Mrs Treves, *d* of Rt Hon. Lord Salmon; three step *s* one step *d*. *Educ:* Lincoln Sch.; Jesus Coll., Cambridge (MA); Sch. of Oriental and African Studies, London Univ. Served War, RA, 1939–46. Solicitor, 1948; Treasury Solicitor's Dept, 1954–62; PLA, 1962–66; Man. Dir, Tees and Hartlepool Port Authority, 1966–77; Chm., English Indust. Estates Corp., 1977–83. Member: National Dock Labour Bd, 1972–77; National Ports Council, 1980–81; Chm., British Ports Assoc., 1983–85. *Publications:* Hedingham Harvest, 1977; various articles. *Recreation:* music. *Address:* 4 Boderton Mews, Burton Park, Duncton, Petworth GU28 0LS; La Baume, 30700 Serviers, France. *Club:* Oxford and Cambridge.
See also P. H. Robinson.

ROBINSON, Hon. (Arthur Napoleon) Raymond, SC; President, Trinidad and Tobago, since 1997; *b* 16 Dec. 1926; *s* of late James Alexander Andrew Robinson, Headmaster, and Emily Isabella Robinson; *m* 1961, Patricia Rawlins; one *s* one *d*. *Educ:* Bishop's High Sch., Tobago; St John's Coll., Oxford (Hon. Fellow 1988). LLB (London); MA (PPE) Oxon. Called to Bar, Inner Temple; in practice, 1957–61. Treas., People's Nat. Movt (governing Party) 1956; Mem. Federal Parlt, 1958; MHR for Tobago East, 1961–71 and 1976–80; Minister of Finance, 1961–66; Dep. Political Leader of Party, 1966; Actg Prime Minister (during his absence), April and Aug. 1967; Minister of External Affairs, Trinidad and Tobago, 1967–70; Chm., Democratic Action Congress, 1971–86; Chm., Tobago House of Assembly, 1980–86; Leader, Nat. Alliance for Reconstruction, 1986–92; Prime Minister of Trinidad and Tobago, 1986–91. Member: Legal Commn on US Leased Areas under 1941 Agreement, 1959; Industrial Develt Corp., 1960; Council, Univ. of West Indies, 1960–62. Dir, Foundn for establishment of an Internat. Criminal Court, 1972–87. Member: UN Expert Gp on Crime and the Abuse of Power, 1979; Adv. Council, Nuclear Age Peace Foundn, 1994–; Pres. and Exec. Mem., Parliamentarians for Global Action, 1993–95. Hon. DCL Obafemi Awolowo Univ., Nigeria, 1991. Dist. Internat. Criminal Law Award, Internat. Criminal Court Foundn, 1977; Dist. Human Develt Award, Internat. Conf. on Human Rights and Humanitarian Law, UN Affiliate, 1983; Commendation Award, and Freeman, City of a Thousand Oaks, Calif, 1987; Dist. Service Award, Calif Lutheran Univ., 1987; Individual of the Year Award, Friends of Tobago Liby Cttee, 1995. Freeman: LA, 1988; Caracas, 1990. KStJ 1992. Gran Cordon, Orden de El Libertador (Venezuela), 1990; Chief of Ile Ife (Nigeria), 1991. *Publications:* The New Frontier and the New Africa, 1961; Fiscal Reform in Trinidad and Tobago, 1966; The Path of Progress, 1967; The Teacher and Nationalism, 1967; The Mechanics of Independence, 1971; Caribbean Man, 1986; articles and addresses. *Address:* 21 Ellerslie Park, Maraval, Trinidad and Tobago; (office) Robinson Street, Scarborough, Trinidad and Tobago.

ROBINSON, Basil William, FBA 1981; retired; *b* 20 June 1912; *o c* of William Robinson and Rebecca Frances Mabel, *d* of Rev. George Gilbanks; *m* 1st, 1945, Ailsa Mary Stewart (*d* 1954); 2nd, 1958, Oriel Hermione Steel; one *s* one *d*. *Educ:* Winchester (Exhibitioner); CCC Oxford. BA 1935; MA, BLitt, 1938. Asst Keeper, Victoria and Albert Museum, 1939. Min. of Home Security, 1939–40. Served as Captain, 2nd Punjab Regt, India, Burma, Malaya, 1943–46. Deputy Keeper, V&A Museum, 1954, Keeper, Dept of Metalwork, 1966–72, Keeper Emeritus, 1972–76. Pres., Royal Asiatic Soc., 1970–73; Vice-Pres., Arms and Armour Soc., 1953; Hon. Pres., Tō-ken Soc. of Great Britain, 1967–93. FSA 1974. *Publications:* A Primer of Japanese Sword-blades, 1955; Persian Miniatures, 1957; Japanese Landscape Prints of the 19th Century, 1957; A Descriptive Catalogue of the Persian Paintings in the Bodleian Library, 1958; Kuniyoshi, 1961; The Arts of the Japanese Sword, 1961, 2nd edn, 1971; Persian Drawings, 1965; part-author, vols 2 and 3, Catalogue of Persian MSS and Miniatures in the Chester Beatty Library, 3 vols, 1958–62; Persian Miniature Painting, 1967; Persian Paintings in the India Office Library, 1976; (ed. and jt author) Islamic painting in the Keir Collection, 1976; Japanese Sword-fittings in the Baur Collection, 1980; Persian Paintings in the John Rylands Library, 1980; Kuniyoshi: the Warrior Prints, 1982 (Uchiyama Meml Prize, Japan Ukiyoe Soc.); Persian Painting and the National Epic (Hertz Lecture, British Acad.), 1983; (jtly) The Aldrich Book of Catches, 1989; Fifteenth Century Persian Painting (Kevorkian Lectures, NY Univ.), 1991; Collection Jean Pozzi, 1992; Persian Paintings in the Collection of the Royal Asiatic Society, 1998; numerous booklets, articles and reviews on Persian and Japanese art. *Recreations:* catch singing (founder and Chairman, Aldrich Catch Club); cats. *Address:* 41 Redcliffe Gardens, SW10 9JH. *Club:* Hurlingham.

ROBINSON, Bill; *see* Robinson, P. W.

ROBINSON, Brian Gordon, CBE 1996; QFSM 1992; FIFireE; Commissioner for Fire and Emergency Planning (formerly Chief Officer, then Chief Fire Officer and Chief Executive), London Fire Brigade, since 1991; *b* 21 April 1947; *s* of Gordon and Theodora Robinson, Colchester, Essex; *m* 1996, Charmian Lesley Houslander-Green. FIFireE 1992. Joined London Fire Brigade, 1968; Accelerated Promotion Course, 1974, Sen. Course Dir, 1982, Fire Service Coll.; Divl Comdr, London, 1983; Asst Chief Officer, 1985; Dep. Chief Officer, 1990. OStJ 1992. *Recreation:* golf. *Address:* London Fire Brigade Headquarters, 8 Albert Embankment, SE1 7SD. *T:* (020) 7587 4000.

ROBINSON, Air Vice-Marshal Brian Lewis; Sole Executive, Belmont Aviation (formerly Senior Partner, Belmont Consultants), since 1991; *b* 2 July 1936; *s* of Frederick Lewis Robinson and Ida (*née* Croft); *m* 1961, Ann Faithfull; one *s* one *d*. *Educ:* Bradford Grammar Sch. Served, 1956–76: 74 Sqn; Oxford Univ. Air Sqn; 73 Sqn; Canberra Trials and Tactical Evaluation Unit; Directorate of Flight Safety, MoD; RAF Staff Coll.; RAF Valley; 2 ATAF Germany; Canadian Forces Comd and Staff Coll., and 411 Air Reserve Sqn, Toronto; Chief Instr, 4 Flying Trg Sch., 1976–78, OC, 1978–80, RAF Valley; Internat. Mil. Staff HQ, NATO, Brussels, 1980–82; Defence and Air Attaché, Moscow, 1983–86; Dir of Orgn and Quartering, RAF, MoD, 1986–88; RAF Long-term Deployment Study, 1988; AOC Directly Administered Units, and AO Admin, HQ Strike Command, 1989–91. Display pilot (Gnat), Kennet Aviation, 1997–; Flying Instr, Bristol Flying Centre, 1997–; Mem., British Precision Flying Team, Krakow, 1998. Editor, Flight Safety section, Air Clues, 1967–69. Mem., RAF and British Bobsleigh teams, 1967–74. Gov., Edgehill Coll., Bideford, 1997–. FIMgt 1979; FRAeS 2000. *Recreations:* travel, skiing, aerobatic display pilot. *Address:* 22 Thackeray Road, Clevedon, Som BS21 7JQ. *T:* (office) (01275) 874434.
See also Sir J. C. N. Wakeley, Bt.

ROBINSON, Christopher John, CVO 1992 (LVO 1986); Organist, Director of Music, and Fellow, St John's College, Cambridge, since 1991; *b* 20 April 1936; *s* of late Prebendary John Robinson, Malvern, Worcs; *m* 1962, Shirley Ann, *d* of H. F. Churchman, Sawston, Cambs; one *s* one *d*. *Educ:* St Michael's Coll., Tenbury; Rugby; Christ Church, Oxford (BMus); MA (Oxon and Cantab). FRCO; Hon. RAM. Assistant Organist of Christ Church, Oxford, 1955–58; Assistant Organist of New College, Oxford, 1957–58; Music Master at Oundle School, 1959–62; Assistant Organist of Worcester Cathedral, 1962–63; Organist and Master of Choristers: Worcester Cathedral, 1963–74; St George's Chapel, Windsor Castle, 1975–91. Conductor: City of Birmingham Choir, 1963–June 2002; Oxford Bach Choir, 1977–97; Leith Hill Musical Festival, 1977–80. Pres., RCO, 1982–84. Hon. Fellow, Univ. of Central England (formerly Birmingham Poly.), 1990. Hon. MMus Birmingham, 1987. *Recreations:* watching cricket, travel. *Address:* St John's College, Cambridge CB2 1TP. *Club:* MCC.

ROBINSON, Sir Christopher Philipse, 8th Bt *cr* 1854, of Toronto; *b* 10 Nov. 1938; *s* of Christopher Robinson, QC (*d* 1974) (*g s* of 1st Bt) and Neville Taylor (*d* 1991), *d* of Rear-Adm. Walter Rockwell Gherardi, USN; S kinsman, Sir John Beverley Robinson, 7th Bt, 1988; *m* 1962, Barbara Judith, *d* of late Richard Duncan; two *s* (and one *s* decd). *Heir:* *s* Peter Duncan Robinson, *b* 31 July 1967. *Address:* Kirks Ferry, 460 RR1, Chelsea, QC J0X 1N0, Canada.

ROBINSON, Prof. Colin, FSS, FInstPet; Professor of Economics, University of Surrey, since 1968; Editorial Director, Institute of Economic Affairs, since 1992; *b* 7 Sept. 1932; *s* of late James Robinson and Elsie (*née* Brownhill); *m* 1st, 1957, Olga West; two *s*; 2nd, 1983, Eileen Marshall; two *s* two *d*. *Educ:* Univ. of Manchester (BA Econ). FSS 1970; FInstPet 1985. Economist, Procter and Gamble, 1957–60; Economist, subseq. Head of Economics Dept, Esso Petroleum Co., 1960–66; Econ. Advr, Natural Gas, Esso Europe, 1966–68. Mem., Monopolies and Mergers Commn, 1992–98. Fellow, Soc. of Business Economists, 2000. Outstanding Contribution to the Profession Award, Internat. Assoc. for Energy Economics, 1998. *Publications:* Business Forecasting, 1970; (with Jon Morgan) North Sea Oil in the Future, 1978; (with Eileen Marshall) Can Coal Be Saved?, 1985; Energy Policy, 1993; papers on energy economics in learned jls. *Recreations:* walking, music, home improvements. *Address:* Institute of Economic Affairs, 2 Lord North Street, SW1P 3LB.

ROBINSON, Ven. David; *see* Robinson, Ven. W. D.

ROBINSON, Prof. David Antony, PhD; Vice Chancellor and President, Monash University, since 1997; *b* 24 July 1941; *s* of Harry Robinson and Marjorie Newcombe Robinson (*née* Patchett); *m* 1st, 1965, Marjorie Rose Collins (marr. diss. 1970); 2nd, 1976, Yvonne Ann Salter; one *s*. *Educ:* Royal Masonic Schs; University Coll., Swansea (BA, PhD 1967). University College, Swansea: Res. Asst, Dept of Sociol., 1964–67; Res. Fellow, DHSS Med. Sociol. Res. Centre, 1967–71; Lectr, then Sen. Lectr, DHSS-MRC Addiction Res. Unit, Inst. of Psychiatry, Univ. of London, 1974–80; University of Hull: Sen. Lectr and Actg Dir, 1980–82, Dir, 1982–91, Inst. for Health Studies; Prof. of Health Studies, 1984–91; Hd of Dept, Social Policy and Professional Studies, 1985–86; Dean, Sch. of Social and Pol Scis, 1986–89; Pro Vice-Chancellor, 1989–91; Co-Dir, ESRC

Addiction Res. Centre, Univs of Hull and York, 1983–88; Dir, WHO Collaborating Centre for Res. and Trng in Psycho-social and Econ. Aspects of Health, 1986–91; Vice-Chancellor and Pres., Univ. of S Australia, 1992–96. Member: Editl Bd, Brit. Jl of Addiction, 1978–89; Editl Adv. Bd, Sociol. of Health and Illness, 1987–90. Member: Exec. Council of Soc. for Study of Addictions, 1979–82; Exec. Cttee, Nat. Council on Alcoholism, 1979–82; Exec. Cttee, Nat. Council on Gambling, 1980–87; Health Services Res. Cttee, MRC, 1981–84; Social Affairs Cttee, ESRC, 1982–85. Member: Australian Vice Chancellors Cttee, 1992–, Dir, 1995–; Business/Higher Educn Round Table, 1992– (Dir, 1995–98); Australian Higher Educn Industrial Assoc., 1992–97 (Mem., Exec. Cttee, 1993–97; Vice Pres., 1995–97). Director: Open Learning Agency of Australia Pty Ltd, 1994–; Foundn for Family and Private Business, 1997–; Monash Univ. Sunway Campus Malaysia Sdn Bhd, 1998–. Chm. Council, Victorian Inst. of Forensic Mental Health, 1998–. FAIM 1993. FRSA 1990. *Publications:* (jtly) Hospitals, Children and their Families, 1970; The Process of Becoming Ill, 1971; Patients, Practitioners and Medical Care: aspects of medical sociology, 1973, 2nd edn 1978; From Drinking to Alcoholism: a sociological commentary, 1976; (ed jtly) Studies in Everyday Medical Life, 1976; (with S. Henry) Self-help and Health: mutual aid for modern problems, 1977; Talking Out of Alcoholism: the self-help process of Alcoholics Anonymous, 1979; (with Y. Robinson) From Self-help to Health: a guide to self-help groups, 1979; (ed) Alcohol Problems: reviews, research and recommendations, 1979; (with P. Tether) Preventing Alcohol Problems: a guide to local action, 1986; (ed jtly) Local Action on Alcohol Problems, 1989; (ed jtly) Controlling Legal Addictions, 1989; (ed jtly) Manipulating Consumption: information, law and voluntary controls, 1990; (with A. Maynard et al) Social Care and HIV–AIDS, 1993; contrib. numerous pamphlets, book chapters and papers in learned and professional jls. *Recreations:* walking, golf, cinema. *Address:* Vice Chancellor's Office, Monash University, Clayton, Vic 3168, Australia. *T:* (3) 99052000.

ROBINSON, (David) Duncan; Director and Marlay Curator, Fitzwilliam Museum, Cambridge, since 1995; Professorial Fellow, Clare College, Cambridge, 1995–Oct. 2002; Master, Magdalene College, Cambridge, from Oct. 2002; *b* 27 June 1943; *s* of Tom and Ann Robinson; *m* 1967, Elizabeth Anne Sutton; one *s* two *d.* *Educ:* King Edward VI Sch., Macclesfield; Clare Coll., Cambridge (MA); Yale Univ. (Mellon Fellow, 1965–67; MA). Asst Keeper of Paintings and Drawings, 1970–76, Keeper, 1976–81, Fitzwilliam Museum, Cambridge; Fellow and Coll. Lectr, Clare Coll., Cambridge, 1975–81; Dir, Yale Center for British Art, New Haven, Conn, and Chief Exec., Paul Mellon Centre for Studies in British Art, London, 1981–95; Adjunct Prof. of History of Art, and Fellow of Berkeley Coll., Yale Univ., 1981–95. Mem. Cttee of Management, Kettle's Yard, Cambridge Univ., 1970–81, 1995– (Chm., Exhibns Cttee, 1970–81). Member: Art Panel, Eastern Arts Assoc., 1973–81 (Chm., 1979–81); Arts Council of GB, 1981 (Mem., 1978–81, Vice-Chm., 1981, Art Panel); Museums and Collections Cttee, English Heritage, 1996–; Assoc. of Art Mus. Dirs (USA), 1982–88; Bd of Managers, Lewis Walpole Library, Farmington Ct, USA, 1982–95; Council of Management, The William Blake Trust, 1983–; Vis. Cttee, Dept of Paintings Conservation, Metropolitan Museum of Art, NY, 1984–94; Walpole Soc., 1983– (Mem. Council, 1985–87, 1995–); Connecticut Acad. of Arts and Scis, 1991–95; Univ. Museums Gp, 1995– (Sec., 1997–99); Adv. Council, Paul Mellon Centre for Studies in British Art, 1997–; Arts and Humanities Res. Bd, 1998–; Chm., Art and Artifacts Indemnity Adv. Panel (USA), 1992–94 (Mem., 1991). Member, Board of Directors: New Haven Colony Historical Soc., 1991–94; Amer. Friends of Georgian Gp, 1992–95. Gov., Yale Univ. Press, 1987–95; Trustee: Yale Univ. Press, London, 1990–; Charleston Trust (USA), 1990–92; Fitzwilliam Mus. Trust, 1995–. Governor: SE Museums Service, 1997–99; Gainsborough's House Soc., 1998–. Pres., Friends of Stanley Spencer Gall., Cookham, 1998–; Vice-Pres., NADFAS, 2000–. FRSA 1990. Organised Arts Council exhibitions: Stanley Spencer, 1975; William Nicholson, 1980. *Publications:* Companion Volume to the Kelmscott Chaucer, 1975, re-issued as Morris, Burne-Jones and the Kelmscott Chaucer, 1982; Stanley Spencer, 1979, rev. edn 1990; (with Stephen Wildman) Morris & Company in Cambridge, 1980; Town, Country, Shore & Sea: English Watercolours from van Dyck to Paul Nash, 1982; Man and Measure: the paintings of Tom Wood, 1996; The Yale Center for British Art: a tribute to the genius of Louis I. Kahn, 1997; catalogues; articles and reviews in Apollo, Burlington Magazine, etc. *Address:* Fitzwilliam Museum, Cambridge CB2 1RB. *T:* (01223) 332925. *Clubs:* Knickerbocker (NY); Elizabethan (New Haven).

ROBINSON, David Julien; film critic and festival director; *b* 6 Aug. 1930; *s* of Edward Robinson and Dorothy Evelyn (*née* Overton). *Educ:* Lincoln Sch.; King's Coll., Cambridge (BA Hons). Associate Editor, Sight and Sound, and Editor, Monthly Film Bulletin, 1956–58; Programme Dir, NFT, 1959; Film Critic: Financial Times, 1959–74; The Times, 1973–92; Editor, Contrast, 1962–63. Vis. Prof. of Film, Westfield Coll., Univ. of London. Director: Garrett Robinson Co., 1987–88; The Davids Film Co., 1988–. Guest Dir, Edinburgh Film Fest., 1989–91; Director: Channel 4 Young Film Maker of the Year Comp., Edinburgh Film Fest., 1992–95; Pordenone Silent Film Fest., Italy, 1997–. Has curated exhibns, incl. Musique et Cinéma muet, Musée d'Orsay, Paris, 1995. Films produced and directed: Hetty King — Performer, 1969; (Co-dir) Keeping Love Alive, 1987; (Co-dir) Sophisticated Lady, 1989. *Publications:* Hollywood in the Twenties, 1969; Buster Keaton, 1969; The Great Funnies, 1972; World Cinema, 1973, 2nd edn 1980 (US edn The History of World Cinema, 1974, 1980); Chaplin: the mirror of opinion, 1983; Chaplin: his life and art, 1985; (ed and trans.) Luis Buñuel (J. F. Aranda); (ed and trans.) Cinema in Revolution (anthology); (ed jtly) The Illustrated History of the Cinema, 1986; Music of the Shadows, 1990; Masterpieces of Animation 1833–1908, 1991; Richard Attenborough, 1992; Georges Méliès, 1993; Lantern Images: iconography of the magic lantern 1440–1880, 1993; Sight and Sound Chronology of the Cinema, 1994–95; Musique et cinéma muet, 1995; Charlot—entre rires et larmes, 1995; Peepshow to Palace, 1995; (jtly) Light and Image: incunabula of the motion picture, 1996; Expanding Vision, 2000. *Recreations:* collecting optical toys, model theatres. *Address:* 96–100 New Cavendish Street, W1M 7FA. *T:* (020) 7580 4959; 1 Winifreds Dale, Cavendish Road, Bath BA1 2UD. *T:* (01225) 420305.

ROBINSON, Derek, CBE 1979; Fellow of Magdalen College, Oxford, 1969–99, now Emeritus; Senior Research Officer, Oxford Institute of Economics and Statistics, 1961–99; *b* 9 Feb. 1932; *s* of Benjamin and Mary Robinson; *m* 1956, Jean Evelyn (*née* Lynch); one *s* one *d.* *Educ:* Barnsley Holgate Grammar Sch.; Ruskin Coll., Oxford; Lincoln Coll., Oxford. MA (Oxon), DipEcPolSci (Oxon). Civil Service, 1948–55. Sheffield Univ., 1959–60; Senior Research Officer, Oxford Inst. of Economics and Statistics, 1961 . Economic Adviser, Nat. Bd for Prices and Incomes, 1965–67; Sen. Economic Adviser, Dept of Employment and Productivity, 1968–70; Dep. Chm., Pay Bd, 1973–74; Chm., SSRC, 1975–78. Mem., British Library Bd, 1979–82. Visiting Professor: Cornell Univ., 1983; Univ. of Hawaii, 1983. Chairman: Oxfordshire Dist Manpower Cttee, 1980–83 (Oxf. and S Bucks, 1975–79); Cttee of Inquiry into the remuneration of members of local authorities, 1977; Chilterns Area Bd, Manpower Services Commn Special Programmes, 1978–79. Inter-regional Adviser on Wage Policy, ILO, 1986–88. Mem., Internat. Reference Panel to Presidential Comprehensive Labour Market Commn, S Africa, 1995–96. *Publications:* Non-Wage Incomes and Prices Policy, 1966; Wage Drift, Fringe Benefits and Manpower Distribution, 1968; Workers' Negotiated Savings Plans for Capital Formation, 1970; (ed) Local Labour Markets and Wage Structures, 1970; Prices and Incomes Policy: the Austrian Experience (with H. Suppanz), 1972; Incomes Policy and Capital Sharing in Europe, 1973; (with J. Vincens) Research into Labour Market Behaviour, 1974; (with K. Mayhew *et al*) Pay Policies for the Future, 1983; Introduction to Economics, 1986; Monetarism and the Labour Market, 1986; Civil Service Pay in Africa, 1990; contributor to Bulletin of Oxford Univ. Inst. of Economics and Statistics; Industrial Relations Jl, etc. *Address:* 56 Lonsdale Road, Oxford OX2 7EP. *T:* (01865) 552276. *Club:* Reform.

ROBINSON, Derek Anthony, DPhil; Hon. Senior Research Fellow, Science Museum, London, since 1999; *b* 21 April 1942; *s* of late Charles Frederick Robinson and of Mary Margaret Robinson; *m* 1965, Susan Gibson (*d* 1991); two *s.* *Educ:* Hymers Coll., Hull; The Queen's Coll., Oxford (BA 1963; MA, DPhil 1967). Post-doctoral Res. Fellow, Dept of Chemistry, Univ. of Reading, 1967–69; Mem. scientific staff, Molecular Pharmacology Unit of MRC, Cambridge, 1969–72; Sen. Asst in Res., Dept of Haematol Medicine, Cambridge Univ. Med. Sch., 1972–74; Science Museum: Asst Keeper I, Dept of Chem., 1974–77; Dep. Keeper (formerly Asst Keeper I), Wellcome Mus. of History of Medicine, and Sec. of Adv. Council, 1977–78; Keeper, Dept of Museum Services, 1978–87; Keeper, Dept of Physical Scis, later Head of Sci. Gp, then Head of Phys. Scis and Engrg Gp, 1987–98; Asst Dir (actg) and Hd of Collections, 1998–99. Mem., British Nat. Cttee for History of Sci., Medicine and Technology, 1987–88; Mem., CGLI, 1984–; Dir, Bd, Mus. Documentation Assoc., 1989–92. Trustee, Nat. Gas Mus., 1999–. *Publications: contributions to:* 2nd edn Acridines, ed R. M. Acheson, 1973; Vol. VI, The History of Technology, ed T. I. Williams, 1978; Cambridge General Encyclopaedia, ed D. Crystal, 1990; Making of the Modern World: milestones of science and technology, ed N. Cossons, 1992; Instruments of Science: an historical encyclopaedia, ed R. F. Bud and D. J. Warner, 1998; Atti del Covegno, 2001; papers on heterocyclic chemistry, molecular pharmacol., and leukaemia chemotherapy, in Jl Chem. Soc., Brit. Jl Pharmacol., and Biochem. Trans. *Recreations:* living and gardening in France, travel, walking. *Address:* 3 Broadwater Avenue, Letchworth, Herts SG6 3HE. *T:* (01462) 686961; *e-mail:* DARSRFSCM@aol.com. *Club:* Athenæum.

ROBINSON, Dr Derek Charles, FRS 1994; Director, UKAEA Fusion (formerly Research Director, UKAEA Government Division, Fusion), since 1992 (Culham Science Centre Director, since 1998); *b* 27 May 1941; *s* of Alexander Robinson and Grace Kitchen; *m* 1968, Marion Quarmby; one *d.* *Educ:* Queen Elizabeth Sch., Kirkby Lonsdale; Manchester Univ. (BSc, PhD). FInstP. AERE Harwell, 1965–68; Vis. Scientist, I. V. Kurchatov Inst. of Atomic Energy, Moscow, 1968–69; research at UKAEA Culham Lab., 1970–78; Vis. Scientist, Tokyo, Nagoya and S Australia, 1978–79; Group Leader, 1979–86, Div. Head, 1986–92, Culham Lab. Member: Council, JET, 1996–2001 (Mem. Sci. Council, 1983–); Sci. Adv. Bd, Max Planck Inst. für Plasma Physik, 1988– (Chm., 1997–); Tech. Adv. Cttee, Internat. Thermonuclear Exp. Reactor, 1991–; Conseil Scientifique, CEA, 1994–99; Consultative Cttee for Fusion Prog., 1996–; Chm., European Fusion Physics Cttee, 2000–. Vice Pres., Inst. of Physics, 2001– (Bd Mem., 1999–, Chm., 2001–, Inst. of Physics Publishing). Alfvén Lect., Swedish Royal Acad. of Scis, 1996. C. V. Boys Prize, 1979, Guthrie Medal and Prize, 1998, Inst. of Physics. *Publications:* contribs to learned jls. *Recreations:* plantsman, photography, hill walking. *Address:* The Thatched Cottage, Church Street, Appleford, Abingdon, Oxon OX14 4PA. *T:* (01235) 848500.

ROBINSON, Sir Dominick Christopher L.; *see* Lynch-Robinson.

ROBINSON, Rt Rev. Donald William Bradley, AO 1984; Archbishop of Sydney and Metropolitan of New South Wales, 1982–93; *b* 9 Nov. 1922; *s* of Rev. Richard Bradley Robinson and Gertrude Marston Robinson (*née* Ross); *m* 1949, Marie Elizabeth Taubman; three *s* one *d.* *Educ:* Sydney Church of England Gram. Sch.; Univ. of Sydney (BA); Queens' Coll., Cambridge (MA). Australian Army, 1941–45, Lieut Intell. Corps, 1944. Deacon 1950, Sydney; priest 1951; Curate, Manly, NSW, 1950–52; St Philip's, Sydney, 1952–53; Lecturer: Moore Coll., 1952–81 (Vice-Principal, 1959–72); Sydney Univ., 1964–81; Asst Bishop, Diocese of Sydney (Bishop in Parramatta), 1973–82. Hon. ThD Aust. Coll. of Theology, 1979. *Address:* 1 Jubilee Avenue, Pymble, NSW 2073, Australia. *T:* (2) 94493033.

ROBINSON, Duncan; *see* Robinson, David D.

ROBINSON, Emma-Jane; University Librarian, University of London Library, since 1994; *b* 19 Aug. 1953; *d* of late Harold Frederick Wensley Cory and of Yvonne Margaret Cory (*née* Hales); *m* 1974, David John Robinson. *Educ:* Westonbirt Sch.; University Coll. of Wales, Aberystwyth (BSc). ALA 1981. Asst Librarian, then Sub-Librarian, Univ. of London Liby, 1989–94. Dir, London and SE Reg. (regl library bureaux), 1994–. Member: Consortium of Univ. Res. Libraries, 1994–; Consortium of European Res. Libraries, 1994–; Res. Libraries Gp, 1994–; BL Arts, Humanities and Social Scis Adv. Bd, 1997–. FRSA 1995. *Publications:* articles in professional jls. *Recreations:* riding, walking, botanising, archaeologising. *Address:* 101 Colindeep Lane, Colindale, NW9 6DD; University of London Library, Senate House, Malet Street, WC1E 7HU. *T:* (020) 7862 8410.

ROBINSON, Eric Embleton; Director, Lancashire Polytechnic (formerly Preston Polytechnic), 1982–90; *b* 12 March 1927; *s* of Cyril Robinson and Florence Mary Embleton. *Educ:* local authority schools, Nelson and Colne, Lancs; London Univ. (MSc). Teaching, Prescot Grammar Sch., 1948, Acton Tech. Coll., 1949–56, Brunel Coll., 1956–62, Enfield Coll., 1962–70; Dep. Dir, NE London Polytechnic, 1970–73; Principal, Bradford Coll., 1973–82. Pres., Assoc. of Teachers in Tech. Instns, 1962; Exec. Mem., Nat. Union of Teachers, 1961–67; Member: Burnham Cttees, 1961–67; Nat. Council for Training and Supply of Teachers, 1964–66; Minister's Working Party on Polytechnics, 1965–66; Equal Opportunities Commn, 1976–81; CNAA, 1976–82; UNESCO Nat. Commn, 1975–78. Vice Pres., Socialist Educn Assoc., 1966–. Hon. Advr, Beijing Inst. of Business, 1987–; Hon. Vis. Prof., Wolverhampton University (formerly Wolverhampton Polytechnic), 1990–. Hon. Fellow, Sheffield Hallam Univ. (Sheffield City Polytechnic, 1990). Hon. DEd CNAA, 1990. *Publications:* The New Polytechnics, 1968; numerous articles and papers. *Address:* 5 Millfield Road, Chorley, Lancs PR7 1RF. *T:* (01257) 415099. *Club:* Savile.

ROBINSON, (Francis) Alastair (Lavie); Group Vice-Chairman, Barclays Bank, 1992–96; non-executive Director: RMC plc, since 1996; Marshall of Cambridge (Holdings) Ltd, since 1996; Portman Building Society, since 1998; *b* 19 Sept. 1937; *s* of late Stephen and Patricia Robinson; *m* 1961, Lavinia Elizabeth Napier; two *d.* *Educ:* Eton. Nat Service, 4th/7th Royal Dragoon Guards, 1956–58 (2nd Lieut). Mercantile Credit: management trainee, 1959; Gen. Manager, 1971; Mem. Board, 1978; Chief Exec. Officer and Pres., Barclays American, USA, 1981; Regional Gen. Manager, Asia-Barclays International, 1984; Barclays Bank: Dir Personnel, 1987; Exec. Dir, UK Ops, 1990–92; Exec. Dir, Banking Div., 1992–96. *Recreations:* music, country pursuits.

ROBINSON, Prof. Francis Christopher Rowland, PhD; Professor of History of South Asia, University of London, since 1990; Vice-Principal (Research and Enterprise), Royal Holloway, University of London, since 1997; *b* Southgate, 23 Nov. 1944; *s* of late Leonard Robinson and Joyce Robinson (*née* King); *m* 1971, Patricia Courtenay Hughes; one *s* one *d*. *Educ:* County Grammar Sch. for Boys, Bexhill-on-Sea; Trinity Coll., Cambridge (MA, PhD). Prize Fellow, Trinity Coll., Cambridge, 1969–73; Royal Holloway College, then Royal Holloway and Bedford New College, University of London: Lectr in History, 1973–85; Reader, 1985–90; Hd of Dept, 1990–96; Mem., Council, 1991–; Mem., Academic Cttee, 1994–, Council, 1995–98, London Univ. Vis. Prof., S Asia Program, 1982 and 1986, Near East Program, 1985, Jackson Sch. of Internat. Studies, Univ. of Washington; Directeur d'Etudes Associé, Ecole des Hautes Etudes en Sciences Sociales, Paris, 1985. Member, Board of Management: Inst. of Histl Research, 1994–99; Inst. of Commonwealth Studies, 1994–99. Pres., RAS, 1997–2000 (Vice-Pres., 2000–); Mem. Council, Soc. for S Asian Studies, 1998–. Trustee, Charles Wallace (Pakistan) Trust, 1999–. FRSA 1997. Iqbal Centenary Medal (Pakistan), 1978. *Publications:* Separatism among Indian Muslims: the politics of the United Provinces' Muslims 1860–1923, 1974, 2nd edn 1993; (with F. Harcourt) Twentieth Century World History: a select bibliography, 1979; Atlas of the Islamic World since 1500, 1982; (with P. R. Brass) Indian National Congress and Indian Society 1885–1985, 1987; Varieties of South Asia Islam, 1988; (ed) Cambridge Encyclopedia of India, Pakistan, Bangladesh, Sri Lanka, 1989; (ed) Cambridge Illustrated History of the Islamic World, 1996; Islam and Muslim History in South Asia, 2000; The 'Ulama of Farangi Mahall and Islamic Culture in South Asia, 2001; contrib. Modern Asian Studies, S Asia, Jl of Islamic Studies, Encyclopedia of Islam, Indian Sociology, etc. *Recreations:* ball games, gardening, people, books, travel, food and wine. *Address:* Vice-Principal's Office, Royal Holloway, University of London, Egham, Surrey TW20 0EX. *T:* (01784) 443995. *Clubs:* Athenæum; Hawks.

ROBINSON, Geoffrey; *see* Robinson, A. G.

ROBINSON, Geoffrey; MP (Lab) Coventry North West, since March 1976; *b* 25 May 1938; *s* of Robert Norman Robinson and Dorothy Jane Robinson (*née* Skelly); *m* 1967, Marie Elena Giorgio; one *s* one *d*. *Educ:* Emanuel School; Cambridge and Yale Univs. Labour Party Research Assistant, 1965–68; Senior Executive, Industrial Reorganisation Corporation, 1968–70; Financial Controller, British Leyland, 1971–72; Managing Director, Leyland Innocenti, Milan, 1972–73; Chief Exec., Jaguar Cars, Coventry, 1973–75; Chief Exec. (unpaid), Meriden Motor Cycle Workers' Co-op, 1978–80 (Dir, 1980–82). Chm., TransTec PLC, 1986–97. Dir, W Midlands Enterprise Bd, 1980–84. Opposition spokesman on science, 1982–83, on regional affairs and industry, 1983–86; HM Paymaster General, 1997–98. *Publication:* The Unconventional Minister: my life inside New Labour, 2000. *Recreations:* reading, architecture, gardens, football. *Address:* House of Commons, SW1A 0AA. *T:* (020) 7219 3000.

ROBINSON, Dr Geoffrey Walter, CBE 1998; FREng, FIEE, FBCS; Director General and Chief Executive, Ordnance Survey, 1998–99; *b* 9 Nov. 1945; *s* of late George Robinson and Edith Margaret (*née* Wilson); *m* 1967 Edwina Jones; one *s* one *d*. *Educ:* Aireborough Grammar Sch.; Nottingham Univ. (BSc 1st Cl. Maths; PhD). IBM UK: Lab. posts, 1969–82; Manager of Scientific Centre, 1982–84; Technical Progs Advr, 1984–85; Technical Dir, 1986–88; Dir, Laboratories, 1988–92, 1994–96; Vice Pres., Networking Software Div., 1994–96; Dir of Technol., 1996–97; Chm., Transarc Corp., 1994–96. Chief Advr on Sci. and Technol., DTI, 1992–94. Dep. Chm., Foundn for Sci. and Technol., 1998–2000. Member: SERC, 1992–94; NERC, 1992–94; PPARC, 1994–98; CCLRC, 1995–98; Bd, QAA, 1997–2000; Bd, British Geol Survey, 2001–. Liveryman: Co. of Inf. Technologists, 1992; Scientific Instrument Makers' Co., 1996. Gov., King Alfred's Coll., Winchester, 1993–99 (Hon. DTech 1992). FBCS 1994 (Pres., 1995–96); FIEE 1994 (Vice Pres., 1998–2000); FREng (FEng 1994). FRSA 1992. DUniv Leeds Metropolitan, 1997. *Publications:* articles on science, technol. and society. *Recreation:* music. *Address:* Fardale, Hookwood Lane, Ampfield, Romsey, Hants SO51 9BZ. *T:* (023) 8026 1837, *Fax:* (023) 8027 1926; *e-mail:* geoff_robinson@attglobal.net. *Club:* Athenæum.

ROBINSON, Gerrard Jude; Chairman, Arts Council of England, since 1998; Director, Granada plc, since 2001; *b* 23 Oct. 1948; *s* of Anthony and Elizabeth Ann Robinson; *m* 1st, 1970, Maria Ann Borg (marr. diss. 1990); one *s* one *d*; 2nd, 1990, Heather Peta Leaman; one *s* one *d*. *Educ:* St Mary's Coll., Castlehead. FCMA 1991. Works Accountant, Lesney Products, 1970–1974; Financial Controller, Lex Industrial Distribution and Hire, 1974–80; Coca Cola: Finance Dir, 1980–81; Sales and Mkting Dir, 1981–83; Man. Dir, 1983–84; Man. Dir, Grand Metropolitan Contract Services, 1984–87; Chief Exec., Compass Gp plc, 1987–91; Chief Exec., 1991–96, Chm., 1996–2000, Granada Gp plc; Chairman: LWT, 1994–96; ITN, 1995–97; BSkyB, 1995–98; Granada Compass plc, 2000–01. *Recreations:* golf, opera, chess, ski-ing, reading, music. *Address:* Granada plc, London Television Centre, Upper Ground, SE1 9LT; Arts Council of England, 14 Great Peter Street, SW1P 3NQ. *Club:* Wisley Golf.

ROBINSON, Sir Ian, Kt 2000; FREng, FIChemE; Chairman: Amey plc, since 2001; Scottish Enterprise, since 2001; Deputy Chairman, Hilton Group, since 2001; *b* 3 May 1942; *s* of Thomas Mottram Robinson and Eva Iris Robinson (*née* Bird); *m* 1967, Kathleen Crawford Leay; one *s* one *d*. *Educ:* Leeds Univ. (BSc); Harvard Univ. FIChemE 1982; FREng (FEng 1994). With Kellogg International Co. Ltd, 1964–72; Managing Director: Ralph M. Parsons Co. Ltd, 1972–86; John Brown Engrgs & Constructors, 1986–92; Dir and Chm., Engrg Div., Trafalgar House plc, 1992–95; Chief Exec., Scottish Power plc, 1995–2001. *Recreations:* golf, gardening. *Address:* Amey plc, 24 Hanover Square, W1S 1JD. *Club:* Royal Automobile.

ROBINSON, Iris; MP (DemU) Strangford, since 2001; Member (DemU) Strangford, Northern Ireland Assembly, since 1999; *b* 6 Sept. 1949; *d* of Joseph and Mary Collins; *m* 1970, Peter David Robinson, *qv*; two *s* one *d*. *Educ:* Knockbreda Intermediate Sch.; Cregagh Tech. Coll. Mem. (DemU) Castlereagh BC, 1989– (Mayor 1992, 1995, 2000). *Recreation:* interior design. *Address:* House of Commons, SW1A 0AA; (constituency office) 2(B) James Street, Newtownards, Northern Ireland BT23 4DY. *T:* (028) 9182 7701.

ROBINSON, Jancis Mary, (Mrs N. L. Lander), MW; wine writer and broadcaster; *b* 22 April 1950; *d* of late Thomas Edward Robinson and of Ann Sheelagh Margaret Robinson (*née* Conacher); *m* 1981, Nicholas Laurence Lander; one *s* two *d*. *Educ:* Carlisle and County High Sch. for Girls; St Anne's Coll., Oxford (MA). Editor, Wine & Spirit, 1976–80; Founder and Editor, Drinker's Digest (subseq. Which? Wine Monthly), 1977–82; Editor, Which? Wine Guide, 1980–82; Sunday Times Wine Corresp., 1980–86; Evening Standard Wine Corresp., 1987–88; Financial Times Wine Corresp., 1989–; freelance journalism, particularly on wine, food and people, 1980–; freelance television and radio broadcasting, on various subjects, 1983–; Writer/Presenter: The Wine Programme, 1983 (Glenfiddich Trophy), 1985, 1987; Jancis Robinson Meets . . ., 1987; Matters of Taste, 1989, 1991; Vintners' Tales, 1992, 1998; Jancis Robinson's Wine Course, 1995 (Glenfiddich Trophy); The Food Chain, 1996; Taste, 1999; wine judging and lecturing, 1983–; Wine Consultant, British Airways, 1995–. Dir, Eden Productions Ltd, 1989–. DUniv Open, 1997. *Publications:* The Wine Book, 1979, rev. edn 1983; The Great Wine Book, 1982 (Glenfiddich Award); Masterglass, 1983, rev. edn 1987; How to Choose and Enjoy Wine, 1984; Vines, Grapes and Wines, 1986 (André Simon Meml Prize, Wine Guild Award, Clicquot Book of the Year); Jancis Robinson's Adventures with Food and Wine, 1987; Jancis Robinson on the Demon Drink, 1988; Vintage Timecharts, 1989; (ed) The Oxford Companion to Wine, 1994 (6 internat. awards), 2nd edn 1999; Jancis Robinson's Wine Course, 1995; Jancis Robinson's Guide to Wine Grapes, 1996; Confessions of a Wine Lover (autobiog.), 1997; Jancis Robinson's Wine Tasting Workbook, 2000; Jancis Robinson's Concise Wine Companion, 2001; (with Hugh Johnson) The World Atlas of Wines, 5th edn 2001. *Recreations:* wine, food and words. *Address:* c/o Peters, Fraser & Dunlop, Drury House, 34–43 Russell Street, WC2B 5HA.

ROBINSON, Jane; *see* Morrice, J.

ROBINSON, John Harris, FREng, FIChemE; Chairman: Railtrack, since 2001; UK Coal (formerly RJB Mining) plc, since 1997; George Wimpey plc, since 1999 (non-executive Director, since 1998); *b* 22 Dec. 1940; *s* of Thomas and Florence Robinson; *m* 1963, Doreen Alice Gardner; one *s* one *d*. *Educ:* Woodhouse Grove Sch.; Birmingham Univ. (BSc). CEng 1968, FREng (FEng 1998); FIChemE 1983. ICI plc, 1962–65; Fisons plc, 1965–70; PA Consulting Gp, 1970–75; Woodhouse and Rixson, 1975–79; Smith & Nephew plc: Man. Dir, Healthcare Div., 1979–82; Dir, 1982–89; Dep. Chief Exec., 1989–90; Chief Exec., 1990–97; Chm., 1997–99; Chm., Low & Bonar PLC, 1997–2001. Non-exec. Dir, Delta plc, 1993–2001. Chm., Healthcare Sector Gp, DTI, 1996–2001; Mem., Industrial Develt Adv. Bd, DTI, 1998–2001. Mem. Council, CBI, 1991–99 (Chm., Technol. and Innovation Cttee, 1998–2001). Gov., Hymers Coll., Hull, 1983–; Chm. Council and Pro-Chancellor, Hull Univ., 1998–; Mem., Cttee of Univ. Chairmen, 1998–. President: IChemE, 1999; Inst. of Mgt, 2001. CIMgt 1991; FRSA 1992. Hon. DEng Birmingham, 2000; DUniv Bradford, 2000. *Recreations:* golf, cricket, theatre. *Address:* 35 Marsham Court, Marsham Street, SW1P 4JY. *T:* (020) 7834 6838. *Clubs:* Athenæum; Brough Golf (E Yorks).

ROBINSON, Sir John (James Michael Laud), 11th Bt *cr* 1660; DL; Chairman, Northampton General Hospital NHS Trust, 1994–99; *b* 19 Jan. 1943; *s* of Michael Frederick Laud Robinson (*d* 1971) and Elizabeth (*née* Bridge); *S* grandfather, 1975; *m* 1968, Gayle Elizabeth (*née* Keyes); two *s* one *d*. *Educ:* Eton; Trinity Coll., Dublin (MA, Economics and Political Science). Chartered Financial Analyst. Chm., St Andrews Hosp., Northampton, 1984–94. Pres., British Red Cross, Northants Br., 1982–90. DL Northants, 1984. *Heir:* *s* Mark Christopher Michael Villiers Robinson, *b* 23 April 1972. *Address:* Cranford Hall, Cranford, Kettering, Northants NN14 4AL.

ROBINSON, Very Rev. (John) Kenneth; Dean of Gibraltar, since 2000; Archdeacon of Gibraltar, since 1994; *b* 17 Dec. 1936; *s* of John Robinson and Elizabeth Ellen Robinson (*née* Blackburn); *m* 1965, Merrylyn Kay (*née* Young); one *s* one *d*. *Educ:* Balshaw's Grammar Sch., Leyland, Lancs; KCL (BD 1961). Ordained deacon, 1962, priest 1963; Assistant Curate: St Chad, Poulton-le-Fylde, 1962–65; Lancaster Priory, 1965–66; Chaplain, St John's Army Children's Sch., Singapore, 1966–68; Vicar, Holy Trinity, Colne, Lancs, 1968–70; Dir of Educn, dio. Windward Is, WI, 1971–74; Vicar, St Luke, Skerton, Lancaster, 1974–81; Area Sec., USPG, 1981–91; Minor Canon, St Edmundsbury Cathedral, 1982–91; Chaplain, Greater Lisbon, Portugal, 1991–2000. *Recreations:* swimming, crossword puzzles, cooking. *Address:* The Deanery, Bomb House Lane, Gibraltar. *T:* 78377.

ROBINSON, John Martin Cotton, FSA; antiquary; Partner, Historic Buildings Consultants, since 1988; *b* 10 Sept. 1948; *s* of John Cotton Robinson and Ellen Anne Cecilia Robinson, *e d* of George Adams, Cape Town, S Africa. *Educ:* Fort Augustus Abbey; St Andrews Univ. (MA 1970); Oriel Coll., Oxford (DPhil 1974). FSA 1979. Historic Buildings Div., GLC, 1974–86; Librarian to Duke of Norfolk, 1978–. Fitzalan Pursuivant Extraordinary, 1982–88; Maltravers Herald Extraordinary, 1988–. Heraldic Advr, NT, 1996–. Vice-Chm., Georgian Gp, 1990–; Chm., Art and Architecture Cttee, Westminster Cathedral, 1996–; Member: Prince of Wales Restoration Cttee, Windsor Castle, 1993–94; NW Cttee, NT, 1994–; Trustee, Abbot Hall Art Gall., 1990–. KM 1980. Architectural Editor, Survey of London, 1978–80. *Publications:* The Wyatts, 1979; Georgian Model Farms, 1980; Dukes of Norfolk, 1982; Latest Country Houses, 1983; Cardinal Consalvi, 1987; (with Thomas Woodcock) Oxford Guide to Heraldry, 1988; Temples of Delight, 1990; Guide to Country Houses of the North West, 1991; Treasures of English Churches, 1995. *Address:* Beckside House, Barbon, Carnforth, Lancs LA6 2LT. *T:* (office) (020) 7831 4398, *Fax:* (office) (020) 7831 8831. *Clubs:* Travellers, Beefsteak, Pitt, XV, Roxburghe (Sec., 1990–).

ROBINSON, Keith; *see* Robinson, L. K.

ROBINSON, Dr Keith; Chief Executive, Wiltshire County Council, since 1996; *b* 12 July 1951; *s* of Wes and Eileen Robinson; *m* 1976, Anne Elizabeth Wilkinson; one *s* one *d*. *Educ:* Sidney Sussex Coll., Cambridge (MA); Durham Univ. (MA); Manchester Univ. (PhD). Dept of Educn and Science, 1975–85; Leics CC, 1985–88; Bucks CC, 1988–93; Wilts CC, 1993–. *Recreations:* jazz, running. *Address:* County Hall, Trowbridge, Wilts BA14 8JF. *T:* (01225) 713100.

ROBINSON, Very Rev. Kenneth; *see* Robinson, Very Rev. J. K.

ROBINSON, Kenneth Ernest, CBE 1971; MA, FRHistS; *b* 9 March 1914; *o s* of late Ernest and Isabel Robinson, Plumstead, Kent; *m* 1938, Stephanie (*d* 1994), *o d* of late William Wilson, Westminster; one *s* one *d*. *Educ:* Monoux Grammar School, Walthamstow; Hertford College, Oxford (Scholar, 1st Cl. PPE; 1st Cl. Mod. Hist.; Beit Senior Schol. in Colonial History); London School of Economics. Colonial Office, 1936; Asst Sec. 1946; resigned 1948. Fellow of Nuffield Coll. (Hon. Fellow, 1984) and Reader in Commonwealth Govt, Oxford, 1948–57; Dir, Inst. of Commonwealth Studies and Prof. of Commonwealth Affairs, Univ. of London, 1957–65 (Hon. Life Mem., 1980–); Vice-Chancellor, Univ. of Hong Kong, 1965–72; Hallsworth Res. Fellow, Univ. of Manchester, 1972–74; Dir, Commonwealth Studies Resources Survey, Univ. of London, 1974–76. Leverhulme Res. Fellow, 1952–53; Vis. Lectr, Sch. of Advanced Internat. Studies, Johns Hopkins Univ., 1954; Carnegie Travel Grant, East, Central and S Africa, 1960; Reid Lectr, Acadia Univ., 1963; Vis. Prof., Duke Univ., NC, 1963; Callander Lectr, Aberdeen, 1979. Editor, Jl of Commonwealth Political Studies, 1961–65; Special Commonwealth Award, ODM, 1965. Member: (part-time) Directing Staff, Civil Service Selection Bd, 1951–56, Assessor Panel, 1973–77; Colonial Economic Res. Cttee, 1949–62; Colonial SSRC, 1958–62; Inter-Univ. Council for Higher Educn Overseas, 1973–79; Mem. Council: Overseas Develt Inst. 1960–65; RIIA, 1962–65; Internat. African Inst., 1960–65; African Studies Assoc., UK, 1963–65, 1978–81; ACU, 1967–68; Hong Kong Management Assoc., 1965–72; Chinese Univ. of Hong Kong, 1965–72; Univ. of Cape Coast, 1972–74; Royal Commonwealth Soc., 1974–87 (Vice Pres., 1984–); Royal African Soc., 1983–89 (Pres., 1989–96); Life Mem. Ct, Univ. of Hong Kong, 1972.

Governor, LSE, 1959–65. Corresp. Mem., Académie des Sciences d'Outre-Mer, Paris. Hon. LLD Chinese Univ. of Hong Kong, 1969; Hon. DLitt, Univ. of Hong Kong, 1972; DUniv Open, 1978. JP Hong Kong, 1967–72. *Publications:* (with W. J. M. Mackenzie) Five Elections in Africa, 1960; (with A. F. Madden) Essays in Imperial Government presented to Margery Perham, 1963; The Dilemmas of Trusteeship, 1965; (with W. B. Hamilton & C. D. Goodwin) A Decade of the Commonwealth 1955–64 (USA), 1966. Contrib. to Africa Today (USA), 1955; Africa in the Modern World (USA), 1955; University Cooperation and Asian Development (USA), 1967; L'Europe du XIXe et du XXe Siècle, Vol. 7 (Italy), 1968; Experts in Africa, 1980; Perspectives on Imperialism and Decolonisation, 1984; papers in learned jls; *festschriften:* Imperialism, the State, and the Third World, ed M. Twaddle, 1992; Decolonisation and the International Community, 1993. *Address:* 52 The Cloisters, Pegasus Grange, Whitehouse Road, Oxford OX1 4QQ. *T:* (01865) 725517. *Clubs:* Royal Commonwealth Society, Lansdowne; Hong Kong.

ROBINSON, Kenneth William; Member (UU) Antrim East, Northern Ireland Assembly, since 1998; *b* Belfast, 2 June 1942; *s* of Joseph Robinson and Anne Elizabeth (*née* Semple); *m* 1964, Louisa Morrison; three *s*. *Educ:* Whitehouse Primary Sch.; Ballyclare High Sch.; Stranmillis Coll. (Teacher's Cert. 1963); Queen's Univ., Belfast (BEd 1979). Principal Teacher: Lisfearty Primary Sch., 1975–77; Argyle Primary Sch., 1977–80; Cavehill Primary Sch., 1980–96. Mem., and Vice-Chm. Educn Cttee, N Eastern Educn and Liby Bd, 1985–93. Mem. (UU), Newtownabbey BC, 1985– (Mayor, 1991–92; Vice Chm., Econ. Develt Cttee, 1995–); Mem., Newtownabbey Dist Partnership Bd, 1996–. Mem., Newtownabbey Volunteer Bureau, 1985–. Chm., S Antrim Unionist Assoc., 1985–87. Governor: E Antrim Inst. Higher and Further Educn, 1985–93; Whiteabbey Primary Sch., 1985–; Hollybank Primary Sch., 1985–. Vice-Chm., Newtownabbey-Dorsten Twinning Assoc., 2001–. *Recreations:* foreign travel, caravanning, historical research, Association Football, swimming. *Address:* 5 Sycamore Close, Jordanstown, Newtownabbey, Co. Antrim BT37 0PL. *T:* (028) 9086 6056.

ROBINSON, Lee Fisher, CEng; Chairman, HMC Technology plc, since 1983; Director: HMC Technology (Asiatic) Ltd, since 1997; Roro Trading Ltd, since 1982; *b* 17 July 1923; *m* 1st, 1944; three *d*; 2nd, 1976, June Edna Hopkins. *Educ:* Howard Sch.; Cardiff Tech. College. CEng, MICE; MCIArb. Royal Engrs, Sappers and Miners, IE, 1942–45. Turriff Const. Corp. Ltd, HBM (BCC), 1963; Man. Dir, Power Gas Corp. Ltd, 1964; Chief Exec. and Dep. Chm., Turriff Construction Corp., 1970–73. Director: Davy-Ashmore Ltd, 1970; Combustion Systems (NRDC), 1972–96 (Chm., 1978); Redwood Internat. (UK) Ltd, 1972; Altech SA, 1976–96; Protech SA, 1976–96; BCS Ltd, 1976–96; Charterhouse Strategic Development Ltd, 1976–80 (Gp Indust. Adviser, Charterhouse Gp); Ingeco Laing SA, 1977–96; RTR (Oil Sands) Alberta, 1977–96; RTR Canada Ltd, 1977–96; RTR SA (also Chief Exec.), 1977–96; RTL SA (also Vice-Pres.), 1977–96; Thalassa (North Sea) Ltd, 1980–96; Marcent Natural Resources Ltd (Man. Dir), 1980–96; Hydromet Mineral Co., 1983–96; Solvex Corp., 1988–96; Chairman: Graesser (Contractors) Ltd, 1979–96; Biotechna Ltd, 1982–96; ABG Ltd, 1993–96; Bio-Electrical Ltd, 1993–96; Chm. and Chief Exec. Officer, Biotechna Environmental Ltd, 1994–96. Consultant, Internat. Management Consultants, 1972–96. Chm., Warren Spring Adv. Bd, 1969–72; Mem. Adv. Council for Technology, 1968–69. Mem., Academy of Experts, 1996. *Publications:* Cost and Financing of Fertiliser Projects in India, 1967; various articles. *Recreations:* badminton, sailing. *Address:* Flat 3, Athenaeum Hall, Vale-of-Health, NW3 1AP. *Club:* Wig and Pen.

ROBINSON, (Leonard) Keith, CBE 1981; DL; management consultant, 1985–87; County Chief Executive, Hampshire County Council, 1973–85; Clerk of Lieutenancy, 1973–85; *b* 2 July 1920; *m* 1948, Susan May Tomkinson; two *s* two *d*. *Educ:* Queen Elizabeth's Grammar Sch., Blackburn; Victoria Univ. of Manchester (LLB). Solicitor. RAFVR, 1940–46 (Navigator, Sqdn-Ldr). Asst Solicitor, City and County of Bristol, 1948–55; Dep. Town Clerk, Birkenhead Co. Borough Council, 1955–66; Town Clerk, Stoke-on-Trent City Council, 1966–73. Association of County Councils: Mem., Officers Adv. Gp, 1974–83 (Chm., 1977–82); Adviser, Policy Cttee, 1975–82; Adviser, Local Govt Finance Cttee, 1976–85; Chm., Assoc. of County Chief Execs, 1975–77. Member: W Mids Econ. Planning Council, 1967–73; Keele Univ. Council, 1968–73; Central Cttee for Reclamation of Derelict Land, 1971–74; Quality Assce Council, BSI, 1973–77; Job Creation Programme Action Cttee for London and SE, 1976–77; District Manpower Cttee, 1980–83; Adv. Council for Energy Conservation, 1982–84; Local Authorities' Mutual Investment Trust, 1982–83; Hillier Arboretum Management Cttee, 1985–99 (Sec., 1977–85); Southern Arts, 1985–91; Exec. Cttee, Hampshire Develt Assoc., 1985–91; Asst Comr, Local Govt Boundary Commn, 1986–91. Mem. Exec. Cttee, Hampshire Gardens Trust, 1985–; Dir, Salisbury Playhouse, 1979–93; Vice-Chm., Nuffield Theatre Bd, 1985–95; Trustee, New Theatre Royal (Portsmouth) Ltd, 1976–; Pres., Winchester Dramatic Soc., 1984–95. Mem., Barton Stacey PCC, 1997–2001 (Chm., Church Appeal Cttee). DL Hants, 1985. *Publications:* contrib. local govt and legal jls. *Recreations:* fly-fishing, theatre, photography, gardening. *Address:* Bransbury Mill Cottage, Bransbury, Barton Stacey, Winchester, Hants SO21 3QJ. *Club:* MCC.

ROBINSON, Mark; Member (DemU) South Belfast, Northern Ireland Assembly, since 1998; *b* 12 May 1959; *s* of Desmond and Evelyne Robinson. *Educ:* Knockbreda High Sch.; Castlereagh Coll. of Further Educn (HNC). Mechanical engr, 1977–89; Gen. Manager, 1989–95; Managing Director: DCR Engrg, 1995–; Woodstock Glazing, 1995–. Mem. (DemU) Castlereagh BC, 1997–. *Recreations:* golf, musical theatre. *Address:* South Belfast DUP Advice Centre, 215A Lisburn Road, Belfast BT9 7EJ. *T:* (028) 9022 5969.

ROBINSON, Mark Noel Foster; Executive Director, Commonwealth Press Union, since 1997; *b* 26 Dec. 1946; *s* of late John Foster Robinson, CBE, TD and Margaret Eve Hannah Paterson; *m* 1982, Vivien Radclyffe (*née* Pilkington); one *s* one *d*. *Educ:* Harrow School; Christ Church, Oxford. MA Hons Modern History. Called to the Bar, Middle Temple, 1975. Research Assistant to Patrick Cormack, MP, 1970–71; Special Asst to US Congressman Hon. F. Bradford Morse, 1971–72; Special Asst to Chief of UN Emergency Operation in Bangladesh, 1972–73; Second Officer, Exec. Office, UN Secretary-General, 1974–77; Asst Dir, Commonwealth Secretariat, 1977–83. Consultant, 1987, Dir, 1988–91, non-exec. Dir, 1991–94, Leopold Joseph & Sons Ltd; non-exec. Dir, Leopold Joseph Hldgs, 1994–95. MP (C): Newport West, 1983–87; Somerton and Frome, 1992–97; contested (C): Newport West, 1987; Somerton and Frome, 1997. PPS to Sec. of State for Wales, 1984–85; Parly Under Sec. of State, Welsh Office, 1985–87; PPS to Minister for Overseas Develt and to Parly Under-Sec. of State, FCO, 1992–94, to Sec. of State for Foreign and Commonwealth Affairs, 1994–95, to Chief Sec. to Treasury, 1995–97. Member: Foreign Affairs Select Cttee, 1983–84; Welsh Affairs Cttee, 1992–97. Chm., UN Parly Gp, 1992–98 (Hon. Sec., 1983–85; Vice Chm., 1996–97); Mem. Cttee, British American Parly Gp, 1996–97. Mem., Commonwealth Develt Corp., 1988–92; Chm., Council for Educn in the Commonwealth, 1999–. Mem. Council, Winston Churchill Meml Trust, 1993–. Fellow, Industry and Parlt Trust, 1985. Member: RUSI, 1984; RIIA, 1984. FIMgt (FBIM 1983); FRSA 1990. *Recreations:* include the countryside and fishing. *Clubs:* Brooks's, Pratt's, Travellers.

ROBINSON, Mary; United Nations High Commissioner for Human Rights, since 1997; *b* 21 May 1944; *d* of Aubrey and Tessa Bourke; *m* 1970, Nicholas Robinson; two *s* one *d*. *Educ:* Trinity Coll. Dublin (MA, LLB 1967; Hon. Fellow 1991); Harvard Law Sch. (LLM 1968). Called to the Bar, King's Inns, Dublin, 1967 (Hon. Bencher, 1991), Middle Temple, 1973 (Hon. Bencher, 1991); SC 1980. Reid Prof. of Constitutional and Criminal Law, 1969–75, Lectr in EC Law, 1975–90, TCD. Mem., Irish Senate, 1969–89; Pres. of Ireland, 1990–97. Member: Adv. Bd, Common Market Law Review, 1976–90; Internat. Commn of Jurists, 1987–90; Adv. Cttee, Inter-Rights, 1984–90. Chancellor, Dublin Univ., 1998–. MRIA 1992; Mem., Amer. Phil Soc., 1998. Hon. Fellow: Hertford Coll., Oxford, 1999; LSE, 1999. Hon. FRCOG 1995; Hon. FRCPsych; Hon. FRCPI; Hon. FRCSI; Hon. FIEI. DCL Oxford (by diploma), 1993; hon. doctorates: Basle; Brown; Cambridge; Columbia; Costa Rica; Coventry; Dublin; Dublin City; Dublin Inst. of Technol.; Essex; Fordham; Harvard; Leuven; Liverpool; London; Melbourne; Mongolia; Montpellier; Northeastern; NUI; Poznan; QUB; Rennes; St Andrews; Schweitzer Internat., Berne; Seoul; Toronto; Uppsala; Wales; Yale. *Address:* Palais des Nations, United Nations, 1211 Geneva 10, Switzerland.

ROBINSON, Michael John, CMG 1993; HM Diplomatic Service; Senior Political Adviser, OSCE Mission to Yugoslavia, since 2001 (on secondment); *b* 19 Dec. 1946; *s* of George Robinson and Beryl Florence Naldrett Robinson; *m* 1971, Anne Jamieson Scott; two *s* two *d*. *Educ:* Cheadle Hulme Sch.; Worcester Coll., Oxford (BA Hons Mod. Langs). Third Sec., FCO, 1969; Russian lang. student, 1969; Third, subseq. Second, Sec., Moscow, 1970; Second, subseq. First, Sec., Madrid, 1972; FCO, 1977; UK Delegn to CSCE, Madrid, 1980; First Sec. and Head of Chancery, Madrid, 1981; Chef de Cabinet to Sec. Gen., OECD, Paris (on secondment), 1982; Dep. Head, UK Delegn to UNESCO, Paris, 1985; First Sec., subseq. Counsellor, FCO, 1986; Dep. Head of Mission and Consul-Gen., subseq. Chargé d'Affaires, Belgrade, 1990; Dep. Gov., Gibraltar, 1995–98; Pol Advr, OSCE Presence in Albania, Tirana (on secondment), 1999–2001. Vis. Fellow, RIIA, 1994. *Publication:* Managing Milosevic's Serbia, 1995. *Recreations:* reading, music, travel. *Address:* c/o Foreign and Commonwealth Office, SW1A 2AH. *Clubs:* Royal Over-Seas League; Royal Gibraltar Yacht.

ROBINSON, Air Vice-Marshal Michael Maurice Jeffries, CB 1982; *b* 11 Feb. 1927; *s* of Dr Maurice Robinson and Muriel (*née* Jeffries); *m* 1952, Drusilla Dallas Bush; one *s* two *d*. *Educ:* King's Sch., Bruton; Queen's Coll., Oxford; RAF Coll., Cranwell. psa 1961, jssc 1965. MA History, Univ. of West of England, 1994. Commnd, 1948; 45 Sqdn, Malaya, 1948–51; CFS, 1953–55; OC 100 Sqdn, 1962–64; Comd, RAF Lossiemouth, 1972–74; Asst Comdt, RAF Coll., Cranwell, 1974–77; SASO No 1 Gp, 1977–79; Dir Gen. of Organisation (RAF), 1979–82, retd. Wing Comdr 1961, Gp Captain 1970, Air Cdre 1976, Air Vice-Marshal 1980. *Recreations:* golf, gardening, going to the opera. *Address:* HSBC, 1 Market Place, Wells, Somerset BA5 2RN. *Club:* Royal Air Force.

ROBINSON, Michael R.; *see* Rowan-Robinson, G. M.

ROBINSON, (Moureen) Ann, (Mrs Peter Robinson); Chair, Gas and Electricity Consumers Council, since 2000; *d* of William and Winifred Flatley; *m* 1961, Peter Crawford Robinson. DHSS, 1969–74; Central Policy Review Staff, 1974–77; nurses and midwives pay, educn and professional matters, 1981–85; liaison with Health Authorities, NHS planning and review, 1985–86; social security operations, 1986–93; Dir of Policy and Planning, Benefits Agency, DSS, 1990–93; Chief Exec., The Spastics Soc., then Scope, 1993–95; Head, Govt Consultancy Computer Sciences Corp., 1995–96; Dir-Gen., British Retail Consortium, 1997–99; Chairman: Gas Consumers Council, 2000; London Electricity Consumer Cttee, 2000. Chm., Victim Support London, 1999–; Trustee, Foundn for Credit Counselling, 2000–. FRSA 1992. *Recreations:* walking, fine wine, bridge, fun tennis. *Address:* 1 Heathfield Road, Maidstone, Kent ME14 2AD; 29 Upper Berkeley Street, W1H 7PG.

ROBINSON, Ven. Neil; Archdeacon of Suffolk, 1987–94; *b* 28 Feb. 1929; *s* of James and Alice Robinson; *m* 1956, Kathlyn Williams; two *s* two *d*. *Educ:* Penistone Grammar School; Univ. of Durham (BA, DipTh). Curate of Holy Trinity Church, Hull, 1954–58; Vicar of St Thomas, South Wigston, Leicester, 1958–69; Rector and RD of Market Bosworth, Leicester, 1969–83; Residentiary Canon of Worcester Cathedral, 1983–87. *Recreation:* hill walking. *Address:* Skell Green, 16 Mallorie Court, Ripon, N Yorks HG4 2QG. *T:* (01765) 603075.

ROBINSON, Neil; Director of Programmes, Border Television, since 2000; *b* 25 April 1958; *s* of Arthur and Margery Robinson; *m* 1988, Susie Elizabeth Campbell; one *s*. *Educ:* Anfield Comprehensive Sch. Journalist: S Yorks Times, 1977–79; Evening Chronicle, Newcastle, 1979–86; Border Television: News Ed., 1986–87; Producer (various programmes), 1987–88; Head of News and Current Affairs, 1988–90; Controller of Programmes, 1990–2000. Dir, Cumbria Inward Investment Agency Ltd, 1997–. European Bd Mem., Co-op. Internat. de la Recherche et d'Actions en Matière de Communication, 1998–. Dir, NW Media Charitable Trust Ltd, 1998–99. Member: Northern Production Fund Panel, Northern Arts, 1993–; Cttee, BAFTA Scotland, 1998–. Mem., RTS, 1988; FRSA 1995. *Address:* Fayrefield, High Bank Hill, Kirkoswald, Cumbria CA10 1EZ. *Club:* Groucho.

ROBINSON, Oswald Horsley, CMG 1983; OBE 1977; HM Diplomatic Service, retired; *b* 24 Aug. 1926; *s* of Sir Edward Stanley Gotch Robinson, CBE, FSA, FBA, and Pamela, *d* of Sir Victor Horsley, CB, FRS; *m* 1954, Helena Faith, *d* of Dr F. R. Seymour; two *s* one *d*. *Educ:* Bedales Sch.; King's Coll., Cambridge. Served RE, 1943–48. Joined FO, 1951; served: Rangoon and Maymyo, 1954; FO, 1958; Mexico and Guatemala, 1961; Quito and Bogotá, 1963; FO (later FCO), 1965; Georgetown, Guyana, 1973; Bangkok, 1976; FCO, 1979–84. Dir, RCC Pilotage Foundn, 1985–95. *Publications:* (compiled) Atlantic Spain and Portugal, 1988; *edited:* Ports and Anchorages of the Antilles, 1991; North Africa, 1991; A Baltic Guide, 1992; Faeroes, Iceland and Greenland, 1994; Cruising Notes on the South Atlantic Coast of South America, 1996; Chile: Atacama Desert to Tierra del Fuego, 1998; Mediterranean Spain: part 1, 1998, part 2, 1999. *Recreation:* sailing. *Address:* Dunn House, The Green, Long Melford, Suffolk CO10 9DU. *Club:* Royal Cruising.

ROBINSON, Dr Patrick William, (Bill); Head UK Business Economist, Corporate Finance and Recovery, PricewaterhouseCoopers, since 1999; *b* 6 Jan. 1943; *s* of Harold Desmond Robinson and Joyce Grover; *m* 1st, 1966, Heather Jackson (*d* 1995); two *s* one *d*; 2nd, 1997, Priscilla Stille. *Educ:* Bryanston Sch.; St Edmund Hall, Oxford; DPhil Sussex 1969; MSc LSE 1971. Economic Asst, 10 Downing Street, 1969–70; Cabinet Office, 1970–71; Economic Adviser, HM Treasury, 1971–74; Head of Div., European Commn, 1974–78; Sen. Res. Fellow, London Business Sch., 1979–86; Adviser, Treasury and Civil Service Cttee, 1981–86; Dir, Inst. for Fiscal Studies, 1986–91; econ. columnist, The Independent, 1989–91; Special Advr to Chancellor of Exchequer, 1991–93; Dir, London Economics, 1993–99. Mem., Retail Prices Index Adv. Cttee, 1988–91. Editor: Exchange Rate Outlook, LBS, 1979–86; Economic Outlook, LBS, 1980–86; IFS Green Budget, 1987–91. *Publications:* Medium Term Exchange Rate Guidelines for Business Planning,

1983; Britain's Borrowing Problem, 1993; numerous articles. *Recreations:* bassoon playing, opera, bridge, ski-ing, windsurfing. *Address:* PricewaterhouseCoopers, 1 Embankment Place, WC2N 6NN. *T:* (020) 7213 5437; *e-mail:* dr.bill.robinson@uk.pwcglobal.com. *Club:* Reform.

ROBINSON, Peter; Director, Tootal Ltd, 1973–91; *b* 18 Jan. 1922; *s* of Harold Robinson and Jane Elizabeth Robinson; *m* Lesley Anne, step *d* of Major J. M. May, TD; two *s* two *d*. *Educ:* Prince Henry's Sch., Otley; Leeds Coll. of Technology (Diploma in Printing). Mem., Inst. of Printing. Management Trainee, 1940–41; flying duties, RAFVR, 1942–46; Leeds Coll. of Technol., 1946–49; Asst Manager, Robinson & Sons Ltd, Chesterfield, 1949–53; Works Dir and Man. Dir, Taylowe Ltd, 1953–62; Dir, Hazell Sun, 1964; British Printing Corporation, subseq. BPC: Dir, 1966–68; Man. Dir, 1969–75; Chm. and Chief Exec., 1976–82; Director: Chromoworks Ltd; Petty & Sons Ltd; Purnell & Sons Ltd; Radio Times Ltd; Hazells Offset Ltd; Taylowe Ltd. Formerly Council Mem., PIRA. CIMgt. *Recreations:* military history, cricket, golf. *Address:* 20 Links Road, Flackwell Heath, High Wycombe, Bucks HP10 9LY.

ROBINSON, Peter Damian, CB 1983; Deputy Secretary, Lord Chancellor's Department, 1980–86; *b* 11 July 1926; *s* of late John Robinson and Jill Clegg (*née* Easten); *m* 1st, 1956, Mary Katinka Bonner (*d* 1978), Peterborough; one *d* (and one *d* decd); 2nd, 1985, Mrs Sheila Suzanne Gibbins (*née* Guille). *Educ:* Corby Sch., Sunderland; Lincoln Coll., Oxford. MA. Royal Marine Commandos, 1944–46. Called to Bar, Middle Temple, 1951; practised common law, 1952–59; Clerk of Assize, NE Circuit, 1959–70; Administrator, NE Circuit, 1970–74; Circuit Administrator, SE Circuit, 1974–80; Dep. Clerk of the Crown in Chancery, Lord Chancellor's Dept, 1982–86. Advr on Hong Kong Judiciary, 1986. Member, Home Office Departmental Cttee on Legal Aid in Criminal Proceedings (the Widgery Cttee), 1964–66; Chm., Interdeptl Cttee on Conciliation, 1982–83. *Recreations:* reading, the countryside, antiques. *Address:* 15 Birklands Park, St Albans AL1 1TS.

ROBINSON, Peter David; MP (DemU) Belfast East, since 1979 (resigned seat Dec. 1985 in protest against Anglo-Irish Agreement; re-elected Jan. 1986); Member (DemU) Belfast East, Northern Ireland Assembly, since 1998; *b* 29 Dec. 1948; *s* of David McCrea Robinson and Sheliah Robinson; *m* 1970, Iris Collins (*see* I. Robinson); two *s* one *d*. *Educ:* Annadale Grammar School; Castlereagh Further Education College. Gen. Secretary, Ulster Democratic Unionist Party, 1975–79, Dep. Leader, 1980–87. Member: (DemU) Belfast E, NI Assembly, 1982–86; NI Forum, 1996–. Member, Castlereagh Borough Council, 1977–; Deputy Mayor, 1978; Mayor of Castlereagh, 1986. Member: Select Cttee on NI, 1994–; All-Party Cttee on Shipbuilding, 1992–. Minister for Regl Develt, NI Assembly, 1999–2000. Mem., NI Sports Council, 1986–. *Publications:* (jtly) Ulster—the facts, 1982; booklets include: The North Answers Back, 1970; Capital Punishment for Capital Crime, 1978; Ulster in Peril, 1981; Their Cry Was "No Surrender", 1989; The Union Under Fire, 1995. *Recreations:* golf, bowling. *Address:* 51 Gransha Road, Dundonald, Northern Ireland BT16 0HB; Strandtown Hall, 96 Belmont Avenue, Belfast BT4 3DE; *e-mail:* probin1690@aol.com.

ROBINSON, Peter James, FCIS, FCIB; Group Chief Executive, Forester UK, since 1998; *b* 28 April 1941; *s* of Percival Albert Robinson and Lillian Caroline (*née* Pantling); *m* 1st, 1963 (marr. diss.); twin *s* one *d*; 2nd, 1984, Janice Helen Jones; two *d*. *Educ:* Erith Co. Grammar Sch.; City of London Poly. FCIS 1967; FCIB 1967. Woolwich Building Society: mgt trainee, 1963–68; PA to Gen. Managers, 1968–70; Ops and Mkting Manager, 1970–72; Co. Sec., 1972–75; Asst Gen. Manager (Develt), 1975–81; Gen. Manager (Ops), 1981–86; Dep. Chief Exec. and Dir, 1986–91; Man. Dir, 1991–95; Gp Chief Exec., Woolwich Building Soc., 1996; management consultant, 1996–98. Chm., Metropolitan Assoc. of Building Socs, 1992. Freeman, City of London, 1982. MInstD 1988; CIMgt 1991. *Publications:* contrib. articles to Finance Gazette, Economist, Mgt Today, various newspapers. *Recreations:* cricket, golf, gardening, dogs. *Address:* Quakers, Brasted Chart, Kent TN16 1LY. *Clubs:* Royal Automobile, MCC.

ROBINSON, Prof. Peter Michael, FBA 2000; Tooke Professor of Economic Science and Statistics, London School of Economics and Political Science, since 1995 (Professor of Econometrics, 1984–95); Leverhulme Trust Personal Research Professor, since 1998; *b* 20 April 1947; *s* of Maurice Allan Robinson and Brenda Margaret (*née* Ponsford); *m* 1981, Wendy Rhea Brandmark; one *d*. *Educ:* Brockenhurst Grammar Sch.; University Coll. London (BSc); London School of Economics (MSc); Australian National Univ. (PhD). Lectr, LSE, 1969–70; Asst Prof. 1973–77, Associate Prof. 1977–79, Harvard Univ.; Associate Prof., Univ. of British Columbia, 1979–80; Prof., Univ. of Surrey, 1980–84. Fellow, Econometric Soc., 1989; FIMS 2000. Co-Editor: Econometric Theory, 1989–91; Econometrica, 1991–96; Jl of Econometrics, 1997–. *Publications:* (ed with M. Rosenblatt) Time Series Analysis, 1996; articles in books, and in learned jls, incl. Econometrica, Annals of Statistics. *Recreation:* walking. *Address:* Department of Economics, London School of Economics and Political Science, Houghton Street, WC2A 2AE. *T:* (020) 7955 7516.

ROBINSON, Philip; Assistant Chief Executive (Policy and Corporate Support), City of Bradford Metropolitan District Council, since 2000; *b* 2 March 1949; *s* of late Clifford and Vera Robinson; *m* 1974, Irene Langdale. *Educ:* Grange Grammar Sch., Bradford. IPFA, IRRV. City of Bradford Metropolitan District Council: Principal Accountant, 1982; Asst Dir of Finance, 1985; Dir of Finance, 1987; Strategic Dir (Corporate Services), 1995–2000. *Recreations:* sport, music, theatre. *Address:* City of Bradford Metropolitan District Council, City Hall, Bradford BD1 1HY. *T:* (01274) 754330.

ROBINSON, Philip Henry; Trustee, Canterbury Cathedral (1980) Pension Plan, since 1999; Member, Estates Committee, Canterbury Cathedral, 1993–99; *b* 4 Jan. 1926; *s* of Arthur Robinson and Frances M. Robinson; *m* 1st, 1959, Helen Wharton (marr. diss. 1979); one *s* one *d*; 2nd, 1985, Mrs A. L. D. Baring; two step *s*. *Educ:* Lincoln Sch.; Jesus Coll., Cambridge (Exhibr, MA); Sch. of Oriental and African Studies, London Univ.; NY Univ. Graduate Sch. of Business Admin. Member, Gray's Inn. Royal Navy, 1944–47; N. M. Rothschild & Sons, 1950–54; Actg Sec., British Newfoundland Corp., Montreal, 1954–56; Asst Vice-Pres., J. Henry Schroder Banking Corp., New York, 1956–61; J. Henry Schroder Wagg & Co. Ltd, 1961; Director: J. Henry Schroder Wagg & Co. Ltd, 1966–85; Siemens Ltd, 1967–86; Schroders & Chartered Ltd Hong Kong, 1971–85; Schroder International Ltd, 1973–85 (Exec. Vice-Pres., 1977–85); Standard Chartered PLC, 1986–91 (Chm., Audit Cttee, 1989–91); Chairman: Schroder Leasing Ltd, 1979–85; Sunbury Investment Co. Ltd, 1985–94; Berkertex Hldgs Ltd, 1987–88; Man. Trustee, Municipal Mutual Insurance Ltd, 1977–92 (Dep. Chm., 1992). Dir and Chm., Audit Cttee, CLF Municipal Bank, 1993–96; Dir, Capital Re Corp., NY, 1993–99 (Chm., Audit Cttee, 1994–98). Mem., Nat. Coal Board, 1973–77. Hon. Treasurer, Nat. Council for One Parent Families, 1977–79. *Recreations:* music, tennis. *Address:* Stone Hall, Great Mongeham, Deal, Kent CT14 0HB. *Club:* Brooks's.
See also A. G. Robinson.

ROBINSON, Hon. Raymond; *see* Robinson, Hon. A. N. R.

ROBINSON, Robert Henry; writer and broadcaster; *b* 17 Dec. 1927; *o s* of Ernest Redfern Robinson and Johanna Hogan; *m* 1958, Josephine Mary Richard; one *s* two *d*. *Educ:* Raynes Park Grammar Sch.; Exeter Coll., Oxford (MA). Editor of Isis, 1950. TV columnist, Sunday Chronicle, 1952; film and theatre columnist, Sunday Graphic, and radio critic, Sunday Times, 1956; editor Atticus, Sunday Times, 1960; weekly column, Private View, Sunday Times, 1962; film critic, Sunday Telegraph, 1965. Writer and presenter of TV programmes: Picture Parade, 1959; Points of View, 1961; Divided We Stand, 1964; The Look of the Week, 1966; Reason to Believe?, The Fifties, 1969; Chm., Call My Bluff, Ask The Family, 1967; The Book Programme, Vital Statistics, 1974; Word for Word, 1978; The Book Game, 1983 and 1985; Behind The Headlines, 1989–; films for TV: Robinson's Travels - the Pioneer Trail West, 1977; B. Traven: a mystery solved, 1978; From Shepherd's Bush to Simla, 1979; Robinson Cruising, 1981; The Auden Landscape, 1982; Robinson Country, 1983, 1987, 1993; In Trust—Houses and Heritage, 1986; The Magic Rectangle, 1986; presenter of: BBC radio current affairs programme Today, 1971–74; Chm., Brain of Britain, 1973–; Chm., Stop the Week, 1974–92; Ad Lib, 1989–; devised and presented: Conversations with Strangers, 1997; Divided We Stand, 1998; Odd Obits, 1999. Mem., Kingman Cttee on the teaching of the English Language, 1987–88. Pres., Johnson Soc. of Lichfield, 1982. Radio Personality of the Year: Radio Industries Club, 1973; Variety Club of GB, 1980. *Publications:* (ed) Poetry from Oxford, 1951; Landscape with Dead Dons, 1956; Inside Robert Robinson (essays), 1965; (contrib.) To Nevill Coghill from Friends, 1966; The Conspiracy, 1968; The Dog Chairman, 1982; (ed) The Everyman Book of Light Verse, 1984; Bad Dreams, 1989; Prescriptions of a Pox Doctor's Clerk, 1990; Skip All That, 1996; The Club, 2000. *Address:* 16 Cheyne Row, SW3 5HL. *Club:* Garrick.

ROBINSON, Prof. Roger James, FRCP, FRCPCH; Professor of Paediatrics, United Medical and Dental Schools of Guy's and St Thomas's Hospitals (formerly Guy's Hospital Medical School), University of London, 1975–90, now Emeritus; *b* 17 May 1932; *s* of Albert Edward and Leonora Sarah Robinson; *m* 1962, Jane Hippisley Packham; two *s* one *d*. *Educ:* Poole Grammar Sch.; Balliol Coll., Oxford (Brackenbury schol.; MA, DPhil, BM, BCh); PhD (English) Aberdeen, 1998. FRCP 1975; FRCPCH 1996. Lectr of Christ Church, Oxford, 1953; appts at Radcliffe Infirmary, Oxford, National Hosp., Queen Square, and Hammersmith Hosp., 1960–66; Visiting Fellow, Harvard, 1967; Sen. Lectr, Inst. of Child Health, Hammersmith Hosp., 1967; Cons. Paediatrician, Guy's Hosp., 1971. Hon. Fellow, Dept of English, Aberdeen Univ., 1996–2000. Associate Ed., BMJ, 1990–. *Publications:* Brain and Early Behaviour: development in the fetus and infant, 1969; (jtly) Medical Care of Newborn Babies, 1972; papers on paediatrics and child neurology, and on James Beattie, the poet. *Recreations:* literature (especially poetry), theatre, walking, canoeing. *Address:* 60 Madeley Road, Ealing, W5 2LU.

ROBINSON, Stella; *see* Robson, S.

ROBINSON, Stephen Joseph, OBE 1971; FRS 1976; FREng, FIEE; FInstP; Director, Royal Signals and Radar Establishment, Ministry of Defence, 1989–91, retired (Deputy Director, 1985–89); *b* 6 Aug. 1931; *s* of Joseph Allan Robinson and Ethel (*née* Bunting); *m* 1957, Monica Mabs Scott; one *s* one *d*. *Educ:* Sebright Sch., Wolverley; Jesus Coll., Cambridge (MA Natural Sciences). RAF, 1950–51. Mullard Res. Labs, 1954–72; MEL Div., Philips Industries (formerly MEL Equipment Co. Ltd), 1972–79; Product Dir, 1973–79; Man. Dir, Pye TVT Ltd, 1980–84. Vis. Prof., Birmingham Univ., 1990–91. Mem. Council, Royal Soc., 1982–. *Recreations:* sailing, ski-ing.

ROBINSON, Rev. Thomas Hugh, CBE 1989; Rector, St Peter's, Cleethorpes, 1998–99; *b* Murree, India, 11 June 1934; *s* of Lt-Col James Arthur Robinson, OBE and Maud Loney Robinson; *m* 1959, Mary Elizabeth Doreen Clingan; two *s* one *d*. *Educ:* Bishop Foy School, Waterford; Trinity Coll., Dublin (BA 1955, MA 1971). Pres., Univ. Philosophical Soc., 1955–56. Deacon 1957, priest 1958; Curate, St Clement's, Belfast, 1957–60; Chaplain, Missions to Seamen, Mombasa, 1961–64; Rector of Youghal, Diocese of Cork, 1964–66; CF, 1966–89; DACG, 2 Armoured Div., 1977–80; Senior Chaplain: RMCS, 1980–82; Eastern Dist, 1982–84; 1st British Corps, 1984–85; BAOR, 1985–86; Dep. Chaplain Gen. to the Forces, 1986–89; Team Rector, Cleethorpes, 1990–98. QHC 1985–89. *Recreations:* travel, photography. *Address:* Brailes View House, Landgate, Blockley, Moreton in Marsh, Glos GL56 9BX. *T:* (01386) 701189; *e-mail:* brailesview@hotmail.com.

ROBINSON, Tony; actor and writer; Vice-President, British Actors' Equity, 1996–2000; *b* 15 Aug. 1946; *s* of Leslie Kenneth Robinson and Phyllis Joan Robinson; one *s* one *d*. *Educ:* Wanstead Co. High Sch.; Central Sch. of Speech and Drama. Numerous appearances as child actor, incl. original stage version of Oliver!; theatre dir, 1968–78; work with Chichester Festival Th., RSC and NT; nationwide tour of 40 Years On, 1997; *television* includes: Joey (documentary); Baldrick in Blackadder (4 series), 1983–89; Sheriff of Nottingham in Maid Marian and Her Merry Men (4 series) (also writer); My Wonderful Life (3 series), 1997–99; presenter of TV programmes, incl. Blood and Honey (OT series) (also writer); Time Team (9 series); The Good Book Guide (series); Hospital Watch; documentaries in Africa for Comic Relief; writer for TV: Fat Tulip's Garden; Odysseus: the greatest hero of them all; *film:* The Never Ending Story III. Mem., Labour Party NEC, 2000–. Hon. MA Bristol, 1999. RTS and BAFTA awards; Internat. Prix Jeunesse. *Publications:* for children: Boodicaa and the Romans, 1989; Robert the Incredible Chicken, 1989; Keeping Mum/Driving Ambition, 1992; Hit Plays, 1992; Blood and Honey: story of Saul and David, 1993; The Kings and Queens of England, 1999; Maid Marian and Her Merry Men series: How the Band Got Together, 1989; Beast of Bolsover, 1990; Whitish Knight, 1990; Rabies in Love, 1991; Worksop Egg Fairy, 1991; It Came From Outer Space, 1992; with Richard Curtis: Odysseus Goes Through Hell, 1996; Odysseus, Superhero!, 1996; Theseus, Monster-killer!, 1996. *Recreations:* politics, Bristol City Football Club. *Address:* c/o Kate Feast Management, 10 Primrose Hill Studios, Fitzroy Road, NW1 8TR.

ROBINSON, Victor, CEng, FIChemE; Vice-President, Fédération Européenne d'Associations Nationales d'Ingénieurs, since 1992; *b* 31 July 1925; *s* of Arthur Worsley Robinson and Nellie (*née* Halliwell); *m* 1948, Sadie Monica (*née* Grut); one *s* five *d*. *Educ:* Manchester Grammar Sch.; Cambridge Univ. (MA); Admin. Staff Coll., Henley. CEng, FIChemE 1960. Simon Carves Ltd: R&D Proj. Engrg, 1945; Technical Dir, 1961; Dir, 1964; Man. Dir Overseas Ops and Dir, Sim-Chem Ltd and subsid. cos, 1966; Man. Dir, Turriff Taylor Ltd, 1974–76; Dir, Davy Internat. Projects, 1976–85; Industrial Adviser, Dept of Trade (on secondment from Davy Corp. Ltd), 1978–81. *Recreation:* fell and alpine walking. *Address:* 32 Guilford Avenue, Surbiton, Surrey KT5 8DG.

ROBINSON, Vivian; QC 1986; a Recorder, since 1986; *b* 29 July 1944; *s* of late William and of Ann Robinson; *m* 1975, Louise Marriner; one *s* two *d*. *Educ:* Queen Elizabeth Grammar School, Wakefield; The Leys School, Cambridge; Sidney Sussex College, Cambridge (BA). Called to the Bar, Inner Temple, 1967 (Bencher, 1991). Liveryman, Gardeners' Co., 1976– (Mem., Court of Assistants, 1989–; Master, 2000–01). *Address:* Queen Elizabeth Building, Temple, EC4Y 9BS. *Clubs:* Garrick, Royal Automobile, MCC, Pilgrims.

ROBINSON, Sir Wilfred (Henry Frederick), 3rd Bt *cr* 1908; Staff, Diocesan College School, Rondebosch, South Africa, 1950–77, Vice-Principal, 1969–77; *b* 24 Dec. 1917; *s* of Wilfred Henry Robinson (*d* 1922) (3rd *s* of 1st Bt), and Eileen (*d* 1963), *d* of Frederick St Leger, Claremont, SA; *S* uncle, Sir Joseph Benjamin Robinson, 2nd Bt, 1954; *m* 1946, Margaret Alison Kathleen, *d* of late Frank Mellish, MC, Cape Town, SA; one *s* two *d*. *Educ:* Diocesan Coll., Rondebosch; St John's Coll., Cambridge, MA 1944. Served War of 1939–45, Devonshire Regt and Parachute Regt, Major. Finance Officer, Soc. of Genealogists, 1980–92. *Heir: s* Peter Frank Robinson [*b* 23 June 1949; *m* 1988, Alison Jane, *e d* of D. Bradley, Rochester, Kent; three *d*]. *Address:* 37 Riverview Gardens, SW13 8QZ.

ROBINSON, Ven. (William) David; Archdeacon of Blackburn, 1986–96, now Emeritus; *b* 15 March 1931; *s* of William and Margaret Robinson; *m* 1955, Carol Averil Roma Hamm; one *s* one *d*. *Educ:* Queen Elizabeth's Grammar School, Blackburn; Durham Univ. (MA, DipTh). Curate: Standish, 1958–61; Lancaster Priory (i/c St George), 1961–63; Vicar, St James, Blackburn, 1963–73; Diocesan Stewardship Adviser, Blackburn, and Priest-in-charge, St James, Shireshead, 1973–86; Hon. Canon, Blackburn Cathedral, 1975–86; Vicar of Balderstone, 1986–87. *Recreation:* fell walking. *Address:* 21 Westbourne Road, Warton, Carnforth, Lancs LA5 9NP. *T:* (01524) 720591.

ROBINSON, William Good; Deputy Secretary, Department of the Civil Service, Northern Ireland, 1978–80, retired; *b* 20 May 1919; *s* of William Robinson and Elizabeth Ann (*née* Good); *m* 1947, Wilhelmina Vaughan; two *d*. *Educ:* Clones High Sch.; Queen's Univ. of Belfast (BScEcon, BA). Served War, RAF, 1941–46 (Flt Lieut, Navigator). Entered NI Civil Service, 1938; Min. of Labour and National Insurance, NI, 1946–63; Principal, Min. of Home Affairs, NI, 1963; Asst Sec., 1967; Sen. Asst Sec., NI Office, 1973. *Recreations:* do-it-yourself, reading history. *Address:* Stormochree, 47 Castlehill Road, Belfast BT4 3GN. *T:* (028) 9020 7386.

ROBINSON, Rt Rev. William James; Hon. Assistant, St George's Cathedral, Kingston, since 1982; *b* 8 Sept. 1916; *s* of Thomas Albert Robinson and Harriet Mills; *m* 1946, Isobel Morton; one *s* three *d*. *Educ:* Bishop's Univ., Lennoxville, PQ (BA Theology). Deacon, 1939; priest, 1940; Asst Curate in Trenton, 1939–41; Rector of: Tweed and Madoc, 1941–46, Tweed and N Addington, 1946–47; Napanee, 1948–53; St Thomas' Church, Belleville, 1953–55; St John's Church, Ottawa, 1955–62; Church of Ascension, Hamilton, 1962–67; St George's Church, Guelph, 1967–70. Canon of Christ Church Cathedral, Hamilton, 1964–68; Archdeacon of Trafalgar (Niagara Diocese), 1968–70; Bishop of Ottawa, 1970–81; retired. Hon. DCL Bishop's Univ., Lennoxville, 1973. *Recreations:* woodworking and gardening. *Address:* 168 Inverness Crescent, Kingston, ON K7M 6N7, Canada. *T:* (613) 5497599.

ROBINSON, William Rhys Brunel; Under Secretary, Overseas Division, Department of Employment, 1980–89; *b* 12 July 1930; *s* of late William Robinson and Elizabeth Myfanwy Robinson (*née* Owen); *m* 1988, Pamela Mary Hall. *Educ:* Chepstow Secondary Grammar Sch.; St Catherine's Soc., Oxford (MA,BLitt). Entered Min. of Labour, 1954; Asst Private Sec. to Minister, 1958–59; Principal, Min. of Labour, 1959; Asst Sec., 1966; London Sch. of Economics, 1972–73 (MSc Industrial Relations, 1973); Asst Sec., Trng Services Agency, 1973–75; Dep. Chief Exec., Employment Service Agency, 1975–77; Under-Sec. and Dir of Establishments, Dept of Employment, 1977–80. Chm., Governing Body, ILO, 1986–87. FSA 1978; FRHistS 1991. *Publications:* articles in historical jls. *Recreation:* historical research. *Address:* 7 Shere Avenue, Cheam, Surrey SM2 7JU. *T:* (020) 8393 3019.

ROBISON, Shona; Member (SNP) North East Scotland, Scottish Parliament, since 1999; *b* 26 May 1966; *d* of Robin and Dorothy Robison. *Educ:* Alva Acad.; Glasgow Univ.; Jordanhill Coll. Sen. Community Worker, City of Glasgow Council, 1993–99. Scottish Parliament: Sec., SNP Parly Gp, 1999–; Mem., Equal Opportunities Cttee, 1999–2000; Dep. Shadow Minister, Health and Community Care Cttee. Contested (SNP) Dundee E, 1997. *Address:* Scottish Parliament, Edinburgh EH99 1SP.

ROBLES, Marisa, FRCM; harpist; Professor of Harp, Royal College of Music, since 1971; *b* 4 May 1937; *d* of Cristobal Robles and Maria Bonilla; *m* 1985, David Bean; two *s* one *d* by previous marriage. *Educ:* Madrid National Sch.; Royal Madrid Conservatoire. Prof. of Harp, Royal Madrid Conservatoire, 1958–60. Recitals and solo appearances with major orchestras in UK, Europe, Africa, Canada, USA, South America, Japan, China and Australia. Mem., UK Harp Assoc. Recordings include concerti by Handel, Dittersdorf, Boildieu, Debussy, Rodrigo, Moreno-Buendia, solo repertoire by Beethoven, Mozart, Fauré, Hasselmans, Tournier, Guridi and others, and chamber music by Alwyn, Roussel, Britten, Ravel, Debussy and others. Hon. Royal Madrid Conservatoire 1958; Hon. RCM 1973; FRCM 1983. *Recreations:* theatre, gardening, indoor plants, family life in general. *Address:* 38 Luttrell Avenue, Putney, SW15 6PE. *T:* (020) 8785 2204. *Club:* Royal Over-Seas League.

ROBLIN, Ven. Graham Henry, OBE 1983; Vicar, Bere Regis and Affpuddle with Turnerspuddle, 1993–2001; *b* 18 Aug. 1937; *s* of Ewart and Marjorie Roblin; *m* 1964, Penelope Ann Cumberlege; one *s* one *d*. *Educ:* Cathedral Sch., Exeter; King's Coll., Taunton; King's Coll., London (AKC). Deacon, 1962; priest, 1963; Curate of St Helier, Southwark, 1962–66; joined Army Chaplaincy Service, 1966; Dep. Asst Chaplain Gen., Hong Kong, 1979–81; Dep. Asst Chaplain Gen., 2nd Armd Div., 1981–83; Warden, RAChD Centre, Bagshot Park, 1983–86; Senior Chaplain: 1st British Corps, 1986–87; BAOR, 1987–89; Dep. Chaplain Gen. to Forces, 1989–93; Archdeacon to the Army, 1990–93, Archdeacon Emeritus, 1994–. QHC 1987–93. Freeman, City of London, 2000. *Recreation:* writing. *Address:* Croft Cottage, High Street, Yetminster, Sherborne, Dorset DT9 6LF.

ROBOROUGH, 3rd Baron *cr* 1938, of Maristow; **Henry Massey Lopes;** Bt 1805; *b* 2 Feb. 1940; *s* of 2nd Baron Roborough and Helen (decd), *o d* of Lt-Col E. A. F. Dawson; *S* father, 1992; *m* 1st, 1968, Robyn Zenda Carol (marr. diss. 1986), *e d* of John Bromwich; two *s* two *d*; 2nd, 1986, Sarah Anne Pipon, 2nd *d* of Colin Baker; two *d*. *Educ:* Eton. ARICS. Late Lt Coldstream Guards. Farmer, managing Maristow Estate, Plymouth. Racehorse owner and breeder. *Heir: s* Hon. Massey John Henry Lopes [*b* 22 Dec. 1969; *m* 1996, Jean, *d* of Peter George Underwood, Supreme Court of Tasmania; one *s*]. *Club:* Turf.

ROBOTTOM, Dame Marlene (Anne), DBE 2000; Headteacher, Mulberry School for Girls, Tower Hamlets, London, since 1991; *b* 10 July 1950; *d* of Alan Joseph Robottom and Patricia Anne Robottom (*née* Gilkes). *Educ:* Coll. of All Saints, London (CertEd 1971); NE London Poly. (BEd 1981); Poly. of E London (MSc 1989). Tower Hamlets, subseq. Mulberry School: Teacher, 1971–72; Dep. Head of Dept, 1972–77; Hd of Dept, 1977–78; Hd of House, 1979–80; Hd of House and Second Dep. Headteacher, 1980–87; First Dep. Headteacher (Curriculum), 1987–90. *Recreations:* theatre, music, the arts. *Address:* Mulberry School for Girls, Richard Street, Commercial Road, E1 2JP. *T:* (020) 7790 6327. *Club:* Institute of Directors.

ROBSON, Agnes; Principal Establishment Officer and Head of Corporate Services, Scottish Executive, since 2000; *b* 6 Oct. 1946; *d* of John Wight and Agnes Margaret Wight (*née* Stark); *m* 1969, Godfrey Robson (marr. diss.); one *s*. *Educ:* Holy Cross Acad., Edinburgh; Edinburgh Univ. (MA Hons Politics and Mod. Hist.). Civil Servant, Dept of Employment, 1968–79; joined Scottish Office, 1985: Industry Department: Head: Energy Div., 1988–89; Nuclear Energy Div., 1989–90; Urban Policy Div., 1990–92; Dir, Primary Care, NHS Mgt Exec., Health Dept, 1992–2000. *Recreations:* opera, contemporary Scottish painting. *Address:* Scottish Executive Corporate Services, 16 Waterloo Place, Edinburgh EH1 3DN. *T:* (0131) 244 3938.

ROBSON, Alan; General Secretary, Confederation of Shipbuilding and Engineering Unions, since 1993; *b* 24 Dec. 1941; *s* of John William Robson and Bridgit Robson; *m* 1964, Joyce Lydia. *Educ:* Ellison C of E Sch. Fitter-turner, 1958–90; Asst Gen. Sec., AEU, 1990–93. *Recreations:* reading, supporting the arts, football. *Address:* 20 York Avenue, Jarrow, Tyne and Wear NE32 5LT. *T:* (0191) 421 6883. *Clubs:* Labour, Elmfield, Ex-Service Men's (Jarrow).

ROBSON, Brian Ewart, CB 1985; FSA, FRHistS; Deputy Under-Secretary of State (Personnel and Logistics), Ministry of Defence, 1984–86; *b* 25 July 1926; 2nd *s* of late Walter Ewart Robson; *m* 1962, Cynthia Margaret (*d* 1997), *o d* of late William James Scott, Recife, Brazil; two *d*. *Educ:* Steyning Grammar Sch.; Varndean Sch., Brighton; The Queen's Coll., Oxford (BA Modern History). FRHistS 1995; FSA 1997. Royal Sussex Regt and Kumaon Regt, Indian Army, 1944–47. Air Min., 1950; Asst Private Sec. to Sec. of State for Air, 1953–55; Principal, 1955; Asst Sec., 1965; Imperial Defence Coll., 1970; Mem., UK Delegn to UN Law of the Sea Conf., Venezuela, 1974; Ecole Nationale d'Administration, Paris, 1975; Ministry of Defence: Asst Under-Sec. of State (Supply and Orgn), 1976–80, (Operational Requirements), 1980–82; Dep. Under-Sec. of State (Army), 1982–84. Technical Advr, Price Waterhouse, 1986–89. Member: Central Finance Bd of C of E, 1985–95; Chichester Diocesan Finance Bd, 1986–94. Comr, Royal Hosp., 1982–85; Chm., Soc. for Army Historical Res., 1993–98; Member Council: Army Records Soc., 1984–89, 1993–; Nat. Army Museum, 1982–93; Trustee, Imperial War Museum, 1984–86. Chm. Govs, Duke of York's Royal Mil. Sch., 1982–85; Governor: Welbeck Coll., 1982–84; Whitelands Coll., 1988–95; Roehampton Inst., 1991–95. *Publications:* Swords of the British Army, 1975, 2nd edn 1996; The Road to Kabul: the Second Afghan War 1878–1880, 1986; Roberts in India: military papers of Lord Roberts, 1993; Fuzzy Wuzzy: the campaigns in the Eastern Sudan 1884–85, 1993; Onward and Upward: a history of Varndean 1884–1975, 1993; Sir Hugh Rose and the Central India Campaign 1858, 2000; numerous articles on weapons and military history. *Recreations:* military history, cricket, travel. *Address:* 17 Woodlands, Hove, East Sussex BN3 6TJ. *T:* (01273) 505803. *Club:* Oxford Union.

ROBSON, David Ernest Henry; QC 1980; a Recorder of the Crown Court (NE Circuit), since 1979; *b* 1 March 1940; *s* of late Joseph Robson and of Caroline Robson. *Educ:* Robert Richardson Grammar Sch., Ryhope; Christ Church, Oxford (MA). Called to the Bar, Inner Temple, 1965 (Profumo Prize, 1963), Bencher, 1988. NE Circuit, 1965–. Artistic Dir, Royalty Studio Theatre, Sunderland, 1986–88. Pres., Herrington Burn YMCA, Sunderland 1987–. *Recreations:* acting, Italy. *Address:* Whitton Grange, Whitton, Rothbury, Northumberland NE65 7RL. *T:* (01669) 620929. *Club:* County (Durham).

ROBSON, Elizabeth; *see* Howlett, E.

ROBSON, Prof. Elizabeth Browel; Galton Professor of Human Genetics, University College London, 1978–93; *b* 10 Nov. 1928; *d* of Thomas Robson and Isabella (*née* Stoker); *m* 1955, George MacBeth, writer (marr. diss. 1975, he *d* 1992). *Educ:* Bishop Auckland Girls' Grammar Sch.; King's Coll., Newcastle upon Tyne; BSc Dunelm; PhD London, 1954; Dip. History of Art, Univ. of London, 2000. *Educ:* Rockefeller Fellowship, Columbia Univ., New York City, 1954–55; external scientific staff of MRC (London Hosp. Med. Coll. and King's Coll. London), 1955–62; Member and later Asst Director, MRC Human Biochemical Genetics Unit, University Coll. London, 1962–78; Hd, Dept of Genetics and Biometry, UCL, 1978–90. Jt Editor, Annals of Human Genetics, 1978–93. *Publications:* papers on biochemical human genetics and gene mapping in scientific jls. *Address:* 44 Sheen Road, Richmond, Surrey TW9 1AW.

ROBSON, Elizabeth Carol; HM Diplomatic Service; Deputy Director, Ditchley Foundation, since 1998 (on special leave); *b* 14 Jan. 1955; *d* of James Henry Robson and Laura Robson (*née* Jacobson). *Educ:* Carlisle and County High Sch.; York Univ. (BA Physics 1977). Entered Diplomatic Service, 1977; Latin America floater, 1980–81; Russian lang. trng, 1981–82; Ulaanbaator, 1983; Moscow, 1983–84; FCO, 1984; UKMIS, Geneva, 1987–92; Asst Head, SE Asia Dept, 1992–95; Head, Transcaucasus and Central Asia Unit, 1995–96; Counsellor, Consul-Gen. and Dep. Head of Mission, Stockholm, 1996–98. *Recreations:* diverse, including cooking, antiques, art, cinema, travel, visiting historic sites and houses, reading. *Address:* Ditchley Park, Enstone, Chipping Norton, Oxon OX7 4ER.

ROBSON, Eric; freelance writer and broadcaster, since 1979; farmer, since 1987; *b* 31 Dec. 1946; *s* of James Walter Robson and Agnes Gourlay Robson; *m* 1st, 1976, Mary Armstrong (marr. diss. 1984); one *s* one *d*; 2nd, 1988, Annette Steinhilber; one *s* two *d*. *Educ:* Carlisle Grammar Sch. Border TV, 1966–; BBC TV and Radio, 1976–; BBC outside broadcast commentator, Trooping the Colour, the Cenotaph, handover of Hong Kong; Chm., Gardeners' Question Time, BBC Radio, 1995–; documentary producer and presenter. Chm., Striding Edge Ltd, 1994–. *Publications:* Great Railway Journeys of the World, 1981; Northumbria, 1998. *Recreations:* painting, fell walking, cooking, avoiding housework. *Address:* Crag House Farm, Wasdale, Cumbria CA19 1UT. *T:* (01946) 726301. *Clubs:* Farmers'; St Augustine's Working Men's (Carlisle).

ROBSON, Euan Macfarlane; Member (Lib Dem) Roxburgh and Berwickshire, Scottish Parliament, since 1999; *b* 17 Feb. 1954; *m* 1984, Valerie Young; two *d*. *Educ:* Univ. of Newcastle upon Tyne (BA Hons History 1976); Univ. of Strathclyde (MSc Political Sci. 1984). Teacher, King Edward VI Sch., Morpeth, 1977–79; Dep. Sec., Gas Consumers' Northern Council, Newcastle upon Tyne, 1981–86; Scottish Manager, Gas Consumers' Council, 1986–99. Mem. (L/All), Northumberland CC, 1981–89 (Chm., Highways Cttee, 1988–89; Hon. Alderman, 1989); L/All Gp Sec., 1981–87. Contested (L/All) Hexham, 1983, 1987. Lib Dem Rural Affairs spokesman, 1998–99, Justice and Home Affairs spokesman, 1999–2001, Scottish Parlt; Dep. Minister for Parlt, Scottish Exec., 2001–. River Tweed Comr, 1994–. Founding Mem., Consumer Safety Internat.; Life Mem., Nat. Trust for Scotland. *Publications:* The Consumers' View of the 1990 EU Gas Appliances' Directive, 1991; George Houston: nature's limner, 1997. *Recreation:* angling. *Address:* Elmbank, Tweedsyde Park, Kelso, Roxburghshire TD5 7RF. *T:* (01573) 225279.

ROBSON, Frank Elms, OBE 1991; Consultant, Winckworth Sherwood (formerly Winckworth & Pemberton), Solicitors, Oxford and Westminster, since 1998 (Partner, 1962–98; Senior Partner, 1990–94); *b* 14 Dec. 1931; *s* of Joseph A. Robson and Barbara

Robson; *m* 1958, Helen (*née* Jackson) four *s* one *d*. *Educ:* King Edward VI Grammar Sch., Morpeth; Selwyn Coll., Cambridge (MA). Admitted solicitor, 1954. Registrar, Dio. Oxford, 1970–2000; Joint Registrar, Province of Canterbury, 1982–2000. Chm., Ecclesiastical Law Soc., 1996–; Vice-Chm., Legal Adv. Commn, Gen. Synod of C of E, 1990–. DCL Lambeth, 1991. *Recreations:* walking, clocks, following Oxford United. *Address:* 2 Simms Close, Stanton St John, Oxford OX9 1HB. *T:* (01865) 351393.

ROBSON, Godfrey; Director of Health Policy, Scottish Executive, since 2000; *b* 5 Nov. 1946; *s* of late William James Robson and of Mary Finn; *m* (marr. diss.); one *s*. *Educ:* St Joseph's Coll., Dumfries; Edinburgh Univ. (MA). Joined Scottish Office, 1970; Pvte Sec. to Parly Under-Sec. of State, 1973–74, to Minister of State, 1974; Prin. Pvte Sec. to Sec. of State for Scotland, 1979–81; Assistant Secretary: Roads and Transport, 1981–86; Local Govt Finance, 1986–89; Under Sec., 1989; Scottish Fisheries Sec., 1989–93; Under Sec., Industrial Expansion, subseq. Economic and Industrial Affairs, 1993–2000. Dir, Lloyds TSB Scotland, 2001–. *Recreations:* walking, travel by other means, reading history. *Address:* 50 East Trinity Road, Edinburgh EH5 3EN. *T:* (0131) 552 9519.

ROBSON, Prof. Sir (James) Gordon, Kt 1982; CBE 1977; MB, ChB; FRCS; FRCA; Professor of Anaesthetics, University of London, Royal Postgraduate Medical School and Hon. Consultant, Hammersmith Hospital, 1964–86, retired; Chairman, Advisory Committee on Distinction Awards, 1984–94; *b* Stirling, Scot., 18 March 1921; *o s* of late James Cyril Robson and Freda Elizabeth Howard; *m* 1st, 1945, Dr Martha Graham Kennedy (*d* 1975); one *s*; 2nd, 1984, Jennifer Kilpatrick. *Educ:* High Sch. of Stirling; Univ. of Glasgow. FRCS 1977. RAMC, 1945–48 (Captain). Sen. Registrar in Anaesthesia, Western Inf., Glasgow, 1948–52; First Asst, Dept of Anaesthetics, Univ. of Durham, 1952–54; Cons. Anaesth., Royal Inf., Edinburgh, 1954–56; Wellcome Res. Prof. of Anaesth., McGill Univ., Montreal, 1956–64. Consultant Advr in Anaesthetics to DHSS, 1975–84; Hon. Consultant in Anaesthetics to the Army, 1983–88. Royal College of Surgeons: Master, Hunterian Inst., 1982–88. Mem. Bd of Faculty of Anaesthetists, 1968–85 (Dean of Faculty, 1973–76); Mem. Council, 1973–81, 1982–88 (a Vice-Pres., 1977–79); Chm., Jt Cttee on Higher Trng of Anaesthetists, 1973–76; Member: AHA, Ealing, Hammersmith and Hounslow, 1974–77 (NW Met. RHB, 1971–74); Chief Scientists' Res. Cttee and Panel on Med. Res., DHSS, 1973–77; Neurosciences Bd, MRC, 1974–77; Clin. Res. Bd, MRC (Chm. Grants Cttee II), 1969–71; Mem. Council, RPMS (Vice-Chm. Academic Bd, 1973–76; Chm. 1976–80); Mem., Rock Carling Fellowship Panel, 1976–78; Vice-Chm., Jt Consultants' Cttee, 1974–79. Special Trustee, Hammersmith Hosp., 1974–77; Chm., Cttee of Management, Inst. of Basic Med. Scis, 1982–85; Hon. Sec., Conf. of Med. Royal Colls and Their Faculties, UK, 1976–82; Examiner, Primary FFARCS, 1967–73; Member: Editorial Bd (and Cons. Editor), British Jl of Anaesthesia, 1965–85; Edit. Bd, Psychopharmacology; Council, Assoc. of Anaesths of GB and Ire., 1973–84; Physiol. Soc., 1966–; Cttee of AA, 1979–91; Hon. Mem., Assoc. of Univ. Anaesths (USA), 1963–; President: Scottish Soc. of Anaesthetists, 1985–86; RSocMed, 1986–88. Royal National Life-boat Institution: Mem. Cttee of Mgt, 1988–; Life Vice-Pres., 1996 (a Vice-Pres., 1992–); Mem., Med. and Survival Cttee, 1981– (Chm., 1988–91). Sir Arthur Sims Commonwealth Trav. Prof., 1968; Visiting Prof. to many med. centres, USA and Canada; Lectures: Wesley Bourne, McGill Univ., 1965; First Gillies Meml, Dundee, 1978; 2nd Gilmartin, Faculty of Anaesthetists, RCSI, 1986; Morrell Mackenzie, Inst. of Laryngology, 1989; (first) J. D. Robertson Meml, Edinburgh Univ., 1992. Hon. FFARACS 1968; Hon. FFARCSI 1980; Hon. FDSRCS 1979; Hon. FRCP(C) 1988; Hon. FRSocMed 1989; Hon. FRCPSGlas 1993. Hon. DSc: McGill, 1984; Glasgow, 1991. Joseph Clover Medal and Prize, Fac. of Anaesths, RCS, 1972; John Snow Medal, Assoc. of Anaesthetists of GB and Ireland, 1986. *Publications:* on neurophysiol., anaesthesia, pain and central nervous system mechanisms of respiration, in learned jls. *Recreations:* golf, wet fly fishing.

ROBSON, Prof. James Scott, MD; FRCP, FRCPE; Professor of Medicine, University of Edinburgh, 1977–86, now Emeritus; Consultant Physician, and Physician in charge, Medical Renal Unit, Royal Infirmary, Edinburgh, 1959–86; *b* 19 May 1921; *s* of William Scott Robson, FSA and Elizabeth Hannah Watt; *m* 1948, Mary Kynoch MacDonald, MB ChB, FRCPE, *d* of late Alexander MacDonald, Perth; two *s*. *Educ:* Edinburgh Univ. (Mouat Schol.). MB ChB (Hons) 1945, MD 1946; FRCPE 1960, FRCP 1977. Captain, RAMC, India, Palestine and Egypt, 1945–48. Rockefeller Student, NY Univ., 1942–44; Rockefeller Res. Fellow, Harvard Univ., 1949–50. Edinburgh University: Sen. Lectr in Therapeutics, 1959; Reader, 1961; Reader in Medicine, 1968. Hon. Associate Prof., Harvard Univ., 1962; Merck Sharp & Dohme Vis. Prof., Australia, 1968. External examnr in medicine to several univs in UK and overseas. Mem., Biomed. Res. Cttee, SHHD, 1979–84; Chm., Sub-cttee in Medicine, Nat. Med. Consultative Cttee, 1983–85. Pres., Renal Assoc., London, 1977–80. Hon. Mem., Australasian Soc. of Nephrology. Sometime Mem. Editl Bd, and Dep. Chm., Clinical Science, 1969–73, and other med. jls. *Publications:* (ed with R. Passmore) Companion to Medical Studies, vol. 1, 1968, 3rd edn 1985; vol. 2, 1970, 2nd edn 1980; vol. 3, 1974; contribs on renal physiology and disease to med. books, symposia and jls. *Recreations:* gardening, theatre, reading, writing, contemporary art of Scotland. *Address:* 1 Grant Avenue, Edinburgh EH13 0DS. *T:* (0131) 441 3508. *Club:* New (Edinburgh).

ROBSON, Sir John (Adam), KCMG 1990 (CMG 1983); HM Diplomatic Service, retired; Ambassador to Norway, 1987–90; *b* 16 April 1930; *yr s* of Air Vice-Marshal Adam Henry Robson, CB, OBE, MC; *m* 1958, Maureen Molly, *er d* of E. H. S. Bullen; three *d*. *Educ:* Charterhouse; Gonville and Caius Coll., Cambridge (Major Scholar). BA 1952, MA 1955, PhD 1958. Fellow, Gonville and Caius Coll., 1954–58; Asst Lectr, University Coll. London, 1958–60. HM Foreign Service (later Diplomatic Service), 1961; Second Sec., British Embassy, Bonn, 1962–64; Second, later First, Secretary, Lima, 1964–66; First Sec., British High Commn, Madras, 1966–69; Asst Head, Latin American Dept, FCO, 1969–73; Head of Chancery, Lusaka, 1973–74; RCDS, 1975; Counsellor, Oslo, 1976–78; Head of E African Dept, FCO, and Comr for British Indian Ocean Territory, 1979–82; Ambassador to Colombia, 1982–87. Leader, UK Delegn, Conf. on Human Dimension, CSCE, 1990–91. Panel Mem., Home Office Assessment Consultancy Unit, 1992–2000. Chm. Mgt Cttee, Seven Springs Cheshire Home, 1992–96; Mem. Internat. Cttee, Cheshire Foundn, 1996–2000. Mem. Ct, Kent Univ., 1990–99. Chm., Anglo-Norse Soc., 1998–. Royal Order of Merit (Norway), 1988. *Publications:* Wyclif and the Oxford Schools, 1961; articles in historical jls. *Recreation:* gardening. *Address:* Biggenden Oast, Paddock Wood, Tonbridge, Kent TN12 6ND. *Club:* Oxford and Cambridge.

ROBSON, Rev. John Phillips, LVO 1999; Chaplain to the Queen, since 1993; Chaplain of the Queen's Chapel of the Savoy and Chaplain of the Royal Victorian Order, since 1989; *b* 22 July 1932; *s* of Thomas Herbert and Nellie Julia Robson. *Educ:* Hele's School, Exeter; Brentwood School; St Edmund Hall, Oxford (Liddon Exhibnr 1954); King's College London (AKC 1958). Deacon 1959, priest 1960; Curate, Huddersfield Parish Church, 1959–62; Asst Chaplain 1962–65, Senior Chaplain 1965–80, Christ's Hospital, Horsham; Senior Chaplain of Wellington College, Berks, 1980–89. *Recreations:* golf, cinema, theatre. *Address:* The Queen's Chapel of the Savoy, Savoy Hill, Strand, WC2R 0DA. *T:* (020) 7836 7221. *Club:* Garrick.

ROBSON, Prof. Peter Neville, OBE 1983; FRS 1987; FREng; Professor of Electronic and Electrical Engineering, University of Sheffield, 1968–96, now Emeritus; *b* 23 Nov. 1930; *s* of Thomas Murton and Edith Robson; *m* 1957, Anne Ross Miller Semple; one *d*. *Educ:* Cambridge Univ. (BA); PhD Sheffield. FIEE, FIEEE, FREng (FEng 1983). Res. Engr, Metropolitan Vickers Electrical Co., Manchester, 1954–57; Lectr 1957–63, Sen. Lectr 1963–66, Sheffield Univ.; Res. Fellow, Stanford Univ., USA, 1966–67; Reader, University Coll. London, 1967–68. *Publications:* Vacuum and Solid State Electronics, 1963; numerous papers on semiconductor devices and electromagnetic theory. *Address:* Department of Electronic and Electrical Engineering, Sheffield University, Mappin Street, Sheffield S1 3JD. *T:* (0114) 222 5131.

ROBSON, Air Vice-Marshal Robert Michael, OBE 1971; freelance journalist; sheep farmer, 1987–96; *b* 22 April 1935; *s* of Dr John Alexander and Edith Robson; *m* 1959, Brenda Margaret (*née* Croysdill); one *s* two *d*. *Educ:* Sherborne; RMA Sandhurst. Commissioned 1955; RAF Regt, 1958; Navigator Training, 1959; Strike Squadrons, 1965; Sqdn Comdr, RAF Coll., 1968; Defence Adviser to British High Comr, Sri Lanka, 1972; Nat. Defence Coll., 1973; CO 27 Sqdn, 1974–75; MoD staff duties, 1978; CO RAF Gatow, 1978–80; ADC to the Queen, 1979–80; RCDS 1981; Dir of Initial Officer Training, RAF Coll., 1982–84; Dir of Public Relations, RAF, 1984–87; Hd, RAF Study of Officers' Terms of Service, 1987; retired. Chairman: Turbo (UK) Ltd, 1995–; Fuel Mechanics Ltd, 1995–97; Dir, Advanced Technology Industries Ltd, 1993–97; Chm., Prince's Trust, Lincs, 1993–96; Dir and Chm., Witham Hall Trust, 1995–; Gov., Witham Hall Sch., 1988– (Chm. Govs, 1995–). FIMgt (FBIM 1980). *Recreations:* fly fishing, golf. *Club:* Royal Air Force.

ROBSON, Robert William, CBE 1991; Manager, Newcastle United FC, since 1999; *b* 18 Feb. 1933; *s* of Philip and Lilian Robson; *m* 1955, Elsie Mary Gray; three *s*. *Educ:* Langley Park Primary Sch.; Waterhouses Secondary Mod. Sch., Co. Durham. Professional footballer: Fulham FC, 1950–56 and 1962–67; West Bromwich Albion FC, 1956–62; twenty appearances for England; Manager: Vancouver FC, 1967–68; Fulham FC, 1968–69; Ipswich Town FC, 1969–82 (FA Cup Winners, 1978; UEFA Cup Winners, 1981); England Assoc. Football Team, and Nat. Coach, 1982–90; Manager, PSV Eindhoven, Netherlands, 1990–92 (Dutch Champions, 1990–91, 1991–92; Super Cup Winners, 1999); Head Coach: Sporting Lisbon, Portugal, 1992–93; Futebol Clube Do Porto, Portugal, 1994–96 (Portuguese Champions, 1994–95, 1995–96; Portuguese Cup Winners, 1995; Super Cup Winners, 1994, 1995); Coach, Barcelona FC, 1996–98 (Spanish Super Cup, 1996; Eur. Cup Winners Cup, 1997; Spanish Cup, 1997); Head Coach, PSV Eindhoven, Netherlands, 1998–99. Hon. MA UEA, 1997. *Publications:* Time on the Grass (autobiog.), 1982; with Bob Harris: So Near and Yet So Far: Bobby Robson's World Cup diary, 1986; Against The Odds, 1990; An Englishman Abroad, 1998. *Recreations:* golf, squash, reading, gardening. *Address:* c/o Newcastle United Football Club, St James' Park, Newcastle upon Tyne NE1 4ST.

ROBSON, Stella; Chair, Northern Sinfonia Board, since 1998; *b* 18 Feb. 1935; *d* of Charles Moreton Marchinton and Margaret Maude Backhouse; *m* 1998, Frank Robson; one *s* one *d* by a previous marriage. *Educ:* Aireborough Grammar Sch.; Princess Mary High Sch., Halifax; Univ. of Leeds (BA Hons English 1956). Housing Officer: Joseph Rowntree Village Trust, York, 1956–57; Rotherham BC, 1957–59; Students Accommodation Officer, King's Coll., Newcastle, 1959–63; Chair, Northern Arts, 1990–98. Mem., Arts Council of England, 1993–98. Trustee, Northern Music Trust, 2000–. Mem. Bd, Darlington Housing Assoc., 2001. Member (Lab): Darlington BC, 1972–79, 1995–; Durham CC, 1981–97 (Hon. Alderman, 1997). *Recreations:* walking, the arts. *Address:* 57 Pinewood Crescent, Heighington Village, Newton Aycliffe DL5 6RR.

ROBSON, Sir Stephen Arthur, (Sir Steve), Kt 2000; CB 1997; PhD; Second Permanent Secretary, Finance, Regulation and Industry, HM Treasury, 1997–2001; *b* 30 Sept. 1943; *s* of Arthur Cyril Robson and Lilian Marianne (*née* Peabody); *m* 1974, Meredith Hilary Lancashire; two *s*. *Educ:* Pocklington Sch.; St John's Coll., Cambridge (MA, PhD); Stanford Univ., USA (MA). Joined Civil Service (HM Treasury), 1969; Private Sec. to Chancellor of the Exchequer, 1974–76; seconded to Investors in Industry plc, 1976–78; Under Sec., Defence Policy and Material Gp, 1987–89, Public Enterprises and Privatisation Gp, 1990–93; Dep. Sec., Industry and Financial Instns, later Finance, Regulation and Industry, 1993–97. Non-executive Director: Royal Bank of Scotland, 2001–; Cazenove, 2001–; Partnerships UK. *Recreation:* sailing. *Club:* Bosham Sailing.

ROCARD, Michel Louis Léon; Member (Party of European Socialists), European Parliament, since 1994; Prime Minister of France, 1988–91; *b* 23 Aug. 1930; *s* of late Yves Rocard and of Renée (*née* Favre); *m* 1st; one *s* one *d*; 2nd, 1972, Michèle Legendre (marr. diss.); two *s*. *Educ:* Lycée Louis-le-Grand, Paris; Univ. of Paris (Nat. Sec., Association des étudiants socialistes, 1953–55); Ecole Nationale d'Administration, 1956–58. Inspecteur des Finances, 1958; Econ. and Financial Studies Service, 1962; Head of Econ. Budget Div., Forecasting Office, 1965; Sec.-Gen., Nat. Accounts Commn, 1965. Nat. Sec., Parti Socialiste Unifié, 1967–73; candidate for Presidency of France, 1969; Deputy for Yvelines, 1969–73, 1978–81, 1986–93; Minister of Planning and Regl Develt, 1981–83; Minister of Agriculture, 1983–85; Mem., Senate, 1995–97. Chm., Employment and Social Affairs Cttee, EP, 1999–. Joined Parti Socialiste, 1974: Mem., Exec. Bureau, 1975–81 and 1986–88; Nat. Sec. in charge of public sector, 1975–79; First Sec., 1993–94. Mayor, Conflans-Sainte-Honorine, 1977–94. *Publications:* Le PSU et l'avenir socialiste de la France, 1969; Des militants du PSU présentés par Michel Rocard, 1971; Questions à l'Etat socialiste, 1972; Un député, pour quoi faire?, 1973; (jtly) Le Marché commun contre l'Europe, 1973; (jtly) L'Inflation au cœur, 1975; Parler vrai, 1979; A l'épreuve des faits: textes politiques 1979–85, 1986; Le coeur à l'ouvrage, 1987; Un pays comme le nôtre, 1989; L'art de la Paix, 1997; Les moyens d'en sortir, 1997; Le français langue des Droits de l'Homme?, 1998; Mes idées pour demain, 2000; Entretiens, 2001. *Address:* 266 boulevard St Germain, 75007, Paris, France.

ROCH, Rt Hon. Sir John (Ormond), Kt 1985; PC 1993; a Lord Justice of Appeal, 1993–2000; *b* 19 April 1934; *s* of Frederick Ormond Roch and Vera Elizabeth (*née* Chamberlain); *m* 1st, 1967, Anne Elizabeth Greany (*d* 1994); three *d*; 2nd, 1996, Mrs Susan Angela Parry. *Educ:* Wrekin Coll.; Clare Coll., Cambridge (BA, LLB). Called to Bar, Gray's Inn, 1961, Bencher, 1985; QC 1976; a Recorder, 1975–85; a Judge of the High Court of Justice, QBD, 1985–93; Presiding Judge, Wales and Chester Circuit, 1986–90. Gov. and Mem. Mgt Cttee, RNLI, 1996–. *Recreations:* sailing, music. *Clubs:* Dale Yacht, Bar Yacht.

ROCH, Muriel Elizabeth Sutcliffe, BA; Headmistress, School of S Mary and S Anne, Abbots Bromley, Staffs, 1953–77; *b* 7 Sept. 1916; *d* of late Rev. Sydney John Roch, MA Cantab, Pembroke and Manchester. *Educ:* Manchester High Sch.; Bedford Coll., London; Hughes Hall, Cambridge. Teaching appointments at: Devonport High School, 1939–41; Lady Manners, Bakewell, 1941–44; Howells School, Denbigh, 1944–47; Talbot Heath, Bournemouth, 1947–53. *Recreations:* music, travel. *Address:* Northdown Cottage, Lamphey, Pembroke SA71 5PL. *T:* (01646) 672577. *Club:* University Women's.

ROCHAT, Dr Philippe Henri Pierre; Executive Director, Air Transport Action Group, Geneva; *b* 19 Oct. 1942; *m* 1967, Catherine Dupuy; two *s* one *d*. *Educ:* Gymnase de Lausanne; Lausanne Univ. (LLB 1966; LLD 1974). Journalist and reporter, Swiss Radio–TV, 1967–74; Asst to Dep. Dir, Federal Office for Civil Aviation, Bern, 1975–77; Admin. and Commercial Dir, Geneva Airport, 1977–85; International Civil Aviation Organisation Council: Alternate Rep. of Belgium, 1985–86; Rep. of Switzerland, 1986–89; Dir, Mkting and Envmt, Geneva Airport, 1989–91; Sec. Gen., ICAO, 1991–97; consultant, Geneva Internat. Airport; Chm., Swiss World Airways. Air Law Professor: Geneva Univ.; Lausanne Univ. *Publications:* articles, reports and lectures on civil aviation and envmt, airports' structure and mgt, challenges in civil aviation, etc. *Recreations:* ski-ing, tennis, hiking, various cultural activities. *Address:* c/o Air Transport Action Group, PO Box 49, 1215 Geneva 15, Switzerland.

ROCHDALE, 2nd Viscount *cr* 1960; **St John Durival Kemp;** Baron 1913; *b* 15 Jan. 1938; *s* of 1st Viscount Rochdale, OBE and Elinor Dorothea Pease, CBE, JP (*d* 1997); *S* father, 1993; *m* 1st, 1960, Serena Jane Clark-Hall (marr. diss. 1974); two *s* two *d*; 2nd, 1976, Elizabeth Anderton. *Educ:* Eton. *Heir: s* Hon. Jonathan Hugo Durival Kemp [*b* 10 June 1961; *m* 1994, Mingxian Zhu]. *Address:* Rosetrees, Lingholm, Keswick, Cumbria CA12 5TZ.

ROCHDALE, Archdeacon of; *see* Ballard, Ven. A. E.

ROCHE, family name of **Baron Fermoy.**

ROCHE, Rt Rev. Arthur; Auxiliary Bishop of Westminster, (RC), and Titular Bishop of Rusticiana, since 2001; *b* 6 March 1950; *s* of Arthur Francis Roche and Frances Roche (*née* Day). *Educ:* Christleton Hall, Chester; English Coll., Valladolid; Pontifical Gregorian Univ., Rome (STL). Ordained priest, 1975; Asst Priest, Holy Rood, Barnsley, 1975–77; Sec. to Rt Rev. Gordon Wheeler, Bishop of Leeds, 1977–82; Vice-Chancellor, 1979–89, Financial Administrator, 1986–90, dio. of Leeds; Asst Priest, Leeds Cathedral, 1982–89; Parish Priest, St Wilfrids's, Leeds, 1989–91; Spiritual Dir, Venerable English Coll., Rome, 1992–96; Gen. Sec. to Catholic Bps' Conf. of England and Wales, 1996–2001. Co-ordinator of the Papal Visit to York, 1982. Prelate of Honour to Pope John Paul II. *Recreations:* gardening, walking, travel. *Address:* (office) Archbishop's House, Ambrosden Avenue, SW1P 1QJ. *T:* (020) 7798 9033.

ROCHE, Barbara Maureen; MP (Lab) Hornsey and Wood Green, since 1992; Minister of State, Cabinet Office, since 2001; *b* 13 April 1954; *d* of late Barnett Margolis and of Hannah (*née* Lopes Dias); *m* 1977, Patrick Roche; one *d*. *Educ:* JFS Comprehensive Sch., Camden; Lady Margaret Hall, Oxford (BA). Called to the Bar, Middle Temple, 1977. Parly Under-Sec. of State, DTI, 1997–98; Financial Sec., HM Treasury, 1999; Minister of State, Home Office, 1999–2001. *Recreations:* theatre, detective fiction. *Address:* House of Commons, SW1A 0AA. *T:* (020) 7219 3000. *Club:* Wood Green Labour.

ROCHE, Sir David (O'Grady), 5th Bt *cr* 1838 of Carass, Limerick; FCA; *b* 21 Sept. 1947; *s* of Sir Standish O'Grady Roche, 4th Bt, DSO, and of Evelyn Laura, *d* of Major William Andon; *S* father, 1977; *m* 1971, Hon. (Helen) Alexandra Briscoe Frewen, *d* of 3rd Viscount Selby; one *s* one *d* (and one *s* decd). *Educ:* Wellington Coll., Berks; Trinity Coll., Dublin. Chairman: Baltic Forest Lines Ltd, 1998–; Linda Investments Ltd, Estonia, 2000–. Liveryman, Co. of Saddlers, 1970. *Heir: s* David Alexander O'Grady Roche, *b* 28 Jan. 1976. *Address:* Bridge House, Starbotton, Skipton, N Yorks BD23 5HY. *T:* (01756) 760863; 20 Lancaster Mews, W2 3QE; *email:* sir.david@uk.com. *Clubs:* Buck's; Kildare Street and University (Dublin); Royal Yacht Squadron.

ROCHE, Sir Henry John, (Sir Harry), Kt 1999; Chairman, Press Association, since 1995 (non-executive Director, since 1988); *b* 13 Jan. 1934; *s* of Henry Joseph Roche and Mary Ann Roche; *m* 1st, 1956, Shirley May Foreman (marr. diss. 1986); three *s*; 2nd, 1986, Heather Worthington. *Educ:* George Mitchell Sch., Leyton; Watford Coll. of Technol. (HND Printing Technol.). Apprentice engraver, until 1959; worked on shopfloor of Daily Mirror, 1959–69; Dep. Prodn Controller, Daily Mirror, 1969–70; Northern Prodn Controller, Mirror Gp Newspapers, Manchester, 1970–73; Prodn Dir, 1973–77, Man. Dir, 1977–85, Manchester Evening News; Man. Dir, The Guardian, 1985–88; Chm. and Chief Exec., Guardian Media Gp Plc, 1988–96; Chm., GMTV, 1989–92. Director: Johnston Press plc, 1993– (Dep. Chm., 1995–); Jazz FM (formerly Golden Rose Communications) plc, 1995– (Chm., 1999–). Chairman: Press Standards Bd of Finance Ltd, 1991–; Orgn for Promoting Understanding in Society, 1998–; Dep. Chm., Printers Charitable Corp., 1996–2000 (Dir, 1985–2000; Pres., 1993). Mem. Council, CPU, 1988–. FIOP 1993 (Pres., 1996–98). Freeman, City of London, 1993. *Recreations:* golf, ski-ing, music (particularly jazz). *Clubs:* Royal Automobile; Dunham Forest Golf and Country (Cheshire).

ROCHE, Patrick John; Member, Lagan Valley, Northern Ireland Assembly (UKU, 1998–99, NIU, since 1999); *b* 1940; *m*. *Educ:* Trinity Coll., Dublin (BA Hons Econs and Politics); Durham Univ. (MA Politics). Posts in banking, 1957–66; Lectr in Economics and Philosophy of Religion, 1972–. *Publications:* (ed jtly) The Northern Ireland Question: myth and reality, 1991, perspectives and policies, 1995, Unionism, nationalism and partition, 1999; (jtly) An Economics Lesson for Irish Nationalists, 1996; The Appeasement of Terrorism and the Belfast Agreement, 2000; publications on political and econ. issues. *Recreation:* squash. *Address:* (home) 4 Pinehill Road, Bangor, Co. Down BT19 6SA; (office) Parliament Buildings, Stormont, Belfast BT4 3XX. *T:* (028) 9052 1994.

ROCHESTER, 2nd Baron, of the 4th creation, *cr* 1931, of Rochester in the County of Kent; **Foster Charles Lowry Lamb;** DL; *b* 7 June 1916; *s* of 1st Baron Rochester, CMG, and Rosa Dorothea (*née* Hurst); *S* father, 1955; *m* 1942, Mary Carlisle (*d* 2000), *yr d* of T. B. Wheeler, CBE; two *s* one *d* (and one *d* decd). *Educ:* Mill Hill; Jesus College, Cambridge. MA. Served War of 1939–45: Captain 23rd Hussars; France, 1944. Joined ICI Ltd, 1946: Labour Manager, Alkali Div., 1955–63; Personnel Manager, Mond Div., 1964–72. Pro-Chancellor, Univ. of Keele, 1976–86. Chairman: Cheshire Scout Assoc., 1974–81; Governors of Chester Coll., 1974–83. DL Cheshire, 1979. DUniv Keele, 1986. *Heir: s* Hon. David Charles Lamb [*b* 8 Sept. 1944; *m* 1969, Jacqueline Stamp; two *s*. *Educ:* Shrewsbury Sch.; Univ. of Sussex]. *Address:* 337 Chester Road, Hartford, Northwich, Cheshire CW8 1QR. *T:* (01606) 74733. *Clubs:* Reform, National Liberal, MCC; Hawks (Cambridge).

See also Hon. T. M. Lamb.

ROCHESTER, Bishop of, since 1994; **Rt Rev. Dr Michael Nazir-Ali;** *b* 19 Aug. 1949; *s* of James and Patience Nazir-Ali; *m* 1972, Valerie Cree; two *s*. *Educ:* St Paul's School and St Patrick's Coll., Karachi; Univ. of Karachi (BA 1970, Econs and Sociology); Fitzwilliam Coll. and Ridley Hall, Cambridge; St Edmund Hall, Oxford (BLitt 1974; Hon. Fellow, 1999). MLitt Cantab 1976; MLitt Oxon 1981; PhD Aust. Coll. of Theol. (Univ. of NSW) with Centre for World Religions, Harvard, 1983. Assistant: Christ Church, Cambridge, 1970–72; St Ebbe's, Oxford, 1972–74; Burney Lectr in Islam, Cambridge, 1973–74; Tutorial Supervisor in Theology, Univ. of Cambridge, 1974–76; Assistant, Holy Sepulchre, Cambridge, 1974–76; Tutor, then Sen. Tutor, Karachi Theol Coll., 1976–81; Assoc. Priest, Holy Trinity Cathedral, Karachi, 1976–79; Priest-in-charge, St Andrew's, Akhtar Colony, Karachi, 1979–81; Provost of Lahore Cathedral, 1981–84; Bishop of Raiwind, Pakistan 1984–86; Asst to Archbp of Canterbury, Co-ordinator of Studies and Editor for Lambeth Conf., 1986–89; Director-in-Residence, Oxford Centre for Mission Studies, 1986–89; Gen. Sec., CMS, 1989–94; Canon Theologian, Leicester Cathedral, 1992–94. Took seat in H of L, 1999. Mem., HFEA, 1998– (Chm., Ethics Cttee, 1998–). Sec., Archbp's Commn on Communion and Women in the Episcopate (Eames Commn), 1988–; Chm., Wkg Party on Women in Episcopate; Archbishops' nominee, CCBI, 1990–94; Chm., C of E Mission Theol Adv. Gp, 1992–2001; Member: ARCIC II, 1991–; C of E Bd of Mission, 1991–94, 1996–; Archbps' Council, 2001–; House of Bishops' Standing Cttee, 2001–; Anglican-Roman Catholic Jt Working Gp, 2001–. Mem. Bd, Christian Aid, 1987–97. Vis. Prof., Univ. of Greenwich, 1997–. *Publications:* Islam: a Christian perspective, 1983; Frontiers in Muslim-Christian Encounter, 1987; Martyrs and Magistrates: toleration and trial in Islam, 1989; From Everywhere to Everywhere, 1990; Mission and Dialogue, 1995; The Mystery of Faith, 1995; Citizens and Exiles: Christian faith in a plural world, 1998; *edited:* Working Papers for the Lambeth Conference, 1988; The Truth shall Make you Free: report of the Lambeth Conference, 1988; Trustworthy and True: Pastoral letters from the Lambeth Conference, 1988; articles and contribs to jls. *Recreations:* cricket, hockey, table tennis, reading detective fiction, humour and poetry, writing fiction and poetry. *Address:* Bishopscourt, Rochester, Kent ME1 1TS. *T:* (01634) 842721.

ROCHESTER, Dean of; *see* Shotter, Very Rev. E. F.

ROCHESTER, Archdeacon of; *see* Lock, Ven. P. H. D'A.

ROCHESTER, Prof. George Dixon, FRS 1958; FInstP; Professor of Physics, University of Durham, 1955–73, now Professor Emeritus; *b* 4 Feb. 1908; *s* of Thomas and Ellen Rochester; *m* 1938, Idaline, *o d* of Rev. J. B. and Mrs Bayliffe; one *s* one *d*. *Educ:* Wallsend Secondary Sch. and Technical Inst.; Universities of Durham, Stockholm and California. BSc, MSc, PhD (Dunelm). Earl Grey Memorial Scholar, Armstrong College, Durham University, 1926–29; Earl Grey Fellow, at Stockholm Univ., 1934–35; Commonwealth Fund Fellow at California Univ., 1935–37; Manchester University: Asst Lectr, 1937–46; Lectr, 1946–49; Sen. Lectr, 1949–53; Reader, 1953–55. Scientific Adviser in Civil Defence for NW Region, 1952–55. (Jt) C. V. Boys Prizeman of the Physical Society of London, 1956; Symons Memorial Lecturer of the Royal Meteorological Soc., 1962. Member: Council CNAA, 1964–74; Council, British Assoc. for Advancement of Science, 1971–72; Council, Royal Soc., 1972–74; Chm., NE Branch, Inst. of Physics, 1972–74. Second Pro-Vice-Chancellor, Univ. of Durham, 1967–69, Pro-Vice-Chancellor, 1969–70. Hon. DSc: Newcastle upon Tyne, 1973; CNAA, 1975; Hon. Fellow, Newcastle upon Tyne Polytechnic, 1977. Methodist. *Publications:* (with J. G. Wilson) Cloud Chamber Photographs of the Cosmic Radiation, 1952; scientific papers on spectroscopy, cosmic rays, history of the strange particles, and Durham astronomy. *Recreations:* outdoor activities, history of physics and astronomy. *Address:* 18 Dryburn Road, Durham DH1 5AJ. *T:* (0191) 3864796.

ROCHESTER, Terence Anthony, CB 1997; Acting Chief Executive, Confederation of Construction Clients, since 2000; *b* 30 May 1937; *s* of Arthur Alfred Rochester and Winifred Mabel Rochester (*née* Smith); *m* 1966, Margaret Alexandra Fleming; one *s* one *d*. *Educ:* Southwest Essex Sch. FICE; FIStructE; FIHT. British Rail, 1953–59, 1961–65; Nat. Service, 2nd Lieut, RE, 1959–61; joined Dept of Transport, 1965; various posts, 1965–87; Director: Transport Eastern Region, 1987–89; Transport W Midlands Region, 1989–90; Construction Programme, W Midlands, 1990–91; Chief Highway Engineer, 1991–94; Civil Engrg and Envmtl Policy Dir, 1994–96, Quality Services Dir, 1996–97, Highways Agency. Chairman: Tech. Cttee B/525 Bldg and Civil Engrg Structures, BSI, 1997–2000; Construction Clients' Forum, 1997–2000; Mem., Govt Cttee on Thaumasite, 1998–99. Res. Fellow, Transport Res. Foundn. Pres., CIRIA, 1998–2001; Hon. Mem., British PIARC. Trustee, Severn Bridges Trust. Liveryman, Co. of Paviors. *Recreations:* music, walking, dogs (own Dalmatian), DIY. *Address:* Confederation of Construction Clients, 7th Floor, 1 Warwick Row, SW1E 5ER.

ROCK, David Annison, PPRIBA; FCSD; President, Royal Institute of British Architects, 1997–99; Partner, Camp 5, since 1992; *b* 27 May 1929; *s* of Thomas Henry Rock and Muriel Rock (*née* Barton); *m* 1st, 1954, Daphne Elizabeth Richards (marr. diss. 1986); three *s* two *d*; 2nd, 1989, Lesley Patricia Murray. *Educ:* Bede Grammar Sch., Sunderland; King's Coll., Durham (BArch 1952; CertTP 1953). ARIBA 1953, FRIBA 1967; MSIAD 1963, FCSD 1978. 2nd Lieut, RE, 1953–55. With Basil Spence and Partners, 1952–53 and 1955–58; David Rock Architect, 1958–59; Associate Partner, 1959–64, Equity Partner, 1964–71, Grenfell Baines & Hargreaves, later Building Design Partnership; Chm. and Man. Dir, Rock Townsend, 1971–92. Inventor, Workspace concept (sharing by several firms of central support services in a building), 1971; first RIBA/ARCUK approved Archt Developer, 1973. Major projects include: Bumpus Bookshop, W1, 1958; Univ. of Surrey Develt Plan, 1965; UN HQ and Austrian Nat. Conf. Centre, Vienna, 1970; Middlesex Poly., Bounds Green, 1975–88; (with Ralph Erskine) The London Ark, Hammersmith, 1993. Graham Willis Vis. Prof., Univ. of Sheffield, 1990–92. Founder Chairman and Director: 5 Dryden Street Collective, 1971–82; Barley Mow Workspace Ltd, 1973–92; Joint Founder: Construction Industry Council, 1986; Urban Design Alliance, 1997. Royal Institute of British Architects: Mem./Chm., Architecture Award Bds for 14 UK Regs, 1960–77; Mem., Vis. Bds, 20 univs and polys, 1973–81; Mem. Council, 1970–76, 1986–88, 1995–2001; Vice-Pres., 1987–88, 1995–97. Member: Architecture Bd, CNAA, 1975–81; Housing the Arts Cttee, Arts Council of GB, 1981–84; Lottery Awards Panel, Sports Council, 1995–97; Specialist Assessor, HEFCE, 1994–95; Hd, Lottery Architecture Unit, Arts Council of England, 1995–99. Chm., Soc. of Architect Artists, 1986–92; Vice Pres., Architects Benevolent Soc., 2000–; Trustee, Montgomery Sculpture Trust, 2000–. *Solo painting exhibitions:* Durham, and Covent Garden, 1977; Ditchling, 1994. Hon. AIA 1998. Glover Medal, Northern Architectl Assoc., 1950; Soane Medallion, 1954, Owen Jones Studentship prize, 1960, RIBA; President's Medal, AIA, 1998. *Publications:* Vivat Ware!: strategies to enhance a historic town, 1974; The Grassroot Developers: a handbook for town development trusts, 1979; *illustrated:* B. Allsopp, Decoration and Furniture, 1950; D. Senior, Your Architect, 1964; articles and reviews in prof. and technical pubns, 1961–. *Recreations:* work, painting, watching TV sport. *Address:* Camp 5, The Beeches, 13 London Road, Harleston, Norfolk IP20 9BH. *T:* and *Fax:* (01379) 854897; *e-mail:* rockc5@talk21.com.

ROCK, Prof. Paul Elliot, FBA 2000; Professor of Social Institutions, London School of Economics and Political Science, since 1995; *b* 4 Aug. 1943; *s* of Ashley Rock and Charlotte (*née* Dickson); *m* 1965, Barbara Ravid (*d* 1998); two *s*. *Educ:* London School of Economics (BScSoc); Nuffield Coll., Oxford (DPhil). London School of Economics: Asst Lectr, 1967; Lectr, 1970; Sen. Lectr, 1976; Reader in Sociology, 1980; Reader in Social Institutions, 1981; Prof. of Sociology, 1986–95; Dir, Mannheim Centre for Study of

Criminology and Criminal Justice, 1992–95. Vis. Prof., Princeton Univ., 1974–75; Vis. Schol., Ministry of Solicitor Gen. of Canada, 1981–82; Fellow, Center for Advanced Study of Behavioral Scis, Stanford, Calif, 1996. FRSA 1997. *Publications:* Making People Pay, 1973; Deviant Behaviour, 1973; The Making of Symbolic Interactionism, 1979; (with D. Downes) Understanding Deviance, 1982, 2nd edn 1988, rev. 1998; A View from the Shadows, 1986; Helping Victims of Crime, 1990; The Social World of an English Crown Court, 1993; Reconstructing a Women's Prison, 1996; After Homicide, 1998. *Address:* London School of Economics and Political Science, Houghton Street, Aldwych, WC2A 2AE. *T:* (020) 7955 7296.

ROCKEFELLER, David; banker; *b* New York City, 12 June 1915; *s* of John Davison Rockefeller, Jr and Abby Greene (Aldrich) Rockefeller; *m* 1940, Margaret, *d* of Francis Sims McGrath, Mount Kisco, NY; two *s* four *d*. *Educ:* Lincoln School of Columbia University's Teachers College; Harvard Coll. (BS); London School of Economics; Univ. of Chicago (PhD). Sec. to Mayor Fiorello H. LaGuardia, 1940–41; Asst Regional Dir, US Office of Defense Health and Welfare Services, 1941. Served in US Army, N Africa and France, 1942–45 (Captain). Joined Chase National Bank, NYC, 1946; Asst Manager, Foreign Dept, 1946–47; Asst Cashier, 1947–48; Second Vice-Pres., 1948–49; Vice-Pres., 1949–51; Senior Vice-Pres., 1951–55; Chase Manhattan Bank (merger of Chase Nat. Bank and Bank of Manhattan Co.): Exec. Vice Pres., 1955–57; Dir, 1955–81; Vice-Chm., 1957–61; Pres. and Chm., Exec. Cttee, 1961–69; Chm. of Bd and Chief Exec. Officer, 1969–81; Chairman: Chase Internat. Investment Corp., 1961–75; Chase Internat. Adv. Cttee, 1980–2000; Rockefeller Brothers Fund Inc., 1981–87; The Rockefeller Group Inc., 1983–95; Rockefeller Center Properties Inc., 1985–92. Director: Internat. Exec. Service Corps (Chm., 1964–68); NY Clearing House, 1971–78; Center for Inter-American Relations (Chm. 1966–70); Overseas Develt Council; US-USSR Trade and Econ. Council, Inc.; Chairman: Rockefeller Univ., 1950–75; NYC Partnership, 1979–88; Hon. Chm., Americas Soc.; Hon. N America Chm., Trilateral Commn; Member: Council on Foreign Relations; Exec. Cttee, Museum of Modern Art (Chm., 1962–72, 1987–93); Harvard Coll. Bd of Overseers, 1954–60, 1962–68; Urban Develt Corp., NY State, Business Adv. Council, 1968–72; US Adv. Cttee on Reform of Internat. Monetary System, 1973–; Sen. Adv. Gp, Bilderberg Meetings; US Exec. Cttee, Dartmouth Conf.; Bd, Inst. of Internat. Economics. Director: Downtown-Lower Manhattan Assoc., Inc. (Chm., 1958–65); Internat. House, NY, 1940–63; Morningside Heights Inc., 1947–70 (Pres., 1947–57, Chm., 1957–65); B. F. Goodrich Co., 1956—64; Equitable Life Assce Soc. of US, 1960–65. Trustee: Univ. of Chicago, 1947–62 (Life Trustee, 1966); Carnegie Endowment for Internat. Peace, 1947–60; Council of the Americas (Chm., 1965–70, 1983–92); Historic Hudson Valley (formerly Sleepy Hollow Restorations), 1981–. Member: American Friends of LSE; US Hon. Fellows, LSE; Founding Mem., Business Cttee for the Arts; Hon. Mem., Commn on White House Fellows, 1964–65; Hon. Chm., Japan Soc. World Brotherhood Award, Jewish Theol Seminary, 1953; Gold Medal, Nat. Inst. Social Sciences, 1967; Medal of Honor for city planning, Amer. Inst. Architects, 1968; C. Walter Nichols Award, NY Univ., 1970; Reg. Planning Assoc. Award, 1971. Hon. LLD: Columbia Univ., 1954; Bowdoin Coll., 1958; Jewish Theol Seminary, 1958; Williams Coll., 1966; Wagner Coll., 1967; Harvard, 1969; Pace Coll., 1970; St John's Univ., 1971; Middlebury, 1974; Univ. of Liberia, 1979; Rockefeller Univ., 1980; Hon. DEng: Colorado Sch. of Mines, 1974; Univ. of Notre Dame, 1987. Holds civic awards. Grand Croix, Legion of Honour, France, 2000 (Grand Officer, 1955); Order of Merit of the Republic, Italy; Order of the Southern Cross, Brazil; Order of the White Elephant and Order of the Crown, Thailand; Order of the Cedar, Lebanon; Order of the Sun, Peru; Order of Humane African Redemption, Liberia; Order of the Crown, Belgium; National Order of Ivory Coast; Grand Cordon, Order of Sacred Treasure, Japan, 1991. *Publications:* Unused Resources and Economic Waste, 1940; Creative Management in Banking, 1964. *Recreation:* sailing. *Address:* 30 Rockefeller Plaza, New York, NY 10112, USA. *Clubs:* Century, Harvard, River, Knickerbocker, Links, University, Recess (New York); New York Yacht.

See also L. S. Rockefeller.

ROCKEFELLER, James Stillman; President and Director, Indian Spring Land Co.; Vice-President and Director, Indian Rock Corp.; *b* New York, 8 June 1902; *s* of William Goodsell Rockefeller and Elsie (*née* Stillman); *m* 1925, Nancy Carnegie; two *s* two *d*. *Educ:* Yale University (BA). With Brown Bros & Co., NYC, 1924–30; joined National City Bank of New York (later First Nat. City Bank; now Citibank, NA), 1930; Asst Cashier, 1931; Asst Vice-Pres. 1933; Vice-Pres., 1940–48; Sen. Vice-Pres., 1948–52; Exec. Vice-Pres., 1952; Pres. and Director, 1952–59; Chairman, 1959–67; former director of several Fortune 500 cos. Rep. Greenwich (Conn.) Town Meeting, 1933–42. Served as Lieutenant-Colonel in US Army, 1942–46. Member Board of Overseers, Memorial Hospital for Cancer and Allied Diseases, NY; Trustee of Estate of William Rockefeller; Trustee American Museum of National History. Olympic Gold Medal for rowing, 1924. *Address:* One Indian Spring Road, Greenwich, CT 06831–4430, USA. *Clubs:* Down Town Assoc., Union League, University (New York); Metropolitan (Washington, DC); Field, Round Hill (Greenwich, Conn).

ROCKEFELLER, Laurance Spelman, Hon. OBE 1971; philanthropist; Director, Rockefeller Center Inc., 1936–78 (Chairman, 1953–56, 1958–66); *b* New York, 26 May 1910; *s* of John Davison Rockefeller, Jr, FRS and Abby Greene Aldrich; *m* 1934, Mary French; one *s* three *d*. *Educ:* Lincoln School of Teachers College; Princeton University (BA). War service, Lt-Comdr, USNR, 1942–45. Chm. Emeritus and Trustee, Jackson Hole Preserve Inc., 1997– (Pres., 1940–87; Chm. and Trustee, 1987–96); Chairman: Citizens' Adv. Council on Environmental Quality, 1969–73 (Mem., 1973–79); Meml Sloan-Kettering Cancer Center, 1960–82 (Hon. Chm., 1982–); NY Zool Soc., 1970–75 (Hon. Chm., 1975–); Woodstock Resort Corp.; Woodstock Foundn, 1968–97 (Chm. Emeritus, 1997–); Dir, Eastern Air Lines, 1938–60, 1977–81, Adv. Dir, 1981–87; Mem. Bd of Dirs, Readers' Digest Assoc., 1973–93; Pres., Palisades Interstate Park Commn, 1970–77 (Comr Emeritus, 1978–); Adv. Trustee, Rockefeller Bros Fund, 1982–85 (Founding Trustee; Chm., 1958–80; Vice-Chm., 1980–82); Charter Trustee, Princeton Univ.; Trustee: Alfred P. Sloan Foundn, 1950–82; Greenacre Foundn; Sleepy Hollow Restorations, 1975–87 (Chm., 1981–85); Hist. Hudson Valley, 1987– (Chm. Emeritus, 1997–); Hon. Trustee, Nat. Geog. Soc.; Life Mem., Mass Inst. of Technology; Dir, Community Blood Council of Gtr NY; Mem., Nat. Cancer Adv. Bd, 1972–79; Chairman: Outdoor Recreation Resources Review Commn, 1958–65; Hudson River Valley Commn, 1956–66; 1965 White House Conf. on Nat. Beauty; Delegate UN Conf. on Human Environment, 1972. Mem., Amer. Conservation Assoc. (Pres., 1958–80; Chm., 1980–85; Hon. Chm., 1985–); Hon. Dir, Nat. Wildflower Center, 1988–. Holds numerous awards, medals and hon. degrees. Comdr, Royal Order of the Lion, Belgium, 1950; US Medal of Freedom, 1969; Congressional Gold Medal, 1990. *Address:* Room 5600, 30 Rockefeller Plaza, New York, NY 10112, USA. *Clubs:* Boone and Crockett, River, Princeton, Lotos, University, Brook, Cosmos, Knickerbocker, Capitol Hill (New York City); Sleepy Hollow (Tarrytown).

See also David Rockefeller.

ROCKEY, Patricia Mary, (Mrs D. C. Rockey); *see* Broadfoot, P. M.

ROCKHAMPTON, Bishop of, since 1996; **Rt Rev. Ronald Francis Stone;** *b* Armadale, Vic, 10 Sept. 1938; *s* of late Allan Francis Stone and Beatrice Rose Stone (*née* Hubber); *m* 1964, Lisbeth Joan Williams; two *s* one *d*. *Educ:* Caulfield South High Sch.; Caulfield Tech. Coll.; Taylors' Coll., Melbourne; St John's Coll., Morpeth, NSW (ThL 1963). Rector of Kerang, 1969–83; Canon, All Saints Cathedral, Bendigo, 1979–82; Archdeacon of Bendigo, 1983–92; VG, Diocese of Bendigo, 1983–92; Provincial Officer, Province of Victoria, 1988–92; Asst Bishop of Tasmania, 1992–96. Convener, Gen. Synod Rural Ministry Task Gp, 1991–98; Mem., Gen. Synod Ministry and Trng Commn, 1991–98. Chm. Bd of Dirs, Anglican Superannuation Australia, 1999–. Editor, The Anglican Gazette, 1997–. *Publication:* contrib. paper on rural ministry to Bush Telegraph. *Recreations:* gardening, philately, furniture restoration, golf, music, radio broadcasting. *Address:* PO Box 8307, Allenstown, Qld 4700, Australia. *T:* (7) 49273188. *Club:* Rockhampton.

ROCKLEY, 3rd Baron *cr* 1934; **James Hugh Cecil;** Director, Kleinwort Benson Group, 1986–98 (Chairman, 1993–96); *b* 5 April 1934; *s* of 2nd Baron Rockley, and Anne Margaret (*d* 1980), *d* of late Adm. Hon. Sir Herbert Meade-Featherstonhaugh, GCVO, CB, DSO; *S* father, 1976; *m* 1958, Lady Sarah Primrose Beatrix, *e d* of 7th Earl Cadogan, MC; one *s* two *d*. *Educ:* Eton; New Coll., Oxford. Wood Gundy & Co. Ltd, 1957–62; Kleinwort Benson Ltd, 1962–96. Chairman: Dartford River Crossing, 1988–93; Kleinwort Develt Fund, 1990–93; Midland Expressway, 1992–93; Director: Equity and Law, 1980–91; Christies Internat., 1989–98; Cobham (formerly FR Gp), 1990–; Abbey National, 1990–99; Foreign and Colonial Investment Trust, 1992–; Cadogan Gp Ltd, 1996–; Dusco (UK) Ltd, 1996–2000; Hypo Foreign & Colonial Mgt (Hldgs) Ltd, 1996–99. Mem., Design Council, 1987–93; Trustee, Nat. Portrait Gall., 1981–88. Chm. of Govs, Milton Abbey Sch., 2000–. *Heir: s* Hon. Anthony Robert Cecil [*b* 29 July 1961; *m* 1988, Katherine Jane, *d* of G. A. Whalley; one *s* two *d*]. *Address:* Lytchett Heath, Poole, Dorset BH16 6AE. *T:* (01202) 622228.

ROCKLIFFE, Victor Paul L.; *see* Lunn-Rockliffe.

ROCKLIN, David Samuel; Chairman, Norton Opax, 1973–89; *b* 15 Aug. 1931; *s* of Alfred Rocklin and Ada Rebecca Rocklin; *m* 1955, Dorothy Ann; two *s* two *d*. *Educ:* Heles School, Exeter. Managing Director, Norton Opax, 1969–73. *Recreations:* books, travel, music, painting, good food and conversation.

RODD, family name of **Baron Rennell.**

RODDA, James, (Jim), FCA; Financial Director, National Film and Television School, since 1996; *b* 16 Aug. 1945; *s* of George Rodda and Ruby (*née* Thompson); *m* 1967, Angela Hopkinson; one *s* two *d*. *Educ:* Maldon Grammar Sch.; Reading Univ. (BA Hons); Leicester Univ. FCA 1971. Spicer and Pegler, 1967–71; Coopers and Lybrand, 1971–77; Thomas Cook Group, 1977–84; Lonconex Group, 1984–85; Mercantile Credit, 1985–86; London Commodity Exchange, 1986–91; Dir of Finance and Admin, House of Commons, 1991–96. *Recreations:* rambling, music. *Address:* National Film and Television School, Beaconsfield Studios, Station Road, Beaconsfield, Bucks HP9 1LG. *T:* (01494) 671234.

RODDA, Dr John Carrol, FRMetS; President, International Association of Hydrological Sciences, 1995–2001; *b* 15 Aug. 1934; *s* of late J. Allen Rodda and Eleanor M. Rodda; *m* 1961, Annabel Brailsford Edwards; two *s*. *Educ:* UCW, Aberystwyth (BSc 1956; DipEd 1957; PhD 1960; DSc 1979). FRMetS 1961; MCIWEM 1976. DSIR Res. Fellow, 1960–62, Hydrologist, 1962–65, Hydraulics Res. Station, Wallingford; Hd, Catchment Res., Inst. Hydrology, Wallingford, 1965–69 and 1970–72; Consultant, WMO, Geneva, 1969–70 (on secondment); Head: Envmtl Pollution and Resources Unit, Directorate Gen. of Res., DoE, 1972–74; Data Acquisition Br., Water Data Unit, Reading, DoE, 1974–82; Asst Dir, Inst. Hydrology, Wallingford, 1982–88; Dir, Hydrology and Water Resources Dept, WMO, Geneva, 1988–95. Visiting Professor: Dept of Geog., Univ. of Strathclyde, 1976–79; Internat. Inst. for Infrastructure, Hydraulics & Envmt, Delft, 1976–97; Univ. of Perugia, 1983; Hon. Prof., Inst. Geog. and Earth Scis, Univ. of Wales, Aberystwyth, 1995–. Ed., 1972–79, Sec.-Gen., 1979–87, Internat. Assoc. Hydrological Scis; Sec./Treas., ICSU/Union Internat. des Assocs et Organismes Techniques Cttee on Water Res., 1982–87; Mem., Scientific Cttee on Water Res., ICSU, 1991–95; Mem. Exec. Cttee, IUGG, 1995–2001. UN International Decade for Natural Disaster Reduction: Member: Prep. Cttee, 1988–90; Scientific and Tech. Cttee, 1990–95; Chm., UN Admin. Co-ordinating Cttee, Sub-cttee on Water Resources, 1990–92; Chairman: Prog. Rev. Gp IV, Centre for Ecol. and Hydrol., NERC, 1996–2000; Commn on Water, World Humanities Action Trust, 1998–2000; Mem., Bd of Govs, World Water Council, 1999–2001. Mem., Amer. Geophysical Union, 1960; Hon. Member: British Hydrological Soc., 1983; Amer. Water Resources Assoc., 1992; Hungarian Hydrological Soc., 1992. Chm., Oxon Agenda 21 Planning Gp, 1997–2001; Mem. Bd, Trust for Oxon's Envmt, 1998–. Hugh Robert Mill Prize, RMetS, 1980. *Publications:* (jtly) Systematic Hydrology, 1976; (ed) Facets of Hydrology, 1976, Facets of Hydrology II, 1985 (trans. Russian); (jtly) Global Water Resource Issues, 1994; (ed jtly) Land Surface Processes in Hydrology: trials and tribulations of modeling and measurement, 1997. *Recreations:* walking, music, golf, environment. *Address:* Ynyslas, Brightwell cum Sotwell, Wallingford, Oxon OX10 0RG; *e-mail:* 106201.1774@compuserve.com. *Club:* Goring and Streatley Golf.

RODDICK, Anita Lucia, OBE 1988; Founder, and Co-Chairman since 1998, The Body Shop; *b* 23 Oct. 1942; *d* of Henry Perilli and Gilda de Vita; *m* 1970, (Thomas) Gordon Roddick; two *d*. *Educ:* Maude Allen Secondary Modern Sch. for Girls; Newton Park Coll. of Educn, Bath. 1962–76: worked in library of Internat. Herald Tribune, Paris; Teacher of History and English; worked in Women's Rights Dept, ILO, at UN, Geneva; owned and managed restaurant and hotel; opened first br. of The Body Shop, Brighton, 1976, Man. Dir, to 1994, Chief Exec., 1994–98. Trustee: The Body Shop Foundn, 1990–; New Acad. of Business, 1996–; Patron: START, 1987–; Schumacher Coll. for Human Scale Educn, 1991–; Assoc. for Creation Spirituality, 1994–; Findhorn Coll. of Internat. Educn, 1995–; Body and Soul, 1996. DUniv: Sussex, 1988; Open, 1995; Hon. LLD: Nottingham, 1990; New England Coll., 1991; Victoria, Canada, 1995; Hon. DSc Portsmouth, 1994; Hon. DBA Kingston, 1996. Veuve Clicquot Business Woman of the Year, 1984; County NatWest Retailer of the Year, 1988; Global 500 award, UNEP, 1989; World Vision Award, 1991; Internat. Banksia Envmtl Award, 1993; Botwinick Prize in Business Ethics, 1994. *Publications:* Body and Soul, 1991; Business as Unusual, 2000. *Address:* The Body Shop International PLC, Watersmead, Littlehampton, W Sussex BN17 6LS; *e-mail:* info@bodyshop.co.uk.

RODDICK, (George) Winston; QC 1986; Counsel General to National Assembly for Wales, since 1998; a Recorder, since 1987; *b* Caernarfon, 2 Oct. 1940; *s* of William and Aelwen Roddick; *m* 1966, Cennin Parry; one *s* one *d*. *Educ:* Sir Huw Owen GS, Caernarfon; Tal Handak, Malta; University Coll. London (LLB, LLM). Called to the Bar, Gray's Inn, 1968, Bencher, 1997. Member: Gen. Council of the Bar, 1992–95; Professional Conduct Cttee of the Bar, 1994–96; Employed Barristers Cttee, Bar Council, 2000–; Chm., Bristol and Cardiff Chancery Bar Assoc., 1996–. Hon. Recorder,

Caernarfon, 2001. Mem., ITC, 1998. Member: Welsh Language Bd, 1988–93; Lord Chancellor's Adv. Cttee on Statute Law, 1999–; Standing Cttee on use of Welsh lang. in legal proceedings, 1999–. Mem. Editl Bd, Cambridge Jl of Financial Crime, 1995–; Mem. Editl Bd, Wales Law Jl. Gov., Ysgol y Wern Sch., Cardiff, 1991–99. Pres., Cantorian Creigian, 2000–. Vice Pres., Caernarfon Male Voice Choir, 1994–. Patron, Caernarfon RFC, 1994–. Hon. Fellow, Univ. of Wales, Aberystwyth, 1999. *Recreations:* walking the countryside, fishing. *Address:* National Assembly for Wales, Cathays Park, Cardiff CF10 3NQ. *T:* (home) (029) 2075 9376. *Club:* Caernarfon Sailing.

RODDIE, Prof. Ian Campbell, CBE 1988; TD 1967; FRCPI; part-time consultant, International Finance Corporation/African Project Development Facility/World Bank, Washington, since 1989; Dunville Professor of Physiology, Queen's University, Belfast, 1964–87, now Emeritus; *b* 1 Dec. 1928; *s* of Rev. J. R. Wesley Roddie and Mary Hill Wilson; *m* 1st, 1958, Elizabeth Ann Gillon Honeyman (decd); one *s* three *d*; 2nd, 1974, Katherine Ann O'Hara (marr. diss.); one *s* one *d*; 3rd, 1987, Janet Doreen Saville (*née* Lennon). *Educ:* Methodist Coll., Belfast; Queen's Univ., Belfast. Malcolm Exhibnr, 1951, McQuitty Schol., 1953; BSc (1st cl. Hons Physiol.), MB BCh, BAO, MD (with gold medal), DSc; MRCPI; MRIA. Major RAMC (T&AVR); OC Med. Sub-unit, QUB OTC, retd 1968. Resident MO, Royal Victoria Hosp., Belfast, 1953–54; Queen's University, Belfast: Lectr in Physiology, 1954–60; Sen. Lectr, 1961–62; Reader, 1962–64; Dep. Dean, 1975–76, Dean, 1976–81, Faculty of Medicine; Pro-Vice-Chancellor, 1983–87; Head of Med. Educn, 1990–94, and Dep. Med. Dir, 1991–94, King Khalid Nat. Guard Hosp., Jeddah. Consultant Physiologist: NI Hosps Authority, 1962–72; Eastern Health Bd, NI, 1972–88. Staff Consultant, Asian Develt Bank, Manila, 1987–88. Harkness Commonwealth Fund Fellow, Univ. of Washington, Seattle, 1960–61; Visiting Professor: Univ. of NSW, 1983–84; Chinese Univ. of Hong Kong, 1988–90; Res. Fellow, Japan Soc. for Promotion of Science, Matsumoto, Japan, 1984. External Examiner: Univs of Aberdeen, Baghdad, Benghazi, Birmingham, Bristol, Glasgow, Ireland, Jeddah, Jos, Lagos, Leeds, London, Sheffield, Southampton, Zimbabwe; RCS, RCSE, RCPGlas, RCSI. Chief Reg. Sci. Advr for Home Defence, NI, 1977–88; Member: Home Defence Sci. Adv. Conf., 1977–88; Eastern Area Health and Social Services Bd, NI, 1976–81; Physiol Systems Bd, MRC, 1974–76; Med. Adv. Cttee, Cttee of Vice-Chancellors and Principals, 1976–81; GMC, 1979–81; GDC, 1979–81. President: Royal Acad. of Medicine in Ireland, 1985–88; Biol Scis Sect., Royal Acad. of Medicine in Ireland, 1964–66; Ulster Biomed. Engrg Soc., 1979–83; Chm. Cttee, Physiol Soc., 1985–88 (Mem. Cttee, 1966–69; Hon. Mem., 1989). Arris and Gale Lectr, RCS, 1962. Conway Bronze Medal, Royal Acad. of Medicine in Ireland, 1977. *Publications:* Physiology for Practitioners, 1971, 2nd edn 1975; Multiple Choice Questions in Human Physiology, 1971, 5th edn 1996; The Physiology of Disease, 1975; papers on physiology and pharmacology of vascular, sudorific and lymphatic systems. *Address:* Casa Matias, Apartment 11, Coto Real, Fase III, Lomas del Marbella Club, 29600 Marbella, Málaga, Spain. *T:* (95) 2857004, *Fax:* (95) 2827489; *e-mail:* icroddie@mercuryin.es.

RODECK, Prof. Charles Henry, DSc; FRCOG, FRCPath, FMedSci; Professor of Obstetrics and Gynaecology, University College London, since 1990; *b* 23 Aug. 1944; *s* of Heinz and Charlotte Rodeck; *m* 1971, Elisabeth (*née* Rampton); one *s* one *d*. *Educ:* University College London (BSc Anatomy 1966); UCH Med. Sch. (MB BS 1969); DSc (Med) London 1991. MRCOG 1975; FRCOG 1987; FRCPath 1994. House appts to 1975; King's College Hospital Medical School: Registrar, 1975; Lectr, 1976; Sen. Lectr/Consultant, 1978; Dir, Harris Birthright Res. Centre for Fetal Medicine, 1983–86; Prof., Inst. of Obstetrics and Gynaecol., RPMS, Queen Charlotte's and Chelsea Hosp., 1986–90. Member, Council: Obst. and Gyn. Sect., RSocMed; British Assoc. of Perinatal Med.; RCOG, 1991–92, 1996–2001 (Chm., Subspeciality Bd, 1989–92); Mem., Working Party on Antenatal Diagnosis, RCP, 1986–89; Chm., Steering Gp for Fetal Tissue Bank, MRC, 1989–92; Mem., EEC Working Party on Chorion Villus Sampling, 1983–85; Mem., Antenatal Screening Subgroup, DoH. Examr, RCOG and Univs of Aberdeen, Brussels, Dublin, Leiden, London, Nottingham, Oxford, Reading, Singapore, Stockholm; Visiting Professor: USA Univs; Hong Kong Univ. Pres., Internat. Fetal Medicine and Surgery Soc., 1986; Chm., Assoc. of Profs of Obst. and Gyn., 1995–; Chm., Fedn of Assocs of Clinical Profs; Pres., Internat. Soc. for Prenatal Diagnosis; Mem. or Hon. Mem., med. socs Europe and USA; Founder FMedSci 1998. Mem., editl bds of professional jls, UK and overseas; Editor for Europe, Prenatal Diagnosis, 1985–. *Publications:* (ed) Prenatal Diagnosis, 1984; (ed) Fetal Diagnosis of Genetic Defects, 1987; (ed) Fetal Medicine, 1989; (co-ed) Prenatal Diagnosis and Screening, 1992; (co-ed) Fetus and Neonate, 1993; (co-ed) Fetal Medicine: basic science and clinical practice, 1999; articles on prenatal diagnosis and fetal medicine. *Recreations:* stroking the cats, looking out of aeroplanes. *Address:* Department of Obstetrics and Gynaecology, University College London, 86–96 Chenies Mews, WC1E 6HX. *T:* (020) 7209 6059. *Club:* Athenæum.

RODEN, 10th Earl of, *cr* 1771 (Ire.); **Robert John Jocelyn;** Baron Newport 1743; Viscount Jocelyn 1755; Bt 1665; *b* 25 Aug. 1938; *s* of 9th Earl of Roden and Clodagh Rose (*d* 1989), *d* of Edward Robert Kennedy; *S* father, 1993; *m* 1st, 1970, Sara Cecilia (marr. diss. 1982), *d* of Brig. Andrew Dunlop; one *d*; 2nd, 1986, Ann Margareta Maria, *d* of Dr Gunnar Henning; one *s*. *Educ:* Stowe. *Heir: s* Viscount Jocelyn, *qv*.

RODENBURG, Patricia Anne, (Patsy); Head of Voice: Guildhall School of Speech and Drama, since 1981; Royal National Theatre, since 1990; *b* 2 Sept. 1953; *d* of Marius Rodenburg and Margaret Rodenburg (*née* Moody). *Educ:* St Christopher's Sch., Beckenham; Central Sch. of Speech and Drama. Voice Tutor, Royal Shakespeare Co., 1981–90; Head of Voice, Stratford Fest. Theatre, Canada, 1984–85; Associate: Michael Howard Studios, NY, 1994–; Royal Court Theatre, 1999–; Founding Dir, Voice and Speech Centre, London, 1989–; works regularly with Almeida Theatre, Shared Experience, Cheek-by-Jowl, Théâtre de Complicité, Donmar Warehouse; works extensively in theatre, TV and radio throughout Europe, N America, Australia, Africa and Asia with major theatre and opera cos. Distinguished Vis. Prof., Southern Methodist Univ., Dallas, 1987–. *Publications:* The Right to Speak, 1992; The Need for Words, 1993; The Actor Speaks, 1997; Speaking Shakespeare, 2002. *Recreations:* travelling, reading. *Address:* c/o Royal National Theatre, South Bank, SE1 9PX.

RODERICK, Caerwyn Eifion; Councillor, South Glamorgan County Council, 1980–96; *b* 15 July 1927; *m* 1952, Eirlys Mary Lewis; one *s* two *d*. *Educ:* Maes-y-Dderwen County Sch., Ystradgynlais; University Coll. of North Wales, Bangor. Asst Master, Caterham Sch., Surrey, 1949–52; Sen. Master, Chartesey Sch., LCC, 1952–54; Sen. Maths Master, Boys' Grammar Sch., Brecon, 1954–57; Method Study Engineer, NCB, 1957–60; Sen. Maths Master, Hartridge High Sch., Newport, Mon, 1960–69; Lecturer, Coll. of Educn, Cardiff, 1969–70. MP (Lab) Brecon and Radnor, 1970–79; PPS to Rt Hon. Michael Foot. Dist Officer, NUT, 1980–91. Mem. Council: UC, Cardiff; formerly Mem. Council, RCVS. *Address:* 29 Charlotte Square, Rhiwbina, Cardiff CF4 6NE. *T:* (029) 2062 8269.

RODERICK, Edward Joseph; Group Chief Executive, Christian Salvesen PLC, since 1997; *b* 23 Oct. 1952; *s* of Edward Deakin Roderick and Joan Roderick; *m* 1974, Denise Ann Rowan; two *s*. *Educ:* De La Salle Grammar Sch., Liverpool. National/International CPC. FILog 1992. B&I Line, 1972–87 (Head, UK Freight Ops, 1984–87); Man. Dir, Alexandra Molyneux Transport, 1987–88; BET plc, 1988–90: Man. Dir, IFF, 1988–90; Gp Dir, UTCH Ltd, 1988–90; Director: UTL Ltd, 1988–90; Seawheel, 1988–90; Gen. Manager, UK and Iberia, Bell Lines, 1990–92; Divl Man. Dir, Hays Network Distbn and other directorships in Hays plc, 1992–95; Man. Dir, Industrial Div., 1996–97, Man. Dir, Logistics UK and Europe, 1997, C. Salvesen PLC. Director: Road Haulage Assoc., 1998–2000; Freight Transport Assoc., 2000–. Dir, Northern Ballet Theatre, 1997–. MInstD 1987; CIMgt 2000. *Recreations:* golf, opera, ballet, swimming, wife and family. *Address:* Campbell House, Northampton Road, Higham Ferrers, Rushden, Northants NN10 6AL. *T:* (01933) 419148.

RODGER OF EARLSFERRY, Baron *cr* 1992 (Life Peer), of Earlsferry in the District of North East Fife; **Alan Ferguson Rodger;** PC 1992; FBA 1991; a Lord of Appeal in Ordinary, since 2001; *b* 18 Sept. 1944; *er s* of Prof. Thomas Ferguson Rodger and Jean Margaret Smith Chalmers. *Educ:* Kelvinside Acad., Glasgow; Glasgow Univ. (MA, LLB, LLD); New Coll., Oxford (MA (by decree), DPhil; DCL). Dyke Jun. Res. Fellow, Balliol Coll., Oxford, 1969–70 (Hon. Fellow, 1999); Fellow, New Coll., Oxford, 1970–72; Mem., Faculty of Advocates, 1974; Clerk of Faculty, 1976–79; QC (Scot.) 1985; Advocate Depute, 1985–88, Home Advocate Depute, 1986–88; Solicitor-Gen. for Scotland, 1989–92; Lord Advocate, 1992–95; a Senator of the Coll. of Justice in Scotland, 1995–96; Lord Justice-Gen. of Scotland and Lord-President of the Court of Session, 1996–2001. Member: Mental Welfare Commn for Scotland, 1981–84; UK Delegn to CCBE, 1984–89; Acad. of European Private Lawyers, 1994–. Maccabaean Lectr, British Acad., 1991. FRSE 1992. Hon. Bencher: Lincoln's Inn, 1992; Inn of Court of NI, 1998. Hon. Mem., SPTL, 1992; Corresp. Mem., Bayerische Akad. der Wissenschaften, 2001. Pres., Holdsworth Club, 1998–99. Hon. LLD: Aberdeen, 1999; Edinburgh, 2001. *Publications:* Owners and Neighbours in Roman Law, 1972 (asst editor) Gloag and Henderson's Introduction to the Law of Scotland, 10th edn, 1995; articles mainly on Roman Law. *Recreation:* walking. *Address:* House of Lords, SW1A 0PW. *Clubs:* Athenæum, Caledonian.

RODGER, Rt Rev. Patrick Campbell; an Assistant Bishop, Diocese of Edinburgh, 1986–2000; *b* 28 Nov. 1920; *s* of Patrick Wylie and Edith Ann Rodger; *m* 1952, Margaret Menzies Menzies, MBE (*d* 1989); one *s* (and one *s* decd). *Educ:* Cargilfield; Rugby; Christ Church, Oxford (Hon. Student, 1990); Westcott House, Cambridge. Deacon, 1949; priest, 1950; Asst Curate, St John's Church, Edinburgh, 1949–51, and Chaplain to Anglican Students in Edinburgh, 1951–54. Study Secretary, SCM of Gt Brit. and Ire., 1955–58; Rector, St Fillan's, Kilmacolm, with St Mary's Bridge of Weir, 1958–61; Exec. Sec. for Faith and Order, World Council of Churches, 1961–66; Vice-Provost, St Mary's Cathedral, Edinburgh, 1966–67; Provost, 1967–70; Bishop of Manchester, 1970–78; Bishop of Oxford, 1978–86; Mem., House of Lords, 1974–86. Chm., Churches' Unity Commn, 1974–78; Pres., Conf. of European Churches, 1974–86. *Publications:* The Fourth World Conference on Faith and Order, Montreal (ed), 1964; Songs in a Strange Land, 1989. *Recreations:* music and walking. *Address:* 12 Warrender Park Terrace, Edinburgh EH9 1EG. *T:* (0131) 229 5075. *Club:* New (Edinburgh).

RODGERS, family name of **Baron Rodgers of Quarry Bank**.

RODGERS OF QUARRY BANK, Baron *cr* 1992 (Life Peer), of Kentish Town in the London Borough of Camden; **William Thomas Rodgers;** PC 1975; Chairman, Advertising Standards Authority, 1995–2001; Leader, Liberal Democrats, House of Lords, 1998–2001; *b* 28 Oct. 1928; *s* of William Arthur and Gertrude Helen Rodgers; *m* 1955, Silvia, *d* of Hirsch Szulman; three *d*. *Educ:* Sudley Road Council Sch.; Quarry Bank High School, Liverpool; Magdalen College, Oxford. General Secretary, Fabian Society, 1953–60. Contested: (Lab) Bristol West, March 1957; (SDP) Stockton N, 1983; (SDP/Alliance) Milton Keynes, 1987. MP (Lab 1962–81, SDP 1981–83) Stockton-on-Tees, 1962–74, Teesside, Stockton, 1974–83; Parly Under-Sec. of State: Dept of Econ. Affairs, 1964–67, Foreign Office, 1967–68; Leader, UK delegn to Council of Europe and Assembly of WEU, 1967–68; Minister of State: BoT, 1968–69; Treasury, 1969–70; MoD, 1974–76; Sec. of State for Transport, 1976–79. Chm., Expenditure Cttee on Trade and Industry, 1971–74. Vice-Pres., SDP, 1982–87. Dir-Gen., RIBA, 1987–94. Borough Councillor, St Marylebone, 1958–62. Hon. FRIBA 1994; Hon. FIStructE 1993. *Publications:* Hugh Gaitskell, 1906–1963 (ed), 1964; (jt) The People into Parliament, 1966; The Politics of Change, 1982; (ed) Government and Industry, 1986; Fourth Among Equals, 2000; pamphlets, etc. *Address:* 43 North Road, N6 4BE.

RODGERS, Sir (Andrew) Piers (Wingate), 3rd Bt *cr* 1964, of Groombridge, Kent; Director, The Type Museum, London, 2001; Secretary, Royal Academy of Arts, London, 1982–96; *b* 24 Oct. 1944; second *s* of Sir John Rodgers, 1st Bt and Betsy (*d* 1998), *y d* of Francis W. Aikin-Sneath; *S* brother, 1997; *m* 1979, Marie Agathe Houette (marr. diss. 2000); two *s*; one *d* by Ilona Medvedeva. *Educ:* Eton Coll.; Merton Coll., Oxford (BA 1st Cl. Honour Mods, Prox. acc. Hertford and De Paravicini Prizes). J. Henry Schroder Wagg & Co. Ltd, London, 1967–73: Personal Asst to Chairman, 1971–73; Director, International Council on Monuments and Sites (ICOMOS), Paris, 1973–79; Consultant, UNESCO, Paris, 1979–80; Member, Technical Review Team, Aga Khan Award for Architecture, 1980, 1983; Secretary, UK Committee of ICOMOS, 1981. FRSA 1973. Mem. Bd, Warburg Inst., Univ. of London, 1993–98. Mem., Court of Assts, Masons' Co., 1982–. Chevalier de l'Ordre des Arts et des Lettres (France), 1987; Chevalier de l'Ordre National du Mérite (France), 1991; Cavaliere dell'Ordine al Merito della Repubblica Italiana, 1992. *Publications:* articles on protection of cultural heritage. *Recreations:* music, Real tennis, Islamic art. *Heir: s* Thomas Rodgers, *b* 18 Dec. 1979. *Address:* Peverell, Bradford Peverell, Dorset DT2 9SE. *Clubs:* Brooks's, Pratt's, MCC.

RODGERS, Bríd; Member (SDLP) Upper Bann, since 1998, and Minister for Agriculture and Rural Development, since 1999, Northern Ireland Assembly; *b* 20 Feb. 1935; *d* of Tom Stratford and Josephine (*née* Coll); *m* 1960, Antoin Rodgers; three *s* three *d*. *Educ:* St Louis Convent, Monaghan; University Coll., Dublin (BA Hons Mod. Langs; Higher DipEd). Exec. Mem., NI Civil Rights Assoc., 1970–71. Mem., Irish Senate, 1983–87. Mem. (SDLP), Craigavon BC, 1985–93. Social Democratic and Labour Party: Vice Chair, 1976–78; Chair, 1978–80; Gen. Sec., 1981–83; Delegate to Brooke/Mayhew Talks, 1991–92; elected in Upper Bann to Negotiations, 1996, Chair, Negotiating Team, 1996–98; Dep. Leader, 2001–. Contested (SDLP) Tyrone West, 2001. *Recreations:* reading, music, golf. *Address:* 34 Kilmore Road, Lurgan, Co. Armagh BT67 9BP. *T:* (028) 3832 2140.

RODGERS, Joan, CBE 2001; soprano; *b* 4 Nov. 1956; *d* of Thomas and Julia Rodgers; *m* 1988, Paul Daniel, *qv*; two *d*. *Educ:* Univ. of Liverpool (BA Hons Russian); RNCM. FRNCM. Kathleen Ferrier Meml Scholarship, 1981. Début, Aix-en-Provence, 1982; Covent Garden début, 1984; NY Met. début, 1995; has appeared with all major British opera cos; has worked with many conductors, incl. Barenboim, Solti, Abbado, Rattle, Gardiner, Colin Davis, Andrew Davis, Salonen, Mehta, Harnoncourt; Mozart rôles incl. Susanna, Zerlina, Ilia, Fiordiligi, Elvira, Sandrina, Countess; other rôles incl. Cleopatra in

Giulio Cesare, Ginevra in Ariodante, Tatyana in Eugene Onegin, Mélisande, Theodora, Governess in The Turn of the Screw, Marschallin in Der Rosenkavalier, Blanche in The Carmelites; regular recitals and concert performances in London, Australia, Vienna, Madrid, Los Angeles, New York, Chicago, Paris and Brussels; many recordings. *Recreations:* walking, spending time with my family. *Address:* c/o Ingpen & Williams Ltd, 26 Wadham Road, SW15 2LR.

RODGERS, Dr Patricia Elaine Joan; Permanent Secretary, Ministry of Tourism, Commonwealth of the Bahamas, since 1995; *b* 13 July 1948; *d* of late Dr Kenneth V. A. Rodgers, OBE and Anatol C. Rodgers, MBE. *Educ:* Univ. of Aberdeen (MA Hons English, 1970); Inst. of Internat. Relations, St Augustine, Trinidad (Dip. in Internat. Relns (Hons) 1972); Inst. Univ. des Hautes Etudes Internationales, Geneva (PhD 1977). Joined Ministry of Foreign Affairs, Nassau, Bahamas, 1970; Minister-Counsellor, Washington, 1978–83; Actg High Comr to Canada, 1983–86, High Comr, 1986–88; High Comr to UK, 1988–92, also Ambassador (non-resident) to: FRG and Belgium, 1988–92, to EC and France, 1989–92; Perm. Rep. to IMO, 1991–92; Chief of Protocol, Min. of For. Affairs, 1993–94. *Publication:* Mid-Ocean Archipelagos and International Law: a study of the progressive development of international law, 1981. *Recreations:* folk painting, gourmet cooking, theatre. *Address:* Ministry of Tourism, PO Box N3701, Market Plaza, Bay Street, Nassau, Bahamas.

RODGERS, Sir Piers; *see* Rodgers, Sir A. P. W.

RODLEY, Sir Nigel (Simon), KBE 1998; PhD; Professor of Law, University of Essex, since 1994; *b* 1 Dec. 1941; *s* of John Peter Rodley (*né* Hans Israel Rosenfeld) and Rachel Rodley (*née* Kantorowitz); *m* 1967, Lyn Bates. *Educ:* Clifton Coll.; Univ. of Leeds (LLB 1963); Columbia Univ. (LLM 1965); New York Univ. (LLM 1970); Univ. of Essex (PhD 1993). Asst Prof. of Law, Dalhousie Univ., 1965–68; Associate Economic Affairs Officer, UN HQ, NY, 1968–69; Vis. Lectr in Pol Sci., New Sch. for Social Res., NY, 1969–72; Res. Fellow, NY Univ. Center for Internat. Studies, 1970–72; Founder and Hd, Legal Office, Amnesty Internat., 1973–90; Vis. Lectr in Law, 1973–90, Res. Fellow, 1983, LSE; Reader in Law, Univ. of Essex, 1990–94. Special Rapporteur on Torture, UN Commn on Human Rights, 1993–2001; Mem., UN Human Rights Cttee, 2001–. Hon. LLD Dalhousie, 2000. *Publications:* (ed jtly) International Law in the Western Hemisphere, 1974; (jtly) Enhancing Global Human Rights, 1979; The Treatment of Prisoners under International Law, 1987, 2nd edn 1999; (ed) To Loose the Bands of Wickedness: international intervention in defence of human rights, 1992; (ed jtly) International Responses to Traumatic Stress, 1996; numerous articles in learned jls and contribs to books. *Recreations:* music, theatre, cinema, crosswords, walking. *Address:* Department of Law, University of Essex, Wivenhoe Park, Colchester CO4 3SQ. *T:* (01206) 872562; (home) 1 Meyrick Crescent, Colchester CO2 7QX. *T:* (01206) 570732.

RODNEY, family name of **Baron Rodney**.

RODNEY, 10th Baron *cr* 1782; **George Brydges Rodney;** Bt 1764; *b* 3 Jan. 1953; *o s* of 9th Baron Rodney and of Régine, *d* of Chevalier Pangaert d'Opdorp, Belgium; *S* father, 1992; *m* 1996, Jane, *d* of Hamilton Rowan Blakeney; one *s*. *Educ:* Eton. *Heir: s* Hon. John George Brydges Rodney, *b* 5 July 1999. *Address:* 38 Pembroke Road, W8 6NU.

RODOTÀ, Antonio; Director General, European Space Agency, since 1997; *b* Cosenza, Italy, 24 Dec. 1935; *s* of Carlo Rodotà and Maria Cristofaro; *m* 1965, Barbara Salvini; one *s* two *d*. *Educ:* Rome Univ. (BSc Electronic Engrg 1959). Asst Lectr in Radio Engrg, Univ. of Rome, 1959–61; with SISPRE SpA (Italy), 1959–65; Italian delegate to NATO, Paris, 1965–66; Selenia: Head, Electronic Design Gp, 1966–71; i/c engrg, Radar and Systems Div., 1971–76, Head of Div., 1976–80; Dir Gen., CNS (Compagnia Nazionale Satelliti) SpA, 1980–83; Joint Managing Director: Selenia Spazio SpA, 1983–90; Alenia Spazio SpA, 1990–95 (Man. Dir, 1995–96); Alenia Spazio SpA incorporated into Finmeccanica, 1996: Head, Space Div., 1996–97. Chm. and Man. Dir, Quadrics Supercomputer World Ltd. Formerly Dir, several aerospace firms, incl. Arianespace. Vice-Chm., Defence and Space Gp, Italian Nat. Assoc. of Electrical Industries; Mem., Managing Cttee, Italian Aerospace Assoc. Mem., High-Performance Computer Gp, Italian Min. of Res. FRAeS 1997. *Recreations:* ski-ing, tennis, classical music. *Address:* European Space Agency, 8–10 rue Mario Nikis, 75738 Paris Cedex, France.

RODRIGUES, Sir Alberto, Kt 1966; CBE 1964 (OBE 1960; MBE (mil.) 1948); ED; Senior Unofficial Member Executive Council, Hong Kong, 1964–74; former Pro-Chancellor and Chairman of Executive Council, University of Hong Kong; *b* 5 Nov. 1911; *s* of late Luiz Gonzaga Rodrigues and late Giovanina Remedios; *m* 1940, Cynthia Maria da Silva; one *s* two *d*. *Educ:* St Joseph's College and University of Hong Kong. MB BS Univ. of Hong Kong, 1934; FRCPE 1988. Post graduate work, London and Lisbon, 1935–36; Medical Practitioner, 1937–40; also Medical Officer in Hong Kong Defence Force. POW, 1940–45. Medical Practitioner, 1945–50; Post graduate work, New York, 1951–52; Resident, Winnipeg Maternity Hosp. (Canada), 1952–53; General Medical Practitioner, Hong Kong, 1953. Member: Urban Council (Hong Kong), 1940–41; 1947–50; Legislative Council, 1953–60; Executive Council, 1960–74. Med. Superintendent, St Paul's Hospital, 1953. Director: Jardine Strategic Hldgs (formerly Jardine Securities), 1969; Lap Heng Co. Ltd, 1970; HK & Shanghai Hotels Ltd, 1969; Peak Tramways Co. Ltd, 1971; Li & Fung Ltd, 1973; HK Commercial Broadcasting Co. Ltd, 1974; Hong Kong and Shanghai Banking Corporation, 1974–76. Officer, Ordem de Cristo (Portugal), 1949; Chevalier, Légion d'Honneur (France), 1962; Knight Grand Cross, Order of St Sylvester (Vatican), 1966. *Recreations:* cricket, hockey, tennis, swimming, badminton. *Address:* c/o University of Hong Kong, Pokfulam Road, Hong Kong. *Clubs:* Hong Kong Jockey, Hong Kong Country, Lusitano, Recreio (all Hong Kong).

RODRIGUES, Christopher John; Director and Chief Executive, Bradford & Bingley plc (formerly Building Society), since 1996; *b* 24 Oct. 1949; *s* of Alfred John Rodrigues and Joyce Margaret Rodrigues (*née* Farron-Smith); *m* 1976, Priscilla Purcell Young; one *s* one *d*. *Educ:* University College Sch.; Jesus Coll., Cambridge (BA Econs and Hist.; Pres., Cambridge Univ. Boat Club, 1971; rowing Blue, 1970 and 1971); Harvard Business Sch. (Baker Scholar; MBA 1976). With Spillers Foods, London, 1971–72; Foster Turner & Benson, London, 1972–74; McKinsey & Co., London, 1976–79; American Express, NY and London, 1979–88; Thos Cook Gp, 1988–95 (Chief Exec., 1992–95). Non-exec. Dir, Energis PLC, 1997–. Non-exec. Dir, FSA, 1997–. Exec. Cttee, NT, 1994–. FRSA 1994. Steward, Henley Royal Regatta, 1998–. *Recreations:* cooking, ski-ing, rowing, shooting, opera, ballet. *Address:* Bradford & Bingley plc, Croft Road, Crossflatts, Bingley, W Yorks BD16 2UA. *T:* (01274) 554426. *Clubs:* Arts; Leander Rowing (former Chm.) (Henley); Hawks (Cambridge); Century (Harvard).

RODRÍGUEZ IGLESIAS, Gil Carlos; President, Court of Justice of European Communities, since 1994; *b* 26 May 1946; *m* 1972, Teresa Díez Gutierrez; two *d*. *Educ:* Oviedo Univ. (LLL 1968); Madrid Autonomous Univ. (doctorate 1975). Internat. law asst, then Lectr, Oviedo, Freiburg, Madrid Autonomous and Madrid Complutense Univs, 1969–82; Professor: Madrid Complutense Univ., 1982–83; Granada Univ., 1983–86; Judge, EC Court of Justice, 1986–94. Hon. Bencher, Gray's Inn, 1995. Hon. Dr: Univ. of Turin, 1996; Univ. of Babes-Bolyai' Cluj-Napoca, Romania, 1996; Univ. of Saarbrücken, Germany, 1997. Encomienda de la Orden de Isabel la Católica (Spain), 1976; Cruz de Honor de la Orden de San Raimundo de Peñafort (Spain), 1986. *Publications:* El régimen juridico de los monopolios de Estado en la Comunidad Económica Europea, 1976; various articles and studies on EC law and internat. law. *Address:* Court of Justice of the European Communities, Plateau du Kirchberg, 2925, Luxembourg. *T:* 43032265 and 43032200, *Fax:* 43032777.

RODWELL, Daniel Alfred Hunter; QC 1982; **His Honour Judge Rodwell;** a Circuit Judge, since 1986; *b* 3 Jan. 1936; *s* of late Brig. R. M. Rodwell, AFC, and Nellie Barbara Rodwell (*née* D'Costa); *m* 1967, Veronica Ann Cecil; two *s* one *d*. *Educ:* Munro Coll., Jamaica; Worcester Coll., Oxford, 1956–59 (BA Law). National service, 1954–56; 2/Lieut 1st West Yorks, PWO, 1955; TA, 1956–67: Captain and Adjt 3 PWO, 1964–67. Called to Bar, Inner Temple, 1960. A Deputy Circuit Judge, 1977; a Recorder, 1980–86. *Recreations:* gardening, sailing. *Address:* Aylesbury Crown Court, 38 Market Square, Aylesbury, Bucks HP20 1DX. *T:* (01296) 434401.

RODWELL, Sheila Anne; *see* Bingham, S. A.

ROE, Anthony Maitland, DPhil; CChem, FRSC; Executive Secretary, Council of Science and Technology Institutes, 1987–94; *b* 13 Dec. 1929; *s* of late Percy Alex Roe and Flora Sara Roe (*née* Kisch); *m* 1958, Maureen, *d* of late William James Curtayne and of Kathleen (*née* Wigfull); two *s* one *d*. *Educ:* Harrow Sch.; Oriel Coll., Oxford (BA, MA, DPhil). ARIC 1955; FRSC, CChem 1976. Commnd Intell. Corps, 1955–57. Univ. of Rochester, NY, 1957–59; Sen. Chemist, Smith Kline & French Res. Inst., 1959–65; Hd of Chemistry Gp, Smith Kline & French Labs Ltd, 1965–78; Dir of Chemistry, Smith Kline & French Res. Ltd, 1978–86. Royal Society of Chemistry: Mem. Council, 1982–85, 1987–91; Vice-Pres., Perkin Div., 1986–88; Chm., Heterocyclic Gp, 1986–88; Chm., 'Chemistry in Britain' Management Cttee, 1987–91. Founder Cttee Mem., Soc. for Drug Res., 1966–77; Member: Bd for Science, BTEC, 1985–88; Parly and Scientific Cttee, 1987–94. Chm., Welwyn Hatfield CAB, 1996–2000. *Publications:* research papers, patents and reviews in field of organic and medicinal chem. *Recreations:* listening to music, walking, good food and wine. *Address:* 10 Lodge Drive, Hatfield, Herts AL9 5HN. *T:* (01707) 265075.

ROE, Chang Hee; Senior Advisor, Federation of Korean Industries, since 1998; *b* 25 Feb. 1938; *m* 1963, Chung Ja Lee; one *s* one *d*. *Educ:* Seoul Nat. Univ., Korea (BA Econ 1960). Joined Min. of Foreign Affairs, 1960: Instructor ROK Air Force Acad., 1962–66; Dir of Legal Affairs, 1968–69; First Sec., Korean Embassy, Canada, 1969–72; Private Sec. to Minister of Foreign Affairs, 1972–73; Dir, Treaties Div., 1973–75; Counsellor, Sweden, 1975–78; Dep. Dir-Gen., American Affairs Bureau, 1978–80; Dir-Gen., Treaties Bureau, 1980–82; Minister and Dep. Chief of Mission, USA, 1982–85; Ambassador to Nigeria, 1985–88; Sen. Protocol Sec. to Pres., 1988–91; Ambassador and Perm. Rep. to UN, 1991–92; Vice Minister of Foreign Affairs, 1992–93; Ambassador to UK, 1993–96; Ambassador at Large, 1996–98. Guest Prof., Hanseo Univ., Korea, 1998–2001. *Recreations:* golf, ski-ing. *Address:* Hanyang Apt 62-606, Apkujong-dong, Kangnam-gu, Seoul 135–110, Korea.

ROE, Geoffrey Eric; Managing Director, FR Aviation Group, since 2000; Director, Cobham plc, since 1997; Chairman: National Jet Systems, Australia, and National Air Support, Australia, since 2000; *b* 20 July 1944; *s* of Herbert William Roe and Florence Roe (*née* Gordon); *m* 1968, Elizabeth Anne Ponton; one *s* one *d*. *Educ:* Tottenham Grammar School. Min. of Aviation, 1963; Finance (R&D) Br., 1963–67; Asst Private Sec. to Sir Ronald Melville, 1967–69; Exports and Internat. Relations Div., Min. of Technology, 1969–74; Guided Weapons Contracts Branch, 1974–76; seconded British Aerospace, 1976–78; Rocket Motor Exec., 1978–81; Asst Dir Contracts (Air), 1981–86; Dir of Contracts (Underwater Weapons), 1986–89; Head, Material Co-ord. (Naval), 1989–90; Principal Dir, Navy and Nuclear Contracts, 1990–91; Director-General: Defence Contracts, MoD, 1991–95; Commercial, MoD, 1995; Aircraft Systems 2, 1995–96. Director: FR Aviation Services Ltd, 2000–; FBS Ltd, 2000–; Air Tanker Ltd, 2000–; FBH Ltd, 2000–. Dir, SBAC, 1998–. *Recreations:* ski-ing, fell-walking, sailing, private flying. *Address:* FR Aviation Ltd, Bournemouth International Airport, Christchurch, Dorset BH23 6NE.

ROE, Howard Stanley James, DSc; Director, Southampton Oceanography Centre, NERC and the University of Southampton, since 1999; *b* 23 May 1943; *s* of Eric James Roe and Freda Mary Roe (*née* Perkins); *m* 1970, Heather Anne Snelling; one *s* two *d*. *Educ:* Bedford Sch.; University Coll. London (BSc 1st Cl. Hons Zool. 1965; DSc Biol Oceanography 1998). Natural Environment Research Council: Scientific Officer, Whale Res. Unit, 1965–68; transferred to Biol. Dept, Nat. Inst. Oceanography, 1968; Project Co-ordinator for develt of Southampton Oceanography Centre, 1989–95; Hd, George Deacon Div., Inst. Oceanographic Scis, later Southampton Oceanography Centre, 1993–99 (Dep. Dir, 1997–99). Mem., Challenger Soc. for Marine Sci. *Publications:* contrib. numerous papers and reports to jls, etc, dealing with whale biology, biological oceanography and develt of sampling technol. *Recreations:* fishing, gardening, travel, amateur dramatics. *Address:* Southampton Oceanography Centre, Empress Dock, Southampton SO14 3ZH; Barton Mere, Barton Court Avenue, New Milton, Hants BH25 7HD. *T:* (01425) 622092. *Clubs:* Little Ship; Christchurch Angling.

ROE, James Kenneth; Director, Jupiter International (formerly Jupiter Tyndall) Group, 1993–2000; Member, Monopolies and Mergers Commission, 1993–99; *b* 28 Feb. 1935; *s* of late Kenneth Alfred Roe and Zirphie Norah Roe (*née* Luke); *m* 1958, Marion Audrey Keyte (*see* M. A. Roe); one *s* two *d*. *Educ:* King's Sch., Bruton. National Service commn, RN, 1953–55. Joined N. M. Rothschild & Sons, 1955; Director, 1970–92. Chm., China Investment Trust, 1993–98; Dep. Chm., Innovations Gp (formerly Kleeneze Holdings), 1985–96; Director: Rothschild Trust Corp., 1970–95; Jupiter European Investment Trust, 1990–2000; GAM Selection Inc., 1992–; Ronson (formerly Halkin Holdings), 1993–98 (Chm., 1993–97); Microvitec, 1993–97; Fleming Income and Capital Investment Trust, 1995–; Whitehall Fund Managers Ltd, 1998–; European Growth and Income Trust, 2000–; New Star Enhanced Income Trust, 2001–. FRSA 1991; FInstD 1993. *Recreations:* walking, reading, theatre, opera. *Clubs:* Brooks's, MCC.

ROE, Marion Audrey; MP (C) Broxbourne, since 1983; *b* 15 July 1936; *d* of William Keyte and Grace Mary (*née* Bocking); *m* 1958, James Kenneth Roe, *qv*; one *s* two *d*. *Educ:* Bromley High Sch. (GPDST); Croydon High Sch. (GPDST); English Sch. of Languages, Vevey. Member: London Adv. Cttee, IBA, 1978–81; Gatwick Airport Consultative Cttee, 1979–81; SE Thames RHA, 1980–83. Member (C): Bromley Borough Council, 1975–78; for Ilford N, GLC, 1977–86 (Cons. Dep. Chief Whip, 1978–82). Contested (C) Barking, 1979. Parly Private Secretary to: Parly Under-Secs of State for Transport, 1985; Minister of State for Transport, 1986; Sec. of State for Transport, 1987; Parly Under Sec. of State, DoE, 1987–88. Member, Select Committee: on Agriculture, 1984–85; on Social

Services, 1988–89; on Procedure, 1990–92; on Sittings of the House, 1991–92; Chairman: Select Cttee on Health, 1992–97; H of C Admin. Cttee, 1997– (Mem., 1991–97); Mem., Speaker's Panel of Chairmen, 1997–. Vice Chairman: All-Party Fairs and Showgrounds Gp, 1992– (Jt Chm., 1989–92); All-Party Parly Garden Club, 1995–; All-Party Gp on Alcohol Misuse, 1997–; Chm., All-Party Hospice Gp, 1992– (Sec., 1990–92); Jt Chm., All-Party Gp on Breast Cancer, 1997–; Chairman: Cons. Back bench Horticulture and Markets Sub-Cttee, 1989–97; Cons. Back bench Social Security Cttee, 1990–97; Vice-Chairman: Cons. Back bench Environment Cttee, 1990–97; Cons. Parly Health Cttee, 1997–99; 1922 Cttee, 2001– (Mem. Exec., 1992–94; Sec., 1997–2001); Sec., Cons. Back bench Horticulture Cttee, 1983–85; Jt Sec., Cons. Back bench Party Orgn Cttee, 1985; British-Canadian Parly Gp, 1991– (Vice Chm., 1997–); Adv. Cttee on Women's Employment, Dept of Employment, 1989–92; Substitute Mem., UK Delegn to Parly Assemblies of Council of Europe and WEU, 1989–92; Member, Executive Committee: UK Br., CPA, 1997–; British Gp, IPU, 1997–98 (Vice Chm., 1998–). Vice-Pres., Women's Nationwide Cancer Control Campaign, 1985–87, 1988–; Patron, UK Nat. Cttee for UN Develt Fund for Women, 1985–87; Gov., Research into Ageing Trust, 1988–97; Managing Trustee, Parly Contributory Pension Fund, 1990–97. Fellow, Industry and Parlt Trust, 1990. Hon. MIHort, 1993. Freeman, City of London, 1985; Liveryman, Gardeners' Co., 1993–. *Recreations:* ballet, opera. *Address:* House of Commons, SW1A 0AA.

ROE, Dame Raigh (Edith), DBE 1980 (CBE 1975); JP; Director, Airlines of Western Australia, 1981–90; World President, Associated Country Women of the World, 1977–80; *b* 12 Dec. 1922; *d* of Alwyn and Laura Kurts; *m* 1941, James Arthur Roe; three *s. Educ:* Perth Girls' Sch., Australia. Country Women's Association: State Pres., 1967–70; National Pres., 1969–71. World Ambassador, WA Council, 1978–; Hon. Ambassador, State of Louisiana, USA, 1979–. Comr, ABC, 1978–83; Nat. Dir (Aust.), Queen Elizabeth II Silver Jubilee Trust for Young Australians, 1978–94. JP Western Australia, 1966. Australian of the Year, 1977; Brooch of Merit, Deutscher Landfrauenverband, Fed. Republic of Germany, 1980. *Address:* 6/131 Broadway, Nedlands, WA 6009, Australia. *T:* (9) 3891262.

ROE, Air Chief Marshal Sir Rex (David), GCB 1981 (KCB 1977; CB 1974); AFC; retired 1981; *b* 1925; *m* 1948, Helen Sophie (*née* Nairn) (*d* 1981); one *s* two *d. Educ:* City of London Sch.; London University. Joined RAF 1943; trained in Canada; served with Metropolitan Fighter Sector, No 11 Group, 203 Sqn, 1950–51; Sch. of Maritime Reconnaissance, 1951–53; Central Flying School and Flying Training Units, 1953–55; Commanded RNZAF Central Flying School, 1956–58; RAF Staff College, 1959; Commanded No 204 Sqn, 1960–62; College of Air Warfare, 1962–64; SASO No 18 (Maritime) Gp, 1964–67; Stn Comdr RAF Syerston, 1967–69; Director of Flying Trng, 1969–71; RCDS, 1971; Deputy Controller Aircraft (C), MoD (Procurement Executive), 1972–74; SASO HQ Near East Air Force, 1974–76; AOC-in-C Training Comd, 1976–77; AOC-in-C, Support Command, 1977–78; Air Mem. for Supply and Organisation, 1978–81. *Recreations:* reading, Rugby football. *Address:* c/o Lloyds TSB, 7 Pall Mall, SW1Y 5NA. *Club:* Royal Air Force.

ROEBUCK, Roy Delville; Barrister-at-law; *b* Manchester, 25 Sept. 1929; *m* 1957, Dr Mary Ogilvy Adams (*d* 1995); one *s. Educ:* various newspapers; Inns of Court Sch. of Law; Univ. of Leicester (LLM 1997; MA 2000). Called to the Bar, Gray's Inn, 1974. Served RAF (National Service), 1948–50 (FEAF). Journalist, Stockport Advertiser, Northern Daily Telegraph, Yorkshire Evening News, Manchester Evening Chronicle, News Chronicle, Daily Express, Daily Mirror and Daily Herald, 1950–66; freelance, 1966–; columnist, London Evening News, 1968–70. Contested (Lab): Altrincham and Sale, 1964 and Feb. 1965; Leek, Feb. 1974. MP (Lab) Harrow East, 1966–70; Member, Select Committee: on Estimates, 1968–70; on Parly Comr, 1968–70; PA to Rt Hon. George Wigg, Paymaster-Gen., 1966–67; Advr to Lord Wigg, Pres. of Betting Office Licensees Assoc., 1975–83. Founder Mem., Labour Common Market Safeguards Cttee, 1967. Member: Islington CHC, 1988–92; Bd of Governors, Moorfields Eye Hospital, 1984–88. Fellow, Atlantic Council, 1993–. Governor, Thornhill Sch., Islington, 1986–88. *Recreations:* tennis, ski-ing, music, reading Hansard and the public prints. *Address:* 12 Brooksby Street, N1 1HA. *T:* (020) 7607 7057; Bell Yard Chambers, 116–118 Chancery Lane, WC2A 1PP. *T:* (020) 7306 9292. *Clubs:* Royal Automobile, Royal Over-Seas League.

ROEG, Nicolas Jack, CBE 1996; film director; *b* 15 Aug. 1928; *s* of Jack Roeg and Gertrude Silk; *m* 1st, 1957, Susan (marr. diss.), *d* of Major F. W. Stephen, MC; four *s*; 2nd, Theresa Russell; two *s. Educ:* Mercers' Sch. Fellow, BFI, 1994–. Hon. DLitt Hull, 1995. Original story of Prize of Arms; Cinematographer: The Caretaker, 1963; Masque of the Red Death, 1964; Nothing But the Best, 1964; A Funny Thing Happened on the Way to the Forum, 1966; Fahrenheit 451, 1966; Far From the Madding Crowd, 1967; Petulia, 1968, etc; 2nd Unit Director and Cinematographer: Lawrence of Arabia, 1962; Judith, 1965; Co-Dir, Performance, 1968; Director: Walkabout, 1970; Don't Look Now, 1972; The Man who Fell to Earth, 1975; Bad Timing, 1979; Eureka, 1983; Insignificance, 1985; Castaway, 1986; Track 29, 1987; Aria, 1987; Sweet Bird of Youth, 1989; Witches, 1990; Cold Heaven, 1991; Heart of Darkness, 1993; Two Deaths, Hotel Paradise, Full Body Massage, 1995; Samson and Delilah, 1996; Exec. Producer, Without You I'm Nothing, 1989; screenplays: Ivanhoe, Kiss of Life, 1999; Night Train, 2001. *Address:* c/o ICM, Oxford House, 76 Oxford Street, W1R 1RB.

ROFF, Derek Michael, OBE 1972; HM Diplomatic Service, retired; *b* 1 Aug. 1932; *m* 1957, Diana Susette Barrow; three *s. Educ:* Royal Grammar Sch., Guildford; St Edmund Hall, Oxford (BA). National Service with The Cameronians (Scottish Rifles) and King's African Rifles, 1952–54. ICI Ltd, 1958–67; entered Foreign Office, 1967; Consul (Economic), Frankfurt, 1968; First Sec., UK Delegn to the European Communities, Brussels, 1970; Consul (Economic), Düsseldorf, 1973; First Sec., FCO, 1977; Counsellor, FCO, 1981–92. Regl Dir, BESO, 1993–97. Mem., Internat. Cttee, Leonard Cheshire, 1997–.

ROGAN, family name of **Baron Rogan**.

ROGAN, Baron *cr* 1999 (Life Peer), of Lower Iveagh in the county of Down; **Dennis Robert David Rogan;** Managing Director, Dennis Rogan Associates, since 1978; Chairman, Ulster Unionist Party, since 1996; *b* 30 June 1942; *s* of Robert Henderson Rogan and Florence Rogan; *m* 1968, Lorna Elizabeth Colgan; two *s. Educ:* Wallace High Sch., Lisburn; Belfast Inst. of Technol.; Open Univ. (BA). Moygashel Ltd, 1960–69; Wm Ewart & Co., 1969–72; Lamont Holdings plc, 1972–78; Chairman: (exec.) Associated Processors Ltd, 1985–; Drury Communications Ltd, 1996–; DCL Gp Ltd, 2001–; Director: Northern Ireland Events Co., 1996–; Independent News & Media (Northern Ireland) Ltd, 2000–. Chm., Lisburn Unit of Mgt, Eastern Health Bd, 1984–85. Chairman: Ulster Young Unionist Council, 1968–69; S Belfast UU Constituency Assoc., 1992–96. Patron, Somme Assoc., 2000–. *Recreations:* Rugby football, oriental carpets, gardening. *Address:* 31 Notting Hill, Belfast BT9 5NS. *T:* (028) 9066 2468. *Club:* Ulster Reform (Belfast).

ROGAN, Rev. Canon John; Chaplain of St Mark's, Lord Mayor's Chapel, Bristol, since 1999; Canon Residentiary, 1983–93, and Chancellor, 1989–93, Bristol Cathedral (Precentor, 1983–89), Canon Emeritus since 1993; *b* 20 May 1928; *s* of William and Jane Rogan; *m* 1953, Dorothy Margaret Williams; one *s* one *d. Educ:* Manchester Central High School; St John's Coll., Univ. of Durham. BA 1949, MA 1951; DipTheol with distinction, 1954; BPhil 1981. Education Officer, RAF, 1949–52. Asst Curate, St Michael and All Angels, Ashton-under-Lyne, 1954–57; Chaplain, Sheffield Industrial Mission, 1957–61; Secretary, Church of England Industrial Cttee, 1961–66; Asst Secretary, Board for Social Responsibility, 1962–66; Vicar of Leigh, Lancs, 1966–78; Sec., Diocesan Bd for Social Responsibility, 1967–74, Chm. 1974–78; Rural Dean of Leigh, 1971–78; Hon. Canon of Manchester, 1975–78; Provost, St Paul's Cathedral, Dundee, 1978–83; Bishop's Adviser in Social Responsibility, dio. Bristol, 1983–93. *Publications:* (ed jtly) Principles of Church Reform: Thomas Arnold, 1962; (ed) Bristol Cathedral: history and architecture, 2000. *Recreations:* medieval life, walking, music. *Address:* 84 Concorde Drive, Bristol BS10 6PX.

ROGERS, family name of **Baron Rogers of Riverside**.

ROGERS OF RIVERSIDE, Baron *cr* 1996 (Life Peer), of Chelsea in the Royal Borough of Kensington and Chelsea; **Richard George Rogers,** Kt 1991; RA 1984 (ARA 1978); RIBA; architect; Chairman, Richard Rogers Architects Ltd, London and Tokyo; Director, River Café Restaurant, London; *b* 23 July 1933; *s* of Dada Geiringer and Nino Rogers; *m* 1961, Su Rogers; three *s*; *m* 1973, Ruth Elias; two *s. Educ:* Architectural Assoc. (AA Dipl.); Yale Univ. (MArch; Fulbright and Yale Scholar). Reith Lectr, 1995. Winner of numerous internat. competitions incl. for Centre Pompidou, Paris, 1971–77; Lloyd's HQ, City of London, 1978. Major internat. work includes: *masterplanning:* Royal Docks, London, 1984–86; Potsdamer Platz, Berlin, 1991; Shanghai Pu Dong District, 1992; Parc BIT, Mallorca, 1994; Greenwich Peninsula Masterplan, 1997–; E Manchester, 1999; Singapore, 2001; *airports and HQ buildings:* PA Technology, Cambridge, 1975–83; PA Technology, Princeton, NJ, 1984; Marseille Airport, 1992; Channel 4 HQ, London, 1994; European Court of Human Rights, Strasbourg, 1995; Law Courts, Bordeaux, 1998; VR Techno offices and lab., Gifu, Japan, 1998; 88 Wood Street, London, 1999; Millennium Experience, Greenwich, 1999; Montevetro Housing, Battersea, 2000; Lloyd's Register of Shipping, London, 2000. *Current projects include:* masterplanning, 5th Terminal, Heathrow Airport; New Area Terminal, Barajas, Madrid Airport; Paddington Basin, London; Bullring, Barcelona; L'Hospitalet Business Park, Barcelona; Antwerp Law Courts. *Exhibitions worldwide include:* Royal Acad.; Mus. of Modern Art, NY; Louisiana Mus., Copenhagen. Teaching posts include: AA, London; Cambridge Univ.; Yale; UCLA. Chairman: Nat. Housing Tenants Resource Centre; Architecture Foundn, 1991–2001; Tate Gall. Trust, 1984–88; Govt Urban Task Force, 1998; Vice-Chm., Arts Council of England, 1994–97; Mem., UN Architects' Cttee; Mem., Urban Strategies Adv. Council, Barcelona; Trustee: London First; UK Bd, Médecins du Monde. Hon. Mem., Royal Inst. of Architects, Scotland, 1999; Hon. FAIA. Hon. DrRCA. Royal Gold Medal for Arch., 1985; Thomas Jefferson Meml Foundn Medal in Architecture, 1999; Praemium Imperiale, 2000. Chevalier de la Légion d'Honneur, France, 1986. Subject of several television documentaries and jl articles on architecture. *Publications:* Richard Rogers + Architects, 1985; A+U: Richard Rogers 1978–1988, 1988; Architecture: a modern view, 1990; (jtly) A New London, 1992; Cities for a Small Planet (Reith Lectures), 1997; Richard Rogers: the complete works, vol. 1, 1999, vol. 2, 2001; (with Anne Power) Cities for a Small Country, 2000; *relevant publications:* Richard Rogers, a biography, by Bryan Appleyard, 1986; Richard Rogers, by Kenneth Powell, 1994; The Architecture of Richard Rogers, by Deyan Sudjic, 1994; Richard Rogers Partnership, by Richard Burdett, 1995. *Recreations:* friends, art, architecture, travel, food. *Address:* (office) Thames Wharf, Rainville Road, W6 9HA. *T:* (020) 7385 1235.

ROGERS, Rt Rev. Alan Francis Bright, MA; Hon. Assistant Bishop, diocese in Europe, since 1996; *b* 12 Sept. 1907; *s* of Thomas and Alice Rogers, London, W9; *m* 1st, 1932, Millicent Boarder (*d* 1984); two *s*; 2nd, 1985, Barbara Gower. *Educ:* Westminster City Sch.; King's Coll., London; Leeds Univ.; Bishop's Coll., Cheshunt (Kitchener Schol., 1926–30). Curate of St Stephen's, Shepherds Bush, 1930–32; Holy Trinity, Twickenham, 1932–34; Civil Chaplain, Mauritius, 1934–49; Archdeacon of Mauritius, 1946–49; Commissary to Bishop of Mauritius, 1949–59; Vicar of Twickenham, 1949–54; Proctor in Convocation, 1951–59; Vicar of Hampstead, 1954–59; Rural Dean of Hampstead, 1955–59; Bishop of Mauritius, 1959–66; Suffragan Bishop of Fulham, 1966–70; Suffragan Bishop of Edmonton, 1970–75; Priest-in-Charge: Wappenham, 1977–80; Abthorpe with Slapton, 1977–83; Hon. Asst Curate, St Mary's, Twickenham, 1985–2000. An Hon. Assistant Bishop: of Peterborough, 1975–84; Dio. of London (Kensington Area), 1985–91. Chm., Archbishops' Bd of Examiners, USPG, 1972–83. MA Lambeth 1959. *Publications:* Threads of Friendship (autobiog.), 1989; Walking with God as a Friend, 1990. *Recreations:* crosswords, theatre-going, listening to tapes, especially poetry. *Address:* 20 River Way, Twickenham, Middx TW2 5JP. *T:* (020) 8894 2031. *Club:* Royal Over-Seas League.

ROGERS, Alan James, MA; Headmaster, Wellington School, since 1990; *b* 30 March 1946; *s* of William James Albert Rogers and Beatrice Gwendolyn Rogers (*née* Evans); *m* 1968, Sheila Follett; one *s* two *d. Educ:* Humphry Davy Grammar Sch., Penzance; Jesus Coll., Oxford (MA). Asst Master, Pangbourne Coll., 1969–73; Head of Geography and Geology, Arnold Sch., Blackpool, 1973–78; Head of Geography, Wellington Coll., 1978–82; Second Master and Dep. Headmaster, Wellington Sch., 1982–90. *Publications:* articles on geographical educn in UK and Commonwealth jls. *Recreations:* alpine environments, tor collecting, sports, house restoration. *Address:* Wellington School, Wellington, Som TA21 8NT. *T:* (01823) 668800.

ROGERS, Allan Ralph, FGS; *b* 24 Oct. 1932; *s* of John Henry Rogers and Madeleine Rogers (*née* Smith); *m* 1955, Ceridwen James; one *s* three *d. Educ:* University College of Swansea (BSc Hons Geology). Geologist, UK, Canada, USA, Australia, 1956–63; Teacher, 1963–65; Tutor-organiser, WEA, 1965–70, District Sec., 1970–79. Vis. Prof., Univ. of Glamorgan, 1997–. MP (Lab) Rhondda, 1983–2001. Opposition spokesman: on defence, 1987–92; on foreign affairs, 1992–94. Mem., Intelligence and Security Cttee, 1994–2001. European Parliament: Mem. (Lab) SE Wales, 1979–84; Vice-Pres., 1979–82. *Recreation:* all sports. *Address:* 8 Ingram Close, Juxon Street, SE11 6NN. *Club:* Workmen's (Treorchy).

ROGERS, Anthony Gordon; JP; Hon. Mr Justice Rogers; Vice-President of the Court of Appeal, Hong Kong, since 2000; *b* 16 Feb. 1946; *s* of late Gordon Victor Rogers and of Olga Elena Rogers; *m* 1970, Barbara Ann Zimmern; one *s* two *d. Educ:* Beaumont Coll. Called to the Bar, Gray's Inn, 1969; practised at the Bar: London, 1970–76; Hong Kong, 1976–93; QC (Hong Kong) 1984; Judge of the High Court, 1993–97, Judge of the Court of Appeal, 1997–2000, Hong Kong. Chm., Hong Kong Bar Assoc., 1990, 1991. Mem., Basic Law Consultative Cttee, 1985–90; Chm., Standing Cttee on Company Law Reform, 1994–. JP Hong Kong 1988. Sec., Hong Kong Br., China Rowing Assoc., 1995–. *Recreations:* rowing, music, keeping the family happy. *Address:* The High Court, 38

Queensway, Hong Kong. *T:* 28254306, *Fax:* 25523327. *Clubs:* Oriental, Thames Rowing; Hong Kong, Hong Kong Jockey, Hong Kong Country, Shek-O, Lion Rock Rowing (Hong Kong); Sydney Rowing, Cruising Yacht (Australia).

ROGERS, Maj.-Gen. Anthony Peter Vernon, OBE 1985; consultant in law of war; *b* 10 July 1942; *s* of Kenneth David Rogers and Eileen (*née* Emmott); *m* 1965, Anne-Katrin Margarethe, *d* of Dr Ewald Lembke; two *d. Educ:* Highgate Sch.; Coll. of Law; Liverpool Univ. (LLM 1994). Admitted Solicitor, 1965. Commnd as Capt., Army Legal Services, 1968; served HQ BAOR, Command Legal Aid Section, BAOR, MoD, SHAPE, HQ UKLF, 3 and 1 Armoured Divs; Col Army Legal Services 2, MoD, 1989–92; Brig. Legal, HQ BAOR, 1992–94; Dir, Army Legal Services, 1994–97, retd. Vice Pres., Internat. Soc. for Mil. Law and Law of War, 1994–97; Mem., Internat. Inst. of Humanitarian Law, 1992–99 (Chm., Cttee for Mil. Instruction, 1993–97). Fellow: Lauterpacht Res. Centre for Internat. Law, Univ. of Cambridge, 1999–; Human Rights Centre, Univ. of Essex, 1999–. FRSA 1995. *Publications:* Law on the Battlefield, 1996; (jtly) ICRC Model Manual on The Law of Armed Conflict, 1999; (co-ed) Joint Service Manual on The Law of Armed Conflict, 2000; articles on law of war. *Recreations:* music, the arts, playing the piano (especially as accompanist), walking (preferably in mountains), cricket. *Address:* c/o Directorate of Army Legal Services, Trenchard Lines, Upavon, Wilts SN9 6BE. *T:* (01980) 615966.

ROGERS, General Bernard William; General, United States Army, retired; Supreme Allied Commander, Europe, 1979–87; *b* 16 July 1921; *s* of late Mr and Mrs W. H. Rogers; *m* 1944, Ann Ellen Jones; one *s* two *d. Educ:* Kansas State Coll.; US Mil. Acad. (BS); Oxford Univ. (Rhodes Scholar; BA, MA); US Army Comd Staff Coll., Fort Leavenworth, Kansas; US Army War Coll., Carlisle Barracks, Pa. CO 3rd Bn, 9th Inf. Regt, 2nd Inf. Div., Korea, 1952–53; Bn Comdr 1st Bn, 23rd Inf., 2nd Inf. Div., Fort Lewis, Washington, 1955–56; Comdr, 1st Battle Gp, 19th Inf., Div. COS, 24th Inf. Div., Augsburg, Germany, 1960–61; Exec. Officer to Chm., Jt Chiefs of Staff, Washington, DC, 1962–66; Asst Div. Comdr, 1st Inf. Div., Republic of Vietnam, 1966–67; Comdt of Cadets, US Mil. Acad., 1967–69; Comdg Gen., 5th Inf. Div., Fort Carson, Colo, 1969–70; Chief of Legislative Liaison, Office of Sec. to the Army, Washington, DC, 1971–72; Dep. Chief of Staff for Personnel, Dept of the Army, Washington, DC, 1972–74; Comdg Gen., US Army Forces Comd, Fort McPherson, Ga, 1974–76; Chief of Staff, US Army, Washington, DC, 1976–79. Hon. Fellow, University Coll., Oxford, 1979. Hon. LLD: Akron, 1978; Boston, 1981; Hon. DCL Oxon, 1983. Dist. Graduate Award, US Mil. Acad., 1995; George C. Marshall Medal, US Army Assoc., 1999. *Publications:* Cedar Falls-Junction City: a Turning Point, 1974; contribs to: Foreign Affairs, RUSI, 1982; Strategic Review, NATO's Sixteen Nations, 1983; Europa Archiv, Defense, NATO Review, 1984; Europäische Wehrkunde, Rivista Militaire, 1985; The Adelphi Papers, 1986; Soldat und Technik, 1987. *Recreations:* golf, reading. *Address:* 1467 Hampton Ridge Drive, McLean, VA 22101, USA.

ROGERS, Surgeon Rear-Adm. (D) Brian Frederick, CB 1980; Director of Naval Dental Services, 1977–80; *b* 27 Feb. 1923; *s* of Frederick Reginald Rogers, MIMechE, MIMarE, and Rosa Jane Rogers; *m* 1946, Mavis Elizabeth (*née* Scott); one *s* two *d. Educ:* Rock Ferry High Sch.; Liverpool Univ. (LDS 1945). House Surgeon, Liverpool Dental Hosp., 1945; joined RNVR, 1946; transf. to RN, 1954; served HMS Ocean, 1954–56 and HMS Eagle, 1964–66; Fleet Dental Surg. on staff of C-in-C Fleet, 1974–77; Comd Dental Surg. to C-in-C Naval Home Comd, 1977. QHDS 1977. *Recreations:* European touring, photography, DIY. *Address:* 22 Trerieve, Downderry, Torpoint, Cornwall PL11 3LY. *T:* (01503) 250526; Montana roja, Lanzarote, Canary Islands. *T:* (28) 517150.

ROGERS, Prof. C(laude) Ambrose, FRS 1959; Astor Professor of Mathematics, University College, London, 1958–86, now Emeritus; *b* 1 Nov. 1920; *s* of late Sir Leonard Rogers, KCSI, CIE, FRS; *m* 1952, Mrs J. M. Gordon, *widow* of W. G. Gordon, and *d* of F. W. G. North; two *d. Educ:* Berkhamsted School; University Coll., London; Birkbeck Coll., London. BSc, PhD, DSc (London, 1941, 1949, 1952). Experimental officer, Ministry of Supply, 1940–45; lecturer and reader, University College, London, 1946–54; Prof. of Pure Mathematics, Univ. of Birmingham, 1954–58. Mem. Council, Royal Soc., 1966–68 and 1983–84; Pres., London Mathematical Soc., 1970–72; Chm., Jt Mathematical Council, 1982–84. *Publications:* Packing and Covering, 1964; Hausdorff Measures, 1970, rev. edn 1998; articles in various mathematical journals. *Recreation:* string figures. *Address:* Department of Mathematics, University College, WC1E 6BT; 8 Grey Close, NW11 6QG. *T:* (020) 8455 8027.

ROGERS, Ven. David Arthur; Archdeacon of Craven, 1977–86; *b* 12 March 1921; *s* of Rev. Canon Thomas Godfrey Rogers and Doris Mary Cleaver Rogers (*née* Steele); *m* 1951, Joan Malkin; one *s* three *d. Educ:* Saint Edward's School, Oxford (scholar); Christ's College, Cambridge (exhibitioner). BA 1947, MA 1952. War service with Green Howards and RAC, 1940–45; Christ's Coll. and Ridley Hall, Cambridge, 1945–49; Asst Curate, St George's, Stockport, 1949–53; Rector, St Peter's, Levenshulme, Manchester, 1953–59; Vicar of Sedbergh, Cautley and Garsdale, 1959–79; Rural Dean of Sedbergh and then of Ewecross, 1959–77; Hon. Canon of Bradford Cathedral, 1967. *Address:* Borrens, Leck, via Carnforth, Lancs LA6 2JG. *T:* (01524) 271616.

ROGERS, David Bryan, CB 1984; Deputy Secretary and Director General, Board of Inland Revenue, 1981–89; *b* 8 Sept. 1929; *s* of Frank Rogers and Louisa Rogers; *m* 1955, Marjory Geraldine Gilmour Horribine; one *s* two *d. Educ:* Grove Park, Wrexham; University Coll., London (BA Classics). Inspector of Taxes, 1953; Principal Inspector, 1968; Sen. Principal Inspector, 1976; Under Sec. and Dir of Operations, Bd of Inland Revenue, 1978–81. Mem. Council, UCL, 1983–93. *Recreations:* piano, organ, singing, reading.

ROGERS, Eric William Evan, DSc(Eng); FRAeS; Deputy Director (A), Royal Aircraft Establishment, Farnborough, Hants, 1978–85; *b* 12 April 1925; *o s* of late W. P. Rogers, Southgate, N London; *m* 1950, Dorothy Joyce Loveless (*d* 2000); two *s* one *d. Educ:* Southgate County Grammar Sch.; Imperial Coll., London. FCGI, DIC. Aerodynamics Div., NPL, 1945–70 (Head of Hypersonic Research, 1961); Aerodynamics Dept, RAE, 1970 (Head, 1972). *Publications:* various papers on aerodynamics and on industrial aerodynamics, in ARC (R and M series), RAeS jls and elsewhere. *Recreations:* music, history. *Address:* 64 Thetford Road, New Malden, Surrey KT3 5DT. *T:* (020) 8942 7452.

ROGERS, Sir Frank (Jarvis), Kt 1988; Director, Telegraph Group Ltd (formerly Daily Telegraph, then The Telegraph, plc), since 1985 (Deputy Chairman, 1986–95); Director, EMAP plc (formerly East Midland Allied Press), 1971–91 (Chairman, 1973–90); *b* 24 Feb. 1920; *s* of Percy Rogers and Elsie Mary (*née* Jarvis); *m* 1949, Esma Holland (*d* 1998); two *d*; *m* 2001, Sheena Phillips. *Educ:* Wolstanton Grammar School. Journalist, 1937–49; Military Service, 1940–46; Gen. Man., Nigerian Daily Times, 1949–52; Manager, Argus, Melbourne, 1952–55; Man. Dir, Overseas Newspapers, 1958–60; Dir, Daily Mirror, 1960–65; Man. Dir, IPC, 1965–70. Chairman: Nat. Newspaper Steering Gp, 1970–72; Newspaper Publishers Assoc. Ltd, 1990–97 (Vice-Chm., 1968–69; Dir, 1971–73); European Publishers Council, 1991–; Reuters Founders Share Co., 1998–99. Adviser on Corporate Affairs, The Plessey Co. Ltd, 1973–81. Mem., British Exec. Cttee, Internat. Press Inst., 1988– (Chm., 1978–88). Mem. Council and Chm., Exec. Cttee, Industrial Soc., 1976–79; Chm. Council, Industry and Parliament Trust, 1979–81; Mem. Council, Advertising Standards Authority, 1985–90. *Recreations:* motoring, golf. *Address:* Greensleeves, Loudwater Drive, Rickmansworth, Herts WD3 4HJ.

ROGERS, (George) Stuart L.; *see* Lawson-Rogers.

ROGERS, Very Rev. John; Dean of Llandaff, 1993–99, now Emeritus; *b* 27 Nov. 1934; *s* of William Harold and Annie Mary Rogers; *m* 1972, Pamela Mary Goddard; one *s* one *d. Educ:* Jones' W Monmouth Sch., Pontypool; St David's Coll., Lampeter (BA 1955); Oriel Coll., Oxford (BA 1957; MA 1960); St Stephen's House, Oxford, 1957–59. Ordained deacon, 1959, priest, 1960; Assistant Curate: St Martin's, Roath (dio. of Llandaff), 1959–63; St Sidwell's, Lodge, with Holy Redeemer, Ruimveldt, Guyana, 1963–67; Vicar: Holy Redeemer, Ruimveldt, Guyana, 1967–69; Wismar and Lower Demerara River Missions, 1969–71; Caldicot, 1971–77; Monmouth, 1977–84; Rector, Ebbw Vale, 1984–93. Rural Dean: Monmouth, 1981–84; Blaenau Gwent, 1986–93; Canon of St Woolos Cathedral, 1988–93. *Recreations:* gardening, beer and wine making. *Address:* Fron Lodge, Llandovery SA20 0LJ.

ROGERS, Prof. (John) Michael, DPhil; FSA; FBA 1988; Khalili Professor of Islamic Art, School of Oriental and African Studies, University of London, 1991–2000, now Emeritus; *b* 25 Jan. 1935. *Educ:* Ulverston Grammar Sch.; Corpus Christi Coll., Oxford (MA, DPhil). FSA 1974. Robinson Sen. Student, Oriel Coll., Oxford, 1958–61; Tutor in Philosophy, Pembroke and Wadham Colls, Oxford, 1961–65; Asst, then Associate, Prof. of Islamic Art and Archaeol., Center for Arabic Studies, Amer. Univ. in Cairo, 1965–77; Dep. Keeper, Dept of Oriental Antiquities, BM, 1977–91. Vis. Sen. Res. Fellow, Merton Coll., Oxford, 1971–72; Vis. Res. Fellow, New Coll., Oxford, 1998; Slade Prof. of Fine Art, Oxford Univ., 1991–92. Pres., British Inst. of Persian Studies, 1993–96. Corresp. Mem., Deutsches Archäologisches Inst., Berlin, 1988. Order of the Egyptian Republic, 2nd cl., 1969. *Publications:* The Spread of Islam, 1976; Islamic Art and Design 1500–1700, 1983; (with R. M. Ward) Süleyman the Magnificent, 1988; Mughal Painting, 1993; Empire of the Sultans: Ottoman art in the Khalili collection, 1995; numerous articles on hist. and archaeol. of Islamic Turkey, Egypt, Syria, Iran and Central Asia. *Recreations:* walking, music, botany. *Address:* School of Oriental and African Studies, Thornhaugh Street, Russell Square, WC1H 0XG. *Club:* Beefsteak.

ROGERS, John Michael Thomas; QC 1979; **His Honour Judge John Rogers;** a Circuit Judge, since 1998. *Educ:* Rydal Sch.; Birkenhead Sch.; Fitzwilliam House, Cambridge (MA, LLB). Called to Bar, Gray's Inn, 1963, Bencher 1991. A Recorder, 1976–98. Leader, Wales and Chester Circuit, 1990–92. *Recreations:* farming, gardening. *Address:* Chester Crown Court, The Castle, Chester CH1 2AN. *Clubs:* Reform; Pragmatist's (Wirral); Ruthin Rugby Football.

ROGERS, Air Chief Marshal Sir John (Robson), KCB 1982; CBE 1971; FRAeS; Executive Chairman, RAC Motor Sports Association, 1989–98; *b* 11 Jan. 1928; *s* of B. R. Rogers; *m* 1955, Gytha Elspeth Campbell; two *s* two *d. Educ:* Brentwood Sch.; No 1 Radio Sch., Cranwell; Royal Air Force Coll., Cranwell. OC 56(F) Sqdn, 1960–61; Gp Captain, 1967; OC RAF Coningsby, 1967–69; Air Commodore, 1971; Dir of Operational Requirements (RAF), 1971–73; Dep. Comdt, RAF Coll., 1973–75; RCDS, 1976; Air Vice-Marshal, 1977; Dir-Gen. of Organisation, RAF, 1977–79; AOC Training Units, RAF Support Comd, 1979–81; Air Mem. for Supply and Organisation, MoD, 1981–83; Controller Aircraft, MoD PE, 1983–86, retired. Director: British Car Auctions, 1986–90; First Technology Gp, 1986–93. FRAeS 1983. *Recreation:* motor racing. *Address:* c/o Lloyds TSB, 27 High Street, Colchester, Essex. *Clubs:* Royal Automobile (Vice-Chm., 1990–98; Life Vice Pres., 1999), Royal Air Force.

ROGERS, His Honour John Willis; QC 1975; a Circuit Judge, 1991–99; a Deputy Circuit Judge, 1999–2001; *b* 7 Nov. 1929; *s* of late Reginald John Rogers and late Joan Daisy Alexandra Rogers (*née* Willis); *m* 1952, Sheila Elizabeth Cann; one *s* one *d. Educ:* Sevenoaks Sch.; Fitzwilliam House, Cambridge (MA). Called to Bar, Lincoln's Inn, 1955 (Cholmeley Schol.); Bencher, 1984. 1st Prosecuting Counsel to Inland Revenue, SE Circuit, 1969–75; a Recorder, 1974–91. Hon. Recorder, City of Canterbury, 1985–2000. Chm., Adv. Cttee on Conscientious Objectors, 1991–99. Hon. Freeman, City of Canterbury, 2001. *Recreations:* cricket, gardening, change ringing, flying. *Address:* c/o 3 Serjeants' Inn, Temple, EC4Y 1BQ. *Clubs:* Garrick, MCC, Band of Brothers.

ROGERS, Malcolm Austin, DPhil; FSA; Ann and Graham Gund Director, Museum of Fine Arts, Boston, Mass, since 1994; *b* 3 Oct. 1948; *s* of late James Eric Rogers and Frances Anne (*née* Elsey). *Educ:* Oakham School; Magdalen College, Oxford (Open Exhibnr); Christ Church, Oxford (Senior Scholar). Violet Vaughan Morgan Prize, 1967; BA (Eng. Lang. and Lit. 1st cl.), 1969; MA 1973; DPhil 1976. National Portrait Gallery: Asst. Keeper, 1974–83; Dep. Keeper, 1983–85; Keeper, 1985–94; Dep. Dir, 1983–94. Cttee to visit Harvard Univ. Art Museums, 1997–. Freeman, City of London, 1992; Liveryman, Girdlers' Co., 1992. *Publications:* Dictionary of British Portraiture, 4 vols (ed jtly), 1979–81; Museums and Galleries of London, 1983, 3rd edn 1991; William Dobson, 1983; John and John Baptist Closterman: a catalogue of their works, 1983; Elizabeth II: portraits of sixty years, 1986; Camera Portraits, 1989; Montacute House, 1991; (with Sir David Piper) Companion Guide to London, 1992; (ed) The English Face, by Sir David Piper, 1992; Master Drawings from the National Portrait Gallery, 1993; articles and reviews in Burlington Magazine, Apollo, TLS. *Recreations:* food and wine, opera, travel. *Address:* 540 Chestnut Hill Avenue, Brookline, MA 02445, USA. *T:* (617) 2320214. *Clubs:* Beefsteak; Algonquin (Hon. Mem.), Wednesday Evening Club of 1777, Odd Volumes (Boston).

ROGERS, Martin Hartley Guy; HM Diplomatic Service, retired; *b* 11 June 1925; *s* of late Rev. Canon T. Guy Rogers and Marguerite Inez Rogers; *m* 1959, Jean Beresford Chinn; one *s* three *d. Educ:* Marlborough Coll.; Jesus Coll., Cambridge. CRO, 1949; 2nd Sec., Karachi, 1951–53; CRO, 1953–56 and 1958–60; seconded to Govt of Fedn of Nigeria, 1956–57; ndc 1960–61; 1st Sec., Ottawa, 1961–62; Adviser to Jamaican Min. of External Affairs, 1963; CRO, later Commonwealth Office, 1963–68; Dep. High Comr, Bombay, 1968–71, Kaduna, 1972–75; High Comr, The Gambia, 1975–79; on loan to CSSB as Asst Dir, 1979–85. *Recreation:* bridge. *Address:* Croftside, Harrow Road East, Dorking, Surrey RH4 2AX. *T:* (01306) 883789.

ROGERS, Martin John Wyndham, OBE 2000; Director, Fellowships in Religious Education for Europe, since 2001; Associate Fellow, Harris Manchester College (formerly Manchester College), Oxford, since 1991; *b* 9 April 1931; *s* of late John Frederick Rogers and Grace Mary Rogers; *m* 1957, Jane Cook; two *s* one *d. Educ:* Oundle Sch.; Heidelberg Univ.; Trinity Hall, Cambridge (MA); MA Oxon 1995. Henry Wiggin & Co., 1953–55; Westminster School: Asst Master, 1955–60; Sen. Chemistry Master, 1960–64; Housemaster, 1964–66; Under Master and Master of the Queen's Scholars, 1967–71; Headmaster of Malvern Coll., 1971–82; Chief Master, King Edward's Sch., Birmingham, Headmaster of the Schs of King Edward VIth in Birmingham, 1982–91; Dir, Farmington

Inst. for Christian Studies, 1991–2001. Seconded as Nuffield Research Fellow (O-level Chemistry Project), 1962–64; Salter's Company Fellow, Dept of Chemical Engrg and Chemical Technology, Imperial Coll., London, 1969. Chairman: Curriculum Cttee of HMC, GSA and IAPS, 1979–86; HMC, 1987; Mem. Council, GPDST, 1991–93. Chm., European Council, Nat. Assocs of Indep. Schs, 1994–97. Mem. Council, Birmingham Univ., 1985–92. Governor: Oundle Sch., 1988–2001; Westonbirt Sch., 1991–97; Elmhurst Ballet Sch., 1991–95; English Coll., Prague, 1991–. Chm., Millwood Educn Trust, 2001–; Trustee: Sandford St Martin Trust, 1994–; Smallpeice Trust, 2000–. *Publications:* John Dalton and the Atomic Theory, 1965; Chemistry and Energy, 1968; Gas Syringe Experiments, 1970; (co-author) Chemistry: facts, patterns and principles, 1972; Editor: Foreground Chemistry Series, 1968; Farmington Papers, 1993–2001. *Address:* Eastwards, 24 Millwood End, Long Hanborough, Oxon OX29 8BX. *Club:* East India, Devonshire, Sports and Public Schools.

ROGERS, Maurice Arthur Thorold; Secretary, Royal Institution, 1968–73; Joint Head, Head Office Research and Development Department, ICI, 1962–72; *b* 8 June 1911; *s* of A. G. L. Rogers; *g s* of Prof. J. E. Thorold Rogers; *m* 1947, Margaret Joan (*née* Craven) one *s* two *d*. *Educ:* Dragon Sch.; Westminster Sch.; University Coll., London. 1st Class hons BSc (Chem.) UCL 1932, PhD (Chem.) 1934. Chemist, ICI Dyestuffs Div., 1934–45; Head of Academic Relations Dept, 1946–58; Head of Head Office Research Dept, ICI, 1958–62. *Publications:* numerous papers in: Jl of Chem. Soc.; Nature; etc. *Recreations:* climbing, gardening, china restoration, conservation of countryside. *Address:* The Skippet, Mount Skippet, Ramsden, Oxford OX7 3AP. *T:* (01993) 868253.

ROGERS, Michael; *see* Rogers, J. M.

ROGERS, Nigel David; free-lance singer, conductor and teacher; Professor of Singing, Royal College of Music, since 1979; *b* 21 March 1935; *m* 1961, Frederica Bement Lord (*d* 1992); one *d*. *Educ:* Wellington Grammar Sch.; King's Coll., Cambridge (MA). Studied in Italy and Germany. Professional singer, 1961–; began singing career in Munich with group Studio der frühen Musik. Is a leading specialist in field of Baroque music, of which he has made over 70 recordings from Monteverdi to Schubert; gives concerts, recitals, lectures and master classes in many parts of world; most acclaimed role in opera as Monteverdi's Orfeo. Formed vocal ensemble Chiaroscuro, to perform vast repertory of Italian Baroque music, 1979, later extended to include Chiaroscuro Chamber Ensemble and Chiaroscuro Baroque Orch. Has lectured and taught at Schola Cantorum Basiliensis, Basle, Switzerland. Hon. RCM 1981. *Publications:* chapter on Voice, Companion to Baroque Music (ed J. A. Sadic), 1991; articles on early Baroque performance practice in various periodicals in different countries. *Address:* Chestnut Cottage, East End, Newbury, Berks RG20 0AB. *T:* and *Fax:* (01635) 253319.

ROGERS, Maj.-Gen. Norman Charles, FRCS 1949; consultant surgeon, retired; *b* 14 Oct. 1916; *s* of Wing Comdr Charles William Rogers, RAF, and Edith Minnie Rogers (*née* Weaver); *m* 1954, Pamela Marion (*née* Rose); two *s* one *d*. *Educ:* Imperial Service Coll.; St Bartholomew's Hosp. MB, BS London; MRCS, LRCP 1939. Emergency Commn, Lieut RAMC, Oct. 1939; 131 Field Amb. RAMC, Dunkirk (despatches, 1940); RMO, 4th Royal Tank Regt, N Africa, 1941–42; Italy, 1942–43 (POW); RMO 1st Black Watch, NW Europe, 1944–45 (wounded, despatches twice). Ho. Surg., St Bartholomew's Hosp., 1946–47; Registrar (Surgical) Appts, Norwich, 1948–52; Sen. Registrar Appts, Birmingham, 1952–56; granted permanent commn, RAMC, 1956; surgical appts in mil. hospitals: Chester, Dhekelia (Cyprus), Catterick, Iserlohn (BAOR), 1956–67; Command Consultant Surgeon, BAOR, 1967–69; Dir, Army Surgery, 1969–73; QHS, 1969–73. Clin. Supt, 1975–80, and Consultant, 1973–81, Accident and Emergency Dept, Guy's Hosp; Civilian Consultant Surgeon: BMH Iserlohn, 1983–86; BMH Munster, 1986. *Publications:* contribs on surgical subjects. *Address:* 110 Mill Street, Kidlington OX5 2EF.

ROGERS, Parry; see Rogers, T. G. P.

ROGERS, Paul; actor; *b* Plympton, Devon, 22 March 1917; *s* of Edwin and Dulcie Myrtle Rogers; *m* 1st, 1939, Jocelyn Wynne (marr. diss. 1955); two *s*; 2nd, 1955, Rosalind Boxall; two *d*. *Educ:* Newton Abbot Grammar School, Devon. Michael Chekhov Theatre Studio, 1936–38. First appearance on stage as Charles Dickens in Bird's Eye of Valour, Scala, 1938; Stratford-upon-Avon Shakespeare Memorial Theatre, 1939; Concert Party and Colchester Rep. Co. until 1940. Served Royal Navy, 1940–46. Colchester Rep. Co. and Arts Council Tour and London Season, Tess of the D'Urbervilles, 1946–47; Bristol Old Vic, 1947–49; London Old Vic (incl. tour S Africa and Southern Rhodesia), 1949–53; also at Edinburgh, London and in USA, 1954–57; London, 1958; tour to Moscow, Leningrad and Warsaw, 1960. Roles with Old Vic include numerous Shakespearean leads; Gloucester, in King Lear, 1989. Other parts include: Sir Claude Mulhammer in The Confidential Clerk, Edinburgh Festival and Lyric, London, 1953; Lord Claverton in The Elder Statesman, Edinburgh Fest. and Cambridge Theatre, London, 1958; Mr Fox in Mr Fox of Venice, Piccadilly, 1959; Johnny Condell in One More River, Duke of York's and Westminster, 1959; Nickles in JB, Phœnix, 1961; Reginald Kinsale in Photo Finish, Saville, 1962; The Seagull, Queen's, 1964; Season of Goodwill, Queen's, 1964; The Homecoming, Aldwych, 1965; Timon of Athens, Stratford-upon-Avon, 1965; The Government Inspector, Aldwych, 1966; Henry IV, Stratford-upon-Avon, 1966; Max in The Homecoming, New York, 1967 (Tony Award and Whitbread Anglo-American Award); Plaza Suite, Lyric, 1969; The Happy Apple, Apollo, 1970; Sleuth, St Martin's, 1970, NY, 1971 and 1974; Othello, Nat. Theatre Co., Old Vic, 1974; Heartbreak House, Nat. Theatre, 1975; The Marrying of Ann Leete, Aldwych, 1975; The Return of A. J. Raffles, Aldwych, 1975; The Zykovs, Aldwych, 1976; Volpone, The Madras House, Nat. Theatre, 1977; Eclipse, Royal Court, 1978; You Never Can Tell, Lyric, Hammersmith, 1979; The Dresser, New York, 1981, 1982; The Importance of Being Earnest, A Kind of Alaska, Nat. Theatre, 1982; The Apple Cart, Theatre Royal, Haymarket, 1986; Danger: Memory!, Hampstead, 1988; Other People's Money, Lyric, 1990. Appears in films and television. *Publication:* a Preface to Folio Soc. edition of Shakespeare's Love's Labour's Lost, 1959. *Recreations:* gardening, carpentry, books. *Address:* 9 Hillside Gardens, Highgate, N6 5SU. *T:* (020) 8340 2656.

ROGERS, Peter Brian, CBE 2001; Chief Executive, Independent Television Commission, 1996–2000; *b* 8 April 1941; *s* of late William Patrick Rogers and Margaret Elizabeth Rogers; *m* 1966, Jean Mary Bailey; one *s* two *d*. *Educ:* De La Salle Grammar Sch., Liverpool; Manchester Univ. (1st Cl. Hons BAEcon; Cobden Prize); London Sch. of Econs and Pol. Science, London Univ. (MSc Econs). Tax Officer, Inland Revenue, 1959–67; Res. Associate, Manchester Univ., 1967–68; Econ. Adviser, HM Treasury, 1968–73; Sen. Econ. Adviser, Central Policy Review Staff, Cabinet Office, 1973–74; Dir of Econ. Planning, Tyne and Wear CC (on secondment from Central Govt), 1974–76; Sen. Econ. Adviser, DoE, 1976–79; Dep. Chief Exec., Housing Corp., 1979–82; Dir of Finance, IBA, 1982–90; Dep. Chief Exec. and Dir of Finance, ITC, 1991–96. Dir, Channel Four Television Co., 1982–92. *Recreations:* woodwork, cycling. *Address:* Thorphinsty House, Cartmell Fell, Grange over Sands, Cumbria LA11 6NF. *T:* (01539) 552515; *e-mail:* peter.rogers@primex.co.uk.

ROGERS, Peter Richard; Master of Costs (formerly Taxing) Office, Supreme Court, since 1992; *b* 2 April 1939; *s* of Denis Roynan Rogers and Lucy Gwynneth (*née* Hopwood); *m* 1966, Adrienne Winifred Haylock. *Educ:* Bristol Univ. (LLB Hons). Solicitor of the Supreme Court. Articled Clerk, then solicitor, Turner Kenneth Brown (formerly Kenneth Brown Baker Baker) (solicitors), 1961–92; Partner, 1968–92; Dep. Supreme Court Taxing Master, 1991–92. Mem., London No 13 Legal Aid Cttee, 1980–92. General Editor, Greenslade on Costs, 1999– (Consulting Editor, 1995–99). *Publication:* (jtly) Rogers and Bacon's Costs Law Reports, 1997. *Recreations:* weather, steam and other railways, environmental concerns. *Address:* Supreme Court Costs Office, Cliffords Inn, Fetter Lane, EC4A 1DQ. *T:* (020) 7936 6224. *Club:* Wig and Pen.

ROGERS, Peter Standing; JP; Member (C) North Wales, National Assembly for Wales, since 1999; *b* 2 Jan. 1940; *s* of late Harold Rogers and of Joan Thomas; *m* 1973, Margaret Roberts; two *s*. *Educ:* Prenton Secondary Sch., Birkenhead; Cheshire Sch. of Agriculture. Farm Manager, 1962–65; Sales Manager, Ciba Geigy UK, 1965–72; self-employed farmer, 1972–. JP Ynys Môn, 1990. *Recreations:* sports, all rural activities. *Address:* Bodrida, Brynsiencyn, Anglesey LL61 6NZ. *Clubs:* Old Birkonians (Birkenhead); Welsh Crawshays Rugby.

ROGERS, Raymond Thomas, CPhys, FInstP; Managing Director, Dragon Health International, since 1997; *b* 19 Oct. 1940; *s* of late Thomas Kenneth Rogers and of Mary Esther Rogers (*née* Walsh); *m* 1964, Carmel Anne Saunders; two *s* one *d*. *Educ:* Gunnersbury Grammar Sch.; Birmingham Univ. (BSc). CPhys, FInstP 1962. Basic Med. Physicist, London Hosp., 1962–66; Sen. Med. Physicist, Westminster Hosp., 1966–70; Department of Health and Social Security, later Department of Health: PSO, Scientific and Tech. Br., 1970; Supt Engr, then Dir 1984; Asst Sec., Health Inf. Br., 1984–91; Under Sec., and Exec. Dir Information Mgt Gp, 1991–97. FRSA 1997. *Publications:* contribs to scientific jls and books. *Recreations:* trekking, opera, science, peace. *Address:* One Bannisters Road, Onslow Village, Guildford, Surrey GU2 5RA. *T:* (01483) 573078.

ROGERS, Col Richard Annesley C.; *see* Coxwell-Rogers.

ROGERS, Richard Ian; Director, Company Law and Investigations, Department of Trade and Industry, since 1997; *b* 10 June 1947; *s* of Charles Murray Rogers and Aileen Mary Seton Rogers (*née* Hole); *m* 1970, Alice Monroe; one *s* one *d*. *Educ:* Monkton Combe Sch.; Queens' Coll., Cambridge (BA). Prison Asst Gov., 1969–72; Brent Family Service Unit, 1972–77; Civil Service, 1977–: Depts of Prices and Consumer Protection, of Trade, and of Industry; Department of Trade and Industry: British Steel Privatisation, 1986–88; Projects and Export Policy, 1989–92; Telecoms Policy, 1992–93; Sen. Staff Mgt, 1993–97; Chm., Company Law Review Steering Gp, 1998–2001. *Recreations:* mountains, music and opera, books, heavy gardening, motorcycling. *Address:* Department of Trade and Industry, 1 Victoria Street, SW1H 0ET.

ROGERS, (Thomas Gordon) Parry, CBE 1991; Director, The Plessey Co. plc, 1976–86; *b* 7 Aug. 1924; *s* of late Victor Francis Rogers and Ella (*née* May); *m* 1st, 1947, Pamela Mary (*née* Greene) (marr. diss. 1973); one *s* seven *d*; 2nd, 1973, Patricia Juliet (*née* Curtis); one *s* one *d*. *Educ:* West Hartlepool Grammar Sch.; St Edmund Hall, Oxford. MA; CIPD, CIMgt; FRSA; FInstD. Served RAC and RAEC, 1944–47. Procter & Gamble Ltd, 1948–54; Mars Ltd, 1954–56; Hardy Spicer Ltd, 1956–61 (Dir, 1957–61); IBM United Kingdom Ltd, 1961–74 (Dir, 1964–74); The Plessey Co. plc, 1974–86; Chairman: Percom Ltd, 1984–94; ECCTIS 2000 Ltd, 1989–97; Director: MSL Gp Internat. Ltd, 1970–78; ICL plc, 1977–79; Hobsons Publishing plc, 1985–90; Butler Cox plc, 1985–91; Norman Broadbent Internat. Ltd, 1985–90; Ocean Group plc, 1988–94; Future Perfect (Counselling) Ltd, 1986–92; PRIMA Europe Ltd, 1987–93; BNB Resources plc, 1990–94. Chm., Plessey Pension Trust, 1978–86; Trustee, BNB Resources Pension Trust, 1991–94. Chairman: BTEC, 1986–94; SW London Coll. HEC, 1989–91; IT Skills Agency, 1984–96; Salisbury HA, 1986–90; Commn on Charitable Fundraising, NCSS, 1970–76; Member: Employment Appeal Tribunal, 1978–87; Standing Cttee on Pay Comparability, 1980–81; Nat. Steering Gp, Trng and Vocational Educn Initiative, MSC, 1983–86; CBI/BIM Panel on Mgt Educn, 1968–78; CBI Employment Policy Cttee, 1980–86; Rev. Team, Children and Young Persons Benefits, DHSS, 1984–85; Oxford Univ. Appts Cttee, 1972–87; Member Council: CRAC, 1965–94; ISCO, 1988–95; Inst. of Manpower Studies, 1970–86; Indust. Participation Assoc., 1972–86; Inst. of Dirs, 1980–95 (Chm., 1985–88; Vice Pres., 1988–95); Inst. of Personnel Management, 1954– (Pres., 1975–77); EEF, 1980–86; Econ. League, 1982–86; E Europe Trade Council, 1982–85. Governor: Ashridge Management Coll., 1985–94; Warminster Sch., 1989–99; St Mary's Sch., Shaftesbury, 1991–94. Trustee, Ella Rogers Music Trust. Patron, Dorset Chamber Orch.; Freeman, City of London, 1987; Mem., Information Technologists' Co., 1987–. *Publications:* The Recruitment and Training of Graduates, 1970; contribs on management subjects to newspapers and jls. *Recreations:* birdwatching, golf, tennis, photography, listening to music. *Address:* St Edward's Chantry, Bimport, Shaftesbury, Dorset SP7 8BA. *T:* (01747) 852789. *Clubs:* Savile; Sherborne Golf.

ROGERSON, Rt Rev. Barry; *see* Bristol, Bishop of.

ROGERSON, Nicolas; Chairman, Global Workplace plc; Partner, Concept2Profit Ltd; *b* 21 May 1943; *s* of late Hugh and Olivia Rogerson; *m* 1998, Hon. Caroline Elizabeth Tamara Le Bas (*d* 2001), *er d* of Baron Gilbert, *qv*. *Educ:* Cheam Sch.; Winchester Coll.; Magdalene Coll., Cambridge. Staff Journalist, Investors Chronicle, 1964–65; Executive, Angel Court Consultants, 1966–68; formed Dewe Rogerson, 1969: Chief Exec., Dewe Rogerson Gp, 1969–99 (Dep. Chm., 1969–88); Chm., Dewe Rogerson Internat., 1985–99. Appeals Chm., King George's Fund for Sailors. *Recreations:* sailing, ski-ing, Real tennis, field sports, languages and European history. *Clubs:* City of London, Turf, Beefsteak, Royal Thames Yacht.

ROGERSON, Paul; Chief Executive, Leeds City Council, since 1999; *b* 10 June 1948; *s* of late John Rogerson and of Hilda Rogerson (*née* Hepworth); *m* 1971, Eileen Kane; four *s* two *d*. *Educ:* De La Salle Coll., Sheffield; Manchester Univ. (LLB, MA Econ). Called to the Bar, Gray's Inn, 1971; Lectr, Univ. of Leeds, 1969–75; Principal Legal Officer: Barnsley MBC, 1975–78; Kirklees MDC, 1978–89; Asst Dir/Chief Legal Officer, 1989–95, Exec. Dir, 1995–99, Leeds CC. Vis. Prof., Univ. of Louisville, USA, 1972–73. Jt Gen. Ed., Local Govt Law Reports, 1999–. *Recreation:* family and friends. *Address:* Civic Hall, Leeds LS1 1UR. *T:* (0113) 247 4554.

ROGERSON, Philip Graham; Chairman, Viridian Group plc, since 1999 (Deputy Chairman, 1998); *b* 1 Jan. 1945; *s* of Henry and Florence Rogerson; *m* 1968, Susan Janet Kershaw; one *s* two *d*. *Educ:* William Hulme's Grammar Sch., Manchester. FCA 1968. Dearden, Harper, Miller & Co., Chartered Accountants, 1962–67; Hill Samuel & Co. Ltd, 1967–69; Thomas Tilling Ltd, 1969–71; Steetley Ltd, 1971–72; J. W. Chafer Ltd, 1972–78; with ICI plc, 1978–92 (General Manager, Finance, 1989–92); British Gas, later BG plc: Man. Dir, Finance, 1992–94; Exec. Dir, 1994–98; Dep. Chm., 1996–98. Non-executive Chairman: Pipeline Integrity Internat., 1998–; Bertram Gp Ltd, 1999–; United Engineering Forgings Ltd, 1999–; KBC Advanced Technologies plc, 1999–; Project

Telecom plc, 2000–; non-exec. Dep. Chm., Aggreko, 1997–; non-executive Director: Leeds Permanent Bldg Soc., then Halifax Bldg Soc., now Halifax plc, 1994–98; Limit plc, 1997–2000; Internat. Public Relations, 1997–98; Wates City of London Properties, 1998–2001; British Biotech, 1999–; Octopus Capital plc, 2000–; CopperEye Ltd, 2001–. Trustee, Changing Faces, 1997–. *Recreations:* golf, tennis, theatre.

ROGG, Lionel; organist and composer; Professor of Organ and Improvisation, Geneva Conservatoire de Musique, since 1961; *b* 1936; *m* Claudine Effront; three *s*. *Educ:* Conservatoire de Musique, Geneva (1st prize for piano and organ). Concerts or organ recitals on the five continents. Records include works by Alain, Buxtehude (complete organ works; Deutscher Schallplatten Preis, 1980), Couperin and Martin; also complete works of J. S. Bach (Grand Prix du Disque, 1970, for The Art of the Fugue). *Compositions:* Acclamations, 1964; Chorale Preludes, 1971; Partita, 1975; Variations on Psalm 91, 1983; Cantata "Geburt der Venus", 1984; Introduction, Ricerare and Toccata, 1985; Two Etudes, 1986; Monodies, 1986; Psalm 92, 1986; Piece for Clarinette, 1986; Face-à-face for two pianos, 1987; Organ Concerto, 1991. DèsL Univ. de Genève, 1989. *Publication:* Eléments de Contrepoint, 1969. *Address:* Conservatoire de Musique, Place Neuve, Geneva, Switzerland; 38A route de Troinex, 1234 Vessy-Genève, Switzerland.

ROH, Tae Woo, Hon. GCMG 1989; President of Republic of Korea, 1988–93; *b* 4 Dec. 1932; *m* 1959, Kim-Ok-Sook; one *s* one *d*. *Educ:* Korean Military Academy; Republic of Korea War College. Commander, Capital Security, 1978, Defence Security, 1980; retd as Army General; Minister of State for Nat. Security and Foreign Affairs, 1981; Minister of Sports, and of Home Affairs, 1982; President: Seoul Olympic Organizing Cttee, 1983; Asian Games Organizing Cttee, 1983; Korean Olympic Cttee, 1984. Mem., Nat. Assembly and Pres., Ruling Democratic Justice Party, 1985. Hon. Dr George Washington Univ., 1989. Order of Nat. Security Merit (Sam Il Medal) (Korea), 1967; Grand Order of Mugunghwa (Korea), 1988; foreign decorations, incl. France, Germany, Kenya, Paraguay. *Publications:* Widaehan pot'ongsaram ui shidae (A great era of the ordinary people), 1987, trans. Japanese, 1988; Korea: a nation transformed, 1990. *Recreations:* tennis, swimming, golf, music, reading.

ROHMER, Eric, (Maurice Henri Joseph Schérer); French film director and writer; *b* 21 March 1920; *s* of Désiré Schérer and Jeanne Monzat; *m* 1957, Thérèse Barbet. *Educ:* Paris. Teacher, 1942–55; journalist, 1951–55. Film critic, Revue du cinéma, Arts, Temps Modernes, La Parisienne, 1949–63; Jt Founder, La Gazette du cinéma (also former Jt Editor). Dir of educnl films for French television, 1964–70. Co-Dir, Société des Films du Losange, 1964–. Films include (director and writer): Charlotte et son steak (short film), 1951; Le signe du lion, 1959; La boulangère de Monceau (short film), 1962; La collectionneuse, 1966; Ma nuit chez Maud, 1969 (prix Max Ophüls, 1970); Le genou de Claire, 1970 (prix Louis-Delluc, prix Méliès, 1971); L'amour l'après-midi, 1972; La Marquise d'O, 1976; Perceval le Gallois, 1978; Le beau mariage, 1982; Pauline à la plage, 1982; Les nuits de la pleine lune, 1984; Le rayon vert (Lion d'or, Venice Film Fest., prix de la critique internationale), 1986; L'ami de mon amie, 1988; Conte de Printemps, 1989; Conte d'Hiver, 1992; L'Arbre, le maire et le médiathèque, 1993; Rendezvous in Paris, 1996; Conte d'Eté, 1996; Conte d'Automne, 1999; L'Anglaise et le Duc, 2001. Best Dir Award, Berlin Film Fest., 1983; Lifetime Achievement Award, Venice Film Fest., 2001. *Publications:* Alfred Hitchcock, 1973; Charlie Chaplin, 1973; Six contes moraux, 1974; L'organisation de l'espace dans le "Faust" de Murnau, 1977; The Taste for Beauty (essays), 1992; De Mozart en Beethoven, 1996. *Address:* Les Films du Losange, 22 avenue Pierre 1er de Serbie, 75116 Paris, France.

ROHRER, Dr Heinrich; IBM Research Division, Zurich Research Laboratory, 1963–97, and IBM Fellow, 1986–97; *b* 6 June 1933; *s* of Henrich and Katharina Rohrer; *m* 1961, Rose-Marie Egger; two *d*. *Educ:* Federal Inst. of Technology, ETH, Zürich (Dr. sc. nat); PhD 1960. Post-doctoral Fellow, Rutgers Univ., 1961–63; joined IBM Res. Div. as Res. Staff Mem., 1963; then various managerial posts. Vis. Scientist, Univ. of Calif. at Santa Barbara, 1974–75. Mem. Bd, Swiss Fed. Insts of Technol., 1993–. Mem., Swiss Acad. of Technical Scis, 1988; For. Associate, US Acad. of Sci., 1988; Hon. Member: Swiss Physical Soc., 1990; Swiss Assoc. of Engrs and Architects, 1991; Zurich Physical Soc., 1992. Hon. Fellow, RMS, 1988. Hon. Dr: Rutgers, 1987; Marseille, 1988; Madrid, 1988; Tsukuba, Japan, 1994; Wolfgang Goethe Univ., Frankfurt, 1996; Tohoku, Japan, 2000. (Jtly) King Faisal Internat. Prize for Science, 1984; (jtly) Hewlett Packard Europhysics Prize, 1984; (jtly) Nobel Prize in Physics, 1986; (jtly) Cresson Medal, Franklin Inst., Philadelphia, 1987. *Recreations:* ski-ing, hiking, gardening. *Address:* Rebbergstrasse 9d, 8832 Wollerau, Switzerland.

ROITH, Oscar, CB 1987; FREng, FIMechE; Deputy Chairman, British Maritime Technology, since 1997 (Director, since 1987); Chief Engineer and Scientist, Department of Trade and Industry, 1982–87; *b* London, 14 May 1927; *s* of late Leon Roith and Leah Roith; *m* 1950, Irene Bullock; one *d*. *Educ:* Gonville and Caius Coll., Cambridge (minor schol.; Mech. Scis Tripos; MA). FIMechE 1967; FREng (FEng 1983); Eur Ing 1988. CBIM. FRSA. Research Dept, Courtaulds, 1948; Distillers Co. Ltd: Central Engrg Dept, 1952; Engrg Manager, Hull Works, 1962; Works Manager, 1968, Works Gen. Manager, 1969, BP Chemicals, Hull; General Manager: Engrg and Technical, BP Chemicals, 1974; Engrg Dept, BP Trading, 1977; Chief Exec. (Engrg), BP Internat., 1981. Dir, Trueland Ltd, 1987–. Mem., Yorks and Humberside Economic Planning Council, 1972–74. Comr, Royal Commn for Exhibition of 1851, 1988–98. Chm., Mech. and Electrical Engrg Requirements Bd, 1981–82; Member: Mech. Engrg and Machine Tools Requirements Bd, 1977–81; (non-exec.) Res. Cttee. British Gas, 1987–96; ACORD, 1982–87; ACARD, 1982–87; Process Plant EDC, NEDO, 1979–82; SERC, 1982–87; NERC, 1982–87; Bd (part-time), LRT, 1988–95; Chm., Res. Adv. Gp, PCFC, 1989–92. Pres., IMechE, 1987–88 (Dep. Pres., 1985–87; Mem. Council, 1981–92; Mem., Process Engrg Gp Cttee, 1962–68); Dep. Chm. Council, Foundn for Science and Technol., 1988–95; Hon. Sec., Mech. Engrg, Council of Fellowship of Engrg, 1988–91. Hon. Prof., Dept of Mgt Sci., Univ. of Stirling, 1992–95; Hon. Fellow, Univ. of Brighton, 1992. Governor: Brighton Polytechnic, 1988–91; ICSTM, 1990–98. Hon. DSc West of England, 1993. *Recreations:* cricket, gardening, walking. *Address:* 20 Wraymill House, Wraymill Park, Batts Hill, Reigate, Surrey RH2 0LJ. *T:* (01737) 779633. *Club:* Athenæum.

ROITT, Prof. Ivan Maurice, FRS 1983; Emeritus Professor of Immunology, since 1992, and Joint Head, Immunoprotein Engineering Group, since 1991, University College London; Professor, 1968–92, and Head of Department of Immunology, 1968–92, and of Rheumatology Research, 1984–92, University College and Middlesex School of Medicine (formerly Middlesex Hospital Medical School); *b* 30 Sept. 1927; *e s* of Harry Roitt; *m* 1953, Margaret Auralie Louise, *d* of F. Haigh; three *d*. *Educ:* King Edward's Sch., Birmingham; Balliol Coll., Oxford (exhibnr; BSc 1950; MA 1953; DPhil 1953; DSc 1968). FRCPath 1973. Res. Fellow, 1953, Reader in Immunopathol., 1965–68, Middlesex Hosp. Med. Sch. Chm., WHO Cttee on Immunolog. Control of Fertility, 1976–79; Mem., Biol. Sub-Cttee, UGC. Mem., Harrow Borough Council, 1963–65; Chm., Harrow Central Lib. Assoc., 1965–67. Florey Meml Lectr, Adelaide Univ., 1982. Hon. FRCP 1995. (Jtly) Van Meter Prize, Amer. Thyroid Assoc., 1957; Gairdner Foundn Award, Toronto, 1964. *Publications:* Essential Immunology, 1971, 10th edn 2001; (jtly) Immunology of Oral Diseases, 1979; (jtly) Immunology, 1985, 6th edn 2001; (jtly) Current Opinion in Immunology (series), 1989–93; (jtly) Clinical Immunology, 1991; Slide Atlas of Essential Immunology, 1992; (with Peter J. Delves) Encyclopedia of Immunology, 1992, 2nd edn 2000; (ed jtly) Medical Microbiology, 1993, 2nd edn 1998; 263 contribs to learned scientific jls. *Recreations:* tennis, golf, clarinet (modest), piano (very modest), banjo (subliminal), the contemporary novel, models of public debate. *Address:* Royal Free and University College London, Department of Immunology, Windeyer Institute of Medical Sciences, Cleveland Street, W1T 4JF.

ROKISON, Kenneth Stuart; QC 1976; a Judge of the Courts of Appeal of Jersey and Guernsey, since 2000; a Deputy High Court Judge; *b* 13 April 1937; *s* of late Frank Edward and late Kitty Winifred Rokison; *m* 1973, Rosalind Julia (*née* Mitchell); one *s* two *d*. *Educ:* Whitgift School, Croydon; Magdalene College, Cambridge (BA 1960). Called to the Bar, Gray's Inn, 1961, Bencher, 1985. A Recorder, 1989–94. *Recreation:* acting. *Address:* Ashcroft Farm, Gadbrook, Betchworth, Surrey RH3 7AH. *T:* (01306) 611244.

ROLAND, Prof. Martin Oliver, DM; FRCP, FRCGP; Professor of General Practice, Manchester University, since 1992; Director, National Primary Care Research and Development Centre, since 1999; *b* 7 Aug. 1951; *s* of Peter Ernest Roland and Margaret Eileen Roland; *m* 1st, 1971, Gillian Chapman; one *s*; 2nd, 1979, Rosalind Thorburn; two *s* one *d*. *Educ:* Rugby Sch.; Merton Coll., Oxford (BA 1972; BM BCh 1975; DM 1989). MRCP 1978, FRCP 2001; FRCGP 1994. Lectr in Gen. Practice, St Thomas's Hosp. Med. Sch., 1979–83; Dir of Studies in Gen. Practice, Cambridge Univ. Sch. of Clinical Medicine, 1987–92. Member: MRC Health Services Research Bd, 1992–96 (Chm. and Mem. MRC Council, 1994–96); Standing Med. Adv. Cttee, DoH, 2001–. FMedSci 2000. *Publications:* contribs on gen. practice, hosp. referrals, back pain, quality of care and out of hours care. *Recreations:* walking, opera. *Address:* National Primary Care Research and Development Centre, University of Manchester, Williamson Building, Oxford Road, Manchester M13 9PL. *T:* (0161) 275 7659.

ROLFE; *see* Neville-Rolfe.

ROLFE, Hume B.; *see* Boggis-Rolfe.

ROLFE, Mervyn James, CBE 2000; JP, DL; FSAScot; Member, since 1995, Convener of Economic Development and Depute Leader, since 1999, Dundee City Council; *b* 31 July 1947; *s* of Raymond Rolfe and late Margaret Rolfe; *m* 1977, Christine Margaret Tyrell; one *s*. *Educ:* Buckhaven High Sch., Fife; Dundee Univ. (MEd Hons); Abertay Dundee Univ. (MSc). FSAScot 1993. Civil servant, MSC, 1977–83; Co-ordinator, Dundee Resources Centre for Unemployed, 1983–87. Tayside Regional Council: Councillor, 1986–96; Convener of Educn, 1986–94; Depute Leader, 1990–94; Opposition Leader, 1994–96; Lord Provost and Lord-Lieut of Dundee, 1996–99. Dir, Scottish Enterprise Tayside, 1992–96, 1999–. Member: General Teaching Council Scotland, 1986–96; Exec., COSLA, 1990–96. Mem. Court, Dundee Univ., 1986–2000. FRSA 1992. JP 1988, DL 1999, Dundee. OStJ 1997. *Recreations:* reading, music, local history, golf. *Address:* 17 Mains Terrace, Dundee DD4 7BX. *T:* (01382) 450073.

ROLFE, William David Ian, PhD; FRSE, FGS, FMA; Keeper of Geology, National Museums of Scotland, 1986–96; *b* 24 Jan. 1936; *s* of late William Ambrose Rolfe and Greta Olwen Jones; *m* 1960, Julia Mary Margaret, *d* of late Capt. G. H. G. S. Rayer, OBE; two *d*. *Educ:* Royal Liberty Grammar Sch., Romford; Birmingham Univ. (BSc 1957; PhD 1960). FGS 1960; FMA 1972; FRSE 1983. Demonstrator in Geol., UC of N Staffs, 1960; Fulbright Schol., and Asst Curator, Mus. of Comparative Zool., Harvard Coll., Cambridge, Mass, 1961–62; Geol. Curator, Univ. Lectr, then Sen. Lectr in Geol., Hunterian Mus., Univ. of Glasgow, 1962–81; Dep. Dir, 1981–86. Vis. Scientist, Field Mus. of Natural Hist., Chicago, 1981. Mem., Trng Awards Cttee, NERC, 1980–83. President: Palaeontol Assoc., 1992–94 (Vice-Pres., 1974–76); Soc. Hist. Natural Hist., 1996–99 (Vice-Pres., 1987). Geological Society of Glasgow: Ed., Scottish Jl of Geol., 1967–72; Pres., 1973–76; Geological Society: Editl Chm., Journal, 1973–76; Chm., Conservation Cttee, 1980–85; Murchison Fund, 1978; Tyrrell Res. Fund, 1982; Coke Medal, 1984; Edinburgh Geological Society: Pres., 1989–91; Clough Medal, 1997. FRSA 1985. *Publications:* (ed) Phylogeny and Evolution of Crustacea, 1963; Treatise on Invertebrate Paleontology, part R, 1969; Geological Howlers, 1980; papers on fossil phyllocarid crustaceans and palaeontol., esp. other arthropods, and hist. of 18th century natural sci. illustration. *Recreations:* visual arts, walking, swimming, music. *Address:* 4A Randolph Crescent, Edinburgh EH3 7TH. *T:* (0131) 226 2094.

ROLFE JOHNSON, Anthony, CBE 1992; tenor; *b* 5 Nov. 1940; *m* (marr. diss.); two *s*; *m* Elisabeth Jones Evans; one *s* two *d*. Has performed at Glyndebourne, Covent Garden, Hamburg State Opera, La Scala Milan, Royal Albert Hall, Coliseum, Queen Elizabeth Hall, Aldeburgh Festival, Royal Festival Hall, Barbican Centre, Wigmore Hall, Salzburg Festival, Metropolitan NY. Has appeared with all major British orchestras and with Chicago Symphony Orchestra, Boston Symphony Orchestra, New York Philharmonic Orchestra and others. *Current rôles include:* Ulisse, Orfeo (Monteverdi), Idomeneo, Aschenbach, Peter Grimes, Lucio Silla, Tamino. *Address:* c/o Askonas Holt, Lonsdale Chambers, 27 Chancery Lane, WC2A 1PF.

ROLL, family name of **Baron Roll of Ipsden**.

ROLL OF IPSDEN, Baron *cr* 1977 (Life Peer), of Ipsden in the County of Oxfordshire; **Eric Roll,** KCMG 1962 (CMG 1949); CB 1956; Director of the Bank of England, 1968–77; Joint Chairman, S. G. Warburg & Co. Ltd, 1983–87 (Chairman, 1974–83; Deputy Chairman, 1967–74); President, S. G. Warburg Group Plc, 1987–95; Senior Adviser, UBS Warburg (formerly SBC Warburg, then Warburg Dillon Read), since 1995; *b* 1 Dec. 1907; *yr s* of Mathias and Fany Roll; *m* 1934, Winifred (*d* 1998), *o d* of Elliott and Sophia Taylor; two *d*. *Educ:* on the Continent; Univ. of Birmingham (BCom 1928; PhD 1930; Gladstone Memorial Prize, 1928; Univ. Research Scholarship, 1929). Prof. of Economics and Commerce, Univ. Coll. of Hull, 1935–46 (leave of absence 1939–46). Special Rockefeller Foundation Fellow, USA, 1939–41. Member, later Dep. Head, British Food Mission to N America, 1941–46; UK Dep. Member and UK Exec. Officer, Combined Food Board, Washington, until 1946; Asst Sec., Ministry of Food, 1946–47; Under-Secretary, HM Treasury (Central Economic Planning Staff), 1948; Minister, UK Delegation to OEEC, 1949. Deputy Head, United Kingdom Delegation to North Atlantic Treaty Organization, Paris, 1952; Under Secretary Ministry of Agriculture, Fisheries and Food, 1953–57; Executive Dir, International Sugar Council, 1957–59; Chm., United Nations Sugar Conf., 1958; Deputy Secretary, Ministry of Agriculture, Fisheries and Food, 1959–61; Deputy Leader, UK Delegation for negotiations with the European Economic Community, 1961–63; Economic Minister and Head of UK Treasury Delegation, Washington, 1963–64, also Exec. Dir for the UK International Monetary Fund and International Bank for Reconstruction and Development; Permanent Under-Sec. of State, Dept of Economic Affairs, 1964–66. Chm., subseq. Hon. Chm., Book Development Council, 1967–. Independent Mem., NEDC, 1971–80. Chm.,

Bilderberg Meetings, 1986–89. Director: Times Newspapers Ltd, 1967–80; Times Newspapers Holdings Ltd, 1980–83; also other Directorships; President: Mercury Securities Ltd, 1985–87 (Chm., 1974–84); Mercury Internat. Gp, 1985–87. Chancellor, Univ. of Southampton, 1974–84. Hon. DSc Hull, 1967; Hon. DSocSci Birmingham, 1967; Hon. LLD Southampton, 1974. Grosses Goldene Ehrenzeichen mit Stern (Austria), 1979; Comdr 1st Cl., Order of the Dannebrog (Denmark), 1981; Officier, Légion d' Honneur, 1984; Grand Cordon, Order of the Sacred Treasure (Japan), 1993; Grand Cross, Order of Merit (Italy), 2000. *Publications:* An Early Experiment in Industrial Organization, 1930; Spotlight on Germany, 1933; About Money, 1934; Elements of Economic Theory, 1935; Organized Labour (collaborated), 1938; The British Commonwealth at War (collaborated), 1943; A History of Economic Thought, 1954, 5th edn 1992; The Combined Food Board, 1957; The World After Keynes, 1968; The Uses and Abuses of Economics, 1978; (ed) The Mixed Economy, 1982; Crowded Hours (autobiog.), 1985; Where Did We Go Wrong?, 1995; Where Are We Going?, 2000; articles in Economic Jl, Economica, American Economic Review, etc. *Recreations:* reading, music. *Address:* D2 Albany, Piccadilly, W1V 9RG. *Club:* Brooks's.

ROLLAND, Lawrence Anderson Lyon, PPRIBA; PPRIAS; FRSE; Chairman/ Consultant, Hurd Rolland Partnership; President of Royal Institute of British Architects, 1985–87; *b* 6 Nov. 1937; *s* of Lawrence Anderson Rolland and Winifred Anne Lyon; *m* 1960, Mairi Melville; two *s* two *d.* *Educ:* George Watson Boys' College, Edinburgh; Duncan of Jordanstone College of Art. Diploma of Art (Architecture) 1959; ARIBA 1960; FRIAS 1965 (Pres., RIAS, 1979–81); FRSE 1989. Sen. Partner, L. A. Rolland & Partners, subseq. Robert Hurd and Partners, then The Hurd Rolland Partnership, 1959–97. Founder Mem., Scottish Construction Industry Group, 1979–81; Mem., Bldg EDC, NEDC, 1982–88. Mem. Bd, Architects' Registration Bd, 1996– (Chm., Qualifications Adv. Gp, 2000–). Architect for: The Queen's Hall, concert hall, Edinburgh; restoration and redesign of Bank of Scotland Head Office (original Architect, Sibbald, Reid & Crighton, 1805 and later, Bryce, 1870); much housing in Fife's royal burghs; British Golf Museum, St Andrews; General Accident Life Assurance, York; redesign, Council Chamber, GMC. Archtl Consultant, RSE. Chairman: RIBA Educn Trust Fund, 1981–; RIBA Educn Funds Cttee; Gen. Trustee, Church of Scotland (Chm., Adv. Cttee on Artistic Matters, 1986–). Chm. Bd. of Govs, Duncan of Jordanstone Coll. of Art, 1993–94; Chm. Court, Univ. of Dundee, 1997– (Mem., 1993–). FRSA 1988. Winner of more than 20 awards and commendations from Saltire Soc., Stone Fedn, Concrete Soc., Civic Trust, Europa Nostra, RIBA, and Times Conservation Award. *Recreations:* music, fishing, food, wine, cars. *Address:* Rossend Castle, Burntisland, Fife KY3 0DF. *T:* (01592) 873535. *Club:* Reform.

ROLLINSON, Timothy John Denis; Head of Policy and Practice Division, Forestry Commission, Edinburgh, since 2000; *b* 6 Nov. 1953; *s* of William Edward Denis Rollinson and Ida Frances Rollinson (*née* Marshall); *m* 1975, Dominique Christine Favardin; one *s* two *d.* *Educ:* Chigwell Sch.; Edinburgh Univ. (BSc Hons). MICFor 1978, FICFor 1995. Forestry Commission: District Officer: Kent, 1976–78; New Forest, 1978–81; Head of: Growth and Yield Studies, 1981–88; Land Use Planning, 1988–90; Parly and Policy Div., 1990–93; Sec., 1994–97; Chief Conservator, England, 1997–2000. Chm., Forest Res. Co-ordination Cttee, 2000–; Pres., Inst. of Chartered Foresters, 2000–. *Publications:* Thinning Control in British Woodlands, 1985; articles in forestry jls. *Recreations:* golf, tennis, swimming, food, France. *Address:* Forestry Commission, 231 Corstorphine Road, Edinburgh EH12 7AT. *T:* (0131) 314 6424. *Club:* Craigmillar Park Golf (Edinburgh).

ROLLO, family name of **Lord Rollo**.

ROLLO, 14th Lord *cr* 1651; **David Eric Howard Rollo;** Baron Dunning 1869; *b* 31 March 1943; *s* of 13th Lord Rollo and of Suzanne Hatton; *S* father, 1997; *m* 1971, Felicity Anne Christian, *o d* of Lt-Comdr J. B. Lamb; three *s.* *Educ:* Eton. Late Captain Grenadier Guards. *Heir:* *s* Master of Rollo, *qv.* *Address:* 20 Draycott Avenue, SW3 3AA. *Clubs:* Cavalry and Guards, Turf.

ROLLO, Master of; Hon. James David William Rollo; *b* 8 Jan. 1972; *s* and *heir* of Lord Rollo, *qv;* *m* 2001, Sophie Sara, *d* of Hubert de Castella.

ROLLO, James Maxwell Cree, CMG 1998; Professor of European Economic Integration, University of Sussex, and Co-Director, Sussex European Institute, since 1999; *b* 20 Jan. 1946; *s* of late James Maxwell Cree Rollo and of Alice Mary (*née* Killen); *m* 1970, Sonia Ann Halliwell; one *s* one *d.* *Educ:* Gourock High Sch.; Greenock High Sch.; Glasgow Univ. (BSc); London School of Economics (MSc Econ). Asst Economist, 1968–75, Economic Advr, 1975–79, MAFF; Economic Advr, FCO, 1979–81; Sen. Economic Advr, ODA, 1981–84; Dep. Head, Economic Advrs, FCO, 1984–89; Dir, Internat. Econs Programme, RIIA, 1989–93; Chief Economic Advr, FCO, 1993–98. Dir, ESRC Res. Prog., One Europe or Several?, 2001–. Special Prof., Univ. of Nottingham, 1996–99. Trustee, Spitalfields Centre. *Publications:* The New Eastern Europe: Western responses, 1990; (with John Flemming) Trade, Payments and Adjustment in Central and Eastern Europe, 1992; articles in learned jls. *Recreations:* eating, cooking, books, performing arts, talking shop with other economists. *Address:* Sussex European Institute, Arts A, University of Sussex, Falmer, Brighton BN1 9SH. *T:* (01273) 877297, *Fax:* (01273) 678571; *e-mail:* j.rollo@sussex.ac.uk.

ROLLS, Prof. Edmund Thomson, DPhil, DSc; Professor of Experimental Psychology, University of Oxford, since 1996; Fellow and Tutor in Psychology, Corpus Christi College, Oxford, since 1973; *b* 4 June 1945; *s* of Eric Fergus Rolls and May Martin Rolls (*née* Thomson); *m* 1969, Barbara Jean Simons (marr. diss. 1983); two *d.* *Educ:* Hardye's Sch., Dorchester; Jesus Coll., Cambridge (BA Preclinical Medicine 1967; MA); Queen's Coll., Oxford (Thomas Hardy Schol.); Magdalen Coll., Oxford (DPhil 1971); DSc Oxon 1986. Oxford University: Fellow by Exam., Magdalen Coll., 1969–73; Lectr in Exptl Psychol., 1973–96. Associate Dir, MRC Oxford IRC for Cognitive Neurosci., 1990–. Member: Soc. for Neurosci.; Physiological Soc.; Exptl Psychol. Soc. Secretary: Eur. Brain and Behaviour Soc., 1973–76; Council, Eur. Neurosci. Assoc., 1985–88; Membre d'Honneur, Société Française de Neurologie, 1994; Mem., Academia Europea. Canadian Commonwealth Fellow, 1980–81. Spearman Medal, BPsS, 1977. *Publications:* The Brain and Reward, 1975; (with B. J. Rolls) Thirst, 1982; (with A. Treves) Neural Networks and Brain Function, 1998; (jtly) Introduction to Connectionist Modelling of Cognitive Processes, 1998; The Brain and Emotion, 1999. *Recreations:* yachting, windsurfing, music, including opera. *Address:* Corpus Christi College, Oxford OX1 4JF. *T:* (01865) 271348, *Fax:* (01865) 310447; *e-mail:* Edmund.Rolls@psy.ox.ac.uk.

ROMAIN, Rabbi Dr Jonathan Anidjar; Minister, Maidenhead Synagogue, since 1980; *b* 24 Aug. 1954; *s* of Daniel and Gabrielle Romain; *m* 1981, Sybil Sheridan; four *s.* *Educ:* University Coll. London (BA Hons); Univ. of Leicester (PhD 1990). Semicha/Rabbinic Ordination, Leo Baeck Coll., London. Trustee, Family Policy Studies Centre, 1999–. *Publications:* Signs and Wonders, 1985; The Jews of England, 1988; Faith and Practice, 1991; Tradition and Change, 1995; Till Faith us to Part, 1996; Renewing the Vision, 1996; Your God Shall Be My God, 2000. *Recreations:* completing a never-ending family tree, preaching what I think I ought to practise. *Address:* Grenfell Lodge, Ray Park Road, Maidenhead, Berks SL6 8QX. *T:* (01628) 673012.

ROMAIN, Roderick Jessel Anidjar; Metropolitan Stipendiary Magistrate, 1972–83; *b* 2 Dec. 1916; *s* of late Artom A. Romain and Winifred (*née* Rodrigues); *m* 1947, Miriam (*d* 1991), *d* of late Semtob Sequerra; one *s* one *d.* *Educ:* Malvern Coll.; Sidney Sussex Coll., Cambridge. Called to the Bar, Middle Temple, 1939. Commissioned from HAC to 27th Field Regt, RA, 1940. Served War of 1939–45; France and Belgium, also N Africa and Italy, JAG Staff, 1943–45; JA at Neuengamme War Crimes Trial. Admitted a Solicitor, 1949, in practice as Partner, in Freke Palmer, Romain & Gassman, until 1972; recalled to Bar, 1973; a Dep. Circuit Judge, 1975–78.

ROMAINE, Prof. Suzanne, PhD; Merton Professor of English Language, and Fellow of Merton College, Oxford University, since 1984. *Educ:* Bryn Mawr Coll., Penn (AB); Edinburgh Univ. (MLitt); PhD Birmingham Univ. Lectr in Linguistics, Birmingham Univ., 1979–84. *Publications:* Socio-historical Linguistics: its status and methodology, 1982; Sociolinguistic Variation in Speech Communities, 1982; Language of Children and Adolescents, 1984; Pidgin and Creole Languages, 1988; Bilingualism, 1989; (ed) Language in Australia, 1991; Language Education and Development, 1992; Language in Society: introduction to sociolinguistics, 1994; (ed) Cambridge History of the English Language, vol; IV, 1998; Communicating Gender, 1999; (with D. Nettle) Vanishing Voices, 2000. *Address:* Merton College, Oxford OX1 4JD.

ROMANES, Professor George John, CBE 1971; PhD; Professor of Anatomy, 1954–84, and Dean of Faculty of Medicine, 1979–83, Edinburgh University; Professor of Anatomy, Royal Scottish Academy, since 1983; *b* 2 Dec. 1916; *s* of George Romanes, BSc, AMICE, and Isabella Elizabeth Burn Smith; *m* 1945, Muriel Grace Adam (*d* 1992), Edinburgh; four *d.* *Educ:* Edinburgh Academy; Christ's College, Cambridge (BA, PhD); Edinburgh University (MB, ChB). Marmaduke Sheild Scholar in Human Anatomy, 1938–40; Demonstrator in Anatomy, Cambridge, 1939; Beit Memorial Fellow for Medical Research, Cambridge, 1944–46; Lectr in Neuroanatomy, Edinburgh, 1946; Prof. of Anatomy, Edinburgh, 1954. Commonwealth Fund Fell., Columbia Univ., NY, 1949–50. Chm., Bd of Management, Edinburgh Royal Infirmary, 1959–74. Mem. Anatomical Soc. of Gt Brit. and Ireland; Mem. Amer. Assoc. of Anatomists; Assoc. Mem. Amer. Neurological Assoc. FRSE 1955; FRCSE 1958. Hon. DSc Glasgow, 1983. *Publications:* (ed) Cunningham's Textbook and Manuals of Anatomy; various papers on the anatomy and development of the nervous system in Jl of Anatomy and Jl of Comparative Neurology. *Recreations:* angling and curling. *Address:* Camus na Feannag, Kishorn, Strathcarron, Ross-shire IV54 8XA. *T:* (01520) 733273.

ROMANOW, Hon. Roy John; QC (Can.); Head, Commission on Future of Health Care in Canada, since 2001; *b* 1939; *s* of Mike and Tekla Romanow; *m* 1967, Eleanore Boykowich. *Educ:* Univ. of Saskatchewan (Arts and Law degrees). First elected to Saskatchewan Legislative Assembly, 1967; MLA (NDP) Saskatoon-Riversdale, 1967–82, 1986–2001; Dep. Premier, 1971–82; Attorney General, 1971–82; Minister of Intergovtl Affairs, 1979–82; Opposition House Leader for NDP Caucus, 1986; Leader, Saskatchewan NDP, 1987–2001; Premier, Saskatchewan, 1991–2001. *Publication:* (jtly) Canada Notwithstanding, 1984. *Address:* Commission on the Future of Health Care in Canada, Box 160, Station Main, Saskatoon, SK S7K 3KA, Canada.

ROME, Alan Mackenzie, OBE 1997; FRIBA, FSA; architect in private practice, since 1960; *b* 24 Oct. 1930; *s* of John and Evelyn Rome; *m* 1956, Mary Lilyan Barnard; one *s* one *d.* *Educ:* King's Sch., Bruton; Royal West of England Academy Sch. of Architecture (DipArch 1955). FRIBA 1971; FSA 1979. Pupil in office of Sir George Oatley, 1947–49; Nat. Service, RE, 1949–50; Asst to Stephen Dykes Bower at Westminster Abbey, 1955–60; Associate Architect with Michael Torrens and Alan Crozier Cole, 1960–64. Former Architect to Deans and Chapters of Bristol, Truro, Leicester, Peterborough, Salisbury, St Edmundsbury and Wells Cathedrals, Bath and Glastonbury Abbeys, St Mary Redcliffe, Bristol, and other churches in Somerset, Devon and Wilts; Architect Emeritus, Lancing Coll. Chapel. Member: Council for the Care of Churches, 1972–96 (Mem., Organs Adv. Cttee, 1991–96); Churches Conservation Trust (formerly Redundant Churches Fund), 1980–99; Cttee of Hon. Consulting Architects, Historic Churches Preservation Trust, 1990–; Bath and Wells DAC, 1978–. Occasional Lectr, Bath and Bristol Univs. *Publications:* (jtly) Bristol Cathedral History and Architecture; papers and addresses on architectural subjects. *Recreations:* walking, sketching, music. *Address:* 11 Mayfair Avenue, Nailsea, N Somerset BS48 2LR. *T:* (01275) 853215.

ROMNEY, 7th Earl of, *cr* 1801; **Michael Henry Marsham;** Bt 1663; Baron of Romney, 1716; Viscount Marsham, 1801; *b* 22 Nov. 1910; *s* of Lt-Col the Hon. Reginald Hastings Marsham, OBE (*d* 1922) (2nd *s* of 4th Earl) and Dora Hermione (*d* 1923), *d* of late Charles North; *S* cousin, 1975; *m* 1939, Frances Aileen (*d* 1995), *o d* of late Lt-Col James Russell Landale, IA. *Educ:* Sherborne. Served War of 1939–45, Major RA. Pres., Marine Soc., 1990–. *Heir:* *cousin* Julian Charles Marsham [*b* 28 March 1948; *m* 1975, Catriona Ann, *d* of Lt-Col Robert Christie Stewart, *qv;* two *s* one *d*]. *Address:* Wensum Farm, West Rudham, King's Lynn, Norfolk PE31 8SZ. *T:* (01485) 528249.

ROMSEY, Lord; Norton Louis Philip Knatchbull; *b* 8 Oct. 1947; *s* and *heir* of Baron Brabourne, *qv* and of Countess Mountbatten of Burma, *qv;* *m* 1979, Penelope Meredith Eastwood; one *s* one *d* (and one *d* decd). *Educ:* Dragon School, Oxford; Gordonstoun; University of Kent (BA Politics). *Heir:* *s* Hon. Nicholas Louis Charles Norton Knatchbull, *b* 15 May 1981. *Address:* Broadlands, Romsey, Hants SO51 9ZD. *T:* (01794) 505030.

RONALD, Edith, (Mrs Edmund Ronald); *see* Templeton, Mrs Edith.

RONALDSHAY, Earl of; Robin Lawrence Dundas; Director: Redcar Racecourse Ltd (formerly Redcar Race Co.), since 1989; Catterick Racecourse Co., since 1988; Fine Art Commissions Ltd, since 1997; Dundas Estates Ltd, since 1999; *b* 5 March 1965; *s* and *heir* of Marquess of Zetland, *qv;* *m* 1997, Heather Hoffman; four *d* (incl. twins). *Educ:* Harrow; Royal Agricl Coll., Cirencester. Man. Dir, Musks Ltd, 1993–99. Mem., Richmond Burgage Pastures Cttee, 2000–. Trustee, Trebetherick Estate Club, 1995–. Chm., Aske Parish Council, 1998–. *Recreations:* tennis, golf. *Club:* Slainte Mhah.

RONAY, Egon; Founder of the Egon Ronay hotel and restaurant guides (taken over by the Automobile Association, 1985, purchased by Leading Guides Ltd, 1992, all publishing rights reverted to Egon Ronay, 1997); *m* 1967, Barbara Greenslade; one *s,* and two *d* of previous marr. *Educ:* School of Piarist Order, Budapest; Univ. of Budapest (LLD); Academy of Commerce, Budapest. Dip. Restaurateurs' Guild, Budapest; FHCIMA. After univ. degree, trained in kitchens of family catering concern; continued training abroad, finishing at Dorchester Hotel, London; progressed to management within family concern of 5 restaurants, of which eventually he took charge; emigrated from Hungary, 1946; Gen. Manager, Princes Restaurant, Piccadilly, then Society Restaurant, Jermyn Street, followed by 96 Restaurant, Piccadilly; opened own restaurant, The Marquee, SW1, 1952–55;

started eating-out and general food, wine and tourism weekly column in Daily Telegraph and later Sunday Telegraph, 1954–60, also eating-out guide, 1957; weekly dining out column in Evening News, 1968–74; fortnightly gastronomic column, Sunday Times, 1986–92; Ed.-in-Chief, Egon Ronay Recommends (BAA Airports magazine), 1992–94. Constant team surveyance of catering and rating, BAA's 7 airports, 1992–. Founder and Pres., British Acad. of Gastronomes, 1983–; Mem. l'Académie des Gastronomes, France, 1979; Founding Vice Pres., Internat. Acad. of Gastronomy, 1985. Lifetime Achievement Award, Carlton London Restaurant Awards, 1999. Médaille de la Ville de Paris, 1983; Chevalier de l'Ordre du Mérite Agricole, 1987. *Publications:* Egon Ronay's Guide to Hotels and Restaurants, annually, 1956–85; Egon Ronay's Just A Bite, annually, 1979–85; Egon Ronay's Pub Guide, annually, 1980–85; Egon Ronay's Guide to 500 Good Restaurants in Europe's main cities, annually, 1983–85; The Unforgettable Dishes of My Life, 1989; various other tourist guides to Britain and overseas, to ski resorts in Europe, to Scandinavian hotels and restaurants and to eating places in Greece.

RONAYNE, Prof. Jarlath, PhD; FRSC, FTSE; Vice-Chancellor and President, Victoria University of Technology, Melbourne, since 1991; *b* 3 Sept. 1938; *s* of late Michael Ronayne and Anne Ronayne (*née* Kenny); *m* 1st, 1965, Rosalind Hickman (marr. diss. 1994); two *s*; 2nd, 1995, Margaret Francis. *Educ:* Trinity Coll., Dublin (BA 1965; MA 1968; Hon. Fellow 1997); St John's Coll., Cambridge (PhD 1968). FRSC 1988; FTSE 1995. Lecturer: Dept of Applied Sci., Wolverhampton Poly., 1968–70; Dept of Sci. and Technol. Policy, Manchester Univ., 1970–74; Sen. Lectr, then Dir, Sci. Policy Res. Centre, Sch. of Sci., Griffith Univ., Brisbane, 1974–77; University of New South Wales: Prof. of Hist. and Philosophy of Sci., 1977–91; Hd of Dept of Hist. and Philosophy of Sci., 1977–83; Dean, Faculty of Arts, 1983–84; Pro-Vice-Chancellor, 1984–88; Dep. Vice-Chancellor, 1988–91; Prof. Emeritus, 1991. Hon. Prof., Shanghai Inst. Tourism, 1993; Vis. Fellow, Oriel Coll., Oxford, 1999. Member: Internat. Council on Sci. Policy Studies, 1984–; Exec. Cttee, Australian Higher Educn Industrial Assoc., 1996–; Bd, Communications Law Centre, Sydney, 1996–; Standing Cttee on Internat. Matters, AVCC, 1998– (Leader, AVCC Delegn to India, 1998). Consultant to Commonwealth Dept of Employment, Educn and Youth Affairs, 1998. Mem., Victorian Educn Ministry Delegns to SE Asia and S America, 1998. Mem. Bd, VU Singapore Pty Ltd, 1999–. FAIM 1989. Member Board: Melba Conservatorium of Music, Melbourne, 1995–; Playbox Theatre Co., Melb., 2000–. Manoel de Vilhena Award, Malta, 1999. *Publications:* Guide to World Science: Australia and New Zealand, 1975; (jtly) Science, Technology and Public Policy, 1979; Science in Government: a review of the principles and practice of science policy, 1983; Science and Technology in Australasia, Antarctica and Pacific Islands, 1989; From First Fleet to Federation: Trinity College, Dublin – law, education and politics in colonial Australia, 2001; contrib. numerous jl articles in chemistry and sci. policy, and book chapters in chemistry, hist. of sci. and sci. policy. *Recreations:* sailing, reading, especially 19th century Irish history. *Address:* Office of the Vice-Chancellor, Victoria University of Technology, PO Box 14428, Melbourne City Mail Centre, Vic 8001, Australia. *T:* (3) 96884010. *Club:* Oxford and Cambridge.

RONE, Ven. James; Archdeacon of Wisbech, since 1995; *b* 28 Aug. 1935; *s* of James and Bessie Rone; *m* 1st, 1956, Ivy Mylchreest (*née* Whitby) (*d* 1970); one *s* one *d*; 2nd, 1976, Mary Elizabeth (*née* Angove). *Educ:* Skerry's Coll., Liverpool; St Stephen's House, Oxford. FSCA 1971. RAMC, 1953–56. Accountant, ICI Ltd, 1957–64; Hawker Siddeley Dynamics, 1964–65; Subsidiary co. dir and Sec., Reed International, 1965–71; Gp Chief Accountant, Leigh & Sillavan, 1971–73; Finance Officer, Oxford Diocesan Bd of Finance, 1973–79. Ordained deacon 1980, priest 1981; Curate, Stony Stratford, dio. of Oxford, 1980–82; Vicar, SS Peter and Mary Magdalene, Fordham and Rector of Kennett, 1982–89; Canon Residentiary, Ely Cathedral, 1989–95. Mem., Gen. Synod of C of E, 1995–. MInstD. *Recreations:* walking, Rugby (now non-playing), classical music, theatre, good food and wine. *Address:* Archdeacon's House, 24 Cromwell Road, Ely, Cambs CB6 1AS. *T:* (01353) 662909, *Fax:* (01353) 662056. *Club:* Carlton.

RONEY, Peter John; Managing Director, Consumer Financial Services, Great Universal Stores PLC, since 1998; *b* 12 Oct. 1949. *Educ:* Durham Univ. (BA Hons Pol. and Econs). Investment Manager, Derbys CC; Chief Investment Officer, S Yorks CC; Chief Exec., Combined Actuarial Performance Services Ltd; Man. Dir, Halifax Financial Services Ltd; Chief Exec., Save & Prosper Gp Ltd, 1996–98. *Address:* Universal House, Devonshire Street, Manchester M60 6EL.

RONSON, Gerald Maurice; Chief Executive: Heron Corporation PLC; Heron International PLC; Chairman and Chief Executive, Snax 24 Corporation Ltd; *b* 27 May 1939; *s* of Henry and Sarah Ronson; *m* 1967, Gail; four *d*. Chief Executive: Heron Corp. PLC, 1976– (Chm., 1978–93); Heron International PLC, 1983– (Chm., 1983–93). Ambassador of Druse community on Mount Carmel. *Recreation:* yachting. *Address:* Heron House, 19 Marylebone Road, NW1 5JL. *T:* (020) 7486 4477. *Club:* Royal Southern Yacht (Southampton).

ROOCROFT, Amanda Jane; soprano; *b* 9 Feb. 1966; *d* of Roger Roocroft and Valerie Roocroft (*née* Metcalfe); *m* 1999, David Gowland; two *s*. *Educ:* Southlands High Sch.; Runshaw Tertiary Coll.; Royal Northern Coll. of Music. Début as Sophie in Der Rosenkavalier, WNO, 1990; has sung at Glyndebourne, Royal Opera House, English Nat. Opera, Bayerische Staatsoper, BBC Promenade Concerts, Edinburgh Internat. Fest.; rôles include: Fiordiligi in Così fan Tutte; Donna Elvira in Don Giovanni; Pamina in Die Zauberflöte; Giulietta in I Capuleti e I Montecchi; Mimi in La Bohème; Amelia in Simon Boccanegra; title rôle in Katya Kabanova; Desdemona in Otello; title rôle in Jenufa. *Address:* c/o Ingpen & Williams Ltd, 26 Wadham Road, SW15 2LR. *T:* (020) 8874 3222, *Fax:* (020) 8877 3113.

ROOK, Peter Francis Grosvenor; QC 1991; a Recorder, since 1995; *b* 19 Sept. 1949; *s* of Dr Arthur James Rook and Frances Jane Elizabeth Rook (*née* Knott); *m* 1978, Susanna Marian Tewson; one *s* two *d*. *Educ:* Charterhouse; Trinity College, Cambridge (Open Exhibnr; MA Hist.); Bristol Univ. (Dip. Soc. Studies). Called to the Bar, Gray's Inn, 1973, Bencher, 2000; 2nd Standing Counsel to Inland Revenue at Central Criminal Court and Inner London Courts, 1981, 1st Standing Counsel, 1989; Asst Recorder, 1990–95. *Publication:* Rook and Ward on Sexual Offences, 1990, 2nd edn 1997. *Recreations:* tennis, squash, cricket, theatre, growing tropical plants. *Address:* 18 Red Lion Court, EC4A 3EB. *T:* (020) 7520 6000. *Clubs:* MCC; Coolhurst Lawn Tennis and Squash.

ROOKE, Daphne Marie; author; *b* 6 March 1914; *d* of Robert Pizzey and Marie Knevitt; *m* 1937, Irvin Rooke; one *d*. *Educ:* Durban, S Africa. Hon. DLit Univ. of Natal, 1997. *Publications:* A Grove of Fever Trees, 1950, repr. 1989; Mittee, 1951, repr. 1987; Ratoons, 1953, repr. 1990; The South African Twins, 1953; The Australian Twins, 1954; Wizards' Country; The New Zealand Twins, 1957; Beti, 1959; A Lover for Estelle, 1961; The Greyling, 1962; Diamond Jo, 1965; Boy on the Mountain, 1969; Double Ex!, 1970; Margaretha de la Porte, 1974; A Horse of his Own, 1976. *Recreation:* walking. *Address:* 54 Regatta Court, Oyster Row, Cambridge CB5 8NS. *T:* (01223) 314293.

ROOKE, Sir Denis (Eric), OM 1997; Kt 1977; CBE 1970; BSc (Eng.); FRS 1978; FREng; Chairman, British Gas plc (formerly British Gas Corporation and earlier, The Gas Council), 1976–89 (Deputy Chairman, 1972–76); Chancellor, Loughborough University (formerly Loughborough University of Technology), since 1989; *b* 2 April 1924; *yr s* of F. G. Rooke; *m* 1949, Elizabeth Brenda, *d* of D. D. Evans, Ystradgynlais, Brecon; one *d*. *Educ:* Westminster City Sch.; Addey and Stanhope Sch.; University Coll., London (Fellow, 1972). FREng (FEng 1977). Served with REME, UK and India, 1944–49 (Major). Joined staff of S Eastern Gas Bd as Asst Mechanical Engr in coal-tar by-products works, 1949; Dep. Man. of works, 1954; seconded to N Thames Gas Bd, 1957, for work in UK and USA on liquefied natural gas; mem. technical team which sailed in Methane Pioneer on first voyage bringing liquefied natural gas to UK, 1959; S Eastern Gas Bd's Development Engr, 1959; Development Engr, Gas Council, 1960; Mem. for Production and Supplies, 1966–71. Chm., CNAA, 1978–83; Member: Adv. Council for R&D, 1972–77; Adv. Council for Energy Conservation, 1974–77; Offshore Energy Technology Bd, 1975–78; BNOC, 1976–82; NEDC, 1976–80; Energy Commn, 1977–79. President: IGasE, 1975; Assoc. for Science Educn, 1981; Fellowship of Engineering, 1986–91; BAAS, 1990; Inst. of Quality Assce, 1990–92. Foreign Associate, NAE, 1987. Chm., Science Museum, 1995 (Trustee, 1983–95); Comr, Royal Commn for Exhibn of 1851, 1984–2001. Hon. Sen. Fellow, RCA, 1991. Hon. DSc: Salford, 1978; Leeds, 1980; City, 1985; Durham, 1986; Cranfield Inst. of Technol., 1987; London, 1991; Loughborough Univ. of Technol., 1994; Cambridge, 2000; Hon. DTech CNAA, 1986; Hon. LLD Bath, 1987; Hon. DEng: Bradford, 1989; Liverpool, 1994; DUniv Surrey, 1990. KStJ 1989. Rumford Medal, Royal Soc., 1986; Prince Philip Medal, Royal Acad. of Engrg, 1992. *Publications:* papers to Instn of Gas Engrs, World Power Conf., World Petroleum Conf., etc. *Recreations:* photography, listening to music. *Address:* 23 Hardy Road, Blackheath, SE3 7NS. *Clubs:* Athenæum, English-Speaking Union.

ROOKE, His Honour Giles Hugh, TD 1963; QC 1979; DL; a Circuit Judge, 1981–2001; Resident Judge, Canterbury, 1995–2001; *b* 28 Oct. 1930; *s* of late Charles Eustace Rooke, CMG, and Irene Phyllis Rooke; *m* 1968, Anne Bernadette Seymour, *d* of His Honour John Perrett; three *s* one *d* (and one *s* decd). *Educ:* Stowe; Exeter Coll., Oxford (MA). Kent Yeomanry, 1951–61, Kent and County of London Yeomanry, 1961–65 (TA), Major. Called to Bar, Lincoln's Inn, 1957; practised SE Circuit, 1957–81; a Recorder of the Crown Court, 1975–81. Hon. Recorder of Margate, 1980–2001. Mem. Council, Univ. of Kent at Canterbury, 1997–; Hon. Sen. Fellow, Univ. of Kent at Canterbury Law Sch., 1999–. DL Kent, 2001. *Address:* St Stephen's Cottage, Bridge, Canterbury CT4 5AH. *T:* (01227) 830298.

ROOKE, James Smith, CMG 1961; OBE 1949; Grand Decoration of Honour in Gold, of the Austrian Republic, 1981; Chief Executive, British Overseas Trade Board, 1972–75; HM Diplomatic Service, retired; Lecturer, Diplomatic Academy, Vienna, 1980–97; *b* 6 July 1916; *s* of Joseph Nelson Rooke and Adeline Mounser (*née* Woodgate); *m* 1938, Maria Theresa Rebrec, Vienna; one *s* two *d*. *Educ:* Workington Grammar Sch.; University College, London; Vienna Univ. Apptd to Dept of Overseas Trade, 1938. Military service, 1940–45, KRRC and AEC. Second Secretary (Commercial), British Embassy, Bogotá, 1946; UK Delegation to ITO Conf., Havana, 1947; Dep. UK Commercial Rep., Frankfurt, 1948; First Secretary (Commercial), British Embassy, Rome, 1951; Consul (Commercial), Milan, 1954; Deputy Consul-General (Commercial), New York, 1955–59; HM Counsellor (Commercial) British Embassy, Berne, 1959–63, Rome, 1963–66; Minister (Commercial), British High Commn, Canberra, 1966–68; Minister (Economic), British Embassy, Paris, 1968–72. *Recreation:* climbing. *Address:* Flotowgasse 26/3/1, 1190 Vienna, Austria. *Club:* East India, Devonshire, Sports and Public Schools.

ROOKE, Brig. Vera Margaret, CB 1984; CBE 1980; RRC 1973; Matron-in-Chief (Army) and Director of Army Nursing Services, 1981–84; *b* 21 Dec. 1924; *d* of late William James Rooke and Lily Amelia Rooke (*née* Cole). *Educ:* Girls' County Sch., Hove, Sussex. Addenbrooke's Hosp., Cambridge (SRN); Royal Alexandra Children's Hosp., Brighton (RSCN); St Helier Hosp., Carshalton (Midwifery). Joined Queen Alexandra's Royal Army Nursing Corps, 1951; appointments include: service in military hospitals, UK, Egypt, Malta, Singapore; Staff Officer in Work Study; Liaison Officer, QARANC, MoD, 1973–74; Assistant Director of Army Nursing Services and Matron: Military Hosp., Hong Kong, 1975; Royal Herbert Hosp. and Queen Elizabeth Military Hosp., Woolwich, 1976–78; Dep. Dir, Army Nursing Services, HQ UKLF, 1979–80. QHNS, 1981–84. Lt-Col 1972, Col 1975, Brig. 1981. *Recreations:* gardening, walking, cookery, opera. *Address:* c/o Lloyds TSB, 208 Portland Road, Hove, Sussex.

ROOKER, Baron *cr* 2001 (Life Peer), of Perry Barr in the County of West Midlands; **Jeffrey William Rooker;** PC 1999; CEng; Minister of State, Home Office, since 2001; *b* 5 June 1941; *m* 1972, Angela. *Educ:* Handsworth Tech. Sch.; Handsworth Tech. Coll.; Warwick Univ. (MA); Aston Univ. (BScEng). CEng, FIEE; MIMgt. Apprentice toolmaker, King's Heath Engrg Co. Ltd, Birmingham, 1957–63; student apprentice, BLMC, 1963–64; Asst to Works Manager, Geo. Salter & Co., West Bromwich, 1964–65, Assembly Manager, 1965–67; Prodn Manager, Rola Celestion Ltd, Thames Ditton and Ipswich, 1967–70; Industrial Relations and Safety Officer, Metro-Cammell, Birmingham, 1971; Lectr, Lanchester Polytechnic, Coventry, 1972–74. MP (Lab) Birmingham, Perry Barr, Feb. 1974–2001. Opposition spokesman on social services, 1979–80, on social security, 1980–83, on treasury and economic affairs, 1983–84, on housing, 1984–87, on local government, 1987–88, on health and social services, 1990–92, on higher educn, 1992–93; Dep. Shadow Leader of H of C, 1994–97; Minister of State: MAFF, 1997–99; DSS, 1999–2001. Mem., Public Accounts Cttee, 1989–91. Chair, Labour Campaign for Electoral Reform, 1989–95. Mem. Council, Instn of Prodn Engrs, 1975–81. Hon. DSc Aston, 2001. *Address:* House of Lords, SW1A 0PW. *T:* (home) (0121) 686 8688.

ROOKS, Robert John; Command Secretary, RAF Personnel and Training Command, since 1999; *b* 20 Nov. 1948; *s* of Ronald Sidney Rooks and Daisy Rooks; *m* 1970, Elizabeth Lewis; one *s* one *d*. *Educ:* Hardye's Sch., Dorchester; Liverpool Univ. (BEng Hons). Spacecraft Design Engr, BAC, 1970–72; Ministry of Defence, 1972–: Admin Trainee, Chief Exec. Dockyards, 1972–73; Adjutant Gen. Secretariat, 1973–74; Size, Shape and Cost of RAF Prog., Defence Secretariat, 1974–75; Private Sec. to Chief of Defence Procurement, 1975–78; Fighting Vehicles and Engrg, Equipment Secretariat, 1978–80; RAF Ops, Defence Secretariat, 1980–83; Mgt Services Orgn, 1983–85; Finance Mgt and Planning, 1985–88, Head, 1988–90, Controller Aircraft Secretariat; Head of: Adjutant Gen. Secretariat 2, 1990–93; Civilian Mgt (Personnel) 1, 1993–97; Dir of Orgn and Mgt, 1998–99. *Recreations:* sailing, travel, IT. *Address:* Headquarters, Personnel and Training Command, RAF Innsworth, Gloucester GL3 1EZ. *T:* (01452) 712612. *Club:* Royal Air Force.

ROOLEY, Anthony; lutenist; Artistic Director: The Consort of Musicke, since 1969; Musica Oscura, since 1993; *b* 10 June 1944; *s* of Madge and Henry Rooley; *m* 1967, Carla Morris; three *d*; one *s* by Emma Kirkby, *qv*. *Educ:* Royal Acad. of Music. LRAM (Performers). Recitals in Europe, USA, Middle East, Japan, S America, New Zealand, Australia; radio and TV in UK, Europe and USA; numerous recordings, British and

German. Hon. FRAM 1990. *Publications:* Penguin Book of Early Music. 1982; Performance—revealing the Orpheus within, 1990. *Recreations:* food, wine, gardening, philosophy. *Address:* 13 Pages Lane, N10 1PU.

ROOME, Maj. Gen. Oliver McCrea, CBE 1973; Vice Lord-Lieutenant, Isle of Wight, 1987–95; *b* 9 March 1921; *s* of late Maj. Gen. Sir Horace Roome, KCIE, CB, CBE, MC, DL, late Royal Engineers; *m* 1947, Isobel Anstis, *d* of Rev. A. B. Jordan; two *s* one *d. Educ:* Wellington Coll. Commissioned in Royal Engineers, 1940. Served War: UK, Western Desert, Sicily, Italy, 1939–45. Various appts, UK, Far and Middle East, Berlin, 1946–68; IDC, 1969; Director of Army Recruiting, 1970–73; Chief, Jt Services Liaison Organisation, Bonn, 1973–76; retired. Col Comdt, RE, 1979–84. County Comr, Scouts, Isle of Wight, 1977–85. DL Isle of Wight, 1981–96; High Sheriff of the Isle of Wight, 1983–84. *Recreations:* sailing, youth activities. *Address:* The White Cottage, Hill Lane, Freshwater, Isle of Wight PO40 9TQ. *Clubs:* Army and Navy, Royal Ocean Racing, Royal Cruising; Royal Yacht Squadron.

ROONEY, Maureen Gowran, OBE 1996; National Women's Officer, Amalgamated Engineering & Electrical Union, since 1990; Co-Chair, Women's National Commission, 1993–95; *b* Blantyre, Lanarks, 27 April 1947; *d* of James Cunningham and Mary Conroy Cunningham; *m* 1966, Philip Rooney; one *s* three *d. Educ:* Elmwood Convent, Bothwell. Hairdresser, 1963–66; machine operator, Hoover plc, 1974–90. Mem., Gen. Council, 1990–, Exec. Council, 1999–, TUC; Mem., Labour Party NEC's Women's Cttee, 1989–. Vice-Pres., Nat. Childminders' Assoc., 1994–96; Bd of Mgt, Adult Literacy and Basic Skills Unit, 1992–95. *Recreations:* music, reading, cinema, theatre, knitting, walking. *Address:* 84 Goodhart Way, West Wickham, Bromley, Kent BR4 0EY. *Club:* Blantyre Miners Welfare.

ROONEY, Michael John, RA 1991 (ARA 1990); Head of Painting, Royal Academy Schools, 1991–95; *b* 5 March 1944; *s* of Elisabeth and John Rooney; *m* 1st, 1967, Patricia Anne Lavender (marr. diss. 1984); one *s* one *d*; 2nd, 1988, Alexandra Grascher, Vienna; one *s. Educ:* primary and secondary schools; Sutton Sch. of Art; Wimbledon Sch. of Art (NDD); Royal Coll. of Art (MA RCA, ARCA); British Sch. at Rome (Austin Abbey Major Award). Part-time lectr, various art colls; artist-in-residence, Towner Art Gall., Eastbourne, 1983; one man exhibns in Holland, Austria, London, Edinburgh and other UK locations; jt exhibns in Chicago, NY, Portland (Oregon), and throughout Europe and UK; commissions include: painting for FT Centenary, 1988; London Transport Poster, 1990; tapestry for TSB Ltd, Birmingham, 1991; work in public collections: Sussex; Cumbria; Birmingham; Punta del Este, Uruguay; London; Govt Art Collection. Chm., Soc. of Painters in Tempera. Prizes include: Calouste Gulbenkian Printmakers' Award, 1984; John Player Portrait Award, Nat. Portrait Gallery, 1985; RA Summer Exhibn Awards, 1986, 1988, 1989; Chichester Arts Prize, 1995. *Recreations:* cooking, travel. *Address:* The Old Sorting House, 19 Alder Road, Mortlake, SW14 8ER. *T:* (020) 8876 0459. *Club:* Chelsea Arts.

ROONEY, Terence Henry; MP (Lab) Bradford North, since Nov. 1990; *b* 11 Nov. 1950; *s* of Eric and Frances Rooney; *m* 1969, Susanne Chapman; one *s* two *d. Educ:* Buttershaw Comprehensive Sch.; Bradford Coll. Formerly: commercial insurance broker; Welfare Rights Advice Worker, Bierley Community Centre. Councillor, Bradford City, 1983–91 (Dep. Leader, 1990). *Address:* c/o House of Commons, SW1A 0AA.

ROOSE-EVANS, James Humphrey; freelance theatre director and author; non-stipendiary Anglican priest; *b* 11 Nov. 1927; *s* of Jack Roose-Evans and Catharina Primrose Morgan. *Educ:* Univ. of Oxford (MA). Started career in repertory, as an actor; Artistic Dir, Maddermarket Theatre, Norwich, 1954–55 (dir. English première of The Language of Flowers, 1955); Faculty of Julliard Sch. of Music, NY, 1955–56; on staff of RADA, 1956–; founded Hampstead Theatre, 1959; Resident Dir, Belgrade Theatre, Coventry, 1961. Regularly tours USA, lecturing and leading workshops. Productions directed include: *Hampstead Theatre*: The Square, 1963; The Little Clay Cart (also adapted), 1964; Adventures in the Skin Trade, world première, The Two Character Play, world première, Letters from an Eastern Front (also adapted), 1966; An Evening with Malcolm Muggeridge (also devised), 1966; *West End*: Cider with Rosie (also adapted), Private Lives, 1963; An Ideal Husband, 1966; The Happy Apple, 1967; 84 Charing Cross Road (also adapted), 1981 (Best Dir, Drama award), NY 1982 (awards for Best Play and Best Dir, 2001); Seven Year Itch, 1986; The Best of Friends, 1988 (also prod Comédie des Champs-Elysées, Paris, 1989); Temptation, 1990; Irving (also jt author with Barry Turner), 1995; Legend of Pericles, 1996; *other productions:* Venus Observed, Chichester, 1992; Pericles, 2000, Macbeth, 2001, Ludlow Fest. Author, Re: Joyce!, West End, 1991. Consultant, Theatre Mus. Founder and Chm., Bleddfa Trust-Centre for Caring and the Arts, Powys, 1974–. Columnist (Something Extra), Woman, 1986–88. Ordained priest, 1981. *Publications:* adaptation of The Little Clay Cart, by King Sudraka, 1965; Directing a Play, 1968; Experimental Theatre, 1970, 4th rev. edn, 1988; London Theatre, 1977; play version of 84 Charing Cross Road, by Helene Hanff, 1983; Inner Journey, Outer Journey, 1987, rev. edn 1998 (US as The Inner Stage, 1990); (introd. and ed) Darling Ma: the letters of Joyce Grenfell, 1988; The Tale of Beatrix Potter, 1988; (with Maureen Lipman) Re:Joyce!, 1988; (introd and ed) The Time of My Life: wartime journals of Joyce Grenfell, 1989; (trans.) Obey, On the Edge of Midnight, 1989; Passages of the Soul: ritual today, 1994; Cider with Rosie (stage adaptation), 1994; One Foot on the Stage (biog. of Richard Wilson), 1996; Eminently Victorian: the story of Augustus Hare (play), 1996; Loving without Tears (stage adaptation of Molly Keane novel), 1996; *for children:* The Adventures of Odd and Elsewhere, 1971; The Secret of the Seven Bright Shiners, 1972; Odd and the Great Bear, 1973; Elsewhere and the Gathering of the Clowns, 1974; The Return of the Great Bear, 1975; The Secret of Tippity-Witchit, 1975; The Lost Treasure of Wales, 1977. *Recreations:* gardening, writing. *Address:* c/o Sheil Land Associates, 43 Doughty Street, WC1N 2LF. *Clubs:* Garrick, Dramatists.

ROOT, Rev. Canon Howard Eugene; Preceptor of Malling Abbey, since 1993; *b* 13 April 1926; *s* of Howard Root and Flora Hoskins; *m* 1952, Celia (MA Lambeth), *e d* of Col R. T. Holland, CBE, DSO, MC; two *s* two *d. Educ:* Univ. of Southern California (BA 1945; Fellow, 1945–47); St Catherine's Soc., Oxford (BA 1951; MA 1970); Magdalen Coll., Oxford; Ripon Hall, Oxford; Magdalene Coll., Cambridge (MA 1953). Instructor, American Univ., Cairo, 1947–49; Sen. Demy, Magdalen Coll., Oxford, and Liddon Student, 1951–53. Deacon, 1953; Priest, 1954. Curate of Trumpington, 1953; Asst Lectr in Divinity, Cambridge, 1953–57; Lectr, 1957–66; Fellow, Emmanuel Coll., Cambridge, 1954–66, Chaplain, 1954–56, Dean, 1956–66; Prof. and Hd of Dept of Theology, Univ. of Southampton, 1966–81; Dir, Anglican Centre, Rome, and Counsellor on Vatican affairs to Archbishop of Canterbury, 1981–91; St Augustine Canon, Canterbury Cathedral, 1980–91, Canon Emeritus, 1991–. Wilde Lectr, Oxford Univ., 1957–60; Senior Denyer and Johnson Scholar, Oxford, 1963–64; Bampton Lectr, Univ. of Oxford, 1972; Pope Adrian VI Chair, Univ. of Louvain, 1979; Vis. Prof., Pontificial Gregorian Univ., Rome, 1984–91. Exam. Chaplain to Bishops of Ripon, 1959–76, Southwark, 1964–81, Bristol, 1965–81, Winchester, 1971–81, and Wakefield, 1977–81; Commissary to Bishop in Jerusalem, 1976–. Delegated Anglican Observer at Second Vatican Council, 1963–65; Consultant, Lambeth Conf., 1968 and 1988. Chm., Archbishops' Commn on Marriage, 1968–71; Member: Academic Council, Ecumenical Inst., Jerusalem, 1966–81; Anglican-RC Preparatory Commn, 1967–68; Archbishops' Commn on Christian Doctrine, 1967–74; Anglican-Roman Catholic Internat. Commn, 1969–81. Hon. Chaplain, Winchester Cathedral, 1966–67; Canon Theologian of Winchester, 1967–80. Mem., BBC/ITV Central Religious Adv. Cttee, 1971–75. Jt Editor, Jl of Theol Studies, 1969–74. Corresp. Fellow, 1993–97, Fellow, 1997–, Pontifical Internat. Marian Acad., Rome. *Address:* 26 St Swithun Street, Winchester, Hants SO23 9HU. *Club:* Brooks's.

ROOT, Jane; Controller, BBC2, since 1999; *b* 18 May 1957; *e d* of James William Root and Kathleen Root. *Educ:* Sussex Univ.; London Coll. of Printing. Manager, Cinema of Women (Film Distribn Co.), 1981–83; freelance journalist and film critic, 1981–83; Lectr in Film Studies, UEA, 1981–84; Researcher, Open the Box, Beat Productions, 1983; Co-Creator, The Media Show, 1986; Jt Founder and Jt Man. Dir, Wall to Wall Television, 1987–96; Head of Independent Commng Gp, BBC, 1997–98. Mem., Exec. Cttee, Edinburgh TV Fest. (Chair, 1995). *Publications:* Pictures of Women: sexuality, 1981; Open the Box: about television, 1983. *Recreations:* reading, travel. *Address:* BBC Television Centre, Wood Lane, W12 7RJ. *T:* (020) 8225 6918.

ROOTES, family name of **Baron Rootes**.

ROOTES, 3rd Baron *cr* 1959; **Nicholas Geoffrey Rootes;** author and freelance copywriter; Managing Director, Nick Rootes Associates Ltd, since 1997; *b* 12 July 1951; *s* of 2nd Baron Rootes and of Marian, *d* of Lt-Col H. R. Hayter, DSO and *widow* of Wing Comdr J. H. Slater, AFC; *S* father, 1992; *m* 1976, Dorothy Anne Burn-Forti (*née* Wood); one step *s* one step *d. Educ:* Harrow Sch. Trustee, Rootes Charitable Trust, 1992–; Patron, Assoc. of Rootes Car Clubs, 1993–. *Publications:* The Drinker's Companion, 1987; Doing a Dyson, 1996. *Recreations:* ski-ing, fly-fishing. *Heir: cousin* William Brian Rootes [*b* 8 Nov. 1944; *m* 1969, Alicia, *y d* of Frederick Graham Roberts, OBE; two *d*]. *Address:* 2 Cedars Road, Barnes SW13 0HP. *T:* (020) 8876 6965. *Club:* Ski of Great Britain.

ROOTS, Guy Robert Godfrey; QC 1989; *b* 26 Aug. 1946; *s* of late William Lloyd Roots, QC and Elizabeth Colquhoun Gow (*née* Gray); *m* 1975, Caroline (*née* Clarkson); three *s. Educ:* Winchester College; Brasenose College, Oxford (MA). Called to the Bar, Middle Temple, 1969, Harmsworth Scholar, 1970, Bencher, 2000. Chm., Planning and Envmt, Bar Assoc., 2000–. Fellow, Soc. of Advanced Legal Studies, 1998–. Liveryman, Drapers' Co., 1972. *Publications:* (ed) Ryde on Rating, 1986; (ed) Butterworths' Compulsory Purchase and Compensation Service, 1999. *Recreations:* sailing, fishing, ski-ing, photography, woodworking. *Address:* 2 Mitre Court Buildings, Temple, EC4Y 7BX. *T:* (020) 7583 1380; *e-mail:* clerks@2mcb.co.uk. *Club:* Itchenor Sailing.

ROOTS, Paul John; Director of Industrial Relations, Ford Motor Co. Ltd, 1981–86, retired; *b* 16 Oct. 1929; *s* of John Earl and Helen Roots; *m* 1951, Anna Theresa Pateman; two *s* two *d. Educ:* Dormers Wells Sch.; London Sch. of Economics; Open Univ. BA Hons 1993; Cert. in Personnel Admin. CIPM; CIMgt. RN, 1947–54: service in Korean War. Personnel Officer, Brush Gp, 1955; Labour Officer, UKAEA, 1956, Labour Manager, 1959; Ford Motor Co. Ltd: Personnel Manager, Halewood, 1962; Forward Planning Manager, 1966; Labour Relations Manager, 1969; Dir of Employee Relations, 1974. Vice-Pres., IPM, 1981–83. Chairman: CBI Health and Safety Policy Cttee, 1984–; CBI Health and Safety Consultative Cttee, 1984–; Member: Council of Management, CBI Educn Foundn, 1981–; CBI Working Party on the Employment of Disabled People, 1981–; CBI Employment Policy Cttee, 1983–; CBI Council, 1984–; Engrg Industry Training Bd, 1985–. *Publications:* (jtly) Communication in Practice, 1981; (jtly) Corporate Personnel Management, 1986; Financial Incentives for Employees, 1988; articles in personnel management jls. *Recreations:* riding, theatre, music.

ROOTS, William; Chief Executive and Director of Finance, City of Westminster, 1994–2000; *b* 12 April 1946; *s* of William Roots and Violet (*née* Frost); *m* 1st, 1963, Norma Jane Smith (marr. diss.); one *s* one *d*; 2nd, 1980, Susan Grace Sharratt; two *s. Educ:* Wandsworth Sch. Sun Life Assce Soc., 1962–64; joined GLC as trainee, 1964; Hd of Budget, 1980; London Borough of Southwark: Head of: Exchequer, 1980–81; Finance, 1982–82; Director of Finance: London Borough of Bexley, 1982–90; City of Westminster, 1990–94. Mem., CIPFA 1970. *Recreations:* sport (esp. Rugby), relaxing with friends, films. *e-mail:* billroots@hotmail.com.

ROPER; *see* Trevor-Roper.

ROPER, family name of **Baron Roper**.

ROPER, Baron *cr* 2000 (Life Peer), of Thorney Island in the City of Westminster; **John Francis Hodgess Roper;** Liberal Democratic Chief Whip, House of Lords, since 2001; Hon. Professor, Institute for German Studies, University of Birmingham, since 1999; *b* 10 Sept. 1935; *e s* of late Rev. Frederick Mabor Hodgess Roper and of Ellen Frances (*née* Brockway); *m* 1959, (Valerie) Hope, *er d* of late Rt Hon. L. John Edwards, PC, OBE, MP, and late Mrs D. M. Edwards; one *d. Educ:* William Hulme's Grammar Sch., Manchester; Reading Sch.; Magdalen Coll., Oxford; Univ. of Chicago. Nat. Service, commnd RNVR, 1954–56; studied PPE, Oxford, 1956–59 (Pres. UN Student Assoc., 1957; organised Univ. referendum on Nuclear Disarmament); Harkness Fellow, Commonwealth Fund, 1959–61; Research Fellow in Economic Statistics, Univ. of Manchester, 1961; Asst Lectr in Econs, 1962–64, Lectr 1964–70, Faculty Tutor 1968–70; RIIA: Editor of International Affairs, 1983–88; Head of Internat. Security Programme, 1985–88, and 1989–90; Dir of Studies, 1988–89; Associate Fellow, 1996–; Hd, WEU Inst. for Security Studies, Paris, 1990–95. Vis. Prof., Coll. of Europe, Bruges, 1997–2000. Contested: (Lab) High Peak (Derbys), 1964; (SDP) Worsley, 1983. MP (Lab and Co-op 1970–81, SDP 1981–83) Farnworth, 1970–83; PPS to Minister of State, DoI, 1978–79; opposition front bench spokesman on defence, 1979–81; Social Democrat Chief Whip, 1981–83. Vice-Chairman: Anglo-German Parly Gp, 1974–83; Anglo-Benelux Parly Gp, 1979–83; Chm., British-Atlantic Gp of Young Politicians, 1974–75. Council of Europe: Consultant, 1965–66; Mem., Consultative Assembly, 1973–80; Chm., Cttee on Culture and Educn, 1979–80; Mem., WEU Assembly, 1973–80; Chm., Cttee on Defence Questions and Armaments, WEU, 1977–80. Hon. Treasurer, Fabian Soc., 1976–81; Chairman: Labour Cttee for Europe, 1976–80; GB/East Europe Centre, 1987–90; Council on Christian Approaches to Defence and Disarmament, 1983–89; Mem., Internat. Commn on the Balkans, 1995–96. Research Adviser (part-time), DEA in NW, 1967–69. Director: Co-op. Wholesale Soc., 1969–74; Co-op Insurance Soc., 1973–74. Pres., Gen. Council, UNA, 1972–78; Mem. Council, Inst. for Fiscal Studies, 1975–90; Mem. Gen. Adv. Council, IBA, 1974–79. Vice-Pres., Manchester Statistical Soc., 1971–. Trustee, Hist. of Parlt Trust, 1974–84. *Publications:* Towards Regional Co-operatives, 1967; The Teaching of Economics at University Level, 1970; The Future of British Defence Policy, 1985; (ed with Karl Kaiser) British–German Defence Co-operation, 1988; (ed with Yves Boyer) Franco-British Defence Co-operation, 1988; (ed with Nicole Gnesotto) Western Europe and the Gulf, 1992; (ed with Nanette Gantz) Towards a New

Partnership, 1993; (ed with Laurence Martin) Towards a Common Defence Policy, 1995. *Recreations:* reading, travel. *Address:* House of Lords, SW1A 0PW. *T:* (020) 7219 3114. *Club:* Oxford and Cambridge.

See also Sir J. C. Jenkins, Rev. G. E. H. Roper.

ROPER, Brian Anthony; Vice-Chancellor and Chief Executive, University of North London, since 1994; *b* 15 Dec. 1949; *s* of Harold Herbert Albert Roper and Elizabeth Roper (*née* Rooney); *m* 1971, Margaret Patricia Jones; one *s* one *d. Educ:* UWIST (BSc Hons Econs 1971); Univ. of Manchester (MA Econs 1973). FSS 1988. Tutor in Econs, UWIST, 1971–72; Lectr in Econs, Teeside Poly., 1973–75; Sen. Lectr, then Principal Lectr, Leicester Poly., 1975–80; Hd, Sch. of Econs, Dean, Faculty of Social Scis and Asst Dir, Resources, Newcastle upon Tyne Poly., 1980–90; Dep. Vice Chancellor Acad. Affairs and Dep. Chief Exec., Oxford Poly., subseq. Oxford Brookes Univ., 1991–94. FIMgt (FBIM 1987). FRSA 1994. *Publications:* contrib. Econ. Theory and Policy, Higher Educn Policy and Mgt. *Recreations:* Rugby Union, Italian opera, Impressionist painting, hill-walking. *Address:* University of North London, 166–220 Holloway Road, N7 8BD. *T:* (020) 7753 5181. *Club:* Tynedale Rugby Football.

ROPER, Rev. Geoffrey Edward Hodgess; Associate General Secretary (Free Churches), and Secretary, Free Churches Group, Churches Together in England, since 2001; *b* 24 April 1940; *y s* of late Rev. Frederick Mabor Hodgess Roper and of Ellen Frances (*née* Brockway); *m* 1967, Janice Wakeham; one *s* one *d. Educ:* Christ's Hosp.; Magdalen Coll., Oxford (MA (PPE and Theol.)); Mansfield Coll., Oxford. Ordained 1965; Minister: Trinity Congregational Church, Ifield, Crawley, 1965–71; Streatham Congregational Church, 1971–78 (URC from 1972); Seaford URC, 1978–85; Christ Church, Chelmsford, 1985–95. Gen. Sec., Free Church Fed. Council, later Free Churches' Council, 1996–2001. Sec., URC Deployment Cttee, 1978–84; URC Ecumenical Officer: Sussex East, 1979–85; Essex, 1986–95. Mem., Churches' Millennium Gp, 1995–2000; Sec., Gen. Body of Dissenting Ministers and Deputies of the Three Denominations, 1998–. Mem., Eastbourne CHC, 1980–85 (Vice-Chm., 1983–84). British Isles Mem., Exec. Cttee, Leuenberg Doctrinal Conversations of Reformed and Lutheran Churches in Europe, 1987–94. Dir, Highway Trust, 1977–94. Dir, British and Internat. Sailors' Soc., 1999–. Chm. of Cttee, Friends of Dr Williams's Library, 1991–. Trustee, St George's Chapel, Heathrow Airport, 1999–. *Recreation:* listening. *Address:* 27 Tavistock Square, WC1H 9HH. *T:* (020) 7387 8413.

See also Baron Roper.

ROPER, Michael, CB 1992; FRHistS; Keeper of Public Records, 1988–92; *b* 19 Aug. 1932; *s* of Jack Roper and Mona Roper (*née* Nettleton); *m* 1957, Joan Barbara Earnshaw; one *s* one *d. Educ:* Heath Grammar Sch., Halifax; Univ. of Manchester (BA, MA; Langton Fellow). Registered Mem., Soc. of Archivists, 1987. Public Record Office: Asst Keeper, 1959–70; Principal Asst Keeper, 1970–82; Records Admin Officer, 1982–85; Dep. Keeper of Public Records, 1985–88. Lectr (part time) in Archive Studies, UCL, 1972–87, Hon. Res. Fellow, 1988–; Dist. Visitor, Univ. of BC, 1994; Vis. Prof., Surugadai Univ., Japan, 1999. Sec., Adv. Council on Public Records, 1963–68; Vice-President: Soc. of Archivists, 1992– (Vice-Chm., 1983–84; Chm., 1985–86; Pres., 1989–92); British Records Soc., 1988–; RHistS, 1989–93 (Hon. Treas., 1974–80); Sec.-Gen., Internat. Council on Archives, 1988–92 (Sec. for Standardization, 1984–88; Hon. Mem., 1992); Hon. Sec., Assoc. of Commonwealth Archivists and Records Managers, 1996–2000. Chairman: Voices from the Past, 1992–95; English Record Collections, 1994–. Ext. Examr, Nat. Univ. of Ireland, 1982–86, Univ. of Liverpool, 1986–89, Univ. of London, 1988–93. Chm., Judy Segal Trust, 1990–98; Hon. Treasurer, Bethlem Art & Hist. Collections Trust, 1995–. Hon. DLitt Bradford, 1991. *Publications:* Yorkshire Fines 1300–1314, 1965; Records of the Foreign Office 1782–1939, 1969; (with J. A. Keene) Planning, Equipping and Staffing a Document Reprographic Service, 1984; Guidelines for the Preservation of Microforms, 1986; Directory of National Standards Relating to Archives Administration and Records Management, 1986; Planning, Equipping and Staffing an Archival Preservation and Conservation Service, 1989; Geresye to Jersey: the record endures, 1991; Records of the War Office and Related Departments 1660–1964, 1998; contribs to learned jls. *Recreations:* listening to music, gardening, walking the dog. *Address:* Sherwood House, Vicarage Road, Roxwell, Chelmsford, Essex CM1 4NY.

ROPER, Robert Burnell, CB 1978; Chief Land Registrar, 1975–83 (Deputy Chief Land Registrar, 1973–75); *b* 23 Nov. 1921; *s* of late Allen George and Winifred Roper; *m* 1948, Mary Brookes; two *s. Educ:* King's College Sch., Wimbledon; King's Coll., London. LLB (Hons) 1941. Called to Bar, Gray's Inn, 1948. Served War, RAF, 1942–46. Miners' Welfare Commn, 1946–48; Nat. Coal Bd, 1948–49; Treasury Solicitor's Dept, 1949–50; HM Land Registry, 1950–83. *Publications:* (Ruoff and Roper) The Law and Practice of Registered Conveyancing, 3rd edn 1972, to 6th (loose-leaf) edn 1991–; Consulting Editor on Land Registration matters for Encyclopaedia of Forms and Precedents (4th edn). *Recreations:* gardening, watching sport. *Address:* 11 Dukes Road, Lindfield, Haywards Heath, West Sussex RH16 2JH.

ROPER, Prof. Warren Richard, FRS 1989; FRSNZ 1984; Professor of Chemistry, University of Auckland, New Zealand, since 1984; *b* 27 Nov. 1938; *m* 1961, Judith Delcie Catherine Miller; two *s* one *d. Educ:* Nelson Coll., Nelson, NZ; Univ. of Canterbury, Christchurch, NZ (MSc, PhD). FNZIC. Postdoctoral Res. Associate, Univ. of N Carolina, 1963–65; Lectr in Chemistry, Univ. of Auckland, 1966. Vis. Lectr, Univ. of Bristol, 1972; Pacific W Coast Inorganic Lectr, 1982; Brotherton Vis. Res. Prof., Univ. of Leeds, 1983; Visiting Professor: Univ. de Rennes, 1984, 1985; Stanford Univ., 1988. Mellor Lectr, NZ Inst. of Chemistry, 1985; Centenary Lectr and Medallist, RSC, 1988; Glenn T. Seaborg Lectr, Univ. of Calif., Berkeley, 1995. Fellow, Japan Soc. for Promotion of Science, 1992. RSC Award in Organometallic Chemistry, 1983; ICI Medal, NZ Inst. of Chemistry, 1984; Hector Medal, Royal Soc. of NZ, 1991; 12th Inorganic Award, Royal Australian Inst. of Chemistry, 1992. *Publications:* over 150 sci. papers in internat. jls. *Recreations:* music, espec. opera, walking. *Address:* 26 Beulah Road, Auckland 10, New Zealand. *T:* (9) 4786940.

ROPER-CURZON, family name of **Baron Teynham.**

ROPNER, David; *see* Ropner, W. G. D.

ROPNER, Sir John (Bruce Woollacott), 2nd Bt *cr* 1952; *b* 16 April 1937; *s* of Sir Leonard Ropner, 1st Bt, MC, TD, and Esmé (*d* 1996), *y d* of late Bruce Robertson; *S* father, 1977; *m* 1st, 1961, Anne Melicent (marr. diss. 1970), *d* of late Sir Ralph Delmé-Radcliffe; two *d*; 2nd, 1970, Auriol (marr. diss. 1993; she *m* 1997, Marquess of Linlithgow, *qv*), *d* of late Captain Graham Lawrie Mackeson-Sandbach, Caerllo, Llangernyw; one *s* two *d*; 3rd, 1996, Diana Nicola, *d* of Peter Agnew. *Educ:* Eton; St Paul's School, USA. High Sheriff, N Yorks, 1991. *Recreation:* field sports. *Heir: s* Henry John William Ropner, *b* 24 Oct. 1981. *Address:* Thorp Perrow, Bedale, Yorks DL8 2PR.

See also Viscount Knutsford.

ROPNER, Sir Robert Douglas, 4th Bt *cr* 1904; *b* 1 Dec. 1921; *o s* of Sir (E. H. O.) Robert Ropner, 3rd Bt; *S* father, 1962; *m* 1943, Patricia Kathleen, *d* of W. E. Scofield, W. Malling, Kent; one *s* one *d. Educ:* Harrow. Formerly Captain, RA. *Heir: s* Robert Clinton Ropner, FCA [*b* 6 Feb. 1949; *m* 1978, Diana Felicia Abbott; one *s* one *d* (twins)]. *Address:* Rose Cottage, Swaffham Prior, Cambridge CB5 0LD.

ROPNER, (William Guy) David; Director, Ropner PLC, 1953–94 (Chairman, 1973–85); *b* 3 April 1924; *s* of late Sir William Guy Ropner and Lady (Margarita) Ropner; *m* 1st, 1955, Mildred Malise Hare Armitage (marr. diss. 1978); one *d* three *s*; 2nd, 1985, Hon. Mrs Charlotte M. Taddei; one *s. Educ:* Harrow. FICS 1953. Served War, 1942–47: 2nd Lieut RA, Essex Yeomanry; Captain 3rd Regt, RHA. Joined Sir R. Ropner and Co. Ltd, 1947; dir of various Ropner PLC gp cos, 1953–94. Member: Lloyd's, 1952–91; Gen. Cttee, Lloyd's Register of Shipping, 1961–94; Pres., Gen. Council of British Shipping, 1979–80; Chairman: Deep Sea Tramp Section, Chamber of Shipping, 1970–72; Lights Adv. Cttee, GCBS, 1978–87; Merchant Navy Welfare Bd, 1980–94; Cleveland & Durham Industrial Council, 1980–94; Dir, British Shipowners Assoc., 1954–89. *Recreations:* country and garden pursuits. *Club:* St Moritz Tobogganing.

ROQUES, (David) John (Seymour); Chairman, Portman Building Society, since 1999 (Director, since 1995); *b* 14 Oct. 1938; *s* of late Frank Davy Seymour Roques and of Marjorie Mabel Hudson; *m* 1963, Elizabeth Anne Mallender; two *s* one *d. Educ:* St Albans Sch. Mem., Inst. of Chartered Accountants of Scotland, 1962. Touche Ross & Co., later Deloitte & Touche: Partner, 1967; Partner in charge, Midlands region, 1973; Partner in charge, Scottish region, 1978; Partner in charge, London office, 1984; Man. Partner, 1990; Sen. Partner and Chief Exec., 1990–99. Non-executive Director: British Nuclear Fuels, 1990–; BBA Gp plc, 1999–; Premier Farnell plc, 1999–. Member: Financial Reporting Review Panel, 1991–94; Financial Reporting Council, 1996–. FRSA. *Recreations:* Rugby football, racing, opera, gardening. *Address:* Portman Building Society, 40 Portman Square, W1H 9FH. *Clubs:* Edgbaston Golf, Harewood Downs Golf.

RORKE, Prof. John, CBE 1979; PhD; FRSE; FIMechE; Professor of Mechanical Engineering, 1980–88, and Vice-Principal, 1984–88, Heriot-Watt University, now Professor Emeritus; *b* 2 Sept. 1923; *s* of John and Janet Rorke; *m* 1948, Jane Craig Buchanan; two *d. Educ:* Dumbarton Acad.; Univ. of Strathclyde (BSc, PhD). Lectr, Strathclyde Univ., 1946–51; Asst to Engrg Dir, Alexander Stephen & Sons Ltd, 1951–56; Technical Manager, subseq. Gen. Man., and Engrg Dir, Wm Denny & Bros Ltd, 1956–63; Tech. Dir, subseq. Sales Dir, Man. Dir, and Chm., Brown Bros & Co. Ltd (subsid. of Vickers Ltd), 1963–78; Man. Dir, Vickers Offshore Engrg Gp, 1978; Dir of Planning, Vickers Ltd, 1979–80. Chairman: Orkney Water Test Centre Ltd, 1987–94; Environment and Resource Technology Ltd, 1991–94. Pres., Instn of Engineers and Shipbuilders in Scotland, 1985–87. Hon. DEng Heriot-Watt, 1994. *Recreations:* golf, bridge. *Address:* 3 Barnton Park Grove, Edinburgh EH4 6HG. *T:* (0131) 336 3044. *Club:* Bruntsfield Links Golfing Society (Edinburgh).

ROSCOE, Alexis Fayrer; *see* Brett-Holt, A. F.

ROSCOE, Dr Ingrid Mary, FSA; Vice Lord-Lieutenant, West Yorkshire, since 2001; Editor, Gunnis Dictionary of British Sculptors, since 2000; *b* 27 May 1944; *d* of late Dr Arthur Allen and Else (*née* Markenstam) and adopted *d* of late Brig. Kenneth Hargreaves; *m* 1963, John Richard Marshall Roscoe; one *s* two *d. Educ:* St Helen's, Northwood; Univ. of Leeds (BA; PhD 1990). FSA 1998. Lectr in Sculpture Hist., Univ. of Leeds, 1990–96. Co. Rep., NACF, 1972–93; Ed., Ch Monuments Jl, 1993–2000. Mem., Exec. Cttee, Walpole Soc., 2000–. Chm. Trustees, 1996–, High Steward, 2000–, Selby Abbey; Trustee, Martin House Childrens' Hospice, 1989–98. *Publications:* contrib. articles to Apollo, Gazette-des-Beaux Arts, Grove Dictionary of Art, Walpole Soc. Jl, Jl of LTS, DNB, etc. *Recreations:* reading, walking, grandchildren. *Address:* North Deighton Manor, Wetherby, Yorks LS22 4EN. *T:* (01937) 582910.

ROSCOE, (John) Gareth; barrister; Consultant Adviser, Department of Trade and Industry, 1999–2001; *b* 28 Jan. 1948; *s* of late John Roscoe and Ann (*née* Jones); *m* 1st, 1970, Helen Jane Taylor (marr. diss. 1979); one *d*; 2nd, 1980, Alexis Fayrer Brett-Holt, *qv*; one *s* one *d. Educ:* Manchester Warehousemen and Clerks' Orphan Schools (now Cheadle Hulme Sch.); Stretford Tech. Coll.; London Sch. of Economics and Political Science (LLB). Called to the Bar, Gray's Inn, 1972; in practice, 1972–75; Legal Asst 1975–79, Sen. Legal Asst 1979, DoE; Law Officers' Dept, Attorney-General's Chambers, 1979–83; Asst Solicitor, 1983–87, Dep. Solicitor, 1987–89, DoE; Dir, BBC Enterprises Ltd, 1989–96; Legal Advr to the BBC, 1989–98; Company Sec., BBC Worldwide Ltd, 1996–98. Non-exec. Dir, Optimum NHS Trust, 1995–97. Mem., Gen. Council of the Bar, 1987–90. Member: Adv. Cttee, Centre for Communications and Information Law, UCL, 1991–; Legal Cttee, EBU, 1989–98. *Recreations:* music, horology, motorcycling. *Address:* 18 College Gardens, Dulwich, SE21 7BE. *T:* (020) 8693 5680. *Club:* Athenæum.

ROSE, Alan Douglas, AO 1994; President, Australian Law Reform Commission, since 1994; *b* 3 May 1944; *s* of late Willfred Allen Rose and Hazel Agnes Rose (*née* Heinemann-Mirre); *m* 1966, Helen Elizabeth Haigh; two *d. Educ:* Univ. of Queensland (BA 1966; LLB Hons 1969); LSE, Univ. of London (LLM 1979). Barrister, Supreme Court of Queensland, 1973; Dep. Sec., Dept of Prime Minister and Cabinet, 1982–86; Sec. to Aust. Dept of Community Services, 1986–87; Associate Sec. and Sec. to Aust. Attorney-Gen. Dept, 1987–94. Affiliate, Aust. Securities Inst. *Publications:* articles in legal jls and works on public admin. *Recreations:* surfing, ski-ing, reading, travelling. *Address:* Australian Law Reform Commission, 131 York Street, Sydney, NSW 2000, Australia. *T:* (2) 62577029; PO Box 1995, Canberra City, ACT 2601, Australia. *T:* (2) 92846301.

ROSE, Anthea Lorrainne, (Mrs H. D. Rose); Chief Executive, Association of Chartered Certified Accountants (formerly Chartered Association of Certified Accountants), 1993–May 2002; *b* 2 Dec. 1946; *d* of Philip Brown and Muriel (*née* Seftor); *m* 1971, Hannan David Rose. *Educ:* St Hugh's Coll., Oxford (MA Mod. Hist.). Administrator, Open Univ., 1968–69; Personnel Officer, Beecham Pharmaceuticals, 1969–71; Administrator, Univ. of Kent, 1971–77; Chartered Association of Certified Accountants, later Association of Chartered Certified Accountants, 1977–: Under Sec., 1982–88; Dep. Chief Exec., 1988–93. *Recreations:* travel, food, wine, preparing for my retirement. *Address:* (until May 2002) 29 Lincoln's Inn Fields, WC2A 3EE. *T:* (020) 7242 6855.

ROSE, (Arthur) James, CBE 1996; Director of Inspection, Office for Standards in Education, 1994–99; *m* 1960, Pauline; one *d. Educ:* Kesteven College; Leicester University. HM Chief Inspector for Primary Educn, DES, subseq. DFE, 1986–92; Dep. Dir of Inspection, OFSTED, 1992–94. *Address:* Greenwey, Bunch Lane, Haslemere, Surrey GU27 1ET. *T:* and *Fax:* (01428) 651627.

ROSE, Aubrey, CBE 1997 (OBE 1986); Deputy Chairman, Commission for Racial Equality, 1995 (Commissioner, 1991–95); consultant with Ross & Craig, since 1996; *b* 1 Nov. 1926; *s* of Solomon Rosenberg and Esther Rosenberg (*née* Kurtz); *m* 1954, Sheila

Ray Glassman; one *s* one *d* (and one *s* decd). *Educ:* at various grammar schs incl. Central Foundn Sch., London. Admitted as solicitor, 1952; Sen. Partner, 1971–91. Chm., Legal Cttee, CRE, 1993–95. Founder Mem. and Treas., Commonwealth Human Rights Initiative, 1990–. Dep. Chm., British Caribbean Assoc., 1990–; Jt Chm., Indian-Jewish Assoc., 1996–. Sen. Vice-Pres., Bd of Deputies of British Jews, 1991–97; Chm., Jewish Wkg Gp on Envmt, 1991–; Jt Patron, New Assembly of Churches, 1993–. Trustee, Project Fullemploy, 1994–. FRSA 1993. Freeman, City of London, 1965. DUniv N London, 2000. *Publications:* Judaism and Ecology, 1992; Jewish Communities of the Commonwealth, 1993; Journey into Immortality, 1997; Brief Encounters of a Legal Kind, 1997. *Recreations:* gardening, walking, various sports, writing, reading, lecturing, listening to music, being a grandfather. *Address:* 14 Pagitts Grove, Hadley Wood, Herts EN4 0NT. *T:* (020) 8449 2166.

ROSE, Barry, MBE 1981; editor and publisher; Chairman, Barry Rose Law Publishers Ltd, since 1970; *b* 17 July 1923; *s* of late William George Rose and Beatrice Mary (*née* Castle); *m* 1963, Dorothy Jean Colthrup, *d* of Lt-Col W.R. Bowden; one *d*. Chm., own group of companies, 1970–97. Editor: Justice of the Peace and Local Government Review, 1944–72; Justice of the Peace, 1972–74; Local Government Review, 1972–76; law and local govt oriented periodicals. Member: Chichester RDC, 1951–61; West Sussex CC, 1952–73 (Leader, Cons. Group, 1967–72; Alderman, 1972); Pagham Parish Council, 1952–62; Bognor Regis UDC, 1964–68; Hon. Editor, Rural District Review, 1959–63; Mem., RDCA, 1960–63, CCA 1968–72; Chm., SE Area Cons. Local Govt Adv. Cttee, 1969–73; Pres., Assoc. of Councillors, 1975–86 (Treasurer, 1960–69; Chm., Exec. Cttee, 1969–75); posts in Cons. Party, 1945–74, incl. Constituency Chm., Chichester, 1961–69; Pres., Chichester Div., Young Conservatives, 1959–69. Contested (Alternative C) Old Bexley and Sidcup, 1992. Publisher, Centre for Policy Studies, 1974–76. Sometime publisher: Parly All-Party Penal Affairs Gp; Magistrates' Assoc.; NACRO; Council for Science and Society. Liveryman, Stationers' Co., 1974. FRSA 1960; FRSocMed 1998. Hon. Life Mem., Justices' Clerks' Soc., 1985. *Publications:* Change of Fortune (play), 1950; Funny Business (play), 1951; England Looks at Maud, 1970; A Councillor's Work, 1971; History of the Poll Tax, 1993; (as Peter Barton) Encounter by Moonlight (novel), 2001; Anecdotage, 2002. *Recreations:* entertaining and being entertained. *Address:* Courtney Lodge, Sylvan Way, Bognor Regis, West Sussex PO21 2RS. *T:* (01243) 829902. *Clubs:* Athenæum, Garrick, MCC, Oxford and Cambridge.

ROSE, Barry Michael, OBE 1998; FRSCM; FRAM; Master of the Music, St Albans Abbey, 1988–97; *b* 24 May 1934; *s* of late Stanley George Rose and Gladys Mildred Rose; *m* 1965, Elizabeth Mary Ware; one *s* two *d*. *Educ:* Sir George Monoux Grammar Sch., Walthamstow; Royal Acad. of Music (ARAM). FRSCM 1973; FRAM 1989. First Organist and Master of the Choristers, new Guildford Cathedral, 1960–74; Sub-Organist, St Paul's Cath., 1974–77; Master of the Choir, 1977–84; Master of the Choirs, The King's School, Canterbury, 1985–88. Music Adviser to Head of Religious Broadcasting, BBC, 1970–90. Hon. DMus City, 1991; MUniv Surrey, 1992. *Recreation:* collecting and restoring vintage fountain-pens. *Address:* Level Crossing, Milking Lane, Draycott, Somerset BS27 3TL. *T:* and *Fax:* (01934) 744838; *e-mail:* brose80648@aol.com.

ROSE, Brian; HM Diplomatic Service, retired; *b* 26 Jan. 1930; *s* of Edwin and Emily Rose; *m* 1952, Audrey Barnes; one *d*. *Educ:* Canford Sch., Dorset. MIL 1983. Intelligence Corps, 1948–50. Min. of Food, 1950–54; CRO, 1954; Peshawar, 1955–56; Ottawa, 1958–61; Kingston, Jamaica, 1962–65; Rome, 1966; Zagreb, 1966–68; Zomba, Malawi, 1968–71; FCO, 1971–74; Düsseldorf, 1974–77; E Berlin, 1977–78; Zürich, 1978–82; Consul-Gen., Stuttgart, 1982–85; Commercial and Econ. Counsellor, Helsinki, 1985–88. *Recreations:* tennis, music. *Club:* Travellers.

ROSE, Major Charles Frederick, CBE 1988 (MBE 1968); CEng, FICE; independent consultant in railway engineering and safety, 1989–98; *b* 9 July 1926; *s* of Charles James Rose and Ida Marguerite Chollet; *m* 1956, Huguette Primerose Lecoultre; one *s* one *d*. *Educ:* Xaverian Coll., Brighton; Royal School of Military Engineering, 1951–52 and 1957–59. Student engineer, Southern Railway Co., 1942–46; commnd RE, 1947; service with mil. railways, Palestine and Egypt, 1947–51; with a Field Sqdn in Germany, 1952–53; Engr SO, Korea, 1953–54; Instructor: Mons Officer Cadet Sch., 1954–57; Transportation Centre, Longmoor, 1959–62; OC a Field Sqdn, Germany, 1962–64; Instr, Royal Sch. of Mil. Engrg, 1964–66; Engr, RE road construction project, Thailand, 1966–68; Inspecting Officer of Railways, MoT, 1968–82; Chief Inspecting Officer of Railways, Dept of Transport, 1982–88. Chm., Anglo-French Channel Tunnel Safety Authy, 1987–89. *Recreations:* hill walking, foreign travel, music. *Address:* Hollybank, Shadyhanger, Godalming, Surrey GU7 2HR. *T:* (01483) 416429.

ROSE, Christine B.; *see* Brooke-Rose.

ROSE, Rt Hon. Sir Christopher (Dudley Roger), Kt 1985; PC 1992; **Rt Hon. Lord Justice Rose;** a Lord Justice of Appeal, since 1992; Vice-President, Court of Appeal (Criminal Division), since 1997; *b* 10 Feb. 1937; *s* of late Roger and Hilda Rose, Morecambe; *m* 1964, Judith, *d* of late George and Charlotte Brand, Didsbury; one *s* one *d*. *Educ:* Morecambe Grammar Sch.; Repton; Leeds Univ.; Wadham Coll., Oxford (Hon. Fellow, 1993). LLB and Hughes Prize, Leeds, 1957; 1st cl. hons BCL 1959, Eldon Scholar 1959, Oxon. Lectr in Law, Wadham Coll., Oxford, 1959–60; called to Bar, Middle Temple, 1960 (Bencher, 1983; Treas., 2002); Bigelow Teaching Fellow, Law Sch., Univ. of Chicago, 1960–61; Harmsworth Scholar, 1961; joined Northern Circuit, 1961; QC 1974; a Recorder, 1978–85; a Judge of the High Court, QBD, 1985–92; Presiding Judge, Northern Circuit, 1987–90. Chm., Criminal Justice Consultative Council, 1994–2000. Mem., Senate of Inns of Court and Bar, 1983–85. *Recreations:* playing the piano, listening to music, travel. *Address:* Royal Courts of Justice, Strand, WC2A 2LL. *Club:* Garrick.

ROSE, Clifford; *see* Rose, F.C.

ROSE, Sir Clive (Martin), GCMG 1981 (KCMG 1976; CMG 1967); HM Diplomatic Service, retired; *b* 15 Sept. 1921; *s* of late Rt Rev. Alfred Carey Wollaston Rose and Lois Juliet (*née* Garton); *m* 1946, Elisabeth Mackenzie, *d* of late Rev. Cyril Lewis, Gilston; two *s* three *d*. *Educ:* Marlborough College; Christ Church, Oxford (MA). Rifle Bde, 1941–46 (Maj.; despatches): served in Europe, 1944–45; India, 1945; Iraq, 1945–46. CRO, 1948; Office of Deputy High Comr, Madras, 1948–49; Foreign Office, 1950–53; UK High Commn, Germany, 1953–54; British Embassy, Bonn, 1955; FO, 1956–59; 1st Sec. and HM Consul, Montevideo, 1959–62; FO, 1962–65; Commercial Counsellor, Paris, 1965–67; Imp. Defence Coll., 1968; Counsellor, British Embassy, Washington, 1969–71; Asst Under-Sec. of State, FCO, 1971–73; Ambassador and Head, British Delegn to Negotiations on Mutual Reduction of Forces and Armaments and Associated Measures in Central Europe, Vienna, 1973–76; Dep. Secretary, Cabinet Office, 1976–79; Ambassador and UK Permanent Rep. on North Atlantic Council, 1979–82. Lectr to RCDS, 1979–87 (Mem., Adv. Bd, 1985–91). Consultant, Control Risks Gp, 1983–95; Dir, Control Risks Information Services Ltd, 1986–93 (Chm., 1991–93). Pres., Emergency Planning Assoc. (formerly Assoc. of Civil Defence and Emergency Planning Officers), 1987–93; Vice-Patron, RUSI, 1993–2001 (Chm. Council, 1983–86; Vice-Pres., 1986–93). Vice-Pres., Suffolk Preservation Soc., 1988– (Chm., 1985–88). FRSA 1982; Hon. FICD 1989. *Publications:* Campaigns Against Western Defence: NATO's adversaries and critics, 1985, 2nd edn 1986; The Soviet Propaganda Network, 1988; The Unending Quest: a search for ancestors, 1996. *Recreations:* gardening, reading Trollope, family history. *Address:* Chimney House, Lavenham, Suffolk CO10 9QT.

ROSE, David Edward; independent film and television producer; *b* 22 Nov. 1924; *s* of Alvan Edward Rose and Gladys Frances Rose; *m* 1st, 1952, Valerie Edwards (*d* 1966); three *s* three *d*; 2nd, 1966, Sarah Reid (marr. diss. 1988); one *d*, and one step *s* one step *d* adopted; 3rd, 2001, Karin Bamborough. *Educ:* Kingswood Sch., Bath; Guildhall Sch. of Music and Drama. Repertory Theatre, 1952; Ballets Jooss, and Sadler's Wells Theatre Ballet, 1954; BBC Television, 1954–81 (in production and direction; Head of Television Training, 1969; Head of Regional Television Drama, 1971–81); Sen. Commng Editor (Fiction), 1981–88, Hd of Drama, 1988–90, Channel Four TV. Member: BAFTA; Eur. Film Acad. Prix Italia TV Award (for film Medico), 1959; BAFTA Producer and Director's Award, (for Z Cars (prod original series)), 1963; BFI Award (for Film on Four and work of new writers and directors), 1985; Desmond Davies Award, BAFTA, 1987; Prix Roberto Rossellini (for Channel Four Television), Cannes Film Fest., 1987; Critics Circle Special Film Award, 1987; Gold Medal, RTS, 1988; BAFTA Fellowship, 1999.

ROSE, Donald Henry Gair, LVO 1982; HM Diplomatic Service, retired; Consul-General, Jedda, 1983–86; *b* 24 Sept. 1926; *m* 1950, Sheila Munro; three *s*. HM Forces, 1944–48; Scottish Office, 1948–66; Commonwealth Office, 1966; Nairobi, 1967; Tripoli, 1971; First Sec., Cairo, 1974–77; FCO, 1977–79; High Comr, Kiribati, 1979–83. *Address:* 11 Buckstone Gardens, Edinburgh EH10 6QD.

ROSE, Dr Frank Clifford, FRCP; Director, London Neurological Centre, and Hon. Consulting Neurologist, Charing Cross Hospital, since 1991; *b* 29 Aug. 1926; *s* of James and Clare Rose; *m* 1963, Angela Juliet Halsted; three *s*. *Educ:* King's Coll., London; Westminster Hosp. Med. Sch.; Univ. of California, San Francisco; Hôpital de la Salpêtrière, Paris. MB BS London; DCH; MRCS; FRCP 1971 (LRCP 1949, MRCP 1954). Medical Registrar, Westminster Hosp., 1955; Resident MO, National Hosp., Queen Square, 1957; Sen. Registrar, Dept of Neurology, St George's Hosp., 1960; Consultant Neurologist: Medical Ophthalmology Unit, St Thomas' Hosp., 1963–85; Moor House Sch. for Speech Disorders, 1965–70; Physician i/c, Dept. of Neurology, Regl Neuroscis Centre, Charing Cross Hosp., 1965–91; Dir, Academic Unit of Neuroscis, Charing Cross and Westminster Med. Sch., 1985–91; Prof. Associate, Dept of Health Scis, Brunel Univ., 1991–. PMO, Allied Dunbar (formerly Hambro Life) Assurance Co., 1970–96. Mem., Wkg Pty on Stroke, RCP, 1988; Chairman: European Stroke Prevention Study, 1981–88; Res. Adv. Cttee, Assoc. for Res. in Multiple Sclerosis, 1987–91; Internat. Amyotrophic Lateral Sclerosis/Motor Neurone Disease Res. Foundn, 1987–90; Motor Neurone Disease Assoc., 1988–90 (Med. Patron, 1978–90; Scientific Advr, 1990–91); Ind. Doctors Forum, 1994–96; Ciba Epilepsy Res. Award, 1997; President: Med. Soc. London, 1983–84 (Treas., 1984–89; Internat. Sec., 1995–); Assurance Med. Soc., 1983–85; Section of Neurology, RSM, 1990–91; Sec.-Treas. Gen., World Fedn of Neurology, 1989–98; Trustee: Migraine Trust (Chm., 1988–96); The Way Ahead Appeal, 1986–91. Examr in Clinical Pharmacology and Therapeutics, Univ. of London. Lettsomian Lectr, Med. Soc. London, 1979; Guest Lectr, Scandinavian Migraine Soc., 1983. Hon. Member: Neurol Soc. of Thailand, 1992; Austrian Soc. of Neurol., 1992; Hon. Life Mem., Internat. Headache Soc., 1997. Harold Wolff Award, 1981 and 1984, and Distinguished Clinician Award, 1986, Amer. Assoc. for the Study of Headache; Louis Boshes Award, Northwestern Univ., Chicago, 1994. Sen. Editor, Neuroepidemiology, 1991– (Dep. Editor, 1982–83; Editor, 1984–90); Editor: World Neurology, 1990–98; Jl of Hist. of Neuroscis, 1992–96; Co-editor, Headache Qly, 1991–. *Publications:* (jtly) Hypoglycaemia, 1965, 2nd edn, 1981 (Japanese trans., 1988); (jtly) Basic Neurology of Speech, 1970, 3rd edn 1983; (ed) Physiological Aspects of Clinical Neurology, 1976; (ed) Medical Ophthalmology, 1976; (ed) Motor Neurone Disease, 1977; (ed) Clinical Neuroimmunology, 1978; (ed) Paediatric Neurology, 1979; (jtly) Optic Neuritis and its Differential Diagnosis, 1979; (ed jtly) Progress in Stroke Research 1, 1979; (ed jtly) Progress in Neurological Research, 1979; (jtly) Migraine: the facts, 1979 (Spanish trans., 1981); (ed) Clinical Neuroepidemiology, 1980; (ed) Animal Models of Neurological Disorders, 1980; (ed jtly) Research Progress in Parkinson's Disease, 1981; (ed) Metabolic Disorders of the Nervous System, 1981; (ed jtly) Progress in Migraine Research 1, 1981; (jtly) Stroke: The Facts, 1981 (Dutch trans., 1982); (ed jtly) Historical Aspects of the Neurosciences, 1982; (ed jtly) Cerebral Hypoxia in the Pathogenesis of Migraine, 1982; (ed) Advances in Stroke Therapy, 1982; (ed) Advances in Migraine Research and Therapy, 1982; (ed) Research Progress in Epilepsy, 1982; (ed jtly) Immunology of Nervous System Infections, 1983; (ed) The Eye in General Disease, 1983; (ed jtly) Progress in Stroke Research 2, 1983; (ed) Research Progress in Motor Neurone Disease, 1984; (ed) Progress in Migraine Research 2, 1984; (ed) Progress in Aphasiology, 1985; (ed) Modern Approaches to the Dementias (2 vols), 1985; (ed jtly) Neuro-oncology, 1985; (ed) Migraine: clinical and research advances, 1985; Handbook of Clinical Neurology: headache, 1986; (ed) Stroke: epidemiological, therapeutic and socio-economic aspects, 1986; (jtly) Atlas of Clinical Neurology, 1986 (Japanese trans., 1989); (ed jtly) Multiple Sclerosis: diagnostic, immunological and therapeutic aspects, 1987; (ed) Advances in Headache Research, 1987; (ed) Parkinson's Disease: clinical and research advances, 1987; (ed jtly) Physiological Aspects of Clinical Neuro-ophthalmology, 1987; (jtly) Answers to Migraine, 1987; (ed jtly) Aphasia, 1988; (ed) The Management of Headache, 1988; (ed jtly) Neuromuscular Stimulation, 1989; (ed) James Parkinson, his life and times, 1989; (ed) Control of the Hypothalamic-Pituitary-Adrenal Axis, 1989; (ed) New Advances in Headache Research, 1989; (ed) Neuroscience across the Centuries, 1989; (ed jtly) Clinical Trial Methodology in Stroke, 1989; (ed jtly) Amyotrophic Lateral Sclerosis: new advances in toxicology and epidemiology, 1990; (ed) Progress in Clinical Neurologic Trials: amyotrophic lateral sclerosis, 1990; (ed) New Advances in Headache Research 2, 1991; (ed) Parkinson's Disease and the Problems of Clinical Trials, 1992; (ed) Molecular Genetics and Neurology, 1992; (ed) Advances in Clinical Neuropharmacology, 1993; (ed) ALS: from Charcot to the present and into the future, 1994; (ed) New Advances in Headache Research 3, 1994; (ed) Tropical Neurology, 1996; Towards Migraine 2000, 1996; A Short History of Neurology: the British contribution 1660–1910, 1999; Multiple Sclerosis at Your Fingertips, 2000; Twentieth Century Neurology: the British contribution, 2001; Neurology of the Arts, 2002; papers in neurological and gen. med. jls. *Recreations:* travel, reading, wine, bridge. *Address:* London Neurological Centre, 110 Harley Street, W1G 7JG. *T:* (020) 7935 3546, *Fax:* (020) 7935 4172. *Clubs:* Royal Society of Medicine, Savile.

ROSE, Gerald Gershon, PhD; CChem, FRSC; Director, Thornton Research Centre, Shell Research Ltd, 1975–80; *b* 4 May 1921; *m* 1945, Olive Sylvia; one *s* two *d*. *Educ:* Hendon County Grammar Sch.; Imperial Coll. of Science and Technology (BSc, ARCS, DIC, PhD). Joined Shell Group, 1944; served in refineries, Stanlow, Trinidad, Singapore and South Africa; General Manager, Shell/BP South Africa Petroleum Refineries, 1963; Manufacturing and Supply Director, Shell/BP Service Co., 1968; Manager, Teesport

Refinery, 1971. *Recreations:* golf, tennis, gardening. *Address:* The Tithe Barn, Great Barrow, Chester, Cheshire CH3 7HW. *T:* (01829) 40623.

ROSE, Graham Hunt; a Master of the Supreme Court (Queen's Bench Division), since 1992; *b* 15 July 1937; *er s* of late William Edward Hunt Rose and Mary Musgrave Rose (*née* Kent); *m* 1962, Malvinia Ann Saunders (marr. diss. 1988); three *s*. *Educ:* Canford Sch.; University Coll., Oxford (MA). Nat. Service, RA, 1955–57: commnd 1956; active service, 1957. Called to the Bar, Inner Temple, 1961; practised at the Bar, 1961–92, Western Circuit. Jt Editor, Civil Procedure (formerly Supreme Court Practice), 1992–. *Recreations:* most ball games, mountaineering, gardening. *Address:* Royal Courts of Justice, Strand, WC2A 2LL. *Clubs:* Travellers; Parkstone Golf.

ROSE, Prof. Harold Bertram; Emeritus Professor of Finance, London Graduate School of Business Studies, since 1996 (Esmée Fairbairn Chair, 1965–75; Visiting Professor of Finance, since 1975); *b* 9 Aug. 1923; *s* of late Isaac Rose and Rose Rose (*née* Barnett); *m* 1st, 1949, Valerie Frances Anne Chubb (marr. diss. 1974); three *s* one *d*; 2nd, 1974, Diana Mary Campbell Scarlett; one *s* one *d*. *Educ:* Davenant Foundn Sch.; LSE (BCom). Served with RA in Britain, India and Burma, 1942–45 (Captain). Head of Econ. Intell. Dept, Prudential Assce Co., Ltd, 1948–58; Sen. Lectr, then Reader, in Business Finance, LSE, 1958–65; Member: Council, Consumers' Assoc., 1958–63; Central Adv. Council on Primary Educn (Plowden Cttee), 1963–65; Business Studies Cttee, SSRC, 1967–68, and Univ. Grants Cttee, 1968–69; Reserve Pension Bd, 1973–75; HM Treasury Inquiry into Value of Pensions, 1980; Special Adviser to: H of C Treasury and Civil Service Cttee, 1980–81; DoI, 1980–81. Gp Economic Advr, Barclays Bank, 1975–88. Director: Economist Newspaper, 1969–71; Abbey National Building Soc., 1975–83. Mem., Retail Prices Adv. Cttee, 1985–89. Trustee, IEA, 1975–98 (Chm., 1995–98); Trustee and Treas., Inst. for Study of Civil Soc., 2000–. Gov., The Hall Sch., 1987–95. *Publications:* The Economic Background to Investment, 1959; Disclosure in Company Accounts, 1963; Management Education in the 1970's, 1970; various papers in econ. and financial jls. *Address:* 33 Dartmouth Park Avenue, NW5 1JL. *T:* (020) 7485 7315; *e-mail:* rose@nws.u-net.com. *Club:* Reform.

ROSE, Gen. Sir (Hugh) Michael, KCB 1994; CBE 1986; DSO 1995; QGM 1981; Adjutant General, 1995–97; Aide de Camp General to the Queen, 1995–97; *b* 5 Jan. 1940; *s* of late Lt-Col Hugh Vincent Rose, IA and of Mrs Barbara Phoebe Masters (*née* Allcard); *m* 1968, Angela Raye Shaw; two *s*. *Educ:* Cheltenham College; St Edmund Hall, Oxford (2nd Cl. Hons PPE; Hon. Fellow, 1995); Staff College; RCDS. Commissioned Gloucestershire Regt, TAVR, 1959; RAFVR, 1962; Coldstream Guards, 1964; served Germany, Aden, Malaysia, Gulf States, Dhofar, N Ireland (despatches), Falkland Is (despatches); BM 16 Para. Bde, 1973–75; CO 22 SAS Regt, 1979–82; Comd 39 Inf. Bde, 1983–85; Comdt, Sch. of Infantry, 1987–88; DSF, 1988–89; GOC NE Dist and Comdr 2nd Inf. Div., 1989–91; Comdt, Staff Coll., 1991–93; Comdr, UK Field Army and Insp. Gen. of TA, 1993–94; Comdr, UN Protection Force, Bosnia-Herzegovina, 1994–95; Dep. C-in-C, Land Comd, 1995. Col, Coldstream Guards, 1999–. Hon. Col, Oxford Univ. OTC, 1995–2000. Hon. DLitt Nottingham, 1999. Comdr, Legion of Honour (France), 1995. *Publication:* Fighting for Peace, 1998. *Recreations:* sailing, ski-ing. *Address:* c/o Regimental HQ Coldstream Guards, Wellington Barracks, Birdcage Walk, SW1E 6HQ. *Club:* Special Forces (Pres.).

ROSE, Jack, CMG 1963; MBE 1954; DFC 1942; *b* 18 Jan. 1917; *s* of late Charles Thomas Rose; *m* 1st, 1940, Margaret Valerie (*d* 1966), 2nd *d* of late Alec Stuart Budd; two *s*; 2nd, 1967, Beryl Elizabeth, 4th *d* of late A. S. Budd. *Educ:* Shooters Hill School; London University. Served RAF, 1938–46 (Wing Commander); served in fighter, fighter/bomber and rocket firing sqdns; France, 1940 and 1944; Battle of Britain; Burma, 1944–45. Joined Colonial Administrative Service, N Rhodesia, 1947; Private Secretary to Governor of Northern Rhodesia, 1950–53; seconded to Colonial Office, 1954–56; Administrative posts, Northern Rhodesia, 1956–60; Administrator, Cayman Islands (seconded), 1960–63; Assistant to Governor, British Guiana, 1963–64 (Actg Governor and Dep. Governor for periods). Member: Professional and Technical 'A' Whitley Council for Health Services, 1965–75 (Chm., 1973–75); Gen. Whitley Council for Health Services, 1973–75. Secretary: Chartered Soc. of Physiotherapy, 1965–75; Salmon and Trout Assoc., 1975–79 (Vice-Pres., 1980–). Chm., Burford Charity Trustees, 1994–. *Recreation:* writing. *Address:* The Little House, 178 The Hill, Burford, Oxon OX18 4QY. *T:* (01993) 822553.

ROSE, James; *see* Rose, A. J.

ROSE, Jeffrey David, CBE 1991; Chairman of the Royal Automobile Club, 1981–98 (Deputy Chairman, 1979–81); *b* 2 July 1931; *s* of late Samuel and Daisy Rose; *m* 1st, 1958, Joyce (*née* Clompus) (marr. diss.); one *s* two *d*; 2nd, 1999, Helga Maria Wiederschwinger Dusauzay. *Educ:* Southend High Sch.; London Sch. of Econs and Pol. Science. Nat. Service, RA, 1950–52 (Lieut). Chm., RAC Motoring Services, 1980–98; Vice Chm., British Road Fedn, 1982–98; Vice President: Fédn Internationale de l'Automobile, 1983–93 and 1994–96 (Hon. Vice Pres., 1996–); Inst. of the Motor Industry, 1992–98; RAC Motor Sports Council, 1994–98; Chm., Commonwealth Motoring Conf., 1988–98; Member: Council, Inst. of Advanced Motorists, 1987–94; Adv. Council, Prince's Youth Business Trust, 1992–2000. Chm., Trustees, British Brain and Spine Foundn, 1995–; Trustee, Brooklands Mus., 1991–. FIMI 1989. Liveryman, Worshipful Co. of Coachmakers and Coach Harness Makers, 1981– (Mem. Court, 1995–). *Recreations:* walking, dining, music. *Address:* Albany, Piccadilly, W1V 9RP. *Clubs:* Royal Automobile (Life Mem.; Vice-Pres., 1998–), Brooks's, MCC.

ROSE, John Edward Victor, FRAeS; Chief Executive, Rolls-Royce, since 1996; *b* 9 Oct. 1952; *s* of (Wentworth) Victor Rose and late Doris Rose (*née* Bridge); *m* 1979, Emma Felicity Granville; two *s* one *d*. *Educ:* Charterhouse Sch.; Univ. of St Andrews (MA Hons Psychology). FRAeS 1993. Board Mem., Rolls-Royce, 1992–. *Recreations:* ski-ing, sailing, diving, golf, theatre, arts. *Address:* Rolls-Royce plc, 65 Buckingham Gate, SW1E 6AT. *T:* (020) 7222 9020. *Club:* Hurlingham.

ROSE, John Raymond; Clerk of Standing Committees, House of Commons, 1987–91; *b* 22 April 1934; *s* of late Arthur Raymond Rose and Edith Mary Rose, Merstham, Surrey and Minehead, Somerset; *m* 1st, 1961, Vivienne (marr. diss. 1991), *d* of late Charles Dillon Seabrooke, IoW; one *s* one *d*; 2nd, 1991, Dr Betty Webb, *d* of late Ernest Julian Webb, Statesville, NC, USA. *Educ:* Marlborough; Trinity Hall, Cambridge (Major Scholar in Classics; Law Tripos 1st Cl. Hons, Pts I and II). 2nd Lieut DCLI, Belize and Jamaica, 1953–55. Clerk's Department, House of Commons, 1958–91: Clerk of Select Cttees on Estimates (Sub-Cttee), Public Accounts, Violence in the Family, Race Relations, Abortion, European Community Secondary Legislation, Foreign Affairs, 1959–87. Vis. Kenan Prof., Meredith Coll., NC, USA, 1981. Fellow, Industry and Parlt Trust, 1987. Freeman, City of London, 1959; Liveryman, Salters' Co., 1959. *Recreations:* travel, walking, cycling, gardening, bridge. *Address:* 220 Hillcrest Road, Raleigh, NC 27605, USA. *T:* (919) 8283443; 4 St James's Square, Bath BA1 2TR. *T:* (01225) 481115.

ROSE, Joyce Dora Hester, CBE 1981; JP, DL; Chairman, Council and Executive, Magistrates' Association, 1990–93; *b* 14 Aug. 1929; *d* of late Abraham (Arthur) Woolf and Rebecca Woolf (*née* Simpson); *m* 1953, Cyril Rose; two *s* one *d*. *Educ:* King Alfred Sch., London; Queen's Coll., London; in N America. Chm., Watford Magistrates' Court, 1990–94 (Dep. Chm., Juvenile Panel, 1968–91, Family Proceedings (formerly Domestic) Panel, 1982–99 (Chm., 1979–82)); Member: Herts Magistrates' Courts Cttee, 1973–95; Herts Probation Cttee, 1971–95. Pres., 1979–80, Chm., 1982–83, Liberal Party; Pres. and Chm., Women's Liberal Fedn, 1972, 1973; Mem., Lib Dem Federal Appeals Panel, 1994–. Mem., Women's Nat. Commn, 1981–87 (Mem. Exec., 1985–87); former Mem., Nat. Exec., UK Cttee for UNICEF (Vice-Chm., 1968–70). Board Member: Apex Trust, 1994–; Herts Care Trust, 1995–99; SW Herts Hospice Charitable Trust (Peace Hospice), 1996–; Herts Family Mediation Service, 1996–. Hon. LLD Hertfordshire, 1992. JP Herts, 1963; DL Herts, 1990. *Address:* 2 Oak House, 101 Ducks Hill Road, Northwood, Middx HA6 2WQ. *T:* (01923) 821385, *Fax:* (01923) 840515. *Club:* National Liberal.

ROSE, Ven. Judith; *see* Rose, Ven. K. J.

ROSE, Judith Ann; *see* Goffe, J. A.

ROSE, Sir Julian (Day), 4th Bt *cr* 1909, of Hardwick House, and 5th Bt *cr* 1872, of Montreal; *b* 3 March 1947; 3rd and *o* surv. *s* of Sir Charles Henry Rose, 3rd Bt and of Phoebe, *d* of 2nd Baron Phillimore (*d* 1947); *S* father, 1966, and cousin, Sir Francis Cyril Rose, 4th Bt, 1979; *m* 1976, Elizabeth Goode Johnson, Columbus, Ohio, USA; one *s* one *d*. *Educ:* Stanbridge School. Actor/asst dir, Players' Theatre of New England, 1973–79; Co-founder, Inst. for Creative Develt, Antwerp, 1978–83. Co-ordinator, Organic Farming practice, Hardwick Estate, 1984–. Chm., Assoc. of Rural Businesses in Oxfordshire, 1995–; Member: Council, Soil Assoc., 1984–; Agricl Panel, Intermediate Technology Develt Gp, 1984–87; Bd, UK Register of Organic Food Standards, Food From Britain, 1987–90; BBC Rural and Agricl Affairs Adv. Cttee, 1991–; Adv. Cttee, Food and Farming, Thames Valley Univ., 1994–; Agricl and Rural Economy Cttee, CLA, 1999–. Rural Economy Advr, SE of England Develt Agency, 1999–. Trustee: SAFE Alliance, 1995–; Dartington Trust, 1996–2000. Agricl Correspondent, Environment Now, 1989–90. *Publication:* (contrib.) Town and Country, 1999. *Heir:* *s* Lawrence Michael Rose, *b* 6 Oct. 1986. *Address:* Hardwick House, Whitchurch-on-Thames, Oxfordshire RG8 7RB.

ROSE, Ven. (Kathleen) Judith; Archdeacon of Tonbridge, 1996–Aug. 2002; *b* 14 June 1937; *d* of Cuthbert Arthur Rose and Margaret Rose; *m* 1991, David Ernest Gwyer (*d* 2000); two step *d*. *Educ:* Sexey's Grammar Sch., Blackford; Seale Hayne Agricl Coll. (NDD 1960); St Michael's House Theol Coll., Oxford (DipTh 1966); London Bible Coll. (BD(Hons)). Agriculture, 1953–64; Parish Worker, Rodbourne Cheney Parish Church, 1966–71; ordained deaconess, 1976, deacon, 1987, priest, 1994; Parish Worker, then Deaconess, St George's Church, Leeds, 1973–81; Chaplain, Bradford Cathedral, 1981–85; Minister responsible for St Paul's Parkwood, Gillingham, 1986–90; Chaplain to Bishop of Rochester, 1990–95. Rural Dean of Gillingham, 1988–90. *Publications:* Sunday Learning for All Ages, 1982; (contrib.) Women in Ministry, 1991; (contrib.) Women Priests: the first years, 1996; (contrib.) A Time and A Season, 2000. *Recreations:* gardening, walking, home-making. *Address:* (until Aug. 2002) 3 The Ridings, Blackhurst Lane, Tunbridge Wells, Kent TN2 4RU. *T:* (01892) 520660; (from Aug. 2002) 4 Glebelands Close, Cheddar, Somerset BS27 3XP.

ROSE, Kenneth Vivian, CBE 1997; FRSL; writer; *b* 15 Nov. 1924; *s* of Dr J. Rose, MB, ChB. *Educ:* Repton Sch.; New Coll., Oxford (scholar; MA). Served Welsh Guards, 1943–46; attached Phantom, 1945. Asst master, Eton Coll., 1948; Editorial Staff, Daily Telegraph, 1952–60; founder and writer of Albany column, Sunday Telegraph, 1961–97. *Publications:* Superior Person: a portrait of Curzon and his circle in late Victorian England, 1969; The Later Cecils, 1975; William Harvey: a monograph, 1978; King George V, 1983 (Wolfson Award for History, 1983; Whitbread Award for Biography, 1983; Yorkshire Post Biography of the Year Award, 1984); Kings, Queens and Courtiers: intimate portraits of the Royal House of Windsor, 1985; (contrib.) Founders and Followers: literary lectures on the London Library, 1992; contribs to Dictionary of National Biography. *Address:* 38 Brunswick Gardens, W8 4AL. *T:* (020) 7221 4783. *Clubs:* Beefsteak, Pratt's.

ROSE, Col Lewis John, OBE 1990; Vice Lord-Lieutenant of Bedfordshire, 1991–98; *b* 18 Aug. 1935; *s* of Reginald George Rose and Mary Agnes Rose; *m* 1st, 1964, Aileen Beth Robertson (marr. diss. 1974); two *s*; 2nd, 1978, Gillian Mary King; one step *s* one step *d*. *Educ:* Bedford Sch.; College of Law. Served RA, 1954–56; Beds Yeomanry, later Herts & Beds Yeomanry, 1956–67. In practice as solicitor, 1962–. Comdt, Beds ACF, 1976–90; Chm., Beds TA&VR Cttee, 1991–94; Vice Chm. (Mil.), E Anglia TA&VRA, 1994–99. President: Beds Small-bore Shooting Assoc., 1992–; Bedford Distict Scout Council, 1975–. DL Bedfordshire, 1981. *Recreations:* shooting, rowing (Pres., Bedford Rowing Club, 1988–91). *Address:* 11 Woodlands Close, Cople, Beds MK44 3UE. *T:* (01234) 838210. *Club:* Leander (Henley on Thames).

ROSE, Mark Willson; Agent General for British Columbia in London, 1992–95; *b* 5 March 1924; *s* of Mark C. Rose and Mildred Willson; *m* 1947, Isabel Phillips; three *d*. *Educ:* Univ. of British Columbia (BScA); Univ. of Western Washington, USA (MEd). Teacher in Okanagan, 1949; Dist Supervisor for New Westminster schools, 1958; University of British Columbia: Faculty of Educn, 1962 (Mem. Policy Council); Mem. Bd of Alumni Assoc. Exec.; Professor Emeritus 1983. Alderman, Coquitlam, 1966–67; MP (NDP) for Fraser Valley W, then Mission-Port Moody, 1968–83; Mem., standing and special cttees, incl. culture, communications, agriculture, the Constitution and alternative energy, to 1978; Chm., NDP Parly Caucus, 1979–83; MLA (NDP) for Coquitlam-Moody, British Columbia, 1983–91; Opposition House Leader, 1986–91; Mem., parly cttee to review and reform Standing Orders; Mem., Speaker's Bd of Internal Economy. Mem., Rotary Club, London. Freeman, City of London, 1993. *Recreations:* music, travel, handyman, renovations, landscaping. *Clubs:* Royal Over-Seas League (Hon.); University of British Columbia Faculty.

ROSE, Gen. Sir Michael; *see* Rose, Gen. Sir H. M.

ROSE, Norman John, FRICS, FCIArb; Member, Lands Tribunal, since 1998; *b* 22 Oct. 1943; *s* of late Jack Rose and Margaret Rose (*née* de Groot); *m* 1968, Helena de Mesquita; three *s*. *Educ:* Christ's Coll., Finchley; Coll. of Estate Management (BSc (Est. Man.); Valuation Prize). FRICS 1976; FCIArb 1977. Gerald Eve & Co., 1964–71; Partner, de Groot Collis, 1971–91; Dir of Valuation, Chesterton, 1992–98. *Address:* Lands Tribunal, 48/49 Chancery Lane, WC2A 1JR. *T:* (020) 7947 7200.

ROSE, Paul (Bernard); HM Coroner, London Southern District, since 1988; *b* 26 Dec. 1935; *s* of Arthur and Norah Rose; *m* 1957, Eve Marie-Thérèse; two *s* one *d*. *Educ:* Bury Gram. Sch.; Manchester Univ.; Gray's Inn. LLB (Hons) Manch., 1956; Barrister-at-Law, 1957. Legal and Secretarial Dept, Co-op. Union Ltd, 1957–60; Lectureship, Dept of Liberal Studies, Royal Coll. of Advanced Technology, Salford, 1961–63; Barrister-at-

Law, 1963–88; Asst Recorder (formerly Dep. Circuit Judge), 1974–88; Immigration Adjudicator (part-time), Hatton Cross, 1987– (Special Adjudicator, 1993–). MP (Lab) Manchester, Blackley, 1964–79; PPS to Minister of Transport, 1967–68; Opposition Front Bench Spokesman, Dept of Employment, 1970–72. Chairman: Parly Labour Home Office Group, 1968–70; Parly Labour Employment Group, 1974–79; Campaign for Democracy in Ulster, 1965–73. Delegate to Council of Europe and WEU, 1968–69; Vice-Chm., Labour Cttee for Europe, 1977–79. Mem., Campaign for Electoral Reform, 1975–. Founder Mem., SDP (Brent Area Sec., 1981–82). Chm., NW Regional Sports Council, 1966–68. Member: Coroners' Soc. (Pres., SE Coroners Soc., 1996–97); Medico-Legal Soc. AIL. *Publications:* Handbook to Industrial and Provident Societies Act, 1960; Guide to Weights and Measures Act 1963, 1965; The Manchester Martyrs, 1970; Backbencher's Dilemma, 1981; The Moonies' Unmasked, 1981; (jt) A History of the Fenian Movement in Britain, 1982; contrib. to many periodicals on political and legal topics. *Recreations:* sport, theatre, languages, travel. *Address:* Coroner's Court, Barclay Road, Croydon CR9 3NE.

ROSE, Prof. Richard, FBA 1992; Director and Professor of Public Policy, Centre for the Study of Public Policy, Strathclyde University, since 1976; *b* 9 April 1933; *o s* of Charles Imse and late Mary Conely Rose, St Louis, Mo, USA; *m* 1956, Rosemary J., *o d* of late James Kenny, Whitstable, Kent; two *s* one *d*. *Educ:* Clayton High Sch., Mo; Johns Hopkins Univ., BA (Double distinction, Phi Beta Kappa) comparative drama, 1953; London Sch. of Economics, 1953–54; Oxford University, 1957–60, DPhil (Lincoln and Nuffield Colls). Political public relations, Mississippi Valley, 1954–55; Reporter, St Louis Post-Dispatch, 1955–57; Lecturer in Govt, Univ. of Manchester, 1961–66; Prof. of Politics, Strathclyde Univ., 1966–82. Consultant Psephologist, The Times, Independent Television, Daily Telegraph, STV, UTV etc., 1964–. American SSRC Fellow, Stanford Univ., 1967; Vis. Lectr in Political Sociology, Cambridge Univ., 1967; Dir, ISSC European Summer Sch., 1973. Sec., Cttee on Political Sociology, Internat. Sociological Assoc., 1970–85; Founding Mem., European Consortium for Political Res., 1970; Member: US/UK Fulbright Commn, 1971–75; Eisenhower Fellowship Programme, 1971. Guggenheim Foundn Fellow, 1974; Visiting Scholar: Woodrow Wilson Internat. Centre, Washington DC, 1974; Brookings Inst., Washington DC, 1976; Amer. Enterprise Inst., Washington, 1980; Fiscal Affairs Dept, IMF, Washington, 1984; Visiting Professor: European Univ. Inst., Florence, 1977, 1978; Central European Univ., Prague, 1992–95; Instituto Ortega y Gasset, Madrid, 2000; Visitor, Japan Foundn, 1984; Hinkley Prof., Johns Hopkins Univ., 1987; Guest Prof., Wissenschaftsentrum, Berlin, 1988–90; Research Associate: UN Eur. Centre for Social Welfare Policy and Res., 1992–; Centre for Study of Democracy, Univ. of Westminster, 1998–2000; Fellow, Max-Planck Transformation Process Gp, Berlin, 1996; Wei Lun Prof., Chinese Univ. of Hong Kong, 2000. Ransone Lectr, Univ. of Alabama, 1990. Consultant Chm., NI Constitutional Convention, 1976; Mem., Home Office Working Party on Electoral Register, 1975–77. Co-Founder, British Politics Gp, 1974–; Convenor, Work Gp on UK Politics, Political Studies Assoc., 1976–88; Mem. Council, Internat. Political Science Assoc., 1976–82; Keynote Speaker, Aust. Inst. of Political Science, Canberra, 1978; Steering Cttee, World Values Study, 1995; Transparency Internat. Index Construction Cttee, 1998–. Technical Consultant: OECD; World Bank; Internat. Inst. for Democracy and Electoral Assistance, Stockholm; Council of Europe; Dir, ESRC (formerly SSRC) Res. Programme, Growth of Govt, 1982–86; UNDP Cons. to Pres. of Colombia, 1990, Scientific Advr, Paul Lazarsfeld Soc., Vienna, 1991–. Mem. Council, Scottish Opera Ltd, 1992–. Hon. Vice-Pres., Political Studies Assoc., UK, 1986. Editor, Jl of Public Policy, 1985–. Foreign Member: Finnish Acad. of Science and Letters, 1985; Amer. Acad. of Arts and Scis, 1994. Amex Internat. Econs Prize, 1992; Lasswell Award in Public Policy, Policy Studies Orgn, USA, 1999; Lifetime Achievement Award, UK Pol Studies Assoc., 2000. Subject of prog. in Man of Action series, BBC Radio 3, 1974. *Publications:* The British General Election of 1959 (with D. E. Butler), 1960; Must Labour Lose? (with Mark Abrams), 1960; Politics in England, 1964, 5th edn 1989; (ed) Studies in British Politics, 1966, 3rd edn 1976; Influencing Voters, 1967; (ed) Policy Making in Britain, 1969; People in Politics, 1970; (ed, with M. Dogan) European Politics, 1971; Governing Without Consensus: an Irish perspective, 1971; (with T. Mackie) International Almanack of Electoral History, 1974, 3rd edn 1991; (ed) Electoral Behavior: a comparative handbook, 1974; (ed) Lessons from America, 1974; The Problem of Party Government, 1974; (ed) The Management of Urban Change in Britain and Germany, 1974; Northern Ireland: a time of choice, 1976; Managing Presidential Objectives, 1976; (ed) The Dynamics of Public Policy, 1976; (ed, with D. Kavanagh) New Trends in British Politics, 1977; (ed with J. Wiatr) Comparing Public Policies, 1977; What is Governing?: Purpose and Policy in Washington, 1978; (ed, with G. Hermet and A. Rouquié) Elections without Choice, 1978; (with B. G. Peters) Can Government Go Bankrupt?, 1978; (ed with W. B. Gwyn) Britain: progress and decline, 1980; Do Parties Make a Difference?, 1980, 2nd edn 1984; (ed) Challenge to Governance, 1980; (ed) Electoral Participation, 1980; (ed with E. Suleiman) Presidents and Prime Ministers, 1980; Understanding the United Kingdom, 1982; (with I. McAllister) United Kingdom Facts, 1982; (ed with P. Madgwick) The Territorial Dimension in United Kingdom Politics, 1982; (ed with E. Page) Fiscal Stress in Cities, 1982; Understanding Big Government, 1984; (with I. McAllister) The Nationwide Competition for Votes, 1984; Public Employment in Western Nations, 1985; (with I. McAllister) Voters Begin to Choose, 1986; (with D. Van Mechelen) Patterns of Parliamentary Legislation, 1986; (ed with R. Shiratori) The Welfare State East and West, 1986; Ministers and Ministries, 1987; (with T. Karran) Taxation by Political Inertia, 1987; The Post-Modern President: the White House meets the world, 1988, 2nd edn 1991; Ordinary People in Public Policy, 1989; (with I. McAllister) The Loyalty of Voters: a lifetime learning model, 1990; Lesson-Drawing in Public Policy: a guide to learning across time and space, 1993; (with P. L. Davies) Inheritance in Public Policy: change without choice in Britain, 1994; What is Europe?, 1996; (with S. White and I. McAllister) How Russia Votes, 1997; (with W. Mishler and C. Haerpfer) Democracy and Its Alternatives, 1998; (ed jtly) A Society Transformed?: Hungary in time-space perspective, 1999; International Encyclopedia of Elections, 2000; The Prime Minister in a Shrinking World, 2001; contribs to academic journals in Europe and America; trans. into eighteen foreign languages; broadcasts on comparative politics and public policy. *Recreations:* architecture (historical, Britain; modern, America), music, writing. *Address:* Centre for the Study of Public Policy, University of Strathclyde, Livingstone Tower, Glasgow G1 1XH. *T:* (0141) 548 3217, *Fax:* (0141) 552 4711; Bennochy, 1 East Abercromby Street, Helensburgh, Argyll G84 7SP, *T:* (01436) 672164, *Fax:* (01436) 673125. *Clubs:* Reform; Cosmos (Washington DC).

ROSE, Prof. Steven Peter Russell, PhD; FIBiol; Professor of Biology and Director, Brain and Behaviour Research Group, Open University, since 1969; *b* 4 July 1938; *s* of Lionel Sydney Rose and Ruth Rose (*née* Waxman); *m* 1961, Hilary Ann Chantler; two *s*. *Educ:* Haberdashers' Aske's Sch., Hampstead; King's Coll., Cambridge (BA); Inst. of Psychiatry, Univ. of London (PhD). FIBiol 1970. Beit Meml and Guinness Res. Fellow, New Coll., Oxford, 1961–63; NIH Res. Fellow, Istituto Superiore di Sanita, Rome, 1963–64; MRC Res. Staff, Dept of Biochem., Imperial Coll., London, 1964–69. Vis. Sen. Res. Fellow, ANU, 1977; Vis. Schol., Harvard Univ., 1980; Distinguished Res. Prof., Univ. of Minn, 1992; Osher Fellow, Exploratorium, San Francisco, 1993; Vis. Prof., UCL, 1999–; Jt Gresham Prof. of Physic, 1999–. FRSA 1980. Anokhin Medal, Russia, 1990; Sechenov Medal, Russia, 1992; Ariens Kappers Medal, Netherlands Royal Acad. of Sci., Amsterdam, 1999. *Publications:* The Chemistry of Life, 1966, 3rd edn 1991; (with Hilary Rose) Science and Society, 1969; The Conscious Brain, 1973; No Fire No Thunder, 1984; (jtly) Not in our Genes, 1984; The Making of Memory, 1992 (Science Book Prize, COPUS, 1993); Lifelines, 1997; (ed) From Brains to Consciousness?, 1998; (ed with Hilary Rose) Alas, Poor Darwin, 2000; numerous edited books, res. papers and scholarly articles. *Address:* Biology Department, The Open University, Milton Keynes MK7 6AA.

ROSE, Stuart Alan Ransom; Chief Executive, Arcadia plc, since 2000; *b* 17 March 1949; *s* of Harry Ransom Rose and Margaret Ransom Rose; *m* 1973, Jennifer Cook; one *s* one *d*. *Educ:* St. Joseph's Convent, Dar-es-Salaam; Bootham Sch., York. With Marks & Spencer plc, 1971–89, Commercial Exec., Europe; Chief Executive: Multiples, Burton Gp plc, 1989–97; Argos plc, 1998; Booker plc, 1998–2000; Iceland Group plc, 2000. *Recreations:* flying, wine. *Address:* (office) Colegrave House, 70 Berners Street, W1T 3NL. *T:* (020) 7927 1801. *Club:* Groucho.

ROSE, William Michael; His Honour Judge Rose; a Circuit Judge, since 1998; *b* 12 July 1949; *s* of Laurence Melville Rose and Anita Rose; partner since 1981, Susan Lawe. *Educ:* Haberdashers' Aske's Sch., Elstree; Univ. of Southampton (LLB Hons). Called to the Bar, Middle Temple, 1972; Asst Recorder, 1992–94; a Recorder, 1994–98. Dir of Studies, Judicial Studies Bd, 2002–. Mem., Bd of Examrs, Council of Legal Educn/Inns of Court Sch. of Law, 1990–. Hon. Vice Pres., Travel and Tourism Lawyers Assoc. Editl Advr, ICSL Manual on Civil Litigation, annually, 1990–; Mem. Editl Bd, Judicial Studies Board Jl, 2000–; Ed., Blackstone's Civil Practice, 2000–. *Publications:* Pleadings Without Tears, 1990, 5th edn 1999; (ed) Blackstone's Guide to the Civil Procedure Rules, 1999. *Recreations:* music, reading, computers, powerboating, photography. *Address:* c/o Wandsworth County Court, 76–78 Upper Richmond Road, Putney, SW15 2SU.

ROSEBERY, 7th Earl of, *cr* 1703; **Neil Archibald Primrose;** DL; Bt 1651; Viscount of Rosebery, Baron Primrose and Dalmeny, 1700; Viscount of Inverkeithing, Baron Dalmeny and Primrose, 1703; Baron Rosebery (UK), 1828; Earl of Midlothian, Viscount Mentmore, Baron Epsom, 1911; *b* 11 Feb. 1929; *o* surv. *s* of 6th Earl of Rosebery, KT, PC, DSO, MC, and Eva Isabel Marian (Eva Countess of Rosebery, DBE) (*d* 1987), *d* of 2nd Baron Aberdare; *S* father, 1974; *m* 1955, Alison Mary Deirdre, *d* of late Ronald William Reid, MS, FRCS; one *s* four *d*. *Educ:* Stowe; New Coll., Oxford. DL Midlothian, 1960. *Heir: s* Lord Dalmeny, *qv*. *Address:* Dalmeny House, South Queensferry, West Lothian EH30 9TQ.

ROSEN, Charles; pianist; *b* New York, 5 May 1927; *s* of Irwin Rosen and Anita Gerber. *Educ:* studied piano with Mr and Mrs Moriz Rosenthal; Princeton Univ. (PhD). Début, NY, 1951. His many recordings include: first complete recording of Debussy Etudes, 1951; late keyboard works of Bach, 1969; last six Beethoven Sonatas, 1970; Schumann piano works; Diabelli Variations; also works by Liszt, Elliott Carter, Boulez, etc. Eliot Norton Prof. of Poetry, Harvard Univ., 1980; George Eastman Vis. Prof., Oxford Univ., 1987–88; Prof. of Music, Univ. of Chicago, 1991–96. Hon. MusD: Trinity Coll., Dublin, 1976; Cambridge, 1992; Hon. DMus Durham, 1980. *Publications:* The Classical Style, 1971; Schoenberg, 1976; Sonata Forms, 1980; (with H. Zerner) Romanticism and Realism: the mythology of nineteenth century art, 1984; The Romantic Generation, 1995. *Recreations:* music, books. *Address:* c/o Owen/White Management, Top Floor, 59 Lansdowne Place, Hove, East Sussex BN3 1FL. *T:* (01273) 727127, *Fax:* (01273) 328128.

ROSEN, Rabbi Jeremy, PhD; Professor of Jewish Studies, since 1991, and President, since 1994, Faculty for Comparative Study of Religions, Wilrijk, Belgium; Principal, Yakar Study Centre, London, since 1999; *b* 11 Sept. 1942; *s* of Rabbi Kopul Rosen and Bella Rosen; *m* 1st, 1971, Vera Giuditta Zippel (marr. diss. 1987); two *s* two *d*; 2nd, 1988, Suzanne Kaszirer. *Educ:* Carmel Coll.; Pembroke Coll., Cambridge (MA); Mir Academy, Jerusalem. Minister, Bulawayo Hebrew Congregation, Rhodesia, 1966; Minister, Giffnock Hebrew Congregation, Scotland, 1968–71; Headmaster, 1971–84, Principal, 1983–84, Carmel Coll; Minister, Western Synagogue, subseq. (following amalgamation in 1990 with Marble Arch Synagogue) Marble Arch Western Synagogue, 1985–93. Chief Rabbi's Rep. on Inter-Faith Affairs, 1987–91. Mem. Bd, Centre Européen Juif d'Information, Brussels, 1991–. Trustee, Yakar Educn Foundn, 1990–2000. *Publication:* Exploding Myths that Jews Believe, 2001. *Address:* 2 Egerton Gardens, NW4 4BA. *T:* (020) 8202 5551.

ROSEN, Prof. Michael, CBE 1990; FRCA; FRCOG; FRCS; Consultant Anaesthetist, South Glamorgan Health Authority, since 1961; Hon. Professor, University of Wales College of Medicine, 1986–93; President, College of Anaesthetists, 1988–91 (Dean of the Faculty of Anaesthetists, Royal College of Surgeons, 1988); *b* 17 Oct. 1927; *s* of Israel Rosen and Lily Hyman; *m* 1955, Sally Cohen; two *s* one *d*. *Educ:* Dundee High Sch. (Dux, 1944); St Andrews Univ. (MB ChB 1949). FRCA (FFARCS 1957); FRCOG 1989; FRCS 1994. House appts, Bolton, Portsmouth and Bradford, 1949–52; served RAMC, 1952–54; Registrar Anaesthetist, Royal Victoria Infirmary, Newcastle upon Tyne, 1954–57; Sen. Registrar, Cardiff, 1957–60; Fellow, Case Western Reserve Univ., Ohio, 1960–61. Member: GMC, 1989–; Clinical Standards Adv. Gp, 1991–94. Mem. Bd, College (formerly Faculty) of Anaesthetists, RCS, 1978–94; Pres., Assoc. of Anaesthetists of GB and Ire, 1986–88 (Mem. Council, 1972–91; formerly Sec. and Treasurer); Founder Academician, European Acad. of Anaesthesiol., 1972 (Treas., 1985–91; Hon. Mem., 1996); Chm., Obstetric Anaesthesia Cttee, World Fedn of Socs of Anaesthesia, 1980–88; Exec. Officer and Treas., World Fedn of Socs of Anesthesiologists, 1992–2000. Hon. Mem., French and Australian Socs of Anaesthetists; Hon. FFARCSI 1990; Hon. Fellow, Acad. of Medicine, Malaysia, 1989. Hon. LLD Dundee, 1996. Sir Ivan Magill Gold Medal, Assoc. of Anaesthetists, 1993. *Publications:* Percutaneous Cannulation of Great Veins, 1981, 2nd edn 1992; Obstetric Anaesthesia and Analgesia: safer practice, 1982; Patient-Controlled Analgesia, 1984; Tracheal Intubation, 1985; Awareness and Pain in General Anaesthesia, 1987; Ambulatory Anaesthesia, 1991; Quality Measures for the Emergency Services, 2001. *Recreations:* family, reading, opera. *Address:* 45 Hollybush Road, Cardiff CF23 6TZ. *T:* and *Fax:* (029) 2075 3893; *e-mail:* mirosen@compuserve.com.

ROSEN, Michael Wayne, PhD; poet and author; BBC Radio presenter, since 1989; *b* 7 May 1946; *s* of Harold Rosen and Connie Ruby Isakofsky; *m* 1st, 1976, Susanna Steele (marr. diss. 1987); one *s* (and one *s* decd); 2nd, 1987, Geraldine Clark (marr. diss. 1997); one *s*, and two step *d*; one *d* with Emma-Louise Williams. *Educ:* Wadham Coll., Oxford (BA); Reading Univ. (MA); Univ. of N London (PhD 1997). BBC general trainee, 1969–73; freelance, 1973–, incl. BBC Radio 4, World Service, Radio 3; Word of Mouth, Radio 4, 1998–. Sunday Times NUS Drama Fest. Award for Best New Play, 1968; Glenfiddich Award for Best Radio Programme on subject of food, 1996; Eleanor Farjeon Award for Distinguished Services to Children's Literature, 1997. *Publications:* include: Backbone, 1968; Mind Your Own Business, 1974; Quick, Let's Get Out of Here, 1983;

Don't put Mustard in the Custard, 1985; The Hypnotiser, 1988; We're Going on a Bear Hunt, 1989 (Smarties Award for Best Children's Book of Year, 1990); You Wait Till I'm Older Than You, 1996; Michael Rosen's Book of Nonsense, 1997; (ed) Classic Poetry, 1998; Rover, 1999; Centrally Heated Knickers, 2000; Shakespeare, His Work and His World, 2001. *Recreations:* Arsenal Football Club, politics, general arts. *Address:* c/o Peters Fraser & Dunlop, 503/4 The Chambers, Chelsea Harbour, SW10 0XF. *T:* (020) 7344 1000.

ROSEN, Murray Hilary; QC 1993; a Recorder, since 2000; *b* 26 Aug. 1953; *s* of Joseph and Mercia Rosen; *m* 1975, Lesley Samuels; one *s* three *d. Educ:* St Paul's Sch.; Trinity Coll., Cambridge (MA). FCIArb 1999. Called to the Bar, Inner Temple, 1976; Mem., Lincoln's Inn *ad eundem.* Chm., Bar Sports Law Gp, 1998–. *Recreations:* books, music, cricket. *Address:* 11 Stone Buildings, Lincoln's Inn, WC2A 3TG. *T:* (020) 7831 6381.

ROSENBERG, Michael Anthony; a District Judge (Magistrates' Courts) (formerly Provincial Stipendiary Magistrate), South Yorkshire, since 1993; *b* 6 March 1943; *s* of late Harry Rosenberg and Gertrude Rosenberg (*née* Silver); *m* 1969, Gillian Anne Wolff; two *s. Educ:* Hymers Coll., Hull; Law Soc. Joined Myer Wolff & Co., Hull, 1961: articled clerk, 1963–68; qualified as solicitor, 1969; Asst Solicitor, 1970–73; Jt Sen. Partner, 1973–93. *Recreations:* sport, gardening, music, humour. *Address:* The Old School House, Main Road, Scalby, Gilberdyke, E Yorks HU15 2UU. *T:* (Barnsley Magistrates' Court) (01226) 320020.

ROSENBERG, Pierre Max; Member, Académie française, since 1995; President-Director, Louvre Museum, Paris, 1994–2001; *b* Paris, 13 April 1936; *s* of Charles Rosenberg and Gertrude (*née* Nassauer); *m* 1981, Béatrice de Rothschild. *Educ:* Lycée Charlemagne, Paris; Law Faculty, Paris (Licence); Louvre Sch., Paris (Dip.). Chief Curator, Dept of Paintings, Louvre Mus., 1982–94. Member: Hist. of French Art Soc. (Pres., 1982–84); French Hist. of Art Cttee (Pres., 1984–96). *Publications:* Chardin, 1979, 2nd edn 1999; Peyron, 1983; Watteau, 1984; Fragonard, 1987; La Hyre, 1988; Les frères Le Nain, 1993; Poussin, 1994; Watteau: catalogue raisonné des dessins, 1996; Georges de la Tour, 1997; exhibn catalogues. *Address:* 35 rue de Vaugirard, 75006 Paris, France.

ROSENBERG, Richard Morris; Chairman and Chief Executive Officer, BankAmerica Corporation and Bank of America NT&SA, 1990–96; *b* 21 April 1930; *s* of Charles Rosenberg and Betty (*née* Peck); *m* 1956, Barbara C. Cohen; two *s. Educ:* Suffolk Univ. (BS 1956); Golden Gate Univ. (MBA 1962; LLB 1966). Served from Ensign to Lieut, USNR, 1953–59. Publicity Assistant, Crocker-Anglo Bank, San Francisco, 1959–62; Wells Fargo Bank: Banking Services Officer, 1962–65; Asst Vice Pres., 1965–68; Vice Pres., Marketing Dept, 1968; Vice Pres., Dir of Marketing, 1969; Sen. Vice Pres., Marketing and Advertising Div., 1970–75; Exec. Vice Pres., 1975–80; Vice Chm., 1980–83; Vice Chm., Crocker Nat. Corp., 1983–85; Pres., Chief Op. Officer and Dir, Seafirst Corp., 1986–87; Pres. and Chief Op. Officer, Seattle-First Nat. Bank, 1985–87; Vice Chm., BankAmerica Corp., 1987–90. Director: Airborne Express; Northrop Corp.; SBC Communications; past Chm., Mastercard Internat. Member: Bd of Dirs, Marin Ecumenical Housing Assoc.; Bd of Trustees, CIT. Mem., State Bar of Calif. Jewish. *Recreations:* tennis, avid reader, history. *Address:* BankAmerica Corporation, 555 California Street CA5-705-11-01, San Francisco, CA 94104, USA. *T:* (415) 9537963. *Clubs:* Rainier (Seattle); Hillcrest (Los Angeles).

ROSENBLUM, Prof. Robert; Professor of Fine Arts, New York University, USA, since 1967; Curator, Guggenheim Museum, New York, since 1996; *b* 24 July 1927; *m* 1977, Jane Kaplowitz; one *s* one *d. Educ:* Queens Coll., Flushing, NY (BA); Yale Univ. (MA); New York Univ. (PhD); Oxford Univ. (MA). Prof. of Art and Archaeology, Princeton Univ., USA, 1956–66; Slade Prof. of Fine Art, Oxford Univ., 1971–72. Fellow, Amer. Acad. of Arts and Scis, 1984. Frank Jewett Mather Award for Art Criticism, 1981. *Publications:* Cubism and Twentieth-Century Art, 1960; Transformations in Late Eighteenth Century Art, 1967; Jean-Auguste-Dominique Ingres, 1967; Frank Stella, 1971; Modern Painting and the Northern Romantic Tradition: Friedrich to Rothko, 1975; French Painting, 1774–1830 (exhibn catalogue), 1975; Andy Warhol: Portraits of the Seventies, 1979; (with H. W. Janson) Nineteenth Century Art, 1984; The Dog in Art from Rococo to Post-Modernism, 1988; The Romantic Child from Runge to Sendak, 1988; Paintings in the Musée d'Orsay, 1989; The Jeff Koons Handbook, 1992; (with H. Geldzahler) Andy Warhol Portraits, 1993; Mel Ramos: Pop images, 1994; The Paintings of August Strindberg: the structure of chaos, 1995; On Modern American Art, 1999; 1900: art at the crossroads, 2000; articles in learned jls: Art Bulletin; Burlington Magazine; Jl of the Warburg and Courtauld Institutes; La Revue de l'Art, etc. *Address:* Department of Fine Arts, New York University, New York, NY 10003, USA. *T:* (212) 9988180.

ROSENBROCK, Prof. Howard Harry, DSc; FRS 1976; FREng, FIEE, FIChemE; Professor of Control Engineering, 1966–87, now Emeritus, Vice-Principal, 1977–79, University of Manchester Institute of Science and Technology, (UMIST); Science Research Council Senior Fellow, 1979–83; *b* 16 Dec. 1920; *s* of Henry Frederick Rosenbrock and Harriett Emily (*née* Gleed); *m* 1950, Cathryn June (*née* Press); one *s* two *d. Educ:* Slough Grammar Sch.; University Coll. London. BSc, PhD; Fellow 1978. Served War, RAFVR, 1941–46. GEC, 1947–48; Electrical Research Assoc., 1949–51; John Brown & Co., 1951–54; Constructors John Brown Ltd, 1954–62 (latterly Research Manager); ADR, Cambridge Univ., 1962–66. Mem. Council, IEE, 1966–70, Vice-Pres., 1977–78; Pres., Inst. of Measurement and Control, 1972–73; Member: Computer Bd, 1972–76; SRC Engineering Bd, 1976–78; SERC/ESRC Jt Cttee, 1981–85. Hon. FInstMC. Hon. DSc Salford, 1987. *Publications:* (with C. Storey) Computational Techniques for Chemical Engineers, 1966; (with C. Storey) Mathematics of Dynamical Systems, 1970; State-space and Multivariable Theory, 1970; Computer-aided Control System Design, 1974; (ed) Designing Human-centred Technology, 1989; Machines with a Purpose, 1990; contribs Proc. IEE, Trans IChemE, Proc. IEEE, Automatica, Internat. Jl Control, etc. *Recreations:* microscopy, photography, 17th and 18th Century literature. *Address:* Linden, Walford Road, Ross-on-Wye, Herefordshire HR9 5PQ. *T:* (01989) 565372, *Fax:* (01989) 767485.

ROSENFELD, Alfred John, CB 1981; Deputy Secretary, 1979–82, and Principal Finance Officer, 1976–82, Department of Transport; *b* 27 Feb. 1922; *s* of late Ernest Rosenfeld and late Annie Jeanette Rosenfeld (*née* Samson); *m* 1955, Mary Elisabeth (*née* Prudence); two *s* one *d. Educ:* Leyton County High Sch. Entered Public Trustee Office, 1938. Served War, Fleet Air Arm, 1942–46. Min. of Civil Aviation, 1947 (later, Min. of Transport, and Dept of Environment); Private Sec. to Jt Parliamentary Sec., 1958–59; Asst Sec., 1967; Under-Sec., 1972. Special Advr to Envmt Cttee, H of C, 1983–96. Mem., Shoreham Port Authority, 1983–92 (Dep. Chm., 1984–89; Chm., 1990–92). *Recreations:* chess, bridge, gardening. *Address:* 33 Elmfield Road, Chingford, E4 7HT. *T:* (020) 8529 8160.

ROSENKRANZ, Franklin Daniel, (Danny); Chief Executive, BOC Group plc, 1996–99; *b* 28 May 1945; *s* of Manfred and Hendel Rosenkranz; *m* 1990, Catherine Ann Eisenklam. *Educ:* UMIST (BSc Chem. Engrg 1967); Univ. of Waterloo, Canada (MASc 1969); Manchester Business Sch. (DipBA 1970). Plessey Radar, 1970–73; BOC, later BOC Group plc: Monitoring Manager, 1973–74; Business Manager, Industrial, Sparklets, 1974–76; UK Manager, 1976–78, Gen. Manager, 1978–81, BOC Sub Ocean Services; Business Develt Dir, 1982–83, Man. Dir, 1983–90, Edwards High Vacuum; Chief Exec., Vacuum Technology and Distribution Services, 1990–94; Man. Dir, 1994–96; Dir, 1994–99. Non-exec. Dir, 3i. *Recreations:* reading, music, theatre, sport, gardening.

ROSENTHAL, Jack Morris, CBE 1994; writer; *b* 8 Sept. 1931; *s* of Samuel and Leah Rosenthal; *m* 1973, Maureen Lipman, *qv*; one *s* one *d. Educ:* Colne Grammar School; Sheffield Univ. (BA Eng. Lit. and Lang). *Television:* writer of over 250 productions, incl. That Was the Week That Was, 1963; 129 episodes of Coronation Street, 1961–69; The Evacuees, 1975; Bar Mitzvah Boy, 1976; Ready When You Are, Mr McGill, 1976; Spend Spend Spend, 1977; The Knowledge, 1979; P'tang Yang Kipperbang, 1982; Mrs Capper's Birthday, 1985; London's Burning, 1986; Fools on the Hill, 1986; Day to Remember, 1986; And a Nightingale Sang, 1989; Bag Lady, 1989; Sleeping Sickness, 1991; 'Bye, 'Bye, Baby, 1992; Wide-Eyed and Legless, 1993; Moving Story, 1994; Eskimo Day, 1996; Cold Enough for Snow, 1997; *stage:* five plays, incl. Smash!, 1981; *films:* seven feature films including: Lucky Star, 1980; Yentl, 1983 (co-written with Barbra Streisand); The Chain, 1985; Captain Jack, 1999. Hon. MA Salford, 1994; Hon. LittD: Manchester, 1995; Sheffield, 1998. BAFTA Writer's Award, 1976; RTS Writer's Award, 1976; RTS Hall of Fame, 1993. *Publications:* (contrib.) The Television Dramatist, 1973; (anthology) First Love, 1984; numerous TV plays. *Recreations:* work, frying fish, polishing almost anything tarnished, playing the violin in enforced privacy, checking Manchester United's score, minute by minute, on teletext. *Address:* c/o Casarotto Ramsay Ltd, National House, 60–66 Wardour Street, W1V 3HP. *T:* (020) 7287 4450. *Club:* Dramatists'.

ROSENTHAL, Maureen Diane, (Mrs J. M. Rosenthal); *see* Lipman, M. D.

ROSENTHAL, Norman Leon; Exhibitions Secretary, Royal Academy of Arts, since 1977; *b* 8 Nov. 1944; *s* of Paul Rosenthal and Kate Zucker; *m* 1989, Manuela Beatriz Mena Marques, *d* of Francisco Mena and Manuela Marques de Mena, Madrid; two *d. Educ:* Westminster City Grammar School; University of Leicester. BA Hons History. Librarian, Thomas Agnew & Sons, 1966–68; Exhibitions Officer, Brighton Museum and Art Gallery, 1970–71; Exhibition Organiser, ICA, 1974–76; organiser of many exhibns including: Art into Society, ICA, 1974; A New Spirit in Painting, RA, 1981; Zeitgeist, West Berlin, 1982; German Art of the Twentieth Century, RA, London and Staatsgalerie, Stuttgart, 1985–86; Italian Art of the Twentieth Century, RA, 1989; Metropolis, Berlin, 1991; American Art in the Twentieth Century, Martin-Gropius Bau, Berlin, and RA, 1993; Charlotte Salomon, RA, 1998; Apocalypse, RA, 2000. TV and radio broadcasts on contemporary art. Member: Opera Bd, Royal Opera House, 1995–99; Bd, Palazzo Grassi, Venice, 1995–. Hon. Fellow RCA, 1987. Chevalier, l'Ordre des Arts et des Lettres, 1987; Cavaliere Ufficiale, Order of Merit (Italy), 1992; Cross, Order of Merit (Germany), 1993. *Recreations:* music, especially opera. *Address:* The Royal Academy of Arts, Burlington House, Piccadilly, W1V 0DS. *T:* (020) 7300 8000.

ROSENTHAL, Thomas Gabriel; publisher, writer and broadcaster; Chairman: André Deutsch Ltd, 1984–98 (joined as Joint Chairman and Joint Managing Director, 1984; Chief Executive, 1987–96); Bridgewater Press Ltd, since 1997; *b* 16 July 1935; *o s* of late Dr Erwin I. J. Rosenthal and Elisabeth Charlotte (*née* Marx); *m* Ann Judith Warnford-Davis; two *s. Educ:* Perse Sch., Cambridge; Pembroke Coll., Cambridge (Exhibnr, MA). Served RA, 1954–56, 2nd Lieut; subseq. Lieut Cambridgeshire Regt (TA). Joined Thames and Hudson Ltd, 1959; Man. Dir, Thames & Hudson Internat., 1966; joined Martin Secker & Warburg Ltd as Man. Dir, 1971; Dir, Heinemann Gp of Publishers, 1972–84; Man. Dir, William Heinemann International Ltd, 1979–84; Chairman: World's Work Ltd, 1979–84; Heinemann Zsolnay Ltd, 1979–84; William Heinemann Ltd, 1980–84; Martin Secker & Warburg Ltd, 1980–84; Kaye & Ward Ltd, 1980–84; William Heinemann, Australia and SA, 1981–82; Frew McKenzie (Antiquarian Booksellers), 1985–93; Pres., Heinemann Inc., 1981–84. Art Critic: The Listener, 1963–66; The New Statesman, 2001–. Chm., Soc. of Young Publishers, 1961–62; Member: Cambridge Univ. Appts Bd, 1967–71; Exec. Cttee, NBL, 1971–74; Trans. Panel, Arts Council, 1988–94; Cttee of Management, Amateur Dramatic Club, Cambridge (also Trustee); Council, RCA, 1982–87; Exec. Council, ICA, 1987–99 (Chm., 1996–99); Council, Friends of ENO; Trustee, Phoenix Trust. Mem. Editl Bd, Logos, 1989–93. *Publications:* Monograph on Jack B. Yeats, 1964; (with Alan Bowness) Monograph on Ivon Hitchens, 1973; (with Ursula Hoff) Monograph on Arthur Boyd, 1986; A Reader's Guide to European Art History, 1962; A Reader's Guide to Modern American Fiction, 1963; The Art of Jack B. Yeats, 1993; introdns to paperback edns of Theodore Dreiser's The Financier, The Titan and Jennie Gerhardt; programme essays for Royal Opera House, ENO and WNO; articles in The Times, Guardian, TLS, THES, Punch, Music Magazine, London Magazine, Encounter, New Statesman, Jl of Brit. Assoc. for Amer. Studies, Studio Internat., Modern Painters, Art Rev., DNB, Bookseller, Nature, Prospect, etc. *Recreations:* opera, bibliomania, looking at pictures, reading other publishers' books, watching cricket. *Address:* Flat 7, Huguenot House, 19 Oxendon Street, SW1Y 4EH. *T:* (020) 7839 3589, *Fax:* (020) 7839 0651. *Clubs:* Garrick, MCC.

ROSEVEARE, Robert William, CBE 1977; Secretary, 1967–83, and Managing Director for administrative affairs, 1971–83, British Steel Corporation; *b* Mandalay, Burma, 23 Aug. 1924; *s* of W. L., (Bill), and Marjory Roseveare; *m* 1954, Patricia Elizabeth, *d* of Guy L. Thompson, FRCS, Scarborough; one *s* three *d. Educ:* Gresham's Sch., Holt; St John's Coll., Cambridge. Served in Fleet Air Arm, 1943–46. Entered Home Civil Service, 1949. Asst Private Sec. to Minister of Fuel and Power, 1952–54; Cabinet Office, 1958–60; British Embassy, Washington, 1960–62; Asst Sec., Ministry of Power, 1964; seconded to Organising Cttee for British Steel Corporation, 1966; left Civil Service, 1971; Dir, BSC, 1969–71; Non-exec. Dir, Community Industry Ltd, 1983–91. Mem. Exec. Cttee, Hereford Diocesan Bd of Finance, 1986–95. *Recreations:* hill-walking, bird-watching, music. *Address:* Old Pasture, Hillfield Drive, Ledbury, Herefordshire HR8 1BH. *T:* (01531) 632913.

ROSEWARN, John; Secretary, Royal Institution of Naval Architects, 1989–97; *b* 14 Jan. 1940; *s* of Ernest and Frances Beatrice Rosewarn; *m* 1963, Josephine Rita Mullis; two *s. Educ:* Westminster City Sch. Royal Institution of Naval Architects, 1958–97: Administrator, 1958–65; Chief Clerk, 1965–75; Asst Sec., 1975–84; Sen. Asst. Sec., 1984–89. Freeman, City of London, 1976. *Recreations:* sailing, DIY, reading. *Address:* Little Fisher Farm, South Mundham, Chichester, West Sussex PO20 6ND.

ROSIER, Rt Rev. Stanley Bruce, AM 1987; Rector of St Oswald's, Parkside, diocese of Adelaide, 1987–94, retired; *b* 18 Nov. 1928; *s* of S. C. and A. Rosier; *m* 1954, Faith Margaret Alice Norwood; one *s* three *d. Educ:* Univ. of WA; Christ Church, Oxford. Asst Curate, Ecclesall, Dio. of Sheffield, 1954; Rector of: Wyalkatchem, Dio. of Perth, 1957; Kellerberrin Dio. of Perth, 1964; Auxiliary Bishop in Diocese of Perth, Western Australia, 1967–70; Bishop of Willochra, 1970–87. *Recreation:* natural history. *Address:* 5A Fowlers Road, Glenunga, SA 5064, Australia. *T:* (8) 83795213.

ROSIN, (Richard) David, FRCS, FRCSE; Consultant in General Surgery and Surgical Oncology, St Mary's Hospital, London, since 1980; *b* 29 April 1942; *s* of late Isadore Rowland Rosin and Muriel Ena Rosin (*née* Wolff); *m* 1971, Michelle Shirley Moreton; one *s* two *d*. *Educ:* St George's Jesuit Coll., Zimbabwe; Westminster Hosp. Sch. of Medicine, Univ. of London (MB, MS). Westminster Hospital: House Physician, subseq. House Surg., 1966–67; Sen. House Officer in Clin. Pathology, 1968, Surgical Rotation, 1969–71; Sen. Registrar, 1975–79; Ship's Surg., P & O Lines, 1967; Sen. House Officer, Birmingham Accident Hosp., 1969; Registrar: Sutton Hosp., Surrey, 1971–73; St Helier's Hosp., Carshalton, 1973–74; Clin. Asst, St Mark's Hosp., London, 1974–75; Sen. Registrar, Kingston Hosp., 1975–77; Vis. Lectr, Univ. of Hong Kong, 1978–79; Clin. Dir of Surgery, St Charles' Hosp., 1990–92; Chm., Div. of Surgery, St Mary's Hosp., London, 1992–96. Consultant Surg., King Edward VII's Hosp. for Officers, 1995–96. Chm. DTI Cttee, Operating Room of Year 2010, 1995–2000. Regl Advr, NW Thames Region, RCSE, 1990–; Member: Council, RCS, 1994– (Penrose-May Tutor, 1985–90; Arris and Gale Lectr, 1978; Hunterian Prof., 1987; Arnott Lectr, 1991); RSM, 1975 (Pres., Clin. Section, 1982–83, Surgery Section, 1992–93); Surgical Res. Soc., 1980; British Assoc. of Surgical Oncology, 1980; British Soc. of Gastroenterology, 1980; Melanoma Study Gp, 1988 (Hon. Sec., 1986–89, Pres., 1989–92); Soc. of Minimally Invasive Gen. Surgs, 1991 (Founder and Hon. Sec.); Hunterian Soc., 1994; Internat. Coll. of Surgs, 1992–. Fellow: Assoc. of Surgs of GB and Ire., 1975; Assoc. of Endoscopic Surgs of GB and Ire. (Mem. Council, 1995–); Assoc. of Upper Gastro-Intestinal Surgs of GB and Ire., 1997. Mem. Council, Marie Curie Foundn, 1984–92. Sir Ernest Finch Meml Lectr, Sheffield, 2000. Freeman, City of London, 1972; Liveryman: Soc. of Apothecaries, 1971; Co. of Barber Surgeons, 1978. Series Ed., Minimal Access textbooks, 1993–. *Publications:* (ed jtly) Cancer of the Bile Ducts and Pancreas, 1989; (ed jtly) Head and Neck Oncology for the General Surgeon, 1991; (ed jtly) Diagnosis and Management of Melanoma in Clinical Practice, 1992; (ed) Minimal Access Medicine and Surgery: principles and practice, 1993; (ed) Minimal Access General Surgery, 1994; (ed) Minimal Access Surgical Oncology, 1995; (co-ed) Minimal Access Thoracic Surgery, 1998; papers in jls and contribs to books. *Recreations:* all sport, particularly golf; opera, music, theatre, history of medicine and surgery, travelling. *Address:* 2 St Simon's Avenue, Putney, SW15 6DU. *T:* (020) 8788 6147; 80 Harley Street, W1G 7HL. *T:* (020) 7631 3447, *Fax:* (020) 7224 0645; *e-mail:* rdrosin@uk-consultants.com.uk. *Clubs:* Garrick, MCC, Roehampton; New Zealand Golf (Weybridge).

ROSINDELL, Andrew; MP (C) Romford, since 2001; *b* Romford, 17 March 1966; *s* of Frederick William Rosindell and Eileen Rosina Rosindell (*née* Clark). *Educ:* Rise Park Jun. and Infant Sch; Marshalls Park Secondary Sch. Researcher and freelance journalist, and Res. Asst to Vivian Bendall, MP, 1986–97; Dir, 1997–99, Internat. Dir, 1999–2001, Eur. Foundn. Mem., London Accident Prevention Council, 1990–95. Mem. (C) Havering BC, 1990– (Vice-Chm., Housing Cttee, 1996–97); Chm., N Romford Community Area Forum, 1998–. Mem., Deregulation and Regulatory Reform Select Cttee, 2001–; Sec. Gibraltar, Falkland Is and Australia/NZ All Party gps, 2001–. Joined Cons. Party and Young Conservatives, 1981; Chairman: Romford YC, 1983–84; Gtr London YC, 1987–88; Nat. YC, 1993–94; Eur. YC, 1993–97; Mem., Nat. Union Exec. Cttee, Cons. Party, 1986–88 and 1992–94; Chm., Romford Cons. Assoc., 1998–2001; Chm., Internat. Young Democrat Union, 1998–. Contested (C): Glasgow Provan, 1992; Thurrock, 1997. Gov., Dame Tipping C of E Sch., Havering-atte-Bower, 1990–. *Publication:* (jtly) Defending Our Great Heritage, 1993. *Recreations:* Staffordshire bull terriers, travel, swimming. *Address:* House of Commons, SW1A 0AA. *T:* (020) 7219 8475; (home) 1 Pettits Close, Romford, Essex RM1 4EB. *T:* (01708) 761186; (constituency office) 85 Western Road, Romford, Essex RM1 3LS. *T:* (01708) 766700, 761583. *Clubs:* Romford Conservative and Constitutional; RAFA; East Anglian Staffordshire Bull Terrier (Hon. Mem.).

ROSLING, Derek Norman, CBE 1988; FCA; Vice-Chairman, Hanson PLC, 1973–93; *b* 21 Nov. 1930; *s* of Norman and Jean Rosling; *m* (marr. diss. 1982); two *s* one *d*; *m* 2000, Julia Catherine Crookston; one step *s*. *Educ:* Shrewsbury Sch. ACA 1955, FCA 1962. Professional practice, 1956–65; Hanson PLC, 1965–94. FRSA 1990. *Recreations:* golf, sailing, theatre. *Address:* Little Salterns, Bucklers Hard, Beaulieu, Hants SO42 7XE. *T:* (01590) 616307. *Clubs:* Royal Yacht Squadron (Cowes); Royal Southampton Yacht; Brokenhurst Manor Golf.

ROSLING, Peter Edward, CMG 1987; LVO 1972; HM Diplomatic Service, retired; *b* 17 June 1929; *s* of Peregrine Starr and Jessie Rosling; *m* 1950, Kathleen Nuell; three *s*. *Educ:* grammar school. Served Royal Navy, 1948–50. HM Diplomatic Service, 1946; Belgrade, Innsbruck, Cape Town, Rome (NATO Defence College), FCO; Consul-Gen., Zagreb, 1980–83; High Comr, Lesotho, 1984–88. EC Monitor, EC Monitoring Mission, Croatia, 1991. Mem. Council, British Commonwealth Ex-Services League, 1988–. *Recreations:* tennis, walking, bridge. *Address:* Southernhay, Vaughan Way, Dorking, Surrey RH4 3DR.

ROSOMAN, Leonard Henry, OBE 1981; RA 1969 (ARA 1960); FSA; Tutor, Royal College of Art, 1957–78; *b* 27 Oct. 1913; *s* of Henry Rosoman; *m* 1963, Jocelyn (marr. diss. 1969), *d* of Bertie Rickards, Melbourne, Australia. *Educ:* Deacons Sch., Peterborough; Durham Univ. Teacher of Drawing and Painting, Reimann Sch. of Art, London, 1938–39; Official War Artist to Admiralty, 1943–45; Teacher: Camberwell Sch. of Art, London, 1948–56; (Mural Painting) Edinburgh Coll. of Art, 1948–56; Chelsea School of Art, 1956–57. One Man Shows: St George's Gallery, London, 1946 and 1949; Roland, Browse and Delbanco Gallery, London, 1954, 1957, 1959, 1965 and 1969; Fine Art Soc., 1974, 1978, 1983, 1990. Works bought by: HM Govt, Arts Council, British Council, York Art Gall., Contemporary Art Soc., Adelaide Art Gallery, V&A Museum, Lincoln Center, NY. Executed large mural paintings for: Festival of Britain, 1951; British Pavilion, Brussels World Fair, 1958; Harewood House, 1959; Lambeth Palace Chapel, 1988, 1992. Hon. ARCA; HRSW; FRPS. *Recreation:* travelling as much as possible. *Address:* 7 Pembroke Studios, Pembroke Gardens, W8 6HX. *T:* (020) 7603 3638. *Clubs:* Arts, Chelsea Arts.

ROSPIGLIOSI, family name of **Earl of Newburgh**.

ROSS, Rt Hon. Lord; Donald MacArthur Ross; PC 1985; Chairman, Judicial Studies Committee, Scotland, since 1997; a Senator of the College of Justice, Scotland, and Lord of Session, 1977–97; Lord Justice Clerk and President of the Second Division of the Court of Session, 1985–97; Lord High Commissioner, General Assembly, Church of Scotland, 1990 and 1991; *b* 29 March 1927; *s* of late John Ross, solicitor, Dundee; *m* 1958, Dorothy Margaret, *d* of late William Annand, Kirriemuir; two *d*. *Educ:* Dundee High School; Edinburgh University. MA (Edinburgh) 1947; LLB with distinction (Edinburgh) 1951. National Service with The Black Watch (RHR), 2nd Lt, 1947–49. Territorial Service, 1949–58, Captain. Advocate, 1952; QC (Scotland) 1964; Vice-Dean, Faculty of Advocates of Scotland, 1967–73; Dean, 1973–76; Sheriff Principal of Ayr and Bute, 1972–73. Dep. Chm., Boundary Commn for Scotland, 1977–85. Member: Scottish Cttee of Council on Tribunals, 1970–76; Cttee on Privacy, 1970; Parole Bd for Scotland, 1997–. Mem. Court, Heriot-Watt Univ., 1978– (Chm., 1984–90). FRSE 1988 (Mem. Council, 1997–99, Vice Pres., 1999–). Hon. LLD: Edinburgh, 1987; Dundee, 1991; Abertay Dundee, 1994; Aberdeen, 1998. DUniv Heriot-Watt, 1988. *Recreations:* gardening, walking, travelling. *Address:* 33 Lauder Road, Edinburgh EH9 2JG. *T:* (0131) 667 5731. *Club:* New (Edinburgh).

ROSS, Rear Adm. Alastair Boyd, CB 1999; CBE 1995; Clerk to Worshipful Company of Drapers, since 2000; *b* 29 Jan. 1947; *s* of Joseph Charles Patrick Ross and Shirley Carlile (*née* Stoddart); *m* 1977, Heather Judy Currie; two *d*. *Educ:* Radley Coll.; BRNC, Dartmouth. Joined RN, 1965; commnd 1968; specialised in aviation; flew as Anti-Submarine Warfare helicopter observer, 1970–80; commanded: HMS Brinton, 1977–79; HMS Falmouth, 1983–85; HMS Edinburgh, 1988–89; RCDS 1990; Capt., HMS Osprey, 1991–93; Comdr, NATO Standing Naval Force, Mediterranean (Adriatic Ops), 1993–94; Dir Overseas (ME and Africa), MoD, 1994–96; Asst Dir Ops, Internat. Mil. Staff, NATO HQ, 1996–99. Mem., RNSA, 1984–. *Recreations:* sailing, golf. *Address:* Drapers' Hall, Throgmorton Avenue, EC2N 2DQ. *Clubs:* Farmers', Royal Navy of 1765 and 1785.

ROSS, Rev. Dr Andrew Christian, FRHistS; Senior Lecturer in Ecclesiastical History, University of Edinburgh, 1966–99; Principal of New College and Dean of the Faculty of Divinity, 1978–84; *b* 10 May 1931; *s* of George Adams Ross and Christian Glen Walton; *m* 1953, Isabella Joyce Elder; four *s* (one *d* decd). *Educ:* Dalkeith High Sch.; Univ. of Edinburgh (MA, BD; PhD 1968; DLitt 1998); Union Theol Seminary, New York (STM). Served Royal Air Force, Pilot Officer, then FO, 1952–54. Ordained Minister of Church of Scotland, 1958; Minister, Church of Central Africa Presbyterian (Malaŵi), 1958–65; Chm., Lands Tribunal of Nyasaland, then Malaŵi Govt, 1963–65; Vice-Chm., Nat. Tenders Bd of Nyasaland, then Malaŵi, 1963–65. Sen. Studentship in African History, Univ. of Edinburgh, 1965–66; Mem. Court of Univ. of Edinburgh, 1971–73, Chm. Student Affairs Cttee of the Court, 1977–83. Kerr Lectr, Glasgow Univ., 1984; Coll. Lectr, Assembly's Coll., Belfast, 1985. Visiting Professor: Univ. of Witwatersrand, 1984; Dartmouth Coll., USA, 1992; Univ. of Malaŵi, 1997; Res. Fellow, Yale Univ., 1994. FRHistS 1996. *Publications:* chapter in: The Zambesian Past, 1965; Religion in Africa, 1965; Witchcraft and Healing, 1969; David Livingstone and Africa, 1973; Malaŵi, Past and Present, 1974; introd. and ed for micro film-prodn: Life and Work in Central Africa 1885–1914, 1969; The Records of the UMCA 1859–1914, 1971; John Philip: missions, race and politics in South Africa, 1986; A Vision Betrayed: the Jesuits in Japan and China 1542–1742, 1994; Blantyre Mission and Malaŵi, 1996; contribs to Union Qly Rev., New Left Rev., Scottish Historical Rev. *Recreation:* watching soccer. *Address:* 27 Colinton Road, Edinburgh EH10 5DR. *T:* (0131) 447 5987.

ROSS, Anthony Lee, (Tony); author and illustrator; *b* 10 Aug. 1938; *s* of Eric Turle Lee Ross and Effie Ross (*née* Griffiths); *m* 1st, 1961, Carole D'Arcy (marr. diss. 1971); 2nd, 1971, Joan Spokes (marr. diss. 1976); 3rd, 1979, Zoe Goodwin. *Educ:* Helsby Grammar Sch.; Liverpool Art Sch. (NDD, ATD). Advertising work, 1962–65; Sen. Lectr, Manchester Poly., 1965–86; children's author, illustrator and film-maker, 1972–; books published in UK, Europe, USA, Japan, Australia, Korea and S America. *Publications: picture books include:* Towser (series), 1984; I'm Coming to Get You, 1984; I Want My Potty (series), 1986; Oscar Got The Blame, 1987; Super Dooper Jezebel, 1988; I Want a Cat, 1989; A Fairy Tale, 1991; Don't Do That, 1991; Through the Looking Glass, 1992, and Alice's Adventures in Wonderland, 1993, abridged from Lewis Carroll; The Shop of Ghosts, from G. K. Chesterton, 1994; *books illustrated include:* Eric Morcambe, The Reluctant Vampire, 1982; Willis Hall, Vampire Park, 1983; Michael Palin, Limericks, 1985; Roald Dahl, Fantastic Mr Fox, 1988; Simon Brett, How to be a Little Sod, 1992; Michael Morpurgo, Red Eyes at Night, 1998; series: Ian Whybrow, Little Wolf, 1985; Jeanne Willis, Dr Xargle, 1988; Richmal Crompton, Meet Just William, 1999; Astrid Lindgren, Pippi Longstocking, 2000. *Recreations:* sailing, gentle sports. *Address:* Lake House, Leek Old Road, Sutton, Macclesfield, Cheshire SK11 0HZ. *T:* (01260) 252271. *Club:* Chelsea Arts.

ROSS, Rt Hon. Donald MacArthur; *see* Ross, Rt Hon. Lord.

ROSS, Donald Nixon, FRCS; Consultant Thoracic Surgeon, Guy's Hospital, 1958–78, now Emeritus; Consultant Surgeon, National Heart Hospital, 1963–93 (Senior Surgeon, 1967); *b* 4 Oct. 1922; *m* 1956, Dorothy Curtis; one *d*; *m* 2001, Barbara Cork. *Educ:* Boys' High Sch., Kimberley, S Africa; Univ. of Capetown (BSc, MB, ChB 1st Cl. Hons, 1946). FRCS 1949; FACC 1973; FACS 1976. Sen. Registrar in Thoracic Surgery, Bristol, 1952; Res. Fellow, 1953, Sen. Thoracic Registrar, 1954, Guy's Hosp.; Dir, Dept of Surgery, Inst. of Cardiology, 1970. Hon. FRSocMed 1996; Hon. FRCSI 1984; Hon. FRCS Thailand, 1987. Hon. DSc CNAA, 1982. Clement Price Thomas Award, RCS, 1983. Order of Cedar of Lebanon, 1975; Order of Merit (1st cl.) (West Germany), 1981; Royal Order (Thailand), 1994. *Publications:* A Surgeon's Guide to Cardiac Diagnosis, 1962; (jtly) Medical and Surgical Cardiology, 1968; (jtly) Biological Tissue in Heart Valve Replacement, 1972; contrib. BMJ, Lancet, Proc. RSM, Annals Royal Coll. Surg., Amer. Jl Cardiol. *Recreations:* Arabian horse breeding, horseriding, gardening. *Address:* 35 Cumberland Terrace, Regent's Park, NW1 4HP. *T:* (020) 7935 0756; (office) 25 Upper Wimpole Street, W1M 7TA. *T:* (020) 7935 8805. *Clubs:* Garrick; Kimberley (SA).

ROSS, Duncan Alexander, CBE 1993; CEng, FIEE; Chairman, Southern Electric plc (formerly Southern Electricity Board), 1984–93, retired; *b* 25 Sept. 1928; *s* of William Duncan Ross and Mary Ross; *m* 1958, Mary Buchanan Clarke Parsons; one *s* one *d*. *Educ:* Dingwall Academy; Glasgow Univ. (BSc Elec. Engrg). CBIM. Various engineering posts, South of Scotland Electricity Board, 1952–57; engineering, commercial and management posts, Midlands Electricity Board, 1957–72; Area Manager, South Staffs Area, 1972–75, Chief Engineer, 1975–77; Dep. Chm., 1977–81, Chm., 1981–84, South Wales Electricity Bd. Mem., Electricity Council, 1981–90. *Recreations:* golf, ski-ing. *Address:* Winterfold, Dovers Orchard, Hoo Lane, Chipping Campden, Glos GL55 6AZ. *T:* and *Fax:* (01386) 841797.

ROSS, Ernest; MP (Lab) Dundee West, since 1979; *b* Dundee, July 1942; *m*; two *s* one *d*. *Educ:* St John's Jun. Secondary Sch. Quality Control Engineer, Timex Ltd. Mem., MSF (formerly AUEW (TASS)). Mem., Select Cttee on Foreign Affairs, 1997–99; Chm., All-Party Poverty Gp, 1997–. Chm. Bd of Govs, Westminster Foundn for Democracy, 1997–. *Address:* House of Commons, SW1A 0AA.

ROSS, Prof. Graham Garland, PhD, FRS 1991; Professor of Theoretical Physics, Oxford University, since 1992; Fellow of Wadham College, Oxford, since 1983. *Educ:* Aberdeen Univ. (BSc); Durham Univ. (PhD); MA Oxon. Rutherford Atlas Res. Fellow, Pembroke Coll., Oxford, 1981–83; Lectr, 1983–90, Reader and SERC Sen. Res. Fellow in Theoretical Physics, 1990–92, Oxford Univ. *Address:* Department of Physics, 1 Keble Road, Oxford OX1 3NP. *T:* (01865) 273990; Woodcock Cottage, Lincombe Lane, Boars Hill, Oxford OX1 5DX.

ROSS, Hugh Robert; Chief Executive, United Bristol Healthcare NHS Trust, since 1995; *b* 21 April 1953; *s* of Robert James Ross and Marion Bertha Ross (*née* Maidment);

m 1981, Margaret Catherine Hehir; one *s* one *d*. *Educ:* Univ. of Durham (BA Pol. and Sociol.); London Business Sch. (MBA). Fellow, IHSM, 1987. Admin. Trainee, NHS, 1976–78; Asst Adminr, Princess Margaret Hosp., Swindon, 1978–80; Asst Adminr, 1980–81, Patient Services Officer, 1981–83, Westminster Hosp.; Dep. Adminr, 1983–84, Dir of Operational Services, 1984–86, St Bartholomew's Hosp.; Unit General Manager: City Unit, Coventry, 1986–90; Leicester Gen. Hosp., 1990–92; Chief Exec., Leicester Gen. Hosp. NHS Trust, 1993–95. *Recreations:* sport, travel, real ale, rock music. *Address:* 40 Alma Road, Clifton, Bristol BS8 2DB. *T:* (0117) 974 4987.

ROSS, James Hood; Chairman: Littlewoods Organisation, 1996–April 2002; National Grid Group plc, since 1999; *b* 13 Sept. 1938; *s* of Thomas Desmond Ross and Lettice Ferrier Ross (*née* Hood); *m* 1964, Sara Blanche Vivian Purcell; one *s* two *d*. *Educ:* Sherborne Sch.; Jesus Coll., Oxford (BA Hons Modern Hist.); Manchester Business Sch. (Dip. with distinction). British Petroleum, 1962–92: Gen. Manager, Corporate Planning, 1981–85; Chief Exec., BP Oil Internat., 1986–88; Chm. and Chief Exec., BP America, 1988–91; a Man Dir, BP, 1991–92; Chief Exec. and Dep. Chm., Cable and Wireless, 1992–96. *Recreations:* gardening, travel, swimming, golf. *Address:* National Grid Group plc, 15 Marylebone Road, NW1 5JD. *T:* (020) 7312 5721.

ROSS, Sir (James) Keith, 2nd Bt *cr* 1960; RD 1967; MS, FRCS; FRCSE; Consultant Emeritus, Southampton and Southwest Hampshire Health Authority, 1990; *b* 9 May 1927; *s* of Sir James Paterson Ross, 1st Bt, KCVO, FRCS, and Marjorie Burton Townsend (*d* 1978); *S* father, 1980; *m* 1956, Jacqueline Annella Clarke; one *s* three *d*. *Educ:* St Paul's School; Middlesex Hospital. MB BS 1950; MS 1965; FRCS 1956; FRCSE 1989. House Surgeon, Registrar, Sen. Registrar, Middlesex Hosp., 1950–67. Surgn Lieut, RNVR, 1952–54; Surg. Lt Comdr, RNR, retd 1972. Heller Fellowship, San Francisco, 1959; Registrar, Brompton Hosp., 1958, 1960. Consultant Thoracic Surgeon, Harefield and Central Middx Hosps, 1964–67; Consultant Surgeon, Nat. Heart Hosp., 1967–72; Consultant Cardiac Surgeon: Wessex Region, 1972–90; King Edward VII Hosp., Midhurst, 1978–92. Hunterian Prof., 1961, Mem. Council, 1986–94, RCS; Pres., Soc. of Cardiothoracic Surgeons, 1988. Hallet Prize, RCS, 1952; Bruce Medal, RCSE, 1989. *Publications:* on cardiac surgery in appropriate medical jls. *Recreations:* fly fishing, golf, painting. *Heir:* *s* Andrew Charles Paterson Ross, *b* 18 June 1966. *Address:* Moonhills Gate, Exbury Road, Beaulieu, Hants SO42 7YS. *T:* (01590) 612104. *Clubs:* Arts, MCC; Royal Lymington Yacht.

ROSS, Jane Angharad; *see* Watts, J. A.

ROSS, John Alexander, CBE 1993; FRAgS; Chairman, Dumfries and Galloway Primary Care NHS Trust, since 2000; *b* 19 Feb. 1945; *m* 1967, Alison Jean Darling; two *s* one *d*. *Educ:* Mahaar Primary Sch., Stranraer; George Watson's Coll., Edinburgh. FRAgS 1993. National Farmers' Union of Scotland: Convener, Hill Farming Sub-cttee, 1984–90; Wigtown Area Pres., 1985–86; Convener, Livestock Cttee, 1987–90; Vice-Pres., 1986–90; Pres., 1990–96. Comr, Meat & Livestock Commn, 1996–March 2002; Chm., Scotch Quality Beef and Lamb Assoc. Ltd, 1997–2000. Dir, NFU Mutual Insurance Soc., 1996–. Dir, Animal Diseases Res. Assoc., 1986–. Chm., Dumfries and Galloway Health Bd, 1997–2000. Chm., Stranraer Sch. Council, 1980–89. Session Clerk, Portpatrick Parish Church, 1975–80; Elder, C of S. *Recreations:* golf, curling. *Address:* Low Auchenree, Portpatrick, Stranraer DG9 8TN. *T:* (01776) 810259. *Club:* Farmers'.

ROSS, John Graffin, QC 2001; a Recorder, since 1974; *b* 9 March 1947; *s* of late James Ross and of Eileen Ross; *m* 1973, Elizabeth Patricia Alexandra Layland; Umtali Boys' High Sch., Southern Rhodesia; University Coll. of Rhodesia and Nyassaland (LLB; LLM (ext.) London Univ.). Called to the Bar, Inner Temple, 1971; Asst Recorder, 1990–94. *Publication:* (contrib) Pittaway and Hammerton, Professional Negligence Cases, 1998. *Recreations:* music, bridge, riding, golf, ski-ing. *Address:* c/o No 1 Serjeants' Inn, Fleet Street, EC4Y 1LH. *T:* (020) 7415 6666. *Club:* Golf (Valderrama).

ROSS, Jonathan Steven; broadcaster; *b* 17 Nov. 1960; *m* 1988, Jane Goldman; three *c*. *Educ:* Sch. of Slavonic and E European Studies, Univ. of London (BA History). Formerly researcher, Channel 4; founding co-Producer, Channel X. Television includes: chat shows: The Last Resort (deviser and associate producer with Alan Marke), 1987; One Hour with Jonathan Ross, 1990; Tonight with Jonathan Ross, 1990; The Late Jonathan Ross, 1996; presenter: The Incredibly Strange Film Show, 1988–89; Jonathan Ross Presents; For One Week Only, 1991; Gag Tag; In Search Of...; The Big Big Talent Show; Film 1999–; panel games: (host) It's Only TV...But I Like It, 1999–; (team mem.) They Think it's all Over, 1999–. Radio presenter, 1987–. *Address:* c/o Off the Kerb Productions, 3rd Floor, Hammer House, 113–117 Wardour Street, W1F 0UN.

ROSS, Kenneth Alexander; Sheriff of South Strathclyde, Dumfries and Galloway at Dumfries, since 2000; President, Law Society of Scotland, 1994–95 (Vice-President, 1993–94); *b* 21 April 1949; *s* of Alexander Cree Ross and Mary Hamilton Ross (*née* M'Lauchlan); *m* 1972, Morag Laidlaw; one *s* one *d*. *Educ:* Hutcheson's GS, Glasgow; Edinburgh Univ. (LLB (Hons) 1971). Pres., Edinburgh Univ. Union, 1970–71. Partner, M'Gowans, later Gillespie, Gifford & Brown, solicitors, Dumfries, 1975–97. Temp. Sheriff, 1987–97; Sheriff of Lothian and Borders at Linlithgow, 1997–2000. Mem. Council, Law Soc. of Scotland, 1987–96. Contested (C): Kilmarnock, Feb. 1974; Galloway, Oct. 1974. *Recreations:* gardening, golf, ski-ing, walking. *Address:* Slate Row, Auchencairn, Castle Douglas, Kirkcudbrightshire DG7 1QL. *Clubs:* Auchencairn Curling, Dumfries and County Golf.

ROSS, Lt-Col Sir Malcolm; *see* Ross, Lt-Col Sir W. H. M.

ROSS, Margaret Beryl C.; *see* Clunies Ross.

ROSS, Michael David, CBE 2001; FFA; Chief Executive, Scottish Widows plc (formerly Managing Director, then Group Chief Executive, Scottish Widows' Fund and Life Assurance Society), since 1991; Joint Deputy Group Chief Executive, Lloyds TSB Group plc, since 2000; *b* 9 July 1946; *s* of Patrick James Forrest Ross and Emily Janet (*née* Forsyth); *m* 1973, Pamela Marquis Speakman. *Educ:* Daniel Stewart's Coll., Edinburgh. FFA 1969. Joined Scottish Widows', 1964, as Trainee Actuary; Asst Gen. Manager, 1986–88; Actuary, 1988; Gen. Manager, 1988–90; Dep. Man. Dir, 1990–91. Chm., Scottish Financial Enterprise, 1999– (Dep. Chm., 1998). CIMgt (CBIM 1991). *Publications:* contrib. Trans. Faculty of Actuaries. *Recreations:* golf, curling, ski-ing, gardening. *Address:* (office) 69 Morrison Street, Edinburgh EH3 8BW. *T:* (0131) 655 6186. *Clubs:* Caledonian; Mortonhall Golf.

ROSS, Nicholas David, (Nick Ross); broadcaster and journalist; *b* 7 Aug. 1947; *s* of late John Caryl Ross and of Joy Dorothy Ross; *m* 1985, Sarah Caplin; three *s*. *Educ:* Wallington County Grammar Sch.; Queen's Univ., Belfast (BA Hons Psychol). Broadcaster, BBC N Ireland, 1971–72; Radio 4: reporter, Today, World at One, 1972–75; presenter, The World Tonight, Newsdesk, 1972–74, World at One, 1982, Call Nick Ross, 1986–97, Gulf News, 1991; producer and dir, TV documentaries, 1979–81; presenter, BBC TV: Man Alive, Man Alive Debates, Out of Court, 1975–82; Breakfast Time, Fair Comment, Star Memories, 60 Minutes, 1982–85; Watchdog, 1985–86; Crimewatch UK, 1984–; Westminster with Nick Ross, 1994–97; political party confs, 1996; Campaign Roadshow, 1997; So You Think You're A Good Driver, 1999–; The Syndicate, 2000; Nick Ross debates, 2000; indep. TV incl. A Week in Politics, Ch 4, 1986–88. Member: Cttee on the Ethics of Gene Therapy, DoH, 1991–93; Gene Therapy Adv. Cttee, DoH, 1993–96; Wider Working Gp on Health of the Nation, DoH, 1992–; Nuffield Council on Bioethics, 1999–; NHS Action Team, 2000–; Nat. Bd for Crime Prevention, 1993–96; Crime Prevention Agency, 1996–99; Property Crime Task Force, 1999–; Victim Support Adv. Bd, 1991–; Crime Concern Adv. Bd, 1991–; COPUS, 1991–96 (Chm., Sci. Book Prize, 1993); President: SANEline, 1990–; Tacade, 1996–; Healthwatch, 1990–; Vice-Pres., Patients' Assoc., 1991–93; Vice-Chm., Nat. Road Safety Campaign, RoSPA, 1990–93. Ambassador, WWF, 2000–. FRSA 1994; FRSocMed 1998. *Recreations:* ski-ing, scuba diving, influencing public policy. *Address:* BBC, White City, W12 7TS. *T:* (020) 8752 5050, *Fax:* (020) 7792 9200; *e-mail:* nickross@lineone.net.

ROSS, Peter Michael; barrister; a Recorder, since 2000; *b* 24 June 1955; *s* of Michael and Colleen Ross; *m* 1979, Julie Anna Ibbetson; two *s* one *d*. *Educ:* John Hampden GS, High Wycombe; Venerable English Coll., Gregorian Univ., Rome (PhB 1975); Coll. of Law. Admitted solicitor, 1980; called to the Bar, Inner Temple, 2000. Articles of clerkship, Allan Janes & Co., 1976–79; Court Clerk, High Wycombe Magistrates' Court, 1979–81; Thames Valley Police: Asst Prosecuting Solicitor, 1981–82; Sen. Prosecuting Solicitor, 1982–84; Principal Prosecuting Solicitor, 1984–86; Sen. Crown Prosecutor, 1986–87, Br. Crown Prosecutor, 1987–90, CPS Aylesbury; Br. Crown Prosecutor, N London CPS, 1990–93; Asst Chief Crown Prosecutor (Ops), CPS London, 1993–96; Dir, Office for Supervision of Solicitors, 1996–99; an Asst Recorder, 1999–2000. *Recreations:* field sports, gardening. *Address:* 13 King's Bench Walk, Temple, EC4Y 7EN.

ROSS, Prof. Richard Lawrence; Professor of Film, Hochschule für Fernsehen und Film, Munich, since 1992; Head of Diploma Course and Deputy to Director, National Film and Television School, 1998–2000; *b* 22 Dec. 1935; *s* of Lawrence Sebley Ross and Muriel Ross; *m* 1957, Phyllis Ellen Hamilton; one *s* one *d*. *Educ:* Westland High School, Hokitika, NZ; Canterbury University College, NZ. Exchange Telegraph, 1958–60; Visnews Ltd, 1960–65; BBC TV News, 1965–80; Prof. of Film and TV, then of Film, RCA, 1980–89; Co-Chm. (with Milos Forman) Grad. Film Dept, Columbia Univ., NY, 1989–90; Chm., Grad. Film Dept, NY Univ., 1990–92; Sen. Lectr in Film, 1995–96, Hd, Curriculum Planning, 1996–98, Nat. Film and TV Sch. Visiting Professor: Jerusalem Film and TV Sch., 1992–; Deutsche Film- und Fernsehakad., Berlin, 1993–. Consultant Dir, Film Educn, 1986–89; Dir, Nat. Youth Film Foundn, 1988–89. Consultant: Univ. Sains, Penang, Malaysia, 1984–; Calouste Gulbenkian Foundn, Lisbon, 1983–85. Chm., Educn Cttee, British Film Year, 1985–86; Exec. Mem., Centre Internat. de Liaison des Ecoles de Cinéma et de Télévision, 1990–95 (Chm., Short Film Project, 1990–95). Fellow in Fine Arts, Trent Polytechnic, 1970–72. Fellow, RCA, 1981–89. *Publications:* Strategy for Story-Telling (2 vols), 1992; Triangle (The Creative Partnership), vol. 1, 1998, vol. 2, 2001, vol. 3, 2002. *Recreations:* walking in London, eating in France, talking and drinking anywhere. *Address:* *e-mail:* dickross@dircon.co.uk.

ROSS, Richard Y.; *see* Younger-Ross.

ROSS, Robert; *see* Ross, W. R. A.

ROSS, Robert, MA, FLS; Keeper of Botany, British Museum (Natural History), 1966–77; *b* 14 Aug. 1912; *e s* of Robert Ross, Pinner, Middx; *m* 1939, Margaret Helen Steadman; one *s* three *d*. *Educ:* St Paul's Sch.; St John's Coll., Cambridge. Asst Keeper, British Museum (Natural History), 1936; Principal Scientific Officer, 1950; Deputy Keeper, 1962. Royal Microscopical Society: Hon. Librarian, 1947–51; Hon. Editor, 1953–71; Vice-Pres., 1959–60. Administrator of Finances, Internat. Assoc. of Plant Taxonomy, 1964–69; Sec., Gen. Cttee for Plant Nomenclature, 1964–69, Chm., 1969–81. President: British Phycological Soc., 1969–71; Quekett Microscopical Club, 1974–76; Pres., Internat. Soc. for Diatom Res., 1994–96 (Vice-Pres., 1992–94). *Publications:* various papers in scientific jls on botanical subjects. *Recreations:* morris dancing (Bagman, Morris Ring, 1946–50), country dancing, gardening. *Address:* The Garden House, Evesbatch, Bishop's Frome, Worcester WR6 5BD. *T:* (01531) 640366.

See also A. F. Stevens.

ROSS, Lt-Gen. Sir Robert (Jeremy), (Sir Robin), KCB 1994 (CB 1992); OBE 1978; Chairman, SSAFA Forces Help, since 2000; Deputy Chairman, Development Group, since 1996; *b* 28 Nov. 1939; *s* of Gerald and Margaret Ross; *m* 1965, Sara (*née* Curtis); one *s* one *d*. *Educ:* Wellington Coll.; Corpus Christi Coll., Cambridge (MPhil). Entered RM, 1957; Commando and Sea Service, 1959–69; Army Staff Coll., 1970; Commando Service, 1971–78; Instr, Army Staff Coll., 1978–79; CO 40 Commando RM, 1979–81; RCDS 1982; MoD, 1984–86; Comdr 3 Commando Bde, 1986–88; Maj.-Gen. RM Trng, Reserve and Special Forces, 1988–90; Maj.-Gen. RM Commando Forces, 1990–93; CGRM, 1993–96. Mem., Internat. Investment Council of S Africa, 2000–. Liveryman, Plaisterers' Co., 1996 (Mem. Court, 2000–). Comdr, Legion of Merit (USA), 1993. *Recreations:* shooting, fishing, walking. *Club:* Army and Navy.

ROSS, Sophie, (Mrs R. P. Ross); *see* Mirman, S.

ROSS, Tessa Sarah; Head of Drama, Channel 4, since 2000; *b* 26 July 1961; *d* of E. Leonard Ross and Sharon F. Ross (*née* Kingsley), MBE; *m* 1987, Mark Scantlebury; two *s* one *d*. *Educ:* Somerville Coll., Oxford (BA Hons, MA Oriental Studies (Chinese)). Literary Agent, Anthony Shiel Associates, 1986–88; Script Editor, BBC Scotland, 1988–89; Hd of Develt, British Screen Finance, 1990–93; Independent Commng Exec., 1993–97, Hd of Independent Commng, 1997–2000, BBC TV Drama. *Address:* Channel 4, 124 Horseferry Road, SW1P 2TX. *T:* (020) 7396 4444. *Club:* Groucho.

ROSS, Timothy David M.; *see* Melville-Ross.

ROSS, Victor; Chairman, Reader's Digest Association Ltd, 1978–84; *b* 1 Oct. 1919; *s* of Valentin and Eva Rosenfeld; *m* 1st, 1944, Romola Wallace; two *s*; 2nd, 1970, Hildegard Peiser. *Educ:* schs in Austria, Germany and France; London Sch. of Economics. Served in Army, 1942–45. Journalist and writer, 1945–55; joined Reader's Digest, 1955; Man. Dir and Chief Exec., 1972–81. Dir, Folio Soc., 1985–89. Pres., Assoc. of Mail Order Publishers, 1979–80, 1983–84; Mem., Data Protection Tribunal, 1985–95. Hon. Fellow, Inst. of Direct Marketing, 1995. Mackintosh Medal for Advertising, Advertising Assoc., 1989. *Publications:* A Stranger in my Midst, 1948; Tightrope, 1952; Basic British, 1956. *Recreations:* collecting books, fishing. *Address:* Worten Mill, Great Chart, Kent TN23 3BS.

ROSS, Lt-Col Sir (Walter Hugh) Malcolm, KCVO 1999 (CVO 1994); OBE 1988; Comptroller, Lord Chamberlain's Office, since 1991 (Assistant Comptroller, 1987–91); *b* 27 Oct. 1943; *s* of Col Walter John Macdonald Ross, CB, OBE, MC, TD and Josephine May (*née* Cross); *m* 1969, Susie, *d* of Gen. Sir Michael Gow, *qv*; one *s* two *d*. *Educ:* Eton Coll.; Royal Military Acad., Sandhurst. Served in Scots Guards, 1964–87; Management Auditor, The Royal Household, 1987–89. Sec., Central Chancery of the Orders of

Knighthood, 1989–91. An Extra Equerry to the Queen, 1988–. Mem., Queen's Body Guard for Scotland, Royal Company of Archers, 1981–. Freeman, City of London, 1994. *Address:* Netherhall, Bridge-of-Dee, Castle-Douglas, Kirkcudbrightshire DG7 2AA. *Clubs:* Pratt's; New (Edinburgh).

See also W. R. A. Ross.

ROSS, (Walter) Robert (Alexander), FRICS; Secretary and Keeper of the Records, Duchy of Cornwall, since 1997; *b* 27 Feb. 1950; *s* of Col Walter John Macdonald Ross, CB, OBE, MC, TD and Josephine May Ross (*née* Cross); *m* 1985, Ingrid Wieser; one *s* one *d. Educ:* Eton Coll.; Royal Agricl Coll., Cirencester. FRICS 1982. Chartered Surveyor, Buccleuch Estates Ltd, Selkirk, 1972–73; joined Savills, 1973: Partner, 1982–86; Dir, 1986–97. *Address:* 10 Buckingham Gate, SW1E 6LA. *T:* (020) 7834 7346. *Clubs:* Boodle's, Farmers.

ROSS, William; *b* 4 Feb. 1936; *m* 1974, Christine; three *s* one *d.* MP (UU) Londonderry, Feb. 1974–83, Londonderry East, 1983–2001 (resigned seat Dec. 1985 in protest against Anglo-Irish Agreement; re-elected Jan. 1986); contested (UU) Londonderry E, 2001. *Recreations:* fishing, shooting. *Address:* Hillquarter, Turmeel, Dungiven, Northern Ireland BT47 4SL. *T:* (028) 7774 1428, *Fax:* (028) 7774 2291. *Club:* Northern Counties (Londonderry).

ROSS, William Mackie, CBE 1987; TD 1969; DL; MD; FRCS; FRCSE; FRCR; retired; Consultant Radiotherapist, Northern Regional Health Authority, 1953–87; Lecturer in Radiotherapy, University of Newcastle upon Tyne, 1973–87; *b* 14 Dec. 1922; *s* of Harry Caithness Ross and Catherine Ross; *m* 1948, Mary Burt; one *s* two *d. Educ:* Durham and Newcastle. MB, BS 1945; MD 1953. FRCS 1956; FRCR 1960; FRCSE 1994. Trainee in Radiotherapy, 1945–51; National Service, 1951–53; RAMC TA, 1953–72; Col, CO 201 Gen. Hosp., 1967–72, Hon. Col, 1977–82. President: Section of Radiology, RSM, 1978; British Inst. of Radiology, 1979; North of England Surgical Soc., 1983; Royal Coll. of Radiologists, 1983–86. Hon. FACR, 1986. DL Northumberland, 1971–74, Tyne and Wear, 1974. *Publications:* articles on cancer, its causation and treatment. *Address:* 62 Archery Rise, Durham City DH1 4LA. *T:* (0191) 3869256.

ROSS GOOBEY, Alastair, CBE 2000; Chairman, Hermes Focus Asset Management Ltd, since 2002; *b* 6 Dec. 1945; *s* of late George Henry Ross Goobey and of Gladys Edith (*née* Menzies); *m* 1969, Sarah Georgina Mary Stille; one *s* one *d. Educ:* Marlborough Coll.; Trinity Coll., Cambridge (MA Econs). With Kleinwort Benson, 1968–72; Hume Holdings Ltd, 1972–77; Investment Manager, Pension Fund, Courtaulds Ltd, 1977–81; Dir, Geoffrey Morley & Partners Ltd, 1981–85; Special Advr to Chancellor of Exchequer, HM Treasury, 1986–87 and 1991–92; Chief Investment Strategist, James Capel & Co., 1987–93; Chief Exec., Hermes Pensions Mgt Ltd, 1993–2001. Director: Scottish Life, 1978–86; Cheltenham and Gloucester Building Soc., 1989–91 and 1992–97; TR Property Investment Trust plc, 1994–; Chm., John Wainwright & Co. Ltd, 1997–. Pres., Investment Property Forum, 1995–; Chm., Private Finance Panel, 1996–97 (Mem., 1995–97). Member: Pensions Law Rev. Cttee (Goode Cttee), 1992–93; Council of Lloyd's, 1997–; Member: Adv. Cttee on Film Finance, 1995–96; Investment Cttee, Nat. Gallery, 1996–; Opera Bd, Royal Opera House, 1995–97; Council, Nat. Opera Studio Foundn, 1996–. Trustee: Royal Opera House Pension Fund, 1995–; Jean Sainsbury Royal Opera House Fund, 1997–. Liveryman, Gold and Silver Wyre Drawers' Co. FRSA. Contested (C) Leicester West, 1979. Hon. RICS; Hon. FIA. *Publications:* The Money Moguls, 1987; (ed jtly) Kluwer Handbook on Pensions, 1988; Bricks & Mortals, 1992, rev. edn 1993. *Recreations:* music, cricket, writing, broadcasting (The Board Game, Radio 4). *Address:* (office) Lloyds Chambers, 1 Portsoken Street, E1 8HZ. *T:* (020) 7702 0888. *Clubs:* Reform, MCC; Bottesford Cricket (Leics).

ROSS-MUNRO, Colin William Gordon; QC 1972; *b* 12 Feb. 1928; *s* of late William Ross-Munro and of Adela Chirgwin; *m* 1958, Janice Jill Pedrana; one step *d. Educ:* Lycée Français de Londres; Harrow Sch.; King's Coll., Cambridge. Served in Scots Guards and in Army Education Corps. Called to the Bar, Middle Temple, 1951 (Master of the Bench, 1983). *Recreations:* tennis and travel. *Address:* (home) 46 Thames Quay, Chelsea Harbour, SW10 0UY; Blackstone Chambers, Blackstone House, Temple, EC4Y 9BW.

ROSS RUSSELL, Graham; Chairman, UK Business Incubation, since 1997; *b* 3 Jan. 1933; *s* of Robert Ross Russell and Elizabeth Ross Russell (*née* Hendry); *m* 1963, Jean Margaret Symington; three *s* one *d. Educ:* Loretto; Trinity Hall, Cambridge (BA; Hon. Fellow, 2000); Harvard Business School (MBA; Frank Knox Fellow, 1958–60). Sub Lieut, RNVR, 1951–53 (Mediterranean Fleet). Merchant banking: Morgan Grenfell & Co. and Baring Brothers, 1956–58; Philip Hill Higginson Erlanger, 1960–63; Stockbroker, Laurence Prust & Co., 1963–90, Partner, 1965; Chm., Laurence Prust & Co. Ltd, 1986–88. Chairman: Braham Miller Group, 1981–84; C. C. F. Hldgs, 1988–90; EMAP, 1990–94 (Dir, 1970–94); Tunnel Services Ltd, 1991–; Securities Inst., 1992–2000; Foreign and Colonial PEP Investment Trust plc, 1993–; Advent Venture Capital Trust plc, 1996–; Enterprise Panel, 1997–; non-executive Director: 3i UK Select Investment Trust (formerly Investment Trust of Guernsey) plc, 1995–; Fordath, 1971–84; Foster Braithwaite, 1988–96; Nasdaq (Europe) (formerly EASDAQ) SA, 1995–98 (Pres., 2000–01, and Mem., Market Authy); Barlow Internat., 1997–; Barloworld plc, 1998–; Bamboo Investments plc, 2000–. Dir, SIB, 1989–93; Mem. Council, Internat. Stock Exchange, subseq. London Stock Exchange, 1973–91 (Dep. Chm., 1984–88; Chairman: Pre-emption Gp, 1987–; Rev. Cttee on Initial Public Offers, 1989–90). Comr, Public Works Loan Bd, 1980–95; Chm., Domestic Promotions Cttee, British Invisible Exports Council, 1987–91. Mem. Council, Crown Agents Foundn, 1997–. Chm. Govs, Sutton's Hosp., Charterhouse, 1996–. Pres., Trinity Hall Assoc., 1994–95. *Publications:* occasional articles in esoteric financial and fiscal jls. *Recreations:* tennis, golf, reading. *Address:* 30 Ladbroke Square, W11 3NB. *T:* (020) 7727 5017. *Clubs:* Athenæum; Hawks (Cambridge); Woodpeckers (Oxford and Cambridge).

ROSS-WAWRZYNSKI, Dana; Headmistress, Altrincham Grammar School for Girls, since 1999; *b* 24 March 1951; *d* of Richard and Pauline Ross; *m* 1974, Jack Wawrzynski; two *s. Educ:* Glasgow Univ. (BSc Hons 1975); Strathclyde Univ. (MSc 1976); Manchester Univ. (NPQH 1999). Teacher, Loreto Sixth Form Coll., Manchester, 1977–81; Hd of Lower Sch. Sci., Central High Sch. for Boys, Manchester, 1981–82; Hd of Sci., St Joseph's High Sch. for Girls, Manchester, 1982–84; Dep. Headteacher, Abraham Moss High Sch. and N Manchester Coll., 1984–90; Dep. Headteacher, All Hallows High Sch., Macclesfield, 1990–98. *Publications:* sex educn booklet, papers. *Recreations:* classical music, hill walking, reading, ski-ing. *Address:* Altrincham Grammar School for Girls, Cavendish Road, Bowdon, Altrincham, Cheshire WA14 2NL. *T:* (0161) 928 0827.

ROSSANT, Dr Janet, FRS 2000; FRSC; Professor, Department of Molecular and Medical Genetics, since 1988, University Professor, since 2001, University of Toronto; Senior Scientist, since 1985, and Co-head, since 1998, Program in Development and Fetal Health, Samuel Lunenfeld Research Institute; *b* 13 July 1950; *d* of Leslie and Doris Rossant; *m* 1977, Alex Bain; one *s* one *d. Educ:* St Hugh's Coll., Oxford (BA, MA 1972); Darwin Coll., Cambridge (PhD 1976). Beit Meml Fellow, Univ. of Oxford, 1975–77; Asst Prof., 1977–82, Associate Prof., 1982–85, Brock Univ., St Catharines, Ont.; Associate Prof., Univ. of Toronto, 1985–88. FRSC 1996. *Publications:* (with R. A. Pedersen) Experimental Approaches to Mammalian Development, 1986; contrib. numerous articles to peer-reviewed jls. *Recreations:* running, cooking, theatre. *Address:* Samuel Lunenfeld Research Institute, Mount Sinai Hospital, 600 University Avenue, Toronto, ON M5G 1X5, Canada.

ROSSDALE, Rt Rev. David Douglas James; *see* Grimsby, Bishop Suffragan of.

ROSSE, 7th Earl of, *cr* 1806; **William Brendan Parsons;** Bt 1677; Baron Oxmantown 1792; *b* 21 Oct. 1936; *s* of 6th Earl of Rosse, KBE, and Anne (*d* 1992), *o d* of Lt-Col Leonard Messel, OBE; *S* father, 1979; *m* 1966, Alison Margaret, *er d* of Major J. D. Cooke-Hurle, Startforth Hall, Barnard Castle, Co. Durham; two *s* one *d. Educ:* Aiglon Coll., Switzerland; Grenoble Univ.; Christ Church, Oxford (BA 1961; MA 1964). 2nd Lieut, Irish Guards, 1955–57. UN Official 1963–80, appointed successively to Ghana, Dahomey, Mid-West Africa, Algeria, as first UN Volunteer Field Dir (in Iran) and UN Disaster Relief Co-ordinator (in Bangladesh). Govt of Ireland: Mem., Adv. Council on Develt Co-operation, 1984–89; Dir, Agency for Personal Service Overseas, 1986–90. Founder and Dir, Birr Scientific and Heritage Foundn (resp. for creation of Ireland's Historic Science Centre), 1985–; Director: Historic Irish Tourist Houses and Gardens Assoc., 1980–91; Lorne House Trust, 1993–; Trustee, Tree Register of British Isles, 1989–. Lord of the Manor: Womersley and Woodhall, Yorks; Newtown, Parsonstown and Roscomroe, Ireland. FRAS; Hon. FIEI. *Heir: s* Lord Oxmantown, *qv. Address:* (home) Birr Castle, Co. Offaly, Ireland. *T:* (509) 20023.

See also Earl of Snowdon.

ROSSER, Richard Andrew; JP; General Secretary, Transport Salaried Staffs' Association, since 1989; *b* 5 Oct. 1944; *s* of Gordon William Rosser and Kathleen Mary (*née* Moon); *m* 1973, Sheena Margaret (*née* Denoon); two *s* one *d. Educ:* St Nicholas Grammar Sch., Northwood. BScEcon London (external degree), 1970. MCIT 1968. Clerk, London Transport, 1962–65; PA to Operating Man. (Railways), LTE, 1965–66; joined full staff of TSSA, 1966: Res. Officer, 1966–74; Asst, London Midland Div. Sec., 1974–76; Finance and Organising Officer, 1976–77; London Midland Region Div. Sec., 1977–82; Asst Gen. Sec., 1982–89. Non-exec. Dir, Strategy Bd for Correctional Services, 2000–. Councillor, London Bor. of Hillingdon, 1971–78 (Chm., Finance Cttee, 1974–78); contested (Lab) Croydon Central, Feb. 1974. Mem., NEC, Labour Party, 1988–98; Vice-Chair, 1996–97, Chair, 1997–98, Labour Party. JP Middlesex, 1978 (Chm., Uxbridge Bench, 1996–). *Recreations:* walking, music, reading The Guardian, and hoping for success for Watford FC. *Address:* Transport Salaried Staffs' Association, Walkden House, 10 Melton Street, NW1 2EJ. *T:* (020) 7387 2101.

ROSSI, Sir Hugh (Alexis Louis), Kt 1983; consultant in environmental law with Simmons and Simmons, solicitors, 1991–97; *b* 21 June 1927; *m* 1955, Philomena Elizabeth Jennings; one *s* four *d. Educ:* Finchley Catholic Gram. Sch.; King's Coll., Univ. of London (LLB; FKC 1986). Solicitor with Hons, 1950. Member: Hornsey Borough Coun., 1956–65; Haringey Council, 1965–68; Middlesex CC, 1961–65. MP (C) Hornsey, 1966–83, Hornsey and Wood Green, 1983–92; Govt Whip, Oct. 1970–April 1972; Europe Whip, Oct. 1971–1973; a Lord Comr, HM Treasury, 1972–74; Parly Under-Sec. of State, DoE, 1974; opposition spokesman on housing and land, 1974–79; Minister of State: NI Office, 1979–81; for Social Security and the Disabled, DHSS, 1981–83. Chm., Select Cttee on the Environment, 1983–92. Dep. Leader, UK Delegn to Council of Europe and WEU, 1972–73 (Mem., 1970–73). Non-exec. Dir, Iveco NV, 1989–; Consultant, Wimpey Environmental Ltd, 1993–95. Vice President: (UK), Adv. Cttee on Protection of the Seas, 1992–; Nat. Soc. for Clean Air, 1985–. Chairman: UNA (UK), 1992–96; Italian Hosp., London, 1988–89, Italian Hosp. Fund, 1990–; Assoc. of Papal Orders in GB of Pius IX, St Gregory and St Sylvester, 1989–99; Historic Chapels Trust, 1992–; Trustee, Trust House Charitable Foundn (formerly Mem., Forte Council), 1992–. Hon. FCIWEM 1990; Hon. Fellow, Inst. Wastes Management, 1993. Knight of Holy Sepulchre, 1966; KCSG 1985. *Publications:* Guide to the Rent Act, 1974; Guide to Community Land Act, 1975; Guide to Rent (Agriculture) Act, 1976; Guide to Landlord and Tenant Act, 1987; Guide to Local Government Acts 1987 and 1988, 1988.

See also M.-L. E. Rossi.

ROSSI, Marie-Louise Elizabeth; Chief Executive, International Underwriting Association of London, since 1998; *b* 18 Feb. 1956; *d* of Sir Hugh Rossi, *qv. Educ:* St Paul's Girls' Sch.; St Anne's Coll., Oxford (BA Hons Lit. Hum., MA; Treas., Oxford Union, 1978). Hogg Robinson Gp plc, 1979–87; Asst Dir, Sedgwick Gp plc, 1987–90; Consultant, Tillinghast-Towers Perrin, mgt consultants and actuaries, 1990–93; Chief Exec., London Internat. Insurance and Reinsurance Market Assoc., 1993–98. Member: Lloyd's, 1985–97 (Underwriting Mem., 1985–91); Gen. Cttee, Lloyd's Register of Shipping, 2000–. Mem. (C), Westminster CC, 1986–94 (Chm., Educn Cttee, 1989–92). Chairman: Bow Gp, 1988–89 (Trustee, 1996–99); Foreign Affairs Forum, Conservative Party, 1993–96; Chm. Orgn Cttee, Pro Euro Cons. Party, 1999–. Trustee and Director: Foundn for Young Musicians, 1990–; Orch. of St John's Ltd, 1995–99. Mem. Governing Council, Nottingham Univ., 2001–. MIEx 1991; MIRM 1996. FRSA 1993. Hon. Citizen, City of Baltimore, Md, 1994. *Address:* London Underwriting Centre, 3 Minster Court, Mincing Lane, EC3R 7DD. *T:* (020) 7617 4444. *Clubs:* Carlton, Special Forces.

ROSSITER, Rt Rev. (Anthony) Francis, OSB; Abbot President of the English Benedictine Congregation, since 1985 (Second Assistant, 1976–85); *b* 26 April 1931; *s* of Leslie and Winifred Rossiter. *Educ:* St Benedict's, Ealing; Sant Anselmo, Rome (LCL). Priest, 1955; Second Master, St Benedict's School, 1960–67; Abbot of Ealing, 1967–91; Vicar for Religious, Archdiocese of Westminster, 1969–88; Pres., Conf. of Major Religious Superiors of England and Wales, 1970–74; Pro-Primate, Benedictine Confedn, 1995–96 (Mem., Abbot Primate's Council, 1988–98). Hon. DD St Vincent Coll., Pa, 1988. *Address:* Ealing Abbey, W5 2DY. *T:* (020) 8862 2100.

ROSSLYN, 7th Earl of, *cr* 1801; **Peter St Clair-Erskine;** Bt 1666; Baron Loughborough, 1795; a Commander, Metropolitan Police, since 2000; *b* 31 March 1958; *s* of 6th Earl of Rosslyn, and of Athenais de Mortemart, *o d* of late Duc de Vivonne; *S* father, 1977; *m* 1982, Helen, *e d* of Mr and Mrs C. R. Watters, Christ's Hospital, Sussex; two *s* two *d. Educ:* Eton; Bristol Univ. Metropolitan Police, 1980–94; Thames Valley Police, 1994–2000. Elected Mem., H of L, 1999. Trustee, Dunimarle Museum. Dir, Ludgrove Sch. Trust. *Heir: s* Lord Loughborough, *qv. Address:* House of Lords, SW1A 0PW. *Club:* White's.

ROSSMORE, 7th Baron *cr* 1796; **William Warner Westenra;** *b* 14 Feb. 1931; *o s* of 6th Baron Rossmore and Dolores Cecil (*d* 1981), *d* of late Lieut-Col James Alban Wilson, DSO, West Burton, Yorks; *S* father, 1958; *m* 1982, Valerie Marion, *d* of Brian Tobin; one *s. Educ:* Eton; Trinity Coll., Cambridge (BA). 2nd Lieut, Somerset LI. Co-founder, Coolemine Therapeutic Community, Dublin. *Recreations:* drawing, painting. *Heir: s* Hon. Benedict William Westenra, *b* 6 March 1983. *Address:* Rossmore Park, Co. Monaghan, Eire. *T:* 81947.

ROSSOR, Prof. Martin Neil, MD, FRCP; Consultant Neurologist, St Mary's Hospital and National Hospital for Neurology and Neurosurgery, London, since 1986; Professor of Clinical Neurology, Institute of Neurology, University College London, since 1998,; *b* 24 April 1950; *s* of Bruce and Eileen Rossor; *m* 1973, Eve Lipstein; two *s* one *d*. *Educ:* Watford Boys' Grammar Sch.; Jesus Coll., Cambridge (MA, MD); King's College Hosp. Med. Sch. (MB BChir). FRCP 1990. Clinical Scientist, MRC Neurochemical Pharmacology Unit, 1978–82; Registrar, 1982–83, Sen. Registrar, 1983–86, Nat. Hosp. for Nervous Diseases and King's Coll. Hosp.; Clinical Dir, Medical Specialities, St Mary's Hosp., 1989–92; Sen. Lectr, Inst. of Neurology, 1992–98; Clin. Dir for Neurology, Nat. Hosp. for Neurology and Neurosurgery, 1994–98. Liveryman, Soc. of Apothecaries, 1978– (Mem., Ct of Assistants, 1999–). *Publications:* Unusual Dementias, 1992; (with J. Growdon) Dementia, 1998; papers on Alzheimer's disease and related dementias. *Recreations:* English literature, equestrian sports, sailing. *Address:* The National Hospital for Neurology and Neurosurgery, Queen Square, WC1N 3BG. *T:* (020) 7837 3611. *Club:* Athenæum.

ROSSWALL, Prof. Thomas; Director, International Foundation for Science, since 2000; *b* 20 Dec. 1941; *s* of Axel Rosswall and Britta (*née* Lindroth). *Educ:* Univ. of Uppsala (BSc 1966). Asst, Dept of Biochemistry, Univ. of Uppsala, 1967–70; Res. Asst, Dept of Microbiol., Swedish Univ. of Agricl Scis, 1970–76; Programme Officer, Swedish Council for Planning and Co-ordination of Research, 1976–80; Researcher, 1980–82, Asst Prof., 1982–84, Associate Prof., 1984, Dept of Microbiol., Swedish Univ. of Agricl Research; Prof., Dept of Water and Envmtl Studies, Univ. of Linköping, 1984–92; Exec. Dir, Internat. Geosphere-Biosphere Prog., 1987–94; Rector, 1994–2000, Prof., 2000–, Swedish Univ. of Agricl Scis. Prof., Stockholm Univ., 1992–2000; Dir, Internat. Secretariat, System for Analysis, Res. and Trng, Washington, 1992–93. Mem., Academia Europaea, 1989; Fellow: Royal Swedish Acad. of Scis, 1989; Royal Swedish Acad. of Agric. and Forestry, 1995; Royal Acad. of Arts and Scis of Uppsala, 1999. *Publications:* edited: Systems Analysis in Northern Coniferous Forests, 1971; (jtly) IBP Tundra Biome Procs 4th International Meeting on Biological Productivity of Tundra, 1971; Modern Methods in the Study of Microbial Ecology, 1973; (jtly) Structure and Function of Tundra Ecosystems, 1975; Nitrogen Cycling in West African Ecosystems, 1980; (jtly) Terrestrial Nitrogen Cycles: processes, ecosystems strategies and management impacts, 1981; (jtly) Nitrogen Cycling in South-East Asian Wet Monsoonal Ecosystems, 1981; (jtly) The Nitrogen Cycle, 1982; (jtly) Nitrogen Cycling in Ecosystems of Latin America and the Caribbean, 1982; (jtly) Scales and Global Change: spatial and temporal variability of biospheric and geospheric processes, 1988; (jtly) Ecology of Arable Land: the role of organism in carbon and nitrogen cycling, 1989; 100 papers in scientific jls. *Address:* (office) Grev Turegatan 19, 11438 Stockholm, Sweden.

ROST, Peter Lewis; energy consultant; *b* 19 Sept. 1930; *s* of Frederick Rosenstiel and Elisabeth Merz; *m* 1961, Hilary Mayo; two *s* two *d*. *Educ:* various primary schs; Aylesbury Grammar Sch. National Service, RAF, 1948–50; Birmingham Univ. (BA Hons Geog.), 1950–53. Investment Analyst and Financial Journalist with Investors Chronicle, 1953–58; firstly Investment Advisor, 1958, and then, 1962, Mem. London Stock Exchange, resigned 1977. MP (C) Derbys SE, 1970–83, Erewash, 1983–92. Secretary: Cons. Parly Trade and Industry Cttee, 1972–73; Cons. Parly Energy Cttee, 1974–77; Select Cttee on Energy, 1979–92. Treasurer, Anglo-German Parly Gp, 1974–92; Jt Chm., Alternative and Complementary Medicine Parly Gp, 1989–92. Chairman: Major Energy Users' Council, 1992–95; Utility Buyers' Forum, 1995–98; Vice-Pres., Combined Heat and Power Assoc. (Hon. Life Mem.). FRGS (Mem. Council, 1980–83); Fellow, Industry and Parlt Trust, 1987; Companion, Inst. of Energy, 1992. Freeman, City of London. Grand Cross, Order of Merit, Germany, 1979. *Publications:* papers on energy. *Recreations:* tennis, ski-ing, gardening, antique map collecting. *Address:* Norcott Court, Berkhamsted, Herts HP4 1LE. *T:* (01442) 866123, *Fax:* (01442) 865901.

ROSTOW, Prof. Eugene Victor; Sterling Professor of Law, Yale University, 1938–84, now Emeritus; Distinguished Visiting Research Professor, National Defense University, since 1992; *b* 25 Aug. 1913; *s* of Victor A. and Lillian H. Rostow; *m* 1933, Edna B. Greenberg; two *s* one *d*. *Educ:* Yale Coll.; King's Coll., Cambridge (LLD 1962); Yale Law Sch. Practised law, New York, 1937–38; Yale Law Faculty, 1938–; Prof. of Law, 1944–84; Dean of Law Sch., 1955–65. Dist. Vis. Res. Prof. of Law and Diplomacy, Nat. Defense Univ., Washington, 1984–90, 1992–. Asst to Asst Sec. of State Acheson, 1942–44; Asst to Exec. Sec., Econ. Commn for Europe, UN, Geneva, 1949–50; Under-Sec. of State for Political Affairs, 1966–69. Dir, Arms Control and Disarmament Agency, 1981–83. Pres., Atlantic Treaty Assoc., 1973–76. Pitt Prof., Cambridge, 1959–60; Eastman Prof., Oxford, 1970–71; Dist. Fellow, US Inst. of Peace, 1990–92. Dir, American Jewish Cttee, 1972–74; Chm. Exec. Cttee, Cttee on the Present Danger (Washington), 1976–81, 1987–. Hon. LLD Boston, 1976. Dist. Civilian Service Medal, US Army, 1990. Chevalier, Legion of Honour (France), 1960; Grand Cross, Order of the Crown (Belgium), 1969. *Publications:* A National Policy for the Oil Industry, 1948; Planning for Freedom, 1959; The Sovereign Prerogative, 1962; Law, Power and the Pursuit of Peace, 1968; (ed) Is Law Dead?, 1971; Peace in the Balance, 1972; The Ideal in Law, 1978; Toward Managed Peace, 1993; A Breakfast for Bonaparte, 1994; contribs to legal and economic jls. *Address:* Peru, Vermont 05152, USA. *T:* (802) 8246627; 1315 4th Street SW, Washington, DC 20024, USA. *Clubs:* Century (New York); Elizabethan (New Haven); Cosmos (Washington).
See also W. W. Rostow.

ROSTOW, Walt Whitman; Professor of Political Economy, University of Texas at Austin, Texas, 1969–77, now Professor Emeritus; *b* 7 Oct. 1916; 2nd *s* of Victor and Lillian Rostow; *m* 1947, Elspeth, *o d* of Milton J. and Harriet Vaughan Davies; one *s* one *d*. *Educ:* Yale (BA 1936; PhD 1940); Oxford (Rhodes Scholar). Social Science Research Council Fellow, 1939–40; Instructor, Columbia Univ., 1940–41; Office Strategic Services, 1941–45 (Army of the United States, 1943–45, Major; Legion of Merit; Hon. OBE); Assistant Chief Division German-Austrian Economic Affairs, Department of State, 1945–46; Harmsworth Professor American History, Oxford, 1946–47; Special Assistant to Executive Secretary, Economic Commission for Europe, 1947–49; Pitt Professor of American History, Cambridge, 1949–50; Professor of Economic History, Massachusetts Institute of Technology, 1950–61; Deputy Special Assistant to the President (USA) for National Security Affairs, Jan. 1961–Dec. 1961; Counselor and Chairman, Policy Planning Council, Department of State, 1961–66; US Mem., Inter-Amer. Cttee on Alliance for Progress, 1964–66; Special Assistant to the President, The White House, 1966–69. Chm. and Chief Exec. Officer, Austin Project, 1992–2000. Member: Royal Economic Society, England; American Academy of Arts and Sciences, 1957; Amer. Philos. Soc.; Massachusetts Historical Soc. Hon. LLD: Carnegie Inst. of Tech., Pittsburgh, 1962; Univ. Miami, 1965; Univ. Notre Dame, 1966; Middlebury Coll., 1967; Jacksonville Univ., 1974. Presidential Medal of Freedom, with distinction, 1969. *Publications:* The American Diplomatic Revolution, 1947; Essays on the British Economy of the Nineteenth Century, 1948; The Process of Economic Growth, 1952; (with A. D. Gayer and A. J. Schwartz) The Growth and Fluctuation of the British Economy, 1790–1850, 1953, new edn 1975; (with A. Levin and others) The Dynamics of Soviet Society, 1953; (with others) The Prospects for Communist China, 1954; (with R. W. Hatch) An American Policy in Asia, 1955; (with M. F. Millikan) A Proposal: Key to An Effective Foreign Policy, 1957; The Stages of Economic Growth, 1960, 3rd edn 1990; The United States in the World Arena, 1960; The Economics of Take-off into Sustained Growth (ed), 1963; View from the Seventh Floor, 1964; A Design for Asian Development, 1965; Politics and the Stages of Growth, 1971; The Diffusion of Power, 1972; How It All Began: origins of the modern economy, 1975; The World Economy: history and prospect, 1978; Getting from Here to There, 1978; Why the Poor Get Richer and the Rich Slow Down, 1980; Pre-Invasion Bombing Strategy: General Eisenhower's Decision of March 25, 1944, 1981; The Division of Europe after World War II: 1946, 1981; British Trade Fluctuations 1868–1896: a chronicle and a commentary, 1981; Europe after Stalin: Eisenhower's Three Decisions of March 11, 1953, 1982; Open Skies: Eisenhower's proposal of July 21, 1955, 1982; The Barbaric Counter-Revolution, 1983; Eisenhower, Kennedy and Foreign Aid, 1985; The United States and the Regional Organization of Asia and the Pacific 1965–85, 1985; Rich Countries and Poor Countries: reflections from the past, lessons for the future, 1987; Essays on a Half Century: ideas, policies and action, 1988; History, Policy and Theory: essays in interaction, 1989; Theorists of Economic Growth from David Hume to the Present, with a Perspective on the Next Century, 1990; The Great Population Spike and After: reflections on the 21st century, 1998; various articles contributed to: The Economist, Economic Journal, Economic History Review, Journal of Econ. History, American Econ. Review, etc. *Address:* 1 Wild Wind Point, Austin, TX 78746, USA. *Clubs:* Elizabethan (New Haven, Conn, USA); Cosmos (Washington, DC).
See also E. V. Rostow.

ROSTROPOVICH, Mstislav, Hon. KBE 1987; 'cellist; Music Director and Conductor, National Symphony Orchestra, Washington, 1977–94; *b* 1927; *m* 1955, Galina Vishnevskaya, *qv*; two *d*. *Educ:* State Conservatoire, Moscow. Has played in many concerts in Russia and abroad from 1942; first performance of Shostakovich's 'cello concerto (dedicated to him), Edinburgh Festival, 1960. Series of concerts with London Symphony Orchestra under Gennadi Rozhdestvensky, Festival Hall, 1965 (Gold Medal); first perf. Britten's third cello suite, Aldeburgh, 1974. Pres., Evian Fest., 1987–. Mem. Union of Soviet Composers, 1950–78, 1990–. Holds over 30 honorary degrees including Hon. MusD: St Andrews, 1968; Cambridge, 1975; Harvard, 1976; Yale, 1976; Oxon, 1980. Lenin Prize, 1964; Premium Imperiale (Japan), 1992. US Presidential Medal of Freedom, 1987; Commandeur de la Légion d'Honneur (France), 1987. *Address:* c/o Jonathan Brill, CAMI, 165 West 57th Street, New York, NY 10019, USA. *T:* (212) 8419599, *Fax:* (212) 8419525.

ROTA, Anthony Bertram; Managing Director, Bertram Rota Ltd, antiquarian booksellers, since 1967; *b* 24 Feb. 1932; *s* of Cyril Bertram Rota and Florence Ellen Rota (*née* Wright); *m* 1957, Jean Mary Foster Kendall; two *s*. Entered family business, 1952. Vis. Distinguished Fellow, Univ. of Tulsa, 1988. President: Antiquarian Booksellers' Assoc., 1971–72; Internat. League of Antiquarian Booksellers, 1988–91. DeGolyer Medal, Southern Methodist Univ., 1988. *Publications:* Points at Issue, 1984; Life in a London Bookshop, 1989; The Changing Face of Antiquarian Bookselling 1950–2000 AD, 1995; Apart from the Text, 1998; Books in the Blood: memoirs, 2001; articles on book-collecting and bibliography in British and American jls. *Recreations:* cinema, opera, theatre, concerts, watching cricket, walking. *Address:* 31 Long Acre, WC2E 9LT. *T:* (020) 7836 0723. *Clubs:* Garrick; Grolier (NY).

ROTBLAT, Sir Joseph, KCMG 1998; CBE 1965; MA, DSc (Warsaw); PhD (Liverpool); DSc (London); FRS 1995; FInstP; Professor of Physics in the University of London, at St Bartholomew's Hospital Medical College, 1950–76, now Emeritus; Physicist to St Bartholomew's Hospital, 1950–76; President, Pugwash Conferences on Science and World Affairs, 1988–97, now Emeritus; *b* 4 Nov. 1908; *e s* of late Z. Rotblat, Warsaw. *Educ:* University of Warsaw, Poland. Research Fellow of Radiological Laboratory of Scientific Society of Warsaw, 1933–39; Asst Director of Atomic Physics Institute of Free Univ. of Poland, 1937–39; Oliver Lodge Fellow of Univ. of Liverpool, 1939–40; work on atomic energy at Liverpool Univ. and Los Alamos, New Mexico, 1939–44; Lecturer and afterwards Senior Lecturer in Dept of Physics, Liverpool Univ., 1940–49; Director of Research in nuclear physics at Liverpool Univ., 1945–49. Treasurer, St Bartholomew's Hosp. Med. Coll., 1974–76; Vice-Dean, Faculty of Sci., London Univ., 1974–76. Member: Adv. Cttee on Med. Res., WHO, 1972–75; WHO Management Gp, 1984–90; Canberra Commn, 1995–96. Ed., Physics in Medicine and Biol., 1960–72. Sec.-Gen., Pugwash Confs on Science and World Affairs, 1957–73; Chm., British Pugwash, 1978–88. Pres., Hosp. Physicists' Assoc, 1969–70; Pres., British Inst. of Radiology, 1971–72 (Hon. Mem., 1990). Mem. Governing Body of Stockholm Internat. Peace Res. Inst., 1966–71. Pres., Internat. Youth Sci. Forum, 1972–74. Vis. Prof. of Internat. Relations, Univ. of Edinburgh, 1975–76; Bertrand Russell Peace Lects, 1998; Dag Hammarskjöld Lectr, 2001. Member, Polish Academy of Sciences, 1966; Hon. Foreign Member: Amer. Acad. of Arts and Sciences, 1972; Ukraine Acad. of Scis, 1994; For. Mem., Czechoslovak Acad. of Scis, 1988. Hon. Freeman, London Bor. of Camden, 1996; Hon. Citizen, Seoul, 2001. Hon. FRSE 1998; Hon. FRCR 1998; Hon. FMedSci 2000; Hon. FInstP 2001. Hon. Fellow: UMIST, 1985; QMW, 1996. Hon. DSc: Bradford, 1973; Liverpool, 1989; City, 1996; Slovak Acad. of Sciences, 1996; Acadia, 1998; Richmond, 1998; (Medicine) London, 2001; Dr *hc* Moscow, 1988. Bertrand Russell Soc. Award, 1983; Gold Medal, Czechoslovak Acad. of Sciences, 1988; Albert Einstein Peace Prize, 1992; Nobel Peace Prize, 1995; Copernicus Medal, Polish Acad. of Sciences, 1996; Jamnalal Bajaj Peace Award, Jamnalal Bajaj Foundn, Bombay, 1999; Toda Peace Prize, Toda Inst., Hawaii, 2000. Commander, Order of Merit (Polish People's Republic), 1987; Order of Cyril and Methodius (1st Cl.) (Bulgaria), 1988; Kt Commander's Cross, OM (Germany), 1989; Kt Comdr's Cross and Star, Order of Polonia Restituta (Poland), 1998. *Publications:* Progress in Nuclear Physics, 1950; (with Chadwick) Radio-activity and Radioactive Substances, 1953; Atomic Energy, a Survey, 1954; Atoms and the Universe, 1956; Science and World Affairs, 1962; Aspects of Medical Physics, 1966; Pugwash, the First Ten Years, 1967; Scientists in the Quest for Peace, 1972; Nuclear Reactors: to breed or not to breed, 1977; Nuclear Energy and Nuclear Weapon Proliferation, 1979; Nuclear Radiation in Warfare, 1981; Scientists, The Arms Race and Disarmament, 1982; The Arms Race at a Time of Decision, 1984; Nuclear Strategy and World Security, 1985; World Peace and the Developing Countries, 1986; Strategic Defence and the Future of the Arms Race, 1987; Coexistence, Co-operation and Common Security, 1988; Verification of Arms Reductions, 1989; Nuclear Proliferation: technical and economic aspects, 1990; Global Problems and Common Security, 1990; Towards a Secure World in the 21st Century, 1991; Striving for Peace, Security and Development in the World, 1992; A Nuclear-Weapon-Free World: Desirable? Feasible?, 1993; A World at the Crossroads: new conflicts, new solutions, 1994; Towards a War-free World, 1995; World Citizenship: allegiance to humanity, 1996; Nuclear Weapons: the road to zero, 1998; papers on nuclear physics and radiation biology in Proceedings of Royal Society, Radiation Research, Nature, etc. *Recreations:* recorded music, travel. *Address:* 8 Asmara Road, West Hampstead, NW2 3ST. *T:* (020) 7435 1471. *Club:* Athenæum.

ROTH, Andrew; Director, Parliamentary Profiles, since 1955; *b* NY, 23 April 1919; *s* of Emil and Bertha Roth; *m* 1949, Mathilda Anna Friederich (marr. diss. 1984); one *s* one *d*.

Educ: City Coll. of NY (BSS); Columbia Univ. (MA); Harvard Univ. Reader, City Coll., 1939; Res. Associate, Inst. of Pacific Relations, 1940; US Naval Intell., 1941–45 (Lieut, SG); Editorial Writer, The Nation, 1945–46; Foreign Corresp., Toronto Star Weekly, 1946–50; London Corresp., France Observateur, Sekai, Singapore Standard, 1950–60; Political Correspondent: Manchester Evening News, 1972–84; New Statesman, 1984–97. Ed., Westminster Confidential, 1955–. DUniv Open, 1993. *Publications:* Japan Strikes South, 1941; French Interests and Policies in the Far East, 1942; Dilemma in Japan, 1945 (UK 1946); The Business Background of MPs, 1959, 7th edn 1980; The MPs' Chart, 1967, 5th edn 1979; Enoch Powell: Tory Tribune, 1970; Can Parliament Decide . . ., 1971; Heath and the Heathmen, 1972; Lord on the Board, 1972; The Prime Ministers, Vol. II (Heath chapter), 1975; Sir Harold Wilson: Yorkshire Walter Mitty, 1977; Parliamentary Profiles, 4 vols, 1984–85, 5th series 1998–2000; New MPs of '92, 1992; Mr Nice Guy and His Chums, 1993; New MPs of '97, 1997. *Recreations:* sketching, jazz-dancing. *Address:* 34 Somali Road, NW2 3RL. *T:* (office) (020) 7435 6673, (020) 7222 5884, *Fax:* (020) 7222 5889.

ROTH, Prof. Klaus Friedrich, FRS 1960; Emeritus Professor, University of London; Hon. Research Fellow, Department of Mathematics, University College London, since 1996; *b* 29 Oct. 1925; *s* of late Dr Franz Roth and Mathilde Roth (*née* Liebrecht); *m* 1955, Melek Khairy, BSc, PhD. *Educ:* St Paul's Sch.; Peterhouse, Cambridge (BA 1945; Hon. Fellow, 1989); University College, London (MSc 1948; PhD 1950; Fellow, 1979). Asst Master, Gordonstoun School, 1945–46. Member of Dept of Mathematics, University College, London, 1948–66; title of Professor in the University of London conferred 1961; Prof. of Pure Maths (Theory of Numbers), 1966–88, Vis. Prof. in Dept of Maths, 1988–96, Fellow, 1999, Imperial College, London. Visiting Lecturer, 1956–57, Vis. Prof., 1965–66, at Mass Inst. of Techn., USA. Foreign Hon. Mem., Amer. Acad. of Arts and Scis, 1966. Hon. FRSE 1993. Fields Medal awarded at International Congress of Mathematicians, 1958; De Morgan Medal, London Math. Soc., 1983; Sylvester Medal, Royal Soc., 1991. *Publications:* papers in various mathematical jls. *Recreations:* chess, cinema, ballroom dancing. *Address:* 24 Burnsall Street, SW3 3ST. *T:* (020) 7352 1363; Colbost, 16A Drummond Road, Inverness IV2 4NB. *T:* (01463) 712595.

ROTH, Prof. Sir Martin, Kt 1972; MD; FRCP; FRCPsych; FRS 1996; DPM; Professor of Psychiatry, University of Cambridge, 1977–85, now Emeritus; Fellow, Trinity College, Cambridge, since 1977; *b* Budapest, 6 Nov. 1917; *s* of late Samuel Simon and Regina Roth; *m* 1945, Constance Heller; three *d*. *Educ:* Davenant Foundn Sch.; University of London, St Mary's Hospital. FRCP 1958. MA Cantab; MD Cantab 1984. Formerly: Senior Registrar, Maida Vale, and Maudsley Hosps; Physician, Crichton Royal Hosp., Dumfries; Director of Clinical Research, Graylingwell Hosp.; Prof. of Psychological Medicine, Univ. of Newcastle upon Tyne, 1956–77. Royal College of Physicians: Examiner in Medicine, 1962–64, 1968–72; Mem. Council, 1968–71. Visiting Assistant Professor, in the Department of Psychiatry, McGill University, Montreal, 1954; Consultant, WHO Expert Cttee on Mental Health Problems of Ageing and the Aged, 1958; Member: Med. Cons. Cttee, Nuffield Provincial Hosp. Trust, 1962; Central Health Services Council, Standing Med. Adv. Cttee, Standing Mental Health Adv. Cttee, DHSS, 1966–75; Scientific Adv. Cttee, CIBA Foundn, 1970–; Syndic of Cambridge Univ. Press, 1980–87. Mayne Vis. Prof., Univ. of Queensland, 1968; Albert Sterne Vis. Prof., Univ. of Indiana, 1976; first Andrew Woods Vis. Prof., Univ. of Iowa, 1976; Vis. Prof., Swedish univs, 1979–80. Adolf Meyer Lectr, Amer. Psychiatric Assoc., 1971; Linacre Lectr, St John's Coll., Cambridge, 1984. Pres., Section of Psychiatry, RSM, 1968–69; Member: MRC, 1964–68; Clinical Research Board, MRC, 1964–70; Hon. Dir, MRC Group for study of relationship between functional and organic mental disorders, 1962–68. FRCPsych (Foundn Fellow; Pres., 1971–75; Hon. Fellow, 1975); Distinguished Fellow, Amer. Psychiatric Assoc., 1972; FMedSci 2001. Hon. FRCPSGlas. Corresp. Mem., Deutsche Gesellschaft für Psychiatrie und Nervenheilkunde; Hon. Mem., Société Royale de Médecine Mentale de Belgique. Hon. Fellow: Amer. Coll. Neuropsychopharmacology; Canadian Psychiatric Assoc., 1972; Australian and New Zealand College of Psychiatry, 1974. Hon. ScD TCD, 1977; Hon. DSc Indiana, 1993. Burlingame Prize, Royal Medico Psychol Assoc., 1951; First Prize, Anna Monika Foundn, 1977; Paul Hoch Prize, Amer. Psychopathological Assoc., 1979; Gold Florin, City of Florence, 1979; Gold Medal, Soc. of Biological Psychiatry, 1980; Kesten Prize, Univ. of Southern Calif, 1983; Sandoz Prize, Internat. Assoc. of Gerontology, 1985; Gold Medal, Max-Planck Inst., 1986; Camillo Golgi Award in Neuroscience, Italian Acad. of Neuroscience, 1993; Lifetime Achievement Medal, Soc. of Biological Psychiatry, 1996. Hon. Citizen, Salamanca, Spain, 1975. Co-Editor: British Jl of Psychiatry, 1967; Psychiatric Developments, 1983–89. *Publications:* (with Mayer-Gross and Slater) Clinical Psychiatry, 1954, (with Slater) rev. 3rd edn 1977 (trans. Spanish, Italian, Portuguese, Chinese); (with L. Iversen) Alzheimer's Disease and Related Disorders, 1986; (with J. Kroll) The Reality of Mental Illness, 1986; (jtly) CAMDEX: the Cambridge examination for mental disorders of the elderly, 1988; (ed jtly) Handbook of Anxiety, Vols I–V, 1988, 1990, 1992; papers on psychiatric aspects of ageing, depressive illness, anxiety states, in various psychiatric and medical journals. *Recreations:* music, literature, conversation, travel. *Address:* Trinity College, Cambridge CB2 1TQ.

ROTH, Peter Marcel; QC 1997; a Recorder, since 2000; *b* 19 Dec. 1952; *s* of Stephen Jeffery Roth and Eva Marta Roth. *Educ:* St Paul's Sch.; New Coll., Oxford (Open Schol.; BA 1974; MA 1986); Law Sch., Univ. of Pennsylvania (Thouron Fellow; LLM 1977). Called to the Bar, Middle Temple, 1977 (Harmsworth Schol.); in practice at the Bar, 1979–. Vis. Associate Prof., Law Sch., Univ. of Pennsylvania, 1987. Jt Chair, Bench and Bar Cttee, United Jewish Israel Appeal, 1997–. Chair, Insurance Wkg Party, Terrence Higgins Trust, 1989–94. Gen. Ed., Bellamy & Child's European Community Law of Competition, 1996–. *Publications:* articles in legal jls. *Recreations:* travel, music. *Address:* Monckton Chambers, 4 Raymond Buildings, Gray's Inn, WC1R 5BP.

ROTHERMERE, 4th Viscount *cr* 1919, of Hemsted, co. Kent; **Jonathan Harold Esmond Vere Harmsworth;** Bt 1910; Baron 1914; Chairman, Daily Mail and General Trust plc, since 1998; *b* 3 Dec. 1967; *s* of 3rd Viscount Rothermere and his 1st wife, Patricia Evelyn Beverley (*née* Matthews; *d* 1992); *S* father, 1998; *m* 1993, Claudia, *d* of T. J. Clemence; one *s* two *d*. *Heir:* *s* Hon. Vere Richard Jonathan Harold Harmsworth; *b* 20 Oct. 1994. *Address:* (office) Northcliffe House, 2 Derry Street, W8 5TT.

ROTHERWICK, 3rd Baron *cr* 1939, of Tylney, Southampton; **Herbert Robin Cayzer;** Bt 1924; *b* 12 March 1954; *s* of 2nd Baron Rotherwick and Sarah-Jane (*d* 1978), *o d* of Sir Michael Nial Slade, 6th Bt; *S* father, 1996; *m* 1982, Sara Jane (marr. diss. 1994), *o d* of Robert James McAlpine; two *s* one *d*; *m* 2000, Tania, *d* of Christopher Fox; one *s*. *Educ:* Harrow. Lieut, Life Guards. Exec. Mem., PFA, 1997–. Elected Mem., H of L, 1999. Pres., Gen. Aviation Awareness Council, 1997–. *Heir:* *s* Hon. Herbert Robin Cayzer, *b* 10 July 1989. *Address:* Cornbury Park, Charlbury, Oxford OX7 3EH.

ROTHES, 21st Earl of, *cr* before 1457; **Ian Lionel Malcolm Leslie;** Lord Leslie 1445; Baron Ballenbreich 1457; *b* 10 May 1932; *o s* of 20th Earl of Rothes and Beryl (*d* 1994), *o d* of J. Lionel Dugdale; *S* father, 1975; *m* 1955, Marigold, *o d* of Sir David M. Evans Bevan, 1st Bt; two *s*. *Educ:* Eton. Sub-Lt RNVR, 1953. *Heir:* *s* Lord Leslie, *qv*. *Address:* Tanglewood, West Tytherley, Salisbury, Wilts SP5 1LX.

ROTHSCHILD, family name of **Baron Rothschild**.

ROTHSCHILD, 4th Baron *cr* 1885; **Nathaniel Charles Jacob Rothschild,** Bt 1847; GBE 1998; Chairman, 1992–98, National Heritage Memorial Fund (administering Heritage Lottery Fund, 1995–98); Chairman: Five Arrows Ltd, since 1980; RIT Capital Partners plc; *b* 29 April 1936; *e s* of 3rd Baron Rothschild, GBE, GM, FRS and Barbara, *o d* of St John Hutchinson, KC; *S* father, 1990; *m* 1961, Serena Mary, *er d* of late Sir Philip Gordon Dunn, 2nd Bt; one *s* three *d*. *Educ:* Eton; Christ Church, Oxford. BA 1st cl. hons History. Chm., 1971–96, now Pres., J. Rothschild Hldgs, subseq. St James's Place Capital. Chm., Bd of Trustees, National Gallery, 1985–91. Pres., Inst. of Jewish Affairs, 1992–. Mem. Council, RCA, 1986– (Sen. Fellow, 1992). Hon. FBA 1998. Hon. PhD Hebrew Univ. of Jerusalem, 1992. Hon. Fellow, City of Jerusalem, 1992. Comdr, Order of Henry the Navigator (Portugal), 1985. *Heir:* *s* Hon. Nathaniel Victor James Rothschild [*b* 12 July 1971; *m* 1995, Annabelle, *d* of Max and Elizabeth Neilson]. *Address:* 14 St James's Place, SW1A 1NP. *T:* (020) 7493 8111.

See also E. Rothschild.

ROTHSCHILD, Edmund Leopold de, CBE 1997; TD; Director, N M Rothschild & Sons Limited, since 1975 (Partner since 1946, Senior Partner, 1960–70, Chairman, 1970–75); *b* 2 Jan. 1916; *s* of late Lionel Nathan de Rothschild and Marie Louise Beer; *m* 1st, 1948, Elizabeth Edith Lentner (*d* 1980); two *s* two *d*; 2nd, 1982, Anne, JP, *widow* of J. Malcolm Harrison, OBE. *Educ:* Harrow Sch.; Trinity Coll., Cambridge. Major, RA (TA). Served France, North Africa and Italy, 1939–46 (wounded). Deputy Chairman: Brit. Newfoundland Corp. Ltd, 1963–69; Churchill Falls (Labrador) Corp. Ltd, 1966–69. Mem., Asia Cttee, BNEC, 1970–71, Chm., 1971. Trustee, Queen's Nursing Inst.; Mem. Council, Royal Nat. Pension Fund for Nurses; Pres., Res. into Ageing. Pres., Assoc. of Jewish Ex-Servicemen and Women; Vice-Pres., Council of Christians and Jews. Governor, Tech. Univ. of Nova Scotia. Hon. LLD Memorial Univ. of Newfoundland, 1961; Hon. DSc Salford, 1983. Order of the Sacred Treasure, 1st Class (Japan), 1973. *Publications:* Window on the World, 1949; A Gilt-Edged Life: memoir, 1998. *Recreations:* gardening, fishing. *Address:* New Court, St Swithin's Lane, EC4P 4DU. *T:* (020) 7280 5000; Exbury House, Exbury, Southampton SO4 1AF. *T:* (023) 8089 3145. *Clubs:* White's, Portland.

See also L. D. de Rothschild.

ROTHSCHILD, Emma, CMG 2000; Fellow, since 1988, and Co-Director, Centre for History and Economics, since 1991, King's College, Cambridge; *b* 16 May 1948; *d* of 3rd Baron Rothschild, GBE, GM, FRS and of Lady Rothschild, MBE (*née* Teresa Mayor); *m* 1991, Prof. Amartya Kumar Sen, *qv*. *Educ:* Somerville Coll., Oxford (MA); Massachusetts Inst. of Technology (Kennedy Schol. in Econs). Associate Professor: of Humanities, MIT, 1978–80; of Science, Technology and Society, MIT, 1979–88; Dir de Recherches Invité, Ecole des Hautes Etudes en Sciences Sociales, Paris, 1981–82. Mem., OECD Gp of Experts on Science and Technology in the New Socio-Economic Context, 1976–80; OECD Sci. Examiner, Aust., 1984–85. Member: Govg Bd, Stockholm Internat. Peace Res. Inst., 1983–93; Govg Bd, Stockholm Envmt Inst., 1989–93; Bd, Olof Palme Meml Fund (Stockholm), 1986–; Royal Commn on Environmental Pollution, 1986–94; Bd, British Council, 1993–98; Bd, UN Foundn, 1998–; Council for Sci. and Technol., 1998–; Chairman: UN Res. Inst. for Social Develt, 1999–; Rothschild Archive Trust, 1999–; Kennedy Meml Trust, 2000–. *Publications:* Paradise Lost: the Decline of the Auto-Industrial Age, 1973; Economic Sentiments, 2001; articles in learned and other jls. *Address:* King's College, Cambridge CB2 1ST.

ROTHSCHILD, Sir Evelyn de, Kt 1989; Chairman, N M Rothschild & Sons Limited; *b* 29 Aug. 1931; *s* of late Anthony Gustav de Rothschild; *m* 1973, Victoria Schott; (marr. diss. 2000) two *s* one *d*; *m* 2000, Lynn Forester. *Educ:* Harrow; Trinity Coll., Cambridge. Chairman: Economist Newspaper, 1972–89; United Racecourses Ltd, 1977–94. Chm., British Merchant Banking and Securities Houses Assoc. (formerly Accepting Houses Cttee), 1985–89. *Recreations:* art, racing.

ROTHSCHILD, Baron Guy (Edouard Alphonse Paul) de; Officier de la Légion d'Honneur, 1959; *b* 21 May 1909; *s* of late Baron Edouard de Rothschild and late Baronne de Rothschild (*née* Germaine Halphen); *m* 1st, 1937, Baronne Alix Schey de Koromla (marr. diss. 1956; she *d* 1982); one *s*; 2nd, 1957, Baronne Marie-Hélène de Zuylen de Nyevelt (who *m* 1st, Comte François de Nicolay; she *d* 1996); one *s* and one step *s*. *Educ:* Lycées Condorcet et Louis le Grand, Facultés de Droit et des Lettres (Licencié en Droit). Served War of 1939–45 (Croix de Guerre). Chevalier du Mérite Agricole, 1948. Associé de MM de Rothschild Frères, 1936–67; President: Compagnie du Chemin de Fer du Nord, 1949–68; Banque Rothschild, 1968–78; Société Imétal, 1975–79. Mem., Société d'Encouragement, 1950–92. *Publications:* The Whims of Fortune (autobiog.), 1985; Mon ombre Siamoise, 1993; Le Fantôme de Léa, 1998. *Recreation:* haras et écurie de courses, golf. *Address:* 2 rue Saint-Louis-en-l'Isle, 75004 Paris, France. *Clubs:* Nouveau Cercle, Automobile Club de France.

ROTHSCHILD, Leopold David de, CBE 1985; Director, N M Rothschild & Sons Limited, since 1970 (Partner, 1956–70); *b* 12 May 1927; *yr s* of Lionel de Rothschild and Marie Louise Beer. *Educ:* Bishops Coll. Sch., Canada; Harrow; Trinity Coll., Cambridge. Director of Bank of England, 1970–83. Chairman: Anglo Venezuelan Soc., 1975–78; English Chamber Orchestra and Music Soc. Ltd, 1963–2001; Bach Choir, 1976–99; Music Adv. Cttee, British Council, 1986–93; Council, RCM, 1988–99 (FRCM 1977). Trustee, Science Mus., 1987–98; Mem. Council, Winston Churchill Meml Trust, 1990–. DUniv York, 1991. Order of Francisco de Miranda, 1st cl. (Venezuela), 1978; Gran Oficial, Order of Merit (Chile), 1993; Ordem Nacional do Cruzeiro do Sul (Brazil), 1993; Encomienda, Order of Aztec Eagle (Mexico), 1994. *Recreations:* music, walking, industrial archaeology. *Address:* New Court, St Swithin's Lane, EC4P 4DU. *T:* (020) 7280 5000. *Clubs:* Brooks's; Royal Yacht Squadron.

See also E. L. de Rothschild.

ROTHSCHILD, Hon. Dame Miriam (Louisa), (Hon. Dame Miriam Lane), DBE 2000 (CBE 1982); FRS 1985; *b* 5 Aug. 1908; *e d* of Hon. N. C. Rothschild, 2nd *s* of 1st Baron Rothschild and Rozsika de Wertheimstein; *m* 1943, Capt. George Lane, MC (marriage dissolved, 1957); one *s* three *d* (and one *s* one *d* decd). *Educ:* home. Member: Zoological and Entomological Research Coun.; Marine Biological Assoc.; Royal Entomological Soc.; Systematics Assoc.; Soc. for Promotion of Nature Reserves, etc.; Ed., Novitates Zoologica, 1938–41; Mem., Publications Cttee, Zoological Soc.; Foreign Office, 1940–42; Trustee, British Museum of Natural History, 1967–75. Mem., Amer. Acad. of Arts and Scis. Vis. Prof. in Biology, Royal Free Hosp. Romanes Lectr, Oxford, 1985. Hon. Fellow, St Hugh's Coll., Oxford. Hon. DSc: Oxford, 1968; Gothenburg, 1983; Hull, 1984; Northwestern (Chicago), 1986; Leicester, 1987; Open Univ., 1989; Essex, 1998; Cambridge, 1999. Floral Medal, Lynn Soc., 1968; Wigglesworth Gold Medal, Royal Entomol Soc., 1982; Silver Medal, Internat. Soc. of Chemical Ecology,

1989; VMH 1991; Bloomer Award, Linnean Soc.; Mendel Award, Czech Sci. Acad., 1993. Defence Medal (1940–45). *Publications:* Catalogue Rothschild Collection of Fleas (British Museum): vol. I 1953, vol. II 1956, vol. III 1962,vol. IV 1966, vol. V 1971, vol. VI 1983; (with Theresa Clay) Fleas, Flukes and Cuckoos, 1952; (with Clive Farrell) The Butterfly Gardener, 1983; Dear Lord Rothschild (biog.), 1983; (with Prof. Schlein and Prof. Ito) Atlas of Insect Tissue, 1985; Animals & Man, 1986; Butterfly Cooing Like a Dove, 1991; The Rothschilds Gardens, 1996; Rothschild's Reserves, 1997; 300 contribs to scientific jls. *Recreations:* natural history, conservation. *Address:* Ashton Wold, Peterborough PE8 5LZ. *Clubs:* Queen's, Entomological.

ROTHSTEIN, Saul; Solicitor to the Post Office, 1976–81; *b* 4 July 1920; *s* of late Simon Rothstein and late Zelda Rothstein; *m* 1949, Judith Noemi (*née* Katz); two *d. Educ:* Church Institute Sch., Bolton; Manchester Univ (LLB). Admitted solicitor, 1947. War service, RAF, 1941–46 (Flt-Lt). Entered Solicitor's Dept, General Post Office, 1949, Asst Solicitor, 1963; Director, Advisory Dept, Solicitor's Office, Post Office, 1972–76. *Recreations:* chamber music, walking, travel. *Address:* 9 Templars Crescent, Finchley, N3 3QR. *T:* (020) 8346 3701.

ROTHWELL, Margaret Irene, CMG 1992; HM Diplomatic Service, retired; Ambassador to Côte d'Ivoire, 1990–97, and concurrently to the Republic of Niger, the People's Democratic Republic of Burkina and Liberia; *b* 25 Aug. 1938; *d* of Harry Rothwell and Martha (*née* Goedecke). *Educ:* Southampton Grammar School for Girls; Lady Margaret Hall, Oxford (BA LitHum). Foreign Office, 1961; Third, later Second Secretary, UK Delegn to Council of Europe, Strasbourg, 1964; FO, 1966; Second Sec. (Private Sec. to Special Representative in Africa), Nairobi, 1967; Second, later First Sec., Washington, 1968; FCO, 1972; First Sec. and Head of Chancery, Helsinki, 1976; FCO, 1980; Counsellor and Hd of Trng Dept, FCO, 1981–83; Counsellor, Consul-Gen. and Head of Chancery, Jakarta, 1984–87; Overseas Inspectorate, FCO, 1987–90. Reviewer, Quinquennial Review of the Marshall Aid Commemoration Commn, 1998; UK Rep., Jt US/UK Commn on Student Travel Exchanges, 1998; voluntary work for Govt of Rwanda, 2001. Hon. LLD Southampton, 1994. *Recreations:* travel, gardening, cooking, tennis. *Address:* Hill House, Knapp, Ampfield, Romsey, Hants SO51 9BT.

ROUCH, Peter Christopher; QC 1996; *b* 15 June 1947; *s* of Rupert Trevelyan Rouch and Doris Linda Rouch; *m* 1980, Carol Sandra Francis; one *s* one *d. Educ:* UCW, Aberystwyth (LLB). Called to the Bar, Gray's Inn, 1972. *Recreations:* golf, ski-ing, fishing, cinema, music. *Address:* Church View, 9 Mayals Road, Mayals, Swansea SA3 5BT; 20 Archery Close, W2 2BE. *Club:* Cardiff and County (Cardiff).

ROUGIER, Maj.-Gen. Charles Jeremy, CB 1986; FICE; Director, Royal Horticultural Society's Garden, Rosemoor, 1988–95; *b* 23 Feb. 1933; *s* of late Lt-Col and Mrs C. L. Rougier; *m* 1964, Judith Cawood Ellis; three *s* one *d. Educ:* Marlborough Coll.; Pembroke Coll., Cambridge (MA). FICE 1986. Aden, 1960; Instructor, RMA Sandhurst, 1961–62; psc 1963; MA to MGO, 1964–66; comd 11 Engineer Sqn, Commonwealth Bde, 1966–68; jssc 1968; Company Comd, RMA Sandhurst, 1969–70; Directing Staff, Staff Coll., Camberley, 1970–72; CO 21 Engineer Regt, BAOR, 1972–74; Staff of Chief of Defence Staff, 1974–77; Commandant, Royal Sch. of Military Engineering, 1977–79; RCDS 1980; COS, Headquarters Northern Ireland, 1981; Asst Chief of General Staff (Trng), 1982–83; Dir of Army Training, 1983–84; Chm., Review of Officer Training and Educn Study, 1985; Engr-in-Chief (Army), 1985–88, retd. Col Comdt, RE, 1987–92. Mem. (part-time), Lord Chancellor's Panel of Ind. Inspectors, 1988–. Gold Veitch Meml Medal, RHS, 1995. *Recreations:* hill walking, DIY, gardening. *Address:* c/o Lloyds TSB, 5 High Street, Bideford, Devon EX39 2AD. *Club:* Army and Navy.

ROUGIER, Hon. Sir Richard George, Kt 1986; **Hon. Mr Justice Rougier;** Judge of the High Court of Justice, Queen's Bench Division, since 1986; *b* 12 Feb. 1932; *s* of late George Ronald Rougier, CBE, QC, and Georgette Heyer, novelist; *m* 1st, 1962, Susanna Allen Flint (*née* Whitworth) (marr. diss. 1996); one *s*; 2nd, 1996, Mrs Judy Williams. *Educ:* Marlborough Coll.; Pembroke Coll., Cambridge (Exhibr, BA). Called to Bar, Inner Temple, 1956, Bencher 1979. QC 1972; a Recorder, 1973–86; Presiding Judge, Midland and Oxford Circuit, 1990–94. *Recreations:* fishing, golf, bridge. *Address:* Royal Courts of Justice, WC2A 2LL. *Clubs:* Garrick; Rye Golf; Sunningdale Golf.

ROULSTONE, Brig. Joan Margaret; Director, Women (Army), 1992–94; Aide-de-Camp to the Queen, 1992–95; *b* 7 Nov. 1945; *d* of Eric Laurie Frank Tyler and Jessie Tyler (*née* Louise); *m* 1971, Peter John Roulstone. *Educ:* seven schools worldwide. Commnd, WRAC, 1964; UK and BAOR, 1965–78; resigned 1978, reinstated, 1980; UK, 1980–86; Corps Recruiting and Liaison Officer, WRAC, 1986–87; Chief G1/G4 NE Dist and 2nd Inf. Div., 1988–89; Comd WRAC, UKLF, 1990–91. *Address:* c/o Barclays Bank, Priestpopple, Hexham, Northumberland NE46 1PE.

ROUND, Prof. Nicholas Grenville, FBA 1996; Hughes Professor of Hispanic Studies, University of Sheffield, since 1994; *b* 6 June 1938; *s* of Isaac Eric Round and Laura Christabel (*née* Poole); *m* 1966, Ann Le Vin; one *d. Educ:* Boyton CP Sch., Cornwall; Launceston Coll.; Pembroke Coll., Oxford. BA (1st cl. Hons, Spanish and French) 1959; MA 1963; DPhil 1967. MITI 1990. Lecturer in Spanish, Queen's Univ. of Belfast, 1962–71, Reader, 1971–72; Warden, Alanbrooke Hall, QUB, 1970–72; Stevenson Prof. of Hispanic Studies, Glasgow Univ., 1972–94. Mem., Exec. Cttee, Strathclyde Region Labour Party, 1986–94. Pres., Assoc. Internat. de Galdosistas, 1999. Officer, Order of Isabel the Catholic (Spain), 1990. *Publications:* Unamuno: Abel Sánchez: a critical guide, 1974; The Greatest Man Uncrowned: a study of the fall of Alvaro de Luna, 1986; trans., Tirso de Molina, Damned for Despair, 1986; (ed) Re-reading Unamuno, 1989; On Reasoning and Realism: three easy pieces, 1991; Libro llamado Fedrón, 1993; (ed) Translation Studies in Hispanic Contexts, 1998; contribs to: Mod. Lang. Review, Bulletin Hispanic Studies, Proc. Royal Irish Academy, etc. *Recreations:* reading, music, all aspects of Cornwall. *Address:* Department of Hispanic Studies, The University, Sheffield S10 2TN. *T:* (0114) 222 4401. *Club:* (Hon. Life Mem.) Students' Union (Belfast).

ROUNDS, Helen; *see* Edwards, H.

ROUNTREE, His Honour Peter Charles Robert; a Circuit Judge, 1986–2001; *b* 28 April 1936; *s* of late Francis Robert George Rountree, MBE and Mary Felicity Patricia Rountree, MBE (*née* Wilson); *m* 1968, Nicola Mary (*née* Norman-Butler) (marr. diss. 1996); one *s* one step *d. Educ:* Uppingham School; St John's College, Cambridge (MA). Called to the Bar, Inner Temple, 1961; a Recorder, April–July 1986. *Recreations:* sailing, golf, tennis. *Clubs:* Boodle's, Pratt's, Royal Automobile, Royal Yacht Squadron, Royal London Yacht; Rye Golf, New Zealand Golf.

ROUS, family name of **Earl of Stradbroke**.

ROUSE, Jonathan Mark; Chief Executive, Commission for Architecture and the Built Environment, since 2000; *b* 23 May 1968; *s* of James Clement Rouse and Barbara Jean Rouse (*née* Fowler); *m* 1991, Heulwen Mary Evans. *Educ:* Univ. of Manchester (LLB); Univ. of Nottingham (MBA Finance Dist.); Univ. of N London (MA Dist.). Principal Policy Officer, Ealing BC, 1992–93; Policy Analyst, Energy Saving Trust, 1993–94; Private Sec. to Housing Minister, 1994–95; Policy and Communications Manager, English Partnerships, 1995–98; Sec., Govt Urban Task Force, 1998–99. Hon. RIBA 2001. *Recreations:* saxophone, hiking, cinema. *Address:* Commission for Architecture and the Built Environment, 16th Floor, Tower Building, 11 York Road, SE1 7NX. *Clubs:* Queen's Park Rangers Football; Nottingham Ambassadors.

ROUSE, Ruth Elizabeth; High Commissioner for Grenada in United Kingdom, since 1999 and to South Africa, since 2000; Ambassador-Designate to France, and High Commissioner-Designate to Nigeria, since 2001; *b* 30 Jan. 1963. *Educ:* German Foundn for Internat. Develt, Berlin (Dip. Internat. Relns and Econ. Co-operation 1987); Diplomatic Acad. of London, PCL, (Post-Grad. Prog. in Diplomacy, Practice, Procedures, Dynamics 1989); Carleton Univ., Canada (BA French and Spanish 1996). Ministry of Foreign Affairs, Grenada: Desk Officer (Africa and ME Affairs), Political and Economic Affairs Div., 1982–83; Protocol Officer, Protocol and Consular Div., 1983–90; Second Sec. (Protocol, Culture and Develt), Orgn of Eastern Caribbean States, High Commn, Ottawa, 1990–96; Chief of Protocol, 1996–99. Perm Rep., IMO, 2000–. Mem., Nat. Celebrations Cttee, Grenada, 1996; Governor: Commonwealth Inst., 1999–; Commonwealth Foundn, 1999–. Independence Award for Exemplary Public Service, 1998. *Recreations:* reading, travelling, Caribbean cooking, tennis, designing (art), photography, meeting people of different cultures, communications (radio/television), music (piano). *Address:* High Commission for Grenada, 1 Collingham Gardens, SW5 0HW. *T:* (020) 7373 7809, *Fax:* (020) 7370 7040; *e-mail:* grenada@high-commission.freeserve.co.uk; (home) 93 Dale Wood Road, Petts Wood, Orpington, Kent BR6 0BY. *T:* (01689) 823127, *Fax:* (01689) 896442; *e-mail:* ruthelizabethrouse@hotmail.com; Westerhall, St David's, Grenada. *T:* 4435316. *Clubs:* Royal Over-Seas League, Royal Commonwealth Society.

ROUSSEAU, Prof. George Sebastian, PhD; Research Professor of English, De Montfort University, since 1999; *b* 23 Feb. 1941; *s* of Hyman Victoire Rousseau and Esther (*née* Zacuto). *Educ:* Amherst Coll., USA (BA 1962); Princeton Univ. (MA 1964; PhD 1966). Princeton University: Osgood Fellow in English Lit., 1965–66; Woodrow Wilson Dissertation Fellow, 1966; Instructor, then Asst Prof., Harvard Univ., 1966–68; University of California, Los Angeles: Asst Prof. of English, 1968–69; Associate Prof., 1969–76; Prof., 1976–94; Regius Prof. of Eng. Lit., and Dir, Thomas Reid Inst., Aberdeen Univ., 1994–98. Fulbright Res. Prof., W Germany, 1970; Cambridge University: Hon. Fellow, Wolfson Coll., 1974–75; Overseas Fellow, 1979; Vis. Fellow Commoner, Trinity Coll., 1982; Sen. Fulbright Res. Schol., Sir Thomas Browne Inst., Netherlands, 1983; Vis. Exchange Prof., King's Coll., Cambridge, 1984; Clark Liby Prof., Univ. of Calif, 1985–86; Sen. Fellow, NEH, 1986–87; Vis. Fellow and Waynflete Lectr, Magdalen Coll., Oxford, 1993–94. Book reviewer, NY Times (Sunday), 1967–. FRSocMed 1967; FRSA 1973. *Publications:* (with M. Hope Nicolson) This Long Disease My Life: Alexander Pope and the sciences, 1968; (with N. Rudenstine) English Poetic Satire, 1969; (ed jtly) The Augustan Milieu: essays presented to Louis A. Landa, 1970; (ed jtly) Tobias Smollett: bicentennial essays presented to Lewis M. Knapp, 1971; (ed) Organic Form: the life of an idea, 1972; Goldsmith: the critical heritage, 1974; (with R. Porter) The Ferment of Knowledge: studies in the historiography of science, 1980; The Letters and Private Papers of Sir John Hill, 1981; Tobias Smollett: essays of two decades, 1982; (ed) Science and the Imagination: the Berkeley Conference, 1987; (with R. Porter) Sexual Underworlds of the Enlightenment, 1987; (with P. Rogers) The Enduring Legacy: Alexander Pope Tercentenary Essays, 1988; (with R. Porter) Exoticism in the Enlightenment, 1990; The Languages of Psyche: mind and body in enlightenment thought, 1990; Perilous Enlightenment: pre- and post-modern discourses—sexual, historical, 1991; Enlightenment Crossings: pre- and post-modern discourses—anthropological, 1991; Enlightenment Borders: pre- and post-modern discourses—medical, scientific, 1991; (jtly) Hysteria Before Freud, 1993; (with Roy Porter) Gout: the patrician malady, 1998; contrib. numerous articles to learned jls and mags. *Recreations:* chamber music, opera, ski-ing, walking, hiking. *Address:* Osterley House, Wellshead, Harwell, Didcot, Oxfordshire OX11 0HD. *T:* (01235) 221222; *e-mail:* gsr@dmu.ac.uk.

ROUSSEL, (Philip) Lyon, OBE 1974; Controller, Arts Division, British Council, 1979–83; retired; *b* 17 Oct. 1923; *s* of late Paul Marie Roussel and Beatrice (*née* Cuthbert; later Lady Murray); *m* 1959, Elisabeth Mary, *d* of Kenneth and Kathleen Bennett; one *s* one *d. Educ:* Hurstpierpoint Coll.; St Edmund Hall, Oxford (MA, Cert. Public and Social Admin); Chelsea Sch. of Art. Served Indian Army in Parachute Regt, 1942–46 (Major); Parachute Regt (TA), 1946–50. Sudan Political Service, 1950–55; Principal, War Office, 1955–56; Associated Newspapers, 1956–57; British Council, 1960–83: India, 1960–67 (Regional Rep., Western and Central India, 1964–67); Dir, Scholarships, 1967–71; Rep. and Cultural Attaché, British Embassy, Belgium and Luxembourg, 1971–76; Europalia-Great Britain Festival Cttee, 1973; Cultural Attaché (Counsellor), British Embassy, Washington, 1976–79. Sponsorship Consultant, National Theatre, 1983–84. Member: Fest. of India Cttee, 1981–82; British Adv. Cttee, Britain Salutes New York, 1981–83; Bd, The Hanover Band, 1984–87; Common Room, Wolfson Coll., Oxford, 1988 (Chm., Arts Soc., 2000–). Hon. Organiser, Poppy Appeal, Woodstock Br., Royal British Legion, 1991–97 (Cert. of Appreciation, 1997). FRGS 1981; FRSA 1979. *Recreations:* painting, looking at pictures, travel, tennis, golf and a barn in France. *Address:* 26 High Street, Woodstock, Oxford OX20 1TG. *Clubs:* Athenæum; Oxford Union; Woodstock Tennis; North Oxford Golf.

ROUSSOS, Stavros G.; Secretary General, Ministry of Foreign Affairs, Greece, 1980–82, retired; *b* 1918; *m*; two *s* one *d. Educ:* Univ. of Lyons (LèsL); Univ. of Paris (LèsL, LèsScPol, LLD). Entered Greek Diplomatic Service as Attaché, Min. of Foreign Affairs, 1946; Mem., Greek Delegn to Gen. Assembly of UN, 1948 and 1954–55; Sec. to Permanent Mission of Greece to UN in New York, 1950; Consul, Alexandria, 1955; i/c Greek Consulate General, Cairo, 1956; Counsellor, 1959; Min. of Foreign Affairs, 1959–61; Mem., Perm. Delegn of Greece to EEC, Brussels, 1962; Perm. Rep. to EEC, 1969; Dir-Gen., Econ. and Commercial Affairs, Min. of Foreign Affairs, 1972; Ambassador of Greece to UK, 1974–79; Alternate Sec. Gen., Min. of Foreign Affairs, 1979–80. Grand Comdr, Order of Phoenix; Commander: Order of Belgian Crown; Order of Merit of Egypt. *Publication:* The Status of Dodecanese Islands in International Law, 1940 (Paris). *Address:* 5 Loukianou Street, Athens 10675, Greece.

ROUT, Leslie; Director General, National Kidney Research Fund and Kidney Foundation, 1992–97; *b* 5 Dec. 1936; *s* of James Rout and Ada Elizabeth Rout; *m* 1957, Josephine Goodley; one *s* one *d. Educ:* Queens, Wisbech. Police cadet, 1952–54; Nat. Service, 1954–56; Police Service, 1956–89: served in all depts; attained rank of Comdr Ops; awarded 6 commendations. FIMgt. *Recreations:* music, history, travel. *Address:* Top Barn, 21 Ermine Street, Little Stukeley, Huntingdon PE17 5BE.

ROUT, Owen Howard, FCIB; Executive Director (UK Operations), Barclays PLC and Barclays Bank PLC, 1987–90; Chairman: Barclays Financial Services Ltd, 1988–90; Starmin plc, 1990–93 (Deputy Chairman, 1993–94); *b* 16 April 1930; *s* of Frederick Owen and Marion Rout; *m* 1954, Jean (*née* Greetham); two *d. Educ:* Grey High Sch., Port Elizabeth, SA. ACIS. Dir, Barclays Bank UK Ltd, 1977–87; Gen. Man., Barclays PLC and Barclays Bank PLC, 1982–87. Chairman: Barclays Insurance Services Co. Ltd, 1982–85; Barclays Insurance Brokers International Ltd, 1982–85; Mercantile Gp, 1989–92; Director: Spreadeagle Insurance Co. Ltd, 1983–85; Baric Ltd, 1982–84; Albaraka Internat. Bank, 1990–93. Chartered Institute of Bankers: Mem. Council, 1985–90; Treas., 1986–90. Mem., Supervisory Bd, Banking World Magazine, 1986–90. Mem., Bd of Govs, Anglia Polytechnic Univ., 1993–. *Recreations:* watching sport—Rugby and cricket, playing golf, listening to music, gardening. *Club:* Saffron Walden Golf.

ROUTH, Donald Thomas; Under Secretary, Department of the Environment, 1978–90; *b* 22 May 1936; *s* of Thomas and Flora Routh; *m* 1961, Janet Hilda Allum. *Educ:* Leeds Modern Sch. Entered WO, Northern Comd, York, as Exec. Officer, 1954; Nat. Service, RN, 1954–56; Higher Exec. Officer, Comd Secretariat, Kenya, 1961–64; Asst Principal, Min. of Housing and Local Govt, 1964–66; Asst Private Sec. to Minister, 1966–67; Principal, 1967; on loan to Civil Service Selection Bd, 1971; Asst Sec., DoE, 1972; Under Sec., 1978; Regional Dir, West Midlands, 1978–81; Hd of Construction Industries Directorate, 1981–85; Dir of Senior Staff Management, 1985–86; Controller, The Crown Suppliers, 1986.

ROUTLEDGE, Alan, CBE 1979; *b* 12 May 1919; *s* of late George and of Rose Routledge, Wallasey, Cheshire; *m* 1949, Irene Hendry, Falkirk, Stirlingshire; one *s* (and one *s* decd). *Educ:* Liscard High Sch., Wallasey. Served Army, Cheshire (Earl of Chester's) Yeomanry, 1939–46. Control Commn for Germany, 1946–51; Diplomatic Wireless Service of FO (now Foreign and Commonwealth Office), 1951–79: Head, Cypher and Signals Branch, 1962; Head, Commns Planning Staff, 1973; Head, Commns Ops Dept, 1979; retired FCO, 1979. *Recreations:* English history, cricket, golf. *Address:* 15 Ilford Court, Elmbridge, Cranleigh, Surrey GU6 8TJ. *T:* (01483) 276669. *Clubs:* Civil Service; Old Liscardians.

ROUTLEDGE, (Katherine) Patricia, OBE 1993; actress; *b* 17 Feb. 1929; *d* of Isaac Edgar Routledge and Catherine (*née* Perry). *Educ:* Birkenhead High Sch.; Univ. of Liverpool; Bristol Old Vic Theatre Sch.; Guildhall Sch. of Music. *Theatre* appearances include: A Midsummer's Night Dream, Liverpool Playhouse, 1952; The Duenna, Westminster, 1954; musical version, The Comedy of Errors, Arts, 1956; The Love Doctor, Piccadilly, 1959; revue, Out of My Mind, Lyric, Hammersmith, 1961; Little Mary Sunshine, Comedy, 1962; Virtue in Danger, Mermaid, transf. Strand, 1963; How's the World Treating You?, Hampstead Theatre Club, 1965, New Arts, transf. Wyndham's, Comedy and Broadway, 1966; Darling of the Day, George Abbott, NY, 1967 (Antoinette Perry Award); The Caucasian Chalk Circle, The Country Wife, and The Magistrate, Chichester Fest., 1969; Cowardy Custard, Mermaid, 1972; Dandy Dick, Chichester Fest., transf. Garrick, 1973; 1600 Pennsylvania Avenue, Mark Hellinger, NY, 1976; Pirates of Penzance, NY, 1980; Noises Off, Savoy, 1981; When the Wind Blows, Whitehall, 1983; Richard III, RSC, 1984–85; Candide, Old Vic, 1988–89 (Laurence Olivier Award); Come for the Ride (one-woman show), Playhouse, 1989; Carousel, NT, 1992; The Rivals, Albery, 1994; Beatrix, Chichester, 1996, transf. Greenwich, 1997; The Importance of Being Earnest, Chichester, transf. Haymarket, 1999, Savoy, 2001; *television* appearances include: Doris and Doreen, 1978; A Woman of No Importance, 1982; Victoria Wood As Seen on TV, 1983–86; Marjorie and Men, 1985; A Lady of Letters, 1988; Keeping Up Appearances, 1990–; Hetty Wainthropp Investigates, 1996–; Miss Fozzard finds her Feet, 1998; many radio plays. *Address:* c/o Marmont Management Ltd, Langham House, 308 Regent Street, W1R 5AL.

ROUX, Michel André; Director and Chef de Cuisine, since 1967; *b* 19 April 1941; *s* of late Henry Roux and of Germaine Triger; *m* 1984, Robyn (Margaret Joyce); one *s* two *d* by previous marr. *Educ:* Ecole Primaire, Saint Mande; Brevet de Maîtrise (Pâtisserie). Apprenticeship, Pâtisserie Loyal, Paris, 1955–57; Commis Pâtissier-Cuisinier, British Embassy, Paris, 1957–59; Commis de Cuisine with Miss Cécile de Rothschild, Paris, 1959–60; Military service, 1960–62, at Versailles and Colomb Bechar, Sahara; Chef with Miss Cécile de Rothschild, 1962–67; came to England, 1967; restaurants opened: Le Gavroche, 1967; Le Poulbot, 1969; Waterside Inn, 1972; Gavvers, 1981. Mem., UK Br., Académie Culinaire de France, 1984–. TV series, At Home with the Roux Brothers, 1988. Numerous French and British prizes and awards, including: Médaille d'Or, Cuisiniers Français, 1972; Restaurateur of the Year, Caterer & Hotelkeeper, 1985; Personnalité de l'Année, Gastronomie dans le Monde, Paris, 1985; Culinary Trophy, Assoc. of Maîtres-Pâtissiers La Saint Michel, 1986; (with Albert Roux) Men of the Year (Radar), 1989. Chevalier, National Order of Merit (France), 1987; Officer, Order of Agricultural Merit (France), 1987; Chevalier, Order of Arts and of Letters (France), 1990. *Publications:* Life is a Menu (autobiog.), 2000; with Albert Roux: New Classic Cuisine, 1983 (French edn, 1985); The Roux Brothers on Pâtisserie, 1986; At Home with the Roux Brothers, 1988; French Country Cooking, 1989; Cooking for Two, 1991; Desserts: a lifelong passion, 1994; Sauces, 1996. *Recreations:* shooting, walking, skiing. *Address:* The Waterside Inn, Ferry Road, Bray, Berks SL6 2AT. *T:* (01628) 620691; 1 Bettoney Vere, Bray, Berks SL6 2BA. *Club:* The Benedicts.

ROWALLAN, 4th Baron *cr* 1911; **John Polson Cameron Corbett;** Director: Rowallan Holdings, since 1991; Rowallan Activity Centre Ltd, since 1991; Rowallan Ltd, since 1997; *b* 8 March 1947; *s* of 3rd Baron Rowallan and of his 1st wife, Eleanor Mary Boyle; *S* father, 1993; *m* 1st, 1971, Jane Green (marr. diss. 1983); one *s* one *d*; 2nd, 1984, Sandrew Bryson (marr. diss. 1994); one *s* one *d*; 3rd, 1995, Claire Dinning; one step *s* one step *d*. *Educ:* Cothill House; Eton Coll.; RAC, Cirencester. Chartered Surveyor, 1972–; farmer, 1975–; equestrian centre owner. Area Rep. Judge, BSJA, 1982–; Dir, BSJA, 1998–. Commentator at equestrian events. Contested (C): Glasgow, Garscadden, Oct. 1974; Kilmarnock, 1979. Former Member All Party Groups on: Mental Health; Clinical Depression; Arts and Heritage; Alternative Medicine; Racing and Bloodstock; Rwanda and Genocide; Conservation; Advertising; Epilepsy; introduced Mental Health (Amendment) Act 1998 to H of L. Mem., Greenway Cttee. Dir, SANE, 1998–. Patron, Depression Alliance, 1998–. Chairman: Lochgoin Covenanters Trust, 1977–; Charity Shopping Day Trust, 1999–2001. *Recreations:* commentating, ski-ing. *Heir:* *s* Hon. Jason William Polson Cameron Corbett [*b* 21 April 1972; *m* 2000, Anna, *d* of Chris Smedley]. *Address:* Meiklemosside, Fenwick, Ayrshire KA3 6AY. *T:* (01560) 600769.

ROWAN, Patricia Adrienne, (Mrs Ivan Rowan); journalist; Editor, The Times Educational Supplement, 1989–97; *d* of late Henry Matthew Talintyre and Gladys Talintyre; *m* 1960, Ivan Settle Harris Rowan; one *s. Educ:* Harrow County Grammar School for Girls. Time & Tide, 1952–56; Sunday Express, 1956–57; Daily Sketch, 1957–58; News Chronicle, 1958–60; Granada Television, 1961–62; Sunday Times, 1962–66; TES, 1972–97. Bd of Trustees, Nat. Children's Bureau, 1997–. Hon. Fellow, Inst. of Educn, London Univ., 1997. Hon. FRSA 1989. *Publications:* What Sort of Life?, 1980; (contrib.) Education—the Wasted Years?, 1988. *Recreations:* cookery, gardening. *Address:* Park View, Nupend, Horsley, Stroud, Glos GL6 0PY. *Club:* Reform.

See also D. G. Talintyre.

ROWAN-ROBINSON, Prof. (Geoffrey) Michael, PhD; FInstP; Professor of Astrophysics, Blackett Laboratory, and Head, Astrophysics Group, Imperial College, University of London, since 1993; *b* 9 July 1942; *s* of John Christopher Rowan-Robinson and Audrey Christine (*née* Wynne); *m* 1978, Mary Lewin (*née* Tubb); one *d*, and two step *s. Educ:* Eshton Hall Sch., Gargrave, Yorks; Pembroke Coll., Cambridge (BA 1963); Royal Holloway Coll., London (PhD 1969). FInstP 1992. Queen Mary, later Queen Mary and Westfield College, London: Asst Lectr in Maths, QMC, 1967–69; Lectr, 1969–78; Reader in Astronomy, 1978–87; Prof. of Astrophysics, 1987–93. Royal Soc. and Academia dei Lincei Vis. Res. Fellow, Univ. of Bologna, 1969, 1971, 1976; Vis. Res. Fellow, Univ. of Calif, Berkeley, 1978–79. Member: Exec. Cttee, IAU Commn 47 on Cosmology, 1976–79; Sci. Team for Infrared Astronomical Satellite, 1977–84; Astronomy Wkg Gp, ESA, 1985–88; Space Sci. Prog. Bd, BNSC, 1988–91. Chm., Time Allocation Cttee, Isaac Newton Gp, 1988–91; Member, Time Allocation Committee: ESA's Infrared Space Observatory mission, 1993–96; Hubble Space Telescope, 1995, 2000. Co-investigator, Infrared Space Observatory Photometer, ESA, 1996–99; Principal Investigator, European Large Area ISO Survey, 1995–2000. Chm., Res. Assessment Panel for Astronomy, PPARC, 1994–97. Mem., RAS, 1965–. Mem., Scientists for Global Responsibility, 1992–; Vice-Chm., Scientists Against Nuclear Arms, 1988–92. Chm., Hornsey Lab. Party, 1971–72. Governor: Creighton Comp. Sch., 1971–78; Fortismere Comp. Sch., 1985–88. *Publications:* Cosmology, 1977, 3rd edn 1996; Cosmic Landscape, 1979; The Cosmological Distance Ladder, 1985; Fire and Ice: the nuclear winter, 1985; Our Universe: an armchair guide, 1990; Ripples in the Cosmos, 1993; Nine Numbers of the Cosmos, 1999; numerous research papers in astronomical jls, articles and book reviews. *Recreations:* poetry, politics, going to the theatre, music, especially Liszt, golf. *Address:* Astrophysics Group, Blackett Laboratory, Imperial College, Prince Consort Road, SW7 2BZ. *T:* (020) 7594 7530.

ROWE, Prof. Adrian Harold Redfern, FDSRCS; Professor of Conservative Dentistry, University of London, at Guy's Hospital, 1971–91, now Professor Emeritus; Dean of Dental Studies, 1985–89, Dean of Dental Sch., 1989–91, and Head of Department of Conservative Dental Surgery, 1967–91, United Medical and Dental Schools of Guy's and St Thomas' Hospitals (Hon. Fellow, 1997); *b* 30 Dec. 1925; *y s* of late Harold Ridges Rowe and Emma Eliza (*née* Matthews), Lymington, Hants; *m* 1951, Patricia Mary Flett; three *s. Educ:* King Edward VI Sch., Southampton; Guy's Hosp. Dental Sch. (BDS 1948, distinguished in Surgery, Op. Dental Surgery, Dental Surgery and Orthodontics; distinguished in Dental Anatomy, 2nd BDS, 1946); MDS London, 1965. FDSRCS 1954; MCCDRCS, 1989. Nat. Service, RADC, 1949–50. Guy's Hospital Dental School: part-time practice and teaching, 1950–63; Sen. Lectr, 1963–67; Hon. Consultant, 1966–; Univ. Reader, 1967–71; London University: Chm., Bd of Studies in Dentistry, 1980–83; Mem., Senate, 1981–83. Member: Lewisham and N Southwark DHA, 1986–90; Special HA, 1986–90. Member: Dental Sub-Cttee, UGC, 1974–83; Council, Medical Defence Union, 1977–96; Specialist Adv. Cttee in Restorative Dentistry, 1979–85; Bd, Faculty in Dental Surgery, RCS, 1980–93 (Vice Dean, 1987); Faculty Advr for SE Thames reg., RCS, 1983–89; President: British Endodontic Soc., 1964 (Hon. Mem., 1974); British Soc. for Restorative Dentistry, 1978 (Hon. Mem., 1991). Past examiner in dental surgery in Univs of Belfast, Birmingham, Cardiff, Colombo, Dublin, Dundee, Edinburgh, Lagos, London, Malaysia, Malta, Manchester, Nairobi, Newcastle and Singapore; Statutory Exam. of GDC; Examnr for Licence and Fellowship exams of RCS and for Fellowship of RCSI. Dir, Medical Sickness Annuity and Life Assce Soc., 1987–95. Governor: UMDS of Guy's and St Thomas' Hosps, 1985–91; Eastman Dental Hosp., 1986–90. Freeman, City of London, 1990; Liveryman, Soc. of Apothecaries, 1995–. Hon. FKC 1998. Colyer Gold Medal, Faculty in Dental Surgery, RCS, 1993. *Publications:* Companion to Dental Studies, vol. I: Book I, Anatomy, Biochemistry and Physiology, 1982; Book II, Dental Anatomy and Embryology, 1981; vol. II, Clinical Methods, Medicine, Pathology and Pharmacology, 1988; vol. III, Clinical Dentistry, 1986; contrib. to British and foreign dental jls. *Recreations:* golf, DIY, gardening. *Address:* Manor Lodge, Manor Mews, Ringwould, Deal, Kent CT14 8HT. *T:* (01304) 375487.

See also O. J. T. Rowe.

ROWE, Andrew John Bernard; *b* 11 Sept. 1935; *s* of John Douglas Rowe and Mary Katharine Storr; *m* 1st, 1960, Alison Boyd (marr. diss.); one *s*; 2nd, 1983, Sheila L. Finkle, PhD; two step *d. Educ:* Eton Coll.; Merton Coll., Oxford (MA). Sub Lt RNVR, 1954–56. Schoolmaster, 1959–62; Principal, Scottish Office, 1962–67; Lectr, Edinburgh Univ., 1967–74; Consultant to Voluntary Services Unit, Home Office, 1974; Dir, Community Affairs, Cons. Central Office, 1975–79; self-employed consultant and journalist, 1979–83. MP (C) Mid Kent, 1983–97, Faversham and Mid Kent, 1997–2001. PPS to Minister for Trade, 1992–95. Chm., Parly Panel for Personal Social Services, 1986–92; Member: Public Accounts Cttee, 1995–97; Internat. Develt Cttee, 1997–2001. Chm. Steering Cttee, UK Youth Parlt, 1998–2001. *Publications:* Democracy Renewed, 1975; pamphlets and articles incl. Somewhere to Start. *Recreations:* fishing, reading, theatre. *Address:* Tithe Barn, The Street, Detling, Maidstone ME14 3JU.

ROWE, Bridget; Content Director, Yava, since 2000; *b* 16 March 1950; *d* of late Peter and Myrtle Rowe; *m*; one *s. Educ:* St Michael's School, Limpsfield. Editor, Look Now, 1971–76; Editor, Woman's World, 1976–81; Asst Editor, The Sun, 1981–82; Editor: Sunday Magazine, 1982–86; Woman's Own, 1986–90; TV Times, 1990–91; Sunday Mirror, 1991–92; Editor, 1992–96, Man. Dir, 1995–98, The People; Man. Dir, 1995–98, and Editor, 1997–98, Sunday Mirror; Dir of Communications, Nat. Magazines, 1998–99. *Recreations:* football, shopping.

ROWE, Helen; *see* Cresswell, H.

ROWE, Owen John Tressider, MA; retired; *b* 30 July 1922; *e s* of late Harold Ridges Rowe and Emma E. Rowe (*née* Matthews), Lymington, Hampshire; *m* 1946, Marcelle Ljufliny Hyde-Johnson (*d* 1986); one *s* one *d. Educ:* King Edward VI School, Southampton; Exeter College, Oxford (Scholar, MA); 1st Cl. Hons in Classical Hon. Mods, 1942. Served War of 1939–45, Lieut in Roy. Hampshire Regt, 1942–45. 1st Cl. Hons in Lit Hum, Dec. 1947; Assistant Master: Royal Grammar School, Lancaster, 1948–50; Charterhouse, 1950–60 (Head of Classical Dept); Officer Comdg Charterhouse CCF, 1954–60; Headmaster: Giggleswick School, 1961–70; Epsom College, 1970–82; Head of Classics, St John's Sch., Leatherhead, 1982–87. Governor, Chinthurst Sch., Tadworth, 1980–. *Recreations:* Rotary, gardening, playing the recorder. *Address:* 8 Pine Hill, Epsom KT18 7BG. *Club:* Rotary (Epsom).

See also A. H. R. Rowe.

ROWE, Rear-Adm. Patrick Barton, CBE 1990; LVO 1975; Deputy Master and Chairman of the Board, Trinity House, since 1996; Chairman, General Lighthouse Authority, since 1996; *b* 14 April 1939; *e s* of Captain G. B. Rowe, DSC, RN and Doreen Rowe (*née* Robarts), Liphook, Hants; *m* 1964, Alexandra, *e d* of Alexander Mellor, OBE; one *s* one *d. Educ:* Wellington College; RNC Dartmouth. FRIN. Served Far East Fleet, 1960–65; specialised in Navigation, 1966; navigation appts, 1966–70; Comd, HMS Soberton, 1970–71; Army Staff Coll., 1972; Navigation Officer, HM Yacht Britannia,

1973–75; Comd, HMS Antelope, 1977–79; Naval Staff appts, 1979–82; Comd, HMS Keren, 1983; Comd, HMS Liverpool, 1983–85; RN Presentation Team, 1985–86; Commodore, Clyde, 1986–88; RCDS 1989; Mil. Deputy, Defence Export Services, 1990–92; Clerk to the Worshipful Co. of Leathersellers, 1993–96. Liveryman: Shipwrights' Co., 1993–; Leathersellers' Co., 1996–; Hon. Liveryman, Master Mariners' Co., 1996. MIPD. *Recreations:* sailing, ski-ing. *Address:* c/o Lloyds TSB, Bishop's Waltham, Southampton SO32 1GS. *Clubs:* Army and Navy; Royal Yacht Squadron.

ROWE, Prof. Peter John, PhD; Professor of Law, Lancaster University, since 1995; *b* 5 Aug. 1947; *s* of late Major Dennis Rowe and of Anne (*née* Nesbitt); *m* 1970, Anne Murland, *d* of D. A. White, OBE and J. C. White; one *s* one *d*. *Educ:* Methodist Coll., Belfast; Queen's Univ. Belfast (LLB); University College London (LLM); Univ. of Liverpool (PhD). Called to the Bar, Lincoln's Inn, 1979. Appts at Anglia Poly., 1970–77 and Lancashire Poly., 1977–79; University of Liverpool, 1979–95: Prof. of Law, 1988–95; Head of Dept of Law, 1988–93. Dir of Legal Studies, Cayman Islands Law Sch., 1982–84. Chm., Ind. Tribunal Service, (pt-time) 1989–94, 1996– (full-time) 1995. Chm., UK Gp, Internat. Soc. for Mil. Law and Law of War, 1990–98. *Publications:* (with S. Knapp) Evidence and Procedure in the Magistrates' Court, 1983, 3rd edn 1989; (ed with C. Whelan) Military Intervention in Democratic Societies, 1985; Defence: the legal implications, military law and the laws of war, 1987; (ed) The Gulf War 1990–91, in International and English Law, 1993; contrib. on War and Armed Conflict to Halsbury's Laws of England, vol. 49(i); articles in learned jls. *Recreations:* sailing, hill-walking, buying at auction. *Address:* Department of Law, Lancaster University, Lancaster LA1 4YW.

ROWE, Prof. Peter Noël, DSc (Eng); FREng, FIChemE; Ramsay Memorial Professor of Chemical Engineering, and Head of Department, University College London, 1965–85, now Professor Emeritus; *b* 25 Dec. 1919; *e s* of Charles Henry Rowe and Kate Winifred (*née* Storry); *m* 1952, Pauline Garmirian; two *s*. *Educ:* Preston Grammar Sch.; Manchester Coll. of Technology; Imperial Coll., London. Princ. Scientific Officer, AERE, Harwell, 1958–65. Crabtree Orator, 1980. Vis. Prof., Univ. Libre de Bruxelles, 1988, 1995. Advr, HEFCE, 1992– (Chm., Assessment Panel, 1992, 1996). Non-exec. Dir, Bentham Fine Chemicals, 1985–; Consultant, SERC, 1990–. Pres., IChemE, 1981–82; Hon. Sec., Fellowship of Engrg, 1982–85. FCGI 1983. Hon. Fellow, UCL, 1993. Hon. DSc Brussels, 1978. *Publications:* scientific articles in Trans IChemE, Chem. Eng. Science, etc. *Address:* Pamber Green, Upper Basildon, Reading, Berks RG8 8PG. *T:* (01491) 671382.

ROWE, Peter Whitmill, MA; Schoolteacher at Kent College, Canterbury, 1983–90, retired; *b* 12 Feb. 1928; British; *s* of Gerald Whitmill Rowe, chartered accountant, one-time General Manager of Morris Commercial Cars Ltd; *m* 1952, Bridget Ann Moyle; two *s* one *d*. *Educ:* Bishop's Stortford College; St John's College, Cambridge. BA 1950; MA (Hons) 1956. VI Form History Master, Brentwood School, Essex, 1951–54; Senior History Master, Repton School, Derbys, 1954–57; Headmaster: Bishop's Stortford Coll., Herts, 1957–70; Cranbrook Sch., Kent, 1970–81; teacher, Williston-Northampton Sch., Mass., USA, 1981–83. JP Bishop's Stortford, 1968–70, Cranbrook, 1971–81. *Recreations:* literature, music, cricket, golf.

ROWE, Richard Brian; District Judge (formerly Registrar) of the High Court (Family Division), 1979–98; *b* 28 April 1933; *s* of Charles Albert Rowe and Mabel Florence Rowe; *m* 1959, Shirley Ann Symons; two *d*. *Educ:* Greenford County Grammar Sch.; King's Coll., London Univ. (LLB Hons). National Service, RAF, 1952–54. High Court (Probate, Divorce and Admiralty Div.), 1954–66; Land Commn, 1966–69; Lord Chancellor's Office, 1969–75; Sec., High Court (Family Div.), 1975–79. Mem., Booth Cttee on Matrimonial Causes Procedure, 1982–85. Chm., AFA, 1995–2001 (Life Vice-Pres., 1991). *Publications:* (ed) Rayden on Divorce, 10th edn, 1967; (ed) Tristram and Coote's Probate Practice, 25th edn, 1978, to 28th edn, 1995. *Recreations:* most sports. *Address:* c/o Principal Registry of the Family Division, First Avenue House, 42–49 High Holborn, WC1V 6NP.

ROWE, Robert Stewart, CBE 1969; Director, Leeds City Art Gallery and Temple Newsam House, 1958–83 (and also of Lotherton Hall, 1968–83); *b* 31 Dec. 1920; *s* of late James Stewart Rowe and late Mrs A. G. Gillespie; *m* 1953, Barbara Elizabeth Hamilton Baynes; one *s* two *d*. *Educ:* privately; Downing Coll., Cambridge; Richmond Sch. of Art. Served RAF, 1941–46. Asst Keeper of Art, Birmingham Museum and Art Gallery, 1950–56; Dep. Dir, Manchester City Art Galls, 1956–58. Pres., Museums Assoc., 1973–74; Member: Adv. Council, V&A Mus., 1969–74; Arts Council of GB, 1981–86; Fine Arts Adv. Cttee, British Council, 1972–84; Chm., Bar Convent Museum Trust, York, 1986–91; Trustee, Henry Moore Sculpture Trust, 1983–95. Liveryman, Worshipful Co. of Goldsmiths. Hon. LittD Leeds, 1983. *Publications:* Adam Silver, 1965; articles in Burlington Magazine, Museums Jl, etc. *Recreations:* gardening, reading. *Address:* Grove Lodge, Shadwell, Leeds LS17 8LB. *T:* (0113) 265 6365.

ROWE, Dr Roy Ernest, CBE 1977; FREng; consultant; Director General, Cement and Concrete Association, 1977–87; *b* 26 Jan. 1929; *s* of Ernest Walter Rowe and Louisa Rowe; *m* 1954, Lillian Anderson; one *d*. *Educ:* Taunton's Sch., Southampton; Pembroke Coll., Cambridge (MA, ScD). FICE, FIStructE; FREng (FEng 1979). Cement and Concrete Association, later British Cement Association: Research Engineer, 1952–57; Head, Design Research Dept, 1958–65; Dir, R&D, 1966–77. Chm., Engrg Res. Commn, SERC, 1991–93. President: IStructE, 1983–84; Comité Euro-Internat. du Béton, 1987–98. Hon. Mem., Amer. Concrete Inst., 1978; For. Associate, Nat. Acad. of Engineering, USA, 1980. Hon. DEng Leeds, 1984. *Publications:* Concrete Bridge Design, 1962, 3rd impr. 1972; numerous papers in technical and professional jls. *Recreations:* fell walking, listening to music. *Address:* 15 Hollesley Road, Alderton, Woodbridge, Suffolk IP12 3BX. *T:* (01394) 411096.

ROWE-BEDDOE, Sir David (Sydney), Kt 2000; Chairman, Wales Millennium Centre, since 2001; *b* 19 Dec. 1937; *s* of late Sydney Rowe-Beddoe and Dolan Rowe-Beddoe (*née* Evans); *m* 1st, 1964, Malinda Collison (marr. diss. 1982); three *d*; 2nd, 1984, Madeleine Harrison. *Educ:* Cathedral Sch., Llandaff; Stowe Sch.; St John's Coll., Cambridge (MA); Harvard Univ. Grad. Sch. of Business Admin (PMD). Served RN, Sub-Lt, RNVR, 1956–58, Lieut, RNR, 1958–66. Thomas de la Rue & Company, 1961–76: Chief Executive, 1971–76; Exec. Dir, De la Rue Co. plc, 1974–76; Revlon Inc., NY, 1976–81; President: Latin America and Caribbean, 1976–77; Europe, ME and Africa, 1977–81; Pres. and Chief Exec. Officer, Ges. für Trendanalysen, 1981–87; Director: Morgan Stanley-GFTA Ltd, 1983–91; Cavendish Services Ltd, 1987–94 (Chm., 1987–94); American Banknote Corp., 1990–; Development Securities plc, 1994–2000; GFTA Analytics, 1997–. Chairman: WDA, 1993–2001; Develt Bd for Rural Wales, 1994–98; N Wales Econ. Forum, 1996–; Mid Wales Partnership, 1996–; SE Wales Econ. Forum, 1999–; Wales N America Business Council, 1999–; Member: Welsh Economic Council, 1994–96; UK Regl Policy Forum, 1999–; Pres., Welsh Centre for Internat. Affairs, 1999–. Dir, Welsh Internat. Film Fest. Ltd, 1998–2000; President: Celtic Film Festival, 2000; Internat. Musical Eisteddfod, 2000. Mem., Prince of Wales' Cttee, 1994–97; Patron, Prince's Trust Bro, 1997–. Gov., WCMD, 1993– (Chm., 2000–). Liveryman, Broderers' Co., 1993. FInstD 1993; FRSA 1993. Hon. Wales Coll. Newport, 1998; Cardiff Univ. DUniv Glamorgan, 1997. R… theatre, country pursuits. *Address:* Wales Millennium Centre, Bay Chambe… Street, Cardiff CF10 5GG. *T:* (029) 2040 2000, *Fax:* (029) 2040 2001. *Club…* Cardiff & County; Brook (New York); Automobile (Monaco).

ROWE-HAM, Sir David (Kenneth), GBE 1986; JP; chartered accountant, since 196…; Lord Mayor of London, 1986–87; Consultant to Touche Ross & Co., 1984–93; *b* 19 Dec. 1935; *o s* of late Kenneth Henry and of Muriel Phyllis Rowe-Ham; *m* Sandra Celia (*née* Nicholls), *widow* of Ian Glover; three *s*. *Educ:* Dragon School; Charterhouse. FCA. Commnd 3rd King's Own Hussars. Mem., Stock Exchange, 1964–84; Sen. Partner, Smith Keen Cutler, 1972–82. Chairman: Asset Trust plc, 1982–89; Jersey General Investment Trust Ltd, 1988–89; Olayan Europe Ltd, 1989–; Brewin Dolphin Hldgs PLC, 1992–; APTA Healthcare PLC, 1994–96; Coral Products PLC, 1995–; Jt Chm., Gradus Group PLC, 1995–97; Regional Dir (London), Lloyds Bank plc, 1985–91; Director: W. Canning plc, 1981–86; Savoy Theatre Ltd, 1986–98; Williams PLC, 1992–2000; CLS Hldgs plc, 1994–99; Chubb plc, 2000–. Pres., Crown Agents Foundn, 1996–. Chm., Adv. Panel, Guinness Flight Unit Trust Managers Ltd, 1987–99. Alderman, City of London, Ward of Bridge and Bridge Without, 1976–; Sheriff, City of London, 1984–85; HM Lieut, City of London, 1987–. Court Member: City Univ., 1981–86 (Chancellor, 1986–87); Worshipful Co. of Chartered Accountants in England and Wales (Master, 1985–86); Worshipful Co. of Wheelwrights; Hon. Mem., Worshipful Co. of Launderers; Mem. Ct, HAC. Gov., Royal Shakespeare Co.; Trustee, Friends of D'Oyly Carte. Pres., Black Country Mus. Develt Trust. Chm., Birmingham Municipal Bank, 1970–72; Mem., Birmingham CC, 1965–72. Chm., Political Council, Junior Carlton Club, 1977; Dep. Chm., Political Cttee, Carlton Club, 1977–79. Mem., Lord's Taverners. Governor, Christ's Hospital. JP City of London, 1976 (Chief Magistrate, 1986–87; Supp. List, 1994–). Hon. DLitt City Univ., 1986. KJStJ 1986. Commandeur de l'Ordre Mérite, France, 1984; Commander, Order of the Lion, Malaŵi, 1985; Order of the Aztec Eagle (Cl. II), Mexico, 1985; Order of King Abdul Aziz (Cl. 1), 1987; Grand Officer, Order of Wissam Alouite, Morocco, 1987; Order of Diego Losada, Caracas, Venezuela, 1987; Pedro Ernesto Medal, Rio de Janeiro, 1987. *Recreation:* theatre. *Address:* 140 Piccadilly, W1J 7NS. *Club:* Carlton.

ROWELL, Anthony Aylett, CMG 1992; Consultant (Southern Africa), Kroll Associates, since 1998; *b* 10 Jan. 1937; *s* of Geoffrey William and Violet Ella Aylett Rowell; *m* 1st, 1965, Bridget Jane Reekie (marr. diss. 1985); one *s* one *d*; 2nd, 1985, Caroline Anne Edgcumbe. *Educ:* Marlborough. With British American Tobacco, 1959–65; HM Diplomatic Service, 1966–93: 2nd Sec., Lusaka, 1968–69; 1st Secretary: FCO, 1969; Bucharest, 1970–73; FCO, 1974–78; Nicosia, 1979–80; FCO, 1981–85; Counsellor: Nairobi, 1985–90; Pretoria, 1990–93. Pol Advr (Southern Africa), Racal Radio Group UK, 1993; Dir, Racal Electronics SA Ltd, 1994; Pol Advr (Southern Africa), Racal Electronics PLC, 1996–97. *Recreations:* tennis, badminton, hiking, photography, fine wines. *Address:* Bracken Cottage, Cross Hands, Devauden, Chepstow, Gwent NP16 6NS.

ROWELL, Rt Rev. Dr (Douglas) Geoffrey; *see* Gibraltar in Europe, Bishop of.

ROWELL, Jack, OBE 1998; Chairman, Celsis plc, 1997–98 and since 2000 (Chief Executive, 1998–2000); Managing Director, Bristol Rugby Ltd, since 2000 (Director, 1998–2000); *s* of late Edwin Cecil Rowell and Monica Mary Rowell (*née* Day); *m* 1969, Susan, *d* of Alan Cooper; two *s*. *Educ:* West Hartlepool Grammar Sch.; St Edmund Hall, Oxford (MA). FCA 1964. With Procter & Gamble to 1976; Lucas Ingredients, Bristol, 1976–88; Chief Exec., Golden Wonder, 1988–92; Exec. Dir, Dalgety, 1993–94; Chairman: Lyon Seafoods Ltd, 1994–; Marlat Bennetts Internat. Ltd, 1994–99; Dolphin Computer Services Ltd, 1994–99; OSI Ltd, 1995–99; Pilgrim Foods Ltd, 1995–; Dir, Oliver Ashworth Gp, 1997–98. Played for Gosforth RFC, later Newcastle Gosforth (Captain, later coach; Cup winners, 1976); coach, Bath RFC, 1977–94: Cup winners 8 times, League winners 5 times, Middlesex Sevens winners, 1994; Manager, England RFU Team, 1994–97. Hon LLD Bath, 1994.

ROWELL, Prof. John Martin, DPhil; FRS 1989; Professor, Materials Research Institute, Northwestern University, since 1997; *b* 27 June 1935; *s* of Frank L. and P. E. Rowell; *m* 1959, Judith A. Harte; two *s* one *d*. *Educ:* Wadham Coll., Oxford (BSc, MA; DPhil 1961). Bell Telephone Labs, 1961–84; Bell Communications Research, 1984–89; Conductus Inc., 1989–95. Member: Acad. of Scis, 1994; Acad. of Engrg, 1995. Fellow, Amer. Physical Soc., 1974. Fritz London Meml Low Temperature Physics Prize, 1978. *Publications:* about 100 pubns in jls. *Address:* 102 Exeter Drive, Berkeley Heights, NJ 07922, USA. *T:* (908) 4646994.

ROWLAND, Rev. Prof. Christopher Charles; Dean Ireland's Professor of the Exegesis of Holy Scripture, and Fellow of Queen's College, University of Oxford, since 1991; *b* Doncaster, 21 May 1947; *s* of Eric Rowland and Frances Mary Lawson; *m* 1969, Catherine Rogers; three *s* one *d*. *Educ:* Doncaster Grammar Sch.; Christ's Coll., Cambridge; Ridley Hall, Cambridge; BA 1969, PhD 1975, Cantab. Ordained deacon, 1975, priest 1976. Lectr in Religious Studies, Univ. of Newcastle upon Tyne, 1974–79; Curate: St James', Benwell, 1975–78; All Saints', Gosforth, 1978–79; Asst Lectr in Divinity, 1983–85, Lectr in Divinity, 1985–91, Univ. of Cambridge; Fellow and Dean, Jesus Coll., Cambridge, 1979–91. *Address:* Queen's College, Oxford OX1 4AW.

ROWLAND, Sir David; *see* Rowland, Sir J. D.

ROWLAND, David Powys; Stipendiary Magistrate, Mid Glamorgan (formerly Merthyr Tydfil), 1961–89, retired; *b* 7 Aug. 1917; *s* of late Henry Rowland, CBE, Weston-super-Mare; *m* 1st, 1946, Joan (*d* 1958), *d* of late Group Capt. J. McCrae, MBE, Weston-super-Mare; one *s* one *d*; 2nd, 1961, Jenny (marr. diss. 1977), *d* of late Percival Lance, Swanage, and *widow* of Michael A. Forester-Bennett, Alverstoke; one *s* one *d* (and one step-*d*); 3rd, 1980, Diana, *d* of late W. H. Smith, Cannock, and *widow* of Lt-Col W. D. H. McCardie, S Staffs Regt (two step-*d*). *Educ:* Cheltenham Coll.; Oriel Coll., Oxford (BA). Lieut, Royal Welch Fusiliers, 1940–46. Called to Bar, Middle Temple, 1947. Deputy Chairman: Glamorgan QS, 1961–71; Breconshire QS, 1964–71. Mem. Nat. Adv. Council on Training of Magistrates, 1964–73. *Recreations:* fly-fishing, gardening. *Address:* Holmdale, Cwmdu, Crickhowell, Powys NP8 1RY. *T:* (01874) 730635.

ROWLAND, Prof. F(rank) Sherwood, PhD; Donald Bren Research Professor of Chemistry, University of California at Irvine, since 1994 (Professor of Chemistry, since 1964); *b* 28 June 1927; *m* 1952, Joan Lundberg; one *s* one *d*. *Educ:* Ohio Wesleyan Univ. (AB 1948); Univ. of Chicago (MS 1951; PhD 1952). Chemistry Instr, Princeton Univ., 1952–56; Asst Prof., 1956–58, Associate Prof., 1958–63, Prof., 1963–64, of Chemistry, Univ. of Kansas; Chm. of Chemistry Dept, 1964–70, Daniel G. Aldrich, Jr, Prof. of Chemistry, 1985–89, Donald Bren Prof. of Chemistry, 1989–94, Univ. of Calif at Irvine. Discovered (with Dr Mario J. Molina) that chlorofluorocarbon gases deplete the ozone layer of the stratosphere. Member: NAS, 1978– (Foreign Sec., 1994–); AAAS (Pres., 1992; Chm. Bd, 1993; Fellow); Acid Rain Peer Review Panel, US Office of Science and Tech., 1982–84; International Association of Meteorology and Atmospheric Physics: Member:

Commn on Atmospheric Chemistry and Global Pollution, 1979–91; Ozone Commn, 1980–88 (Hon. Life Mem., 1996); Jt Chm., Dahlem Conf. on Our Changing Atmosphere, Germany, 1987. Fellow: APS; Amer. Geophysical Union. Numerous hon. degrees and awards. (Jtly) Nobel Prize in Chemistry, 1995. *Publications:* on atmospheric chemistry, radio-chemistry and chemical kinetics. *Address:* Department of Chemistry, University of California, 571 Rowland Hall, Irvine, CA 92697–2025, USA. *T:* (949) 8246016, *Fax:* (949) 8242905.

ROWLAND, Geoffrey Robert; QC (Guernsey) 1993; HM Attorney-General for Guernsey, since 1999; *b* 5 Jan. 1948; *s* of Percy George Rowland and Muriel Florence (*née* Maunder); *m* 1972, Diana Janet Caryl; two *s*. *Educ:* Elizabeth Coll., Guernsey; Univ. of Southampton; Univ. of Caen. Called to the Bar, Gray's Inn, 1970; called to the Guernsey Bar, 1971; in private practice as advocate, Guernsey, 1971–91; Sen. Partner, Collas Day and Rowland, 1984–91; Solicitor General for Guernsey, 1992–99. Vice-Chm., Guernsey Financial Services Commn, 1988–92. Chairman: Guernsey Press Co. Ltd, 1990–92; TSB Foundn for CI, 1990–92. Provincial Grand Master, Guernsey and Alderney, United Grand Lodge, Freemasons of England, 2000–. *Recreations:* ski-ing, reading history, international travel. *Address:* Armorica, L'Ancresse, Guernsey, CI GY3 5JR. *T:* (01481) 247494.

ROWLAND, Sir (John) David, Kt 1997; President, Templeton College, Oxford, since 1998; Chairman and Chief Executive, National Westminster Bank plc, 1999–2000 (Joint Deputy Chairman, 1998–99); *b* 10 Aug. 1933; *s* of Cyril Arthur Rowland and Eileen Mary Rowland; *m* 1st, 1957, Giulia Powell (marr. diss. 1991); one *s* one *d*; 2nd, 1991, Diana Louise Matthews (*née* Dickie). *Educ:* St Paul's School; Trinity College, Cambridge (MA Natural Sciences). Joined Matthews Wrightson and Co., 1956, Dir, 1965; Dir, Matthews Wrightson Holdings, 1972; Dep. Chm., 1978–81, Chm., 1981–87, Stewart Wrightson Holdings plc; Dep. Chm., Willis Faber plc, 1987–88; Chief Exec., 1988–92, Chm., 1989–92, Sedgwick Gp plc; Chm of Lloyd's, 1993–97. Chm., Westminster Insurance Agencies, 1981–88; Dir, Sedgwick Lloyd's Underwriting Agencies, 1988–92. Director: Project Fullemploy, 1973–88; Fullemploy Gp Ltd, 1989–90; Non-executive Director: Royal London Mutual Insurance Soc., 1985–86; S. G. Warburg Gp, 1992–95; Somerset House Ltd, 1997–; NatWest Gp, 1998–. Mem. Council, Lloyd's, 1987–90; Mem., President's Cttee, Business in the Community, 1986–92 (Mem., City of London section, 1983–86). Vice-Pres., British Insurance and Investment Brokers' Assoc. (formerly British Insurance Brokers' Assoc.), 1980–; Member of Council: Industrial Soc., 1983–88; Contemporary Applied Arts, subseq. British Crafts Centre, 1985–92; Council of Industry and Higher Educn, 1990–92. Member: Council, Templeton Coll. (Oxford Centre for Management Studies), 1980– (Chm., 1985–92); Governing Bd, City Res. Project, 1991–92; Governor: Coll. of Insurance, 1983–85; St Paul's Schs, 1991. Hon. FIA; Hon. Fellow, Cardiff Univ., 1999. Hon. MA Oxford, 1993; Hon. DPhil London Guildhall, 1996; Hon. DSc City, 1997. Lloyd's Gold Medal, 1996. *Recreations:* family, admiring my wife's garden, golf, running slowly. *Address:* 6 Danbury Street, N1 8JU. *T:* (020) 7359 6444; Giffords Hall, Wickhambrook, Newmarket, Suffolk CB8 8PQ. *T:* (01440) 820221. *Clubs:* Brooks's, MCC; Royal and Ancient Golf (St Andrews), Royal St George's (Sandwich), Royal Worlington and Newmarket Golf, Sunningdale Golf.

ROWLAND, John Peter; QC 1996; barrister; *b* 17 Jan. 1952; *s* of Peter Rowland and Marion Rowland (*née* Guppy); *m* 1979, Juliet Hathaway; three *s* two *d*. *Educ:* Univ. of Western Australia (BEc Hons); King's Coll., London (LLB Hons). Pilot Officer, RAAF (Reserves), 1970–72; Sen. Tutor and Lectr in Econs, Univ. of Western Australia, 1973–74; Lectr in Economics, WA Inst. of Technology, 1974–75; called to the Bar, Middle Temple, 1979; admitted to practice, NSW, 2001. *Recreations:* cricket, walking, ski-ing. *Address:* 4 Pump Court, Temple, EC4Y 7AN. *T:* (020) 7353 2656. *Club:* Theberton Cricket.

ROWLAND, Mark; Social Security Commissioner and Child Support Commissioner, since 1993; *b* 20 July 1953; *s* of Sqdn Leader Bernard Rowland and late Elizabeth Rowland (*née* Cuerden); *m* 1977, Eileen Cleary; two *d*. *Educ:* Ampleforth Coll.; Univ. of Warwick (LLB Hons). Called to the Bar, Gray's Inn, 1975; Welfare rights adviser, CPAG, 1975–78; private practice at the Bar, 1979–93; part-time Chm., social security, medical and disability appeal tribunals, 1988–93; Dep. Social Security Comr, 1992–93; Chm., registered homes tribunal, 1995–. *Publications:* (ed jtly) Rights Guide to Non-means-tested Benefits, 2nd edn 1978, 14th edn 1991; The Industrial Injuries Scheme, 1983; Medical and Disability Appeal Tribunals: the Legislation, 1993, 3rd edn 1998; (ed jtly) Social Security Tribunals: the legislation, 2000, 2nd edn as Social Security Legislation, 2001; papers on social security law. *Recreations:* railways, military history, social history, gardening. *Address:* Office of the Social Security and Child Support Commissioners, Harp House, 83 Farringdon Street, EC4A 4DH. *T:* (020) 7353 5145.

ROWLAND, His Honour Robert Todd; QC 1969; County Court Judge of Northern Ireland, 1974–90; President, Lands Tribunal for Northern Ireland, 1983–90; part-time Chairman, Value Added Tax Tribunals, 1990–94; *b* 12 Jan. 1922; *yr s* of late Lt-Col Charles Rowland and Jean Rowland; *m* 1952, Kathleen, *er d* of late H. J. Busby, Lambourn, Berks; two *s*. *Educ:* Crossley and Porter Sch., Halifax, Yorks; Ballyclare High Sch.; Queen's Univ. of Belfast (LLB 1948). Called to Bar of N Ireland, 1949; Mem., Bar Council, 1967–72. Served 2nd Punjab Regt, IA, in India, Assam, Burma, Thailand, Malaya, 1942–46. Counsel to Attorney-Gen. for N Ireland, 1966–69; Sen. Crown Prosecutor for Co. Tyrone, 1969–72; Vice-Pres., VAT Tribunal for N Ireland, 1972–74. Served on County Court Rules Cttee, 1965–72; Chairman: War Pensions Appeal Tribunal, 1962–72; Commn of Inquiry into Housing Contracts, 1978; Member: Bd of Governors, Strathearn Sch., 1969–89; Legal Adv. Cttee, Gen. Synod of Church of Ireland, 1975–89. Chancellor, dioceses of Armagh, and Down and Dromore, 1978–89. *Recreations:* fly-fishing, golf, hill-walking. *Address:* The Periwinkle, 25 Back Lane, South Luffenham, Oakham, Rutland LE15 8NQ. *Club:* Flyfishers'.

ROWLAND-JONES, Prof. Sarah Louise, (Mrs R. T. Walton), DM; FRCP; Professor of Immunology, University of Oxford, since 2000; Research Student, Christ Church, Oxford, since 1997; *b* 8 Nov. 1959; *d* of Timothy Louis Rowland-Jones and Kathleen Norah Rowland-Jones; *m* 1988, Dr Robert Thompson Walton. *Educ:* Girton Coll., Cambridge (BA 1st Cl. Hons 1980; MA 1984); Green Coll., Oxford (BM BCh 1983; DM 1995). MRCP 1986, FRCP 1999. Postgrad. med. trng in gen. medicine and infectious diseases, Oxford, London (St George's and Brompton Hosps) and Sheffield, 1983–89; Molecular Immunology Group, Oxford: MRC Trng Fellow, 1989–92; MRC clinician scientist, 1992–95; MRC Sen. Fellow, 1995–2000. Hon. Consultant in Infectious Diseases, Churchill Hosp., Oxford, 1995–. FMedSci 2000. Elizabeth Glaser Scientist Award, Paediatric Aids Foundation, 1997. *Publications:* (ed with A. J. McMichael) Lymphocytes: a practical approach, 2000; contrib. papers to Nature, Nature Medicine, Immunity, The Lancet, Jl Exptl Medicine, Jl Immunology, Jl Virology, etc. *Recreations:* scuba diving, travel, gardening, collecting art deco, good wine and good company. *Address:* Human Immunology Unit, Institute of Molecular Medicine, John Radcliffe Hospital, Headington, Oxford OX3 9DS. *T:* (01865) 222316; 53 Jack Straw's Lane, Headington, Oxford OX3 0DW.

ROWLANDS, Christopher John, FCA; Chief Executive, The Television Corporation, 1998–2001; *b* 29 Aug. 1951; *s* of late Wilfrid John Rowlands and of Margaretta (*née* Roberts); *m* 1978, Alison Mary Kelly; twin *d*. *Educ:* Roundhay Sch., Leeds; Gonville and Caius Coll., Cambridge (MA Econ). FCA 1975. Peat Marwick Mitchell: articled clerk, 1973–75; CA, 1975; Manager, 1981; seconded as Partner, Zambia, 1981–83; Sen. Manager, London, 1983–85; Asda Group plc: Controller, business planning, Asda Stores, 1985–86; Divl Dir, Gp Finance, 1986–88; Dep. Man. Dir and Finance Dir, Asda Gp/Property Develt and Investment cos, 1988–92; Gp Finance Dir, 1992–93, Chief Exec., 1993–97, HTV Gp plc. Mem. Council, ITVA, 1993–97 (Chm., Engrg Policy Gp, 1993–96). CIMgt 1995. FRSA 1995. *Recreations:* family, theatre, church, reading, ski-ing, tennis, travel. *Fax:* (020) 7478 7404.

ROWLANDS, David, CB 1991; Director General, Railways, Aviation, Logistics and Maritime Transport (formerly Railways, Aviation and Shipping), Department for Transport, Local Government and the Regions (formerly Department of the Environment, Transport and the Regions), since 1997; *b* 31 May 1947; *s* of George and Margaret Rowlands; *m* 1975, Louise Marjorie Brown; two *s*. *Educ:* St Mary's Coll., Crosby; St Edmund Hall, Oxford. Entered Civil Service, 1974; Private Sec. to Minister of State for Industry, 1978–80; Principal, Dept of Trade, then of Transport, 1980–84; Asst Sec., 1984–90, Under Sec., 1990–93, Dept of Transport; Dep. Sec., Dept of Transport, later DETR, then DTLR, 1993–. *Address:* Department for Transport, Local Government and the Regions, 76 Marsham Street, SW1P 4DR.

ROWLANDS, Edward; *b* 23 Jan. 1940; *e s* of W. S. Rowlands; *m* 1968, Janice Williams, Kidwelly, Carmarthenshire; two *s* one *d*. *Educ:* Rhondda Grammar Sch.; Wirral Grammar Sch.; King's Coll., London. BA Hons History (London) 1962. Research Asst, History of Parliament Trust, 1963–65; Lectr in Modern History and Govt, Welsh Coll. of Adv. Technology, 1965–66. MP (Lab): Cardiff North, 1966–70; Merthyr Tydfil, April 1972–1983, Merthyr Tydfil and Rhymney, 1983–2001. Parliamentary Under-Secretary of State: Welsh Office, 1969–70, 1974–75; FCO, 1975–76; Minister of State, FCO, 1976–79; Opposition spokesman on energy, 1980–87; Mem., Select Cttee on Foreign Affairs, 1987–2001; Chm., Jt Cttee (inquiring into strategic export controls) of Select Cttees on Defence, Internat. Develt, and Trade and Industry, 1999–2001. Chm., History of Parliament Trust, 1993–. Member: Governing Body, Commonwealth Inst., 1980–92; Academic Council, Wilton Park, 1983–92. A Booker Prize Judge, 1984. *Publications:* various articles. *Recreations:* music, golf. *Address:* 5 Park Crescent, Thomastown, Merthyr Tydfil, Mid Glamorgan CF47 0EU. *T:* (01685) 384912.

ROWLANDS, Rev. Canon John Henry Lewis; Team Rector, Rectorial Benefice of Whitchurch, since 2001 (Vicar, 1997–2001); Chaplain of Whitchurch Hospital, since 1997; *b* 16 Nov. 1947; *s* of William Lewis and Elizabeth Mary Rowlands; *m* 1976, Catryn Meryl Parry Edwards; one *s* two *d*. *Educ:* Queen Elizabeth Grammar Sch., Carmarthen; St David's University Coll., Lampeter (BA); Magdalene Coll., Cambridge (MA); Durham Univ. (MLitt); Wescott House, Cambridge. Ordained deacon, 1972, priest, 1973 (St David's Cathedral); Curate, Rectorial Benefice of Aberystwyth, 1972–76; Chaplain, St David's University Coll., Lampeter, 1976–79; Youth Chaplain, dio. of St David's, 1976–79; Dir, Academic Studies, St Michael's Coll., Llandaff, 1979–84, Sub-Warden, 1984–88, Warden, 1988–97. Lectr, Faculty of Theology, University Coll., Cardiff, later Univ. of Wales Coll. of Cardiff, then Univ. of Wales, Cardiff, 1979–97, Asst Dean, 1981–83; Dean, Faculty of Divinity: Univ. of Wales, 1991–95; Univ. of Wales, Cardiff, 1993–97. Diocesan Dir of Ordinands, Dio. Llandaff, 1985–88; Exmng Chaplain to Archbishop of Wales, 1987–91; Sec., Doctrinal Commn of the Church in Wales, 1987–94. Hon. Canon, 1990–97, Residentiary Canon, 1997–, Llandaff Cathedral. Chaplain, Whitchurch Br., RBL, 1997–. Pres., Diwinyddiaeth (Soc. of Theol. Grads, Univ. of Wales), 1989–92. Member: (*ex officio*) Governing Body of the Church in Wales, 1988–97; Court, Univ. of Wales, 1988–94; Court, Univ. of Wales Coll. of Cardiff, 1988–97; Academic Bd, Univ. of Wales, 1991–94; Council, Llandaff Cathedral Sch., 1991–. Fellow, Woodard Corp., 1993. *Publications:* (ed) Essays on the Kingdom of God, 1986; Church, State and Society 1827–45, 1989; Doing Theology, 1996. *Recreations:* beachcombing, racket games, auctioneering, antique markets. *Address:* The Rectory, 6 Penlline Road, Whitchurch, Cardiff CF14 2AD. *T:* (029) 2062 6072; *e-mail:* vicar@parishofwhitchurch.org.uk.

ROWLANDS, John Kendall, FSA; Keeper, Department of Prints and Drawings, British Museum, 1981–91; *b* 18 Sept. 1931; *s* of Arthur and Margaret Rowlands; *m* 1st, 1957, Else A. H. Bachmann (marr. diss. 1981); one *s* two *d*; 2nd, 1982, Lorna Jane Lowe; one *d*. *Educ:* Chester Cathedral Choir Sch.; King's Sch., Chester; Gonville and Caius Coll., Cambridge. MA Cantab 1959; MA Oxon; FSA 1976. Asst Keeper, Dept of Art, City Mus. and Art Gall., Birmingham, 1956–60; Editor, Clarendon Press, Oxford, 1960–65; Asst Keeper, 1965–74, Dep. Keeper, 1974–81, Dept of Prints and Drawings, British Museum. Mem. Adv. Cttee, Collected Works of Erasmus, 1979–. *Publications:* David Cox Centenary Exhibition Catalogue, 1959; Graphic Work of Albrecht Dürer, 1971; Bosch, 1975; Rubens: drawings and sketches . . . , 1977; Urs Graf, 1977; Hercules Segers, 1979; Bosch, the Garden of Earthly Delights, 1979; German Drawings from a Private Collection, 1984; Master Drawings and Watercolours in the British Museum: from Fra Angelico to Henry Moore, 1984; The Paintings of Hans Holbein the Younger, 1985; The Age of Dürer and Holbein, 1988; Drawings by German Artists in the British Museum: 15th century, and 16th century by artists born before 1530, 1993; contribs to specialist journals, Festschriften. *Recreations:* rustic pursuits, music making. *Address:* Brant House, Brant Broughton, Lincs LN5 0SL. *T:* (01400) 272184. *Club:* Beefsteak.

ROWLANDS, (John) Martin, CBE 1980; Secretary for Civil Service, Hong Kong Government, 1978–85; *b* 20 July 1925; *s* of late John Walter Rowlands and Mary Ace Maitland (*née* Roberts); *m* 1956, Christiane Germaine Madeleine Lacheny; two *d*. *Educ:* Charterhouse; Selwyn Coll., Cambridge (MA). Military service, 1943–47 (Captain, 3rd Royal Indian Artillery Field Regt, HQ XV Indian Corps, HQ ALFSEA). HMOCS, Hong Kong Admin. Service, 1952–85: Dep. Dir of Urban Services, 1966–68; Principal Asst Colonial Sec., 1968–71; Dep. Sec. for Home Affairs, 1971–74; Dir of Immigration, 1974–78; Mem., Hong Kong Legislative Council, 1978–84. *Recreations:* railways, bird-watching. *Address:* Flat 3, 15 Collingham Road, SW5 0NU. *Clubs:* Hong Kong, Hong Kong Jockey (Hong Kong).

ROWLANDS, Air Marshal Sir John (Samuel), GC 1943 KBE 1971 (OBE 1954); Consultant, Civil Aviation Administration, since 1981; *b* 23 Sept. 1915; *s* of late Samuel and Sarah Rowlands; *m* 1942, Constance Wight; two *d*. *Educ:* Hawarden School; University of Wales (BSc Hons). Joined RAFVR, 1939; permanent commission in RAF, 1945. British Defence Staff, Washington, 1961–63; Imperial Defence College, 1964; Royal Air Force College, Cranwell, 1965–68; First Director General of Training, RAF, 1968–70; AOC-in-C, RAF Maintenance comd, 1970–73; Asst Principal, Sheffield Polytechnic, 1974–80. *Recreations:* photography, tennis, motoring. *Club:* Royal Air Force.

ROWLANDS, Martin; *see* Rowlands, J. M.

ROWLANDS, Martyn Omar, FCSD, FIM; Chairman, Martyn Rowlands Design Consultants Ltd, 1960–88; retired; *b* 27 July 1923; *s* of Edward and Mildred Rowlands; *m* 1st, 1951, Ann Patricia (*d* 1974); two *s* one *d*; 2nd, 1978 (marr. diss. 1986). *Educ:* Eltham Coll.; Central Sch. of Art and Design. FCSD (FSIAD 1960); FIM (FPRI 1973). Served War, RAF, 1940–45: India and Burma. Central Sch. of Art and Design, 1946–49; Head of Indust. Design, Ekco Plastics, 1954–59; started own design consultancy, 1959. Past Pres., SIAD (now CSD). *Recreation:* photography.

ROWLATT, Penelope Anne, PhD; Publisher, Medicine Today, since 2001; *b* 17 May 1936; *d* of Theodore Alexander Maurice Ionides and Anne Joyce Ionides (*née* Cooke); *m* 1961, Charles Rowlatt; one *s* three *d*. *Educ:* King Alfred Sch.; Somerville Coll., Oxford (BA 1959); Imperial Coll., London (PhD 1963); London Sch. of Economics (MSc 1973). Chief Economist, Economic Models Gp of Cos, 1975–76; Economist, NIESR, 1976–78; Economic Advr, HM Treasury, 1978–86; Sen. Economic Advr, Dept of Energy, 1986–88; Director: Nat. Economic Res. Associates, 1988–98; Europe Economics, 1998–2001. Member: Retail Prices Adv. Cttee, 1991–94; Royal Commn on Envmtl Pollution, 1996–2000; Steering Gp, Performance and Innovation Unit Project, Cabinet Office, 1999; Better Regulation Task Force, 2000–. Treas., REconS, 1999–. *Publications:* Group Theory and Elementary Particles, 1966; Inflation, 1992; papers in learned jls on nuclear physics and economics. *Recreations:* walking, sailing, eating and drinking. *Address:* 10 Hampstead Hill Gardens, NW3 2PL. *Club:* Reform.

ROWLEY, Sir Charles (Robert), 7th Bt *cr* 1836; *b* 15 March 1926; *s* of Sir William Joshua Rowley, 6th Bt and Beatrice Gwendoline, *d* of Rev. Augustus George Kirby; *S* father, 1971; *m* 1952, Astrid, *d* of Sir Arthur Massey, CBE; one *s* one *d*. *Educ:* Wellington. *Heir: s* Richard Charles Rowley [*b* 14 Aug. 1959; *m* 1989, Alison (marr. diss. 1999), *d* of late Henry Bellingham, and of Mrs Ian Baillie; two *s*]. *Address:* 21 Tedworth Square, SW3 4DR; Naseby Hall, Northamptonshire NN6 6DP.

ROWLEY, Frederick Allan, CMG 1978; OBE 1959; MC 1945; Major (retd); HM Diplomatic Service, retired; *b* 27 July 1922; *m* 1951, Anne Crawley; one *s* three *d*. *Educ:* Haig Sch., Aldershot. Served War of 1939–45: Ranks, 8th Worcs Regt (TA), 1939–40; Emergency Commnd Officer, 5th Bn, 10th Baluch Regt (KGVO), Jacob's Rifles, Indian Army, Burma Campaign (MC), June 1941–Nov. 1948. At partition of India, granted regular commn (back-dated, 1942) in Worcestershire Regt, but retd (wounded), sub. Major. Joined HM Diplomatic Service, Nov. 1948: served (with brief periods in FO) in: Egypt; Ethiopia; Turkey; Burma; Singapore; Australia; Malaysia; FCO 1971–72; Under-Sec., N Ireland Office (on secondment), 1972–73; Counsellor, FCO, 1973–79. Joint Services Staff College (jssc), 1959. *Recreations:* cricket, golf. *Clubs:* Army and Navy; MCC.

ROWLEY, Geoffrey William, CBE 1989; Town Clerk, City of London, 1982–91; *b* 9 Sept. 1926; *s* of George Frederick Rowley and Ellen Mary Rowley; *m* 1950, Violet Gertrude Templeman; one *s* one *d*. *Educ:* Owens School. FCIPD (FIPM 1974). Served War, Royal Marines, 1944–47. Corporation of the City of London, 1947–: Head, Personnel Sect., 1965–74; Dep. Town Clerk, 1974–82. Trustee, Silver Jubilee Walkway Trust, 1992–. Liveryman, Basketmakers' Co. (Prime Warden, 1990–91). Hon. Fellow, City of London Poly, subseq. London Guildhall Univ., 1991. DCL *hc* City, 1989. Order of White Rose, Finland, 1969; Order of Orange Nassau, Holland, 1982; Légion d'Honneur, France, 1985. OStJ 1987. *Recreations:* sport: badminton, cricket and soccer as a spectator. *Address:* 3 Wensley Avenue, Woodford Green, Essex IG8 9HE. *T:* (020) 8504 6270.

ROWLEY, Keith Nigel; QC 2001; *s* of James and Eva Rowley; *m* 1986, Chantal Anna MacKenzie; one *s* one *d*. *Educ:* King's Coll., London (LLB). Called to the Bar, Gray's Inn, 1979; in practice at Chancery Bar, 1980–. *Recreations:* classical music, gardening, theatre, wine. *Address:* 11 Old Square, Lincoln's Inn, WC2A 3TS. *T:* (020) 7430 0341. *Club:* Hurlingham.

ROWLEY, Peter, MC 1944; Vice President, Leonard Cheshire Foundation, since 1993 (Chairman, 1982–90); Chairman, Cheshire Homes European Regional Council, 1990–94; *b* 12 July 1918; *s* of late Roland and Catherine Isabel Rowley; *m* 1940, Ethnea Louis Florence Mary Howard Kyan; four *d*. *Educ:* Wembley County Sch.; University Coll., Oxford (MA). Served War of 1939–45: Queen's Westminster Rifles, 1938–39; 14th Bn Sherwood Foresters, 1940–46; Adjt, Middle East, N Africa; Company Comdr, Italy; Bde Major 13 Bde, 1944–45; GSOII 8 Corps, 1945–46. Admitted Solicitor, Titmuss Sainer & Webb, 1950; Sen. Partner, 1981–83, retd. Member, Law Society Land Law Cttee, 1970–87. Liveryman, Distillers Co., 1975. *Address:* Underlea, 34 Radnor Cliff, Folkestone, Kent CT20 2JL. *T:* (01303) 248689. *Club:* Royal Automobile.

ROWLEY-CONWY, family name of **Baron Langford**.

ROWLEY HILL, Sir George Alfred; *see* Hill.

ROWLING, Joanne Kathleen, OBE 2000; writer of children's books; *b* 31 July 1965; *d* of Peter John Rowling and late Anne Rowling; *m* 1992; one *d*. *Educ:* Univ. of Exeter (BA 1986). Author of the Year, British Book Awards, 2000. *Publications:* Harry Potter and the Philosopher's Stone, 1997 (Smarties Prize, 1997; filmed, 2001); Harry Potter and the Chamber of Secrets, 1998 (Smarties Prize, 1998; Children's Book Award, Scottish Arts Council, 1999); Harry Potter and the Prisoner of Azkaban, 1999 (Smarties Prize, 1999; Whitbread Children's Book of the Year, 2000); Harry Potter and the Goblet of Fire, 2000 (WH Smith Children's Book of the Year, Children's Book Award, Scottish Arts Council, 2001). *Address:* c/o Christopher Little Literary Agency, Ten Eel Brook Studios, 125 Moore Park Road, SW6 4PS.

ROWLINSON, Sir John (Shipley), Kt 2000; DPhil; FRS 1970; FREng, FRSC, FIChemE; Dr Lee's Professor of Physical Chemistry, Oxford University, 1974–93, now Emeritus; Fellow of Exeter College, Oxford, since 1974; *b* 12 May 1926; *er s* of late Frank Rowlinson and Winifred (*née* Jones); *m* 1952, Nancy Gaskell; one *s* one *d*. *Educ:* Rossall School (Scholar); Trinity College, Oxford (Millard Scholar; BSc, MA, DPhil; Hon. Fellow, 1992). Research Associate, Univ. of Wisconsin, USA, 1950–51; ICI Research Fellow, Lecturer, and Senior Lecturer in Chemistry, University of Manchester, 1951–60; Prof. of Chemical Technology, London Univ. (Imperial Coll.), 1961–73. Mary Upson Prof. of Engrg, 1988, Andrew D. White Prof.-at-large, 1990–96, Cornell Univ. Lectures: Liversidge, Chem. Soc., 1978; von Hofmann, Gesell. Deutscher Chem., 1980; Faraday, 1983, Lennard-Jones, 1985, RSC; Guggenheim, Reading Univ., 1986; T. W. Leland, Rice Univ., Houston, Texas, 1990; Rossini, IUPAC, 1992; Dreyfus, Dartmouth Coll., 1993; Birch, ANU, 1994. Pres., Faraday Div., Chem. Soc., 1979–81; Hon. Treas., Faraday Society, 1968–71; Vice-Pres., Royal Instn of GB, 1974–76, 1993–95; Physical Sec. and Vice-Pres., Royal Soc., 1994–99. Member, Sale Borough Council, 1956–59. FREng (FEng 1976). Hon. FCGI 1987. Hon. For. Mem., Amer. Acad. of Arts and Scis, 1994. Meldola Medal, Roy. Inst. of Chemistry, 1954; Marlow Medal, Faraday Soc., 1957; Leverhulme Medal, Royal Soc., 1993. *Publications:* Liquids and Liquid Mixtures, 1959, (jtly) 3rd edn, 1982; The Perfect Gas, 1963; Physics of Simple Liquids (joint editor), 1968; (trans. jtly) The Metric System, 1969; (jtly) Thermodynamics for Chemical Engineers, 1975; (jtly) Molecular Theory of Capillarity, 1982; (ed) J. D. van der Waals, On the Continuity of the Gaseous and Liquid States, 1988; (jtly) Record of the Royal Society 1940–1989, 1993; (jtly) Van der Waals and Molecular Science, 1996; papers in scientific journals. *Recreation:* mountaineering. *Address:* 12 Pullens Field, Headington, Oxford OX3 0BU. *T:* (01865) 767507; Physical and Theoretical Chemistry Laboratory, South Parks Road, Oxford OX1 3QZ. *T:* (01865) 270829. *Club:* Alpine.

ROWNTREE CLIFFORD, Rev. Paul; *see* Clifford.

ROWSELL, Edmund Lionel P.; *see* Penning-Rowsell.

ROWSON, John Anthony; Director, Royal & Sun Alliance Insurance Group (formerly Royal Insurance Holdings), 1994–2000; *b* 6 May 1930; *s* of Thomas Herbert Rowson and Hilda Elizabeth Rowson; *m* 1st, 1955, Elizabeth Mary (*née* Fiddes) (marr. diss. 1980); two *s* one *d*; 2nd, 1989, Molly Lesley (*née* Newman). *Educ:* Beckenham Grammar Sch.; College of Law. Admitted Solicitor, 1959. Partner, Herbert Smith, 1960, Sen. Partner, 1988–93. Dir, Glaxo Trustees Ltd, 1992–96 (Chm., 1994–96). Master, Solicitors' Co., and Pres., City of London Law Soc., 1992–93. FRSA 1993. *Recreations:* tennis, golf, ski-ing, music. *Address:* 112 Rivermead Court, Ranelagh Gardens, SW6 3SB. *Clubs:* Athenæum, Royal Automobile; Hurlingham; New Zealand Golf.

ROWTHORN, Prof. Robert Eric; Professor of Economics, Cambridge University, since 1991; Fellow, King's College, Cambridge, since 1991; *b* 20 Aug. 1939; *s* of Eric William Rowthorn and Eileen Rowthorn; *m* 1981, Amanda Jane Wharton; one *s* one *d*. *Educ:* Newport High Sch. for Boys; Jesus Coll., Oxford (BA, BPhil, MA). University of Cambridge: Res. Fellow, Churchill Coll., 1964–65; College Lectr, King's Coll., 1965–66; Asst Lectr, 1966–71; Lectr, 1971–82; Reader in Economics, 1982–91. *Publications:* International Big Business, 1971; Capitalism, Conflict and Inflation, 1980; (with J. Wells) De-industrialisation and Foreign Trade, 1987; (with N. Wayne) Northern Ireland: the political economy of conflict, 1988; (ed jtly) The Role of the State in Economic Change, 1995; (ed jtly) Democracy and Efficiency in the Economic Enterprise, 1996; (ed jtly) Transnational Corporations and the Global Economy. *Recreations:* swimming, reading, scuba-diving. *Address:* King's College, Cambridge CB2 1ST.

ROXBURGH, Iain Edge; Chief Executive and Town Clerk, Coventry City Council, since 1989; *b* 4 Nov. 1943; *s* of John and Irene Roxburgh; *m* 1965, Tessa Breddy; two *s*. *Educ:* William Hulme's Grammar Sch., Manchester; Imperial Coll., London (BSc Eng, MSc, DIC). ACGI; CEng; MICE. Civil Engineer and transport planner, 1965–80; Greater London Council: Dep. Head of Personnel Services, 1981–83; Dir of Admin, 1983–85; Dep. Sec., AMA, 1985–89. Pres., Coventry and Warwicks Inst. of Mgt. FRSA. *Recreations:* photography, motor cycling, walking, ski-ing. *Address:* Council House, Earl Street, Coventry CV1 5RR. *T:* (024) 7683 1100.

ROXBURGH, Prof. Ian Walter; Professor of Mathematics and Astronomy, since 1987, Director, Astronomy Unit, since 1983, Queen Mary and Westfield (formerly Queen Mary) College, London; *b* 31 Aug. 1939; *s* of Walter McRonald Roxburgh and Kathleen Joyce (*née* Prescott); *m* 1960, Diana Patricia (*née* Dunn); two *s* one *d*. *Educ:* King Edward VII Grammar Sch., Sheffield; Univ. of Nottingham (BSc Mathematics 1st Cl. Hons); Univ. of Cambridge (PhD); Elected Res. Fellow, Churchill Coll., Cambridge, 1963; Asst Lectr, Mathematics, 1963–64, Lectr, 1964–66, KCL; Reader in Astronomy, Univ. of Sussex, 1966–67; Queen Mary, later Queen Mary and Westfield College, London University: Prof. of Applied Maths, 1967–87; Hd, Dept of Applied Maths, 1978–84; Hd, Sch. of Math. Scis, 1984–95; Pro-Principal, 1987. Chm., Cttee of Heads of Univ. Depts of Maths and Stats, 1988–93. Chercheur associé, Observatoire de Paris. Contested: (L) Walthamstow W, 1970; (SDP) Ilford N, 1983. *Publications:* articles in Monthly Notices RAS, Astrophys. Jl, Astronomy and Astrophysics, Jl Geophysical Res., Phil. Trans Royal Soc., Gen. Relativity and Gravitation, Jl Physics A., Foundations of Physics, Nature, Solar Physics, Brit. Jl for the Philosophy of Science. *Recreations:* politics, economics, philosophy. *Address:* 37 Leicester Road, Wanstead, E11 2DW. *T:* (020) 8989 7117.

ROXBURGH, Rt Rev. James William; Assistant Bishop, Diocese of Liverpool, since 1991; *b* 5 July 1921; *s* of James Thomas and Margaret Roxburgh; *m* 1949, Marjorie Winifred (*née* Hipkiss); one *s* one *d*. *Educ:* Whitgift School; St Catharine's Coll., Cambridge (MA); Wycliffe Hall, Oxford. Deacon 1944, priest 1945; Curate: Christ Church and Holy Trinity, Folkestone, 1944–47; Handsworth, Birmingham, 1947–50; Vicar: St Matthew, Bootle, 1950–56; Drypool, Hull, 1956–65; Barking, 1965–77; Archdeacon of Colchester, 1977–83; Bishop Suffragan, later Area Bishop of Barking, 1983–90. Canon of Chelmsford, 1972–77. Pro-Prolocutor, Convocation of Canterbury, 1977–83. Pres. Barking Rotary Club, 1976–77. Hon. Freeman, Barking and Dagenham, 1990. *Recreations:* travel, philately. *Address:* 53 Preston Road, Southport, Merseyside PR9 9EE. *T:* (01704) 542927. *Club:* Royal Commonwealth Society.

ROXBURGH, Vice-Adm. Sir John (Charles Young), KCB 1972 (CB 1969); CBE 1967; DSO 1943; DSC 1942 (Bar, 1945); *b* 29 June 1919; *s* of Sir (Thomas) James (Young) Roxburgh, CIE and Mona Heymerdinguer; *m* 1942, Philippa, 3rd *d* of late Major C. M. Hewlett, MC; one *s* one *d*. *Educ:* RNC, Dartmouth. Naval Cadet, 1933; Midshipman, 1937; Sub-Lt 1939; Lt 1941; Lt-Comdr 1949; Comdr 1952; Capt. 1958; Rear-Adm. 1967; Vice-Adm. 1970. Served in various ships, 1937–39; joined Submarine Br., 1940; served in ops off Norway, in Bay of Biscay and Mediterranean, 1940–42; comd HM Submarines H43, United and Tapir, 1942–45 in ops in Mediterranean and off Norway; HMS Vanguard, 1948–50; comd HM Submarine Turpin, 1951–53; HMS Triumph, 1955; HMS Ark Royal, 1955–56; comd HMS Contest, 1956–58; Brit. Jt Services Mission, Wash., 1958–60; comd 3rd Submarine Sqdn and HMS Adamant, 1960–61; idc 1962; Dep. Dir of Defence Plans (Navy), MoD, 1963–65; comd HMS Eagle, 1965–67; Flag Officer: Sea Training, 1967–69; Plymouth, 1969; Submarines, and NATO Comdr Submarines, E Atlantic, 1969–72, retired 1972. Chm., Grovebell Group Ltd, 1972–75. Mem. Management Cttee, The Freedom Assoc., 1978–85. Pres., Royal Naval Benevolent Trust, 1978–84. Mem., Friends of Hong Kong Cttee, 1986 (Chm., 1987–95). Co. Councillor, Surrey, 1977–81. *Recreations:* golf, sailing, walking, music. *Address:* Oakdene, Wood Road, Hindhead, Surrey GU26 6PT. *T:* (01428) 605600. *Clubs:* Army and Navy; Liphook Golf, Woking Golf.

ROXBURGHE, 10th Duke of, *cr* 1707; **Guy David Innes-Ker;** Baron Roxburghe 1600; Earl of Roxburghe, Baron Ker of Cessford and Cavertoun, 1616; Bt (NS) 1625; Viscount Broxmouth, Earl of Kelso, Marquis of Bowmont and Cessford, 1707; Earl Innes (UK), 1837; *b* 18 Nov. 1954; *s* of 9th Duke of Roxburghe, and Margaret Elisabeth (*d* 1983) (who *m* 1976, Jocelyn Olaf Hambro, *qv*), *d* of late Frederick Bradshaw McConnel; *S* father, 1974; *m* 1st, 1977, Lady Jane Meriel Grosvenor (*see* Lady J. M. Dawnay) (marr. diss. 1990); two *s* one *d*; 2nd, 1992, Virginia, *d* of David Wynn-Williams; one *s* one *d*. *Educ:* Eton; RMA Sandhurst (Sword of Honour, June 1974); Magdalene Coll., Cambridge (BA (Land Economy) 1980; MA 1984). Commnd into Royal Horse Guards/1st Dragoons, 1974;

RARO 1977. Mem., Jockey Club. Mem., Fishmongers' Co.; Freeman of City of London, 1983. *Recreations:* shooting, fishing, golf, racing, ski-ing. *Heir: s* Marquis of Bowmont, *qv*. *Address:* Floors Castle, Kelso TD5 7RW. *T:* (01573) 224288. *Clubs:* Turf, White's.

ROY, Andrew Donald; economist; *b* 28 June 1920; *er s* of late Donald Whatley Roy, FRCS, FRCOG, and late Beatrice Anne Roy (*née* Barstow); *m* 1947, Katherine Juliet Grove-White (*d* 2001); one *s* two *d*. *Educ:* Malvern Coll.; Sidney Sussex Coll., Cambridge. Maths Trip. Pt I 1939 and Econ. Trip. Pt II 1948, Class I hons. 1939–45: served Royal Artillery, in UK, India and Burma (8 Medium Regt; Adjt, 1942–44). Cambridge Univ.: Asst Lecturer, 1949–51; Lecturer, 1951–64; Jun. Proctor, 1956–57; Sidney Sussex Coll.: Fellow, 1951–64; Tutor, 1953–56; Sen. Tutor, 1956–62; Financial Bursar, 1959–61. HM Treasury: Economic Consultant, 1962; Sen. Economic Adviser, 1964; Under-Sec. (Economics), 1969–72; Under-Sec., DTI, 1972–74, MoD, 1974–76; Chief Economic Adviser, DHSS, 1976–80. Consultant, NIESR, 1981–83. Governor, Malvern Coll., 1960–. *Publications:* British Economic Statistics (with C. F. Carter), 1954; articles in economic and statistical jls. *Address:* 15 Rusholme Road, Putney, SW15 3JX. *T:* (020) 8789 3180. *Club:* Oxford and Cambridge.

ROY, Prof. Arthur Douglas, FRCS, FRCSE, FRCSGlas, FRCSI; FACS; Chief of Surgical Services, Ministry of Health, Sultanate of Oman, 1985–88, and Professor of Surgery, Sultan Qaboos University, 1986–88, retired; Professor Emeritus, Queen's University of Belfast, 1985; *b* 10 April 1925; *s* of Arthur Roy and Edith Mary (*née* Brown); *m* 1st, 1954, Monica Cecilia Mary Bowley; three *d*; 2nd, 1973, Patricia Irene McColl. *Educ:* Paisley Grammar Sch.; Univ. of Glasgow (MB, ChB, Commendation). RAMC, 1948–50; Surgical Registrar posts in Glasgow and Inverness, 1950–54; Sen. Surgical Registrar, Aylesbury and Oxford, 1954–57; Cons. Surgeon and Hon. Lectr, Western Infirmary, Glasgow, 1957–68; Foundn Prof. of Surgery, Univ. of Nairobi, 1968–72; Prof. of Surgery, QUB, 1973–85. Non-exec. Dir, Exeter Dist Community NHS Trust, 1991–. Mem. Council, RCSE, 1979–85; Pres., Devon and Exeter Med. Soc., 1994–95 (Vice-Pres., 1993–94). *Publications:* Lecture Notes in Surgery: tropical supplement, 1975; various papers on gastro-enterology, endocrine surgery, tropical medicine, etc. *Recreations:* sailing, gliding, gardening. *Address:* Garden House, Old Feniton Village, near Honiton, Devon EX14 0BE. *T:* (01404) 850055. *Club:* Devon and Somerset Gliding.

ROY, Frank; MP (Lab) Motherwell and Wishaw, since 1997; *b* 29 Aug. 1958; *s* of James Roy and Esther McMahon; *m* 1977, Ellen Foy; one *s* one *d*. *Educ:* St Joseph's High Sch.; Our Lady's High Sch., Motherwell; Motherwell Coll. (HNC Mktg); Glasgow Caledonian Univ. (BA Consumer and Mgt Studies 1994). Steelworker, Ravenscraig Steelworks, Motherwell, 1977–91; PA to Helen Liddell, MP, 1994–97. *Recreations:* gardening, reading, football. *Address:* House of Commons, SW1A 0AA. *T:* (020) 7219 3000.

ROY, Paul David; Executive Vice President and Co-President, Investment Banking and Global Markets, Merrill Lynch & Co., since 2001; *b* 8 May 1947; *s* of Vernon Alfred Roy and Elsie Florence Roy; *m* 1985, Susan Mary Elkies; five *s* one *d*. *Educ:* Trinity Sch., Croydon; Liverpool Univ. (BA Hons Econs). Partner: Morton Bros (Stockbrokers), 1974–77; Kemp-Gee & Co., 1977–87; Jt Man. Dir, Citicorp Scrimgeour Vickers, 1987–89; Man. Dir, Smith New Court (UK), 1989–95; Chief Exec., Smith New Court plc, 1995; Man. Dir Equities, Europe, Middle East and Africa, 1995–98, Sen. Vice-Pres. and Head of Global Equities, 1998–2001, Merrill Lynch & Co. *Recreations:* art, golf, tennis, fishing, watching school matches. *Address:* Merrill Lynch International, 20 Farringdon Road, EC1M 3NH. *Club:* City of London.

ROY, Sheila; Group Director of Healthcare Services, Westminster Health Care, since 2000; owner, Sheila Roy & Associates, 1996; *b* 27 Feb. 1948; *d* of late Bertie and of Dorothy Atkinson; *m* 1970, Robert Neil Roy. *Educ:* BA Open Univ.; RGN; DN (London); Cert Ed Leeds Univ.; RNT; PMD Harvard Business Sch. Milton Keynes Health Authority: Dir, Nursing Studies, 1983–86; Actg Chief Nursing Officer and Dir, Nursing Studies, Feb.–May 1986; Dist Nursing Advr and Dir, Nurse Educn, Hillingdon HA, 1986–88; Dir of Nursing Management and Res., NW Thames RHA, 1988–91; Dir, Newchurch & Co., 1991–96. Non-exec. Dir, Meditech Gp Ltd, 1996–. *Recreations:* riding, tennis, sailing. *Address:* The Pyghtle, Thurleigh Road, Milton Ernest, Beds MK44 1RF. *T:* (01234) 823402, *Fax:* (01234) 824857; *e-mail:* sroy33@aol.com. *Club:* Harvard Business.

ROYCE, David Nowill; Director-General, Institute of Export, 1980–85; *b* 10 Sept. 1920; *s* of late Bernard Royce and Ida Christine (*née* Nowill); *m* 1942, Esther Sylvia Yule (*d* 2001); two *s* one *d*. *Educ:* Reading School; Vienna University. Served HM Forces, 1940–46. Major, Intelligence Corps, 1946; Asst Principal, Foreign Office, German Section, 1948; Foreign Service, 1949; First Secretary: Athens, 1953; Saigon, 1955; Foreign Office, 1957; Head of Chancery, Caracas, 1960; Counsellor (Commercial), Bonn, 1963; Counsellor (Commercial) and Consul-Gen., Helsinki, 1967–68; Commercial Inspector, FCO, 1969–71; Dir for Co-ordination of Export Services, DTI, 1971–73; Under-Secretary: Overseas Finance and Planning Div., Dept of Trade, 1973–75; CRE 3 and Export Develt Divs, Dept of Trade, 1975–77; Export Develt Div., Dept of Trade, 1977–80. Hon. Fellow, Inst. of Export, 1985. *Publication:* Successful Exporting for Small Businesses, 1990. *Recreation:* gardening. *Address:* 5 Sprimont Place, SW3 3HT. *T:* (020) 7589 9148. *Club:* Hurlingham.

ROYCE, (Roger) John; QC 1987; a Recorder, since 1986; *b* 27 Aug. 1944; *s* of J. Roger Royce and Margaret A. Royce (*née* Sibbald); *m* 1979, Gillian Wendy Adderley; two *s* one *d*. *Educ:* The Leys Sch., Cambridge; Trinity Hall, Cambridge (BA). Qualified as Solicitor, 1969; called to the Bar, Gray's Inn, 1970, Bencher, 1997; a Dep. High Ct Judge, QBD, 1993–; Leader, Western Circuit, 1998–2001. Cambridge Hockey Blue, 1965, 1966; Captain Somerset Hockey, 1976; Austrian qualified ski instructor. *Recreations:* cricket, ski-ing, golf, collecting corkscrews. *Address:* Guildhall Chambers, Broad Street, Bristol BS1 2HG. *T:* (0117) 927 3366. *Clubs:* Hawks (Cambridge); St Enodoc Golf.

ROYDEN, Sir Christopher (John), 5th Bt *cr* 1905; Associate Director, Greig Middleton & Co. Ltd, since 1996; *b* 26 Feb. 1937; *s* of Sir John Ledward Royden, 4th Bt, and Dolores Catherine (*d* 1994), *d* of late Cecil J. G. Coward; *S* father, 1976; *m* 1961, Diana Bridget, *d* of Lt-Col J. H. Goodhart, MC; two *s* one *d*. *Educ:* Winchester Coll.; Christ Church, Oxford (MA). Duncan Fox & Co. Ltd, 1960–71; Spencer Thornton & Co., 1971–88: Partner, 1974–86; Dir, 1986–88; Associate Dir, Gerrard Vivian Gray Ltd, 1988–96. *Recreations:* fishing, shooting, gardening. *Heir: s* John Michael Joseph Royden [*b* 17 March 1965; *m* 1989, Lucilla, *d* of J. R. Stourton; two *d*]. *Address:* Flat 2, 8 Nevern Square, SW5 9NW. *Club:* Boodle's.

ROYDS, Rev. John Caress, MA Cantab; *b* 1920; 3rd *s* of Rev. Edward Thomas Hubert Royds, BA. *Educ:* Monkton Combe School, Bath; Queens' College, Cambridge (BA II 1 hons History, 1947). Military service with British and Indian Armies, 1940–46. Assistant master, Bryanston School, Dorset, 1947–61, House-master, 1951–61; Headmaster: General Wingate School, Addis Ababa, 1961–65; Uppingham Sch., 1965–75. Deacon, 1974; Priest, 1975; Dir of Educn for Peterborough diocese, 1976–81; Vicar of St James's, Northampton, 1981–85; with CMS, Peshawar, Pakistan, 1985–86. *Address:* 16B Donaldson Road, Salisbury SP1 3DA.

ROYLE, family name of **Baron Fanshawe of Richmond**.

ROYLE, Rev. Canon Roger Michael; freelance broadcaster and writer, since 1979; Chaplain, Southwark Cathedral, since 1993; *b* 30 Jan. 1939; *s* of Reginald and Agnes Royle. *Educ:* St Edmund's Sch., Canterbury; King's Coll. London (AKC 2nd Class Hons). Curate, St Mary's, Portsea, Portsmouth, 1962–65; Sen. Curate, St Peter's, Morden, 1965–68; Succentor, Southwark Cathedral, 1968–71; Warden of Dorney Parish, Eton Coll. Project, 1971–74; Conduct, Eton Coll., 1974–79; Chaplain, Lord Mayor Treloar Coll., 1990–92. MA Lambeth, 1990. *Publications:* A Few Blocks from Broadway, 1987; Royle Exchange, 1989; To Have and to Hold, 1990; Picking up the Pieces, 1990; Mother Teresa: her life in pictures, 1992; Between Friends, 2001. *Recreations:* theatre, music, patience, cooking. *Address:* Southwark Cathedral, Montague Close, SE1 9DA.

ROYLE, Timothy Lancelot Fanshawe, FCIM; Director, Wellmarine Reinsurance Brokers, since 1976; *b* 24 April 1931; *s* of Sir Lancelot Carrington Royle, KBE, and Barbara Rachel Royle; *m* 1958, Margaret Jill Stedeford; two *s* one *d*. *Educ:* Harrow; Mons Mil. Acad. FCIM (FInstM 1977). Commnd 15th/19th King's Royal Hussars, 1949, Inns of Court Regt, TA, 1951–63. Joined Hogg Robinson Gp, 1951; Man. Dir, 1980–81. Chairman: Control Risks Group, 1975–91; Berry Palmer & Lyle, 1984–91; Hemotex Holdings, 1991–93; Director: Imperio Reinsurance Co. (UK), 1989–97; Imperio Holdings Ltd, 1995–97. Mem., Insce Brokers Regulatory Council, 1989–94. Member: Church Assembly of C of E, 1965–70; Gen. Synod of C of E, 1985–; Church Comr, 1966–83. Director: Christian Weekly Newspapers, 1997–2001 (Chm., 1979–97); Lindley Educn Trust, 1998– (Chm., 1970–98). Trustee: Ridley Hall, Cambridge, 1976–; Wycliffe Hall, Oxford, 1976–; Charinco, 1977–; Charishare, 1977–; Intercontinental Church Soc., 1977–. Freeman, City of London, 1976; Member: Marketors' Co., 1977; Insurers' Co., 1979. Councillor (C) Cotswold DC, 1999–. *Recreations:* country pursuits, ski-ing. *Address:* Icomb Place, near Stow on the Wold, Cheltenham, Glos GL54 1JD. *Clubs:* Cavalry and Guards, MCC; St Moritz Tobogganing (St Moritz).

See also Baron Fanshawe of Richmond.

ROZARIO, Most Rev. Michael; *see* Dhaka, Archbishop of, (RC).

ROZARIO, Patricia Maria, OBE 2001; soprano; *b* Bombay; *m*; two *c*. *Educ:* Guildhall Sch. of Music (Gold Medal; Maggie Teyte Prize). Performances include: Werther, Opera North, 1985; Idomeneo, Royal Opera House, 1985; Coronation of Poppea, Kent Opera, 1986; Golem, 1989; title rôle, world première, Mary of Egypt, Aldeburgh, 1992; The Duel of Tancredi and Clorinda, 1993; Depart in Peace (tour), 1998; numerous concerts and recitals in UK, France and Germany. Recordings include Schubert songs, Tavener's Akhmatova songs. *Address:* c/o Askonas Holt Ltd, Lonsdale Chambers, 27 Chancery Lane, WC2A 1PF.

ROZENBERG, Joshua Rufus; Legal Editor, The Daily Telegraph, since 2000; *b* 30 May 1950; *s* of late Zigmund and Beatrice Rozenberg; *m* 1974, Melanie Phillips; one *s* one *d*. *Educ:* Latymer Upper Sch., Hammersmith; Wadham Coll., Oxford (MA 1976). Solicitor's articled clerk, 1972; admitted Solicitor, 1976; trainee journalist, BBC, 1975; Legal Affairs Correspondent, 1985–97, Legal and Constitutional Affairs Correspondent, 1997–2000, BBC News. Hon. LLD Hertfordshire, 1999. *Publications:* Your Rights and the Law (with Nicola Watkins), 1986; The Case for the Crown, 1987; The Search for Justice, 1994; Trial of Strength, 1997. *Recreations:* my family and my computer, ideally in that order. *Address:* The Daily Telegraph, 1 Canada Square, E14 5DT. *T:* (020) 7538 6498; *e-mail:* joshua.rozenberg@telegraph.co.uk. *Club:* Garrick.

ROZENTAL, Andrés; Ambassador-at-Large and Special Presidential Envoy, Mexico, since 2000; President, Rozental y Asociados, since 1997; *b* 27 April 1945; *s* of Leonid Rozental and Neoma Gutman; *m* 1971, Vivian Holzer; two *d*. *Educ:* Univ. of Bordeaux (Dip. French 1962); Univ. of the Americas (BA 1965); Univ. of Pennsylvania (MA 1966). Joined Foreign Service, 1967; Alternate Perm. Rep. to OAS, Washington, 1971–74; Counsellor, London, 1974–76; Prin. Advr to the Minister, 1977–79; Dir-Gen. of Diplomatic Service, 1979; Dir-Gen. for N American Affairs, 1979–82; Ambassador: to UN, Geneva, 1982–83; to Sweden, 1983–88; Sen. Vice-Pres., Banco Nacional de México, 1988; Dep. Foreign Minister, 1988–94; Amb. to Court of St James's, 1995–97. Orders include: Polar Star (Sweden), 1983; Civil Merit (Spain), 1991; Order of Merit (France), 1993. *Publications:* (jtly) Paradoxes of a World in Transition, 1993; (jtly) The United Nations Today: a Mexican vision, 1994; Mexican Foreign Policy in the Modern Age, 1994; (jtly) Foreign Ministries: change and adaptation, 1997. *Recreations:* swimming, sailing, hiking. *Address:* (home) Virreyes 1360, Col. Lomas de Chapultepec, 11000 México DF, México. *T:* (5) 2025347.

ROZHDESTVENSKY, Gennadi Nikolaevich; Founder, Artistic Director and Chief Conductor, State Symphony Orchestra of Ministry of Culture, Russia (New Symphony Orchestra), 1983–92; Chief Conductor, Royal Stockholm Philharmonic Orchestra, 1991–95; Professor of Conducting, Moscow State Conservatoire, since 1965; *b* 4 May 1931; *m* Victoria Postnikova, concert pianist. Studied piano at Moscow Conservatoire; started conducting at 18. Bolshoi Theatre: Asst Conductor, 1951; Conductor, 1956–60; Principal Conductor, 1965–70; Artistic Dir, 2000–01. Chief Conductor, USSR Radio and Television Symphony Orchestra, 1960–74; Chief Conductor: Stockholm Philharmonic Orchestra, 1974–77; BBC Symphony Orchestra, 1978–81; Moscow Chamber Opera, 1974–83; Vienna Symphony Orchestra, 1981–83. Guest conductor, Europe, Israel, America, Far East, Australia. Lenin Prize, 1970; People's Artist, USSR, 1972; Order of Red Banner of Labour, 1981. *Recreation:* music. *Address:* c/o Allied Artists Agency, 42 Montpelier Square, SW7 1JZ. *Club:* Athenæum.

RUANE, Christopher Shaun; MP (Lab) Vale of Clwyd, since 1997; *b* 18 July 1958; *s* of late Michael Ruane, labourer, and of Esther Ruane, dinner lady; *m* 1994, Gill, *d* of Joe and Phil Roberts; two *d*. *Educ:* Blessed Edward Jones Comp. Sch., Rhyl; UCW Aberystwyth (BSc); Liverpool Univ. (PGCE); Glamorgan Univ. (Dip. Media Educn); UCW Bangor (Dip.). Teacher, Ysgol Mair RC Primary Sch., Rhyl, 1982–97 (Dep. Hd, 1991–97). Mem. (Lab) Rhyl Town Council, 1988–97. Contested (Lab) Clwyd NW, 1992. Mem., Welsh Affairs Select Cttee, 1999–. *Address:* House of Commons, SW1A 0AA.

RUAUX, Gillian Doreen, (Mrs W. D. Partington); Her Honour Judge Ruaux; a Circuit Judge, since 1993; *b* 25 March 1945; *d* of late Charles Edward Ruaux and Denise Maud Ruaux (*née* Le Page); *m* 1968, William Derek Partington; one *d*. *Educ:* Bolton Sch.; Univ. of Manchester (LLB Hons, LLM). Called to the Bar, Gray's Inn, 1968; practised at the Bar, Manchester, 1968–93. *Recreations:* theatre, opera, horse-racing, cookery. *Address:* Bolton Combined Court Centre, Blackhorse Street, Bolton, Greater Manchester BL1 1SU. *Club:* Bolton Old Links Golf.

RUBBIA, Prof. Carlo; physicist; Senior Physicist, European Organisation for Nuclear Research, since 1993 (Director-General, 1989–93); *b* 31 March 1934; *s* of Silvio and Bice

Rubbia; *m* Marisa; one *s* one *d.* *Educ:* Scuola Normale Superiore, Pisa; Univ. of Pisa (Dr 1957). Research Fellow, Columbia Univ., 1958–59; Lectr, Univ. of Rome, 1960–61; CERN, 1960– (head of team investigating fundamental particles on proton-antiproton collider); scientist, Fermi Nat. Accelerator Lab., USA, 1969–73; Higgins Prof. of Physics, Harvard Univ., 1971–88. Member: Papal Acad. of Science, 1985–; Amer. Acad. of Arts and Sciences, 1985; Accademia dei XL; Accademia dei Lincei; European Acad. of Sciences; Ateneo Veneto; Foreign Member: Royal Soc.; Soviet Acad. of Scis, 1988; US Nat. Acad. of Scis; Polish Acad. of Scis. Hon. Doctorates: Boston, Chicago, Geneva, Genoa, Northwestern, Udine, Carnegie-Mellon, Loyola, Sofia, Moscow, Chile, Padova, Madrid, Rio de Janeiro, La Plata and Oxford Universities. Gold Medal, Italian Physical Soc., 1983; Lorenzo il Magnifico Prize for Sciences, 1983; Achille de Gasperi Prize for Sciences, 1984; Nobel Prize for Physics (jtly), 1984; Leslie Prize for exceptional achievements, 1985; Castiglioni di Sicilia Prize, 1985; Carlo Capodieci Gold Medal, 1985; Jesolo d'Oro, 1986. Knight Grand Cross, Italy; Officer, Legion of Honour, France, 1989. *Publications:* papers on nuclear physics: weak force quanta (W–, W+ and Z particles, intermediate vector bosons); proton-antiproton collision; sixth quark. *Address:* CERN, 1211 Geneva 23, Switzerland.

RUBEN, Prof. David-Hillel; Director, New York University in London, since 1999; *b* 25 July 1943; *s* of Blair S. Ruben and Sylvia G. Ruben; *m* 1968, Eira (*née* Karlinsky); one *s* two *d.* *Educ:* Dartmouth Coll. (BA); Harvard Univ. (PhD). Tutor in Philosophy, Univ. of Edinburgh, 1969; Lecturer in Philosophy: Univ. of Glasgow, 1970–75; Univ. of Essex, 1975–79; Lectr, 1979–82, Sen. Lectr, 1982–84, City Univ.; Prof. of Philosophy, LSE, 1984–98; Dir, Jews' Coll., London, later London Sch. of Jewish Studies, 1998–99. Phi Beta Kappa, 1964. *Publications:* Marxism and Materialism, 1977, 2nd edn 1979; Metaphysics of the Social World, 1985; Explaining Explanation, 1990; (ed) Explanation, 1994; articles in phil. jls. *Address:* New York University in London, 6 Bedford Square, WC1B 3RA. *T:* (020) 7907 3200.

RUBENS, Bernice Ruth; writer and director of documentary films, since 1957; *m* 1947, Rudi Nassauer (*d* 1997); two *d.* *Educ:* University of Wales, Cardiff (BA, Hons English; Fellow 1982; Hon. DLitt 1991). Followed teaching profession, 1950–55. American Blue Ribbon award for documentary film, Stress, 1968. *Publications:* Set on Edge, 1960; Madame Sousatzka, 1962 (filmed, 1989); Mate in Three, 1965; The Elected Member, 1969 (Booker Prize, 1970); Sunday Best, 1971; Go Tell the Lemming, 1973; I Sent a Letter to my Love, 1975 (filmed, 1981); The Ponsonby Post, 1977; A Five Year Sentence, 1978; Spring Sonata, 1979; Birds of Passage, 1981; Brothers, 1983; Mr Wakefield's Crusade, 1985 (televised, 1992); Our Father, 1987; Kingdom Come, 1990; A Solitary Grief, 1991; Mother Russia, 1992; Autobiopsy, 1993; Yesterday in the Back Lane, 1995; The Waiting Game, 1997; I, Dreyfus, 1999; Milwaukee, 2001. *Recreation:* plays piano and 'cello. *Address:* 213A Goldhurst Terrace, NW6 3ER. *T:* (020) 7625 4845.

RUBENS, Prof. Robert David, MD; FRCP; Professor of Clinical Oncology, Guy's, King's and St Thomas' School of Medicine of King's College London (formerly United Medical and Dental Schools of Guy's and St Thomas' Hospitals), University of London, since 1985; Consultant Physician in Medical Oncology, Guy's Hospital, since 1975; *b* 11 June 1943; *s* of Joel Rubens and Dinah Rubens (*née* Hasseck); *m* 1970, Margaret Chamberlin; two *d.* *Educ:* King's Coll., London (BSc); St George's Hosp. Med. Sch. (MB, BS); MD London. FRCP 1984. House and Registrar appts, St George's, Brompton, Hammersmith and Royal Marsden Hosps, 1968–72; Clin. Res. Fellow, ICRF Labs, 1972–74; Dir, ICRF Clinical Oncology Unit, Guy's Hosp., 1985–97. Chm., EORTC Breast Cancer Co-op. Gp, 1991–94. Examr, RCP, 1987–93. Editor-in-Chief, Cancer Treatment Reviews, 1993–. *Publications:* A Short Textbook of Clinical Oncology, 1980; Bone Metastases: diagnosis and treatment, 1991; Cancer and the Skeleton, 2000; ed and contrib. books and papers on cancer and other med. subjects. *Recreations:* golf, bridge. *Address:* 5 Currie Hill Close, Wimbledon, SW19 7DX. *Clubs:* Athenæum; Royal Wimbledon Golf.

RUBERTI, Prof. Antonio, FIEEE; MP (Left Democratic Party), Rome, since 1995; Professor of System Theory, La Sapienza University, Rome, since 1962; *b* Aversa, Italy, 24 Jan. 1927; *m* 1955, Luisa Andreozzi; one *s* three *d.* *Educ:* Naples Univ. (Laurea in electrical engrg). FIEEE 1985. La Sapienza University, Rome: Head, Engrg Faculty, 1973–76; Rector, 1976–87. Minister for Co-ordination of Scientific and Technol Research and for Research and Univs, 1987–92; MP (Italian Socialist Party), Rome-Latina-Frosinone-Viterbo, 1992; Mem., CEC, then Eur. Commn, 1993–95 (a Vice-Pres., 1993). Ordre National de la Légion d'Honneur (France), 1982; Leonardo da Vinci Medal (Italy), 1989. *Publications:* numerous scientific works on control and system theory, essays, books and encyclopedia articles on university policy concerning research and problems of technol innovation. *Address:* Via San Calepodio 36, 00152 Roma, Italy; Palazzo Montecitorio, Roma, Italy. *T:* (6) 67603905, *Fax:* (6) 67609948.

RUBERY, Dr Eileen Doris, CB 1998; Senior Research Associate, Judge Institute of Management Studies, University of Cambridge, since 1997; Senior Research Fellow and Registrar of the Roll, Girton College, Cambridge, since 2000 (Visiting Senior Fellow, 1997–2000); *b* 16 May 1943; *d* of James and Doris McDonnell; *m* 1969, Philip Huson Rubery; one *d.* *Educ:* Westcliff High Sch. for Girls; Sheffield Univ. Med. Sch. (MB ChB Hons); Cambridge Univ. (PhD). FRCR; FRCPath; FFPHM. Royal Infirmary, Sheffield, 1966–67; MRC Res. Fellow, Dept of Biochem., Cambridge, 1967–71; Meres' Sen. Student, St John's Coll., Cambridge, 1971–73; Addenbrooke's Hospital, Cambridge: Registrar in Radiotherapy and Oncology, 1973–76; Sen. Registrar, 1976–78; Wellcome Sen. Clinical Res. Fellow, 1978–83; Hon. Consultant, 1978–83; Sen. Res. Fellow and Dir of Med. Studies, Girton Coll., 1981–83; SMO (Toxicology), DHSS, 1983–88; Department of Health: PMO, 1988–89; SPMO and Hd of Med. Div., Communicable Disease and Immunisation, 1989–91; SPMO and Hd of Health Promotion Med. Div., 1991–95; Under Sec. and Hd of Health Aspects of Envmtl and Food Div., 1995–97; Under Sec. and Hd of Protection of Health Div., 1996–99. Mem., Professional Conduct Cttee, GMC, 2000–. QHP, 1993–96. *Publications:* (ed) Indications for Iodine Prophylaxis following a Nuclear Accident, 1990; (ed) Medicine: a degree course guide, 1974–83; papers on public health, food safety, health promotion, professionals and public sector incl. policy making and the management of uncertainty, in professional jls. *Recreations:* visiting Venice, reading Proust, Renaissance and Medieval art, opera, Wagner, Ruskin. *Address:* Judge Institute of Management Studies, University of Cambridge, Trumpington Street, Cambridge CB2 1AG. *T:* (01223) 766293, *Fax:* (01223) 766330; Girton College, Huntingdon Road, Cambridge CB3 0JG, *T:* (01223) 337025; *e-mail:* e.rubery@jims.cam.ac.uk.

RUBERY, Reginald John; His Honour Judge Rubery; a Circuit Judge, since 1995; *b* 13 July 1937; *s* of Reginald Arthur Rubery and Phyllis Margaret (*née* Payne); *m* 1st, 1961, Diana Wilcock Holgate (marr. diss.); one *s*; 2nd, 1974, Frances Camille Murphy; one step *d.* *Educ:* Wadham House, Hale, Cheshire; King's Sch., Worcester. Admitted Solicitor, 1963; Partner: Whitworths, Manchester, 1966–72; Taylor Kirkman & Mainprice, 1972–78; County Court and Dist Registrar, then District Judge, 1978–95; Asst Recorder, 1987–91; a Recorder, 1991–95; Judge, St Helena Court of Appeal, 1997–; Justice of Appeal, Falkland Is, British Indian Ocean Territory, British Antarctic Territory. Chm. (pt-time) Immigration Appeal Tribunal, 1998–. Mem., Manchester City Council, 1968–71. Hon. Sec., Manchester Law Soc., 1974–78. *Recreations:* golf, swimming, gardening. *Address:* Birkby, Charnes Road, Ashley, Market Drayton, Shropshire TF9 4LQ. *Clubs:* Lansdowne; Hale Golf, Nefyn Golf, Market Drayton Golf.

RUBIN, Prof. Peter Charles, DM; FRCP; Professor of Therapeutics, since 1987, and Dean, Faculty of Medicine and Health Sciences, since 1997, University of Nottingham; *b* 21 Nov. 1948; *s* of late Woolf Rubin and Enis Rubin; *m* 1976, Dr Fiona Logan; one *s* one *d.* *Educ:* Redruth Grammar Sch.; Emmanuel Coll., Cambridge (MA); Exeter Coll., Oxford (DM 1980). FRCP 1989. Jun. hosp. posts, Stoke on Trent, 1974–77; American Heart Assoc. Fellow, Stanford Med. Center, 1977–79; Sen. Registrar (Medicine and Clinical Pharmacology), Glasgow, 1979–82; Wellcome Trust Sen. Fellow in Clinical Sci., Glasgow, 1982–87; Chm., Dept of Medicine, Univ. of Nottingham, 1991–97. *Publications:* Lecture Notes on Clinical Pharmacology, 1981, 6th edn 2000; Prescribing in Pregnancy, 1987, 3rd edn 2000; Hypertension in Pregnancy, 1988, 2nd edn 2000. *Recreations:* sport, walking, music. *Address:* Dean's Office, Medical School, Queen's Medical Centre, Nottingham NG7 2UH. *T:* (0115) 970 9380. *Club:* Oxford and Cambridge.

RUBIN, Robert E(dwin); Chairman of the Executive Committee, Citigroup, since 1999; Secretary of the United States Treasury, 1995–99; *b* 29 Aug. 1938; *s* of Alexander Rubin and Sylvia Rubin (*née* Seiderman); *m* 1963, Judith Leah Oxenberg; two *s*. . *Educ:* Harvard (AB *summa cum laude* 1960); LSE, London Univ.; Yale Univ. (LLB 1964). Admitted to NY Bar, 1965; Associate, Cleary, Gottlieb, Steen & Hamilton, 1964–66; Goldman, Sach & Co.: Associate, 1966–70; Partner, 1971; Mem. Mgt Cttee, 1980; Vice Chair and Co-Chief Operating Officer, 1987–90; Sen. Partner and Co-Chair, 1990–93; Asst to the Pres. on econ. policy and Head, Nat. Econ. Council, Exec. Office of US President, 1993–95. Member, Board of Directors: Chicago Bd of Options Exchange, Inc., 1972–76; NY Futures Exchange, 1979–85; Center for Nat. Policy, 1982–93 (Vice Chair, 1984); NY Stock Exchange, Inc., 1991–93 (Mem., Regulatory Adv. Cttee, 1988–90); NYC Partnership Inc., 1991–93 (also Partner). Member: Adv. Cttee on Tender Offers, 1983, Adv. Cttee on Market Oversight and Financial Services, 1991–93, Securities and Exchange Commn; NY Adv. Cttee on Internat. Capital Markets, Federal Reserve Bank, 1989–93; Mayor's Council of Econ. Advrs, 1990. Trustee: Amer. Ballet Theatre Foundn, 1969–93; Mt Sinai Hosp., 1977 (Vice-Chm., 1986); Collegiate Sch., 1978–84; Station WNET-TV, 1985–93; Carnegie Corp., NY, 1990–93; Harvard Mgt Co. Inc., 1990–93. Hon. DHL Yeshiva, 1996. Nat. Assoc. of Christians and Jews Award, 1977; Dist. Leadership in Govt Award, Columbia Business Sch., 1996; Finance Minister of the Year Award, Euromoney mag., 1996. *Recreation:* fly fishing. *Address:* Citigroup Inc., 153 East 53rd Street, New York, NY 10043, USA. *Clubs:* Harvard (NYC); Century Country (Purchase).

RUBIN, Stephen Charles; QC 2000; *b* 14 March 1955; *s* of Joseph Rubin and Shirley Rubin (*née* Dank); *m* 1985, Jayne Anne Purdy; two *s* two *d.* *Educ:* Merchant Taylors' Sch., Northwood; Brasenose Coll., Oxford (Open Exhibnr; MA Jurisp.). Called to the Bar, Middle Temple, 1977; in practice at the Bar, 1979–. Mem., Professional Conduct and Complaints Cttee, Bar Council, 1994–99. *Recreations:* contemporary art, tennis, ski-ing, golf. *Address:* Fountaiin Court Chambers, Temple, EC4Y 9DH.

RUBINS, Jack, FIPA; Chairman, Osprey Communications plc, since 1993 (non-executive Chairman, 1999–2000; Chief Executive, 1993–95); *b* 4 Aug. 1931; *m* 1962, Ruth Davids; three *s.* *Educ:* Northern Polytechnic (Architecture). Chm. and Chief Exec., DFS Dorland Advertising, 1976–87; Chm. and Chief Exec., McCann Erickson Gp UK, 1990–91; Chm., SMS Communications, 1991–93. *Recreations:* philately, golf. *Address:* Danehurst, 34 Northwick Circle, Harrow, Middx HA3 0EE.

RUBINSTEIN, Hilary Harold; Chairman, Hilary Rubinstein Books (Literary Agents), since 1992; *b* 24 April 1926; *s* of H. F. and Lina Rubinstein; *m* 1955, Helge Kitzinger; three *s* one *d.* *Educ:* Cheltenham Coll.; Merton Coll., Oxford (MA). Editorial Dir, Victor Gollancz Ltd, 1952–63; Special Features Editor, The Observer, 1963–64; Dep. Editor, The Observer Magazine, 1964–65. Partner, later Director, 1965–92, Chm. and Man. Dir, 1983–92, A. P. Watt Ltd. Mem. Council, ICA, 1976–92; Trustee, Open Coll. of the Arts, 1987–96. Founder-editor, The Good Hotel Guide (published in USA as Europe's Wonderful Little Hotels and Inns), 1978–2000. *Publications:* The Complete Insomniac, 1974; Hotels and Inns, an Oxford anthology, 1984. *Recreations:* hotel-watching, reading in bed. *Address:* 32 Ladbroke Grove, W11 3BQ. *T:* (020) 7727 9550, *Fax:* (020) 7221 5291; *e-mail:* hrubinstein@becb.net.

RUBINSTEIN, Prof. Nicolai, FBA 1971; FRHistS; Professor of History, Westfield College, London University, 1965–78, now Emeritus; *b* 13 July 1911; *s* of Bernhard and Irene Rubinstein; *m* 1954, Ruth Kidder Olitsky. *Educ:* Univs of Berlin and Florence. LittD Florence. Lectr, UC Southampton, 1942–45; Lectr, 1945–62, Reader, 1962–65, Westfield Coll., Univ. of London. Corresp. Mem., Accad. Toscana La Colombaria, 1976; Hon. Fellow: Warburg Inst., 1985; Westfield Coll., 1986. Hon. Diploma di perfezionamento, Scuola Normale Superiore, Pisa, 1991. Serena Medal, British Acad., 1974; Premio Internazionale Galileo Galilei, 1985; Fiorino d'oro, Florence, 1990; Premio della Cultura della Presidenza del Consiglio, 1993. Hon. Citizen, Florence, 1991. *Publications:* The Government of Florence under the Medici 1434–94, 1966, 2nd edn 1997; (ed) Florentine Studies: politics and society in Renaissance Florence, 1968; Gen. Editor, Letters of Lorenzo de'Medici and ed vol. 3, 1977, and vol. 4, 1981; The Palazzo Vecchio 1298–1532, 1995; articles in Jl of Warburg and Courtauld Insts, Italian Studies, Archivio Storico Italiano, Rinascimento, etc. *Address:* 16 Gardnor Mansions, Church Row, NW3 6UR. *T:* (020) 7435 6995.

RUBYTHON, Eric Gerald, CBE 1978; Member of Aerospace Board, British Aerospace, 1977–83, retired (Deputy Chief Executive of Aircraft Group, 1977–82); *b* 11 Feb. 1921; *s* of Reginald Rubython and Bessie Rubython; *m* 1943, Joan Ellen Mills. Joined Hawker Aircraft Ltd, 1948; Co. Sec., 1953; Exec. Dir, 1959; Dir and Gen. Man., 1960; Divl Dir and Gen. Man., Hawker Blackburn Div., 1963; Hawker Siddeley Aviation: Commercial Dir, 1965; Dir and Gen. Manager, 1970; Chm. and Man. Dir, 1977. *Recreations:* golf, gardening. *Address:* 1230 San Julian Drive, Lake San Marcos, CA 92069–4807, USA.

RUCK, Peter Frederick C.; *see* Carter-Ruck.

RUCK-KEENE, John Robert, CBE 1977 (MBE 1946); TD 1950; Secretary General, Royal Society of Chemistry, 1980–81; *b* 2 Jan. 1917; *s* of late Major Robert Francis Ruck Keene, OBE, and Dorothy Mary (*née* Chester); *m* 1951, Beryl M Manistre; two *s.* *Educ:* Eton; Trinity Coll., Cambridge (BA 1938, MA 1955). Commissioned TA, Oxford and Bucks LI, 1939; served UK and NW Europe, 1939–45 (Major 1944, MBE 1946). First appointment with Chemical Society, 1946; General Secretary, 1947–80, when the Royal Society of Chemistry was formed by unification under Royal Charter of The Chemical

Society and The Royal Institute of Chemistry, 1 June 1980. Hon. FRSC, 1982. *Address:* Flat 28, Archer Court, 43 Chesham Road, Amersham, Bucks HP6 5UL. *T:* (01494) 727123.

RUCKER, Jeffrey Hamilton; His Honour Judge Rucker; a Circuit Judge, since 1988; *b* 19 Dec. 1942; *s* of late Charles Edward Sigismund Rucker and Nancy Winifred Hodgson; *m* 1965, Caroline Mary Salkeld; three *s*. *Educ:* St Aubyn's, Rottingdean; Charterhouse. Called to the Bar, Middle Temple, 1967; a Recorder, 1984; a Circuit Judge, assigned to SE Circuit, 1988. Mem. Council of Govs, UMDS of Guy's and St Thomas', 1991–98. *Recreations:* sailing, ski-ing, music. *Address:* Southwark Crown Court, 1 English Grounds, off Battlebridge Lane, SE1 2HU.

RUDD, Sir (Anthony) Nigel (Russell), Kt 1996; DL; Chairman, Pilkington plc, since 1995 (Director, since 1994); non-executive Chairman, Kidde, since 2000; *b* 31 Dec. 1946; *m* 1969, Lesley Elizabeth (*née* Hodgkinson); two *s* one *d*. *Educ:* Bemrose Grammar Sch., Derby. FCA. Qualified Chartered Accountant 1968; Divl Finance Dir, London & Northern Group, 1970–77; Chairman: C. Price & Son Ltd, 1977–82; Williams Holdings (later Williams plc), 1982–2000; Dep. Chm., Raine Industries, 1992–94 (non-exec. Chm., 1986–92); non-executive Chairman: Pendragon PLC, 1989–; East Midlands Electricity, 1994–97 (Dir, 1990–97); non-executive Director: Williams Management Services, 1985–96; Westminster Securities, 1987–96; Gartmore Value Investment, 1989–93; Gartmore, 1993–96; Derby Pride, 1993–98; Mithras Investment Trust, 1994–98; Barclays Bank, 1996–. Member: European Round Table of Industrialists, to 2001; Council, CBI, 1999–. Freeman, City of London; Mem, Chartered Accountants' Co. DL Derbys, 1996. Hon. DTech Loughborough, 1998; DUniv Derby, 1998. *Recreations:* golf, ski-ing, theatre, field sports. *Address:* c/o Kidde plc, Pentagon House, Sir Frank Whittle Road, Derby DE21 4XA. *T:* (01332) 202020.

RUDD, Norman Julian Peter Joseph; His Honour Judge Rudd; a Circuit Judge, since 1988; *b* 12 May 1943; *s* of Norman Arthur Rudd and Winifred Rudd; *m* 1968, Judith Margaret Pottinger; three *s*. *Educ:* Paston Sch., N Walsham, Norfolk; University Coll. London (LLB, LLM). Called to the Bar, Inner Temple, 1969; Asst Recorder, 1982–87, Head of Chambers, 1982–87; a Recorder, 1987. Trustee, New Forest Commoning Trust, 1993– (Chm., 1993–98); Chm., Northern Commoners Assoc. (New Forest), 1999–. *Recreations:* farming, shooting. *Address:* The Courts of Justice, London Road, Southampton SO9 5AF.

RUDD-JONES, Derek, CBE 1981; PhD; Director, Glasshouse Crops Research Institute, Littlehampton, Sussex, 1971–86; *b* 13 April 1924; 2nd *s* of late Walter Henry Jones and late Doris Mary, *er d* of H. Rudd Dawes; *m* 1948, Joan, 2nd *d* of late Edward Newhouse, Hong Kong, and Malvern, Worcs; two *s* one *d*. *Educ:* Whitgift; Repton; Emmanuel Coll., Cambridge. BA, MA, PhD (Cantab); FIBiol; FIHort. Agricultural Research Council, postgrad. student, Botany Sch., Univ. of Cambridge, 1945–48; Plant Pathologist, E African Agric. and Forestry Research Org., Kenya, 1949–52; Nat. Research Council, Postdoctoral Fellow, Univ. of Saskatchewan, Saskatoon, Canada, 1952–53. ICI Ltd, Akers Research Laboratory, The Frythe, Welwyn, Herts, 1953–56; Jealott's Hill Research Station, Bracknell, Berks, 1956–59; Scientific Adviser to Sec., Agricl Research Council, 1959–71; Foundn Chm., 1968–72, Managing Editor, 1986–93, British Crop Protection Council (Mem., 1968–86); Pres., Section K, BAAS, 1981–82; Mem., Scientific Cttee, RHS, 1985–96; formerly Mem., Adv. Cttee on Pesticides and Other Toxic Chemicals. Vis. Fellow, Univ. of Southampton, 1975–86. Governor, Chichester (formerly W Sussex) Inst. of Higher Educn, 1980–95; Trustee, Thomas Phillips Price Trust, 1988–93. *Publications:* papers in scientific journals. *Recreations:* gardening, riding, fly-fishing. *Address:* Bignor Park Cottage, near Pulborough, West Sussex RH20 1HQ. *Club:* Farmers'.

RUDDEN, Prof. Bernard (Anthony), LLD; FBA 1995; Professor of Comparative Law, University of Oxford, 1979–99, now Emeritus; Fellow of Brasenose College, Oxford, 1979–99, now Emeritus; *b* 21 Aug. 1933; *s* of John and Kathleen Rudden; *m* 1957, Nancy Campbell Painter; three *s* one *d*. *Educ:* City of Norwich Sch.; St John's Coll., Cambridge. LLD Cantab; DCL Oxon; PhD Wales. Solicitor. Fellow and Tutor, Oriel Coll., Oxford, 1965–79. Hon. LLD McGill, 1991. *Publications:* Soviet Insurance Law, 1966; The New River, 1985; Basic Community Cases, 1987, 2nd edn 1997; co-author or editor of: The Law of Mortgages, 1967; Source-Book on French Law, 1973, 3rd edn 1991; Basic Community Laws, 1980, 7th edn 1999; The Law of Property, 1982, 2002; Comparing Constitutions, 1995; contrib. periodical pubns. *Address:* 15 Redinnick Terrace, Penzance TR18 4HR. *T:* (01736) 360395. *Club:* Oxford and Cambridge.

RUDDOCK, Alan Stephen Dennis; Editor, The Scotsman, 1998–2000; *b* 21 July 1960; *s* of John and Doreen Ruddock; *m* 1986, Jacqueline Kilroy; three *s*. *Educ:* Coll. of St Columba, Dublin; TCD (BA 1983). Reporter: Business Day, Johannesburg, 1984–86; Today newspaper, 1986–89; Business Editor, Sunday Tribune, Dublin, 1989–92; Sunday Times, 1992–96; Man. Editor, Sunday Express, 1996; Projects Editor, Mirror Gp Newspapers, 1996–98. *Recreations:* watching sport, ski-ing, tennis. *Address:* Rathmore Park, Tullow, Co. Carlow, Ireland. *T:* (503) 61179.

RUDDOCK, Rev. Canon Bruce; *see* Ruddock, Rev. Canon R. B.

RUDDOCK, Joan Mary; MP (Lab) Lewisham, Deptford, since 1987; *b* 28 Dec. 1943; *d* of Ken and Eileen Anthony. *Educ:* Pontypool Grammar Sch. for Girls; Imperial Coll., Univ. of London (BSc; ARCS). Worked for Shelter, national campaign for the homeless, 1968–73; Dir, Oxford Housing Aid Centre, 1973–77; Special Programmes Officer with unemployed young people, MSC, 1977–79; Organiser, CAB, Reading, 1979–86. Chairperson, CND, 1981–85, a Vice Chairperson, 1985–86. Opposition spokesperson: on transport, 1989–92; on home affairs, 1992–94; on envmtl protection, 1994–97; Parly Under-Sec. of State for Women, DSS, 1997–98. Active in politics and pressure groups, and mem. of anti-racist concerns, throughout working life. Hon. Fellow: Goldsmiths Coll., Univ. of London, 1996; Laban Centre, 1996. Frank Cousins' Peace Award, TGWU, 1984. *Publications:* CND Scrapbook, 1987; co-author of pubns on housing; (contrib.): The CND Story, 1983; Voices for One World, 1988. *Recreations:* music, travel, gardening. *Address:* c/o House of Commons, SW1 0AA.

RUDDOCK, Rev. Canon (Reginald) Bruce; Residentiary Canon of Worcester Cathedral, since 1999; *b* 17 Dec. 1955; *s* of Reginald and Hilary Ruddock; *m* 1983, Vivien Chrismas. *Educ:* Hurstpierpoint Coll., Sussex; Guildhall Sch. of Music and Drama (AGSM); Chichester Theol Coll.; Southampton Univ. (Cert. Theol.). Ordained deacon, 1983, priest, 1984; Asst Curate, St Mary's, Felpham with St Nicholas, Middleton-on-Sea, 1983–86; Priest-in-Charge, St Wilfrid's Church, Parish of St Mary, Portsea, 1986–88; Vicar, St Michael's, Barnes, 1988–95; Dir, Anglican Centre in Rome, and Archbishop of Canterbury's Counsellor for Vatican Affairs, 1995–99. Hon. Canon, Amer. Cathedral, Paris, 1996. *Recreations:* music, cricket, art, theatre. *Address:* 15A College Green, Worcester WR1 2LH.

RUDENSTINE, Neil Leon; Chairman, Art STOR, Andrew W. Mellon Foundation, since 2001; President Emeritus, Harvard University, since 2001; *b* 21 Jan. 1935; *s* of Harry Rudenstine and Mae Esperito Rudenstine; *m* 1960, Angelica Zander; one *s* two *d*. *Educ:* Princeton Univ. (BA 1956); New Coll., Oxford (BA 1959; MA 1963; Hon. Fellow, 1992); Harvard Univ. (PhD 1964). Instructor, English and American Lit. and Lang., Harvard Univ., 1964–66, Asst Prof. 1966–68; Princeton University: Associate Prof., English Dept, 1968–73; Dean of Students, 1968–72; Prof. of English, 1973–88; Dean of College, 1972–77; Provost, 1977–88, Provost Emeritus, 1988–; Exec. Vice-Pres., Andrew W. Mellon Foundn, 1988–91; Pres., and Prof. of English and Amer. Lit. and Lang., Harvard Univ., 1991–2001. Hon. Fellow, Emmanuel Coll., Cambridge, 1991. Hon. DPhil: Princeton, 1989; Yale, 1992. Hon. DCL Oxford, 1998. *Publications:* Sidney's Poetic Development, 1967; (ed with George Rousseau) English Poetic Satire: Wyatt to Byron, 1972; (with William Bowen) In Pursuit of the PhD, 1992; Pointing Our Thoughts, 2001. *Address:* A. W. Mellon Foundation, 140E 62nd Street, NY. *T:* (212) 838 8400.

RUDGE, Sir Alan (Walter), Kt 2000; CBE 1995 (OBE 1987); PhD; FRS 1992; FREng; Chairman: ERA Technology Ltd, since 1997; ERA Foundation, since 2001; Chief Executive Officer, MSC Cellular, since 2001; *b* 17 Oct. 1937; *s* of Walter Thomas Rudge and Emma (*née* McFayden); *m* 1969, Jennifer Joan Minott; one *s* one *d*. *Educ:* Hugh Myddelton Sch.; London Polytechnic; Univ. of Birmingham (PhD ElecEng). FIEE, FIEEE; FREng (FEng 1984). Res. Engr, Illinois Inst. of Technol. Res. Inst., 1968–71; Lectr, Electronic and Elec. Engrg Dept, Univ. of Birmingham, 1971–74; Engrg Adviser, Illinois Inst. of Technol. Res. Inst., 1974–79; Man. Dir, Era Technology Ltd, 1979–86; BT (formerly British Telecom): Dir, Research and Technology, 1987–89; Group Technology and Develt Dir, 1989–90; Mem. Main Bd, 1989–97; Man. Dir, Develt and Procurement, 1990–95; Dep. Gp Man. Dir, 1995–96; Dep. Chief Exec., 1996–97; Chm., WS Atkins plc, 1997–2001. Non-executive Director and Member Board: British Maritime Technology Ltd, 1984–89; Ricardo Consulting Engrs PLC, 1985–89; BT&D Technologies Ltd, 1987–93; Telecom Securicor Cellular Radio, 1989–90; MCI (USA), 1995–96; LucasVarity plc, 1997–99; Marconi (formerly GEC) plc, 1997–; GUS plc, 1997–; MSI Cellular Investment Hldgs BV, 1998–; non-exec. Chm., Metapath Software Internat. Inc., 1999–2000. Vis. Prof., Queen Mary and Westfield Coll. (formerly QMC), Univ. of London, 1985–. Pres., AIRTO, 1986. Pres., IEE, 1993–94 (Vice Chm., 1989–91; Dep. Pres., 1991; Mem., Electronics Divl Bd, 1980–89, Chm., 1984; Faraday Medal, 1991); Chairman: Learned Soc. Bd, 1989–91; EPSRC, 1994–99; Senate, Engrg Council, 1996–99; Member: Systems and Electronics Bd, MoD Defence Scientific Adv. Council, 1981–87; CBI Res. and Technol. Cttee, 1980–86; ACOST, 1987–90; Council, DRA, then DERA, MoD, 1991–96; Council for Sci. and Technology, 1993–97. Chairman: Bd of Trustees, British Retinitis Pigmentosa Soc., 1996–; Bd of Mgt, Royal Commn for Exhibn of 1851, 2001– (Mem., 1997–). Member, Council: QMW, 1991–93; Royal Instn, 1992–95. Freeman, City of London; Liveryman, Engineers' Co., 1998–. Hon. FIEE 2000. Hon. Fellow, UCL, 1998. Hon. DEng: Birmingham, 1991; Bradford, Portsmouth, 1994; Nottingham Trent, 1995; Hon. DSc: Strathclyde, 1992; Bath, Loughborough, 1995; Westminster, 1996; DUniv Surrey, 1994. Duncan Davies Meml Medal, R&D Soc., 1998; Founder's Medal, IEEE, 1998. *Publications:* The Handbook of Antenna Design, vol. 1 1982, vol. 2 1983; papers in sci. and tech. jls on antennas, microwaves and satellite communications. *Recreations:* sailing, cycling, reading. *Address:* Tanners Barn, Brockham Lane, Brockham, Betchworth, Surrey RH3 7JW. *Clubs:* Athenæum, Royal Automobile, Royal Ocean Racing; Royal Southampton Yacht, Royal Southern Yacht.

RUDIN, Toni Richard Perrott; Secretary, Magistrates' Association, 1986–93; *b* 13 Oct. 1934; *s* of Richard William Rudin and Sarah Rowena Mary Rudin (*née* Perrott); *m* 1958, Heather Jean (*née* Farley); one *s* three *d*. *Educ:* Bootham Sch.; Millfield Sch.; RMA Sandhurst; Army Staff Coll.; Coll. of Law, Guildford. Commissioned Royal Artillery, 1954; served BAOR, Cyprus, UK; MoD, 1967–69; Battery Comdr and 2 i/c 26th Field Regt, RA, BAOR, 1969–72; MoD, 1972–75; retired, 1975. Solicitor, 1978; private practice as solicitor, 1978–80; Press and Public Relations, Law Soc., 1980–86. Pt-time Chm., Pensions Appeal Tribunals, 1994. Gen. Comr of Income Tax, 1995–97. *Recreations:* 19th century history, riding, house renovation. *Address:* The Old Workshop, 8 London Road, Uppingham, Rutland LE15 9TJ. *T:* (01572) 822999.

RUDKIN, (James) David; playwright; *b* 29 June 1936; *s* of David Jonathan Rudkin and Anne Alice Martin; *m* 1967, Alexandra Margaret Thompson; one *s* two *d* (and one *s* decd). *Educ:* King Edward's Sch., Birmingham; St Catherine's Coll., Oxford (MA). *Screenplays:* Testimony, 1987; December Bride, 1991; The Woodlanders, 1996; *opera libretti:* Broken Strings, 1992; (with Jonathan Harvey) Inquest of Love, 1993; *radio plays:* The Lovesong of Alfred J. Hitchcock, 1993; The Haunting of Mahler, 1994. *Publications:* plays: Afore Night Come, 1963; (trans.) Moses and Aaron, 1965; The Grace of Todd (orig. opera libretto), 1969; Cries from Casement as his Bones are Brought to Dublin (radio), 1974; Penda's Fen (film), 1975; Burglars (for children), 1976; Ashes, 1978; (trans.) Hippolytus, 1980; The Sons of Light, 1981; The Triumph of Death, 1981; (trans.) Peer Gynt, 1983; The Saxon Shore, 1986; (trans.) When We Dead Waken, 1989; (trans.) Rosmersholm, 1990; articles, reviews etc. for Encounter, Drama, Tempo, Theatre Res. Internat. *Recreations:* piano, geology, anthropology, languages, swimming, bridge. *Address:* c/o Casarotto Ramsay Ltd, 60–66 Wardour Street, W1V 4ND. *T:* (020) 7287 4450, *Fax:* (020) 7287 9128.

RUDKIN, Walter Charles, CBE 1981; Director of Economic Intelligence, 1973–81, of Economic and Logistic Intelligence, 1982, Ministry of Defence; retired; *b* 22 Sept. 1922; *e s* of Walter and Bertha Rudkin; *m* 1950, Hilda Mary Hope; two *s*. *Educ:* Carre's Grammar Sch., Sleaford; UC Hull. BSc (Econ) London. Served with RAF, 1942–46. Lectr, Dept of Econs and Econ. History, Univ. of Witwatersrand, 1948–52. Entered Min. of Defence, 1954; appts incl. Hong Kong, 1956–59; Junior Directing Staff, Imperial Defence Coll., 1962–64; Cabinet Office, 1968–71. *Recreation:* fishing. *Address:* 9 Speen Place, Speen, Newbury, Berks RG14 1RX. *T:* (01635) 49244. *Club:* Royal Commonwealth Society.

RUDLAND, Margaret Florence; Headmistress, Godolphin and Latymer School, since 1986; *b* 15 June 1945; *d* of Ernest George and Florence Hilda Rudland. *Educ:* Sweyne School, Rayleigh; Bedford College, Univ. of London (BSc); Inst. of Education (PGCE). Asst Mathematics Mistress, Godolphin and Latymer Sch., 1967–70; VSO, Ilorin, Nigeria, 1970–71; Asst Maths Mistress, Clapham County Sch., 1971–72; Asst Maths Mistress and Head of Dept, St Paul's Girls' Sch., 1972–83; Deputy Headmistress, Norwich High Sch., GPDST, 1983–85. Pres., GSA, 1996 (Chm., Educn Cttee, 1993–94). Member Council: Nightingale Fund, 1989– (Chm., 1998–); UCL, 1998–. Governor: St Margaret's Sch., Bushey, 1997–; Merchant Taylors' Sch., Northwood, 2000–. *Recreations:* opera, cinema, travel. *Address:* The Godolphin and Latymer School, Iffley Road, Hammersmith, W6 0PG. *T:* (020) 8741 1936.

RUDMAN, Michael Edward; theatre director and producer; Artistic Director, Sheffield Theatres (Crucible and Lyceum), 1992–94; *b* Tyler, Texas, 14 Feb. 1939; *s* of M. B.

Rudman and Josephine Davis; *m* 1963, Veronica Anne Bennett (marr. diss. 1981); two *d*; *m* 1983, Felicity Kendal, *qv* (marr. diss. 1994); one *s*. *Educ:* St Mark's Sch., Texas; Oberlin Coll. (BA *cum laude* Govt); St Edmund Hall, Oxford (MA). Pres., OUDS, 1963–64. Asst Dir and Associate Producer, Nottingham Playhouse and Newcastle Playhouse, 1964–68; Asst Dir, RSC, 1968; Artistic Director: Traverse Theatre Club, 1970–73; Hampstead Theatre, 1973–78 (Theatre won Evening Standard Award for Special Achievement, 1978); Associate Dir, Nat. Theatre, 1979–88; Dir, Lyttelton Theatre (National), 1979–81; Dir, Chichester Festival Theatre, 1990. Mem., Bd of Dirs, Hampstead Theatre, 1979–89. *Plays directed* include: *Nottingham Playhouse:* Changing Gear, Measure for Measure, A Man for All Seasons, 1965; Julius Caesar, She Stoops to Conquer, Who's Afraid of Virginia Woolf, Death of a Salesman, 1966; Long Day's Journey into Night, 1967; Lily in Little India, 1968; *RSC Theatregoround:* The Fox and the Fly, 1968; *Traverse Theatre:* Curtains (transf. Open Space, 1971), Straight Up (transf. Piccadilly, 1971), A Game called Arthur (transf. Theatre Upstairs, 1971), Stand for my Father, (with Mike Wearing) A Triple Bill of David Halliwell plays, 1970; The Looneys, Pantagleize, 1971; Carravagio Buddy, Tell Charlie Thanks for the Truss, The Relapse, 1972; *Hampstead Theatre:* Ride across Lake Constance (transf. Mayfair), A Nightingale in Bloomsbury Square, 1973; The Black and White Minstrels, The Show-off, The Connection, The Looneys, 1974; Alphabetical Order (transf. May Fair), 1975; Clouds, 1977 (transf. Duke of York's, 1978); Cakewalk, Beyond a Joke, Gloo-Joo (transf. Criterion), 1978; Making it Better (transf. Criterion), 1992; *National Theatre:* For Services Rendered (televised, 1980), Death of a Salesman, 1979; Thee and Me, The Browning Version/Harlequinade, Measure for Measure, 1980; The Second Mrs Tanqueray, 1981; Brighton Beach Memoirs (transf. Aldwych), The Magistrate, 1986; Six Characters in Search of an Author, Fathers and Sons, Ting Tang Mine, Waiting for Godot, 1987; *Chichester:* The Merry Wives of Windsor, Rumours, 1990; Mansfield Park, 1996; The Admirable Crichton, 1997; Tallulah!, 1997; Our Betters, 1997; *Sheffield:* A Midsummer Night's Dream, 1992; Donkeys' Years, (with Robert Delamere) Jane Eyre, Hamlet, Mansfield Park, 1993; The Grapes of Wrath, 1994; *West End:* Donkeys Years, Globe, 1976; Taking Steps, Lyric, 1980; Camelot, 1982; The Winslow Boy, 1983; The Dragon's Tail, Apollo, 1985; Exclusive, Strand, 1989; Fallen Angels, Apollo, 2000; *Gate Theatre, Dublin:* The Heiress, 1997; *New York:* The Changing Room, 1973 (Drama Desk Award); Hamlet, 1976; Death of a Salesman, 1984 (Tony Award for Best Revival); Measure for Measure, 1993; Have you spoken to any Jews lately?, 1995. *Address:* c/o Peter Murphy Esq., Curtis Brown Group, 162–168 Regent Street, W1R 5TA. *T:* (020) 7396 6600. *Clubs:* Royal Automobile; Royal Mid-Surrey Golf.

RUDOE, Wulf, CB 1975; *b* 9 March 1916; *m* 1942, Ellen Trilling; one *s* one *d*. *Educ:* Central Foundation School; Peterhouse, Cambridge (Open Schol. and Research Schol.). Mathematics Tripos Pt III, 1938, Distinction. Royal Aircraft Establishment, 1939. Operational Research, RAF, 1939–45. Operational Research in Building Industry, Min. of Works, 1946–48, Principal Scientific Officer 1948; Board of Trade, Statistician 1948, Chief Statistician 1952; Dir of Statistics and Research, DHSS (formerly Min. of Health), 1966–76; Asst Sec., Price Commn, 1976–79; Adviser to Govt of Ghana, 1980–81. Fellow Inst. of Statisticians; Mem. Council, 1962–78, Hon. Treasurer, 1965–74, Vice-Pres., 1974–75 and 1976–77, Roy. Statistical Soc. *Recreations:* walking, travel, languages. *Address:* 72 North End Road, NW11 7SY. *T:* (020) 8455 2890.

RUE, Dame (Elsie) Rosemary, DBE 1989 (CBE 1977); Regional General Manager, 1984–88, and Regional Medical Officer, 1973–88, Oxford Regional Health Authority; *b* 14 June 1928; *d* of Harry and Daisy Laurence; divorced; two *s*. *Educ:* Sydenham High Sch.; Univ. of London; Oxford Univ. Med. School. (MB, BS 1951). DCH 1962; MRCP 1972, FRCP 1977; FFPHM (FFCM 1972); MPCPsych 1975, FRCPSych 1980, Hon. FRCPsych 1990; FRCGP *ad eundem* 1982; FRCS 1994. Gen. Practitioner, 1952–58; Public Health Service, 1958–65; Hospital Service, 1965–73; SAMO, Oxford RHB, 1971. President: Faculty of Community Medicine, 1986–89; BMA, 1990–91; Past-Pres., Medical Women's Fedn. Hon. Fellow, Green Coll., Oxford, 1985. Hon. MA Oxford, 1988. *Publications:* papers on gen. practice, women in medicine, ward design, community hosps, health services, individuals requiring security. *Address:* 2 Stanton St John, Oxford OX33 1ET.

RUFFLE, Mary, (Mrs Thomas Ruffle); *see* Dilnot, M.

RUFFLES, Philip Charles, CBE 2001; RDI 1997; FRS 1998; FREng, FRAeS, FIMechE; Director, Engineering and Technology, Rolls-Royce plc, 1997–2001; *b* 14 Oct. 1939; *s* of Charles Richard Ruffles and Emily Edith Ruffles; *m* 1967, Jane Connor; two *d*. *Educ:* Sevenoaks Sch.; Bristol Univ. (BSc 1st Cl. Mech. Engrg 1961). FRAeS 1985; FREng (FEng 1988); FIMechE 1989. Rolls-Royce: trainee, 1961–63; technical appts, 1963–77; Chief Engr, RB211-22B, RB211-524, 1977–81; Head of Engrg, Small Engines, 1981–84; Dir, Technol. & Design Engrg, 1984–89; Technical Dir, 1989–91; Dir of Engrg, Aerospace Gp, 1991–96. Member: Defence Scientific Adv. Council, 1990–93; Technol. Foresight Defence and Aerospace Panel, 1994–97; LINK Bd (OST), 1995–98; Council for Central Lab. of Res. Councils, 1998–. Member Council: Royal Acad. Engrg, 1994–97; RAeS, 1995–. FRSA 1998. Liveryman, Engineers' Co., 1998. Hon. DEng: Bristol, 1995; Birmingham, 1998; Hon. DSc City, 1998. Ackroyd Stuart Prize, 1987, Gold Medal, 1996, RAeS; MacRobert Award, Royal Acad. of Engrg, 1996; James Clayton Prize, IMechE, 1998; Duncan Davies Meml Medal, R & D Soc., 2000. *Publications:* contrib. to numerous learned jls on engrg and technol. topics. *Recreations:* Rugby, D-I-Y. *Address:* Rolls-Royce plc, PO Box 31, Derby DE24 8BJ. *T:* (01332) 249701.

RUFFLEY, David Laurie; MP (C) Bury St Edmunds, since 1997; *b* 18 April 1962; *s* of Jack Laurie Ruffley, solicitor and Yvonne Grace (*née* Harris). *Educ:* Bolton Boys' Sch.; Queens' Coll., Cambridge (Exhibnr, 1981, Foundn Scholar, 1983; Histl Tripos pt 1, Law Tripos pt 2, BA 1985, MA 1988). Articled clerk and Solicitor with Coward Chance, then Clifford Chance, 1985–91; Special Advr to Sec. of State for Educn and Science, 1991–92, to Home Sec., 1992–93, to Chancellor of the Exchequer, 1993–96; Economic Consultant, Cons. Party, 1996–97; Vice-Pres., Small Business Bureau, 1996–. Member: Select Cttee on Public Admin, 1997–99; Select Cttee on Treasury Affairs, 1998–; Secretary: Finance Cttee, 1999–; Home Affairs Cttee, 2000–. Governor: Marylebone Sch., 1992–94; Pimlico Sch., 1994–96; Bolton Boys' Sch., 1997–99. Patron: Bury St Edmunds Town Trust; Bury St Edmunds and Dist Football League; Bury St Edmunds Constitl Club; W Suffolk Voluntary Assoc. for the Blind. *Recreations:* football, golf, film, thinking. *Address:* House of Commons, SW1A 0AA. *Clubs:* Athenæum; Moreton Hall Community Assoc.; Suffolk Golf and Country, Stowmarket FC.

RUGBY, 3rd Baron *cr* 1947, of Rugby, Co. Warwick; **Robert Charles Maffey;** farmer; *b* 4 May 1951; *s* of 2nd Baron Rugby and of Margaret Helen, *d* of late Harold Bindley; *S* father, 1990; *m* 1974, Anne Penelope, *yr d* of late David Hale; two *s*. *Educ:* Brickwall House Sch., Northiam. *Recreations:* shooting, woodwork and metal work. *Heir:* *s* Hon. Timothy James Howard Maffey, *b* 23 July 1975.

RUGG, Prof. Michael Derek, PhD; Professor of Cognitive Neuroscience and Wellcome Trust Principal Research Fellow, University College London, since 1998; *b* 23 Sept. 1954; *s* of Derek and Brenda Rugg; *m* 1976, Elizabeth Jackson; one *s*. *Educ:* Univ. of Leicester (BSc Psychol; PhD 1979). FRSE 1996. Res. Fellow, Dept of Psychology, Univ. of York, 1978–79; University of St Andrews: Lectr in Psychology, 1979–88; Reader, 1988–92; Prof., 1992–98; Head, Sch. of Psychology, 1992–94. Hon. Res. Fellow, Inst. of Neurology, 1994–98. Member: DoH Wkg Gp on Organophosphates, 1998–99; Govt Ind. Expert Gp on Mobile Phones, 1999–2000; Prog. mgt cttee, mobile telecomm. and health res. prog.; Adv. gp on non-ionising radiation, NRPB. *Publications:* (ed with A. D. Milner) Neuropsychology of Consciousness, 1991; (ed with M. G. H. Coles) Electrophysiology of Mind, 1995; (ed) Cognitive Neuroscience, 1996; numerous articles in neuropsychology and related fields in learned jls. *Recreations:* rock climbing, ski-ing, mountaineering, 20th century novels, music. *Address:* Institute of Cognitive Neuroscience, University College London, Alexandra House, 17 Queen Square, WC1N 3AR.

RUGGIERO, Renato, Hon. KCMG 1980; Minister of Foreign Affairs, Italy, since 2001; *b* Naples, 9 April 1930; *s* of Antonio Ruggiero and Lucia (*née* Rubinacci); *m* 1956, Paola Tomacelli Filomarino; two *s* one *d*. *Educ:* Univ. of Naples (degree in law 1953). Joined Italian diplomatic service; served Sao Paulo, Moscow, Washington, Belgrade and Brussels; Chef de Cabinet of Pres., 1969–73, Dir-Gen. for Regional Policies, 1973–77, EC; Foreign Ministry, Rome, 1978–80; Ambassador to EEC, 1980–84; Dir-Gen. for Econ. Affairs, 1984–85, Sec. Gen., 1985–87, Foreign Ministry; Foreign Trade Minister, 1987–91; Dir-Gen., WTO, 1995–99; Vice-Chm., Salomon Smith Barney Internat., 2000–01. Dir and adviser, various Italian, European and American cos, 1991–95. KCSG 1997. Cavalierato di Gran Croce (Italy), 1985; Grand Cordon, Order of the Sacred Treasure (Japan), 1991. *Recreations:* sailing, hiking. *Address:* Ministry of Foreign Affairs, Piazzale della Farnesia 1, 00194 Rome, Italy.

RUGGLES-BRISE, Col Sir John Archibald, 2nd Bt *cr* 1935; CB 1958; OBE (mil.) 1945; TD; JP; Lord-Lieutenant of Essex, 1958–78; first Pro-Chancellor, University of Essex, 1964–79; *b* 13 June 1908; *er s* of Colonel Sir Edward Archibald Ruggles-Brise, 1st Bt, MC, TD, DL, JP, MP, and Agatha (*d* 1937), *e d* of J. H. Gurney, DL, JP, of Keswick Hall, Norfolk; *S* father, 1942. *Educ:* Eton. Served AA Comd, 1939–45 (comd 1st 450 Mixed HAA Regt, and 2nd AA Demonstration and User Trials Regt); formed and comd 599 HAA Regt, 1947. Member of Lloyd's. Pres., CLA, 1957–59 (helped promote Game Fair); Church Comr, 1959–64; Chm., Council of the Baronetage, 1958–63. Formerly Chm. Promotion Cttee, 1959, then Chm. Council, Univ. of Essex. Patron, Essex Agricl Soc., 1970–78. Liveryman, Spectacle Makers' Co., 1948–. DL 1945, JP 1946, Vice-Lieutenant, 1947, Co. Essex. Hon. Freeman of Chelmsford. Governor of Felsted and Chigwell Schools, 1950–75. DUniv Essex, 1980. KStJ. *Recreation:* shooting. *Heir:* *nephew* Timothy Edward Ruggles-Brise [*b* 11 April 1945; *m* 1975, Rosemary Craig; three *s* two *d*]. *Address:* Spains Hall, Finchingfield, Essex CM7 4PF. *T:* (01371) 810266.

RÜHE, Volker; Member of Bundestag, since 1976; Minister of Defence, Germany, 1992–98; *b* 25 Sept. 1942; *m*; three *c*. *Educ:* Univ. of Hamburg. School teacher, Hamburg, 1968–76. Joined CDU, 1963; Mem., Hamburg City Council, 1970–76; Gen. Sec., CDU, 1989–92. *Address:* Bundeshaus, Platz der Republik, 11011 Berlin, Germany.

RUHFUS, Dr Jürgen, Officer's Cross, Order of Merit, Federal Republic of Germany, 1983; Hon. KBE 1978; *b* 4 Aug. 1930; three *d*. *Educ:* Universities of Munich, Münster and Denver, USA. Joined Federal Foreign Office, Bonn, 1955; Consulate General: Geneva, 1956–57; Dakar, 1958–59; Embassy, Athens, 1960–63; Dep. Spokesman of Federal Foreign Office, 1964, Official Spokesman, 1966; Ambassador to Kenya, 1970–73; Asst Under-Secretary, Federal Foreign Office, 1973–76; Adviser on Foreign Policy and Defence Affairs to Federal Chancellor Helmut Schmidt, 1976–80; Ambassador to UK, 1980–83; Head of Political Directorate-General (dealing with Third World and other overseas countries), Federal Foreign Office, Dec. 1983–June 1984; State Sec., Federal Foreign Office, FRG, 1984–87; Ambassador to USA, 1987–92; Chm., Deutsch-Englische Ges., 1993–98; Mem., Supervisory Bd, Adam Opel AG, 1993–2001. *Recreations:* golf, tennis, skiing, shooting. *Address:* Ettenhausener Strasse 23a, 53229 Bonn, Germany.

RUHNAU, Heinz; Chairman, Deutsche Lufthansa, 1982–91; *b* Danzig, 5 March 1929; *m* Edith Loers; three *d*. Dip. in Business Administration, 1954; Head, personal office of Chm., IG-Metall, Frankfurt; Regional Dir, IG-Metall, Hamburg, 1956–65; Mem., Supervisory Bd, Hapag Lloyd; Head of Dept of Internal Affairs and Mem., Senate of Free Hanseatic City of Hamburg, 1965–73; Mem., Exec. Bd, COOP, 1973; State Sec., Ministry of Transport, 1974–82; Mem., Supervisory Bd, Vereinigte Tanklager und Transportmittel, Hamburg and Hapag Lloyd. Chm., Assoc. of European Airlines, 1988. Federal Grand Cross of Merit, 1980, with Star, 1989, FRG.

RULE, Brian Francis; Director General of Information Technology Systems, Ministry of Defence, 1985–94; Chairman, Emeritus Plus Ltd, 1994–98; *b* 20 Dec. 1938; *s* of late Sydney John Rule and Josephine Rule, Pen-y-ffordd, near Chester; *m* 1993, Irene M. Rees, Pembs. *Educ:* Daniel Owen Sch., Mold; Loughborough Univ. of Technology (MSc). Engineer, de Havilland Aircraft Co., 1955–59; Res. Assistant, Loughborough Univ., 1963–65; Lectr, Univ. of Glasgow, 1965–67; University of Aberdeen: Lectr, 1967–70; Sen. Lectr, 1970–72; Dir of Computing, 1972–78; Dir, Honeywell Information Systems Ltd, 1978–79; Dir of Scientific Services, NERC, 1979–85. *Publications:* various papers in scientific jls. *Recreations:* motoring, antique clocks. *Address:* c/o Lloyds TSB, 14 Castle Street, Cirencester, Glos GL7 1QJ.

RULE, Margaret Helen, (Mrs A. W. Rule), CBE 1983; FSA; Consultant, Mary Rose Trust, 1994–98 (Research Director, 1983–94); *b* 27 Sept. 1928; *d* of Ernest Victor and Mabel Martin; *m* 1949, Arthur Walter Rule; one *s*. *Educ:* Univ. of London. FSA 1967. Dir of Excavations, Chichester Civic Soc., 1961–79; Hon. Curator, Fishbourne Roman Palace and Museum, 1968–79; Archaeol Dir, Mary Rose Trust, 1979–82. Hon. Fellow, Portsmouth Polytechnic, 1982. Hon. DLitt Liverpool, 1984; Hon. DSc Portsmouth, 1999. Reginald Mitchell Medal, Stoke-on-Trent Assoc. of Engrs, 1983. *Publications:* Chichester Excavations 1, 1967; The Mary Rose, 1982; A Gallo-Roman Trading Vessel from Guernsey, 1993; Life at Sea: Tudors and Stuarts, 1994; many papers in jls in Britain and USA. *Recreations:* anything in or on the water. *Address:* Crofton, East Bracklesham Drive, Bracklesham Bay, W Sussex PO20 8JW.

RUMALSHAH, Rt Rev. Munawar Kenneth, (Mano); General Secretary, United Society for the Propagation of the Gospel, since 1998; an Assistant Bishop of Southwark, since 1999; *b* 16 June 1941; *s* of Ven. Inayat and Mrs Akhtar Rumalshah; *m* 1st, 1966, Rosalind Andrews; two *d*; 2nd, 1984, Sheila Benita Biswas; one *d*. *Educ:* Punjab Univ. (BSc 1960); Serampur Univ. (BD 1965); Karachi Univ. (MA 1968); Cambridge Univ. (PGCE 1986). Ordained deacon, 1965, priest, 1966; Curate: Holy Trinity Cathedral, Karachi, 1965–69; St Edmund Roundhay, Leeds, 1970–73; Area Sec., and Asst Home Sec., CMS, 1973–78; Educn Sec., BCC, 1978–81; Priest-in-charge, St George, Southall, 1981–88; Presbyter, St John's Cathedral, and Lectr, Edwarde's Coll., Peshawar, 1989–94; Bishop of Peshawar, 1994–98. Mem., Archbp of Canterbury's Commn on Urban Priority Areas, 1984–86. Jt Ed., Lambeth Conf., 1998. *Publications:* Focus on Pakistan, 1989, 4th edn 1999; Being a Christian in Pakistan, 1998. *Recreations:* watching cricket, music, reading, travel. *Address:* (office) Partnership House, 157 Waterloo Road, SE1 8XA. *T:* (020) 7928 8681.

RUMBELOW, Arthur Anthony; QC 1990; a Recorder, since 1988; a Deputy High Court Judge (Family Division), since 2001; *b* Salford, Lancs, 9 Sept. 1943; *er s* of Arthur Rumbelow and Theresa (*née* Lucketti); *m*; three *d*. *Educ:* Salford Grammar Sch.; Queens' Coll., Cambridge (Squire Schol.; BA 1966). Called to the Bar, Middle Temple, 1967 (Harmsworth Exhibnr, Astbury Schol.). Chairman: Medical Appeal Tribunal, 1988–; Mental Health Rev. Tribunal, 2000–. Mem., Rochdale MBC, 1982–84. *Recreations:* wine, theatre, Rugby, collecting. *Address:* 28 St John Street, Manchester M3 4DJ. *T:* (0161) 834 8418; 1 Serjeant's Inn, Temple, EC4Y 1NH. *T:* (020) 7583 1355.

RUMBELOW, (Roger) Martin, CEng; non-executive director and consultant, since 1996; *b* 3 June 1937; *s* of Leonard Rumbelow and Phyllis (*née* Perkins); *m* 1965, Marjorie Elizabeth Glover. *Educ:* Cardiff High Sch.; Bristol Univ. (BSc); Cranfield Inst. of Technol. (MSc). CEng 1966. National Service, RAF Pilot, 1955–57. British Aircraft Corporation, 1958–74: Dep. Prodn Controller, 1967–73; Concorde Manufg Project Manager, 1973–74; Department of Trade and Industry, 1974–96: Principal, 1974–78; Asst Sec., 1978–86; Under Sec., 1987–96; Services Management Div., 1987–92; Head, Electronics and Engrg Div., 1992–96. *Recreations:* singing, opera, theatre, computing, amateur radio, electronics, tennis. *Club:* Royal Air Force.

RUMBLE, Peter William, CB 1984; Chief Executive, Historic Buildings and Monuments Commission, (English Heritage), 1983–89; Director-General, Union of European Historic Houses Associations, 1991–94; *b* 28 April 1929; *s* of Arthur Victor Rumble and Dorothy Emily (*née* Sadler); *m* 1953, Joyce Audrey Stephenson; one *s* one *d*. *Educ:* Harwich County High Sch.; Oriel Coll., Oxford (MA). Entered Civil Service, 1952; HM Inspector of Taxes, 1952; Principal, Min. of Housing and Local Govt, 1963; Asst Sec., 1972, Under Sec., 1977, DoE. Member: Architectural Heritage Fund, 1984–98 (Vice-Chm., 1992–98); Cttee, Southern Region, NT, 1990–96; Churches Conservation Trust (formerly Redundant Churches Fund), 1991–99; Rep., Church Heritage Forum, 1997–99. Trustee, Amer. Friends of English Heritage, 1988–94. *Recreations:* music, pottery. *Address:* 11 Hillside Road, Cheam, Surrey SM2 6ET. *T:* (020) 8643 1752.

RUMBLES, Michael John; Member (Lib Dem) West Aberdeenshire and Kincardine, Scottish Parliament, since 1999; *b* 10 June 1956; *s* of Samuel and Joan Rumbles; *m* 1985, Pauline Sillars; two *s*. *Educ:* Univ. of Wales (MSc Econ). Commissioned RAEC, 1979–94 (Major); Team Leader in Business Management, Aberdeen Coll., 1995–99. *Recreations:* family, hill walking. *Address:* Kinloch House, Birse, Aboyne, Aberdeenshire AB34 5BY. *T:* (01339) 886841.

RUMBOLD, Rt Hon. Dame Angela (Claire Rosemary), DBE 1992 (CBE 1981); PC 1991; a Vice Chairman, Conservative Party, 1995–97 (a Deputy Chairman, 1992–95); *b* 11 Aug. 1932; *d* of late Harry Jones, FRS; *m* 1958, John Marix Rumbold; two *s* one *d*. *Educ:* Perse Sch. for Girls; Notting Hill and Ealing High Sch.; King's Coll., London. Founder Member, National Assoc. for the Welfare of Children in Hospital, and National Chairman, 1974–76. Councillor, Royal Borough of Kingston upon Thames, 1974–83; Chm., Council, Local Educn Authorities, 1979–80. Mem., Doctors and Dentists Review Body, 1979–81. Co-Chm., Women's Nat. Commn, 1986–90. MP (C) Merton, Mitcham and Morden, June 1982–1983, Mitcham and Morden 1983–97; contested (C) Mitcham and Morden, 1997. PPS to Financial Sec. to the Treasury, 1983, to Sec. of State for Transport, 1983–85; Parly Under Sec. of State, DoE, 1985–86; Minister of State, DES, 1986–90, Home Office, 1990–92. Mem., Social Services Select Cttee, 1982–83. Chairman: Minerva Fund, GDST, 1993–; GBGSA, 2001–; Mem., Church Schs Co., 2000–. Chairman of Governors: Mill Hill Sch. Foundn, 1994–; Wimbledon High Sch., 1999–; Governor: Danes Hill Prep. Sch., 1998–; More House Sch., 2000–. Freeman, City of London, 1988. *Recreations:* swimming, cinema, reading, ballet.

RUMBOLD, Sir Henry (John Sebastian), 11th Bt *cr* 1779; Partner, Dawson Cornwell, since 1991; *b* 24 Dec. 1947; *s* of Sir Horace Anthony Claude Rumbold, 10th Bt, KCMG, KCVO, CB, and Felicity Ann Rumbold (*née* Bailey); *S* father, 1983; *m* 1978, Frances Ann (*née* Hawkes, formerly wife of Julian Berry). *Educ:* Eton College; College of William and Mary, Virginia, USA (BA). Articled Stileman, Neate and Topping, 1975–77; admitted solicitor, 1977; asst solicitor, Stileman, Neate and Topping, 1977–79; Partner, 1979–81; joined Stephenson Harwood, 1981, Partner, 1982–91. *Recreations:* riding, shooting, reading. *Heir: cousin* Charles Anton Rumbold [*b* 7 Feb. 1959; *m* 1967, Susan, *er d* of J. M. Tucker]. *Address:* 19 Hollywood Road, SW10 9HT. *T:* (020) 7352 9148; Hatch House, Tisbury, Wilts SP3 6PA. *T:* (01747) 870622. *Clubs:* Boodle's, Brooks's, Groucho.

RUMBOLD, Sir Jack (Seddon), Kt 1984; QC (Zanzibar) 1963; President of the Industrial Tribunals, England and Wales, 1979–84, retired; *b* 5 March 1920; *s* of William Alexander Rumbold and Jean Lindsay Rumbold (*née* Mackay), Christchurch, NZ; *m* 1st, 1949, Helen Suzanne, *d* of Col J. B. Davis, Wanganui, NZ; two *d*; 2nd, 1970, Veronica Ellie Hurt (*née* Whigham). *Educ:* St Andrew's Coll., NZ; Canterbury Univ., NZ (LLB 1940); Brasenose Coll., Oxford (Rhodes Schol.; BCL 1948). Served Royal Navy, Lieut RNZNVR, 1941–45 (despatches). Called to Bar, Inner Temple, 1948; Crown Counsel, Kenya, 1957, Sen. Crown Counsel, 1959; Attorney General, Zanzibar, 1963; Legal Adviser, Kenya Govt, 1964–66; Academic Director, British Campus of Stanford Univ., USA, 1966–72; Chairman of Industrial Tribunals (part-time), 1968; (full-time) 1972; Regional Chairman (London South), 1977. FRSA 1985. *Recreations:* books, music; formerly cricket (Oxford Blue). *Address:* 5 Church Row, Moore Park Road, SW6 2JW; Le Mas du Vallon, Le Brulat du Castellet, Var 83330, France. *Clubs:* Garrick, MCC.

RUMFITT, Nigel John; QC 1994; a Recorder, since 1995; *b* 6 March 1950; *s* of Alan Regan Rumfitt and late Dorothy Rumfitt (*née* Ackroyd); *m* 1984, Dorothy Pamela Pouncey. *Educ:* Leeds Modern Sch.; Pembroke Coll., Oxford (MA, BCL). Teaching Associate, Northwestern Univ. Sch. of Law, Chicago, 1972–73; called to the Bar, Middle Temple, 1974; Asst Recorder, 1991–95. *Recreations:* ski-ing, wind-surfing, travel, reading, Francophilia. *Address:* 7 Bedford Row, WC1R 4BU. *T:* (020) 7242 3555.

RUNACRES, Eric Arthur; *b* 22 Aug. 1916; *s* of Arthur Selwyn Runacres and Mildred May (*née* Dye); *m* 1950, Penelope Jane Elizabeth Luxmoore; one *s* one *d*. *Educ:* Dulwich College; Merton College, Oxford (Postmaster; 1st cl. hons Lit. Hum. 1939). Commissioned Royal Engineers, Oct. 1939; served UK, Malta, Middle East, India, 1939–46 (Major). J. & P. Coats Ltd, 1946–48. Entered HM Foreign Service, 1948; First Secretary, 1951–53. British Productivity Council, 1954–71 (Deputy Director, 1959–71, and Secretary, 1962–71); Vice-Chm., OECD, Cttee on National Productivity Centres, 1960–66; Exec. Director, Commonwealth Agricultural Bureaux, 1973–77; Consultant, Industrial Facts & Forecasting Ltd, 1978–81. *Recreation:* European thought and literature. *Address:* Gables, Radbone Hill, Over Norton, Oxon OX7 5RA. *T:* (01608) 643264.

RUNCIMAN, family name of **Viscount Runciman of Doxford**.

RUNCIMAN OF DOXFORD, 3rd Viscount, *cr* 1937; **Walter Garrison Runciman, (Garry),** CBE 1987; FBA 1975; Bt 1906; Baron Runciman, 1933, of Shoreston; Chairman: Andrew Weir and Co. Ltd, since 1991; Runciman Investments Ltd, since 1990; Fellow, Trinity College, Cambridge, since 1971; President, British Academy, since 2001; *b* 10 Nov. 1934; *o s* of 2nd Viscount Runciman of Doxford, OBE, AFC, AE and Katherine Schuyler (*d* 1993), *y d* of late William R. Garrison, New York; *S* father, 1989; *m* 1963, Ruth (*see* Viscountess Runciman of Doxford); one *s* two *d*. *Educ:* Eton (Oppidan Schol.); Trinity Coll., Cambridge (Schol.; Fellow, 1959–63, 1971–). National Service, 1953–55 (2/Lt, Grenadier Guards); Harkness Fellow, 1958–60; part-time Reader in Sociology, Univ. of Sussex, 1967–69; Vis. Prof., Harvard Univ., 1970; Vis. Fellow, Nuffield Coll., Oxford, 1979–87 (Hon. Fellow, 1998). Lectures: Radcliffe-Brown, British Acad., 1986; Spencer, Oxford Univ., 1986; Chorley, London Univ., 1993; ESRC, 1993; T. H. Marshall, Southampton Univ., 1994; British Acad., 1998. Chm., Walter Runciman plc, 1976–90. Treas., Child Poverty Action Gp, 1972–97; Member: SSRC, 1974–79; Securities and Investments Board, 1986–97 (a Dep. Chm., 1990–97); British Library Bd, 1999–; Dep. Chm., FSA, 1997–98. Pres., Gen. Council of British Shipping, 1986–87 (Vice-Pres., 1985–86). Chm., Royal Commn on Criminal Justice, 1991–93. Hon. Foreign Mem., Amer. Acad. of Arts and Sciences, 1986. Hon. DSc (SocScis) Edinburgh, 1992; DUniv York, 1994; Hon. DLitt Oxford, 2000. *Publications:* Plato's Later Epistemology, 1962; Social Science and Political Theory, 1963, 2nd edn 1969; Relative Deprivation and Social Justice, 1966, 2nd edn 1972; Sociology in its Place, and other essays, 1970; A Critique of Max Weber's Philosophy of Social Science, 1972; A Treatise on Social Theory: vol. I, 1983, vol. II, 1989, vol. III, 1997; Confessions of a Reluctant Theorist, 1989; The Social Animal, 1998; articles in academic jls. *Heir: s* Hon. David Walter Runciman, PhD [*b* 1 March 1967; *m* 1997, Beatrice, (Bee), *yr d* of A. N. Wilson, *qv* and Katherine Duncan-Jones, *qv*; one *s*]. *Address:* 44 Clifton Hill, NW8 0QG. *Club:* Brooks's.

RUNCIMAN OF DOXFORD, Viscountess; Ruth Runciman, DBE 1998 (OBE 1991); Chairman, Mental Health Act Commission, 1994–98; *b* 9 Jan. 1936; *o d* of Joseph Hellmann and Dr Ellen Hellmann; *m* 1st, 1959, Denis Mack Smith, *qv* (marr. diss. 1962); 2nd, 1963, Viscount Runciman of Doxford, *qv*; one *s* two *d*. *Educ:* Roedean Sch., Johannesburg; Witwatersrand Univ. (BA 1956); Girton Coll., Cambridge (BA 1958). Chm., Ind. Inquiry into Misuse of Drugs Act 1971, 1997–2000; Member: Adv. Council on Misuse of Drugs, 1974–95; Press Complaints Commn, 1998–. Council Mem., Nat. Assoc. of CAB, 1978–83; Outreach advice worker, Kensington CAB, 1988–; Chm., Nat. AIDS Trust, 2000– (Trustee, 1989–93); Dep. Chm., Prison Reform Trust, 1981–. Trustee: Prince's Trust Volunteers, 1989–94; Mental Health Foundn, 1990–96; Pilgrim Trust, 1999–; Sainsbury Centre for Mental Health, 2001–. Dir, ENO, 1978–83. Hon. Fellow, Univ. of Central Lancs, 2000. Hon. LLD De Montfort, 1997. *Recreations:* tennis, gardening. *Address:* 44 Clifton Hill, NW8 0QG.

RUNDELL, Richard John; His Honour Judge Rundell; a Circuit Judge, since 2001; *b* 29 July 1948; *s* of Norman Henry Rundell and Pamela Anne Rundell; *m* 1969, Yvonne Doreen Lipinski; two *s*. *Educ:* Chelmsford Tech. High Sch.; Mid Essex Tech. Coll., Chelmsford (LLB London). Called to the Bar, Gray's Inn, 1971; barrister in practice, S Eastern Circuit, 1972–2001; a Recorder, 1996–2001. *Recreations:* cricket, choral music, opera, gardening. *Address:* c/o Circuit Administrator, Midland Circuit, The Priory Courts, 33 Bull Street, Birmingham B4 6DW. *T:* (0121) 681 3206.

RUNDLE, Hon. Anthony Maxwell; MHA (L) Braddon, Tasmania, since 1986; Shadow Minister for Energy, since 1998, and for Small Business, since 2001; *b* 5 March 1939; *s* of M. J. Rundle; *m* Caroline Watt; two *d*. *Educ:* Launceston Church Grammar Sch. Journalist, Australian Associated Press, London, 1961–62; Eric White & Associates Public Relns, London, 1963–68; journalist, Tasmanian TV, 1979. Govt Whip, Tas, 1986; Speaker, House of Assembly, 1988–89; Shadow Minister for Tourism and for Transport, 1989–92; Minister: for Forests and for Mines, 1992–93; assisting Premier on Econ. Develt, 1992–93; for Public Sector Mgt, 1993–96; for Finance, 1993–95; for Employment and for Racing and Gaming, 1993–95; assisting Premier on State Develt and Resources, 1993–96; for Energy, 1995–96; Treasurer, 1993–98, and Premier of Tasmania, 1996–98; Leader of the Opposition, 1998–99; Shadow Minister for Tourism, for Nat. Parks & Public Lands, and for Planning & Inland Fisheries, 1999–2001. Chm., Port Devonport Authy, 1982–87. *Recreations:* yachting, tennis, fishing. *Address:* Parliament House, Hobart, Tas 7000, Australia. *Club:* Royal Yacht of Tasmania.

RUNDLE, Christopher John Spencer, OBE 1983; HM Diplomatic Service, retired; Research Counsellor, Foreign and Commonwealth Office, 1991–98; *b* 17 Aug. 1938; *s* of late Percy William and Ruth Rundle (*née* Spencer); *m* 1970, Qamar Said; one *d*. *Educ:* Cranbrook Sch.; St John's Coll., Cambridge (MA). Served HM Forces, 1957–59. Central Asian Res. Centre, 1962–63; joined Diplomatic Service, 1963; Tehran, 1967–68; Oriental Sec., Kabul, 1968–70; FCO, 1970–75; seconded to Cabinet Office, 1975–77; First Secretary: FCO, 1977–81; Tehran, 1981–84; FCO, 1985. Member Council, British Inst. of Persian Studies, 1990–2001. Hon. Fellow, Centre for Middle Eastern and Islamic Studies, Durham Univ., 2001. *Publications:* papers in academic jls, inc. Durham Middle East Papers. *Recreations:* sports, foreign films and literature. *Address:* 16 Buckingham Gardens, West Molesey, Surrey KT8 1TH.

RUNDLE, John Louis, AM 1981; JP; Agent-General for South Australia, 1980–85; *b* 11 Jan. 1930; *s* of late J. A. Rundle; *m* Elizabeth Phillipa, *d* of John P. Little, Melbourne; one *s* one *d*. *Educ:* Rostrevor Coll. Formerly Senior Partner, J. C. Rundle & Co., and Rundle, Parsons & Partners; Former Chairman: J. C. Rundle Holdings Pty Ltd; Seacliff Investments Pty Ltd; Thevenard Hotel Pty Ltd; former Director: Commonwealth Accommodation & Catering Service Ltd; Mallen & Co. Ltd; Commercial & Domestic Finance Ltd. Former Member: Nat. Employers Ind. Council (Dep. Chm., 1979–80); Confed. of Aust. Industry (Mem. Bd, 1978–80); State Develt Council, SA; Ind. Relations Adv. Council, SA; Adv. Curriculum Bd, SA; Council, Royal AA of SA. Pres., Junior Chambers, Adelaide, 1957, SA, 1958, Australia, 1959; Vice-Pres., JCI, 1960, 1963, Exec. Vice-Pres., 1964, World Pres., 1965, Pres. Senate, 1966; Councillor, Adelaide Chamber of Commerce, 1956–57, 1961–72, Vice-Pres., 1968–70, Dep. Pres., 1970–72; Vice-Pres., Chamber of Commerce & Industry, SA, 1973–75, Dep. Pres., 1975–77, Pres. 1977–79 (Chm., Commerce Div., 1973, 1974; Chm., Ind. Matters Cttee); Exec. Mem., Aust. Chamber of Commerce, 1980. Councillor: Red Cross Soc., SA Div., 1957–63 (Chm., Junior Red Cross, 1961–62); Burnside City Council, 1962–64; President: Assoc. of Indep. Schools of SA, 1972–75; Nat. Council of Indep. Schools, 1975–77; Chm., Bd of Governors, Rostrevor Coll., 1967–77. Mem. Central Council, Royal Over-Seas League, 1988–93. Freeman, City of London, 1981. JP SA, 1956. KHS 1989. *Address:* 230 Victoria Grove, 254 Greenhill Road, Glenside, SA 5065, Australia. *Clubs:* East India; Naval Military and Air Force (Adelaide).

RUNGE, Charles David; Hon. Secretary, Royal Agricultural Society of the Commonwealth, since 2000; Chief Executive, Royal Agricultural Society of England, 1992–2000; *b* 24 May 1944; *s* of Sir Peter Runge and late Hon. Fiona Margaret Stewart (*née* Macpherson), *d* of 1st Baron Strathcarron, PC, KC; *m* 1st, 1969, Harriet (marr. diss. 1979), *d* of late John Bradshaw; one *s* one *d*; 2nd, 1981, Jil, *d* of late John Liddell, Greenock; one *d*. *Educ:* Eton; Christ Church, Oxford (MA Nat. Scis); Manchester Business Sch. Tate & Lyle: Man. Dir, Transport, 1977–79; Chief Exec., Refineries, 1979–81; Man. Dir, Agribusiness, 1983–86; Dir of Corporate Affairs, 1986–87; Chief Exec., MMB, 1988–92. *Recreations:* music, walking, fishing. *Address:* Little Finings, Lane End, High Wycombe, Bucks HP14 3LP; Royal Agricultural Society of the Commonwealth, 2 Grosvenor Gardens, SW1W 0DH. *Clubs:* Boodle's, Royal Anglo-Belgian, Farmers'.

RUPERT'S LAND, Metropolitan of; *see* Saskatoon, Archbishop of.

RUPERT'S LAND, Bishop of, since 2000; **Rt Rev. Donald David Phillips;** *m* Nancy. *Educ:* Univ. of Western Ontario (BSc 1976, MSc 1979); Huron Coll., Univ. of Western Ontario (MDiv 1981). Ordained deacon, 1981, priest, 1981; incumbent, Lac La Biche, Alberta, 1981–84; Priest in charge, St Thomas Ch, Fort McMurray and St Paul's Ch, Fort Chipewyan, Alberta, 1984–87; incumbent, St Michael and All Angels, Moose Jaw, Sask, 1987–92; Ministries Develt Co-ordinator, 1992–96, Exec. Officer, 1997–2000, Dio. Qu'Appelle. Hon. Asst, Parish of St Matthew, Regina, Sask, 1992–2000. *Address:* (office) 935 Nesbitt Bay, Winnipeg, MB R3T 1W6, Canada. *T:* (204) 453 6248, *Fax:* (204) 452 3915; *e-mail:* dphillips@rupertsland.anglican.ca.

RUSBRIDGE, Brian John, CBE 1984; exhibition and training consultant, since 1998; Director, Association of Exhibition Organisers, 1992–98; Secretary, Local Authorities' Conditions of Service Advisory Board (and all Local Authority National Negotiating Councils), 1973–87; *b* 10 Sept. 1922; *s* of late Arthur John and Leonora Rusbridge, Appleton, Berks; *m* 1951, Joyce, *d* of late Joseph Young Elliott, Darlington; two *s*. *Educ:* Willowfield Sch., Eastbourne; Univ. of Oxford Dept of Social and Admin. Studies (Dip. Social Admin.). Served War of 1939–45, Lieut RNVR. Personnel Manager, Imperial Chemical Industries (Teesside), 1949; British Railways Board: Dir of Industrial Relations, 1963; Divisional Manager, London, 1970. Ed., Municipal Year Book, 1987–94; Dir, Newman Books Ltd, 1991–94. CIPD; MCIT. FRSA. *Recreations:* walking, golf. *Address:* 19 Beauchamp Road, East Molesey, Surrey KT8 0PA. *T:* (020) 8979 4952.

RUSBRIDGER, Alan Charles; Editor, The Guardian, since 1995; *b* 29 Dec. 1953; *s* of G. H. Rusbridger and late B. E. Rusbridger (*née* Wickham); *m* 1982, Lindsay Mackie; two *d*. *Educ:* Cranleigh Sch.; Magdalene Coll., Cambridge (MA). Reporter, Cambridge Evening News, 1976–79; reporter, columnist and feature writer, The Guardian, 1979–86; TV Critic, The Observer, 1986–87; Washington Corresp., London Daily News, 1987; Editor, Weekend Guardian, 1988–89; The Guardian: Features Editor, 1989–93; Dep. Editor, 1993–95. Editor of the Year: Granada TV What the Papers Say Awards, 1996; Newspaper Focus Awards, 1996; Nat. Newspaper Editor, Newspaper Industry Awards, 1996; Editors' Editor, Press Gazette, 1997; Freedom of the Press Award, London Press Club, 1998. *Recreations:* music, painting, golf. *Address:* The Guardian, 119 Farringdon Road, EC1R 3ER. *T:* (020) 7278 2332, *Fax:* (020) 7239 9997. *Clubs:* Garrick, Soho House; Nairn Golf.

RUSBY, Vice-Adm. Sir Cameron, KCB 1979; LVO 1965; *b* 20 Feb. 1926; *s* of late Captain Victor Evelyn Rusby, CBE, RN, and Mrs Irene Margaret Rusby; *m* 1948, Marion Elizabeth Bell; two *d*. *Educ:* RNC, Dartmouth. Midshipman 1943; specialised in communications, 1950; CO HMS Ulster, 1958–59; Exec. Officer, HM Yacht Britannia, 1962–65; Dep. Dir, Naval Signals, 1965–68; CO HMS Tartar, 1968–69; Dep. ACOS (Plans and Policy), staff of Allied C-in-C Southern Europe, 1969–72; Sen. Naval Off., WI, 1972–74; Rear-Adm. 1974; ACDS (Ops), 1974–77; Vice-Adm. 1977; Flag Officer Scotland and N Ireland, 1977–79; Dep. Supreme Allied Comdr, Atlantic, 1980–82. Chief Exec., Scottish SPCA, 1983–91. Dir, World Soc. for the Protection of Animals, 1986–98 (Life Vice Pres., 1998). Dir, Freedom Food Ltd, 1994–2000. Vice Pres., King George's Fund for Sailors, 1996–. *Recreations:* sailing, country pursuits. *Club:* New (Edinburgh).

RUSE, David John; Assistant Director, Lifelong (formerly Lifetime) Learning, Westminster City Council, since 1999; *b* 24 Aug. 1951; *s* of Ronald Frank and Betty Irene Ruse; *m* 1975, Carole Anne Lawton; two *d*. *Educ:* Birmingham Coll. of Commerce. ALA 1973. Bath Municipal Libraries, 1969–70; Asst Librarian, London Borough of Havering, 1972–77; Branch Librarian, London Borough of Barking and Dagenham, 1977–81; Asst Dir, Library Assoc., 1981–89; Head, Planning and Review, Berks CC, 1989–93; Asst Dir, Leisure and Libraries, Westminster CC, 1993–99. Mem., Inst. of Leisure and Amenity Mgt. *Publications:* chapters in various librarianship books; various articles in professional library press. *Recreations:* social history of railways, reading, music, countryside matters. *Address:* City Hall, Victoria Street, SW1E 6QP. *T:* (020) 7641 2496.

RUSH, Ann Patricia; Director, Migraine Trust, since 1992; *b* 17 March 1948; *d* of Peter Deshaw and Hanni Adele Gray; *m* 1969, Charles Anthony Rush; one *s* one *d*. *Educ:* Ursuline Convent; LSE (MSc). The Observer, 1966–68; RABI, 1969–76; CR Associates, 1974–88; Ed., Migraine News, 1989–96; Dep. Dir, Migraine Trust, 1990–92. Trustee, Neurological Alliance, 1999–2001. *Publication:* Migraine, 1996. *Recreations:* family, reading, sailing. *Address:* 36 Mayfield Road, Weybridge, Surrey KT13 8XB.

RUSH, Most Rev. Francis Roberts, DD; RC Archbishop of Brisbane, 1973–91; *b* 11 Sept. 1916; *s* of T. J. Rush. *Educ:* Christian Brothers' Coll., Townsville; Mt Carmel, Charters Towers; St Columba's Coll., Springwood; Coll. de Propaganda Fide, Rome. Assistant Priest, Townsville, Mundingburra and Ingham; Parish Priest, Abergowrie and Ingham; Bishop of Rockhampton, 1960–73. *Address:* Verona Villa, 169 Seventeen Mile Rocks Road, Oxley, Brisbane, Qld 4075, Australia.

RUSHDIE, (Ahmed) Salman, FRSL; writer; *b* 19 June 1947; *s* of Anis Ahmed Rushdie and Negin Rushdie (*née* Butt); *m* 1976, Clarissa Luard (marr. diss. 1987); one *s*; *m* 1988, Marianne Wiggins (marr. diss. 1993); *m* 1997, Elizabeth West; one *s*. *Educ:* Cathedral Sch., Bombay; Rugby Sch.; King's Coll., Cambridge (MA (Hons) History). Hon. Prof., MIT, 1993; Dist. Fellow in Lit., UEA, 1995. Hon. DLitt Bard Coll., 1995. Arts Council Literature Bursary Award; Kurt Tucholsky Prize, Sweden, 1992; Prix Colette, Switzerland, 1993; Austrian State Prize for European Literature, 1994. *Films for TV:* The Painter and the Pest, 1985; The Riddle of Midnight, 1988. *Publications:* Grimus, 1975; Midnight's Children, 1981 (Booker Prize for Fiction, 1981; James Tait Black Meml Book Prize; E-SU Literary Award; Booker of Bookers Prize, 1993); Shame, 1983 (Prix du Meilleur Livre Etranger, 1984); The Jaguar Smile: a Nicaraguan journey, 1987; The Satanic Verses, 1988 (Whitbread Novel Award; German Author of the Year Award, 1989); Haroun and the Sea of Stories, 1990 (Writers' Guild Award); Imaginary Homelands (essays), 1991; The Wizard of Oz, 1992; East, West, 1994; The Moor's Last Sigh (Whitbread Novel Award; British Book Awards Author of the Year), 1995; (ed with Elizabeth West) The Vintage Book of Indian Writing, 1947–97, 1997; The Ground Beneath Her Feet, 1999; Fury, 2001; contribs to many journals. *Address:* c/o Wylie Agency (UK) Ltd, 4–8 Rodney Street, N1 9JH.

RUSHFORD, Antony Redfern, CMG 1963; consultant on constitutional, international and commonwealth law; *b* 9 Feb.; *m* 1975, June Jeffrey, *widow* of Roy Eustace Wells; one step *s* one step *d*. *Educ:* Taunton Sch.; Trinity Coll., Cambridge (BA 1948; LLM (LLB 1948); MA 1951). FRSA. RAFVR, 1942 (active service, 1943–47, reserve, 1947–59); Sqdn Ldr, 1946. Solicitor, 1944–57 (distinction in Law Soc. final exams, 1942); Called to the Bar, Inner Temple, 1983. Asst Solicitor, E. W. Marshall Harvey & Dalton, 1948. Home Civil Service, Colonial Office, 1949–68; joined HM Diplomatic Service, 1968; CO, later FCO, retd as Dep. Legal Advr (Asst Under-Sec. of State), 1982. Crown Counsel, Uganda, 1954; Principal Legal Adviser, British Indian Ocean Territory, 1983; Attorney-Gen., Anguilla, and St Helena, 1983; Legal Adviser for Commonwealth Sec.-Gen. to Governor-Gen. of Grenada, Mem. Interim Govt, Attorney-Gen., and JP, Grenada, 1983; consultancies: FCO (special duties), 1982; Commonwealth Sec.-Gen., St Kitts and Nevis independence, 1982–83, St Lucia treaties, 1983–85; E Caribbean courts, 1983; maritime legislation for Jamaica, Internat. Maritime Orgn, 1983 and 1985; constitutional advr, Govt of St Kitts and Nevis, and Govt of St Lucia, 1982–85. Has drafted many constitutions for UK dependencies and Commonwealth countries attaining independence; presented paper on constitutional develt to meeting of Law Officers from Smaller Commonwealth Jurisdictions, IoM, 1983. UK deleg. or advr at many constitutional confs and discussions; CO Rep., Inst. of Advanced Legal Studies; participant, Symposium on Federalism, Chicago, 1962; Advr, Commonwealth Law Ministers Conf., 1973. Lectr, Overseas Legal Officers Course, 1964; Special Examnr, London Univ., 1963, 1987; a dir of studies, RIPA (Overseas Services Unit), and also associate consultant on statute law, 1982–86. Mem. Editl Bd, Inst. of Internat. Law and Econ. Develt, Washington, 1977–82. Co. Sec., Forwardstrike Ltd, 1997–. Foundn Mem. Exec. Council, Royal Commonwealth Soc. for the Blind, 1969–81, 1983–99 (Hon. Legal Counsellor, 1984–; Indiv. Mem., 1998–); Hon. Sec., Services Race Club, Hong Kong, 1946–47. Member: Glyndebourne Fest. Soc., 1950–96; Inst. of Advanced Motoring, 1959–73; Commonwealth Lawyers Assoc., 1982–90; Commonwealth Assoc. of Legislative Counsel, 1984–; Commonwealth Magistrates and Judges Assoc., 1986–90; Anglo-Arab Assoc., 1990–; Saudi-British Soc., 1990–. Governor, Taunton Sch., 1948–. CStJ 1989 (Hon. Legal Counsellor, 1978–93; Mem., Chapter-Gen., 1983–94). *Address:* Flat 5, 50 Pont Street, Knightsbridge, SW1X 0AE. *T:* (020) 7589 4235; (chambers) 12 King's Bench Walk, Temple, EC4Y 7EL. *T:* (020) 7353 5692/6. *Clubs:* Royal Commonwealth Society; Polish Air Force Association.

RUSHTON, Ian Lawton, FIA, FCII, FSS; Chairman, Hackney Empire Ltd, since 1994; Vice Chairman, Royal Insurance Holdings plc, 1991–93 (Group Chief Executive, 1989–91); *b* 8 Sept. 1931; *s* of Arthur John and Mabel Lilian Rushton; *m* 1st, 1956, Julia Frankland (decd); one *d*; 2nd, 1986, Anita Spencer; one step *s* one step *d*. *Educ:* Rock Ferry High Sch., Birkenhead; King's Coll., London (BSc Mathematics). FIA 1959; FCII 1961. Served RAF, 1953–56 (Flt-Lieut). Royal Insurance, 1956–93: Dep. Gen. Man. (UK), 1972; Exec. Vice Pres., Royal US, 1980; Gen. Man. Royal UK, 1983; Exec. Dir and Gp Gen. Man., Royal Insurance plc, 1986. Chairman: Fire Protection Assoc., 1983–87; Assoc. of British Insurers, 1991–93; Vice Pres., Inst. of Actuaries, 1986–89. FRSA. *Recreations:* golf, gardening, theatre, music. *Address:* Flat 136, 3 Whitehall Court, SW1A 2EL.

RUSHTON, Prof. Julian Gordon, DPhil; West Riding Professor of Music, University of Leeds, since 1982; *b* 22 May 1941; *s* of Prof. William A. H. Rushton and Marjorie Rushton; *m* 1968, Virginia S. M. Jones (marr. diss. 2000); two *s*. *Educ:* Trinity Coll., Cambridge (BA 1963; BMus 1965; MA 1967); Magdalen Coll., Oxford (DPhil 1970). Lecturer in Music: UEA, 1968–74; and Fellow, King's Coll., Cambridge, 1974–81. Chm., Editl Bd, Musica Britannica, 1993–. Pres., Royal Musical Assoc., 1994–99. Corres. Mem., Amer. Musicol Soc., 2000. *Publications:* W. A. Mozart: Don Giovanni, 1981, 2nd edn 1990; The Musical Language of Berlioz, 1983; Classical Music: a concise history, 1986; W. A. Mozart: Idomeneo, 1993; Berlioz: Romeo et Juliette, 1994; Elgar: Enigma Variations, 1999; The Music of Berlioz, 2001; contrib. to Music & Letters, Music Analysis, Cambridge Opera Jl, Musical Times, Elgar Soc. Jl. *Recreations:* literature, walking to work, marmalade making. *Address:* Department of Music, University of Leeds, Leeds LS2 9JT. *T:* (0113) 233 2579; *e-mail:* j.g.rushton@leeds.ac.uk; 362 Leymoor Road, Golcar, Huddersfield HD7 4QF.

RUSHWORTH, Dr (Frank) Derek; Headmaster, Holland Park School, London, 1971–85; *b* 15 Sept. 1920; *s* of late Frank and Elizabeth Rushworth, Huddersfield; *m* 1941, Hamidah Begum, *d* of late Justice S. Akhlaque Hussain, Lahore, and Edith (*née* Bayliss), Oxford; three *d*. *Educ:* Huddersfield Coll.; St Edmund Hall, Oxford (Schol.; BA 1942, MA 1946); Doctorate of Univ. of Paris (Lettres), 1947. Served 6th Rajputana Rifles, Indian Army, 1942–45 (Major); began teaching, 1947; Head of Modern Languages: Tottenham Grammar Sch., 1953; Holland Park Sch., 1958; Head of Shoreditch Sch., London, 1965. Chairman: Associated Examining Board, French Committee, 1964–74; Schools Council, 16+ Examination Feasibility Study (French), 1971–75; Pres., London Head Teachers' Assoc., 1985. Governor, Holland Park Sch., 1990–95. *Publications:* Our French Neighbours, 1963, 2nd edn 1966; French text-books and language-laboratory books; articles in French Studies, Modern Languages, also educnl jls. *Recreation:* photography. *Address:* 25c Lambolle Road, NW3 4HS. *T:* (020) 7794 3691.

RUSSELL; *see* Hamilton-Russell, family name of Viscount Boyne.

RUSSELL, family name of **Duke of Bedford, Earl Russell, Baron Ampthill, Baron de Clifford** and **Baron Russell of Liverpool**.

RUSSELL, 5th Earl *cr* 1861; **Conrad Sebastian Robert Russell,** FBA 1991; Viscount Amberley 1861; Professor of British History, King's College London, since 1990; *b* 15 April 1937; *s* of 3rd Earl Russell, OM, FRS and Patricia Helen, *d* of H. E. Spence; *S* half brother, 1987; *m* 1962, Elizabeth Franklyn Sanders; two *s*. *Educ:* Merton College, Oxford (BA 1958, MA 1962; Sir Henry Savile Fellow, 1994); MA Yale 1979. FRHistS 1971. Lectr in History, Bedford College, London, 1960–74, Reader, 1974–79; Prof. of History, Yale Univ., 1979–84; Astor Prof. of British History, UCL, 1984–90. Ford Lectr, Univ. of Oxford, 1987–88; Trevelyan Lectr, Univ. of Cambridge, 1995. Takes Liberal Democrat whip, H of L; elected Mem., H of L, 1999. *Publications:* The Crisis of Parliaments: English History 1509–1660, 1971; (ed) The Origins of the English Civil War, 1973; Parliaments and English Politics 1621–1629, 1979; The Causes of the English Civil War, 1990; Unrevolutionary England 1603–1642, 1990; The Fall of the British Monarchies 1637–1642, 1991; Academic Freedom, 1993; An Intelligent Person's Guide to Liberalism, 1999; articles in jls. *Recreations:* swimming, uxoriousness, cricket. *Heir:* *s* Viscount Amberley, *qv*. *Address:* Department of History, King's College, Strand, WC2R 2LS.

RUSSELL OF LIVERPOOL, 3rd Baron *cr* 1919; **Simon Gordon Jared Russell;** *b* 30 Aug. 1952; *s* of Captain Hon. Langley Gordon Haslingden Russell, MC (*d* 1975) (*o s* of 2nd Baron), and of Kiloran Margaret, *d* of late Hon. Sir Arthur Jared Palmer Howard, KBE, CVO; *S* grandfather, 1981; *m* 1984, Dr Gilda Albano, *y d* of late Signor F. Albano and of Signora Maria Caputo-Albano; two *s* one *d*. *Educ:* Charterhouse; Trinity Coll.,

Cambridge; INSEAD, Fontainebleau, France. *Heir:* *s* Hon. Edward Charles Stanley Russell, *b* 2 Sept. 1985.

RUSSELL, Alan Keith, OBE 2000; Chairman, Dresden Trust, since 1993; charity administrator, consultant and writer; *b* 22 Oct. 1932; *s* of late Keith Russell and Gertrude Ann Russell; *m* 1959, Philippa Margaret Stoneham; two *s* one *d*. *Educ:* Ardingly Coll.; Lincoln Coll., Oxford (BA; MA Econ and Pol Sci. 1956); DPhil Oxon 1962; Cert. in Architectural Hist., Oxford Univ. Dept for Contg Educn/Oxford Brookes, 1997; Postgrad. Dip. in Historic Conservation, Oxford Brookes, 1998. Colonial Office, ODM, FCO, 1959–69, 1972–75; CS Coll., 1969–71; Dir, Inter University Council for Higher Educn Overseas, 1980–81; sen. official, Commn of EC, 1976–79, 1981–86, 1988–89; Fellow, Lincoln Coll., Oxford and Sen. Res. Associate, Queen Elizabeth House, 1986–88; manager of civic improvement trust, 1990–92. Cross of Order of Merit (Germany), 1997. *Publications:* ed, The Economic and Social History of Mauritius, 1962; Liberal Landslide: the General Election of 1906, 1973; contrib. Edwardian Radicalism, 1974; The Unclosed Eye (poems), 1987; Dresden: a city reborn, 1999; (ed) Dresden, 2000; articles on trade and development, on Germany and on Europe. *Recreations:* conservation and town planning, German and European history, services for the mentally handicapped. *Address:* 9 Oaklands Court, Somerstown, Chichester, W Sussex PO19 4AF.

RUSSELL, Sir (Alastair) Muir, KCB 2001; FRSE; Permanent Secretary, Scottish Executive, since 1999; *b* 9 Jan. 1949; *s* of Thomas Russell and Anne Muir; *m* 1983, Eileen Alison Mackay, *qv*. *Educ:* High Sch. of Glasgow; Univ. of Glasgow (BSc Nat. Phil.). Joined Scottish Office, 1970; seconded as Sec. to Scottish Development Agency, 1975–76; Asst Sec., 1981; Principal Private Sec. to Sec. of State for Scotland, 1981–83; Under Sec., 1990; seconded to Cabinet Office, 1990–92; Under Sec. (Housing), Scottish Office Envmt Dept, 1992–95; Dep. Sec., 1995; Sec. and Hd of Dept, Scottish Office Agric., Envmt and Fisheries Dept, 1995–98; Permanent Under-Sec. of State, Scottish Office, 1998–99. Non-exec. Dir, Stagecoach Hldgs, 1992–95. FRSE 2000; CIMgt 2001. Hon. LLD Strathclyde, 2000; DUniv Glasgow, 2001. *Recreations:* music, food, wine. *Address:* Scottish Executive, St Andrew's House, Regent Road, Edinburgh EH1 3DG. *T:* (0131) 244 4026. *Clubs:* Royal Commonwealth Society, Caledonian; New (Edinburgh).

RUSSELL, (Albert) Muir (Galloway), CBE 1989; QC (Scot.) 1965; Sheriff of Grampian, Highland and Islands (formerly Aberdeen, Kincardine and Banff) at Aberdeen and Stonehaven, 1971–91; *b* 26 Oct. 1925; *s* of Hon. Lord Russell; *m* 1954, Margaret Winifred, *o d* of T. McW Millar, FRCS(E), Edinburgh; two *s* two *d*. *Educ:* Edinburgh Academy; Wellington College; Brasenose College, Oxford. BA (Hons) Oxon, 1949; LLB (Edin.), 1951. Lieut, Scots Guards, 1944–47. Member of Faculty of Advocates, 1951–. *Recreation:* golf. *Address:* Tulloch House, Aultbea, Ross-shire IV22 2JA. *T:* (01445) 731325. *Club:* Royal Northern (Aberdeen).

RUSSELL, Alexander William, CB 1996; strategic consultant on public service reform and fiscal management; Commissioner, 1985–98, and Deputy Chairman, 1993–98, HM Customs and Excise; *b* 16 Oct. 1938; *s* of late William and Elizabeth W. B. Russell (*née* Russell); *m* 1st, 1962, Elspeth Rae (*d* 1996); *m* 2nd, 1999, Patricia Sebbelov. *Educ:* Royal High Sch., Edinburgh; Edinburgh Univ. (MA Hons); Manitoba Univ. (MA). Assistant Principal, Scottish Development Dept, 1961–64; Private Sec. to Parliamentary Under Secretary of State, Scottish Office, 1961–65; Principal, Regional Development Div. and Scottish Development Dept, 1965–72; Principal Private Sec. to Secretary of State for Scotland, 1972–73; Asst Secretary: Scottish Development Dept, 1973–76; Civil Service Dept, 1976–79; Under-Secretary: Management and Personnel Office (formerly CSD), 1979–82; Hd of Treasury MPO Financial Management Unit, 1982–85; Dir Orgn, HM Customs and Excise, 1985–90, Dir Customs, 1990–93, HM Customs and Excise. Chm., Europro, 1999–; Dir and Mem. Bd, SITPRO, 1999–. Co-coordinator, Tax Mgt Res. network, Univ. of Bath. *Address:* 293 Lauderdale Tower, Barbican, EC2Y 8BY. *T:* (020) 7638 3054.

RUSSELL, Andrew Victor Manson; Executive Director, Association for Spina Bifida and Hydrocephalus, since 1991; *b* 7 Dec. 1949; *s* of Manson McCausland Russell and Margaret Ivy Russell; *m* 1974, Susan Elizabeth Aykroyd; one *s* one *d*. *Educ:* Dartington Hall; Fitzwilliam Coll., Cambridge Univ. (MA). NSMHC, 1974–85; General Manager, Eastern Div., Royal MENCAP Soc., 1985–91. *Recreations:* sailing, music. *Address:* c/o ASBAH House, 42 Park Road, Peterborough PE1 2UQ. *T:* (01733) 555988.

RUSSELL, Anna; International Concert Comedienne; *b* 27 Dec. 1911; *d* of Col C. Russell-Brown, CB, DSO, RE, and Beatrice M. Tandy; single. *Educ:* St Felix School, Southwold; Royal College of Music, London. Folk singer, BBC, 1935–40; Canadian Broadcasting Corp. programmes, 1942–46; Radio interviewer, CBC, 1945–46; Debut, Town Hall, New York, as concert comedienne, 1948; Broadway show, Anna Russell and her Little Show, 1953; Towns of USA, Canada, Great Britain, Australia, New Zealand, the Orient and South Africa, 1948–60. Television, Radio Summer Theatre, USA; recordings, Columbia Masterworks. Resident in Australia, 1968–75. Mayfair Theatre, London, 1976. *Publications:* The Power of Being a Positive Stinker (NY); The Anna Russell Song Book; I'm Not Making This Up, You Know (autobiog.). *Recreation:* gardening. *Address:* 70 Anna Russell Way, Unionville, ON L3R 3X3, Canada. *Club:* Zonta International (USA, Toronto Branch, Internat. Mem.).

RUSSELL, Rt Rev. Anthony John; *see* Ely, Bishop of.

RUSSELL, Anthony Patrick; QC 1999; a Recorder, 1993–96 and since 2001; *b* 11 April 1951; *s* of late Dr Michael Hibberd Russell and of Pamela Russell (*née* Eyre). *Educ:* King's Sch., Chester; Pembroke Coll., Oxford (MA). Called to the Bar, Middle Temple, 1974; in practice at the Bar, Northern Circuit, 1974–; Standing Counsel to Inland Revenue, 1994–96. Mem., Gen. Council of the Bar, 1987–94. *Recreations:* music, especially singing, the countryside. *Address:* Peel Court Chambers, 45 Hardman Street, Manchester M3 3PL. *T:* (0161) 832 3791. *Club:* Oxford and Cambridge.

RUSSELL, Rev. Arthur Colin, CMG 1957; ED; MA; *b* 2 Nov. 1906; *e s* of late Arthur W. Russell, OBE, WS; *m* 1939, Elma (*d* 1967), *d* of late Douglas Strachan, Hon. RSA; three *d*. *Educ:* Harrow; Brasenose College, Oxford (Heberden Scholar). Called to the Bar, Inner Temple, 1939. Cadet, Gold Coast (now Ghana), 1929; Asst Dist Comr, 1930; Dist Comr, 1940; Judicial Adviser, 1947; Senior, 1951; Regional Officer, 1952; Permanent Sec., Min. of Education and Social Welfare, 1953; Governor's Secretary, 1954; Chief Regional Officer, Ashanti, 1955–57, retd. Trained for the Ministry, 1957–59; Ordained (Church of Scotland), 1959; Parish Minister, Aberlemno, 1959–76; retd. District Councillor, Angus District, 1977–84. *Publications:* Stained Glass Windows of Douglas Strachan, 1972, 2nd edn 1994; Gold Coast to Ghana, 1996. *Address:* Balgavies Lodge, by Forfar, Angus DD8 2TH. *T:* (01307) 818571.

RUSSELL, Sir (Arthur) Mervyn, 8th Bt *cr* 1812, of Swallowfield, Berkshire; *b* 7 Feb. 1923; *s* of Sir Arthur Edward Ian Montagu Russell, 6th Bt, MBE, and his 2nd wife, Cornélie, *d* of Maj. Jacques de Bruijn, Amsterdam; *S* half-*b*, 1993; *m* 1st, 1945, Ruth Holloway (marr. diss.); one *s*; 2nd, 1956, Kathleen Joyce Searle; one *s*. *Heir:* *s* Stephen Charles Russell [*b* 12 Jan. 1949; *m* 1974, Dale Frances Markstein; one *d*].

RUSSELL, Barbara Winifred, MA; Headmistress, Berkhamsted School for Girls, 1950–71; *b* 5 Jan. 1910; *er d* of Lionel Wilfred and Elizabeth Martin Russell. *Educ:* St Oran's School, Edinburgh; Edinburgh University; Oxford University, Dept of Education. History Mistress, Brighton and Hove High School, 1932–38; Senior History Mistress, Roedean School, 1938–49. *Recreations:* reading, gardening. *Club:* East India, Devonshire, Sports and Public Schools.

RUSSELL, Cecil Anthony Francis; Director of Intelligence, Greater London Council, 1970–76; *b* 7 June 1921; *s* of late Comdr S. F. Russell, OBE, RN retd and late Mrs M. E. Russell (*née* Sneyd-Kynnersley); *m* 1950, Editha May (*née* Birch); no *c*. *Educ:* Winchester Coll.; University Coll., Oxford (1940–41, 1945–47). RNVR, 1941–45. Civil Service, 1949–70: Road Research Lab., 1949–50; Air Min., 1950–62; Dep. Statistical Adviser, Home Office, 1962–67; Head of Census Div., General Register Office, 1967–70. FSS. *Recreation:* ocean sailing. *Address:* Pagan Hill, Whiteleaf, Princes Risborough, Bucks HP27 0LQ. *T:* (01844) 343655. *Clubs:* Cruising Association; Ocean Cruising.

RUSSELL, Sir Charles (Dominic), 4th Bt *cr* 1916, of Littleworth Corner, Burnham, co. Buckingham; antiquarian bookseller, trading as Russell Rare Books, since 1978; *b* 28 May 1956; *o s* of Sir Charles Ian Russell, 3rd Bt and Rosemary Lavender Russell (*née* Prestige) (*d* 1996); *S* father, 1997; *m* 1986, Sarah Chandor (marr. diss. 1995); one *s*. *Educ:* Worth Sch. *Heir:* *s* Charles William Russell, *b* 8 Sept. 1988. *Club:* Garrick.

RUSSELL, Christine Margaret; JP; MP (Lab) City of Chester, since 1997; *b* 25 March 1945; *d* of John Alfred William Carr and Phyllis Carr; *m* 1971, Dr James Russell (marr. diss. 1991); one *s* one *d*. *Educ:* Spalding High Sch.; London Sch. of Librarianship (ALA). PA to Brian Simpson, MEP, 1992–94. Mem. (Lab) Chester CC, 1980–97 (Chair, Develt). Co-ordinator, Mind Advocacy Scheme, 1995–97. JP 1980. *Recreations:* film, visual arts, walking, football. *Address:* House of Commons, SW1A 0AA.

RUSSELL, Christopher; *see* Russell, R. C. G.

RUSSELL, Clare Nancy; Vice Lord-Lieutenant for Banffshire, since 1998; estate owner and rural land manager, Ballindalloch, since 1979; *b* 4 Aug. 1944; *d* of Sir Ewan Macpherson-Grant, 6th Bt, and Lady Macpherson-Grant; *m* 1967, Oliver Henry Russell; two *s* one *d*. *Educ:* in Scotland. Professional florist, Head Decorator, Constance Spry, 1962–65; Sec. to Fourth Clerk at the Table, H of C, 1965–67; Dir, Craigo Farms Ltd, 1970–; living at Ballindalloch, 1978–; opened Ballindalloch Castle to public, 1993. Mem., Moray Health Council, 1986–91. Mem. Council, NT for Scotland, 1985–88; Dist Organiser, Moray and Banff, 1980–93; Mem. Exec. Cttee, 1987–93, Scotland's Garden Scheme. Chm., Queen Mary's Clothing Guild, 1990–93 (started Queen Mary's Clothing Guild in Scotland, 1986). Mem. Bd, Children's Hospice Assoc., Scotland, 1995–. Sunday Sch. teacher, Inveraven Ch, 1982–94. DL Banffshire, 1991–98. *Publications:* Favourite Recipes, Dried Flowers and Pot Pourri from Ballindalloch Castle, 1993; Favourite Puddings from Ballindalloch Castle, 1995; Favourite First Courses from Ballindalloch Castle, 1996; Favourite Recipes from Ballindalloch Castle, 1998. *Recreations:* dog-handling, gardening, flower arranging, piano, tapestry, knitting, cooking, historic houses, antiques. *Address:* Ballindalloch Castle, Banffshire AB37 9AX. *T:* (01807) 500206. *Club:* Sloane.

RUSSELL, Dan Chapman; Sheriff of South Strathclyde, Dumfries and Galloway at Hamilton, since 1992; *b* 25 Dec. 1939; *s* of William Morris Russell and Isabella Ritchie Stein Scott; *m* 1969, Janet McNeil; three *d*. *Educ:* Airdrie Acad.; Glasgow Univ. (MA 1960; LLB 1963). Qualified as Solicitor, 1963; in private practice, 1963–92; Partner, Bell, Russell & Co., Solicitors, Airdrie, 1965–92. Temp. Sheriff, 1976–78 and 1985–92. Reporter, Airdrie Children's Panel, 1972–75. Mem. Council, Law Soc. of Scotland, 1975–84; Dean, Airdrie Soc. of Solicitors, 1986–88. *Recreations:* golf, bridge, walking. *Address:* Sheriff Court, Almada Street, Hamilton ML3 6AA. *T:* (01698) 282957.

RUSSELL, Rt Rev. David Hamilton; *see* Grahamstown, Bishop of.

RUSSELL, Sir David Sturrock W.; *see* West-Russell.

RUSSELL, Rev. David Syme, CBE 1982; MA, DD, DLitt; President, Baptist Union of Great Britain and Ireland, 1983–84 (General Secretary, 1967–82); *b* 21 Nov. 1916; second *s* of Peter Russell and Janet Marshall Syme; *m* 1943, Marion Hamilton Campbell; one *s* one *d*. *Educ:* Scottish Baptist Coll., Glasgow; Trinity Coll., Glasgow; Glasgow Univ. (MA, BD, DLitt, Hon. DD); Regent's Park Coll., Oxford Univ. (MA, MLitt; Hon. Fellow, 1995). Minister of Baptist Churches: Berwick, 1939–41; Oxford, 1943–45; Acton, 1945–53. Principal of Rawdon Coll., Leeds, and lectr in Old Testament languages and literature, 1953–64; Joint Principal of the Northern Baptist College, Manchester, 1964–67. Moderator, Free Church Federal Council, 1974–75. Pres., European Baptist Fedn, 1979–81. Mem., Central Cttee, WCC, 1968–83; Vice-Pres., BCC, 1981–84. Hon. DD McMaster, 1991. *Publications:* Between the Testaments, 1960; Two Refugees (Ezekiel and Second Isaiah), 1962; The Method and Message of Jewish Apocalyptic, 1964; The Jews from Alexander to Herod, 1976; Apocalyptic: Ancient and Modern, 1978; Daniel (The Daily Study Bible), 1981; In Journeyings Often, 1982; From Early Judaism to Early Church, 1986; The Old Testament Pseudepigrapha: patriarchs and prophets in early Judaism, 1987; Daniel: an active volcano, 1989; Poles Apart: the Gospel in creative tension, 1990; Divine Disclosure: an introduction to Jewish apocalyptic, 1992; Prophecy and the Apocalyptic Dream: protest and promise, 1994; contrib. to Encyc. Britannica, 1963. *Recreation:* woodwork. *Address:* 7 Cedar Court, Glenavon Park, Stoke Bishop, Bristol BS9 1RL. *T:* (0117) 968 1131.

RUSSELL, Prof. Donald Andrew Frank Moore, FBA 1971; Fellow, St John's College, Oxford, 1948–88, now Emeritus; Professor of Classical Literature, Oxford, 1985–88; *b* 13 Oct. 1920; *s* of Samuel Charles Russell (schoolmaster) and Laura Moore; *m* 1967, Joycelyne Gledhill Dickinson (*d* 1993). *Educ:* King's College Sch., Wimbledon; Balliol Coll., Oxford (MA 1946); DLitt Oxon 1985. Served War: Army (R Signals and Intelligence Corps), 1941–45. Craven Scholar, 1946; Lectr, Christ Church, Oxford, 1947; St John's College, Oxford: Tutor, 1948–84, Dean, 1957–64; Tutor for Admissions, 1968–72; Reader in Class. Lit., Oxford Univ., 1978–85. Paddison Vis. Prof., Univ. of N Carolina at Chapel Hill, 1985; Vis. Prof. of Classics, Stanford Univ., 1989, 1991. Co-editor, Classical Quarterly, 1965–70. *Publications:* Commentary on Longinus, On the Sublime, 1964; Ancient Literary Criticism (with M. Winterbottom), 1972; Plutarch, 1972; (with N. G. Wilson) Menander Rhetor, 1981; Criticism in Antiquity, 1981; Greek Declamation, 1984; (ed) Antonine Literature, 1990; Commentary on Dio Chrysostom, Orations, 7, 12, 36, 1992; (trans.) Plutarch: selected essays and dialogues, 1993; (trans.) Libanius, Imaginary Speeches, 1996; Quintilian, 2001; articles and reviews in classical periodicals. *Address:* 35 Belsyre Court, Oxford OX2 6HU. *T:* (01865) 556135.

RUSSELL, Edwin John Cumming, FRBS 1978; sculptor; *b* 4 May 1939; *s* of Edwin Russell and Mary Elizabeth Russell; *m* 1964, Lorne McKean; two *d*. *Educ:* Brighton Coll. of Art and Crafts; Royal Academy Schs (CertRAS). *Works:* Crucifix, limewood, pulpit, St Paul's Cathedral, 1964; St Catherine, lead, Little Cloister, Westminster Abbey, 1966; St Michael, oak, Chapel of St Michael and St George, St Paul's Cath., 1970; Bishop Bubwith, W Front Wells Cath., 1980; sundials: Jubilee Dolphin Dial, bronze, Nat. Maritime Mus., Greenwich, 1978; 3m, Sultan Qaboos Univ., Oman, 1986; Botanical Armillery, Kew Gardens, 1987; 5m, bronze, Parliament Square, Dubai, 1988; Forecourt sculpture, Rank Xerox Internat. HQ, 1989; shopping centre sculpture: Mad Hatter's Tea Party play sculpture, granite, Warrington, 1984; Lion and Lamb, teak, Farnham, 1986; public works: Suffragette Meml, 1968; 1st Gov. of Bahamas, Sheraton Hotel, Nassau, 1968; Lewis Carroll commemorative sculpture, Alice and the White Rabbit, Guildford, 1984; Panda, marble, WWF Internat. HQ, 1988; private collections: Goodwood House; Sir Robert McAlpine & Sons Ltd; Rosehaugh Stanhope Developments; Arup Associates; Bovis; YRM International; Trafalgar House plc; Cementation International; John Laing Construction; John Mowlem & Co.; ARC; Worshipful Co. of Stationers; City of London Grammar Shool. Royal Academy Gold Medal for Sculpture, 1960; Otto Beit Medal for sculpture, RBS, 1991. *Recreation:* philosophy. *Address:* Lethendry, Polecat Valley, Hindhead, Surrey GU26 6BE. *T:* (01428) 605655.

RUSSELL, Eileen Alison, (Lady Russell); *see* Mackay, E. A.

RUSSELL, Francis Mark; Chairman, B. Elliott plc, 1975–87 (Chief Executive, 1972–83); *b* 26 July 1927; *s* of W. Sidney and Beatrice M. Russell; *m* 1950, Joan Patricia Ryan; two *s* three *d*. *Educ:* Ratcliffe Coll., Leicester; Clare Coll., Cambridge (MA). CIMgt. Palestine Police, 1946–48; Director: S. Russell & Sons Ltd, 1959; B. Elliott & Co. Ltd, 1967; Chief Executive, 1969, Dir, 1969–88, Chm., 1975–87, Goldfields Industrial Corporation; Dep. Chm., B. Elliott & Co. Ltd, 1971; Dir, Johnson & Firth Brown plc, 1982–92. *Recreations:* golf, gardening. *Address:* Armour Barn, Stockwell Lane, Meadle, Aylesbury, Bucks HP17 9UG. *T:* (01844) 275861. *Clubs:* Aldeburgh Golf; Denham Golf.

RUSSELL, Sir George, Kt 1992; CBE 1985; Chairman: 3i Group plc, 1993–2001 (Director, 1992–2001); Camelot Group plc, 1995–2002; *b* 25 Oct. 1935; *s* of William H. Russell and Frances A. Russell; *m* 1959, Dorothy Brown; three *d*. *Educ:* Gateshead Grammar Sch.; Durham Univ. (BA Hons). ICI, 1958–67 (graduate trainee, Commercial Res. Officer, Sales Rep., and Product Sales Man.); Vice President and General Manager: Welland Chemical Co. of Canada Ltd, 1968; St Clair Chemical Co. Ltd, 1968; Man. Dir, Alcan UK Ltd, 1976; Asst Man. Dir, 1977–81, Man. Dir, 1981–82, Alcan Aluminium (UK) Ltd; Man. Dir and Chief Exec., British Alcan Aluminium, 1982–86; Chief Exec., 1986–92, Chm., 1989–93, non-exec. Chm., 1993–97, Marley plc. Chairman: Luxfer Holdings Ltd, 1976–78; Alcan UK Ltd, 1978–82; Northern Develt Co., 1994–99; Director: Alcan Aluminiumwerke GmbH, Frankfurt, 1977–82; Northern Rock plc (formerly Bldg Soc.), 1985–; Alcan Aluminium Ltd, 1987–2000; Taylor Woodrow, 1992–; British Alcan plc, 1997–2001. Chairman: ITN, 1987–88; IBA, 1988–92 (Mem., 1979–86); ITC, 1991–96; Cable Authy, 1989–90; Dep. Chm., Channel Four TV, 1987–88. Visiting Professor, Univ. of Newcastle upon Tyne, 1978. Member: Board, Northern Sinfonia Orchestra, 1977–80; Northern Industrial Development Board, 1977–80; Washington Development Corporation, 1978–80; Board, Civil Service Pay Research Unit, 1980–81; Megaw Inquiry into Civil Service Pay, 1981; Widdicombe Cttee of Inquiry into Conduct of Local Authority Business, 1985. Trustee, Beamish Develt Trust, 1985–90. Hon. DEng Newcastle upon Tyne, 1985; Hon. DBA Northumbria, 1992; Hon. LLD: Sunderland, 1995; Durham, 1997. *Recreations:* tennis, bird watching. *Address:* c/o 4th Floor, Nedbank House, 20 Abchurch Lane, EC4N 7BB. *Club:* Garrick.

RUSSELL, Gerald Francis Morris, MD, FRCP, FRCPE, Hon. FRCPsych; Professor of Psychiatry, Institute of Psychiatry, University of London, and Physician, Bethlem Royal and Maudsley Hospital, 1979–93, now Professor Emeritus; Director, Eating Disorders Unit, The Priory Hayes Grove Hospital, since 1993; *b* Grammont, Belgium, 12 Jan. 1928; 2nd *s* of late Maj. Daniel George Russell, MC, and late Berthe Marie Russell (*née* De Boe); *m* 1950, Margaret Taylor, MB, ChB; three *s*. *Educ:* Collège St Jean Berchmans, Brussels; George Watson's Coll., Edinburgh (Dux); Univ. of Edinburgh (Mouat Schol. in Practice of Physic). MD (with commendation), 1957; DPM; FRCPE 1967; FRCP 1969; Hon. FRCPsych (FRCPsych 1971). RAMC Regimental Med. Off., Queen's Bays, 1951–53; Neurological Registrar, Northern Gen. Hosp., Edin., 1954–56; MRC Clinical Res. Fellow, 1956–58; Inst. of Psychiatry, Maudsley Hospital: 1st Asst, 1959–60; Senior Lectr, 1961–70; Dean, 1966–70; Bethlem Royal and Maudsley Hospital: Physician, 1961–70; Mem. Bd of Governors, 1966–70; Mem., Special Health Authority, 1979–90; Prof. of Psychiatry, Royal Free Hosp. Sch. of Medicine, 1971–79. Chairman: Educn Cttee, Royal Medico-Psychological Assoc., 1970 (Mem. Council, 1966–71); Sect. on Eating Disorders, World Psychiatric Assoc., 1989–99; Assoc. of Univ. Teachers of Psychiatry, 1991–94; Sec. of Sect. of Psychiatry, Roy. Soc. Med., 1966–68 (Pres., 1998–99); Special Interest Gp on Eating Disorders, RCPsych, 1995–99; Mem., European Soc. for Clinical Investigation, 1968–72; Pres., Soc. for Psychosomatic Res., 1989–91. Corr. Fellow, Amer. Psychiatric Assoc., 1967–2000. Member Editorial Boards: British Jl of Psychiatry, 1966–71; Psychological Medicine, 1970–2000; Jl Neurology, Neurosurgery and Psychiatry, 1971–75; Medical Education, 1975–84; Internat. Jl of Eating Disorders, 1981–. Mem., 1942 Club, 1978–. *Publications:* contrib. to Psychiatrie der Gegenwart, vol. 3, 1975; (ed jtly with L. Hersov and contrib.) Handbook of Psychiatry, vol. 4, The Neuroses and Personality Disorders, 1984; (contrib. and ed jtly) Anorexia Nervosa and Bulimic Disorders: current perspectives, 1985; (contrib.) Oxford Textbook of Medicine, 2nd edn, 1987; (contrib.) Handbook of Treatment for Eating Disorders, 2nd edn, 1997; (contrib.) New Oxford Textbook of Psychiatry, 2000; articles in med. jls on psychiatry, disorders of eating, dyslexia, education and neurology. *Recreations:* art galleries, language, photography. *Address:* The Priory Hayes Grove Hospital, Prestons Road, Hayes, Kent BR2 7AS.

RUSSELL, Graham R.; *see* Ross Russell.

RUSSELL, Ven. (Harold) Ian (Lyle); Archdeacon of Coventry, 1989–2000; Chaplain to the Queen, since 1997; *b* 17 Oct. 1934; *s* of Percy Harold and Emma Rebecca Russell; *m* 1961, Barbara Lillian Dixon; two *s* one *d*. *Educ:* Epsom College; London Coll. of Divinity (BD, ALCD). Shell Petroleum Co., 1951–53; RAF, Jan. 1953; RAF Regt, Nov. 1953–1956; London Coll. of Divinity, 1956–60; ordained, 1960; Curate of Iver, Bucks, 1960–63; Curate-in-charge of St Luke's, Lodge Moor, Parish of Fulwood, Sheffield, 1963–67; Vicar: St John's, Chapeltown, Sheffield, 1967–75; St Jude's, Mapperley, Nottingham, 1975–89. *Recreations:* walking, photography, sport, gardening. *Address:* 5 Old Acres, Woodborough, Nottingham NG14 6ES. *T:* (0115) 965 3543. *Club:* Royal Air Force.

RUSSELL, Prof. Ian John, FRS 1989; Professor of Neurobiology, Sussex University, since 1987; *b* 19 June 1943; *s* of Philip William George Russell and Joan Lillian Russell; *m* 1968, Janice Marion Russell; one *s* one *d*. *Educ:* Chatham Technical Sch.; Queen Mary Coll., London (BSc Zoology); Univ. of British Columbia (NATO Student; MSc Zool.); Univ. of Cambridge (SRC Student; Trinity Hall Res. Student; PhD Zool.). Res. Fellowship, Magdalene Coll., Cambridge, 1969–71; SRC Res. Fellowship, Cambridge, 1969–71; Royal Soc. Exchange Fellowship, King Gustav V Res. Inst., Stockholm, 1970–71; University of Sussex: Lectr in Neurobiology, 1971–79; Reader in Neurobiology, 1979–80 and 1982–87; MRC Sen. Res. Fellow, 1980–82, 1995–98. *Publications:* on the neurobiology of hearing, in learned jls. *Recreations:* hockey, windsurfing, reading, music, gardening, walking. *Address:* Little Ivy Cottage, Waldron, Heathfield, East Sussex TN21 0QX. *T:* (01435) 813382.

RUSSELL, James Francis Buchanan; QC (NI) 1968; **His Honour Judge Russell;** County Court Judge of Northern Ireland, 1978–97; *b* 7 July 1924; *e s* of John Buchanan Russell and Margaret Bellingham Russell; *m* 1946, Irene McKee; two *s* one *d* (and one *d* decd). *Educ:* King's Sch., Worcester; St Andrews Univ.; Queen's Univ., Belfast (LLB). Served Royal Air Force, 1941–47. Called to Bar, NI, 1952; Crown Prosecutor: Co. Fermanagh, 1970; Co. Tyrone, 1974; Co. Londonderry, 1976; Recorder of Belfast, 1995–97. Bencher, Inn of Court, N Ireland, 1972–78 and 1988–, Treasurer, 1977. Member, Standing Advisory Commn on Human Rights, 1974–78; Chairman, Pensions Appeal Tribunal, N Ireland, 1970–99. *Recreations:* golf, gardening. *Address:* 5 Grey Point, Helen's Bay, Co. Down, Northern Ireland BT19 1LE. *T:* (028) 9185 2249. *Clubs:* Royal Air Force; Royal Belfast Golf.

RUSSELL, Prof. James Knox, MD; ChB; FRCOG; Emeritus Professor of Obstetrics and Gynæcology, University of Newcastle upon Tyne, since 1982; Dean of Postgraduate Medicine, 1968–77; Consultant Obstetrician, Princess Mary Maternity Hospital, Newcastle upon Tyne, 1956–82, now Hon. Consultant; Consultant Gynæcologist, Royal Victoria Infirmary, Newcastle upon Tyne, 1956–82, now Hon. Consultant; *b* 5 Sept. 1919; *s* of James Russell, Aberdeen; *m* 1944, Cecilia V. Urquhart, MD, DCH, *o d* of Patrick Urquhart, MA; three *d*. *Educ:* Aberdeen Grammar School; University of Aberdeen. MB, ChB 1942, MD 1954, Aberdeen; MRCOG 1949; FRCOG 1958. Served War, 1943–46, as MO in RAF, UK and Western Europe. First Assistant to Prof. of Obstetrics and Gynæcology, Univ. of Durham, 1950; Senior Lecturer in Obstetrics and Gynæcology, Univ. of Durham, 1956; Prof., first at Durham, then at Newcastle upon Tyne, 1958–82. Hon. Obstetrician, MRC Unit on Reproduction and Growth; Examiner in Obstetrics and Gynæcology, Univs of London, Birmingham, Manchester, Belfast, Aberdeen, Liverpool, RCOG, CMB, Tripoli and Kuala Lumpur; Presiding Examiner, CMB, Newcastle upon Tyne; Consultant in human reproduction, WHO. Commonwealth Fund Fellow 1962. Visiting Professor: New York, 1974; South Africa, 1978; Kuala Lumpur, 1980, 1982; Oviedo, Spain, 1987; Graham Waite Meml Lectr, Amer. Coll. of Obstetricians and Gynaecologists, Dallas, 1982. *Publications:* Teenage Pregnancy: Medical, Social and Educational Aspects, 1982; various papers, editorials and articles on obstetrical and gynæcological subjects and medical education to learned journals, newspapers and magazines. *Recreations:* writing, gardening, curing and smoking bacon, eels, salmon, etc. *Address:* Newlands, Tranwell Woods, Morpeth, Northumberland NE61 6AG. *T:* (01670) 515666.

RUSSELL, Jeremy Jonathan; QC 1994; *b* 18 Dec. 1950; *s* of Sidney Thomas Russell and Maud Eugenie Russell; *m* 1987, Gillian Elizabeth Giles; one *s* one *d*. *Educ:* Watford Boys' GS; City of London Poly. (BA); LSE (LLM). Lectr in Law, City of London Poly., 1973–80; called to the Bar, Middle Temple, 1975; in practice, 1977–. Lloyd's Salvage Arbitrator, 2000. CEDR accredited mediator, 2001. *Recreations:* reading, gliding, classic cars. *Address:* 4 Essex Court, Temple, EC4Y 9AJ.

RUSSELL, John, CBE 1975; Art critic, The New York Times, since 1974 (Chief Art Critic, 1982–90); *b* 22 Jan. 1919; *o s* of Isaac James Russell and Harriet Elizabeth Atkins; *m* 1st, 1945, Alexandrine Apponyi (marr. diss., 1950); one *d*; 2nd, 1956, Vera Poliakoff (marr. diss., 1971; she *d* 1992); 3rd, 1975, Rosamond Bernier. *Educ:* St Paul's Sch.; Magdalen Coll., Oxford (MA). Hon. Attaché, Tate Gall., 1940–41; MOI, 1941–43; Naval Intell. Div., Admty, 1943–46. Regular contributor, The Sunday Times, 1945–, art critic, 1949–74. Mem. art panel, Arts Council, 1958–68. Organised Arts Council exhibns: Modigliani, 1964, Rouault, 1966 and Balthus, 1968 (all at Tate Gallery); Pop Art (with Suzi Gablik), 1969 (at the Hayward Gallery); organised Vuillard exhibn (Toronto, Chicago, San Francisco), 1971. Hon. Fellow, Royal Acad. of Arts, 1989; Mem., Amer. Acad. of Arts and Letters, 1996. Frank Jewett Mather Award (College Art Assoc.), 1979; Mitchell Prize for Art Criticism, 1984. Grand Medal of Honour (Austria), 1972; Officier de l'Ordre des Arts et des Lettres, 1975; Order of Merit, Fed. Repub. of Germany, 1982; Chevalier, Légion d'Honneur, 1986. *Publications:* books include: Shakespeare's Country, 1942; British Portrait Painters, 1945; Switzerland, 1950; Logan Pearsall Smith, 1950; Erich Kleiber, 1956; Paris, 1960, new and enlarged edn, 1983; Seurat, 1965; Private View (with Bryan Robertson and Lord Snowdon), 1965; Max Ernst, 1967; Henry Moore, 1968; Ben Nicholson, 1969; Pop Art Redefined (with Suzi Gablik), 1969; The World of Matisse, 1970; Francis Bacon, 1971; Edouard Vuillard, 1971; The Meanings of Modern Art, 1981, new and enlarged edn 1990; Reading Russell, 1989; London, 1994; Matisse: father and son, 1999. *Recreations:* reading, writing, Raimund (1790–1836). *Address:* 166 East 61st Street, New York, NY 10021, USA. *Clubs:* Century, Knickerbocker (New York).
See also N. T. Grimshaw.

RUSSELL, John Harry; Chairman and Chief Executive, Duport plc, 1981–86; *b* 21 Feb. 1926; *s* of Joseph Harry Russell and Nellie Annie Russell; *m* 1951, Iris Mary Cooke; one *s* one *d*. *Educ:* Halesowen Grammar Sch. FCA; CIMgt. War Service, RN. Joseph Lucas Ltd, 1948–52; Vono Ltd (Duport Gp Co.), 1952–59; Standard Motors Ltd, 1959–61; rejoined Duport Gp, 1961: Man. Dir, Duport Foundries Ltd, 1964; Dir, Duport Parent Bd, 1966; Chm., Burman & Sons Ltd (formerly part of Duport), 1968–72; Chief Exec., Duport Engrg Div., 1972–73; Dep. Gp Man. Dir, 1973–75; Gp Man. Dir, 1975–80, Dep. Chm., 1976–81, Duport Ltd. Chm., Blagg plc, 1994–95; non-exec. Dir, Birmingham Local Bd, Barclays Bank Ltd, 1976–88. Chm., Black Country Museum Trust Ltd, 1988–99. Liveryman, Worshipful Co. of Glaziers and Freeman and Citizen of London, 1976. *Recreations:* reading, music, antiques. *Address:* 442 Bromsgrove Road, Hunnington, Halesowen, West Midlands B62 0JL.

RUSSELL, Ken; film director since 1958; *b* 3 July 1927; *m* Shirley Kingdom (marr. diss. 1978); five *c*; *m* 1984, Vivian Jolly; one *s* one *d*; *m* 1992, Hetty Baines (marr. diss. 1997); one *s*. Merchant Navy, 1945; RAF, 1946–49. Ny Norsk Ballet, 1950; Garrick Players, 1951; free-lance photographer, 1951–57; Film Director, BBC, 1958–66; free-lance film director, 1966–. Vis. Prof. of Film Studies, Southampton Inst., 1996–. *Films for TV:* Elgar; Bartok; Debussy; Henri Rousseau; Isadora Duncan; Delius; Richard Strauss; Clouds of Glory; The Planets; Vaughan Williams; ABC of British Music (Emmy award); The Mystery of Dr Martinù; The Secret Life of Arnold Bax; Classic Widows; *television serial:* Lady Chatterley, 1993; *films:* French Dressing, 1964; The Billion Dollar Brain, 1967; Women in Love, 1969; The Music Lovers, 1970; The Devils, 1971; The Boy Friend, 1971; Savage Messiah, 1972; Mahler, 1973; Tommy, 1974; Lisztomania, 1975; Valentino, 1977; Altered States, 1981; Crimes of Passion, 1985; Gothic, 1987; (jtly) Aria, 1987; Salome's Last Dance, 1988; Lair of the White Worm, 1989; The Rainbow, 1989; Whore,

1991; Lion's Mouth, 2000; *opera:* The Rake's Progress, Florence, 1982; Madam Butterfly, Spoleto, 1983; La Bohème, Macerata, 1984; Faust, Vienna, 1985; Princess Ida, ENO, 1992; Salome, Bonn, 1993. Screen Writers Guild Award for TV films Elgar, Debussy, Isadora and Dante's Inferno. *Publications:* A British Picture (autobiog.), 1989; Fire Over England, 1993; Mike and Gaby's Space Gospel (novel), 1999. *Recreations:* music, walking.

RUSSELL, Sir Mark; *see* Russell, Sir R. M.

RUSSELL, Sir Mervyn; *see* Russell, Sir (Arthur) M.

RUSSELL, Prof. Michael Anthony Hamilton, FRCP, FRCPsych; Hon. Consultant and Head of Tobacco Research Section, National Addiction Centre, Institute of Psychiatry, University of London, 1997–March 2002, then Emeritus Consultant (Professor of Addiction, 1992–98, now Emeritus); *b* 9 March 1932; *s* of late James Hamilton Russell and of Hon. Kathleen Mary (*née* Gibson); *m* 1962, Audrey Ann Timms; two *s*. *Educ:* Diocesan Coll., Cape Town; University Coll., Oxford (BA Physiol. 1954; MA); Guy's Hosp., London (BM BCh 1957). FCP (SA) 1963; MRCP 1964, FRCP 1982; DPM 1968; FRCPsych 1980. Junior hospital appointments: Guy's Hosp., 1957–58; in Medicine, Cardiology and Pathology, Groote Schuur Hosp., Cape Town and King Edward VII Hosp., Durban, 1959–63; Sen. Med. Registrar, Groote Schuur Hosp., 1963–64; travel, incl. 6 months as Med. Registrar, Ruttonjee TB Sanatorium, Hong Kong, 1964–65; Trainee Registrar in Psychiatry, 1965–68, Sen. Registrar, 1968–69, Maudsley Hosp.; Institute of Psychiatry: Res. Worker, 1969–71; Lectr, 1971–73; Sen. Lectr, 1973–85; Reader, 1985–92. Hon. Consultant Psychiatrist: Maudsley Hosp., 1973–; UCH, 1996–. Mem., Ext. Scientific Staff, MRC, 1978–98; built up ICRF Health Behaviour Unit at Inst. of Psychiatry, 1988–96, moved to UCL, 1996, Hon. Dir, 1988–97, Hon. Consultant, 1997–. Invited Lect., Royal Stat. Soc., 1974; Robert Philip Lect., RCPE, 1978. No-tobacco Medal, WHO, 1989; Alton Ochsner Award, Amer. Coll. Chest Physicians, 1996; Ove Ferno Award, Soc. Res. on Nicotine and Tobacco, 1998. *Publications:* numerous contribs to scientific books and jls on: nicotine psychopharmacology, pharmacokinetics and dependence; regulation of nicotine intake by smokers; motivational typologies of smoking; effect of cigarette prices on consumption; smoking in children; passive smoking; less harmful cigarettes; nicotine replacement and other treatments in clinic, workplace, primary care and medical practice settings. *Recreations:* reading, travel, watersports, oil paintings. *Address:* 14 Court Lane Gardens, Dulwich, SE21 7DZ.

RUSSELL, Michael William; Member (SNP) Scotland South, Scottish Parliament, since 1999; *b* 9 Aug. 1953; *s* of late Thomas Stevenson Russell and of Jean Marjorie Russell (*née* Haynes); *m* 1980, Cathleen Ann Macaskill; one *s*. *Educ:* Marr Coll., Troon; Edinburgh Univ. (MA 1974). Creative Producer, Church of Scotland, 1974–77; Dir, Cinema Sgire, Western Isles Islands Council, 1977–81; Founder and Dir, Celtic Film and Television Fest., 1981–83; Exec. Dir, Network Scotland Ltd, 1983–91; Dir, Eala Bhan Ltd, 1991–; Chief Exec., SNP, 1994–99. Opposition front bench spokesman for: Parlt, 1999–2000; children and educn, 2000–. *Publications:* (ed) Glasgow: the book, 1990; (ed) Edinburgh: a celebration, 1992; A Poem of Remote Lives: the enigma of Werner Kissling, 1997; In Waiting: travels in the shadow of Edwin Muir, 1998. *Recreation:* tending my Argyll garden. *Address:* Feorlean, Glendaruel, Argyll PA22 3AH.

RUSSELL, Muir; *see* Russell, A. M. G.

RUSSELL, Sir Muir; *see* Russell, Sir A. M.

RUSSELL, Ven. Norman Atkinson; Archdeacon of Berkshire, since 1998; *b* 7 Aug. 1943; *s* of Norman Gerald Russell and Olive Muriel Russell (*née* Williamson); *m* 1974, Victoria Christine Jasinska; two *s*. *Educ:* Royal Belfast Academical Instn; Churchill Coll., Cambridge (BA 1965; MA 1969); London Coll. of Divinity (BD London 1970). Articled Clerk, Coopers & Lybrand, 1966–67; ordained deacon, 1970, priest, 1971; Curate: Christ Church with Emmanuel, Clifton, Bristol, 1970–74; Christ Church, Cockfosters, and pt-time Chaplain, Middx Poly., 1974–77; Rector, Harwell with Chilton, 1977–84; Priest in Charge: St James, Gerrards Cross, 1984–88; St James, Fulmer, 1985–88; Rector, Gerrards Cross and Fulmer, 1988–98; RD, Amersham, 1996–98. Vice-Chm., Ecumenical Council for Corporate Responsibility, 1999–. *Publication:* Censorship, 1972. *Recreations:* downland walking, watching Rugby football. *Address:* Foxglove House, Love Lane, Donnington, Newbury, Berks RG14 2JG. *T:* (01635) 552820.

RUSSELL, Pam; *see* Ayres, P.

RUSSELL, Hon. Sir Patrick; *see* Russell, Hon. Sir T. P.

RUSSELL, Prof. Sir Peter (Edward Lionel Russell), Kt 1995; DLitt; FBA 1977; King Alfonso XIII Professor of Spanish Studies, Oxford, 1953–81; *b* 24 Oct. 1913; *er s* of Hugh Bernard Wheeler and late Rita Muriel (*née* Russell), Christchurch, NZ; adopted surname Russell by deed poll, 1929. *Educ:* Cheltenham College; Queen's College, Oxford (DLitt 1981; Hon. Fellow, 1990). Lecturer of St John's College, 1937–53 and Queen's College, 1938–45. Enlisted, 1940; commissioned (Intelligence Corps) Dec. 1940; Temp. Lt-Col, 1945; specially employed in Caribbean, W Africa and SE Asia, 1942–46. Fellow of Queen's College, 1946–53, and Univ. Lectr in Spanish Studies, 1946–53; Fellow of Exeter Coll., 1953–81, Emeritus Fellow, 1981; Taylorian Special Lectr, Oxford, 1983; Visiting Professor: Univ. of Virginia, 1982; Univ. of Texas, 1983, 1987; Johns Hopkins Univ., 1986; Vanderbilt Univ., 1987. Member: Portuguese Academy of History, 1956; Real Academia de Buenas Letras, Barcelona, 1972; UGC Cttee on Latin-American Studies in British Univs, 1962–64. FRHistS. Premio Antonio de Nebrija, Univ. of Salamanca, 1989. Comdr, Order of Isabel the Catholic (Spain), 1989; Comdr, Order of the Infante Dom Henrique (Portugal), 1993. *Publications:* As Fontes de Fernão Lopes, 1941; The English Intervention in Spain and Portugal in the Time of Edward III and Richard II, 1955 (Portuguese edn 2000); Prince Henry the Navigator, 1960; (with D. M. Rogers) Hispanic Manuscripts and Books in the Bodleian and Oxford College Libraries, 1962; (ed) Spain: a Companion to Spanish Studies, 1973, Spanish edn, 1982; Temas de la Celestina y otros estudios (del Cid al Quijote), 1978; Prince Henry the Navigator: the rise and fall of a culture hero, 1984; Traducción y traductores en la Península Ibérica 1400–1550, 1985; Cervantes, 1985; La Celestina, 1991; Portugal, Spain and the African Atlantic 1343–1490, 1995; Prince Henry the Navigator: a life, 2000; articles and reviews in Modern Language Review, Medium Aevum, Bulletin of Hispanic Studies, etc. *Recreation:* reading travel literature. *Address:* 23 Belsyre Court, Woodstock Road, Oxford OX2 6HU. *T:* (01865) 556086. *Club:* Oxford and Cambridge.

RUSSELL, Most Rev. Philip Welsford Richmond; *b* 21 Oct. 1919; *s* of Leslie Richmond Russell and Clarice Louisa Russell (*née* Welsford); *m* 1945, Violet Eirene, *d* of Ven. Dr. O. J. Hogarth, sometime Archdeacon of the Cape; one *s* three *d*. *Educ:* Durban High Sch.; Rhodes Univ. College (Univ. of South Africa), BA 1948; LTh 1950. Served War of 1939–45; MBE 1943. Deacon, 1950; Priest, 1951; Curate, St Peter's, Maritzburg, 1950–54; Vicar: Greytown, 1954–57; Ladysmith, 1957–61; Kloof, 1961–66; Archdeacon of Pinetown, 1961–66; Bishop Suffragan of Capetown, 1966–70; Bishop of Port Elizabeth, 1970–74; Bishop of Natal, 1974–81; Archbishop of Cape Town and Metropolitan of Southern Africa, 1981–86. *Recreation:* walking. *Address:* 400 Currie Road, Durban, Natal 4001, South Africa.

RUSSELL, Robert Christopher Hamlyn, CBE 1981; formerly Director, Hydraulics Research Station, Department of the Environment (formerly Ministry of Technology), 1965–81; *b* Singapore, 1921; *s* of late Philip Charles and Hilda Gertrude Russell; *m* 1950, Cynthia Mary Roberts; one *s* two *d*. *Educ:* Stowe; King's Coll., Cambridge. Asst Engineer: BTH Co., Rugby, 1944; Dunlop Rubber Co., 1946; Sen. Scientific Officer, later PSO, then SPSO, in Hydraulics Research Station, 1949–65. Visiting Prof., Univ. of Strathclyde, 1967. *Publications:* Waves and Tides, 1951; papers on civil engineering hydraulics. *Address:* 29 St Mary's Street, Wallingford, Oxfordshire OX10 0ET. *T:* (01491) 837323.

RUSSELL, Robert Edward, (Bob); MP (Lib Dem) Colchester, since 1997; *b* 31 March 1946; *s* of Ewart Russell and Muriel Russell (*née* Sawdy); *m* 1967, Audrey Blandon; twin *s* one *d* (and one *d* decd). *Educ:* Myland Primary Sch., Colchester; St Helena Secondary Modern Sch., Colchester; NE Essex Technical Coll. Reporter, Essex County Standard and Colchester Gazette, 1963–66; News Editor, Braintree & Witham Times, 1966–68; Editor, Maldon & Burnham Standard, 1968–69; Sub-Editor, London Evening News, 1969–72; Sub-Editor, London Evening Standard, 1972–73; Press Officer, Post Office Telecommunications, subseq. British Telecom (Eastern Reg.), 1973–85; Publicity Officer, Univ. of Essex, 1986–97. Mem., Colchester BC, 1971– (Lab 1971–81, SDP 1981–88, Lib Dem 1988–) (Mayor, 1986–87). *Recreations:* promoting the interests of the town of Colchester, watching Colchester United. *Address:* Corporate House, Queen Street, Colchester CO1 2PG. *Club:* Colchester United Football.

RUSSELL, Sir (Robert) Mark, KCMG 1985 (CMG 1977); HM Diplomatic Service, retired; *b* 3 Sept. 1929; *s* of Sir Robert E. Russell, CSI, CIE; *m* 1954, Virginia Mary Rogers; two *s* two *d*. *Educ:* Trinity Coll., Glenalmond; Exeter Coll., Oxford (MA). Hon. Mods cl. 2, Lit. Hum. cl. 1. Royal Artillery, 1952–54; FO, 1954–56; 3rd, later 2nd Sec., HM Legation, Budapest, 1956–58; 2nd Sec., Berne, 1958–61; FO, 1961–65; 1st Sec., 1962; 1st Sec. and Head of Chancery, Kabul, 1965–67; 1st Sec., DSAO, 1967–69; Counsellor, 1969; Dep. Head of Personnel (Ops) Dept, FCO, 1969–70; Commercial Counsellor, Bucharest, 1970–73; Counsellor, Washington, 1974–78, and Head of Chancery, 1977–78; Asst Under Sec. of State, FCO and Dep. Chief Clerk and Chief Inspector, HM Diplomatic Service, 1978–82; Ambassador to Turkey, 1983–86; Dep. Under-Sec. of State (Chief Clerk), FCO, 1986–89. Chairman: Margaret Blackwood Housing Assoc., 1990–98; Scottish Trust for the Physically Disabled, 1990–98; Centre for Maritime and Industrial Safety Technol. Ltd, 1992–. *Recreations:* travel, music. *Address:* 20 Meadow Place, Edinburgh EH9 1JR. *Club:* New (Edinburgh).

RUSSELL, (Ronald) Christopher (Gordon), FRCS; Consultant Surgeon: Middlesex Hospital, since 1975; King Edward VII Hospital, since 1985; *b* 15 May 1940; *s* of Rognvald Gordon Russell and Doris Isa Russell (*née* Troup); *m* 1965, Mary Ruth Pitcher; two *s* (and one *s* decd). *Educ:* Epsom College; Middlesex Hosp. Med. Sch. (MB BS, MS). Sen. Lectr in Surgery, St Mary's Hosp., 1973–75. Member Council: Med. Defence Union, 1996–; RCS, 1999– (Chm., Ct of Examnrs, 1997–99); Pres., Assoc. of Upper Gastrointestinal Surgeons, 1998–2000; Pres., Assoc. of Surgeons of GB and Ire., 2001–May 2002. Chm., British Jl of Surgery Soc. Ltd, 1996–; Associate Editor, 1978, Co-Editor, 1986–91, British Jl of Surgery; Gen. Editor, Operative Surgery, 1986–. *Publications:* (ed) Recent Advances in Surgery, vol. XI 1982, vol. XII 1985, vol. XIII 1991; (ed jtly) Bailey & Love Textbook of Surgery, 1991–; numerous contribs to surgical and gastroenterological jls. *Recreation:* travel. *Address:* 149 Harley Street, W1G 6DE; Little Orchards, 6 Layters Way, Gerrards Cross SL9 7QY. *T:* (01753) 882264. *Club:* Royal Society of Medicine.

RUSSELL, Rudolf Rosenfeld; a Recorder of the Crown Court, 1980–97; *b* 5 Feb. 1925; *s* of Robert and Johanna Rosenfeld; *m* 1952, Eva Maria Jaray; one *s*. *Educ:* Bryanston Sch.; Worcester Coll., Oxford (MA). Service in RAF, 1943–46. Called to the Bar, Middle Temple, 1950. *Recreations:* walking, music, skiing. *Address:* 197 Roehampton Lane, SW15 4HN. *T:* (020) 8288 9925.

RUSSELL, Stephen George; Chief Executive, The Boots Co., since 2000; *b* 13 March 1945; *s* of Llandel and Olive Russell; *m* 1969, Elizabeth Jane Brook; one *s* one *d*. *Educ:* Tiffin Sch., Kingston upon Thames; Trinity Hall, Cambridge (BA Hons Classics). Joined Boots 1967; Dir of Merchandise, Boots The Chemists, 1988–92; Managing Dir, Do It All Ltd, 1992–95; Man. Dir, Boots The Chemists, 1995–2000; Jt Gp Man. Dir, Boots Co., 1997–2000. Non-executive Director: Woolwich plc, 1998–2000; Barclays Bank plc, 2000–. *Recreations:* sport, classical music, opera, reading. *Address:* Boots Co. plc, 1 Thane Road West, Beeston, Notts NG90 4HQ. *Club:* Hawks (Cambridge).

RUSSELL, Terence Francis; Sheriff of North Strathclyde at Kilmarnock, since 1983; *b* 12 April 1931; *s* of Robert Russell and Catherine Cusker Russell; *m* 1965, Mary Ann Kennedy; two *d*. *Educ:* Glasgow Univ. (BL). Qualified as Solicitor, 1955; practised in Glasgow, 1955–58 and 1963–81; Solicitor in High Court, Bombay, 1958–63. Sheriff of N Strathclyde, and of Grampian, Highland and Islands, 1981–83. *Recreations:* gardening, travel.

RUSSELL, Thomas, CMG 1980 CBE 1970 (OBE 1963); HM Overseas Civil Service, retired; Representative of the Cayman Islands in UK, 1982–2000; *b* 27 May 1920; *s* of late Thomas Russell, OBE, MC and Margaret Thomson Russell; *m* 1951, Andrée Irma Désfossés (*d* 1989); one *s*. *Educ:* Hawick High Sch.; St Andrews Univ.; Peterhouse, Cambridge. MA St Andrews; Dip. Anthrop. Cantab. War Service, Cameronians (Scottish Rifles), 1941; 5th Bn (Scottish), Parachute Regt, 1943: served in N Africa and Italy; POW, 1944; Captain 1945; OC Parachute Trng Company, 1946. Cambridge Univ., 1946–47. Colonial Admin. Service, 1948; District Comr, British Solomon Is Protectorate, 1948; Asst Sec., Western Pacific High Commn, Fiji, 1951; District Comr, British Solomon Is Protectorate, 1954–56; seconded Colonial Office, 1956–57; Admin. Officer Class A, 1956; Dep. Financial Sec., 1962; Financial Sec., 1965; Chief Sec. to W Pacific High Commn, 1970–74; Governor of the Cayman Islands, 1974–81. Chairman: Welfare Cttee, British Commonwealth Ex Services League, 1993–; Dependent Territories Assoc., 1997–98; Mem. Council, Pacific Islands Soc. of UK and Ire., 1986– (Chm., 1982–86). FRAI. *Recreations:* anthropology, archæology. *Address:* Hassendean, Gattonside, Melrose, TD6 9NA. *Clubs:* Royal Commonwealth Society, Caledonian.

RUSSELL, Rt Hon. Sir (Thomas) Patrick, Kt 1980; PC 1987; a Lord Justice of Appeal, 1987–96; *b* 30 July 1926; *s* of late Sidney Arthur Russell and Elsie Russell; *m* 1951, Doreen (Janie) Ireland; two *d*. *Educ:* Urmston Grammar Sch.; Manchester Univ. (LLB). Served in Intelligence Corps and RASC, 1945–48. Called to Bar, Middle Temple, 1949, Bencher, 1978; Prosecuting Counsel to the Post Office (Northern Circuit), 1961–70; Asst Recorder of Bolton, 1963–70; Recorder of Barrow-in-Furness, 1970–71; QC 1971; a Recorder of the Crown Court, 1972–80; Leader, 1978–80, Presiding Judge, 1983–87, Northern Circuit; a Judge of the High Court of Justice, QBD, 1980–86. A Justice of the Court of

Appeal, Gibraltar, 1998–99. Mem. Senate, Inns of Court and Bar, 1978–80. Mem., Lord Justice James Cttee on Distribution of Criminal Business, 1973–76. Pres., Manchester and Dist Medico-Legal Soc., 1978–79 (Patron, 1987); Vice-Pres., Lancs CCC, 1980–98 and 2001– (Pres., 1999–2001). Hon. LLD Manchester, 1988. *Recreation:* cricket. *Address:* Oakfield, 65 Crofts Bank Road, Urmston, Manchester M41 0UB.

RUSSELL, William Martin, (Willy); author since 1971; *b* 23 Aug. 1947; *s* of William and Margery Russell; *m* 1969, Ann Seagroatt; one *s* two *d.* *Educ:* St Katharine's Coll. of Educn, Liverpool, 1970–73 (Cert. of Educn). Ladies' Hairdresser, 1963–69; Teacher, 1973–74; Fellow in Creative Writing, Manchester Polytechnic, 1977–78. Founder Mem., and Dir, Quintet Films; Hon. Dir, Liverpool Playhouse. *Theatre:* Blind Scouse (3 short plays), 1971–72; When the Reds (adaptation), 1972; John, Paul, George, Ringo and Bert (musical), 1974; Breezeblock Park, 1975; One for the Road, 1976; Stags and Hens, 1978; Educating Rita, 1979; Blood Brothers (musical), 1983; Our Day Out (musical), 1983; Shirley Valentine, 1986; *television plays:* King of the Castle, 1972; Death of a Young, Young Man, 1972; Break In (for schools), 1974; Our Day Out, 1976; Lies (for schools), 1977; Daughters of Albion, 1978; Boy with Transistor Radio (for schools), 1979; One Summer (series), 1980; *radio play:* I Read the News Today (for schools), 1976; *screenplays:* Band on the Run, 1979 (not released); Educating Rita, 1981; Shirley Valentine, 1988; Dancing Through the Dark, 1989. Hon. MA Open Univ., 1983; Hon. DLit Liverpool, 1990. *Publications:* Breezeblock Park, 1978; One for the Road, 1980, rev. edn 1985; Educating Rita, 1981; Our Day Out, 1984; Stags and Hens, 1985; Blood Brothers, 1985 (also pubd as short non-musical version for schools, 1984); Shirley Valentine, 1989; The Wrong Boy (novel), 2000; several other plays included in general collections of plays; songs and poetry. *Recreations:* playing the guitar, composing songs, gardening, cooking. *Address:* c/o Casarotto Company Ltd, 60–66 Wardour Street, W1V 3HP. *T:* (020) 7287 4450. *Club:* Athenæum (Liverpool).

RUSSELL BEALE, Simon; *see* Beale.

RUSSELL-DAVIS, John Darelan, FRICS; chartered surveyor, retired; *b* 23 Dec. 1912; *s* of Edward David Darelan Davis, FRCS, and Alice Mildred (*née* Russell); *m* 1st, 1938, Barbarina Elizabeth Graham Arnould (*d* 1985); one *s* one *d*; 2nd, 1986, Gaynor, *widow* of Lt-Col A. V. Brooke-Webb, RA. *Educ:* Stowe Sch.; Germany; Coll. of Estate Management, London. FRICS 1934. Served War, HAC, 1939; commnd RA, 1940; Captain 1942; mentioned in despatches, 1945. Partner, C. P. Whiteley & Son, Chartered Surveyors, 1938; Sen. Partner, Whiteley, Ferris & Puckridge, and Kemsley, Whiteley & Ferris, City of London, 1948–72. Mem., Lands Tribunal, 1972–77. Royal Instn of Chartered Surveyors: formerly Mem. Council (twice); Chm., City branch, 1959; Hon. Treasurer, Benevolent Fund. Mem., East Grinstead UDC, 1957–60 (Vice-Chm., 1960). Formerly: Mem. Council, Wycombe Abbey Sch.; Trustee, Cordwainer and Bread Street Foundn; Mem. Court, Turners Co. (Renter-Warden, 1975). *Recreation:* Somerset and Dorset countryside. *Address:* 171 Goose Hill, Bower Hinton, Martock, Somerset TA12 6LJ. *T:* (01935) 822307. *Clubs:* Army and Navy; Somerset CC.

RUSSELL-JOHNSTON, family name of **Baron Russell-Johnston.**

RUSSELL-JOHNSTON, Baron *cr* 1997 (Life Peer), of Minginish in Highlands; **David Russell Russell-Johnston,** Kt 1985; *b* 28 July 1932; *s* of late David Knox Johnston and Georgina Margaret Gerrie Russell; name changed to Russell-Johnston by Deed Poll, 1997; *m* 1967, Joan Graham Menzies; three *s.* *Educ:* Carbost Public Sch.; Portree High Sch.; Edinburgh Univ. (MA). Commissioned into Intelligence Corps (Nat. Service), 1958; subseq., Moray House Coll. of Educn until 1961; taught in Liberton Secondary Sch., 1961–63. Research Asst, Scottish Liberal Party, 1963–64. MP (L 1964–88, LibDem 1988–97) Inverness, 1964–83, Inverness, Nairn and Lochaber, 1983–97. Mem., Select Cttee of Privileges, 1988–92; Lib Dem spokesman: on foreign affairs, 1988–89; on European Community affairs, 1988–97; on East-West relations, 1992–94; on Central and Eastern Europe, 1994–97. Chm., Scottish Liberal Party, 1970–74 (Vice-Chm., 1965–70), Leader, 1974–88; Dep. Leader, Social and Liberal Democrats, 1988–92; Pres., Scottish Liberal Democrats, 1988–94. Mem., UK Delegn to European Parlt, 1973–75 and 1976–79, Vice Pres., Political Cttee, 1976–79; Mem., UK Delegn to Council of Europe and WEU, 1988; Council of Europe: Chm., Cttee on Culture and Educn, 1996–97; Ldr, Liberal, Democrat and Reform Gp, 1994; Pres., Parly Assembly, 1999–. Contested (L) Highlands and Islands, European Parly elecn, 1979, 1984. Chm., All Party Scottish Gaelic Parly Gp; Vice Chm., Europe Gp; Vice-President: Liberal Gp; European Lib Dem and Reform Parties, 1990–92; Liberal Internat., 1994–; Secretary: UK-Falkland Is Parly Gp; British–Hong Kong Parly Gp; Treasurer, All Party Photography Gp. Mem., Royal Commission on Local Govt in Scotland, 1966–69. *Publications:* (pamphlet) Highland Development, 1964; (pamphlet) To Be a Liberal, 1972; Scottish Liberal Party Conf. Speeches, 1979 and 1987. *Recreations:* reading, photography, shinty (Vice Chief, Camanachd Assoc., 1987–90). *Address:* House of Lords, SW1A 0PW. *Club:* Scottish Liberal (Edinburgh).

RUSSELL-JONES, Maj. Gen. (Peter) John, OBE 1988; Army Adviser to BAE SYSTEMS, since 2001; *b* 31 May 1948; *s* of Peter Rathbone Russell-Jones and Margaret Silis Russell-Jones; *m* 1976, Stella Margaret Barrett; one *s* one *d.* *Educ:* Wellington Coll.; RMCS (BScEng Hons 1972). Commnd RE, 1968; Regtl duty, 1972–79; Army Staff Coll., 1979–80; MA to Master Gen. of the Ordnance, 1986–88; CO 23 Engr Regt, 1988–90; Col, Defence Policy, MoD, 1990–91; Comdt, Royal Mil. Sch. of Engrg, 1992–95; rcds, 1995; Dir, Internat. Orgns, MoD, 1996–97; ACDS, Operational Requirements (Land Systems), MoD, 1997–99; Capability Manager (Manoeuvre), MoD, 1999–2001. *Recreations:* sport, military history, travel, rock and roll, family. *Address:* Regimental HQ RE, Brompton Barracks, Chatham, Kent ME4 4UG.

RUSSELL-SMITH, Penelope, LVO 2000; Press Secretary to the Queen, since 2000; *b* 22 oct. 1956; *d* of Denham William Russell-Smith and Barbara Cynthia Russell-Smith. *Educ:* Sherborne Sch. for Girls; Girton Coll., Cambridge (MA). Dep. Editor, Whitaker's Almanack, 1980–81; Editor of Navy and Army publications, MoD, 1982–84; MoD Press Office, 1984–88; Chief Press Officer, Dept of Transport, 1988–90; on secondment as Press Officer, EU Desk, News Dept, FCO, 1990–93; Asst Press Sec., 1993–97, Dep. Press Sec., 1997–2000, to the Queen. *Recreations:* embroidery, walking, holidaying without a mobile phone. *Address:* c/o Press Office, Buckingham Palace, SW1A 1AA. *T:* (020) 7930 4832.

RUSSELL VICK, Arnold Oughtred; *see* Vick.

RUSSILL, Patrick Joseph; Director of Music, London Oratory, since 1999; Head of Choral Direction and Church Music, since 1997, and Professor of Organ, since 1999, Royal Academy of Music; *b* 9 Sept. 1953; *e s* of John Leonard Russill and Vera Mary Russill (*née* Clarke); *m* 1979, Jane Mary Rogers; two *s* three *d.* *Educ:* Shaftesbury Grammar Sch.; New Coll., Oxford (Organ Schol.; BA 1st Cl. Hons 1975; MA). ARCO 1971. Asst Organist, 1976–77, Organist, 1977–99, London Oratory; Dir, Oxford Chamber Choir, 1976–79; organist for Papal Mass, Wembley Stadium, 1982; Prof. of Acad. Studies, 1982–87, Hd of Ch Music, 1987–97, RAM; Director: London Oratory Jun. Choir, 1984–; Europa Singers of London, 1985–89. RFH recital début, 1986; appearances as organist and conductor in UK, Europe, Near East and Asia; has made recordings. Visiting Lecturer: St George's Coll., Jerusalem, 1994–95; Malmö Coll. of Music, Sweden, 1994; Vis. Lectr, 1999, Vis. Prof. of Choral Direction, 2001–, Leipzig Hochschule für Musik und Theater. Ext. Examr, UEA, 1991–97; Ext. Moderator, Archbps' Cert., Guild of Ch Musicians, 1997–. Mem. Council, RCO, 1996–. Member Committee: Organ Adv. Gp, Soc. of St Gregory, 1978–; Ch Music Soc., 1990–; Churches Initiative for Music Educn, 1993–; Organists' Benevolent League, 1994–. Trustee: Friends of St Marylebone Music, London, 1993–; Nicholas Danby Trust, 1998–. Organ restoration consultant, incl. St Dominic's Priory, London, 1992, Ely Cathedral, 1997–2001. Hon. Patron, Herbert Howells Soc., 1993. Hon. RAM 1993 (Hon. ARAM 1989); Hon. FGCM 1997. *Publications:* (musical ed.) The Catholic Hymn Book, 1998; (contrib.) The Cambridge Companion to the Organ, 1998; (ed) Sweelinck and Howells choral works; contrib. articles and reviews in Gramophone, Musical Times, Organists' Rev., Choir and Organ, British Inst. Organ Studies Jl, RCO Year Book. *Recreations:* family photography, rural open air. *Address:* 65 Sandford Avenue, Wood Green, N22 5EJ.

RUSSON, David, CPhys, FInstP; Deputy Chief Executive, British Library, 1996–2001; *b* 12 June 1944; *s* of Thomas Charles Russon and Violet Russon (*née* Jarvis); *m* 1967, Kathleen Mary Gregory; one *s* two *d.* *Educ:* Wellington Grammar Sch.; University College London (BSc); Univ. of York. CPhys, FInstP 2000. Various appts, Office for Scientific and Technical Information, DES, 1969–74; British Library: R & D Dept, 1974–75; Lending Div., 1975–85; Dir, Document Supply Centre, 1985–88; Dir Gen., Sci., Technol. and Industry, later Boston Spa, 1988–96; Mem., British Liby Bd, 1988–2001. Pres., Internat. Council for Scientific and Technical Information, 1995–2001 (Vice Pres., 1992–95). FRSA; FIInfSc. *Publications:* contribs to professional jls of library and inf. science. *Recreations:* golf, village tennis and badminton. *Address:* March House, Tollerton, York YO61 1QQ. *T:* (01347) 838253.

RUST, Susan Esther; *see* Golombok, S. E.

RUSTON, Rt Rev. John Harry Gerald, OGS; Bishop of St Helena, 1991–99; *b* 1 Oct. 1929; *s* of late Alfred Francis Gerald Ruston and Constance Mary (*née* Symonds). *Educ:* Berkhamsted Sch.; Sidney Sussex Coll., Cambridge (BA 1952; MA 1956); Ely Theol Coll. Ordained deacon 1954, priest 1955; joined OGS, 1955; Asst Curate, St Andrew's, Leicester, 1954–57; Tutor, Cuddesdon Coll., Oxford, 1957–61; Asst Curate, All Saints, Cuddesdon, 1957–61; Asst Priest, St Francis, Sekhukhuniland, Transvaal, dio. of Pretoria, 1962–70; Principal, St Francis's Coll., Sekhukhuniland, 1967–70; Canon, Pretoria, 1968–76; Sub-Dean, Pretoria, 1970–76; Archdeacon of Bloemfontein, 1976–83; Warden, Community of St Michael and All Angels, and Chaplain, St Michael's Sch., Bloemfontein, 1976–83; consecrated Bishop, 1983; Bishop Suffragan, Pretoria, 1983–91. *Recreation:* music (composition and adaptation for 3-part singing). *Address:* Braehead House, Auburn Road, Kenilworth, Cape Town 7708, South Africa.

RUTHERFORD, Andrew; DL; **His Honour Judge Rutherford;** a Circuit Judge, since 1995; *b* 25 March 1948; *s* of Robert Mark Rutherford and Alison Wellington (*née* Clark); *m* 1994, Lucy Elizabeth Bosworth; two *d.* *Educ:* Clifton Coll.; Exeter Univ. (LLB). Called to the Bar, Middle Temple, 1970; Asst Recorder, 1990–93; Recorder, 1993–95. DL Somerset, 2000. *Address:* c/o Lord Chancellor's Department, Western Circuit Office, Bridge House, Sion Place, Clifton, Bristol BS8 4BN. *Club:* Bath and County.

RUTHERFORD, Derek Thomas Jones, CBE 1994; FCA; Commissioner for Administration and Finance, Forestry Commission, 1984–90; financial and management accounting consultant, 1990–96; *b* 9 April 1930; *s* of late Sydney Watson Rutherford and Elsie Rutherford; *m* 1956, Kathleen Robinson; one *s* four *d.* *Educ:* Doncaster Grammar School. Practising accountant and auditor, 1955–59; Company Sec./Accountant, P. Platt & Sons, 1959–61; Retail Accountant, MacFisheries, 1961–63; Factory Management Accountant, then Company Systems Manager, T. Wall & Son (Ice Cream), 1963–70; Dir of Finance, Alfa-Laval Co., 1970–74; Group Financial Dir, Oxley Printing Group, 1974; HMSO: Chief Accountant, Publications Group, 1975–76; Dir, Management Accounting Project, 1976–77; Dir of Finance and Planning Div., 1977–83; Principal Estabt and Finance Officer, 1983–84. *Recreations:* reading, gardening, home computing. *Address:* 3 Berkeley Gardens, Bury St Edmunds, Suffolk IP33 3JW. *T:* (01284) 767279. *Club:* Royal Air Force.

RUTHERFORD, Frederick John; District Judge (Magistrates' Courts), Humberside, since 2001; *b* Kelso, 6 Aug. 1954; *s* of Frederick George Rutherford and late Isabella Rutherford; *m* 1997, Jayne Louise Curry; one *s* two *d.* *Educ:* Heckmondwike Grammar Sch.; Leicester Univ. (LLB Hons). Articled Clerk, 1976–78, Asst Solicitor, 1978–80, Partner, 1980–89, Inesons, Solicitors, Cleckheaton; Partner, Jordans, Solicitors, Dewsbury, 1989–2000. *Recreations:* reading, walking, gardening, fly fishing.

RUTHERFORD, (Herman) Graham, CBE 1966; QPM 1957; DL; Chief Constable of Surrey, 1956–68; retired, 1968; *b* 3 April 1908; *m* 1940, Dorothy Weaver (*d* 1987); two *s* one *d* (and one *s* decd). *Educ:* Grammar School, Consett, County Durham. Metropolitan Police, 1929–45; Chief Constable: of Oxfordshire, 1945–54; of Lincolnshire, 1954–56. Barrister, Gray's Inn, 1941. Served Army, Allied Military Government, 1943–45, Lt-Colonel. DL Surrey, 1968. *Address:* Hankley Farm, Elstead, Surrey GU8 6LJ. *T:* (01252) 702200.

RUTHERFORD, Jessica Marianne Fernande, FSA; Head of Libraries and Museums, and Director of the Royal Pavilion (Brighton and Hove), since 1996; *b* 7 Feb. 1949; *d* of Raymond Denys Rutherford and Simone Genvieve (*née* Michaud). *Educ:* Brighton and Hove High Sch.; Manchester Univ. (BA Hons Hist. of Art); Sussex Univ. (PGCE). V&A Mus., 1974; Royal Pavilion, Art Gallery and Museums, Brighton: Keeper of Decorative Art, 1974–85; Principal Keeper, Royal Pavilion, 1985–87; Asst Dir (Collections), 1987–92; Head of Mus and Dir, Royal Pavilion, 1992–96. Mem. Steering Cttee, Nat. Report on Mus. Educn, Dept of Nat. Heritage, 1994–. Decorative Arts Society: Sec., 1975–85; Trustee, 1992–; Mem. Council, Charleston Trust, 1992–; Sec. to Trustees and Governors, Friends of Royal Pavilion, Art Gall. and Museums, 1992–. Sussex University: Mem. Council, 1995–; Dir, Gardner Arts Centre, 1996–98; Trustee, The Barlow Collection, 1996–. FRSA 1998. *Publications:* Art Nouveau, Art Deco and the Thirties: the furniture collections at Brighton Museum, 1983; (jtly) Art Nouveau, Art Deco and the Thirties: the ceramic, glass and metalwork collections at Brighton Museum, 1986; The Royal Pavilion: the palace of George IV, 1995; *chapters in:* James Tissot, 1984; The Crace Firm of Royal Decorators 1768–1900, 1990; Country House Lighting, 1992; articles and reviews for learned jls. *Recreations:* travel, historic houses, film. *Address:* The Royal Pavilion, Brighton, E Sussex BN1 1EE. *T:* (01273) 292560.

RUTHERFORD, Thomas, CBE 1982; Chairman, North Eastern Electricity Board, 1977–89, retired; *b* 4 June 1924; *s* of Thomas and Catherine Rutherford; *m* 1950, Joyce Foreman; one *s* one *d.* *Educ:* Tynemouth High Sch.; King's Coll., Durham Univ. BSc(Hons); CEng, FIEE. Engrg Trainee, subseq. Research Engr, A Reyrolle & Co. Ltd,

Hebburn-on-Tyne, 1943–49; North Eastern Electricity Bd: various engrg and commercial appts, 1949–61; Personal Asst to Chm., 1961–63; Area Commercial Engr, then Area Engr, Tees Area, 1964–69; Dep. Commercial Man., 1969–70; Commercial Man., 1970–72; Chief Engr, 1972–73; Dep. Chm., 1973–75; Chm., SE Electricity Board, 1975–77. *Address:* 76 Beach Road, Tynemouth, Northumberland NE30 2QW. *T:* (0191) 257 1775.

RUTHNASWAMY, Elizabeth Kuanghu, (Mrs Vincent Ruthnaswamy); *see* Han Suyin.

RUTHVEN; *see* Hore-Ruthven, family name of Earl of Gowrie.

RUTHVEN OF CANBERRA, Viscount; Patrick Leo Brer Hore-Ruthven; Operations Director, Camphor Ltd; *b* 4 Feb. 1964; *s* and *heir* of 2nd Earl of Gowrie, *qv*; *m* 1990, Julie Goldsmith; one *s*. *Heir: s* Hon. Heathcote Patrick Cornelius Hore-Ruthven, *b* 28 May 1990.

RUTLAND, 11th Duke of, *cr* 1703; **David Charles Robert Manners;** Marquess of Granby 1703; Earl of Rutland 1525; Baron Manners of Haddon 1679; Baron Roos of Belvoir 1896; *b* 8 May 1959; *er s* of 10th Duke of Rutland, CBE and of Frances Helen (*née* Sweeny); *S* father, 1999; *m* 1992, Emma, *d* of John Watkins; one *s* three *d*. Mem. Civilian Cttee, ATC Sqdn, Grantham. Member: CLA Cttee for Leicestershire/Rutland; HHA (Chm., E Midlands Area, 1995–99). Game Conservancy. President: Notts Rifle Assoc.; Ex-Aircrew Assoc., Grantham and Dist Br. Parish Councillor, Knipton, Belvoir and Harston. Freeman, City of London; Liveryman, Gunsmiths' Co. *Recreations:* shooting, fishing, flying when I can. *Heir: s* Marquis of Granby, *qv*. *Address:* Belvoir Castle, Grantham, Lincs NG32 1PD. *T:* (01476) 870246. *Clubs:* Turf; Annabel's.

RUTT, Rev. (Cecil) Richard, CBE 1973; MA; *b* 27 Aug. 1925; *s* of Cecil Rutt and Mary Hare Turner; *m* 1969, Joan Mary Ford. *Educ:* Huntingdon Grammar School; Kelham Theol. Coll.; Pembroke Coll., Cambridge. RNVR, 1943–46. Deacon, 1951; Priest, 1952. Asst Curate, St George's, Cambridge, 1951–54; Dio. of Korea, 1954; Parish Priest of Anjung, 1956–58; Warden of St Bede's House Univ. Centre, Seoul, 1959–64; Rector of St Michael's Seminary, Oryu Dong, Seoul, 1964–66; Archdeacon, West Kyonggi (Dio. Seoul), 1965–66; Asst Bishop of Taejon, 1966–68; Bishop of Taejon, 1968–74; Bishop Suffragan of St Germans, 1974–79; Hon. Canon, St Mary's Cathedral, Truro, 1974–79; Bishop of Leicester, 1979–90. Received into RC Ch, 1994, ordained priest, 1995; Hon. Asst, St Mary Immaculate, Falmouth; Hon. Canon, Plymouth Cathedral Chapter, 2001. Associate Gen. Sec., Korean Bible Soc., 1964–74; Episcopal Sec., Council of the Church of SE Asia, 1968–74; Commissary, dio. of Taejon, 1974–90; Pres., Roy. Asiatic Soc., Korea Br., 1974. Chairman: Adv. Council on Relations of Bishops and Religious Communities, 1980–90; Bishop of Truro's Adv. Gp on Services in Cornish, 1975–79 and Ecumenical Adv. Gp (formerly Adv. Gp on Services in Cornish), 1990–; Mem., Anglican/Orthodox Jt Doctrinal Discussions, 1983–89. Bard of the Gorsedd of Cornwall, Cornwhylen, 1976 (Chaplain, 1993–97). Hon. Fellow, Northumbrian Univs' E Asia Centre, 1990. Hon. DLitt Confucian Univ., Seoul, 1974. Tasan Cultural Award (for writings on Korea), 1964. ChStJ 1978. Order of Civil Merit, Peony Class (Korea), 1974. *Publications:* (ed) Songgonghoe Songga (Korean Anglican Hymnal), 1961; Korean Works and Days, 1964; P'ungnyu Han'guk (in Korean), 1965; (trans.) An Anthology of Korean Sijo, 1970; The Bamboo Grove, an introduction to Korean Sijo poetry, 1971; James Scarth Gale and his History of the Korean People, 1972; The Green People (translations of Korean poet, Yi Unsang), 1973; Virtuous Women, three masterpieces of traditional Korean fiction, 1974; A History of Handknitting, 1987; The Book of Changes (Zhouyi): a Bronze Age document translated with introduction and notes, 1996; (with K. L. Pratt) Korea: an historical and cultural dictionary, 1999; (contrib.) The Path to Rome, ed D. Longenecker, 1999; contribs on Korean classical poetry and history to Trans Royal Asiatic Soc. (Korea Br.) and various Korean publications. *Address:* 3 Marlborough Court, Falmouth, Cornwall TR11 2QU. *T:* (01326) 312276.

RUTTER, Prof. Arthur John; Emeritus Professor, Imperial College, University of London (Professor of Botany, 1967–79 and Head of Department of Botany and Plant Technology, 1971–79); *b* 22 Nov. 1917; *s* of late W. Arthur Rutter, CBE, FRIBA and Amy, *d* of William Dyche, BA, Cardiff; *m* 1944, Betsy Rosier Stone (*d* 1978); two *s* one *d*. *Educ:* Royal Grammar Sch., Guildford; Imperial Coll. of Science and Technology. ARCS, BSc, PhD, FIBiol. Mem., ARC team for selection of oil-seed crops and develt selective herbicides, 1940–45; Asst Lectr, Imperial Coll., 1945, Lectr 1946; Reader in Ecology, Univ. of London, 1956. Vis. Prof., Univ. of the Panjab, Pakistan, 1960–61. *Publications:* papers, mainly in Annals of Botany, Jl of Ecology, Jl of Applied Ecology on water relations of plants, forest hydrology and effects of atmospheric pollution on trees. *Recreations:* gardening, walking. *Address:* 10 Thursby Road, Woking, Surrey GU21 3NZ. *T:* (01483) 765009.

RUTTER, Sir Frank (William Eden), KBE 1986 (CBE 1981); general medical practitioner; *b* 5 June 1918; *s* of Edgar and Nellie Rutter; *m* 1947, Mary Elizabeth Milton; six *d*. *Educ:* Welsh National Sch. of Medicine, Cardiff; Westminster Hosp. Med. Sch., London. MRCGP, FRCGP, MRCS, LRCP; DipObst. RAMC (Airborne Forces), 1942–46; OC 195 (Parachute) Field Ambulance, 1946. Chm., Health Cttee, Cardiff RDC, 1960–62; Member: Auckland Hosp. Bd, 1971–88 (Chm., 1974–88); Auckland Area Health Bd, 1988–89; Pres., Hosp. Bds Assoc., NZ, 1977–81 and 1983–85; Chairman, National Advisory Committee: Cancer Treatment Services, 1978–89; Organ Imaging Services, 1982–89; Life-Mem., NZ National Multiple Sclerosis Soc. Patron, South Island Airedale Terrier Club, 1989–93. CStJ 1989. Silver Jubilee Medal, 1977. *Recreation:* watching development of fourteen grandchildren. *Address:* 266 Meola Road, Point Chevalier, Auckland, New Zealand. *T:* (9) 8542544.

See also J. C. Rutter.

RUTTER, Dr (James) Michael; Director of Veterinary Medicines, since 1989, and Chief Executive, Veterinary Medicines Directorate, since 1990, Ministry of Agriculture, Fisheries and Food; *b* 20 Aug. 1941; *s* of late James and Lily Rutter; *m* 1967, Jacqueline Patricia Watson; one *d*. *Educ:* Kendal Grammar Sch.; Univ. of Edinburgh (BVM&S 1964; BSc 1965; PhD 1967). MRCVS 1964. Res. Schol., 1964–67, Res. Asst, 1967–69, Univ. of Edinburgh; Institute for Research on Animal Diseases, later Institute for Animal Health: Vet. Res. Officer, 1969–73; Principal Vet. Res. Officer, 1973–84 (on secondment to DES, 1975–78); Head: Dept of Microbiol., 1984–89; Compton Lab., 1986–89. Expert Consultant: ODA; FAO; WHO. Member: Cttee for Vet. Medicinal Products, EC, 1991–99; Mgt Bd, Eur. Medicines Evaluation Agency, 1996–. *Publications:* Perinatal Ill Health in Calves, 1973; Pasteurella and Pasteurellosis, 1989; contrib. numerous papers to scientific jls. *Recreations:* gardening, outdoor sports, theatre, ballet, music. *Address:* Veterinary Medicines Directorate, Woodham Lane, New Haw, Addlestone, Surrey KT15 3LS. *T:* (01932) 338301.

RUTTER, His Honour John Cleverdon; a Circuit Judge, 1972–92 (a Senior Circuit Judge, 1990–92); *b* 18 Sept. 1919; 2nd *s* of late Edgar John Rutter; *m* 1951, Jill (*d* 1993), *d* of late Maxwell Duncan McIntosh; one *s* one *d*. *Educ:* Cardiff High Sch.; Univ. Coll., of SW of England, Exeter (Open Schol.); Keble Coll., Oxford. MA Oxon; LLB London. Royal Artillery, 1939–46; commnd 1941; served overseas. Called to the Bar, Lincoln's Inn, 1948; practised Wales and Chester Circuit, 1948–66, Stipendiary Magistrate for City of Cardiff, 1966–71. A Legal Member, Mental Health Review Tribunal for Wales Region, 1960–66. An Assistant Recorder of: Cardiff, 1962–66; Merthyr Tydfil, 1962–66; Swansea, 1965–66; Dep. Chm., Glamorgan QS, 1969–71. *Recreations:* walking, reading. *Address:* Law Courts, Cardiff.

See also Sir F. W. E. Rutter.

RUTTER, John Milford; composer and conductor; *b* 24 Sept. 1945; *s* of Laurence Frederick and Joan Mary Rutter; *m* 1980, JoAnne Redden; one *s* (and one *s* decd), and one step *d*. *Educ:* Highgate Sch.; Clare Coll., Cambridge (MA, MusB; Hon. Fellow, 2001). Fellow and Director of Music, Clare Coll., Cambridge, 1975–79; Founder and Director, Cambridge Singers, 1981–. Hon. FGCM 1988; Hon. Fellow, Westminster Choir Coll., Princeton, 1980. DMus Lambeth, 1996. *Publications:* compositions include choral pieces, anthems and carols, 1969–. *Address:* Old Laceys, St John's Street, Duxford, Cambridge CB2 4RA. *T:* (01223) 832474, *Fax:* (01223) 836723.

RUTTER, Michael; *see* Rutter, J. M.

RUTTER, Sir Michael (Llewellyn), Kt 1992; CBE 1985; MD; FRCP, FRCPsych, FMedSci; FRS 1987; Professor of Child Psychiatry, 1973–98, Professor of Developmental Psychopathology, since 1998, University of London Institute of Psychiatry; *b* 15 Aug. 1933; *s* of Llewellyn Charles Rutter and Winifred Olive Rutter; *m* 1958, Marjorie Heys; one *s* two *d*. *Educ:* Moorestown Friends' Sch., USA; Wolverhampton Grammar Sch.; Bootham Sch., York; Birmingham Univ. Med. Sch. (MB ChB 1955, MD Hons 1963). MRCS 1955; LRCP 1955, MRCP 1958, FRCP 1972; FRCPsych 1971. Training in paediatrics, neurology and internal medicine, 1955–58; Maudsley Hosp., 1958–61; Nuffield Med. Travelling Fellow, Albert Einstein Coll. of Medicine, NY, 1961–62; Mem., Sci. Staff, MRC Social Psych. Res. Unit, 1962–65; University of London Institute of Psychiatry: Sen. Lectr, then Reader, 1966–73; Hon. Dir, MRC Child Psychiatry Unit, 1984–98; Dir, Social, Genetic and Develtl Psychiatry Res. Centre, 1994–98. Fellow, Center for Advanced Study in Behavioral Scis, Stanford, Calif, 1979–80. Lectures: Goulstonian, RCP, 1973; Salmon, NY Acad. of Medicine, 1979; Adolf Meyer, Amer. Psych. Assoc., 1985; Maudsley, RCPsych, 1986. Pres., Soc. for Res. in Child Develt, 1999–2001 (Pres.-elect, 1997–99). Gov., 1996–, Dep. Chm., 1999–, Wellcome Trust; Trustee: Nuffield Foundn, 1992–; Jacobs Foundn, 1998–; Novartis Foundn, 1999–; One Plus One, 2001–. Founding Mem., Acad. Europaea, 1988; Founder FMedSci 1998; Foreign Associate Member: Inst. of Medicine, Nat. Acad. of Scis, USA, 1988; US Nat. Acad. of Educn, 1990; Foreign Hon. Mem., Amer. Acad. of Arts and Scis, 1989. FKC 1998. Hon. Prof., Amsterdam Univ., 2001. Hon. FBPsS 1978; Hon. Fellow: Amer. Acad. of Pediatrics, 1981; RSocMed 1996; Hon. FRCPCH 1996. Hon. DSSc Univ. of Leiden, 1985; Hon. Dr Leuven, 1990; Hon. DSc: Birmingham, 1990; Chicago, 1991; Minnesota, 1993; Ghent, 1994; Warwick, 1999; E Anglia, 2000; Hon. MD Edinburgh, 1990; Hon. DPsych Jyväskylä, Finland, 1996; DUniv N London, 2000. Numerous awards, UK and USA. *Publications:* Children of Sick Parents, 1966; (jtly) A Neuropsychiatric Study in Childhood, 1970; (ed jtly) Education, Health and Behaviour, 1970; (ed) Infantile Autism, 1971; Maternal Deprivation Reassessed, 1972, 2nd edn 1981; (ed jtly) The Child with Delayed Speech, 1972; Helping Troubled Children, 1975; (jtly) Cycles of Disadvantage, 1976; (ed jtly) Child Psychiatry, 1977, 2nd edn as Child and Adolescent Psychiatry, 1985, 3rd edn, 1994; (ed jtly) Autism, 1978; Changing Youth in a Changing Society, 1979; (jtly) Fifteen Thousand Hours: secondary schools and their effects on children, 1979; (ed) Scientific Foundations of Developmental Psychiatry, 1981; A Measure of Our Values: goals and dilemmas in the upbringing of children, 1983; (jtly) Lead Versus Health, 1983; (jtly) Juvenile Delinquency, 1983; (ed) Developmental Neuropsychiatry, 1983; (ed jtly) Stress, Coping and Development, 1983; (ed jtly) Depression in Young People, 1986; (jtly) Treatment of Autistic Children, 1987; (ed jtly) Language Development and Disorders, 1987; (jtly) Parenting Breakdown: the making and breaking of inter-generational links, 1988; (ed jtly) Assessment and Diagnosis in Child Psychopathology, 1988; (ed) Studies of Psychosocial Risk: the power of longitudinal data, 1988; (ed jtly) Straight and Devious Pathways from Childhood to Adulthood, 1990; (ed jtly) Biological Risk Factors for Psychosocial Disorders, 1991; (jtly) Developing Minds: challenge and continuity across the life span, 1993; (ed jtly) Development Through Life: a handbook for clinicians, 1994; (ed jtly) Stress, Risk and Resilience in Children and Adolescents: processes, mechanisms and interventions, 1994; (ed jtly) Psychosocial Disorders in Young People, 1995; (jtly) Behavioural Genetics, 3rd edn, 1997; (jtly) Antisocial Behaviour by Young People, 1998. *Recreations:* fell walking, tennis, wine tasting, theatre, family. *Address:* 190 Court Lane, Dulwich, SE21 7ED. *Club:* Royal Society of Medicine.

RUTTER, Trevor John, CBE 1990 (OBE 1976); Assistant Director General, British Council, 1990–91, retired; *b* 26 Jan. 1934; *s* of late Alfred Rutter and Agnes Rutter (*née* Purslow); *m* 1959, Josephine Henson; one *s*. *Educ:* Monmouth Sch.; Brasenose Coll., Oxford (BA). National Service, Army, 1955–57. British Council, Indonesia, W Germany (Munich), London, 1959–66; First Secretary, Foreign Office, 1967; British Council, 1968–91: Representative: Singapore, 1968–71; Thailand, 1971–75; various appointments, London, 1975–85, including: Head, Home Div., 1980; Asst Dir Gen., 1981–85; Rep. in W Germany, 1986–90. *Address:* 1 Gill's Nursery, Totnes, Devon TQ9 5DG.

RUTTLE, (Henry) Stephen (Mayo); QC 1997; *b* 6 Feb. 1953; *s* of His Honour Henry Samuel Jacob Ruttle and Joyce Mayo Ruttle (*née* Moriarty); *m* 1985, Fiona Jane Mitchell-Innes; two *s* two *d*. *Educ:* Westminster Sch. (Queen's Schol.); Queens' Coll., Cambridge (BA Hons Eng. Lit. and Law). Called to the Bar, Gray's Inn, 1976; in practice at the Bar, 1976–; now practising substantially as commercial mediator (CEDR accredited mediator, 1998). *Recreations:* fly-fishing, the countryside, mountains, oak furniture. *Address:* Brick Court Chambers, 7–8 Essex Street, WC2R 3LD. *T:* (020) 7379 3550, (020) 7520 9871. *Club:* Flyfishers'.

RYAN, Prof. Alan James, FBA 1986; Fellow, since 1969, Warden, since 1996, New College, Oxford; Professor of Politics, University of Oxford, since 1997; *b* 9 May 1940; *s* of James William Ryan and Ivy Ryan; *m* 1971, Kathleen Alyson Lane; one *d*. *Educ:* Christ's Hospital; Balliol Coll., Oxford. Lectr in Politics, Univ. of Keele, 1963–66, Univ. of Essex, 1966–69; Lectr in Politics, 1969–78, Reader, 1978–87, Univ. of Oxford; Prof. of Politics, Princeton Univ., 1988–96. Visiting Professor in Politics: City University of New York, 1967–68; Univs of Texas, 1972, California, 1977, the Witwatersrand, 1978; Vis. Fellow, ANU, 1974, 1979; Mellon Fellow, Inst. for Advanced Study, Princeton, 1991–92; de Carle Lectr, Univ. of Otago, 1983. Official Mem., CNAA, 1975–80. Delegate, Oxford Univ. Press, 1983–87. *Publications:* The Philosophy of John Stuart Mill, 1970, 2nd edn 1987; The Philosophy of the Social Sciences, 1970; J. S. Mill, 1975; Property and Political Theory, 1984; (ed jtly) The Blackwell Encyclopaedia of Political Thought, 1987; Property, 1987; Bertrand Russell: a political life, 1988; John Dewey and the High Tide of American Liberalism, 1995; Liberal Anxieties and Liberal Education, 1998. *Recreations:*

dinghy sailing, long train journeys. *Address:* Warden's Lodgings, New College, Oxford OX1 3BN. *Club:* Oxford and Cambridge.

RYAN, (Christopher) Nigel (John), CBE 1977; freelance writer; Chairman, TV-am News, 1989–92 (Director, 1985–92); *b* 12 Dec. 1929; *s* of late Brig. C. E. Ryan, MC, RA; *m* 1984, Susan Anne Crewe (marr. diss.), *qv*. *Educ:* Ampleforth Coll.; Queen's Coll., Oxford (MA). Joined Reuters, London, 1954; Foreign Corresp., 1957–60; joined Independent Television News, 1961, Editor, 1968–71, Editor and Chief Executive, 1971–77; Vice-Pres., NBC News, America, 1977–80; Dir of Progs, Thames Television, 1980–82. Silver Medal, Royal Television Soc., 1970; Desmond Davis Award, 1972. *Publications:* A Hitch or Two in Afghanistan, 1983; (jtly) The Scholar and the Gypsy, 1992; trans. novels from French by Georges Simenon and others. *Address:* 4 Cleveland Square, W2 6DH. *T:* (020) 7723 8552. *Club:* Beefsteak.

RYAN, Maj.-Gen. Denis Edgar, CB 1987; Director of Army Education, 1984–87; *b* 18 June 1928; *s* of late Reginald Arthur Ryan and of Amelia (*née* Smith); *m* 1955, Jean Mary Bentley; one *s* one *d*. *Educ:* Sir William Borlase School, Marlow; King's College, London (LLB). Commissioned RAEC, 1950; served BAOR, 1950–54; Instr, RMA Sandhurst, 1954–56; Adjt, Army Sch. of Educn, 1957–59; Staff Coll., 1960; served in Cyprus, Kenya and UK, 1961–67; CAES, HQ 4 Div., BAOR, 1968–70; Cabinet Office, 1970–72; TDA, Staff Coll., 1972–75; Col GS MoD, 1976–78; Chief Education Officer: HQ SE Dist, 1978–79; HQ BAOR, 1979–82; Comd, Education, UK, 1982–84. Col Comdt, RAEC, 1990–92; Dep. Col Comdt, AGC, 1992–93. *Recreations:* cricket, tennis, Rugby, music, theatre. *Club:* Army and Navy.

RYAN, Sir Derek (Gerald), 4th Bt *cr* 1919, of Hintlesham, Suffolk; architect; *b* 25 March 1954; *s* of Sir Derek Gerald Ryan, 3rd Bt and of Penelope Anne Hawkings; *S* father, 1990; *m* (marr. diss.); *m* 1997, Roberta Tonn. *Educ:* Univ. of California at Berkeley (BAED 1977). Washington State Architect License #4296, 1984; NCARB Certificate #32,269, 1984. *Recreations:* ski-ing, guitar. *Heir: cousin* Desmond Maurice Ryan [*b* 16 Sept. 1918; *m* 1942, Margaret Catherine, *d* of A. H. Brereton; three *s*]. *Address:* 111 South Jackson Street, Seattle, WA 98104, USA. *T:* (206) 2235555.

RYAN, Gerard Charles; QC 1981; a Recorder of the Crown Court, 1984–98; *b* 16 Dec. 1931; *er s* of Frederick Charles Ryan, Hove, and Louie Violet Ryan (*née* Ball); *m* 1960, Sheila Morag Clark Cameron, *qv*; two *s*. *Educ:* Clayesmore Sch.; Brighton Coll.; Pembroke Coll., Cambridge (Exhibnr; MA). Served RA, 1955–57 (Lieut). Called to the Bar, Middle Temple, 1955, Bencher, 1988; Harmsworth Scholar, 1956. Chm., Tribunal of Inquiry into Loscoe (Derbyshire) gas explosion, 1986–87. Chairman: Soc. of Sussex Downsmen, 1977–80; Murray Downland Trust, 1993–. *Publication:* (with A. O. B. Harris) Outline of the Law of Common Land, 1967. *Recreations:* conservation, growing trees and other plants, walking. *Address:* 13 Westmoreland Place, SW1V 4AA; 2 Harcourt Buildings, Temple, EC4Y 9DB. *T:* (020) 7353 8415. *Club:* Oxford and Cambridge.

RYAN, Joan Marie; MP (Lab) Enfield North, since 1997; *b* 8 Sept. 1955; *d* of late Michael Joseph Ryan and of Dolores Marie Ryan (*née* Joyce); partner, Martin Hegarty; one *s* one *d*. *Educ:* City of Liverpool Coll. of Higher Educn (BA Hons 1979); South Bank Poly. (MSc 1983); Avery Hill Coll. (PGCE 1984). Sociology, Soc. Sci. and Religious Studies Teacher, and Hd of Year, Hurlingham and Chelsea Secondary Sch., Fulham, 1984–89; Head of Pastoral Educn, Hawksmoor Sixth Form Coll., Fulham, 1989–94; Head of Humanities, William Morris Acad., Hammersmith, 1994–97. Mem. (Lab), Barnet LBC, 1990–98. *Recreations:* visiting historic buildings, swimming, cinema. *Address:* House of Commons, SW1A 0AA. *T:* (020) 7219 6502.

RYAN, John; Senior Lecturer in Management Studies, Napier University; *b* 30 April 1940; *m* 1964, Eunice Ann Edmonds; two *s*. *Educ:* Lanark Grammar School; Glasgow University (MA, MBA). Member, National Association of Labour Student Organisations, 1958–62; formerly Youth Organiser, Lanark City Labour Party; Member, Executive Committee, North Paddington Labour Party, 1964–66. Contested (Lab) Buckinghamshire South, 1964; MP (Lab) Uxbridge, 1966–70. Member, Fabian Society, 1961; Dir, Tribune Publications Ltd, 1969. Mem., Inst. of Marketing; Associate Member: Market Res. Soc.; Inst. of Mgt. *Recreations:* golf, walking. *Address:* Napier Business School, 219 Colinton Road, Edinburgh EH14 1DJ. *T:* (0131) 455 5004, *Fax:* (0131) 455 5046.

RYAN, Most Rev. Laurence; *see* Kildare and Leighlin, Bishop of (RC).

RYAN, Nigel; *see* Ryan, C. N. J.

RYAN, Peter James, QPM 1991; Commissioner of Police for New South Wales, since 1996; *b* 18 May 1944; *s* of late Lawrence Joseph Ryan and of Margaret Jane (*née* Stephenson); *m* 1985, Adrienne Margaret Butterworth; two *d*. *Educ:* Newman Coll., Preston; Univ. of Lancaster (BA Hons); Preston Poly. (DMS); Open Univ. (MSc). FIPM 1994. Lancs Constabulary, 1963–83; Metropolitan Police, 1983–84; Asst Chief Constable, N Yorks Police, 1984–88; Dep. Chief Constable, Durham Constabulary, 1988–90; Chief Constable, Norfolk, 1990–93; Nat. Dir of Police Trng and Comdt Police Staff Coll., 1993–96. Sec., 1991–92, Chm., 1992–93, Personnel & Trng Cttee, ACPO. Mem., BTEC, 1985–88. Vis. Fellow, UEA Sch. of Educn, 1993–; Grad., FBI Nat. Exec. Inst., 1994. Pres., Assoc. of Eur. Police Colls, 1996; Vice Pres., Police Mutual Assurance Soc., 1994–96. Asst Dir Gen., St John Ambulance, 1995. FIMgt 1980. Hon. LLD Macquarie, 2000. OStJ 1995. *Publications:* contrib. Police Jl and similar professional jls. *Recreations:* occasional golf, riding, water-colour painting, reading. *Address:* (office) Avery Building, 14–24 College Street, Darlinghurst, NSW 2010, Australia. *Clubs:* Royal Air Force; Royal Sydney Yacht Squadron.

RYAN, Sheila Morag Clark, (Mrs G. C. Ryan); *see* Cameron, S. M. C.

RYAN, Prof. Terence John, DM; FRCP; Clinical Professor of Dermatology, Oxford University, 1992–97, now Emeritus Professor; Fellow, Green College, 1979–97, now Emeritus Fellow; *b* 24 July 1932; *s* of Gerald John Ryan and Kathleen May (*née* Knight); *m* 1968, Trudie Anne Merry; one *s* one *d*. *Educ:* numerous schs including: Michael Hall (Rudolf Steiner); Brickwall Sch., Northiam; Worcester Coll., Oxford (BM, BCh 1957; DM 1977). FRCP 1975. Capt. RAMC, 1955–60: Officer i/c Dept of Dermatol. and ENT Surgery, Colchester Mil. Hosp.; Radcliffe Infirmary, Oxford: Hse Officer, 1958; Registrar and Sen. Registrar in Dermatol., 1962–68; Lectr and Sen. Lectr, Inst. of Dermatol., London Univ., 1967–71; Dept of Dermatol., RPMS, 1968–71; Lectr in Dermatology, Oxford Univ., 1971–92. Cons. Dermatologist, 1969–97, Hon. Cons., 1997–, Oxon HA. Vis. Prof., Brookes Univ., Oxford, 1991–; Adjunct Prof., Jefferson Univ., Philadelphia, 1988–. Med. Advr, St Francis Leprosy Guild, 1987–. Promoter, Sine Lepra and Healthy Skin for All programmes, Internat. League of Dermatologists, 1987–2002; Dir, Fuel Initiatives Resources Strategies Technologies, 1998–. Pres., Section of Dermatol., RSocMed, 1990. Mem., Internat. Cttee of Dermatol., 1987–; Pres., Internat. Soc. for Dermatol., 1994–99 (Hon. Pres., 1999); Chm., Internat. Foundn for Dermatol., 1997–. Trustee: Oxford Internat. Biomedical Centre, 1999–; Arts Dyslexia Trust, 1999–; British Skin Foundn, 1999. Hon. Mem., various foreign nat. socs of dermatol. KStJ 1984 (County Surgeon Comr, then Comdr, SJAB, Oxon). *Publications:* (contrib.) Oxford Textbook of Medicine, 3rd edn 1995, 5th edn 2002; contrib. textbooks of dermatology and numerous in field of blood supply, dermatology and internat. dermatological policy. *Recreations:* painting water-colours, flowers, piano playing, foreign travel. *Address:* Oxford Centre for Healthcare Research and Development, 44 London Road, Headington, Oxford OX3 7PD; Hill House, Abberbury Road, Iffley, Oxford OX4 4EU. *T:* (01865) 777041.

RYAN, Dr Thomas Anthony, (Tony); Chairman, Irelandia Investments, since 1994; Director, Ryanair, since 1996 (Chairman, 1996–98); *b* 2 Feb. 1936; *m*; three *s*. *Educ:* Christian Brothers Sch., Thurles, Co. Tipperary; North Western Univ., Chicago. Aer Lingus, 1956–75, incl. sen. mgt positions in Ireland and US; founder: GPA Gp, 1975–93; Ryanair Gp, 1985. Mem., Bd of Govs, Nat. Gall. of Ireland. Hon. Mem., Univ. of Limerick Foundn, 1986. Hon. LLD: TCD, 1987; NUI, 1987; Limerick, 1992. *Recreations:* farming, horse breeding in Co. Kildare.

RYAN, Prof. William Francis, DPhil; FSA; FBA 2000; Librarian, Warburg Institute, since 1976, and Professor of Russian Studies, School of Advanced Study, since 2000, University of London; *b* 13 April 1937; *s* of William Gerard Ryan and Marjorie Ellen Ryan; *m* 1st, 1963, Marina Guterman (marr. diss. 1970); two *d*; 2nd, 1986, Janet Margaret Hartley; one *s* one *d*. *Educ:* Bromley GS for Boys; Oriel Coll., Oxford (MA; DPhil 1970). FSA 1972. Editor, Clarendon Press, Oxford, 1963–65; Asst Curator, Mus. of Hist. of Science, Oxford, 1965–67; Lectr in Russian Lang. and Lit., SSEES, London Univ., 1967–76. *Publications:* (with Peter Norman) The Penguin Russian Dictionary, 1995; The Bathhouse at Midnight: an historical survey of magic and divination in Russia, Stroud and University Park PA, 1999. *Address:* 61 Rodway Road, Bromley, Kent BR1 3JP. *T:* (020) 8466 1718.

RYCROFT, Prof. Michael John, PhD; Proprietor, Cambridge Atmospheric, Environmental and Space Activities and Research Consultancy, since 1998; Professor, International Space University, France, since 1995 (now part-time); *b* 15 July 1938; *s* of late John Lambert Rycroft and Molly Elizabeth Rycroft (*née* Riglen); *m* 1967, Mary Cheeseright; three *s*. *Educ:* Merchant Taylors' School, Northwood; Imperial Coll., London (BSc Hons Physics); Churchill Coll., Cambridge (PhD Met. Physics). CPhys, MInstP; CMath, FIMA; FRAS. Lectr, Dept of Physics, Univ. of Southampton, 1966–79; Head, Atmospheric Scis Div., NERC British Antarctic Survey, Cambridge, 1979–90; Prof. of Aerospace, 1990–94, Hd, Coll. of Aeronautics, 1990–92, Cranfield Inst. of Technol., subseq. Cranfield Univ. Visiting Professor: Dept. of Physics, Univ. of Houston, 1974–75; Cranfield Univ., 1995–; De Montfort Univ., 1998–. Gen. Sec., Eur. Geophysical Soc., 1996–. Member: Internat. Acad. of Astronautics, 1986; Council of Sen. Fellows, De Montfort Univ., 1999–. MAE 2000. Editor-in-Chief, Jl of Atmospheric and Solar-Terrestrial Physics, 1989–99. Hon. DSc De Montfort, 1998. *Publications:* (with D. Shapland) Spacelab: research in Earth orbit, 1984; (ed) Cambridge Encyclopedia of Space, 1990; 230 pubns on atmospheric and space sci. and related fields. *Recreations:* music, gardening, hill walking, wining and dining. *Address:* Bassett Mead, 35 Millington Road, Cambridge CB3 9HW. *T:* (01223) 353839; *Fax:* (01223) 303839; *e-mail:* michael.j.rycroft@ukgateway.net.

RYCROFT, Sir Richard (John), 8th Bt *cr* 1784, of Calton, Yorkshire; *b* 15 June 1946; *s* of Cdre Henry Richard Rycroft, OBE, DSC, RN, 4th *s* of 5th Bt, and Penelope Gwendoline Rycroft (*née* Evans-Lombe); *S* cousin, 1999. *Educ:* Sherborne. Dep. Launching Authority, Burnham-on-Crouch RNLI Lifeboat. *Recreations:* sailing, listening to jazz, Burmese cats. *Heir: cousin* Francis Edward Rycroft [*b* 4 Aug. 1950; *m* 1975, Cherry Willmott; one *s* one *d*]. *Club:* Royal Corinthian Yacht.

RYDER, family name of **Earl of Harrowby** and of **Barons Ryder of Eaton Hastings** and **Ryder of Wensum**.

RYDER OF EATON HASTINGS, Baron *cr* 1975 (Life Peer), of Eaton Hastings, Oxfordshire; **Sydney Thomas Franklin, (Don), Ryder,** Kt 1972; Chairman, National Enterprise Board, 1975–77; *b* 16 Sept. 1916; *s* of John Ryder; *m* 1950; one *s* one *d*. *Educ:* Ealing. Editor, Stock Exchange Gazette, 1950–60; Jt Man. Dir, 1960–61, Sole Man. Dir, 1961–63, Kelly Iliffe Holdings, and Associated Iliffe Press Ltd; Dir, Internat. Publishing Corp., 1963–70; Man. Dir, Reed Paper Gp, 1963–68; Chm. and Chief Executive, Reed International Ltd, 1968–75; Dir, MEPC Ltd, 1972–75. Industrial Advr to the govt, 1974. Member: British Gas Corp., 1973–78; Reserve Pension Bd, 1973; Council and Bd of Fellows, BIM, 1970; Court and Council, Cranfield Inst. of Technology, 1970–74; Council, UK S Africa Trade Assoc., 1974; Nat. Materials Handling Centre (Pres., 1970–77); Council, Industrial Soc., 1971; NEDC, 1976–77. Vice-Pres., RoSPA, 1973. *Recreations:* sailing, chess. *Address:* House of Lords, SW1A 0PW.

RYDER OF WENSUM, Baron *cr* 1997 (Life Peer), of Wensum in the co. of Norfolk; **Richard Andrew Ryder,** OBE 1981; PC 1990; *b* 4 Feb. 1949; *s* of Richard Stephen Ryder, JP, DL, and Margaret MacKenzie; *m* 1981, Caroline, MBE, *o d* of Sir David Stephens; one *d* (one *s* decd). *Educ:* Radley; Magdalene Coll., Cambridge (BA Hons History, 1971). Partner, M. Ryder and Sons; journalist; Chm., Eastern Counties Radio, 1997–. Political Secretary: to Leader of the Opposition, 1975–79; to Prime Minister, 1979–81. Contested (C) Gateshead E, Feb. and Oct., 1974. MP (C) Mid Norfolk, 1983–97. Parliamentary Private Secretary: to Financial Sec. to the Treasury, 1984; to Sec. of State for Foreign and Commonwealth Affairs, 1984–86; an Asst Govt Whip, 1986–88; Parly Under-Sec. of State, MAFF, 1988–89; Econ. Sec. to HM Treasury, 1989–90; Paymaster General, 1990; Parly Sec. to HM Treasury and Govt Chief Whip, 1990–95. Chm., Cons. Foreign and Commonwealth Council, 1984–89. *Address:* House of Lords, SW1A 0PW.

RYDER, Edward Alexander, CB 1992; HM Chief Inspector of Nuclear Installations, Health and Safety Executive, 1985–91; Joint Chairman and Head of UK Delegation, Channel Tunnel Safety Authority, 1992–97; *b* 9 Nov. 1931; *s* of Alexander Harry and Gwendoline Gladys Ryder; *m* 1956, Janet; one *s* one *d*. *Educ:* Cheltenham Grammar School; Bristol University (BSc). CPhys; FInstP. Flying Officer, RAF, 1953–55; Engineer, GEC Applied Electronics Labs, 1955–57; Control Engineer, Hawker Siddeley Nuclear Power Co., 1957–61; Sen. Engineer, CEGB, 1961–71; Principal Inspector, then Superintending Inspector, HM Nuclear Installations Inspectorate, 1971–80; Head of Hazardous Installations Policy Branch, 1980–85, Head of Nuclear Installations Policy Branch, 1985, HSE. Sec., Adv. Cttee on Major Hazards, 1980–85. Chairman: HSC Working Gp on Ionising Radiations, 1987–91; IAEA Nuclear Safety Standards Adv. Gp, 1988–93; Mem., Intergovtl Commn for Channel Tunnel, 1992–97. Organiser, Shiplake and Dunsden Area, RBL Poppy Appeal, 1996–. Mem., Shiplake Parish Council, 1999– (Vice-Chm., 2000–). *Recreations:* golf—or is it nature study, concertgoing. *Address:* Pinewood, Baskerville Lane, Lower Shiplake, Henley on Thames, Oxon RG9 3JY.

RYDER, Eric Charles, MA, LLB; Barrister; Professor of English Law in the University of London (University College) 1960–82, now Professor Emeritus; *b* 28 July 1915; *er s* of late Charles Henry Ryder, solicitor, Hanley, Staffs, and of Ellen Miller; *m* 1941, Nancy Winifred Roberts. *Educ:* Hanley High School; Gonville and Caius College, Cambridge (scholar). BA (Law Tripos Parts I and II, 1st Cl.), 1936; LLB (1st Cl.) 1937; MA 1940; Tapp Law Scholar, Gonville and Caius College, 1937; called to Bar, Gray's Inn, 1937; practice at Chancery Bar. Ministry of Food, 1941–44; Lecturer in Law, King's College, Newcastle upon Tyne, 1944; Dean of Faculty of Law, Univ. of Durham, 1947–60; Professor of Law, Univ. of Durham (King's College), 1953–60. Practised as conveyancing counsel, Newcastle upon Tyne, 1944–53. *Publications:* Hawkins and Ryder on the Construction of Wills, 1965; contrib. to legal periodicals. *Address:* 9 Arlington Court, Kenton Avenue, Gosforth, Newcastle upon Tyne NE3 4JR. *T:* (0191) 285 1172.

RYDER, Ernest Nigel, TD 1996; QC 1997; a Recorder, since 2000; *b* 9 Dec. 1957; *s* of Dr John Buckley Ryder, TD and Constance Ryder; *m* 1990, Janette Lynn Martin; one *d.* *Educ:* Bolton Sch.; Peterhouse, Cambridge (MA 1983). Merchant banker, Grindley Brandt & Co., 1979; called to the Bar, Gray's Inn, 1981; Asst Recorder, 1997–2000; Northern Circuit. Counsel, N Wales Tribunal of Inquiry, 1996–99. Asst Boundary Comr, 2000–. Chm., Manchester Reg., Family Law Bar Assoc., 2000–. Commnd Duke of Lancaster's Own Yeomanry, 1981; Sqdn Leader, 1990; Sqdn Leader, Royal Mercian and Lancastrian Yeomanry, 1992. *Recreations:* listening, walking. *Address:* Deans Court Chambers, 24 St John Street, Manchester M1 4DF. *T:* (0161) 214 6000. *Club:* Royal Commonwealth Society.

RYDER, Janet; Member (Plaid Cymru) North Wales, National Assembly for Wales, since 1999; *b* Sunderland, 21 June 1955; *m* Peter; two *s* one *d.* *Educ:* Northern Counties Coll. of Educn (Teacher's Cert. (Dist.)); Open Univ. (BA Hist./Arts). Teacher: Little Weighton Co. Primary Sch., E Riding of Yorks, 1980–83; St Bede's Catholic Primary Sch., Hull, 1987–88; Coleford Primary Sch., Hull (i/c Religious and Moral Educn), 1988–89; Bransholme Youth Club, Hull. Member: N Wales Fire Authy, 1995–99; Bd, Denbighshire Voluntary Services Council, 1995–99. Mem., voluntary gps, incl. Strategic Planning Gp for People with a Learning Difficulty. Member (Plaid Cymru): Rhuthun Town Council, 1992– (Mayor, 1998–2000); Denbighshire CC, 1994–99 (mem., various cttees; Chairman: Children and Families Sub-cttee, 1995–98; Denbigh Early Years Partnership, 1996–98; Denbigh Plan Partnership). Mem., Nat. Exec., Plaid Cymru, 1993–99. *Address:* National Assembly for Wales, Cardiff Bay, Cardiff CF99 1NA. *T:* (029) 2089 8250; (constituency) 20 Chester Street, Wrexham LL13 8BG. *T:* (01978) 313909; *e-mail:* janet.ryder@wales.gsi.gov.uk.

RYDER, John; QC 2000; a Recorder, since 2000; *m* 1989, Carolyn Espley; one *d.* *Educ:* Monmouth Sch. Called to the Bar, Inner Temple, 1980; Asst Recorder, 1997–2000. *Recreations:* riding, ski-ing, opera. *Address:* 6 King's Bench Walk, Temple, EC4Y 7DR. *Club:* Travellers.

RYDER, Dr Peter, CB 1994; consultant in environmental information services, since 1996; General Secretary, Royal Meteorological Society, since 2001; *b* 10 March 1942; *s* of Percival Henry Sussex Ryder and Bridget (*née* McCormack); *m* 1965, Jacqueline Doris Sylvia Rigby; two *s* one *d.* *Educ:* Yorebridge Grammar Sch., Askrigg; Univ. of Leeds (BSc 1963; PhD 1966). Research Asst, Physics Dept, Univ. of Leeds, 1966–67; Meteorological Office, 1967–96: Asst Dir, Cloud Physics Res, 1976–82; Asst Dir, Systems Develt, 1982–84; Dep. Dir, Observational Services, 1984–88; Dep. Dir, Forecasting Services, 1988–89; Dir of Services, 1989–90; Dep. Chief Exec. and Dir of Ops, then Man. Dir (Ops), 1990–96. Royal Meteorological Society: Mem. Council, 1980–83; Mem., Qly Jl Editing Cttee, 1981–84. Mem., Thames Regl Flood Defence Cttee, EA, 1997–. William Gaskell Meml Medal, RMetS, 1981; L. G. Groves Meml Prize for Meteorology, MoD, 1982. *Publications:* papers in learned jls on experimental atmospheric physics and meteorology. *Recreations:* gardening, walking, fishing, photography. *Address:* 8 Sherring Close, Bracknell, Berks RG42 2LD.

RYDER, Dr Richard Hood Jack Dudley; author, campaigner; Director of Animal Welfare Studies, International Fund for Animal Welfare, 1997–2000; *b* 3 July 1940; *s* of late Major D. C. D. Ryder, JP and Vera Mary (*née* Cook); *m* 1974, Audrey Jane Smith (marr. diss. 1999); one *s* one *d.* *Educ:* Sherborne Sch.; Cambridge Univ. (MA; PhD 1993); Edinburgh Univ. (DCP); Columbia Univ., NY (Fellow). AFBPsS; FZS. Sen. Clinical Psychologist, Warneford Hosp., Oxford, 1967–84; Principal Clin. Psychologist, St James Hosp., Portsmouth, 1983–84. Chm., Oxford Div. of Clin. Psych., 1981–83; Member: Oxford Regional Adolescent Service, 1971–84; DHSS Health Adv. Service, 1977–78. Royal Society for Prevention of Cruelty to Animals: Mem. Council, 1972– (Chm., 1977–79; Vice Chm., 1990–91); Dep. Treas., 2000–01; Chairman: Political Cttee, 1979–80; Animal Experimentation Adv. Cttee, 1983–85; Public Relns and Campaign Cttee, 1990–91; Scientific Cttee, 1992–; Internat. Cttee, 1999–. Dep. Chm., Cttee on Welfare of Animals in Psychology, BPsS, 2001–. Political Consultant, 1991–93, Dir, 1993–97, Political Animal Lobby Ltd. Founder Mem., Gen. Election Co-ordinating Cttee on Animal Protection, 1978; Prog. Organiser, IFAW, 1984–91; UK Delegate, Eurogroup, 1980. Chm., Liberal Animal Welfare Gp, 1981–88; Member: Liberal Party Council, 1983–87; Liberal Party Policy Panels on defence, health, home affairs, Eur. affairs, foreign affairs, environment, 1981–88; contested (L): Buckingham, 1983; Teignbridge, 1987. Pres., Lib. Democrats Animal Protection Gp, 1989–91. Chairman: Teignbridge NSPCC, 1984–87; Teignbridge Home Start, 1987–89. Mellon Prof., Tulane Univ., New Orleans, 1996. Broadcaster and writer on psychological, ethical, political and animal protection subjects. FRSA 1992. *Publications:* Speciesism, 1970; Victims of Science, 1975, 2nd edn 1984; (ed) Animal Rights—a Symposium, 1979; Animal Revolution: changing attitudes to speciesism, 1989, 2nd edn 2000; Painism, 1990; (ed) Animal Welfare and the Environment, 1992; The Political Animal, 1998; Painism: a modern morality, 2001. *Recreations:* trees, opera, vodka martinis. *Clubs:* National Liberal, Royal Over-Seas League.

RYDILL, Prof. Louis Joseph, OBE 1962; FREng; RCNC; Consultant in Naval Ship Design, since 1986; Professor of Naval Architecture, University College London, 1981–85, now Emeritus Professor; *b* 16 Aug. 1922; *s* of Louis and Queenie Rydill; *m* 1949, Eva (*née* Newman); two *d.* *Educ:* HM Dockyard Sch., Devonport; RNEC Keyham; RNC Greenwich; Royal Corps of Naval Constructors. FRINA (Gold Medallist); FREng (FEng 1982). Asst Constructor, 1946–52; Constructor, 1952–62, incl. Asst Prof. of Naval Architecture, RNC Greenwich, 1953–57; Chief Constructor, 1962–72, incl. Prof. of Naval Architecture, RNC Greenwich and UCL, 1967–72; Asst Dir Submarines, Constructive, 1972–74; Dep. Dir Submarines (Polaris), 1974–76; Dir of Ship Design and Engrg (formerly Warship Design), MoD, 1976–81. Hon. Res. Fellow, UCL, 1974; Vis. Prof., US Naval Acad., Annapolis, Md, 1985–86. Silver Jubilee Medal, 1977. *Publication:* (jtly) Concepts in Submarine Design, 1993. *Recreations:* literature, theatre, jazz and other music. *Address:* The Lodge, Entry Hill Drive, Bath BA2 5NJ. *T:* (01225) 427888.

RYKWERT, Prof. Joseph, MA (Cantab), DrRCA; Paul Philippe Cret Professor of Architecture, University of Pennsylvania, 1988–98, now Emeritus; *b* 5 April 1926; *s* of Szymon Rykwert and Elizabeth Melup; *m* 1st, 1960 (marr. diss. 1967); 2nd, 1972, Anne-Marie Sandersley; one *s* one *d.* *Educ:* Charterhouse; Bartlett Sch. of Architecture; Architectural Assoc. Lectr, Hochschule für Gestaltung, Ulm, 1958; Librarian and Tutor, Royal Coll. of Art, 1961–67; Prof. of Art, Univ. of Essex, 1967–80; Lectr on Arch., 1980–85, Reader, 1985–88, Univ. of Cambridge. Bollingen Fellow, Inst. for Arch. and Urban Studies, NY, 1969–71; Sen. Fellow, Council of Humanities, Princeton Univ., 1971; Visiting Professor: Institut d'Urbanisme, Univ. of Paris, 1974–76; Princeton Univ., 1977; Andrew Mellon Vis. Prof., Cooper Union, NY, 1977; Slade Prof. of Fine Art, Cambridge Univ., 1979–80; Vis. Fellow, Darwin Coll., Cambridge, 1979–80; Mem., Trinity Hall, Cambridge, 1980–; Sen. Fellow, Center for the Advanced Studies in the Visual Arts. Nat. Gall. of Art, Washington; Vis. Prof., Univ. of Louvain, 1981–84; George Lurcy Vis. Prof., Columbia, 1986; Sen. Schol., Getty Res. Inst. in Hist. of Art and Humanities, 1992–93. Pres., Comité Internat. des Critiques d'Architecture, 1996–. Mem. Commn, Venice Biennale, 1974–78. Consultant, Min. of Urban Develt and Ecology, Republic of Mexico, 1986–88. Co-ed., RES (Anthropology and Aesthetics), 1981–. Member: Accademia Clementina, 1992; Accademia di S Luca, 1993; Polish Acad. of Arts and Scis, 1998. Hon. DSc: Edinburgh, 1995; Bath, 2000; Hon. Dr Córdoba, Argentina, 1998. Alfred Jurzykowski Foundn Award, 1990. Chevalier des Arts et des Lettres, 1984. *Publications:* The Golden House, 1947; (ed) The Ten Books of Architecture, by L. B. Alberti (annotated edn of Leoni trans. of 1756), 1955, new translation from Latin, as On the Art of Building in Ten Books, 1988; The Idea of a Town, 1963, 3rd edn 1988; Church Building, 1966; On Adam's House in Paradise, 1972, 2nd edn 1982; (ed) Parole nel Vuoto, by A. Loos, 1972; The First Moderns, 1980; The Necessity of Artifice, 1981; (with Anne Rykwert) The Brothers Adam, 1985; The Dancing Column, 1996; The Seduction of Place, 2000; contrib. Arch. Rev., Burlington Mag., Lotus. *Recreations:* rare. *Address:* 26A Wedderburn Road, NW3 5QG. *Club:* Savile.

RYLAND, Timothy Richard Godfrey Fetherstonhaugh; His Honour Judge Ryland; a Circuit Judge, since 1988; a Judge at Central London County Court, since 1994; *b* 13 June 1938; *s* of late Richard Desmond Fetherstonhaugh Ryland and Frances Katharine Vernon Ryland; *m* 1991, Jean Margaret Muirhead. *Educ:* St Andrew's Coll.; TCD. BA (Moderatorship), LLB. Called to Bar, Gray's Inn, 1961. Dep. Circuit Judge, 1978; a Recorder, 1983–88. *Recreations:* opera, wine. *Clubs:* Lansdowne; Kildare Street and University (Dublin).

RYLE, Evelyn Margaret; consultant and author; *b* 26 March 1947; *d* of Paul McConnell Cassidy and Emily Margaret Cassidy (*née* Wright); *m* 1975, Anthony E. Ryle, OBE; one *s* one *d.* *Educ:* King's Park Sch., Glasgow; Univ. of Glasgow (MA Hons; Dip. Management Studies). Dexion-Comino Internat., 1969; commnd WRAF; Flight Lieut, accountant officer, 1973; financial systems analyst: Dexion Gp, 1975; Southern Electricity, 1976; Departments of Trade and Industry, 1977–96; British Steel Corp. Finance; Commercial Relations and Exports; Consumer Affairs; Vehicles Div.; Dep. Dir, IT Services, 1987; Head, Educn and Trng Policy, 1990; seconded to Design Council as Dir-Gen., 1993; Dir, Business Competitiveness, Govt Office for London, 1995–96; Mem., CSSB Panel of Chairs, 1996–99. Mem., Finance Cttee, 1996– (Chair, 2001–), Mem., Exec., 1999–, Charter 88. FRSA. *Recreations:* family, music, gardening, needlework, walking. *Address:* *e-mail:* evelyn.ryle@virgin.net. *Club:* Royal Air Force.

RYLE, Michael Thomas; Clerk of Committees, House of Commons, 1987–89, retired; *b* 30 July 1927; *s* of Peter Johnston Ryle and Rebecca Katie (*née* Boxall); *m* 1952, Bridget Moyes; one *s* two *d.* *Educ:* Newcastle upon Tyne Royal Grammar Sch.; Merton Coll., Oxford (1st Cl. Hons PPE, 1951; MA). Served RA, 1946–48 and TA, 1950–57. Entered Clerk's Dept, House of Commons, 1951; served in various offices; Clerk of Overseas Office, 1979–83; Principal Clerk, Table Office, 1983–84; Clerk of the Journals, 1985–87; attached Nova Scotia Legislature, 1976. Consultant/advr, Belarus, Slovakian, Ukrainian and other parlts in E Europe, 1995–97. Chm., Lib Dem Wkg Gp on Reform of H of C, 1996. Member: Study of Parlt Gp, 1964– (Founding Mem.; Chm., 1975–78; Pres., 1986–94); Council, Hansard Soc., 1974–94 (Mem. and Sec., Commn on the Legislative Process, 1991–93); Council, RIPA, 1982–88; Lambeth HMC, 1960–64. Governor, St Thomas' Hosp., 1964–74. Hon. Res. Fellow, Univ. of Exeter, 1990–. Mem., Exec. Cttee, 1991–, Vice-Chm., 2000–, Exmoor Soc. *Publications:* (ed with S. Walkland) The Commons in the Seventies, 1977, 2nd edn, as The Commons Today, 1981; (contrib.) The House of Commons in the Twentieth Century, 1979; (ed with P. G. Richards) The Commons Under Scrutiny, 1988; (with J. A. G. Griffith) Parliament, 1989, 2nd edn 2002; contrib. to books on parly practice and procedure; articles in Pol Qly, Parly Affairs, The Table, etc. *Recreations:* cricket, golf, bridge, watching birds. *Address:* Jasmine Cottage, Winsford, Minehead, Somerset TA24 7JE. *T:* and *Fax:* (01643) 851317; *e-mail:* mbryle@lineone.net.

RYMAN, John; *b* 7 Nov. 1930. *Educ:* Leighton Park; Pembroke College, Oxford. Inns of Court Regt (TA), 1948–51. Called to the Bar, Middle Temple, 1957. Harmsworth Law Scholar. MP (Lab): Blyth, Oct. 1974–1983; Blyth Valley, 1983–87. Mem. Council, Assoc. of the Clergy, 1976. *Recreation:* Horses.

RYRIE, Sir William (Sinclair), KCB 1982 (CB 1979); Chairman, Baring Emerging Europe Trust plc, since 1994; *b* 10 Nov. 1928; *s* of Rev. Dr Frank Ryrie and Mabel Moncrieff Ryrie (*née* Watt); *m* 1st, 1953, Dorrit Klein (marr. diss. 1969); two *s* one *d*; 2nd, 1969, Christine Gray Thomson; one *s.* *Educ:* Mount Hermon Sch., Darjeeling; Heriot's Sch., Edinburgh; Edinburgh Univ. MA 1st cl. hons History, 1951. Nat. Service, 1951–53: Lieut, Intell. Corps, Malaya, 1952–53 (despatches). Colonial Office, 1953; seconded to Uganda, 1956–58; Principal 1958; transf. to Treasury, 1963; Asst Sec., internat. monetary affairs, 1966–69; Principal Private Sec. to Chancellor of Exchequer, 1969–71; Under-Sec., Public Sector Gp, HM Treasury, 1971–75; Econ. Minister, Washington, and UK Exec. Dir, IMF and IBRD, 1975–79; 2nd Perm. Sec. (Domestic Economy Sector), HM Treasury, 1980–82; Permanent Sec., ODA, FCO, 1982–84; Exec. Vice-Pres. and Chief Exec., IFC at World Bank, 1984–93; Dep. Chm., Commonwealth Develt Corp., 1994–98. Vice Chm., ING Barings Hldg Co., 1995–98. Director: Barings plc, 1994–95; First NIS Regl Fund, 1994–99; W. S. Atkins plc, 1994–2001; Ashanti Goldfields Co. Ltd, 1995–2000. Dir, CARE Britain, 1994–. Pres., Edinburgh Univ. Develt Trust, 1994–99. Mem., Gp of 30, 1992–. FRSA 1993. *Publication:* First World, Third World, 1995. *Recreations:* photography, walking. *Address:* Hawkwood, Hawkwood Lane, Chislehurst, Kent BR7 5PW. *Club:* Reform.

S

SAATCHI, family name of **Baron Saatchi**.

SAATCHI, Baron *cr* 1996 (Life Peer), of Staplefield in the county of West Sussex; **Maurice Saatchi;** Partner, M & C Saatchi Agency, since 1995; *b* 21 June 1946; *s* of late Daisy and Nathan Saatchi; *m* 1984, Josephine Hart; one *s*, and one step *s*. *Educ:* London School of Economics and Political Science (1st class BSc Econ). Co-Founder of Saatchi & Saatchi Co., 1970, Chm., 1985–94. Chm., Megalomedia PLC, 1995–.Opposition spokesman on Treasury affairs, H of L, 1999–. A Trustee, Victoria and Albert Mus., 1988–96; Mem. Council, RCA, 1997–2000. Governor, LSE, 1996–. *Publication:* The Science of Politics, 2001. *Address:* (office) 36 Golden Square, W1R 4EE. *T:* (020) 7543 4500.
See also C. Saatchi.

SAATCHI, Charles; Founder, Saatchi & Saatchi Co., 1970–93; Partner, M & C Saatchi Agency, since 1995; *b* 9 June 1943. *Educ:* Christ's Coll., Finchley. *Address:* (office) 36 Golden Square, W1R 4EE. *T:* (020) 7543 4500.

SABATINI, Lawrence John; retired; Assistant Under Secretary of State, Ministry of Defence, 1972–79; *b* 5 Dec. 1919; *s* of Frederick Laurence Sabatini and Elsie May Sabatini (*née* Friggens); *m* 1947, Patricia Dyson; one *s* one *d*. *Educ:* Watford Grammar School. Joined HM Office of Works, 1938. Army service, 1940–46: commnd in RTR, 1943: service in NW Europe with 5 RTR. Asst Principal, Min. of Works, 1947; Asst Private Sec. to Minister of Works, 1948–49; Principal, 1949; Principal Private Sec. to Ministers of Defence, 1958–60; Asst Sec., MoD, 1960; Defence Counsellor, UK Delegn to NATO, on secondment to Diplomatic Service, 1963–67. *Recreations:* gardening, photography, music. *Address:* 44a Batchworth Lane, Northwood, Mddx HA6 3DT. *T:* (01923) 823249. *Club:* MCC.

SABBEN-CLARE, James Paley; Headmaster, Winchester College, 1985–2000; *b* 9 Sept. 1941; *s* of late Ernest Sabben-Clare and Rosamond Dorothy Mary Scott; *m* 1969, Geraldine Mary Borton, LLB; one *s* one *d*. *Educ:* Winchester College (Scholar); New College, Oxford (Scholar; 1st Class Classical Hon. Mods and Greats, 1964; MA). Asst Master, Marlborough College, 1964–68; Vis. Fellow, All Souls College, Oxford, 1967–68; Winchester College, 1968–2000: Head of Classics Dept, 1969–79; Second Master, 1979–85. Chm., HMC, 1999. Governor: Oundle Sch.; British Sch., Paris. *Publications:* Caesar and Roman Politics, 1971, 2nd edn 1981; Fables from Aesop, 1976; The Culture of Athens, 1978, 2nd edn 1980; Winchester College, 1981, 2nd edn 1988; (contrib.) Winchester: history and literature, 1992; contribs to educnl and classical jls. *Recreations:* Italian opera, mountains, furniture making, living in Dorset. *Address:* Sandy Hill Barn, Corfe Castle, Dorset BH20 5JF. *T:* (01929) 481080.

SABIN, Paul Robert; DL; Chief Executive, Leeds Castle, since 1998; *b* 29 March 1943; *s* of Robert Reginald and Dorothy Maude Sabin; *m* 1965, Vivien Furnival; one *s* two *d*. *Educ:* Oldbury Grammar Sch. DMS Aston Univ.; CPFA (IPFA 1966). West Bromwich CBC, 1961–69; Redditch Develt Corp., 1969–81, Chief Finance Officer, 1975–81; City of Birmingham, 1981–86: City Treas., 1982–86; Dep. Chief Exec., 1984–86; Chief Exec., Kent CC, 1986–97. MIMgt (MBIM 1967); FRSA 1988; FTS 2000. DL Kent, 2001. *Recreations:* fine books, music. *Address:* Leeds Castle, near Maidstone, Kent ME17 1PL.

SABINE, Peter Aubrey, DSc; FRSE, FRSA, FIMM; CEng, CGeol, FGS; Deputy Director (Chief Scientific Officer, Chief Geologist), British Geological Survey (formerly Institute of Geological Sciences), 1977–84; *b* 29 Dec. 1924; *s* of Bernard Robert and Edith Lucy Sabine; *m* 1946, Peggy Willis Lambert, MSc, FBCS, FRSA, FSS; one *s*. *Educ:* Brockley County Sch.; Chelsea Polytechnic; Royal Coll. of Science, Imperial Coll., London (BSc, ARCS (1st Cl. Geol.; Watts medal) 1945); PhD 1951, DSc 1970, London. Apptd Geological Survey of Gt Britain as Geologist, 1945; Geological Museum, 1946–50; in charge Petrographical Dept, Geol Survey and Museum, 1950, Chief Petrographer, 1959; Asst Dir, S England and Wales, 1970; Chief Geochemist, 1977; Dep. Dir, 1977–84. Sec., Geol Soc. of London, 1959–66, Vice-Pres., 1966–67, 1982–84 (Lyell Fund, 1955; Sen. Fellow, 1994); International Union of Geological Sciences: Mem. Commn on Systematics of Igneous Rocks, 1969–; Mem. Commn on Systematics in Petrology, 1980–96 (Chm., 1984–92; Vice-Chm., 1992–96); Chief UK Deleg., 1980–84; Mem. Council, 1980–92; Member Council: Geologists' Assoc., 1966–70; Mineralogical Soc., 1950–53; Instn of Mining and Metallurgy, 1976–80; Mineral Industry Res. Orgn, 1983–86; Member: DTI Chem. and Mineral Research Requirements Bd, 1973–82; Minerals, Metals Extraction and Reclamation Cttee, 1981–84; EEC Cttees on minerals and geochemistry; Cttee of Dirs of W European Geolog. Surveys, 1978–84; Chm., Sub-Cttee on geochem. and cosmochem. of British Nat. Cttee for Geology, 1977–86. Royal Institution: Visitor, 1979–82; Mem., Audit Cttee, 1987–90 (Chm., 1989–90). Fellow, Mineralogical Soc., 1999; FMSA 1959; FBCartS 1996. *Publications:* Chemical Analysis of Igneous Rocks (with E. M. Guppy), 1956; (with D. S. Sutherland) Petrography of British Igneous Rocks, 1982; (jtly) Classification of Igneous Rocks, 1989; numerous scientific contribs in Mem. Geol. Surv., Qly Jl Geol. Soc., Mineral. Mag., Phil. Trans Roy. Soc., etc. *Recreations:* gardening, genealogy. *Address:* Lark Rise, Camp Road, Gerrards Cross, Bucks SL9 7PF. *T:* (01753) 891529. *Clubs:* Athenæum; Geological Society (Hon. Mem.).

SACHRAJDA, Prof. Christopher Tadeusz Czeslaw, PhD; FRS 1996; Professor of Physics, University of Southampton, since 1990; *b* 15 Nov. 1949; *s* of Czeslaw Sachrajda and Hanna Teresa Sachrajda (*née* Grabowska); *m* 1974, Irena Czyzewska; two *s* one *d*. *Educ:* Finchley GS; Univ. of Sussex (BSc); Imperial Coll. of Sci. and Technol. (PhD 1974). CPhys, FInstP 1989. Harkness Fellow, Stanford Linear Accelerator Center, Stanford Univ., 1974–76; Fellow and Staff Mem., CERN, 1976–79 (Scientific Associate, 1986–87 and 1995–96); Department of Physics, University of Southampton: Lectr, 1979–86; Sen. Lectr, 1986–88; Reader, 1988–89; Hd of Dept of Physics and Astronomy, 1997–99. Sen. Fellow, SERC and PPARC, 1991–96. Mem. Council, PPARC, 1998–. *Publications:* numerous research and review articles on theory of elementary particles. *Recreations:* family, tennis, philately (early Polish), walking. *Address:* Department of Physics and Astronomy, University of Southampton, Southampton SO17 1BJ. *T:* (023) 8059 2105; *e-mail:* cts@hep.ph.soton.ac.uk; (home) 20 Radway Road, Southampton SO15 7PW. *Club:* Portswood Lawn Tennis (Southampton).

SACHS, Andrew; actor and writer; *b* 7 April 1930; *s* of Hans and Katharina Sachs; *m* 1962, Melody Good; two *s* one *d*. *Educ:* Zinnowald Sch., Berlin; William Ellis Sch., London. Nat. service, RAC, 1949–51. Started acting career in rep., 1948–49, 1951–56; *theatre* includes: as actor: Whitehall farces, 1958–61; A Voyage Round My Father, Haymarket, 1971; Habeas Corpus, Lyric, 1973; Jumpers, Aldwych, 1985; Kafka's Dick, Royal Court, 1986; Wild Oats, RNT, 1995; Enoch Arden, Steinway Hall, London, NY, 1998 and arts fests, 1998–; Life After Fawlty (tour), 2001; pantomimes, UK and Canada; writer, Made in Heaven, Chichester Fest., 1975; *television* includes: as actor: The Tempest, 1979; History of Mr Polly (serial), 1979; series: Fawlty Towers, 1975, 1979; Every Silver Lining, 1993; Jack of Hearts, 1999; Attachments, 2000, 2001; commentaries for TV documentaries; as actor and co-writer of series: The Galactic Garden, 1984; When in Spain, 1987; Berliners, 1988; *radio* includes: as actor, Heart of a Dog, 1988 (Sony Best Actor Award, 1989); as writer: numerous plays and series, incl. The Revenge, 1978 (Ondas Prize, Radio Barcelona, 1979); audio-cassettes (Talkies Award, for best actor, 1999); *films:* Nicholas Nickleby, 1946; Hitler–the Last Ten Days, 1972; Taxandria, 1989; Mystery of Edwin Drood, 1992. *Address:* c/o Richard Stone Partnership, 2 Henrietta Street, WC2E 8PS. *T:* (020) 7497 0849.

SACHS, Prof. Leo, PhD; FRS 1997; Otto Meyerhof Professor of Biology, Weizmann Institute of Science, Rehovot, Israel, since 1952; *b* 14 Oct. 1924; *s* of Elias and Louise Sachs; *m* 1970, Pnina Salkind; one *s* three *d*. *Educ:* City of London Sch.; Univ. of Wales, Bangor (BSc 1948; Hon. Fellow, 1999); Trinity Coll., Cambridge (PhD 1951). Research Scientist in Genetics, John Innes Inst., 1951–52; Weizmann Institute of Science, Rehovot, Israel: Res. Scientist, 1952–; estabd Dept of Genetics and Virology, 1960; Head, Dept of Genetics, 1962–89; Dean, Faculty of Biol., 1974–79. Fogarty Internat. Scholar, US NIH, 1972; Harvey Lecture, Rockefeller Univ., 1972. Member: EMBO, 1965; Israel Acad. of Scis and Humanities, 1975. Foreign Associate, NAS, 1995; Foreign Mem., Academia Europaea, 1998. Hon. Dr Bordeaux, 1985; Hon. DrMed Lund, 1997. Israel Prize for Natural Scis, 1972; Rothschild Prize in Biol Scis, 1977; Wolf Prize in Medicine, 1980; Bristol-Myers Award for Distinguished Achievement in Cancer Res., 1983; Wellcome Foundn Prize, Royal Soc., 1986; Alfred P. Sloan Prize, General Motors Cancer Res. Foundn, 1989; Warren Alpert Foundn Prize, Harvard Med. Sch., 1997. *Publications:* published papers on blood cell develt, cancer res. and control of growth and differentiation in various scientific jls. *Recreations:* music, museums. *Address:* Department of Molecular Genetics, Weizmann Institute of Science, Rehovot 76100, Israel. *T:* (8) 9343970, *Fax:* (8) 9344108.

SACHS, Hon. Sir Michael (Alexander Geddes), Kt 1993; **Hon. Mr Justice Sachs;** a Judge of the High Court of Justice, Queen's Bench Division, since 1993; *b* 8 April 1932; *s* of Dr Joseph Sachs, MB, ChB, DPH, and Mrs Ruby Mary Sachs (*née* Ross); *m* 1957, Patricia Mary (*née* Conroy); two *s* two *d*. *Educ:* Sedbergh; Manchester Univ. (LLB 1954). Admitted solicitor, 1957. Partner in Slater, Heelis & Co., Solicitors, Manchester, 1962–84. A Recorder, 1980–84; a Circuit Judge, 1984–93. Pres., Manchester Law Soc., 1978–79; Chm., Greater Manchester Legal Services Cttee, 1977–81; Member: No 7 (NW) Area, Legal Aid Cttee, 1966–80 (Chm., 1975–76); Council, Law Soc., 1979–84 (Chm., Standing Cttee on Criminal Law, 1982–84); Court, Univ. of Manchester, 1977–84. Hon. Bencher, Middle Temple, 1993; Hon. Mem., Law Soc., 1993. Hon. LLD Manchester, 1994. KSS 1980. *Address:* Royal Courts of Justice, WC2A 2LL.

SACKS, The Chief Rabbi Dr Jonathan Henry; Chief Rabbi of the United Hebrew Congregations of the British Commonwealth of Nations, since 1991; *b* 8 March 1948; *s* of late Louis David Sacks and Louisa (*née* Frumkin); *m* 1970, Elaine (*née* Taylor); one *s* two *d*. *Educ:* Christ's Coll., Finchley; Gonville and Caius Coll., Cambridge (MA 1972; Hon. Fellow, 1993); New Coll., Oxford; PhD London, 1981. Rabbinic Ordination: Jews' Coll., London, 1976; Yeshivat Etz Hayyim, London, 1976. Lectr in Moral Philosophy, Middlesex Polytechnic, 1971–73; Jews' College, London: Lectr in Jewish Philosophy, 1973–76; Lectr on the Talmud and in Phil., 1976–82; apptd (first) Sir Immanuel (now Lord) Jakobovits Prof. of Modern Jewish Thought, 1982–90; Dir, Rabbinic Faculty, 1983–90; Principal, 1984–90; Rabbi: Golders Green Synagogue, 1978–82; Marble Arch Synagogue, 1983–90. Member (Univ. of London): Bd of Phil., 1985–90; Bd of Studies in Oriental Languages and Literature, 1985–90; Bd of Studies in Theology and Religious Studies, 1986–90. Member: Theol. and Religious Studies Bd, CNAA, 1984–87; Central Religious Adv. Cttee, BBC and IBA, 1987–90. Visiting Professor: Univ. of Essex, 1989–90; Hebrew Univ. in Jerusalem, 1999–; KCL, 1999–. BBC Reith Lectr, 1990. Associate Pres., Conf. of European Rabbis, 2000–. Editor, L'Eylah: A Journal of Judaism Today, 1984–90. FKC 1993. Hon. DD Cantab, 1993; DUniv Middlesex, 1993; Hon. PhD Haifa, 1996; Hon. LLD Liverpool, 1997; Hon. Dr: Yeshiva, NY, 1997; St Andrews, 1997. Jerusalem Prize, 1995. *Publications:* Torah Studies, 1986; (ed) Tradition and Transition: essays presented to Sir Immanuel Jakobovits, 1986; Traditional Alternatives, 1989; Tradition in an Untraditional Age, 1990; The Persistence of Faith, 1991; Argument for the Sake of Heaven, 1991; (ed) Orthodoxy Confronts Modernity, 1991; Crisis and Covenant, 1992; One People? Tradition, Modernity and Jewish Unity, 1993; Will we have Jewish grandchildren?, 1994; Faith in the Future, 1995; Community of Faith, 1996; The Politics of Hope, 1997; Morals and Markets, 1999; Celebrating Life, 2000; Radical

Then, Radical Now, 2001; articles, booklets and book reviews. *Address:* (office) 735 High Road, N12 0US. *T:* (020) 8343 6301, *Fax:* (020) 8343 6310; *e-mail:* info@chiefrabbi.org.

SACKS, Oliver Wolf; neurologist and writer; Clinical Professor of Neurology, Albert Einstein College of Medicine, since 1985; *b* London, 9 July 1933; *s* of Samuel Sacks and Muriel Elsie Landau Sacks. *Educ:* St. Paul's Sch.; Queen's Coll., Oxford (BA 1954; BM BCh 1958; Hon. Fellow, 1999); Middlesex Hosp. Med. Sch. (MA 1956). Jun. med. posts, Middlesex Hosp., 1959–60, Mount Zion Hosp., San Francisco, 1961–62; Resident in Neurology and Neuropathology, UCLA, 1962–65; Fellow, Neurology and Neurochemistry, 1965–66, Instructor in Neurology, 1966–75, Albert Einstein Coll. of Medicine, NY; Consulting Neurologist: Headache Unit, Montefiore Hosp., NY, 1966–68; Bronx Psychiatric Center, NY, 1966–91; Beth Abraham Hosp., NY, 1966–; Little Sisters of the Poor Hosp., NY, 1971–; Asst Prof., 1975–78, Associate Prof., 1978–85, in Neurology, Albert Einstein Coll. of Medicine; Adjunct Prof. of Neurology, NY Univ. Med. Center, 1992–. Member: Amer. Acad. of Neurology, 1962– (Presidential Citation, 1991); NY Inst. for the Humanities, 1984–; Soc. for Neurosci., 1992–. Guggenheim Fellow, 1989; Fellow: Amer. Acad. of Arts and Letters, 1996; NY Acad. of Scis, 1999. Hon. Fellow, Cowell Coll., Univ. of Calif, 1987; Hon. Mem. Amer. Neurological Assoc., 1992. Hon. DHumLit: Georgetown Univ., Washington, DC, 1990; Coll. of Staten Island, NY, 1991; Hon. DSc: Tufts Univ., Mass, 1991; NY Med. Coll., 1991; Bard Coll., NY, 1992; Hon. LLD Queen's Univ. at Kingston, Ont, 2001.Oskar Pfisker Award, Amer. Psychiatric Assoc., 1988; Harold D. Vursell Meml Award, Amer. Acad. and Inst. of Arts and Letters, 1989; Communicator of the Year Award, RNID, 1991; George S. Polk Award, 1994. *Publications:* Migraine, 1970, 2nd edn 1993; Awakenings, 1973, 2nd edn 1990 (Hawthornden Prize, 1975; filmed, 1990); A Leg to Stand On, 1984, 2nd edn 1993; The Man Who Mistook His Wife For a Hat, 1985; Seeing Voices: a journey into the world of the deaf, 1989; An Anthropologist on Mars: seven paradoxical tales, 1995; The Island of the Colorblind, and Cycad Island, 1996; Uncle Tungsten: memories of a chemical boyhood, 2001; papers, contribs to books and jls chiefly on neurology and neuroscience. *Address:* 2 Horatio Street #3G, New York, NY 10014, USA. *T:* (212) 6338373.

SACKUR, Stephen John; Washington Correspondent, BBC, since 1997; *b* 9 Jan. 1964; *s* of Robert Neil Humphrys Sackur and Sallie Caley; *m* 1992, Zina Sabbagh; two *s* one *d*. *Educ:* Emmanuel Coll., Cambridge (BA Hons Hist. 1985). Reporter, Hebden Bridge Times, 1981–82; Henry Fellow, Harvard Univ., 1985–86; BBC: Producer, Current Affairs, 1986–89; Foreign Affairs Corresp., 1989–92; ME Corresp., Cairo, 1992–95; Jerusalem Corresp., 1995–97. *Publication:* On the Basra Road, 1991. *Recreations:* books, films, sports, family adventures. *Address:* c/o BBC Newsgathering, BBC TV Centre, W12 7RJ. *T:* (020) 8743 8000.

SACKVILLE, family name of **Earl De la Warr**.

SACKVILLE, 6th Baron *cr* 1876; **Lionel Bertrand Sackville-West;** *b* 30 May 1913; *s* of late Hon. Bertrand George Sackville-West, *y b* of 4th Baron and Eva Adela Mabel Inigo (*d* 1936), *d* of late Maj.-Gen. Inigo Richmond Jones, CB, CVO; *S* cousin, 1965; *m* 1st, 1953, Jacobine Napier (*d* 1971), *widow* of Captain John Hichens, RA, and *d* of J. R. Menzies-Wilson; five *d*; 2nd, 1974, Arlie, Lady de Guingand (marr. diss. 1983; she *d* 1991); 3rd, 1983, Jean, *widow* of Sir Edward Imbert-Terry, 3rd Bt. *Educ:* Winchester; Magdalen Coll., Oxford. Formerly Capt. Coldstream Gds; served War, 1939–42 (POW). Member of Lloyd's, 1949. *Heir: nephew* Robert Bertrand Sackville-West [b 10 July 1958; *m* 1st, 1985, Catherine Dorothea Bennett (marr. diss. 1992); *m* 1994, Margot Jane MacAndrew; one *d*]. *Address:* Knole, Sevenoaks, Kent TN15 0RP.

See also Sir M. E. S. Imbert-Terry, Bt.

SACKVILLE, Hon. Thomas Geoffrey, (Tom); Chief Executive, International Federation of Health Plans (formerly International Federation of Health Funds), since 1998; *b* 26 Oct. 1950; 2nd *s* of 10th Earl De La Warr (*d* 1988) and of Anne Rachel, *o d* of Geoffrey Devas, MC, Hunton Court, Maidstone; *m* 1979, Catherine Theresa, *d* of Brig. James Windsor Lewis; one *s* one *d*. *Educ:* St Aubyn's, Rottingdean, Sussex; Eton Coll.; Lincoln Coll., Oxford (BA). Deltec Banking Corp., New York, 1971–74; Grindlays Bank Ltd, London, 1974–77; Internat. Bullion and Metal Brokers (London) Ltd, 1978–83. MP (C) Bolton West, 1983–97; contested (C) same seat, 1997. PPS to Minister of State at the Treasury, 1985, to Minister for Social Security, 1987–88; an Asst Govt Whip, 1988–90; a Lord Comr of HM Treasury (Govt Whip), 1990–92; Parliamentary Under-Secretary of State: DoH, 1992–95; Home Office, 1995–97. Sec., All-Party Cttee on Drug Misuse, 1984–88. Dir, NewMedia Investors, 1997. *Address:* International Federation of Health Plans, 46–48 Grosvenor Gardens, SW1W 0EB.

SACKVILLE-WEST, family name of **Baron Sackville**.

SADEQUE, Shahwar; educational and ICT consultant, since 1996; a Governor, BBC, 1990–95; *b* 31 Aug. 1942; *d* of late Ali Imam and of Akhtar Imam; *m* 1962, Pharhad Sadeque; one *s* one *d*. *Educ:* Dhaka Univ., Bangladesh (BSc 1st Cl. Hons Physics); Bedford Coll., London (MPhil Physics); Kingston Poly. (MSc Inf. Technol.). MBCS 1991. Computer Programmer with BARIC Services Ltd, 1969–73; Teacher, Nonsuch High Sch., Sutton, 1974–84; research in computer integrated manufacture incorporating vision systems and artificial intelligence, Kingston Univ. (formerly Poly.), 1985–92. Member: Commn for Racial Equality, 1989–93; VAT Tribunals (England and Wales), 1991–; (pt-time) Income and Corporation Tax Tribunals, 1992–; SCAA, 1993–97; NCET, 1994–97; Metropolitan Police Cttee, 1995–2000; Cttee on Ethical Issues in Medicine, RCP, 1998–; Wkg Gp on operational and ethical guidelines (tissue collections), MRC, 1998–; Good Practice in Consent Adv. Gp, DoH, 2000–; Wkg Pty on Healthcare-related Res. in Developing Countries, Nuffield Council on Bioethics, 2000–; Lord Chancellor's Adv. Council on Public Records, 1999–. Foreign and Commonwealth Office: Member: Panel 2000, 1998; Marshall Aid Commemoration Commn, 1998–; Special Rep. of Sec. of State, FCO, 1998–. Member: Bd, Waltham Forest HAT, 1991–; Council, C&G, 1995–; Bd of Govs, Kingston Univ., 1995–. Gov., Res. into Ageing, 1998–2001; Trustee: Windsor Leadership Trust, 1998–; Immigration Adv. Service, 2000–. FRSA 1994–2000. *Publications:* papers (jointly): Education and Ethnic Minorities, 1988; Manufacturing—towards the 21st Century, 1988; A Knowledge-Based System for Sensor Interaction and Real-Time Component Control, 1988. *Recreations:* collecting thimbles and perfume bottles, cooking Indian-style, passion for keeping up-to-date with current affairs. *e-mail:* Shahwar.Sadeque@BTInternet.com.

SADGROVE, Very Rev. Michael; Dean (formerly Provost) of Sheffield, since 1995; *b* 13 April 1950; *s* of Ralph and Doreen Sadgrove; *m* 1974, (Elizabeth) Jennifer Suddes; one *s* three *d*. *Educ:* UCS; Balliol Coll., Oxford (BA (Maths and Philosophy, Theology) 1972; MA 1975); Trinity Coll., Bristol. Ordained, deacon, 1975, priest, 1976; Lectr in OT studies, 1977–82, Vice-Principal, 1980–82, Salisbury and Wells Theol College; Vicar, Alnwick, Northumberland, 1982–87; Canon Residentiary, Precentor and Vice-Provost, Coventry Cathedral, 1987–95. Bishops' Inspector of Theol Colls and Courses, 1982– (Sen. Inspector, 1997–). Chairman: Precentors' Conf. of England and Wales, 1991–94; Church Men in the Midlands, 1991–95; Mem., Cathedrals Fabric Commn for England, 1996–. Chm., Sheffield Common Purpose, 1996–99. FRSA 1997. *Publications:* A Picture of Faith, 1995; contributor to: Studia Biblica, 1978; Reflecting the Word, 1989; Lion Handbook of the World's Religions, 1982, 2nd edn 1994; Rethinking Marriage, 1993; Coventry's First Cathedral, 1994; The Care Guide, 1995; Calling Time, 2000; Creative Chords, 2001; articles and reviews in theol jls. *Recreations:* music (piano, organ, singing), arts, classical literature, walking the north-east of England, riding Sheffield's trams, travels in Burgundy, European issues. *Address:* The Cathedral, Sheffield S1 1HA. *T:* (0114) 275 3434, *Fax:* (0114) 278 0244; *e-mail:* dean@sheffield-cathedral.org.uk.

SADIE, Stanley (John), CBE 1982; writer on music; Music Critic for The Times, 1964–81, thereafter freelance; Editor: The Musical Times, 1967–87; The New Grove Dictionary of Music and Musicians, 1970–2000; Master Musicians series, since 1976; *b* 30 Oct. 1930; *s* of David Sadie and Deborah (*née* Simons); *m* 1st, 1953, Adèle Bloom (*d* 1978); two *s* one *d*; 2nd, 1978, Julie Anne Vertrees; one *s* one *d*. *Educ:* St Paul's Sch.; Gonville and Caius Coll., Cambridge Univ. (MA, PhD, MusB). Prof., Trinity Coll. of Music, London, 1957–65. President: Royal Musical Assoc., 1989–94 (Vice-Pres., 1985–89; Mem., 1957–); Internat. Musicological Soc., 1992–97 (Mem., 1955–; Directorium, 1987–92); Member: Critics' Circle, 1963–; American Musicological Soc., 1970–; Hon. Corresp. Mem., 1994. Chm., Handel House Trust, 1994–96 (Pres., 1996–). Writer and broadcaster on musical subjects, *circa* 1955–; Music Consultant, Man and Music, Granada TV, 1984–89; editor of many edns of 18th-century music, 1955–; Series Editor, Man and Music, 8 vols, 1989–93. Hon. RAM 1981; Hon. FRCM 1994. Hon. DLitt Leicester, 1981. *Publications:* Handel, 1962; Mozart, 1966; Beethoven, 1967; Handel, 1968; (with Arthur Jacobs) Pan Book of Opera/The Opera Guide, 1964, new edns 1969, 1984; Handel Concertos, 1973; (ed) The New Grove Dictionary of Music and Musicians, 1980, rev. edn 2001; Mozart (The New Grove Biographies), 1982; (ed) New Grove Dictionary of Musical Instruments, 1984; (with Alison Latham) The Cambridge Music Guide, 1985, US edn 1993 (trans. German, French and Swedish); Mozart Symphonies, 1986; (ed with H. Wiley Hitchcock) The New Grove Dictionary of American Music, 1986; (ed) The Grove Concise Dictionary of Music, 1988, rev. edn 1994; (ed) History of Opera, 1989; (ed with H. M. Brown) Performance Practice, 1989; (ed with D. W. Krummel) Music Printing and Publishing, 1989; (ed) The New Grove Dictionary of Opera, 1992; (ed) Wolfgang Amadè Mozart: essays on his life and works, 1996; (ed) New Grove Book of Operas, 1996; contrib. The Musical Times, Gramophone, Opera, Music and Letters, Musical Quarterly, Proc. Roy. Musical Assoc. *Recreations:* watching cricket, drinking (mainly wine and coffee), bridge, travel, reading. *Address:* The Manor, Cossington, Bridgwater, Somerset TA7 8JR. *T:* (01278) 723655, *Fax:* (01278) 723656; *e-mail:* s.sadie@ukgateway.net.

SADLER, Ven. Anthony Graham; Archdeacon of Walsall, since 1997; *b* 1 April 1936; *s* of Frank and Hannah Sadler; unmarried. *Educ:* Bishop Vesey's Grammar Sch.; The Queen's Coll., Oxford (MA); Lichfield Theol Coll. Ordained deacon, 1962, priest, 1963; Asst Curate, St Chad, Burton upon Trent, 1963–65; Vicar: All Saints, Rangemore and St Mary, Dunstall, 1965–72; St Nicholas, Abbots Bromley, 1972–79; St Michael, Pelsall, 1979–90; Rural Dean of Walsall, 1982–90; Priest-in-charge of Uttoxeter, Bramshall, Gratwich, Marchington Kingstone, Marchington Woodlands, Checkley, Stramshall and Leigh, and Leader of the Uttoxeter Area of Ministry Develt, 1990–97; Rector of Uttoxeter, 1997. Prebendary, 1987–97, Hon. Canon, 1997–, Lichfield Cathedral. *Recreations:* music, painting. *Address:* The Archdeacon's House, 10 Paradise Lane, Pelsall, Walsall, West Midlands WS3 4NH. *T:* (01922) 445353, *Fax:* (01922) 445354.

SADLER, Anthony John; Archbishops' Appointments Secretary, since 1996; *b* 2 Oct. 1938; *s* of David James Sadler and Joan Sybil (*née* Alt); *m* 1966, Marie-José Lucas; three *d*. *Educ:* Bedford Sch.; Magdalene Coll., Cambridge (MA). Personnel Manager, Hawker Siddeley Aviation, Hatfield, 1964–75; Asst Personnel Controller, Rank Orgn, 1975–78; Employee Relns Manager, Lloyds Bank Internat., 1978–83; Dir, Gp Human Resources, Minet plc, 1983–92. Vice-Pres., Internat. IPM, 1981–83; Chm., Staff Mgt Assoc., 1989–91. Chm., Southwark Welcare Centenary Appeal Cttee, 1993–95. Chm., S London Industrial Mission, 1980–82. Church Warden, St Luke, Kew, 1976–88. CIPD (CIPM 1983). *Publication:* Human Resource Management: developing a strategic approach, 1995. *Recreations:* divided between London (theatre, classical music, gardening) and Ile de Ré, France (cycling, bird-watching, swimming). *Address:* 343 Sandycombe Road, Richmond, Surrey TW9 3NA. *T:* (020) 8940 3626. *Club:* Army and Navy.

SADLER, Joan; Principal, Cheltenham Ladies' College, 1979–87; *b* 1 July 1927; *d* of Thomas Harold Sadler and Florence May Sadler. *Educ:* Cambridgeshire High Sch.; Univ. of Bristol (BA Hons (History); DipEd; MEd 1998). Downe House, Cold Ash, Newbury, Berks: Asst History teacher, 1950–56; Head of History Dept, 1956–58; Heriots Wood School, Stanmore, Mddx: Head of History Dept, 1958–68; Sen. Mistress, 1966–68; Headmistress, Howell's School, Denbigh, 1968–79. Chairman: Boarding Schools' Assoc., 1983–85; Independent Schools' Curriculum Cttee, 1986; Trustee: Central Bureau for Educnl Visits and Exchanges; Common Entrance Examination for Girls' Schools. Hon. Freewoman: City of London; Drapers' Co., 1979. FRSA. *Recreations:* music, theatre, travel, reading. *Address:* Locke's Cottage, Caudle Green, Cheltenham, Glos GL53 9PR.

SADLER, John Stephen, CBE 1982; *b* 6 May 1930; *s* of late Bernard and Phyllis Sadler; *m* 1952, Ella (*née* McCleery); three *s*. *Educ:* Reading Sch.; Corpus Christi Coll., Oxford (MA 1st cl. PPE). Board of Trade, 1952–54; Treasury, 1954–56; Board of Trade, 1956–60; British Trade Commissioner, Lagos, Nigeria, 1960–64; Board of Trade, 1964–66. John Lewis Partnership Ltd, 1966–89: Finance Dir, 1971–87; Dep. Chm., 1984–89. Chairman: Water Res. Centre, subseq. WRC, 1989–93; West End Bd, Royal & Sun Alliance (formerly Sun Alliance) Insurance Gp, 1991–2001; UK Bd, Australian Mutual Provident Soc. and London Life, 1991–96; Pearl Gp PLC, 1994–96; Argent Gp PLC, 1997–2001; Dir, Debenham Tewson & Chinnock Hldgs plc, 1987–2000. Dir, IMRO, 1987–94; Chm., Authorised Conveyancing Practitioners Bd, 1991–93; Mem., Monopolies and Mergers Commn, 1973–85. Special Advr, Ofgem, 1996–2001. Trustee, British Telecommunications Staff Superannuation Scheme, 1983–98. *Publication:* report of enquiry into media promotion. *Recreations:* golf, boating. *Address:* Riverlea, The Warren, Caversham, Reading RG4 7TQ. *Clubs:* Oriental, Lansdowne; Caversham Heath Golf.

SAFFMAN, Prof. Philip Geoffrey, FRS 1988; Theodor von Kármán Professor of Applied Mathematics and Aeronautics, California Institute of Technology, since 1995 (Professor of Applied Mathematics, 1964–95); *b* 19 March 1931; *s* of Sam Ralph Saffman and Sarah Rebecca Leviten; *m* 1954, Ruth Arion; one *s* two *d*. *Educ:* Roundhay Sch., Leeds; Trinity Coll., Cambridge (BA, MA, PhD). Prize Fellow, Trinity Coll., Cambridge, 1955–59; Asst Lectr, Applied Math., Cambridge, 1958–60; Reader in Applied Math., King's Coll. London, 1960–64. Fellow, Amer. Acad. of Arts and Scis, 1978. *Publications:* Vortex Dynamics, 1992; numerous papers in sci. jls. *Recreations:* hiking, camping. *Address:* 399 Ninita Parkway, Pasadena, CA 91106, USA.

SAGAN, Françoise; pen-name of Françoise Quoirez; authoress; *b* France, 21 June 1935; *y c* of Paul Quoirez; *m* 1958, Guy Schoeller (marr. diss. 1960); *m* 1962, Robert James

Westhoff (marr. diss.); one *s*. *Educ:* convent and private school. Published first novel at age of 18. Has written some songs and collaborated in scheme for ballet Le Rendez-vous Manqué, produced Paris and London, 1958. *Publications:* Bonjour Tristesse, 1954; Un Certain Sourire, 1956 (filmed, 1958); Dans un mois, dans un an, 1957 (Those Without Shadows, 1958); Aimez-vous Brahms . . . , 1959 (1960); Château en Suède (play), 1960; Les Violons, parfois . . . (play), 1961; La Robe Mauve de Valentine (play), 1963; Bonheur, impair et passe (play), 1964; Toxique ... (trans. 1965); La Chamade, 1965 (trans. 1966) (film, 1970); Le Cheval Evanoui (play), 1966; L'Echarde, 1966; Le Garde du cœur, 1968 (The Heart-Keeper, 1968); Un peu de soleil dans l'eau froide, 1969 (Sunlight and Cold Water, 1971); Un piano dans l'herbe (play), 1970; Des bleus à l'âme, 1972 (Scars on the Soul, 1974); Zaphorie (play), 1973; Lost Profile, 1976; Silken Eyes (short stories), 1977; The Unmade Bed, 1978; Le Chien Couchant, 1980; La femme fardée, 1981 (The Painted Lady, 1982); The Still Storm, 1984; Incidental Music (short stories), 1985; Avec mon meilleur souvenir (With Fondest Regards), 1986; Un sang d'aquarelle, 1987; Dear Sarah Bernhardt, 1989; (with W. Denker) The Eiffel Tower, 1989; La Laisse, 1989 (The Leash); Les Faux-fuyants, 1991 (The Evasion, 1993); Répliques, 1992; Oeuvres (collected works), 1993; ----- et toute ma sympathie (essays), 1993; Un Chagrin de Passage, 1994; Le Miroir égaré, 1996; Dernière l'épaule . . . , 1998. *Address:* c/o Editions Julliard, 24 avenue Marceau, 75008 Paris, France.

SAGE, Stephen Paul; Chief Executive, FCO Services, Foreign and Commonwealth Office, since 2000; *b* 3 June 1953; *s* of late Ivor John Sage and Kathleen Gwendoline Sage (*née* Jeffrey); *m* 1982, Anne Jennifer Mickleburgh; two *s* one *d*. *Educ:* Bristol Grammar Sch.; Peterhouse, Cambridge (BA Hons Classics 1974; MA). MCIPS 1993. John Henderson Sports, 1976–78; Crown Agents, 1978–80; Department of the Environment, 1980–93: Private Sec. to Housing Minister, 1984–85; Controller, Merseyside Task Force, 1989–93; Chief Exec., The Buying Agency, 1993–2000. Mem. Cttee, Pierhead Housing Assoc., 1994–. *Recreations:* reading, music, Alfa Romeos. *Address:* FCO Services, Foreign and Commonwealth Office, Hanslope Park, Hanslope MK19 7BH. *Club:* Bristol City Football.

SAID, Prof. Edward W., PhD; University Professor, English and Comparative Literature, Columbia University, since 1992; *b* 1 Nov. 1935; *m* 1970, Mariam Cortas; one *s* one *d*. *Educ:* Princeton Univ. (AB 1957); Harvard Univ. (AM 1960; PhD 1964). Columbia University: Instructor in English, 1963–65; Asst Prof. of English and Comparative Literature, 1967–69; Prof., 1969–77; Parr Prof., 1977–89; Old Dominion Foundn Prof. in Humanities, 1989–92. Reith Lectr, 1993. *Publications:* Joseph Conrad and the Fiction of Autobiography, 1966; Beginnings: intention and method, 1975; Orientalism, 1978; The Question of Palestine, 1979; (ed) Literature and Society, 1980; Covering Islam, 1981; The World, the Text and the Critic, 1983; After the Last Sky, 1986; (ed jtly) Blaming the Victims, 1988; Musical Elaborations, 1991; Culture and Imperialism, 1993; The Politics of Dispossession, 1994; Representations of the Intellectual, 1994; Peace and Its Discontents: Gaza to Jericho 1993–1995, 1996; Out of Place: a memoir, 1999. *Address:* 602 Philosophy Hall, Department of English, Columbia University, New York, NY 10027, USA.

SAINSBURY, family name of **Barons Sainsbury of Preston Candover** and **Sainsbury of Turville**.

SAINSBURY OF PRESTON CANDOVER, Baron *cr* 1989 (Life Peer), of Preston Candover in the county of Hampshire; **John Davan Sainsbury,** KG 1992; Kt 1980; President, J Sainsbury plc, since 1992 (Vice-Chairman, 1967–69; Chairman, 1969–92; Director, 1958–92); *b* 2 Nov. 1927; *e s* of Baron Sainsbury; *m* 1963, Anya Linden, *qv*; two *s* one *d*. *Educ:* Stowe School; Worcester College, Oxford (Hon. Fellow 1982). Dir, Royal Opera House, Covent Garden, 1969–85 (Chm., 1987–91); Chairman: Friends of Covent Garden, 1969–81; Benesh Inst. of Choreology, 1986–87; Bd of Trustees, Dulwich Picture Gall., 1994–2000; Govs, Royal Ballet, 1995– (Gov., 1987–); Governor: Royal Ballet Sch., 1965–76, and 1987–91; Royal Opera House Trust, 1974–84 and 1987–97. Dir, The Economist, 1972–80; Jt Hon. Treas., European Movt, 1972–75; Pres., British Retail Consortium, 1993–97 (Mem. Council, Retail Consortium, 1975–79); Member: Nat. Cttee for Electoral Reform, 1976–85; President's Cttee, CBI, 1982–84. Vice Patron, Contemporary Arts Soc. (Hon. Sec., 1965–71; Vice Chm., 1971–74); Trustee: Nat. Gall., 1976–83; Westminster Abbey Trust, 1977–83; Tate Gall., 1982–83; Rhodes Trust, 1984–98. Dir, Friends of the Nelson Mandela Children's Fund, 1996–2000. Pres., Sparsholt Coll., Hants, 1993–2000. Hon. Bencher, Inner Temple, 1985. FIGD 1973. Hon. DScEcon London, 1985; Hon. DLitt South Bank, 1992; Hon. LLD Bristol, 1993; Hon. DEconSc Cape Town, 2000. Albert Medal, RSA, 1989. *Address:* c/o Stamford House, Stamford Street, SE1 9LL. *T:* (020) 7695 6000. *Clubs:* Garrick, Beefsteak.
See also Rt Hon. Sir T. A. D. Sainsbury.

SAINSBURY OF PRESTON CANDOVER, Lady; *see* Linden, Anya.

SAINSBURY OF TURVILLE, Baron *cr* 1997 (Life Peer), of Turville in the co. of Buckinghamshire; **David John Sainsbury;** Parliamentary Under-Secretary of State, Department of Trade and Industry, since 1998; *b* 24 Oct. 1940; *s* of Sir Robert Sainsbury and of Lisa Ingeborg (*née* Van den Bergh); *m* 1973, Susan Carole Reid; three *d*. *Educ:* King's Coll., Cambridge (BA); Columbia Univ., NY (MBA). Joined J. Sainsbury, 1963; Finance Dir, 1973–90; Dep. Chm., 1988–92; Chm., 1992–98; Chief Exec., 1992–97. Member: Cttee of Review of the Post Office (Carter Cttee), 1975–77; IPPR Commn on Public Policy and British Business, 1995–97. Trustee, Social Democratic Party, 1982–90; Mem. Governing Body, London Business Sch., 1985– (Chm., 1991–98); Chm. Transition Bd, Univ. for Industry, 1998–99. Hon. FREng (Hon. FEng 1994). Hon. LLD Cambridge, 1997. *Publications:* Government and Industry: a new partnership, 1981; (with Christopher Smallwood) Wealth Creation and Jobs, 1987.

SAINSBURY, Edward Hardwicke, TD 1945; consultant; Partner, Dawson, Hart & Co., Uckfield, 1961–92 (ceased to practice, 1993), retired; District Notary Public, Uckfield, since 1965; *b* 17 Sept. 1912; *e s* of Henry Morgan Sainsbury, and *g s* of James C. Hardwicke, a pioneer of technical and other education in S Wales; *m* 1946, Ann, 2nd *d* of late Kenneth Ellis, Tunbridge Wells; one *s* one *d*. *Educ:* Cardiff High School; University of S Wales and Monmouth. Solicitor in private practice, 1935–; commissioned (TA) 1936; Prosecuting Solicitor, Cardiff, 1938, Sen. Pros. Solicitor, 1939. Served War of 1939–45; Adjutant, 77th HAA Regt, 1940; comd 240 HAA Battery Gibraltar, 1944; demobilised Nov. 1945. Hong Kong: Asst Crown Solicitor, 1946; commissioner for revision of the laws of Hong Kong, 1947; magistrate, 1948; registrar, High Court, 1949; sen. magistrate, Kowloon, 1951; Barrister, Inner Temple, 1951; Land Officer and sen. crown counsel, Hong Kong, 1952; legal draftsman, Nigeria, 1953; Principal Legal Draftsman, Fed. of Nigeria, 1958. President, Commonwealth Parliamentary Assoc., Southern Cameroons, 1959–63. Judge, High Court of Lagos, 1960–63, and of Southern Cameroons, 1961–63; Speaker, House of Assembly, 1958–63, Chm., Public Service Commn, 1961–63, Southern Cameroons. *Publication:* (jointly) Revised Laws of Hong Kong, 1948. *Recreations:* squash (a memory), golf. *Address:* 35 Allington Road, Newick, Lewes, East Sussex BN8 4NB. *T:* (01825) 723682.

SAINSBURY, Jeffrey Paul, FCA; chartered accountant; Executive Manager, Computershare Services plc, since 2000; Lord Mayor of Cardiff, 1991–92; *b* 27 June 1943; *s* of Capt. Walter Ronald Sainsbury and Joan Margaret Slamin; *m* 1967, Janet Elizabeth Hughes; one *s* one *d*. *Educ:* Cardiff High Sch. FCA 1966. Partner, Pannell Kerr Forster, 1969–94; Man. Dir, Exchange Registrars Ltd, 1994–2000. Mem., Cardiff CC, 1969–96. Member: S Glamorgan HA, 1987–91; Bd, Cardiff Bay Develt Corp., 1991–2000. Chm., New Theatre, Cardiff, 1983–87. Chm., S Glam TEC, 1996–99; Dep. Chm., TEC SE Wales, 1999–2000. Gov., WCMD, 1995–2001. FRSA 1997. OStJ 1997. *Recreations:* cooking, music, theatre, sport. *Address:* 6 Druidstone House, Druidstone Road, St Mellons, Cardiff CF3 6XF. *Club:* Cardiff & County.

SAINSBURY, Prof. (Richard) Mark, FBA 1998; Stebbing Professor of Philosophy, King's College London, since 1989; *b* 2 July 1943; *s* of Richard Eric Sainsbury and Freda Margaret Sainsbury (*née* Horne); *m* 1970, Gillian McNeill Rind (separated); one *s* one *d*. *Educ:* Sherborne Sch.; Corpus Christi Coll., Oxford (MA, DPhil). Lecturer in Philosophy: Magdalen Coll., Oxford, 1968–70; St Hilda's Coll., Oxford, 1970–73; Brasenose Coll., Oxford, 1973–75; Univ. of Essex, 1975–78; Bedford Coll., Univ. of London, 1978–84; King's College London: Lectr in Philosophy, 1984–87; Reader in Philosophy, 1987–89. Leverhulme Sen. Res. Fellow, 2000–Sept. 2002. Editor of Mind, 1990–2000. *Publications:* Russell, 1979; Paradoxes, 1988, 2nd edn 1995; Logical Forms, 1991, 2nd edn 2000. *Recreation:* baking bread. *Address:* Philosophy Department, King's College London, WC2R 2LS; *e-mail:* mark.sainsbury@kcl.ac.uk.

SAINSBURY, Rt Rev. Roger Frederick; *see* Barking, Area Bishop of.

SAINSBURY, Rt Hon. Sir Timothy (Alan Davan), Kt 1995; PC 1992; Chairman: Somerset House Trust (formerly Somerset House Ltd), since 1997; Pendennis Shipyard (Holdings) Ltd, since 1999; Marlborough Tiles Ltd, since 1999; *b* 11 June 1932; *y s* of Baron Sainsbury; *m* 1961, Susan Mary Mitchell; two *s* two *d*. *Educ:* Eton; Worcester Coll., Oxford (MA; Hon. Fellow 1982). Dir, J. Sainsbury, 1962–83; non-exec. Dir, J. Sainsbury plc, 1995–99. Chm., Council for the Unit for Retail Planning Information Ltd, 1974–79. MP (C) Hove, Nov. 1973–1997. PPS to Sec. of State for the Environment, 1979–83, to Sec. of State for Defence, 1983; a Govt Whip, 1983–87; Parly Under-Sec. of State for Defence Procurement, 1987–89; Parly Under-Sec. of State, FCO, 1989–90; Minister of State, DTI, 1990–94 (Minister for Trade, 1990–92, for Industry, 1992–94). Pres., Cons. Friends of Israel, 1997– (Parly Chm., 1994–97). Mem. Council, RSA, 1981–83. Hon. ARICS 1994; Hon. FRIBA 1994. *Address:* Suite 2.3 Buckingham Court, 78 Buckingham Gate, SW1E 6PE.
See also Baron Sainsbury of Preston Candover, S. A. Woodward.

SAINT, Prof. Andrew John; Professor of Architecture, University of Cambridge, since 1995; *b* 30 Nov. 1946; *s* of Arthur James Maxwell Saint and late Elisabeth Yvetta Saint (*née* Butterfield); three *d*. *Educ:* Christ's Hosp.; Balliol Coll., Oxford. Part-time Lectr, Univ. of Essex, 1971–74; Architectural Editor, Survey of London, 1974–86; Historian, London Div., English Heritage, 1986–95. Hon. FRIBA 1993. *Publications:* Richard Norman Shaw, 1976; The Image of the Architect, 1983; Towards a Social Architecture, 1987. *Address:* Department of Architecture, University of Cambridge, 1 Scroope Terrace, Cambridge CB2 1PX. *T:* (01223) 332964; *e-mail:* ajs61@cam.ac.uk; (home) 14 Denny Crescent, SE11 4UY. *T:* (020) 7735 3863.

SAINT, Dora Jessie, MBE 1998; (*pen name* Miss Read); writer, since 1950; *b* 17 April 1913; *d* of Arthur Gunnis Shafe and Grace Lilian Shafe; *m* 1940, Douglas Edward John Saint; one *d*. *Educ:* Bromley County Sch.; Homerton Coll., Cambridge. Teaching in Middlesex, 1933–40; occasional teaching, 1946–63. *Publications:* Village School, 1955; Village Diary, 1957; Storm in the Village, 1958; Thrush Green, 1959; Fresh from the Country, 1960; Winter in Thrush Green, 1961; Miss Clare Remembers, 1962; Chronicles of Fairacre, 1963; Over the Gate, 1964; Market Square, 1965; Village Christmas, 1966; Fairacre Festival, 1968; News from Thrush Green, 1970; Tiggy, 1971; Emily Davis, 1971; Tyler's Row, 1972; The Christmas Mouse, 1973; Farther Afield, 1974; Battles at Thrush Green, 1975; No Holly for Miss Quinn, 1976; Village Affairs, 1977; Return to Thrush Green, 1978; The White Robin, 1979; Village Centenary, 1980; Gossip from Thrush Green, 1981; Affairs at Thrush Green, 1983; Summer at Fairacre, 1984; At Home in Thrush Green, 1985; The School at Thrush Green, 1987; The World of Thrush Green, 1988; Mrs Pringle, 1989; Friends at Thrush Green, 1990; Celebrations at Thrush Green, 1992; Farewell to Fairacre, 1993; Tales from a Village School, 1994; Early Days, 1995; The Year at Thrush Green, 1995; A Peaceful Retirement, 1996; *for children:* Hobby Horse Cottage, 1958; Hob and the Horse-Bat, 1965; The Red Bus Series, 1965; *non-fiction:* Country Bunch (anthology), 1963; Miss Read's Country Cooking, 1969; *autobiography:* A Fortunate Grandchild, 1982; Time Remembered, 1986. *Recreations:* theatre-going, reading. *Address:* c/o Michael Joseph Ltd, Penguin Group (UK), 80 Strand, WC2R 0RL.

ST ALBANS, 14th Duke of, *cr* 1684; **Murray de Vere Beauclerk;** Earl of Burford, Baron of Heddington, 1676; Baron Vere of Hanworth, 1750; Hereditary Grand Falconer of England; Hereditary Registrar, Court of Chancery; Partner, Burford & Co., chartered accountants, since 1981; *b* 19 Jan. 1939; *s* of 13th Duke of St Albans, OBE and Nathalie Chatham, *d* of P. F. Walker (later Mrs Nathalie C. Eldrid, *d* 1985); *S* father, 1988; *m* 1st, 1963, Rosemary Frances Scoones (marr. diss. 1974); one *s* one *d*; 2nd, 1974, Cynthia Theresa Mary, *d* of late Lt-Col W. J. H. Howard, DSO and formerly wife of Sir Anthony Robin Maurice Hooper, 2nd Bt. *Educ:* Tonbridge. Chartered Accountant, 1962. Gov.-Gen., Royal Stuart Soc., 1989–. Pres., Beaufort Opera, 1991–. *Heir:* *s* Earl of Burford, *qv*. *Address:* 16 Ovington Street, SW3 2JB. *Club:* Hurlingham.

ST ALBANS, Bishop of, since 1995; **Rt Rev. Christopher William Herbert;** *b* 7 Jan. 1944; *s* of Walter Meredith Herbert (who *m* 1950, Dorothy Margaret Curnock) and late Hilda Lucy (*née* Dibbin); *m* 1968, Janet Elizabeth Turner; two *s*. *Educ:* Monmouth School; St David's Coll., Lampeter (BA); Univ. of Bristol (PGCE); Wells Theol Coll. Asst Curate, Tupsley, Hereford, 1967–71; Asst Master, Bishop's Sch., Hereford, 1967–71; Adv in Religious Educn, 1971–76, Dir of Educn, 1976–81, Dio. of Hereford; Vicar, St Thomas on the Bourne, Farnham, Surrey, 1981–90; Archdeacon of Dorking, 1990–95. Dir, Post-ordination Training, Dio. of Guildford, 1984–90; Hon. Canon of Guildford, 1984–95. *Publications:* The New Creation, 1971; A Place to Dream, 1976; St Paul's: A Place to Dream, 1981; The Edge of Wonder, 1981; Listening to Children, 1983; On the Road, 1984; Be Thou My Vision, 1985; This Most Amazing Day, 1986; The Question of Jesus, 1987; Alive to God, 1987; Ways into Prayer, 1987; Help in your Bereavement, 1988; Prayers for Children, 1993; Pocket Prayers, 1993; The Prayer Garden, 1994; Words of Comfort, 1994; Pocket Prayers for Children, 1999. *Recreations:* walking, cycling, reading, gardening, writing unpublished novels. *Address:* Abbey Gate House, St Albans, Herts AL3 4HD. *T:* (01727) 853305.

ST ALBANS, Dean of; *see* Lewis, Very Rev. C. A.

ST ALBANS, Archdeacon of; *see* Cheetham, R. I.

ST ALDWYN, 3rd Earl *cr* 1915; **Michael Henry Hicks Beach;** Bt 1619; Viscount St Aldwyn 1906; Viscount Quenington 1915; Managing Director, International Fund Marketing (UK) Ltd, since 1994; *b* 7 Feb. 1950; *s* of 2nd Earl St Aldwyn, GBE, TD, PC and Diana Mary Christian Smyly (*d* 1992), *o d* of Henry C. G. Mills; S father, 1992; *m* 1982, Gilda Maria, *o d* of Barão Saavedra, Copacabana, Rio de Janeiro; two *d. Educ:* Eton; Christ Church, Oxford (MA). *Heir: b* Hon. David Seymour Hicks Beach [*b* 25 May 1955; *m* 1993, Kate, *d* of Michael Henriques; one *s* two *d*]. *Address:* 17 Hale House, 34 De Vere Gardens, W8 5AQ. *T:* (020) 7937 6223, *Fax:* (020) 7937 3756; Williamstrip Park, Coln St Aldwyns, Cirencester, Glos GL7 5AT; International Fund Marketing (UK) Ltd, 5th Floor, Suite 7A, Berkeley Square House, Berkeley Square, W1J 6BY. *T:* (020) 7616 7400, *Fax:* (020) 7616 7411.

ST ANDREWS, Earl of; George Philip Nicholas Windsor; *b* 26 June 1962; *s* of HRH the Duke of Kent and HRH the Duchess of Kent; *m* 1988, Sylvana Tomaselli; one *s* two *d. Educ:* Eton (King's Scholar); Downing College, Cambridge. Attached to FCO, 1987–88. Specialist, Christie's (Books and Manuscripts Dept), 1996–98. Trustee: GB-Sasakawa Foundn, 1995–; SOS Children's Villages UK, 1999–. Patron: Assoc. for Internat. Cancer Res., 1995–; Princess Margarita of Romania Trust, 1997–. *Heir: s* Lord Downpatrick, *qv. Address:* York House, St James's Palace, SW1A 1BQ.
See under Royal Family.

ST ANDREWS AND EDINBURGH, Archbishop of, (RC), since 1985; **Most Rev. Keith Michael Patrick O'Brien;** *b* Ballycastle, Co. Antrim, 17 March 1938; *s* of late Mark Joseph O'Brien and Alice Mary (*née* Moriarty). *Educ:* schools in Ballycastle, Dumbarton and Edinburgh; Edinburgh Univ. (BSc 1959, DipEd 1966); St Andrew's Coll., Drygrange; Moray House Coll. of Education, Edinburgh. Ordained Priest, 1965; pastoral appointments: Holy Cross, Edinburgh, 1965–66; St Bride's, Cowdenbeath, 1966–71 (while Chaplain and teacher of Maths and Science, St Columba's High Sch., Cowdenbeath and Dunfermline); St Patrick's, Kilsyth, 1972–75; St Mary's, Bathgate, 1975–78. Spiritual Director, St Andrew's Coll., Drygrange, 1978–80; Rector of St Mary's Coll., Blair, Aberdeen, 1980–85. *Address:* St Bennet's, 42 Greenhill Gardens, Edinburgh EH10 4BJ. *T:* (0131) 447 3337.

ST ANDREWS, DUNKELD AND DUNBLANE, Bishop of, since 1995; **Rt Rev. Michael Harry George Henley,** CB 1991; *b* 16 Jan. 1938; *s* of Eric Edward Henley and Evelyn Agnes Henley (*née* Lilly); *m* 1965, Rachel Jean (*née* Allen); two *d. Educ:* St Marylebone Grammar Sch.; St John's Hall, London (LTh). Ordained deacon, 1961, priest, 1962; Curate, St Marylebone Parish Ch., 1961–64; Chaplain: RN, 1964–68; St Andrews Univ., 1968–72; Royal Hosp. Sch., 1972–74; RN, 1974–93 (Chaplain of the Fleet, Archdeacon for RN and Dir Gen. Naval Chaplaincy Services, 1989–93; Archdeacon Emeritus of the Fleet); Priest i/c, Holy Trinity, Pitlochry, 1994–95. Hon. Canon, Holy Trinity Cathedral, Gibraltar, 1989–93. QHC 1989–93. *Recreations:* golf, fishing. *Address:* Afton House, St Andrews, Fife KY16 9DJ. *Clubs:* Army and Navy; Leander (Henley); County and City (Perth); Royal and Ancient Golf (St Andrews); Royal Perth Golfing Society.

ST ANDREWS, DUNKELD AND DUNBLANE, Dean of; *see* MacAlister, Very Rev. R. G. L.

ST ASAPH, Bishop of, since 1999; **Rt Rev. John Stewart Davies;** *b* 28 Feb. 1943; *s* of John Edward Davies and Dorothy Stewart Davies (*née* Jones); *m* 1965, Joan Patricia Lovatt; two *s. Educ:* St John's Sch., Leatherhead; UCNW, Bangor (BA Hebrew); Westcott House, Cambridge; Queens' Coll., Cambridge (MLitt 1974). Journalism, 1960–68; ordained deacon, 1974, priest, 1975; Curate, Hawarden, 1974–78; Vicar: Rhosymedre, 1978–87; Mold, 1987–92; Archdeacon of St Asaph, 1991–99. *Recreations:* hill walking, cycling. *Address:* Esgobty, St Asaph, Denbighshire LL17 0TW.

ST ASAPH, Dean of; *see* Potter, Very Rev. C. N. L.

ST AUBYN, family name of **Baron St Levan**.

ST AUBYN, Nicholas Francis; *b* 19 Nov. 1955; *s* of Hon. Piers St Aubyn, MC, *heir* to 4th Baron St Levan, *qv*, and late Mary St Aubyn (*née* Bailey-Southwell); *m* 1980, Jane Mary Brooks; two *s* three *d. Educ:* Eton Coll.; Trinity Coll., Oxford (MA PPE). With J. P. Morgan, 1977–86; Kleinwort Benson, 1986–87; American Internat. Gp, 1987–89; Gemini Clothescare, 1989–93; Fitzroy Joinery, 1993–. Founding Mem., London Internat. Futures Market, 1982–84. MP (C) Guildford, 1997–2001; contested same seat, 2001. Mem., Select Cttee on Educn and Employment, 1997–2001. MInstD. *Recreations:* riding, shooting, swimming, sailing. *Clubs:* Brooks's; Surrey County (Guildford); Cornish, Mounts Bay Sailing.

ST AUBYN, Major Thomas Edward, CVO 1993; DL; FRGS; Lieutenant, HM Body Guard of Honourable Corps of Gentlemen at Arms, 1990–93 (Clerk of the Cheque and Adjutant, 1986–90); *b* 13 June 1923; *s* of Hon. Lionel Michael St Aubyn, MVO, and Lady Mary St Aubyn; *m* 1953, Henrietta Mary, *d* of Sir Henry Studholme, 1st Bt; three *d. Educ:* Eton. Served in King's Royal Rifle Corps, 1941–62; Italian Campaign, 1944–45; Adjt 1st KRRC, 1946–48; seconded to Sudan Defence Force in rank of Bimbashi, 1948–52; leader of Tibesti Mountain Expedn in Chad, 1957; Bde Adjt Green Jackets Bde, 1960–62. Mem., HM Body Guard, 1973–. High Sheriff of Hampshire, 1979–80; DL Hampshire, 1984. FRGS 1959. *Recreations:* shooting, fishing. *Address:* West Leigh House, Nether Wallop, Stockbridge, Hants SO20 8EY. *T:* (01264) 782914. *Club:* Army and Navy.

ST AUBYN, Sir William M.; *see* Molesworth-St Aubyn.

ST CLAIR; family name of **Lord Sinclair**.

ST CLAIR, Malcolm Archibald James; *b* 16 Feb. 1927; *o s* of late Maj.-Gen. George James Paul St Clair, CB, CBE, DSO and late Charlotte Theresa Orme Little; *m* 1955, Mary-Jean Rosalie Alice, *o d* of Wing-Comdr Caryl Liddell Hargreaves, Broadwood House, Sunningdale; two *s* one *d. Educ:* Eton. Served with Royal Scots Greys, 1944–48. Formerly Hon. Sec. to Sir Winston Churchill. Contested (C) Bristol South-East, 1959; MP (C) Bristol South-East, 1961–63. Lt Col Comdg, Royal Gloucestershire Hussars (TA), 1967–69. High Sheriff Glos, 1972. *Address:* Long Newnton Priory, Tetbury, Glos GL8 8RR. *Club:* White's.

ST CLAIR, William Linn, FBA 1992; FRSL; author; Fellow, Trinity College, Cambridge, since 1998 (Visiting Fellow Commoner, 1997); *b* 7 Dec. 1937; *s* of late Joseph and Susan St Clair, Falkirk; two *d. Educ:* Edinburgh Acad.; St John's Coll., Oxford. FRSL 1973. Admiralty and MoD, 1961–66; First Sec., FCO, 1966–69; transferred to HM Treasury, 1969, Under Sec., 1990–92; Consultant to OECD, 1992–95, to EC, 1997. Visiting Fellow: All Souls Coll., Oxford, 1981–82; Huntington Library, Calif, 1985; Fellow, All Souls Coll., Oxford, 1992–96. Member: Cttee, London Liby, 1996–2000; Council, British Acad., 1996–2000. Internat. Pres., Byron Soc. Thalassa Forum award for culture, Greece, 2000. *Publications:* Lord Elgin and the Marbles, 1967, 3rd edn 1998; That Greece Might Still Be Free, 1972 (Heinemann prize); Trelawny, 1978; Policy Evaluation: a guide for managers, 1988; The Godwins and the Shelleys, 1989 (Time Life prize and Macmillan silver pen); Executive Agencies: a guide to setting targets and measuring performance, 1992; (ed with Irmgard Maassen) Conduct Literature for Women, 1500–1640, 2000. *Recreations:* old books, Scottish hills. *Address:* 52 Eaton Place, SW1X 8AL. *Clubs:* Athenæum, PEN.

ST CLAIR-ERSKINE, family name of **Earl of Rosslyn**.

ST CLAIR-FORD, Sir James (Anson), 7th Bt *cr* 1793, of Ember Court, Surrey; *b* 16 March 1952; *s* of Capt. Sir Aubrey St Clair-Ford, 6th Bt, DSO, RN and of Anne, *o d* of Harold Cecil Christopherson; *S* father, 1991; *m* 1st, 1977, Jennifer Margaret (marr. diss. 1984), *yr d* of Commodore Robin Grindle, RN; 2nd, 1987, Mary Anne, *er d* of His Honour Nathaniel Robert Blaker, QC. *Educ:* Wellington; Bristol Univ. *Heir: cousin* Colin Anson St Clair-Ford [*b* 19 April 1939; *m* 1964, Gillian Mary, *er d* of Rear Adm. Peter Skelton, CB; two *d*].

ST CYRES, Viscount; John Stafford Northcote; *b* 15 Feb. 1957; *s* and *heir* of 4th Earl of Iddesleigh, *qv*; *m* 1983, Fiona Caroline Elizabeth (marr. diss. 1999), *d* of P. Wakefield, Barcelona, and Mrs M. Hattrell, Burnham, Bucks; one *s* one *d*; *m* 2000, Maria Ann Akaylar. *Educ:* Downside Sch.; RAC Cirencester. *Heir: s* Hon. Thomas Stafford Northcote, *b* 5 Aug. 1985.

ST DAVIDS, 3rd Viscount *cr* 1918; **Colwyn Jestyn John Philipps;** Baron Strange of Knokin, 1299; Baron Hungerford, 1426; Baron de Moleyns, 1445; Bt 1621; Baron St Davids, 1908; *b* 30 Jan. 1939; *s* of 2nd Viscount St Davids and Doreen Guinness (*d* 1956), *o d* of late Captain Arthur Jowett; *S* father, 1991; *m* 1965, Augusta Victoria Correa Larrain, *d* of late Don Estanislao Correa Ugarte; two *s. Educ:* Haverfordwest Grammar Sch.; Sevenoaks Sch.; King's Coll., London (Cert. Advanced Musical Studies, 1989). Nat. Service, 1958–60; commnd 2nd Lt Welsh Guards. Securities Agency Ltd, 1960–65; Mem., Stock Exchange, 1965–93; Maguire Kingsmill and Co., 1965–68; Partner, Kemp-Gee and Co., later Scrimgeour Kemp-Gee and Co., 1971; Director: Citicorp Scrimgeour Vickers (Securities) Ltd, 1985–88; Greig Middleton & Co. Ltd, 1989–90, 1994–99. Mem. Bd, Milford Haven Port Authority, 1997–. A Lord in Waiting (Govt Whip), 1992–94; a Dep. Speaker, H of L, 1995–99. Mem., Baden-Powell Fellowship, 1985–. Mem. Council, Univ. of Wales, Lampeter, 1995–99; Gov., WCMD, 1996–2000. Liveryman: Musicians' Co., 1971–; Welsh Livery Guild, 1997. *Recreations:* music, literature, natural history. *Heir: s* Hon. Rhodri Colwyn Philipps, *b* 16 Sept. 1966. *Clubs:* Garrick; Cardiff and County (Cardiff).

ST DAVIDS, Bishop of; *no new appointment at time of going to press.*

ST DAVIDS, Dean of; *see* Evans, Very Rev. J. W.

ST EDMUNDSBURY, Dean of; *see* Atwell, Very Rev. J. E.

ST EDMUNDSBURY AND IPSWICH, Bishop of, since 1997; **Rt Rev. (John Hubert) Richard Lewis;** *b* 10 Dec. 1943; *s* of John Wilfred and Winifred Mary Lewis; *m* 1968, Sara Patricia Hamilton; two *s* (and one *s* decd). *Educ:* Radley; King's Coll., London (AKC). Curate of Hexham, 1967–70; Industrial Chaplain, Diocese of Newcastle, 1970–77; Communications Officer, Diocese of Durham, 1977–82; Agricultural Chaplain, Diocese of Hereford, 1982–87; Archdeacon of Ludlow, 1987–92; Bishop Suffragan of Taunton, 1992–97. Prebendary, Wells Cathedral, 1992–97. Nat. Chm., Small Farmers' Assoc., 1984–88. Mem., Gen. Synod of C of E, 1987–92. *Publication:* (ed jtly) The People, the Land and the Church, 1987. *Recreations:* bricklaying, bumble bees, kit car building. *Address:* Bishop's House, 4 Park Road, Ipswich IP1 3ST.

ST GEORGE, Sir John (Avenel Bligh), 10th Bt *cr* 1766 (Ire.), of Athlone, co. Westmeath; *b* 18 March 1940; *s* of Sir George Bligh St George, 9th Bt and of Mary Somerville St George (*née* Sutcliffe); *S* father, 1995; *m* (marr. diss.); two *d*; *m* 1981, Linda, *d* of Robert Perry; two *s. Heir: s* Robert Alexander Bligh St George; *b* 17 Aug. 1983. *Address:* 2 Curzon Street, Ibstock, Leics LE67 6LA.

ST GERMANS, 10th Earl of, *cr* 1815; **Peregrine Nicholas Eliot;** Baron Eliot 1784; *b* 2 Jan. 1941; *o s* of 9th Earl of St Germans, and Helen Mary (*d* 1951), *d* of late Lieut-Col Charles Walter Villiers, CBE, DSO, and Lady Kathleen Villiers; *S* father, 1988; *m* 1st, 1964, Hon. Jacquetta Jean Frederika Lampson (marr. diss. 1989), *d* of 1st Baron Killearn and Jacqueline Aldine Lesley (*née* Castellani); three *s*; 2nd, 1992, Elizabeth Mary Williams (marr. diss. 1996). *Educ:* Eton. *Recreation:* mucking about. *Heir: s* Lord Eliot, *qv. Address:* Port Eliot, St Germans, Cornwall PL12 5ND. *Clubs:* Pratt's; Cornish Club 1768.

ST GERMANS, Bishop Suffragan of, since 2000; **Rt Rev. Royden Screech;** *b* 15 May 1953; *s* of Raymond Kenneth Screech and Gladys Beryl Screech; *m* 1988, Angela May Waring; no *c. Educ:* Cotham Grammar Sch.; King's Coll. London (BD 1974, AKC 1974); St Augustine's Coll., Canterbury. Ordained deacon, 1976, priest, 1977; Curate, St Catherine, Hatcham, 1976–80; Vicar, St Antony, Nunhead, 1980–87; Priest-in-charge, St Silas, Nunhead, 1982–87; Rural Dean, Camberwell, 1984–87; Vicar, St Edward, New Addington, 1987–94; Selection Sec., 1994–97, Sen. Selection Sec., 1997–2000, ABM, subseq. Ministry Div., Archbishops' Council. *Recreations:* opera, holidays in Italy, Coronation Street. *Address:* 32 Falmouth Road, Truro, Cornwall TR1 2HX. *T:* (01872) 273190.

ST HELENA, Bishop of, since 1999; **Rt Rev. John William Salt,** OGS; *b* 30 Oct. 1941; *s* of William Edward and Jenny Salt. *Educ:* Kelham Theol Coll.; London Univ. (DipTh). Ordained deacon, 1966, priest, 1967; Curate, St Matthew's, Barrow-in-Furness, 1966–69; dio. of Lesotho, 1970–77; dio. of Kimberley and Kuruman, 1977–89; Dean of Zululand, 1989–99. *Recreations:* music, walking, reading. *Address:* Bishopsholme, PO Box 62, Island of St Helena, South Atlantic Ocean. *T:* 4471, *Fax:* 4330.

ST HELENS, 2nd Baron *cr* 1964; **Richard Francis Hughes-Young;** *b* 4 Nov. 1945; *s* of 1st Baron St Helens, MC, and Elizabeth Agnes (*d* 1956), *y d* of late Captain Richard Blakiston-Houston; *S* father, 1980; *m* 1983, Mrs Emma R. Talbot-Smith; one *s* one *d. Educ:* Nautical College, Pangbourne. *Heir: s* Henry Thomas Hughes-Young, *b* 7 March 1986.

ST JOHN, family name of **Earl of Orkney** of **Viscount Bolingbroke** and of **Baron St John of Bletso**.

ST JOHN OF BLETSO, 21st Baron *cr* 1558; **Anthony Tudor St John;** Bt 1660; financial consultant to Merrill Lynch, London, since 1989; Chairman: Eurotrust International, since 1993; Governing Board, Certification International, since 1995; Business Development Director, Globix Corp., since 1998; solicitor; *b* 16 May 1957; *s* of 20th Baron St John of Bletso, TD, and of Katharine, *d* of late A. G. von Berg; *S* father, 1978; *m* 1994, Dr Helen Westlake; two *s* one *d. Educ:* Diocesan College, Rondebosch, Cape; Univ. of Cape Town (BSocSc 1977, BA (Law) 1978); Univ. of S Africa (BProc

1982); London Univ. (LLM 1983). An Extra Lord-in-Waiting to the Queen, 1998–. Cross-bencher in House of Lords, specific interests foreign affairs, envmtl protection, sport, financial services, European monetary union. Vice Chm., Parly South Africa Gp; Mem., EU Select Cttee A on Trade, Finance and Foreign Affairs, 1996–99; elected Mem., H of L, 1999. Pres., Friends of Television Trust for the Envmt. Trustee: Tusk; S African Educn Foundn. *Recreations:* golf, tennis and ski-ing; bridge. *Heir: s* Hon. Oliver Beauchamp St John, *b* 11 July 1995. *Address:* c/o House of Lords, SW1A 0AA. *Clubs:* Hurlingham; Royal Cape Golf, Wisley Golf.

ST JOHN OF FAWSLEY, Baron *cr* 1987 (Life Peer), of Preston Capes in the County of Northamptonshire; **Norman Antony Francis St John-Stevas;** PC 1979; FRSL 1966; Master, Emmanuel College, Cambridge, 1991–96, Life Fellow, 1996; Chairman: Royal Fine Art Commission, 1985–99; Royal Fine Art Commission Educational Trust, since 1985; Grand Bailiff and Head of the Military and Hospitaller Order of St Lazarus of Jerusalem in England and Wales, since 2000; author, barrister and journalist; *b* London, 18 May 1929; *o s* of late Stephen S. Stevas, civil engineer and company director, and late Kitty St John O'Connor; unmarried. *Educ:* Ratcliffe; Fitzwilliam, Cambridge (Hon. Fellow 1991); Christ Church, Oxford; Yale. Scholar, Clothworkers Exhibnr, 1946, 1947; BA (Cambridge) (1st cl. hons in law), 1950, MA 1954; President, Cambridge Union, 1950; Whitlock Prize, 1950; MA 1952, BCL 1954 (Oxon); Sec. Oxford Union, 1952; DLitt Oxon 1994; LittD Cantab, 1994. Barrister, Middle Temple, 1952; Blackstone and Harmsworth schol., 1952; Blackstone Prize, 1953. Lecturer, Southampton University, 1952–53, King's Coll., London, 1953–56, tutored in jurisprudence, Christ Church, 1953–55, and Merton, 1955–57, Oxford. Founder member, Inst. of Higher European Studies, Bolzano, 1955; PhD (Lond.) 1957; Yorke Prize, Cambridge Univ., 1957; Fellow Yale Law School, 1957; Fulbright Award, 1957; Fund for the Republic Fellow, 1958; Dr of Sc. of Law (Yale), 1960; Lecture tours of USA, 1958–68. Regents' Prof., Univ. of California at Santa Barbara, 1969; Regents' Lectr, Univ. of Calif at La Jolla, 1984. Legal Adviser to Sir Alan Herbert's Cttee on book censorship, 1954–59; joined The Economist, 1959, to edit collected works of Walter Bagehot and became legal, ecclesiastical and political correspondent. Contested (C) Dagenham, 1951; MP (C) Chelmsford, 1964–87. Mem. Shadow Cabinet, 1974–79, and Opposition Spokesman on Educn, 1975–78, Science and the Arts, 1975–79; Shadow Leader of the House, 1978–79; Parly Under-Sec. of State, DES, 1972–73; Min. of State for the Arts, DES, 1973–74; Chancellor of the Duchy of Lancaster, Leader of the House of Commons and Minister for the Arts, 1979–81. Sec., Cons. Parly Home Affairs Cttee, 1969–72; Vice-Chm., Cons. Parly N Ireland Cttee, 1972–74; Mem. Executive, Cons. Parly 1922 Cttee, 1971–72 and 1974; Vice Chm., Cons. Group for Europe, 1972–75; Member: Cons. Nat. Adv. Cttee on Policy, 1971; Fulbright Commission, 1961; Parly Select Cttee: on Race Relations and Immigration, 1970–72; on Civil List, 1971–73; on Foreign Affairs, 1983–89; Deleg., Council of Europe and WEU, 1967–71; Head, British delegn to Helsinki Cultural Forum, Budapest, 1985. Chm., New Bearings for the Re-Establishment, 1970–. Hon. Sec., Fedn of Cons. Students, 1971–73, Hon. Vice-Pres. 1973. Chm., Booker McConnell Prize, 1985. Mem. Council: RADA, 1983–88; Nat. Soc. for Dance, 1983–; Nat. Youth Theatre, 1983– (Patron, 1984–); RCA, 1985–; Mem., Pontifical Council for Culture, 1987–92; Patron, Medieval Players, 1984–89; Dir, N. M. Rothschild Trust, 1990–98; Trustee: Royal Philharmonic Orch., 1985–88; Philharmonic Orch., 1988–; Royal Soc. of Painters in Watercolours, 1984; Decorative Arts Soc., 1984–. Editor The Dublin (Wiseman) Review, 1961. Vice Pres., Les Amis de Napoléon III, 1974; Mem., Académie du Second Empire, 1975. Hon. FRIBA 1990; Presidential Fellow, Aspen Inst., 1980; Hon. Fellow, St Edmund's College, Cambridge, 1985. Romanes Lectr, Oxford, 1987. DD (*hc*) Univ. of Susquehanna, Pa, 1983; DLitt (*hc*): Schiller Univ., 1985; Bristol Univ., 1988; Hon. LLD: Leicester, 1991; Notre Dame, 1999; Hon. DArts De Montfort, 1996. Silver Jubilee Medal, 1977. SBStJ. Gran Ufficiale, Order of Merit (Italian Republic), 1989 (Commendatore, 1965). GCKLJ 1976 (KSLJ 1963). *Publications:* Obscenity and the Law, 1956; Walter Bagehot, 1959; Life, Death and the Law, 1961; The Right to Life, 1963; Law and Morals, 1964; The Literary Works of Walter Bagehot, vols I, II, 1966, The Historical Works, vols III, IV, 1968, The Political Works, vols V, VI, VII and VIII, 1974, The Economic Works, vols IX, X and XI, 1978, Letters and Miscellany, vols XII, XIII, XIV and XV, 1986; The Agonising Choice, 1971; Pope John Paul II, his travels and mission, 1982; The Two Cities, 1984; contrib. to: Critical Quarterly, Modern Law Review, Criminal Law Review, Law and Contemporary Problems, Twentieth Century, Times Lit. Supp., Dublin Review. *Recreations:* reading, talking, listening (to music), travelling, walking, appearing on television, sleeping. *Address:* The Old Rectory, Preston Capes, Daventry, Northants NN11 3TE; 7 Brunswick Place, The Regent's Park, NW1 4PS; Emmanuel College, Cambridge CB2 3AP. *Clubs:* White's, Garrick, Pratt's, Arts (Hon. Mem., 1980), The Other; Hawks (Cambridge) (Hon. Mem., 1993); Emmanuel Boat (Pres., 1993–).

ST JOHN, Rt Rev. Andrew Reginald; an Assistant Bishop, Diocese of Melbourne (Bishop of the Western Region), since 1995; *b* 16 Feb. 1944; *s* of Reginald and Leila St John. *Educ:* Wesley Coll., Melbourne; Melbourne Univ. (LLB 1966); Trinity Coll., Melbourne (ThSchol 1971); Gen. Theol Seminary, New York (STM 1984). Barrister and solicitor, Supreme Court of Victoria, 1967. Ordained priest, 1972; Precentor, St Paul's Cathedral, Melbourne, 1975–78; Vicar: St Mary's, E Chadstone, 1978–84; Holy Trinity, Kew, 1984–95. Hon. DD Gen. Theol Seminary, NY, 1995. *Recreations:* reading, gardening, opera. *Address:* 364 Shannon Avenue, Newtown, Vic 3220, Australia. *T:* (3) 52298625. *Clubs:* Melbourne, Melbourne Cricket (Melbourne).

ST JOHN, Lauren; freelance golf writer, since 1990; *b* 21 Dec. 1966; *d* of Errol Antonie Kendall and Margaret May Dutton Kendall. *Educ:* Roosevelt High Sch., Harare, Zimbabwe; Harare Poly. (Dip. Journalism). Sub-editor, Resident Abroad magazine, 1987; journalist, Today's Golfer, 1988–89; Golf Correspondent, Sunday Times, 1994–98. Mem., Assoc. of Golf Writers, 1989–. *Publications:* Shooting at Clouds: inside the European golf tour, 1991; Seve: the biography, 1993, 2nd edn 1997; Out of Bounds: inside professional golf, 1995; Greg Norman: the biography, 1998; Walkin' After Midnight: a journey to the heart of Nashville, 2000; articles in Sunday Times, Independent. *Recreations:* music, art, literature, golf, horse riding, green issues.

ST JOHN, Oliver Beauchamp, CEng, FRAeS; Chief Scientist, Civil Aviation Authority, 1978–82; *b* 22 Jan. 1922; 2nd *s* of late Harold and Ella Margaret St John; *m* 1945, Eileen (*née* Morris); three *s*. *Educ:* Monkton Combe Sch.; Queens Coll., Cambridge (MA); London Univ. (External) (BSc). Metropolitan Vickers, Manchester, 1939; Royal Aircraft Estabt, Farnborough, from 1946, on automatic control of fixed-wing aircraft and helicopters; Supt, Blind Landing Experimental Unit, RAE, Bedford, 1966; Director of Technical Research & Development, CAA, 1969–78. Queen's Commendation for Valuable Services in the Air, 1956. *Publication:* A Gallimaufry of Goffering: a history of early ironing implements, 1982. *Recreations:* mountaineering, early music, instrument making. *Address:* The Old Stables, Manor Farm Barns, East Hagbourne OX11 9ND. *T:* (01235) 818437.

ST JOHN-BROOKS, Dr Caroline; Editor, Times Educational Supplement, 1997–2000; *b* 24 March 1947; *d* of Maj. Julian Gordon de Renzy St John-Brooks and Diana Wintersladen; *m* 1972, Roger Hampson; one *s* one *d*. *Educ:* Royal Sch., Bath; Thornbury Grammar Sch., Glos; Trinity Coll., Dublin (BA Hons); Univ. of Ulster (MA); Univ. of Bristol (PhD 1981). Lecturer: Portrush Hotel and Catering Coll., 1971–73; Bristol Poly., 1976–79; Educn Corresp., New Society, 1979–87; Educn Ed., Sunday Times, 1987–91; Asst Editor, TES, 1991–94; Administrator, Centre for Educnl Research and Innovation, OECD, Paris, 1994–97. *Publications:* Schools Under Scrutiny, 1995; Mapping the Future: young people and career guidance, 1996; Parents As Partners in Schooling, 1997. *Address:* 1 Grove Hall, West Grove, Greenwich, SE10 8QT. *T:* (020) 8469 0703.

ST JOHN-MILDMAY, Sir Walter (John Hugh), 11th Bt *cr* 1772, of Farley, Southampton; *b* 3 Sept. 1935; *s* of Michael Paulet St John-Mildmay (*d* 1993), *gggs* of Sir Henry Paulet St John-Mildmay, 3rd Bt, and Joan Elizabeth (*née* Stockley; *d* 1977); *S* kinsman, Rev. Sir (Aubrey) Neville St John-Mildmay, 10th Bt, who *d* 1955, after which Btcy was dormant until revived, 1998. *Educ:* Wycliffe Coll.; Emmanuel Coll., Cambridge (BA 1958); Hammersmith Coll. of Art and Building; RAC Cirencester. *Heir: b* Michael Hugh Paulet St John-Mildmay [*b* 28 Sept. 1937; *m* 1965, Mrs Crystal Margaret Ludlow; two *s* one *d*]. *Address:* 9 Lansdown Crescent, Bath BA1 5EX.

ST JOHN PARKER, Michael, MA (Cantab); Headmaster, Abingdon School, Oxfordshire, 1975–2001; *b* 21 July 1941; *s* of Rev. Canon J. W. Parker; *m* 1965, Annette Monica Ugle; two *s* two *d*. *Educ:* Stamford Sch.; King's Coll., Cambridge. Asst Master: Sevenoaks Sch., 1962–63; King's Sch., Canterbury, 1963–69; Winchester Coll., 1969–75; Head of History Dept, Winchester Coll., 1970–75. Schoolmaster Student, Christ Church, Oxford, 1984. Member: Council, Hansard Soc., 1972–; Marsh Cttee on Politics and Industry, 1978–79. Chm., Midland Div., HMC, 1984. Governor: St Helen's Sch., 1975–83; Christ Church Cathedral Sch.; Cokethorpe Sch. (Chm., 1990); Josca's Sch. *Publications:* The British Revolution—Social and Economic History 1750–1970, 1972; The Martlet and the Griffen, 1997; various pamphlets and articles. *Recreations:* old buildings, music, books, gardens. *Clubs:* Athenæum, East India; Leander.

ST JOHN WILSON, Sir Colin Alexander; *see* Wilson.

ST JOHN'S (Newfoundland), Archbishop of, (RC), since 1991; **Most Rev. James Macdonald,** DD, CSC; *b* 28 April 1925; *s* of Alexander and Mary Macdonald. *Educ:* St Joseph's Univ., 1944–45. Ordained priest, 1953. Congregation of the Holy Cross: Mission Bank, 1954–56; Dir, Holy Cross Minor Seminary, St Joseph's, NB, 1956–62; Sec., Provincial Council, 1956–63; Dir of Vocations, 1962–63; Superior, Holy Cross House of Studies, 1964–69; Asst Provincial, 1966–72; Pastor, St Michael's, Waterloo, Ont., 1969–77; Dean, Waterloo County Priests, dio. of Hamilton, 1974–77; Aux. Bishop of Hamilton, 1978–82; Bishop of Charlottetown, 1982–91. *Address:* PO Box 37, St John's, NF A1C 5H5, Canada.

ST JOHNSTON, Colin David; Managing Director, PRO NED (Promotion of Non-Executive Directors), 1989–95; *b* 6 Sept. 1934; *s* of Hal and Sheilagh St Johnston; *m* 1958, Valerie Paget; three *s* one *d*. *Educ:* Shrewsbury Sch.; Lincoln Coll., Oxford. Booker McConnell Ltd, 1958–70; Ocean Transport and Trading Ltd, 1970–88: Dir, 1974–88; Dep. Gp Chief Exec., 1985–88; Man. Dir, Ocean Cory, 1976–85; non-Executive Director, FMC plc, 1981–83. Mem. Council: Royal Commonwealth Society for the Blind, 1967–95; Industrial Soc., 1981–96; Trustee, Frances Mary Buss Foundn, 1981–95; Governor: Camden Sch., 1974–96; Arnold House Sch., 1993– (Chm., 1995–). *Recreations:* music, Real and lawn tennis. *Address:* 30 Fitzroy Road, NW1 8TY. *T:* (020) 7722 5932. *Club:* MCC.

ST JOHNSTON, Sir Kerry, Kt 1988; Chairman, Tri Anchors Ltd, since 1993; Director, International Multimedia Corporation Ltd, since 2001; *b* 30 July 1931; *s* of late George Eric St Johnston and Viola Rhona Moriarty; *m* 1st, 1960, Judith Ann Nichols; two *s* one *d*; 2nd, 1980, Charlotte Ann Taylor, *d* of late John Scott Limnell Lyon and Patricia Marjorie Hambro. *Educ:* Summer Fields, Oxford; Eton Coll.; Worcester Coll., Oxford (MA Jurisprudence). Joined Ocean Steamship Co. Ltd, 1955, Man. Dir 1963; Overseas Containers Ltd: Founder Dir, 1965; Commerical Dir, 1966; Jt Man. Dir, 1969; Dep. Chm., 1973; Pres. and Chief Exec. Officer, Private Investment Co. for Asia (PICA), SA, Singapore, 1977–82; Chm. and Chief Exec., P & O (formerly Overseas) Containers Ltd, 1982–89. Chairman: Wilrig AS, 1989–92; NM Funds Mgt (Europe) Ltd, 1993–95; Freightliner Ltd, 1996–2001. Director: Royal Insurance, 1973–76; TR Pacific, then Henderson TR Pacific, Investment Trust, 1982–2000; Lloyds Bank Internat. Ltd, 1983–85; P&OSNCo., 1986–89; Diehl and St Johnston Ltd, 1989–91; OTAL Hldgs Ltd, 1997–99. President: Gen. Council of British Shipping, 1987–88; CIT, 1989–90. *Recreations:* trout fishing, gardening. *Address:* The Garden House, 26 Clapham Common North Side, SW4 0RL. *Clubs:* Boodle's, Beefsteak, White's.

SAINT LAURENT, Yves (Henri Donat); Officier de la Légion d'Honneur, 1995; couturier; *b* 1 Aug. 1936; *s* of Charles and Lucienne-Andrée (Wilbaux) Mathieu Saint Laurent. *Educ:* Lycée d'Oran. Collaborator, 1954, then successor of Christian Dior, 1957–60; Dir, Société Yves Saint Laurent, 1962–. *Exhibitions:* Metropolitan Mus. of Art, NY, 1983; Fine Arts Mus., Beijing, 1985; Musée des Arts de la Mode, Paris, 1986; House of Painters of the USSR, Moscow, 1986; Hermitage Mus., Leningrad, 1987; Art Gall. of NSW, Sydney, 1987; Sezon Mus. of Art, Tokyo, 1990. *Costume design: for theatre:* Le Mariage de Figaro, 1964; Delicate Balance, 1967; *for ballet:* Cyrano de Bergerac, 1959; Adage et Variations, 1965; Notre Dame de Paris, 1965; Scheherazade, 1973; *for films:* The Pink Panther, 1962; Belle de Jour, 1967; La Chamade, 1968; La Sirène du Mississippi (with Catherine Deneuve), 1969; L'affaire Stavisky, 1974; *stage sets and costumes:* Les Chants de Maldoror, 1962; Spectacle Zizi Jeanmaire, 1961, 1963, 1968; Revue Zizi Jeanmaire, 1970, 1972, 1977; L'Aigle à deux têtes, 1978. Celebration of 40 yrs of fashion creation with a show of 300 models at Stade de France before Football World Cup Final, 1998. Neiman-Marcus Award for fashion, 1958; Oscar from Harper's Bazaar, 1966; Internat. Award, Council of Fashion Designers of America, 1982; Best Fashion Designer Oscar, 1985. *Publication:* La Vilaine Lulu, 1967. *Address:* (office) 5 avenue Marceau, 75116 Paris, France.

ST LEGER, family name of **Viscount Doneraile**.

ST LEVAN, 4th Baron *cr* 1887; **John Francis Arthur St Aubyn,** DSC 1942; Bt 1866; landowner and company director; Vice Lord-Lieutenant of Cornwall, 1992–94; *b* 23 Feb. 1919; *s* of 3rd Baron St Levan, and Hon. Clementina Gwendolen Catharine Nicolson (*d* 1995), *o d* of 1st Baron Carnock; *S* father, 1978; *m* 1970, Susan Mary Marcia, *d* of late Maj.-Gen. Sir John Kennedy, GCMG, KCVO, KBE, CB. *Educ:* Eton Coll.; Trinity Coll., Cambridge (BA). Served RNVR, 1940–46 (Lieut). Admitted a Solicitor, 1948. High Sheriff of Cornwall, 1974; DL Cornwall, 1977. President: Friends of Plymouth City Museums and Art Gallery, 1985–2000; St Ives Soc. of Artists, 1979–; Penwith NT Assoc., 1987–; Penwith and Isles of Scilly Dist Scout Council, 1991–; W Cornwall Br., STA, 1994–; Cornish Maritime Trust, 1996–; Vice President: Royal Bath and West and Southern Counties Soc., 1984– (Pres., 1983); Royal Cornwall Agricl Assoc., 1980– (Pres., 1979); Minack Theatre, 1989–; London Cornish Assoc., 1997– (Pres., 1987–97); Patron:

Penzance YMCA; Cornwall Br., Normandy Veterans' Assoc.; Truro Naval Assoc., 1995–; Hon. Patron, Penzance Sea Cadet Corps. Bard of Cornwall, 1995. FRSA 1974. KStJ 1998. *Publication:* Illustrated History of St Michael's Mount, 1974. *Recreation:* sailing. *Heir: b* Hon. (Oliver) Piers St Aubyn, MC [*b* 12 July 1920; *m* 1948, Mary (*d* 1987), *e d* of late Bailey Southwell; two *s* one *d*]. *Address:* St Michael's Mount, Marazion, Cornwall TR17 0HT. *Clubs:* Brooks's; Royal Yacht Squadron.

ST OSWALD, 6th Baron *cr* 1885, of Nostell, co. York; **Charles Rowland Andrew Winn;** landowner; *b* 22 July 1959; *s* of 5th Baron St Oswald and of Charlotte Denise Eileen Winn, *d* of Wilfred Haig Loyd; *S* father, 1999; *m* 1985, Louise Alexandra, *yr d* of Stewart Mackenzie Scott; one *s* one *d*. *Educ:* New Sch., King's Langley. *Recreations:* shooting, walking. *Heir: s* Hon. Rowland Charles Sebastian Henry Winn, *b* 15 April 1986. *Address:* Nostell Priory Estate Office, Doncaster Road, Nostell, Wakefield, W Yorkshire WF4 1QD. *T:* (01924) 862221.

ST PAUL'S, Dean of; *see* Moses, Very Rev. J. H.

ST VINCENT, 7th Viscount *cr* 1801; **Ronald George James Jervis;** *b* 3 May 1905; *o surv. s* of 6th Viscount and Marion Annie (*d* 1911), *d* of James Brown, JP, Orchard, Carluke, Scotland; *S* father, 1940; *m* 1945, Phillida, *o d* of Lt-Col R. H. Logan, Taunton; two *s* one *d*. *Educ:* Sherborne. JP Somerset, 1950–55. *Heir: s* Hon. Edward Robert James Jervis [*b* 12 May 1951; *m* 1977, Victoria Margaret, *o d* of Wilton J. Oldham, St Peter, Jersey; one *s* one *d*]. *Address:* Les Charrieres, St Ouen, Jersey, CI.

SAINTY, Sir John Christopher, KCB 1986; Clerk of the Parliaments, 1983–90, retired; *b* 31 Dec. 1934; *s* of late Christopher Lawrence Sainty and Nancy Lee Sainty (*née* Miller); *m* 1965, (Elizabeth) Frances Sherlock; three *s*. *Educ:* Winchester Coll.; New Coll., Oxford (MA). FSA; FRHistS. Clerk, Parlt Office, House of Lords, 1959; seconded as Private Sec. to Leader of House and Chief Whip, House of Lords, 1963; Clerk of Journals, House of Lords, 1965; Res. Asst and Editor, Inst. of Historical Research, 1970; Reading Clerk, House of Lords, 1974. Mem., Royal Commn on Historical MSS, 1991–. Sen. Res. Fellow, Inst. of Historical Res., 1994–. *Publications:* Treasury Officials 1660–1870, 1972; Officials of the Secretaries of State 1660–1782, 1973; Officials of the Boards of Trade 1660–1870, 1974; Admiralty Officials 1660–1870, 1975; Home Office Officials, 1782–1870, 1975; Colonial Office Officials 1794–1870, 1976; (with D. Dewar) Divisions in the House of Lords: an analytical list 1685–1857, 1976; Officers of the Exchequer, 1983; A List of English Law Officers, King's Counsel and Holders of Patents of Precedence, 1987; The Judges of England 1272–1990, 1993; (with R. O. Bucholz) Officials of the Royal Household 1660–1837, vol. 1 1997, vol. 2 1998; Peerage Creations 1649–1800, 1998; articles in Eng. Hist. Rev., Bull. Inst. Hist. Research. *Address:* 22 Kelso Place, W8 5QG. *T:* (020) 7937 9460. *Club:* Brooks's.

SAKMANN, Prof. Bert, MD; Director, Department of Cell Physiology, Max-Planck-Institut für medizinische Forschung, Heidelberg, since 1989; Professor of Physiology, Medical Faculty, University of Heidelberg, since 1990; *b* Stuttgart, 12 June 1942; *m* 1970, Dr Christiane Wülfert; two *s* one *d*. *Educ:* Univ. of Tübingen; Univ. of Munich; University Hosp., Munich; Univ. of Göttingen (MD). Research Asst, Max-Planck-Institut für Psychiatrie, Munich, 1969–70; British Council Fellow, Dept of Biophysics, UCL, 1971–73; Max-Planck-Institut für biophysikalische Chemie, University of Göttingen: Res. Asst, 1974–79; Res. Associate, Membrane Biology Gp, 1979–82; Head, Membrane Physiology Unit, 1983–85; Dir 1985–87, Prof. 1987–89, Dept of Cell Physiology. Lectures: Yale, 1982; Washington Univ., Seattle, 1986, 1990; Univ. of Miami, 1989; Liverpool Univ., 1990; Univ. of Rochester, NY, 1991. Foreign Member: Royal Soc., 1994; Nat. Acad., USA, 1993. Numerous prizes and awards; (jtly) Nobel Prize for Physiology, 1991. *Publications:* (contrib.) The Visual System: neurophysiology, biophysics and their clinical applications, 1972; (contrib.) Advances in Pharmacology and Therapeutics, 1978; (contrib. and ed with E. Neher) Single Channel Recording, 1983; (contrib.) Membrane Control of Cellular Activity, 1986; (contrib.) Calcium and Ion Channel Modulation, 1988; (contrib.) Neuromuscular Junction, 1989; numerous articles in jls incl. Annual Rev. Physiol., Jl Physiol., Nature, Proc. Nat. Acad. Scis, Pflügers Archiv., Jl Exptl Physiol., Neuron, FEBS Lett., Science, Eur. Jl Biochem., Proc. Royal Soc., Jl Cell Biol. *Recreations:* tennis, ski-ing, music, reading. *Address:* Max-Planck-Institut für medizinische Forschung, Jahnstrasse 29, 69120 Heidelberg, Germany. *T:* (6221) 486460.

SAKO, Prof. Mari, PhD; P & O Professor of International Business, University of Oxford, since 1997; Fellow, Templeton College, Oxford, since 1997; *b* Japan, 12 June 1960; *d* of Kanzo Sako and Akemi Sako; *m* 1983, Sumantra Chakrabarti, *qv*; one *d*. *Educ:* Lady Margaret Hall, Oxford (BA Hons); London Sch. of Econs (MSc); PhD London 1990. Researcher, Technical Change Centre, London, 1984–86; London School of Economics and Political Science: Lectr in Modern Japanese Business, 1987–92; Lectr in Industrial Relns, 1992–94; Reader, 1994–97. Fellow, Japanese Soc. for Promotion of Sci., Kyoto Univ., 1992; Japan Foundn Fellow, Tokyo Univ., 1997. *Publications:* (with R. Dore) How the Japanese Learn to Work, 1989, rev. edn 1998; Prices, Quality and Trust: inter-firm relations in Britain and Japan, 1992; (ed with H. Sato) Japanese Labour and Management in Transition, 1997; (jtly) Are Skills the Answer?, 1998. *Recreation:* music. *Address:* Saïd Business School, University of Oxford, Park End Street, Oxford OX1 1HP. *T:* (01865) 288800.

SALAS, Dame Margaret Laurence, (Dame Laurie), DBE 1988; QSO 1982; *b* 8 Feb. 1922; *d* of Sir James Lawrence Hay, OBE and late Davidina Mertel (née Gunn); *m* 1946, Dr John Reuben Salas, FRCSE, FRACS; two *s* four *d*. *Educ:* Christchurch; Univ. of New Zealand (BA). Teacher, audiometrist in Med. practice. National Council of Women of NZ: legislative and parly work; Nat. Sec., 1976–80; Nat. Vice-Pres., 1982–86; Vice-Convener, Internat. Council, Women's Cttee on Develt, 1985–94; Nat. Sec., Women's Internat. League for Peace and Freedom, 1985–90; Pres., UNA, NZ, 1988–92; Vice-Pres., World Fedn of UNAs, 1993–2000; Member: Public Adv. Cttee, Disarmament and Arms Control, 1987–96; Nat. Cons. Cttee on Disarmament (Chair, 1979–90); Adv. Cttee, External Aid and Develt, 1986–88; Standing Cttee, NZ Inst. of Internat. Affairs, 1989–; Educn Cttee, Alcoholic Liquor Adv. Council, 1976–81; Nat. Review Cttee on Social Studies, Educn Dept; Cttee, SCF, 1970–76; Nat. Commn, UN Internat. Year of the Child, 1978–80; UN Internat. Year of Peace, Aotearoa Cttee, (Vice-Chair, 1986); NZ Cttee, Council for Security, Co-operation in Asia and Pacific, 1994–. Pres., Wellington Branch, NZ Fedn of Univ. Women, 1970–72; repr. NZ, overseas meetings. Silver Jubilee Medal, 1977; NZ Commemoration Medal, 1990. *Publication:* Disarmament, 1982. *Recreations:* choral and classical music, enjoying extended family. *Address:* 2 Raumati Terrace, Khandallah, Wellington 4, New Zealand. *T:* (4) 4793415.

See also Sir David Hay, Sir Hamish Hay.

SALCEDO-BASTARDO, José Luis; writer and diplomat; *b* Carúpano, Venezuela, 15 March 1926; *s* of Joaquin Salcedo-Arocha and Catalina Salcedo-Arocha (*née* Bastardo); *m* 1968, Maria Cecilia Avila; four *s*. *Educ:* Central Univ. of Venezuela; Univ. of Paris; London Sch. of Economics. Teacher of social sciences, 1945; Chief Editor, Nat. Magazine of Culture, 1948–50; Asst Lectr, Central Univ., 1949; Founder Rector, Univ. of Santa Maria, Caracas, 1953; Senator for State of Sucre, 1958; Mem., Senate Foreign Relations Cttee; Ambassador to Ecuador, 1959–61; to Brazil, 1961–63; Prof. of Sociology, Central Univ., 1964; Pres., Nat. Inst. of Culture and Fine Arts, 1965–67; Vice-Pres., Supreme Electoral Council, 1970–74; Ambassador to France, 1974–76; Minister, Secretariat of the Presidency, 1976–77; Minister of State for Sci., Tech. and Culture, 1977–79; Ambassador to UK, 1984–87, to GDR, 1987–90. Member, councils and commns, S America and Europe. *Publications:* Through the Sociological World of Cecilio Acosta, 1945; In Pursuit of Glory, 1947; Vision and Revision of Bolívar, 1957; Biography of Don Egidio Montesinos, 1957; Thesis for Union, 1963; Basis for Cultural Action, 1965; Fundamental History of Venezuela, 1970; Conscience of the Present, 1971; Carabobo: nationality and history, 1972; Bolívar: a continent and its destiny, 1972 (26 edns, trans into 12 langs); The First Duty, 1973; To Make History Unpolitical, 1973; Of History and Duties, 1975; Bolívar and San Martín, 1975; A Transparent Man, 1976; Crucible of Americanism, 1979; Ideological and Literary Concordances in Bolívar, 1981; Andrés Bello: an American, 1982; Bolivarian Repetition, 1983; Andrés Eloy Blanco For the Young, 1983; Simón Bolívar, 1983; Bolívar, Ideas and People, 1994; Man and Men, 1994. *Recreation:* travelling abroad. *Address:* PO Box 2777, Caracas 1010, Venezuela.

SALEM, Daniel Laurent Manuel; Chairman, The Condé Nast Publications Ltd, London, 1968–97; *b* 29 Jan. 1925; *s* of Raphael Salem and Adriana Gentili di Giuseppe; *m* 1950, Marie-Pierre Arachtingi. *Educ:* Harvard Univ., Cambridge, Mass (BA, MA). Served Free French Forces, 1943–45. Exec. Asst, Lazard Frères & Co., New York, 1946–50; exec. positions, The Condé Nast Publications Inc., New York, 1950–60, Vice-Pres., 1965–86, Dep. Chm., 1986–92; Vice Pres., Banque Paribas, Paris, 1961–65; Chm., Condé Nast International Inc., 1971–91. Chairman: Mercury Selected Trust, 1974–96; Mercury Offshore Selected Trust, 1979–96; Philharmonia Trust Ltd, 1985–92. Officier, Legion of Honour (France), 1997; Commendatore, Order of Merit (Italy), 1988. *Recreations:* music, bridge, chess, golf. *Address:* 3 Ennismore Gardens, SW7 1NL. *T:* (020) 7584 0466. *Clubs:* White's, Portland; Harvard (New York City).

SALES, (Donald) John; gardens consultant; Chief Gardens Adviser, then Head of Gardens, The National Trust, 1974–98; *b* 1 May 1933; *s* of Frederic Donald Sales and Alice Elizabeth (*née* Burrell); *m* 1958, Lyn Thompson; three *s*. *Educ:* Westminster City Sch.; Kent Horticultural Coll.; Royal Botanic Gardens, Kew. MHort (RHS) 1957; FIHort 1984. Lectr in Horticulture, Writtle Agricl Coll., Chelmsford, 1958–70 (Fellow, 1998); Horticulturist (Asst to Gardens Advr), NT, 1971–74. Medal of Honour, Internat. Castles Inst., 1991; VMH, RHS, 1992; Inst. of Horticulture Award for Outstanding Services to Horticulture, 1996. *Publications:* West Country Gardens, 1980; A Year in the Garden, 2001; contrib. articles in Country Life. *Recreations:* gardening, photography, walking, music, ballet, the arts generally. *Address:* Covertside, Perrott's Brook, Cirencester, Glos GL7 7BW. *T:* (01285) 831537; (office) *T:* and *Fax:* (01285) 831116.

SALFORD, Bishop of, (RC), since 1997; **Rt Rev. Terence John Brain;** *b* 19 Dec. 1938; *s* of Reginald John Brain and Mary Cooney. *Educ:* Cotton Coll., North Staffordshire; St Mary's Coll., Oscott, Birmingham. Ordained priest, 1964; Asst Priest, St Gregory's, Longton, 1964–65; mem. of staff, Cotton Coll., 1965–69; Hosp. Chaplain, St Patrick's, Birmingham, 1969–71; Archbishop's Secretary, Birmingham, 1971–82; Parish Priest: Bucknall, Stoke-on-Trent, 1982–88; St Austin's, Stafford, 1988–91; Auxiliary Bishop of Birmingham, 1991–97. RC Bishop for Prisons, 1994–. Chm., RC Bishops' Social Welfare Cttee, 1992–. Episcopal Advr, Nat. Council of Lay Assocs, 1993–. *Recreations:* crossword puzzles, water colour painting. *Address:* Wardley Hall, Worsley, Manchester M28 2ND.

SALINGER, Jerome David; American author; *b* New York City, 1 Jan. 1919; *m* 1953, Claire Douglas (marr. diss. 1967); one *s* one *d*. *Educ:* Manhattan public schools; Military Academy, Paris. Served with 4th Infantry Division, US Army, 1942–46 (Staff Sergeant). Travelled in Europe, 1937–38. Started writing at age of 15; first story published, 1940. *Publications:* The Catcher in the Rye, 1951; For Esme-with Love and Squalor, 1953; Franny and Zooey, 1962; Raise High the Roof Beam, Carpenters and Seymour: an Introduction, 1963. *Address:* c/o Harold Ober Associates, 425 Madison Avenue, New York, NY 10017–1110, USA.

SALINGER, Pierre (Emil George); politician, journalist; independent public relations counselor, since 1996; International Consultant, ABC News, American Broadcasting Company, since 1993; *b* San Francisco, 14 June 1925; *s* of Herbert and Jehanne Salinger; *m* 1st; one *s* one *d* (and one *s* decd); 2nd, 1957, Nancy Brook Joy (marr. diss., 1965); 3rd, 1965, Nicole Gillmann (marr. diss. 1988), Paris, France; one *s*; 4th, 1989, Nicole Beauvillain. *Educ:* Lowell High School, San Francisco; State Coll., San Francisco; Univ. of San Francisco. Served War, 1942–45, with US Navy. With San Francisco Chronicle, 1942–55; Guest Lectr, Mills Coll., Calif, 1950–55; Press Officer, Democratic Presidential Campaign (Calif), 1952; West Coast Editor, Contributing Editor, Collier's Magazine, 1955–56; Investigator, Senate Labor Rackets Cttee, 1957–59; Press Sec. to President Kennedy (when Senator), 1959–61, and to President of the United States, 1961–64; appointed to serve as a US Senator, 4 Aug. 1964–2 Jan. 1965; Roving Editor, L'Express, Paris, 1973–78; ABC News: Correspondent, Paris, 1978–79; Paris Bureau Chief, 1979–87; Chief Foreign Corresp., 1983–93; Sen. Ed., Europe, 1988–93. Vice Chm., Burson Marsteller, 1993–96; Vice Pres., Continental Airlines, Continental Air Services, 1965–68. Trustee, Robert F. Kennedy Meml Foundn; Hon. Chm., Bd of Trustees, American Coll. in Paris. Mem., Legion of Honour, 1978; US Navy and Marine Corps Medal, 1946. *Publications:* articles on county jail conditions in California, 1953; A Tribute to John F. Kennedy, Encyclopedia Britannica, 1964; With Kennedy, 1966; A Tribute to Robert F. Kennedy, 1968; For the Eyes of the President Only, 1971; Je suis un Americain, 1975; La France et le Nouveau Monde, 1976; America Held Hostage—the secret negotiations, 1981; (with Leonard Gross) The Dossier, 1984; (with Robert Cameron) Above Paris, 1985; (with Leonard Gross) Mortal Games, 1988; (with Eric Laurent) La Guerre du Golfe: le dossier secret, 1990; P.S.: a memoir, 1995; John F. Kennedy, Commander in Chief, 1997. *Address:* 3904 Hillandale Ct NW, Washington, DC 20007, USA.

SALISBURY, 6th Marquess of, *cr* 1789; **Robert Edward Peter Gascoyne-Cecil;** DL; Baron Cecil, 1603; Viscount Cranborne, 1604; Earl of Salisbury, 1605; Captain Grenadier Guards; High Steward of Hertford since 1972; *b* 24 Oct. 1916; *s* of 5th Marquess of Salisbury, KG, PC, FRS, and Elizabeth Vere (*d* 1982), *e d* of late Lord Richard Cavendish, PC, CB, CMG; *S* father, 1972; *m* 1945, Marjorie Olein (Mollie), *d* of late Captain Hon. Valentine Wyndham-Quin, RN; four *s* one *d* (and one *s* decd). MP (C) Bournemouth West, 1950–54. Pres., Monday Club, 1974–81. DL Dorset, 1974. *Heir: s* Viscount Cranborne, *qv*. *Address:* Hatfield House, Hatfield, Herts AL9 5NF.

SALISBURY, Bishop of, since 1993; **Rt Rev. David Staffurth Stancliffe;** *b* 1 Oct. 1942; *s* of late Very Rev. Michael Staffurth Stancliffe; *m* 1965, Sarah Loveday Smith; one *s* two *d*. *Educ:* Westminster School; Trinity College, Oxford (MA); Cuddesdon Theological College. Assistant Curate, St Bartholomew's, Armley, Leeds, 1967–70;

Chaplain to Clifton Coll., Bristol, 1970–77; Canon Residentiary of Portsmouth Cathedral, Diocesan Director of Ordinands and Lay Ministry Adviser, 1977–82; Provost of Portsmouth, 1982–93. Member: Gen. Synod, 1985–; Liturgical Commn, 1986– (Chm., 1993–); Cathedrals' Fabric Commn, 1991–2001. Pres., Council, Marlborough Coll., 1994–. DLitt Portsmouth, 1993. *Recreations:* old music, Italy. *Address:* South Canonry, 71 The Close, Salisbury, Wilts SP1 2ER. *T:* (01722) 334031; *e-mail:* dsarum@eluk.co.uk.

See also M. J. Stancliffe.

SALISBURY, Dean of; *see* Watson, Very Rev. D. R.

SALISBURY, David Maxwell, CB 2001; FRCP, FRCPCH, FFPHM; Principal Medical Officer, Department of Health, since 1986; *b* 10 Aug. 1946; *s* of Dr Steven Salisbury and Judith Grace Vivien Salisbury; *m* 1974, Anne Harvey; one *s* one *d*. *Educ:* Epsom Coll.; Royal London Hosp., Univ. of London (MB BS 1969). FRCP 1992; FRCPCH 1997; FFPHM 1998. Sir William Coxen Res. Fellow, Dept of Paediatrics, Univ. of Oxford, 1973–75; Paediatric Registrar, John Radcliffe Hosp., Oxford, 1976–77; Sen. Registrar, Great Ormond Street Hosp. for Children, 1977–85; Consultant Paediatrician, New Cross Hosp., Wolverhampton, 1985–86. Freeman, City of London; Liveryman, Soc. of Apothecaries. *Publications:* contrib. jls and textbooks on immunisation, infectious disease, paediatrics and neonatology. *Recreations:* destructive gardening (lawns, logs and hedges), sailing. *Address:* Pound Cottage, Brightwell-cum-Sotwell, Wallingford OX10 0QD. *T:* (01491) 837209.

SALISBURY, David Murray; Chief Executive, Schroders, 2000–01; *b* 18 Feb. 1952; *s* of Norman Salisbury and Isobel Sutherland Murray; *m* 1977, Lynneth Mary Jones; two *d*. *Educ:* Harrow Sch.; Trinity Coll., Oxford (MA). Joined J. Henry Schroder Wagg & Co. Ltd, 1974; Chief Exec., Schroder Capital Management International Inc., 1986–97; Jt Chief Exec., 1995–97, Chm., 1997–2000, Schroder Investment Management Ltd; Dir, Schroders PLC, 1998–2001. Dir, Dimensional Fund Advisers Inc., 1991–96. Gov., Harrow Sch., 1996–99. *Recreations:* tennis, ski-ing. *Address:* The Dutch House, West Green, Hartley Wintney, Hants RG27 8JN.

SALISBURY, John; *see* Caute, J. D.

SALISBURY, Sir Robert (William), Kt 1998; educational consultant, Northern Ireland; Director of Partnerships, University of Nottingham, since 1999; *b* 21 Oct. 1941; *s* of Ernest Arthur Salisbury and Vera Ellen Salisbury; *m* 1975, Rosemary D'Arcy (Principal, Drumragh Coll., Omagh, NI); three *s*. *Educ:* Henry Mellish Sch., Nottingham; Kesteven Trng Coll., Lincs (Teacher's Cert.); Nottingham Univ. (CFPS); Loughborough Univ. (MA). Geography teacher, Holgate Sch., Hucknall, Notts, 1962–64; study in Europe, 1964–66; Second in English, Kimberley Comp. Sch., Notts, 1973–77; Head of Humanities and of 6th Form, Gedling Comp. Sch., Notts, 1977–83; Dep. Head, Alderman White Comp. Sch., Notts, 1983–89; Headteacher, Garibaldi Sch., Mansfield, 1989–99. Vis. Prof., Sch. of Educn, Nottingham Univ., 1998. Chief Examr, JMB/NEAB, 1979–90. Formerly Ind. Chm., NE Lincs Educn Action Zone. Chm., Sherwood Partnership. Associate Advr, Industrial Soc., 1992–; Mem. Adv. Council, Carlton Television; Educn Advr, Centre for British Teaching. Regl Chm., Teaching Awards Trust, 1998–; Chairman, Trustees: Fathers Direct, 1998–; Sherwood Coalfield Develt Trust, 1999–; Trustee, Drugs Abuse Resistance Educn, 1997–. Nat. and internat. speaker, 1992–. FRSA 1998. *Publications:* Series Ed., Humanities textbooks, 1988; Marketing for Schools Guide, 1993; contrib. numerous articles on educational issues, also on fishing and country matters; freelance articles for The Times and TES. *Recreations:* trout and salmon fishing, travel, gardening. *Address:* Grange Court, Moyle Road, Newtownstewart, Omagh, Co. Tyrone BT78 4AP. *T:* (028) 8166 2441.

SALISSE, John Joseph, CBE 1986; Director, Marks and Spencer, 1968–85; *b* 24 March 1926; *s* of Joseph and Anne Salisse; *m* 1949, Margaret Horsfield; one *d*. *Educ:* Portsmouth Grammar Sch. Marks and Spencer, 1944–85. Chairman: CBI Distributive Trades Survey Cttee, 1983–86; St Enoch Management Centre Ltd, 1986–97; Jt London Tourism Forum, 1986–97; London Enterprise Agency, 1983–88; Retail Consortium, 1986–92; Director: London Tourist Bd, 1984–97 (Vice-Chm., 1989–97); City Shops, 1986–88; Fullemploy, 1984–86; Allied Internat. Designers, 1986–87. Jt Treas., European Movement, 1982–86; Member: CBI Council, 1984–89; Cttee, Amer. European Community Assoc., 1983–90; Nat. Employers' Liaison Cttee, 1987–92; Cttee on Commerce and Distribution, 1988–93; Council for Charitable Support, 1986–89; Inst. of Dirs; Trustee, London Educn Business Partnership, 1986–92; Dir, CECD, 1986–93 (Vice-Pres., 1989–93). Hon. Vice Pres., Magic Circle, 1975– (Hon. Sec., 1965–86); Hon. Life Mem., Acad. of Magical Arts and Scis, America, 1979. Freeman, City of London, 1992. *Publications:* (jtly) A Candid View of Maskelyne's 1916–17, 1995; various contribs to Magic literature. *Recreations:* golf, theatre, history of magic, collecting Victorian theatre programmes. *Address:* 12 Hampstead Way, NW11 7LS. *Clubs:* Savage, Magic Circle, Highgate Golf; Magic Castle (Los Angeles).

SALJE, Prof. Ekhard Karl Hermann, PhD; FRS 1996; FInstP, FGS; Professor of Mineralogy and Petrology, since 1994, and Head of Department of Earth Sciences, since 1998, Cambridge University (Professor of Mineral Physics, 1992–94); President, Clare Hall, Cambridge, since 2001; *b* Hanover, Germany, 26 Oct. 1946; *s* of Gerhard Salje and Hildegard (*née* Drechsler); *m* 1980, Elisabeth Démaret; one *s* four *d*. *Educ:* Univ. of Hanover (PhD 1972); MA Cantab 1986. FInstP 1996; FGS 1997. University of Hanover: Lectr in Physics, 1972–75; Habilitation in Crystallography, 1975; Prof. of Crystallography, 1978–86; Hd, Dept of Crystallography and Petrology, 1983–86; Mem., Senate, 1980–82; Lectr, Cambridge Univ., 1987–92; Fellow, Darwin Coll., Cambridge, 1987–2001. Associate Prof. of Physics, Univ. of Paris, 1981; Prof. invité in Physics, Grenoble Univ., 1990–91; Mombushu Vis. Prof., Nagoya, Japan, 1996; Visiting Professor: Le Mans Univ., France, 1998, 2000; Bilbao Univ., Spain, 1999. Advr to British, French, German and EU scientific orgns. Fellow, Leopoldina German Acad. of Natural Sci., 1994. Schlumberger Medal, 1988; G. Werner Medal, Mineralogical Soc., Germany, 1995; Humboldt Prize, Humboldt Foundn, Germany, 1999. FRSA 1996. *Publications:* Physical Properties and Thermodynamic Behaviour of Minerals, 1987; Phase Transitions in ferroelastic and co-elastic crystals, 1991; Application of Landau Theory for the Analysis of Phase Transitions in Minerals, 1992; numerous res. papers in solid state physics, crystallography and mineralogy. *Recreations:* painting, music. *Address:* The President's House, Clare Hall, 1 Herschel Road, Cambridge CB3 9AL.

SALLON, Christopher Robert Anthony; QC 1994; a Recorder, since 1996; *b* 3 May 1948; *s* of late Alexander and Alice Sallon; *m* 1971, Jacqueline Gould; two *s*. Called to the Bar, Gray's Inn, 1973, Eastern Caribbean, 1994. Bar Council: South Eastern Circuit Rep., 1992–94; Member: Professional Conduct Cttee, 1992–93; Public Affairs Cttee, 1994–97; Dir, Public Affairs, 1995–. Fellow, American Bd of Criminal Lawyers, 1997. Mem. Bd, Counsel Magazine, 1995–. *Recreations:* swimming, cycling, music. *Address:* Doughty Street Chambers, 11 Doughty Street, WC1N 2PG. *T:* (020) 7404 1313.

SALMON, Charles Nathan; QC 1996; *b* 5 May 1950; *s* of His Honour Judge Cyril Salmon, QC and of Patrice Salmon; *m* 1981, Vanessa Clewes; one *s*. *Educ:* Carmel Coll.; University Coll. London (LLB Hons 1971). Travelled through Asia and SE Asia, 1971–73, worked as rubber tapper in Malaysia; called to the Bar, Middle Temple, 1972; volunteer, ME war, 1973; in practice as barrister, 1974–. *Recreations:* reading about Middle East history, 2nd World War and Italian Risorgimento, travel, collecting 18th century Japanese woodcuts and contemporary European paintings. *Address:* 1 Hare Court, Temple, EC4Y 7BE. *T:* (020) 7353 5324.

SALMON, Michael John; Vice Chancellor, Anglia Polytechnic University, 1992–95, now Emeritus Professor; Chairman, Essex Rivers Healthcare NHS Trust, since 1995; *b* 22 June 1936; *o s* of Arthur and May Salmon; *m* 1st, 1958, Angela Cookson (marr. diss. 1973); one *s*; 2nd, 1973, Daphne Bird (*d* 1996); one *s*; 3rd, 1998, Sheila Frances Sisto. *Educ:* Roundhay Sch., Leeds; Leeds Univ.; Leicester Univ. Served RAF, 1957–62; commnd 1957. Teaching posts: Letchworth Coll. of Technology, 1962–65; Leeds Coll. of Technology, 1965–68; Barking Regional Coll., 1968–71; Head of Dept, NE London Poly., 1971–77; Dep. Dir, Chelmer Inst., 1977–83; Dir, Essex Inst., 1983–89; Director: Anglia HEC, 1989–91; Anglia Poly., 1991–92. Member: CNAA, 1970–92; IBA Educn Adv. Council, 1973–81; Electricity Industry Trng Council, 1971–74; PCFC, 1989–93; CBI (Eastern Region) Council, 1990–93; Gen. Optical Council, 1999–. Dir, Essex TEC, 1990–93; Chm., 1998, Vice-Chm., 1999–, InterCollege, Essex. Member: Court, Essex Univ., 1987–; Acad. Cttee, RCM, 1994–; Governor: Norwich Sch. of Art and Design, 1996– (Chm. Govs, 1998–); King Edward VI GS, Chelmsford, 1995–. Director: Proshare, 1991–93; Mid-Essex NHS Hosp. Trust, 1993–95. Chm., Tendring Community Develt Forum, 1998–. Vice Patron, Helen Rollason Cancer Appeal. FIMgt (FBIM 1983); FRSA 1984. Hon. Fellow: Limburg Poly., Netherlands, 1993; Fachhochschule für Wirtschaft, Berlin, 1994. *Address:* Barberries, Runsell Lane, Danbury, Essex CM3 4NY. *T:* (01245) 223734.

SALMON, Nicholas Robin, FREng, FIMechE; Executive Vice President, ALSTOM, since 2001; *b* 13 June 1952; *s* of Keneth Salmon and Winifred Elsie Salmon (*née* Martin); *m* 1976, Deirdre Ann Thompson Hardy; two *d*. *Educ:* Bristol Univ. (BSc (Hons) Mech. Engrg 1973). Grad. trainee, 1969–74, Project Engr, 1974–77, CEGB; Project Manager, China Light and Power Co. Ltd (Hong Kong), 1977–88; Dir and Gen. Manager, Power Station Projects Div., GEC Turbine Generators Ltd, 1988–93; Dep. Man. Dir, Power Stn Projects Div. and Gas Turbine and Diesel Div., GEC Alsthom, 1993–94; Chief Exec., Babcock Internat. Gp plc, 1994–97; Man. Dir, Power Generation Div., GEC Alsthom, 1997–99; Executive Vice President: ABB ALSTOM Power, 1999–2000; ALSTOM Power, 2000–01. FREng (FEng 1995). *Recreations:* latent—sailing, ski-ing, bridge. *Address:* ALSTOM, 25 avenue Kléber, Paris 75795 Cedex 16, France. *T:* (1)47552430. *Club:* Royal Hong Kong Yacht.

SALMON, Paul Raymond, FRCPE, FRCP; independent consultant Physician and Gastroenterologist, since 1989; *b* 11 July 1936; *s* of late Harold William Salmon and Blanche Percy Salmon (*née* Piper); *m* 1st, 1962 (marr. diss. 1980); one *s* one *d*; 2nd, 1984, Diana Frances Lawrence. *Educ:* Epsom Coll.; Middx Hosp. Sch. of Medicine, Univ. of London (BSc Hons Anatomy 1958). MRCS 1961; MRCPE 1966, FRCPE 1977; MRCP 1967, FRCP 1978. House Physician and House Surgeon, 1962, Casualty MO, 1963–64, Middlesex Hosp.; House Physician, London Chest Hosp., 1963; Sen. House Physician, Ipswich and E Suffolk Hosp., 1964–65; Med. Registrar, Princess Margaret Hosp., Swindon, 1965–66; Res. Registrar in Gastroenterology, Bristol Royal Infirmary, 1967–68; Lectr in Medicine, 1969–73, Sen. Lectr in Medicine, 1974–79, Univ. of Bristol; Hon. Sen. Registrar, United Bristol Hosps, 1969–73; Hon. Consultant Physician, Bristol Health Dist, 1974–79; Consultant Physician, UCH, and Sen. Clin. Lectr in Gastroenterology, Sch. of Medicine, UCL, 1978–89; Consultant Physician, Middlesex Hosp., 1985–89. Annual Foundn Lectr, British Soc. for Digestive Endoscopy, 1979; Poona Orator, Indian Gastroenterology Soc., 1984. FDS Examr, RCS, 1982–88. Pres., Eur. Laser Assoc., 1981–85; Member: British Soc. of Gastroenterology, 1969–; Chelsea Clin. Soc., 1986– (Mem. Council, 2000–); Independent Doctors Forum, 1989–. FRSocMed 1986. Freeman, City of London, 1985; Liveryman: Co. of Farriers, 1986; Soc. of Apothecaries, 1993. Privilegiate *hc* St Hilda's Coll., Oxford, 1996. Several teaching films (Dip., Marburg Film Fest., 1977, Silver Award, BMA Film Competition, 1983). *Publications:* Fibreoptic Endoscopy, 1974; (ed) Topics in Modern Gastroenterology, 1976; (jtly) Radiological Atlas of Biliary and Pancreatic Disease, 1978; (ed) Ranitidine, 1982; (ed) Advances in Gastrointestinal Endoscopy, 1984; (ed) Key Developments in Gastroenterology, 1988; 200 contribs to books, scientific papers and review articles. *Recreations:* golf, music, ski-ing, travel, angling. *Address:* 2d Melbury Road, W14 8LP. *T:* (020) 7602 3311, *Fax:* (020) 7602 2562; 80 Harley Street, W1G 7HL. *T:* (020) 7486 7939, *Fax:* (020) 7224 0645; *e-mail:* prsalmon@email.msn.com. *Clubs:* Athenæum, Roehampton; Stoke Poges Golf.

SALMON, Peter; Director of Sport, BBC, since 2000; *b* 15 May 1956; *s* of Patrick and Doreen Salmon; three *s*; *m* 2001, Sarah Lancashire. *Educ:* Univ. of Warwick (BA English and European Lit.). VSO, 1977; Min. of Overseas Develt, 1978; Chatham News, 1979–81; BBC, 1981–93: Series Producer, Crimewatch UK; Editor, Nature; Exec. Producer, 999, and The Wrong Trousers; Head of TV Features, BBC Bristol; Controller of Factual Programmes, Channel 4, 1993–96; Dir of Programmes, Granada TV, 1996–97; Controller, BBC 1, 1997–2000. *Recreations:* music, football, cycling, museums. *Address:* BBC Television, Wood Lane, W12 0AX. *T:* (020) 8225 8755.

SALMON, Very Rev. Thomas Noel Desmond Cornwall; Dean of Christ Church, Dublin, 1967–88; *b* Dublin, 5 Feb. 1913; *s* of Francis Allen Cornwall Salmon, BDS, and Emma Sophia, *d* of Dr Hamilton Jolly, Clonroche, Co. Wexford; unmarried. *Educ:* privately; Trinity College, Dublin; BA 1935, MA, BD. Deacon 1937; Priest 1938. Curate Assistant: Bangor, Co. Down, 1937–40; St James' Belfast, 1940–42; Larne, Co. Antrim, 1942–44; Clerical Vicar, Christ Church Cathedral, 1944–45; Curate Assistant, Rathfarnham, Dublin, 1945–50; Incumbent: Tullow, Carrickmines, 1950–62; St Ann, Dublin, 1962–67. Asst Lectr in Divinity School, TCD, 1945–63; Examining Chaplain to Archbishop of Dublin, 1949–96. *Recreations:* in younger days Rugby football (Monkstown FC Dublin) and swimming; now walking, gardening and reading. *Address:* 3 Glenageary Terrace, Lower Glenageary Road, Dun Laoghaire, Co. Dublin. *T:* 2800101.

SALMOND, Alexander Elliot Anderson; MP (SNP) Banff and Buchan, since 1987; *b* 31 Dec. 1954; *s* of Robert F. F. Salmond and Mary S. Milne; *m* 1981, Moira F. McGlashan. *Educ:* Linlithgow Acad.; St Andrews Univ. (MA Hons). Govt Econ. Service, 1980; Asst Agricl and Fisheries Economist, DAFS, 1978–80; Energy Economist, Royal Bank of Scotland plc, 1980–87. Scottish National Party: Mem. Nat. Exec., 1981–; Vice-Chair (Publicity), 1985–87; Sen. Vice-Convener (Dep. Leader) (formerly Sen. Vice-Chair), 1987–90; Nat. Convener, 1990–2000. SNP parly spokesperson on energy, treasury and fishing, 1987–88, on economy, energy, environment and poll tax, 1988–97, on constitution and fishing, 1997–. Mem. (SNP) Banff & Buchan, Scottish Parlt, 1999–2001; Ldr of the Opposition, 1999–2000. Columnist, Herald, News of the World,

Press & Journal. *Publications:* articles and conference papers on oil and gas economics; contribs to Scottish Government Yearbook, Fraser of Allander Economic Commentary, Petroleum Review, Opec Bulletin, etc. *Address:* House of Commons, SW1A 0AA; 17 Maiden Street, Peterhead, Aberdeenshire AB42 1EE.

SALMOND, Dame Anne; *see* Salmond, Dame M. A.

SALMOND, Prof. George Peacock Copland, PhD; Professor of Molecular Microbiology, University of Cambridge, since 1996; Fellow, Wolfson College, Cambridge, since 2000; *b* 15 Nov. 1952; *s* of John Brown Salmond and Joan Tennant Lambie Salmond (*née* Copland); *m* 1975, Christina Brown Adamson (marr. diss. 1985); partner, Carolyn Ann Alderson; one *d*. *Educ:* Whitburn Primary Sch.; Bathgate Acad.; Whitburn Acad.; Univ. of Strathclyde (BSc 1st cl. Hons Microbiology); Univ. of Warwick (PhD Bacterial Genetics); MA Cantab. Postdoctoral Res. Fellow, Dept of Molecular Biology, Univ. of Edinburgh, 1977–80; Lectr in Microbiology, Biological Lab., Univ. of Kent at Canterbury, 1980–83; Lectr in Microbiology, 1983–89, Sen. Lectr, 1989–93, Prof., 1993–96, Dept of Biological Scis, Univ. of Warwick. Member: Scientific Adv. Bd, NSC Technologies, USA, 1996–; Plants and Microbial Scis Cttee, BBSRC, 1999–. Mem. Council, Soc. for Gen. Microbiology, 1997–. UK Sen. Ed., Jl of Molecular Microbiology and Biotechnology, 1998–; Member Editorial Board: Molecular Microbiology, 1988–97; Molecular Plant Pathology–On Line, 1996–; Microbiology, 1999–2000; Molecular Plant Pathology, 1999–; Associate Editor: European Jl of Plant Pathology, 1992–98; Molecular Plant-Microbe Interactions, 1993–98. *Publications:* many res. articles on molecular microbiology and bacterial genetics, incl. studies on bacterial cell div., molecular phytopathology, carbapenem antibiotics, quorum sensing, bacterial virulence and protein secretion in learned jls. *Recreations:* driving a sports car, cooking, reading poetry, good wines and malt whiskies, comedy; avoiding hysterical media spins. *Address:* Department of Biochemistry, University of Cambridge, Tennis Court Road, Cambridge CB2 1QW. *T:* (01223) 333650.

SALMOND, Dame (Mary) Anne, DBE 1995 (CBE 1988); PhD; FRSNZ; Professor of Social Anthropology and Maori Studies, since 1992, and Pro Vice-Chancellor (Equal Opportunity), since 1997, University of Auckland; *b* 16 Nov. 1945; *d* of Jack Thorpe and Joyce Thorpe; *m* 1971, Jeremy Salmond; two *s* one *d*. *Educ:* Univ. of Auckland (BA 1966; MA 1st cl. 1966); Univ. of Pennsylvania (PhD 1972). FRSNZ 1990. Post-grad. Schol., Univ. of Auckland, 1968; Fulbright Schol., 1969; Nuffield Fellow, 1980–81; Capt. James Cook Fellow, RSNZ, 1987. Henry Myers Lectr, RAI, 1996. Elsdon Best Meml Gold Medal, Polynesian Soc., 1976; Wattie Book of Year Awards, 1977, 1981, 1991; Nat. Book Award (non-fiction), 1991; Ernest Scott Prize, Melbourne Univ., 1992, 1997. *Publications:* Hui: a study of Maori ceremonial gatherings, 1975, 7th edn 1994; Amiria: the life story of a Maori woman, 1976, 3rd edn 1994; Eruera: the teachings of a Maori Elder, 1980; Two Worlds: first meetings between Maori and Europeans 1642–1772, 1991, 2nd edn 1993; Between Worlds: early Maori-European exchanges 1773–1815, 1997. *Recreations:* gardening, tennis, reading, family and friends. *Address:* 14 Glen Road, Devonport, Auckland, New Zealand. *T:* (9) 4452573.

SALOLAINEN, Pertti Edvard; Grand Cross, Order of the Lion of Finland, 1994; Ambassador of Finland to the Court of St James's, since 1996; *b* 19 Oct. 1940; *s* of Edvard Paavali Salolainen and Ella Elisabet Salolainen; *m* 1964, Anja Sonninen; one *s* one *d*. *Educ:* Helsinki Sch. of Economics (MSc Econ 1969). TV newsreader and editor, then producer, 1962–66, London Correspondent, 1966–69, Finnish Broadcasting Co.; London Editor, BBC Finnish Sect., 1966; Head of Dept, Finnish Employers' Confedn, 1969–89; Minister for Foreign Trade, Finland, 1987–95; Dep. Prime Minister of Finland, 1991–95; Ministerial Chm., Finland-EU membership negotiations, 1991–95. Chm., Conservative Party of Finland, 1991–94. Freeman, City of London, 1998. Internat. Conservation Award, WWF, 1990. Grand Cross, Nordstjerna Order (Sweden), 1996; Grand Cross, nat. orders of Germany, Austria and Hungary. *Recreations:* bird-watching, nature photography, tennis. *Address:* Embassy of Finland, 38 Chesham Place, SW1X 8HW. *T:* (020) 7838 6200. *Clubs:* Athenæum, Travellers.

SALONEN, Esa-Pekka; conductor and composer; Music Director, Los Angeles Philharmonic Orchestra, since 1992; *b* 30 June 1958; *s* of Raimo Salonen and Pia Salonen; *m* 1991, Jane Price; one *s* two *d*. *Educ:* Sibelius Acad., Helsinki. Principal Conductor, Swedish Radio Symphony Orch., 1985–95; Artistic Dir, Helsinki Fest., 1995–96. Principal Guest Conductor, Philharmonia Orch., 1985–94. Mem., Royal Swedish Music Acad., 1991; FRCM 1995. Opera Award, 1995, Conductor Award, 1997, Royal Philharmonic Soc.; numerous record and composition awards. Pro Finlandia Medal (Finland), 1992; Litteris et Artibus Medal (Sweden), 1996; Officier de l'ordre des Arts et des Lettres (France), 1998. *Compositions include:* Saxophone Concerto, 1980; Giro, 1982–97; YTA I, 1982, II, 1985 and III, 1986; FLOOF, 1990; MIMO II, 1992; LA Variations, 1996; Gambit, 1998; Five Images after Sappho, 1999; Mania, 2000; Foreign Bodies, 2001. *Address:* Van Walsum Management, 4 Addison Bridge Place, W14 8XP. *T:* (020) 7371 4343, *Fax:* (020) 7371 4344.

SALOP, Archdeacon of; *see* Hall, Ven. J. B.

SALSBURY, Peter Leslie; Chief Executive, Marks & Spencer plc, 1999–2000; Director, TR Property Investment Trust, since 1997; *b* 20 June 1949; *s* of Joseph Leslie Salsbury and Sylvia Olive (*née* Cook); *m* 1987, Susan Elizabeth Gosling; one *s* from previous *m*. *Educ:* Bancroft Sch.; London Sch. of Econs (BSc Econ). Joined Marks & Spencer, 1970: mgt trainee in stores, 1970–73; merchandiser, Head Office, 1973–76; Merchandise Manager, 1976–82; Exec., 1982–85; Sen. Exec., 1985–86; Divisional Director: Homeware Gp, 1986–88; Ladieswear Gp, 1988–90; Dir, Personnel, 1990–93, and Store Ops, 1993–94; Man. Dir, 1994–99. Non-exec. Dir, NORWEB plc, 1992–95. Mem., Govt Better Regulation Task Force, 1997–99. Council, Inst. of Employment Studies, 1995–; Mem. Council, C&G, 1997–. *Address:* TR Property Investment Trust, 4 Broadgate, EC2M 2DA.

SALT, George, FRS 1956; ScD; Fellow of King's College, Cambridge, since 1933; Reader in Animal Ecology, University of Cambridge, 1965–71, now Emeritus; *b* Loughborough, 12 Dec. 1903; *s* of late Walter Salt and Mary Cecilia (*née* Hulme); *m* 1939, Joyce Laing, Newnham Coll. and Stockton-on-Tees; two *s*. *Educ:* Crescent Heights Collegiate Inst., Calgary; Univ. of Alberta (BSc); Harvard Univ. (SM, SD); Univ. of Cambridge (PhD, ScD). National Research Fellow, Harvard Univ., 1927–28; Entomologist, Imperial Inst. Entom, 1929–31; Royal Soc. Moseley Research Student, 1932–33; Univ. Lectr in Zoology, Cambridge, 1937–65; Dean, 1939–45, Tutor for Advanced Students, 1945–51, King's Coll., Cambridge. Visiting Prof. Univ. of California, Berkeley, 1966. On biological expedns in NW Canada and Rocky Mts, Cuba, Republic of Colombia, E Africa, Pakistan. Murchison Grant, RGS, 1951. *Publications:* The Cellular Defence Reactions of Insects, 1970; papers in scientific jls on insect parasitism and ecology. *Recreations:* mountaineering, gardening, calligraphy and palaeography. *Address:* King's College, Cambridge CB2 1ST.

SALT, Rear-Adm. James Frederick Thomas George, CB 1991; *b* 19 April 1940; *s* of Lieut Comdr George Salt (lost in 1939–45 War in command HMS Triad, 1940) and Lillian Bridget Lamb; *m* 1975, Penelope Mary Walker; four *s*. *Educ:* Wellington College; RNC Dartmouth (1958–59). Served Far East, Mediterranean, South Atlantic and home waters; commanded HM Sub. Finwhale, 1969–71; 2 i/c HM Sub. Resolution (Polaris), 1973–74; Comd HM Nuclear Sub. Dreadnought, 1978–79; Comd HMS Sheffield, 1982 (sank Falklands); Comd HMS Southampton, 1983; ACOS Ops C-in-C Fleet, 1984–85; Dir, Defence Intell., 1986–87; Sen. Naval Mem., Directing Staff, RCDS, 1988–90; ACNS (Gulf War), 1990–91; Mil. Dep., Defence Export Services, 1992–97. Hd of Marketing, Colebrand Ltd, 1998–2000. Master, Cordwainers' Co., 2000–01. *Recreations:* sailing, ski-ing, gardening. *Address:* Birdham Pool, Chichester, West Sussex PO20 7BB.

SALT, Rt Rev. John William; *see* St Helena, Bishop of.

SALT, Sir Patrick (Macdonnell), 7th Bt *cr* 1869, of Saltaire, Yorkshire; *b* 25 Sept. 1932; *s* of Sir John Salt, 4th Bt and Stella Houlton Jackson (*d* 1974); *S* brother, 1991; *m* 1976, Ann Elizabeth Mary Kilham Roberts, *widow* of Denys Kilham Roberts, OBE. *Educ:* Summer Fields, Oxford; Stowe Sch. Dir, Cassidy Davis Members Agency Ltd, 1983–92. *Recreation:* fishing. *Heir: cousin* Daniel Alexander Salt [*b* 15 Aug. 1943; *m* 1968, Merchide, *d* of Dr Ahmad Emami; two *d*]. *Address:* Hillwatering Farmhouse, Langham, Bury St Edmunds, Suffolk IP31 3ED. *T:* (01359) 259367.

SALT, Sir (Thomas) Michael (John), 4th Bt *cr* 1899; *b* 7 Nov. 1946; *s* of Lt-Col Sir Thomas Henry Salt, 3rd Bt, and Meriel Sophia Wilmot, *d* of late Capt. Berkeley C. W. Williams and Hon. Mrs Williams, Herringston, Dorchester; *S* father, 1965; *m* 1971, Caroline, *er d* of Henry Hildyard; two *d*. *Educ:* Eton. *Heir: b* Anthony William David Salt [*b* 5 Feb. 1950; *m* 1978, Olivia Anne, *yr d* of Martin Morgan Hudson; two *s*]. *Recreations:* cricket, shooting. *Address:* Shillingstone House, Shillingstone, Dorset DT11 0QR. *Club:* Boodle's.

SALTER, Harry Charles, CMG 1983; DFC 1945; Director, Financing of Community Budget, European Economic Community, 1973–82, retired; *b* 29 July 1918; *er s* of late Harry Arnold Salter and Irene Beatrice Salter; *m* 1st, 1946, Anne Hooper (marr. diss. 1980); one *d*; 2nd, 1983, Mrs Janet Watford (marr. diss. 1999). *Educ:* St Albans Sch. Entered Ministry of Health, 1936. Served War, Royal Artillery, 1939–46 (despatches, DFC). Asst Sec., Min. of Health, 1963; Under-Sec., DHSS, 1971–73. *Recreations:* living, golf, bridge, chess, cooking. *Address:* 27 Streatley Lodge, Pegasus Grange, White House Road, Oxford OX1 4QF. *T:* (01865) 201856.

SALTER, Ian George; Principal, SG Investment Management Ltd; a Deputy Chairman, London Stock Exchange, since 1990; *b* Hobart, Tasmania, 7 March 1943; *s* of Desmond and Diane Salter. *Educ:* Hutchins Sch., Hobart, Tasmania. AASA. Member: Hobart Stock Exchange, 1965–69; London Stock Exchange, 1970–; Principal, Strauss Turnbull, subseq. Société Générale Strauss Turnbull (Investment Advisers Ltd), now SG (formerly Socgen) Investment Management Ltd, 1978–. Mem., Stock Exchange Council, 1980–91, subseq. London Stock Exchange Bd, 1991–. DTI Inspector, 1984–87. Chm., Emdex Trade PLC, 2001–. Mem., Bd, British Youth Opera, 1998–2000. *Recreations:* opera, travel, gardening. *Address:* SG Investment Management Ltd, 41 Tower Hill, EC3N 4SG. *T:* (020) 7597 3204.

SALTER, Martin John; MP (Lab) Reading West, since 1997; *b* 19 April 1954; *s* of Raymond and Naomi Salter. *Educ:* Univ. of Sussex. Co-ordinator, Reading Centre for Unemployed; Reg. Manager, Co-operative Home Services. Mem., Reading BC (Dep. Leader). Contested (Lab) Reading E, 1987. *Address:* House of Commons, SW1A 0AA.

SALTER, Patience Jane; *see* Wheatcroft, P. J.

SALTER, Richard Stanley; QC 1995; a Recorder, since 2000; *b* 2 Oct. 1951; *s* of late Stanley James Salter and Betty Maud Salter (*née* Topsom); *m* 1991, Shona Virginia Playfair Cannon. *Educ:* Harrow County Sch. for Boys; Balliol Coll., Oxford (MA); Inns of Court Sch. of Law. Called to the Bar, Inner Temple, 1975, Bencher, 1991; pupil to Sir Henry Brooke, 1975–76; in practice at Commercial Bar, 1976–; an Asst Recorder, 1997–2000. Member: Council of Legal Educn, 1990–96; Advocacy Studies Bd, 1996–. Chm., Bd of Examnrs for Bar Vocational Course, 1992–93. Gov., Inns of Court Sch. of Law, 1996–. Consulting Ed., All England Commercial Cases, 1999–. *Publications:* (contrib.) Banks, Liability and Risk, 1991, 3rd edn 2001; (contrib.) Banks and Remedies, 1992, 2nd edn 1999; Guarantee and Indemnity, Halsbury's Laws of England, Vol. 20, 4th edn 1993; (ed) Legal Decisions Affecting Bankers, vols 12–14, 2001. *Recreations:* books, music, theatre, cricket. *Address:* 3 Verulam Buildings, Gray's Inn, WC1R 5NT. *T:* (020) 7831 8441. *Clubs:* Savile; Shoscombe Village Cricket.

SALTHOUSE, Edward Charles, PhD; CEng, FIEE; Master of University College, Durham University, 1979–98; *b* 27 Dec. 1935; *s* of Edward Salthouse, MBE, and Mrs Salthouse (*née* Boyd); *m* 1961, Denise Kathleen Margot Reid; two *s*. *Educ:* Campbell Coll., Belfast; Queen's University of Belfast (BSc, PhD). Lecturer in Electrical Engrg, Univ. of Bristol, 1962–67; University of Durham: Reader in Elec. Engrg Science, 1967–79; Chairman, Board of Studies in Engrg Science, 1976–79; Dean, Faculty of Science, 1982–85; First Chm., School of Applied Science and Engrg, 1985–87; Pro-Vice-Chancellor, 1985–88. Sec., Scottish Industrial Heritage Soc., 1998–. *Publications:* papers on electrical insulation in Proc. IEE and other appropriate jls. *Recreations:* industrial archaeology, photography. *Address:* Shieldaig, Hume, Kelso TD5 7TR.

SALTHOUSE, Leonard; Assistant Under Secretary of State, Ministry of Defence, 1977–87; *b* 15 April 1927; *s* of late Edward Keith Salthouse and Dorothy Annie (*née* Clark); *m* 1950, Kathleen May (*née* Spittle); one *s* one *d*. *Educ:* Queen Elizabeth Grammar Sch., Atherstone, Warwickshire; University Coll. London (BScEcon). Home Civil Service: Asst Principal, Min. of Fuel and Power, 1950–55; Principal, Air Min., then Min. of Defence, 1955–66; Asst Sec., 1966–77. *Recreations:* gardening, music. *Address:* Highfield, 115 Cross Oak Road, Berkhamsted, Herts HP4 3HZ. *T:* (01442) 877809.

SALTON, Prof. Milton Robert James, FRS 1979; Professor and Chairman of Microbiology, New York University School of Medicine, 1964–90, now Emeritus Professor; *b* 29 April 1921; *s* of Robert Alexander Salton and Stella Salton; *m* 1951, Joy Marriott; two *s*. *Educ:* Univ. of Sydney (BSc Agr. 1945); Univ. of Cambridge (PhD 1951, ScD 1967). Beit Meml Res. Fellow, Univ. of Cambridge, 1950–52; Merck Internat. Fellow, Univ. of California, Berkeley, 1952–53; Reader, Univ. of Manchester, 1956–61; Prof. of Microbiology, Univ. of NSW, Australia, 1962–64. Hon. Mem., British Soc. for Antimicrobial Chemotherapy, 1983. Docteur en Médecine, Dhc, Université de Liège, 1967. *Publications:* Microbial Cell Walls, 1960; The Bacterial Cell Wall, 1964; Immunochemistry of Enzymes and their Antibodies, 1978; β-Lactam Antibiotics, 1981; (ed jtly) Antibiotic Inhibition of Bacterial Cell Surface Assembly and Function, 1988. *Address:* Department of Microbiology, New York University School of Medicine, 550 First Avenue, New York, NY 10016, USA. *Club:* Oxford and Cambridge.

SALTOUN, Lady (20th in line) *cr* 1445, of Abernethy; **Flora Marjory Fraser;** Chief of the name of Fraser; *b* 18 Oct. 1930; *d* of 19th Lord Saltoun, MC, and Dorothy (*d* 1985), *e d* of Sir Charles Welby, 5th Bt; *S* father, 1979; *m* 1956, Captain Alexander Ramsay of Mar, Grenadier Guards retd (*d* 2000), *o s* of late Adm. Hon. Sir Alexander Ramsay, GCVO, KCB, DSO, and The Lady Patricia Ramsay, CI, VA, CD; three *d*. Elected Mem., H of L, 1999. *Heiress: d* Hon. Katharine Ingrid Mary Isabel Fraser [*b* 11 Oct. 1957; *m* 1980, Captain Mark Malise Nicolson, Irish Guards; one *s* two *d*]. *Address:* Inverey House, Braemar, Aberdeenshire AB35 5YB.

SALUSBURY-TRELAWNY, Sir John Barry; *see* Trelawny.

SALVADOR PINHEIRO, João de Deus; *see* Pinheiro.

SALVAGE, Jane Elizabeth; Nursing Director, Emap Healthcare, since 2000; international healthcare consultant; *b* 6 Aug 1953; *d* of Robert Salvage and Patricia Grutchfield; *m* 1995, Nareman Taha Wahab. *Educ:* Newnham Coll., Cambridge (BA Hons); Royal Holloway and Bedford New Coll., London (MSc). RGN 1978; Staff Nurse, London Hosp., 1978–80; worked on British nursing jls, and Ed., Sen. Nurse, 1980–88; Dir, Nursing Develt Prog., King's Fund, London, 1988–91; Regl Advr for Nursing and Midwifery, European Reg., WHO, 1991–95; Editor, 1996–97, Editor-in-Chief, 1997–99, Nursing Times. Associate, Newnham Coll., Cambridge, 1993; Vis. Prof., Sheffield Univ., 1999. First Hon. Mem., Romanian Nurses Assoc., 1992. Hon. LLD Sheffield, 1996. *Publications:* The Politics of Nursing, 1985; (ed) Models for Nursing, Vol. 1 1986, Vol. 2 1990; Nurses at Risk, 1988, 2nd edn 1999; (ed) Nurse Practitioners, 1991; (ed) Nursing in Action, 1993; (ed) Nursing Development Units, 1995; (ed) Nursing in Europe, 1997; contrib. numerous articles. *Recreations:* friendship, travel, reading, swimming, cooking and eating, walking, theatre, opera, watching football. *Address:* 2 Church Cottages, Piddinghoe, near Newhaven, E Sussex BN9 9AP.

SALVESEN, (Charles) Hugh, PhD; HM Diplomatic Service; Deputy Head, Economic Policy Department, Foreign and Commonwealth Office, since 2000; *b* 10 Sept. 1955; *s* of John and Eelin Salvesen; *m* 1983, Emilie Maria Ingenhousz; two *s* (one *d* decd). *Educ:* Loretto Sch., Musselburgh; Christ's Coll., Cambridge (MA, PhD). Joined Diplomatic Service, 1982; FCO, 1982–84; First Sec., BMG, Berlin, 1984–85; Bonn, 1985–88; FCO, 1988–93; Argentina, 1993–96; Dep. High Comr, NZ, 1996–2000. *Address:* Foreign and Commonwealth Office, King Charles Street, SW1A 2AH.

SALVIDGE, Paul; Director, Employment Relations, Department of Trade and Industry, 1998–2000; *b* 22 Aug. 1946; *s* of Herbert Stephen and Winifred Alice Elisabeth Salvidge; *m* 1972, Heather Margaret (*née* Johnson); one *d*. *Educ:* Cardiff High School; Birmingham Univ. (LLB). Ministry of Power, 1967; Dept of Trade and Industry, 1972; Asst Secretary, 1982; Under Sec., 1989.

SALZ, Anthony Michael Vaughan; Joint Senior Partner, Freshfields Bruckhaus Deringer, since 2000; *b* 30 June 1950; *s* of Michael H. Salz and Veronica Edith Dorothea Elizabeth Salz (*née* Hall); *m* 1975, Sally Ruth Hagger; one *s* two *d*. *Educ:* Summerfields Sch., Oxford; Radley Coll.; Exeter Univ. (LLB Hons). Admitted Solicitor, 1974; Kenneth Brown Baker Baker, 1972–75; joined Freshfields, 1975, Partner, 1980, Sen. Partner, 1996–2000; seconded to Davis Polk & Wardwell, NY, 1977–78. Chm., Tate Gall. Corporate Adv. Gp, 1997–. Dir, Taro Foundn. Trustee, Eden Project. FRSA 1996. *Publications:* contrib. to various legal books and jls. *Recreations:* golf, fly-fishing, watching sports (including Southampton FC), tennis, walking, theatre, contemporary art. *Address:* (office) 65 Fleet Street, EC4Y 1HS. *T:* (020) 7936 4000. *Clubs:* Walbrook, MCC; Berkshire Golf, Trevose Golf.

SAMARAKOON, Hon. Neville Dunbar Mirahawatte; Chief Justice, Democratic Socialist Republic of Sri Lanka, 1977–84; *b* 22 Oct. 1919; *s* of Alfred Charles Warnabarana Wickremasinghe Samarakoon and Rajapaksa Wasala Mudiyanselage Chandrawati Mirahawatte Kumarihamy; *m* 1949, Mary Patricia Mulholland; one *s* two *d*. *Educ:* Trinity Coll., Kandy; University Coll., Colombo; Law Coll., Colombo. Enrolled as Advocate, 1945; Crown Counsel, Attorney-General's Dept, 1948–51; reverted to Private Bar, 1951; QC 1968. Member: Bar Council, 1964–77; Disciplinary Bd for Lawyers 1971–74, 1976, 1977. Chairman: Judicial Service Commn, 1978–84; Council of Legal Educn.

SAMARANCH, Juan Antonio; Marqués de Samaranch, 1991; President, International Olympic Committee, 1980–2001 (Member, 1966; Hon. Life President, 2001); *b* 17 July 1920; *s* of Francisco Samaranch and Juana Torello; *m* 1955, Maria Teresa Salisachs Rowe (*d* 2000); one *s* one *d*. *Educ:* Instituto Superior Estudios de Empresas, Barcelona; German College; Higher Inst. of Business Studies, Barcelona. Industrialist, Bank Consultant; Pres., Barcelona Diputacion, 1973–77; Ambassador to USSR and to People's Republic of Mongolia, 1977–80. Mem., Spanish Olympic Cttee, 1954 (Pres., 1967–70); Nat. Deleg. for Physical Educn and Sport. Pres., Caja de Ahorros y de Pensiones de Barcelona. Holds numerous decorations and various honorary degrees from different univs. *Publications:* Deporte 2000, 1967; Olympic Message, 1980; Olympic Review. *Recreation:* philately. *Address:* International Olympic Committee, Château de Vidy, 1007 Lausanne, Switzerland. *T:* (21) 6216111.

SAMBLES, Prof. John Roy, PhD; FInstP; Professor of Physics, Exeter University, since 1991; *b* 14 Oct. 1945; *s* of Charles Henry Sambles and Georgina (*née* Deeble); *m* 1966, Sandra Elizabeth Sloman; two *s* one *d*. *Educ:* Callington Grammar Sch., Cornwall; Imperial Coll., London Univ. (BSc 1st Cl. Hons Physics 1967; ARCS; PhD 1970; DIC). FInstP 1988. Res. Fellow, Imperial Coll., London, 1970–72; Exeter University: Lectr in Physics, 1972–85; Sen. Lectr, 1985–88; Reader, 1988–91. George Gray Medal, British Liquid Crystal Soc., 1998. *Publications:* numerous papers in learned scientific jls, incl. works on liquid crystals, diffractive optics, melting, electron microscopy, resistivity of thin samples, molecular electronics and surface plasmons. *Recreations:* writing poetry, local Methodist preacher. *Address:* School of Physics, University of Exeter, Exeter, Devon EX4 4QL. *T:* (01392) 264103; Rivendell, Pope's Lane, Lapford, Crediton, Devon EX17 6QU. *T:* (01363) 83075.

SAMBROOK, Prof. Joseph Frank, PhD; FRS 1985; Director, Peter MacCallum Cancer Institute, Melbourne, since 1995; *b* 1 March 1939; *s* of Thomas Sambrook and Ethel Gertrude (*née* Lightfoot); *m* 1st, 1960, Thelma McGrady (marr. diss. 1984); two *s* one *d*; 2nd; 1986, Mary-Jane Gething; one *d*. *Educ:* Liverpool Univ. (BSc 1962); Australian Nat. Univ. (PhD 1965). Res. Fellow, John Curtin Sch. of Med. Res., ANU, 1965–66; Postdoctoral Fellow, MRC Lab. of Molecular Biol., 1966–67; Jun. Fellow, Salk Inst. for Biol Studies, 1967–69; Sen. Staff Investigator, 1969–77, Asst Dir, 1977–85, Cold Spring Harbor Lab.; Prof. and Chm., Dept of Biochemistry, Southwestern Medical Center, Dallas, 1985–91; Dir, McDermott Center for Human Growth and Develt, Southwestern Med. Sch., Dallas, 1991–94. *Publications:* contribs to learned jls. *Recreation:* music. *Address:* Peter MacCallum Cancer Institute, St Andrews Place, East Melbourne, Vic 3002, Australia. *T:* (3) 96561513, *Fax:* (3) 96561411; 115 George Street, East Melbourne, Vic 3002, Australia.

SAMBROOK, Richard Jeremy; Director, BBC News, since 2001; *b* 24 April 1956; *s* of Michael Sambrook and Joan Sambrook (*née* Hartridge); *m* 1987, Susan Fisher; one *s* one *d*. *Educ:* Maidstone Sch. for Boys; Reading Univ. (BA); Birkbeck Coll., London Univ. (MSc). Trainee journalist, Thomson Newspapers, 1977–80; joined BBC, 1980: Radio News, 1980–84; TV News, 1984–87; Dep. Ed., Nine O'Clock News, 1988–92; News Editor, BBC News, 1992–96; Head, Newsgathering, 1996–99; Dep. Dir, BBC News, 1999–2001. Member: RTS, 1992–; BAFTA, 1996–. FRSA. *Recreations:* walking, squash, music. *Address:* BBC TV Centre, Wood Lane, W12 7RJ. *T:* (020) 8576 7178.

SAMPAIO, Jorge Fernando Branco de, Hon. GCVO 1993; President of Portugal, since 1996; *b* Lisbon, 18 Sept. 1939; *s* of António Arnaldo de Carvalho Sampaio and Fernanda Bensaúde Branco de Sampaio; *m* Maria José Ritta; one *s* one *d*. *Educ:* Law Sch., Univ. of Lisbon. Practised as a lawyer, specialising in defending political prisoners. Sec. of State for External Co-operation, 1975; MP, Lisbon, 1979–84; Speaker, Socialist Parly Gp, 1987–88; Mem., Council of State, 1989–92; Mayor of Lisbon, 1989–95. Founder, Intervenção Socialista, 1975; joined Socialist Party, 1978: Mem., Nat. Secretariat, 1979–92; Dir, Internat. Dept, 1986–87; Sec. Gen., 1989–92. Mem., European Human Rights Commn, Council of Europe, 1979–84. Numerous decorations, including: Grand Officer, Order of Prince Henry (Portugal), 1983; Grand Cross, Order of Orange Nassau (Netherlands), 1990. *Publications:* A Festa de um Sonho, 1991; A Look on Portugal, 1995; numerous articles on political issues. *Recreations:* music, golf. *Address:* Presidência da República, Palácio de Belém, 1349–022 Lisbon, Portugal.

SAMPLES, Reginald McCartney, CMG 1971; DSO 1942; OBE 1963; HM Diplomatic Service, retired; *b* 11 Aug. 1918; *o s* of late William and Jessie Samples; *m* 1947, Elsie Roberts Hide (*d* 1999); two *s* one step *d*. *Educ:* Rhyl Grammar Sch.; Liverpool Univ. (BCom). Served, 1940–46; RNVR (Air Branch); torpedo action with 825 Sqn against German ships Scharnhorst, Gneisenau and Prinz Eugen in English Channel (wounded, DSO); Lieut (A). Central Office of Information (Economic Editor, Overseas Newspapers), 1947–48. CRO (Brit. Inf. Services, India), 1948; Economic Information Officer, Bombay, 1948–52; Editor-in-Chief, BIS, New Delhi, 1952; Dep.-Dir, BIS, New Delhi, 1952–56; Dir, BIS, Pakistan (Karachi), 1956–59; Dir, BIS, Canada (Ottawa), 1959–65, OBE; Counsellor (Information) to Brit. High Comr, India, and Dir, BIS, India (New Delhi), 1965–68; Asst Under-Sec. of State, Commonwealth Office, 1968; Head of British Govt Office, and Sen. British Trade Comr, Toronto, 1969; Consul-Gen., Toronto, 1974–78. Asst Dir, Royal Ontario Museum, 1978–83. Volunteer recording books for the blind, Canadian Nat. Inst. for the Blind, 1983–. *Recreations:* watching tennis, ballet. *Address:* Belmont House, Apartment 508, 52 McMurrich Street, Toronto, ON M5R 3T3, Canada. *Clubs:* Naval; Queens (Toronto).

SAMPRAS, Peter; tennis player; *b* 12 Aug. 1971; *s* of Sam and Georgia Sampras; *m* 2000, Bridgette Wilson. Professional tennis player, 1988–; won US Open, 1990 (youngest winner), 1993, 1995, 1996, 1999; Australian Open, 1994, 1997; Wimbledon, 1993, 1994, 1995, 1997, 1998, 1999, 2000; ATP World Champion, 1991, 1994, 1996, 1997, 1999; Davis Cup player. Member: American Cancer Soc. Public Awareness Council; Board, Tim and Tom Gullikson Foundation; Founder, Aces for Charity Fund. *Recreations:* golf, basketball, Formula 1 racing. *Address:* c/o 200 ATP Tour Boulevard, Ponte Vedra Beach, FL 32082, USA. *T:* (904) 2858000.

SAMPSON, Anthony (Terrell Seward); writer and journalist; *b* 3 Aug. 1926; *s* of Michael Sampson and Phyllis, *d* of Sir Albert Seward, FRS; *m* 1965, Sally, *d* of Dr P. G. Bentlif, Jersey, and of Mrs G. Denison-Smith, Islip, Oxon; one *s* one *d*. *Educ:* Westminster School; Christ Church, Oxford. Served with Royal Navy, 1944–47; Sub-Lieut, RNVR, 1946. Editor of Drum Magazine, Johannesburg, 1951–55; Editorial staff of The Observer, 1955–66; Associate Prof., Univ. of Vincennes, Paris, 1968–70; Chief American Corresp., The Observer, 1973–74. Contributing Editor, Newsweek, 1977–; Editorial Conslt, The Brandt Commn, 1978–79; Editor, The Sampson Letter, 1984–86. Presenter and narrator: The Midas Touch (BBC2), 1990; The Two-Edged Sword (BBC2), 1991. Chm., Soc. of Authors, 1992–94. Trustee, Scott Trust (Guardian/Observer), 1993–96; Mem., Internat. Adv. Bd, Independent Newspapers (S Africa), 1995–. *Publications:* Drum, a Venture into the New Africa, 1956; The Treason Cage, 1958; Commonsense about Africa, 1960; (with S. Pienaar) South Africa: two views of Separate Development 1960; Anatomy of Britain, 1962; Anatomy of Britain Today, 1965; Macmillan: a study in ambiguity, 1967; The New Europeans, 1968; The New Anatomy of Britain, 1971; The Sovereign State: the secret history of ITT, 1973; The Seven Sisters, 1975 (Prix International de la Presse, Nice, 1976); The Arms Bazaar, 1977; The Money Lenders, 1981; The Changing Anatomy of Britain, 1982; Empires of the Sky, 1984; (with Sally Sampson) The Oxford Book of Ages, 1985; Black and Gold: tycoons, revolutionaries and apartheid, 1987; The Midas Touch, 1989; The Essential Anatomy of Britain, 1992; Company Man, 1995; The Scholar Gypsy: the quest for a family secret, 1997; Mandela: the authorised biography, 1999. *Recreations:* vertical gardening, opera. *Address:* 10 Hereford Mansions, Hereford Road, W2 5BA. *T:* (020) 7727 4188, *Fax:* (020) 7221 5738; Quarry Garden, Wardour, Tisbury, Wilts SP3 6HR, *T:* (01747) 870407. *Clubs:* Beefsteak, Groucho, Academy, Grillions.

SAMPSON, Sir Colin, Kt 1993; CBE 1988; QPM 1978; DL; HM Chief Inspector of Constabulary for Scotland, 1991–93; *b* 26 May 1929; *s* of James and Nellie Sampson; *m* 1953, Kathleen Stones; two *s*. *Educ:* Stanley Sch., Wakefield; Wakefield Technical Coll.; Univ. of Leeds (Criminology). Joined Police Force, 1949; served mainly in the CID (incl. training of detectives), at Dewsbury, Skipton, Doncaster, Goole, Wakefield, Huddersfield, Rotherham, Barnsley; Comdt, Home Office Detective Trng Sch., Wakefield, 1971–72; Asst Chief Constable, West Yorks, 1973; Dep. Chief Constable, Notts, 1976; Chief Constable, W Yorks, 1983–89; HM Inspector of Constabulary, 1989–90 (for NE England, 1990). Advr on police matters to govt of Namibia, 1989–93. Vice Pres., Yorkshire Soc., 1983–. Freeman, City of London, 1990. DL West Yorks, 1994. DUniv Bradford, 1988; Hon. LLD Leeds, 1990. KStJ 1998. *Recreations:* choral music, walking, gardening. *Address:* Cliffside, Riviera Drive, Sewerby Village, East Yorks YO15 1EL.

SAMS, Jeremy Charles; composer; translator; director; *b* 12 Jan. 1957; *s* of Eric Sams and Enid (*née* Tidmarsh); one *s*. *Educ:* Magdalene Coll., Cambridge (BA); Guildhall Sch. of Music. Freelance pianist, 1977–82; director: *theatre* includes: Entertaining Mr Sloane, Greenwich, 1992; Wind in the Willows, Tokyo, 1993, Old Vic, 1995; Neville's Island, Apollo, 1994; Wild Oats, RNT, 1995; Passion, Queen's, 1996; Marat/Sade, RNT, 1997; Enter the Guardsman, Donmar, 1997; Two Pianos, Four Hands, Birmingham Rep, and Comedy, 1999; Spend! Spend! Spend!, Piccadilly, 1999; Noises Off, RNT, 2000, transf. Piccadilly, 2001; What the Butler Saw, Theatre Royal, Bath, and tour, 2001; *opera:* The Reluctant King, Opera North, 1994; *translations* include: The Rehearsal, Almeida and Garrick, 1991 (Time Out Award); Becket, Theatre Royal Haymarket, 1991; The Miser, NT; Les Parents Terribles, RNT and NY, 1990; Mary Stuart, RNT, 1996; The Magic Flute, Macbeth, Figaro's Wedding, La Bohème, ENO; Merry Widow, Royal Opera, 1997; A Fool and His Money, Nottingham Playhouse and Birmingham Rep, 1998; Colombe, Salisbury Playhouse, 1999; The Rhinegold, ENO, 2001; *adaptations* include: Waiting in the Wings, NY, 1999; composer of numerous scores: *theatre* includes: Kean,

Old Vic, 1990; for RSC: Temptation, The Tempest, Measure for Measure, Merry Wives of Windsor, Midsummer Night's Dream; for RNT: Ghetto (also lyrics); Wind in the Willows (also lyrics); Arcadia; *television:* Persuasion, 1996 (Award for Original TV Music, BAFTA); Have Your Cake, 1997. *Publications:* (ed) Wild Oats, 1995; *translations:* Molière, The Miser, 1991; Anouilh, The Rehearsal, 1991; Cocteau, Les Parents Terribles, 1995; Schiller, Mary Stuart, 1996; Anouilh, Becket, 1997; Lehár, The Merry Widow, 2000. *Address:* c/o The Agency, 24 Pottery Lane, W11 4LZ.

SAMSON, Prof. Thomas James, (Jim), PhD; FBA 2000; Professor of Music, Royal Holloway , University of London, from Feb. 2002; *b* 6 July 1946; *s* of Edward Samson and Matilda Jayne (*née* Smyth); partner, Dr Susan Jane Rogers. *Educ:* Queen's Univ., Belfast (BMus); UC, Cardiff, (MMus; PhD 1972). Res. Fellow in Humanities, Univ. of Leicester, 1972–73; University of Exeter: Lectr in Music, 1973–87; Reader in Musicology, 1987–92; Prof. of Musicology, 1992–94; Stanley Hugh Badock Prof. of Music, Univ. of Bristol, 1994–2002. Order of Merit, Ministry of Culture (Poland), 1990. *Publications:* Music in Transition: a study of tonal expansion and early atonality 1900–1920, 1977, 3rd edn 1993; The Music of Szymanowski, 1980; The Music of Chopin, 1985, 2nd edn 1994 (trans. German 1991); (ed) Chopin Studies, 1988; (ed) The Late Romantic Era: Vol. VII, Man and Music, 1991; Chopin: the Four Ballades, 1992; (ed) The Cambridge Companion to Chopin, 1992; (ed with J. Rink) Chopin Studies 2, 1994; Chopin, 1996; (ed) The Cambridge History of Nineteenth-Century Music, 2002. *Recreations:* farming, astronomy. *Address:* Edbury Farm, Pennymoor, Tiverton, Devon EX16 8LR. *T:* (01363) 866234; Department of Music, Royal Holloway, University of London, Egham, Surrey TW20 0EX.

SAMSOVA, Galina; producer; Teacher with the company in the Royal Ballet; *b* Stalingrad, 1937; *d* of a Byelorussian; *m* 1st, Alexander Ursuliak; 2nd, André Prokovsky. *Educ:* the Ballet Sch., Kiev (pupil of N. Verekundova). Joined Kiev Ballet, 1956 and became a soloist; Canadian Ballet, 1961; created chief rôle in Cendrillon, Paris 1963 (Gold Medal for best danseuse of Paris Festival). Ballerina, Festival Ballet, 1964–73; headed the group of André Prokovsky, The New London Ballet, (disbanded in 1977, revived for 3 new productions, The Theatre Royal, York, 1979); a Principal Dancer, Sadler's Wells Royal Ballet, subseq. Birmingham Royal Ballet, 1980–91; Artistic Dir, Scottish Ballet, 1991–97; has danced principal rôles in Sleeping Beauty, Nutcracker, Giselle, Swan Lake, Anna Karenina, and other classical ballets; danced in Europe, Far East and USA. Produced: Sequence from Paquita, Sadler's Wells, 1980; (with Peter Wright) Swan Lake, Sadler's Wells, 1983, Covent Garden, 1991, Royal Swedish Ballet, 2001; Giselle, London City Ballet, 1986; Les Sylphides, Birmingham Royal Ballet, 1992; Sleeping Beauty, Scottish Ballet, 1994, Tulsa Ballet, USA, 2000; Swan Lake, Scottish Ballet, 1995.

SAMUEL, family name of **Viscounts Bearsted** and **Samuel**.

SAMUEL, 3rd Viscount *cr* 1937, of Mount Carmel and of Toxteth, Liverpool; **David Herbert Samuel,** OBE 1996; Professor of Physical Chemistry, Weizmann Institute of Science, Rehovot, Israel, 1967–87, Emeritus Professor of Physical Chemistry since 1987; *b* 8 July 1922; *s* of 2nd Viscount Samuel, CMG, and Hadassah (*d* 1986), *d* of Judah Goor (Grasovsky); *S* father, 1978; *m* 1st, 1950, Esther Berelowitz; one *d*; 2nd, 1960, Rinna Dafni (*née* Grossman); one *d*; 3rd, 1980, Veronika Engelhardt Grimm; 4th, 1997, Eve Black. *Educ:* Balliol Coll., Oxford (MA 1948); Hebrew Univ. (PhD 1953). Served War of 1939–45 (despatches); Captain RA, in India, Burma and Sumatra. Weizmann Institute of Science, Rehovot, Israel: Member of Staff, 1949–87, of Isotope Dept, 1949–86, of Dept of Neurobiology, 1986–; Dir, Center for Neurosciences and Behavioural Research, 1978–87; Head, Chemistry Gp, Science Teaching Dept, 1967–83; Dean, Faculty of Chemistry, 1971–73; Chm., Bd of Studies in Chemistry, Feinberg Grad. Sch., 1968–74. Post-doctoral Fellow, Chem. Dept, UCL, 1956; Res. Fellow, Chem. Dept, Harvard Univ., 1957–58; Res. Fellow, Lab. of Chemical Biodynamics (Lawrence Radiation Lab.), Univ. of California, Berkeley, 1965–66; Vis. Prof., Sch. of Molecular Scis, Univ. of Warwick, 1967; Royal Soc. Vis. Prof., MRC Neuroimmunology Unit, Zoology Dept, UCL, 1974–75; Vis. Prof., Pharmacol. Dept, Yale Sch. of Medicine, 1983–84; McLaughlin Prof., Sch. of Medicine, McMaster Univ., 1984; Vis. Prof., Dept of Chemistry, Univ. of York, 1995–96, 1997. Member: Adv. Bd, Bat-Sheva de Rothschild Foundn for Advancement of Science in Israel, 1970–83; Bd, US-Israel Educnl (Fulbright) Foundn, 1969–74 (Chm., 1974–75); Bd, Israel Center for Scientific and Technol Information, 1970–74; Scientific Adv. Cttee and Bd of Trustees of Israel Center for Psychobiol., 1973–; Acad. Adv. Cttee, Everyman's (Open) Univ., 1976–83; Bd of Govs, Bezalel Acad. of Arts and Design, 1977–; Council, Israel Chemical Soc., 1977–83; Internat. Brain Res. Org. (IBRO), 1977–; Israel Exec. Cttee, America-Israel Cultural Foundn, 1978–89 (Chm., 1986–89); Bd of Governors, Tel Aviv Museum, 1980–; Cttee on Teaching of Chemistry, IUPAC, 1981–89; Anglo-Israel Assoc., 1985– (Chm., Colloquia, 1997–); British Israel Arts Foundn, 1986–98; Bd of Trustees, Menninger Foundn, USA, 1988–; Soc. of Manufacturing Engrs, 1989–94; Fibre Soc., 1990–94. Pres., Shenkar Coll. of Textile Technology and Fashion, 1987–94. Former Member, Editorial Board: Jl of Labelled Compounds & Radiopharmaceuticals; Alzheimer Disease and Associated Disorders; Brain Behaviour and Immunity. Scopus Award, Hebrew Univ. of Jerusalem, 2000. *Publications:* Memory: how we use it, lose it and can improve it, 1999; more than 300 papers, reviews and parts of collective volumes on isotopes, physical chemistry, reaction mechanisms, neurochemistry, psychopharmacology, animal behavior, education and the history and teaching of science. *Heir: b* Hon. Dan Judah Samuel [*b* 25 March 1925; *m* 1st, 1957, Nonni (Esther) (marr. diss. 1977), *d* of late Max Gordon, Johannesburg; one *s* two *d*; 2nd, 1981, Heather, *d* of Angus and Elsa Cumming, Haywards Heath; one *s* one *d*]. *Address:* Weizmann Institute of Science, Rehovot 76100, Israel. *T:* (8) 9344229; (home) 1/4 Pinhas Rosen Street, Herzlia 46590, Israel. *T:* (9) 9553242.

SAMUEL, Adrian Christopher Ian, CMG 1959; CVO 1963; *b* 20 Aug. 1915; *s* of late George Christopher Samuel and Alma Richards; *m* 1942, Sheila, *er d* of late J. C. Barrett, Killiney, Co. Dublin; three *s* one *d*. *Educ:* Rugby Sch.; St John's Coll., Oxford. Entered HM Consular Service, 1938; served at Beirut, Tunis and Trieste. Served War, 1940–44, in Royal Air Force. Returned to HM Foreign Service and served at HM Embassies in Ankara, Cairo and Damascus; First Secretary, 1947; Counsellor, 1956; Principal Private Secretary to the Secretary of State for Foreign Affairs, Oct. 1959–63; Minister at HM Embassy, Madrid, 1963–65; resigned 1965. Director: British Chemical Engrg Contractors Assoc., 1966–69; British Agrochemicals Assoc., 1972–78; Dir-Gen., Groupement Internat. des Assocs Nats de Fabricants de Pesticides (GIFAP), 1978–79. *Publication:* An Astonishing Fellow: a life of Sir Robert Wilson, KMT, MP, 1986. *Recreations:* golf, reading. *Address:* The Laundry House, Handcross, near Haywards Heath, West Sussex RH17 6HQ. *T:* (01444) 400717. *Club:* Garrick.

SAMUEL, Gillian Patricia; Director (formerly General Manager) of Corporate Communications, P & O Nedlloyd Ltd, since 1998; *b* 19 Oct. 1945; *d* of Harry Martin Samuel and Kathleen Joyce Samuel (*née* Drake). *Educ:* Edmonton Co. Grammar Sch.; Exeter Univ. (BA Hons Hist.). Current Affairs Gp, BBC TV, 1968–70; Plessey Co., 1970–72; Department of: Nat. Savings, 1972–75; Industry, later DTI, 1975–87; Dir of Information, Dept of Transport, 1987–92; Press Sec. and Chief of Information, 1992–97, Sen. Advr, Internal Communications Develt, 1997–98, MoD. Trustee, Inst. for Citizenship, 1999–. *Recreations:* walking, keep fit. *Address:* P & O Nedlloyd Ltd, Beagle House, Braham Street, E1 8EP.

SAMUEL, Sir John (Michael Glen), 5th Bt *cr* 1898; Chairman, Synergy Management Services Ltd, since 1983; *b* 25 Jan. 1944; *o s* of Sir John Oliver Cecil Samuel, 4th Bt, and of Charlotte Mary, *d* of late R. H. Hoyt, Calgary, Canada; *S* father, 1962; *m* 1st, 1966, Antoinette Sandra, *d* of late Captain Antony Hewitt, RE, 2nd SAS Regt, and of Mrs K. A. H. Casson, Frith Farm, Wolverton, Hants; two *s*; 2nd, 1982, Mrs Elizabeth Ann Molinari, *y d* of late Major R. G. Curry, Bournemouth, Dorset. *Educ:* Radley; London Univ. Director: Enfield Automotive, 1967–70; Advanced Vehicle Systems Ltd, 1971–78; Chm., Electric Auto Corp. (USA), 1978–83. *Recreation:* motor racing. *Heir: s* Anthony John Fulton Samuel, *b* 13 Oct. 1972.

SAMUEL, Richard Christopher, CMG 1983; CVO 1983; HM Diplomatic Service, retired; Ambassador to Latvia, 1991–93; *b* Edinburgh, 8 Aug. 1933; *m* 1986, Frances Draper; one *s* one *d*. *Educ:* Durham Sch.; St John's Coll., Cambridge (BA). Royal Navy, 1952–54. FO, 1957–58; Warsaw, 1958–59; Rome, 1960–63; FO, 1963; Private Sec. to Parly Under-Sec. of State, 1965–68; Hong Kong, 1968–69; 1st Sec. and Head of Chancery: Singapore, 1969–71; Peking, 1971–73; Counsellor, Washington, 1973–76; Head of Far Eastern Dept, FCO, 1976–79; Counsellor (Commercial), Moscow, 1980–82; Minister and Dep. High Comr, New Delhi, 1982–85; Under-Sec. for Asia and the Oceans, ODA, FCO, 1986–88; on loan to Inter-Amer. Develt Bank, Washington, as Exec. Dir for UK/Western Europe, 1988–91. Hd, CSCE Resident Mission, Moldova, 1994; Head, OSCE Resident Mission: Estonia, 1995; Latvia, 1997–98. Diplomatic Adviser: to UN Special Envoy, Inter-Tajik negotiations in Ashkhabad, 1995–96; to EU Justice and Home Affairs Mission to Central Asia, 1997. *Address:* 41 Northumberland Place, W2 5AS. *T:* and *Fax:* (020) 7229 8357.

SAMUELS; *see* Turner-Samuels.

SAMUELS, Hon. Gordon (Jacob), AC 1987; CVO 2000; Governor of New South Wales, 1996–2001; *b* 12 Aug. 1923; *s* of Harry Samuels and Zelda Selina (*née* Glass); *m* 1957, Jacqueline Kott; two *d*. *Educ:* University Coll. Sch., London; Balliol Coll., Oxford (MA). Served War, 1942–46; Capt. 96th (Royal Devon Yeomanry) Field Regt, RA. Called to the Bar: Inner Temple, 1948; NSW, 1952; Teaching Fellow in Jurisprudence, Sydney Univ. Law Sch., 1952–56; QC NSW 1964, Vic, 1965; Challis Lectr in Pleading, Sydney Univ. Law Sch., 1964–70; Judge: Supreme Court of NSW, 1972–92; Court of Appeal, 1974–92; independent arbitrator, referee and mediator, 1992–96. Chairman: Law Reform Commn of NSW, 1993–96; Mediator Accreditation Bd, Australian Commercial Disputes Centre, 1994–96; Sen. Comr, Commn of Inquiry into Australian Secret Intelligence Service, 1994–95; Pres., Australian Security Appeals Tribunal, 1980–90. Mem., NSW Migrant Employment and Qualifications Bd, 1989–95 (Chm., 1992–95). President: NSW Bar Assoc., 1971–72; Acad. of Forensic Scis, 1974–76; Australian Soc. of Legal Phil., 1976–79. Chancellor, Univ. of NSW, 1976–94. Mem., Bd of Govs, Law Foundn of NSW, 1992–94 (Chm., 1992–93). Hon. LLD Sydney, 1994; Hon. DSc NSW, 1994. *Recreations:* reading, music, theatre. *Address:* 38 Evans Street, Bronte, NSW 2024, Australia. *Club:* Australian (Sydney).

SAMUELS, John Edward Anthony; QC 1981; **His Honour Judge Samuels;** a Circuit Judge, since 1997; *b* 15 Aug. 1940; *s* of late Albert Edward Samuels, solicitor, Reigate, Surrey; *m* 1967, Maxine (*née* Robertson), JP; two *s*. *Educ:* Charterhouse; Perugia; Queens' Coll., Cambridge (MA). Commnd, Queen's Royal Regt (TA), 1959; Lieut, Queen's Royal Surrey Regt (TA), 1961–67. Chairman, Cambridge Univ. United Nations Assoc., 1962. Called to Bar, Lincoln's Inn, 1964 (Mansfield Schol., 1963; Bencher, 1990); South Eastern Circuit; a Dep. High Court Judge, 1981–97; a Recorder, 1985–97. Asst Parly Boundary Comr, 1992–95. Member: Senate of the Inns of Court and the Bar, 1983–86; Bar Council, 1992–97; Council of Legal Educn, 1983–90; Chm., Jt Regulations Cttee, Inns' Council and Bar Council, 1987–90. Mem. Cttee, Council of HM Circuit Judges, 2001–. Co-opted Mem., ILEA Education Cttee, 1964–67; Jt Chm., ILEA Disciplinary Tribunals, 1977–87; Alternate Chm., Burnham Cttee, 1981–87; Lay Chm., NHS Complaints Panels, 1996–97; Mem., Criminal Injuries Compensation Appeal Panel, 1997. Member: Richmond, Twickenham and Roehampton HA, 1982–85; Kingston and Richmond FPC, 1982–86. Trustee: Richmond Parish Lands Charity, 1986–96 (Chairman: Educn Cttee, 1987–89; Property Cttee, 1987–95); Prisoners' Educn Trust, 2000–. *Publications:* Action Pack: counsel's guide to chambers' administration, 1986, 2nd edn 1988; contributor to Halsbury's Laws of England, 4th edn. *Recreations:* conservation, restoration, serendipity. *Address:* c/o Blackfriars Crown Court, Pocock Street, SE1 0BJ. *T:* (020) 7922 5800.

SAMUELS, Prof. Michael Louis, FRSE; Professor of English Language, University of Glasgow, 1959–89; *b* 1920; *s* of late Harry Samuels, OBE, MA, barrister-at-law, and Céline Samuels (*née* Aronowitz), London; *m* 1950, Hilary, *d* of late Julius and Ruth Samuel, Glasgow; one *d*. *Educ:* St Paul's School; Balliol College, Oxford. Domus Exhibitioner in Classics, Balliol College, Oxford, 1938–40 and 1945–47; MA 1947 (First Class Hons English Lang. and Lit.). Worked for Air Ministry (Maintenance Command), 1940–45. Research Fellow, University of Birmingham, 1947–48; Assistant in English Language, University of Edinburgh, 1948–49; Lecturer in English Language, Univ. of Edinburgh, 1949–59. Chm., Scottish Studentships Selection Cttee, 1975–88. FRSE 1989. *Publications:* Linguistic Evolution, 1972; (ed jtly) A Linguistic Atlas of Late Medieval English, 1987; (jtly) Middle English Dialectology, 1989; (with J. J. Smith) The English of Chaucer, 1989; contribs to: Approaches to English Historical Linguistics, 1969; So Meny people Longages and Tonges (presented to A. McIntosh), 1981; Middle English Studies (presented to N. Davis), 1983; Proc. 4th Internat. Conf. on English Historical Linguistics, 1985; Explanation and Linguistic Change, 1987; A Companion to Piers Plowman, 1988; articles and reviews in linguistic and literary jls. *Address:* 4 Queen's Gate, Dowanhill, Glasgow G12 9DN. *T:* (0141) 334 4999.

SAMUELSON, Sir (Bernard) Michael (Francis), 5th Bt *cr* 1884; *b* 17 Jan. 1917; *s* of Sir Francis Henry Bernard Samuelson, 4th Bt, and Margaret Kendall (*d* 1980), *d* of H. Kendall Barnes; *S* father, 1981; *m* 1952, Janet Amy, *yr d* of Lt-Comdr L. G. Elkington, RN retd, Chelsea; two *s* two *d*. *Educ:* Eton. Served War of 1939–45 with RA and Leicestershire Regt (despatches). *Heir: s* James Francis Samuelson [*b* 20 Dec. 1956; *m* 1987, Caroline Anne Woodley; two *d*]. *Address:* Harborne, Hailsham Road, Stone Cross, Pevensey, East Sussex BN24 5AS. *T:* (01323) 760487.

SAMUELSON, Prof. Paul Anthony; Institute Professor, Massachusetts Institute of Technology, 1966–86, now Emeritus; Shinsei Bank Visiting Professor of Political Economy, Center for Japan—US Business and Economic Studies, New York University; *b* Gary, Indiana, 15 May 1915; *m* 1st, 1938, Marion Crawford (*d* 1978); four *s* (inc. triplets) two *d*; 2nd, 1981, Risha Claypool. *Educ:* Univs of Chicago (BA) and Harvard (MA, PhD). SSRC Predoctoral Fellow, 1935–37; Soc. of Fellows, Harvard, 1937–40; Guggenheim

Fellow, 1948–49; Ford Faculty Research Fellow, 1958–59; Hoyt Vis. Fellow, Calhoun Coll., Yale, 1962; Carnegie Foundn Reflective Year, 1965–66. MIT: Asst Prof. of Econs, 1940; Assoc. Prof. of Econs, 1944; Staff Mem., Radiation Lab., 1944–45; Prof. of Econs, 1947; Prof. of Internat. Economic Relations (part-time), Fletcher Sch. of Law and Diplomacy, 1945. Consultant: to Nat. Resources Planning Bd, 1941–43; to Rand Corp., 1948–75; to US Treasury, 1945–52, 1961–74; to Johnson Task Force on Sustained Prosperity, 1964; to Council of Econ. Advisers, 1960–68; to Federal Reserve Bd, 1965–; to Congressional Budget Office, 1974–. Economic Adviser to Senator, Candidate and President-elect John F. Kennedy, informal adviser to President Kennedy. Member: War Prodn Bd and Office of War Mobilization and Reconstruction, 1945; Bureau of the Budget, 1952; Adv. Bd of Nat Commn on Money and Credit, 1958–60; Research Adv. Panel to President's Nat. Goals Commn, 1959–60; Research Adv. Bd Cttee for Econ. Develt, 1960; Nat. Task Force on Econ. Educn, 1960–61; Sen. Advr, Brookings Panel on Econ. Activity. Contrib. Editor and Columnist, Newsweek, 1966–81. Vernon F. Taylor Vis. Dist. Prof., Trinity Univ., Texas, 1989. Lectures: Stamp Meml, London, 1961; Wicksell, Stockholm, 1962; Franklin, Detroit, 1962; Gerhard Colm Meml, NYC, 1971; Davidson, Univ. of New Hampshire, 1971; 12th John von Neumann, Univ. of Wisconsin, 1971; J. Willard Gibbs, Amer. Mathematical Soc., 1974; 1st Sulzbacher, Columbia Law Sch., 1974; John Diebold, Harvard Univ., 1976; Alice Bourneauf, Boston Coll., 1981; Horowitz, Jerusalem and Tel Aviv, 1984; Marschak Meml, UCLA, 1984; Olin, Univ. of Virginia Law Sch., 1989; Joseph W. Martin Commemorative, Stonehill Coll., 1990; Lionel Robbins Meml, Claremont Coll., 1991. Corresp. Fellow, British Acad., 1960; Fellow: Amer. Philosoph. Soc.; Econometric Soc. (Mem. Council; Vice-Pres. 1950; Pres. 1951); Member: Amer. Acad. Arts and Sciences; Amer. Econ. Assoc. (Pres. 1961; Hon. Fellow, 1965); Phi Beta Kappa; Commn on Social Sciences (NSF), 1967–70; Internat. Econ. Assoc. (Pres. 1965–68; Hon. Pres. 1968–); Nat. Acad. of Sciences, 1970–; Omicron Delta Epsilon, Bd of Trustees (Internat. Honor Soc. in Econ.). Hon. Fellow: LSE; Peruvian Sch. of Economics, 1980. Hon. LLD: Chicago, 1961; Oberlin, 1961; Boston Coll., 1964; Indiana, 1966; Michigan, 1967; Claremont Grad. Sch., 1970; New Hampshire, 1971; Seton Hall, 1971; Keio, Tokyo, 1971; Harvard, 1972; Gustavas Adolphus Coll., 1974; Univ. of Southern Calif, 1975; Univ. of Rochester, 1976; Univ. of Pennsylvania, 1976; Emmanuel Coll., 1977; Stonehill Coll., 1978; Widener, 1982; Indiana Univ. of Pennsylvania, 1993; Hon. DLitt: Ripon Coll., 1962; Northern Michigan Univ., 1973; Valparaiso Univ., 1987; Columbia Univ., 1988; Hon DSc: E Anglia, 1966; Massachusetts, 1972; Rhode Is., 1972; City Univ. of London, 1980; Tufts Univ., 1988; Hon. LHD Williams Coll., 1971; *Dhc*: Université Catholique de Louvain, 1976; Catholic Univ. at Riva Aguero Inst., Lima, 1980; Universidad Nacional de Educación a Distancia, Madrid, 1989; Universidad Politénica de Valencia, 1991; DUniv New Univ. of Lisbon, 1985. David A. Wells Prize, Harvard, 1941; John Bates Clark Medal, Amer. Econ. Assoc., 1947; Medal of Honor, Univ. of Evansville, 1970; Nobel Prize in Econ. Science, 1970; Albert Einstein Commemorative Award, 1971; Alumni Medal, Chicago Univ., 1983; Britannica Award, 1989; Medal and Hon. Mem., Club of Economics and Management, Valencia, Spain, 1990; Gold Scanno Prize in Economy, Naples, Italy, 1990; Nat. Medal of Science, USA, 1996. *Publications:* Foundations of Economic Analysis, 1947, enlarged edn 1982; Economics, 1948, (with Paul A. Samuelson and William D. Nordhaus) 12th edn 1985, 17th edn 2001 (trans. 40 langs, 1948); (jtly) Linear Programming and Economic Analysis, 1958 (trans. French, Japanese); Readings in Economics, 1955; The Collected Scientific Papers of Paul A. Samuelson (ed J. E. Stiglitz), vols I and II, 1966, vol. III (ed R. C. Merton), 1972, vol. IV (ed H. Nagatani and K. Crowley), 1977, vol. V (ed K. Crowley), 1986; co-author, other books in field, papers in various jls, etc. *Recreation:* tennis. *Address:* Department of Economics, Massachusetts Institute of Technology E52–383, Cambridge, MA 02139, USA. *T:* (617) 2533368, *Fax:* (617) 2530560.

SAMUELSON, Sir Sydney (Wylie), Kt 1995; CBE 1978; first British Film Commissioner, 1991–97; President, 1990–95, Senior Consultant, 1998–2000, Samuelson Group PLC (Chairman and Chief Executive, 1966–90); *b* 7 Dec. 1925; 2nd *s* of G. B. and Marjorie Samuelson; *m* 1949, Doris (*née* Magen); three *s*. *Educ:* Irene Avenue Council Sch., Lancing, Sussex. Served RAF, 1943–47. From age 14, career devoted to various aspects of British film industry: cinema projectionist, 1939–41; asst film editor, 1942–43; asst film cameraman, cameraman and dir of documentary films and television, 1947–59; founded company to service film, TV and, later, audio-visual prodn organisations, supplying cameras and other technical equipment, with purchase of first camera, 1954; continued filming as technician on locations throughout world until 1959, when activities concentrated on expanding the company. Permanent Trustee, 1973– and Chm. Bd of Management, 1976–, BAFTA (Vice-Chm. Film, 1971–73; Chm. of Council, 1973–76; Mem., Business Bd, 1994–; Michael Balcon Award, 1985; Fellow, 1993); Chairman: BAFTA—Shell UK Venture, 1988–91; British Cinematography Scholarships Trust, 1999–; Member: BECTU History Project, 1995–; Exec. Cttee, Cinema and Television Veterans (Pres., 1980–81); Council and Exec. Cttee, Cinema and TV Benevolent Fund, 1969–92 (Trustee, 1982–89; Pres., 1983–86). Hon. Mem., Brit. Soc. of Cinematographers (Governor, 1969–79; 1st Vice-Pres., 1976–77; award for Outstanding Contribution to Film Industry, 1967; special award for services to UK film prodn sector as British Film Comr, 1997); Associate Mem., Amer. Soc. of Cinematographers, 1981–96; Hon. Life Mem., BECTU, 1990 (Mem., ACTT, 1947); Fellow, BFI, 1997; Hon. Life Fellow, BKSTS–The Moving Image Soc., 1995 (Patron, 1997–); Hon. Member: Guild of British Camera Technicians (Trustee, 1993–); Guild of Film Prodn Execs, 1996–. Hon. Technical Advr, Royal Naval Film Corp.; Member, Advisory Board: Northern Media Sch., 1996–; Assoc. of Film Comrs Internat., 1999–. Pres., UK Friends of Akim (Israel Assoc. for Mentally Handicapped); Vice Pres., Muscular Dystrophy Campaign; Patron, Young Persons Concert Foundn. Dr (*hc*) Sheffield Hallam, 1996. Award of Merit, Guild of Film Prodn Execs, 1986; Lifetime achievement award, Birmingham Internat. Film and TV Festival, 1997; Howard Dutch Horton Award, Assoc. of Film Comrs Internat., 1997. *Recreations:* listening to music, vintage motoring, veteran jogging (finished a mere 13,006 places behind the winner, London Marathon 1982). *Address:* 31 West Heath Avenue, NW11 7QJ. *T:* (020) 8455 6696, *Fax:* (020) 8458 1957; *e-mail:* sydneysam@compuserve.com.

SAMUELSSON, Prof. Bengt Ingemar; Professor of Medical and Physiological Chemistry, Karolinska Institutet, Stockholm, since 1972; Chairman, Nobel Foundation, Stockholm, since 1993; Special Adviser to Commissioner for Research and Education, European Commission, since 1995; *b* Halmstad, Sweden, 21 May 1934; *s* of Anders and Stina Samuelsson; *m* 1958, Inga Karin Bergstein; one *s* one *d* (and one *d* decd). *Educ:* Karolinska Institutet (DMedSci 1960, MD 1961). Res. Fellow, Harvard Univ., 1961–62; Asst Prof. of Med. Chemistry, Karolinska Inst, 1961–66; Prof., Royal Vet. Coll., Stockholm, 1967–72; Chm., Dept of Chemistry, 1973–83, Dean of Med. Faculty, 1978–83, Pres., 1983–95, Karolinska Inst, Stockholm. Vis. Prof., Harvard, 1976; T. Y. Shen Vis. Prof. in Med. Chem., MIT, 1977; Walker-Ames Prof., Washington Univ., 1987. Lectures include: Shirley Johnson Meml, Philadelphia, 1977; Sixth Annual Marrs McLean, Houston, 1978; Harvey, NY, 1979; Lane Medical, Stanford Univ., 1981; Eighth Annual Sci. in Med., Univ. of Washington, 1981; Arthur C. Corcoran Meml, Cleveland, Ohio, 1981; Kober, Assoc. of Amer. Physicians, 1982; Brown-Razor, Rice Univ., Houston, 1984; Solomon A. Berson Meml, Mount Sinai Sch. of Medicine, NY, 1984; Angelo Minich, Venice, 1988; Hans Neurath, Univ. of Washington, 1990; Dunham, Harvard Med. Sch., 1990; First Fogarty Internat., NIH, 1992. Member: Nobel Assembly, Karolinska Inst., 1972– (Chm., 1990); Nobel Cttee for Physiol. or Medicine, 1984–89 (Chm., 1987–89); Swedish Govt Res. Adv. Bd, 1985–88; Nat. Commn on Health Policy, 1987–90; ESTA, 1995–. Member: Royal Swedish Acad. of Scis, 1981–; Mediterranean Acad., Catania, 1982–; US Nat. Acad. of Scis, 1984; French Acad. of Scis, 1989; Royal Soc., 1990; Royal Nat. Acad. of Medicine, Spain, 1991; Hon. Prof., Bethune Univ. of Med. Scis, China, 1986; Hon. Member: Amer. Soc. of Biological Chemists, 1976; Assoc. of American Physicians, 1982; Swedish Med. Assoc., 1982; Italian Pharmacological Soc., 1985; Acad. Nac. de Medicina de Buenos Aires, 1986; Internat. Soc. of Haematology, 1986; Spanish Soc. of Allergology and Clinical Immunology, 1989; Foreign Hon. Member: Amer. Acad. of Arts and Scis, 1982–; Internat. Acad. of Science, ICSD; Founding Mem., Academia Europaea, 1988. Hon. DSc: Chicago, 1978; Illinois, 1983; DUniv: Rio de Janeiro, 1986; Buenos Aires, 1986; Complutense, Madrid, 1991; Milan, 1993; Louisiana State, 1993. Nobel Prize in Physiology or Medicine (jtly), 1982; numerous awards and prizes. *Publications:* papers on biochemistry of prostaglandins, thromboxanes and leukotrienes. *Address:* Department of Medical Biochemistry and Biophysics, Karolinska Institutet, 17177 Stockholm, Sweden. *T:* (8) 7287600.

SAMWORTH, David Chetwode, CBE 1985; DL; Chairman, Samworth Brothers Ltd (formerly Gorran Foods Ltd), since 1984 (Director since 1981); *b* 25 June 1935; *s* of Frank and Phyllis Samworth; *m* 1969, Rosemary Grace Cadell; one *s* three *d*. *Educ:* Uppingham Sch. Chm., Pork Farms Ltd, 1968–81; Director: Northern Foods Ltd, 1978–81; Imperial Gp, 1983–85; (non-exec.) Thorntons plc, 1988–94. Chm., Meat and Livestock Commn, 1980–84. Member: Leicester No 3 HMC, 1970–74; Trent RHA, 1974–78, 1980–84. President: RASE, 2000–01; Leics Agricl Soc., 1996–99; Young Enterprise, Leics, 2001–. Chm. Trustees, Uppingham Sch., 1995–99. DL Leics, 1984, High Sheriff, Leics, 1997. *Recreation:* tennis. *Address:* PO Box 9, Melton Mowbray, Leics LE13 0XH.

SANBERK, Özdem; Director, TESEV (Turkish economic and social studies foundation), since 2000; *b* 1938; *m* Sumru Sanberk; one *d*. *Educ:* Faculty of Law, Univ. of Istanbul. Joined Turkish Ministry of Foreign Affairs, 1963; Dep. Perm. Deleg. to OECD, Paris, and to UNESCO, Paris, 1980–83; Dep. Dir-Gen. for Bilateral Economic Affairs, Min. of Foreign Affairs, 1983–85; Advr for external relations to Prime Minister, 1985–87; Ambassador and Perm Deleg. to EC, 1987; Under-Sec., Min. of Foreign Affairs, 1991; Ambassador to UK, 1995–2000. Numerous foreign orders. *Address:* TESEV, Fenerl. Türbe Sok. No 6, 80830 Rumeli Hisarüstü, Istanbul, Turkey. *T:* (212) 2873213. *Club:* Cavalry and Guards.

SANCTUARY, Gerald Philip; Secretary, National Union of Journalists Provident Fund, 1984–95; *b* 22 Nov. 1930; *s* of late John Cyril Tabor Sanctuary, MD and Maisie Toppin Sanctuary (*née* Brooks); *m* 1956, Rosemary Patricia L'Estrange, Dublin; three *s* two *d*. *Educ:* Bryanston Sch.; Law Soc.'s Sch. of Law. National Service Pilot, 1953–55; Asst Solicitor, Kingston, 1955–56; Partner in Hasties, Solicitors, Lincoln's Inn Fields, 1957–62; Field Sec., Nat. Marriage Guidance Council, 1963–65, Nat. Secretary 1965–69; Exec. Dir, Sex Information and Educn Council of US, 1969–71; Sec., Professional and Public Relations, The Law Soc., 1971–78; Exec. Dir, Internat. Bar Assoc., 1978–79; Legal Adviser and Regional and Local Affairs Dir, Mencap, 1979–84. Regl PR Consultant, E of England Reg., Prince's Trust, 2000–. Hon. Treas., GAPAN, 1986–. Editor, Law Soc. series, It's Your Law, 1973–79. Regular broadcaster on radio. *Publications:* Marriage Under Stress, 1968; Divorce — and After, 1970, 2nd edn 1976; Before You See a Solicitor, 1973, 2nd edn 1983; After I'm Gone—what will happen to my Handicapped Child?, 1984, 2nd edn 1991; contrib., Moral Implications of Marriage Counselling, 1971; Vie Affective et Sexuelle, 1972; Loss Prevention Manual, 1978; The English Legal Heritage, 1979; booklets: Fishpool Street—St Albans, 1984; Tudor St Albans; St Albans and the Wars of the Roses, 1985; The Romans in St Albans, 1986; The Monastery at St Albans, 1987; Shakespeare's Globe Theatre, 1992; Abbey Theatre, St Albans, 1993. *Recreations:* amateur drama, organising murder mystery weekends; woodland owner. *Address:* 99 Beechwood Avenue, St Albans, Herts AL1 4XU. *T:* (01727) 842666.

SANDARS, Christopher Thomas; Director General (Central Budget) (formerly Assistant Under-Secretary of State (General Finance)), Ministry of Defence, since 1997; *b* 6 March 1942; *s* of late Vice-Adm. Sir Thomas Sandars, KBE, CB and Lady Sandars; *m* 1966, Elizabeth Anne Yielder; three *s* one *d*. *Educ:* Oundle Sch.; Corpus Christi Coll., Cambridge (Trevelyan Schol.; Foundation Schol.). Joined MoD, 1964; Asst Private Sec. to Minister of State, 1967–69; Central Policy Review Staff, Cabinet Office, 1971–74; Private Sec. to Minister of State, 1975–77; Hd, General Finance Div. 1, 1977–80; Hd, Defence Secretariat 13, 1980–84; RCDS, 1985; Hd, Secretariat 9 (Air), 1986–90; Asst Under-Sec. of State, MoD, 1990–95; Fellow, Center for Internat. Affairs, Harvard Univ., 1995–96. *Publication:* America's Overseas Garrisons: the leasehold empire, 2000. *Recreations:* tennis, badminton, gardening, theatre. *Address:* Ministry of Defence, Main Building, Whitehall, SW1A 2HB.

SANDARS, Nancy Katharine, FBA 1984; FSA; archaeologist; *b* 29 June 1914; *d* of Edward Carew Sandars and Gertrude Annie Sandars (*née* Phipps). *Educ:* at home; Wychwood School, Oxford; Inst. of Archaeology, Univ. of London (Diploma 1949); St Hugh's College, Oxford (BLitt 1957). Archaeological research and travel in Europe, 1949–69; British School at Athens, 1954–55; Elizabeth Wordsworth Studentship, St Hugh's College, Oxford, 1958–61; travelled in Middle East, 1957, 1958, 1962, 1966; conferences, lectures (Prague, Sofia, McGill Univ.); excavations in British Isles and Greece. *Publications:* Bronze Age Cultures in France, 1957; The Epic of Gilgamesh, an English version, 1960; Prehistoric Art in Europe, 1967, rev. edn 1985; Poems of Heaven and Hell from Ancient Mesopotamia, 1971; The Sea-Peoples: warriors of the ancient Mediterranean, 1978; Grandmother's Steps: poems, 2001; articles on David Jones, painter and poet. *Recreations:* walking, translating, looking at pictures. *Address:* The Manor House, Little Tew, Chipping Norton, Oxford OX7 4JF. *Club:* University Women's.

SANDARS, Prof. Patrick George Henry; Professor of Experimental Physics and Student of Christ Church, Oxford University, since 1978; *b* 29 March 1935; *s* of late P. R. and A. C. Sandars; *m* 1959, P. B. Hall; two *s*. *Educ:* Wellington Coll.; Balliol Coll., Oxford (MA, DPhil). Oxford University: Weir Junior Research Fellow, University Coll., and ICI Research Fellow, Clarendon Laboratory, 1960–63; Tutorial Fellow, Balliol Coll., and Univ. Lectr, 1964–72; Reader in Physics, 1972–77; Head of Clarendon Lab., 1987–90; Hd, Atomic and Laser Physics, 1990–95; Junior Proctor, 1971–72. *Address:* 3 Hawkswell Gardens, Oxford OX2 7EX. *T:* (01865) 558535.

SANDBANK, Charles Peter, FREng; Deputy Director of Engineering, BBC, 1985–91; Broadcasting Technology Adviser, Department of Trade and Industry, since 1993; *b* 14 Aug. 1931; *s* of Gustav and Clare Sandbank; *m* 1955, Audrey Celia; one *s* two *d*. *Educ:* Bromley Grammar Sch.; London Univ. (BSc, DIC). FREng (FEng 1983); FIEE, FInstP. Prodn Engr, 1953–55, Develt Engr, 1955–60, Brimar Valve Co.; Develt Section Head,

STC Transistor Div., 1960–64; Head of Electron Devices Lab., 1964–68, Manager, Communication Systems Div., 1968–78, Standard Telecommunication Laboratories; Head of BBC Research Dept, 1978–84; Asst Dir of Engrg, 1984–85, Asst to Dir of Engrg, 1991–93, BBC. Mem. Council: IEE, 1978–81, 1989–92 (Chairman: Electronics Divisional Bd, 1979–80; London Centre, 1991–92); Royal TV Soc., 1983–86, 1989–92; Chairman: EBU New Systems and Services Cttee, 1984–89; EBU High Definition TV Cttee, 1981–84; EUREKA High Definition Television Project Adv. Bd, 1988–94; Jt Technical Cttee, EBU/Eur. Telecommunications Standards Inst., 1990–93; DTI Cttee for Enhanced Definition TV, 1990–; DCMS/DTI Electronic Cinema Cttee, 2000–; Bureau mem., EBU Tech. Cttee, 1989–93. Ext. Examr, London Univ., 1982–89. Royal Acad. of Engrg Vis. Prof. of Information Systems Design, Univ. of Bradford, 1995–. Dir, Snell and Wilcox Ltd, 1993–97. Chm., Internal Cttee of Inquiry into Legionnaires Disease Outbreak at Broadcasting House, London, 1988. Liveryman, Scientific Instrument Makers' Co., 1988–. Fellow, SMPTE, 1989; FBKSTS 1991; FRTS; FRSA. DUniv Surrey, 1994. *Publications:* Optical Fibre Communication Systems, 1980; Digital Television, 1990; papers and patents (about 200) on semiconductor devices, integrated circuits, solid-state bulk effects, compound semiconductors, micro-waves, electron-phonon interactions, navigational aids, electro-optics and broadcasting technology. *Recreations:* boatbuilding, sailing, film-making, music, garden-watching. *Address:* Grailands, Beech Road, Reigate, Surrey RH2 9NA. *T:* (office) (020) 7215 1825. *Club:* Royal Norfolk and Suffolk Yacht.

SANDBERG, family name of **Baron Sandberg**.

SANDBERG, Baron *cr* 1997 (Life Peer), of Passfield in the co. of Hampshire; **Michael Graham Ruddock Sandberg,** Kt 1986; CBE 1982 (OBE 1977); Chairman: The Hongkong and Shanghai Banking Corporation, 1977–86; The British Bank of the Middle East, 1980–86; *b* 31 May 1927; *s* of Gerald Arthur Clifford Sandberg and Ethel Marion Sandberg; *m* 1954, Carmel Mary Roseleen Donnelly; two *s* two *d. Educ:* St Edward's Sch., Oxford. 6th Lancers (Indian Army) and First King's Dragoon Guards, 1945. Joined The Hongkong and Shanghai Banking Corp., 1949. Director: Pricoa Group; Broadstreet Inc. Mem. Exec. Council, Hong Kong, 1978–86. Steward, Royal Hong Kong Jockey Club, 1972–86, Chm., 1981–86; Treasurer, Univ. of Hong Kong, 1977–86. FCIB (FIB 1977; Vice Pres. 1984–87); FRSA 1983. Freeman, City of London; Liveryman, Co. of Clockmakers. Hon. LLD: Hong Kong, 1984; Pepperdine, 1986. *Publication:* The Sandberg Watch Collection, 1998. *Recreations:* horse racing, bridge, cricket, horology. *Address:* 100 Piccadilly, W1V 9FN; Domaine de la Haute Germaine, Ste Marguerite, Le Broc, Alpes Maritimes, France. *Clubs:* Cavalry and Guards, Portland, White's, MCC; Surrey CC (Pres. 1988), Hampshire CC.

SANDELL, Terence, (Terry), OBE 1991; Director, Visiting Arts (formerly Visiting Arts Office of Great Britain and Northern Ireland), since 1994; *b* 8 Sept. 1948; *s* of James William Sandell and Helen Elizabeth McCombie; *m* 1984, Kate Ling; two *s. Educ:* Watford Grammar Sch. for Boys; Univ. of Nottingham (BA Hons); Univ. of Edinburgh; City Univ. (MA). VSO, Berber, N Sudan, 1970–72. Joined British Council, 1974: Asst Rep. Dir, Omdurman Centre, Sudan, 1974–78; Regional Officer, Soviet Union and Mongolia, London, 1978–81; 1st Sec. (Cultural), British Embassy, Moscow, 1981–83; Asst Rep., Vienna, 1983–86, Rep. 1986–89; Projects Manager, Soviet Union, London, 1989; Dir, Soviet Union/CIS, and Cultural Counsellor, British Embassy, Moscow, 1989–92; attachment to Dept of Arts Policy and Management, City Univ., 1992–93; Consultant, Arts Policy Develt, British Council, 1993–94. Chairman, Council of Europe Review of Cultural Policy: Russian Fedn, 1995–96; Romania, 1998–99; Georgia, 2000–; Azerbaijan, 2000–. Special Lectr, Dept of Slavonic Studies, Univ. of Nottingham, 1993–99. *Recreations:* walking, literature, theatre, travel. *Address:* 1A Shepherd Street, W1J 7HJ.

SANDELSON, Neville Devonshire; Barrister-at-Law; public affairs and business consultant; Deputy Chairman, Westminster and Overseas Trade Services Ltd, since 1985; Co-Founder, 1988, President, since 1990, The Radical Society (Co-Chairman, 1988–90); Executive Director, Profundis Ltd, since 1989; *b* Leeds, 27 Nov. 1923; *s* of late David I. Sandelson, OBE, and Dora Sandelson, (*née* Lightman); *m* 1959, Nana Karlinski, Neuilly sur Seine, France; one *s* two *d. Educ:* Westminster School; Trinity College, Cambridge; MA. Called to Bar, Inner Temple, 1946; for some years director of local newspaper and book publishing cos and producer of TV documentary programmes until resuming practice at Bar, 1964. Dep. Circuit Judge and Asst Recorder, 1977–85. Mem. London County Council, 1952–58. Travelled extensively in USA, Middle East, Asia and Europe. Contested (Lab): Ashford (Kent) 1950, 1951 and 1955; Beckenham (by-election) 1957; Rushcliffe 1959; Heston & Isleworth 1966; SW Leicester (by-election) 1967; Chichester 1970; (SDP) Hayes and Harlington, 1983. MP (Lab 1971–81, SDP 1981–83) Hayes and Harlington, June 1971–83; Founder Mem., SDP, 1981, resigned 1987. Parly spokesman on NI, 1981–82, and on the arts, 1982–83; Vice-Chm., All-Party Productivity Gp; Sec., All-Party Theatre Gp; Jt Sec., British-Greek Parly Gp; Sec., British Gibraltar Parly Gp; Vice-Chm., Afghanistan Parly Support Cttee. Promoted, as a Private Mem's Bill, the Matrimonial Proceedings (Polygamous Marriages) Act, 1972. Member: Council, Nat. Cttee for Electoral Reform, 1977–88 (resigned); Nat. Council of European Movement, 1985–; Exec. Cttee, Wider Share Ownership Council, 1979–92; founder Mem., Manifesto Gp, 1975–80 (Hon. Treas.). Mem. Ct, Brunel Univ., 1975–81. *Address:* 71 Valiant House, Vicarage Crescent, SW11 3LX. *T:* and *Fax:* (020) 7223 5211; Villecelle, 34240 Lamalou-les-Bains, France. *T:* and *Fax:* 467952502. *Club:* Reform.

SANDER, Audrey Olga Helen; Her Honour Judge Sander; a Circuit Judge, since 1995; *b* 10 Nov. 1936; *d* of Ernest Sander and Marian Sander; *m* 1963, Prof. Adrian Gale; one *s* two *d. Educ:* St Paul's Girls' Sch.; Somerville Coll., Oxford (MA Jurisprudence). Called to the Bar, Gray's Inn, 1960; in practice at the Bar, 1960–77; Editl Asst, Legal Action Gp, 1978–83; admitted solicitor, 1986; practised as solicitor, 1986–95 (at Gill Akaster, 1989–95); Asst Recorder, 1990–94; Recorder, 1994–95. Legal Mem., Mental Health Rev. Tribunals, 1992–; Mem., Parole Bd of England and Wales, 2000–. *Address:* Plymouth Combined Court Centre, Armada Way, Plymouth, Devon PL1 2ER.

SANDERLING, Kurt; conductor; *b* 19 Sept. 1912; *m* 1st, 1941, Nina Bobath; one *s*; 2nd, 1963, Barbara Wagner; twin *s. Educ:* privately. Conductor: Leningrad Philharmonic Orch., 1941–60; East Berlin Symphony Orch., 1960–95. Guest conductor of many orchs in Europe and N America. *Address:* Am Iderfenngraben 47, 13156 Berlin, Germany.

SANDERS, Adrian Mark; MP (Lib Dem) Torbay, since 1997; *b* 25 April 1959; *s* of John and Helen Sanders; *m* 1992, Alison Nortcliffe. *Educ:* Torquay Boys' Grammar Sch. Vice Pres., Nat. League of Young Liberals, 1985. Campaigns Officer, Assoc. of Liberal Councillors, 1986–89; Parly Officer, Lib Dem Whips' Office, 1989–90; Res. Officer, Assoc. of Lib Dem Councillors, 1990–92; Project Officer, Paddy Ashdown, MP, 1992–93; Policy Officer, NCVO, 1993–94; Grants Advr, Southern Assoc. of Voluntary Action Gps for Europe, 1994. Mem. (L) Torbay BC, 1984–86. Contested (Lib Dem): Torbay, 1992; Devon and Plymouth East, EP elecn, 1994. Lib Dem spokesman on local govt and housing (on housing, 1997–, and on local govt, 1999–); a Lib Dem Whip, 1997–2001. Chm., All Pty Diabetes Gp, 1997–. *Address:* House of Commons, SW1A 0AA.

SANDERS, Cyril Woods, CB 1959; Lord of the Manor of Kavenham-Stoke-Wereham and Wretton in Norfolk; *b* 21 Feb. 1912; *er s* of Cyril Sturgis Sanders and Dorothy (*née* Woods); *m* 1944, Kate Emily Boyes, *qv*; one *s* three *d. Educ:* St Paul's Sch.; Queen's Coll., Oxford. BA Oxon 1934, Lit. Hum. Joined General Post Office as Assistant Principal, 1934; transferred to Board of Trade, 1935; retired from Dept of Trade and Industry (formerly Bd of Trade) as Under-Secretary, 1972.

SANDERS, Prof. Dale, PhD, ScD; FRS 2001; Professor of Biology, University of York, since 1992; *b* 13 May 1953; *s* of Leslie G. D. Sanders and Daphne M. Sanders; *m* 1983, Marcelle Mekies (marr. diss. 2001); three *d. Educ:* Hemel Hempstead Grammar Sch.; Univ. of York (BA); Darwin Coll., Cambridge (PhD 1978, ScD 1993). James Hudson Brown Res. Fellow, 1978–79, Post-doctoral Res. Associate, 1979–83, Sch. of Medicine, Yale Univ.; University of York: Lectr, 1983–89; Reader, 1989–92. Nuffield Foundn Sci. Res. Fellow, 1989–90; Royal Soc./Leverhulme Trust Sen. Res. Fellow, 1997–98. President's Medal, Soc. for Exptl Biol., 1987; Körber Eur. Sci. Award, 2001. *Publications:* numerous refereed articles in learned jls. *Address:* Biology Department, PO Box 373, University of York, Heslington, York YO10 5DD. *T:* (01904) 432825.

SANDERS, Donald Neil, AO 1994; CB 1983; Chairman, H-G Ventures Ltd, 1995–2000; *b* Sydney, 21 June 1927; *s* of L. G. and R. M. Sanders; *m* 1952, Betty Elaine, *d* of W. B. and E. M. Constance; four *s* one *d. Educ:* Wollongong High Sch.; Univ. of Sydney (BEc). Commonwealth Bank of Australia, 1943–60; Australian Treasury, 1956; Bank of England, 1960; Reserve Bank of Australia, 1960–87: Supt, Credit Policy Div., Banking Dept, 1964–66; Dep. Manager: Banking Dept, 1966–67; Res. Dept, 1967–70; Aust. Embassy, Washington DC, 1968; Chief Manager: Securities Markets Dept, 1970–72; Banking and Finance Dept, 1972–74; Adviser and Chief Manager, Banking and Finance Dept, 1974–75; Dep. Governor and Dep. Chm., 1975–87; Commonwealth Bank of Australia: Chief Exec., 1987–92; Man. Dir, 1991–92; Man. Dir, Commonwealth Banking Corp., 1987–91. Director: Queensland Investment Corp., 1992–98; Lend Lease Corp. Ltd, 1992–99; Australian Chamber Orch. Ltd, 1993–99; MLC Ltd, 1994–99. *Address:* Somerset, Taralga Road, via Goulburn, NSW 2580, Australia.

SANDERS, Prof. Ed Parish, FBA 1989; Arts and Sciences Professor of Religion, Duke University, since 1990; *b* 18 April 1937; *s* of Mildred Sanders (*née* Parish) and Eula Thomas Sanders; *m* 1st, 1963, Becky Jill Hall (marr. diss. 1978); one *d*; 2nd, 1996, Rebecca N. Gray. *Educ:* Texas Wesleyan College (BA); Southern Methodist Univ. (BD); Union Theological Seminary, NY (ThD). Asst Prof. of Religious Studies, McMaster Univ., 1966–70, Associate Prof., 1970–74, Prof., 1974–88; Dean Ireland's Prof. of Exegesis of Holy Scripture, Oxford Univ., 1984–89. Visiting Professor: Jewish Theol. Seminary, 1980; Chair of Judeo-Christian Studies, Tulane Univ., 1980; Walter G. Mason Dist. Vis. Prof., Coll. of William and Mary in Virginia, 1981; Vis. Fellow Commoner, Trinity Coll., Cambridge, 1982. Donnellan Lectr, TCD, 1982. *Publications:* The Tendencies of the Synoptic Tradition, 1969; Paul and Palestinian Judaism, 1977, 2nd edn 1981; (ed) Jewish and Christian Self-Definition, vol. I, The Shaping of Christianity in the Second and Third Centuries, 1980, vol. II, Aspects of Judaism in the Graeco-Roman Period, 1981, vol. III, Self-Definition in the Graeco-Roman World, 1982; Paul, The Law and the Jewish People, 1983; Jesus and Judaism, 1985, 3rd edn 1987; (ed) Jesus, The Gospels and the Church, 1987; (with Margaret Davies) Studying the Synoptic Gospels, 1989; Jewish Law from Jesus to the Mishnah, 1990; Paul, 1991; Judaism: practice and belief 63 BCE to 66 BCE, 1992; The Historical Figure of Jesus, 1993; articles in NT Studies, Jl of Biblical Literature, Harvard Theol. Review, Jewish Quarterly Review. *Address:* Department of Religion, Duke University, Durham, NC 27708, USA.

SANDERS, Prof. Jeremy Keith Morris, FRS 1995; Professor, since 1996, and Head, since 2000, Department of Chemistry, Cambridge University; Fellow of Selwyn College, Cambridge, since 1976; *b* 3 May 1948; *s* of Sidney Sanders and Sylvia (*née* Rutman); *m* 1972, Louise Elliott; one *s* one *d. Educ:* Imperial Coll., London (BSc, ARCS Chem. 1969); PhD 1972, MA 1974, Cantab. FRSC, CChem. Junior Res. Fellow, Christ's Coll., Cambridge, 1972; NATO/EMBO Fellow, Stanford Univ., 1972–73; Cambridge University: Demonstrator, 1973–78; Lectr in Chemistry, 1978–92; Reader in Chemistry and Asst Hd, Dept of Chemistry, 1992–96; Dep. Hd, Dept of Chem., 1998–2000; Mem. Council, 1999–; Chm., Allocations Cttee, 1999–2000. FRSA 1997. Associate Ed., New Jl of Chemistry, 1998–2000; Chm. Editl Bd, Chem. Soc. Reviews, 2000–. Pfizer Awards, Pfizer plc, 1984, 1988; Royal Society of Chemistry: Meldola Medal, 1975; Hickinbottom Award, 1981; Josef Loschmidt Prize, 1994; Pedler Lect. and Medal, 1996. *Publications:* (with B. K. Hunter) Modern NMR Spectroscopy, 1987, 2nd edn 1993; contribs to chem. and biochem. jls. *Recreations:* family, cooking, music, walking. *Address:* University Chemical Laboratory, Lensfield Road, Cambridge CB2 1EW. *T:* (01223) 336411, *Fax:* (01223) 336017; *e-mail:* jkms@cam.ac.uk.

SANDERS, Rear-Adm. Jeremy Thomas, CB 1994; OBE 1982; JP; Commander British Forces, Gibraltar, 1992–94; *b* 23 Nov. 1942; *s* of late Thomas Sanders and Pauline (*née* Woodfield-Smith); *m* 1966, Judith Rosemary Jones; two *d. Educ:* Norwood Sch., Exeter; Pangbourne Coll. BRNC, Dartmouth, 1960; appts include: Lieut i/c HMS Chilcompton and Kellington, 1968–69; long communications course, HMS Mercury, 1970; Lt Comdr on staff of Flag Officer, Submarines, 1974–76; Comdr i/c HMS Salisbury, 1977–78; ndc 1979; SO Ops to Flag Officer, 1st Flotilla, 1981–83; Capt., 8th Frigate Sqdn and i/c HMS Andromeda, 1985–87; Dir, Maritime Tactical Sch., 1987–89; Chief Naval Signal Officer, 1989–90; Dir, Naval Warfare, 1990–92. JP S Hants 1997. *Recreations:* rambling and hill walking, cabinet making, growing vegetables, cricket. *Club:* MCC.

SANDERS, John Derek, OBE 1994; Director of Music, Cheltenham Ladies' College, 1968–97; Organist and Master of the Choristers, Gloucester Cathedral, 1967–94; *b* 26 Nov. 1933; *s* of Alderman J. T. Sanders, JP, CA and Mrs E. M. Sanders (*née* Trivett); *m* 1967, Janet Ann Dawson; one *s* one *d. Educ:* Felsted Sch., Essex; Royal Coll. of Music; Gonville and Caius Coll., Cambridge. ARCM 1952; FRCO 1955; MusB 1956; MA 1958. Dir of Music, King's Sch., Gloucester, and Asst Organist, Gloucester Cathedral, 1958–63; Organist and Master of the Choristers, Chester Cathedral, 1964–67. Conductor: Gloucestershire Symphony Orchestra, 1967–94; Gloucester Choral Soc., 1967–94. Conductor of Three Choirs Festival, triennially, 1968–94. Pres., Cathedral Organists' Assoc., 1990–92; Mem. Council, RCO, 1979–94, and 1996–2000. Liveryman, Co. of Musicians, 1987. Freeman, City of London, 1986. DMus Lambeth, 1990. Hon. FRSCM 1991. *Publications:* Festival Te Deum, 1962; Soliloquy for Organ, 1977; Toccata for Organ, 1979; Te Deum Laudamus, 1985; Jubilate Deo, 1986; Two Prayers, 1988; A Canticle of Joy, 1991; The Reproaches, 1993; St Mark Passion, 1993. *Recreations:* gastronomy, travelling. *Address:* Ridge Cottage, Upton Bishop, Ross-on-Wye, Herefordshire HR9 7UD. *T:* (01989) 780482.

SANDERS, John Leslie Yorath; HM Diplomatic Service, retired; *b* 5 May 1929; *s* of late Reginald Yorath Sanders and Gladys Elizabeth Sanders (*née* Blything); *m* 1953, Brigit Mary

Lucine Altounyan (*d* 1999); one *s* two *d*. *Educ:* Dulwich Coll. Prep. Sch.; Cranleigh School. Higher Dip. in Furniture Prodn and Design, London Coll. of Furniture, 1982. Nat. Service in HM Forces (RA), 1948–50; entered HM Foreign Service, 1950; FO, 1950–52; MECAS, Lebanon, 1953; Damascus, 1954–55; Bahrain, 1955–56; Vice-Consul, Basra, 1956–60; Oriental Sec., Rabat, 1960–63; FO, 1964–67; 1st Sec., Beirut, 1968–70; 1st Sec. and Head of Chancery, Mexico City, 1970–73; Counsellor, Khartoum, 1973–75; Counsellor, Beirut, 1975–76; Dir of Res., FCO, 1976–78; Ambassador to Panama, 1978–80. *Publication:* contrib. to Archaeologia Aeliana. *Recreations:* genealogy, music. *Address:* 122 Bay View Road, Northam, Bideford, N Devon EX39 1BJ.

SANDERS, Sir John Reynolds M.; *see* Mayhew-Sanders.

SANDERS, Kate Emily Tyrrell, (Mrs C. W. Sanders); *see* Boyes, K. E. T.

SANDERS, Michael David, FRCS, FRCP, FRCOphth; Consultant Ophthalmologist, National Hospital for Neurology and Neurosurgery, 1969–99; *b* 19 Sept. 1935; *s* of Norris Manley Sanders and Gertrude Florence Sanders (*née* Hayley); *m* 1969, Thalia Margaret Garlick; one *s* one *d*. *Educ:* Tonbridge Sch.; Guy's Hosp., Univ. of London (MB BS). DO RCS/RCP; FRCS 1967; FRCP 1977; FRCOphth 1990. Guy's Hosp., 1954–60; Moorfields Eye Hosp., 1964–67; Univ. of California, San Francisco, 1967–68; Consultant Ophthalmologist, St Thomas' Hosp., 1972–96. Civilian Consultant, RAF, 1975–2000; Dep. Hospitallier, St John Ophthalmic Hosp., Jerusalem, 1992. Visiting Professor: Mayo Clinic, 1979; Univ. of New South Wales, 1982; NY Eye and Ear Infirmary, 1995. Lectures: Middlemore, Birmingham and Midlands Eye Hosp., 1985; Percival J. Hay Meml, N of England Ophthalmol Soc., 1986; Ida Mann, Oxford Univ., 1987; Sir Stewart Duke Elder, Ophthalmol. Soc. UK, 1987; Lettsomian, Med. Soc. London, 1988; Sir William Bowman, RCOphth, 1996; Montgomery, Irish Coll. of Ophthalmologists, 1997. Trustee, Frost Charitable Trust, 1974–96 (Chm., 1996–); Med. Advr, Iris Fund for Prevention of Blindness, 1982–97 (Mem. Council, 1997–); Pres., Internat. Neuro-Ophthalmology Soc., 1990– (Mem. Council, 1974–). *Publications:* Topics in Neuro-Ophthalmology, 1978; Computerised Tomography in Neuro-Ophthalmology, 1982; Common Problems in Neuro-Ophthalmology, 1997. *Recreations:* golf, collecting. *Address:* Chawton Lodge, Chawton, near Alton, Hants GU3 1SL. *T:* (01420) 86681; 9 Alma Terrace, Allen Street, W8 6QY. *T:* (020) 7937 7955. *Clubs:* Royal Air Force, Hurlingham; Hankley Common Golf (Farnham).

SANDERS, Nicholas John, CB 1998; PhD; Director for Higher Education, Department for Education and Skills (formerly for Education and Employment), since 1999; *b* 14 Sept. 1946; *s* of Ivor and Mollie Sanders; *m* 1971, Alison Ruth Carter; one *s* one *d*. *Educ:* King Edward's Sch., Birmingham; Magdalene Coll., Cambridge (MA, PhD). Joined DES, subseq. Dept for Educn, then DFEE, 1971; Principal Private Sec. to Sec. of State, 1974–75; Private Sec. to Prime Minister, 1978–81; Prin. Finance Officer, 1989–93; Hd, Teachers Br., 1993–95; Dir, Teachers, Funding and Curriculum, 1995–99. *Address:* Department for Education and Skills, Sanctuary Buildings, Great Smith Street, SW1P 3BT. *T:* (020) 7925 5000.

SANDERS, Peter Basil, CBE 1993; Chief Executive, Commission for Racial Equality, 1988–93 (Director, 1977–88); *b* 9 June 1938; *s* of Basil Alfred Horace Sanders and Ellen May Sanders (*née* Cockrell); *m* 1st, 1961, Janet Valerie (*née* Child) (marr. diss. 1984); two *s* one *d*; 2nd, 1988, Anita Jackson. *Educ:* Queen Elizabeth's Grammar Sch., Barnet; Wadham Coll., Oxford (MA, DPhil). Administrative Officer, Basutoland, 1961–66; Research in Oxford for DPhil, 1966–70; Officer, Min. of Defence, 1971–73; Race Relations Bd: Principal Conciliation Officer, 1973–74; Dep. Chief Officer, 1974–77. *Publications:* Lithoko: Sotho Praise-Poems (ed jtly and trans. with an Introd. and Notes), 1974; Moshoeshoe, Chief of the Sotho, 1975; The Simple Annals: the history of an Essex and East End family, 1989; (ed jtly) Race Relations in Britain: a developing agenda, 1998; The Last of the Queen's Men: a Lesotho experience, 2000. *Address:* The Old Post Office, High Street, Widdington, Saffron Walden, Essex CB11 3SG. *T:* (01799) 540273.

SANDERS, Raymond Adrian; Social Security Commissioner, 1986–99; a Child Support Commissioner, 1993–99; *b* 13 May 1932; *s* of Leslie Harry Sanders and Beatrice Sanders; *m* 1st, 1961, Anna Margaret Burton (marr. diss.); one *s*; 2nd, 1985, Virginia Varnell Dunn; three *d*. *Educ:* Auckland Univ. (LLB); London School of Economics (LLB). Barrister and Solicitor, New Zealand, 1956–66; Partner in Jackson, Russell and Co., Barristers and Solicitors, Auckland, NZ, 1962–66; part-time Lectr 1960–66 and Examiner 1961–66, Auckland Univ.; Solicitor, Allen and Overy, London, 1967–71; practising barrister, 1971–73; DHSS, 1973–74, 1975–84; Law Officers' Dept, 1974–75. Legal Advr to Warnock Inquiry (Human Fertilisation and Embryology), 1982–84; Regional Chm., Social Security and Medical Appeal Tribunals, 1984–86. *Publications:* Credit Management (jtly) 1966; Building Contracts and Practice, 1967. *Recreations:* theatre, music, cycling, tennis. *Address:* 7 Melville Road, Barnes, SW13 9RH.

SANDERS, Sir Robert (Tait), KBE 1980; CMG 1974; HMOCS; Secretary to the Cabinet, Government of Fiji, 1970–79; Treaties Adviser, Government of Fiji, 1985–87; *b* 2 Feb. 1925; *s* of late A. S. W. Sanders and Charlotte McCulloch; *m* 1951, Barbara, *d* of G. Sutcliffe; two *s* (and one *s* decd). *Educ:* Canmore Public Sch., Dunfermline; Dunfermline High Sch.; Fettes Coll., Edinburgh; Cambridge Univ. (Major Open Classical Schol., Pembroke Coll., 1943; John Stewart of Rannoch Schol. in Latin and Greek, 1947; 1st cl. Hons, Pts I and II of Classical Tripos); London Sch. of Economics, 1949–50; SOAS, 1949–50. Served War, 1943–46: Lieut, 1st Bn the Royal Scots, India and Malaya. Sir Arthur Thomson Travelling Schol., 1948; Sir William Browne Medal for Latin Epigram, 1948; MA (Cantab) 1951. Joined HM Overseas Civil Service, Fiji, as Dist Officer, 1950; Sec. to Govt of Tonga, 1956–58; Sec., Coconut Commn of Enquiry, 1963; MLC, Fiji, 1963–64; Sec. for Natural Resources, 1965–67; Actg Sec. Fijian Affairs, and Actg Chm. Native Lands and Fisheries Commn, 1967; MEC, Fiji, 1967; Sec. to Chief Minister and to Council of Ministers, 1967; apptd Sec. to Cabinet, 1970, also Sec. for Foreign Affairs, 1970–74, Sec. for Home Affairs, 1972–74 and Sec. for Information, 1975–76. Mem., Internat. Cttee, Stirling Univ., 1991–93. Fiji Independence Medal, 1970; 25th Anniversary of Fiji's Independence Medal, 1995. *Publications:* Interlude in Fiji, 1963; Fiji Treaty List, 1987; articles in Corona, jl of HMOCS. *Recreations:* languages, travel, golf, music, hill-walking. *Address:* 6 Park Manor, Crieff PH7 4LJ. *Club:* Royal Scots (Edinburgh).

SANDERS, Roger Benedict; His Honour Judge Sanders; a Circuit Judge, since 1987; Resident Judge, Harrow Crown Court, since 1999; *b* 1 Oct. 1940; *s* of late Maurice and Lilian Sanders; *m* 1st, 1969, Susan Brenner (marr. diss. 1992); two *s* (one *d* decd); 2nd, 1998, Dee Connolly, *e d* of John and Mary Connolly. *Educ:* Highgate School. Co-founder, Inner Temple Debating Soc., 1961, Chm. 1962. Called to the Bar, Inner Temple, 1965; South Eastern Circuit. Metropolitan Stipendiary Magistrate, 1980–87; a Recorder, 1986–87. A Chm., Inner London Juvenile Courts, 1980–87; Chm., Legal Cttee, Inner London Juvenile Panel, 1983–86; First Chm., No 1 (London S) Regional Duty Solicitor Cttee, 1984–85; Member: Inner London Magistrates' Training Panel, 1983–87; Mental Health Review Tribunal, 1990–2000; Middx Probation Cttee, 1999–2001. Chairman, Walker School Assoc. (Southgate), 1976, 1977; Schools' Debating Assoc. Judge, 1976–93. Mem., Haringey Schools Liaison Group, 1979. Hon. Fellow, Univ. of E London, 1993. *Address:* Harrow Crown Court, Hailsham Drive, Harrow, Middx HA1 4TU. *T:* (020) 8424 2294.

SANDERS, Sir Ronald (Michael), KCN 2001; CMG 1997; Senior Ambassador with Ministerial rank, Antigua and Barbuda, 1999; High Commissioner for Antigua and Barbuda in London, 1984–87, and since 1995; non-resident Ambassador to France and Germany, since 1996; *b* Guyana, 26 Jan. 1948; *m* 1975, Susan Indrani (*née* Ramphal). *Educ:* Sacred Heart RC Sch., Guyana; Boston Univ., USA; Sussex Univ. Gen. Man., Guyana Broadcasting Service, 1973–76; Communication Cons. to Pres., Caribbean Develt Bank, Barbados, 1977; Cons. to Govt of Antigua, 1977–81; Advr to For. Minister of Antigua and Barbuda, 1981–82; Dep. Perm. Rep. to UN, 1982–83; Ambassador to UNESCO and EEC, 1983–87, to FRG, 1986–87; Vis. Fellow, Oxford Univ., 1988–89; Advr to Govt of Antigua and Barbuda, 1989–91; Internat. relns consultant to Prime Minister of Antigua and Barbuda, 1994–96. Director: Swiss Amer. Nat. Bank, Antigua, 1990–97; Guyana Telephone and Telegraph Co., 1991–97; Innovative Communications Corp., USA, 1998–; consultant, Internat. Relns, Atlantic Tele Network, USA, 1989–97. Member: Inter-Govtl Council, Internat. Prog. for Develt of Communications, UNESCO, 1983–87; Exec. Bd, UNESCO, 1985–87; RIIA, 1987–; Internat. Inst. of Communications, 1984–. *Publications:* Broadcasting in Guyana, 1977; Antigua and Barbuda: transition, trial, triumph, 1984; (ed) Inseparable Humanity—an anthology of reflections of Shridath Ramphal, Commonwealth Secretary-General, 1988; several contribs to internat. jls on communication, Antarctica, also political commentaries. *Recreations:* reading, cinema. *Address:* High Commission for Antigua and Barbuda, 15 Thayer Street, W1M 5LD. *Clubs:* Royal Automobile, St James's.

SANDERS, Prof. Roy, FRCS; consultant plastic surgeon, since 1974; Consultant, since 1974 at: Mount Vernon Centre for Plastic Surgery; Royal National Orthopaedic Hospital; Luton and Dunstable Hospital; Humana Hospital; Bishops Wood Hospital, Northwood; *b* 20 Aug. 1937; *s* of Leslie John Sanders and Marguerite Alice (*née* Knight); *m* 1st, 1961, Ann Ruth Costar (marr. diss.); two *s* one *d*; 2nd, 1984, Fleur Annette Chandler, Baroness von Balajthy. *Educ:* Hertford Grammar Sch.; Charing Cross Hosp. Med. Sch. (BSc Hons Anatomy, MB, BS). LRCP 1962; FRCS 1967. Various hosp. appts; Sen. Lectr in Plastic Surgery, London Univ. and Hon. Cons. Plastic Surgeon, Mt Vernon Centre for Plastic Surgery, 1972–74; Cons. Plastic Surgeon, St Andrew's Hosp., Billericay and St Bart's Hosp., 1974–76; Hon. Sen. Lectr, London Univ., 1976–93; Hd, Service Dept, Plastic Maxillo-Facial and Oral Surgery, Mt Vernon Hosp., 1986–; Vis. Prof., UCL, 1993–. Sec., Brit. Assoc. Aesthetic Plastic Surgeons, 1984–87; Pres., Brit. Assoc. Plastic Surgeons, 1993 (Sec., 1987–90). OC Light Cavalry, HAC, 1996–. *Publications:* scientific pubns in med. jls and textbooks. *Recreations:* equestrian pursuits, watercolour painting, books. *Address:* 82 Portland Place, W1B 1NS. *T:* (020) 7580 3541; 77 Harley Street, W1N 1DE. *T:* (020) 7935 7417; Upper Rye Farm, Moreton-in-Marsh, Glos GL56 9AB. *T:* (01608) 650542. *Clubs:* Athenæum, Garrick, Honourable Artillery Company, Royal Society of Medicine.

SANDERS, William George, CB 1991; CEng, FRINA; RCNC; Head of Royal Corps of Naval Constructors, 1986–91; Director General, Submarines, Ministry of Defence (PE), 1985–91; *b* 22 Jan. 1936; *s* of George and Alice Irene Sanders; *m* 1956, Marina Charlotte Burford; two *s* one *d*. *Educ:* Public Secondary Sch., Plymouth; Devonport Dockyard Tech. Coll.; RN Coll., Greenwich. Asst Constructor, Ship Dept, Admiralty, 1961–68; FNCO Western Fleet, 1968–70; Constructor, Ship Dept, MoD (Navy), 1970–77; Principal Naval Overseer, Scotland, 1977–79; Marconi Space and Defence Systems, 1979–81; Project Director, Type 23, 1981–83; DG Future Material Projects (Naval), MoD (PE), 1983–85. *Recreations:* golf, painting, gardening. *Address:* 11 Chestnut Grange, Park Lane, Corsham, Wilts SN13 9XR. *T:* (01249) 701558.

SANDERSON, family name of **Baron Sanderson of Bowden**.

SANDERSON OF AYOT, 2nd Baron *cr* 1960, title disclaimed by the heir, Dr Alan Lindsay Sanderson, 1971.

SANDERSON OF BOWDEN, Baron *cr* 1985 (Life Peer), of Melrose in the District of Ettrick and Lauderdale; **Charles Russell Sanderson,** Kt 1981; DL; Chairman, Clydesdale Bank PLC, since 1999 (Director, 1986–87 and since 1994; Deputy Chairman, 1996–98); *b* 30 April 1933; *s* of Charles Plummer Sanderson and Martha Evelyn Gardiner; *m* 1958, Frances Elizabeth Macaulay; one *s* two *d* (and one *s* decd). *Educ:* St Mary's Sch., Melrose; Trinity Coll., Glenalmond; Scottish Coll. of Textiles, Galashiels; Bradford Coll. (now Bradford Univ.). Commnd Royal Signals, 1952; served: 51 (Highland) Inf. Div. Signal Regt TA, 1953–56, KOSB TA, 1956–58. Partner, Chas P. Sanderson, Wool and Yarn Merchants, Melrose, 1958–87; Chairman: Edinburgh Financial Trust (formerly Yorkshire & Lancashire Investment Trust), 1983–87; Shires Investment Trust, 1984–87; Hawick Cashmere Co., 1991–; Scottish Mortgage & Trust, 1993– (Mem. Bd, 1991–); Scottish Pride plc, 1994–97; Director: United Auctions, 1992–99; Edinburgh Woollen Mills, 1993–97; Watson & Philip, 1993–99; Morrison Construction Group, 1995–2000. Minister of State, Scottish Office, 1987–90. Chairman, Roxburgh, Selkirk and Peebles Cons. and Unionist Assoc., 1970–73; Scottish Conservative Unionist Association: Chm. Central and Southern Area, 1974–75; Vice-Pres. 1975–77; Pres. 1977–79; Vice-Chm. Nat. Union of Cons Assocs, 1979–81 (Mem. Exec. Cttee, 1975–); Chm. Exec. Cttee, Nat. Union of Cons. Assocs, 1981–86; Member: Cons. Party Policy Cttee, 1979–86; Standing Adv. Cttee of Parly Candidates, 1979–86 (Vice-Chm. with responsibility for Europe, 1980–81); Chm., Scottish Cons. Party, 1990–93. Chm., Scottish Peers Assoc., 1998–2000. Deacon, Galashiels Manufrs Corp., 1976; Chm., Eildon Housing Assoc., 1978–82. Mem. Court, Napier Univ., 1994–2001; Governor, St Mary's Sch., Melrose, 1977–87; Mem. Council, Trinity Coll., Glenalmond, 1982 (Chm., 1994–2000). Comr, Gen. Assembly of Ch. of Scotland, 1972. Mem. Court, Framework Knitters' Co., 2000–. DL Roxburgh, Ettrick and Lauderdale, 1990. *Recreations:* golf, fishing, amateur operatics (Past Pres., Producer and Mem. Melrose Amateur Operatic Soc.). *Address:* Becketts Field, Bowden, Melrose, Roxburgh TD6 0ST. *T:* (01835) 822736. *Clubs:* Caledonian; Hon. Co. of Edinburgh Golfers (Muirfield).

SANDERSON, Prof. Alexis Godfrey James Slater; Spalding Professor of Eastern Religions and Ethics, and Fellow of All Souls College, Oxford University, since 1992; *b* 28 June 1948; *e s* of J. J. Sanderson, Houghton-le-Spring. *Educ:* Royal Masonic Sch., Watford; Balliol Coll., Oxford (BA 1971). Oxford University: Domus Sen. Schol., Merton Coll., 1971–74; Platnauer Jun. Res. Fellow, Brasenose Coll., 1974–77; Univ. Lectr in Sanskrit, 1977–92; Fellow of Wolfson Coll., 1977–92, Fellow Emeritus, 1992. *Address:* All Souls College, Oxford OX1 4AL.

SANDERSON, Bryan Kaye, CBE 1999; Chairman: Learning and Skills Council, since 2000; BUPA, since 2001; *b* 14 Oct. 1940; *s* of Eric and Anne Sanderson; *m* 1966, Sirkka Kärki; one *s* one *d*. *Educ:* Dame Allan's Sch., Newcastle upon Tyne; LSE (BSc Econ.); Dip. Business Studies, IMEDE Lausanne, 1973. VSO Peru, 1962–64; British Petroleum, 1964; Sen. BP rep., SE Asia and China, 1984–87; Chief Exec. Officer, BP Nutrition, 1987–90;

CEO, BP Chemicals, then Chief Exec., BP Amoco Chemicals, 1990–2000; Man. Dir, British Petroleum, then BP Amoco, 1992–2000. Non-exec. Dir, Corus (formerly British Steel), 1994–; Chairman: Sunderland FC plc, 1998–; Sunderland Urban Regeneration Co., 2001–. Pres., CEFIC, 1998–2000. Member: Adv. Gp to the Labour Party on industrial competition policy, 1997–98; DTI Adv. Gp on competitiveness, 1997–; DTI Co. Law Steering Gp, 1998–; DTI Industrial Develt Adv. Bd, 2000–. Gov., LSE, 1997– (Vice-Chm. Govs, 1998–). Hon. DBA: Sunderland, 1998; York, 1999. *Recreations:* reading, golf, walking, gardening. *Address:* Learning and Skills Council, Cheylesmore House, Quinton Road, Coventry CV1 2WT; BUPA House, 15–19 Bloomsbury Way, WC1A 2BA. *T:* (020) 7656 2338. *Club:* Hampstead Golf.

SANDERSON, Charles Denis; HM Diplomatic Service, retired; Fellow, St Peter's College, Oxford, 1985–96, now Emeritus; *b* 18 Dec. 1934; *s* of Norman and Elsie Sanderson; *m* 1960, Mary Joyce Gillow; one *s* two *d*. *Educ:* Bishopshalt Sch., Hillingdon, Mddx; Pembroke Coll., Oxford (MA). National Service, 1953–55; Oxford, 1955–58; British Petroleum Co. Ltd, 1958–64; Second, later First Secretary, Commonwealth Relations Office, 1964–67; First Sec., Kingston, and concurrently, Haiti, 1967–70; Acting Consul, Port au Prince, 1969; First Sec., Head of Chancery and Consul, Panama, 1970–73; First Sec., FCO, 1973–75; Consul (Commercial), British Trade Development Office, New York, 1975–77; Dep. Consul General and Director Industrial Development, New York, 1977–79; Counsellor, Caracas, 1979–84; Hd, W Indian and Atlantic Dept, FCO, 1984–85. Domestic Bursar, 1985–92, Bursar, 1992–96, St Peter's Coll., Oxford. *Address:* Gilletts Farm, Asthall Leigh, Oxford OX29 9PX. *T:* (01993) 878455. *Club:* Royal Commonwealth Society.

SANDERSON, Eric Fenton; Managing Director, Kwik-Fit Insurance Services Ltd, since 2000 (Director, since 1999); *b* 14 Oct. 1951; *s* of Francis Kirton Sanderson and Margarita Shand (*née* Fenton); *m* 1975, Patricia Ann Shaw; three *d*. *Educ:* Morgan Acad., Dundee; Univ. of Dundee (LLB); Harvard Business Sch. (AMP). FCIBS (MCIBS 1991). Touche Ross & Co., CA, 1973–76; CA 1976; British Linen Bank Group Ltd, 1976–97: Corporate Finance Div., 1976–84; Dir, British Linen Bank and Head, Corporate Finance Div., 1984–89; Chief Exec., 1989–97; Chief Exec., Bank of Scotland Treasury Services PLC, 1997–99. Non-executive Director: Airtours plc (Dep. Chm., 2001–); DLR Ltd; Mem., BRB, 1991–94. *Recreations:* tennis, photography, gardening. *Address:* Kwik-Fit Insurance Services Ltd, 2 Forrest Gate, Tannochside Business Park, Uddingston G71 5PG. *Club:* New (Edinburgh).

SANDERSON, Sir Frank (Linton), 3rd Bt *cr* 1920, of Malling Deanery, South Malling, Sussex; *b* 21 Nov. 1933; *s* of Sir Bryan Sanderson, 2nd Bt and Annette Laskowska (*d* 1967); *S* father, 1992; *m* 1961, Margaret Ann, *o d* of late John Cleveland Maxwell, New York, USA; two *s* three *d* (incl. twin *d*). *Educ:* Stowe; Univ. of Salamanca. RNVR, 1950–65. J. H. Minet & Co. Ltd, 1956–93 (Dir, 1985); Dir, Knott Hotels Co. of London, 1965–75; Dir and Chm., Humber Fertilisers plc, 1972–88. Underwriting Mem. of Lloyd's, 1957–88. Mem., Chichester Dio. Synod, 1980–93. Master, Worshipful Co. of Curriers, 1993–94. *Heir: s* David Frank Sanderson [*b* 26 Feb. 1962; *m* 1990, Fiona Jane Ure]. *Address:* Grandturzel Farm, Burwash, East Sussex TN19 7DE. *Clubs:* Naval, City of London, Farmers'.

SANDERSON, George Rutherford, CBE 1978; British Council Representative, Spain, and Cultural Attaché, British Embassy, Madrid, 1976–79; *b* 23 Nov. 1919; *er s* of late George Sanderson and Edith Mary Sanderson, Blyth, Northumberland; *m* 1947, Jean Cecilia, *d* of late James C. McDougall, Chesterfield, Derbyshire; two *s*. *Educ:* Blyth Grammar Sch.; Univ. of London (BA 1st Cl. Hons French and Italian). War Service, 1940–46: RA, Malta and Egypt (Major). British Council, 1949–79: Actg Dir, Anglo Argentine Cultural Inst., La Plata, Argentina, 1949; Dir, Tucuman, Argentina, 1950–52; Asst Rep., Santiago, Chile, 1952–58; Dep. Area Officer, Oxford, 1958–62; Reg. Dir, and Dir Anglo Argentine Cultural Assoc., Rosario, Argentina, 1962–66; Asst Rep., Buenos Aires, 1966–69; Reg. Dir, and Dir Anglo Brazilian Cultural Soc., São Paulo, Brazil, 1969–72; Dir, Drama and Music Dept, and Dep. Controller, Arts Div., 1973; Educnl Attaché, British Embassy, Washington, 1973–76; Administering Officer, The Kennedy Scholarships and Knox Fellowships, ACU, 1979–82. *Recreations:* art, reading. *Address:* Leafield House, Holton, Oxford OX33 1PZ. *T:* (01865) 872526. *Club:* Athenæum.

SANDERSON, Lt-Gen. John Murray, AC 1994 (AO 1991; AM 1985); Governor of Western Australia, since 2000; *b* 4 Nov. 1940; *s* of John Edward, (Jack), Sanderson and (Dorothy) Jean Sanderson; *m* 1962, Viva Lorraine; one *s* two *d*. *Educ:* Bunbury High Sch., WA; Royal Mil. Coll., Duntroon; Royal Melbourne Inst. of Technol. (FRMIT). FIEAust. Australian Army: Comdr of Sqdn, Vietnam, 1970–71; Sen. Instructor, Sch. of Mil. Engrg, 1972; Instructor, Staff Coll., Camberley, UK, 1976–78; Comdr, 1st Field Engrg Regt, 1979–80; MA to CGS, 1982; Dir of Army Plans, 1982–85; Comdr, 1st Bde, 1986–88; Chief of Staff, Land HQ, 1989; Asst Chief, Defence Forces Develt, 1989–91; Mil. Comdr, UN Transitional Authy, Cambodia, 1992–93; Comdr, Jt Forces Aust., 1993–95; CGS, 1995–97; Chief of Aust. Army, 1997–98. *Address:* Government House, St George's Terrace, Perth, WA 6000, Australia.

SANDERSON, Dr Michael David; Chief Executive, Engineering and Marine Training Authority, since 1995; *b* 7 June 1943; *s* of Arthur Joseph Sanderson and Betty (*née* Potter); *m* 1967, Mariana Welly Madinaveitia; one *s* one *d*. *Educ:* Strode's Sch., Egham; Univ. of Reading (BSc Hons Chem. 1964); Univ. of Leeds (PhD 1968). With Wilkinson Sword: Research Scientist, 1968–71; Technical Manager, 1971–73; Technical Dir, 1973–79; Internat. Marketing Dir, 1979–82; Engrg Dir, AMF Legg, 1982–84; with Lansing Bagnall: Export Dir, 1984–87; Gp Dir, UK Market, 1987–89; Jt Man. Dir, Lansing Linde, 1989–90; Man. Dir, AWD Bedford, 1990–91; Chief Exec., BSI, 1991–93; Chief Exec., Nat. Assoc. of Goldsmiths and Sec. Gen., Internat. Confedn of Jewellers, 1994–95. Pres., Inst. of Supervision and Mgt, 1995–99; Chairman: Action for Engrg, Task Force 3, 1995–96; Output Standards Adv. Cttee, Engrg Professors Council, 2000–; Nat. Chm., Women into Sci. and Engrg Campaign, 2001–; Dep. Nat. Chm., Inst. Materials Management, 1991–93; Member Council: Inst. of Materials, 1993–96; Inst. of Logistics, 1988–94; Inst. of Quality Assurance, 1997–2001; Foundn for Sci. and Technol., 2000–. Mem., Benchmarking Forum, Amer. Soc. for Trng and Develt, 1999–. Trustee: Business Dynamics; Scottish Council of NTOs, 1999–; EdExcel Foundn, 2001–. Mem. Court, Cranfield Univ., 1996–. Mem., Editorial Bd, TQM Magazine, 1993–. Freeman, City of London, 1995; Freeman, 1994–96, Liveryman, 1996–, Mem. Court, 2000–, Clockmakers' Co. *Publications:* contribs to learned jls on surface chemistry, thin surface films, materials management, quality and general management topics. *Recreation:* books. *Address:* 31 Murray Mews, NW1 9RH. *T:* (020) 7284 3155, *Fax:* (020) 7267 9453; *e-mail:* sandersonmm@netscape.net. *Clubs:* Athenæum, Wig and Pen.

SANDERSON, Rev. Peter Oliver; Vicar of All Saints' Episcopal Church, Storm Lake, Iowa, 1991–2000; *b* 26 Jan. 1929; *s* of Harold and Doris Sanderson; *m* 1956, Doreen Gibson; one *s* one *d* (and one *s* decd). *Educ:* St Chad's College, Durham Univ. (BA, DipTh). Asst Curate, Houghton-le-Spring, Durham Diocese, 1954–59; Rector, Linstead and St Thomas Ye Vale, Jamaica, 1959–63; Chaplain, RAF, 1963–67; Vicar, Winksley-cum-Grantley and Aldfield-with-Studley, Ripon, 1967–74; Vicar, St Aidan, Leeds, 1974–84; Provost of St Paul's Cathedral, Dundee, 1984–91. *Recreations:* gardening, music, reading. *Address:* 201 1st Avenue North, Apt 405, Iowa City, IA 52245, USA.

SANDERSON, Very Rev. Roy; *see* Sanderson, Very Rev. W. R.

SANDERSON, Roy, OBE 1983; National Secretary, Federation of Professional Associations Section, Amalgamated Engineering and Electrical Union, 1992–93; *b* 15 Feb. 1931; *s* of George and Lillian Sanderson; *m* 1951, Jean (*née* Booth); two *s* (and one *s* decd). *Educ:* Carfield Sch., Sheffield. Electrical, Electronic Telecommunication & Plumbing Union: Convenor, Lucas Aerospace, Hemel Hempstead, 1952–67; Asst Educn Officer, 1967–69; Nat. Officer, 1969–87; Nat. Sec., Electrical and Engrg Staff Assoc., 1987–92. Non-exec. Dir, UKAEA, 1987–96. Member: Armed Forces Pay Review Body, 1987–93; Economic and Social Cttee, EU, 1990–98; Industrial Tribunals, 1992–99; Employment Appeal Tribunal, 1995–. *Recreations:* golf, snooker; supporter of Watford Football Club. *Address:* 24 Harborough Road North, Kingsthorpe, Northampton NN2 8LU.

SANDERSON, Very Rev. (William) Roy; Parish Minister at Stenton and Whittingehame, 1963–73; Extra Chaplain to the Queen in Scotland, since 1977 (Chaplain, 1965–77); *b* 23 Sept. 1907; *er s* of late Arthur Watson Sanderson, Leith, and late Ethel Catherine Watson, Dundee; *m* 1941, Annie Muriel Easton, Glasgow; three *s* two *d*. *Educ:* Cargilfield Sch.; Fettes Coll.; Oriel Coll., Oxford; Edinburgh University. BA 1929, MA 1933, Oxon. Ordained, 1933. Asst Minister, St Giles' Cath., Edin., 1932–34; Minister: at St Andrew's, Lochgelly, 1935–39; at the Barony of Glasgow, 1939–63. Moderator: Glasgow Presbytery, 1958; Haddington and Dunbar Presbytery, 1972–74; Convener of Assembly Cttees: on Religious Instruction of Youth, 1950–55; on Deaconesses, 1956–61; Panel of Doctrine, 1960–65; on Gen. Administration, 1967–72. Convener of Business Cttee and Leader of General Assembly of the Church of Scotland, 1965–66, 1968–72. Moderator of Gen. Assembly of the Church of Scotland, May 1967–May 1968. Chm., BBC Scottish Religious Advisory Committee, 1961–71; Member Central Religious Advisory Cttee of BBC and ITA, 1961–71. Governor, Fettes Coll., Edinburgh, 1967–76. Hon. DD Glasgow, 1959. *Publication:* Responsibility (Moderatorial address), 1967. *Recreations:* cooking, reading. *Address:* 1a York Road, North Berwick, East Lothian EH39 4LS. *T:* (01620) 892780.

SANDFORD, 2nd Baron *cr* 1945, of Banbury; **Rev. John Cyril Edmondson,** DSC 1942; *b* 22 Dec. 1920; *e s* of 1st Baron Sandford; *S* father, 1959; *m* 1947, Catharine Mary Hunt; two *s* two *d*. *Educ:* Eton Coll.; Royal Naval Coll., Dartmouth; Westcott House, Cambridge. Served War of 1939–45: Mediterranean Fleet, 1940–41; Home Fleet, 1942; Normandy Landings, 1944 (wounded); Mediterranean Fleet, HMS Saumarez, 1946 (wounded). Staff of RN Coll., Dartmouth, 1947–49; HMS Vengeance, 1950; HMS Cleopatra, 1951–52; Staff Commander-in-Chief Far East, 1953–55; Commander of Home Fleet Flagship, HMS Tyne, 1956; retired 1956. Ordained in Church of England, 1958; Parish of St Nicholas, Harpenden, 1958–63; Exec. Chaplain to Bishop of St Albans, 1965–68. Conservative Peer in H of L, 1959–99; Opposition Whip, 1966–70; Parly Sec., Min. of Housing and Local Govt, June–Oct. 1970; Parliamentary Under-Secretary of State: DoE, 1970–73; DES, 1973–74. Dir, Ecclesiastical Insce Office, 1977–89. Chairman: Cttee to review the condition and future of National Parks in England and Wales, 1971; Standing Conf. of London and SE Regl Planning Authorities, 1981–89. A Church Comr, 1982–89. Chairman: Hertfordshire Council of Social Service, 1969–70; Church Army, 1969–70; Community Task Force, 1975–82; Redundant Churches Cttee, 1982–88; Founder Chm., Pilgrims Assoc., 1982–88; Mem., Adv. Council on Penal Reform, 1968–70. President: Anglo-Swiss Soc., 1974–84; Council for Environmental Educn, 1974–84; Assoc. of District Councils, 1980–86; Offa's Dyke Assoc., 1980–84; Countrywide Holidays Assoc., 1982–86; Vice-Pres., YHA, 1979–90. Founder Trustee, WaterAid, 1981 (Council Mem., 1984; Vice Pres., 1991). Founder, Sandford Award for Heritage Educn, 1978; inaugurated Heritage Educn Trust, 1982. Hon. Fellow, Inst. of Landscape Architects, 1971. *Heir: s* Hon. James John Mowbray Edmondson [*b* 1 July 1949; *m* 1st, 1973, Ellen Sarah, *d* of Jack Shapiro, Toronto; one *d*; 2nd, 1986, Linda, *d* of Mr and Mrs Wheeler, Nova Scotia; one *s*]. *Address:* 27 Ashley Gardens, Ambrosden Avenue, Westminster, SW1P 1QD. *T:* (020) 7834 5722. *Clubs:* Ski of Great Britain, Camping and Caravan, Caravan, Stroke.

SANDFORD, Arthur; DL; Consultant: Pannone & Partners, since 1998; Amey plc, since 1998; Chairman, Christie Hospital NHS Trust, since 1999; *b* 12 May 1941; *s* of Arthur and Lilian Sandford; *m* 1963, Kathleen Entwistle; two *d*. *Educ:* Queen Elizabeth's Grammar Sch., Blackburn; University Coll., London (LLB Hons (Upper 2nd Class)). Preston County Borough Council: Articled Clerk to Town Clerk, 1962–65; Asst Solicitor, 1965–66; Sen. Asst Solicitor, 1966–68; Asst Solicitor, Hants CC, 1969–70; Nottinghamshire County Council: Second Asst Clerk, 1970–72; First Asst Clerk, 1972–74; Dep. Dir of Admin, 1973–75; Dir of Admin, 1975–77; Dep. Clerk and County Sec., 1977–78; Clerk and Chief Exec., 1978–89; Chief Executive: Football League, 1990–92; Manchester CC, 1992–98. DL Notts, 1990. *Recreations:* watching sport, gardening. *Address:* 7 Mersey Meadows, Manchester M20 2GB. *T:* (0161) 446 2574.

SANDFORD, Prof. Cedric Thomas; Professor of Political Economy, University of Bath, 1965–87, now Professor Emeritus; Director of Bath University Centre for Fiscal Studies, 1974–86; *b* 21 Nov. 1924; *s* of Thomas Sandford and Louisa (*née* Hodge); *m* 1945, Evelyn Belch (*d* 1982); one *s* one *d*; *m* 1984, Christina Privett; one *d*. *Educ:* Manchester Univ. (BAEcon 1948, MAEcon 1949); London Univ. (BA History (external) 1955). Undergraduate, Manchester Univ., 1942–43 and 1946–48; RAF, 1943–46 (Pilot). Graduate Research Schol., Univ. of Manchester, 1948–49; Lectr, Burnley Municipal Coll., 1949–60; Sen. Lectr, subseq. Head of General and Social Studies Dept, Bristol Coll. of Science and Technology, 1960–65; Head of Sch. of Humanities and Social Sciences, Univ. of Bath, 1965–68, 1971–74, 1977–79. Visiting Prof., Univ. of Delaware, USA, 1969; Visiting Fellow: ANU, 1981, 1985; Univ. of Melbourne, 1990; Univ. of Newcastle, NSW, 1994. Mem., Meade Cttee on Reform of Direct Tax System, 1975–78; Consultant: Fiscal Div., OECD, 1976–79, 1985–87; Irish Commn on Taxation, 1982–85; World Bank, 1986; UN 1986; IMF 1989, 1992; Nat. Audit Office, 1992–94; UK Inland Revenue, 1995–97. Partner, Fiscal Publications, 1989–. *Publications:* Taxing Inheritance and Capital Gains (Hobart Paper 32, IEA), 1965, 2nd edn 1967; Economics of Public Finance, 1969, 4th edn 1992; Realistic Tax Reform, 1971, Taxing Personal Wealth, 1971; (sen. editor and jt author) Case Studies in Economics (3 vols), 1971, 2nd edn 1977; National Economic Planning, 1972, 2nd edn 1976; Hidden Costs of Taxation, 1973; (jtly) An Accessions Tax, 1973; (jtly) An Annual Wealth Tax, 1975; Social Economics, 1977; (jtly) Grants or Loans?, 1980; (jtly) The Costs and Benefits of VAT, 1981; The Economic Framework, 1982; (jtly) Tax Policy-Making in the United Kingdom, 1983; (jtly) The Irish Wealth Tax: a study in economics and politics, 1985; Taxing Wealth in New Zealand, 1987; (jtly) Administrative and Compliance Costs of Taxation, 1989; (jtly) The Compliance Costs of Business Taxes in New Zealand, 1992; Successful Tax Reform: lessons from an analysis of tax reform in six countries, 1993; (jtly) Key Issues in Tax Reform, 1993; (jtly) More Key Issues in Tax Reform, 1995; (jtly) Tax Compliance Costs:

measurement and policy, 1995; (jtly) Further Key Issues in Tax Reform, 1998; Why Tax Systems Differ: a comparative study of the political economy of taxation, 2000; numerous articles in wide range of learned jls. *Recreations:* fishing, gardening, busking. *Address:* Old Coach House, Fersfield, Perrymead, Bath BA2 5AR. *T:* (01225) 832683.

SANDFORD, Jeremy; writer, journalist, musician; *s* of late Christopher Sandford, owner/director of the Golden Cockerel Press, and Lettice Sandford, wood engraver, craft worker; *m* 1st, 1956, Nell Dunn (marr. diss. 1986); three *s*; 2nd, 1988, Philippa Finnis. *Educ:* Eton; Oxford. Executive Mem., Gypsy Council. Formerly editor, Romano Drom (Gypsy newspaper); author/researcher of many plays and documentaries for radio, stage and television. Screen Writers' Guild of Gt Britain Award, 1967, 1971; Prix Italia prize for TV drama, 1968; Critics Award for TV drama, 1971. *Publications:* Synthetic Fun, 1967; Cathy Come Home, 1967; Whelks and Chromium, 1968; Edna the Inebriate Woman, 1971; Down and Out in Britain, 1971; In Search of the Magic Mushrooms, 1972; Gypsies, 1973; Tomorrow's People, 1974; Prostitutes, 1975; Smiling David, 1975; Figures and Landscapes, 1991; Castle by the Sea, 1998; Spirit of the Gypsies, 1999; Rokkering to the Gorjios, 1999; contribs to Guardian, Sunday Times, etc. *Recreations:* painting, traditional and Romany Gypsy music (accordion and Irish whistle), travel, mountain exploration, riding, wandering, windsurfing, wondering, festivals, holistic educational camps, sacred circle dance. *Address:* Hatfield Court, Hatfield, Leominster, Herefordshire HR6 0SD.

SANDFORD, Kenneth Leslie, CMG 1974; retired barrister; *b* 14 Aug. 1915; *s* of Albert Edgar Sandford and Barbara Ivy (*née* Hill); *m* 1946, Airini Ethel Scott Sergel; one *s* one *d* (and one *d* decd). *Educ:* King's Coll., Auckland, NZ; Auckland University Coll. LLB 1938. Served War: 34 Bn (NZ), rank of Captain, 1940–45. Barrister and Solicitor, 1939–72; Crown Solicitor (Hamilton), 1950–72; Chm., Accident Compensation Commn (NZ), 1972–80. *Publications:* Dead Reckoning, 1955; Dead Secret, 1957; Mark of the Lion, 1962. *Recreation:* cricket (Pres. NZ Cricket Council, 1971–73). *Address:* 1523 Kawakawa Bay, RD5 Papakura, New Zealand.

SANDFORD, Rear-Adm. Sefton Ronald, CB 1976; *b* 23 July 1925; *s* of Col H. R. Sandford and Mrs Faye Sandford (*née* Renouf); *m* 1st, 1950, Mary Ann Prins (*d* 1972); one *s*; 2nd, 1972, Jennifer Rachel Newell; two *d*. *Educ:* St Aubyns, Rottingdean, 1934–38; Royal Naval Coll., Dartmouth, 1939–42. Served War: went to sea, July 1942; commanded HMMTB 2017, Lieut, 1946–47; ADC to Comdr British Forces, Hong Kong (Lt-Gen. Sir Terence Airey), 1952–53; commanded HMS Teazer (rank Comdr), 1958; Staff of Imperial Defence Coll., 1963–65; comd HMS Protector, Captain, 1965–67; Naval Attaché, Moscow, 1968–70; comd HMS Devonshire, 1971–73; ADC to the Queen, 1974; Flag Officer, Gibraltar, 1974–76. A Younger Brother of Trinity House, 1968. *Recreations:* cricket, sailing, fishing, photography. *Address:* St Christophe, 47400 Villeton, France. *T:* 553790852. *Clubs:* Marylebone Cricket (MCC); Royal Yacht Squadron (Cowes).

SANDHURST, 5th Baron *cr* 1871; **(John Edward) Terence Mansfield,** DFC 1944; *b* 4 Sept. 1920; *er s* of 4th Baron Sandhurst, OBE, and Morley Victoria (*née* Upcher; *d* 1961); *S* father, 1964; *m* 1947, Janet Mary, *er d* of late John Edward Lloyd, NY, USA; one *s* one *d*. *Educ:* Harrow. Served RAFVR, 1939–46: Bomber Command (as Navigator and Bombing Leader): 149 Sqdn, 1941; 419 (RCAF) Sqdn, 1942; 12 Sqdn, 1943–45. 1946–55: Metropolitan Special Constabulary 'C' Div., Sergeant, 1949–52; long service medal, 1955. Hon. ADC to Lieutenant-Governor of Jersey, 1969–74. *Recreation:* golf. *Heir: s* Hon. Guy Rhys John Mansfield, *qv*. *Educ:* Harrow; Oriel Coll., Oxford (MA). Called to Bar, Middle Temple, 1972]. *Address:* La Volière, Les Ruisseaux, St Brelade, Jersey JE3 8DD. *Clubs:* Royal Air Force, MCC; United (Jersey).

See also Earl of Macclesfield.

SANDIFORD, Rt Hon. Sir Lloyd Erskine, KA 1999; PC (Barbados); PC 1989; JP; Prime Minister of Barbados, 1987–94; *b* 24 March 1937; *s* of Cyril and Eunice Sandiford; *m* 1963, Angelita P. Ricketts; one *s* two *d*. *Educ:* Coleridge/Parry Sec. Sch.; Harrison Coll.; Univ. of WI, Jamaica (BA Hons English); Univ. of Manchester (MAEcon). Assistant Master: Modern High Sch., Barbados, 1956–57; Kingston Coll., Jamaica, 1960–61; Asst Master, 1963–64, Sen. Graduate Master, 1964–66, Harrison Coll., Barbados; part-time Tutor and Lectr, Univ. of the WI, Barbados, 1963–65; Asst Tutor, Barbados Community Coll., 1976–86. Democratic Labour Party, Barbados: Mem., 1964–; Asst Sec., 1966–67; Gen. Sec., 1967–68; (first) Vice-Pres., 1972–74; Pres., 1974–75; Vice-Pres., 1975–76; Founder, Acad. of Politics. Member: Senate, 1967–71; House of Assembly, St Michael South, 1971–99; Personal Asst to the Prime Minister, 1966–67; Minister: of Educn, 1967–71; of Educn, Youth Affairs, Community Develt and Sport, 1971–75; of Health and Welfare, 1975–76; Dep. Leader of Opposition, 1978–86; Dep. Prime Minister and Minister of Educn and Culture, 1986–87; Minister: for Civil Service, 1987–94; of Finance and Economic Affairs, 1987–93; of Economic Affairs, 1993–94; of Tourism and Internat. Transport, 1994. Dist. Fellow, Univ. of WI, Barbados. Order of the Liberator (Venezuela), 1987. *Publications:* Books of Speeches 1987–1994; The Essence of Economics, 1997; Politics and Society in Barbados and the Caribbean, 2000; *poems:* Ode to the Environment; When She Leaves You; (contrib.) Business, Government and Society, ed Monya Anyadike-Danes. *Address:* Hillvista, Porters, St James, Barbados, West Indies.

SANDIFORD, Peter, OBE 1992; Director, Spain, British Council, since 1999; *b* 23 May 1947; *s* of Jack Sandiford and Joan Mary Sandiford; *m* 1970, Yvonne Kay Haffenden; one *s* one *d*. *Educ:* Watford Grammar Sch. for Boys; University College London (BSc Hons Anthropology 1969). VSO Volunteer, Malawi, 1965–66; Archaeologist, MPBW, 1969–70; British Council: Asst Dir, Singapore, 1971–75; Regl Dir, Munich, 1975–82; Dir, Mgt Services Dept, London, 1982–86; Dir, Israel, 1986–94; Regl Dir, East and Southern Europe, 1994–96, Americas, 1996–98, London. *Recreations:* amateur radio (call sign G3STF), sailing, hiking. *Address:* c/o British Council, 10 Spring Gardens, SW1A 2BN.

SANDILANDS, family name of **Baron Torphichen**.

SANDIS, Alexandros C.; Ambassador of Greece to the Court of St James's, since 2000; *b* Alexandria, Egypt, 29 Aug. 1947; *s* of Constantinos and Maria Sandis; *m* 1969, Anastasia Tsagarakis; one *s* one *d*. *Educ:* Univ. of Athens (BA Pol and Econ. Scis). Joined Ministry of Foreign Affairs, Athens, 1971: Attaché, 1971–73; New Delhi, 1973–77; Nicosia, 1977-83; Perm. Delegn to EC, Brussels, 1983–88; Dir, EU Affairs Dept, Athens, 1989-91; Ambassador to: Zimbabwe, 1991–93; Cyprus, 1993–97; Italy, 1997–2000. Greek Govt Rep. at Cyprus Talks, 1997–. Grand Cross, Order of Makarios III (Greece), 1993; Comdr, Order of Greek Orthodox Patriarchate of Alexandrea, 1995. *Recreations:* history, music, theatre, football. *Address:* Embassy of Greece, 1A Holland Park, W11 3TP. *T:* (020) 7313 8924. *Club:* Travellers.

SANDISON, Alexander, (Alec), FCCA; charity management and finance consultant, since 1994; *b* 24 May 1943; *s* of late Alexander Sandison and Mary Roscoe; *m* 1st, 1968, Janet Firmager (marr. diss.); 2nd, 1977, Merralyn Martin (*née* Hill) (marr. diss.); two *s*; 3rd, 1994, Susan Dixon. *Educ:* Cambs High Sch.; Trinity Sch. of John Whitgift, Croydon. FCCA 1975 (ACCA 1970). Commercial Union Assce Co., 1962–63; John Mowlem PLC, 1964–71 (Gp Financial Accountant, 1970–71); Chief Accountant: and Co. Sec., J. E. Freeman & Co., 1972–73; Wings Ltd, 1973–78; Divl Financial Dir, Doulton Glass Inds, 1978–80; Sec. for Finance and Corporate Controller, RICS, 1980–90; Chief Exec., Surveyors Holdings Ltd, 1985–89; Chm., Imaginor Systems Ltd, 1989–90; Director: Cruse-Bereavement Care, 1990–91; Finance and Admin, Prince's Trust and Royal Jubilee Trusts, 1992–94. Mem. Charities Panel, Chartered Assoc. of Certified Accountants. Trustee: ACCA Benevolent Assoc., 1999–; Islington Volunteers Centre, 1999–. *Publications:* People to People: course notes, 1985; Watton-at-Stone Village Guide, 1989; contribs to learned jls, brainteasers and poetry. *Recreations:* voluntary social work; reading, writing; avoiding involvement with and conversations about sport. *Address:* 38 Grange Rise, Codicote, Hitchin, Herts SG4 8YR. *T:* (07958) 643472.

SANDISON, James Sinclair, FCA; freelance financial and management consultant, 1998–2000; *b* 22 June 1936; *s* of William Robert Sandison and Evelyn Gladys Sandison; *m* 1978, Jeannette Avery Keeble; one *s* one *d*. *Educ:* John Lyon Sch., Harrow. FCA 1958. Nat. Service, 2nd Lt, 1958–60. Franklin, Wild & Co., 1953–58; Touche Ross & Co., 1960–62; British Relay Wireless and Television Ltd, 1962–66; joined Dexion Gp, 1966: Gp Controller, 1975–76; Finance Dir, Dexion Ltd, 1977–91; Royal Society for Encouragement of Arts, Manufactures and Commerce: Dir of Finance and Admin, 1991–96; Acting Dir, 1996–97. FRSA 1998. Mem. Develt Bd, Chelsea Physic Garden. *Recreations:* reading, tennis, gardening, cinema, fairground organs, history of London. *Address:* 33 Montagu Road, Highcliffe, Christchurch, Dorset BH23 5JT.

SANDLE, Prof. Michael Leonard, DFA; FRBS 1994; sculptor; Professor of Sculpture, Akademie der Bildenden Künste, Karlsruhe, Germany, 1980–99; *b* 18 May 1936; *s* of Charles Edward Sandle and Dorothy Gwendoline Gladys (*née* Vernon); *m* 1971, Cynthia Dora Koppel (marriage annulled 1974); *m* 1988, Demelza Spargo; one *s* one *d*. *Educ:* Douglas High Sch., IOM; Douglas Sch. of Art and Technol.; Slade Sch. of Fine Art (DFA 1959). ARA 1982, RA 1989, resigned 1997. Studied painting and printmaking, Slade Sch. of Fine Art, 1956–59; changed to sculpture, 1962; various teaching posts in Britain, 1961–70, including Lectr, Coventry Coll. of Art, 1964–68; resident in Canada, 1970–73; Vis. Prof., Univ. of Calgary, Alberta, 1970–71; Vis. Associate Prof., Univ. of Victoria, BC, 1972–73; Lectr in Sculpture, Fachhochschule für Gestaltung, Pforzheim, W Germany, 1973–77, Prof., 1977–80. Sen. Res. Fellow, De Montfort Univ., 1996–2001. Has participated in exhibns in GB and internationally, 1957–, including: V Biennale, Paris, 1966; Documenta IV, Kassel, W Germany, 1968 and Documenta VI, 1977. Work in public collections, including: Arts Council of GB, Tate Gall.; Australian Nat. Gall., Canberra; Met. Mus., NY; Stzüki Mus., Lodz; Nat. Gall., Warsaw; Wilhelm Lehmbruck Mus., Duisburg, W Germany. Designed: Malta Siege Bell Meml, Valetta, 1992; Seafarers Meml, for Internat. Maritime Orgn's HQ, London, 2001. Nobutaka Shikanai Special Prize, Utsukushi-Ga-Hara Open-Air Mus., Japan, 1986; Henry Hering Meml Medal, Nat. Sculpture Soc. of Amer., 1995.

SANDLER, Prof. Merton, MD; FRCP, FRCPath, FRCPsych; Professor of Chemical Pathology, Royal Postgraduate Medical School, Institute of Obstetrics and Gynaecology, University of London, 1973–91, Professor Emeritus, since 1991; Consultant Chemical Pathologist, Queen Charlotte's Maternity Hospital, 1958–91; *b* 28 March 1926; *s* of late Frank Sandler and Edith (*née* Stein), Salford, Lancs; *m* 1961, Lorna Rosemary, *d* of late Ian Michael and Sally Grenby, Colindale, London; two *s* two *d*. *Educ:* Manchester Grammar Sch.; Manchester Univ. (MB ChB 1949; MD 1962). FRCPath 1970 (MRCPath 1963); FRCP 1974 (MRCP 1955); FRCPsych 1986. Jun. Specialist in Pathology, RAMC (Captain), 1951–53. Research Fellow in Clin. Path., Brompton Hosp., 1953–54; Lectr in Chem. Path., Royal Free Hosp. Sch. of Med., 1955–58. Visiting Professor: Univ. of New Mexico, 1983; Chicago Med. Sch., 1984; Univ. of S Fla, 1988. Recognized Teacher in Chem. Path., 1960–91; extensive examining experience for various Brit. and for. univs and Royal Colls; Mem. Standing Adv. Cttee, Bd of Studies in Path., Univ. of London, 1972–76 (also Mem. Chem. Path. Sub-Cttee, 1973–91); Chm., Academic Bd, 1972–73, Bd of Management, 1975–84, Inst. of Obst. and Gyn.; Governor: Brit. Postgrad. Med. Fedn, 1976–78; Queen Charlotte's Hosp. for Women, 1978–84; Council Mem. and Meetings Sec., Assoc. of Clin. Pathologists, 1959–70; Mem. Council, Collegium Internat. Neuro-Psycho-pharmacologicum, 1982–90. Various offices in: RSM, incl. Hon. Librarian, 1987–93, and Pres. Section of Med. Exper. Med. and Therapeutics, 1979–80; Brit. Assoc. for Psychopharm., incl. Pres., 1980–82 (Hon. Mem., 1993); British Assoc. for Postnatal Illness (Pres., 1980–); office in many other learned socs and grant-giving bodies, incl. Med. Adv. Councils of Migraine Trust, 1975–80 (Chm., Scientific Adv. Cttee, 1985–91; Trustee, 1987–91), Schizophrenia Assoc. of GB, 1975–78, Parkinson's Disease Soc., 1981–97 (Trustee, 1994–97); Chm. of Trustees, Nat. Soc. for Res. into Mental Health, 1983–. Pres., W London Medico-Chirurgical Soc., 1996–97. Chm. and Sec., Biol Council Symposium on Drug Action, 1979; Sec., Mem. Bd of Management and Chm. Awards Subcttee, Biological Council, 1983–91; Member, Executive Committee: Marcé Soc., 1983–86; Med. Council on Alcoholism, 1987–90; Sec. and Mem. Council, Harveian Soc. of London, 1979–89 (Vice Pres., 1990; Pres., 1991–92); Mem. Council of Management and Patron, Helping Hand Orgn, 1981–87. Organiser or Brit. rep. on org. cttees of many nat. and internat. meetings incl. Internat. Chm., 6th Internat. Catecholamine Congress, 1987. For. Corresp. Mem., Amer. Coll. of Neuropsychopharm., 1975; Hon. Member: Indian Acad. of Neuroscis, 1982; Hungarian Pharmacological Soc., 1985. Jt Editor: British Jl of Pharmacology, 1974–80; Clinical Science, 1975–77; Jl of Neural Transmission, 1979–82; Jt Editor-in-Chief, Jl of Psychiatric Research, 1982–93, and present or past Mem. Editorial Bds of 17 other sci. jls; eponymous lectures to various learned socs incl. 1st Cumings Meml, 1976, James E. Beall II Meml, 1980, Biol Council Lecture and Medal, 1984; F. B. Smith Meml, 1995; Jane Chomet Meml, 1997; Marcia Wilkinson, 2001; provision of Nat. Monoamine Ref. Laboratory Service, 1976–91. Dr *hc* Semmelweis Univ. of Medicine, Budapest, 1992. Anna Monika Internat. Prize (jtly), for Res. on Biol Aspects of Depression, 1973; Gold Medal, Brit. Migraine Assoc., 1974; Senator Dr Franz Burda Internat. Prize for Res. on Parkinson's Disease, 1988; Arnold Friedman Distinguished Clinician Researcher Award, 1991; British Assoc. for Psychopharmacology/Zeneca Lifetime Achievement Award, 1999. *Publications:* Mental Illness in Pregnancy and the Puerperium, 1978; The Psychopharmacology of Aggression, 1979; Enzyme Inhibitors as Drugs, 1980; Amniotic Fluid and its Clinical Significance, 1980; The Psychopharmacology of Alcohol, 1980; The Psychopathology of Anticonvulsants, 1981; Nervous Laughter, 1990; Parkinson's Disease, 1993; *jointly:* The Adrenal Cortex, 1961; The Thyroid Gland, 1967; Advances in Pharmacology, 1968; Monoamine Oxidases, 1972; Serotonin—New Vistas, 1974; Sexual Behaviour: Pharmacology and Biochemistry, 1975; Trace Amines and the Brain, 1976; Phenolsulphotransferase in Mental Health Research, 1981; Tetrahydroisoquinolines and β-Carbolines, 1982; Progress towards a Male Contraceptive, 1982; Neurobiology of the Trace Amines, 1984; Psychopharmacology and Food, 1985; Neurotransmitter Interactions, 1986; Progress in Catecholamine Research, 1988; Design of Enzyme Inhibitors as Drugs, Vol. 1, 1989, Vol. 2, 1994; Migraine: a spectrum of ideas, 1990; 5-Hydroxytryptamine in Psychiatry, 1991; Monoamine Oxidase: basic and clinical aspects,

1993; Genetic Research in Psychiatry, 1992; Migraine–Pharmacology and Genetics, 1996; Wine: a scientific exploration, 2002; numerous research pubns on aspects of biologically-active monoamine metabolism. *Recreations:* reading, listening to music, travel. *Address:* 33 Park Road, East Twickenham, Middlesex TW1 2QD. *T:* (020) 8892 9085, *Fax:* (020) 8891 5370. *Club:* Athenæum.

SANDLER, Ronald Arnon; Chairman: Computacenter plc, since 2001; Kyte Group, since 2000; *b* 5 March 1952; *s* of Bernard Maurice Sandler and Carla Sandler; *m* 1977, Susan Lee; two *s*. *Educ:* Milton Sch., Bulawayo; Queens' Coll., Cambridge (MA); Stanford Univ., USA (MBA). Boston Consulting Gp Inc., 1976–84, Dir 1983–84; Sen. Vice Pres., Booz Allen & Hamilton Inc., 1984–88; Chm., Chalcon Ltd, 1989–93; Chm. and Chief Exec., Martin Bierbaum Gp plc, 1990–93; Chief Executive: Exco plc, 1993–94; Lloyd's of London, 1995–99; Chief Operating Officer, NatWest Gp, 1999–2000. Non-exec. Dir, Greenalls Gp plc, 1998–2000. Trustee, Royal Opera House, 1999–. *Recreations:* golf, ski-ing, guitar playing. *Address:* 5 Southside, Wimbledon, SW19 4TG. *T:* (020) 8946 1179. *Club:* Coombe Hill Golf.

SANDON, Viscount; Dudley Adrian Conroy Ryder; chartered surveyor; *b* 18 March 1951; *s* and *heir* of Earl of Harrowby, *qv*; *m* 1st, 1977, Sarah Nichola Hobhouse Payne (*d* 1994), *d* of Captain Anthony Payne; three *s* one *d*; 2nd, 1998, Mrs Caroline J. Coram James (*née* Marks). *Educ:* Eton; Univ. of Newcastle upon Tyne; Magdalene Coll., Cambridge (MA). FRICS. Exec. Dir, Compton Street Securities Ltd, 1988–. Governor, John Archer Sch., Wandsworth, 1986–88. Pres., Staffordshire Soc., 1995–97. Patron, Guild of Handicraft Trust, 1991–. *Recreations:* shooting, fell walking, music, study of fine art and architecture. *Heir:* *s* Hon. Dudley Anthony Hugo Coventry Ryder, *b* 5 Sept. 1981. *Address:* Sandon Estate Office, Sandon, Stafford ST18 0DA.

SANDS, John Robert; Chief Executive, Pubmaster Ltd, since 1996 (Managing Director, 1991–96); *b* 8 Oct. 1947; *s* of John Sands and Jane Caroline Sands (*née* Reay); *m* 1969, Susan Elizabeth; two *s* two *d*. J. W. Cameron & Co. Ltd: Trng and Develt Manager, 1980–81; Tied Trade Dir, 1981–84; Trade Dir, 1984–85; Managing Director: Cameron Inns, 1985–88; and CEO, Tollemache & Cobbold Breweries Ltd, 1988–89; Brent Walker Inns and Retail, 1989–91. *Recreations:* ski-ing, keep fit, playing guitar and banjo, playing mahjong, watching Newcastle United FC. *Address:* Pubmaster Ltd, Greenbank, Hartlepool TS24 7QS. *T:* (01429) 266699.

SANDS, Roger Blakemore; Clerk Assistant, House of Commons, since 2001; *b* 6 May 1942; *s* of late Thomas Blakemore Sands and Edith Malyon (Betty) Sands (*née* Waldram); *m* 1966, Jennifer Ann Cattell; two *d*. *Educ:* University Coll. Sch., Hampstead; Oriel Coll., Oxford (scholar; MA LitHum). A Clerk, House of Commons, 1965–; Sec. to H of C Commn and Clerk to H of C (Services) Cttee, 1985–87; Clerk of Overseas Office, 1987–91; Clerk of Select Cttees and Registrar of Members' Interests, 1991–94; Clerk of Public Bills, 1994–97; Clerk of Legislation, 1998–2001. Trustee: History of Parlt Trust, 2001– (Sec., 1974–80); Industry and Parlt Trust, 2001–; Chm, Study of Parlt Group, 1993–95. *Recreations:* gardening, listening to music, walking, occasional golf. *Address:* House of Commons, SW1A 0AA. *T:* (020) 7219 3311.

SANDS SMITH, David; development administrator, since 2001; *b* 19 April 1943; *s* of late Arthur S. Smith and Eileen Annie Smith; *m* 1966, Veronica Harris; one *s* one *d*. *Educ:* Brighton Coll. of Technology, Dept of Technical Co-operation, 1963–71. 2nd Sec., British High Commn, Kuala Lumpur, 1971–75; Overseas Development Administration: Principal: European Community Dept, 1975–80; Zimbabwe Desk, 1980–85; Asst Head, 1985–88, Head, 1988–90, European Community Dept; Head, British Develt Div. in Eastern Africa, 1990–93; UK Perm. Rep., FAO, World Food Programme and IFAD, 1993–97; Head: Procurement, Appts and NGOs Dept, DFID, 1997–99; Develt Policy Dept, DFID, 1999–2001. *Recreations:* running, windsurfing, tennis. *Address:* 42 Ballard Drive, Ringmer, East Sussex BN8 5NU. *T:* (01273) 813143.

SANDWICH, 11th Earl of, *cr* 1660; **John Edward Hollister Montagu;** Viscount Hinchingbrooke and Baron Montagu of St Neots, 1660; editor and researcher; *b* 11 April 1943; *er s* of (Alexander) Victor (Edward Paulet) Montagu; *S* to disclaimed Earldom of father, 1995; *m* 1968, Caroline, *o d* of late Canon P. E. C. Hayman, Beaminster, Dorset; two *s* one *d*. *Educ:* Eton; Trinity College, Cambridge. Inf. Officer, 1974–85, Res. Officer, 1985–86, Mem., Bd, 1999–, Christian Aid; Editor, Save the Children Fund, 1987–92; Consultant, CARE Britain, 1987–93; Mem. Council, Anti-Slavery Internat., 1997–. Chm., Britain Afghanistan Trust, 1995–; Trustee, TSW Telethon Trust, 1987–91; Managing Trustee, St Francis Sch., Dorset, 1987–92; Gov. Beaminster Sch., 1996–. Pres., Earl of Sandwich, 2001–. Jt Administrator, Mapperton Estate, 1982–. Crossbencher, H of L, 1995–; elected Mem., H of L, 1999. Pres., Samuel Pepys Club. *Publications:* The Book of the World, 1971; Prospects for Africa's Children, 1990; Children at Crisis Point, 1992; (ed jtly) Hinch: a celebration of Viscount Hinchingbrooke, MP 1906–1995, 1997. *Heir:* *s* Viscount Hinchingbrooke, *qv*. *Address:* Mapperton House, Beaminster, Dorset DT8 3NR.

SANDYS, 7th Baron *cr* 1802; **Richard Michael Oliver Hill;** DL; Captain of the Yeomen of the Guard (Deputy Government Chief Whip, House of Lords), 1979–82; Landowner; *b* 21 July 1931; *o s* of 6th Baron Sandys, Lt-Col, RE, and Cynthia Mary (*d* 1990), *o d* of late Col F. R. T. T. Gascoigne, DSO; *S* father, 1961; *m* 1961, Patricia Simpson Hall, *d* of late Captain Lionel Hall, MC. *Educ:* Royal Naval College, Dartmouth. Lieutenant in The Royal Scots Greys, 1950–55. A Lord in Waiting, 1974; an Opposition Whip, H of L, 1974–79. FRGS. DL Worcestershire, 1968. *Heir:* Marquess of Downshire, *qv*. *Address:* Ombersley Court, Droitwich, Worcestershire WR9 0HH. *T:* (01905) 620220. *Club:* Cavalry and Guards.

SANÉ, Pierre Gabriel; Secretary General, Amnesty International, since 1992; *b* 7 May 1948; *s* of Nicolas Sané and Therese Carvalho; *m* 1981, Ndeye Sow; one *s* one *d*. *Educ:* LSE (MSc in Public Admin and Public Policy); Ecole Supérieure de Commerce, Bordeaux (MBA); Carleton Univ., Canada (doctoral studies in pol scis). Regl Dir, Internat. Develt Research Centre, Ottawa, Canada, 1978–92. *Address:* (office) 1 Easton Street, WC1X 0DW.

SANGER, David John, FRAM, FRCO; organ recitalist, composer, teacher; *b* 17 April 1947; *s* of Stanley Charles Sanger and Ethel Lillian Florence Sanger (*née* Woodgate). *Educ:* Eltham Coll.; Royal Acad. of Music, London (FRAM). ARCM, FRCO. Royal Academy of Music: Prof. of Organ, 1982–89; Chm., Organ Dept, 1987–89; Vis. Prof. of Organ, 1989–; freelance teaching at Cambridge and Oxford Univs, 1976–. Guest Prof., Royal Danish Acad. of Music, 1991–93; Vis. Tutor in Organ Studies, RNCM, 1991–. Perfs at the Proms and RFH; internat. tours as soloist, notably in Scandinavia; masterclasses, lectures and seminars. Jury Mem., internat. organ competitions in St Albans, Paisley, Speyer, Biarritz, Alkmaar and Odense. Consultant: new organ, Exeter Coll., Oxford; restoration of Usher Hall organ, Edinburgh. Numerous recordings. Winner, international organ competition: St Albans, 1969; Kiel, 1972. *Publications:* Play the Organ, vol. 1, 1990, vol. 2, 1993; (ed) organ works of Willan, 1990, Pepusch, 1994, and Lefébure-Wély, 2 vols, 1994; numerous compositions for organ and choir; articles for Organists' Review, The Organ. *Recreations:* racquet sports, swimming, fell-walking. *Address:* Old Wesleyan Chapel, Embleton, Cumbria CA13 9YA. *T:* (01768) 776628.

SANGER, Frederick, OM 1986; CH 1981; CBE 1963; PhD; FRS 1954; on staff of Medical Research Council, 1951–83; *b* 13 Aug. 1918; *s* of Frederick Sanger, MD, and Cicely Sanger; *m* 1940, M. Joan Howe; two *s* one *d*. *Educ:* Bryanston; St John's College, Cambridge. BA 1939; PhD 1943. From 1940, research in Biochemistry at Cambridge University; Beit Memorial Fellowship for Medical Research, 1944–51; at MRC Lab. of Molecular Biol., Cambridge, 1961–83; Fellowship at King's College, Cambridge, 1954. (Hon. Fellow 1983). For. Hon. Mem., Amer. Acad. of Arts and Sciences, 1958; Hon. Mem. Amer. Society of Biological Chemists, 1961; Foreign Assoc., Nat. Acad. of Sciences, 1967. Hon. DSc: Leicester, 1968; Oxon, 1970; Strasbourg, 1970; Cambridge, 1983. Corday-Morgan Medal and Prize, Chem. Soc., 1951; Nobel Prize for Chemistry, 1958, (jointly) 1980; Alfred Benzon Prize, 1966; Royal Medal, Royal Soc., 1969; Sir Frederick Gowland Hopkins Meml Medal, 1971; Gairdner Foundation Annual Award, 1971, 1979; William Bate Hardy Prize, Cambridge Philosophical Soc., 1976; Hanbury Meml Medal, 1976; Copley Medal, Royal Soc., 1977; Horwitz Prize, Albert Lasker Award, 1979; Biochem. Analysis Prize, German Soc. Clin. Chem., 1980; Gold Medal, RSM, 1983. *Publications:* papers on Chemistry of Insulin and Nucleic Acid Structure in Biochemical and other journals. *Address:* Far Leys, Fen Lane, Swaffham Bulbeck, Cambridge CB5 0NJ.

SANGSTER, Nigel; QC 1998; a Recorder, since 2000; *b* 16 Feb. 1955; *s* of Dr H. B. Singh and Irene Singh (*née* Carlisle), JP. *Educ:* Repton; Leeds Univ. (LLB Hons). Called to the Bar, Middle Temple, 1976; Head of Chambers, St Pauls Chambers, Leeds, 1995–; Asst Recorder, 1997–2000. Mem., Bar Council, 1994–. *Address:* St Pauls Chambers, St Pauls House, Park Square, Leeds LS1 2ND. *T:* (0113) 245 5866; 23 Essex Street, WC2R 3AS. *T:* (020) 7413 0353.

SANGSTER, Robert Edmund; *b* 23 May 1936; *o c* of late Mr Vernon Sangster and of Mrs Sangster. *Educ:* Repton Coll. Chairman: Vernons Orgn, 1980–88; Sangster Gp, 1988–. Owner of: The Minstrel (won Derby, 1977); Alleged (won Prix de l'Arc de Triomphe, 1977, 1978); Jaazeiro (won Irish Derby, 1978); Detroit (won Prix de l'Arc de Triomphe, 1980); Beldale Ball (won Melbourne Cup, 1980); Kings Lake (won Irish 2,000 Guineas, 1981); Our Paddy Boy (won Australian Jockey Club Cup, 1981); Golden Fleece (won Derby, 1982); Assert (won Irish Sweeps Derby, and French Derby, 1982); Lomond (won 2,000 Guineas, 1983); Caerleon (won French Derby, 1983); El Gran Señor (won 2,000 Guineas, Irish Sweeps Derby, 1984); Sadler's Wells (won Irish 2,000 Guineas, 1984); Gildoran (won Ascot Gold Cup, 1984, 1985, Goodwood Cup, 1984); Law Society (won Irish Derby, 1985); Committed (won Prix de l'Abbaye de Longchamp; Champion European Sprinter); Royal Heroine (Champion Grass Mare, USA, 1984); Marooned (won Sydney Cup, 1986); Prince of Birds (won Irish 2,000 Guineas, 1988); Rodrigo de Triano (won 2,000 Guineas and Irish 2,000 Guineas, 1992); Las Meninas (won 1,000 Guineas, 1994); Turtle Island (won Irish 2,000 Guineas, 1994); Riverina Charm (Champion, Australia); Kostroma (Champion, USA); Royal Heroine (Champion, USA); Revoque (Champion European Two Year Old). Leading winning race-horse owner, 1977, 1978, 1982, 1983 and 1984 seasons; owner of 741 Stakes winners, 1977–. *Recreation:* golf. *Address:* Manton House, Manton House Estate, Marlborough, Wilts SN8 1PN. *Club:* Jockey.

SANKEY, John Anthony, CMG 1983; HM Diplomatic Service, retired; Secretary General, Society of London Art Dealers, 1991–96; *b* 8 June 1930; *m* 1958, Gwendoline Putman; two *s* two *d*. *Educ:* Cardinal Vaughan Sch., Kensington; Peterhouse, Cambridge (Classical Tripos Parts 1 and 2, Class 1; MA). 1st (Singapore) Regt, RA (2nd Lieut), 1952. Colonial Office, 1953–61; UK Mission to United Nations, 1961–64; Foreign Office, 1964–68; Guyana, 1968–71; Singapore, 1971–73; NATO Defence Coll., Rome, 1973; Malta, 1973–75; The Hague, 1975–79 (Gov., British Sch. in the Netherlands); FCO, 1979–82; High Comr, Tanzania, 1982–85; UK Perm. Rep. to UN Office, Geneva, 1985–90. Leader, British Govt Delegn to Internat. Red Cross Conf., 1986. Dir, Internat. Art and Antiques Loss Register Ltd, 1993–96. Trustee, Tanzania Develt Trust, 1997–. Sir Evelyn Wrench Lectr, ESU, 1990. KHS 1996. *Publications:* (contrib.) The United Kingdom—the United Nations, 1990; The Conscience of the World, 1995; articles on Victorian sculpture and art dealing. *Recreations:* nineteenth century sculpture. *Address:* 108 Lancaster Gate, W2 3NW.

SANKEY, Vernon Louis; Chairman, Gala Group Holdings plc, since 2000; *b* 9 May 1949; *s* of late Edward Sankey and Marguerite Elizabeth Louise (*née* van Maurik); *m* 1976, Elizabeth, *d* of Tom Knights; three *s* one *d* (of whom one *s* one *d* are twins). *Educ:* Harrow School; Oriel Coll., Oxford (MA Mod. Langs). Joined Reckitt & Colman, 1971: Mgt Trainee, 1971–74; Asst Manager, Finance and Planning, 1974–76; Dir, Planning and Develt, Europe, 1976–78; General Manager, Denmark, 1978–80; PA to Chm. and Chief Exec., 1980–81; Man. Dir, France, 1981–85; Man. Dir, Colman's of Norwich, 1985–89; Chm. and Chief Exec. Officer, Reckitt & Colman Inc., USA, 1989–92; Chief Exec., 1992–99. Chm., The Really Effective Develt Co. Ltd, 2000–; Deputy Chairman: Photo-Me Internat. plc, 2000–; Beltpacker plc, 2000–; non-executive Director: Pearson, 1993–; Allied Zurich plc, 1998–; Zurich Allied AG, 1998–; Zurich Financial Services AG, 2000–; Member: Internat. Adv. Bd, Korn/Ferry Internat., 1994–; Adv. Bd, Proudfoot UK. Mem. Bd, Grocery Manufacturers of Amer., 1995–99; Mem., Marketing Soc., 1995–99. Member: Listed Cos Adv. Cttee, London Stock Exchange, 1997–99; Bd, Food Standards Agency, 2000–. FIMgt 1992; MInstD 1995. FRSA. *Recreations:* jogging, tennis. *Address:* Gala Group Holdings plc, New Castle House, Castle Boulevard, Nottingham NG7 1FT. *Club:* Leander (Henley).

SANKEY, William Patrick F.; *see* Filmer-Sankey.

SANSOM, Bruce Edward; Principal Dancer, Royal Ballet Co., 1987–2000; *b* 8 Sept. 1963; *s* of Dr Bernard Sansom and Prudence Sansom. *Educ:* Royal Ballet Sch. Joined Royal Ballet Co., 1982; Soloist, 1985; also danced with San Francisco Ballet Co., 1991–92 season. Has danced principal rôles in all major ballets, incl. La Fille Mal Gardée, Swan Lake, Giselle, The Nutcracker, Manon, Sleeping Beauty, La Bayadère, Cinderella, The Dream, Romeo and Juliet, Scènes de Ballet, Manon; leading rôles created for him in a number of ballets including Galanteries, Still Life at the Penguin Café, Pursuit, Piano, Prince of the Pagodas, Tombeaux. Mem., Cttee of Mgt, Friends of Covent Garden. Time Out Award for performances with Royal Ballet, 1990. *Recreations:* shooting, opera, contemporary art, Parson Jack Russell terriers. *Address:* c/o San Francisco Ballet, 455 Franklin Street, San Francisco, CA 94109, USA.

SANT, Hon. Dr Alfred; MP (Lab) Malta, since 1987; Leader of the Opposition, Malta, since 1998; *b* 28 Feb. 1948; *s* of Joseph and Josephine Sant; one *d*. *Educ:* Univ. of Malta (BSc, MSc); Inst. Internat. d'Admin Publique, Paris (Dip.); Boston Univ. (MBA); Harvard Univ. (DBA). Res. Fellow, Harvard Business Sch. First Sec., Malta Mission to EEC, Brussels, 1970–75; Man. Dir, Medina Consulting Gp, 1979–80; Dep. Chm., Malta Develt

Corp., 1980–82. Leader, Labour Party, 1992–; Prime Minister of Malta, 1996–98. *Publications: novels:* L-Ewwel Weraq tal-Bajtar, 1968; Silg fuq Kemmuna, 1982; Bejgh u Xiri, 1984; *dramas:* Min hu Evelyn Costa?, 1982; Fid-Dell tal-Katidral, 1994. *Recreations:* listening to classical music, walking. *Address:* 18A Victory Street, B'Kara, Malta.

SANTER, Jacques; Member (EPP) for Luxembourg, European Parliament, since 1999; *b* 18 May 1937; *m* Danièle Binot; two *s*. *Educ:* Athénée de Luxembourg; Paris Univ.; Strasbourg Univ.; Inst. d'Etudes Politiques, Paris. DenD. Advocate, Luxembourg Court of Appeal, 1961–65; Attaché, Office of Minister of Labour and Social Security, 1963–65; Govt Attaché, 1965–66; Christian Socialist Party: Parly Sec., 1966–72; Sec.-Gen., 1972–74; Pres., 1974–82; Sec. of State for Cultural and Social Affairs, 1972–74; Mem., Chamber of Deputies, 1974–79; MEP, 1975–79 (a Vice-Pres., 1975–77); Minister of Finance, Labour and Social Security, Luxembourg, 1979–84; Prime Minister of Luxembourg, 1984–94; Pres. of Govt, Minister of State and Minister of Finance, 1984–89; Minister for Cultural Affairs, 1989–94; Pres., EC, 1995–99. *Address:* European Parliament, Rue Wiertz, 1047 Brussels, Belgium.

SANTER, Rt Rev. Mark; *see* Birmingham, Bishop of.

SANTOMARCO, Oona Tamsyn; *see* King, O. T.

SAOUMA, Edouard; Director-General of the Food and Agriculture Organization of the United Nations, Rome, 1976–93; agricultural engineer and international official; *b* Beirut, Lebanon, 6 Nov. 1926; *m* Inés Forero; one *s* two *d*. *Educ:* St Joseph's University Sch. of Engineering, Beirut; École Nat. Supérieure d'Agronomie, Montpellier, France. Director: Tel Amara Agric. Sch., 1952–53; Nat. Centre for Farm Mechanization, 1954–55; Sec. Gen., Nat. Fedn of Lebanese Agronomists, 1955; Dir-Gen., Nat. Inst. for Agricl Res., 1957–62; Mem. Gov. Bd, Nat. Grains Office, 1960–62; Minister of Agric., Fisheries and Forestry, 1970. Food and Agric. Organization of UN: Dep. Regional Rep. for Asia and Far East, 1962–65; Dir, Land and Water Develt Div., 1965–75; Dir-Gen., 1976, re-elected 1981, 1987. Hon. Prof. of Agronomy, Agricl Univ. of Beijing, China. Said Akl Prize, Lebanon; Chevalier du Mérite Agricole, France; Grand Cross: Order of the Cedar, Lebanon; Ordre National du Chad; Ordre Nat. du Ghana; Ordre National de Haute Volta; Mérito Agrícola of Spain; Orden Nacional al Mérito, Colombia; Kt Comdr, Order of Merit, Greece; Order of Agricl Merit, Colombia; Gran Oficial, Orden de Vasco Nuñez de Balboa, Panamá; Orden al Mérito Agrícola, Peru; Order of Merit, Egypt; Order of Merit, Mauritania; Grand Officier: Ordre de la République, Tunisia; Ordre National, Madagascar; Ordre de Commandeur, Ouissan Alouite, Morocco. Dr (*hc*): Univ. of Bologna, Italy; Agric. Univ. La Molina, Peru; Univ. of Seoul, Republic of Korea; Univ. of Uruguay; Univ. of Jakarta, Indonesia; Univ. of Warsaw; Univ. of Los Baños, Philippines; Punjab Agricultural Univ., India; Faisalabad Agricultural Univ., Pakistan; Univ. of Agricl Scis of Gödöllö, Hungary; Univ. Nacional Autónoma, Nicaragua; Univ. of Florence, Italy; Univ. of Gembloux, Belgium; Univ. of Prague, Czechoslovakia; Catholic Univ. of America; Univ. of Bologna, Italy; Agricl Inst., Mongolia. Accademico Corrispondente, Accademià Nazionale di Agricultura, Bologna, Italy. *Publications:* technical publications on agriculture. *Address:* POB H0210, Baabda, Lebanon.

SAPHIR, Nicholas Peter George; Chairman, Agricultural Forum, since 2001; *b* 30 Nov. 1944; *s* of Emanuel Saphir and Ann (*née* Belikoff); *m* 1971, Ena Bodin; one *s*. *Educ:* City of London Sch.; Manchester Univ. (LLB Hons). Called to the Bar, Lincoln's Inn, 1967. Chm., Hunter Saphir, 1987–97; Director: Bodin & Nielsen Ltd, 1975–; Albert Fisher Gp PLC, 1993–97; non-executive Director: Dairy Crest Ltd, 1987–93; San Miguel SA (Argentina), 1993–98, 2001–. Chm., CCAHC, 1980–83; Founder Chm., Food From Britain, 1983–87; Mem., Food and Drink EDC, 1984–87; Chm., British Israel Chamber of Commerce, 1991–94. Pres., Fresh Produce Consortium, 1997–2000. *Recreations:* farming, carriage driving. *Address:* Heronden, Chart Hill, Chart Sutton, Kent ME17 3EZ. *T:* (01622) 843892, *Fax:* (01622) 844361. *Club:* Farmers.

SAPIN, Michel Marie; Minister for the Civil Service and Administrative Reform, France, since 2000; Mayor, Argenton-sur-Creuse (Indre), since 1995; *b* 9 April 1952; *m* 1982, Yolande Millan; three *s*. *Educ:* Ecole Normale Supérieure de la rue d'Ulm (MA Hist., post-grad. degree Geog.); Institut d'Etudes Politiques de Paris; Ecole Nationale d'Administration. Joined Socialist Party, 1975; National Assembly: Socialist Deputy of the Indre, 1981–86, of Hauts-de-Seine, 1986–91; Sec., 1983–84; Vice-Pres., 1984–85, 1988; Vice-Chm., Socialist Gp, 1987–88; Pres., Commn of Law, 1988–91. Minister-Delegate of Justice, 1991–92; Minister of the Economy and Finance, 1992–93; Mem., Monetary Policy Council, Bank of France, 1994–95. City Cllr, Nanterre, 1989–94; Regl Cllr, Ile de France, 1992–94; Gen. Cllr of the Indre, 1998; Pres., 1998, Vice-Pres., 2000–01, Centre Regl Council. First Vice-Pres., Assoc. of Regions of France, 1998–2000. *Address:* 9 rue Dupertuis, 36200 Argenton-sur-Creuse, France.

SAPPER, Alan Louis Geoffrey; Founder and Chief Executive, Interconnect AV, since 1991; General Secretary, Association of Cinematograph, Television and Allied Technicians, 1969–91; *b* 18 March 1931; *y s* of late Max and Kate Sapper; *m* 1959, Helen Rubens; one *s* one *d*. *Educ:* Upper Latymer Sch.; Univ. of London. Botanist, Royal Botanic Gardens, Kew, 1948–58; Asst Gen. Sec., 1958–64, Dep. Gen. Sec., 1967–69, Assoc. of Cinematograph, Television and Allied Technicians; Gen. Sec., Writers' Guild of Great Britain, 1964–67. Mem. General Council, Trades Union Congress, 1970–84 (Chm., 1982). President: Confedn of Entertainment Unions, 1970–91; Internat. Fedn of Audio-Visual Workers, 1974–94; Sec., Fedn of Film Unions, 1968–91; Treas., Fedn of Broadcasting Unions, 1968–91; Member: British Copyright Council, 1964–74; British Screen Adv. Council, 1985–. Governor: BFI, 1974–94; Nat. Film School, 1980–95; Hammersmith Hosp., 1965–72; Ealing Coll. of Higher Educn, 1976–78. Dir, Ealing Studios, 1994–. Chm., League for Democracy in Greece, 1970–. *Publications:* articles, short stories; stage plays, On Licence, Kith and Kin; TV play, The Return, 1961. *Recreations:* taxonomic botany, hill walking, politics and human nature. *Address:* 3 Boston Gardens, Chiswick, W4 2QJ. *T:* (020) 8742 8313.

SARAMAGO, José; writer; *b* Azinhaga, Portugal, 16 Nov. 1922; *s* of José de Sousa and Maria da Piedade; *m* 1st, 1944, Ilda Reis (marr. diss. 1970; she *d* 1998); one *c*; 2nd, 1998, Pilar de Río. Formerly car mechanic, admin. civil servant, and metal co. worker; with Estúdios Cor until 1971; translator of Colette, Tolstoy, Maupassant, Baudelaire, etc, 1955–81; political commentator and cultural editor, Diário de Lisboa, 1972–75; Asst Ed., Diário de Nóticias, 1975. Nobel Prize for Literature, 1998. *Publications: fiction:* Terra do Pecado, 1947; Manual de Pintura e Caligrafia, 1977 (trans. Manual of Painting and Calligraphy); Objecto Quase (short stories), 1978; Levantado do Chão, 1980; Memorial do Convento, 1982 (trans. Baltasar and Blimunda); O Ano da Morte de Ricardo Reis, 1984 (trans. The Year of the Death of Ricardo Reis); A Jangada de Pedra, 1986 (trans. The Stone Raft); História do Cerco de Lisboa, 1989 (trans. The History of the Siege of Lisbon); O Evangelho Segundo Jesus Cristo, 1991 (trans. The Gospel According to Jesus Christ); Ensaio Sobrea a Cegueira, 1995 (trans. Blindness); Todos os Nomes, 1997 (trans. All the Names); El Amor Posible, 1998; The Tale of the Unknown Island, 1999; *poetry:* Os Poemas Possíveis, 1966; Provavelmente Alegria, 1970; O Ano de 1993, 1975; *plays:* A Noite, 1979; Que Farei com este Livro?, 1980; A Segunda Vida de Francisco de Assisi, 1987; In Nomine Dei, 1993; *essays:* Deste Mundo e do Outro, 1971; A Bagagem do Viajante, 1973; Os Opiniões que o D. L. Teve, 1974; Os Apontamentos, 1976; Viagem a Portugal, 1981; *journals:* Cadernos de Lanzarote, 5 Vols, 1994–. *Address:* Los Topes 3, 35572 Tias, Lanzarote, Canary Islands.

SAREI, Sir Alexis Holyweek, Kt 1987; CBE 1981; PhD; Premier of North Solomons Provincial Government, Papua New Guinea, 1976–80 and 1985–88; *b* 25 March 1934; *s* of late Joseph Nambong and Joanna Mota; *m* 1972, Claire Dionne; three *s* three *d* (all adopted). *Educ:* PNG Primary to Tertiary, 1949–66; Rome Univ., 1968–71 (PhD Canon Law). RC Priest, 1966–72; Secretary to Chief Minister, PNG, 1972–73; District Comr, 1973–75; Advisor to Bougainville people, 1975–76; High Comr in UK, 1980–83. PNG Independence Medal 1977; CBE for work in Provincial Govt, pioneering work in the system in PNG. Successor to his uncle, Gregory Moah, as Chief of Clan, Petisuun. *Publication:* The Practice of Marriage Among the Solos, Buka Island, 1974. *Recreations:* music, sketching, golf, swimming, sports. *Address:* 8039 Adoree Street, Downey, CA 90242, USA.

SARELL, Captain Richard Iwan Alexander, DSO 1939; RN retd; *b* 22 Feb. 1909; *s* of late Philip Charles Sarell; *m* 1961, Mrs Ann Morgan (*née* Keenlyside). *Educ:* Royal Naval Coll., Dartmouth. Entered RNC Dartmouth, 1922; Comdr 1943; Capt. 1948; specialised in Gunnery, 1934; DSO for action against enemy submarines while in command of HMS Broke, 1939; despatches, 1943. Naval Attaché, Moscow and Helsinki, 1949–51; student Imperial Defence Coll., 1952; Defence Research Policy Staff, 1954; retd 1957. *Recreation:* fishing. *Address:* 43 Rivermead Court, Ranelagh Gardens, SW6 3RX.

SARGANT, Naomi Ellen, (Lady McIntosh of Haringey); writer and consultant; *b* 10 Dec. 1933; *d* of late Tom Sargant, OBE, and of Marie Cerny (*née* Hlouskova); *m* 1st, 1954, Peter Joseph Kelly; one *s*; 2nd, 1962, Andrew Robert McIntosh (now Baron McIntosh of Haringey, *qv*); two *s*. *Educ:* Friends' Sch., Saffron Walden, Essex; Bedford Coll., London (BA Hons Sociology). Social Surveys (Gallup Poll) Ltd, 1955–67; Sen. Lectr in Market Res., Enfield Coll. of Technol., 1967–69; Open University: Sen. Lectr in Res. Methods, 1970–75; Reader in Survey Research, 1975–78; Head, Survey Res. Dept, Inst. of Educnl Technol., 1972–81; Pro Vice-Chancellor (Student Affairs), 1974–78; Prof. of Applied Social Research, 1978–81; Sen. Commng Editor for Educnl Programming, Channel 4, 1981–89; Acting Chief Exec., Open Poly., 1990. Vis. Prof. in Higher Educn (part-time), Univ. of Mass, Amherst, 1974–75; Vis. Prof., Open Univ. Quality Support Centre, 1995–. Councillor, and Chm. Children's Cttee, London Bor. of Haringey, 1964–68; Vice-Chm., London Boroughs Trng Cttee (Social Services), 1966–68. Chm., National Gas Consumers' Council, 1977–80. Pres., Nat. Soc. for Clean Air, 1981–83. Member: Council and Exec. Cttee, Social Work Adv. Service, 1966–68; Local Govt Trng Bd, 1967–68; Energy Commn, 1978–79; Commn on Energy and the Environment, 1978–81; Nat. Consumer Council, 1978–81; Adv. Council for Adult and Continuing Educn, 1977–83; Council, Bedford Coll., Univ. of London, 1977–83; Council, Polytechnic of the South Bank, 1982–86; Exec. Cttee, Nat. Inst. of Adult and Continuing Educn, 1986–89, 1992–; Gov., Haringey Coll., 1984–87; Pro-Chancellor, Univ. of E London HEC, 1992–94 (Vice-Chm., Poly. of E London HEC, 1989–92); Gov., NE London Poly., 1987–89. Vice Chm., Film, TV and Video Panel, Arts Council of GB, 1986–90; Vice-Chair: NCVO, 1992–98; Open Coll. of the Arts, 1998–. Chm., Great Ormond Street Hosp. for Children NHS Trust, 1997–2000. Trustee: Nat. Extension Coll., 1975–97; Charities Aid Foundn, 1992– (Vice Chm., Grants Council, 1995–2000). Mem. RTS, 1982–. FRSA 1991. Hon. Fellow RCA, 1988. *Publications:* A Degree of Difference, 1976 (New York 1977); (with A. Woodley) The Door Stood Open, 1980; Learning and 'Leisure', 1991; Learning for a Purpose, 1993; (with A. Tuckett) Pandora's Box, 1997; The Learning Divide, 1997; The Learning Divide Revisited, 2000. *Recreation:* gardening. *Address:* 27 Hurst Avenue, N6 5TX. *T:* (020) 8340 1496, *Fax:* (020) 8348 4641.

SARGEANT, Frank Charles Douglas, CMG 1972; HM Diplomatic Service, retired 1977; *b* 7 Nov. 1917; *s* of late John Sargeant and Anna Sargeant; *m* 1946, Joan Adene Bickerton; one *s* one *d*. *Educ:* Lincoln; St Catharine's Coll., Cambridge. MA Cantab, Natural Sciences. Cadbury Bros. Ltd, 1939. Served War: Army, 1939–46; Lt-Col, Royal Signals. Imperial Chemical Industries Ltd, 1947–48. HM Diplomatic Service: Curacao, 1948; The Hague, 1951; Kuwait, 1954; Foreign Office, 1957 (First Sec. 1958); First Sec., Head of Chancery and Consul, Mogadishu, 1959; First Sec. (Commercial) Stockholm, 1962–66; First Sec., Head of Chancery, Colombo, and Consul for the Maldive Islands, 1967; Counsellor, 1968; Consul-General, Lubumbashi, 1968–70; Dep. High Comr, Dacca, 1970–71; Sen. Officers' War Course, RN Coll., Greenwich, 1971–72; Consul Gen., Lyons, 1972–77 (Doyen of the Consular Corps). *Recreations:* shooting, fishing. *Address:* 2 Impasse de la Vierge, Usclas du Bosc, 34700 Lodève, France.

SARGEANT, Rt Rev. Frank Pilkington; an Hon. Assistant Bishop, Diocese in Europe and Diocese of Manchester, since 1999; *b* 12 Sept. 1932; *s* of John Stanley and Grace Sargeant; *m* 1958, Sally Jeanette McDermott; three *s* two *d*. *Educ:* Boston Grammar School; Durham Univ., St John's Coll. and Cranmer Hall (BA, Dip Theol); Nottingham Univ. (Diploma in Adult Education). National Service Commission, RA (20th Field Regt), 1955–57. Assistant Curate: Gainsborough Parish Church, 1958–62; Grimsby Parish Church, and Priest-in-Charge of St Martin's, Grimsby, 1962–67; Vicar of North Hykeham and Rector of South Hykeham, 1967–73; Residentiary Canon, Bradford Cathedral, 1973–77; Archdeacon of Bradford, 1977–84; Bishop Suffragan of Stockport, 1984–94; head of the Archbishop of Canterbury's staff (with title of Bishop at Lambeth), 1994–99, and Asst Bishop, dio. of Canterbury, 1995–99; retired 1999. President: Retired Clergy Assoc., 2000–; Actors' Church Union, 1995–. *Address:* 32 Brotherton Drive, Trinity Gardens, Salford M3 6BH. *T:* (0161) 839 7045; *e-mail:* franksargeant68@hotmail.com.

SARGENT, Anthony; *see* Sargent, D. A.

SARGENT, Dick; *see* Sargent, J. R.

SARGENT, (Donald) Anthony; General Director, Music Centre Gateshead, since 2000; *b* 18 Dec. 1949; *s* of Sir Donald Sargent, KBE, CB and Mary (*née* Raven); *m* 1st, 1978, Sara Gilford (marr. diss.); 2nd, 1986, Caroline Gant; one *d*. *Educ:* King's Sch., Canterbury; Oriel Coll., Oxford (Open Exhibnr); Magdalen Coll., Oxford (Choral Schol.); Christ Church Coll., Oxford (Choral Schol.; MA Hons PPE). Various prodn and presentation posts, BBC Radio and TV, 1974–86 (Manager, Concert Planning, 1982–86); Artistic Projects Dir, S Bank Centre, London, 1986–89; Hd of Arts, Birmingham CC, 1989–99; Partnerships and Prog. Develt Manager, BBC Music Live, 1999–2000. FRSA 1999. Hon. Fellow, Birmingham Conservatoire, 1999. *Publications:* contrib. miscellaneous periodical and professional articles. *Recreations:* problem solving, fresh air, laughing. *Address:* (home) 6 Winchester Terrace, Summerhill Square, Newcastle upon Tyne NE4 6EH; (office) PO Box 254, Gateshead NE8 1FP.

SARGENT, Prof. John Reid, PhD; FRSE; FIBiol; Professor of Biological Science, University of Stirling, since 1986; Director, Natural Environment Research Council Unit of Aquatic Biochemistry, University of Stirling, 1986–98; *b* 12 Oct. 1936; *s* of Alex and Annie Sargent; *m* 1961, Elizabeth Jean Buchan; two *d. Educ:* Buckie High Sch.; Robert Gordon's Coll., Aberdeen; Aberdeen Univ. (BSc 1st Cl. Hons, PhD). FIBiol 1983; FRSE 1986. Res. Fellow, Middlesex Hosp. Med. Sch., 1961–64; Lectr, Biochem. Dept, Univ. of Aberdeen, 1964–69; PSO, then SPSO, then Dir, NERC Inst. of Marine Biochem., 1970–85; Stirling University: Head of Dept of Biol Science, 1985–89; Head of Sch. of Natural Scis, 1989–93. Bond Gold Medal, Amer. Oil Chemists' Soc., 1971. *Publications:* numerous research pubns in biochem. and marine biol., esp. on marine lipids and polyunsaturated fatty acids. *Recreations:* sailing, ski-ing, golf. *Address:* Institute of Aquaculture, Faculty of Natural Sciences, University of Stirling, Stirling FK9 4LA. *T:* (01786) 473171.

SARGENT, John Richard, (Dick); *b* 22 March 1925; *s* of John Philip Sargent and Ruth (*née* Taunton); *m* 1st, 1949, Anne Elizabeth Haigh (marr. diss. 1980); one *s* two *d*; 2nd, 1980, Hester Mary Campbell. *Educ:* Dragon Sch., Oxford; Rugby Sch.; Christ Church, Oxford (MA). Fellow and Lectr in Econs, Worcester Coll., Oxford, 1951–62; Econ. Consultant, HM Treasury and DEA, 1963–65; Prof. of Econs, Univ. of Warwick, 1965–73 (Pro-Vice-Chancellor, 1971–72), Hon. Prof., 1974–81. Vis. Prof. of Econs, LSE, 1981–82; Gp Economic Adviser, Midland Bank Ltd, 1974–84; Houblon-Norman Res. Fellow, Bank of England, 1984–85. Member: Doctors and Dentists Rev. Body, 1972–75; Armed Forces Pay Rev. Body, 1972–86; Channel Tunnel Adv. Gp, 1974–75; SSRC, 1980–85; Pharmacists Review Panel, 1986–; Pres., Société Universitaire Européenne de Recherches Financières, 1985–88. Editor, Midland Bank Rev., 1974–84. *Publications:* British Transport Policy, 1958; (ed with R. C. O. Matthews) Contemporary Problems of Economic Policy, 1983; articles in various economic jls, and in vols of conf. papers etc. *Recreation:* work. *Address:* Trentham House, Fulbrook, Burford, Oxon OX18 4BL. *T:* (01993) 823525. *Club:* Reform.

SARGENT, Prof. Roger William Herbert, FREng; Courtaulds Professor of Chemical Engineering, Imperial College, 1966–92, now Emeritus; Senior Research Fellow, Imperial College, since 1992; *b* 14 Oct. 1926; *s* of Herbert Alfred Sargent and May Elizabeth (*née* Gill); *m* 1951, Shirley Jane Levesque (*née* Spooner); two *s. Educ:* Bedford Sch.; Imperial Coll., London (FIC 1994). BSc, ACGI, PhD, DScEng, DIC; FIChemE, FIMA; FREng (FEng 1976). Design Engineer, Société l'Air Liquide, Paris, 1951–58; Imperial College: Sen. Lectr, 1958–62; Prof. of Chem. Engrg, 1962–66; Dean, City and Guilds Coll., 1973–76; Head of Dept of Chem. Engrg and Chem. Technology, 1975–88; Dir of Interdisciplinary Res. Centre in Process Systems Engrg, 1989–92. Member: Engrg and Technol. Adv. Cttee, British Council, 1976–89 (Chm., 1984–89); Technol. Subcttee, UGC, 1984–88. Pres., Instn of Chem. Engrs, 1973–74; For. Associate, US Nat. Acad. of Engrg, 1993. FRSA 1988. Hon. FCGI 1977. Dhc: Institut Nat. Polytechnique de Lorraine, 1987; Univ. de Liège, 1996; Hon. DSc Edinburgh, 1993. *Publications:* contribs to: Trans Instn Chem. Engrs, Computers and Chemical Engrg, Jl of Optimization Theory and Applications, SIAM Jl of Optimization, Mathematical Programming, Internat. Jl of Control, etc. *Address:* Mulberry Cottage, 291A Sheen Road, Richmond, Surrey TW10 5AW. *T:* (020) 8876 9623.

SARGENT, Prof. Wallace Leslie William, FRS 1981; Ira S. Bowen Professor of Astronomy, California Institute of Technology, since 1981; *b* 15 Feb. 1935; *s* of Leslie William Sargent and Eleanor (*née* Denniss); *m* 1964, Anneila Isabel Cassells, PhD; two *d. Educ:* Scunthorpe Tech. High Sch. (first pupil to go to univ., 1953); Manchester Univ. (BSc Hons, MSc, PhD). Research Fellow in Astronomy, California Inst. of Tech., 1959–62; Sen. Research Fellow, Royal Greenwich Observatory, 1962–64; Asst Prof. of Physics, Univ. of California, San Diego, 1964–66; California Institute of Technology: Asst Prof. of Astronomy, 1966–68, Associate Prof., 1968–71, Professor, 1971–81; Executive Officer for Astronomy, 1975–81 and 1996–97; Dir, Palomar Observatory, 1997–2000. Lectures: George Darwin, RAS, 1987; Thomas Gold, Cornell Univ., 1995; Sackler Dist., Harvard Univ., 1995; Sackler Prize, Univ. of California, Berkeley, 1996; Henry Norris Russell, AAS, 2001. Fellow, American Acad. of Arts and Sciences, 1977; Associate, RAS, 1998. Warner Prize, American Astronomical Soc., 1968; Dannie Heineman Prize, 1991; Bruce Gold Medal, Astronomical Soc. of the Pacific, 1994. *Publications:* many papers in learned jls. *Recreations:* reading, gardening, mountain walking, watching sports. *Address:* Astronomy Dept 105–24, California Institute of Technology, Pasadena, CA 91125, USA. *T:* (626) 3954055; 400 South Berkeley Avenue, Pasadena, CA 91107, USA. *T:* (626) 7956345. *Club:* Athenæum (Pasadena).

SARGESON, Prof. Alan McLeod, FRS 1983; Professor of Inorganic Chemistry, Australian National University, 1978–95, now Emeritus; *b* 13 Oct. 1930; *s* of late H. L. Sargeson; *m* 1959, Marietta, *d* of F. Anders; two *s* two *d. Educ:* Maitland Boys' High Sch.; Sydney Univ. (BSc, PhD, DipEd). FRACI; FAA. Lectr, Chem. Dept, Univ. of Adelaide, 1956–57; Res. Fellow, John Curtin Sch. of Med. Research, ANU, 1958, Fellow 1960; Sen. Fellow, then Professorial Fellow, 1969–78, Res. Sch. of Chemistry, ANU. For. Mem., Royal Danish Acad. of Science, 1976; For. Hon. Mem., Amer. Acad. of Arts and Sci., 1998; For. Associate, US Nat. Acad. of Science, 1996. DSc *hc* Sydney, 1990; Copenhagen, 1996; Bordeaux, 1997. *Address:* Research School of Chemistry, Australian National University, Canberra, ACT 0200, Australia.

SARGINSON, Edward William; retired from Civil Service, 1976; with Confederation of British Industry until 1982; *b* 22 May 1919; *s* of Frederick William and Edith Sarginson; *m* 1944, Olive Pescod; one *s* one *d. Educ:* Barrow-in-Furness Grammar School. Entered Civil Service, War Office, 1936; served Infantry, 1939–46; Principal, Min. of Supply, 1955; Asst Sec., Min. of Aviation, 1965; Asst Under Sec. of State, MoD (PE), 1972–76. Voluntary work: with Childline, 1987–89; with Victim Support, 1990–91. *Recreations:* gardening, bowls. *Address:* 41 Kendall Avenue South, Sanderstead, Surrey CR2 0QR. *T:* (020) 8660 4476.

SARK, Seigneur of; *see* Beaumont, J. M.

SARKIS, Angela Marie, CBE 2000; Chief Executive, Church Urban Fund, since 1996; *b* 6 Jan. 1955; *d* of Rupert Sadler and Hazel Sadler (*née* McDonald); *m* 1980, Edward Tacvor Sarkis; one *s* one *d. Educ:* Cottesmore Sch., Nottingham; Clarendon Coll. of Further Educn, Nottingham; Leeds Univ. (BA Theol./Sociol.); Leicester Univ. (Dip. Social Work and CQSW). Probation Officer, Middx Probation Service, 1979–89; Unit Manager, Brent Family Services Unit, 1989–91; Asst Dir, Intermediate Treatment Fund, 1991–93; Dir, DIVERT Trust, 1993–96. Advr, Social Exclusion Unit, Cabinet Office, 1997–; Mem., H of L Appts Commn, 2000–. Mem. Council, Howard League for Penal Reform, 1998–. Mem., Housing and Neighbourhood Cttee, Joseph Rowntree Foundn, 1997–. Mem. Council, Evangelical Alliance, 1995–99; Vice-Pres., African and Caribbean Evangelical Alliance, 1996–; Mem., Leadership Team, Brentwater Evangelical Ch, NW2, 1990–94. Mem. Cttee, Assoc. Charitable Foundns, 1995–99; Trustee: BBC Children in Need, 1995–; Inst. Citizenship Studies, 1995–97; Notting Hill Housing Trust, 1995–97. Trustee: Single Homeless Housing Project, NW10, 1980–87; Learie Constantine Youth Club, NW2, 1980–90; Single Mothers Project, NW10, 1984–90; Tavistock Youth Club, NW10, 1985–90. *Recreations:* gardening, family, singing. *Address:* Church Urban Fund, 1 Millbank, SW1P 3JZ. *T:* (020) 7898 1647.

SARMADI, Morteza; Ambassador of the Islamic Republic of Iran to the Court of St James's, since 2000; *b* July 1954; *m* 1982, Fatemeh Hosseini; four *d. Educ:* Sharif Univ. (BS Metallurgy); Tehran Univ. Joined Ministry of Foreign Affairs, Tehran, 1981: Dir Gen., Press and Inf., 1982–89; Deputy Foreign Minister: for Communication, 1989–97; Eur. and American and CIS Countries' Affairs, 1997–2000. Special Rep. to Caspian Sea Legal Regime; Sen. Mem., Delegn for Iran and Iraq Peace Negotiation. Has participated in numerous confs internationally. Trustee Member: Islamic Thought Foundn; Islamic Republic News Agency; Islamic High Council of Propagation Policy; Inst. for Political and Internat. Studies. *Recreations:* reading, watching TV, swimming, spending time with the family. *Address:* Embassy of Iran, 16 Prince's Gate, SW7 1PT.

SAROOP, Narindar, CBE 1982; Director, International Operations, C2 Resolutions Group, since 2000; *b* 14 Aug. 1929; *e s* of Chaudhri Ram Saroop, Ismaila, Rohtak, India and late Shyam Devi; *m* 1st, 1952, Ravi Gill (marr. diss. 1967), *o surv. c* of the Sardar and Sardarni of Premgarh, India; two *d* (one *s* decd); 2nd 1969, Stephanie Denise, *yr d* of Alexander and Cynthia Amie Cronopulo, Zakynthos, Greece. *Educ:* Aitchison Coll. for Punjab Chiefs, Lahore; Indian Military Acad., Dehra Dun. Served as regular officer, 2nd Royal Lancers (Gardner's Horse) and Queen Victoria's Own The Poona Horse; retired, 1954. Management Trainee, Yule Catto, 1954; senior executive and Dir of subsidiaries of various multinationals, to 1976; Hon. Administrator, Oxfam Relief Project, 1964; Director: Devi Grays Insurance Ltd, 1981–84; Capital Plant International Ltd, 1982–86. Adviser: Develt, Clarkson Puckle Gp, 1976–87; Banque Belge, 1987–91; Cancer Relief Macmillan Fund, 1992–95; Nat. Grid plc, 1993; Coutts & Co., 1995–98. Mem., BBC Adv. Council on Asian Programmes, 1977–81. Pres., Indian Welfare Soc., 1983–92. Member Council: Freedom Assoc., 1978–86; Internat. Social Services, 1981–91; Inst. of Directors, 1983–93; Founder Mem., Tory Asians for Representation Gp, 1984–85; Mem. Adv. Council, Efficiency in Local Govt, 1984. Contested (C) Greenwich, 1979 (first Asian Tory Parliamentary candidate this century); Founder and 1st Chm., UK Anglo Asian Cons. Soc., 1976–79, 1985–86; Vice Chm., Cons. Party Internat. Office, 1990–92. Councillor, Kensington and Chelsea, 1974–82; initiated Borough Community Relations Cttee (Chm., 1975–77, 1980–82); Chm., Working Party on Employment, 1978; Founder and Chm., Durbar Club, 1981–. Mem., V & A Mus. Appeal Cttee, 1994–95. Hon. Mem., Clan Moncreiffe, 2000. *Publications:* In Defence of Freedom (jtly), 1978; A Squire of Hindoostan, 1983. *Recreations:* keeping fools, boredom and socialism at bay. *Address:* 25 de Vere Gardens, W8 5AN. *Clubs:* Beefsteak, Cavalry and Guards, Pratt's; Puffin's (Edinburgh); Imperial Delhi Gymkhana; Royal Bombay Yacht, Royal Calcutta Golf.

SARWAR, Mohammad; MP (Lab) Glasgow Govan, since 1997; *b* 18 Aug. 1952; *s* of Mohammed and Rashida Abdullah Sarwar; *m* 1976, Perveen Sarwar; three *s* one *d. Educ:* Univ. of Faisalabad (FSC; BA). Shopkeeper, 1976–83; Dir, United Wholesale Ltd, 1983–97. Member (Lab): Glasgow DC, 1992–96; Glasgow CC, 1995–97. First ethnic minority MP in Scotland; first Muslim MP in Britain. *Recreation:* relaxing with family and friends. *Address:* House of Commons, SW1A 0AA. *T:* (020) 7219 3000; (constituency) 247 Paisley Road West, Glasgow G51 1NE. *T:* (0141) 427 5250, *Fax:* (0141) 427 5938; *e-mail:* sarwar@sarwar.org.uk.

SASKATCHEWAN, Bishop of, since 1993; **Rt Rev. Anthony John Burton;** *b* 11 Aug. 1959; *s* of Peter Michael Burton and Rachel Wood Greaves; *m* 1989, Anna Kristine Erickson; one *s* one *d. Educ:* Trinity Coll., Toronto Univ. (BA (Hons) 1982); King's Coll., Dalhousie Univ.; Wycliffe Hall, Oxford (BA, MA). Ordained deacon, 1987, priest, 1988; Curate, St John the Baptist, N Sydney, Nova Scotia, 1987–88; Rector, Trinity Church, Sydney Mines, 1988–91; Rector and Canon Residentiary, Cathedral Church of St Alban the Martyr, Saskatchewan, 1991–93; Dean of Saskatchewan, 1991–94. Hon. DD King's Coll., Halifax, 1994. *Publications:* (contrib.) Anglican Essentials: reclaiming faith in the Anglican Church of Canada, 1995; contrib. to Machray Rev. *Recreations:* walking, tyrannizing the clergy. *Address:* Synod Office, 1308 Fifth Avenue East, Prince Albert, SK S6V 2H7, Canada. *T:* (306) 7632455, *Fax:* (306) 7645172.

SASKATOON, Archbishop of, since 2000; **Most Rev. Thomas Oliver Morgan;** Metropolitan of the Ecclesiastical Province of Rupert's Land, since 2000; *b* 20 Jan. 1941; *s* of Charles Edwin Morgan and Amy Amelia (*née* Hoyes); *m* 1963, Lillian Marie (*née* Textor); two *s* one *d. Educ:* Univ. of Saskatchewan (BA 1962); King's College, London (BD 1965); Tyndale Hall, Bristol (GOE 1966). Curate, Church of the Saviour, Blackburn, Lancs, 1966–69; Rector: Porcupine Plain, Sask, Canada, 1969–73; Kinistino, 1973–77; Shellbrook, 1977–83; Archdeacon of Indian Missions, Saskatchewan, 1983–85; Bishop of Saskatchewan, 1985–93; Bishop of Saskatoon, 1993–. Hon. DD Coll. of Emmanuel and St Chad, Saskatoon, 1986. *Address:* PO Box 1965, Saskatoon, SK S7K 3S5, Canada.

SASSOON, Prof. Donald, PhD; Professor of Comparative European History, Queen Mary, University of London, since 1997; *b* 25 Nov. 1946; *s* of Joseph Isaac Sassoon and Doris Sassoon (*née* Bardak); *m* 1973, Anne Showstack (marr. diss. 1987); one *d. Educ:* schools in Paris, Milan and Tunbridge Wells; University Coll. London (BSc Econ 1969); Pennsylvania State Univ. (MA 1971); Birkbeck Coll., Univ. of London (PhD 1977). Lectr in Hist., 1979–89, Reader in Hist., 1989–97, Westfield Coll., then QMW, Univ. of London. Nuffield Social Sci. Fellow, 1997–98; Vis. Prof., Univ. of Trento, 1999; Leverhulme Maj. Res. Fellow, 2000–; Sen. Res. Fellow, New York Univ., 2001. Literary Ed., Political Qly, 2000–. *Publications:* The Strategy of the Italian Communist Party, 1981; Contemporary Italy: politics, economy and society since 1945, 1986, 2nd edn 1997; One Hundred Years of Socialism: the West European Left in the Twentieth Century, 1996 (Deutscher Meml Prize 1997); Mona Lisa: the history of the world's most famous painting, 2001; contribs to jls. *Recreations:* travel, classical music, country walking. *Address:* Department of History, Queen Mary, University of London, Mile End Road, E1 4NS; *e-mail:* d.sassoon@qmw.ac.uk.

SATCHELL, Keith; Group Chief Executive, Friends Provident plc (formerly Friends Provident Life Office), since 1997; *b* 3 June 1951; *s* of Dennis Joseph Satchell and Joan Betty Satchell; *m* 1972, Hazel Burston; two *s* one *d. Educ:* Univ. of Aston (BSc). FIA 1976. With Duncan C. Fraser, 1972–75; UK Provident, 1975–86 (latterly as Marketing Man.); Friends Provident, 1986–: Gen. Manager, 1987–97; Dir, 1992 . *Recreations:* soccer, golf, ski-ing, theatre.

SATCHWELL, Sir Kevin Joseph, Kt 2001; Headmaster, Thomas Telford School, since 1991; *b* 6 March 1951; *e s* of late Joseph Satchwell and of Pauline Satchwell; *m* 1975, Maria Bernadette Grimes; one *s* one *d. Educ:* Wodensborough High Sch.; Wednesbury Boys' High Sch.; Shoreditch Coll. of Technology (Cert Ed London Univ. 1973); Open Univ. (BA 1977; AdvDip Educn Mgt 1978). Teacher, Cantril High Sch., Liverpool, 1973–79; Dep. Head, Brookefield Sch., Liverpool, 1979–87; Headteacher, Moseley Park Sch., Wolverhampton, 1987–90. Member: NCET, 1994–96; City Technology Colls Principals' Forum, 1991– (Chm., 1997); Chm., W Midlands Consortium for School Centred Initial

Teacher Trng, 1993–. *Recreations:* family, squash, junior football coaching. *Address:* Thomas Telford School, Old Park, Telford TF3 4NW. *T:* (01952) 200000.

SATOW, Rear-Adm. Derek Graham, CB 1977; *b* 13 June 1923; *y s* of late Graham F. H. Satow, OBE, and Evelyn M. Satow (*née* Moore); *m* 1944, Patricia E. A. Penaliggon; two *d. Educ:* Oakley Hall Sch.; Haileybury Coll.; Royal Naval Engineering Coll. CEng, FIMechE, FIMarE. HMS Ceylon, 1945–46; RNC, Greenwich, 1946–48; HMS Duke of York, 1948–49; RAE Farnborough, 1949–51; HMS Newcastle, 1951–53 (despatches, 1953); Naval Ordnance and Weapons Dept, Admiralty, 1953–59; Dir of Engineering, RNEC, 1959–62; HMS Tiger, 1962–64; Asst and Dep. Dir of Marine Engineering, MoD, 1964–67; IDC, 1968; Captain, RNEC, 1969–71; Dir, Naval Officer Appointments (Eng), MoD, 1971–73; Chief Staff Officer, Technical, later Engineering, to C-in-C Fleet, 1974–76; Dep. Dir-Gen., Ships, MoD, 1976–79; Chief Naval Engr Officer, 1977–79. Comdr, 1955; Captain, 1964; Rear-Adm., 1973.

SATTERTHWAITE, Rt Rev. John Richard, CMG 1991; Bishop of Gibraltar in Europe, 1980–93; an Assistant Bishop, diocese of Carlisle, since 1994; *b* 17 Nov. 1925; *s* of William and Clara Elisabeth Satterthwaite. *Educ:* Millom Grammar Sch.; Leeds Univ. (BA); Coll. of the Resurrection, Mirfield. History Master, St Luke's Sch., Haifa, 1946–48; Curate: St Barnabas, Carlisle, 1950–53; St Aidan, Carlisle, 1953–54; St Michael Paternoster Royal, London, 1955–59, Curate-in-Charge, 1959–65; Guild Vicar, St Dunstan-in-the-West, City of London, 1959–70. Gen. Sec., Church of England Council on Foreign Relations, 1959–70 (Asst Gen. Sec., 1955–59); Gen. Sec., Archbp's Commn on Roman Catholic Relations, 1965–70; Bishop Suffragan of Fulham, 1970; Bishop of Gibraltar, 1970; known as Bishop of Fulham and Gibraltar until creation of new diocese, 1980. Hon. Canon of Canterbury, 1963–71; ChStJ 1972 (Asst ChStJ 1963); Hon. Canon of Utrecht, Old Catholic Church of the Netherlands, 1969. Holds decoration from various foreign churches. *Recreations:* fell walking, music. *Address:* 25 Spencer House, St Paul's Square, Carlisle, Cumbria CA1 1DG. *T:* (01228) 594055. *Club:* Athenæum.

SAUER, Fernand Edmond; Director for Public Health Policy, Directorate General for Health and Consumer Protection, European Commission, since 2000; *b* 14 Dec. 1947; *s* of Ferdinand Sauer and Emilie Scherer Sauer; *m* 1971, Pamela Sheppard; one *s* two *d. Educ:* Univ. of Strasbourg (pharmacist, 1971); Paris II Univ. (Masters in European Law, 1977). Hosp. Pharmacist, Reunion Island, 1972–73; Pharmaceutical Insp., Health Min., France, 1974–79; European Commission: Adminr, 1979–85; Head of Pharmaceuticals, 1986–94; Exec. Dir, Eur. Agency for the Evaluation of Medicinal Products, 1994–2000. Mem., Faculty of Pharmacy, London Univ., 1996–. Hon. Fellow, RPSGB, 1996. Chevalier de l'Ordre du Mérite (France), 1990; Chevalier de la Légion d'Honneur (France), 1998. *Publications:* various articles and publications on pharmaceutical regulation. *Recreation:* jogging. *Address:* (office) Bâtiment Jean Monnet, Rue Alcide de Gasperi, 2920 Luxembourg.

SAUGMAN, Per Gotfred, Hon. OBE 1990; Knight of the Order of Dannebrog; Chairman, Blackwell Scientific Publications Ltd, Oxford, 1972–92 (Managing Director, 1954–87); *b* 26 June 1925; *s* of Emanuel A. G. Saugman and Esther (*née* Lehmann); *m* 1950, Patricia (*née* Fulford); two *s* one *d* (and one *s* decd). *Educ:* Gentofte Grammar Sch.; Commercial Coll., Copenhagen. Bookselling and publishing training in Denmark, Switzerland and England, 1941–49; Sales Manager, Blackwell Scientific Publications Ltd, 1952; Director, University Bookshops (Oxford) Ltd, 1963–92; Mem. Board, B. H. Blackwell Ltd, 1964–92; Chairman: William George's Sons Ltd, Bristol, 1965–92; Oxford Illustrators Ltd, 1968–; Blackwell North America, Inc., 1975–92; Ejnar Munksgaard Publishers Ltd, Copenhagen, 1967–92; Kooyker Boekhandel Leiden, 1973–92; Oxford Shutter Co. Ltd, 1994–98. Member Council: International Publishers' Assoc., 1976–79; Publishers' Assoc. of GB and Ireland, 1977–82; President, Internat. Group of Scientific, Technical and Medical Publishers, 1977–79. Chairman: Oxford Round Table, 1953–55; Sunningwell Sch. of Art, 1972–. Chm. Trustees, City of Oxford Orch., 2000. Hon. Mem., British Ecological Soc., 1960–; Governor: Oxford Polytechnic, 1972–85; Dragon Sch., Oxford, 1975–2000; Headington Sch., Oxford, 1988–. Fellow, St Cross Coll., Oxford, 1978; Hon. MA Oxford, 1978; Hon. Fellow, Green Coll., Oxford, 1981. Chevalier, Order of Icelandic Falcon, 1984. *Publications:* From the First Fifty Years, 1989, 2nd edn 1992; The Way I Think it Was (autobiog.), 1992; Ejnar Munksgaard: a biography, 1992, 2nd edn 1997; The Way it Was (autobiog.), 1994. *Recreations:* reading, art—English watercolours, golf. *Address:* Hollen House, Buckland, Faringdon, Oxon SN7 8QN. *T:* (01367) 870570, *Fax:* (01367) 870590. *Clubs:* Athenæum, Royal Automobile; Frilford Golf (Oxford).

SAUL, Hon. David John; JP; PhD; financial consultant; President, Fidelity International Bermuda Ltd, 1984–99, retired; Premier of Bermuda, 1995–97; *b* 27 Nov. 1939; *s* of late John Saul and Sarah Saul; *m* 1963, Christine Hall; one *s* one *d. Educ:* Queen's Univ., Canada (BA); Univ. of Toronto (MEd, PhD); Nottingham Univ. (CertEd); Loughborough Univ. of Tech. (DipEd). Perm. Sec. for Educn, 1972–76, Financial Sec., 1976–81, Bermuda Govt; Chief Admin Officer, Edmund Gibbons Ltd, 1982–84; MP (United Bermuda Party) Devonshire South, 1989–97; Minister of Finance, Bermuda, 1989–95. Pres., Fidelity Internat. Ltd, 1984–95; Exec. Vice Pres., Fidelity Investments, Worldwide, 1990–95; Director: Fidelity Internat. Ltd, 1984–; Lombard Odier (Bermuda) Ltd, 1995–. Director: Bermuda Monetary Authority, 1987–89, 1998–99; Bermuda Track and Field Assoc., 1987–; London Steamship Owners Mutual Assoc., 1989–. Trustee, Bermuda Underwater Exploration Inst., 1992–99 (Life Trustee, 1999). *Recreations:* running, scuba, fishing, kayaking, stalking, collecting Bermuda stamps, Bermuda currency notes, and sea shells. *Address:* Rocky Ledge, 18 Devonshire Bay Road, Devonshire DV 07, Bermuda. *T:* 2365087. *Clubs:* Explorers' (New York); Mid Ocean, Royal Hamilton Amateur Dinghy (Bermuda).

SAUL, Roger John; Chairman and Chief Executive, Mulberry Co., since 1971; *b* 25 July 1950; *s* of Michael and Joan Saul; *m* 1977, Monty Cameron; three *s. Educ:* Kingswood Sch., Bath; Westminster Coll., London. Founded Mulberry Co., 1971 (Queen's Award to Industry for Export, 1979, 1989 and 1996); launched Mulberry at Home, 1991; opened Charlton House Hotel and Mulberry Restaurant, 1997. Chm., London Designer Collections, 1976–80. Mem., RHS. Classic Designer of Year, British Fashion Council, 1992. *Publication:* Mulberry at Home, 1992. *Recreations:* gardening, tennis, ski-ing, historic car racing (Mem., Vintage Sports Car Club), 6m yacht racing. *Address:* Mulberry Co. (Design) Ltd, Kilver Court, Shepton Mallet, Somerset BA4 5NF. *Club:* Mark's.

SAUL, Prof. (Samuel) Berrick, CBE 1992; PhD; Executive Chairman, Universities and Colleges Admissions Service, 1993–97; Vice Chancellor, University of York, 1979–93; *b* 20 Oct. 1924; *s* of Ernest Saul and Maud Eaton; *m* 1953, Sheila Stenton; one *s* one *d. Educ:* West Bromwich Grammar Sch.; Birmingham Univ. (BCom 1949, PhD 1953). National Service, 1944–47 (Lieut Sherwood Foresters). Lectr in Econ. History, Liverpool Univ., 1951–63; Edinburgh University: Prof. of Econ. History, 1963–78; Dean, Faculty of Social Sciences, 1970–75; Vice Principal, 1975–77; Actg Principal, 1978. Rockefeller Fellow, Univ. of Calif (Berkeley), and Columbia Univ., 1959; Ford Fellow, Stanford Univ., 1969–70. Vis. Prof., Harvard Univ., 1973. Chairman: Central Council for Educn and Trng in Social Work, 1986–93; Standing Conf. on Univ. Entrance, 1986–93; Vice-Chm., Commonwealth Scholarship Commn, 1993–2000. Hon. LLD York, Toronto, 1981; Hon. Dr *hc* Edinburgh, 1986; DUniv York, 1994. *Publications:* Studies in British Overseas Trade 1870–1914, 1960; The Myth of the Great Depression, 1969; Technological Change: the US and Britain in the 19th Century, 1970; (with A. S. Milward) The Economic Development of Continental Europe 1780–1870, 1973; (with A. S. Milward) The Development of the Economies of Continental Europe 1850–1914, 1977. *Recreations:* fell walking, travel, music. *Address:* 39 Drome Road, Copmanthorpe, York YO23 3TG. *T:* (01904) 701011.

SAULL, Rear-Adm. (Keith) Michael, CB 1982; FCIT; Chairman, New Zealand Ports Authority, 1984–88; *b* 24 Aug. 1927; *s* of Harold Vincent Saull and Margaret Saull; *m* 1952, Linfield Mabel (*née* Barnsdale); two *s* one *d. Educ:* Altrincham Grammar Sch.; HMS Conway. Royal Navy, 1945–50; transferred to Royal New Zealand Navy, 1951; commanded HMNZ Ships: Kaniere, Taranaki, Canterbury, 1956–71; Naval Attaché, Washington DC, 1972–75; RCDS 1976; Commodore, Auckland, 1978; Chief of Naval Staff, RNZN, 1980–83. Vice Patron, Royal NZ Coastguard Fedn, 1987–2000. *Recreations:* golf, fishing, sailing.

SAULTER, Paul Reginald; Managing Director, Heritage of Industry (formerly Cornwall of Mine) Ltd, since 1989; *b* 27 Aug. 1935; *s* of Alfred Walter Saulter and Mabel Elizabeth Oliver. *Educ:* Truro Sch.; University Coll., Oxford. MA. Admin. Asst, Nat. Council of Social Service, 1960–63; Sen. Asst and Principal, CEGB, 1963–65; Dep. Head, Overseas Div., BEAMA, 1965–69; Dir, Internat. Affairs, ABCC, 1969–73; Sec.-Gen., British Chamber of Commerce in France, 1973–81; Chief Executive: Manchester Chamber of Commerce and Industry, 1981–85; Assoc. of Exhibn Organisers, 1985–86; Administrator, St Paul's, Knightsbridge, 1987–95. Mgt consultant, 1986–89; Exhibn Advr, London Chamber of Commerce, 1986–88. Secretary: For. Trade Working Gp, ORGALIME, 1967–69; Council of British Chambers of Commerce in Continental Europe, 1977–80; Member: Export Promotion Cttee, CBI, 1983–86; Bd, Eur. Fedn of Assocs of Industrial and Technical Heritage, 1999–. Member: RHS; Trevithick Soc., 1986–; Assoc. for Industrial Archaeology; Newcomen Soc., 1995– (Mem. Council, 1995–98, 1999–Oct. 2002). *Recreations:* walking, music, theatre, researching Cornish mining history, industrial archaeology. *Address:* Rye, Sussex.

SAUMAREZ, family name of **Baron de Saumarez**.

SAUMAREZ SMITH, Dr Charles Robert, FSA; Director, National Portrait Gallery, since 1994; *b* 28 May 1954; *s* of late William Hanbury Saumarez Smith, OBE and of Alice Elizabeth Harness Saumarez Smith (*née* Raven); *m* 1979, Romilly Le Quesne Savage; two *s. Educ:* Marlborough Coll.; King's Coll., Cambridge (BA 1st cl. History of Art 1976; MA 1978); Henry Fellow, Harvard, 1977; Warburg Inst. (PhD 1986). FSA 1997. Christie's Res. Fellow in Applied Arts, Christ's Coll., Cambridge, 1979–82; Asst Keeper with resp. for V&A/RCA MA course in history of design, 1982–90, Head of Res., 1990–94, V & A. Vis. Fellow, Yale Center for British Art, 1983; Benno Forman Fellow, Winterthur Mus., 1988; South Square Fellow, RCA, 1990. Member, Executive Committee: Design History Soc., 1985–89; Soc. of Architectural Historians, 1987–90; Assoc. of Art Historians, 1990–94; London Library, 1992–96; Member, Advisory Council: Paul Mellon Centre for British Studies, 1995–; Warburg Inst., 1997–; Inst. of Historical Research, 1999–; Mem. Council, Museums Assoc., 1998–. Trustee: Soane Monuments Trust, 1988–; Charleston, 1993–. FRSA 1995. Hon. Fellow, RCA, 1991; Hon. FRIBA 2000. Hon. DLitt UEA, 2001. *Publications:* The Building of Castle Howard, 1990 (Alice Davis Hitchcock Medallion); Eighteenth Century Decoration, 1993; The National Portrait Gallery, 1997. *Address:* National Portrait Gallery, St Martin's Place, WC2H 0HE. *T:* (020) 7312 2400, *Fax:* (020) 7306 0064; *e-mail:* csaumarezsmith@npg.org.uk.

SAUNDERS, Albert Edward, CMG 1975; OBE 1970; HM Diplomatic Service, retired; Ambassador to the United Republic of Cameroon and the Republic of Equatorial Guinea, 1975–79; *b* 5 June 1919; *s* of late Albert Edward and Marie Marguerite Saunders; *m* 1945, Dorothea Charlotte Mary Whittle (*d* 1985); one *s* one *d. Educ:* yes. Westminster Bank Ltd, 1937. Royal Navy, 1942–45: last appt, Asst Chief Port Security Officer, Middle East. Apptd to British Embassy, Cairo, 1938 and 1945; Asst Information Officer, Tripoli, 1949; Asst Admin. Officer, Athens, 1951; Middle East Centre for Arabic Studies, 1952; Third Sec., Office of UK Trade Comr, Khartoum, 1953; Third Sec. (Information), Beirut, 1954; POMEF, Cyprus, 1956; FO, 1957; Second Sec. (Oriental), Baghdad, 1958; FO, 1959; Vice-Consul, Casablanca, 1963; Second Sec. (Oriental), Rabat, 1963; Consul, Jerusalem, 1964; First Sec., FO, 1967; Chancery, Baghdad, 1968; Head of Chancery and Consul, Rabat, 1969; Counsellor and Consul General in charge British Embassy, Dubai, 1972; Chargé d'Affaires, Abu Dhabi, 1972 and 1973; RN War Coll., Greenwich, 1974, sowc, 1975. *Recreation:* iconoclasm (20th Century). *Address:* 3 Deanhill Road, SW14 7DQ.

SAUNDERS, Andrew Downing; *b* 22 Sept. 1931; *s* of Lionel Edward Saunders; *m* 1st, 1961, Hilary Jean (*née* Aikman) (marr. diss. 1980); two *s* one *d*; 2nd, 1985, Gillian Ruth Hutchinson; one *d. Educ:* Magdalen Coll. Sch., Oxford; Magdalen Coll., Oxford (MA). FSA, FRHistS, FSAScot, MIFA. Joined Ancient Monuments Inspectorate, 1954; Inspector of Ancient Monuments for England, 1964; Chief Inspector of Ancient Monuments and Historic Buildings, DoE, subseq. English Heritage, 1973–89. Pres., Royal Archaeol Inst., 1993–96; Vice-Pres., Hendon and Dist Archaeol Soc.; Chm., Fortress Study Gp, 1995–2001; Member: Internat. Fortress Council; Exec. Cttee, Council for British Archaeology; Scientific Council, Europa Nostra/Internat. Castles Inst. Chm. Adv. Panel, Defence of Britain Project, Council for British Archaeology, 1996–. Hon. Res. Fellow, Exeter Univ., 2000–01. Editor, Fortress: the Castles and Fortifications Qly, 1989–94. *Publications:* ed jtly and contrib., Ancient Monuments and their Interpretation, 1977; Fortress Britain, 1989; Devon and Cornwall, 1991; Channel Defences, 1997; excavation reports on various Roman and Medieval sites and monuments, papers on castles and artillery fortification in various archæological and historical jls; guidebooks to ancient monuments. *Recreations:* opera, sailing. *Address:* The Crest, The Hill, Cranbrook, Kent TN17 3AH. *Club:* Athenæum.

SAUNDERS, Andrew William, CB 1998; Director, Communications-Electronics Security Group, 1991–98; *b* 26 Oct. 1940; *s* of late Joseph and of Winifred Saunders; *m* 1964, Josephine Sharkey; one *s* two *d. Educ:* Wolverhampton Grammar Sch.; Christ Church, Oxford (MA). Joined Civil Service, GCHQ, 1963: Principal, 1968; Asst Sec., 1978; Counsellor, Washington, 1983–86 (on secondment); Under Sec., 1991. *Recreations:* earthly pleasures and practicalities, especially narrow-boating. *Address:* c/o Barclays Bank PLC, 128 High Street, Cheltenham, Glos GL50 1EL.

SAUNDERS, Christopher John, MA; Headmaster, Lancing College, 1993–98; *b* 7 May 1940; *s* of R. H. Saunders and G. S. Saunders (*née* Harris); *m* 1973, Cynthia Elizabeth Stiles; one *s* one *d. Educ:* Lancing Coll.; Fitzwilliam Coll., Cambridge (MA); PGCE Wadham Coll., Oxford. Assistant Master, Bradfield College, 1964–80 (Housemaster, 1972–80); Headmaster, Eastbourne Coll., 1981–93. Mem. Council, FA. *Recreations:* music, bridge, theatre, gardening, soccer (Oxford Blue 1963), cricket (Oxford Blue 1964), golf, people. *Address:* Folly Bottom, Scottalls Lane, Hampstead Norreys, Thatcham, Berks RG18 0RT. *T:* (01635) 200222. *Clubs:* MCC; Hawks (Cambridge).

SAUNDERS, Dame Cicely (Mary Strode), OM 1989 DBE 1980 (OBE 1967); FRCP, FRCS; Chairman, St Christopher's Hospice, since 1985 (Medical Director, 1967–85); *b* 22 June 1918; *d* of Gordon Saunders and Mary Christian Knight; *m* 1980, Prof. Marian Bohusz-Szyszko (*d* 1995), *s* of Antoni Bohusz-Szyszko, Wilno, Poland. *Educ:* Roedean Sch.; St Anne's Coll., Oxford (Hon. Fellow, 1987); St Thomas's Hosp. Med. Sch.; Nightingale Sch. of Nursing. SRN 1944; MB, BS, 1957; MA 1960 (BA (war degree) 1945). FRCP 1974 (MRCP 1968); FRCN 1981; FRCS 1986. Founded St Christopher's Hospice, 1967 (St Christopher's has been a Registered Charity since 1961 and was opened as a Hospice in 1967). Mem., MRC, 1976–79; Dep. Chm., Attendance Allowance Bd, 1979–85. Hon. Consultant, St Thomas' Hosp., 1985. AIMSW 1947. Freedom of London Boroughs: Bromley, 1987; Lewisham, 2000. Hon. FRCPsych 1988; Hon. Fellow: Sheffield City Polytechnic, 1983; Newnham Coll., Cambridge, 1986; Guy's and St Thomas' Med. Schs (UMDS), 1993; Liverpool John Moores, 1998; Middlesex Univ., 2000. Hon. DSc: Yale, 1969; London, 1983; Glasgow, 1990; Durham, 1995; McGill, 1997; Dr of Medicine, Lambeth, 1977; Hon. MD Belfast, 1984; DUniv: Open, 1978; Middlesex, 2000; Hon. LLD: Columbia, NY, 1979; Leicester, 1983; DHL Jewish Theological Seminary of America, 1982; DU Essex, 1983; Hon. DCL: Canterbury, 1984; Cambridge, 1986; Oxford, 1986; Hon. Dr Med. TCD, 1988. Gold Medal, Soc. of Apothecaries of London, 1979; Gold Medal, BMA, 1987; Templeton Foundation Prize, 1981; Conrad N. Hilton Humanitarian Prize, 2001. DSG 1996. *Publications:* Care of the Dying, 1960, 2nd edn 1977; (ed) The Management of Terminal Disease, 1978, 3rd edn 1993; (ed jtly) Hospice: the living idea, 1981; Living with Dying, 1983, 2nd edn 1989; (ed) St Christopher's in Celebration, 1988; Beyond the Horizon, 1990; (ed) Hospice and Palliative Care, 1990; various papers on terminal care. *Recreations:* theology, ethics, classical music. *Address:* St Christopher's Hospice, 51–59 Lawrie Park Road, Sydenham, SE26 6DZ. *T:* (020) 8778 9252.

SAUNDERS, Air Vice-Marshal David John, CBE 1986; FIMechE; FRAeS; FILog; Vice President, Airinmar Ltd, since 1999; *b* 12 June 1943; *s* of John Saunders and Nina Saunders (*née* Mabberley); *m* 1966, Elizabeth Jane Cairns; one *s* one *d. Educ:* Commonweal Grammar Sch.; RAF College; Cranfield Inst. of Technology. BSc, MSc; CEng, FRAeS 1993; FILog 1997. Joined RAF 1961; management appts, 1966–85; Station Comdr, RAF Sealand, 1983; ADC to HM the Queen, 1984–86; Command Mechanical Engineer, HQ RAF Germany, 1986; Dir of Engineering Policy (RAF), MoD, 1989–91; ACDS (Logistics), 1991–93; Hd of RAF Mobility Study, 1993; AO Engrg and Supply, 1993–97. *Recreations:* hill walking, cross country ski-ing, off-road cycling, fishing. *Address:* St John's Coach House, St John's Street, Lechlade, Glos GL7 3AT. *Club:* Royal Air Force.

SAUNDERS, David John; Regional Director, Government Office for the South East, since 1998; *b* 4 Aug. 1953; *s* of James and Margaret Saunders; *m* 1975, Elizabeth Jean Hodgson; two *s* two *d. Educ:* Royal Grammar Sch., Guildford; Kingston Poly. (BSc Chemistry and Business Studies); Aston Univ. (PhD Applied Business Studies 1978). Joined DTI, 1978; Private Sec. to Sec. of State, 1981–82, to Parly Under Sec. of State, 1982–84; seconded to OFT, 1984–87; British Steel privatisation, 1987–88; Export Promotion, 1988–95; Sec., BOTB, 1990–95; Director: Nuclear Power Privatisation Team, 1995–96; Oil and Gas Directorate, 1996–98. *Recreations:* swimming, cycling, surfing, cinema, keeping track of my teenage children. *Address:* (office) Bridge House, 1 Walnut Tree Close, Guildford, Surrey GU1 4GA. *T:* (01483) 882260.

SAUNDERS, David Martin St George; HM Diplomatic Service, retired; *b* 23 July 1930; *s* of late Hilary St George Saunders and Helen (*née* Foley); *m* 1960, Patricia, *d* of James Methold, CBE; one *s* one *d. Educ:* Marlborough Coll.; RMA Sandhurst; Staff Coll., Quetta, Pakistan. Commnd Welsh Guards, 1950; Staff Captain Egypt, 1954–56; Asst Adjt, RMA Sandhurst, 1956–58; Adjt 1st Bn Welsh Guards, 1958–60; GSO III War Office, 1960–62; sc 1962–63; Company Comdr 1st Bn Welsh Guards, 1964; GSO II British Defence Liaison Staff, Canberra, 1965–67; Guards Depot, Pirbright, 1967–68; joined Foreign Service, 1968; Consul (Economic), Johannesburg, 1970–73; First Secretary: FCO, 1973–74; Dakar, 1974–76; FCO, 1976–77; Pretoria, 1977–79; The Hague, 1979–83; Counsellor, FCO, 1983–90. *Recreations:* military history, shooting, cinema, bridge, the wines of Burgundy. *Address:* 18 Garfield Road, SW11 5PN.

SAUNDERS, David William, CB 1989; Counsel to the Chairman of Committees, House of Lords, since 1999; *b* 4 Nov. 1936; *s* of William Ernest Saunders and Lilian Grace (*née* Ward); *m* 1963, Margaret Susan Rose Bartholomew. *Educ:* Hornchurch Grammar Sch.; Worcester Coll., Oxford (MA). Admitted solicitor, 1964. Joined Office of Parly Counsel, 1970; Dep. Parly Counsel, 1978–80; Parly Counsel, 1980–94 and 1996–99; Second Parly Counsel, 1994–96; with Law Commn, 1972–74, 1986–87. *Recreations:* flying, golf, bridge. *Address:* Highfields, High Wych, Sawbridgeworth, Herts CM21 0HX. *T:* (01279) 724736. *Club:* Oxford and Cambridge.

SAUNDERS, Prof. Derek William, CBE 1986; Professor of Polymer Physics and Engineering, Cranfield Institute of Technology, 1967–87, retired 1988, Emeritus Professor, since 1989; Director, Science and Engineering Research Council/Department of Industry Teaching Company Scheme, 1981–88; *b* 4 Dec. 1925; *s* of Alfred and Elizabeth Hannah Saunders; *m* 1949, Mahalah Harrison; three *s* two *d. Educ:* Morley Grammar Sch.; Imperial Coll., Univ. of London. PhD, ARCS, FInstP, FIM, CEng, CPhys. Building Res. Stn, Garston, 1945–47; British Rubber Producers Res. Assoc., 1947–51; Royal Instn, 1951–54; British Rayon Res. Assoc., 1954–60; Cranfield Inst. of Technology: Sen. Lectr 1960, subseq. Reader; Head of Materials Dept, 1969–81; Pro-Vice-Chancellor, 1973–76. Chm. Council, Plastics Inst., 1973–75; Chm. Council, 1975–76, Pres., 1983–85 and 1990–91, Plastics and Rubber Inst.; Vice-Pres., Inst. of Materials, 1992–94. Mem. Harpur Trust (Bedford Charity), 1968–88. Hon. DTech CNAA, 1990. *Publications:* chapters in several books on polymeric materials; sci. papers in various learned jls. *Address:* 98 Topcliffe Road, Thirsk, N Yorks YO7 1RY. *T:* (01845) 523344.

SAUNDERS, Ernest Walter, MA; President, Stambridge Management (formerly Associates), since 1992; *b* 21 Oct. 1935; *m* 1963, Carole Ann Stephings; two *s* one *d. Educ:* Emmanuel Coll., Cambridge (MA). Man. Dir, Beecham Products Internat., and Dir, Beecham Products, 1966–73; Chm., European Div., Great Universal Stores, 1973–77; Pres., Nestlé Nutrition SA, and Mem. Worldwide Management Cttee, Nestlé SA, Vevey, Switzerland, 1977–81; Chm., Beechnut Corp., USA, 1977–81; Chief Exec., 1981–87, Chm., 1986–87, Arthur Guinness & Sons plc, later Guinness PLC; Chairman: Arthur Guinness Son & Co. (Great Britain), 1982–87; Guinness Brewing Worldwide, 1982–87. Dir, Brewers' Soc., 1983. Dir, Queens Park Rangers Football & Athletic Club, 1983. *Recreations:* skiing, tennis, football.

SAUNDERS, James; playwright; *b* Islington, 8 Jan. 1925; *s* of Walter Percival Saunders and Dorcas Geraldine (*née* Warren); *m* 1951, Audrey Cross; *s* two *d. Educ:* Wembley County Sch.; Southampton Univ. *Plays:* Moonshine, 1955; Alas, Poor Fred, The Ark, 1959; Committal, Barnstable, Return to a City, 1960; A Slight Accident, 1961; Double Double, 1962; Next Time I'll Sing to You (Evening Standard Drama Award), The Pedagogue, Who Was Hilary Maconochie?, 1963; A Scent of Flowers, Neighbours, 1964; Triangle, Opus, 1965; A Man's Best Friend, The Borage Pigeon Affair, 1969; After Liverpool, 1970; Games, Savoury Meringue, 1971; Hans Kohlhaas, 1972; Bye Bye Blues, 1973; The Island, 1975; Bodies, 1977; Birdsong, 1979; Fall, 1981; Emperor Waltz, 1983; Scandella, 1985; Menocchio, 1985 (BBC Radio Play Award, 1986); Making it Better, 1992; Retreat, 1995; Lancelot, 2000; *stage adaptations:* The Italian Girl, 1968; The Travails of Sancho Panza, 1969; A Journey to London, 1973; Player Piano, 1978; Random Moments in a May Garden, 1980; The Girl in Melanie Klein, 1980; *television:* Watch Me I'm a Bird, 1964; Bloomers, 1979 (series); television adaptations of works by D. H. Lawrence, Henry James, H. E. Bates and R. F. Delderfield; *screenplays:* Sailor's Return; The Captain's Doll. Arts Council of GB Drama Bursary, 1960; Writers' Guild TV Adaptation Award, 1966; Arts Council Major Bursary, 1984. *Address:* c/o Casarotto Ramsay Ltd, 60–66 Wardour Street, W1V 3HP.

SAUNDERS, Jennifer; actress, writer; *b* 6 July 1958; *m* Adrian Edmondson; three *d. Educ:* Central Sch. of Speech and Drama. *Theatre:* An Evening with French and Saunders (nat. tour), 1989; Me and Mamie O'Rourke, Strand, 1993; French and Saunders Live – 2000, Apollo Hammersmith, 2000; *television:* Ab Fab The Last Shout, 1996; Mirrorball, 2000; *series:* The Comic Strip Presents…, 1982–90; Girls on Top, 1985–87; French and Saunders (5 series); Absolutely Fabulous, 1993, 1994, 1995 (Emmy Award, 1993) and 2001; Let Them Eat Cake, 1999; *films:* The Supergrass, 1984; Muppet Treasure Island, 1996; In the Bleak Midwinter, 1996; Maybe Baby, 2000. *Publications:* (with Dawn French) A Feast of French and Saunders, 1992; Absolutely Fabulous: the scripts, 1993; Absolutely Fabulous: Continuity, 2001. *Address:* c/o Peters, Fraser & Dunlop, Drury House, 34-43 Russell Street, WC2B 5HA.

SAUNDERS, Sir John (Anthony Holt), Kt 1972; CBE 1970; DSO 1945; MC 1944; Chairman, Hongkong and Shanghai Banking Corporation, 1962–72; *b* 29 July 1917; *m* 1942, Enid Mary Durant Cassidy (*d* 1996); two *d. Educ:* Bromsgrove Sch. War Service, 1940–45; OCTU Sandhurst (Belt of Honour); N Africa, Sicily and Italy. Lived in Hong Kong 1950–72; MEC Hong Kong Govt, 1966–72. Chm. of Stewards, Royal Hong Kong Jockey Club, 1967–72.

SAUNDERS, John Henry Boulton; QC 1991; a Recorder, since 1990; *b* 15 March 1949; *s* of Kathleen Mary Saunders and Henry G. B. Saunders; *m* 1975, Susan Mary Chick; one *s* two *d. Educ:* Uppingham School; Magdalen College, Oxford (BA). Called to the Bar, Gray's Inn, 1972. *Recreations:* music, sailing. *Address:* 4 Fountain Court, Steelhouse Lane, Birmingham B4 6DR. *T:* (0121) 236 3476.

SAUNDERS, Prof. Kenneth Barrett, MD, DSc; FRCP; Professor of Medicine, St George's Hospital Medical School, 1980–95, now Emeritus; *b* 16 March 1936; *s* of Harold N. Saunders and Winifred F. Saunders (*née* Gadge); *m* 1961, Philippa Mary Harrison; one *s* one *d. Educ:* Kingswood Sch., Bath; Trinity Hall, Cambridge (MA 1966; MD 1966); St Thomas's Hosp. Med. Sch.; DSc London 1995. FRCP 1978. Sen. Lectr, then Reader in Medicine, Middx Hosp. Med. Sch., 1972–80; Dean, Fac. of Medicine, London Univ., 1990–94. Member: GMC, 1992–95; Jt Planning and Adv. Cttee, 1990–94; Jt Cttee on Higher Med. Trng, 1990–94. Hon. Consultant Physician to the Army, 1994–97. Chm., Assoc. of Clinical Profs of Medicine, 1993–95. Royal College of Physicians: Tudor Edwards Lectr, 1987; Procensor, 1986–87; Censor, 1987–88. Member: Governing Body, BPMF, 1990–96; Council, Sch. of Pharmacy, London Univ., 1990–96. Hon. Treas., Hellenic Soc., 1998–. *Publications:* Clinical Physiology of the Lung, 1977; various papers on respiratory science and medicine. *Recreations:* English and classical literature (especially Homer), squash rackets, golf. *Address:* 77 Lee Road, Blackheath, SE3 9EN. *T:* (020) 8852 8138. *Clubs:* Royal Automobile, Academy; Royal Blackheath Golf.

SAUNDERS, Kenneth Herbert; Chief Architect, Commission for the New Towns, 1976–82, retired; *b* 5 April 1915; *s* of William James Saunders and Anne Elizabeth Baker; *m* 1940, Kathleen Bettye Fortune (*d* 1981); one *s* one *d. Educ:* elementary sch., Worthing; Sch. of Art, Worthing; Brighton Coll. of Art. ARIBA 1940. Served War: RA Iraq and Persia; OCTU Bengal Sappers and Miners, India and Burma; Major RE ALFSEA, SORE II, 1940 (mentioned in despatches). Articled pupil, 1933; Dept of Architecture, Bor. of Worthing, 1936; City Architect's Dept, Portsmouth, 1937–39, 1946–49; Crawley Develt Corporation: Architect, 1949; Sen. Architect, 1952; Asst Chief Architect, 1958; Commission for New Towns: Asst Chief Architect, 1962; Exec. Architect, 1965; Manager (Crawley), 1978–80. *Recreations:* architecture, buildings. *Address:* Longthorpe, 22 Goffs Park Road, Crawley, West Sussex RH11 8AY. *T:* (01293) 521334.

SAUNDERS, Matthew John, MBE 1998; FSA; Secretary, Ancient Monuments Society, since 1977; *b* 12 April 1953; *s* of John William Saunders and Joyce Mary Saunders. *Educ:* Latymer Sch., Edmonton; Corpus Christi Coll., Cambridge (MA Hist. and Hist. of Architecture 1974). FSA 1980. Editorial Asst, Whitaker's Almanack, 1975; Sec., SAVE Britain's Heritage, 1976–77; Asst Sec., Ancient Monuments Soc., 1976. Sec., Jt Cttee of Nat. Amenity Socs, 1982–; Hon. Dir, Friends of Friendless Churches, 1993–; Trustee, Historic Chapels Trust, 1993–95; Member: Historic Bldgs and Land Cttee, Heritage Lottery Fund, 1999– (Mem., Places of Worship Adv. Cttee, 1995–98); Fabric Adv. Cttee, St Paul's Cathedral, 2001. Vice President: Ecclesiological Soc., 1994–; Men of the Stones, 2000; Enfield Preservation Soc., 1999. IHBC 1998. *Publications:* (contrib.) Railway Architecture, 1979; (contrib.) The Architectural Outsiders, 1985; The Historic Home Owner's Companion, 1987; (contrib.) Concerning Buildings, 1996. *Recreations:* music, travel, photography, good food. *Address:* (office) St Ann's Vestry Hall, 2 Church Entry, EC4V 5HB. *T:* (020) 7236 3934.

SAUNDERS, Sir Peter, Kt 1982; Chairman and Managing Director, Peter Saunders Group Ltd; Director: West End Theatre Managers Ltd; Theatre Investment Fund Ltd; Theatre Investment Finance Ltd; *b* 23 Nov. 1911; *s* of Ernest and Aletta Saunders; *m* 1st, 1959, Ann Stewart (*d* 1976); no *c*; 2nd, 1979, Catherine Baylis (*née* Imperiali dei Principi di Francavilla) (Katie Boyle); no *c. Educ:* Oundle Sch.; Lausanne. Film cameraman, film director, journalist and press agent; served War of 1939–45 (Captain); started in theatrical production, 1947; has presented over 100 plays incl. The Mousetrap, which has run since 1952 (became world's longest ever run, Dec. 1971, he produced it from 1952 until 1994 when he gave up active theatrical production); other West End productions include: Fly Away Peter; The Perfect Woman; Breach of Marriage; My Mother Said; The Hollow; Witness for the Prosecution; The Manor of Northstead; Spider's Web; The Water Gipsies; The Bride and the Bachelor; Subway in the Sky; Verdict; The Trial of Mary Dugan; The Unexpected Guest; A Day in the Life Of; And Suddenly it's Spring; Go Back For Murder; You Prove It; Fit To Print; Rule of Three; Alfie; The Reluctant Peer; Hostile Witness; Every Other Evening; Return Ticket; Arsenic and Old Lace; Justice Is A Woman; As You Like It; Oh Clarence!; On A Foggy Day; The Jockey Club Stakes; Move Over Mrs Markham; Lover; Cockie; Double Edge; A Murder is Announced; The Family Reunion; Cards On The Table; in 1971 acquired Volcano Productions Ltd., whose productions include No Sex Please, We're British; The Mating Game; Lloyd George Knew My Father;

At The End Of The Day; Touch Of Spring; Betzi; operated repertory at Royal Artillery Theatre, Woolwich, 1951, and at Prince of Wales Theatre, Cardiff, 1956; in 1958, took over a long lease of the Ambassadors Theatre; bought the Duchess Theatre, 1961, and sold it in 1968; held a long lease of the St Martin's Theatre, 1968–94; bought the Vaudeville Theatre, 1969, and sold it in 1983; bought the Duke of York's Theatre, 1976 and sold it in 1979 to Capital Radio on condition that it remained a live theatre in perpetuity; has produced more than 1500 programmes for Radio Luxembourg; an original Dir, Yorkshire Television; Mem. consortium awarded London Gen. Radio Station by IBA, which became Capital Radio, 1973. Life Pres., Theatre Investment Fund, 1995; Vice-President: Actors' Benevolent Fund, 1972–; Royal General Theatrical Fund Assoc., 1985–; Mem. Bd, SOLT (formerly Mem. Exec. Council, SWET), 1954– (Pres. 1961–62 and 1967–69; Vice Pres., 1988–93; Hon. Vice Pres., 1999); Mem. Council, Theatrical Management Assoc., 1958–64; Pres., Stage Golfing Soc., 1963; Pres., Stage Cricket Club, 1956–65. Life Mem., Dogs Home Battersea Assoc., 1988. Governor, Christ's Hosp. Silver Heart award, Variety Club of GB, 1955. *Publications:* The Mousetrap Man (autobiog.), 1972; Scales of Justice (play), 1978. *Recreations:* cricket, chess, bridge, photography, music of George Gershwin, telephoning, collecting wills. *Address:* Monkswell, Canons Close, The Bishops Avenue, N2 0BH. *Club:* MCC.

SAUNDERS, Peter Gordon; media consultant, since 1991; *b* 1 July 1940; *s* of late Gordon and of Winifred Saunders; *m* 1964, Teresa Geraldine Metcalf; two *d. Educ:* Newport High Sch. for Boys, Gwent; London Sch. of Econs and Pol Science (BScEcon 1961). Reporter, Gloucestershire Echo, 1961–63; Sports Reporter, Sunderland Echo, 1963–64; Sub-Editor: Yorkshire Post, 1964; The Birmingham Post, 1964–69; Lectr in Journalism, Cardiff Coll. of Commerce, 1969–70; The Birmingham Post, 1971–90: successively Dep. Chief Sub-Editor, Chief Sub-Editor, Asst Editor, Exec. Editor; Editor, 1986–90. *Recreations:* Rugby Union, reading, rhythm and blues, golf. *Address:* Well Cottage, West Street, Kingham, Oxon OX7 6YQ. *T:* and *Fax:* (01608) 659010; *e-mail:* petersaund@aol.com.

SAUNDERS, Raymond; Secretary, British Museum (Natural History), 1976–87; *b* 24 July 1933; *s* of late Herbert Charles Saunders and Doris May (*née* Kirkham-Jones); *m* 1959, Shirley Marion (*née* Stringer); two *s. Educ:* Poole Grammar Sch. WO, 1950; Air Min., 1956; Min. of Land and Natural Resources, 1966; Land Commn, 1967; Treasury, 1968; CSD, 1969. *Recreations:* reading biographies, gardening, sport (now as spectator). *Address:* High Trees, 24 Landguard Manor Road, Shanklin, Isle of Wight PO37 7HZ.

SAUNDERS, Richard; Partnership Consultant, Christ's Hospital, 1993–96; *b* 4 July 1937; *s* of late Edward E. Saunders and Betty Saunders; *m* 1st, 1961, Suzannah Rhodes-Cooke (marr. diss.); one *s*; 2nd, 1970, Alison Fiddes. *Educ:* St Edmund's Sch., Hindhead; Uppingham. FRICS 1965. National Service, commnd The Life Guards, 1958–60. Jun. Partner, Richard Ellis, Chartered Surveyors, 1966–69; formed Richard Saunders & Partners, 1969; Baker Harris Saunders, 1977; Chm., Baker Harris Saunders Group, 1986–92; Director: Herring Baker Harris, 1992–93; (non-exec.) Herring Baker Harris Gp, 1992–93. Chm., City Br., RICS, 1979–80; Pres., Associated Owners of City Properties, 1985–87; Member: Council, British Property Fedn, 1974–90 (Hon. Treas., 1974–85); Bd, Gen. Practice Finance Corp., 1984–89. Chairman: Barbican Residential Cttee, 1979–81; Barbican Centre Cttee, 1983–86; Metropolitan Public Gardens Assoc., 1984–90; Governor: Bridewell Royal Hosp. and King Edward's Sch., Witley, 1976–93; St Edmund's Sch., Hindhead, 1979–93 (Chm., 1979–87); (also Almoner), Christ's Hosp., 1980–93; Royal Star and Garter Home, 1984–. Mem., Court of Common Council, Corp. of London, 1975–2000; Deputy for Ward of Candlewick, 1983–2000; Liveryman: Clothworkers Co., 1960– (Warden, 1989; Master, 2001–July 2002); Co. of Chartered Surveyors, 1979–93; Church Warden, St Lawrence Jewry-by-Guildhall, 1984–; Sheriff, City of London, 1987–88. *Recreations:* instant gardening, music, golf, tennis. *Address:* 13 Caroline Place, W2 4AW. *T:* (020) 7727 1637; The Old Rectory, Bagendon, Cirencester, Glos GL7 7DU. *Clubs:* City Livery, Cavalry and Guards, MCC.

SAUNDERS, Prof. Wilfred Leonard, CBE 1982; FLA; Director, University of Sheffield Postgraduate School of Librarianship and Information Science, 1963–82, now Professor Emeritus; *b* 18 April 1920; *s* of Leonard and Annie Saunders; *m* 1946, Joan Mary Rider, *er d* of late Major W. E. Rider; two *s. Educ:* King Edward's Grammar Sch. for Boys, Camp Hill, Birmingham; Fitzwilliam House, Univ. of Cambridge (MA). FLA 1952. Served War: France, 1940; N Africa, 1942–43; Italy, 1943–46; Captain Royal Signals. Library Asst, Birmingham Reference Library, 1936–39; Dep. Lib., Inst. of Bankers, 1948–49; Lib., Univ. of Birmingham Inst. of Educn, 1949–56; Dep. Lib., Univ. of Sheffield, 1956–63; 12 months' secondment to UNESCO as Expert in Educnl Documentation, Uganda, 1962; Univ. of Sheffield: Prof. of Librarianship and Inf. Science, 1968; Dean, Faculty of Educnl Studies, 1974–77. Visiting Professor: Pittsburgh Univ. Grad. Sch. of Library and Inf. Sciences, 1968; UCLA, 1985; Commonwealth Vis. Fellow, Australia, 1969; (1st) Elsie O. and Philip Sang Internat. Lectr, Rosary Grad. Sch. of Library Science, USA, 1974. UK Rep., Internat. Fedn for Documentation/Training of Documentalists Cttee, 1966–70; Hon. Consultant, E Africa Sch. of Librarianship, Makerere Univ., 1967–73; numerous overseas consultancy and adv. missions. Mem. Council, Library Assoc., 1979–83 (Pres. 1980); Member: Council, ASLIB, 1965–71, 1972–78; British Council, 1970 (Mem., Libraries Adv. Panel, 1970–87, Chm. 1975–81); Bd of Librarianship, CNAA, 1966–79; Library Adv. Council (England), 1970–73; Adv. Cttee, British Library Ref. Div., 1975–80; *ad hoc* Cttee on Educn and Trng (Gen. Inf. Prog.), UNESCO, 1978–85; Adv. Cttee, British Library R&D Dept, 1980–88; British Library Adv. Council, 1981–84; Adv. Council on Public Records, 1986–91; Chairman: Jt Consultative Cttee of Library Assoc., Aslib, SCONUL, Soc. of Archivists and IInfSc, 1980–81; Library and Information Services Council (formerly Library Adv. Council for Eng.), 1981–84. Hon. FIInfSc 1977; Hon. FCP 1983. Hon. LittD Sheffield, 1989. *Publications:* (ed) The Provision and Use of Library and Documentation Services, 1966; (ed) Librarianship in Britain Today, 1967; (with H. Schur and Lisbeth J. Pargeter) Education and Training for Scientific and Technological Library and Information Work, 1968; (ed) University and Research Library Studies, 1968; (with W. J. Hutchins and Lisbeth J. Pargeter) The Language Barrier: a study in depth of the place of foreign language materials in the research activity of an academic community, 1971; (ed) British Librarianship Today, 1977; (with E. M. Broome) The Library and Information Services of the British Council, 1977; Guidelines for Curriculum Development in Information Studies, 1978; Professional Education for Library and Information Work in the Socialist Republic of Macedonia, 1982; Post-graduate Training for Information Specialists (Venezuela), 1984; An Evaluation of Education for Librarianship in New Zealand, 1987; Towards a Unified Professional Organization for Library and Information Science and Services, 1989; Dunkirk Diary of a Very Young Soldier (autobiog.), 1989; jl articles and res. reports. *Recreations:* gardening, walking, listening to music, book collecting. *Address:* 30 Endcliffe Glen Road, Sheffield S11 8RW.

SAUNDERS WATSON, Comdr (Leslie) Michael (Macdonald), CBE 1993; RN (retired); DL; Chairman: British Library Board, 1990–93; Kettering General Hospital NHS Trust, 1993–99; *b* 9 Oct. 1934; *s* of Captain L. S. Saunders, DSO, RN (retd), and Elizabeth Saunders (*née* Culme-Seymour); *m* 1958, Georgina Elizabeth Laetitia, *d* of Adm. Sir William Davis, GCB, DSO; two *s* one *d. Educ:* Eton; BRNC, Dartmouth. Joined Royal Navy, 1951; specialised in Communications (Jackson Everett Prize); Comdr 1969; retired, 1971, on succession to Rockingham Castle Estate. Pres., Historic Houses Assoc., 1982–88 (Dep. Pres., 1978–82; Chm., Tax and Parly Cttee, 1975–82); Chairman: Northamptonshire Assoc. Youth Clubs, 1977–91 (Pres., 1997–); Heritage Educn Year, 1977; Corby Community Adv. Gp, 1979–86; Ironstone Royalty Owners Assoc., 1979–91; Nat. Curriculum History Wkg Gp, 1988–90; Heritage Educn Trust, 1988–99; Modern Records Centre Adv. Cttee, Warwick Univ., 1993–98; Public Affairs Cttee, ICOMOS UK, 1994–98; Friends of British Library, 1994—2000; Vice-Chm., Northamptonshire Small Industries Cttee, 1974–79; Member: British Heritage Cttee, BTA, 1978–88; Northamptonshire Enterprise Agency, 1986–90; Country Landowners' Association: Member: Taxation Cttee, 1975–90; Exec. Cttee, 1977–82, 1987–92; Legal and Land Use Cttee, 1982–87; F and GP Cttee, 1994–98; Chairman: Northamptonshire Branch, 1981–84; Game Fair Local Cttee, 1997. Director: Lamport Hall Preservation Trust, 1978–91; English Sinfonia, 1981–2000. Trustee: Royal Botanic Gdns, Kew, 1983–91 (Chm., Bldgs and Design Cttee, 1985–91); Nat. Heritage Meml Fund, 1987–96. Chm., Governors Lodge Park Comprehensive Sch., 1977–82; Trustee, Oakham Sch., 1975–77. FSA 2001; FRSA 1986. High Sheriff, 1978–79, DL 1979–, Northamptonshire. Hon. DLitt: Warwick, 1991; Leicester, 1997. *Recreations:* sailing, music, gardening. *Address:* The Manor House, Ashley Road, Stoke Albany, Market Harborough, Leicestershire LE16 8PL. *Club:* Brooks's (Manager, 1994–99).

SAUVAGNARGUES, Jean Victor, Commander, Légion d'Honneur, Croix de Guerre avec palme (1939–45); Hon. GCMG 1976; Commander of the National Order of Merit; French Ambassador; former Foreign Minister; *b* Paris, 2 April 1915; *s* of Edmond Sauvagnargues and Alice Caplan; *m* 1948, Lise Marie L'Evesque; two *s* two *d. Educ:* Higher Normal Sch.; Dip., Political Science Sch.; Univ. (German) (Agrégé). Attaché, Embassy, Bucharest, 1941. Served War with Free French Forces, 1943 (Army, June 1944–May 1945). Cabinet of: the High Commn, Beirut, 1943; M Massigli, 1944; Gen. de Gaulle, 1945–46; Specialist on German questions, Quai d'Orsay, 1947–55; Cabinet of M Pinay, 1955. In negotiations about the Saar, Jan.-June 1956; Ambassador to Ethiopia, 1956–60; Director, African and Middle-Eastern Affairs, Min. of Foreign Affairs, 1960–62; Ambassador to: Tunisia, 1962–70; the Federal Republic of Germany, Bonn, 1970–74; Minister for Foreign Affairs, France, 1974–76; Ambassadeur de France, 1976; Ambassador to UK, 1977–81. *Address:* 14 avenue Pierre 1er de Serbie, 75116 Paris, France.

SAUVAIN, Stephen John; QC 1995; *b* 3 June 1949; *s* of Alan Sauvain and Norah Sauvain; *m* 1980, Christine McLean; two *s*, and one step *s. Educ:* King Edward VII Grammar Sch., King's Lynn; Sidney Sussex Coll., Cambridge (MA, LLB). Lectr in Law, Univ. of Manchester, 1971–78; called to the Bar, Lincoln's Inn, 1977; in practice as barrister, 1978–. *Publications:* Highway Law, 1988, 2nd edn 1997; (ed) Encyclopedia of Highway Law and Practice. *Address:* 40 King Street, Manchester M2 6BA. *T:* (0161) 832 9082.

SAVAGE, Caroline Le Quesne; *see* Lucas, C.

SAVAGE, Sir Ernest (Walter), Kt 1979; FCA; company director, retired; *b* 24 Aug. 1912; *s* of Walter Edwin Savage and Constance Mary Sutton; *m* 1938, Dorothy Winifred Nicholls; one *s* one *d. Educ:* Brisbane Grammar School; Scots Coll., Warwick, Qld. In public practice as chartered accountant, 1940–76; retd as Sen. Partner of Coopers & Lybrand, Queensland. Chairman, Bank of Queensland, 1960–84; Director of several other public companies, retired. Institute of Chartered Accountants in Australia: Mem. Queensland State Council, 1951–74 (Chm. three years); Nat. Council, 1961–73; Aust. Pres., 1968–70; elected Life Member, 1978. Hon. Consul for Norway at Brisbane, 1950–76. Chairman: Queensland Govt Cttee of Review of Business Regulations, 1985–86; Public Sector Review Cttee, 1987. Member: Bd of Governors, Cromwell Univ. Coll., 1950–77 (Chm. 1958–67); Faculty of Commerce and Economics, Univ. of Queensland, 1960–67; Bd of Advanced Education, 1978–82 (Finance Cttee, 1974–83); Salvation Army Adv. Bd, 1981–92. Trustee, Leukaemia Foundn, 1983–; Chm., Geriatric Medical Foundn, 1986–94. Knight 1st class, Order of St Olav (Norway), 1966. *Recreation:* brick and concrete work. *Address:* Forest Place, R42/35b Blunder Road, Durack, Qld 4077, Australia. *T:* (7) 33722669. *Clubs:* Queensland, Brisbane (Brisbane).

SAVAGE, Francis Joseph, CMG 1996; LVO 1986; OBE 1989; HM Diplomatic Service; Governor, British Virgin Islands, since 1998; *b* Preston, Lancs, 8 Feb. 1943; *s* of Francis Fitzgerald Savage and late Mona May Savage (*née* Parsons); *m* 1966, Veronica Mary McAleenan; two *s. Educ:* Holy Cross Convent, Broadstairs; St Stephen's Sch., Welling, Kent; NW Kent Coll., Dartford. Joined FO, 1961; served in: Cairo, 1967–70; Washington, 1971–73; Vice-Consul, Aden, 1973–74; FCO, 1974–78; Vice-Consul, then Consul (Commercial), Düsseldorf, 1978–82; Consul, Peking, 1982–86; First Sec. (Consular), Lagos, and Consul for Benin, 1987–90; First Sec., FCO, 1990–93; Counsellor, 1993; Governor of Montserrat, 1993–97. Member: Catenian Assoc., 1991–; Montserrat Nat. Trust, 1993–97; Montserrat Cricket Assoc., 1993–97. *Recreations:* cricket, volcano watching, hurricane dodging, travel, golf, meeting people. *Address:* c/o Foreign and Commonwealth Office, SW1A 2AH. *Clubs:* Royal Over-Seas League, Royal Commonwealth Society; Kent CC; Peking Cricket.

SAVAGE, Prof. (Richard) Nigel, PhD; Chief Executive, College of Law of England and Wales, since 1996; *b* 27 May 1950; *s* of Jack and Joan Savage; *m* 1976, Linda Jane Sherwin; two *s. Educ:* Edward Cludd Sch., Southwell; Newark Tech. Coll.; Manchester Poly. (BA 1st cl. 1972); Univ. of Sheffield (LLM 1974); Univ. of Strathclyde (PhD 1980). Lectr, Univ. of Strathclyde, 1974–83; Principal Lectr, Nottingham Poly., 1983–85; Prof., 1985–96, and Dean and Founding Man. Dir, 1989–96, Nottingham Law Sch. *Publications:* Business Law, 1987, 2nd edn (with R. Bradgate) 1993; (with R. Bradgate) Commercial Law, 1991; articles in business and legal jls. *Recreation:* cricket. *Address:* Station House, Station Lane, Farnsfield, Notts NG22 8LB. *T:* (01623) 882412. *Club:* Reform.

SAVAGE, Thomas Hixon, CBE 1990; Chairman: North American Trust Co., 1992–95; A. G. Simpson Automotive Inc.; *b* Belfast, 21 Nov. 1928; *s* of Thomas Hixon Savage and Martha Foy Turkington; *m* 1st, 1950, Annie Gloria Ethel Gilmore (marr. diss. 1975); one *s* two *d*; 2nd, 1976, Evelyn Phyllis Chapman. *Educ:* Belfast High Sch.; Indian Army Officers' Trng Coll.; Univ. of Toronto Dept of Extension (Indust. Management). Chm., ITT Canada, 1990–93; Chm., Abbey Life Insurance Co., Canada; formerly Chief Industrial Engineer: Union Carbide; Dunlop Canada; W. J. Gage Co.; Hallmark Greeting Cards; Electric Reduction Co.; Director: Acklands; Samuel Manu-Tech; Mem. Adv. Bd, Accenture (formerly Andersen Consulting). Former Mem., Policy Cttee, Business Council on Nat. Issues; Business Co-Chm., Canadian Labour Market & Productivity Center, 1990. Dir, Nat. Retinitis Pigmentosa Eye Res. Foundn, Canada; Chairman: Bd of Govs, West Park Hosp., 1991–94; Adv. Bd, Canadian Inst. of Management, 1971 (Life Mem.); Adv. Bd, Boys' and Girls' Clubs of Canada; NI Partnership in Canada. *Recreation:* golf. *Address:* c/o Hixon-Savage and Associates, 41 Abilene Drive, Etobicoke, ON M9A 2N1, Canada. *Clubs:* Ontario (Toronto); Lambton Golf and Country (Islington).

SAVAGE, (Thomas) William, CMG 1993; HM Diplomatic Service, retired; Counsellor, Foreign and Commonwealth Office, 1984–93; *b* Knockloughrim, Co. Derry, 21 Nov. 1937; *s* of late Hugh Murray Savage and Anna Mary Savage (*née* Whyte); *m* 1966, Gloria Jean Matthews; three *d*. *Educ:* Sullivan Upper Sch., Holywood, Co. Down; Queen's Univ., Belfast (BA (Hons), DipEd); LSE. Vice-Pres. and Sec., 1961–64, Pres., 1964–66, Nat. Union of Students; journalist, ITN, 1967; joined Diplomatic Service, 1968; Dar es Salaam, 1970–73; First Sec., FCO, 1973; Counsellor, on loan to Cabinet Office, 1981. *Recreations:* amateur drama, golf, topiary. *Club:* Tanganyika Golfing Society.

SAVAGE, Wendy Diane, FRCOG; Senior Lecturer in Obstetrics and Gynaecology, St Bartholomew's and the Royal London School of Medicine and Dentistry, Queen Mary and Westfield College (formerly London Hospital Medical College), University of London, 1977–2000; *b* 12 April 1935; *d* of William George Edwards and Anne (*née* Smith); *m* 1960, Miguel Babatunde Richard Savage (marr. diss. 1973); two *s* two *d*. *Educ:* Croydon High School for Girls; Girton Coll., Cambridge (BA); London Hosp. Med. Coll. (MB BCh); MSc (Public Health), LSHTM, 1997. MRCOG 1971, FRCOG 1985. Res. Fellow, Harvard Univ., 1963–64; MO, Nigeria, 1964–67; Registrar: Surgery and Obst. and Gynaec., Kenya, 1967–69; Obst. and Gynaec., Royal Free Hosp., 1969–71; venereology, abortion work, family planning, Islington, 1971–73; Specialist in obst. and gynaec., family planning and venereology, Gisborne, NZ 1973–76; Lectr, London Hosp., 1976–77. Hon. Vis. Prof., Middx Univ., 1991–. Contract as Hon. Cons. suspended for alleged incompetence, April 1985 — reinstated by unanimous vote of DHA after exoneration by HM61/112 Enquiry, July 1986. Mem., GMC, 1989–94, 1995–. *Publications:* Hysterectomy, 1982; (with Fran Reader) Coping with Caesarean Section and other difficult births, 1983; A Savage Enquiry — who controls childbirth?, 1986; (jtly) Caesarean Birth in Britain, 1993; papers on abortion, sexually transmitted disease, ultrasound, sex in pregnancy, cervical cytology, medical education. *Recreations:* playing piano duets, reading. *Address:* 19 Vincent Terrace, N1. *T:* and *Fax:* (020) 7837 7635; *e-mail:* w.savage@qmw.ac.uk.

SAVAGE, William; *see* Savage, T. W.

SAVARESE, Signora Fernando; *see* Elvin, Violetta.

SAVERNAKE, Viscount; Thomas James Brudenell-Bruce; *b* 11 Feb. 1982; *s* and *heir* of Earl of Cardigan, *qv*. *Educ:* Radley Coll. *Address:* Savernake Lodge, Savernake Forest, Marlborough, Wilts SN8 3HP.

SAVIDGE, Malcolm Kemp; MP (Lab) Aberdeen North, since 1997; *b* 9 May 1946; *s* of late David Gordon Madgwick Savidge and Jean Kirkpatrick Savidge (*née* Kemp). *Educ:* Wallington County Grammar Sch., Surrey; Aberdeen Univ. (MA); Aberdeen Coll. of Educn (Teaching Cert.). Production Control and Computer Asst, Bryans Electronics Ltd, 1970–71; Teacher: Greenwood Dale Secondary Sch., Nottingham, 1971; Peterhead Acad., 1972–73; Teacher of Maths, Kincorth Acad., Aberdeen, 1973–97. Mem. (Lab) Aberdeen City Council, 1980–96 (Dep. Leader, 1994–96). Contested (Lab) Kincardine and Deeside, Nov. 1991 and 1992. Governor: Robert Gordon's Inst. of Technol., 1980–88; Aberdeen Coll. of Educn, 1980–87. Hon. Fellow, Robert Gordon Univ., 1997. *Recreation:* exploring "life, the Universe and everything". *Address:* House of Commons, SW1A 0AA; 13F Belmont Road, Aberdeen AB25 3SR.

SAVILE, family name of **Earl of Mexborough**.

SAVILE, 3rd Baron *cr* 1888; **George Halifax Lumley-Savile;** DL; JP; *b* 24 Jan. 1919; *s* of 2nd Baron Savile, KCVO and Esme Grace Virginia (*d* 1958), *d* of J. Wolton; *S* father, 1931. *Educ:* Eton. Served in 1939–45 War in Duke of Wellington's Regiment, and attached Lincolnshire Regiment during the Burma Campaigns. DL W Yorks, 1954. Is Patron of two livings. Owns about 18,000 acres. JP Borough of Dewsbury, 1955. CStJ 1982. *Recreations:* music and shooting. *Heir: nephew* John Anthony Thornhill Lumley-Savile, *b* 10 Jan. 1947. *Address:* Gryce Hall, Shelley, Huddersfield HD8 8LP. *T:* (01484) 602774; Walshaw, Hebden Bridge, Yorks HX7 7AX. *T:* (01422) 842275. *Clubs:* Brooks's, Sloane.

SAVILE, Sir James (Wilson Vincent), Kt 1990; OBE 1971; TV and radio personality; *b* 31 Oct. 1926. *Educ:* St Anne's, Leeds. Presenter: Radio One Weekly Show, 1969–89; Independent Radio weekly show, 1989–; television: Jim'll Fix It, making dreams come true, No 1 in the ratings every year, 1975–94; Mind How You Go, road safety show; Top of the Pops. Man of many parts but best known as a voluntary helper at Leeds Infirmary, Broadmoor Hospital, and Stoke Mandeville where he raised twelve million pounds to rebuild the National Spinal Injuries Centre. Fellow of Cybernetics, Reading Univ., 1990. Hon. FRCR 1997. Hon. LLD Leeds, 1986. Hon. KCSG (Holy See), 1982; Bronze and Gold medals, SMO, St John of Jerusalem. *Publications:* As It Happens (autobiog.), 1975; Love is an Uphill Thing (autobiog.), 1975; God'll Fix It, 1978. *Recreations:* running, cycling, wrestling. *Address:* National Spinal Injuries Centre, Stoke Mandeville Hospital, Aylesbury, Bucks HP21 8AL. *T:* (01296) 395353. *Club:* Athenæum.

SAVILL, His Honour David Malcolm; QC 1969; a Senior Circuit Judge and Resident Judge, Leeds Combined Court Centre, 1991–96 (a Circuit Judge, 1984–91); *b* 18 Sept. 1930; *s* of late Lionel and of Lisbeth Savill; *m* 1955, Mary Arnott (*née* Eadie), JP, *d* of late Lady Hinchcliffe and step *d* of late Hon. Sir (George) Raymond Hinchcliffe; one *s* two *d*. *Educ:* Marlborough Coll. (Pres., Marlburian Club, 1996–97); Clare Coll., Cambridge. 2nd Lieut Grenadier Guards, 1949–50. BA (Hons) Cambridge, 1953. Called to the Bar, Middle Temple, 1954 (Bencher, 1977); Mem., Senate of Inns of Court and the Bar, 1976, 1980–83. A Recorder, 1972–84 (Hon. Recorder, Leeds, 1993–96); Chancellor: diocese of Bradford, 1976–99; diocese of Ripon, 1987–92; Leader, NE Circuit, 1980–83. Chairman: Adv. Cttee on Conscientious Objectors, 1978–91; W Yorks Criminal Justice Liaison Cttee, 1992–96. *Recreations:* travel, golf, gardening. *Address:* 11 King's Bench Walk, Temple, EC4Y 7EQ. *Clubs:* MCC; Aldwoodley Golf.

SAVILL, Prof. John Stewart, PhD; FRCP, FRCPE; Professor of Medicine, University of Edinburgh Medical School, Director of University of Edinburgh/MRC Centre for Inflammation Research, and Hon. Consultant Physician in Renal and General Medicine, Royal Infirmary of Edinburgh, since 1998; *b* 25 April 1957; *s* of Peter Edward Savill and Jean Elizabeth Savill (*née* Garland); *m* 1979, Barbara Campbell; two *s*. *Educ:* St Catherine's Coll., Oxford (BA 1st cl. Hons Physiol Scis 1978); Sheffield Univ. Med. Sch. (MB ChB Hons 1981); Royal Postgrad. Med. Sch., London (PhD 1989). MRCP 1984, FRCP 1994; FRCPE 2000. Jun. med. posts in Sheffield, Nottingham and London, 1981–85; Department of Medicine, Royal Postgraduate Medical School, Hammersmith Hospital: Registrar in Renal Medicine, 1985–86; MRC Training Fellow, 1986–89; Sen. Registrar in Renal Medicine 1989–90; Wellcome Trust Sen. Res. Fellow in Clin. Sci., Hon. Sen. Lectr and Consultant Physician, 1990–93; Prof. in Medicine and Hd, Div. of Renal and Inflammatory Disease, 1993–98, Hd of Sch., 1997–98, Sch. of Med. and Surgical Scis, Univ. of Nottingham Faculty of Medicine and Health Scis. Founder FMedSci 1998 (Chm., Wkg Party on Career Structure and Prospects for Clinical Scientists in UK, 1999–2000). Presidential Award, Soc. of Leukocyte Biology of USA, 1989, 1990; Milne-Muehrcke Award, Nat. Kidney Foundn, USA, 1992. *Publications:* papers on cell death in inflammation. *Recreations:* hockey, cricket, real ale. *Address:* Department of Clinical and Surgical Sciences (Internal Medicine), Royal Infirmary of Edinburgh, Edinburgh EH3 9YW. *T:* (0131) 536 2238. *Clubs:* West Bridgford Hockey, Wilson's Cricket.

SAVILL, Colonel Kenneth Edward, CVO 1976; DSO 1945; DL; Member, HM Bodyguard of Hon. Corps of Gentlemen at Arms, 1955–76 (Lieutenant, 1973–76; Standard Bearer, 1972–73); *b* 8 August 1906; *o s* of Walter Savill, Chilton Manor, Alresford and May, *d* of Major Charles Marriott; *m* 1935, Jacqueline (*d* 1980), *o d* of Brig. John Salusbury Hughes, MC; two *d* (and one *d* decd). *Educ:* Winchester College; RMC Sandhurst. Commissioned, 12th Royal Lancers, 1926; 1st King's Dragoon Guards, 1936; The Queen's Bays, 1947. Served War of 1939–45, France, 1939–40; N Africa and Italy, 1943–45; Col 1950; retd 1953. High Sheriff of Hampshire, 1961; DL Hampshire, 1965. Col, 1st The Queen's Dragoon Guards, 1964–68. *Address:* Chilton Manor, Alresford, Hants SO24 9TX. *T:* (01256) 389246. *Club:* Cavalry and Guards.

SAVILL, Peter David; Chairman, British Horseracing Board, since 1998; *b* 30 July 1947; *s* of Harry and Betty Savill; *m* 1996, Ruth Pinder; one *s* two *d*. *Educ:* Ampleforth Coll.; Downing Coll., Cambridge (LLB 1969). Trainee, Doyle Dane Bernbach, Advertising Agency, 1969–70; Special Projects Manager, Admaster Corp., 1970–71; Asst to Chm., Barclay Securities, 1971–75; President: P & D International, 1975–91; International Voyager Publications, 1980–91; Shorex International, 1991–95; Chm., North South Net, 1985–98. Chm., Plumpton Racecourse, 1998–. Director: Horserace Totalisator Bd, 1998–; Horserace Betting Levy Bd, 1998–99. *Recreations:* golf, horse racing, sport. *Address:* Springfield House, Kilbride, Wicklow, Co. Wicklow, Ireland. *Club:* Turf.

SAVILL, Rosalind Joy, CBE 2000; FSA; Director, The Wallace Collection, since 1992; *b* 12 May 1951; *d* of Dr Guy Savill and Lorna (*née* Williams); one *d*. *Educ:* Wycombe Abbey Sch.; Châtelard Sch., sur-Montreux; Univ. of Leeds (BA Hons 1972); Study Centre, London (Dip in Fine and Decorative Arts 1973). Ceramics Dept, V&A Mus., 1973–74; The Wallace Collection: Museum Asst, 1974–78; Asst to Dir, 1978–92. Guest Scholar, J. Paul Getty Mus., 1985. Mem. Council, Attingham Trust, 1980–92; Member: Nat. Trust Arts Panel, 1995–; Art Adv. Cttee, Nat. Mus and Galls of Wales, 1997–; Museums and Collections Adv. Cttee, English Heritage, 1998–; Registration Cttee, Museums and Galls Commn, 1999–; Adv. Cttee, Royal Mint, 1999–. Trustee: Somerset House Trust, 1997–; Campaign for Museums, 1999–. Pres., French Porcelain Soc., 1999– (Chm., 1988–94). Gov., Camden Sch. for Girls, 1996–. FSA 1990; FRSA 1990. Nat. Art Collections Award for Scholarship, 1990. *Publications:* The Wallace Collection Catalogue of Sèvres Porcelain, 3 vols, 1988; (contrib.) Treasure Houses of Britain, 1985; Boughton House, 1992; Versailles: tables royales, 1993; articles in Apollo, Burlington Mag., Antologia di Belle Arti, J. Paul Getty Mus. Jl, Ars Ceramica, Antique Collector. *Recreations:* music, birds, wildlife, gardens. *Address:* The Wallace Collection, Hertford House, Manchester Square, W1U 3BN. *T:* (020) 7224 2155.

SAVILLE, family name of **Baron Saville of Newdigate**.

SAVILLE OF NEWDIGATE, Baron *cr* 1997 (Life Peer), of Newdigate in the co. of Surrey; **Mark Oliver Saville,** Kt 1985; PC 1994; a Lord of Appeal in Ordinary, since 1997; *b* 20 March 1936; *s* of Kenneth Vivian Saville and Olivia Sarah Frances Gray; *m* 1961, Jill Gray; two *s*. *Educ:* St Paul's Primary Sch., Hastings; Rye Grammar Sch.; Brasenose Coll., Oxford (BA, BCL; Hon. Fellow, 1998). Nat. Service, 2nd Lieut Royal Sussex Regt, 1954–56; Oxford Univ., 1956–60 (Vinerian Schol. 1960); called to Bar, Middle Temple, 1962 (Bencher, 1983); QC 1975; Judge of the High Court, QBD, 1985–93; a Lord Justice of Appeal, 1994–97. Hon. LLD London Guildhall, 1997. *Recreations:* sailing, flying, computers. *Address:* House of Lords, SW1A 0PW.

SAVILLE, Clive Howard; Chief Executive, UKCOSA: Council for International Education, since 1997; *b* 7 July 1943; *m* 1967, Camille Kathleen Burke. *Educ:* Bishop Gore Grammar Sch., Swansea; University Coll., Swansea (BA). Joined DES as Asst Principal, 1965; Grade 3, DES, then DFE, later DFEE, 1987–97. Vis. Associate, Center for Studies in Higher Educn, Univ. of California, Berkeley, 1987. Member: Exec. Cttee, Nat. Literary Trust, 1997–; British Accreditation Council for Ind. Further and Higher Educn, 1998–. Gov., Morley Coll., 1999–. *Address:* 9–17 St Albans Place, N1 0NX. *T:* (020) 7226 3762, *Fax:* (020) 7226 3373; *e-mail:* c.saville@ukcosa.org.uk.

SAVILLE, Prof. John; Emeritus Professor of Economic and Social History, University of Hull; *b* 2 April 1916; *o s* of Orestes Stamatopoulos, Volos, Greece, and Edith Vessey (name changed by deed poll to that of step-father, 1937); *m* 1943, Constance Betty Saunders; three *s* one *d*. *Educ:* Royal Liberty Sch.; London Sch. of Economics. 1st Cl. Hons BSc (Econ) 1937. Served War, RA, 1940–46; Chief Scientific Adviser's Div., Min. of Works, 1946–47; Univ. of Hull, 1947–82, Prof. of Economic and Social History, 1972–82. Leverhulme Emeritus Fellow, 1984–86. Mem., British Communist Party, 1934–56; Chm., Oral Hist. Soc., 1976–87; Convenor, Northern Marxist Historians Gp, 1986–95; Vice-Chm., and then Chm., Soc. for Study of Labour Hist., 1974–82; Mem. Exec. Cttee and Founder-Mem., Council for Academic Freedom and Democracy, 1971–81, Chm. 1982–89; Chm., Economic and Social Hist. Cttee, SSRC, 1977–79. Trustee, Michael Lipman Trust, 1977–93. Vice-Chm., Friends of the Brynmor Jones Library, Hull Univ., 1988–. FRHistS 1973. *Publications:* Ernest Jones, Chartist, 1952; Rural Depopulation in England and Wales 1851–1951, 1957; 1848, The British State and the Chartist Movement, 1987; The Labour Movement in Britain: a commentary, 1988; The Politics of Continuity: British Foreign Policy and the Labour Government 1945–46, 1993; The Consolidation of the Capitalist State, 1994; numerous articles; Co-Editor: (with E. P. Thompson) Reasoner and New Reasoner, 1956–59; (with Asa Briggs) Essays in Labour History, 1960, 1971, 1977; (with Ralph Miliband) Socialist Register (annual, 1964–90); (with Joyce M. Bellamy) Dictionary of Labour Biography, 1972–2000. *Recreations:* working for socialism, looking at churches. *Address:* 152 Westbourne Avenue, Hull HU5 3HZ. *T:* (01482) 343425.

SAVOURS; *see* Campbell-Savours, family name of Baron Campbell-Savours.

SAWARD, Rev. Canon Michael John; Treasurer and Canon Residentiary of St Paul's Cathedral, 1991–2000, Canon Emeritus, since 2001; *b* 14 May 1932; *s* of late Donald and Lily Saward; *m* 1956, Jackie, *d* of late Col John Atkinson, DSO, OBE, and Eileen Atkinson, MBE; one *s* three *d*. *Educ:* Eltham Coll.; Bristol Univ. (BA Theology). 2nd Lieut, RA, 1950–52, RWAFF (Nat. Service). Deacon 1956, priest 1957; curacies in Croydon, 1956–59, and Edgware, 1959–64; Sec., Liverpool Council of Churches, 1965–67; C of E Radio and Television Officer, 1967–72; Vicar: St Matthew, Fulham, 1972–78; Ealing, 1978–91; Prebendary of St Paul's Cathedral, 1985–91. Mem., General Synod, 1975–95 (Mem., House of Clergy Standing Cttee, 1981–86); a Church Comr, 1978–93 (Member: Redundant Churches Cttee, 1978–81; Houses Cttee, 1981–88; Bd of Govs, 1986–93; Pastoral Cttee, 1988–93); Chairman: C of E Pensions Measure Revision Cttee, 1987–88; Care of Cathedrals (Supplementary Provisions) Measure Revision Cttee,

1992–93; Billy Graham Mission '89 Media Task Gp, 1988–89; Member: Lambeth Conf., Preparatory Cttee, 1967–68; Archbishops' Council on Evangelism, 1975–78; C of E Evangelical Council, 1976–93; Nat. Partners in Mission Wkg Party, 1979–81; Dioceses Commn, 1981–89; Council, CPAS, 1992–98. Sec., Gen. Synod Broadcasting Commn, 1970–73. Trustee: Hartlebury Castle Trust, 1983–88; Church Urban Fund, 1989–90; Christian Evidence Soc., 1992–98. Mem. Council, Trinity Theol Coll., 1974–78; Mem., RTS, 1970–72. Gov., St Paul's Cathedral (formerly Choir) Sch., 1991–2000. Chm., Jubilate Hymns Ltd, 1999–2001. Journalist, broadcaster, lectr, reviewer. Winston Churchill Travelling Fellowship, 1984. Freeman, City of London, 1993; Liveryman, Co. of Gardeners, 1997–2001. Words Editor: Hymns for Today's Church, 1974–82; Sing Glory, 1997–99. Chairman, Panel of Judges: St Paul's Cathedral Millennium Hymn Competition, 1997–99; The Times Preacher of the Year Comp., 2000. Prizewinner: Southern TV Hymn for Britain competition, 1966; BBC-TV Songs of Praise new hymn competition, 1985; Polly Bond journalism award (USA), 1990. *Publications:* Leisure, 1963 (Norwegian edn 1971); Christian Youth Groups, 1965; Cracking the God-Code, 1974, 3rd edn 1989 (USA edn 1974, Chinese and Swedish edns 1976); And So To Bed?, 1975; God's Friends, 1978; All Change, 1983; Evangelicals on the Move, 1987; These Are The Facts, 1997; A Faint Streak of Humility, 1999; contribs to books including: Broadcasting, Society and the Church, 1973; Christian Initiation, 1991; Prayers for Today's World, 1993; Has Keele Failed?, 1995; The Post Evangelical Debate, 1997; 366 Graces, 1999, and to 130 hymnbooks worldwide; author of 90 hymns. *Recreations:* reading (esp. military history), music, cricket, travel, food and drink, writing hymns. *Address:* 6 Discovery Walk, E1W 2JG. *T:* (020) 7702 1130. *Club:* Athenæum (Mem., General Cttee, 1997–2000).

SAWDY, Peter Bryan; Director: Griffin International Ltd, since 1988; Yule Catto PLC, since 1990; Lazard Birla Indian Investment Fund plc, since 1994; *b* 17 Sept. 1931; *s* of Alfred Eustace Leon Sawdy and Beatrice Sawdy; *m* 1st, 1955, Anne Stonor (marr. diss. 1989; she *d* 1995); two *d*; 2nd, 1989, Judith Mary Bowen. *Educ:* Ampleforth Coll.; Regent St Polytechnic; LSE. Trainee, Brooke Bond Ltd, 1952; Chm., Brooke Bond Ceylon Ltd, 1962–65; Director: Brooke Bond Ltd, 1965–68; Brooke Bond Liebig Ltd, 1968–75; Brooke Bond Group: Man. Dir, 1975–77; Gp Chief Exec., 1977–81; Dep. Chm. and Gp Chief Exec., 1981–85. Chm., Costain Gp, 1990–93; Dep. Chm., Hogg Gp, 1992–94 (Dir, 1986–). *Recreations:* golf, opera, collecting modern first editions. *Address:* 13 Clarendon Street, SW1V 2EN. *Clubs:* Naval and Military; Royal Ashdown Golf (Forest Row), Royal Mid-Surrey Golf (Richmond).

SAWERS, David Richard Hall; writer; *b* 23 April 1931; *s* of late Edward and Madeline Sawers; unmarried. *Educ:* Westminster Sch.; Christ Church, Oxford (MA). Research Asst to Prof. J. Jewkes, Oxford Univ., 1954–58; Journalist, The Economist, 1959–64; Vis. Fellow, Princeton Univ., 1964–65; Econ. Adviser, Min. of Aviation and of Technology, 1966–68; Sen. Econ. Adviser, Min. of Technology, Aviation Supply, and DTI, 1968–72; Under-Sec., Depts of Industry, Trade and Prices and Consumer Protection, 1972–76; Under-Sec., Depts of Environment and Transport, 1976–83; Principal Res. Fellow, Technical Change Centre, 1984–86. *Publications:* (with John Jewkes and Richard Stillerman) The Sources of Invention, 1958; (with Ronald Miller) The Technical Development of Modern Aviation, 1968; Competition in the Air, 1987; Should the Taxpayer Support the Arts, 1993; (contrib.) Markets and the Media, 1996; (contrib.) Does the Past Have a Future?: the political economy of heritage, 1998; articles in daily press and journals. *Recreations:* listening to music, looking at pictures, gardening. *Address:* 10 Seaview Avenue, Angmering-on-Sea, Littlehampton BN16 1PP. *T:* (01903) 779134.

SAWERS, (Robert) John, CMG 1996; HM Diplomatic Service; Ambassador to Egypt, since 2001; *b* 26 July 1955; *s* of Colin Simon Hawkesley Sawers and Daphne Anne Sawers; *m* 1981, Avril Helen Shelley Lamb; two *s* one *d*. *Educ:* Beechen Cliff Sch., Bath; Univ. of Nottingham (BSc Hons Physics and Philosophy). FCO 1977; served Sana'a, 1980; Damascus, 1982; FCO, 1984; Private Sec. to Minister of State, FCO, 1986; Pretoria/Cape Town, 1988; Head, European Community Dept (Presidency), 1991; Principal Private Sec. to Sec. of State for Foreign and Commonwealth Affairs, 1993–95; Career Develt Attachment, Harvard Univ., 1995–96; Counsellor, Washington, 1996–99; Private Sec. (Foreign Affairs) to the Prime Minister, 1999–2001 (on secondment). *Recreations:* sport, films, family. *Address:* c/o Foreign and Commonwealth Office, SW1A 2AH.

SAWFORD, Philip Andrew; MP (Lab) Kettering, since 1997; *b* 26 June 1950; *s* of John and Audrey Sawford; *m* 1971, Rosemary Stokes; two *s*. *Educ:* Ruskin Coll., Oxford (Dip. Soc.); Univ. of Leicester (BA Hons). Manager, Phoenix Training, Wellingborough. Member (Lab): Desborough Town Council, 1977–97; Kettering BC, 1979–83, 1991–97 (Leader). Contested (Lab) Wellingborough, 1992. *Recreations:* playing guitar, reading. *Address:* 46 Federation Avenue, Desborough, Northants NN14 2NX.

SAWKO, Prof. Felicjan, DSc; Professor of Civil Engineering and Head of Department at the Sultan Qaboos University, Oman, 1986–95, now Emeritus Professor; *b* 17 May 1937; *s* of Czeslaw Sawko and Franciszka (*née* Nawrot); *m* 1960, Genowefa Stefania (*née* Bak); four *s* one *d*. *Educ:* Leeds Univ. (BSc Civil Engrg, 1958; MSc 1960; DSc 1973). Engr, Rendel Palmer & Tritton, London, 1959–62; Lectr, 1962–67, Reader, 1967, Leeds University; Prof. of Civil Engrg, Liverpool Univ., 1967–86. Henry Adams Award, IStructE, 1980. *Publications:* (ed) Developments in Prestressed Concrete, Vols 1 and 2, 1968; (with Cope and Tickell) Numerical Methods for Civil Engineers, 1981; some 70 papers on computer methods and structural masonry. *Recreations:* travel, bridge (Dir, Liverpool Bridge Club, 1998–), numismatics. *Address:* 23 Floral Wood, Liverpool L17 7HR. *T:* (0151) 727 0913.

SAWYER, Baron *cr* 1998 (Life Peer), of Darlington in the co. of Durham; **Lawrence Sawyer, (Tom);** *b* 12 May 1943. Dep. Gen. Sec., NUPE, later UNISON, 1981–94; Gen. Sec., Labour Party, 1994–98. Mem., NEC, Labour Party, 1981–94 and 1999–; Chm., Labour Party, 1990–91. Director (non-executive): Reed Executive, 1999–; Investors in People UK. Vis. Prof., Cranfield Sch. of Mgt. *Address:* House of Lords, SW1A 0PW.

SAWYER, Anthony Charles, CB 1999; fiscal expert, International Monetary Fund, since 1999; Commissioner, 1991–99, and Director Operations Prevention, 1994–99, HM Customs and Excise; *b* 3 Aug. 1939; *s* of Charles Bertram and Elizabeth Sawyer; *m* 1962, Kathleen Josephine McGill; two *s* one *d*. *Educ:* Redhill Tech. Coll., Surrey. Nat. Service, RA, 1960. Underwriter, Northern Assurance Group, 1962; Customs and Excise, 1964–99: Collector, Edinburgh, 1984; Dep. Dir, 1988, Dir, 1991, Outfield. Dir, Customs Annuity and Benevolent Fund, 1998–. Non-exec. Dir, Retail Banking Bd, Royal Bank of Scotland, 1994–97. FIMgt 1996; FInstD 1997. FRSA 1994. *Recreations:* walking, cricket, sailing. *Clubs:* National Liberal; Royal Scots (Edinburgh).

SAWYER, Hon. Dame Joan (Augusta), DBE 1997; Chief Justice of the Bahamas, since 1996; *b* 26 Nov. 1940; *m* 1962, Geoffrey Sawyer; one *s*. *Educ:* London Univ. (LLB 1973). Clerk, 1958–68; HEO (Public Service), 1968–73; called to the Bar, Gray's Inn, 1973; Asst Crown Counsel, 1973–78; acting Stipendiary and Circuit Magistrate, 1978; Sen. Counsel, 1979–83; acting Dir, Legal Affairs, 1983; Counsel, Central Bank of the Bahamas, 1984–88; Justice, 1988–95, Sen. Justice, 1995–96, Supreme Court of Bahamas. Patron, Girls Brigade Council. *Publications:* articles in Bahamian Review. *Recreations:* reading, sewing, serious theatre, gardening, embroidering. *Address:* Bahamas Supreme Court, PO Box N-8167, Nassau, Bahamas. *T:* 3569101, 3564234.

SAXBEE, Rt Rev. John Charles; *see* Lincoln, Bishop of.

SAXBY, Robin Keith; Chairman and Chief Executive Officer, ARM Holdings plc (formerly Advanced RBC Machines Ltd), since 1991; *b* 4 Feb. 1947; *s* of Keith William Saxby and Mary Saxby; *m* 1970, Patricia Susan Bell; one *s* one *d*. *Educ:* Univ. of Liverpool (BEng Electronics 1968). R&D engr, Rane Bush Murphy, 1968–72; Sen. Engr, Pyte TMC, 1972–73; Sales Engr, then System Strategy Manager, Europe, Motorola Semiconductors, 1973–84; Chief Exec., Henderson Security Systems, 1984–86; Man. Dir, ES2 Ltd, 1986–91. Vis. Prof., Dept of Electronics, Univ. of Liverpool. FRSA; CIMgt. Hon. FIEE. Hon. DEng 2000. *Publications:* (contrib.) Electronic Engineers' Reference Book, 1983; Microcomputer Handbook, 1985; (contrib.) Advances in Information Technology, 1998. *Recreations:* tennis, ski-ing, music, swimming, astronomy, genealogy. *Address:* ARM Holdings plc, Liberty House, Moorbridge, Maidenhead, Berks SL6 8LT.

SAXON, Prof. David Harold, DPhil, DSc; CPhys, FInstP; FRSE; Kelvin Professor of Physics, since 1990, Vice Dean, Physical Sciences, since 2000, University of Glasgow (Head, Department of Physics and Astronomy, 1996–2001); *b* 27 Oct. 1945; *s* of Rev. Canon Eric Saxon and Ruth (*née* Higginbottom); *m* 1968, Margaret Flitcroft; one *s* one *d*. *Educ:* Manchester Grammar Sch.; Balliol Coll., Oxford (MA, DSc); Jesus Coll., Oxford (DPhil). CPhys 1985; FInstP 1985; FRSE 1993. Jun. Res. Fellow, Jesus Coll., Oxford, 1968–70; Res. Officer, Nuclear Physics Dept, Oxford, 1969–70; Res. Associate, Columbia Univ., NY, 1970–73; Rutherford Appleton Laboratory, Oxford: Res. Associate, 1974–75; SSO, 1975–76; PSO, 1976–89; Grade 6, 1989–90. Member, SERC Committees: Particle Physics Experiment Selection Panel, 1989–92; Particle Physics, 1991–94 (Chm., 1992–94); Nuclear Physics Bd, 1992–93; Particles, Space & Astronomy Bd, 1993–94. Member Council: PPARC, 1997–2001 (Chairman: Particle Physics Cttee, 1994–95; Public Understanding of Sci. Panel, 1997–2001); CCLRC, 2000–01 (Chm., Particle Physics Users Adv. Cttee, 1998–). Chairman: 27th Internat. Conf. on High Energy Physics, 1994; Scottish Univs Summer Schs in Physics, 1997–; Member: CERN Scientific Policy Cttee, Geneva, 1993–98; Physics Res. Cttee, Deutsches Elektronen Synchrotron, Hamburg, 1993–99; Res. Assessment Panel (Physics), Higher Educn Funding Councils, 1996; MRC Scientific Adv. Gp on Technology, 1999; Discipline Hopping Panel, 2000. FRSA 1997. *Recreation:* staying close to home. *Address:* Department of Physics and Astronomy, University of Glasgow, Glasgow G12 8QQ. *T:* (0141) 330 4673.

SAXON, David Stephen, PhD; President Emeritus, University of California; Hon. Chairman of the Corporation, Massachusetts Institute of Technology, 1990–95 (Chairman, 1983–90); *b* 8 Feb. 1920; *s* of Ivan Saxon and Rebecca Moss; *m* 1940, Shirley Goodman; six *d*. *Educ:* Massachusetts Institute of Technology (BS 1941; PhD 1944). Massachusetts Institute of Technology: Res. physicist, Radiation Lab., 1943–46; Philips Labs, 1946–47. Univ. of California at Los Angeles: Mem. of Faculty, 1947–75; Prof. of Physics, 1958–75; Chm. of Dept, 1963–66; Dean of Physical Sciences, 1966–68; Vice-Chancellor, 1968–75; Provost, Univ. of California, 1974–75, Pres., 1975–83. Guggenheim Fellow, 1956–57 and 1961–62; Fulbright grant, 1961–62. Vis. Prof., Univ. of Paris, Orsay, France, 1961–62; Vis. scientist, Centre d'Etudes Nucléaires, France, 1968–69; Vis. Research Fellow, Merton Coll., Oxford, 1981; consultant to research organisations, 1948–. Special research into theoretical physics: nuclear physics, quantum mechanics, electromagnetic theory and scattering theory. Dir, Eastman Kodak Co., 1983–90. Fellow: Amer. Acad. of Arts and Scis; Amer. Phys. Soc.; Member: Amer. Phil Soc.; Amer. Assoc. Physics Teachers; Amer. Inst. Physics; Amer. Assoc. for the Advancement of Science; Technical Adv. Council for Ford Motor Co., 1979–; Corp. of MIT, 1977–; Dir, Houghton Mifflin Co., 1984–90. Recipient of several honorary degrees. Member: Phi Beta Kappa; Sigma Pi Sigma; Sigma Xi. Royal Order of the Northern Star (Nordstjärnan), 1979. *Publications:* Elementary Quantum Mechanics, 1968; The Nuclear Independent Particle Model (with A. E. S. Green and T. Sawada), 1968; Discontinuities in Wave Guides (with Julian Schwinger), 1968; Physics for the Liberal Arts Student (with William B. Fretter), 1971. *Address:* University of California, Los Angeles, Department of Physics, Knudsen Hall Room 3145J, 405 Hilgard Avenue, Los Angeles, CA 90095-1547, USA.

SAXTON, Robert Louis Alfred, DMus; FGSM; University Lecturer, Oxford University, and Tutor and Fellow in Music, Worcester College, Oxford, since 1999; *b* 8 Oct. 1953; *s* of Jean Augusta Saxton (*née* Infield) and Ian Sanders Saxton. *Educ:* Bryanston Sch.; St Catharine's Coll., Cambridge (MA); Worcester Coll., Oxford (BMus; DMus 1992). FGSM 1987. Lectr, Bristol Univ., 1984–85; Fulbright Arts award, 1985; Vis. Fellow, Princeton Univ., 1986; Head of Composition: GSMD, 1990–98; RAM, 1998–99; Vis. Fellow in Composition, Bristol Univ., 1995–. Artistic Dir, Opera Lab, 1994–; Associate Dir, Performing Arts Labs, 1998–; Pres., Brunel Ensemble, 1995–. Hon. Pres., Assoc. of English Singers and Speakers, 1997–. Mem., Site Develt Bd, South Bank Centre, 1997–. Patron, Bristol Univ. Music Soc., 1998–. Finalist, BBC Young Composers' Comp., 1973; First Prize, Gaudeamus Music Fest., Holland, 1975; early works at ISCM Fest., Bonn, 1977, Royan Fest., 1977; later works, majority recorded, include: The Ring of Eternity, 1983; Concerto for Orchestra, 1984; The Circles of Light, 1985; The Child of Light (carol), 1985; The Sentinel of the Rainbow, 1984; Viola Concerto, 1986; Night Dance, 1986–87; I Will Awake the Dawn, 1987; In the Beginning, 1987; Elijah's Violin, 1988; Chacony, 1988; Music to celebrate the Resurrection of Christ, 1988; Violin Concerto, Leeds Fest., 1990; Caritas (opera with libretto by Arnold Wesker), 1990–91; Paraphrase on Mozart's Idomeneo, 1991; At the Round Earth's Imagined Corners (anthem), 1992; 'Cello Concerto, 1992; Psalm—a song of ascents, 1992; O Sing unto the Lord a new song (anthem), 1993; Fantazia, 1993; Canticum Luminis, 1994; A Yardstick to the Stars, 1994; Ring, Time, 1994; Songs, Dances, Ellipses, 1997; Prayer before Sleep, 1997; Music for St Catharine, 1998; Miniature Dance for a Marionette Rabbi, 1999; Sonata for solo 'cello on a theme of Sir William Walton, 1999; The Dialogue of Zion and God, 2000; works commissioned by: Fires of London, London Sinfonietta, BBC, LSO, ECO, Aldeburgh Fest., Cheltenham Fest., Opera North, LPO, RPO, City of London Fest./St Paul's Cathedral, Leeds Fest. *Publications:* The Process of Composition from Detection to Confection, 1998; all compositions; contribs TLS, Musical Times, etc. *Recreations:* reading, theatre, cinema, studying history, watching cricket. *Address:* c/o Chester Music, 8–9 Frith Street, W1V 5TZ. *T:* (020) 7434 0066; University of York Music Press, Department of Music, University of York, Heslington, York YO10 5DD. *T:* (01904) 432434, *Fax:* (01904) 432450.

SAY, Rt Rev. Richard David, KCVO 1988; DD (Lambeth) 1961; an Assistant Bishop, diocese of Canterbury, since 1988; *b* 4 Oct. 1914; *s* of Commander Richard Say, OBE, RNVR, and Kathleen Mary (*née* Wildy); *m* 1943, Irene Frances (OBE 1980, JP 1960), *e d* of Seaburne and Frances Rayner, Exeter; one *s* two *d* (and one *s* decd). *Educ:* University

Coll. Sch.; Christ's College, Cambridge (MA); Ridley Hall, Cambridge. Ordained deacon, 1939; priest, 1940. Curate of Croydon Parish Church, 1939–43; Curate of St Martin-in-the-Fields, London, 1943–50; Asst Sec. Church of England Youth Council, 1942–44; Gen. Sec., 1944–47; Gen. Sec. British Council of Churches, 1947–55; Church of England delegate to World Council of Churches, 1948, 1954 and 1961. Select Preacher, University of Cambridge, 1954 and University of Oxford, 1963; Rector of Bishop's Hatfield, 1955–61; Hon. Canon of St Albans, 1957–61; Bishop of Rochester, 1961–88; High Almoner to HM the Queen, 1970–88. Domestic Chaplain to Marquess of Salisbury and Chaplain of Welfield Hospital, 1955–61; Hon. Chaplain of The Pilgrims, 1968–. Entered House of Lords, 1969. Chaplain and Sub-Prelate, Order of St John, 1961. Mem., Court of Ecclesiastical Causes Reserved, 1984–93. Dep. Pro-Chancellor, 1977–83, Pro-Chancellor, 1983–93, Kent Univ.; Governor, University Coll. Sch., 1980–88. A Vice-Pres., UNA of GB, 1986–; Pres., Friends of Kent Churches, 1988–. Chm., Age Concern, England, 1986–89 (Vice Pres., 1990–94; Patron, 1994–). Freeman of City of London, 1953; Hon. Freeman: of Tonbridge and Malling, 1987; of Rochester upon Medway, 1988. Hon. Member: Smeatonian Soc., 1977; Instn of Royal Engineers, 1987. Hon. DCL Kent, 1987. *Recreations:* walking, travel. *Address:* 23 Chequers Park, Wye, Ashford, Kent TN25 5BB. *T:* (01233) 812720. *Club:* Oxford and Cambridge.

SAYCE, Roy Beavan, FRICS, FAAV; FRAC; Director, RPS Group (formerly Rural Planning Services) PLC, Didcot, 1980–88; *b* 19 July 1920; *s* of Roger Sayce, BScAgric, NDA, and Lilian Irene Sayce; *m* 1949, Barbara Sarah (*née* Leverton) (marr. diss. 1990); two *s*. *Educ:* Culford, Royal Agricultural Coll. (MRAC; Silver Medal 1948; FRAC 1999). FRICS 1949; FAAV 1978. Univ. of London, 1938–40. Served War, Intell., RAFVR, 1940–46. Agricultural Land Service: Asst Land Comr, Chelmsford, 1949–50; Sen. Asst Land Comr, Norwich, 1950–63; Divl Land Comr, Oxford, 1963–71; Reg. Surveyor, Land Service, Agric. Develt and Adv. Service, Bristol, 1971–76; Chief Surveyor, Land Service, Agric. Develt and Adv. Service, MAFF, 1977–80. Royal Instn of Chartered Surveyors: Mem., Gen. and Divl Councils, 1970–80; Divl Pres., Land Agency and Agric. Div., 1973–74. Chm., Farm Buildings Information Centre, 1980–85. Governor, Royal Agric. Coll., Cirencester, 1975–88. Fellow, RAC, 1999. Hon. Mem., CAAV, 1978. *Publications:* Farm Buildings, 1966; (contrib.) Walmsley's Rural Estate Management, 1969; The History of the Royal Agricultural College, 1992; A Rural Surveyor, 2000. *Recreations:* golf, historical writing. *Address:* 13 Haywards Close, Wantage, Oxon OX12 7AT. *T:* (01235) 223266. *Clubs:* Civil Service; Frilford Heath Golf.

SAYE AND SELE, 21st Baron *cr* 1447 and 1603; **Nathaniel Thomas Allen Fiennes;** DL; *b* 22 Sept. 1920; *s* of Ivo Murray Twisleton-Wykeham-Fiennes, 20th Baron Saye and Sele, OBE, MC, and Hersey Cecilia Hester, *d* of late Captain Sir Thomas Dacres Butler, KCVO; *S* father, 1968; *m* 1958, Mariette Helena, *d* of Maj.-Gen. Sir Guy Salisbury-Jones, GCVO, CMG, CBE, MC; two *s* one *d* (and two *s* decd). *Educ:* Eton; New College, Oxford. Served with Rifle Brigade, 1941–49 (despatches twice). Chartered Surveyor. Partner in firm of Laws and Fiennes. Regl Dir, Lloyds Bank, 1982–90. Trustee, Ernest Cook Trust, 1960–95 (Chm. Trustees, 1965–92). DL Oxfordshire, 1979. Fellow, Winchester Coll., 1967–83. *Heir:* *s* Hon. Martin Guy Fiennes [*b* 27 Feb. 1961; *m* 1996, Pauline Kang Chai Lian, *o d* of Kang Tiong Lam; two *s*]. *Address:* Broughton Castle, Banbury, Oxon OX15 5EB. *T:* (01295) 262624.

See also Very Rev. Hon. O. W. Fiennes.

SAYEED, Dr (Abulfatah) Akram, OBE 1976; FRCPE, FRCGP; General Medical Practitioner in Leicester, since 1963; Hon. Adviser in UK to Ministry of Health, Government of Bangladesh, since 1991; Chairman, Overseas Doctors' Association in UK, 1993–96; *b* Bangladesh, 23 Nov. 1935; *s* of late Mokhles Ahmed, school teacher; registered British; *m* 1959, Hosne-ara Ali, *d* of M. S. Ali; two *s* one *d*. *Educ:* St Joseph's Sch., Khulna; Dacca Univ. MB, BS 1958. FODA 1985; FRIPHH 1991; FRSH 1991; FCPS (Bangladesh) 1991; FRCPE 1994; FRCGP 1997 (MRCGP 1992). Editor, Dacca Med. Coll. Jl and Magazines, 1957–58; Lit. Sec., Students Union. Went to USA, 1960; resident in Britain from 1961. Mem. Staff, Leicester Royal Infirmary, 1964–89; Member: Leics Local Medical Cttee, 1977–; Leics Family Practitioner Cttee, 1982–87; Leics Med. Adv. and Audit Gp. Member: DHSS Working Party on Asian Health Gp, 1979; DHSS Adv. Council on Violence Against NHS Staff, 1986–89; Home Office Statutory Adv. Council on Community and Race Relations, 1983–88; Health Care Planning Team, Leics HA, 1984–86; Policy Planning (formerly Unit Management) Team, Leics Central Unit, 1986–; Gen. Optical Council, 1994–98. British Medical Association: Mem., 1979–; Mem. Gen. Med. Services Cttee, 1993–97; Pres., Leics Div., 1993–94; Fellow, 1995; Visitor, Council, 1994–96; Mem., GMC, 1999–. Co-founder, Nat. Fedn of Pakistani Assocs in GB, 1963; Adviser, NCCI, 1965–68; Founder Member: Leicester Council for Community Relations, 1965; British-Bangladesh Soc.; Member: Community Relations Commn, 1968–77; E Midlands Adv. Cttee, CRE, 1978–; Regl Inner City Task Force, 1991–; Stop Rickets Campaign (Chm., Leicester Campaign); Central Exec. Council, Bangladesh Med. Assoc. in UK; Hon. Med. Advr in UK, Min. of Health, Govt of Bangladesh; Chm., Standing Conf. of Asian Orgns in UK, 1973–77 (Vice-Chm., 1970–73; Pres., 1977–90); Hon. Sec., Inst. of Transcultural Health Care, 1985–93; Pres., Pakistan Assoc., Leics, 1965–71. Pres., Leicester Med. Soc. Mem., BBC Asian Programme Adv. Cttee, 1972–77. Special interest in problems of Asians; initiated study of problems of second generation Asians (CRE report Between Two Cultures); Overseas Doctors' Association: Founder Chm., 1975, Sponsor Chm., 1975; Gen. Sec., 1975–77; Vice-Pres., 1979–84; Vice-Chm., 1984–90; Chm., Annual Reps Meeting, 1990–93; Nat. Chm., 1993–96; Fellow, 1985; Member Editorial Board: ODA News Review, 1986–96; Ethnicity and Health. FRSocMed 1981; Associate Mem., MJA. Attended First World Conf. on Muslim Educn, Mecca, 1977; has done much work with disaster funds, etc. *Publications:* (ed jtly) Asian Who's Who, 1975–76, 10th edn 1996–97; contribs on socio-med. aspects of Asians in Britain to various jls. *Recreations:* gardening, reading, stamp collecting. *Address:* Ramna, 2 Mickleton Drive, Leicester LE5 6GD. *T:* (0116) 241 6703. *Clubs:* Royal Over-Seas League, Royal Commonwealth Society.

SAYEED, Jonathan; MP (C) Mid Bedfordshire, since 1997; *b* 20 March 1948; *m* 1980, Nicola Anne Parkes Power; two *s*. *Educ:* Britannia Royal Naval Coll., Dartmouth; Royal Naval Engrg Coll., Manadon. Chairman, Ranelagh Ltd, 1992–96; Trng Div., Corporate Services Group plc, 1996–97. MP (C) Bristol E, 1983–92; contested (C) same seat, 1992. PPS to Paymaster General and Minister of State for NI, 1991–92. Vice-Chm., 1987–91, Chm., 1991–92, Cons. Backbench Shipping and Shipbuilding Cttee; Dep. Chm., All Party Maritime Group, 1987–92; Member: Environment Select Cttee, 1987–92; Defence Select Cttee, 1988–91; Chairman's Panel, 1999–. Pres., Bristol E Cons. Assoc., 1995–. Pres., Bristol West Indian Cricket Club, 1986–. Member: RYA; RNSA. *Recreations:* golf, yachting, riding, classical music, architecture. *Address:* House of Commons, SW1A 0AA. *Clubs:* Carlton; Highgate Golf.

SAYER, Guy Mowbray, CBE 1978; JP; retired banker; *b* 18 June 1924; *yr s* of late Geoffrey Robley and Winifred Lily Sayer; *m* 1951, Marie Anne Sophie, *o d* of late Henri-Marie and Elisabeth Mertens; one *s* two *d*. *Educ:* Mill Mead Prep. Sch.; Shrewsbury School. FCIB (FIB 1971). Royal Navy, 1942–46. Joined Hongkong & Shanghai Banking Corp., 1946; Gen. Man. 1969; Exec. Dir 1970; Dep. Chm. 1971; Chm., 1972–77. Treas., Hong Kong Univ., 1972–77. Mem., Exchange Fund Adv. Cttee, Hong Kong, 1971–77. MLC, 1973–74, MEC, 1974–77, Hong Kong. JP Hong Kong, 1971. Hon. LLD Hong Kong, 1978. Liveryman, Innholders' Co. (Master, 2000–01). *Recreations:* golf, walking. *Address:* 5 Pembroke Gardens, W8 6HS. *T:* (020) 7602 4578. *Clubs:* Oriental, MCC; Royal Wimbledon Golf; West Sussex Golf; Hong Kong, Shek O Country (Hong Kong).

SAYER, John Raymond Keer, MA; Director and Hon. Secretary, Developing Services for Teaching in Europe, since 1997; Chairman, GTC (England and Wales) Trust, since 2000; *b* 8 Aug. 1931; *s* of Arthur and Hilda Sayer; *m* 1955, Ilserose (*née* Heyd); one *s* one *d*. *Educ:* Maidstone Grammar Sch.; Brasenose Coll., Oxford (Open Scholar; MA). FBIM 1979. Taught languages, 1955–63; Dep. Head, Nailsea Sch., Somerset, 1963–67; Headmaster, Minehead Sch., Somerset, 1967–73; Principal, Banbury Sch., 1973–84; Vis. Fellow, Univ. of London Inst. of Educn, 1985–92 (Dir, Educn Management Unit, 1987–90); Dir, E. C. Tempus Projects: Developing Schs for Democracy in Europe, Oxford Univ., 1991–2000; Co-Dir, European Sch. of Educnl Mgt, 1991–96. Chairman: Reform of Assessment at Sixteen-Plus, 1972–75; External Relations Cttee, Headmasters' Assoc., 1974–77; Secondary Heads Association: Mem. Exec., 1978–86; Press and Publications Officer, 1978–79, 1982–84; Pres., 1979–80. Chm., Jt Council of Heads, 1981; Member: Exec., UCCA, 1975–84; Schools Panel, CBI, 1975–82; Heads Panel, TUC, 1975–80; National Adv. Council on Educn for Industry and Commerce, 1974–77; Adv. Cttee on Supply and Educn of Teachers, 1982–85. Hon. Sec., 1990–94, Vice-Chm., 1994–2000, GTC (England and Wales). Trustee and Mem. Exec., Education 2000, 1983–89 (Hon. Sec., 1987–89); Mem. Exec., Schools Curriculum Award, 1986–91. Hon. Prof., Russian Fedn Min. of Educn (Perm State Pedagogical Univ.), 1998–. *Publications:* (ed) The School as a Centre of Enquiry, 1975; (ed) Staffing our Secondary Schools, 1980; (ed) Teacher Training and Special Educational Needs, 1985; What Future for Secondary Schools?, 1985; Secondary schools for All?, 1987, 2nd edn 1994; (ed) Management and the Psychology of Schooling, 1988; Schools and External Relations, 1989; Managing Schools, 1989; Towards the General Teaching Council, 1989; The Future Governance of Education, 1993; Developing Schools for Democracy in Europe, 1995; (ed) Developing Teaching for Special Needs in Russia, 1999; (ed with K. Van der Wolf) Opening Schools to All, 1999; (ed with J. Vanderhoeven) School Choice, Equity and Social Exclusion, 2000; (ed with J. Vanderhoeven) Reflection for Action, 2000; The General Teaching Council, 2000; (ed) Opening Windows to Change, 2001; frequent contribs on educnl topics to learned jls and symposia. *Recreation:* postal history. *Address:* 8 Northmoor Road, Oxford OX2 6UP. *T:* (01865) 556932.

SAYER, Robert; Senior Partner, Sayer Moore & Co., since 1983; President, Law Society, 1999–2000 (Vice-President, 1995–96 and 1998–99); *b* 16 Jan. 1952; *s* of Kenneth Albert Ernest Sayer and Ellen Sayer; *m* 1997, Cathy Hunt. *Educ:* Salvatorian Coll., Harrow Weald, Middx; Swansea Univ. (BA Hons). Admitted Solicitor, 1979. Law Society: Dep. Vice Pres., 1997–98; Treas., 1997–99. Hon. Mem., Inst. of Advanced Legal Studies. *Publications:* numerous articles in legal jls. *Recreations:* sailing, walking. *Address:* (office) 190 Horn Lane, W3 6PL. *T:* (020) 8993 7571. *Club:* Naval and Military.

SAYERS, Prof. Bruce McArthur, PhD, DScEng; FREng, FIEE; Professor Emeritus of Computing Applied to Medicine, and Senior Research Fellow, Imperial College of Science, Technology and Medicine, since 1993; *b* 6 Feb. 1928; *s* of John William McArthur Sayers and Mabel Florence Sayers (*née* Howe); *m* 1951, R Woolls Humphery. *Educ:* Melbourne Boys' High School; Univ. of Melbourne (MSc); Imperial College, Univ. of London (PhD, DIC, DScEng; FIC 1996). FREng (FEng 1990). Biophysicist, Baker Med. Research Inst. and Clinical Research Unit, Alfred Hosp., Melbourne, 1949–54; Imperial College, London: Research Asst, 1955–56; Philips Elec. Ltd Research Fellow, 1957; Lectr, 1958; Senior Lectr, 1963; Reader, 1965; Prof. of Electrical Engrg Applied to Medicine, 1968–84; Head of Dept of Electrical Engrg, 1979–84; Prof. of Computing Applied to Medicine and Head of Dept of Computing, 1984–89; Kobler Prof. of the Management of IT, and Dir, Centre for Cognitive Systems, 1990–93; Dean, City and Guilds Coll., 1984–88, and 1991–93, Fellow, 1996. Pres., Section of Measurement in Medicine, Royal Soc. of Medicine, 1971–72; Hon. Consultant, Royal Throat, Nose and Ear Hosp., 1974–93; UK rep., Bio-engineering Working Group, EEC Cttee for Med. Res., 1976–80; Temp. Adviser, WHO, 1970–76, 1981–87 and 1995–; Member: WHO Adv. Cttee for Health Res., 1988–94 and 1997–2000 (Vice Chm., 1990–92); Engrg Adv. Cttee, Science Mus., 1987–93. Consultant: Data Laboratories, 1968–80; Data Beta, 1981–93; Advent Eurofund, 1981–89; Shinan Investment Services SA, Switzerland, 1984–87; Advent Capital Ltd, 1985–89; Neuroscience Ltd, 1985–90; Transatlantic Capital (Biosciences) Fund, 1985–; Director: Imperial Software Technology Ltd, 1984–90; Imperial Information Technology Ltd, 1986–90. Former Visiting Prof., Univs of Melbourne, Rio de Janeiro, McGill, Toronto. Travelling Lectr: Nuffield Foundn-Nat. Research Council, Canada, 1971; Inst. of Electron. and Radio Engrs, Australia, 1976. Member: (PC nominee), Academic Adv. Council, 1988–96, Council, 1994–96, Buckingham Univ.; Internat. Academic Cttee on Energy Studies, Ecole Polytechnique Fédérale de Lausanne, 1989–98; Scientific Council, Internat. Center of Biocybernetics, Warsaw, 1993–99; Steering Gp, Internat. Centre for Advanced Studies in Health Sci., Univ. of Ulm, 2000–. FCGI 1983 (Pres., City and Guilds Coll. Assoc., 1995–96). Hon. Fellow, British Cybernetics Soc., 1986. Hon. Foreign Mem., Medico-Chirurgical Soc. of Bologna, 1965; Hon. Member, Eta Kappa Nu (USA), 1980. Freeman of the City of London, 1986; Liveryman, Scientific Instrument Makers' Co., 1986. *Publications:* papers, mainly on biomedical signals and control systems, epidemiology, cardiology and audiology. *Recreations:* lazing around the Languedoc, music. *Address:* 40 Queen's Gate, SW7 5HR. *T:* (020) 7581 3690; La Payrastrié, 81360 Montredon-Labessonnié, France. *T:* 563751018. *Club:* Athenæum.

SAYERS, Michael Patrick; QC 1988; a Recorder of the Crown Court, since 1986; *b* 28 March 1940; *s* of Major Herbert James Michael Sayers, RA (killed on active service, 1943) and late Joan Sheilah de Courcy Holroyd (*née* Stephenson); *m* 1976, Mrs Moussie Brougham (*née* Hallstrom); one *s* one *d*, and one step *s*. *Educ:* Harrow School; Fitzwilliam College, Cambridge (Evelyn Rothschild Scholar; MA). Called to the Bar, Inner Temple, 1970, Bencher, 1994; Junior, Central Criminal Court Bar Mess, 1975–78; Supplementary Prosecuting Counsel to the Crown, Central Criminal Court, 1977–88. Mem. Cttee, Barristers' Benevolent Assoc., 1991–. Vice-Pres., Harrow Assoc., 1999– (Chm., 1992–97). *Recreations:* shooting, stalking, theatre, Sweden. *Address:* 2 King's Bench Walk, Temple, EC4Y 7DE. *T:* (020) 7353 1746; 1 Pembroke Villas, W8 6PG. *T:* (020) 7937 6033. *Clubs:* Garrick, Pratt's; Queen's, Swinley Forest Golf.

SAYERS, Ross Edward; Chairman: Innogy Holdings plc, since 2000; Associated British Ports, from April 2002; *b* 1 Sept. 1941; *s* of Stanley and Grace Sayers; *m* 1964, Glenda Seath; two *s*. *Educ:* Auckland GS; Auckland Univ. (Dip. Business and Industrial Admin); Harvard Univ. (AMP). FCA 1962. Man. Dir, Holeproof NZ Ltd, 1958–75; Partner, McElroy Speakman & Co., 1976–77; Gen. Manager, Ops, Feltex NZ, 1977–83; Man. Dir, NZ Breweries, 1983–86; Chairman and Chief Executive: NZ Railways Corp., 1986–88; State Rail Authy of NSW, 1988–92; Man. Dir and CEO, China Light and

Power Co., subseq. CLP Hldgs, 1993–2000. NZ Commemoration Medal, 1990. *Recreations:* walking, photography. *Address:* (office) Windmill Hill Business Park, Whitehill Way, Swindon, Wilts SN5 6PB. *T:* (01793) 893030. *Clubs:* Athenæum, Royal Automobile.

SAYLE, Alexei David; actor, comedian, writer; *b* 7 Aug. 1952; *s* of Joseph Henry Sayle and Malka Sayle; *m* 1974, Linda Rawsthorn. *Educ:* Alsop GS, Liverpool; Southport Coll. of Art; Chelsea Sch. of Art (DipAD); Garnett Coll. (CertEd). Compère: Comedy Store Club, 1979–80; Comic Strip Club, 1980–81; *television series:* Young Ones, 1982–84; Alexei Sayle's Stuff (also writer), 1988–89, 1991; The Gravy Train, 1990; All New Alexei Sayle Show (also writer), 1994–95; Alexei Sayle's Merry-go-round, 1998; Arabian Nights, 2000; *films include:* Gorky Park, 1983; Indiana Jones and the Last Crusade, 1989; Swing, 1998. Columnist: Independent, Car; formerly on Observer, Time Out, Sunday Mirror. Hon Prof., Thames Valley Univ., 1995. *Publications:* Train to Hell, 1982; Geoffrey the Tube Train and the Fat Comedian, 1987; Great Bus Journeys of the World, 1988; Barcelona Plates (short stories), 2000; The Dog Catcher (short stories), 2001. *Recreation:* walking. *Address:* c/o Mayer & Eden, 34 Kingly Court, W1R 5LE. *T:* (020) 7434 1242. *Club:* Chelsea Arts.

SAYNOR, John, CMG 1992; JP; Secretary and Director-General, Commonwealth War Graves Commission, 1989–92; *b* 28 Sept. 1930; *s* of Charles Herbert Saynor and Emily Saynor (*née* Mundie); *m* 1954, Jennifer Ann Nelson; two *s. Educ:* Doncaster Grammar Sch. Commnd RASC, 1949–51. Post Office, 1951–69; Dept for National Savings, 1969–74; Commonwealth War Graves Commn, 1974–92. Mem. Bd, High Wycombe YMCA (Chm., 1992–98; Vice-Chm., 1998–2000); Mem. Cttee, Flackwell Heath Age Concern, 1998–. JP Berks, 1983. *Recreations:* gardening, golf, bridge, travel, painting. *Address:* 12 The Meadows, Flackwell Heath, High Wycombe, Bucks HP10 9LX. *T:* (01628) 523459.

SCACCHI, Greta; actress. *Films* include: Heat and Dust, 1983; The Coca Cola Kid, 1985; Burke & Wills; Defence of the Realm, 1986; Good Morning Babylon, 1987; A Man in Love, 1988; White Mischief, 1988; Love and Fear (Les Trois Soeurs), 1990; Presumed Innocent, 1990; Fires Within, 1991; Shattered, 1991; Turtle Beach, 1992; The Player, 1992; Salt on our Skin; The Browning Version, 1994; Jefferson in Paris, 1994; Country Life, 1994; Emma, 1996; The Serpent's Kiss; The Red Violin, 1999; Cotton Mary, 1999; Tom's Midnight Garden, 2000; *television:* The Ebony Tower, 1984; Dr Fischer of Geneva; Waterfront (Best Actress, Penguin and Golden Logie Awards, Australia); Rasputin (Emmy for best-supporting actress), 1996; The Odyssey, 1997; Macbeth, 1997; *stage:* Cider with Rosie, Phoenix Arts, Leicester, 1982; Times Like These, Bristol Old Vic, 1985; Airbase, Oxford Playhouse, 1986; Uncle Vanya, Vaudeville, 1988; The Doll's House, Fest. of Perth, 1991; Miss Julie, 1992, Simpatico, 1996, Sydney Theatre Co.; The Guardsman, Albery, 2000. *Address:* c/o Conway van Gelder, 3rd Floor, 18–21 Jermyn Street, SW1Y 6HP.

SCADDING, Dr John William, FRCP; Consultant Neurologist: National Hospital for Neurology and Neurosurgery, since 1982 (Medical Director, 1993–96); Whittington Hospital, since 1982; *b* 17 June 1948; *s* of late Prof. John Guyett Scadding, FRCP; *m* 1st, 1975, Glenis Kathleen Dawes (marr. diss. 1986); one *s* one *d*; 2nd, 1994, Maureen Ann Clarke-Darby (marr. diss. 1997); 3rd, 2000, Stella Veronica Tan Su-Ming. *Educ:* University College London and UCH Med. Sch. (BSc 1st Cl. Hons, MB BS, MD). Jun. hosp. posts at UCH, Hammersmith, Brompton, Royal Free and National Hosps, 1972–82; Res. Fellow, UCL and Royal Free Hosp. Sch. of Medicine, 1978–80. Hon. Sen. Lectr, Inst. of Neurology, 1982–. Hon. Neurologist: St Luke's Hosp. for the Clergy, 1983–; Royal Soc. of Musicians, 1996–; Civilian Consultant Adviser, MoD, 1989–; Civilian Consultant Neurologist to RN, 1993–, to RAF, 1997–. *Publications:* research papers on mechanisms of pain in neurological disease; contribs to learned jls. *Recreations:* music (pianist), mountain walking. *Address:* National Hospital for Neurology and Neurosurgery, Queen Square, WC1N 3BG. *T:* (020) 7837 3611.

SCAIFE, Geoffrey Richard, CB 1999; Chief Executive, Birmingham Health Authority, since 2000; *b* 12 Jan. 1949; *m* 1971, Janet Elizabeth Woodward; two *s* two *d. Educ:* Workington GS. DHSS, 1968–71, 1975–83; seconded to Prime Minister's Private Office, 1971–74; Mersey RHA, 1983–93, Chief Exec., 1989–93; Chief Exec., Mgt Exec. for NHS in Scotland, Scottish Office, then Scottish Exec., DoH, 1993–2000. Mem. Bd, Nat. Develt Team for People with Learning Disabilities, 1992–95. *Address:* Birmingham Health Authority, St Chad's Court, 213 Hagley Road, Edgbaston, Birmingham B16 9RG.

SCALES, Prof. John Tracey, OBE 1986; FRCS, LRCP; CIMechE; Hon. Director, 1988–93 and Director, Pressure Sore Prevention, 1994–97, RAFT Institute of Plastic Surgery (formerly Department of Research in Plastic Surgery), Regional Plastic and Oral Surgery Centre, Mount Vernon Hospital; Professor of Biomedical Engineering, Institute of Orthopaedics, University of London, 1974–87, now Emeritus; *b* 2 July 1920; *s* of late W. L. Scales and E. M. Scales (*née* Tracey); *m* 1945, Cecilia May (*d* 1992), *d* of late A. W. Sparrow; two *d. Educ:* Haberdashers' Aske's Sch., Hampstead; King's Coll., London; Charing Cross Hosp. Med. Sch. MRCS, LRCP 1944; FRCS 1969. CIMechE 1966. Captain RAMC, 1945–47. Casualty Officer and Resident Anaesthetist, Charing Cross Hosp., 1944; Royal National Orthopaedic Hosp., Stanmore: House Surgeon, 1944–45 and 1947–49; MO i/c Plastics Res. Unit, 1949–50; Hon. Registrar, 1950–52; Hon. Sen Registrar, 1952–57; Lectr i/c Plastics Res. Unit, Inst. of Orth., Stanmore, 1951–52; Sen. Lectr i/c Plastics Res. Unit (re-named Dept. of Biomechanics and Surg. Materials, 1956; re-named Dept of Biomed. Engrg, 1968), Inst. of Orth., Univ. of London, 1952–68; Consultant in Orthopaedic Prosthetics, 1958–68, in Biomedical Engrg, 1968–87, Royal Nat. Orthopaedic Hosp., Stanmore and London (Hon. Consultant); Reader in Biomed. Engrg, Dept of Biomed. Engrg, Inst. of Orth., Univ. of London, 1968–74; Consultant in Biomed. Engrg, Mt Vernon Hosp., Northwood, 1969–85; Consultant, Royal Orthopaedic Hosp., Birmingham, 1978–87. Vis. Prof., Biomed. Centre, Cranfield Univ., 1997–98. Chairman: BSI Cttee on Orthopaedic Joint-replacements, 1981–91; ISO Cttee on Bone and Joint Replacements; Member: IMechE Engrg in Medicine Gp, 1966–91 (Founder Mem.); Adv. Panel on Med. Engrg, National Fund for Res. into Crippling Diseases (Chm., 1981–85); British Orth. Res. Soc., 1962–; Biol Engrg Soc., 1960– (Founder Mem.); Eur. Soc. of Biomaterials, 1974– (Founder Mem.); Hon. Member: Eur. Soc. of Biomechanics, 1976– (Former Pres., Founder Mem.); British Assoc. of Plastic Surgeons, 1993–. Ext. Examiner, Univ. of Surrey, 1969–84, and other univs. Freeman, City of London, 1995. FRSocMed 1950; Companion Fellow, British Orth. Assoc., 1959 (Sen. Companion Fellow, 1994); FBES 1994; FIPEM 1995. Thomas Henry Green Prize in Surgery, Charing Cross Hosp. Med. Sch., 1943; Robert Danis Prize, Internat. Soc. of Surgery, Brussels, 1969; James Berrie Prize, RCS, 1973; Clemson Univ. Award, USA, 1974; S. G. Brown Award, Royal Soc., 1974; A. A. Griffith Silver Medal, Materials Science Club, 1980; Jackson Burrows Medal, Royal Nat. Orthopaedic Hosp., Stanmore, 1985; Don Julius Groen Prize, IMechE, 1988. Kentucky Colonel, 1986. Member Editorial Board: Engineering in Medicine; Clinical Materials, 1986–; Wounds, 1989–. Research includes development of: polymeric orthopaedic splints and appliances, 1945–81; bone and joint prostheses and joint replacements, using metals and polymers, 1949–87; British cuirass respirator, 1950–53; Airstrip, 1954–59; air support systems for prevention of pressure sores, 1960–82. *Publications: chapters in:* Modern Trends in Surgical Materials, ed Gillis, 1958; Aspects of Medical Physics, ed Rotblat, 1966; Surgical Dressings and Wound Healing, ed Harkiss, 1971; (and ed jtly) Bed Sore Biomechanics, 1976; Surgical Dressings in the Hospital Environment, ed Turner and Brain, 1976; Treatment of Burns, ed Donati, Burke and Bertelli, 1976; Scientific Foundations of Orthopaedics and Traumatology, ed Owen, Goodfellow and Bullough, 1980; also jt author of chapters in med. books; contrib. Proc. RSM, Proc. IMechE, Proc. Physiol Soc., BMJ, Jl of Bone and Jt Surg., Lancet, Nature, and other med. and scientific jls; contrib. conf. and symposia reports. *Recreations:* walking dogs, Goss china. *Address:* Fairbanks, Riverview Road, Pangbourne, Berks RG8 7AU. *T:* (0118) 9843568, *Fax:* (0118) 9844945.

SCALES, Neil; Chief Executive and Director General, Merseytravel, since 1999; *b* 24 June 1956; *s* of Gordon and Joyce Scales; *m* 1983, June Bradley; one *s* one *d. Educ:* Sunderland Poly. (BSc 1981; MSc 1984; DMS 1986); Open Univ. (MBA 1991). Apprentice, Sunderland Corp. Transport, 1972–76; engrg posts, Tyne & Wear PTE, 1976–86; Chief Engr, 1986–88, Dir of Engrg, 1988–90, Greater Manchester Buses; Man. Dir, Northern Counties, 1990–96; Greater Manchester PTE, 1996; consultant, private sector, 1997–99; Dir of Customer Services, Merseytravel, 1999. *Recreations:* Sunderland FC, tutoring with Open University. *Address:* Merseytravel, 24 Hatton Garden, Liverpool L3 2AN. *T:* (0151) 330 1101.

SCALES, Prunella, (Prunella Margaret Rumney West), CBE 1992; actress; *d* of John Richardson Illingworth and Catherine Scales; *m* 1963, Timothy Lancaster West, *qv*; two *s. Educ:* Moira House, Eastbourne; Old Vic Theatre School, London; Herbert Berghof Studio, New York (with Uta Hagen). Repertory in Huddersfield, Salisbury, Oxford, Bristol Old Vic, etc; seasons at Stratford-on-Avon and Chichester Festival Theatre; plays on London stage include: The Promise, 1967; Hay Fever, 1968; It's a Two-Foot-Six-Inches-Above-The-Ground-World, 1970; The Wolf, 1975; Breezeblock Park, 1978; Make and Break, 1980; An Evening with Queen Victoria, 1980; The Merchant of Venice, 1981; Quartermaine's Terms, 1981; Big in Brazil, 1984; When We Are Married, 1986; Single Spies (double bill), 1988; The School for Scandal, 1990; Long Day's Journey into Night, 1991; Mother Tongue, 1992; The Birthday Party, 1999; A Day in the Death of Joe Egg, 2001; regional theatre: Happy Days, Leeds, 1993; The Matchmaker, Chichester, 1993; Staying On, nat. tour, 1997; The Cherry Orchard, Oxford Playhouse, 2000; *films include:* Howard's End, 1992; Second Best, 1993; Wolf, 1994; An Awfully Big Adventure, 1994; An Ideal Husband, 1999; Ghost of Greville Lodge; *television:* Fawlty Towers (series), 1975, 1978; Grand Duo, The Merry Wives of Windsor, 1982; Mapp and Lucia (series), 1985–86; Absurd Person Singular, 1985; The Index Has Gone Fishing, What the Butler Saw, 1987; After Henry (series), 1988, 1990; The Rector's Wife, Fair Game, 1994; Dalziel & Pascoe, 1996; Signs and Wonders, Lord of Misrule, Breaking the Code, 1997; frequent broadcasts, readings, poetry recitals and fringe productions. Has directed plays at Bristol Old Vic, Arts Theatre, Cambridge, Billingham Forum, Almost Free Theatre, London, Nottingham Playhouse, Palace Theatre, Watford, W Yorks Playhouse, Leeds, Nat. Theatre of WA, Perth, and taught at several drama schools. Pres., CPRE, 1997–. Hon DLitt: Bradford, 1995; East Anglia, 1996. *Recreation:* gardening. *Address:* c/o Jeremy Conway, 18–21 Jermyn Street, SW1Y 6HP.

See also S. A. J. West.

SCALIA, Antonin; Associate Justice, United States Supreme Court, since 1986; *b* 11 March 1936; *s* of S. Eugene Scalia and Catherine Louise (*née* Panaro); *m* 1960, Maureen McCarthy; five *s* four *d. Educ:* Georgetown Univ. (AB 1957); Fribourg Univ., Switzerland; Harvard (LLB 1960; Sheldon Fellow, 1960–61). Admitted to Ohio Bar, 1962, to Virginia Bar, 1970. Associate, Jones, Day, Cockley & Reavis, Cleveland, 1961–67; Associate Prof., 1967–70, Prof., 1970–74, Univ. of Virginia Law Sch.; Gen. Counsel, Office of Telecommunications, Exec. Office of Pres., 1971–72; Chm., Admin. Conf. US, Washington, 1972–74; Asst Attorney Gen., US Office of Legal Counsel, Justice Dept, 1974–77; Prof., Law Sch., Chicago Univ., 1977–82; Judge, US Court Appeals (DC Circuit), 1982–86. American Bar Association: Mem. Council, 1974–77, Chm., 1981–82, Section Admin. Law; Chm., Conf. Section, 1982–83. Jt Editor, Regulation Magazine, 1979–82. *Address:* US Supreme Court, 1 First Street NE, Washington, DC 20543, USA.

SCALLY, Dr Gabriel John, FFPHM; Regional Director of Public Health, South West Region, NHS Executive, Department of Health, since 1996; *b* 24 Sept. 1954; *s* of Bernard Gabriel Scally and Maureen Scally (*née* Hopkins); *m* 1990, Rona Margaret Campbell; two *d. Educ:* St Mary's Grammar Sch., Belfast; Queen's Univ., Belfast (MB, BCh, BAO 1978); London Sch. of Hygiene and Tropical Medicine, Univ. of London (MSc 1982). MFPHM 1984, FFPHM 1991; MFPHMI 1992; MRCGP 1993. Trainee in Gen. Practice, 1980–81; Sen. Tutor, Dept of Community Medicine, QUB, 1984–86; Consultant in Public Health Medicine, 1986–88, Chief Admin. MO and Dir of Public Health, 1989–93, Eastern Health and Social Services Bd, Belfast; Regional Director of Public Health: SE Thames RHA, 1993–94; South and West RHA, 1994–96. Member: NI Bd for Nursing, Health Visiting and Midwifery, 1988–93; Council, BMA, 1985–86, 1988–89 (Chm., Jun. Mems Forum, 1988–89); GMC, 1989–99. *Publications:* papers on med. res. and health policy in med. jls. *Recreations:* sailing, traditional and contemporary Irish music, theatre. *Address:* 11 Dowry Square, Bristol BS8 4SH. *T:* (0117) 926 8510.

SCANLAN, Dorothy, (Mrs Charles Denis Scanlan); *see* Quick, Dorothy.

SCANLAN, Prof. John Oliver, PhD, DSc; FIEEE, FIEE, FIMA, FIEI; Professor of Electronic Engineering, University College Dublin, since 1973; President, Royal Irish Academy, 1993–96; *b* 20 Sept. 1937; *s* of John and Hannah Scanlan; *m* 1961, Ann Weadock. *Educ:* University Coll. Dublin (BE, ME); Leeds Univ. (PhD); NUI (DSc). FIMA 1971; FIEE 1972; FIEEE 1976; FIEI 1980. Lectr, 1963–68, Prof. of Electronic Engrg, 1968–73, Univ. of Leeds. Dir, Telecom Eireann, 1984–97. MRIA 1977 (Sec., 1981–89). Editor, Internat. Jl of Circuit Theory and Applications, 1973–. *Publications:* Analysis and Synthesis of Tunnel Diode Circuits, 1966; Circuit Theory, vol. I, 1970, (with R. Levy) vol. II, 1973; numerous contribs to learned jls. *Recreations:* golf, music. *Address:* Department of Electronic and Electrical Engineering, University College Dublin, Dublin 4, Ireland. *T:* 2693244.

SCANLAN, Michael; Senior Partner, Russells Gibson McCaffrey (formerly Russells), Solicitors, Glasgow, since 1982; President, Law Society of Scotland, 1999–2000 (Vice-President, 1998–99); *b* 6 June 1946, *s* of William Scanlan and Agnes (Nancy) Scanlan; *m* 1971, Margaret Denvir; one *s. Educ:* St Aloysius Coll., Glasgow; Glasgow Univ. Apprentice, T. F. Russell & Co., 1965–71; admitted solicitor, 1971; Asst, 1971–73, Partner, 1973–82, T. F. Russell & Co., subseq. Russells. Lectr in Evidence and Procedure, Strathclyde Univ., 1979–85. Ext. Examr in Evidence and Procedure, Glasgow Univ., 1982–85. Temp. Sheriff, 1986–96. *Recreations:* golf, reading, music. *Address:* Russells Gibson McCaffrey, 13 Bath Street, Glasgow G2 1HY; Willowfield, Kirkintilloch Road, Lenzie, Glasgow G66 4LW.

SCANLON, family name of **Baron Scanlon**.

SCANLON, Baron *cr* 1979 (Life Peer), of Davyhulme in the County of Greater Manchester; **Hugh Parr Scanlon;** President, Amalgamated Union of Engineering Workers, 1968–78; Member, British Gas Corporation, 1976–82; *b* 26 Oct. 1913; *m* 1943, Nora; two *d. Educ:* Stretford Elem. Sch.; NCLC. Apprentice, Instrument Maker, Shop Steward-Convener, AEI, Trafford Park; Divisional Organiser, AEU, Manchester, 1947–63; Member: Exec. Council, AEU, London, 1963–67; TUC Gen. Council, 1968–78; TUC Econ. Cttee, 1968–78. Member: NEDC, 1971–; Metrication Bd, 1973–78; NEB, 1977–79; Govt Cttee of Inquiry into Teaching of Maths in Primary and Secondary Schs in England and Wales, 1978–; Chm., Engineering Industry Training Bd, 1975–82. Vice-Pres., Internat. Metalworkers' Fedn, 1969–78; Pres., European Metal Workers' Fedn, 1974–78. Hon. DCL Kent, 1988. *Recreations:* golf, swimming, gardening. *Address:* 23 Seven Stones Drive, Broadstairs, Kent CT10 1TW. *Club:* Eltham Warren Golf.

SCANLON, Mary Elizabeth; Member (C) Highlands and Islands, Scottish Parliament, since 1999; *b* 25 May 1947; *d* of John Charles Campbell and Anne Campbell (*née* O'Donnell); *m* 1970, James Scanlon; one *s* one *d. Educ:* Univ. of Dundee (MA Econ/Pol 1982). Civil Service Administrator; Lecturer: Dundee Inst. of Technology, 1982–85; Perth Coll., 1985–88; Lectr in Econs, Dundee Coll. of Technology, 1988–94; Lectr in Econs and Business Studies, Inverness Coll., 1994–99. *Recreations:* hill walking, swimming, gardening. *Address:* 25 Miller Street, Inverness IV2 3DN. *T:* (01463) 718951.

SCANNELL, Vernon, FRSL; free-lance author, poet and broadcaster, since 1962; *b* 23 Jan. 1922. *Educ:* elementary schools; Leeds Univ. Served with Gordon Highlanders (51st Highland Div.), ME and Normandy, 1940–45; Leeds Univ. (reading Eng. Lit.), 1946–47; various jobs incl. professional boxer, 1945–46, English Master at Hazelwood Prep. Sch., 1955–62. Southern Arts Assoc. Writing Fellowship, 1975–76; Vis. Poet, Shrewsbury Sch., 1978–79; Res. Poet, King's Sch. Canterbury, Michaelmas Term 1979. FRSL 1960. Granted a civil list pension, 1981, for services to literature. *Publications: novels:* The Fight, 1953; The Wound and the Scar, 1953; The Big Chance, 1960; The Face of the Enemy, 1961; The Shadowed Place, 1961; The Dividing Night, 1962; The Big Time, 1965; The Dangerous Ones (for children), 1970; A Lonely Game (for younger readers), 1979; Ring of Truth, 1983; Feminine Endings, 2000; *poetry:* The Masks of Love, 1960 (Heinemann Award, 1960); A Sense of Danger, 1962; Walking Wounded: poems 1962–65, 1968; Epithets of War: poems 1965–69, 1969; Mastering the Craft (Poets Today Series) (for children), 1970; (with J. Silkin) Pergamon Poets, No 8, 1970; Selected Poems, 1971; The Winter Man: new poems, 1973; The Apple Raid and other poems (for children), 1974 (Cholmondeley Poetry Prize, 1974); The Loving Game, 1975 (also in paperback); New and Collected Poems 1950–80, 1980; Winterlude and other poems, 1982; Funeral Games and other poems, 1987; The Clever Potato (for children), 1988; Soldiering On: poems of military life, 1989; Love Shouts and Whispers (for children), 1990; A Time for Fires, 1991; Travelling Light (for children), 1991; Collected Poems 1950–93, 1994; The Black and White Days, 1996; Views and Distances, 2000; *edited:* (with Ted Hughes and Patricia Beer) New Poems: a PEN anthology, 1962; Sporting Literature: an anthology, 1987; *criticism:* Not Without Glory: poets of World War II, 1976; How to Enjoy Poetry, 1982; How to Enjoy Novels, 1984; *autobiography:* The Tiger and the Rose, 1971; A Proper Gentleman, 1977; Argument of Kings, 1987; Drums of Morning, 1992. *Recreations:* listening to radio (mainly music), drink, boxing (as a spectator), films, reading, learning French, loathing Tories and New Labour. *Address:* 51 North Street, Otley, W Yorks LS21 1AH. *T:* (01943) 467176.

SCARASCIA-MUGNOZZA, Carlo; Hon. President: International Centre for Advanced Mediterranean Agronomic Studies, Paris, since 1988 (President, 1983–87); Council of State, Italy, since 1990 (Member, 1977–90); President, Accademia Nazionale di Danza, Rome, since 1968; *b* Rome, 19 Jan. 1920. Mem., Italian Chamber of Deputies, for Lecce-Brindisi-Taranto, 1953; Vice-Pres., Christian Democrat Party Gp, 1958–62; Leader, Italian Delegn to UNESCO, 1962; Secretary of State: for Educn, 1962–63; for Justice, June 1963–Dec. 1963; Mem., European Parliament, 1961–72, Chm., Political Cttee, 1969–72; a Vice-Pres., EEC, 1972–77. Mem., Accademia Agricoltura di Francia. *Address:* Via Timavo 32, 00195 Rome, Italy. *T:* (6) 37351379.

SCARBOROUGH, Vernon Marcus; HM Diplomatic Service; Resident Deputy High Commissioner, Tarawa, Republic of Kiribati, since 2000; *b* 11 Feb. 1940; *s* of George Arthur Scarborough and Sarah Florence Scarborough (*née* Patey); *m* 1966, Jennifer Bernadette Keane; three *d. Educ:* Brockley County Grammar Sch.; Westminster Coll. Passport Office, FO, 1958–61, CRO 1961; served Dacca, Karachi, Brussels, Bathurst, later Banjul, FCO, Muscat and Lagos; Kuala Lumpur, 1983–86 (First Sec., 1984); FCO, 1986; Chargé d'Affaires, San Salvador, 1987–90; Consul, Auckland, 1990–94; Dep. High Comr, Suva, and Ambassador to Palau, Federated States of Micronesia and Marshall Is, 1995–2000. *Recreations:* photography, golf, vintage vehicles. *Address:* c/o Foreign and Commonwealth Office, King Charles Street, SW1A 2AH; Broadoaks, 29 Erica Way, Copthorne, W Sussex RH10 3XG. *Clubs:* Royal Commonwealth Society, Model A Club of Great Britain; Fiji, Defence, Fiji Golf, Returned Servicemen's and Ex-Servicemen's Association (Suva).

SCARBROUGH, 12th Earl of, *cr* 1690; **Richard Aldred Lumley;** Viscount Lumley (Ire.), 1628; Baron Lumley, 1681; Viscount Lumley, 1690; Lord-Lieutenant of South Yorkshire, since 1996 (Vice Lord-Lieutenant, 1990–96); *b* 5 Dec. 1932; *o s* of 11th Earl of Scarbrough, KG, PC, GCSI, GCIE, GCVO, and Katharine Isobel, Dowager Countess of Scarbrough, DCVO (*d* 1979), *d* of late R. F. McEwen; *S* father, 1969; *m* 1970, Lady Elizabeth Ramsay (Lady of the Bedchamber to Queen Elizabeth the Queen Mother), *d* of 16th Earl of Dalhousie, KT, GCVO, GBE, MC; two *s* one *d. Educ:* Eton; Magdalen College, Oxford. 2nd Lt 11th Hussars, 1951–52; formerly Lt Queen's Own Yorkshire Dragoons. ADC to Governor and C-in-C, Cyprus, 1956. Hon. Col, 1st Bn The Yorkshire Volunteers, 1975–88. President: Northern Area, Royal British Legion, 1984–93; York Georgian Soc., 1985–92; Northern Assoc. of Building Socs (formerly Yorkshire and North Western Assoc. of Building Socs), 1985–95. Mem., Royal Commn on Historical MSS, 1994–. Trustee, Leeds Castle Foundn, 1983–. Hon. RIBA, Yorks Region. Hon. LLD Sheffield, 2001. DL S Yorks, 1974. *Heir: s* Viscount Lumley, *qv. Address:* Sandbeck Park, Maltby, Rotherham, S Yorks S66 8PF. *T:* (01302) 742210. *Clubs:* White's, Pratt's; Jockey (Newmarket).
See also Lady Grimthorpe.

SCARD, Dennis Leslie; General Secretary, Musicians' Union, 1990–2000; *b* 8 May 1943; *s* of late Charles Leslie Scard and Doris Annie (*née* Farmer); *m* 1st, (marr. diss); two *s;* 2nd, 1993, Linda Perry. *Educ:* Lascelles Co. Secondary Sch.; Trinity Coll. of Music, London (Hon. Fellow, 1997). Professional horn player, 1962–85, performed with leading symphony and chamber orchestras. Part-time instrumental teacher, London Borough of Hillingdon, 1974–85. Musicians' Union: Chm., Central London Br., 1972–85; Mem., Exec. Cttee, 1979–85; full-time Official, Birmingham, 1985–90. Mem., TUC Gen. Council, 1990–2001. Member Board: Symphony Hall, Birmingham; Trinity Coll. of Music (Chair, Alumni Assoc.). FRSA 1992. *Recreations:* music, home wine making, walking, theatre. *Address:* 6 Cranborne Avenue, Meads, Eastbourne BN20 7TS. *T:* and *Fax:* (01323) 648364.

SCARDINO, Marjorie Morris, DJur; Chief Executive, Pearson plc, since 1997; *b* 25 Jan. 1947; *d* of Robert Weldon and Beth Morris (*née* Lamb); *m* 1974, Albert James Scardino; two *s* one *d. Educ:* Baylor Univ. (BA); Univ. of San Francisco (DJur). Partner, Brannen Wessels & Searcy, 1976–85; Pres., Economist Newspaper Gp Inc., 1985–93; Worldwide Man. Dir, Economist Intelligence Unit, NY, 1992–93; Chief Exec., Economist Gp, 1993–97. *Address:* Pearson plc, 3 Burlington Gardens, W1X 1LE.

SCARFE, Gerald, RDI 1989; artist; *b* 1 June 1936; *m* Jane Asher, *qv;* two *s* one *d. Educ:* scattered (due to chronic asthma as a child). Punch, 1960; Private Eye, 1961; Daily Mail, 1966; Sunday Times, 1967–; cover artist to illustrator, Time Magazine, 1967; animation and film directing for BBC, 1969–; artist, New Yorker, 1993–. Has taken part in exhibitions: Grosvenor Gall., 1969 and 1970; Pavillon d'Humour, Montreal, 1967 and 1971; Expo '70, Osaka, 1970; six sculptures of British Character, Millennium Dome, 2000. One-man exhibitions of sculptures and lithographs: Waddell Gall., New York, 1968 and 1970; Grosvenor Gall., 1969; Vincent Price Gall., Chicago, 1969; National Portrait Gall., 1971; retrospective exhibn, Royal Festival Hall, 1983; drawings: Langton Gall., 1986; Chris Beetles Gall., 1989; Gerald Scarfe Meets Walt Disney, MOMI, 1997; Gerald Scarfe, The Art of Hercules, Z Gall., NY, 1997; Nat. Portrait Gall., 1998; Cleveland Gall., 1998. Animated film for BBC, Long Drawn Out Trip, 1973 (prizewinner, Zagreb); Dir, Scarfe by Scarfe, BBC (BAFTA Award, 1987); Designer and Dir, animated sequences in film, The Wall, 1982; designer: Who's A Lucky Boy?, Royal Exchange, Manchester, 1984; Orpheus in the Underworld, ENO, 1985; Born Again, Chichester, 1990; The Magic Flute, Los Angeles, 1993, Houston, Texas, 1997, Seattle, 1999; An Absolute Turkey, Globe, 1994 (Olivier Award for best costumes); Mind Millie For Me, Haymarket, 1996; Fantastic Mr Fox, Los Angeles Opera, 1998; production designer, Hercules (Walt Disney film), 1995–97; costume designer, Peter and the Wolf, Holiday on Ice and world tour. *Publications:* Gerald Scarfe's People, 1966; Indecent Exposure (ltd edn), 1973; Expletive Deleted: the life and times of Richard Nixon (ltd edn), 1974; Gerald Scarfe, 1982; Father Kissmass and Mother Claws, 1985; Scarfe by Scarfe (autobiog), 1986 (televised, 1987); Scarfe's Seven Deadly Sins, 1988; Scarfe's Line of Attack, 1988; Scarfeland: a lost world of fabulous beasts and monsters, 1989; Scarfe on Stage, 1992; Scarfeface, 1993; Hades: the truth at last, 1997. *Recreations:* drawing, painting and sculpting. *Address:* c/o ICM, Oxford House, 76 Oxford Street, W1N 0AX.

SCARFE, Jane; *see* Asher, J.

SCARGILL, Arthur; General Secretary, Socialist Labour Party; President, National Union of Mineworkers, since 1981 (General Secretary, 1992); *b* 11 Jan. 1938; *o c* of Harold and Alice Scargill; *m* 1961, Anne, *d* of Elliott Harper; one *d. Educ:* Worsbrough Dale School; White Cross Secondary School; Leeds Univ. Miner, Woolley Colliery, 1953; Mem., NUM branch cttee, 1960; Woolley branch deleg. to Yorks NUM Council, 1964; Mem., Nat. Exec., 1972, Pres., 1973, Yorks NUM. Mem., TUC Gen. Council, 1986–88. Member: Young Communists' League, 1955–62; Co-op Party, 1963; Labour Party, 1966–95; Socialist Labour Party, 1996; CND. Contested (Socialist Lab): Newport East, 1997; Hartlepool, 2001. *Address:* Socialist Labour Party, 9 Victoria Road, Barnsley, S Yorks S70 2BB.

SCARLETT, family name of **Baron Abinger.**

SCARLETT, His Honour James Harvey Anglin; a Circuit Judge, 1974–89; *b* 27 Jan. 1924; *s* of Lt-Col James Alexander Scarlett, DSO, RA, and Muriel Scarlett, *d* of Walter Blease; unmarried. *Educ:* Shrewsbury Sch.; Christ Church, Oxford (MA). Barrister-at-law. Served War, Royal Artillery (Lieut), 1943–47. Called to the Bar, Inner Temple, 1950. A Recorder of the Crown Court, 1972–74. Malayan Civil Service, 1955–58. *Recreation:* gardening. *Address:* Chilmington Green, Great Chart, near Ashford, Kent TN23 3DP. *Clubs:* Athenæum; Athenæum (Liverpool).

SCARLETT, John McLeod, CMG 2001; OBE 1987; HM Diplomatic Service, retired; Chairman, Joint Intelligence Committee, and Intelligence Co-ordinator, Cabinet Office, since 2001; *b* 18 Aug. 1948; *s* of late Dr James Henri Stuart Scarlett and of Clara Dunlop Scarlett; *m* 1970, Gwenda Mary Rachel Stilliard; one *s* three *d* (and one *s* decd). *Educ:* Epsom Coll.; Magdalen Coll., Oxford (MA). Joined HM Diplomatic Service, 1971; Third Sec., FCO, 1971, Nairobi, 1973–74; lang. student, 1974–75; Second, later First, Sec., Moscow, 1976–77; First Secretary: FCO, 1977–84; Paris, 1984–88; FCO, 1988–91; Counsellor: Moscow, 1991–94; FCO, 1994–2001. *Recreations:* history, medieval churches, family. *Address:* c/o Cabinet Office, 70 Whitehall, SW1A 2AS. *Club:* Oxford and Cambridge.

SCARMAN, family name of **Baron Scarman.**

SCARMAN, Baron *cr* 1977 (Life Peer), of Quatt in the county of Salop; **Leslie George Scarman;** PC 1973; Kt 1961; OBE 1944; a Lord of Appeal in Ordinary, 1977–86; *b* 29 July 1911; *s* of late George Charles and Ida Irene Scarman; *m* 1947, Ruth Clement Wright; one *s. Educ:* Radley College; Brasenose College, Oxford. Classical Scholar, Radley, 1925; Open Classical Scholar, Brasenose Coll., 1930; Hon. Mods 1st cl., 1932; Lit. Hum. 1st cl., 1934; Harmsworth Law Scholar, Middle Temple, 1936, Barrister, 1936; QC 1957. A Judge of the High Court of Justice, Probate, Divorce, and Admiralty Div., later Family Div., 1961–73; a Lord Justice of Appeal, 1973–77. Chairman: Law Commn, 1965–73; Council of Legal Educn, 1973–76; President: Constitutional Reform Centre, 1984–; Citizen Action Compensation Campaign, 1988–. Chm., Univ. of London Court, 1970–86 (Dep. Chm., 1966–70); Chancellor, Univ. of Warwick, 1977–89. Vice-Chm., Statute Law Cttee, 1967–72. Pres., Senate of Inns of Court and Bar, 1976–79. Mem. Arts Council, 1968–70, 1972–73; Vice-Chm., ENO, 1976–81. Pres., RIPA, 1981–89. Hon. Fellow: Brasenose College, Oxford, 1966; Imperial Coll., Univ. of London, 1975; UCL, 1985; LSE, 1985; Leeds, 1987; Brunel, 1988. Hon. LLD: Exeter, 1965; Glasgow, 1969; London, 1971; Keele, 1972; Freiburg, 1973; Warwick, 1974; Bristol, 1976; Manchester, 1977; Kent, 1981; Wales, 1985; QUB, 1990; Dundee, 1990; Hon. DCL: City, 1980; Oxon, 1982. RAFVR, 1940–45; Chm., Malcolm Clubs, RAF. Order of Battle Merit (Russia), 1945. *Publications:* Pattern of Law Reform, 1967; English Law—The New Dimension, 1975. *Recreations:* gardening, walking. *Address:* House of Lords, SW1A 0PW. *Club:* Royal Air Force.

SCARONI, Paolo; Group Chief Executive, Pilkington plc, since 1997; *b* 28 Nov. 1946; *s* of Bruno and Clementina Boniver Scaroni; *m* 1974, Francesca (*née* Zanconato); two *s* one *d. Educ:* Luigi Bocconi Commercial Univ., Milan (Dr Econs); Columbia Univ., NY (MBA). Sales Manager, 1968–70, TBA Supervisor, 1970–71, Chevron; Associate, McKinsey & Co., 1972–73; Saint-Gobain, 1973–85; Financial Dir, Italy, 1973–78; General Delegate: Venezuela, Colombia, Equador, and Peru, 1978–81; Italy, 1981–84; Pres., Flat Glass Div. (world-wide), France, 1984–85; Exec. Vice-Pres., Techint, Italy, 1985–96; Pres., Automotive Products Worldwide, Pilkington plc, 1996–98. Non-executive Director: Burmah Castrol plc, 1998–2000; BAE SYSTEMS, 2000–; Alstom, 2001–. Mem., Eur. Round Table of Industrialists, 2001–. Mem., Bd of Overseers, Columbia Business Sch., 1996–. *Publication:* (jtly) Professione Manager, 1985. *Recreations:* reading, ski-ing, golf. *Address:* Pilkington plc, Prescot Road, St Helens WA10 3TT. *T:* (01744) 28882. *Club:* Royal Automobile.

SCARSDALE, 4th Viscount *cr* 1911; **Peter Ghislain Nathaniel Curzon;** Bt (Scot.) 1636, (Eng.) 1641; Baron Scarsdale 1761; *b* 6 March 1949; *s* of 3rd Viscount Scarsdale and his 1st wife, Solange Yvonne Palmyre Ghislaine Curzon (*née* Hanse); *S* father, 2000; *m* 1983, Mrs Karen Osborne (marr. diss. 1996); one *d. Educ:* Ampleforth. *Heir: b* Hon. David James Nathaniel Curzon [*b* 3 Feb. 1958; *m* 1981, Ruth Linton; one *s* one *d*].

SCHAFF, Alistair Graham; QC 1999; *b* 25 Sept. 1959; *s* of John Schaff and Barbara Schaff (*née* Williams); *m* 1991, (Marie) Leona Burley; one *s* one *d. Educ:* Bishop's Stortford Coll.; Magdalene Coll., Cambridge (MA 1st Cl. Jt Hons History and Law). Called to the Bar, Inner Temple, 1983; in practice at the Bar, 1983–. *Recreations:* family life, foreign travel, history, spectator sport. *Address:* 7 King's Bench Walk, Temple, EC4Y 7DS. *T:* (020) 7583 0404.

SCHAFFTER, Ernest Merill James; Secretary, Royal Aeronautical Society, 1973–82 (Deputy Secretary, 1970–73); Director, Engineering Sciences Data Unit Ltd, 1975–82; *b* 1922; *er s* of late Dr Charles Merill Schaffter and of Bertha Grace Brownrigg, of the CMS in Isfahan, Iran; *m* 1951, Barbara Joy, *o c* of Alfred Bennett Wallis and Hilda Frances Hammond; three *d. Educ:* Trent Coll., Nottinghamshire; King's Coll., Cambridge. BA 1950, MA 1955. Served War: RAF, as Pilot with Coastal and Transport Command, Flt Lt, 1941–46. De Havilland Aircraft Co., Hatfield, as Aerodynamicist and Engr, 1950–54; Marshall's Flying Sch., Cambridge, as Engr, 1954–60; Marshall of Cambridge (Eng) Ltd, as Personal Asst to Chief Designer and later as Design Office Manager, 1960–70. Freeman, GAPAN, 1978. FRAeS, AFAIAA, AFCASI, FIMgt. *Address:* 43 Speldhurst Road, W4 1BX. *T:* (020) 8723 1728, *Fax:* (020) 8995 0708.

SCHALLER, George Beals; Vice President, Wildlife Conservation Society, New York, since 2001; *b* 26 May 1933; *m* 1957 Kay Morgan; two *s. Educ:* Univ. of Alaska (BA, BS 1955); Univ. of Wisconsin (PhD 1962). Fellow, Center for Advanced Study in the Behavioral Sciences, Stanford Univ., 1962–63; Res. Associate, Johns Hopkins Univ., 1963–66; Wildlife Conservation (formerly NY Zoological) Society, 1966–: Dir of Internat. Progs, 1972–88; Dir for Sci., 1988–2001. *Publications:* The Mountain Gorilla, 1963; The Year of the Gorilla, 1964; The Deer and the Tiger, 1967; The Serengeti Lion, 1972; Serengeti: a kingdom of predators, 1972; Golden Shadows, Flying Hooves, 1973; Mountain Monarchs: wild sheep and goats of the Himalaya, 1977; Stones of Silence, 1980; (with Chinese co-authors) The Giant Pandas of Wolong, 1985; The Last Panda, 1993; Tibet's Hidden Wilderness, 1997; Wildlife of the Tibetan Steppe, 1998. *Recreations:* watching wildlife, photography. *Address:* Wildlife Conservation Society, 185th Street and Southern Boulevard, Bronx, NY 10460, USA.

SCHALLY, Dr Andrew Victor; Distinguished Medical Research Scientist, Veterans Administration Medical Center, New Orleans, since 1999 (Chief of Endocrine, Polypeptide and Cancer Institute, 1962–99 and Senior Medical Investigator, 1973–99); Professor of Medicine, since 1967, and Head, Section of Experimental Medicine, since 1978, Tulane University School of Medicine, New Orleans (Associate Professor, 1962–67); *b* Wilno, Poland, 30 Nov. 1926; US Citizen (formerly Canadian Citizen); *s* of Casimir and Maria Schally; *m* 1st, 1956, Margaret White (marr. diss.); one *s* one *d*; 2nd, 1976, Ana Maria Comaru. *Educ:* Bridge of Allan, Scotland (Higher Learning Cert.); London (studied chemistry); McGill Univ., Montreal, Canada (BSc Biochem., 1955; PhD Biochem., 1957). Res. Assistant: Dept of Biochem., Nat. Inst. for Med. Res., MRC, Mill Hill, 1949–52; Endocrine Unit, Allan Meml Inst. for Psych., McGill Univ., Montreal, 1952–57; Baylor University Coll. of Medicine, Texas Med. Center: Res. Associate, Dept of Physiol., 1957–60; Asst Prof. of Physiol., Dept of Physiol., and Asst Prof. of Biochem., Dept of Biochem., 1960–62. Member: Endocrine Soc., USA; AAAS; Soc. of Biol Chemists; Amer. Physiol Soc.; Soc. for Experimental Biol. and Med.; Amer. Assoc. for Cancer Res.; Amer. Soc. for Reproductive Medicine; Internat. Brain Res. Org.; Nat. Acad. of Medicine, Mexico; Nat. Acad. of Medicine, Brazil; Nat. Acad. of Medicine, Venezuela; Nat. Acad. of Scis (US); Hungarian Acad. of Scis; Acad. of Scis, Russia, 1991; Acad. of Medicine, Poland, 1995. Hon. Member: Chilean Endocrine Soc.; Mexican Soc. of Nutrition and Endocrinol.; Acad. of Med. Sciences of Cataluna and Baleares; Endocrine Soc. of Madrid; Polish Soc. of Internal Med.; Endocrine Soc. of Ecuador; Endocrine Soc. of Peru. Dr *hc* State Univ. of Rio de Janeiro, 1977; Rosario, Argentina, 1979; Univ. Peruana Cayetano Heredia, Lima, 1979; Univ. Nat. de San Marcos, Lima, 1979; MD *hc* Tulane, 1978; Cadiz, 1979; Univ. Villareal-Lima, 1979; Copernicus Med. Acad., Cracow, 1979; Chile, 1979; Buenos Aires, 1980; Salamanca, 1981; Complutense Univ., Madrid, 1984; Pécs Univ., 1986; Autónoma, Madrid, 1994; Alcala, Madrid, 1996; Hon. DSc McGill, 1979; Hon. Dr Université René Descartes, Paris, 1987; Hon. Dr rer. nat. Regensburg Univ., 1992; Hon. Dr Nat. Sci. Salzburg, 1997; Hon. Dr Federal Univ. Porto Alegre, Brazil, 1998. Nobel Prize in Physiology or Medicine, 1977. Veterans Administration: William S. Middleton Award, 1970; Exceptional Service Award and Medal, 1978. Van Meter Prize, Amer. Thyroid Assoc., 1969; Ayerst-Squibb Award, US Endocrine Soc., 1970; Charles Mickle Award, Faculty of Med., Univ. of Toronto, 1974; Gairdner Foundn Internat. Award, Toronto, 1974; Edward T. Tyler Award, 1975; Borden Award, Assoc. of Amer. Med. Colls, 1975; Albert Lasker Basic Med. Res. Award, 1975; Spanish Pharmaceutical Soc., 1977; Laude Award, 1978; Heath Meml Award from M. D. Anderson Tumour Inst., 1989. Member Editorial Board: Life Sciences, 1980–; Peptides, 1980–; The Prostate, 1985–. *Publications:* (compiled and ed with William Locke) The Hypothalamus and Pituitary in Health and Disease, 1972; over 2000 other pubns (papers, revs, books, abstracts). *Address:* Quadrant F, 7th Floor Veterans Administration Medical Center, 1601 Perdido Street, New Orleans, LA 70146, USA. *T:* (504) 5895230.

SCHAMA, Prof. Simon Michael, CBE 2001; University Professor, Columbia University, since 1997; art critic, New Yorker, since 1995; *b* 13 Feb. 1945; *s* of Arthur Osias Schama and Gertrude Steinberg Schama; *m* 1983, Virginia Papaioannou; one *s* one *d. Educ:* Christ's Coll., Cambridge (BA 1966; MA 1969; Hon. Fellow, 1995). Fellow and Dir of Studies in History, Christ's Coll., Cambridge, 1966–76; Fellow and Tutor in Modern History, Brasenose Coll., Oxford, 1976–80; Mellon Prof. of History, 1980–90, and Kenan Prof., 1990–93, Harvard Univ.; Old Dominion Foundation Prof. in the Humanities, Columbia Univ., 1993–96. Writer and presenter, A History of Britain, BBC TV Series, 2000, 2001. *Publications:* Patriots and Liberators: revolution in the Netherlands 1780–1813, 1978; Two Rothschilds and the Land of Israel, 1979; The Embarrassment of Riches: an interpretation of Dutch culture in the Golden Age, 1987; Citizens: a chronicle of the French Revolution, 1989; Dead Certainties (Unwarranted Speculations), 1991; Landscape and Memory, 1995; Rembrandt's Eyes, 1999; A History of Britain, vol. 1, 3000 BC–AD 1603, 2000, vol. 2, The British Wars 1603–1776, 2001. *Recreations:* Bordeaux wine, gardening, Brazilian music. *Address:* Department of History, Fayerweather Hall, Columbia University, New York, NY 10027, USA. *T:* (212) 8544593. *Club:* Century (New York).

SCHAPERA, Prof. Isaac, MA (Cape Town) 1925; PhD (London) 1929; DSc (London) 1939; FBA 1958; FRSSAf 1934; Emeritus Professor, University of London (London School of Economics), 1969; *b* Garies, South Africa, 23 June 1905; 3rd *s* of late Herman and Rose Schapera. *Educ:* S African Coll. Sch., Cape Town; Universities of Cape Town and London. Prof. of Social Anthropology, Univ. of Cape Town, 1935–50; Prof. of Anthropology, Univ. of London (LSE), 1950–69, now Emeritus; Hon. Fellow, 1974. Visiting Professor: Univ. of Chicago, 1948; Univ. of Toronto, 1953. Many anthropological field expeditions to Bechuanaland Protectorate, 1929–50. Chairman Association of Social Anthropologists of the British Commonwealth, 1954–57; President, Royal Anthropological Inst., 1961–63. Hon. DLitt: Cape Town, 1975; Botswana, 1985; Hon. LLD Witwatersrand, 1979. *Publications:* The Khoisan Peoples of South Africa, 1930; A Handbook of Tswana Law and Custom, 1938; Married Life in an African Tribe, 1940; Native Land Tenure in the Bechuanaland Protectorate, 1943; Migrant Labour and Tribal Life, 1948; The Ethnic Composition of Tswana Tribes, 1952; The Tswana, 1953; Government and Politics in Tribal Societies, 1956; Praise Poems of Tswana Chiefs, 1965; Tribal Innovators, 1970; Rainmaking Rites of Tswana Tribes, 1971; Kinship Terminology in Jane Austen's Novels, 1977; Editor: Western Civilization and the Natives of South Africa, 1934; The Bantu-speaking Tribes of South Africa, 1937; David Livingstone's Journals and Letters, 1841–56 (6 vols), 1959–63; David Livingstone: South African Papers 1849–1853, 1974; contrib. to many learned journals. *Address:* 157 White House, Albany Street, NW1 3UP.

SCHAPIRO, Isabel Margaret; *see* Madariaga, I. M. de.

SCHARPING, Rudolf; Member, Bundestag, since 1994; Minister of Defence, since 1998; Deputy Chairman, Social Democratic Party of Germany, since 1995 (Chairman, 1993–95); Chairman, Social Democratic Party of Europe, since 1994; *b* Niederelbert, Westerwald, 2 Dec. 1947. *Educ:* Univ. of Bonn. State Chm. and Nat. Dep. Chm., Jusos (Young Socialists), 1966; joined SPD, 1966; Rhineland-Palatinate: Mem., State Parlt, 1975–94; Leader, SPD, 1985–91; Leader of Opposition, 1987–91; Minister-Pres., 1991–94; Leader of Opposition, 1994–98. *Address:* Bundeshaus, Platz der Republik, 11011 Berlin, Germany.

SCHÄUBLE, Dr Wolfgang; Member of Bundestag, since 1972; Chairman: CDU/CSU Parliamentary Group, Germany, 1991–2000; CDU Germany, 1998–2000; *b* 18 Sept. 1942; *s* of Karl Schäuble and Gertrud (*née* Göhring); *m* 1969, Ingeborg Hensle; one *s* three *d. Educ:* Univ. of Freiburg; Univ. of Hamburg (Dr jur 1971). Tax Revenue Dept, State of Baden-Württemberg, 1971–72; solicitor, 1978–84; Parly Sec., CDU/CSU, 1981–84; Federal Minister and Head of Federal Chancellery, 1984–89; Federal Minister of the Interior, 1989–91. Chairman: CDU Cttee on Sports, 1976–84; Working Gp, European Border Regions, 1979–82. Grosskreuz des Verdienstordens der Bundesrepublik Deutschland, 1990. *Publications:* Der Vertrag, 1991; Und der Zukunft zugewandt, 1994; Mitten im Leben, 2000. *Recreation:* classical music. *Address:* (office) c/o Bundeshaus, Platz der Republik, 11011 Berlin, Germany.

SCHAUFUSS, Peter; ballet dancer, producer, choreographer, director; *b* 26 April 1950; *s* of late Frank Schaufuss and Mona Vangsaae, former solo dancers with Royal Danish Ballet. *Educ:* Royal Danish Ballet School. Apprentice, Royal Danish Ballet, 1965; soloist, Nat. Ballet of Canada, 1967–68; Royal Danish Ballet, 1969–70; Principal, London Festival Ballet, 1970–74; NY City Ballet, 1974–77; Principal, National Ballet of Canada, 1977–83; Artistic Dir, London Fest. Ballet, later English Nat. Ballet, 1984–90; Dir of Ballet, Deutsche Oper, Berlin, 1990–93; Ballet Dir, Royal Danish Ballet, 1994–95; Founder Dir, Peter Schaufuss Ballet, 1997–. Guest appearances in Austria, Canada, Denmark, France, Germany, Greece, Israel, Italy, Japan, Norway, S America, Turkey, UK, USA, USSR; Presenter, Dancer, BBC, 1984; numerous TV appearances. Roles created for him in: Phantom of the Opera; Orpheus; Verdi Variations; The Steadfast Tin Soldier; Rhapsodie Espagnole. Produced ballets: La Sylphide (London Fest. Ballet, Stuttgart Ballet, Roland Petit's Ballet de Marseille, Deutsche Oper Berlin, Teatro Comunale, Florence, Vienna State Opera, Opernhaus Zurich, Teatro dell' Opera di Roma, Hessisches Staatstheater, Wiesbaden, Ballet du Rhin, Royal Danish Ballet, Ballet West); Napoli (Nat. Ballet of Canada, Teatro San Carlo, English Nat. Ballet); Folktale (Deutsche Oper Berlin); Dances from Napoli (London Fest. Ballet); Bournonville (Aterballetto); The Nutcracker (English Nat. Ballet, Deutsche Oper, Berlin); Giselle, Sleeping Beauty, Swan Lake, Tchaikovsky Trilogy (Deutsche Oper, Berlin). Staging for Ashton's Romeo and Juliet, and prod. and choreog. Hamlet, Royal Danish Ballet, 1996; produced and/or choreographed, for Peter Schaufuss Ballet, new versions of: Swan Lake, Sleeping Beauty, The Nutcracker, 1997; Hamlet, Romeo and Juliet, 1998; The King, Manden der Onskede Sig en Havudsigt, 1999; Midnight Express, The Three Presents, 2000; Hans Christian Andersen, 2001. Solo award, 2nd Internat. Ballet Competition, Moscow, 1973; Star of the Year, Munich Abendzeitung, 1978; Evening Standard and SWET ballet award, 1979; Manchester Evening News theatre award, 1986; Lakerolprisen, Copenhagen, 1988; Berlin Co. award, Berlinerzeitung, 1991; Edinburgh Festival Critics' Prize, 1991. Knight of the Dannebrog (Denmark), 1988; Officier de l'Ordre de la Couronne (Belgium), 1995. *Recreation:* boxing. *Address:* c/o Papoutsis Representation Ltd, 18 Sundial Avenue, SE25 4BX.

SCHEEL, Walter; Grand Cross First Class of Order of Merit of Federal Republic of Germany; President of the Federal Republic of Germany, 1974–79; *b* 8 July 1919; *m* 1969, Dr Mildred Wirtz (*d* 1985); one *s* two *d*, and one *s* of previous *m*; *m* 1988, Barbara Wiese. *Educ:* Reform Gymnasium, Solingen. Served in German Air Force, War of 1939–45. Mem. of Bundestag, 1953–74; Federal Minister for Economic Co-operation, 1961–Oct. 1966, Vice-President of Bundestag, 1967–69; Vice-Chancellor and Foreign Minister, 1969–74. Mem., Landtag North Rhine Westphalia, 1950–54; Mem. European Parlt, 1958–61 (Vice-Chm., Liberal Gp; Chm., Cttee on Co-operation with Developing Countries). Free Democratic Party: Mem., 1946; Mem. Exec. Cttee for North Rhine/Westphalia, 1953–74; Mem. Federal Exec., 1956–74; Chm., 1968–74; Hon. Pres., 1979. Holds numerous hon. degrees and foreign decorations. *Publications:* Konturen einer neuen Welt, 1965; Formeln deutscher Politik, 1968; Warum Mitbestimmung und wie—eine Diskussion, 1970; Reden und Interviews, 1969–79; Vom Recht des anderen, 1977; Die Zukunft der Freiheit, 1979; Wen schmerzt noch Deutschlands Teilung?, 1986. *Address:* Flemingstrasse 107, 81925 München, Germany.

SCHEELE, Sir Nicholas Vernon, KCMG 2001; Chief Operating Officer and President, Ford Motor Company, since 2001; *b* 3 Jan. 1944; *s* of Werner James Scheele and Norah Edith Scheele (*née* Gough); *m* 1967, Rosamund Ann Jacobs; two *s* one *d. Educ:* Durham Univ. (BA). Purchasing, Supply, Procurement, Ford of Britain, 1966–78; Ford of US: Purchasing, Supply, Procurement Management, 1978–83; Dir, Supply Policy and Planning, 1983–85; Dir, Body and Chassis Parts Purchasing, 1985–88; Pres., Ford of Mexico, 1988–91; Vice-Chm., Jan.–April 1992, Chm. and Chief Exec., 1992–99, Jaguar Cars; Sen. Vice-Pres., April–July 1999, Chm., July 1999–2001, Ford of Europe; Mem. Supervisory Bd, Ford Werke AG, 1999–2001; Vice-Pres. for N America, Ford Motor

Co., 2001. Dir, W Midlands Radio, 2000–. Member Council: Midlands Region, Inst. of Dirs, 1994–99; SMMT, 1992–99; President: Motor and Allied Trades Benevolent Fund, 1996–97; Coventry and Warwicks Partnership; Midlands Business of the Year, 1996; Chm., Business in the Arts, West Midlands, 1997–99. Chairman: Prince of Wales Business and Envmt Cttee, 1999–; Manufacturing Theme Gp, Foresight, 2020, 1999–. Member, Advisory Board: British American Chamber of Commerce, 1995–99; Fulbright Commn, 1995–99; Member, Board of Advisors: Coventry Univ., 1995–; Durham Univ., 1996–. Life Mem., NSPCC (Chm., Coventry Centenary Appeal, 1994–96); mem. charity bds and cttees devoted to children's welfare, community relns and indust. regeneration. Hon. RCM. Hon. FIMechE 2000. Gold Medal: IMI Castrol, 1999; IMechE, 2000; Carmen's Co., 2000. 5 hon. doctorates. *Publications:* articles on manufg efficiency, quality, envmtl affairs, and youth employment and trng. *Recreations:* reading, classical music, tennis, squash. *Address:* Ford Motor Company, 1 American Road, Dearborn, MI 48126, USA. *Clubs:* Royal Automobile; Catawba Island (Great Lakes).

SCHERER, Paul Joseph; Managing Director, 1982–95, Chairman, 1995–96, Transworld Publishers Ltd; *b* 28 Dec. 1933; *s* of François Joseph Scherer and Florence (*née* Haywood); *m* 1959, Mary Fieldus; one *s* three *d*. *Educ:* Stonyhurst Coll. National Service, commnd BUFFS (Royal E Kent Regt), 1952–54. Bailey Bros & Swinfen, 1954–56; Jun. Editor, G. Bell & Sons, 1956–58; Sales Man., Penguin Books, 1958–63; Gp Sales Dir, Paul Hamlyn, 1963–68; William Collins Sons & Co.: Man. Dir, Internat. Div., 1968–77; Pres., Collins & World USA, 1974–75; Man. Dir, Mills & Boon, 1977–82; Sen. Vice Pres., Bantam Doubleday Dell Publishing Gp Inc., 1990–98; Chm., Curtis Brown Gp, 1996–. Director: Bloomsbury Publishing plc, 1993–; Book Tokens Ltd, 1995–. Member Board: Book Develt Council, 1971–74; Book Marketing Council, 1977–84 (Chm., 1982–84); British Library, 1996–2000; Mem. Council, Publishers Assoc., 1982–84 and 1989–94 (Pres., 1991–93); Pres., Book Trade Benevolent Soc., 1995–99. Trustee, Whizz-Kidz, 1996– (Chm., 1998–2000). Founding Chm., Unicorn Sch., Kew, 1970–73; Gov., Worth Sch., 1993–96. *Recreation:* laughing at my own jokes. *Address:* 43A Cheyne Court, SW3 5TS. *T:* (020) 7376 7570. *Clubs:* Garrick, Hurlingham.

SCHERMERS, Prof. Dr Henry Gerhard; Professor of Law, University of Leiden, 1978–June 2002; *b* 27 Sept. 1928; *s* of Petrus Schermers and Amelia M. Gooszen; *m* 1957, Hotsche A. C. Tans; one *s* two *d*. *Educ:* Leiden Univ. (LLM 1953; LLD 1957). Ministry of Foreign Affairs: Internat. Orgns Dept, 1953–56; Asst Legal Advr, 1956–63; University of Amsterdam: Lectr in Internat. Law, 1963–65; Prof. of Law, 1965–78. Visiting Professor: Ann Arbor, Michigan, 1968; Louisiana, 1981; QMC, 1988; Oxford, 1996. Mem., Eur. Commn of Human Rights, 1981–96. Corresp. Fellow, British Acad., 1990; Mem., Inst. de Droit Internat., 1989. Chief Editor, Common Market Law Review, 1978–93. Dr (*hc*): Edinburgh, 1993; Osnabrück, 1994. Kt of Netherlands Lion, 1984; Comdr, Order of Oranje Nassau, 1993; Officer: Crown of Belgium, 1962; Ordre des Palmes Académiques (France), 1998. *Publications:* International Institutional Law, 1972, 3rd edn 1995; Judicial Protection in the European Communities, 1976, 5th edn 1991; numerous articles in Common Market Law Review and professional jls. *Recreations:* hiking, ski-ing, carpentry. *Address:* Herengracht 15, 2312 LA Leiden, Netherlands. *T:* (71) 5124294.

SCHIEMANN, Rt Hon. Sir Konrad Hermann Theodor, Kt 1986; PC 1995; **Rt Hon. Lord Justice Schiemann;** a Lord Justice of Appeal, since 1995; *b* 15 Sept. 1937; *s* of Helmuth and Beate Schiemann; *m* 1965, Elisabeth Hanna Eleonore Holroyd-Reece; one *d*. *Educ:* King Edward's Sch., Birmingham; Freiburg Univ.; Pembroke Coll., Cambridge (Schol.; MA, LLB; Hon. Fellow, 1998). Served Lancs Fusiliers, 1956–58 (commnd, 1957). Called to Bar, Inner Temple, 1962 (Bencher, 1985; Reader, 2002); Junior Counsel to the Crown, Common Law, 1978–80; QC 1980; a Recorder of the Crown Court, 1985–86; a Justice of the High Court, QBD, 1986–95. Chairman of panel conducting Examinations in Public of: North-East Hants and Mid Hants Structure Plans, 1979; Merseyside Structure Plan, 1980; Oxfordshire Structure Plan, 1984. Mem., Parole Bd, 1990–92 (Vice-Chm., 1991–92). Member Advisory Board: Centre for Eur. Legal Studies, Cambridge Univ., 1996–; Centre of Eur. Private Law, Münster Univ., 1999–. Mem. Council of Mgt, British Inst. of Internat. and Comparative Law, 2000–. Patron, Busoga Trust, 1999– (Chm., 1989–99); Trustee, St John's, Smith Square, 1990– (Chm., 1994–). Dir, Acad. of Ancient Music, 2001–; Gov., English Nat. Ballet, 1995–2001. *Publications:* contrib. English and German legal books and jls. *Recreations:* music, reading. *Address:* c/o Royal Courts of Justice, Strand, WC2A 2LL.

SCHIFF, András; concert pianist; *b* 21 Dec. 1953; *s* of Odon Schiff and Klara Schiff (*née* Csengeri). *Educ:* Franz Liszt Academy of Music, Budapest; with Prof. Pal Kadosa, Ferenc Rados and Gyorgy Kurtag; private study with George Malcolm. Artistic Dir, September Chamber Music Fest., Mondsee, Austria, 1989–98. Regular orch. engagements include: NY Philharmonic, Chicago Symphony, Vienna Phil., Concertgebouw, Orch. de Paris, London Phil., London Symph., Philharmonia, Royal Phil., Israel Phil., Philadelphia, Washington Nat. Symph.; major festival performances include: Salzburg, Lucerne, Edinburgh, Aldeburgh, Tanglewood. Recordings include: extensive Bach repertoire (Grammy Award for recording of English Suites, 1990); all Mozart Piano Sonatas; all Mozart Piano Concertos; all Schubert Sonatas; all Bartok Piano Concertos; all Beethoven Piano Concertos; Lieder records with Peter Schreier, Robert Holl and Cecilia Bartoli. Prizewinner, Tchaikovsky competition, Moscow, 1974 and Leeds comp., 1975; Liszt Prize, 1977; Premio, Accademia Chigiana, Siena, 1987; Wiener Flotenuhr, 1989; Bartok Prize, 1991; Instrumentalist of the Year, Internat. Classical Music Awards, 1993; Claudio Arrau Meml Medal, 1994; Instrumentalist of the Year, Royal Philharmonic Soc., 1994; Kossuth Prize, 1996; Deutsche Schallplattenkrik, 1996; Leonie Sonnings Music Prize, Copenhagen, 1997. *Recreations:* literature, languages, soccer. *Address:* c/o Harrison Operations Ltd, The Orchard, Market Street, Charlbury, Oxon OX7 3PJ.

SCHIFF, Heinrich; conductor; 'cellist; *b* Gmunden, Austria, 18 Nov. 1951. Studied with Tobias Kühne and André Navarra; attended Hans Swarovsky's conducting class. Joined professional orchestras, 1986; Chief Conductor and Guest Conductor of numerous orchestras in Austria, Finland, Germany, Holland, Sweden, Switzerland, UK, USA; also opera director. Principal Conductor: Musikcollegium, Winterthur, 1995–; Copenhagen Philharmonic Orchestra, 1995–. Numerous recordings.

SCHIFFRIN, Prof. David Jorge, PhD; FRSC; Brunner Professor of Physical Chemistry, University of Liverpool, since 1990; *b* 8 Jan. 1939; *s* of Bernardo Schiffrin and Berta Kurlat Schiffrin; *m* 1965, Margery Watson; one *s* one *d*. *Educ:* Univ. of Buenos Aires (BSc); Univ. of Birmingham (PhD). FRSC 1997. Lectr in Physical Chemistry, Univ. of Buenos Aires, 1966; Asst Technical Manager, CIABASA, Buenos Aires, 1967; Lectr in Physical Chemistry, Chemistry Dept, Univ. of Southampton, 1968–72; Head of Applied Electrochemistry Div., Nat. Inst. of Technology, Buenos Aires, 1972–77; Manager and Dir, Wolfson Centre for Electrochemical Science, 1979–90, Sen. Lectr, Chemistry Dept, 1988–90, Univ. of Southampton. Mem., IUPAC, 1995–. Foreign Mem., Finnish Soc. of Scis and Letters, 1996. Electrochemistry Medal and Prize, RSC, 2001. Mem. Editl Bd, Jl of Electroanalytical Chemistry, 1997–. *Publications:* numerous articles in jls; chapters in books. *Recreations:* hill walking, music, photography. *Address:* Chemistry Department, University of Liverpool, Liverpool L69 7ZD. *T:* (0151) 794 3574.

SCHILD, Geoffrey Christopher, CBE 1993; PhD; DSc; FRCPath, FRCPE; FIBiol; Director, National Institute for Biological Standards and Control, since 1985; *b* 28 Nov. 1935; *s* of Christopher and Georgina Schild; *m* 1961, Tora Madland; two *s* one *d*. *Educ:* High Storrs Sch., Sheffield; Univ. of Reading (BSc Hons 1954; DSc 1993); Univ. of Sheffield (PhD 1963). FIBiol 1978; FRCPath 1993; FRCPE 1998. Hon. MRCP 1995. Res. Fellow 1961–63, Lectr in Virology 1963–67, Univ. of Sheffield; National Institute for Medical Research: Mem., Scientific Staff of MRC, 1967–75; Dir, World Influenza Centre, 1970–75; Hd, Div. of Virology, Nat. Inst. for Biol Standards, 1975–85; Dir, MRC Directed Prog. of AIDS Res., 1987–95. Chm., WHO Steering Cttee on Biomed. Res. on AIDS, 1987–90; Member: WHO Scientific Adv. Gp on Vaccine Develt, 1991–; Strategic Planning Task Force, Internat. Children's Vaccine Initiative, 1996. Vice Chm. Bd of Trustees, UNDP Internat. Vaccine Inst., Seoul, 1995–. Freeman, City of London, 1989. *Publications:* Influenza, the Virus and the Disease, 1975, 2nd edn 1985; some 300 original res. papers on virology in learned jls. *Recreations:* hill walking, music, ornithology. *Address:* National Institute for Biological Standards and Control, Blanche Lane, South Mimms, Potters Bar, Hertfordshire EN6 3QG. *T:* (01707) 654753.

SCHLESINGER, Arthur (Meier), Jr; writer; educator; Schweitzer Professor of the Humanities, City University of New York, 1966–95, now Emeritus; *b* Columbus, Ohio, 15 Oct. 1917; *s* of late Arthur Meier and of Elizabeth Bancroft Schlesinger; *m* 1st, 1940, Marian Cannon (marr. diss. 1970); two *s* two *d*; 2nd, 1971, Alexandra Emmet; one *s*. *Educ:* Phillips Exeter Acad. AB (Harvard), 1938; Henry Fellow, Peterhouse, Cambridge, 1938–39. Soc. of Fellows, Harvard, 1939–42; US Office of War Information, 1942–43; US Office of Strategic Services, 1943–45; US Army, 1945. Mem. Adlai Stevenson Campaign Staff, 1952, 1956. Professor of History, Harvard University, 1954–61 (Associate, 1946–54); Special Assistant to President Kennedy, 1961–63. Film Reviewer: Show, 1962–65; Vogue (US), 1966–70; Saturday Review, 1977–80; Amer. Heritage, 1981. Member of Jury, Cannes Film Festival, 1964. Holds 32 honorary doctorates, incl. DLitt Oxford, 1987. Mem. of numerous Socs and Instns; Pres., Amer. Acad. of Arts and Letters, 1981–84; Chancellor, Amer. Acad., 1985–88. Pulitzer Prize: History, 1946; Biography, 1966; Nat. Book Award for Biog., 1966 (for A Thousand Days: John F. Kennedy in the White House), 1979 (for Robert Kennedy and His Times); Amer. Acad. of Arts and Letters, Gold Medal for History, 1967; National Humanities Medal, 1998; U Thant Award for Internat. Understanding, 1998. Commander, Order of Orange-Nassau (Netherlands), 1987; Ordem del Libertador (Venezuela), 1995. *Publications:* Orestes A. Brownson: a Pilgrim's Progress, 1939; The Age of Jackson, 1945; The Vital Center, 1949, (in UK) The Politics of Freedom, 1950; The General and the President (with R. H. Rovere), 1951; (co-editor) Harvard Guide to American History, 1954; The Age of Roosevelt: I: The Crisis of the Old Order, 1957; II: The Coming of the New Deal, 1958; III: The Politics of Upheaval, 1960; Kennedy or Nixon, 1960; The Politics of Hope, 1963; (ed with Morton White) Paths of American Thought, 1963; A Thousand Days: John F. Kennedy in the White House, 1965; The Bitter Heritage: Vietnam and American Democracy 1941–1966, 1967; The Crisis of Confidence: ideas, power & violence in America, 1969; (ed with F. L. Israel) History of American Presidential Elections, 1971; The Imperial Presidency, 1973; (ed) History of US Political Parties, 1973; Robert Kennedy and His Times, 1978; The Cycles of American History, 1986; The Disuniting of America, 1991; A Life in the 20th Century: vol. I, Innocent Beginnings, 2000; articles to magazines and newspapers. *Recreations:* theatre, movies, tennis. *Address:* 455 E 51st Street, New York, NY 10022, USA. *Clubs:* Century, Knickerbocker (New York).

SCHLESINGER, John Richard, CBE 1970; film director; *b* 16 Feb. 1926; *s* of late Bernard Schlesinger, OBE, MD, FRCP and Winifred Henrietta (*née* Regensburg). *Educ:* Uppingham; Balliol Coll., Oxford (BA; Hon. Fellow 1981). Associate Dir, Nat. Theatre, 1973–88. Mem., Theatre Dirs' Guild of GB, 1983–. Directed: *films:* for Monitor and Tonight (BBC TV), 1958–60; Terminus, for British Transport Films, 1960 (Golden Lion Award, Venice Film Fest., 1961); A Kind of Loving, 1961 (Golden Bear Award, Berlin Film Festival, 1962); Billy Liar, 1962–63; Darling, 1964–65 (NY Critics Award); Far from the Madding Crowd, 1966–67; Midnight Cowboy, 1968–69 (Academy Award for Best Dir; Soc. of TV and Film Acad. Award for Best Dir; Dir's Guild of America Award); Sunday, Bloody Sunday, 1971 (Soc. of TV and Film Acad. Award for Best Dir; David di Donatello Award); contrib. Visions of Eight, 1973; Day of the Locust, 1975; Marathon Man, 1976; Yanks, 1978 (New Evening Standard Award, 1980); Honky Tonk Freeway, 1980; The Falcon and the Snowman, 1984; The Believers, 1987; Madame Sousatzka, 1988 (screenplay with Ruth Prawer Jhabvala); Pacific Heights, 1991; The Innocent, 1994; Eye for an Eye, 1995; The Next Best Thing, 2000; *television:* Separate Tables, 1982; An Englishman Abroad, 1983 (BAFTA Award, Broadcasting Press Guild Award, Barcelona Film Fest. Award and Nat. Bd of Review Award, 1984); A Question of Attribution, 1991 (BAFTA Award); Cold Comfort Farm, 1995 (film, 1996); Sweeney Todd, 1997; The Next Best Thing, 2000. *plays:* No, Why, for RSC, 1964; Timon of Athens, and Days in the Trees, for RSC, 1964–66; I and Albert, Piccadilly, 1972; Heartbreak House, 1975, Julius Caesar, 1977, and True West, 1981, for Nat. Theatre; *opera:* Les Contes d'Hoffmann, 1980 (SWET Award, 1981), and Der Rosenkavalier, 1984, for Covent Garden; Un Ballo in Maschera, for Salzburg Fest., 1989; Peter Grimes, for La Scala, Milan and LA Opera, 2000. Fellow, BAFTA, 1995. David di Donatello Special Award, 1980; Shakespeare Prize, FVS Foundn of Hamburg, 1981; Outstanding Achievement in Directing, Hollywood Film Fest., 1999. *Recreations:* gardening, travel, music, antiques. *Address:* c/o Duncan Heath, ICM, 76 Oxford Street, W1R 1RB.

SCHLUTER, Prof. Dolph, PhD; FRS 1999; Professor of Zoology, University of British Columbia, since 1996; *b* 22 May 1955; *s* of Antoine Schluter and Magdalena Schluter; *m* 1993, Andrea Lawson; one *d*. *Educ:* Univ. of Guelph, Ont (BSc Wildlife Biol. 1977); Univ. of Michigan (PhD Ecol. and Evolution 1983). NSERC Postdoctoral Fellow, Zool. Dept, UBC and Univ. of Calif, Davis, 1983–85; Zoology Department, University of British Columbia: NSERC Univ. Res. Fellow, 1985–89; Asst Prof., 1989–91; Associate Prof., 1991–96. E. W. R. Steacie Meml Fellow, NSERC, 1993; Izaak Walton Killam Meml Faculty Res. Fellow, UBC, 1996; Scholar-in-Residence, Peter Wall Inst. of Advanced Studies, UBC, 1999. Vice-Pres., American Soc. Naturalists, 1999 (President's Award, 1997). Charles A. McDowell Medal, UBC, 1995. *Publications:* (ed with R. Ricklefs) Species Diversity in Ecological Communities: historical and geographical perspectives, 1993; The Ecology of Adaptive Radiation, 2000; contrib. chapters in books; contrib. numerous articles to Science, Nature, Evolution, American Naturalist, Ecology, Proc. Royal Soc., Philosophical Trans Royal Soc. *Address:* Zoology Department, University of British Columbia, 6270 University Boulevard, Vancouver, BC V6T 1Z4, Canada. *T:* (604) 8222387, *Fax:* (604) 8222416; *e-mail:* schluter@zoology.ubc.ca.

SCHMIDHUBER, Peter Michael; Member, Commission of the European Communities, 1987–94; lawyer; *b* 15 Dec. 1931; *s* of Jakob Schmidhuber and Anna (*née* Mandlmayr); *m* 1960, Elisabeth Schweigart; one *d*. *Educ:* Univ. of Munich (MA Econs 1955). Qualified as lawyer, 1960. Mem. Bd, Deutsche Bundesbank, 1995–. Member:

Bundestag, 1965–69 and 1972–78; Bundesrat, Bavarian Parliament, 1978–87 (Bavarian Minister of State for Federal Affairs). Mem., CSU. *Address:* Wiesengrund 1b, 81243 Munich, Germany.

SCHMIDT, Benno Charles, Jr; Chairman of the Board, Edison Schools, since 1998 (President and Chief Executive, The Edison Project, 1992–98); *b* 20 March 1942; *s* of Benno Charles Schmidt and Martha Chastain; *m* 1980, Helen Cutting Whitney; one *s* two *d. Educ:* Yale Univ. (BA 1963; LLB 1966). Mem., DC Bar, 1968; Law Clerk to Chief Justice Earl Warren, 1966–67; Special Asst Atty Gen., Office of Legal Counsel, US Dept of Justice, Washington, 1967–69; Harlan Fiske Stone Prof. of Constitutional Law, Columbia Univ., 1969–86, Dean of Law School, 1984–86; Professor of Law, and President, Yale Univ., 1986–92. Hon. Bencher, Gray's Inn, 1988. Hon. degrees: LLD Princeton, 1986; DLitt Johns Hopkins, 1987; LLD Harvard, 1987. Hon. AM, 1989. *Publications:* Freedom of the Press Versus Public Access, 1974; (with A. M. Bickel) The Judiciary and Responsible Government 1910–1921, 1985. *Address:* Edison Schools, 521 5th Avenue, New York, NY 10175, USA. *T:* (212) 3091611.

SCHMIDT, Helmut H. W.; Chancellor, Federal Republic of Germany, 1974–82; Member of Bundestag, Federal Republic of Germany, 1953–61, and 1965–87; Publisher, Die Zeit, since 1983; *b* 23 Dec. 1918; *s* of Gustav Lentfält Schmidt and Ludovica Schmidt; *m* 1942, Hannelore Glaser; one *d. Educ:* Univ. of Hamburg. Diplom-Volkswirt, 1949. Manager of Transport Administration, State of Hamburg, 1949–53; Social Democratic Party: Member, 1946–; Mem. Federal Executive, 1958–83; Chm., Parly Gp, 1967–69; Vice-Chm. of Party, 1968–84; Senator (Minister) for Domestic Affairs in Hamburg, 1961–65; Minister of Defence, 1969–72; Minister of Finance and Economics, 1972; Minister of Finance, 1972–74. Hon LLD: Newberry Coll., S Carolina, 1973; Johns Hopkins Univ., 1976; Cambridge, 1976; Hon. DCL Oxford, 1979; Hon. Doctorate: Harvard, 1979; Sorbonne, 1981; Georgetown, 1986; Scranton, Pennsylvania, 1987; Bergamo, 1989; Keio, Tokyo, 1991; Nat. Chung-Hsing, Taipei, 1992; Potsdam, Haifa, 2000. Athinai Prize for Man and Mankind, Onassis Foundn, Greece, 1986. *Publications:* Defence or Retaliation, 1962; Beiträge, 1967; Balance of Power, 1971; Auf dem Fundament des Godesberger Programms, 1973; Bundestagsreden, 1975; Kontinuität und Konzentration, 1975; Als Christ in der politischen Entscheidung, 1976; (with Willy Brandt) Deutschland 1976—Zwei Sozialdemokraten im Gespräch, 1976; Der Kurs heisst Frieden, 1979; Freiheit verantworten, 1980; Pflicht zur Menschlichkeit, 1981; A Grand Strategy for the West, 1985; Menschen und Mächte, 1987 (trans. as Men and Powers, 1989); Die Deutschen und ihre Nachbarn, 1990; Handeln fur Deutschland, 1993; Das Jahr der Entscheidung, 1994; Weggefährten, 1996; Jahrhundertwende, 1998; Allgemeine Erklärung der Menschenpflichten, 1998; Globalisierung, 1998; Auf der Suche nach einer öffentlichen Moral, 1998; Die Selbstbehauptung Europas, 2000. *Recreations:* sailing, chess, playing the organ. *Address:* c/o Deutscher Bundestag, Platz der Republik, 11011 Berlin, Germany.

SCHMIDT, Prof. Michael Norton, FRSL; Director, Writing School, since 1998, and Professor of English, since 2000, Manchester Metropolitan University; Founder, and Editorial and Managing Director, Carcanet Press Ltd, since 1969; *b* 2 March 1947; *s* of Carl Bernhardt Schmidt and Elizabeth Norton Schmidt (*née* Hill); *m* 1979, Claire Harman (marr. diss. 1989); two *s* one *d. Educ:* Harvard Univ.; Wadham Coll., Oxford (BA 1969; MA). Manchester University: Gulbenkian Fellow of Poetry, 1970–73; Special Lectr, Poetry, 1973–92; Sen. Lectr in Poetry, 1992–98. Founder and Ed., PN Rev. (formerly Poetry Nation), 1971–; Poetry Ed., Grand Street (NY), 1998–2000. FRSL 1994. *Publications: criticism:* Fifty Modern British Poets: an introduction, 1979; Fifty English Poets 1300–1900: an introduction, 1979; Reading Modern Poetry, 1989; Lives of the Poets, 1998; The Story of Poetry, 2001; *translations:* (with E. Kissam) Flower and Song: Aztec poetry, 1977; On Poets and Others, by Octavio Paz, 1986; *poetry anthologies* include: Eleven British Poets, 1980; The Harvill Book of 20th Century Poetry in English, 1999; *fiction:* The Colonist, 1983; The Dresden Gate, 1988; *poetry* includes: New and Selected Poems, 1997. *Address:* Carcanet Press Ltd, Conavon Court, Blackfriars Street, Manchester M3 5BQ. *Club:* Savile.

SCHNEIDER, Dr William George, OC 1977; FRS 1962; FRSC 1951; Research Consultant, National Research Council of Canada, Ottawa, since 1980 (President, 1967–80); *b* Wolseley, Saskatchewan, 1 June 1915; *s* of Michael Schneider and Phillipina Schneider (*née* Kraushaar); *m* 1940, Jean Frances Purves; two *d. Educ:* University of Saskatchewan; McGill University; Harvard University. BSc 1937, MSc 1939, University of Saskatchewan; PhD (in physical chem.), 1941, McGill Univ. Research physicist at Woods Hole Oceanographic Inst., Woods Hole, Mass, USA, 1943–46 (US Navy Certificate of Merit, 1946). Joined Nat. Research Council, Division of Pure Chemistry, Ottawa, 1946; Vice-President (Scientific), 1965–67. Pres., Internat. Union of Pure and Applied Chemistry, 1983–85. Chemical Inst. of Canada Medal, 1961, Montreal Medal, 1973; Henry Marshall Tory Medal, RSC, 1969. Hon. DSc: York, 1966; Memorial, 1968; Saskatchewan, 1969; Moncton, 1969; McMaster, 1969; Laval, 1969; New Brunswick, 1970; Montreal, 1970; McGill, 1970; Acadia, 1976; Regina, 1976; Ottawa, 1978; Hon. LLD: Alberta, 1968; Laurentian, 1968. *Publications:* (with J. A. Pople and H. J. Bernstein) High Resolution Nuclear Magnetic Resonance, 1959; scientific papers in chemistry and physics research jls. *Recreations:* tennis, ski-ing. *Address:* #2–65 Whitemarl Drive, Ottawa, ON K1L 8J9, Canada. *T:* (613) 7489742.

SCHOFIELD, Prof. Andrew Noel, MA, PhD (Cantab); FRS 1992; FREng, FICE; Professor of Engineering, Cambridge University, 1974–98, now Professor Emeritus; Fellow of Churchill College, Cambridge, 1963–66 and since 1974; *b* 1 Nov. 1930; *s* of late Rev. John Noel Schofield and Winifred Jane Mary (*née* Eyles); *m* 1961, Margaret Eileen Green; two *s* two *d. Educ:* Mill Hill Sch.; Christ's Coll., Cambridge. John Winbolt Prize, 1954. Asst Engr, in Malawi, with Scott Wilson Kirkpatrick and Partners, 1951. Cambridge Univ.: Demonstrator, 1955, Lectr, 1959, Dept of Engrg. Research Fellow, California Inst. of Technology, 1963–64. Univ. of Manchester Inst. of Science and Technology: Prof. of Civil Engrg, 1968; Head of Dept of Civil and Structural Engrg, 1973. Chm., Andrew N. Schofield & Associates Ltd, 1984–2000. Rankine Lecture, ICE British Geotechnical Soc., 1980. Chm., Tech. Cttee on Centrifuge Testing, Int. Soc. for Soil Mech. and Foundn Engrg, 1982–85. FREng (FEng 1986). James Alfred Ewing Medal, ICE, 1993. US Army Award, Civilian Service 1979. *Publications:* (with C. P. Wroth) Critical State Soil Mechanics, 1968; (ed with W. H. Craig and R. G. James and contrib.) Centrifuges in Soil Mechanics, 1988; (ed with J. R. Gronow and R. K. Jain and contrib.) Land Disposal of Hazardous Waste, 1988; papers on soil mechanics and civil engrg. *Address:* 9 Little St Mary's Lane, Cambridge CB2 1RR. *T:* (01223) 314536; *e-mail:* ans@eng.cam.ac.uk.

SCHOFIELD, Derek; Hon. Mr Justice Schofield; Chief Justice of Gibraltar, since 1996; a Recorder, since 2000; *b* 20 Feb. 1945; *s* of John Schofield and Ethelena Schofield (*née* Calverley); *m* 1st, 1967, Judith Danson (marr. diss.); one *s* one *d*; 2nd, 1983, Anne Wangeci Kariuki; one *s* one *d. Educ:* Morecambe Grammar Sch.; NAJCA Dip. in Magisterial Law, 1966. English Magisterial Service, 1961–74; called to the Bar, Gray's Inn, 1970; Kenya: Resident Magistrate, 1974–78; Sen. Resident Magistrate, 1978–82; Puisne Judge, 1982–87; Judge of Grand Court, Cayman Islands, 1988–96; Asst Recorder, 1997–2000. *Recreations:* travel, reading. *Address:* Supreme Court, Gibraltar. *T:* 78808. *Club:* Royal Gibraltar Yacht.

SCHOFIELD, Grace Florence; Regional Nursing Officer to the South West Thames Regional Health Authority, 1974–82, retired; *b* 24 Feb. 1925; *d* of Percy and Matilda Schofield. *Educ:* Mayfield Sch., Putney; University College Hosp. (SRN, SCM); Univ. of London (Dip. in Nursing); Royal College of Nursing (Dip. in Nursing Admin. (Hosp.)). Asst Matron, Guy's Hosp., 1960–61; Dep. Matron, Hammersmith Hosp., 1962–66; Matron, Mount Vernon Hosp. Northwood, and Harefield Hosp., Harefield, 1966–69; Chief Nursing Officer, University Coll. Hosp., 1969–73. *Address:* 42 Briarwood Road, Stoneleigh, Epsom, Surrey KT17 2LY.

SCHOFIELD, Kenneth Douglas, CBE 1996; Executive Director, European Golf Tour, Professional Golfers' Association, since 1975; *b* 3 Feb. 1946; *s* of late Douglas Joseph and Jessie Schofield (*née* Gray); *m* 1968, Evelyn May Sharp; two *d. Educ:* Auchterarder High Sch. Associate, Savings Bank Inst., 1966. Joined Trustee Savings Bank, Perth, 1962: Br. Manager, Dunblane, 1969–71; George Simms Public Relations Co., 1971–74; Sec., PGA European Tour, 1975. Order of Merit, Royal Spanish Golf Fedn, 1993. *Publication:* Pro Golf: the official PGA European Tour Media Guide, 1972–1975. *Recreations:* golf, cricket, soccer, walking. *Address:* Riding Cottage, 2 The Riding, Woodham, Woking, Surrey GU21 5TA. *T:* (office) (01344) 842881. *Clubs:* Caledonian; Wentworth Golf; Crieff Golf; Auchterarder Golf; Royal and Ancient Golf (St Andrews).

SCHOFIELD, Prof. Malcolm, FBA 1997; Professor of Ancient Philosophy, University of Cambridge, since 1998; Fellow, St John's College, Cambridge, since 1972; *b* 19 April 1942; *er s* of Harry Schofield and Ethel Schofield (*née* Greenwood); *m* 1970, Elizabeth Milburn; one *s. Educ:* St Albans Sch.; St John's Coll., Cambridge; Balliol Coll., Oxford. Asst Prof. of Classics, Cornell Univ., 1967–69; Dyson Res. Fellow in Greek Culture, Balliol Coll., Oxford, 1970–72; Cambridge University: Lectr in Classics, 1972–89; Reader in Ancient Philosophy, 1989–98; Mem., Gen. Bd, 1991–94 and 1999–; Chm. Council, Sch. of Arts and Humanities, 1993–94; Chm. Faculty Bd of Classics, 1997–98; Mem., Univ. Council, 1997–; St John's College: Dean, 1979–82; Tutor, 1982–89; Pres., 1991–95. Chm., Benchmarking Gp for Classics and Ancient History, QAA, 1999–2000. Editor, Phronesis, 1987–92. Hon. Sec., Classical Assoc., 1989–. Hon. Citizen, Rhodes, 1992. *Publications:* (ed jtly) Articles on Aristotle, 4 vols, 1975–79; (ed jtly) Doubt and Dogmatism, 1980; An Essay on Anaxagoras, 1980; (ed with M. Nussbaum) Language and Logos, 1982; (ed jtly) Science and Speculation, 1982; (with G. S. Kirk and J. E. Raven) The Presocratic Philosophers, 2nd edn, 1983; (ed with G. Striker) The Norms of Nature, 1986; The Stoic Idea of the City, 1991; (ed with A. Laks) Justice and Generosity, 1995; Saving the City, 1999; (ed jtly) The Cambridge History of Hellenistic Philosophy, 1999; (ed with C. J. Rowe) The Cambridge History of Greek and Roman Political Thought, 2000. *Address:* St John's College, Cambridge CB2 1TP. *T:* (01223) 338644.

SCHOFIELD, Michael, CBE 1999; Chairman, Dorset Community NHS Trust, 1996–2001; *b* 30 Jan. 1941; *s* of Edward Ronald Schofield and Edna Schofield (*née* Davies); *m* 1st, 1971, Patricia Ann Connell (marr. diss. 1982); two *s*; 2nd, 1989, Angela Rosemary Tym. *Educ:* Manchester Grammar Sch.; Exeter Coll., Oxford (BA Mod. Hist. 1962); Manchester Univ. (Dip. Social Admin). Asst House Gov., General Infirmary, Leeds, 1969–72; Asst Sec., United Liverpool Hosps, 1972–74; Dep. Dist Administrator, Liverpool Central and Southern NHS Dist, 1974–76; Area Administrator, 1976–86, and Chief Exec., 1985–86, Rochdale HA; Dir, Health Services Mgt Unit, Univ. of Manchester, 1987–95; Chm., Bradford Community NHS Trust, 1992–96. Mem., EOC, 1997–2000. Chm., Nat. Assoc. of Health Authorities and Trusts, 1995–97. Pres., IHSM, 1990–91. Mem. Council, RPSGB, 1999–. *Publications:* (jtly) The Future Healthcare Workforce, First Report, 1996, Second Report, 1999. *Recreations:* golf, music, gardening. *Address:* 8 Gravel Lane, Charlton Marshall, Blandford Forum, Dorset DT11 9NS. *T:* (01258) 450588. *Clubs:* Royal Society of Medicine; Broadstone golf (Dorset).

SCHOFIELD, Neill; consultant in vocational education and training, since 1996; *b* 2 Aug. 1946; *m* 1969, Carol; two *d. Educ:* Univ. of Leeds (BA Econs 1967); QMC, Univ. of London (MSc 1975). DoE, 1970–78; Dept of Energy, 1978–82; Department of Employment, later Department for Education and Employment, 1982–96: Director: Business and Enterprise, 1990–92; Quality Assurance, 1992–93; Training, Infrastructure and Employers Div., 1994–96. *Recreations:* walking, theatre, family. *Address:* 3 Dobcroft Close, Sheffield S11 9LL. *T:* (0114) 236 3978.

SCHOFIELD, Dr Roger Snowden, FRHistS; FBA 1988; FSS; Senior Research Associate, Cambridge Group for the History of Population and Social Structure, Economic and Social Research Council, 1994–98 (Director, 1974–94); Fellow of Clare College, Cambridge, since 1969; *b* 26 Aug. 1937; *s* of Ronald Snowden Schofield and Muriel Grace Braime; *m* (marr. diss.); one *d. Educ:* Leighton Park Sch., Reading; Clare Coll., Cambridge (BA (History); PhD 1963). FRHistS 1970; FSS 1987. Hon. Reader in Historical Demography, Univ. of Cambridge, 1991–98. Vis. Prof., Div. of Humanities and Social Scis, CIT, 1992–94. Member: Computing Cttee, SSRC, 1970–75; Stats Cttee, SSRC, 1974–78; Software Provision Cttee, UK Computer Bd, 1977–79. Mem., Population Investigation Cttee, 1976– (Treas., 1987–); British Society for Population Studies: Mem., Council, 1979–87; Treas., 1981–85; Pres., 1985–87. *Publications:* (with E. A. Wrigley) The Population History of England 1541–1871: a reconstruction, 1981, repr. with introd. essay, 1993; (ed with John Walter) Famine, Disease, and the Social Order in Early Modern Society, 1989; (jtly) English Population History from Family Reconstitution, 1580–1837, 1997; contrib. to Population Studies, Jl of Interdisciplinary Hist., Jl of Family Hist. *Address:* Clare College, Cambridge CB2 1TL. *T:* (01223) 333267.

SCHOLAR, Sir Michael (Charles), KCB 1999 (CB 1991); President, St John's College, Oxford, since 2001; *b* 3 Jan. 1942; *s* of Richard Herbert Scholar and Mary Blodwen Scholar; *m* 1964, Angela Mary (*née* Sweet); three *s* (one *d* decd). *Educ:* St Olave's Grammar School, Bermondsey; St John's College, Cambridge (PhD, MA; Hon. Fellow, 1999); Univ. of California at Berkeley. ARCO. Loeb Fellow, Harvard Univ., 1967; Asst Lectr in Philosophy, Leicester Univ., 1968; Fellow, St John's College, Cambridge, 1969; HM Treasury, 1969; Private Sec. to Chief Sec., 1974–76; Barclays Bank International, 1979–81; Private Sec. to Prime Minister, 1981–83; Under Secretary, HM Treasury, 1983–87, Dep. Sec., 1987–93; Permanent Secretary: Welsh Office, 1993–96; DTI, 1996–2001. Chm., Civil Service Sports Council, 1998–2001. Fellow, Univ. of Wales, Aberystwyth, 1996. Hon. Dr Glamorgan, 1999. *Recreations:* playing the piano and organ, walking. *Address:* St John's College, Oxford OX1 3JP.

SCHOLEFIELD, Susan Margaret, CMG 1999; Executive Director, Defence Procurement Agency, Ministry of Defence, since 2000; *b* 9 May 1955; *d* of John and Millicent Scholefield; *m* 1977 (marr. diss. 1981); one *s. Educ:* Blackheath High Sch.; Somerville Coll., Oxford (MA); Univ. of Calif, Berkeley (MA). Joined MoD, 1981; on secondment to Ecole Nationale d'Admin, Paris, 1985–86; Principal, MoD, 1986–92

(Private Sec. to Chief of Defence Procurement, 1990–92); Asst Sec., Efficiency Unit, Cabinet Office (on secondment), 1992–95; Head, Balkans Secretariat, MoD, 1995–98; Asst Sec., NI Office (on secondment), 1998–2000; Under Sec., MoD, 2000. *Recreations:* reading, music, theatre, gardening. *Address:* c/o Ministry of Defence, Abbey Wood, Bristol BS34 8JH.

SCHOLES, Hon. Gordon Glen Denton, AO 1993; MHR for Corio (Victoria), Australia, 1967–93; *b* 7 June 1931; *s* of Glen Scholes and Mary Scholes; *m* 1957, Della Kathleen Robinson; two *d. Educ:* various schs. Loco-engine driver, Victorian Railways, 1949–67. Councillor, Geelong City, 1965–67; Pres., Geelong Trades Hall Council, 1965–66. House of Representatives: Chm. cttees, 1973–75; Speaker, 1975–76; Shadow Minister for Defence, 1977–83; Minister for Defence, 1983–84; Minister for Territories, 1984–87. Amateur Boxing Champion (Heavyweight), Vic, 1949. *Recreations:* golf, reading. *Address:* 20 Stephen Street, Newtown, Vic 3220, Australia.

SCHOLES, Hubert, CB 1977; a Commissioner of Customs and Excise, 1978–81; *b* 22 March 1921; *s* of late Hubert Scholes and Lucy (*née* Carter); *m* 1949, Patricia Caldwell (*d* 1999); one *s. Educ:* Shrewsbury Sch.; Balliol Coll., Oxford. Served RA, 1940–45. Asst Principal, Min. of Fuel and Power, 1946; Principal, 1950; Ministry of Housing and Local Govt, 1956–57; Principal Private Sec. to Minister of Power, 1959–62; Asst Sec., 1962; Under-Sec., Min. of Power, subseq. Min. of Technol., DTI and Dept of Industry, 1968–78. Specialist Advr to H of C Employment Cttee, 1981–82. *Address:* 5A Lancaster Avenue, Farnham, Surrey GU9 8JY. *T:* (01252) 723992.

SCHOLES, Mary Elizabeth, (Mrs A. I. M. Haggart), OBE 1983; SRN; Chief Area Nursing Officer, Tayside Health Board, 1973–83; *b* 8 April 1924; *d* of late John Neville Carpenter Scholes and Margaret Elizabeth (*née* Hines); *m* 1983, Most Rev. Alastair Iain Macdonald Haggart (*d* 1998). *Educ:* Wyggeston Grammar Sch. for Girls, Leicester; Leicester Royal Infirmary and Children's Hosp. (SRN 1946); Guy's Hosp., London (CMB Pt I Cert. 1947); Royal Coll. of Nursing, London (Nursing Admin (Hosp.) Cert. 1962). Leicester Royal Infirmary and Children's Hospital: Staff Nurse, 1947–48; Night Sister, 1948–50; Ward Sister, 1950–56; Night Supt, 1956–58; Asst Matron, 1958–61; Asst Matron, Memorial/Brook Gen. Hosp., London, 1962–64; Matron, Dundee Royal Infirm. and Matron Designate, Ninewells Hosp., Dundee, 1964–68; Chief Nursing Officer, Bd of Management for Dundee Gen. Hosps and Bd of Man. for Ninewells and Associated Hosps, 1968–73. Pres., Scottish Assoc. of Nurse Administrators, 1973–77. Member: Scottish Bd, Royal Coll. of Nursing, 1965–70; Gen. Nursing Council for Scotland, 1966–70, 1979–; Standing Nursing and Midwifery Cttee, Scotland, 1971–74 (Vice-Chm., 1973–74); UK Central Council for Nursing, Midwifery and Health Visiting, 1980–84; Management Cttee, State Hosp., Carstairs, 1983–92; Scottish Hosp. Endowments Res. Trust, 1986–96; Chm., Scottish National Bd for Nursing, Midwifery and Health Visiting, 1980–84. *Recreations:* travel, music. *Address:* 14/2 St Margaret's Place, Edinburgh EH9 1AY. *Club:* Royal Over-Seas League.

SCHOLES, Prof. Myron S., PhD; Professor of Law, Stanford University, since 1983; *b* 1941; *m*; *c. Educ:* McMaster Univ.; Univ. of Chicago. Instr, Univ. of Chicago Business Sch., 1967–68; Asst Prof., 1968–72, Associate Prof., 1972–73, MIT Mgt Sch.; University of Chicago: Associate Prof., 1973–75; Prof., 1975–79; Dir, Center for Res. in Security Prices, 1975–81; Edward Eagle Brown Prof. of Finance, 1979–82; Frank E. Buck Prof. of Finance, 1988, Emeritus 1996, and Sen. Res. Fellow, Hoover Inst., 1988–, Stanford Univ. Man. Dir, Salomon Bros, 1991–93; Partner, Long-Term Capital Management, 1994–99 (Limited Partner, 1999–); Oak Hill Capital Management, 1999–. (Jtly) Nobel Prize for Economics, 1997. *Publication:* (jtly) Taxes and Business Strategy: a planning approach, 1992. *Address:* Stanford University Graduate School of Business, Stanford, CA 94305, USA.

SCHOLES, Rodney James; QC 1987; a Recorder, since 1986; *b* 26 Sept. 1945; *s* of late Henry Scholes and Margaret Bower; *m* 1977, Katherin Elizabeth (*née* Keogh); two *s* (and one *s* decd). *Educ:* Wade Deacon Grammar Sch., Widnes; St Catherine's Coll., Oxford (scholar) (BA; BCL). Lincoln's Inn: Hardwicke Schol., 1964; Mansfield Schol., 1967; called to the Bar, 1968, Bencher, 1997. Mem., Northern Circuit, 1968–. *Recreations:* watching Rugby football, dog walking. *Address:* Byrom Street Chambers, 12 Byrom Street, Manchester M3 4PP. *T:* (0161) 829 2100, *Fax:* (0161) 829 2101; 22 Old Buildings, Lincoln's Inn, WC2A 3UJ. *T:* (020) 7831 0222.

SCHOLEY, Sir David (Gerald), Kt 1987; CBE 1976; Senior Advisor, UBS Warburg (formerly Warburg Dillon Read), since 1997; Deputy Chairman, Anglo-American, since 1999; *b* 28 June 1935; *s* of Dudley and Lois Scholey; *m* 1960, Alexandra Beatrix, *d* of Hon. George and Fiorenza Drew, Canada; one *s* one *d. Educ:* Wellington Coll., Berks; Christ Church, Oxford. Nat Service, RAC, 9th Queen's Royal Lancers, 1953–55; 3/4 CLY (Sharpshooters); Metropolitan Special Constabulary (Thames Div.). Thompson Graham & Co. (Lloyd's brokers), 1956–58; Dale & Co. (Insce brokers), Canada, 1958–59; Guinness Mahon & Co. Ltd, 1959–64; joined S. G. Warburg & Co. Ltd, 1965, Dir, 1967, Dep. Chm., 1977, Jt Chm., 1980–84, Chm., 1985–95; Chm., SBC Warburg, July–Nov. 1995; Sen. Advr, IFC, Washington, 1996–. Director: Mercury Securities plc, 1969 (Chm., 1984–86); Orion Insurance Co. Ltd, 1963–87; Stewart Wrightson Holdings Ltd, 1972–81; Union Discount Co. of London, Ltd, 1976–81; Bank of England, 1981–98; British Telecom plc, 1986–94; Chubb Corp., 1991–; General Electric Co., 1992–95; J. Sainsbury plc, 1996–2000; Vodafone Group (formerly Vodafone Airtouch) plc, 1997–; Close Bros, 1999– (Chm., 1999–). Mem., Export Guarantees Adv. Council, 1970–75 (Dep. Chm. 1974–75); Chm., Construction Exports Adv. Bd, 1975–78; Member: Inst. Internat. d'Etudes Bancaires, 1976–94 (Pres., 1988); Cttee on Finance for Industry, NEDO, 1980–87; Council, IISS, 1984–93 (Hon. Treas., 1984–90); Industry and Commerce Gp, SCF, 1989–95; President's Cttee, BITC, 1988–91; Ford Foundn Adv. Gp on UN Financing, 1992–93; London First, 1993–96; Bd of Banking Supervision, 1996–98. Dir, INSEAD, 1989– (Chm., UK Council, 1992–97; Chm., Internat. Council, 1995–). A Gov., BBC, 1994–2000; Mem. Adv. Council, LSO, 1998–. Trustee: Glyndebourne Arts Trust, 1989–; Nat. Portrait Gallery, 1992–. Governor: Wellington Coll., 1977–89, 1996–; NIESR, 1984–; LSE, 1993–96. FRSA. Hon. DLitt London Guildhall, 1993. *Address:* (office) 1 Finsbury Avenue, EC2M 2PP.

SCHOLEY, Dr Keith Douglas; Head, Natural History Unit, BBC, since 1998; *b* 24 June 1957; *s* of Douglas and Jeannie Scholey; *m* 1985, Elizabeth Sara Potter; two *s. Educ:* Reed's Sch., Surrey; Univ. of Bristol (BSc Hons; PhD 1982). Postgrad. res., Bristol Univ., 1978–81; joined BBC, 1982: researcher, 1982–85; TV asst producer, 1985–88; TV producer, 1989–93; editor, TV series, 1993–98. *Recreations:* flying (private pilot's licence), scuba diving, sailing, photography. *Address:* BBC Natural History Unit, Broadcasting House, Whiteladies Road, Bristol BS8 2LR. *T:* (0117) 974 2114.

SCHOLEY, Sir Robert, Kt 1987; CBE 1982; FREng; Chairman, British Steel plc (formerly British Steel Corporation), 1986–92; *b* 8 Oct. 1921; *s* of Harold and Eveline Scholey; *m* 1946, Joan Methley; two *d. Educ:* King Edward VII Sch. and Sheffield Univ. Associateship in Mech Engrg; FREng (FEng 1990). United Steel Companies, 1947–68; British Steel Corporation, 1968–92: Dir and Chief Executive, 1973–86; Dep. Chm., 1976–86. Dir, Eurotunnel Bd, 1987–94. Mem., HEFCE, 1992–95. Pres., Eurofer, 1985–90. Chm., Internat. Iron and Steel Inst., 1989–90; Pres., Inst. of Metals, 1989–90. Hon. DEng Sheffield, 1987; Hon. DSc Teeside, 1995. *Recreations:* outdoor life, history.

SCHOLL, Andreas; countertenor; *b* Germany, 1967. *Educ:* Schola Cantorum Basiliensis, Switzerland (Dip. in Ancient Music). Former chorister, Kiedricher Chorbuben, Germany. Début internat. recital, Théâtre de Grévin, Paris, 1993; opera début in Handel's Rodelinda, Glyndebourne, 1998; appears regularly with Les Arts Florissants, Akad. für Alte Musik Berlin, Orch. of the Age of Enlightenment and other baroque ensembles. Teaches at Schola Cantorum Basiliensis. Composes and records pop music; prizewinning recordings include works by Vivaldi and Caldara, and English folk and lute songs. *Address:* c/o Harrison Parrott Ltd, 12 Penzance Place, W11 4PA.

SCHOLTE, Nicholas Paul; Chief Executive, Prescription Pricing Authority, since 1999; *b* 6 May 1959; *s* of Christiaan and Sylvia Joyce Scholte; partner, Iris Monika Esters; one *s* one *d. Educ:* Chesterfield Grammar Sch.; Manchester Univ. (BA Hons Politics). Law Society: Exec. Officer, 1981–85; Sen. Exec. Officer, 1985–86; Finance Manager, 1986–89; Legal Aid Board: Gp Manager (NE), 1990–96; Business Systems Dir, 1996–99. *Recreations:* sailing, ballet, literature, football. *Address:* Prescription Pricing Authority, Bridge House, 152 Pilgrim Street, Newcastle upon Tyne NE1 6SN. *T:* (0191) 203 5209.

SCHOLTENS, Sir James (Henry), KCVO 1977 (CVO 1963); Director, Office of Government Ceremonial and Hospitality, Department of the Prime Minister and Cabinet, Canberra, 1973–80, retired; Extra Gentleman Usher to the Queen, since 1981; *b* 12 June 1920; *s* of late Theo F. J. Scholtens and late Grace M. E. (*née* Nolan); *m* 1945, Mary Maguire, Brisbane; one *s* five *d. Educ:* St Patrick's Marist Brothers' Coll., Sale, Vic. Served War, RAAF, 1943–45. Joined Aust. Public Service, 1935; PMG's Dept, Melbourne, 1935; Dept of Commerce, Melb., 1938; transf. to Dept of Commerce, Canberra, 1941; Dept of Prime Minister, Canberra: Accountant, 1949; Ceremonial Officer, 1954; Asst Sec., Ceremonial and Hospitality Br., 1967. Dir of visits to Australia by the Sovereign and Members of the Royal Family, Heads of State, Monarchs and Presidents, and by Heads of Govt and Ministers of State. *Address:* 34 Teague Street, Cook, Canberra, ACT 2614, Australia. *T:* (2) 62510125. *Clubs:* Canberra, Southern Cross (Canberra); Royal Automobile of Australia (Sydney).

SCHOLZ, Prof. Dr Rupert; Professor of Public Law, Institut für Politik und öffentliches Recht, University of Munich, since 1981; *b* 23 May 1937; *s* of Ernst and Gisela Scholz (*née* Merdas); *m* 1971, Dr Helga Scholz-Hoppe. *Educ:* Abitur, Berlin; studied law and economics, Berlin and Heidelberg; Dr Jur., Univ. of Munich. Prof., Univ. of Munich, taught in Munich, Berlin, Regensburg, Augsburg; Public Law Chair, Berlin and Munich, 1978. Senator of Justice, Land Berlin, 1981; Acting Senator for Federal Affairs; Mem., Bundesrat, 1982; Mem., N Atlantic Assembly, 1982; Senator for Federal Affairs, Land Berlin, 1983; MHR, Berlin, and Senator for Justice and Federal Affairs, 1985; Federal Minister of Defence, FRG, 1988–89; Mem., German Bundestag, 1990–. *Publications:* numerous papers in jurisp., German policy, foreign policy, economic policy. *Address:* Institut für Politik und öffentliches Recht, Universität München, Ludwigstrasse 28, 80539 München, Germany.

SCHOPPER, Prof. Herwig Franz; Professor of Physics, University of Hamburg, 1973–89, now Emeritus; *b* 28 Feb. 1928; *s* of Franz Schopper and Margarete Hartmann; *m* 1949, Dora Klara Ingeborg (*née* Stieler); one *s* one *d. Educ:* Univ. of Hamburg. Dip. Phys. 1949, Dr rer nat 1951. Asst Prof. and Univ. Lectr, Univ. of Erlangen, 1954–57; Prof., Univ. of Mainz, 1957–60; Prof., Univ. of Karlsruhe and Dir of Inst. for Nuclear Physics, 1961–73; Chm., Scientific Council, Kerforschungszentrum, Karlsruhe, 1967–69; Chm., Deutsches Elektronen Synchrotron particle physics Lab., Hamburg, 1973–80; European Organisation for Nuclear Research (CERN): Res. Associate, 1966–67; Head, Dept of particle physics and Mem., Directorate for experimental prog., 1970–73; Chm., Intersecting Storage Ring Cttee, 1973–76; Mem., Sci. Policy Cttee, 1979–80; Dir-Gen., 1981–88. Chm., Assoc. of German Nat. Research Centres, 1978–80; Mem., Scientific Council, IN2P3, Paris; Advr, UNESCO, 1994–. President: German Physical Soc., 1992–94; European Physical Soc., 1995–97. Member: Akad. der Wissenschaften Leopoldina, Halle; Joachim Jungius Gesellschaft, Hamburg; Sudetendeutsche Akad. der Wissenschaft, 1979; Acad. Scientiarium et Artium, Vienna, 1993; MAE 1992; Corresp. Mem., Bavarian Acad. of Scis, 1981; Hon. Mem., Hungarian Acad. of Scis, 1995. Foreign FInstP 1996. Dr *hc*: Univ. of Erlangen, 1982; Univ. of Moscow, 1989; Univ. of Geneva, 1989; Univ. of London, 1989; Jt Inst. of Nuclear Res., Dubna, 1998; Inst. of High Energy Physics, Russia, 1999. Physics Award, Göttinger Akad. der Wissenschaft, 1957; Carus Medal, Akad. Leopoldina, 1958; Ritter von Gerstner Medal, 1978; Sudetendeutscher Kulturpreis, 1984; Golden Plate Award, Amer. Acad. of Achievement, 1984; Gold Medal, Weizmann Inst., 1987; Wilhelm Exner Medal, Gewerbeverein, Austria, 1991; Purkyne Meml Medal, Czech Acad. of Scis, 1994; 650 Years Jubilee Medal, Charles Univ., Prague, 1998. Grosses Bundesverdienstkreuz (FRG), 1989; Friendship Order of Russian Pres., 1996. *Publications:* Weak Interactions and Nuclear Beta Decay, 1966; Matter—Antimatter, 1989; papers on elementary particle physics, high energy accelerators, relation of science and society. *Recreations:* music, gardening. *Address:* c/o CERN, 1211 Geneva 23, Switzerland. *T:* (22) 7675350.

SCHOUVALOFF, Alexander, MA; *b* 4 May 1934; *s* of Paul Schouvaloff (professional name Paul Sheriff) and Anna Schouvaloff (*née* Raevsky); *m* 1st, Gillian Baker; one *s*; 2nd, 1971, Daria Chorley (*née* de Mérindol). *Educ:* Harrow Sch.; Jesus Coll., Oxford (MA). Asst Director, Edinburgh Festival, 1965–67; Dir, North West Arts Assoc., 1967–74; Founder Curator, Theatre Mus., V & A Mus., 1974–89; Director: Rochdale Festival, 1971; Chester Festival, 1973. Sec. Gen., Société Internat. des Bibliothèques et des Musées des Arts du Spectacle, 1980–90; Cttee Mem. for Dance Div., NY Public Liby for Performing Arts, 1993–. Trustee, London Archives of the Dance, 1976–. BBC Radio plays: Summer of the Bullshine Boys, 1981; No Saleable Value, 1982. Cross of Polonia Restituta, 1971. *Publications:* Place for the Arts, 1971; Summer of the Bullshine Boys, 1979; (with Victor Borovsky) Stravinsky on Stage, 1982; (with April FitzLyon) A Month in the Country, 1983; (with Catherine Haill) The Theatre Museum, 1987; Theatre on Paper, 1990; Léon Bakst: The Theatre Art, 1991; Imperial Domes: Russian Orthodox Churches built outside Russia before the Revolution, 2001; catalogues: Thyssen-Bornemisza Collection (set and costume designs), 1987; The Art of Ballets Russes (the Serge Lifar collection of theater designs, costumes, and paintings at the Wadsworth Atheneum), 1998. *Recreations:* France, Italy. *Address:* 10 Avondale Park Gardens, W11 4PR. *T:* (020) 7727 7543. *Club:* Garrick.

SCHRAM, Prof. Stuart Reynolds; Professor of Politics (with reference to China) in the University of London, School of Oriental and African Studies, 1968–89, now Emeritus; Research Associate, Harvard University, since 1989; *b* Excelsior, Minn, 27 Feb. 1924; *s* of Warren R. Schram and Nada Stedman Schram; *m* 1972, Marie-Annick Lancelot; one *s. Educ:* West High Sch., Minneapolis, Minn; Univ. of Minnesota (BA, 1944); Columbia Univ. (PhD 1954). Dir, Soviet and Chinese Section, Centre d'Etude des Relations Internationales, Fondation Nationale des Sciences Politiques, Paris, 1954–67; Head,

Contemporary China Inst., SOAS, 1968–72. *Publications:* Protestantism and Politics in France, 1954; The Political Thought of Mao Tse-Tung, 1963, rev. edn 1969; Le marxisme et l'Asie 1853–1964, 1965, rev. and enl. English edn 1969; Mao Tse-tung, 1966; Ideology and Policy in China since the Third Plenum, 1978–84, 1984; (ed) The Scope of State Power in China, 1985; (ed) Foundations and Limits of State Power in China, 1987; The Thought of Mao Tse-tung, 1989; (ed) Mao's Road to Power: Revolutionary Writings 1912–1949, vol. I 1992, vol. II 1994, vol. III 1995, vol. IV 1997, vol. V 1999, vols VI and VII, 2002. *Recreations:* concert- and theatre-going, walking in the country, fishing. *Address:* John King Fairbank Center for East Asian Research, Harvard University, 1737 Cambridge Street, Cambridge, MA 02138, USA.

SCHRAMEK, Sir Eric (Emil) von; *see* von Schramek.

SCHREIBER, family name of **Baron Marlesford**.

SCHREIER, Sir Bernard, Kt 2000; mechanical engineer; Chairman, CP Holdings Ltd. Pres., IIC Industries Inc., NY; Chm., Danubius Hotels RT, Hungary; Dep. Chm., Bank Leumi (UK) plc. Hon. Fellow, UCL. Queen's Award for Export, 1976; Jubilee Award, Israel, 1998. Officer's Cross, Order of Hungarian Republic, 1998. *Address:* CP Holdings Ltd, CP House, Otterspool Way, Watford, Herts WD2 8HG.

SCHREMPP, Jürgen E.; Chairman, Board of Management, DaimlerChrysler AG, since 2000 (Joint Chairman, 1998–2000); *b* 15 Sept. 1944. *Educ:* Univ. for Applied Scis, Offenburg. Apprentice motor mechanic, Mercedes-Benz Dealership, Freiburg, 1961–64; joined Daimler-Benz AG, 1967; Mercedes-Benz of South Africa: Manager, Service Div., 1974–80; Mem., Bd of Mgt, 1980–82, 1984–87; Vice Pres., 1984; Pres., 1985–87; Pres., Euclid Inc., USA (subsidiary of Daimler-Benz AG), 1982–84; Daimler-Benz Board of Management: Dep. Mem., 1987–89; Mem., 1989–95; Chm., 1998; Pres. and CEO, Daimler-Benz Aerospace AG, 1989–95. *Address:* DaimlerChrysler, Epplestrasse 225, 70546 Stuttgart, Germany. *T:* (711) 1794326.

SCHREUDER, Prof. Deryck Marshall, DPhil; FAHA; Vice-Chancellor, and President (formerly Principal), University of Western Australia, since 1998; *b* 19 Jan. 1942; *s* of Peter Jurian and Jean Margaret Schreuder; *m* 1965, Patricia Anne Pote; three *s*. *Educ:* Llewellin High Sch., Zambia; Univ. of Rhodes, S Africa (BA Hons); DPhil Oxon 1964. FAHA 1985. Rhodes Schol. from Central Africa, 1964–67; Kennedy Fellow of Modern Hist., New Coll., Oxford, 1967–69; Prof. of Hist., and Hd of Dept, Trent Univ., Ontario, 1970–79; Challis Prof. of Hist., Univ. of Sydney, 1980–93 (Dep. Chm., Acad. Bd, 1984–85); on secondment as Associate Dir, Humanities Res. Centre, ANU, 1992–93; Dep. Vice-Chancellor (Acad.), Macquarie Univ., 1993–95; Vice-Chancellor, Univ. of Western Sydney, 1995–98; Emeritus Prof., Macquarie Univ. and Univ. of Western Sydney, 1998. Res. Fellow, Res. Sch. of Social Scis, ANU, 1976–77. Member: Aust. Res. Grants Cttee, 1986–92; Commn on Commonwealth Studies, 1995–97. President: Aust. Hist. Assoc., 1985–86; Aust. Acad. Humanities, 1992–95 (Vice-Pres., 1989–90). Associate Ed., New DNB, 1995–. *Publications:* Gladstone and Kruger: Liberal Government and Colonial Home Rule (1880–85), 1969; The Scramble for Southern Africa (1877–95), 1981; (jtly) The Rise of Colonial Nationalism: Australia, New Zealand, Canada and South Africa first assert their nationality 1880–1914, 1988; (ed jtly) The Commonwealth and Australia in World Affairs, 1990; (ed jtly) History and Social Change: the G. A. Wood Memorial Lectures 1949–91, 1991; (ed) Imperialisms, 1991; A Letter from Sydney: history and the post-Colonial society (J. M. Ward Memorial Lecture), 1991; (ed jtly) History at Sydney, 1992; (ed) The Humanities and the Creative Nation, 1995; (ed jtly) Africa Today, 1997. *Recreations:* gardening, jogging, writing history. *Address:* Office of the Vice-Chancellor, University of Western Australia, Nedlands, WA 6907, Australia. *T:* (8) 93802801. *Clubs:* Royal Over-Seas League; Weld (Perth); Universities and Schools (Sydney).

SCHREYER, Rt Hon. Edward Richard, CC 1979; CMM 1979; CD 1979; PC 1984; High Commissioner for Canada in Australia, and concurrently Ambassador to Vanuatu, 1984–88; *b* Beausejour, Man., 21 Dec. 1935; *s* of John and Elizabeth Schreyer, a pioneer family of the district; *m* 1960, Lily, *d* of Jacob Schulz, MP; two *s* two *d*. *Educ:* Beausejour, Manitoba; United Coll., Winnipeg; St John's Coll., Winnipeg, Univ. of Manitoba (BA, BEd, MA). While at university served as 2nd Lieut, COTC, Royal Canadian Armored Corps, 1954–55. Member, Legislative Assembly of Manitoba, 1958; re-elected, 1959 and 1962; MP: for Springfield, 1965; for Selkirk, 1968; chosen as Leader of New Democratic Party in Manitoba, 1969, and resigned seat in House of Commons; MLA for Rossmere and Premier of Manitoba, 1969–77; Minister of: Dominion-Provincial Relns, 1969–77; Hydro, 1971–77; Finance, 1972–74; re-elected MLA, 1977; Governor-Gen. and C-in-C of Canada, 1979–84. Prof. of Political Science and Internat. Relns, St John's Coll., Univ. of Manitoba, 1962–65. Distinguished Vis. Prof., Univ. of Winnipeg, 1989–90; Vis. Prof., Simon Fraser Univ., Vancouver, 1991; Distinguished Fellow, Inst. for Integrated Energy Systems, Univ. of Victoria, 1992–94; Univ. of BC, 1995–. Director: Perfect Pacific Investments, 1989–; China International Trade and Investment Corp., Canada, 1991–; Saskatchewan Energy Conservation and Develt Authy, 1993–; Alternate Fuel Systems Inc. (Calgary), 1994–; Cephalon Oil & Gas Resource Corp. (Calgary), 1994–. Chm., Canadian Shield Foundn, 1984–; Member: Internat. Assoc. of Energy Economists; CPA; IPU. Hon. LLD: Manitoba, 1979; Mount Allison, 1983; McGill, 1984; Simon Fraser, 1984; Lakehead, 1985; Hon. Dr Sci. Sociale Ottawa, 1980. *Recreations:* reading, golf, sculpting, woodworking. *Address:* 250 Wellington Center, Unit 401, Winnipeg, MB R3M 0B3, Canada. *T:* (204) 9897580, *Fax:* (204) 9897581. *Clubs:* Rideau (Ottawa); York, Upper Canada (Toronto).

SCHREYER, Michaele, PhD; Member, European Commission, since 1999; Member (Green Party) State Parliament of Berlin, since 1991; *b* Cologne, 9 Aug. 1951. *Educ:* Univ. of Cologne (Dip. Econs and Sociology 1976); Univ. of Berlin (PhD 1983). Research Assistant: Inst. for Public Finances and Social Policy, Free Univ. of Berlin, 1977–82; Green Party, Bundestag, 1983–87; Researcher, Inst. for Econ. Res., 1987–88. Minister for Urban Develt and Envmtl Protection, State Govt of Berlin, 1989–90; Chair, Green Party Gp, State Parlt of Berlin, 1998–. *Address:* European Commission, rue de la Loi 200, 1049 Brussels, Belgium.

SCHRIEFFER, Prof. John Robert, PhD; University Professor, Florida State University, and Chief Scientist, National High Magnetic Field Laboratory, since 1992; University Eminent Scholar Professor, State of Florida University System, since 1995; *b* Oak Park, Ill, 31 May 1931; *s* of John Henry Schrieffer and Louise Anderson; *m* 1960, Anne Grete Thomsen; one *s* two *d*. *Educ:* MIT(BS); Univ. of Illinois (MS, PhD). Nat. Sci. Foundn Fellow, Univ. of Birmingham, and Niels Bohr Inst. for Theoretical Physics, Copenhagen, 1957–58; Asst Prof., Univ. of Chicago, 1957–59; Asst Prof., Univ. of Illinois, 1959–60, Associate Prof., 1960–62; Univ. of Pennsylvania: Mem. Faculty, 1962–79; Mary Amanda Wood Prof. of Physics, 1964–79; University of California, Santa Barbara: Prof. of Physics, 1980–91; Chancellor's Prof., 1984–91; Dir, Inst. for Theoretical Physics, 1984–89. Guggenheim Fellow, Copenhagen, 1967. Member: Nat. Acad. Scis; Amer. Acad. of Arts and Scis; Amer. Philos. Soc.; Amer. Phys Soc. (Vice-Pres., 1994; Pres.-elect, 1995; Pres., 1996); Danish Royal Acad. Sci.; Acad. of Sci. of USSR, 1989. Hon. ScD: Technische Hochschule, Munich, 1968; Univ. of Geneva, 1968; Univ. of Pennsylvania, 1973; Illinois Univ., 1974; Univ. of Cincinnati, 1977; Hon. DSc Tel-Aviv Univ., 1987. Buckley Prize, Amer. Phys Soc., 1968; Comstock Prize, Nat. Acad. Scis, 1968; (jtly) Nobel Prize for Physics, 1972; John Ericsson Medal, Amer. Soc. of Swedish Engineers, 1976; Nat. Medal of Science, USA, 1985. *Publications:* Theory of Superconductivity, 1964; articles on solid state physics and chemistry. *Recreations:* painting, gardening, wood working. *Address:* NHMFL/FSU, 1800 E Paul Dirac Drive, Tallahassee, FL 32310, USA.

SCHRÖDER, Gerhard; Member, Bundestag, 1980–86 and since 1998; Chancellor, Federal Republic of Germany, since 1998; Chairman, Social Democratic Party, Germany, since 1999; *b* 7 April 1944; *m* 1998, Doris Köpf. *Educ:* Univ. of Göttingen. Apprentice retailer, 1959–61; qualified as lawyer, 1976; in practice, Hannover, 1978–90. Member, Supervisory Board: Volkswagen AG, 1994–98; Norddeutsche Landesbank, 1994–98; EXPO 2000 Hannover GmbH, 1994–98. Joined SPD, 1963; Mem. for Hannover Bezirk, Lower Saxony Landtag, 1977–98; Chm., SPD Gp, 1986–90; Prime Minister, Lower Saxony, 1990–98. Sozialdemokratische Partei Deutschlands: Nat. Chm., Young Socialists, 1978–80; Member: Exec. Cttee, Hannover, 1977–99 (constituency Chm., 1983–93); NEC, 1986–99; Presiding Council, 1989–99; Chm., Lower Saxony Br., 1994–98. *Address:* Bundeskanzleramt, Willy Brandt Strasse 1, 10557 Berlin, Germany.

SCHUBERT, Sir Sydney, Kt 1985; Chairman, Daikyo Group Australia, since 1998 (Chief Executive, 1988–98); Co-ordinator General and Permanent Head, 1982–88, Director General, 1987–88, Premier's Department, Government of Queensland, Australia; *b* 22 March 1928; *s* of Wilhelm F. Schubert and Mary A. Price; *m* 1961, Maureen Kistle; two *d*. *Educ:* Univ. of Queensland; Univ. of Durham. Queensland Government: Civil Engr, 1950; Dep. Chief Engr, Main Roads Dept, 1965–69; Chief Engr Dept., 1969–72; Dep. Co-ordinator General, 1972–76. Director: Jupiters, 1988–92 (Dep. Chm., 1990–92); Coffey Internat., 1990–; APN Hldgs, 1992–; Victoria Hotels Pty Ltd (Christchurch), 1990–; Premier Hotels Pty Ltd (Christchurch), 1990–; Christchurch Casinos Pty Ltd, 1992–. Chancellor, Bond Univ., 1987–89. Mem., Gt Barrier Reef Marine Park Authy, 1978–88; Deputy Chairman: Brisbane Exposition and S Bank Redevelt Authy, 1984–88; Qld Cultural Centre Trust, 1986–88. Member: Bd of Management, Graduate Sch. of Management, Univ. of Queensland, 1985–88; Exec. Council, Australia Japan Assoc. Qld, 1988–90. Eisenhower Fellow, Aust., 1972. FIE(Aust); Hon. Fellow, Aust. Instn of Engrs. *Recreation:* golf. *Address:* 15 Apex Street, Clayfield, Brisbane, Qld 4011, Australia. *Clubs:* Queensland, Royal Queensland Golf.

SCHÜELEIN-STEEL, Danielle Fernande, (Danielle Steel); writer; *b* 14 Aug. 1947; *d* of John and Norma Schüelein-Steel; *m*; one *d*; *m* 1977, Bill Toth; (one *s* decd); *m* 1981, John Traina (marr. diss.); one *s* four *d*. *Educ:* Lycée Français, NYC; Parsons Sch. of Design, NY; Univ. of New York. Vice-Pres. of Public Relations and New Business, Supergirls Ltd, 1968–71; copywriter, Grey Advertising Agency, 1973–74. *Publications: fiction:* Going Home, 1973; Now and Forever, 1978; The Promise, 1978; Golden Moments, 1979; Season of Passion, 1980; Summer's End, 1980; The Ring, 1980; To Love Again, 1981; Palomino, 1981; Loving, 1981; Remembrance, 1981; A Perfect Stranger, 1982; Once in a Lifetime, 1982; Crossings, 1982; Changes, 1983; Thurston House, 1983; Full Circle, 1984; Secrets, 1985; Family Album, 1985; Wanderlust, 1986; Fine Things, 1987; Kaleidoscope, 1987; Zoya, 1988; Star, 1989; Daddy, 1989; Message from Nam, 1990; Heartbeat, 1991; No Greater Love, 1991; Jewels, 1992; Mixed Blessings, 1992; Vanished, 1993; Accident, 1994; The Gift, 1994; Wings, 1994; Lightning, 1995; Five Days in Paris, 1995; Malice, 1996; Silent Honor, 1996; The Ranch, 1997; The Ghost, 1997; Special Delivery, 1997; The Long Road Home, 1998; The Klone and I, 1998; Mirror Image, 1998; Bittersweet, 1999; Granny Dan, 1999; Irresistible Forces, 1999; The Wedding, 2000; The House on Hope Street, 2000; Journey, 2000; Lone Eagle, 2001; Leap of Faith, 2001; *non-fiction:* (contrib.) Having a Baby, 1984; His Bright Light: the story of Nick Traina, 1998; *poetry:* Love, 1981; several children's books. *Address:* c/o Dell Publishing, 1540 Broadway, New York, NY 10036, USA.

SCHULTZ, Rt Rev. Bruce Allan; Bishop of Grafton, NSW, 1985–98; *b* 24 May 1932; *s* of Percival Ferdinand and Elsie Amelia Schultz; *m* 1962, Janet Margaret Gersbach; two *s* two *d* (and one *s* decd). *Educ:* Culcairn High School; St Columb's Hall and St John's Coll., Morpeth. ThL (ACT) 1960. Sheep and wheat property, Manager–Owner, 1950–57. Theolog. student, 1957–60; deacon 1959, priest 1960, dio. Riverina; Asst Priest, Broken Hill, 1961–63; Priest-in-charge, Ariah Park, Ardlethan and Barellan with Weethalle, 1964–67; Rector: Deniliquin, 1967–73; Gladstone, dio. Rockhampton, 1973–79; Archdeacon and Commissary of Rockhampton, 1975–79; Rector of Grafton and Dean of Christ Church Cathedral, 1979–83; Asst Bishop of Brisbane (Bishop for the Northern Region), 1983–85. Nat. Chm., Anglican Boys' Soc. in Australia, 1987–94; Episcopal overseer, Cursillo Movement in Australia, 1987–95; Chm., NSW Provincial Commn on Christian Educn, 1989; Bd Mem., Australian Bd of Missions, 1988–95; Chm., Nat. Home Mission Fund, 1999–. *Recreations:* family, fishing, tennis, water ski-ing, gardening. *Address:* 11 Carwoola Crescent, Mooloolaba, Qld 4557, Australia. *Clubs:* Mooloolaba Surf Life Saving, Mooloolaba Bowls, Coast Guard (Mooloolaba).

SCHUMACHER, Michael; racing driver; *b* 3 Jan. 1969; *m* 1995, Corinna Betsch; one *s* one *d*. Formula 3, 1983–90; European and World Champion, 1990; Formula 1, 1991–; Benetton-Ford team, 1991–95; Ferrari team, 1995–; Drivers' World Champion, 1994, 1995, 2000, 2001. *Publication:* (jtly) Formula for Success, 1996. *Address:* c/o Weber Management GmbH, Traenkenstrasse 11, 70597 Stuttgart, Germany. *T:* (711) 726460.

SCHUSTER, Rt Rev. James Leo; Assistant Bishop of George, since 1980; *b* 18 July 1912; *s* of Rev. Harold Vernon Schuster and Elsie Jane (*née* Roberton); *m* 1951, Ilse Henriette Emmy Gottschalk; three *s* two *d* (and one *s* decd). *Educ:* Lancing; Keble Coll., Oxford. Deacon, 1937; Priest, 1938; Asst Missioner, Clare Coll. Mission, Rotherhithe, 1937–38; Chaplain St Stephen's House, Oxford, 1938–40; CF (EC), 1940–46; wounded, 1942; despatches, 1943. Chaplain, St Stephen's House, Oxford, 1946–49; Principal St Bede's Coll., Umtata, 1949–56; Bishop of St John's, 1956–79; Archdeacon of Riversdale, 1980–86; Rector of Swellendam, 1980–87. *Address:* PO Box 285, 19 Aanhuizen Street, Swellendam 6740, South Africa.

SCHWARTZ, Melvin, PhD; I. I. Rabi Professor of Physics, Columbia University, New York, since 1994; *b* 2 Nov. 1932; *s* of Harry Schwartz and Hannah Schwartz (*née* Shulman); *m* 1953, Marilyn Fenster; one *s* two *d*. *Educ:* Columbia College, NY (AB 1953); Columbia Univ., NY (PhD 1958). Associate Physicist, Brookhaven Nat. Lab., 1956–58; Asst Prof., Associate Prof. and Prof. of Physics, Columbia Univ., 1958–66; Prof. of Physics, 1966–83, Consulting Prof., 1983–, Stanford Univ.; Associate Dir for High Energy and Nuclear Physics, Brookhaven Nat. Lab., NY, 1991–94. Chief Exec. Officer, Digital Pathways Inc., 1970–91. Mem., Nat. Acad. of Scis, 1975. Hughes Prize, 1964; (jtly) Nobel Prize in Physics, 1988. *Publication:* Principles of Electrodynamics, 1972. *Recreations:* ski-ing, photography, woodworking. *Address:* PO Box 5068, Ketchum, ID 83340–5068, USA.

SCHWARZ, Cheryl Lynn; *see* Studer, C. L.

SCHWARZ, Gerard; conductor; Music Director; Royal Liverpool Philharmonic Orchestra, since 2001; *b* NJ, 19 Aug. 1947; *m* 1984, Jody Greitzer; two *s* two *d. Educ:* Juilliard Sch., NYC. Conductor, 1966–: Music Director: Erick Hawkins Dance Co., 1967–72; SoHo Ensemble, 1969–75; Eliot Field Dance Co., NYC, 1972–78; NY Chamber SO, 1977–; LA Chamber Orch., 1976–86; Music Advr, 1983–84, Principal Conductor, 1984–85, Music Dir, 1985–2001, Seattle SO. Estabd Music Today, 1981, Music Dir, 1981–89; Music Advr, Mostly Mozart Fest., NYC, 1982–84 (Music Dir, 1984–); Artistic Advr, Tokyo Bunkamura's Orchard Hall, 1994–; operatic conducting début with Washington Opera, 1982, with Seattle Opera, 1986. Guest Conductor with major orchestras in N America, Europe, Australia and Japan. Has made numerous recordings. Hon. DMus: Juilliard Sch.; Puget Sound; Hon. DFA: Farleigh Dickinson; Seattle. Ditson Conductor's Award, Columbia Univ., 1989; Conductor of Year, Musical America Internat. Directory of Performing Arts, 1994. *Address:* Royal Liverpool Philharmonic Orchestra, Philharmonic Hall, Hope Street, Liverpool L1 9BP.

SCHWARZ-BART, André; French writer; *b* Metz, Lorraine, France, 23 May 1928; 2nd *s* of parents from Poland; *m* 1961, Simone Schwarz-Bart; two *c. Educ:* self-educated; Trades Sch., Sillac; Sorbonne. Joined French Resistance at 15. Has worked in factories as a fitter and in Les Halles, Paris, while writing; has travelled to Israel, Africa and to the West Indies. *Publications:* Le Dernier des Justes, 1959 (Prix Goncourt, 1959; Eng. trans., 1960); (with Simone Schwarz-Bart) Un plat de porc aux bananes vertes, 1967 (Jerusalem Prize, 1967); La Mulâtresse Solitude, 1972 (Eng. trans., A Woman Named Solitude, 1973). *Address:* c/o Editions du Seuil, 27 rue Jacob, 75261 Paris Cedex 06, France.

SCHWARZKOPF, Dame Elisabeth, (Dame Elisabeth Legge-Schwarzkopf), DBE 1992; soprano; *b* Jarotschin/Poznan, 9 Dec. 1915; *o d* of Oberschulrat Friedrich Schwarzkopf and Elisabeth (*née* Fröhlich); holds dual UK/Austrian nationality; *m* 1953, Walter Legge (*d* 1979). *Educ:* High School for Music, Berlin; studied with Lula Mysz-Gmeiner, Dr Heinrich Egenolf and Maria Ivogün-Raucheisen. Début at Deutsches Opernhaus, Berlin, 1938; has appeared at Vienna State Opera, 1943–49 and 1958–65; Royal Opera House, Covent Garden, 1948–50; La Scala, Milan, 1948–63; San Francisco Opera, 1955; Chicago Opera, etc; at reopening of Bayreuth Festival, 1951, Salzburg Festival, 1947–64. Film, Der Rosenkavalier (Salzburg Festival), 1961. *Roles:* Rosina (Barber of Seville), Blondchen, Konstanze (Entführung aus dem Serail), Susanna, Contessa (Le Nozze di Figaro), Donna Elvira (Don Giovanni), Fiordiligi (Così fan Tutte), Pamina (Die Zauberflöte), Marzelline, Leonore (Fidelio), Violette (Traviata), Gilda (Rigoletto), Alice (Falstaff), Musetta, Mimi (Bohème), Cio-sio-san (Madam Butterfly), Liù (Turandot), Manon (Manon), Eva (Meistersinger), Elsa (Lohengrin), Elisabeth (Tannhäuser), Mélisande (Pelléas and Mélisande), Iole (Herakles), Anne (Rake's Progress), Margarethe (Faust), Mařenka (Bartered Bride), Ännchen, Agathe (Freischütz), Nedda (Pagliacci), Zerbinetta (Ariadne auf Naxos), Sophie, Marschallin (Rosenkavalier), Madeleine (Capriccio). Many recordings incl. 16 complete operas, six complete operettas, symphonies, lieder and arias. Hon. Member: Royal Swedish Acad. for Arts and Sciences; Accad. S Cecilia, Roma; RAM; Wiener Staatsoper; Corres. Mem., Bayerischer Akad. der Künste. Hon. Senator, Carl Maria von Weber Music Sch., Dresden. Hon. Prof., Baden-Württemberg. MusD (*hc*) Cambridge, 1976; Hon. DMus Amer. Univ. Washington, DC, 1982; Hon. DMus Glasgow, 1990. Lilli Lehmann Medal, Salzburg, 1950; first Premio Orfeo d'oro, Mantua; Hugo Wolf Ges. Medal, Vienna, 1973; Premio Viotti, Vercelli, 1991; UNESCO Mozart Medal, Paris, 1991; Litteris et Artibus Medal, Sweden; Kammersängerin, Austria; Mozart Medal, Frankfurt; Grosses Bundesverdienstkreuz with star, Germany, 1995; Order of Merit for Sci. and the Arts (Germany), 1983; 1st class Order of Dannebrog, Denmark; Commandeur, Ordre des Arts et des Lettres, France. *Publication:* (ed) On and Off the Record: a memoire of Walter Legge, 1982.

SCHWARZKOPF, Gen. H. Norman, Hon. KCB 1991; Commander, Allied Forces, Gulf War, Jan.–Feb. 1991; Commander in Chief, US Central Command, MacDill Air Force Base, Florida, 1988–91; *b* 22 Aug. 1934; *s* of Herbert Norman Schwarzkopf and Ruth (*née* Bowman); *m* 1968, Brenda Holsinger; one *s* two *d. Educ:* Bordentown Mil. Inst.; Valley Forge Mil. Acad. (football schol.); US Mil. Acad., West Point; Univ. of S Calif (MME 1964). Commnd 2nd Lieut. Inf. and airborne trng, Fort Benning, Ga; 101st Airborne Div., Fort Campbell, Ky; Teacher, Mil. Acad., West Point, 1964 and 1966–68; Task-Force Advr, S Vietnamese Airborne Div., 1965; Comdr, 1st Bn, 6th Inf., 198th Inf. Bde, Americal Div., 1969–73; Dep. Comdr, 172nd Inf. Bde, Fort Richardson, Alaska, 1974–76; Comdr, 1st Bde, 9th Inf. Div., Fort Lewis, Wash, 1976–78; Dep. Dir of Plans, US Pacific Comd, Camp Smith, Hawaii, 1978–80; Asst Div. Comdr, 8th Mechanized Inf. Div., W Germany, 1980–82; Dir, Military-Personnel Management, Office of Dep. Chief of Staff for Personnel Management, Office of Dep. Chief of Staff for Personnel, Washington, DC, 1982–83; Comdr, 24th Mechanized Inf. Div., Fort Stewart, Ga, 1983–85; Comdr, US Ground Forces and Dep. Comdr, Jt Task Force, Grenada op. Oct. 1983; Asst Dep. Chief of Staff, Army Ops, Washington DC, 1985–86; Comdr, I Corps, Fort Lewis, Wash, 1986–87; Dep. Chief for Ops and Plans, Washington, DC, 1987–88. DSM with oak leaf cluster; DFC; Silver Star with 2 oak leaf clusters; Bronze Star with 3 oak leaf clusters; Purple Heart with oak leaf cluster; Congressional Gold Medal, 1991. *Publication:* (with Peter Petre) It Doesn't Take a Hero (autobiog.), 1992. *Address:* c/o Marvin Josephson, International Creative Management, 40 West 57th Street, New York, NY 10019–4001, USA.

SCHWEBEL, Stephen Myron; President, Administrative Tribunal, International Monetary Fund, since 1994; *b* 10 March 1929; *s* of Victor Schwebel and Pauline Pfeffer Schwebel; *m* 1972, Louise Killander; two *d. Educ:* Harvard Coll. (BA); Trinity Coll., Cambridge (Frank Knox Meml Fellow); Yale Law Sch. (LLB). Attorney, White & Case, 1954–59; Asst Prof. of Law, Harvard Law Sch., 1959–61; Asst Legal Advr, State Dept, 1961–66; Exec. Dir, Amer. Soc. of Internat. Law, 1967–73; Dep. Legal Advr, State Dept, 1973–81; Judge, 1981–2000, Pres., 1997–2000, Internat. Court of Justice. Burling Prof. of Internat. Law, Sch. of Advanced Internat. Studies, Johns Hopkins Univ., 1967–81. Member: UN Internat. Law Commn, 1977–81; Panel of Arbitrators and Panel of Conciliators, ICSID, 2001–. Hon. Bencher, Gray's Inn, 1998. Weill Medal, NY Univ. Sch. of Law, 1992; Medal of Merit, Yale Law Sch., 1997; Manley O. Hudson Medal, Amer. Soc. of Internat. Law, 2000. *Publications:* The Secretary-General of the United Nations, 1952; International Arbitration: three salient problems, 1987; Justice in International Law, 1994. *Recreations:* music, walking. *Address:* 1917 23rd Street NW, Washington, DC 20008, USA. *T:* (202) 2323114; Cady Brook Farm, PO Box 356, South Woodstock, Vermont 05071, USA. *T:* (802) 4571358. *Clubs:* Athenæum; Harvard (New York); Cosmos (Washington).

SCHWEITZER, Louis; Chairman and Chief Executive Officer, Renault, since 1992; *b* Geneva, 8 July 1942; *s* of late Pierre-Paul Schweitzer; *m* 1972, Agnès Schmitz; two *d. Educ:* Institut d'Etudes Politiques, Paris; Faculté de Droit, Paris; Ecole Nationale d'Administration, Paris. Inspectorate of Finance, 1970–74; special assignment, later Dep. Dir, Min. of Budget, 1974–81; Chief of Staff: to Minister of Budget, 1981–83; of Industry and Research, 1983; to Prime Minister, 1984–86; Régie Renault: Vice-Pres. for Finance and Planning, 1986–90; Chief Finance Officer, 1988–90; Exec. Vice-Pres., 1989–90; Pres. and Chief Operating Officer, 1990–92. Prof., Inst. d'Etudes Politiques de Paris, 1982–86. Director: Inst Français des Relations Internats, 1989–; BNP, 1993–; Philips, 1997–; EDF, 1999–; Volvo, 2001–. Officier: Légion d'Honneur (France), 1998; Ordre National du Mérite (France), 1992. *Address:* Renault, 13–15 Quai Alphonse Le Gallo, 92513 Boulogne-Billancourt cedex, France.

SCHWEITZER, Prof. Miguel; Minister for Foreign Affairs, Chile, 1983; *b* 22 July 1940; *s* of Miguel Schweitzer and Cora Walters; *m*; two *s* one *d. Educ:* The Grange School, Santiago (preparatory and secondary schooling); Law School, Univ. of Chile (law degree). Doctorate in Penal Law, Rome, 1964–65; Professor of Penal Law: Law Sch., Univ. of Chile, 1966; High Sch. of Carabineros (Police), 1968, 1970 and from 1974; Director, Dept of Penal Sciences, Univ. of Chile, 1974–76; Chile's Alternate Representative with the Chilean Delegn to UN, 1975, 1976, 1978; Ambassador on special missions, 1975–80; Chilean Delegate to OAS, 1976–78; Ambassador to UK, 1980–83. *Publications:* El Error de Derecho en Materia Penal (Chile), 1964; Sull elemento soggettivo nel reato di bancarotta del l'imprenditore (Rome), 1965; Prospectus for a Course on the Special Part of Penal Law (USA), 1969. *Recreations:* music, reading, golf, tennis, Rugby. *Address:* Floor 15, Miraflores 178, Santiago, Chile; *e-mail:* msw@schweitzer.cl. *Clubs:* Union; Prince of Wales Country (Santiago).

SCICLUNA, Martin Anthony, FCA; Chairman, Deloitte & Touche, since 1995; *b* 20 Nov. 1950; *s* of late William Scicluna and Miriam Scicluna; *m* 1979 (marr. diss. 2000); two *s* one *d. Educ:* Berkhamsted Sch., Herts; Univ. of Leeds (BCom). FCA 1983 (ACA 1977). Joined Deloitte & Touche (formerly Touche Ross & Co.), 1973; Partner, 1982; Head, London Audit, 1990–95; Mem., Bd of Partners, 1991–; Mem. Bd Dirs and Governance Cttee, Deloitte Touche Tohmatsu, 1999–. Chm., Accounting and Reporting Working Gp, and Mem., Steering Gp, Company Law Review, 1999–2001. Chm., London Soc. Chartered Accountants in England and Wales, 1989–90; Institute of Chartered Accountants in England and Wales: Mem. Council, 1990–95; Chm., Auditing Cttee, 1990–95. Mem., City Adv. Gp, CBI, 1996–. Trustee, Understanding Industry, 1999–; Mem. Bd of Trustees, WellBeing, 2000. Member: Sailability Develt Bd, RYA, 2000–; Adv. Council, CRC, 1999–. Freeman, City of London, 1993; Liveryman, Co. of Chartered Accountants in England and Wales, 1993. FRSA 1996. CIMgt 1996. *Recreations:* tennis, gardening, wine. *Address:* (office) Stonecutter Court, 1 Stonecutter Street, EC4A 4TR.

SCICLUNA, Martin Leonard Andrew; Director of Finance and Infrastructure, PricewaterhouseCoopers, Malta, since 1999; *b* 16 Nov. 1935; *s* of Richard Hugh Scicluna and Victoria Mary (*née* Amato-Gauci); *m* 1st, 1960, Anna Judith Brennand (marr. diss. 1988); one *s*; 2nd, 1989, Loraine Jean Birnie; two step *d. Educ:* St Edward's Coll., Cottonera, Malta; RMA, Sandhurst. Royal Malta Artillery, 1953–65 (commnd 1955); transferred to RA, 1965–74 (Army Staff Coll., 1965). Joined Civil Service, MoD, 1974; Principal: Naval Personnel Div., 1974–76; Naval and Army Defence Secretariats, 1976–80; Asst Sec., 1980; Hd, Air Force Logistics Secretariat, 1980–83; Dep. Chief, Public Relns, 1983–85; Hd, Gen. Staff Secretariat, 1985–89; RCDS, 1989; Hd, Manpower Resources and Progs, 1990–91; Hd, Resources and Progs (Management Planning), 1991; Asst Under Sec. of State (Adjt Gen.), MoD, 1992; on secondment to FCO, UK delegn to NATO, 1993–95; Ambassador of Malta to NATO, 1996; Advr on Defence Policy to the PM of Malta, 1996–99. 1992–93: Chm. of Comrs, Duke of York's Royal Mil. Coll.; Comr, Royal Hosp., Chelsea; Commissioner: Queen Victoria Sch., Dunblane; Welbeck Coll., Notts; Chm., of Trustees, Army Welfare Fund; Trustee: Nat. Army Mus.; Army Benevolent Fund; Pres., Nat. Trust of Malta, 2001–. Chm. Bd of Govs, St Edward's Coll., 2000–. *Recreations:* painting, theatre, watching sport, other sedentary pursuits. *Address:* c/o Barclays Bank plc, 212 Regent's Street, W1A 4BP; Dar San Martin, Triq Il-Bali Guarena, Qrendi ZRQ 07, Malta. *T:* 689532.

SCLATER, Prof. John George, PhD; FRS 1982; Professor, Scripps Institution of Oceanography, University of California at San Diego, since 1991; *b* 17 June 1940; *s* of John George Sclater and Margaret Bennett Glen; *m* 1st, 1968, Fredrica Rose Felcyn; two *s*; 2nd, 1985, Paula Ann Edwards (marr. diss. 1985); 3rd, 1992, Naila Gloria Cortez. *Educ:* Carlekemp Priory School; Stonyhurst College; Edinburgh Univ. (BSc); Cambridge Univ. (PhD 1966). Research Scientist, Scripps Instn of Oceanography, 1965; Massachusetts Institute of Technology: Associate Prof., 1972; Professor, 1977; Dir, Jt Prog. in Oceanography and Oceanographic Engrg with Woods Hole Oceanographic Instn, 1981; Prof., Dept of Geol Scis, and Associate Dir, Inst. for Geophysics, 1983–91, Shell Dist. Prof., 1983–88, Univ. of Texas at Austin. Guggenheim Fellow, 1998–99. Fellow Geological Soc. of America; Fellow Amer. Geophysical Union; Mem., US Nat. Acad. of Scis, 1989. Rosenstiel Award in Oceanography, Rosenstiel Sch., Univ. of Miami, 1979; Bucher Medal, Amer. Geophysical Union, 1985. *Recreations:* running, swimming, golf. *Address:* Scripps Institution of Oceanography, La Jolla, CA 92093–0215, USA.

SCLATER, John Richard, CVO 1999; Chairman, Foreign & Colonial Investment Trust PLC, since 1985 (Director, since 1981); *b* 14 July 1940; *s* of Arthur William Sclater and Alice Sclater (*née* Collett); *m* 1st, 1967, Nicola Mary Gloria Cropper (marr. diss.); one *s* (one *d* decd); 2nd, 1985, Grizel Elizabeth Catherine Dawson, MBE. *Educ:* Charterhouse; Gonville and Caius Coll., Cambridge (schol., 1st Cl. Hons History Tripos, BA, MA); Commonwealth Fellow, 1962–64; Yale Univ. (MA 1963); Harvard Univ. (MBA 1968). Glyn, Mills & Co., 1964–70; Dir, Williams, Glyn & Co., 1970–76; Man. Dir, Nordic Bank, 1976–85 (Chm., 1985); Dir, 1985–87, Jt Dep. Chm., 1987, Guinness Peat Gp PLC; Dir and Dep. Chm., 1985–87, Chm., 1987, Guinness Mahon & Co. Ltd; Chairman: Graphite (formerly Foreign & Colonial) Enterprise Trust PLC, 1986–; Foreign & Colonial Ventures Ltd, 1989–98; Berisford plc, 1990–2000 (Dir, 1986–2000); Hill Samuel Bank Ltd, 1992–96 (Dir, 1990–96; Vice-Chm., 1990–92); Graphite (formerly Foreign & Colonial) Private Equity Trust PLC, 1994–; Union (formerly Union Discount Co. of London) plc, 1996 (Dir, 1981–96, Dep. Chm., 1986–96); Finsbury (formerly Reabourne Merlin) Life Sciences Investment Trust plc, 1997–; Argent Group Europe Ltd, 1998–; Pres., Equitable Life Assce Soc., 1994–2001 (Dir, 1985–2002); Deputy Chairman: Yamaichi International (Europe) Ltd, 1985–97; Millennium & Copthorne Hotels PLC, 1996–; Grosvenor Gp Hldgs Ltd (formerly Grosvenor Estate Hldgs), 1999– (Dir, 1989–); Director: Berner, Nicol & Co. Ltd, 1968–; James Cropper PLC, 1972–; Holker Estates Co. Ltd, 1974–; F & C Group (Hldgs) Ltd, 1989–2001; Fuel Tech (Europe), 1990 98; Angerstein Underwriting Trust PLC, 1995–96; Wates Group Ltd, 1999–; Member, London Bd of Halifax Building Soc., 1983–90. Mem., City Taxation Cttee, 1973–76. Chm., Assoc. of Consortium Banks, 1980–82. Mem., City Adv. Gp, CBI, 1988–99. Trustee, Grosvenor Estate, 1973–; Mem. Council, Duchy of Lancaster, 1987–2000. First Church Estates Comr, 1999–2001; Mem., Archbishops' Council and Gen. Synod, C of E, 1999–2001. Governor: Internat. Students House, 1976–99; Brambletye Sch. Trust, 1976–. Freeman, City of London, 1992; Liveryman, Goldsmiths' Co., 1992–. *Recreations:* country pursuits. *Address:* Sutton Hall, Barcombe, near Lewes, Sussex BN8 5EB. *T:*

(01273) 400450, *Fax:* (01273) 401086; *e-mail:* john.sclater@talk21.com. *Clubs:* Brooks's, Pratt's; University Pitt (Cambridge); Sussex.

SCLATER-BOOTH, family name of **Baron Basing**.

SCOBIE, Kenneth Charles, CA; Chairman, Chemring, since 1997; *b* 29 July 1938; *s* of Charles Scobie and Shena (*née* Melrose); *m* 1973, Adela Jane Hollebone; one *s* one *d*. *Educ:* Daniel Stewart's Coll., Edinburgh; Edinburgh Univ. CA 1961. Romanes-Munro, CA, 1956–61; BMC (Scotland) Ltd, 1961–63; Rolls-Royce Ltd, 1963–66; Robson Morrow & Co., 1966–70; Black & Decker, 1971–72; Vavasseur South Africa Ltd, 1972–76; H. C. Sleigh Ltd, 1979–83; Blackwood Hodge plc, 1984–90; Dep. Chm. and Chief Exec., Brent Walker Group, 1991–93; Chairman: Lovells Confectionery Ltd, 1991–98; William Hill Group, 1992–93; Allied Leisure, 1994–2000; Dep. Chm., Addis, 1993–94; Dir, Postern Exec. Gp., 1991–97. Non-exec. Director: Albrighton plc., 1990–93; Gartmore Venture Capital, 1993–98. Chm. Exec. Bd, Scottish Rugby Union, 2000–. CIMgt (CBIM 1987). *Recreations:* sport, Bridge. *Address:* Path Hill House, Path Hill, Goring Heath, Oxon RG8 7RE. *T:* (0118) 9842417. *Clubs:* London Scottish Football (Pres., 1987–); Huntercombe Golf; Durban (S Africa).

SCOBLE, Christopher Lawrence; Assistant Under-Secretary of State, Home Office, 1988–95; *b* 21 Nov. 1943; *s* of Victor Arthur Oliphant Scoble and Mabel Crouch; *m* 1972, Florence Hunter; one *s* one *d*. *Educ:* Kent Coll., Canterbury; Corpus Christi Coll., Oxford. Asst Principal, Home Office, 1965; Private Sec. to Minister of State, Welsh Office, 1969–70; Home Office: Principal, 1970; Sec. to Adv. Council on the Penal System, 1976–78; Asst Sec., 1978; Asst Under-Sec. of State, Broadcasting and Miscellaneous Dept, 1988–91, Establishment Dept, 1991–94, Police Dept, 1994–95. Vice-Chm., Media Policy Cttee, Council of Europe, 1985–87. CS (Nuffield and Leverhulme) Travelling Fellowship, 1987–88. *Publications:* Fisherman's Friend: a life of Stephen Reynolds, 2000; (ed) A Poor Man's House, by Stephen Reynolds, 2001. *Address:* The School House, Church Lane, Sturminster Newton, Dorset DT10 1DH. *T:* (01258) 473491; Hallandsgatan 46, 11857 Stockholm, Sweden. *T:* (8) 6434877.

SCOFIELD, (David) Paul, CH 2001; CBE 1956; actor; *b* 21 Jan. 1922; *s* of Edward H. and M. Scofield; *m* 1943, Joy Parker (actress); one *s* one *d*. *Educ:* Varndean Sch. for Boys, Brighton. Theatre training, Croydon Repertory, 1939; London Mask Theatre School, 1940. Shakespeare with ENSA, 1940–41; Birmingham Repertory Theatre, 1942; CEMA Factory tours, 1942–43; Whitehall Theatre, 1943; Birmingham Repertory, 1943–44–45; Stratford-upon-Avon, 1946–47–48. Mem., Royal Shakespeare Directorate, 1966–68. Associate Dir, Nat. Theatre, 1970–71. London theatres: Arts, 1946; Phoenix, 1947; Adventure Story, and The Seagull, St James's, 1949; Ring Round the Moon, Globe, 1950; Much Ado About Nothing, Phœnix, 1952; The River Line, Edin. Fest., Lyric (Hammersmith), Strand, 1952; John Gielgud's Company, 1952–53: Richard II, The Way of the World, Venice Preserved, etc; A Question of Fact, Piccadilly, 1953–54; Time Remembered, Lyric, Hammersmith, New Theatre, 1954–55; Hamlet, Moscow, 1955; Paul Scofield-Peter Brook Season, Phœnix Theatre, 1956; Hamlet, The Power and the Glory, Family Reunion; A Dead Secret, Piccadilly Theatre, 1957; Expresso Bongo, Saville Theatre, 1958; The Complaisant Lover, Globe Theatre, 1959; A Man For All Seasons, Globe Theatre, 1960, New York, 1961–62; Coriolanus and Love's Labour's Lost, at Shakespeare Festival Season, Stratford, Ont., 1961; King Lear: Stratford-on-Avon, Aldwych Theatre, 1962–63, Europe and US, 1964; Timon of Athens, Stratford-on-Avon, 1965; The Government Inspector, also Staircase, Aldwych, 1966; Macbeth, Stratford-on-Avon, 1967, Russia, Finland, 1967, Aldwych, 1968; The Hotel in Amsterdam, Royal Court, 1968; Uncle Vanya, Royal Court, 1970; Savages, Royal Court and Comedy, 1973; The Tempest, Wyndhams, 1975; Dimetos, Comedy, 1976; The Family, Royal Exchange, Manchester, and Haymarket, 1978; I am Not Rappaport, Apollo, 1986–87; Exclusive, Strand, 1989; Heartbreak House, Haymarket, 1992; *National Theatre:* The Captain of Kopenick, The Rules of the Game, 1971; Volpone, The Madras House, 1977; Amadeus, 1979; Othello, 1980; Don Quixote, A Midsummer Night's Dream, 1982; John Gabriel Borkman, 1996. *Films:* The Train, 1964; A Man for All Seasons, 1966 (from the play); Bartleby, King Lear, 1971; Scorpio, 1973; A Delicate Balance, 1974; Nineteen Nineteen, 1985; When the Whales Came, 1989; Henry V, 1989; Hamlet, 1991; Utz, 1992; Quiz Show, 1995; The Little Riders, 1995; The Crucible, 1997; *TV films:* Anna Karenina, 1985; The Attic, 1988; *TV serial:* Martin Chuzzlewit, 1994. Hon. LLD Glasgow, 1968; Hon. DLit Kent, 1973; Hon. DLitt: Sussex, 1985; St Andrews, 1998. Shakespeare prize, Hamburg, 1972; Shakespeare Birthday Award, Shakespeare Birthday Celebrations Cttee, Stratford-upon-Avon, 1999. *Relevant publication:* Paul Scofield, by J. C. Trewin, 1956. *Address:* The Gables, Balcombe, W Sussex RH17 6ND. *Club:* Athenæum.

SCOLES, Prof. Giacinto, FRS 1997; Donner Professor of Science, Princeton University, since 1987; *b* 2 April 1935; *m* 1964, Giok-Lan Lim; one *d*. *Educ:* Univ. of Genova (DChem 1959; Libera docenza 1968). Asst Prof., 1960–61 and 1964–68, Associate Prof., 1968–71, Physics Dept, Univ. of Genova; Res. Associate, Kamerlingh-Onnes Lab., Univ. of Leiden, 1961–64; Prof. of Chemistry and Physics, Univ. of Waterloo, Canada, 1971–86. Hon. DPhys Genova, 1996. *Publications:* Atomic and Molecular Beam Methods, vol. 1, 1988, vol. 2, 1992; The Chemical Physics of Atomic and Molecular Clusters, 1990; contribs to learned jls. *Address:* Department of Chemistry, Frick Laboratory, Princeton University, Princeton, NJ 08544–1009, USA. *T:* (609) 2585570.

SCOON, Sir Paul, GCMG 1979; GCVO 1985; OBE 1970; Governor General of Grenada, 1978–92; *b* 4 July 1935; *m* 1970, Esmai Monica McNeilly (*née* Lumsden); two step *s* one step *d*. *Educ:* St John's Anglican Sch., Grenada; Grenada Boys' Secondary Sch.; Inst. of Education, Leeds; Toronto Univ. BA, MEd. Teacher, Grenada Boys' Secondary Sch., 1953–67. Chief Educn Officer, 1967–68, Permanent Sec., 1969, Secretary to the Cabinet, 1970–72, Grenada; Dep. Director, Commonwealth Foundn, 1973–78. Governor, Centre for Internat. Briefing, Farnham Castle, 1973–78; Vice-Pres., Civil Service Assoc., Grenada, 1968; Co-founder and former Pres., Assoc. of Masters and Mistresses, Grenada. *Recreations:* reading, tennis. *Address:* PO Box 180, St George's, Grenada. *T:* 4402180.

SCORER, Philip Segar; Consultant solicitor, Burton & Co., Lincoln, since 1991 (Partner, 1952–91); *b* 11 March 1916; *s* of late Eric W. Scorer and Maud Scorer (*née* Segar); *m* 1950, Monica Smith; one *s* three *d*. *Educ:* Repton. Admitted Solicitor, 1938; London County Council Legal Dept, 1938–40. Served War, Army (Royal Signals: War Office, SHAEF and BAS, Paris), 1940–46. Solicitors' Dept, New Scotland Yard, 1947–51; Clerk of the Peace, City of Lincoln, 1952–71; Under-Sheriff of Lincolnshire, 1954–96, of Humberside, 1974–96; Asst Under-Sheriff of Lincolnshire, 1996–; a Recorder, 1976–83. Pres., Under Sheriffs Assoc., 1978–84. Hon. Solicitor, Lincoln and Dist CAB, 1966–2000. *Address:* (office) Stonebow, Lincoln LN2 1DA. *T:* (01522) 523215. *Club:* National Liberal.

SCORSESE, Martin; American film director; *b* 17 Nov. 1942; *s* of Charles Scorsese and Catherine (*née* Cappa); *m* 1st, 1965, Laraine Marie Brennan (marr. diss.); one *d*; 2nd, Julia Cameron (marr. diss.); one *d*; 3rd, 1979, Isabella Rosellini (marr. diss. 1983); 4th, 1985, Barbara DeFina; *m* 1999, Helen Morris; one *d*. *Educ:* Univ. of New York (BS 1964; MA 1966). Faculty Asst, 1963–66, Lectr, 1968–70, Dept of Film, Univ. of New York; dir and writer of documentaries. *Films* include: Who's That Knocking At My Door? (also writer), 1968; Mean Streets (also co-writer), 1973; Alice Doesn't Live Here Any More, 1974; Taxi Driver (Palme d'or, Cannes Film Fest.), 1976; New York, New York, 1977; The Last Waltz (also actor), 1978; Raging Bull, 1980; After Hours, 1985 (Best Dir Award, Cannes Film Fest., 1986); The Color of Money, 1986; acted in 'Round Midnight, 1986; The Last Temptation of Christ, 1988; Goodfellas, 1990; Cape Fear, 1992; The Age of Innocence, 1993; Bringing out the Dead, 1999; producer: Mad Dog and Glory, 1993; Naked in New York, 1994; Casino, 1996; Kundun, 1998. *Address:* c/o Artists Management Group, 9465 Wilshire Boulevard, Suite 519, Los Angeles, CA 90212, USA.

SCOTFORD, Garth Barrie, OBE 1994; QFSM 1982; County Manager, Berkshire County Council, 1993–96; *b* 28 Oct. 1943; *s* of Albert Edward Scotford and Louisa Emily Jane Scotford (*née* Leach); *m* 1st, 1964, Gillian Avril Patricia Constable (*d* 1999); one *s* two *d*; 2nd, 2000, Caroline Susan James. *Educ:* Reading Grammar Sch. Joined Fire Service, 1961: served in Reading, Liverpool, Hants and Gtr Manchester; Chief Fire Officer, Berks, 1984–93, retd. FIFireE 1977 (Pres., 1985). *Recreations:* opera, bridge, American football, golf. *Address:* 1 Park Avenue, Wokingham, Berks RG40 2AJ. *T:* (01734) 780359.

See also *J. E. Scotford.*

SCOTFORD, John Edward, CBE 1993; Treasurer, Hampshire County Council, 1983–97; *b* 15 Aug. 1939; *s* of Albert and Louisa Scotford; *m* 1962, Marjorie Clare Wells; one *s*. *Educ:* Reading Grammar Sch. CPFA. Reading County Borough Council, 1955–62; Coventry County Borough Council, 1962–65; Hampshire CC, 1965–97; Dep. County Treasurer, 1977–83. Public Works Loan Comr, 1992–96. Pres., CIPFA, 1996–97. Freeman, City of London, 1995. *Address:* Stable Lodge, Garden Close, Leatherhead, Surrey KT22 8LU.

See also *G. B. Scotford.*

SCOTHERN, Mark Francis; Director, Derby Council for Voluntary Service, since 1999; *b* 2 July 1960; *s* of late Norman Scothern and of Joan Scothern; *m* 1998, Caroline Fiske. *Educ:* Austin Friars Sch., Carlisle; MBA Norwich Univ. Business Sch., 2000. Co-ordinator, Thamesdown Housing Link, 1984–88; Policy Officer, CHAR (Housing Campaign for Single People), 1988–91; Dir, Crisis (formerly Crisis at Christmas), 1991–96; Develt Man., Shelter, 1997–98; Associate, Rho Delta, mgt consultancy, 1998–99. *Recreations:* film, contemporary music, food, biographies, sleep. *Address:* Derby Council for Voluntary Service, 4 Charnwood Street, Derby DE1 2GT. *T:* (01332) 346266.

SCOTHORNE, Prof. Raymond John, BSc, MD Leeds; MD Chicago; FRSE; FRCSGlas; Regius Professor of Anatomy, University of Glasgow, 1972–90, now Emeritus; *b* 1920; *s* of late John and Lavinia Scothorne; *m* 1948, Audrey, *o d* of late Rev. Selwyn and Winifred Gillott; one *s* two *d*. *Educ:* Royal Grammar School, Newcastle upon Tyne; Universities of Leeds and Chicago, BSc (Hons) 1st cl. (Leeds), 1941; MD (Chicago), Rockefeller Student, 1941–43; MB (Hons) 1st cl. (Leeds), 1944; MD (with Distinction) (Leeds), 1951. Demonstrator and Lecturer in Anatomy, 1944–50, Univ. of Leeds; Sen. Lecturer in Anatomy, 1950–60, Univ. of Glasgow; Prof., Univ. of Newcastle upon Tyne, 1960–72. Hon. Sec., Anat. Soc. of Great Britain and Ireland, 1967–71, Pres., 1971–73; Hon. Fellow, British Assoc. of Clinical Anatomists (Pres., 1986–88); Mem., Med. Sub-Cttee, UGC, 1967–76. Hon. Member: Assoc. des Anatomistes; Amer. Assoc. of Clinical Anatomists. Struthers Prize and Gold Medal in Anatomy, Univ. of Glasgow, 1957. Anatomical Editor, Companion to Medical Studies; Editor, Clinical Anatomy, 1987–2001. *Publications:* chapter on Peripheral Nervous System in Hamilton's Textbook of Anatomy, 2nd edn, 1975; chapters on Early Development, on Tissue and Organ Growth, on Skin and on the Nervous System in Companion to Medical Studies, 3rd edn, 1985; chapter on Development and Structure of Liver in Pathology of the Liver, 1979, 4th edn 2001; chapter on Respiratory System in Cunningham's Textbook, 12th edn, 1981; chapter on Development of Spinal Cord and Vertebral Column in Surgery of the Spine, 1992; papers on embryology, histology and tissue transplantation. *Address:* Southernknowe, Linlithgow, West Lothian EH49 6BQ. *T:* (01506) 842463.

SCOTLAND OF ASTHAL, Baroness *cr* 1997 (Life Peer), of Asthal in the co. of Oxfordshire; **Patricia Janet Scotland;** PC 2001; QC 1991; Parliamentary Secretary, Lord Chancellor's Department, since 2001; *m* 1985, Richard Mawhinney; two *s*. *Educ:* London Univ. (LLB). Called to the Bar, Middle Temple, 1977, Bencher, 1997; Mem., Antigua Bar; a Recorder, 2000. Parly Under-Sec. of State, FCO, 1999–2001. Former Mem., Commn for Racial Equality; Mem., Millennium Commn, 1994. *Address:* House of Lords, SW1A 0PW.

SCOTT, family name of **Earl of Eldon** and **Baron Scott of Foscote**.

SCOTT; *see* Hepburne-Scott, family name of Lord Polwarth.

SCOTT; *see* Maxwell Scott and Maxwell-Scott.

SCOTT; *see* Montagu Douglas Scott, family name of Duke of Buccleuch.

SCOTT OF FOSCOTE, Baron *cr* 2000 (Life Peer), of Foscote in the county of Buckinghamshire; **Richard Rashleigh Folliott Scott,** Kt 1983; PC 1991; a Lord of Appeal in Ordinary, since 2000; *b* 2 Oct. 1934; *s* of Lt-Col C. W. F. Scott, 2/9th Gurkha Rifles and Katharine Scott (*née* Rashleigh); *m* 1959, Rima Elisa, *d* of Salvador Ripoll and Blanca Korsi de Ripoll, Panama City; two *s* two *d*. *Educ:* Michaelhouse Coll., Natal; Univ. of Cape Town (BA); Trinity Coll., Cambridge (BA, LLB). Bigelow Fellow, Univ. of Chicago, 1958–59. Called to Bar, Inner Temple, 1959, Bencher, 1981. In practice, Chancery Bar, 1960–83; QC 1975; Attorney Gen., 1980–83, Vice-Chancellor, 1987–91, Duchy and County Palatine of Lancaster; Judge of the High Court of Justice, Chancery Div., 1983–91; a Lord Justice of Appeal, 1991–94; Vice-Chancellor, Supreme Court, 1994–2000; Head of Civil Justice, 1995–2000. Inquiry into defence related exports to Iraq and related prosecutions, 1992–96. Chm. of the Bar, 1982–83 (Vice-Chm., 1981–82). Editor-in-Chief, Supreme Court Practice, 1996–. Hon. Member: Amer. Bar Assoc., 1983; Canadian Bar Assoc., 1983. Hon. LLD: Birmingham, 1996; Buckingham, 1999. *Publications:* articles in legal jls. *Recreations:* hunting, tennis, bridge, ten grandchildren, formerly Rugby (Cambridge Blue, 1957). *Address:* House of Lords, SW1A 0PW. *Clubs:* Hawks (Cambridge); Vanderbilt Racquet.

SCOTT OF NEEDHAM MARKET, Baroness *cr* 2000 (Life Peer), of Needham Market in the co. of Suffolk; **Rosalind Carol Scott;** *b* 10 Aug. 1957; *d* of Kenneth Vincent and Carol Jane Leadbeater; one *s* one *d*. *Educ:* Whitby Grammar Sch.; Univ. of East Anglia. Member (Lib Dem) Mid Suffolk DC, 1991–94; Suffolk CC, 1993– (Gp Leader, 1997–2000). Mem., UK delegn to EU Cttee of the Regions. Vice Chm., LGA Transport Exec. Contested (Lib Dem) Eastern Region, EP elecns, 1999. *Recreations:* walking, travel. *Address:* House of Lords, SW1A 0PW. *Club:* Royal Commonwealth Society.

SCOTT, Alan James, CVO 1986; CBE 1982; Governor, Cayman Islands, 1987–92; *b* 14 Jan. 1934; *er s* of Rev. Harold James Scott and Mary Phyllis Barbara Scott; *m* 1st, 1958, Mary Elizabeth Ireland (*d* 1969); one *s* two *d*; 2nd, 1971, Joan Hall; one step *s* two step *d*. *Educ:* King's Sch., Ely; Selwyn Coll., Cambridge Univ. Suffolk Regt, Italy and Germany, 1952–54. HMOCS, 1958–87: Fiji: Dist Officer, 1958; Estabts Officer, 1960; Registry of Univ. of S Pacific, 1968; Controller, Organisation and Estabts, 1969; Hong Kong: Asst Financial Sec., 1971; Prin. Asst Financial Sec., 1972; Sec. for CS, 1973; MLC, 1976–85; Sec. for Housing, and Chm. Hong Kong Housing Authy, 1977; Sec. for Information, 1980; Sec. for Transport, 1982; Dep. Chief Sec., 1985–87. President: Fiji AAA, 1964–69; Hong Kong AAA, 1978–87. *Recreations:* boule, golf, dilatory travel, writing.

SCOTT, Prof. Alastair Ian, FRS 1978; FRSE 1981; Davidson Professor of Chemistry and Biochemistry, Texas A & M University, since 1981; *b* 10 April 1928; *s* of William Scott and Nell Florence (*née* Newton); *m* 1950, Elizabeth Wilson (*née* Walters); one *s* one *d*. *Educ:* Glasgow Univ. (BSc, PhD, DSc). Postdoctoral Fellow, Ohio State Univ., 1952–53; Technical Officer, ICI (Nobel Div.), 1953–54; Postdoctoral Fellow, London and Glasgow Univs, 1954–57; Lectr, Glasgow Univ., 1957–62; Professor: Univ. of British Columbia, 1962–65; Univ. of Sussex, 1965–68; Yale Univ., 1968–77; Texas A&M Univ., 1977–80; Edinburgh Univ., 1980–83 (Forbes Prof., 1980–81). Lectures: Karl Folkers, Wisconsin Univ., 1964; Burger, Virginia Univ., 1975; Benjamin Rush, Pennsylvania Univ., 1975; 5 colls, Mass, 1977; Andrews, NSW Univ., 1979; Dreyfus, Indiana Univ., 1983; Centenary, RSC, 1994; Gottlieb Meml, Univ. of Illinois, 1995; Bakerian, Royal Soc., 1996. FAAAS 1988. Hon. Mem., Pharmaceutical Soc. of Japan, 1985. Hon. MA Yale, 1968; Hon. DSc: Coimbra, 1990; Paris, 1992. Corday-Morgan Medallist, Chemical Soc., 1964; Natural Products Res. Award, Royal Soc. Chem., 1995; Ernest Guenther Medallist, 1976, Cope Scholar Award, 1992, Amer. Chem. Soc.; Res. Achievement Award, Amer. Soc. of Pharmacognosy, 1993; Tetrahedron Prize, Pergamon, 1995; Robert A. Welch Award in Chem., R. A. Welch Foundn, Houston, Tex, 2000. *Publications:* Interpretation of Ultraviolet Spectra of Natural Products, 1964; (with T. K. Devon) Handbook of Naturally Occurring Compounds, 1972; numerous pubns in learned jls. *Recreations:* music, gardening. *Address:* Department of Chemistry, Texas A & M University, 3255 Tamu College Station, TX 77843–3255, USA. *T:* (979) 8453243. *Club:* Athenæum.

SCOTT, Allan; *see* Shiach, A. G.

SCOTT, Andrew John, FMA; CEng; Head, National Railway Museum, since 1994; *b* 3 June 1949; *s* of late Cyril John Scott and of Gertrude Ethel (*née* Miller); *m* 1972, Margaret Anne Benyon, JP, BA. *Educ:* Bablake Sch., Coventry; Univ. of Newcastle upon Tyne (BSc Civil Engrg 1970; MSc Mining Engrg 1971). CEng, MICE 1976. AMA 1987, FMA 1993. Practising civil engr, 1972–84; Actg Dir, W Yorks Transport Mus., 1984–86; Keeper of Technol., Bradford City Museums, 1986–87; Dir, London Transport Mus., 1988–94. Mem., North Eastern Locomotive Preservation Gp, 1967– (Cttee Mem., 1972–84); Council Member: Assoc. of Indep. Museums, 1991–; Internat. Assoc. of Transport Museums, 1992– (Vice Pres., 1999–); Vice-Chm., Assoc. of British Transport and Engrg Museums, 1992–. Director: FNRM Enterprises Ltd, 1994–; York Tourism Bureau, 1995– (Chm., 1999–). Trustee, Friends of London Tspt Mus., 1994–; Exec. Mem., Friends of Nat. Rlwy Mus., 1994–; Pres., London Underground Railway Soc., 1995–96. *Publications:* North Eastern Renaissance, 1991; (with C. Divall) Making Histories in Transport Museums, 2001; contrib. to railway and museological jls and books. *Recreations:* travel, railways, ecclesiastical architecture. *Address:* National Railway Museum, Leeman Road, York YO26 4XJ. *T:* (01904) 686200. 10A Moreton Avenue, Harpenden, Herts AL5 2ET; *e-mail:*a.scott@nmsi.ac.uk

SCOTT, Anthony Douglas, TD 1972; chartered accountant in public practice; *b* 6 Nov. 1933; *o s* of Douglas Ernest and Mary Gladys Scott; *m* 1962, Irene Robson; one *s* one *d*. *Educ:* Gateshead Central Technical Secondary Sch. Articled to Middleton & Middleton, also J. Stanley Armstrong, Chartered Accountants, Newcastle upon Tyne, 1952–57; National Service, WO Selection Bd, 1957–59; Accountant with Commercial Plastics Ltd, 1959; joined ICI Ltd (Agricl Div), 1961; seconded by ICI to Hargreaves Fertilisers Ltd, as Chief Accountant, 1966; ICI Ltd (Nobel Div.) as Asst Chief Acct, 1970; seconded by ICI to MoD as Dir-Gen. Internal Audit, 1972–74. Dir of Consumer Credit, Office of Fair Trading, 1974–80. Chief Exec. and Dir, CoSIRA, 1981–88. Chm., Teesside Soc. of Chartered Accts, 1969–70; Mem. Cttee, London Chartered Accountants, 1974–79. Chm., Jt Working Party on Students' Societies (ICAE&W), 1979–80. Mem., Smaller Firms Council, CBI, 1983–86. TA (17th (later 4th) Bn Para. Regt (9 DLI) TA, 44 Para. Bde (TA) and 6th (V) Bn Royal Anglian Regt), 1959–91, Major. *Publications:* Accountants Digests on Consumer Credit Act 1974, 1980; Accountants Digest on Estate Agents Act 1979, 1982. *Recreations:* antiquary, walking, gardening. *Address:* 2 Oakfield Road, Harpenden, Herts AL5 2NE. *T:* (01582) 763067.

SCOTT, Sir Anthony (Percy), 3rd Bt *cr* 1913; *b* 1 May 1937; *s* of Sir Douglas Winchester Scott, 2nd Bt, and of Elizabeth Joyce, *d* of W. N. C. Grant; *S* father, 1984; *m* 1962, Caroline Theresa Anne, *er d* of Edward Bacon; two *s* one *d*. *Educ:* Harrow; Christ Church, Oxford. Barrister, Inner Temple, 1960. *Recreation:* racing. *Heir: s* Henry Douglas Edward Scott, *b* 26 March 1964. *Address:* 13 King's Quay, Chelsea Harbour, SW10 0UX.

SCOTT, Brough; *see* Scott, J. B.

SCOTT, Dame Catherine Margaret Mary; *see* Scott, Dame M.

SCOTT, Sir (Charles) Peter, KBE 1978 (OBE 1948); CMG 1964; HM Diplomatic Service, retired; *b* 30 Dec. 1917; *er s* of late Rev. John Joseph Scott and late Dorothea Scott (*née* Senior); *m* 1954, Rachael, *yr d* of C. W. Lloyd Jones, CIE; one *s* two *d*. *Educ:* Weymouth Coll.; Pembroke Coll., Cambridge. Indian Civil Service: Probationer, 1939; appointed to Madras Presidency, 1940; Asst Private Sec. to Viceroy, 1946–47. Entered HM Diplomatic Service, 1947, Second Sec., Tokyo, 1948; First Sec., 1949; Foreign Office, 1950; Private Sec. to Gen. Lord Ismay at NATO, Paris, 1952; First Sec., Vienna, 1954; First Sec. at British Information Services, NY, 1956; Counsellor and Consul-General, Washington, 1959; Student at IDC, 1962; Head of UK Mission to European Office of the United Nations, Geneva, 1963; Minister at HM Embassy, Rome, 1966–69; Temp. Vis. Fellow at Centre for Contemporary European Studies, Univ. of Sussex, 1969–70; Asst Under Sec. of State, FCO, 1970–75; Ambassador to Norway, 1975–77. Private Sec., 1978–79, Treasurer, 1979–81, to HRH Prince Michael of Kent. *Recreations:* walking, and such as offer. *Address:* 284 Kew Road, Kew, Richmond, Surrey TW9 3DU. *T:* (020) 8948 4262. *Clubs:* Oxford and Cambridge; Hawks (Cambridge).

SCOTT, Charles Thomas, FCA; Chairman, Cordiant Communications Group plc, since 1997; *b* 22 Feb. 1949. FCA 1979. Binder Hamlyn, 1967–72; ITEL Internat. Corp., 1972–77; IMS Internat. Inc., 1978–89; Saatchi & Saatchi Co. plc, later Cordiant plc, 1990–97: Chief Exec., 1993–95; Chm., 1995–97. *Recreations:* golf, tennis, sport in general. *Address:* Cordiant Communications Group plc, 121–141 Westbourne Terrace, W2 6JR.

SCOTT, Prof. Clive, DPhil; FBA 1994; Professor of European Literature, University of East Anglia, since 1991; *b* 13 Nov. 1943; *s* of Jesse Scott and Nesta Vera Scott (*née* Morton); *m* 1st, 1965, Elizabeth Anne (*née* Drabble) (marr. diss.); one *s* one *d*; 2nd, 1984, Marie-Noëlle Guillot; two *s*. *Educ:* St John's Coll., Oxford (MA, MPhil, DPhil). University of East Anglia: Asst Lectr, 1967–70; Lectr, 1970–88; Reader, 1988–91. *Publications:* French Verse-Art: a study, 1980; Anthologie Eluard, 1983; A Question of Syllables: essays in nineteenth-century French verse, 1986; The Riches of Rhyme: studies in French verse, 1988; Vers Libre: the emergence of free verse in France 1886–1914, 1990; Reading the Rhythm: the poetics of French free verse 1910–1930, 1993; The Poetics of French Verse: studies in reading, 1998; The Spoken Image: photography and language, 1999; Translating Baudelaire, 2000. *Address:* School of English and American Studies, University of East Anglia, University Plain, Norwich NR4 7TJ. *T:* (01603) 456161.

SCOTT, Rt Rev. Colin John Fraser; Bishop Suffragan of Hulme, 1984–98; *b* 14 May 1933; *s* of late Kenneth Miller Scott and Marion Edith Scott; *m* 1958, Margaret Jean MacKay; one *s* two *d*. *Educ:* Berkhamsted School; Queens' College, Cambridge (MA); Ridley Hall, Cambridge. Curate: St Barnabas, Clapham Common, 1958–61; St James, Hatcham, 1961–64; Vicar, St Mark, Kennington, 1964–71; Vice-Chm., Southwark Diocesan Pastoral Cttee, 1971–77; Team Rector, Sanderstead Team Ministry, 1977–84. Chm., Council for the Care of Churches, 1994–98. *Address:* The Priest House, Prior Park Road, Ashby de la Zouch, Leics LE65 1BH. *T:* (01530) 564403.

SCOTT, Prof. Dana Stewart, FBA 1976; Hillman University Professor of Computer Science, Philosophy and Mathematical Logic, Carnegie Mellon University, since 1981; *b* Berkeley, Calif, 11 Oct. 1932; *m* 1959, Irene Schreier; one *d*. *Educ:* Univ. of Calif, Berkeley (BA); Princeton Univ. (PhD). Instructor, Univ. of Chicago, 1958–60; Asst Prof., Univ. of Calif, Berkeley, 1960–63; Associate Prof. and Prof., Stanford Univ., 1963–69; Prof., Princeton, 1969–72; Prof. of Mathematical Logic, Oxford Univ., 1972–81. Visiting Professor: Amsterdam, 1968–69; Linz, 1992–93; Guggenheim Fellow, 1978–79. Mem., US Nat. Acad. of Scis, 1988. *Publications:* papers on logic and mathematics in technical jls. *Address:* School of Computer Science, Carnegie Mellon University, 5000 Forbes Avenue, Pittsburgh, PA 15213-3890, USA.

SCOTT, Sir David; *see* Scott, Sir W. D. S.

SCOTT, Sir David (Aubrey), GCMG 1979 (KCMG 1974; CMG 1966); HM Diplomatic Service, retired 1979; *b* 3 Aug. 1919; *s* of late Hugh Sumner Scott and Barbara E. Scott, JP; *m* 1941, Vera Kathleen, *d* of late Major G. H. Ibbitson, MBE, RA; two *s* one *d*. *Educ:* Charterhouse; Birmingham University (Mining Engrg). Served War of 1939–45, Royal Artillery, 1939–47; Chief Radar Adviser, British Military Mission to Egyptian Army, 1945–47, Major. Appointed to CRO, 1948; Asst Private Secretary to Secretary of State, 1949; Cape Town/Pretoria, 1951–53; Cabinet Office, 1954–56; Malta Round Table Conf., 1955; Secretary-General, Malaya and Caribbean Constitutional Confs, 1956; Singapore, 1956–58; Monckton Commn, 1960; Dep. High Comr, Fedn of Rhodesia and Nyasaland, 1961–63; Imperial Defence College, 1964; Dep. High Comr, India, 1965–67; British High Comr to Uganda, and Ambassador (non-resident) to Rwanda, 1967–70; Asst Under-Sec. of State, FCO, 1970–72; British High Comr to New Zealand, and Governor, Pitcairn Is., 1973–75; HM Ambassador to Republic of S Africa, 1976–79. Chairman: Ellerman Lines plc, 1982–83; Nuclear Resources Ltd, 1984–88; Director: Barclays Bank International Ltd, 1979–85; Mitchell Cotts plc, 1980–86; Delta Metal Overseas Ltd, 1980–83; Bradbury Wilkinson plc, 1984–86; Consultant, Thomas De La Rue & Co. Ltd, 1986–88. Pres., Uganda Soc. for Disabled Children, 1984–2000; Vice-Pres., UK South Africa Trade Assoc., 1980–85. Mem., Manchester Olympic Bid Cttee, 1989–93. Gov., Sadler's Wells Trust, 1984–89. Trustee, John Ellerman Foundn, 1979–2000 (Chm., 1997–2000). Freeman, City of London, 1982; Liveryman, Shipwrights' Co., 1983. *Publications:* Ambassador in Black and White, 1981; contrib. DNB. *Recreations:* music, birdwatching. *Address:* Wayside, Moushill Lane, Milford, Surrey GU8 5BQ. *T:* (01483) 421935. *Club:* Royal Over-Seas League (Chm., 1981–86; Vice-Pres., 1986–98; Pres., 1998–).

See also Sir R. D. H. Scott, Sir J. B. Unwin.

SCOTT, David Gidley; Registrar of the High Court in Bankruptcy, 1984–96; *b* 3 Jan. 1924; *s* of late Bernard Wardlaw Habershon Scott, FRIBA and Florence May Scott; *m* 1948, Elinor Anne, *d* of late Major Alan Garthwaite, DSO, MC, and Mrs Garthwaite; two *s* two *d*. *Educ:* Sutton Valence School (scholarship); St John's College, Cambridge (exhibnr, MA, LLM). Army service, 1942–47, Royal Engineers; Assault RE European theatre, 1944–45 (wounded); Acting Major, Palestine. Called to the Bar, Lincoln's Inn, 1951; practised Chancery Bar, 1951–84. *Recreation:* choral singing. *Address:* 45 Benslow Lane, Hitchin, Herts SG4 9RE. *T:* (01462) 434391.

SCOTT, David Ian; Group Human Resources Director, United Utilities PLC, since 1998; *b* 2 May 1953; *s* of Daniel McAlees and Jean Scott; *m* 1999, Ingrid Ann Blackford-Swaries. *Educ:* Lancaster Univ. (BA Hons English and French). Pilot Officer, RAF, 1971–74. Post Office Telecommunications, later British Telecommunications: Personnel Manager, 1975–80; Ops Manager, 1980–87; Personnel Manager, 1987–89; Gp Industrial Relns Manager, 1989–95; Personnel Dir, Gp HQ, 1995; Dir of Personnel, HM Prison Service, 1995–98. MIPD 1992. *Recreations:* sport, motoring. *Address:* United Utilities PLC, Group Corporate Centre, Dawson House, Great Sankey, Warrington WA5 3LW; 26 Merchants Quay, Salford, Lancs M5 2XR. *T:* (0161) 877 7584.

SCOTT, David Richard Alexander, FCA; Managing Director, Channel Four Television Corporation, since 1997; *b* 25 Aug. 1954; *s* of R. I. M. Scott, OBE and Daphne Scott (*née* Alexander); *m* 1981, Moy Barraclough; one *s* one *d*. *Educ:* Wellington Coll. FCA 1979. Chartered Accountant, Peat Marwick Mitchell & Co., 1972–81; Channel Four Television: Controller of Finance, 1981–88; Dir of Finance, 1988–97. *Recreations:* sailing, walking, film, opera, bridge. *Address:* Channel Four Television Corporation, 124 Horseferry Road, SW1P 2TX. *T:* (020) 7306 8730. *Club:* Guards Polo.

SCOTT, Derek John; Economic Adviser to the Prime Minister, since 1997; *b* 17 Jan. 1947; *s* of John William Scott and Alice Isabel Scott (*née* Heal); *m* 1985, Elinor Mary Goodman, *qv*. *Educ:* Liverpool Univ. (BA Hons); London Sch. of Econs (MSc Econ); Birkbeck Coll., Univ. of London (MSc Econ). Special Advr to Denis Healey, 1977–79; Econ. Advr to James Callaghan, 1979–81; Internat. Policy Advr, Shell Internat., 1982–86; Dir, European Economics, Barclays de Zoete Wedd, 1986–97. *Address:* 80 Denbigh Street, SW1V 2EX.

SCOTT, Douglas Andrew Montagu-Douglas-, OBE 1994; Chief Executive and Director, Cancer Relief Macmillan Fund, 1987–95; *b* 21 June 1930; *s* of late Col C. A. Montagu-Douglas-Scott, DSO and Lady Victoria Haig, *d* of Field Marshal 1st Earl Haig, KT, GCB, OM, GCVO, KCIE; *m* 1st, 1954, Bridget George (marr. diss. 1976), *d* of Air Vice-Marshal Sir Robert George, KCMG, KCVO, KBE, CB, MC; two *d* (one *s* decd); 2nd, 1977, Daphne Shortt (marr. diss. 2000), *d* of Dr Cyril Shortt, Winchcombe. *Educ:* Eton; RMA, Sandhurst. Commnd Irish Guards, 1950. ADC to Gov. of S Australia,

1953–55; Tubemakers of Australia, 1955–63; TI Group, 1963–83: Dir, Accles & Pollock Ltd, 1966–76; Man. Dir, TI Chesterfield Ltd, 1976–81; Dir, TI Gp Overseas Ops, 1981–83; Recruitment Consultant, PE Internat. plc, 1984–87. Director: S Warwicks Gen. Hosps NHS Trust, 1995–97; Global Cancer Concern, 1995–2000; CLIC, 1997–2000; Compton Hospice, 1995–99. *Recreations:* painting, shooting, gardening, opera. *Address:* Stonefield, Bemersyde, Melrose TD6 9DP. *T:* (01835) 824123. *Clubs:* White's, Pratt's, MCC; New (Edinburgh).

SCOTT, Prof. Douglas Frederick Schumacher; Professor of German in the University of Durham (late Durham Colleges), 1958–75, now Emeritus Professor; *b* Newcastle under Lyme, Staffs, 17 Sept. 1910; *o s* of Frederick Scott and Magdalena (*née* Gronbach); *m* 1942, Margaret (*d* 1972), *o d* of late Owen Gray Ellis, Beaumaris, Anglesey, and Helen (*née* Gibbs); two *d. Educ:* Queen Mary's Grammar School, Walsall, Staffs; Dillman-Realgymnasium Stuttgart, Germany; University of Tübingen, Göttingen (Dr phil.); University College, London (MA). Part-time Assistant, German Dept, University Coll., London, 1935–37; Lecturer in charge German Dept, Huddersfield Technical Coll., 1937–38; Lecturer in German, King's Coll., Newcastle, 1938–46; released for service with Friends' Ambulance Unit, 1940–46; Lecturer in German, King's Coll., London, 1946–49; Reader and Head of Dept of German, The Durham Colls, 1949–58. *Publications:* Some English Correspondents of Goethe, 1949; W. v. Humboldt and the Idea of a University, 1960; Luke Howard: his correspondence with Goethe and his continental journey of 1816, 1976; articles and reviews on German lit. and Anglo-German literary relations in various English and German journals. *Recreations:* music, travel. *Address:* 6 Fieldhouse Terrace, Durham DH1 4NA. *T:* (0191) 386 4518.

SCOTT, Douglas Keith, (Doug Scott), CBE 1994; *b* Nottingham, 29 May 1941; *s* of George Douglas Scott and Edith Joyce Scott; *m* 1962, Janice Elaine Brook (marr. diss. 1988); one *s* two *d*; *m* 1993, Sharavati, (Sharv), Prabhu; two *s. Educ:* Cottesmore Secondary Modern Sch.; Mundella Grammar Sch., Nottingham; Loughborough Teachers' Trng Coll. (Teaching Certificate). Began climbing age of 12, British crag climbing, and most weekends thereafter; visited the Alps age of 17 and every year thereafter; first ascent, Tarso Teiroko, Tibest Mts, Sahara, 1965; first ascents, Cilo Dag Mts, SE Turkey, 1966; first ascent, S face Koh-i-Bandaka (6837 m), Hindu Kush, Afghanistan, 1967; first British ascent, Salathé Wall, El Capitain, Yosemite, 1971; 1972: Spring, Mem., European Mt Everest Expedn to SW face; Summer, first ascent, E Pillar of Mt Asgard, Baffin Island Expedn; Autumn, Mem., British Mt Everest Expedn to SW face; first ascent, Changabang (6864 m), 1974; first ascent, SE spur, Pic Lenin (7189 m), 1974; reached summit of Mt Everest, via SW face, with Dougal Haston, as Members, British Everest Expedn, 24th Sept. 1975 (first Britons on summit); first Alpine ascent of S face, Mt McKinley (6226 m), via new route, British Direct, with Dougal Haston, 1976; first ascent, East Face Direct, Mt Kenya, 1976; first ascent, Ogre (7330 m), Karakoram Mountains, 1977; first ascent, N Ridge route, Kangchenjunga (8593 m), without oxygen, 1979; first ascent, N Summit, Kussum Kangguru, 1979; first ascent, N Face, Nuptse, 1979; Alpine style, Kangchungtse (7640 m), 1980; first ascent Shivling E Pillar, 13-day Alpine Style push, 1981; Chamlang (7366 m) North Face to Central Summit, with Rheinhold Messner, 1981; first ascent, Pungpa Ri (7445 m), 1982; first ascent Shishapangma South Face (8046 m), 1982; first ascent, Lobsang Spire (Karakoram), and ascent Broad Peak (8047 m), 1983; Mt Baruntse (7143 m), first ascent, East Summit Mt Chamlang (7287 m), and traverse over unclimbed central summit Chamlang, Makalu SE Ridge, Alpine Style, to within 100 m of summit, 1984; first Alpine style ascent, Diran (7260 m), 1985; first ascent of rock climbs in S India, 1986; first ascent of rock climbs, Wadi Rum, Jordan, 1987; Mt Jitchu Drake (Bhutan) (6793 m), South face first ascent of peak, Alpine style, 1988; first ascent, Indian Arete Latok III, 1990; first ascent, Hanging Glacier Peak South (6294 m), via South Ridge, 1991; first British ascent of Chimtarga (5482 m), Fanskiye Mountains, Tadzhikistan, 1992; first ascent Dhromo Central summit (6855 m), via South pillar, Alpine style, with Roger Mear, 1998. Pres., Alpine Climbing Gp, 1976–82; Vice-Pres., British Mountaineering Council, 1994–97. A vegetarian, 1978–. Hon. MA: Nottingham, 1991; Loughborough, 1993; Hon. MEd Nottingham Trent, 1995. *Publications:* Big Wall Climbing, 1974; (with Alex MacIntyre) Shishapangma, Tibet, 1984; Himalayan Climber, 1992; contrib. to Alpine Jl, Amer. Alpine Jl, Mountain Magazine and Himal Magazine. *Recreations:* rock climbing, photography, organic gardening. *Address:* Chapel House, Low Cotehill, Carlisle CA4 0EL. *T:* (01228) 562358. *Clubs:* Alpine (Pres., 1999–); Alpine Climbing Group; Nottingham Climbers'.

SCOTT, Edward John Rankin; Chairman, John Swire & Sons Ltd, since 1998; *b* 3 Jan. 1939; *s* of late Lt-Col C. R. Scott, KRRC and Elizabeth Meade, *d* of 5th Earl of Clanwilliam; *m* 1997, Angela Brice; one *d. Educ:* Eton; McGill Univ. (BA Hons). Joined Swire Group, 1960: Swire Hong Kong, 1964–65; Swire Japan, 1965–67; Man. Dir, 1971–76, Chm., 1976–97, John Swire & Sons Pty Ltd; Dir, Swire Pacific, 1993–. Director: Brick & Pipe Industries, 1975–81 (Chm., 1981–88); Cathay Pacific Airways, 1976–; Steamships Trading Co., 1979–96 (Chm., 1997–); United States Cold Storage, 1981–85 (Chm., 1985–2001); James Finlay Ltd, 1991–. Chairman: Internat. Assoc. of Refrigerated Warehousemen, Washington, 1988 (Dir, 1985–89); Australia and NZ Trade Adv. Cttee, 1997–. *Recreations:* fishing, farming. *Address:* Swire House, 59 Buckingham Gate, SW1E 6AJ. *T:* (020) 7834 7717. *Clubs:* White's, MCC; Melbourne; Union, Australian Jockey (Sydney).

SCOTT, Edward McM.; *see* McMillan-Scott.

SCOTT, Most Rev. Edward Walter, CC 1978; Archbishop, and Primate of All Canada, 1971–86; *b* Edmonton, Alberta, 30 April 1919; *s* of Tom Walter Scott and Kathleen Frances Ford; *m* 1942, Isabel Florence Brannan; one *s* three *d. Educ:* Univ. of British Columbia; Anglican Theological Coll. of BC. Vicar of St Peter's, Seal Cove, 1943–45; SCM Secretary, Univ. of Manitoba, 1945–59; Staff of St John's Coll., Winnipeg, 1947–48; Rector: St John the Baptist, Fort Garry, 1949–55; St Jude's, Winnipeg, 1955–60; Dir, Diocesan Council for Social Service, Diocese of Rupert's Land, and Priest Dir of Indian Work, 1960–64; Associate Sec., Council for Social Service, Anglican Church of Canada, 1964–66; Bishop of Kootenay, 1966–71. Moderator of Executive and Central Cttees, WCC, 1975–83; Pres., Canadian Council of Churches, 1985. Mem. Commonwealth Eminent Persons Gp on South Africa, Dec. 1985–June 1986. DD Lambeth, 1986; Hon. DD: Anglican Theol Coll., BC, 1966; Trinity Coll., Toronto, 1971; Wycliffe Coll., Toronto, 1971; Huron Coll., Ont., 1973; United Theol Coll., Montreal, 1971; Renison Coll., Waterloo; Coll. of Emmanuel & St Chad, Saskatoon, 1979; Univ. of Victoria Coll., Toronto, 1986; Queen's Univ., Kingston, 1987; Hon. DCL St John's Coll., Winnipeg, 1971; Hon. STD: Dio. Theol Coll., Montreal, 1973; Thorneloe Coll., Ont., 1974; Hon. LLD York, 1987. Human Relations Award, Canadian CCJ, 1987. *Recreation:* carpentry. *Address:* 1177 Yonge Street, Unit 208, Toronto, ON M4T 2Y4, Canada.

SCOTT, Elinor Mary, (Mrs D. J. Scott); *see* Goodman, E. M.

SCOTT, Esme, (Lady Scott), CBE 1985; WS; Chair, Volunteer Centre UK, 1993–96; *b* 7 Jan. 1932; *d* of David Burnett, SSC and Jane Burnett (*née* Thornton); *m* 1st, 1956, Ian Macfarlane Walker, WS (*d* 1988); one *s*; 2nd, 1990, Sir Kenneth Scott, *qv*; one step *s* one step *d. Educ:* St George's School for Girls, Edinburgh; Univ. of Edinburgh (MA, LLB). NP; Mem., Law Soc. of Scotland; Vice-Pres., Inst. of Trading Standards Admin. Lectr in Legal Studies, Queen Margaret College, Edinburgh, 1977–83. Voluntary worker, Citizens' Advice Bureau, 1960–85; Chm., Scottish Assoc. of CABx, 1986–88. Comr, Equal Opportunities Commn, 1986–90. Chm., Scottish Consumer Council, 1980–85; Vice-Chm., Nat. Consumer Council, 1984–87; Chm., Volunteer Development Scotland, 1989–92; Member: Expert Cttee, Multiple Surveys and Valuations (Scotland), 1982–84; Working Party on Procedure for Judicial Review of Admin. Action, 1983–84; Cttee on Conveyancing, 1984; Scottish Cttee, Council on Tribunals, 1986–92; Social Security Adv. Cttee, 1990–96; Direct Mail Services Standards Bd, 1990–95; Privacy Adv. Cttee, Common Services Agency, 1990–95. SIB, 1991–93; Monopolies and Mergers Commn, 1992–95; Exec. Cttee, NCVO, 1993–95; Member: Court, Edinburgh Univ., 1989–92; Council, St George's Sch. for Girls, 1989–96. FRSA. *Recreation:* crosswords. *Address:* 13 Clinton Road, Edinburgh EH9 2AW. *T:* (0131) 447 5191. *Club:* New (Edinburgh).

SCOTT, Finlay McMillan, TD 1984; Chief Executive and Registrar, General Medical Council, since 1994; *b* 25 May 1947; *s* of Finlay McMillan Scott and Anne Cameron Robertson Coutts Scott; *m* 1969, Eileen Frances Marshall (marr. diss. 2001); one *s* one *d. Educ:* Greenock High Sch.; Open Univ. (BA Hons); Durham Univ. (MSc). Department of Education and Science, subseq. Department for Education, 1975–94: Head of Pensions Br. and Controller, Darlington, 1983–86; Head of Inf. Systems Br., 1986–90; on secondment: to UFC, 1990–93; to PCFC, 1992–93; to HEFCE, 1992–94; Under Sec., 1990–94. Lt-Col, RAOC, 1989–93, RLC, 1993–95, RARO, 1995–, TA. Member: NIHEC, 1993–; Medical Workforce Standing Adv. Cttee, 1996–. Gov., London Guildhall Univ., 1996–. *Recreation:* hill walking. *Address:* General Medical Council, 178 Great Portland Street, W1N 6JE. *T:* (020) 7915 3563.

SCOTT, (George) Peter; Vice-Chancellor, Kingston University, since 1998; *b* 1 Aug. 1946; *s* of George Edward Grey Scott and Evelyn Mary Scott (*née* Robb); *m* 1968, Cherill Andrea Williams; one *d. Educ:* Merton Coll., Oxford (BA 1st cl. Hons Modern History 1967). Journalist: TES, 1967–69; The Times, 1969–71; Dep. Editor, THES, 1971–73; Vis. Scholar (Harkness Fellow), Grad. Sch. of Public Policy, Univ. of Calif at Berkeley, 1973–74; leader writer, The Times, 1974–76; Editor, THES, 1976–92; Prof. of Education, 1992–97, Pro-Vice-Chancellor, 1996–97, Univ. of Leeds. Hon. Fellow, UMIST, 1992. Hon. LLD Bath, 1992; Hon. DLitt: CNAA, 1992; Grand Valley State Univ., 1999; Hon. PhD Anglia Polytech. Univ., 1998. *Publications:* The Crisis of the University, 1986; Knowledge and Nation, 1990; The New Production of Knowledge, 1994; The Meanings of Mass Higher Education, 1995; Governing Universities, 1996. *Address:* Kingston University, River House, 53–57 High Street, Kingston-upon-Thames KT1 1LQ. *T:* (020) 8547 7010.

SCOTT, Dr Graham Alexander; retired; *b* 26 Nov. 1927; *s* of Alexander Scott and Jessie Scott; *m* 1951, Helena Patricia Margaret Cavanagh; two *s* one *d. Educ:* Daniel Stewart's Coll., Edinburgh; Edinburgh Univ. (MB, ChB). FRCPE, FFCM, DPH. RAAMC, 1951–56 (Dep. Asst Dir, Army Health, 1st Commonwealth Div., Korea, 1953–54). Sen. Asst MO, Stirling CC, 1957–62, Dep. County MO, 1962–65; Scottish Home and Health Department: MO, 1965–68; SMO, 1968–74; PMO, 1974–75; Dep. CMO, 1975–89. Consultant in Public Health Medicine, Borders Health Board, 1990–93. QHP 1987–90. *Recreations:* gardening, walking. *Address:* 5 Eildon Bank, Eildon, Melrose TD6 9HH.

SCOTT, Hilary; Deputy Health Service Ombudsman, since 1999; *b* 9 June 1954; *d* of Stephen and June Scott. *Educ:* Camden Sch. for Girls; Poly. of Central London (BA Hons Social Sci. 1978); Poly. of South Bank (MSc Sociol. of Health and Illness 1986). Nat. Admin. Trainee, NHS, 1978–81; Asst House Gov., St Stephen's Hosp., 1981–83; Dep. Administrator, Brook Gen. Hosp., 1983–86; Outpatient and Diagnostic Services Manager, Northwick Park Hosp., 1986–89; Chief Exec., Enfield & Haringey FHSA, 1989–93; Project Dir, City and E London Family and Community Health Services, 1993–95; Chief Exec., Tower Hamlets Health Care NHS Trust, 1995–99. *Recreations:* family, friends, films, flowers. *Address:* 3 Christchurch Square, E9 7HU.

SCOTT, Sir Ian Dixon, KCMG 1962 (CMG 1959); KCVO 1965; CIE 1947; *b* Inverness, 6 March 1909; *s* of Thomas Henderson Scott, OBE, MICE, and Mary Agnes Dixon, Selkirk; *m* 1937, Hon. Anna Drusilla Lindsay, *d* of 1st Baron Lindsay of Birker, CBE, LLD; one *s* four *d. Educ:* Queen's Royal College, Trinidad; Balliol College, Oxford (MA); London School of Economics. Entered Indian Civil Service, 1932; Indian Political Service, 1935; Assistant Director of Intelligence, Peshawar, 1941; Principal, Islamia College, Peshawar, 1943; Deputy Private Secretary to the Viceroy of India, 1945–47. Dep. Dir of Personnel, John Lewis & Co. Ltd, 1948–50. Appointed to Foreign Service, 1950; First Secretary, Foreign Office, 1950–51; British Legation, Helsinki, 1952; British Embassy, Beirut, 1954; Counsellor, 1956; Chargé d'Affaires, 1956, 1957, 1958; idc 1959; Consul-General, then Ambassador to the Congo, 1960–61; Ambassador to Sudan, 1961–65, to Norway, 1965–68. Chm., Clarksons Holidays Ltd, 1972–73 (Dir, 1969–73). Chm., Suffolk AHA, 1973–77; Member: Council, Dr Barnardo's, 1970–84 (Chm., 1972–78; elected Vice-Pres., 1984–); Bd of Governors, Felixstowe Coll., 1971–84 (Chm., 1972–78); Chm., Indian Civil Service (retd) Assoc., 1977–97 (Hon. Life Pres., 1997). *Publications:* Tumbled House, 1969; A British Tale of Indian and Foreign Service: the memoirs of Sir Ian Scott, 1999. *Recreation:* sailing. *Address:* Leiston Old Abbey Residential Home, Leiston, Suffolk IP16 4RF.

SCOTT, (Ian) Jonathan, CBE 1995; FSA; Deputy Chairman, since 1997 and Trustee, since 1996, Victoria & Albert Museum; *b* 7 Feb. 1940; *s* of Col Alexander Brassey Jonathan Scott, DSO, MC and Rhona Margaret Scott; *m* 1965, Annabella Constance Loudon; two *s* one *d. Educ:* Harrow Sch.; Balliol Coll., Oxford (BA). FSA 1980. Director: Charterhouse Japhet, 1973–80; Barclays Merchant Bank, subseq. Barclays de Zoete Wedd, 1980–92. Chairman: Reviewing Cttee on Export of Works of Art, 1985–95; Acceptance in Lieu Panel, 2000–. Trustee, Imperial War Mus., 1984–98. *Publications:* Piranesi, 1975; Salvator Rosa, 1995. *Recreations:* horses, trees. *Address:* Lasborough Manor, Tetbury, Glos GL8 8UF. *Club:* Brooks's.

SCOTT, Prof. Ian Richard, PhD; Professor of Law (personal chair), University of Birmingham, since 2001 (Barber Professor of Law, 1978–2000); *b* 8 Jan. 1940; *s* of Ernest and Edith Scott; *m* 1971, Ecce Cole; two *d. Educ:* Geelong Coll.; Queen's Coll., Univ. of Melbourne (LLB); King's Coll., Univ. of London (PhD). Barrister and Solicitor, Supreme Court of Victoria; called to Bar, Gray's Inn, 1995. Dir, Inst. of Judicial Admin, 1975–82. Exec. Dir, Victoria Law Foundn, 1982–84; Dean, Faculty of Law, Univ. of Birmingham, 1985–94. Member: Lord Chancellor's Civil Justice Review Body, 1985–88; Policy Adv. Gp, NHS Litigation Authy, 1996–2000; Alternative Dispute Resolution sub-cttee, Civil Justice Council, 1998–; Chm., N Yorks Magistrates' Courts Inquiry, 1989. Non-exec. Dir, Royal Orthopaedic Hosp. NHS Trust, 1995–2000. Hon. Bencher, Gray's Inn, 1988. Fellow, Aust. Inst. of Judicial Admin, 1990. *Recreation:* law. *Address:* Faculty of Law, University of Birmingham, Birmingham B15 2TT. *T:* (0121) 414 6334.

SCOTT, Prof. James, FRCP; FRS 1997; Professor of Medicine and Deputy Vice-Principal of Research, Imperial College School of Medicine, London University, since 1997; *b* 13 Sept. 1946; *s* of Robert Bentham Scott and Iris Olive Scott (*née* Hill); *m* 1976, Diane Marylin Lowe; two *s* one *d*. *Educ:* London Univ. (BSc 1968); London Hosp. Med. Coll. (MB, BS 1971; MSc Biochem. 1978). MRCP 1974, FRCP 1986. House Officer: London Hosp., 1971–72; Hereford Co. Hosp., 1972; Sen. House Officer, Midland Centre for Neurosurgery and Neurol., and Queen Elizabeth Hosp., Birmingham, 1972–73; Registrar in Medicine: General Hosp., Birmingham, 1973–74; Acad. Dept of Medicine, Royal Free Hosp., 1975–76; MRC Res. Fellow and Hon. Sen. Registrar, RPMS and Hammersmith Hosp., 1977–80; European Molecular Biol. Fellow, Dept of Biochem., Univ. of Calif, San Francisco, 1980–83; MRC Clinical Scientist and Hon. Consultant Physician, MRC Clinical Res. Centre and Northwick Park Hosp., 1983–91; Prof. and Chm. of Medicine, RPMS, 1992–97; Dir of Medicine and Chief of Service Med. Cardiology, Hammersmith Hosps NHS Trust, 1994–97; Hon. Consultant Physician, Hammersmith Hosp., 1992–; Hon. Dir, MRC Molecular Medicine Gp, 1992–. Member: RCP Res. Cttee, 1988–91; Assoc. of Physicians of GB and Ireland, 1987; European Molecular Biol. Orgn, 1993–; RSocMed Adv. Cttee, 1999–; Chm., N Thames Higher Merit Award Adv. Cttee, 1996–2000. Lectures include: Humphrey Davy Rolleston, RCP, 1989; Simms, RCP, 1995; Pfizer, Clin. Res. Inst., Montreal; Guest, Japan Atherosclerosis Soc., 1992. Founder FMedSci 1998. Graham Bull Prize, RCP, 1989; Squibb Bristol Myers Award for Cardiovascular Res., 1993. *Publications:* numerous on molecular medicine, molecular genetics, atherosclerosis, RNA modification, RNA editing and gene expression. *Recreations:* family and friends, the twentieth century novel, British Impressionists and modern painting, long distance running, swimming. *Address:* Department of Molecular Medicine, Imperial College School of Medicine, Hammersmith Hospital, Du Cane Road, W12 0NN.

SCOTT, James Alexander, OBE 1987; FCA; Partner, Binder Hamlyn, Chartered Accountants, 1969–98; *b* 30 April 1940; *s* of Douglas McPherson Scott and Mabel Mary (*née* Skepper); *m* 1965, Annette Goslett; three *s* two *d*. *Educ:* Uppingham Sch.; Magdalene Coll., Cambridge (Schol.; MA); London Business Sch. (MSc). Joined Binder Hamlyn, 1961; Man. Partner, London Region, 1980–88; Nat. Man. Partner, 1988–89. Director: Vestey Group Ltd, 1992–; Schroder Exempt Property Unit Trust, 1994–. Chairman, Trustees: Lonmin Superannuation Scheme, 2000–; Scottish and Universal Investments Ltd Gp Pensions and Life Assce Scheme, 2001–. Mem., Agricl Wages Bd for England and Wales, 1971–86; Sec., Review Bd for Govt Contracts, 1969–98; Member: NHS Pharmacists Remuneration Review Panel, 1982; Restrictive Practices Court, 1993–2000. DTI Inspector, Atlantic Computers plc, 1990. *Recreations:* walking, golf, tennis, ski-ing. *Clubs:* Berkshire Golf; St Enodoc Golf.

SCOTT, James Archibald, CB 1988; LVO 1961; FRSE; Deputy Spokesman on trade and industry, Scottish National Party, 1997–99; *b* 5 March 1932; *s* of late James Scott, MBE, and Agnes Bone Howie; *m* 1957, Elizabeth Agnes Joyce Buchan-Hepburn; three *s* one *d*. *Educ:* Dollar Acad.; Queen's Univ. of Ont.; Univ. of St Andrews (MA Hons). FRSE 1993. RAF aircrew, 1954–56. Asst Principal, CRO, 1956; served in New Delhi, 1958–62, and UK Mission to UN, New York, 1962–65; transf. to Scottish Office, 1965; Private Sec. to Sec. of State for Scotland, 1969–71; Asst Sec., Scottish Office, 1971; Under-Sec., Scottish Economic Planning Dept, later Industry Dept for Scotland, 1976–84; Sec., Scottish Educn Dept, 1984–87; Sec., Industry Dept for Scotland, 1987–90; Chief Exec., SDA, 1990–91; Exec. Dir, Scottish Financial Enterprise, 1991–94. Non-exec. Director: Scottish Power plc, 1992–96; Dumyat Investment Trust plc, 1995–2000. Fellow, SCOTVEC, 1990. Chevalier, Ordre National du Mérite (France), 1995. *Recreations:* flying, golf. *Address:* 38 Queen's Crescent, Edinburgh EH9 2BA. *T:* (0131) 667 8417.

SCOTT, Sir James (Jervoise), 3rd Bt *cr* 1962, of Rotherfield Park, Alton, Hants; farmer and landowner; *b* 12 Oct. 1952; *e s* of Lt-Col Sir James Walter Scott, 2nd Bt, and of Anne Constantia (*née* Austin); *S* father, 1993; *m* 1982, Judy Evelyn, *d* of Brian Trafford and Hon. Mrs Trafford; one *s* one *d*. *Educ:* Eton; Trinity Coll., Cambridge (MA). Agricultural journalist, 1977–88. Mem., Hampshire CC, 2001–. *Recreation:* shooting. *Heir: s* Arthur Jervoise Trafford Scott, *b* 2 Feb. 1984. *Address:* Estate Office, Rotherfield Park, East Tisted, Alton, Hampshire GU34 3QL. *T:* (01420) 588207. *Clubs:* White's, Travellers.

SCOTT, James Steel; Professor of Obstetrics and Gynæcology, 1961–89, and Dean of Faculty of Medicine, 1986–89, University of Leeds, now Professor Emeritus; *b* 18 April 1924; *s* of late Dr Angus M. Scott and late Margaret Scott; *m* 1958, Olive Sharpe; two *s*. *Educ:* Glasgow Academy; University of Glasgow. MB, ChB 1946, MD 1959; FRCSEd 1959; FRCOG 1962 (MRCOG 1953); FRCS (*ad eund*) 1986. Service in RAMC, 1947–49. Liverpool University: Obstetric Tutor, 1954; Lecturer, 1958; Senior Lecturer, 1960. *Publications:* contrib. to New Engl. Jl of Medicine, Lancet, BMJ, Jl of Obst. and Gynæc. of Brit. Empire, Amer. Jl of Obstetrics and Gynæcology, etc. *Recreations:* skiing, biography. *Address:* Byards Lodge, Boroughbridge Road, Knaresborough, N Yorks HG5 0LT.

SCOTT, Jean Grant, (Mrs Donald Macleod); Headmistress, South Hampstead High School GDST, 1993–2001; Chairman, Independent Schools Council, since 2001; *b* 7 Oct. 1940; *d* of Dr Duncan W. D. MacLaren and Etta M. MacLaren (*née* Speirs); *m* 1964, John Scott (*d* 1979); two *s*; *m* 2000, Donald Macleod. *Educ:* George Watson's Ladies' Coll., Edinburgh; Wellington Sch., Ayr; Univ. of Glasgow (BSc Hons Zool.); Univ. of London Inst. of Educn (PGCE). Research Biologist: Glaxo Labs Ltd, 1962–65; ICI, Alderley Edge, 1966–67; part-time Lectr in Biol., Newcastle-under-Lyme Coll. of FE, 1969–70; Teacher of Biology: (part-time) Dr Challoner's High Sch., 1970–76; Northgate Grammar Sch., Ipswich, 1976–77; Hd of Biol. and Sen. Mistress, Ipswich High Sch. (GPDST), 1977–86; Headmistress, St George's Sch. for Girls, Edinburgh, 1986–93. *Recreations:* concerts, theatre, film, swimming, ski-ing, loch fishing, travel abroad. *Address:* 3 Merton Rise, NW3 3EN.

SCOTT, Sir John; *see* Scott, Sir P. J. and Scott, Sir W. J.

SCOTT, John; *see* Scott, W. J. G.

SCOTT, (John) Brough; Director, Racing Post, since 1988; Sports Writer, Sunday Telegraph, since 1995; *b* 12 Dec. 1942; *s* of Mason Hogarth Scott and Irene Florence Scott, Broadway, Worcs; *m* 1973, Susan Eleanor MacInnes; two *s* two *d*. *Educ:* Radley College; Corpus Christi, Oxford (BA History). Amateur, then professional, Nat. Hunt jockey, 1962–71 (100 winners, incl. Imperial Cup and Mandarin Chase). ITV presenter, sports programmes and documentaries, 1971–; chief racing presenter, ITV, 1979–85; chief presenter, Channel 4 Racing, 1985–2001. Evening Standard sports correspondent, 1972–74; sports journalist: Sunday Times, 1974–90, 1993–94; The Independent on Sunday, 1990–92. Vice-Pres., Jockeys' Assoc., 1969–71; Trustee: Injured Jockeys Fund; Professional Riders' Insurance Scheme; Racing Welfare. Lord Derby Award, 1978 (racing journalist of the year); Clive Graham Trophy, 1982; Sports Journalist of the Year, 1983; Sports Feature Writer of the Year, 1985, 1991, 1992. *Publications:* World of Flat Racing, 1983; On and Off the Rails, 1984; Front Runners, 1991; Up Front—Willie Carson, 1994; Racing Certainties, 1995. *Recreation:* making bonfires. *Address:* Willow House, 35 High Street, Wimbledon Common, SW19 5BY. *T:* (020) 8946 9671.

SCOTT, Rev. Prof. John Fraser, AO 1990; Vice-Chancellor, La Trobe University, Melbourne, 1977–90; Associate Priest, St George's, Malvern, since 1992; *b* 10 Oct. 1928; *s* of Douglas Fraser Scott and Cecilia Louise Scott; *m* 1956, Dorothea Elizabeth Paton Scott; one *s* three *d*. *Educ:* Bristol Grammar Sch.; Trinity Coll., Cambridge (MA); Melbourne Coll. of Divinity (BD 1994). FIS. Research Asst, Univ. of Sheffield, 1950–53; Asst, Univ. of Aberdeen, 1953–55; Lectr in Biometry, Univ. of Oxford, 1955–65; University of Sussex: Reader in Statistics, 1965–67; Prof. of Applied Statistics, 1967–77; Pro-Vice-Chancellor, 1971–77. Adv. Prof., E China Normal Univ., 1988. Visiting Consultant in Statistics: Nigeria, 1961, 1965; Sweden, 1969; Kuwait, 1973, 1976; Iraq, 1973; Malaysia, 1976. Reader, Church of England, 1971–77; Examining Chaplain to Bp of Chichester, 1974–77; Diocesan Lay Reader, Anglican Dio. of Melbourne, 1977–90; ordained deacon, then priest, 1990; Asst Curate, St George's, E Ivanhoe, 1990–91. Chairman: Jt Cttee on Univ. Statistics, 1978–86; Cttee of Review of Student Finances, 1983; Aust. Univs Industrial Assoc., 1986–; AVCC, 1986–88 (Dep. Chm., 1986, Chm., Wkg Party on Attrition, 1981–86); Council for Chaplains in Tertiary Instns, 1990–94; Member: Grad. Careers Council of Aust., 1980–86; Council, 1986–89, Exec. Cttee, 1986–88, ACU; ABC Victorian State Adv. Cttee, 1978–81; Ethics Cttee, Victorian State Dept of Health, 1990–; Pres., Victorian State Libraries Bd, 1990–96. Dir, LTU Credit Union, 2001–. Editor, Applied Statistics, 1971–76; Mem., Editl Bd, The Statistician, 1987–. DUniv La Trobe, 1990. *Publications:* The Comparability of Grade Standards in Mathematics, 1975; Report of Committee of Review of Student Finances, 1983; papers in JRSS, Lancet, BMJ, Chemistry and Industry, Statistician, etc. *Recreations:* wine, women and song; canals. *Address:* 1/18 Riversdale Road, Hawthorn, Victoria 3122, Australia. *T:* (3) 98191862. *Club:* Melbourne.

SCOTT, John Gavin, FRCO; Organist and Director of Music, St Paul's Cathedral, since 1990; *b* 18 June 1956; *s* of Douglas Gavin Scott and Hetty Scott (*née* Murphy); *m* 1979, Carolyn Jane Lumsden; one *s* one *d*. *Educ:* Queen Elizabeth Grammar Sch., Wakefield; St John's Coll., Cambridge (MA, MusB). Asst Organist, Wakefield Cath., 1970–74; Organ Scholar, St John's Coll., Cambridge, 1974–78; Assistant Organist: Southwark Cath., 1978–85; St Paul's Cath., 1978–85; Sub-Organist, St Paul's Cath., 1985–90. Prof., Royal Acad. of Music, 1988–91. Accompanist, Bach Choir, 1979–91. Hon. RAM 1990; Hon. FGCM 1996. First Prizewinner: Manchester Internat. Organ Fest., 1978; Leipzig Internat. J. S. Bach Competition, 1984. *Recreations:* reading, travel, ecclesiastical architecture. *Address:* 5 Amen Court, EC4M 7BU. *T:* (020) 7248 6868.

SCOTT, John Hamilton; Lord-Lieutenant for Shetland, since 1994; farming in Bressay and Noss; *b* 30 Nov. 1936; *s* of Dr Thomas Gilbert Scott and Elizabeth M. B. Scott; *m* 1965, Wendy Ronald; one *s* one *d*. *Educ:* Bryanston; Cambridge Univ.; Guy's Hosp., London. Shepherd, Scrabster, Caithness, 1961–64. Chm., Woolgrowers of Shetland Ltd, 1981–. Pres., Shetland NFU, 1976; Chairman: Shetland Crofting, Farming and Wildlife Adv. Gp, 1984–95; Shetland Arts Trust, 1993–98; Sail Shetland Ltd, 1997–; Belmont Trust, 1997–; Member: Nature Conservancy Council Cttee for Scotland, 1984–91; NE Regl Bd, Nature Conservancy Council for Scotland, 1991–92, Scottish Natural Heritage, 1992–97. *Recreations:* mountain climbing, Up-Helly-Aa, music. *Address:* Keldabister Banks, Bressay, Shetland ZE2 9EL. *T:* (01595) 820281. *Club:* Alpine.
See also T. H. Scott.

SCOTT, John James, PhD; Financial Adviser, Allied Dunbar, 1995–96; *b* 4 Sept. 1924; *s* of late Col John Creagh Scott, DSO, OBE and Mary Elizabeth Marjory (*née* Murray of Polmaise); *m* 1st, Katherine Mary (*née* Bruce); twin *d*; 2nd, Heather Marguerite (*née* Douglas Brown); 3rd, June Rose (*née* Mackie); twin *s*. *Educ:* Radley (Schol.); Corpus Christi Coll., Cambridge (Schol.); National Inst. for Medical Research, London. War Service, Captain, Argyll and Sutherland Highlanders, 1944–47. BA 1st cl. hons Nat. Sci. Tripos, Pts I and II, 1950, MA 1953, Cantab; PhD London 1954. Senior Lectr in Chem. Pathology, St Mary's Hosp., 1955–61; Mem. Editorial Bd, Biochem. Jl, 1956–61; Mem. Cttee of Biochem. Soc., 1961; Vis. Scientist, Nat. Insts of Health, Bethesda, Md, 1961. Entered Diplomatic Service, 1961; Office of Comr Gen. for SE Asia, Singapore, 1962; Office of Political Adviser to C-in-C, Singapore, 1963; FO, 1966; Counsellor, Rio de Janeiro and Brasilia, 1971; seconded to NI Office as Asst Sec., Stormont, 1974–76; Asst Under-Sec., FCO, 1978–80; Asst Managing Dir, later Commercial Dir, Industrial Engines (Sales) Ltd, Elbar Group, 1980; Man. Dir, Dudmass Ltd, 1983–93; Associate: Trident Life, 1984–85; Save & Prosper Group, 1985–95. Sir Nicholas Bacon Prize, Cambridge, 1950. *Publications:* papers in Biochem. Jl, Proc. Royal Soc. and other learned jls. *Recreations:* botany, photography, music. *Address:* Moat Cottage, Northbeck, Scredington, Sleaford, Lincs NG34 0AD. *Clubs:* Carlton, Institute of Directors; Leander (Henley-on-Thames); Hawks (Cambridge); Ski Club of GB.

SCOTT, Jonathan; *see* Scott, I. J.

SCOTT, Judith Margaret, CEng, FBCS; Chief Executive, British Computer Society, since 1995; *b* 4 Oct. 1942; *d* of Robert Wright and Marjorie Wood; *m* 1972, Gordon Robert Scott; two *d*. *Educ:* St Andrews Univ. (BSc Hons); Cambridge Univ. (Dip. Computer Sci.). Various posts, Computel Systems Ltd (Canada), 1968–79; seconded to Computer/Communications Policy Task Force, Govt of Canada, 1971–72; Manager, Product Mktg, Gandalf Data Inc. (Canada), 1979–82; Dir Corporate Planning, Gandalf Technologies Inc. (Canada), 1982–87; Man. Dir, Gandalf Digital Communications Ltd, UK, 1987–95. Mem., PPARC, 2001–. *Recreation:* orchid growing. *Address:* 3 Winkfield Close, Wokingham, Berks RG41 2EZ. *T:* (0118) 977 1656.

SCOTT, Sir Kenneth (Bertram Adam), KCVO 1990; CMG 1980; an Extra Equerry to the Queen, since 1996; *b* 23 Jan. 1931; *s* of late Adam Scott, OBE, and Lena Kaye; *m* 1st, 1966, Gabrielle Justine (*d* 1977), *d* of R. W. Smart, Christchurch, New Zealand; one *s* one *d*; 2nd, 1990, Esme Walker (*see* Esme Scott); one step *s*. *Educ:* George Watson's Coll., Edinburgh; Edinburgh Univ. MA Hons 1952. Foreign Office, 1954; served in Moscow, Bonn, Washington and Vientiane; Counsellor and Head of Chancery, Moscow, 1971; Sen. Officers' War Course, RNC, Greenwich, 1973; Dep. Head, Personnel Ops Dept, FCO, 1973; Counsellor and Head of Chancery, Washington, 1975; Head of E European and Soviet Dept, FCO, 1977; Minister and Dep. UK Perm. Rep. to NATO, 1979–82; Ambassador to Yugoslavia, 1982–85; Asst Private Sec. to the Queen, 1985–90; Dep. Private Sec. to the Queen, 1990–96. Vice-Chm., Provisional Election Commn for Bosnia and Herzogovina, Sarajevo, 1996. Dep. Chm., Hopetoun House Preservation Trust, 1998–. Trustee, Develt Trust, Edinburgh Univ., 1999–. Gov., George Watson's Coll., 1997–. *Address:* 13 Clinton Road, Edinburgh EH9 2AW. *Clubs:* Royal Over-Seas League (Mem., Central Council, 1996–; Vice Chm., 2000–); New (Edinburgh).

SCOTT, Kenneth Farish, MC 1943 and Bar, 1944; FREng, FICE; Senior Partner, 1977–84, Senior Consultant, 1984–87, Sir Alexander Gibb & Partners; *b* 21 Dec. 1918; *s* of Norman James Stewart and Ethel May Scott; *m* 1945, Elizabeth Mary Barrowcliff; one *s* one *d*. *Educ:* Stockton Grammar School; Constantine Tech. Coll. Served Royal Engineers, 1939–46. Joined Sir Alexander Gibb & Partners, 1946; Resident Engineer, Hydro-Electric Works, Scotland, 1946–52; Chief Rep., NZ, 1952–55, Scotland, 1955–59; Partner 1959, Senior Partner 1977; responsible for design and supervision of construction of major water resource develt projects, incl. Latiyan Dam, 1959–67, Lar Dam 1968–82, Greater Tehran Water Supply, 1959–82; major maritime works incl. modernisation Devonport Dockyard, 1970–80; internat. airports at Tripoli, 1966–70, Bahrain, 1970–72. Pres., Soc. des Ingénieurs et Scientifiques de France (British Section), 1975; Vice-Pres., ICE, 1985–87. Chm., Assoc. of Consulting Engineers, 1976. FREng (FEng 1979). Hon. Mem., Instn of RE, 1982. *Publications:* papers to ICE and International Congress of Large Dams. *Recreations:* sailing, golf, wood working. *Address:* Forest House, Brookside Road, Brockenhurst, Hants SO42 7SS. *T:* (01590) 623531. *Clubs:* Special Forces, Royal Over-Seas League; Royal Southampton Yacht.

SCOTT, Linda Valerie; *see* Agran, L. V.

SCOTT, Malcolm Charles Norman; QC (Scot.) 1991; *b* 8 Sept. 1951; *s* of James Raymond Scott and Marjorie Stewart Simpson. *Educ:* Trinity Coll., Glenalmond; Gonville and Caius Coll., Cambridge (BA 1972); Glasgow Univ. (LLB 1975). Advocate 1978. Dir, Mid Wynd International Investment Trust plc, 1990–. *Recreations:* fishing, ski-ing, hill walking. *Address:* 72 Northumberland Street, Edinburgh EH3 6JG. *Club:* New (Edinburgh).

SCOTT, Dame Margaret, (Dame Catherine Margaret Mary Denton), DBE 1981 (OBE 1977); Founding Director of the Australian Ballet School, 1964–90, retired; *b* 26 April 1922; *d* of John and Marjorie Douglas-Scott; *m* 1953, Derek Ashworth Denton, *qv*; two *s*. *Educ:* Parktown Convent, Johannesburg, S Africa; Graduate Dip. in Visual and Performing Arts, RMIT, 2000. Sadler's Wells Ballet, London, 1940–43; Principal: Ballet Rambert, London and Australia, 1944–49; National Ballet, Australia, 1949–50; Ballet Rambert, and John Cranko Group, London, 1951–53; private ballet teaching, Australia, 1953–61; planned and prepared the founding of the Aust. Ballet Sch., 1962–64. Hon. Life Mem., Australian Ballet Foundn, 1988. Hon. LLD Melbourne, 1989; Hon. DEd RMIT. Life Time Achievement Award: Green Room Awards Assoc., 1998; Aust. Dance Awards, 1998. *Recreations:* music, theatre, garden. *Address:* 816 Orrong Road, Toorak, Melbourne, Vic 3142, Australia. *T:* (3) 98272640. *Club:* Alexandra (Melbourne).

SCOTT, Maurice FitzGerald, FBA 1990; Official Fellow in Economics, Nuffield College, Oxford, 1968–92, now Emeritus Fellow; *b* 6 Dec. 1924; *s* of Colonel G. C. Scott, OBE and H. M. G. Scott; *m* 1953, Eleanor Warren (*née* Dawson) (*d* 1989); three *d*. *Educ:* Wadham Coll., Oxford (MA); Nuffield Coll., Oxford (BLitt). Served RE, 1943–46. OEEC, Paris, 1949–51; Paymaster-General's Office (Lord Cherwell), 1951–53; Cabinet Office, 1953–54; NIESR, London, 1954–57; Tutor in Economics and Student of Christ Church, Oxford, 1957–68; NEDO, London, 1962–63; OECD, Paris, 1967–68. *Publications:* A Study of U.K. Imports, 1963; (with I. M. D. Little and T. Scitovsky) Industry and Trade in Some Developing Countries, 1970; (with J. D. MacArthur and D. M. G. Newbery) Project Appraisal in Practice, 1976; (with R. A. Laslett) Can We get back to Full Employment?, 1978; (with W. M. Corden and I. M. D. Little) The Case against General Import Restrictions, 1980; A New View of Economic Growth, 1989; Peter's Journey, 1998. *Recreation:* walking. *Address:* 11 Blandford Avenue, Oxford OX2 8EA. *T:* (01865) 559115. *Club:* Political Economy (Oxford).

SCOTT, Sir Michael, KCVO 1979 (MVO 1961); CMG 1977; HM Diplomatic Service, retired; *b* 19 May 1923; *yr s* of late John Scott and Kathleen Scott; *m* 1st, 1944, Vivienne Sylvia Vincent-Barwood; three *s*; 2nd, 1971, Jennifer Slawikowski (*née* Cameron Smith), *widow* of Dr George J. M. Slawikowski. *Educ:* Dame Allan's School; Durham Univ. War Service: Durham Light Infantry, 1941; 1st Gurkha Rifles, 1943–47. Joined Colonial Office, 1949; CRO, 1957; First Secretary, Karachi, 1958–59; Deputy High Commissioner, Peshawar, 1959–62; Counsellor and Director, British Information Services in India, New Delhi, 1963–65; Head of E and Central Africa Dept, FCO, 1965–68; Dep. High Comr, British High Commn, Nicosia, 1968–72; RCDS, 1973; Ambassador to Nepal, 1974–77; High Comr in Malaŵi, 1977–79; High Comr in Bangladesh, 1980–81. Sec.-Gen., Royal Commonwealth Soc., 1983–88. Dir, Tiger Mountain Gp (Nepal and India), 1984–93. Mem., Governing Council, ODI, 1983–93; Trustee, Internat. Agricl Trng Programme, 1988–2001. Dep. Chm., Drive for Youth Programme, 1987–93. *Address:* 87A Cornwall Gardens, SW7 4AY. *T:* (020) 7589 6794. *Club:* Oriental.

SCOTT, Maj.-Gen. Michael Ian Eldon, CB 1997; CBE 1987; DSO 1982; Complaints Commissioner, Bar Council, since 1997; *b* 3 March 1941; *s* of Col Eric Scott and Rose-Anne Scott; *m* 1968, Veronica Daniell; one *s* one *d*. *Educ:* Bradfield Coll. Commnd Scots Guards, 1960; Regtl service in UK, E Africa, N Ireland, BAOR; Staff Coll., Camberley, 1974; 2nd MA to CGS, 1975; COS Task Force Delta, 1979; Armed Forces Staff Coll., USA, 1981; CO, 2nd Bn Scots Guards, London, Falklands War and Cyprus, 1981–84; Comd 8th Inf. Bde, N Ireland, 1984–86; RCDS 1987; Dep. Mil. Sec., 1988–93; GOC Scotland and Gov., Edinburgh Castle, 1993–95; Mil. Sec., 1995–97. *Recreations:* travel, visual arts, outdoor pursuits. *Club:* Pratt's.

SCOTT, Michael John; broadcaster; *b* 8 Dec. 1932; *s* of Tony and Pam Scott; *m* 1956, Sylvia Hudson; one *d*. *Educ:* Latymer Upper Sch., Hammersmith; Clayesmore, Iwerne Minster, Dorset. National Service, RAOC, 1951–53. Stagehand with Festival Ballet, and film extra, 1954; TV production trainee, Rank Organization, 1955; Granada TV: joined as floormanager, 1956; Prog. Dir, 1957; Producer/Performer, daily magazine prog., 1963–65; Presenter, Cinema, 1965–68; Exec. Producer, local progs, 1968–73; World in Action interviewer, and producer/performer of other progs, 1974–75; Exec. Producer and Reporter, Nuts and Bolts of the Economy, 1975–78; Dep. Prog. Controller, 1978–79; Prog. Controller, 1979–87; returned to active broadcasting, via live daily programme The Time … The Place, 1987–93. Director: Channel 4 Television Co., 1984–87; Granada TV, 1978–87. *Recreations:* watching the box, jogging, a 1932 Lagonda, a garden. *Address:* Flat 1, 39 Gloucester Walk, W8 4HY. *T:* (020) 7937 3962.

SCOTT, Rt Hon. Sir Nicholas (Paul), KBE 1995 (MBE 1964); PC 1989; JP; *b* 5 Aug. 1933; *e s* of late Percival John Scott; *m* 1st, 1964, Elizabeth Robinson (marr. diss. 1976); one *s* two *d*; 2nd, 1979, Hon. Mrs Cecilia Anne Tapsell, *d* of 9th Baron Hawke; one *s* one *d*. *Educ:* Clapham College. Served Holborn Borough Coun., 1956–59 and 1962–65; contested (C) SW Islington, 1959 and 1964. MP (C): Paddington S, 1966–Feb. 1974; Chelsea, Oct. 1974–1997. PPS to: Chancellor of the Exchequer, Rt Hon. Iain Macleod, 1970; Home Sec., Rt Hon. Robert Carr, 1972–74; Parly Under-Sec. of State, Dept of Employment, 1974; Opposition spokesman on housing, 1974–75; Parly Under Sec. of State, 1981–86, Minister of State, 1986–87, Northern Ireland Office; Minister of State, DHSS, then DSS, 1987–94. Mem., 1922 Exec. Cttee, 1978–81; Dir, London Office, European Cons. Gp in European Parlt, 1974. Nat. Chm., Young Conservatives, 1963 (Vice-Pres., 1988–89); Chm., Conservative Parly Employment Cttee, 1979–81 (Vice-Chm., 1967–72); formerly Nat. Pres., Tory Reform Gp. Chairman: Westminster Community Relations Council, 1967–72; Paddington Churches Housing Assoc., 1970–76; British Atlantic Gp Younger Politicians, 1970–73; Dep. Chm., British Caribbean Assoc.; Mem. Council, Community Service Volunteers; Governor, British Inst. of Human Rights; Dep. Chm., Youthaid, 1977–79. Mem., Cttee, MCC, 1972–75. Churchwarden, St Margaret's, Westminster, 1971–73. Man. Dir, E. Allom & Co., 1968–70; Chm., Creative Consultants Ltd, 1969–79; Director: A. S. Kerswill Ltd, 1970–81; Eastbourne Printers Ltd, 1970–81; Juniper Studios Ltd, 1970–81; Midhurst White Holdings Ltd, 1977–78; Bonusbond Hldgs Ltd, 1980–81; Bonusplan Ltd, 1977–81; Cleveland Offshore Fund Inc., 1970–81; Throgmorton Securities Ltd, 1970–74; Ede & Townsend, 1977–80; Learplan Ltd, 1978–81; Consultant: Campbell-Johnson Ltd, 1970–76; Roulston & Co. Inc., 1970–78; Lombard North Central Ltd, 1971–74; Clevebourne Investments Ltd, 1974–76; Claremont Textiles Ltd, 1974–76; Procter & Gamble Ltd, 1974–78; Hill & Knowlton (UK) Ltd, 1981; Bank of Ireland, 1994–97; Clarke Smith Industries, 1994–96; Tara Television, 1997–; VSO, 1974–76; Council, Bank Staff Assocs, 1968–77. Freeman, City of London, 1979; Liveryman, GAPAN, 1988–. JP London, 1961. *Recreations:* cricket, tennis, golf, flying. *Clubs:* Pratt's, Garrick, Chelsea Arts, MCC, Hurlingham, Queen's; St Enodoc.

SCOTT, Norman Bruce St Clair, CMG 1994; Director, United Nations Secretariat, retired; Director, Diplomatic Studies Programmes, Graduate Institute of International Studies, Geneva, since 1999 (Visiting Professor, 1963–98); Consultant, International Monetary Fund, since 1994; *b* 13 April 1933; *s* of John Reid Scott and Isobel Carmichael-Brown; *m* 1955, Mirjana Matejovic; one *s* one *d*. *Educ:* Glasgow Univ. (MA 1954); Univ. of Belgrade; Univ. of Geneva; Coatbridge Acad. UN Economic Commission for Europe: Sen. Economist, Res. Div., 1966–73; Dir, Technol. Div., 1974–83; Dir, Trade Div., 1983–93; Sen. Dir, Secretariat, retd 1993. Pres., Centre for Res. on Internat. Instns, Geneva, 1986–. *Publications:* numerous essays on comparative economic systems and policies in collective works; contrib. economic and technical jls. *Recreations:* amateur theatre, angling, antique map collecting. *Address:* 2 avenue De Warens, 1203 Geneva, Switzerland. *T:* (22) 3448664; Glower, Birsay, Orkney KW17 2ND. *Clubs:* Athenæum, Oriental.

SCOTT, Sir Oliver (Christopher Anderson), 3rd Bt *cr* 1909 of Yews, Westmorland; Radiobiologist, Richard Dimbleby Cancer Research Department, St Thomas' Hospital, 1982–88; Radiobiologist, 1954–66, Director, 1966–69, British Empire Cancer Campaign Research Unit in Radiobiology; *b* 6 Nov. 1922; *s* of Sir Samuel H. Scott, 2nd Bt and Nancy Lilian (*née* Anderson); *S* father, 1960; *m* 1951, Phoebe Ann Tolhurst; one *s* two *d*. *Educ:* Charterhouse; King's College, Cambridge. Clinical training at St Thomas' Hosp., 1943–46; MRCS, LRCP, 1946; MB, BCh, Cambridge, 1946; MD Cambridge, 1976; Surgeon-Lieutenant RNVR, 1947–49. Dir, Provincial Insurance Co., 1955–64. Hon. Consultant, Inst. of Cancer Res., Sutton, 1974–82. Pres., Section of Oncology, RSM, 1987–88. Mem. Council, Cancer Res. Campaign, 1978–91. Mem., BIR, 1999. Hon. FRCR 1998. High Sheriff of Westmorland, 1966. *Publications:* contributions to scientific books and journals. *Recreations:* music, walking. *Heir:* s Christopher James Scott [*b* 16 Jan. 1955; *m* 1988, Emma, *o d* of Michael Boxhall; two *s* two *d*]. *Address:* 31 Kensington Square, W8 5HH. *T:* (020) 7937 8556. *Club:* Brooks's.

SCOTT, Oliver Lester Schreiner; Emeritus Consultant: Skin Department, Charing Cross Hospital, since 1985 (Physician-in-Charge, 1956–84); South West Metropolitan Regional Hospital Board, since 1985 (Consultant Dermatologist, 1951–84); *b* London, 16 June 1919; *s* of Ralph Lester Scott, FRCSE, and Ursula Hester Schreiner; *m* 1943, Katherine Ogle Branfoot (*d* 1987); two *d*. *Educ:* Diocesan College, Cape Town; Trinity College, Cambridge; St Thomas's Hospital, London. MRCS, LRCP 1942; MA, MB, BChir, (Cantab) 1943; MRCP (London) 1944. FRCP 1964. Med. Specialist, RAF Med. Branch, 1943–46 (Sqn Leader). Consultant, Medical Insurance Agency, 1976–93; Hon. Consultant: Dispensaire Français, 1960–86; King Edward VII Hosp. for Officers, London, 1975–84. Hon. Treas., RSocMed, 1978–82 (Pres., Dermatology Section, 1977–78); Vice-Pres., Royal Medical Foundn of Epsom Coll., 1992– (Hon. Treas., 1978–93); Hon. Mem., British Assoc. of Dermatologists (Pres., 1982–83). Chevalier, l'Ordre National du Mérite, France. *Publications:* section on skin disorders in Clinical Genetics, ed A. Sorsby; medical articles in Lancet, British Journal of Dermatology, etc. *Recreations:* fishing, gardening. *Address:* South Lodge, 7 South Side, Wimbledon Common, SW19 4TL. *T:* (020) 8946 6662.

SCOTT, Paul Henderson, CMG 1974; writer; HM Diplomatic Service, retired 1980; *b* 7 Nov. 1920; *s* of Alan Scott and Catherine Scott (*née* Henderson), Edinburgh; *m* 1953, Beatrice Celia Sharpe; one *s* one *d*. *Educ:* Royal High School, Edinburgh; Edinburgh University (MA, MLitt). HM Forces, 1941–47 (Major RA). Foreign Office, 1947–53; First Secretary, Warsaw, 1953–55; First Secretary, La Paz, 1955–59; Foreign Office, 1959–62; Counsellor, Havana, 1962–64; Canadian National Defence College, 1964–65; British Deputy Commissioner General for Montreal Exhibition, 1965–67; Counsellor and Consul-General, Vienna, 1968–71; Head of British Govt Office, 1971, Consul-Gen., 1974–75, Montreal; Research Associate, IISS, 1975–76; Asst Under Sec., FO (negotiator on behalf of EEC Presidency for negotiations with USSR, Poland and East Germany), 1977; Minister and Consul-General, Milan, 1977–80. Chairman: Adv. Council for the Arts in Scotland, 1981–98; Steering Cttee for a Scottish Nat. Theatre, 1988–; Mem., Constitutional Steering Cttee, which drew up A Claim of Right for Scotland, published 1988; Pres., Saltire Soc., 1996–2001 (Dep. Chm., 1981–95); Member: Council, Nat. Trust for Scotland, 1981–87; Assoc. for Scottish Literary Studies, 1981–; Scots Language Soc., 1981–91; Cockburn Assoc., 1982–85; Council, Edinburgh Internat. Fest., 1984–87; Chm., Friends of Dictionary of Older Scottish Tongue, 1984–; President: Andrew Fletcher Soc., 1988–96; Scottish Centre, PEN Internat., 1992–97. Scottish National Party: Mem., NEC, 1989–97; spokesman on educn and the arts, 1991–97; Vice-Pres., 1992–97; dep. spokesman on Europe and external affairs, 1997–99; contested (SNP): Eastwood, 1992; Lothians, Scottish Parlt, 1999. Convener, Scottish Centre for Econ. and Social Res., 1990–95. Rector, Dundee Univ., 1989–92. Hon. Fellow, Glasgow Univ., 1996. Grosse Goldene Ehrenzeichen, Austria, 1969. *Publications:* 1707: The Union of Scotland and England, 1979; (ed with A. C. Davis) The Age of MacDiarmid, 1980; Walter Scott and Scotland, 1981; (ed) Walter Scott's Letters of Malachi Malagrowther, 1981; (ed) Andrew Fletcher's United and Separate Parliaments, 1982; John Galt, 1985; In Bed with an Elephant, 1985; (ed with George Bruce) A Scottish Postbag, 1986; The Thinking Nation, 1989; Towards Independence, 1991; Andrew Fletcher and the Treaty of Union, 1992; Scotland in Europe: a dialogue with a sceptical friend, 1992; (ed) Scotland: a concise cultural history, 1993; Defoe in Edinburgh and Other Papers, 1995; (ed) Scotland's Ruine: Lockhart of Carnwath's Memoirs, 1995; Scotland: an unwon cause, 1997; Still in Bed with an Elephant, 1998; The Boasted Advantages, 1999; articles and book reviews esp. in Economist, Scotsman and other periodicals. *Recreations:* ski-ing, sailing. *Address:* 33 Drumsheugh Gardens, Edinburgh EH3 7RN. *T:* (0131) 225 1038. *Clubs:* New, Scottish Arts (Edinburgh).

SCOTT, Sir Peter; *see* Scott, Sir C. P.

SCOTT, Peter; *see* Scott, G. P.

SCOTT, Peter Anthony; Managing Director, Peel Holdings plc, since 1985; *b* 24 April 1947; *s* of Barclay and Doris Scott; *m* 1969, Lynne Smithies; one *s* one *d*. *Educ:* Heywood Grammar Sch.; Littleborough High Sch.; Manchester Poly. ACCA 1979. Financial Accountant: Fothergill & Harvey Ltd, 1962–75; Crane Fruehauf Trailers (Oldham) Ltd, 1975–77; Co. Sec., 1977–81, Financial Dir, 1981–85, Peel Hldgs plc. *Address:* Peel Holdings plc, Peel Dome, Trafford Centre, Manchester M17 8PL; (home) 6 Bowling Green Way, Bamford, Rochdale, Lancs OL11 5QQ.

SCOTT, Peter Denys John; QC 1978; Chairman, City Panel on Takeovers and Mergers, since 2000; *b* 19 April 1935; *s* of John Ernest Dudley Scott and Joan G. Steinberg. *Educ:* Monroe High Sch., Rochester, NY, USA; Balliol Coll., Oxford (MA). Second Lieut, RHA, Lieut (TA), National Service, 1955. Called to the Bar, Middle Temple (Harmsworth Scholar), 1960, Bencher, 1984; Standing Counsel: to Dir, Gen. of Fair Trading, 1973–78; to Dept of Employment, 1974–78. Member: Home Sec.'s Cttee on Prison Disciplinary System, 1984; Interception of Communications Tribunal, 1986–; Lord Chancellor's Adv. Cttee on Legal Educn and Conduct, 1991–94; Investigatory Powers Tribunal, 2000–; Chm., Appeal Bd, Inst. of Actuaries, 1995–; a Judicial Tribunal Chm., City Disputes Panel, 1997–. Vice-Chm., Senate of the Inns of Court and the Bar, 1985–86; Chm., General Council of the Bar, 1987; Mem., Senate and Bar Council, 1981–87; Chm., London Common Law Bar Assoc., 1983–85. Chm., Bd of Trustees, Nat. Gall., 2000–. Chairman: N Kensington Amenity Trust, 1981–85; Kensington Housing Trust, 1999–. *Recreations:* gardening, theatre. *Address:* 4 Eldon Road, W8 5PU. *T:* (020) 7937 3301, *Fax:* (020) 7376 1169.

SCOTT, Peter Francis, CBE 1982; retired; *b* 21 Sept. 1917; *s* of Francis C. Scott and Frieda Jager; *m* 1953, Prudence Mary Milligan; one *s* three *d*. *Educ:* Winchester; Oriel Coll., Oxford (BA). Commnd 1st Bn, KRRC; Capt.; served War, 1939–46: with 8th Army in N Africa, Sicily and Italy; with 21st Army Gp in NW Europe. Joined Provincial Insurance Co. Ltd, 1946: Dir, 1946–77; Chm., 1957–77; Pres., 1977; Pres., Sand Aire Ltd, 1997. Former Member: Northern Econ. Planning Council; Careers Res. Adv. Council; Standing Cttee on Museums and Galleries. Former Chairman: Trustees, Brathay Hall; Lake Dist Art Gall. Trust; Kendal Brewery Arts Centre Trust; Mem., Lake Dist Mus. Trust. Chm., Lake Dist Cttee, NT. Dir, National Theatre (Mem., Exec. Cttee); Mem., Council, Northern Arts Assoc. DL, High Sheriff 1963, Westmorland. Freeman of Kendal. Hon. LLD Lancaster. *Address:* Fardel Manor, Ivybridge, Devon PL21 9HT. *T:* (01752) 893039. *Clubs:* Brook's, Garrick.

SCOTT, Sir (Philip) John, KBE 1987; FRCP; FRACP; FRSNZ; Professor of Medicine, University of Auckland, 1975–97, now Emeritus; *b* 26 June 1931; *s* of Horace McD. Scott and Doris A. Scott (*née* Ruddock); *m* 1956, Elizabeth Jane MacMillan; one *s* three *d*. *Educ:* Univ. of Otago (BMedSci; MB, ChB); Univ. of Birmingham (MD). Qual. in medicine, Dunedin, 1955; hosp. and gen. practice experience, Auckland, 1956–58; postgrad. trng, RPMS, London, 1959–60; Queen Elizabeth Hosp. and Univ. of Birmingham, 1960–62; Med. Res. Fellowships, Auckland, 1962–68; Sen. Lectr, Univ. of Otago, based on Auckland Hosp., 1969–72; University of Auckland: Sen. Lectr, 1970–72; Associate Prof., 1973–75; Hd, Dept of Medicine, the Univ.'s Sch. of Medicine, 1979–87. Pres., Royal Soc. of NZ, 1998–2000. Res. interests in lipoprotein metabolism, arterial disease, human nutrition, med. econs and educn, professional ethics. *Publications:* (first author/co-author) articles in sci./med. jls and in press, on aspects of coronary artery disease, atherosclerosis, lipoprotein metabolism, human nutrition, ethical issues. *Recreations:* music, pottery, gardening. *Address:* 64 Temple Street, Meadowbank, Auckland 5, New Zealand. *T:* (9) 5215384.

SCOTT, Primrose Smith; Head of Quality Review, Institute of Chartered Accountants of Scotland, since 1999; Senior Partner, The McCabe Partnership (formerly Primrose McCabe & Co.), 1987–99; *b* 21 Sept. 1940. *Educ:* Ayr Acad. Trained with Stewart Gilmour, Ayr; qualified as CA, 1963; joined Romanes & Munro, Edinburgh, 1964; progressed through manager ranks to Partner, Deloitte Haskins & Sells, 198–87; set up own practice, Linlithgow, 1987; moved practice to Edinburgh, 1997. Dep. Chm., Dunfermline Building Soc., 1998–; non-exec. Dir, Northern Venture Trust PLC, 1995–. Pres., Institute of Chartered Accountants of Scotland, 1994–95. Hon. Treas., Hospitality Industry Trust Scotland, 199–. Fellow, SCOTVEC, 1994. *Recreation:* walking three dogs in Scottish Borders. *Address:* The Cleugh, Redpath, Earlston, Berwicks TD4 6AD. *T:* (01896) 849042.

SCOTT, Sheriff Richard John Dinwoodie; Sheriff of Lothian and Borders at Edinburgh, since 1986; *b* 28 May 1939; *s* of late Prof. Richard Scott and Mary Ellen Maclachlan; *m* 1969, Josephine Moretta Blake; two *d*. *Educ:* Edinburgh Academy; Univ. of Edinburgh (MA, LLB) (Vans Dunlop Schol. in Evidence and Pleading, 1963). Lektor in English, British Centre, Sweden, 1960–61; Tutor, Faculty of Law, Univ. of Edinburgh, 1964–72; admitted to Faculty of Advocates, 1965; Standing Jun. Counsel to Min. of Defence (Air) in Scotland, 1968–77. Sheriff of Grampian, Highland and Islands, at Aberdeen and Stonehaven, 1977–86. Chm., Scottish Assoc. for Study of Delinquency, 1996– (Chm., Aberdeen Branch, 1978–86, Edinburgh Branch, 1993–96); Mem., Working Party on Offenders aged 16–18, 1991–93; Chm., Grampian Victim Support Scheme, 1983–86; Vice Pres., Sheriffs' Assoc., 2001– (Mem. Council, 1979–82 and 1994–); Mem., Sheriff Court Rules Council, 1995–98. Hon. Lectr, Univ. of Aberdeen, 1980–86. *Publications:* various articles in legal jls. *Recreations:* golf, curling, traditional music of Scotland. *Address:* Sheriff Court House, 27 Chambers Street, Edinburgh EH1 1LB.

SCOTT, Ridley; film director; *b* S Shields, 30 Nov. 1937. *Educ:* Royal Coll. of Art. *Films include:* The Duellists, 1976; Alien, 1978; Blade Runner, 1980; Someone to Watch over Me, 1987; Black Rain, 1989; Thelma and Louise, 1991; 1492: Conquest of Paradise, 1992; White Squall, 1996; GI Jane, 1997; Gladiator, 2000; Hannibal, 2001. *Address:* Scott Free, 42–44 Beak Street, W1R 3DA. *T:* (020) 7437 3163.

SCOTT, Robert Avisson; Group Chief Executive, CGNU (formerly CGU) plc, 1998–2001; *b* 6 Jan. 1942; *s* of Robert Milligan Scott and Phyllis Winifred Scott; *m* 1979, Joanne Rose Adams; two *d*. *Educ:* Scots Coll., Wellington, NZ. Associate: Australian Ins. Inst.; Ins. Inst. NZ. South British Insurance Co. Ltd, later NZI Corp. Ltd, then General Accident plc, subseq. CGU plc, then CGNU plc, 1959–2001: Asst Gen. Manager, NZ, 1981–83; Australia: Asst Gen. Manager, 1983–85; Gen. Manager, 1985–87; Chief Gen. Manager, 1987–90; Dep. Gen. Manager, UK, 1990–91, Gen. Manager, 1991–94; Dep. Chief Exec., 1994–96; Gp Chief Exec., 1996 98. Dir, Royal Bank of Scotland plc, 2001–. *Recreations:* sporting interests, walking, do it yourself. *Address:* Axford Lodge, Axford, Hants RG25 2DZ. *T:* (01256) 389259.

SCOTT, Sir Robert (David Hillyer), Kt 1994; Chairman, Greenwich Peninsula Partnership, since 2001; Chief Executive, Liverpool Culture Co., since 2000; *b* 22 Jan. 1944; *s* of Sir David (Aubrey) Scott, *qv*; *m* 1st, 1972, Su Dalgleish (marr. diss. 1995); two *s* one *d*; 2nd, 1995, Alicia Tomalino; two step *d*. *Educ:* Haileybury; Merton Coll., Oxford (Pres., OUDS, 1965–66). Actor, 1966–67; Administrator: 69 Theatre Co., Manchester, 1968–74; Royal Exchange Theatre Trust, 1974–77; Man. Dir, Manchester Theatres Ltd, 1978–96; Chairman: Manchester Olympic Bid Cttee, 1985–93; Manchester Commonwealth Games Bid Cttee, 1993–95; Chief Exec., Greenwich Millennium Trust, 1995–2001. Mem., Central Manchester Develt Corp., 1988–96. Special Projects Dir, Apollo Leisure Gp, 1994–99. Chairman: Cornerhouse Manchester, 1984–95; Granada Foundn, 1993–; Piccadilly Radio, 1993–2001; Tour East London, 1998–2001; S London Econ. Develt Alliance, 1999–; City Bars and Restaurants, 1999–; Director: Royal Exchange Theatre, 1976–94; Hallé Concerts Soc., 1989–94; White Horse Fast Ferries, 1998–; London First, 1999–. Mem. Cttee, Whitworth Art Gall., 1989–95. Chm., Bexley Heritage Trust, 1999–. DL Greater Manchester, 1988–97. Hon. RNCM 1990. Hon Fellow: Manchester Poly., 1987; UMIST, 1989. Hon. MA: Manchester, 1988; Salford, 1991. Officier de l'Ordre des Arts et des Lettres (France), 1991. *Publication:* The Biggest Room in the World, 1976. *Recreations:* food, travel, talking, sport, theatre. *Address:* 11 King William Walk, Greenwich, SE10 9JH. *T:* (020) 8305 1999.

SCOTT, Col Robert Edmond Gabriel, MBE 1959; MC 1953; Director General, Engineering Industries Association, 1981–82; *b* 3 Aug. 1920; *s* of Edmond James and Lilian Kate Scott; *m* 1942, Anna Maria Larkin; two *s*. *Educ:* Roan, Greenwich. Commissioned into Durham Light Inf., 1942; regimental service with this regt in Western Desert, Italy, Korea and Rhine Army, 1942–52; Staff duties, MoD and Eastern Comd, 1952–56; service with W African Frontier Force, 1956–60; comd inf. batt., Home Service, 1960–66; seconded to Diplomatic Service, as Defence Adviser, Lagos, 1966–70; Dep. Comd, W. Midland Dist, 1970–72; retired, 1972. Engineering Industries Association: Export Sec. and Dep. Dir, 1973–77; Dir, 1977–81. *Recreations:* rough shooting, country pursuits, philately. *Address:* Zaria, 22 Crail Close, Wokingham, Berks RG11 2PZ. *T:* (0118) 977 6595.

SCOTT, Prof. Roger Davidson, PhD; CPhys, FInstP; FRSE; Director, Scottish Universities Research and Reactor Centre, 1991–98; Professor of Nuclear Science, University of Glasgow, 1994–98; *b* 17 Dec. 1941; *s* of Alexander N. Scott and Jessie H. Scott (*née* Davidson); *m* 1965, Marion S. McCluckie; two *s* one *d*. *Educ:* Anderson Inst., Lerwick; Univ. of Edinburgh (BSc 1st Cl. Hons Physics; PhD Nuclear Physics). University Demonstrator, Univ. of Edinburgh, 1965–68; Lectr, 1968–88, Depute Dir, 1988–91, Scottish Univs Res. and Reactor Centre. FRSE 1995. *Publications:* articles on nuclear physics and envmtl radioactivity; contribs to learned jls. *Recreations:* watching football, walking wife and dogs, home maintenance. *Address:* 4 Inch Keith, East Kilbride, Glasgow G74 2JZ. *T:* (01355) 229536.

SCOTT, Roger Martin; His Honour Judge Scott; a Circuit Judge, since 1993; *b* 8 Sept. 1944; *s* of Hermann Albert and Sarah Margaret Scott; *m* 1966, Diana Elizabeth Clark; two *s* one *d*. *Educ:* Mill Hill Sch.; St Andrews Univ. (LLB). Called to the Bar, Lincoln's Inn, 1968. *Recreations:* golf, cricket, walking, theatre. *Address:* North Eastern Circuit Administrator's Office, West Riding House, Albion Street, Leeds LS1 5AA. *T:* (0113) 244 1841. *Club:* Yorkshire County Cricket (Leeds).

SCOTT, Stuart Lothian, JD; Chairman and Chief Executive Officer, Jones Lang LaSalle (formerly LaSalle Partners Inc.), since 1990; *b* 21 Aug. 1938; *s* of David G. Scott and Jean Lothian Scott; *m* 1st, 1961, Penelope Spare; four *d*; 2nd, 1971, Elizabeth Love; one *s* one *d*; 3rd, 1982, Anne O'Laughlin; one *d*. *Educ:* Hamilton Coll. (AB 1961); Northwestern Univ. Sch. of Law (JD 1964). Attorney, US Securities and Exchange Commn, 1964–67; Sen. Vice-Pres. and Dir, Arthur Rubloff & Co., 1967–73; Pres., LaSalle Partners Inc., 1973–90. *Recreations:* golf, shooting, fishing (fly), theatre, reading. *Address:* Jones Lang LaSalle, 22 Hanover Square, W1A 2BN. *T:* (020) 7399 5151. *Clubs:* Royal Troon (Scotland); Wisley (Surrey); Pine Valley (NJ); Seminole (Florida); Old Elm (Chicago); Shoreacres (Illinois).

SCOTT, Tavish Hamilton; Member (Lib Dem) Shetland, Scottish Parliament, since 1999; farmer; *b* 6 May 1966; *s* of John Hamilton Scott, *qv*; *m* 1990, Margaret McDonald; two *s* one *d*. *Educ:* Napier Coll., Edinburgh (BA Hons Business Studies). Research Asst to J. R. Wallace, MP, 1989–90; Press Officer, Scottish Lib Dem Party, 1990–92. Mem. (Lib Dem) Shetland Islands Council, 1994–99. Dep. Minister for Parlt, 2000–01. Chm., Lerwick Harbour Trust, 1996–99. *Recreations:* cinema, golf, Up Helly Aa. *Address:* Scottish Parliament, Edinburgh EH99 1SP. *T:* (0131) 348 5815.

SCOTT, Prof. Thomas Frederick McNair, MA Cantab, MD Cantab, MRCS; FRCP; Associate Director of Ambulatory Pediatrics, 1983–85, retired, now Emeritus Professor of Paediatrics, Hahnemann University (Professor of Paediatrics, 1974, Co-ordinator of Ambulatory Care Teaching, 1974–75, and Co-Director of Ambulatory Paediatrics, 1975–83, Hahnemann Medical College and Hospital); Senior Physician, The Children's Hospital of Philadelphia, 1940–69, now Physician Emeritus; *b* 18 June 1901; *e s* of Robert Frederick McNair Scott, MB, ChB (Edin.), and Alice Nystrom; *m* 1936, Mary Dwight Baker, PhD (Radcliffe), *o d* of late Clarence Dwight Baker, Wisconsin, USA; one *s* one *d*. *Educ:* Cheltenham College; Caius College, Cambridge (Scholar). Natural Science Tripos Pt I Class I, Part II (Physiology) Class II; Junior University Entrance Scholarship to St George's Hospital, 1924; Brackenbury Prize in Medicine, 1926; Qualified conjoint board, 1927; MRCP 1928; FRCP 1953; MD (Cantab) 1938; Casualty Officer, House Surgeon, House Physn, Resident Obst. Asst, Medical Registrar, at St George's Hospital, 1927–29; House Physician Queens Hospital for Children, 1930; Research Fellow of Medicine, Harvard University, Mass, USA, 1930–31; Instructor in Pædiatrics Johns Hopkins University, Baltimore, Md, USA, 1931–34; Assistant Resident Physician at Hospital of Rockefeller Institute for Medical Research, New York, USA, working on Virus diseases, 1934–36; Assistant Physician i/c of Children's Out-patients, Lecturer in Children's Diseases, at St George's Hospital, SW1, Assistant Physician at Queens Hospital for Children, E2, 1936–38; Prof. of Pediatrics, Temple Univ. Med. Sch., Philadelphia, 1938–40; Research Prof. of Pediatrics, Univ. of Pennsylvania, 1940–66, Prof. of Paediatrics, 1966–69, now Emeritus. Dist. Service Award, The Children's Hosp. of Philadelphia, 1977; Corp. medal, Hahnemann Med. Coll., 1978; Alumni Award, Children's Hosp. Alumni Orgn, 1989. Elected Faculty Mem., Medical Students' Honor Soc. (AOA), 1981. *Publications:* Papers on Cytology and Blood diseases, Lead poisoning in children, Virus diseases of the central nervous system, Herpes simplex infections, Common exanthemata, History of measles and herpes. *Address:* 2 Franklin Town Boulevard 1605, Philadelphia, PA 19103, USA.

SCOTT, Dame Thora; *see* Hird, Dame T.

SCOTT, Timothy John Whittaker; QC 1995; a Recorder, since 1999; *b* 19 July 1949; *s* of late John Dick Scott and of Helen Scott (*née* Whittaker); *m* 1982, Clare, *d* of Baron Renton, *qv*; one *s* two *d*. *Educ:* Westminster Sch. (Queen's Schol.); New Coll., Oxford (Exhibnr; MA). Journalist, 1970–72; called to the Bar, Gray's Inn, 1975; Asst Recorder, 1995–99. *Publications:* articles on family law topics in specialist jls. *Recreations:* fishing, reading, travel. *Address:* 29 Bedford Row, WC1R 4HE. *T:* (020) 7404 1044. *Club:* Garrick.

SCOTT, Sir (Walter) John, 5th Bt *cr* 1907, of Beauclerc, Bywell St Andrew, Northumberland; farmer, author, columnist and television presenter; *b* 24 Feb. 1948; *s* of

Sir Walter Scott, 4th Bt and Diana Mary (*d* 1985), *d* of J. R. Owen; *m* 1st, 1969, Lowell Patria (marr. diss. 1971), *d* of late Pat Vaughan Goddard, Auckland, NZ; one *d*; 2nd, 1977, Mary Gavin, *d* of Alexander Fairly Anderson, Gartocharn, Dunbartonshire; one *s* one *d*. *Recreations:* field sports. *Heir: s* Walter Samuel Scott, *b* 6 Dec. 1984. *Address:* Billerwell, Bonchester Bridge, Roxburghshire TD9 8JF.

SCOTT, Prof. William, RSA 1984; FRBS; Post-Graduate Course Leader, Edinburgh College of Art, 1997–2000 (Head of Sculpture, 1989–97); *b* 16 Aug. 1935; *s* of George Barclay Scott and Jeanie Stuart Scott (*née* Waugh); *m* 1961, Phyllis Owen Fisher; one *s* two *d*. *Educ:* Edinburgh Coll. of Art (DA 1959); Ecole des Beaux Arts, Paris. FRBS 1994. Prof., Heriot-Watt Univ., 1994. Contributor to: annual exhibns in Scotland; British Art Show, 1979–80; Fifth Biennial of Small Sculptures, Budapest, 1981; Chelsea Harbour Show, 1993; *one-person shows* in galleries and museums, 1971–, incl. Talbot Rice Gall., Edinburgh Univ., 1994; *public commissions* for sculpture include: St Andrews, 1970; Cumbernauld, 1980; Glasgow, 1985 and 1998; sculpture for Sir Alec Douglas-Home at The Hirsel, Coldstream, 1998; sculptures and drawings in *public collections*, including: Aberdeen Art Gall.; Royal Scottish Acad.; Kirkcaldy Gall. and Mus.; Leeds City; Edinburgh City; also work in private collections. Member: Selection Cttee for British Sch. at Rome, 1985–90; Bd of Dirs, Fruit Mkt Gall., Edinburgh, 1981–92; Chm., Scottish Arts Council Awards Panel, 1990–93. Sec., RSA, 1998–. *Recreations:* walking, reading, travel. *Address:* 45 St Clair Crescent, Roslin, Midlothian EH25 9NG. *T:* (0131) 440 2544.

SCOTT, Rear-Adm. Sir (William) David (Stewart), KBE 1977; CB 1974; *b* 5 April 1921; *y s* of Brig. H. St G. Scott, CB, DSO and bar and Ida Christabel Trower Scott (*née* Hogg); *m* 1952, Pamela Dorothy Whitlock; one *s* two *d*. *Educ:* Tonbridge. Naval Cadet, 1938; comd HM Submarines: Umbra, 1944; Vulpine, Satyr, 1945; Andrew, 1953; Thermopylae, 1955; comd HM Ships: Gateshead, 1951; Surprise, 1960; Adamant, 2nd Submarine Sqdn, 1963; Fife, 1969; Trng Comdr, BRNC, Dartmouth, 1956; Fleet Ops Officer, Home Fleet, 1958; US Naval War Coll., 1962; Dep. Dir of Defence Plans, Navy, 1965; Chief of British Navy Staff, Washington, UK Rep. to SACLANT, and Naval Attaché to USA, 1971–73; Deputy Controller, Polaris, 1973–76; Chief Polaris Executive, 1976–80, retd; Comdr 1956; Captain 1962; Rear-Adm. 1971. *Address:* c/o Lloyds TSB, Pall Mall Branch, 8–10 Waterloo Place, SW1Y 4BE.

SCOTT, (William) John (Graham); Member (C) Ayr, Scottish Parliament, since March 2000; *b* 7 June 1951; *s* of William Scott and Elizabeth Haddow Scott; *m* 1975, Charity Nadine Mary Bousfield (*d* 2000); one *s* one *d*. *Educ:* Barhill Primary Sch.; George Watson's Coll.; Edinburgh Univ. (BSc Civil Engrg 1973). Farming in family partnership, 1973–; Partner, family catering business, 1985–2000. Founder Dir, Ayshire Country Lamb Ltd, 1988–93; created Ayrshire Farmers' Mkts, 1999 (Chm., 1999–). Convenor, Hill Farming Cttee, NFU Scotland, 1993–99; Chairman: S of Scotland Regl Wool Cttee, 1996–2000; Ayrshire and Arran Farming Wildlife Adv. Gp, 1993–99. Mem., Petition Cttee, Scottish Parlt, 2000–. Chm., Hill Sheep and Native Woodland Project, Scottish Agricl Coll., 1999–. JP Girvan, 1997. Elder, Ballantrae Ch, 1985–. *Recreations:* curling, geology, bridge. *Address:* Scottish Parliament, George IV Bridge, Edinburgh EH99 1SP. *T:* (0131) 348 5664, *Fax:* (0131) 348 5938; (constituency office) 1 Wellington Square, Ayr KA7 1EN. *T:* (01292) 263991, *Fax:* (01292) 280480.

SCOTT, Rev. Preb. William Sievwright; Vicar, St Mary's, Bourne Street, SW1, since 1991; Prebendary, St Paul's Cathedral, since 2000; *b* 1 Feb. 1946; *s* of David Anderson Harper Scott and Amelia Scott (*née* Sievwright). *Educ:* Harris Acad., Dundee; Edinburgh Theol Coll. Ordained deacon 1970, priest 1971; Curate: St Ninian's, Glasgow, 1971–73; St Francis, Bridgwater, 1973–77; Rector: Shepton Beauchamp, Barrington, Puckington and Stocklinch, 1977–82; Woolavington and Cossington, 1982–84; Chaplain: Community of All Hallow's, Ditchingham, 1984–91; Priory of Our Lady of Walsingham, 1991–. Area Dean of Westminster, 1997–. *Recreations:* music making and listening, reading novels and poetry, conducting retreats. *Address:* 26 Graham Terrace, SW1W 8JH. *T:* (020) 7730 2423. *Club:* Sloane.

SCOTT, William Wootton, CB 1990; Under Secretary, Industry Department for Scotland, 1985–90; *b* 20 May 1930; *s* of Dr Archibald C. Scott and Barbara R. Scott; *m* 1958, Margaret Chandler, SRN; three *s* one *d*. *Educ:* Kilmarnock Academy; Dollar Academy; Glasgow Univ. (MA, 1st Cl. Hons History). National Service in Royal Artillery, 1952–54. Assistant Principal, 1954, Principal, 1958, Min. of Transport and Civil Aviation; Principal Private Sec. to Minister of Transport, 1965–66; Asst Sec., 1966; Regional Controller (Housing and Planning), Northern Regional Office of DoE, 1971–74; joined Scottish Development Dept, 1974, Under Sec., 1978. *Publications:* occasional historical notes. *Recreations:* historical research, music, gardening, reading. *Address:* Whitethorn, Hardgate, Castle Douglas, Kirkcudbrightshire DG7 3LD. *T:* (01556) 660200. *Club:* Royal Commonwealth Society.

SCOTT-BARRETT, Lt-Gen. Sir David (William), KBE 1976 (MBE 1956); MC 1945; GOC Scotland and Governor of Edinburgh Castle, 1976–79; Chairman, Army Cadet Force Association, 1982–96; *b* 16 Dec. 1922; 2nd *s* of late Brig. Rev. H. Scott-Barrett, CB, CBE; *m* 1st, 1948, Marie Elise (*d* 1985), *d* of late Norman Morris; three *s*; 2nd, 1992, Judith, *widow* of Major John Waring. *Educ:* Westminster School. Commnd Scots Guards, 1942; served NW Europe, 3rd Armd Bn Scots Guards; GSO3 Gds Div., 1948; Co. Comdr 2nd Bn Malaya, 1951; GSO2, 1st Div., 1955; DS Camberley, 1961; Comdt Gds Depot, 1963; GSO1, 4th Div. BAOR, 1965; comd 6 Inf. Bde BAOR, 1967; idc 1970; GOC Eastern District, 1971–73; GOC Berlin, 1973–75. Col Comdt, Scottish Div., 1976–79; Hon. Col, 205 (Scottish) Gen. Hosp., RAMC, TAVR, 1981–88. *Club:* Cavalry and Guards.

SCOTT-BOWDEN, Maj.-Gen. Logan, CBE 1972 (OBE 1964); DSO 1944; MC 1944 and Bar 1946; *b* 21 Feb. 1920; *s* of late Lt-Col Jonathan Scott-Bowden, OBE, TD, and Mary Scott-Bowden (*née* Logan); *m* 1950, Helen Jocelyn, *d* of late Major Sir Francis Caradoc Rose Price, 5th Bt, and late Marjorie Lady Price; three *s* three *d*. *Educ:* Malvern Coll.; RMA Woolwich. Commissioned Royal Engineers, 1939; served in War of 1939–45: Norway, 1940; Adjt, 53rd (Welsh) Div. RE, 1941; Liaison Duties in Canada and USA, 1942; Normandy Beach Reconnaissance Team (Major), 1943; OC 17 Fd Co RE, NW Europe, 1944; psc 1945; Singapore, Burma (Bde Maj. 98 Indian Inf. Bde), Palestine, Libya, 1946–51; Korea, 1953; jssc 1956; Arabia, 1958–60 (Lt-Col 1959); CRE 1st Div., BAOR, 1960; Head, UK Land Forces Planning Staff, 1963; Asst Dir, Def. Plans MoD (Col), 1964; Comd Trg Bde RE (Brig.), 1966; Nat. Defence Coll. (India), 1969; Comd Ulster Defence Regiment, 1970–71; Head of British Defence Liaison Staff, India, 1971–74, retd 1974. Col Comdt RE, 1975–80. *Recreations:* ski-ing, travel.

SCOTT-ELLIOT, Aydua Helen, CVO 1970 (MVO 1958); FSA; retired 1970; *b* 11 Dec. 1909; *d* of late Lewis Alexander Scott-Elliot and of Princess Eydua Odescalchi. *Educ:* St Paul's Girls' School and abroad. Temp. Asst Civilian Officer, Admty, 1941–46; Keeper of Prints and Drawings, Royal Library, Windsor Castle, 1946–69. *Publications:* articles in Burlington Magazine, Apollo, Papers of the Bibliographical Soc. of America, etc. *Club:* University Women's.

SCOTT-GALL, Anthony Robert Gall; His Honour Judge Scott-Gall; a Circuit Judge, since 1996; *b* 30 March 1946; *s* of Robert and Daphne Scott-Gall; *m* 1973, Caroline Anne Scott; one *s* one *d*. *Educ:* Stowe Sch.; New Coll., Oxford (BA). Called to the Bar, Middle Temple, 1971; Recorder, 1993. *Recreations:* cricket, Rugby football, gardening, travel, ornithology, history, music. *Address:* 3 Temple Gardens, Temple, EC4Y 9AU. *T:* (020) 7353 3102. *Clubs:* Richmond Football; Armadillos Cricket.

SCOTT-JAMES, Anne Eleanor, (Lady Lancaster); author and journalist; *b* 5 April 1913; *d* of R. A. Scott-James and Violet Brooks; *m* 2nd, 1944, Macdonald Hastings (marr. diss.; he *d* 1982); one *s* one *d*; 3rd, 1967, Sir Osbert Lancaster, CBE (*d* 1986). *Educ:* St Paul's Girls' Sch.; Somerville Coll., Oxford (Class. Schol.). Editorial staff of Vogue, 1934–41; Woman's Editor, Picture Post, 1941–45; Editor, Harper's Bazaar, 1945–51; Woman's Editor, Sunday Express, 1953–57; Woman's Adviser to Beaverbrook Newspapers, 1959–60; Columnist, Daily Mail, 1960–68; freelance journalist, broadcasting, TV, 1968–. Member: Council, RCA, 1948–51, 1954–56; Council, RHS, 1978–82. *Publications:* In the Mink, 1952; Down to Earth, 1971; Sissinghurst: The Making of a Garden, 1975; (with Osbert Lancaster) The Pleasure Garden, 1977; The Cottage Garden, 1981; (with Christopher Lloyd) Glyndebourne—the Gardens, 1983; The Language of the Garden: a personal anthology, 1984; (introd.) Our Village, by Mary Russell Mitford, 1987; The Best Plants for your Garden, 1988; (with Ray Desmond) The British Museum Book of Flowers, 1989; (with Clare Hastings) Gardening Letters to My Daughter, 1990; Sketches from a Life (autobiog.), 1993. *Recreations:* reading, gardening, travelling, looking at churches and flowers. *Address:* 78 Cheyne Court, Royal Hospital Road, SW3 5TT.

See also M. M. Hastings.

SCOTT-JOYNT, Rt Rev. Michael Charles; *see* Winchester, Bishop of.

SCOTT-MALDEN, (Charles) Peter, CB 1966; retired civil servant; *b* 29 June 1918; *e s* of late Gilbert Scott Scott-Malden and Phyllis Dorothy Scott-Malden (*née* Wilkinson); *m* 1941, Jean Honor Chamberlain Silver, *yr d* of late Lt-Col J. P. Silver, CBE, DSO, RAMC; two *s* two *d*. *Educ:* Winchester Coll. (Schol.); King's College, Cambridge (major Scholar). Entered Ministry of Transport, 1939. War of 1939–45; RAMC 1940–41; Glider Pilot Regiment, 1942–45. Min. of Transport (later DoE): Asst Sec., 1949; Under-Sec., 1959; Dep. Sec., 1968, retired, 1976. Member: Transport Tribunal, 1978–88; Management Cttee, Hanover Housing Assoc., 1978–93; Nat. Exec. Cttee, Abbeyfield Soc., 1983–90. *Recreations:* music, watching golf. *Address:* 18A Tower Road, Tadworth, Surrey KT20 5QY. *T:* (01737) 215644.

SCOTT-MALDEN, Peter; *see* Scott-Malden, C. P.

SCOTT-SMITH, Catharine Mary, MA Cantab; Principal of Beechlawn Tutorial College, Oxford, 1966–71, retired; *b* 4 April 1912; *d* of Edward Montagu Scott-Smith and Catharine Lorance (*née* Garland). *Educ:* Wycombe Abbey School, Bucks; Girton College, Cambridge. Classics Mistress: St Katharine's School, Wantage, 1933–37; Godolphin School, Salisbury 1937–41; Classics Mistress and house-mistress, Headington School, Oxford, 1941–47, Second Mistress, 1946–47; Classics Mistress and house-mistress, Wycombe Abbey School, Bucks, 1947–55, Second Mistress, 1951–54; Headmistress of Westonbirt School, Tetbury, Gloucestershire, 1955–64. Member Council: Berkhamsted School for Girls; Berkhamsted School; Mem. Exec. Cttee, GBGSA, 1975–78. Pres., Wycombe Abbey School Seniors, 1974–79. *Club:* University Women's.

SCOTT WHYTE, Stuart; *see* Whyte.

SCOTT WRIGHT, Prof. Margaret, PhD; Dean, 1979–84, and Professor, 1979–86, now Emeritus, Faculty of Nursing, University of Calgary; *b* 10 Sept. 1923; *d* of Ebenezer Wright and Margaret Greig Masson. *Educ:* Wallington County Grammar Sch.; Univ. of Edinburgh; St George's and Queen Charlotte's Hosps, London. MA Hons Hist., PhD and Dipl. Med. Services Admin, Edinburgh; SRN and SCM. Research Asst, Unilever Ltd, 1947–50; Student Nurse, St George's Hosp., 1950–53; Student Midwife, Queen Charlotte's Hosp. and E Sussex CC, 1954–55; Staff Nurse and Sister, St George's Hosp., London, 1955–57; Boots Research Fellow in Nursing, Dept of Social Medicine, Univ. of Edinburgh, 1957–61; Rockefeller Fellow, USA, 1961–62; Deputy Matron, St George's Hosp., 1962–64; Matron, Middlesex Hosp., 1965–68; Dir, Dept of Nursing Studies, Univ. of Edinburgh, 1968–71; Prof. of Nursing Studies, Univ. of Edinburgh, 1972–76; Dir and Prof. of Sch. of Nursing, Dalhousie Univ., Nova Scotia, 1976–79. Second Vice-Pres., Internat. Council of Nurses, 1973–77. Margaret Scott Wright Annual Lecture in Nursing Research established in Faculty of Nursing, Univ. of Alberta, 1984. Silver Jubilee Medal, 1977. *Publications:* Experimental Nurse Training at Glasgow Royal Infirmary, 1963; Student Nurses in Scotland, 1968. *Recreations:* walking, music, reading, travel. *Address:* 7 Noverre House, Theatre Street, Norwich NR2 1RG.

SCOULLER, (John) Alan; Head of Industrial Relations, Midland Bank Group, 1975–88; Visiting Professor in Industrial Relations, Kingston University (formerly Kingston Polytechnic), 1988–95; Senior Visiting Fellow, City University Business School, 1989–92; *b* 23 Sept. 1929; *e s* of late Charles James Scouller and Mary Helena Scouller; *m* 1954, Angela Geneste Ambrose; two *s* five *d*. *Educ:* John Fisher Sch., Purley. Army service, Queen's Own Royal W Kent Regt, 1948–58 (Captain). Joined Unilever as management trainee, 1958; Personnel Man., Wall's Ice Cream, 1959–62; Domestos, 1963–66; Holpak, 1966–68; Commercial Plastics and Holpak, 1968–69; left Unilever to join Commn on Industrial Relations, 1969; Dir of Industrial Relations until 1973, full-time Comr, 1973–74. Member: Employment Appeal Tribunal, 1976–2000; Educn Bd, RC Dio. of Westminster, 1990–. FIPD. Governor, Letchworth Garden City Heritage Foundn, 1995–. KSG 1996. *Recreations:* studying employment law, walking, listening to music, looking after grandchildren, cricket. *Address:* Walnut Cottage, 33 Field Lane, Letchworth, Herts SG6 3LD. *T:* (01462) 682781.

SCOURFIELD, Edward Grismond Beaumont D.; *see* Davies-Scourfield.

SCOURSE, Rear-Adm. Frederick Peter, CB 1997; MBE 1972; FREng, FIEE; Nuclear Weapons Safety Advisor, Ministry of Defence, since 1997; Senior Consultant, Devonport Management Ltd, since 1998; Maritime Capability Advisor, Thales; *b* 23 June 1944; *s* of Frederick David John Scourse and late Margaret Elaine Scourse; *m* 1967, Nicolette Jean Somerville West; one *s*. *Educ:* Wells Cathedral Sch.; RN Coll., Dartmouth; Churchill Coll., Cambridge (MA Mech Sci, Elect. Sci). Served HM Ships: Dido, 1963–64; Warspite, 1969–72; Renown, 1974–77; MoD (PE), 1979–82; NDC, 1982–83; MoD (PE), 1983–89; Dir-Gen., Surface Weapons (Navy), 1989–94; Dir-Gen., Surface Ships, 1994–97; Actg Controller of the Navy, 1996–97. Industry Advr, Churchill Coll., Cambridge, 1998–. Vice Chm., Regular Forces Employment Assoc., 1998–. FREng 2000. *Recreations:* fly fishing, singing. *Address:* Valley View, 278a Turleigh, Bradford on Avon BA15 2HH. *Club:* Royal Commonwealth Society.

SCOWCROFT, Gen. Brent, Hon. KBE 1993; President, Forum for International Policy, since 1993; *b* 19 March 1925; *s* of James Scowcroft and Lucile (*née* Ballantyne); *m* 1951,

Marian (Jackie) Horner (*d* 1995); one *d*. *Educ:* Ogden City Schs; US Mil. Acad.; Columbia Univ. (MA 1953; PhD 1967); Lafayette Coll.; Georgetown Univ. Joined Army 1943; qualified pilot 1948; Prof. of Russian History, US Mil. Acad., 1953–57; service in Washington, Yugoslavia, Colorado, Western Hemisphere Region; with Jt Chiefs of Staff, 1970; MA to President, 1972–73; Dep. Asst, 1973–75, and Asst 1975–77 and 1989–93, to successive Presidents, for Nat. Security Affairs; retired from mil. service, 1975; Dir, Council on Foreign Relations, 1983–89; served on major US cttees, commns and bds, 1977–89. Vice-Chm., Kissinger Associates, 1982–89. Chm., CSIS/Pacific Forum, 1993–. Mem. Bd of Visitors, USAF Acad., 1993–. US Medal of Freedom, 1991; numerous Service medals and awards. *Recreation:* ski-ing. *Address:* 6114 Wynnwood Road, Bethesda, MD 20816, USA. *T:* (301) 2291986.

SCOWEN, Sir Eric (Frank), Kt 1973; MD, DSc; FRCP, FRCS, FRCPE, FRCPath, FRPharmS, FRCGP; Director, Medical Professorial Unit, 1955–75; Physician to St Bartholomew's Hospital, 1946–75; Professor of Medicine, University of London, 1961–75 (Reader in Medicine, 1938–61); *b* 22 April 1910; *s* of late Frank Edward Scowen and Eleanor Betsy (*née* Barnes) (*d* 1969). *Educ:* City of London School; St Bartholomew's Hospital Medical College (MD 1935, DSc 1962, London); MA KCL 1988. FRCP 1941; FRCS 1960; FRCPE 1965; FRCPath 1965; FRPharmS 1984; FRCGP 1989. St Bartholomew's Hospital: House Physician, 1931, Second Assistant, 1933, to Medical Professorial Unit; Baly Research Fell. in Clin. Med., 1933; First Asst to Med. Professorial Unit, 1935; Asst Dir of Med. Prof. Unit, and Asst Phys, 1937; Rockefeller Research Fell. to Columbia Univ., New York, 1937. Chairman: Council, Imperial Cancer Research Fund, 1967–82 (Vice-Pres., 1982); British Pharmacopœia Commission, 1963–69; Cttee on Safety of Medicines (formerly Cttee on Safety of Drugs), 1969–80 (Mem., 1963); Cttee on the Review of Medicines, 1975–78; Poisons Bd (Home Office), 1976–83. Chm. Council, Sch. of Pharmacy, Univ. of London, 1979–88 (Hon. Fellow, 1986). FKC 2000. FRSA 2000. Hon. LLD Nottingham, 1979. *Publications:* various in medical and scientific journals. *Address:* Flat 77, 6/9 Charterhouse Square, EC1M 6EX. *T:* (020) 7251 3212. *Club:* Athenæum.

SCRAFTON, Douglas, CMG 1998; HM Diplomatic Service; Foreign Secretary's Special Representative for the Great Lakes region, since 2000; *b* 14 July 1949; *s* of late Douglas Scrafton and of Irene Hilda Kirk (formerly Scrafton, *née* Hammett); *m* 1975, Carolyn Patricia Collison; one *s* one *d*. Joined FCO, 1967; Mem., UK Delegn (later UK Perm. Repn) to EC, 1970–73; Kampala, 1973–74; Mbabane, 1975–77; FCO, 1977–80; Jedda, 1980–82; British Liaison Office, Riyadh, 1982–84; Cairo, 1984–85; FCO, 1985–87; on loan to Cabinet Office, 1987–88; Ottawa, 1989–92; FCO, 1992–94; Ambassador: to Yemen Republic, 1995–97; to Democratic Republic of the Congo, 1998–2000. *Recreations:* photography, reading, gardening. *Address:* c/o Foreign and Commonwealth Office, King Charles Street, SW1A 2AH.

SCRASE-DICKINS, Mark Frederick Hakon, CMG 1991; HM Diplomatic Service, retired; *b* 31 May 1936; *s* of late Alwyne Rory Macnamara Scrase-Dickins and Ingeborg Oscara Frederika Scrase-Dickins; *m* 1969, Martina Viviane Bayley; one *s* one *d* (and one *d* decd). *Educ:* Eton Coll.; RMA, Sandhurst. Commnd Rifle Bde (later Royal Green Jackets), 1956; Malaya, 1956–57 (despatches); ADC to GOC Ghana Army, 1958–59; ADC to Chief of Imperial Gen. Staff, 1959–60; SE Asia, 1962–65; Army Staff Coll., 1967; Hong Kong, 1968–70; transferred to FCO, 1973; Vientiane, 1975; Muscat, 1976; Counsellor: Jakarta, 1983; Riyadh, 1990. *Recreation:* field sports. *Address:* Coolhurst Grange, Horsham, West Sussex RH13 6LE. *T:* (01403) 252416. *Clubs:* White's, Beefsteak, Special Forces.

SCREECH, Rev. Prof. Michael Andrew, FBA 1981; FRSL; Extraordinary Fellow, Wolfson College, Oxford, since 1993; Fellow and Chaplain, All Souls College, Oxford, since 2001 (Senior Research Fellow, 1984–93); *b* 2 May 1926; 3rd *s* of Richard John Screech, MM and Nellie Screech (*née* Maunder); *m* 1956, Anne (*née* Reeve); three *s*. *Educ:* Sutton High Sch., Plymouth; University Coll. London (BA (1st cl. Hons) 1950; Fellow, 1982); University of Montpellier, France; Oxford Ministry Course. DLitt Birmingham, 1959; DLit London, 1982; DLitt Oxon 1990. Other Rank, Intelligence Corps (mainly Far East), 1944–48. Asst, UCL, 1950–51; Birmingham Univ.: Lectr, 1951–58; Sen. Lectr., 1959–61; UCL: Reader, 1961–66; Personal Chair of French, 1966–71; Fielden Prof. of French Language and Lit., London Univ., 1971–84. Ordained deacon, 1993, priest, 1994; Asst Curate (NSM), St Giles with St Philip, and St James with St Margaret, Oxford, 1993–. Visiting Professor: Univ. of Western Ontario, 1964–65; Univ. of New York, Albany, 1968–69; Johnson Prof., Inst. for Research in the Humanities, Madison, Wisconsin, 1978–79; Vis. Fellow, All Souls, Oxford, 1981; Edmund Campion Lectr, Regina, 1985; Wiley Vis. Prof., N Carolina, 1986; Professeur, Collège de France, 1989; Prof. Associé, Paris IV (Sorbonne), 1990; Leverhulme Emeritus Fellow, 1995–98. Member: Cttee, Warburg Inst., 1970–84; Comité d'Humanisme et Renaissance, 1971–; Comité de parrainage des Classiques de l'Humanisme, 1988–; Corresponding Member: Société Historique de Genève, 1988; Acad. des Inscriptions et Belles Lettres, Paris, 2000. Hon. DLitt Exeter, 1993; Hon. D(Th.) Geneva, 1998. Chevalier dans l'Ordre National du Mérite, 1983; Médaille de la Ville de Tours, 1984; Chevalier, Légion d'Honneur, 1992. *Publications:* The Rabelaisian Marriage, 1958, rev. edn trans. French, 1992; L'Evangélisme de Rabelais, 1959, rev. edn trans. English, 1992; Tiers Livre de Pantagruel, 1964; Les épistres et évangiles de Lefèvre d'Etaples, 1964; (with John Jollife) Les Regrets et autres oeuvres poëtiques (Du Bellay), 1966; Marot évangélique, 1967; (with R. M. Calder) Gargantua, 1970; La Pantagrueline Prognostication, 1975; Rabelais, 1980, rev. edn trans. French, 1992; Ecstasy and the Praise of Folly, 1981, rev. edn trans. French, 1991; Montaigne and Melancholy, 1983, rev. edn trans. French, 1992; (prefaces) Erasmus' Annotations on the New Testament (ed Anne Reeve): The Gospels, 1986, Acts, Romans, I and II Corinthians, 1990, Galatians—Revelation, 1993; (ed trans.) Montaigne, An Apology for Raymond Sebond, 1987; (with Stephen Rawles *et al.*) A New Rabelais Bibliography: editions before 1626, 1987; (ed trans.) The Essays of Montaigne, 1991; Some Renaissance Studies, ed. M. Heath, 1992; Clément Marot: a Renaissance poet discovers the Gospel, 1994; Monumental Inscriptions in All Souls College, Oxford, 1997; Laughter at the Foot of the Cross, 1998; Montaigne's Copy of Lucretius, 1998; *edited reprints:* Le Nouveau Testament de Lefèvre d'Etaples, 1970; F. de Billon: Le Fort inexpugnable de l'Honneur du Sexe Femenin, 1970; Opuscules d'Amour par Héroët et autres divins poëtes, 1970; Amyot: Les œuvres morales et meslées de Plutarque, 1971; Warden Mocket of All Souls: Doctrina et Politia Ecclesiae Anglicanae, 1995. *Recreation:* walking. *Address:* 5 Swanston-field, Whitchurch-on-Thames RG8 7HP. *T:* and *Fax:* (0118) 984 2513. *Clubs:* Athenæum; Pangbourne Working Men's.

SCREECH, Rt Rev. Royden; *see* St Germans, Bishop Suffragan of.

SCRIMSHAW, Frank Herbert; *b* 25 Dec. 1917; *s* of late John Leonard Scrimshaw and Jessie Scrimshaw (*née* Sewell), Lincoln; *m* 1950, Joan Olive, *d* of Leslie Stephen Paskall, Felixstowe; one *s*. *Educ:* The City Sch., Lincoln; University Coll., Nottingham. BSc London. Joined Scientific Civil Service, 1939; various posts at RAE, Farnborough, and Blind Landing Experimental Unit, RAF Martlesham Heath, 1939–58; Dir of Scientific Research (Electronics), Min. of Aviation, 1959–61; RRE, Malvern: Head of Guided Weapons Group, 1961–65; Head of Mil. and Civil Systems Dept, 1965–67; Dir Gen., Electronics R&D, Min. of Technology, later MoD, 1967–72; Dep. Dir, RAE, Farnborough, 1972–78, retired. *Address:* 53 Feoffees Road, Somersham, near Huntingdon, Cambs PE28 3JQ. *T:* (01487) 840143.

SCRIVEN, Rt Rev. Henry William; *see* Gilbraltar in Europe, Suffragan Bishop of.

SCRIVEN, Pamela; QC 1992; a Recorder, since 1996; *b* 5 April 1948; *d* of Maurice Scriven and Evelyn Scriven (*née* Stickney); *m* 1973; two *s*. *Educ:* University College London (LLB Hons). Called to the Bar, Inner Temple, 1970 (Bencher, 1995). Chm., Family Law Bar Assoc., 1999–. *Address:* 1 King's Bench Walk, Temple, EC4Y 7DB. *T:* (020) 7583 6266.

SCRIVEN, Wilton Maxwell, AO 1983; Member, Council on the Ageing (Chairman, Seniors Week Committee); *b* 10 Dec. 1924; *m* 1948, Marjorie Reta Shaw; two *s* two *d*. *Educ:* Univ. of Adelaide. BSc; FIEAust. Flying Officer RAAF; served with RAF Sqdn 622 Mildenhall, 1943–45. Engr, PMG's Dept, 1946–64; Regional Dir, Dept of Trade, 1965–66; Chm., Australian Industrial Research and Develt Grants Bd, 1967–68; Dir of Industrial Develt, S Australian Govt, 1969–76; Agent General for S Australia in London, 1977–80; Dir Gen., S Aust. Dept of Premier and Cabinet, 1980–83; Dir Gen., Dept of Lands, SA, 1983–84. Mem. Bd, Investigator Sci. and Technol. Centre, 1992–. *Recreations:* tennis, golf, flute. *Address:* 7 Knightsbridge Road, Leabrook, SA 5068, Australia. *Clubs:* Royal Over-Seas League; Kensington Gardens Tennis (Australia).

SCRIVENER, Anthony Frank Bertram; QC 1975; a Recorder of the Crown Court, 1976–92; *b* 31 July 1935; *s* of late Frank Bertram Scrivener and of Edna Scrivener; *m* 1964, Irén Becze (marr. diss.); one *s* one *d*; *m* 1993, Ying Hui Tan. *Educ:* Kent Coll., Canterbury; University Coll. London (LLB). Called to Bar, Gray's Inn, 1958 (Holt Scholar); Bencher, Lincoln's Inn, 1985. Lectr in Law, Ghana, 1959–61; practice as Junior, 1961–75. Chm., Gen. Council of Bar, 1991 (Vice-Chm., 1990). *Recreations:* tennis, chess, cricket, car racing, taking the dog for a walk. *Address:* 2–3 Gray's Inn Square, WC1R 5JH.

SCRIVENER, Christiane; Commandeur de la Légion d'Honneur, 2001 (Officier, 1995); Médiateur, Société Générale, since 1996; Member, Commission of the European Communities, 1989–95; *b* 1 Sept. 1925; *m* 1944, Pierre Scrivener; one *s* decd. *Educ:* Lycée de Grenoble; Faculté de lettres et de droit de Paris. Dip. Psychol.; Dip. Harvard Business Sch. Directeur Général: l'Assoc. pour l'organisation des Stages en France, 1958–69; l'Assoc. pour l'organisation des missions de coopération technique, 1961–69; l'Agence pour la coopération technique industrielle et économique, 1969–76; Sec. d'Etat à la Consommation, 1976–78; Pres., la Commission chargée d'étudier les problèmes éthiques de la publicité, 1978; Sec. Gen. Adj. du parti républicain, 1978–79; Mem., Parlement européen (UDF), 1979–89; Mem., Conseil d'admin des Assurances Générales de France, 1986–89. Alumni Achievement Award (Harvard Business Sch.), 1976. Officier, Polonia Restituta, 1968; Médaille d'Or du Mérite Européen, 1990; Grand Croix de l'Ordre de Léopold II (Belgium), 1995; Grand Croix de Mérite du Grand Duché de Luxembourg, 1996. *Publications:* L'Europe, une bataille pour l'avenir, 1984; (pour les enfants) L'histoire du Petit Troll, 1986. *Recreations:* ski-ing, tennis, classical music. *Address:* 21 avenue Robert-Schumann, 92100 Boulogne-Billancourt, France.

SCRIVER, Prof. Charles Robert, CC 1997 (OC 1986); GOQ 1997; FRS 1991; FRSC 1973; Alva Professor of Human Genetics, since 1994, Professor of Pediatrics, Faculty of Medicine, and Professor of Biology, Faculty of Science, since 1969, McGill University, Montreal; *b* 7 Nov. 1930; *s* of Walter DeMoulpied Scriver and Jessie Marion (*née* Boyd); *m* 1956, Esther Katherine Peirce; two *s* two *d*. *Educ:* McGill Univ., Montreal (BA *cum laude* 1951, MD, CM *cum laude* 1955). Intern, Royal Victoria Hosp., Montreal, 1955–56; Resident: Royal Victoria and Montreal Children's Hosps, 1956–57; Children's Med. Center, Boston, 1957–58; McLaughlin Travelling Fellow, UCL, 1958–60; Chief Resident in Pediatrics, Montreal Children's Hosp., 1960–61; Asst, Associate Prof., Pediatrics, 1961–69, Markle Schol., 1962–67, McGill Univ. Rutherford Lectr, RSCan, 1983. Associate, 1968–95, Dist. Scientist, 1995–, MRC; Dir, MRC Gp (Med. Genetics), 1982–94; Associate Dir, Can. Genetic Diseases Networks (Centers of Excellence), 1989–98. President: Can. Soc. Clinical Investigation, 1974–75; Soc. Pediatric Res., 1975–76; Amer. Soc. Human Genetics, 1986–87; Amer. Pediatric Soc., 1994–95. FAAAS 1992; Member: Amer. Soc. Clinical Investigation; Assoc. Amer. Physicians; Hon. Member: Brit. Paediatric Assoc.; Soc. Française de Pédiatrie. Wood Gold Medal, McGill Univ., 1955; Mead Johnson Award, 1968, Borden Award 1973, Amer. Acad. Pediatrics; Borden Award, Nutrition Soc. Can., 1969; Allan Award, Amer. Soc. Human Genetics, 1978; G. Malcolm Brown Award, Can. Soc. Clin. Invest., 1979; Gairdner Internat. Award, Gairdner Foundn, 1979; McLaughlin Medal, RSC, 1981; Ross Award, Can. Pediatric Soc., 1990; Award of Excellence, Genetic Soc. of Canada, 1992; Prix du Québec (Wilder Penfield), 1995; Lifetime Achievement Award in Genetics, Birth Defects Foundn, 1997. *Publications:* (jtly) Amino Acid Metabolism and its Disorders, 1973; (ed) The Metabolic Basis of Inherited Disease, 6th edn 1986, 7th edn as The Metabolic and Molecular Bases of Inherited Disease, 1995, 8th edn 2001; numerous res. pubns. *Recreations:* history, music, photography, literature. *Address:* McGill University—Montreal Children's Hospital Research Institute, 2300 Tupper Street, Montreal, QC H3H 1P3, Canada. *T:* (514) 9344418, *Fax:* (514) 9344329; *e-mail:* cscriv@po-box.mcgill.ca; (home) 232 Strathearn N, Montreal West, QC H4X 1Y2, Canada. *T:* (514) 4860742.

SCROGGIE, Alan Ure Reith, CBE 1973 (OBE 1961); QPM 1968; one of HM's Inspectors of Constabulary 1963–75; *b* 1912; *s* of late Col W. R. J. Scroggie, CIE, IMS, Callander, Perthshire; *m* 1940, Shiela Catherine, *d* of late Finlay Mackenzie, Elgin, Morayshire; two *s*. *Educ:* Cargilfield Preparatory Sch.; Fettes Coll.; Edinburgh Univ. (BL). Joined Edinburgh City Police, 1930; Asst Chief Constable of Bucks, 1947–53; Chief Constable of Northumberland, 1953–63. OStJ 1955. *Recreations:* golf, country pursuits, gardening. *Address:* Fowler's Cottage, Abercrombie, by St Monans, Anstruther, Fife KY10 2DE. *Clubs:* Royal and Ancient (St Andrews); Golf House (Elie).

SCROGGS, Cedric Annesley; Chief Executive, Fisons plc, 1992–93; *b* 2 Jan. 1941; *s* of Richard B. H. Scroggs and Vera Wesley Shutte (*née* Coombs); *m* 1964, Patricia Mary Sutherland Ogg; two *s* one *d*. *Educ:* Reading Sch.; St John's Coll., Oxford (Sir Thos White Scholar; BA 1962). Marketing posts: AEI-Hotpoint Ltd, 1962–67; General Foods Ltd, 1967–73; Cadbury Ltd, 1973–76 (Mkting Dir, 1974–76); Mkting Dir, Leyland Cars, 1976–78; Fisons plc: Man. Dir, Scientific Equipment Div., 1979–81; Dir and Div. Chm., 1981. Dep. Chm., Sarginsons plc, 1999–; non-executive Director: Caradon plc, 1988–89; Montpellier Group plc (formerly Y. J. Lovell (Hldgs) plc, then YJL plc), 1990– (Chm., 1999–); Hillingdon Hosp. NHS Trust, 1991–92; Genus plc, 1994–2000 (Dep. Chm., 1995–2000); Huntsworth (formerly Holmes & Marchant Gp) plc, 1997–2000. Advr, Müller Gp, 1997–. Dir, Oxfordshire Mental Healthcare NHS Trust, 1995–2001; Chm., SE Oxon Primary Care Trust, 2001–. President: BEAMA, 1991–92; CBI Nat. Mfg Council, 1992–94; Mem., Milk Mktg Bd, 1991–94. Vis. Fellow, Nuffield Coll., Oxford,

1993. *Recreations:* boating, golf, diving. *Address:* Sotwell Priory, Wallingford, Oxon OX10 0RH. *Clubs:* Royal Automobile; Leander (Henley); Goring and Streatley Golf (Oxon).

SCRUBY, Ven. Ronald Victor, MA; Archdeacon of Portsmouth, 1977–85, now Emeritus; *b* 23 Dec. 1919; 6th *s* of late Thomas Henry Scruby and late Florence Jane Scruby, Norwood Green, Southall, Middx; *m* 1955, Sylvia Tremayne Miles (*d* 1995), *e d* of late Rear-Adm. Roderic B. T. Miles, Trotton, Sussex; two *s* one *d*. *Educ:* Southall Technical Coll.; Trinity Hall, Cambridge. Engineering Apprentice, London Transport, 1936–39. Royal Engineers, 1939–45; Capt. 1943. Trinity Hall, Cambridge, 1945–48; Cuddesdon Coll., Oxford, 1948–50. Asst Curate, Rogate, Sussex, 1950–53; Chaplain, King Edward VII Hosp., Midhurst, 1950–53; Chaplain, Saunders-Roe, Osborne, E Cowes, 1953–58; Vicar of Eastney, Portsmouth, 1958–65; Rural Dean of Portsmouth, 1960–65; Archdeacon of the Isle of Wight, 1965–77. *Address:* Church House, Rogate, Petersfield, Hants GU31 5EA. *T:* (01730) 821784.

SCRUTON, Prof. Roger Vernon; writer and philosopher; *b* 27 Feb. 1944; *s* of John Scruton and Beryl C. Haynes; *m* 1st, 1973, Danielle Laffitte (marr. diss. 1979); 2nd, 1996, Sophie Jeffreys; one *s* one *d*. *Educ:* Jesus Coll., Cambridge (MA, PhD). Called to the Bar, Inner Temple, 1978. Res. Fellow, Peterhouse, 1969–71; Lectr in Philosophy, Birkbeck Coll., London, 1971–79, Reader, 1979–85, Prof. of Aesthetics, 1985–92; Prof. of Philosophy, Boston Univ., Mass, 1992–95. Founder and Dir, The Claridge Press, 1987–. Editor, Salisbury Review, 1982–2000. *Publications:* Art and Imagination, 1974, 2nd edn 1982; The Aesthetics of Architecture, 1979; The Meaning of Conservatism, 1980, 3rd edn 2001; From Descartes to Wittgenstein, 1981, 2nd edn 1995; Fortnight's Anger (novel), 1981; The Politics of Culture, 1981; Kant, 1982; A Dictionary of Political Thought, 1982, 2nd edn 1996; The Aesthetic Understanding, 1983; (with Baroness Cox) Peace Studies: A Critical Survey, 1984; Thinkers of the New Left, 1985; (jtly) Education and Indoctrination, 1985; Sexual Desire, 1986; Spinoza, 1986; A Land held Hostage, 1987; Untimely Tracts, 1987; The Philosopher on Dover Beach (essays), 1990; Francesca (novel), 1991; A Dove Descending and Other Stories, 1991; (ed) Conservative Texts: an anthology, 1992; Xanthippic Dialogues (novel), 1993; Modern Philosophy, 1994; The Classical Vernacular, 1994; An Intelligent Person's Guide to Philosophy, 1996; The Aesthetics of Music, 1997; On Hunting, 1998; (ed with Anthony Barnett) Town and Country, 1998; An Intelligent Person's Guide to Modern Culture, 1998; Animal Rights and Wrongs, 2000; England: an elegy, 2000; contribs to The Times, Guardian, etc. *Recreations:* music, architecture, literature, hunting. *Address:* Sunday Hill Farm, Brinkworth, Wilts SN15 5AS.

See also E. Hodder.

SCRYMGEOUR, family name of **Earl of Dundee**.

SCRYMGEOUR, Lord; Henry David; *b* 20 June 1982; *s* and *heir* of 12th Earl of Dundee, *qv*.

SCUDAMORE, James Marfell; Chief Veterinary Officer, Department for Environment, Food and Rural Affairs (formerly Ministry of Agriculture, Fisheries and Food), since 1997; *b* 24 March 1944; *s* of Leonard John Scudamore and Joan Kathleen Scudamore; *m* 1968, Alison Ceridwen Foulkes. *Educ:* Chester City Grammar Sch.; Liverpool Univ. (BVSc 1967; BSc 1st cl. Hons 1968). Qualified as vet. surg., 1967; Dist Vet. Officer, Kenya, 1968–71; Vet. Res. Officer, Kenya, 1971–74; joined MAFF, 1974: Vet. Investigation Service, 1974–80; Divl Vet. Officer, Tolworth, 1980–84, Taunton, 1984–87; Regl Vet. Officer, S Scotland, 1987–90; Asst Chief Vet. Officer, Edinburgh, 1990–96, Tolworth (Meat Hygiene), 1996–97. *Recreations:* reading, swimming, gardening. *Address:* Department for Environment, Food and Rural Affairs, 1a Page Street, SW1P 4PQ. *T:* (020) 7904 6139.

SCUDAMORE, Peter Michael, MBE 1990; National Hunt jockey, 1979–93; in partnership with trainer, Nigel Twiston-Davies; *b* 13 June 1958; *s* of Michael and Mary Scudamore; *m* 1980, Marilyn Linda Kington; two *s*. *Educ:* Belmont Abbey, Hereford. Champion Jockey, 1981–82 and annually, 1986–93; rode for British Jump Jockeys; winners in Australia, Belgium, Germany, New Zealand, Norway; Leading Jockey, Ritz Club Charity Trophy, Cheltenham Festival, 1986; leading jockey, Cheltenham, 1986, 1987; set new record for number of winners ridden in career, 1989, for number in one season (221), 1989; rode 1,500th winner, 1992; record 1,678 wins on retirement. Racing journalist, Daily Mail, 1993–; Commentator for Nat. Hunt racing, Grandstand, BBC TV, 1993–. *Publication:* Scu: the autobiography of a champion, 1993. *Recreations:* golf, watching sport. *Fax:* (01451) 850995; *e-mail:* Peter.Scu@ic24.net.

SCUDAMORE, Richard Craig; Chief Executive, Football Association Premier League, since 1999; *b* 11 Aug. 1959; *s* of late Kenneth Ronald Scudamore and of Enid Doreen Scudamore (*née* Selman); *m* 1999, Catherine Joanne Ramsey; one *s* one *d*. *Educ:* Kingsfield Sch., Bristol; Nottingham Univ. Regl Dir, BT Yellow Pages, ITT World Directories, 1981–89; Man. Dir, Newspaper and Media Sales Ltd, Ingersoll Publications, 1989–90; Thomson Corporation: Newspaper Gp Sales and Mktg Dir, 1991–94; Asst, then Man. Dir, Scotsman Publications, 1994–95; Sen. Vice Pres., N America, 1995–98; Chief Exec. and Dir, Football League Ltd, 1998–99. *Recreations:* golf, music, children, and of course football. *Address:* FA Premier League, 11 Connaught Place, W2 2ET. *T:* (020) 7298 1607.

SCULLARD, Geoffrey Layton, OBE 1971; HM Diplomatic Service, retired; Head of Accommodation and Services Department, Foreign and Commonwealth Office, 1978–80; *b* 5 July 1922; *s* of late William Harold Scullard and late Eleanor Mary Scullard (*née* Tomkin); *m* 1945, Catherine Margaret Pinington; three *d*. *Educ:* St Olave's Grammar Sch. Joined Foreign Office, 1939. Served War (RAF Signals), 1942–46. Diplomatic service at: Stockholm, Washington, Baghdad, Los Angeles, Moscow. *Recreation:* golf. *Address:* 2 Albury Heights, 8 Albury Road, Guildford, Surrey GU1 2BT. *T:* (01483) 539915. *Clubs:* Civil Service; Bramley Golf.

SCULLY, Prof. Crispian Michael, CBE 2000; MD, PhD; FDSRCPSGlas, FFDRCSI, FDSRCS, FDSRCSE, FRCPath, FMedSci; Dean and Director of Studies and Research, Eastman Dental Institute, University of London, since 1994; Professor of Oral Medicine, Pathology and Microbiology, University of London, since 1993; Professor of Special Needs Dentistry, University College London, since 1998; *b* 24 May 1945; *s* of Patrick and Rosaleen Scully; *m* Zoitsa Boucoumani; one *d*. *Educ:* Univ. of London (BSc, BDS, PhD); Univ. of Glasgow; Univ. of Bristol (MD, MDS). MRCS; LRCP; LDS RCS; FDSRCPSGlas 1979; FFDRCSI 1983; FDSRCS 1988; FDSRCSE 1998; FRCPath 1998. MRC Research Fellow, Guy's Hosp., 1975–78; Lectr, 1979–81, Sen. Lectr, 1981–82, Univ. of Glasgow; Prof. of Stomatology, 1982–93, and Dean, 1982–92, Univ. of Bristol. Hon. Consultant: Inst. of Dental Surgery, subseq. Eastman Dental Inst., London Univ., 1993–; Great Ormond St Hosp., 1998–; Nuffield Orthopaedic Centre, Oxford, 1998–; John Radcliffe Hosp., Oxford, 1998–. Clinical Dir, UC London Hosps NHS Trust, 1995–96. Visiting Professor: Middx Univ., 1998–; UWE, 1998–. Consultant Adviser in Dental Research, DHSS, 1986–98. Member: GDC, 1984–94; Adv. Council for Misuse of Drugs, 1985–89; Chm., Central Examining Bd for Dental Hygienists, 1989–94; Member: Medicines Control Agency Cttee on Dental and Surgical Materials, 1990–93; Standing Dental Adv. Cttee, 1992–99; Adv. Cttee on Infected Health Care Workers, 1991–; Expert Adv. Cttee on Antimicrobial Resistance, 2001–. Chm. Jt Adv. Cttee, Additional Dental Specialities, 1993–99. Sec.-Gen., 1993–, and Vice-Pres., 2000–, Europ. Assoc. for Oral Medicine. Founder FMedSci 1998. Founder, Internat. Fedn of Oral Medicine, 1998. *Publications:* Medical Problems in Dentistry, 1982, 4th edn 1998; (jtly) Multiple Choice Questions in Dentistry, 1985; Handbook for Hospital Dental Surgeons, 1985; (jtly) Slide Interpretation in Oral Disease, 1986; Dental Surgery Assistants' Handbook, 1988; Colour Atlas of Stomatology, 1988, 2nd edn 1996; Colour Aids to Oral Medicine, 1988, 3rd edn 1998; The Dental Patient, 1988; The Mouth and Perioral Tissues, 1989; Patient Care: a dental surgeon's guide, 1989; (jtly) Occupational Hazards in Dentistry, 1990; (jtly) Clinic Virology in Oral Medicine and Dentistry, 1992; (jtly) Medicine and Surgery for Dentistry, 1993, 2nd edn 1999; (jtly) Colour Atlas of Oral Diseases in Children and Adolescents, 1993, 2nd edn 2001; (jtly) Colour Atlas of Oral Pathology, 1995; (jtly) Oxford Handbook of Dental Patient Care, 1998; Handbook of Oral Disease, 1999; (jtly) Dermatology of the Lips, 2000; ABC of Oral Health, 2000; 700 contribs to learned jls. *Recreations:* music, skiing, cycling, windsurfing. *Address:* Eastman Dental Institute, 256 Gray's Inn Road, WC1X 8LD. *T:* (020) 7915 1038.

SCULLY, Sean Paul; artist; *b* Dublin, 30 June 1945; *s* of John Anthony Scully and Holly Scully; *m* Catherine Lee. *Educ:* Croydon Coll. of Art; Newcastle Univ.; Harvard Univ. Lecturer: Harvard Univ., 1972–73; Chelsea Sch. of Art, and Goldsmiths' Sch. of Art, 1973–75; Princeton Univ., 1978–83; Parsons Sch. of Design, NY, 1983–. *Solo exhibitions* include: Rowan Gall., London, 1973, 1975, 1977, 1979, 1981; Tortue Gall., Calif, 1975–76; Nadin Gall., NY, 1979; Mus. für (Sub-) Kultur, Berlin, 1981; retrospective, Ikon Gall., Birmingham, and tour, 1981; David McKee Gall., NY, 1983, 1985–87, 1989–91; Art Inst. of Chicago, 1987; University Art Mus., Univ. of Calif at Berkeley, 1987; Paintings and Works on Paper 1982–88, Whitechapel Art Gall., Neubachhaus, Munich, Palacio Velásquez, Madrid, 1989; Waddington Gall., 1992, 1995; The Catherine Paintings, Mus. of Modern Art, Fort Worth, 1993, Palais de Beaux-Arts, Belgium, 1995, Galérie Nat. de Jeu de Paume, Paris, 1996; *works in public collections* include: Mus. of Modern Art, NY; Tate Gall.; V & A Mus.; Aust. Nat. Gall., Canberra. *Address:* c/o Mayor Rowan Gallery, 31A Bruton Place, W1X 7AB; c/o Diane Villani Editions, 271 Mulberry Street, New York, NY 10012, USA.

SCURR, Dr Cyril Frederick, CBE 1980; LVO 1952; FRCS, FRCA; Hon. Consulting Anaesthetist, Westminster Hospital, since 1985 (Consultant Anaesthetist, 1949–85); Hon. Anaesthetist, Hospital of SS John and Elizabeth, 1952–94, now Emeritus; *b* 14 July 1920; *s* of Cyril Albert Scurr and Mabel Rose Scurr; *m* 1947, Isabel Jean Spiller; three *s* one *d*. *Educ:* King's Coll., London; Westminster Hosp. MB, BS. Served War of 1939–45: RAMC, 1942–47, Major, Specialist Anaesthetist. Faculty of Anaesthetists: Mem. Bd, 1961–77; Dean, 1970–73; Mem. Council, RCS, 1970–73; Pres., Assoc. of Anaesthetists of GB and Ireland, 1976–78; Mem. Health Services Bd, 1977–80; Chm., Scientific Programme, World Congress of Anaesthetists, London, 1968; Pres., 1978–79, Hon. Mem., 1988, Anaesthetics Section, RSocMed; Mem. Adv. Cttee on Distinction Awards, 1973–84; Vice-Chm., Jt Consultants Cttee, 1979–81; past Member: Cttee, Competence to Practise; Standing Med. Adv. Cttee, DHSS. Mem. d'Honneur, Société Française d'Anesthésie et de Réanimation, 1978; Academician, European Acad. of Anaesthesiology, 1978. Frederick Hewitt Lectr, RCS, 1971; Magill Centenary Oration, RCS, 1988. Dudley Buxton Prize, RCS, 1977; Gold Medal, Faculty of Anaesthetists, 1983; John Snow Medal, Assoc. of Anaesthetists of GB and Ireland, 1984. Hon. FFARCSI 1977. *Publications:* Scientific Foundations of Anaesthesia, 1970, 4th edn 1990; (jtly) Drug Mechanisms in Anaesthesia, 1987, 2nd edn 1993. *Recreations:* photography, gardening. *Address:* 16 Grange Avenue, Totteridge Common, N20 8AD. *T:* (020) 8445 7188.

SEABROOK, Air Vice-Marshal Geoffrey Leonard, CB 1965; *b* 25 Aug. 1909; *s* of late Robert Leonard Seabrook; *m* 1949, Beryl Mary (*née* Hughes); one *s* one *d*. *Educ:* King's Sch., Canterbury. Commissioned in RAF (Accountant Branch), 1933; served in: Middle East, 1935–43; Bomber Command, 1943–45; Transport Command, 1945–47; Iraq, 1947–49; Signals Command, 1949–51; Air Ministry Organisation and Methods, 1951–53; Home Command Group Captain Organisation, 1953–56; Far East Air Force, 1957–59; idc 1960; Director of Personnel, Air Ministry, 1961–63; Air Officer Administration, HQ, RAF Tech. Trg Comd, 1963–66; retired June 1966. Air Cdre 1961; Air Vice-Marshal, 1964. Head of Secretarial Branch, Royal Air Force, 1963–66. FCA 1957 (Associate, 1932). *Recreations:* sailing, golf. *Address:* Long Pightle, Piltdown, Uckfield, E Sussex TN22 3XB. *T:* (01825) 722322. *Clubs:* Royal Air Force; Piltdown Golf.

SEABROOK, Graeme; Director (non-executive): P. Cleland Enterprises Ltd, Australia, since 1997; Country Road Ltd, since 1997; *b* 1 May 1939; *s* of Norman and Amy Winifred Seabrook; *m* 1967, Lorraine Ellen Ludlow; one *s* one *d*. G. J. Coles & Co. (later Coles Myer), Australia, 1955; Chief Gen. Manager, G. J. Coles, 1982; acquisition of Myer, 1985; Man. Dir, Discount Stores Group, 1985; Jt Man. Dir, Coles Myer, 1987, resigned 1988; joined Dairy Farm International, Hong Kong and seconded to Kwik Save Group, 1988: Man. Dir, 1988–93, Chief Exec., 1989–93, non-exec. Dir, 1993–96; Man. Dir, Dairy Farm Internat., Hong Kong, 1993–96. Non-exec. Dir, Woolworths Hldgs Ltd, S Africa, 1997–2000. *Recreations:* tennis, photography. *Address:* 26 Victoria Avenue, Canterbury, Vic 3126, Australia.

SEABROOK, Peter John; consultant horticulturist, since 1971; *b* 2 Nov. 1935; *s* of Robert Henry Seabrook and Emma Mary Seabrook (*née* Cottey); *m* 1960, Margaret Ruth Risbey; one *s* one *d*. *Educ:* King Edward VI Grammar Sch., Chelmsford; Essex Inst. of Agric., Writtle (Dip. Hort, MHort). Cramphorn Ltd, 1952–66; Bord Na Mona, 1966–70; Gardening Corresp., Sun, 1977–; Director: Wm Strike Ltd, 1972–95; Roger Harvey Ltd, 1981–99. TV presenter: WGBH TV, Boston, USA, 1975–97; Pebble Mill At One, 1975–86; Gardeners' World, 1976–79; Chelsea Flower Show, (annually) 1976–89; Gardeners' Direct Line, 1982–90; Peter Seabrook's Gardening Week, 1996. Hon. Fellow, Writtle Coll., 1997; Associate of Honour, RHS, 1996. Pearson Meml Medal, Horticultural Trades Assoc., 1985. *Publications:* Shrubs for Your Garden, 1973, 10th edn 1991; Plants for Your Home, 1975; Complete Vegetable Gardener, 1976, 4th edn 1981; Book of the Garden, 1979, 2nd edn 1984; Good Plant Guide, 1981; Good Food Gardening, 1983; Shrubs for Everyone, 1997. *Recreation:* gardening. *Address:* 212A Baddow Road, Chelmsford, Essex CM2 9QR. *T:* (01245) 490201. *Club:* Farmers'.

SEABROOK, Robert John; QC 1983; a Recorder, since 1985; *b* 6 Oct. 1941; *s* of late Alan Thomas Pertwee Seabrook, MBE and Mary Seabrook (*née* Parker); *m* 1965, Liv Karin Djupvik, Bergen, Norway; two *s* one *d*. *Educ:* St George's Coll., Salisbury, Southern Rhodesia; University Coll., London (LLB). Called to the Bar, Middle Temple, 1964, Bencher, 1990. Leader, SE Circuit, 1989–92; Chm., Bar Council, 1994. Member: Criminal Justice Consultative Council, 1995–; Interception of Communications Tribunal, 1996–; Investigatory Powers Tribunal, 2000–. Member: Brighton Fest. Cttee, 1976–86; Court, Univ. of Sussex, 1988–93. Gov., Brighton Coll., 1993– (Chm. of Govs, 1998–). Liveryman, Curriers' Co., 1972– (Master, 1995–96). *Recreations:* travel, listening to music, wine. *Address:* (chambers) 1 Crown Office Row, Temple, EC4Y 7HH. *T:* (020) 7797 7500. *Clubs:* Athenæum, Les Six.

SEABROOKE, George Alfred; consultant in education and training; Director, The Polytechnic, Wolverhampton, 1977–85; *b* 8 Dec. 1923; *s* of late John Arthur Seabrooke and Elsie Seabrooke; *m* 1945, Evelyn Sargent; two *s. Educ:* Keighley Boys' Grammar Sch.; Bradford Technical Coll.; Stoke-on-Trent Tech. Coll.; King's Coll., London Univ. FBIM 1978. National Service, 1946–48. Post Office Engrg Dept, 1940–50; Estate Duty Office, Comrs of Inland Revenue, 1950–56; SW London Coll. of Commerce, 1956–60; Trent Polytechnic, Nottingham (and precursor Colls), 1960–73; Dep. Dir, NE London Polytechnic, 1974–77. *Publications:* Air Law, 1964; contrib. learned jls. *Recreations:* music, cricket, rugby. *Address:* 6 John Trundle Court, Barbican, EC2Y 8DJ.

SEAFIELD, 13th Earl of, *cr* 1701; **Ian Derek Francis Ogilvie-Grant;** Viscount Seafield, Baron Ogilvy of Cullen, 1698; Viscount Reidhaven, Baron Ogilvy of Deskford and Cullen, 1701; *b* 20 March 1939; *s* of Countess of Seafield (12th in line), and Derek Studley-Herbert (who assumed by deed poll, 1939, the additional surnames of Ogilvie-Grant; he *d* 1960); *S* mother, 1969; *m* 1st, 1960, Mary Dawn Mackenzie (marr. diss. 1971), *er d* of Henry Illingworth; two *s*; 2nd, 1971, Leila, *d* of Mahmoud Refaat, Cairo. *Educ:* Eton. *Recreations:* shooting, fishing, tennis. *Heir: s* Viscount Reidhaven, *qv. Address:* Old Cullen, Cullen, Banffshire AB56 4XW. *T:* (01542) 840221. *Club:* White's.

SEAFORD, 6th Baron *cr* 1826, of Seaford, co. Sussex; **Colin Humphrey Felton Ellis;** *b* 19 April 1946; *o s* of Major William Felton Ellis and Edwina (*née* Bond); *S* to Seaford Barony of cousin, 9th Baron Howard de Walden, 1999; *m* 1st, 1971, Susan Magill (marr. diss. 1992); two *s* two *d*; 2nd, 1993, Penelope Mary Bastin. *Educ:* Sherborne; RAC, Cirencester (MRAC 1968). ARICS 1970. *Heir: s* Hon. Benjamin Felton Thomas Ellis, *b* 17 Dec. 1976. *Address:* Bush Farm, West Knoyle, Warminster, Wilts BA12 6AE.

SEAFORD, Very Rev. John Nicholas; Dean of Jersey and Rector of St Helier, since 1993; *b* 12 Sept. 1939; *s* of Nicholas Shtetinin Seaford and Kathleen Dorothy (*née* Longbotham); *m* 1967, Helen Marian Webster; two *s* one *d. Educ:* Radley Coll.; St Chad's Coll., Durham Univ. (BA 1967; DipTh 1968). Ordained deacon, 1968, priest, 1969; Assistant Curate: St Mark, Bush Hill Park, Enfield, 1968–71; St Luke, Winchester, 1971–73; Vicar: Chilworth and North Baddesley, 1973–78; Highcliffe and Hinton Admiral, 1978–93. Hon. Canon, Winchester Cathedral, 1993–. Religious Broadcasting Advr, Channel TV, 1993–. Mem., States of Jersey, 1993–. *Recreation:* walking. *Address:* The Deanery, David Place, St Helier, Jersey JE2 4TE. *T:* (01534) 720001, *Fax:* (01534) 617488.

SEAGA, Rt Hon. Edward Philip George; PC 1982; MP for Western Kingston, since 1962; Leader of the Jamaica Labour Party, since 1974; Chairman, Premium Group, since 1989; *b* 28 May 1930; *s* of late Philip Seaga and of Erna (*née* Maxwell); *m* 1965, Marie Elizabeth (marr. diss. 1995) (*née* Constantine) (Miss Jamaica, 1964); two *s* one *d*; *m* Carla Frances Vendryes, MPA. *Educ:* Wolmers Boys' Sch., Kingston, Jamaica; Harvard Univ., USA (BA Social Science, 1952). Did field research in connection with Inst. of Social and Econ. Res., University Coll. of the West Indies (now Univ. of the WI), Jamaica, on develt of the child, and revival spirit cults, by living in rural villages and urban slums; proposed estabt of Unesco Internat. Fund for Promotion of Culture, 1971, and is founding mem. of its Administrative Council. Nominated to Upper House (Legislative Council), 1959 (youngest mem. in its history); Asst Sec., Jamaica Labour Party, 1960–62; Minister of Develt and Social Welfare, 1962–67; Minister of Finance and Planning, 1967–72, and 1980–89; Leader of Opposition, 1974–80; Prime Minister, 1980–89. Director: Consulting Services Ltd, to 1979; Capital Finance Co. Ltd, to 1979. Hon. LLD: Miami, 1981; Tampa, 1982; S Carolina, 1983; Boston, 1983; Hartford, 1987. Grand Collar, and Golden Mercury Internat. Award, Venezuela, 1981; Grand Cross, Order of Merit of Fed. Rep. of Germany, 1982. Gold Key Award, Avenue of the Americas, NYC, 1981; Environment Leadership Award, UN, 1987; Golden Star Caribbean Award Man of the Year, 1988. Religion Anglican. *Publications:* The Development of the Child; Revival Spirit Cults. *Recreations:* classical music, reading, shooting, hockey, football, cricket, tennis, swimming. *Address:* 24–26 Grenada Crescent, New Kingston, Kingston 5, Jamaica. *Clubs:* Kingston Cricket, Jamaica Gun (Jamaica).

SEAGER, family name of **Baron Leighton of Saint Mellons**.

SEAGER, Major Ronald Frank; RA, retired; Executive Director, RSPCA, 1971–78 (Secretary, 1966–71); Advisory Director, International Society for Protection of Animals; *b* 27 May 1918; *s* of Frank Seager and Lilias K. (*née* Parr); *m* 1941, Josephine, *d* of Rev. R. M. Chadwick; one *s* one *d. Educ:* St Albans School. Royal Artillery (HAC), 1939; commnd, 1941; Italy, 1944–45; seconded Royal Pakistan Artillery, 1949–50; served Korean War, 1953–54; Perm. Pres. Courts Martial, Eastern Command, 1960–63. Joined RSPCA, 1963. *Recreations:* golf, gardening. *Address:* 4 Thornbank Court, Long Street, Sherborne, Dorset DT9 3BS. *T:* (01935) 816223.

SEAGER BERRY, Thomas Henry; Master of the Supreme Court Costs (formerly Taxing) Office, since 1991; Deputy District Judge, Principal Registry, Family Division, since 2000; *b* 29 Jan. 1940; *s* of Thomas Geoffrey Seager Berry, CBE and Ann Josephine Seager Berry. *Educ:* Shrewsbury Sch. Admitted solicitor, 1964; Sherwood & Co., 1964–69 (Partner, 1966–69); Partner, Boodle Hatfield, 1969–91. Pres., London Solicitors Litigation Assoc., 1982–84; Mem. Cttee, Media Soc., 1985–91; Mem. Council, Feathers Clubs Assoc., 1986–. Liveryman, Merchant Taylors' Co., 1967. *Publication:* Longman's Litigation Practice, 1988. *Recreations:* tennis, gardening, wine-tasting, walking. *Address:* Supreme Court Costs Office, Clifford's Inn, Fetter Lane, EC4A 1DQ. *T:* (020) 7947 6158. *Clubs:* Hurlingham, MCC.

SEAGROATT, Conrad; Hon. Mr Justice Seagroatt; a Judge of the Court of First Instance of the High Court (formerly a Judge of the High Court), Hong Kong, since 1995; a Recorder of the Crown Court, since 1980; *s* of late E. G. Seagroatt, Solicitor of the Supreme Court and Immigration Appeals Adjudicator, and of Gray's Inn, and of Barbara C. Seagroatt; *m* Cornelia Mary Anne Verdegaal; five *d. Educ:* Solihull Sch., Warwicks; Pembroke Coll., Oxford (MA Hons Modern History). Admitted Solicitor of the Supreme Court, 1967; called to the Bar, Gray's Inn, 1970, Bencher, 1991; QC 1983; Dep. High Court Judge, 1993–. Member: Senate of the Inns of Court and the Bar, 1980–83; Criminal Injuries Compensation Bd, 1986–94. *Publications:* (contrib.) The Civil Reform Process in Hong Kong, 1999; (Adv. Ed., and contrib.) The Hong Kong White Book, 2001–. *Recreations:* running, fairweather ski-ing. *Address:* High Court, Hong Kong. *Club:* Garrick.

SEAL, Dr Barry Herbert; Chairman, Brookfields International, since 1999; *b* 28 Oct. 1937; *s* of Herbert Seal and Rose Anne Seal; *m* 1963, Frances Catherine Wilkinson; one *s* one *d. Educ:* Heath Grammar Sch., Halifax; Univ. of Bradford (MSc, PhD); European Business Sch., Fontainebleau. CEng. Served RAF, 1955–58. Trained as Chem. Engr, ICI Ltd, 1958–64; Div. Chem. Engr, Murex Ltd, 1964–68; Sen. Engr, BOC Internat., 1968–71; Principal Lectr in Systems, Huddersfield Polytechnic, 1971–79; consultant on microprocessors. Contested (Lab) Harrogate, Oct. 1974; Leader, Bradford MDC Labour Gp, 1976–79. MEP (Lab) Yorks W, 1979–99; contested (Lab) Yorks and the Humber Reg., 1999. European Parliament: Leader, British Lab. Gp, 1988–89; Chm., Econ., Monetary and Industrial Policy Cttee, 1984–87; Chm., delegn to USA, 1998–99. Hon. Freeman, Borough of Calderdale, 2000. *Publications:* papers on computer and microprocessor applications. *Recreations:* walking, reading, films, sailing, flying. *Address:* Brookfields Farm, Brookfields Road, Wyke, Bradford, West Yorks BD12 9LU; *e-mail:* barryseal@hotmail.com.

SEAL, (Karl) Russell; Joint Managing Director, British Petroleum Co. plc, 1991–97; *b* 14 April 1942; *m* 1966, Pauline Hilarie (*née* Edwards); three *s. Educ:* Keele Univ. Joined BP, 1964; NY, 1970–72; Rotterdam, 1976–78; Asst Gen. Manager, Gp Corporate Planning, 1978–80; Chief Exec., Mktg and Refining, Singapore, Malaysia, and Hong Kong, and Sen. Rep., SE Asia, 1980–84; Gen. Manager, BP Oil Trading & Supply Dept, 1984; Chief Exec. and Man. Dir, BP Oil, 1988–95. Non-executive Director: Commonwealth Develt Corp., 1996–; Blue Circle plc, 1996–. Sen. Exec. Prog., Stanford Univ., 1984. *Recreations:* jogging, walking, golf.

SEAL, Richard Godfrey, FRCO; FRSCM; Organist of Salisbury Cathedral, 1968–97; *b* 4 Dec. 1935; *s* of late William Godfrey Seal and of Shelagh Seal (*née* Bagshaw); *m* 1975, Dr Sarah Helen Hamilton; two *s. Educ:* New Coll. Choir Sch., Oxford; Cranleigh Sch., Surrey; Christ's Coll., Cambridge (MA). FRCO 1958; FRSCM 1987. Assistant Organist: Kingsway Hall, London, 1957–58; St Bartholomews the Great, London, 1960–61; Chichester Cathedral (and Dir of Music, Prebendal Sch.), Sussex, 1961–68. DMus Lambeth, 1992. *Address:* The Bield, Flamstone Street, Bishopstone, Salisbury, Wilts SP5 4BZ. *Club:* Crudgemens (Godalming).

SEALE, Sir (Clarence) David, Kt 2000; JP; Chairman and Managing Director, R. L. Seale & Co., since 1969; *b* 11 Dec. 1937; *m* 1961, Margaret Anne Farmer; one *s* three *d. Educ:* Harrison Coll., Barbados. Airline Clerk, 1956–62; Gen. Manager, R. L. Seale & Co., 1962–69. JP Bridgetown, 1978. *Recreation:* horse racing. *Address:* Hopefield Manor, Hopefield, Christ Church, Barbados. *T:* 4280065. *Club:* Barbados Turf (Bridgetown).

SEALE, Sir John Henry, 5th Bt *cr* 1838; RIBA; *b* 3 March 1921; *s* of Sir John Seale, 4th Bt; *S* father, 1964; *m* 1953, Ray Josephine, *d* of Robert Gordon Charters, MC, Christchurch, New Zealand; one *s* one *d. Educ:* Eton; Christ Church, Oxford. Served War of 1939–45: Royal Artillery, North Africa and Italy; Captain, 1945. ARIBA 1951. *Heir: s* John Robert Charters Seale [*b* 17 Aug. 1954; *m* 1996, Michelle, *d* of K. W. Taylor]. *Address:* Slade, Kingsbridge, Devon TQ7 4BL. *T:* (01548) 550226.

SEALEY, Barry Edward, CBE 1990; Chairman, Lothian University Hospitals NHS Trust, 1999–2001; *b* 3 Feb. 1936; *s* of Edward Sealey and Queenie Katherine Sealey (*née* Hill); *m* 1960, Helen Martyn; one *s* one *d. Educ:* Dursley GS; St John's Coll., Cambridge (BA 1958; MA 1991); Harvard Business Sch. (PMD 1968). Christian Salvesen plc, 1958–90: Dir, 1969–90; Man. Dir, 1981–89. Chm., Edinburgh Healthcare NHS Trust, 1993–99. Director: Scottish American Investment Co. plc, 1983–2001; Morago Ltd, 1989–; Queen's Hall (Edinburgh) Ltd, 1990–99; Caledonian Brewing Co. Ltd, 1990–; Wilson Byard plc, 1992–; Interface Graphics Ltd, 1992–99; Optos Plc (formerly Besca Ltd), 1992–; Stagecoach Hldgs plc, 1992–2001; Scottish Equitable Policy Holders Trust Ltd, 1993–; Scottish Equitable, 1993–99; ESI Investors Ltd, 1999–. Dir, Lothian Health Bd, 1999–2001. Mem. Council and Policy Cttee, Industrial Soc., 1990–. Dep. Chm. of Court, Napier Poly., subseq. Univ., 1987–98. *Recreations:* walking, music. *Address:* 4 Castlelaw Road, Edinburgh EH13 0DN. *T:* (0131) 441 2802; *e-mail:* bes@morago.co.uk. *Club:* New (Edinburgh).

SEALY, Austin Llewellyn; Managing Partner, A. Sealy & Co., international business consultancy and management services, since 1996; *b* 17 Sept. 1939; *s* of Kenneth Llewellyn Sealy and Gerdsene Elaine Sealy (*née* Crawford); *m* 1964, Rita Anita Pilgrim; three *s. Educ:* St Mary's Boys' Sch., Barbados; Harrison Coll., Barbados. Banker, 1958–93: Sen. Mgt Official with Barclays Bank PLC in Caribbean; High Comr for Barbados in UK, and Ambassador to Israel, 1993–94. Pres., Nat. Olympic Cttee of Barbados, 1982–96; Hon. Treas., Commonwealth Games Fedn, 1986–; Member: IOC, 1994–; Exec. Council, Assoc. of Nat. Olympic Cttees, 1995–. Silver Crown of Merit (Barbados), 1985. *Recreations:* cricket, tennis, golf. *Address:* Crestview, 35 Highgate Gardens, St Michael, Barbados. *T:* 4272256; A. Sealy & Co., Leamington House, 4th Avenue, Belleville, St Michael, Barbados; *e-mail:* austinsealy@sealygroup.com.

SEALY, Prof. Leonard Sedgwick, PhD; S. J. Berwin Professor of Corporate Law, University of Cambridge, 1991–97, now Emeritus; Life Fellow, Gonville and Caius College, Cambridge, since 1997 (Fellow, 1959–97); *b* 22 July 1930; *s* of Alfred Desmond Sealy and Mary Louise Sealy, Hamilton, NZ; *m* 1960, Beryl Mary Edwards; one *s* two *d. Educ:* Stratford High Sch.; Auckland Univ. (MA, LLM); Gonville and Caius Coll., Cambridge (PhD). Barrister and solicitor, NZ, 1953; in practice at NZ Bar, 1953–55 and 1958–59. Faculty of Law, University of Cambridge: Asst Lectr, 1959–61; Lectr, 1961–91; Tutor, 1961–70, Sen. Tutor, 1970–75, Gonville and Caius Coll. *Publications:* Disqualification and Personal Liability of Directors, 1968, 5th edn 2000; Cases and Materials in Company Law, 1971, 7th edn 2001; Company Law and Commercial Reality, 1984; (with D. Milman) Guide to the 1986 Insolvency Legislation, 1987, 5th edn as Guide to the Insolvency Legislation, 1999; (with R. Hooley) Cases and Materials in Commercial Law, 1994, 2nd edn 1999; (ed with A. G. Guest *et al.*) Benjamin's Sale of Goods, 1974, 5th edn 1997; (General Editor): British Company Law and Practice, 1989; International Corporate Procedures, 1992; Commonwealth Editor, Gore-Browne on Companies, 1997. *Address:* Gonville and Caius College, Cambridge CB2 1TA. *T:* (01223) 332471.

SEAMAN, Christopher; international conductor; Music Director: Naples Philharmonic Orchestra, Florida, since 1993; Rochester Philharmonic Orchestra, New York, since 1998; *b* 7 March 1942; *s* of late Albert Edward Seaman and Ethel Margery Seaman (*née* Chambers). *Educ:* Canterbury Cathedral Choir Sch.; The King's Sch., Canterbury; King's Coll., Cambridge. MA, double first cl. Hons in Music; ARCM, ARCO. Principal Timpanist, London Philharmonic Orch., 1964–68 (Mem., LPO Bd of Dirs, 1965–68); Asst Conductor, 1968–70, Principal Conductor, 1971–77, BBC Scottish Symphony Orchestra; Princ. Conductor and Artistic Dir, Northern Sinfonia Orch., 1974–79; Principal Guest Conductor, Utrecht Symphony Orch., 1979–83; Principal Conductor, BBC Robert Mayer concerts, 1978–87; Conductor-in-Residence, Baltimore SO, 1987–98; also works widely as a guest conductor, and appears in America, Holland, France, Germany, Belgium, Italy, Norway, Spain, Portugal, Czechoslovakia, Israel, Hong Kong, Japan, Australia, New Zealand and all parts of UK. FGSM 1972. *Recreations:* people, reading, walking, theology. *Address:* 25 Westfield Drive, Glasgow G52 2SG.

SEAMAN, Gilbert Frederick, AO 1981; CMG 1967; Chairman, State Bank of South Australia, 1963–83; Deputy Chairman, Electricity Trust of SA, 1970–84; Trustee, Savings Bank of SA, 1973–81; *b* 7 Sept. 1912; *s* of Eli S. Seaman, McLaren Vale, South Australia; *m* 1935, Avenal Essie Fong; one *s* one *d. Educ:* University of Adelaide. BEc, Associate of

University of Adelaide, 1935, High School Teacher, Port Pirie and Unley, 1932–35; South Australian Public Service, 1936–41; Seconded to Commonwealth of Australia as Assistant Director of Manpower for SA, 1941–46; Economist, SA Treasury, 1946–60; Under Treasurer for SA, 1960–72. *Address:* 27 William Street, Hawthorn, SA 5062, Australia. *T:* (8) 82714271.
See also Sir K. D. Seaman.

SEAMAN, Sir Keith (Douglas), KCVO 1981; OBE 1976; Governor of South Australia, 1977–82; *b* 11 June 1920; *s* of late E. S. and E. M. Seaman; *m* 1946, Joan, *d* of F. Birbeck; one *s* one *d*. *Educ:* Unley High Sch.; Univ. of Adelaide (BA, LLB); Flinders Univ. (MA, DipHum). South Australian Public Service, 1937–54; RAAF Overseas HQ, London, 1941–45, Flt-Lieut. Entered Methodist Ministry, 1954: Renmark, 1954–58; Adelaide Central Methodist Mission, 1958–77 (Supt, 1971–77). Sec., Christian Television Assoc. of S Australia, 1959–73; Mem. Executive, World Assoc. of Christian Broadcasting, 1963–70; Director, 5KA, 5AU and 5RM Broadcasting Companies, 1960–77; Chm., 5KA, 5AU and 5RM, 1971–77. Mem., Australian Govt Social Welfare Commn, 1973–76. KStJ 1978. *Recreations:* reading, gardening. *Address:* Victor Harbor, SA 5211, Australia.
See also G. F. Seaman.

SEAMMEN, Diana Jill; Command Secretary, HQ Land Command, since 1998; *b* 24 March 1948. *Educ:* Univ. of Sussex. HM Treasury, 1969–89; Dir, VAT Control, and a Comr, HM Customs and Excise, 1989–91; Asst Under-Sec. of State, Air, 1992, Finance, 1993, MoD (PE), Programmes, 1994, MoD. *Address:* HQ Land Command, Erskine Barracks, Wilton, Salisbury, Wilts SP2 0AG.

SEAR, Dr John William; Clinical Reader in Anaesthetics, University of Oxford, and Fellow of Green College, Oxford, since 1982; *b* 3 Sept. 1947; *e s* of late Lionel and Ethel Alice Moore, and adoptive *s* of late Frederick Carl William Sear; *m* 1978, Yvonne Margaret Begley; three *s*. *Educ:* Enfield Grammar Sch.; London Hosp. Med. Coll. (BSc, MBBS); Univ. of Bristol (PhD); MA Oxford. FFARCS, FANZCA. Posts in London Hosp., 1972–75; Registrar in Anaesthetics, Royal Devon & Exeter Hosp. and United Bristol Hosps, 1975–77; University of Bristol: MRC Res. Training Fellow and Hon. Sen. Registrar, 1977–80; Lectr in Anaesthetics, 1980–81; Dir of Clinical Studies, Univ. of Oxford, 1995–98. Hon. Consultant Anaesthetist, Oxford Radcliffe Hosp. NHS Trust, 1982–; non-exec. Dir, Nuffield Orthopaedic Centre NHS Trust, 1993–. Member, Editorial Board: British Jl of Anaesthesia, 1989–; Jl of Clinical Anesthesia, USA, 1989–. *Publications:* papers in learned jls. *Recreations:* sport, music, writing. *Address:* 6 Whites Forge, Appleton, Abingdon, Oxon OX13 5LG. *T:* (01865) 863144.

SEARBY, Philip James, CBE 1981; Secretary and Authority Finance Officer, UK Atomic Energy Authority, 1976–84; *b* 20 Sept. 1924; *s* of Leonard James and Lillian Mary Searby; *m* 1955, Mary Brent Dudley; two *s*. *Educ:* Bedford Sch.; Wadham Coll., Oxford (MA). Entered Civil Service, Min. of Nat. Insurance, 1949; Prime Minister's Statistical Branch, 1951; Private Sec. to Paymaster Gen. (Lord Cherwell), 1952; Principal, Atomic Energy Office, 1954. Joined UK Atomic Energy Authority, 1956; Dep. Gen. Sec., Harwell, 1959; Principal Economics and Programmes Officer, 1965; Authority Finance and Programmes Officer, 1971. St Albans Diocesan Reader, 1950. *Recreations:* reading, committee work. *Address:* 5 Borodale, Kirkwick Avenue, Harpenden, Herts AL5 2QW. *T:* (01582) 760837.

SEARBY, Richard Henry; QC (Aust.) 1971; Deputy Chairman, Times Newspapers Holdings Ltd, since 1981; *b* 23 July 1931; *s* of late Henry and Mary Searby; *m* 1962, Caroline (*née* McAdam); three *s*. *Educ:* Geelong Grammar Sch., Corio, Vic; Corpus Christi Coll., Oxford Univ. (MA Hons). Called to Bar, Inner Temple, London, 1956; admitted Barrister and Solicitor, Victoria, Aust., 1956; called to Victorian Bar, 1957; Associate to late Rt Hon. Sir Owen Dixon, Chief Justice of Aust., 1956–59; commenced practice, Victorian Bar, 1959; Independent Lectr in Law relating to Executors and Trustees, Univ. of Melbourne, 1961–72. Director: Equity Trustees Executors & Agency Co. Ltd, 1975–2000 (Chm., 1980–2000); CRA Ltd, then Rio Tinto Ltd, 1977–97; Rio Tinto PLC, 1995–97; Shell Australia Ltd, 1977–98; News Corp. Ltd, 1977–92 (Chm., 1981–91; Dep. Chm., 1991–92); News Ltd, 1977–92 (Chm., 1981–92); News International plc, 1980–92 (Chm., 1981–89); South China Morning Post Ltd, 1986–92 (Chm., 1987–92); Reuters Founders Share Co. Ltd, 1987–93; BRL Hardy Ltd, 1992–; Amrad Corp. Ltd, 1992–; Tandem Australian Ltd, 1992–98; Woodside Petroleum Ltd, 1998–. Member Council: Nat. Library of Australia, 1992–95; Mus. of Victoria, 1993–98. President: Medico-Legal Soc. of Vic, 1986–87; Aust. Inst. of Internat. Affairs, 1993–97. Chancellor, Deakin Univ., 1997–. Chm., Geelong Grammar Sch., 1983–89. *Publication:* (jtly) report on Conciliation and Arbitration Act, 1981. *Recreations:* reading, music, tennis, fishing. *Address:* 23A Hampden Road, Armadale, Vic 3143, Australia. *T:* (3) 95763100. *Clubs:* Melbourne, Australian (Melbourne).

SEARBY, Maj. Gen. Robin Vincent; Senior British Loan Service Officer, Sultanate of Oman, since 2000; *b* 20 July 1947; *s* of late John Henry Searby and Eva Searby; *m* 1976, Caroline Angela Beamish; one *s* two *d*. *Educ:* Leasam House; RMA Sandhurst. Commissioned 9th/12th Royal Lancers, 1968; Directing Staff, Camberley, 1984–87; CO, 9th/12th Royal Lancers, 1987–89; COS to HQ Dir, RAC, 1989–91; Comdr, Armoured 1st (Br) Corps, 1991–93; Comdr, British Forces Bosnia-Hercegovina, 1993; Pres., Regular Commissions Bd, 1994; Chief, Jt Ops (Bosnia), HQ Allied Forces Southern Europe, 1995; GOC 5th Div., 1996–2000. Distinguished Service Medal for Gallantry, Sultanate of Oman, 1975; QCVS 1994. *Recreations:* walking, country sports, reading. *Club:* Cavalry and Guards.

SEARLE, Ronald William Fordham, RDI 1988; AGI; artist; *b* Cambridge, 3 March 1920; *m* 1st, Kaye Webb (marr. diss. 1967; she *d* 1996); one *s* one *d*; 2nd, 1967, Monica Koenig. *Educ:* Cambridge School of Art. Served with 287 Field Co. RE, 1939–46; captured by the Japanese at fall of Singapore, 1942; Prisoner of War in Siam and Malaya, 1942–45; Dept of Psychological Warfare, Allied Force HQ Port Said Ops, 1956. Creator of the schoolgirls of St Trinian's, 1941 (abandoned them in 1953); Cartoonist to Tribune, 1949–51; to Sunday Express, 1950–51; Special Feature artist, News Chronicle, 1951–53; Weekly Cartoonist, News Chronicle, 1954; Punch Theatre artist, 1949–62; Contributor: New Yorker and New York Times, 1966–; Le Monde, 1995–. Designer of commemorative medals for: the French Mint, 1974–; British Art Medal Soc., 1983–. *One Man Exhibitions include:* Leicester Galls, 1948, 1950, 1954, 1957; New York, 1959, 1963, 1969, 1976; Galerie La Pochade, Paris, 1966, 1967, 1968, 1969, 1971; Galerie Gurlitt, Munich, 1967, 1968, 1969, 1970, 1971, 1973, 1976; Grosvenor Gall., London, 1968; Bibliothèque Nat., Paris, 1973; Galerie Carmen Casse, Paris, 1975, 1976, 1977; Staatliche Mus., Berlin, 1976; Rizzoli Gall., NY, Gal. Bartsch & Chariau, Munich, 1981; Cooper-Hewitt Museum, NY, 1984; Neue Galerie Wien, 1985, 1988; Imperial War Museum, BM, 1986; Fitzwilliam Museum, Cambridge, 1987; Mus. of Fine Arts, San Francisco, 1987–88; Heineman Galls, NY, 1994; Wilhelm-Busch Mus., Hanover, 1996, (with Monica Searle), 2001; Galerie Martine Gossieaux, Paris, 2000. *Works in permanent collections:* V&A, BM, Imperial War Museum, Tate Gall.; Bibliothèque Nat., Paris; Wilhelm-Busch Museum, Hanover; Staatlische Mus., Berlin; Cooper-Hewitt Museum, NY; Univ. of Texas, Austin; Mus. of Fine Arts, San Francisco. *Films based on the characters of St Trinian's:* The Belles of St Trinian's, 1954; Blue Murder at St Trinian's, 1957; The Pure Hell of St Trinian's, 1960; The Great St Trinian's Train Robbery, 1966; The Wildcats of St Trinian's, 1980. *Films designed:* John Gilpin, 1951; On the Twelfth Day, 1954 (Acad. Award Nomination); Energetically Yours (USA), 1957; Germany, 1960 (for Suddeutschen RTV); The King's Breakfast, 1962; Those Magnificent Men in their Flying Machines (Animation Sequence), 1965; Monte Carlo or Bust (Animation Sequence), 1969; Scrooge (Animation Sequence), 1970; Dick Deadeye, 1975. *Publications:* Forty Drawings, 1946; Le Nouveau Ballet Anglais, 1947; Hurrah for St Trinian's!, 1948; The Female Approach, 1949; Back to the Slaughterhouse, 1951; John Gilpin, 1952; Souls in Torment, 1953; Rake's Progress, 1955; Merry England, etc, 1956; A Christmas Carol, 1961; Which Way Did He Go?, 1961; Searle in the Sixties, 1964; From Frozen North to Filthy Lucre, 1964; Pardong M'sieur, 1965; Searle's Cats, 1967; The Square Egg, 1968; Take one Toad, 1968; Baron Munchausen, 1960; Hello—where did all the people go?, 1969; Hommage à Toulouse-Lautrec, 1969; Secret Sketchbook, 1970; The Addict, 1971; More Cats, 1975; Drawings from Gilbert and Sullivan, 1975; The Zoodiac, 1977; Ronald Searle (Monograph), 1978; The King of Beasts, 1980; The Big Fat Cat Book, 1982; Illustrated Winespeak, 1983; Ronald Searle in Perspective (monograph), 1984; Ronald Searle's Golden Oldies 1941–61, 1985; To the Kwai—and Back, 1986; Something in the Cellar, 1986; Ah Yes, I Remember It Well ..., 1987; Ronald Searle's Non-Sexist Dictionary, 1988; Slightly Foxed—but still desirable, 1989; Carnet de Croquis: le plaisir du trait, 1992; The Curse of St Trinian's, 1993; Marquis de Sade meets Goody Two-Shoes, 1994; Ronald Searle dans Le Monde, 1998; *in collaboration:* (with D. B. Wyndham Lewis) The Terror of St Trinian's, 1952; (with Geoffrey Willans) Down with Skool, 1953; How to be Topp, 1954; Whizz for Atomms, 1956; The Compleet Molesworth, 1958; The Dog's Ear Book, 1958; Back in the Jug Agane, 1959; (with Kaye Webb) Paris Sketchbook, 1950 and 1957; Looking at London, 1953; The St Trinian's Story, 1959; Refugees 1960, 1960; (with Alex Atkinson) The Big City, 1958; USA for Beginners, 1959; Russia for Beginners, 1960; Escape from the Amazon!, 1964; (with A. Andrews & B. Richardson) Those Magnificent Men in their Flying Machines, 1965; (with Heinz Huber) Haven't We Met Before Somewhere?, 1966; (with Kildare Dobbs) The Great Fur Opera, 1970; (with Irwin Shaw) Paris! Paris!, 1977; (with Simon Rae) The Face of War, 1999; Le théâtre à Paris (1954–1962), 2000; *relevant publications:* Ronald Searle: a biography, by Russell Davies, 1990; Ronald Searle: monograph, ed Gisela Vetter-Liebenow, 1996. *Address:* c/o The Sayle Agency, 11 Jubilee Place, SW3 3TD. *T:* (020) 7823 3883. *Club:* Garrick.

SEARS, Hon. Raymond Arthur William; Judge of the Court of First Instance of the High Court (formerly a Judge of the Supreme Court), Hong Kong, 1986–99; Commissioner of the Supreme Court of Brunei Darussalam, 1987–99; *b* 10 March 1933; *s* of William Arthur and Lillian Sears; *m* 1960 (marr. diss. 1981); one *s* one *d*. *Educ:* Epsom Coll.; Jesus Coll., Cambridge. BA 1956. Lieut RA (TA) Airborne, 1953. Called to Bar, Gray's Inn, 1957. QC 1975; Recorder of the Crown Court, 1977–86. Vice-Chm., Judges' Forum, Internat. Bar Assoc., 1993. Dir, South China Brokerage Ltd. *Recreations:* watching horse-racing, music. *Address:* PO Box 10156, GPO, Hong Kong. *Clubs:* Hong Kong, Hong Kong Jockey (Hong Kong); Sydney Turf.

SEATON, Andrew James; HM Diplomatic Service; Head, China Hong Kong Department, Foreign and Commonwealth Office, since 2000; *b* 20 April 1954; *s* of Albert William Seaton and Joan Seaton (*née* Mackenzie); *m* 1983, Helen Elizabeth Pott; three *s*. *Educ:* Royal Grammar Sch., Guildford; Univ. of Leeds (BA Hons); Beijing Univ. Joined FCO, 1977: Third, later Second, Sec., Dakar, 1979–81; Hd, China Trade Unit, British Trade Commn, Hong Kong, 1982–86; FCO, 1987–92; Asst Hd, Aid Policy Dept, ODA, 1992–95; Trade Counsellor, British Trade Commn, Hong Kong, 1995–97; Dep. Consul-Gen., Hong Kong, 1997–2000. *Recreations:* family, wine, walking. *Address:* c/o Foreign and Commonwealth Office, King Charles Street, SW1A 2AH. *T:* (020) 7270 2648.

SEATON, Prof. Anthony, CBE 1997; MD; FRCP, FRCPE, FFOM, FMedSci; Professor of Environmental and Occupational Medicine, Aberdeen University, since 1988; *b* 20 Aug. 1938; *s* of late Douglas Ronald Seaton and of Julia Seaton; *m* 1962, Jillian Margaret Duke; two *s*. *Educ:* Rossall Sch.; King's Coll., Cambridge (BA, MB, MD); Liverpool Univ. FRCP 1977; FFOM 1982; FRCPE 1985. Jun. med. posts, Liverpool and Stoke-on-Trent, 1962–69; Asst Prof. of Medicine, W Virginia Univ., 1969–71; Consultant Chest Physician, Cardiff, 1971–77; Dir, Inst. of Occupational Medicine, Edinburgh, 1978–90. Chm., Expert Panel on Air Quality Standards, DoE, 1992–. Lectures: Tudor Edwards, RCP, 1996; Baylis, PPP, 1997; Warner, British Occupational Hygiene Soc., 1998; Hunter, FOM, 2000. Founder FMedSci 1998. Editor, Thorax, 1977–81. *Publications:* jointly: Occupational Lung Diseases, 1975, 3rd edn 1995; Crofton and Douglas's Respiratory Diseases, 1989, 2nd edn 2000; Practical Occupational Medicine, 1994; papers in med. literature. *Recreations:* opera, painting. *Address:* 8 Avon Grove, Cramond, Edinburgh EH4 6RF. *T:* (0131) 336 5113; 71 Urquhart Terrace, Aberdeen AB2 1NJ. *T:* (01224) 648947. *Club:* St Andrew Boat.

SEATON, Prof. Michael John, FRS 1967; Professor of Physics, Department of Physics and Astronomy, University College London, 1963–88, now Emeritus; Senior Fellow, Science and Engineering Research Council, 1984–88; *b* 16 Jan. 1923; *s* of late Arthur William Robert Seaton and Helen Amelia Seaton; *m* 1st, 1943, Olive May (*d* 1959), *d* of Charles Edward Singleton; one *s* one *d*; 2nd, 1960, Joy Clarice, *d* of Harry Albert Balchin; one *s*. *Educ:* Wallington Co. Sch., Surrey; University Coll., London (Fellow, 1972). BSc 1948, PhD 1951, London. Dept of Physics, UCL: Asst Lectr, 1950; Lectr, 1953; Reader, 1959; Prof., 1963. Chargé de Recherche, Institut d'Astrophysique, Paris, 1954–55; Univ. of Colorado, 1961; Fellow-Adjoint, Jt Inst. for Laboratory Astrophysics (Nat. Inst. of Standards and Technology and Univ. of Colorado), Boulder, Colo, 1964–. Hon. Mem., Amer. Astronomical Soc., 1983; For. Associate, Amer. Nat. Acad. of Scis, 1986. Pres., RAS, 1979–81, Gold Medal, 1983; Guthrie Medal and Prize, Inst. of Physics, 1984; Hughes Medal, Royal Soc., 1992. Dr *hc* Observatoire de Paris, 1976; Hon. DSc QUB, 1982. *Publications:* papers on atomic physics and astrophysics in various jls. *Address:* Chatsworth, Bwlch, Powys LD3 7RQ. *T:* (01874) 730652.

SEAWARD, Colin Hugh, CBE 1987; HM Diplomatic Service, retired; *b* 16 Sept. 1926; *s* of late Sydney W. Seaward and Molly W. Seaward; *m* 1st, 1949, Jean Bugler (decd); three *s* one *d*; 2nd, 1973, Judith Margaret Hinkley; two *d*. *Educ:* RNC, Dartmouth. Served Royal Navy, 1944–65. Joined HM Diplomatic Service, 1965; served: Accra, 1965; Bathurst (Banjul), 1966; FO, 1968; Rio de Janeiro, 1971; Prague, 1972; FCO, 1973; RNC, Greenwich (sowc), 1976; Counsellor (Econ. and Comm.), Islamabad, 1977–80; Consul-General, Rio de Janeiro, 1980–86, retd; re-employed in FCO, 1987–91. Sec., Anglo-Brazilian Soc., 1992–95 (Hon. Sec., 1986–91). Freeman, City of London, 1987. *Address:* Brasted House, Brasted, Westerham, Kent TN16 1JA.

SEBAG-MONTEFIORE, Harold Henry; Barrister-at-law; Deputy Circuit Judge, 1973–83; *b* 5 Dec. 1924; *e s* of late John Sebag-Montefiore and Violet, *o c* of late James Henry Solomon; *m* 1968, Harriet, *o d* of late Benjamin Harrison Paley, New York; one *d*.

Educ: Stowe; Lower Canada Coll., Montreal; Pembroke Coll., Cambridge (MA). Served War of 1939–45, RAF. Called to Bar, Lincoln's Inn, 1951. Mem., Disciplinary Tribunal, Bar Council. Contested (C) North Paddington, Gen. Elec., 1959; Chm., Conservative Parly Candidates Assoc., 1960–64. Member: LCC, 1955–65 (last Alderman, Co. of London, 1961–65); GLC, for Cities of London and Westminster, 1964–73, First Chm., GLC Arts and Recreation Cttee, 1968–73; Sports Council, 1972–74. Pres., Anglo-Jewish Assoc., 1966–71; Jt Pres., Barkingside Jewish Youth Centre, 1988–94; Mem. Council, Anglo-Netherlands Soc., 1988–2001. Freeman, City of London, and Liveryman, Spectacle Makers' Co. Trustee: Royal Nat. Theatre Foundn; Internat. Festival of Youth Orchestras; Whitechapel Art Gall.; Touro National Heritage, RI; Mem., Cttee of Honour: RAH Centenary; "Fanfare for Europe"; William and Mary Tercentenary; Centenary of Montefiore Hosp., NY. Rode winner of Bar Point-to-Point, 1957 and 1959; Pres., Greater London Horse Show, 1970–73. Chevalier, Légion d'Honneur, 1973. *Publications:* obituaries; book reviews and articles on Polo under *nom-de-plume* of "Marco II". *Recreations:* theatre, travel, collecting conductors' batons. *Clubs:* Garrick, Hurlingham, Pegasus (Pres., 1979).

See also Sir M. W. Hanham, Bt.

SEBASTIAN, Sir Cuthbert (Montraville), GCMG 1996; OBE 1970; MD; Governor-General, St Christopher and Nevis, since 1996; *b* 22 Oct. 1921. *Educ:* Mount Allison Univ., Canada (BSc 1953); Dalhousie Univ., Canada (MD, CM 1958). Pharmacist and Lab. Technician, Cunningham Hosp., St Kitts, 1942–43; RAF, 1944–45; Captain Surg., St Kitts Nevis Defence Force, 1958–80; Medical Superintendent: Cunningham Hosp., 1966; Joseph N. France Gen. Hosp., 1967–80; CMO, St Christopher and Nevis, 1980–83; private medical practitioner, 1983–95. *Recreations:* farming, reading, dancing. *Address:* Government House, Basseterre, St Kitts, W Indies; #6 Cayon Street, Basseterre, St Kitts, West Indies. *T:* 4652315. *Club:* Rotary of St Kitts.

SEBASTIAN, Timothy; freelance writer and journalist; *b* 13 March 1952; *s* of Peter Sebastian, CBE and Pegitha Saunders; *m* 1977, Diane Buscombe; one *s* two *d. Educ:* Westminster School; New College, Oxford. BA (Hons) Mod. Lang. BBC Eastern Europe correspondent, 1979–82; BBC TV News: Europe correspondent, 1982–84; Moscow correspondent, 1984–85; Washington correspondent, 1986–89. Presenter, Hardtalk, BBC TV, 1997–. TV journalist of the year, 1982, Interviewer of the Year, 2000, 2001, RTS; Richard Dimbleby Award, BAFTA, 1982. *Publications:* Nice Promises, 1985; I Spy in Russia, 1986; *novels:* The Spy in Question, 1988; Spy Shadow, 1989; Saviour's Gate, 1990; Exit Berlin, 1992; Last Rights, 1993; Special Relations, 1994; War Dance, 1995; Ultra, 1997. *Address:* BBC TV Centre, W12 7RT.

SEBER, Andrew James; County Education Officer, Hampshire County Council, since 1998; *b* 18 Sept. 1950; *s* of Philip George Seber and Helen Kathleen Seber (*née* Medhurst); *m* 1972, Sally Elizabeth Tyrrill; one *s* one *d. Educ:* East Barnet Grammar Sch.; Hertford Coll., Oxford (MA Biochemistry); Univ. of York; Middlesex Poly. (PGCE 1977). Science Teacher: City of Leeds Sch., 1973–74; Hayes Manor Sch., 1974–79; Education Officer: Ealing LBC, 1979–81; Bucks CC, 1981–83; Hants CC, 1983–98; City Educn Officer, Portsmouth CC, 1998. Director: Southern Careers Ltd, 1996–; South Central Connexions, 2001–; Chm., Southern Strategic Partnership for Lifelong Learning, 2000–; Advr, Service Children's Educn, 2000–. Member: Nat. Council, Soc. of Educn Officers, 2000–; Local Learning and Skills Council, 2001–. *Publications:* contribs to educnl jl. *Recreations:* family, theatre. *Address:* Hampshire County Council, The Castle, Winchester, Hants SO23 8UG. *T:* (01962) 846400.

SEBRIGHT, Sir Peter Giles Vivian, 15th Bt *cr* 1626, of Besford, Worcs; *b* 2 Aug. 1953; *s* of Sir Hugo Giles Edmund Sebright, 14th Bt and of Deirdre Ann, *d* of late Major Vivian Lionel Slingsby Bethell; *S* father, 1985; *m* 1st, 1977, Regina Maria (marr. diss.), *d* of Francis Steven Clarebrough, Melbourne; one *s*; 2nd, Madeleine; one *s* one *d. Heir: s* Rufus Hugo Giles Sebright; *b* 31 July 1978.

SECCOMBE, family name of **Baroness Seccombe**.

SECCOMBE, Baroness *cr* 1991 (Life Peer), of Kineton in the County of Warwickshire; **Joan Anna Dalziel Seccombe,** DBE 1984; Deputy Opposition Chief Whip, House of Lords, since 2001; *b* 3 May 1930; *d* of Robert John Owen and Olive Barlow Owen; *m* 1950, Henry Lawrence Seccombe; two *s. Educ:* St Martin's Sch., Solihull. Member: Heart of England Tourist Bd, 1977–81 (Chm., Marketing Sub-Cttee, 1979–81); Women's Nat. Commn, 1984–90; Chm., Lord Chancellor's Adv. Cttee, 1975–93. Mem. Exec., 1975–97, Vice-Chm., 1984–87, Chm., 1987–88, Nat. Union of Cons. and Unionist Assocs; Chairman: W Midlands Area Cons. Women's Cttee, 1975–78; Cons. Women's Nat. Cttee, 1981–84; Cons. Party Social Affairs Forum, 1985–87; Dep. Chm., W Midlands Area Cons. Council, 1979–81; Vice-Chm., with special responsibility for women, Cons. Party, 1987–97. Mem., W Midlands CC, 1977–81 (Chm., Trading Standards Cttee, 1979–81). An Opposition Whip, H of L, 1997–2001. Governor, 1988–2001, Dep. Chm., 1994–2001, Nuffield Hosps; Chm. Trustees, Nuffield Hosps Pension Scheme, 1992–2000. JP Solihull, 1968–2000 (Chm., 1981–84). *Recreations:* golf, ski-ing. *Address:* Linden Cottage, The Green, Little Kineton, Warwicks CV35 0DJ. *T:* (01926) 640562. *Club:* St Enedoc Golf (Pres., 1992–).

See also Hon. Sir J. A. D. Owen.

SECCOMBE, Sir (William) Vernon (Stephen), Kt 1988; JP; Chairman, Plymouth Hospitals NHS Trust, 1993–98; former electrical contractor; *b* 14 Jan. 1928; *s* of Stephen Seccombe and Edith Violet (*née* Smith); *m* 1950, Margaret Vera Profit; four *s. Educ:* Saltash Grammar Sch.; Plymouth and Devonport Tech. Coll. Mem., E Cornwall Water Bd, 1960–74 (Vice-Chm., 1963–66; Chm., 1966–69); Chairman: Cornwall and Isles of Scilly DHA, late AHA, 1981–82; S Western RHA, 1983–90; Plymouth HA, 1990–93; Dep. Comr, 1970–79, Comr, 1979–82, Western Area Traffic Comrs. Member: Saltash BC, 1953–74 (Chairman: Works Cttee, 1956–62; Finance and Estabs Cttee, 1963–74; Mayor, 1962–63); Caradon DC, 1973–79 (Vice-Chm., 1973–76; Chm., 1976–78). Governor, Saltash Comprehensive Sch., 1970–81 (Chm., 1974–78). JP SE Cornwall, 1970. *Recreations:* industrial and local archaeology, genealogy (Pres., Cornwall Family History Soc., 1995–). *Address:* Hawks Park House, Hawks Park, Saltash, Cornwall PL12 4SP.

SECKER-WALKER, Prof. Lorna Margaret, PhD; Professor of Cancer Cytogenetics, Royal Free Hospital School of Medicine, 1993–97, Emeritus since 1997; *b* 17 Nov. 1933; *d* of late William Elmer Lea and Margaret Violet Lea (*née* Rees); *m* 1957, David Secker-Walker; one *s* three *d. Educ:* numerous schs; St Anne's Coll., Oxford (BA 1955; MA 1959); Inst. of Orthopaedics, London Univ. (PhD 1961). FRCPath 1996. Res. Fellow, MRC Unit for bone seeking isotopes, Oxford, 1955–56; Post-grad. Scholarship, Louvain Univ., Belgium, 1956–57; Royal Marsden Hospital, 1967–84; Non-clinical Lectr in cytogenetics of leukaemia; Gordon Jacobs, MRC and Leukaemia Res. Fund Fellowhips; Royal Free Hospital School of Medicine: Lectr, 1984–85; Sen. Lectr, 1985–93. Member Editorial Board: Acta Haematological, 1988–2000; Cancer Genetics and Cytogenetics, 1987–97; Leukemia, 1994–. Chm., UK Cancer Cytogenetics Gp, 1988–97; Dir, Leukaemia Res. Fund Leukaemia Cytogenetics Gp and UK Cancer Cytogenetics Gp karyotype database in Acute Lymphoblastic Leukaemia, 1992–97; Mem. Fac., European Sch. of Haematol., 1986–95. Advr to MRC on cytogenetics of leukaemia, 1985–97. Member: Brit. Soc. Haematol., 1975; Internat. Soc. Hematol., 1976; Genetical Soc., 1976; RSocMed, 1984; Assoc. of Clin. Cytogeneticists, 1984; Amer. Soc. Hematol., 1994; European Haematol. Assoc., 1994; European Soc. Human Genetics, 1994. *Publications:* Chromosomes and Genes in Acute Lymphoblastic Leukemia, 1997; chapters in: Postgraduate Haematology, 3rd edn 1989, 4th edn 1998; Haematological Oncology, 1994; over 100 articles in scientific and med. jls. *Recreations:* theatre, opera, travel, jigsaw puzzles. *Address:* 5 Chalcot Square, NW1 8YB. *T:* (020) 7722 6467.

SECKERSON, Edward Stuart; music critic, writer and broadcaster; Chief Opera Critic and General Music Critic, The Independent, since 1991; *b* 27 July 1947; *s* of William Douglas Seckerson and Daphne Lilian (*née* Beard). *Educ:* Spender Park Sch.; private studies music and drama. BBC Gramophone Liby, 1966–69; Marketing Assistant, Decca Record Co., 1969–72; professional actor, 1972–80; music journalist, 1980–; contributor to: music mags incl. Classical Music, Hi-Fi News & Record Rev., BBC Music Mag., Gramophone; newspapers: The Guardian; The Times; Chief Music Critic, Sunday Correspondent, 1989–90. Radio and TV: contrib. BBC Radio 2, 3, 4 and World Service; commentator, Cardiff Singer of the World, BBC TV, 1991, 1993, 1995, 1997. *Publications:* Mahler: his life and times, 1984; Viva Voce: conversations with Michael Tilson Thomas, 1994. *Recreations:* music, literature, cinema, theatre. *Address:* 16 Dalebury Road, SW17 7HH. *T:* (020) 8672 4340.

SECONDÉ, Sir Reginald (Louis), KCMG 1981 (CMG 1972); CVO 1968 (MVO 1957); HM Diplomatic Service, retired; Ambassador to Venezuela, 1979–82; *b* 28 July 1922; *s* of late Lt-Col Emile Charles Secondé and Doreen Secondé (*née* Sutherland); *m* 1951, Catherine Penelope, *d* of late Thomas Ralph Sneyd-Kynnersley, OBE, MC and late Alice Sneyd-Kynnersley; one *s* two *d. Educ:* Beaumont; King's Coll., Cambridge. Served, 1941–47, in Coldstream Guards: N Africa and Italy (despatches); Major. Entered Diplomatic Service, 1949; UK Delegn to the UN, New York, 1951–55; British Embassy: Lisbon, 1955–57; Cambodia, 1957–59; FO, 1959–62; British Embassy, Warsaw, 1962–64; First Secretary and later Political Counsellor, Rio de Janeiro, 1964–69; Head of S European Dept, FCO, 1969–72; Royal Coll. of Defence Studies, 1972–73; Ambassador to Chile, 1973–76, to Romania, 1977–79. *Address:* Gosfield Hall, Apt 14, Gosfield, Halstead, Essex CO9 1SF. *T:* (01787) 477191. *Club:* Cavalry and Guards.

SECRETAN, Lance Hilary Kenyon; consultant, lecturer, journalist, author and entrepreneur, since 1981; Founder and President, The Secretan Center Inc., since 1972; President, Thaler Resources Ltd, since 1981; *b* 1 Aug. 1939; *s* of late Kenyon and Marie-Therese Secretan; *m* 1st, 1961, Gloria Christina (marr. diss. 1990; she *d* 2000); two *d* (and one *d* decd); 2nd, 1993, Patricia Edith Sheppard. *Educ:* Los Cocos, Argentina; Italia Conti, London; St Peters, Bournemouth; Univ. of Waterloo, Canada; Univ. of Southern California (MA in International Relations, *cum laude*); LSE (PhD in International Relations). Sales Manager, J. J. Little and Ives, Toronto, 1959; Analyst, Toronto Stock Exchange, 1960; Sales Manager, Office Overload Co. Ltd, 1960–67; Man. Dir, Manpower Ltd Gp of Cos, UK, Ireland, Middle East and Africa, 1967–81. Prof. of Entrepreneurship, McMaster Univ., 1981–82; Vis. Prof., York Univ., Toronto, 1983–84; Special Goodwill Ambassador for Canadian Assoc., UNEP, 1989–93; Chm. Adv. Bd, 1997 Special Olympics World Winter Games. *Publications:* How to be an Effective Secretary, 1972; From Guns to Butter, 1983; Managerial Moxie, 1985, rev. edn 1992; The State of Small Business in Ontario, 1986; The Masterclass, 1988; The Way of the Tiger, 1989; The Personal Masterclass, 1991; Living the Moment, 1992; Reclaiming Higher Ground, 1996; Inspirational Leadership, 1999. *Recreations:* life, music, ski-ing, Mother Earth. *Address:* 1137 Cataract Road, RR2, Alton, ON L0N 1A0, Canada; 38 Chester Terrace, Regent's Park, NW1 4ND. *Club:* Mensa.

SEDAT, Elizabeth Helen, (Mrs J. W. Sedat); *see* Blackburn, E. H.

SEDCOLE, Cecil Frazer, FCA; a Vice Chairman, Unilever PLC, 1982–85; *b* 15 March 1927; *s* of late William John Sedcole and Georgina Irene Kathleen Bluett (*née* Moffatt); *m* 1962, Jennifer Bennett Riggall; one *s* one *d. Educ:* Uppingham Sch., Rutland. FCA 1952; CBIM 1982. Joined Unilever Group of Cos, 1952: Dir, Birds Eye Foods, 1960–66; Vice-Chairman: Langnese-Iglo, Germany, 1966–67; Frozen Products Gp, Rotterdam, 1967–71; Dir, Unilever PLC and Unilever NV, 1974–85; Chm., UAC International, 1976–79; Mem., 1971–75, Chm., 1979–85, Overseas Cttee, Unilever; Dir, Tate & Lyle, 1982–90; Dep. Chm., Reed International, 1985–87. Mem., BOTB, 1982–86; Mem. Bd, Commonwealth Devlt Corp., 1984–88. Trustee, Leverhulme Trust, 1982–97. Governor: Bedales Sch., 1983–90; Queen Elizabeth's Foundn for Disabled People, 1993–. *Recreation:* golf. *Address:* Beeches, Tyrrell's Wood, Leatherhead, Surrey KT22 8QH. *Club:* Royal Air Force.

SEDDON, (Edward) Jeremy; Chief Executive, British Invisibles, 1997–2001; *b* 14 April 1941; *s* of Col Roland Nelson Seddon, OBE and Dorothy Ida Kathleen Seddon (*née* Canning); *m* 1975, Prudence Mary Clarke; one *s* two *d. Educ:* King's Sch., Bruton; Southampton Univ. (BScEng). Associated Electrical Industries, 1958–68; Dalgety Ltd, 1968–73; Barclays Merchant Bank, then BZW Ltd, 1973–97: Dir, Barclays Development Capital, 1978–87; Head, BZW Privatisation and Govt Adv. Practice, 1987–95; Chm., BZW & Barclays India, 1995–97. Mem., Competition Commn, 1998–. *Recreations:* gardening, music, sailing. *Address:* The Meadow House, Toys Hill, Westerham, Kent TN16 1QE. *T:* (01732) 750699. *Clubs:* Royal Thames Yacht, Special Forces.

SEDDON, Richard Harding, PhD; RWS 1976 (ARWS 1972); ARCA; artist and writer; President, Royal Watercolour Society, 1995–96; *b* 1 May 1915; *s* of Cyril Harding Seddon; *m* 1946, Audrey Madeline Wareham. *Educ:* King Edward VII School; Roy. Coll. of Art; Univ. of Reading (PhD 1946). Demonstrator in Fine Art, Univ. of Reading, 1944; Extra-Mural Staff Tutor in Fine Art, Univ. of Birmingham, 1947; Director, Sheffield City Art Galleries, 1948–63; Curator, Ruskin Collection, 1948–63; Dir of Art History and Liberal Studies, Sch. of Design and Furniture, Buckinghamshire Coll. of Higher Educn, 1963–80. Hon. Advisory Panel, Hereford Art Galls, 1948; Arts Council Selection Bd (Art Students Exhib.), 1947; Pres. Ludlow Art Soc., 1947–67; Hon. Member: Sheffield Soc. of Artists; Oxford Folk Art Soc.; Sheffield Photographic Soc.; Mem., Oxford Bureau for Artists in War-time, 1940; Chm. Selection Cttee, Nottingham Artists Exhibition, 1953; Guest Speaker Educational Centres Association Annual Conference, 1951; West Riding Artists Exhibition Selection Committee, 1956; Northern Young Artists Exhibition Selection Committee, 1958; Member Sheffield Univ. Court; Sheffield Diocesan Advisory Cttee, 1948. Exhibitor at: RA; NEAC; RI; RBA; Internat. Artists; Architectural Assoc.; RIBA; National Gallery (War Artists) 1943; Leicester Galleries; Redfern Galleries. Official acquisitions: V. & A. Museum, 1939; Pilgrim Trust, 1942; Imperial War Museum (War Artists), 1943, 1956 (ten paintings); Graves Gall., Sheffield, 1943 and 1956; Atkinson Gall., Southport, 1953; Reading Art Gall., 1956; Leeds Education Cttee Collection, 1956. Extra Mural and Univ. Extension lectr on art to Univs of Oxford, Birmingham, London and Sheffield, 1948–; initiated Sheffield Conference on Nation's Art Treasures, 1958; FMA, 1951–74; Mem. Yorkshire Fed. Museums and Art Galls, 1948 (Committee 1952 and

1957, President, 1954–55, Vice-President, 1955–56); Secretary Yorks Museums Regional Fact Finding Committee, 1959; National Art Collections Fund Rep. for Yorks, 1954–63; Judge for Wakefield Art Galls Open Art Competition, 1984. Hon. Adviser to Co. of Cutlers in Hallamshire, 1950–64; Dep. Chm., Sheffield Design Council for Gold, Silver and Jewelry Trades, 1960; Mem. BBC '51 Soc., 1960; Mem. Govg Council, Design and Res. Centre, 1960; Mem. Art Adv. Cttee Yorks Area Scheme for Museums and Art Galleries, 1963; Art Critic: Birmingham Post, 1963–71; Yorkshire Post, 1974–92; Jl Fedn of British Artists, 1975–83; Mem. Recognised Panel of London Univ. Extension Lectrs, 1964; Mem. Council and Hon. Treasurer, 1976, Trustee, 1983–86, RWS; Hon. Artist Mem., RI, 1996; Hon. Treas., Artists' League of GB, 1984–86. Hon. Mem., Mark Twain Soc., USA, 1976. War Service with RAOC Field Park, France, 1940 (King's Badge); facilities by War Office Order to make war drawings in Maginot Line, 1940. *Publications:* The Technical Methods of Paul Nash (Memorial Vol.), 1949; The Artist's Vision, 1949; The Academic Technique of Oil Painting, 1960; A Hand Uplifted (war memoirs), 1962; Art Collecting for Amateurs, 1964; (ed) Dictionary of Art Terms, 1981; The Artist's Studio Book, 1983; articles on fine art for Jl of Aesthetics (USA), Burlington Magazine, Apollo, The Studio, The Connoisseur, Arch. Review, The Artist, The Antique Collector and daily press; lectures on art in England and abroad; criticisms; book reviews; broadcasts. *Recreation:* gardening. *Address:* 6 Arlesey Close, Putney, SW15 2EX. *T:* (020) 8788 5899.

SEDGEMORE, Brian Charles John; MP (Lab) Hackney South and Shoreditch, since 1983; *b* 17 March 1937; *s* of Charles John Sedgemore, fisherman; *m* 1964 (marr. diss.); one *s*. *Educ:* Newtown Primary Sch.; Heles Sch.; Oxford Univ. (MA). Diploma in public and social administration. Called to Bar, Middle Temple, 1966. RAF, 1956–58; Oxford, 1958–62. Administrative Class, Civil Service, Min. of Housing and Local Govt, 1962–66 (Private Sec. to R. J. Mellish, MP, then junior Minister of Housing, 1964–66). Practising barrister, 1966–74. MP (Lab) Luton West, Feb. 1974–1979; PPS to Tony Benn, MP, 1977–78. Researcher, Granada TV, 1980–83. *Publications:* The How and Why of Socialism, 1977; Mr Secretary of State (fiction), 1979; The Secret Constitution, 1980; Power Failure (fiction), 1985; Big Bang 2000, 1986; Pitiless Pursuit (fiction), 1994; Insider's Guide to Parliament, 1995; one time contributor to Britain's top satirical magazine. *Recreation:* sleeping on the grass. *Address:* 71 Riverside Close, Hackney, E5 9SR; House of Commons, SW1A 0AA.

SEDGMAN, Francis Arthur, AM 1980; Lawn Tennis Champion: Australia, 1949, 1950; USA, 1951, 1952; Wimbledon, 1952; Italy, 1952; Asia, 1952; Professional Tennis Player since 1953; *b* Victoria, Australia, 29 Oct. 1927; *m* 1952, Jean Margaret Spence; four *d*. *Educ:* Box Hill High School, Vic, Australia. First played in the Australian Davis Cup team, 1949; also played in winning Australian Davis Cup team, 1950, 1951, 1952. With John Bromwich, won Wimbledon doubles title, 1948; with Kenneth McGregor, won the Australian, French, Wimbledon and American doubles titles in the same year (1951), the only pair ever to do so; with Kenneth McGregor also won Australian, French and Wimbledon doubles titles, 1952; with Doris Hart, won French, Wimbledon and US mixed doubles titles, 1952. Last male player to win three titles at Wimbledon in one year, 1952. Director of many private companies. USA Hall of Fame, 1987; Australian Hall of Fame, 1988. *Publication:* Winning Tennis, 1955. *Recreations:* golfing, racing. *Address:* 19 Bolton Avenue, Hampton, Victoria 3188, Australia. *T:* (3) 95986341. *Clubs:* All England Lawn Tennis and Croquet, Queen's; Melbourne Cricket (Melbourne); Kooyong Tennis; Grace Park Tennis; Victoria Amateur Turf, Victoria Racing; Royal Melbourne Golf, Carbine (Melbourne); Mornington Racing (Mem. Cttee); Sanctuary Cove Country.

SEDGWICK, (Ian) Peter; Chairman, Schroders, since 2000 (Deputy Chairman, 1995–2000); *b* 13 Oct. 1935; *m* 1956, Verna Mary Churchward; one *s* one *d*. National Westminster Bank, 1952–59; Ottoman Bank, 1959–69; J. Henry Schroder Wagg & Co., 1969–89; Chief Exec., Schroder Investment Management, 1985–95; Schroders, 1987–; Pres. and CEO, Schroders Inc., NY, 1996–2000; Chm., Schroder & Co. Inc., NY, 1996–2000; Vice Pres., Equitable Life Assurance Soc., 1995–2001. *Recreations:* golf, theatre, grandchildren.

SEDGWICK, Nina, (Mrs A. R. M. Sedgwick); *see* Milkina, N.

SEDGWICK, Peter; *see* Sedgwick, I. P.

SEDGWICK, Peter Norman; Vice-President, and Member of Management Committee, European Investment Bank, since 2000; *b* 4 Dec. 1943; *s* of late Norman Victor Sedgwick and of Lorna Clara (*née* Burton); *m* 1984, Catherine Jane, *d* of Mr and Mrs B. D. T. Saunders; two *s* two *d*. *Educ:* Westminster Cathedral Choir Sch.; Downside; Lincoln Coll., Oxford (MA PPE, BPhilEcon). HM Treasury: Economic Asst, 1969; Economic Adviser, 1971; Sen. Economic Adviser, 1977; Under Sec., 1984; Hd of Internat. Finance Gp, 1990–94; Hd of Educn, Trng and Employment Gp, 1994–95; Dep. Dir, Public Services (formerly Public Spending) Directorate, 1995–99. Chm. 1979–84, Mem. Develt Cttee 1984–, London Symphony Chorus. *Recreation:* singing. *Address:* European Investment Bank, 100 Boulevard Konrad Adenauer, 2950 Luxembourg.

SEDLEY, Prof. David Neil, PhD; FBA 1994; Laurence Professor of Ancient Philosophy, University of Cambridge, since 2000; Fellow, Christ's College, Cambridge, since 1976; *b* 30 May 1947; *s* of William Sedley and Rachel Sedley (*née* Seifert); *m* 1973, Beverley Anne Dobbs; two *s* one *d*. *Educ:* Westminster Sch.; Trinity Coll., Oxford (BA Lit. Hum. 1969; MA 1973); University Coll. London (PhD 1974). Dyson Jun. Res. Fellow in Greek Culture, Balliol Coll., Oxford, 1973–75; University of Cambridge: Asst Lectr in Classics, 1975–78; Lectr, 1978–89; Reader in Ancient Philosophy, 1989–96; Prof. of Ancient Philosophy, 1996–2000. Townsend Lectr, Cornell Univ., 2001. Foreign Hon. Mem., Amer. Acad. of Arts and Scis, 1998. Editor: Classical Qly, 1986–92; Oxford Studies in Ancient Philosophy, 1998–. *Publications:* (with A. A. Long) The Hellenistic Philosophers, 2 vols, 1987; Lucretius and the Transformation of Greek Wisdom, 1998; articles in classical and philosophical jls and collaborative vols. *Recreations:* cinema, vegetable growing. *Address:* Christ's College, Cambridge CB2 3BU. *T:* (01223) 334910; 97 Hills Road, Cambridge CB2 1PG. *T:* (01223) 368845.

See also Rt Hon. Sir S. J. Sedley.

SEDLEY, Rt Hon. Sir Stephen (John), Kt 1992; PC 1999; **Rt Hon. Lord Justice Sedley;** a Lord Justice of Appeal, since 1999; *b* 9 Oct. 1939; *s* of William and Rachel Sedley; *m* 1st, 1968, Ann Tate (marr. diss. 1995); one *s* two *d*; 2nd, 1996, Teresa, (Tia) (*née* Chaddock). *Educ:* Mill Hill Sch. (entrance schol.); Queens' Coll., Cambridge (open schol./exhibnr; BA Hons 1961). Freelance writer, interpreter, musician, translator, 1961–64; called to the Bar, Inner Temple, 1964, Bencher, 1989; QC 1983; a Judge of the High Court of Justice, QBD, 1992–99; Pres., Nat. Reference Tribunals for the Coalmining Industry, 1983–88. Chm., Sex Discrimination Cttee, Bar Council, 1992–95. Pres., British Inst. of Human Rights, 2000–. *Ad hoc* judge, European Court of Human Rights, 2000. Vis. Professorial Fellow, Warwick Univ., 1981; Vis. Fellow, 1987, Vis. Prof., 1997, Osgoode Hall Law Sch., Canada; Distinguished Visitor, Hong Kong Univ., 1992; Hon. Professor: Univ. of Wales, Cardiff, 1993–; Univ. of Warwick, 1994–; Vis. Fellow, Victoria Univ. of Wellington, NZ, 1998; Judicial Visitor, UCL, 1999–. Lectures: Bernard Simons Meml, 1994; Paul Sieghart Meml, 1995; Radcliffe (with Lord Nolan), 1996; Laskin, 1997; Hamlyn, 1998; Lord Morris of Borth-y-Gest, 1999. A Dir, Public Law Project, 1989–93; Hon. Vice-Pres., Administrative Law Bar Assoc., 1992–. Mem., Internat. Commn on Mercenaries, Angola, 1976. Sec., Haldane Soc., 1964–69. Hon. Fellow, Inst. for Advanced Legal Studies, 1997. Hon. Dr N London, 1996; Hon. LLD: Nottingham Trent, 1997; Bristol, 1999; Warwick, 1999. *Publications:* (trans.) From Burgos Jail, by Marcos Ana and Vidal de Nicolas, 1964; (ed) Seeds of Love (anthology), 1967; Whose Child? (report of inquiry into death of Tyra Henry), 1987; (ed) A Spark in the Ashes: writings of John Warr, 1992; (with Lord Nolan) The Making and Remaking of the British Constitution (Radcliffe Lectures), 1997; Freedom, Law and Justice (Hamlyn Lectures), 1999; contributed: Orwell: inside the myth, 1984; Civil Liberty, 1984; Police, the Constitution and the Community, 1986; Challenging Decisions, 1986; Public Interest Law, 1987; Civil Liberties in Conflict, 1988; Law in East and West, 1988; Citizenship, 1991; Administrative Law and Government Action, 1994; Frontiers of Legal Scholarship, 1995; Law Society and Economy, 1997; Human Rights for the 1990s, 1997; The Golden Metwand and the Crooked Cord (essays for Sir William Wade), 1998; Freedom of Expression and Freedom of Information (essays for Sir David Williams), 2000; Judicial Review in International Perspective (essays for Lord Slynn of Hadley), 2000; Discriminating Lawyers, 2000; contrib. DNB: Missing Persons; London Review of Books, Public Law, Modern Law Review, Jl of Law and Soc., Civil Justice Qly, Law Qly Review, Industrial Law Jl, Eur. Human Rights Law Rev. *Recreations:* carpentry, music, cycling, walking, changing the world. *Address:* c/o Royal Courts of Justice, Strand, WC2A 2LL.

See also D. N. Sedley.

SEDOV, Leonid Ivanovich; 6 Orders of Lenin, Hero of Socialist Labour, USSR; Professor, Moscow University, since 1937; Chief of Department of Hydrodynamics, since 1941; Member, Russian Academy of Sciences; *b* 14 Nov. 1907; *m* 1931, Galya Tolstova; one *s* one *d*. *Educ:* Moscow University. Chief Engineer, Associate Chief lab., N.E. Zhukovsky Aerohydrodynamic Inst., Moscow, 1930–47; Vice-President, International Astronautical Federation, 1962–80 (Pres., 1959–61); Internat. Astronautical Acad., 1980–. Hon. Member: American Academy of Arts and Sciences; Internat. Astronautical Acad.; Serbian Academy, Belgrade; Tech. Academy, Finland; For. Associate, Acad. of Sciences, Paris; Academia Leopoldina. Hon. doctorates from many foreign universities. Medal of Obert; State Prize; Chaplygin Prize; Lomonosov Prize; Lyapunov Medal; Guggenheim Award; Van Allen Award. Commandeur de la Légion d'Honneur (France). *Publications:* Theory of Plane Flow of Liquids, 1939; Plane Problems of Hydrodynamics and Aerodynamics, 1950, 1966, 1980; Similarity and Dimensional Methods in Mechanics, 1944, 1951, 1953, 1957, 1960, 1965, 1967, 1977, 1995; Introduction into the Mechanics of Continua, 1962; Mechanics of Continuous Media, 2 vols, 1970, 1973, 1976, 1983–84, 1996; Thoughts about Science and Scientists, 1980; (with A. G. Tsypkin) Fundamentals of Electromagnetical and Gravitational Macroscopic Theories, 1989; numerous articles. *Address:* Moscow University, Zone I, kv 84, Vorobrevy Gory, Moscow 119899, Russia.

SEED, John Junior, CEng, FIEE; Chief Executive, South Western Electricity plc, 1992–95; *b* 25 Oct. 1938; *s* of John Seed and Elizabeth (*née* Earley); *m* 1961, Maureen Syder; two *d*. *Educ:* City of Norwich Grammar Sch.; Norwich City Coll. CEng 1972; FIEE 1986. Eastern Electricity: Dist Manager, Bury St Edmunds, 1976–80; Area Manager, Suffolk, 1980–82; Dir of Engrg, 1982–86; Dep. Chm., S Western Electricity Bd, 1986–90; Man. Dir, S Western Electricity plc, 1990–92. Director: Royal United Hosp. Trust, 1991–97; United Utilities plc, 1996–; British Smaller Companies VCT plc, 1996–; Prism Rail plc, 1996–2000; Weston Attenas Ltd, 2001–; Chairman: Great Western Assured Growth plc, 1991–97; Windelectric Ltd, 1996–99; Rebus Group plc, 1997–99; Warren Associates Ltd, 1998–2001. CIMgt (FBIM 1980). *Recreations:* golf, walking, bridge.

SEED, Rev. Michael Joseph Steven, SA; STD; Chaplain, Westminster Cathedral, since 1985; Ecumenical Officer, Archdiocese of Westminster, since 1988; *b* 16 June 1957; adopted *s* of late Joseph Seed and Lillian Seed (*née* Ramsden). *Educ:* St Mary's Coll., Aberystwyth; St Joseph's Coll., Cork; Missionary Inst., Mill Hill; Washington Theol Inst., Md; Catholic Univ. of America, Washington (MDiv. 1984); Heythrop Coll.; Pontifical Lateran Univ., Rome (STL 1987; STD 1989); Polish Univ., London (PhD 1991). Entered Franciscan Friars of the Atonement, 1979; final profession, 1985; ordained priest, 1986; Chaplain, Westminster Hosp., 1986–90; Officiating Chaplain to the Forces, Wellington Barracks, 1990–2000. Chaplain, Soc. of Useless Information, 1998. For. Corresp. Academician, Historical Inst. of Dom Luiz I (Portugal), 1998. Cross of Merit in Gold (Poland), 1988; Order of Orthodox Hospitallers (Cyprus), 1988; Ecclesiastical Kt of Grace, Sacred and Mil. Constantinian Order of St George (Naples), 1989; Kt of Justice for Merit, Mil. Order of the Collar, 2001. *Publications:* I Will See You in Heaven, 1991; (contrib.) Sons and Mothers, 1996; (contrib.) Faith, Hope and Chastity, 1999; Will I See You in Heaven?, 1999; Assurance, 2000; Letters from the Heart, 2000. *Recreations:* politicans, pizza, Zwinglianism. *Address:* Clergy House, 42 Francis Street, SW1P 1QW. *T:* (020) 7798 9055.

SEED, Nigel John; QC 2000; a Recorder, since 2000; *b* 30 Jan. 1951; *s* of Thomas Robertson Seed and Joan Hall Seed (*née* Evison). *Educ:* Ellesmere Port Grammar Sch. for Boys; St Chad's Coll., Durham (BA 1972). Called to the Bar, Inner Temple, 1978; Mem., Western Circuit, 1981–; Asst Recorder, 1995–2000. Chancellor, Dio. of Leicester, 1989–; Deputy Chancellor: Dio. of Salisbury, 1992–97; Dio. of Norwich, 1992–98. *Recreations:* walking, cooking, eating and drinking. *Address:* 3 Paper Buildings, Temple, EC4Y 7EU. *T:* (020) 7583 8055. *Club:* Athenæum.

SEED, Ven. Richard Murray Crosland; Archdeacon of York, since 1999; Rector of Micklegate and Bishophill Junior, since 2000; *b* 9 May 1949; *s* of Denis Briggs Seed and Mary Crosland Seed (*née* Barrett); *m* 1974, Jane Margaret Berry; one *s* three *d*. *Educ:* St Philip's Sch., Burley-in-Wharfedale; Edinburgh Theol Coll.; Leeds Univ. (MA). Deacon 1972, priest 1973; Asst Curate, Christ Church, Skipton, 1972–75, Baildon, 1975–77, Dio. Bradford; Team Vicar, Kidlington, Oxford, 1977–80; Chaplain, HM Detention Centre, Campsfield House, 1977–80; Vicar of Boston Spa, Dio. York, 1980–99; Priest-in-charge: Clifford, 1989–99; Thorp Arch with Walton, 1998–99. Mem., Gen. Synod of C of E, 2000–. Chm., Diocesan Redundant Churches Cttee. Founder Chm. and Chaplain, Martin House Hospice for Children, 1980–. *Publication:* (contrib.) Appointed for Growth, 1994. *Recreations:* swimming, travel, Byzantine studies, monastic spirituality, walking dogs. *Address:* Holy Trinity Rectory, Micklegate, York YO1 6LE. *T:* (01904) 623798, *Fax:* (01904) 628155.

SEEL, Derek, FDSRCS; FRCS; FRCA; Dental Postgraduate Dean, University of Bristol, 1986–98; *b* 2 April 1932; *s* of William Alfred and Olive Seel; *m* 1960, Gillian Henderson. *Educ:* Stockport Sch.; Manchester Univ. Inst. of Dental Surgery (BDS). MOrthRCS; FRCS 1994; FRCA 1995. General dental practice, 1956–62; orthodontic trainee, 1962–68; Lectr in Orthodontics, Bristol Univ., 1967–69; Consultant Orthodontist, Univ. of Wales Coll. of Medicine, 1969–94; Consultant in Orthodontics, Welsh RHA, 1969–94. Dean, Faculty of Dental Surgery, RCS, 1990–92. Hon. Diploma in Gen. Dental

Practice, RCS 1994. C. F. Ballard Medal, Consultant Orthodontists' Gp, 1992; Colyer Gold Medal, RCS, 1994. *Recreations:* music, ski-ing, photography. *Address:* 20 Blenheim Road, Bristol BS6 7JP. *T:* (0117) 973 6635; *e-mail:* derek.seel@which.net.

SEELY, family name of **Baron Mottistone**.

SEELY, Sir Nigel (Edward), 5th Bt *cr* 1896; Dorland International; *b* 28 July 1923; *s* of Sir Victor Basil John Seely, 4th Bt and of Sybil Helen, *d* of late Sills Clifford Gibbons; *S* father, 1980; *m* 1949, Loraine, *d* of late W. W. Lindley-Travis; three *d*; *m* 1984, Trudi Pacter, *d* of Sydney Pacter. *Educ:* Stowe. *Heir: half-b* Victor Ronald Seely [*b* 1 Aug. 1941; *m* 1972, Annette Bruce, *d* of Lt-Col J. A. D. McEwen; one *s* one *d*]. *Address:* 3 Craven Hill Mews, W2 3DY. *Clubs:* Buck's; Royal Solent.

SEENEY, Leslie Elon Sidney, OBE 1978; Director General (formerly General Secretary), National Chamber of Trade, 1971–87; *b* 19 Jan. 1922; *s* of Sidney Leonard and Daisy Seeney, Forest Hill; *m* 1947, Marjory Doreen Greenwood, Spalding; one *s*. *Educ:* St Matthews, Camberwell. RAFVR, 1941–46 (Flt Lt, Pilot). Man. Dir, family manufg business (clothing), 1946–63, with other interests in insce and advertising. Mem., West Lewisham Chamber of Commerce, 1951, subseq. Sec. and Chm.; Delegate to Nat. Chamber of Trade, 1960; joined NCT staff, 1966. Mem., Home Office Standing Cttee on Crime Prevention, 1971–87. Council Member: (founding) Retail Consortium, 1971–87; Assoc. for Prevention of Theft from Shops, 1976–87. Fellow, Soc. of Assoc. Executives, 1970. *Publications:* various articles. *Recreations:* genealogy, travel, photography. *Address:* 60 Stanley Drive, Sutton Bridge, Spalding, Lincs PE12 9XQ. *T:* (01406) 359236.

SEETO, Sir (James Hip) Ling, Kt 1988; MBE 1975; Managing Director, Lingana Pty Ltd, Port Moresby, Papua New Guinea, since 1965; Director and part owner, Kwila Insurance Co., Port Moresby, since 1978; *b* 19 June 1933; *s* of Yeeying Seeto and Kamfoung Mack; *m* 1960, Anna Choiha Peng; two *s*. *Educ:* Rabaul Public Sch., PNG; Mowbray House Sch., Sydney, Australia; Trinity Grammar Sch., Sydney. Pings Co., Rabaul, PNG, 1954–58; Shell Co., Rabaul, 1958–62; Rabaul Metal Industries, Rabaul, 1962–64. Former Board Member: Nat. Investment and Develt Authy, PNG; PNG Develt Bank; Harbors Board; Water Resources Bd of PNG; Salvation Army Adv. Bd, PNG. A Youth Leader, Rabaul Methodist Ch., 1954–60. Silver Jubilee Medal, 1977; PNG Independence Medal, 1986. *Recreations:* golf, swimming, gardening, cooking. *Address:* PO Box 1756, Boroko, National Capital District, Papua New Guinea. *T:* (office) 254966, (home) 211873. *Clubs:* Cathay (Port Moresby) (Patron); Port Moresby Golf.

SEEYAVE, Sir René (Sow Choung), Kt 1985; CBE 1979; Group Chairman, Happy World Ltd, since 1986 (Group Managing Director, 1968–86); *b* 15 March 1935; *s* of late Antoine Seeyave, CBE and Lam Tung Ying; *m* 1961, Thérèse How Hong; one *s* four *d*. *Educ:* Royal College, Port Louis, Mauritius. Chm., Happy World Foods (formerly Mauritius Farms) Ltd, 1974–. Chm., Electricity Adv. Cttee, 1972–76. Vice Chairman: Mauritius Employers' Fedn, 1972; Mauritius Broadcasting Corp., 1980–81. Director: Mauritius Development Investment Trust Ltd, 1968–; Swan Insurance Co. Ltd, 1969–; Mauritius Marine Authority, 1980–95. Mauritius Res. Council, 1997–. Vice-Chm. Council, Univ. of Mauritius, 1985–87. Hon. Pres., Heen Foh Soc., 1991–. *Address:* Happy World Ltd, Level 8, Happy World House, 37 Sir William Newton Street, Port Louis, Mauritius. *T:* 2086886, *Fax:* 2086699. *Clubs:* Mauritius Gymkhana, Port Louis City.

SEGAL, Prof. Anthony Walter, MD; PhD, DSc; FRCP, FMedSci; FRS 1998; Charles Dent Professor of Medicine, University College London, since 1986; *b* 24 Feb. 1944; *s* of Cyril Segal and late Doreen (*née* Hayden); *m* 1966, Barbara Miller; three *d*. *Educ:* Univ. of Cape Town (MB, ChB; MD 1974); PhD 1979, DSc 1984, London. FRCP 1987. Internship, Groote Schuur Hosp., SA, 1968–69; Sen. House Officer, Registrar and Sen. Registrar in Medicine, Hammersmith Hosp., 1970–76; Registrar and Clinical Scientist, Northwick Park Hosp. and Clinical Res. Centre, 1971–79; Wellcome Trust Sen. Clinical Fellow, UCL, 1979–86; Hon. Consultant Physician, UCH, 1979–. Founder FMedSci 1998. *Publications:* contribs on biochemistry, cell biology, immunology and gastroenterology. *Recreations:* golf, sculpture, painting, theatre, music, dining. *Address:* Department of Medicine, Rayne Institute, 5 University Street, WC1E 6JJ. *T:* (020) 7679 6175. *Club:* Highgate Golf.

SEGAL, Ben; *see* Segal, J. B.

SEGAL, Prof. Erich; Adjunct Professor of Classics, Yale University, 1981–88; Hon. Research Fellow, Classics, University College London, 1982; *b* 16 June 1937; *s* of Samuel M. Segal, PhD, DHL and Cynthia Shapiro Segal; *m* 1975, Karen James; two *d* (one *s* decd). *Educ:* Harvard (Boylston Prize 1957, Bowdoin Prize 1959; AB 1958, AM 1959, PhD 1965). Teaching Fellow, Harvard, 1959–64; Lectr in Classics, Yale, 1964, Asst Prof., 1965–68, Associate Prof., 1968–73; Vis. Prof. in Classics: Munich, 1973; Princeton, 1974–75; Tel Aviv, 1976–77; Vis. Prof. in Comp. Lit., Dartmouth, 1976–78; Wolfson College, Oxford: Vis. Fellow, 1979–80; Supernumerary Fellow, 1982–88; Mem. Common Room, 1984–; Hon. Fellow, 1999. Member: Acad. of Literary Studies, USA, 1981; Nat. Adv. Council, 1970–72, Exec. Cttee, 1971–72, Peace Corps, USA (Presidential Commendation for Service to Peace Corps, 1971). Lectures: Amer. Philological Assoc., 1971, 1972; Amer. Comparative Lit. Assoc., 1971; German Classical Assoc., 1974; Boston Psychoanalytic Inst., 1974; Istituto Nazionale del Dramma Antico, Sicily, 1975; Brit. Classical Assoc., 1977; William Kelley Prentice Meml, Princeton, 1981; Inaugural Andrea Rosenthal Meml, Brown Univ., 1992. Author and narrator, The Ancient Games, 1972; TV commentator, ABC–TV, US, radio commentator in French, RTL Paris, Olympic Games, 1972 and 1976. Screenplays include: The Beatles' Yellow Submarine, 1968; The Games, 1969; Love Story, 1970 (Golden Globe Award, 1970); Oliver's Story, 1978; Man, Woman and Child, 1983. Mem., Authors Guild, 1970–. (With Mother Teresa and Peter Ustinov) Premio San Valentin di Terni, 1989. Chevalier de l'Ordre des Arts et des Lettres (France), 1998. *Publications:* Roman Laughter: the comedy of Plautus, 1968, rev. edn 1987; (ed) Euripides: a collection of critical essays, 1968; (ed and trans.) Plautus: Three Comedies, 1969, rev. edn 1985; (ed) Oxford Readings in Greek Tragedy, 1983; (ed with Fergus Millar) Caesar Augustus: seven aspects, 1984; (ed) Plato's Dialogues, 1985; Oxford Readings in Aristophanes, 1996; (ed and trans.) Plautus: Four Comedies, 1996; Death of Comedy, 2001; Oxford Readings in Menander, Plautus and Terence, 2002; *novels:* Love Story, 1970; Fairy Tale (for children), 1973; Oliver's Story, 1977; Man, Woman and Child, 1980; The Class, 1985 (Prix Deauville, France, and Premio Bancarella Selezione, Italy, 1986); Doctors, 1988; Acts of Faith, 1992; Prizes, 1995; Only Love, 1997; articles and reviews in Amer. Jl of Philology, Classical World, Harvard Studies in Classical Philology, Classical Review, Greek, Roman and Byzantine Studies, TLS, New York Times Book Review, New Republic, The Independent, Washington Post. *Recreations:* swimming, walking. *Address:* Wolfson College, Oxford OX2 6UD. *T:* (01865) 274100. *Club:* Athenæum.

SEGAL, Graeme Bryce, DPhil; FRS 1982; Senior Research Fellow, All Souls College, Oxford, since 1999; *b* 21 Dec. 1941; *s* of Reuben Segal and Iza Joan Harris; *m* 1962, Desley Rae Cheetham (marr. diss. 1972). *Educ:* Sydney Grammar School; Univ. of Sydney (BSc 1962); Univ. of Cambridge; Univ. of Oxford (MA, DPhil 1967). Oxford University: Junior Res. Fellow, Worcester Coll., 1964–66; Junior Lectr in Mathematics, 1965–66; Fellow, St Catherine's Coll., 1966–90; Reader in Maths, 1978–89; Prof. of Maths, 1989–90; Lowndean Prof. of Astronomy and Geometry, and Fellow, St John's Coll., Cambridge, 1990–99. Mem., Inst. for Advanced Study, Princeton, 1969–70. Editor, Topology, 1970–90. *Publications:* (with A. Pressley) Loop Groups, 1986; articles in learned jls. *Address:* All Souls College, Oxford OX1 4AL. *T:* (01865) 279379.

SEGAL, Prof. Judah Benzion, (Ben), MC 1942; FBA 1968; Professor of Semitic Languages in the University of London, School of Oriental and African Studies, 1961–79, now Emeritus; *b* 21 June 1912; *s* of Prof. Moses H. Segal and Hannah Leah Segal; *m* 1946, Leah (*née* Seidemann); two *d*. *Educ:* Magdalen College School, Oxford; St Catharine's College, Cambridge. Jarrett Schol., 1932; John Stewart of Rannoch Schol., in Hebrew, 1933; 1st Cl. Oriental Langs Tripos, 1935; Tyrwhitt Schol. and Mason Prizeman, 1936; BA (Cambridge), 1935; MA 1938. Colours, Cambridge Univ. Boxing Club, 1935, 1936. Mansel Research Exhibitioner, St John's Coll., Oxford, 1936–39; James Mew Schol., 1937; DPhil (Oxon.), 1939. Deputy Assistant Director, Public Security, Sudan Government, 1939–41; served War of 1939–45, GHQ, MEF, 1942–44, Captain; Education Officer, British Military Administration, Tripolitania, 1945–46. Head of Dept of Near and Middle East, Sch. of Oriental and African Studies, 1961–68 (Hon. Fellow 1983); Visiting Lectr, Ain Shams Univ., Cairo, 1979; Res. Fellow, Hebrew Univ., Jerusalem, 1980; Leverhulme Emeritus Fellowship, S India, 1981. Principal, Leo Baeck Coll., 1982–85, Pres., 1985–. Mem., Council of Christians and Jews; President: North Western Reform Synagogue; British Assoc. for Jewish Studies, 1980; Vice-Pres., Reform Synagogues of GB, 1985–91. Freedom, City of Urfa, Turkey, 1973. *Publications:* The Diacritical Point and the Accents in Syriac, 1953; The Hebrew Passover, 1963; Edessa, 1970; Aramaic Texts From North Saqqara, 1983; A History of the Jews of Cochin, 1993; Aramaic and Mandaic Incantation Bowls in the British Museum, 2000; Whisper Awhile, 2000; articles in learned periodicals. *Recreations:* walking, meditation. *Address:* 17 Hillersdon Avenue, Edgware, Middx HA8 7SG. *T:* (020) 8958 4993.

SEGAL, Michael John; District Judge (formerly Registrar), Principal Registry, Family Division, since 1985; *b* 20 Sept. 1937; *s* of Abraham Charles Segal and Iris Muriel (*née* Parsons); *m* 1963, Barbara Gina Fluxman; one *d*. *Educ:* Strode's Sch., Egham. Called to the Bar, Middle Temple, 1962. Practised at Bar, Midland and Oxford Circuit, 1962–84. Mem., Civil and Family Cttee, Judicial Studies Bd, 1990–94. Editor, Family Div. section, Butterworth's Cost Service, 1987–; Jt Editor, Supreme Court Practice, 1991–94. *Recreation:* living in the past. *Address:* 28 Grange Road, N6 4AP. *T:* (020) 8348 0680.

SEGALL, Anne Celia, (Mrs D. H. Evans); Economics Correspondent, Daily Telegraph, since 1985; *b* 20 April 1948; *d* of John Segall and Marsha (*née* Greenberg); *m* 1973, David Howard Evans, *qv*; two *s*. *Educ:* St Paul's Girls' Sch., London; St Hilda's Coll., Oxford (BA Hons PPE 1969). Banking correspondent: Investors' Chronicle, 1971–76; The Economist, 1976–80; Daily Telegraph, 1981–85. Wincott Award for Financial Journalism, 1975. *Recreations:* swimming, reading, theatre. *Address:* 24 Pembroke Gardens, W8 6HU. *T:* (office) (020) 7538 5000. *Clubs:* Roehampton; Riviera Golf (France).

SEGAR, Christopher Michael John; HM Diplomatic Service; Head of Aviation, Maritime, Science and Energy Department, Foreign and Commonwealth Office, since 2001; *b* 25 Nov. 1950; *s* of Cyril John Segar and Margery (*née* Angliss). *Educ:* Sevenoaks Sch.; Sidney Sussex Coll., Cambridge (BA Hons). VSO, Cameroun, 1969; joined FCO, 1973; MECAS, 1974–76; Third, later Second Sec., Dubai, 1976–79; FCO, 1979–84; Head of Chancery and Consul, Luanda, 1984–87; UK Delgn to OECD, Paris, 1987–90; Dep. Head of Mission and Consul Gen., Baghdad, 1990–91; on secondment to MoD, 1991–94; Commercial Counsellor: Riyadh, 1994–97; Peking, 1997–2001. *Recreations:* music, travel, squash. *Address:* c/o Foreign and Commonwealth Office, King Charles Street, SW1A 2AH. *Club:* Oxford and Cambridge.

SEIFERT, Robin, (also known as **Richard**); JP; FRIBA; Principal R. Seifert and Partners, Architects, since 1934; *b* 25 Nov. 1910; *s* of William Seifert; *m* 1939, Josephine Jeanette Harding; two *s* one *d*. *Educ:* Central Foundation Sch., City of London; University College, London (DipArch), Fellow, 1971. Commenced architectural practice, 1934. Corps of Royal Engineers, 1940–44; Indian Army, 1944–46; Hon. Lt-Col, 1946; Certif. for Meritorious Services Home Forces, 1943. Returned to private practice, 1948. Designed: ICI Laboratories, Dyestuffs Div., Blackley, Manchester; The Times Newspapers building, Printing House Square; Centre Point, St Giles Circus; Drapers Gardens, Nat. West. Bank Tower, City; The Royal Garden Hotel, Kensington; Tolworth Towers, Surbiton; Guiness Mahon Bank, Gracechurch Street; HQ of ICT, Putney; Kellogg House, Baker Street; Dunlop House, King Street, St James's; BSC Res. Labs, Middlesbrough; Britannia Hotel; Park Tower Hotel; London Heathrow Hotel; Sobell Sports Centre; ATV Centre, Birmingham; Central Television Complex, Nottingham; International Press Centre; Metropolitan Police HQ, Putney; Wembley Conference Centre; Princess Grace Hospital, Marylebone Road; Princess Margaret Hospital, Windsor; Churchill Hospital, Harrow; BUPA Hospital, Bushey; The Pirate Castle, Camden; British Rail HQ Offices, Euston Station. RIBA Architectural Exhibition (depicting 50 years of practice), Heinz Gall., 1984. Member: MoT Road Safety Council, 1969 (now disbanded); Home Office Cttee of Management, Housing Assoc. for Discharged Offenders; (part-time) British Waterways Bd, 1971–74; Council, RIBA, 1971–74. FRSA 1976. Liveryman, Glaziers' Co. City of London. JP Barnet, 1969. *Recreations:* chess, violin. *Address:* Eleventrees, Milespit Hill, Mill Hill, NW7 2RS. *T:* (020) 8959 3397. *Clubs:* Army and Navy, City Livery, Arts.

SEIFTER, Pavel, PhD; Ambassador of the Czech Republic to the Court of St James's, since 1997; *b* 27 May 1938; *s* of Karel and Anna Seifter; *m* 1st, 1966, Jana Macenaverová; one *d*; 2nd, 1986, Lenka Urbanová; 3rd, 1999, Lesley Chamberlain. *Educ:* Charles Univ., Prague (Hist., Czech Lang. and Lit. degree 1961; PhD Hist. 1968); Centre Universitaire Européen, Nancy, France (postgrad. study). Lectr in Hist., Charles Univ., Prague, 1964–68; translator, window cleaner, editor of dissident histl publications, 1969–89; Deputy Director: Inst. of Contemporary Hist., Prague, 1990–91; Inst. of Internat. Relns, Prague, 1991–92; Dir, Foreign Policy Dept, Office of Pres. of Czech Republic, 1993–97. Fellow: CISAC, Stanford Univ., 1992; Uppsala Univ., 1992. *Address:* 26 Kensington Palace Gardens, W8 4QY. *T:* (020) 7243 1115. *Clubs:* Athenæum, Travellers.

SEIGNORET, Sir Clarence (Henry Augustus), GCB 1985; OBE 1966; Award of Honour, Dominica, 1993; President of the Commonwealth of Dominica, 1983–93; *b* 25 Feb. 1919; *s* of Clarence Augustus Seignoret and Violet Elizabeth (*née* Riviere); *m* 1950; two *s*. *Educ:* Dominica Grammar Sch.; Balliol Coll., Oxford. Civil Servant, 1936–77: Permanent Sec., 1956–67; Sec. to Cabinet, Hd of Civil Service, 1967–77; Administrator's Dep., Governor's Dep., Actg Pres. on six occasions, 1966–83. Exec. Sec., Dominica Assoc. of Industry and Commerce, 1980–83. Pres., Internat. Develt and Management Ltd, 1994–. Mem., Girl Guide Council of Dominica. Patron: Community Hostels Inc.; Nat. Develt Foundn of Dominica; Dominica Special Olympics. Kt Comdr Grand Cross of Grace, Order of Imperial Russian Order of St John of Jerusalem Ecumenical (Kt of Malta), 1992. Collar of Order of the Liberator (Simon Bolivar), Venezuela, 1987. *Recreations:*

agriculture, horticulture. *Address:* 24 Cork Street, Roseau, Commonwealth of Dominica, West Indies. *T:* (office) 4498777; (home) 4482108. *Clubs:* Lions Club of Dominica (Hon. Mem.), Rotary Club of Dominica (Hon. Mem.).

SEIPP, Walter, Dr jur; Chairman, Supervisory Board, Commerzbank AG, 1991–99, now Hon. Chairman; *b* 13 Dec. 1925. *Educ:* Univ. of Frankfurt (Law studies); final legal examination and doctorate in Law, 1950–53. Military Service, 1943–45. Deutsche Bank AG, 1951–74: Exec. Vice Pres., 1970–74; Vice Chm., UBS–DB Corp., New York, 1972–74; Westdeutsche Landesbank Girozentrale, 1974–81: Mem. Bd, 1974–81, and Dep. Chm. of the Bd, 1977–81; Chm., Bd of Man. Dirs, Commerzbank AG, 1981–91. Pres., Internat. Monetary Conf., 1987–88. *Publications:* multiple. *Address:* (office) Kaiserplatz, 60311 Frankfurt/Main, Germany. *T:* (69) 13620.

SEITZ, Raymond George Hardenbergh; Vice Chairman, Lehman Brothers, since 1996 (a Senior Managing Director, 1995–96); *b* Hawaii, 8 Dec. 1940; *s* of Maj.-Gen. John Francis Regis Seitz and Helen Johnson Hardenbergh; two *s* one *d*; *m* 1985, Caroline Richardson. *Educ:* Yale University (BA History 1963). Joined Foreign Service, Dept of State, 1966; served Montreal, Nairobi, Bukavu, Zaire, 1966–72; Staff Officer, later Director, Secretariat Staff, Washington, Special Asst to Dir Gen., Foreign Service, 1972–75; Political Officer, London, 1975–79; Dep. Exec. Sec., Washington, 1979–81; Senior Dep. Asst Sec., Public Affairs, Washington, 1981–82; Exec. Asst to Secretary George P. Shultz, Washington, 1982–84; Minister and Dep. Chief of Mission, US Embassy, London, 1984–89; Asst Sec. for European and Canadian Affairs, State Dept, Washington, 1989–91; Ambassador to UK, 1991–94. Trustee: Nat. Gall., 1996–; Royal Acad., 1996–. Benjamin Franklin Medal, RSA, 1996. Kt Comdr's Cross (Germany), 1991. *Publication:* Over Here (memoir), 1998. *Address:* Lehman Brothers International (Europe), One Broadgate, EC2M 7HA.

SEKERS, David Nicholas Oliver, OBE 1986; FMA; Director of the Regions, National Trust, since 1998; *b* 29 Sept. 1943; *s* of Sir Nicholas Sekers, MBE and Lady Sekers; *m* 1965, Simone, *er d* of Moran Caplat, *qv*; one *d*. *Educ:* Eton: Worcester College, Oxford (BA). West Cumberland Silk Mills, 1965–73, Dir, 1968–73; Dir, Gladstone Pottery Museum (Museum of the Year 1976), 1973–78; Museum Dir, Quarry Bank Mill (Museum of the Year 1984), 1978–89; Dir, NT Southern Reg., 1989–98. Mem., Crafts Council, 1984–86; Chm., Assoc. of Independent Museums, 1987–89. *Publications:* (booklet) Role of Museum Trustees, 1987; other booklets on Staffordshire pottery and the Potteries; articles for museum jls. *Recreations:* growing vegetables, fell-walking. *Address:* c/o National Trust, 36 Queen Anne's Gate, SW1H 9AS. *T:* (020) 7222 9251. *Club:* Garrick.

SELBORNE, 4th Earl of, *cr* 1882; **John Roundell Palmer,** KBE 1987; FRS 1991; DL; Baron Selborne, 1872; Viscount Wolmer, 1882; Chancellor, Southampton University, since 1996; President, Royal Geographical Society (with the Institute of British Geographers), 1997–2000; *b* 24 March 1940; *er s* of William Matthew, Viscount Wolmer (killed on active service, 1942), and of Priscilla (who *m* 1948, Hon. Peter Legh, later 4th Baron Newton (*d* 1992); she *m* 1994, Frederick Fryer), *d* of late Captain John Egerton-Warburton; *S* grandfather, 1971; *m* 1969, Joanna Van Antwerp, PhD, *yr d* of Evan Maitland James, *qv*; three *s* one *d*. *Educ:* Eton; Christ Church, Oxford (MA). Chm., AFRC, 1983–90 (Mem., 1975–90; Vice-Chm., 1980–83); Vice-Chm., Apple and Pear Develt Council, 1969–73; Mem., Hops Mkting Bd, 1972–82 (Chm., 1978–82); Pres., British Crop Protection Council, 1977–80; Chm., SE Regl Panel, MAFF, 1979–83. Member: Royal Commn on Environmental Pollution, 1993–98; Govt Panel on Sustainable Develt, 1994–97. Chm., UK Chemical Stakeholder Forum, 2000–. Chairman: H of L Select Cttee on Sci. and Technol., 1993–97; Sub-Cttee D (Agric. and Food), H of L Select Cttee on European Communities, 1991–93; Sub-Cttee D (Agric., Food, Envmt and Consumer Affairs), H of L Select Cttee on EU, 1999–; elected Mem., H of L, 1999; Pres., Parly and Scientific Cttee, 1997–2000. Director: Agricl Mortgage Corp., 1990– (Chm., 1995–); Lloyds Bank, 1994–95; Lloyds TSB Gp, 1995–. Chm., Jt Nature Conservation Cttee, 1991–97. President: South of England Agric. Soc., 1984; RASE, 1988; Royal Bath & West Agricl Soc., 1995; Vice-President: Foundn for Sci. and Technol., 1994–; RSPB, 1996–. Trustee, Royal Botanic Gardens, Kew, 1993–98. Treas., Bridewell Royal Hosp. (King Edward's Sch., Witley), 1972–83. Mem., Hampshire County Council, 1967–74. FIBiol 1984; FRAgS 1986; FLS, 1994. Master, Mercers' Co., 1989–90. JP Hants 1971–78; DL Hants 1982. Hon. LLD Bristol, 1989; Hon. DSc: Cranfield, 1991; UEA, 1996; Southampton, 1996. *Heir: s* Viscount Wolmer, *qv*. *Address:* Temple Manor, Selborne, Alton, Hants GU34 3LR. *T:* (01420) 473646. *Club:* Brooks's.

SELBY, 6th Viscount *cr* 1905, of the City of Carlisle; **Christopher Rolf Thomas Gully;** *b* 18 Oct. 1993; *s* of 5th Viscount Selby and of his 1st wife, Charlotte Cathrine Brege; *S* father, 2001. *Heir: great-uncle* Hon. James Edward Hugh Grey Gully [*b* 17 March 1945; *m* 1971, Fiona Margaret Mackenzie; two *s*].

SELBY, Bishop Suffragan of, since 1991; **Rt Rev. Humphrey Vincent Taylor;** *b* 5 March 1938; *s* of late Maurice Humphrey Taylor and Mary Patricia Stuart Taylor (*née* Wood, later Pearson); *m* 1965, Anne Katharine Dart; two *d*. *Educ:* Harrow School; Pembroke College, Cambridge (MA); London University (MA). Nat. Service Officer, RAF, 1956–58; Cambridge 1958–61; College of the Resurrection, Mirfield, 1961–63; Curate in London, 1963–66; Rector of Lilongwe, Malawi, 1967–71; Chaplain, Bishop Grosseteste Coll., Lincoln, 1971–74; Sec. for Chaplaincies in Higher Education, Gen. Synod Bd of Education, 1974–80; Mission Programmes Sec., USPG, 1980–84; Sec., USPG, 1984–91. Hon. Canon of Bristol Cathedral, 1986–91; Provincial Canon of Southern Africa, 1989–. Moderator, Conf. for World Mission, BCC, 1987–90; Chairman: Internat. and Develt Affairs Cttee, Archbps' Council, 1996–; Northern and Yorkshire Adv. Cttee on Spiritual Care and Chaplaincy, 1997–. *Recreations:* music, gardening. *Address:* 10 Precentor's Court, York YO1 7EJ. *T:* (01904) 656492.
See also R. M. Thornley-Taylor.

SELBY, Prof. Peter John, CBE 2001; MD; Professor of Cancer Medicine, and Consultant Physician, St James's University Hospital, Leeds, since 1988; Director, Imperial Cancer Research Fund Cancer Medicine Research Unit, Leeds, since 1993; Lead Clinician, Leeds Cancer Centre, since 1997; *b* 10 July 1950; *s* of Joseph Selby and Dorothy Selby (*née* Cross); *m* 1972, Catherine Elisabeth, *d* of Peter Thomas; one *s* one *d*. *Educ:* Lydney Grammar Sch.; Christ's Coll., Cambridge (MA; MB BChir; MD 1980). Registrar, Fellow and Sen. Lectr (Consultant), Royal Marsden Hosp. and Inst. Cancer Res., 1977–88; Dir, Clin. Res., ICRF, 1997–2001. Dir, Nat. Cancer Res. Network, 2001–. Pres., British Oncol Soc., 1992–94. *Publications:* Hodgkin's Disease, 1987; Confronting Cancer: Care and Prevention, 1993; Cancer in Adolescents, 1995; Malignant Lymphomas, 2000. *Recreations:* reading, music, jogging, watching sport. *Address:* 17 Park Lane, Roundhay, Leeds LS8 2EX. *Club:* Leeds United Football.

SELBY, Rt Rev. Peter Stephen Maurice; *see* Worcester, Bishop of.

SELDON, Anthony Francis, PhD; FRHistS; Headmaster, Brighton College, since 1997; *b* 2 Aug. 1953; *s* of Arthur Seldon, *qv*; *m* 1982, Joanna Pappworth; one *s* two *d*. *Educ:* Tonbridge Sch.; Worcester Coll., Oxford (MA 1980); London School of Economics (PhD 1981); KCL (PGCE 1983); MBA Poly. of Central London 1989. FRHistS 1992. Res. Fellow and Tutor, London School of Economics, 1980–81; Consultant Historian, Rio Tinto Zinc, 1981–83; Head of Politics, Whitgift Sch., 1983–86; Co-founder, 1987, and first Dir, 1987–89, Inst. of Contemporary British History; Head of History and Gen. Studies, Tonbridge Sch., 1989–92; Dep. Headmaster, 1993–97, acting Headmaster, 1997, St Dunstan's Coll. FRSA 1990. Series Ed., Making Contemporary Britain, 1988. Co-founder: Contemporary Record, 1987 (Ed., 1987–95); Modern Hist. Rev., 1988 (Ed., 1989–92); Twentieth Century British Hist., 1989 (Consulting Ed., 1989–91); Contemp. European Hist., 1989 (Consulting Ed., 1989–90). *Publications:* Churchill's Indian Summer, 1981; (jtly) By Word of Mouth, 1983; (ed) Contemporary History, 1987; (ed jtly) Ruling Performance, 1987; (ed) Political Parties since 1945, 1988; (ed jtly) Thatcher Effect, 1989; (jtly) Politics UK, 1991; (ed jtly) Conservative Century, 1994; (ed jtly) Major Effect, 1994; (ed jtly) The Heath Government 1970–74, 1996; (ed jtly) Contemporary History Handbook, 1996; (ed jtly) Ideas That Shaped Postwar Britain, 1996; (ed) How Tory Governments Fall: the Conservative Party in power since 1783, 1996; Major: a political biography, 1997; 10 Downing Street: the illustrated history, 1999; (jtly) Britain under Thatcher, 1999; (jtly) The Powers Behind the Prime Minister, 1999; The Foreign Office: an illustrated history of the place and the people, 2000; (ed) The Blair Effect, 2001. *Recreations:* drama, sport, writing, old sports cars. *Address:* Headmaster's House, Brighton College, E Sussex BN2 2AL. *T:* (01273) 704201. *Club:* Reform.

SELDON, Arthur, CBE 1983; economist and writer; a Founder President, Institute of Economic Affairs, since 1990; Founder Editor, Economic Affairs, 1980; *b* 29 May 1916; *m* (Audrey) Marjorie, *d* of Wilfred Willett and Eileen Willett (*née* Stenhouse); three *s*. *Educ:* Dempsey St Elementary Sch., Stepney; Raine's Foundation Sch. (State Scholar); LSE. BCom 1937 (1st cl. hons). Army service in Africa and Italy, 1942–45. Editor, Store, 1946–49; Tutor, Univ. of London Commerce Degree Bureau, 1946–56; economist in industry, 1949–1959; Staff Examr, LSE, 1956–66; Editorial Dir, Inst. of Economic Affairs, 1957–88; Chm., Liberal Party Cttee on the Aged, 1948–49; Mem., BMA Cttee on Health Financing, 1968–70; Adviser, Australian Cabinet Cttee on Welfare, 1968; Vice-Pres., Mont Pèlerin Soc., Switzerland, 1980–86 (first Hon. Fellow, 1996); Founder Trustee, Social Affairs Unit, 1980. Hon. DSocSc Univ. Francisco Marroquin, Guatemala, 1998; Hon. DSc Buckingham, 1999. *Publications:* Pensions in a Free Society, 1957; (jtly) Advertising in a Free Society, 1959; Pensions for Prosperity, 1960; (jtly) Everyman's Dictionary of Economics, 1965, 2nd edn 1976; After the NHS, 1968; The Great Pensions Swindle, 1970; Charge, 1977; (jtly) Over-ruled on Welfare 1963–78, 1979; Corrigible Capitalism, Incorrigible Socialism, 1980; Wither the Welfare State, 1981; Socialism Explained, 1983 (US edn as Socialism: the grand delusion, 1986); (ed) The New Right Enlightenment, 1985; The Riddle of the Voucher, 1986; (jtly) Welfare Without the State, 1987; Capitalism, 1990 (Fisher Prize, 1991); The State is Rolling Back, 1994; (contrib.) Democracy and Public Choice: essays in honour of Gordon Tullock, ed C. K. Rowley, 1987; The Dilemma of Democracy, 1998; The Retreat of the State: nurturing the soul of society, 1998; (jtly) Government: whose obedient servant?, 2000. *Recreations:* writing, cricket, opera, parties for non-conformists. *Address:* The Thatched Cottage, Godden Green, Sevenoaks, Kent TN15 0HR. *T:* (01732) 761499.
See also Anthony Seldon.

SELF, William Woodard; writer, since 1990; *b* 26 Sept. 1961; *s* of late Prof. Peter John Otter Self and of Elaine Self (*née* Rosenbloom); *m* 1st, 1989, Katharine Sylvia Chancellor (marr. diss. 1997); one *s* one *d*; 2nd, 1997, Deborah Jane Orr; one *s*. *Educ:* Exeter Coll., Oxford (BA Hons). Freelance cartoonist, 1982–88; Publishing Dir, Cathedral Publishing, 1988–90; contributing editor, London Evening Standard mag., 1993–95; columnist: Observer, 1995–97; The Times, 1998–99; Independent on Sunday, 1999–. *Publications:* The Quantity Theory of Insanity, 1991; Cock & Bull, 1992; My Idea of Fun, 1993; Grey Area, 1994; Junk Mail, 1995; The Sweet Smell of Psychosis, 1996; Great Apes, 1997; Tough Tough Toys for Tough Tough Boys, 1998; Sore Sites, 2000; How the Dead Live, 2000; Perfidious Man, 2000; Feeling Frenzy, 2001. *Recreation:* walking. *Address:* c/o David Godwin Associates, 14 Goodwins Court, WC2N 4LL. *T:* (020) 7240 9992. *Clubs:* Groucho, Colony Room.

SELIGMAN, Madron; *see* Seligman, R. M.

SELIGMAN, Sir Peter (Wendel), Kt 1978; CBE 1969; BA; FIMechE; *b* 16 Jan. 1913; *s* of late Dr Richard Joseph Simon Seligman and of Hilda Mary Seligman; *m* 1937, Elizabeth Lavinia Mary Wheatley; two *s* three *d* (and one *d* decd). *Educ:* King's Coll. Sch., Wimbledon; Harrow Sch.; Kantonschule, Zürich; Caius Coll., Cambridge. Joined APV Co. Ltd, as Asst to Man. Dir, 1936; appointed Dir, 1939; Man. Dir, 1947; Dep. Chm., 1961; Chm., APV Holdings Ltd, 1966–77. Director: St Regis International Ltd, 1973–83 (Vice-Chm., 1981–83); EIBIS International Ltd, 1980–90; Bell Bryant Pty Ltd, 1976–80; St Regis ACI Pty Ltd, 1980–84. Mem., Engineering Industries Council, 1975–77. Chm., Nat. Ski Fedn of GB, 1977–81. *Recreations:* travelling, carpentry, DIY. *Address:* 8 Bluecoat Pond, Christ's Hospital, near Horsham, West Sussex RH13 7NW. *T:* (01403) 275331, *Fax:* (01403) 275332. *Clubs:* Hawks (Cambridge); Ski of Great Britain (Invitation Life Mem.); Kandahar Ski (Chm., 1972–77; Hon. Mem.).
See also R. M. Seligman.

SELIGMAN, (Richard) Madron, CBE 1994; *b* 10 Nov. 1918; 4th *s* of late Dr Richard Seligman, FCGI, FIM, and Hilda Mary (*née* MacDowell); *m* 1947, Nancy-Joan, *d* of Julian Marks; three *s* one *d*. *Educ:* Rokeby Sch., Wimbledon; Harrow Sch.; Balliol Coll., Oxford (BA (Hons) PPE; MA). Oxford Univ. ski team, 1938–39; President, Oxford Union, 1940. Served war, 6th Armoured Divisional Signals, N Africa and Italy, 1941–46, Major 1945. Chm., Incinerator Company, Eaton Socon, 1960–88. MEP (C) Sussex W, 1979–94. Vice Pres., European Energy Foundn, 1982–94. Hon. Treas., Cons. Animal Welfare Gp, 1996–. Chm. UK Br., Confédn Européenne des Anciens Combattants, 1989–. *Recreations:* tennis, ski-ing, gardening, piano, sailing. *Address:* Mile Ash, Tower Hill, Horsham, West Sussex RH13 7AG. *T:* (01403) 240075. *Clubs:* Royal Thames Yacht, Royal Institute of International Affairs, MCC.
See also Sir Peter Seligman.

SELKIRK, Earldom of (*cr* 1646); title disclaimed by 11th Earl (*see under* Selkirk of Douglas, Baron).

SELKIRK OF DOUGLAS, Baron *cr* 1997 (Life Peer), of Cramond in the City of Edinburgh; **James Alexander Douglas-Hamilton;** PC 1996; QC (Scot.) 1996; Member (C) Lothians, Scottish Parliament, since 1999; *b* 31 July 1942; 2nd *s* of 14th Duke of Hamilton, and *b* of 15th Duke of Hamilton, *qv*; renounced claim to Earldom of Selkirk, 1994, prior to succession being determined, 1996; *m* 1974, Hon. Priscilla Susan Buchan, *d* of 2nd Baron Tweedsmuir, CBE, CD, and late Baroness Tweedsmuir of Belhelvie, PC; four *s* (incl. twins). *Educ:* Eton College; Balliol Coll., Oxford (MA, Mod. History; Oxford Boxing Blue, 1961; Pres., Oxford Univ. Cons. Assoc., 1963; Pres., Oxford Union Soc., 1964); Edinburgh Univ. (LLB, Scots Law). Advocate at Scots Bar and Procurator Fiscal Depute, 1968–72. Town Councillor, Murrayfield-Cramond, Edinburgh, 1972–74. MP

(C) Edinburgh West, Oct. 1974–1997; contested (C) same seat, 1997. Scottish Conservative Whip, 1977; a Lord Comr of HM Treasury, and Govt Whip for Scottish Cons. Mems, 1979–81; PPS to Foreign Office Minister, 1983–86, to Sec. of State for Scotland, 1986–87; Parly Under-Sec. of State for Home Affairs and the Envmt, 1987–92, for Educn and Housing, 1992–95, Scottish Office; Minister of State for Home Affairs and Health, Scottish Office, 1995–97. Captain Cameronian Co., 2 Bn Low Vols RARO, 1974–92. Hon. Air Cdre, No 2 (City of Edinburgh) Maritime HQ Unit, 1994–99; Hon. Air Cdre, 603 (City of Edinburgh) Sqn, RAAF, 1999–; Pres., Internat. Rescue Corps, 1995. Hon. Pres., Scottish Amateur Boxing Assoc., 1975–99; President: Royal Commonwealth Soc. in Scotland, 1979–87; Scottish Council, UNA, 1981–87. Mem. Royal Co. of Archers, Queen's Body Guard for Scotland. *Publications:* Motive for a Mission: The Story Behind Hess's Flight to Britain, 1971; The Air Battle for Malta: the diaries of a fighter pilot, 1981, 2nd edn 1990; Roof of the World: man's first flight over Everest, 1983; The Truth About Rudolf Hess, 1993. *Recreations:* golf, forestry. *Heir (to disclaimed earldom):* *s* Hon. John Andrew Douglas-Hamilton, Master of Selkirk; *b* 8 Feb. 1978. *Address:* House of Lords, SW1A 0PW. *Clubs:* Pratt's; New (Edinburgh); Hon. Company of Edinburgh Golfers.

SELL, Anthony Lawrence, CBE 1999; Chief Executive, British Tourist Authority, 1993–98; *b* 19 April 1943; *s* of late Richard Geoffrey Sell and Zena Warren Sell (*née* Goddard); *m* 1975, Susan Constance; two *s* one *d*. *Educ:* Berkhamsted; Christ's Coll., Cambridge (Open Schol., MA); Univ. of Wisconsin (Fulbright Schol.); London Business Sch. (MSc). ICI Organics Div., 1965–67; Booz Allen & Hamilton Internat., 1969–73; Internat. Investment Corp. for Yugoslavia, 1973–74; Foseco Internat. Exports, 1974–78; Man. Dir, Kemwell, 1978–82; Commercial Dir, Metalchem Internat., 1982–86; Exec. Dir, Boosey & Hawkes plc, 1986–89; Pres.-Dir-Gen., Buffet Crampon SA, 1986–88; Man. Dir, Continental Europe, Thomas Cook Gp, 1989–93 (Pres., Chm., Mem., Thomas Cook subsidiaries, France, Switzerland, Netherlands, Italy, Sweden, Czechoslovakia). Mem., London Tourist Bd, 1993–98. Chm., Soc. of Ticket Agents and Retailers, 1997. Gov., Warwick Sch., 1983–85. FRSA. *Recreations:* rowing, music, the clarinet. *T:* (020) 8748 9272. *Club:* Mortlake Boat.

SELLARS, John Ernest, CBE 1994; CEng; CMath, FIMA; MRAeS; Chief Executive, Business and Technology (formerly Business and Technician) Education Council, 1983–94; *b* 5 Feb. 1936; *s* of late Ernest Buttle Sellars and Edna Grace Sellars; *m* 1958, Dorothy Beatrice (*née* Morrison); three *d*. *Educ:* Wintringham Grammar Sch., Grimsby; Manchester Univ. (BSc, MSc). Research Engineer, English Electric (GW) Ltd, 1958–61; Lectr, Royal College of Advanced Technology (now Univ. of Salford), 1961–67; Head of Mathematics, Lanchester College of Technology, Coventry, 1967–71; Head of Computer Science, Lanchester Polytechnic, Coventry/Rugby, 1971–74; Chief Officer, Business Educn Council, 1974–83. Member: Bd, Nat. Adv. Body for Public Sector Higher Educn, 1982–88; BBC School Broadcasting Council for UK, 1982–87; City Technology Colls Trust, 1989–94; Engrg and Technol. Adv. Cttee, British Council, 1990–95; Engrg Council, 1994–95 (Mem., Standing Cttee for Engrg Profession, 1994–95); British Accreditation Council for Indep., Further and Higher Educn, 1999–. Mem. Exec. Cttee, RoSPA, 1994–. Governor, London Guildhall Univ., 1994–2000. Trustee, Gatsby Technical Educn Project, 1999–. FInstD. Hon. FCP 1989. DUniv Sheffield Hallam, 1994; Hon. DTech London Guildhall, 2001. *Publications:* papers on mathematics, computer science and business educn. *Recreation:* walking. *Address:* 306 Cassiobury Drive, Watford WD1 3AW. *Clubs:* Reform, MCC.

SELLARS, Peter; American opera and theatre director; *b* 27 Sept. 1957. *Educ:* Phillips Acad., Mass; Harvard Univ. (BA 1980). Artistic Director: Boston Shakespeare Co., 1983–84; American Nat. Theater at Kennedy Center for the Performing Arts, 1984–; LA Fest., 1990, 1993. Prof. of World Arts and Cultures, UCLA. *Productions* include: Armida, Monadnock Music Fest., 1981; The Mikado, Lyric Opera of Chicago, 1983; Così fan tutte, Castle Hill Fest., Mass, 1984; The Electrification of the Soviet Union, Glyndebourne Touring Opera, 1987; Nixon in China, Houston, 1987, ENO 2000; Die Zauberflöte, Glyndebourne, 1990; The Persians, Edinburgh Fest., 1993; Pelléas and Mélisande, Amsterdam, 1993; The Merchant of Venice, Barbican, 1994; Mathis der Maler, Royal Opera House, 1995; Theodora, Glyndebourne, 1996; The Rake's Progress, 1996, El Niño, 2000, Châtelet, Paris. *Address:* American National Theater, Kennedy Center, Washington, DC 20566, USA.

SELLERS, Basil Alfred; Chairman, Sellers Group, since 1987; *b* 19 June 1935; *s* of William Alfred Sellers and Irene Ethel Sellers (*née* Freemantle); *m* 2nd, 1980, Gillian Clare Heinrich; two *s* one *d* from previous marr. *Educ:* King's College, Adelaide, SA. Clerk, State Bank of SA, 1952; Clerk, Cutten & Harvey, Adelaide, 1954–69 (Investment Advr, 1969); owner, Devon Homes, SA, 1970; bought Ralph Symonds Ltd, 1975 (Man. Dir); Chm., Gestetner plc, 1987–94. *Recreations:* cricket, art, music. *Address:* (office) 10 Stratton Street, W1X 5FD. *T:* (020) 7546 8636. *Clubs:* MCC, Cricketers'; University (Australia).

SELLERS, Geoffrey Bernard, CB 1991; Parliamentary Counsel, since 1987; *b* 5 June 1947; *s* of late Bernard Whittaker Sellers and Elsie (*née* Coop); *m* 1971, Susan Margaret Faulconbridge (*d* 1995); two *s* two *d*. *Educ:* Manchester Grammar Sch. (Scholar); Magdalen Coll., Oxford (Mackinnon Scholar; BCL 1st Cl. Hons; MA). Called to the Bar, Gray's Inn, 1971 (Macaskie Scholar). Legal Assistant: Law Commn, 1971; Commn on Industrial Relations, 1971–74; joined Office of Parly Counsel, 1974; with Law Commn, 1982–85, and 1991–93; with Inland Revenue, 1996–99. *Address:* (office) 36 Whitehall, SW1A 2AY. *Club:* Royal Automobile.

SELLERS, John Marsland; Parliamentary Counsel, since 1998; *b* 15 July 1951; *s* of late Bernard Whittaker Sellers and Elsie (*née* Coop); *m* 1975, Patricia Susan Burns; two *s*. *Educ:* Manchester Grammar Sch.; Magdalen Coll., Oxford (BA, BCL). Lecturer: Lincoln Coll., Oxford, 1973–75; LSE, 1975–77; Articled Clerk, 1977-80, Solicitor, 1980–83, Freshfields; Asst Parly Counsel, 1983–88; Sen. Asst Parly Counsel, 1988–91; Dep. Parly Counsel, 1991–98; on secondment to Law Commn, 1998–2001. *Address:* Office of the Parliamentary Counsel, 36 Whitehall, SW1A 2AY. *T:* (020) 7210 2586.

See also G. B. Sellers.

SELLERS, Philip Edward, CBE 2001; Deputy Chairman, Powerleague Ltd, since 1999; *b* 20 March 1937; *s* of George Edward and Helen Sellers; *m* 1962, Brenda Anne Bell; two *s*. *Educ:* Ernest Bailey Grammar School, Matlock; CIPFA. Local Govt, 1953–72; Controller of Audit, British Gas Corp., 1972–76; Finance Dir, North Thames Gas, 1976–80; Dir of Finance and Planning, British Rail Board, 1980–84; Board Mem. for Corporate Finance and Planning, Post Office, 1984–89. Mem., Postel Property Cttee, 1992–94; non-exec. Dir, Postel Investment Management, 1994–95; Trustee, Post Office Pension Funds, 1985–99. Non-executive Chairman: CSL Group, 1989–93; ICL Outsourcing Ltd (formerly CFM Group Ltd, then ICL/CFM), 1989–99; Pegasus Group plc, 1992–2000; Inner City Enterprises, 1992–98; Powerleague Soccer Centres Ltd (formerly Powerplay Supersoccer Ltd), 1995–99; Workplace Technologies plc, 1995–99; Alexander Mann Associates Ltd, 1997–; non-exec. Dir, Etam Gp, 1991–98. UK rep., IFAC Public Sector Cttee, 1987–90; Philip Sellers Communications and Consultancy, 1989–. Mem., NCC Impact Adv. Bd, 1989–92. Pres., CIPFA, 1985–86; Chm., Nationalised Industries Finance Panel, 1986–89; Chm., Audit Cttee, DTI, 1994–. Non-exec. Dir, London Festival Orch., 1994–98. *Recreations:* tennis, ski-ing. *Address:* Yarrimba, 31 Howards Thicket, Gerrards Cross, Bucks SL9 7NT. *T:* (01753) 893489.

SELLERS, Robert Firth, ScD; FRSE; MRCVS; consultant on foreign animal diseases; *b* 9 June 1924; *s* of Frederick Sellers and Janet Walkinshaw Shiels; *m* 1951, Margaret Peterkin; one *s* one *d*. *Educ:* Christ's Hospital; Gonville and Caius Coll., Cambridge (MA, ScD); Royal (Dick) School of Veterinary Studies, Edinburgh (PhD, BSc). FIBiol. Served War, Royal Artillery, 1943–46. Research Institute (Animal Virus Diseases), Pirbright, 1953–58; Wellcome Research Laboratories, Beckenham, 1958–62; Instituto Venezolano de Investigaciones Cientificas, Venezuela, 1962–64; Animal Virus Research Institute, Pirbright, 1964–84, Dep. Dir, 1964–79, Dir, 1979–84; Consultant, Foreign Animal Disease Unit, Agriculture, Canada, 1985–88. J. T. Edwards Meml Medal, 1976. *Publications:* papers on animal viruses in scientific jls. *Recreation:* archaeology. *Address:* 4 Pewley Way, Guildford, Surrey GU1 3PY.

SELLIER, Robert Hugh, FICE; Chief Executive, Y. J. Lovell, 1991–95; *b* 15 Nov. 1933; *s* of Major Philip Joseph Sellier and Lorna Geraldine Sellier (*née* Luxton); *m* 1st, 1963, Cynthia Ann Dwelly (*d* 1985); one *d*; 2nd, 1987, Gillian Dalley (*née* Clark). *Educ:* St Joseph's Coll., Oxford; King's Coll., Durham Univ. (BScCivEng). FIHT. Man. Dir, New Ideal Homes, 1972–74; Dep. Man. Dir, Cementation International, 1974–79; Man. Dir, Cementation Construction, 1979–83; Chm., Cementation Gp of Companies, 1983–86; Gp Man. Dir, George Wimpey, 1986–91. Non-exec. Dir, Hyder plc, 1993–2000. *Recreations:* ski-ing, shooting, scuba, flying. *Address:* Field House, Skeynes Park, Lingfield Road, Edenbridge, Kent TN8 5HN. *T:* (01732) 864860, *Fax:* (01732) 864861.

SELLORS, Sir Patrick (John) Holmes, KCVO 1999 (LVO 1990); FRCS, FRCOphth; Surgeon-Oculist to the Queen, 1980–99; Ophthalmic Surgeon, King Edward VIIth Hospital for Officers, 1975–99; *b* 11 Feb. 1934; *s* of Sir Thomas Holmes Sellors, DM, MCh, FRCP, FRCS; *m* 1961, Gillian Gratton Swallow; two *s* one *d*. *Educ:* Rugby Sch.; Oriel Coll., Oxford; Middlesex Hosp. Med. School. MA Oxon; BM, BCh Oxon 1958; FRCS 1965; FRCOphth 1990. Registrar, Moorfields Eye Hosp., 1962–65; recognised teacher in Ophthalmology, St George's Hosp., 1966; Ophthalmic Surgeon: St George's Hosp., 1965–82 (Hon., 1983); Croydon Eye Unit, 1970–94; Surgeon-Oculist to HM Household, 1974–80; Hon. Consultant Ophthalmic Surgeon, St Luke's Hosp. for the Clergy, 1983–96. Sec. to Ophthalmic Soc. of UK, 1970–72; Examr for Diploma of Ophthalmology, 1974–77; Pres., Ophthalmology Section, RSocMed, 1992–94; Vice-Pres., Coll. of Ophthalmologists, 1992–96 (Mem. Council, 1988–96); Member, Council: Faculty of Ophthalmologists, 1977–88; Med. Defence Union, 1977–; Gen. Optical Council, 1978–96. Dep. Master, Oxford Congress, 1991. *Publications:* (jtly) Outline in Ophthalmology, 1985, 2nd edn 1994; articles in BMJ and Trans OSUK. *Recreations:* gardening, golf. *Address:* The Summer House, Sandy Lane, West Runton, Cromer, Norfolk NR27 9NB.

SELLS, Oliver Matthew; QC 1995; a Recorder of the Crown Court, since 1991; *b* 29 Sept. 1950; *s* of late Sir David Perronet Sells and Beryl Cecilia Sells (*née* Charrington); *m* 1986, Lucinda Jane, *d* of late Gerard William Mackworth-Young and Lady Eve Mackworth-Young; one *s* one *d*. *Educ:* St Peter's, Seaford; Wellington Coll.; Coll. of Law, London. Mem., Hon. Soc. of Inner Temple, 1969–; called to the Bar, Inner Temple, 1972, Bencher, 1996; SE Circuit, 1974–; Supplementary Counsel to the Crown, 1981–86. Member: Gen. Council of the Bar, 1977–80 and 1986–91; Commonwealth Law Assoc.; Hon. Mem., Amer. Bar Assoc.; Dir, Music for Charity. *Recreations:* shooting, cricket, fishing. *Address:* 5 Paper Buildings, Temple, EC4Y 7HB. *T:* (020) 7583 6117. *Clubs:* Boodle's, MCC; Norfolk (Norwich).

SELLS, Robert Anthony, FRCS, FRCSE; Consultant Surgeon and Director of Transplantation, Royal Liverpool University Hospital (formerly Liverpool Royal Infirmary), since 1970; *b* 13 April 1938; *s* of Rev. William Blyth Sells and Eleanor Mary Sells; *m* 1st, 1964, Elizabeth Lucy Schryver (marr. diss. 1976); two *s* one *d*; 2nd, 1977, Pauline Gilchrist Muir; two *s*. *Educ:* Christ's Hosp. Sch., Horsham; Guy's Hosp. Med. Sch., Univ. of London (MB BS). FRCS 1966; FRCSE 1966. Lecturer, Department of Surgery: Guy's Hosp. Med. Sch., 1966–67; Univ. of Cambridge, 1967–69; MRC Travelling Schol., Univ. of Harvard, 1969–70; Dir of Surgery, Royal Liverpool Univ. Hosp., 1997–99; Hon. Prof. of Surgery and Immunology, Univ. of Liverpool, 1998–. Vis. Professor: Detroit Univ., 1977; Adelaide Univ., 1984; Minnesota Univ., 1984–85; London Univ., 1998. Gen. Sec. and Pres., British Transplantation Society, 1978–86; Mem. Council, Chm. of Ethics Cttee and Vice Pres., The Transplantation Soc., 1986–94; Vice Pres., Inst. of Med. Ethics, 1986–; Co-Founder and Chm., Internat. Forum for Transplant Ethics, 1995–; Pres., Liverpool Med. Instn, 1997–98 (Mem., 1972–). Principal Conductor and Musical Dir, Crosby SO, 1982–; Hon. Pres., Aberwheeler Show, 1995. FRSA 1996; Hon. Fellow, Amer. Soc. of Transplant Surgeons, 1978–. *Publications:* (ed jtly) Transplantation Today, 1983; (ed jtly) Organ Transplantation: Current Clinical and Immunological Concepts, 1989; papers on transplantation and bioethics in med. jls. *Recreations:* collecting Victorian pickle jars, orchestral and choral conducting. *Address:* Cil Llwyn, Bodfari, Denbighshire LL16 4HY. *T:* (01745) 710296; (office) (0151) 706 3491. *Clubs:* Moynihan Chirurgical Travelling (Pres., 2000–01), Twenty (Liverpool).

SELOUS, Andrew Edmund Armstrong; MP (C) Bedfordshire South West, since 2001; *b* 27 April 1962; *s* of Gerald Selous and Miranda Selous (*née* Casey); *m* 1993, Harriet Marston; three *d*. *Educ:* London Sch. of Econs (BSc Econ). ACII 1993. Great Lakes Re (UK) PLC, 1991–2001. Served TA, HAC and RRF, 1981–94. *Recreation:* family life. *Address:* House of Commons, SW1A 0AA. *Clubs:* Leighton Buzzard Conservative, Dunstable Conservative.

SELSDON, 3rd Baron *cr* 1932, of Croydon; **Malcolm McEacharn Mitchell-Thomson;** Bt 1900; banker; *b* 27 Oct. 1937; *s* of 2nd Baron Selsdon (3rd Bt, *cr* 1900), DSC; *S* father, 1963; *m* 1st, 1965, Patricia Anne (marr. diss.), *d* of Donald Smith; one *s*; 2nd, 1995, Gabrielle Tesseron (*née* Williams). *Educ:* Winchester College. Sub-Lieut, RNVR. Deleg. to Council of Europe and WEU, 1972–78. C. T. Bowring Gp, 1972–76; Midland Bank Group, 1976–90: EEC Advr, 1979–85; Public Finance Advr, 1985–90. Dir of various companies. Chm., Committee for Middle East Trade (COMET), 1979–86; Member: BOTB, 1983–86; E European Trade Council, 1985 87. Pres., British Exporters Assoc., 1990–98. Elected Mem., H of L, 1999. Chm., Greater London and SE Regional Council for Sport and Recreation, 1977–83. *Recreations:* rackets, squash, tennis, lawn tennis, ski-ing, sailing. *Heir:* *s* Hon. Callum Malcolm McEacharn Mitchell-Thomson, *b* 7 Nov. 1969. *Address:* c/o House of Lords, SW1A 0PW. *Club:* MCC.

SELTEN, Prof. Reinhard J., PhD; Professor of Economics, University of Bonn, 1984–96, now Emeritus; *b* 5 Oct. 1930; *s* of Adolf Selten and Käthe Selten; *m* 1959, Elisabeth. *Educ:* Univ. of Frankfurt (Dip. Maths; PhD Maths 1961). Asst posts in econs, Frankfurt, 1975–67; Vis. Prof., Schs of Business Admin, Univ. of Calif., Berkeley, 1967–68; privat docent, econs, Frankfurt, 1968–69; Professor of Economics: Berlin,

1969–72; Bielefeld, 1972–84. Hon. PhD (Economics): Bielefeld, 1991; Frankfurt, 1992. (Jtly) Nobel Prize in Economics, 1994. Bundesverdienstkreuz am Band mit Stern (Germany). *Publications:* Preispolitik der Mehrproduktenunternehmung in der Statischen Theorie, 1970; (with T. H. Marschak) General Equilibrium with Price Making Firms, 1974; Models of Strategic Rationality, 1988; (with John C. Harsanyi) A General Theory of Equilibrium Selection in Games, 1988. *Recreation:* hiking. *Address:* Hardtweg 23, 53639 Königswinter, Germany. *T:* (2223) 23610.

SELVARATNAM, Vasanti Emily Indrani, (Mrs P. Capewell); QC 2001; a Recorder, since 2000; *b* 9 April 1961; *d* of George H. Selvaratnam and Wendy L. Selvaratnam (*née* Fairclough); *m* 1989, Phillip Capewell; one *s. Educ:* King's Coll., London (AKC 1982; LLB Hons 1982, LLM 1st Cl. 1984); Inns of Court Sch. of Law. Called to the Bar, Middle Temple, 1983; in practice as barrister, specialising in commercial and shipping law, 1985–; Asst Recorder, Western Circuit, 1999–2000. *Recreations:* fine dining, foreign travel, horse riding. *Address:* (chambers) 4 Field Court, Gray's Inn, WC1R 5EF. *T:* (020) 7440 6900. *Club:* Phyllis Court (Henley-on-Thames).

SELVEY, Michael Walter William; Cricket Correspondent, The Guardian, since 1987; *b* 25 April 1948; *s* of late Walter Edwin Selvey and of Edith Milly Selvey; *m* 1st, 1970, Mary Evans (marr. diss. 1991); one *d*; 2nd, 1992, Sarah (*née* Taylor); two *s* one *d* (triplets). *Educ:* Battersea Grammar Sch.; Univ. of Manchester (BSc Geog.); Emmanuel Coll., Cambridge (Cert Ed). Professional cricketer: Middlesex, 1972–82; Glamorgan, 1983–84 (Capt.); played 3 Tests for England: two *v* West Indies, 1976; one *v* India, 1977. Journalist, Guardian, 1985–. *Publication:* The Ashes Surrendered, 1989. *Recreations:* golf, fitness, cooking, real ale, crosswords, garden, children. *Address:* c/o The Guardian, 119 Farringdon Road, EC1R 3ER. *T:* (020) 7278 2332. *Club:* Woburn Golf and Country.

SELWOOD, Maj.-Gen. David Henry Deering; His Honour Judge Selwood; a Circuit Judge, since 1992; Resident Judge, Portsmouth Crown Court, since 1996; *b* 27 June 1934; *s* of late Comdr George Deering Selwood, RN, and Enid Marguerite Selwood (*née* Rowlinson); *m* 1973, Barbara Dorothea (*née* Hütter); three *s* one *d. Educ:* Kelly Coll., Tavistock; University College of the South-West; Law Society's School of Law. Articled to G. C. Aldhouse, Esq., Plymouth, 1952–57; admitted Solicitor 1957; National Service, RASC 2/Lieut, 1957–59; private practice, Plymouth, 1959–61; TA 4 Devons, Lieut, 1959–61; commnd Army Legal Services Staff List, 1961; service on legal staffs, MoD, Headquarters: BAOR, MELF, FARELF, UKLF, Land Forces Cyprus, 1961–85; Brig., Legal, HQ BAOR, 1986–90; Dir of Army Legal Services, MoD, 1990–92. Asst Recorder, SE Circuit, 1980, Recorder, 1985–92. Dep. Col Comdt, AGC, 1996–. Hon. Advocate, US Court of Military Appeals, 1972–. *Publications:* (jtly) Criminal Law and Psychiatry, 1987; (ed jtly) Crown Court Index, 1996–. *Address:* c/o Barclays Bank, PO Box 87, Winchester, Hants SO23 8TN. *Club:* Army and Navy.

SEMKEN, John Douglas, CB 1980; MC 1944; Legal Adviser to the Home Office, 1977–83; *b* 9 Jan. 1921; *s* of Wm R. Semken and Mrs B. R. Semken (*née* Craymer); *m* 1952, Edna Margaret, *yr d* of T. R. Poole; three *s. Educ:* St Albans Sch.; Pembroke Coll., Oxford (MA, BCL). Solicitor's articled clerk, 1938–39. Commnd in Sherwood Rangers Yeo., 1940; 1st Lieut 1941, Captain 1942, Major 1944; 8th Armd Bde, N Africa, 1942–43; Normandy beaches to Germany, 1944. Called to Bar, Lincoln's Inn, 1949; practised at Chancery Bar, 1949–54; joined Legal Adviser's Br., Home Office, 1954; Mem., Criminal Law Revision Cttee, 1980–83. Silver Star Medal (USA), 1944. *Address:* 4 Mariner's Court, Victoria Road, Aldeburgh IP15 5EH. *T:* (01728) 453754.

SEMMENS, Victor William; Partner, Eversheds Solicitors (Chairman, 1989–96; Director of International Business, since 1998); *b* 10 Oct. 1941; *s* of Ronald William Semmens and Cecile Maude Semmens; *m* 1964, Valerie Elizabeth Norton; two *s. Educ:* Blundell's. Qualified Solicitor, 1964; Partner, Wells & Hurd, subseq. Eversheds, Nottingham, 1968–. *Recreations:* golf, tennis, ski-ing. *Address:* 1 Royal Standard Place, Nottingham NG1 6FZ. *T:* (0115) 950 7000. *Club:* Combined Services (Notts).

SEMPER, Very Rev. Colin (Douglas); Canon of Westminster, 1987–97; *b* 5 Feb. 1938; *s* of William Frederick and Dorothy Anne Semper; *m* 1962, Janet Louise Greaves; two *s. Educ:* Lincoln School; Keble College, Oxford (BA); Westcott House, Cambridge. Curate of Holy Trinity with St Mary, Guildford, 1963–66; Recruitment and Selection Sec., ACCM, 1966–69; Head of Religious Programmes, BBC Radio, and Deputy Head of Religious Broadcasting, BBC, 1969–82; Provost of Coventry Cathedral, 1982–87. Hon. Chaplain, 1985–, Freeman, 1991, Liveryman, 1991–, Feltmakers' Co. *Recreations:* travel, reading modern novels, canals. *Address:* 8 Thames Mews, Old Town, Poole, Dorset BH15 1JY.

SEMPILL, family name of **Baron Sempill**.

SEMPILL, 21st Baron *cr* 1489; **James William Stuart Whitemore Sempill;** Sales and Marketing Manager, Angus Distillers plc, since 2001; Director: Scotch Embassy Ltd, since 1995; Malt Masterclass, Edinburgh, since 1997; Holyrood Strategy, Edinburgh, since 1998; *b* 25 Feb 1949; *s* of Lady Sempill (20th in line), and Lt-Col Stuart Whitemore Chant-Sempill (*d* 1991); *S* mother, 1995; *m* 1977, Josephine Ann Edith, *e d* of J. Norman Rees, Kelso; one *s* one *d. Educ:* The Oratory School; St Clare's Hall, London (BA Hons History, 1971); Hertford Coll., Oxford. Gallaher Ltd, 1972–80; PA to Man. Dir, Sentinel Engineering Pty Ltd, Johannesburg, 1980–81; Manager, TWS Public Relations Company, Johannesburg, 1981–83; investment manager, Alan Clarke and Partners, 1982–83; Marketing Manager, S African Breweries, 1983–86; Account Director: Bates Wells (Pty), 1986; Partnership in Advertising, Johannesburg, 1988–90; Client Service Dir, Ogilvy & Mather, Cape Town, 1990–92; Trade Marketing Dir, 1993–95, Dir, Special Projects, 1995, Scottish & Newcastle. Chm., Edinburgh N and Leith Cons. Assoc., 1999–2001. Contested (C) Edinburgh N and Leith, Scottish Parly elecn, 1999. *Heir: s* Master of Sempill, *qv. Club:* New (Edinburgh).

SEMPILL, Master of; Hon. Francis Henry William Forbes Sempill; *b* 4 Jan. 1979; *s* and *heir* of Baron Sempill, *qv. Educ:* Western Province Prep. Sch., Cape Town; Merchiston Castle Sch., Edinburgh; Napier Univ., Edinburgh. *Recreations:* cricket, swimming, tennis. *Address:* 3 Vanburgh Place, Edinburgh EH6 8AE.

SEMPLE, Prof. Andrew Best, CBE 1966; VRD 1953; Professor of Community and Environmental Health (formerly of Public Health), University of Liverpool, 1953–77, now Professor Emeritus; *b* 3 May 1912; *m* 1941, Jean (*née* Sweet); one *d. Educ:* Allan Glen's School, Glasgow; Glasgow Univ. MB, ChB 1934, MD 1947, DPH 1936, Glasgow. FFCM 1972. Various hospital appointments, 1934–38; Asst MOH and Deputy Medical Superintendent, Infectious Diseases Hosp., Portsmouth, 1938–39; Asst MOH and Asst School Medical Officer, Blackburn, 1939–47 (interrupted by War Service); Senior Asst MOH, Manchester, 1947–48; Deputy MOH, City and Port of Liverpool, 1948–53, MOH and Principal Sch. Med. Officer, 1953–74; Area MO (teaching), Liverpool AHA, 1974–77. Served War of 1939–46; Surgeon Commander, RNVR; Naval MOH, Western Approaches, Malta and Central Mediterranean. Chm. Council and Hon. Treasurer, RSH, 1963. QHP 1962. *Publications:* various regarding infectious disease, poı etc. *Address:* Kelvin, 433 Woolton Road, Gateacre, Liverpool L25 4SY. 2081.

SEMPLE, Andrew Greenlees; *b* 16 Jan. 1934; *s* of late William Hugh Sem Madeline, *d* of late E. H. Wood, Malvern, Worcs; *m* 1st, 1961, Janet Elizabeth Wha 1993); one *s* one *d*; 2nd, 2000, Susan Lucy Jacobs. *Educ:* Winchester Coll.; St John's Co Cambridge (MA). Entered Min. of Transport and Civil Aviation, 1957; Private Sec. to Permanent Sec., 1960–62; Principal, 1962; Asst Sec., 1970; Private Sec. to successive Secs of State for the Environment, 1972–74; Under Sec., DoE, 1976; Principal Finance Officer, PSA, DoE, 1980–83; Sec., Water Authorities Assoc., 1983–87; Man. Dir, Anglian Water Authority, 1987–89; Gp Man. Dir, 1989–90, Vice-Chm., 1990–92, Anglian Water plc. Mem., Bd, Eureau, 1983–92. Chm., Huntingdonshire Enterprise Agency, 1990–2001. Mem. Council, and Chm. Activities Cttee, Garden History Soc., 1997–. Governor: Huntingdonshire Regl Coll., 1992–; Kimbolton Sch., 2001–. Hon. Mem., IWO (AWO, 1988). FCIWEM 1994. *Recreations:* reading, gardens, watching cricket. *Address:* 14 Druce Road, SE21 7DW. *T:* (020) 8693 8202; 3 Church Lane, Covington, Cambs PE18 0RT. *T:* (01480) 860497. *Club:* Surrey CC.

SEMPLE, Sir John (Laughlin), KCB 2000 (CB 1993); Head of Northern Ireland Civil Service, 1997–2000; Second Permanent Under-Secretary of State, Northern Ireland Office, 1998–99; Secretary to the Executive Committee, Northern Ireland Assembly, 1999–2000; *b* 10 Aug. 1940; *s* of late James E. Semple and of Violet E. G. Semple; *m* 1970, Maureen Anne Kerr; two *s* one *d. Educ:* Campbell Coll., Belfast; Corpus Christi Coll., Cambridge (MA). BScEcon London. Joined Home CS as Asst Principal, Min. of Aviation, 1961; transf. to NI CS, 1962; Asst Principal, Mins of Health and Local Govt, Finance, and Health and Social Services, 1962–65; Dep. Principal, Min. of Health and Social Services, 1965; Principal: Min. of Finance, 1968; Min. of Community Relations, 1970–72; Asst Sec. (Planning), Min. of Develt, 1972; Asst Sec. (Housing), DoE, 1977–79; Under Sec. (Housing), DoE for N Ireland, 1979–83; Under Sec., 1983–88, Permanent Sec., 1988–97, Dept of Finance and Personnel for NI. Mem., Consumer Council for Postal Services. *Recreations:* golf, tennis, gardening.

SEMPLE, Prof. Stephen John Greenhill, MD, FRCP; Emeritus Professor, University College London, since 1991; Visiting Professor of Medicine, Imperial College School of Medicine (at Charing Cross Hospital), since 1991; Hon. Consultant Physician, Hammersmith Hospitals NHS Trust, since 1991; *b* 4 Aug. 1926; *s* of late John Edward Stewart and Janet Semple; *m* 1961, Penelope Ann, *y d* of Sir Geoffrey Aldington, KBE, CMG; three *s. Educ:* Westminster; London Univ. MB, BS, 1950, MD 1952, FRCP 1968. Research Asst, St Thomas' Hosp. Med. Sch., 1952; Jun. Med. Specialist, RAMC, Malaya, 1953–55; Instr, Med. Sch., Univ. of Pennsylvania, USA, 1957–59; St Thomas' Hosp. Medical Sch.: Lectr, 1959; Sen. Lectr, 1961; Reader, 1965; Prof. in Medicine, 1969; Prof. of Medicine, The Middlesex Hosp. Medical Sch., 1970–87; Prof. of Medicine, and Head, Dept of Medicine, UCL, 1987–91. *Publications:* Disorders of Respiration, 1972; articles in: Lancet, Jl Physiol. (London), Jl Applied Physiol. *Recreations:* tennis, music. *Address:* White Lodge, 3 Claremont Park Road, Esher, Surrey KT10 9LT. *T:* (01372) 465057. *Club:* Queen's.

SEN, Prof. Amartya Kumar, Bharat Ratna, 1999; Hon. CH 2000; FBA 1977; Master of Trinity College, Cambridge, since 1998; Lamont University Professor Emeritus, Harvard University, since 1998; *b* 3 Nov. 1933; *s* of late Dr Ashutosh Sen, Dhaka, and of Amita Sen, Santiniketan, India; *m* 1st, 1960, Nabaneeta Dev (marr. diss. 1975); two *d*; 2nd, 1978, Eva Colorni (*d* 1985); one *s* one *d*; 3rd, 1991, Emma Rothschild, *qv. Educ:* Calcutta Univ.; Cambridge Univ. MA, PhD. Prof. of Economics, Jadavpur Univ., Calcutta, 1956–58; Trinity Coll., Cambridge: Prize Fellow, 1957–61; Staff Fellow, 1961–63; Hon. Fellow, 1991; Professor of Economics: Delhi Univ., 1963–71 (Chm., Dept of Economics, 1966–68, Hon. Prof., 1971–); LSE, 1971–77; Oxford Univ., 1977–80; Fellow, Nuffield College, Oxford, 1977–80 (Associate Mem., 1980–89; Hon. Fellow, 1998); Drummond Prof. of Political Economy, and Fellow, All Souls Coll., Oxford, 1980–88; Prof. of Economics and Philosophy, 1987–97 and Lamont Univ. Prof., 1988–97, Harvard Univ. Hon. Dir, Agricultural Economics Research Centre, Delhi, 1966–68 and 1969–71. Res. Advr, World Inst. for Develt Econ. Res., Helsinki, Finland, 1985–93. Vis. Professor: MIT, 1960–61; Univ. of Calif at Berkeley, 1964–65; Harvard Univ., 1968–69; Andrew D. White Professor-at-large, Cornell Univ., 1978–84. Chm., UN Expert Gp Meeting on Role of Advanced Skill and Technology, New York, 1967. President: Develt Studies Assoc., 1980–82; Econometric Soc., 1984 (Fellow 1968–, Vice-Pres. 1982–83); Internat. Economic Assoc., 1986–89; Indian Econ. Assoc., 1989; Amer. Econ. Assoc., 1994; Soc. for Social Choice and Welfare, 1993–94; Vice-Pres., Royal Economic Soc., 1988– (Mem. Council, 1977–87); Trustee, Inst. for Advanced Study, Princeton, 1987–94. Foreign Hon. Mem., Amer. Acad. of Arts and Sciences, 1981; Hon. Mem., Amer. Econ. Assoc., 1981. Hon. FRSE; Hon. Fellow: Inst. of Social Studies, The Hague, 1982; LSE, 1984; IDS, Sussex Univ., 1984; SOAS, London Univ., 1998; Darwin Coll., Cambridge, 1998. Hon. DLitt: Saskatchewan, 1980; Visva-Bharati, 1983; Georgetown, 1989; Jadavpur, Kalyani, 1990; Williams Coll., City of London Poly., 1991; New Sch. for Social Res., NY, Calcutta, 1992; Syracuse, 1994; Oxford, 1996; Bard Coll., 1997; Leicester, Kingston, Columbia, 1998; UEA, Nottingham, Heriot-Watt, 1999; Allahabad, Assam, Strathclyde, 2000; Hon. DHumLit: Oberlin Coll., 1993; Wesleyan, 1995; McGill, 1998; Hon. DSc: Bath, 1984; Edinburgh, 1995; Dhaka, 1999; Assam Agricl, Birmingham, 2000; DSocSc Chinese Univ. of HK, 1999; DU: Essex, 1984; Rabindra Bharati, 1998; Dr *hc*: Caen, 1987; Bologna, 1988; Univ. Catholique de Louvain, 1989; Athens Univ. of Econs and Business, 1991; Valencia, Zurich, 1994; Antwerp, 1995; Stockholm, 1996; Kiel, 1997; Padua, 1998; Athens, Méditerranée (Marseille), 1999; Hon. LLD: Tulane, 1990; Queen's Univ., Kingston, Ont., 1993; Harvard, 2000. Agnelli Internat. Prize, 1990; Alan Shawn Feinstein World Hunger Award, 1990; Nobel Prize for Economics, 1998. Grand Cross, Order of Scientific Merit (Brazil), 2000. *Publications:* Choice of Techniques, 1960, 3rd edn 1968; Growth Economics, 1970; Collective Choice and Social Welfare, 1971; On Economic Inequality, 1973; Employment, Technology and Development, 1975; Poverty and Famines: an essay on entitlement and deprivation, 1981; (ed with Bernard Williams) Utilitarianism and Beyond, 1982; Choice, Welfare and Measurement, 1982; Resources, Values and Development, 1984; Commodities and Capabilities, 1985; On Ethics and Economics, 1987; The Standard of Living, 1987; (with Jean Drèze) Hunger and Public Action, 1989; (ed with Jean Drèze) The Political Economy of Hunger, 3 vols, 1990–91; Inequality Re-examined, 1992; (with Jean Drèze) India: economic development and social opportunity, 1995; Development as Freedom, 1999; articles in various jls in economics, philosophy, political science, decision theory, demography and law. *Address:* Master's Lodge, Trinity College, Cambridge CB2 1TQ.

SEN, Emma; *see* Rothschild, Emma.

SENDAK, Maurice Bernard; writer and illustrator of children's books; theatrical designer; Artistic Director, The Night Kitchen, national children's theater; *b* 10 June 1928; *yr s* of Philip Sendak and Sarah (*née* Schindler). *Educ:* Lafayette High School, Brooklyn;

Art Students' League, NY. Worked part-time at All American Comics; window display work with Timely Service, 1946–48, F. A. O. Schwartz, 1948–50; illustrated over 50 books by other writers, 1951–. Retrospective one-man exhibitions: Sch. of Visual Arts, NY, 1964; Ashmolean, Oxford, 1975; Amer. Cultural Center, Paris, 1978. *Stage designs:* The Magic Flute, Houston, 1980; The Cunning Little Vixen, NY, 1981; The Love of Three Oranges, Glyndebourne, 1982; Where the Wild Things Are, NT, 1984; L'enfant et les sortilèges, L'Heure espagnole, Glyndebourne, 1987. Hon. RDI 1986. *Publications:* Kenny's Window, 1956; Very Far Away, 1957; The Sign on Rosie's Door, 1960; Nutshell Library set, 1962; Where the Wild Things Are, 1963 (Amer. Liby Assoc. Caldecott Medal, 1964; opera, by Oliver Knussen, Glyndebourne, 1984); Higglety Pigglety Pop!, 1967; Hector Protector, 1967; In the Night Kitchen, 1971; (with Charlotte Zolotow) Rabbit and the Lovely Present, 1971; Pictures, 1972; Maxfield Parrish Poster Book, 1974; (with Matthelo Margolis) Some Swell Pup, 1976; Charlotte and the White Horse, 1977; (ed) Disney Poster Book, 1977; Seven Little Monsters, 1977; (with Doris Orgel) Sarah's Room, 1977; Very Far Away, 1978; Outside Over There, 1981; (with Frank Corsaro) The Love for Three Oranges, 1984; (with Ralph Manheim) Nutcracker, 1984; Dear Mili, 1988; Caldecott and Company (essays), 1989; We are all in the Dumps with Jack and Guy, 1993. *Address:* c/o HarperCollins, 10 East 53rd Street, New York, NY 10022, USA.

SENIOR, (Alan) Gordon, CBE 1981; CEng, FICE, FIStructE; Managing Partner, Gordon Senior Associates, Engineering and Management Consultants, since 1980; *b* 1 Jan. 1928; *s* of late Oscar Senior and Helen Senior (*née* Cooper); *m* 1st, 1955, Sheila Lockyer (marr. diss. 1961); 2nd, 1968, Lawmary Mitchell (marr. diss. 1978); one *s*. *Educ:* Normanton Grammar School; Leeds Univ. (BSc 1948, MSc 1949). J. B. Edwards (Whyteleafe) Ltd, 1949–51; Oscar Faber & Partners, Consulting Engineers, 1951–54; W. S. Atkins & Partners, Consulting Engineers, 1954–80: Technical Dir, 1967; Man. Dir of Atkins Research and Development, 1972; Director, W. S. Atkins & Partners, 1976. Chairman: Surface Engineering and Inspection Ltd, 1983–86; Masta Corp. Ltd, 1987–92; Aptech Ltd, 1988–89; Director: Ansen Offshore Consultants Ltd and McMillan Sloan & Partners, 1981–84; Armstrong Technology Services Ltd, 1986. Member, Navy Dept Advisory Cttee on Structural Steels, 1967–71. Science and Engineering Research Council: Mem., Engineering Bd, 1974–78; Chm., Transport and Civil Engineering Cttee, 1974–78; Chm., Marine Technology Management Cttee, 1980–83. Department of Trade and Industry: Mem., Ship and Marine Technology Requirements Bd, and Chm., Marine Technology Cttee, 1976–81; Mem., Maritime Technology Cttee, 1981–86; Chm., Adv. Cttee on Resources from the Sea, 1983–86. Member: Dept of Energy Programme Cttee, Offshore Energy Technology Bd, 1978–85; HSE Offshore Safety and Tech. Bd, 1985–92. Chm., Greenwich Forum, 1991–; Vice-Pres. and Chm. of Council, Soc. for Underwater Technology, 1979–81. Chm., Industrial Science and Technology Ltd, 1997–. *Publications:* (co-author) Brittle Fracture of Steel Structures, 1970; papers on welding, fatigue, brittle fracture, design of steel structures, computer aided design, renewable energy from the sea, and future developments offshore and in the oceans. *Recreations:* food and wine, travel, music, opera, ski-ing. *Address:* 3 Briar Patch, Charterhouse, Godalming, Surrey GU7 2JB. *T:* (01483) 417781, *Fax:* (01483) 427781; *e-mail:* agsenior@aol.com. *Club:* Athenæum.

SENIOR, Gordon; *see* Senior, A. G.

SENIOR, Olive Edith; JP, MPhil, SRN; consultant in clinical risk, 1995–2000; Regional Nursing Officer, Trent Regional Health Authority, 1973–86; Fellow, Nottingham University, 1988–95; *b* 26 April 1934; *d* of Harold and Doris Senior, Mansfield, Notts. *Educ:* Harlow Wood Orthopaedic Hosp., 1949–52; St George's Hosp., Hyde Park Corner, 1952–56; City Hosp., Nottingham (Pt I, CMB 1956); Nottingham Univ. (HV Cert. 1957, MPhil 1978). Health Visitor, Notts CC, 1958–60; St George's Hosp., London (Ward Sister), 1960–63; S Africa, June-Dec. 1963; Forest Gate Hosp., London (SCM), 1964; St Mary's Hosp., Portsmouth (Asst Matron/Night Supt), 1964–66; NE Metropolitan Regional Hosp. Bd (Management Services), 1966–71; Chief Nursing Officer, Nottingham and Dist. HMC, 1971–73. Member: Local Res. Ethics Cttee, N Notts HA, 1998–; N Notts Community Health Council, 2001–. Secretary of State Fellow, 1973. JP Nottingham Guildhall, 1973. *Publications:* An Analysis of Nurse Staffing Levels in Hospitals in the Trent Region (1977 Data), 1978; Dependency and Establishments, 1979; contrib. to Nursing Times (Determining Nursing Establishments). *Address:* 94 Oak Tree Lane, Mansfield, Notts NG18 3HL. *Club:* Nottingham University (Nottingham).

SENNITT, John Stuart; His Honour Judge Sennitt; a Circuit Judge, since 1994; *s* of late Stuart Osland Sennitt and Nora Kathleen Sennitt; *m* 1966, Janet Ann; one *s* two *d*. *Educ:* Culford Sch., Bury St Edmunds; St Catharine's Coll., Cambridge (MA, LLB). Admitted Solicitor, 1961; Partner, Wild, Hewitson & Shaw, Cambridge, 1963–83; County Court Registrar, then Dist Judge, 1983–94; Asst Recorder, 1988–92; a Recorder, 1992–94. *Address:* Cambridge County Court, Bridge House, Bridge Street, Cambridge CB2 1UA.

SENSI, His Eminence Cardinal (Giuseppe M.); *b* 27 May 1907. Ordained, 1929; Sec. of Apostolic Nunciature in Roumania, 1934–38; Secretary and Auditor of Apostolic Nunciature in Switzerland, 1938–46; Councillor of Apostolic Nunciature in Belgium, 1946–47; Chargé d'Affaires of the Holy See in Prague, 1948–49; Councillor in the Secretariat of State of His Holiness, 1949–53; Permanent Observer of the Holy See at UNESCO in Paris, 1953–55; apptd Nuncio Apostolic to Costa Rica, May 1955, and consecrated Titular Archbishop of Sardi, July 1955; Apostolic Delegate to Jerusalem, 1957; Apostolic Nuncio to Ireland, 1962–67; Apostolic Nuncio to Portugal, 1967–76; Cardinal, 1976. Chevalier, Grand Cross SMO Malta, 1959; Grand Cross, Santi Maurizio e Lazzaro, 1975; Grand Cross, Ordre Militaire du Christ (Portugal), 1976; Grand Cross, Ordre Equestre du St Sepolcre de Gerusalemme, 1978. Hon. Mem., Accademia Cosentina, 1976. *Address:* Piazza S Calisto 16, 00153 Rome, Italy. *T:* (6) 6987265/6987388/5897827.

SENTAMU, Rt Rev. John Mugabi Tucker; *see* Stepney, Area Bishop of.

SENTANCE, Dr Andrew William; Chief Economist, British Airways, since 1998; *b* 17 Sept. 1958; *s* of William Thomas Wulfram Sentance and Lillian Sentance (*née* Bointon); *m* 1985, Anne Margaret Penfold; one *s* one *d*. *Educ:* Eltham Coll., London; Clare Coll., Cambridge (BA Hons, MA); London Sch. of Econs (MSc Econ; PhD 1988). Manager, Petrocell Ltd, 1980–81; with NCB, 1982–83; Confederation of British Industry: Head, Econ. Policy, 1986–89; Dir, Econ. Affairs, 1989–93; London Business School: Sen. Res. Fellow, 1994–95; Dir, Centre for Economic Forecasting, 1995–98. Chief Economic Advr, British Retail Consortium, 1995–98. Member: HM Treasury Panel of Independent Forecasters, 1992–93; various statistical adv. cttees, 1988–. Mem., Adv. Bd, Air Transport Action Gp, 2000–. Vis. Prof. of Econs, Royal Holloway, Univ. of London, 1998–; Vis. Prof., Coll. of Aeronautics, Cranfield Univ., 2001–. Dep. Chm., Soc. of Business Economists, 2000– (Mem. Council, 1991–; Chm., 1995–2000). Trustee: Harvest Help, 1996–; Anglo-German Foundn, 2001–. Ed., London Business Sch. Econ. Outlook, 1994–98. *Publications:* numerous articles in books and jls on current economic issues. *Recreations:* playing piano, guitar and organ, listening to music. *Address:* British Airways plc, Waterside, Harmondsworth UB7 0GB. *T:* (020) 8738 6813.

SEOKA, Rt Rev. Johannes Thomas; *see* Pretoria, Bishop of.

SEPHTON, Craig Gardner; QC 2001; *b* 7 Dec. 1957; *s* of Bruce and Betty Sephton; *m* 1985, Colette (marr. diss.); three *s*. *Educ:* Ecclesbourne Sch., Duffield; Lincoln Coll., Oxford (MA, BCL). Called to the Bar, Middle Temple, 1981. *Recreations:* swimming, mountaineering, music. *Address:* 24 St John Street, Manchester M3 4DF. *T:* (0161) 214 6000.

SEPÚLVEDA, Bernardo, Hon. GCMG 1985; Foreign Affairs Adviser to President of Mexico, since 1993; *b* 14 Dec. 1941; *s* of Bernardo Sepúlveda and Margarita Amor; *m* 1970, Ana Yturbe; three *s*. *Educ:* Univ. of Mexico (Law Degree *magna cum laude*, 1964); Queens' Coll., Cambridge (LLB 1966; Hon. Fellow, 1990). Prof. of Internat. Law, El Colegio de México, 1967–81; Dep. Dir Gen. for Legal Affairs to Secretary of the Presidency, 1968–70; Asst Sec. for Internat. Affairs, Min. of the Treasury, 1976–80; Principal Advisor on Internat. Affairs to the Minister of Planning and Budget, 1981; Ambassador to USA, 1982; Minister of Foreign Relations, Mexico, 1982–88; Ambassador to UK, 1989–93. Dr *hc*: Univ. of San Diego, Calif, 1982; Univ. of Leningrad, 1987. Principe de Asturias Prize, Spain, 1984; Simón Bolívar Prize, UNESCO, 1985. Grand Cross, Order of: Civil Merit (Spain), 1979; Isabel the Catholic (Spain), 1983; Southern Cross (Brazil), 1983; Boyacá (Colombia), 1984; Merit (FRG), 1984; Liberator San Martín (Argentina), 1984; Vasco Núñez de Balboa (Panama), 1984; Manuel Amador Geurrero (Panama), 1985; Christ (Portugal), 1985; Crown (Belgium), 1985; Quetzal (Guatemala), 1986; Prince Henry the Navigator (Portugal), 1986; Sun (Peru), 1987; Rio Branco (Brazil), 1988; Grand Officier, Nat. Order of Legion of Honour (France), 1985; also orders and decorations from Korea, Venezuela, Poland, Yugoslavia, Greece, Japan, Egypt and Jamaica. *Publications:* The United Nations: dilemma at 25, 1970; Foreign Investment in Mexico, 1973; Transnational Corporations in Mexico, 1974; articles on internat. law in prof. jls. *Recreations:* reading, music. *Address:* Rocas 185, México, DF 01900, México. *T:* (5) 6520641. *Clubs:* Brooks's, Travellers.

SERAFÍN, David; *see* Michael, I. D. L.

SERENY, Gitta; writer; *b* 13 March 1923; *d* of Gyula and Margit Serényi; *m* 1948, Donald Honeyman; one *s* one *d*. *Educ:* Vienna Realgymnasium Luithlen; Stonar House Sch., Sandwich, Kent; Reinhardt-Seminar, Vienna; Sorbonne, Univ. of Paris. *Publications:* The Medallion (novel), 1957; *non-fiction:* The Case of Mary Bell, 1972; Into That Darkness, 1974; The Invisible Children, 1984; Albert Speer, His Battle With Truth, 1995; Cries Unheard, 1998; The German Trauma: experiences and reflections 1938–2001, 2001; contrib. features and series to newspapers and periodicals, incl. The Times and The Independent, Die Zeit, Dagens Nyheter, and NY Review of Books. *Recreations:* swimming, hiking, reading. *Address:* c/o Tessa Sayle Literary Agency, 11 Jubilee Place, SW3 3TE.

SERGEANT, John; Political Editor, ITN, since 2000; *b* 14 April 1944; *s* of Ernest Sergeant and Olive Sergeant (now Stevens); *m* 1969, Mary Smithies; two *s*. *Educ:* Millfield Sch., Street; Magdalen Coll., Oxford (BA Hons PPE). Appeared in On the Margin, BBC TV, 1966–67; Reporter, Liverpool Daily Post and Echo, 1967–70; BBC: Reporter, 1970–81: reported from 25 countries, incl. conflicts in Vietnam, Cyprus, Israel, Lebanon, Rhodesia and NI; acting Corresp., Dublin, Paris and Washington; Presenter, current affairs progs, Radio 4, incl. Today, World at One, PM; Political Corresp., 1981–88; Chief Political Corresp., 1988–2000; has appeared on numerous TV and radio progs, incl. Have I Got News for You, Room 101, Call My Bluff, News Quiz, Quote Unquote, etc. Most Memorable TV Broadcast award, British Press Guild, 1991; Best Individual TV Contributor, Voice of the Listener and Viewer, 1999. *Publication:* Give Me Ten Seconds (memoirs), 2001. *Recreations:* sailing, listening to classical music. *Address:* ITN, Press Gallery, House of Commons, SW1A 0AA. *T:* (020) 7219 3334.

SERGEANT, Sir Patrick (John Rushton), Kt 1984; City Editor, Daily Mail, 1960–84; Founder, 1969, and Chairman, 1985–92, Euromoney Publications (Managing Director, 1969–85); *b* 17 March 1924; *s* of George and Rene Sergeant; *m* 1952, Gillian Anne Wilks, Cape Town; two *d*. *Educ:* Beaumont Coll. Served as Lieut, RNVR, 1945. Asst City Editor, News Chronicle, 1948; Dep. City Editor, Daily Mail, 1953. Director: Associated Newspapers Group, 1971–83; Daily Mail General Trust, 1983–; (non-exec.) Euromoney Institutional Investor plc (formerly Euromoney Publications), 1992–. Domus Fellow, St Catherine's Coll., Oxford, 1988. Freeman, City of London, 1987. Wincott Award, Financial Journalist of the Year, 1979. *Publications:* Another Road to Samarkand, 1955; Money Matters, 1967; Inflation Fighters Handbook, 1976. *Recreations:* skiing, tennis, swimming, talking. *Address:* One The Grove, Highgate Village, N6 6JU. *T:* (020) 8340 1245. *Clubs:* Royal Automobile; All England Lawn Tennis and Croquet.

SERGIEVO, Bishop of, since 1993; **Rt Rev. Basil Alfred Herbert Ernst Osborne;** Assistant Bishop, Russian Orthodox Diocese of Sourozh, since 1993; Vicar General, since 1997; *b* 12 April 1938; *s* of Alexander W. R. Osborne and Josephine Gerringer; *m* 1962, Rachel Vida Spitzer (*d* 1991); two *s* one *d*. *Educ:* State Univ. of New York at Buffalo (BA (Classics), 1963); Univ. of Cincinnati, Ohio (PhD (Classics), 1969). Ordained deacon, 1969, priest, 1973; consecrated bishop, 1993. A Pres., Churches Together in England, 1993–98; Chm., Oxfordshire Ecumenical Council, 1997–98. Chm. Bd of Dirs, Inst. for Orthodox Christian Studies, Cambridge, 1999–. Editor, Sourozh: A Journal of Orthodox Life and Thought, 1980–. Phi Beta Kappa, 1963. *Publications:* The Light of Christ, 1992, 2nd edn 1996; Speaking of the Kingdom, 1993. *Address:* 94a Banbury Road, Oxford OX2 6JT. *T:* (01865) 512701.

SERIÈS, Sir Emile; *see* Seriès, Sir J. M. E.

SERIÈS, Sir (Joseph Michel) Emile, Kt 1978; CBE 1974; FCIS, FAIA, FSCA, FREconS, FInstD, FRSA; Chairman, Flacq United Estates Ltd and WEAL Group (West East Ltd), since 1968 (General Manager, 1968–96); *b* 29 Sept. 1918; *s* of late Emile Seriès and Julie (*née* Langlois); *m* 1942, Rose-Aimée Jullienne; two *s* two *d*. *Educ:* Royal Coll., Mauritius; London Univ. MCom Delhi Commercial Univ., 1967. FIMgt; FCCS 1958. Accounts Dept, General Electric Supply Co. of Mauritius Ltd, 1936–52 (final position, Chief Acct); Chief Acct and Econ. Adviser, Union Flacq Sugar Estate Ltd and Flacq United Estates Ltd, 1952–61; Manager, Union Flacq Sugar Estate Ltd, 1961–68. Chairman: Rogers & Co. Ltd; Alcohol & Molasses Co. Ltd; Compagnie Mauricienne de Commerce Ltd. Director: Maur. Commercial Bank Ltd; Anglo-Maur. Assurance Society Ltd, and other cos in Mauritius. Past President: Maur. Chamber of Agriculture; Maur. Sugar Industry Research Inst. Member: Maur. Sugar Producers' Assoc.; Maur. Sugar Syndicate; Amer. Management Assoc., New York; National Assoc. of Accts, New York. Chevalier de l'Ordre National du Mérite (France), 1978; Chevalier de la Légion d'Honneur, 1988. *Recreations:* sailing, photography, classical music. *Address:* Flacq United Estates Ltd, Union Flacq, Mauritius. *T:* 532583 and 535535; c/o Weal House, Port Louis, Mauritius. *Clubs:* Dodo, Mauritius Turf, Mauritius Gymkhana, Le Morne Anglers', Grand'Baie Yacht (Mauritius).

SERJEANT, Graham Roger, CMG 1981; MD; FRCP; Chairman, Sickle Cell Trust of Jamaica, since 1986; *b* 26 Oct. 1938; *s* of Ewart Egbert and Violet Elizabeth Serjeant; *m* 1965, Beryl Elizabeth, *d* of late Ivor Edward King, CB, CBE. *Educ:* Sibford Sch., Banbury; Bootham Sch., York; Clare Coll., Cambridge (BA 1960, MA 1965); London Hosp. Med. Sch.; Makerere Coll., Kampala. MB BChir 1963, MD 1971, Cantab; MRCP 1966, FRCP 1977. House Physician: London Hosp., 1963–64; Royal United Hosp., Bath, 1965–66; RPMS, 1966; Med. Registrar, University Hosp. of WI, 1966–67; Wellcome Res. Fellow, Dept of Medicine, Univ. of WI, 1967–71; Medical Research Council: Mem., Scientific Staff, Abnormal Haemoglobin Unit, Cambridge, 1971–72; Epidemiology Res. Unit, Jamaica, 1972–74; Dir, MRC Labs, Jamaica, 1974–99. Hon., Prof. of Clin. Epidemiology, Univ. of WI, 1981–99, now Emeritus. Pres., Caribbean Orgn of Sickle Cell Assocs, 1997–2000. Gold Musgrave Medal, Inst. of Jamaica, 1995; Pelican Award, Univ. of WI, 1995; Vice-Chancellor's Award for Excellence, 1999. Dist. Res. Award, Caribbean Health Res. Council, 1999. Hon. CD (Jamaica), 1996. *Publications:* The Clinical Features of Sickle Cell Disease, 1974; Sickle Cell Disease, 1985, 3rd edn 2001; Guide to Sickle Cell Disease, 2001; approx. 400 papers on the nat. hist. of sickle cell disease, in med. jls. *Recreation:* squash. *Address:* Sickle Cell Trust, 14 Milverton Crescent, Kingston 6, Jamaica, WI. *T:* 9272311, *Fax:* 9700074; *e-mail:* grserjeant@cwjamaica.com.

SERJEANT, William Ronald, FRHistS; County Archivist, Suffolk, 1974–82, retired; Vice-President, Society of Archivists, since 1988 (President, 1982–88); Hon. Archivist to the Lords de Saumarez and Tollemache, and to the British Association for Local History; *b* 5 March 1921; *s* of Frederick William and Louisa (*née* Wood); *m* 1961, Ruth Kneale (*née* Bridson); one *s*. *Educ:* Univ. of Manchester (BA Hons History); Univ. of Liverpool (Dip. Archive Admin. and Study of Records). Archivist/Librarian: Univ. of Sheffield, Sheffield City Library, Liverpool Record Office, 1952–56; Librarian/Archivist, Manx Nat. Library and Archives, Dep. Dir, Manx Mus. and Nat. Trust, 1957–62; County Archivist, Notts, 1962–70; Jt County Bor. and County Archivist, Ipswich and E Suffolk, 1970–74. Member: Lord Chancellor's Adv. Council on Public Records, 1982–88; Suffolk Heraldry Soc., 1982–; Member, Executive Committee: Suffolk Local History Council, 1970–; Ipswich Film Soc., 1974–; Council Member: Suffolk Inst. of Archeology and History, 1970–90; Suffolk Records Soc., 1970–; British Records Soc., 1974–2001; Ipswich Building Preservation Trust, 1988–; British Assoc. for Local History, 1994–97 (Mem. Publications Cttee, 1988– (Chm., 1988–92)); Trustee, Leiston Long Shop Steam Museum, 1983–. Editor: Jl of the Manx Museum, 1957–62; The Suffolk Review, 1970–82; The Blazon (Suffolk Heraldry Soc.), 1984–88. *Publications:* The History of Tuxford Grammar School, 1969; (ed) Index to the Probate Records of the Court of the Archdeacon of Suffolk 1444–1700, 1979–80; (ed) Index to the Probate Records of the Court of the Archdeacon of Sudbury 1354–1700, 1984; articles in county and other local history periodicals. *Recreations:* walking, participation in local historical and heraldic studies and activities, theatre and cinema going; any gaps filled by reading novels. *Address:* 51 Derwent Road, Ipswich, Suffolk IP3 0QR. *T:* (01473) 728997.

SERLE, Anna Catherine; *see* Southall, A. C.

SERMON, (Thomas) Richard, FCIS; Chairman: Gryphon Corporate Counsel, since 1996; Shandwick Consultants Ltd, since 1996; *b* 25 Feb. 1947; *s* of Eric Thomas Sermon and Marjorie Hilda (*née* Parsons); *m* 1970, Rosemary Diane, *yr d* of Thomas Smith; one *s* one *d*. *Educ:* Nottingham High Sch. FCIS 1972. Crest Hotels, 1969–74; Good Relations Gp, 1974–79; Chief Exec., 1979–87, Chm., 1987–90, Shandwick Consultants; Man. Dir, Shandwick Consulting Gp, 1987–88; Chief Executive: Shandwick Europe, 1988–90; Shandwick International, 1990–96; public relns advr, Goldman Sachs Internat., 1992–96. Director: Wrightson Wood Associates, 1994–; Jardine Lloyd Thompson Gp, 1996–; Newmond, 1997–; Appointed Mem., PPP, 1993–98. Mem., Nat. Adv. Council on Employment of People with Disabilities, 1994–98. Mem. Council, C & G, 1993– (Mem. Exec. Cttee, 1999–; Hon. Mem., 1999). Vice-President: RADAR, 1987–; Providence Row, 1999–; Mem. Exec. Cttee, Fedn of London Youth Clubs (formerly London Fedn of Clubs for Young People), 1994– (Hon. Treas., 1995–96; Chm., 1996–). Dir, City of London Sinfonia, 1995–. Chm., The Home Improvement Trust, 1997–. Freeman, City of London, 1968; Member, Court of Assistants: Wheelwrights' Co., 1990– (Master, 2000–01); Chartered Secretaries and Administrators' Co., 1991–. *Address:* Friars Well, Aynho, Banbury, Oxon OX17 3BG. *T:* (01869) 810284. *Clubs:* City of London, City Livery.

SEROTA, family name of **Baroness Serota**.

SEROTA, Baroness *cr* 1967 (Life Peer), of Hampstead in Greater London; **Beatrice Serota,** DBE 1992; JP; a Deputy Speaker, House of Lords, since 1985; *b* 15 Oct. 1919; *m* 1942, Stanley Serota, BSc (Eng), FICE; one *s* one *d*. *Educ:* John Howard School; London School of Economics (BSc (Econ); Hon. Fellow, 1976). Member: Hampstead Borough Council, 1945–49; LCC for Brixton, 1954–65 (Chm., Children's Cttee, 1958–65); GLC for Lambeth, 1964–67 (Chief Whip). Baroness in Waiting, 1968–69; Minister of State (Health), Dept of Health and Social Security, 1969–70; Prin. Dep. Chm. of Cttees, and Chm., European Communities Select Cttee, H of L, 1986–92; Mem., Public Service Select Cttee, H of L, 1996–98. Founder Chm., Commn for Local Admin, 1974–82; Member: Adv. Council in Child Care, and Central Training Council in Child Care, 1958–68; Adv. Council on Treatment of Offenders, 1960–64; Longford Cttee on "Crime—A Challenge to us all", 1964; Royal Commn on Penal System, 1964–66; Latey Cttee on Age of Majority, 1965–67; Adv. Council on Penal System, 1966–68, 1974–79 (Chm., 1976–79); Seebohm Cttee on Organization of Local Authority Personal Social Services, 1966–68; Community Relations Commn, 1970–76; BBC Complaints Commn, 1975–77; Governor, BBC, 1977–82. JP Inner London (West Central Division). Peerage conferred for services to children. Hon. DLitt Loughborough, 1983. *Recreations:* needlepoint, gardening, collecting shells. *Address:* The Coach House, 15 Lyndhurst Terrace, NW3 5QA.

See also Sir N. A. Serota.

SEROTA, Daniel; QC 1989; **His Honour Judge Serota;** a Circuit Judge, since 1999; *b* 27 Sept. 1945; *s* of Louis and N'eema Serota; *m* 1970; two *d*. *Educ:* Carmel Coll.; Jesus Coll., Oxford (MA). Called to the Bar, Lincoln's Inn, 1969; a Recorder, 1989–99. *Address:* Milton Keynes County Court, 351 Silbury Boulevard, Witan Gate East, Milton Keynes MK9 2DT. *T:* (01908) 668855.

SEROTA, Sir Nicholas (Andrew), Kt 1999; Director of the Tate Gallery, since 1988; *b* 27 April 1946; *s* of Stanley Serota and Beatrice Serota (*see* Baroness Serota); *m* 1st, 1973, Angela Mary Beveridge (marr. diss. 1995); two *d*; 2nd, 1997, Teresa Gleadowe; two step *d*. *Educ:* Haberdashers' Aske's Sch., Hampstead and Elstree; Christ's Coll., Cambridge (BA); Courtauld Inst. of Art, London (MA). Regional Art Officer and Exhibn Organiser, Arts Council of GB, 1970–73; Dir, Museum of Modern Art, Oxford, 1973–76; Dir, Whitechapel Art Gallery, 1976–88. Chm., Visual Arts Adv. Cttee, British Council, 1992–98 (Mem., 1976–98); Comr, Commn for Architecture and the Built Envmt, 1999–. Trustee: Public Art Develt Trust, 1983–87; Architecture Foundn, 1991–99. Sen. FRCA 1996. Hon. Fellow: QMC 1988; Goldsmiths' Coll., Univ. of London, 1994. Hon. FRIBA 1992. Hon. DLitt: City, 1990; Plymouth, 1993; Keele, 1994; Exeter, 2000; London Inst., 2001; Surrey, 1997; South Bank, 1996; Hon. Dr Arts City of London Polytechnic, 1990. *Publication:* Experience or Interpretation: the dilemma of museums of modern art, 1996. *Address:* Tate Gallery, Millbank, SW1P 4RG. *T:* (020) 7887 8004.

SERPELL, Sir David Radford, KCB 1968 (CB 1962); CMG 1952; OBE 1944; Member, British Railways Board, 1974–82; *b* 10 Nov. 1911; 2nd *s* of Charles Robert and Elsie Leila Serpell, Plymouth; *m* 1st, Ann Dooley (marr. diss.); three *s*; 2nd, Doris Farr. *Educ:* Plymouth Coll.; Exeter Coll., Oxford (Hon. Fellow, 1992); Univ. of Toulouse (DèsL); Syracuse University, USA; Fletcher School of Law and Diplomacy, USA. (Fell.) Imp. Economic Cttee, 1937–39; Min. of Food, 1939–42; Min. of Fuel and Power, 1942–45; Under-Sec., HM Treasury, 1954–60; Dep. Sec., MoT, 1960–63; Second Sec., BoT, 1963–66; Second Permanent Sec., 1966–68; Second Sec., Treasury, 1968; Permanent Secretary: MoT, 1968–70; DoE, 1970–72. Private Sec. to Parly Sec., Ministry of Food, 1941–42; Principal Private Sec. to Minister of Fuel and Power, 1942–45. Chairman: Nature Conservancy Council, 1973–77; Ordnance Survey Review Cttee, 1978–79; Cttee on the Review of Railway Finances, 1982; Member: NERC, 1973–76; Council, National Trust, 1973–77. *Recreation:* walking. *Address:* 25 Crossparks, Dartmouth, Devon TQ6 9HP. *T:* (01803) 832073. *Club:* Oxford and Cambridge.

SERVAN-SCHREIBER, Prof. Jean-Jacques; engineer, author, politician; Professor of Strategic Thinking and Chairman, International Committee, Carnegie-Mellon University, since 1985; *b* Paris, 13 Feb. 1924; *s* of late Emile Servan-Schreiber, journalist, and Denise Bresard; *m*; four *s*. *Educ:* Ecole Polytechnique, Paris. Served as US-trained fighter pilot, Free French Air Force, World War II. Diplomatic Editor of Le Monde, 1948–53; Founder and Editor of weekly news-magazine, L'Express, 1953–73. Deputy for Lorraine, French National Assembly, 1970–78; Minister of Reforms, June 1974. Pres., Region of Lorraine, 1975–78. Pres., Radical Party, 1971–79; Chm., World Center for Computer Literacy, Paris, 1981–85. Holds military cross for valour, with bar. *Publications:* Lieutenant en Algérie, 1957 (Lieutenant in Algeria); Le Défi américain, 1967 (The American Challenge); Le Manifeste Radical, 1970 (The Radical Alternative); Le Défi mondial, 1980 (The World Challenge); The Chosen and the Choice, 1988; Passions, 1992; Les Fossoyeurs, 1993 (The Gravediggers). *Address:* 37 avenue du Roule, Neuilly/Seine 92200, France.

SERVICE, Alastair Stanley Douglas, CBE 1995; writer, historian and campaigner; *b* 8 May 1933; *s* of late Douglas William Service and Evelyn Caroline (*née* Sharp); *m* 1st, 1959, Louisa Anne Hemming (*see* L. A. Service) (marr. diss. 1984); one *s* one *d*; 2nd, 1992, Zandria Madeleine Pauncefort. *Educ:* Westminster Sch.; Queen's Coll., Oxford. Midshipman, RNR, 1952–54. Trainee, Lazard Bros, 1956–58; Director: McKinlay, Watson and Co. Ltd, Brazil, USA and London, 1959–64 (export finance); Seeley, Service and Co. Ltd (publishers), 1965–79; Municipal Journal Ltd, 1970–78. Hon. Parly Officer: Abortion Law Reform Assoc., organising MPs' and Peers' support of Abortion Act, 1964–67; Divorce Law Reform Union, organising support of Divorce Reform Act, 1967–69; Chm., Birth Control Campaign, organising support of NHS (Family Planning) Amendment Act, 1972, and NHS Reorganisation Act, 1973 (made vasectomy and contraception available free from NHS); involved in other parly campaigns, incl.: Town and Country Amenities Act, 1974; Children's Act, 1975; Public Lending Right for Authors; One-Parent Families. Nat. Chm., 1975–80, Gen. Sec., 1980–89, FPA; Vice-Chm., Health Educn Council, 1976–87; Dep. Chm. (Sec. of State appointee), Health Educn Authy, 1987–89. Chairman: Wilts and Bath Health Commn, 1992–96; Wessex RHA, 1993–94 (non-exec. Dir, 1989–93; Vice-Chm., 1992–93); Wilts HA, 1996–2000; Wilts NHS and Local Govt Strategic Forum, 1996–2000. Member: Nat. Cttee, Population Concern, 1973– (Chm., 1975–79); Nat. Cttee, Victorian Soc., 1975–95 (Chm., Publications Cttee, 1982–89); Hon. Sec., Action for River Kennet, 1991–. Trustee, Prince of Wales's Foundn for Architecture, 1999–; Chm., Prince's Regeneration Through Heritage Gp, 2000–. *Publications:* A Birth Control Plan for Britain (with Dr John Dunwoody and Dr Tom Stuttaford), 1972; The Benefits of Birth Control—Aberdeen's Experience, 1973; Edwardian Architecture and its Origins, 1975; Edwardian Architecture, 1977; The Architects of London from 1066 to Present Day, 1979; London 1900, 1979; (with Jean Bradbery) Megaliths of Europe, 1979; Lost Worlds, 1981; Edwardian Interiors, 1982; series editor, The Buildings of Britain, 1981–84, and author, Anglo-Saxon and Norman Buildings vol., 1982; Victorian and Edwardian Hampstead, 1989; The Standing Stones of Europe, 1993; Sky Speaker (opera libretto), 1999; articles in Arch. Rev., Guardian, Oldie, etc. *Recreations:* looking at buildings (old, new and megalithic), opera (esp. Verdi and Bellini), cycling, Dalmatian dogs, et al. *Address:* Swan House, Avebury, Wilts SN8 1RA. *Club:* Garrick.

SERVICE, Louisa Anne, OBE 1997; Joint Chairman: The Hemming Group (formerly The Municipal Group) of Companies, since 1976; Hemming Publishing Ltd, since 1987; *d* of late Henry Harold Hemming, OBE, MC, and Alice Louisa Weaver, OBE; *m* 1959, Alastair Stanley Douglas Service, *qv* (marr. diss. 1984); one *s* one *d*. *Educ:* private and state schs, Canada, USA and Britain; Ecole des Sciences Politiques, Paris; St Hilda's Coll., Oxford (BA and MA, PPE). Export Dir, Ladybird Appliances Ltd, 1957–59; Municipal Journal Ltd and associated cos: Financial Dir, 1966; Dep. Chm., 1974; Chm., Merchant Printers Ltd, 1975–80; Dir, Brintex Ltd, 1965–; Dir, Glass's Information Services Ltd, 1971, Dep. Chm. 1976–81, Chm., 1982–95. Member: Dept of Trade Consumer Credit Act Appeals Panel, 1981–; Cttee of Magistrates, 1985–88; FIMBRA Appeals Panel, 1988–92; Solicitors Complaints Bureau, 1992–93. JP Inner London Juvenile Courts, 1969–2001; Chm., Hackney Youth Court, 1975–82, Westminster Juvenile Ct, 1982–88, Hammersmith and Fulham Juvenile Court, 1988–94, Camden Youth and Family Proceedings Ct, 1994–; JP Inner London (5) PSD, 1980–; Chairman: Exec. Cttee, Inner London Juvenile Courts, 1977–79; Inner London Juvenile Liaison Cttee, 1986–88 (Mem., 1980–86); Member: working party on re-org. of London Juvenile Courts, 1975; Inner London Family Proceedings Courts, 1991–; Inner London Youth Courts, 1992–; Inner London Magistrates' Cts Cttee, 1995–2001; Vice-Chm., Paddington Probation Hostel, 1976–86. Corres. mem., SDP Policy Gp on Citizens' Rights, 1982–89. Mem., St Hilda's Coll. Develt Adv. Cttee, 1996–; Dir, 1997–, Chm., 2001–, Jacqueline du Pré Music Building Ltd. Dir, Opera Circus Ltd, 2000–. Chm. Council, Mayer-Lismann Opera Workshop, 1976–91; Hon. Sec., Women's India Assoc. of UK, 1967–74. Dir, Arts Club Ltd, 1981–84; Member Council: Friends of Covent Garden, 1982–; Haydn-Mozart Soc., 1988–93; Chm., Youth & Music, 1990–2001(Dir, 1988–90); Mem., E-SU Music Cttee, 1984–91, 1997–2001. Mem. Adv. Bd, Rudolf Kempe Soc., 2000–. Trustee, Performing Arts Labs, 1996–99. *Publications:* articles on a variety of subjects. *Recreations:* travel, and attractive and witty people including my family. *Address:* c/o Hemming Publishing Ltd, 32 Vauxhall Bridge Road, SW1V 2SS. *T:* (020) 7973 6404.

See also J. H. Hemming.

SERVICE, Prof. Robert John, PhD; FBA 1998; Fellow, St Antony's College, Oxford, since 1998; *b* 29 Oct. 1947; *s* of Matthew Service and Janet Service (*née* Redpath); *m* 1975, Adele Biagi; two *s* two *d*. *Educ:* Northampton Town and County Grammar Sch. for Boys; King's Coll., Cambridge (Douton Open Schol. in Classics; BA 1970; MA 1971); Univ. of

Essex (MA Govt and Politics 1971; PhD 1977). British Council Exchange Res. Student, Leningrad, 1973–74; Lectr in Russian Studies, Univ. of Keele, 1975–84; School of Slavonic and East European Studies, University of London: Lectr in Hist., 1984–87; Reader in Soviet Hist. and Politics, 1987–91; Prof. of Russian Hist. and Politics, 1991–98; Chairman: Hist. Dept, 1987–90; Acad. Assembly, 1990–92; Grad. Studies, 1993–97. *Publications:* The Bolshevik Party in Revolution, 1979; Lenin: a political life, Vol. 1 1985, Vol. 2 1991, Vol. 3 1995; The Russian Revolution 1900–1927, 1986, 3rd rev. edn 1999; A History of Twentieth-Century Russia, 1997; Lenin: a biography, 2000. *Recreations:* walking, bicycling. *Address:* 6 Braydon Road, N16 6QB. *T:* (020) 8809 1800.

SERWOTKA, Mark Henryk; General Secretary elect, Public and Commercial Services Union, 2001–May 2002, General Secretary from June 2002; *b* 26 April 1963; *s* of Henryk Josef Serwotka and Audrey Phylis Serwotka; *m* 2001, Ruth Louise Cockroft; one *s* one *d*. *Educ:* St Margaret's RC Primary Sch., Aberdare; Bishop Hedley RC Comprehensive Sch., Merthyr Tydfil. Admin Officer, DHSS, 1980–2001. *Recreations:* sport (golf, football), reading, walking. *Address:* (office) 160 Falcon Road, SW11 2LN; 39 Vivian Road, Sheffield S5 6WJ. *T:* (0114) 243 5497.

SESHADRI, Prof. Conjeevaram Srirangachari, PhD; FRS 1988; Director, Chennai Mathematical Institute (formerly Dean, School of Mathematics, SPIC Science Foundation, then SPIC Mathematic Institute), since 1989; *b* 29 Feb. 1932; *s* of C. Srirangachari and Chudamani; *m* 1962, Sundari; two *s*. *Educ:* Loyola College, Madras (BA Hons Maths Madras Univ. 1953); PhD Bombay Univ. 1958. Tata Institute of Fundamental Research: Student, 1953; Reader, 1961; Professor, 1963; Senior Professor, 1975–84; Sen. Prof., Inst. of Math. Scis, Madras, 1984–89. *Publications:* Fibres Vectorials sur les courtes algébriques, Asterisque, 96, 1982; Introduction to the Theory of Standard Monomials, 1985. *Recreation:* south Indian classical music. *Address:* Chennai Mathematical Institute, 92 G. N. Chetty Road, Chennai 600 017, India. *T:* (44) 8284232, 8284251; (home) (44) 4951198.

SESSIONS, John; *see* Marshall, J. G.

SESSIONS, John Lionel; His Honour Judge Sessions; a Circuit Judge, since 1992; Judge Advocate of the Fleet, since 1995; *b* 8 Jan. 1941; *s* of Geoffrey and Anita Sessions; *m* 1967, Patrizia Corinna Sanminiatelli; one *s* two *d*. *Educ:* King Edward's Sch., Birmingham; BRNC, Dartmouth. Joined RN, 1959; served in HM Ships incl. Venus, Roebuck, Protector, Agincourt and Leopard; Naval interpreter in Italian, 1966; Comdr, 1976; retd 1981. Called to the Bar, Middle Temple, 1972; in practice (Common Law), 1981–92; Recorder, 1989–92. Hon. Legal Advr, Assoc. of Wrens and WRNS Benevolent Trust, 1995–; Member: Civil and Family Cttee, Judicial Studies Bd, 1996–99; Civil Justice Council, 1998–2000; Assoc. of Italian-Speaking Jurists, 1989–. Grand Registrar, United Grand Lodge of England, 1996–98. *Publication:* Naval Interpreters' Handbook (Italian), 1974. *Recreation:* sailing. *Address:* 2 Harcourt Buildings, Temple, EC4Y 9DB. *Clubs:* Anchorites; Bar Yacht; Royal London Yacht (Cowes).

SETCHELL, Marcus Edward, FRCSE, FRCS, FRCOG; Surgeon-Gynaecologist to the Queen, since 1990; Consultant Obstetrician and Gynaecologist, Whittington Hospital NHS Trust, since 2000; *b* 4 Oct. 1943; *s* of late Eric Hedley Setchell and Barbara Mary (*née* Whitworth); *m* 1973, Dr Sarah French; two *s* two *d*. *Educ:* Felsted Sch.; Gonville and Caius Coll., Cambridge; St Bartholomew's Hosp. MA, MB BChir. Consultant Obstetrician and Gynaecologist, St Bartholomew's and Homerton Hosps, 1975–2000, now Hon. Consultant; Hon. Consultant Gynaecologist: King Edward VII Hosp. for Officers, 1982– (Chm. Med. Cttee, 1998–); St Luke's Hosp. for Clergy, 1983–. Convener, Scientific Meetings, 1989–92, Mem. Council, 1994–2000, Chm., Consumers' Forum, 1995–98, RCOG; Mem., Council, 1990–94, Pres., Section of Obstetrics and Gynaecology, 1994–95, RSocMed. *Publications:* (with R. J. Lilford) Multiple Choice Questions in Obstetrics and Gynaecology, 1985, 3rd edn 1996, 4th edn (with B. Thilaganathan) 2001; (contrib.) Ten Teachers in Obstetrics and Gynaecology, 13th edn 1980–16th edn 1995; (with E. E. Philipp) Scientific Foundations of Obstetrics and Gynaecology, 1991; (with C. N. Hudson Shaw) Textbook of Operative Gynaecology, 5th edn, 2001. *Recreations:* tennis, ski-ing, gardening, walking. *Address:* 149 Harley Street, W1N 2DE. *T:* (020) 7935 4444. *Clubs:* Royal Society of Medicine, St Albans Medical, Soho House.

SETH, Vikram, Hon. CBE 2001; writer; *b* 20 June 1952; *s* of Premnath and Leila Seth. *Educ:* Doon Sch., Dehradun, India; Tonbridge Sch., Kent; Corpus Christi Coll., Oxford (MA Hons PPE; Hon. Fellow 1994); Stanford Univ., Calif (MA Econs); Nanjing Univ., China. Sen. Editor, Stanford Univ. Press, 1985–86. Chevalier, Ordre des Arts et des Lettres (France), 2001. *Publications:* Mappings (poems), 1982; From Heaven Lake: travels through Sinkiang and Tibet, 1983; The Humble Administrator's Garden (poems), 1985; The Golden Gate (novel in verse), 1986; All You Who Sleep Tonight (poems), 1990; Three Chinese Poets: translations of Wang Wei, Li Bai and Du Fu, 1992; Arion and the Dolphin (libretto), 1994; Beastly Tales From Here and There (fables in verse), 1992; A Suitable Boy (novel), 1992; An Equal Music (novel), 1999. *Recreations:* music, Chinese calligraphy, swimming. *Address:* c/o Giles Gordon, Curtis Brown Ltd, 37 Queensferry Street, Edinburgh EH2 4QS. *T:* (0131) 225 1286, *Fax:* (0131) 225 1290.

SETINC, Marjan; Ambassador of Slovenia to the Court of St James's, and to Ireland, since 1998; *b* 15 May 1949; *s* of late Martin Setinc and Ana Setinc; *m* 1973, Marta Bartol; one *s* one *d*. *Educ:* Atlantic Coll., S Wales; Univ. of Ljubljana (BA Psychol.); London Sch. of Econs (MSc). Researcher, TUC of Slovenia, 1974–80; Sen. Researcher, Educnl Res. Inst., Ljubljana, 1980–92. MP (Liberal Democracy) Brezice, Slovenia, 1992–96; Mem., Culture and Educn, Sci. and Technol. and Foreign Affairs Select Cttees; Chm., EU Affairs Select Cttee. Rep. of Slovenia, OSCE Parly Delegn, IPU Delegn and Delegn to EU Parlt; Chm., Parly delegns to various bilateral confs. Member: Gen. Assembly for Slovenia, Internat. Assoc. for Evaluation of Educnl Achievement, 1989; Exec. Cttee, Eur. Educnl Res. Assoc., 1996; Nat. Stats Council, 1996. Mem., London Diplomatic Assoc., 1998. Ed., School Field jl, 1989–. *Publications:* Social Conflicts and Strikes, 1975; Public Opinion on Political Decision-Making, 1980; The Averageachieving Curriculum: comparative assessment of pre-university mathematics in Slovenia, 1991; (jtly) Knowldge for Entering the 21st Century, Maths and Natural Sciences: comparison of the achievements of school children aged 14 to 15, in 45 countries, 1997; contrib. numerous articles and papers to scientific jls. *Recreations:* tennis, mountain walking, chess. *Address:* Embassy of the Republic of Slovenia, 11–15 Wigmore Street, W1H 9LA. *T:* (020) 7495 7777, *Fax:* (020) 7495 7776; *e-mail:* slovene-embassy.london@virgin.net. *Clubs:* Travellers, Farmers'.

SETON, Sir Charles Wallace, 13th Bt *cr* 1683 (NS), of Pitmedden, Aberdeenshire; *b* 25 Aug. 1948; *s* of Charles Wallace Seton (*d* 1975) and of Joyce (*née* Perdunn); *S* uncle, 1998; *m* 1974, Rebecca (marr. diss. 1994), *d* of Robert Lowery; one *d*. *Heir:* *b* Bruce Anthony Seton [*b* 29 April 1957; *m* 1991, Paula Harper; one *s* one *d*].

SETON, Sir Iain (Bruce), 13th Bt *cr* 1663 (NS), of Abercorn; *b* 27 Aug. 1942; *s* of Sir (Christopher) Bruce Seton, 12th Bt and of Joyce Vivien, *d* of late O. G. Barnard; *S* father, 1988; *m* 1963, Margaret Ann, *d* of Walter Charles Faulkner; one *s* one *d*. *Educ:* Colchester and Chadacre. Farming until 1972; mining, 1972–. *Heir:* *s* Laurence Bruce Seton [*b* 1 July 1968; *m* 1990, Rachel, *d* of Jeffery Woods; two *d*]. *Address:* Bellavista, PO Box 253, Bridgetown, WA 6255, Australia. *T:* (97) 611349.

SETON, Lady, (Julia), OBE 1989; VMH; (Julia Clements, professionally); author, speaker, international floral art judge; flower arrangement judge for RHS and National Association of Flower Arrangement Societies; *d* of late Frank Clements; *m* 1962, Sir Alexander Hay Seton, 10th Bt, of Abercorn (*d* 1963); no *c*. *Educ:* Isle of Wight; Zwicker College, Belgium. Organised and conducted first Judges' School in England at Royal Horticultural Society Halls; has since conducted many other courses for judges all over Europe. VMH, RHS, 1974. *Publications:* Fun with Flowers; Fun without Flowers; 101 Ideas for Flower Arrangement; Party Pieces; Flower Arranging for All Occasions, 1993; Flower Arrangements in Stately Homes; Julia Clements' Gift Book of Flower Arranging; Flowers in Praise; The Art of Arranging a Flower, etc; My Life with Flowers, 1993. *Address:* 122 Swan Court, SW3 5RU. *Clubs:* Women's Press, Royal Anglo-Belgian.

SETSHOGO, Boithoko Moonwa; Managing Director, Merchandising Associates Pty Ltd; Chairman, Via Afrika Pty Ltd; *b* Serowe, 16 June 1941; *m* 1971, Jennifer Tlalane; two *d*. *Educ:* Moeng Coll.; Univ. of Botswana, Lesotho and Swaziland (BA). District Officer, Kanye, 1969–70; First Sec., High Commn, London, 1970–72; Clerk to the Cabinet, 1972–73; Under-Sec., Min. of Commerce and Industry, 1973–75; High Comr of Botswana in London, 1975–78; Dir of Inf. and Broadcasting, 1978–80. Dir, Aeriel Services (Botswana) Pty. *Address:* (office) PO Box 73, Gaborone, Botswana.

SETTRINGTON, Lord; Charles Henry Gordon-Lennox; *b* 20 Dec. 1994; *s* and *heir* of Earl of March and Kinrara, *qv*.

SEVER, (Eric) John; *b* 1 April 1943; *s* of Eric and Clara Sever. *Educ:* Sparkhill Commercial School. Travel Executive with tour operator, 1970–77. MP (Lab) Birmingham, Ladywood, Aug. 1977–1983; PPS to the Solicitor General, 1978–79. Contested (Lab) Meriden, 1983. *Recreations:* theatre, cinema, reading.

SEVERIN, Prof. Dorothy Virginia Sherman, PhD; FSA; Gilmour Professor of Spanish, University of Liverpool, since 1982; *b* 24 March 1942; *d* of Wilbur B. and Virginia L. Sherman; marr. diss.; one *d*. *Educ:* Harvard Univ. AB 1963; AM 1964; PhD 1967. FSA 1989. Teaching Fellow and Tutor, Harvard Univ., 1964–66; Vis. Lectr, Univ. of W Indies, 1967–68; Asst Prof., Vassar Coll., 1968; Lectr, Westfield Coll., London Univ., 1969–82; Pro-Vice-Chancellor, Univ. of Liverpool, 1989–92. Member: NI Higher Educn Council, 1993–; Res. Panel, British Acad. Humanities Res. Council, 1994–96. Vis. Associate Prof., Harvard Univ., 1982; Visiting Professor: Columbia Univ., 1985; Yale Univ., 1985; Univ. of Calif, Berkeley, 1996. Mem. Cttee, Asociación Hispánica de Literatura Medieval, 1997–99; Trustee, MHRA, 1998–. Editor, Bulletin of Hispanic Studies, 1982–; Mem. Edtl Bd, Hispanic Rev., Celestinesca. *Publications:* (ed) de Rojas, La Celestina, 1969; Memory in La Celestina, 1970; (ed) Diego de San Pedro, La pasión trobada, 1973; (ed) La Lengua de Erasmo romançada por muy elegante estilo, 1975; The Cancionero de Martínez de Burgos, 1976; (ed with K. Whinnom) Diego de San Pedro, Poesía (Obras completas III), 1979; (ed with Angus MacKay) Cosas sacadas de la Historia del rey Juan el Segundo, 1982; (ed) Celestina, trans. James Mabbe (Eng./Spanish text), 1987; (ed) Celestina (Spanish edn), 1987; Tragicomedy and Novelistic Discourse in Celestina, 1989; Cancionero de Oñate-Castañeda, 1990; ADMYTE: The Paris Cancioneros, 1993, 2nd edn 1999 (PN2 with M. Garcia, PN9, PN13 with F. Maguire); Witchcraft in Celestina, 1995; Animals in Celestina, 1999; Two Spanish Cancioneros: The Colombina (LB3) and Egerton (SV2), 2000; contribs to learned jls incl. Hispanic Rev., Romance Philology, Medium Aevum, MLR and THES. *Address:* Department of Hispanic Studies, Modern Languages Building, The University, Chatham Street, Liverpool L69 7ZR. *T:* (0151) 794 2773/4.

SEVERIN, (Giles) Timothy; author, traveller and historian; *b* 25 Sept. 1940; *s* of Maurice Watkins and Inge Severin; *m* 1966, Dorothy Virginia Sherman (marr. diss. 1979); one *d*. *Educ:* Tonbridge School; Keble Coll., Oxford. MA, BLitt. Commonwealth Fellow, USA, 1964–66. Expeditions: led motorcycle team along Marco Polo route, 1961; R Mississippi by canoe and launch, 1965; Brendan Voyage from W Ireland to N America, 1977; Sindbad Voyage from Oman to China, 1980–81; Jason Voyage from Iolkos to Colchis, 1984; Ulysses Voyage from Troy to Ithaca, 1985; first Crusade route by horse to Jerusalem, 1987–88; travels by horse in Mongolia, 1990; N Pacific voyage by bamboo sailing raft, 1993; Moluccan Islands voyage by traditional sailing prahu, 1996. Hon. DLitt Dublin, 1997. Founders Medal, RGS; Livingstone Medal, RSGS; Sykes Medal, RSAA. *Publications:* Tracking Marco Polo, 1964; Explorers of the Mississippi, 1967; The Golden Antilles, 1970; The African Adventure, 1973; Vanishing Primitive Man, 1973; The Oriental Adventure, 1976; The Brendan Voyage, 1978; The Sindbad Voyage, 1982; The Jason Voyage, 1985; The Ulysses Voyage, 1987; Crusader, 1989; In Search of Genghis Khan, 1991; The China Voyage, 1994; The Spice Islands Voyage, 1997; In Search of Moby Dick, 1999. *Address:* Timoleague, Co. Cork, Eire. *T:* (23) 46127, *Fax:* (23) 46233.

SEVERN, David; *see* Unwin, David Storr.

SEVERN, Prof. Roy Thomas, CBE 1992; FREng, FICE; Professor of Civil Engineering, Bristol University, 1968–95, now Emeritus; *b* 6 Sept. 1929; *s* of Ernest Severn and Muriel Woollatt; *m* 1957, Hilary Irene Saxton; two *d*. *Educ:* Deacons School, Peterborough; Imperial College (DSc). Lectr, Imperial College, 1949–54; Royal Engineers (Survey), 1954–56; Bristol University: Lectr, 1956–65; Reader, 1965–68; Dean of Faculty of Engrg, 1970–73 and 1991–94; Pro-Vice Chancellor, 1981–84. Pres., ICE, 1991. FREng (FEng 1981). *Publications:* (ed) Engineering Structures: developments in the twentieth century, 1983; contribs to Procs of ICE, Jl Earthquake Eng. and Structural Dynamics. *Recreations:* sailing, gardening, cricket. *Address:* 49 Gloucester Road, Rudgeway, Bristol BS35 3SF. *T:* (01454) 412027.

SEVERNE, Air Vice-Marshal Sir John (de Milt), KCVO 1988 (LVO 1961); OBE 1968; AFC 1955; Extra Equerry to the Queen, since 1984; *b* 15 Aug. 1925; *s* of late Dr A. de M. Severne, Wateringbury, Kent; *m* 1951, Katharine Veronica, *d* of late Captain V. E. Kemball, RN (Retd); three *d*. *Educ:* Marlborough. Joined RAF, 1944; Flying Instr, Cranwell, 1948; Staff Instr and PA to Comdt CFS, 1950–53; Flt Comdr No 98 Sqdn, Germany, 1954–55; Sqdn Comdr No 26 Sqdn, Germany, 1956–57; Air Min., 1958; Equerry to Duke of Edinburgh, 1958–61; psa 1962; Chief Instr No 226 Operational Conversion Unit (Lightning), 1963–65; jssc 1965; Jt HQ, ME Comd, Aden, and Air Adviser to the South Arabian Govt, 1966–67; DS, JSSC, 1968; Gp Captain Organisation, HQ Strike Comd, 1968–70; Stn Comdr, RAF Kinloss, 1971–72; RCDS 1973; Comdt, Central Flying School, RAF, 1974–76; Air Cdre Flying Trg, HQ RAF Support Comd, 1976–78; Comdr, Southern Maritime Air Region, Central Sub-Area Eastern Atlantic Comd, and Plymouth Sub-Area Channel Comd, 1978–80; retd 1980; recalled as Captain of the Queen's Flight, 1982–89. ADC to The Queen, 1972–73. Hon. Air Cdre, No 3 (Co. of Devon) Maritime HQ Unit, RAuxAF, 1990–95. President: SW Area, RAFA,

1981–95; Queen's Flight Assoc., 1990–2000; CFS Assoc., 1993–98; Taunton and dist Br., ESU, 1996–. Won King's Cup Air Race, British Air Racing Champion, 1960. Pres., RAF Equitation Assoc., 1976–79 (Chm. 1973); Chm., Combined Services Equitation Assoc., 1977–79 (Vice-Chm., 1976). DL Somerset, 1991–2001. *Club:* Royal Air Force.

SEWARD, Guy William; QC 1982; *b* 10 June 1916; *s* of late William Guy Seward and Maud Peacock; *m* 1946, Peggy Dearman. *Educ:* Stationers' Sch. Called to the Bar, Inner Temple, 1956. FRVA 1948. Chairman: Medical Service Cttee, 1977–81; Examination in Public, Devon Structure Plan, 1980; E Herts Health Authority, 1982–90; Member: Mid-Herts HMC, 1966–70; Napsbury HMC, 1970–74 (Chm., 1972–74); Bd of Governors, UCH, 1970–74; Herts AHA, 1974–82 (Vice Chm., 1980–82); Herts FPC, 1974–82; Council, Rating and Valuation Assoc., 1983. Freeman, City of London, 1949. *Publications:* (jtly) Enforcement of Planning Control, 1956; (jtly) Local Government Act, 1958; Howard Roberts Law of Town and Country Planning, 1963; (jtly) Rent Act, 1965; (jtly) Land Commission Act, 1967; (jtly) Leasehold Reform, 1967. *Recreations:* travel, gardening. *Address:* Stocking Lane Cottage, Ayot St Lawrence, Welwyn, Herts AL6 9BW. *Club:* Garrick.

SEWARD, Dame Margaret (Helen Elizabeth), DBE 1999 (CBE 1994); Chief Dental Officer, Department of Health, since 2000; *b* 5 Aug. 1935; *d* of Dr Eric Oldershaw and Gwen Oldershaw; adopted, 1938, by John Hutton Mitchell and Marion Findlay Mitchell; *m* 1962, Prof. Gordon Seward, CBE; one *s* one *d*. *Educ:* Latymer Sch., Edmonton; London Hosp. Med. Coll. Dental Sch. (BDS Hons 1959; MDS 1970). FDSRCS 1962; MCCDRCS 1989. Dental practice: Highlands Hosp., 1962–64; Cheshunt Community Clinic, 1969–75; Royal London Hosp., 1980–94. Sen. Res. Fellow, BPMF, Univ. of London, 1975–77. Member: GDC, 1976–99; Bd, Faculty of Dental Surgery, RCS, 1980–94 (Vice-Dean, 1990). President: Section of Odontology, RSM, 1991; BDA, 1993–94; GDC, 1949–99. Editor: Brit. Dental Jl, 1979–92; Internat. Dental Jl, 1990–2000. Dir, Teamwork Project, DoH, 1991–95; Ind. Dir, Quality Assessment Agency, 1997–2000. Chm., Communication Cttee, FDI, 1984–89. Hon. Pres., Women in Dentistry, 1989–92; Hon. Member: Amer. Dental Assoc., 1992; Amer. Coll. of Dentists, 1994. Chm. Govs, Latymer Sch., 1984–94. Hon. FDSRCSE 1995; Hon. Fellow, QMW, 1997. Hon. DDSc Newcastle, 1995; Hon DDS Birmingham, 1995. *Publications:* Disturbances Associated with the Eruption of the Primary Dentition, 1969; Provision of Dental Care by Women Dentists in England and Wales, 1975, 2nd survey 1985; numerous articles in learned jls, UK and internationally. *Recreations:* cooking, entertaining, housework! *Address:* Department of Health, Richmond House, 79 Whitehall, SW1A 2NS. *Club:* Royal Society of Medicine.

SEWARD, William Richard, RCNC; General Manager, HM Dockyard, Portsmouth, 1975–79, retired; *b* 7 Feb. 1922; *s* of William and Gertrude Seward, Portsmouth; *m* 1946, Mary Deas Ritchie; one *d*. *Educ:* Portsmouth Dockyard Techn. Coll.; RNC Greenwich; Royal Corps of Naval Constructors. Asst Constructor, HM Dockyard, Rosyth, 1945–47; Constructor, Naval Construction Dept, Admty, 1947–58; Admty Constructor Overseer, Birkenhead, 1958–63; Chief Constructor, MoD (N), 1963–70; Prodn Man., HM Dockyard, Chatham, 1970–73, Gen. Manager, 1973–75. *Recreations:* reading, music, caravanning, hill walking. *Club:* Civil Service.

SEWEL, family name of **Baron Sewel**.

SEWEL, Baron *cr* 1995 (Life Peer), of Gilcomstoun in the District of the City of Aberdeen; **John Buttifant Sewel,** CBE 1984; PhD; *b* 15 Jan 1946; *s* of late Leonard Buttifant Sewel and of Hilda Ivy Sewel (*née* Brown). *Educ:* Hanson Boys' Grammar Sch., Bradford; Univ. of Durham (BA 1967); UC, Swansea (MSc (Econ) 1970); Univ. of Aberdeen (PhD 1977). Res. Asst, Dept of Sociology and Anthropology, UC, Swansea, 1967–69; University of Aberdeen: Res. Fellow, Dept of Politics, 1969–72, Depts of Educn and Political Economy, 1972–75; Lectr, 1975; Sen. Lectr, 1988; Prof., Regl Centre for Study of Econ. and Social Policy, 1991–97; Dean: Econ. and Social Scis, 1988–95; Social Scis and Law, 1995–96; Vice-Principal, 1994–96 and 1999–. Mem., City of Aberdeen DC, 1974–84 (Leader, 1977–80). Parly Under-Sec. of State, Scottish Office, 1997–99. Pres., COSLA, 1982–84. Member: Accounts Commn for Scotland, 1987–96; Scottish Constitutional Commn, 1994–95. *Publications:* Colliery Closure and Social Change, 1975; Education and Migration, 1976; (with F. W. Bealey) The Politics of Independence: a study of a Scottish town, 1981; (jtly) The Rural Community and the Small School, 1983; articles and chapters on sociology and politics. *Recreations:* hill walking, ski-ing, watching cricket. *Address:* Birklands, Kilduthie, Raemoir, Banchory, Kincardineshire AB31 5QU. *T:* (01330) 844545.

SEWELL, James Reid, OBE 2001; FSA; City Archivist (formerly Deputy Keeper of Records), Corporation of London, since 1984; *b* 12 April 1944; *s* of late James Campbell Sewell and of Iris Eveleen Sewell (*née* Reid). *Educ:* High Sch., Glasgow; Univ. of Glasgow (MA Hons Hist.); University Coll. London (Dip. Archive Admin). FSA 1979. Asst Archivist, Durham Co. Record Office, 1967–70; Asst Dep. Keeper, Corp. of London Records Office, 1970–84. Chm. and Pres., Section of Municipal Archives, Internat. Council on Archives, 1992–2000 (Mem. Cttee, 1986–92). Fellow, Guildhall Wine Acad., 1993. *Publications:* (with W. A. L. Seaman) The Russian Journal of Lady Londonderry 1836–37, 1973; The Artillery Ground and Fields in Finsbury, 1977; contrib. articles to various professional jls. *Recreations:* tennis, orchid growing, wine. *Address:* Corporation of London Records Office, PO Box 270, Guildhall, EC2P 2EJ. *T:* (020) 7332 1250. *Club:* Shirley Park Lawn Tennis (Hon. Sec., 1983-98).

SEWELL, Thomas Robert McKie; HM Diplomatic Service, retired; Contributing Editor, Informa Group Publishing plc, since 1991; international grains consultant; *b* 18 Aug. 1921; *s* of late O. B. Fane Sewell and late Frances M. Sewell (*née* Sharp); *m* 1955, Jennifer Mary Sandeman; one *d* (and one *d* decd). *Educ:* Eastbourne Coll.; Trinity Coll., Oxford (Schol., Heath Harrison Prize, MA); Lausanne and Stockholm Univs (Schol.). HM Forces, 1940–45 (despatches); Major. Entered Foreign Service, 1949; Second Sec., Moscow, 1950–52; FO, 1952–55; First Sec., 1954; Madrid, 1955–59; Lima, 1959–61; Chargé d'Affaires, 1960; FO, 1961–63; Counsellor and Head of Chancery, Moscow, 1964–66; Diplomatic Service Rep. at IDC, 1966; Head of Associated States, West Indies and Swaziland Depts, Commonwealth Office, 1967–68; Head of N American and Caribbean Dept, FCO, 1968–70; Asst Sec., MAFF, 1970–81; UK Rep. to Internat. Wheat Council, 1972–81. Chm., World Grain Conf., Brussels, 1990. Contested: (C) Greater Manchester Central, EP elecn, 1984; (Referendum) Weston-super-Mare, 1997. Vis. Fellow, Hubert H. Humphrey Inst. of Public Affairs and Dept of Agricl and Applied Econs, Univ. of Minnesota, 1985. Chm., Training the Teachers of Tomorrow Trust, 1987–. *Publications:* (with John de Courcy Ling) Famine and Surplus, 1985; The World Grain Trade, 1992; Grain-Carriage by Sea, 1998; The Global Grain Market, 2000. *Recreations:* international trail riding, inland waterways cruising. *Clubs:* Farmers', Airborne.

SEWELL, Maj.-Gen. Timothy Patrick T.; *see* Toyne Sewell.

SEYCHELLES, Bishop of, since 1979; **Rt Rev. French Kitchener Chang-Him;** Archbishop of the Indian Ocean, 1984–95; *m* 1975, Susan Talma; twin *d*. *Educ:* Lichfield Theolog. Coll.; St Augustine's Coll., Canterbury; Trinity Coll., Univ. of Toronto (LTh 1975). Deacon, Sheffield, 1962; priest, Seychelles,1963; Curate of Goole, 1962–63; Rector of Praslin, Seychelles, 1963–66 and 1969–71; Asst Priest, St Leonard's, Norwood, Sheffield, 1967–68; Vicar General, Seychelles, 1972–73; Rector, S Mahé Parish, 1973–74; Archdeacon of Seychelles, 1973–79; Priest-in-charge, St Paul's Cathedral, Mahé, 1977–79; Dean, Province of the Indian Ocean, 1983–84. DD (*hc*) Trinity Coll., Toronto, 1991. *Address:* Box 44, Victoria, Mahé, Seychelles. *T:* 224242, *Fax:* 224296; *e-mail:* angdio@sey.net.

SEYMOUR, family name of **Marquess of Hertford** and **Duke of Somerset**.

SEYMOUR, Lord; Sebastian Edward Seymour; *b* 3 Feb. 1982; *s* and *heir* of 19th Duke of Somerset, *qv*. *Address:* Berry Pomeroy, Totnes, Devon TQ9 6NJ.

SEYMOUR, David; Legal Adviser to the Home Office, since 2000; *b* 24 Jan. 1951; *s* of Graham Seymour and late Betty (*née* Watson); *m* 1972, Elisabeth Huitson; one *s* two *d*. *Educ:* Trinity Sch., Croydon; Queen's Coll., Oxford (Open Exhibn; BA Jurisprudence 1972; MA 1977); Fitzwilliam Coll., Cambridge (LLB 1974). Law clerk, Rosenfeld, Meyer & Susman (Attorneys), Beverly Hills, Calif, 1972–73; called to the Bar: Gray's Inn (Holt Schol.), 1975, Bencher, 2001; NI, 1997; pupillage, 1975–76; Legal Advr's Br., Home Office, 1976–97; Principal Asst Legal Advr, 1994; Dep. Legal Advr, 1996; Legal Sec. to the Law Officers, 1997–2000. Vis. Lectr in European Human Rights Law, Univ. of Conn Sch. of Law, 1986. Mem., Review of Criminal Justice System in NI, 1998–2000. *Recreations:* hockey, squash, walking. *Address:* c/o Home Office, 50 Queen Anne's Gate, SW1H 9AT. *Club:* MCC.

SEYMOUR, Julian Roger, CBE 2001; Director, New Star Hedge Fund, since 1998; *b* 19 March 1945; *s* of Evelyn Roger Seymour and Rosemary Evelyn Seymour (*née* Flower); *m* 1984, Diana Elizabeth Griffith; one *s* one *d*. *Educ:* Eton. Director: Collett, Dickinson, Pearce Ltd, 1969–79; Robert Fox Ltd, 1980–85; Dir, Corporate Finance, Lowe Gp PLC, 1985–91; Dir, Lady Thatcher's Private Office, 1991–2000. Non-executive Director: Chime Communications PLC, 1990–; Indonesia Fund PLC, 1995–2001. Comr, English Heritage, 1992–98. *Recreations:* gardening, shooting. *Address:* 37 Surrey Lane, SW11 3PA.

SEYMOUR, Lynn, CBE 1976; ballerina; *b* Wainwright, Alberta, 8 March 1939; *d* of E. V. Springbett; *m* 1st, 1963, Colin Jones, photo-journalist (marr. diss.); 2nd, 1974, Philip Pace; three *s*; 3rd, 1983, Vanya Hackel (marr. diss.). *Educ:* Vancouver; Sadler's Wells Ballet School. Joined Sadler's Wells Ballet Company, 1957; Deutsche Oper, Berlin, 1966; Artistic Dir, Ballet of Bavarian State Opera, Munich, 1979–80; has danced with Royal Ballet, English Nat. Ballet, Berliner Ballet, and Adventures in Motion Pictures. *Roles created:* Adolescent, in The Burrow, Royal Opera House, 1958; Bride, in Le Baiser de la Fée, 1960; Girl, in The Invitation, 1960; Young Girl, in Les Deux Pigeons, 1961; Principal, in Symphony, 1963; Principal, in Images of Love, 1964; Juliet, in Romeo and Juliet, 1964; Albertine, BBC TV, 1966; Concerto, 1966; Anastasia, 1966; Flowers, 1972; Side Show, 1972; A Month in the Country, 1976; Five Brahms Waltzes in the manner of Isadora Duncan, 1976; mother, in Fourth Symphony, 1977; Mary Vetsera, in Mayerling, 1978; Take Five, 1978. *Other appearances include:* Danses Concertantes; Solitaire; La Fête Etrange; Sleeping Beauty; Swan Lake; Giselle (title-role); Cinderella; Das Lied von der Erde; The Four Seasons; Voluntaries; Manon, Sleeping Beauty, Dances at a Gathering, The Concert, Pillar of Fire, Romeo and Juliet (Tudor, Nureyev and Cranko), Las Hermañas, Moor's Pavane, Auriole, Apollon, Le Corsaire, Flower Festival, La Sylphide (Sylph and Madge), A Simple Man, Onegin. *Choreography for:* Rashomon, for Royal Ballet Touring Co., 1976; The Court of Love, for SWRB, 1977; Intimate Letters, 1978 and Mac and Polly, for Commonwealth Dance Gala, 1979; Boreas, and Tattoo, for Bavarian State Opera Ballet, 1980; Wolfi, for Ballet Rambert, 1987; Bastet, for SWRB, 1988. A Time to Dance (film), 1986. *Publication:* Lynn: leaps and boundaries (autobiog.), 1984.

SEYMOUR, Sir Michael Patrick Culme-, 6th Bt *cr* 1809, of Highmount, co. Limerick and Friery Park, Devonshire; Vice President, Swisscargo, Singapore, since 1998; *b* 28 April 1962; *s* of Major Mark Charles Culme-Seymour and of his 3rd wife, Patricia June, *d* of Charles Reid-Graham; *S* cousin, 1999; *m* 1986, Karin Fleig; two *s*. *Heir:* *s* Michael Culme-Seymour; *b* 5 Oct. 1986. *Address:* 18-04 Wisma Atria, Orchard Road, Singapore. *Club:* British (Singapore).

SEYMOUR, Richard William; QC 1991; **His Honour Judge Seymour;** a Circuit Judge, since 2000; a Judge of the Technology and Construction Court, since 2000; *b* 4 May 1950; *e s* of late Albert Percy and of Vera Maud Seymour; *m* 1971, Clare Veronica, BSS, MSc, *d* of Stanley Victor Peskett, *qv*; one *s* one *d*. *Educ:* Brentwood Sch.; Royal Belfast Academical Instn; Christ's Coll., Cambridge (schol.; BA 1971; MA 1975). Holker Jun. Exhibn, 1970, Holker Sen. Schol., 1972, Gray's Inn; called to the Bar, Gray's Inn, 1972. Asst Recorder, 1991–95; Recorder, 1995–2000. Pres., Mental Health Review Tribunals, 2000. *Publications:* (ed jtly) Kemp and Kemp, The Quantum of Damages, 4th edn 1975; legal chapters in: Willis and Willis, Practice and Procedure for the Quantity Surveyor, 8th edn 1980; Willis and George, The Architect in Practice, 6th edn 1981. *Recreations:* archaeology, walking, foreign travel. *Address:* St Dunstan's House, 133–137 Fetter Lane, EC4A 1HD. *T:* (020) 7947 6331.

SEYMOUR, Richard William; Founder and Director, Seymour Powell, since 1984; *b* 1 May 1953; *s* of Bertram Seymour and Annie Irene (*née* Sherwood); *m* 1980, Anne Margaret Hart; one *s* one *d*. *Educ:* Central Sch. of Art & Design (BA); Royal Coll. of Art (MA). Advertising Creative Dir, Blazelynn Advertising, London, 1978–81; film prodn designer, with Anton Furst, later Seymour Furst, 1981–83; freelance designer working on advertising and new product develt projects, 1982–83; Founder, with R. Powell, Seymour Powell (product and transportation design consultancy), 1984 (clients incl. BR, Yamaha, Casio). Vis. Prof. of Product and Transportation Design, RCA, 1995–. Trustee, Design Mus., London, 1994–. Contrib. to TV progs and children's progs featuring design and future thinking. Pres., D&AD, 1999 (Mem., Exec. Cttee, 1997–). FRSA 1993; FCSD 1993. Awards include: Best Overall Design and Product Design (for Norton F1 motorcycle), Design Week Awards, 1990; Silver Awards (for Technophone Cellular Phone), 1991, and (for MuZ Scorpion motorcycle), 1993, and President's Award (for outstanding contribn to design), 1995, D&AD; Product Design Award, BBC Design Awards, 1994. *Publication:* (with M. Palin) The Mirrorstone (Smarties Design Award, Hatchard's Top Ten Author's Award), 1986. *Recreations:* Early English music, cello, motorcycling. *Address:* Seymour Powell, The Chapel, Archel Road, W14 9QH. *T:* (020) 7381 6433. *Clubs:* Bluebird, Chelsea Arts.

SEYS-LLEWELLYN, His Honour John Desmond; a Circuit Judge (formerly a County Court Judge), 1971–85; *b* 3 May 1912; *s* of Charles Ernest Llewellyn, FAI and Hannah Margretta Llewellyn, of Cardiff; *m* 1st, 1939, Elaine (*d* 1984), *d* of H. Leonard Porcher, solicitor, and Mrs Hilda Porcher, JP, of Pontypridd; three *s*; 2nd, 1986, Mrs Joan Banfield James (*d* 2001), *d* of R. H. Cumming, JP, of Plymouth. *Educ:* Cardiff High

School; Jesus College, Oxford; Exhibitioner, MA. Joined Inner Temple, 1936. War Service, RTR, 1940–46 (Captain). Called to the Bar, Inner Temple, in absentia OAS, 1945; Profumo Prizeman, 1947; practised on Wales and Chester Circuit, 1947–71; Local Insurance Appeal Tribunal, 1958–71; Dep. Chm., Cheshire QS, 1968–71; joined Gray's Inn, *ad eundem*, same day as youngest son, 1967. Contested Chester Constituency (L), 1955 and 1956. *Recreations:* languages, travel, archaeology, art galleries, music, swimming, English Setter. *Address:* Little Chetwyn, Green Pastures, Gresford, Clwyd LL12 8RT. *T:* (01978) 856818. *Club:* Athenæum (Liverpool).

SHACKLE, Prof. Christopher, PhD; FBA 1990; Professor of Modern Languages of South Asia, University of London, since 1985; *b* 4 March 1942; *s* of late Francis Mark Shackle and Diana Margaret Shackle (*née* Harrington, subseq. Thomas); *m* 1st, 1964, Emma Margaret Richmond (marr. diss.); one *s* two *d*; 2nd, 1988, Shahrukh Husain; one *s* one *d*. *Educ:* Haileybury and ISC; Merton College, Oxford (BA 1963); St Antony's College, Oxford (DipSocAnthrop 1965; BLitt 1966); PhD London, 1972. School of Oriental and African Studies, University of London: Fellow in Indian Studies, 1966; Lectr in Urdu and Panjabi, 1969; Reader in Modern Languages of South Asia, 1979; Pro-Dir for Academic Affairs, 1997–; Chm., Section H3, 1999–. Mem. Council, British Acad., 1995–96. *Publications:* Teach Yourself Punjabi, 1972; (with D. J. Matthews) An Anthology of Classical Urdu Love Lyrics, 1972; The Siraiki Language of Central Pakistan, 1976; Catalogue of the Panjabi and Sindhi Manuscripts in the India Office Library, 1977; A Guru Nanak Glossary, 1981; An Introduction to the Sacred Language of the Sikhs, 1983; The Sikhs, 1984; (with D. J. Matthews and S. Husain) Urdu Literature, 1985; (with R. Snell) Hindi and Urdu since 1800, 1990; (with Z. Moir) Ismaili Hymns from South Asia, 1992; (with R. Snell) The Indian Narrative, 1992; (with S. Sperl) Qasida Poetry in Islamic Asia and Africa, 1996; (with J. Majeed) Hali's Musaddas, 1997; (with N. Awde) Treasury of Indian Love Poetry, 1999; (with G. Singh and A. Mandair) Sikh Religion, Culture and Ethnicity, 2001; numerous articles. *Address:* Department of South Asia, School of Oriental and African Studies. Thornhaugh Street, Russell Square, WC1H 0XG. *T:* (020) 7637 2388.

SHACKLETON, Fiona Sara; Personal Solicitor to the Prince of Wales and to Prince William of Wales and Prince Harry of Wales, since 1996; Partner, Payne Hicks Beach, since 2001; *b* 26 May 1956; *d* of Jonathan Philip Charkham, *qv* and Moira Elizabeth Frances Charkham; *m* 1985, Ian Ridgeway Shackleton; two *d*. *Educ:* Francis Holland Sch.; Benenden Sch.; Univ. of Exeter (LLB 1977). Articled Clerk, Herbert Smith, 1978–80; admitted solicitor, 1980; Partner, Brecher & Co., 1981–84; Farrer & Co., 1984–2000 (Partner, 1987–2000). Inaugural Mem., Internat. Acad. of Matrimonial Lawyers, 1986–. Gov., Benenden Sch., 1985–. *Publication:* (with Olivia Timbs) The Divorce Handbook, 1992. *Recreations:* listening to music, particularly opera, cooking, calligraphy, bridge. *Address:* 10 New Square, Lincoln's Inn, WC2A 3QG. *T:* (020) 7465 4300.

SHACKLETON, Keith Hope; artist and naturalist; President, Society of Wildlife Artists, 1978–83; Chairman, Artists League of Great Britain; *b* 16 Jan. 1923; *s* of W. S. Shackleton; *m* 1951, Jacqueline Tate; two *s* one *d*. *Educ:* Oundle. Served RAF, 1941–46. Civil Pilot and Dir, Shackleton Aviation Ltd, 1948–63; natural history programmes for television, 1964–68; joined naturalist team aboard MS Lindblad Explorer, 1969. Pres., Royal Soc. of Marine Artists, 1973–78. Member: RGS; Zool Soc. of London; NZ Antarctic Soc. Vice Pres., Wildfowl and Wetlands Trust, 1994–. Trustee, UK Antarctic Heritage Trust, 1997–. Hon. LLD Birmingham, 1983. *Publications:* Tidelines, 1951; Wake, 1953; Wild Animals in Britain, 1959; Ship in the Wilderness, 1986; Wildlife and Wilderness, 1986; Keith Shackleton: an autobiography in paintings, 1998; illustrations for books. *Recreations:* small Boat Sailing, exploration field work. *Address:* Woodley Wood Farm, Woodleigh, Devon TQ7 4DR. *Club:* Itchenor Sailing.

SHACKLETON, Sir Nicholas (John), Kt 1998; PhD; FRS 1985; Director, Institute for Quaternary Research, Department of Earth Sciences, University of Cambridge, since 1995 (Director, Sub-Department of Quaternary Research, 1988–95); Fellow of Clare Hall, since 1980; *b* 23 June 1937; *s* of Prof. Robert Millner Shackleton, FRS; *m* 1986, Vivien Anne Law, *qv*. *Educ:* Cranbrook Sch.; Clare Coll., Cambridge (BA, PhD); ScD Cantab 1984. Cambridge University: Senior Asst in Research, 1965–72, Asst Dir of Res., 1972–87, Reader, 1987–91, Prof., 1991–, sub-dept of Quaternary Res.; Research Fellow, Clare Hall, 1974–80, Official Fellow, 1980–. Sen. Vis. Res. Fellow, Lamont Doherty Geol Observatory of Columbia Univ., 1974–75. Hon. LLD Dalhousie, 1996; Hon. DPhil Stockholm, 1997. Founding Mem., Academia Europaea, 1988. Carus Medal, Deutsche Akad. der Naturforscher Leopoldina, 1985; Sheppard Medal, SEPM, 1985; Lyell Medal, Geol Soc. of London, 1987; Huntsman Award, Bedford Inst. of Oceanography, Canada, 1991; Crafoord Prize, Royal Swedish Acad. of Scis, 1995; Woolaston Medal, Geol Soc. of London, 1996; Milankovitch Medal, European Geophysical Soc., 1999. *Publications:* numerous articles on marine geology, geological history of climate, etc; articles in New Grove Dictionary of Music and Musicians. *Recreations:* clarinet playing, researching history of clarinet, Thai food. *Address:* 12 Tenison Avenue, Cambridge CB1 2DY. *T:* (01223) 311938; Godwin Laboratory, Pembroke Street, Cambridge CB2 3SA.

SHACKLETON, Vivien Anne, (Lady Shackleton); *see* Law, V. A.

SHACKLETON BAILEY, David Roy; *see* Bailey.

SHAFER, Prof. Byron Edwin, PhD; Glenn B. and Cleone Orr Hawkins Professor of Political Science, University of Wisconsin, Madison, since 2001; *b* 8 Jan. 1947; *s* of Byron Henry Shafer and Doris Marguerite (*née* Von Bergen); *m* 1981, Wanda K. Green; one *s*. *Educ:* Yale Univ. (BA Magna Cum Laude, Deptl Hons in Pol. Sci. with Excep. Dist. 1968); Univ. of California at Berkeley (PhD Pol. Sci. 1979). Resident Scholar, Russell Sage Foundn, USA, 1977–84; Associate Prof. of Pol. Sci., Florida State Univ., 1984–85; Andrew W. Mellon Prof. of American Govt, Univ. of Oxford, 1985–2001; Fellow, 1985–2001, now Emeritus, and Actg Warden, 2000–01, Nuffield Coll., Oxford. Hon. MA Oxford, 1985. E. E. Schattschneider Prize, 1980, Franklin L. Burdette Prize, 1990, Jack L. Walker Award, 1997, Amer. Pol. Sci. Assoc. *Publications:* Presidential Politics, 1980; Quiet Revolution: the struggle for the Democratic Party and the shaping of post-reform politics, 1983; Bifurcated Politics: evolution and reform in the National Party Convention, 1988; Is America Different?, 1991; The End of Realignment?: interpreting American electoral eras, 1991; The Two Majorities: the issue context of modern American politics, 1995; Postwar Politics in the G-7, 1996; Present Discontents: American politics in the very late twentieth century, 1997, Partisan Approaches to Postwar American Politics, 1998; articles in learned jls. *Recreations:* furniture restoration, gardening, livestock management. *Address:* Department of Political Science, College of Letters and Science, University of Wisconsin, 1050 Bascom Mall, Madison, WI 53706, USA.

SHAFFER, Anna; *see* Wintour, A.

SHAFFER, Elinor Sophia, PhD; FBA 1995; Senior Research Fellow, School of Advanced Study, University of London, since 1998 (Fellow, 1997–98); *b* 6 April 1935; *d* of Vernon Cecil Stoneman and Helene Dorothy Stoneman (*née* Nieschlag); *m* 1964, Brian M. Shaffer; two *s*. *Educ:* Chicago Univ. (BA 1954); St Hilda's Coll., Oxford (BA 1958; MA 1962); PhD Columbia Univ., NY, 1966; MA Cantab 1968. Fellow, Columbia Univ., 1961–63; Instr, 1963–64, Asst Prof., 1964–65, Dept of English, Univ. of Calif, Berkeley; Res. Fellow, Clare Hall, Cambridge, 1968–71; Lectr, 1971–77, Reader in English and Comparative Lit., 1977–97, UEA. Visiting Professor: Brown Univ., 1983–84; Zurich Univ., 1986; Stanford Univ., 1988; Vis. Lectr, Free Univ., Berlin, 1979; Study Fellow, ACLS, 1971; Leverhulme Fellowship, 1976; Research Fellow: Humanities Res. Centre, ANU, 1982; Humanities Res. Inst., Univ. of Calif, 1991; Dist. Fellow, Eur. Humanities Res. Centre, Oxford, 1995–; Vis. Fellow, All Souls Coll., Oxford, 1996. Editor, Comparative Criticism, 1979–; Gen. Editor, Reception of British Authors in Europe, 1997–. *Publications:* 'Kubla Khan' and The Fall of Jerusalem: the mythological school in Biblical criticism and secular literature 1770–1880, 1975; Erewhons of the Eye: Samuel Butler as painter, photographer and art critic, 1988; The Third Culture: literature and science, 1998; (ed) Coleridge's Writings: On Criticism, vol. 2, 2002; Coleridge's Literary Theory, 2002; *chapters in:* The Coleridge Connection, 1990; Romanticism and the Sciences, 1990; Aesthetic Illusion: theoretical and historical approaches, 1990; Reflecting Senses: perception and appearance in literature, culture and the arts, 1994; Milton, the Metaphysicals and Romanticism, 1994; Apocalypse Theory and the Ends of the World, 1995; Boydell's Shakespeare Gallery, 1996; Transports: imaginative geographies 1600–1830, 1996; Coleridge and the Science of Life, 2001; Shaping Victorian Biography, 2001; many lectures, reviews and contribs to learned jls. *Recreations:* theatre, travelling, photography, wine. *Address:* 9 Cranmer Road, Cambridge CB3 9BL. *T:* (01223) 357406.

SHAFFER, Sir Peter (Levin), Kt 2001; CBE 1987; FRSL; playwright; *b* 15 May 1926; *s* of Jack Shaffer and Reka Shaffer (*née* Fredman). *Educ:* St Paul's School, London; Trinity College, Cambridge. Literary Critic, Truth, 1956–57; Music Critic, Time and Tide, 1961–62. Cameron Mackintosh Vis. Prof. of Contemporary Theatre, and Fellow, St Catherine's Coll., Oxford Univ., 1994. Mem., European Acad. of Yuste (Cervantes Seat), 1998. Hon. DLitt St Andrews, 1999. Hamburg Shakespeare Prize, 1989; William Inge Award for Distinguished Achievement in the American Theatre, 1992. *Stage Plays:* Five Finger Exercise, prod. Comedy, London, 1958–60, and Music Box Theatre, NY, 1960–61 (Evening Standard Drama Award, 1958; NY Drama Critics Circle Award (best foreign play), 1959–60); (double bill) The Private Ear (filmed 1966) and The Public Eye, produced, Globe, London, 1962, Morosco Theater, New York 1963 (filmed 1972); The Merry Roosters Panto (with Joan Littlewood and Theatre Workshop) prod. Wyndham's Theatre, Christmas, 1963; The Royal Hunt of the Sun, Nat. Theatre, Chichester Festival, 1964, The Old Vic, and Queen's Theatres, 1964–67, NY, 1965–66 (filmed 1969); Black Comedy, Nat. Theatre, Chichester Fest., 1965, The Old Vic and Queen's Theatres, 1965–67; as double bill with White Lies, NY, 1967, Shaw, 1976; The White Liars, Lyric, 1968; The Battle of Shrivings, Lyric, 1970; Equus, Nat. Theatre, 1973–74, Plymouth Theatre, NY, 1976, Albery Theatre, 1976–77 (NY Drama Critics' and Antoinette Perry Awards) (filmed 1977); Amadeus, Nat. Theatre, 1979 (Evening Standard Drama Award, Plays and Players Award, London Theatre Critics Award), Broadhurst Theatre, NY, 1980 (Antoinette Perry Award, Drama Desk Award), Her Majesty's, 1981 (filmed 1984, Acad. Award, Golden Globe Award, Los Angeles Film Critics Assoc. Award, Premi David di Donatello, 1985); Yonadab, Nat. Theatre, 1985; Lettice and Lovage, Globe, 1987, Barrymore Theatre, NY, 1990 (Evening Standard Drama Award for Best Comedy, 1988); The Gift of the Gorgon, Barbican, 1992, transf. Wyndhams, 1993; Whom Do I Have the Honour of Addressing?, Chichester, 1996. Plays produced on television and sound include: The Salt Land (ITV), 1955; Balance of Terror (BBC TV), 1957; Whom Do I Have the Honour of Addressing? (radio), 1989, etc. *Recreations:* music, architecture. *Address:* c/o MacNaughton Lord Ltd 2000, Douglas House, 16–18 Douglas Street, SW1P 4PB. *T:* (020) 7834 4646. *Club:* Garrick.

SHAFTESBURY, 10th Earl of, *cr* 1672; **Anthony Ashley-Cooper;** Bt 1622; Baron Ashley 1661; Baron Cooper of Paulet, 1672; *b* 22 May 1938; *o s* of Major Lord Ashley (*d* 1947; *e s* of 9th Earl of Shaftesbury, KP, PC, GCVO, CBE) and Françoise Soulier; *S* grandfather, 1961; *m* 1st, 1966, Bianca Maria (marr. diss. 1976), *o d* of late Gino de Paolis; 2nd, 1976, Christina Eva, *o d* of Ambassador Nils Montan; two *s*. *Educ:* Eton; Christchurch, Oxford. Chm., London Philharmonic Orchestra Council, 1966–80. Dir, PKL Gp, 1989–96. Vice-Pres., British Butterfly Conservation Soc., 1992–; Pres., Hawk and Owl Trust, 1996–2000. Hon. Pres., Shaftesbury Soc., 1961–97. (Jtly) Nat. Duke of Cornwall's Award for Forestry and Conservation, Royal Forestry Soc., 1992. Hon. Citizen, South Carolina, USA, 1967. Patron of seven livings. *Recreations:* mountains, music, ecology. *Heir: s* Lord Ashley, *qv*. *Address:* St Giles, Wimborne, Dorset BH21 5NA. *T:* (01725) 517312. *Clubs:* Turf, MCC.

SHAGARI, Alhaji Shehu Usman Aliyu; President of Nigeria and Commander-in-Chief of the Armed Forces, 1979–83; *b* April 1925; *s* of Magaji Aliyu; *m* 1946; three *s* three *d*. *Educ:* Middle Sch., Sokoto; Barewa Coll., Kaduna; Teacher Trg Coll., Zaria. Teacher of science, Sokoto Middle Sch., 1945–50; Headmaster, Argungu Sen. Primary Sch., 1951–52; Sen. Visiting Teacher, Sokoto Prov., 1953–58. Entered politics as Mem. Federal Parl., 1954–58; Parly Sec. to Prime Minister, 1958–59; Federal Minister: Economic Develt, 1959–60; Establishments, 1960–62; Internal Affairs, 1962–65; Works, 1965–66; Sec., Sokoto Prov. Educl Develt Fund, 1966–68; State Comr for Educn, Sokoto Province, 1968–70; Fed. Comr for Econ. Develt and Reconstruction, 1970–71; for Finance, 1971–75. Mem., Constituent Assembly, Oct. 1977–83; Mem., Nat. Party of Nigeria. *Publications:* (poetry) Wakar Nijeriya, 1948; Dun Fodia, 1978; (collected speeches) My Vision of Nigeria, 1981. *Recreations:* Hausa poetry, reading, farming, indoor games.

SHAKER, Mohamed Ibrahim, PhD; Order of the Arab Republic of Egypt (Second Grade), 1976; Order of Merit (Egypt) (First Grade), 1983; Advisor, Regional Technology & Software Engineering Centre, Cairo, since 1997; Chairman, Egyptian Council for Foreign Affairs, since 1999; *b* 16 Oct. 1933; *s* of Mahmoud Shaker and Zeinab Wasef; *m* 1960, Mona El Kony; one *s* one *d*. *Educ:* Cairo Univ. (Lic. en Droit); Inst. of Internat. Studies, Geneva (PhD). Representative of Dir-Gen. of IAEA to UN, New York, 1982–83; Amb. and Dep. Perm. Rep. of Egypt to UN, New York, 1984–86; Amb. to Austria, 1986–88; Hd of Dept of W Europe, Min. of For. Affairs, Cairo, 1988; Ambassador of the Arab Republic of Egypt to UK, 1988–97. President: Third Review Conf. of the Parties to the Treaty on Non-Proliferation of Nuclear Weapons, Geneva, 1985; UN Conf. for the Promotion of Internat. Co-operation in the Peaceful Uses of Nuclear Energy, Geneva, 1987; Member: UN Sec. General's Adv. Bd on Disarmament, 1993–98 (Chm., 1995–98); Core Gp of Prog. for Promotion of Non-Proliferation of Nuclear Weapons, 1987–97. *Publications:* The Nuclear Non-Proliferation Treaty: origin and implementation 1959–1979, 1980; several articles. *Recreations:* tennis, music. *Address:* 9 Aziz Osman Street, Zamalek, Cairo, Egypt; Regional Technology and Software Engineering Centre, 11A Hassan Sabry Street, Zamalek, Cairo, Egypt; Egyptian Council for Foreign Affairs, 120 Mohie Edlin Abou Elez Street, Mohandesseen, Cairo, Egypt. *Clubs:* Royal Automobile, Queen's (Member); Guizera Sporting (Cairo).

SHAKERLEY, Sir Geoffrey (Adam), 6th Bt *cr* 1838; Managing Director, Photographic Records Ltd, since 1970; *b* 9 Dec. 1932; *s* of Sir Cyril Holland Shakerley, 5th Bt, and

Elizabeth Averil (MBE 1955; *d* 1990), *d* of late Edward Gwynne Eardley-Wilmot; *S* father, 1970; *m* 1st, 1962, Virginia Elizabeth (*d* 1968), *d* of W. E. Maskell; two *s*; 2nd, 1972, Lady Elizabeth Georgiana, *d* of late Viscount Anson and Princess Georg of Denmark; one *d*. *Educ:* Harrow; Trinity College, Oxford. *Publications:* Henry Moore Sculptures in Landscape, 1978; The English Dog at Home, 1986. *Heir: s* Nicholas Simon Adam Shakerley, *b* 20 Dec. 1963. *Address:* Brent House, North Warnborough, Hants RG29 1BE.

SHAKESPEARE, John William Richmond, CMG 1985; LVO 1968; HM Diplomatic Service, retired; *b* 11 June 1930; *s* of late Dr W. G. Shakespeare; *m* 1955, Lalage Ann, *d* of late S. P. B. Mais; three *s* one *d*. *Educ:* Winchester; Trinity Coll., Oxford (Scholar, MA). 2nd Lieut Irish Guards, 1949–50. Lectr in English, Ecole Normale Supérieure, Paris, 1953–54; on editorial staff, Times Educational Supplement, 1955–56 and Times, 1956–59; entered Diplomatic Service, 1959; Private Sec. to Ambassador in Paris, 1959–61; FO, 1961–63; 1st Sec., Phnom-Penh, 1963–64; 1st Sec., Office of Polit. Adviser to C-in-C Far East, Singapore, 1964–66; Dir of British Information Service in Brazil, 1966–69; FCO, 1969–73; Counsellor and Consul-Gen., Buenos Aires, 1973–75; Chargé d'Affaires, Buenos Aires, 1976–77; Head of Mexico and Caribbean Dept, FCO, 1977–79; Counsellor, Lisbon, 1979–83; Ambassador to Peru, 1983–87, to Kingdom of Morocco, 1987–90. Mem., Sensitivity Review Unit, FCO, 1991–. Chm., Morgan Grenfell Latin American Cos Trust, 1994–2000; Latin Amer. Consultant, Clyde & Co., 1991–. Chm., Anglo-Portuguese Soc., 1994–97. Officer, Order of Southern Cross (Brazil), 1968. *Recreations:* tennis, gardening, music (light), poetry. *Address:* 10 South End Row, Kensington, W8 5BZ. *Club:* Garrick.
See also N. W. R. Shakespeare.

SHAKESPEARE, Nicholas William Richmond; author and journalist; *b* 3 March 1957; *s* of J. W. R. Shakespeare, *qv*; *m* 1999, Gillian Johnson; one *s*. *Educ:* Dragon Sch., Oxford; Winchester Coll.; Magdalene Coll., Cambridge (MA English). BBC TV, 1980–84; Dep. Arts and Literary Editor, The Times, 1985–87; Literary Editor: London Daily News, 1987–88; Daily Telegraph, 1988–91; Sunday Telegraph, 1989–91; film critic, Illustrated London News, 1989. Work for TV includes: writer and narrator: The Evelyn Waugh Trilogy; Mario Vargas Llosa; Iquitos; For the Sake of the Children (Christopher Award, USA); Return to the Sacred Ice; In the Footsteps of Bruce Chatwin; presenter, Cover to Cover. FRSL 1999. *Publications:* The Men who would be King, 1984; Londoners, 1986; The Vision of Elena Silves, 1989 (Somerset Maugham Prize, Betty Trask Award, 1990); The High Flyer, 1993; The Dancer Upstairs, 1995 (American Liby Assoc. Award, 1997); Bruce Chatwin, 1999. *Recreations:* travelling, drawing. *Address:* 71 Oxford Gardens, W10 5UJ. *Club:* Beefsteak.

SHAKESPEARE, Sir Thomas William, 3rd Bt *cr* 1942, of Lakenham, City of Norwich; (known professionally as Dr Tom Shakespeare); Director of Outreach, Policy, Ethics and Life Sciences Research Institute, Newcastle University, since 1999; *b* 11 May 1966; *er s* of Sir William Geoffrey Shakespeare, 2nd Bt and of Susan Mary Shakespeare (*née* Raffel); *S* father, 1996; unmarried; one *d* by Lucy Ann Broadhead; one *s* by Judy Brown. *Educ:* Pembroke Coll., Cambridge (BA (Hons) 1987); King's Coll., Cambridge (PhD 1994). Printer, Cambridge Free Press, 1987–88; Administrator, The Works Theatre Co-operative, 1988–89; Lectr, Univ. of Sunderland, 1993–95; Res. Fellow, Univ. of Leeds, 1996–99. Mem., Working Party on the ethics of res. on genes and behaviour, Nuffield Council on Bioethics, 2000–June 2002. Vice-Chair, Gateshead Voluntary Orgns Council, 1993–96; Chair, Northern Disability Arts Forum, 1993–95. Vice-Chm., Northern Arts Bd, 1998–99 (Mem., 1995–99 and 2000–); Mem., Tyneside Cinema Bd, 1995–97. *Publications:* (jtly) The Sexual Politics of Disability, 1996; The Disability Reader, 1998; (jtly) Exploring Disability, 1999; Help, 2000; various articles in academic jls. *Recreations:* film appreciation and production, reading, flirting. *Heir: b* James Douglas Geoffrey Shakespeare [*b* 12 Feb. 1971; *m* 1996, Alison (*née* Lusby)]. *Address:* 13 Wood Terrace, Bill Quay, Gateshead NE10 0UD. *T:* (0191) 495 0405.

SHALIKASHVILI, Gen. John Malchase David; Chairman, Joint Chiefs of Staff, USA, 1993–97; *b* Poland, 27 June 1936; *s* of Dimitri Shalikashvili and Maria Shalikashvili (*née* Ruediger); *m* 1st, 1963, Gunhild Bartsch (*d* 1965); 2nd, 1966, Joan Zimpelman; one *s*. *Educ:* Bradley Univ. (BS Mech Eng 1958); George Washington Univ. (MS Internat. Affairs 1970); Officer Candidate Sch. Commissioned Artillery, 1959; served USA, Germany, Vietnam, Korea, Italy; Office of DCS for Ops, 1981–84 and 1986–87; Asst Div. Comdr, 1st Armd Div., 1984–86; Commanding Gen., 9th Inf. Div., 1987–89; Dep. C-in-C, US Army Europe and 7th Army, 1989–91; Asst to Chm., Jt Chiefs of Staff, 1991–92; Supreme Allied Comdr, Europe, and C-in-C, US European Command, 1992–93. *Address:* 55 Chapman Loop, Steilacooh, WA 98388, USA.

SHALLICE, Prof. Timothy, PhD; FRS 1996; Professor of Psychology, since 1990, and Director, Institute of Cognitive Neuroscience, since 1996, University College London; *b* 11 July 1940; *s* of Sidney Edgar Shallice and Doris Dronsfield Shallice; *m* 1987, Maria Anna Tallandini. *Educ:* St John's Coll., Cambridge (BA 1961); University Coll. London (PhD 1965). Asst Lectr in Psychol., Univ. of Manchester, 1964–65; Lectr in Psychol., UCL, 1966–72; Sen. Res. Fellow in Neuropsychol., Inst. Neurology, London, 1972–77; Scientist, MRC Applied Psychol. Unit, 1978–90. Prof. of Cognitive Neurosci., Scuola Internazionale Superiore di Studi Avanzati, Trieste, 1994–. Mem., Conseil Scientifique de la Fondation Fyssen, 1995–; MAE, 1996. Founder FMedSci 1998. Hon. Dr: Univ. Libre de Bruxelles, 1992; London Guildhall, 1999. President's Award, BPsS, 1991. *Publications:* From Neuropsychology to Mental Structure, 1988; (with D. Plaut) Connectionist Modelling in Cognitive Neuropsychology, 1994. *Recreations:* e-mail chess, mountain walking, cinema, theatre. *Address:* Institute of Cognitive Neuroscience, University College London, Alexandra House, 17 Queen Square, WC1N 3AR. *T:* (020) 7387 7050.

SHAMS-UD DOHA, Aminur Rahman; Minister for Foreign Affairs, Government of the People's Republic of Bangladesh, 1982–84; Publisher and Editor-in-Chief: Dialogue Publications Ltd, Dhaka; Dialogue, international English weekly, since 1988; *b* 24 Jan. 1929; *m*; two *s*; *m* 1981, Wajiha Moukaddem. *Educ:* Calcutta and Dacca Univs (BSc Hons; BA). Commnd 2nd Lieut, Pakistan Artillery, 1952; Sch. of Artillery and Guided Missiles, Ft Sill, Okla, USA, 1957–58; Gen. Staff Coll., Quetta, 1962; GS Inf. Bde HQ, 1963; RMCS, Shrivenham, 1964–65; Sen. Instr, Gunnery, 1965; GS GHQ, 1965–66; retired, 1968 (Major). Editor and Publisher, Inter-Wing, Rawalpindi, 1968–71; Gen. Sec., Awami League, Rawalpindi, 1969–71, and Mem. Working Cttee; Ambassador of Bangladesh to: Yugoslavia and Roumania, 1972–74; Iran and Turkey, 1974–77; High Comr for Bangladesh in UK, 1977–82; Minister for Information, Bangladesh, March–June 1982. Member and Leader of Bangladesh delegns to numerous internat., Islamic and Commonwealth meetings. Associate Mem., Inst. of Strategic Studies, London. C-in-C's Commendation, 1964; several military awards and decorations. Order of the Lance and Flag, Cl. 1 (Yugoslavia); Order of Diplomatic Service, Gwanha Medal (S Korea). *Publications:* Arab-Israeli War, 1967; The Emergence of South Asia's First Nation State; Aryans on the Indus (MS); In the Shadow of the Eagle and the Bear (MS). *Recreations:* sport (selected for all India Trials, London Olympics, 1948), writing, gardening. *e-mail:* amindoha@aol.com. *Clubs:* English-Speaking Union, Royal Over-Seas League.

SHAND, Major Bruce Middleton Hope, MC 1940, and Bar 1942; Vice Lord-Lieutenant, East Sussex, 1974–92; *b* 22 Jan. 1917; *s* of late P. Morton Shand; *m* 1946, Rosalind Maud (*d* 1994), *d* of 3rd Baron Ashcombe; one *s* two *d*. *Educ:* Rugby; RMC, Sandhurst. 2nd Lieut 12th Royal Lancers, 1937; Major 1942; wounded and PoW 1942; retd 1947. Exon, Queen's Body Guard of the Yeomen of the Guard, 1971, Ensign, 1978–85, Adjutant and Clerk of the Cheque, 1985–87. Joint or Acting Master, Southdown Fox Hounds, 1956–75. DL Sussex, 1962. *Publication:* Previous Engagements, 1991. *Recreation:* gardening. *Address:* Stourpaine Cottage, Stourpaine, near Blandford, Dorset DT11 8TQ. *T:* (01258) 459436. *Club:* Cavalry and Guards.
See also Lady Howe of Idlicote.

SHAND, Rt Rev. David Hubert Warner; Assistant Bishop and Bishop in Geelong, Diocese of Melbourne, Archbishop's Provincial Assistant, 1985–88; *b* 6 April 1921; *s* of late Rev. Canon Rupert Warner Shand and Madeleine Ethel Warner Shand; *m* 1946, Muriel Jean Horwood Bennett; one *s* three *d*. *Educ:* The Southport Sch., Queensland; St Francis' Theological Coll., Brisbane (ThL, 2nd Cl. Hons); Univ. of Queensland (BA, 2nd Cl. Hons). Served War, AIF, 1941–45: Lieut, 1942. St Francis' Coll., Brisbane, 1946–48. Deacon, 1948; priest, 1949; Asst Curate, Lutwyche. Served in Parishes: Moorooka, Inglewood, Nambour, Ipswich; Org. Sec., Home Mission Fund, 1960–63; Rural Dean of Ipswich, 1963–66; Dio. of Brisbane: Chaplain CMF, 1950–57; Vicar, Christ Church, South Yarra, 1966–69; St Andrew's, Brighton, 1969–73; Rural Dean of St Kilda, 1972–73; Dio. of Melbourne: consecrated Bishop, St Paul's Cathedral, Melbourne, Nov. 1973; Bishop of St Arnaud, 1973–76 (when diocese amalgamated with that of Bendigo); Vicar of St Stephen's, Mt Waverley, 1976–78; Bishop of the Southern Region, 1978–85. Chm., Gen. Bd of Religious Educn, 1974–84. *Recreation:* carpentry. *Address:* 40 Volitans Avenue, Mount Eliza, Vic 3930, Australia.

SHAND, John Alexander Ogilvie; His Honour Judge Shand; DL; a Circuit Judge, since 1988; *b* 6 Nov. 1942; *s* of late Alexander Shand and Marguerite Marie Shand; *m* 1st, 1965, Patricia Margaret (*née* Toynbee) (marr. diss.); two *s* one *d*; 2nd, 1990, Valerie Jean (*née* Bond). *Educ:* Nottingham High Sch.; Queens' Coll., Cambridge (MA, LLB; Chancellor's Medal for Law 1965). Called to the Bar, Middle Temple, 1965 (Harmsworth Scholarship); practised on Midland and Oxford Circuit (Birmingham), 1965–71 and 1973–81 (Dep. Circuit Judge, 1979); a Recorder, 1981–88. Chm. of Industrial Tribunals (Birmingham Reg.), 1981–88. Fellow and Tutor, Queens' Coll., Cambridge, 1971–73. Chancellor: Dio. Southwell, 1981–; Dio. Lichfield, 1989–. DL Staffs, 1998. *Publications:* (with P. G. Stein) Legal Values in Western Society, 1974; contrib. various articles in Cambridge Law Jl. *Address:* c/o Court Group Manager's Office, Stafford Combined Court Centre, Victoria Square, Stafford ST16 2QQ. *T:* (01785) 610801.

SHANKAR, Pandit Ravi; Presidential Padma Vibhushan Award, 1980; Bharat Ratna, 1999; musician and composer; MP (Member of Rajya Sabha) India, since 1986; *b* 7 April 1920; *m* 1989, Sukanya Rajan; two *d* (one *s* decd). Studied with brother Uday Shankar in Paris, 1930, with Ustad Allaudin Khan in Maihar, 1938–. Music Dir, All-India Radio, 1949–56; music and choreography for ASIAD 82 (Asian Games, New Delhi, 1982). Fellow, Sangeet Natak Akademi, 1977 (President's Award, 1962); Member, Nat. Acad. for Recording Arts and Sciences, 1966. Over 50 recordings, including recordings with Yehudi Menuhin, Jean-Pierre Rampal, Philip Glass, and others. Has received hon. doctorates in letters and arts from California, 1968; Colgate, NY, 1972; Rabindra Bharati, Calcutta; Benares Hindu Univ.; New England Conservatory of Music; Univ. of Delhi; Univ. of Calcutta, Deshikottam Award, 1982. Praemium Imperiale, 1997. *Compositions:* Indian ragas; music for ballet, and films incl. Gandhi, 1983; Concertos for sitar and orch., No 1, 1971, No 2, 1981; Ghanashyam—A Broken Branch, 1989. *Publications:* My Music My Life, 1968; Raga Mala (autobiog.), 1997. *Recreations:* films, people, music, theatre. *Address:* c/o Tennant Artists, Unit 2, 39 Tadema Road, SW10 0PY; Ravi Shankar Institute of Performing Arts, New Delhi.

SHANKS, Duncan Faichney, RSA 1990 (ARSA 1972); RGI 1982; RSW 1987; artist; *b* 30 Aug. 1937; *s* of Duncan Faichney Shanks and Elizabeth Clark; *m* 1966, Una Brown Gordon. *Educ:* Glasgow School of Art; DA (Post Diploma) 1960. Travelling scholarship to Italy, 1961; part-time teacher, Glasgow Sch. of Art, 1963–79; full-time artist, 1979–. *Recreations:* classical and contemporary music.

SHANKS, Ian Alexander, PhD; FRS 1984; FREng; FRSE; Head of Engineering Sciences, Unilever plc, since 2001; *b* 22 June 1948; *s* of Alexander and Isabella Affleck (*née* Beaton); *m* 1971, Janice Smillie Coulter; one *d*. *Educ:* Dumbarton Acad.; Glasgow Univ. (BSc); Glasgow Coll. of Technology (PhD); CEng, MIEE 1983, FIEE 1990; FREng (FEng 1992). Projects Manager, Scottish Colorfoto Labs, 1970–72; Research Student, Portsmouth Polytechnic, 1972–73 (liquid crystal displays); RSRE, Malvern, 1973–82 (displays and L-B films); Unilever Research, 1982, Principal Scientist, 1984–86 (electronic biosensors); Chief Scientist, THORN EMI plc, 1986–94; Divl Sci. Advr, Unilever Res., 1994–2000. Vis. Prof. of Electrical and Electronic Engrg, Univ. of Glasgow, 1985–. Chm., Inter-Agency Cttee for Marine Sci. and Technol., 1991–93; Member: Opto-electronics Cttee, Rank Prize Funds, 1985–; Science Consultative Gp, BBC, 1989–91; ABRC, 1990–93. A Vice-Pres. and Mem. Council, Royal Soc., 1989–91. FRSE 2000. Paterson Medal and Prize, Inst. of Physics, 1984; Best Paper Award, Soc. for Inf. Display, 1983. *Publications:* numerous sci. and tech. papers; numerous patents. *Recreations:* music, horology. *Address:* Kings Close, 11 Main Road, Biddenham, Bedford MK40 4BB.

SHANKS, Prof. Robert Gray, (Robin), CBE 1997; MD, DSc; FRCP, FRCPI, FRCPE; Whitla Professor of Therapeutics and Pharmacology, 1977–98, now Emeritus, and Pro-Vice-Chancellor, 1991–98, Queen's University, Belfast; *b* 4 April 1934; *s* of Robert Shanks and Mary Anne Shanks (*née* Gray); *m* 1960, Denise Isabelle Sheila Woods (*d* 1998); four *d*; *m* 2000, Mary Carson. *Educ:* Queen's Univ., Belfast (MD; DSc). MRIA. RMO, Royal Victoria Hosp., Belfast, 1958–59; Res. Fellow, Medical Coll. of Georgia, 1959–60; Lectr in Physiology, QUB, 1960–62; Pharmacologist, ICI, 1962–66; Queen's University, Belfast: Sen. Lectr, Therapeutics and Pharmacology, 1967–72; Prof., Clinical Pharmacology, 1972–77; Dean, Faculty of Medicine, 1986–91; Consultant Physician, Belfast City and Royal Victoria Hosps, 1967–98. FACP. Hon. LLD QUB, 1999. *Publications:* papers in scientific jls. *Recreations:* golf, gardening, cooking. *Address:* 19 Magheralave Park North, Lisburn, Northern Ireland BT28 3NL. *T:* (028) 9266 5426.

SHANNON, 9th Earl of, *cr* 1756; **Richard Bentinck Boyle;** Viscount Boyle, Baron of Castle-Martyr, 1756; Baron Carleton (GB), 1786; late Captain Irish Guards; Director of companies; *b* 23 Oct. 1924; *o s* of 8th Earl of Shannon; *S* father, 1963; *m* 1st, 1947, Catherine Irene Helen (marr. diss. 1955), *d* of the Marquis Demetrio Imperiali di Francavilla; 2nd, 1957, Susan Margaret (marr. diss. 1979), *d* of late J. P. R. Hogg; one *s* two *d*; 3rd, 1994, Almine, *d* of late Rocco Catorsia de Villiers, Cape Town. *Educ:* Eton College. A Dep. Speaker and Dep. Chm. of Cttees, House of Lords, 1968–78; Chm., British-Armenian All-Party Parly Gp, 1992–99. Dir, Cttee of Dirs of Res. Assocs,

1969–85; Sec. and Treas., Fedn of Eur. Indust. Co-operative Res. Orgns, 1971–86; President: Architectural Metalwork Assoc., 1966–74; Kent Br., BIM, 1970–87; Vice-President: Aslib, 1974; British Hydromechanics Res. Assoc., 1975–87; Foundn for Sci. and Tech. (founding Chm., 1977–83); IWA. Hon. Pres., Foundn for the Educn of the Underachieving and Dyslexic. FRSA, FIMgt, FBHI. Provincial Grand Master, Masonic Province of Surrey, 1967–99. *Heir:* *s* Viscount Boyle, *qv*. *Address:* Pimm's Cottage, Man's Hill, Burghfield Common, Berks RG7 3BD. *Club:* White's.

SHANNON, Alan David; Permanent Secretary, Department of Higher and Further Education, Training and Employment, Northern Ireland, since 1999; *b* 11 Jan. 1949; *s* of Samuel and Florence Shannon; *m* 1972, Christine Montgomery; one *s* two *d*. *Educ:* Belfast Royal Acad.; Queen's Univ., Belfast (BA Hons 1971). Joined NI Civil Service as Asst Principal, 1971; Min. of Agriculture (NI), 1971–82; Cabinet, British Mem. of European Court of Auditors, Luxembourg, 1982–85; Hd of Efficiency Scrutiny, Health Service, NI Dept of Finance and Personnel, 1985–86; Northern Ireland Office: Hd of Police Div., 1986–90; Hd of Probation, Juveniles and Compensation Div., 1990–92; Chief Exec., NI Prison Service, 1992–98; Principal Estabt and Finance Officer, NI Office, 1998–99. *Recreations:* tennis, gardening, local history, music. *Address:* (office) Adelaide House, 39–49 Adelaide Street, Belfast BT2 8FD. *T:* (028) 9025 7833.

SHANNON, David William Francis, PhD; Chief Scientist, Department of Environment, Food and Rural Affairs (formerly Ministry of Agriculture, Fisheries and Food), since 1986; *b* 16 Aug. 1941; *s* of late William Francis Shannon and Elizabeth (*née* Gibson); *m* 1967, Rosamond (*née* Bond); one *s* one *d*. *Educ:* Wallace High Sch., Lisburn, NI; Queen's Univ., Belfast (BAgr, PhD); DMS Napier Coll., Edinburgh, 1976. Poultry Res. Centre, ARC, Edinburgh, 1967; study leave; Dept of Animal Science, Univ. of Alberta, Edmonton, 1973–74; Hd of Nutrition Sect., Poultry Res. Centre, AFRC, 1977, Dir, 1978. Member: AFRC, 1986–94; BBSRC, 1995–; NERC, 1995–; Pres., UK Br., World's Poultry Science Assoc., 1986–90. Chm., Exec. Council, CAB Internat., 1988–91. Mem. Court, Cranfield Univ., 1996–. FRSA 1996. *Publications:* contribs to learned jls on poultry science and animal nutrition. *Recreations:* golf, bridge. *Address:* Department of Environment, Food and Rural Affairs, Cromwell House, Dean Stanley Street, SW1P 3JH. *T:* (020) 7238 1645.

SHANNON, (Richard) James; Member (DemU) Strangford, Northern Ireland Assembly, since 1998; *b* Omagh, 25 March 1955; *s* of Richard James Shannon and Mona Rebecca Rhoda Shannon; *m* 1987, Sandra George; three *s*. *Educ:* Ballywalter Primary Sch.; Coleraine Academical Instn. Served UDR, 1974–75 and 1976–77; 102 Light Air Defence Regt, RA, 1978–89. Ards Borough Council: Mem. (DemU), 1985–; Mayor, 1991–92; Alderman, 1997–. Mem., NI Forum, 1996–98. GSM (NI) 1974. *Recreations:* field sports, football. *Address:* Strangford Lodge, 40 Portaferry Road, Kircubbin, Co. Down BT22 2RY. *T:* (028) 9178 8581.

SHAPCOTT, Sidney Edward, CEng, FIEE, FInstP; Director-General, Airborne Weapons and Electronic Systems, Ministry of Defence, 1976–80; *b* 20 June 1920; *s* of late Percy Thomas and Beatrice Shapcott; *m* 1943, Betty Jean Richens (*d* 1999); two *s* one *d*. *Educ:* Hele's School, Exeter; King's College, London. BSc. Joined Air Defence Experimental Establishment, 1941; various appointments in Min. of Supply and Min. of Aviation, 1941–62; DCSO, 1963; Dir of Projects, ESRO, 1963–65; Min. of Defence, Navy Dept, 1965–75; CSO, 1968; Dep. Dir, Admiralty Surface Weapons Establishment, 1968–72; Dir, Underwater Weapon Projects, Admiralty Underwater Weapons Establishment, Portland, 1972–75. Defence Engrng Consultant, 1981–85. *Address:* 23 Upper Churston Rise, Seaton, Devon EX12 2HD. *T:* (01297) 21545.

SHAPER, Prof. (Andrew) Gerald, FRCP; FRCPath; FFPHM; Professor of Clinical Epidemiology and Head of Department of Public Health and Primary Care, Royal Free Hospital School of Medicine, University of London, 1975–92, now Professor Emeritus; *b* 9 Aug. 1927; *s* of Jack and Molly Shaper; *m* 1952, Lorna June Clarke; one *s*. *Educ:* Univ. of Cape Town (MB ChB); DTM&H with Milne Medal (Liverpool). Ho. Phys./Surg., Harare, 1952; SHO, Trop. Diseases Unit, Sefton Gen. Hosp., Liverpool, and Res. Asst, Liverpool Sch. of Trop. Med., 1953–54; Registrar: Clatterbridge Gen. Hosp., 1954–55; Hammersmith Hosp. and Post Grad. Med. Sch., 1955–56; Lectr, Sen. Lectr, Reader in Medicine and Prof. of Cardiovascular Disease, Makerere Univ. Med. Sch., Kampala, 1957–69; Mem. Sci. Staff, MRC Social Medicine Unit, LSHTM, 1970–75; Hon. Cons. Phys. (Cardiology), UCH, 1975–87; Hon. Consultant in Community Medicine, subseq. Public Health Medicine, Hampstead HA, 1975–92. RCP Milroy Lectr, 1972; Pickering Lectr, British Hypertension Soc., 1993. Chm., Jt Wkg Party of RCP and Brit. Cardiac Soc. on Prevention of Coronary Heart Disease, 1976; Member: DHSS Cttee on Med. Aspects of Water Quality, 1978–84; DHSS Cttee on Med. Aspects of Food Policy, 1979–83; Chairman: MRC Health Services Res. Panel, 1981–86; Heads of Academic Depts of Public Health (formerly Community) Medicine, 1987–90; Vice-Chm., Nat. Heart Forum, 1995–98; Member: WHO Expert Adv. Panel on Cardiovascular Disease, 1975–; DHSS Central Health Monitoring Unit Steering Gp, 1989–91. Elected Mem., Commonwealth Caribbean MRC, 1986–98. Alwyn Smith Prize Medal, FPHM, 1991. *Publications:* (ed) Medicine in a Tropical Environment, 1972; (ed) Cardiovascular Disease in the Tropics, 1974; Coronary Heart Disease: risks and reasons, 1988. *Recreations:* walking, second-hand/antiquarian books, theatre. *Address:* 8 Wentworth Hall, The Ridgeway, Mill Hill, NW7 1RJ. *T:* (020) 8959 8742; 2 Church Hill, Fremington, Barnstaple, N Devon EX31 3BH. *T:* (01271) 373913.

SHAPIRO, Dr Bernard Jack, OC 1999; Principal and Vice-Chancellor, McGill University, Montreal, since 1994; *b* 8 June 1935; *s* of Maxwell Shapiro and Mary Tafler; *m* 1957, Dr Phyllis Schwartz; one *s* one *d*. *Educ:* McGill Univ. (Schol.; BA Hons Econs and Pol Sci. 1956); Harvard Univ. (MAT Social Sci.; EdD Measurement and Stats 1967). Vice-Pres., William Barbara Corp., 1956–61; Res. Fellow, Educnl Testing Service, 1963; Res. Asst/Associate, Educnl Res. Council of America, 1965–67; Boston University: Asst Prof., 1967–71; Associate Prof., 1971–76; Chm., Dept of Humanistic and Behavioral Studies, 1971–74; Associate, Sch. of Educn, 1974–76; University of Western Ontario: Dean, Faculty of Educn and Prof. of Educn, 1976–78; Vice-Pres. (Academic) and Provost, 1978–80; Dir, Ont Inst. for Studies in Educn, 1980–86; Deputy Minister, Ontario: of Educn, 1986–89; of Skills Develt, 1988–89; Dep. Sec. of Cabinet, Ont, 1989–90; Deputy Minister: and Sec., Mgt Bd, 1990–91; of Colls and Univs, 1991–93; Prof. of Educn and Public Policy, Univ. of Toronto, 1992–94. Co-Chm., Nat. Adv. Cttee on Educn Stats, 1987–89. Chm., Governing Bd, OECD Centre for Educnl Res. and Innovation, 1984–86. President: Canadian Soc. for Study of Educn, 1983–84; Social Sci. Fedn of Canada, 1985–86; Conf. of Rectors and Principals of Quebec Univs, 1997–99. Hon. LLD: McGill, 1988; Toronto, 1994; Ottawa, 1995; Yeshiva, 1996; McMaster, 1997; Montreal, 1998; Edinburgh, 2000; Glasgow, 2001; Bishop's, 2001. *Address:* McGill University, 845 Sherbrooke Street West, # 506, Montreal, QC H3A 2T5, Canada. *T:* (514) 3984180.

SHAPIRO, Dr Harold Tafler; Professor of Economics and Public Affairs, Woodrow Wilson School, Princeton University, since 1988; *b* Montreal, 8 June 1936; *m* Vivian; four *d*. *Educ:* McGill Univ. (Lieut Governor's Medal; BA 1956); Graduate Sch., Princeton (PhD Econ 1964). University of Michigan: Asst Prof. of Economics, 1964; Associate Prof., 1967; Prof., 1970–88; Vice-Pres. for Acad. Affairs and Chm., Cttee on Budget Admin, 1977; President, 1980–88; President, Princeton Univ., 1988–2001, now Emeritus. Director: Dow Chemical Co.; Nat. Bureau of Economic Research; Member: Conference Board Inc.; Bretton Woods Cttee; Govt-Univ.-Industry Res. Round-table; Inst. of Medicine, Nat. Acad. of Scis; German-Amer. Acad. Council; Council of Advrs to Pres. Bush on Sci. and Technology, 1990–92. Member, Board of Directors: DeVry Inst., 2001; Hastings Center, 2001–; HCA, 2001–. Mem., Amer. Philosophical Soc.; Fellow, Amer. Acad. of Arts and Scis. Trustee: Alfred P. Sloan Foundn; Univs Res. Assoc.; Univ. of Pa Med. Center; Educnl Testing Service. *Address:* Woodrow Wilson School, Princeton University, Princeton, NJ 08544, USA.

SHAPLAND, Prof. Joanna Mary, DPhil; Professor of Criminal Justice, and Director, Institute for the Study of the Legal Profession, University of Sheffield, since 1993; *b* 17 Feb. 1950; *d* of late Brig. John C. C. Shapland and Mary W. Shapland (*née* Martin, now Moberly); *m* 1978, Dr John Patrick George Mailer; one *s*. *Educ:* Croydon High Sch.; St Hilda's Coll., Oxford (BA 1971); Darwin Coll., Cambridge (Dip. Criminol. 1972); Wolfson Coll., Oxford (DPhil 1975). CPsychol 1989; Chartered Forensic Psychologist, 1993. Home Office Res. Fellow in Criminology, KCL, 1975–78; Res. Fellow, Centre for Criminol. Res., Oxford Univ., 1978–88; Jun. Res. Fellow, 1979–83, Res. Fellow, 1983–88, Wolfson Coll., Oxford; Sheffield University: Sen. Res. Fellow, Centre for Criminol. and Socio-Legal Studies, 1988–89; Lectr, 1989–91, Sen. Lectr, 1991–93, Dept of Law. Cons. Expert, Select Cttee on Victim and Criminal and Social Policy, Council of Europe, 1982–87; Indep. Assessor, Review of Criminal Justice in NI, 1998–2000. Jt Ed., Internat. Review of Victimology, 1989–; Ed, British Jl of Criminology, 1990–98. *Publications:* Between Conviction and Sentence: the process of mitigation, 1981; *jointly:* Victims in the Criminal Justice System, 1985; Policing by the Public, 1988; Developing Vocational Legal Training for the Bar, 1990; Violent Crime in Small Shops, 1993; Arson in Schools, 1993; Studying for the Bar, 1995; Drug Usage and Drugs Prevention, 1993; Organising UK Professions: continuity and change, 1994; Starting Practice, 1995; Pupillage and the Vocational Course, 1995; Milton Keynes Criminal Justice Audit: the detailed report, 1996; Professional Bodies' Communications with Members and Clients, 1996; Affording Civil Justice, 1998; Good Practice in Pupillage, 1998; Social Control and Policing: the public/private divide, 1999. *Recreations:* gardening, music, tapestry. *Address:* Institute for the Study of the Legal Profession, University of Sheffield, Crookesmoor Building, Conduit Road, Sheffield S10 1FL. *T:* (0114) 222 6712.

SHAPLAND, Maj.-Gen. Peter Charles, CB 1977; MBE 1960; MA; Senior Planning Inspector, Department of the Environment, 1980–93; *b* 14 July 1923; *s* of late F. C. Shapland, Merton Park, Surrey; *m* 1954, Joyce Barbara Shapland (*née* Peradon); two *s*. *Educ:* Rutlish Sch., Merton Park; St Catharine's Coll., Cambridge. Served War: commissioned Royal Engineers, 1944; QVO Madras Sappers and Miners, Indian Army, 1944–47. Served United Kingdom, Middle East (Canal Zone) and Cyprus, 1948–63. Attended Staff Coll., 1952; jssc, 1960. Lt-Col, 1965; comd in Aden, 1965–67; Brig., Dec. 1968; comd 30 Engineer Bde. Attended Royal Coll. of Defence Studies, 1971. Dep. Comdr and Chief of Staff, HQ SE Dist, 1972–74; Maj.-Gen. 1974; Dir, Volunteers Territorials and Cadets, MoD (Army), 1974–78, retired. Hon. Col, 73 Engineer Regt, TA, 1979–89; Col Comdt, RE, 1981–86. Vice Pres., CCF Assoc., 1997– (Chm., 1982–96). Pres., Instn of Royal Engrs, 1982–87. Mem., Worshipful Co. of Painter-Stainers, 1983–. *Publications:* contribs to Royal Engineers' Jl. *Recreations:* sailing, swimming. *Clubs:* Royal Ocean Racing; Royal Engineer Yacht (Chatham).

SHAPS, Simon; Managing Director, Granada Content, since 2001; *b* 10 Sept. 1956; *m*. *Educ:* Magdalene Coll., Cambridge (BA 1979). Researcher, Thames TV, 1982–83; London Weekend Television: researcher, 1983–90; Head of Current Affairs, 1990–93; Controller, Factual Progs, 1993–96; Dir of Progs, 1996–97; Dir of Progs, Granada TV, 1997–2000; Managing Director: Granada Prodns, 2000; Granada Broadband, 2000–01. *Address:* Granada Media, Upper Ground, SE1 9LT. *T:* (020) 7261 3297.

SHARIF, Mohammad Nawaz; Prime Minister of Pakistan, 1990–93, and 1997–99; *b* 25 Dec. 1949; *m* Kalsoom Nawaz Sharif; two *s* two *d*. *Educ:* St Anthony Sch., Lahore; Government Coll., Lahore; University Law Coll., Lahore. Finance Minister, Govt of Punjab, 1981–85; Chief Minister, Punjab, 1985–90; Leader of the Opposition, Nat. Assembly of Pakistan, 1993–97. *Recreations:* sports, especially cricket. *Address:* 180-H, Model Town, Lahore, Pakistan.

SHARKEY, Colum John, CMG 1984; MBE 1973; HM Diplomatic Service, retired; *b* 9 June 1931; *s* of late Andrew Sharkey and late Sarah Josephine Sharkey (*née* Whelan); *m* 1962, Olivia Anne (*née* Brassil); two *s* one *d*. Commonwealth Relations Office, 1954; served in New Delhi, 1955, Calcutta, 1956–58; Second Secretary: Dacca, 1959–61; Melbourne, 1962–66; Montevideo, 1967–68 (joined HM Diplomatic Service, 1968); First Sec. and Consul, Asuncion, 1969; First Sec., Montevideo, 1971; seconded to Dept of Trade, 1972–74; Consul, Vancouver, 1974–78; Consul-Gen., Bilbao, 1978–81; Ambassador to Honduras, 1981–84 and non-resident Ambassador to El Salvador, 1982–84; Head of British Interests Section, Buenos Aires, 1984–87; Ambassador to Bolivia, 1987–89, to Uruguay, 1989–91, retd, then re-engaged as Personnel Assessor, FCO, 1991–93. *Recreations:* travel, golf.

SHARLAND, (Edward) John; HM Diplomatic Service, retired; High Commissioner, the Seychelles, 1992–95; *b* 25 Dec. 1937; *s* of late William Rex Sharland and Phyllis Eileen Sharland (*née* Pitts); *m* 1970, Susan Mary Rodway Millard; four *d*. *Educ:* Monmouth Sch.; Jesus Coll., Oxford. BA Hons History; MA. FO, 1961–62; Bangkok, 1962–67; Far Eastern Dept, FCO, 1967–69; Dep. Perm. Rep. to UNIDO and Dep. Resident Rep. to IAEA, Vienna, 1969–72; Bangkok, 1972–75; Montevideo, 1976–79; Cultural Relations Dept, FCO, 1979–82; Consul-Gen., Perth, 1982–87; Consul-Gen., Cleveland, 1987–89; High Comr, PNG, 1989–91. *Recreations:* tennis, bridge, stamp collecting. *Address:* 21 Maidstone Road, Lenham, Kent ME17 2QH. *Club:* Royal Bangkok Sports.

SHARMAN, family name of **Baron Sharman**.

SHARMAN, Baron *cr* 1999 (Life Peer), of Redlynch in the county of Wiltshire; **Colin Morven Sharman,** OBE 1979; FCA; Deputy Chairman, Aegis Group, since 1999; Chairman, Aegis plc, since 2000; *b* 19 Feb. 1943; *s* of late Col Terence John Sharman and of Audrey Emmiline Sharman (*née* Newman); *m* 1966, Angela M. Timmins; one *s* one *d*. *Educ:* Bishops Wordsworth Sch., Salisbury. FCA 1977. Qualified as Chartered Accountant with Woolgar Hennel & Co., 1965; joined Peat Marwick Mitchell, later KPMG Peat Marwick, then KPMG, 1966; Manager, Frankfurt office, 1970–72; The Hague, 1972–81 (Partner 1973, Partner i/c, 1975); London, 1981–99; Sen. Partner (Nat. Mkting and Industry Gps), 1987–90; Sen. Mgt Consultancy Partner, 1989–91; Sen. Regl Partner (London and SE), 1990–93; Sen. Partner, 1994–98; Chm., KPMG International, 1997–99. Director: AEA Technol.; Young & Co.'s Brewery plc; BG Internat. plc, 2000–; Chm., Le Gavroche Restaurant. Mem., Lib Dem Business Adv. Forum; Chm., DTI

Foresight Crime Prevention Panel; Dir, Britain in Europe. Mem., Industrial Soc. CIMgt. Liveryman, Co. of Gunmakers, 1992. *Publication:* (jtly) Living Culture, 2001. *Recreations:* shooting, sailing, opera, wine and food. *Address:* House of Lords, SW1A 0PW. *Clubs:* Reform, Flyfishers'; Bembridge Sailing.

SHARMAN, Maj.-Gen. Alan George, CEng, FIMechE; Director General, Defence Manufacturers' Association, since 1997; *b* 14 May 1942; *s* of late Major Frederick Sharman and Margaret (*née* Watkins); *m* 1st, 1967, Caroline Anne Lister (marr. diss.); one *d*; 2nd, 1977, Juanita Jane Lawson; one *s* one *d*. *Educ:* Hutton Grammar Sch.; Welbeck Coll.; RMA, Sandhurst; Army Staff Coll. CEng, FIMechE 1989. Commnd REME, 1962; served Aden and Oman, 1963; Elec. and Mech. Engr, The Life Guards, Singapore, 1967–68; Comd Allied Comd Europe Mobile Force (Land) Workshop, 1978–79; Mil. Sec's Dept, MoD, 1979–80; Comdr Maintenance, 1 (Br) Corps Troops, 1984; Col Elec. and Mech. Engr 7, 1985–87; Project Manager, Logistic Vehicles, MoD (PE), 1987–89; Prog. Dir, Tank Systems, MoD (PE), 1991–95; Dir Gen. Land Systems, MoD (PE), 1995–96. Mem., DTI Defence and Aerospace Cttee, 1998–. Col Comdt, REME, 1996–. Chm., Auto. Div., IMechE, 1996. *Recreations:* sailing, photography, family. *Address:* (office) Marlborough House, Grayshott, Surrey GU26 6LG. *Club:* Army and Navy.

SHARMAN, Evelyn Janet, (Jane), CBE 1998; *b* 5 July 1943; *d* of Kenneth Blair Austin Dobson and Evelyn Barbara Dobson (*née* Phillips); *m* 1972, John Matthew Reid Sharman; two *s*. *Educ:* St Andrews Univ. (MA 1st Cl. Hons Mod. and Med. *Address:* History); Bryn Mawr Coll., USA. Asst Principal, MPBW then DoE, 1968–72; Principal, DoE, 1972–85 (incl. secondment to Cabinet Office and Royal Commn on Envmtl Pollution); English Heritage: Head, Ancient Monuments Div., 1985–89; Actg Dir of Conservation, 1989–91; Dir of Conservation, 1991–96; Acting Chief Exec., 1996–97. Sec., Historic Buildings Council, 1981–84. Chm., Architectural Heritage Fund, 2001–. Trustee: Chatham Historic Dockyard Trust, 1997–; Royal Artillery Museums, 1998–; Historic Royal Palaces Trust, 1998–. *Recreations:* reading, travelling.

SHARMAN, Mark Brian; Director of Broadcasting, Sky Networks, BSkyB Ltd, since 2000; *b* 2 Jan. 1950; *s* of Stanley Sharman and Beryl Sharman; *m* 1981, Patricia; two *s*. *Educ:* John Port Grammar Sch., Etwall, Derby. Reporter, Derby Evening Telegraph, 1967–71; Sports Sub-Editor, Birmingham Evening Mail, 1971–76; Asst Producer, ATV Birmingham, 1976–77; Prog. Ed., Sport, LWT, 1977–81; Controller of News and Sport, TVS, Southampton, 1981–88; Man. Dir, Chrysalis Television, 1988–92; Dir of Progs, London News Network, 1992–94; Dep. Man. Dir, Sky Sports, 1994–98; Controller of Sport, Channel 4, 1998–2000. *Recreations:* watching my sons play Rugby and soccer, walking in the New Forest. *Address:* BSkyB Ltd, Grant Way, Isleworth, Middx TW7 5QD. *T:* (020) 7805 8383.

SHARMAN, Peter William, CBE 1984; Director, 1974–95 and Chief General Manager, 1975–84, Norwich Union Insurance Group; *b* 1 June 1924; *s* of William Charles Sharman and Olive Mabel (*née* Burl); *m* 1946, Eileen Barbara Crix; one *s* two *d*. *Educ:* Northgate Grammar Sch., Ipswich; Edinburgh Univ. MA 1950; FIA 1956. War service as Pilot, RAF. Joined Norwich Union Insce Gp, 1950; Gen. Man. and Actuary, 1969. Chairman: Life Offices' Assoc., 1977–78; British Insurance Assoc., 1982–83. *Recreation:* golf. *Address:* 28B Eaton Road, Norwich NR4 6PZ. *T:* (01603) 451230.

SHARP, family name of **Baroness Sharp of Guildford**.

SHARP OF GUILDFORD, Baroness *cr* 1998 (Life Peer), of Guildford in the co. of Surrey; **Margaret Lucy Sharp;** *b* 21 Nov. 1938; *d* of Osmund and Sydney Mary Ellen Hailstone; *m* 1962, Thomas Sharp, *qv*; two *d*. *Educ:* Tonbridge Girls' Grammar Sch.; Newnham Coll., Cambridge (BA 1960; MA 1962). Asst Principal, Bd of Trade and HM Treasury, 1960–63; Lectr in Economics, LSE, 1963–72; (pt-time) Guest Fellow, Brookings Instn, Washington, DC, 1973–76; Econ. Advr, NEDO, 1977–81; Res. Fellow, Sussex European Res. Centre, 1981–84, Sen. Fellow, Sci. Policy Res. Unit, 1984–99, Univ. of Sussex. Mem., Lib Dem Federal Policy Cttee, 1992–. Contested: (SDP/Alliance) Guildford, 1983 and 1987; (Lib Dem) Guildford, 1992 and 1997. Lib Dem front bench spokesman on educn, H of L, 2000–. *Publications:* The State, the Enterprise and the Individual, 1974; The New Biotechnology: European Governments in search of a strategy, 1985; (ed) Europe and the New Technologies, 1985; (with Geoffrey Shepherd) Managing Change in British Industry, 1986; (ed with Peter Holmes) Strategies for New Technologies, 1987; (with Claire Shearman) European Technological Collaboration, 1987; (ed jtly) Technology and the Future of Europe, 1992; (with John Peterson) Technology Policy in the European Union, 1998; many articles in learned jls dealing with science and technology policy. *Recreations:* reading, walking, theatre. *Address:* 96 London Road, Guildford, Surrey GU1 1TH. *T:* (01483) 572669; *e-mail:* sharpm@parliament.uk.

SHARP, Sir Adrian, 4th Bt *cr* 1922, of Warden Court, Maidstone, Kent; *b* 17 Sept. 1951; *s* of Sir Edward Herbert Sharp, 3rd Bt and of Beryl Kathleen, *d* of Leonard Simmons-Green; *S* father, 1986; *m* 1st, 1976, Hazel Patricia Bothwell (marr. diss. 1986), *o d* of James Trevor Wallace; 2nd, 1994, Denise, *o d* of Percy Edward Roberts; one *s*. *Heir:* *s* Hayden Sean Sharp, *b* 27 Aug. 1994. *Address:* 47 Libertas Avenue, Tableview, Cape Town 7441, South Africa.

SHARP, His Honour Alastair George, MBE 1945; ERD 1996; QC 1961; DL; a Circuit Judge (formerly Judge of County Courts), 1962–84; Liaison Judge, Durham County Magistrates Courts, 1972–84; *b* 25 May 1911; *s* of late Alexander Sharp, Advocate in Aberdeen, and of late Mrs Isabella Sharp, OBE; *m* 1940, Daphne Sybil (*d* 2000), *d* of late Maj. Harold Smithers, RGA, and late Mrs Connor; one *s* two *d*. *Educ:* Aberdeen Grammar School; Fettes; Clare College, Cambridge (Archdeacon Johnson Exhibitioner in Classics). BA 1933, 1st Class Hons Classical Tripos Part II, Aegrotat Part I. Boxed Cambridge Univ., 1931–32; Cambridge Union Debating Team in America, 1933. On staff of Bonar Law College, Ashridge, 1934–35; Barrister, Middle Temple, 1935; Harmsworth Law Scholar; North Eastern Circuit, 1936. Dep. Chm. of Agricultural Land Tribunal, Northern Area, 1958–62; Asst Recorder of Huddersfield, 1958–60; Recorder of Rotherham, 1960–62; Dep. Chm., N Riding Yorks QS, 1959–65; Dep. Chm., 1965–70, Chm., 1970–71, Durham QS. Chm., Washington New Town Licensed Premises Cttee, 1966–78; Jt Pres., Council of Circuit Judges, 1979. Commissioned, The Gordon Highlanders, Feb. 1939; served War of 1939–45: Staff Coll., 1943; 2nd Bn The London Scottish, 1943; Gen. Staff, War Office, 1944–45, Temp. Major. Governor, Sherburn Hosp. Charity, 1972–81. Mem. Board, Faculty of Law, Durham Univ., 1976–84. DL Co. Durham, 1973. *Recreations:* gardening, music, hill walking. *Address:* High Point, Western Hill, Durham DH1 4RG; The Old Kennels, Tomintoul, Banffshire AB37 9EN. *Club:* Durham County.

See also Baron Mackie of Benshie, Sir R. L. Sharp.

SHARP, Christopher Francis; QC 1999; *b* 17 Sept. 1952; *s* of late (Charles Vyvyan) Peter Sharp and of (Lilian) Corona Sharp (*née* Bradshaw); *m* 1978, Sarah Margot Cripps, JP; one *s* one *d*. *Educ:* Canford Sch., Dorset; Worcester Coll., Oxford (MA). Called to the Bar, Inner Temple, 1975; Mem., Western Circuit; founder mem., St John's Chambers, Bristol, 1978 (Dep. Hd, 1988–2000, Hd of Chambers, 2000–). Founder Chm., Bristol Family Law Bar Assoc., 1990–96. *Publications:* articles in legal jls. *Recreations:* family holidays, Real tennis, ski-ing, sailing. *Address:* St John's Chambers, Small Street, Bristol BS1 1DW. *Clubs:* Bar Yacht, Bristol and Bath Tennis, Chew Valley Lake Sailing.

SHARP, Dr John, OBE 1994; Headmaster of Rossall School, 1973–87; *b* 18 Dec. 1927; *o s* of late Alfred and May Sharp, North Ives, Oxenhope, Keighley; *m* 1950, Jean Prosser; one *s* two *d*. *Educ:* Boys' Grammar Sch., Keighley; Brasenose Coll., Oxford (MA, MSc, DPhil). RAF Educn Br., 1950–52; research at Oxford, 1952–54; Marlborough College: Asst Master, 1954–56; Senior Chemistry Master, 1956–62; Senior Science Master, 1959–62; Headmaster, Christ Coll., Brecon, 1962–72. Co-opted Mem., Oxford and Cambridge Schools Examn Bd, 1966–74; Selected Mem., Breconshire Educn Cttee, 1966–72; Co-opted Mem., Lancs Educn Cttee, 1974–81; Divisional Chm., HMC, SW 1971 and NW 1977–78; Chm., HMC Acad. Policy Sub-Cttee, 1982–85. Chm., Independent Schs' Jt Council Accreditation and Consultancy Service, 1987–93; Governor: City Technology Coll., Kingshurst, Solihull, 1989–96; Christ Coll., Brecon, 1992–99 (Chm., 1993–99). *Publications:* contrib. Anal. Chim. Acta. *Recreations:* fishing, photography, roses and shrubs. *Address:* Wood End Cottage, St Michael's, Tenbury Wells, Worcs WR15 8TG. *Club:* East India.

SHARP, Sir Kenneth (Johnston), Kt 1984; TD 1960; Partner, Baker, Tilly & Co. (formerly Howard, Tilly), Chartered Accountants, 1983–89; *b* 29 Dec. 1926; *s* of late Johnston Sharp and Ann Sharp (*née* Routledge); *m* 1955, Barbara Maud Keating; one *s*. *Educ:* Shrewsbury Sch.; St John's Coll., Cambridge (MA). ACA 1955, FCA 1960. Partner, Armstrong, Watson & Co., Chartered Accountants, 1955–75; Head, Govt Accountancy Service and Accountancy Advr to DoI, 1975–83. Indian Army, 1945–48; TA, 251st (Westmorland and Cumberland Yeo.) Field Regt RA, 1948–62; 2nd-in-Comd, 1959–62. Inst. of Chartered Accountants: Mem. Council, 1966–83; Vice-Pres., 1972–73; Dep. Pres., 1973–74; Pres., 1974–75. Master, Co. of Chartered Accountants in England and Wales, 1979–80. Mem., Governing Body, Shrewsbury Sch., 1976–95. JP Carlisle, 1957–73. *Publications:* The Family Business and the Companies Act 1967, 1967; articles in professional accountancy press. *Recreation:* gardening. *Address:* Roseland House, Marine Parade, St Mawes, Cornwall TR2 5DW.

SHARP, Sir Leslie, Kt 1996; QPM 1986; Chief Constable of Strathclyde Police, 1991–95; *b* 14 May 1936; *s* of George James Sharp and Lily Mabel (*née* Moys); *m* 1st, 1956, Maureen (*née* Tyson) (decd); two *d*; 2nd, 1985, Audrey (*née* Sidwell); two *d*. *Educ:* University Coll. London (LLB). MRC, 1952–54; Nat. Service, Mddx Regt, 1954–56; Metropolitan Police, 1956–80; Asst Chief Constable, 1980–83, Dep. Chief Constable, 1983–88, W Midlands Police; Chief Constable, Cumbria Constab., 1988–91. Hon. LLD Strathclyde, 1995. *Recreations:* angling, watercolour painting, gardening. *Address:* 1 Woolton Lodge Gardens, Woolton Hill, Newbury, Berks RG20 9SU.

SHARP, Dr Lindsay Gerard; Director, National Museum of Science & Industry, since 2000; *b* 22 Aug. 1947; *s* of Clifford Douglas Sharp and late Olive Dora Sharp; *m* 1st, 1968, Margaret Mary Sommi (marr. diss. 1979); one *s*; 2nd, 1981, Robyn Catherine Peterson; one *d*. *Educ:* Wadham Coll., Oxford (BA 1st cl. Hons 1969); Queen's Coll., Oxford (DPhil 1976). Clifford Norton Res. Fellow, Queen's Coll., Oxford, 1972–75; Asst Keeper, Pictorial Collection, Science Mus., 1976–78; Dep. Dir, then Dir, Mus. of Applied Arts and Scis, Sydney, 1978–88; Director: Entertainment and Leisure, Merlin Internat. Properties, Sydney, 1988–90; The Earth Exchange, Sydney, 1990–93; consultant, Asia and Australasia, 1990–93; Sen. Mus. Consultant and Dep. Dir, Mus. of Creativity Project, Milken Family Foundn, Santa Monica, 1993–97; Pres. and CEO, Royal Ontario Mus., Toronto, 1997–2000. *Recreations:* reading, garden design, music, opera, film, wine collection, travel, cultural and architectural history, bio-diversity, sustainability and cultural diversity issues. *Address:* 20 Pond Place, SW3 6QJ. *T:* (020) 7589 7882; Science Museum, Exhibition Road, SW7 2DD. *Club:* York (Toronto).

SHARP, Hon. Mitchell William; PC (Can.) 1963; CC 1999 (OC 1983); Personal adviser to the Prime Minister of Canada, since 1993; *b* 11 May 1911; *s* of Thomas Sharp and Elizabeth (*née* Little); *m* 1938, Daisy Boyd (decd); one *s*; *m* 1976, Jeannette Dugal (decd); *m* 2000, Jeanne d'Arc Labrecque. *Educ:* University of Manitoba; London School of Economics. Statistician, Sanford Evans Statistical Service, 1926–36; Economist, James Richardson & Sons Ltd, 1937–42; Officer, Canadian Dept of Finance, Ottawa, 1942–51; Director Economic Policy Division, 1947–51; Associate Deputy Minister, Canadian Dept Trade and Commerce, 1951–57; Dep. Minister, 1957–58; Minister, 1963–65; elected to Canadian House of Commons, 1963; Minister of Finance, 1965–68; Sec. of State for External Affairs, 1968–74; Pres., Privy Council, 1974–76; Govt Leader in House of Commons, 1974–76; resigned from Parliament, 1978. Comr, Northern Pipeline Agency, 1978–88; Policy Associate, Strategicon Inc., Ottawa, 1988–93. Vice-Pres., Brazilian Traction, Light & Power Co., Toronto, 1958–62. Hon. Dip., Royal Conservatory of Music, 1998; Hon. LLD: Univ. of Manitoba, 1965; Univ. of Western Ontario, 1977; Carleton Univ., 1994; McMaster Univ., 1995; Hon. DrSocSci Ottawa, 1970. *Recreations:* music, walking. *Address:* 2–140 Rideau Terrace, Ottawa, ON K1M 0Z2, Canada. *T:* (613) 7451117.

SHARP, Prof. Phillip Allen, PhD; Institute Professor, Center for Cancer Research, Massachusetts Institute of Technology, since 1999 (Salvador E. Luria Professor, 1992–99); *b* 6 June 1944; *s* of Joseph W. Sharp and Katherin (*née* Colvin); *m* 1964, Ann Christine Holcombe; three *d*. *Educ:* Union Coll., Barbourville, Ky (BA 1966); Univ. of Illinois (PhD 1969). NIH Postdoctoral Fellow, CIT, 1969–71; Sen. Res. Investigator, Cold Spring Harbor Lab., NY, 1972–74; Massachusetts Institute of Technology: Associate Prof., 1974–79; Prof. of Biol., 1979–86; Class of '41 Prof., 1986–87; John D. MacArthur Prof., 1987–92; Associate Dir, 1982–85, Dir, 1985–91, Hd, Dept of Biol., 1991–99, Center for Cancer Res. Biogen, Inc.: Co-founder and Mem., Scientific and Director Bds, 1978–; Chm., Scientific Bd, 1987–. Member, Editorial Board: Cell, 1974–95; Jl Virol., 1974–86; Molecular and Cellular Biol., 1974–85; RNA, 1995–. Nobel Prize in Physiology or Medicine, 1993. *Publications:* numerous scientific articles in jls and other pubns. *Recreations:* reading, fishing at summer house in Maine. *Address:* Center for Cancer Research, Room E17–529, Massachusetts Institute of Technology, 40 Ames Street, Cambridge, MA 02139–4307, USA. *T:* (617) 2536421.

SHARP, Sir Richard (Lyall), KCVO 1982; CB 1977; Ceremonial Officer, Management and Personnel Office (formerly Civil Service Department), 1977–82; *b* 27 March 1915; *s* of late Alexander Sharp, Advocate, Aberdeen, and late Mrs Isabella Sharp, OBE; *m* 1950, Jean Helen, *er d* of late Sir James Crombie, KCB, KBE, CMG; two *s* two *d* (and one *d* decd). *Educ:* Fettes Coll.; Aberdeen Univ.; Clare Coll., Cambridge. MA with 1st Class Hons Classics, Aberdeen 1937; BA with 1st Class in Classical Tripos pt II, Cambridge 1939. Served Royal Northumberland Fusiliers, 1939–46 (POW, Singapore and Siam, 1942–45). Principal, HM Treasury, 1946; Private Sec. to Chancellor of Exchequer, 1948–50 and to Minister of State for Economic Affairs, 1950; UK Treasury and Supply Delegn, Washington, 1952–56; Asst Sec., 1954; IDC, 1961; Under-Secretary: Nat. Bd for Prices and Incomes, 1966–68; HM Treasury, 1968–77. *Recreations:* playing the viola, viticulture, gardening. *Address:* Home Farm House, Briston, Melton Constable, Norfolk

NR24 2HN. *T:* (01263) 860445.
See also Baron Mackie of Benshie, A. G. Sharp.

SHARP, Robert Charles, CMG 1971; Director of Public Works, Tasmania, 1949–71; *b* 20 Sept. 1907; *s* of Robert George Sharp and Gertrude Coral (*née* Bellette); *m* 1st, 1935, Margaret Fairbrass Andrewartha (*d* 1975); one *d*; 2nd, 1978, Marie, widow of Alan C. Wharton, St Albans, Herts. *Educ:* Univ. of Tasmania. BE 1929. Bridge Engr, Public Works, 1935. Enlisted RAE (Major): comd 2/4 Aust. Field Sqdn RAE, 1942; 1 Aust. Port Mtce Co. RAE, 1943; HQ Docks Ops Gp, 1944. Chief Engr, Public Works, 1946; State Co-ordinator of Works, 1949–71. *Address:* The Coach House, Wickwood Court, Sandpit Lane, St Albans, Herts AL1 4BP; 594 Sandy Bay Road, Hobart, Tasmania 7005, Australia. *Club:* Athenæum.

SHARP, Robin; *see* Sharp, Sir S. C. R.

SHARP, Robin John Alfred, CB 1993; Director, Global Environment, Department of the Environment, 1994–95; *b* 30 July 1935; *s* of Robert Arthur Sharp and Yona Maud (*née* Brazier); *m* 1963, Anne Elizabeth Davison. *Educ:* Brentwood Sch.; Brasenose Coll., Oxford (MA); Wesley House, Cambridge (BA). Methodist Minister, West Mersea, 1960–62; Theol Colls Sec., SCM, 1962–65; Minister, Paddington, 1965–66. Principal, Min. of Housing and Local Govt and DoE, 1966–72; Asst Sec., 1972; Special Advr to Chancellor of Duchy of Lancaster, Cabinet Office, 1972; Department of the Environment: Road Safety Div., 1972–75; Housing Div., 1975–81; Under Sec., 1981; Public Housing and Right to Buy, 1981–86; Local Govt, 1986–91; Dir of Rural Affairs, 1991–94. Chairman: European Sustainable Use Gp, IUCN, 1997–; New Renaissance Gp, 1997–; Vice Pres., BTCV, 1997–. Trustee, Fauna and Flora Internat., 1995– (Company Sec., 2000–). Chm., Brent Cttee, Paddington Churches Housing Assoc., 1998–. *Publications:* (jtly) Preparing for the Ministry of the 1970's, 1964; (jtly) Worship in a United Church, 1964; (contrib.) British Environmental Policy and Europe, 1998. *Recreations:* bird-watching, walking, concert-going, travel. *Address:* 30 Windermere Avenue, NW6 6LN. *T:* (020) 8969 0381.

SHARP, Sir Sheridan (Christopher Robin), 4th Bt *cr* 1920, of Heckmondwike, co. York, (known as **Mr Robin Sharp**); independent writer and consultant, since 1992; *b* 25 April 1936; *s* of Reginald Sharp (*d* 1969), 3rd *s* of Sir Milton Sheridan Sharp, 1st Bt and Doris Eve (*née* Faulder; *d* 1985); *S* cousin, 1996; *m* 1st, 1958, Sheila Aileen Moodie (marr. diss. 1967); 2nd, 1969, Anna Maria, *d* of N. H. Saverio Rossi, Rome; one *s* one *d*. *Educ:* Rugby Sch. News Ed., United Press, Montreal, 1956–58; Reuters, London, 1959–60; Correspondent, Australian Broadcasting Corp., 1961–71; Head of Public Affairs, Oxfam, London, 1973–77; Dir of Information, Soc. for Internat. Develt, Rome, 1978–81; Sec. Gen., World Food Assembly, 1983–86; Internat. Inst. for Envmnt and Develt, 1986–92; freelance consultant and Dir of Res., Right Livelihood Award, 1993–. FRSA. *Publications:* Whose Right to Work?, 1976; (with C. Whittemore), Europe and the World Without, 1977; Burkina Faso: new life for the Sahel?, 1990; Senegal: a state of change, 1994. *Heir:* *s* Fabian Alexander Sebastian Sharp, *b* 5 Nov. 1973.

SHARP, Thomas, (Tom), CBE 1987; retired; General Manager, Names' Interests, Lloyd's of London, 1987–91; *b* 19 June 1931; *s* of late William Douglas Sharp and Margaret Sharp (*née* Tout); *m* 1962, Margaret Lucy Hailstone (*see* Baroness Sharp of Guildford); two *d*. *Educ:* Brown Sch., Toronto; Abbotsholme Sch., Derbs; Jesus Coll., Oxford. BoT and DTI (with short interval HM Treasury), 1954–73; Counsellor (Commercial), British Embassy, Washington, 1973–76; Dept of Trade, 1976–79; Dept of Industry, 1979–83; DTI, 1983–87. Member (Lib Dem): Surrey CC, 1989– (Chm., Social Services Cttee, 1993–95); Guildford BC, 1991–99. *Address:* 96 London Road, Guildford, Surrey GU1 1TH. *T:* (01483) 572669.

SHARP, William Johnstone, CB 1983; Controller and Chief Executive, Her Majesty's Stationery Office and Queen's Printer of Acts of Parliament, 1981–86; *b* 30 May 1926; *s* of Frederick Matthew and Gladys Evelyn Sharp; *m* 1952, Joan Alice Clark, MBE, *d* of Arnold and Violet Clark. *Educ:* Queen Elizabeth Grammar Sch., Hexham; Emmanuel Coll., Cambridge (MA). Army Service, Reconnaissance Corps, Durham LI and Staff, 1944–48. Entered Min. of Transport, 1949; Private Sec. to Perm. Sec., 1951–53; Principal, Min. of Civil Aviation, 1953; Asst Sec., Min. of Transport, 1962; Under-Sec., DoE, 1970; Controller of Supplies, PSA, 1976–80. FRSA 1984. Hon. Life Member: Nat. State Printing Assoc. (USA), 1987; Internat. Govt Printers Assoc., 1988. *Recreation:* the Turf. *Address:* 43 Friars Quay, Norwich NR3 1ES. *T:* (01603) 624258.

SHARPE, Brian Sidney; Consultant, financial and marketing presentation, since 1985; *b* 12 Feb. 1927; *s* of S. H. Sharpe and Norah Sharpe; *m* 1967, Susan Lillywhite; two *s*. *Educ:* Haberdashers' Aske's Sch., Hampstead; Guildhall Sch. of Music and Drama. Royal Fusiliers (att. Forces Broadcasting Service), 1945–48; BBC: Announcer, Midland Region, 1955; Television Presentation, 1956; Producer, African Service, External Services, 1957; Senior Producer: Overseas Talks and Features, 1965; The Financial World Tonight, Radio 4, 1974; Money Programme, Sept–Dec. 1979; on secondment as Exec. Dir, City Communications Centre, 1976–79; Director: Charles Barker Lyons, 1980–85; Charles Barker City, 1983–85. Town Councillor (Lib Dem), 1986–2000, Town Mayor, 1991–92, Godalming; Bor. Councillor (Lib Dem), Waverley, 1987–99. *Publications:* How Money Works (with A. Wilson), 1975; several articles on corporate and other forms of communication. *Recreations:* offshore fishing, music. *Address:* 26 Hallam Road, Godalming, Surrey GU7 3HW. *T:* (01483) 421551.

SHARPE, Prof. David Thomas, OBE 1986; FRCS; Consultant Plastic Surgeon, St Luke's Hospital, Bradford, Bradford Royal Infirmary, Royal Halifax Infirmary and Huddersfield Royal Infirmary, since 1985; Director, Plastic Surgery and Burns Research Unit, since 1986, and Professor in Plastic and Reconstructive Surgery, since 1996, University of Bradford; *b* 14 Jan. 1946; *s* of Albert Edward Sharpe and Grace Emily Sharpe; *m* 1971, Patricia Lilian Meredith; one *s* two *d*. *Educ:* Grammar School for Boys, Gravesend; Downing Coll., Cambridge (MA); Clin. Med. Sch., Oxford (MB BChir); FRCS 1975. Ho. Surg., Radcliffe Inf., Oxford, 1970–71; Senior House Officer: Plastic Surgery, Churchill Hosp., Oxford, 1971–72; Accident Service, Radcliffe Inf., 1972; Pathology, Radcliffe Inf., 1972–73; Gen. Surgery, Royal United Hosp., Bath, 1973–75; Plastic Surgery, Welsh Plastic Surgery Unit, Chepstow, 1976; Registrar, Plastic Surgery: Chepstow, 1976–78; Canniesburn Hosp., Glasgow, 1978–80; Sen. Registrar, Plastic Surgery, Leeds and Bradford, 1980–84; Visiting Consultant Plastic Surgeon: Yorkshire Clinic, Bradford, 1985–; BUPA Hosp., Elland, W Yorks, 1985–; Cromwell Hosp., London, 1985–. Chm., Breast Special Interest Gp, British Assoc. of Plastic Surgeons, 1997–. Pres., British Assoc. of Aesthetic Plastic Surgeons, 1997–99. Inventor and designer of med. equipment and surgical instruments and devices; exhibitor, Design Council, London, 1987. British Design Award, 1988; Prince of Wales Award for Innovation and Production, 1988. *Publications:* chapters, leading articles and papers on plastic surgery topics, major burn disaster management, tissue expansion and breast reconstruction. *Recreations:* painting, shooting, flying. *Address:* Hazelbrae, Calverley, Leeds LS28 5QQ. *T:* (0113) 257 0027; *e-mail:* profsharpe@hotmail.com.

SHARPE, John Herbert S.; *see* Subak-Sharpe.

SHARPE, Thomas Anthony Edward; QC 1994; *b* 21 Dec. 1949; *e s* of late James Sharpe, MC, Maxwelltown, Dumfriesshire and of Lydia de Gegg, Donauworth, Germany; *m* 1st, 1974, Sheena M. Carmichael (marr. diss. 1987), *o d* of Lord Carmichael of Kelvingrove, and of Catherine McIntosh Carmichael, *qv*; one *s* one *d*; 2nd, 1988, Phillis M. Rogers, *y d* of late W. P. Rogers; one *s* one *d*. *Educ:* Trinity Hall, Cambridge (MA). Called to the Bar, Lincoln's Inn, 1976; Fellow in Law, Wolfson and Nuffield Coll., Oxford, 1979–88; in practice at the Bar, 1987–. Exec. Dir (part-time), Inst. for Fiscal Studies, 1981–87. Chm., New London Orch., 1998–2000; Trustee, Musicians' Benevolent Fund, 1999–. *Publications:* monographs and articles in law jls on competition law, utility regulation and EC law. *Recreations:* opera, ballet, children, ski-ing. *Address:* 1 Essex Court, Temple, EC4Y 9AR. *T:* (020) 7583 2000, *Fax:* (020) 7583 0118. *Club:* Reform.

SHARPE, Thomas Ridley; novelist; *b* 30 March 1928; *s* of Rev. George Coverdale Sharpe and Grace Egerton Sharpe; *m* 1969, Nancy Anne Looper; three *d*. *Educ:* Lancing College; Pembroke Coll., Cambridge (MA). National service, Royal Marines, 1946–48. Social worker 1952, teacher 1952–56, photographer 1956–61, in S Africa; Lecturer in History, Cambridge Coll. of Arts and Technology, 1963–71; full time novelist, 1971–. Lauréat, Le Grand Prix de l'Humour Noir, Paris, 1986; Légion de l'Humour, Assoc. for Promotion of Humour in Internat. Affairs, Paris, 1986. *Publications:* Riotous Assembly, 1971; Indecent Exposure, 1973; Porterhouse Blue, 1974 (televised, 1987); Blott on the Landscape, 1975 (televised, 1985); Wilt, 1976 (filmed, 1989); The Great Pursuit, 1977; The Throwback, 1978; The Wilt Alternative, 1979; Ancestral Vices, 1980; Vintage Stuff, 1982; Wilt on High, 1984; Grantchester Grind, 1995; The Midden, 1996. *Recreations:* gardening, photography. *Address:* 38 Tunwells Lane, Great Shelford, Cambridge CB2 5LJ.

SHARPE, Prof. William Forsyth; STANCO 25 Professor of Finance, Stanford University, 1995–99, now Emeritus (Timken Professor of Finance, 1970–89; Professor of Finance, 1993–95); *b* 16 June 1934; *s* of Russell Thornley Sharpe and Evelyn Jillson Maloy; *m* 1st, 1954, Roberta Ruth Branton; one *s* one *d*; 2nd, 1986, Kathryn Peck. *Educ:* UCLA (AB 1955; MA 1956; PhD 1961). Economist, Rand Corp., 1957–61; University of Washington: Asst Prof. of Economics, 1961–63; Associate Prof., 1963–67; Prof., 1967–68; Prof., Univ. of California, Irvine, 1968–70. Pres., William F. Sharpe Associates, 1986–92. Chm., Financial Engines Inc., 1996–. DHumLit De Paul, 1997. Graham and Dodd Award, 1972, 1973, 1986, 1988, 1998, Nicholas Molodovsky Award, 1989, Financial Analysts Fedn; (jtly) Nobel Prize in Economics, 1990; UCLA Medal, 1998. *Publications:* Economics of Computers, 1969; Portfolio Theory and Capital Markets, 1970; Investments, 1978, 6th edn 1999; Fundamentals of Investments, 1989. *Recreations:* sailing, opera, music. *Address:* Graduate School of Business, Stanford University, Stanford, CA 94305-5015, USA. *T:* (415) 7254876.

SHARPLES, family name of **Baroness Sharples**.

SHARPLES, Baroness *cr* 1973 (Life Peer); **Pamela Sharples;** Director, TVS, 1981–90 and 1991–93; *b* 11 Feb. 1923; *o d* of late Lt-Comdr K. W. Newall and of Violet (who *m* 2nd, Lord Claud Hamilton, GCVO, CMG, DSO); *m* 1st, 1946, Major R. C. Sharples, MC, Welsh Guards (later Sir Richard Sharples, KCMG, OBE, MC, assassinated 1973); two *s* two *d*; 2nd, 1977, Patrick D. de Laszlo (*d* 1980); 3rd, 1983, Robert Douglas Swan (*d* 1995). *Educ:* Southover Manor, Lewes; Florence. WAAF, 1941–46. Mem., Review Body on Armed Forces Pay, 1979–81. Trustee, Wessex Med. Trust, 1997–. *Recreations:* gardening, fishing, tennis, golf. *Address:* 60 Westminster Gardens, SW1P 4JG. *T:* (020) 7821 1875; Well Cottage, Higher Coombe, Shaftesbury, Dorset SP7 9LR. *T:* (01747) 852971.
See also Hon. C. J. Sharples.

SHARPLES, Adam John; Director, Public Spending (formerly Deputy Director, Public Services Directorate), HM Treasury, since 1998; *b* 1 Feb. 1954; *s* of Frederick Sharples and Margaret (*née* Robertson); *m* 1982, Barbara Bleiman; one *s* one *d*. *Educ:* Corpus Christi Coll., Oxford (BA PPE 1975); Queen Mary Coll., London Univ. (MSc Econs 1977). Economist, Labour Party, 1978–83; Head of Res., NUPE, 1983–88; HM Treasury: Principal, 1988; Head: Tax Policy Team, 1992–96; Transport Team, 1996–97; Public Enterprise Partnerships Team, 1997–98. FRSA 2000. *Recreations:* family, football, guitar, cooking. *Address:* HM Treasury, Parliament Street, SW1P 3AG. *T:* (020) 7270 4499; *e-mail:* Adam.Sharples@hm-treasury.gov.uk.

SHARPLES, Hon. Christopher John; Director, Unigestion (UK) Ltd, since 2000; *b* 24 May 1947; *s* of Sir Richard Sharples, KCMG, OBE, MC and of Baroness Sharples, *qv*; *m* 1975, Sharon Joanne Sweeny, *d* of late Robert Sweeny, DFC and Joanne Sweeny; one *s* two *d*. MSI 1992. VSO, India, 1965–66; C. Czarnikow Ltd (commodity brokers), 1968–72; Co-founder and Dir, Inter-Commodities Ltd, 1972 (renamed GNI Ltd, 1984; Chm., 1994–96); Director: GNI Holdings Ltd, 1984–2000; GNI Wallace Ltd, 1986–97; Founder Director and Chairman: ICV Ltd, 1981–98; Intercom Data Systems (renamed RoyalBlue Ltd), 1982–90; Chairman: GH Asset Management Ltd, 1991–94; Datastream Internat. Ltd, 1996–98; Lombard Street Research, 1997–2000; Membertrack Ltd, 1999–2000; Director: Gerrard Vivian Gray, 1994–98; Hiscox Dedicated Insurance Fund, 1995–96; Digital River Inc., 1998–2000. Member: Adv. Panel to SIB, 1986–87; City Panel on Takeovers and Mergers, 1991–95; Association of Futures Brokers and Dealers, 1987–92: Chairman: Rules Cttee, 1987–91; F and GP Cttee, 1987–91; Chm., Securities and Futures Authority, 1991–95 (Chairman: Exec. Cttee, 1991–95; Capital Rules Cttee, 1991–95; Finance Cttee, 1991–95). International Petroleum Exchange: Dir, 1981–87; Dep. Chm., 1986–87; Mem., Public Relns Cttee, 1981–87; Member: Public Relns Cttee, London Commodity Exchange, 1983–96; Clearing Cttee, LIFFE, 1982–87; Taxation Cttee, British Fedn of Commodity Assocs, 1985–87; London Markets Adv. Gp on Regulation, 1986–87. *Recreations:* sailing, tennis, flying. *Address:* Unigestion Ltd, 105 Piccadilly, W1V 9FN. *Clubs:* White's; Royal Yacht Squadron; Royal Bermuda Yacht.

SHARPLES, Air Vice-Marshal Christopher John, QHP 1995; FFOM; Director General, RAF Medical Services, since 1997; *b* 9 April 1942; *s* of Arthur Victor Sharples and Alma Alice Sharples; *m* 1965, Barbara Anne Edwards; one *s* one *d*. *Educ:* Ashville Coll.; King's Coll., London; St George's Hosp. Med. Sch.; LSHTM (MSc 1981). MRCS, LRCP 1966; DAvMed 1972; MFOM 1980, FFOM 1991. Cadet, RAF Med., 1963; MO, RAF, 1967–; Consultant in Occupational Medicine, 1984–. Vice-Pres., Peterborough RFC. FRAeS 1999 (MRAeS 1979); FRSocMed 1994. Cade Medal, RCS, 1979. CStJ 1999. Silver Jubilee Medal, 1977. *Publications:* MoD papers in preventive medicine and occupational and aviation medicine. *Recreations:* country, golf, Rugby football. *Address:* One Black Swan Spinney, Wansford, Peterborough, Cambs PE8 6LE. *T:* (01780) 782246. *Club:* Royal Air Force.

SHARPLES, Florence Elizabeth; Executive Director, Young Women's Christian Association of Great Britain, 1987–93 (National General Secretary, 1978–87); *b* 27 May 1931; *d* of late Flying Officer Albert Sharples, RAFVR, and Kathleen (*née* Evans). *Educ:*

Alice Ottley Sch., Worcester; Homerton Coll., Cambridge (Teachers' Cert.); King's Coll., London (Cert. Prof. in Religious Knowledge). Head of Religious Education: Bruton Sch. for Girls, Somerset, 1953–57; Loughton High Sch., Essex, 1957–60; Housemistress, Headington Sch., Oxford, 1960–66; Headmistress, Ancaster House, Bexhill, Sussex, 1966–78. Vice Pres., World YWCA, 1995–99. Reader, dio. of Oxford, 1994–. Former Mem., New Philharmonia Chorus. *Recreation:* the theatre.

SHARPLES, Sir James, Kt 1996; QPM 1989; DL; Chief Constable, Merseyside Police, 1989–98. Lancashire Constabulary, 1964–74; Greater Manchester Police, 1974–82; Asst Chief Constable, 1982–85, Dep. Chief Constable, 1985–88, Avon and Somerset Constabulary; Dep. Chief Constable, Merseyside Police, 1988–89. DL Merseyside, 1997. *Address:* c/o Merseyside Police HQ, PO Box 59, Liverpool L69 1JD.

SHARPLEY, Ven. Roger Ernest Dion; Archdeacon of Hackney and Vicar of Guild Church of St Andrew, Holborn, 1981–92; *b* 19 Dec. 1928; *s* of Frederick Charles and Doris Irene Sharpley; unmarried. *Educ:* Dulwich College; Christ Church, Oxford (MA); St Stephen's House, Oxford. Deacon, 1954; Priest, 1955; Curate of St Columba, Southwick, 1954–60; Vicar of All Saints', Middlesbrough, 1960–81; Curate-in-charge, St Hilda with St Peter, Middlesbrough, 1964–72; RD of Middlesbrough, 1970–81; Canon and Prebendary of York Minster, 1974–81; Priest-in-charge, St Aidan, Middlesbrough, 1979–81. Chaplain, Grey Coll., Durham Univ., 1996–98. *Address:* 2 Hill Meadows, High Shincliffe, Durham DH1 2PE. *T:* (0191) 3861908.

SHARPSTON, Eleanor Veronica Elizabeth; QC 1999; practising Barrister; Fellow in Law, King's College, Cambridge, since 1992; Senior Fellow, Centre for European Legal Studies, Cambridge, since 1998; *b* 13 July 1955; *d* of Charles Sharpston and Pauline Sharpston (*née* Bryant); *m* 1991, David John Lyon (*d* 2000). *Educ:* St Paul's Girls' Sch. (Schol.); Bedales Sch. (Schol.); Konservatorium der Stadt Wien, Vienna; King's Coll., Cambridge (BA 1st Cl. Hons 1976; MA 1979); Inns of Court Sch. of Law; Corpus Christi Coll., Oxford (Squash Blue, 1978; Rowing Blue, 1978, 1979, 1980; Pres., Oxford Univ. Women's Boat Club, 1978–79 and 1979–80). Called to the Bar: Middle Temple, 1980; Republic of Ireland, 1986; Gibraltar, 1999; Hong Kong, 2001; in practice as Barrister, specialising in EU and ECHR law, Brussels, 1981–87, London, 1990–; référendaire (legal sec.) to Advocate Gen. (later Judge) Sir Gordon Slynn at Court of Justice of EC, Luxembourg, 1987–90; Lectr and Dir of Eur. Legal Studies, UCL, 1990–92; Univ. Lectr, 1992–98, Affiliated Lectr, 1998–, Cambridge. *Publications:* Interim and Substantive Relief in Claims Under Community Law, 1993; contrib. articles to Eur. Law Rev. and Common Market Law Rev. *Recreations:* theatre, classical music, European literature, sailing square riggers, rowing, squash, scuba diving, ski-ing. *Address:* (chambers) 4 Paper Buildings, Temple, EC4Y 7EX. *T:* (020) 7353 3366, *Fax:* (020) 7353 5778; King's College, Cambridge CB2 1ST. *T:* (01223) 331436. *Club:* Leander (Henley).

SHATTOCK, David John, CBE 1995; QPM 1985; Personal Advisor to Prime Minister of Mauritius, 1998–2000; Chief Constable, Avon and Somerset Constabulary, 1989–98; *b* 25 Jan. 1936; *s* of Herbert John Shattock and Lucy Margaret Shattock; *m* 1973, Freda Thums; three *s*. *Educ:* Sir Richard Huish's Sch., Taunton. Joined as Constable, final post Asst Chief Constable, Somerset and Bath, later Avon and Somerset Constabulary, 1956–82; Deputy Chief Constable: Wilts Constab., 1983–85; Dyfed-Powys Police, 1985–86; Chief Constable, Dyfed-Powys Police, 1986–89. Hon. MA Bristol, 1998; Hon. LLD UWE, 1999. OStJ 1989. *Recreations:* racket sports, particularly badminton, antique restoration, keeping fit, horse riding. *Clubs:* Bristol Shakespeare, Bristol Savages (Bristol).

SHATTOCK, Sir Gordon, Kt 1985; Vice-Chairman, VDC plc, since 1990 (Director, 1982–98); Divisional Bursar, Western Division, and Hon. Fellow, Woodard Schools, since 1988; *b* 12 May 1928; *s* of Frederick Thomas and Rose May Irene Shattock; *m* 1952, Jeanne Mary Watkins (*d* 1984); one *s* one *d*; *m* 1988, Mrs Wendy Sale. *Educ:* Hele's Sch., Exeter; Royal Veterinary Coll., London. MRCVS. Senior Partner, St David's Vet. Hosp., Exeter, 1954–84. Mem., Exeter HA, 1987–93. Fellow of Woodard Corp., 1973–88; Executive Member: Animal Health Trust, 1978–99; GBA, 1986–89; Mem. of Council, Guide Dogs for the Blind, 1985–97; Chairman: Grenville Coll., 1982–88; Exeter Cathedral Music Foundn Trust, 1987–. Pres., Old Heleans' Soc., 1999–. FRSocMed 1987; FRSA 1990. Hon. FRVC 1994; Hon. Mem., BVA, 1989. Farriers' Company: Liveryman, 1978–; Mem. Ct of Assistants, 1986–; Master, 1992. Jun. Grand Warden, United Grand Lodge of England, 1997–98. *Publications:* contrib. to Jl Small Animal Practice; papers to British Veterinary Assoc. *Recreation:* gardening. *Address:* Bowhill, Riverside Road, Topsham, Exeter EX3 0LR. *T:* (01392) 876655, *Fax:* (01392) 875588.

SHAUGHNESSY, family name of **Baron Shaughnessy**.

SHAUGHNESSY, 3rd Baron *cr* 1916, of Montreal; **William Graham Shaughnessy,** CD 1955; Director: Arbor Memorial Services Inc., Toronto, since 1972; Eurogas Corporation, Calgary, since 1995; *b* 28 March 1922; *s* of 2nd Baron Shaughnessy and Marion (*d* 1936), *d* of late R. K. Graham, Montreal; *S* father, 1938; *m* 1944, Mary Whitley (*d* 1999), *o d* of late John Whitley, Copthorne House, Letchworth; one *s* two *d* (and one *s* decd). *Educ:* Bishop's Coll. Sch. and Bishop's Univ., Lennoxville, Canada; BA 1941; MSc Columbia Univ., NY, 1947. Dir, Canada-UK Chamber of Commerce, 1981–. Member: Jt Cttee on Statutory Instruments, H of L, 1984–99; Delegated Powers Scrutiny Cttee, H of L, 1992–96. Trustee: The Last Post Fund Inc., Canada; Canada Meml Foundn (UK). Major (retd), Canadian Grenadier Guards; served NW Europe in World War II (despatches). *Heir:* *s* Hon. Michael James Shaughnessy, *b* 12 Nov. 1946. *Address:* 27 Melton Court, Old Brompton Road, South Kensington, SW7 3JQ. *Clubs:* Cavalry and Guards; University (Montreal).

SHAVE, Alan William, CVO 1994; OBE 1991; HM Diplomatic Service, retired; businessman; Representative for Bolivia, British Executive Service Overseas, since 1996; *b* 3 Nov. 1936; *s* of late William Alfred Shave and of Emily Shave; *m* 1961, Lidia Donoso Bertolotto; one *s* one *d*. *Educ:* George Green's Grammar sch., Poplar. Cert., Nat. Council of Journalists, E London Advertiser, 1953–57; Nat. Service, RAF, 1957–59; Journalist: Greenock Telegraph, 1960; Bristol Evening World, 1961; Asst Information Officer, COI, 1961; joined CRO, 1961; Salisbury, Rhodesia, 1961–62; Dar es Salaam, 1962–64; Sydney, 1964–66; La Paz, 1966–70; FCO, 1970–72; Santiago, 1972–76; Consul (Commercial): Barcelona, 1977–81; Milan, 1981–84; First Sec., FCO, 1984–88; Dep. Hd of Mission and Consul, La Paz, 1988–92; Governor of Anguilla, 1992–95. *Recreations:* cycle racing, ornithology, travel. *Address:* Casilla 3-35183, San Miguel (Calacoto), La Paz, Bolivia; *e-mail:* awshave@latinwide.com.

SHAVE, Kenneth George, CEng, FIMechE; Member, London Transport Executive, 1967–73, retired; *b* 25 June 1908; *s* of George Shave and Frances Larkin; *m* 1935, Doris May Stone; one *s* one *d*. *Educ:* St Paul's School. Apprenticed London General Omnibus Company, 1925; Rolling Stock Engineer, East Surrey Traction Company, 1930; London Transport: Asst Divisional Engineer, 1935; Divisional Engineer, 1948; Rolling Stock Engineer, 1956; Chief Mechanical Engineer, 1965. CStJ 1971 (OStJ 1963). *Recreations:* golf, bridge, gardening. *Address:* 19 Hillcrest Lane, Scaynes Hill, Haywards Heath, West Sussex RH17 7PH.

SHAW, family name of **Barons Craigmyle** and **Shaw of Northstead**.

SHAW OF NORTHSTEAD, Baron *cr* 1994 (Life Peer), of Liversedge in the County of West Yorkshire; **Michael Norman Shaw,** Kt 1982; JP; DL; *b* 9 Oct. 1920; *e s* of late Norman Shaw; *m* 1951, Joan Mary Louise, *o d* of Sir Alfred L. Mowat, 2nd Bt; three *s*. *Educ:* Sedbergh. Chartered Accountant. MP (L and C) Brighouse and Spenborough, March 1960–Oct. 1964; MP (C) Scarborough and Whitby, 1966–74, Scarborough, 1974–92. PPS to Minister of Labour, 1962–63, to Sec. of State, Dept of Trade and Industry, 1970–72, to Chancellor of the Duchy of Lancaster, 1973. Mem., UK Delegn to European Parlt, 1974–79. FCA. JP Dewsbury, 1953; DL W Yorks, 1977. *Address:* Duxbury Hall, Liversedge, W Yorkshire WF15 7NR. *T:* (01924) 402270. *Club:* Carlton.

SHAW, Angela Brigid L.; *see* Lansbury, A. B.

SHAW, Maj.-Gen. Anthony John, CB 1988; CBE 1985; Director General, Army Medical Services, 1988–90, retired; *b* 13 July 1930; *s* of late Lt Col W. A. Shaw, MC and Mrs E. Shaw (*née* Malley); *m* 1961, Gillian Shaw (*née* Best); one *s* one *d*. *Educ:* Epsom College; Clare College, Cambridge (MA; MB BChir); Westminster Hosp. MRCS; LRCP 1954; D(Obst)RCOG 1956; DTM&H 1961; FFCM 1983; FRCP 1989. Casualty Officer, Westminster Hosp.; House Surgeon and Obst. House Officer, Kingston Hosp., 1955–56; Commissioned Lieut RAMC, 1956; Staff College, 1963; served in UK, Malta, Berlin, BAOR, MoD, Malaya, Nepal, Penang, Cameron Highlands; CO 28 Field Ambulance, 1969–70; Chief Instructor, RAMC Training Centre, 1970–72; Nat. Defence Coll., 1973; ADGMS, MoD, 1973–76; CO Cambridge Mil. Hosp., 1977–79; Comdr Med. 2 Armd Div., BAOR, 1979–81; Comdr Med. SE Dist., 1981; Dir of Med. Supply, MoD, 1981–83; DDGAMS, 1983–84; Dir, Army Community and Occupational Medicine, 1983–87; Comdr Medical Servs, UKLF, 1984–87. QHP 1983–90. Member: BMA; Board of Faculty of Community Medicine, 1983–87. Pres., Standing Med. Bd, Aldershot, 1995–. Fellow, Med. Soc. of London, 1988. CStJ 1989. *Recreations:* sailing, gardening, music, military history, golf. *Club:* Army and Navy.

SHAW, Antony Michael Ninian; QC 1994; a Recorder, since 2000; *b* 4 Oct. 1948; *s* of Harold Anthony Shaw and Edith Beatrice Sandbach (*née* Holmes); *m* 1983, Louise Göta Faugust; one *s* two *d*. *Educ:* King's Sch., Canterbury; Trinity Coll., Oxford (Schol.; BA Juris. 1969). Researcher in Law, Bedford Coll., London, 1972–74; called to the Bar, Middle Temple, 1975; Astbury Scholar, 1975; an Asst Recorder, 1997–2000. Head of Chambers, 4 Brick Court, 1988–99. Major cases: Guinness; Eagle Trust; Polly Peck; BCCI; Butte Mining; Alliance. Vice Chm., Fees and Legal Aid Cttee, Gen. Council of the Bar, 1995–97. Gov., Internat. Students House, 1999–. *Publications:* contrib. Halsbury's Laws of England, 1977; (ed jtly) Archbold: Criminal Pleading, Evidence and Practice, 1991–; contrib. various law jls. *Recreations:* history, most literature. *Address:* 18 Red Lion Court, EC4A 3EB. *T:* (020) 7520 6000.

SHAW, Sir Barry; *see* Shaw, Sir C. B.

SHAW, Prof. Bernard Leslie, FRS 1978; Professor of Chemistry, 1971–94, Research Professor, since 1995, University of Leeds; *b* Springhead, Yorks, 28 March 1930; *s* of Thomas Shaw and Vera Shaw (*née* Dale); *m* 1951, Mary Elizabeth Neild; two *s* (and one *s* decd). *Educ:* Hulme Grammar Sch., Oldham; Univ. of Manchester (BSc, PhD). Sen. DSIR Fellow, Torry Research Station, Aberdeen, 1953–55; Scientific Officer, CDEE, Porton, 1955–56; Technical Officer, ICI Ltd, Akers Research Labs, Welwyn, 1956–61; Lectr, Reader, and Prof., Univ. of Leeds, 1962–. Visiting Professor: Univ. of Western Ontario, 1969; Carnegie Mellon Univ., 1969; ANU, 1983; Univ. of Auckland, 1986; Univ. of Strasbourg, 1993. Liversidge Lectr, 1987–88, Ludwig Mond Lectr, 1992–93, Sir Edward Frankland Prize Lectr, 1996, RSC. Member: Royal Soc. Cttees; RSC Cttees; SERC (formerly SRC) Chem. Cttee, 1975–78, 1981–84 (and Inorganic Panel, 1977–78, Co-operative Grants Panel, 1982–84); Tilden Lectr and Prizewinner, 1975; Chem. Soc. Medal and Prize for Transition Metal Chem., 1975. *Publications:* Transition Metal Hydrides, 1967; (with N. Tucker) Organotransition Metal Chemistry, and Related Aspects of Homogeneous Catalysis, 1973; numerous original papers and reviews in chem. jls, several patents. *Recreations:* pottery, music, walking, gardening. *Address:* School of Chemistry, The University of Leeds, Leeds LS2 9JT. *T:* (0113) 233 6402.

SHAW, Brian Hamilton; Director and Chief Executive, Britannic Assurance plc, since 1997; *b* 26 April 1942; *s* of late Dennis Hamilton Shaw and of Peggy Shaw (now Dolan). *Educ:* King Edward's Sch., Birmingham. FIA 1966. Nat. Farmers' Union Mutual Insurance Soc., 1960–63; joined Britannic Assurance, 1963: Dir and Gen. Manager, 1979–86; Dir, Gen. Manager and Actuary, 1986–97. *Recreation:* sports. *Address:* Vicarage Farmhouse, Pillerton Hersey, Warwicks CV35 0QA. *T:* (01789) 740423. *Club:* Royal Automobile.

SHAW, Sir Brian (Piers), Kt 1986; Chairman, Port of London Authority, 1993–2000 (Member of the Authority, 1987–2000); *b* 21 March 1933; *s* of Percy Augustus Shaw and Olive Shaw (*née* Hart); *m* 1962, Penelope Reece; three *s*. *Educ:* Wrekin Coll.; Corpus Christi Coll., Cambridge (MA). National Service (2nd Lieut, Cheshire Regt), 1951–53. Called to Bar, Gray's Inn, 1957, Bencher, 1992. Joined Pacific Steam Navigation Co., Liverpool, 1957; Company Secretary, 1960; Company Sec., Royal Mail Lines, London, 1961; Dir, Royal Mail Lines, 1968–87; Furness Withy & Co.: Manager, 1969; Dir, 1973; Man. Dir, 1977–87; Chm., 1979–90; Chairman: Shaw Savill & Albion Co., 1973–87; ANZ Grindlays Bank, 1987–95; Director: Overseas Containers Ltd, 1972–80; Nat. Bank of NZ, 1973–77 (London Board, 1977–80; Chm., London Adv. Cttee, 1980–84); New Zealand Line, 1974–79; Grindlays Bank, 1977–85; Orient Overseas (Holdings), 1980–91; ANZ Holdings (UK), 1985–87; Enterprise Oil, 1986–98; Walter Runciman, 1988–90; Andrew Weir, 1991–; Henderson plc, 1998–2000; Centrica plc, 1999–. Mem., Gen. Cttee, Lloyd's Register of Shipping, 1974–2000; Chairman: Internat Chamber of Shipping, 1987–92; Council of European and Japanese Nat. Shipowners' Assocs (CENSA), 1979–84; Pres., Gen. Council of British Shipping, 1985–86. Automobile Association: Mem. Cttee, 1988–99; Treas., 1990–93; Vice-Chm., 1992–95; Chm., 1995–99. Pres., New Zealand Soc., 1979–80; Chm., Cook Soc., 1995. Prime Warden, Shipwrights' Co., 1993–94; Freeman, Watermen and Lightermen's Co., 1994; Elder Brother, Trinity House, 1989–. *Recreations:* golf, music, theatre, cricket. *Address:* The Coach House, Biddestone, Wilts SN14 7DQ. *T:* (01249) 713112; 3A Lansdowne Road, W11 3AL. *T:* (020) 7221 4066. *Clubs:* Brooks's, MCC; Denham Golf.

SHAW, Carolyn Janet; Headmistress, St Mary's School, Calne, since 1996; *b* 24 April 1947; *d* of Norman and Mary Carey; *m* 1974, Dr Charles Drury Shaw; one *s* one *d*. *Educ:* Goldsmiths' Coll., Univ. of London (BA Hons 1970); Liverpool Univ. (PGCE 1971). English Teacher, La Sainte Union Convent, Bath, 1972–74; Head of English, Mount Saint Agnes Acad., Bermuda, 1974–77; English Teacher and Univ. Advr, Cheltenham Ladies'

Coll., 1989–96. *Recreations:* reading, walking, travel. *Address:* St Mary's School, Calne, Wilts SN11 0DF. *T:* (01249) 857200. *Club:* University Women's.

SHAW, Sir (Charles) Barry, Kt 1980; CB 1974; QC 1964; DL; Director of Public Prosecutions for Northern Ireland, 1972–89; *b* 12 April 1923; *s* of late Ernest Hunter Shaw and Sarah Gertrude Shaw, Mayfield, Balmoral, Belfast; *m* 1964, Jane (*née* Phillips). *Educ:* Inchmarlo House, Belfast; Pannal Ash Coll., Harrogate; The Queen's Univ. of Belfast (LLB). Served War: commissioned RA, 97 A/Tk Regt RA, 15th (Scottish) Div., 1942–46. Called to Bar of Northern Ireland, 1948, Bencher 1968; called to Bar, Middle Temple, 1970, Hon. Bencher, 1986. DL Co. Down, 1990. *Address:* c/o Royal Courts of Justice, Belfast, Northern Ireland BT1 3NX.

SHAW, Prof. C(harles) Thurstan, CBE 1972; FBA 1991; Professor of Archaeology, University of Ibadan, 1963–74; *b* 27 June 1914; 2nd *s* of late Rev. John Herbert Shaw and Grace Irene (*née* Woollatt); *m* Gilian Ione Maud (*d* 1992), *e d* of late Edward John Penberthy Magor and Gilian Sarah (*née* Westmacott); two *s* three *d*. *Educ:* Blundell's Sch.; Sidney Sussex Coll., Cambridge (Hon. Fellow 1994); Univ. of London Inst. of Education. 1st cl. hons Arch. and Anthrop. Tripos 1936, MA, PhD Cantab; DipEd London. FRAI 1938; FSA 1947. Curator, Anthropology Museum, Achimota Coll., Gold Coast, 1937–45; Cambs Educn Cttee, 1945–51; Cambridge Inst. of Educn, 1951–63; Dir of Studies, Archaeol. and Anthrop., Magdalene Coll., Cambridge, 1976–79. Vis. Fellow, Clare Hall, Cambridge, 1973; Vis. Prof., Northwestern Univ., USA, 1969; Vis. Res. Prof., Ahmadu Bello Univ., 1975–78; Visiting Lecturer: Harvard, 1975; Yale, 1979; Calgary, 1980; Hans Wolff Meml Lectr, Indiana Univ., 1984. Founder and Editor: W African Archaeological Newsletter, 1964–70; W African Jl of Archaeology, 1971–75. Mem. Perm. Council, Internat. Union of Pre- and Proto-historic Sciences, 1965–74; Vice-Pres., Panafrican Congress on Prehistory and Study of Quaternary, 1966–77; Dir, and Mem. Exec. Cttee, World Archaeol Congress, 1986–89. Founder, and Chm., Icknield Way Assoc., 1984–89, Pres., 1989–; Pres., Prehistoric Soc., 1986–90. Mem. Council, Univ. of Ibadan, 1969–71. Hon. DSc: Univ. of Nigeria, 1982; Ibadan, 1989. Amaury Talbot Prize, Royal Anthrop. Inst., 1970 and 1978; Gold Medal, Soc. of Antiquaries, 1990. Onuna-Ekwulu Ora of Igbo-Ukwu, 1972; Onyofuonka of Igboland, 1989; Onuna Ekwulu Nri, 1989; Olokun-Ayala of Ife, 1991. *Publications:* Excavation at Dawu, 1961; Archaeology and Nigeria, 1964; (with J. Vanderburg) Bibliography of Nigerian Archaeology, 1969; (ed) Nigerian Prehistory and Archaeology, 1969; Igbo-Ukwu: an account of archaeological discoveries in eastern Nigeria, 2 vols, 1970; Discovering Nigeria's Past, 1975; Why 'Darkest' Africa?, 1975; Unearthing Igbo-Ukwu, 1977; Ancient People and Places: Nigeria, 1978; (with S. G. H. Daniels) Excavations at Iwo Eleru, Ondo State, Nigeria, 1988; (with K. D. Aiyedun) Prehistoric Settlement and Subsistence in the Kaduna Valley, Nigeria, 1989; (ed jtly) The Archaeology of Africa, 1993; *festschrift:* (ed jtly) Africa: the challenge of archaeology, 1998; numerous articles on African archaeology and prehistory in jls. *Recreations:* walking, music, calligraphy. *Address:* 26 Kingsdale Court, Peacocks, Great Shelford, Cambridge CB2 5AT. *T:* (01223) 842283. *Clubs:* Athenæum; Explorers' (New York).

SHAW, Prof. Charles Timothy, CEng; Professor of Mining, Imperial College, London, since 1980 (Head of Department of Mineral Resources Engineering, 1980–85; Dean, Royal School of Mines, 1991–95); *b* 4 Oct. 1934; *s* of Charles John and Constance Olive Shaw (*née* Scotton); *m* 1962, Tuulike Raili Linari-Linholm; one *s* two *d*. *Educ:* Univ. of Witwatersrand (BSc(Mining) 1956); McGill Univ. (MSc(Applied) (Mineral Exploration) 1959). Mine Manager's, Mine Overseer's and Mine Surveyor's Certs of SA; Chartered Engineer. Johannesburg Consolidated Investment Co. Ltd (JCI): numerous positions at various levels, 1960–67; Head of Computer Div., 1967–70; Manager, 1970–72 (as such an appointed dir of 14 cos incl. Consolidated Murchison Ltd and Alternate Dir of 9 cos); Consulting Engr, Consolidated Murchison Ltd, Randfontein Estates Gold Mining Co. (Wits.) Ltd and Shangani Mining Corp. (Zimbabwe), 1972–74; Consulting Engr and Alternate Dir, Rustenburg Platinum Mines Ltd, 1974–76; Chief Consulting Engr and Alternate Dir, Johannesburg Consolidated Investment Co. Ltd, also Man. Dir, Western Areas Gold Mining Co. Ltd, 1976–77; Associate Prof., Virginia Polytechnic Inst. and State Univ., 1977–80. Rep. for JCI on Technical Adv. Cttee of SA Chamber of Mines, 1974–77; Alternate Mem. for Gold Producers Cttee, 1976–77. Sec. Gen., Soc. of Mining Professors, 1990–; Member Council: InstnMM, 1981–88; IMinE, 1989– (Pres., S Counties Br., 1988–89). Hon. PhD Miskolc, Hungary, 1995; Hon. Dr Moscow State Mining Univ., 1999. *Publications:* (with J. R. Lucas) The Coal Industry: Industry Guides for Accountants, Auditors and Financial Executives, 1980; papers both in technical literature and in house at Johannesburg Consolidated Investment Co. Ltd. *Recreations:* golf, mining history. *Address:* T. H. Huxley School of Environment, Earth Science and Engineering, Imperial College, SW7 2AZ.

SHAW, Christopher Thomas; Senior Programme Controller, Channel 5, since 2000; *b* 19 June 1957; *s* of John Denis Bolton Shaw and Isabel Shaw (*née* Löewe); *m* 2001, Martha Catherine Kearney. *Educ:* Westminster Sch.; Balliol Coll., Oxford (BA Hons Modern Hist.). Independent Radio News, 1980–85; ITN, 1985–89; Sen. Prog. Ed., Sky News, 1989–91; Foreign Ed., Channel 4 News, 1991–93; Programme Ed., News At Ten, 1993–95; Exec. Producer, ITN Factual, 1995–96; Ed., Channel 5 News, 1996–98; Controller, News, Current Affairs and Documentaries, Channel 5, 1998–2000. *Recreations:* travel, watching football, archaeology. *Address:* c/o Channel 5 Broadcasting, 22 Long Acre, WC2E 9LY. *T:* (020) 7421 7123.

SHAW, Colin Don, CBE 1993; writer and lecturer; Director, Broadcasting Standards Council, 1988–96; *b* 2 Nov. 1928; *s* of late Rupert M. Shaw and Enid F. Shaw (*née* Smith); *m* 1955, Elizabeth Ann, *d* of late Paul Bowker; one *s* two *d*. *Educ:* Liverpool Coll.; St Peter's Hall, Oxford (MA). Called to the Bar, Inner Temple, 1960. Nat. Service, RAF, 1947–49. Joined BBC as Radio Drama Producer, North Region, 1953; Asst, BBC Secretariat, 1957–59; Asst Head of Programme Contracts Dept, 1959–60; Sen. Asst, BBC Secretariat, 1960–63; special duties in connection with recruitment for BBC2, 1963; Asst Head of Programmes, BBC North Region, 1963–66; various posts in TV Programme Planning, ending as Head of Group, 1966–69; Secretary to the BBC, 1969–72, Chief Secretary, 1972–76; Dir of Television, IBA, 1977–83; Dir, Programme Planning Secretariat, ITCA, 1983–87. Vis. Fellow, Europ. Inst. for the Media, Düsseldorf, 1985–98; Vis. Lectr, Annenberg Sch. of Communications, Univ. of Pa, 1988; Manchester University: Hon. Lectr in Educn, 1994–96; Hon. Prof., 1996–99. Member: Arts Council of GB, 1978–80 (Chairman: Arts Council Research Adv. Gp, 1978–80; Housing the Arts Cttee, 1979–80; Touring Cttee, 1980); Home Office Working Party on Fear of Crime, 1990. Trustee, Internat. Inst. of Communications, 1983–89; Governor, E-SU of the Commonwealth, 1976–83; Chm., Bd of Governors, Hampden House Sch., 1972–77. FRTS 1987. *Publications:* Deciding what we watch: taste, decency and media ethics in the UK and the USA, 1999; several radio plays and a stage-play for children. *Recreations:* going to the theatre, reading. *Address:* Lesters, Little Ickford, Aylesbury, Bucks HP18 9HS. *T:* (01844) 339225.

SHAW, David; Executive Director, International Badminton Federation, 1992–98; *b* 19 Oct. 1936; *s* of Thomas Young Boyd Shaw and Elizabeth Shaw; *m* 1961, Margaret Esmé Bagnall; one *s* one *d*. *Educ:* Univ. of Birmingham (BA (Hons) Geography); Univ. of Sussex (Adv. Dip. Educnl Technology). Education Officer in Royal Air Force, final rank Sqn Ldr, 1960–76; Training Adviser to North Western Provincial Councils, 1976–78; Gen. Sec., British Amateur Athletic Bd, 1978–81; Gen. Sec., ITCA, then Dir, Indep. Television Assoc., 1981–92. Represented Great Britain in Athletics (3000 metres steeplechase), 1958; British Universities Cross-Country Champion, 1959. *Recreations:* reading, hill-walking, geographical research. *Club:* Royal Air Force.

SHAW, Prof. David Aitken, CBE 1989; FRCP, FRCPE; Professor of Clinical Neurology, University of Newcastle upon Tyne, 1976–89, now Emeritus; *b* 11 April 1924; *s* of John James McIntosh Shaw and Mina Draper; *m* 1960, Jill Parry; one *s* two *d*. *Educ:* Edinburgh Academy; Edinburgh Univ. MB ChB (Edin) 1951; FRCPE 1968; FRCP (Lond.) 1976. Served as Lieut RNVR, 1943–46. Hospital appts, Edinburgh Royal Infirmary, 1951–57; Lectr, Inst. of Neurology, Univ. of London, 1957–64; Mayo Foundation Fellow, 1962–63; University of Newcastle upon Tyne: Sen. Lectr, 1964–76; Public Orator, 1976–79; Dean of Medicine, 1981–89. Mem., GMC, 1979–94. Hon. FCST 1988. *Publications:* (with N. E. F. Cartlidge) Head Injury, 1981; chapters in books and scientific articles in medical jls. *Recreations:* golf and fishing. *Address:* The Coach House, 82 Moor Road North, Newcastle upon Tyne NE3 1AB. *T:* (0191) 285 2029.

SHAW, David Lawrence, FCA; chartered accountant; Founder and Chairman, Sabrelance Ltd, corporate finance advisers; *b* 14 Nov. 1950; *m* 1986, Dr Lesley Brown; one *s* one *d*. *Educ:* King's Sch., Wimbledon; City of London Polytechnic. FCA 1974. Coopers & Lybrand, 1971–79; County Bank, 1979–83. Chairman: RRI PLC, 1994–2000; 2020 Strategy Ltd, 1997–; Dep. Chm., The Adscene Group PLC, 1986–99. Mem., Political, Communications and Marketing Cttee, City Gp for Smaller Quoted Cos, 1997–. Mem., Royal Borough of Kingston upon Thames Council, 1974–78. Contested (C) Leigh, 1979; MP (C) Dover, 1987–97; contested (C) same seat, 1997. Chm., Bow Gp, 1983–84 (Founder, Transatlantic Conf., 1982); Mem., Social Security Select Cttee, 1991–97; Jt Chm., All Party Cttee on Dolphins, 1989–97; Chm., Cons. Backbench Smaller Businesses Cttee, 1990–97 (Sec., 1987–90); Vice Chm., Cons. Backbench Finance Cttee, 1991–97 (Hon. Sec., 1990–91). Vice-Chm., Kingston and Malden Cons. Assoc., 1979–86. *Address:* 66 Richborne Terrace, SW8 1AX; *e-mail:* david@davidshaw.net.

SHAW, Maj.-Gen. Dennis, CB 1991; CBE 1983 (OBE 1978); FIMechE; Director General Electrical and Mechanical Engineering (Army), 1988–91; *b* 11 May 1936; *s* of Nathan Shaw and Frances Ellen (*née* Cookson); *m* 1955, Barbara Tate; two *d*. *Educ:* Humberstone Foundn Sch.; Scunthorpe Grammar Sch.; Royal Military Coll. of Science. BScEng 1st Cl. Hons, London. Commd into REME, 1956; served in Cyprus, 1957–58, and with 3 Commando Bde, Far East, 1963–66; sc Shrivenham and Camberley, 1967–68; Staff of High Commn, Ottawa, 1969–70; comd 1 Corps Troops Workshop, W Germany, 1971–72; Dep. Asst Adjt Gen., MoD, 1972–74; NDC Latimer, 1974–75; comd Commando Logistic Regt, RM, 1975–78; Instr, Ghana Armed Forces Staff Coll., Accra, 1978–80; ACOS in Comd HQ, 1981–83; served Logistic Executive (Army), 1983; RCDS 1984; ACOS, HQ UKLF, 1985–87. Col Comdt, REME, 1991–95. Dir, Greig Fester Group Services Ltd, 1994–96 (Gp Advr, 1992–96). Liveryman, Turners' Co., 1990–(Clerk, 1996–97). Freeman, City of London, 1990. *Recreations:* golf, motoring. *Address:* c/o Royal Bank of Scotland, Laurie House, Victoria Road, Farnborough, Hants GU14 7NR. *Club:* Gainsborough Golf.

SHAW, Dr Dennis Frederick, CBE 1974; Fellow, 1957, Professorial Fellow, 1977, Emeritus Fellow, 1992, Keble College, Oxford; Keeper of Scientific Books, Bodleian Library, Oxford, 1975–91; *b* 20 April 1924; 2nd *s* of Albert Shaw and Lily (*née* Hill), Teddington; *m* 1949, Joan Irene, *er d* of Sidney and Maud Chandler; one *s* three *d*. *Educ:* Harrow County Sch.; Christ Church, Oxford. BA 1945, MA 1950, DPhil 1950. FInstP 1971, CPhys; FZS. Jun. Sci. Officer, MAP, 1944–46; Res. Officer in Physics, Clarendon Lab., Oxford, 1950–57, Sen. Res. Officer 1957–64; Univ. Lectr in Physics, Oxford, 1964–75. Vis. Prof. of Physics and Brown Foundn Fellow, Univ. of the South, Tennessee, 1974. Hon. Mem., Internat. Assoc. of Technol Univ. Libraries, 1992 (Sec., 1983–85; Pres., 1986–90); International Federation of Library Associations: Chm., Cttee for Sci. and Technol. Libys, 1987–91 (Mem., 1985–87); Finance Officer, Special Libraries Div., 1991–93; Mem., Press Cttee, ICSU, 1991–. Mem., Oxford City Council, 1963–67; Chm., Oxford City Civil Emergency Cttee, 1966–67; Member: Home Office Sci. Adv. Council, 1966–78; Home Defence Sci. Adv. Cttee, 1978–95; Hebdomadal Council, 1980–89; Chairman: Oxford Univ. Delegacy for Educnl Studies, 1969–73; Home Office Police Equipment Cttee, 1969–70; Home Office Police Sci. Develt Cttee, 1971–74. Member: Amer. Phys. Soc., 1957; NY Acad. of Scis, 1981. Gov., Christ's Hosp., 1980– (Almoner, 1980–98). Freeman, City of London, 1997. *Publications:* An Introduction to Electronics, 1962, 2nd edn 1970; A Review of Oxford University Science Libraries, 1977, 2nd edn 1981; (ed) Information Sources in Physics, 1985, 3rd edn 1994; (ed jtly) Electronic Publishing in Science, 1996; papers in sci. jls. *Recreations:* riding, gardening, enjoying music. *Address:* Keble College, Oxford OX1 3PG. *T:* (01865) 272727. *Club:* Oxford and Cambridge.

SHAW, Rev. Douglas William David; Professor of Divinity, 1979–91, and Principal, St Mary's College, 1986–92, University of St Andrews; *b* 25 June 1928; *s* of William David Shaw and Nansie Smart. *Educ:* Edinburgh Acad.; Loretto; Ashbury Coll., Ottawa; Univs of Cambridge and Edinburgh. MA (Cantab), BD (Edin.), LLB (Edin.). WS. Practised law as Partner of Davidson and Syme, WS, Edinburgh, 1953–57. Ordained Minister of Church of Scotland, 1960; Asst Minister, St George's West Church, Edinburgh, 1960–63; Official Observer of World Alliance of Reformed Churches at Second Vatican Council, Rome, 1962. University of Edinburgh: Dean, Faculty of Divinity, and Principal, New College, 1974–78; Lectr in Divinity, 1963–79; Dean, Faculty of Divinity, Univ. of St Andrews, 1983–86. Croall Lectr, New Coll., Edinburgh, 1983; Alexander Robertson Lectr, Univ. of Glasgow, 1991–92. Editor, Theology in Scotland, 1994–. Hon. DD Glasgow, 1991. *Publications:* Who is God? 1968, 2nd edn 1970; The Dissuaders, 1978; trans. from German: F. Heyer: The Catholic Church from 1648 to 1870, 1969; (ed) In Divers Manners—a St Mary's Miscellany, 1990; Dimensions—Literary and Theological, 1992; various articles in theological jls. *Recreations:* squash (Scottish Amateur Champion, 1950–51–52), golf. *Address:* 4 Alexandra Court, St Andrews, Fife KY16 9XH. *T:* (01334) 477254. *Clubs:* New (Edinburgh); Royal and Ancient (St Andrews); Luffness New; Edinburgh Sports.

SHAW, Very Rev. Duncan; JP; PhD; Minister Emeritus of the parish of Craigentinny, Edinburgh; *b* 27 Jan. 1925; *e s* of Neil Shaw (Mac Gille Chainnich), master carpenter, and Mary Thompson Borthwick; *m* 1st, 1955, Ilse (*d* 1989), *d* of Robert Peiter and Luise Else Mattig, Dusseldorf; one *s* two *d*; 2nd, 1991, Prof. Anna Libera, DrPhil, *d* of Prof. Luigi Dallapiccola and Dr Laura Coen Luzzatto, Florence. *Educ:* Univ. of Edinburgh (PhD). Served REME, TA(WR), 1943–47 (Warrant Officer, cl. I 1946). Minister of parish: of St Margaret, Dumbiedykes, Edinburgh, 1951–59, of Craigentinny, Edinburgh, 1959–97.

Scottish Rep. of Aktion Sühnezeichen, Berlin, 1966–71; Chm. of Bd, St Andrew Press, 1967–74; Editorial Dir, 1974–2000, Man Dir, 2000–, Edina Press, Edinburgh; Chm., IMS Trust and Instant Muscle (Scotland) plc, 1988–92; Dir, Instant Muscle plc, London, 1988–95. Dir, Centre for Theological Exploration Inc. USA, 1989–95. Trustee: Nat. Museum of Antiquities of Scotland, 1974–85; Edinburgh Old Town Charitable Trust, 1989–; Luigi and Laura Dallapiccola Foundn, 1997–. Pres., Scottish Record Soc., 1998– (Treas., 1964–97); Founder and Chm. of Council, Scottish Soc. for Reformation History, 1980–2000. University of Edinburgh: Sec. of Gen. Council, 1965–93; Sen. Hume Brown Prizeman for Scottish History, 1965; Visiting Fellow, Inst. for Advanced Studies in the Humanities, 1975; part-time Lectr in Theological German, Faculty of Divinity, 1975–81; Sec., Gen. Council Trust, 1982–90; Dr *hc* 1990. Guest Prof., Lancaster Theolog. Seminary and Vis. Lectr, Princeton Theolog. Seminary, USA, 1967; Hastie Lectr in Divinity, Univ. of Glasgow, 1968–71; Visiting Lecturer: Univ. of Munich, 1980; Univ. of Heidelberg, 1983; McGill Univ., Montreal, 1984; Univ. of Mainz, 1991; St Andrew's Coll., Laurenburg, USA, 1999. Member of Advisory Commitee: Christian Peace Conf., Prague, 1960–68; Conf. of European Churches, 1970–86 (acted as Gen. Sec., 1971). Hon. Mem., United Church of Berlin Brandenburg, 1969; Mem. of Cons. Cttee, Selly Oak Colls, Birmingham, 1976–87; Moderator, Presbytery of Edinburgh, 1978; Moderator, Gen. Assembly of Church of Scotland, 1987–88. Freeman, City of London, 1990; Liveryman, Scriveners' Co., 1990. JP 1974; Chm., City of Edinburgh Justices Cttee, 1984–87. KStJ 1983 (Mem., Chapter Gen., 1984–93, Chancellor of Scotland, 1986–92, Order of St John). ThDr *hc* Comenius Faculty of Theology, Charles Univ., Prague, 1969. Patriarchal Cross of Romanian Orthodox Church, 1978; Bundesverdienstkreuz, 1st cl., 1980; Com. al Merito Melitense (SMO Malta), 1987; Order of St Sergius, 1987, Order of St Vladimir, 1997, Russian Orthodox Church. *Publications:* The General Assemblies of the Church of Scotland 1560–1600: their Origins and Development, 1964; (contrib. and ed) Reformation and Revolution: Essays presented to Principal Emeritus Hugh Watt, 1967; Inauguration of Ministers in Scotland 1560–1600, 1968; (contrib. and ed) John Knox: A Quartercentenary Reappraisal, 1975; Knox and Mary, Queen of Scots, 1980; (contrib. foreword and supervised translation) Zwingli's Thought: New Perspectives (by G. W. Locher), 1981; (contrib. and ed with I. B. Cowan) The Renaissance and Reformation in Scotland: Essays in Honour of Gordon Donaldson, 1983; A Voice in the Wilderness, 1995; Valedictory Address, 1997; (contrib.) Die Zürcher Reformation: Ausstrahlungen und Rückwirkungen, 2000; contribs to learned jls. *Address:* 4 Sydney Terrace, Edinburgh EH7 6SL. *T:* (0131) 669 1089; 12 Castelnau Gardens, Arundel Terrace, SW13 8DU. *T:* (020) 8746 3087. *Club:* Highland (Inverness).

SHAW, Elizabeth Angela; Director, Musikansky, since 1998; *b* 5 June 1946; *d* of John Edward Comben and Irene (*née* Thomson); *m* 1st, 1970, Graham Shaw (marr. diss. 1985); two *s* one *d*; 2nd, 1993, Adrian Carter. *Educ:* Sydenham High School. Executive Officer: Home Office, 1965–68; FCO, 1968–70; DSS, 1970–72; Department of Health and Social Security: HEO (Develt), 1972–77; Principal, 1977–84; Asst Sec., 1984–87; Dir of Finance, Planning and Marketing, Civil Service Coll., 1987–90; Head of Staff Develt, DoH, 1990–91; Exec. Dir, Charity Commn, 1991–96. Chair: COMPAID Trust, 1997–99; St Michael's Fellowship, 1997–99. *Recreations:* music, literature, walking, riding, family.

SHAW, Fiona Mary, Hon. CBE 2001; actress; *b* 10 July 1958; *d* of Dr Denis Joseph Wilson and Mary Teresa Wilson (*née* Flynn), MSc; adopted Shaw as stage name. *Educ:* University Coll. Cork (BA); Royal Acad. of Dramatic Art (Hons Dip.; Bancroft Gold medal; Tree Prize; Ronson Award). *Theatre* includes: The Rivals, 1983; RSC, 1985–88: Philistines; As You Like It; Les Liaisons Dangereuses; Mephisto; Much Ado About Nothing; The Merchant of Venice; Hyde Park; The Taming of the Shrew; New Inn; Electra (title rôle); Mary Stuart, Greenwich, 1988; As You Like It, Old Vic, 1989; The Good Person of Sichuan, NT, 1989; Hedda Gabler (title rôle), Dublin and Playhouse, 1991; Machinal, NT, 1993; Footfalls, Garrick, 1994; Richard II, The Way of the World, RNT, 1995; The Waste Land, Brussels and Dublin Fests, NY, 1996, Wilton's Music Hall, London, 1997, Adelaide, 1998; The Prime of Miss Jean Brodie, RNT, 1998; Medea, Abbey Th., Dublin, 2000, Queen's, 2001; *films* include: My Left Foot, 1988; The Mountains of the Moon, 1988; Three Men and a Little Lady, 1990; London Kills Me, 1991; Super Mario Brothers, 1993; Undercover Blues, 1993; Jane Eyre, 1994; Anna Karenina, 1996; The Butcher Boy, 1996; The Avengers, 1997; The Last September, 2000; Harry Potter and the Philosopher's Stone, 2001; *television* includes: Fireworks for Elspeth, 1983; Persuasion, 1994; The Waste Land, 1995; Gormenghast, 2000; Mind Games, 2000. Hon. Prof. of Drama, TCD, 1997. Hon. LLD NUI, 1996; DUniv Open, 1998; Hon. Dr TCD, 2001. London Theatre Critics' Award, 1989, 1992; Best Actress, Olivier Awards, 1989, 1994; Best Actress, Evening Standard Awards, 1993. *Publications:* Players of Shakespeare, 1987; Clamerous Voices, 1988; Conversations with Actresses, 1990. *Recreations:* travel, reading, walking, thinking, snorkling. *Address:* c/o ICM, Oxford House, 76 Oxford Street, W1N 0AX.

SHAW, (Francis) Michael; Managing Director, 1985–93, Executive Vice Chairman, 1993–94, Britannia Building Society; *b* 12 Aug. 1936; *s* of Joseph Stanley Shaw and Irene Shaw (*née* Weldrake); *m* 1960, Margaret Elinor Russum; two *d*. *Educ:* Rotherham Grammar Sch. Qualified as chartered accountant, 1957. National Service, RAF, 1958–60; Peat Marwick Mitchell & Co., Sheffield, 1960–61; Company Sec. and Accountant, John Speed & Co., 1961–67; Chief Accountant, Eastern Counties Building Soc., 1967–74; Britannia Building Society: Chief Accountant, 1974–77; Gen. Manager, 1977–83; Chief Gen. Manager, 1983–85. Chm., BSA, 1992–93; Pres., N Staffs Chamber of Commerce, 1993–95. *Recreations:* golf, foreign travel, photography. *Club:* Leek Golf.

SHAW, Dr Gavin Brown, CBE 1981; FRCP, FRCPE, FRCPGlas; Consultant Physician, Southern General Hospital, Glasgow, 1956–84, Hon. Consultant, since 1984; *b* 24 May 1919; *s* of Gavin Shaw and Christian Douglas Cormack; *m* 1943, Margaret Mabon Henderson (*d* 1990); one *d* (and one *s* one *d* decd). *Educ:* Glasgow Academy; Glasgow Univ., 1936–42 (BSc, MB ChB). President, Students' Representative Council, 1940–41. House Phys. to Sir J. W. McNee, 1942; Temporary Surg.-Lieut, RNVR, 1942–45; Asst Phys., Southern Gen. Hosp., Glasgow, 1948–56. Actg post-Grad. Dean., Glasgow Univ., 1983–84. Royal College of Physicians and Surgeons of Glasgow: Hon. Sec., 1957–65; Visitor, 1977–78; Pres., 1978–80. Mem., West Regional Hosp. Bd, 1971–74; Chairman: Greater Glasgow Med. Adv. Cttee, 1973–76; Jt Cttee for Higher Med. Trng, 1979–83; Specialty Adviser in Medicine, W of Scotland Post-Graduate Cttee, 1971–83. Mem., GMC, 1982–89. Hon. FACP 1979; Hon. FRCPI 1979; Hon. FRCPsych 1980; Hon. FRCGP 1980. *Publications:* (ed jtly) Cardiac Resuscitation and Pacing, 1964; occasional contributor to BMJ, Brit. Heart Jl, Lancet, Practitioner, Amer. Heart Jl, Scottish Med. Jl. *Recreations:* walking, gardening, bird watching and one-time sailor, listening to music, painting, reading. *Address:* 31 St Germains, Bearsden, Glasgow G61 2RS. *T:* (0141) 942 4553. *Club:* Royal Scottish Automobile.

SHAW, Rev. Canon Geoffrey Norman; Hon. Canon Emeritus of Christ Church Cathedral, Oxford, since 1989 (Hon. Canon, 1985–89); *b* 15 April 1926; *s* of Samuel Norman Shaw and Maud Shaw; *m* 1st, 1948, Cynthia Brown (*d* 1997); one *s* two *d*; 2nd, 1998, Margaret Dorothy Thurlow. *Educ:* Holgate Grammar Sch., Barnsley; Jesus Coll., Oxford (MA); Wycliffe Hall, Oxford. Asst Curate, St Mary, Rushden, 1951–54; Vicar of St Paul, Woking, 1954–62; Rector of St Leonards-on-Sea, Sussex, 1962–68; Asst Master, Ecclesfield Grammar Sch., Sheffield, 1968–69; Head of Religious Educn and Classics, Silverdale Sch., Sheffield, 1969–72; Vice-Principal, Oak Hill Theol Coll., Southgate, 1972–79; Principal, Wycliffe Hall, Oxford, 1979–89. Hon. Asst Chaplain, Kingham Hill Sch., 1992–. *Recreations:* bird watching, walking, golf, music. *Address:* 15A West Street, Kingham, Oxon OX7 6YF. *T:* (01608) 658006.

SHAW, Geoffrey Peter; QC 1991; *b* 19 April 1944; *s* of late James Adamson Shaw and Hilda Gargett Shaw (*née* Edwards); *m* 1985, Susan Cochrane. *Educ:* Worksop College, Notts; Worcester College, Oxford (BA, BCL). Teaching Fellow, Univ. of Chicago Law Sch., 1966; Arden Scholar of Gray's Inn, 1967; called to the Bar, Gray's Inn, 1968. *Recreations:* walking, travel, gardening. *Address:* 1 Brick Court, Temple, EC4Y 9BY. *T:* (020) 7353 8845.

SHAW, Sir (George) Neville B.; *see* Bowman-Shaw.

SHAW, Sir John (Calman), Kt 1995; CBE 1989; CA; FRSE; Governor, Bank of Scotland, 1999–2001(non-executive Director,1990–2001; Deputy Governor, 1991–99); *b* 10 July 1932; *m* 1960, Shirley Botterill; three *d*. *Educ:* Strathallan Sch.; Edinburgh Univ. BL; FCMA, MBCS, JDipMA. National Service, RAF, 1955–57. Partner in Graham, Smart & Annan (later Deloitte, Haskins & Sells), 1960, Sen. Edinburgh Partner, 1980–87. Pres., Inst. of Chartered Accountants of Scotland, 1983–84. Johnstone Smith Prof. of Accountancy (pt-time appt), 1977–82, Vis. Prof., 1986–, Glasgow Univ. Chairman: Scottish American Investment Co. PLC (formerly Trust), 1991–2001 (Dir, 1986–); US Smaller Cos Investment Trust, 1991–99 (Dir, 1991–); TR European Growth Trust PLC, 1998– (Dir, 1992); Director: Scottish Metropolitan Property plc, 1994–2000; Scottish Mortgage and Trust PLC, 1982–2001; Templeton Emerging Markets Investment Trust plc, 1994–; Templeton Latin America Investment Trust plc, 1994–. Chairman: SHEFC, 1992–98; Scottish Financial Enterprise, 1995–99 (Exec. Dir, 1986–90); Scottish Science Trust, 1998–; Edinburgh Technology Fund, 1999–; Member: Scottish Industrial Develt Adv. Bd, 1987–95; Bd, Scottish Enterprise, 1990–98; Financial Reporting Council, 1990–96; UFC, 1991–93; HEFCE, 1992–94; Scottish Econ. Council, 1996–98. Chm., David Hume Inst., 1995–. Dep. Chm., Edinburgh Fest. Soc., 1991–2000. Dr *hc* Edinburgh, 1998; Hon. LLD: Glasgow, 1998; Abertay Dundee, 1998; St Andrews, 1999; Hon. DEd Napier, 1999. Receiver General, The Priory of Scotland of Most Venerable Order of St John, 1992–; KStJ 1992. *Publications:* (ed) Bogie on Group Accounts (3rd edn), 1973; The Audit Report, 1980; (jtly) Information Disclosure and the Multinational Corporation, 1984; numerous articles in Accountant's Magazine and Accounting and Business Research and Accountancy, etc. *Recreations:* opera, theatre, walking. *Address:* Tayhill, Dunkeld PH8 0BA. *Clubs:* Caledonian; New (Edinburgh); Western (Glasgow).

SHAW, John Campbell; Managing Director: Amberton Shaw, since 1997; Stannifer Group Holdings, since 1998; *b* 2 Aug. 1949; *s* of late John C. B. Shaw and of May B. Shaw; *m*; two *d*. *Educ:* Grosvenor High Sch., Belfast; QUB (BSc Hons in Urban Geography); Heriot-Watt Univ. (MSc in Town & Country Planning). Lanarkshire CC, 1973–75; Motherwell DC, 1975–78; East Kilbride Development Corporation, 1978–95: Head of Planning, 1982; Tech. Dir, 1986; Man. Dir, 1990–95; Bd Mem., Lanarkshire Develt Agency, 1991–95. *Recreation:* sport. *Address:* Stannifer Group Holdings Ltd, Ryon Hill Park, Warwick Road, Stratford upon Avon CV37 0UX.

SHAW, John Frederick, CB 1996; Director of Corporate Affairs, National Health Service Executive, 1993–96; *b* 7 Dec. 1936; *s* of James Herbert and Barbara Shaw; *m* 1964, Ann Rodden; two *s* one *d*. *Educ:* Loretto Sch., Musselburgh; Worcester Coll., Oxford (MA). National Service, 2/Lieut KOYLI, 1955–57. Church Comrs, 1960–62; Industrial Christian Fellowship, 1962–63; HQ Staff, VSO, 1963–73; Principal (Direct Entry), DHSS, 1973, Asst Sec. 1978; Under Sec., DHSS, then DoH, 1987–93. Chairman: REACH, 1988–92; Nat. Family Mediation, 1996–2001; Rickmansworth Waterways Trust, 1997–; UK Transplant Support Services Authority, 1998–2001; Nat. Centre for Volunteering, 1999– (Trustee, 1996–, Chm. Trustees, 1998–); Mem. Council, Patients' Assoc., 1998–99 (Vice-Chm., 1996–98). Lay Mem., GMC, 1996–. *Recreations:* church activities, singing, gardening. *Address:* Hyde House, West Hyde, Rickmansworth, Herts WD3 9XH.

SHAW, John Michael, MC 1940; QC 1967; Barrister-at-Law; Regional Chairman of Industrial Tribunals, 1972–84; *b* 14 Nov. 1914; *yr s* of late M. J. Shaw (killed in action, 1916); *m* 1940, Margaret L. (*d* 1997), *yr d* of Robert T. D. Stoneham, CBE; two *s* two *d*. *Educ:* Rugby; Worcester Coll., Oxford. Called to the Bar, Gray's Inn, 1937. Served War of 1939–45 (Major): commissioned Royal Fusiliers, 1940. *Recreation:* gardening.

SHAW, Sir John Michael Robert B.; *see* Best-Shaw.

SHAW, Jonathan Rowland; MP (Lab) Chatham and Aylesford, since 1997; *b* 3 June 1966; *s* of Alan James Shaw and Lesbia Virginia Percival Shaw; *m* 1990, Susan Lesley Gurmin; one *s* one *d*. *Educ:* Vinters Boys' Sch., Maidstone; Bromley Coll., Kent (Cert. in Social Services). Social Worker, Kent Social Services, 1990–97. *Recreations:* walking, cooking, reading. *Address:* c/o House of Commons, SW1A 0AA.

SHAW, Dr Kenneth Martin, FRCP; Senior Consultant Physician and Associate Clinical Director, Medicine, and Director, Department of Diabetes and Endocrinology, Portsmouth Hospitals NHS Trust (formerly Portsmouth and South East Hants Health District), since 1979; *b* 20 April 1943; *s* of late Frank Shaw and Gwen (*née* Mosson); *m* 1968, Phyllis Dixon; two *s*. *Educ:* City of Norwich Sch.; Downing Coll., Cambridge (BA 1965, MA 1969; BChir 1968, MB 1969; MD 1979); University Coll. Hosp., London. FRCP 1985. MRC Res. Fellow, Dept of Clin. Pharmacol., UCH Med. Sch., 1971–72; Sen. Registrar, 1973–77, Resident Asst Physician, 1977–78, UCH, London; Postgrad. Clin. Tutor, Univ. of Southampton, 1983–90; Dir, R&D, Portsmouth Hosps NHS Trust, and R&D Support Unit and Portsmouth R&D Consortium, Sch. of Postgrad. Medicine, Univ. of Portsmouth (at Queen Alexandra's Hosp.), 1995–. Vis. Prof., Portsmouth Univ., 1996–. Editor-in-Chief, Practical Diabetes Internat., 1992–. Royal College of Physicians: Member: Jt Speciality Cttee for Endocrinol. and Diabetes, 1998–; Adv. Panel for Service Rev. Visits, 2000–; Mem., Med. Adv. Cttee, 1982–86, Vice Chm., Specialist Care Cttee, 1998–, British Diabetic Assoc.; Chm., Wessex Diabetes and Endocrinol. Assoc., 1989–96. Member: Eur. Assoc. for Study of Diabetes, 1980–; Amer. Diabetes Assoc., 1995–; Internat. Diabetes Fedn, 1995–; Founding Mem., Trustee and Hon. Treas., Assoc. of British Clin. Diabetologists, 1996–. FRSocMed 1972; Scientific FZS 1974. Mem., Harveian Med. Soc. of London, 1969–. UK Hosp. Diabetes Team Award, 1998. *Publications:* Complications of Diabetes, 1996; contrib. chapters in books; contrib. numerous rev. articles and peer-reviewed original scientific articles. *Recreations:* golf, opera. *Address:* Castle Acre, Hospital Lane, Portchester, Hants PO16 9QP.

SHAW, Dr Mark Robert; Keeper of Geology and Zoology, National Museums of Scotland, since 1996; *b* 11 May 1945; *s* of William Shaw and Mabel Courtenay Shaw (*née* Bower); *m* 1970, Francesca Dennis Wilkinson; two *d*. *Educ:* Dartington Hall Sch.; Oriel Coll., Oxford (BA 1968; MA, DPhil 1972). Res. Assistant, Manchester Univ., 1973–76; Univ. Res. Fellow, Reading Univ., 1977–80; Asst Keeper, Dept of Natural History, 1980–83, Keeper of Natural History, 1983–96, Royal Scottish Mus., subseq. Nat. Museums of Scotland. *Publications:* contribs (mainly on parasitic wasps) to entomological jls. *Recreations:* field entomology, family life. *Address:* 48 St Alban's Road, Edinburgh EH9 2LU. *T:* (0131) 667 0577.

SHAW, Martin; actor; *b* 21 Jan. 1945; two *s* one *d*. *Educ:* Great Barr Sch., Birmingham; LAMDA. *Stage* includes: appearances at Royal Court and National Theatre; West End: Are You Lonesome Tonight, Phoenix, 1985; The Big Knife, Albery, 1987; Other People's Money, Lyric 1990; Betrayal, 1991; An Ideal Husband, Globe, 1992, Haymarket, 1996 (Best Actor Award, NY Drama Desk, 1996), 1997, transf. Gielgud, and Albery, 1998, Haymarket, and Lyric, 1999; Rough Justice, Apollo, 1994; *television* includes, 1968–: The Professionals; The Chief, 1994; title rôle in Rhodes, 1996; The Scarlet Pimpernel, 1999; Always and Everyone, later A & E, 1999–. *Recreation:* flies own antique biplane. *Address:* c/o Ken McReddie, 91 Regent Street, W1R 7TB.

SHAW, Group Captain Mary Michal, RRC 1981; Director and Matron-in-Chief, Princess Mary's Royal Air Force Nursing Service, and Deputy Director, Defence Nursing Services (Operations and Plans), 1985–88; *b* 7 April 1933; *d* of Ven. Archdeacon Thorndike Shaw and Violet Rosario Shaw. *Educ:* Wokingham Grammar School for Girls. SRN 1955, Royal Berkshire Hosp., Reading; SCM 1957, Central Middlesex Hosp., London and Battle Hosp., Reading; PMRAFNS, 1963–88; QHNS, 1985–88. OStJ 1974. *Recreations:* gardening, home crafts. *Address:* 33 Whiting Street, Bury St Edmunds, Suffolk IP33 1NP. *T:* (01284) 705836.

SHAW, Max S.; *see* Stuart-Shaw.

SHAW, Michael; *see* Shaw, F. M.

SHAW, Michael Hewitt, CMG 1990; foreign affairs adviser and consultant; HM Diplomatic Service, retired; *b* 5 Jan. 1935; *s* of late Donald Shaw and Marion (*née* Hewitt); *m* 1963, Elizabeth Rance; three *d* (and one *d* decd). *Educ:* Sedbergh; Clare College, Cambridge (MA); UCL (MA 1992). HM Forces, 1953. HMOCS Tanganyika, 1959–62; joined Diplomatic Service, 1963; served The Hague, FCO and Vientiane, 1964–68; First Sec., FCO, 1968–72, Valletta, 1972–76, FCO, 1976–82, Brussels, 1982–84; Counsellor, Brussels, 1984–86, FCO, 1986–95. *Recreations:* cricket, theatre, travel, historical research. *Address:* The Close, Marley Common, Haslemere, Surrey GU27 3PT; *e-mail:* mhshaw@supanet.com. *Clubs:* Army and Navy, MCC.

SHAW, Sir Neil (McGowan), Kt 1994; Chairman: Tate & Lyle PLC, London, 1986–98 (Director, 1975–98; Chief Executive, 1986–92); Tate & Lyle Holdings, 1981–98; Tate & Lyle Industries, 1981–98; Tunnel Refineries, 1982–98 (Director, 1981–98); Vice-Chairman: Redpath Industries, 1981–98 (Director, 1972–98); A. E. Staley Manufacturing Co., 1988–98; *b* 31 May 1929; *s* of late Harold LeRoy Shaw and Fabiola Marie Shaw; *m* 1952, Audrey Robinson (marr. diss.); two *s* three *d*; *m* 1985, Elizabeth Fern Mudge-Massey. *Educ:* Knowlton High Sch.; Lower Canada Coll., Canada. Trust Officer, Crown Trust Co., Montreal, 1947–54; Merchandising Manager, Canada & Dominion Sugar Co. (later Redpath Industries Ltd), Montreal, 1954–66; Vice Pres., Canada & Dominion Sugar Co., Toronto, 1967–72; Pres., Redpath Industries Ltd, 1972–80; Gp Man. Dir, Tate & Lyle PLC, 1980–86. Director: Americare Corp., 1980–96; Alcantara, 1983–98; Canadian Imperial Bank of Commerce (Toronto), 1986–2000; United Biscuits (Hldgs), 1988–97. Dir, World Sugar Res. Orgn, 1982–97 (Chm., 1994–96); Gov., World Food and Agro Forum, 1988–96. Chairman: Business in the Community, 1991–94; Assoc. of Lloyd's Members, 1992–94. Dir and Gov., United World Coll. of Atlantic, 1997–2000. Gov., Montreal Gen. Hosp. Hon. Fellow, RHBNC, 1995. Hon. LLD E London, 1997. *Recreations:* sailing, ski-ing, golfing. *Clubs:* Brooks's; Toronto, Toronto Golf (Toronto).

SHAW, Sir Neville B.; *see* Bowman-Shaw.

SHAW, Nicholas Glencairn B.; *see* Byam Shaw.

SHAW, Peter Alan, CB 2000; Director-General, Youth, Department for Education and Skills, since 2001; *b* 31 May 1949; *s* of late Frank Shaw and Ursula Lister Shaw (*née* Dyson); *m* 1975, Frances Willcox; two *s* one *d*. *Educ:* Bridlington Sch.; Durham Univ. (BSc Geography); Bradford Univ. (MSc Traffic Eng. and Planning); Regent Coll., Univ. of British Columbia (Master in Christian Studies). FIHT. Department of Education and Science, subseq. Department for Education, then Department for Education and Employment, then Department for Education and Skills, 1972–: Private Sec. to Perm. Sec., 1975–76; Principal Private Sec. to Sec. of State, 1979–81; Asst Sec., 1981–91; on loan to HM Treasury, 1985–86; Press Sec. to DES Sec. of State, 1988–89; Grade 3, 1991–98; on loan to Depts of the Envmt and Transport as Regl Dir, Northern Reg., 1991–93; Dir of Estabts and Personnel, 1993–94; Dir of Services (personnel, analytical and inf. systems), 1994–95; Leader, Sen. Mgt Review, 1995; Dir, Sch. Places, Buildings and Governance, 1995–97; Dir, Finance, 1997–98; Grade 2, 1998–; Director-General: Finance and Analytical Services, 1998–2000; Employment, Equality and Internat. Relations, 2000–01. Hon. Vis. Prof., Educn Dept, Univ. of Durham, 1997–. Member: Council, St John's Coll., Durham Univ., 1993–; Governing Body, Goldalming Sixth Form Coll., 1996–. Anglican Lay Reader, 1972–, Selector for Lay Readers in Trng, 1997–, Mem., Ministerial Adv. Council, dio. of Guildford. FRSA. *Recreations:* walking, travelling. *Address:* Department for Education and Skills, Sanctuary Buildings, Great Smith Street, SW1P 3BT. *T:* (020) 7925 6943.

SHAW, Captain Peter Jack, CBE 1990; RN (retd); General Secretary, British Group Inter-Parliamentary Union, 1979–90; Consultant to President, Interparliamentary Council, 1991–93; *b* Geelong, Australia, 27 Oct. 1924; *s* of late Jack and Betty Shaw; *m* 1951, Pauline, *e d* of Sir Frank Madge, 2nd Bt, and Lady (Doris) Madge, East Grinstead; one *s* one *d*. *Educ:* Watford Grammar School; RNC Dartmouth; RN Staff Coll. Greenwich; NATO Defence Coll., Paris. FIL 1957. War service in HM Ships Kenya, Resolution, Quadrant, Kelvin, incl. Malta and Russian Convoys and Normandy invasion; comd HM Ships Venus, Carron, Vigilant, 1958–61; Staff, C-in-C Portsmouth and MoD, 1961–65; SHAPE, Paris and Mons, 1966–68; Comdr, RN Coll. Greenwich, 1968–70; Defence and Naval Attaché, The Hague, 1971–73; Captain of Port and Queen's Harbourmaster, Plymouth, 1973–76; Captain of Port, Chatham, 1976–79. MBIM. *Recreations:* international relations, foreign languages, domestic pursuits. *Address:* Woodside, Rogate, Petersfield, Hants GU31 5DJ. *T:* (01730) 821344.

SHAW, Prof. Richard Wright, CBE 1997; Vice-Chancellor and Principal, University of Paisley, 1992–2001 (Principal, Paisley College, 1987–92); *b* 22 Sept. 1941; *s* of late George Beeley Shaw and Bella Shaw; *m* 1965, Susan Angela Birchley; two *s*. *Educ:* Lancaster Royal Grammar Sch.; Sidney Sussex Coll., Cambridge (MA). Leeds University: Asst Lectr in Management, 1964–66; Lectr in Econs, 1966–69; Stirling University: Lectr in Econs, 1969–75; Sen. Lectr, 1975–84; Head of Dept of Econs, 1982–84; Paisley College: Head, Dept of Econs and Management and Prof., 1984–86; Vice Principal, 1986–87. Convenor, Cttee of Scottish Higher Educn Principals, 1996–98. Member: Scottish Economic Council, 1995–98; Scottish Business Forum, 1998–99. Fellow, SCOTVEC, 1995; FRSA. *Publications:* (with C. J. Sutton) Industry and Competition, 1976; articles in Jl Industrial Econs, Scottish Jl Pol Econ., Managerial and Decision Econs. *Recreations:* walking, listening to music, sketching and painting. *Address:* Drumbarns, 18 Old Doune Road, Dunblane, Perthshire FK15 9AG.

SHAW, Sir Robert, 7th Bt *cr* 1821; *b* Nairobi, Kenya, 31 Jan. 1925; *s* of Sir Robert de Vere Shaw, 6th Bt, MC, and Joan (*d* 1967), *d* of Thomas Cross; *S* father, 1969; *m* 1954, Jocelyn, *d* of late Andrew McGuffie, Swaziland; two *d*. *Educ:* Harrow; Univs of Oklahoma and Missouri, USA. RN, 1943–47 (Lieut RN retd). BS Civil Eng. Oklahoma, 1962; MS Civil Eng. Missouri, 1964; Professional Engineer, Alberta, now retired; Mem., Assoc., of Prof. Engrs, Geologists and Geophysicists of Alberta. *Recreation:* sailing. *Heir:* *n* Charles de Vere Shaw [*b* 1 March 1957; *m* 1985, Sonia, *e d* of Thomas Geoffrey Eden; one *s* one *d*]. *Address:* 234 40th Avenue SW, Calgary, AB T2S 0X3, Canada.

SHAW, Prof. Robert Wayne, MD; FRCSE; FRCOG; Postgraduate Dean, Medical and Dental Education, Eastern Deanery, University of Cambridge, since 2001; *b* 25 June 1946; *s* of Arthur Stanley Shaw and Margery Maude Shaw (*née* Griffiths); *m* 1980, Mary Philomena McGovern; one *s* one *d*. *Educ:* Priory Grammar Sch., Shrewsbury; Birmingham Univ. Med. Sch. (MB ChB 1969; MD 1975). FRCSE 1978; MRCOG 1977, FRCOG 1993. Lectr, 1975–79, and Sen. Lectr, 1979–81, in Obstetrics and Gynaecology, Birmingham Univ.; Sen. Lectr, Edinburgh Univ., 1981–83; Prof., Royal Free Hosp. Sch. of Medicine, 1983–92; Prof. and Head of Acad. Dept of Obstetrics and Gynaecology, Univ. of Wales Coll. of Medicine, 1992–2001. Vice-Pres., 1995–98, Pres., 1998–2001, RCOG. Founder FMedSci 1998. Hon. Fellow, Finnish Gynaecological Soc., 1992. *Publications:* (ed jtly) Gynaecology, 1992, 2nd edn, 1997; (ed) Endometriosis: current management, 1995; over 300 articles on gynaecological reproductive medicine. *Recreations:* sailing, hill walking. *Address:* PGMDE, Eastern Deanery, Block 3, Ida Darwin Site, Fulbourn, Cambridge CB1 5EE. *Club:* Athenæum.

SHAW, Prof. Rory James Swanton, MD; FRCP; Professor of Respiratory Medicine, Imperial College School of Medicine, since 1997; Medical Director, Hammersmith Hospitals NHS Trust, since 1998; *b* 5 Jan. 1954; *s* of late Dr James Brian Shaw, OBE and of Irma Valerie Shaw, JP; *m* 1991, Sarah Margaret Foulkes; two *d*. *Educ:* Bedford Sch.; St Bartholomew's Hosp. Med. Sch. (BSc 1974; MB BS 1977); MD 1985, MBA 1995, London. MRCP 1979, FRCP 1993. Sen. Lectr, St Mary's Hosp. Med. Sch., Imperial Coll., and Consultant Physician in Respiratory Medicine, 1989–97. *Publications:* articles on tuberculosis and asthma in learned jls. *Address:* Medical Director's Office, Hammersmith Hospital, Du Cane Road, W12 0HS. *T:* (020) 8383 3370.

SHAW, Sir Roy, Kt 1979; Secretary General of the Arts Council of Great Britain, 1975–83; *b* 8 July 1918; *s* of Frederick and Elsie Shaw; *m* 1946, Gwenyth Baron; five *s* two *d*. *Educ:* Firth Park Grammar School, Sheffield; Manchester Univ. BA(Hons). Newspaper printing department 'copy-holder', 1937; newspaper publicity, 1938; Library Asst, Sheffield City Library, 1939; Cataloguer, Manchester Univ. Library, 1945; Organizing Tutor, WEA, 1946; Adult Educn Lectr, Leeds Univ., 1947; Warden, Leeds Univ. Adult Educn Centre, Bradford, 1959; Professor and Dir of Adult Educn, Keele Univ., 1962. Vis. Prof., Centre for Arts, City Univ., London, 1977–83. Theatre critic, The Tablet, 1990–2000. Hon. DLitt: City, 1978; Southampton, 1984; DUniv Open, 1981. *Publications:* The Arts and the people, 1987; (ed) The Spread of Sponsorship, 1993; contrib. chapters to: Trends in English Adult Education, 1959; The Committed Church, 1966; Your Sunday Paper, 1967; over 170 articles and book chapters on cultural policy, adult education and the mass media. *Recreations:* reading, theatre, opera, films, concerts and art galleries, swimming, watching the best of television—and sometimes, for clinical reasons, the worst. *Address:* 48 Farrer Road, N8 8LB. *T:* (020) 8348 1857. *Club:* Arts.

SHAW, Roy Edwin, OBE 1991; Council Member, London Borough of Camden, since 1964; Mayor of Camden, 1999–2000; *b* 21 July 1925; *s* of Edwin Victor and Edith Lily Shaw. Hampstead Borough Council, 1956–62; St Pancras Borough, 1962–65; Camden Borough Council: Chm., Planning Cttee, 1967–68; Chm., Finance Cttee, 1971–74; Chief Whip and Dep. Leader, 1965–73; Leader, 1975–82; Dep. Leader, 1990–94. Vice-Chm., AMA, 1979–83; Dep. Chm. and Leader of Labour Party, London Boroughs Assoc.; Dep. Leader, London Fire and Civil Defence Authy, 1999–2000; Vice-Chm., London Fire and Emergency Planning Authy, 2000–. Part-time Mem., London Electricity Bd, 1977–83; Member: Transport Users Consultative Cttee for London, 1974–80; Adv. Cttee on Local Govt Audit, 1979–82; Audit Commn, 1983–91; Consult. Council on Local Govt Finances, 1978–84. Chm., Camden Trng Centre, 1990–99. *Recreations:* listening to music; entertaining attractive women. *Address:* Town Hall, Euston Road, NW1 2RU. *T:* (020) 7278 4444.

SHAW, Sir Run Run, Kt 1977; CBE 1974; Founder and Chairman, Shaw Organisation, since 1963; Founder and Chairman, Shaw Foundation, since 1973; *b* 14 Oct. 1907; *m* 1st, 1932, Lily Wong Mee Chun (decd); two *s* two *d*; 2nd, 1997, Lee Mong-lan (Mona Fong). Left China for Singapore and began making films and operating cinemas, 1927; left Singapore for Hong Kong and built Shaw Movietown, making and distributing films, 1959. Pres., Hong Kong Red Cross Soc., 1972–98. Chairman: Hong Kong Arts Festival, 1974–88; Bd of Governors, Hong Kong Arts Centre, 1978–88; Television Broadcasts Ltd, 1980–. Chinese University of Hong Kong: Mem. Council, 1977–92; Chm., Bd of Trustees, United Coll., 1983–92; Founder, Shaw Coll., 1986. Appointed by Govt of People's Republic of China, Hong Kong Advr, 1992–97, Mem., Preparatory Cttee, 1995–98. Hon. LLD Hong Kong Univ., 1980; Hon. Dr Soc. Scis: Chinese Univ. of Hong Kong, 1981; Univ. of E Asia, Macau, 1985; Hon. DLitt: Sussex, 1987; Hong Kong Baptist Coll., 1990; Hon. DSc City Poly., Hong Kong, 1988; Hon. DHL SUNY at Stony Brook, 1989; Hon. DCL Oxford, 1992; Hon. DBA Hong Kong Poly., 1991. Queen's Badge, Red Cross, 1982; Montblanc de la Culture Award, 1993. Comdr, Order of the Crown of Belgium, 1989; Chevalier, Légion d'Honneur (France), 1991. *Address:* Shaw House, Lot 220 Clear Water Bay Road, Kowloon, Hong Kong. *T:* 27198371.

SHAW, Stephen Arthur, PhD; Prisons Ombudsman, since 1999; *b* 26 March 1953; *s* of late Walter Arthur Shaw and of Gwendolyn Primrose Shaw (*née* Cottrell); *m* 1977, Christine Elizabeth Robinson; partner, Jane Angela Skinner; two *s*. *Educ:* Rutlish Sch., Merton; Univ. of Warwick (BA 1974); Univ. of Leeds (MA 1976); Univ. of Kent (PhD 1979). Lectr in Further Educn, Mid-Kent Coll. of Technology, 1977–79; Researcher, NACRO, 1979–80; Research Officer, Home Office, 1980–81; Dir, Prison Reform Trust, 1981–99. *Publications:* numerous contribs to jls. *Recreations:* playing with my children, watching Fulham FC. *Address:* Prisons Ombudsman's Office, Ashley House, 2 Monck Street, SW1P 2BQ. *T:* (020) 7276 2876.

SHAW, Thurstan; *see* Shaw, C. T.

SHAW, Prof. William V., MD; Founder and Chief Scientific Officer, PanTherix Ltd, 1998–2000; *b* Philadelphia, Pennsylvania, 13 May 1933. *Educ:* Williams Coll., Williamstown, Mass (BA Chemistry 1955); Columbia Univ., New York (MD 1959). Diplomate: Amer. Bd of Med. Examrs, 1960; Amer. Bd of Internal Med., 1968 (Examiner, 1970). Appts, Presbyterian Hosp., New York, Nat. Heart Inst., Bethesda, Maryland, and Columbia Univ., New York, until 1966; Asst Prof. of Medicine, Columbia Univ., New York, 1966–68; University of Miami School of Medicine, Miami, Florida: Associate Prof. of Medicine and Biochemistry, 1968–73; Chief, Infectious Diseases, 1971–74; Prof. of Medicine, 1973–74; Leicester University: Prof. of Biochemistry, 1974–97; Prof. of Chemical Microbiology, 1997–98. Hon. Prof. of Biochemistry, Univ. of Glasgow, 1998–. Vis. Scientist, MRC Lab. of Molecular Biology, Cambridge, Eng., 1972–74. Member: MRC Cell Biology and Disorders Bd, 1976–80 (Bd Chm. and Mem. Council, 1978–80); Science Council, Celltech Ltd, 1980–89 (Chm., 1983–89); Lister Inst. Sci. Adv. Cttee, 1981–85 (Chm., 1997–2000); AFRC, 1990–94. Member: Amer. Soc. for Clinical Investigation, 1971; Infectious Disease Soc. of Amer., 1969; Amer. Soc. of Biol Chemists; Biochem. Soc. (UK); Amer. Soc. for Microbiology; Soc. for Gen. Microbiology (UK). *Publications:* contribs to professional works and jls in microbial biochemistry and molecular enzymology. *Address:* PO Box 83, Sunset, ME 04683, USA.

SHAW-STEWART, Sir Houston (Mark), 11th Bt *cr* 1667; MC 1950; TD; DL; Vice Lord-Lieutenant, Strathclyde Region (Eastwood, Renfrew and Inverclyde Districts), 1980–95; *b* 24 April 1931; *s* of Sir Guy Shaw-Stewart, 9th Bt, MC, and Diana (*d* 1931), *d* of late George Bulteel; *S* brother, 1980; *m* 1982, Lucinda Victoria, *yr d* of Alexander Fletcher, Old Vicarage, Wighill, near Tadcaster; one *s*. *Educ:* Eton. Joined Coldstream Guards, 1949; served as 2/Lt Royal Ulster Rifles, Korea, 1950 (MC); joined Ayrshire Yeomanry, 1952; retired, 1969; Hon. Col A (Ayrshire Yeomanry) Sqdn, Queen's Own Yeomanry RAC, TA, 1984–87. Member of the Royal Company of Archers, Queen's Body Guard for Scotland. Joint Master, Lanark and Renfrewshire Foxhounds, 1974–79. DL Renfrewshire, 1970. *Recreations:* hunting, shooting and racing. *Heir: s* Ludovic Houston Shaw Stewart *b* 12 Nov. 1986. *Address:* Ardgowan, Inverkip, Renfrewshire PA16 0DW. *T:* (01475) 521226. *Clubs:* White's, Turf, Pratt's.

SHAWCROSS, family name of **Baron Shawcross**.

SHAWCROSS, Baron *cr* 1959 (Life Peer), of Friston; **Hartley William Shawcross;** PC 1946; GBE 1974; Kt 1945; QC 1939; Special Adviser, Morgan Guaranty Trust of New York, 1965–94 (Chairman, International Advisory Council, 1967–74); Director, Hawker Siddeley Group, 1968–82; Director, The Observer, 1981–93; *b* 4 Feb. 1902; *s* of John Shawcross, MA, and Hilda Shawcross; *m* 1st, 1924, Rosita Alberta Shyvers (*d* 1943); 2nd, 1944, Joan Winifred Mather (*d* 1974); two *s* one *d*; 3rd, 1997, Mrs Monique Huiskamp. *Educ:* Dulwich Coll.; abroad. Certificate of Honour for 1st place in Bar Final; called to Bar, Gray's Inn, 1925 (Bencher, 1939); practised on Northern Circuit. Sen. Law Lectr, Liverpool Univ., 1927–34. Chm., Enemy Aliens Tribunal, 1939–40; left practice at Bar for War Service, 1940; Chief Prosecutor for UK before Internat. Military Tribunal at Nuremberg. Asst Chm. of E Sussex QS, 1941; Recorder of Salford, 1941–45; Dep. Regional Comr, South-Eastern Region, 1941; Regional Comr, North-Western Region, 1942–45; Recorder of Kingston-upon-Thames, 1946–61; retired from practice at Bar, 1958. MP (Lab) St Helens, 1945–58; Attorney-General, 1945–51; Pres., BoT, April–Oct. 1951. A Principal Deleg. for UK to Assemblies of UN, 1945–49; a UK Mem., Permanent Court of Arbitration at The Hague, 1950–67. Independent Chm., Kent District Coal Mining Board, 1940–45; Chairman: Catering Wages Commn, 1943–45; Bar Council, 1952–57; Royal Commn on the Press, 1961–62; MRC, 1961–65; Internat. Law Section of British Inst. of Internat. and Comparative Law; Justice (British Br. of Internat. Commn of Jurists), 1956–72; Panel on Take-overs and Mergers, 1969–80; Press Council, 1974–78; ICC Commn on Unethical Practices, 1976. President: Rainer Foundn (formerly London Police Court Mission), 1951–71; British Hotels and Restaurants Assoc., 1959–71. Member: Home Secretary's Adv. Council on Treatment of Offenders, 1944–45; Council, Internat. Law Assoc., 1958–74; Exec. Cttee, Internat. Commn of Jurists, 1959. Hon. Member: Bar Council; Amer. and New York Bar Assoc.; Fellow, Amer. Bar Foundn. Director: Shell Transport and Trading Co., 1961–72; EMI Ltd, 1965–81; Rank-Hovis-McDougall Ltd, 1965–79; Caffyns Motors Ltd, 1965–93; Morgan et Cie International SA, 1966–77; Morgan et Cie SA, 1967–90; Times Newspapers Ltd, 1967–74; Upjohn & Co Ltd, 1967–76 (Chm.); Birmingham Small Arms Co. Ltd, 1968–73 (Chm., 1971–73); European Enterprises Development Co. SA, 1970–78 (Chm., 1973–78); Chairman: Dominion Lincoln Assurance Co. Ltd, 1969–76; Thames Television Ltd, 1969–74; London and Continental Bankers, 1974–80; Chm. Bd of Governors, Dulwich Coll.; Member: Court, London Univ., 1958–74; Council and Exec. Cttee, Sussex Univ., 1959– (Pro-Chancellor, 1960–65; Chancellor, 1965–85); Council, Eastbourne Coll., 1965–70. Hon. FRCS 1981; Hon. FRCOG 1978. Hon. degrees from Universities of Bristol, Columbia, Hull, Lehigh, Liverpool, London, Loughborough, Massachusetts, Michigan. JP Sussex, 1941–68. Chm., Soc. of Sussex Downsmen, 1962–75. Knight Grand Cross, Imperial Iranian Order of Homayoon, 1st Cl., 1974. *Publication:* Life Sentence: the memoirs of Hartley Shawcross, 1995. *Recreation:* sailing. *Address:* Cowbeech Farm, Cowbeech, East Sussex BN27 4JF. *Clubs:* Pratt's, Garrick; Travellers (Paris); Royal Cornwall Yacht (Falmouth); Royal Yacht Squadron (Cowes); New York Yacht (US).

See also Hon. O. Polizzi, Hon. W. H. H. Shawcross.

SHAWCROSS, Roger Michael; His Honour Judge Shawcross; a Circuit Judge, since 1993; *b* 27 March 1941; *s* of Michael and Friedel Shawcross; *m* 1969, Sarah Broom; one *s* one *d*. *Educ:* Radley Coll.; Christ Church, Oxford (MA). Called to the Bar, Gray's Inn, 1967; a Recorder, 1985–93. *Recreations:* playing tennis, following most other sports, history, literature, music, cinema, travel, admiring my wife's gardening skills.

SHAWCROSS, Valerie; Member (Lab) Lambeth and Southwark, London Assembly, and e-envoy, Greater London Authority, since 2000; Chairman, London Fire and Emergency Planning Authority, since 2000; *b* 9 April 1958; *d* of Alfred Shawcross and Florence Shawcross (*née* Cooke); *m* 1983, Alan Frank Neil Parker, *qv* (separated 1998). *Educ:* Univ. of Liverpool (BA Hons Pol Theory and Instns 1980); Inst. of Education, Univ. of London (MA Educn 1986). Sabbatical Officer, Liverpool Univ. Guild of Undergraduates, 1980–81; UK Council for Overseas Students' Affairs, 1981–84; ILEA, 1984–86; World Univ. Service (UK), 1986; Commonwealth Secretariat, 1987–91; freelance appointments, 1992–: NFWI, Labour Party, Westminster Foundn for Democracy, Body Shop Internat., Public Policy Unit, Infolog. Mem. (Lab), Croydon LBC, 1994–2000 (Chair of Educn, 1995, Dep. Leader, 1997, Leader, 1997–2000). Mem., Labour Party, 1979–. *Recreation:* poetry. *Address:* Greater London Authority, Romney House, 43 Marsham Street, SW1P 3PY. *T:* (020) 7983 4000; *e-mail:* valerie.shawcross@london.gov.uk.

SHAWCROSS, Hon. Mrs William; *see* Polizzi, Hon. Olga.

SHAWCROSS, Hon. William (Hartley Hume); writer and broadcaster; *b* 28 May 1946; *s* of Baron Shawcross, *qv*; *m* 1st, 1971, Marina Sarah Warner, *qv*; one *s*; 2nd, 1981, Michal Levin; one *d*; 3rd, 1993, Hon. Olga Polizzi, *qv*. *Educ:* Eton; University Coll., Oxford. Chm., Article 19, Internat. Centre on Censorship, 1986–97; Mem. Bd, Internat. Crisis Gp, 1995–. *Publications:* Dubcek, 1970; Crime and Compromise, 1974; Sideshow: Kissinger, Nixon and the destruction of Cambodia, 1979; The Quality of Mercy: Cambodia, holocaust and modern memory, 1984; The Shah's Last Ride, 1989; Kowtow: a plea on behalf of Hong Kong, 1989; Murdoch, 1992; Cambodia's New Deal, 1994; Deliver Us from Evil, 2000. *Recreations:* walking, sailing. *Address:* Friston Place, East Dean, E Sussex BN20 0AH. *T:* (020) 7289 8089. *Club:* St Mawes Sailing.

SHAWE-TAYLOR, Desmond Philip; Director, Dulwich Picture Gallery, since 1996; *b* 30 Sept. 1955; *s* of late Brian Newton Shawe-Taylor and Jocelyn Cecilia Shawe-Taylor; *m* 1987, Rosemary Gillian North; two *s* one *d*. *Educ:* Shrewsbury Sch.; University Coll., Oxford; Courtauld Inst. of Art, London. Lectr, History of Art Dept, Nottingham Univ., 1979–96. *Publications:* Genial Company: the theme of genius in eighteenth-century British portraiture, 1987; The Georgians: eighteenth-century portraiture and society, 1990; Dramatic Art: theatrical paintings from the Garrick Club, 1997; Rembrandt to Gainsborough: masterpieces from Dulwich Picture Gallery, 1999. *Recreation:* playing the piano. *Address:* 13 Chestnut Road, SE27 9EZ. *T:* (020) 8766 6633.

SHAWYER, Eric Francis, CBE 1998; FICS; Chairman, E. A. Gibson Shipbrokers Ltd, 1988–2000; Chairman, Baltic Exchange, 1996–98 (Director, 1991–98); *b* 17 July 1932; *m* 1956, Joyce Patricia Henley; one *s* one *d*. Joined E. A. Gibson Shipbrokers, 1948; Dir, 1963–; Man. Dir, 1969–98. Chairman: Worldscale Assoc. (London) Ltd, 1979–96; London Tanker Brokers Panel Ltd, 1990–96; Director: Maersk Air Ltd, 1994–; Maersk Air Hldg Ltd, 1994–. FICS 1994 (Pres., 1996). Freeman, City of London, 1980; Liveryman, Co. of Shipwrights, 1981 (Mem., Ct of Assts); Freeman, Co. of Watermen and Lightermen, 1989. *Address:* Souvenir, Woodlands Road, Bromley, Kent BR1 2AE.

SHAWYER, Peter Michael, FCA; Managing Partner, Deloitte & Touche, since 1999; *b* 11 Sept. 1950; *s* of Edward William Francis Shawyer and Marjorie Josephine Shawyer; *m* 1979, Margot Bishop; one *s* one *d*. *Educ:* Enfield GS; Univ. of Sheffield (BA Hons). FCA 1975. Touche Ross & Co., subseq. Deloitte & Touche, 1972–: admitted Partner, 1982; Tax Partner, 1982–84; Group Partner, a Tax Group, 1984–93; Partner in charge of Tax Dept, 1993–95; Partner in charge of London Office, 1995–99; Member of Board: Deloitte & Touche, UK; Deloitte & Touche, Central Europe. Member: UK Exec. Gp; Europe-Africa Mgt Gp; European Tax Leader. *Recreation:* golf. *Address:* Deloitte & Touche, Stonecutter Court, 1 Stonecutter Street, EC4A 4TR. *T:* (020) 7303 5764. *Club:* Hadley Wood Golf.

SHCHASNY, Uladzimir; Chairman, National Commission of Republic of Belarus for UNESCO, since 2001; *b* 25 Nov. 1948; *s* of Ryhor and Nadzeya Shchasny; *m* 1972, Lyudmila Kazakova (marr. diss. 1993). *Educ:* Minsk State Linguistic Univ. (grad. 1972). Interpreter for USSR Min. of Geology, Pakistan, 1969–70, 1972–74; Lectr, Minsk State Inst. of Foreign Languages, 1975–77; Translation Service, UN Secretariat, NY, 1978–82; joined Min. of Foreign Affairs, Belarus, 1983; Press Dept and Dept of Internat. Orgns, 1983–91; Asst to Minister for Foreign Affairs, 1991–92; Dir, Dept of Bilateral Co-operation, 1992–93; Chargé d'Affaires, 1993–94, Counsellor Minister, 1994–95, Lithuania; Ambassador of the Republic of Belarus to the UK and to the Republic of Ireland, 1995–2000; Dir, Dept of Bilateral Relations with CIS Countries, Min of For. Affairs, 2000–01. *Publications:* numerous translations of works of English and Urdu writers into Belarusian; articles in Belarusian jls. *Recreation:* antique map collecting. *Address:* Ministry of Foreign Affairs, ul. Lenina 19, Minsk, Belarus.

SHEA, Michael Sinclair MacAuslan, CVO 1987 (LVO 1985); DL; PhD; author and broadcaster; *b* 10 May 1938; *s* of late James Michael Shea and Mary Dalrymple Davidson MacAuslan, North Berwick; *m* 1968, Mona Grec Stensen, Oslo; two *d*. *Educ:* Gordonstoun Sch.; Edinburgh Univ. (MA, PhD Econs). FO, 1963; Inst. of African Studies, Accra, Ghana, 1963; FO, 1964; Third, later Second Sec., CRO, 1965; Second, later First Sec. (Econ.), Bonn, 1966; seconded to Cabinet Office, 1969; FO, 1971; Head of Chancery, Bucharest, 1973; Dep. Dir Gen., Brit. Inf. Services, New York, 1976; Press Sec. to the Queen, 1978–87. Dir of Public Affairs, Hanson PLC, 1987–92; Chairman: Connoisseurs Scotland, 1992–98; Nordic UK Ltd, 1999–; non-executive Director: Caledonian Newspaper Publishing, 1993–96; P & A Gp, 1989–; Murray International Trust, 1992–. Scottish Mem., ITC, 1996–. Vis. Prof., Strathclyde Univ. Grad. Business Sch., 1991–99. Trustee, Nat. Galls of Scotland, 1992–99; Chm., Royal Lyceum Theatre Co., 1998–. Gov., Gordonstoun Sch., 1988–99. Vice-Chm., Foundn for Skin Res., 1993–. DL Edinburgh, 1996. *Publications:* Britain's Offshore Islands, 1981; Maritime England, 1981; Tomorrow's Men, 1982; Influence: how to make the system work for you, 1988; Leadership Rules, 1990; Personal Impact: the art of good communication, 1993; Spin Doctor, 1995; To Lie Abroad, 1996; The British Ambassador, 1996; State of the Nation, 1997; Berlin Embassy, 1998; The Primacy Effect, 1998; Spin off, 2000; (as Michael Sinclair): Sonntag, 1971; Folio Forty-One, 1972; The Dollar Covenant, 1974; A Long Time Sleeping, 1976; The Master Players, 1978; (with David Frost): The Mid-Atlantic Companion, 1986; The Rich Tide, 1986. *Recreations:* writing, sailing. *Address:* 1A Ramsay Garden, Edinburgh EH1 2NA. *Club:* Garrick.

SHEARER, Rt Hon. Hugh Lawson, OJ 1990; PC 1969; President, Bustamante Industrial Trade Union, Jamaica, since 1977; *b* 18 May 1923; *m* 1998, Dr Denise Eldemire. *Educ:* St Simons Coll., Jamaica. Journalist on weekly newspaper, Jamaica Worker, 1941–44, subseq. Editor. Apptd Asst Gen. Sec., Bustamante Industrial TU, 1947, Island Supervisor, 1953–67, Vice-Pres., 1960–79 (on leave of absence, 1967–72). Mem. Kingston and St Andrew Corp. Council, 1947; MHR for West Kingston, 1955–59; MLC, later Senator, 1962–67; Leader of Govt Business in Senate, 1962–67; MP SE Clarendon, 1967–93; Prime Minister of Jamaica, 1967–72; Minister of Defence and of External Affairs, 1967–72; Leader of the Opposition, 1972–74; Dep. Prime Minister, and Minister of For. Affairs and For. Trade, 1980–89; Leader, Jamaica Labour Party, 1967–74. Chm., Jt Trade Unions Res. Develt Centre, 1992; Pres., Jamaica Confedn of Trade Unions, 1994. Patron, Nat. Council of Senior Citizens, 1997–. Hon. Dr of Laws: Howard Univ., Washington, 1968; Univ. of WI, Jamaica, 1994. *Address:* Bustamante Industrial Trade Union, 98–100 Duke Street, Kingston, Jamaica.

SHEARER, Janet Sutherland; *see* Avonside, Lady.

SHEARER, Magnus MacDonald; JP; Lord-Lieutenant of Shetland, 1982–94; Managing Director, J. & M. Shearer Ltd (Est. 1919), 1960–85; *b* 27 Feb. 1924; *s* of late Lt-Col Magnus Shearer, OBE, TD, JP, and Flora MacDonald Stephen; *m* 1949, Martha Nicolson Henderson, *d* of late Captain John Henderson, DSM, and late Martha Nicolson; one *s*. *Educ:* Anderson Educational Institute, Shetland; George Watson's Coll., Edinburgh. Served RN in Atlantic, Mediterranean and Far East, 1942–46. 2nd Lieut, RA (TA), 1949; Captain, TARO, 1959. Hon. Consul: for Sweden in Shetland and Orkney, 1958–94; for Federal Republic of Germany in Shetland, 1972–87. Mem., Lerwick Harbour Trust, 1960–75 (Chm., 1967–72); Hon. Sec., RNLI Lerwick Stn, 1968–92; Mem. Lerwick Town Council, 1963–69; JP 1969, DL 1973, Shetland. Knight 1st Class, Royal Order of Vasa (Sweden), 1969; Officer 1st Class, Order of Merit (Federal Republic of Germany), 1983; Officer 1st Class, Order of Polar Star (Sweden), 1983. *Recreations:* reading, bird watching, ships. *Address:* 4 Queen's Place, Lerwick, Shetland ZE1 0BZ. *T:* (01595) 696612.

SHEARER, Moira, (Lady Kennedy); writer; *b* Dunfermline, Fife, 17 Jan. 1926; *d* of Harold King; *m* 1950, Sir Ludovic Kennedy, *qv*; one *s* three *d*. *Educ:* Dunfermline High School; Ndola, N Rhodesia; Bearsden Acad., Scotland. Professional training: Mayfair Sch.; Nicolas Legat Studio. Début with International Ballet, 1941; joined Sadler's Wells Ballet, 1942, during following ten years danced all major classic roles and full repertoire of revivals and new ballets; first ballerina rôle in Sleeping Beauty, Royal Opera House, Covent Gdn, 1946; created rôle of Cinderella, 1948; Carmen, with Roland Petit, Théâtre Marigny, 1950; George Balanchine's Ballet Imperial, Covent Garden, 1950; Titania in Old Vic production of A Midsummer Night's Dream (Edin. Festival, 1954, and tour of US and Canada); American tours with Sadler's Wells Ballet, 1949, 1950–51. Toured as Sally Bowles in I am a Camera, 1955; joined Bristol Old Vic, 1955; Major Barbara, Old Vic, 1956; Man of Distinction, Edin. Fest., 1957; Madame Ranevskaya in The Cherry Orchard, Royal Lyceum, Edin., 1977; Judith Bliss in Hay Fever, Royal Lyceum, 1978; Elizabeth Lowry, in A Simple Man (Gillian Lynne's ballet for L. S. Lowry's centenary), BBC TV, 1987; Juliana Bordereau in The Aspern Papers, Citizens Th., Glasgow, 1994. Recorded: Thomas Hardy's Tess of the D'Urbervilles, 1977; Muriel Spark's The Ballad of Peckham Rye, BBC Radio 4, 1982; Dame Ninette de Valois' short stories, Acad. of Sound and Vision, 1990. Member: Scottish Arts Council, 1971–73; BBC Gen. Adv. Council, 1970–77; Dir, Border TV, 1977–82. Toured US, lecturing on history of ballet and Sergei Diaghilev, 1973; regular lecturing in England and Wales. Lectured and gave recitals on three world cruises, Queen Elizabeth II. Poetry and prose recitals, Edinburgh Festivals, 1974 and 1975; now in regular performance with Ludovic Kennedy, and harpist Gillian Tingay. *Films:* Ballerina in The Red Shoes (première, 1948); Tales of Hoffmann, 1950; Story of Three Loves, 1952; The Man Who Loved Redheads, 1954; Peeping Tom, 1960; Black Tights, 1961. Regular book reviewer for Daily and Sunday Telegraphs. *Publications:* Balletmaster: a dancer's view of George Balanchine, 1986 (USA 1987); Ellen Terry (biog.), 1998.

SHEARING, George Albert, OBE 1996; jazz pianist and composer; *b* 13 Aug. 1919; *s* of James Philip Shearing and Ellen Amelia Shearing (*née* Brightman); *m* 1st, 1941, Beatrice Bayes (marr. diss.); one *d*; 2nd, Eleanor Geffert. *Educ:* Linden Lodge Sch. for the Blind, London. Founded and performed with George Shearing Quintet, 1949–78; has also led other jazz ensembles. Composed Lullaby of Birdland, 1952, and many other popular songs. Member of Board: Guide Dogs for the Blind; Hadley Sch. for the Blind; Nat. Braille Press. Has made many recordings, 1939–. Hon. DMus: Westminster Coll., Salt Lake City, 1975; Hamilton Coll., NY, 1994. Golden Plate Award, American Acad. of Achievement, 1968. *Address:* c/o Joan Shulman, 103 Avenue Road, Suite 301, Toronto, Ont M5R 2GR, Canada.

SHEARLOCK, Very Rev. David John; Dean and Rector of St Mary's Cathedral, Truro, 1982–97, now Dean Emeritus; *b* 1 July 1932; *s* of Arthur John Shearlock and Honora Frances Hawkins; *m* 1959, Jean Margaret Marr; one *s* one *d*. *Educ:* Univ. of Birmingham (BA); Westcott House, Cambridge. Assistant Curate: Guisborough, Yorks, 1957–60; Christchurch Priory, Hants, 1960–64; Vicar: Kingsclere, 1964–71; Romsey Abbey, 1971–82; Diocesan Director of Ordinands (Winchester), 1977–82; Hon. Canon of Winchester, 1978–82. FRSA 1991; FRGS 1992; ARSCM 1998. *Publications:* The Practice of Preaching, 1990; When Words Fail: God and the world of beauty, 1996. *Address:* 3 The Tanyard, Shadrack Street, Beaminster, Dorset DT8 3BG. *T:* (01308) 863170.

SHEARMAN, Rt Rev. Donald Norman, OBE 1978; *b* 6 Feb. 1926; *s* of late S. F. Shearman, Sydney; *m* 1952, Stuart Fay, *d* of late Chap. F. H. Bashford; three *s* three *d*. *Educ:* Fort St and Orange High Schools; St John's Theological College, Morpeth, NSW. Served War of 1939–45: air crew, 1944–46. Theological College, 1948–50. Deacon, 1950; Priest, 1951. Curate: of Dubbo, 1950–52; of Forbes, and Warden of St John's Hostel, 1953–56; Rector of Coonabarabran, 1957–59; Director of Promotion and Adult Christian Education 1959–62; Canon, All Saints Cathedral, Bathurst, 1962; Archdeacon of Mildura and Rector of St. Margaret's, 1963; Bishop of Rockhampton, 1963–71; Chairman, Australian Board of Missions, Sydney, 1971–73; Bishop of Grafton, 1973–85; Asst Bishop, dio. of Brisbane, 1989–91. ChStJ 1989. *Address:* 123 Turner Street, Scarborough, Qld 4020, Australia.

SHEARMAN, Prof. John Kinder Gowran, PhD; FBA 1976; Adams University Professor, Harvard University, since 1994; *b* 24 June 1931; *s* of late Brig. C. E. G. Shearman; *m* 1957, Jane Dalrymple Smith; one *s* three *d*; *m* 1998, Kathryn Brush. *Educ:* St Edmund's, Hindhead; Felsted; Courtauld Inst., London Univ.; BA, PhD 1957. Lectr, Courtauld Inst., 1957–67; Research Fellow, Inst. for Advanced Study, Princeton, 1964; Reader, Courtauld Inst., 1967–74, Prof. of the History of Art, 1974–79 (Dep. Dir, 1974–78); Prof., Dept of Art and Archaeology, Princeton Univ., 1979–87 (Chm., 1979–85); Prof. of Fine Arts, Harvard Univ., 1987–94 (Chm. of Dept, 1990–93). Member: Accademia del Disegno, Florence, 1979; Amer. Acad. of Arts and Scis, 1993; Accademia di S Luca, Rome, 1995. Serena Medal, British Acad., 1979. *Publications:* Andrea del Sarto, 1965; Mannerism, 1967, 8th edn 1990; Raphael's Cartoons, 1972; Catalogue of the Early Italian Paintings in the Collection of HM the Queen, 1983; Funzione e Illusione, 1983; Only Connect …, 1992; contribs to British, French, German, American jls. *Recreations:* sailing, music. *Address:* 3 Clement Circle, Cambridge, MA 02138, USA. *Club:* Bembridge Sailing.

SHEARS, Philip Peter; QC 1996; a Recorder, since 1990; *b* 10 May 1947; *m* 1990, Sarah; two *s* one *d* by previous marriage. *Educ:* Leys Sch., Cambridge; Nottingham Univ. (LLB); St Edmund's Coll., Cambridge (LLB). Called to the Bar, Middle Temple, 1972; Mem., Midland and Oxford Circuit. *Recreations:* sailing, France. *Address:* 7 Bedford Row, WC1R 4BU. *T:* (020) 7242 3555. *Club:* Royal London Yacht.

SHEBBEARE, Thomas Andrew, (Tom), CVO 1996; Chief Executive, The Prince's Trust, since 1999 (Executive Director, The Prince's Trust and Secretary, The Royal Jubilee Trusts, 1988–99); *b* 25 Jan. 1952; *s* of late Robert Austin Shebbeare and of Frances Dare Graham; *m* 1976, Cynthia Jane Cottrell; one *s* one *d*. *Educ:* Malvern Coll.; Univ. of Exeter (BA Politics). World University Service (UK), 1973–75; Gen. Sec., British Youth Council, 1975–80; Administrator, Council of Europe, 1980–85; Exec. Dir, European Youth Foundn, 1985–88. Trustee: Inst. for Citizenship Studies, 1991–; Nations Trust (S Africa), 1995–; Director: Gifts in Kind UK; Skills Festival Co. Ltd. *Recreations:* family, cooking, food and drink. *Address:* (office) 18 Park Square East, NW1 4LH. *T:* (020) 7543 1234.

SHEDDEN, Alfred Charles; Chariman, Halladale Group plc, since 2001; *b* 30 June 1944; *s* of Alfred Henry Shedden and Jane Murray Shedden; *m* 1st, 1968, Rosalyn Terris; one *s*; 2nd, 1978, Irene McIntyre; one *d*. *Educ:* Aberdeen Univ. (MA, LLB). Mem., Law Soc. of Scotland. McGrigor Donald: apprentice, 1967; Partner, 1971; Managing Partner, 1985–92; Sen. Partner, 1993–2000. Non-executive Director: Standard Life Assurance Co., 1992–99; Scottish Financial Enterprise, 1988–99; Martin Currie Japan Investment Trust plc, 1996–; Scottish Metropolitan Property plc, 1998–2000; Burn Stewart Distillers plc, 2000–; Iomart Group plc, 2000–; Murray Internat. Trust plc. Mem., Scottish FEFC, 1999–. *Recreations:* Scottish art, football spectator. *Address:* 17 Beaumont Gate, Glasgow G12 9ED. *T:* (0141) 339 4979.

SHEDDEN, Rev. John, CBE 1998; Minister, Hawick Wilton with Teviothead, since 1998; *b* 23 June 1943; *s* of Robert Blair Arnott Shedden and Grace Roberts (*née* Henderson); *m* 1965, Jeannie Lillian Gilling; one *s* one *d*. *Educ:* Johnstone High Sch.; Univ. of St Andrews (BD Hons; Dip. in Pastoral and Social Studies). Asst Minister, Paisley Abbey, 1970–72; ordained 1971; Parish Minister, Thornhill, Dumfries, 1972–75; Social Welfare Officer, Salisbury, Rhodesia, 1975–76; Chaplain, RN, 1977–84; Minister, St Mark's, Moose Jaw, Sask., 1984–86; Chaplain, RAF, 1986–98; Principal Chaplain, Church of Scotland and Free Churches, RAF, 1994–98. QHC 1994–98. *Recreations:* hill-walking, D-I-Y, reading, radio. *Address:* Wilton Manse, Wilton Hill Terrace, Hawick TD9 8BE; 8 Millwell Park, Innerleithen, Peebles EH44 6JF; *e-mail:* reverend@stbprofessionals.com.

SHEEHAN, Albert Vincent; Sheriff of Tayside, Central and Fife, since 1983; *b* 23 Aug. 1936; *s* of Richard Greig Sheehan and May Moffat; *m* 1965, Edna Georgina Scott Hastings (*d* 2000); two *d*. *Educ:* Bo'ness Acad.; Edinburgh Univ. (MA 1957; LLB 1959). Admitted as Solicitor, 1959. 2nd Lieut, 1st Bn The Royal Scots (The Royal Regt), 1960; Captain, Directorate of Army Legal Services, 1961. Depute Procurator Fiscal, Hamilton, 1961–71; Sen. Depute Procurator Fiscal, Glasgow, 1971–74; Depute Crown Agent for Scotland, 1974–79; Asst Solicitor, Scottish Law Commn, 1979–81; Sheriff of Lothian and Borders, 1981–83. Leverhulme Fellow, 1971. *Publications:* Criminal Procedure in Scotland and France, 1975; Criminal Procedure, 1990. *Recreations:* naval history, travel, legal history. *Address:* Sheriff's Chambers, Sheriff Court House, Falkirk FK1 4AR.

SHEEHAN, Gen. John Joseph, USMC; Supreme Allied Commander, Atlantic and Commander-in-Chief, US Atlantic Command, 1994–97; *b* 23 Aug. 1940; *s* of John J. Sheehan and Ellen Sheehan; *m* Margaret M. Sullivan; one *s* three *d*. *Educ:* Boston Coll. (BA English 1962); Georgetown Univ. (MA Govt 1985). Joined USMC, 1960; various postings, incl. Vietnam; Amphibious Warfare Sch., 1969–70; Airborne Corps, 1970–71; 2nd Marine Div., 1971–73; Naval War Coll., 1974–75; HQ USMC, 1975–78; 1st Marine Air Wing, 1978–79; Nat. War Coll., 1979–80; 1st Marine Bde, 1980–83; Jt Staff, 1983–84; Office of Sec. of Defense, 1984–86; 2nd Marine Div., 1986–88; 4th Marine Exped. Bde, 1988–89; HQ USMC, 1989–91; US Naval Forces Central Comd, 1991; US Atlantic Comd, 1991–93; Jt Staff, 1993–94. Numerous gallantry and other Service awards. Grand Cross, Norwegian Order of Merit, 1996. *Publications:* contribs to Joint Forces Qly. *Recreations:* golf, tennis, gardening. *Clubs:* Military Order of the Carabao, Ancient and Honorable Artillery Company of Massachusetts.

SHEEHY, Rev. Jeremy Patrick, DPhil; Principal, St Stephen's House, Oxford, since 1996; *b* 31 Oct. 1956; *s* of Eric Sheehy and Noreen Patricia Sheehy. *Educ:* Trinity Sch. of John Whitgift; Bristol Grammar Sch.; King Edward's Sch., Birmingham; Magdalen Coll., Oxford (BA (Jurisprudence Cl. 1)); St Stephen's House, Oxford (BA (Theol. Cl. 1)); MA 1981, DPhil 1990, Oxon. Ordained deacon 1981; priest 1982; Assistant Curate: St Barnabas, Erdington, 1981–83; St Gregory, Small Heath, 1983–84; Dean of Divinity, Chaplain and Fellow, New Coll., Oxford, 1984–90; Vicar, St Margaret, Leytonstone, 1990–96; Priest in charge, St Andrew, Leytonstone, 1993–96. Chm., Oxford Partnership for Theol Educn and Trng, 1999–2001. Guardian, Shrine of Our Lady of Walsingham, 1997–. Gov., Quainton Hall Sch., Harrow, 1998–. *Recreations:* hill-walking, cooking. *Address:* St Stephen's House, Marston Street, Oxford OX4 1JX. *T:* (01865) 247874.

SHEEHY, Sir Patrick, Kt 1991; Chairman, B.A.T Industries, 1982–95; *b* 2 Sept. 1930; *s* of Sir John Francis Sheehy, CSI and Jean Newton Simpson; *m* 1964, Jill Patricia Tindall; one *s* one *d*. *Educ:* Australia; Ampleforth Coll., Yorks. Served Irish Guards, 1948–50; rank on leaving 2nd Lieut. Joined British-American Tobacco Co., 1950, first appt in Nigeria; Ghana, 1951; Reg. Sales Manager, Nigeria, 1953; Ethiopian Tobacco Monopoly, 1954; Marketing Dir, Jamaica, 1957; Barbados, 1961; Marketing Advr, London, 1962; Gen. Man., Holland, 1967; Mem., Gp Bd, 1970; Mem., Chm.'s Policy Cttee, and Chm., Tobacco Div. Bd, 1975; Dep. Chm., 1976–81, Vice-Chm., 1981–82, B.A.T Industries; Chm., British-American Tobacco Co., 1976–82. *Address:* 11 Eldon Road, W8 5PU. *T:* (020) 7937 6250.

SHEEN, Sir Barry (Cross), Kt 1978; a Judge of the High Court of Justice, Queen's Bench Division (Admiralty Court), 1978–93; *b* 31 Aug. 1918; 2nd *s* of late Ronald Sheen, FCA; *m* 1st, 1946, Diane (*d* 1986), *d* of late C. L. Donne, MD; three *s*; 2nd, 1988, Helen Ursula, *widow* of Philip Spink; two step *d*. *Educ:* Haileybury College, Hill School (USA); Trinity Hall, Cambridge (MA). Served in RNVR, 1939–46; Commanding Officer, HMS Kilkenzie (corvette), 1943–45. Called to Bar, Middle Temple, 1947, Master of the Bench, 1971, Reader, 1990; Member Bar Council, 1959–63; QC 1966. Junior Counsel to Admiralty, 1961–66; a Recorder of the Crown Court, 1972–78. On Panel of Wreck Comrs (Eng.) under Merchant Shipping Acts, 1966–78; Mem., Panel of Lloyd's Arbitrators in Salvage Cases, 1966–78, Appeal Arbitrator, 1977–78. Presided over Inquiry into Zeebrugge ferry disaster, 1987; Vice-Pres., British Maritime Law Assoc., 1979–93. Life Governor, Haileybury (Pres., Haileybury Soc., 1982); Hon. Mem., Assoc. of Average Adjusters, 1979– (Chm., 1986). Liveryman, Shipwrights' Co. Younger Brother, Trinity House, 1993–. Hon. FNI 1993. *Recreations:* golf, bowls, travel, carpentry. *Address:* 107 Rivermead Court, Ranelagh Gardens, SW6 3SB. *T:* (020) 7731 7275. *Clubs:* Hurlingham, Pilgrims; Royal Wimbledon Golf.

SHEERMAN, Barry John; MP (Lab) Huddersfield, since 1983 (Huddersfield East, 1979–83); *b* 17 Aug. 1940; *s* of late Albert William Sheerman and Florence Sheerman (*née* Pike); *m* 1965 Pamela Elizabeth (*née* Brenchley); one *s* three *d*. *Educ:* Hampton Grammar Sch.; LSE. BSc (Economics) Hons; MSc Hons. Lectr, Univ. Coll. of Swansea, 1966–79. An opposition front bench spokesman on: employment, dealing with training, small business and tourism, 1983–88; home affairs, dealing with police, prisons, crime prevention, drugs, civil defence and fire service, 1988–92; disabled people's rights, 1992–94. Mem., Public Accounts Cttee, 1981–83; Co-Chm., Educn and Employment Select Cttee, 1999– (Chm., Sub-Cttee on Educn, 1999–); Chairman: Parly Adv. Council on Transport Safety, 1981–; Labour Campaign for Criminal Justice, 1989–92; Co-Chm., Parly Manufg Industry Gp, 1993–; Vice-Chm., Parly Univ. Gp, 1994–. Chm. Parly Gps for Urban Mines, 1995–, and for Manufg, Design and Innovation, 1999–; Chm., Cross-Party Adv. Gp on Preparation for EMU, 1998–. Mem., Sec. of State for Trade and Industry's Manufg Task Force, 1999–. Chairman: World Bank Business Partnerships for Develt Cttee, 2001–; Global Road Safety Partnership, 2001–. FRSA; FRGS 1989. *Publications:* (jtly) Harold Laski: a life on the Left, 1993; pamphlets on education and training, tourism, and justice. *Address:* House of Commons, SW1A 0AA. *Club:* Royal Commonwealth Society.

SHEFFIELD, 8th Baron; *see under* Stanley of Alderley, 8th Baron;

SHEFFIELD, Bishop of, since 1997; **Rt Rev. John Nicholls;** *b* 16 July 1943; *s* of late James William and Nellie Nicholls; *m* 1969, Judith Dagnall; two *s* two *d*. *Educ:* Bacup and Rawtenstall Grammar School; King's Coll., London (AKC); St Boniface Coll., Warminster. Curate, St Clement with St Cyprian, Salford, 1967–69; Curate, 1969–72, Vicar 1972–78, All Saints and Martyrs, Langley, Manchester; Dir of Pastoral Studies, Coll. of the Resurrection, Mirfield, 1978–83; Canon Residentiary of Manchester Cathedral, 1983–90; Suffragan Bishop of Lancaster, 1990–97. Hon. Fellow, Univ. of Central Lancashire, 1997. *Publication:* (jtly) A Faith Worth Sharing? A Church Worth Joining?, 1995. *Recreations:* music (listening and singing), reading, films. *Address:* Bishopscroft, Snaithing Lane, Sheffield, S Yorks S10 3LG. *Club:* Royal Over-Seas League.

SHEFFIELD, Dean of; *see* Sadgrove, Very Rev. Michael.

SHEFFIELD, Archdeacon of; *see* Blackburn, Ven. R. F.

SHEFFIELD, Graham Edward; Artistic Director, Barbican Centre, since 1995; *b* 12 Feb. 1952; *s* of Gordon and Jacqueline Sheffield; *m* 1979, Ann Roberta Morton; two *s*. *Educ:* Tonbridge Sch.; Edinburgh Univ. (BMus Hons 1975). Producer, then Sen. Producer, Music Dept, BBC Radio 3, 1976–90; Music Dir, South Bank Centre, 1990–95. Mem. Council, Royal Philharmonic Soc., 1999–; Sec., Internat. Soc. for Performing Arts, 2000–. *Recreations:* piano, golf, ski-ing, travel, fine wine. *Address:* 42 Woodland Gardens, N10 3UA. *T:* (020) 8883 0213. *Club:* MCC.

SHEFFIELD, (John) Julian (Lionel George); DL; Deputy Chairman, Guardian Royal Exchange, 1988–99 (Director, 1981–99); Chairman, Portals Group (formerly Portals Holdings PLC), 1979–95 (Director, 1969–95); *b* 28 Aug. 1938; *s* of John Vincent Sheffield, *qv*; *m* 1961, Carolyn Alexander Abel Smith; three *s* one *d*. *Educ:* Eton Coll.; Christ's Coll., Cambridge. Joined Portals Ltd, 1962. Director: Norcros, 1974–96 (Chm., 1989–93); Tex Hldgs, 1985–93; Newbury Racecourse, 1988–; Inspec, 1994–99. Mem., Economic and Commercial Cttee, EEF, 1974–90. Member: Council, St John's Sch., Leatherhead, 1966–96; Bd of Govs, N Foreland Lodge, 1987–97 (Chm., 1992–97). Trustee: Henry Smith's Charity, 1971– (Chm., 1997–); Winchester Cathedral Trust, 1984–; Hosp. of St Cross and Almshouse of Noble Poverty, 1996–. High Sheriff, 1998, DL 2001, Hants. *Recreations:* outdoor sports, collecting. *Address:* Spring Pond, Laverstoke Lane, Whitchurch, Hants RG28 7PD. *T:* (01256) 895130. *Clubs:* White's, MCC.

SHEFFIELD, John Vincent, CBE 1984; Chairman, Norcros Ltd, 1956–81; *b* 11 Nov. 1913; *y s* of Sir Berkeley Sheffield, 6th Bt; *m* 1st, 1936, Anne (*d* 1969), *d* of Sir Lionel Faudel-Phillips, 3rd Bt; one *s* three *d*; 2nd, 1971, Mrs France Crosthwaite, *d* of Brig.-Gen. Goland Clarke, CMG, DSO. *Educ:* Eton; Magdalene College, Cambridge (MA). Private Secretary to Minister of Works, 1943–44; Chairman: Portals Ltd, 1968–78; Atlantic Assets Trust Ltd, 1972–83. Chm., BEC, 1980–83; Vice-Chm., BTEC, 1983. High Sheriff of Lincolnshire, 1944–45. *Address:* New Barn House, Laverstoke, Whitchurch, Hants RG28 7PF. *T:* (01256) 893187. *Club:* White's.

See also J. J. L. G. Sheffield.

SHEFFIELD, Sir Reginald (Adrian Berkeley), 8th Bt *cr* 1755; DL; Director, Normanby Estate Co. Ltd, since 1983, and other companies; *b* 9 May 1946; *s* of Edmund Charles Reginald Sheffield, JP, DL (*d* 1977) and Nancie Miriel Denise (*d* 1997), *d* of Edward Roland Soames; *S* uncle, 1977; *m* 1st, 1969, Annabel Lucy Veronica (marr. diss.), *d* of late T. A. Jones; two *d*; 2nd, 1977, Victoria Penelope, *d* of late R. C. Walker, DFC; one *s* two *d*. *Educ:* Eton. Member of Stock Exchange, 1973–75. Vice-Chm., S Humberside Business Advice Centre Ltd, 1984–. Pres., S Humberside CPRE, 1985–96; Member: Cttee, Lincs Br., CLA, 1987–99; Taxation Cttee, CLA, 1989–95; Central Transport Consultative Cttee (NE Reg.), 1988–94; Rail Users Consultative Cttee for NE England, 1994–97. Mem. (C) for Ermine Ward, Humberside County Council, 1985–93. Pres., Scunthorpe United Football Club, 1982–94. Pres., Scunthorpe and Dist, Victim Support Scheme, 1989–. DL Humberside, now Lincs, 1985. *Heir: s* Robert Charles Berkeley Sheffield, *b* 1 Sept. 1984. *Address:* Estate Office, Normanby, Scunthorpe, N Lincs DN15 9HS. *T:* (01724) 720618; *e-mail:* norestate@fsbdial.co.uk. *Clubs:* White's, Pratt's; Lincolnshire (Sleaford).

SHEFTON, Prof. Brian Benjamin, FBA 1985; FSA 1980; Professor of Greek Art and Archaeology, University of Newcastle upon Tyne, 1979–84, now Emeritus; *b* 11 Aug. 1919; *yr s* of late Prof. I. Scheftelowitz (Cologne, Germany, until 1933 and Oxford) and Frieda (*née* Kohn); *m* 1960, Jutta Ebel of Alingsås, Sweden; one *d*. *Educ:* Apostelngymnasium, Cologne; St Lawrence Coll., Ramsgate; Magdalen Coll. Sch., Oxford; Oriel Coll., Oxford (Open Scholar, 1938; Hon. Mods Greek and Latin Lit. 1940; Lit Hum 1947, Class I). War service, HM Forces (change of name), 1940–45. Sch. Student, British Sch. at Athens, 1947; Derby Scholar, Oxford, 1948; Bishop Fraser Scholar, Oriel Coll., Oxford, 1949, in Aegean to 1950; excavated at Old Smyrna; Lectr in Classics, University Coll., Exeter, 1950–55; Lectr in Greek Archaeology and Ancient History, 1955, Sen. Lectr, 1960, Reader, 1974–79, King's Coll., Univ. of Durham (later Univ. of Newcastle upon Tyne). Established and directed Univ.'s Greek Museum (renamed Shefton Mus. of Greek Art and Archaeology, 1994), 1956–84, Hon. Advr, 1985–; Trustee, Oriental Mus., Durham Univ., 1989–93. Vis. Res. Fellow, Merton Coll., Oxford, 1969; British Acad. Vis. Scholar to Albania, 1973; Munro Lectr, Edinburgh Univ., 1974; British Acad. European Exchange Fellow, Marburg Univ., 1975; German Academic Exchange Fellow, Marburg and Cologne, 1976; Leverhulme Res. Fellow, 1977; Webster Meml Lectr, Stanford Univ., 1981; Vis. Prof. of Classical Archaeology, Vienna Univ. (winter), 1981–82; British Council Vis. Scholar to Soviet Union, 1982, to Spain, 1985; Jackson Knight Meml Lectr, Exeter Univ., 1983; Leverhulme Emeritus Fellow, 1984–86; Balsdon Sen. Fellow, British Sch. at Rome, 1985; Vis. Scholar, J. Paul Getty Museum, 1987; British Academy Exchange Fellow, Jerusalem, 1993. Mem., German Archaeological Inst., 1961; Foreign Mem., Inst. of Etruscan and Italic Studies, Florence, 1990. Hon. Dr.phil Cologne, 1989. Aylwin Cotton Award, 1977; Kenyon Medal, British Acad., 1999. *Publications:* History of Greek Vase Painting (with P. Arias and M. Hirmer), 1962; Die rhodischen Bronzekannen, 1979; chapters in: Perachora II, 1962; Phoenizier im Westen, 1982; The Eye of Greece, 1982; Das Kleinaspergle, 1988; Cyprus and the East Mediterranean in the Iron Age, 1989; The Rogozen Treasure, 1989; Kotinos, 1992; Cultural Transformations and Interactions in Eastern Europe, 1993; The Archaeology of Greek Colonization, 1994; Social Complexity and the Development of Towns in Iberia, 1995; Italy in Europe: economic relations 700BC–AD50, 1995; Sur les traces des Argonautes, 1996; Céramique et peinture grecques: modes d'emploi, 1999; I Piceni, 1999; Periplous, 2000; Heuneburg XI, 2000; articles in British and foreign periodicals. *Recreations:* music, travel. *Address:* 24 Holly Avenue, Jesmond, Newcastle upon Tyne NE2 2PY. *T:* (0191) 281 4184.

SHEGOG, Rev. Preb. Eric Marshall; Communications Adviser, Diocese of Europe, since 2000; *b* 23 July 1937; *s* of George Marshall Shegog and Helen (*née* Whitefoot); *m* 1961, Anne Thomas; two *s* one *d*. *Educ:* Leigh Grammar School; College of St Mark and St John; Whitelands College; Lichfield Theol College; City Univ. (MA). CertEd London; DipTh London. Asst Master, Holy Trinity Primary Sch., Wimbledon, 1960–64; Asst Curate, All Saints, Benhilton, 1965–68; Asst Youth Adviser, Dio. of Southwark, 1968–70; Vicar, St Michael and All Angels, Abbey Wood, 1970–75; Town Centre Chaplain, Sunderland, 1976–83; Head of Religious Broadcasting, IBA, 1984–90; Dir of Communications, C of E, 1990–97; Dir of Communications, 1997–2000 and Acting Gen. Sec., 1999–2000, Dio. of London; Prebendary, St Paul's Cathedral, 1997–2000, now Emeritus. Chairman: BBC Adv. Cttee for NE, 1980–83; Mgt Cttee, Churches TV Centre, 1997–; Dir, World Assoc. for Christian Communication, 1990–93 (Vice-Chm., Eur. Region, 1990–93). Chm., Age Concern Sunderland, 1980–83. FRSA 1992. *Publications:* (jtly) Religious Television: controversies and conclusions, 1990; (jtly) Religious Broadcasting in the 90s, 1991; (contrib.) Elvy, Opportunities and Limitations in Religious Broadcasting, 1991; (contrib.) The Communication of Values, 1993. *Recreations:* gardening, opera, walking. *Address:* 9 Colbron Close, Ashwell, Herts SG7 5TH. *T:* (01462) 743251.

SHEHADIE, Sir Nicholas (Michael), AC 1990; Kt 1976; OBE 1971; Managing Director, Nicholas Shehadie Pty Ltd, since 1959; *b* 15 Nov. 1926; *s* of Michael and Hannah Shehadie; *m* 1957, Dr Marie Roslyn Bashir, AO; one *s* two *d*. *Educ:* Sydney. Elected Alderman, City of Sydney, Dec. 1962; Dep. Lord Mayor, Sept. 1969–73; Lord Mayor of Sydney, Sept. 1973–75. Chm., Special Broadcasting Services, to 2000. Rugby Union career: Captained NSW and Australia; played 30 Internationals and 6 overseas tours; Mem., Barbarians'. Chm., Sydney Cricket Ground, 1990–. *Recreations:* Rugby, surfing, horse racing, bowls. *Address:* 118 Old Canterbury Road, Lewisham, Sydney, NSW 2049, Australia. *Clubs:* Randwick Rugby, Tattersall's (Sydney).

SHEIKHOLESLAMI, Prof. Ali Reza, PhD; Soudavar Professor of Persian Studies, Oxford University, since 1990; Fellow, Wadham College, Oxford, since 1990; *b* 21 July 1941; *s* of Ali Soltani Sheikholeslami and Shah-Zadeh Mansouri; *m* 1996, Scheherezade Vigeh. *Educ:* Columbia Univ., NY (BA); Northwestern Univ. (MA); UCLA (PhD). Asst Prof. of Pol Sci., Univ. of Washington, Seattle, 1975–85; Res. Fellow, Harvard Univ., 1987–88; Iranian Fellow, St Antony's Coll., Oxford, 1988–90. *Publications:* Political Economy of Saudi Arabia, 1984; The Structure of Central Authority in Qajar Iran 1876–1896, 1996; articles on 19th and 20th Century Persia in jls and book chapters. *Recreations:* reading, travelling. *Address:* Wadham College, Oxford OX1 3PN. *T:* (01865) 278200, 278223.

SHEIL, Brenda Margaret Hale, (Lady Sheil); barrister; Member, Radio Authority, 1994–99; *o d* of late Rev. Forde Patterson and Elizabeth Bell Patterson (*née* Irwin); *m* 1979, Sir John (Joseph) Sheil, *qv*; one *s*. *Educ:* Armagh Girls' High Sch.; Trinity Coll., Dublin (BA (Mod) Legal Science; LLB 1966; MA 1990). Called to the Bar, NI, 1976, Ireland, 1995; Government Service (Legal): Min. of Home Affairs, NI, 1967–72; NI Office, 1972–79; Head, Legal Div., NI Court Service, Lord Chancellor's Dept, 1979–80. Chm. (part time), Industrial Tribunals, 1984–87. Member: Secretariat of Anglo-Irish Law Commn, 1973–74; Indep. Commn for Police Complaints, 1988–90. Mem., Gen. Consumer Council, NI, 1985–88. Mem., Standing Cttee, Gen. Synod of Church of Ireland, 1988– (Lay Hon. Sec., 1999–); Lay Rep., Ch of Ireland, ACC, 1994–2000. Governor, Royal Sch., Armagh, 1992–. *Recreations:* horses (Hon. Sec., Tynan and Armagh Hunt, 1973–), gardening, travel, golf. *Address:* Bar Library, Royal Courts of Justice, Belfast BT1 3JF.

SHEIL, Hon. Sir John (Joseph), Kt 1989; **Hon. Mr Justice Sheil;** a Judge of the High Court of Northern Ireland, since 1989; *b* 19 June 1938; *yr* twin *s* of late Hon. Mr Justice (Charles Leo) Sheil and Elizabeth Josephine Sheil (*née* Cassidy); *m* 1979, Brenda Margaret Hale Patterson (*see* B. M. H. Sheil); one *s*. *Educ:* Clongowes Wood Coll.; Queen's Univ. Belfast (LLB); Trinity Coll., Dublin (MA). Called to Bar: NI, 1964 (Bencher 1988), QC 1975; Gray's Inn, 1974 (Hon. Bencher, 1996); Ireland, 1976. Chairman: Mental Health Rev. Tribunal, 1985–87; Fair Employment Appeals Bd, 1986–89; Mem., Standing Adv. Commn on Human Rights, 1981–83. Senator, QUB, 1987–99. *Recreations:* golf, travel. *Address:* Royal Courts of Justice, Belfast BT1 3JY.

SHEINWALD, Sir Nigel (Elton), KCMG 2001 (CMG 1999); HM Diplomatic Service; Ambassador and UK Permanent Representative to the European Union, Brussels, since 2000; *b* 26 June 1953; *s* of Leonard and Joyce Sheinwald; *m* 1980, Dr Julia Dunne; three *s*. *Educ:* Harrow Co. Sch. for Boys; Balliol Coll., Oxford (BA Classics 1976). Joined HM Diplomatic Service, 1976; Japan Desk, FCO, 1976–77; Russian lang. trng, 1977–78; Third, later Second Sec., Moscow, 1978–79; Rhodesia/Zimbabwe Dept, FCO, 1979–81; E European and Soviet Dept, FCO, 1981–83; First Sec., Washington, 1983–87; Deputy Head: Policy Planning Staff, FCO, 1987–89; European Community Dept (Internal), FCO, 1989–92; Counsellor and Hd of Chancery, UK Perm. Rep. to EU, Brussels, 1993–95; Hd of News Dept, FCO, 1995–98; Dir, EU, FCO, 1998–2000. *Recreations:* reading, music. *Address:* c/o Foreign and Commonwealth Office, King Charles Street, SW1A 2AH. *T:* (020) 7270 3098.

SHELDON, family name of **Baron Sheldon.**

SHELDON, Baron *cr* 2001 (Life Peer), of Ashton-under-Lyne in the County of Greater Manchester; **Robert Edward Sheldon;** *b* 13 Sept. 1923; *m* 1st, 1945, Eileen Shamash (*d* 1969); one *s* one *d*; 2nd 1971, Mary Shield. *Educ:* Elementary and Grammar Schools; Engineering Apprenticeship; Technical Colleges in Stockport, Burnley and Salford; WhSch 1944. Engineering diplomas; external graduate, London University. Contested (Lab) Withington, Manchester, 1959; MP (Lab) Ashton-under-Lyne, 1964–2001. Chm., Labour Parly Economic Affairs and Finance Group, 1967–68; Opposition front bench spokesman on Civil Service and Machinery of Govt, also on Treasury matters, 1970–74; Minister of State, CSD, March-Oct. 1974; Minister of State, HM Treasury, Oct. 1974–June 1975; Financial Sec. to the Treasury, 1975–79; Opposition front bench spokesman on Treasury matters, 1981–83; Chairman: Public Accounts Cttee, 1983–97 (Mem., 1965–70, 1975–79); Standards and Privileges Cttee, 1997–2001; Liaison Cttee, 1997–2001; Public Accounts Commn, 1997–2001; Dep. Chm., All Party Arts and Heritage Gp, 1997–2001; Member: Public Expenditure Cttee (Chm. Gen. Sub-Cttee), 1972–74; Select Cttee on Treasury and Civil Service, 1979–81 (Chm., Sub-Cttee); Fulton Cttee on the Civil Service, 1966–68. Chm., NW Gp of Labour MPs, 1970–74. *Address:* 2 Ryder Street, SW1Y 6QB.

SHELDON, Bernard, CB 1981; *b* 14 June 1924; *s* of Gerald Walter Sheldon and Doris Sheldon (*née* Hopkins); *m* 1951, Dorothy Kirkland (*d* 1999); one *s* two *d*. *Educ:* Hurstpierpoint Coll. (Scholar). War service, N Atlantic and Pacific, 1943–46 (Lieut RNVR). Called to the Bar, Middle Temple, 1949. Joined Colonial Legal Service, 1951; Federal Counsel and Dep. Public Prosecutor, Fedn of Malaya, 1951–59; Legal Adviser: Pahang, 1953; Kedah and Perlis, 1955–59; War Office, 1959–67; MoD, 1967–87, retired 1987. Badlishah Decoration for Loyalty, Kedah, 1959. *Recreation:* chess. *Address:* c/o Lloyds TSB, 64 High Street, Epsom, Surrey KT19 8AT.

SHELDON, Hon. Sir Gervase; *see* Sheldon, Hon. Sir J. G. K.

SHELDON, Harold; Chairman, Batley Sports Development Council, 1965–2000; Vice Chairman, Kirklees District Sports Council, 1974–2000; *b* 22 June 1918; *s* of Charles Edwin Sheldon and Lily Sheldon (*née* Taylor); *m* 1941, Bessie Sheldon (*née* Barratt); two *s* one *d*. HM Forces, 1939–45 (Sgt; wounded D Day landings). Local Government: elected Batley Borough Council, 1953; Mayor of Batley, 1962–63; W Yorkshire County Council, 1973–86 (Chm., 1976–77), re-elected 1977, 1981; Mem., Kirklees MDC, 1987–98 (Mayor, 1994–95). Mem., W Yorks Police Authy, 1989–95 (Vice-Chm., 1992–95). Mem., Yorks and Humberside Council for Sport and Recreation, 1977–86 and 1991–98; President: Batley Boys' Club (Founder Mem.), 1975–2000; Batley CAB, 1987–92; Batley Sports for the Disabled Assoc., 1987–96. *Address:* 5 Norfolk Avenue, Carlton Grange, Batley, West Yorkshire WF17 7AR. *T:* (01924) 504019.

SHELDON, John Denby, OBE 2000; Joint General Secretary, Public and Commercial Services (formerly Public Services, Tax and Commerce) Union, 1996–2000; *b* 31 Jan. 1941; *s* of Frank and Doreen Sheldon; *m* 1976; two *s*. *Educ:* Wingate County Primary and West Leeds High School. Oxford Univ. Diploma in Social Studies. Post Office Engineer, 1957–68; student, Ruskin Coll., 1968–70; full time Trade Union Official, Instn of Professional Civil Servants, 1970–72; Civil Service Union: National Officer, 1972–78; Deputy Gen. Sec., 1978–82; Gen. Sec., 1982–88; Dep. Gen. Sec., 1988–93, Gen. Sec., 1993–96, Nat. Union of Civil and Public Servants. *Recreations:* cricket; Rugby League as spectator; family. *Address:* 2 Wincroft Road, Reading, Berks RG4 7HH. *T:* (0118) 947 7810.

SHELDON, Sir (John) Gervase (Kensington), Kt 1978; a Judge of the High Court, Family Division, 1978–88; an Additional Judge of the High Court, 1988–93; *b* 4 Oct. 1913; *s* of John Henry Sheldon, MD, DPH, and Eleanor Gladys Sheldon, MB, BS; *m* 1st, 1940, Patricia Mary Mardon; one *s*; 2nd, 1960, Janet Marguerite Seager; two *s* one *d*. *Educ:* Winchester Coll.; Trinity Coll., Cambridge (MA; 1st Cl. Hons Law). Barrister-at-Law, called Lincoln's Inn, 1939 (Cert. of Honour, Cholmeley Schol.), Bencher, 1978. Served RA (TA), 1939–45 (despatches twice): Egypt, N Africa, Italy; Major, RA, 1943. A Circuit Judge (formerly a County Court Judge), 1968–78; Presiding Judge, Western Circuit, 1980–84. *Recreation:* family and home. *Address:* Little Hopton, 7 Beech Avenue, Lower Bourne, Farnham, Surrey GU10 3JZ. *T:* (01252) 792035. *Club:* MCC.

SHELDON, Mark Hebberton, CBE 1997; Chairman, PPP healthcare medical trust, since 1999 (Governor, since 1998); President of The Law Society, 1992–93; *b* 6 Feb. 1931; *s* of late George Hebberton Sheldon and Marie Sheldon (*née* Hazlitt); *m* 1971, Catherine Ashworth; one *s* one *d*. *Educ:* Wycliffe Coll.; Corpus Christi Coll., Oxford (BA Jurisprudence (Hons), MA; Hon. Fellow, 1995). National Service, 1949–50, TA, 1950–54, Royal Signals (Lieut). Linklaters & Paines: articled clerk, 1953–56; Asst Solicitor, 1957–59; Partner, 1959–93, Sen. Partner, 1988–91, Jt Sen. Partner, 1991–93, Consultant, 1994–96. Resident Partner, New York, 1972–74. Mem. Council 1978–, Treas. 1981–86, Vice-Pres., 1991–92, Law Soc.; Mem. Court 1975–, Master 1987–88, City of London Solicitors' Co.; Pres., City of London Law Soc., 1987–88. Hon. Bencher, Inner Temple, 1993. Chm., Bar Council Working Party on Barristers' Rights to Conduct Litigation, 1999–2000. Nominated Mem., Council of Corp. of Lloyd's, 1989–90; Member: Financial Reporting Council, 1990–98; Cadbury Cttee on Financial Aspects of Corporate Governance, 1991–95; Financial Law Panel, 1993–98; Council, Justice, 1993–; Sen. Salaries Rev. Body, 1994–99; Panel of Conciliators, Internat. Centre for Investment Disputes, 1995–; Adv. Panel, Inst. for Socio-Legal Studies, Univ. of Oxford, 1995–. Dir, Coutts & Co., 1996–98. Hon. Member: Canadian Bar Assoc., 1993–; SPTL, 1993–. Trustee, Oxford Inst. of Legal Practice, 1993–. Gov., Yehudi Menuhin Sch., 1996–. Chm., Corpus Assoc., 1983–89. *Recreations:* music, English water-colours, wine, swimming. *Address:* 5 St Albans Grove, W8 5PN. *T:* (020) 7460 7172, *Fax:* (020) 7938 4771. *Clubs:* Travellers, City of London, Hurlingham.

SHELDON, Peter, FCA; Chairman, BATM Advanced Communications Ltd, since 1999 (Director, 1998–99); President, United Synagogue, since 1999; *b* 11 June 1941; *s* of Izydor Schuldenfrei and Regina Schuldenfrei; surname changed to Sheldon by Deed Poll, 1964; *m* 1965, Judith Marion Grunberger; two *s* one *d*. *Educ:* Kilburn Grammar Sch. FCA 1969. Partner: Alfred N. Emanuel & Co., Chartered Accountants, 1963–70; Bright, Grahame Murray, Chartered Accountants, 1970–71; Director: UDS Gp Plc, 1971–83; Hambros Bank, 1983–85; World of Leather Plc, 1985–97; Geo Interactive Media Gp Ltd, 1996–98. Chm., Stirling Gp Plc, 1990–94; Dir, Kindertec Ltd, 1997–. JP Haringey, 1979–90 and 1997–. *Recreations:* theatre, travel, walking, grandchildren. *Address:* 34 Fairholme Gardens, Finchley, N3 3EB. *T:* (020) 7349 9462.

SHELDON, Richard Michael; QC 1996; *b* 29 Sept. 1955; *s* of Ralph Maurice Sheldon and Ady Sheldon (*née* Jaudel); *m* 1983, Helen Mary Lake; two *s* one *d*. *Educ:* Maidenhead Grammar Sch.; Jesus Coll., Cambridge (MA). Called to the Bar, Gray's Inn, 1979. *Publication:* contrib. Halsbury's Laws of England. *Recreations:* music, bassoon. *Address:* 3/4 South Square, Gray's Inn, WC1R 5HP. *T:* (020) 7696 9900.

SHELDRICK, Prof. George Michael, PhD; FRS 2001; Professor of Structural Chemistry, University of Göttingen, since 1978; *b* 17 Nov. 1942; *s* of George and Elizabeth M. Sheldrick; *m* 1968, Katherine E. Herford; two *s* two *d*. *Educ:* Huddersfield New Coll.; Jesus Coll., Cambridge (MA; PhD 1966). University of Cambridge: Demonstrator, 1966–71, Lectr, 1971–78, Dept of Inorganic, Organic and Theoretical Chm.; Fellow, Jesus Coll., 1966–78. Mem., Akademie der Wissenschaften zu Göttingen, 1989. Mineral Sheldrickite named after him, 1996. Meldola Medal, 1970, Corday-Morgan Medal, 1978, Award for Structural Chem., 1981, RSC; Leibniz Prize, Deutsche Forschungsgemeinschaft, 1987; Patterson Prize, Amer. Crystallographic Assoc., 1993; Carl-Hermann Medal, Deutsche Ges. für Kristallographie, 1999. *Publications:* numerous papers in scientific jls. *Recreations:* tennis, chess. *Address:* Lehrstuhl für Strukturchemie, Tammannstrasse 4, 37077 Göttingen, Germany. *T:* (551) 393021.

SHELFORD, William Thomas Cornelius; Senior Partner, CMS Cameron McKenna, Solicitors; *b* 27 Jan. 1943; *s* of late Cornelius William Shelford and of Helen Beatrice Hilda (*née* Schuster); *m* 1971, Annette Heap Holt; two *s* one *d*. *Educ:* Eton Coll.; Christ Church, Oxford (MA Jurisprudence). Partner, 1970–, Sen. Partner, 1990–, Cameron Markby Hewitt, later Cameron McKenna. *Recreations:* gardening, walking, ski-ing. *Address:* Mitre House, 160 Aldersgate Street, EC1A 4DD. *T:* (020) 7367 3000. *Clubs:* Brooks's, City of London.

SHELLAM, Fiona Juliet; *see* Stanley, F. J.

SHELLARD, Maj.-Gen. Michael Francis Linton, CBE 1989; Comptroller, Royal Artillery Institution, since 2001; *b* 19 Aug. 1937; *s* of Norman Shellard and Stella (*née* Linton); *m* 1960, Jean Mary Yates; one *s* one *d*. *Educ:* Queen's Coll., Taunton; RMA, Sandhurst. Commnd, RA, 1957; Staff Coll., Camberley, 1969; NDC, Latimer, 1974; GSO1 MO4, MoD, 1975–76; CO 22 AD Regt, 1977–79; Col, 1983; Brig., 1985; Comd 1st Artillery Bde and Dortmund Garrison, 1985–88; Comdr Artillery, 1st British Corps, 1990–92. Dir, NATO Area, Short Brothers plc, 1992–94; Chief Exec, Regular Forces Employment Assoc., 1994–2001. Col Comdt, RA, 1993–; Hon. Col 22nd Regt, RA, 1993–2000. Chairman: RA Historical Affairs Cttee, 1994–; RA Historical Trust, 1994–. Dir, RA Museums Ltd, 1997–. Gov., Queen's Coll., Taunton, 1989–. *Recreations:* golf, bird watching, gardening. *Address:* c/o HSBC, High Street, Amesbury, Wilts SP4 7DN. *Club:* Army and Navy (Chm., 2000–).

SHELLEY, Alan John; Senior Partner, Knight, Frank & Rutley, 1983–92; *b* 7 Aug. 1931; *s* of Stanley and Ivy Shelley; *m* 1958, Josephine (*née* Flood); one *s* one *d*. *Educ:* People's College, Nottingham. FRICS. Senior Partner, Knight, Frank & Rutley (Nigeria), 1965. General Commissioner of Income Tax, 1984–. Chairman: W Africa Cttee, 1985–97; Mansfield Settlement, 1992–2000. Mem. Ct of Governors, Royal Shakespeare Theatre, 1990–. *Recreations:* theatre, squash. *Address:* Thatch Farm, Glaston, Rutland LE15 9BX. *T:* (01572) 822396. *Clubs:* Oriental, MCC.

SHELLEY, Howard Gordon; concert pianist and conductor; Music Director and Principal Conductor, Uppsala Chamber Orchestra, Sweden, since 2000; *b* 9 March 1950; *s* of Frederick Gordon Shelley and Katharine Anne Taylor; *m* 1975, Hilary Mary Pauline Macnamara; one *s*, and one step *s*. *Educ:* Highgate Sch.; Royal College of Music (ARCM Hons 1966; Foundn Schol. 1967–71); Boise Schol. 1971–72; ARCO 1967. Studied with Vera Yelverton, Harold Craxton, Kendall Taylor, Lamar Crowson and Ilona Kabos. Recital début, Wigmore Hall, 1971; televised Henry Wood Prom début, 1972; conducting début, London Symphony Orch., Barbican, 1985; Associate Conductor, 1990–92, Principal Guest Conductor, 1992–98, London Mozart Players. Internat. solo career extending over five continents; performed world's first complete exposition of solo piano works of Rachmaninov, Wigmore Hall, 1983; soloist, 100th anniv. of Henry Wood Proms, 1995. Discography includes: Rachmaninov solo works (8 vols), Rachmaninov two-piano works, Rachmaninov Complete Piano Concertos, Mozart, Hummel and Mendelssohn Piano Concertos (conductor/soloist), Chopin, Schumann recitals, Schubert recital on fortepiano, piano concertos of Alwyn, Gershwin, Tippett, Vaughan Williams, Howard Ferguson, Szymanowski, Korngold, Rubbra, Carwithen, Balakirev, Messiaen and Peter Dickinson; Mozart and Schubert symphonies (conductor). 2 piano partnership with Hilary Macnamara, 1976–. Presenter, conductor and pianist, TV documentary on Ravel (Gold Medal, NY Fests Awards), 1998. Chappell Gold Medal and Peter Morrison Prize, 1968, Dannreuther Concerto Prize, 1971, RCM; Silver Medal, Co. of Musicians, 1971. *Address:* c/o Caroline Baird Artists, Pinkhill House, Oxford Road, Farmoor, Oxon OX2 9NN; *e-mail:* caroline@cbartists.com.

SHELLEY, James Edward, CBE 1991; Secretary to Church Commissioners, 1985–92; *b* 1932; *s* of Vice-Adm. Richard Shelley and Eve Cecil; *m* 1956, Judy Grubb; two *s* two *d*. *Educ:* Eton; University College, Oxford (MA). Joined Church Commissioners' staff, 1954; Under Secretary General, 1976–81; Assets Secretary, 1981–85. Dir, Save & Prosper, 1987–94. *Recreations:* country pursuits. *Address:* Mays Farm House, Ramsdell, Tadley, Hants RG26 5RE. *T:* (01256) 850770.

SHELLEY, Sir John (Richard), 11th Bt *cr* 1611; (professionally Dr J. R. Shelley); general medical practitioner; Partner, Drs Shelley, Doddington and Gibb, Health Centre, South Molton, Devon; *b* 18 Jan. 1943; *s* of John Shelley (*d* 1974), and of Dorothy, *d* of Arthur Irvine Ingram; *S* grandfather, 1976; *m* 1965, Clare, *d* of Claud Bicknell, *qv*; two *d*. *Educ:* King's Sch., Bruton; Trinity Coll., Cambridge (BA 1964, MA 1967); St Mary's Hosp., London Univ. MB, BChir 1967; DObstRCOG 1969; MRCGP 1978. Partner in Drs Harris, Barkworth, Savile, Shelley and Gurney, Eastbourne, Sx, 1969–74; Partnership, Health Centre, S Molton, 1974–. Member: Exeter Diocesan Synod for South Molton Deanery, 1976–79; BMA; CLA; NFU. *Heir:* *b* Thomas Henry Shelley [*b* 3 Feb. 1945; *m* 1970, Katherine Mary Holton (marr. diss. 1992); three *d*]. *Address:* Health Centre, 9–10 East Street, South Molton, Devon EX36 3BZ; Shobrooke Park, Crediton, Devon EX17 1DG. *T:* (01769) 573101.

SHELTON, Gen. Henry Hugh; Chairman, Joint Chiefs of Staff, USA, 1997–2001; *b* 2 Jan. 1942; *s* of late Hugh Shelton and of Sarah Shelton (*née* Laughlin); *m* 1963, Carolyn L. Johnson; three *s*. *Educ:* N Carolina State Univ. (BS Textiles 1963); Auburn Univ., Alabama (MS Pol Sci.); Harvard Univ.; Air Comd and Staff Coll., Alabama; Nat. War Coll., Washington. Entered US Army, 1963: active duty assignments in US, Hawaii and Vietnam (2 tours), 1963–87; Dep. Dir for Ops, Nat. Mil. Comd Center, Jt Chiefs of Staff, Washington, 1987–88; Chief, Current Ops, Jt Chiefs of Staff, 1988–89; Assistant Division Commander, 101st Airborne Division (Air Assault): Fort Campbell, Kentucky, 1989–90; Operations Desert Shield and Desert Storm, Saudi Arabia, 1990–91; Fort Campbell, March–May 1991; Commanding General: 82nd Airborne Div., Fort Bragg, NC, 1991–93; XVIII Airborne Corps and Fort Bragg, 1993–96 (i/c Jt Task Force, Operation Uphold Democracy, Haiti, 1994); Lt-Gen. 1993; Gen. 1996; C-in-C, US Special Ops Comd, MacDill Air Force Base, Fla, 1996–97. Mem., Council on Foreign Relns, 1998–. Mem., Assoc. of US Army, 1983–. Gov., American Red Cross, 1998–. Purple Heart, 1967; Bronze Star Medal: (with V device), 1967; (with three Oak Leaf Clusters), 1968, 1969, 1991; MSM (with two Oak Leaf Clusters), 1979, 1982, 1983; Legion of Merit (with Oak Leaf Cluster), 1985, 1991; DSM 1994; Defense DSM (with two Oak Leaf Clusters), 1989, 1994, 1997. *Publications:* contrib0. to Harvard Internat. Rev., Armed Forces Jl, Nat. Defense, Special Warfare, Jt Force Qly, Qly Mil. Rev. *Recreations:* jogging, woodworking, reading, playing guitar. *Address:* c/o The Pentagon, Room 2E872, Washington, DC 20318–9999, USA. *T:* (703) 6979121.

SHELTON, Shirley Megan, (Mrs W. T. Shelton); Editor, Home & Freezer Digest, 1988–90; *b* 8 March 1934; *d* of Lt-Col T. F. Goodwin; *m* 1960, William Timothy Shelton; one *s* two *d*. *Educ:* various schs. Home Editor 1970–75, Assistant Editor, 1975–78, Editor, 1978–82, Woman and Home magazine. *Address:* 59 Croftdown Road, NW5 1EL. *T:* (020) 7485 4936.

SHELTON, Sir William (Jeremy Masefield), Kt 1989; MA Oxon; *b* 30 Oct. 1929; *s* of late Lt-Col R. C. M. Shelton, MBE, St Saviour's, Guernsey, and Mrs R. E. P. Shelton (*née* Coode), London Place, Oxford; *m* 1960, Anne Patricia, *o d* of John Arthur Warder, CBE; one *s* one *d*. *Educ:* Radley Coll.; Tabor Academy, Marion, Mass; Worcester Coll., Oxford; Univ. of Texas, Austin, Texas. Colman, Prentis & Varley Ltd, 1952–55; Corpa, Caracas, Venezuela, 1955–60; Managing Director: CPV (Colombiana) Ltd, Bogota, Colombia, 1960–64; CPV (International) Ltd, 1967–74 (Dir, 1964); Grosvenor Advertising Ltd, 1969–74 (Dir, 1964); Chairman: Fletcher, Shelton, Delaney & Reynolds Ltd, 1974–81; GGK London Ltd, 1984–86; Dir, Access to Justice Ltd, 1995–97. Member for Wandsworth, GLC, 1967–70; Chief Whip, on ILEA, 1968–70. MP (C) Clapham, 1970–74, Streatham, 1974–92; contested (C) Streatham, 1992. PPS to Minister of Posts and Telecommunications, 1972–74; PPS to Rt Hon. Margaret Thatcher, MP, 1975; Parly Under-Sec. of State, DES, 1981–83. Mem., Council of Europe and WEU, 1987–92. *Recreations:* golf, reading, painting. *Address:* Upton Downs House, near Burford, Oxon OX18 4LY. *T:* (01993) 823537. *Club:* Carlton.

SHELVEY, (Elsie) Miriam; a District Judge (Magistrates' Court) (formerly Provincial Stipendiary Magistrate), Greater Manchester, since 1999; *b* 23 Aug. 1955; *d* of Francis

James Dunn and Edith Elsie Dunn; *m* 1977, Peter Anthony Shelvey; one *d*. *Educ:* Liverpool Univ. (LLB). Admitted Solicitor, 1979; Partner, Silverman Livermore, 1980–99. *Recreation:* gardening. *Address:* Manchester City Magistrates' Court, Crown Square, Manchester M60 1PR. *T:* (0161) 832 7272.

SHENFIELD, Dame Barbara (Estelle), DBE 1986; Chairman, Women's Royal Voluntary Service, 1981–88 (Vice Chairman, 1976–81); *d* of George and Jane Farrow, Bearwood, Staffs; *m* 1st, Flt-Lt Gwilym Ivor Lewis, RAF (killed in action); one *s*; 2nd, Arthur A. Shenfield (*d* 1990); one *s*. *Educ:* Langley High Sch., Worcs; Univ. of Birmingham (Hons Social and Political Science). Lectr in Soc. Studies, Univ. of Birmingham, 1945–56; Lectr, Dept of Econs and Soc. Studies, Bedford Coll., London Univ., 1959–65; Academic Dir, UC at Buckingham, 1972–73. Visiting Professor: Michigan State Univ., 1960; Temple Univ., Philadelphia, 1974; Distinguished Vis. Prof., Rockford Coll., Ill, 1969–71, 1974. Consultant, US Dept of Labor, 1964; Dir, PEP Study of Co. Bds' Soc. Responsibilities, 1965–68. Member: UK Govt Cttee on Local Taxation, 1965–66; UK Govt Cttee on Abuse of Welfare Services, 1971–73; Govt Review Team on Social Security, 1984–85. Chairman: Nat Exec., Nat. Old People's Welfare Council (now Age Concern), 1971–73; Friends of the Imperial War Mus., 1991–; Pornography and Violence Res. Trust, 1996–. Trustee, Social Affairs Unit, 1990–. DUniv Buckingham, 1987. *Publications:* Social Policies for Old Age, 1957; The Social Responsibilities of Company Boards, 1971; The Organisation of a Voluntary Service, 1972; Myths of Social Policy, 1975; monographs and articles on gerontological and other social subjects. *Recreations:* gardening, music. *Address:* 22 Lower Sloane Street, SW1W 8BJ. *T:* (020) 7730 5810.

SHENKIN, Prof. Alan, PhD; FRCP, FRCPath, FRCPGlas; Professor of Clinical Chemistry, University of Liverpool, since 1990; Hon. Consultant and Clinical Director, since 1990, Director of Research and Development, since 1998, Royal Liverpool and Broadgreen University Hospitals NHS Trust; *b* 3 Sept. 1943; *s* of Louis Shenkin and Miriam Shenkin (*née* Epstein); *m* 1967, Leonna Estelle Delmonte; one *s* two *d*. *Educ:* Hutchesons Boys' Grammar Sch.; Univ. of Glasgow (BSc Hons; MB ChB 1969; PhD 1974). FRCPath 1990; FRCPGlas 1990; FRCP 1993. Lectr in Biochem., Univ. of Glasgow, 1970–74; Sen. Registrar in Clinical Biochem., Glasgow Royal Infirmary, 1974–78; Royal Soc. Eur. Exchange Fellow, Karolinska Inst., Stockholm, 1976–77; Consultant in Clinical Biochem., Glasgow Royal Infirmary, 1978–90. Chm., Specialty Adv. Cttee on Chemical Pathology, RCPath, 1995–98; Chairman: Royal Med. Colls Intercollegiate Gp on Nutrition, 1996–; JCHMT Sub-Cttee on Metabolic Medicine, 2001–. Pres., Assoc. Clinical Biochemists, 2000–; Hon. Treas., Eur. Soc. Parenteral and Enteral Nutrition, 1988–92. Hon. Associate, British Dietetic Assoc., 1989; Hon. Member: Czechoslovakian Med. Soc., 1990; Czechoslovakian Soc. for Parenteral and Enteral Nutrition, 1990. Mem., Scotch Malt Whisky Soc. 650th Anniversary Jubilee Medal, Charles Univ., 1998. *Publications:* contrib. res. papers, book chapters and conf. proc. on trace elements and vitamins in nutritional support, and metabolic response to illness. *Recreations:* golf, word games, malt whisky, travel. *Address:* 10 Rockbourne Green, Woolton, Liverpool L25 4TH. *T:* (0151) 428 9756. *Club:* Lee Park Golf (Liverpool).

SHENNAN, Robert Duncan James; Controller, BBC Radio Five Live, since 2000; *b* 18 March 1962; *s* of Joseph and Margaret Shennan; *m* 1987, Joanne Margaret Melford; two *s* one *d*. *Educ:* Lancaster Royal Grammar Sch.; Corpus Christi Coll., Cambridge (BA Hons English Lit. 1984). Journalist, Hereward Radio, 1984–87; BBC: Radio Sport: Producer, 1987–90; Asst Editor, 1990–92; Editor, 1992–94; Head, 1994–97; Head of Sport (TV and Radio), 1997–2000. *Recreations:* sport, literature, my children. *Address:* Fairbanks, 30 Amersham Road, High Wycombe, Bucks HP13 6QU. *T:* (01494) 459216.

SHEPARD, Giles Richard Carless, CBE 1994; Managing Director, Ritz Hotel (London) Ltd, since 1995; *b* 1 April 1937; *er s* of late Richard S. H. Shepard, MC, TD; *m* 1966, Peter Carolyn Fern Keighley; one *s* one *d*. *Educ:* Heatherdown, Ascot; Eton (King's Scholar); Harvard Business School (PMD 1967). Commissioned Coldstream Guards, 1955–60. Director: Charrington & Co., 1960–64; H. P. Bulmer & Co., 1964–70; Managing Director: Findlater Mackie, Todd, 1967–70; Westminster & Country Properties, 1970–76; Savoy Hotel plc, 1979–94; Director: Dorchester Hotel, 1972–76; Savoy Hotel, 1976–79; Guinness Mahon & Co. Ltd, 1994–98; Longshot Ltd, 1994–; Chm., Searcy Tansley & Co. Ltd, 1995–. Dir, Kleinwort Develt Fund, 1990–. Mem., Adv. Council for the Royal Parks, 1993–98; Hon. Catering Advr to the Army, 1994–. Member Council: Union Jack Club, 1980–; King Edward VII's Hosp. (Sister Agnes) (formerly King Edward VII's Hosp. for Officers), 1995–; RUSI, 1995–97. Chairman: City and Guilds of London Art Sch.; Heritage of London Trust, 1996–. Mem., Court of Assistants, Fishmongers' Co. (Prime Warden, 1987–88); High Sheriff of Greater London, 1986–87. Governor, Gresham's School, Holt, 1980–. *Recreations:* gardening, shooting, embroidery. *Address:* Wallop House, Nether Wallop, near Stockbridge, Hants SO20 8HE. *Clubs:* White's, Pratt's, Beefsteak, Boodle's.

SHEPHARD, Rt Hon. Gillian (Patricia); PC 1992; MP (C) South West Norfolk, since 1987; *b* 22 Jan. 1940; *d* of Reginald and Bertha Watts; *m* 1975, Thomas Shephard; two step *s*. *Educ:* North Walsham High Sch. for Girls; St Hilda's Coll., Oxford (MA Mod. Langs; Hon. Fellow, 1991). Educn Officer and Schools Inspector, 1963–75; Lectr, Cambridge Univ. Extra-Mural Bd, 1965–87. Councillor, Norfolk CC, 1977–89 (Chm. of Social Services Cttee, 1978–83, of Educn Cttee, 1983–85); Chairman: W Norfolk and Wisbech HA, 1981–85; Norwich HA, 1985–87; Co-Chm., Women's Nat. Commn, 1990–91. PPS to Economic Sec. to the Treasury, 1988–89; Parly Under Sec. of State, DSS, 1989–90; Minister of State, HM Treasury, 1990–92; Sec. of State for Employment, 1992–93; Minister of Agric., Fisheries and Food, 1993–94; Sec. of State for Educn, later Educn and Employment, 1994–97; Shadow Leader, H of C, 1997; Opposition front bench spokesman on the envmt, transport and the regions, 1997–99. Dep. Chm., Conservative Party, 1991–92. Vice Pres., Hansard Soc., 1997–. Mem., Franco-British Council, 1997–; Chm., Cons. Friends of Israel, 1997–. Mem. Council, Univ. of Oxford, 2000–. *Publication:* Shephard's Watch, 2000. *Recreations:* music, gardening, France. *Address:* House of Commons, SW1A 0AA. *T:* (constituency office) (01366) 385072.

SHEPHEARD, Sir Peter (Faulkner), Kt 1980; CBE 1972; PPRIBA, MRTPI, PPILA; architect, town planner and landscape architect in private practice since 1948 (with Bridgwater & Shepheard, later Shepheard, Epstein & Hunter, until 1989, now solo); Professor of Architecture and Environmental Design, Graduate School of Fine Arts, University of Pennsylvania, since 1971; *b* 11 Nov. 1913; *s* of Thomas Faulkner Shepheard, FRIBA, Liverpool; *m* 1943, Mary Bailey; one *s* one *d*. *Educ:* Birkenhead Sch.; Liverpool Sch. of Architecture. BArch. (1st Cl. Hons) Liverpool, 1936; Univ. Grad. Scholar in Civic Design, 1936–37. Asst to Derek Bridgwater, 1937–40; Min. of Supply, Royal Ordnance Factories, 1940–43; Min. of Town and Country Planning: technical officer, first on Greater London Plan (Sir Patrick Abercrombie's staff), later on research and master plan for Stevenage New Town, 1943–47. Dep. Chief Architect and Planner, Stevenage Develt Corp., 1947–48. Vis. Prof., Landscape Architecture, 1959 and 1962–71, and Dean of Fine Arts, 1971–79, Univ. of Pennsylvania. Member: Nat. Parks Commn, 1966–68; Countryside Commn, 1968–71; Royal Fine Art Commn, 1968–71. Artistic Advr, Commonwealth War Graves Commn, 1977–. Works include: housing and schools for GLC and other authorities; Landscape of part of Festival of Britain South Bank Exhibition, London, 1951; Master plan and buildings for University of Lancaster; work for the Universities of Keele, Liverpool, Oxford, and Ghana, and for Winchester College; gardens in England and USA. President: RIBA, 1969–71; Architectural Association, 1954–55; Inst. of Landscape Architects, 1965–66. Master, Art Workers' Guild, 1984. RIBA Distinction in Town Planning, 1956. Hon. FRAIC; Hon. FAIA. *Publications:* Modern Gardens, 1953; Gardens, 1969; various articles, lectures and broadcasts on architecture and landscape; drawings and illustrations of architecture and other things; illustr. A Book of Ducks, and Woodland Birds (King Penguins). *Recreations:* music and poetry; drawing, gardening and the study of natural history. *Address:* 21 Well Road, NW3 1LH. *T:* (020) 7435 3019. *Club:* Athenæum.

SHEPHERD, family name of **Baron Shepherd**.

SHEPHERD, 3rd Baron *cr* 1946, of Spalding, co. Lincoln; **Graeme George Shepherd;** *b* 6 Jan. 1949; *er s* of 2nd Baron Shepherd, PC and Allison (*née* Redmond); *S* father, 2001; *m* 1971, Eleanor; one *s*. *Heir:* *s* Hon Patrick Malcolm Shepherd.

SHEPHERD, Alan Arthur, CBE 1984; PhD; FREng, FInstP; Director, Ferranti plc, 1981–94; *b* 6 Sept. 1927; *s* of Arthur and Hannah Shepherd; *m* 1953, Edith Hudson; two *d*. *Educ:* Univ. of Manchester (BSc, MSc, PhD). FREng (FEng 1986). Lectr, Physics Dept, Univ. of Keele, 1950–54; Ferranti Ltd: Chief Engineer, Electronic Components Div., 1954–67; Gen. Manager, Instrument Dept, 1967–70; Gen. Manager, Electronic Components Div., 1970–78; Man. Dir, Ferranti Electronics, 1978–87; Dep. Man. Dir, Ops, Ferranti, then Ferranti Internat. Signal plc, 1987–89; Chm., Ferranti California Group of Cos, 1978–87. Hon. Fellow, UMIST, 1988. J. J. Thomson Medal, IEE, 1985. *Publication:* The Physics of Semiconductors, 1957. *Recreations:* golf, swimming, photography. *Address:* 6 Southern Crescent, Bramhall, Cheshire SK7 3AH. *T:* (0161) 439 2824. *Club:* St James's (Manchester).

SHEPHERD, Archie; HM Diplomatic Service, retired; Counsellor and Head of Migration and Visa Department, Foreign and Commonwealth Office, 1977–80; *b* 2 Nov. 1922; *s* of William Shepherd and Edith (*née* Browning); *m* 1959, Dorothy Annette Walker; one *s*. *Educ:* Torquay Grammar Sch. Prison Commission, 1939; served War, RAF, 1942–46. Foreign Office, 1949; Asst Political Agent and Vice Consul, Muscat, 1951–53; FO, 1954–55; Second Sec., UK Delegn to United Nations, Geneva, 1956–57; HM Consul: Warsaw, 1958–60; Rabat, 1960–62; FO, 1963–67; Consul, Cape Town, 1968–72; First Sec. (Commercial), Beirut, 1973–75. *Recreations:* tennis, gardening. *Address:* 9 Oaks Way, Kenley, Surrey CR8 5DT. *T:* (020) 8660 1299. *Clubs:* Civil Service, Royal Commonwealth Society.

SHEPHERD, Sir Colin (Ryley), Kt 1996; Director, Haigh Engineering Company Ltd, since 1963; *b* 13 Jan. 1938; *s* of late T. C. R. Shepherd, MBE; *m* 1966, Louise, *d* of late Lt-Col E. A. M. Cleveland, MC; three *s*. *Educ:* Oundle; Caius Coll., Cambridge; McGill Univ., Montreal. RCN, 1959–63. MP (C) Hereford, Oct. 1974–1997; contested (C) same seat, 1997. PPS to Sec. of State for Wales, 1987–90. Jt Sec., Cons. Parly Agr. Fish. and Food Cttee, 1975–79, Vice-Chm., 1979–87, 1991–92; Member: Select Cttee on H of C Services, 1979–92; Select Cttee on H of C Finance and Services, 1993–97; Sec., Cons. Parly Hort. Sub-Cttee, 1976–87; Chairman: Library Sub-Cttee, 1983–91; Catering Cttee, 1991–97. Chm., UK Br., CPA, 1991–94 (Mem. Exec. Cttee, 1986–97; Treas., 1991–93, Chm., 1993–96, Internat. Exec. Cttee). Council Mem., RCVS, 1983–99; Governor, Commonwealth Inst., 1989–97. Fellow, Industry and Parlt Trust, 1985. *Address:* Manor House, Ganarew, Monmouth NP25 3SU. *T:* (01600) 890220. *Clubs:* Naval, Royal Commonwealth Society.

SHEPHERD, David; *see* Shepherd, R. D.

SHEPHERD, Prof. James, PhD; FRCPath, FRCPGlas, FMedSci; FRSE; Professor, and Head of Department of Pathological Biochemistry, University of Glasgow and Glasgow Royal Infirmary, since 1988; *b* 8 April 1944; *s* of James Bell Shepherd and Margaret McCrum Shepherd (*née* Camick); *m* 1969, Janet Bulloch Kelly; one *s* one *d*. *Educ:* Hamilton Acad.; Glasgow Univ. (BSc Hons 1965; MB ChB Hons 1968; PhD 1972). MRCPath 1982, FRCPath 1994; FRCPGlas 1990. Lectr in Biochemistry, Univ. of Glasgow, 1969–72; Lectr, 1973–77, Sen. Lectr and Hon. Consultant, 1977–88, Dept of Pathological Biochemistry, Univ. of Glasgow and Glasgow Royal Infirmary; Clin. Dir, Labs, Glasgow Royal Infirmary, 1993–. Asst Prof. of Medicine, Methodist Hosp., Houston, Texas, 1976–77; Vis. Prof. of Medicine, Cantonal Hosp., Geneva, 1984. Dir, W Scotland Coronary Prevention Study, 1989–96; Chairman: European Atherosclerosis Soc., 1993–96 (Chm., Congress, 2001); Prospective Study of Pravastatin in the Elderly at Risk, 1997–; Mem., Internat. Atherosclerosis Soc., 1977–. FRSE 1996; Founder FMedSci, 1998. *Publications:* (jtly) Lipoproteins in Coronary Heart Disease, 1986; (jtly) Atherosclerosis: developments, complications and treatment, 1987; Lipoprotein Metabolism, 1987; (ed jtly) Coronary Risks Revisited, 1989; (ed jtly) Human Plasma Lipoproteins, 1989; (ed jtly) Preventive Cardiology, 1991; (ed jtly) Lipoproteins and the Pathogenesis of Atherosclerosis, 1991; (ed jtly) Cardiovascular Disease: current perspectives on the Asian-Pacific region, 1994; (jtly) Clinical Biochemistry, 1995; (jtly) Lipoproteins in Health and Disease, 1999; (jtly) Statins in Perspective, 1999; Atherosclerosis Annual, 2001. *Recreations:* travel, walking, art appraisal. *Address:* (home) 17 Barriedale Avenue, Hamilton ML3 9DB. *T:* (01698) 428359; (office) Institute of Biochemistry, Royal Infirmary, Glasgow G4 0SF. *T:* (0141) 552 0689.

SHEPHERD, James Rodney; Under-Secretary, Department of Trade and Industry (formerly Department of Industry), 1980–89, retired; *b* 27 Nov. 1935; *s* of Richard James Shepherd and Winifred Mary Shepherd. *Educ:* Blundell's; Magdalen Coll., Oxford (PPE; Diploma in Statistics). National Inst. of Economic and Social Res., 1960–64; Consultant to OECD, 1964; HM Treasury, 1965–80 (Under-Sec., 1975–80). *Publications:* articles in technical jls.

SHEPHERD, Sir John (Alan), KCVO 2000; CMG 1989; HM Diplomatic Service; Ambassador to Italy, since 2000; *b* 27 April 1943; *s* of William (Mathieson) Shepherd and (Elsie) Rae Shepherd; *m* 1969, Jessica Mary Nichols; one *d*. *Educ:* Charterhouse; Selwyn Coll., Cambridge (MA); Stanford Univ., Calif (MA). Merchant Navy, 1961; HM Diplomatic Service, 1965–: CO, 1965–66; MECAS, Lebanon, 1966–68; 3rd Sec., Amman, 1968–70; 2nd Sec., Rome, 1970–73; 1st Secretary: FCO, 1973–76; The Hague, 1977–80; First Sec., 1980–82, Counsellor and Hd of Chancery, 1982–84, Office of UK Rep. to EEC, Brussels; Head of European Community Dept (External), FCO, 1985–87; Ambassador to Bahrain, 1988–91; Minister, Bonn, 1991–96; Dir, Middle East and North Africa, FCO, 1996–97; Dep. Under-Sec. of State, FCO, 1997–2000. *Recreations:* hills, birds, tennis. *Club:* Oxford and Cambridge.

SHEPHERD, John Dodson, CBE 1979; Regional Administrator, Yorkshire Regional Health Authority, 1977–82, retired; *b* 24 Dec. 1920; *s* of Norman and Elizabeth Ellen Shepherd; *m* 1948, Marjorie Nettleton; one *s* two *d. Educ:* Barrow Grammar School. RAF, 1940–46: N Africa, Italy, Middle East, 1943–46. Asst Sec., Oxford RHB, 1956–58; Dep. Sec., Newcastle upon Tyne HMC, 1958–62; Sec., East Cumberland HMC, 1962–67; Sec., Liverpool RHB, 1967–73; Reg. Administrator, Mersey RHA, 1973–77. Pres., Inst. of Health Service Administrators, 1974–75 (Mem. Council, 1969–78). Trustee, Leonard Cheshire Foundn, 1989–95. *Recreations:* golf, music. *Address:* 14 Leconfield Garth, Follifoot, Harrogate HG3 1NF. *T:* (01423) 870520. *Clubs:* Harrogate Golf, Harrogate Rotary (Pres., 1990–91).

SHEPHERD, Prof. John Graham, PhD; FRS 1999; CMath, FIMA; Professor of Marine Sciences, since 1994 and Director, Earth System Modelling Initiative, since 1999, University of Southampton; *b* 24 Aug. 1946; *s* of Ian Alastair Shepherd and Eileen Alice Mary Shepherd; *m* 1968, Deborah Mary Powney; two *s. Educ:* Pembroke Coll., Cambridge (MA); Cavendish Lab., Cambridge (PhD 1971). FIMA 1989; CMath 1991. Res. Officer, CEGB, 1970–74; MAFF Fisheries Lab, Lowestoft, 1974–94, Dep. Dir and Hd, Fish Stock Mgt Div., 1989–94; Dir, Southampton Oceanography Centre, NERC, 1994–99. Vis. Sen. Res. Associate, Lamont-Doherty Geol Observatory, Columbia Univ., NY, 1978–79. FRGS 1994; Pres., Challenger Soc., 2000–Aug. 2002. *Publications:* numerous professional articles on marine science, fish stock assessment and fishery mgt. *Recreations:* rowing, music, walking. *Address:* Southampton Oceanography Centre, European Way, Southampton SO14 3ZH. *T:* (023) 8059 6256. *Club:* Lowestoft Rowing.

SHEPHERD, Sister Margaret Ann; Member, Religious Congregation (RC) of Our Lady of Sion; Director, Council of Christians and Jews, since 1999; *b* 26 April 1944; *d* of Alfred and Alice Shepherd. *Educ:* Maria Assumpta Coll. of Educn (DipEd); Open Univ. (BA); Leo Baeck Coll. (Dip. Jewish Studies 1980); King's Coll., London (MTh Biblical Studies). Teacher of English (part time) during noviciate period; teacher, English and religious studies: Our Lady of Sion Boarding Sch., Shropshire, 1969–70; Our Lady of Sion Sen. Sch., Worthing, 1970–77; full time rabbinical studies, 1977–80; Study Centre for Christian Jewish Relations: Team Mem., 1980–86; Dir, 1986–89; Council of Christians and Jews: Educn Officer, 1989–93; Dep. Dir, 1993–98. *Publications:* (contrib.) Dialogue with a Difference, ed Tony Bayfield and Marcus Braybrooke, 1992; (contrib.) Splashes of Godlight, ed Terence Copley, 1997; (contrib.) The Holocaust and the Christian World, 2000; contrib. to The Month. *Recreations:* visiting art galleries and exhibitions, music, painting, poetry, browsing in second hand bookshops, spending time with friends. *Address:* Council of Christians and Jews, Camelford House, 87–89 Albert Embankment, SE1 7TP. *T:* (020) 7820 0090. *Club:* New Cavendish.

SHEPHERD, Richard Charles Scrimgeour; MP (C) Aldridge-Brownhills, since 1979; *b* 6 Dec. 1942; *s* of late Alfred Reginald Shepherd and Davida Sophia Wallace. *Educ:* LSE; Johns Hopkins Univ. (Sch. of Advanced Internat. Studies). Director: Shepherd Foods (London) Ltd, 1970–; Partridges of Sloane Street Ltd, 1972–. Mem., SE Econ. Planning Council, 1970–74. Underwriting Mem. of Lloyds, 1974–94. Mem., Treasury and Civil Service Select Cttee, 1979–83; Secretary: Cons. Parly Industry Cttee, 1980–81; Cons. Parly European Cttee, 1980–81. Parly Co-Vice Chm., Campaign for Freedom of Inf., 1989–. Sponsor, Liberty, 2001–. Court of Govs, LSE. Backbencher of the Year, Spectator, 1987; Special Award, Campaign for Freedom of Information, 1988; Parliamentarian of the Year, Spectator, 1995. *Recreations:* book collecting; searching for the Home Service on the wireless. *Address:* House of Commons, SW1A 0AA. *Clubs:* Carlton, Beefsteak, Chelsea Arts.

SHEPHERD, (Richard) David, OBE 1980; artist; *b* 25 April 1931; *s* of Raymond Oxley Shepherd and Margaret Joyce Shepherd (*née* Williamson); *m* 1957, Avril Shirley Gaywood; four *d. Educ:* Stowe. Art trng under Robin Goodwin, 1950–53; started career as aviation artist (Founder Mem., Soc. of Aviation Artists). Exhibited, RA, 1956; began painting African wild life, 1960. First London one-man show, 1962; painted 15 ft reredos of Christ for army garrison church, Bordon, 1964; 2nd London exhibn, 1965; Johannesburg exhibns, 1966 and 1969; exhibn, Tryon Gall., London, 1978. Painted: HE Dr Kaunda, President of Zambia, 1967; HM the Queen Mother for King's Regt, 1969; HE Sheikh Zayed of Abu Dhabi, 1970; 3rd London exhibn, 1971. Auctioned 5 wildlife paintings in USA and raised sufficient to purchase Bell Jet Ranger helicopter to combat game poaching in Zambia, 1971; painted Tiger Fire, for Operation Tiger, 1973; presented with 1896 steam locomotive by Pres. Kenneth Kaunda of Zambia (its return to Britain subject of BBC TV documentary, Last Train to Mulobezi); purchased 2 main line steam locomotives from BR, 1967 (92203 Black Prince, 75209 The Green Knight); Founder Chm., E Somerset Railway. BBC made 50-minute colour life documentary, The Man Who Loves Giants, 1970; series, In Search of Wildlife, in which he is shown tracking down and painting endangered species, Thames TV, 1988. Established The David Shepherd Conservation Foundn, 1984. Mem. of Honour, World Wildlife Fund, 1979. FRGS 1989; FRSA 1986. Hon. DFA, Pratt Inst., New York, for services to wildlife conservation, 1971; Hon. DSc Hatfield Polytechnic, 1990. OStJ 1996. Order of the Golden Ark, Netherlands, for services to wildlife conservation (Zambia, Operation Tiger, etc), 1973. *Publications:* Artist in Africa, 1967; (autobiog.) The Man who Loves Giants, 1975; Paintings of Africa and India, 1978; A Brush with Steam, 1983; David Shepherd: the man and his paintings, 1985; An Artist in Conversation, 1992; David Shepherd: my painting life, 1995. *Recreations:* driving steam engines, raising money for wildlife. *Address:* Brooklands Farm, Hammerwood, East Grinstead, West Sussex RH19 3QA. *T:* (01342) 302480.

SHEPHERD, Richard Thorley, FRCPath; Senior Lecturer in Forensic Medicine and Head of Forensic Medicine Unit, St George's Hospital Medical School, since 1996; *b* 20 Sept. 1952; *s* of George and Lucy Shepherd; *m* 1978, Jane Caroline Malcolm; one *s* one *d. Educ:* University Coll. London (BSc Hons); St George's Hosp. Med. Sch. (MB BS 1977). DMJ 1984; FRCPath 1997. Lectr in Forensic Medicine, St George's Hosp. Med. Sch., 1981–86; Lectr in Forensic Medicine, 1986–88, Sen. Lectr, 1988–96, UMDS of Guy's and St Thomas' Hosps. Asst Ed., Medico-Legal Jl, 1986–97. *Recreation:* flying light aircraft. *Address:* Forensic Medicine Unit, St George's Hospital Medical School, SW17 0RE. *T:* (020) 8725 0015. *Club:* Athenaeum.

SHEPHERD, Rt Rev. Ronald Francis; Hon. Assisting Bishop for the Development of Mission in the Borrego Region, Diocese of San Diego, California, 2000; *b* 15 July 1926; *s* of Herbert George Shepherd and Muriel Shepherd (*née* Grant); *m* 1952, Ann Alayne Dundas, *d* of Rt Hon. R. S. Dundas; four *s* two *d. Educ:* Univ. of British Columbia (BA Hons 1948); King's Coll., London (AKC 1952). Fellow, Coll. of Preachers, Washington, DC, 1972. Curate, St Stephen's, Rochester Row, London SW, 1952–57; Rector: St Paul's, Glanford, Ont, 1957–59; All Saints, Winnipeg, 1959–65; Dean and Rector: All Saints Cathedral, Edmonton, 1965–69; Christ Church Cathedral, Montreal, 1970–83; Rector, St Matthias, Victoria, 1983–84; Bishop of British Columbia, 1985–92. Hon. DDiv. St John's Coll., Winnipeg, 1988. *Recreations:* reading, gardening, walking. *Address:* Easter Hill, 110 Ensilwood, Salt Spring Island, BC V8K 1N1, Canada. *T:* (604) 5371399.

SHEPHERD, William Stanley; Managing Director, Civic Investments Ltd; *b* 12 March 1910; *s* of W. D. Shepherd; *m* 1942, Betty, *d* of late T. F. Howard, MP for Islington South, 1931–35; two *s.* Served in Army, War of 1939–45. A managing director of businesses which he has established; MP (C): Bucklow Div. of Cheshire, 1945–50; Cheadle Div. of Cheshire, 1950–66. Mem., Select Committee on Estimates; Joint Hon. Sec. Conservative Parliamentary Committee in Trade and Industry, 1945–51. Joined SDP, 1982. Hon. Mem., Valuers Institution. FREconS. *Address:* (office) Civic Investments Ltd, 77 George Street, W1H 5PL. *T:* (020) 7486 7580; (home) 33 Queens Grove, St John's Wood, NW8. *T:* (020) 7722 7526. *Club:* Savile.

SHEPHERDSON, Prof. John Cedric, ScD; FBA 1990; FIMA; H. O. Wills Professor of Mathematics, Bristol University, 1977–91, now Emeritus; *b* 7 June 1926; *s* of Arnold Shepherdson and Elsie (*née* Aspinall); *m* 1957, Margaret Smith; one *s* two *d. Educ:* Manchester Grammar Sch.; Trinity Coll., Cambridge (BA, MA, ScD). Asst Experimental Officer, Aerodynamics and Maths Div., NPL, 1946; Bristol University: Asst Lectr in Maths, 1946–49; Lectr, 1949–55; Reader, 1955–63; Prof. of Pure Maths, 1964–77. Mem., Inst. for Advanced Study, Princeton, 1953–54; Vis. Associate Prof., 1958–59, Vis. Prof., 1966–67, Univ. of Calif at Berkeley; Vis. Prof., Monash Univ., 1971, 1986, 1991, 1992, 1994, 1996; Vis. Scientist, IBM Res. Labs, Yorktown Heights, NY, 1973, 1975, 1979; Guest, Technische Hochschule, Zürich, 1988. *Publications:* papers in mathematical, logical and computer sci. jls. *Recreations:* walking, ski-ing, squash, cycling, board-sailing, occasional climbing. *Address:* Oakhurst, North Road, Leigh Woods, Bristol BS8 3PN. *T:* (0117) 973 5410; *e-mail:* john.shepherdson@bris.ac.uk. *Clubs:* Fell & Rock Climbing (Lake District); Bristol Corinthian Yacht.

SHEPLEY, Christopher John; Chief Planning Inspector and Chief Executive, Planning Inspectorate Agency, Department for Transport, Local Government and the Regions and National Assembly for Wales (formerly Department of the Environment, then of the Environment, Transport and the Regions, and Welsh Office), since 1994; *b* 27 Dec. 1944; *s* of George Frederick Shepley and Florence Mildred Shepley (*née* Jepson); *m* 1st, 1967, Jennifer Webber (marr. diss. 1992); one *s* one *d*; 2nd, 1998, Janet Winifred Molyneux. *Educ:* Stockport Grammar Sch.; LSE (BA Hons Geography); Univ. of Manchester (DipTP). MRTPI. Manchester City Council, 1966–73; Greater Manchester County Council, 1973–85 (Dep. County Planning Officer, 1984–85); Plymouth City Council: City Planning Officer, 1985–92; Dir of Develt, 1992–94. Mem., Architecture Adv. Gp, Arts Council of England, 1992–. Pres., RTPI, 1989. Hon. Vis. Prof., Univ. of Manchester Dept of Planning and Landscape, 1990–94. FRSA. Hon. DSc West of England, 2001. *Publications:* The Grotton Papers, 1979; (contrib.) Plymouth: a maritime city in transition, 1990; articles in planning and local govt jls. *Recreations:* music, watching sport, travel, walking. *Address:* Planning Inspectorate, 4/14 Eagle Wing, Temple Quay House, 2 The Square, Temple Quay, Bristol BS1 6PN. *T:* (0117) 372 8963. *Club:* Manchester United Football.

SHEPPARD, family name of **Baron Sheppard of Liverpool.**

SHEPPARD OF DIDGEMERE, Baron *cr* 1994 (Life Peer), of Roydon in the County of Essex; **Allen John George Sheppard,** KCVO 1998; Kt 1990; Chairman, Grand Metropolitan plc, 1987–96 (Chief Executive, 1986–93); *b* 25 Dec. 1932; *s* of John Baggott Sheppard and Lily Marjorie Sheppard (*née* Palmer); *m* 1st, 1959, Peggy Damaris (*née* Jones) (marr. diss. 1980); 2nd, 1980, Mary (*née* Stewart). *Educ:* Ilford County School; London School of Economics (BSc Econ). FCMA, FCIS, ATII. Ford of Britain and Ford of Europe, 1958–68; Rootes/Chrysler, 1968–71; British Leyland, 1971–75; Grand Metropolitan, 1975–96. Non. Exec. Dir, later Chm., UBM Group, 1981–85; Chm., Mallinson-Denny Group, 1985–87. Chairman: McBride Ltd, 1993–; Group Trust (formerly Group Development Capital Trust) PLC, 1994–2001; Unipart, 1996–; GB Railways, 1996–; Deputy Chairman: Meyer Internat., 1992–94 (non-exec. Dir, 1989–94); Brightreasons Group PLC, 1994–96; part time Mem., BR Board, 1985–90; Director: Bowater, 1993–94; High-Point Rendel Gp plc, 1997–; OneClickHR PLC (formerly Visual Business Tools), 1999–; Gladstone PLC, 1999–; Nyne (formerly Zolon) plc, 1999–; Transware plc, 2001–. Chm., Adv. Bd, British American Chamber of Commerce, 1991–94; Vice-Pres., BITC (Dep. Chm., 1989–94; Chm., 1994–97); Dep. Chm., Internat. Business Leaders Forum, 1990–95; Member: Nat. Trng Task Force, 1989–92; NEDC, 1990–92. Chairman: Bd of Trustees, Prince's Youth Business Trust, 1990–94; Prince's Trust Council, 1995–98; Mem. Exec. Cttee, Animal Health Trust. Chm., London First, 1992–; Co-Chair, London Pride Partnership, 1994–99; Dir, London Develt Partnership; Mem. Bd, Blue Cross. Vice-President: United Response; Brewers & Licensed Retailers' Assoc. Mem., Bd of Management, Conservative Party, 1993–98. Governor, LSE, 1989–; Chancellor, Middlesex Univ., 2000–. CIMgt (CBIM 1982; Gold Medal, 1994); FRSA. Hon. FCGI 1993; Hon. Fellow, London Business Sch., 1993. Hon. Dr: Internat. Management Centre, 1989; South Bank Univ., 1994; Brunel, 1994; East London, 1997; Westminster, 1998; Middlesex, 1999; LSE, 2001. *Publications:* Your Business Matters, 1958; Maximunium Leadership, 1995; articles in professional jls. *Recreations:* gardens, reading, red setter dogs. *Address:* 20 Cockspur Street, SW1Y 5BL.

SHEPPARD OF LIVERPOOL, Baron *cr* 1998 (Life Peer), of West Kirby in the co. of Merseyside; **Rt Rev. David Stuart Sheppard;** Bishop of Liverpool, 1975–97; *b* 6 March 1929; *s* of late Stuart Morton Winter Sheppard, Solicitor, and Barbara Sheppard; *m* 1957, Grace Isaac; one *d. Educ:* Sherborne; Trinity Hall, Cambridge (MA; Hon. Fellow, 1983); Ridley Hall Theological Coll. Asst Curate, St Mary's, Islington, 1955–57; Warden, Mayflower Family Centre, Canning Town, E16, 1957–69; Bishop Suffragan of Woolwich, 1969–75. Chairman: Evangelical Urban Training Project, 1968–75; Peckham Settlement, 1969–75; Martin Luther King Foundn, 1970–75; Urban Ministry Project, 1970–75; Area Bd for Merseyside, MSC, 1978–85; Central Religious Adv. Cttee for BBC and IBA, 1989–93; Gen. Synod Bd for Social Responsibility, 1991–96; Churches' Enquiry into Unemployment and the Future of Work, 1995–97; Vice-Chm., Archbishop of Canterbury's Commn on Urban Priority Areas, 1983–85. Nat. Pres., Family Service Units, 1987–97. Chm. (alternating with Archbp of Liverpool), Liverpool Inst. of Higher Educn, later Liverpool Hope UC, 1982–97. Cricket: Cambridge Univ., 1950–52 (Captain 1952); Sussex, 1947–62 (Captain 1953; Pres., Sussex CCC, 2001); England (played 22 times) 1950–63 (Captain 1954). Freedom, City of Liverpool, 1995. Hon. LLD Liverpool, 1981; Hon. DTech Liverpool Polytechnic, 1987; Hon. DD: Cambridge, 1991; Exeter, 1998; Birmingham, 1999; Wales, 2000; DUniv Open, 1999. *Publications:* Parson's Pitch, 1964; Built as a City, 1974; Bias to the Poor, 1983; The Other Britain (Richard Dimbleby Lecture), 1984; with Most Rev. D. Worlock: Better Together, 1988; With Christ in the Wilderness, 1990; With Hope in Our Hearts, 1994. *Recreations:* family, reading, music, gardening, reading Wisden, singing in choir. *Address:* Ambledown, 11 Melloncroft Drive, West Kirby, Merseyside CH48 2JA.

SHEPPARD, Francis Henry Wollaston; General Editor, Survey of London, 1954–82, retired; *b* 10 Sept. 1921; *s* of late Leslie Alfred Sheppard; *m* 1st, 1949, Pamela Gordon Davies (*d* 1954); one *s* one *d*; 2nd, 1957, Elizabeth Fleur Lees; one *d. Educ:* Bradfield; King's Coll., Cambridge (MA); PhD London. FRHistS. Asst Archivist, West Sussex CC,

Chichester, 1947–48; Asst Keeper, London Museum, 1948–53. Mayor of Henley on Thames, 1970–71; Pres., Henley Symphony Orchestra, 1973–76. Visiting Fellow, Leicester Univ., 1977–78; Alice Davis Hitchcock Medallion of Soc. of Architectural Historians of Gt Britain, 1964. *Publications:* Local Government in St Marylebone 1688–1835, 1958; London 1808–1870: The Infernal Wen, 1971; Brakspear's Brewery, Henley on Thames, 1779–1979, 1979; The Treasury of London's Past, 1991; London: a history, 1998; (ed) Survey of London, Vols XXVI–XLI, 1956–83. *Address:* 10 Albion Place, West Street, Henley on Thames, Oxon RG9 2DT. *T:* (01491) 574658.

SHEPPARD, Maurice Raymond, RWS; painter; President, Royal Society of Painters in Water-Colours, 1984–87; *b* 25 Feb. 1947; *s* of late Wilfred Ernest Sheppard and of Florence Hilda (*née* Morris). *Educ:* Loughborough; Kingston upon Thames (Dip AD Hons 1970); Royal College of Art (MA 1973). ARWS 1974, RWS 1977, Vice-Pres., 1978–83, Trustee, 1983–95; NEAC 2000. One man exhibitions: New Grafton Gallery, 1979; Christopher Wood Gall., 1989; inaugural exhibn of L'Institut Europ. de l'Aquarelle, Brussels, 1986; works in: Royal Library, Windsor; BM; Contemporary Art Soc. for Wales; V&A; Nat. Museum of Wales; Beecroft Museum and Art Gallery, Southend; Birmingham City Mus. and Art Gallery; Glynn Vivian Mus., Swansea; Nat. Library of Wales; Tullie House, Carlisle; watercolour: The Golden Valley (for film, Shadowlands, 1993). British Instn Award, 1971; David Murray Landscape Award, 1972; Geoffrey Crawshay Meml Travelling Schol., Univ. of Wales, 1973. *Publications:* articles and essays in jls and catalogues; *relevant publication:* Maurice Sheppard, RWS, by Felicity Owen (Old Watercolour Society Club, vol. 59, 1984). *Recreations:* cycling, a small garden, the pursuit of quiet. *Address:* Mole Bridge Cottage, 14 Apsley Street, Rusthall Common, Tunbridge Wells, Kent TN4 8NU. *T:* (01892) 513405.

SHEPPARD, Prof. Michael Charles, PhD; FRCP; William Withering Professor of Medicine, since 2000 (Professor of Medicine, since 1986), Head of Department of Medicine, since 1992, and of Division of Medical Sciences, since 1998, University of Birmingham; *b* 24 Jan. 1947; *s* of Kenneth Alfred and Eileen Maude Sheppard; *m* 1973, Judith Elaine James; two *s* one *d*. *Educ:* Univ. of Cape Town (MB, ChB; PhD 1979). MRCP 1974, FRCP 1985. Wellcome Trust Sen. Lectr, Dept of Medicine, Birmingham Univ., 1982–86; Hon. Consultant Physician, Queen Elizabeth Hosp., Birmingham, 1982–. Founder FMedSci, 1998; Sir Arthur Sims RCS Commonwealth Travelling Professor, 1999. *Publications:* numerous contribs to learned jls and works on clinical and experimental endocrinology. *Recreations:* coastal walking, sport, glass and porcelain collecting. *Address:* Department of Medicine, Queen Elizabeth Hospital, Edgbaston, Birmingham B15 2TH. *T:* (0121) 627 2380. *Club:* Edgbaston Priory (Birmingham).

SHEPPARD, Prof. Norman, FRS 1967; Professor of Chemical Sciences, University of East Anglia, Norwich, 1964–86, now Emeritus; *b* 16 May 1921; *s* of Walter Sheppard and Anne Clarges Sheppard (*née* Finding); *m* 1949, Kathleen Margery McLean; two *s* one *d* (and one *s* decd). *Educ:* Hymers Coll., Hull; St Catharine's Coll., Cambridge. BA Cantab 1st cl. hons 1943; PhD and MA Cantab 1947. Vis. Asst Prof., Pennsylvania State Univ., 1947–48; Ramsay Memorial Fellow, 1948–49; Senior 1851 Exhibn, 1949–51; Fellow of Trinity Coll., Cambridge and Asst Dir of Research in Spectroscopy, Cambridge Univ., 1955–64. *Publications:* scientific papers on spectroscopy and surface chemistry in Proc. Roy. Soc., Faraday Trans., Jl Chem. Soc., Spectrochimica Acta, etc. *Recreations:* architecture, classical music, philosophy of science, walking. *Address:* 5 Hornor Close, Norwich NR2 2LY. *T:* (01603) 453052.

SHEPPARD, Maj.-Gen. Peter John, CB 1995; CBE 1991 (OBE 1982); Controller (Chief Executive), Soldiers, Sailors, Airmen and Families Association—Forces Help, since 1996; *b* 15 Aug. 1942; *s* of Kenneth Wescombe Sheppard and Margaret Sheppard; *m* 1964, Sheila Elizabeth Bell; one *s* one *d*. *Educ:* Welbeck Coll.; RMA Sandhurst; RMCS (BScEng 1st Class Hons London Univ.). Commnd Royal Engineers, 1962; Staff Coll., 1974 (psc); British Embassy, Washington, 1975; OC 29 Field Sqn, 1977 (despatches 1978); GSO1 Mil. Ops, MoD, 1980; CO 35 Engineer Regt, 1982; ACOS, HQ 1st (BR) Corps, 1984; Comdr Corps RE, 1st (BR) Corps, 1986; Dir, Army Plans and Programmes, MoD, 1989; COS HQ BAOR, 1991; Dir Gen. Logistic Policy (Army), MoD, 1993; COS HQ QMG, 1994. Special Advr, H of C Defence Select Cttee, 1997–2001. Chm., RE Officers Widows Soc., 2000–. Gov., Royal Sch., Hampstead, 1997– (Chm., Bd of Govs, 1999–). *Publications:* contribs to RE Jl, NATO's 16 Nations, Officer mag. *Recreations:* golf, philately, travel. *Address:* c/o Lloyds TSB, 3 Allendale Place, Tynemouth, Tyne and Wear NE30 4RA. *Club:* Army and Navy.

SHEPPERD, Sir Alfred (Joseph), Kt 1989; Chairman and Chief Executive: Wellcome plc, 1986–90; The Wellcome Foundation Ltd, 1977–90; Chairman, Burroughs Wellcome Co., 1986–90; *b* 19 June 1925; *s* of Alfred Charles Shepperd and Mary Ann Williams; *m* 1950, Gabrielle Marie Yvette Bouloux; two *d*. *Educ:* Archbishop Tenison's Sch.; University Coll., London (BSc Econ; Fellow, 1986). Rank Organisation, 1949; Selincourt & Sons Ltd, 1963; Chamberlain Group, 1965; Managing Director, Keyser Ullmann Industries Ltd, 1967; Dir, Keyser Ullmann Ltd, 1967; Financial Dir, Laporte Industries Ltd, 1971, Wellcome Foundation Ltd, 1972; Director: Anglia Maltings (Holdings) Ltd, 1972–97; Mercury Asset Management Group (formerly Holdings) Ltd, 1987–96; Isoscelles plc, 1991–93; Oxford Instruments plc, 1991–95; National Transcommunications Ltd, 1992–96; Dep. Chm., Zoo Ops Ltd, 1988–91. Mem., ACOST, 1989–93. Member: Adv. Bd, British-Amer. Chamber of Commerce, 1988–96; Governing Body, Internat. Chamber of Commerce UK, 1988–96. Mem. and Gov., Adv. Panel, Inst. of Intellectual Property, 1986–96; Governor: NIESR, 1981–90; Royal Agricl Soc. of England, 1977–90. Chm., Barts NHS Trust, 1991–93. Commendatore della Repubblica, Italy, 1983; Encomienda al Merito de Sanidad, Spain, 1988; Comdr, Order of Leopold II, Belgium, 1989. *Club:* County (Guildford).

SHEPPERSON, Prof. George Albert, CBE 1989; William Robertson Professor of Commonwealth and American History, University of Edinburgh, 1963–86, now Emeritus; *b* 7 Jan. 1922; *s* of late Albert Edward Shepperson and Bertha Agnes (*née* Jennings); *m* 1952, Joyce Irene (*née* Cooper); one *d*. *Educ:* King's Sch., Peterborough; St John's Coll., Cambridge (Schol.; 1st Class Hons: English Tripos, Pt I, 1942; Historical Tripos, Pt II, 1947); 1st Cl. CertEd (Cantab), 1948. Served War, commnd Northamptonshire Regt, seconded to KAR, 1942–46. Edinburgh University: Lectr in Imperial and American History, 1948, Sen. Lectr, 1960, Reader, 1961; Dean of Faculty of Arts, 1974–77. Visiting Professor: Roosevelt and Chicago Univs, 1959; Makerere Coll., Uganda, 1962; Dalhousie Univ., 1968–69; Rhode Is Coll., 1984; Vis. Scholar, W. E. B. DuBois Inst. for Afro-American Res., Harvard Univ., 1986–87; Lectures: Herskovits Meml, Northwestern Univ., 1966 and 1972; Livingstone Centenary, RGS, 1973; Soc. of the Cincinnati, State of Virginia, 1976; Sarah Tryphena Phillips, in Amer. Lit. and Hist., British Acad., 1979; Rhodes Commem., Rhodes Univ., 1981; Alan Graham Meml, Queen's Univ., Belfast, 1992. Chairman: British Assoc. for American Studies, 1971–74; Mungo Park Bicentenary Cttee, 1971; David Livingstone Documentation Project, 1973–89; Commonwealth Inst., Scotland, 1973–89; Mem., Marshall Aid Commemoration Commn, 1976–88. FEIS 1990. DUniv: York, 1987; Edinburgh, 1991. Jt Editor, Oxford Studies in African Affairs, 1969–85. *Publications:* Independent African: John Chilembwe, 1958, 5th edn 1987; David Livingstone and the Rovuma, 1964; many articles and chapters in learned jls, collaborative vols and encycs. *Recreations:* reading, music. *Address:* 15 Farleigh Fields, Orton Wistow, Peterborough PE2 6YB. *T:* (01733) 238772.

SHER, Sir Antony, KBE 2000; actor, writer; *b* 14 June 1949; *s* of late Emmanuel and of Margery Sher. *Educ:* Sea Point Boys' Junior and High Schools, Cape Town; Webber-Douglas Acad. of Dramatic Art, London, 1969–71. Repertory seasons at Liverpool Everyman, Nottingham Playhouse and Royal Lyceum, Edinburgh; John, Paul, George, Ringo and Bert; Teeth and Smiles; Goose-Pimples; Torch Song Trilogy, Albery, 1985; National Theatre: True West; The Trial, The Resistable Rise of Arturo Ui, 1991; Uncle Vanya, 1992; Stanley, 1996; Royal Shakespeare Co.: Associate Artist, 1982–; Richard III, Merchant of Venice, Twelfth Night, King Lear, The Revenger's Tragedy, Molière, Tartuffe, Hello and Goodbye, Maydays, Red Noses, Singer, Tamburlaine the Great, Travesties, Cyrano de Bergerac, The Winter's Tale, Macbeth; Titus Andronicus, Johannesburg and RNT, 1995; Mahler's Conversion, Aldwych, 2001; *films:* Shadey, 1986; Mark Gertler; The Young Poisoner's Handbook, 1995; Wind in the Willows, 1996; Alive and Kicking, 1996; Mrs Brown, 1997; Shakespeare in Love, 1999; *television series:* The History Man, 1982; The Land of Dreams, 1990; *television film:* Genghis Cohn, 1994. Hon. DLitt Liverpool, 1998. Best Actor Awards: Drama Magazine, 1984; Laurence Olivier, 1985, 1997; London Standard, 1985; TMA, 1995; Evening Standard Peter Sellers Film Award, 1998. *Publications:* Year of the King, 1985; Middlepost (novel), 1988; Characters (paintings and drawings), 1989; Changing Step (TV filmscript), 1989; The Indoor Boy (novel), 1991; Cheap Lives (novel), 1995; (with Greg Doran) Woza Shakespeare!, 1996; The Feast (novel), 1998; Beside Myself (memoir), 2001. *Address:* c/o Paul Lyon-Maris, ICM, Oxford House, 76 Oxford Street, W1N 0AX. *T:* (020) 7636 6565.

SHER, Samuel Julius; QC 1981; a Recorder, since 1987; *b* 22 Oct. 1941; *s* of Philip and Isa Phyllis Sher; *m* 1965, Sandra Maris; one *s* two *d*. *Educ:* Athlone High Sch., Johannesburg; Univ. of the Witwatersrand (BComm, LLB); New Coll., Oxford (BCL). Called to the Bar, Inner Temple, 1968, Bencher, 1988. *Recreation:* tennis. *Address:* 12 Constable Close, NW11 6TY. *T:* (020) 8455 2753.

See also V. H. Sher.

SHER, Victor Herman, (Harold), CA (SA); Chief Executive, Amalgamated Metal Corporation Plc, since 1992 (Group Managing Director, 1988–92); *b* 13 Jan. 1947; *s* of Philip Sher and Isa Phyllis Sher; *m* 1979, Molly Sher; one *s* three *d*. *Educ:* King Edward VII Sch., Johannesburg; Univ. of the Witwatersrand, Johannesburg (BComm). Chartered Accountant, Fuller, Jenks Beechcroft, 1972–73; Amalgamated Metal Corporation: Taxation Manager, 1973; Finance Manager, 1977; Dir of Corporate Finance, 1978; Dir of Corporate Treasury, 1981; Finance Dir, 1983; Finance and Trading Dir, 1986. Chm. of Trustees, Amalgamated Metal Corp. Pension Scheme, 1983–91 (Trustee, 1978). *Recreation:* tennis. *Address:* 42 Southway, Hampstead Garden Suburb, NW11 6SA. *T:* (020) 8455 6160.

See also S. J. Sher.

SHERBOK, Dan. C.; *see* Cohn-Sherbok.

SHERBORNE, Area Bishop of, since 2001; **Rt Rev. Timothy Martin Thornton;** *b* 14 April 1957; *s* of John and Mary Thornton; *m* 1978, Siân Evans; one *s* one *d*. *Educ:* Southampton Univ. (BA Theol. 1978); St Stephen's House, Oxford (Cert. Theol.); KCL (MA Ecclesl Hist. 1997). Ordained deacon, 1980, priest, 1981; Asst Curate, Todmorden, Dio. Wakefield, 1980–83; Priest i/c, Walsden, 1983–85; Chaplain, UC Cardiff, 1985–87; Bishop's Chaplain: Wakefield, 1987–91; London, 1991–94; Principal, N Thames Ministerial Trng Course, 1994–98; Vicar of Kensington, 1998–2001. *Address:* Sherborne House, Tower Hill, Iwerne Minster, Blandford Forum, Dorset DT11 8NH. *T:* (01258) 857659.

SHERBORNE, Archdeacon of; *see* Wheatley, Ven. P. C.

SHERBORNE, Montague; QC 1993; *b* 2 Dec. 1930; *s* of Abraham and Rose Sherborne; *m* 1963, Josephine Valerie Jay; two *s* one *d*. *Educ:* East Ham Grammar Sch.; New Coll., Oxford (BA Hons PPE); London Univ. (PGCE). Teaching, E London, 1954–58; called to the Bar, Middle Temple, 1960 (Harmsworth Schol.). *Recreations:* bridge, Chinese food, singing, amateur dramatics. *Address:* 3 Raymond Buildings, Gray's Inn, WC1R 5BH. *T:* (020) 7831 3833.

SHERBOURNE, Stephen Ashley, CBE 1988; Diector, Chime Communications plc, since 2001; *b* 15 Oct. 1945; *s* of late Jack and Blanche Sherbourne. *Educ:* Burnage Grammar Sch., Manchester; St Edmund Hall, Oxford (BA PPE). Hill Samuel, 1968–70; Conservative Research Dept, 1970–75: Head of Economic Section, 1973–74; Asst Dir, 1974–75; Head of Rt Hon. Edward Heath's Office, 1975–76; Gallaher, 1978–82; Special Adviser to Rt Hon. Patrick Jenkin, (then) Sec. of State for Industry, 1982–83; Political Sec. to the Prime Minister, 1983–88; Sen. Corporate Communications Consultant, Lowe Bell Communications, 1988–92; Man. Dir, Lowe Bell Consultants, subseq. Bell Pottinger Consultants, 1992–99; Chm., Lowe Bell Political, subseq. Bell Pottinger Public Affairs, 1994–2001. *Recreations:* cinema, tennis, music. *Club:* Reform.

SHERBROOKE, Archbishop of, (RC), since 1996; **Most Rev. Mgr André Gaumond;** *b* 3 June 1936. *Educ:* Ste Anne de la Pocatière, PQ (BA); St Paul's Seminary, Ottawa (LTh); Institut Catholique, Paris (LPh). Teacher of Philosophy: Ste Anne de la Pocatière, 1966–69; Coll. d'Enseignment Général et Professionel de la Pocatière, 1969–80; Parish Priest, St Pamphile and St Omer, PQ, 1980–85; Bishop of Ste Anne de la Pocatière, 1985–95; Coadjutor Archbishop of Sherbrooke, 1995–96. *Recreation:* golf. *Address:* 130 rue de la Cathédrale, Sherbrooke, QC J1H 4M1, Canada.

SHERFIELD, 2nd Baron *cr* 1964, of Sherfield-on-Loddon, Southampton; **Christopher James Makins;** President, Atlantic Council of the United States, since 1999; *b* 23 July 1942; *er s* of 1st Baron Sherfield, GCB, GCMG, FRS and Alice Brooks (*d* 1985), *e d* of Hon. Dwight Davis; *S* father, 1996; *m* 1975, Wendy Cortesi; one *d*. *Educ:* Winchester; New Coll., Oxford. Fellow, All Souls Coll., Oxford, 1963–77. HM Diplomatic Service, 1964–75. Sen. Vice-Pres., Aspen Inst., 1989–97. *Heir: b* Hon. Dwight William Makins [*b* 2 March 1951; *m* 1983, Penelope Jane, *d* of D. R. L. Massy Collier]. *Address:* 3034 P Street NW, Washington, DC 20007, USA.

SHERIDAN, Christopher Julian; Chairman, Yorkshire Building Society, since 2001 (non-executive Director, since 1995); *b* 18 Feb. 1943; *s* of late Mark Sheridan and of Olive Maud Sheridan (*née* Hobbs); *m* 1972, Diane Virginia (*née* Wadey); one *d*. *Educ:* Berkhamsted School. Joined Samuel Montagu & Co., 1962; Dir, 1974; Managing Dir, 1981; Chief Exec., 1984–94; Dep. Chm., 1988–94. Mem., Partnership Board, Lovells (formerly Lovell White Durrant), 1996–. Non-executive Director: Hanover Acceptances Ltd, since 1995; Prudential Bache International Bank, since 1996; Minerva plc, since 1996;

Willmott Dixon Ltd, since 1999; Standard Bank Ltd, since 1999. *Recreations:* theatre, travel, tennis. *Club:* Buck's.

SHERIDAN, James; MP (Lab) West Renfrewshire, since 2001; *b* 24 Nov. 1952; *s* of Frank and Annie Sheridan; *m* 1977, Jean McDowell; one *s* one *d*. *Educ:* St Pius Secondary Sch., Drumchapel, Glasgow. Worked in manufacturing industry since leaving school, 1967; full-time Trade Union Official, TGWU, 1998–99. *Recreations:* leisure activities, current affairs. *Address:* 31 Park Glade, Erskine, Renfrewshire PA8 7HH. *T:* (0141) 561 3892.

SHERIDAN, Prof. Lionel Astor, PhD, LLD; Professor of Law, University College, Cardiff, 1971–88 (Acting Principal, 1980 and 1987); retired; *b* 21 July 1927; *s* of Stanley Frederick and Anne Agnes Sheridan; *m* 1948, Margaret Helen (*née* Béghin); one *s* (one *d* decd). *Educ:* Whitgift Sch., Croydon; University College London (LLB 1947; LLD 1969); Queen's Univ., Belfast (PhD 1953). Called to the Bar, Lincoln's Inn, 1948. Part-time Lectr, Univ. of Nottingham, 1949; Lectr, QUB, 1949–56; Prof. of Law, Univ. of Singapore (formerly Univ. of Malaya in Singapore), 1956–63; Prof. of Comparative Law, QUB, 1963–71. Hon. LLD Univ. of Singapore, 1963. *Publications:* Fraud in Equity, 1957; Constitutional Protection, 1963; Rights in Security, 1974; Injunctions and Similar Orders, 1999; *jointly:* The Cy-près Doctrine, 1959; Constitution of Malaysia, 1961, 4th edn 1987; Malaya, Singapore, The Borneo Territories, 1961; Equity, 1969, 3rd edn 1987; Survey of the Land Law of Northern Ireland, 1971; The Modern Law of Charities, 1971, 4th edn 1992; The Law of Trusts, 10th edn 1974, 12th edn 1993; The Comparative Law of Trusts in the Commonwealth and the Irish Republic, 1976; Digest of the English Law of Trusts, 1979; papers in jls. *Recreations:* reading, theatre-going. *Address:* Cherry Trees, Broadway Green, St Nicholas, Vale of Glam CF5 6SR. *T:* (01446) 760403. *Club:* Athenæum.

SHERIDAN, Peter; QC 1977; *b* 29 May 1927; *s* of Hugo and Marie Sheridan. *Educ:* eight schools; Lincoln Coll., Oxford Univ. BA Hons, 1950. Called to the Bar, Middle Temple, 1955, Bencher, 1988. *Recreations:* motor cars, archery. *Address:* 11 Stone Buildings, Lincoln's Inn, WC2A 3TG. *T:* (020) 7831 6381; 17 Brompton Square, SW3 2AD. *T:* (020) 7584 7250; Pile Oak Lodge, Donhead St Andrew, Wilts SP7 9EU. *T:* (01747) 828484.

SHERIDAN, Roderick Gerald, OBE 1978; MVO 1968; HM Diplomatic Service, retired; Consul-General, Barcelona and Andorra, 1977–80; *b* 24 Jan. 1921; *s* of late Sir Joseph Sheridan; *m* 1942, Lois Mary (*née* Greene); one *s* one *d*. *Educ:* Downside Sch.; Pembroke Coll., Cambridge. Served War, Coldstream Guards, N Africa and Italy, 1940–46. HM Overseas Colonial Service: Zanzibar and Cyprus, 1946–60; retd as District Comr, Nicosia; HM Diplomatic Service, 1960–: First Sec., Cyprus, 1960–63; Foreign Office, 1964–66; First Sec., Brasilia, 1966–69; FO, 1969–70; Head of Chancery, Oslo, 1970–73; Consul, Algeciras, 1973–77. Hon. Vice-Consul, Menorca, 1983–93. *Recreations:* tennis, golf, skiing.

SHERIDAN, Susan Elizabeth; *see* Norman, S. E.

SHERIDAN, Tommy; Member (Scot Socialist) Glasgow, Scottish Parliament, since 1999. Columnist, Daily Record. Mem. (Scot Mil Lab) Glasgow Council, 1992–. Contested (Scot Mil Lab) Glasgow Pollok, 1992. Former Pres., Anti-Poll Tax Fedn. *Address:* Scottish Parliament, Edinburgh EH99 1SP; 261c Linthaugh Road, Pollok, Glasgow G53 5YE.

SHERLOCK, Barry; *see* Sherlock, E. B. O.

SHERLOCK, David Christopher, FCSD; Chief Inspector of Adult Learning and Chief Executive, Adult Learning Inspectorate, since 2000; *b* 6 Nov. 1943; *s* of Frank Ernest Sherlock and Emily Edna (*née* Johnson); *m* 1st, 1970, Jean Earl; 2nd, 1976, Cynthia Mary (*née* Hood); one *s* one *d*. *Educ:* Rutlish Sch., Merton, Newcastle upon Tyne; College of Art and Industrial Design, Univ. of Nottingham (BA, MPhil). Nottingham Coll. of Art, 1966–70; Trent Polytechnic, 1970–74; Dep. Dir, Nat. College of Art and Design, Dublin, 1975–80; Principal, Winchester Sch. of Art, 1980–87; Exec. Chm., Hampshire Consortium for Art, Design and Architecture, 1985–87; Head of Central Saint Martin's Coll. of Art and Design and Asst Rector, London Inst., 1988–91; Dir of Develt, RCA, 1991–93; Sen. Inspector, Art, Design and Performing Arts, and for SE England, FEFCE, 1993–97; Chief Inspector and Chief Exec., Training Standards Council, 1997–2001; FRSA. *Recreations:* sailing, mountain biking. *Address:* Adult Learning Inspectorate, 101 Lockhurst Lane, Coventry CV6 5SF; Poplar Farm, West Tytherley, Salisbury SP5 1NR. *Club:* Royal Southern Yacht (Hamble).

SHERLOCK, (Edward) Barry (Orton), CBE 1991; Chairman, Life Assurance and Unit Trust Regulatory Organisation, 1986–96; *b* 10 Feb. 1932; *s* of Victor Edward and Irene Octavia Sherlock; *m* 1955, Lucy Trerice Willey; two *d*. *Educ:* Merchant Taylors' School; Pembroke College, Cambridge (MA 1st cl. Hons Maths). FIA. Joined Equitable Life Assurance Society, 1956; qualified actuary, 1958; Asst Actuary, 1962; Asst Gen. Manager, 1968; Gen. Manager and Actuary, 1972–91; Dir, 1972–94. Director: USS Ltd, 1978–96 (Dep. Chm., 1993–96); M & G Group, 1994–96; Medical Defence Union Ltd, 1994–96. Institute of Actuaries: Hon. Sec., 1978–80; Vice-Pres., 1981–84. Chairman: Life Offices' Assoc., 1985; Life Insurance Council, Assoc. of British Insurers, 1985–86. Trustee, Harvest Help, 1993–96. Liveryman, Co. of Actuaries. *Recreations:* music, gardening. *Club:* Actuaries'.

SHERLOCK, Kathryn Jane; *see* Parminter, K. J.

SHERLOCK, Maeve Christina Mary, OBE 2000; Adviser to the Chancellor of the Exchequer, since 2000; *b* 10 Nov. 1960; *d* of William and Roisin Sherlock. *Educ:* Our Lady's Convent, Abingdon; Univ. of Liverpool (BA Hons Sociol. 1984); Open Univ. (MBA 1997). Treas., Univ. of Liverpool Guild, 1984–85; National Union of Students: Exec. Officer, 1985–86; Treas., 1986–88; Pres., 1988–90; Dep. Dir, 1990–91, Dir, 1991–97, Council for Internat. Educn; Dir, NCOPF, 1997–2000. Mem., Exec. Bd, Eur. Assoc. for Internat. Educn, 1994–97. Dir, Endsleigh Insce, 1986–90. Member: Court, Univ. of Warwick, 1993–95; Assembly, Greenwich Univ., 1995–97; Gov., Sheffield Hallam Univ., 1997–2000. Trustee, Nat. Family and Parenting Inst., 1999–2000. DUniv Sheffield Hallam, 2000. *Recreations:* politics, books, restaurants, films, theatre. *Address:* c/o Council of Economic Advisers, HM Treasury, Parliament Street, SW1P 3AG.

SHERLOCK, Nigel; Chief Executive, Wise Speke, since 1993; Director, Brewin Dolphin Holdings plc, since 1998; Lord-Lieutenant, County of Tyne and Wear, since 2000; *b* 12 Jan. 1940; *s* of late Horace Sherlock and Dorothea Sherlock (*née* Robinson); *m* 1966, Helen Diana Frances Sigmund; two *s* one *d*. *Educ:* Barnard Castle Sch.; Univ. of Nottingham (BA Law). Dir, Ockham Hldgs, 1993–98; non-executive Director: London Stock Exchange, 1995–2001; Skipton Bldg Soc., 1998–. Mem. Bd, 1993–, non-exec. Dep. Chm., 1995–, Assoc. of Private Client Investment Managers and Stockbrokers. Mem. Council, NE Regl Chamber of Commerce, 1997– (Pres., 2000–01). Member: Council, Nat. Assoc. of Pension Funds, 1988–90; C of E Pension Bd, 1988–. Mem., Bishop's Council, Dio. Newcastle, 1975–94; Hon. Financial Advr to Dean and Chapter of Durham Cathedral, 1997–. Patron, Northumbrian Coalition Against Crime, 2001– (Vice-Patron, 1995–2001). Founder Mem., Community Foundn of Tyne and Wear, 1988 (Vice-Pres., 2001–). Member: Council, Univ. of Newcastle upon Tyne, 1984– (Chm., 1993–); Council, St John's Coll., Univ. of Durham, 1984–95 (Hon. Fellow, 1997); Bd of Govs, Royal GS, Newcastle upon Tyne, 1998– (Chm., 2000–). Member: Bd, Fundraising Cttee, N Music Trust, 2000– (Chm.); Bd, Northern Sinfonia Orchestral Soc., 1974–95 (Chm., 1990–95); Northern Sinfonia Develt Trust, 1980–2001 (Trustee, 1980–2001; Chm., 1981–2001). Pres., Northumberland Co. Scouts, 2000– (Mem. Council, 1980–98, Chm., 1990–97). Co-Pres., RFCA, N of England, 2001–. Trustee: Bede Monastery Mus. Trust, 1980–90 (Chm., 1985–90); William Leech Charity, 1990–. Hon. Brother, Trinity House, Newcastle upon Tyne, 1995–. FSI 1999; FRSA 1994; CIMgt 2000. High Sheriff, 1990–91, DL, 1995–2000, Tyne and Wear. Freeman, City of London, 2000; Liveryman, Scriveners' Co., 2000–; Freeman, City of Newcastle, 1985. *Recreations:* family, the countryside, leisurely ski-ing, listening to music, theatre. *Address:* 14 North Avenue, Gosforth, Newcastle upon Tyne NE3 4DS. *T:* (0191) 285 4379; Wise Speke, Commercial Union House, 39 Pilgrim Street, Newcastle upon Tyne NE1 6RQ. *T:* (0191) 279 7300. *Clubs:* Brooks's, City of London; New (Edinburgh); Northern Counties (Newcastle upon Tyne).

SHERLOCK, Prof. Dame Sheila (Patricia Violet), DBE 1978; MD; FRCP, FRCPE; FRS 2001; Professor of Medicine, University of London, at the Royal Free Hospital School of Medicine, since 1959; *b* 31 March 1918; *d* of late Samuel Philip Sherlock and Violet Mary Catherine Beckett; *m* 1951, David Geraint James, *qv*; two *d*. *Educ:* Folkestone County Sch.; Edinburgh Univ. Ettles Scholar, 1941; Beit Memorial Research Fellow, 1942–47; Rockefeller Fellow, Yale University, USA, 1948. Physician and Lecturer in Medicine, Postgraduate Medical School of London, 1948–59. RCP Lectures: Bradshaw, 1961; Rolleston, 1968; Lumleian, 1978; Harveian, 1985. RCP: Councillor, 1964–68; Censor, 1970–72; Senior Censor and Vice-Pres., 1976–77. Mem. Senate, Univ. of London, 1976–81. Hon. Member: Gastro-enterological Societies of America, 1963, Australasia, 1965, Mexico, 1968, Czechoslovakia, 1968, Yugoslavia, 1981, Sweden, 1983; Assoc. of Amer. Physicians, 1973; Assoc. of Alimentary Surgeons, 1973; Alpha Omega Alpha Assoc., 1992. Hon. FACP; Hon. FRCPC; Hon. FRACP 1984; Hon. FRCPI; Hon. FRCPS 1986; Hon. FRCS 1989. Hon. DSc: City Univ. of NY, 1977; Yale Univ., USA, 1983; Edinburgh, 1985; London, 1989; Cambridge, 1995; Hon. MD: Lisbon, 1981; Oslo, 1981; Leuven, 1984; Barcelona, 1991; Mainz, 1991; TCD, 1992; Valladolid, 1994; Wisconsin, 1995; Santiago de Chile, 1995; Padua, 1996; Toronto, 1996; Oviedo, 1998; Hon. LLD Aberdeen, 1982. William Cullen Prize, 1962 (shared); Jimenez-Diaz Prize, 1980; Thannhauser Prize, 1980; Fothergill Gold Medal, Med. Soc. of London, 1983; Gold Medal, BMA, 1985. *Publications:* Diseases of the Liver and Biliary System, 1955, 11th edn 2001; papers on liver structure and function in various medical journals, since 1943. *Recreations:* cricket, travel. *Address:* 41 York Terrace East, NW1 4PT. *T:* (020) 7486 4560, (020) 7431 4589.

SHERMAN, Sir Alfred, Kt 1983; journalist; public affairs advisor in private practice; co-founder, Centre for Policy Studies, 1974 (Director of Studies until 1984); *b* 10 Nov. 1919; *m* 1958, Zahava (*d* 1993), *d* of Dr Gideon Levin; one *s*. Served in International Brigade, Spanish Civil War, 1937–38; war of 1939–45 in field security and occupied enemy territory administration. Mem., economic adv. staff of Israeli Govt, in 1950s; leader writer, Jewish Chronicle; various appts with Daily Telegraph, 1965–86, as leader writer 1977–86. Consultant to Pres. Radovan Karadžic of the Serbian Republic in Bosnia-Herzogovina, 1993–94. Chm., Lord Byron Foundn for Balkan Studies, Arizona, 1995–. Vis. Fellow, LSE, 1983–85. Broadcaster. Councillor, RBK&C, 1971–78. FRSA 1996. *Publications:* Local Government Reorganisation and Industry, 1970; Councils, Councillors and Public Relations, 1973; Local Government Reorganization and the Salary Bill, 1974; (with D. Mallam) Waste in Wandsworth, 1976; Crisis Calls for a Minister for Denationalization, 1980; The Scott Report, 1981; (introd.) The Grenada Documents, ed Brian Crozier, 1987; (contrib.) Revisionism, 1961; Communism and Arab Nationalism: a reappraisal; Capitalism and Liberty; Our Complacent Satirists; Political Violence in Britain; contribs to newspapers and periodicals. *Address:* 14 Malvern Court, Onslow Square, SW7 3HU. *T:* (020) 7581 4075; *e-mail:* shermania@compuserve.com. *Club:* Reform.

SHERMAN, Sir Louis, (Sir Lou Sherman), Kt 1975; OBE 1967; JP; Chairman, Housing Corporation, 1977–80; Deputy Chairman, Harlow Development Corporation. Initiated Lea Valley Regional Park Authority. Mayor of Hackney, 1961. Chm., London Boroughs Assoc., 1971–78. JP Inner London Area. *Recreations:* politics, reading, talking.

SHERRARD, Michael David; QC 1968; Director, Middle Temple Advocacy, since 1994; a Recorder of the Crown Court, 1974–93; *b* 23 June 1928; *er s* of late Morris and Ethel Sherrard; *m* 1952, Shirley (artist), *d* of late Maurice and Lucy Bagrit; two *s*. *Educ:* King's Coll., London. LLB 1949. Called to Bar, Middle Temple, 1949 (Bencher 1977; Treas., 1996); Mem., Inner Temple, 1980; Mem. Senate, 1977–80. Mem., SE Circuit, 1950. Mem., Winn Cttee on Personal Injury Litigation, 1966; Mem. Council, Justice, British Section, Internat. Commn of Jurists, 1974–2000; Dept of Trade Inspector, London Capital Group, 1975–77; Chm., Normansfield Hosp. Inquiry, 1977–78; Comr for trial of local govt election petitions (under Representation of the People Act 1949), 1978–80. Mem., Bar Assoc. of NYC, 1986–94. FRSA 1991. *Recreations:* oriental art, travel, listening to opera. *Address:* Middle Temple Treasury, 2 Plowden Building, Middle Temple Lane, EC4Y 9AT. *T:* (020) 7427 4815; 26 Eton Avenue, Hampstead, NW3 3HL. *T:* (020) 7431 0713.

SHERRATT, Brian Walter, OBE 1995; Headmaster, Great Barr School, since 1984; *b* 28 May 1942; *er s* of Walter Eric Sherratt and Violet Florence Sherratt (*née* Cox-Smith); *m* 1966, (Pauline) Brenda Hargreaves; two *s* two *d*. *Educ:* Univ. of Leeds (BA Hons 1964, PGCE 1965); Inst. of Educn, Univ. of London (AcDipEd 1973, MA 1976). Asst Master, Normanton GS, 1965–67; Hd, Religious Studies Dept, Selby GS, 1967–70; Avery Hill College of Education: Sen. Lectr in Religious Studies and Warden, 1970–73 (Sen. Warden, 1972–73); Warden, Mile End Teachers' Centre, 1971–73; concurrently Asst Master, Kidbrooke Sch., London, 1970–71; Sen. Master, 1973–76, Dep. Headmaster, 1976–79, Sandown Court Sch., Tunbridge Wells; Headmaster and Warden, Kirk Hallam Sch. and Community Centre, Ilkeston, Derbys, 1979–84. Mem. Court, 1986–90, Hon. Lectr, Sch. of Educn, 1988–, Univ. of Birmingham. Member: Centre for Policy Studies, 1994–; Politeia, 1995–; Civitas, 2000–. Chairman: Eco-Schs Adv. Panel, 1997–2001; Green Code for Schs Adv. Panel, 1998–2001; non-executive Director: Going for Green, 1996– (Mem., Organising Cttee, 1994–96); Envmtl Campaigns, 1998– (Trustee, Pension Fund, 1999–). FIMgt 1984; FRSA 1984. Queen Mother's Birthday Award for the Envmt, 1999. *Publications:* Gods and Men: a survey of world religions, 1971; Local Education Authorities Project, 1988; Opting for Freedom: a stronger policy on grant-maintained schools, 1994; Grant-Maintained Status: considering the options, 1994; (jtly) A Structured Approach to School and Staff Development: from theory to practice, 1996; (jtly) Headteacher Appraisal, 1997; (jtly) Radical Educational Policies and Conservative Secretaries of State, 1997; (jtly) Policy, Leadership and Professional Knowledge in

Education, 1999; contrib. to TES, etc. *Recreations:* opera, buildings, reading, antiques. *Address:* Great Barr School, Aldridge Road, Birmingham B44 8NU. *T:* (0121) 366 6611, *Fax:* (0121) 366 6007; *e-mail:* headmaster@greatbarr.bham.sch.uk; Oakhurst, 17 Lenton Road, The Park, Nottingham NG7 1DQ. *T:* (0115) 941 8766.

SHERRATT, Prof. David John, PhD; FRS 1992; FRSE; Iveagh Professor of Microbiology, and Fellow, Linacre College, Oxford, since 1994; *b* 14 June 1945; *m* 1st, 1968, Susan Bates (marr. diss. 1992); one *s* two *d*; 2nd, 1992, Dr Lidia Kamilla Arciszewska; one *d*. *Educ:* Manchester Univ. (BSc 1st Cl. Biochem. 1966); Edinburgh Univ. (PhD Molecular Biol. 1969). FRSE 1984. Post-doctoral Fellow, Univ. of California, 1969–71; Lectr in Microbial Genetics, Univ. of Sussex, 1971–80; Prof. of Genetics, Inst. of Genetics, Glasgow Univ., 1980–93. Mem., EMBO, 1983. *Publications:* scientific papers and reviews; editor of several jls. *Recreations:* variety of outdoor pursuits. *Address:* Linacre College, Oxford OX1 3JA.

SHERRIN, Edward George, (Ned), CBE 1997; film, theatre and television producer, presenter, director and writer; *b* Low Ham, Som, 18 Feb. 1931; *s* of late T. A. Sherrin and D. F. Sherrin (*née* Drewett). *Educ:* Sexey's Sch., Bruton; Exeter Coll., Oxford; Gray's Inn. Producer: ATV, Birmingham, 1955–57; BBC TV, 1957–66 (prod. and dir. That Was The Week That Was). Produced films: The Virgin Soldiers (with Leslie Gilliat) 1968; Every Home Should Have One, 1969; (with Terry Glinwood) Up Pompeii, 1971; Up the Chastity Belt, 1971; Girl Stroke Boy, 1971; Rentadick, 1971; Up the Front, 1972; The National Health, 1972; acted in film: Orlando, 1993; TV plays (with Caryl Brahms) include: Little Beggars; Benbow was his Name; Take a Sapphire; The Great Inimitable Mr Dickens; Feydeau Farces; plays (with Caryl Brahms): No Bed for Bacon; Cindy-Ella or I Gotta Shoe, 1962–63; The Spoils, 1968; Nicholas Nickleby, 1969; Sing a Rude Song, 1970; Fish out of Water, 1971; Liberty Ranch, 1972; Nickleby and Me, 1975; Beecham, 1980; The Mitford Girls, 1981; Oh, Kay! (new book with Tony Geiss), 1984; directed: Come Spy with Me, Whitehall, 1967; (and appeared in) Side by Side by Sondheim, Mermaid, 1976, NY 1977; Only in America (with D. Yakir), Roundhouse, 1980; Noël, Goodspeed, USA, 1981; Mr & Mrs Nobody, Garrick, 1986; Jeffrey Bernard is Unwell, Apollo, 1989, Old Vic, 1999; Same Old Moon, Nuffield, Southampton, 1990; Bookends, Apollo, 1990; Our Song, Apollo, 1992; A Passionate Woman, Comedy, 1994; Salad Days, Vaudeville, 1996; Good Grief, touring, 1998; Bing Bong, touring, 1999; A Saint She Ain't, King's Head, Islington, 1999, Apollo, 2000; directed and co-adapted: The Ratepayers' Iolanthe, QEH, 1984 (Olivier Award); The Metropolitan Mikado, QEH, 1985; Small Expectations, QEH, 1986; dir, The Sloane Ranger Revue, Duchess, 1985; scripted (with A. Beaton) Ziegfeld, London Palladium, 1988. TV appearances include: Song by Song, BBC and Yorkshire TV series; Quiz of the Week, BBC; The Rather Reassuring Programme, ITV; We Interrupt this Week, PBS, NY; Friday Night Saturday Morning, BBC-2; Countdown, Channel 4; radio appearances: Midweek (host), Medium Dry Sherrin, Extra Dry Sherrin, And So to Ned; Loose Ends; Counterpoint. Governor, BFI, 1980–84. Guild of TV Producers and Directors' Awards; Ivor Novello Award, 1966. *Publications:* (with Caryl Brahms) Cindy-Ella or I Gotta Shoe, 1962; Rappell 1910, 1964; Benbow was his Name, 1967; Ooh la! la! (short stories), 1973; After You Mr Feydeau, 1975; A Small Thing—Like an Earthquake (memoirs), 1983; (with Caryl Brahms) Song by Song, 1984; Cutting Edge, 1984; (with Neil Shand) 1956 and all that, 1984; (with Caryl Brahms) Too Dirty for the Windmill, 1986; Loose Neds, 1990; Theatrical Anecdotes, 1991; Ned Sherrin in his Anecdotage, 1993; (ed) The Oxford Dictionary of Humorous Quotations, 1995; Scratch an Actor (novel), 1996; Sherrin's Year (diary), 1996; many songs. *Address:* c/o Casarotto Ramsay Ltd, 60–66 Wardour Street, W1V 3HP. *T:* (020) 7287 4450.

SHERRINGTON, Prof. David, PhD; FRS 1994; FInstP; Wykeham Professor of Physics, University of Oxford, since 1989; Fellow, New College, Oxford, since 1989; *b* 29 Oct. 1941; *s* of James Arthur Sherrington and Elfreda (*née* Cameron); *m* 1966, Margaret Gee-Clough; one *s* one *d*. *Educ:* St Mary's Coll.; Univ. of Manchester (BSc 1st Cl. Hons Physics, 1962; PhD Theoretical Physics, 1966). FInstP 1974; Asst Lectr in Theoretical Physics, 1964–67, Lectr, 1967–69, Univ. of Manchester; Asst Res. Physicist, UCSD, 1967–69, Lectr in Theor. Solid State Phys, 1969–74, Reader in Theor. Solid State Phys, 1974–83, Prof. of Phys, 1983–89, Imperial Coll., Univ. of London; Cadre Supérieur, Inst Laue Langevin, Grenoble, France, 1977–79; Ulam Scholar, Los Alamos Nat. Lab., USA, 1995–96. Bakerian Lect., Royal Soc., 2001. Fellow, Amer. Physical Soc., 1985. Editor, Advances in Physics, 1984–; Hon. Editor, Jl of Physics A: Mathematical and General, 1989–93. Hon. MA Oxford, 1989. *Publications:* (ed jtly) Phase Transitions in Soft Condensed Matter, 1990; (ed jtly) Spontaneous Formation of Space-Time Structures and Criticality, 1991; (ed jtly) Phase Transitions and Relaxation in Systems with Competing Energy Scales, 1993; (ed jtly) Physics of Biomaterials: fluctuations, self-assembly and evolution, 1995; (ed jtly) Dynamical properties of unconventional magnetic systems, 1998; papers in learned jls. *Recreations:* wine tasting, travel, theatre, walking, ski-ing. *Address:* 53 Cumnor Hill, Oxford OX2 9EY.

SHERRINGTON, Air Vice-Marshal Terence Brian, CB 1997; OBE 1984; Director Welfare, RAF Benevolent Fund, since 1998 (Director Administration, 1997); *b* 30 Sept. 1942; *s* of Thomas and Edna Sherrington; *m* 1969, Anne Everall; one *s* one *d*. *Educ:* Ottershaw Sch.; Westminster Technical Coll. Commnd RAF, 1963; served Aden, Sharjah, Germany and UK, 1963–78; RAF Staff College, 1979; MoD, 1980–81; OC Admin Wing, RAF Leuchars, 1981–83; OC, RAF Hereford, 1983–85; RCDS, 1986; Sen. Officer Admin, HQ 11 Gp, 1987–88; Dir of Personnel (Ground), MoD, 1988–91; AOA and AOC Support Units, RAF Support Comnd, 1992–93; Head, RAF Admin. Br., 1992–97; AO Admin and AOC Directly Administered Units, Strike Comd, 1994–97. Mem. Council, Wycombe Abbey Sch., 1998–. Freeman, Tallow Chandlers' Co., 1998–. FIMgt. *Recreations:* fishing, golf, Rugby. *Address:* c/o Lloyds TSB, Shipston-on-Stour, Warwicks CV36 4AJ. *Club:* Royal Air Force.

SHERRY, Prof. Norman, FRSL 1985; writer; Mitchell Distinguished Professor of Literature, Trinity University, San Antonio, Texas, since 1983; *b* 6 July 1935; *m* 1st, 1960, Sylvia Brunt (marr. diss. 1990); 2nd, 1990, Carmen Flores (marr. diss. 1996); one *s* one *d*. *Educ:* Univ. of Durham (BA Eng Lit); Univ. of Singapore (PhD). Lectr, Univ. of Singapore, 1961–66; Lectr and Sen. Lectr, Univ. of Liverpool, 1966–70; Prof. of English, Univ. of Lancaster, 1970–82. Fellow, Humanities Research Center, N Carolina, 1982; Guggenheim Fellow, 1989–90. *Publications:* Conrad's Eastern World, 1966; The Novels of Jane Austen, 1966; Charlotte and Emily Bronte, 1969; Conrad's Western World, 1971; Conrad and his World, 1972; (ed) Conrad: the Critical Heritage, 1973; (ed) An Outpost of Progress and Heart of Darkness, 1973; (ed) Lord Jim, 1974; (ed) Nostromo, 1974; (ed) The Secret Agent, 1974; (ed) The Nigger of Narcissus, Typhoon, Falk and Other Stories, 1975; (ed) Joseph Conrad: a commemoration, 1976; The Life of Graham Greene, vol. I, 1904–1939, 1989, vol. II, 1939–1955, 1994 (Edgar Allan Poe Award, Britannica Book of the Year, 1990); contribs to Review of English Studies, Notes & Queries, Modern Language Review, TLS, Observer, The Daily Telegraph, The Guardian, The Independent, Sunday Times, New York Times, Literary Review. *Recreations:* reading, writing, jogging, body building. *Address:* Trinity University, 715 Stadium Drive, San Antonio, TX 78212, USA.

SHERSTON-BAKER, Sir Robert (George Humphrey), 7th Bt *cr* 1796, of Dunstable House, Richmond, Surrey; *b* 3 April 1951; *o s* of Sir Humphrey Sherston-Baker, 6th Bt and Margaret Alice (*m* 2nd, Sir Ronald Leach, GBE; she *d* 1994), *o d* of Henry William Binns; *S* father, 1990; *m* 1991, Vanessa, *y d* of C. E. A. Baird; one *s* one *d*. *Heir: s* David Arbuthnot George Sherston-Baker; *b* 24 Nov. 1992. *Address:* Wealden House, North Elham, Kent CT4 6UY.

SHERVAL, Rear-Adm. David Robert, CB 1989; CEng; FIMechE; FIMarE; Chief Surveyor and Deputy General Manager, The Salvage Association, 1990–98; *b* 4 July 1933; *s* of William Robert Sherval (HMS Hood, 1941), and Florence Margaret Sherval (*née* Luke); *m* 1961, Patricia Ann Phillips; one *s* one *d*. *Educ:* Portsmouth Southern Grammar School. Artificer Apprentice, 1950; BRNC Dartmouth, 1951; Training: at sea, HM Ships Devonshire, Forth and Glasgow, 1951–52 and 1955; RNEC, 1952–53, 1956; served: HM Ships Eagle, Tiger, Hampshire, HM Dockyard Gibraltar and HMY Britannia, 1957–68; BRNC, 1968–70; HMS Juno, 1970–72; NDC, 1972–73; Naval Plans, MoD, 1973–75; Staff of FO Sea Training, 1975–76; Naval Op. Requirements, MoD, 1976–77; NATO Defence Coll., Rome, 1979; ACOS (Intell.) to SACLANT, 1979–82; Fleet Marine Engineer Officer, 1982–84; Dir, Naval Logistic Planning, 1984–85; ADC to the Queen, 1985; CSO (Engrg) to C-in-C Fleet, 1985–87; Dir Gen. Ship Refitting, 1987–89. *Recreation:* music.

SHERWIN, Glynn George; Head of Corporate Finance, Sheffield City Council, 1998–2001; *b* 27 Feb. 1948; *s* of George Sherwin and Lilian Sherwin (*née* Billingham); *m* 1969, Janet Heather Broomhead Ferguson; one *s* two *d*. *Educ:* Firth Park Grammar Sch., Sheffield; Chesterfield Coll. of Technol. CPFA (Hons Final) 1971. Various posts, Sheffield CBC, 1966–74; Sheffield City Council: Principal Accountant, 1974–79; Chief Develt Officer, 1979–88; Asst City Treas., 1988–94; Dep. City Treas., 1994–98. Project Examr, 1978–83, Sen. Project Examr, 1983–86, Chartered Inst. Public Finance and Accountancy. *Recreations:* jogging, keep fit, reading, cinema, theatre. *Address:* 4 Melford Glen, Sheffield S10 5SU.

SHERWOOD, Bishop Suffragan of, since 1989; **Rt Rev. Alan Wyndham Morgan;** *b* 22 June 1940; *s* of A. W. Morgan; *m* 1965, Margaret Patricia, *d* of W. O. Williams; one *s* one *d*. *Educ:* Boys' Grammar School, Gowerton; St David's Coll., Lampeter (BA 1962); St Michael's Coll., Llandaff. Deacon 1964, priest 1965; Assistant Curate: Llangyfelach with Morriston, 1964–69; Cockett, 1969–72; St Mark with St Barnabas, Coventry, 1972–73; Team Vicar, St Barnabas, Coventry East, 1973–77; Bishop's Officer for Social Responsibility, Diocese of Coventry, 1978–83; Archdeacon of Coventry, 1983–89. Mem., Gen. Synod, 1980–89. Vice-Pres., NCVO, 1989–93 (Chm., 1986–89); Chairman: Dio. of Southwell Ministry Gp, 1989–97; Dio. of Southwell Social Housing Gp, 1990–; Lay Training Partnership, Dio. of Southwell, 1998–2001; Wkg Pty on Future of the Family, Bd of Social Responsibility, 1993–95; Notts Child Care Forum, 1993–99; Regl Awards Cttee, Nat. Lottery Charities Bd, 1999–2000 (Chm., E Midlands Regl Adv. Panel, 1995–99); Coalfields Regeneration Trust, 1999–; Member: N Notts HA Local Res. Ethics Cttee, 1990–97; Governing Council, Family Policy Studies Gp, 1994–99; Dep. Prime Minister's Coalfield Task Force, 1997–98; Mansfield Area Strategic Partnership (formerly Mansfield Partnership Task Force), 1998–; President: Notts Help the Homeless, 1990–; Mansfield Disabled Inf. Advice Line, 1994–; Director: Greater Nottingham TEC, 1991–95; N Notts TEC, 1995–2001; Notts Enterprise, 2001–. Trustee, Charities Aid Foundn, 1997–. *Address:* Dunham House, Westgate, Southwell, Notts NG25 0JL.

SHERWOOD, James Blair; Founder and President, Sea Containers Group, Bermuda and London, since 1965; Chairman: Orient-Express Hotels, since 1987; GE Senco SRL, since 1998; Neptune Maritime Ltd, since 1999; *b* 8 Aug. 1933; *s* of William Earl Sherwood and Florence Balph Sherwood; *m* 1977, Shirley Angela Masser Cross; two step *s*. *Educ:* Yale Univ. (BA Economics 1955). Lieut US Naval Reserve, Far East service, afloat and ashore, 1955–58. Manager, French Ports, later Asst General Freight Traffic Manager, United States Lines Co., Le Havre and NY, 1959–62; Gen. Manager, Container Transport Internat. Inc., NY and Paris, 1963–64. In partnership with Mark Birley, established Harry's Bar Club in London, 1979. Restored, and brought into regular service, the Venice Simplon-Orient-Express, 1982. Trustee, Solomon R. Guggenheim Foundn, 1989–. *Publication:* James Sherwood's Discriminating Guide to London, 1975, 2nd edn 1977. *Recreations:* sailing, tennis, skiing. *Address:* Hinton Manor, Hinton Waldrist, Oxon SN7 8SA. *T:* (01865) 820260. *Clubs:* Hurlingham, Pilgrims.

SHERWOOD, (Peter) Louis (Michael); Chairman: Clerical Medical Investment Group, since 2000; Govett European Technology and Income Trust plc (formerly First Ireland Investment Co.), since 1999; Director, Hbos, since 2001; *b* 27 Oct. 1941; *s* of Peter Louis Sherwood and Mervyn Sherwood (*née* de Toll); *m* 1970, Nicole Dina; one *s* two *d*. *Educ:* New Coll., Oxford (BA 1963; MA 1966); Stanford Univ. (MBA 1965). Morgan Grenfell & Co., Corporate Finance Officer, 1965–68; Asst to Chm., Fine Fare (Supermarkets), 1968–69; Man. Dir, Melias (Fine Fare subsid.), 1969–72; Dir, Anglo-Continental Investment & Finance Co., 1972–79; Sen. Vice-Pres. for Development, Grand Union Co., USA, 1979–85; Pres., Great Atlantic & Pacific Tea Co., USA, 1985–88; Chm. and Chief Exec., Gateway Foodmarkets, 1988–89; Chairman: HTV Gp, 1991–97 (Dir, 1990–97); HTV West, 1997–99. Director: RoK Property Solutions (formerly EBC Gp plc), 1990–; Clerical Medical Investment Group (formerly Clerical Medical & General Life Assurance Soc.), 1990– (Dep. Chm., 1996–2000); Halifax Bldg Soc., subseq. Halifax Gp plc, 1997–2001. *Recreations:* mountain walking, collecting fine wine. *Address:* 10 College Road, Clifton, Bristol BS8 3HZ. *Club:* Lansdowne.

SHERWOOD, (Robert) Antony (Frank), CMG 1981; Assistant Director-General, British Council, 1977–81, retired; *b* 29 May 1923; *s* of Frank Henry Sherwood and Mollie Sherwood (*née* Moore); *m* 1953, Margaret Elizabeth Simpson; two *s* two *d*. *Educ:* Christ's Hospital; St John's Coll., Oxford (BA 1949, MA 1953). War service, RAF, 1942–46. Apptd to British Council, 1949; served in Turkey, Nigeria (twice), Syria, Uganda, Somalia and at HQ. Help the Aged: Vice-Chm., Internat. Cttee, 1982–88, Chm., 1988–92; Trustee, 1988–94; Mem. Council and Exec. Cttee, HelpAge Internat., 1983–93; Hon. PRO, Surrey Voluntary Service Council, 1982–88. Vice-Chm., Management Cttee, Guildford Inst. of Univ. of Surrey, 1993–97 (Chm., Finance Cttee, 1988–93). *Publication:* (ed) Directory of Statutory and Voluntary Health, Social and Welfare Services in Surrey, 1987. *Recreations:* travel, genealogy and family history, reading. *Address:* 18 Rivermount Gardens, Guildford, Surrey GU2 4DN. *T:* (01483) 538277.

SHERWOOD, Prof. Thomas, FRCP, FRCR; Professor of Radiology, 1978–94, Clinical Dean, 1984–96, University of Cambridge, now Professor Emeritus; Fellow of Girton College, Cambridge, since 1982; *b* 25 Sept. 1934; *m* 1961, Margaret Gooch; two *s* one *d*. *Educ:* Frensham Heights Sch.; Guy's Hospital, London. MA; DCH. Consultant Radiologist, Hammersmith Hospital and St Peter's Hospitals, 1969–77. Chm. Govs, Frensham Heights Sch., 1996–2000. Ombudsman, The Lancet, 1996–2001. *Publications:*

Uroradiology, 1980; Roads to Radiology, 1983; Blow the Wind Southerly, 1988; papers in medical and radiological jls, 1964–. *Recreations:* music, reading and writing. *Address:* 19 Clarendon Street, Cambridge CB1 1JU.

SHESTOPAL, Dawn Angela, (Mrs N. J. Shestopal); *see* Freedman, D. A.

SHETH, Pranlal, CBE 1994; Director: One World International (formerly One World Online) Ltd, since 1995; Victim Support Ltd, since 1995; Member, Independent Television Commission, 1991–95; *b* 20 Dec. 1924; *s* of Purashotam Virji Sheth and Sakarben Sheth; *m* 1951, Indumati Sheth; one *s* one *d*. Called to the Bar, Lincoln's Inn, 1962. Journalist, Kenya, 1943–52; Chm., Nyanza Farmers' Cooperative Soc., 1954–60; Mem., Central Agriculture Bd, Kenya, 1963–66; Chm., Asian Hosp. Authority, 1964–66; Mem., Economic Planning and Develt Council, Kenya, 1964–66. Group Sec., 1971, Legal Advr and Dir, 1985–88, Abbey Life Gp of Cos; Chm. Adv. Bd, Abbey Ethical Unit Trust, 1988–96; Legal Dir, Hartford Europe Gp of Cos, 1977–86; Director: Abbey Life Assurance Co. Ltd, 1977–89; Ambassador Life Assce Co. Ltd, 1980–88; Abbey Life Assurance (Ireland), 1981–85; Reed Exec. plc, 1990–93; Chairman: Sense Internat. Ltd, 1998–; Channel East TV, 1999–; Go Education plc, 2000–. Gp Sec., ITT cos in UK, 1983–86. Chairman: Asian Business Initiatives, 1997–; Unity Radio, 1997–; Mem. Bd, Notting Hill Housing Trust, 1997–; Advr, Supervisory Bd, One World Europe BV, Maastricht, 1998–2000. Director: Round House Arts Centre, 1986–90; Pan-Centre for Inter-Cultural Arts, 1998–; Member: BBC Consultative Gp on Commerce, Industry and Finance, 1986–89; BBC Asian Progs Adv. Cttee, 1986–89; IBA, 1990. Founder, and Chief Editor, Gujarat Samachar Weekly, 1972–73; Mem., N Metropolitan Conciliation Cttee, Race Relations Bd, 1973–77; a Dep. Chm., CRE, 1977–80; Vice Pres., UKIAS, 1986–93. Trustee: Project Fullemploy (Charitable Trust), 1977–89; Assoc. of Asian Women, 1979–; Find Your Feet, 1980–2000; Runnymede Trust, 1987–1998; Urban Trust, 1987–2000; Windsor Fellowship, 1988–; Womankind Worldwide Trust, 1989–96; One World Broadcasting Trust, 1991–; Gujarati Literary Acad., 1992–; Immigrants Aid Trust, 1988–; Uniting Britain Trust, 1997–; National Primary Trust, 1998–; Mem. Oxfam Council, 1993–94, Assembly, 1994– (Mem. Shops and Premises Cttee, 1988–93); Vice-Patron, UK Assoc., Internat. Year of the Child, 1978–80; Patron: Internat. Centre for Child Studies; CRE Race in Media Awards, 1992–2001; Ruth Hayman Trust, 2001–. Chm., One World Internat. Foundn, 1999–. Dir, Shelter, 1987–91; Hon. Legal Advr and Mem. Exec. Cttee, Nat. Assoc. of Victim Support Schemes, 1988–95 (Mem. Adv. Bd, 1995–). FInstD 1977; FIMgt (FBIM 1980); FRSA 1999. Mem., Bd of Dirs, Univ. (formerly Poly.) of N London, 1979–2000. Mem. Editorial Adv. Panel, Equal Opportunities Review, 1984. *Address:* 70 Howberry Road, Edgware, Mddx HA8 6SY; *e-mail:* pransheth@aol.com. *Clubs:* Royal Over-Seas League, Royal Commonwealth Society.

SHEUMACK, Rt Rev. Colin Davies; Bishop of Gippsland, 1987–94; *b* 9 Feb. 1929; *s* of Joseph Sheumack and Gwladys (*née* Davies); *m* 1951, Ena Beryl Dickson (*d* 1994); one *s* three *d*, and one adopted *d*. *Educ:* Tingha Central and Inverell High School; Moore Theological Coll. (ThL 2nd cl. Hons). Deacon 1952, priest 1953, Canberra Goulburn; Rector: Kemeruka, 1954–59; Kyabram, Vic., 1959–67; Archdeacon of Bendigo, 1967–83; Vicar General, 1968–83; Dean of Bathurst, 1983–87. Registrar of Melbourne, 1994; Administrator, Dio. Carpentaria, 1995–96. Chairman: SPCK Aust., 1992–; Nat. Anglican Men's Soc., 1994–; Nat. Home Missions Fund, 1997–99; Samaritan Foundn, 1997–. *Recreations:* gardening, fishing. *Address:* 12 Nijorie Close, Kincumber, NSW 2251, Australia. *T:* (2) 43683860. *Clubs:* Nat. Roads and Motoring Assoc. (Sydney); Royal Automobile of Victoria (Melbourne); Avoca Beach Bowling.

SHEVARDNADZE, Eduard Amvrosiyevich, Hon. GCMG 2000; President of Georgia, since 1995; *b* Georgia, 25 Jan. 1928; christened Georgi, 1992, but continues to be known as Eduard. *Educ:* Pedagogical Institute, Kutaisi. Mem., CPSU, 1948–91; Sec., Komsomol Cttee in Kutaisi, 1952–56, of Georgia, 1956–61; 1st Sec., Regional Party Cttee, Mtsheta, 1961–63, Tbilisi, 1963–64; Minister of Internal Affairs, Georgia, 1964–72; 1st Sec., Republican Party Cttee, Georgia, 1972–85; Mem., Politburo, 1985–91; Minister of Foreign Affairs, USSR, 1985–90, 1991; founder, Movement for Democratic Reform, 1991; Chm., Georgian State Council, 1992; Chm., Supreme Council and Head of State, Georgia, 1992–95. Hon. doctorates from Harvard, Boston, Emory and Providence, USA and Trieste, Italy. Order of Lenin (five times); Hero of Socialist Labour (twice); Order of Red Banner of Labour. *Publication:* The Future Belongs to Freedom, 1991. *Address:* Chancellery of the President of Georgia, 7 Ingorovka Street, Tbilisi 380034, Georgia.

SHEWRY, Prof. Peter Robert, CBiol, FIBiol; Director (formerly Head) of Long Ashton Research Station (Institute of Arable Crops Research) and Professor of Agricultural Sciences, University of Bristol, since 1989; *b* 19 March 1948; *s* of late Robert Thomas Shewry and Mary Helen Shewry; *m* 1969, Rosemary Willsdon; one *s* one *d*. *Educ:* Bristol Univ. (BSc, PhD, DSc). Postdoctoral Res. Fellow, Westfield Coll., Univ. of London, 1972; Rothamsted Experimental Station: Res. Scientist, 1974; Head of Biochem. Dept, 1986. *Publications:* (ed with Steven Gutteridge) Plant Protein Engineering, 1992; (ed) Barley: genetics, biochemistry, molecular biology and biotechnology, 1992; (ed with A. K. Stobart) Seed Storage Compounds, 1993; (ed jtly) Protein Phosphorylation in Plants, 1996; (ed jtly) Engineering Crop Plants for Industrial End Uses, 1998; (ed with R. Casey) Seed Proteins, 1999; (ed with A. S. Tatham) Wheat Gluten, 2000; (ed jtly) Biotechnology of Cereals, 2001; numerous papers in sci. jls on plant genetics, biochem. and molecular biol. *Address:* IACR-Long Ashton Research Station, Long Ashton, Bristol BS41 9AF. *T:* (01275) 392181.

SHIACH, Allan George; film writer (as Allan Scott) and producer; Chairman: Macallan-Glenlivet plc, 1980–96; Rafford Films Ltd, since 1983; *b* Elgin; *er s* of late Gordon Leslie Shiach, WS and Lucy Sybil (*née* De Freitas); *m* 1966, Kathleen Swarbreck; two *s* one *d*. *Educ:* Gordonstoun Sch.; L'Ecole des Roches; McGill Univ. (BA). Writer of TV and radio drama, 1965–72; screenwriter and co-writer of films, including: Don't Look Now, 1975; Joseph Andrews, 1977; Martin's Day, 1980; D.A.R.Y.L., 1984; Castaway, 1985; A Shadow on the Sun, 1987; The Witches, 1989; Cold Heaven, 1990; Two Deaths, 1994; In Love and War, 1996; The Preacher's Wife, 1996; Regeneration, 1997; also Producer or Exec. Producer: Cold Heaven, 1991; Shallow Grave, 1994; Two Deaths, 1995; True Blue, 1996; Grizzly Falls, 1999; The Match, 1999. Dir, Scottish Media Group plc (formerly Scottish Television plc), 1993–. Mem., BBC Broadcasting Council (Scotland), 1987–90; Chairman: Writers' Guild of GB, 1989 and 1990; Scottish Film Council, 1991–97; Scottish Film Prodn Fund, 1992–; Scottish Screen, 1997–98; Governor, BFI, 1993–. Mem., Amer. Acad. of Motion Picture Arts & Scis, 1991–. Mem. Council, Scotch Whisky Assoc., 1983–96. Liveryman, Distillers' Co., 1989–. *Recreations:* writing, cooking, tennis. *Address:* Rafford Films Ltd, Clareville House, 26–27 Oxendon Street, SW1Y 4DL. *T:* (020) 7839 1800, *Fax:* (020) 7839 3600. *Club:* Savile.

SHIACH, Gordon Iain Wilson; Sheriff of Lothian and Borders, at Edinburgh, 1984–97, also at Peebles, 1996–97; *b* 15 Oct. 1935; *o s* of late Dr John Crawford Shiach, FDS, QHDS, and Florence Bygott Wilson; *m* 1962, Margaret Grant Smith; one *d* (and one *d* decd). *Educ:* Lathallan Sch.; Gordonstoun Sch.; Edinburgh Univ. (MA, LLB); Open Univ. (BA Hons). Admitted to Faculty of Advocates, 1960; practised as Advocate, 1960–72; Tutor, Dept of Evidence and Pleading, Univ. of Edinburgh, 1963–66; Clerk to Rules Council of Court of Session, 1963–72; Standing Jun. Counsel in Scotland to Post Office, 1969–72; Sheriff of: Fife and Kinross, later Tayside, Central and Fife, at Dunfermline, 1972–79; Lothian and Borders at Linlithgow, 1979–84; Hon. Sheriff at Elgin, 1986–. Member: Council, Sheriffs' Assoc., 1989–95 (Pres., 1993–95); Bd, Lothian Family Conciliation Service, 1989–93; Standing Cttee on Criminal Procedure, 1989–93; Parole Bd for Scotland, 1990–99 (Vice-Chm., 1995–99); Council, Faculty of Advocates, 1993–95; Shrieval Training Gp, 1994–95; Review Gp on Social Work Nat. Standards for Throughcare, 1994–95. Chairman: The Scottish Soc., 1992–93; Edinburgh Sir Walter Scott Club, 1995–98. *Recreations:* walking, swimming, music, art, theatre, film. *Clubs:* New, Scottish Arts (Edinburgh).

SHIELD, Leslie, TD; DL; a Recorder of the Crown Court, 1980–91; *b* 8 May 1916; *s* of Tom Shield and Annie Maud Shield; *m* 1941, Doris Leather; one *s*. *Educ:* Cowley Sch., St Helens; Univ. of Liverpool (LLB 1936, LLM 1938). Qualified solicitor, 1939, admitted 1945. Served War, 1939–46: commnd 5th Bn Prince of Wales' Volunteers (S Lancs) Regt; demob., Major. Entered into gen. practice as solicitor, 1946. DL Merseyside, 1976. *Recreations:* gardening (particular interest, orchids), music. *Address:* 185 Higher Lane, Rainford, St Helens, Merseyside WA11 8NF. *T:* (01744) 882708.

SHIELDS, Prof. Carol Ann, OC 1998; Professor, University of Manitoba, 1980–2000, now Emerita; Chancellor, University of Winnipeg, 1996–2000, now Emerita; *b* 2 June 1935; *d* of Robert Warner and Inez Warner (*née* Sellgren); *m* 1957, Donald Shields; one *s* four *d*. *Educ:* Hanover Coll. (BA 1957); Univ. of Ottawa (MA 1975). Lecturer: Univ. of Ottawa, 1977–88; Univ. of BC, 1978–79. Mem., Royal Soc. of Canada, 1997. Hon. degrees from: Univ. of Ottawa, 1995; Univ. of Winnipeg, 1996; Hanover Coll., Queen's Univ., Univ. of BC, 1997; Concordia Univ., Univ. of Toronto, 1998; Carleton Univ., Wilfrid Laurier Univ., Mount St Vincent Univ., 2000. Marian Engel Award, Toronto, 1990. *Publications:* Small Ceremonies, 1976 (Canadian Authors' Award, 1976); The Box Garden, 1977; Happenstance, 1980; A Fairly Conventional Woman, 1982; Various Miracles, 1985; Swann, 1987 (Arthur Ellis Award, 1987); The Orange Fish, 1989; The Republic of Love, 1992; The Stone Diaries, 1993 (Gov. Gen's Award, 1993; Nat. Book Critics Circle Award, Lire Prize, France, Pulitzer Prize, 1995); Coming to Canada: Poems, 1993; Departures and Arrivals, 1993; Thirteen Hands (play), 1993; Fashion, Power, Guilt and the Charity of Families, 1995; Larry's Party, 1997 (Orange Prize, UK, 1998); Anniversary, 1998; Dressing up for the Carnival, 2000; (with Blanche Howard) A Celibate Season, 2000; Jane Austen, 2001. *Recreations:* theatre, France, literary theory. *Address:* 990 Terrace Avenue, Victoria, BC V8S 3V3, Canada. *Club:* PEN International.

SHIELDS, Elizabeth Lois; Lecturer, Medieval Studies Department, University of York, since 1995; *b* 27 Feb. 1928; *d* of Thomas Henry Teare and Dorothy Emma Elizabeth Roberts-Lawrence; *m* 1961, David Cathro Shields. *Educ:* Whyteleafe Girls' Grammar School; UCL (BA Hons Classics); Avery Hill College of Education (Cert Ed); MA York 1988. Asst Teacher, St Philomena's Sch., Carshalton, 1954–59; Head of Department: Jersey Coll. for Girls, 1959–61; Whyteleafe Girls' Grammar Sch., 1961–62; Trowbridge Girls' High Sch., 1962–64; St Swithun's, Winchester, 1964–65; Queen Ethelburga's, Harrogate, 1967–69; Malton Sch., N Yorks, 1976–86; Univ. of York (on secondment), 1985–86 (Medieval Studies). Mem., Ryedale DC, 1980– (Chm., 1989–90; Chm., Community Services Cttee). Contested (L) Howden, 1979, Ryedale, 1983, 1992; MP (L) Ryedale, May 1986–87. Lib Dem spokesman on envmt, Yorks and Humberside Reg., 1989–; Chm., Yorks and Humberside Lib Dem Candidates' Assoc., 1992–97; President: Lib Dems in Ryedale Constituency, 1995–; Yorks and Humberside Lib Dem Regl Party, 1998–. Chm., Ryedale Housing Assoc., 1990–91; President: Ryedale Motor Neurone Disease Assoc., 1990–; Ryedale Cats' Protection League, 1991–. *Publication:* A Year to Remember, 1996. *Recreations:* gardening, music, travel. *Address:* Firby Hall, Kirkham Abbey, Westow, York YO60 7LH. *T:* (01653) 618474. *Club:* National Liberal.

SHIELDS, (Leslie) Stuart; QC 1970; a Recorder of the Crown Court, 1972–91; *b* 15 May 1919; *m* 1st, 1941, Maureen Margaret McKinstry (*d* 1989); two *s* two *d* (and one *s* decd); 2nd, 1990, Barbara Diana Lloyd. *Educ:* St Paul's School; Corpus Christi College, Oxford. Paid Local Sergeant, Oxford and Buckinghamshire Light Infantry, 1945–47. Called to the Bar, Middle Temple, 1948; Bencher, 1977. Member: Criminal Injuries Compensation Bd, 1981–92; Independent Review Body for Coal Industry, 1985–90. *Recreations:* music, travel. *Address:* Devereux Chambers, Devereux Court, Temple, WC2R 3JJ.

SHIELDS, Michael; *see* Shields, R. M. C.

SHIELDS, Sir Neil (Stanley), Kt 1964; MC 1946; management consultant and company director; Chairman, Commission for the New Towns, 1982–95 (Chairman designate, 1981–82); *b* 7 Sept. 1919; *o s* of late Archie Shields and Mrs Hannah Shields; *m* 1970, Gloria Dawn Wilson. Member of Honourable Artillery Company 1939–. Served in Royal Artillery, 1939–46; commnd 1940; Major 1943. Chairman: Anglo Continental Investment & Finance Co., 1965–74; Standard Catalogue Co., 1976–84; Holcombe Hldgs, 1978–84; Trianco Redfyre, 1979–84; Director: Chesham Amalgamations & Investments, 1964–84; Continental Bankers Agents, 1965–74; Central and Sheerwood, 1969–84; Newton Chambers & Co., 1972–84; Paxall Engineering, 1976–79. London Transport (formerly London Regional Transport): Mem. Bd, 1986–93; Chm., 1988–89, Dep. Chm., 1989–93; Chm., Property Bd, 1986–95. Prospective candidate (C) North St Pancras 1947 and contested by-election 1949. Chairman: Camden Conservative Cttee, 1965–67; Hampstead Conservative Assoc., 1954–65 (Vice-Chm., 1951–54); Hon. Treas. 1965–67; National Union of Conservative and Unionist Assocs: Chm. of London Area, 1961–63 (Vice-Chm., 1959–61); Mem. of National Executive, 1955–59, 1961–67, 1968–69; Hampstead Borough Council: Mem. 1947–65; Deputy Leader, 1952–61; Chm. of Works Cttee, 1951–55; Chm. of Finance Cttee, 1955–59. Mem. Council, Aims of Industry, 1976–. Chm., WNCCC/Cancer Aware Develt Task Force, 1996–98; Vice-Pres., Women's Nationwide Cancer Control Campaign, 1998–. Governor, Bedford Coll., London Univ., 1983–85. Freeman, City of London, 1993; Mem., Ct of Assts, Guild of Freemen, 1998–. Hon. RICS (Hon. MRICS 1993). *Recreations:* reading, music, wining and dining. *Address:* 12 London House, Avenue Road, NW8 7PX. *Clubs:* Carlton, HAC.

SHIELDS, Sir Robert, Kt 1990; DL; MD, FRCS, FRCSE, FRCPS, FRCPE; Professor of Surgery, University of Liverpool, 1969–96; Consultant Surgeon, Royal Liverpool Hospital and Broadgreen Hospital, 1969–96; President, Royal College of Surgeons of Edinburgh, 1994–97; *b* 8 Nov. 1930; *o s* of late Robert Alexander Shields and Isobel Dougall Shields; *m* 1957, Grace Marianne Swinburn; one *s* two *d*. *Educ:* John Neilson Institution, Paisley; Univ. of Glasgow. MB, ChB 1953 (Asher-Asher Medal and MacLeod Medal); MD (Hons and Bellahouston Medal) 1965; FRCSE 1959; FRCS 1966; FRCPS 1993; FRCPE 1996. House appts, Western Infirmary, Glasgow, 1953–54; RAMC, Captain attached 1 Bn Argyll and Sutherland Highlanders, 1954–56; RAMC (TA), Major (Surg. Specialist) attached 7 Bn A and SH, 1956–61. Hall Fellow, Univ. of Glasgow, 1957–58; Mayo Foundn Fellow, 1959–60; Lectr in Surgery, Univ. of Glasgow, 1960–63;

Sen. Lectr and Reader in Surgery, Welsh Nat. Sch. of Medicine, 1963–69; Dean, Faculty of Medicine, Univ. of Liverpool, 1982–85. Mem., GMC, 1982–94. Royal College of Surgeons: Mem., Ct of Examrs, 1980–86; Mem. Bd, Hunterian Inst., 1986–94; Zachary Cope Lectr, 1992; Vice Chm., Royal Liverpool Univ. Hosp. Trust, 1992–95 (non-exec. Trustee, 1991–95); Member: Liverpool AHA (T) (Chm., Area/Univ. Liaison Cttee), 1974–78; Mersey RHA, 1982–85 (Vice-Chm., 1985; Regl Advr, 1986–94); Liverpool Med. Instn (Vice-Pres., 1983–84; Pres., 1988–89); Council, RCSE, 1985–98 (Regent, 1999–); MRC, 1987–91 (Member: Cell Bd, 1974–77; Strategy Cttee, 1987–91); Exec. Cttee, Council of Military Educn Cttees of Univs of UK, 1990–94; Vice-Chm., Specialist Trng Authy, Med. Royal Colls, 1996–97. Member: Surgical Research Soc. (Hon. Sec. 1972–76 and Pres. 1983–85); British Soc. of Gastroenterology (Mem. Council, 1984–86; Pres., 1990–91; Hon. Mem., 1998–); N of England Gastroent. Soc. (Pres., 1981–83); Internat. Surgical Gp; James IV Assoc. of Surgeons, 1986– (Dir, 1991–96; Pres., 1994–96); Assoc. of Surgs of GB and Ire. (Mem. Council 1966–69; Pres., 1986–87); Council, European Surgical Assoc., 1995–98; Chm., Med. Adv. Cttee, British Liver Trust (formerly British Liver Foundn), 1991–94; Vice-Chm., Brit. Jl of Surgery Soc., 1989–95. Member: Panel of Assesssors, Nat. Health and Med. Res. Council of Commonwealth and Australia, 1983–; List of Assessors for Cancer Grants, Anti-Cancer Council of Vic, Australia, 1986–. Chm., Merseyside, Lancashire and Cheshire Council on Alcoholism, 1992–94. Marjorie Budd Prof., Univ. of Bristol, 1983; Wilson Wang Vis. Prof., Chinese Univ. of Hong Kong, 1990; Wellcome Prof., Coll. of Medicine of S Africa, 1991. Former Visiting Prof., Univs of Toronto, Virginia, Witwatersrand, Rochester (NY), Hong Kong, Calif, Yale, and Examiner in Surgery, Univs of Glasgow, Edinburgh, Dundee, Leicester, Sheffield, Cambridge, Lagos, Amman, Riyadh, Malta; Dist. Lectr, Alpha Omega Alpha Assoc., 1994. Mem. Bd of Advrs in Surgery, London Univ., 1983–. Member: Editorial Board: Gut, 1969–76; Brit. Jl of Surgery, 1970–85, 1989–95; Internat. Editl Bd, Current Practice in Surgery, 1989–. Hon. Col Liverpool Univ. OTC, 1994–2001. DL Merseyside, 1991. Founder FMedSci 1998. Hon. FACS 1990; Hon. FCSSA 1991; Hon. FCSHK 1995; Hon. FRCSI 1996; Hon. FRACS 1997; Hon. Fellow: Amer. Surgical Assoc., 1993; Acad. Medicine of Singapore, 1996; Hon. Mem., Indian Assoc. of Surgeons, 1993. Hon. DSc Wales, 1990. Moynihan Medal, Assoc. of Surgs of GB and Ire., 1966. *Publications:* (ed jtly): Surgical Emergencies II, 1979; Textbook of Surgery, 1983; Gastrointestinal Emergencies, 1992; contribs to medical and surgical jls relating to surgery and gastroenterology. *Recreations:* sailing and walking. *Address:* 81 Meols Drive, West Kirby, Wirral CH48 5DF. *T:* (0151) 632 3588; Ardlaraig, Tayvallich, Lochgilphead, Argyll PA31 8PJ. *T:* (01546) 870308. *Club:* Army and Navy.

SHIELDS, (Robert) Michael (Coverdale); Chief Executive, North West Regional Development Agency, since 1999; *b* 23 Jan. 1943; *s* of Thomas and Dorothy Shields; *m* 1965, Dorothy Jean Dennison; two *s* one *d*. *Educ:* Durham Johnston Grammar Tech. Sch.; Durham Univ. (BSc Hons); Newcastle Univ. (DipTP). MRTPI. Planning Departments: Newcastle upon Tyne, 1964–65; Durham CC, 1965–69; Nottingham, 1969–73; Dep. Dir of Planning, Leeds City Council, 1973–78; City Tech. Services Officer and Dep. Chief Exec., Salford City Council, 1978–83; Chief Executive: Trafford BC, 1983–87; Trafford Park Devett Corp., 1987–98. Dir, Innvotec North West Trust Ltd, 1998–. Gov., Altrincham Grammar Sch.; Pro Chancellor and Chm. Council, Salford Univ. *Recreations:* family, books. *Address:* North West Regional Development Agency, New Town House, Buttermarket Street, Warrington, Cheshire WA1 2LF.

SHIELDS, Stuart; *see* Shields, L. S.

SHIERLAW, Norman Craig; Senior Partner, N. C. Shierlaw & Associates (Stock and Sharebrokers), 1968–87; Chairman, Swiss Partners (Stock and Sharebrokers), 1987–91; *b* 17 Aug. 1921; *s* of Howard Alison Shierlaw and Margaret Bruce; *m* 1944, Patricia Yates (*d* 1987); two *d*; *m* 1989, Barbara Jean Lacey. *Educ:* Pulteney Grammar Sch., Adelaide; St Peter's Coll., Adelaide; Univ. of Adelaide (BE). Assoc. Mem. Australian Inst. Mining and Metallurgy; FSASM; Mining Manager's Certificate. War Service, AIF, 1941–45 (War Service medals). Mining Engr with North Broken Hill Ltd, 1949–58; Sharebroker's Clerk, 1959–60; Partner, F. W. Porter & Co. (Sharebrokers), 1960–68. Chairman: Australian Development Ltd, 1981–83 (Dir, 1959–81); Burmine Ltd, 1990–92 (Dir, 1985–90); Director: Poseidon Ltd, 1968–77; North Flinders Mines Ltd, 1969–77; Nobelex NL, 1974–80; Palm Springs Ltd, 1987–; Gympie Eldorado Gold Mines, 1993–97; Cooper's Brewery Ltd, 1995–97. FAIM 1971. *Recreations:* golf, tennis. *Clubs:* Naval, Military and Air Force, Kooyonga Golf (Adelaide).

SHIFFNER, Sir Henry David, 8th Bt *cr* 1818; company director; *b* 2 Feb. 1930; *s* of Major Sir Henry Shiffner, 7th Bt, and Margaret Mary (*d* 1987), *er d* of late Sir Ernest Gowers, GCB, GBE; *S* father, 1941; *m* 1st, 1949, Dorothy Jackson (marr. diss. 1956); one *d* (and one *d* decd); 2nd, 1957, Beryl (marr. diss. 1970), *d* of George Milburn, Saltdean, Sussex; one *d*; 3rd, 1970, Joaquina Ramos Lopez. *Educ:* Rugby; Trinity Hall, Cambridge. *Heir: cousin* George Frederick Shiffner [*b* 3 August 1936; *m* 1961, Dorothea Helena Cynthia, *d* of late T. H. McLean; one *s* one *d*].

SHIFFNER, Rear-Adm. John Robert, CB 1995; Director, MSI-Defence Systems Ltd, since 1996; *b* 30 Aug. 1941; *s* of late Captain John Scarlett Shiffner, RN and Margaret Harriet Shiffner (*née* Tullis); *m* 1969, Rosemary Tilly; two *s* one *d*. *Educ:* Sedbergh Sch.; BRNC Dartmouth; RNEC Manadon; RNC Greenwich (BSc). CEng, FIMarE. Joined RN, 1959; served in HM Ships Centaur, Glamorgan, Andromeda, Zulu; Staff Marine Engineer Officer, CBNS Washington, 1980; RCDS 1983; MoD Procurement Executive: Project Manager, Type 42 Destroyer/Aircraft Carrier, 1984–86; Dir, Mechanical Engineering, 1987–88; Captain, Britannia RNC, Dartmouth, 1989–91; ADC to the Queen, 1989–91; COS to C-in-C Naval Home Comd, 1991–93; Dir Gen. Fleet Support (Equipment and Systems), MoD, 1993–95. Director: GEC Marine, 1996–98; Marconi Electronic Systems, 1997–99. MInstD. *Recreations:* golf, sailing, country pursuits, garden taming. *Address:* Westholme, Redlap, Dartmouth, S Devon TQ6 0JR. *Club:* Royal Yacht Squadron (Cowes).

SHIGEHARA, Kumiharu; Deputy Secretary-General, Organisation for Economic Co-operation and Development, 1997–99; *b* 5 Feb. 1939; *s* of Seizaburo Shigehara and Rutsu (*née* Tanabe); *m* 1965, Akiko Yoshizawa; one *s* one *d*. *Educ:* Law Sch., Univ. of Tokyo (Hozumi Hon. Award, 1960). Joined Bank of Japan, 1962; joined OECD, 1970: Principal Administrator, 1971–72; Hd, Monetary Div., 1972–74; Councillor on policy planning, and Advr on Internat. Finance, Bank of Japan, 1974–80; Dep. Dir, Gen. Econs Br., OECD, 1980–82; Manager of Res., Inst. for Monetary and Econ. Studies, Bank of Japan, 1982–87, Dep. Dir, 1987; Dir, Gen. Econs Br., OECD, 1987–89; Dir, Inst. for Monetary and Econ. Studies, Bank of Japan, 1989–92; Hd, Econs Dept and Chief Economist, OECD, 1992–97. Hon. Dr Econs Liège, 1998. *Publications:* The Rôle of Monetary Policy in Demand Management (with Niels Thygesen), 1975; Stable Economic Growth and Monetary Policy, 1991; New Trends in Monetary Theory and Policy, 1992. *Recreations:* tennis, golf. *Address:* 4-7-11-1104 Seta, Setagaya-ku, Tokyo, Japan. *T:* (3) 3709 7969.

SHILLING, (Hugh) David (V.); artist, designer; President, David Shilling, since 1976; *b* 27 June 1954; *s* of late Ronald and Gertrude Shilling. *Educ:* Colet Court; St Paul's Sch., Hammersmith. Founded David Shilling, 1976. Sen. Consultant on design, ITC, UNCTAD and GATT, 1990. One person shows in UK and worldwide, 1979–, including: NT and Crafts Council, 1979; Ulster, Worthing, Plymouth, Leeds, Cheltenham, Durham, Salisbury, Chester and Edinburgh Museums; LA Co. Mus., 1982; Moscow, 1989; Sotheby's, Stockholm, 1992; Salama-Caro Gall., London, 1993; Rio de Janeiro, 1993; Manila, 1994; Brit. Embassy, Paris, 1995; British Council, Cologne, 1995, and Delhi and Bombay, 1996; War Child/Pavarotti, Modena, 1995; Royal Shakespeare Theatre, Stratford upon Avon, 1996; Dubai, 1999; work in permanent collections: Metropolitan Mus., NY, LA Co. Mus., Philadelphia Mus. of Art, Musée de l'Art Decoratif, Paris, V&A Mus. Pres. for Life, Valdivia, Ecuador, 1993. Freeman, Gold and Silver Wyre Drawers, 1975. *Publication:* Thinking Rich, 1986. *Address:* 5 Homer Street, W1H 1HN. *T:* (020) 7262 2363. *Club:* City Livery.

SHILLINGFORD, Arden; *see* Shillingford, R. A. C.

SHILLINGFORD, (Romeo) Arden (Coleridge), MBE 1977; Permanent Secretary, Ministry of Legal Affairs, Commonwealth of Dominica, 1992; *b* 11 Feb. 1936; *s* of Stafford Shillingford and Ophelia Thomas, step *d* of Hosford Samuel O'Brien and *d* of Clarita (*née* Hunt), Roseau, Dominica; *m* 1st, Evelyn Blanche Hart; one *s* one *d*; 2nd, Maudline Joan Green; three *s*. *Educ:* Wesley High Sch., Roseau Boys' Sch., Dominica; grammar school; School of Law. Member, Hon. Soc. Inner Temple. Joined Dominican Civil Service, 1957, after brief period as solicitor's clerk; junior clerk, various Govt Depts, Dominica, 1957–59; Clerk of Court, then Chief Clerk, Magistrates' Office, 1960–61; joined staff, Eastern Caribbean Commn, London, on secondment from Dominican CS, 1965; served variously as Migrants' Welfare Officer, Students' Officer, Asst Trade Sec. and PA to Comr, 1968–71; Admin. Asst, Consular and Protocol Affairs, 1973–78 (actg Comr, several occasions, 1975–78); High Comr in UK, 1978–85 (concurrently non-resident Ambassador to France, Spain, Belgium, W Germany and EEC, Brussels, and Perm. Rep. to UNESCO); Perm. Sec., Min. of Community Develt and Social Affairs, Dominica, 1985–92. Mem., Bd of Trustees, Dominica Conservation Assoc., 1989–92. Past Member, numerous cttees and *ad hoc* bodies for West Indian Immigrant Welfare and Education; Dep. Chm., Bd of Governors, W Indian Students' Centre, 1970–75, Chm., 1976–79; Member, West India Cttee (Vice-Pres. 1979–). Liaison Officer, Victoria League for Commonwealth Friendship; Founder-Mem. and Vice-Chm., Jaycees (Dominica Jun. Chamber of Commerce); Mem., Nat. Scouts Council Assoc. *Recreations:* cricket, collecting authentic folk music, swimming.

SHILTON, Peter, OBE 1991 (MBE 1986); footballer; *b* 18 Sept. 1949; *s* of Les and May Shilton; *m* 1970, Sue. *Educ:* King Richard III Sch., Leicester. Goalkeeper; started playing, 1964, for Leicester City; scored a goal, 1967; Stoke City, 1974; Nottingham Forest, 1977; Southampton, 1982; Derby County, 1987; Plymouth Argyle, 1992–95 (player-manager); Leyton Orient, 1996; 1,000 League appearances (record), 1996; first played for England, 1970; 125 England caps (record); final appearance, World Cup, 1990. PFA Footballer of the Year, 1978. *Address:* Hubbards Cottage, Bentley Lane, Maxstoke, near Coleshill B46 2QR.

SHIMMON, Ross Michael, OBE 2000; FLA; Secretary General, International Federation of Library Associations and Institutions, since 1999; *b* 10 Jan. 1942; *s* of late John Ross Shimmon and Eileen Margaret Shimmon; *m* 1967, Patricia, *d* of late Ronald George Hayward, CBE; one *s* two *d*. *Educ:* St John's Coll., Southsea; Poly. of North London; Coll. of Librarianship, Wales. FLA 1972 (Hon. FLA 2000). Liby Assistant, Portsmouth City Libraries, 1960; Asst Librarian, 1962, Area Librarian, Havant, 1964, Hants County Liby; Lectr, Southampton Coll. of Technol., 1964; Librarian (Tech. Assistant), London Bor. of Bexley, 1966; Professional Assistant to Library Advisers, DES, 1968; Lectr, Coll. of Librarianship, Wales, 1970; Services Librarian, Preston Poly., 1975; Head, Liby Studies Dept, Admin. Coll. of PNG, 1979; Library Association: Sec. for Manpower and Educn, 1984; Dir, Professional Practice, 1988; Chief Exec., 1992–99. Member: Adv. Council, 1992–99, Adv. Cttee, 1994–99, British Council; BookAid Internat. Council, 1994–99; Adv. Cttee, Liby and Inf. Stats Unit, Univ. of Loughborough, 1997–99; Cttee on Freedom of Access to Information and Freedom of Expression, IFLA, 1998–99; Adv. Council on Libraries, 1999; Design Gp, Museums, Libraries and Archives Council, 1999. Pres., Eur. Bureau of Liby, Inf. and Documentation Assocs, 1992–95. Hon. Mem. PNG Liby Assoc., 1983. Member: Adv. Cttee, Archival Sci.; Internat. Jl on Recorded Information. *Publications:* Reader in Library Management, 1976; conf. papers and contribs to liby jls. *Recreations:* cricket, photography, railways (prototype and model). *Address:* (office) POB 95312, 2509 CH The Hague, Netherlands; 7 Nobel Court, Faversham, Kent ME13 7SD.

SHINGLES, Godfrey Stephen, (Geoff), CBE 1987; CEng, FIEE; FBCS; Chairman, Imagination Technologies (formerly VideoLogic) Group PLC, since 1995; *b* 9 April 1939; *s* of Sidney and Winifred Shingles; *m*; two *s*; *m* 1997, Frances Margaret Mercer; one *d*. *Educ:* Paston Sch., N Walsham; Leeds Univ. (BSc). Joined Digital UK, 1965; Chm., Digital Equipment Co. Ltd, 1991–94 (Man. Dir, 1983–91; Chief Exec., 1991–93). Vice-Pres., Digital Equipment Corp., 1981–92. Chm., Nanomagnetics Ltd; non-executive Director: Interregnum; Authoriszor Inc.; Udate.com. FInstD. Freeman, City of London. *Recreations:* sailing, cricket, Rugby, golf, ski-ing. *Address:* Imagination Technologies Group PLC, Home Park Estate, Kings Langley, Herts WD4 8LZ. *Clubs:* Royal Ocean Racing, MCC.

SHINNIE, Prof. Peter Lewis; Professor of Archæology, in the University of Calgary, 1970–80, now Emeritus; *b* 18 Jan. 1915; *s* of late Andrew James Shinnie, OBE; *m* 1st, 1940, Margaret Blanche Elizabeth Cloake (marr. diss. 1970; she *d* 1995); two *s* one *d*; 2nd, 1971, Ama Nantwi. *Educ:* Westminster Sch.; Christ Church, Oxford. Served War with RAF, 1939–45. Temp. Asst Keeper, Ashmolean Museum, 1945; Asst Commissioner for Archæology, Sudan Government, 1946; Commissioner for Archæology, Sudan Govt, 1948; Director of Antiquities, Uganda, 1956; Prof. of Archæology: Univ. of Ghana, 1958–66; Univ. of Khartoum, 1966–70. Corresp. FBA 1999; FSA. Hon. LLD Calgary, 1983. *Publications:* Excavation at Soba, 1955; Medieval Nubia, 1954; Ghazali: A Monastery in Northern Sudan, 1960; Meroe-Civilization of the Sudan, 1967; The African Iron Age, 1971; Debeira West, 1978; (with R. J. Bradley) The Capital of Kush, 1980; (ed with R. Haaland) African Iron Working: ancient and traditional, 1985; (with F. J. Kense) Archaeology in Gonja: excavations at Daboya, 1989; Early Asante, 1995; Ancient Nubia, 1996; articles in Journal of Egyptian Archæology, Sudan Notes and Records, Kush. *Recreations:* reading, photography, travelling in Greece. *Address:* Department of Archæology, University of Calgary, Calgary, AB T2N 1N4 Canada. *T:* (403) 2205227.

SHINWELL, Sir (Maurice) Adrian, Kt 1996; DL; NP; solicitor; Senior Partner, Kerr Barrie (formerly Kerr, Barrie & Duncan), Glasgow, since 1991; *b* 27 Feb. 1951; *s* of late Maurice Shinwell and Andrina (*née* Alexander); *m* 1973, Lesley McLean; two *s* one *d*. *Educ:* Hutchesons' Boys' Grammar Sch.; Glasgow Univ. (LLB). NP 1976. MCIArb 1999 (ACIArb 1990). Admitted solicitor, 1975; Solicitor-Mediator, 1994–. Mem., Children's Panel, 1973–77. Part-time Tutor, Law Faculty, Glasgow Univ., 1980–84. Mem., Central Adv. Cttee on Justices of the Peace, 1996–99. Scottish Conservative & Unionist

Association: Mem., 1975–; Mem., Scottish Council, 1982–98; Chairman: Eastwood Assoc., 1982–85; Cumbernauld & Kilsyth Assoc., 1989–91; Scottish Cons. Candidates' Bd, 1997–2000; Vice-Pres., 1989–92; Pres., 1992–94; architect of re-organisation, 1992–93; Member: Gen. Purposes Cttee, 1993–98; Scottish Exec. and Scottish Council, 1998–2000. Vice Chm., JP Adv. Cttee, E Renfrewshire, 2000–. Dir, St Leonards Sch., St Andrews, 2000–. DL Renfrewshire, 1999. *Recreations:* family, politics. *Address:* Sarona, South Road, Busby, Glasgow G76 8JB. *T:* (office) (0141) 221 6844.

SHIPLEY, Debra Ann; MP (Lab) Stourbridge, since 1997; *b* 22 June 1957. *Educ:* Oxford Poly. (BA Hons); MA London. Writer and lecturer, history, critical studies and architecture. *Publications:* 17 books on subjects including architecture, museums, heritage, travel. *Recreations:* walking, reading, cooking. *Address:* House of Commons, SW1A 0AA.

SHIPLEY, Jane; Her Honour Judge Shipley; a Circuit Judge, since 2000; *b* 5 Jan. 1952; *m* 1977, David; two *d*. *Educ:* Maltby Grammar Sch. (Head Girl); St Hugh's Coll., Oxford (Pres., Law Soc.; MA). Called to the Bar, Gray's Inn, 1974; in practice, Leeds, NE Circuit, 1974–2000. Asst Recorder, 1991–95; Recorder, 1995–2000. *Recreation:* gardening. *Address:* Sheffield Combined Court Centre, 50 West Bar, Sheffield S3 8PH.

SHIPLEY, Rt Hon. Jennifer (Mary); PC 1998; MP (Nat. Party) for Rakaia (formerly Ashburton), since 1987; *b* 4 Feb. 1952; *d* of Rev. Len Robson and Adele Robson; *m* 1973, Burton Shipley; one *s* one *d*. *Educ:* Marlborough Coll., NZ; Christchurch Coll. of Educn (Dip. Teaching). Primary Sch. Teacher, 1972–77; farmer in partnership, 1973–88. MEC, NZ, 1990–99; Minister: of Social Welfare, 1990–93; of Women's Affairs, 1990–99; of Health, 1993–96; of State Services, of Transport, i/c Accident Rehabilitation and Compensation Insurance, for State Owned Enterprises, and i/c Radio NZ, 1996–97; i/c Security Intelligence Service, 1997–99; Prime Minister, 1997–99; Chair, Security and Intelligence Cttee, 1997–99; Leader of the Opposition, 1999–2001. *Recreations:* gardening, walking, water sports. *Address:* Parliament Buildings, Wellington, New Zealand.

SHIPLEY DALTON, Duncan Edward; Member (UU) Antrim South, Northern Ireland Assembly, since 1998; barrister-at-law; *b* 7 Nov. 1970; *s* of Kenneth Shipley and Susan Iris Dalton, BSc, MA, PhD. *Educ:* Carisbrooke, Isle of Wight; Univ. of Essex (LLB Hons); Queen's Univ., Belfast (CPLS 1996); BL Inn of Court of NI 1996. Called to the Bar, N Ireland, 1996. 7th (City of Belfast) Bn, Royal Irish Regt, 1994–98. *Recreations:* reading (history and politics), karate, computers. *Address:* Parliament Buildings, Stormont, Belfast BT4 3XX. *T:* (028) 9052 0317.

SHIRE, Rabbi Dr Michael Jonathan; Director, Centre for Jewish Education, since 1990 (Deputy Director, 1988–90); *b* 15 Dec. 1957; *s* of Dr Heinz Shire and Ruth Shire; *m* 1991, Rabbi Marcia Plumb; one *d*. *Educ:* George Dixon Sch., Birmingham; University Coll. London (BA Hons 1981); Hebrew Union Coll., USA (MA 1983; PhD 1996); Leo Baeck Coll. (MA 1995). Dir of Educn, Temple Beth Hillel, Calif, 1983–88. Ordained, 1996. *Publications:* The Illuminated Haggadah, 1998; L'Chaim, 2000; The Jewish Prophet, 2002. *Recreations:* theatre, contemporary architecture, the men's movement, modern fiction. *Address:* Centre for Jewish Education, 80 East End Road, N3 2SY. *T:* (020) 8349 5620.

SHIRLEY, family name of **Earl Ferrers**.

SHIRLEY, Malcolm Christopher, CEng; Director General, Engineering Council, since 1998; *b* 10 April 1945; *s* of late Leonard Noel Shirley and Edith Florence Shirley (*née* Bullen); *m* 1970, Lucilla Rose Geary Dyer; three *s*. *Educ:* Churcher's Coll., Petersfield; BRNC Dartmouth; RNEC Plymouth (BSc 1969). CEng 1973; FIMarE 1981. Royal Navy: served HMS Manxman, HMS Triumph, HMS Zulu, HMS Rapid, HMS Eastbourne, 1970–74; Sen. Engr, HM Yacht Britannia, 1975–77; RNSC Greenwich, 1977; Staff, Dir Gen. Ships, 1977–79; HMS Coventry, 1980–82; Asst Naval Attaché, Paris, 1982–84; staff appts, MoD Naval Staff, 1984–86, 1990–92; Nat. Rep. SHAPE, NATO, 1992–94; Cdre, 1994; Naval Manpower Study Leader, 1994–95; CO HMS Sultan, 1995–98. Mem., RNSA, 1967. Freeman, City of London, 1999; Liveryman, Engineers' Co., 1999. Assoc. of Cape Horners, 1974. *Recreations:* sailing, music. *Address:* Greyhound Cottage, Freshford, Bath BA3 6BT. *T:* (01225) 722424. *Clubs:* National Liberal; Royal Yacht Squadron.

SHIRLEY, Dame (Vera) Stephanie, (Steve), DBE 2000 (OBE 1980); FREng; FBCS; Life President, Xansa (formerly F.I. Group) PLC; *b* 16 Sept. 1933; *d* of late Arnold Buchthal and Mrs Margaret Brook (formerly Buchthal, *née* Schick); name changed to Brook on naturalisation, 1951; *m* 1959, Derek George Millington Shirley; (one *s* decd). *Educ:* Sir John Cass Coll., London. BSc (Spec.) London 1956. FBCS 1971; CEng 1990. PO Res. Stn, Dollis Hill, 1951–59; CDL (subsid. of ICL), 1959–62; F International Group, later F.I. Group, 1962–93 (Founder Dir and Chief Exec., 1962–87; Settlor FI Shareholders' Trust, 1981); Director: AEA Technology Plc, 1992–2000; Tandem Computers Inc., 1992–97; John Lewis Partnership plc, 1999–. Member: Computer, Systems and Electronics Requirements Bd, 1979–81; Electronics and Avionics Requirements Bd, 1981–83; Open Tech, MSC, 1983–86; Council, Industrial Soc., 1984–90; NCVQ, 1986–89. Pres., British Computer Soc., 1989–90; Vice Pres., C&G, 2000–. Consulting Editor on information processing, J. Wiley & Sons, 1978–87. Member: Council, Duke of Edinburgh's Seventh Commonwealth Study Conf., 1991–92; British-N American Cttee, 1992–2001. Chm., Women of Influence, 1993. Trustee, Help The Aged, 1987–90; Patron: Disablement Income Gp, 1989–2001; Centre for Tomorrow's Co., 1997–; Founder: The Kingwood Trust, 1993; The Shirley Foundn, 1996; Prior's Court Foundn, 1998. Master, Information Technologists' Co., 1992 (Liveryman, 1992); Freeman, City of London, 1987. CIMgt (CBIM 1984); FRSA 1985; FREng 2001. Hon. FCGI 1989. Hon. Fellow: Manchester Metropolitan Univ. (formerly Poly.), 1989; Staffordshire Univ. (formerly Poly.), 1991; Sheffield Hallam Univ., 1992; Foundn Fellow, Balliol Coll., Oxford, 2001. Hon. DSc: Buckingham, 1991; Aston, 1993; Nottingham Trent, 1994; Southampton Inst., 1994; Hon. DTech: Loughborough, 1991; Kingston, 1995; DUniv: Leeds Metropolitan, 1993; Derby, 1997; London Guildhall, 1998; Stirling, 2000; Hon. DLitt de Montfort, 1993; Hon. DBA: West of England, 1995; City, 2000. Recognition of Information Technology Achievement Award, 1985; Gold Medal, Inst. of Mgt, 1991; Mountbatten Medal, IEE, 1999. US Nat. Women's Hall of Fame, 1995. *Publications:* articles in prof. jls, reviews, proc. of confs, and papers. *Recreation:* sleep. *Address:* 47 Thames House, Phyllis Court Drive, Henley-on-Thames, Oxon RG9 2NA. *T:* (01491) 579004, *Fax:* (01491) 574995; *e-mail:* steve.shirley@dial.pipex.com.

SHIRLEY-QUIRK, John Stanton, CBE 1975; bass-baritone singer; Member, Voice Faculty, Peabody Conservatory, Baltimore, since 1991; *b* 28 Aug. 1931; *s* of Joseph Stanley and Amelia Shirley-Quirk; *m* 1st, 1955, Patricia Hastie (*d* 1981); one *s* one *d*; 2nd, 1981, Sara V. Watkins (*d* 1997); one *s* one *d* (and one *d* decd). *Educ:* Holt School, Liverpool; Liverpool University. Violin Scholarship, 1945; read Chemistry, Liverpool Univ., 1948–53; BSc (Hons), 1952; Dipl. in Educn 1953; became professional singer, 1961. Officer in Education Br., RAF, 1953–57. Asst Lectr in Chemistry, Acton Technical Coll., 1957–61; Lay-clerk in St Paul's Cathedral, 1961–62. First Appearance Glyndebourne Opera in Elegy for Young Lovers, 1961; subseq. 1962, 1963. Sang in first performance of Curlew River, 1964, The Burning Fiery Furnace, 1966, The Prodigal Son, 1968, Owen Wingrave, 1970, Death in Venice, 1973, Confessions of a Justified Sinner, 1976, The Ice Break, 1977. Has sung world wide. First American tour, 1966; Australian tour, 1967; first appearance Metropolitan Opera, NY, 1974. Has made numerous recordings: operas, songs, cantatas, etc. Mem. Voice Faculty, Carnegie-Mellon Univ., Pittsburgh, 1994–98. Mem. Court, Brunel Univ., 1977–. Hon. RAM 1972; Hon. DMus Liverpool, 1976; DUniv Brunel, 1981. Liverpool Univ. Chem. Soc. Medal, 1965; Sir Charles Santley Meml Gift, Worshipful Co. of Musicians, 1969. *Recreations:* trees, canals, clocks. *Address:* 6062 Red Clover Lane, Clarksville, MD 21029–1272, USA.

SHIRRAS, Ven. Edward Scott; Vicar, Christ Church, Winchester, 1992–2001; *b* 23 April 1937; *s* of Edward Shirras and Alice Emma Shirras (*née* Morten); *m* 1962, Pamela Susan Mackenzie; two *s* two *d*. *Educ:* Sevenoaks School; St Andrews Univ. (BSc); Union Coll., Schenectady, NY, USA; Clifton Theolog. Coll., Bristol. Curate: Christ Church, Surbiton Hill, 1963–66; Jesmond Parish Church, Newcastle upon Tyne, 1966–68; Church Pastoral Aid Society: Youth Sec., 1968–71; Publications Sec., 1971–74; Asst Gen. Sec., 1974–75; Vicar of Christ Church, Roxeth, dio. London, 1975–85; Area Dean of Harrow, 1982–85; Archdeacon of Northolt, 1985–92. *Recreations:* transport photography (Scottish), Aberdeen FC. *Address:* 4 Culham Close, Abingdon, Oxon OX14 2AS. *T:* (01235) 550381; *e-mail:* shirras@ukgateway.net.

SHIVAS, Mark; film and television producer; *b* 24 April 1938; *s* of James Dallas Shivas and Winifred Alice Lighton (*née* Bristow). *Educ:* Whitgift School; Merton College, Oxford (MA Law). Asst Editor, Movie Magazine, 1962–64; freelance journalist; joined Granada TV, 1964, Director-Producer, 1965–68; Producer of Drama, 1969–88, Head of Drama, 1988–93, Head of Films, 1993–97, BBC TV; Creative Dir, Southern Pictures, 1979–81. Productions include: The Six Wives of Henry VIII (BAFTA awards, Prix Italia), The Evacuees (BAFTA and Emmy awards), Casanova, The Glittering Prizes, Rogue Male, Professional Foul (BAFTA award), Telford's Change, On Giant's Shoulders (Emmy award), Talking Heads 2, Telling Tales; for Channel 4: The Price, What if it's Raining?, The Storyteller (Emmy award); feature films include: Moonlighting, 1982; A Private Function, 1984; The Witches, 1988; Truly, Madly, Deeply, 1991; Enchanted April, 1991; The Snapper, 1993; Priest, 1995; Small Faces, 1996; Jude, 1996; Regeneration, 1997; Hideous Kinky, 1998; The Claim, 2000. *Publications:* articles in art jls. *Recreations:* Italy, gardens, swimming, cycling, moviegoing. *Address:* 38 Gloucester Mews, W2 3HE. *T:* (020) 7723 4678, *Fax:* (020) 7262 1415.

SHOCK, Sir Maurice, Kt 1988; Rector, Lincoln College, Oxford, 1987–94, Hon. Fellow, 1995; *b* 15 April 1926; *o s* of Alfred and Ellen Shock; *m* 1947, Dorothy Donald (*d* 1998); one *s* three *d*. *Educ:* King Edward's Sch., Birmingham; Balliol Coll., Oxford (MA); St Antony's Coll., Oxford. Served Intell. Corps, 1945–48. Lectr in Politics, Christ Church and Trinity Coll., Oxford, 1955–56; Fellow and Praelector in Politics, University Coll., Oxford, 1956–77, Hon. Fellow, 1986; Estates Bursar, 1959–74; Vice-Chancellor, Leicester Univ., 1977–87. Sen. Treasurer, Oxford Union Soc., 1954–72 (Trustee, 1988–); Member: Franks Commn of Inquiry into the University of Oxford, 1964–66; Hebdomadal Council, Oxford Univ., 1969–75; Chairman: Univ. Authorities Panel, 1980–85; CVCP, 1985–87. Vis. Prof. of Govt, Pomona Coll., 1961–62, 1968–69. Member: ESRC, 1981–85; GMC, 1989–94; a Governing Trustee, 1980–, Chm., 1988–, Nuffield Provincial Hosps Trust. Hon. Vice-Pres., Political Studies Assoc., 1989. Review Panel on Machinery of Government of Jersey, 1999–2000. Hon. FRCP 1989. Hon. LLD Leicester, 1987. *Publications:* The Liberal Tradition; articles on politics and recent history. *Recreations:* gardening, theatre. *Address:* 4 Cunliffe Close, Oxford OX2 7BL.

SHOENBERG, Prof. David, MBE 1944; FRS 1953; Professor of Physics, Cambridge University and Head of Low Temperature Physics Group, Cavendish Laboratory, 1973–78, now Emeritus; Life Fellow of Gonville and Caius College; *b* 4 Jan. 1911; *s* of Isaac and Esther Shoenberg; *m* 1940, Catherine Félicitée Fischmann; one *s* two *d*. *Educ:* Latymer Upper School, W6; Trinity College, Cambridge (Scholar). PhD 1935; Exhibition of 1851 Senior Student, 1936–39; Research in low temperature physics, 1932–, in charge of Royal Soc. Mond Laboratory, 1947–73; Univ. Lectr in Physics, 1944–52; Univ. Reader in Physics, 1952–73; UNESCO Adviser on Low Temperature Physics, NPL of India, 1953–54. Mellon Prof., Univ. of Pittsburgh, 1962; Gauss Prof., Univ. of Göttingen, 1964; Visiting Professor: Univ. of Maryland, 1968; Univ. of Toronto, 1974; Univ. of Waterloo, 1977; Lectures: Guthrie, 1961; Rutherford Meml, India and Sri Lanka, 1980; Krishnan Meml, New Delhi, 1988. Hon. Foreign Mem., Amer. Acad. of Arts and Sciences, 1982. Dr (*hc*) Univ. of Lausanne, 1973. Fritz London Award for Low Temperature Physics, 1964; Hughes Medal, Royal Soc., 1995. *Publications:* Superconductivity, 1938, revised edn, 1952; Magnetism, 1949; Magnetic Oscillations in Metals, 1984; (ed jtly) Kapitza in Cambridge and Moscow, 1990; scientific papers on low temperature physics and magnetism. *Address:* 2 Long Road, Cambridge CB2 2PS; Cavendish Laboratory, Madingley Road, Cambridge CB3 0HE. *T:* (01223) 337389.

SHONE, Very Rev. John Terence; Team Vicar, Cullercoats Team, Marden St Hilda, Diocese of Newcastle, 1989–2000; retired; *b* 15 May 1935; *s* of late Arthur Shone and E. B. Shone; *m* 1st, 1958, Ursula Ruth Buss (marr. diss.); three *s*; 2nd, 1987, Annette Simmons, *d* of late William Caterer and Ada Caterer. *Educ:* St Dunstan's College; Selwyn Coll., Cambridge (BA 1958, MA 1962); Lincoln Theological Coll.; Newcastle Univ. (MA 1992). Deacon 1960, priest 1961, London; Curate, St Pancras Parish Church, 1960–62; Chaplain, St Andrew's Cathedral, Aberdeen, 1962–65; Chaplain to Anglican Students, Aberdeen, 1962–68; Lectr, Aberdeen Coll. of Education, 1965–68; Exam. Chaplain to Bishop of Aberdeen, 1966–68; Vicar, St Andrew and St Luke, Grimsby, 1968–69; Rector, St Saviour, Bridge of Allan, 1969–86; Chaplain, Stirling Univ., 1969–80; Priest i/c, St John's, Alloa, 1977–85, and St James', Dollar, 1981–86; Canon, St Ninian's Cathedral, Perth, 1980–82; Dean, 1982–89, Dean Emeritus, 2000, United Dio. of St Andrews, Dunkeld and Dunblane; Diocesan R & D Officer, 1986–89. *Address:* 29 Redwell Place, Alloa, Clackmannanshire FK10 2BT. *T:* (01259) 215113.

SHOOTER, Prof. Eric Manvers, FRS 1988; Professor of Neurobiology, Stanford University, since 1975; *b* 18 April 1924; *s* of Fred and Pattie Shooter; *m* 1949, Elaine Staley Arnold; one *d*. *Educ:* Gonville and Caius Coll., Cambridge (BA 1945; MA 1950; PhD 1950; ScD 1986); DSc London 1964. Senior Scientist, Brewing Industry Research Foundn, 1950–53; Lectr in Biochem., University Coll. London, 1953–63; Stanford University: Associate Prof. of Genetics, 1963–68; Prof. of Genetics and Prof. of Biochem., 1968–75; Prof. and Chm. of Neurobiol., 1975–87. Macy Faculty Scholar, Univ. of Geneva, 1974–75. Foreign Assoc., Inst. of Medicine, Nat. Acad. of Scis, USA, 1989; Fellow: American Acad. of Arts and Scis, 1993; AAAS, 1998. Wakeman Award, 1988; Ralph W. Gerard Prize in Neuroscience, 1995; Bristol-Myers Squibb Award for Dist. Achievement in Neurosci. Res., 1997. *Publications:* (associate editor) Annual Review of Neuroscience, vols 6–21, 1983–; numerous papers in sci jls. *Address:* Department of Neurobiology, Stanford University School of Medicine, Stanford, CA 94305–5125, USA. *T:* (650) 7236638.

SHOOTER, Prof. Reginald Arthur, CBE 1980; Emeritus Professor of Medical Microbiology, London University, since 1981; *b* 1916; *s* of Rev. A. E. Shooter, TD and M. K. Shooter; *m* 1946, Jean Wallace, MB, ChB; one *s* three *d. Educ:* Mill Hill Sch.; Caius Coll., Cambridge; St Bartholomew's Hosp. BA 1937; MB, BChir 1940; MRCS, LRCP 1940; MA 1941; MD 1945; MRCP 1961; FRCP 1968; FRCS 1977; FRCPath 1963 (Vice-Pres., 1971–74). After various Hosp. appts became Surgeon Lieut, RNVR. Appointments at St Bartholomew's Hospital from 1946; Rockefeller Travelling Fellow in Medicine, 1950–51; Reader in Bacteriology, 1953–61, Prof. of Medical Microbiology, 1961–81, Univ. of London; Bacteriologist to St Bartholomew's Hosp., 1961–81 and Dean, Medical Coll., 1972–81. Member: City and E London AHA (T), 1974–81; Gloucester HA, 1981–85; Chm., Regional Computing Policy Steering Gp, SW RHA, 1983–85. Mem., Public Health Lab. Service Bd, 1970–82; Chm., Dangerous Pathogens Adv. Gp, 1975–81. Mem., Scientific Adv. Council, Stress Foundn, 1981–90. Governor: St Bartholomew's Hosp., 1972–74; Queen Mary Coll., 1972–81; Trustee: Mitchell City of London Trust, 1958–82; Jenner Trust, 1989–. Mem. Court, City Univ., 1972–81. Pybus Medal, N of England Surg. Soc., 1979. Asst Editor, British Jl of Exp. Pathology, 1953–58; Hon. Editor, RSocMed, 1960–65. *Publications:* books, and articles in medical journals. *Recreations:* archaeology, gardening, fishing. *Address:* Eastlea, Back Edge Lane, The Edge, Stroud, Glos GL6 6PE. *T:* (01452) 812408.

SHORE OF STEPNEY, Lady; *see* Shore, E. C.

SHORE, David Teignmouth, OBE 1982; FREng; Director (Technical), APV PLC, 1984–88; *b* 15 Nov. 1928; *e s* of Geoffrey and Cecilia Mary Shore; *m* 1950, Pamela Goodge; one *s* two *d. Educ:* Tiffin Boys' Sch., Kingston; Imperial Coll., London (MSc(Eng)). FIMechE 1967; FIChemE 1970; FIFST 1970; FCGI 1979; FREng (FEng 1979). Engrg apprenticeship, 1944–47; Thermal Engr, Foster Wheeler Ltd, 1953–54; APV Co. Ltd: Research Engr, 1950–52; Process Develt Engr, 1954–65; Research Dir, 1965–77; Man. Dir, 1977–82; Chm., 1982–84; Divisional Dir, APV Holdings PLC, 1982–84. Chm., British Food Manufg Industries Res. Assoc., 1984–87; Chm. Engrg Bd, 1985–89 and Mem. Council, 1985–89, SERC; Member: Bd of Advisers in Chemical Engrg, Univ. of London, 1983–; Bd of Food Studies, Univ. of Reading, 1984–93; Jt Delegacy for Food Res. Inst., Reading, 1985–; Council, Univ. of Reading, 1987–93. *Publications:* technical articles on rheology, heat transfer and food process engrg in learned jls. *Recreations:* walking, astronomy, wine-making. *Address:* Hembury, Garratts Lane, Banstead, Surrey SM7 2EA. *T:* (01737) 353721.

SHORE, Dr Elizabeth Catherine, CB 1980; Hon. Senior Lecturer, Charing Cross and Westminster Medical School, 1993–97; *b* 19 Aug. 1927; *d* of Edward Murray Wrong and Rosalind Grace Smith; *m* 1948, Peter David Shore (later Baron Shore of Stepney, PC; he *d* 2001); one *s* two *d* (and one *s* decd). *Educ:* Newnham Coll., Cambridge; St Bartholomew's Hospital; BA Hons Open 1999. MRCP, FRCP; MRCS, FFCM, DRCOG. Joined Medical Civil Service, 1962; Dep. Chief Medical Officer, DHSS, 1977–85. Dean of Postgrad. Medicine, NW Thames Reg., 1985–93; Assoc. Dean of Postgrad. Med. Educn, N Thames Reg., 1993–95. Mem., GMC, 1989–94 (Member: Standards Cttee, 1989–91; Professional Conduct Cttee, 1991–93; Educnl Cttee, 1992–93; Prelim. Proceeding Cttee, 1993). Pres., Med. Women's Fedn, 1990–92 (Chm., Careers Cttee, 1989–95); Chair: BMA Career Progress Cttee, 1994–96; BMA Working Party on Exodus of Doctors, 1996–97. Mem. Council, PSI, 1992–. Trustee, Child Accident Prevention Trust, 1985–91 (Chm., Council and Professional Cttee, 1985–90). Editor, Medical Woman, 1992–97. *Recreations:* reading, cookery, swimming in rough seas. *Address:* 23 Dryburgh Road, SW15 1BN.

SHORE, Jack; President, Royal Cambrian Academy of Art, 1977–83; *b* 17 July 1922; *s* of Frank and Maggie Shore; *m* 1970, Olive Brenda Williams; one *s* one *d. Educ:* Accrington and Manchester Schools of Art. Lectr, Blackpool School of Art, 1945–60; Head, Chester Sch. of Art, 1960–81. Paintings in public and private collections, including USA. RCamA 1962 (ARCamA 1961). Jubilee Medal, 1977. *Recreations:* gardening, enjoyment of music. *Address:* 11 St George's Crescent, Queens Park, Chester CH4 7AR. *T:* (01244) 675017.

SHORROCK, John Michael; QC 1988; a Recorder of the Crown Court, since 1982; *b* 25 May 1943; *s* of late James Godby Shorrock and Mary Patricia Shorrock (*née* Lings); *m* 1971, Marianne (*née* Mills); two *d. Educ:* Clifton College, Bristol; Pembroke College, Cambridge. MA. Called to the Bar, Inner Temple, 1966, Bencher, 1995; practising on Northern Circuit, 1966–: Junior, 1968; Sec., Exec. Cttee, 1981–85. Member: Criminal Injuries Compensation Bd, 1995–2000; Criminal Injuries Compensation Appeals Panel, 1996–. Gov., William Hulme's Grammar Sch., 1999–. *Recreations:* walking, gardening, opera, theatre, cinema. *Address:* 45 Hardman Street, Manchester M3 3HA. *T:* (0161) 832 3791.

SHORT, family name of **Baron Glenamara**.

SHORT, Bernard David, CBE 1995; Head of Further Education Support Unit, Department for Education and Employment (formerly Department for Education), 1993–96; *b* 9 June 1935; *s* of late Bernard Charles and of Ethel Florence Short; *m* 1960, Susan Yvonne Taylor; two *s* one *d. Educ:* St Edmund Hall, Oxford (MA). Served The Royal Scots, 1953–56 (commnd 1954). Taught at Ingiliz Erkek Lisesi, Istanbul, Turkey, 1960–63; Lectr, Univ. of Kyushu, Japan, 1963–65; Asst Lectr, Garretts Green Technical Coll., Birmingham, 1966–67; Lectr, Bournville Coll. of Further Educn, Birmingham, 1967–71; Sen. Lectr, Henley Coll. of Further Educn, Coventry, 1971–73; Head, Dept of Gen. Studies, Bournville Coll., Birmingham, 1973–76; HM Inspectorate of Schools, 1976–93: Inspector, 1976; Staff Inspector, 1984; Chief Inspector, Further Education, 1986. Chm. of Govs, Bournville Coll., Birmingham, 2000–. FRSA 1991. *Publications:* A Guide to Stress in English, 1967; Humour, 1970. *Recreations:* music, gardening, boats.

SHORT, Rt Hon. Clare; PC 1997; MP (Lab) Birmingham, Ladywood, since 1983; Secretary of State for International Development, since 1997; *b* 15 Feb. 1946; *d* of late Frank Short and of Joan Short; *m* 1981, Alexander Ward Lyon (*d* 1993), sometime MP for York; one *s* by previous marriage. *Educ:* Keele Univ.; Leeds Univ. (BA Hons Political Sci.). Home Office, 1970–75; Dir, All Faiths for One Race, Birmingham, 1976–78; Dir, Youth Aid and the Unemployment Unit, 1979–83. Chm., All Party Parly Gp on Race Relations, 1985–86; Mem., Home Affairs Select Cttee, 1983–85; front bench spokesperson on employment, 1985–88, on social security, 1989–91, on envmtl protection, 1993, on women, 1993–95, on transport, 1995–96, on overseas develt, 1996–97. Mem., Labour Party NEC, 1988–98. *Publications:* Talking Blues: a study of young West Indians' views of policing, 1978; Handbook of Immigration Law, 1978; Dear Clare … this is what women think about Page 3, 1991. *Recreations:* family and friends, swimming. *Address:* House of Commons, SW1A 0AA. *T:* (020) 7219 3000.

SHORT, Prof. David Somerset, MD, FRCP, FRCPE; Clinical Professor in Medicine, University of Aberdeen, 1983, now Emeritus; Hon. Consultant Physician, Aberdeen Royal Infirmary, since 1983 (Consultant Physician, 1960–83); *b* 6 Aug. 1918; *s* of Latimer James Short, MD, DPH, Bristol, and Mabel Annie Wood, SRN, Nottingham; *m* 1948, Joan Anne McLay, BSc, MB, ChB, Cardiff; one *s* four *d. Educ:* Bristol Grammar Sch.; Cambridge Univ.; Bristol Royal Hospitals. MD 1948; PhD 1957; FRCP 1964; FRCPE 1966. Served with RAMC, 1944–47; Registrar, Southmead Hosp., Bristol, 1947–49; Sen. Registrar, National Heart Hosp. and London Hosp., 1950–54; Lecturer in Medicine, Middlesex Hosp., 1955–59. Physician to the Queen in Scotland, 1977–83. *Publications:* Medicine as a Vocation, 1978, 2nd edn 1987; The Medical Consultation, 1995; Real Success, 1998; contribs to medical journals, mainly on cardiovascular and pulmonary diseases. *Recreations:* touring, music. *Address:* 48 Victoria Street, Aberdeen, Scotland AB10 1PN. *T:* (01224) 645853.

SHORT, Rt Rev. Kenneth Herbert, AO 1988; Dean of Sydney (St Andrew's Cathedral), 1989–92; *b* 6 July 1927; *s* of Cecil Charles Short and Joyce Ellen Begbie; *m* 1950, Gloria Noelle Funnell; one *s* two *d. Educ:* Moore Theological Coll. (ThL and Moore Coll. Dipl.). Commissioned AIF, 1946; with BCOF, 1946–48; theological training, 1949–52; ordained Anglican Ministry, 1952; Minister in Charge, Provisional Parish of Pittwater, 1952–54; with CMS in Tanzania, E Africa, 1955–64; Chaplain, Tabora 1955, Mwanza 1955–59; founding Principal, Msalato Bible School, 1961–64; Gen. Secretary, CMS NSW Branch, 1964–71, including Sec. for S America; Canon of St Andrew's Cathedral, Sydney, 1970–75; Exam. Chaplain to Archbishop of Sydney, 1971–82; Rector of St Michael's, Vaucluse, 1971–75; Archdeacon of Wollongong and Camden, 1975–79; Chaplain General (CE), Australian Army, 1979–81; Bishop of Wollongong, Dio. of Sydney, 1975–82, Acting Bishop, 1993 and 1999; Anglican Bishop to Aust. Defence Force (Army, Navy and Air Force), 1979–89; Bishop of Parramatta, Dio. of Sydney, 1982–89; Assistant, St John's Shaughnessy, Vancouver, Dio. of New Westminster, 1992–93 and 1995–96. Acting Gen. Sec., CMS Victoria, 1997, NSW, 1998. ChStJ 1989. *Publications:* Guidance, 1969; (contrib.) Evangelism and Preaching in Secular Australia, 1989. *Recreations:* rock fishing, reading, walking, wood turning. *Address:* 16 Chapman Street, Kiama, NSW 2533, Australia. *T:* (2) 42321261.

SHORT, Nigel David; professional chess player; *b* 1 June 1965; *s* of David Malcolm Short and Jean Short (*née* Gaskill); *m* 1987, Rhea Argyro, *d* of Nikolaos Karageorgiou; one *d. Educ:* Bolton Sch. British chess champion: 1979 (equal first), 1984, 1987, 1991; internat. master 1980; grandmaster 1984; world championship candidate, 1985–93 (finalist, 1992, defeating Anatoly Karpov in semi-final). Resigned from FIDE, 1993 and formed Professional Chess Assoc. (with Gary Kasparov), 1993. *Recreation:* guitar.

SHORT, Peter, BA; IPFA; financial management consultant, since 1995; *b* 21 June 1945; *s* of Christopher John Grewcock Short and Isabella Short; *m* 1967, Eileen Short (*née* Makin); one *s* one *d. Educ:* South Shields Grammar Sch.; Univ. of Exeter (2nd Cl. Hons, Div. 1, Modern Economic History). IPFA (1st place Final, 1970). Local Govt Accountant with Manchester City Council, 1967–73; Leeds City Council, 1973–78; Dir of Finance, South Tyneside MDC, 1978–83; City Treas., Manchester CC, 1983–89; Dep. Chief Exec. and Dir of Finance, Greater Manchester Buses Ltd, 1989–93; Man. Dir, Gtr Manchester Buses South Ltd, 1993–95. *Recreations:* reading, walking, caravanning, avoiding household maintenance, planning to walk the Pennine Way. *Address:* 2 Netherwood Road, Northenden, Manchester M22 4BQ.

SHORT, Mrs Renee; *m*; two *d. Educ:* Nottingham County Grammar Sch.; Manchester Univ. Freelance journalist. Member: Herts County Council, 1952–67; Watford RDC, 1952–64; West Herts Group Hosp. Management Cttee; former Chm. Shrodell's Hosp., Watford. Governor: Watford Coll. of Technology; Watford Grammar Sch. Contested (Lab) St Albans, 1955, Watford, 1959. MP (Lab) Wolverhampton NE, 1964–87; TGWU sponsored Member of Parliament. Member: Delegation to Council of Europe, 1964–68; Estimates Cttee, 1964–69; Expenditure Cttee, 1970–79 (Chm., Social Services and Employment Sub-Cttee); Chairman: Select Cttee for Social Services, 1979–87; Parly and Scientific Cttee, 1982–85 (Vice-Pres., 1986; Life Mem.); Associate Mem., Parly IT Cttee, 1987–. Vice-Chm., Parly East-West Trade Gp, 1968–87; Chairman: British-GDR Parly Gp, 1972–87; British-Soviet Parly Gp 1984–87 (Sec., 1972–84); Pres., British-Romanian Friendship Assoc. Mem., Nat. Exec. Cttee of Labour Party, 1970–81, 1983–88. Member: MRC, 1988–93; Research in Patients Cttee, RCP, 1988–91; IVF Cttee, BMA, 1988–91; AIDS Study Gp, Inst. of Medical Ethics, 1989–91; Special Hosps Services Authority, 1991–. National President: Nursery Schools Assoc., 1970–80; Campaign for Nursery Educn, 1970–83; Pres., Action for the Newborn, 1988–; Vice-President: Women's Nat. Cancer Control Campaign; Health Visitors' Assoc. Patron, Rescare, 1990–. Mem., Roundhouse Theatre Council; Chm., Theatres' Advisory Council, 1974–80. Hon. Fellow, Wolverhampton Polytechnic, 1987; Hon. FRCPsych 1988; Hon. MRCP 1989. *Publication:* The Care of Long Term Prisoners, 1979.

SHORT, Robin; *see* Short, William Robert.

SHORT, Roger Guy, MVO 1971; HM Diplomatic Service; HM Consul General, Istanbul, since 2001; *b* 9 Dec. 1944; *s* of Harold Short and Alice Ames Short (*née* Fox); *m* 1971, Sally Victoria Taylor; one *s* two *d. Educ:* Malvern; University Coll., Oxford (schol.; BA Lit.Hum.; MA). Served FCO and Ankara, 1967–78; Consul (Commercial), Rio de Janeiro, 1978–80; Head of Chancery, Ankara, 1981–84; Counsellor and Dep. Head of Permanent Under-Sec. of State's Dept, FCO, 1984–86; Head of Chancery and Consul-Gen., Oslo, 1986–90; Head of Personnel Services Dept, FCO, 1990–94; Ambassador to Bulgaria, 1994–98; COS, Office of High Rep., Sarajevo, 1999–2000. *Recreations:* music, classical studies, languages, wine. *Address:* c/o Foreign and Commonwealth Office, SW1A 2AH.

SHORT, Prof. Roger Valentine, FRCOG; FRS 1974; FRSE; FRCVS; FAA; Wexler Professorial Fellow, Department of Perinatal Medicine, University of Melbourne, since 1996; *b* 31 July 1930; *s* of F. A. and M. C. Short, Weybridge; *m* 1st, 1958, Dr Mary Bowen Wilson (marr. diss. 1981); one *s* three *d*; 2nd, 1982, Prof. Marilyn Bernice Renfree; two *d. Educ:* Sherborne Sch.; Univs of Bristol (BVSc, MRCVS), Wisconsin (MSc) and Cambridge (PhD, ScD). FRSE 1974; FRCVS 1976; FAA 1984; FRCOG 1991. Mem., ARC Unit of Reproductive Physiology and Biochemistry, Cambridge, 1956–72; Fellow, Magdalene Coll., Cambridge, 1962–72; Lectr, then Reader, Dept of Veterinary Clinical Studies, Cambridge, 1961–72; Dir, MRC Unit of Reproductive Biology, Edinburgh, 1972–82; Prof. of Reproductive Biology, Monash Univ., Australia, 1982–95. Hon. Prof., Univ. of Edinburgh, 1976–82. Chm., Bd of Dirs, Family Health Internat., NC, USA, 1984–90. Fellow, American Acad. of Arts and Scis. Hon. DSc: Guelph, 1988; Bristol, 1997. *Publications:* (ed, with C. R. Austin) Reproduction in Mammals, vols 1–8, 1972–80, 2nd edn vols 1–5, 1982–86; (ed, with D. T. Baird) Contraceptives of the Future, 1976; contrib. Jl Endocrinology, Jl Reproduction and Fertility, Jl Zoology, Lancet, Nature. *Recreations:* gardening, wildlife, history of biology. *Address:* Department of Perinatal Medicine, Royal Women's Hospital, 132 Grattan Street, Melbourne, Vic 3053, Australia.

SHORT, Maj.-Gen. William Robert, (Robin), CB 1999; Operations Director, PHC Ltd, since 1999; Chairman, Royal Army Medical Corps Association, since 1999; *b* 30 March 1942; *s* of Dr Andrew Galbraith Short and Dr Helen Greig Short (*née* Dunlop); *m* 1967, Annette Pamela Barrow; three *s. Educ:* Glasgow High Sch.; Glasgow Univ. (MB

ChB). RMO, 1 Black Watch, RHR, 1969–72; 19 Field Ambulance, RAMC, 1972–73; RAMC Trg Centre, 1973–76; Army Staff Coll., 1976–77 (psc); S02, Med. HQ 1 (BR) Corps, 1978–81; CO, 3 Armd Field Ambulance, RAMC, 1981–84; Chief Instr, RAMC Trg Centre, 1984–86; Comdr Med. 1 Armd Div., 1986–88; Col, Ops and Plans, 1988–91, Dir Med. Ops and Logistics, 1991–94, Defence Med. Services Directorate; Comdr, Med. HQ Land Comd, 1994–96; DGAMS, 1996–99. QHP, 1996–99. CStJ 1997 (OStJ 1971). *Recreations:* gardening, ski-ing, collecting cigarette cards (cartophily). *Address:* Beeswing, 26 Orchard Road, Farnborough, Hants GU14 7PR.

SHORTIS, Maj.-Gen. Colin Terry, CB 1988; CBE 1980 (OBE 1977; MBE 1974); General Officer Commanding North West District, 1986–89; *b* 18 Jan. 1934; *s* of late Tom Richardson Shortis and Marna Evelyn Shortis (*née* Kenworthy); *m* 1957, Sylvia Mary, *o d* of H. C. A. Jenkinson; two *s* two *d*. *Educ:* Bedford School. Enlisted Army 1951; 2nd Lieut Royal Fusiliers, 1953; transf. to Dorset Regt, 1955; served Hong Kong, Korea, Suez Canal Zone, Sudan, BAOR, Aden, Singapore and British Guiana, 1953–63; Instructor, Sch. of Infantry, 1964–65; Staff Coll., 1966; Co. Comdr, 1st Devonshire and Dorset, 1967–73; served Malta, NI, Belize, Cyprus, BAOR, CO 1974–77; Directing Staff, Staff Coll., 1977; Comdr, 8 Infantry Brigade, 1978–80; RCDS 1981; Comdr, British Mil. Adv. and Training Team, Zimbabwe, 1982–83; Dir of Infantry, 1983–86. Col Comdt, The Prince of Wales Div., 1983–88; Col, Devonshire and Dorset Regt, 1984–90. *Recreation:* sailing. *Address:* Hart House, 52 Fore Street, Topsham, Exeter EX3 0HW. *Club:* Army and Navy.

SHORTRIDGE, Jon Deacon; Permanent Secretary, National Assembly for Wales, since 1999; *b* 10 April 1947; *s* of late Eric Creber Deacon Shortridge and Audrey Joan Shortridge (*née* Hunt); *m* 1972, Diana Jean Gordon; one *s* one *d*. *Educ:* Chichester High Sch.; St Edmund Hall, Oxford (MA); Edinburgh Univ. (MSc). Min. of Housing, then Countryside Commn, subseq. DoE, 1969–75; Shropshire County Planning Dept, 1975–84; Welsh Office: Principal, 1984–88, Pvte Sec. to Sec. of State for Wales, 1987–88; Asst Sec., 1988–92; G3, 1992–97; Dir of Economic Affairs, 1997–99; Perm. Sec., 1999. *Recreations:* sailing, tennis, walking, rowing, modern history. *Address:* National Assembly for Wales, Crown Buildings, Cathays Park, Cardiff CF1 3NQ. *T:* (029) 2082 3289.

SHORVON, Prof. Simon David, MD; FRCP; Professor in Clinical Neurology, Institute of Neurology, University College London, since 1995; Hon. Consultant Neurologist, National Hospital for Neurology and Neurosurgery (formerly for Nervous Diseases), since 1983; *b* 17 June 1948; *s* of late Hyam Joseph Shorvon, DPM and of Mary Barbara Shorvon (*née* Bensusan Butt), MRCPsych; *m* 1st, 1984, Penelope Farmer (marr. diss.); 2nd, 1999, Dr Lynne Soon Li Low; one *s*. *Educ:* City of London Sch.; Trinity Coll., Cambridge (BA 1970; MB BChir 1974; MA 1974; MD 1983); St Thomas' Hosp. Med. Sch. MRCP 1975, FRCP 1990. Jun. med. and academic appts, Oxford, Manchester, KCH, Maudsley Hosp., and Nat. Hosp for Nervous Diseases, 1973–83; Vis. Scientist, Univ. of Virginia, 1981; Sen. Lectr, 1983–92, Reader in Neurology, 1992–95, Chm., Dept of Clin. Neurology, 1998–, Inst. of Neurology, UCL; Dir, Nat. Neurosci. Inst., Singapore, 2000–. Med. Dir, Nat. Soc. for Epilepsy, 1989–98. Member: Med. Panel, DVLA, 1987–; Disability Living Allowance Bd, 1994–96. International League Against Epilepsy: Mem., Exec. Cttee; Vice-Pres., 1993–; Information Officer, 1997–, Mem., edtl bds, internat. learned jls; Guarantor, Brain, 1998–. *Publications:* Neurological Emergencies, 1989; Status Epilepticus: its clinical form and treatment in children and adults, 1994; (ed jtly) Magnetic Resonance Scanning and Epilepsy, 1994; (ed jtly) Epilepsy, 2nd edn 1995; Clinical Epilepsy, 1995; (ed jtly) The Treatment of Epilepsy, 1996; Handbook of Epilepsy Treatment, 2000; contribs to epilepsy, epidemiology and clin. neurology in learned jls. *Recreation:* the liberal arts. *Address:* Department of Clinical Neurology, Institute of Neurology, University College London, Queen Square, WC1N 3BG. *T:* (020) 7837 3611; *e-mail:* s.shorvon@ion.ucl.ac.uk.

SHOSTAK, Raymond Jon; Director, Children, Schools and Families Service, Hertfordshire County Council, since 2001; *b* 2 July 1949; *s* of late Jerome M. Shostak and Alma (*née* Stern); *m* 1980, Gill Rivaz; one *s* one *d*. *Educ:* Nanuet Jun. Sen. High Sch.; Syracuse Univ. (BA Hons); Univ. of Southern Calif (MSc). Teacher: Isbell Jun. High Sch., Santa Paula, Calif, 1971–73; Leggatts Sch., Watford, Herts, 1973–74; Dep. Warden, 1974, Warden, 1975–83, SW Herts Teachers' Centre, Herts CC; Sen. Staff Inspector, Notts CC Adv. Inspection Service, 1983–86; Asst Dir of Educn and Chief Advr, W Sussex CC, 1989–96; Ofsted Inspector, 1993–; Head, Pupil Performance Team, Sch. Effectiveness Div., DFEE, 1996–97; Dir of Educn, Herts CC, 1997–2001. Dir, Herts TEC, 1997–2001; Board Member: QCA, 2001–; Herts Learning and Skills Council, 2001–; Chm., Wallenberg Centre for Improvement in Educn, Univ. of Cambridge, 1998–. Mem., Eastern Region NHS Childrens Task Force, 2001. Sec., Soc. of Chief Inspectors and Advrs, 1992–96. Vis. Fellow (part-time), Sussex Univ., 1996–. FRSA 1993. *Recreations:* family, ski-ing, tennis, photography, woodturning. *Address:* Hertfordshire County Council, County Hall, Hertford, Herts SG13 8DF. *T:* (01992) 555700.

SHOTTER, Very Rev. Edward Frank; Dean of Rochester, since 1989; *b* 29 June 1933; *s* of late Frank Edward Shotter and Minnetta Shotter (*née* Gaskill); *m* 1978, Jane Edgcumbe; two *s* one *d*. *Educ:* Humberstone Foundation School, Clee; Durham Univ. School of Architecture; St David's Coll., Lampeter, Univ. of Wales (BA 1958); St Stephen's House, Oxford. Deacon 1960, priest 1961; Curate of St Peter, Plymouth, 1960–62; Intercollegiate Sec., SCM, London, 1962–66; Director of Studies, London Medical Group, 1966–89; Director, Inst. of Medical Ethics, 1974–89 (Amulree Fellow, 1991–; Vice Pres., 1999–); Chaplain to Univ. of London, 1969–89; Prebendary of St Paul's Cathedral, 1977–89. Leverhulme Sen. Educnl Fellowship, 1976–79. Chairman: Cttee on Welfare of Czechoslovak Med. Students in Britain, 1968–69; Educn Sub-Cttee, Faculty of History and Phil. of Medicine, Apothecaries Soc., 1976–81; Church, Commerce and Industry Project, 1991–95: N Kent NHS Chaplaincy Service, 1993–96; Jt Chm., Kent Police Ecumenical Chaplaincy Cttee, 1993–; Force Chaplain, Kent Co. Constab., 1996–. Member: SCM Trust Assoc. Exec., 1965–79; Univ. Chaplains' Cttee, C of E Bd of Educn, 1968–70; Archbishop of Canterbury's Counsellors on Foreign Relations, 1971–82; BCC East/West Relations Adv. Cttee, 1971–81; Liberal Party Foreign Affairs Panel (Chm. East Europe Sub-Cttee), 1974–81; St Christopher's Hospice Educn Cttee, 1982–89; Wking Party on ethics of med. involvement in torture, 1989–91; Chm., IME working party on ethics of prolonging life and assisting death, 1991–98; Chm., Univ. of Greenwich Res. Ethics Cttee, 1995–. Chairman: Medway Enterprise Agency, 1993–98; Medway Business Support Partnership, 1994–96; Medway Business Point Ltd, 1996–98. Dir, Firmstart Medway Ltd, 1991–. C of E rep. on Churches Council of Health and Healing, 1975–76. Mem., Gen. Synod of C of E, 1994–; Sec., Assoc. of English Cathedrals, 1994–; Mem., Church Heritage Forum, 1999–. Chm., HMS Cavalier Meml Steering Gp, 2000–. Chm., Governing Body, King's School, Rochester, 1989–; Pres., St Bartholomew's Hosp., Rochester, 1989–. Founder, Jl of Medical Ethics, 1975. FRSocMed 1976. Patriarchal Cross, Romanian Orthodox Church, 1975. *Publications:* (ed) Matters of Life and Death, 1970; (with K. M. Boyd and B. Callaghan, SJ) Life Before Birth, 1986. *Recreations:* hill walking, domestic architecture. *Address:* The Deanery, Rochester, Kent ME1 1TG. *T:* (01634) 844023, *Fax:* (01634) 401410. *Club:* Reform.

SHOTTON, Dr Keith Crawford, CEng, FIEE; CPhys, FInstP; technical project and recruitment consultant; Head of Management and Technology Services Division, Department of Trade and Industry, 1994–96; *b* 11 Sept. 1943; *s* of William Crawford Shotton and Mary Margaret Shotton (*née* Smith); *m* 1969, Maria Elizabeth Gonszor; two *d*. *Educ:* Newcastle upon Tyne Royal Grammar Sch.; Trinity Coll., Cambridge (Schol.; MA, PhD). CPhys, FInstP 1982; CEng, FIEE 1988. Post-doctoral Fellow (laser physics and spectroscopy), NRCC, 1969–71; National Physical Laboratory: mem. team measuring speed of light, 1971–77; Head, Ultrasonics Metrology Unit, 1977–80; Head, Marketing and Inf. Services, 1980–84; DCSO, Supt, Div. of Radiation Sci. and Acoustics, 1984–87; Department of Trade and Industry: Dir, Radio Technology, Radio Communications Div., 1987–90; Hd, IT Div., 1990–92; Hd, Inf. and Manufg Technols Div., 1992–93; Hd, Technol. Progs and Services Div., 1993–94. *Publications:* papers in sci. jls, principally in spectroscopy, laser physics, ultrasonics and instrumentation. *Recreations:* walking, sailing, motor cars, food.

SHOVELTON, Prof. David Scott, FDSRCS; Professor of Conservative Dentistry, University of Birmingham, 1964–89, Professor Emeritus, since 1990; Honorary Consultant in Conservative Dentistry, Central Birmingham Health Authority, since 1989; *b* 12 Sept. 1925; *s* of Leslie Shovelton, LDSRCS, and Marion de Winton (*née* Scott); *m* 1949, Pearl Holland; two *s*. *Educ:* The Downs Sch., Colwall; King's Sch., Worcester; Univ. of Birmingham (BSc, LDS, BDS). House Surg., Birmingham Dental Hosp., 1951; gen. dental practice, Evesham, Worcs, 1951; Dental Officer, RAF, 1951–53; Birmingham University: Lectr in Operative Dental Surg., 1953–60; Sen. Lectr, 1960–64; Dir, 1974–78, Dep. Dir, 1982–84, Dental Sch.; Consultant Dental Surgeon, Utd Birmingham Hosps, subseq. Central Birmingham HA, 1960–89. Vis. Asst Prof. of Clin. Dentistry, Univ. of Alabama, 1959–60. Hon. Cons. Dental Surg., Birmingham Reg. Hosp. Bd, 1962–74. Pres., British Soc. for Restorative Dentistry, 1970–71 (Vice-Pres., 1968–70 and 1971–72). Consultant, Commn on Dental Practice, Fédn Dentaire Internat., 1972–79; Consultant Adviser in Restorative Dentistry, DHSS, 1983–89. Member: Gen. Dental Council, 1974–89; Birmingham Area Health Authority (Teaching), 1973–79; Cttee of Management, Sch. for Dental Therapists, 1977–80; Jt Cttee for Higher Trng in Dentistry, 1979–84 (Chm., Specialist Adv. Cttee in Restorative Dentistry, 1979–84); Standing Dental Adv. Cttee, 1982–88; Bd, Faculty of Dental Surgery, RCS, 1983–91; Jt Dental Cttee of MRC, Health Depts and SERC, 1984–87; Cttee of Enquiry into unnecessary dental treatment, 1984–85. Ext. Examnr in dental subjects, univs and colls, 1968–94. *Publications:* Inlays, Crowns and Bridges (jtly), 1963, 5th edn 1993 (trans. Portuguese 1991); articles in med. and dental jls, 1957–89. *Recreations:* music, learning about wine, gardening. *Address:* 86 Broad Oaks Road, Solihull, West Midlands B91 1HZ. *T:* (0121) 705 3026. *Club:* Royal Air Force.

SHOVELTON, Dame Helena, DBE 1999; Chair, Audit Commission, 1998–2001 (Member, 1995–2001); *b* 28 May 1945; *d* of Denis George Richards, *qv*; *m* 1968, Walter Patrick Shovelton, *qv*. *Educ:* North London Collegiate Sch.; Regent St Poly. (HND Business Studies); Strathclyde Univ. (MBA 1998). Manager, Tunbridge Wells and Dist CAB, 1987–94. National Association of Citizens Advice Bureaux: Council Mem., 1989–90; Vice-Chm., 1990–94; Chm., 1994–99. Member: Local Govt Commn, 1995–98 (Dep. Chm., 1996–98); Banking Code Standards Bd (formerly Ind. Review Body for Banking and Mortgage Lending Codes), 1997–2000; Competition (formerly Monopolies and Mergers) Commn, 1997–; Better Regulation Task Force, 1997–99; Nat. Lottery Commn, 1999–2000. Chm., Independent Review Panel on Continuing Care, E Sussex, Brighton and Hove HA, 1996–97. Non-exec. Dir, Energy Saving Trust, 1998–. Trustee, RAF Benevolent Fund, 1997–. FRSA 1995. *Recreations:* looking at the garden, reading. *Address:* 63 London Road, Tunbridge Wells, Kent TN1 1DT. *T:* (01892) 533919.

SHOVELTON, (Walter) Patrick, CB 1976; CMG 1972; FCIT; Adviser: Maersk Co., since 1996 (Director, 1985; Vice-Chairman, 1987–95); Maersk Air, since 1995 (Director, 1993–95); *b* 18 Aug. 1919; *s* of late S. T. Shovelton, CBE, and May Catherine (*née* Kelly), cousin of Patrick and Willie Pearse, Irish patriots; *m* 1st, 1942, Marjorie Lucy Joan Manners (marr. diss. 1967); one *d*; 2nd, 1968, Helena Richards (*see* Dame Helena Shovelton). *Educ:* Charterhouse; Keble Coll., Oxford (scholar of both). Rep. Oxford Univ. at Eton Fives. Served in RA and RHA, 1940–46; DAAG, War Office, 1945–46. Entered Administrative Civil Service as Asst Principal, Min. of War Transport, 1946; Principal 1947; Admin. Staff College, 1951; Private Sec. to Secretary of State for Co-ordination of Transport, Fuel and Power, 1951–53; Asst Sec., Road Transport, 1957; transferred to Min. of Aviation, 1959; IDC, 1962; Under Secretary, 1966; transferred to Min. of Technology, 1966, and to DTI, 1970; Mem., UK Negotiating Team for entry into EEC, 1970–72; Deputy Secretary: DTI, 1972–74; Dept of Prices and Consumer Protection, 1974–76; Dept of Trade, 1976–78; led UK Negotiating Team for Bermuda 2, 1977; Dir-Gen., Gen. Council of British Shipping, 1978–85; Dir, British Airports Authy, 1982–85. Chm., Birmingham Executive, later European, Airways, 1988–93. William and Mary Tercentenary Trust: Chairman: Maritime Cttee, 1985–89; Finance and Sponsorship Cttee, 1988–89. Council, CIT, 1982–85; Advr, Inquiries into EEC Maritime Transport Policy H of L, 1985–86, into Merchant Shipping, H of C, 1986–88. Brancker Lectr (civil aviation), 1979; Grout Lectr (shipping), 1985. Founder and Chm., Friends of Tunbridge Wells and Rusthall Commons, 1991–98. Officer, Order of Orange-Nassau (Netherlands), 1989. *Recreations:* competitive golf, reading, opera, bridge. *Clubs:* Brooks's; Jesters; Royal Ashdown Forest Golf, Rye Golf, Hampstead Golf, Seniors Golf; Tunbridge Wells & Counties Bridge, West Kent Bridge.

SHOWALTER, Prof. Elaine, PhD; Professor of English and Avalon Foundation Professor of Humanities, Princeton University, since 1984; *b* 21 Jan. 1941; *d* of Paul Cottler and Violet Rottenberg; *m* 1963, English Showalter; one *s* one *d*. *Educ:* Bryn Mawr Coll. (BA 1962); Univ. of California, Davis (PhD 1970). Departments of English: Douglass Coll., 1966–78; Rutgers Univ., 1966–84. Pres., Modern Language Assoc. of America, 1998. *Publications:* A Literature of Their Own, 1977; The Female Malady, 1985; Sexual Anarchy, 1990; Sister's Choice: tradition and change in American women's writing, 1991; (jtly) Hysteria Beyond Freud, 1993; Hystories: hysterical epidemics and modern culture, 1997; Inventing Herself: claiming a feminist intellectual heritage, 2001. *Address:* 119 Snowden Lane, Princeton, NJ 08540, USA. *T:* (609) 9240832. *Club:* Princeton (NY).

SHRAPNEL, Norman; Parliamentary Correspondent of the Guardian, 1958–75; *b* 5 Oct. 1912; *yr s* of Arthur Edward Scrope Shrapnel and Rosa Brosy; *m* 1940, Mary Lilian Myfanwy Edwards; two *s*. *Educ:* King's School, Grantham. Various weekly, evening and morning newspapers from 1930; Manchester Guardian (later the Guardian) from 1947, as reporter, theatre critic and reviewer; contributor to various journals. Political Writer of the Year Award (the Political Companion), 1969. *Publications:* A View of the Thames, 1977; The Performers: politics as theatre, 1978; The Seventies, 1980. *Recreations:* walking, music. *Address:* Laburnum Cottage, Far Oakridge, Stroud, Glos GL6 7PB.

SHREEVE, Ven. David Herbert; Archdeacon of Bradford, 1984–99, now Emeritus; *b* 18 Jan. 1934; *s* of Hubert Ernest and Ivy Eleanor Shreeve; *m* 1957, Barbara (*née* Fogden);

one *s* one *d.* *Educ:* Southfield School, Oxford; St Peter's Coll., Oxford (MA); Ridley Hall, Cambridge. Asst Curate, St Andrew's Church, Plymouth, 1959–64; Vicar: St Anne's, Bermondsey, 1964–71; St Luke's, Eccleshill, 1971–84; RD of Calverley, 1978–84. Mem., Gen. Synod and Proctor in Convocation, 1977–90, 1993–98; Mem., Dioceses Commn, 1988–98. Hon. Canon of Bradford Cathedral, 1983–84. *Recreations:* walking, camping, travel, photography. *Address:* 26 Kingsley Drive, Harrogate, N Yorks HG1 4TJ. *T:* (01423) 886479.

SHRESTHA, Surya Prasad; Ambassador of Nepal to the Court of St James's, 1992–97; *b* 1 March 1937; *s* of late L. P. Shrestha and Mrs G. K. Shrestha; *m* 1958, Ginni Baba Shrestha; two *s* two *d.* *Educ:* Tribhuvan Univ. (MA Pol Sci.); LSE (Dip. Econs and Social Admin). Joined HM Govt service, Nepal, 1958; Section Officer, Parlt Secretariat and Min. of Develt, 1958–63; Under Secretary: Min. of Home and Panchayat, 1963–65; Election Commn, 1965–66; Jt Zonal Comr, 1970–74, Zonal Comr, 1974–78, Bagmati Zone; Actg Sec., Home and Panchayat Min., 1978–79; Sec. of Industry and Commerce, 1979–83; Jt Mem., Nat. Planning Commn, 1983–85; Chief Election Comr, 1985–92. Prabal Gorkha Dakshin Bahu, III Cl. (Nepal), 1966, Prasiddha, II Cl., 1976; Trishakti Patta, Vikhyat, III Cl. (Nepal), 1973, Suvikhyat, II Cl., 1991. FRGS 1996. *Recreations:* reading, gardening. *Address:* PO Box 2482, Chha–403, Maharajgung, Kathmandu, Nepal.

SHREWSBURY, Bishop Suffragan of, since 2001; **Rt Rev. Alan Gregory Clayton Smith;** *b* 14 Feb. 1957; *s* of late Frank Eric Smith and of Rosemary Clayton Smith. *Educ:* Trowbridge Grammar Sch.; Univ. of Birmingham (BA Theol. 1978; MA 1979); Wycliffe Hall, Oxford. Ordained deacon, 1981, priest, 1982; Assistant Curate: St Lawrence, Pudsey, 1981–82; St Lawrence and St Paul, Pudsey, 1982–84; Chaplain, Lee Abbey Community, Devon, 1984–90; Diocesan Missioner, Lichfield, 1990–97; Team Vicar, St Matthew's, Walsall, 1990–97; Archdeacon, Stoke-upon-Trent, 1997–2001. Chm. Bd, Lee Abbey Household Communities, 1996–; Hon. Canon, Lichfield Cathedral, 1997–. *Recreations:* classical music, travel, squash, ski-ing. *Address:* Athlone House, 68 London Road, Shrewsbury SY2 6PG.

SHREWSBURY, Bishop of, (RC), since 1995; **Rt Rev. Brian Michael Noble;** *b* 11 April 1936; *s* of Thomas Joseph and Cecelia Noble. *Educ:* Ushaw Coll., Durham. Ordained priest for RC Diocese of Lancaster, 1960; parish appts, 1960–72; Chaplain, Lancaster Univ., 1972–80; Lectr, Pontificio Collegio Beda, Rome, 1980–87; Parish Priest, St Benedict's, Whitehaven, and Dean of West Cumbria, 1987–95. Canon of Lancaster Cath. Chapter, 1994. *Recreations:* music, poetry, natural history, walking. *Address:* Laburnum Cottage, 97 Barnston Road, Barnston, Wirral CH61 1BW.

SHREWSBURY AND WATERFORD, 22nd Earl of, *cr* 1442 and 1446; **Charles Henry John Benedict Crofton Chetwynd Chetwynd-Talbot;** DL; Baron Talbot, 1733; 7th Earl Talbot, Viscount Ingestre, 1784; Premier Earl on the Rolls of England and Ireland, Hereditary Great Seneschal or Lord High Steward of Ireland; Lord Dungarvan; director and landowner; *b* 18 Dec. 1952; *s* of 21st Earl of Shrewsbury and Waterford, and of Nadine, *yr d* of late Brig.-Gen. C. R. Crofton, CBE; *S* father, 1980; *m* 1974, Deborah, *o d* of Noel Hutchinson; two *s* one *d.* *Educ:* Harrow. Director: Britannia Building Soc., 1984–92 (Dep. Chm., 1987–89; Jt Dep. Chm., 1989–92); Richmount Enterprise Zone Managers, 1988–94. Mem. Exec. Cttee, Staffs Br., Game Conservancy Trust, 1988–. Pres., Staffordshire Soc., 1989–91; Vice-Pres., Midland & West Assoc. of Building Socs, 1984–92; Pres., BSA, 1993–97. Chm., Firearms Consultative Cttee, 1994–99. Chancellor, Univ. of Wolverhampton, 1993–99. Elected Mem., H of L, 1999. President: British Inst. of Innkeeping, 1996–97; Staffs & Birmingham Agricl Soc., 2000–01. Patron: St Giles Hospice, Lichfield, 1988–; Staffs Br., BRCS, 1989–92. Hon. President: Shropshire Bldg Preservation Trust, 1984–; Lord Roberts Wkshops and SSAFA (Wolverhampton Br.), 1987–; Staffs Small Bore Rifle Assoc., 1988–; Hon. Vice-Pres., Rugeley Rugby FC. Hon. Pres., Shropshire Hospice, 1983–88. Patron of 11 livings. DL Stafford, 1994. Hon. LLD Wolverhampton, 1994. *Recreations:* shooting, fishing. *Heir:* *s* Viscount Ingestre, *qv.* *Address:* Wanfield Hall, Kingstone, Uttoxeter, Staffs ST14 8QT.

SHRIMPLIN, John Steven; consultant, since 1994; Member, European Space Agency Appeals Board, since 2000; *b* 9 May 1934; *s* of late John Reginald Shrimplin and Kathleen Mary (*née* Stevens); *m* 1957, Hazel Baughen; two *s.* *Educ:* Royal Grammar Sch., Colchester; King's Coll., London (BSc Maths). Joined RAE, Farnborough, 1956; Defence Operational Analysis Estabt, 1966; JSSC, 1970; Weapons Dept, RAE, 1971; Defence R&D Staff, British Embassy, Washington, 1972; Asst Dir, Future Systems, Air Systems Controllerate, MoD PE, 1974; Asst Chief Scientist, RAF, 1978; Head of Weapons Dept, RAE, 1983; Dep. Hd, British Defence Staff, and Minister/Counsellor, Defence Equipment, British Embassy, Washington, DC, 1985–88; Dir, Defence Science (Studies), MoD, 1988–91; Dep. Dir Gen. and Dir, Space Technol., BNSC, 1991–94. UK Rep., Eur. Space Policy Cttee, 1994–99. FRAeS 1993. *Recreations:* travel, camping, walking. *Address:* c/o National Westminster Bank, 2 Alexandra Road, Farnborough, Hants GU14 6BZ.

SHRIMSLEY, Bernard; journalist; *b* 13 Jan. 1931; *er s* of John and Alice Shrimsley, London; *m* 1952, Norma Jessie Alexandra, *d* of Albert and Maude Porter, Southport; one *d.* *Educ:* Kilburn Grammar School, Northampton. Press Association, 1947–48; Southport Guardian, 1948–49 and 1951–53; RAF, 1949–51; Daily Mirror, 1953–58 and 1961–68; Sunday Express, 1958–61; Editor, Daily Post, Liverpool, 1968–69; Dep. Editor, 1969–72, Editor, 1972–75, The Sun; Editor, News of the World, and Dir, News Group Newspapers Ltd, 1975–80; Editor-designate (subseq. Editor), The Mail on Sunday, and Dir (subseq. Vice-Chm.), The Mail on Sunday Ltd, 1980–82; Asst Editor, 1983–86, Associate Editor, 1986–96, Daily Express; media consultant, Referendum Party, 1996–97; leader writer, Press Gazette, 1999–. Member: Press Council, 1989–90 (Jt Vice-Chm., 1990); Defence, Press and Broadcasting Cttee, 1989–93. Mem. judging panel, British Press Awards, 1988–. *Publications:* The Candidates, 1968; Lion Rampant, 1984 (US Book of the Month Choice). *Club:* Garrick.

SHRIMSLEY, Robert Gideon; Chief Political Correspondent, Financial Times, since 2000; *b* 21 Sept. 1964; *s* of late Anthony Shrimsley and of Yvonne Shrimsley; *m* 1997, Reeve Lewis; one *s.* *Educ:* St Nicholas Preparatory Sch.; University College Sch.; London Sch. of Economics (BSc Econs 1985). Reporter: Darlington Evening Despatch, 1986; Kentish Times, 1986–88; Sunday Telegraph, 1988–89; Reporter, 1989–92, political staff, 1992–95, Daily Telegraph; Lobby Corresp., Financial Times, 1995–96; Chief Pol Corresp., Daily Telegraph, 1996–2000. *Recreations:* cinema, reading, comedy clubs, watching QPR, spending time with my family. *Address:* (office) Financial Times, 1 Southwark Bridge, SE1 9HL. *T:* (020) 7873 3000, (020) 7219 6892.

SHRIVER, (Robert) Sargent; Partner, 1971–86, Lawyer Of Counsel, Fried, Frank, Harris, Shriver & Jacobson, since 1986; Chairman, Special Olympics International, since 1990 (President, 1984–90); *b* Westminster, Md, 9 Nov. 1915; *s* of Robert Sargent and Hilda Shriver; *m* 1953, Eunice Mary Kennedy; four *s* one *d.* *Educ:* parochial schools, Baltimore; Canterbury School, New Milford, Conn.; Yale College; Yale University. BA (*cum laude*) 1938; LLB 1941; LLD 1964. Apprentice Seaman, USNR, 1940; Ensign, 1941. Served War of 1941–45: Atlantic and Pacific Ocean Areas aboard battleships and submarines; Lt-Comdr, USNR. Admitted to: New York Bar, 1941; Illinois Bar, (retd) 1959; US Supreme Court, 1966; District of Columbia Bar, 1971. With legal firm of Winthrop, Stimson, Putnam & Roberts, NYC, 1940–41; Asst Editor, Newsweek, 1945–46; associated with Joseph P. Kennedy Enterprises, 1946–48; Asst Gen. Man., Merchandise Mart, 1948–61; President: Chicago Bd of Educn, 1955–60; Catholic Interracial Council of Chicago, 1954–59; Dir, Peace Corps, Washington, 1961–66; Dir, Office of Economic Opportunity (resp. for develt of Head Start, Job Corps, VISTA Community Action, Legal Services for the Poor, etc), and Special Asst to Pres. Johnson, 1964–68; US Ambassador to France, 1968–70. Vice-Presidential candidate (Democrat), Nov. 1972. Democrat; Roman Catholic. US Presidential Medal of Freedom, 1994; Franklin D. Roosevelt Freedom From Want Award, 1994. *Address:* Suite 500, 1325 G Street NW, Washington, DC 20005, USA.

SHRUBSOLE, Alison Cheveley, CBE 1982; Principal, Homerton College, Cambridge, 1971–85; Fellow of Hughes Hall, Cambridge, 1974; *b* 7 April 1925; *d* of Rev. Stanley and Mrs Margaret Shrubsole; *m* 1983, George Huntly Hilton Brown. *Educ:* Milton Mount Coll.; Royal Holloway Coll., London Univ. (BA Hons); Inst. of Education (Postgraduate Cert. in Educn); MA Cantab. FCP. Teaching in schools in South London, 1946–50; Lectr and Sen. Lectr, Stockwell Coll., 1950–57; Principal: Machakos Training Coll., Kenya, 1957–62; Philippa Fawcett Coll., London SW16, 1963–71. DUniv Open, 1985. *Recreations:* music, architecture, travel, gardening, cooking. *Address:* 4 Chancellor House, Mount Ephraim, Tunbridge Wells, Kent TN4 8BT; Cortijo Abulagar, Rubite, Granada, Spain.

SHTAUBER, Dr Zvi; Ambassador of Israel to the Court of St James's, since 2001; *m* Nitza Rousso; two *s* one *d.* *Educ:* Fletcher Sch. of Law and Diplomacy; Harvard Business Sch.; Hebrew Univ. of Jerusalem. Mem., Israel Defence Force, 1970–95; Vice-Pres., Ben Gurion Univ. of Negev, 1996–99; Foreign Policy Advr to Prime Minister of Israel, 1999–2000. *Address:* Embassy of Israel, 2 Palace Green, W8 4QB. *T:* (020) 7957 9500.

SHUCKBURGH, Sir Rupert (Charles Gerald), 13th Bt *cr* 1660, of Shuckburgh, Warwickshire; *b* 12 Feb. 1949; *s* of Sir Charles Gerald Stewkley Shuckburgh, 12th Bt, TD and Nancy Diana Mary, OBE (*d* 1984), *o d* of late Captain Rupert Lubbock, RN; *S* father, 1988; *m* 1st, 1976, Judith (marr. diss. 1987), *d* of W. G. Mackaness; two *s*; 2nd, 1987, Margaret Ida, *d* of late W. Evans. *Heir:* *s* James Rupert Charles Shuckburgh, *b* 4 Jan. 1978. *Address:* Shuckburgh Hall, Daventry, Northants NN11 6DT. *Club:* Farmers'.

SHUFFREY, Ralph Frederick Dendy, CB 1983; CVO 1981; Deputy Under-Secretary of State and Principal Establishment Officer, Home Office, 1980–84; *b* 9 Dec. 1925; *s* of late Frederick Arthur Shuffrey, MC and Mary Shuffrey (*née* Dendy); *m* 1953, Sheila, *d* of late Brig. John Lingham, CB, DSO, MC, and Juliet Judd; one *s* one *d.* *Educ:* Shrewsbury; Balliol Coll., Oxford. Served Army, 1944–47 (Captain). Entered Home Office, 1951; Private Sec. to Parly Under-Sec. of State, 1956–57; Private Sec. to Home Sec., 1965–66; Asst Sec., 1966–72; Asst Under-Sec. of State, 1972–80. Chairman: The Cranstoun Projects Ltd, 1988–97; Fire Service Res. and Trng Trust, 1989–. Hon. Sec., Soc. for Individual Freedom, 1985–89. *Address:* Flat D, Campden House, 29 Sheffield Terrace, W8 7ND. *Club:* Reform.

SHULL, Prof. Clifford Glenwood, PhD; Professor of Physics, Massachusetts Institute of Technology, 1955–86, now Emeritus Professor; *b* 23 Sept 1915; *s* of David H. and Daisy B. Shull; *m* 1941, Martha-Nuel Summer; three *s.* *Educ:* Carnegie Inst. of Technology (BS 1937); New York Univ. (PhD 1941). Research Physicist: The Texas Co., 1941–46; Oak Ridge Nat. Lab., 1946–55. Hon. ScD New York, 1997. Buckley Prize, Amer. Phys. Soc., 1956; Humboldt Sen. US Scientist Award, 1980; Aminoff Prize, Royal Swedish Acad. of Scis, 1993; (jtly) Nobel Prize for Physics, 1994. *Publications:* numerous scientific articles. *Address:* 4 Wingate Road, Lexington, MA 02421, USA. *T:* (781) 8628627.

SHULMAN, Alexandra; Editor, British Vogue, since 1992; *b* 13 Nov. 1957; *d* of Milton Shulman, *qv* and Drusilla Beyfus, *qv*; *m* 1994, Paul, *s* of late Rev. Dr Robert W. Spike, NY; one *s.* *Educ:* St Paul's Girls' Sch.; Sussex Univ. (BA Social Anthropology). Tatler: Commissioning Editor, 1982–84; Features Editor, 1984–87; Sunday Telegraph: Editor, Women's Page, 1987; Dep. Editor, 7 Days Mag., 1987–88; Features Editor, Vogue, 1988–90; Editor, GQ, 1990–92. Trustee, Nat. Portrait Gall. and Arts Foundn. *Address:* Condé Nast Publications, Vogue House, Hanover Square, W1R 0AD. *T:* (020) 7499 9080.

SHULMAN, Drusilla Norman; *see* Beyfus, Drusilla N.

SHULMAN, Milton; writer, journalist, critic; *b* Toronto; *s* of late Samuel Shulman, merchant, and of Ethel Shulman; *m* 1956, Drusilla Beyfus, *qv*; one *s* two *d.* *Educ:* Univ. of Toronto (BA); Osgoode Hall, Toronto. Barrister, Toronto, 1937–40. Armoured Corps and Intelligence, Canadian Army, 1940–46 (despatches, Normandy, 1945); Major. Film critic, Evening Standard and Sunday Express, 1948–58; book critic, Sunday Express, 1957–58; theatre critic, Evening Standard, 1953–91; TV critic, Evening Standard, 1964–73; columnist, social and political affairs, Daily Express, 1973–75; film critic, Vogue Magazine, 1975–87; columnist, art affairs, Evening Standard, 1991–96. Executive producer and producer, Granada TV, 1958–62; Asst Controller of Programmes, Rediffusion TV, 1962–64. Mem., Adv. Council, British Theatre Museum, 1981–83. Mem. Panel of Judges, Evening Standard Drama Awards, 1955–. Regular panel mem., Stop the Week, BBC Radio 4. IPC Award, Critic of the Year, 1966. *Publications:* Defeat in the West, 1948; How To Be a Celebrity, 1950; The Ravenous Eye, 1973; The Least Worst Television in the World, 1973; Marilyn, Hitler and Me (memoirs), 1998; Voltaire, Goldberg and Others, 1999; It Takes All Sorts, 2001; *children's books:* Preep, 1964; Preep in Paris, 1967; Preep and The Queen, 1970; *novel:* Kill Three, 1967; *novel and film story:* (with Herbert Kretzmer) Every Home Should Have One, 1970. *Recreations:* modern art, history, tennis. *Address:* 51 Eaton Square, SW1W 9BE. *T:* (020) 7235 7162. *Clubs:* Garrick, Chelsea Arts, Hurlingham.

See also Marquis of Normanby, A. Shulman.

SHULTZ, George Pratt; Secretary of State, United States of America, 1982–89; Distinguished Fellow, Hoover Institution, since 1989; *b* New York City, 13 Dec. 1920; *s* of Birl E. Shultz and Margaret Pratt; *m* 1946, Helena Maria O'Brien (*d* 1995); two *s* three *d*; *m* 1997, Charlotte Mailliard Swig. *Educ:* Princeton Univ., 1942 (BA Econ); Massachusetts Inst. of Technology, 1949 (PhD Industrial Econ). Served War, US Marine Corps, Pacific, 1942; Major, 1945. Faculty, MIT, 1949–57; Sen. staff economist, President's Council of Economic Advisers, 1955–56 (on leave, MIT); Univ. of Chicago, Graduate Sch. of Business: Prof. of Industrial Relations, 1957–68; Dean, 1962–69; Prof. of Management and Public Policy, Stanford Univ., Graduate Sch. of Business, 1974. Secretary of Labor, 1969–July 1, 1970; Dir, Office of Management and Budget, 1970–72; Secretary of the Treasury, 1972–74; Exec. Vice-Pres., Bechtel Corp., 1974–75, Pres. 1975–77; Vice-Chm., Bechtel Corp., 1977–81 (Dir); Pres., Bechtel Group Inc., San Francisco, 1981–82. Chairman: President's Economic Policy Adv. Bd, 1981–82; Internat.

Council, J. P. Morgan, 1989–; Adv. Council, Inst. of Internat. Studies, 1989–. Director: General Motors Corp., 1981–82, 1989–91; Boeing Corp., 1989–93; Bechtel Gp Inc., 1989–; Tandem Computers Inc., 1989–92; Chevron Corp., 1989–93; Gulfstream Aerospace Corp., 1992–99; AirTouch Communications, 1994–98; Gilead Scis, 1996–; Charles Schwab & Co. Inc., 1997–; Unext.com, 2000–; Mem., GM Corporate Adv. Council. Chm., State of California Gov's Econ. Policy Adv. Bd, 1995–98. Hon. Dr of Laws: Notre Dame Univ., 1969; Loyola Univ., 1972; Pennsylvania, 1973; Rochester, 1973; Princeton, 1973; Carnegie-Mellon Univ., 1975; Columbia, 2001. *Publications:* Pressures on Wage Decisions, 1951; The Dynamics of a Labor Market (with C. A. Myers), 1951; Labor Problems: cases and readings (with J. R. Coleman), 1953; Management Organization and the Computer (with T. L. Whisler), 1960; Strategies for the Displaced Worker (with Arnold R. Weber), 1966; Guidelines, Informal Controls, and the Market Place (with Rober Z. Aliber), 1966; Workers and Wages in the Urban Labor Market (with Albert Rees), 1970; Leaders and Followers in an Age of Ambiguity, 1975; Economic Policy Beyond the Headlines (with Kenneth W. Dam), 1977, 2nd edn 1998; Turmoil and Triumph: my years as Secretary of State, 1993. *Recreations:* golf, tennis. *Address:* Hoover Institution, Stanford University, Stanford, CA 94305–6010, USA.

SHURMAN, Laurence Paul Lyons; Banking Ombudsman, 1989–96; *b* 25 Nov. 1930; *s* of Joseph and Sarah Shurman; *m* 1963, Mary Seamans (*née* McMullan); two *s* one *d*. *Educ:* Newcastle upon Tyne Royal Grammar Sch.; Magdalen Coll., Oxford (MA). Solicitor. Articles, John H. Sinton & Co., Newcastle, 1954–57; Assistant Solicitor: Haswell Croft, Newcastle, 1957–58; Hall Brydon, London, 1958–60; Kaufman & Siegal, London, 1960–61; Partner: Shurman & Bindman, Solicitors, London, 1961–64; Shurman & Co., London, 1964–67; Kingsley Napley, London, 1967–89 (Managing Partner, 1975–89). Legal Mem., Mental Health Review Tribunal, 1976–94; Chm., Portman Gp (drinks industry) Complaints Panel, 1997–; Mem. Council, Justice, 1973–. Lectures: Gilbart, 1990; Ernest Sykes Meml, 1991. Pres., City of Westminster Law Soc., 1980–81; Chm., British and Irish Ombudsman Assoc., 1993–95. Vice-Chm., Disciplinary Cttee, Assoc. of Chartered Certified Accountants, 1998–2000. Member: Mgt Cttee, Care and Repair England, 1998–; Council, RSAS Age Care, 1998–. Governor: Channing Sch., 1985– (Vice-Chm., 1988–); Newcastle upon Tyne Royal Grammar Sch., 1991–2001. Pres., Highgate Literary and Scientific Inst., 1998–. *Publications:* The Practical Skills of the Solicitor, 1981, 2nd edn 1985; contributor on Mental Health Tribunals in Vol. 26 of Atkin's Encyc. of Court Forms, 2nd edn 1985. *Recreations:* reading, fell walking, swimming, law reform. *Address:* 14 Southwood Avenue, N6 5RZ. *T:* (020) 8348 5409. *Club:* Leander (Henley).

SHUTLER, (Ronald) Rex (Barry), CB 1992; FRICS; FAAV; Chairman, Leasehold Valuation Tribunal and Rent Assessment Panel, since 1999 (Vice President, 1994–99); *b* 27 June 1933; *s* of Ronald Edgar Coggin Shutler and Helena Emily Shutler (*née* Lawes); *m* 1958, Patricia Elizabeth Longman; two *s*. *Educ:* Hardye's, Dorchester. Articled pupil and assistant, chartered surveyors, Dorchester, 1952–59; joined Valuation Office (Inland Revenue), 1959; District Valuer, Hereford and Worcester, 1970; Superintending Valuer, Wales, 1976; Dep. Chief Valuer, 1984–88; Chief Valuer, then Chief Exec., Valuation Office Agency, 1988–94. FRICS 1972; FAAV 1962; Hon. FSVA 1994. *Recreations:* golf, country pursuits, gardening. *Address:* (office) Whittington House, 19–30 Alfred Place, WC1E 7LR. *T:* (020) 7446 7779. *Club:* Bank House Golf & Country.

SHUTT, family name of **Baron Shutt of Greetland**.

SHUTT OF GREETLAND, Baron *cr* 2000 (Life Peer), of Greetland and Stainland in the county of West Yorkshire; **David Trevor Shutt,** OBE 1993; FCA; Consultant, Bousfield Waite & Co., Halifax, since 1994 (Partner, 1970–94); *b* 16 March 1942; *s* of Edward Angus Shutt and Ruth Satterthwaite Shutt (*née* Berry); *m* 1965, Margaret Edith; two *s* one *d*. *Educ:* Pudsey Grammar Sch. FCA 1969. Smithson Blackburn & Co., Leeds: Articled Clerk, 1959–64; Audit Clerk, 1964–66; Taxation Asst, Bousfield Waite & Co., Halifax, 1967–70. Mem. (L then Lib Dem) Calderdale MBC, 1973–90 and 1995– (Mayor, 1982–83). Dir, Joseph Rowntree Reform Trust Ltd, 1975– (Vice Chm.); Trustee, Joseph Rowntree Charitable Trust, 1985–. Treas., Inst. for Citizenship, 1995–. Contested: (L): Sowerby, 1970, Feb. and Oct. 1974, 1979; (L/Alliance): Calder Valley, 1983, 1987; (Lib Dem): Pudsey, 1992. Freeman of Calderdale, 2000. Paul Harris Fellow, Rotary Club, 1999. Citoyen d'honneur, Commune de Riorges (France), 1983. *Recreations:* transport, travel. *Address:* Woodfield, 197 Saddleworth Road, Greetland, Halifax, West Yorkshire HX4 8LZ. *T:* (01422) 375276. *Club:* Penn.

SHUTTLE, Penelope (Diane); writer and poet; *b* 12 May 1947; *d* of Jack Frederick Shuttle and Joan Shepherdess Lipscombe; *m* Peter Redgrove, *qv*; one *d*. *Educ:* Staines Grammar Sch.; Matthew Arnold County Secondary Sch., Mddx. Radio plays: The Girl who Lost her Glove, 1975 (Jt 3rd Prize Winner, Radio Times Drama Bursaries Comp., 1974); The Dauntless Girl, 1978. Poetry recorded for Poetry Room, Harvard Univ. Arts Council Awards, 1969, 1972 and 1985; Greenwood Poetry Prize, 1972; E. C. Gregory Award for Poetry, 1974. *Publications: novels:* An Excusable Vengeance, 1967; All the Usual Hours of Sleeping, 1969; Wailing Monkey Embracing a Tree, 1974; Rainsplitter in the Zodiac Garden, 1976; Mirror of the Giant, 1979; *poetry:* Nostalgia Neurosis, 1968; Midwinter Mandala, 1973; Photographs of Persephone, 1973; Autumn Piano, 1973; Songbook of the Snow, 1973; Webs on Fire, 1977; The Orchard Upstairs, 1980; The Child-Stealer, 1983; The Lion from Rio, 1986; Adventures with my Horse, 1988; Taxing the Rain, 1992; Building a City for Jamie, 1996; Selected Poems, 1998; A Leaf out of his Book, 1999; *with Peter Redgrove:* The Hermaphrodite Album (poems), 1973; The Terrors of Dr Treviles (novel), 1974; The Wise Wound (psychology), 1978, 5th edn 1999; Alchemy for Women, 1995. *Recreations:* listening to music, Hatha Yoga, walking, reading, contemplation. *Address:* c/o David Higham Associates Ltd, 5–8 Lower John Street, Golden Square, W1R 4HA.

SHUTTLEWORTH, 5th Baron *cr* 1902, of Gawthorpe; **Charles Geoffrey Nicholas Kay-Shuttleworth,** Bt 1850; JP; Lord-Lieutenant and Custos Rotulorum of Lancashire, since 1997; *b* 2 Aug. 1948; *s* of 4th Baron Shuttleworth, MC, and Anne Elizabeth (*d* 1991), *er d* of late Col Geoffrey Phillips, CBE, DSO; *S* father, 1975; *m* 1975, Mrs Ann Mary Barclay, *d* of James Whatman, MC; three *s*. *Educ:* Eton. Partner, Burton, Barnes & Vigers, Chartered Surveyors, 1977–96; National & Provincial Building Society: Dir, 1983–96; Chm., 1994–96; Director: Burnley Bldg Soc., 1978–82 (Vice-Chm., 1982); Rank Foundn, 1993–; Abbey National plc, 1996– (Dep. Chm., 1996–99). Chairman: Rural Develt Commn, 1990–97; Lancs Small Industries Cttee, COSIRA, 1978–83; Lancs Youth Clubs Assoc., 1980–86, Pres., 1986–; Member: Skelmersdale Develt Corp., 1982–85; NW Regional Cttee, National Trust, 1980–89; Council, CBI, 1993–96; Council, Duchy of Lancaster, 1998–. President: Royal Lancashire Agricl Soc., 1985–86, 2000–01; Assoc. of Lancastrians in London, 1986–87 and 1997. Vice-Pres., TAVRA, NW, 1997–. Chm., Yorkshire Dales Millennium Trust, 2000–. Mem. Council, Lancaster Univ., 1990–93; Governor, Giggleswick Sch., 1981– (Chm., 1984–97). Hon. Fellow, Univ. of Central Lancs, 1996. Hon. Colonel: 4th (V) Bn, Queen's Lancs Regt, 1996–99; Lancastrian and Cumbrian Vol., 1999–. FRICS. JP 1997, DL Lancs, 1986. KStJ 1997 (Pres., Council for Lancs, 1997–). *Heir: s* Hon. Thomas Edward Kay-Shuttleworth, *b* 29 Sept. 1976. *Address:* Leck Hall, Carnforth, Lancs LA6 2JF; 14 Sloane Avenue, SW3 3JE. *Clubs:* Brooks's, MCC.

SIAGURU, Sir Anthony (Michael), KBE 1990; Chairman, Port Moresby Stock Exchange, since 1998; *b* 4 Nov. 1946; *s* of Khaisir Petrus Siaguru and Kandambi Maria Krakemoine; *m* 1972, Wilhelmina Isikini; three *s*. *Educ:* Marist Brothers' Sch., Wewak and Ashgrove; Univ. of Papua New Guinea (Law); Harvard Univ. (Public Admin). Entered Foreign Service as Cadet Diplomat, 1972; Permanent Sec., Foreign Affairs and Trade, 1975–80; MP, 1982; Minister for: Public Service, 1982–84; Youth and Develt, 1985; Dep. Sec.-Gen. (Pol) of the Commonwealth, 1990–95. Partner, Blake Dawson Waldron, 1988–90 and 1996–97; Chm., South Pacific Games Foundn, 1989–90. Columnist, PNG Post Courier, 1988–90 and 1996–. Fulbright Scholar, 1980. FRSA 1992. *Publications: contributions to:* Ethics in Government, 1983; The United States' Dilemma, 1983; The Red Orchestra, 1987; Ethics of Public Decision Making, 1987. *Recreations:* gardening, tennis, fishing. *Address:* PO Box 5917, Boroko, NCD, Papua New Guinea. *Clubs:* Reform; Papua (Port Moresby).

SIBBETT, Prof. Wilson, CBE 2001; PhD; FRS 1997; FInstP; FRSE; Wardlaw Professor of Natural Philosophy, since 1997 (Professor, since 1985) and Director of Research, School of Physics and Astronomy, since 1994, University of St Andrews; *b* 15 March 1948; *s* of John Sibbett and Margaret (*née* McLeister); *m* 1979, Barbara Anne Brown; three *d*. *Educ:* Ballymena Tech. Coll.; Queen's Univ., Belfast (BSc 1st Cl. Hons Physics); Imperial Coll., London (PhD Laser Physics 1973). FInstP 1986. Blackett Laboratory, Imperial College, London: Postdoctoral Res. Asst, 1973–77; Lectr in Physics, 1977–84; Reader, 1984–85; University of St Andrews: Head, Physics Dept, 1985–88; Chm., Physics and Astronomy Dept, 1988–94. Mem., EPSRC, 1998–2001. Mem., St Andrews Rotary Club. FRSE 1988; Fellow, Optical Soc. of America, 1998. Hubert Schardin Gold Medal for Res. in Ultrafast Lasers and Diagnostics, 1978; C. V. Boys Prize and Medal for Exptl Physics, Inst. of Physics, 1993; Rank Prize for Optoelectronics, 1997. *Publications:* numerous on laser physics and related diagnostic techniques in internat. scientific jls. *Recreations:* golf, gardening, DIY. *Address:* School of Physics and Astronomy, University of St Andrews, North Haugh, St Andrews, Fife KY16 9SS. *T:* (01334) 463100. *Club:* Royal and Ancient Golf (St Andrews).

SIBERRY, John William Morgan; Under-Secretary, Welsh Office, 1963–73, retired; Secretary to Local Government Staff Commission for Wales, and NHS Staff Commission for Wales, 1973–75; *b* 26 Feb. 1913; *s* of late John William and Martha (*née* Morgan) Siberry; *m* 1949, Florence Jane Davies (*d* 1995); one *s* one *d*. *Educ:* Porth County School, Rhondda; Univ. Coll. Cardiff. Entered Civil Service as Asst Principal, Unemployment Assistance Board (later Nat. Assistance Board), 1935; Principal, 1941; Asst Sec., 1947; transferred to Min. of Housing and Local Govt as Under-Sec., 1963; Welsh Secretary, Welsh Office and Office for Wales of the Ministry of Housing and Local Government, 1963–64. Chm., Working Party on Fourth Television Service in Wales, 1975. *Address:* Northgates, 59 Pwllmelin Road, Llandaff, Cardiff CF5 2NG. *T:* (029) 2056 4666.

See also W. R. Siberry.

SIBERRY, William Richard; QC 1989; a Recorder, since 2000; *b* 11 Dec. 1950; *s* of John William Morgan Siberry, *qv*; *m* 1976, Julia Christine Lancaster. *Educ:* King's Coll., Taunton; Pembroke Coll., Cambridge (MA, LLB). Fellow, Pembroke Coll., Cambridge, 1973–75. Called to the Bar, Middle Temple, 1974; Asst Recorder, 1997–2000. *Recreations:* music, gardening, walking, photography, North West Highlands of Scotland. *Address:* Essex Court Chambers, 24 Lincoln's Inn Fields, WC2A 3ED. *T:* (020) 7813 8000. *Club:* Royal Automobile.

SIBLEY, Dame Antoinette, (Dame Antoinette Corbett), DBE 1996 (CBE 1973); Prima Ballerina, The Royal Ballet, Covent Garden; President, Royal Academy of Dancing, since 1991 (Vice-President, 1989–91); guest coach, Royal Ballet, since 1991; *b* 27 Feb. 1939; *d* of Edward G. Sibley and Winifred M. Sibley (*née* Smith); *m* 1964, M. G. Somes, CBE (marr. diss. 1973; he *d* 1994); *m* 1974, Panton Corbett; one *s* one *d*. *Educ:* Arts Educational Sch. and Royal Ballet Sch. 1st performance on stage as Student with Royal Ballet at Covent Garden, a swan, Jan. 1956; joined company, July 1956; has appeared with the company or as guest artist in most opera houses worldwide. Leading role in: Swan Lake, Sleeping Beauty, Giselle, Coppelia, Cinderella, The Nutcracker, La Fille Mal Gardée, Romeo and Juliet, Harlequin in April, Les Rendezvous, Jabez and the Devil (created the role of Mary), La Fête Etrange, The Rake's Progress, Hamlet, Ballet Imperial, Two Pigeons, La Bayadère, Symphonic Variations, Scènes de Ballet, Lilac Garden, Daphnis and Chloe, Pas de Quatre (Dolin's), Konservatoriett, A Month in the Country, Raymonda Act III, The Dream (created Titania), Laurentia, Good Humoured Ladies, Aristocrat in Mam'zelle Angot, Façade, Song of the Earth, Monotones (created role), Jazz Calendar (created Friday's Child), Enigma Variations (created Dorabella), Thais (created pas de deux), Anastasia (created Kshessinska), Afternoon of a Faun, Triad (created the Girl), Pavanne (created pas de deux), Manon (created title role), Soupirs (created pas de deux), L'invitation au voyage (created), Impromptu (created pas de deux), Varii Capricci (created La Capricciosa), Fleeting Figures (created rôle). *Film:* The Turning Point, 1978. *Relevant publications:* Classical Ballet—the Flow of Movement, by Tamara Karsavina, 1962; Sibley and Dowell, by Nicholas Dromgoole and Leslie Spatt, 1976; Antoinette Sibley, 1981, photographs with text by Mary Clarke; Reflections of a Ballerina, by Barbara Newman, 1986. *Recreations:* gardening, opera, reading. *Address:* c/o Royal Academy of Dancing, 36 Battersea Square, SW11 3RA.

SIBSON, Prof. Robin, PhD; Chief Executive, Higher Education Statistics Agency, since 2001; *b* 4 May 1944; *o s* of late Robert Sibson and Florence Elizabeth Sibson (*née* Worth); *m* 1975, Heather Gail Gulliver; two *s*. *Educ:* Sutton County Grammar Sch.; King's Coll., Cambridge (Schol., Sen. Schol., Prizeman; Wrangler, Maths Tripos Pt II, 1965; Dist. Maths Tripos Part III, 1966; BA 1966; A. M. P. Read Schol., 1966; Smith's Prize, 1968; MA, PhD 1970). CStat 1993. Fellow, King's Coll., 1968–76, Lectr in Math. Stats, 1971–76, Univ. of Cambridge; University of Bath: Prof. of Stats, 1976–94; Head, Sch. of maths, 1979–82; Sci. Area Chm., 1984–87; Pro-Vice-Chancellor, 1989–94; Vice-Chancellor, Univ. of Kent at Canterbury, 1994–2001. Member: various SSRC/ESRC and SERC cttees, 1980–85; Science Bd, SERC, 1986–89; Commonwealth Scholarship Adv. Panel, 1976–86; Wildfowl Trust Sci. Adv. Cttee, 1979–83; Bd, Higher Educn Stats Agency, 1996–; UK Acad. Mem., Higher Educn and Res. Cttee, Council of Europe, 1997– (Mem. Bureau, 2000–); Scientific Sec., Bernoulli Soc. for Math. Stats and Probability, 1985–87. Mem. Corp., Canterbury Coll., 1995–2001. *Publications:* (with N. Jardine) Mathematical Taxonomy, 1971; papers in learned jls *Recreation:* natural history. *Address:* Higher Education Statistics Agency, 18 Royal Crescent, Cheltenham GL50 3DA.

SIDAWAY, Ven. Geoffrey Harold; Archdeacon of Gloucester, since 2000; *b* 28 Oct. 1942; *s* of Harold and Margaret Sidaway; *m* 1970, Margaret Bates; two *s* one *d*. *Educ:* Kelham Theol Coll. Ordained deacon, 1966, priest, 1967; Curate: Beighton, Derby, 1966–70; St Mary and All Saints, Chesterfield, 1970–72; Vicar, St Bartholomew, Derby, 1972–77; Chaplain to E Midlands Ordination Course, 1974–77; Vicar: St Martin,

Maidstone, 1977–86; Bearstead and Thurnham, 1986–2000. Rural Dean, Sutton, 1992–99; Hon. Canon, Canterbury Cathedral, 1994–2000. Mem., Gen. Synod of C of E, 1995–2000. *Recreations:* cooking, gardening, walking, showing labradors. *Address:* Glebe House, Church Road, Maisemore, Gloucester GL2 8EY.

SIDDALL, Jonathan Charles; Director, Sports Dispute Resolution Panel Ltd, since 1999; *b* 6 July 1954; *s* of John Siddall and Joan Siddall; *m* 1988, Nicola Ann Glover; two *d*. *Educ:* Rugby Sch.; Univ. of Birmingham (LLB Hons 1976). Called to the Bar, Middle Temple, 1978; Accredited Mediator, CEDR, 1999. Pupillage, 1979–80; in-house Lawyer, Internat. Mgt Gp, 1980–83; Gen. Sec., British Univs Sports Fedn, 1984–86; Sec., Cumberland Lawn Tennis Club, 1987–90; Sec. and Campaign Co-ordinator, Law Aid Trust, 1990–91; Dep. Sec., LTA, 1992–98. MInstD 1999. *Recreations:* golf, tennis, squash, ski-ing, running, gardening. *Address:* Sports Dispute Resolution Panel Ltd, Francis House, Francis Street, SW1P 1DE. *T:* (020) 7854 8590. *Clubs:* Cumberland Lawn Tennis; Jesters; Highgate Golf; Hunstanton Golf.

SIDDALL, Sir Norman, Kt 1983; CBE 1975; DL; FREng; Member of the National Coal Board, 1971–83, Deputy Chairman 1973–82, Chairman 1982–83; *b* 4 May 1918; *s* of late Frederick and Mabel Siddall; *m* 1943, Pauline, *d* of late John Alexander and Edith Arthur; two *s* one *d*. *Educ:* King Edward VII School, Sheffield; Sheffield Univ. (BEng). National Coal Board: Production Manager, No 5 Area, East Midlands Div., 1951–56; General Manager, No 5 Area, East Midlands Div., 1956–57; General Manager, No 1 Area, East Midlands Div., 1957–66; Chief Mining Engineer, 1966–67; Dir Gen. of Production, 1967–71. Former Mem., Midland Cos Instn of Engrs (Silver Medal, 1951; Past Pres.). Chartered Engineer; FIMinE; CIMgt. DL Notts, 1987. Hon. DSc Nottingham, 1982. National Association of Colliery Managers: Silver Medal, 1955; Bronze Medal, 1960; Coal Science Lecture Medal, 1972; CGLI Insignia Award in Technology (*hc*), 1978; Instn Medal, IME, 1982; Krupinski Medal, 1982. *Publications:* articles in professional journals. *Address:* Brentwood, High Oakham Road, Mansfield, Notts NG18 5AJ.

SIDDELEY, family name of **Baron Kenilworth**.

SIDDELEY, Randle; *see* Kenilworth, 4th Baron.

SIDDIQI, Prof. Obaid, Padma Bhushan 1984; FRS 1984; FIASc 1968; FNA 1977; Professor Emeritus, Tata Institute of Fundamental Research, National Centre for Biological Sciences, Bangalore; *b* 7 Jan. 1932; *s* of M. A. Qadeer Siddiqi and Umme Kulsum; *m* 1955, Asiya Siddiqi; two *s* two *d*. *Educ:* Univ. of Aligarh (MSc); Univ. of Glasgow (PhD). Lecturer, Aligarh Univ., 1954–57; Indian Agricl Res. Inst., 1957–58; Dept of Genetics, Glasgow Univ., 1958–61; Cold Spring Harbor Lab., NY, 1961; Univ. of Pennsylvania, 1961–62; Tata Inst. of Fundamental Research: Fellow, 1962; Prof. of Molecular Biol., 1972–95; Dir, Nat. Centre for Biol Scis, Bangalore, 1992–99. Vis. Associate, Yale Univ., 1966; Vis. Prof., MIT, 1970–71; CIT Gosney Fellow, 1971–72; Sherman Fairchild Distinguished Scholar, 1981–82; Fellow, Third World Acad. of Sciences, Trieste, 1986; Vis. Fellow, 1997, and Life Mem., Clare Hall, Cambridge. Hon. DSc: Aligarh, 1984; Banaras Hindu, 1986. *Publications:* (co-ed) Development and Neurobiology of Drosophila, 1981; several papers in learned jls on genetics and neurobiology. *Recreations:* music, tennis, photography. *Address:* Tata Institute of Fundamental Research, National Centre for Biological Sciences, GKVK Campus, Bangalore 560065, India. *T:* (80) 3636420, ext. 2110, *Fax:* (80) 3636662; *e-mail:* osiddiqi@ncbs.res.in; (home) 382 RMV Extension Stage II, Bangalore 560094, India. *T:* (080) 3411372.

SIDDLE, Prof. Kenneth, PhD; Professor of Molecular Endocrinology, University of Cambridge, since 1990; Fellow, Churchill College, Cambridge, since 1982; *b* 30 March 1947; *s* of Fred and Vera Siddle; *m* 1st, 1971, Yvonne Marie Kennedy (marr. diss. 1994); one *s*; 2nd, 1996, Anne Elizabeth Willis; one *s*. *Educ:* Morecambe Grammar Sch.; Downing Coll., Cambridge (BA 1969). MA, PhD 1973. Lectr, Dept Medical Biochemistry, Welsh Nat. Sch. Med., Cardiff, 1971–78; Meres Sen. Student for Med. Research, St John's Coll., Cambridge, 1978–81; Wellcome Lectr, Dept Clinical Biochem., Univ. of Cambridge, 1981–90. Vis. Scientist, Joslin Diabetes Center and Harvard Med. Sch., 1989–90. Hon. Treas., Cambridge Univ. CC, 1990–. Chm. Editl Bd, Biochemical Jl, 1995–99. *Publications:* articles in biochem. jls. *Recreations:* mountaineering (especially Munro bagging), cricket, bird watching, vegetable gardening. *Address:* 6 Church Street, Wing, Oakham, Rutland LE15 8RS. *T:* (01572) 737675. *Clubs:* Hawks (Cambridge); Lancashire County Cricket.

SIDDLE, Oliver Richard, CB 1995; OBE 1983; General Manager, Enterprises Group, and Assistant Director-General, British Council, 1992–96; retired; *b* 11 March 1936; *s* of George Siddle and Grace (*née* Hatfield); *m* 1964 (marr. diss. 1995); one *s* one *d*. *Educ:* Hymers Coll., Hull; Queen's Coll., Oxford (BA 2nd Cl. Hons Mod. Hist. 1959). Joined British Council, 1961: Budget Dept, 1961–63; Poland, 1963–65; Argentina, 1965–68; Nigeria, 1968–70; Mgt Trng, Heriot-Watt Univ., 1970–71; Staff Trng Dept, 1971–74; Dir, Budget Dept, 1974–76; Representative: Peru, 1976–80; Hong Kong, 1980–85; Malaysia, 1985–87; Gen. Manager, Direct Teaching, 1987–92. *Recreations:* hill-walking, gardening, drawing. *Address:* 24320 La Tour Blanche, France.

SIDELL, Ron Daniel; architect; Sidell Gibson Partnership (private practice), since 1970; *b* 20 April 1941; *s* of Daniel Sidell and Dorothy Eady; *m* Sally Hodgson; one *d*. *Educ:* Canterbury Coll. of Architecture; York Univ. Projects in London and Germany include: Unilever, Lloyds, Casenove, Prudential, Rothschilds, European Bank and Civic Bldgs; Crown Jewel House and Windsor Castle reconstruction. Winner: Grand Buildings Trafalgar Square Internat. Competition, 1986; City of Winchester Central Redevelt Proposal Comp., 1989. *Recreations:* just about most things. *Address:* (office) Fitzroy Yard, Fitzroy Road, Primrose Hill, NW1 8TF. *T:* (020) 7722 5009.

SIDEY, Air Marshal Sir Ernest (Shaw), KBE 1972; CB 1965; MD, ChB, FFCM, DPH; Director-General, Chest, Heart and Stroke Association, 1974–85; *b* 2 Jan. 1913; *s* of Thomas Sidey, Alyth, Perthshire; *m* 1946, Doreen Florence, *y d* of late Cecil Ronald Lurring, Dalkey, Ireland; one *d* (and one *d* decd). *Educ:* Morgan Acad., Dundee; St Andrews Univ. Commissioned in RAF, 1937. Served in Burma Campaign during War of 1939–45. Recent appts include: Chief, Med. Adv. Staff, Allied Air Forces Central Europe, 1957–59; PMO: Flying Trg Comd, 1961–63; Middle East Comd, 1963–65; Transport Command, 1965–66; DDGMS, RAF, 1966–68. PMO, Strike Command, 1968–70; Dir-Gen., RAF Med. Services, 1971–74; QHS 1966–74. Governor, Royal Star and Garter Home, 1974–86. *Recreations:* racing, golf, bridge. *Address:* Callums, Tugwood Common, Cookham Dean, Berks SL6 9TU. *T:* (01628) 483006. *Club:* Royal Air Force.

SIDEY, Thomas Kay Stuart, CMG 1968; Founder Patron, Wickliffe Press Ltd, since 1993 (Managing Director, 1961–83; Executive Chairman, 1983–93); Barrister and Solicitor, NZ, since 1932; *b* 8 Oct. 1908; *s* of Sir Thomas Kay Sidey; *m* 1933, Beryl, *d* of Harvey Richardson Thomas, Wellington, NZ; one *s* one *d*. *Educ:* Otago Boys' High School; Univ. of Otago (LLM; Hon LLD, 1978). Served War of 1939–45 (despatches): 2nd NZEF; 4 years, Middle East and Italy, rank of Major. Dunedin City Council, 1947–50, 1953–65, 1968–83; Dep. Mayor, 1956–59, 1968–77; Mayor, 1959–65. Mem., Univ. of Otago Council, 1947–83, Pro-Chancellor, 1959–70, Chancellor, 1970–76. Past President: Dunedin Chamber of Commerce; Automobile Assoc., Otago; Trusteebank Otago; NZ Library Assoc.; Otago Old People's Welfare Council; Otago Boys' High Sch. Old Boys' Soc. *Recreations:* fishing, boating, ski-ing. *Address:* 190 Beacon Point Road, Wanaka, New Zealand. *T:* (3) 4775694. *Club:* Dunedin (Dunedin, NZ).

SIDMOUTH, 7th Viscount *cr* 1805; **John Tonge Anthony Pellew Addington;** *b* 3 Oct. 1914; *s* of 6th Viscount Sidmouth and of Gladys Mary Dever (*d* 1983), *d* of late Thomas Francis Hughes; *S* father, 1976; *m* 1st, 1940, Barbara Mary (*d* 1989), *d* of Bernard Rochford, OBE; one *s* five *d* (and one *s* decd); 2nd, 1993, Mrs Thérèse Pollen. *Educ:* Downside School (Scholar); Brasenose Coll., Oxford (Scholar). Colonial Service, E Africa, 1938–54. Mem. Council and Chm. Glasshouse Cttee, Nat. Farmers Union, 1962–69; Member: Agricultural Research Council, 1964–74; Central Council for Agricultural Cooperation, 1970–73. Mem., Select Cttee on European Communities, 1984–87. Pres., Nat. Council on Inland Transport, 1978–84. Trustee, John Innes Foundation, 1974–89. Chm. of Governing Body, Glasshouse Crops Research Inst., 1981–84. Knight of Malta, 1962. *Recreation:* gardening. *Heir: s* Hon. Jeremy Francis Addington [*b* 29 July 1947; *m* 1st, 1970, Grete Henningsen; one *s* one *d*; 2nd, 1986, Una Coogan; one *s* two *d*]. *Address:* 12 Brock Street, Bath, Avon BA1 2LW. *T:* (01225) 301946.

SIDNEY, family name of **Viscount De L'Isle**.

SIEFF, Hon. Sir David (Daniel), Kt 1999; Director, Marks and Spencer plc, 1972–97 (non-executive Director, 1997–2001); Chairman, Newbury Racecourse plc, since 1998 (Member of Board, since 1988); *b* 22 March 1939; *s* of Baron Sieff of Brimpton, OBE, and late Rosalie Cottage; *m* 1962, Jennifer Walton; two *s*. *Educ:* Repton. Joined Marks & Spencer, 1957. Pt-time Mem., NFC, 1972–78; non-exec. Chm., FIBI Bank (UK) Plc (formerly First Internat. Bank of Israel (UK) Ltd), 1994–. Chm., British Retail Consortium, 1998–. Chairman, North Metropolitan Conciliation Cttee of Race Relations Board, 1969–71; Vice-Chm., Inst. of Race Relations, 1971–72; Member: Policy Studies Inst. (formerly PEP), 1976–84; Bd, Business in the Community; Council, Industrial Soc., 1975–90. Governor: Weizmann Inst. of Science, Rehovot, Israel, 1978– (Chm. Exec. Cttee, UK Foundn, 1984–2000); Shenkar Coll. of Textile Technology (Israel), 1980–; Hon. Pres., British ORT, 1983–. Trustee, Glyndebourne Arts Trust, 1971–2000. Pres., Racehorse Owners Assoc., 1975–78; Chairman: Racing Welfare Charities, 1988–2000; Community Fund (formerly Nat. Lottery Charities Bd), 1994–99; Member: Jockey Club, 1977–; Horserace Totalisator Bd, 1991–98; British Horseracing Bd, 1998–. FRSA 1989. *Address:* 47 Baker Street, W1U 8EP. *T:* (020) 7935 4422. *Club:* White's.

SIEGBAHN, Prof. Kai Manne Börje; Professor of Physics, University of Uppsala, 1954–84; *b* 20 April 1918; *s* of Manne Siegbahn and Karin Siegbahn (*née* Högbom); *m* 1944, Anna-Brita (*née* Rhedin); three *s*. *Educ:* Univ. of Uppsala (BSc 1939; Licentiate of Philosophy 1942); Univ. of Stockholm (Dr of Philosophy 1944). Research Associate, Nobel Inst. of Physics, 1942–51; Prof. of Physics, Royal Inst. of Technology, Stockholm, 1951–54. Founder, and Editor 1957, Internat. Jl of Nuclear Instruments and Methods in Physics Res. Member: Roy. Swedish Acad. of Sci.; Roy. Swedish Acad. of Engrg Scis; Roy. Soc. of Sci.; Roy. Acad. of Arts and Sci. of Uppsala; Roy. Physiographical Soc. of Lund; Societas Scientiarum Fennica; Norwegian Acad. of Sci.; Roy. Norwegian Soc. of Scis and Letters; Nat. Acad. of Sciences; Pontifical Acad. of Sci.; European Acad. of Arts, Scis and Humanities. Hon. Mem. Amer. Acad. of Arts and Scis; Membre de Comité des Poids et Mesures, Paris; Pres., IUPAP, 1981–84. Dr of Science, *hc* Durham, 1972; Basel, 1980; Liège, 1980; Upsala Coll., East Orange, NJ, 1982; Sussex, 1983. Lindblom Prize, 1945; Björkén Prize, 1955, 1977; Celsius Medal, 1962; Sixten Heyman Award, 1971; Harrison Howe Award, 1973; Maurice F. Hasler Award, 1975; Charles Frederick Chandler Medal, 1976; Torbern Bergman Medal, 1979; (jtly) Nobel Prize for Physics, 1981; Pittsburgh Award of Spectroscopy, 1982; Röntgen Medal, 1985; Fiuggi Award, 1986; Humboldt Award, 1986; Premio Castiglione Di Sicilia, 1990. *Publications:* Beta- and Gamma-Ray Spectroscopy, 1955; Alpha-, Beta- and Gamma-Ray Spectroscopy, 1965; ESCA—Atomic, Molecular and Solid State Structure Studied by Means of Electron Spectroscopy, 1967; ESCA Applied to Free Molecules, 1969; Some Current Problems in Electron Spectroscopy, 1983; around 400 scientific papers. *Recreations:* tennis, skiing and music. *Address:* Institute of Physics, University of Uppsala, Box 530, 751 21 Uppsala, Sweden. *T:* (18) 146963.

SIEGERT, Air Vice-Marshal Cyril Laurence, CB 1979; CBE 1975; MVO 1954; DFC 1944; AFC 1954; *b* 14 March 1923; *s* of Lawrence Siegert and Julia Ann Siegert; *m* 1948, Shirley Berenice Dick; two *s* two *d*. *Educ:* Fairlie High School; St Kevin's Coll., Oamaru; Victoria Univ. of Wellington. Joined RNZAF, 1942; served in UK with Nos 299 and 190 Sqdns; on loan to BOAC, 1945–47; Berlin airlift, 1949; NZ, 1952–54; NZ Defence Staff, Washington, 1954–56; RAF Staff Coll., 1957; NZ, 1958–62; Comdt, RNZAF's Command and Staff Sch., 1962; RAF Coll. of Air Warfare, 1963; Singapore, 1963–65; CO, No 3 Battlefield Support Sqdn and RNZAF Transport Wing, 1965–69; AOC RNZAF Ops Group, 1969–70; IDC 1970; RNZAF Air Staff, 1971; Chief of Staff, ANZUK Joint Force HQ, Singapore, 1971–73; Dep. Chief of Defence Staff (Policy), 1973–76; Chief of Air Staff, RNZAF, 1976–79. Gen. Manager, Marine Air Systems, 1980–84; Mem., Air Services Licensing Authority, 1980–87. *Recreations:* fishing, tramping, gardening. *Address:* 46 Wyndrum Avenue, Lower Hutt, New Zealand.

SIEGHART, Mary Ann Corinna Howard; Assistant Editor, The Times, since 1988; *b* 6 Aug. 1961; *d* of Paul Sieghart and Felicity Ann Sieghart (*née* Baer); *m* 1989, David Prichard; two *d*. *Educ:* Cobham Hall; Bedales Sch.; Wadham Coll., Oxford (MA). Occasional feature and leader writer (part-time), Daily Telegraph, 1980–82; Eurobond Correspondent and Lex Columnist, Financial Times, 1982–86; City Editor, Today, 1986; Political Correspondent, Economist, 1986–88; The Times: Opinion Page Editor, 1988–91; Arts Editor, 1989–90; Political Leader Writer, 1990–; acting Editor on Sundays, 1997–99; columnist, 1998–. Television: presenter: The World This Week; The Brains Trust; The Big Picture Show; Powerhouse; radio: presenter, The Week in Westminster; guest interviewer, Start the Week. Founding Cttee Mem., Women in Journalism, 1995–98; Member: Adv. Council and Steering Cttee, New Europe, 1999–; Social Studies Adv. Bd, Oxford Univ., 1999–. Trustee, Nat. Heritage Meml Fund, 1997–. Vice Pres., Nat. Assoc. for Gifted Children, 1996–. Mem., Shadow Bd, New Deal for Communities, N Fulham, 2001–. Laurence Stern Fellow, Washington Post, 1984. Harold Wincott Young Financial Journalist of the Year, 1983; Commended, Young Journalist of the Year, British Press Awards, 1983. *Recreations:* reading, rollerblading, architecture, music, travel to remote places, doodling. *Address:* (office) 1 Pennington Street, E98 1TA. *T:* (020) 7782 5000. *Club:* Groucho.

SIEPMANN, Mary Aline, (Mary Wesley), CBE 1995; FRSL; writer; *b* 24 June 1912; *d* of Col Harold Mynors Farmar, CMG, DSO and Violet Hyacinth (*née* Dalby); *m* 1st, 1937, 2nd Baron Swinfen (marr. diss. 1945); two *s*; 2nd, 1952, Eric Siepmann (*d* 1970);

one *s. Educ:* at home (governesses); LSE (Hon. Fellow 1994). FRSL 1997. DUniv Open, 1993; Hon. DLitt Exeter, 1993. *Publications:* Speaking Terms (for children), 1968; The Sixth Seal (for children), 1968; Haphazard House (for children), 1983; Jumping the Queue, 1983; The Camomile Lawn, 1984; Harnessing Peacocks, 1985; The Vacillations of Poppy Carew, 1986; Not That Sort of Girl, 1987; Second Fiddle, 1988; A Sensible Life, 1990; A Dubious Legacy, 1993; An Imaginative Experience, 1994; Part of the Furniture, 1997; (with Kim Sayer) Part of the Scenery, 2001. *Recreation:* reading. *Address:* c/o Transworld Publishers, 61–63 Uxbridge Road, W5 5SA.

SIGMON, Robert Leland; lawyer; *b* Roanoke, Va, 3 April 1929; *s* of Ottis Leland Sigmon and Aubrey Virginia (*née* Bishop); *m* 1st, 1963, Marianne Rita Gellner (marr. diss.); 2nd, 1992, Jean Mary Anderson. *Educ:* Univ. of Virginia; Sorbonne; London Sch. of Economics. BA, DrJur. Member of the Bar: US Supreme Court; Court of Appeals, Second and District of Columbia Circuits; Virginia; District of Columbia. Vice-Pres., Pilgrims Soc. of GB, 1993– (Chm., Exec. Cttee, 1977–93); Founder Member: Associates of the Victoria and Albert Museum, 1976 (Dir, 1976–87); Amer. and Internat. Friends of V&A Mus. (Trustee, 1985–2000). Mem., Council of Management, British Inst. of Internat. and Comparative Law, 1982–. Trustee: American Sch. in London, 1977–91; Magna Carta Trust, 1984–94; Vice-Chm., Mid-Atlantic Club of London, 1977–96; Vice-Pres., European-Atlantic Gp, 1978–94; Member: Exec. Cttee, Amer. Soc. in London, 1969– (Chm. 1974); Amer. Soc. of Internat. Law; Selden Soc.; Guild of St Bride's Church, Fleet Street; Ends of the Earth; Gov., E-SU, 1984–90. Chevalier du Tastevin. *Publications:* contribs to legal periodicals. *Recreations:* collecting antiquarian books, oenology. *Address:* 2 Plowden Buildings, Middle Temple, EC4Y 9AS. *T:* (020) 7583 4851. *Club:* Reform.

SIGURDSSON, Niels P.; Ministry of Foreign Affairs, Iceland, 1990–96; *b* Reykjavik, 10 Feb. 1926; *s* of Sigurdur B. Sigurdsson and Karitas Einarsdóttir; *m* 1953, Olafia Rafnsdóttir; two *s* one *d. Educ:* Univ. of Iceland (Law). Joined Diplomatic Service 1952; First Sec., Paris Embassy, 1956–60; Dep. Permanent Rep. to NATO and OECD, 1957–60; Dir, Internat. Policy Div., Min. of Foreign Affairs, Reykjavik, 1961–67; Delegate to UN Gen. Assembly, 1965; Ambassador and Permanent Rep. of Iceland to N Atlantic Council, 1967–71. Ambassador: to Belgium and EEC, 1968–71; to UK, 1971–76; to Fed. Republic of Germany, 1976–78; Ministry of Foreign Affairs, Reykjavik, 1979–84; Ambassador to Norway, 1985–89. *Recreations:* swimming, riding. *Address:* Sólheimar 15, 104 Reykjavík, Iceland.

SIKORA, Prof. Karol, FRCP, FRCR; Professor of Clinical Oncology, Imperial College School of Medicine (formerly Royal Postgraduate Medical School), Hammersmith Hospital, since 1986; *b* 17 June 1948; *s* of Witold Karol Sikora and Thomasina Sikora; *m* 1974, Alison Mary Rice; one *s* two *d. Educ:* Dulwich Coll.; Corpus Christi Coll., Cambridge (MA, MB, BChir, PhD); Middlesex Hospital. Middlesex Hosp., 1972; Hammersmith Hosp., 1973; MRC Clinical Fellow, Lab. for Molecular Biol., Cambridge, 1974–77; Clinical Fellow, Stanford Univ., 1978–79; Dir, Ludwig Inst. for Cancer Research, Cambridge, 1980–86; Dep. Dir (Clinical Res.), ICRF, 1995–97; Chief, WHO Cancer Prog., Lyon, France, 1997–99. Vice Pres., Global Clinical Res. (Oncology), Pharmacia Corp, 1999–. *Publications:* Monoclonal Antibodies, 1984; Interferon, 1985; Cancer: a student guide, 1988; (ed jtly) Treatment of Cancer, 1990, 4th edn 2001; Fight Cancer, 1990; Genes and Cancer, 1990; contrib. Gene Therapy. *Recreations:* boating, travelling, rock climbing. *Address:* Department of Cancer Medicine, Hammersmith Hospital, W12 0HS. *T:* (020) 8383 3060. *Clubs:* Athenæum, Polish Hearth.

SILBER, Dr Evelyn Ann, FMA; Director, Hunterian Museum and Art Gallery, University of Glasgow, since 2001; *b* 22 May 1949; *d* of late Martin Helmut Silber and Mavis Evelyn (*née* Giles). *Educ:* Hatfield Girls' Grammar Sch.; New Hall, Cambridge (MA); Univ. of Pennsylvania (MA); Clare Hall, Cambridge (PhD). Guide, Hatfield House, 1965–70; Thouron Fellow, Univ. of Penn., 1972–73; copy-writer and media controller, Associated Book Publishers, 1973–74; publicity manager, Addison Wesley Publishers, 1974–75; Leverhulme Res. Fellow in Hist. of Art, 1975–76; Lectr, Hist. of Art, Glasgow Univ., 1978; Birmingham Museum and Art Gallery: Asst Keeper (Fine Art), 1979–82; Dep. Keeper (Painting and Sculpture), 1982–85; Birmingham Museums and Art Gallery: Asst Dir, Public Services, 1985–94; Head of Central Museums, 1994–95; Dir, Leeds Mus and Galls, 1995–2001. Mem. Council, Ikon Gall., 1981–88. Mem. Bd, Cultural Heritage NTO (formerly Museums Trng Inst.), 1996–. FMA 1996; FRSA 2000. *Publications:* The Sculpture of Epstein, 1986; (with T. Friedman) Jacob Epstein Sculpture and Drawings, 1987; Gaudier-Brzeska: Life and Art, 1996. *Recreations:* travel, music, walking, gardening. *Address:* Hunterian Museum, University Avenue, Glasgow G12 8QQ. *Club:* Royal Over-Seas League.

SILBER, Hon. Sir Stephen (Robert), Kt 1999; **Hon. Mr Justice Silber;** a Judge of the High Court of Justice, Queen's Bench Division, since 1999; *b* 26 March 1944; *s* of late J. J. Silber and of Marguerite Silber; *m* 1982, Lucinda, *d* of Lt-Col David St John Edwards, retd; one *s* one *d. Educ:* William Ellis Sch.; University Coll. London; Trinity Coll., Cambridge. Called to Bar, Gray's Inn, 1968, Bencher, 1994; in practice, 1969–94; QC 1987; a Recorder, 1987–99; a Dep. High Court Judge, 1995–99. Law Comr for England and Wales, 1994–99. Mem., Criminal Law Cttee, Judicial Studies Bd, 1994–99. *Recreations:* photography, walking, music, watching sport, theatre. *Address:* Royal Courts of Justice, Strand, WC2A 2LL.

SILBERSTON, Prof. (Zangwill) Aubrey, CBE 1987; Professor of Economics, University of London, at Imperial College, 1978–87, now Emeritus, and Head of Department of Social and Economic Studies, 1981–87; Senior Research Fellow, Management School, Imperial College, since 1987; *b* 26 Jan. 1922; *s* of Louis and Polly Silberston; *m* 1st, 1945, Dorothy Marion Nicholls (marr. diss.); one *s* (one *d* decd); 2nd, 1985, Michèle Ledić. *Educ:* Hackney Downs Sch., London; Jesus Coll., Cambridge. MA (Cantab); MA (Oxon). Courtaulds Ltd, 1946–50; Kenward Res. Fellow in Industrial Admin, St Catharine's Coll., Cambridge, 1950–53; University Lectr in Economics, Cambridge, 1953–71; Fellow, 1958–71, Dir of Studies in Econs, 1965–71, St John's Coll., Cambridge; Chm., Faculty Bd of Econs and Politics, Cambridge, 1966–70; Official Fellow in Econs, 1971–78, and Dean, 1972–78, Nuffield Coll., Oxford. Rockefeller Fellow, Univ. of Calif, Berkeley, 1959–60; Visiting Professor: Queensland Univ., 1977; Univ. of the South, Sewanee, 1984. Member: Monopolies Commn, 1965–68; Board of British Steel Corp., 1967–76; Departmental Cttee on Patent System, 1967–70; Econs Cttee, SSRC, 1969–73; Royal Commn on the Press, 1974–77; Restrictive Practices Ct, 1986–92; Royal Commn on Environmental Pollution, 1986–96; Biotechnol. Adv. Commn, Stockholm Envmt Inst., 1993–97; Council of Experts, Intellectual Property Inst., 1992–. Dir, Brussels Office, London Economics, 1992–; Economic Adviser, CBI, 1972–74; Specialist Advr, Eur. Communities Cttee, H of L, 1993; Chm., Assoc. of Learned Societies in the Social Sciences, 1985–87; President: Section F, British Assoc., 1987; Confedn of European Economic Assocs, 1988–90 (Vice-Pres., 1990–92); Vice-Pres., REconS, 1992– (Sec.-Gen., 1979–92). *Publications:* Education and Training for Industrial Management, 1955; (with G. Maxcy) The Motor Industry, 1959; (jtly)Economies of Large-scale Production in British Industry, 1965; (jtly) The Patent System, 1967; (with C. T. Taylor) The Economic Impact of the Patent System, 1973; (ed) Industrial Management: East and West, 1973; (with A. Cockerill) The Steel Industry, 1974; (jtly) Microeconomic Efficiency and Macroeconomic Performance, 1983; The Multi-Fibre Arrangement and the UK Economy, 1984; (jtly) British Manufacturing Investment Overseas, 1985; The Economic Importance of Patents, 1987; (ed) Technology and Economic Progress, 1989; Patent Policy: is the pharmaceutical industry a special case?, 1989; (with Michèle Ledić) The Future of the Multi-Fibre Arrangement, 1989; (ed with Gianna Boero) Environmental Economics, 1995; (jtly) Beyond the Multifibre Arrangement, 1995; (with C. Raymond) The Changing Industrial Map of Europe, 1996; PR China's Textile and Clothing Sector and its Export Potential, 1999; articles in Econ. Jl, Bulletin of Oxford Inst. of Statistics, Oxford Economic Papers, Jl of Royal Statistical Society. *Recreations:* music, ballet. *Address:* 53 Prince's Gate, SW7 2PG. *T:* (020) 7594 9354. *Club:* Travellers.

SILJA, Anja; German opera singer; *b* Berlin, 17 April 1940; parents both actors; *m* 1980, Christoph von Dohnányi, *qv*; one *s* two *d*. Started career at age 10; first opera engagement, Staatstheater Braunschweig, 1956; débuts: Stuttgart State Opera, Frankfurt Opera, 1958; Bayreuth Fest. (Senta in The Flying Dutchman), 1960; has appeared widely in USA, Japan and Europe, in all major opera houses, incl. Salzburg, and Glyndebourne Fest. (début, 1989); repertoire includes: all major Wagner rôles, Salome, Lulu, Fidelio, Elektra, Carmen, The Merry Widow, Jenůfa, The Makropulos Case, etc. Has made recordings and videos. *Address:* c/o Artists Management Zürich/Rita Schütz, Rütistrasse 52, 8044 Zürich, Switzerland.

SILK, Rt Rev. David; *see* Silk, Rt Rev. R. D., Bishop of Ballarat.

SILK, Dennis Raoul Whitehall, CBE 1995; MA; Warden of Radley College, 1968–91; Chairman, Test and County Cricket Board, 1994–96; *b* 8 Oct. 1931; 2nd *s* of late Rev. Dr Claude Whitehall Silk and Mrs Louise Silk; *m* 1963, Diana Merilyn, 2nd *d* of W. F. Milton, Pitminster, Somerset; two *s* two *d. Educ:* Christ's Hosp.; Sidney Sussex Coll., Cambridge (Exhibr). MA (History) Cantab. Asst Master, Marlborough Coll., 1955–68 (Housemaster, 1957–68). JP Abingdon, 1972–89. *Publications:* Cricket for Schools, 1964; Attacking Cricket, 1965. *Recreations:* antiquarian, literary, sporting (Blues in cricket (Capt. Cambridge Univ. CC, 1955) and Rugby football). *Address:* Sturts Barn, Huntham Lane, Stoke St Gregory, Taunton, Somerset TA3 6EG. *T:* (01823) 490348. *Clubs:* East India, Devonshire, Sports and Public Schools, MCC (Pres., 1992–94); Hawks (Cambridge).

SILK, Prof. Joseph Ivor, PhD; FRS 1999; Savilian Professor of Astronomy, Oxford University, since 1999; Fellow, New College, Oxford, since 1999; *b* 3 Dec. 1942; *s* of Philip and Sylvie Silk; *m* 1968, Margaret Wendy Kuhn (marr. diss. 1998); two *s*; *m* 2001, Jacqueline Riffault. *Educ:* Clare Coll., Cambridge (MA 1963); Harvard Univ. (PhD 1968). Research Fellow: Inst. of Astronomy, Cambridge Univ., 1968–69; Princeton Univ. Observatory, 1969–70; University of California at Berkeley: Prof. of Astronomy, 1970–; Miller Res. Prof., 1980–81; Prof. of Physics, 1988–. Alfred P. Sloan Foundn Fellow, 1972–74; Guggenheim Fellow, 1975–76; Leon Lectr, Univ. of Penn, 1984; Hooker Dist. Vis. Prof., McMaster Univ., 1987; Bearden Vis. Prof., Johns Hopkins Univ., 1994; Sackler Fellow, Inst. Astronomy, Cambridge, 1997; Tercentenary Fellow, Emmanuel Coll., Cambridge, 1997; Blaise-Pascal Prof., Inst. d'Astrophysique, Paris, 1997–98; Biermann Lectr, Max-Planck Inst. für Astrophys., Garching, 1997. FAAAS 1987; Fellow, APS, 1996. Hon. Mem., French Physical Soc., 1997. *Publications:* The Big Bang, 1980, 3rd edn 2001; (jtly) Star Formation, 1980; The Left Hand of Creation, 1983, rev. edn 1994, Cosmic Enigmas, 1994; A Short History of the Universe, 1994; contrib. numerous articles to refereed jls. *Recreation:* ski-ing. *Address:* Physics Department (Astrophysics), Nuclear and Astrophysics Laboratory, Keble Road, Oxford OX1 3RH. *T:* (01865) 273300; New College, Oxford OX1 3BN.

SILK, Prof. Michael Stephen, PhD; Professor of Greek Language and Literature, King's College, London, since 1991; *b* 11 June 1941; *s* of Norman and Ada Silk; *m* 1964, Laurel Evans; one *s* two *d. Educ:* King Edward's Sch., Birmingham; St John's Coll., Cambridge (BA 1964; MA 1967; PhD 1969). Res. Fellow, St John's Coll., Cambridge, 1967–70; King's College, London: Lectr in Classics, 1970–85; Reader in Classics, 1985–91; Head, Dept of Classics, 1993–97. Leverhulme Major Res. Fellowship, 2000–. Co-founder and co-editor, Dialogos, 1994–99. *Publications:* Interaction in Poetic Imagery, 1974; (with J. P. Stern) Nietzsche on Tragedy, 1981, rev. edn 1983; Homer: the Iliad, 1987; (ed) Tragedy and the Tragic: Greek theatre and beyond, 1996; Aristophanes and the Definition of Comedy, 2000; articles and reviews in classical and literary jls and collections. *Recreations:* poetry, jazz, standard popular songs, cricket. *Address:* Department of Classics, King's College London, Strand, WC2R 2LS. *T:* (020) 7848 2627.

SILK, Rt Rev. (Robert) David; *see* Ballarat, Bishop of.

SILK, Robert K.; *see* Kilroy-Silk.

SILKE, William James; Justice of Appeal, Supreme Court of Hong Kong, 1981–94; Vice-President, Court of Appeal, 1987–94; *b* 21 Sept. 1929; *s* of William Joseph Silke and Gertrude (*née* Delany). *Educ:* Dominican Convent, Wicklow; Xavier Sch., Donnybrook; King's Inns, Dublin. Called to Irish Bar (South Eastern Circuit, Leinster Bar), 1955; Magistrate, North Borneo/Malaysia, 1959; Registrar, High Court in Borneo (Sabah-Sarawak), 1965; Puisne Judge, 1966; retired under compensation scheme during Malaysianisation, 1969; Hong Kong: Magistrate, 1969; President, Tenancy Tribunal, 1971; Acting Asst Registrar, High Court, 1972; President, Lands Tribunal, 1974; Judge, District Court, 1975; Judicial Commissioner, State of Brunei, 1978–91, Negara Brunei Darusalam, 1998–; Judge of the High Court, 1979; Non-Permanent Judge, Court of Final Appeal, 1997–. Mem., Royal Dublin Soc., 1996–. *Recreations:* horse racing/breeding, music, travel. *Address:* 16 Seabank Court, Marine Parade, Sandycove, Co. Dublin. *T:* (1) 2808739, *Fax:* (1) 2808372. *Clubs:* Royal Over-Seas League; Stephen's Green (Dublin); Royal Sabah Turf (Sabah, Malaysia); Hong Kong, Hong Kong Jockey (Hong Kong).

SILKIN; 2nd Baron, *cr* 1950, of Dulwich [disclaimed his peerage for life, 1972]; *see under* Silkin, Arthur.

SILKIN, Arthur; Lecturer in Public Administration, Civil Service College, Sunningdale, 1971–76, on secondment from Department of Employment; retired 1976; *b* 20 Oct. 1916; *e s* of 1st Baron Silkin, PC, CH; *S* father, 1972, as 2nd Baron Silkin, but disclaimed his peerage for life; *m* 1969, Audrey Bennett. *Educ:* Dulwich College; Peterhouse, Cambridge (BA 1938); Dip. in Govt Admin, 1959; Dip. in Hist. of Art, 1990, Dip. in Eng. Lit., 2000, London Univ. Served 1940–45, Royal Air Force (A and SD Branch), Pilot Officer, 1941, subsequently Flying Officer. Entered Ministry of Labour and National Service, 1939; 2nd Secretary, British Embassy, Paris; First Secretary: High Commissioner's Office, Calcutta, 1960–61; British Embassy, Dakar, May 1962–Mar. 1964; British Embassy, Kinshasa, 1964–66. *Publications:* contrib. to Public Administration, Political Qly. *Address:* Cuzco, 33 Woodnook Road, SW16 6TZ. *T:* (020) 8677 8733.

SILLARS, James; management consultant; Assistant to Secretary-General, Arab-British Chamber of Commerce, since 1993; *b* Ayr, 4 Oct. 1937; *s* of Matthew Sillars; *m* 1st, 1957; one *s* one *d*; 2nd, 1981, Mrs Margo MacDonald, *qv*. *Educ:* Newton Park Sch., Ayr; Ayr Academy. Former official, Fire Brigades Union; Past Member Ayr Town Council and Ayr County Council Educn Cttee. Head of Organization and Social Services Dept, Scottish TUC, 1968–70. Full-time Labour Party agent, 1964 and 1966 elections. Contested (SNP): Linlithgow, 1987; Glasgow, Govan, 1992. MP: (Lab) South Ayrshire, March 1970–1976, (SLP) 1976–79; (SNP) Glasgow, Govan, Nov. 1988–1992. Among the founders of the Scottish Labour Party, Jan. 1976. Man. Dir, Scoted Ltd, 1980–83. Especially interested in education, social services, industrial relations, development policies. *Publications:* Scotland—the Case for Optimism, 1986; Labour Party pamphlets on Scottish Nationalism; Tribune Gp pamphlet on Democracy within the Labour Party. *Recreations:* reading, golf. *Address:* 97 Grange Loan, Edinburgh EH9 2ED.

SILLARS, Margo; *see* MacDonald, M.

SILLERY, William Moore; DL; Headmaster, Belfast Royal Academy, 1980–2000; *b* 14 March 1941; *s* of William and Adeline Sillery; *m* 1963, Elizabeth Margaret Dunwoody; two *d*. *Educ:* Methodist Coll., Belfast; St Catharine's Coll., Cambridge. Head of Modern Languages, Belfast Royal Academy, 1968, Vice-Principal 1974, Deputy Headmaster 1976. Educnl Advr, Ulster Television, 1985–94. Chm., Ministerial Working Party on Modern Langs in NI Curriculum, 1991; Member: NI Cttee, UFC, 1989–93; Belfast Educn and Liby Bd, 1994–97; Cttee, HMC, 1998–99; Chm., Irish Div., HMC, 1998–99. Lay Mem., Solicitors' Disciplinary Tribunal, NI, 1999–. DL Belfast, 1997. *Recreations:* golf, bridge. *Address:* Ardmore, 15 Saintfield Road, Belfast BT8 7AE. *T:* (028) 9064 5260. *Clubs:* East India; Belvoir Park (Belfast).

SILLITO, Prof. Adam Murdin, PhD; Professor of Visual Science, since 1987, and Director, since 1991, Institute of Ophthalmology, University College London; *b* 31 March 1944; *s* of Adam Cheswardine Sillito and Jean Mary Sillito, Amington, Tamworth; *m* Sharon Pascoe; one *s* one *d*. *Educ:* Univ. of Birmingham (MRC Schol.; BSc, PhD). Res. Fellow, Dept of Physiol., Univ. of Birmingham, 1968–70; Sir Henry Wellcome Travelling Fellow, Dept of Physiol., Johns Hopkins Med. Sch., Baltimore, 1970–71; Lectr, 1971–79, Wellcome Trust Sen. Lectr, 1979–82, Med. Sch., Birmingham; Prof. and Hd of Dept of Physiol., UC, Cardiff, 1982–87. Mem. Editl Bd, Jl Physiol., 1979–86; Co-Ed., Exptl Brain Res., 1989–; Mem., Adv. Cttee, Plenum Press Cerebral Cortex series, 1991–. Non-exec. Dir, Moorfields NHS Trust, 1994– (Mem. Bd, Moorfields Eye Hosp., 1992–94). Medical Research Council: Member: Neurosci. Grants Cttee, 1982–86; Neurosci. Bd, 1991–95; Non-clinical Trng and Career Develt Panel, 1993–95. Chairman: Res. Cttee, BPMF, 1990–94; Electrophysiol. Panel, Prog. Cttee, ARVO, 1996–99; Member: Surgery Task Force—Technol. Transfer of Minimal Access Surgery, ACOST Med. Res. and Health Cttee, 1992; Human Frontiers Fellowship Panel, 1994–98. Chm., Brain Res. Assoc., 1980–83; Member: Physiol Soc. (Mem. Cttee, 1982–86); IBRO; British Neurosci. Assoc.; Soc. for Neurosci.; Assoc. for Res. in Vision and Ophthalmology (Mem., Prog. Cttee, 1996–99); Eur. Neurosci. Assoc. Founder FMedSci, 1998. Hon. Fellow, UCL. *Publications:* (ed jtly) Progress in Brain Research, 1990; Mechanisms of the GABA Action in the Visual System, 1992; (ed with G. Burnstock) Nervous Control of the Eye, 2000; numerous contribs to learned jls on mechanisms of vision. *Recreations:* dreaming of better things, learning and speculating. *Address:* Institute of Ophthalmology, University College London, Bath Street, EC1V 9EL. *T:* (020) 7608 6805, *Fax:* (020) 7608 6852; *e-mail:* a.sillito@ucl.ac.uk.

SILLITOE, Alan; writer since 1948; *b* 4 March 1928; *s* of Christopher Sillitoe and Sabina (*née* Burton); *m* 1959, Ruth Fainlight; one *s* one *d*. *Educ:* various elementary schools in Nottingham. Raleigh Bicycle Factory, 1942; air traffic control asst, 1945–46; wireless operator, RAF, 1946–49. Lived in France and Spain, 1952–58. Vis. Prof. of English, De Montfort Univ., 1994–97. FRGS. Hon. Fellow, Manchester Polytechnic, 1977. Hon. DLitt: Nottingham Poly., 1990; Nottingham Univ., 1994; De Montfort Univ., 1998. *Publications: novels:* Saturday Night and Sunday Morning, 1958 (Authors' Club Award for best first novel of 1958; filmed, 1960, play, 1964); The General, 1960 (filmed 1967 as Counterpoint); Key to the Door, 1961; The Death of William Posters, 1965; A Tree on Fire, 1967; A Start in Life, 1970; Travels in Nihilon, 1971; Raw Material, 1972; The Flame of Life, 1974; The Widower's Son, 1976; The Storyteller, 1979; Her Victory, 1982; The Lost Flying Boat, 1983; Down from the Hill, 1984; Life Goes On, 1985; Out of the Whirlpool, 1987; The Open Door, 1989; Last Loves, 1990; Leonard's War: a love story, 1991; Snowstop, 1993; The Broken Chariot, 1998; The German Numbers Woman, 1999; Birthday, 2001; *stories:* The Loneliness of the Long Distance Runner, 1959 (Hawthornden Prize; filmed, 1962); The Ragman's Daughter, 1963 (filmed, 1972); Guzman, Go Home, 1968; Men, Women and Children, 1973; The Second Chance, 1981; The Far Side of the Street, 1988; Collected Stories, 1995; Alligator Playground, 1997; *poetry:* The Rats and Other Poems, 1960; A Falling Out of Love, 1964; Love in the Environs of Voronezh, 1968; Storm and Other Poems, 1974; Snow on the North Side of Lucifer, 1979; Sun before Departure, 1984; Tides and Stone Walls, 1986; Collected Poems, 1993; *for children:* The City Adventures of Marmalade Jim, 1967; Big John and the Stars, 1977; The Incredible Fencing Fleas, 1978; Marmalade Jim at the Farm, 1980; Marmalade Jim and the Fox, 1985; *travel:* Road to Volgograd, 1964; (with Fay Godwin) The Saxon Shore Way, 1983; (with David Sillitoe) Nottinghamshire, 1987; Leading the Blind, 1995; *plays:* (with Ruth Fainlight) All Citizens are Soldiers, 1969; Three Plays, 1978; *essays:* Mountains and Caverns, 1975; *autobiography:* Life Without Armour, 1994; *miscellaneous:* Every Day of the Week, 1987. *Recreations:* travel, shortwave wireless telegraphy listening. *Address:* 14 Ladbroke Terrace, W11 3PG. *Club:* Savage.

SILLS, Beverly, (Mrs P. B. Greenough); Chairman, Lincoln Center for the Performing Arts, since 1994; Director, New York City Opera, 1979–88; former leading soprano, New York City Opera and Metropolitan Opera; *b* 25 May 1929; *d* of late Morris Silverman and of Sonia Bahn; *m* 1956, Peter B. Greenough; one *s* one *d*. *Educ:* Professional Children's Sch., NYC; privately. Vocal studies with Estelle Liebling, piano with Paulo Gallico. Operatic debut, Philadelphia Civic Opera, 1947; San Francisco Opera, 1953; New York City Opera, 1955; Vienna State Opera, 1967; Teatro Colón, Buenos Aires, 1968; La Scala, Milan, 1969; Teatro San Carlo, Naples, 1970; Royal Opera, Covent Garden, London, 1970; Deutsche Oper, W Berlin, 1971; NY Metropolitan Opera, 1975, etc. Repeated appearances as soloist with major US symphony orchestras; English orchestral debut with London Symphony Orch., London, 1971; Paris debut, orchestral concert, Salle Pleyel, 1971. Repertoire includes title roles of Norma, Manon, Lucia di Lammermoor, Maria Stuarda, Daughter of Regiment, Anna Bolena, Traviata, Lucrezia Borgia, Thais, Louise, Cleopatra in Giulio Cesare, Elizabeth in Roberto Devereux, Tales of Hoffmann, Elvira in Puritani, Rosina in Barber of Seville, Norina in Don Pasquale, Pamira in Siege of Corinth; created title role, La Loca, San Diego Opera, 1979. Subject of BBC-TV's Profile in Music (Nat. Acad. of TV Arts and Sciences Emmy Award, 1975); other TV includes: Sills and Burnett at the Met, 1976; Hostess/Commentator for Young People's Concerts, NY Philharmonic, 1977; Moderator/Hostess, Lifestyles with Beverly Sills, 1976, 1977 (Emmy 1978). Hon. DMus: Temple Univ., 1972; New York Univ., 1973; New England Conservatory, 1973; Harvard Univ., 1974. Woman of the Year, Hasty Pudding Club, Harvard, 1974; Handel Medallion, NYC; US Presidential Medal of Freedom. *Publications:* Bubbles: a self-portrait, 1976; (autobiog. with Lawrence Linderman) Beverly, 1987. *Recreations:* fishing, bridge. *Address:* c/o Edgar Vincent, Vincent & Farrell Associates Inc., 481 Eighth Avenue, Suite 740, New York, NY 10001. *T:* (212) 643 9987, *Fax:* (212) 642 8636.

SILSOE, 2nd Baron *cr* 1963; **David Malcolm Trustram Eve,** Bt 1943; QC 1972; Barrister, Inner Temple, since 1955; *b* 2 May 1930; *er* twin *s* of 1st Baron Silsoe, GBE, MC, TD, QC, and Marguerite (*d* 1945), *d* of late Sir Augustus Meredith Nanton, Winnipeg; *S* father, 1976; *m* 1963, Bridget Min, *d* of Sir Rupert Hart-Davis; one *s* one *d*. *Educ:* Winchester; Christ Church, Oxford (MA); Columbia Univ., New York. 2nd Lt, Royal Welch Fusiliers, 1949–50; Lieut, Queen Victoria's Rifles (TA), 1950–53. Bar Auditor, Inner Temple, 1965–70; Bencher, 1970. *Recreations:* music, singing. *Heir:* *s* Hon. Simon Rupert Trustram Eve, *b* 17 April 1966. *Address:* Neals Farm, Wyfold, Reading, Berks RG4 9JB. *Club:* Ski of Great Britain.

SILUNGWE, Hon. Annel Musenga; Hon. Mr Justice Silungwe; Judge of the High Court and acting Judge of the Supreme Court, Namibia, since 1999; Judge, Court of Appeal, Seychelles, since 1992; *b* 10 Jan. 1936; *s* of late Solo Musenga Silungwe and Janet Nakafunda Silungwe; *m* 1960, Abigail Nanyangwe; one *s* four *d*. *Educ:* Council of Legal Educn; Univ. of Zambia (LLM 1977). Called to the Bar, Inner Temple, 1966; State Counsel, Zambia, 1974; Judge of the High Court, Zambia, 1971–73; Minister of Legal Affairs and Attorney-General, 1973–75; Chief Justice of Zambia, 1975–92; Dir, Justice Trng Centre, Ministry of Justice, Namibia, 1994–99. Chairman: Judicial Services Commn, 1975–92; Council of Legal Educn, 1975–92; Council of Law Reporting, 1975–92. Award of Merit, Rotary Internat. Dist 9210, 1989. *Publications:* contrib. learned jls. *Recreations:* music, photography, reading, golf. *Address:* High Court, Private Bag 13179, Windhoek, Namibia. *T:* (office) (61) 227927, *Fax:* (61) 221686, *T:* and, *Fax:* (home) (61) 242705.

SILVER, Clinton Vita, CBE 1993; Chairman, British Fashion Council, 1994–97; Deputy Chairman, 1991–94, and Managing Director, 1990–94, Marks & Spencer plc; *b* 26 Sept. 1929; *s* of Sidney (Mick) Silver and Mina Silver (*née* Gabriel); *m* 1973, Patricia Ann (Jill) Vernon; one *s* one *d*. *Educ:* Upton House Sch.; Southampton Univ. (BSc Econ). Nat. Service, 1950–52. Joined Marks & Spencer, 1952; Alternate Dir, 1974; Dir, 1978. Director: Hillsdown Hldgs, 1994–98; Pentland Group plc, 1994–99; Tommy Hilfiger Corp., 1994–. Member: Bd, Youth and Music, 1987–99 (Patron, 1999–2000); Southampton Univ. Develt Trust, 1992–; Chm., Israel/Diaspora Trust, 1989–; Trustee, Jewish Assoc. for Business Ethics, 1995– (Chm. Trustees, 1995–97). CIMgt 1991; CompTI 1994. Hon. DLitt Southampton, 1997. *Recreations:* gardening, music. *Clubs:* Athenæum; Phyllis Court (Henley-on-Thames).

SILVER, Prof. Ian Adair; Professor of Comparative Pathology, University of Bristol, 1970–93, Emeritus Professor of Pathology, since 1993; Adjunct Professor of Neurology, University of Pennsylvania, since 1977; *b* 28 Dec. 1927; *s* of Captain George James Silver and Nora Adair Silver; *m* 1st, 1950, Dr Marian Scrase (*d* 1994), *d* of Dr F. J. Scrase; two *s* two *d*; 2nd, 1996, Prof. Maria Erecińska, *d* of Prof. K Ereciński. *Educ:* Rugby School; Corpus Christi Coll., Cambridge (BA, MA); Royal Veterinary Coll. MRCVS 1952, FRCVS 1990. University of Cambridge: Univ. Demonstrator, Zoology, 1952–57; Univ. Lectr, Anatomy, 1957–70; Official Fellow and Coll. Lectr, Churchill Coll., 1965–70; Sen. Tutor for Advanced Students, Churchill Coll., 1966–70; University of Bristol: Hd, Dept of Path., later Path. and Microbiol., 1982–93; Dean, Faculty of Medicine, 1987–90; Chm., Inst. of Clinical Neurosis, 2000–. Chm., Southmead Health Services NHS Trust, Bristol, 1992–99. Vis. Fellow, Weitzmann Inst., Rehovot, 1963; Vis. Prof., Louisiana Tech. Univ., 1973; Royal Soc. Vis. Prof., Fed. Univ. of Rio de Janeiro, 1977. Mem., SERC Biol. Scis Cttee, 1975–80; President: Internat. Soc. for O_2 Transport to Tissue, 1976 and 1986; RCVS, 1985–86 and 1987 (Sen. Vice-Pres., 1986–87 and 1987–88). RAgS Silver Medal, 1952; Sir Frederick Hobday Meml Medal, British Equine Vet. Assoc., 1982; Dalrymple-Champneys Medal, BVA, 1984. *Publications:* Editor of scientific books, 1971–; numerous articles in scientific jls. *Recreations:* farming, exploring, fishing, DIY. *Address:* Department of Anatomy, School of Veterinary Science, University of Bristol, Southwell Street, Bristol BS2 8EJ. *T:* (0117) 928 8362.

SILVER, Prof. Peter Hele S.; *see* Spencer-Silver.

SILVERLEAF, (Alexander) Michael; QC 1996; *b* 2 Nov. 1953; *s* of David and Rachel Silverleaf; partner since 1985, Joanne Ruth Welch; four *d*. *Educ:* King's Coll. Sch., Wimbledon; Imperial Coll. (BSc Physics 1975). Called to the Bar, Gray's Inn, 1980; practice in Intellectual Property; Junior Counsel to HM Treasury in Patent Matters, 1991–96. *Publication:* (with John Drysdale) Passing Off Law and Practice, 1986, 2nd edn 1995. *Address:* 11 South Square, Gray's Inn, WC1R 5EY. *T:* (020) 7405 1222.

SILVERMAN, Prof. Bernard Walter, FRS 1997; Henry Overton Wills Professor of Mathematics, since 1999, and Provost, Institute for Advanced Studies, since 2000, University of Bristol; *b* 22 Feb. 1952; *s* of Elias and Helen Silverman; *m* 1985, Dr Rowena Fowler; one *s*. *Educ:* City of London Sch.; Jesus Coll., Cambridge (MA, PhD, ScD); Southern Theol Educn and Trng Scheme (BTh). CStat. Research Fellow, Jesus Coll., Cambridge, 1975–77; Calculator Develt Manager, Sinclair Radionics, 1976–77; Weir Fellow, University Coll., Oxford, and Jun. Lectr, Oxford Univ., 1977–78; University of Bath: Lectr, Reader, and Prof. of Statistics, 1978–93; Head, Sch. of Math. Scis, 1988–91; Prof. of Stats, Univ. of Bristol, 1993–. Various vis. appts at foreign univs, 1978–; Fellow, Center for Advanced Study in Behavioral Scis, Stanford, 1997–98. Pres., Inst. of Mathematical Stats, 2000–01. Ordained deacon, 1999, priest, 2000; Hon. Curate, St Paul's Clifton, and St Mary's, Cotham, Bristol, 1999–; Proctor in Convocation, Gen. Synod of C of E, 2000–. Awards from UK and USA. *Publications:* Density Estimation for Statistics and Data Analysis, 1986; (with P. J. Green) Nonparametric Regression and Generalized Linear Models, 1994; (with J. O. Ramsay) Functional Data Analysis, 1997; numerous papers in learned jls. *Recreations:* opera, theatre, family, talking. *Address:* Institute for Advanced Studies, University of Bristol, Royal Fort House, Bristol BS8 1UJ. *T:* (0117) 928 9172; *e-mail:* b.w.silverman@bristol.ac.uk.

SILVERMAN, Prof. Hugh Richard, OBE 2000; Professor of Architecture, University of Wales, Cardiff (formerly University of Wales College of Cardiff), 1986–99, now Emeritus (Head of Welsh School of Architecture, 1986–97); *b* 23 Sept. 1940; *m* 1963, Kay Sønderskov-Madsen; two *d*. *Educ:* Edinburgh Univ. (MSc Soc. Sci). Lectr, then Sen. Lectr, Univ. of Bristol, 1971–82. Partner, Alec French Partnership, Architects, Bristol, 1984–86. Built project, 1 Bridewell St, Bristol, 1985 (RIBA Regl Award). Mem. Board, Cardiff Bay Develt Corp., 1990–2000. FRSA 1989. *Address:* 15 Clifton Vale, Bristol BS8 4PT.

SILVERSTONE, Judith Anne; *see* Hunt, J. A.

SILVESTER, Frederick John; public affairs consultant; Chairman and Managing Director, Advocacy (formerly Advocacy Partnership) Ltd, 1986–2000; *b* 20 Sept. 1933; *s* of William Thomas Silvester and Kathleen Gertrude (*née* Jones); *m* 1971, Victoria Ann, *d* of James Harold and Mary Lloyd Davies; two *d*. *Educ:* Sir George Monoux Grammar Sch.; Sidney Sussex Coll., Cambridge. Called to the Bar, Gray's Inn, 1957. Teacher, Wolstanton Grammar School, 1955–57; Political Education Officer, Conservative Political Centre, 1957–60. Member, Walthamstow Borough Council, 1961–64; Chairman, Walthamstow West Conservative Association, 1961–64. Contested (C) Manchester, Withington, 1987. MP (C): Walthamstow West, Sept. 1967–70; Manchester, Withington, Feb. 1974–1987. An Opposition Whip, 1974–76; PPS to Sec. of State for Employment, 1979–81, to Sec. of State for NI, 1981–83. Member: Public Accounts Cttee, 1983–87; Procedure Cttee, 1983–87; Exec., 1922 Cttee, 1985–87; Vice-Chm., Cons. Employment Cttee, 1976–79. Sen. Associate Dir, J. Walter Thompson, 1970–88. *Address:* 27 King Edward Walk, SE1 7PR.

SIM, Andrew Fraser; Consultant, Kennedys, solicitors, since 1999; *b* 27 Nov. 1948; *s* of Donald Fraser Sim and Pamela Jean Sim; *m* 1975, Antonia Rolfe Tweedie Aitken; two *s* one *d*. *Educ:* Haileybury Coll., Herts; City of London Poly. (BA Business Law). Admitted Solicitor. British Railways Board: Asst Solicitor, 1975; Head of Litigation, 1982; Dep. Solicitor, 1986–93; Solicitor, 1993–99. *Recreation:* the countryside. *Address:* (office) Longbow House, 14–20 Chiswell Street, EC1Y 4TW.

SIMCOX, Richard Alfred, CBE 1975 (MBE 1956); Hon. Member of the British Council; *b* 29 March 1915; *s* of Alfred William and Alice Simcox; *m* 1951, Patricia Elisabeth Gutteridge; one *s* two *d*. *Educ:* Gonville and Caius Coll., Cambridge. BA Class. Tripos. Served with N Staffs Regt, 1939–43; British Council from 1943: Rep. in Jordan, 1957–60; in Libya, 1960; in Jordan (again), 1960; Cultural Attaché, British Embassy, Cairo, 1968–71; British Council Representative, Iran, 1971–75. Governor, Gabbitas-Thring Educnl Trust. *Recreations:* gardening, philately. *Address:* 105 Edburton Avenue, Brighton, E Sussex BN1 6EQ. *T:* (01273) 561748.

SIMEON, Sir Richard (Edmund Barrington), 8th Bt *cr* 1815, of Grazeley, Berkshire; PhD; Professor of Political Science and Law, University of Toronto, since 1990; *b* 2 March 1943; *s* of Sir John Simeon, 7th Bt and of Anne Robina Mary (*née* Dean); *S* father, 1999; *m* 1st, 1966, Agnes Joan Weld (marr. diss. 1990); one *s* one *d*; 2nd, 1992, Maryetta Cheney. *Educ:* Univ. of British Columbia (BA Hons 1964); Yale Univ. (MA 1966; PhD 1968). Queen's University, Kingston, Ont: Asst Prof., 1968; Assoc. Prof., 1972–76; Dir, Inst. of Intergovtl Relns, 1976–83; Prof. of Political Studies, 1976–90; Dir, Sch. of Public Admin, 1985–90. Res. Co-ordinator, Royal Commn on the Econ. Union and Canada's Develt Prospects, 1983–85; Vice Chm., Ontario Law Reform Commn, 1988–96. Vis. Prof., Essex Univ., 1975–76; Vis. Prof. of Public Law, Univ. of Cape Town, 1997 and 2000; William Lyon Mackenzie King Prof. of Canadian Studies, Harvard Univ., 1998. *Publications:* Federal-Provincial Diplomacy: the making of recent policy in Canada, 1972; (jtly) Small Worlds: provinces and parties in Canadian political life, 1983; (jtly) State, Society and the Development of Canadian Federalism, 1991; (jtly) Degrees of Freedom: Canada and the United States in a changing world, 1997; ed numerous other works; contribs to jls. *Heir: s* Stephen George Barrington Simeon [*b* 29 Oct. 1970; *m* 1996, Michelle Owens; two *c*]. *Recreations:* walking, canoeing. *Address:* (home) 20 Biggar Avenue, Toronto, ON M6H 2N4, Canada. *T:* (416) 6563919; *e-mail:* rsimeon@chass.utoronto.ca.

SIMEONE, Reginald Nicola, CBE 1985; FRMetS; Adviser to the Chairman, Nuclear Electric plc, 1990–96; *b* 12 July 1927; *s* of late Nicola Francisco Simeone, FCIS, and Phyllis Simeone (*née* Iles); *m* 1954, Josephine Frances Hope; two *s*. *Educ:* Raynes Park Grammar Sch.; St John's Coll., Cambridge (Schol.; MA). FRMetS 1993. Instr Lieut, Royal Navy, 1947–50; Admiralty: Asst Principal, 1950–55; Principal, 1955–59; UKAEA: Finance Br., 1959–61; Economics and Programmes Br., 1961–65; Chief Personnel Officer, AWRE, 1965–69; Principal Estabts Officer, 1970–76; Authority Personnel Officer, 1976–84; Comptroller of Finance and Administration, 1984–86; Bd Mem., 1987–88; Advr to the Chm., 1988–90. Chm., Atomic Energy Constabulary Police Cttee, 1986–90; Exec. Vice Pres., European Atomic Energy Soc., 1987–90. *Recreations:* travel, theatre, opera, ballet, music. *Address:* 31 Portsmouth Avenue, Thames Ditton, Surrey KT7 0RU.

SIMEONS, Charles Fitzmaurice Creighton, MA; Consultant: Environmental Control, Market and Behavioural Studies, Health and Safety at Work, Electronic Information Technology, Communications with Government, technical programmes for conferences and annual events in internat. chemical control, London and Washington; Director, Action Learning Trust, 1978–82; *b* 22 Sept. 1921; *s* of Charles Albert Simeons and Vera Hildegarde Simeons; *m* 1st, 1945, Rosemary (*née* Tabrum) (*d* 1991); one *s* one *d*; 2nd, 1991, Constance Anne Dowson (*née* Restell). *Educ:* Oundle; Queens' Coll., Cambridge. Royal Artillery with 8th Indian Div., 1942–45, HQ RA E African Comd and Northern Comd (Major). Man. Dir, supplier to photographic industry, 1957–70. MP (C) Luton, 1970–Feb. 1974. Chm., Luton Cons. Assoc., 1960–63. President: Luton, Dunstable and District Chamber of Commerce, 1967–68; Rotary Club of Luton, 1960; District Gov., Rotary International, 1967–68; Mem., Rotary Club of Holt, 1992; Advisor, Eastern Area, Prince's Youth Business Trust, 1994–2000; Chm. of cttees raising funds for disabled and cancer research and for National Children's Homes; Chm., Kelling Hosp. Gala, 1996–97, 2000; Member: Nat. Appeals Cttee, Cancer Res. Campaign, 1977–78; Children in Danger Campaign, 1985–90. Chm., Adv. Cttee, Rotary Internat. Bd on Environmental Research and Resources, 1973–74; Vice Pres., Nat. Industrial Material Recovery Assoc., 1972–77; Member: Internat. Cttee, Water Pollution Control Federation, Washington, DC, 1974–77; Customer Consultative Cttee, Anglian Water, 1984–89, Thames Water, 1986–89; Eastern Customer Services Cttee, Water Services, 1990–96; Council, Smaller Business Assoc., 1974–76; ABCC Small Firms Panel; Chm., Central Govt Cttee, Union of Independent Cos. Member: N Norfolk Public Plenary Gp, 1998–2000; N Norfolk Healthwatch, 2000–. Founder Chm., Friends of Pensthorpe Waterfowl Trust, 1993–95 (Founder Patron of Trust, 1990). Hon. Mem., Inst. of Water Pollution Control, 1973. Liveryman: Co. of Feltmakers (Master, 1987–88); Co. of Water Conservators, 2000 (Mem., 1991). Guild of Freemen of City of London. FIIM; FRSA. Hon. FIWEM. Pres., Old Oundelian Club, 1976–77; Hon. Secretary: 8th Indian Clover Club, 1984–; Manchester Artillery 52nd Field Regt RA Officers' Reunion, 1998–. Patron, Luton Area, Dunkirk Veterans, 1995–2000 (Pres., 1965–95). JP Luton, 1959–74; DL Beds, 1987. *Publications:* Energy Research in Western Europe, 1976; Coal: its role in tomorrow's technology, 1978; Water as a Source of Energy, 1980; A Review of Chemical Response Data Bases in Europe and the United States, 1985; Studies on Incidents Involving Chemicals on Board Ship, in Port, and at Sea in Europe and the United States, 1985; Data Bases capable of response to Chemical Incidents Worldwide, 1986. *Recreations:* watching football, cricket, gardening. *Address:* Mill Leet, High Street, Cley-next-the-Sea, Norfolk NR25 7RR. *T:* (01263) 740772, *Fax:* (01263) 741198; *e-mail:* charles.simeons@btinternet.com. *Club:* City Livery.

SIMHA, Maj.-Gen. Bharat Kesher; Tri Sakti Patta, 1st Class; Gorkha Dakchhina Bahu, 1st Class; Nepal Kirtimaya Shreepad, 3rd Class; Ambassador of Nepal to the Court of St James's, 1988–92, concurrently accredited to Finland, Iceland, Sweden, Norway and Denmark; *b* 15 Aug. 1934; *s* of Lt-Gen. Dharma Bahadur Simha and Chaitanya Rajya Laxmi Simha; *m* 1955, Teeka Rajya Laxmi Rana; three *s*. *Educ:* Durbar High Sch., Kathmandu; Col Brown's Cambridge Sch., Dehradun; Indian Mil. Acad., Dehradun (grad. 1954). Commnd into Royal Nepalese Army, 1952; appts as Adjt, Co. Comdr, ADC to C-in-C, 1954–55; various courses in England, 1956; attached BAOR, 1956; Instr, Sch. of Inf., 1957–59; GSO 3 Directorate of Mil. Ops and Staff Duties, also ADC to C-in-C, 1960; Mem., Nepal–China Jt Boundary Commn, 1960–63; sc Camberley, 1964 (grad.); Resident Mil. Attaché, UK, with accreditation to France, W Germany, Belgium, Netherlands, Sweden, 1964–67; Dir of Mil. Intelligence, 1967–68; Para Overall Comdr, 1968–70; Dir of Res. and Planning, 1970; Asst Dir of Mil. Ops and Staff Duties, 1971; Dir of Mil. Trng, 1972–73; Officiating Dir of Mil. Ops and Staff Duties, 1974; Master-Gen. of Ordnance, 1975; Comdr, No 4 Bde, 1975–77; Dir, Mil. Ops, Staff Duties, Res. and Planning, 1978–80; Adjt-Gen., 1980; QMG, 1982–83; CGS, 1983–85 (retired); ADC Gen. to King of Nepal, 1986. Mem. Exec. Cttee, Pashupati Area Develt Trust, 1987–. Sen. Vice Pres., World Hindu Fedn, 1998–. Army Long Service Medal. Comdr OM (France), 1966; OM (Jugoslavia), 1974; Grand Cross: Order of the Lion of Finland, 1989; Order of the Dannebrog (Denmark), 1989. *Recreations:* hunting, jogging, squash, tennis, trekking. *Address:* Dharma Ashram, CHHA 3/150 Kaldhara, Kathmandu 16, PO Box 257, Nepal. *T:* (1) 251472, *Fax:* (1) 419625. *Club:* Tribhuwan Army Officers (Kathmandu).

SIMINOVITCH, Dr Louis, CC 1989 (OC 1980); PhD, FRS 1980; FRSC 1965; Director, Samuel Lunenfeld Research Institute of Mount Sinai Hospital (formerly Mount Sinai Hospital Research Institute), University of Toronto, 1983–94, now Director Emeritus; *b* Montreal, PQ, 1 May 1920; *s* of Nathan Siminovitch and Goldie Watchman; *m* 1944, Elinore, *d* of late Harry Faierman; three *d*. *Educ:* McGill Univ. (BSc 1941, PhD 1944; Arts and Sci. schol. 1939, Sir William McDonald schol. 1940, Anne Molson prize in Chem. 1941). With NRC at Ottawa and Chalk River, Ont., 1944–47; NRC Studentship and Fellowship, 1942–44; Canadian Royal Soc. Fellowship, 1947–49; with Centre Nat. de la Recherche Scientifique, Paris, 1949–53; Nat. Cancer Inst. Canadian Fellowships, 1953–55; Connaught Med. Res. Labs, Univ. of Toronto, 1953–56. Head of Div. of Biolog. Research, Ontario Cancer Inst., Toronto, 1963–69; Chm., Dept of Med. Cell Biology, Univ. of Toronto, 1969–72; Chm., Dept of Med. Genetics, 1972–79, Univ. Prof., 1976–85, Special Advr to Dean on Res., 1994–, Toronto Univ. Founding Mem. and Pres., Editorial Bd, Science Forum, 1966–79; Pres., Canadian Cell Biology Soc., 1967. Member: Bd of Dirs, Nat. Cancer Inst. of Canada, 1975–85 (Pres., 1982–84); Nat. Bd of Dirs, Canadian Cancer Soc., 1981–84; Bd, Ontario Cancer Treatment and Res. Foundn, 1979–94; Scientific Adv. Cttee, Connaught Res. Inst., 1980–84; Alfred P. Sloan, Jr, Selection Cttee, General Motors Cancer Res. Foundn, 1980–81, 1983–84; Health Res. and Develt Council of Ont, 1983–86. Chairman: Scientific Advisory Committee: Ontario Cancer Treatment and Res. Foundn, 1985–; Loeb Inst. for Med. Res., Ottawa, 1988–; Rotman Res. Inst., Toronto, 1988–; Phagetech, 1998–; Scientific Advisory Board: Bioniche Inc., 1996–98; Cytochroma Inc., 1999–; Member, Scientific Advisory Committee: Montreal Neurol Inst., 1992– (Mem., Neuro. Adv. Council, 1997–); Glycodesign, 1996–; Member, Scientific Advisory Board: Apoptogen Inc., 1995–; Univ. Medical Discoveries Inc., 1996–; GeminX, 1997–; Genesense Technologies Inc., 1998–; Ottawa Gen. Hosp. Res. Inst., 1998–. Member: Med. Discoveries Fund, Ontario, 1994–; Scientific/Med. Adv. Bd, Hybrisens Ltd, 1995–; Program Adv. and Sci. Adv. Cttee, Tanenbaum Chairs, Univ. of Toronto, 1995–; Bd, Premier's Res. Excellence Awards Prog., 1998–. Member: Bd of Dirs, Ottawa Civic Hosp. & Loeb Res. Inst. Corp., 1996–; Bd, Baycrest Centre for Geriatric Care, Toronto, 1998– (Consultant to Vice-Pres. Res. and Co-Chm. Res. Adv. Cttee, 1994–; Chm., Sci. Adv. Cttee, KLARU, 1997–). Founding Editor, Cell, 1973–81; Ed., Jl of Molecular and Cellular Biology, 1980–90; Member Editorial Board: Jl Cancer Surveys (London), 1980–89; Somatic Cell and Molecular Genetics, 1984–. Hon. DSc: Meml Univ., Newfoundland, 1978; McMaster Univ., 1978; Hon. Dr: Univ. of Montreal, 1990; McGill Univ., Montreal, 1990; Univ. of Western Ont, London, 1990; Univ. of Toronto, 1995. Flavelle Gold Medal, RSC, 1978; Univ. of Toronto Alumni Assoc. Award, 1978; Izaak Walton Killam Meml Prize, 1981; Gairdner Foundn Wightman Award, 1981; Medal of Achievement Award, Institut de Recherches Cliniques de Montreal, 1985; Environmental Mutagen Society Award, Baltimore, Maryland, 1986; R. P. Taylor Award, Canadian Cancer Soc., Nat. Cancer Inst., 1986; Distinguished Service Award, Canadian Soc. for Clinical Investigation, 1990; Toronto Biotechnol. Initiative Community Service Award, 1991; Canadian Medical Hall of Fame, 1997. Silver Jubilee Medal, 1977; Gov.-Gen.'s Commemorative Medal for 125th Anniversary of Canadian Confedn, 1992. Has specialised in the study of bacterial and somatic cell genetics. *Publications:* many contribs to scientific and learned journals. *Address:* c/o Samuel Lunenfeld Research Institute of Mount Sinai Hospital, 600 University Avenue, Toronto, ON M5G 1X5, Canada; Apt 805, 130 Carlton Street, Toronto, ON M5A 4K3, Canada.

SIMITIS, Konstantinos, DJur; MP (PASOK) Piraeus, since 1985; Prime Minister of Greece, since 1996; Leader, Panhellenic Socialist Movement, since 1996; *b* Athens, 23 June 1936; *s* of George Simitis and Fani Cristopoulou; *m* Daphne Arkadiou; two *d*. *Educ:* Univ. of Marburg (DJur 1959); LSE. Lawyer of the Supreme Court, 1961; Reader in Law, Univ. of Konstanz, Germany, 1971; Prof. of Commercial Law and Civil Law, Justus Liebig Univ., Germany, 1971–75; Prof. of Commercial Law, Panteion Univ. of Political and Social Scis, Athens, 1977. Member: Nat. Council, Panhellenic Liberation Movt, 1970; PASOK, 1974–. Minister: of Agriculture, 1981–85; of Nat. Econ., 1985–87; of Educn and Religious Affairs, 1989–90; of Industry and Commerce, 1993–95. *Publications:* The Structural Opposition, 1979; Policy for Economic Stabilisation, 1989; Nationalistic Populism or National Strategy?, 1992; Towards a Vigorous Society, Towards a Vigorous Greece, 1995; books and articles on legal and econ. matters. *Address:* Office of the Prime Minister, Leoforos Vassilissis Sophias 15, 10674 Athens, Greece.

SIMKINS, Charles Anthony Goodall, CB 1968; CBE 1963; *b* 2 March 1912; *s* of Charles Wyckens Simkins; *m* 1938, Sylvia, *d* of Thomas Hartley, Silchester, Hants; two *s* one *d*. *Educ:* Marlborough; New Coll., Oxford (1st Class Hons Mod. Hist.). Barrister, Lincoln's Inn, 1936; served 1939–45 as Captain, Rifle Bde (POW); attached War Office (later MoD), 1945–71; idc, 1958. *Publication:* (with Sir Harry Hinsley) British Intelligence in the Second World War: vol. IV, security and counter-intelligence, 1990. *Address:* The Cottage, 94 Broad Street, near Guildford, Surrey GU3 3BE. *T:* (01483) 572456. *Clubs:* Naval and Military, MCC; Woking Golf.

SIMMERS, Graeme Maxwell, CBE 1998 (OBE 1982); Chairman, Scottish Sports Council, 1992–99; *b* 2 May 1935; *s* of W. Maxwell Simmers and Gwen Simmers; *m* 1965, Jennifer Roxburgh; two *s* two *d*. *Educ:* Glasgow Acad.; Loretto Sch. CA 1959. National Service, commnd Royal Marines, 1959–61. Sen. Partner, S. Easton Simmers & Co., 1960–86; Dir, Scottish Highland Hotels Gp, 1962–92 (Chm., 1972–92). Mem., Scottish Tourist Bd, 1979–86; British Hospitality Association (formerly British Hotels & Restaurants Association): Chm., Bd of Management, 1987–88; Mem. Nat. Exec.,

1991–97. Dir, Forth Valley Acute Hosps NHS Trust. Governor: Loretto Sch., 1968–2000 (Chm., 1992–99); Queen's Coll., Glasgow, 1989–93. Hon. Col, RM Reserve, Scotland, 2000–. Treasurer and Elder, Killearn Kirk. *Address:* Kincaple, Boquhan, Balfron, Glasgow G63 0RW. *Clubs:* All England Lawn Tennis; Royal & Ancient Golf (Chm., Championship Cttee, 1988–91; Captain, 2001–); Prestwick Golf, Loch Lomond Golf.

SIMMONDS, Andrew John; QC 1999; *b* 9 May 1957; *s* of late Ernest Simmonds and of Sybil Simmonds; *m* 1981, Kathleen Moyse; one *d. Educ:* Sevenoaks Sch., Kent; St John's Coll., Cambridge (MA). Called to the Bar, Middle Temple, 1980. *Recreations:* alpine skiing, fitness training. *Address:* 5 Stone Buildings, Lincoln's Inn, WC2A 3XT. *T:* (020) 7242 6201.

SIMMONDS, John Andrew; Registrar in Bankruptcy, High Court of Justice, since 1993; *b* 8 March 1939; *s* of Frank Andrew Simmonds and Eugenie Marie Alexandra (*née* Longyear); *m*; one *s. Educ:* Holloway Grammar Sch. Admitted solicitor, 1968; Partner, Stafford Clark & Co., 1971–93. Mem., Insolvency Practitioners Tribunal, 1987–. *Publications:* Statutory Demands: use and abuse, 1992; contributions to: Report by Lord Justice Otton, Litigants in Person in the High Court, 1995–96; Report by Mr Justice Ferris, Insolvency Practitioner Renumeration, 1999–2000. *Address:* Parkhill Road, NW3.

SIMMONDS, Rt Hon. Dr Kennedy Alphonse; PC 1984; Prime Minister, Federation of St Christopher (St Kitts) and Nevis, 1983–95; *b* 12 April 1936; *s* of Bronte Clarke and Arthur Simmonds; *m* 1976, Mary Camella (*née* Matthew); three *s* two *d. Educ:* St Kitts and Nevis Grammar School; Leeward Islands Scholar, 1954; Univ. of West Indies (studies in Medicine), 1955–62. Senior Bench Chemist, Sugar Assoc. Res. Lab., St Kitts, 1955; Internship, Kingston Public Hosp., 1963; medical practice, St Kitts, Anguilla and Nevis, 1964–66; postgrad. studies, Princess Margaret Hosp., Bahamas, 1966; Resident in Anaesthesiology, Pittsburgh, 1968–69; medical practice, St Kitts, 1969–80; Premier of St Christopher (St Kitts) and Nevis, 1980–83. Foundn Mem., People's Action Movement Opposition Party, 1965, Pres., People's Action Movement, 1976. Fellow, Amer. Coll. of Anaesthesiology, 1970. *Recreations:* tennis, cricket, football, video taping. *Address:* PO Box 167, Earle Morne Development, Basseterre, St Kitts, West Indies.

SIMMONDS, Mark Jonathan Mortlock; MP (C) Boston and Skegness, since 2001; *b* 12 April 1964; *s* of Neil Mortlock Simmonds and Mary Griffith Simmonds; *m* 1994, Lizbeth Josefina Hanomancin; two *d. Educ:* BSc Hons. MRICS 1987. With Savills, 1986–88; Partner, Strutt & Parker, 1988–96; Dir, C. B. Hillier Parker, 1996–98; Man. Dir, 1998–2001, Chm., 2001–, Mortlock Simmonds. *Recreations:* family, Rugby, tennis, history, reading. *Address:* House of Commons, SW1A 0AA. *T:* (020) 7219 8143. *Club:* Naval and Military.

SIMMONDS, Posy; freelance illustrator/cartoonist, since 1969; *b* 9 Aug. 1945; *d* of late Reginald A. C. Simmonds and Betty Cahusac; *m* 1974, Richard Hollis. *Educ:* Queen Anne's Sch., Caversham; L'Ecole des Beaux Arts, Paris; Central Sch. of Art and Design, London (BA Art and Design). Cartoonist: The Guardian, 1977–87, 1988–90, 1992–; The Spectator, 1988–90. Exhibitions: The Cartoon Gall. (formerly the Workshop), 1974, 1976, 1979, 1981, 1982, 1984; Mus. of Modern Art, Oxford, 1981; Manor House Mus. & Art Gall., Ilkley, 1985. TV documentary, Tresoddit for Easter, 1991. Hon. DArt Plymouth, 1993. Cartoonist of the Year: Granada TV/What The Papers Say, 1980; British Press Awards, 1981; Nat. Art Liby Illustrations Award, 1998. *Publications:* Bear Book, 1969; Mrs Weber's Diary, 1979; True Love, 1981; Pick of Posy, 1982; (illustrator) Daisy Ashford, The Young Visiters, 1984; Very Posy, 1985; Fred, 1987 (filmed as Famous Fred, 1997); Pure Posy, 1987; Lulu and the Flying Babies, 1988; The Chocolate Wedding, 1990; (illustrator) Hilaire Belloc, Matilda, who told such Dreadful Lies, 1991; Mustn't Grumble, 1993; Bouncing Buffalo, 1994; F-Freezing ABC, 1995; (illustrator) Hilaire Belloc, Cautionary Tales, 1998; Gemma Bovery, 1999; Lavender, 2002. *Address:* c/o Peters, Fraser & Dunlop, Drury House, 34–43 Russell Street, WC2B 5HA. *T:* (020) 7344 1000.

See also R. J. Simmonds.

SIMMONDS, Richard James, CBE 1996; farmer and forester; Chairman, Independent Transport Commission, since 1999; *b* 2 Aug. 1944; *s* of late Reginald A. C. Simmonds and Betty Cahusac; *m* 1967, Mary (*née* Stewart); one *s* two *d. Educ:* Trinity Coll., Glenalmond. Councillor, Berkshire CC (Chm. of Environment, Property, Transport, and Development Cttees), 1973–79. National Vice-Chm. of Young Conservatives, 1973–75; Founding Vice-Chm. of Young European Democrats, 1974; Personal Asst to Rt Hon. Edward Heath, 1973–75; MEP (C) Midlands W, 1979–84, Wight and Hampshire E, 1984–94; PPS to Sir James Scott-Hopkins, Leader of European Democratic Gp, European Parlt, 1979–82; Cons. spokesman on youth and educn, European Parlt, 1982–84, on budget control, 1984–87; Whip, 1987–89; Chief Whip, 1992–94. Mem., Agric., Fisheries, Food and Rural Develt Cttee, 1992–94; Expert Advr, Eur. Commn, 1997–. Fellow of Parly & Industry Trust. Chm., Countryside Commn, 1995–99. Mem. Council, PDSA, 1995–. Founding Pres., Mounted Games Assoc. of GB, 1984–; President: Royal E Berks Agricl Assoc., 1995; Jersey Cattle Soc., 1997. Fellow, Waitangi Foundn, NZ, 1996. Chm. of Governors, Berkshire Coll. of Agriculture, 1979–92; Mem. Adv. Cttee, Centre for Agric. Strategy, Reading Univ., 1998–. ARAgS 1997. *Publications:* The Common Agricultural Policy—a sad misnomer, 1979; An A to Z of Myths and Misunderstandings of the European Community, 1981, 3rd edn 1993; (jtly) Cork Declaration on Rural Development, 1996; European Parliamentary report on farm animal welfare, 1985, 1987, 1990; report on prodn, processing, politics and potential of NZ meat (P4 report), 1996. *Recreations:* resisting bureaucracy, getting things done. *Address:* Dyars, Cookham Dean, Berkshire SL6 9PJ. *Clubs:* Ancient Britons, Tamworth; OPB Sailing (Hon. Cdre, 1999–).

See also Posy Simmonds.

SIMMONS, Alan Gerald; His Honour Judge Simmons; a Circuit Judge, since 1990; *b* 7 Sept. 1936; *s* of late Maurice Simmons and Sophie Simmons (*née* Lasserson); *m* 1961, Mia, *d* of late Emanuel and Lisa Rosenstein; one *s* one *d. Educ:* Bedford Modern Sch.; Quintin Sch. RAF, 1956–58. Director: Aslon Labs; Record Productions (Surrey); Ashcourt. Called to the Bar, Gray's Inn, 1968 (Lee Essay Prize; Holker Sen Exhibn); SE Circuit; Assistant Recorder, 1985; Recorder, 1989. Mem., Mental Health Rev. Tribunal, 1993–2000. Member: Board of Deputies of British Jews, 1982–88; Council, United Synagogue, 1979–93. *Recreations:* music, reading, fencing.

SIMMONS, Fr Eric, CR; Prior of St Michael's Priory, Burleigh Street, London, 1993–98; *b* 1930. *Educ:* Univ. of Leeds. BA (Phil) 1951. Coll. of the Resurrection, Mirfield, 1951; deacon, 1953, priest, 1954; Curate of St Luke, Chesterton, 1953–57; Chaplain, University Coll. of N Staffordshire, 1957–61; licensed to officiate: Dio. Wakefield, 1963–65 and 1967–; Dio. Ripon, 1965–67; Warden and Prior of Hostel of the Resurrection, Leeds, 1966–67; subseq. Novice Guardian, CR, looking after young Community members; Superior, Community of the Resurrection, Mirfield, Yorks, 1974–87; permission to officiate, Dio. London, 1989–98; the Community is an Anglican foundation engaged in evangelism and teaching work, based in Yorkshire but with work in Southern Africa. *Address:* House of the Resurrection, Mirfield, W Yorks WF14 0BN.

SIMMONS, Guy Lintorn, LVO 1961; HM Diplomatic Service, retired; *b* 27 Feb. 1925; *s* of late Captain Geoffrey Larpent Simmons, RN and Frances Gladys Simmons (*née* Wright); *m* 1951, Sheila Jacob; three *d. Educ:* Bradfield Coll.; Oriel Coll., Oxford. RAF, 1943–46; CRO, 1949; 2nd Sec., British High Commn: Lahore, 1950; Dacca, 1952; CRO, 1954–58 and 1964–66; 1st Sec.: Bombay, 1958; New Delhi, 1961; Commercial Counsellor: New Delhi, 1966–68; Cairo, 1968–71; Head of Trade Policy Dept, FCO, 1971–73; Diplomatic Service Inspectorate, 1973–76; Commercial Counsellor, Copenhagen, 1976–79; Consul-General: Karachi, 1979–82; Montreal, 1982–84; FCO, 1984–90. Chm., Crouch End Open Space, 1992–94. *Recreations:* the arts, travel, country pursuits. *Address:* 29 Wood Vale, N10 3DJ. *Club:* Sind (Karachi).

SIMMONS, Prof. Ian Gordon, PhD, DLitt; FSA; FBA 1997; Professor of Geography, University of Durham, 1981–2001 (part-time, 1999–2001); *b* 22 Jan. 1937; *s* of Charles Frederick Simmons and Christina Mary Simmons (*née* Merrills); *m* 1962, Carol Mary Saunders; one *s* one *d. Educ:* UCL (BSc 1959; PhD 1962); Durham Univ. (DLitt 1990). Lectr, 1962–70, Sen. Lectr, 1970–76, Reader, 1976–77, in Geography, Univ. of Durham; Prof. of Geography, Univ. of Bristol, 1977–81. ACLS Postdoctoral Fellow, Univ. of Calif at Berkeley, 1964–65; Churchill Meml Travelling Fellow, 1970–71. Chm., Benchmarking Panel for Geography, QAA, 1999–; Mem. Geog. Panel, RAE, 1996–2001. FSA 1980; MAE 1994. *Publications:* Changing the Face of the Earth, 1989, 2nd edn 1996; Earth, Air and Water, 1993; Interpreting Nature, 1993; Environmental History, 1993; The Environmental Impact of Later Mesolithic Cultures, 1996; Humanity and Environment: a cultural ecology, 1997; An Environmental History of Great Britain, 2001; chapters in edited collections and about 100 papers in learned jls. *Recreations:* music, poetry. *Address:* Science Laboratories, South Road, Durham DH1 3LE. *T:* (0191) 374 2464, *Fax:* (0191) 374 2456; *e-mail:* i.g.simmons@durham.ac.uk.

SIMMONS, Jean; film actress; *b* London, 31 Jan. 1929; *m* 1950, Stewart Granger (marr. diss. 1960; he *d* 1993); one *d*; *m* 1960, Richard Brooks (marr. diss. 1977; he *d* 1992); one *d. Educ:* Orange Hill Sch.; Aida Foster School of Dancing. First film appearance in Give Us the Moon, 1942; minor parts in Cæsar and Cleopatra, The Way to the Stars, etc., 1942–44; since then has appeared in numerous British films, including: Great Expectations, Black Narcissus, Hungry Hill, Uncle Silas, Hamlet (Best Actress Award, Venice Film Festival, 1950), So Long at the Fair, The Blue Lagoon, Trio, Adam and Evalyn, Clouded Yellow; The Grass is Greener, 1960; Life at the Top, 1965; Say Hello to Yesterday, 1971; began American film career, 1950; American films include: Androcles and the Lion, Young Bess, The Actress, Desirée, Footsteps in the Fog, Guys and Dolls, This Could be the Night, Spartacus, Elmer Gantry, All the Way Home; Divorce, American Style, 1967; The Happy Ending, 1970; The Thorn Birds, 1982 (Emmy award, 1983); How to Make an American Quilt, 1996; television includes: Down at the Hydro, 1982. Musical: A Little Night Music, Adelphi, 1975. Outstanding Film Achievement Award, Italy, 1989. Comdr, Order of Arts and Letters (France), 1990. *Address:* c/o A. Morgan Maree, Jr & Assoc., Inc., 4727 Wilshire Boulevard, Suite 600, Los Angeles, CA 90010–3875, USA.

SIMMONS, John Barry Eves, OBE 1987; VMH 1986; Curator: Castle Howard Arboretum Trust, since 1997; Royal Botanic Gardens, Kew, 1972–95; *b* 30 May 1937; *s* of Alfred John and Gladys Enid Simmons; *m* 1958, Valerie Lilian Dugan; two *s* one *d. Educ:* Harrow County Grammar Sch.; Herts Coll. of Agric. and Hort.; Regent Street Polytechnic; Sch. of Horticulture, Kew. MHort, FIHort; FIBiol, CBiol. Royal Botanic Gardens, Kew: Supervisor, Tropical Propagation Unit, 1961–64; Asst Curator, Temperate Section, 1964–68; Deputy Curator, 1968–72. Chm., Nat. Council for Conservation of Plants and Gardens, 1994–97 (Mem. Council, 1985–97; Vice-Chm., 1991–94; Pres., Norfolk Gp, 1993–); Member: RHS Award and Judging Cttees, 1969–; Longwood Gardens (Pennsylvania) Visiting Cttee, 1984–91; Westonbirt Arboretum Consultative Cttee, 1986–; Chm., Bedgebury Pinetum Consultative Cttee, 1992–; Dir, Flora for Fauna, 1997–2000; Trustee, Stanley Smith (UK) Horticultural Trust, 1994–. Pres., Inst. of Horticulture, 1987–88. Gov., Writtle Agricl Coll., 1990–93. *Publications:* The Life of Plants, 1974, 2nd edn 1990; (series editor) Kew Gardening Guides, 1987–; (gen. editor) Kew Gardens Book of Indoor Plants, 1988; (jtly) The Gardens of William Morris, 1998; (jtly) English Plants for your Garden, 2000; ed and contrib. to learned jls. *Recreations:* photography, walking, gardening (own garden!).

SIMMONS, Marion Adèle; QC 1994; a Recorder, since 1998; *b* 11 April 1949; *d* of late Sidney Simmons and of Bella Simmons (*née* Byer). *Educ:* Hendon County Grammar Sch.; Queen Mary Coll., Univ. of London (LLB Hons, LLM). Called to the Bar, Gray's Inn, 1970 (Bencher, 1993); Asst Recorder, 1990–98. Asst Boundary Comr, 2000–; Legal Mem., Restricted Cases Panel, Mental Health Review Tribunal, 2000–. Vice Chm., Appeals Cttee, ICAEW, 2000–. *Address:* 3/4 South Square, Gray's Inn, WC1R 5HP. *T:* (020) 7696 9900.

SIMMONS, Air Marshal Sir Michael (George), KCB 1989 (CB 1988); AFC 1976; Secretary, Humane Slaughter Association and Council of Justice for Animals, 1992–2000; *b* 8 May 1937; *s* of George and Thelma Simmons; *m* 1964, Jean Aliwell; two *d. Educ:* Shrewsbury Sch.; RAF Coll., Cranwell. Commissioned 1958; No 6 Squadron, Cyprus, 1959–61; ADC to AOC-in-C FTC, 1961–64; No 39 Sqdn, Malta, 1964–66; No 13 Sqdn, Malta, 1966–67; No 51 Sqdn, Wyton, 1967–69; RN Staff Coll., 1970; MoD, 1971–72; OC No XV Sqdn, Germany, 1973–76; MoD, 1976–79; OC RAF Cottesmore, 1980–82; MoD, 1982–84; SASO, HQ Strike Comd, 1984–85; AOC No 1 Gp, RAF, 1985–87; ACAS, 1987–89; Dep. Controller Aircraft, MoD, 1989–92. ADC to the Queen, 1980–81. Mem. Council, RAF Benevolent Fund, 1994–. Chm. Bd of Govs, Duke of Kent Sch., 1994–96. *Recreations:* clock repairing, gardening, golf. *Club:* Royal Air Force.

SIMMONS, Peter Patrick; High Commissioner for Barbados in the United Kingdom, since 1995; *b* 13 April 1942; *s* of late Kenneth G. Simmons and of Sybil Louise Simmons; *m* 1968, Rosalind Cecelia Hinds; one *s* one *d. Educ:* London Sch. of Journalism (Diploma); New York State Univ. (BA); Univ. of WI, St Augustine (Cert. Govt Admin). Sub-Editor, Barbados Advocate, 1961–73; Min. of Foreign Affairs, London, NY, Bridgetown, 1963–76; Asst Registrar, Univ. of WI, Cave Hill Campus, 1976–79; Dep. Perm. Rep. and Chargé d'Affaires, Barbados Mission to UN, 1979–82; Chief Develt Planner, Min. of Finance and Planning, 1982–84; Dir of Communications, Barbados, 1984–86; Political Specialist, US Embassy, Bridgetown, 1986–91; Chm., SBG Develt Corp., 1991–94. ITV documentary: The Red Legs of Barbados, 1986. *Publications:* Red Legs: class and colour contradictions in Barbados, 1976; (with Sir Garfield Sobers) The Changing Face of Cricket, 1995. *Recreations:* reading, public affairs, cricket, cooking, walking. *Address:* High Commission for Barbados, 1 Great Russell Street, WC1B 3JY. *T:* (020) 7631 4975; Pembroke House, 9 Roehampton Gate, SW15 5JR. *T:* (020) 8878 0260.

SIMMONS, Richard John, CBE 1995; FCA; Senior Partner, Andersen (formerly Arthur Andersen), 1996–2001, Senior Adviser, since 2002; *b* 2 June 1947; *s* of John Eric Simmons and Joy Mary Simmons (*née* Foat); *m* 1993, Veronica Sinkins; one *s* one *d. Educ:* Moseley GS, Birmingham; London School of Economics (BSc Econs); Haas Business Sch., Univ. of California, Berkeley. FCA 1971. Joined Arthur Andersen, subseq. Andersen, 1968;

Partner, 1979–2001. Asst Sec, Internat. Accounting Standards Cttee, 1973–75. Non-executive Director: Cranfield Information Technology Inst., 1987–89; Westminster Forum Ltd, 1999–; Chm., Chameleon Nursery Ltd, 2002–. Chairman: Bow Gp, 1980–81; CBlu Adv. Council, 2000–; Mem., Shadow Nat. Accounts Commn, 2000–. Mem., Develt Bd, Royal Acad. of Arts, 1995–. *Recreations:* horse racing, tennis, gardening. *Address:* Andersen, 1 Surrey Street, WC2R 2PS. *Club:* Carlton (Hon. Treas., Political Cttee, 1995).

SIMMONS, Prof. Robert Malcolm, FRS 1995; Professor of Biophysics, King's College London, since 1983; *b* 23 Jan. 1938; *s* of Stanley Laurence Simmons and Marjorie Amys; *m* 1967, Mary Ann (Anna) Ross; one *s* one *d*. *Educ:* King's College London (BSc Physics 1960; FKC 1996); Royal Institution (PhD London 1965); University College London (MSc Physiol. 1967). CBiol, FIBiol 2000. Department of Physiology, University College London: Sharpey Scholar, 1967–70; Lectr, 1970–79; MRC Res. Fellow, 1979–81; King's College London: MRC Cell Biophysics Unit, 1981–83; Associate Dir, 1983–91; Head of Dept of Biophysics, 1983–88; Head of Div. of Biomolecular Scis, 1988–91; Hon. Dir, MRC Muscle and Cell Motility Unit, 1991–; Dir, Randall Centre (formerly Randall Inst.), 1995–. *Publications:* (ed) Muscular Contraction, 1992; contribs on physiol. and biophys to learned jls. *Recreations:* music, fishing. *Address:* Randall Centre, King's College London, New Hunt's House, Guy's Campus, SE1 1UL. *Club:* Athenæum.

SIMMONS, Sir Stanley (Clifford), Kt 1993; FRCS, FRCOG; Consultant Obstetrician and Gynaecologist, Windsor, 1965–92; *b* 28 July 1927; *s* of Lewis Alfred and Ann Simmons; *m* 1956, Ann Wine; one *s* three *d*. *Educ:* Hurstpierpoint Coll.; St Mary's Hosp., London Univ. (MB BS 1951). FRCS 1957, FRCOG 1971. National Service, Royal West African Frontier Force, 1953–55. Resident MO, Queen Charlotte's Hosp. and Chelsea Hosp. for Women, 1955–56; Registrar, St Mary's Hosp. Paddington, 1957–59; Sen. Registrar, St Thomas' Hosp., 1960–64. Member: GMC, 1975–84; Council, RCOG, 1971–72, 1973–78, 1982– (Vice-Pres., 1986; Sen. Vice-Pres., 1987; Pres., 1990–93); Council, RCS (co-opted), 1984–86; President: Hosp. Consultants and Specialists Assoc., 1972; Windsor Med. Soc., 1983; Section of Obst. and Gyn., RSocMed, 1985. Hon. FRCSE 1994; Hon. FRACOG 1992; Hon. FACOG 1993; Hon. Fellow, Inst. of Gynaecologists, RCPI, 1993. *Publications:* (jtly) General Surgery in Gynaecological Practice, 1974; contribs to med. jls. *Recreations:* flying, sailing, golf, ski-ing, painting. *Address:* 23 Chapel Square, Virginia Park, Virginia Water, Surrey GU25 4SZ. *T:* (01344) 844029. *Clubs:* Royal Society of Medicine, Royal Ocean Racing; Wentworth.

SIMMONS, Tom Christopher; Town Clerk, Corporation of London, since 1998; *b* 29 Oct. 1942; *s* of Tom Francis Simmons and Mary Simmons; *m* 1971, Barbara Loxley; one *s*. *Educ:* Nottingham Univ. (BA Law 1963). Admitted Solicitor, 1968. Borough Sec., Chelmsford BC, 1973–83; Dep. Town Clerk, 1983–95, City Sec., 1996–98, Corp. of London. Sec., Mus. of London, 1990–; Clerk: Nat. Crime Squad Authy, 1998–; Nat. Criminal Intelligence Service Authy, 1998–. *Recreations:* water colour painting, gardening, walking. *Address:* Guildhall, EC2P 2EJ. *T:* (020) 7332 1400.

SIMMS, Sir Neville (Ian), Kt 1998; FREng, FICE, FCIOB; Chairman, Carillion plc, since 1999 (Chief Executive, 1999–2000); *b* 11 Sept. 1944; *s* of late Arthur Neville Simms and of Anne Davidson Simms (*née* McCulloch). *Educ:* Queen Elizabeth's GS, Crediton; Univ. of Newcastle upon Tyne (BSc 1st cl. Hons 1966); Univ. of Glasgow (MEng 1971). CEng 1970; FICE 1995; FCIOB 1995; FREng (FEng 1996). Structural Engr, Ove Arup and Partners, 1966–69; joined Tarmac plc as Sect. Engr, Roads Div., Tarmac Civil Engrg, 1970; Chief Exec., Tarmac Construction Ltd, 1988–92; Gp Chief Exec., 1992–99, Dep. Chm., 1994–99, Tarmac plc. Chm., Internat. Power, 2000–; Dir, Bank of England, 1995–; non-executive Director: Courtaulds, 1994–98; Private Finance Panel Ltd, 1994–99; National Power, 1998–2000. Chm., BITC (W Midlands), 1998–; Member: New Deal Task Force, 1999–; Trade Partners UK-Business Adv. Panel, 2001–. Gov., Ashridge Mgt Coll., 2000–. MInstD 1995; CIMgt 1992; FRSA 1992. Hon. DTech Wolverhampton Univ., 1997; Dr *hc* Edinburgh, 2000. *Address:* (office) Birch Street, Wolverhampton WV1 4HY. *T:* (01902) 422431.

SIMON, family name of **Viscount Simon**, and of **Barons Simon of Glaisdale, Simon of Highbury** and **Simon of Wythenshawe**.

SIMON, 3rd Viscount *cr* 1940; **Jan David Simon;** a Deputy Speaker, House of Lords, since 1999; *b* 20 July 1940; *o s* of 2nd Viscount Simon, CMG; *S* father, 1993; *m* 1969, Mary Elizabeth, *d* of late John J. Burns, Sydney, NSW; one *d*. *Educ:* Westminster; Sch. of Navigation, Univ. of Southampton; Sydney Tech. Coll. Dep. Chm. of Cttees, H of L, 1998–; Mem., Select Cttee on Procedure of H of L, 1999–; elected Mem., H of L, 1999. *Heir:* none. *Address:* House of Lords, SW1A 0PW.

SIMON OF GLAISDALE, Baron *cr* 1971 (Life Peer), of Glaisdale, Yorks; **Jocelyn Edward Salis Simon;** PC 1961; Kt 1959; DL; a Lord of Appeal in Ordinary, 1971–77; *b* 15 Jan. 1911; *s* of Frank Cecil and Claire Evelyn Simon, 51 Belsize Pk, NW3; *m* 1st, 1934, Gwendolen Helen (*d* 1937), *d* of E. J. Evans; 2nd, 1948, Fay Elizabeth Leicester, JP, *d* of Brig. H. G. A. Pearson; three *s*. *Educ:* Gresham's School, Holt; Trinity Hall, Cambridge (Exhibitioner). Called to Bar, Middle Temple, 1934 (Blackstone Prizeman). Served War of 1939–45; commissioned RTR, 1939; comd Spec. Service Sqn, RAC, Madagascar, 1942; Burma Campaign, 1944; Lieut-Col. 1945. Resumed practice at Bar, 1946; KC 1951. MP (C) Middlesbrough West, 1951–62; Mem. of the Royal Commission on the Law relating to Mental Illness and Mental Deficiency, 1954–57. Jt Parly Under-Sec. of State, Home Office, 1957–58; Financial Sec. to the Treasury, 1958–59; Solicitor-General, 1959–62. President, Probate, Divorce and Admiralty Div. of the High Court of Justice, 1962–71. Elder Brother, Trinity House, 1975. Hon. Fellow, Trinity Hall, Cambridge, 1963. DL NR (now North) Yorks, 1973. Hon. Dr en Droit Laval, 1961; Hon. LLD Cambridge, 1994. *Publications:* Change is Our Ally, 1954 (part); Rule of Law, 1955 (part); The Church and the Law of Nullity, 1955 (part). *Address:* c/o House of Lords, SW1A 0PW.

See also Hon. P. C. H. Simon.

SIMON OF HIGHBURY, Baron *cr* 1997 (Life Peer), of Canonbury in the London Borough of Islington; **David Alec Gwyn Simon,** Kt 1995; CBE 1991; Adviser, Cabinet Office, since 1999; Member, Prodi Group advising on Enlargement Implications, European Union, since 1999; *b* 24 July 1939; *s* of late Roger Albert Damas Jules Simon and of Barbara (*née* Hudd); *m* 1st, 1964, Hanne (*née* Mohn) (marr. diss. 1987); two *s*; 2nd, 1992, Sarah (*née* Roderick Smith). *Educ:* Christ's Hospital; Gonville and Caius College, Cambridge (MA Hons); MBA INSEAD. Joined BP 1961; a Man. Dir, 1985–97, CEO, 1992–95 and Chm., 1995–97, BP. A Dir, Bank of England, 1995–97. Minister of State, HM Treasury and DTI, 1997–99. Director: (Adv.), Unilever, 2000–; Morgan Stanley Dean Witter (Europe), 2000–; Fortis, 2001–; Suez Group, 2001–. Member: International Council and UK Adv. Bd, INSEAD, 1985–; President's Cttee, CBI, 1992–97; Vice Chm., European Round Table, 1993–97; Trustee, Cambridge Univ. Foundn, 1991–. Hon. DSc(Econ) Hull, 1990; D*hc* Univ. of N London, 1995; Hon. LLD Bath, 1998. *Recreations:* golf, books, music. *Address:* House of Lords, SW1A 0PW. *Clubs:* Athenæum, Brooks's.

SIMON OF WYTHENSHAWE, 2nd Baron *cr* 1947, of Didsbury; **Roger Simon;** *b* 16 Oct. 1913; *S* father, 1960 (but does not use the title and wishes to be known as Roger Simon); *m* 1951 (Anthea) Daphne May; one *s* one *d*. *Educ:* Gresham's School; Gonville and Caius College, Cambridge. *Heir:* *s* Hon. Matthew Simon, *b* 10 April 1955. *Address:* Oakhill, Chester Avenue, Richmond, Surrey TW10 6NP.

See also B. Simon.

SIMON, Prof. Brian; Emeritus Professor of Education, University of Leicester; *b* 26 March 1915; *yr s* of 1st Baron Simon of Wythenshawe and Shena D. Potter; *m* 1941, Joan Home Peel; two *s*. *Educ:* Gresham's Sch., Holt; Schloss Schule, Salem; Trinity Coll., Cambridge; Inst. of Educn, Univ. of London. MA. Pres., Nat. Union of Students, 1939–40; Royal Corps of Signals, GHQ Liaison Regt (Phantom), 1940–45; teaching Manchester and Salford schs, 1945–50; Univ. of Leicester: Lectr in Educn, 1950–64; Reader, 1964–66; Professor, 1966–80; Dir, Sch. of Educn, 1968–70, 1974–77. Chairman: History of Educn Soc., 1976–79; Internat. Standing Conf. for Hist. of Educn, 1979–82; President: British Educn Res. Assoc., 1977–78; Council for Educational Advance, 1991–. Mem., Nat. Acad. of Educn, USA, 1992–. Editor, Forum (for discussion of new trends in educn), 1958–90; Jt Editor, Students Library of Education, 1966–77. Dr *hc* Cath. Univ. of Leuven, 1980; DUniv Open, 1981; Hon. DEd UWE, 1997; Hon. DLitt: Warwick, 1998; Leicester, 2000; Hon. LLD Manchester, 1999. *Publications:* A Student's View of the Universities, 1943; Intelligence Testing and the Comprehensive School, 1953; The Common Secondary School, 1955; (ed) New Trends in English Education, 1957; (ed) Psychology in the Soviet Union, 1957; Studies in the History of Education 1780–1870, 1960; (ed, with Joan Simon) Educational Psychology in the USSR, 1963; (ed) The Challenge of Marxism, 1963; (ed) Non-streaming in the Junior School, 1964; Education and the Labour Movement 1870–1920, 1965; (ed) Education in Leicestershire 1540–1940, 1968; (with D. Rubinstein) The Evolution of the Comprehensive School 1926–66, 1969 (revised edn 1973); (with Caroline Benn) Half-Way There: Report on the British Comprehensive School Reform, 1970 (revised edn 1972); Intelligence, Psychology and Education, 1971 (revised edn 1978); (ed) The Radical Tradition in Education in Britain, 1972; The Politics of Educational Reform 1920–1940, 1974; (ed with Ian Bradley) The Victorian Public School, 1975; (with Maurice Galton) Inside the Primary Classroom, 1980; Progress and Performance in the Primary Classroom, 1980; (ed with William Taylor) Education in the Eighties, the central issues, 1981; (ed with John Willcocks) Research and Practice in the Primary Classroom, 1981; Does Education Matter?, 1985; (ed with Detlef Müller and Fritz Ringer) The Rise of the Modern Educational System, 1987; Bending the Rules: the Baker "reform" of education, 1988; (ed) The Search for Enlightenment: the working class and adult education in the twentieth century, 1989; Education and the Social Order 1940–1990, 1991; What Future for Education?, 1992; (ed with Clyde Chitty) Education Answers Back, 1993; (with Clyde Chitty) SOS Save Our Schools, 1993; The State and Educational Change: essays in the history of education and pedagogy, 1994; In Search of a Grandfather: Henry Simon of Manchester 1835–1899, 1997; A Life in Education (autobiog.), 1998; The Monument at Murg, 1998; Henry Simon's Children, 1999. *Address:* 11 Pendene Road, Leicester LE2 3DQ. *T:* (0116) 270 5176.

SIMON, Claude (Henri Eugène); French writer and vine grower; *b* Madagascar, 10 Oct. 1913; *s* of Antoine Simon and Suzanne (*née* Denamiel); *m* 1978, Réa Karavas. *Educ:* Collège Stanislas, Paris. Jury Mem., Prix Médicis, 1968–70. Nobel Prize for Literature, 1985. *Publications:* Le tricheur, 1945; La corde raide, 1947; Gulliver, 1952; Le sacre du printemps, 1954; Le vent, 1957; L'herbe, 1958 (trans. The Grass, 1961); La route des Flandres (Prix de l'Express), 1960 (trans. The Flanders Road, 1962); Le palace, 1962 (trans. 1964); Histoire (Prix Médicis), 1967 (trans. 1969); La bataille de Pharsale, 1969 (trans. The Battle of Pharsalus, 1971); Orion aveugle, 1970; Les corps conducteurs, 1971 (trans. Conducting Bodies, 1975); Triptyque, 1973 (trans. 1977); Leçon de choses, 1975; Les Géorgiques, 1981 (trans. 1985); L'Acacia, 1989; Photographies, 1992; Le Jardin des Plantes, 1997; Le Tramway, 2001; articles in journals. *Address:* c/o Editions de Minuit, 7 rue Bernard-Palissy, 75006 Paris, France.

SIMON, Neil; playwright; *b* NYC, 4 July 1927; *s* of Irving and Mamie Simon; *m* 1st, 1953, Joan Baim (*d* 1973); 2nd, 1973, Marsha Mason; 3rd, 1987, Diane Lander. *Educ:* De Witt Clinton High Sch.; entered Army Air Force Reserve training programme as an engineering student at New York University; discharged with rank of corporal, 1946. Went to New York Offices of Warner Brothers Pictures to work in mail room. Hon. LHD Hofstra Univ., 1981; Dr *hc* Williams Coll., 1984. *Screenplays include:* After The Fox (produced 1966); Barefoot in the Park, 1967; The Odd Couple, 1968; The Out-of-Towners, 1970; Plaza Suite, 1971; The Last of the Red Hot Lovers, 1972; The Heartbreak Kid, 1973; The Prisoner of 2nd Avenue, 1975; The Sunshine Boys, 1975; Murder by Death, 1976; The Goodbye Girl, 1977; The Cheap Detective, 1978; California Suite, 1978; Chapter Two, 1979; Seems Like Old Times, 1980; Only When I Laugh, 1981; I Ought To Be In Pictures, 1982; Max Dugan Returns, 1983; adapt. Lonely Guy, 1984; The Slugger's Wife, 1984; Brighton Beach Memoirs, 1986; Biloxi Blues, 1988; The Marrying Man, 1991; Broadway Bound (TV film), 1992; Lost in Yonkers, 1993; Jake's Women (TV film), 1996; The Odd Couple II, 1998; other films based on his stage plays: Come Blow Your Horn, 1963; Sweet Charity, 1969; The Star-Spangled Girl, 1971. *Plays produced:* Come Blow Your Horn, 1961 (publ. 1961); (jtly) Little Me, 1962 (publ. 1979), rev. version 1982, West End 1984; Barefoot in the Park, 1963 (publ. 1964); The Odd Couple, 1965 (publ. 1966), West End 1996; (jtly) Sweet Charity, 1966 (publ. 1966); The Star-Spangled Girl, 1966 (publ. 1967); Plaza Suite, 1968 (publ. 1969); (jtly) Promises, Promises, 1968 (publ. 1970); Last of the Red Hot Lovers, 1969 (publ. 1970), Criterion, 1979; The Gingerbread Lady, 1970 (publ. 1971); The Prisoner of Second Avenue, 1971 (publ. 1972); The Sunshine Boys, 1972 (publ. 1973); The Good Doctor, 1973 (publ. 1974); God's Favorite, 1974 (publ. 1975); California Suite, 1976 (publ. 1977); Chapter Two, 1977 (publ. 1979), West End 1996; (jtly) They're Playing Our Song, 1979 (publ. 1980); I Ought To Be In Pictures, 1980 (publ. 1981); Fools, 1981 (publ. 1982); Brighton Beach Memoirs, 1983 (publ. 1984), NT, 1986, West End, 1987; Biloxi Blues, 1985 (Tony Award for Best Play, 1985) (publ. 1986); The Odd Couple (female version), 1985 (publ. 1992); Broadway Bound, 1986 (publ. 1988); Rumors, 1988 (publ. 1990), Chichester, 1990; Lost in Yonkers, 1991 (Pulitzer Prize, Tony Award for Best Play, 1991) (publ. 1992), West End, 1992; Jake's Women, 1992 (publ. 1994); (jtly) The Goodbye Girl, 1993; Laughter on the 23rd Floor, 1993 (publ. 1995), West End 1996; London Suite, 1995; Proposals, 1997; The Dinner Party, 2000. *Publication:* Rewrites: a memoir, 1996. *Address:* c/o A. DaSilva, 502 Park Avenue, New York, NY 10022, USA.

SIMON, Paul; American singer and songwriter; *b* 13 Oct. 1941; *s* of Louis and Belle Simon; *m* 1st, Peggy Harper (marr. diss.); one *s*; 2nd, 1983, Carrie Fisher (marr. diss.); 3rd, 1992, Edie Brickell; two *s* one *d*. *Educ:* Queens Coll. (BA Eng. Lit.). Mem., Simon and Garfunkel, 1964–71; solo performer, 1971–. *Songs* include: *with Art Garfunkel:* The Sounds of Silence; Homeward Bound; I Am a Rock; 59th Street Bridge Song (Feelin' Groovy); Scarborough Fair/Canticle; Mrs Robinson; The Boxer; Bridge Over Troubled Water; Cecilia; *solo:* American Tune; Loves Me Like a Rock; Still Crazy After All These Years; 50 Ways to Leave Your Lover; Slip Slidin' Away; Something So Right; Hearts and Bones;

Graceland; You Can Call Me Al; Diamonds on the Soles of her Shoes; Under African Skies; The Rhythm of the Saints; albums include: (with Derek Walcott) Songs from The Capeman, 1997; You're the One, 2000; *films:* performer (with Art Garfunkel) and composer of soundtrack, The Graduate, 1967; actor, Annie Hall, 1977; writer of screenplay and score, One-Trick Pony, 1980; musical, The Capeman (lyrics with Derek Walcott), 1998. Numerous Grammy Awards. *Publication:* At the Zoo, 1991. *Address:* c/o C. Vaughn Hazell, Paul Simon Music, Suite 500, 1619 Broadway, New York, NY 10019, USA.

SIMON, Hon. Peregrine Charles Hugo, FLS; QC 1991; a Recorder, since 1998; *b* 20 June 1950; *s* of Lord Simon of Glaisdale, *qv*, and Fay Elizabeth Leicester, *d* of Brig. Guy Pearson; *m* 1980, Francesca Fortescue Hitchins, *d* of Major Tom Fortescue Hitchins; two *s* two *d*. *Educ:* Westminster School; Trinity Hall, Cambridge (MA). Called to the Bar, Middle Temple, 1973, Bencher, 1999. Mem. Council, Zool Soc., 1992–96 (Vice-Pres., 1995–96). *Address:* Brick Court Chambers, 7–8 Essex Street, WC2R 3LD. *T:* (020) 7379 3550.

SIMON, Robin John Hughes, FSA; art historian; Founding Partner, Draig Publishing, since 1997; Founder and Editor, The British Art Journal, since 1999; Director, Art Journals Ltd, since 1999; *b* 23 July 1947; *s* of Most Rev. (William) Glyn (Hughes) Simon, sometime Archbishop of Wales, and Sarah Sheila Ellen (*née* Roberts); *m* 1st, 1971, Jette Margaret Brooke (*see* J. M. Guillebaud) (marr. diss.); one *s* one *d*; 2nd, 1979, Joanna Christine Ross; one *d*. *Educ:* Cardiff High Sch.; Univ. of Exeter (BA Hons English); Courtauld Inst. of Art (MA Hist. European Art). FSA 1998. Lectr in Hist. of Art and English, Univ. of Nottingham, 1972–78; Historic Bldgs Rep., NT, 1979–80; Dir, Inst. European Studies, London, 1980–90; Editor, Apollo, 1990–97; Hd of Publications, NACF, and Ed., Art Qly, Annual Review, 1997–98. Vis. Lectr in Hist. of Art, Univ. of Warwick, 1978; Vis. Prof. in Hist. of Art and Architecture, Westminster Coll., Fulton, Mo, 1989. Arts Corresp., 1987–90, Art Critic, 1990–, Daily Mail; columnist, Tatler, 1994–. Delmas Foundn Fellow, Venice, 1978. Member: Council, 1991–96, Exec. and Editl Cttee, 1993–96, Walpole Soc.; Adv. Council, Paul Mellon Centre for Studies in British Art, 1993–98; Exec. Cttee, Assoc. of Art Historians, 1993–96; Cttee, Courtauld Assoc. of Former Students, 1992– (Chm., 1998–); Johnson Club, 1995–; Founding Chm., Hogarth Club, 1997–; Patron, Lord Leighton Centenary Trust, 1994–96. *Publications:* (with Alastair Smart) The Art of Cricket, 1983; The Portrait in Britain and America, 1987; (ed) Buckingham Palace: a complete guide, 1993; (ed) The King's Apartments, Hampton Court Palace, 1994; (ed with Gervase Jackson-Stops) The National Trust 1895–1995: 100 great treasures, 1995; (ed) Lord Leighton 1830–1896 and Leighton House, 1996; (ed with Christopher Woodward) A Rake's Progress: from Hogarth to Hockney, 1997; (ed with Rhian Harris) Enlightened Self-interest: the Foundling Hospital and Hogarth, 1997; (ed) Oxford: art and architecture, 1997; articles in Apollo, Burlington Mag., TLS, Papers of Brit. Sch. at Rome, Spectator, Tatler, Opera Now, Country Life, Sunday Times, etc. *Recreations:* cricket (Captain, Poor Fred's XI), music. *Address:* The British Art Journal, 46 Grove Lane, SE5 8ST. *T:* (020) 7787 6944. *Club:* Garrick.

SIMON, Roger; *see* Simon of Wythenshawe barony.

SIMON, Sion Llewelyn; MP (Lab) Birmingham, Erdington, since 2001; *b* 23 Dec. 1968; *s* of Jeffrey Simon and Anne Loverini Simon (*née* Jones; now Owen); *m* 1992, Elizabeth Jane Middleton; two *d*. *Educ:* Handsworth Grammar Sch., Birmingham; Magdalen Coll., Oxford (BA PPE 1990). Res. Asst to George Robertson, MP, 1990–93; Sen. Manager, Guinness plc, 1993–95; freelance, 1995–97; columnist, Daily Telegraph, 1997–2001. *Address:* House of Commons, SW1A 0AA.

SIMON, Tobias Robert Mark, (Toby); JP; Member, London Fire and Emergency Planning Authority, since 2000; *b* 31 May 1948; *s* of Anthony Percival Warwick, (Tim), Simon and Barbara Mary Simon; partner, Mrs Margaret Anne McAlpine; two step *s* one step *d*. *Educ:* Bryanston Sch., Dorset; Trinity Hall, Cambridge (MA); BA Open Univ. 1976. Department of Health and Social Security, 1969–87: Sec., Cttee on Safety of Medicines, 1973–76; Principal, 1973; NHS Personnel, 1978–81, 1983–84; Machinery of Govt Div., MPO, CSD, 1981–83; Sen. Lectr, Civil Service Coll., 1984–87; Sec., Chartered Soc. of Physiotherapy, 1987–96. Gen. Man., Assoc. of Anaesthetists of GB and Ireland, Jan.–Aug. 2000. Chm. Scrutiny Commn, London Fire and Civil Defence Authy, 1999–2000; Mem., Regl Legal Services Cttee for London, 2000–. Mem. (Lab) Enfield LBC, 1998– (Chm., Social Inclusion Scrutiny Panel). Governor: Enfield County Sch., 1996–; Edmonton County Sch., 1999–. FRSA. JP Enfield, 1998. *Recreations:* ski-ing, opera, theatre, books, cycling. *Address:* 73 Wellington Road, Enfield EN1 2PH.

SIMONDS-GOODING, Anthony James Joseph; company director; *b* 10 Sept. 1937; *s* of Major and Mrs Hamilton Simonds-Gooding; *m* 1st, 1961, Fiona (*née* Menzies) (marr. diss. 1982); three *s* two *d* (and one *s* decd); 2nd, 1982, Marjorie Anne, *d* of late William and Wendy Pennock; one step *s*. *Educ:* Ampleforth Coll.; BRNC, Dartmouth. Served RN, 1953–59; Unilever, 1960–73; Marketing Dir, subseq. Man. Dir (UK), finally Gp Man. Dir, Whitbread & Co. plc, 1973–85; Saatchi plc, 1985–87 (Chm. and Chief Exec. of all communication and advertising cos worldwide); Chief Exec., British Satellite Broadcasting, 1987–90. Chairman: Aqueduct Enterprises, 1992–94; Ammirati Puris Lintas, 1994–96; Clark & Taylor (Dir, 1996–99); Director: Robinson and Sons, Chesterfield, 1993–99; Lilliput Group, 1993–94; Community Hosps Gp plc, 1995–2001; Newell & Sorrell, 1996–99; Kunick plc, 1997–; Blick plc, 1997–; CLK.MPL, 1999–. Chm., D&AD, 1992–; Director: ICA, 1992–94; Macmillan Cancer Relief (formerly Cancer Relief Macmillan Fund), 1992–2001; Brixton Prison Bd, 1994–97; Rainbow Trust, 2001–; Sea Cadets Assoc., 2001–. *Recreations:* family, opera, sport, travel, art. *Clubs:* Sloane, Hurlingham.

SIMONET, Henri François; Commander, Order of Leopold, 1974; Member, Belgian Parliament, 1966–92; *b* Brussels, 10 May 1931; *m* 1960, Marie-Louise Angenent; one *s* one *d*. *Educ:* Univ. Libre de Bruxelles (DenD, DèsSc); Columbia Univ., USA. Assistant, Univ. Libre de Bruxelles, 1956–58, now Prof.; Financial Adv., Inst. Nat. d'Etudes pour le Développement du Bas-Congo, 1958–59; Legal Adv., Commn of Brussels Stock Exchange, 1956–60; Dep. Dir, Office of Econ. Programming, 1961; Director of Cabinet: of Min. of Econ. Affairs and Power, 1961–65; of Dep. Prime Minister responsible for co-ordination of Econ. Policy, 1965; Minister of Econ. Affairs, 1972; Vice-Pres., Commn of the European Communities, 1973–77; Foreign Minister, Belgium, 1977–80; Sec. of State, Brussels Regional Economy, 1977–79. Mayor of Anderlecht, 1966–84. Commander, Légion d'Honneur (France), 1985. *Publications:* various books and articles on economics, financial and political topics.

SIMONET, Sir (Louis Marcel) Pierre, Kt 1985; CBE 1980 (OBE 1972); Director and Proprietor, Pharmacie Simonet, since 1955 (founded by father, 1926); *b* 6 March 1934; *s* of Marcel Simonet and Marguerite Simonet. *Educ:* Collège du St Esprit up to Higher School Certificate. Town Council of Curepipe: Mem., 1960; Vice-Chm., 1962; Chm., 1964; 1st Mem. for Curepipe, Legislative Assembly, 1976. Judge Assessor, Permt Arbitration Tribunal, 1984. Dir, Central Electricity Bd, 1972. Chm., Central Housing Authority, 1986–88. Mem., Ex-servicemen's Assoc., 1977; Pres., Widows and Orphans Pension Fund, 1978; Past Pres., Lions Club of Curepipe; Chm., Centre Culturel d'Expression Française (Founder Mem., 1960). Pres., Soc. of St Vincent de Paul. Testimonial, Royal Humane Soc. for life saving, 1962; Chevalier de l'Ordre National du Mérite (France), 1980. *Address:* Queen Mary Avenue, Floreal, Mauritius. *T:* (office) 6763532, (residence) 6865240. *Club:* Mauritius Racing.

SIMONS, (Alfred) Murray, CMG 1983; HM Diplomatic Service, retired; Head of UK Delegation to Negotiations on Mutual Reduction of Armed Forces and Armaments and Associated Measures in Central Europe, at Vienna, 1982–85, with personal rank of Ambassador; *b* 9 Aug. 1927; *s* of late Louis Simons and of Fay Simons; *m* 1975, Patricia Jill, *d* of late David and May Barclay, Westbury on Trym, Bristol; two *s*. *Educ:* City of London Sch.; Magdalen Coll., Oxford (MA). FO, 1951; 3rd Sec., Moscow, 1952–55; FO, 1955–56; Columbia Univ., 1956; 2nd Sec., Bogota, 1957; 1st Sec., Office of Comr-Gen. for SE Asia, Singapore, 1958–61; FO, 1961–64; 1st Sec., British High Commn, New Delhi, 1964–68; FCO, 1968–71; Counsellor, 1969; British Embassy, Washington, 1971–75; Head of SE Asia Dept, FCO, 1975–79; Consul General, Montreal, 1980–82. Pres., John Carpenter Club, 1992–93. Freeman, City of London, 1990. *Recreations:* tennis, theatre. *Address:* 128 Longland Drive, Totteridge, N20 8HL. *T:* (020) 8446 3163.

SIMONS, Prof. John Philip, PhD, ScD; FRS 1989; CChem, FRSC; Dr Lee's Professor of Chemistry, Oxford University, 1993–99, now Emeritus; Fellow of Exeter College, Oxford, 1993–99; *b* 20 April 1934; *s* of Mark Isaac Simons and Rose (*née* Pepper); *m* 1st, 1956, Althea Mary (*née* Screaton) (*d* 1989); three *s*; 2nd, 1992, Elizabeth Ann Corps. *Educ:* Haberdashers' Aske's Hampstead Sch.; Sidney Sussex Coll., Cambridge (BA; PhD 1958; ScD 1975). CChem, FRSC 1975. Chemistry Department, University of Birmingham: ICI Fellow, 1959; Lectr, 1961; Reader in Photochemistry, 1977; Prof. of Photochem., 1979; Prof. of Physical Chemistry, Univ. of Nottingham, 1981–93. Erskine Fellow, Univ. of Canterbury, NZ, 1996; Vis. Prof., Univ. of Pittsburgh, 1998; Vis. Miller Prof., Univ. of Calif, Berkeley, 2000. Lectures: Tilden, RSC, 1983; Pimentel, UC Berkeley, 1998; Spiers, RSC, 1999; Burton, KCL, 2001; Humphrey Davy, Royal Soc., 2001. Vice Pres., and Hon. Sec., 1981–93, Pres., 1993–95, Faraday Div., RSC. Member: Chemistry Cttee, 1983–85, Laser Facility Cttee, 1983–87, SERC; Comité de Direction, CNRS Lab. de Photophysique Moleculaire, Orsay, 1985–90; specially promoted scientific programme panel, NATO, 1985–88; Council, Royal Soc., 1999–2000. Adv. Councillor, Ramsay Meml Fellowship Trust, 1991–. Ed., PhysChemComm, 1998–. Member Editorial Boards: Molecular Physics, 1980–96; Chemical Physics Letters, 1982–99; Jl Chem. Soc. Faraday Trans, 1990–98; Chemical Physics, 1994–; Phys Chem Chem Phys, 1998–. Chemical Dynamics Award, 1994, Polanyi Medal, 1996, RSC. Citoyen Honoraire de la Ville de Toulouse, 1997. *Publications:* Photochemistry and Spectroscopy, 1970; research papers in learned jls of molecular/chemical physics. *Recreations:* writing and reading verse. *Address:* Physical and Theoretical Chemistry Laboratory, South Parks Road, Oxford OX1 3QZ. *T:* (01865) 275400.

SIMONS, Richard Brian; Development Director, New Media Productions, United Broadcasting & Entertainment, since 2000; *b* 5 Nov. 1952; *s* of Harry Simons and Ann Lily Simons (*née* Gold); one *s* one *d*. *Educ:* Royal Grammar Sch., High Wycombe; Exeter Coll., Oxford (BA Hons PPE). Independent Television News Ltd: Trainee TV Journalist, 1974–75; Writer, News at Ten, and Reporter, News at One, 1976–78; Prog. Editor and News Editor, News At One, 1979; Special Progs Producer and Foreign News Editor, also Home News Editor, 1980–84; Head of Investigative Unit, and Associate Producer, D-Day: 40 Years On, 1984; Associate Prod., VE Day: 40 Years On, 1985; Sports Editor, and Mem., ITV Sport Network Cttee, 1985; Editor, World Cup Mexico, 1986; News Editor, 'Vote '87', General Election Results Special, 1986; Special Productions Editor, 1988–90; Develt Dir, First in Fact Ltd, 1991; Commissioning Editor, Factual Progs, 1992–94, Head of Features, 1995–96, Carlton TV; Dir of Progs, Meridian Broadcasting, 1994–2000. *Recreations:* my children, piano, papers and TV for pleasure, tennis. *Address:* (office) 48 Leicester Square, WC2H 7FB.

SIMPLE, Peter; *see* Wharton, Michael B.

SIMPSON, family name of **Baron Simpson of Dunkeld**.

SIMPSON OF DUNKELD, Baron *cr* 1997 (Life Peer), of Dunkeld in Perth and Kinross; **George Simpson,** FCCA; FIMI; FCIT; Chief Executive, Marconi (formerly General Electric Co.) plc, 1996–2001; *b* 2 July 1942; *s* of William Simpson and Elizabeth Simpson; *m* 1964, Eva Chalmers; one *s* one *d*. *Educ:* Morgan Acad., Dundee; Dundee Inst. of Technology. ACIS. Sen. Accountant, Gas Industry, Scotland, 1962–69; Central Audit Man., BLMC, 1969–73; Financial Controller, Leyland Truck and Bus Div., 1973–76; Dir of Accounting, Leyland Cars, 1976–78; Finance and Systems Dir, Leyland Trucks, 1978–80; Managing Director: Coventry Climax Ltd, 1980–83; Freight Rover Ltd, 1983–86; Chief Exec. Officer, Leyland DAF, 1986–88; Man. Dir, 1989–91, Chm., 1991–94, and Chief Exec., 1991–92, Rover Gp; Dep. Chief Exec., BAe, 1992–94 (Dir, 1990–94); Chairman: Ballast Nedam Construction Ltd, 1992–94; Arlington Securities, 1993–94; Chief Exec., Lucas Industries plc, 1994–96. Mem. Supervisory Bd and non-exec. Director: Pilkington plc, 1992–99; Northern Venture Capital, 1992–; Pro Share, 1992–94; ICI plc, 1995–2001; Nestlé SA, 1999–. Member: Exec. Cttee, SMMT, 1986– (Vice Pres., 1986–95, Pres., 1995–96, Council); Senate, Engrg Council, 1996–. Industrial Prof., Warwick Univ., 1991–. *Recreations:* golf, squash and Rugby (now spectating). *Address:* c/o House of Lords, SW1A 0PW. *Clubs:* Royal Birkdale Golf, New Zealand Golf (Weybridge), Gleneagles Golf, Rosemount Golf (Blairgowrie), Pine Valley Golf (NJ); Kenilworth RFC.

SIMPSON, His Honour Alan; a Circuit Judge, 1985–2000; *b* 17 April 1937; *s* of William Henry Simpson and Gladys Simpson; *m* 1965, Maureen O'Shea; one *s* one *d*. *Educ:* Leeds Grammar Sch.; Corpus Christi Coll., Oxford (MA). Called to the Bar, Inner Temple, 1962; a Recorder, 1975–85. Prosecuting Counsel to DHSS, North Eastern Circuit, 1977–85. Admin. Steward, 1994–, Vice-Chm., 2000–, BBB of C. Mem., Sports Disputes Resolution Panel, 2000. *Recreations:* music, books, sport (especially cricket and boxing).

SIMPSON, Alan Francis, OBE 2000; author and scriptwriter since 1951 (in collaboration with Ray Galton, *qv*); *b* 27 Nov. 1929; *s* of Francis and Lilian Simpson; *m* 1958, Kathleen Phillips (*d* 1978). *Educ:* Mitcham Grammar Sch. *Television:* Hancock's Half Hour, 1954–61 (adaptation and trans., Fleksnes, Scandinavian TV, film and stage); Comedy Playhouse, 1962–63; Steptoe and Son, 1962–74 (US TV version, Sanford and Son; Dutch TV, Stiefbeen And Zoon; Scandinavian TV, Albert Och Herbert; Portuguese TV, Camilo & Filho); Galton-Simpson Comedy, 1969; Clochemerle, 1971; Casanova '74, 1974; Dawson's Weekly, 1975; The Galton and Simpson Playhouse, 1976–77; Paul Merton in Galton & Simpson's …, 1996, 1997; *films:* The Rebel, 1960; The Bargee, 1963; The Wrong Arm of the Law, 1963; The Spy with a Cold Nose, 1966; Loot, 1969; Steptoe and Son, 1971; Steptoe and Son Ride Again, 1973; Den Siste Fleksnes (Scandinavia), 1974; Skraphandlarne (Scandinavia), 1975; *theatre:* Way Out in Piccadilly, 1966; The Wind in the Sassafras Trees, 1968; Albert och Herbert (Sweden), 1981; Fleksnes (Norway), 1983;

Mordet pa Skölgatan 15 (Sweden), 1984; *radio:* The Galton & Simpson Radio Playhouse, 1998–99. Awards: Scriptwriters of the Year, 1959 (Guild of TV Producers and Directors); Best TV Comedy Series (Steptoe and Son, 1962, 1963, 1964, 1965 (Screenwriters Guild)); John Logie Baird Award (for outstanding contribution to Television), 1964; Best Comedy Series (Stiefbeen And Zoon, Dutch TV), 1966; Best Comedy Screenplay (Steptoe and Son, Screenwriters Guild), 1972; Best TV Series, Portugal Golden Globe (Camilo & Filho), 1995. *Publications:* (jointly with Ray Galton, *qv*): Hancock, 1961; Steptoe and Son, 1963; The Reunion and Other Plays, 1966; Hancock Scripts, 1974; The Best of Hancock, 1986. *Recreations:* Hampton & Richmond Borough FC (Pres.), gourmet travelling, guest speaking. *Address:* c/o Tessa Le Bars Management, 54 Birchwood Road, Petts Wood, Kent BR5 1NZ. *T:* (01689) 837084.

SIMPSON, Alan John; MP (Lab) Nottingham South, since 1992; *b* 20 Sept. 1948; *s* of Reginald James and Marjorie Simpson; *m* (separated); one *d* two *s*. *Educ:* Bootle Grammar Sch.; Nottingham Poly. (BSc Econ). Asst Gen. Sec., Nottingham Council of Voluntary Service, 1970–72; Develt Officer, Home Office Pilot Programme (Non Custodial Treatment of Offenders), 1972–74; Community Worker, Nottingham Areas Project, 1974–78; Res. and Inf. Officer, Nottingham Racial Equality Council, 1979–92. Cllr, Notts CC, 1985–93. Member: CND; Shelter; Oxfam. *Publications:* (contrib.) Issues in Community Education, 1980; Stacking the Decks: a study of race and council housing, 1981; (contrib.) The Right to a Home, 1984; Cuckoos in the Nest—Task Forces and urban policy, 1988; Against a Rising Tide—racism, Europe and 1992, 1991; Beyond the Famished Road—new policies for common security, 1994. *Recreations:* tennis, football (lifelong supporter, Everton FC), vegetarian cooking, eclectic interest in music and reading. *Address:* 222A Bluebell Hill Road, St Anns, Nottingham NG3 3EA. *T:* (0115) 950 3769.

SIMPSON, Sir Alfred (Henry), Kt 1985; Chief Justice of Kenya, 1982–85; *b* 29 Oct. 1914; *s* of John Robertson Simpson, Dundee; *m* 1941, Hilda Corson Rodgers (*d* 1999); one *d*; *m* 2000, Anne McMillan. *Educ:* Grove Academy; St Andrews University; Edinburgh University. MA St Andrews, 1935; LLB Edinburgh, 1938 and Solicitor. Served in RASC, 1940–46, Middle East and Italy; Military Mission to the Italian Army and Allied Commission, Austria. Legal Officer, BMA, Cyrenaica, 1946–48. Member of the Faculty of Advocates, 1952. Crown Counsel, Singapore, 1948–56; Legal Draftsman, Gold Coast, 1956; Solicitor-General, Ghana, 1957, then Puisne Judge, Supreme Court, 1957–61; Puisne Judge, Combined Judiciary of Sarawak, North Borneo and Brunei, 1962; Senior Puisne Judge, Fedn of Malaysia High Court in Borneo, 1964; Reader, Faculty of Law, ANU, Canberra, 1965; Barrister-at-Law, NSW, 1967; Puisne Judge, High Court of Kenya, 1967–82. *Publications:* (with others) The Laws of Singapore, revised edn, 1955; Memoirs Legal and Otherwise, 1996. *Recreation:* golf. *Address:* 23 Downes Place, Hughes, ACT 2605, Australia. *Clubs:* Royal Commonwealth Society, Royal Over-Seas League; Royal Canberra Golf.

SIMPSON, Alfred Moxon, AC 1978; CMG 1959; Chairman, SA Telecasters Ltd, 1964–92 (Director, 1962–92); *b* 17 Nov. 1910; *s* of late A. A. Simpson, CMG, CBE; *m* 1938, Elizabeth Robson Cleland; one *s*. *Educ:* St Peter's College; University of Adelaide, (BSc). Associate (Commerce) of Univ. of Adelaide, 1940. Dir, Simpson Holdings Ltd, 1939–83 (Chm., 1954–81). Pres. Adelaide Chamber of Commerce, 1950–52; Sen. Vice-Pres. Associated Chambers of Commerce of Aust., 1953–55; Pres. SA Chamber of Manufrs, 1956–58; Pres. Associated Chambers of Manufrs of Aust., 1957–58. Director: Bank of Adelaide, 1952–79; Elder Smith Goldsbrough Mort Ltd, 1954–81; Adelaide Steamship Co. Ltd, 1960–83; QBE Insurance Group Ltd, 1975–83 (Local Dir, 1935). Mem. Hulme Cttee on Rates of Depreciation, 1956; Report on employment security of overseas officers in Papua-New Guinea, 1972, adopted by govt, 1973. Mem. Council, Flinders Univ., 1965–76. *Recreations:* carpentry, lawnmowing. *Address:* 31 Heatherbank Terrace, Stonyfell, SA 5066, Australia. *T:* (8) 311285. *Clubs:* Adelaide, Naval, Military and Airforce, Mt Lofty Ski (Adelaide).

SIMPSON, Prof. (Alfred William) Brian, DCL; FBA 1983; JP; Charles F. and Edith J. Clyne Professor of Law, University of Michigan, since 1987; Professor of Law, University of Kent, 1973–85, now Emeritus; *b* 17 Aug. 1931; *s* of Rev. Canon Bernard W. Simpson and Mary E. Simpson; *m* 1st, 1954, Kathleen Anne Seston (marr. diss. 1968); one *s* one *d*; 2nd, 1969, Caroline Elizabeth Ann Brown; one *s* two *d*. *Educ:* Oakham Sch., Rutland; The Queen's Coll., Oxford (MA 1958, DCL 1976). Nat. Service with Nigeria Regt, RWAFF, 1950–51; E Yorks Regt, TA, 1951–57 (Capt.). Junior Research Fellow, St Edmund Hall, Oxford, 1954–55; Fellow and Tutor, Lincoln Coll., Oxford, 1955–73; Dean: Faculty of Law, Univ. of Ghana, 1968–69; Faculty of Social Sciences, Univ. of Kent, 1975–78; Prof. of Law, Univ. of Chicago, 1984–86. Called to the Bar, Gray's Inn, 1994. Visiting Professor: Dalhousie Univ., 1964; Univ. of Chicago, 1979, 1980, 1982, 1984; Univ. of Michigan, 1985; Goodhart Prof. of Legal Sci., Univ. of Cambridge, 1993–94. Hon. Dep. District Attorney, Denver City, 1982. Member, Deptl Cttee on Obscenity and Film Censorship, 1977–79. Fellow, Amer. Acad. of Arts and Scis, 1993. JP Canterbury and St Augustine's, 1968–. Hon. QC 2001. Hon. Fellow, Lincoln Coll., Oxford, 1995. Hon. DLitt Ghana, 1993. *Publications:* Introduction to the History of the Land Law, 1961, new edn as A History of the Land Law, 1986; (ed) Oxford Essays in Jurisprudence, 2nd Series, 1973; A History of the Common Law of Contract, 1975; Pornography and Politics, 1983; Cannibalism and the Common Law, 1984; (ed) A Biographical Dictionary of the Common Law, 1984; Legal Theory and Legal History: essays on the common law, 1987; Invitation to Law, 1988; In the Highest Degree Odious: detention without trial in wartime Britain, 1992; Leading Cases in the Common Law, 1995; Human Rights and the End of Empire: Britain and the genesis of the European Convention, 2001; articles in legal jls. *Recreations:* sailing, flying. *Address:* University of Michigan Law School, Hutchins Hall, Ann Arbor, MI 48109–1215, USA. *T:* (734) 7630413, *Fax:* (734) 7639375; 36 High Street, Wingham, Canterbury, Kent CT3 1AB. *T:* (01227) 720979; *e-mail:* bsimpson@umich.edu.

SIMPSON, Anthony Maurice Herbert, TD 1973; Member Task Force, later Directorate General, Justice and Home Affairs, European Commission, 1997–2000; *b* 28 Oct. 1935; *y s* of late Lt-Col Maurice Rowton Simpson, OBE, TD, DL and Mrs Renée Claire Simpson; *m* 1961, Penelope Gillian, *d* of late Howard Dixon Spackman; one *s* two *d*. *Educ:* Rugby; Magdalene College, Cambridge. BA 1959, LLM (LLB 1961), MA 1963. Leics and Derbys (PAO) Yeomanry, 1956–59; TA 1956–74, Major 1968. Called to Bar, Inner Temple, 1961; practised Midland and Oxford Circuit, 1961–75; Mem., Legal Service of European Commn, Brussels, 1975–79; MEP (C) Northamptonshire, 1979–94; contested (C) Northamptonshire and Blaby, Eur. Parly elecns, 1994; Quaestor of the European Parlt, 1979–87, and 1989–94; EDG spokesman on develt and co-operation, 1987–89; Mem., Inspectorate-Gen. of Services, Eur. Commn, 1994–96. Contested (C) West Leicester, Feb. and Oct. 1974. Common Market Law Editor, Current Law, 1965–72. *Recreations:* flying, walking, travelling. *Address:* Bassets, Great Glen, Leicestershire LE8 9GQ. *T:* (0116) 259 2386; Avenue Michel-Ange 57, 1000 Brussels, Belgium. *T:* (2) 7364219.

SIMPSON, Prof. Brian; *see* Simpson, Prof. A. W. B.

SIMPSON, Brian; Member (Lab) North West Region, England, European Parliament, since 1999 (Cheshire East, 1989–99); *b* Leigh, Lancs, 6 Feb. 1953; *s* of late John Hartley Simpson and of Freda Simpson; *m* 1975, Linda Jane Gwynn; one *s* two *d*. *Educ:* Golborne Comprehensive Sch., Wigan; W Midlands Coll. of Educn, Walsall (Cert Ed). Teacher, City of Liverpool, 1974–89. Councillor: Merseyside CC, 1981–85; Warrington Bor. Council, 1987–91. *Recreations:* Rugby League, cricket, British and European history, steam railways. *Address:* Gilbert Wakefield House, 67 Bewsey Street, Warrington WA2 7JQ. *T:* (01925) 654074. *Club:* Golborne Sports and Social (Wigan).

SIMPSON, Air Vice-Marshal Charles Ednam; Director (Scotland), Royal Air Force Benevolent Fund, 1989–94; *b* 24 Sept. 1929; *s* of Charles and Margaret Simpson; *m* 1955, Margaret Riddell; two *s* one *d*. *Educ:* Stirling and Falkirk High Schools; Univ. of Glasgow (MB ChB); University of London (MSc). FFOM 1986; MFCM. British Defence Staff, Washington DC, 1975; Dep. Dir, Aviation Medicine, RAF, 1978; CO, RAF Hosp., Wegberg, 1981; CO, Princess Alexandra Hosp., Wroughton, 1982; Dir of Health and Research, RAF, 1984; Asst Surgeon General (Envtl Medicine and Res.), 1985; PMO HQ RAF Strike Comd, 1986–89; QHS 1985–89. HM Comr, Queen Victoria Sch., Dunblane, 1990–2000 (Chm. Bd, 1997–2000). *Recreations:* golf, birdwatching. *Address:* 12 Balmyle Grove, Dunblane, Perthshire FK15 0QB. *T:* (01786) 822191. *Club:* Royal Air Force.

SIMPSON, Commander Cortlandt James Woore, CBE 1956; DSC 1945; retired 1961; *b* 2 Sept. 1911; *s* of late Rear-Admiral C. H. Simpson, CBE, and Edith Octavia (*née* Busby); *m* 1st, Lettice Mary Johnstone; 2nd, Ann Margaret Cubitt; 3rd, Joan Mary Watson; one *d*; 4th, Vanessa Ann Stainton (*née* Heald). *Educ:* St Ronans, Worthing; RN College, Dartmouth; London Univ. (BSc Engineering, Hons). Joined RN (Dartmouth), 1925; Lieut, 1934. Served War of 1939–45 in Home and Mediterranean Fleets; Commander (L), 1948. Summer expeditions to Greenland, 1950, 1951; Leader of British North Greenland Expedition, 1952–54. Polar Medal, 1954; Royal Geographical Society, Founder's Medal, 1955. *Publication:* North Ice, 1957. *Recreations:* mountaineering, sailing, walking. *Address:* Sanctuary Gate, Iddesleigh, Winkleigh, Devon EX19 8SN. *Club:* Alpine.

SIMPSON, David; District Judge (Magistrates' Courts) (formerly Metropolitan Stipendiary Magistrate), since 1993; *b* 29 July 1947; *s* of Albert Edward Simpson and Lily Simpson; *m* 1975, Jane Richards; one *s*. *Educ:* N Cestrian GS, Altrincham; Worthing High Sch. for Boys; King's Coll., London (LLM 1987). Admitted a solicitor, 1974. British Bank of ME, 1966–67; Court Clerk, Magistrates' Court: Worthing, 1967–74; Mansfield, 1975–76; Dep. Clerk, 1976–82, Clerk, 1982–93, to the Justices, Uxbridge. Part-time Immigration Special Adjudicator, 1996–2000. Vice-Pres., Assoc. of Magisterial Officers, 1981–82; Member: Council, Justices' Clerks' Soc., 1987–93; Magisterial Cttee, Judicial Studies Bd, 1990–93; Inner London Magistrates' Courts' Cttee, 1998–2001. *Recreations:* gardening, golf, reading, railways. *Address:* West London Magistrates' Court, 181 Talgarth Road, W6 8DN. *Club:* Eton College Golf.

SIMPSON, David Rae Fisher; Economic Adviser, Standard Life Assurance Co., 1988–2001; *b* 29 Nov. 1936; *s* of late David Ebenezer Simpson and Roberta Muriel Wilson; *m* 1980, Barbara Dianne Goalen, *d* of N. and Mrs G. Inglis, Edinburgh; one *s* (and one step *s* one step *d*). *Educ:* Skerry's Coll.; Edinburgh and Harvard Univs. MA 1st cl. hons Econs Edinburgh; PhD Econs Harvard. Instr in Econs, Harvard Univ., 1963–64; Assoc. Statistician, UN Hdqtrs, NY, 1964–65; Res. Officer, Econ. Res. Inst., Dublin, 1965–67; Lectr in Polit. Economy, UCL, 1967–69; Sen. Lectr in Econs, Univ. of Stirling, 1969–74; University of Strathclyde: Prof. and Dir, Fraser of Allander Inst., 1975–80, Res. Prof., 1980–85; Prof., Dept of Economics, 1985–88. Contested (SNP) Berwick and E Lothian Division, 1970 and Feb. 1974. *Publications:* Problems of Input-Output Tables and Analysis, 1966; General Equilibrium Analysis, 1975; The Political Economy of Growth, 1983; The Challenge of New Technology, 1987; The End of Macro Economics?, 1994; Regulating Pensions, 1996; Re-Thinking Economic Behaviour, 2000; articles in Econometrica, Rev. Econs and Statistics, Scientific American, Spectator. *Recreations:* walking, reading. *Address:* Holmsmill, Broughton, Peeblesshire ML12 6JF.

SIMPSON, David Richard Salisbury, OBE 1989; Founder and Director, International Agency on Tobacco and Health, since 1991; *b* 1 Oct. 1945; *s* of late Richard Salisbury Simpson and of Joan Margaret Simpson (*née* Braund). *Educ:* Merchiston Castle School, Edinburgh. ACA 1969; FCA 1979 (but resigned from Institute, 1981). Teacher at Cadet College, Hasan Abdal, West Pakistan, 1963–64 (VSO). Peat, Marwick, Mitchell & Co., Chartered Accountants, 1964–72; Scottish Director, Shelter, Campaign for the Homeless, 1972–74; Director: Amnesty International (British Section), 1974–79; ASH, 1979–90. Sundry journalism, broadcasting and public lectures. Hon. Consultant, Clin. Trial Service Unit and Epidemiol Studies Unit, Oxford Univ., 1991–. Vis. Prof., LSHTM, 2000–. News Ed., Tobacco Control, 1993–. Trustee, Pier Arts Centre, Stromness, 1994–. Hon. MFPHM 1991. *Publication:* Doctors and Tobacco: medicine's big challenge, 2000. *Recreations:* friends, reading, music, hill-walking, Orkney. *Address:* IATH, Tavistock House, Tavistock Square, WC1H 9LG.

SIMPSON, Lt-Col (Retd) David Sackville Bruce, CBE 1990; Chief Executive, Civil Service Catering Organisation, 1981–91, retired; *b* 18 March 1930; *s* of Henry and Violet Simpson; *m* 1956, Margaret Elizabeth Goslin; two *s* three *d*. *Educ:* Brockley Grammar Sch.; Westminster Technical Coll. FHCIMA. Regular Officer, Army Catering Corps (retd in rank of Lt-Col), 1950–75; Principal Education Catering Organiser, Inner London Education Authority, 1975–81. *Recreations:* golf, squash. *Address:* 1 Tavistock Road, Fleet, Hants GU13 8EH. *T:* (01252) 625795.

SIMPSON, Dennis Charles; business consultant and lecturer; Managing Director, Axtel (UK) Ltd, 1986–88; *b* 24 Oct. 1931; *s* of late Arthur and Helen Simpson; *m* 1st, 1964, Margery Bruce Anderson (marr. diss.); three *s* one *d*; 2nd, 1983, Susan Gaynor Conway-Williams. *Educ:* Manchester Univ. (BA). FInstPS. 2nd Lieut Royal Signals, 1952–54; commercial appts, Philips Electrical Industries, 1956–63; Group Purchasing Manager, STC Ltd, 1963–66; Gp Purchasing Controller, Rank Organisation, 1966–69; Gen. Man., Cam Gears (S Wales) Ltd, 1969–72; Industrial Dir for Wales, Dept of Industry, 1972–75; Industrial Dir for Wales, Welsh Office, 1975–76; Business Agent, Welsh Develt Agency, 1983–85. Chairman: Spencer Harris Ltd, 1976–81; Grainger Hydraulics Ltd, 1976–81; Wellfield Engineering, 1976–81; Director: Beechwood Holdings, 1976–81; Gower Technology Ltd, 1983–87; Video Interactive Systems Ltd, 1983–87; Gower Alarms Ltd, 1985–87; Video Interactive Teaching Aids Ltd, 1985–87. *Recreations:* golf, bridge, reading war histories.

SIMPSON, Edward Alexander, CB 1993; Director, Northern Ireland Court Service, 1987–95; *b* 25 Dec. 1935; *s* of late Robert Simpson and Eva (*née* Graham); *m* 1960, Audrey Gordon; two *s*. *Educ:* Regent House Sch., Newtownards; Queen's Univ., Belfast (BSc Econ). Joined Ministry of Finance, 1953; various posts in Mins of Health and Local Govt and DoE, 1956–77; Asst Sec., Transportation and the Fire Service, 1977–81; Belfast Develt Officer, 1981–87. *Recreations:* golf, walking, wine. *Address:* 28 Londonderry Avenue, Comber, Newtownards BT23 5ES.

SIMPSON, Edward Hugh, CB 1976; FSS 1947; Visiting Research Fellow, University of Warwick, since 1993; Deputy Secretary, Department of Education and Science, 1973–82, retired; *b* 10 Dec. 1922; *o s* of Hugh and Mary Simpson, of Brookfield, Ballymena, Co. Antrim; *m* 1947, Rebecca, *er d* of Sam and Elizabeth Gibson, Ernevale, Kesh, Co. Fermanagh; one *s* one *d*. *Educ:* Coleraine Academical Institution; Queen's Univ., Belfast (BSc (1st cl. Hons Mathematics), 1942); Mathematical Statistics res., Christ's Coll., Cambridge (Scholar), 1945–47. Foreign Office, Bletchley Park, 1942–45; Min. of Education, 1947–50 and 1952–56; HM Treasury, 1950–52; Commonwealth Fund Fellow, USA, 1956–57; Private Sec. to Lord President of Council and Lord Privy Seal, 1957–60; Dep. Dir, Commonwealth Educn Liaison Unit, 1960–62; Sec., Commonwealth Educn Conf., New Delhi, 1962; Asst Sec., DES, 1962–68; Under-Sec., Civil Service Dept, 1968–71, DES, 1971–73. Sen. Hon. Res. Fellow, Birmingham Univ., 1983–88. Chairman: Nat. Assessment Panel, Schools Curriculum Award, 1983–; Educn Grants Adv. Service, 1987–; Gov. and Chm., Professional Cttee, Bishop Grosseteste Coll., Lincoln, 1984–; Trustee, Educn 2000, 1987–. Consultant: Educn Management Information Exchange, 1986–89; Dixons plc, 1987–. FRSA 1991. Hon. LLD Hull, 1992. *Publications:* articles in statistical and educn journals. *Address:* 40 Frays Avenue, West Drayton, Mddx UB7 7AG. *T:* (01895) 443417. *Club:* Athenæum.

SIMPSON, Prof. Elizabeth; Professor of Immunogenetics, Imperial College School of Medicine, London University (formerly Royal Postgraduate Medical School), since 1994; Head of Transplantation Biology Group, MRC Clinical Sciences Centre, Hammersmith Hospital (formerly Clinical Research Centre, Harrow), since 1984; *b* 29 April 1939; *d* of J. H. G. Browne and O. R. Browne (*née* Wood); *m* 1963 (marr. diss. 1973); one *d*. *Educ:* Old Palace Sch. for Girls, Croydon; Girton Coll., Cambridge (BA Nat. Sci. 1960; VetMB 1963; MA 1964). Vet. Surg., private practice, Canada, 1963–65; Res. Virologist, Ottawa, 1965–66; Univ. Demonstrator in Animal Pathology, Cambridge Univ., 1966–69; Research Scientist: NIMR 1969–71; Clin. Res. Centre, Harrow, 1971–1984. Visiting Scientist: All India Inst. Med. Res., Delhi, 1971; Nat. Inst. Health, Bethesda, 1972–73; Jackson Lab., Maine, 1976–. FMedSci 1999. *Publications:* (ed) T Cell Receptors, 1995; reviews and scientific papers on transplantation, immunology and genetics in jls. *Recreations:* reading, writing, talking, listening, walking, sailing, ski-ing. *Address:* Transplantation Biology Group, MRC Clinical Sciences Centre, Imperial College School of Medicine, Hammersmith Hospital, Du Cane Road, W12 0NN. *T:* (020) 8383 8282.

SIMPSON, Sir Gilbert, (Sir Gil), KNZM 2000; QSM 1986; Chief Executive Officer, Aoraki Corp. Ltd, since 1982; *b* 5 April 1948; *m* 1998, Joy Reilly. *Educ:* Christchurch Boys' High Sch. Clerk, Nat. Bank of NZ, 1967–71; Sen. Programmer, NZ Aluminium Shelters, 1971–74; Data Processing Manager, Whitcoulls NZ, 1974–78; formed own co., 1978. Dir, Reserve Bank of NZ, 1997. Pres., Royal Soc. of NZ, 2000. Fellow: NZ Computer Soc., 1998; NZ Inst. Mgt, 1999; NZ Inst. Dirs, 2000. *Recreations:* tramping, flying, railway enthusiast, following cricket and Rugby. *Address:* Aoraki Corp. Ltd, PO Box 20–152, Christchurch, New Zealand. *T:* (3) 3652500.

SIMPSON, Gordon Russell, DSO 1944 and Bar 1945; LVO 1979; TD; stockbroker; Partner, Bell, Cowan & Co. (now Brewin Dolphin Bell Lawrie Ltd), 1938–82; *b* 2 Jan. 1917; 2nd *s* of A. Russell Simpson, WS; *m* 1943, Marion Elizabeth King (*d* 1976); two *s*. *Educ:* Rugby School. Served with 2nd Lothians and Border Horse, 1939–46 (comd 1944–46); Col TA, 1950–52. Chm., Edinburgh Stock Exchange, 1961–63; Chm., Scottish Stock Exchange, 1965–66; Pres., Council of Associated Stock Exchanges, 1971–73; Dep. Chm., Stock Exchange, 1973–78. Chm., General Accident Fire & Life Assurance Corporation Ltd, 1979–87 (Dir, 1967–87). Captain, Queen's Body Guard for Scotland (Royal Company of Archers). Mem. Court, Stirling Univ., 1980–88; Comr, Queen Victoria Sch., 1982–92. DL Stirling and Falkirk Dists (Central Region), 1981–92. *Recreations:* music, ski-ing, archery. *Address:* Arntomie, Port of Menteith, by Stirling FK8 3RD. *Club:* New (Edinburgh).

SIMPSON, Ian; artist and writer; Course Director, Open College of the Arts, 1996–99, now Consultant (East Regional Organizer and Visual Arts Course Leader, 1992–96); *b* 12 Nov. 1933; *s* of Herbert William and Elsie Simpson; *m* 1st, 1958, Joan (*née* Charlton) (marr. diss. 1982); two *s* one *d*; 2nd, 1982, Birgitta Willcocks (*née* Brädde). *Educ:* Bede Grammar Sch., Sunderland; Sunderland Coll. of Art; Royal Coll. of Art. ARCA 1958. Freelance artist and illustrator, 1958–63; Hornsey Coll. of Art: Lectr, 1963–66; Head, Dept of Visual Research, 1966–69; Head, Dept of Co-ordinated Studies, 1969–72; Principal, 1972–86, Head, 1986–88, St Martin's Sch. of Art; Asst Rector, London Inst., 1986–88. Exhibited various exhibns, Britain, USA, etc; one-man exhibn, Cambridge, 1975, Durham, 1977, Blandford, 1985, Chappel, Colchester, 1994. Mem. Council, CNAA, 1974–80 (Chm., Fine Art Bd, 1976–81). Pres., Nat. Soc. for Art Educn, 1976. Consultant, Leisure Study Group Ltd, 1986–87. FSAE 1976; FRSA 1983. *Publications:* Eyeline, 1968; Drawing: seeing and observation, 1973; Picture Making, 1973; Guide to Painting and Composition, 1979; Painters Progress, 1983, repr. as Practical Art School, 1995; Encyclopedia of Drawing Techniques, 1987; The Challenge of Landscape Painting, 1990; The New Guide to Illustration, 1990; Anatomy of Humans, 1991; Collins Complete Painting Course, 1993; Collins Complete Drawing Course, 1994. *Television Programmes:* Eyeline (10 programmes), 1968, 1969; Picture Making (10 programmes), 1973, 1976; Reading the Signs (5 programmes), 1977–78. *Recreations:* reading, music. *Address:* Motts Farm House, Chilton Street, Clare, Sudbury, Suffolk CO10 8QS.

SIMPSON, Ian Christopher; Sheriff of South Strathclyde, Dumfries and Galloway at Airdrie, since 1991 (Floating Sheriff, 1988–91); *b* 5 July 1949; *s* of David F. Simpson and J. O. S. Simpson (M. S. Dickie); *m* 1973, Anne Strang; two *s*. *Educ:* Glenalmond; Edinburgh Univ. (LLB). Admitted Faculty of Advocates, 1974. *Recreations:* golf, dog-walking. *Address:* 30 Cluny Drive, Edinburgh EH10 6DP. *T:* (0131) 447 3363. *Clubs:* Royal and Ancient (St Andrews); Dunbar Golf.

SIMPSON, James; *see* Simpson, W. J.

SIMPSON, Very Rev. James Alexander; Chaplain to the Queen in Scotland, since 1992; Moderator of the General Assembly of the Church of Scotland, 1994–95; *b* 9 March 1934; *s* of Robert and Marion Simpson; *m* 1960, Helen Gray McCorquodale; three *s* two *d*. *Educ:* Glasgow Univ. (BSc Hons 1955; BD 1958); Union Seminary, New York (STM 1959). Minister: Grahamston Church, Falkirk, 1960–66; St John's Renfield Church, Glasgow, 1966–76; Dornoch Cathedral, 1976–97; Interim Minister: Almondbank Tibbermore, Perth, 1997–98; Brechin Cathedral, 1998–99. Hon. DD Aberdeen, 1995. *Publications:* There is a Time To, 1971; Marriage Questions Today, 1975; Doubts Are Not Enough, 1982; Holy Wit, 1986, 3rd edn 1991; Laughter Lines, 1988, 2nd edn 1991; The Master Mind, 1989; History of Dornoch Cathedral, 1989; More Holy Wit, 1990; Keywords of Faith, 1992; Royal Dornoch Golf Club (a pictorial history), 1992; All about Christmas, 1994; The Laugh shall be First, 1998. *Recreation:* golf. *Address:* Dornoch, Perth Road, Bankfoot, Perth PH1 4ED. *Club:* Royal Dornoch Golf (Captain, 1993).

SIMPSON, James Walter Thorburn, RIBA; FRIAS; Partner, Simpson & Brown, Architects, since 1977; *b* 27 July 1944; *s* of Robert Alison Crighton Simpson, TD, FRIBA, and Rosemary Euphemia (*née* Morrison); *m* 1968, Ann Mary Bunney; two *d*. *Educ:* Belhaven Hill Sch.; Trinity Coll., Glenalmond; Edinburgh Coll. of Art (BArch Hons). RIBA 1970; FRIAS 1985. Trained as architect with Ian G. Lindsay and with Sir Bernard Feilden, 1972–77 (work on St Paul's, Norwich and St Giles' Cathedral, Edinburgh); estabd Simpson & Brown, with Stewart Brown, 1977. Building projects in Scotland and NE England, including: St Giles' Cathedral; Alderman Fenwick's House, Newcastle-upon-Tyne; Kinlochmoidart House, Inverness-shire; Rosslyn Castle and Chapel, Midlothian; 26–31 Charlotte Square, Edinburgh. Curator, William Adam Exhibn, Scottish Nat. Portrait Gall., 1989. Surveyor of the Fabric, York Minster, 1994–95. Mem., Ancient Monuments Bd for Scotland, 1984–96. Comr, Royal Commn on Ancient and Historical Monuments of Scotland, 1997–. *Publications:* Vitruvius Scoticus, 1980; The Care of Historic Buildings and Ancient Monuments by Government Departments in Scotland, 1995; The British Standard Guide to the Principles of the Conservation of Historic Buildings, 1998. *Recreations:* playing Scottish small pipes, Amy and Bella—two Norfolk Terriers, thinking about architecture, learning Gaelic. *Address:* (office) St Ninian's Manse, Quayside Street, Edinburgh EH6 6EJ. *T:* (0131) 555 4678; 40 Raeburn Place, Edinburgh EH4 1HL. *T:* (0131) 332 7294.

SIMPSON, Janet Ann; *see* Plant, J. A.

SIMPSON, John Andrew; Chief Editor, Oxford English Dictionary, since 1993; Fellow of Kellogg College (formerly Rewley House), Oxford, since 1991; *b* 13 Oct. 1953; *s* of Robert Morris Simpson and Joan Margaret (*née* Sersale); *m* 1976, Hilary Croxford; two *d*. *Educ:* Dean Close Sch., Cheltenham; Univ. of York (BA Hons English Literature); Univ. of Reading (MA Medieval Studies). Editorial Asst, Supplement to OED, 1976–79; Editor, Concise Oxford Dictionary of Proverbs, 1979–81; Sen. Editor, Supplement to OED, 1981–84; Editor (New Words), OED, 1984–86; Co-editor, OED, 1986–93. Mem., Faculty of English, Univ. of Oxford, 1993–. Editl Consultant, Australian National Dictionary, 1986–88. Vis. Asst Prof., Dept of English, Univ. of Waterloo, Ont, Canada, 1985. Mem., Philolog. Soc., 1994–. Hon. LittD ANU, 1999. *Publications:* (ed) Concise Oxford Dictionary of Proverbs, 1982, 3rd edn 1998; (contrib.) Oxford English, 1986; (contrib.) Words, 1989; (ed) Oxford English Dictionary, 2nd edn (with Edmund Weiner) 1989, 3rd edn (online) 2000–; (contrib.) Wörterbücher: ein internationales Handbuch zur Lexikographie, 1990; (ed with John Ayto) Oxford Dictionary of Modern Slang, 1992; (ed with Edmund Weiner) OED Additions series, vols 1 and 2, 1993, (Gen. Ed.) vol. 3, 1997; articles in Medium Aevum, English Today, and other lexicographical and linguistic publications. *Recreation:* cricket (Holton CC). *Address:* Chestnut Lodge, St Mary's Close, Wheatley, Oxford OX33 1YP. *T:* (office) (01865) 267728; *e-mail:* john.simpson@kellogg.ox.ac.uk.

SIMPSON, Very Rev. John Arthur, OBE 2001; Dean of Canterbury, 1986–2000, now Emeritus; *b* 7 June 1933; *s* of Arthur Simpson and Mary Esther Simpson; *m* 1968, Ruth Marian (*née* Dibbens); one *s* two *d*. *Educ:* Cathays High School, Cardiff; Keble Coll., Oxford (BA, 2nd cl. Mod. History 1956, MA 1960); Clifton Theological Coll. Deacon 1958, priest 1959; Curate: Leyton, 1958–59; Christ Church, Orpington, 1959–62; Tutor, Oak Hill Theol Coll., 1962–72; Vicar of Ridge, Herts, 1972–79; Director of Ordinands and Post-Ordination Training, Diocese of St Albans, 1975–81; Hon. Canon of St Albans Cathedral, 1977–79; Residentiary Canon, St Albans, and Priest-in-charge of Ridge, 1979–81; Archdeacon of Canterbury and Canon Res. of Canterbury Cathedral, 1981–86. Dir, Ecclesiastical Insurance Group (formerly Ecclesiastical Insurance Office), 1983–2000. Chm. Govs, King's Sch., Canterbury, 1986–. Hon. DD Kent, 1994. *Recreations:* travel, theatre, opera. *Address:* Flat D, 9 Earls Avenue, Folkestone, Kent CT20 2HW. *Club:* Athenæum.

SIMPSON, John (Cody Fidler-), CBE 1991; World (formerly Foreign) Affairs Editor, BBC, since 1988; *b* 9 Aug. 1944; *s* of Roy Simpson Fidler-Simpson and Joyce Leila Vivienne Cody; *m* 1965, Diane Jean Petteys (marr. diss. 1995), El Cajon, California; two *d*; *m* 1996, Adèle Krüger. *Educ:* St Paul's School; Magdalene Coll., Cambridge (MA; Hon. Fellow, 1999). FRGS 1990. Reporter, BBC Radio News, 1970; BBC correspondent, Dublin, 1972; Common Market correspondent (based in Brussels), 1975; Southern Africa correspondent (based in Johannesburg), 1977; Diplomatic correspondent, BBC Television News, 1978; BBC Political Editor, 1980; Presenter and Correspondent, BBC-TV News, 1981; Diplomatic Editor, BBC-TV, 1982–88. Associate Editor, The Spectator, 1991–96; columnist, Sunday Telegraph. Hon. DLitt: De Montfort, 1995; Nottingham, 2000. RTS Journalist of the Year, 1990, 2000; BAFTA Award, 1992, 2000. *Publications:* (ed jtly) The Best of Granta, 1966; The Disappeared: voices from a secret war, 1985; Behind Iranian Lines, 1988; Despatches from the Barricades, 1990; From the House of War: Baghdad and the Gulf, 1991; The Darkness Crumbles: the death of Communism, 1992; In the Forests of the Night: drug-running and terrorism in Peru, 1993; (ed) The Oxford Book of Exile, 1995; (jtly) Lifting the Veil: life in revolutionary Iran, 1995; Strange Places, Questionable People (autobiog.), 1998; A Mad World, My Masters: tales from a traveller's life, 2000; *novels:* Moscow Requiem, 1981; A Fine And Private Place, 1983. *Recreations:* collecting obscure books, travelling to obscure places, and returning to Suffolk. *Address:* BBC Television Centre, Wood Lane, W12 7RJ. *T:* (020) 8743 8000. *Clubs:* Athenæum, Garrick, Chelsea Arts; National Yacht (Dun Laoghaire).

SIMPSON, John Ernest Peter, FRCS; Director, Health Management Systems, since 1996; *b* 30 Jan. 1942; *s* of John and Alice Bewick Simpson; *m* 1st, 1964, Valerie Joan Lamb (marr. diss. 1987); one *s* one *d*; 2nd, 1996, Elizabeth Anne Lang. *Educ:* Jesus Coll., Oxford (MA, BM BCh); St Thomas's Hosp. Med. Sch. (Schol.). MFPHM. Surgical training, St Thomas' and Northwich Park Hosps, 1966–78; Lectr, Community Medicine, St Thomas' Hosp., 1974–75; Tutor, King's Fund Coll., 1975–78; Management, Planning Policy and Internat. Divs, DHSS, 1978–88; Regl MO, Mersey RHA, 1988–93; Med. Advr, London Implementation Gp, 1993–96. Past Pres., British Assoc. of Day Surgery. *Publications:* Going Home (from hospital) (ed jtly), 1981; articles on day case surgery and organisation of surgical and other clinical services. *Recreations:* golf, music. *Address:* White Cottage, 21 Clive Road, Esher, Surrey KT10 8PS. *T:* (01372) 470554. *Clubs:* Royal Society of Medicine; Royal Mid Surrey Golf.

SIMPSON, Keith Robert; MP (C) Mid Norfolk, since 1997; *b* 29 March 1949; *s* of Harry Simpson and Jean Simpson (*née* Day); *m* 1984, Pepita Hollingsworth; one *s*. *Educ:* Thorpe Grammar Sch.; Univ. of Hull (BA Hons 1970). Postgrad. res., KCL, 1970–72; Sen. Lectr in War Studies, RMA Sandhurst, 1973–86; Hd of Oversea and Defence Section, Cons. Res. Dept, 1986–88; Special Advr to Sec. of State for Defence, 1988–90; Dir, Cranfield Security Studies Inst., Cranfield Univ., 1991–97. Opposition front bench spokesman on defence, 1998–99; an Opposition Whip, 1999–2001. Sec., Cons. backbench Defence Cttee, 1997–98; Mem., H of C Catering Cttee, 1997–98. Member: RUSI, 1970–; IISS, 1975–; British Commn for Mil. History, 1980–; Council, SSAFA, 1997–. *Publications:* The

Old Contemptibles, 1981; (ed) A Nation in Arms, 1985; History of the German Army, 1985; (ed) The War the Infantry Knew 1914–1919, 1987; Waffen SS, 1990. *Recreations:* collecting books, cinema, visiting restaurants, walking battlefields, observing ambitious people. *Address:* House of Commons, SW1A 0AA. *T:* (020) 7219 4053. *Club:* Norfolk (Norwich).

SIMPSON, Keith Taylor; His Honour Judge Keith Simpson; a Circuit Judge, since 1990; *b* 8 May 1934; *m* 1961, Dorothy Preece; two *s* one *d*. *Educ:* privately; Jesus Coll., Oxford (MA). Called to the Bar, Middle Temple, 1958; joined SE Circuit; general Common Law practice. *Recreations:* walking, gardening, tennis, fishing, reading, opera. *Address:* c/o Crown Court, Barker Road, Maidstone, Kent ME16 8EQ.

SIMPSON, Malcolm Carter; Director of Finance, Leeds City Council, 1978–82, retired; *b* 15 June 1929; *s* of Arthur and Rhoda Simpson; *m* 1st, 1952, Doreen Patricia Wooler; two *d*; 2nd, 1980, Andrea Gillian Blythe. *Educ:* Stanningley Council Sch. DPA; CIPFA. Employed by Leeds CC for whole of working life, 1943–82: Asst Dir of Finance, 1968; Dep. Dir of Finance, 1973. Board Member: Yorks Water Authority, 1983–88; S Yorks Residuary Body, 1985–89. *Recreations:* golf, bridge. *Address:* Swiss Cottage, 44 Millbeck Green, Collingham Bridge, Leeds LS22 5AJ. *T:* (01937) 573917.

SIMPSON, Meg; *see* Hillier, M.

SIMPSON, Rear-Adm. Michael Frank, CB 1985; CEng, FIMechE; FRAeS; Chairman, Aircraft Engineering Division, Hunting Aviation Ltd, 1994–98; *b* 27 Sept. 1928; *s* of Robert Michael Simpson and Florence Mabel Simpson; *m* 1973, Sandra MacDonald (*née* Clift); two *s* one *d*. *Educ:* King Edward VI Sch., Bath; RN Engrg Coll., Manadon. CEng, FIMechE 1983; FRAeS 1983. Joined RN, 1944; qual. as Air Engr Officer, 1956; served in FAA Sqdns, cruisers and carriers; served with US Navy on exchange, 1964–66; Air Engr Officer, HMS Ark Royal, 1970–72; MoD appts, 1972–78; Supt, RN Aircraft Yard, Fleetlands, 1978–80; Cdre, RN Barracks, Portsmouth, 1981–83; Dir Gen. Aircraft (Naval), 1983–85; Dir and Gen. Man., 1985–88, Man. Dir, Field, later Hunting, Airmotive Ltd, 1988–94; Chm., Somet Ltd, 1988. Mem. Council and Dir, SBAC, 1994–98. Chairman: RN/RM Children's Home Management Cttee, 1980–83; RN Athletics Assoc., 1981–83. Mem. Court, Cranfield Inst. of Technology, 1983–86. *Publications:* articles on helicopter engrg in Jl of Naval Engrg; symposium paper on helicopter environmental design, 1975. *Recreations:* sailing, ski-ing, shooting, making things, military history, swimming. *Address:* Keppel, Blackhills, Esher, Surrey KT10 9JW. *Clubs:* Army and Navy; Royal Naval Sailing Association (Captain, Portsmouth Br., 1981–83); Royal Navy Ski.

SIMPSON, Morag; *see* Macdonald, M.

SIMPSON, Dr Patricia Ann, FRS 2000; Wellcome Trust Principal Fellow, Department of Zoology, University of Cambridge, since 2000; *b* 9 Dec. 1945; *d* of James Alfred Simpson and Peggy Anderson Simpson. *Educ:* Univ. of Southampton (BSc Hons); Univ. Pierre et Marie Curie, Paris (DèsSc). Scientific research at: Inst. d'Embryologie et Tératologie Experimentale, Nogent sur Marne, Paris, 1968–72; Center for Pathobiol., Univ. of Calif, Irvine, 1972–74; Centre de Génétique Moleculaire, Gif sur Yvette, France, 1975–80; Inst. de Génétique et de Biologie Moleculaire et Cellulaire, Univ. Louis Pasteur, Strasbourg (Res. Dir, 1981–2000). Silver Medal, CNRS, France, 1993. *Publication:* The Notch Receptors, 1994. *Recreations:* hiking in remote corners of the world, woodwork, boating. *Address:* Department of Zoology, Downing Street, Cambridge CB2 3EJ. *T:* (01223) 336669.

SIMPSON, Peter Robert; His Honour Judge P. R. Simpson; a Circuit Judge, since 1989; Second Judge, Mayor's and City of London Court, since 1994; *b* 9 Feb. 1936; *o s* of late Surg. Capt. (D) Donald Lee Simpson, RN and of Margaret Olive (*née* Lathan); *m* 1st, 1968, Mary Elizabeth (marr. diss. 1994), *y d* of late Thomas Kirton and Frances Florence Cecilia Kirton; two *s*; 2nd, 1995, Megan Elizabeth, *o d* of late Kenneth John Dodd and Melva Dodd. *Educ:* St John's Coll., Southsea, Hants. Admitted Solicitor, 1960; called to the Bar, Inner Temple, 1970, *ad eundem* Lincoln's Inn, 1972. Practised on S Eastern Circuit, then at Chancery Bar, mainly in property and conveyancing matters; a Recorder, 1987–89; London County Courts, 1989–94. Former Mem., Herts and Essex Sessions Bar mess. *Recreations:* playing chess, reading legal and political biographies, dipping into books of history, listening to music, dining out. *Address:* Mayor's and City of London Court, Guildhall Buildings, Basinghall Street, EC2V 5AR. *T:* (020) 7796 5400; 12 New Square, Lincoln's Inn, WC2A 3SW. *T:* (020) 7405 3808. *Club:* Guildhall.

SIMPSON, Richard John, FRCPsych; Member (Lab) Ochil, Scottish Parliament, since 1999; *b* 22 Oct. 1942; *s* of John and Norah Simpson; *m* 1967, Christine McGregor; two *s*. *Educ:* Edinburgh Univ. (MB ChB; DPM). FRCPsych 1994; MRCGP 1996. Pres., Scottish Union of Students, 1967–69. GP, Stirling, 1970–99; Psychiatrist, 1970–99. Hon. Prof., Stirling Univ., 1997. *Publications:* numerous papers and articles in medical research. *Recreations:* watching Rugby, golf. *Address:* Scottish Parliament, Edinburgh EH99 1SP; 49–51 High Street, Alloa FK10 1JF. *T:* (01259) 212518.

SIMPSON, Robert Brian; consultant in interactive media, since 2000; Chairman: Antenna Audio Ltd, since 2001; Empics Ltd, since 2001; *b* 12 Sept. 1944; *s* of Harold and Clara Simpson; *m* 1966, Vivienne Jones; three *s*. *Educ:* Liverpool Inst.; University Coll. London (BA 1966). Asst to Marketing Dir, Holt, Rinehart & Winston (Publishers) Ltd, 1966–68; Asst Develt Manager, later Develt Manager, and Dep. Hd of Inf. Services, Consumers' Assoc., 1968–73; Marketing Manager, Universal News Services Ltd, 1973–74; Marketing Dir, later Man. Dir, University Microfilms Internat. Ltd. 1974–79; Marketing and Develt Manager, later Commercial Manager, Press Assoc., 1979–86; Chief Exec., Universal News Services Ltd, 1986–90; Chm. and Chief Exec., PNA Ltd, 1989–90; Chief Exec., The Press Assoc. Ltd, 1990–2000 (Dir, 1989–2000). Chairman: Two-Ten Communications Ltd, 1990–99; Tellex Monitors Ltd, 1990–99; PA News Ltd, 1994–2000; PA Listings Ltd, 1996–2000; PA WeatherCentre Ltd, 1997–2000; Director: Canada NewsWire, 1986–2000; PA Sporting Life Ltd, 1996–2000; World Assoc. of Newspapers, 1997–2000. Pres., Eur. Alliance of Press Agencies, 1998–99 (Mem., 1990–2000); Mem. Council, CPU, 1995–2000. *Recreations:* music, walking, reading, gardening.

SIMPSON, Robert Watson, (Robin); JP; Director, Brewers and Licensed Retailers Association (formerly Brewers' Society), 1993–98; *b* 14 June 1940; *s* of Robert Simpson and Susan Simpson (*née* Rolland). *Educ:* Perth Academy; University of St Andrews (BSc Hons). Board of Trade (Patent Office), 1962; Dept of Trade (Aviation), 1973; Dept of Industry (Indust. Develt Unit), 1976; Dept of Trade (Shipping), 1979; Department of Trade and Industry: (Management Services and Manpower), 1982; Under Sec., and NE Regl Dir, 1986; Head, Business Task Force Div. (incl. Envmt Unit), 1990–92; Head, Steel, Metals and Minerals Div., 1992. JP 2001. *Recreations:* history, commemorative pottery.

SIMPSON, Robin; *see* Simpson, Robert W.

SIMPSON, Robin Muschamp Garry; QC 1971; *b* 19 June 1927; *s* of Ronald Maitland Simpson, actor and Lila Maravan Simpson (*née* Muschamp); *m* 1st, 1956, Avril Carolyn Harrisson; one *s* one *d*; 2nd, 1968, Mary Faith Laughton-Scott; one *s* one *d*. *Educ:* Charterhouse; Peterhouse, Cambridge (MA). Called to Bar, Middle Temple, 1951, Bencher, 1979; SE Circuit; former Mem., Surrey and S London Sessions; a Recorder of the Crown Court, 1976–86. Mem., CCC Bar Mess. Appeal Steward, British Boxing Bd of Control. *Recreation:* Real tennis. *Address:* 116 Station Road, Barnes, SW13 0NB. *T:* (020) 8878 9898. *Clubs:* Pratt's, MCC.

SIMPSON, Sir Roderick Alexander C.; *see* Cordy-Simpson.

SIMPSON, Prof. Stephen James, PhD; Professor of the Hope Entomological Collections, since 1998, and Associate Head, Department of Zoology, since 2000, University of Oxford; Fellow, Jesus College, Oxford, since 1988; *b* 26 June 1957; *s* of Arthur Leonard and Patricia Simpson; *m* 1984, Lesley Kathryn Dowie; two *s*. *Educ:* C of E Grammar Sch., Brisbane; Univ. of Queensland (BSc Hons 1978); King's Coll., London (PhD 1982); MA Oxon 1986. Univ. of Qld Travelling Schol., 1979–82; University of Oxford: MRC post-doctoral res. asst, Dept of Exptl Psychol., 1982–83; Demonstrator, Dept of Zool., 1983–86; Lectr in Entomol. and Curator, Hope Entomol Collections, 1986–98; Reader in Zool., 1996–98; Fellow, Linacre Coll., 1986–88; Principal Curator, Mus. of Natural Hist., 1989–92. Guest Prof. in Animal Behaviour, Univ. of Basel, 1990; Dist. Vis. Prof., Univ. of Arizona, 1999. Fellow, Wissenschaftskolleg (Inst. for Advanced Study), Berlin, Oct. 2002–. *Publications:* The Right Fly, 1996 (US edn as Angler's Fly Identifier, 1996); Anglers' Flies, 1997; ed books and scientific papers. *Recreations:* fishing, cookery. *Address:* Department of Zoology, University of Oxford, South Parks Road, Oxford OX1 3PS. *T:* (01865) 272976.

SIMPSON, Susan Margaret; *see* Haird, S. M.

SIMPSON, Prof. Thomas James, PhD, DSc; FRS 2001; CChem, FRSC; Professor of Organic Chemistry, University of Bristol, since 1990; *b* 23 Feb. 1947; *s* of Thomas Simpson and Hughina Ross Hay; *m* 1st, 1972, Elizabeth Crosthwaite Nattrass; one *s* one *d*; 2nd, 1987, Prof. Mary Norval. *Educ:* Univ. of Edinburgh (BSc 1st Cl. Hons 1969; Macfarlan-Smith Prize; DSc 1986); Univ. of Bristol (PhD 1973). Sen. Univ. Demonstrator, Dept of Organic Chem., Univ. of Liverpool, 1973–74; Research Fellow: Res. Sch. of Chem., ANU, 1974–76; Dept of Organic Chem., Univ. of Liverpool, 1977–78; Lectr, Dept of Chem., Univ. of Edinburgh, 1978–88; Prof. of Organic Chem., Univ. of Leicester, 1988–89. Mem., Mycotoxins Sub-cttee, MAFF Food Surveillance Gp. Royal Society of Chemistry: Tilden Lectr, 2001; Simonsen Lectr, 2002–; Mem., Perkin Council, 1989–96 (Vice-Pres., 1993–95); Mem., 1989–93, Chm., 1993–96, Perkin Div. Standing Cttee on Meetings; Chm., Editl Bd, Natural Product Reports; Mem., Editl Bd, Chem. in Britain, 1994–. Corday-Morgan Medal and Prize, RSC, 1984. *Publications:* contrib. numerous original papers and review articles. *Recreations:* mountain walking, food and wine. *Address:* School of Chemistry, University of Bristol, Bristol BS8 1TS. *T:* (0117) 928 7656.

SIMPSON, William George; Librarian and College Archivist, Trinity College Dublin, since 1994; *b* 27 June 1945; *s* of William Anion Simpson and Sarah Jane Simpson; *m* 1968, Margaret Lilian Pollard; two *d*. *Educ:* Liverpool Inst.; Univ. of Liverpool (BA 1st class Hons); MA Dublin 1995. ALA. Gilroy Scholar in Semitic Languages, Univ. of Aberdeen, 1968; Asst Librarian, Univ. of Durham, 1969–73; Asst Librarian, Sub-Librarian and Senior Sub-Librarian, John Rylands Univ. Library of Manchester, 1973–85; University Librarian: Surrey, 1985–90; London, 1990–94. Chairman: Guildford Inst., 1987–90; Amer. Studies Library Gp, 1992–94; Mem., Humanities and Social Scis Adv. Cttee, 1991–92, London Adv. Cttee, 1992–94, British Library; Dir, Consortium of University Res. Libraries, 1992–97. Dir, IRIS, 1994–; Member: An Chomhairle Leabharlanna (Liby Council of Ireland), 1995–; Council for Library Co-operation, 1995– (Chm., 1998–2000); Nat. Preservation Adv. Cttee, 1994–96; Nat. Preservation Office Mgt Cttee, 1996– (Chm., 1999–); Chairman: CONUL, 1997–99; Standing Cttee on Legal Deposit, 1999–. Trustee, Worth Library, 1997–. FRAS 1994; FRSA 1988. Jubilee Medal, Charles Univ., Prague, 1998. *Publications:* Libraries, Languages and the Interpretation of the Past, 1988; articles in learned jls and press. *Recreations:* astronomy, genealogy, languages, travel. *Address:* Trinity College Library, College Street, Dublin 2, Ireland. *T:* (1) 6081661; White Cottage, 30 New Road, Milford, Godalming, Surrey GU8 5BE.

SIMPSON, Sir William (James), Kt 1984; Chairman, Health and Safety Commission, 1974–83; *b* Falkirk, 20 May 1920; *s* of William Simpson and Margaret Nimmo; *m* 1942, Catherine McEwan Nicol; one *s*. *Educ:* Victoria Sch. and Falkirk Techn. Sch., Falkirk. Served War of 1939–45, Argyll and Sutherland Highlanders (Sgt). Apprenticed to moulding trade, 1935; returned to foundry, 1946. Mem. Nat. Exec. Council, Amalgamated Union of Foundry Workers, 1955–67; Gen. Sec., AUEW (Foundry Section), 1967–75. Chm. of Labour Party, 1972–73; Member: Race Relations Board; Ct of Inquiry into Flixborough explosion, 1974; Chm., Adv. Cttee on Asbestos, 1976–79. *Publication:* Labour: The Unions and the Party, 1973.

SIMPSON, Prof. (William) James, PhD; Professor of Medieval and Renaissance English, University of Cambridge, since 1999; Fellow, Girton College, Cambridge, since 1989; *b* 16 March 1954; *s* of R. C. Simpson and M. A. Simpson (*née* MacDougall); *m* 1982, Luisella Maria Brunetti; two *s* one *d*. *Educ:* Scotch Coll., Melbourne; Univ. of Melbourne (BA Hons); St Edmund Hall, Oxford (MPhil); Girton Coll., Cambridge (PhD 1996). Lectr in English Lit., Westfield Coll., Univ. of London, 1981–89; Lectr in English, Univ. of Cambridge, and Lectr, Girton Coll., 1989–99. *Publications:* Piers Plowman: an introduction to the B-text, 1990; Sciences and the Self in Medieval Poetry, 1995; contrib. articles to Medium Aevum, Rev. English Studies, Speculum, Traditio, Jl Medieval & Early Modern Studies, etc. *Recreations:* gardening, mountain walking. *Address:* Girton College, Cambridge CB3 0JG. *T:* (01223) 338999; *e-mail:* wjs18@cus.cam.ac.uk.

SIMPSON-JONES, Peter Trevor, CBE 1971; Président d'Honneur, Société Française des Industries Lucas, since 1980 (Président-Directeur Général, 1957–80); *b* 20 March 1914; *s* of Frederick Henry Jones and Constance Agnès Simpson; *m* 1948, Marie-Lucy Sylvain; one *s* one *d*. *Educ:* Royal Navy School. British Chamber of Commerce, France: Vice-Pres., 1967–68 and 1970–72; Pres., 1968–70. Mem., RNSA, 1955–. Chevalier de la Légion d'Honneur, 1948, Officier 1973. *Recreation:* yachting. *Address:* 11 rue Max Blondat, 92 Boulogne-sur-Seine, France. *T:* 48250120. *Clubs:* Special Forces; Polo (Paris).

SIMS, Prof. Andrew Charles Petter, MD; FRCP, FRCPsych, FRCPE; Professor of Psychiatry, since 1979, Chairman, Division of Psychiatry and Behavioural Sciences in Relation to Medicine, 1994–97, University of Leeds; Consultant Psychiatrist, St James's University Hospital, since 1979; *b* 5 Nov. 1938; *s* of late Dr Charles Henry Sims and of Dr Norah Winifred Kennan Sims (*née* Petter); *m* 1964, Ruth Marie Harvey; two *s* two *d*. *Educ:* Monkton Combe Sch.; Emmanuel Coll., Cambridge (MA; MD 1973); Westminster Hosp. DObstRCOG; FRCPsych 1979; FRCPE 1993; FRCP 1997. House Surgeon, Westminster Hosp., 1963–64; Registrar in Psychiatry, Manchester Royal Infirmary,

1966–69; Consultant Psychiatrist, All Saints Hosp., Birmingham, 1971–76; Sen. Lectr, Univ. of Birmingham, 1976–79; Head of Dept of Psychiatry, Univ. of Leeds, 1980–83, 1986–89, 1994–97. Royal College of Psychiatrists: Sub-Dean, 1984–87; Dean, 1987–90; Pres., 1990–93; Dir, Continuing Professional Develt, 1993–97. Chairman: Confidential Inquiry into Homicides and Suicides by Mentally Ill People, 1993–96; Schizophrenia Cttee, Clinical Standards Adv. Gp, DoH, 1994–95; Health Adv. Service 2000, 1997–98. Mem., GMC, 1994–. Hon. FCPS(Pak) 1994; Hon. FCMSA 1997. MD Lambeth, 1995. Editor, Advances in Psychiatric Treatment, 1994–. *Publications:* Neurosis in Society, 1983; Psychiatry (Concise Medical Textbooks), 5th edn (with Sir William Trethowan), 1983, 6th edn (with D. Owens), 1993; (with W. I. Hume) Lecture Notes in Behavioural Sciences, 1984; Symptoms in the Mind: introduction to descriptive psychopathology, 1988 (Italian edn 1993), 2nd edn 1995; (with R. P. Snaith) Anxiety in Clinical Practice, 1988 (German edn 1993); Speech and Language Disorders in Psychiatry, 1995; (with C. Williams) Disorders of Volition, 1999. *Recreations:* gardening, music, theatre, walking. *Address:* Gledholt, Oakwood Grove, Leeds LS8 2PA. *T:* (0113) 206 5646. *Clubs:* Christian Medical Fellowship, Royal Society of Medicine, Athenæum.

SIMS, Prof. Geoffrey Donald, OBE 1971; FREng; Vice-Chancellor, University of Sheffield, 1974–90; *b* 13 Dec. 1926; *s* of Albert Edward Hope Sims and Jessie Elizabeth Sims; *m* 1949, Pamela Audrey Richings; one *s* two *d. Educ:* Wembley County Grammar School; Imperial College of Science and Technology, London. Research physicist, GEC, 1948–54; Sen. Scientific Officer, UKAEA, 1954–56; Lecturer/Senior Lecturer, University College, London, 1956–63; University of Southampton: Prof. and Head of Dept of Electronics, 1963–74; Dean, Faculty of Engrg, 1967–70; Senior Dep. Vice-Chancellor, 1970–72. Member: Council, British Association for the Advancement of Science, 1965–69 (Chm., Sheffield Area Council, 1974–); EDC for Electronics Industry, 1966–75; Adv. Cttee for Scientific and Technical Information, 1969–74; CNAA Electrical Engineering Bd, 1970–73; Planning Cttee for British Library, 1971–73 (Chm., British Library R&D Adv. Cttee, 1975–81); Adv. Council, Science Museum, 1972–84; British Nat. Cttee for Physics, 1972–78; Royal Soc. Cttee on Sci. Information, 1972–81; Electronics Res. Council, 1973–74; Annan Cttee on Future of Broadcasting, 1974–77; Naval Educn Adv. Cttee, 1974–79; Trent RHA, 1975–84; British Council Engrg and Tech. Adv. Cttee, 1976–84 (Chm.); Interim Action Cttee on British Film Industry, 1977–81; EEC Adv. Cttee on Scientific and Technical Trng, 1977–81; Univs Council for Adult and Continuing Educn, 1978–84 (Chm., 1980–84); CNAA, 1979–83; Liaison Cttee on Highly Qualified Technol Manpower, 1979–82; Council, Nat. Inst. of Adult Educn, 1980–84; SRC, later SERC Engrg Bd, 1980–84; Inter Univ. and Polytechnic Council, 1981–91 (IUC and Exec. Cttee, 1974–81; Vice-Chm., IUPC, 1985–91); Cttee for Internat. Co-operation in Higher Educn, 1981–94 (Vice-Chm., 1985–91); EEC Adv. Cttee on Programme Management, 1981–84; BBC Engrg Adv. Cttee, 1981–90 (Chm.); Council, Fellowship of Engrg, 1986–88; Museums and Galleries Commn, 1983–88; Hong Kong City Polytechnic Sub-cttee, 1984–86, Hong Kong Univ. of Sci. and Technol. Sub-cttee, 1987–91, UPGC, Hong Kong; Mem. of Council and Hon. Dep. Treas., ACU, 1984–90; Chm., Council for Commonwealth Educn, 1991–96. UK rep. on Perm. Cttee of Conf. of European Rectors, 1981–84; *ad personem* rep. on Perm. Cttee and Bureau of Conf. of European Rectors, 1984–94; rep. on Liaison Cttee, Rectors' Confs of EEC Mem. States, 1985–90 (Pres., 1987–89). Chairman of Governors: Southampton College of Technology, 1967–69; Southampton Sch. of Navigation, 1972–74; Sheffield High Sch., 1978–85; Fellow, Midland Chapter, Woodard Schools, 1977–97 (Hon. Fellow, 1997); Custos, Worksop Coll., 1984–92. Trustee, Church Burgesses Trust, Sheffield, 1984–, Capital, 1988–89, 1999–2000. FIEE 1963; FCGI 1980; FREng (FEng 1980). Hon. Fellow, Sheffield City Polytechnic, 1990. Hon. DSc: Southampton, 1979; Huddersfield, 2001; Hon. ScD Allegheny Coll., Penn, USA, 1989; Hon. DSc (Eng) QUB, 1990; Hon. LLD: Dundee, 1987; Sheffield, 1991. Symons Medal, ACU, 1991. Founder Mem., 1966, Reviews Editor, 1969–91, Chm., 1987–90, Jl of Materials Science Bd. *Publications:* Microwave Tubes and Semiconductor Devices (with I. M. Stephenson), 1963; Variational Techniques in Electromagnetism (trans.), 1965; numerous papers on microwaves, electronics and education in learned jls. *Recreations:* golf, travel, music. *Address:* Ingleside, 70 Whirlow Lane, Sheffield S11 9QF. *T:* (0114) 236 6196, *Fax:* (0114) 236 6196; *e-mail:* GeoffreyDSims@aol.com. *Club:* Athenæum.

SIMS, Monica Louie, OBE 1971; MA, LRAM, LGSM; Vice President, British Board of Film Classification, 1985–98; *d* of late Albert Charles Sims and Eva Elizabeth Preen, both of Gloucester. *Educ:* Girls' High School, Gloucester; St Hugh's College, Oxford. Tutor in Literature and Drama, Dept of Adult Educn, Hull Univ., 1947–50; Educn Tutor, Nat. Fedn of Women's Institutes, 1950–53; BBC Sound Talks Producer, 1953–55; BBC Television Producer, 1955–64; Editor of Woman's Hour, BBC, 1964–67; Head of Children's Programmes, BBC TV, 1967–78; Controller, BBC Radio 4, 1978–83; Dir of Programmes, BBC Radio, 1983–84; Dir of Prodn, Children's Film and TV Foundn, 1985–97. Chm., Careers Adv. Bd, Univ. of Bristol, 1991–99. Hon. DLitt Bristol, 2000. *Address:* 97 Gloucester Terrace, W2 3HB.

SIMS, Sir Roger (Edward), Kt 1996; JP; *b* 27 Jan. 1930; *s* of late Herbert William Sims and Annie Amy Savidge; *m* 1957, Angela Mathews; two *s* one *d. Educ:* City Boys' Grammar Sch., Leicester; St Olave's Grammar Sch., London. MCInstM. National Service, 1948–50. Coutts & Co., 1950–51; Campbell Booker Carter Ltd, 1953–62; Dodwell & Co. Ltd, 1962–90; Dir, Inchcape International Ltd, 1981–90. Contested (C) Shoreditch and Finsbury, 1966 and 1970. MP (C) Chislehurst, Feb. 1974–1997. PPS to Home Sec., 1979–83. Mem., Nat. Commn of Inquiry into the Prevention of Child Abuse, 1995–96. Mem., GMC, 1989–99. Mem., Central Exec. Cttee, NSPCC, 1980–93. Chm., Bromley Voluntary Sector Trust, 1997–2001. Mem. Chislehurst and Sidcup UDC, 1956–62; JP Bromley, 1960–72 (Dep. Chm. 1970–72); Chm., Juvenile Panel, 1971–72. *Recreations:* swimming; music, especially singing (Mem. Royal Choral Soc., 1950–). *Address:* 68 Towncourt Crescent, Petts Wood, Orpington, Kent BR5 1PJ. *Clubs:* Royal Society of Medicine; Bromley Conservative (Bromley).

SIMS-WILLIAMS, Prof. Nicholas John, PhD; FBA 1988; Professor of Iranian and Central Asian Studies, School of Oriental and African Studies, University of London, since 1994; *b* 11 April 1949; twin *s* of late Rev. M. V. S. Sims-Williams; *m* 1972, Ursula Mary Judith, *d* of late Prof. Hugh Seton-Watson, CBE, FBA; two *d. Educ:* Trinity Hall, Cambridge (BA, MA; PhD 1978). Res. Fellow, Gonville and Caius Coll., Cambridge, 1975–76; Lectr in Iranian Langs, 1976–89, Reader in Iranian Studies, 1989–94, SOAS, Univ. of London. Visiting Professor: Collège de France, 1998–99; Macquarie Univ., 1998–2000; Univ. of Rome 'La Sapienza', 2001. Corresp. Mem., Austrian Acad. of Scis, 1990; Corresp. Etranger, Acad. des Inscriptions et Belles Lettres, Inst de France, 2000. Hirayama Prize for Silk Road Studies, 1996. *Publications:* The Christian Sogdian manuscript C2, 1985 (Prix Ghirshman, Inst. de France, 1988); Sogdian and other Iranian Inscriptions of the Upper Indus, vol. I, 1989, vol. II, 1992; (with James Hamilton) Documents turco-sogdiens du IXe–Xe siècle de Touen-houang, 1990; Partita, 1993; Serenade, 1997; New Light on Ancient Afghanistan: the decipherment of Bactrian, 1997; Bactrian Documents from Northern Afghanistan, vol. I, 2001; contrib. on Iranian and Central Asian langs and culture to learned jls. *Recreation:* music. *Address:* 11 Park Parade, Cambridge CB5 8AL. *T:* (01223) 368903; *e-mail:* ns5@soas.ac.uk.
See also P. P. Sims-Williams.

SIMS-WILLIAMS, Prof. Patrick Philip, PhD; FBA 1996; Professor of Celtic Studies, University of Wales, Aberystwyth (formerly University College of Wales, Aberystwyth), since 1994; *b* 11 April 1949; twin *s* of late Rev. Michael Sims-Williams and Kathleen (*née* Wenborn); *m* 1986, Dr Marged Haycock; one *s* one *d. Educ:* Borden GS, Sittingbourne; Trinity Hall, Cambridge (BA 1972; MA 1975); PhD Birmingham 1980. Cambridge University: Lectr, Dept of Anglo-Saxon, Norse and Celtic, 1977–93; British Acad. Res. Reader, 1988–90; Reader in Celtic and Anglo-Saxon, 1993; Fellow, St John's Coll., 1977–93. O'Donnell Lectr, Oxford Univ., 1981–82, Edinburgh Univ., 1986, Univ. of Wales, 2000–01. Mem., Royal Commn on Ancient and Historical Monuments of Wales, 1998–. Council Member: Irish Texts Soc., 1991–97; Philological Soc., 1997–. Editor, Cambrian Medieval Celtic Studies, 1981–. Gollancz Prize, British Acad., 1992; Antiquity prize, 1998. *Publications:* Religion and Literature in Western England 600–800, 1990; Britain and Early Christian Europe, 1995; Ptolemy: towards a linguistic atlas of the earliest Celtic place-names of Europe, 2000. *Recreations:* music, sailing, carpentry. *Address:* Department of Welsh, University of Wales, Aberystwyth SY23 2AX. *T:* (01970) 622137.
See also N. J. Sims-Williams.

SIMSON, Michael Ronald Fraser, OBE 1966; Secretary of the National Corporation for the Care of Old People, 1948–73; *b* 9 Oct. 1913; *er s* of Ronald Stuart Fraser Simson and Ethel Alice Henderson; *m* 1939, Elizabeth Joan Wilkinson; one *s. Educ:* Winchester Coll.; Christ Church, Oxford. OUAFC 1936 and 1937. Asst Master, West Downs Sch., 1938–40; RNVR, 1941–46; Asst Sec., Nat. Fedn of Housing Socs, 1946–48. Member: Min. of Labour Cttee on Employment of Older Men and Women, 1953–55; Cttee on Local Authority and Allied Personal Social Services (Seebohm Cttee), 1966–68; Supplementary Benefits Commn, 1967–76; Adv. Cttee on Rent Rebates and Rent Allowances, 1973–75, resigned 1975; Personal Social Services Council, 1973–78. *Recreations:* gardening, interested in all forms of sport. *Address:* Beauchamp House, Hatch Beauchamp, Taunton, Somerset TA3 6SG. *T:* (01823) 481427.

SINCLAIR, family name of **Earl of Caithness, Viscount Thurso** and **Baron Sinclair of Cleeve**.

SINCLAIR, 17th Lord *cr* 1449 (Scotland); **Charles Murray Kennedy St Clair,** CVO 1990 (LVO 1953); Major, late Coldstream Guards; Extra Equerry to Queen Elizabeth the Queen Mother since 1953; Lord-Lieutenant, Dumfries and Galloway Region (District of Stewartry), 1982–89 (Vice-Lord-Lieutenant, 1977–82); Member Queen's Body Guard for Scotland (Royal Company of Archers); *b* 21 June 1914; *o s* of 16th Lord Sinclair, MVO, and Violet (*d* 1953), *d* of Col J. Murray Kennedy, MVO; *S* father, 1957; *m* 1968, Anne Lettice, *yr d* of Sir Richard Cotterell, 5th Bt, CBE; one *s* two *d. Educ:* Eton; Magdalene Coll., Cambridge. Served War of 1939–45, Palestine, 1939 (wounded, despatches). Retired as Major Coldstream Guards, 1947. Portcullis Pursuivant of Arms, 1949–57; York Herald, 1957–68, retired. A Representative Peer for Scotland, 1959–63. DL Kirkcudbrightshire, 1969. *Heir: s* Master of Sinclair, *qv. Address:* Knocknalling, St John's Town of Dalry, Castle Douglas, Kirkcudbrightshire, Scotland DG7 3ST. *T:* (01644) 430221.

SINCLAIR, Master of; Hon. Matthew Murray Kennedy St Clair; Director, Saint Property Ltd; *b* 9 Dec. 1968; *s* and *heir* of 17th Lord Sinclair, *qv. Educ:* Glenalmond; RAC Cirencester. MRICS. *Club:* New (Edinburgh).

SINCLAIR OF CLEEVE, 3rd Baron *cr* 1957, of Cleeve, Somerset; **John Lawrence Robert Sinclair;** Founding Member and Secretary, Hackney Local Economic Trading System, since 1992; *b* 6 Jan. 1953; *s* of 2nd Baron Sinclair of Cleeve, OBE, and of Patricia, *d* of late Major Lawrence Hellyer; *S* father, 1985; *m* 1997, Shereen Khan. *Educ:* Winchester College; Manchester Univ. Teaching support staff, an Inner London comprehensive sch., 1984–94. Interest in archaeology. *Recreations:* motor cycling, mime, music.

SINCLAIR, Alexander Riddell; HM Diplomatic Service, retired; *b* 28 Aug. 1917; *s* of Henry W. Sinclair and Mary Turner; *m* 1948, Alice Evelyn Nottingham; three *d. Educ:* Greenock High School. DipCAM. Inland Revenue, 1935–37; Admty, 1938–47 (Comdr RNVR, 1945–46); 2nd Sec., HM Embassy, Moscow, 1947–48; Vice-Consul: Detroit, 1949; Mosul, 1950; FO, 1952; 1st Secretary, HM Embassy: Saigon, 1953–56; Amman, 1957–58; FO, 1959; 1st Sec. (Cultural), Budapest, 1962; FO, 1964; 1st Secretary (Information): Beirut, 1967–70; Rome, 1970–71; Consul-Gen., Genoa, 1972–76; FCO Library, 1977–85. Pres., St Andrews Probus Club, 1997–98. Silver Jubilee Medal, 1977. *Publications:* literary articles in learned jls. *Recreations:* reading, book browsing, walking. *Address:* 2 Ruthven Place, St Andrews, Fife KY16 8SJ. *Club:* Civil Service.

SINCLAIR, Andrew Annandale; author; Managing Director, Timon Films, since 1967; *b* 21 Jan. 1935; *m* 1960, Marianne, *d* of Mr and Mrs Arsène Alexandre; *m* 1972, Miranda, *o d* of Mr and Hon. Mrs George Seymour; one *s*; *m* 1984, Sonia Lady Melchett (*see* S. E. Sinclair), *d* of Dr and Mrs Roland Graham. *Educ:* Eton Coll.; Trinity Coll., Cambridge (BA, PhD); Harvard. Ensign, Coldstream Guards, 1953–55. Harkness Fellow of the Commonwealth Fund, 1959–61; Dir of Historical Studies, Churchill Coll., Cambridge, 1961–63; Fellow of American Council of Learned Societies, 1963–64; Lectr in American History, University Coll., London, 1965–67. Dir/Writer Mem., ACTT. FRSL 1973; Fellow Soc. of American Historians, 1974. Somerset Maugham Literary Prize, 1966. *Film:* (dir) Under Milk Wood, 1971. *Publications:* The Breaking of Bumbo, 1958; My Friend Judas, 1959; The Project, 1960; Prohibition, 1962; The Hallelujah Bum, 1963; The Available Man: Warren E. Harding, 1964; The Better Half, 1964; The Raker, 1965; Concise History of the United States, 1966; Albion Triptych: Gog, 1967, Magog, 1972, King Ludd, 1988; The Greek Anthology, 1967; Adventures in the Skin Trade, 1968; The Last of the Best, 1969; Guevara, 1970; Dylan Thomas: poet of his people, 1975; The Surrey Cat, 1976; The Savage, 1977; Jack: the biography of Jack London, 1977; A Patriot for Hire, 1978; John Ford, 1979; The Facts in the Case of E. A. Poe, 1979; Corsair, 1981; The Other Victoria, 1981; Sir Walter Raleigh and the Age of Discovery, 1984; Beau Bumbo, 1985; The Red and the Blue, 1986; Spiegel, 1987; War Like a Wasp, 1989; (ed) The War Decade, an anthology of the 1940s, 1989; The Need to Give, 1990; The Far Corners of the Earth, 1991; The Naked Savage, 1991; The Strength of the Hills, 1992; The Sword and the Grail, 1993; Francis Bacon: his life and violent times, 1993; In Love and Anger, 1994; Arts and Cultures: the history of the fifty years of the Arts Council of Great Britain, 1995; Jerusalem: the endless crusade, 1996; Death by Fame: a life of Elisabeth Empress of Austria, 1998; The Discovery of the Grail, 1998; Dylan the Bard: a life of Dylan Thomas, 1999; The Secret Scroll, 2001. *Recreations:* old cities, old movies. *Address:* Flat 20, Millennium House, 132 Grosvenor Road, SW1V 3JY.

SINCLAIR, Carolyn Elizabeth Cunningham, (Mrs S. J. Bowen); Director, Constitutional and Community Policy Directorate, and Registrar of the Baronetage, Home Office, since 1996; *b* 13 July 1944; *d* of John Archibald Sinclair and Grace Margaret

Stuart Sinclair (*née* Cunningham); *m* 1979, Stephen John Bowen. *Educ:* Laurel Bank Sch., Glasgow; Brown Univ., RI; Edinburgh Univ. (MA Hist.); Univ. of E Africa (Leverhulme Schol.; MA Pol Sci.). Joined FCO, 1968; Vienna, 1970–73; Private Sec. to Minister of State, 1977–78; transferred to HM Treasury, 1979; Prime Minister's Policy Unit, 1988–92; transf. to Home Office, as Asst Under-Sec. of State, 1992. *Recreations:* gardening, listening to music, reading, seeing friends. *Address:* Home Office, 50 Queen Anne's Gate, SW1H 9AT. *Club:* Royal Automobile.

SINCLAIR, Charles James Francis; Group Chief Executive, Daily Mail and General Trust plc, since 1988; *b* 4 April 1948; *s* of Sir George (Evelyn) Sinclair, *qv*; *m* 1974, Nicola Bayliss; two *s*. *Educ:* Winchester Coll.; Magdalen Coll., Oxford (BA). ACA 1974. VSO, Zambia, 1966–67. Dearden Farrow, CA, 1970; joined Associated Newspapers Holdings, 1975; Asst Man. Dir and Mem. Main Bd, 1986; Man. Dir, 1988 (Associated Newspapers Holdings became the wholly-owned operating subsid. of Daily Mail and General Trust, 1988); Director: Euromoney Institutional Investor PLC, 1985–; Schroders plc, 1990–; Reuters Group plc, 1994–. Chm. of Trustees, Minack Theatre Trust, Porthcurno, Cornwall, 1985–. *Recreations:* opera, fishing, ski-ing. *Address:* Northcliffe House, 2 Derry Street, Kensington, W8 5TT. *Clubs:* Athenæum; Vincent's (Oxford).

SINCLAIR, Sir Clive (Marles), Kt 1983; Chairman, Sinclair Research Ltd, since 1979; *b* 30 July 1940; *s* of late George William Carter Sinclair and of Thora Edith Ella (*née* Marles); *m* 1962, Ann (*née* Trevor Briscoe) (marr. diss. 1985); two *s* one *d*. *Educ:* Boxgrove Prep. Sch., Guildford; Highgate; Reading; St George's Coll., Weybridge. Editor, Bernards Publishers Ltd, 1958–61; Chairman: Sinclair Radionics Ltd, 1962–79; Sinclair Browne Ltd, 1981–85; Cambridge Computer Ltd, 1986–90; Dir, Shaye Communications Ltd, 1986–91. Vis. Fellow, Robinson Coll., Cambridge, 1982–85; Vis. Prof., Dept of Elec. Engrg, Imperial Coll. of Science, Technol. and Medicine, London, 1984–92 (Hon. Fellow, 1984). Chm., British Mensa, 1980–97 (Hon. Pres., 2001–). Hon. Fellow UMIST, 1984. Hon. DSc: Bath, 1983; Warwick, 1983; Heriot-Watt, 1983. Mullard Award, Royal Soc., 1984. *Publications:* Practical Transistor Receivers, 1959; British Semiconductor Survey, 1963. *Recreations:* music, poetry, mathematics, science, poker. *Address:* 1A Spring Gardens, Trafalgar Square, SW1A 2BB. *T:* (office) (020) 7839 6868, *Fax:* (020) 7839 6622, *T:* (home) (020) 7839 7744. *Clubs:* National Liberal, Chelsea Arts.

SINCLAIR of Freswick, Maj.-Gen. David Boyd A.; *see* Alexander-Sinclair.

SINCLAIR, Prof. David Cecil; Emeritus Professor, University of Western Australia; *b* 28 Aug. 1915; *s* of Norman James Sinclair and Annie Smart Sinclair; *m* 1945, Grace Elizabeth Simondson, Melbourne, Vic.; one *s* one *d*. *Educ:* Merchiston Castle Sch.; St Andrews University. MB, ChB (Commendation) St Andrews, 1937; MD (Hons and Rutherford Gold Medal) St Andrews, 1947; MA Oxon, 1948; DSc Western Australia, 1965. Served in RAMC, 1940–46: AMF, 1943–45; Head of Physiology Sect., Aust. Chem. Warfare Research and Experimental Stn, 1943–44; Dep. Chief Supt, Aust. Field Experimental Stn, 1944–45. Sen. Res. Off., Dept of Human Anatomy, Oxford, 1946–49; Univ. Demonstrator in Anatomy, Oxford, 1949–56; Lectr in Anatomy, Pembroke Coll., Oxford, 1950–56; Lectr in Anatomy, Ruskin Sch. of Fine Art, 1950–56; first Prof. of Anatomy, Univ. of W Australia, 1957–64, Dean of Med. Sch., 1964; Regius Prof. of Anatomy, Univ. of Aberdeen, 1965–75; Dir of Postgrad. Med. Educn, Queen Elizabeth II Med. Centre, WA, 1975–80. FRCSE 1966. Life Governor, Aust. Postgrad. Fedn in Medicine, 1983. *Publications:* Medical Students and Medical Sciences, 1955; An Introduction to Functional Anatomy, 1957 (5th edn 1975); A Student's Guide to Anatomy, 1961; Cutaneous Sensation, 1967, Japanese edn 1969; Human Growth after Birth, 1969 (6th edn 1998); Muscles and Fascia (section in Cunningham's Anatomy), 11th edn, 1972, 12th edn, 1981; Basic Medical Education, 1972; The Nerves of the Skin (section in Physiology and Pathophysiology of the Skin, ed Jarrett), 1973; Growth, section in Textbook of Human Anatomy (ed Hamilton), 1976; Mechanisms of Cutaneous Sensation, 1981; Not a Proper Doctor (autobiog.), 1989; Outside the Dissecting Room, 1989; papers on chemical warfare, neurological anatomy, experimental psychology, and medical education; Editor, Jl of Anatomy, 1970–73. *Recreations:* reading, writing, photography, chess problems. *Address:* Flat 3, Netherby, Netherby Road, Cults, Aberdeen AB15 9HL.

SINCLAIR, Douglas, CBE 2001; Chief Executive, Fife Council, since 1999; *b* 28 Jan. 1946; *s* of Douglas Matheson Sinclair and Agnes Jack Sinclair; *m* 1969, Mairi MacPhee; two *d*. *Educ:* Edinburgh Univ. (MA Hons Politics). Admin. Asst, Midlothian, E Lothian and Peebles Social Work Dept, 1969–72; Admin. Officer, Barnardo's, Scotland, 1972–75; Depute Dir of Admin, 1975–78, Dir of Admin, 1978–85, Western Isles Is Council; Chief Executive: Ross and Cromarty Council, 1985–90; Central Regl Council, 1990–95; COSLA, 1995–99. *Recreations:* Scottish literature, music, gardening, walking. *Address:* Fife Council, Fife House, North Street, Glenrothes, Fife KY7 5LT. *T:* (01592) 413999.

SINCLAIR, Maj.-Gen. George Brian, CB 1983; CBE 1975; Engineer-in-Chief (Army), 1980–83; *b* 21 July 1928; *s* of Thomas S. Sinclair and Blanche Sinclair; *m* 1953, Edna Margaret Richardson; two *s* one *d*. *Educ:* Christ's College, Finchley; RMA Sandhurst. Commissioned, Royal Engineers, 1948; served UK, BAOR, Korea, and Christmas Island, 1948–66; Directing Staff, Staff College, Camberley, 1967–69; CRE, Near East, 1970–71; Col GS, HQ 1st British Corps, 1972–74; Nat. Defence Coll., India, 1975; Commandant Royal School of Military Engineering, 1976–77; BGS, Military Operations, MoD, 1978–80. Col Comdt, RE, 1983–91; Hon. Col, Engineer and Transport Staff Corps, 1988–93. Vice Pres., Red R (formerly Register of Engrs for Disaster Relief), 1985–98; Trustee: Imperial War Mus., 1990–2000; RE Museum Foundn, 1993–2001. Mem., Smeatonian Soc. of Civil Engrs, 1985–. Governor, King's Sch., Rochester, 1984–97. Freeman, City of London, 1981. DL Kent, 1996–97. *Publication:* The Staff Corps, The History of the Engineer and Logistic Staff Corps RE, 2001. *Recreations:* hill walking, bird watching and discussion. *Address:* Brockie's Hole, The Croft, St Boswells, Roxburghshire TD6 0AE. *Club:* Army and Navy (Chm., 1995–97; Trustee, 1999–).

SINCLAIR, Sir George (Evelyn), Kt 1960; CMG 1956; OBE 1950; *b* Cornwall, 6 Nov. 1912; 2nd *s* of late F. Sinclair, Chynance, St Buryan, Cornwall; *m* 1st, 1941, Katharine Jane Burdekin (*d* 1971); one *s* three *d*; 2nd, 1972, Mary Violet, *widow* of George Lester Sawday, Saxmundham, Suffolk. *Educ:* Abingdon School; Pembroke College, Oxford (MA; Hon. Fellow, 1986). Entered Colonial Administrative Service, 1936; appointed to Gold Coast Administration; Asst District Comr, 1937. Military service, 1940–43. District Commissioner, Gold Coast, 1943; seconded to Colonial Office, 1943–45; Sec. to Commn on Higher Education in West Africa, 1943–45; returned to Gold Coast, 1945; Senior Assistant Colonial Secretary, 1947; Principal Assistant Secretary, 1950; Regional Officer, Trans-Volta Togoland Region, 1952; Deputy Governor, Cyprus, 1955–60; retired, 1961. MP (C) Dorking, Surrey, Oct. 1964–1979. Member, Parly Select Committees on: Procedure, 1965–66; Race Relations, 1969–70; Overseas Aid, 1969–70; Race Relations and Immigration, 1970–74; Members Interests, 1975; Abortion Act (Amendment) Bill; Joint Secretary: Cons. Parly Commonwealth Affairs Cttee, 1966–68; Cons. Parly Educn Cttee, 1974–79, Vice-Chm., 1974; Member: Intermediate Technology Develt Gp (Vice-Pres., 1966–79; Dir, 1979–82); Nat. Exec. Cttee, UNA (UK Branch), 1968–70; Council, Overseas Services Resettlement Bureau; Council of PDSA, 1964–70; Council, Christian Aid, 1973–78; Steering Cttee, UN/FPA World Conf. of Parliamentarians on population and develt, 1978–79; Vice-Chm., Family Planning Assoc., 1979–81; Consultant: UN Fund for Population Affairs, 1979–82; IPPF, 1979–83; special advr to Global Cttee on Population and Develt, 1982–88. Trustee: Runnymede Trust, 1969–75; Human Rights Trust, 1971–74; Physically Handicapped and Able Bodied (Foundn Trustee), 1973–81; Wyndham Place Trust. Mem., Wimbledon Borough Council, 1962–65. Member, Board of Governors: Abingdon Sch., 1970–87 (Chm., 1971–79); Felixstowe Coll., 1980–87; Campion Sch., Athens, 1983–94; Chm., Assoc. of Governing Bodies of Independent Schools, 1979–84 (Mem., 1973–); Member: Direct Grant Jt Cttee, 1974–80; Indep. Schools Jt Council, 1979–84 (Chm. 1980–83, Dep. Chm., 1984); Council, Oxford Soc., 1982–93. Chm. Planning Office, 1988 Internat. Conf. of Spiritual and Parly Leaders on Human Survival, 1986–88. *Recreations:* golf, fishing. *Address:* Rookery Orchard, Kelsale-cum-Carlton, Saxmundham, Suffolk IP17 2NN; South Minack, Porthcurno, Cornwall TR19 6JU. *Clubs:* Athenæum, Royal Commonwealth Society; Aldeburgh Golf.

See also C. J. F. Sinclair.

SINCLAIR, Hon. Ian David, OC 1979; QC (Can.) 1961; Member, Senate of Canada, 1983–88; *b* Winnipeg, 27 Dec. 1913; *s* of late John David Sinclair and late Lillian Sinclair; *m* 1942, Ruth Beatrice, *d* of Robert Parsons Drennan, Winnipeg; two *s* two *d*. *Educ:* public schs, Winnipeg; Univ. of Manitoba (BA Econs 1937); Manitoba Law School (LLB 1941). Barrister, Guy Chappell & Co., Winnipeg, 1937–41; Lectr in Torts, Univ. of Manitoba, 1942–43; joined Canadian Pacific Law Dept as Asst Solicitor, Winnipeg, 1942; Solicitor, Montreal, 1946; Asst to General Counsel, 1951; General Solicitor, 1953; Vice-Pres. and Gen. Counsel, 1960; Vice-Pres., Law, 1960; Canadian Pacific Railway Co.: Vice-Pres., Dir and Mem. Exec. Cttee, 1961; Pres., 1966; Chief Exec. Officer, 1969; Chm. and Chief Exec. Officer: Canadian Pacific Ltd, 1972–81; Canadian Pacific Enterprises Ltd, 1972–82 (Chm., 1982–84); Director: Canadian Investment Fund, Ltd, 1972–89; Canadian Marconi Co., 1967–; Union Carbide Canada Ltd, 1968–; Public Dir, Investment Dealers Assoc. of Canada, 1984–88; Public Gov., Car Investors Protection Fund, 1990–; Mem., Internat. Adv. Cttee, Chase Manhattan Bank, N America, 1973–87; Trustee, Alliance Global Fund, 1987–. Hon. LLD Manitoba, 1967; Hon. DBA Laval, 1981; Hon. DCL Acadia, 1982. Mem., Canadian Business Hall of Fame. *Club:* Toronto (Toronto).

SINCLAIR, Rt Hon. Ian (McCahon); AC 2001; PC 1977; Chairman, Foundation for Rural and Regional Renewal, since 1999; *b* 10 June 1929; *s* of George McCahon Sinclair and Gertrude Hazel Sinclair; *m* 1st, 1956, Margaret Tarrant (*d* 1967); one *s* two *d*; 2nd, 1970, Rosemary Fenton; one *s*. *Educ:* Knox Grammar Sch., Wahroonga, NSW; Sydney Univ. BA, LLB. Grazier. Mem. Legislative Council, NSW, 1961–63; MP (Nat.) New England, NSW, 1963–98; Minister for: Social Services, 1965–68; Trade and Industry (Minister Assisting Minister), 1966–71; Shipping and Transport, 1968–71; Primary Industry, 1971–72; Leader of House for Opposition, 1974–75; Country Party spokesman for Defence, Foreign Affairs, Law and Agriculture, 1973; Opposition spokesman on primary industry, 1974–75; Leader of House, 1975–79; Minister for: Agriculture and N Territory, Nov.–Dec. 1975; Primary Industry, 1975–79; Special Trade Representations, 1980; Communications, 1980–82; Defence, 1982–83; Leader of the House for the Opposition, 1983–89; Shadow Minister: Defence, 1983–87; Trade and Resources, 1987–89; of State, Jan.–May 1994; Speaker, House of Reps, Australia, 1998. Member Committee: House of Reps Standing Orders, 1974–79, 1980–82, 1983–84; Privileges, 1980–82; Legal and Constitutional Affairs, 1990–98; Jt Foreign Affairs, Defence and Trade, 1990–98 (Chm., 1996–98); Nat. Crime Authority, 1990–98; Member: Jt Standing Cttee on Migration Regulations, 1990–98; Jt Cttee on Corps and Securities, 1990–98; Parly Code of Conduct Working Gp, 1994–96. Perm. Rep., Exec., IPU, 1996–98; Chm., Aust. Parly Gps for UK, PNG, Uruguay and Vietnam, 1996–98. Dep. Leader, 1971–84, Leader, 1984–89, Nat. Party of Australia. Chairman: Australian Constitutional Convention, 1998; Australian Rural Summit, 1999; Co-Chairman: NSW Drugs Summit, 1999; NSW Salinity Summit, 2000. Chm., Harts Australasia Ltd, 1999–. Chairman: Good Beginnings (Australia), 2000–; Australia Taiwan Business Council, 2000–. Pres., Austcare, 2000–. Adjunct Prof. of Social Scis (Pol Sci.), Univ. of New England, 2000–. DUniv New England, 1999. *Address:* Glenclair, Bendemeer, NSW 2355, Australia. *T:* (2) 67696559, *Fax:* (2) 67696666; *e-mail:* iansinclair@ozemail.com.au. *Clubs:* Australian, American, Union (Sydney); Tamworth; Killara Golf.

SINCLAIR, Sir Ian (McTaggart), KCMG 1977 (CMG 1972); QC 1979; Barrister-at-Law; Visiting Professor of International Law, King's College, London, 1989–93; *b* 14 Jan. 1926; *s* of late John Sinclair, company director; *m* 1954, Barbara Elizabeth (*née* Lenton); two *s* one *d*. *Educ:* Merchiston Castle Sch. (Scholar); King's Coll., Cambridge; BA 1948, LLB 1949 (1st cl. hons). Served Intelligence Corps, 1944–47. Called to the Bar, Middle Temple, 1952; Bencher, 1980. Asst Legal Adviser, Foreign Office, 1950–56; Legal Adviser, HM Embassy, Bonn, 1957–60; Asst Legal Adviser, FO, 1960–64; Legal Adviser, UK Mission to the UN, New York, and HM Embassy, Washington, 1964–67; Foreign and Commonwealth Office: Legal Counsellor, 1967–71; Dep. Legal Advr, 1971–72; Second Legal Advr, 1973–75; Legal Advr, 1976–84. Has been Legal Adviser to UK delegn at numerous internat. confs, incl. Geneva Conf. on Korea and Indo-China, 1954, and Brussels negotiations for UK entry into the EEC, 1961–63; Dep. Chm., UK delegn to Law of Treaties Conf., Vienna, 1968–69; Legal Adviser to UK delegn on negotiations for UK entry into EEC, 1970–72; Member: Bureau of European Cttee on Legal Co-operation, Council of Europe, 1979–81; Panel of Conciliators, Annex to Vienna Convention on Law of Treaties, 1981–; Internat. Law Commn, 1981–86; Panel of Arbitrators, Internat. Centre for Settlement of Investment Disputes, 1988–; Panel of Legal Experts under INTELSAT Convention, 1990–96; Perm. Ct of Arbitration, 1992–. Mem., Committee of Management: British Inst. of Internat. and Comparative Law, 1976–; Inst. of Advanced Legal Studies, 1980–84. Associate Mem., Inst de Droit Internat., 1983, elected Mem., 1987; Hon. Mem., Amer. Soc. of Internat. Law, 1987. *Publications:* Vienna Convention on the Law of Treaties, 1973, 2nd edn 1984; International Law Commission, 1987; articles in British Yearbook of International Law, International and Comparative Law Qly and other legal jls. *Recreations:* golf, fishing, watching sea-birds. *Address:* Lassington, Chithurst, Petersfield, Hants GU31 5EU. *T:* (01730) 815370; 10B South Park Road, Wimbledon, SW19 8ST. *T:* (020) 8543 1843; (chambers) Blackstone Chambers, Blackstone House, Temple, EC4Y 9BW. *T:* (020) 7583 1770. *Club:* Athenæum.

SINCLAIR, Isabel Lillias, (Mrs J. G. MacDonald); QC (Scotland) 1964; Sheriff of Lothian and Borders (formerly Roxburgh, Berwick, and Selkirk), 1968–79, now Honorary Sheriff; Honorary Sheriff of Bute; *d* of William Sinclair, Glasgow, and Isabella (*née* Thomson), Glasgow; *m* 1938, J. Gordon MacDonald (decd), BL, Solicitor, Glasgow. *Educ:* Shawlands Academy; Glasgow Univ. MA 1932; BL 1946. Worked as a newspaper-woman from 1932. Admitted to Faculty of Advocates, Edinburgh, 1949. Sheriff-Substitute of Lanarkshire at Airdrie, 1966–68. *Address:* 30 Ravelston Garden, Edinburgh EH4 3LE. *Clubs:* Caledonian, Royal Over-Seas League (Edinburgh).

SINCLAIR, Jeremy Theodorson; Partner, M & C Saatchi, since 1995; *b* 4 Nov. 1946; *s* of Lilian Theodora Sinclair and Donald Alan Forrester Sinclair; *m* 1976, Jacqueline Margaret Metcalfe; two *s* one *d* (and one *s* decd). *Educ:* Rannoch Sch., Perthshire; Watford Art Sch. Saatchi & Saatchi and Co.: Jt Founder, 1970; Dir, 1973–95; Head of Creative Dept, 1973–86; Chairman: UK Agency, 1982–86; Saatchi & Saatchi International, 1986–95. Pres., D&AD, 1987. Chairman: Educn Renaissance Trust, 1999–; Sculpture Acad., 1999–. *Recreations:* philosophy, economics, gardening. *Address:* M & C Saatchi, 36 Golden Square, W1F 9EE. *T:* (020) 7543 4500.

SINCLAIR, Prof. John McHardy; Professor of Modern English Language, University of Birmingham, 1965–2000; President, Tuscan Word Centre, since 1996; *b* 14 June 1933; *s* of late George Ferguson Sinclair and Isabella (*née* Palmer); *m* 1st, Margaret Myfanwy Lloyd; two *s* one *d*; 2nd, Elena Tognini Bonelli; one *s* one *d*. *Educ:* George Heriot's Sch., Edinburgh; Edinburgh Univ. (MA). Served Royal Air Force (Flt-Lt), 1955–58. Lectr, Edinburgh Univ., 1959–65. Adjunct Prof., Shanghai Jiao Tong Univ., 1986–; Hon. Prof. Res. Fellow, Univ. of Glasgow, 1997–. Pres., Trans-European Language Resources Infrastructure, 1997–. Hon. Life Mem., Linguistics Assoc. of GB, 2000. Hon. DPhil Gothenburg, 1998. *Publications:* A Course in Spoken English—Grammar, 1972; (with R. M. Coulthard) Towards an Analysis of Discourse, 1975, 2nd edn 1978; (with D. C. Brazil) Teacher Talk, 1982; Corpus, Concordance, Collocation, 1991; Founding Editor in Chief, Cobuild: Collin's Cobuild English Language Dictionary, 1987; Collins Cobuild English Grammar, 1990. *Address:* Tuscan Word Centre, Vellano 409, 51010 Pescia (PT), Italy. *T:* (0572) 409251, *Fax:* (0572) 409253; *e-mail:* jms@twc.it.

SINCLAIR, Karen; Member (Lab) Clwyd South, National Assembly for Wales, since 1999; *b* 20 Nov. 1952; *m* 1973, Mike Sinclair; one *s* one *d*. *Educ:* Grove Park Girls' Sch., Wrexham. Contracted Care Manager, Wrexham Social Services, 1990–99. CAB Advr, 1995–97. Member (Lab): Glyndwr DC, 1988–95; Denbighshire CC, 1997–99. *Recreations:* family, local politics, horse riding. *Address:* National Assembly for Wales, Cardiff Bay, Cardiff CF99 1NA; (constituency) 6 Oak Mews, Oak Street, Llangollen, Denbighshire LL20 8RP.

SINCLAIR, Air Vice-Marshal Sir Laurence (Frank), GC 1941; KCB 1957 (CB 1946); CBE 1943; DSO 1940 (and Bar, 1943); *b* 13 June 1908; *m* 1941, Valerie (*d* 1990), *d* of Lt-Col Joseph Dalton White; one *s* one *d*. *Educ:* Imperial Service Coll.; RAF Coll. Cranwell. Comd No 110 Sqdn in 1940; Comd RAF Watton, 1941; Comd Tactical Light Bomber Force in North Africa and Italy, 1943–44; ADC to King George VI, 1943–44; subsequently Sen. Air Staff Officer, Balkan Air Force; Imperial Defence Coll., 1947; commanded No 2 Light Bomber Group (Germany), 1948–49; Assistant Commandant RAF Staff College, 1949–50; Commandant, Royal Air Force College Cranwell, 1950–52; Commandant, School of Land/Air Warfare, 1952–53; Asst Chief of the Air Staff (Operations), 1953–55; Comdr British Forces, Arabian Peninsula, 1955–57; Commandant Joint Services Staff College, 1958–60, retired from RAF. Controller of Ground Services, Min. of Aviation, 1960–61; Controller, Nat. Air Traffic Control Services, Min. of Aviation, and MoD, 1962–66. Legion of Merit (American), 1943; Legion of Honour, 1944; Partisan Star (Yugoslavia). *Address:* The Old Prebendal House, Shipton-under-Wychwood, Oxford OX7 6BQ.

SINCLAIR, Martin John; Assistant Auditor General, National Audit Office, since 1999; *b* 24 April 1957; *s* of late Malcolm Sinclair and of Susan Sinclair; *m* 1996, Joke Pouw; one *s* one *d*. *Educ:* Glasgow Univ. (MPhil Town and Regl Planning). CPFA 1985. Joined Nat. Audit Office, 1981 (Mem., Mgt Bd, 1999-). *Recreations:* hill-walking, ski-ing, reading. *Address:* National Audit Office, 157-197 Buckingham Palace Road, SW1W 9SP. *T:* (020) 7798 7180.

SINCLAIR, Rt Rev. Maurice Walter; *see* Northern Argentina, Bishop of.

SINCLAIR, Michael; *see* Shea, M. S. MacA.

SINCLAIR, Sir Patrick (Robert Richard), 10th Bt *cr* 1704 (NS), of Dunbeath, Caithness-shire; barrister; *b* 21 May 1936; s of Alexander Robert Sinclair (Robin) (*d* 1972) (*b* of 8th Bt) and Vera Mabel (*d* 1981), *d* of late Walter Stephings Baxendale; *S* cousin, 1990; *m* 1974, Susan Catherine Beresford Davies, *e d* of Geoffrey Clive Davies, OBE; one *s* one *d*. *Educ:* Winchester; Oriel Coll., Oxford. Nat. Service, RNVR, 1954–56 (Actg Sub-Lieut). Called to the Bar, Lincoln's Inn, 1961, Bencher, 1994; in practice at Chancery Bar. *Recreations:* sailing, tennis. *Heir:* *s* William Robert Francis Sinclair, *b* 27 March 1979. *Address:* 5 New Square, Lincoln's Inn, WC2A 3RJ. *T:* (020) 7404 0404. *Club:* Pin Mill Sailing (Suffolk).

SINCLAIR, Rear-Adm. Peter Ross, AC 1992 (AO (mil.) 1986); Governor of New South Wales, 1990–96; farmer, Flagship Poll Hereford Stud; *b* 16 Nov. 1934; *s* of late G. P. Sinclair; *m* 1957, Shirley, *d* of J. A. McLellan; one *s* two *d*. *Educ:* North Sydney Boys' High Sch.; Royal Aust. Naval Coll.; Royal Coll. of Defence Studies. jssc. Joined RAN 1948; served HM Australian ships Australia, Tobruk, Vengeance, Arunta, Swan, Sydney, Vendetta, Vampire, Penguin, HMS Maidstone, HMS Jutland; CO HMAS Duchess, 1970–72; CO HMAS Hobart, 1974–77; Dir, Naval Plans, 1979–80; Dir-Gen., Mil. Staff Branch, Strategic and Internat. Policy Div., Defence Dept, 1980–82; Chief of Staff, 1983–84; First Comdt, Aust. Defence Force Acad., 1984–86; Maritime Comdr Australia, 1986–90 and Dep. Chief of Naval Staff, 1989. Chm. Council, Order of Australia. Hon. FIEAust 1994; CPEng 1994. DUniv Sydney, 1992. KStJ 1991. *Recreations:* painting, sketching, whittling, reading, cricket, golf, tennis. *Address:* Post Office, Tea Gardens, NSW 2324, Australia.

SINCLAIR, Sonia Elizabeth, (Mrs A. A. Sinclair); Board Member, Royal Court Theatre, since 1974; *b* 6 Sept. 1928; *d* of Col R. H. Graham; *m* 1st, 1947, Hon. Julian Mond, later 3rd Baron Melchett (*d* 1973); one *s* two *d*; 2nd, 1984, Dr Andrew Annandale Sinclair, *qv*. *Educ:* Royal School, Bath. Board Member: NSPCC, 1960–70; Nat. Theatre, then RNT, 1984–94. JP Marylebone, 1962–72. *Publications:* Tell Me, Honestly, 1964; Someone is Missing, 1987; Passionate Quests, 1991. *Recreations:* reading, walking, swimming, foreign travel. *Address:* Flat 20, Millennium House, 132 Grosvenor Road, SW1V 3JY. *T:* (020) 7976 6958.
See also Baron Melchett.

SINCLAIR-LOCKHART, Sir Simon (John Edward Francis), 15th Bt *cr* 1636 (NS); *b* 22 July 1941; *s* of Sir Muir Edward Sinclair-Lockhart, 14th Bt, and of Olga Ann, *d* of late Claude Victor White-Parsons, Hawkes Bay, NZ; *S* father, 1985; *m* 1973, Felicity Edith, *d* of late I. L. C. Stewart, NZ; one *s* one *d* (and one *s* decd). *Heir:* *yr* twin *s* James Lachlan Sinclair-Lockhart, *b* 12 Sept. 1973. *Address:* 62 Muritai Crescent, Havelock North, Hawke's Bay, New Zealand.

SINCLAIR-STEVENSON, Christopher Terence; literary agent, since 1995; *b* 27 June 1939; *s* of late George Sinclair-Stevenson, MBE and Gloria Sinclair-Stevenson; *m* 1965, Deborah Susan (*née* Walker-Smith). *Educ:* Eton Coll.; St John's Coll., Cambridge (MA). Joined Hamish Hamilton Ltd, 1961, Dir, 1970, Man. Dir, 1974–89; Man. Dir, Sinclair-Stevenson Ltd, 1989–92; Publisher, Sinclair-Stevenson, and Editor-in-Chief, Reed Consumer Books, 1992–95; Consultant, Sinclair-Stevenson, 1995–96. *Publications:* The Gordon Highlanders, 1968; Inglorious Rebellion, 1971; The Life of a Regiment, 1974; Blood Royal, 1979; That Sweet Enemy, 1987; (ed) Enjoy!, 2000. *Recreations:* music, travel, food, the written word. *Address:* 3 South Terrace, SW7 2TB. *T:* (020) 7584 8087.

SINDALL, Adrian John, CMG 1993; HM Diplomatic Service, retired; Chairman, Council for British Research in the Levant, since 1997; *b* 5 Oct. 1937; *s* of Stephen Sindall and Clare Mallet; *m* 1st, 1958; one *s* one *d*; 2nd, 1978, Jill Margaret Cowley. *Educ:* Battersea Grammar Sch. FO, 1956–58; ME Centre for Arab Studies, 1958–60; Third Sec. (Commercial), Baghdad, 1960–62; Second Sec., British Embassy, Rabat, 1962–67; First Secretary: FCO, 1967–70; Beirut, 1970–72; First Sec. and Head of Chancery, British Embassy, Lima, 1972–76; FCO, 1976–79; Counsellor, Head of Chancery and Consul-Gen., Amman, 1979–82; Hd of S America Dept, FCO, 1982–85; Consul-Gen., Sydney, 1985–88; ME Marketing Dir, Defence Export Services Orgn, MoD, on secondment, 1988–91; High Comr, Brunei, 1991–94; Ambassador to Syria, 1994–96. Sen. Diplomatic Consultant, Landair Internat. Chairman: Gtr London Fund for the Blind, 1997–99; Internat. Adv. Panel, Nat. Lottery Charities Bd, 1997–; Arab-British Centre, 1997–; Vice-Chm., Medical Aid for Palestinians, 1997–99; Mem. Adv. Bd, Centre for Near and Middle Eastern Studies, 1997–. Member: RIIA; RUSI; RSAA. SPMB (Negara Brunei Darussalam), 1992. *Address:* Steps Cottage, Easton, near Winchester, Hants SO21 1EG. *Club:* Travellers.

SINDALL, Barry John; Headmaster, Colyton Grammar School, Devon, since 1990; *b* 20 Oct. 1945; *s* of Reginald and Kathleen Sindall; *m* 1975, Margaret Eleanor Barker; one *s* one *d*. *Educ:* Univ. of Exeter (MEd). Teacher of Hist., Duncan Bowen Secondary Mod. Sch., Ashford, Kent, 1967-68; Hd of Humanities, R. M. Bailey High Sch., Nassau, Bahamas, 1968-76; Dir of Studies, Colyton GS, 1976-88; Dep. Headteacher, Torquay Boys' GS, 1988-90. FRSA 1994. *Recreations:* amateur dramatics, cricket, fell-walking, ski-ing. *Address:* Colyton Grammar School, Colyford, Colyton, Devon EX24 6HN. *T:* (01297) 552327.

SINDELL, Marion Harwood; Chief Executive, Equal Opportunities Commission, 1979–85; *b* 23 June 1925; *d* of Arthur Barrett Sindell and Ethel Maude Sindell. *Educ:* Lincoln Girls' High Sch.; St Hilda's Coll., Oxford (MA). Solicitor. Deputy Town Clerk: Workington, 1959–64; Nuneaton, 1964–66; Town Clerk, Goole, 1966–74; Chief Exec., Boothferry Bor. Council, 1974–79.

SINDEN, Sir Donald (Alfred), Kt 1997; CBE 1979; actor; *b* 9 Oct. 1923; *s* of Alfred Edward Sinden and Mabel Agnes (*née* Fuller), Sussex; *m* 1948, Diana, *d* of Daniel and Muriel Mahony; one *s* (and one *s* decd). First appearance on stage, 1942, in Charles F. Smith's Co., Mobile Entertainments Southern Area; Leicester Repertory Co., 1945; Memorial Theatre Co., Stratford upon Avon, 1946 and 1947; Old Vic and Bristol Old Vic, 1948; The Heiress, Haymarket, 1949–50; Bristol Old Vic, 1950; Red Letter Day, Garrick, 1951. Under contract to Rank Organisation, 1952–60, appearing in 23 films including The Cruel Sea, Doctor in the House, etc. Returned to theatre, appearing in Odd Man In, St Martin's, 1957; Peter Pan, Scala, 1960; Guilty Party, St Martin's, 1961; Royal Shakespeare Co., playing Richard Plantagenet in Henry VI (The Wars of the Roses), Price in Eh!, etc, 1963 and 1964; British Council tour of S America in Dear Liar and Happy Days, 1965; There's a Girl in my Soup, Globe, 1966; Lord Foppington in The Relapse, RSC, Aldwych, 1967; Not Now Darling, Strand, 1968; RSC, Stratford, 1969 and Aldwych, 1970 playing Malvolio; Henry VIII; Sir Harcourt Courtly in London Assurance, revived at New Theatre, 1972, tour of the USA, 1974 (Drama Desk Award); In Praise of Love, Duchess, 1973; Stockmann in An Enemy of the People, Chichester, 1975; Habeas Corpus, USA, 1975; Benedick in Much Ado About Nothing, King Lear, RSC, Stratford, 1976, Aldwych, 1977 (Variety Club of GB Stage Actor of 1976; Evening Standard Drama Award, Best Actor, 1977); Shut Your Eyes and Think of England, Apollo, 1977; Othello, RSC, Stratford, 1979, Aldwych, 1980; Present Laughter, Vaudeville, 1981; Uncle Vanya, Haymarket, 1982; The School for Scandal, Haymarket and Duke of York's (Eur. tour, 1984), 1983; Ariadne auf Naxos, Coliseum, 1983, 1992, 1997; Two Into One, Shaftesbury, 1984; The Scarlet Pimpernel, Chichester transf. to Her Majesty's, 1985; Major Barbara, Chichester, 1988; Over My Dead Body, Savoy, 1989; Oscar Wilde, Playhouse, 1990; Out of Order, Shaftesbury, 1990, nat. tour, 1990–91, Australia, 1992–93; Venus Observed, Chichester, 1992; She Stoops to Conquer, Queen's, 1993; Hamlet, Gielgud, 1994; Quartet, Albery, 1999; dir, The Importance of Being Earnest, Royalty, 1987; *television series include:* Our Man from St Marks; Two's Company; Discovering English Churches; Never the Twain; has appeared in many films. Assoc. Artist, RSC, 1967–. Member: Council, British Actors Equity Assoc., 1966–77 (Trustee, 1988–); Council, RSA, 1972; Adv. Council, V&A Museum, 1973–80; Arts Council Drama Panel, 1973–77; Leicestershire Educn Arts Cttee, 1974–; BBC Archives Adv. Cttee, 1975–78; London Acad. of Music and Dramatic Art Council, 1976–; Kent and E Sussex Reg. Cttee, National Trust, 1978–82; Arts Council of GB, 1982–86; Chairman: British Theatre Museum Assoc., 1971–77; Theatre Museum Adv. Council, 1973–80; President: Fedn of Playgoers Socs, 1968–93; Royal Theatrical Fund, 1983–; Green Room Benevolent Fund, 1998–; Vice-Pres., London Appreciation Soc., 1960–. FRSA 1966. *Publications:* A Touch of the Memoirs (autobiog.), 1982; Laughter in the Second Act (autobiog.), 1985; (ed) The Everyman Book of Theatrical Anecdotes, 1987; The English Country Church, 1988; (ed) The Last Word, 1994. *Recreations:* theatrical history, architecture, ecclesiology, genealogy, serendipity. *Address:* Number One, NW11 6AY; Rats Castle, TN30 7HX. *Clubs:* Garrick (Trustee, 1980–2000), Beefsteak, MCC.

SINGARES McALMAN, Ariadne Elizabeth; Ambassador of Panama to the Court of St James's, since 2000; *b* Panama, 24 Sept. 1961; *m* Andrew Ian Robinson; one *d*. *Educ:* Knox Sch., Long Island, NY; Le Château Mont-Choisi, Geneva; Stony Brook Univ., NY; Parson Sch. of Design, Manhattan; New York Univ. A designer and personal asst to Gerald Franklin, Canadian designer of haute couture, NY, 1985–88. Member: Breast Cancer Assoc., Race for Life; City Harvest; Meals on Wheels; volunteer, St Lucas Hosp., Manhattan. *Address:* Embassy of Panama, Panama House, Mayfair, 40 Hertford Street, W1Y 7TG.

SINGER, Adam Nicholas; Chief Executive, Telewest Communications plc, since 2000; *s* of Aubrey Edward Singer, *qv*; *m*; three *c*. Formerly posts with BBC, Ten, and Viacom, USA; Dep. Chm., 1992-97, Chm. and Chief Exec., 1998-2000, Flextech plc. Formerly Director: HTV Gp plc; Scottish Television plc; Telewest plc; Tele-Communications Internat.; Director: Scottish Media Gp plc, 1995-; QXL, 2001-. *Address:* Telewest Communications plc, 160 Great Portland Street, W1N 5TB.

SINGER, Aubrey Edward, CBE 1984; Managing Director, White City Films, 1984–96 (Chairman, 1984–94); *b* 21 Jan. 1927; *s* of Louis Henry Singer and late Elizabeth (*née* Walton); *m* 1949, Cynthia Hilda Adams; one *s* two *d* (and one *d* decd). *Educ:* Giggleswick; Bradford Grammar School. Joined film industry, 1944; directed various films teaching armed forces to shoot; worked extensively in Africa, 1946–48; worked on children's films in Austria, 1948–49; joined BBC TV Outside Broadcasts, 1949; TV Producer Scotland,

1951; BBC New York Office, 1953; returned to London as Producer, 1956; produced many scientific programmes; Asst Head of Outside Broadcasts, 1959; Head of Science and Features, 1961; Head of Features Gp, BBC TV, 1967; Controller, BBC 2, 1974–78; Man. Dir, BBC Radio, 1978–82; Dep. Dir-Gen., and Man. Dir, Television, BBC, 1982–84. Chm., Soc. of Film and Television Arts, 1971–73. President: TV and Radio Industries Club, 1984–85; Council, Nat. Mus. of Photography, Film and TV, 1984–96. FRTS 1978 (a Vice-Pres., 1982–88); FRAS; FRSA. Hon. DLitt Bradford, 1984. *Publication:* The Lion and the Dragon, 1992. *Recreations:* walking, talking, archery.

See also A. N. Singer.

SINGER, Sir Hans (Wolfgang), Kt 1994; PhD; Professorial Fellow, Institute of Development Studies, University of Sussex, since 1969, Emeritus Professor, since 1980; *b* 29 Nov. 1910; *s* of Heinrich and Antonia Singer; *m* 1934, Ilse Lina Plaut; one *s* (and one *s* decd). *Educ:* Univ. of Bonn (Econ. Dip. 1931); King's Coll., Cambridge (PhD 1936). Pilgrim Trust Unemployment Enquiry, 1936–38; Manchester Univ., 1938–44; Min. of Town and Country Planning, 1945–46; Glasgow Univ., 1946–47; with United Nations Secretariat, 1947–69: Dir, Econ. Div., UNIDO, 1967–69. Hon. Fellow, Inst. of Social Studies, The Hague, 1978. Hon. DLitt: Sussex, 1990; Santa Fe, Argentina, 1989; Glasgow, 1994; Lisbon, 1994; Innsbruck, 1997. *Publications:* numerous books including: (jtly) Men Without Work, 1938; International Development, Growth and Change, 1964; (with J. Ansari) Rich and Poor Countries, 1977 (trans. Portuguese, 1979, Spanish, 1982), 4th edn 1988; (jtly) Food Aid: the challenge and the opportunity, 1987; (ed jtly) New World Order Series, 12 vols, 1987–92; (with S. Roy) Economic Progress and Prospects in the Third World: lessons of development experience since 1945, 1993; (with K. Raffer) The Foreign Aid Business, 1996; also articles in learned jls. *Recreations:* walking, music, chess. *Address:* Institute of Development Studies, University of Sussex, Brighton, E Sussex BN1 9RE; 18 The Vale, Ovingdean, Brighton, E Sussex BN2 7AB. *T:* (01273) 303567.

SINGER, Harold Samuel; His Honour Judge Harold Singer; a Circuit Judge, since 1984; *b* 17 July 1935; *s* of Ellis and Minnie Singer; *m* 1966, Adèle Berenice Emanuel; one *s* two *d*. *Educ:* Salford Grammar School; Fitzwilliam House, Cambridge (MA). Called to the Bar, Gray's Inn, 1957; a Recorder, 1981–84. Governor, Delamere Forest Sch., 1998–. *Recreations:* music, painting, books, photography.

SINGER, Harry Bruce, OBE 1995; TD 1955; DL; FCA; Senior Partner, Singer & Partners, Chartered Accountants, 1968–87; *b* 21 June 1921; *er s* of Geoffrey and Agnes Singer; *m* 1945, Betty Alison Brittan (*d* 1993); one *s*. *Educ:* Cathedral Sch., Hereford. FCA 1960 (Mem., 1953). Served War: commnd 99th (London Welsh) HAA Regt, RA, 1941; served in UK and NW Europe; Instr, Sch. of AA Artillery, 1945; joined 281 (Glam Yeomanry) Field Regt, RA (TA), 1947; in comd, 1959–62. Pres., S Wales Soc. of Chartered Accountants, 1970–71; Inst. of Chartered Accountants in England and Wales: Mem. Council, 1973–85; Vice Pres., 1979–80; Dep. Pres., 1980–81; Pres., 1981–82. Hon. Treasurer, SSAFA, 1990–96; Trustee, Yeomanry Benevolent Fund, 1995–. Liveryman, Worshipful Co. of Chartered Accountants, 1978–89; Freeman, City of London, 1978. Vice Chm. Wales, TA&VRA, 1984–87. DL Mid Glamorgan, 1985. *Recreations:* golf, foreign travel, Rugby football (originally as player). *Address:* 8 Windsor House, Castle Court, Cardiff CF1 1DG. *Clubs:* Army and Navy; Cardiff and County, Cardiff Golf (Cardiff).

SINGER, Hon Sir (Jan) Peter, Kt 1993; **Hon. Mr Justice Singer;** a Judge of the High Court of Justice, Family Division, since 1993; *b* 10 Sept. 1944; *s* of late Dr Hanus Kurt Singer and Anita Singer; *m* 1970, Julia Mary Caney; one *s* one *d*. *Educ:* King Edward's School, Birmingham; Selwyn College, Cambridge. Called to the Bar, Inner Temple, 1967, Bencher, 1993; QC 1987; a Recorder, 1987–93; NE Circuit Liaison Judge, 1993–2001. Chm., Family Law Bar Assoc., 1990–92 (Sec., 1980–83, Treasurer, 1983–90); Member: Matrimonial Causes Rule Cttee, 1981–85; Senate of Inns of Court and Bar, 1983–86; Law Soc. Legal Aid Cttee, 1984–89; Gen. Council of the Bar, 1990–92. Vice-Pres., European Chapter, Internat. Acad. of Matrimonial Lawyers, 1992–93. Joint Editor: Capitalise (software), 1998–; @ e Glance (software), 2001. *Publications:* (ed jtly) Rayden on Divorce, 14th edn, 1983; (ed jtly) At A Glance, annually 1992–; (Consulting Ed.) Essential Family Practice, annually 2000. *Recreations:* gardening, walking, travel. *Address:* Royal Courts of Justice, Strand, WC2A 2LL.

SINGER, Norbert, CBE 1990; PhD, FRSC; Vice Chancellor, University of Greenwich, 1992–93 (Director, Thames Polytechnic, 1978–92); *b* 3 May 1931; *s* of late Salomon Singer and late Mina Korn; *m* Brenda Margaret Walter, *e d* of Richard and Gladys Walter, Tunbridge Wells, Kent. *Educ:* Highbury County School; Queen Mary Coll., London. BSc, PhD, CChem, FRSC. Research Chemist and Project Leader, Morgan Crucible Co. Ltd, 1954–57; Lecturer, Senior Lectr, Principal Lectr and Dep. Head of Department, Dept of Chemistry, Northern Polytechnic, 1958–70; Head of Dept of Life Sciences 1971–74, Professor of Life Sciences 1972–74, Polytechnic of Central London; Asst Director, then Dep. Director, Polytechnic of North London, 1974–78: Vis. Prof., Univ. of Westminster, 1996–. Council for National Academic Awards: Mem., 1982–88; Chm., Reviews Co-ordination Sub-Cttee, 1984–87; Vice Chm., Cttee for Academic and Institutional Policy, 1985–87; Mem., Accreditation Cttee, 1987–89; Chm., Cttee for CATs, 1990–93. Mem., MSC Nat. Steering Gp, TVEI, 1984–88 (Mem., Quality and Standards Gp, 1987–89). Chairman: Bexley HA, 1993–94; Oxleas (formerly Bexley Community Health) NHS Trust, 1994–2001. Chm., Governing Body, Rose Bruford Coll., 1994–99; Governor: London Inst., 1993–99; Nene Coll., Northants, 1993–97; St Peters C of E Primary Sch., 1995–. Fellow: QMW, 1993; Nene Coll., 1998. Hon. DSc Greenwich, 1993. *Publications:* research papers in electrochemistry, theoretical chemistry and surface chemistry in scientific jls. *Recreations:* walking, reading. *Address:* Croft Lodge, Bayhall Road, Tunbridge Wells, Kent TN2 4TP. *T:* (01892) 523821.

SINGER, Hon. Sir Peter; *see* Singer, Hon. Sir J. P.

SINGER, Philip Francis; QC 1994; a Recorder, since 1989; *b* 1 Dec. 1940; *s* of late Abraham Singer and of Sylvia (*née* Hyman); *m* 1978, Heather Angela Cutt. *Educ:* Bedford Modern Sch.; Bishop's Stortford Coll.; St John's Coll., Cambridge (MA, LLM). Called to the Bar, Inner Temple, 1964. *Address:* 2 Pump Court, Temple, EC4Y 7AH. *T:* (020) 7353 5597.

SINGER, Sara Catherine; *see* Nathan S. C.

SINGER, Susan Honor; Headmistress, Guildford High School, since 1991; *b* 23 Feb. 1942; *d* of late Brig. John James McCully, DSO and of Honor Goad (*née* Ward, now Mrs E. B. Elliott); *m* 1964, Christopher Ronald Morgan Singer; one *s* two *d*. *Educ:* St Mary's, Calne; Open Univ. (BA); Garnett Coll. (PGCE). Set up and ran pre-school playgroup, E Sheen, 1968–74; St Paul's Girls' School: maths teacher, 1980–91; Head of Middle School, 1988–91; Head of Maths, 1990–91. Pres., GSA, 2001. *Recreation:* transatlantic sailing 1907 gaff cutter. *Address:* Guildford High School, London Road, Guildford, Surrey GU1 1SJ. *T:* (01483) 561440; 39 East Sheen Avenue, SW14 8AR. *T:* (020) 8876 4031.

SINGH, Prof. Ajit, PhD; Professor of Economics, Cambridge University, since 1995; Fellow of Queens' College, Cambridge, since 1965 (Senior Fellow since 1992); *b* 11 Sept. 1940; *s* of Gurbachan Singh and Pushpa Singh; *m* 1993, Josephine Bradley. *Educ:* Punjab Univ. (BA); Howard Univ. (MA); Univ. of California at Berkeley (PhD). Queens' College, Cambridge: Asst Lectr, 1965; Dir of Studies in Econs, 1972–94; Univ. Lectr, then Reader, Econs Faculty, Cambridge Univ. Scholl Vis. Prof. of Internat. Econs, Univ. of Notre Dame, USA, 1987–95. Research Consultant: UN Univ., World Inst. of Develt Econ. Res., 1986–92; ILO, 1988–; UNCTAD, 1988–; IFC, 1989–; South Commn, later South Centre, Geneva, 1990–; other adv. positions in Switzerland, Mexico, Tanzania. Founding Editor, Cambridge Jl of Economics, 1977–. *Publications:* (with G. Whittington) Growth, Profitability and Valuation, 1968; Takeovers, 1971; (ed jtly) The State, Markets and Development, 1994; Corporate Financial Patterns in Industrialising Countries, 1995; (jtly) The Effects of Hyper-Inflation on Accounting Ratios, 1997; (ed with C. Howes) Competitiveness Matters: industry and economic performance in the US, 2000; contribs to learned jls. *Recreations:* table tennis, hiking, travel, friends. *Address:* Queens' College, Cambridge CB3 9ET. *T:* (01223) 335200.

SINGH, Gurbux; Chair, Commission for Racial Equality, since 2000; *b* Punjab, India, 4 Dec. 1950; *s* of Parkesh Singh and Shaminder Kaur; *m* Siobhan Maguire; three *s*. *Educ:* Univ. of Sussex (BA Hons Pol Sci.). Housing Specialist, CRC, 1972–77; housing and local govt, CRE, 1977–83; Housing Services, GLC, 1983–85; Dep. Dir of Housing, Brent BC, 1985–87; Dir of Housing, 1987–89, Chief Exec., 1989–2000, Haringey BC. Mem., Home Sec.'s Race Relns Forum, 1998–; Dir, N London TEC, 1990–; Mem. Bd, Food Standards Agency, 2000–. *Recreation:* supporting Wolverhampton Wanderers and the Indian cricket team. *Address:* Commission for Racial Equality, Elliot House, 10–12 Allington Street, SW1E 5EH. *T:* (020) 7932 5352.

SINGH, Indarjit, OBE 1996; JP; CEng; Director, Network of Sikh Organisations (UK), since 1995; *b* 17 Sept. 1932; *s* of Dr Diwan Singh and Kundan K. Singh; *m* 1962, Dr Kanwaljit Kaur; two *d*. *Educ:* Birmingham Univ. (MCom, MBA). CEng 1967; MIMinE 1967. Worked in sen. positions in mining and civil engrg, 1955–75: NCB, 1955–59, 1965–67; manager of mines, India, 1959–65; with Costain, 1967–75; mgt consultant in various areas of local govt, Gtr London, 1975–93; hon. work for Sikh community and in promotion of inter-faith understanding, 1993–. Editor, Sikh Messenger (qly mag.), 1984–. Has made broadcasts on religious and current affairs, incl. Any Questions, Thought for the Day. JP Wimbledon, 1984. UK Templeton Prize for the promotion of inter-faith understanding, 1989; Inter-faith Medallion for services to religious broadcasting, BBC and CCJ, 1991. *Recreations:* writing, broadcasting. *Address:* 43 Dorset Road, Merton Park, SW19 3EZ. *T:* (020) 8540 4148.

SINGH, Kanwar N.; *see* Natwar-Singh.

SINGH, Khushwant; Padma Bhushan, 1974; Barrister-at-law; writer; Member, Rajya Sabha, India, 1980–86; *b* Feb. 1915; *m* Kaval (*née* Malik); one *s* one *d*. *Educ:* Univ. of London (LLB); called to Bar. Practising Lawyer, High Court, Lahore, 1939–47; Min. of External Affairs, of India; PRO Ottawa and London, 1947–51; UNESCO, 1954–56. Visiting Lectr: Oxford (Spalding Trust); USA: Rochester, Princeton, Hawaii, Swarthmore; led Indian Delegn to Writers' Conf., Manila, Philippines, 1965; Guest Speaker at Montreal 'Expo 67'. Has written for many nat. dailies and foreign jls: New York Times; Observer and New Statesman (London); Harper's (USA); Evergreen Review (USA); London Magazine. Editor, The Illustrated Weekly of India, Bombay, 1969–78; Chief Editor, New Delhi, 1979–80; increased circulation of Illustrated Weekly of India from 80,000 to 410,000 in 9 yrs; Editor-in-chief, The Hindustan Times and Contour, New Delhi, 1980–83. *Broadcasting and Television:* All India Radio, BBC, CBC; LP recordings. Awards include: from Punjab Govt: 5,000 rupees and Robe of Honour, for contrib. to Sikh literature; Mohan Singh Award: 1,500 rupees for trans. of Sikh hymns, etc. *Publications: Sikh History and Religion:* The Sikhs, 1953; A History of the Sikhs: vol. i, 1469–1839, 1964; vol. ii, 1839–1964, 1967; Ranjit Singh, Maharajah of the Punjab, 1780–1839, 1963; Fall of the Kingdom of the Punjab; Sikhs Today; (ed) Sunset of the Sikh Empire, by Dr Sita Ram Kohli (posthumous); Hymns of Nanak The Guru; *fiction:* The Mark of Vishnu and other stories, 1951; Train to Pakistan, 1956; I Shall Not Hear the Nightingales, 1961; *stories:* The Voice of God and other stories; Black Jasmine and other stories; A Bride for the Sahib and other stories; (*co-author*): Sacred Writing of the Sikhs; (with Arun Joshi) Shri Ram: a biog., 1969; (with Satindra Singh) Ghadr Rebellion; (with Suneet Veer Singh) Homage to Guru Gobind Singh; *miscellaneous:* Love and Friendship (editor of anthology); Khushwant Singh's India—collection of articles (ed Rahul Singh); Shri Ram—a biography; Delhi—a Profile, 1982; The Sikhs, 1984; (with Kuldip Nayar) Punjab Tragedy, 1984; *translations:* Umrao Jan Ada, Courtesan of Lucknow, by Mohammed Ruswa (with M. A. Husaini); The Skeleton (by Amrita Pritam); Land of the Five Rivers; I Take This Woman, by Rajinder Singh Bedi; Iqbal's Dialogue with Allah (Shikwah and Jawab-e-Shikwah); We Indians. *Recreation:* bird watching. *Address:* 49E Sujan Singh Park, New Delhi 110003, India. *T:* (11) 690159. *Clubs:* Imperial Gymkhana (New Delhi); Bombay Gymkhana (Bombay).

SINGH, Laleshwar Kumar Narayan, CCH 1996; High Commissioner for Guyana in London, since 1993; also non-resident Ambassador to The Netherlands, the Republic of France, the Russian Federation, the Czech Republic and the Holy See; *b* 2 April 1941; *s* of late Mr and Mrs Narayan; *m* 1972, Latchmin Ramrattan; one *s* one *d*. *Educ:* Windsor Forest Govt Sch., Guyana; Indian Educn Trust Coll., Guyana; Univ. of London (ext. student; Intermediate Exam. in Laws); Court Clerk Trng Course. Left Guyana, 1961 to work and study in England; Inner London Magistrates' Courts Service, 1971–93: work in magistrates' courts and Admin Office, Principal Chief Clerk's Office; Personnel Officer, 1988–89. Dean, Caribbean High Comrs; Chm., Exec. Council, CAB Internat. *Address:* Guyana High Commission, 3 Palace Court, Bayswater Road, W2 4LP. *T:* (020) 7229 7684.

SINGH, Margaret Stella, CBE 1996; JP; Chair, Association of District Councils, 1993–95; *b* 10 Aug. 1945; *d* of Edward Richard Jones and Stella Jones; *m* (marr. diss.); one *s* one *d*; *m* 2001, Christopher Cook; one step *d*. Working in and for local govt, 1962–; Mem. (Lab) Reading BC, 1976–95. Lay Mem., W Norfolk Primary Care Trust, 2000–. JP Reading and Sonning, 1998, King's Lynn, 2000. *Recreations:* reading, walking the dogs, listening to people. *Address:* Chiswick House, Creake Road, Burnham Market, Norfolk PE31 8EN.

SINGH, Marsha; MP (Lab) Bradford West, since 1997; *b* 11 Oct. 1954; *s* of Harbans Singh and late Kartar Kaur; *m* 1971, Sital Kaur; one *s* one *d*. *Educ:* Loughborough Univ. (BA Hons Pols and Econs of Modern Europe). With Lloyds Bank, 1976–79; Bradford Community Relations Council, 1979–80; Bradford Law Centre, 1980–83; Directorate of Educn, Bradford Council, 1983–90; Bradford Community Health Trust, 1990–97. *Recreations:* reading, chess, bridge. *Address:* House of Commons, SW1A 0AA.

SINGH, Mota; QC 1978; **His Honour Judge Mota Singh;** a Circuit Judge, since 1982; *b* 26 July 1930; *s* of Dalip Singh and Harnam Kaur; *m* 1950, Swaran Kaur; two *s* one *d*.

Educ: Duke of Gloucester Sch., Nairobi, Kenya; Hon. Soc. of Lincoln's Inn. Called to the Bar, 1956. Left school, 1947; Solicitor's Clerk, Nairobi, 1948–54; Lincoln's Inn, London, 1954–56; Advocate, High Court of Kenya, 1957–65; Alderman, City of Nairobi, 1958–63; Vice-Chm., Kenya Justice; Sec., Law Soc. of Kenya, 1963–64. A Deputy Circuit Judge, 1976–82; a Recorder of the Crown Court, 1979–82. Member: London Rent Assessment Panel, 1965–67; Race Relations Bd, 1968–77; Chm., Immigration Adv. Service, 2000–. Vice-Pres., Family Service Units. Trustee: St George's Hosp., Tooting; Windsor Leadership Trust. Chm., Eur. Sect., World Sikh Council, 1998–. Patron: Anne Frank Foundn; World Council of Faiths; Swami Narayan Temple, Neasden; Asha Foundn; Ben Samuel Trust. Hon. LLD Guru Nanak Dev Univ., Amritsar, 1981. *Recreations:* reading; formerly cricket (represented Kenya). *Address:* Cedarwood, 3 Somerset Road, Wimbledon SW19 5JU. *T:* (020) 8947 2271. *Club:* MCC.

SINGH, Vishwanath Pratap; Prime Minister of India, 1989–90; *b* 25 June 1931; *s* of Raja Bahadur Ram Gopal Singh; *m* 1955, Sita Kumari; two *s*. *Educ:* Poona Univ.; Allahabad Univ. (Vice-Pres., Students Union; LLB); Udip Pratap College, Varanasi (Pres., Students Union). Participated in Bhoodan Movement, 1957, and donated farm, Pasna, Allahabad; Mem. Exec., Allahabad Univ., 1969–71; founded Gopal Vidyalaya, Intermediate Coll., Koraon, Allahabad. Uttar Pradesh appointments: MLA, 1969–71 and 1981–83; Whip, Congress Legislature Party, 1970–71; MLC, 1980–81; Chief Minister, 1980–82; Pres., UP Congress Cttee, 1984. Mem., Lok Sabha, 1971–77, 1980, 1988–89 and 1989–94; Mem., Rajya Sabha, 1983–88; Union Dep. Minister (Commerce), 1974–76; Union Minister of State (Commerce), 1976–77; Union Minister (Commerce), 1983 (also i/c Dept of Supply); Union Finance Minister, 1984–87; Defence Minister, Jan.–April 1987. Founded Jan Morcha, 1987; Pres., Janata Dal, 1988; Convenor, Nat. Front, 1988. *Address:* 1 Teen Murti Marg, New Delhi 110001, India.

SINGHVI, Dr Laxmi Mall; MP (BJP) Rajasthan, Rajya Sabha, since 1998; Senior Advocate, Supreme Court of India, since 1967 (Advocate, 1951–67); *b* 9 Nov. 1931; *s* of D. M. Singhvi and Akal Kaur Singhvi; *m* 1957, Kamla Baid, author; one *s* one *d*. *Educ:* Allahabad Univ. (BA); Rajasthan Univ. (LLB); Harvard Univ. Law Sch. (LLM); Cornell Univ. Law Sch. (SJD). MP, Independent, Lok Sabha, 1962–67; Senior Standing Counsel, State of UP, Union of India, 1967–71; Advocate-Gen., 1972–77. High Comr for India in UK, 1991–97. Mem., Perm. Court of Arbitration, The Hague, 2000; Comr of Inquiry into admin of justice, Trinidad and Tobago, 2000. Dep. Leader, Indian Parly Delegn to CPA, 1964, Leader Parly Delegn, 1966; Chm. and Founder, Inst. of Constitutional and Parly Studies, 1964–. Chairman: Indian Fedn of Unesco Assocs, 1974–; World Colloquium on Legal Aid, 1975; State Bar Council, 1975–77; Indian Nat. Cttee for Abolition of Death Penalty, 1977–; Nat. Sch. of Drama, 1978–82; Supreme Court Law Reforms Cttee, 1981–82; Asian Conf. on Approaches to Human Rights, 1985; Govt of India Cttee on Revitalisation of Rural Local Self-Govt, 1986–87; Govt of India Task Force on Child Labour; Govt of India Cttee on Brain Death and Organ Transplantation, 1991; Founder Chm., 1972, Hon. Patron, 1983, Commonwealth Legal Educn Assoc.; Founder-Pres., Indian Centre for Human Rights Educn and Research, 1980; Pres., World Congress on Human Rights, 1990; Member: UN Human Rights Sub-Commn, Geneva, 1978–82 (Vice-Chm.); Nat. Commn for Unesco; Govt of India Expert Cttee on Legal Aid, 1971–73; Commn on Inf. and Broadcasting, 1964–68; Internat. Forum on Freedoms and Rights of Man, Paris, 1985–. President: Supreme Court Bar Assoc., 1977, 1978, 1980, 1982; Supreme Court Bar Trust, 1981–; Nat. Legal Aid Assoc., 1970–; Indian Centre for Independence of Judges and Lawyers, 1979–; UN Special Rapporteur on Independence of Judges and Lawyers, 1979–; Hon. Mem. and Adv. Panelist, Comparative Const. Law Project and Bicentennial of Amer. Constitution, Amer. Council of Learned Socs, 1986–88. Trustee and Mem. Jury, G. D. Birla Award on Humanism. Life Trustee and Pres., India Internat. Centre; Pres. Emeritus, Authors Guild of India (Pres., 1986–90). Hon. Tagore Law Prof., 1975–; Visiting Professor and Fellow: Univ. of Leicester, 1991–; Univ. of Hull, 1994–. Rede Lectr, Univ. of Cambridge, 1993. Hon. Bencher, Middle Temple, 1987. Hon. LLD: Jabalpur, 1983; Banaras Hindu, 1984; Tamil, Tamilnadu, 1991; Buckingham, 1993; N London, 1993; Osmania, 1994; De Montfort, 1994. Hon. Nyayavacaspati, Gurukul, 1968. *Publications:* Horizons of Freedom, 1969; (ed) Law and Poverty, 1970; Indian Federalism, 1974; Legal Aid, 1985; Law Day, 1985; Independence of Justice, 1985; Jain Declaration on Nature, 1990; Freedom on Trial, 1991; The Evening Sun (poems), 1991; A Third International Covenant for the Prevention of Ecocide, 1991. *Recreations:* theatre, poetry, chess, gardening, classical Indian dance appreciation, archaeology. *Address:* 18 Willingdon Crescent, New Delhi 110001, India. *Club:* Athenæum.

SINGLETON, Barry Neill; QC 1989; *b* 12 April 1946; *s* of late Clifford and Moyna Singleton; *m* 1971, Anne Mary Potter; one *s* two *d*. *Educ:* Downside Sch.; Gonville and Caius Coll., Cambridge (MA). Called to the Bar, Gray's Inn, 1968. *Address:* 1 King's Bench Walk, Temple, EC4Y 7DB. *T:* (020) 7936 1500, *Fax:* (020) 7936 1590.

SINGLETON, Norman, CB 1966; retired civil servant; *b* 21 March 1913; *s* of Charles and Alice Singleton, Bolton, Lancs; *m* 1936, Cicely Margaret Lucas (*d* 2000), Claverdon, Warwick; one *s* two *d*. *Educ:* Bolton School; Emmanuel College, Cambridge. Min. of Labour, 1935; Under-Secretary: Civil Service Pay Research Unit, 1956–60; Min. of Labour, then Dept of Employment and Productivity, 1960–69; Sec., 1969–72, Dep. Chm., 1973–74, Commn on Industrial Relns; Dep. Chm., Central Arbitration Cttee, 1976–85; Arbitrator and Mediator, ACAS, 1976–87. *Publication:* Industrial Relations Procedures, 1976. *Address:* 34 Willoughby Road, Hampstead, NW3 1RU. *T:* (020) 7435 1504.

See also E. A. Woods.

SINGLETON, Roger, CBE 1997; Chief Executive, Barnardo's, since 1984; *b* 6 Nov. 1942; *s* of late Malcolm and Ethel Singleton, Nether Edge, Sheffield; *m* 1966, Ann Hasler; two *d*. *Educ:* City Grammar Sch., Sheffield; Durham Univ. (MA); Bath Univ. (MSc); London Univ. (DipSocStud); Leeds (Cert. Ed.). Accredited Mediator. Appts in care and educn of deprived and delinquent young people, 1961–71; professional adviser to Children's Regional Planning Cttee, 1971–74; Dep. Dir, Dr Barnardo's, 1974–84. Treas., Nat. Council of Voluntary Child Care Organisations, 1996– (Chm., 1990–92); Member: Central Council for Educn and Training in Social Work, 1984–86; Council, Nat. Children's Bureau, 1982–84; Council, Nat. Youth Bureau, 1986–91; Children's Services Strategy Gp, 1996–. Company Dir. CIMgt (FBIM 1982); FRSA 1991. *Publications:* contribs to professional jls. *Recreation:* timber framed buildings. *Address:* Barnardo's, Tanners Lane, Barkingside, Ilford, Essex IG6 1QG. *T:* (020) 8550 8822; *e-mail:* roger.singleton@barnardos.org.uk. *Club:* Reform.

SINGLETON, Valerie, OBE 1994; television broadcaster, travel writer for newspapers and magazines; with BBC, 1962–93; *b* 9 April 1937; *d* of Wing Comdr Denis G. Singleton, OBE and late Eileen Singleton, LRAM. *Educ:* Arts Educational Sch. (3 times Drama Cup); RADA (schol.). Bromley Rep.; commercial voice-overs; TV advertising magazines; joined BBC as announcer, 1962; presenter: Blue Peter, 1962–71; Blue Peter Special Assignments, covering capital cities, islands, famous houses, 1972–75, and Rivers Niagra and Yukon, 1980; Val Meets the VIPs, 1972–75; Nationwide, 1972–78; Tonight, and Tonight in Town, 1978–79; Echoes of Holocaust, documentary, BBC 2, Midweek, Radio 4, 1980; The Money Programme, BBC 2, 1980–88; Radio 4 PM, 1981–93; (jtly) Travel UK, Central TV, 1992; Backdate, Channel 4, 1996; Playback, History Channel, 2 series, 1998, 1999; numerous other radio and TV progs; corporate videos, business confs. Work for British Wildlife Appeal and Dr Barnardo's. *Recreations:* sailing, ski-ing, water ski-ing, photography, exploring London, travelling anywhere, riding, pottering in museums and antique shops. *Address:* c/o Arlington Enterprises, 1-3 Charlotte Street, W1P 1HD. *Clubs:* Hurlingham; Hayling Island Sailing.

SINGLETON, William Brian, CBE 1974; FRCVS; retired; Director, Animal Health Trust, 1977–88; *b* 23 Feb. 1923; *s* of William Max Singleton and Blanche May Singleton; *m* 1947, Hilda Stott; two *s* one *d* (and one *s* decd). *Educ:* Queen Elizabeth Grammar Sch., Darlington; Royal (Dick) Sch. of Vet. Studies, Edinburgh. Vis. Prof. Surgery, Ontario Vet. Coll., Guelph, Canada, 1973–74; Hon. Vet. Advr to Jockey Club, 1977–88. Member: Govt Cttee of Inquiry into Future Role of Veterinary Profession in GB (Chm., Sir Michael Swann), 1971–75; UGC Wkg Pty on Vet. Educn into the 21st Century (Chm., Sir Ralph Riley, FRS), 1987–89. President: British Small Animal Vet. Assoc., 1960–61; RCVS, 1969–70; World Small Animal Vet. Assoc., 1975–77; BEVA, 1988–89. Hon. Diplomate, Amer. Coll. of Vet. Surgeons, 1973; Hon. DVM & S Edinburgh, 1993. Dalrymple-Champneys Award, 1987. *Publications:* Canine Medicine and Therapeutics, 1979; numerous papers on veterinary orthopaedics and comparative medicine. *Recreations:* gardening, sailing, bird watching, horse riding. *Address:* Vine Cottage, Morston Road, Blakeney, Holt, Norfolk NR25 7BE. *T:* (01263) 740246. *Club:* Farmers'.

SINHA, 6th Baron *cr* 1919, of Raipur; **Arup Kumar Sinha;** *b* 23 April 1966; *er s* of 5th Baron Sinha and of Lolita, *d* of Deb Kumar Das; *S* father, 1999; *m* 1993, Deborah Jane Tidswell (marr. diss. 1995). *Heir:* *b* Hon. Dilip Kumar Sinha, *b* 1967.

SINNATT, Maj.-Gen. Martin Henry, CB 1984; *b* 28 Jan. 1928; *s* of Dr O. S. Sinnatt and Mrs M. H. Sinnatt (*née* Randall); *m* 1957, Susan Rosemary Clarke; four *d*. *Educ:* Hitchin Grammar School; Hertford College, Oxford (1 Year Army Short Course); RMA Sandhurst. Commissioned RTR, 1948; served Germany, Korea, UK, Hong Kong, 1948–58; psc 1959; Aden, 1959–62; Germany and UK, 1962–64; MA to C-in-C AFNE, Norway, 1964–66; jssc 1967; Germany and UK, 1967–69; CO 4 RTR, BAOR, 1969–71; Nat. Defence Coll., 1971–72; Comdr RAC, 1 (BR) Corps, BAOR, 1972–74; Dir Operational Requirements MoD, 1974–77; rcds 1978; Dir, Combat Development (Army), 1979–81; Chief of Staff to Live Oak, SHAPE, 1982–84; completed service, 1984. Sen. Exec. and Sec., Kennel Club, 1984–93. *Recreations:* medieval history, gardening, swimming, golf. *Address:* Meadowside Farmhouse, Tulls Lane, Standford, Bordon, Hants GU35 8RB.

SINNOTT, John Brian; Chief Executive, Leicestershire County Council and Clerk of Lieutenancy, since 1994; *b* 11 March 1949; *s* of William John Sinnott and Mary Josephine Sinnott (*née* Foley); *m* 1970, Helen Mary Turner; two *s* two *d*. *Educ:* St Mary's Coll., Crosby; Univ. of Liverpool (MA, Dip. Public Admin). Liverpool CC, 1970–74; PA to Chm. and Leader of Council, Head of Leader's office, Merseyside CC, 1974–86; Management Consultant, Coopers and Lybrand Associates, 1986–87; Leicestershire County Council: Asst, then Sen. Asst, County Clerk, 1987–90; Asst Chief Exec., 1990–92; Dir, Corporate Management, 1992–94. Director: Leics TEC, 1994–2001; Leics Business Point (Business Link), 1995–2001; Leics Develt Agency, 1998–; Heart of the Nat. Forest Foundn, 1998–. Chm., Leics Cricket Bd, 2001–. *Publications:* papers in local govt jls. *Recreations:* sport, cricket literature, history of rock music. *Address:* County Hall, Glenfield, Leicester LE3 8RA. *T:* (0116) 265 6000; 24 Gullet Lane, Kirby Muxloe, Leics LE9 2BL. *Club:* Everton Football.

SINTON, William Baldie, OBE 1999; HM Diplomatic Service: Ambassador to Bolivia, since 2001; *b* 17 June 1946; *s* of late John William Sinton and Isabella McCrae Sinton (*née* Baldie); *m* 1995, Jane S. B. Aryee. *Educ:* Bristol Cathedral Sch.; Kirkcaldy High Sch.; Edinburgh Univ. (MA 1968). Third Sec., FCO, 1968; Third later Second Sec., Prague, 1970; Second later First Sec., UK Delegn to NATO, Brussels, 1973; FCO, 1977–81; First Sec. (Commercial), Algiers, 1981; FCO, 1985–96; Ambassador to Panama, 1996–99; Ambassador to Algeria, 1999–2001. *Address:* c/o Foreign and Commonwealth Office, SW1A 2AH.

SINYOR, Joseph, (Joe); Chief Executive, Newspapers, Trinity Mirror plc, since 2000; *b* 16 Aug. 1957; *s* of Samuel Joseph Sinyor and Claire Sinyor; *m* 1987, Pamela Caroline Nield Collis; two *s* one *d*. *Educ:* Jesus Coll., Cambridge; London Business Sch. (MBA). Corporate Finance Exec., J. Henry Schroder Wagg, 1983–85; Sen. Engagement Manager, McKinsey & Co. Inc., 1985–90; Gp Chief Exec., Pepe Gp plc, 1990–93; Man. Dir, Dillon's Bookstores Ltd, 1994–98; Man. Dir, Sony UK Ltd, 1998–2000. Non-exec. Dir, Channel 4 TV Corp., 1998–. *Recreations:* tennis, opera, ski-ing, walking. *Address:* 70 Sheldon Avenue, N6 4ND; Trinity Mirror plc, One Canada Square, Canary Wharf, E14 5AP.

SIRS, William; JP; General Secretary, Iron and Steel Trades Confederation, 1975–85, retired; *b* 6 Jan. 1920; *s* of Frederick Sirs and Margaret (*née* Powell); *m* 1941, Joan (*née* Clark); one *s* one *d*. *Educ:* Middleton St Johns, Hartlepool; WEA. Steel Industry, 1937–63; Iron and Steel Trades Confedn: Organiser, 1963; Divisional Officer, Manchester, 1970; Asst Gen. Sec., 1973. Member: Iron and Steel Industry Trng Bd, 1973; TUC Gen. Council, 1975–85; Trade Union Steel Industry Cons. Cttee, 1973– (Chm., 1975–) and Jt Accident Prevention Adv. Cttee, 1973; Employment Appeal Tribunal, 1976–; Jt Sec., Jt Industrial Council for Slag Industry, 1973; Exec. Mem., Paul Finet Foundn, European Coal and Steel Community, 1974; Hon. Sec. (British Section), Internat. Metalworkers Fedn, 1975. Mem., Management Cttee, BSC (Industry) Ltd, 1975–. Pres., Northern Home Counties Productivity Assoc., 1985–; Mem. RIIA, 1973. Mem. Council, Winston Churchill Meml Trust, 1985–90. Director (formerly Governor), Oaklands Coll., Herts, 1991–. JP Hartlepool, Co. Durham, later Knutsford, Cheshire, then Herts, 1963. Freeman, City of London, 1984. *Publication:* Hard Labour (autobiog.), 1985. *Recreations:* sailing, squash, swimming, running. *Address:* Hatfield, Hertfordshire.

SISSON, Charles Hubert, CH 1993; writer; *b* 22 April 1914; *s* of late Richard Percy Sisson and Ellen Minnie Sisson (*née* Worlock); *m* 1937, Nora Gilbertson; two *d*. *Educ:* University of Bristol, and in France and Germany. Entered Ministry of Labour as Assistant Principal, 1936; HM Forces, in the ranks, mainly in India, 1942–45; Simon Senior Research Fellow, 1956–57; Dir of Establishments (Under Sec.), Min. of Labour, 1962–68; Dir of Occupational Safety and Health (Under Sec.), Dept of Employment, 1972. FRSL 1975. Hon. DLitt Bristol, 1980. Jt Editor, PN Review, 1976–84. *Publications:* An Asiatic Romance, 1953; The Spirit of British Administration, 1959; Christopher Homm, 1965; Art and Action, 1965; Essays, 1967; English Poetry 1900–1950, 1971, rev. edn 1981; The Case of Walter Bagehot, 1972; (ed) The English Sermon, Vol. II 1650–1750, 1976; David Hume, 1976; (ed) Selected Poems of Jonathan Swift, 1977; The Avoidance of Literature, 1978; (ed) Autobiographical and Other Papers of Philip Mairet, 1981; Anglican Essays,

1983; (ed) Selected Poems of Christina Rossetti, 1984; On the Look-out (autobiog.), 1989; In Two Minds, 1990; (ed) Jeremy Taylor: selected writings, 1990; English Perspectives, 1992; Is There a Church of England?, 1993; (ed) Edgar Allan Poe: Poems and Essays on Poetry, 1995; *poetry:* The London Zoo, 1961; Numbers, 1965; The Discarnation, 1967; Metamorphoses, 1968; In the Trojan Ditch, 1974; The Corridor, 1975; Anchises, 1976; Exactions, 1980; Selected Poems, 1981; Collected Poems, 1984, rev. edn 1998; God Bless Karl Marx!, 1987; Antidotes, 1991; What and Who, 1994; Poems: Selected, 1995; Collected Poems, 1998; *translations:* Versions and Perversions of Heine, 1955; Catullus, 1966; The Poetic Art: a translation of the Ars Poetica of Horace, 1975; The Poem on Nature, 1976; Some Tales of La Fontaine, 1979; The Divine Comedy, 1980; The Song of Roland, 1983; Les Regrets of Joachim du Bellay, 1983; The Aeneid of Virgil, 1986; Britannicus, Phaedra, Athaliah, of Racine, 1987; Collected Translations, 1996. *Address:* Moorfield Cottage, The Hill, Langport, Somerset TA10 9PU. *T:* (01458) 250845.

SISSON, Rosemary Anne; writer since 1929; *b* 13 Oct. 1923; *d* of Prof. C. J. Sisson, MA, DèsL and Vera Kathleen (*née* Ginn). *Educ:* Cheltenham Ladies' Coll.; University Coll., London (BA Hons English); Newnham Coll., Cambridge (MLit). Served War, Royal Observer Corps, 1943–45. Instr in English, Univ. of Wisconsin, 1949; Lecturer in English: UCL, 1950–53; Univ. of Birmingham, 1953–54; Dramatic Critic, Stratford-upon-Avon Herald, 1954–57; after prodn of first play, The Queen and the Welshman, became full-time writer, 1957. Co-Chm., Writers Guild of GB, 1979 and 1980 (Pres., 1995–98); Hon. Sec., Dramatists' Club; Mem., BAFTA (Mem. Council, 1995–98). Laurel Award, for service to writers, 1985; Prince Michael of Kent Award, for services to SSAFA, 1987. *Plays:* The Queen and the Welshman, 1957; Fear Came to Supper, 1958; The Splendid Outcasts, 1959; The Royal Captivity, 1960; Bitter Sanctuary, 1963; Ghost on Tiptoe (with Robert Morley), 1974; The Dark Horse, 1978. Contributed to *TV series:* Catherine of Aragon, in The Six Wives of Henry VIII; The Marriage Game, in Elizabeth R; Upstairs, Downstairs; A Town Like Alice; The Young Indiana Jones Chronicles; *TV scripts:* Irish RM; Seal Morning; The Manions of America; The Bretts (creator of series). *Film scripts* include: Ride a Wild Pony; Escape from the Dark; Candleshoe; Watcher in the Woods; The Black Cauldron (full-length animation film) (all for Walt Disney); The Wind in the Willows (animation film), 1983 (also TV series, 1984). *Other scripts:* Heart of a Nation (Son-et-Lumière), Horse Guards Parade, 1983; Dawn to Dusk, Royal Tournament, 1984; Joy to the World, Royal Albert Hall, 1988–97; Royal Military Tattoo, 2000. *Publications: children's books:* The Adventures of Ambrose, 1951; The Young Shakespeare, 1959; The Young Jane Austen, 1962; The Young Shaftesbury, 1964; *novels:* The Exciseman, 1972; The Killer of Horseman's Flats, 1973; The Stratford Story, 1975; Escape from the Dark, 1976; The Queen and the Welshman, 1979; The Manions of America, 1982; Bury Love Deep, 1985; Beneath the Visiting Moon, 1986; The Bretts, 1987; Footstep on the Stair, 1999; First Love, Last Love, 2002; *poetry:* Rosemary for Remembrance, 1995. *Recreations:* travel, walking, riding, writing poetry. *Address:* 167 New King's Road, Parson's Green, SW6 4SN.

SISSONS, Prof. (John Gerald) Patrick, MD; FRCP, FRCPath; Professor of Medicine, University of Cambridge, and Fellow of Darwin College, since 1988; *b* 28 June 1945; *s* of Gerald William Sissons and Georgina Margaret Cockin; *m* 1971, Jennifer Ann Scovell (marr. diss. 1987); two *d*. *Educ:* Felstead Sch.; St Mary's Hosp. Med. Sch. (MB, MD). FRCP 1983; FRCPath 1995. Hosp. appts, St Mary's, St George's and Hammersmith Hosps, 1968–71; Registrar and Lectr, Dept of Medicine, RPMS, 1972–77; NIH Research Fellow and Asst Mem., Res. Inst. of Scripps Clinic, California, 1977–80; Wellcome Sen. Lectr, Depts of Medicine and Virology, RPMS, 1980–86; Prof. of Infectious Diseases, RPMS, 1987. Founder FMedSci 1998. *Publications:* papers on immunology and pathogenesis of virus infections. *Recreation:* travel. *Address:* Department of Medicine, University of Cambridge Clinical School, Hills Road, Cambridge CB2 2QQ. *T:* (01223) 336849.

SISSONS, Peter George; presenter, BBC TV 10 o'clock news, since 2000; *b* 17 July 1942; *s* of late George Robert Percival Sissons and Elsie Emma Evans; *m* 1965, Sylvia Bennett; two *s* one *d*. *Educ:* Liverpool Inst. High Sch. for Boys; University College Oxford (MA PPE). Independent Television News: graduate trainee, 1964; general reporter, 1967; industrial corresp., 1970; indust. editor, 1972–78; presenter, News at One, 1978–82; presenter: Channel Four News, 1982–89; BBC TV 6 o'clock news, 1989–93; BBC 9 o'clock news, 1993–2000; Chm., BBC TV Question Time, 1989–93. Hon. Fellow, Liverpool John Moores Univ., 1997. Broadcasting Press Guild Award, 1984; RTS Judges' Award, 1988; Newscaster of the Year, TRIC, 2001. *Recreations:* relaxing, supporting Liverpool FC. *Address:* BBC Television Centre, Wood Lane, W12 7RJ. *T:* (020) 8743 8000.

SISSONS, (Thomas) Michael (Beswick); Senior Consultant, The Peters Fraser and Dunlop Group Ltd, since 1999 (Managing Director, 1988–94; Chairman, 1988–99); *b* 13 Oct. 1934; *s* of Captain T. E. B. Sissons (killed in action, 1940) and late Marjorie (*née* Shepherd); *m* 1st, 1960, Nicola Ann Fowler (marr. diss. 1974); one *s* one *d*; 2nd, 1974, Ilze Kadegis (marr. diss. 1992); two *d*; 3rd, 1992, Serena Palmer. *Educ:* Winchester Coll.; Exeter Coll., Oxford (BA 1958, MA 1964). National Service, 2nd Lieut 13/18 Royal Hussars, 1953–55. Lectr in History, Tulane Univ., New Orleans, USA, 1958–59; joined A.D. Peters, Literary Agent, 1959; Dir, 1965, Chm. and Man. Dir, 1973–88, A. D. Peters & Co. Ltd. Pres., Assoc. of Authors' Agents, 1978–81; Director: London Broadcasting Co., 1973–75; Groucho Club plc, 1985–2001; Mem. Council, Consumers Assoc., 1974–77. Board Member: BFSS, 1994–95; Countryside Movt, 1995–97. *Publications:* (ed with Philip French) Age of Austerity, 1963, repr. 1986; (ed) A Countryside for All, 2001. *Recreations:* riding, gardening, cricket, music. *Address:* The White House, Broadleaze Farm, Westcot Lane, Sparsholt, Wantage, Oxon OX12 9PZ. *T:* (01235) 751215, *Fax:* (01235) 751561. *Clubs:* Groucho, MCC (Mem. Cttee, 1984–87, 1993–2000; Chm., Marketing and Public Affairs Sub-Cttee, 1995–2000).

SITWELL, Peter Sacheverell W.; *see* Wilmot-Sitwell.

SITWELL, Sir (Sacheverell) Reresby, 7th Bt *cr* 1808, of Renishaw; DL; *b* 15 April 1927; *s* of Sir Sacheverell Sitwell, 6th Bt, CH and Georgia Louise (*d* 1980), *d* of Arthur Doble; *S* father, 1988; *m* 1952, Penelope, *yr d* of late Col Hon. Donald Alexander Forbes, DSO, MVO; one *d*. *Educ:* Eton College; King's Coll., Cambridge (schol.). Served Grenadier Guards, 1945–48, mainly as Lieut, 2nd Bn, BAOR. Advertising and PR executive, 1948–63; operated vending machines and wholesale wine business, 1963–73. Took over Renishaw and family estates from late uncle, Sir Osbert, 1965. High Sheriff of Derbyshire, 1983; DL Derbyshire 1984. Freedom of City of London, 1984. *Publications:* (with John Julius Norwich and A. Costa) Mount Athos, 1964; Hortus Sitwellianus (epilogue), 1984. *Recreations:* art and architecture, music, travel, photography, racing. *Heir:* *b* Francis Trajan Sacheverell Sitwell [*b* 17 Sept. 1935; *m* 1966, Susanna Carolyn, *d* of Sir Ronald Hibbert Cross, 1st Bt, KCMG, KCVO, PC; two *s* one *d*]. *Address:* Renishaw Hall, Sheffield S21 3WB; 4 Southwick Place, W2 2TN. *T:* (020) 7262 3939. *Clubs:* White's, Brooks's, Pratt's, Society of Dilettanti; Pitt (Cambridge).

SIU, Gordon Kwing-Chue, CBE 1997; JP; Secretary for Planning and Lands, Hong Kong, since 1999; *b* 29 Nov. 1945; *s* of Siu Wood-chuen and Chan Shuk-ming; *m* 1999, Cynthia Wong Lok-yee; two *s* by a previous marriage. *Educ:* Birmingham Univ. (MSocSci). Joined Hong Kong Civil Service, 1966; Sec.-Gen., Office of Members of Exec. and Legislative Councils, 1985; Postmaster Gen., 1988; Comr for Transport, 1989; Dir, New Airport Projects Co-ordination Office, 1992; Secretary for: Economic Services, 1993; Transport, 1996; Hd, Central Policy Unit, 1997. *Recreations:* reading, swimming, golf. *Address:* 9th floor, Murray Building, Garden Road, Hong Kong. *T:* 28482101. *Clubs:* Hong Kong Golf, Hong Kong Jockey.

SIZELAND, Paul Raymond; HM Diplomatic Service; Consul General, Shanghai, since 2000; *b* 19 Feb. 1952; *s* of Raymond Sizeland and Patricia Sizeland (*née* Dudley); *m* 1976, Vasantha, *d* of late James Kanaka and Nancy Jesudasan; two *d*. *Educ:* Dulwich Coll.; Bradford Univ. (BTech Hons Applied Biol. 1975). MIPD 1995. VSO teacher, St Stephen's Coll., Trinidad, 1970–71; Res. Student, Rowett Res. Inst., Aberdeen, 1973–74; CMS volunteer teacher, Ida Scudder Sch., Vellore, S India, 1976–78; Med. Rep. for Essex and Suffolk, Merrell Pharmaceuticals, 1978–80; joined HM Diplomatic Service, 1980; Third Sec., UK Delegn to NATO, Brussels, 1981–84; Commercial Attaché, Doha, 1985–86; Second Sec., FCO, 1986–88; First Sec., Political/Develt, Lagos, 1988–91; Private Sec. to Lord Carrington, Chm., EU Conf. on former Yugoslavia, 1991–92; Head, Career Develt Unit, FCO, 1992–95; Dep. Head, Personnel Mgt Dept, FCO, 1995–96; Dep. Hd of Mission, Bangkok, 1996–2000. *Recreations:* family, Millwall FC supporter, travel, books, music, Kipling Society. *Address:* c/o Foreign and Commonwealth Office, King Charles Street, SW1A 2AH.

SIZER, Prof. John, CBE 1989; DLitt; Chief Executive and Member: Scottish Higher Education Funding Council, since 1992; Scottish Further Education Funding Council, since 1999; *b* 14 Sept. 1938; *s* of Mary and John Robert Sizer; *m* 1965, Valerie Claire Davies; three *s*. *Educ:* Grimsby Coll. of Technology; Univ. of Nottingham (BA); DLitt Loughborough, 1989. FCMA. Teaching Fellow, later Lectr, Univ. of Edinburgh, 1965; Sen. Lectr, London Graduate Sch. of Business Studies, 1968; Loughborough University of Technology: Prof. of Financial Mgt, 1970–96; Vis. Prof., 1996–; Founding Head of Dept of Management Studies, 1971–84; Dean of Sch. of Human and Environmental Studies, 1973–76; Sen. Pro Vice-Chancellor, 1980–82; Dir, Business Sch., 1991–92. Chm., Directing Group, OECD/CERI Programme on Institutional Management in Higher Educn, 1980–84; Mem., UGC, 1984–89 (Chm., Business and Management Studies Sub-Cttee, 1984–89); Advr on Business and Management Studies, and Mem., NI Cttee, UFC, 1989–93; Member: Council, CIMA, 1981–88 (Chairman: Internat. Cttee, 1982–86; Finance Cttee, 1986–88); Nat. Forum for Management Educn and Develt, 1989–95 (Chm., Finance and Resourcing Cttee, 1989–95; Mem., Exec. Cttee, 1989–95); Sci. and Engrg Base Co-ordinating Cttee, 1993–; Foresight Prog. Steering Gp, 1995–2001; Chm., Soc. for Res. into Higher Educn, 1992–93 (Vice Pres., 1995–). Member: Public Sector and Not-for-Profit Cttee, Accounting Standards Bd, 1994–98; Sec. of State for Scotland's Scottish Parlt Financial Issues Adv. Gp, 1998–99. FIMgt; FRSA. *Publications:* An Insight into Management Accounting, 1969, 1979, 1989; Case Studies in Management Accounting, 1974; Perspectives in Management Accounting, 1981; (ed jtly) Resources and Higher Education, 1983; (jtly) A Casebook of British Management Accounting, vol. 1, 1984, vol. 2, 1985; Institutional Responses to Financial Reductions in the University Sector, 1987; numerous articles in accounting, economics, higher educn and management jls. *Recreations:* enjoying Scotland, walking. *Address:* SHEFC, Donaldson House, 97 Haymarket Terrace, Edinburgh EH12 5HD. *T:* (0131) 313 6500.

SKARBEK, Marjorie Shiona, (Countess Skarbek); *see* Wallace, M. S.

SKEAT, Theodore Cressy, BA; Keeper of Manuscripts and Egerton Librarian, British Museum, 1961–72; *b* 15 Feb. 1907; *s* of Walter William Skeat, MA; *m* 1942, Olive Martin (*d* 1992); one *s*. *Educ:* Whitgift School, Croydon; Christ's College, Cambridge. Student at British School of Archaeology, Athens, 1929–31; Asst Keeper, Dept of Manuscripts, British Museum, 1931; Deputy Keeper, 1948. FBA, 1963–80. *Publications:* (with H. I. Bell) Fragments of an Unknown Gospel, 1935; (with H. J. M. Milne) Scribes and Correctors of the Codex Sinaiticus, 1938; The Reigns of the Ptolemies, 1954; Papyri from Panopolis, 1964; Catalogue of Greek Papyri in the British Museum, vol. VII, 1974; (with C. H. Roberts) The Birth of the Codex, 1983; The Reign of Augustus in Egypt, 1993; The Codex Sinaiticus, the Codex Vaticanus and Constantine, 1999; articles in papyrological journals. *Address:* 12 Berkeley Court, 31/33 Gordon Road, W5 2AE. *T:* (020) 8998 9174.

SKEATES, Basil George; Director, Ashdown Gallery, 1985–94; Under Secretary, Department of the Environment, 1980–85; *b* 19 May 1929; *s* of George William Skeates and Florence Rachel Skeates; *m* 1957, Irene Margaret (*née* Hughes); four *s*. *Educ:* Hampton Grammar Sch. RIBA 1955. Mil. Service with RE, W Africa, 1947–49. Architect with LCC schs and special works, 1949–61; Principal Architect: NE Metrop. Reg. Hosp. Bd, 1961–64; MPBW, 1964–71; Superintending Architect, CSD, 1971–73; Asst Dir, Architectural Services, PSA, 1973–75; Dir of Works, PO Services, 1975–80; Dir of Def. Services II, DoE, 1980–85. *Publications:* articles in prof. and technical jls. *Recreation:* designing and making things.

SKEET, Muriel Harvey; International Health Services adviser and consultant, World Health Organisation Headquarters, 1971–96; *b* 12 July 1926; *y d* of late F. W. C. Skeet, Suffolk. *Educ:* privately; Endsleigh House; Middlesex Hosp. SRN, MRSH; FRCN. Gen. Nursing Trg at Middx Hosp., 1946–49; also London Sch. of Hygiene and Tropical Med.; Ward Sister and Admin. Sister, Middx Hosp., 1949–60; Field Work Organiser, Opl Res. Unit, Nuffield Provincial Hosps Trust, 1961–64; Res. Org., Dan Mason Nursing Res. Cttee of Nat. Florence Nightingale Memorial Cttee of Gt Britain and N Ire., 1965–70; Chief Nursing Officer and Nursing Advr, BRCS, and St John of Jerusalem and BRCS Jt Cttee, 1970–78. WHO Res. Consultant, SE Asia, 1970; European Deleg. and First Chm. of Bd of Commonwealth Nurses' Fed., 1971. Leverhulme Fellowship, 1974–75. Member: Hosp. and Med. Services Cttee, 1970; Ex-Services War Disabled Help Cttee, 1970; British Commonwealth Nurses War Memorial Fund Cttee and Council, 1970; Council of Management of Nat. Florence Nightingale Memorial Cttee, 1970; Council of Queen's Inst. of District Nursing, 1970; Royal Coll. of Nursing and Nat. Council of Nurses; RSM, 1980. Fellow RCN, 1977. *Publications:* Waiting in Outpatient Departments (Nuffield Provincial Hospitals Trust), 1965; Marriage and Nursing (Dan Mason NRC), 1968; Home from Hospital (Dan Mason NRC), 1970; Home Nursing, 1975; Manual: Disaster Relief Work, 1977; Back to Our Basic Skills, 1977; Health needs Help, 1977; (jtly) Health Auxiliaries in the Health Team, 1978; Self Care for the People of Developing Countries, 1979; Discharge Procedures, 1980; Notes on Nursing 1860 and 1980, 1980; Emergency Procedures and First Aid for Nurses, 1981; The Third Age, 1982; Providing Continuing Care for Elderly People, 1983; First Aid for Developing Countries, 1983; Protecting the Health of the Elderly, 1983; Know Your Own Body, 1987; Add Life to Years, 1989; Tropical Health: concise notes, 1989; Better Opportunities for Disabled People, 1989;

Care and Maintenance of Hospital Equipment, 1995; various articles in professional jls. *Recreations:* music, opera, painting, reading. *Clubs:* Royal Society of Medicine, Sloane.

SKEET, Sir Trevor (Herbert Harry), Kt 1986; barrister, writer and consultant; *b* 28 Jan. 1918; British; *m* 1st, 1958, Elizabeth Margaret Gilling (*d* 1973); two *s*; 2nd; 1985, Mrs Valerie Anita Edwina Benson. *Educ:* King's College, Auckland; University of New Zealand, Auckland (LLB). Served War of 1939–45, with NZ Engineers (sergeant); 2nd Lieut, NZ Anti-Aircraft (Heavy); Sub-Lieutenant, NZ Roy. Naval Volunteer Reserve; demobilised, 1945. Formerly Barrister and Solicitor of Supreme Court of New Zealand; Barrister, Inner Temple, 1947. Has considerable experience in public speaking. Formerly associated with Commonwealth and Empire Industries Assoc.; Mem. Council, Royal Commonwealth Soc., 1952–55, and 1956–69. Contested (C): Stoke Newington and Hackney, North, Gen. Election, 1951; Llanelly Div. of Carmarthenshire, Gen. Election, 1955; MP (C): Willesden East, 1959–64; Bedford, 1970–83; Bedfordshire North, 1983–97. Mem., Select Cttee on Science and Technol., 1993–97; Vice-Chairman: Cons. Party Power Cttee, 1959–64; Energy Cttee, 1974–77; Chairman: Oil Sub-Cttee, 1959–64; Cons. Party Trade Cttee, 1971–74; Cons. Party Middle East Cttee (Foreign and Commonwealth Affairs), 1973–78; Secretary: All-Party Cttee on Airships, 1971–78; All-Party Gp on Minerals, 1971–97 (Co-Chm., 1979–97); Vice-Pres., Steering Cttee, Parly and Scientific Cttee, 1988–91 (Mem., 1982–97; Sec., 1983–85; Chm., 1985–88); Vice-Chm., British-Japanese and British-Brazilian Gps; Sec., British-Nigerian Gp. Mem., Econ. Cttee, Machine Tool Trades Association for several years; Member Technical Legislation Cttee, CBI. *Publications:* contrib. to numerous journals including New Commonwealth and Mining World, on oil, atomic energy, metals, commodities, finance, and Imperial and Commonwealth development. *Address:* The Gables, Milton Ernest, Bedfordshire MK44 1RS. *T:* (01234) 822307. *Clubs:* Army and Navy, Royal Commonwealth Society.

SKEFFINGTON, family name of **Viscount Massereene and Ferrard**.

SKEGGS, Sir Clifford (George), Kt 1987; JP; FNZIM; Chairman and Chief Executive, Skeggs Group; Director of various public and private companies; Mayor, Dunedin City, 1978–89; *b* 19 March 1931; *s* of George Henry Skeggs and Beatrice Hannah (*née* Heathcote); *m* 1952, Marie Eleanor Ledgerwood; three *s*. *Educ:* Southland Technical Coll., New Zealand. Mem., 1968–80, Chm., 1973–77, Otago Harbour Bd. City Councillor, Dunedin, 1972–77. Mem. Council, Univ. of Otago, 1981–89. FNZIM 1985; Mem., Inst. of Dirs, 1984. JP Dunedin, 1978. OStJ 1987. *Publications:* contrib. fishing and general business publications. *Recreations:* yachting, golf, flying, power boating, squash, keen follower of Rugby. *Address:* Skeggs Group, Box 5657, Dunedin, New Zealand. *Club:* Dunedin (Dunedin).

SKEHEL, Sir John (James), Kt 1996; PhD; FRS 1984; Director, MRC National Institute for Medical Research, since 1987; *b* 27 Feb. 1941; *s* of Joseph and Annie Josephine Skehel; *m* 1962, Anita Varley; two *s*. *Educ:* St Mary's Coll., Blackburn; University College of Wales, Aberystwyth (BSc); UMIST (PhD). Post-doctoral Fellow, Marischal Coll., Aberdeen, 1965–68; Fellow, Helen Hay Whitney Foundn, 1968–71; MRC National Institute for Medical Research: Mem., Scientific Staff, 1971–; Head of Div. of Virology, 1984–87. Dir, World Influenza Centre, 1975–93. Leeuwenhoek Lecture, Royal Soc., 1990. Hon. Prof., Liverpool Polytechnic Sch. of Nat. Sci., 1990; Hon. Prof. of Virology, Glasgow Univ., 1997. Founder FMedSci 1998. Hon. DSc CNAA, 1990. Wilhelm Feldberg prize, Feldberg Foundn, 1986; Robert Koch prize, Robert Koch Foundn, 1987; Prix Louis Jeantet de Médecine, Jeantet Foundn, 1988; Internat. Prize in Virology, ICN Pharmaceuticals, 1992. *Publications:* scientific articles in various jls. *Address:* National Institute for Medical Research, The Ridgeway, Mill Hill, NW7 1AA. *T:* (020) 8959 3666; *e-mail:* mbrenna@nimr.ac.uk.

SKELLETT, Colin Frank, CChem, FRSC; FCIWEM; Chairman: Wessex Water, since 1999; Jarvis plc, since 2000; Vice Chairman, Azurix Services, since 1999; *b* 13 June 1945; *s* of Harry and Ivy Skellett; *m* 1963, Jennifer Trout; two *s* one *d*. *Educ:* City Univ. (MSc). CChem 1971, FRSC 1990. Operational and mgt posts, Wessex Water, 1974–88; Chief Exec., Wessex Water plc, 1988–99. Trustee: WaterAid, 1995–; Money Advice Trust, 2000–. Churchill Fellow, 1983. *Publications:* various technical papers on water and waste water treatment. *Recreations:* walking, theatre, music, charity fundraising. *Address:* (office) Wessex Water, Claverton Down Road, Claverton Down, Bath BA2 7WW. *T:* (01225) 526000.

SKELMERSDALE, 7th Baron *cr* 1828; **Roger Bootle-Wilbraham;** advisor on politics and parliamentary affairs; Director, Broadleigh Nurseries Ltd, since 1991 (Managing Director, 1973–81); *b* 2 April 1945; *o s* of 6th Baron Skelmersdale, DSO, MC, and Ann (*d* 1974), *d* of late Percy Cuthbert Quilter; *S* father, 1973; *m* 1972, Christine Joan, *o d* of Roy Morgan; one *s* one *d*. *Educ:* Eton; Lord Wandsworth Coll., Basingstoke; Somerset Farm Institute; Hadlow Coll. VSO (Zambia), 1969–71; Proprietor, Broadleigh Gardens, 1972; Vice-Chm., Co En Co, 1979–81. A Lord in Waiting (Govt Whip), 1981–86; Parly Under-Sec. of State, DoE, 1986–87; Parly Under-Sec. of State, DHSS, 1987–88, Dept of Social Security, 1988–89, NI Office, 1989–90; House of Lords: Dep. Chm. of cttees, 1991–; Dep. Speaker, 1996–; elected Mem., 1999. President: Somerset Trust for Nature Conservation, 1980–; British Naturalists Assoc., 1980–85. Chm., Stroke Assoc., 1993–. Gov., Castle Sch., Taunton, 1993–97. *Recreations:* gardening, reading, bridge playing. *Heir:* *s* Hon. Andrew Bootle-Wilbraham, *b* 9 Aug. 1977. *Address:* c/o House of Lords, SW1A 0PW.

SKELTON, Rt Rev. Kenneth John Fraser, CBE 1972; an Assistant Bishop, Dioceses of Sheffield and Derby; *b* 16 May 1918; *s* of Henry Edmund and Kate Elizabeth Skelton; *m* 1945, Phyllis Barbara, *y d* of James Emerton; two *s* one *d*. *Educ:* Dulwich Coll.; Corpus Christi Coll., Cambridge (1st Cl. Class. Tripos, Pt 1, 1939; 1st Cl. Theol. Tripos, Pt 1, 1940; BA 1940, MA 1944); Wells Theological Coll. Deacon, 1941; priest, 1942; Curate: Normanton-by-Derby, 1941–43; Bakewell, 1943–45; Bolsover, 1945–46; Tutor, Wells Theol Coll., and Priest-Vicar, Wells Cathedral, 1946–50; Vicar of Howe Bridge, Atherton, 1950–55; Rector, Walton-on-the-Hill, Liverpool, 1955–62; Exam. Chap. to Bp of Liverpool, 1957–62; Bishop of Matabeleland, 1962–70; Asst Bishop, Dio. Durham, Rural Dean of Wearmouth and Rector of Bishopwearmouth, 1970–75; Bishop of Lichfield, 1975–84. Select Preacher, Cambridge Univ., 1971, 1973. *Publications:* Bishop in Smith's Rhodesia, 1985; The Overseas Bishoprics' Fund 1941–1991, 1991. *Recreation:* music. *Address:* 65 Crescent Road, Sheffield S7 1HN. *T:* (0114) 255 1260.

SKELTON, Nicholas David, (Nick); show jumper; *b* 30 Nov. 1957; *s* of David Frank Skelton and Norma Skelton (*née* Brindley); *m* 1982, Sarah Poile; two *s*. Jun. European Champion, 1975; British Champion, 1981, on St James; European Championships: team gold medal, 1985, 1987, 1989, team silver medal, 1991, 1993, 1995, individual bronze medal, 1987; World Championships: team bronze medals, 1982, 1990, 1998, team silver medal, and individual bronze medal, on Apollo, 1986; winner: King George V Gold Cup, on St James, 1984, on Limited Edition, 1993, 1996, on Hopes Are High, 1999; Hickstead Derby, on J Nick, 1987, on Apollo, 1988, 1989; Grand Prix in Britain, Canada, France, Germany, Ireland, USA; Member: Nations Cup team, 1978–2000; Olympic team, 1988, 1992, 1996. Chef d'équipe, British team, Nations Cup, Lisbon, 2001. *Address:* c/o British Show Jumping Association, British Equestrian Centre, Stoneleigh Park, Kenilworth, Warwicks CV8 2LR.

SKELTON, Peter John, OBE 1997; Regional Director, Eastern and Central Africa, and Director, Kenya, British Council, since 1998; *b* 24 Sept. 1949; *s* of John Frederick and Gwendoline Mabel Skelton; *m* 1971, Heather Morrison; one *s* one *d*. *Educ:* Queen Elizabeth's Grammar Sch., Barnet; Durham Univ. (BA Hons Modern Arabic Studies 1971); UCNW, Bangor (PGCE (TEFL) 1973). Desk Officer, FCO, 1971; British Council: Asst Rep., Jordan, 1977–81, Peru, 1982–84; Dep. Rep., Wales, 1984–86, Zambia, 1986–88; Dir, Hamburg, 1989–93, E Jerusalem (West Bank and Gaza), 1993–98. *Recreations:* listening to music, playing guitar, playing tennis, hashing, Tottenham Hotspur. *Address:* British Council, 10 Spring Gardens, SW1A 2BN. *T:* (020) 7930 8466.

SKELTON, Robert William, OBE 1989; Keeper, Indian Department, Victoria and Albert Museum, 1978–88; *b* 11 June 1929; *s* of John William Skelton and Victoria (*née* Wright); *m* 1954, Frances Aird; three *s*. *Educ:* Tiffin Boys' Sch., Kingston-upon-Thames. Joined Indian Section of Victoria and Albert Museum, 1950; Asst Keeper, 1960; Dep. Keeper, 1972; Nuffield Travelling Fellow in India, 1962. Mem. Council: Royal Asiatic Soc., 1970–73, 1975–78, 1988–92; Soc. for S Asian Studies, 1984–94; Trustee: Asia House Trust (London), 1977–; Indian Nat. Trust for Art and Cultural Heritage, UK, 1991–. *Publications:* Indian Miniatures from the XVth to XIXth Centuries, 1961; Rajasthani Temple Hangings of the Krishna Cult, 1973; (jtly) Islamic Painting and Arts of the Book, 1976; (jtly) Indian Painting, 1978; (jtly) Arts of Bengal, 1979; (jtly) The Indian Heritage, 1982; (jtly) Islamic Art in the Keir Collection, 1988; various contribs to art periodicals and conf. proc., 1956–. *Recreations:* chamber music, walking. *Address:* 10 Spencer Road, South Croydon CR2 7EH. *Fax:* (020) 8688 7187.

SKENE, (Karen) Prudence Patricia, (Mrs B. H. Wray), CBE 2000; Chairman: Rambert Dance Company, since 2000; Arvon Foundation, since 2000; *b* 9 Jan. 1944; *d* of Robert Worboys Skene and Phyllis Monica Skene (*née* Langley); *m* 1986, Brian Henry Wray; one step *s* one step *d*. *Educ:* Francis Holland Sch., London. Dep. Administrator, The Round House, Chalk Farm, 1973–75; Ballet Rambert: Administrator, 1975–78; Admin. Dir, 1978–84; Exec. Dir, 1984–86; Exec. Producer, English Shakespeare Co., 1987–90 and 1992; Dir, The Arts Foundn, 1993–98. Dir, Royal United Hosp. Bath NHS Trust, 1999–. Mem., Arts Council of England (formerly Arts Council of GB), 1992–2000 (Chairman: Dance Panel, 1992–96; Lottery Panel, 1996–2000). Vice-Pres., 1985–89, Pres., 1991–92, Theatrical Management Assoc.; Chm., Dancers Resettlement Trust and Vice-Chm., Dancers Resettlement Fund, 1988–92; Dir, Theatre Royal, Bath, 1998–. Trustee: Cardiff Old Liby Trust, 1996–2000; Stephen Spender Meml Fund, 2000–. FRSA 1992. *Recreations:* travel, food, the performing arts. *Address:* 8 Prior Park Buildings, Bath BA2 4NP.

SKERMAN, Ronald Sidney, CBE 1974; Deputy Chairman, Prudential Corporation plc, 1985–87 (Director, 1980–87; Group Chief Actuary, 1979); *b* 1 June 1914; *s* of S. H. Skerman; *m* 1939, Gladys Mary Fosdike (*d* 1998); no *c*. *Educ:* Hertford Grammar School. BA Open Univ., 1989. FIA. Actuarial Trainee with Prudential Assurance Co., 1932; Chief Actuary, 1968–79. Pres., Inst. Actuaries, 1970–72; Chm., Life Offices Assoc., 1973–74; Chm., British Insurers European Cttee, 1972–82; Mem., Royal Commn on Civil Liability, 1973–78. Gold Medal, Inst. of Actuaries, 1980. *Publications:* contrib. Jl Inst. Actuaries. *Recreations:* walking, travel, music. *Address:* 1 Rookes, Little Walden Road, Saffron Walden, Essex CB10 2EP. *T:* (01799) 513158.

SKEWIS, (William) Iain, PhD; consultant; Chief Executive, Enterprise South West Shropshire, since 1999; Director: Event Co. Ltd, since 1993; Development Consultancy Ltd, since 1995; *b* 1 May 1936; *s* of John Jamieson and Margaret Middlemass Skewis; *m* 1963, Jessie Frame Weir; two *s* one *d*. *Educ:* Hamilton Academy; Univ. of Glasgow (BSc, PhD). MCIT 1970; FTS 1987. British Rail, 1961–63; Transport Holding Co., 1963–66; Highlands and Islands Development Bd, 1966–72; Yorkshire and Humberside Development Assoc., 1973–77; Chief Exec., Develt Bd for Rural Wales, 1977–90. Chm., Regl Studies Assoc., 1990–93. Chairman: British Isles Soccer Tournaments Assoc.; Football Assoc. of Wales Premier Cup. *Recreation:* soccer. *Address:* Rock House, The Square, Montgomery, Powys SY15 6PA. *T:* (01686) 668276; Grange Court, Newtownstewart, Omagh, Co. Tyrone, Northern Ireland BT78 4AP. *T:* (028) 8266 2267.

SKIDELSKY, family name of **Baron Skidelsky**.

SKIDELSKY, Baron *cr* 1991 (Life Peer), of Tilton in the County of East Sussex; **Robert Jacob Alexander Skidelsky,** DPhil; FRSL; FRHistS; FBA 1994; Professor of Political Economy, Warwick University, since 1990; *b* 25 April 1939; *s* of late Boris Skidelsky and Galia Sapelkin; *m* 1970, Augusta Mary Clarissa Hope; two *s* one *d*. *Educ:* Brighton Coll.; Jesus Coll., Oxford (BA and MA Mod. Hist.; DPhil; Hon. Fellow, 1997). FRHistS 1973; FRSL 1978. Res. Fellow: Nuffield Coll., Oxford, 1965–68; British Acad., 1968–70; Associate Prof. of History, Sch. of Advanced Internat. Studies, Johns Hopkins Univ., Washington, DC, 1970–76; Head, Dept of History, Philosophy and Eur. Studies, Polytechnic of N London, 1976–78; Prof. of Internat. Studies, Warwick Univ., 1978–90. Dir, Stilwell Financial Inc., 2001–. Dir, 1989–91, Chm., 1991–, Social Market Foundn; Mem., Policy Cttee, SDP, 1988–90. Opposition Spokesman on: Culture, Media and Sport, H of L, 1997–98; Treasury affairs, 1998–99. Chairman: Charleston Trust, 1987–92; Hands Off Reading Campaign, 1994–98. Member: Adv. Council on Public Records, 1988–93; Schools Examinations and Assessment Council, 1992–93. Mem., Bd of Dirs, Moscow Sch. of Pol Studies, 1999–; Governor: Portsmouth Univ., 1994–97; Brighton Coll., 1998–. Hon. DLit Buckingham, 1997. *Publications:* Politicians and the Slump, 1967, 2nd edn 1994; English Progressive Schools, 1969; Oswald Mosley, 1975; (ed) The End of the Keynesian Era, 1977; (ed, with Michael Holroyd) William Gerhardie's God's Fifth Column, 1981; John Maynard Keynes, vol. 1 1883–1920, Hopes Betrayed, 1983, vol. 2 1921–1937, The Economist as Saviour (Wolfson History Prize), 1992, vol. 3 1937–1946, Fighting for Britain (Duff Cooper Prize), 2000; (ed) Thatcherism, 1988; Interests and Obsessions, 1993; The World After Communism, 1995; Keynes, 1996. *Recreations:* opera, ballet, cinema, tennis, table tennis. *Address:* Tilton House, Firle, East Sussex BN8 6LL. *T:* (01323) 811570.

SKILBECK, Diana Margaret; Headmistress, The Queen's School, Chester, 1989–2001; *b* 14 Nov. 1942; *d* of late William Allen Skilbeck and Elsie Almond Skilbeck. *Educ:* Wirral County Grammar School for Girls, Cheshire; Furzedown Coll., London (Teacher's Cert.); BA Hons London (External). Assistant Teacher: Mendell Primary Sch., 1964–67; Gayton Primary Sch., 1967–69; Wirral County Grammar Sch., 1969–74; Head of Geography, Wirral County Grammar Sch., 1974–78; Dep. Headmistress, West Kirby Grammar Sch., 1978–83; Headmistress, Sheffield High School, GPDST, 1983–89. *Recreations:* inland waterways, walking, singing, reading, industrial archaeology.

SKILBECK, Prof. Malcolm; education consultant and writer; Deputy Director (Education), Directorate of Education, Employment, Labour and Social Affairs, Organisation for Economic Co-operation and Development, Paris, 1991–97; *b* 22 Sept. 1932; *s* of Charles Harrison Skilbeck and Elsie Muriel Nash Skilbeck; *m* Helen Connell. *Educ:* Univ. of Sydney (BA); Acad. DipEd London, PhD London; MA Illinois. Secondary school teacher and adult educn teacher, 1958–63; Lectr. Univ. of Bristol, 1963–71; Prof., New Univ. of Ulster, 1971–75; Dir, Australian Curriculum Develt Centre, 1975–81; Dir of Studies, Schs Council for Curriculum and Exams for England and Wales, 1981–83; Prof. of Education, Univ. of London, 1981–85; Prof. and Vice-Chancellor, Deakin Univ., Australia, 1986–91. Consultancies for Unesco, OECD, etc, intermittently, 1967–; active in voluntary organizations concerned with educn for internat. understanding, eg, Chm., World Educn Fellowship, 1981–85. Hon. DLitt NUI. *Publications:* John Dewey, 1970; (jtly) Classroom and Culture, 1976; (jtly) Inservice Education and Training, 1977; A Core Curriculum for the Common School 1982; (ed) Evaluating the Curriculum in the Eighties, 1984; School Based Curriculum Development, 1984; Readings in School-Based Curriculum Development, 1984; Curriculum Reform, 1990; The Vocational Quest, 1994; (jtly) Redefining Tertiary Education, 1998; Access and Equity in Higher Education, 2000; Education for All: 2000 assessment, 2000; numerous contribs to jls, project reports, etc. *Recreations:* gardening, travelling, walking, reading.

SKILTON, Prof. David John; Professor and Head of School of English, Communication and Philosophy, Cardiff University (formerly University of Wales College of Cardiff), since 1988; *b* 10 July 1942; *s* of Henry C. S. Skilton and Iris F. M. Skilton (*née* Redfern); *m* 1st, 1976, Marvid E. G. Kennedy-Finlayson (marr. diss.); 2nd, 1984, Joanne V. Papworth; one *s* one *d*. *Educ:* Tollington Grammar Sch., London; King's Coll., Cambridge (MA, MLitt); Univ. of Copenhagen. Lectr, Glasgow Univ., 1970–80; Professor of English: St David's University Coll., Lampeter, 1980–86; UWIST, 1986–88; Pro Vice-Chancellor, UWCC, 1992–96; Dean, Faculty of Humanities, Cardiff Univ., 1997–99. Mem., Nat. Curriculum English Working Group, 1988–89; Trustee, Roald Dahl Arts Project, 1996–. Literary Adviser to Trollope Soc., 1988–; Editor, Trollope Soc. edn of novels of Anthony Trollope, 1988–99. *Publications:* Anthony Trollope and his Contemporaries, 1972, 2nd edn 1996; Defoe to the Victorians, 1977, 2nd edn 1985; The Early and Mid-Victorian Novel, 1993. *Recreations:* music, Scandinavian culture. *Address:* Cardiff University, Cardiff CF10 3XB. *T:* (029) 2087 4503.

SKINGSLEY, Air Chief Marshal Sir Anthony (Gerald), GBE 1992 KCB 1986 (CB 1983); Deputy Commander-in-Chief, Allied Forces Central Europe, 1989–92, retired; *b* 19 Oct. 1933; *s* of Edward Roberts Skingsley; *m* 1957, Lilwen; two *s* one *d*. *Educ:* St Bartholomew's, Newbury; Cambridge Univ. (BA, MA). Commissioned RAFVR 1954, RAF 1955; several flying appointments, then Flt Comdr 13 Sqdn, 1961–62; OC Ops Sqdn, RAF Akrotiri, 1962–63; RAF Staff Coll., Bracknell, 1964; OC 45 Sqdn, RAF Tengah, Singapore, 1965–67; jssc Latimer, 1968; RAF Project Officer for Tornado in MoD, 1968–71; OC 214 Sqdn, RAF Marham, 1972–74; Station Comdr, RAF Laarbruch, Germany, 1974–76; Hon. ADC to the Queen, 1976–78; Asst Chief of Staff, Offensive Ops, HQ 2nd ATAF, 1977; RCDS 1978; Director of Air Staff Plans, MoD, 1978–80; Asst Chief of Staff, Plans and Policy, SHAPE, 1980–83; Comdt, RAF Staff Coll., Bracknell, 1983–84; ACAS, 1985–86; Air Mem. for Personnel, 1986–87; C-in-C RAF Germany, and Comdr, Second ATAF, 1987–89. Mem., Allgemeine Rheinlaendische Industrie Gesellschaft, 1975. Pres., RAFA, Luxembourg, 1992–; Mem. Adv. Council, Atlantic Council, 1993–. *Recreations:* travel, off-shore sailing, music, golf. *Address:* c/o National Westminster Bank, 43 Swan Street, West Malling, Kent ME19 6HF. *Club:* Royal Air Force.

SKINNER, Prof. Andrew Stewart, FBA 1993; FRSE; Adam Smith Professor of Political Economy, University of Glasgow, 1994–97, now Emeritus (Daniel Jack Professor, 1985–94); *b* 11 Jan. 1935; *s* of late Andrew Paterson Skinner and Isabella Bateman (*nee* Stewart); *m* 1966, Margaret Mary Dorothy Robertson. *Educ:* Glasgow Univ. (MA 1958; BLitt 1960). FRSE 1988. Tutor and Asst Lectr, QUB, 1959–62; Lectr, Queen's Coll., Dundee, Univ. of St Andrews, 1962–64; University of Glasgow: Lectr, 1964–70; Sen. Lectr, 1970–75; Reader, 1975–77; Prof., 1977–85; Dean, Faculty of Social Scis, 1980–83; Clerk of Senate, 1983–90; Vice-Principal, 1991–96. *Publications:* (ed) Sir James Steuart, Principles of Political Economy, 1966; (ed with R. H. Campbell and W. B. Todd) Adam Smith, The Wealth of Nations, 1976; A System of Social Science: papers relating to Adam Smith, 1979, 2nd edn 1996; (with R. H. Campbell) Adam Smith: a short biography, 1982; (ed with P. Jones) Adam Smith Reviewed, 1992. *Recreation:* gardening. *Address:* Department of Political Economy, The University, Glasgow G12 8RT. *T:* (0141) 330 4657; Glen House, Cardross, Dumbarton, Dunbartonshire G82 5ES. *T:* (01389) 841603. *Club:* University (Glasgow).

SKINNER, Angus Mackinnon Cumming; Chief Inspector of Social Work Services for Scotland, Scottish Executive Education Department (formerly Scottish Office), since 1992; *b* 4 Jan. 1950; *s* of Dr Theodore Skinner, OBE and Morag Mackinnon Skinner; *m* (separated 1995); one *s* two *d*. *Educ:* Univ. of Edinburgh (BSc 1971); London Univ. (CQSW 1973); Strathclyde Univ. (MBA 1988). Social Worker, Cheshire and Kent, 1971–75; Social Work Manager, Lothian, 1975–87; Depute Dir, Borders, 1987–91; Chief Social Work Advr, Scottish Office, 1991–92. Gov., Nat. Inst. of Social Work, 1992–. *Publication:* Another Kind of Home, 1992. *Recreations:* family, friends, learning. *Address:* Social Work Services Inspectorate, Victoria Quay, Edinburgh EH6 6QQ. *T:* (0131) 244 5414.

SKINNER, David; Chief Executive, Co-operative Wholesale Society Ltd, 1992–96; *b* 27 Oct. 1931; *s* of late David Skinner and Mary (*née* Davidson); *m* 1st, 1956, Elizabeth Vera Harben (marr. diss. 1976); one *s* one *d*; 2nd, 1996, Morag J. L. Mar (*née* Busby). *Educ:* Gateshead Grammar Sch.; Nottingham Univ. (BSc). Nat. Service, RNVR, 1953–55. Food Divl Manager, Scottish CWS, 1969–73; Co-operative Wholesale Society Ltd: Non Food Controller, 1974–83; Retail Controller and Dep. Chief Exec. (Retail & Services), 1983–92. *Recreations:* comfortable travelling, easy gardening. *Address:* Rowan Tree Cottage, Pannal Road, Follifoot, Harrogate HG3 1DR.

SKINNER, Dennis Edward; MP (Lab) Bolsover, since 1970; *b* 11 Feb. 1932; good working-class mining stock; *m* 1960; one *s* two *d*. *Educ:* Tupton Hall Grammar Sch.; Ruskin Coll., Oxford. Miner, Parkhouse Colliery and Glapwell Colliery, 1949–70. Mem., Nat. Exec. Cttee of Labour Party, 1978–96; Vice-Chm., Labour Party, 1987–88, Chm., 1988–89; Pres., Derbyshire Miners (NUM), 1966–70; Pres., NE Derbs Constituency Labour Party, 1968–71; Derbyshire CC, 1964–70; Clay Cross UDC, 1960–70. *Recreations:* tennis, cycling, walking. *Address:* House of Commons, SW1A 0AA. *T:* (01773) 581027. *Clubs:* Miners' Welfares in Derbyshire; Bestwood Working Men's.

SKINNER, Air Vice-Marshal Graham, CBE 1999 (MBE 1982); CEng, FIMechE; FILT; Visiting Professor, Acquisition and Logistics Unit, Royal Military College of Science, Shrivenham, at Cranfield University, since 2000; *b* 16 Sept. 1945; *s* of late Frederick and Phyllis Skinner; *m* 1969, Margaret Christine Hacon; one *s* one *d*. *Educ:* Hampton Sch.; RAF Tech. Coll., Henlow; Bristol Univ. (BSc); Loughborough Univ. (MSc). CEng 1972; MRAeS 1980; FIMechE 1990; FILT 1997. Commnd Engr Br., RAF, 1964; served at Odiham, Sharjah, Coltishall, Leconfield, Kemble, 1967–78; RAF Staff Coll., Bracknell, 1978; air weapons staff, MoD, London, 1979–83; OC Engrg Wing, RAF Valley, 1983–85; various engrg posts and SO Engrg and Supply, HQ 38 Gp, Strike Comd, 1986–95; Air Cdre, Policy and Plans, HQ Logistics Comd, 1996–97; Dir, Support Mgt (RAF), 1997–99; COS, 1999–2000; last AOC-in-C Logistics Comd, 1999; Mem. Mgt Bd, Defence Logistics Orgn, 1999-2000; retd RAF, 2000. Military Adviser: Marshall Aerospace, Cambridge, 2000–; Barlow Handling, Maidenhead, 2001–; non-exec. Dir, Short Bros plc, Belfast, 2000–; Associate, Rossmore Dempsey and Co. Ltd, 2001–. FIMgt 1983. Freeman, City of London, 2000–; Mem., Co. of Engrs, 2000–. Gov., Hampton Sch., Middx, 2001–. *Publications:* contrib. various articles to professional jls on aerospace engrg and defence logistics. *Recreations:* golf, watercolour painting. *Address:* Rokesly, 63 Sandelswood End, Beaconsfield, Bucks HP9 2AA. *T:* (01494) 672350. *Club:* Royal Air Force.

SKINNER, James John; QC; Social Security Commissioner, 1986–96; a Child Support Commissioner, 1993–96; *b* 24 July 1923; *o s* of late William Skinner, Solicitor, Clonmel, Ireland; *m* 1950, Regina Brigitte Reiss; three *s* two *d*. *Educ:* Clongowes Wood Coll.; Trinity Coll., Dublin; King's Inns, Dublin. Called to Irish Bar, 1946; joined Leinster Circuit; called to English Bar, Gray's Inn, 1950; called to Bar of Northern Rhodesia, 1951; QC (Northern Rhodesia) 1964; MP (UNIP) Lusaka East, 1964–68; Minister of Justice, 1964–65; Attorney-General, 1965–69 (in addition, Minister of Legal Affairs, 1967–68); Chief Justice of Zambia, March-Sept. 1969; Chief Justice of Malaŵi, 1970–85. Grand Comdr, Order of Menelik II of Ethiopia, 1965. *Recreation:* reading. *Address:* 12A Ashley Court, Ashley Road, Epsom, Surrey KT18 5AJ. *T:* (01372) 728299.

SKINNER, Joyce Eva, CBE 1975; retired; *b* 5 Sept. 1920; *d* of Matthew and Ruth Eva Skinner. *Educ:* Christ's Hosp.; Girls' High Sch., Lincoln; Somerville Coll., Oxford. BA 1941, MA 1945. Bridlington Girls' High Sch., 1942–45; Perse Girls' Sch., 1946–50; Keswick Sch., 1950–52; Homerton Coll., Cambridge, 1952–64; Vis. Prof., Queen's Coll., NY, 1955–56; Principal, Bishop Grosseteste Coll., Lincoln, 1964–74; Dir, Cambridge Inst. of Educn, 1974–80; Academic Sec., Universities' Council for Educn of Teachers, 1979–84. Fellow: Hughes Hall, Cambridge, 1974–85; Worcester Coll. of Higher Educn, 1985. Hon. FCP 1971. Hon. DEd CNAA, 1989; Hon. DLitt Hull, 1997. *Recreations:* walking, reading, conversation. *Address:* 26 Rasen Lane, Lincoln LN1 3EY. *T:* (01522) 529483.

SKINNER, Sir Keith; *see* Skinner, Sir T. K. H.

SKINNER, Peter William; Member (Lab) South East Region, England, European Parliament, since 1999 (Kent West, 1994–99); *b* 1 June 1959; *s* of William James Skinner and Jean Theresa Skinner; *m* 1990, Julie Doreen; one *d*, and one step *s* one step *d*. *Educ:* Bradford Univ. (BSc); Warwick Univ. (Post Grad. Cert. in Industl Relns); Greenwich Univ. (PGCE 1992). Industrial Relations Officer, 1982; Trades Union Organiser, 1984; Course Dir for HNC in Business and Finance, North West Kent Coll. of Technol., 1989–94. European Parliament: Member: Employment and Social Affairs Cttee, 1994–; Educn, Culture, Media and Youth Cttee, 1997–; Economic and Monetary Affairs Cttee, 2000–; Health and Safety Rapporteur, 1995–; Lab. spokesman on employment and social affairs, 1996–2000. Mem., Educn and Employment Policy Commn, Lab Party, 1995–. *Address:* (office) 99 Kent Road, Dartford, Kent DA1 2AJ. *T:* (01322) 281500; European Parliament, Rue Wiertz, 1047 Brussels, Belgium.

SKINNER, Prof. Quentin Robert Duthie, FBA 1981; Regius Professor of Modern History, University of Cambridge, since 1996 (Pro-Vice-Chancellor, 1999); Fellow, Christ's College, Cambridge, since 1962 (Vice Master, 1997–99); *b* 26 Nov. 1940; 2nd *s* of late Alexander Skinner, CBE, and Winifred Skinner (*née* Duthie), MA; *m* 2nd, 1979, Susan Deborah Thorpe James, MA, PhD; one *s* one *d*. *Educ:* Bedford Sch.; Gonville and Caius Coll., Cambridge (BA 1962, MA 1965; Hon. Fellow, 1997). Cambridge University: Lectr in History, 1967–78; Prof. of Political Sci., 1978–96; Chm., Faculty of Hist., 1993–95. Visiting Fellow: Research Sch. of Social Science, ANU, 1970, 1994; Humanities Res. Centre, ANU, 1989, 1994; Institute for Advanced Study, Princeton: Mem., School of Historical Studies, 1974–75; longer-term Mem., School of Social Science, 1976–79; Gauss Seminars, Princeton Univ., 1980; Directeur d'Etudes Associé, Ecole des Hautes Etudes, 1987; Professeur Associé, Université Paris X, 1991; Cardinal Mercier Vis. Prof., Univ. of Leuven, 1992; Professeur invité, Collège de France, 1997. Carlyle Vis. Lectr, Univ. of Oxford, 1980–81; Avalon Vis. Lectr, Northwestern Univ., 1995. Mem., Council, British Acad., 1987–90. Foreign Hon. Mem., Amer. Acad. of Arts and Sciences, 1986; For. Mem., Amer. Phil Soc., 1997. MAE 1989. Hon. MRIA 1999. Hon. Fellow, QMW, 1999. Hon. LittD: Chicago, 1992; East Anglia, 1992; Helsinki, 1997; Hon. DLitt Oxford, 2000. *Publications:* (ed jtly and contrib.) Philosophy, Politics and Society, Series 4, 1972; The Foundations of Modern Political Thought, Vol. 1, The Renaissance, 1978; Vol. 2, The Age of Reformation, 1978 (Wolfson Prize, 1979); Machiavelli, 1981; (ed jtly and contrib.) Philosophy in History, 1984; (ed and contrib.) The Return of Grand Theory in the Human Sciences, 1985; (ed jtly and contrib.) The Cambridge History of Renaissance Philosophy, 1988; Meaning and Context: Quentin Skinner and his critics, ed J. H. Tully, 1988; (ed and introd) Machiavelli: The Prince, 1988; (ed jtly and contrib.) Machiavelli and Republicanism, 1990; (ed jtly and contrib.) Political Discourse in Early-modern Britain, 1992; (ed jtly) Milton and Republicanism, 1995; Reason and Rhetoric in the Philosophy of Hobbes, 1996; Liberty Before Liberalism, 1998. *Address:* c/o Christ's College, Cambridge CB2 3BU. *T:* (01223) 334900.

SKINNER, Samuel Knox; lawyer; Chairman, President and Chief Executive Officer, USFreightways Corporation, since 2000; Chairman, transportation.com, since 2000; Co-Chairman, Hopkins & Sutter, since 1998; *b* 10 June 1938; *m* 1989, Mary Jacobs; two *s* one *d*. *Educ:* Univ. of Illinois (BSc); DePaul Univ. Law School. Served as Lieut and Tank Platoon Leader, US Army, 1960–61. IBM Corp., 1961–68; Illinois Northern District: Office of US Attorney, 1968–75; US Attorney, 1975–77; Partner, Sidley & Austin, 1977–89; President's Cabinet as Sec. of Transportation, 1989–91; Chief of Staff to President of USA, 1991–92; Gen. Chm., Republican Nat. Cttee, USA, 1992–93; Pres., Commonwealth Edison Co., subseq. Unicom Corp., 1993–98. *Address:* Suite 4100, 3 1st National Plaza, Chicago, IL 60602, USA.

SKINNER, Sir (Thomas) Keith (Hewitt), 4th Bt *cr* 1912; Director, Reed International, 1980 90; Chairman and Chief Executive, Reed Publishing and Reed Regional Publishing, 1982–90, and other companies; *b* 6 Dec. 1927; *s* of Sir (Thomas) Gordon Skinner, 3rd Bt, and Mollie Barbara (*d* 1965), *d* of Herbert William Girling; *S* father, 1972; *m* 1959, Jill, *d* of Cedric Ivor Tuckett; two *s*. *Educ:* Charterhouse. Managing Director, Thomas Skinner & Co. (Publishers) Ltd, 1952–60; also Director, Iliffe & Co. Ltd, 1958–65; Director, Iliffe-NTP Ltd; Chairman: Industrial Trade Fairs Holdings Ltd, 1977–; Business Press Internat., 1970–84. *Recreations:* publishing, shooting, fishing, gardening, golf. *Heir:* *s* Thomas James Hewitt Skinner, *b* 11 Sept. 1962. *Address:* Wood Farm, Reydon, near Southwold, Suffolk IP18 6SL.

SKIPPER, David John; education consultant, since 1996; Director: Westminster Centre for Education, Independent Schools Joint Council, 1991–96; Secondary Post Graduate Certificate of Education Course by Distance Learning, South Bank University (formerly Polytechnic), 1991–97; *b* 14 April 1931; *s* of late Herbert G. and Edna Skipper; *m* 1955, Brenda Ann Williams; three *s* one *d*. *Educ:* Watford Grammar Sch.; Brasenose Coll., Oxford (2nd Cl. Hons Nat. Science (Chemistry)). Royal Air Force (Short Service Commn) (Education), 1954–57; Assistant Master: Radley Coll., 1957–63; Rugby Sch., 1963–69; Headmaster: Ellesmere Coll., Shropshire, 1969–81; Merchant Taylors' Sch., Northwood, 1982–91. Chairman: ISJC Special Educnl Needs, 1983–91; Soc. of Schoolmasters, 1985–97; Pres., Soc. of Schoolmasters and Schoolmistresses, 1998–. Chm. Governors, Quainton Sch., Harrow, 1993–. Fellow, Midland Div., Woodard Corp., 1996–. Freeman, City of London, 1991; Liveryman, Merchant Taylors' Co., 1991–. *Recreations:* walking, drawing, music, gardening, books. *Address:* 4 St Michael's Green, Lyneal Lane, Welshampton, Ellesmere, Shropshire SY12 0QT. *T:* (01948) 710899.

SKIPWITH, Sir Patrick Alexander d'Estoteville, 12th Bt *cr* 1622; Head of Translation, BRGM, Orléans, since 1996; *b* 1 Sept. 1938; *o s* of Grey d'Estoteville Townsend Skipwith (killed in action, 1942), Flying Officer, RAFVR, and Sofka (*d* 1994), *d* of late Prince Peter Dolgorouky; *S* grandfather, 1950; *m* 1st, 1964, Gillian Patricia (marr. diss. 1970), *d* of late Charles F. Harwood; one *s* one *d*; 2nd, 1972, Ashkhain (marr. diss. 1997), *d* of late Bedros Atikian, Calgary, Alta; 3rd, 1997, Martine Sophie, *d* of Joseph de Wilde, Theillay, France; twin *s*. *Educ:* Harrow; Dublin (MA); London (DIC, PhD). With Ocean Mining Inc., in Tasmania, 1966–67, Malaysia, 1967–69, W Africa, 1969–70; with Min. of Petroleum and Mineral Resources, Saudi Arabia, 1970–71 and 1972–73. Editor, Bureau de Recherches Géologiques et Minières, Jiddah, 1973–86; consultant editor/translator (trading as GeoEdit), 1986–96; Man. Dir, Immel Publishing Ltd, 1988–89. *Heir: s* Alexander Sebastian Grey d'Estoteville Skipwith, *b* 9 April 1969. *Address:* 76 rue de Pont-aux-Moines, 45450 Donnery, France. *Club:* Chelsea Arts.

SKITT, Baden Henry, CBE 1997; BEM 1969; QPM 1990; Member, Criminal Cases Review Commission, since 1997; *b* 5 Dec. 1941; *s* of Frederick Albert Skitt and Laura Kathleen (*née* Oakley). *Educ:* Rugeley Grammar Sch., Staffs; St Paul's Coll., Cheltenham (Dip of PE; CertEd). Schoolmaster, Sir Wilfrid Martineau Sch., Birmingham, 1963–67; Constable to Supt, Birmingham City, later W Midlands, Police, 1967–82; Chief Supt, 1982–84, Comdr, 1984–86, Metropolitan Police; Dep. Chief Constable, Northants, 1986–90; Chief Constable, Herts, 1990–94; Asst Comr, Metropolitan Police, 1994–97. Chm., Personnel and Training Cttee, 1993–96, Chm., Internat. Affairs Adv. Cttee, 1996–97, ACPO. Dir, Police Extended Interviews, 1995–97. Member: Police Adv. Bd, 1993–97; Police Trng Council, 1993–97; Police Advr, Police Negotiating Bd, 1994–96. Dir, Educnl Broadcasting Services Trust; Trustee: Police Convalescent Home, 1995–97; Youth Sport Trust, 1995–97. Advr, N London Common Purpose, 1995–97. Patron, Revolving Doors Agency, 1995–97. *Publications:* (jtly) In Service Training: a new approach, 1974; (jtly) Education 2000, 1984; contrib. to learned jls. *Recreations:* the history and travelling of inland waterways, Rugby football, music. *Address:* Criminal Cases Review Commission, Alpha Tower, Suffolk Street, Queensway, Birmingham B1 1TT.

SKOU, Prof. Jens Christian, MD; Professor, Institute of Biophysics, Aarhus University, 1978–88; *b* Lemvig, Denmark, 8 Oct. 1918; *s* of Magnus Martinus Skou and Ane Margrethe (*née* Knak); *m* 1947, Ellen-Margrethe Nielsen; two *d*. *Educ:* Univ. of Copenhagen (MD 1944); Univ. of Aarhus (DrMedSci 1954). Intern, 1944–45, Resident, 1945–46, Hjørring Hosp.; Resident, Orthopaedic Hosp., Aarhus, 1946–47; Institute of Physiology, Aarhus University: Asst Prof., 1947–54; Associate Prof., 1954–63; Prof. and Chm., Inst. Physiol., 1963–78. Member: Danish Royal Acad. Scis, 1965; Deutsche Acad. der Naturforscher Leopoldina, 1977; EMBO, 1978; For. Associate, US Nat. Acad. of Scis, 1988; For. Hon. Mem., Amer. Acad. of Arts and Scis, 1999; Hon. Member: Japanese Biochem. Soc., 1988; American Physiol. Soc., 1990. Hon. DrMedSci Copenhagen, 1986. Leo Prize, 1954; Novo Prize, 1965; Consul Carlsen Prize, 1973; A. Retzius Gold Medal, Swedish Med. Assoc., 1977; Fernström Foundn Prize, 1985; Prakash Datta Medal, Fedn European Biochem. Socs, 1985; (jtly) Nobel Prize for Chemistry, 1997. *Recreations:* classical music, yachting, ski-ing, fishing. *Address:* Rislundvej 9, 8240 Risskov, Denmark. *T:* 86177918; (office) Institute of Biophysics, Ole Worms Allé 185, 8000C Aarhus, Denmark. *T:* 89422929, *Fax:* 86129599; *e-mail:* jcs@biophys.au.dk.

SKYRME, Sir (William) Thomas (Charles), KCVO 1974; CB 1966; CBE 1953; TD 1949; JP, DL; Chairman, Broadcasting Complaints Commission, 1985–87 (Member, 1981–87); Secretary of Commissions, 1948–77; Vice-President, Magistrates' Association of England and Wales, since 1981 (Member of Council, since 1974; Deputy Chairman, 1977–79; Chairman, 1979–81); *b* 20 March 1913; *s* of Charles G. Skyrme, Hereford, and of Katherine (*née* Smith), Maryland, USA; *m* 1st, 1938, Hon. Barbara Suzanne Lyle (marr. diss. 1953; she *d* 1994), *yr d* of 1st Baron Lyle of Westbourne; one *s* two *d*; 2nd, 1957, Mary (*d* 1999), *d* of Dr R. C. Leaning. *Educ:* Rugby School; New College, Oxford (MA); Universities of Dresden and Paris. Called to the Bar, Inner Temple, 1935, Bencher 1988. Practised in London and on Western Circuit. Served War of 1939–45 in Royal Artillery in Middle East, North Africa and Italy (wounded twice); Lt-Col; Founder and first CO, G Locating Battery, HAC, 1947. Secretary to the Lord Chancellor, 1944. Governor and Member of Committee of Management of Queen Mary's Hosp., London, 1938–48. Mem., Magistrates' Courts Rule Cttee, 1950–66; Chm., Interdepartmental Working Party on Legal Proceedings against Justices and Clerks, 1960; Mem., Interdepartmental Cttee on Magistrates Courts in London, 1961; Life Vice-Pres., Commonwealth Magistrates' and Judges' Assoc. (formerly Commonwealth Magistrates' Assoc.), 1979 (Founder, and first Pres., 1970–79); Chm., Commonwealth Magistrates' Confs, London, 1970, Bermuda, 1972, Nairobi, 1973, Kuala Lumpur, 1975, Tonga, 1976, Jamaica, 1977, Oxford, 1979; Vice-Chm., Adv. Cttee on Training of Magistrates, 1974–80. Hon. Life Mem., Justices' Clerks' Soc., 1979–. A General Comr of Income Tax, 1977–88; Mem., Top Salaries Review Body, 1981–90; Chm., Judicial Salaries Cttee, 1983–90. Chm., Batsford Foundn, 1983–96. Pres., City of London RAOC Assoc., 1987–. Freeman of City of London, 1970; HM Lieut for City of London, 1977–. DL Glos 1983. FRGS. JP (Oxfordshire), 1948, (London), 1952, (Gloucestershire), 1976. *Publications:* The Changing Image of the Magistracy, 1979; History of the Justices of the Peace, 1990; contribs to legal jls. *Recreations:* ski-ing, travel, rifle shooting (captained Oxford University, 1934). *Address:* Amesbury Abbey, Amesbury, Wilts SP4 7EX; Casa Larissa, Klosters, Switzerland. *Clubs:* Army and Navy; Hurlingham.

See also Sir J. G. Waterlow, Bt.

SLABAS, Prof. Antoni Ryszard, DPhil; Professor of Plant Sciences, since 1990, and Director of Research, Department of Biological Sciences, since 1994, University of Durham; *b* 30 July 1948; *s* of Franciszek Slabas and Wiera Ruban. *Educ:* Bishop Thomas Grant Sch.; QMC, Univ. of London (BSc); St Edmund Hall, Oxford (DPhil). Postdoctoral Fellow: Univ. of Sheffield, 1974–75; UCL, 1975–77; Unilever Research Laboratory, Sharnbrook, Bedford: Mem., Basic Studies Unit, 1977–80; Gp Leader, Lipid Enzymology, 1980–85; Section Manager, Protein Chem., 1985–86; Plant Molecular Biol. Prog. Leader, 1986–87; Sen. Molecular Biologist, 1988; Section Manager, Cell Scis, 1989–90. Mem., EC Seeds of Tomorrow Scientific Steering Cttee, 1990–; Agricultural and Food Research Council: Member: Engrg Bd, 1992–94; Plants and Envmt Res. Cttee, 1992–94; Wkg Gp, Protein Sci., 1992; Bd of Metabolic Regulation, 1992–94. Member: Cttee, Biochem. Soc. Lipid Gp, 1984–88; Health and Life Scis Panel, 1994–99, Food Chain and Crops for Industry Panel, 1999–2001, Technol. Foresight Prog., OST; Management Cttee, Agricl Systems Directorate, BBSRC, 1994–98; Governing Body, Scottish Crops Res. Inst., 1995–. Member, Editorial Board: Biochem. Jl, 1989–; Plant Molecular Biol., 1991–. *Publications:* various in area of plant and microbial lipid biochem., enzymology and gene cloning; contrib. Science, Jl Biol Chem., Eur. Jl Biochem., Biochim. Biophys. Acta, Biochem. Jl, etc. *Recreations:* book collecting, classical music, walking, feeding swans by hand. *Address:* Department of Biological Sciences, University of Durham, South Road, Durham DH1 3LE. *T:* (0191) 3743352.

SLABBERT, Dr Frederik Van Zyl; political consultant; Chairman: Adcorp Holdings, since 1998; Metro Cash&Carry, since 2000; *b* 2 March 1940; *s* of Petrus Johannes and Barbara Zacharia Slabbert; *m* 1965, Marié Jordaan (marr. diss. 1983); one *s* one *d*; *m* 1984, Jane Catherine Stephens. *Educ:* Univ. of Stellenbosch. BA, BA (Hons), MA 1964, DPhil 1967. Lectr in Sociology, Stellenbosch Univ., 1964–68; Senior Lecturer: Rhodes Univ., 1969; Stellenbosch Univ., 1970–71; Cape Town Univ., 1972–73; Prof. of Sociology, Univ. of the Witwatersrand, 1973–74. MP (Progressive Federal Party) Claremont, 1974–86; Leader, Official Opposition, S African Parlt, 1979–86. Founder and Dir, Inst. for a Democratic Alternative for South Africa, 1987; Chm., Open Soc. Initiative for Southern Africa. Vis. Prof., Univ. of the Witwatersrand Business Sch., 1988–. *Publications:* South African Society: its central perspectives, 1972; (jtly) South Africa's Options: strategies for sharing power, 1979; The Last White Parliament (autobiog.), 1986; (jtly) Comrades in Business: post-liberation politics in South Africa, 1998; Afrikaner Afrikaan, 1999; contributions to: Change in Contemporary South Africa, 1975; Explorations in Social Theory, 1976; various SPROCAS (Study Project of a Christian in an Apartheid Society) publications. *Recreations:* jogging, swimming, squash, chess. *Address:* Khula Consulting (Pty) Ltd, PO Box 2817, Houghton, 2041, South Africa.

SLACK, Dr Charles Roger, FRS 1989; FRSNZ 1983; Senior Scientist, New Zealand Institute for Crop and Food Research Ltd, 1989–2000; *b* 22 April 1937; *s* of Albert Oram Slack and Eva (*née* Simister); *m* 1963, Pamela Mary Shaw; one *s* one *d*. *Educ:* Audenshaw Grammar Sch., Lancs; Sch. of Agriculture, Univ. of Nottingham (BSc; PhD 1962). Biochemist, David North Plant Res. Centre, CSR Co. Ltd, Brisbane, Australia, 1962–70; Leader, Biochemistry Group, 1970–84, Leader, Crop Physiology Group and Dep. Dir, Plant Physiol. Div., 1984–89, DSIR, NZ; Sen. Scientist, Crop Res. Div., DSIR, NZ, subseq. NZ Inst. for Crop and Food Res. Ltd, 1989. Charles F. Kettering Award for Photosynthesis Res., Amer. Soc. of Plant Physiologists, 1980; Rank Prize for Nutrition, 1981. *Publications:* scientific pubns, mainly on aspects of photosynthesis and plant lipid synthesis. *Recreations:* bird watching, hiking, trout fishing, gardening. *Address:* 30 Ihaka Street, Palmerston North, New Zealand. *T:* (6) 3572966.

SLACK, His Honour George Granville; a Circuit Judge (formerly a County Court Judge), 1966–81; *b* 11 July 1906; *s* of George Edwin and Amy Beatrice Slack; *m* 1st, 1935, Ella Kathleen (*d* 1957), *d* of Henry Alexander Eason; one *d*; 2nd, 1958, Vera Gertrude, *d* of Reginald Ackland Spencer; one *s* one *d*. *Educ:* Accrington Grammar School; London University. BA (Hons History) 1926; LLB 1929; LLM 1932. Called to Bar, Gray's Inn, 1929. Served RAFVR, 1943–46. Judge of Croydon County Court, 1969–75, of Willesden County Court, 1976–81. Contested (L): Twickenham, 1945; Dewsbury, 1950; Chairman: London Liberal Party, 1947–48, 1950–53; Liberal Party Organisation, 1956–57. Sec., Acton Baptist Church, 1954–77. Chm., West Gp Housing Soc. Ltd (West Haven), 1961–94. *Publications:* Slack on War Damage, 1941; Liabilities (War Time Adjustment) Act, 1941; Liability for National Service, 1942. *Address:* 10 Baronsmede, Ealing, W5 4LT. *T:* (020) 8567 8164. *Club:* National Liberal.

SLACK, His Honour John Kenneth Edward, TD 1964; DL; a Circuit Judge, 1977–99; *b* 23 Dec. 1930; *o s* of late Ernest Edward Slack, formerly Chief Clerk Westminster County Court, and late Beatrice Mary Slack (*née* Shorten), Broadstairs; *m* 1959, Patricia Helen, MA Cantab, *o d* of late William Keith Metcalfe, Southport; two *s*. *Educ:* University College Sch., Hampstead; St John's Coll., Cambridge (MA). Captain, RAEC, 1950. Admitted Solicitor, 1957; Partner, Freeborough Slack & Co., 1958–76; Mem. No 1 (later No 14) Legal Aid Area, 1966–69; Deputy Registrar, County Courts, 1969–72; a Recorder of the Crown Court, 1972–77; Pres., Wireless Telegraphy Appeals Tribunal, 1974–77. Captain Club Cricket Conf., 1962–66; Captain Bucks County Cricket Club, 1967–69 (Minor County Champions 1969); Active Vice-Pres., Club Cricket Conf., 1969–77, Pres., 1978. Chm. Council, University Coll. Sch., 1980–87 (Mem., 1974–90). DL Bucks, 1995. *Recreations:* cricket (Cambridge Blue 1954), golf. *Address:* c/o Crown Court, Aylesbury, Bucks HP20 1XD. *Clubs:* Hawks (Cambridge); Beaconsfield Golf.

SLACK, Prof. Paul Alexander, DPhil; FBA 1990; FRHistS; Principal of Linacre College, Oxford, since 1996; Titular Professor of Early Modern Social History, since 1999, and Pro-Vice-Chancellor (Academic Services and University Collections), since 2000, Oxford University; *b* 23 Jan. 1943; *s* of Isaac Slack and Helen (*née* Firth); *m* 1965, Diana Gillian Manby; two *d*. *Educ:* Bradford Grammar Sch.; St John's Coll., Oxford (Casberd Exhibnr and Schol.; 1st cl. Hons Mod. Hist. 1964; MA; DPhil 1972; Hon. Fellow, 1998). FRHistS 1972. A. M. P. Read Schol., Oxford Univ., and Harmsworth Sen. Schol., Merton Coll., Oxford, 1965–66; Jun. Res. Fellow, Balliol Coll., Oxford, 1966–69; Lectr in Hist., York Univ., 1969–72; Oxford University: Fellow and Tutor, 1973–96 (Emeritus Fellow, 1996–), Sub-Rector, 1983, Sen. Tutor, 1984–86 and 1991–92, Exeter Coll.; Reader in Modern Hist., 1990–96; Jun. Proctor, 1986–87; Mem., Hebdomadal Council, 1987–; Chm., Gen. Bd of Faculties, 1995–96; Pro-Vice-Chancellor, 1997–; Delegate, OUP, 2000–. Vis. Prof., Univ. of S Carolina, 1980; Vis. Res. Associate, Rikkyo Univ., Tokyo, 1988. Ford's Lectr in British History, Oxford, 1994–95. Member: Internat. Commn for Hist. of Towns, 1976–; Humanities Res. Bd, 1994–95. Pres., Soc. for Social Hist. of Medicine, 1991; Member, Council: RHistS, 1984–87; British Acad., 1994–95. Editor, Past and Present, 1985–94. *Publications:* (ed with Peter Clark) Crisis and Order in English Towns 1500–1700, 1972; (ed) Poverty in Early Stuart Salisbury, 1975; (with P. Clark) English Towns in Transition 1500–1700, 1976 (Japanese edn 1989); (ed) Rebellion, Popular Protest and the Social Order in Early Modern England, 1984; The Impact of Plague in Tudor and Stuart England, 1985; Poverty and Policy in Tudor and Stuart England, 1988; The English Poor Law 1531–1782, 1990; (ed with T. Ranger) Epidemics and Ideas, 1992; (ed jtly) Public Duty and Private Conscience in Seventeenth-Century England, 1993; From Reformation to Improvement: public welfare in early modern England, 1999; (ed) Environments and Historical Change, 1999; (ed jtly) Civil Histories: essays presented to Sir Keith Thomas, 2000; contribs to learned jls. *Recreations:* opera, fell-walking. *Address:* Linacre College, Oxford OX1 3JA. *T:* (01865) 271650.

SLACK, Stephen; Head, Legal Office of the Church of England and Chief Legal Adviser to the Archbishops' Council, since 2001; Chief Legal Adviser and Registrar, General

Synod of the Church of England, since 2001; Joint Registrar of the Provinces of Canterbury and York, since 2001; *b* 1954; *s* of Thomas and Ada Genary Slack; *m* 1982, Georgiana Sophia (*née* Shaw); one *s* two *d*. *Educ:* Aylesbury Grammar Sch.; Christ Church, Oxford (MA). Solicitor in private practice, 1979–84; Charity Commission: Sen. Lawyer, Liverpool, 1984–89; Hd, Legal Sect., Taunton, 1989–2001. *Address:* Church House, Great Smith Street, SW1P 3NZ.

SLACK, Timothy Willatt, LVO 1995; MA; Principal, St Catharine's Foundation at Cumberland Lodge, 1985–95; *b* 18 April 1928; *yr s* of late Cecil Moorhouse Slack, MC, and Dora Willatt, Beverley, Yorks; *m* 1st, 1957, Katharine (*d* 1993), 2nd *d* of late Walter Norman Hughes, MA, and Jean Sorsbie, Chepstow, Mon; one *s* three *d*; 2nd, 1996, Shuna Ann, *d* of late Lt-Col James Hayton Greenhill Black and Mary Margaret Boden. *Educ:* Winchester Coll.; New Coll., Oxford. Hons. PPE, 1951. Asst, Lycée de Rennes, France, 1951; Asst master, the Salem School, Baden, Germany, 1952; Assistant master, Repton School, 1953–59; Headmaster of Kambawsa College, Taunggyi, Shan State, Burma, 1959–62; Headmaster, Bedales Sch., 1962–74. Chairman, Society of Headmasters of Independent Schools, 1968–70. Dep. Dir, 1975–77, Dir, 1977–83, Wiston House FCO Conf. Centre (incorp. Wilton Park Confs), Steyning; Headmaster, Hellenic Coll. of London, 1983–84. Kurt Hahn Meml Lectr, 1982. Dir, Nat. Tenants Resource Centre, 1993–. Chm. Governors, The Royal Sch., Windsor Great Park, 1988–95. Chm., Round Table Moot, 1994–. Contested (L): Petersfield, Feb. and Oct. 1974; Enfield, Southgate, Dec. 1984; (L/Alliance) Fareham, 1987. *Address:* Hamlet House, Hambledon, Hampshire PO7 4RY.

See also Sir W. W. Slack.

SLACK, Sir William (Willatt), KCVO 1990; MA, MCh, BM, FRCS; Consultant Surgeon, Middlesex Hospital, 1962–91, now Emeritus Surgeon; Senior Lecturer in Surgery, 1962–91, and Dean, 1983–87, Middlesex Hospital Medical School; Dean, Faculty of Clinical Sciences, University College and Middlesex School of Medicine, University College London, 1987–91; also Surgeon: Hospital of St John and St Elizabeth, 1970–88; King Edward VII Hospital for Officers, 1975–91; *b* 22 Feb. 1925; *s* of late Cecil Moorhouse Slack, MC, and Dora Slack (*née* Willatt); *m* 1951, Joan, 4th *d* of late Lt-Col Talbot H. Wheelwright, OBE; two *s* two *d*. *Educ:* Winchester Coll.; New Coll., Oxford; Middlesex Hosp. Med. Sch. Ho. Surg., Surgical Registrar and Sen. Surgical Registrar, Mddx Hosp., 1950–59; Jun. Registrar, St Bartholomew's Hosp., 1953; Fulbright Scholar, R. & E. Hosp., Univ. of Illinois, Chicago, 1959. Surgeon to the Queen, 1975–83; Serjeant Surgeon to the Queen, 1983–90. Hon. Fellow, UCL, 1987. Master, Barbers' Co., 1991–92. *Publications:* various surgical articles in med. jls and textbooks. *Recreations:* skiing, gardening; Oxford blue for Association football, 1946. *Address:* Hillside Cottage, Tower Hill, Stawell, near Bridgwater, Somerset TA7 9AJ. *T:* (01278) 722719.

See also T. W. Slack.

SLADE, Adrian Carnegie, CBE 1988; marketing consultant, since 1991; *b* 25 May 1936; *y s* of late George Penkivil Slade, KC and Mary Albinia Alice Slade; *m* 1960, Susan Elizabeth Forsyth; one *s* one *d*. *Educ:* Eton Coll.; Trinity Coll., Cambridge (BA Law). Pres., Cambridge Footlights, 1959. Writer, J. Walter Thompson, 1959–64; S. H. Benson, 1964–71, Dir, 1970–71; Co-Founder and Managing Director: Slade Monico Bluff Ltd, 1971–75; Slade Bluff & Bigg Ltd, 1975–86; Slade Hamilton Fenech Ltd, 1986–91. Director: Orange Tree Th., Richmond, 1986–98 (Chm., 1991–98); Adzido, 1998–. Trustee, One plus One, 1987–97 (Chm., 1990–97). Mem. (L) Richmond, GLC, 1981–86 (Leader, L/SDP Alliance Gp, 1982–86). Contested: (L) Putney, 1966, Feb. and Oct. 1974; (L/SDP Alliance) Wimbledon, 1987. Pres., Liberal Party, 1987–88; Jt Pres., 1988, Vice-Pres., 1988–89, Liberal Democrats. *Recreations:* music, theatre, films, piano playing, photography. *Address:* 28 St Leonard's Road, SW14 7LX. *T:* (020) 8876 8712.

See also Rt Hon. Sir C. J. Slade, J. P. Slade.

SLADE, Sir Benjamin Julian Alfred, 7th Bt *cr* 1831; Chairman, Shirlstar Container Transport Ltd, since 1973, and director of subsidiary companies; *b* 22 May 1946; *s* of Sir Michael Slade, 6th Bt and Angela (*d* 1959), *d* of Captain Orlando Chichester; *S* father, 1962; *m* 1977, Pauline Carol (marr. diss. 1991), *er d* of Major Claude Myburgh. *Educ:* Millfield Sch. Chm., Pyman Bell (Holding) Ltd. Mem., Worshipful Co. of Ironmongers. Freeman, City of London, 1979. *Recreations:* racing, polo, bridge. *Heir:* none. *Address:* Maunsel, North Newton, Bridgwater, Somerset TA7 0BU. *T:* (01278) 663413; *e-mail:* bensladebt@aol.com; Shirlstar Holdings, 5th Floor, Hayes Gate House, 27-33 Uxbridge Road, Hayes, Middx UB4 0JN. *T:* (020) 7352 1132, *Fax:* (020) 7352 6441; *e-mail:* shirlstar@clara.net. *Clubs:* Turf; Old Somerset Dining (Taunton).

SLADE, Brian John, FInstPS; Director General of Defence Contracts, Ministry of Defence, 1986–91; *b* 28 April 1931; *s* of late Albert Edward Victor Slade and Florence Elizabeth (*née* Eveleigh); *m* 1955, Grace, *d* of late W. McK. Murray and Mary Murray, Ayr; one *s* one *d*. *Educ:* Portsmouth Northern Grammar School; London University. Joined Min. of Supply, 1951; Private Sec. to Permanent Sec., Min. of Aviation, 1962–64; Head of Industrial Personnel Branch, Min. of Technology, 1968–73; Principal Dir of Contracts, Air, MoD, 1982–86. Mem. Synod, Methodist Church, London SW, 1981–90. *Recreations:* cricket, downs walking. *Address:* Doonbank, 16 Greenway, Great Bookham, Surrey KT23 3PA. *T:* (01372) 454359.

SLADE, Rt Hon. Sir Christopher John, Kt 1975; PC 1982; a Lord Justice of Appeal, 1982–91; *b* 2 June 1927; *e s* of late George Penkivil Slade, KC, and Mary Albinia Alice Slade; *m* 1958, Jane Gwenllian Armstrong Buckley, *d* of Rt Hon. Sir Denys Buckley, PC, MBE; one *s* three *d*. *Educ:* Eton (Scholar); New Coll., Oxford (Scholar). Eldon Law Scholar, 1950. Called to Bar, Inner Temple, 1951; joined Lincoln's Inn *ad eundem*, 1954, Bencher, 1973 (Treas., 1994). In practice at Chancery Bar, 1951–75; QC 1965; Attorney General, Duchy of Lancaster and Attorney and Serjeant Within the County Palatine of Lancaster, 1972–75; a Judge of the High Ct, Chancery Division, 1975–82; a Judge of Restrictive Practices Ct, 1980–82, Pres., 1981–82. Member: Gen. Council of the Bar, 1958–62, 1965–69; Senate of Four Inns of Court, 1966–69; Lord Chancellor's Legal Educn Cttee, 1969–71. Master, Ironmongers' Co., 1973. *Address:* 16 Elthiron Road, SW6 4BN. *Club:* Garrick.

See also A. C. Slade, J. P. Slade.

SLADE, Elizabeth Ann; QC 1992; a Recorder, since 1998; *b* 12 May 1949; *d* of late Dr Charles Slade and of Henriette Slade; *m* 1975; two *d*. *Educ:* Wycombe Abbey Sch.; Lady Margaret Hall, Oxford (Exhibnr, MA). Called to the Bar, Inner Temple, 1972, Bencher, 1990, Master of Staff, 1994–98. Asst Recorder, 1995–98; a Dep. High Court Judge, 1998–; additional Judge, Employment Appeal Tribunal, 2000–. Mem. Admin. Tribunal, BIS, 1999–. Chm., Sex Discrimination Cttee, Bar Council, 2000–. Hon. Vice Pres., Employment Law Bar Assoc., 1998 (Chm., 1995–97). Trustee, Free Representation Unit, 1998–. *Publication:* Tolley's Employment Handbook, 1978, to 7th edn (ed jtly) 1991. *Recreations:* theatre, art, music, swimming, walking. *Address:* 11 King's Bench Walk, Temple, EC4Y 7EQ.

SLADE, Julian Penkivil; author and composer since 1951; *b* 28 May 1930; *s* of G. P. Slade, KC. *Educ:* Eton College; Trinity College, Cambridge (BA). Went to Bristol Old Vic Theatre School, 1951; wrote incidental music for Bristol Old Vic production of Two Gentlemen of Verona, 1952; joined Bristol Old Vic Co. as musical director, 1952; wrote and composed Christmas in King St (with Dorothy Reynolds and James Cairncross) Bristol, 1952; composed music for Sheridan's The Duenna, Bristol, 1953; transferred to Westminster Theatre, London, 1954; wrote and composed The Merry Gentleman (with Dorothy Reynolds), Bristol, 1953; composed incidental music for The Merchant of Venice (1953 Stratford season); wrote musical version of The Comedy of Errors for TV, 1954, and for Arts Theatre, London, 1956, revd version for 400th anniv. of first perf. at Gray's Inn, 1994; wrote (with Dorothy Reynolds) Salad Days, Bristol, Vaudeville, 1954, Duke of York's, 1976, Bristol Old Vic, 1994 (adaptation for Yorks TV, 1983, and for 40th birthday recording, BBC, 1994), Vaudeville, 1996; Free as Air, Savoy, London, 1957; Hooray for Daisy!, Bristol, 1959, Lyric, Hammersmith, 1960; Follow that Girl, Vaudeville, London, 1960, revived Theatre Mus., 2000; Wildest Dreams, 1960; Vanity Fair (with Alan Pryce-Jones and Robin Miller), Queen's Theatre, London, 1962, revived Theatre Mus., 2001; Nutmeg and Ginger, Cheltenham, 1963, revived Orange Tree Theatre, Richmond, 1991; Sixty Thousand Nights (with George Rowell), Bristol, 1966; The Pursuit of Love, Bristol, 1967; composed music for songs in: As You Like It, Bristol, 1970; A Midsummer Night's Dream and Much Ado About Nothing, Regent's Park, 1970; adapted A. A. Milne's Winnie The Pooh, Phoenix Theatre, 1970, 1975; (music and lyrics with Aubrey Woods and George Rowell) Trelawny (based on Pinero's Trelawny of the Wells), Bristol, then London West End, 1972; Out of Bounds (book, music and lyrics, based on Pinero's The Schoolmistress), 1973. Composed incidental music for Nancy Mitford's Love in a Cold Climate, Thames TV, 1980; (with Veronica Flint-Shipman and Kit Harvey) musical adaptation of J. M. Barrie's Dear Brutus, 1985; (with Gyles Brandreth) Now We Are Sixty (musical play based on works of A. A. Milne), Arts Theatre, Cambridge, 1986; (with Elizabeth Seal) concert performances of own songs, Easy to Sing, 1986–87; played and sang, gala concert to launch Questfest, Buxton Opera House Festival of Musicals, 1992; (with Eden Phillips) musical stage adaptation of Nancy Mitford's Love in a Cold Climate, 1997; 70th birthday celebration concert, Theatre Mus., 2000. Played and sang for solo record album of own songs, Looking for a Piano, 1981; played for vocal album, Salad Days, 1982. Gold Badge of Merit, British Acad. of Songwriters, Composers and Authors, 1987. *Publications:* Nibble the Squirrel (children's book), 1946; music of: The Duenna, 1954; Salad Days, 1954; Free as Air, 1957; Follow That Girl, 1967; Trelawny, 1974; The Merry Gentleman, 1985. *Recreations:* drawing, going to theatres and cinemas, listening to music. *Address:* 86 Beaufort Street (Ground Floor/Basement), SW3 6BU. *T:* (020) 7376 4480.

See also A. C. Slade, Rt Hon. Sir C. J. Slade.

SLADE, Laurie George; Insurance Ombudsman, 1994–96 and 1999–2000; *b* Nairobi, 12 Feb. 1944; *yr s* of Humphrey Slade and Constance Laing Gordon. *Educ:* Duke of York's Sch., Nairobi; Magdalen Coll., Oxford (MA); London Univ. Inst. of Educn (PGCE). FCIArb 1994. Called to the Bar, Lincoln's Inn, 1966. Worked in professional theatre and TV, Kenya and UK, to 1970; stage management, acting; teaching, 1972–75; Advocate, Kenya High Court, 1975–81; Legal Advr, CIArb and Dep. Registrar, London Court of Internat. Arbitration, 1982–88; Dep. Insurance Ombudsman, 1988–94; Independent Investigator, SIB, then FSA, 1996–99. Mem., Insurance Brokers' Registration Council, 1997–98. Chm., FSA Ombudsman Steering Gp, 1998. Voluntary counsellor, Hounslow Social Services, 1988–94; counselling and psychotherapy practice, 1991–, UKCP Registered Psychoanalyst, 1999. Mem., British and Irish Ombudsman Assoc. Mem., Guild of Psychotherapists; Founder Mem., Internat. Neuro-Psychoanalysis Soc. Wrote plays, Out of Africa, 1988, and Karen's Tale, 1996 (after Karen Blixen). *Publications:* professional papers and contribs to learned jls. *Recreations:* theatre, painting (2 solo exhibns in Kenya, 1974, 1979).

SLADE, Patrick Buxton M.; *see* Mitford-Slade.

SLADE, William Charles; Vice-Principal, 1998–2000, Consultant, 2000–01, King's College London; *b* 20 June 1939; *s* of late Charles Slade and Phyllis (*née* Littlejohns); *m* 1961, Elizabeth Lyn Roberts; two *d*. *Educ:* St Julian's High Sch., Newport, Gwent; UC of Swansea (BSc; Pres., Students' Union, 1960–61). ACMA 1966. Guest Keen Iron and Steel Ltd, 1961–66; Management Accountant: Tunnel Cement Ltd, 1966–71; Pye TMC Ltd, 1971–75; Finance Officer, 1975–77, Sec., 1977–85, Chelsea Coll., Univ. of London; Sec., 1986–98, Mem. Council, 1998–2000, KCL (FKC 1989). Chm., Univ. of London Purchasing Consortium, 1991–94. Mem. Council, Greenacre Sch. for Girls, 1980–95. *Recreations:* theatre, golf, Rugby football. *Address:* Fairway, 1A Links Road, Epsom, Surrey KT17 3PP. *T:* (01372) 742952. *Clubs:* Royal Automobile; Reigate Hill Golf (Reigate).

SLADEN, Teresa; Secretary of the Victorian Society, 1987–93; *b* 16 Sept. 1939; *d* of Robert John Fawcett and Anne (*née* Fairlie Clarke); *m* 1961, David Sladen; one *s* two *d*. *Educ:* Birkbeck Coll., London Univ. (BA Hons Hist. of Art/Italian); Courtauld Inst. (MA Medieval Art and Architecture, 1978). Royal Commn on Historical Monuments, 1978–79; part-time lectr and freelance researcher, 1980–82; Architectural Advr, Victorian Soc., 1983–87. Trustee and Cttee Mem., Mausolea & Monuments Trust, 1997– (Chm., 1998–2000); Vice-Chm., Victorian Soc., 1998–; Member: Southwark DAC, 1993–; Adv. Bd for Redundant Churches, 1999–. *Publications:* (contrib.) The Albert Memorial, 2000; contrib. jl of Garden History. *Recreations:* drawing, 19th century stained glass and painted decoration, 19th century novels.

SLANE, Viscount; Alexander Burton Conyngham; *b* 30 Jan. 1975; *s* and *heir* of Earl of Mount Charles, *qv*.

SLANEY, Prof. Sir Geoffrey, KBE 1984; FRCS; Barling Professor, Head of Department of Surgery, Queen Elizabeth Hospital, Birmingham University, 1971–86, now Emeritus; Hon. Consultant Surgeon: United Birmingham Hospitals and Regional Hospital Board, since 1959; Royal Prince Alfred Hospital, Sydney, since 1981; President, Royal College of Surgeons of England, 1982–86; Hon. Consulting Surgeon Emeritus, City of London and Hackney Health Authority, since 1983; *b* 19 Sept. 1922; *er s* of Richard and Gladys Lois Slaney; *m* 1956, Josephine Mary Davy; one *s* two *d*. *Educ:* Brewood Grammar Sch.; Univs of Birmingham, London and Illinois, USA. MB, ChB (Birmingham) 1947, FRCS 1953, MS (Ill) 1956, ChM (Birmingham) 1961; Hon. FRCSI 1983; Hon. FRACS 1983; Hon. FCSSL 1984; Hon. FACS 1985; Hon. FCSSA 1986; Hon. FRCSCan 1986; Hon. FRCA (Hon. FFARCS 1987). Ho. Surg. and Surgical Registrar, Gen. Hosp. Birmingham, 1947–48. Captain RAMC, 1948–50. Surgical Registrar, Coventry, London and Hackney Hosps, 1950–53; Surgical Registrar, Lectr in Surgery and Surgical Research Fellow, Queen Elizabeth Hosp., Birmingham, 1953–59; Hunterian Prof., RCS, 1961–62; Prof. of Surgery, Univ. of Birmingham, 1966–87. Non-exec. Dir, St Martins Hosps, 1987–. Member: London Adv. Group to Sec. of State, DHSS, 1980–81; Ministerial Adv. Gp on Med. Manpower, 1985–86; Res. Liaison Gp, DHSS, 1979–85; Midlands Med. Appeals Tribunal, 1964–94; Med. Adv. Bd, Internat. Hosp. Gp, 1986–94. Former External Examr in Surgery to Univs of: Newcastle upon Tyne, London, Cambridge,

Oxford, Liverpool, Nat. Univ. of Ireland, Lagos, Zimbabwe, and Licentiate Cttee, Hong Kong; Advisor in Surgery, Univs of Bristol and London. Lectures: Richardson Meml, Massachusetts Gen. Hosp., Boston, USA, 1975; Pybus Meml, Newcastle, 1978; Simpson Smith Meml, London, 1979; Legg Meml, KCH, London, 1982; Chesledon, St Thomas' Hosp., London, 1983; Miles Meml, London, 1983; Berrill Meml, Coventry, 1984; Sandblom, Lund, Sweden, 1984; Sir John Frazer Meml, Edinburgh, 1984; Tung Wah Inaugural, Tung Wah Hosp., Hong Kong, 1986; Sir Ernest Finch Meml, Sheffield, 1986; Hunterian Oration, RCS, 1987; Budd Meml, Bristol, 1987; Annual Guest Lecture, Chicago Surgical Soc., 1987; Barney Brooks Meml, Vanderbilt Univ., Tennessee, 1987; Rutherford-Morison, Newcastle, 1987; Walter C. Mackenzie, Edmonton, 1988; Francis C. Moore, Boston, 1988; Joseph C. Finneran, Indianapolis, 1988; Annual Oration, Osler Club, 1988; Qvist Meml, Royal Free Hosp., 1988; Duke Sesquicentennial, NC, 1988; Telford Meml, Manchester, 1989; (first) Bryan Brooke, Ileostomy Assoc., 1990. Visiting Professor: Durban, Cape Town, Witwatersrand, 1970; Sir Logan Campbell and RACS, NZ, 1977; Univ. of Calif and Cedars-Sinai Hosp., LA, 1978; Pearce Gould, Middlesex Hosp., 1980; McIlrath Guest, Sydney, 1981; G. B. Ong, Univ. of Hong Kong, 1983 (Ong Inaugural Lecture); Foundn Culpepper Prof., Univ. of California, 1984; Madras Med. Coll., and Univ. of Istanbul, 1986; Univ. of Alberta, Edmonton, 1988; Harvard, 1988; Uniformed Services Univ., Bethesda, 1988; Duke Univ., 1988; Wernicke-Marks-Elk, Univ. of Zimbabwe, 1989. Mem. Council, RCS, 1975–87; Member: Moynihan Chirurgical Club (Pres., 1986–87); James IV Assoc. of Surgeons (Pres., 1985–86); Internat. Surgical Gp (Pres., 1985–86); Surgical Research Soc.; Internat. Soc. of Cardio-Vascular Surgeons; Vascular Surgical Soc., GB (Pres., 1974–75); Chm., Assoc. of Profs of Surgery of GB and Ireland, 1979–82. Mem. Council, Univ. of Zimbabwe, 1973–82. Fellow: RSM; Assoc. of Surgeons GB and Ire. (Mem. Council, 1966–76, Treasurer, 1970–76); Assoc. Clinical Anatomists; Amer. Surgical Assoc. Hon. Life Member: Los Angeles Surgical Soc.; Chicago Surgical Soc.; Warren H. Cole Surgical Soc.; William H. Scott Surgical Soc.; Hon. Member: Grey Turner Surgical Club; Assoc. of Surgeons of India. Hon. Freeman, Barbers' Co. Jacksonian Prize and Medal, RCS, 1959; Pybus Meml Medal, NE Surgical Soc., 1978; Miles Medal, Royal Marsden Hosp., 1983; Vanderbilt Univ. Medal, 1987; Brooke Medal, Ileostomy Assoc. of GB and Ireland, 1990. Mem. Editl Bd, British Jl of Surgery, 1970–84; Co-Chief Editor, Jl of Cardio-Vascular Surgery, 1988–92. *Publications:* Metabolic Derangements in Gastrointestinal Surgery (with B. N. Brooke), 1967 (USA); (jtly) Cancer of the Large Bowel, 1991; numerous contribs to med. and surg. jls. *Recreations:* fishing, family, sculpture and carving. *Address:* 23 Aston Bury, Edgbaston, Birmingham B15 3QB. *T:* (0121) 454 0261.

SLANEY, William Simon Rodolph K.; *see* Kenyon-Slaney.

SLATER, Bill; *see* Slater, W. J.

SLATER, Dr David Homfray, CB 1996; Principal Partner, Acona Group, since 2001; *b* 16 Oct. 1940; *m* 1964, Edith Mildred Price; four *d.* *Educ:* University College of Wales Aberystwyth (BSc, PhD). CChem, FRIC, FIChemE, CEng, FInstE. Research Associate, Ohio State Univ., 1966–69; Sen. Res. Fellow, Dept of Chemistry, Univ. of Southampton, 1969–70; Lectr in Combustion, Dept of Chem. Engineering and Chem. Technology, Imperial College London, 1970–75; Cremer and Warner: Sen. Scientist, 1975; Partner, 1979–81; Founding Dir, Technica, 1981–91; Chief Inspector, HM Inspectorate of Pollution, 1991–96; Dir, Pollution Prevention and Control, Envmt Agency, 1996–98; Dir, Oxera Envmtl, 1998–2001. Specialist Advr to Envmt, Transport and Regl Affairs Select Cttee, H of C, 1999–2000; Envmtl Advr, Better Regulation Task Force, Cabinet Office, 2000. Chm., Envmtl Gp, Regulatory Policy Inst., Oxford, 2001–. Associate, Envmtl Change Unit, Oxford Univ., 1999–. Hon. Prof. of Life Sciences, Univ. of Wales, Aberystwyth, 1991. Mem. Court, Cranfield Univ., 1997–. *Publications:* numerous contribs to sci. jls and conference procs. *Recreations:* music, horses. *Club:* Athenæum.

SLATER, Duncan, CMG 1982; HM Diplomatic Service, retired; Chairman, GEC Marconi (Projects) Ltd, since 1995; *b* 15 July 1934; *m* 1972, Candida Coralie Anne Wheatley; one *s* two *d.* Joined FO, 1958; Asst Polit. Agent, Abu Dhabi, 1962–66; First Secretary: Islamabad, 1966; New Delhi, 1966–68; Head of Chancery, Aden, 1968–69; FO, 1969; Special Asst to Sir William Luce, 1970–71; First Sec., UK Representation to EEC, Brussels, 1973–75; UK Resident Rep. to IAEA and UK Perm. Rep. to UNIDO, Vienna, 1975–78; on staff of Government House, Salisbury, Dec. 1979–April 1980; Counsellor and Head of Chancery, Lagos, 1978–81; Ambassador to Oman, 1981–86; Asst Under Sec. of State, FCO, 1986–92; High Comr, Kuala Lumpur, 1992–94. Part-time Lectr, SOAS, Univ. of London. Chm., Res. Inst. for Study of Conflict and Terrorism, 1994–. Vice Pres., British Malaysian Soc. *Recreations:* walking, sailing, skiing, studying Islamic art. *Address:* 15 Marlborough Street, SW3 3PS.

SLATER, Prof. Edward Charles, ScD; FRS 1975; Professor of Physiological Chemistry, University of Amsterdam, The Netherlands, 1955–85; *b* 16 Jan. 1917; *s* of Edward Brunton Slater and Violet Podmore; *m* 1940, Marion Winifred Hutley; one *d.* *Educ:* Melbourne Univ. (BSc, MSc); Cambridge Univ. (PhD, ScD). Biochemist, Australian Inst. of Anatomy, Canberra, Aust., 1939–46; Research Fellow, Molteno Inst., Univ. of Cambridge, UK, 1946–55. Pres., Internat. Union of Biochem., 1988–91. Member: Royal Netherlands Acad. of Science and Letters, 1964; Hollandsche Maatschappij van Wetenschappen, 1970; Hon. Member: Amer. Soc. of Biological Chemists, 1971; Japanese Biochemical Soc., 1973; The Biochemical Soc., 1987; Nederlandse Vereniging voor Biochemie, 1989; For. Mem., Royal Swedish Acad. of Sciences, 1975; Hon. For. Mem., Académie Royal de Méd., Belgium, 1982; Corresponding Member: Acad. Nacional de Ciencas Exactas, Fisicasy Naturales, Argentina, 1973; Australian Acad. of Science, 1985. Hon. DSc Southampton, 1993; Hon. DBiolSci Bari, 1998. Kt, Order of the Netherlands Lion, 1984. *Publications:* Biochimica et Biophysica Acta: story of a biochemical journal, 1986; about 450 contribs to learned jls. *Recreation:* yachting. *Address:* 9 Oaklands, Lymington, Hants SO41 3TH. *T:* (01590) 679455.

SLATER, Prof. Gillian Lesley, (Mrs Ian Huntley), DPhil; CMath, FIMA; Vice-Chancellor, Bournemouth University, since 1994; *b* 13 Jan. 1949; *d* of Leonard William Henry Filtness and Adeline Mary Filtness; *m* 1st, 1970, John Bruce Slater (marr. diss. 1983); two *d;* 2nd, 1988, Ian David Huntley. *Educ:* Sutton High Sch. for Girls; St Hugh's Coll., Oxford (BA 1970; MSc 1971; MA, DPhil 1973). FIMA 1982; CMath 1991. Lectr, Poly. of South Bank, 1973–79; Sen. Lectr, 1979–84, Prin. Lectr, 1984–86, Sheffield City Poly., 1979–86; Head of Dept of Math. and Physics, 1986–89, Asst Dir and Dean of Science and Engrg, 1989–92, Manchester Poly.; Pro-Vice-Chancellor, Manchester Metropolitan Univ., 1992–94. *Publications:* Essential Mathematics for Software Engineers, 1987; (with A. Norcliffe) Mathematics for Software Construction, 1991; numerous articles in learned jls. *Recreation:* listening to classical orchestral music. *Address:* Bournemouth University, Fern Barrow, Poole, Dorset BH12 5BB. *T:* (01202) 595070.

SLATER, James Derrick, FCA; Chairman, Salar Properties Ltd, since 1983; *b* 13 March 1929; *o s* of Hubert and Jessica Slater; *m* 1965, Helen Wyndham Goodwyn; two *s* two *d.* *Educ:* Preston Manor County Sch. Accountant and then Gen. Man. to a gp of metal finishing cos, 1953–55; Sec., Park Royal Vehicles Ltd, 1955–58; Dep. Sales Dir, Leyland Motor Corp. Ltd, 1963; Chm., Slater Walker Securities Ltd, 1964–75; Dir, BLMC, 1969–75. FCA 1963 (ACA 1953). *Publications:* Return to Go, 1977; The Zulu Principle, 1992; Investment Made Easy, 1994; Pep Up Your Wealth, 1994; Beyond the Zulu Principle, 1996; How to Become a Millionaire, 2000; *for children:* Goldenrod, 1978; A. Mazing Monsters, 1979; Grasshopper and the Unwise Owl, 1979; The Boy Who Saved Earth, 1979. *Recreations:* chess, bridge, salmon fishing, table tennis.

SLATER, John Christopher Nash; QC 1987; a Recorder, since 1990; *b* 14 June 1946; *er s* of late Lt-Col Leonard Slater, CBE and Olga Patricia Slater (*née* George); *m* 1971, Jane Schapiro; two *s* one *d.* *Educ:* Sedbergh School; University College, Oxford (MA Hon. Classical Mods 1966 and Jurisprudence 1968). Called to the Bar, Middle Temple, 1969 (Harmsworth Scholar; Bencher, 1996); Hd of Chambers, 1996–99. Assistant Recorder, 1987–90. *Recreations:* golf, acting, travel. *Address:* Crown Office Chambers, One Paper Buildings, Temple, EC4Y 7EP. *T:* (020) 7797 8100; 16 Stormont Road, N6 4NL. *T:* (020) 8348 2725. *Clubs:* Hampstead Golf; Hampstead Cricket.

SLATER, Adm. Sir John Cunningham Kirkwood, (Sir Jock), GCB 1992 (KCB 1988); LVO 1971; DL; First Sea Lord and Chief of Naval Staff, and First and Principal Naval Aide-de-Camp to the Queen, 1995–98; *b* 27 March 1938; *s* of late Dr James K. Slater, OBE, MD, FRCPE and M. C. B. Slater (*née* Bramwell); *m* 1972, Ann Frances, *d* of late Mr and Mrs W. P. Scott of Orkney; two *s.* *Educ:* Edinburgh Academy; Sedbergh. BRNC Dartmouth, 1956–58; served HM Ships Troubridge, Yaxham, HM Yacht Britannia, Cassandra, 1959–64; Comd HMS Soberton, 1965; specialised in navigation, HMS Dryad, 1965–66; HM Ships Victorious and Scarborough (Dartmouth Training Sqdn), 1966–68; Equerry to HM the Queen, 1968–71; Comdr 1971; Comd, HMS Jupiter, 1972–73; Directorate of Naval Ops, MoD, 1973–75; Captain 1976; Comd, HMS Kent, 1976–77; RCDS 1978; Asst Dir of Naval Warfare, MoD, 1979–81; Comd, HMS Illustrious, 1982–83; Captain, Sch. of Maritime Ops and Comd, HMS Dryad, 1983–85; Rear Adm. 1985; ACDS (Policy and Nuclear), 1985–87; Vice-Adm., 1987; Flag Officer, Scotland and NI, and NATO Comdr Northern sub area Eastern Atlantic, Comdr Nore sub area Channel and Naval Base Comdr, Rosyth, 1987–89; Chief of Fleet Support (Mem., Admiralty Bd), 1989–91; Adm. 1991; C-in-C, Fleet, Allied C-in-C, Channel, and Eastern Atlantic, 1991–92; VCDS, 1993–95. Non-executive Director: Vosper Thornycroft Hldgs plc, 1999–; Lockheed Martin UK Ltd, 2000–. Vice Pres., RUSI, 1995–98 (Vice Chm., 1993–95); Member: Bd of Mgt, BNSC, 1986–87; Cttee of Mgt, RNLI, 1999– (Chm., Search and Rescue Cttee, 2001–). Vice-Chm., British Forces Foundn, 1999–; Mem. Council, White Ensign Assoc., 1999–. Trustee, Imperial War Mus., 1999– (Chm., 2001–). Mem., Nat. Youth Orchestra of GB, 1955. Gov., Sedbergh Sch., 1997–. Elder Brother, Trinity Hse, 1995 (Younger Brother, 1978–95). Freeman, City of London, 1989; Liveryman, Shipwrights' Co., 1991. DL Hants, 1999. Hon. DSc Cranfield, 1998. Comdr Legion of Merit (US), 1997. *Recreations:* outdoor. *Address:* c/o Naval Secretary, Victory Building, HM Naval Base, Portsmouth PO1 3LS. *Club:* Army and Navy.

See also P. J. B. Slater.

SLATER, John Fell, CMG 1972; Assistant Secretary, HM Treasury, 1968–82; *b* 3 July 1924; *s* of J. Alan Slater, FRIBA, and Friede R. Slater (*née* Flight); *m* 1951, Susan Baron (*d* 1996); two *s* two *d* (and one *d* decd). *Educ:* Abinger Hill Preparatory Sch.; Leighton Park Sch.; New Coll., Oxford (BA). *Recreations:* gardening, photography. *Address:* 20 Upham Park Road, W4 1PG. *T:* (020) 8995 8299.

SLATER, Dr John Morton; agricultural economic consultant, since 1998; *b* 21 Aug. 1938; *s* of Rev. Percy William Slater and Evelyn Maude Morton Slater; *m* 1972, Susan Mary Black, *d* of Rev. Dr John Ferguson Park and Mary Davis McCaughey Park; two *s* one *d.* *Educ:* Durham Sch.; Univ. of Nottingham (BSc Agric. Sc 1961); Univ. of Toronto (MS Agric. Econ. 1963); Univ. of Illinois (L. J. Norton Meml Fellow; PhD 1965). Lectr, Univ. of Manchester, 1965–70; Consultant, FAO, 1966–67; Ministry of Agriculture, Fisheries and Food: Economic Advr, 1970–84; Head of Econs and Stats (Food) Div., 1984–92; Head of Econs (Internat.) Div., 1992–96; Head of Econs and Stats Gp, 1996–98. Special Advr, H of L Select Cttee on Science and Technol., 1999–2000. Master, Worshipful Co. of Turners, 1999–2000. MRI. *Publication:* (ed) Fifty Years of the National Food Survey 1940–1990, 1991. *Recreations:* cricket, golf, bridge. *Address:* 28 Swains Lane, N6 6QR. *T:* (020) 7485 1238, *Fax:* (020) 7485 1268; *e-mail:* j.slater@slaterconsult.demon.co.uk. *Clubs:* City Livery, United Wards, MCC.

SLATER, Kenneth Frederick, FREng, FIEE; engineering and defence consultant; *b* 31 July 1925; *s* of Charles Frederick and Emily Gertrude Slater; *m* 1965, Marjorie Gladys Beadsworth, Northampton. *Educ:* Hull Grammar Sch.; Manchester Univ. (BSc Tech (Hons)). Admiralty Signal Estab. Extension, 1943–46; RRE, 1949–63; UK Mem., NATO Air Defence Planning Team, 1964; Supt, Radar Div., RRE, 1965–68; Asst Dir of Electronics R&D, Min. of Technology, 1968–70, Dir, 1970–71; Head of various groups, RRE, 1971–76; Dep. Dir, RSRE, 1976–78; Dir, Admiralty Surface Weapons Estab., 1978–84; Dir of Engrg, Marconi Underwater Systems Ltd, 1984–88. Vis. Prof., UCL, 1995–. Liveryman, Engineers' Co., 1992–. FREng (FEng 1985). *Publications:* specialist contribs on Radar to Encyclopaedia Britannica and Encyclopaedic Dictionary of Physics; technical articles. *Recreations:* photography, music. *Address:* Valinor, Blackheath Way, West Malvern WR14 4DR. *T:* (01684) 567641.

SLATER, Prof. Michael Derek, DPhil; Professor of Victorian Literature, Birkbeck College, University of London, 1991–2001, now Emeritus; *b* 29 Dec. 1936; *s* of Jesse Slater and Valentine Blanche (*née* Clément). *Educ:* Reading Sch.; Balliol Coll., Oxford (Goldsmith Schol., Charles Oldham Schol., MA, DPhil 1965). Birkbeck College, University of London: Res. Asst, 1962–65; Asst Lectr in English, 1965–67; Lectr in English, 1967–79; Sen. Lectr, 1979–83; Reader, 1983–91. Dist. Vis. Prof., Ohio State Univ., 1975–76; Visiting Professor: Univ. of Debrecen, Hungary, 1992; Univ. of Kyoto, Japan, 1995. Tennyson Soc. annual Lect., 1997. President: Dickens Soc. of America, 1973; Internat. Dickens Fellowship, 1988–90. Chm. Trustees, Dickens House Mus., 1996–99. Editor, The Dickensian, 1968–77. *Publications:* The Catalogue of the Suzannet Charles Dickens Collection, 1975; (ed) Dickens 1970, 1970; Dickens on America and the Americans, 1978; Dickens and Women, 1983, 2nd edn 1986; (with N. Bentley and N. Burgis) The Dickens Index, 1988; (ed) The Dent Uniform Edition of Dickens's Journalism, Vol. 1 1994, Vol. 2 1996, Vol. 3 1998, (with J. Drew) Vol. 4 2000; The Intelligent Person's Guide to Dickens, 2000. *Recreations:* theatre, travel, visiting literary museums. *Address:* c/o Department of English, Birkbeck College, Malet Street, WC1E 7HX. *T:* (020) 7631 6088.

SLATER, Prof. Nigel Kenneth Harry, PhD; CEng, FIChemE; Professor of Chemical Engineering, Cambridge University, since 2000; Fellow, Fitzwilliam College, Cambridge, 1978–85, and since 2000; *b* 22 March 1953; *s* of Arthur Geoffrey Slater; *m* 1976, Kay Bendle; one *s* two *d.* *Educ:* Bolton Sch.; Sidney Sussex Coll., Cambridge (MA; PhD). CEng 1990; FIChemE 1997. Asst Lectr, 1979–82, Lectr, 1982–85, in Chemical Engrg, Cambridge Univ.; Bioprocessing Section Manager, Unilever Research NL, 1985–90; Head of Bioprocess Dept, Wellcome Foundation Ltd, 1990–95; Prof. and Head of Dept of Chem. Engrg and Applied Chemistry, Aston Univ., 1995–2000. Dir, Birmingham Technology Ltd, 1995–2000; Founder, Cobra Biosciences Ltd, 1997. Chm., Chemical and Pharmaceuticals Directorate, BBSRC, 1993–96; Mem. Governing Body, Silsoe Res. Inst., 1996–2000. Governor, King Edward VI Foundn, 1997–2000. *Publications:* numerous articles in learned science and engrg jls. *Recreations:* golf, socialising, outdoor pursuits. *Address:* Shenstone House, 3 St Bernard's Road, Sutton Coldfield, W Midlands B72 1LE. *T:* (0121) 321 2349.

SLATER, Prof. Peter James Bramwell, FRSE; Kennedy Professor of Natural History, since 1984, and Dean of the Faculty of Science, since 1998, University of St Andrews; *b* 26 Dec. 1942; *s* of Dr James Kirkwood Slater, OBE and Margaret Claire Byrom Slater (*née* Bramwell); *m* 1968, Elisabeth Priscilla Vernon Smith; two *s*. *Educ:* Edinburgh Academy; Glenalmond; Univ. of Edinburgh (BSc 1964; PhD 1968; DSc 1983). FIBiol 1986; FRSE 1991. Shaw Macfie Lang Fellow, 1964–66, Demonstrator in Zoology, 1966–68, Univ. of Edinburgh; Lectr in Biology, Univ. of Sussex, 1968–84; Head, Sch. of Biol and Med. Scis, St Andrews Univ., 1992–97. Chm., Heads of Univ. Biol Scis, 1994–96. Association for Study of Animal Behaviour: Hon. Sec., 1973–78; Hon. Pres., 1986–89; Medallist, 1999. European Editor, Animal Behaviour, 1979–82; Editor: Advances in the Study of Behavior, 1989– (Associate Editor, 1982–88); Science Progress, 1983–89. *Publications:* Sex Hormones and Behaviour, 1978; (ed with T. R. Halliday) Animal Behaviour, 1983; An Introduction to Ethology, 1985; (ed) Collins Encyclopaedia of Animal Behaviour, 1986; (ed with T. R. Halliday) Evolution and Behaviour, 1994; (with C. K. Catchpole) Bird Song: biological themes and variations, 1995; Essentials of Animal Behaviour, 1999; numerous articles in learned jls. *Recreations:* ornithology, writing, listening to music. *Address:* School of Biology, University of St Andrews, Fife KY16 9TS. *T:* (01334) 463500.

See also Sir J. C. K. Slater.

SLATER, William Bell, CBE 1982; VRD 1959; FCIT; Chairman, The Mersey Docks & Harbour Co., 1987–93; Managing Director, The Cunard Steam-Ship Co. plc, 1974–85 (Director, 1971–85 and 1986–88); Director, Trafalgar House plc, 1975–88; *b* 7 Jan. 1925; *s* of William Bell and Mamie Slater; *m* 1950, Jean Mary Kiernan; two *s*. *Educ:* Lancaster Royal Grammar Sch. FCIT 1970. National Service, RM, 1943–47 (Captain, 3rd Commando Bde); RM Reserve, 1949–63 (Lt-Col and CO Merseyside Unit, 1959–63; Hon. Col, 1986–91). Trainee, Thos & Jno Brocklebank Ltd, 1947, Dir 1966–85, also Chm.; Ops Dir, 1968, Dep. Man. Dir, 1969, Man. Dir, 1971–72, Chm. 1972–85, Cunard Brocklebank Ltd. Director: Atlantic Container Line Ltd, 1968–85 (Chm., 1977–78 and 1982–83); Associated Container Transportation (Australia) Ltd, 1974–85 (Chm., 1982–85); Associated Container Transportation Ltd, 1974–85 (Chm., 1982–85); The Mersey Docks & Harbour Co., 1980–93 (Dep. Chm., 1985–87; Chm., 1987–93). External Dir, British Internat. Freight Assoc., 1989–94. Vice-Pres., CIT, 1984–87; Pres., Inst. of Freight Forwarders Ltd, 1987–88. Gen. Comr of Income Tax, 1987–99. Order of El Istiqlal (2nd Cl.), Jordan, 1972. *Recreations:* Rugby and cricket (formerly Senior Club player). *Address:* Gayton Court, 419 Woodham Lane, Woodham, Addlestone, Surrey KT15 3PP. *T:* (01932) 349389. *Club:* Naval.

SLATER, William John, CBE 1998 (OBE 1982); President, British Amateur Gymnastics Association, 1989–2000; Director of National Services, Sports Council, 1984–89; *b* 29 April 1927; *s* of John Rothwell Slater and Ethel May Slater; *m* 1952, Marion Warr; two *s* two *d*. *Educ:* Clitheroe Royal Grammar Sch.; Carnegie Coll. of Physical Educn (Dip. in Phys. Educn); Univ. of Birmingham (BSc). FPEA 1984. Dir of Phys. Educn, Univ. of Liverpool, 1964–70; Dir of Phys. Educn, Univ. of Birmingham, 1970–83. Member: Central Adv. Council for Educn (Newsom Cttee), 1961–63; Cttee of Enquiry into Association Football (Chester Cttee), 1966–68; Sports Council, 1974–83; Nat. Olympic Cttee, 1990–2000. Chairman: Cttee of Advrs, Sports Aid Foundn, 1978–97; West Midlands Council for Sport and Recreation, 1979–83. Wolverhampton Wanderers Football Club, 1952–62; rep. England in Association Football, 1951–60; Olympic Games, Helsinki, 1952; World Cup (Assoc. Football), Sweden, 1958. Hon. MSc Birmingham, 1990. Footballer of the Year, 1960. *Recreations:* games and sports of all kinds.

SLATKIN, Leonard; conductor; music director; Music Director, National Symphony Orchestra, Washington, since 1995; Chief Conductor, BBC Symphony Orchestra, since 2000; *b* Los Angeles, 1 Sept. 1944; *s* of Felix Slatkin and Eleanor Slatkin (*née* Aller); *m* 1986, Linda Hohenfeld; one *s*. *Educ:* Indiana Univ.; LA City Coll.; Juilliard Sch. of Music. Conducting début as Asst Conductor, Youth Symphony Orch. of NY, Carnegie Hall, 1966; Asst Conductor, Juilliard Opera Theater and Dance Dept, 1967; St Louis Symphony Youth Orchestra: Founder, Music Dir and Conductor, 1969–75; Musical Advr, 1984–96; St Louis Symphony Orchestra: Asst Conductor, 1968–71; Associate Conductor, 1971–74; Music Dir and Conductor, 1979–95; Music Dir, New Orleans Philharmonic Symphony, 1977–78; débuts: with Chicago Symphony, NY Philharmonic, Philadelphia Orch., RPO, 1974; with USSR orchs, 1976–77; Tokyo, 1986; Metropolitan Opera, 1991. Guest conductor with orchs throughout world incl. Concertgebouw, English Chamber Orch., LPO, LSO, Vienna State Opera, Stuttgart Opera; Principal Guest Conductor: Minnesota Orch., 1974–79; Philharmonia, 1997–2000. Has made numerous recordings. Mem., Nat. Acad. Recording Arts and Scis, 1985. Holds hon. doctorates. Grammy Awards, 1984, 1991 and 1994. Declaration of Honor (Silver) (Austria), 1986. *Compositions:* The Raven, 1971; Rhymes and Sonnets, 1974; Dialogue for Two Cellos and Orchestra, 1975; Absurd Alphabed-time Stories, 1976; Extensions, 1, 2, 3 and 4, 1973–75. *Address:* National Symphony Orchestra, John F. Kennedy Center, Washington, DC 20566, USA.

SLATTERY, Dr David Antony Douglas, MBE (mil.) 1958; Chief Medical Officer, Rolls-Royce plc, 1973–92; Dean, Faculty of Occupational Medicine, Royal College of Physicians, 1988–91 (Vice-Dean, 1986–88); *b* 28 Jan. 1930; *s* of Rear-Adm. Sir Matthew Slattery, KBE, CB and Mica Mary Slattery (*née* Swain); *m* 1st, 1954, Mary Winifred Miller; two *s* two *d*; 2nd, 1974, Claire Louise McGuinness; one *s*. *Educ:* Ampleforth Coll.; St Thomas' Hosp., London. MB BS; FFOM RCPI 1977; FFOM RCP 1981; FRCP 1986. Capt., RAMC, 1954–58. MO, E Midlands Gas Bd, 1959–69; Manager, Health and Safety, BSC, Rotherham, 1969–73. Special Lectr, Dept of Community Health, Nottingham Univ., 1978–93; Vis. Prof., Dept of Occupational Health, Univ. of Liverpool, 1992–97. Consultant Advr in occupational medicine, RAF, 1987–96; Advr on occupational health policy, Mersey RHA, 1992–94. Dir, Occupational Health Service, Aintree Hosps NHS Trust, 1993–94. Member: Standing Med. Adv. Cttee, DHSS, 1988–91; Adv. Bd, CS Occupational Health Service, 1988–91. Industrial Health Advr, Derbys Br., BRCS, 1976–93. *Publications:* papers on occupational medicine and the employment of the disabled. *Recreations:* history, fishing, people. *Address:* 99 South Quay, Wapping Dock, Liverpool L3 4BW. *T:* (0151) 707 2022. *Club:* Royal Society of Medicine.

SLATYER, Prof. Ralph Owen, AC 1993 (AO 1982); FRS 1975; Distinguished Scholar in Residence, Australian National University, since 1992; *b* 16 April 1929; *s* of Thomas Henry and Jean Slatyer; *m* 1953, June Helen Wade; one *s* two *d*. *Educ:* Univ. of Western Australia (DSc (Agric.). CSIRO Res. Scientist, subseq. Chief Res. Scientist, 1951–67; Prof., Inst. of Advanced Studies, 1967–89, Dir, Res. Sch. of Biol Scis, 1984–89, ANU; Chief Scientist, Dept of Prime Minister and Cabinet, Australia, 1989–92; Mem. and Exec. Officer, Prime Minister's Science Council, 1989–92. Aust. Amb. to UNESCO, 1978–81. Member: Australian Res. Grants Cttee, 1969–72; Nat. Capital Planning Cttee, 1973–76; Aust. Nat. Commn for UNESCO, 1975–78 (Chm., 1976–78); Policy Adv. Council and Bd of Management, Aust. Centre for Internat. Agricl Research, 1981–85; President: Ecol Soc. of Austr., 1969–71; UNESCO Man and the Biosphere Programme, 1977–81; UNESCO World Heritage Cttee, 1981–83; ICSU Sci. Cttee on Problems of the Environment, 1982–85; ANZAAS, 1983; Chairman: Aust. Biol. Resources Study, 1981–84; Australian Science and Technology Council, 1982–87; Co-ordination Cttee on Sci. and Technol., 1989–92; Co-op. Res. Centre for Rainforest Ecology and Mgt, 1993–; Dep. Chm., Nat. Greenhouse Adv. Cttee, 1989–93. FAA 1967; Fellow, Aust. Acad. of Technol Scis and Engrg, 1992. For. Associate, US Nat. Acad. of Sciences, 1976; Hon. For. Mem., Amer. Acad. of Arts and Scis, 1981; For. Mem., Korean Acad. of Scis and Technol., 1996. Hon. DSc: Univ. of WA, 1983; Duke Univ., 1986; Univ. of Qld, 1992; Charles Sturt, 1999. Edgeworth David Medal, 1960; Austr. Medal of Agric. Sci., 1968; ANZAAS Medal, 1991. *Publications:* (with I. C. McIlroy) Practical Microclimatology, 1961; Plant-Water Relationships, 1967; (ed with R. A. Perry) Arid Lands of Australia, 1969; (ed jtly) Photosynthesis and Photorespiration, 1971; (ed) Plant Response to Climatic Factors, 1974; papers in learned jls. *Recreation:* bushwalking. *Address:* 54 Musgrave Street, Yarralumla, ACT 2600, Australia.

SLAUGHTER, Audrey Cecelia, (Mrs C. V. Wintour); writer and freelance journalist; *d* of Frederick George Smith and Ethel Louise Smith; *m* 1st, 1949, W. A. Slaughter (marr. diss.); one *s* one *d*; 2nd, 1979, Charles Vere Wintour, CBE (*d* 1999). *Educ:* Chislehurst High Sch., Stand Grammar Sch., Manchester. Editor, Honey magazine, 1960; founded Petticoat magazine, 1964; columnist, Evening News, 1968; joined National Magazine Co., to edit Vanity Fair, 1969; founded and funded own magazine, Over 21; 1970; after sale to Morgan Grampian, 1972, remained as Dir and Editor until 1979; Associate Editor, Sunday Times, 1979; with husband founded Sunday Express colour magazine, 1981; Founder Editor, Working Woman magazine, 1984–86; Lifestyle Editor, The Independent, 1986–87. *Publications:* Every Man Should Have One (with Margaret Goodman), 1969; Getting Through . . ., 1981; Working Woman's Handbook, 1986; Your Brilliant Career, 1987; Private View (novel), 1990; Blooming (novel), 1992; Unknown Country (novel), 1994. *Recreations:* classical music, theatre, painting.

SLAUGHTER, Giles David, MA; Headmaster, University College School, 1983–96; *b* 11 July 1937; *s* of Gerald Slaughter and Enid Lillian Slaughter (*née* Crane); *m* 1965, Gillian Rothwell Shepherd; three *d*. *Educ:* Royal Masonic School; King's College, Cambridge. MA. Pierrepont School, Frensham, 1961–65; Campbell College, Belfast, 1965–68; Stockport Grammar School, 1968–70; Housemaster, Ormiston House, Campbell Coll., 1970–73; Headmaster, Solihull School, 1973–82. Non-exec. Dir, Heckett MultiServ plc, 1999–. Chm., London and SE, ISIS, 1995–98. Governor: Godolphin and Latymer Sch., 1988–99; Cobham Hall, 1989–2000; Aldwickbury Sch., 1974–; King's Coll. Sch., Wimbledon, 1995–. JP Solihull, 1977–82. *Recreations:* gardening, cricket, golf, theatre. *Address:* 6 Church Lane, Lower Ufford, Woodbridge, Suffolk IP13 6DS.

SLEDGE, Ven. Richard Kitson; Archdeacon of Huntingdon, 1978–96; *b* 13 April 1930; *s* of Sydney Kitson and Mary Sylvia Sledge; *m* 1958, Patricia Henley (*née* Sear); one *s* two *d* (and one *s* decd). *Educ:* Epsom College; Peterhouse, Cambridge (MA). Curate of Emmanuel, Plymouth, 1954–57; Curate-in-charge of St Stephen's, Exeter, 1957–63; Rector: Dronfield, 1963–78; Hemingford Abbots, 1978–89. *Address:* 7 Budge Close, Brampton, Huntingdon, Cambs PE28 4PL. *T:* (01480) 380284.

SLEE, Very Rev. Colin Bruce, OBE 2001; Dean (formerly Provost) of Southwark, since 1994; *b* 10 Nov. 1945; *s* of Herbert Samuel Slee and Miriam Clara May Slee; *m* 1971, Edith Tryon; one *s* two *d*, and one foster *s* one foster *d*. *Educ:* Ealing Grammar Sch.; King's Coll., London (BD, AKC; FKC 2001); St Augustine's Coll., Canterbury. Ordained deacon, 1970, priest, 1971; Curate, St Francis, Heartsease, 1970–73; Curate, Great St Mary's, Cambridge, and Chaplain, Girton Coll., Cambridge, 1973–76; Chaplain and Tutor, KCL, 1976–82; Sub-Dean and Canon Residentiary, St Alban's Abbey, 1982–94. Mem., General Synod, C of E, 1995–. Hon. Chaplain, Shakespeare's Globe Theatre, 1997–. Trustee: Crisis, 1995–; Parents for Children, 1995–. Governor, INFORM, 1985–. Patron: Southwark Fest., 1994–; Home Start, 1994–; British Sch. of Osteopathy, 1997–. *Recreations:* rowing (purple, London Univ., 1967, 1968), gardening, bee keeping. *Address:* Southwark Cathedral, Montague Close, SE1 9DA. *T:* (020) 7407 3708; Provost's Lodging, 51 Bankside, SE1 9JE. *T:* (020) 7928 6414, *Fax:* (020) 7357 7389.

SLEEMAN, His Honour (Stuart) Colin; a Circuit Judge, 1976–86; *s* of Stuart Bertram Sleeman and Phyllis Grace (*née* Pitt); *m* 1944, Margaret Emily, *d* of late William Joseph Farmer; two *s* one *d*. *Educ:* Clifton Coll.; Merton Coll., Oxford (BA 1936, MA 1963). Called to the Bar, Gray's Inn, 1938; Bencher, 1974. World War II: Admin. Officer, Prize Dept, Min. of Economic Warfare, 1939–40; Lt-Col 16th-5th Lancers; Staff Captain: RAC Wing, Combined Trng Centre, 1941; 6th Armoured Div., 1942; Adjt, RAC Range, Minehead, 1942–44; Asst Judge Advocate Gen., HQ Allied Land Forces, SE Asia, 1945. London Corresp., Scottish Law Rev., 1949–54; a Recorder, 1975–76. *Publications:* The Trial of Gozawa Sadaichi and Nine Others, 1948; (with S. C. Silkin) The 'Double Tenth' Trial, 1950. *Recreations:* travel, genealogy. *Address:* West Walls, Cotmandene, Dorking, Surrey RH4 2BL. *T:* (01306) 883616.

See also S. P. Sleeman.

SLEEMAN, Stuart Philip; His Honour Judge Sleeman; a Circuit Judge, since 1993; *s* of His Honour (Stuart) Colin Sleeman, *qv*; *m* 1973, Elisabeth Nina Brann; one *s* two *d*. *Educ:* Cranleigh Sch.; Merton Coll., Oxford (BA Jurisprudence 1969; MA 1972). Called to the Bar, Gray's Inn, 1970; a Recorder, 1986–93. Chm., Old Cranleighan Soc., 1984–97; Gov., Cranleigh Sch., 1989–. *Recreations:* hockey (Oxford Occasionals), music, history (in particular the Reformation).

SLEEP, Wayne Philip Colin, OBE 1998; dancer, actor, choreographer; *b* Plymouth, 17 July 1948. *Educ:* Hartlepool; Royal Ballet Sch. (Leverhulme Scholar). Graduated into Royal Ballet, 1966; Soloist, 1970; Principal, 1973; roles in: Giselle; Dancers at a Gathering; The Nutcracker; Romeo and Juliet; The Grand Tour; Elite Syncopations; Swan Lake; The Four Seasons; Les Patineurs; Petroushka (title role); Cinderella; The Dream; Pineapple Poll; Mam'zelle Angot; 4th Symphony; La Fille mal gardée; A Month in the Country; A Good Night's Sleep (gala); Coppelia, English Nat. Ballet, 1994; chor., with Robert North, David & Goliath; also roles in operas, A Midsummer Night's Dream and Aida; roles created for him by Sir Frederick Ashton, Dame Ninette de Valois, Sir Kenneth MacMillan, Rudolf Nureyev, John Neumeier, Joe Layton and many others. *Theatre:* Ariel in The Tempest, New Shakespeare Co.; title role in Pinocchio, Birmingham Rep.; genie in Aladdin, Palladium; soldier in The Soldier's Tale, QEH, 1980 and 1981; Truffaldino in The Servant of Two Masters; chor. and played lead in The Point, Mermaid; Mr Mistoffelees in Cats, New London, 1981; co-starred in Song and Dance, Palace, 1982, Shaftesbury, 1990 (video, 1984); Cabaret, Strand, 1986; chor. Savoy Suite, 1993; The History of Dance, tour, 1995. Formed own company, DASH, 1980: Chichester Fest., 1980, national tour and Sadler's Wells, 1982, Apollo Victoria and national tour, Christmas season, Dominion, 1983; danced in and jtly choreographed Bits and Pieces, Dominion, 1989; Hollywood and Broadway tour, 1996–97; World of Classical Ballet tour, 1998; has directed several charity galas including 90 Years of Dance, 1995 and Stars of the Night, 1997. Teaches workshops around the world. *Films:* The Virgin Soldiers; The First Great Train Robbery; The Tales of Beatrix Potter, 1971. Chor. films and television, inc. Adam's Rib, Death on the Nile, and appeared in many television progs inc. Dizzy Feet and series, The Hot Shoe Show, 1983, 1984; Tony Lumpkin in She Stoops to Conquer, radio. Patron: Wheelchair Dance Assoc.; Dance Teachers Benevolent Fund; Benesh Dance Inst. Hon. DLitt Exeter. Show Business Personality of the Year, 1983. *Publications:* Variations on Wayne Sleep, 1983; Precious little Sleep (autobiog.), 1996. *Recreation:* entertaining. *Address:* 22 Queensberry Mews West, SW7 2DY.

SLEIGH, Andrew Crofton; Managing Director, Defence Solutions, QinetiQ plc, since 2001; *b* 4 Nov. 1950; *s* of Arthur Ffennell Crofton Sleigh and Margaret Sleigh; *m* 1986, Christine Mattick; one *s* one *d*. *Educ:* Portsmouth Grammar Sch.; Maret Sch., Washington; Havant Grammar Sch.; St Catherine's Coll., Oxford (MA Physics). Superintendent, Pattern Processing and Machine Intelligence Div., RSRE, 1985–90; Director: of Science, Central Staff, MoD, 1990–93; Operation Studies Sector, DRA, 1993–94; Chief Exec., Defence Operational Analysis Centre, MoD, 1994–95; Man. Dir, Centre for Defence Analysis, DERA, 1995–98; Dir Gen. for Inf. and Communications Services, MoD, 1998–2000; Capability Manager for Information Superiority, MoD, 2000–01. Chairman: Malvern Fest. Fringe, 1977–82; Wyvern Trust Ltd, 1984–90. *Publication:* (with O. J. Braddick) The Physical and Biological Processing of Images, 1983. *Recreations:* family, windsurfing, photography, maintaining country cottage and grounds. *Address:* Ministry of Defence, Main Building, Whitehall, SW1A 2HB. *T:* (020) 7218 7445; *e-mail:* Andrew_Sleigh@compuserve.com.

SLEIGHT, Prof. Peter, MD (Cantab), DM (Oxon), FRCP; FACC; Field-Marshal Alexander Professor of Cardiovascular Medicine in the University of Oxford, and Fellow of Exeter College, Oxford, 1973–94, now Emeritus Professor and Fellow; Hon. Consultant Physician, Oxford Health Authority, since 1964; *b* 27 June 1929; *s* of William and Mary Sleight, Boston Spa, Yorks; *m* 1953, Gillian France; two *s*. *Educ:* Leeds Grammar Sch.; Gonville and Caius Coll., Cambridge; St Bartholomew's Hosp., London. Ho. Phys. and Ho. Surg., Med. and Surg. Professorial Units, Bart's, 1953; Sen. Registrar, St George's Hosp., London, 1959–64; Bissinger Fellow, Cardiovascular Research Inst., Univ. of California, San Francisco, 1961–63; MRC Scientific Officer, Depts of Physiology and Medicine, Univ. of Oxford, 1964–66; Consultant Physician, Radcliffe Infirmary, Oxford, 1966–73. Visiting Prof., Univ. of Sydney (Warren McDonald Sen. Overseas Fellow of Aust. Heart Foundn), 1972–73; Hon. Prof. of Medicine, Federal Univ. of Pernambuco, 1975. Civil Consultant in Medicine, RAF, 1985–94. Co-Chm., Heartoutcomes Prevention Evaluation Study Gp, 1995–; Co-Chm., ON TARGET Study Gp, 2000–. Vice Pres., ASH, 1994– (Chm., 1982–93); President: British Hypertension Soc., 1993–95; World Hypertension League, 1995–; Member Council: Internat. Soc. of Hypertension, 1978–86; European Soc. of Cardiology, 1983–88; Hon. Mem., European Soc. of Hypertension, 2001. Mem. Editorial Bd, British Heart Jl, 1976–83; Editor: Jl of Cardiovascular Res., 1983–92; Jl of Cardiovascular Risk, 1994–. Hon. MD Gdansk, 2000. Young Investigators Award, Amer. Coll. of Cardiology, 1963; Evian Prize, 1988; Merck Sharp and Dohme Award, Internat. Soc. of Hypertension, 1990; Galen Medal for Therapeutics, Soc. of Apothecaries, 2000; Sen. Internat. Award, Aspirin Foundn, 2000. *Films:* Control of Circulation; History of Hypertension (Medal, BMA Scientific Film Competition, 1981). *Publications:* Modern Trends in Cardiology, 1976; (ed) Arterial Baroreceptors and Hypertension, 1981; Hypertension, 1982; (ed) Scientific Foundations of Cardiology, 1983; (with D. Eckberg) Human arterial baro reflexes in Health and Disease, 1992; contribs on nervous control of the circulation, hypertension and treatment of myocardial infarction in: Circulation Research; Jl Physiol; Lancet (Chm., Internat. Studies of Infarct Survival). *Recreations:* sailing, golf, travel. *Address:* Wayside, 32 Crown Road, Wheatley, Oxon OX33 1UL. *Club:* Royal Air Force.

SLEIGHT, Sir Richard, 4th Bt *cr* 1920, of Weelsby Hall, Clee; *b* 27 May 1946; *s* of Sir John Frederick Sleight, 3rd Bt and of Jacqueline Margaret, *o d* of late Maj. H. R. Carter, Brisbane, Queensland; *S* father, 1990; *m* 1978, Marie-Thérèse, *o d* of O. M. Stepan; two *s*. *Heir: s* James Alexander Sleight, *b* 5 Jan. 1981. *Address:* c/o National Westminster Bank, 6 High Street, Teddington, Middlesex TW11 8EP.

SLEVIN, Maurice Louis, MD; FRCP; Consultant Physician, Medical Oncology Department, St Bartholomew's and Homerton Hospitals, since 1982; *b* 2 July 1949; *s* of David Slevin and Nita (*née* Rosenbaum); *m* 1st, 1975, Cherry Jacobsohn (marr. diss. 1987); two *d*; 2nd, 1993, Nicola Jane Harris; one *s* one *d*. *Educ:* Univ. of Cape Town (MB ChB 1973; MD 1984). MRCP 1978, FRCP 1989. Registrar in General Medicine, Groote Schuur Hosp., Cape Town, 1977–78; Registrar in Med. Oncology, St Bartholomew's Hosp., 1978–80, Sen. Registrar, 1980–82. Chm. and Trustee, BACUP, 1987–. *Publications:* Randomised Trials in Cancer, 1986; Metastases, 1988; Challenging Cancer: from chaos to control, 1991; Cancer: the facts, 1996; Cancer: how worthwhile is non-curative treatment?, 1998; numerous pubns on clinical oncology, clinical pharmacology and psychosocial oncology. *Address:* Medical Oncology Department, St Bartholomew's Hospital, West Smithfield, EC1A 7BE. *T:* (020) 7606 6662; 149 Harley Street, W1N 1HG. *T:* (020) 7224 0685.

SLIGO, 11th Marquess of, *cr* 1800; **Jeremy Ulick Browne;** Baron Mount Eagle 1760; Viscount Westport 1768; Earl of Altamont 1771; Earl of Clanricarde 1543 and 1800; Baron Monteagle (UK) 1806; *b* 4 June 1939; *s* of 10th Marquess of Sligo and of José Gauche; *S* father, 1991; *m* 1961, Jennifer June, *d* of Major Derek Cooper, Dunlewey, Co. Donegal, and Mrs C. Heber Percy, Pophleys, Radnage; five *d*. *Educ:* St Columba's College, Eire; Royal Agricultural College, Cirencester. *Heir: cousin* Sebastian Ulick Browne, *b* 27 May 1964. *Address:* Westport House, Co; Mayo, Eire.

SLIM, family name of **Viscount Slim**.

SLIM, 2nd Viscount *cr* 1960, of Yarralumla and Bishopston; **John Douglas Slim,** OBE 1973; DL; Chairman, 1976–91, and non-executive Deputy Chairman, since 1991, Peek plc (formerly Peek Holdings); Director, Trailfinders Ltd, since 1984, and a number of other companies; *b* 20 July 1927; *s* of Field Marshal the 1st Viscount Slim, KG, GCB, GCMG, GCVO, GBE, DSO, MC, and Aileen (*d* 1993), *d* of Rev. J. A. Robertson, MA, Edinburgh; *S* father, 1970; *m* 1958, Elisabeth, *d* of Arthur Rawdon Spinney, CBE; two *s* one *d*. *Educ:* Prince of Wales Royal Indian Military College, Dehra Dun. Indian Army, 6 Gurkha Rifles, 1945–48; Argyll and Sutherland Highlanders, 1948; SAS, 1952; Staff. Coll., Camberley, 1961; Brigade Major, HQ Highland Infantry Bde (TA), 1962–64; JSSC 1964; Lt-Col 1967; Comdr, 22 Special Air Service Regt, 1967–70; GSO1 (Special Forces) HQ UK Land Forces, 1970–72; retired 1972. Elected Mem., H of L, 1999. President, Burma Star Association, 1971–. Vice-Pres., Britain-Australia Soc., 1988– (Chm., 1978–84); Vice-Chm., Arab-British Chamber of Commerce and Industry, 1977–96. Master, Clothworkers' Co., 1995–96. FRGS 1983. DL Greater London, 1988. *Heir: s* Hon. Mark William Rawdon Slim [*b* 13 Feb. 1960; *m* 1992, Harriet Laura, *yr d* of Jonathan Harrison; two *s*]. *Address:* House of Lords, Westminster, SW1A 0PW. *Clubs:* White's, Special Forces.

SLINGER, Edward; His Honour Judge Slinger; a Circuit Judge, since 1995; *b* 2 Feb. 1938; *s* of Thomas Slinger and Rhoda (*née* Bradshaw); *m* 1965, Rosalind Margaret Jewitt; two *s* two *d*. *Educ:* Accrington Grammar Sch.; Balliol Coll., Oxford (Dist. Law Mods 1956; BA 1958). Admitted solicitor (with Hons), 1961; Partner, Ramsbottom & Co., Solicitors, Blackburn, 1964–95; Dep. Registrar, 1982–88; Asst Recorder, 1988–92; Recorder, 1992–95. Pres., Blackburn Incorporated Law Assoc., 1986; Member: Immigration Law Sub-cttee, Law Soc., 1990–95; Immigration Appeal Tribunal, 1997–. Lancashire County Cricket Club: Captain, 2nd XI, 1967–75; Mem. Cttee, 1969–99; Trustee, 1978–96; Vice-Chm., 1985–98; Vice-Pres., 2000–. Dep. Chm., Discipline Cttee, TCCB (now ECB), 1990–. Governor: Samlesbury C of E Sch., Lancs, 1986–; Westholme Sch., Blackburn, 1985–. *Recreation:* cricket. *Address:* c/o Court Administrator's Office, Sessions House, Lancaster Road, Preston, Lancs PR1 2PD. *T:* (01772) 821451. *Clubs:* MCC, Lansdowne.

SLIPMAN, Sue, OBE 1994; Director for Social Responsibility, Camelot Group plc, since 1998; *b* 3 Aug. 1949; *d* of Marks Slipman and Doris Barham; one *s*. *Educ:* Stockwell Manor Comprehensive School; Univ. of Wales (BA Hons 1st Class English; Post Graduate Cert Ed); Univs of Leeds and London. Sec. and Nat. Pres., Nat. Union of Students, 1975–78; Mem., Adv. Council for Adult and Continuing Educn, 1978–79; Area Officer, Nat. Union of Public Employees, 1979–85; Director: Nat. Council for One Parent Families, 1985–95; London TEC Council, 1995–96; Gas Consumers' Council, 1996–98. Mem. Exec., NCCL, 1974–75; Vice-Chair, British Youth Council, 1977–78; Chair: Women for Social Democracy, 1983–86; Advice Guidance and Counselling Lead Body, 1992–; Member: Exec. and Chair of Training, 300 Group, 1985–86; Exec., London Voluntary Service Council, 1986; Women's Issues Wkg Gp, Dept of Employment, 1990–94; Better Regulation Task Force, 1997–. Dir, London East TEC, 1990; Trustee, Full Employment UK, 1990–95; Dir, Social Market Foundn, 1992–93. *Publications:* chapter in The Re-Birth of Britain, 1983; Helping Ourselves to Power: a handbook for women on the skills of public life, 1986. *Address:* Camelot Group plc, 20 Cockspur Street, SW1Y 5BL.

SLIVE, Prof. Seymour; Gleason Professor of Fine Arts at Harvard University, 1973–91, Emeritus since 1991; Director, Fogg Art Museum, 1975–82, sometime Elizabeth and John Moors Cabot Director of Harvard Art Museums; *b* Chicago, 15 Sept. 1920; *s* of Daniel Slive and Sonia (*née* Rapoport); *m* 1946, Zoya Gregorovna Sandomirsky; one *s* two *d*. *Educ:* Univ. of Chicago. BA 1943; PhD 1952. Served US Navy, Lieut, CO Small Craft, 1943–46. Instructor in Art History, Oberlin Coll., 1950–51; Asst Prof. and Chm. of Art Dept, Pomona Coll., 1952–54; Asst Prof. 1954–57, Assoc. Prof. 1957–61, Prof., 1961–73, Chm. of Dept 1968–71, Fine Arts, Harvard Univ.; Exchange Prof., Univ. of Leningrad, 1961. Ryerson Lectr, Yale, 1962. Slade Prof. of Fine Art, Univ. of Oxford, 1972–73. Trustee, Solomon R. Guggenheim Foundn, 1978–. FAAAS 1964; Corresp. FBA 1995. For. Mem., Netherlands Soc. of Sciences, 1971. Hon. MA Harvard, 1958; Hon. MA Oxford, 1972. Officer, Order of Orange Nassau, 1962. *Publications:* Rembrandt and His Critics: 1630–1730, 1953; Drawings of Rembrandt, 1965; (with J. Rosenberg and E. H. ter Kuile) Dutch Art and Architecture: 1600–1800, 1965, 2nd edn, 1978; Frans Hals, 3 vols, 1970–74; Jacob van Ruisdael, 1981; Frans Hals, 1989; Dutch Painting: 1600–1800, 1995, 2nd edn 1998; Jacob van Ruisdael: a complete catalogue of his paintings, drawings and etchings, 2001; contribs to learned jls. *Address:* 1 Walker Street Place, Cambridge, MA 02138, USA.

SLOAN, Sir Andrew (Kirkpatrick), Kt 1991; QPM 1983; Chief Constable of Strathclyde, 1985–91; *b* 27 Feb. 1931; *s* of Andrew Kirkpatrick Sloan and Amelia Sarah (*née* Vernon), Kirkcudbright; *m* 1953, Agnes Sofie Storvik, Trondheim, Norway; three *d*. *Educ:* Kirkcudbright Acad.; Dumfries Acad.; Open Univ. (BA). Joined RN as boy seaman, 1947; served at home and abroad in cruisers and submarines, and worked in industry in Norway, 1947–55; joined W Riding Constab., 1955; apptd to CID, 1963; Det. Sgt, Barnsley, 1964; Det. Insp., Reg. Crime Squad, Leeds, 1966; Det. Chief Insp., Goole and Pontefract, 1969; Det. Supt, Reg. Crime Squad, Wakefield, 1970; Chief Supt, Toller Lane Div., Bradford, 1975; Asst Chief Constable, Operations, Lincolnshire Police, 1976–79; National Co-ordinator, Regional Crime Squads of England and Wales, 1979–81; Dep. Chief Constable, Lincs, 1981–83; Chief Constable, Beds, 1983–85. Pres., ACPO (Scotland), 1987–88. *Recreations:* reading, travel, walking, conversation. *Address:* c/o Royal Bank of Scotland, 151 High Street, Dumfries DG1 2RA.

SLOANE, Ian Christopher; HM Diplomatic Service, retired; Executive Director, Prospect Burma, since 1998; *b* 28 Jan. 1938; *s* of Albert Henry Sloane and Ivy Rose (*née* Dennis); *m* 1968, June Barton; two *s*. *Educ:* Lewes Co. Grammar Sch. for Boys; DMS Poly. of Central London 1971. Joined FO, 1956; RAF, 1957–59; FO, 1959–60; MECAS, 1960–61; Vice-Consul: Khartoum, 1961–64; Algiers, 1964–66; Saigon, 1967; 2nd Secretary: Dacca, 1967; Lahore, 1967–70; FCO, 1970–73; UK Disarmament Delegn, Geneva, 1973–74; 1st Sec., Hd of Chancery and Consul, Seoul, 1974–77; 1st Sec. (Econ.), Bonn, 1978–82; W European Dept, FCO, 1983–85; Cultural Attaché, Moscow, 1985; 1st Sec. (Commercial), Ankara, 1986–88; Overseas Estate Dept, FCO, 1989–90; Counsellor and Dep. Consul-Gen, New York, 1990–93; Ambassador to Mongolia, 1994–96. Chm. Bd of Trustees, Electronic Aids for the Blind, 1997–. *Recreations:* tennis, bridge, collecting antique maps, travelling. *Address:* 4 Nursery Way, Heathfield, East Sussex TN21 0UW.

SLOANE, Peter James, PhD; FRSE; Jaffrey Professor of Political Economy, since 1984, Vice Principal, and Dean of Social Sciences and Law, since 1996, University of Aberdeen; *b* 6 Aug. 1942; *s* of John Joseph Sloane and Elizabeth (*née* Clarke); *m* 1969, Avril Mary Urquhart; one *s*. *Educ:* Cheadle Hulme Sch.; Univ. of Sheffield (BAEcon Hons 1964); Univ. of Strathclyde (PhD 1966). FRSE 1997. Asst Lectr in Pol. Econ., Univ. of Aberdeen, 1966–67, Lectr in Pol. Econ., 1967–69; Lectr in Indust. Econs, Univ. of Nottingham, 1969–75; Economic Adviser, Unit for Manpower Studies, Dept of Employment (on secondment), 1973–74; Prof. of Econs and Management, Paisley Coll., 1975–84. Vis. Prof. (Commonwealth Fellow), Faculty of Business, McMaster Univ., Canada, 1978; Vis. Prof., Indiana Univ., 1996. Member: ESRC (formerly SSRC), 1979–85; Mergers Cttee, SHEFC, 1994–97; Council, Scottish Economic Soc., 1983–. Sec., REconS Conf. of Heads of Univ. Depts of Econs, 1990–97. Vice-Pres., Internat. Assoc. of Sports Economists, 2000–. FRSA 1997. *Publications:* (with B. Chiplin) Sex Discrimination in the Labour Market, 1976; (ed) Women and Low Pay, 1980; (with H. C. Jain) Equal Employment Issues, 1981; (with B. Chiplin) Tackling Discrimination, 1982; (with D. Carline *et al*) Labour Economics, 1985; (ed jtly) Low Pay and Earnings Mobility in Europe, 1998; monographs on changing patterns of working hours, discrimination and on sport in the market; articles in learned jls, incl. Econ. Jl, Economica, Econs Letters, Applied Econs, Bull. Econ. Res., Oxford Bull. of Econ. Stats, Scottish Jl of Pol. Econ., British Jl of Indust. Relations, Managerial and Decision Econs, Lab., Lab. Econs, Ind. and Lab. Rels Review, Educn Econs, Nat. Inst. Econ. Review, Jl of Health Econs. *Recreation:* sport. *Address:* Hillcrest, 45 Friarsfield Road, Cults, Aberdeen AB15 9LB. *T:* (01224) 869412. *Clubs:* Royal Commonwealth Society; Aboyne Golf.

SLOGGETT, Jolyon Edward, OBE 1995; CEng, Hon. FIMarE, FRINA, FICS; Secretary, Institute of Marine Engineers, 1986–98; *b* 30 May 1933; *s* of Edward Cornelius Sloggett and Lena May (*née* Norton); *m* 1970, Patricia Marjorie Iverson Ward; two *d*. *Educ:* John Lyon Sch.; Univ. of Glasgow (BSc). CDipAF. William Denny & Brothers Ltd, Leven Shipyard, Dumbarton, 1951–57 and 1959–60. Served, Royal Navy, TA Sub Lieut (E), RNVR, 1957–58; Houlder Brothers & Co. Ltd, 1960–78, Director, 1972–78; Man. Dir, Offshore, British Shipbuilders Corp., 1978–81; Dir, Vickers Shipbuilding Group, 1979–80; Chm., Vickers Offshore (Projects & Development) Ltd, 1979–81; Consultant to Marine and Offshore Industries, 1981–86. Liveryman, Shipwrights' Co. *Publication:* Shipping Finance, 1984, 2nd edn 1998. *Recreations:* sailing, gardening, woodwork. *Address:* Annington House, Steyning, West Sussex BN44 3WA. *T:* (01903) 812259, *Fax:* (01903) 879043; *e-mail:* jolyon@townrow.demon.co.uk.

SLOMAN, Sir Albert (Edward), Kt 1987; CBE 1980; DPhil; Vice-Chancellor of University of Essex, 1962–1987; *b* Launceston, Cornwall, 14 Feb. 1921; *y s* of Albert Sloman; *m* 1948, Marie Bernadette, *d* of Leo Bergeron, Cognac, France; three *d*. *Educ:* Launceston Coll., Cornwall; Wadham Coll., Oxford (Pope Exhibitioner, 1939; Hon. Fellow, 1982). BA Mediæval and Mod. Langs, 1941; MA (Oxon and Dublin); DPhil (Oxon). Served War of 1939–45 (despatches): night-fighter pilot with 219 and 68 squadrons; Flight-Lieut. Lecturer in Spanish, Univ. of California, Berkeley, USA, 1946–47; Reader in Spanish, in charge of Spanish studies, Univ. of Dublin, 1947–53; Fellow TCD, 1950–53; Gilmour Professor of Spanish, University of Liverpool, 1953–62; Dean, Faculty of Arts, 1961–62. Editor of Bulletin of Hispanic Studies, 1953–62. Reith Lecturer, 1963. Chairman: Dept of Education, subseq. British Acad., Studentship Cttee, 1965–87; Cttee of Vice-Chancellors and Principals of UK Univs, 1981–83 (Vice-Chm., 1979–81); Overseas Research Students Fees Support Scheme, 1980–87; Univs' Council for Adult and Continuing Educn, 1984–86; Inter-Univ. and Polytechnic Council, 1985–88; Cttee for Internat. Co-operation in Higher Educn, 1985–88; Selection Cttee of Commonwealth Scholarship Commn, 1986–; Internat. Bd, United World Colls, 1988–92 (Mem., 1985–92); Bd, Univ. of London Inst. of Latin American Studies, 1990–92; Member: Council of Europe Cttee for Higher Educn and Research, 1963–72; Inter-Univ. Council for Higher Educn Overseas, 1964–81; Conf. of European Rectors and Vice-Chancellors, 1965–85 (Pres., 1969–74); Admin. Bd, Internat. Assoc. of Univs, 1965–75 (Vice-Pres., 1970–75); Economic and Social Cttee, EEC, 1973–82; Council, ACU, 1981–87 (Vice-Chm., 1985–87); Commonwealth Scholarship Commn, 1984–93; Bd, British Council, 1985–88. Chm. Bd of Governors, Centre for Inf. on Lang. Teaching and Res., 1979–87; Member: Bd of Governors, Guyana Univ., 1966–92; Cttee of Management, British Inst. in Paris, 1982–97. Pres., Penzance Library, 1990–97. Director: Isys Ltd, 1987–98; Close Brothers Business Expansion Secure Share Account cos, 1992–99. Hon. Doctorate: Nice, 1974; Essex, 1988; Liverpool, 1989. *Publications:* The Sources of Calderón's El Principe constante, 1950; The Dramatic Craftsmanship of Calderón, 1958; A University in the Making, 1964; articles and reviews in Modern Language Review, Bulletin of Hispanic Studies, Hispanic Review, Romance Philology and other journals. *Recreations:* travel, walking. *Address:* 19 Inglis Road, Colchester CO3 3HU. *Club:* Savile.

SLOMAN, Mrs (Margaret) Barbara; Under Secretary, Management and Personnel Office (formerly Civil Service Department), 1975–84, retired; *b* 29 June 1925; *d* of Charles and Margaret Pilkington-Rogers; *m* 1950, Peter Sloman, *qv*; one *s* one *d*. *Educ:* Cheltenham Ladies' Coll.; Girton Coll., Cambridge. BA Hons Classics. FIMgt. Asst Principal, Treasury, 1947, Principal 1954–65; Asst Sec., DES, 1965–69; Asst Sec., Civil Service Dept, 1970–75. *Address:* 11 Lowther Road, SW13 9NX. *T:* (020) 8748 2196.

SLOMAN, Peter; retired; Education Officer, Association of Metropolitan Authorities, 1974–79; *b* Oct. 1919; *s* of H. N. P. and Mary Sloman (*née* Trinder); *m* 1950, Barbara (*see* M. B. Sloman); one *s* one *d*. *Educ:* Winchester Coll.; New Coll., Oxford (BA, MA 1945). War Service (RA), 1939–46; TA, 1951–61. Home Civil Service, 1946–74: Under-Secretary, 1968; Min. (later Dept) of Education; Treasury; Ministries of Defence, Land and Natural Resources, Housing and Local Govt; IDC 1960. Principal Admin. Officer: Newham, 1980–83; Surrey, 1985; Principal Administrator, ACC, 1983–88. *Address:* 11 Lowther Road, SW13 9NX. *T:* (020) 8748 2196.

SLOSS; *see* Butler-Sloss.

SLOT, His Honour Peter Maurice Joseph; a Circuit Judge, 1980–97; *b* 3 Dec. 1932; *s* of Joseph and Marie Slot; *m* 1962, Mary Eiluned Lewis; two *s* three *d*. *Educ:* Bradfield Coll.; St John's Coll., Oxford (MA). Called to Bar, Inner Temple, 1957. A Recorder of the Crown Court, 1974–80. *Recreations:* golf, creating harmony. *Address:* The Red House, Betchworth, Surrey RH3 7DR. *T:* (01737) 842010. *Club:* Walton Heath Golf.

SLYNN OF HADLEY, Baron *cr* 1992 (Life Peer), of Eggington in the County of Bedfordshire; **Gordon Slynn,** Kt 1976; PC 1992; a Lord of Appeal in Ordinary, since 1992; *b* 17 Feb. 1930; *er s* of John and Edith Slynn; *m* 1962, Odile Marie Henriette Boutin. *Educ:* Sandbach Sch.; Goldsmiths' Coll., Univ. of London (BA; Hon. Fellow, 1993); Trinity Coll., Cambridge (Sen. Schol.; Sub-Lector, 1956–61; MA, LLB; Hon. Fellow, 2001). Called to Bar, Gray's Inn, 1956, Bencher, 1970, Treas., 1988. Junior Counsel: Min. of Labour, 1967–68; to the Treasury (Common Law), 1968–74; QC 1974; Leading Counsel to the Treasury, 1974–76. Recorder of Hereford, 1971; a Recorder, and Hon. Recorder of Hereford, 1972–76; a Judge of the High Ct of Justice, QBD, 1976–81; Pres., Employment Appeal Tribunal, 1978–81; an Advocate Gen., 1981–88, a Judge, 1988–92, Court of Justice of EC, Luxembourg. Chairman: H of L Select Sub-Cttee on Eur. Law and Instns, 1992–95; H of L Select Cttee on Public Service, 1996–98. Dist. Global Fellow, NY Univ., 1999; Singhvi Fellow, Raj Loomba Foundn, India, 1999; Lectures include: Bloomfield, Montreal, 1980; Irvine, Cornell, 1984; Leon Ladner, Univ. of BC, 1987; Hamlyn, 1992; Tanner, 1993, Romanes, 1994, Oxford Univ.; Presidential, Roumania, 1995; M. K. Nambyar, India, 1996; Sakkar, India, 1998; John E. James, Mercer, 2001. Chief Steward of Hereford, 1978– (Freedom of the City, 1996). Chm., Exec. Council, Internat. Law Assoc., 1988–; Hon. Vice-Pres., Union Internat. des Avocats, 1976– (Vice-Pres., 1973–76). Mem., Exec. Cttee, Pilgrims, 1992–98, 1999–. Fellow, Internat. Soc. of Barristers, USA; Mem., American Law Inst.; Hon. Member: Canadian Bar Assoc.; Georgia Trial Lawyers' Assoc.; SPTL. Governor: Internat. Students' Trust, 1979–85, and 1992– (Fellow, 1986–); Sadler's Wells Theatre, 1988–95; Chm. Ct of Governors, Mill Hill Sch., 1989–95; Visitor: Mansfield Coll., Oxford, 1995–; Univ. of Essex, 1995–2000. President: Bentham Club, 1992; Holdsworth Club, 1993. Master, Broderers' Co., 1994–95. FCIArb 1995. FKC 1995; Hon. Fellow: UC at Buckingham, 1982; St Andrews Coll., Univ. of Sydney, 1991; Amer. Coll. of Trial Lawyers, 1992; Liverpool John Moores, 1993; U C Northampton, 2001. Hon. LLD: Birmingham, Buckingham, 1983; Exeter, 1985; Univ. of Technol., Sydney, 1991; Bristol Poly. (CNAA), Sussex, 1992; Stetson, USA, 1993; Staffordshire, 1994; Pace, NY, 1995; Pondicherry, Kingston, 1997; Strathclyde, London, 1999; Hon. DCL: Durham, 1989; City 1994; Hon. Dr Juris Saarlandes, 1994; DUniv: Univ. del Museo Social Argentino, 1994; Essex, 2001. Hon. Decanus Legis, Mercer Univ., Ga, 1986; Cordell Hull Medal, Samford Univ., Ala, USA, 1993. Chevalier du Tastevin; Commandeur, Confrérie de St Cunibert; Commandeur d'Honneur, Commanderie du Bon Temps du Médoc et des Graves. KStJ 1998 (OStJ 1992; Prior, England and the Islands, 1999–). Grande Croix de l'Ordre de Mérite (Luxembourg), 1998; Knight Cross, Order of Merit (Poland), 1999; Grand Cross, Order of Merit (Malta), 2001. *Publications:* (contrib.) Halsbury's Laws of England, 4th edn; lectures in legal jls. *Address:* House of Lords, SW1A 0PW. *Clubs:* Beefsteak, Garrick.

SMALE, John Gray; Chairman, Executive Committee of Board of Directors, General Motors Corporation, 1996–2000; *b* 1 Aug. 1927; *s* of Peter John Smale and Vera Gladys (*née* Gray); *m* 1950, Phyllis Anne Weaver; two *s* two *d*. *Educ:* Miami Univ., Oxford, Ohio (BS 1949). Procter & Gamble Company: Pres., 1974–81; Pres. and Chief Exec., 1981–86; Chm. Bd and Chief Exec., 1986–90; Chm., Exec. Cttee of Bd of Dirs, 1990; General Motors: Dir, 1981–92; Chm., 1992–96. Hon. LLD: Kenyon Coll., 1974; Miami, 1979; Xavier, 1986; Hon. DSc DePauw, 1983; Hon. DCL St Augustine's Coll., 1985. *Address:* Procter & Gamble, PO Box 599, Cincinnati, OH 45201–0599, USA. *T:* (513) 9831100. *Clubs:* Queen City, Commercial, Cincinnati Country (Cincinnati).

SMALL, (Charles) John; development consultant, 1985–94; economist; *b* Chengdu, Sichuan, China, 19 Dec. 1919; *s* of Rev. and Mrs Walter Small; *m* 1946, Jean McNeel; four *d*. *Educ:* Ontario Agricultural Coll. (BSA); Univ. of Toronto (BA). LLD *hc* Univ. of Guelph, 1975. Royal Canadian Navy service, 1941–46, in N Atlantic, Mediterranean, Normandy and Australia. Mem., Dept of Trade and Commerce, 1949–55; serving in The Hague as Commercial Sec. (Agriculture), 1950–55; Dept of External Affairs, 1955–84; Chinese studies at Univ. of Toronto, 1956–57; seconded to Dept of Trade and Commerce, and apptd Canadian Govt Trade Comr, Hong Kong, 1958–61; Ottawa, 1961–63; Counsellor, Canadian High Commn, Karachi, 1963–65; Perm. Rep. of Canada to OECD, Paris, concurrently Canadian observer, Council of Europe, Strasbourg, 1965–69; Amb. to Pakistan, 1969–72, concurrently Amb. to Afghanistan; Amb. to People's Repub. of China, 1972–76, concurrently to Socialist Repub. of Viet-Nam, 1975–76; Dep. Sec.-Gen. of the Commonwealth, 1978–83; High Comr to Malaysia and concurrently to Brunei, 1983–84; retd from Foreign Service, 1984. Administrator, Code of Conduct concerning employment practices of Canadian cos operating in South Africa, 1986–90. Chm., Presbyterian World Service and Develt Cttee, 1989–91. Patron, Ex Terra Foundn (Canada/China Dinosaur Project), 1987–. Member: CIIA; Agricl Inst. of Canada; Royal Commonwealth Society, Ottawa. *Recreations:* tennis, golf, swimming.

SMALL, David Purvis, CMG 1988; MBE 1966; HM Diplomatic Service, retired; High Commissioner to Guyana and non-resident Ambassador to Suriname, 1987–90; *b* 17 Oct. 1930; *s* of Joseph Small and Ann (*née* Purvis); *m* 1957, Patricia Kennedy (*d* 1998); three *s*. *Educ:* Our Lady's High Sch., Motherwell. National Service, RAF Transport Comd, 1949–51. Metropolitan Vickers, 1951–53; Clerical Officer, Admiralty, Bath, 1953–55; Exec. Officer, HM Dockyard, Rosyth, 1955–58 and Singapore, 1958–60; Admiralty, London, 1960–61; CRO, 1961; Chief Clerk, Madras, 1962–64; Second Sec., Ibadan, 1964–68; Second, later First Sec. and Head of Chancery, Quito, 1968–73; FCO, 1973–76; Head of Chancery, Dacca, 1976–80; First Sec. (Commercial), Stockholm, 1980–82; Counsellor (Economic and Commercial), Copenhagen, 1982–87. *Recreations:* golf, soccer. *Address:* Ashbank, Strachur, Argyll PA27 8BX. *T:* (01369) 860282. *Club:* Cowal Golf.

SMALL, John; *see* Small, C. J.

SMALL, Prof. John Rankin, CBE 1991; Professor of Accountancy and Finance, Heriot-Watt University, 1967–98, now Emeritus; *b* 28 Feb. 1933; *s* of David and Annie Small; *m* 1957, Catherine Wood; one *s* two *d*. *Educ:* Harris Academy, Dundee; Dundee Sch. of Econs. BScEcon London; FCCA, FCMA, JDipMA. Dunlop Rubber Co., 1956–60; Lectr, Univ. of Edinburgh, 1960–64; Sen. Lectr, Univ. of Glasgow, 1964–67; Heriot-Watt University: Head, Dept of Accountancy and Finance, 1967–90; Dean of Faculty of Econ. and Social Studies, 1972–74; Vice-Principal, 1974–78, 1987–90; Dep. Principal, 1990–94. Director: Edinburgh Instruments Ltd, 1976–; Orkney Water Test Centre, Ltd, 1987–96; Environment and Resource Technology Ltd, 1991–99; Petroleum Science and Technology Ltd, 1992–97; Computer Application Services, 1997–; Mem. Bd, Scottish Homes, 1993–. Chm., Nat. Appeal Panel for Entry to Pharmaceutical Lists (Scotland), 1987–95. Trustee, Nat. Library of Scotland, 1991–99. Pres., Assoc. of Certified Accountants, 1982 (Mem. Council, 1971–99); Member: Educn Cttee, Internat. Fedn of Accountants, 1978–85 (Chm., 1978–82); Commn for Local Authority Accounts in Scotland, 1982–92 (Chm., 1983–92); Chm., Inst. of Offshore Engrg, 1988–90. Hon. DLitt Heriot-Watt, 1996. *Publications:* (jtly) Introduction to Managerial Economics, 1966; (contrib.) Business and Accounting in Europe, 1973; (jtly) Acccounting, 1991; articles in accounting and financial jls on accounting and financial management. *Recreation:* golf. *Address:* 39 Caiystane Terrace, Edinburgh EH10 6ST. *T:* (0131) 445 2638. *Club:* New (Edinburgh).

SMALL, Peter John, CB 1999; Permanent Secretary, Department of Agriculture and Rural Development, Northern Ireland, since 1996; *b* 21 July 1946; *s* of John and Kathleen Small; *m* 1971, Pamela Hanna; two *s*. *Educ:* Univ. of London (LLB ext.). Northern Ireland Civil Service: Dept of Finance and Personnel, 1966–94: Treasury Officer of Accounts, 1986–88; Dir of Personnel, 1988–94; Finance Dir, Dept of Health and Social Services, 1994–96. *Recreations:* golf, gardening, reading, music, soccer. *Address:* Department of Agriculture and Rural Development, Dundonald House, Belfast BT4 3SB. *Club:* Farmers'.

SMALL, Dr Ramsay George; Chief Administrative Medical Officer, Tayside Health Board, 1986–89; *b* 5 Feb. 1930; *s* of Robert Small and Ann Ramsay; *m* 1951, Aileen Masterton; four *s*. *Educ:* Harris Academy, Dundee; Univ. of St Andrews (MB ChB); FFCM; FRCPE; DPH. Asst Medical Officer of Health, Ayr CC, 1958–61; Sen. Asst/PMO, City of Dundee, 1961–74; Community Medicine Specialist, Tayside Health Bd, 1974–86. Convener, Scottish Affairs Cttee, Faculty of Community Medicine, 1983–86. Pres., Baptist Union of Scotland, 1972–73. *Recreations:* music, bird watching, mediaeval ecclesiastical buildings. *Address:* 46 Monifieth Road, Broughty Ferry, Dundee DD5 2RX. *T:* (01382) 778408.

SMALLBONE, Graham; Headmaster, Oakham School, 1985–96; *b* 5 April 1934; *s* of Dr E. G. Smallbone and Jane Mann; *m* 1959, Dorothea Ruth Löw; two *s* two *d*. *Educ:* Uppingham School (music scholar); Worcester College, Oxford (Hadow Scholar; MA; Pres., Oxford Univ. Music Club, 1957). ARCO, ARCM. 2nd Lieut, RA, 1952–54. Asst Master, Oundle Sch., 1958–61; Director of Music: Dean Close Sch., 1961–66; Marlborough Coll., 1967–71; Precentor and Director of Music, Eton, 1971–85. Pres., Music Masters' Assoc., 1975; Warden, Music in Educn Section, ISM, 1977; Pres., International Cello Centre, 1985–2000. Conductor: Cheltenham Chamber Orch., 1963–66; N Wilts Orch., 1966–71; Windsor and Eton Choral Soc., 1971–85. Chm., Peterborough Cathedral Fabric Adv. Cttee, 1990–. Chm. of Govs, Purcell Sch., 1997–. FRSA. *Recreations:* music, golf, photography. *Address:* The Old Manse, 56 High Street, Chinnor, Oxon OX39 4DH. *T:* (01844) 354572.

SMALLEY, Prof. Richard Errett, PhD; Gene and Norman Hackerman Professor of Chemistry, since 1982, and Professor, Department of Physics, since 1990, Rice University; *b* 6 June 1943; *s* of Frank Dudley Smalley and Virginia Smalley (*née* Rhoads); *m* 1968, Judith Grace Sampierj (marr. diss. 1979); one *s*; *m* 1980, Mary Lynn Chapieski (marr. diss. 1994); *m* 1997, JoNell Marie Chauvin. *Educ:* Univ. of Michigan (BS Chemistry 1965); Princeton Univ. (MA Chemistry 1971; PhD Chemistry 1973). Associate, James Franck Inst., Chicago, 1973–76; Asst Prof., subseq. Prof., Rice Univ., 1976–82; Chm., Rice Quantum Inst., 1986–96; Dir, Rice Center for Nanoscale Science and Technology, 1996–. Franklin Medal, Franklin Inst., 1996; (jtly) Nobel Prize for Chemistry, 1996. *Publications:* articles in learned jls. *Address:* Department of Chemistry, Rice University, Mail Stop 100, PO Box 1892, Houston, TX 77251–18921, USA.

SMALLEY, Very Rev. Stephen Stewart; Dean of Chester, 1987–2001; *b* 11 May 1931; *s* of Arthur Thomas Smalley and May Elizabeth Selina Smalley; *m* 1974, Susan Jane Paterson (*d* 1995); one *s* one *d*. *Educ:* Jesus Coll., Cambridge (MA, PhD); Eden Theological Seminary, USA (BD). Assistant Curate, St Paul's, Portman Square, London, 1958–60; Chaplain of Peterhouse, Cambridge, 1960–63; Lectr and Sen. Lectr in Religious Studies, Univ. of Ibadan, Nigeria, 1963–69; Lectr in New Testament, Univ. of Manchester, 1970–77, Sen. Lectr, 1977 (also Warden of St Anselm Hall, 1972–77); Canon Residentiary and Precentor of Coventry Cathedral, 1977–86, Vice-Provost, 1986. Mem., C of E Doctrine Commn, 1981–86. Mem., Studiorum Novi Testamenti Soc., 1965–. Manson Meml Lectr, Univ. of Manchester, 1986. *Publications:* Building for Worship, 1967; Heaven and Hell (Ibadan), 1968; The Spirit's Power (Achimota), 1972; ed, Christ and Spirit in the New Testament, 1973; John: Evangelist and Interpreter, 1978, USA 1984, 2nd edn 1998; 1, 2, 3 John, 1984; Thunder and Love, 1994; numerous articles in learned jls, incl. New Testament Studies, Novum Testamentum, Jl of Biblical Lit. *Recreations:* literature, music, drama, travel. *Address:* The Old Hall, The Folly, Longborough, Glos GL56 0QS. *T:* (01451) 830238. *Clubs:* City, Business, Pitt (Chester).

SMALLMAN, Barry Granger, CMG 1976; CVO 1972; HM Diplomatic Service, retired; Founder, Granger Consultancies, 1984; *b* 22 Feb. 1924; *s* of late C. Stanley Smallman, CBE, ARCM, and Ruby Marian Granger; *m* 1952, Sheila Knight; two *s* one *d*. *Educ:* St Paul's School; Trinity College, Cambridge (Major Scholar, MA). Served War of 1939–45, Intelligence Corps, Australia 1944–46. Joined Colonial Office, 1947; Assistant Private Secretary to Secretary of State, 1951–52; Principal, 1953; attached to United Kingdom Delegation to United Nations, New York, 1956–57, 1958, 1961, 1962; seconded to Government of Western Nigeria, Senior Assistant Secretary, Governor's Office, Ibadan, 1959–60; transferred to CRO, 1961; British Deputy High Comr in Sierra Leone, 1963–64; British Dep. High Comr in NZ, 1964–67; Imp. Defence Coll., 1968; FCO, 1969–71; Counsellor and Consul-Gen., British Embassy, Bangkok, 1971–74; British High Comr to Bangladesh, 1975–78; Resident Diplomatic Service Chm., Civil Service Selection Bd, 1978–81; High Comr to Jamaica and non-resident Ambassador to Haiti, 1982–84. Mem. Governing Council: SPCK, 1984–99 (Vice Chm., 1993–99); Leprosy Mission, 1985–97; St Lawrence Coll., Ramsgate, 1984–97 (Vice-Pres., 1997–); Benenden Sch., 1985–92 (Chm., 1986–92). *Recreations:* tennis, golf, making and listening to music, light verse, bird watching. *Address:* Beacon Shaw, Benenden, Kent TN17 4BU. *T:* (01580) 240625.

SMALLMAN, David Leslie, LVO 1990; HM Diplomatic Service, retired; Historical Records Adviser, Foreign and Commonwealth Office, since 2000; *b* 29 April 1940; *s* of Leslie Alfred Smallman and Millicent Jean (*née* Burton); *m* 1st, 1967 (marr. diss.); one *s*; 2nd, 1979, Sandra Jill (*née* Browne); one step *s* one step *d*. *Educ:* St Clement Danes; Kingston upon Hull Univ.; London Business Sch. MIEx, MIM. RAFVR/RAF, 1958–60. Nat. Assistance Bd, 1961–66; Colonial, later Foreign and Commonwealth, Office, 1966–67; served Rawalpindi, Islamabad, Nicosia, 1967–72; attached DTI, 1973; Singapore, 1973–77; FCO, 1977; Consul, Aden, 1981–83; Head of Chancery, Rangoon, 1983–87; Head of Royal Matters, FCO, 1987–90; Dep. High Comr, Port of Spain, 1990–94; Gov. and C-in-C, St Helena and Dependencies, 1995–99 (first Gov. to visit Nightingale Is, Inaccessible Is and Gough Is.). Pres., St Helena Cricket Assoc., 1995–98 (played for Governor's XI, 1996–98; Patron, 1998–99); Founder, Governor's Cup internat. yacht race. Promoter, internat. sporting links, Louis Glanville Associates, 1999–. *Recreations:* riding, walking, tennis, cricket, water-sports. *Address:* Ivy Bank Farmhouse, Maidford, Northamptonshire NN12 8HT. *Clubs:* MCC; Queen's Park Cricket, Trinidad Union (Trinidad); Royal Cape Yacht (S Africa); St Helena Yacht (Hon. Life Mem.).

SMALLMAN, Prof. Raymond Edward, CBE 1992; FRS 1986; FREng; Hon. Professor of Metallurgy and Materials Science, University of Birmingham, since 1996 (Feeney Professor, 1969–88, Professor, 1988–96); *b* 4 Aug. 1929; *s* of David Smallman and Edith French; *m* 1952, Joan Doreen Faulkner; one *s* one *d*. *Educ:* Rugeley Grammar Sch.; Univ. of Birmingham (BSc, PhD, DSc). FIM 1964; FREng (FEng 1991). AERE Harwell, 1953–58; University of Birmingham: Lectr in Dept of Physical Metallurgy, 1958, Sen Lectr, 1963; Prof. of Phys. Metall., 1964; Head of Dept of Phys. Metall. and Sci. of Materials, 1969–81, of Metallurgy and Materials, 1981–88; Dean of Faculty of Sci. and Eng., 1984–85, of Faculty of Eng., 1985–87; Pro-Vice-Chancellor and Vice-Principal, 1987–92. Visiting Professor: Pennsylvania, 1961; Stanford, 1962; NSW, 1974; Calif, Berkeley, 1978; Cape Town, 1982; Hon. Prof., 1990–, Dist. Lectr, 1999, Univ. of Hong Kong; Van Horn Dist. Lectr, Case Western Reserve Univ., 1978; Edwin Liddiard Lectr, Inst. of Metals, 1991. IUC Consultant, Hong Kong, 1979. Academic Adviser: Ghulam Ishaq Khan Inst. of Engrg Scis and Technol., Topi, Pakistan, 1996–; Hong Kong Univ., 1997–2000. Member: Inter-Services Cttee, MoD, 1965; Metals and Materials Cttee, SRC, 1968–71; Materials Adv. Cttee, MoD, 1971; Cttee, Engrg Profs Conf., 1985; Materials Commn, 1988–91, Council, 1992–94, SERC. President: Birmingham Metallurgical Assoc., 1972–73; Fedn of European Materials Socs, 1994–96 (Vice-Pres., 1992–94); Vice-Pres., Metals Soc., 1980–84 (Chm., Metals Sci Cttee, 1974–84); Member: Council, Inst. of Materials (Vice Pres., 1995–99; Chm., Internat. Affairs Cttee, 1993–96); Lunar Soc., 1991–99; Steering Cttee, Industry '96, W Midlands Festival of Industry and Enterprise, 1993–96. Advr, ACU, 1985–91. Warden, Birmingham Assay Office, 1994–97 (Guardian, 1992–94 and 1997–). Dir, Univ. Hosps Birmingham NHS Trust, 1995–99. Gov., Tettenhall Coll., 1982–. Hon. Foreign Member: China Ordinance Soc., 1992; Czech Soc. for Metal Sci., 1995. Hon. DSc: Wales, 1990; Univ. of Novi Sad, Yugoslavia, 1990; Cranfield, 2001. Sir George Beilby Gold Medal, Inst. of Metals and Chem. Soc., 1969; Rosenhain Medal, Inst. Metals, 1972; Elegant Work Prize, Metals Soc., 1979; Platinum Medal, Inst. of Metals, 1989. *Publications:* Modern Physical Metallurgy, 1962, 4th edn 1985; (jtly) Modern Metallography, 1966; (jtly) Structure of Metal and Alloys, 1969; (jtly) Defect Analysis in Electron Microscopy, 1975; (jtly) Metals and Materials: science, processing and applications, 1994; (jtly) Modern Physical Metallurgy and Materials Engineering, 1999; sci. papers on relationship of microstructure of materials to their properties in learned jls. *Recreations:* writing, travel, friendly golf, bridge. *Address:* 59 Woodthorne Road South, Tettenhall, Wolverhampton WV6 8SN. *T:* and *Fax:* (01902) 752545; *e-mail:* R.E.Smallman@bham.ac.uk. *Clubs:* Athenæum; South Staffordshire Golf.

SMALLRIDGE, Peter William, CBE 1995; Chairman, West Kent Health Authority, since 1998; *b* 8 Aug. 1943; *s* of William Smallridge and Eileen (*née* Wilson); *m* 1965, Margaret Collis; two *s* one *d*. *Educ:* Sutton High Sch.; Chichester High Sch.; North-Western Polytechnic (CSW 1965); LSE (Dip. Mental Health 1970). Sen. Mental Health Social Worker, W Sussex CC, 1965–71; Area Officer, W Sussex Social Services, 1971–73; Sen. Lectr, Croydon Coll., 1973–75; Divl Manager, Social Services, Norfolk CC, 1975–82; Dep. Dir, 1982–83, Dir, 1983–91, Social Services, Warwicks CC; Dir of Social Services, Kent CC, 1991–98. Dir, Initiatives in Care Ltd. Pres., Assoc. of Dirs of Social Services, 1992–93. Nat. Trustee, BRCS, 1997–; Trustee, Smith's Charity, 1999–. *Recreations:* reading, walking, golf, travel. *Address:* Maltmans Hill Barn, Maltmans Hill, Smarden, Kent TN27 8RD.

SMALLWOOD, Anne Hunter, CMG 1976; Commissioner, Board of Inland Revenue, 1973–81; *b* 20 June 1922; *d* of Martin Wilkinson McNicol and Elizabeth Straiton Harper; *m* 1972, Peter Basil Smallwood (*d* 1977). *Educ:* High Sch. for Girls, Glasgow; Glasgow Univ. Entered Inland Revenue, 1943; Min. of Land and Natural Resources, 1964–66; Min. of Housing and Local Govt, 1966; Under-Sec., Inland Revenue, 1971–73. *Address:* 83 Lyncombe Hill, Bath BA2 4PJ.

See also G. P. McNicol.

SMALLWOOD, Christopher Rafton; Partner, Brunswick Group Ltd, since 1998; *b* 13 Aug. 1947; *s* of James Rafton Smallwood and Josephine Smallwood (*née* Mortimer); *m* 1979, Ingeborg Hedwig Eva Wiesler; one *s* one *d*. *Educ:* Lancaster Royal Grammar Sch.; Exeter Coll., Oxford (MA 1st Cl. Hons PPE); Nuffield Coll., Oxford (MPhil Econs). Lecturer in Economics: Exeter Coll., Oxford, 1971-72; Edinburgh Univ., 1972-76; Special Advr, Constitution Unit, Cabinet Office, 1974–75; Econ. Advr, HM Treasury, 1976-81; Dir of Policy, SDP, 1981-83; Chief Economist, British Petroleum plc, 1983-86; Econs Ed., Sunday Times, 1986-89; Strategic Develt Dir, TSB Gp and Dir, TSB Bank, 1989-94; Partner, Makinson Cowell Ltd, 1994-98. *Recreations:* golf, opera, theatre. *Address:* 7 Wool Road, Wimbledon, SW20 0HN. *T:* (020) 8946 7434. *Club:* Reform.

SMALLWOOD, John Frank Monton, CBE 1991; a Church Commissioner, 1966–98 (Member, Board of Governors, 1966–98, and Member, General Purposes Committee, 1968–98); *b* 12 April 1926; *s* of late Frank Theodore and Edith Smallwood; *m* 1952, Jean Margaret Lovell; one *s* two *d*. *Educ:* City of London Sch.; Peterhouse, Cambridge, 1948–51 (MA Classics). Served RAF, 1944–48 (Japanese translation and interrogation). Joined Bank of England, 1951; Private Sec. to Governors, 1959–62; Adviser, 1967; Auditor, 1969; Dep. Chief Accountant, 1974–79. Member: Church Assembly/General Synod, 1965–2000 (Standing Cttee, 1971–96); numerous *ad hoc* Cttees, etc, over years, incl. Wkg Party on State Aid for Churches in use, 1971–96; Central Bd of Finance, 1965–98 (Dep. Vice-Chm. 1972–82); Pensions Bd, 1985–96; Anglican Consultative Council, 1975–87 (Trinidad, 1976, Lambeth Conf., 1978, Canada, 1979, Newcastle, 1981, Singapore, 1987). A Trustee: City Parochial Foundn, 1969–99 (Vice-Chm., 1977–81; Chm., 1981–92); Trust for London, 1986–99 (Chm., 1986–92); Overseas Bishoprics Fund, 1977–99 (Chm., 1992–99); Lambeth Palace Library, 1978–98. Member: Southwark Dio. Bd of Finance, 1962–2000 (Chm. 1975–2000); Southwark Ordination Course Council, 1960–74 and 1980–94 (Vice-Chm., 1980–94); Corp. of Church House Council, 1986–96; Churches' Main Cttee, 1987–96; BCC 1987–90. Lee Abbey Council, 1969–74; Lay Reader, 1983–. *Recreations:* church finances (incl. various financial pamphlets), biographies, family, music, cathedrals, old churches, historic houses, gardens. *Address:* The Willows, Parkgate Road, Newdigate, Dorking, Surrey RH5 5AH. *T:* (01306) 631457.

SMALLWOOD, Trevor, OBE 1995; Chairman, WestCom Media Ltd, since 1999; *b* 4 Nov. 1947; *s* of late Eric Smallwood and of Vera Smallwood; *m* 1986, Caroline Mary Ball; two *s* two *d*. *Educ:* Mexborough Grammar Sch. MCIT. Mgt Trainee, Yorkshire Traction, 1966; National Bus Co., 1970–80; Traffic Manager, Potteries Motor Traction, 1980–82; Man. Dir, Bristol Country Bus, 1983; purchased Badgerline from Dept of Transport, 1986; developed and floated Badgerline, 1993; merged with GRT to become FirstBus, 1995, renamed FirstGroup, 1997, Exec. Chm., 1995–99. Dir, Bristol Water plc, 1999–. Pres., Confedn of Public Transport, 1994. *Recreations:* football, cricket. *Address:* (office) 11 Beaconsfield Road, Weston-super-Mare, N Somerset BS23 1YE.

SMART; *see* de Bernière-Smart.

SMART, (Alexander Basil) Peter, CMG 1990; HM Diplomatic Service, retired; *b* 19 Feb. 1932; *s* of late Henry Prescott Smart and Mary Gertrude Todd; *m* 1955, Joan Mary Cumming; three *s* (incl. twin *s*). *Educ:* Ryhope Grammar Sch., Co. Durham. Commnd RAEC, 1951; Supervising Officer, Educn, Gibraltar Comd, 1951–52; entered HM Foreign (later Diplomatic) Service, 1953; Vice Consul, Duala, 1955; Polit. Office, ME Forces, Cyprus, 1956; 2nd Sec. (Information), Seoul, 1959; News Dept, FO, 1964; Head of Chancery, Rangoon, 1968; FCO, 1971; Head of Communications Technical Services Dept, 1975; Counsellor, 1977–82, and Dep. High Comr, 1981–82, Canberra; Counsellor and Head of Chancery, Prague, 1983–86; High Comr, Seychelles, 1986–89; Ambassador to Fiji, and High Comr (non-resident) to Republic of Nauru and to Tuvalu, 1989–92. FRSA. *Recreations:* wild nature, the arts: looking and listening. *Address:* 715 Willoughby House, Barbican, EC2Y 8BN.

SMART, Andrew, CB 1981; defence consultant, retired 1991; Director, Royal Signals and Radar Establishment, Malvern, 1978–84; *b* 12 Feb. 1924; *s* of late Mr and Mrs William S. Smart; *m* 1949, Pamela Kathleen Stephens; two *s* two *d*. *Educ:* Denny; High Sch. of Stirling; Glasgow Univ. MA 1944. TRE Malvern, 1943; Science 2 Air Min., 1950–53; Guided Weapons Gp, RRE, Malvern, 1953–70 (Head, 1968–70); Dep. Dir (Scientific B), DOAE, 1970; RAE, Farnborough: Head of Weapons Res. Gp, 1972; Head of Weapons Dept, 1973; Dep. Dir (W), 1974–77. *Recreations:* gardening, reading. *Address:* Hill Orchard, Shelsley Drive, Colwall, Malvern, Worcs WR13 6PS. *T:* (01684) 540664.

SMART, Prof. (Arthur David) Gerald, CBE 1991; FRTPI; Emeritus Professor of Urban Planning, University of London, since 1984; Professor of Urban Planning at University College London, 1975–84 and part-time, 1984–87 (Head of Bartlett School of Architecture and Planning, University College London, 1975–80); *b* 19 March 1925; *s* of Dr A. H. J. Smart and A. O. M. Smart (*née* Evans); *m* 1955, Anne Patience Smart (*née* Baxter); two *d*. *Educ:* King's Coll. Choir Sch., Cambridge (chorister); Rugby Sch.; King's Coll., Cambridge; Regent St Polytechnic. MA, DipTP; MRICS, FRSA. Served in The Rifle Brigade, 1943–47 (Captain). Appts in local govt (planning), London, NE England, E Midlands, 1950–63; County Planning Officer, Hants CC, 1963–75; Member: Planning Adv. Gp, 1964–65, Cttee on Public Participation in Planning, 1968–69, Min. of Housing and Local Govt; Planning and Transportation Res. Adv. Council, DoE, 1975–79; Working Party on alternative uses of Historic Buildings, Historic Bldgs Council and BTA, 1979–81; Council, TCPA, 1983–89; Council, RSPB, 1985–90; Governing Body, British Assoc. for Central and East Europe (formerly GB/E Europe Centre), 1985–96; Council, Solent Protection Soc., 1986–; House Builders' Fedn Commn on Inner Cities, 1986–87; occasional Chm., Structure Plans Exams in Public for DoE; Consultant for review of Areas of Outstanding Natural Beauty, Countryside Commn, 1989–90. Chm., Milford-on-Sea Parish Council, 1989–93 (Councillor, 1987–99); Mem. Cttee, Lymington Choral Soc., 1994–. Bowland Award, Areas of Outstanding Natural Beauty Assoc., 1999. *Publications:* (jtly) Landscapes at Risk?, 2001; articles, conf. papers, in books, professional and other jls, booklets and reports. *Recreations:* sailing, ornithology, music, walking. *Address:* 10 Harewood Green, Keyhaven, Lymington, Hants SO41 0TZ. *T:* (01590) 645475. *Clubs:* Royal Lymington Yacht, Keyhaven Yacht (Lymington).

SMART, Edwin; *see* Smart, L. E.

SMART, Professor Sir George (Algernon), Kt 1978; MD, FRCP; Director, British Postgraduate Medical Federation, 1971–78, retired; *b* 16 Dec. 1913; *er s* of A. Smart, Alnwick, Northumb; *m* 1939, Monica Helen Carrick; two *s* one *d. Educ:* Uppingham; Durham Univ., BSc 1935, MB, BS 1937. MD 1939 (Durham); MRCP 1940, FRCP 1952. Commonwealth Fund Fellow, 1948–49. Lectr in Med., Univ. of Bristol, 1946–50; Reader in Medicine, Univ. of Durham, 1950–56; Prof. of Medicine, Univ. of Durham, 1956–68, Univ. of Newcastle upon Tyne, 1968–71 (Post-graduate Sub-Dean, 1962–68, Dean of Medicine, 1968–71). Censor, 1965–67, Senior Censor and Senior Vice-Pres., 1972–73, RCP. Chairman: Review Bd for Overseas Qualified Practitioners, GMC, 1979–82; Cttee of Management, and Med. and Survival Cttee, RNLI, 1979–83. Life Vice Pres., RNLI, 1988. Hon. Fellow, Coll. of Physicians and Surgeons, Pakistan, 1976. *Publications:* contrib. to Price's Textbook of Medicine, and Progress in Clinical Medicine (Daley and Miller); (ed) Metabolic Disturbances in Clinical Medicine, 1958; (co-author) Fundamentals of Clinical Endocrinology, 1969, 2nd edn 1974. *Recreation:* photography. *Address:* Taffrail, Crede Lane, Old Bosham, Chichester, Sussex PO18 8NX.

SMART, Gerald; *see* Smart, A. D. G.

SMART, Sir Jack, Kt 1982; CBE 1976; JP; DL; Chairman, Wakefield District Health Authority, 1982–88; *b* 25 April 1920; *s* of James and Emily Smart; *m* 1941, Ethel King; one *d. Educ:* Altofts Colliery Sch. Miner, 1934–59; Branch Sec., Glasshoughton Colliery, NUM, 1949–59; Mem., Castleford Municipal Borough Council, 1949–74; Mayor of Castleford, 1962–63; Mem., Wakefield City Council, 1973–86 (Leader, 1973–86). Chm., Assoc. of Metropolitan Authorities, 1977–78, 1980–84; Leader of the Opposition Group, AMA, 1978–80. Chm., Wakefield AHA, 1977–81; Mem., Layfield Cttee of Enquiry into Local Govt Finance, 1974–76. Pres., Yorkshire Soc. (1980), 1988–. Hon. Fellow, Bretton Coll., 1983. Hon. Freeman, City of Wakefield, 1985. JP Castleford, 1960; DL West Yorks, 1987. FRSA. *Recreations:* golf, music. *Address:* Churchside, Weetworth, Pontefract Road, Castleford, West Yorks WF10 4QA. *T:* (01977) 554880.

SMART, John Dalziel Beveridge; Lord-Lieutenant of Kincardineshire, since 1999; *b* Edinburgh, 12 Aug. 1932; *s* of George Beveridge Smart and Christina Mary Ann Smart (*née* MacDonald); *m* 1960, Valerie Bigelow Blaber; two *s. Educ:* Harrow; Admin. Staff Coll. Nat. Service, 2nd Lieut, Black Watch, RHR, Korea, 1952; PA to COS, 1953. With J. & J. Smart (Brechin) Ltd, 1953–64 (Dir, 1954–64); Dir, 1964–85, Man. Dir, 1985–87, Don Brothers Buist & Co. Ltd; retd. Chm., British Polyolefin Textile Assoc., 1986–97. Chm., Scottish-American Community Relns Cttee, 1990–93. Mem., Queen's Bodyguard for Scotland (Royal Co. of Archers), 1974. Mem., St Andrews Mgt Inst., 1989–. DL Kincardineshire, 1993–99. Dean, Guildry of Brechin, 1991–93. *Recreations:* shooting, skiing. *Address:* Woodmyre, Edzell, Brechin DD9 7UX. *T:* and *Fax:* (01356) 648416.

SMART, Kenneth Peter Ross, CBE 1996; Chief Inspector of Air Accidents, Department for Environment, Transport and the Regions (formerly Department of Transport), since 1990; *b* 28 April 1946; *s* of Peter Smart and Evelyn Smart (*née* Ross); *m* 1st, 1969, Kathleen Rouse (marr. diss.); one *s* one *d*; 2nd, 1993, Christine Palmer. *Educ:* Coll. of Electronics, Malvern (FTC); Worcester Tech. Coll. (HNC Aero Engrg); Open Univ. (BA). Aircraft Engrg apprentice, Min. of Aviation, 1962–67; Technical Officer, RRE, 1967–75; Inspector of Accidents, Dept of Trade, 1975–82; Principal Inspector of Accidents, 1982–86, Dep. Chief Inspector of Accidents, 1986–90, Dept of Transport. *Recreations:* mountaineering, tennis, sailing, classic motorcycle restoration. *Address:* c/o Air Accidents Investigation Branch, Department for Environment, Transport and the Regions, Berkshire Copse Road, Aldershot, Hants GU11 2HH. *T:* (01252) 510300.

SMART, (Louis) Edwin, JD; Chairman and Chief Executive Officer, Trans World Corporation, 1978–87; Chairman of Executive Committee, Hilton International Co., since 1986 (Chairman of Board, 1978–86); *b* Columbus, Ohio, 17 Nov. 1923; *s* of Louis Edwin Smart and Esther Guthery; *m* 1st, 1944, Virginia Alice Knouff (marr. diss. 1958); one *s* one *d*; 2nd, 1964, Jeanie Alberta Milone; one *s. Educ:* Harvard Coll. (AB *magna cum laude* 1947); Harvard Law Sch. (JD *magna cum laude* 1949). Served to Lieut, USNR, 1943–46. Admitted to NY Bar, 1950; Associate, Hughes, Hubbard & Ewing, NYC, 1949–56; Partner, Hughes, Hubbard & Reed, NYC, 1957–64; Pres., Bendix Internat. and Dir, Bendix Corp. and foreign subsids, 1964–67; Trans World Airlines Inc.: Sen. Vice Pres., External Affairs, 1967–71, Corp. Affairs, 1971–75; Vice Chm. 1976; Chief Exec. Officer, 1977–78; Chm. of Bd, 1977–85; also Dir, Mem. Exec., and Mem. Finance Cttee. Chairman: Canteen Corp., 1973–; Spartan Food Systems Inc., 1979–; former Director: Sonat Inc.; The Continental Corp.; NY Stock Exchange; Trustee, Cttee for Econ. Develt, 1977–. Member: Conf. Bd, 1977–; Amer. Bar Assoc.; NY County Lawyers Assoc.; Phi Beta Kappa; Sigma Alpha Epsilon. *Address:* 535 E 86th Street, New York, NY 10028, USA. *Club:* Marco Polo (NYC).

SMART, Air Vice-Marshal Michael David; Director, Meer Consultants Ltd, since 2000; *b* 18 March 1942; *s* of Gerald Sidney Smart and Keziah Smart (*née* Edwards); *m* 1964, Sheelagh Ann Gent; one *d* (and one *d* decd). *Educ:* Trinity Sch. of John Whitgift, Croydon; BA Open Univ. Joined RAF Secretarial Branch, 1960; jsdc, 1979; Air Sec.'s Branch, 1980–82 and 1983–85; Comd, Admin Wing, RAF Coltishall, 1982–83; CO RAF Hereford, 1985–88; Sen. Personnel Staff Officer, HQ Strike Command, 1988–89; RCDS, 1990; Dir, Ground Training, 1991–92; Air Cdre, Training Support, 1993; Dir of Personnel, 1994–95; C of S to Air Mem. for Personnel, 1995–98. Dir, Govt Services, Arthur Andersen Business Consulting, 1998. *Recreations:* track and field athletics and cross country, travelling, cooking. *Address:* c/o Drummonds Bank, 49 Charing Cross, SW1A 2DX. *Club:* Royal Air Force.

SMART, Peter; *see* Smart, A. B. P.

SMART, Rosamund H.; *see* Horwood-Smart.

SMART, William Norman H.; *see* Hunter Smart.

SMEATON, John Joseph; National Director, Society for the Protection of Unborn Children, since 1996; *b* 20 Feb. 1951; *s* of John Henry Smeaton and Marguerite Amy Smeaton; *m* 1984, Josephine Ann Toner (*née* Clarke); one *s* one *d*, and two step *s. Educ:* Salesian Coll., Battersea; Greyfriars Hall, Oxford (MA Eng. Lang. and Lit.); London Univ. (Cert Ed). English Teacher, 1973–75 (full-time), 1976–78 (part-time), Salesian Coll., Battersea; Head of English, Whitefriars, Cheltenham, 1975–76; part-time volunteer worker, 1976–78, Gen. Sec., 1978–96, SPUC. *Recreations:* reading, enjoying company of my family. *Address:* Society for the Protection of Unborn Children, Phyllis Bowman House, 5/6 St Matthews Street, Westminster, SW1P 2JT. *T:* (020) 7222 5845. *Club:* New Cavendish.

SMEDLEY, Sir (Frank) Brian, Kt 1995; a Judge of the High Court, Queen's Bench Division, 1995–2000; *b* 28 Nov. 1934. *Educ:* West Bridgford Grammar Sch.; London Univ. LLB Hons, 1957. Called to the Bar, Gray's Inn, 1960; Midland Circuit; a Recorder, 1972; QC 1977; a Circuit Judge, 1987–95; Sen. Judge, Sovereign Base Areas, Cyprus, 1991–95 (Dep. Sen. Judge, 1989–91). Judicial Mem., Proscribed Organs Appeal Commn, 2001–. Mem., Senate of the Inns of Court and the Bar, 1973–77. Freeman, City of London, 1990. *Recreations:* travel, music. *Club:* Garrick.

SMEDLEY, George; *see* Smedley, R. R. G. B.

SMEDLEY, Sir Harold, KCMG 1978 (CMG 1965); MBE 1946; HM Diplomatic Service, retired; *b* 19 June 1920; *s* of late Dr R. D. Smedley, MA, MD, DPH, Worthing; *m* 1950, Beryl Mary Harley Brown, Wellington, New Zealand; two *s* two *d. Educ:* Aldenham School; Pembroke College, Cambridge. Served War of 1939–45, Royal Marines. Entered Dominions Office (later Commonwealth Relations Office), 1946; Private Secretary to Permanent Under-Secretary of State, 1947–48; British High Commissioner's Office: Wellington, NZ, 1948–50; Salisbury, Southern Rhodesia, 1951–53; Principal Private Sec. to Sec. of State for Commonwealth Relations, 1954–57; Counsellor, British High Comr's Office: Calcutta, 1957; New Delhi, 1958–60; British High Comr in Ghana, 1964–67; Ambassador to Laos, 1967–70; Asst Under-Sec. of State, FCO, 1970–72; Sec. Gen., Commn on Rhodesian opinion, 1971–72; High Comr in Sri Lanka, and Ambassador to Republic of Maldives, 1972–75; High Comr in NZ and concurrently Governor of Pitcairn Island, 1976–80; High Comr in Western Samoa (non-resident), 1977–80. Chm., London Bd, Bank of NZ, 1983–89. Vice Chm., Victoria League, 1981–90. Pres., Hakluyt Soc., 1987–92. Mem., W Sussex CC, 1989–93. Pres., W Sussex Assoc. for the Blind, 1991–97. *Address:* 11A Beehive Lane, Ferring, Sussex BN12 5NN. *Clubs:* Oxford and Cambridge, Royal Commonwealth Society.

SMEDLEY, (Roscoe Relph) George (Boleyne); Barrister; Counsellor, HM Diplomatic Service, retired; *b* 3 Sept. 1919; *o s* of late Charles Boleyne Smedley and Aimie Blaine Smedley (*née* Relph); *m* 1st, 1947, Muriel Hallaway Murray (*d* 1975), *o d* of late Arthur Stanley Murray; one *s*; 2nd, 1979, Margaret Gerrard Gourlay (*d* 1991), *o c* of late Augustus Thorburn Hallaway and *widow* of Dr John Stewart Gourlay; 3rd, 1993, Marjorie Drummond (*d* 1994), *d* of late John Leonard Haslam and *widow* of David Drummond. *Educ:* King's Sch., Ely; King's Coll., London (LLB). Called to Bar, Inner Temple. Artists Rifles TA; commnd S Lancs Regt, 1940; Indian Army, 1942–46 (Captain); Foreign Office, 1937 and 1946; Foreign Service (subseq. Diplomatic Service): Rangoon, 1947; Maymyo, 1950; Brussels, 1952; Baghdad, 1954; FO, 1958; Beirut, 1963; Kuwait, 1965; FCO, 1969; Consul-Gen., Lubumbashi, 1972–74; British Mil. Govt, Berlin, 1974–76; FCO 1976; Head of Nationality and Treaty Dept, 1977–79. Part-time appointments (since retirement): Adjudicator under Immigration Act 1971; Inspector, Planning Inspectorate, Depts of the Environment and Transport; Dep. Traffic Comr for N Eastern Traffic Area; Legal Mem., Mental Health Review Tribunal; Chm., Rent Assessment Cttee; Mem., No 2 Dip. Service Appeal Bd. Churchwarden; Mem., diocesan and deanery synods. *Recreations:* forestry, reading. *Address:* Garden House, Whorlton, Barnard Castle, Co. Durham DL12 8XQ. *T:* (01833) 627381. *Clubs:* Royal Automobile, Royal Over-Seas League.

SMEDLEY, Susan M.; *see* Marsden, S.

SMEE, Clive Harrod, CB 1997; Chief Economic Adviser to Department of Health, since 1988 (to Department of Health and Social Security, 1984–88 and to Department of Social Security, 1988–89); *b* 29 April 1942; *s* of Victor Woolley Smee and Leila Olive Smee (*née* Harrod); *m* 1975, Denise Eileen Sell; one *s* two *d. Educ:* Royal Grammar Sch., Guildford; LSE (BSc Econ); Indiana Univ. (MBA); Inst. of Commonwealth Studies, Oxford. British Council, Nigeria, 1966–68; Economic Advr, ODM, 1969–75; Sen. Economic Advr, DHSS, 1975–82; Nuffield and Leverhulme Travelling Fellow, USA and Canada, 1978–79; Advr, Central Policy Review Staff, 1982–83; Sen. Economic Advr, HM Treasury, 1983–84. Consultant: NZ Treasury, 1988; NZ Dept of Health, 1991. Chm., OECD Social Policy Working Party, 1987–90; Mem., Internat. Co-ordinating Cttee, Commonwealth Fund, 1998–2001. Vis. Prof. of Econs, Univ. of Surrey, 1995–. *Publications:* articles on economics in learned jls. *Recreations:* running, gardening; Anna, David and Elizabeth. *Address:* c/o Department of Health, Skipton House, 80 London Road SE1 6LW. *T:* (020) 7972 5220.

SMEE, John Charles O.; *see* Odling-Smee.

SMETHAM, Andrew James, MA; Headmaster, The Purbeck School, Wareham, Dorset, since 1985; *b* 22 Feb. 1937; *s* of Arthur James Smetham and Eunice (*née* Jones). *Educ:* Vaynor and Penderyn Grammar Sch., Cefn Coed, Breconshire; King's Coll., Univ. of London (BA (Hons German) 1959, DipEd 1964, MA (Educn) 1968). Assistant Master: Wandsworth Sch., 1960–66; Sedgehill Sch., 1966–70; Dep. Headmaster, Holloway Sch., 1970–74; Headmaster, Wandsworth Sch., 1974–84. *Recreations:* music, walking. *Address:* The Water Barn, East Burton, Wareham, Dorset BH20 6HL. *T:* (01929) 463727.

SMETHURST, (John) Michael, CBE 1996; Deputy Chief Executive, British Library, London, 1995–96; *b* 25 April 1934; *s* of Albert Smethurst and Nelly Smethurst (*née* Kitchin); *m* 1960, Mary Clayworth; one *s* one *d. Educ:* William Hulme's Grammar School, Manchester; Manchester Univ. (BA). ALA. Librarian: Bede Coll., Durham Univ., 1964–66; Inst. of Educn, Newcastle upon Tyne, 1966–69; Dep. Librarian, Univ. of Glasgow, 1969–72; Univ. Librarian, Univ. of Aberdeen, 1972–86; British Library: Dir-Gen., Humanities and Social Sciences, 1986–91; Dir-Gen., London Services, 1991–95; Mem. Bd, 1986–96; Mem., Lending Div. Adv. Cttee, 1976–80; Mem., Adv. Council, 1982–86 (Chm., Bibliog. Services Adv. Cttee, 1983–86). Hon. Res. Fellow, UCL, 1987–. Trustee, Nat. Library of Scotland, 1976–86; Chairman: Library and Inf. Services Cttee (Scotland), 1982–86; SCONUL, 1984–86, 1989–90 (Vice-Chm., 1983–84, 1988; Mem. Council, 1977–80, 1983–92); Brotherton Liby Cttee, Leeds Univ., 1986–98; Consortium of Eur. Res. Libraries, 1992–2000; Member: British Council Libraries Adv. Cttee, 1983–92; Bd, Res. Libraries Gp, USA, 1992–96; UNESCO Commn for Rehabilitation of Russian State Liby, Moscow, 1993–98; Expert Panel, Museums, Libraries, Archives Heritage Lottery Fund, 1996–; UNESCO Consultative Cttee, Qarawiyyin Library Project, Morocco, 1998–99. President: Scottish Liby Assoc., 1983; Friends of Aberdeen Univ. Liby, 1986–; LIBER, 1989–95. Trustee, Lambeth Palace Liby, 1998–. Hon. LittD Sheffield, 1996. *Publications:* papers and articles in professional jls. *Recreations:* music, art, travel, gardening. *Address:* Romney, 72 Grove Road, Tring, Herts HP23 5PB. *Club:* Athenæum.

SMETHURST, Richard Good, MA; Provost, Worcester College, Oxford, since 1991; *b* 17 Jan. 1941; *s* of Thomas Good Smethurst and Madeleine Nora Foulkes; *m* 1964, Dorothy Joan (*née* Mitchenall); two *s* two *d*. *Educ:* Liverpool Coll.; Worcester Coll., Oxford; Nuffield Coll., Oxford. Webb Medley Jun. Schol. 1962; BA 1st Cl. 1963; MA Oxon. Research Fellow: St Edmund Hall, Oxford, 1964–65; Inst. for Commonwealth Studies, Oxford, 1965–66 (Consultant, UN/FAO World Food Program); University of Oxford: Fellow and Tutor in Economics, St Edmund Hall, 1966–67; Fellow and Tutor in Economics, Worcester Coll., and Univ. Lectr in Economics, 1967–76; Dir, Dept for External Studies, and Professorial Fellow, Worcester Coll., 1976–89; Supernumerary Fellow, Worcester Coll., and Chm., Gen. Bd of Faculties, 1989–91. Economic Adviser, HM Treasury, 1969–71; Policy Adviser, Prime Minister's Policy Unit, 1975–76. Dir, IMRO, 1987–99. Member: Adv. Council for Adult and Continuing Educn, DES, 1977–83; Monopolies and Mergers Commn, 1978–89 (Dep. Chm., 1986–89); UGC/NAB Continuing Educn Standing Cttee, 1984–88; Acad. Consultative Cttee, Open Univ., 1986–92; Adv. Bd, Music at Oxford, 1988–94; Chm., Unit for Develt of Adult Continuing Educn, 1991–92. Trustee, Eur. Community Baroque Orch., 1986–93. Mem. Council, Templeton Coll., Oxford (formerly Oxford Management Centre), 1982–; Life Governor, Liverpool Coll., 1968. Foundn Hon. Fellow, Rewley House, Oxford, 1990; Hon. Fellow, St Edmund Hall, Oxford, 1991. *Publications:* Impact of Food Aid on Donor Countries (with G. R. Allen), 1967; contribs to New Thinking About Welfare, 1969; Economic System in the UK, 1977, 2nd edn 1979; New Directions in Adult and Continuing Education, 1979; Continuing Education in Universities and Polytechnics, 1982; contrib. Jl of Development Studies, Oxford Rev. of Educn, Studies in Adult Education. *Recreation:* good food. *Address:* The Provost's Lodgings, Worcester College, Oxford OX1 2HB. *T:* (01865) 278362.

SMETTEM, Colin William; Chairman, North Eastern Region, British Gas Corporation, 1973–76; *b* 1 June 1916; *s* of William Home Smettem and Agnes Grace; *m* 1945, Sylvia Elisabeth (*née* Alcock); two *s* two *d*. Solicitor (Hons) 1938. Asst Solicitor, Scarborough Corp., 1938. Served War, RA, 1939–45: UK, India, Assam; started 14th Army Trng Sch., 1943; GII (Major) at Tactical Trng Centre, India Command, 1944. Asst Town Clerk, Wallasey, 1948; Solicitor, North Western Gas Bd, 1950; Commercial Manager, North Western Gas Bd, 1961, and Mem. Bd, 1965–68; Dep. Chm., Eastern Gas Bd, 1968. Mem., Law Soc. Mem., Rutland DC, 1983–91. CompIGasE 1966. *Address:* The Rookery, Tinwell, Rutland, via Stamford, Lincs PE9 3UJ. *T:* (01780) 753168.

SMIETON, Dame Mary Guillan, DBE 1949; MA Oxon; Permanent Secretary, Ministry of Education, 1959–63, retired; *b* 5 Dec. 1902; *d* of John Guillan Smieton, late librarian and bursar Westminster Coll., Cambridge, and of Maria Judith Toop. *Educ:* Perse Sch., Cambridge; Wimbledon High Sch.; Bedford Coll., London (1 year) (Hon. Fellow, 1971); Lady Margaret Hall. Assistant Keeper, Public Record Office, 1925–28; Ministry of Labour and National Service, 1928–46; on loan to Home Office as General Secretary, Women's Voluntary Services, 1938–40, and to UN as Director of Personnel, 1946–48; Deputy Secretary, Ministry of Labour and National Service, 1955–59 (Under-Secretary, 1946–55). UK representative, Unesco Executive Board, 1962–68. Trustee, British Museum, 1963–73; Chm., Bedford Coll. Council, 1964–70. Member: Advisory Council on Public Records, 1965–73; Standing Commn on Museums and Galleries, 1970–73; Vice Pres., Museums Assoc., 1974–77. Hon. Fellow, Lady Margaret Hall, Oxford, 1959. *Address:* 14 St George's Road, St Margaret's on Thames, Middlesex TW1 1QR. *T:* (020) 8892 9279. *Club:* Oxford and Cambridge.

SMILEY, Lt-Col Sir John (Philip), 4th Bt *cr* 1903, of Drumalis, Larne, Co. Antrim and Gallowhill, Paisley, Co. Renfrew; *b* 24 Feb. 1934; *s* of Sir Hugh Houston Smiley, 3rd Bt and Nancy Elizabeth Louise Hardy (*née* Beaton) (*d* 1999); *S* father, 1990; *m* 1963, Davina Elizabeth, *e d* of late Denis Charles Griffiths; two *s* one *d*. *Educ:* Eton Coll.; RMA Sandhurst. Commnd Grenadier Guards, 1954; ADC to Governor of Bermuda, 1961–62; served in Cyprus, BAOR, Hong Kong; Lt-Col, 1981; retired 1986. Russell Reynolds Associates, 1986–89. Governor, Oundle Sch., 1987–99. Mem., Ct of Assts, Worshipful Co. of Grocers, 1987– (Master, 1992–93). *Recreations:* gardening, travel. *Heir:* *s* Christopher Hugh Charles Smiley [*b* 7 Feb. 1968; *m* 1998, Mrs Clare Annabel Barr Smith, *y d* of Maj. Henry Blosse-Lynch; one *s*]. *Address:* Cornerway House, Chobham, Woking, Surrey GU24 8SW. *T:* (01276) 858992. *Club:* Army and Navy.

SMILEY, Prof. Timothy John, PhD; FBA 1984; Knightbridge Professor of Philosophy, University of Cambridge, 1980–98; Fellow of Clare College, Cambridge, since 1955; *b* 13 Nov. 1930; *s* of Prof. M. T. Smiley and Mrs T. M. Smiley (*née* Browne); *m* 1955, Benita Mary Bentley; four *d*. *Educ:* Ardwyn Grammar Sch., Aberystwyth; Ampleforth Coll.; Fribourg Univ.; Clare Coll., Cambridge (BA 1952, Math. Tripos; MA, PhD 1956). Holt Scholarship, Gray's Inn, 1954; called to the Bar, 1956. Pilot Officer, RAFVR, 1954. Scientific Officer, Air Min., 1955–56; Clare Coll., Cambridge: Res. Fellow, 1955–59; Asst Tutor, 1959–65; Sen. Tutor, 1966–69; Asst Lectr in Phil., Cambridge Univ., 1957–62, Lectr, 1962–79. Vis. Professor: Cornell Univ., 1964; Univ. of Virginia, 1972; Yale Univ., 1975; Univ. of Notre Dame, 1986; Yale Univ., 1990. Sec. for Postgrad. Studies, 1992–94, Mem., Humanities Res. Bd, 1994–96, British Acad. *Publications:* (with D. J. Shoesmith) Multiple-conclusion Logic, 1978; articles in phil and math. jls. *Recreation:* orienteering. *Address:* Clare College, Cambridge CB2 1TL. *T:* (01223) 352152.

SMILLIE, (William) John (Jones); Managing Director, Gatehouse Records, since 1992; *b* 18 Feb. 1940; *s* of late John Smillie and Emily Mary Caroline (*née* Jones). *Educ:* Lauriston Sch., Falkirk; Territorial Sch., Stirling; Stirling High Sch. Scottish hotel family background; trained in all hotel depts in Scotland and Paris, with extensive kitchen work; progressed to management with Edward R. Barnett & Co. Ltd, industrial caterers (now taken over by Grand Metropolitan Gp), resp. for 50 outlets throughout Scotland, England and Wales (Asst Gen. Man., 1964–67); joined House of Commons Catering Dept as Personnel Manager, 1967: Personnel Manager and Asst to Catering Manager, 1970; Gen. Man., 1971; Head of Dept, 1980–91. Mem., Newbury Community Radio Assoc., 1996–; Dir, Newbury Community Radio (Investments) Ltd. Member: British Inst. of Cleaning Science, 1976–; Hine Soc., 1979–; FHCIMA 1979; Fellow, Cookery and Food Assoc., 1967; Founder Mem., Wine Guild of UK, 1984–; Mem., Restaurateurs Assoc. of GB, 1983–; Hon. Member: Assoc. Culinaire Française, 1972; Conseil Culinaire Française de Grande Bretagne, en Reconnaissance des Services Rendus à l'Art Culinaire, 1987. Vice Pres., British Epilepsy Assoc., 1981–. *Publications:* articles for catering trade papers. *Recreations:* theatre, ballet, music, piano, motoring, boating, radio presenting, travel, gourmandise, intervals at the opera, jazz music. *Address:* The Gatehouse, 90 Wimbledon Parkside, SW19 5LT. *T:* (020) 8780 9353, *Fax:* (020) 7823 8905. *Club:* Mortons.

SMIT, Timothy Bartel; Chief Executive, Eden Project, since 1999; Director, Lost Gardens of Heligan, since 1990; *b* 25 Sept. 1954; *s* of Jan Adrianus Bartel Smit and Anthea Margaret Smit (*née* Fairclough); *m* 1978, Laura Candace Pinsent; two *s* one *d*. *Educ:* Cranbrook Sch.; Univ. of Durham (BA Hons Archaeol. and Anthropology). Archaeologist, 1977–78; record producer and composer, 1978–90; with John Nelson discovered, 1990, and restored Heligan estate, Cornwall, now open to visitors and known internationally as Lost Gardens of Heligan (Gardener of Year, Country Life, 1995; Garden of Year, Good Guide to Britain, 1999); Co-Founder, Eden Project, 1994 (scientific instn featuring conservatories inside a 34 acre, 200ft deep clay pit near St Austell). Mem. Bd, Prince's Trust Business Div., 1999–. Hon. MSc Gen. Sci. Plymouth, 1998; Hon. LLD Exeter, 2001. *Publications:* The Lost Gardens of Heligan, 1997 (Illustrated Book of Year, BCA, 1998); The Complete Works: secrets locked in silence, 1999; (with Philip McMillan Browse) The Heligan Vegetable Bible, 2000. *Recreations:* music, reading, scuba diving. *Address:* Treveague, Gorran, St Austell, Cornwall PL26 6NY.

SMITH; *see* Abel Smith.

SMITH; *see* Darwall Smith.

SMITH; *see* Delacourt-Smith.

SMITH; *see* Dixon-Smith, family name of Baron Dixon-Smith.

SMITH; *see* Gordon-Smith.

SMITH; *see* Hamilton-Smith, family name of Baron Colwyn.

SMITH; *see* Hugh Smith.

SMITH; *see* Llewellyn Smith and Llewellyn-Smith.

SMITH; *see* Mackenzie Smith and McKenzie Smith.

SMITH; *see* Spencer Smith and Spencer-Smith.

SMITH; *see* Stewart-Smith.

SMITH; *see* Stuart-Smith.

SMITH, family name of **Viscount Hambleden, Barons Bicester, Kirkhill, Smith of Clifton** and **Smith of Leigh** and **Baroness Smith of Gilmorehill**.

SMITH OF CLIFTON, Baron *cr* 1997 (Life Peer), of Mountsandel, in the co. of Londonderry; **Trevor Arthur Smith,** Kt 1996; FRHistS; Vice-Chancellor, University of Ulster, 1991–99; *b* 14 June 1937; *e s* of late Arthur James Smith and Vera Gladys Smith (*née* Cross); *m* 1st, 1960, Brenda Eustace (marr. diss. 1973); two *s*; 2nd, 1979, Julia Donnithorne (*née* Bullock); one *d*. *Educ:* LSE (BSc Econ 1958). Schoolteacher, LCC, 1958–59; temp. Asst Lectr, Exeter Univ., 1959–60; Research Officer, Acton Soc. Trust, 1960–62; Lectr in Politics, Hull Univ., 1962–67; Queen Mary College, later Queen Mary & Westfield College, London: Lectr, then Sen. Lectr, in Political Studies, 1967–83; Prof., Political Studies, 1983–91; Head of Dept, 1972–85; Dean of Social Studies, 1979–82; Pro-Principal, 1985–87; Sen. Pro-Principal, 1987–89; Sen. Vice-Prin., 1989–91. Vis. Associate Prof., California State Univ., LA, 1969. Director: Job Ownership Ltd, 1978–85; New Society Ltd, 1986–88; Statesman & Nation Publishing Co. Ltd, 1988–90; G. Duckworth & Co., 1990–95. Mem., Tower Hamlets DHA, 1987–91 (Vice Chm., 1989–91); non-exec. Mem., N Yorks HA, 2000–. Vice Pres., Patients' Assoc. of UK, 1988–97. Chm., Conf. of Rectors in Ireland, 1997. Vice-Pres., Political Studies Assoc. of UK, 1989–91 (Chm., 1988–89; Pres., 1991–93); Dep. Pres., Inst. of Citizenship Studies, 1991–; Member: Admin. Bd, Internat. Assoc. of Univs, 1995–96; Editl Bd, Government and Opposition, 1995–; UK Socrates Council, 1993–99 (Chm., 1996–99). Contested (L) Lewisham W, 1959. Lib Dem Spokesman on NI, H of L; Chm., Select Cttee on Animals in Scientific Procedures, H of L, 2001–02; Member: Sci. and Technol. Sub-Cttee on Complementary and Alternative Medicine, 1999–2000; EU Sub-Cttee E (Law and Instns), 2000–. Trustee, Joseph Rowntree Reform (formerly Social Service) Trust, 1975– (Chm., 1987–99); Pres., Belfast Civic Trust, 1995–99; Member Board: Taste of Ulster, 1996–99; Opera NI, 1997–99. Governor: Sir John Cass and Redcoats Sch., 1979–84; Univ. of Haifa, 1985–92; Bell Educnl Trust, 1988–93. Hon. Mem. Senate, Fachhochschule Augsberg, 1994. FRHistS 1986; FICPD 1998. CIMgt (CBIM 1992); FRSA 1994. AcSS 2000. Hon. LLD: Dublin, 1992; Hull, 1993; Belfast, 1995; NUI, 1996; Hon. DHL Alabama, 1998. *Publications:* (with M. Argyle) Training Managers, 1962; (with A. M. Rees) Town Councillors, 1964; Town and County Hall, 1966; Anti-Politics, 1972; (jtly) Direct Action and Democratic Politics, 1972; The Politics of the Corporate Economy, 1979; (with A. Young) The Fixers, 1996; numerous articles. *Address:* House of Lords, SW1A 0PW. *Club:* Reform.

SMITH OF GILMOREHILL, Baroness *cr* 1995 (Life Peer), of Gilmorehill in the City of Glasgow; **Elizabeth Margaret Smith;** DL; *b* 4 June 1940; *d* of Frederick William Moncrieff Bennett and Elizabeth Waters Irvine Shanks; *m* 1967, Rt Hon. John Smith, PC, QC (Scot.), MP (*d* 1994); three *d*. *Educ:* Hutchesons' Girls' Grammar Sch.; Univ. of Glasgow (MA, DipEd). Admin. Asst, 1962–64, Scottish Sec., 1982–88, Great Britain-USSR Assoc.; teacher of French, 1964–68. Mem., Press Complaints Commn, 1995–. Chm., Edinburgh Festival Fringe, 1995; non-executive Director: Scottish Media Group plc (formerly Scottish Television), 1995–97; Deutsche Bank (formerly Deutsche Morgan Grenfell) (Scotland), 1996–; Member: BP Adv. Bd, Scotland, 1996–; Adv Bd, Know How Fund, 1998–99. Member Board: Russo-British Chamber of Commerce, 1996–; Covent Garden Fest., 1997–. Pres., Scottish Opera, 1997–. Trustee: John Smith Meml Trust, 1995–; BHF, 1995–98; ESU, 1995–; Centre for European Reform, 1996–; World Monument Fund, 1996–; Hakluyt Foundn, 1998–2001. Pres., Birkbeck Coll., London, 1998–. DL Edinburgh, 1996. Hon. LLD Glasgow, 1998. *Recreations:* family, cinema, music, theatre, travel. *Address:* House of Lords, SW1A 0PW.

SMITH OF LEIGH, Baron *cr* 1999 (Life Peer), of Wigan in the county of Greater Manchester; **Peter Richard Charles Smith;** Lecturer, Manchester College of Art and Technology, since 1974; *b* 24 July 1945; *s* of Ronald Ernest Smith and Kathleen (*née* Hocken); *m* 1968, Joy Lesley (*née* Booth); one *d*. *Educ:* Bolton Sch.; LSE (BScEcon); Garnett Coll. of Educn (CertEd FE); Salford Univ. (MSc Urban Studies). Lectr, Walbrook Coll., 1969–74. Mem. (Lab) Wigan MBC, 1978– (Chm. Finance, 1982–91; Leader, 1991–). Chm., NW Regl Assembly, 1999– (Vice Chm., 1998–99). Bd Mem., Manchester Airport plc, 1986– (Chm., 1989–90). *Recreations:* gardening, reading political biographies, jazz. *Address:* Mysevin, Old Hall Mill Lane, Atherton, Manchester M46 0RG. *T:* (01942) 676127. *Club:* Hindley Green Labour.

SMITH, Prof. Adam Neil, MD, DSc; FRCSE, FRCPE; retired consultant surgeon; *b* 27 June 1926; *s* of William Blackwood Smith and Janet Elder Robertson; *m* 1953, Sibyl Mary Veitch Johnstone; one *s* three *d*. *Educ:* Lanark Grammar Sch.; Univ. of Glasgow (MB ChB 1948; MD Hons 1959); DSc Edinburgh, 1995. FRCSE 1956; FRCPE 1988; FRSE 1982; FIBiol 1991. Hall Fellow, Univ. of Glasgow, 1949–50; Faulds Fellow, 1950–51; MRC Clinical Research Fellow, 1951–54; Lectr in Surgery, Univ. of Glasgow, 1954–58; St Mark's Hosp., 1958; Sen. Lectr, 1959–63, Reader in Surgery, 1963–91, Univ. of Edinburgh. James IV and Commonwealth Travelling Fellow, 1963. Royal College of Surgeons of Edinburgh: Wade Prof. of Surgical Studies, 1986–97; Vice-Pres., 1991–94;

Medal, 1997. Mem. Council, Assoc. of Coloproctology, 1991–94; President: Pelvic Floor Soc., 1989–92; Scottish Soc. of Coloproctology, 1991–94; Mem., James IV Surgical Assoc. Formerly Ext. Examr, Glasgow, Dundee, Newcastle, overseas. Chm., Clinical Sci. Adv. Body, 1984–94, and Trustee, 1994–, Melville Trust for Cancer Research. *Publications:* Scientific Foundations of Gastroenterology, 1980; (contrib.) Nutrition in the Prevention of Disease, 1989; (contrib.) Clinical Measurements in Coloproctology, 1991; (contrib.) The Large Intestine, 1991; (contrib.) Coloproctology and the Pelvic Floor, 1992; (contrib.) Colorectal Physiology: Faecal Incontinence, 1994; papers in surgical, gastroenterological and cancer jls. *Recreations:* golf, gardening (Mem. Council, Royal Caledonian Horticultural Soc.), art. *Address:* 2 Ravelston House Park, Edinburgh EH4 3LU. *T:* (0131) 332 4077. *Club:* Scottish Arts (Edinburgh).

SMITH, Adrian Charles; His Honour Judge Adrian Smith; a Circuit Judge, since 1996; *b* 25 Nov. 1950; *s* of late Fred Smith and Jenny Smith; *m* 1973, Sallie Ann Palmer (*d* 1994); two *d. Educ:* Blackpool Grammar Sch.; Queen Mary Coll., Univ. of London (LLB (Hons)). Called to the Bar, Lincoln's Inn, 1973; in practice on Northern Circuit, 1974–96; a Recorder, 1994–96. Mem., Liverpool Witness Support Mgt Cttee, 1990–93; Legal Mem., NW Mental Health Review Tribunal, 1994–96. *Recreations:* Italian travel, theatre, fell walking. *Address:* Crown Court, Crown Square, Manchester M3 3FL. *Club:* Waterloo Rugby Union.

SMITH, Adrian Frederick Melhuish, PhD; FRS 2001; Principal, Queen Mary and Westfield College, University of London, since 1998; *b* 9 Sept. 1946; *s* of Claude Herbert Melhuish Smith and late Jean Margaret Eileen Smith (*née* Hunt); one *s. Educ:* Teignmouth Grammar Sch.; Selwyn Coll., Cambridge (MA 1968); University Coll. London (MSc 1969; PhD 1971). Jun. Lectr, 1971–72, Univ. Lectr, 1972–74, in Maths, Univ. of Oxford; Tutorial Fellow in Maths, Keble Coll., Oxford, 1971–74; Lectr in Stats, UCL, 1974–77; Prof. of Mathematical Stats, Univ. of Nottingham, 1977–90; Prof. of Stats, Imperial Coll. of Sci., Technology and Medicine, 1990–98 (Vis. Prof., 1998–). Dir, Imperial College Consultants, 1992–98 (Chm. of Bd, 1996–98). Member: Math. Cttee, SERC, 1985–91 (Chm., 1988–91); Sci. Bd, SERC, 1988–91; Technical Opportunities Panel, EPSRC, 1997–2000; Stats Adv. Cttee, ONS, 1997–99. Pres., Royal Statistical Soc., 1995–97 (Guy Medal in Bronze, 1977, in Silver, 1993). Mem. Governing Body, London Business Sch., 1998–. FIS 1980. *Publications:* (jtly) The Statistical Analysis of Finite Mixture Models, 1985; (jtly) Bayesian Theory, 1994; (trans. jtly) Bruno de Finetti, Theory of Probability, vol. I, 1974, vol. II, 1975; papers in statistical jls. *Recreations:* jazz, opera, cooking. *Address:* 58 Noel Road, N1 8HB. *Club:* Reform.

SMITH, Alan; mining engineer; *b* 19 Jan. 1930; *s* of John Smith and Alice (*née* Williams); *m* 1958, Adele Marguerite (*née* Buckle) (marr. diss. 1986); two *s* two *d. Educ:* Rossall; St Catherine's Soc., Oxford. BSc Leeds 1957. MIMinE 1958. NCB, 1957–64; Principal Sci. Officer, Min. of Power, 1964; Sci. Counsellor, HM Embassy, Paris, 1965–70; Cabinet Secretariat, 1970–71; DTI, 1971–73; Dept of Industry, 1973–74; Sci. and Technol. Counsellor, HM Embassy, Washington, 1975–77; Head of Sci. and Technol. Div., OECD, 1977–80; DTI Research Gp, 1980–84. Exec. Sec., Newcomen Soc., 1988–92. De Laune Lectr, Apothecaries' Soc., 1980. *Publications:* learned articles on steam engines. *Recreation:* engineering history. *Address:* 63 Abbey House, Abbey Road, NW8 9BX.

SMITH, Sir Alan, Kt 1982; CBE 1976; DFC 1941, and Bar 1942; DL; President, Dawson International plc, since 1982; *b* 14 March 1917; *s* of Alfred and Lilian Smith; *m* 1st, 1943, Margaret Stewart Todd (*d* 1971); three *s* two *d*; 2nd, 1977, Alice Elizabeth Moncur. *Educ:* Bede College, Sunderland. Self employed, 1931–36; Unilever Ltd, 1937–39; RAF, 1939–45; Man. Dir, Todd & Duncan Ltd, 1946–60; Chm. and Chief Exec., Dawson International, 1960–82. DL Kinross, 1967. *Recreations:* sailing, swimming. *Address:* Ardgairney House, Cleish, by Kinross, Scotland KY13 7LG. *T:* (01577) 850265. *Club:* Lansdowne.

SMITH, Prof. Alan, DPhil; UNESCO Professor of Education, University of Ulster, since 2000; *b* Belfast, 18 Jan. 1954; *s* of Walter Smith and Barbara Smith (*née* Stanex); *m* 1981, Elaine Steele; two *d. Educ:* Univ. of Ulster (BSc Hons; DPhil 1985). Teacher, NI and Zimbabwe, 1978–84; Research Fellow, Centre for Study of Conflict, Univ. of Ulster, 1985–96; Nuffield Foundn nominee to Integrated Educn Fund, 1992–99. Consultant to Dept of Education, NI, DFID, Council of Europe and World Bank, 1997–. Founding Chm., NI Council for Integrated Educn, 1987–89. Mem., UNESCO Adv. Cttee on Peace, Human Rights and Democracy, Paris, 2000–. Trustee, Speedwell Envmtl Centre, 1990–96. *Publications:* contribs to acad. jls on educn and conflict in NI, peace, human rights and democracy. *Address:* School of Education, University of Ulster, Coleraine, Northern Ireland BT52 1SA. *T:* (028) 7032 4137.

SMITH, Alan Christopher, CBE 1996; Chief Executive, Test and County Cricket Board, 1987–96; *b* 25 Oct. 1936; *s* of Herbert Sidney and Elsie Smith; *m* 1963, Anne Elizabeth Boddy; one *s* one *d. Educ:* King Edward's Sch., Birmingham; Brasenose Coll., Oxford (BA). Played cricket: Oxford Univ. CC, 1958–60 (Captain, 1959 and 1960); Warwicks CCC, 1958–74 (Captain, 1968–74); rep. England in six Test Matches, Australia and NZ, 1962–63. Gen. Sec., Warwicks CCC, 1976–86; England overseas cricket tours: Asst Manager, Australia, 1974–75; Manager: West Indies, 1981; Fiji, NZ and Pakistan, 1984. Mem., England Cricket Selection Cttee, 1969–73, 1982–86; ICC Referee, 1998–. Director: Royds Advertising and Marketing, 1971–86; Aston Villa Football Club plc, 1972–78. President: Brasenose Soc., 1999–2000; OUCC, 2000–. *Recreations:* both football codes, golf, bridge, motoring. *Address:* The Old Farmhouse, Wyck Rissington, Gloucestershire GL54 2PN. *T:* (01451) 820509. *Clubs:* MCC, I Zingari; Vincent's (Oxford); Warwickshire CC, Worcestershire CC, Glamorgan CC.

SMITH, Alan Frederick; Group Managing Director, Anglian Water PLC, 1990–97; *b* 21 July 1944; *s* of Frederick Herbert Smith and Winifred Alice Bella (*née* Farthing); *m* 1966, Judith Mary Forshaw (marr. diss. 1991); one *s* one *d. Educ:* Gosfield Sch., Essex. CIPFA. Trainee, Colchester BC, 1961–66; Ipswich County Borough Council: Sen. Accountant, 1966–72; Asst Treas., 1972–74; Principal Accountant, Anglian Water Authy, 1974–75; Asst Dir of Finance, Southern Water Authy, 1975–80; Dir of Finance, Anglian Water Authy, 1980–89; Dep. Man. Dir and Dir of Finance, Anglian Water PLC, 1989–90. Dir, Peptide Therapeutics Gp. *Recreations:* walking, photography.

SMITH, Rt Rev. Alan Gregory Clayton; *see* Shrewsbury, Bishop Suffragan of.

SMITH, Alan Keith Patrick; Chairman, Mothercare plc (formerly Storehouse plc), since 2000; *b* 17 March 1941; *s* of Ernest and Mary Smith; *m* 1st, 1968, Veronica Soskin (marr. diss.); one *s* one *d*; 2nd, 1983, Joan Peregrine; two *s. Educ:* St Michael's Coll., Leeds; Edinburgh Univ. (MA). Marks & Spencer, 1964–93, Dir, 1978–93; Chief Exec., Kingfisher, 1993–95. Director: Colefax & Fowler, 1993–; Whitehead Mann Gp, 1997–; The Health Clinic, 1998–; Iceland, 2000–. Gov., South Bank Centre, 1995–. *Recreations:* family, wine collecting, walking, cooking. *Address:* Mothercare plc, Cherry Tree Road, Watford, Herts WD2 5SH. *T:* (01923) 241000. *Clubs:* Brooks's, MCC.

SMITH, Alasdair; *see* Smith, M. A. M.

SMITH, Sir Alex; *see* Smith, Sir Alexander M.

SMITH, Alexander; *b* Kilwinning, 2 Dec. 1943. *Educ:* Irvine Royal Acad. Former gardener. Chm., 1983–87, Trade Union Liaison Officer, 1986–88, Cunninghame S CLP; former Chm., Irvine and District Trades Council. MEP (Lab) Scotland S, 1989–99. Member: TGWU (Mem., Regl, Public Service and Political Cttees); Scottish CND; Anti-Apartheid Movement; Amnesty Internat.; Latin American Solidarity Campaign.

SMITH, Prof. Alexander Crampton, (Alex Crampton Smith); Nuffield Professor of Anaesthetics, Oxford University, and Fellow of Pembroke College, Oxford, 1965–79; now Emeritus Professor; *b* 15 June 1917; *s* of William and Mary Elizabeth Crampton Smith; *m* 1953, Marjorie (*née* Mason); three *s*; two *d* by a former marriage. *Educ:* Inverness Royal Acad.; Edinburgh University. Edinburgh Univ., 1935–41. Served War of 1939–45 (Croix de Guerre, despatches), RNVR, 1942–46. Consultant Anaesthetist, United Oxford Hospitals, 1951; Clinical Lectr in Anaesthetics, Oxford Univ., 1961. FFARCS 1953; MA Oxon 1961. Civilian Consultant Anaesthetist to Royal Navy, 1968. Mem. Bd, Faculty of Anaesthetists, 1965–80. Mem. Trustees, Nuffield Medical Benefaction, 1973–92. *Publications:* Clinical Practice and Physiology of Artificial Respiration (with J. M. K. Spalding), 1963; contribs to anaesthetic, medical and physiological jls. *Recreations:* sailing, fishing. *Address:* 10 Horwood Close, Headington, Oxford OX3 7RF. *T:* (01865) 769593.

SMITH, Sir Alexander Mair, (Sir Alex), Kt 1975; Director of various companies; *b* 15 Oct. 1922; *s* of late John S. and Anne M. Smith; *m* 1st, 1944, Muriel (*née* Harris) (*d* 1950); one *d*; 2nd, 1956, Doris Neil (*née* Patrick) (*d* 1980); one *d* (and one *d* decd); 3rd, 1984, Jennifer Lewis (*née* Pearce); two step *s. Educ:* Univ. of Aberdeen. MA (Maths and Nat. Phil.), PhD, FInstP. Physicist, UKAEA, 1952–56; Head of Advanced Research, Rolls Royce Ltd, 1956–67; Dir and Chief Scientist, Rolls Royce & Associates Ltd, 1967–69; Dir, Manchester Polytechnic, 1969–81. Chairman: Cttee of Dirs of Polytechnics, 1974–76; Schools Council, 1975–78; Member: UGC, 1974–76; BBC Gen. Adv. Council, 1978–81; Council, RSA, 1979–84; Vice-Pres., CGLI, 1981–91; Patron, Educnl Inst. of Design, Craft and Technology, 1977–83. Hon. Fellow: Sheffield Poly., 1977; Poly. of Wales, 1983. *Publications:* Lock Up the Swings on Sundays (memoirs), 1998; papers in learned jls. *Recreation:* music. *Address:* Flat 2, 6 Hall Road, Wilmslow, Cheshire SK9 5BW. *T:* (01625) 522011.

SMITH, Alistair; *see* Smith, E. A.

SMITH, Alwyn; *see* Smith, Ernest A.

SMITH, Andreas W.; *see* Whittam Smith.

SMITH, Hon. Sir Andrew (Charles), Kt 2000; **Hon. Mr Justice Andrew Smith;** a Judge of the High Court of Justice, Queen's Bench Division, since 2000; *b* 31 Dec. 1947; *s* of Charles George Smith and Winifrid Smith; *m* 1986, Indu Nathoo; one *s* two *d. Educ:* Wyggeston Grammar Sch. for Boys, Leicester; Wadham Coll., Oxford (BA). Called to Bar, Middle Temple, 1974, Bencher, 1999. QC 1990; a Recorder, 1996–2000. *Address:* Royal Courts of Justice, Strand, WC2A 2LL.

SMITH, Rt Hon. Andrew (David); PC 1997; MP (Lab) Oxford East, since 1987; Chief Secretary to HM Treasury, since 1999; *b* 1 Feb. 1951; *m*; one step *s. Educ:* Reading Grammar Sch.; St John's Coll., Oxford. Joined Labour Party, 1973. Mem., Oxford City Council, 1976–87 (Chairman: Recreation Cttee, 1980–83; Planning Cttee, 1984–87). Opposition spokesman on higher and continuing educn, 1988–92, on Treasury and Economic Affairs, 1992–94, on transport, 1996–97; Shadow Chief Sec. to HM Treasury, 1994–96; Minister of State, DFEE, 1997–99. Contested (Lab) Oxford E, 1983. Chm., Bd, Oxford Brookes Univ. (formerly Oxford Poly.), 1987–93. *Address:* 4 Flaxfield Road, Blackbird Leys, Oxford OX4 5QD; House of Commons, SW1A 0AA.

SMITH, Angela Evans; MP (Lab and Co-op) Basildon, since 1997; an Assistant Government Whip, since 2001; *b* 7 Jan. 1959; *d* of Patrick Joseph Evans and Emily Meikle Evans (*née* Russell); *m* 1978, Nigel J. M. Smith. *Educ:* Chalvedon Comprehensive Sch., Basildon; Leicester Poly. (BA Hons Public Admin). Part-time shop asst, J Sainsbury, 1975–77; Trainee Accountant, Newham LBC, 1981–83; Head of Pol and Public Relations, League Against Cruel Sports, 1983–95; Researcher, Alun Michael, MP, 1995–97. Mem. (Lab) Essex CC, 1989–97. Contested (Lab) Southend W, 1987. PPS to Minister of State, Home Office, 1999–2001. *Address:* House of Commons, SW1A 0AA. *T:* (020) 7219 6273.

SMITH, Anne; Chief Executive, National Asthma Campaign, since 1998; *b* 6 May 1961; *d* of John and Gerry Bradley; *m* 2000, Amahl Smith. *Educ:* Christ's Coll., Cambridge (MA; tennis blue). Product Manager, then Gp Product Manager, Merck Sharp and Dohme Ltd, 1982–89; Allen & Hanburys: Mktg Manager, 1989–94; Business Zone Manager, 1994–96; Glaxo Wellcome UK Ltd, 1989–98: Regl Business Dir, 1994–96; Dir, Respiratory Mktg, 1996–98. *Recreations:* travelling, hill walking, gardening, cycling, tennis. *Address:* National Asthma Campaign, Providence House, Providence Place, N1 0NT. *T:* (020) 7226 2260.

SMITH, Anne; QC (Scot) 1993; *b* 16 March 1955; *d* of John Mather and Jessica Douglas; *m* 1979, David Alexander Smith, WS; one *s* one *d. Educ:* Cheadle Girls' Grammar Sch.; Edinburgh Univ. (LLB Hons). Apprenticeship with Shepherd & Wedderburn WS, 1977–79; pupil of James McGhie, 1979–80; admitted Faculty of Advocates, 1980. *Recreations:* music (piano, flute), aerobics, ski-ing, swimming, gardening, walking. *Address:* Advocates' Library, Parliament House, Edinburgh EH1 1RF. *T:* (0131) 226 5071.

SMITH, Anne Margaret Brearley; *see* Luther, A.M.

SMITH, Annette Dionne K.; *see* Karmiloff-Smith.

SMITH, Lt-Gen. Sir Anthony Arthur D.; *see* Denison-Smith.

SMITH, Anthony David, CBE 1987; President, Magdalen College, Oxford, since 1988; *b* 14 March 1938; *s* of Henry and Esther Smith. *Educ:* Brasenose Coll., Oxford (BA; Hon. Fellow, 1994). BBC TV Current Affairs Producer, 1960–71; Fellow, St Antony's Coll., Oxford, 1971–76; Director, BFI, 1979–88 (Fellow 1988). Bd Mem., Channel Four Television Co., 1980–84. Chairman: Writers and Scholars Educnl Trust, 1989–99 (Mem., 1982–); Jan Hus Educnl Foundn; Mem., Arts Council, 1990–94; Trustee, Cambodia Trust, 1990–99. *Publications:* The Shadow in the Cave: the broadcaster, the audience and the state, 1973, 2nd edn 1976; British Broadcasting, 1974; The British Press since the War, 1976; Subsidies and the Press in Europe, 1977; The Politics of Information, 1978; Television and Political Life, 1979; The Newspaper: an international history, 1979; Newspapers and Democracy, 1980; Goodbye Gutenberg—the newspaper revolution of the 1980's, 1980; The Geopolitics of Information, 1980; The Age of the Behemoths, 1991; From Books to Bytes, 1993; The Oxford Illustrated History of Television, 1995;

Software for the Self: culture and technology, 1996. *Address:* Magdalen College, Oxford OX1 4AU. *T:* (01865) 276000; Albany, Piccadilly, W1V 9RP. *Club:* Grillions.

SMITH, Prof. (Anthony) David, DPhil; Professor of Pharmacology, since 1984, and Deputy Head, Division of Medical Sciences, University of Oxford; Director, Oxford Project to Investigate Memory and Ageing, since 1988; Fellow, Lady Margaret Hall, Oxford, since 1984; *b* 16 Sept. 1938; *s* of Rev. William Beddard Smith and Evelyn Smith; *m* 1st, 1962, Wendy Diana Lee (marr. diss. 1974); one *s* one *d*; 2nd, 1975, Dr Ingegerd Östman; one *s*. *Educ:* Kingswood Sch., Bath; Christ Church, Oxford (Bostock Exhibnr; BA 1963, MA 1966, DPhil 1966). Royal Soc. Stothert Res. Fellow, Oxford, 1966–70; Res. Lectr, Christ Church, Oxford, 1966–71; Wellcome Res. Fellow, Oxford, 1970–71; Univ. Lectr in Pharmacology and Student of Christ Church, 1971–84. Hon. Dir, MRC Anatomical Neuropharmacology Unit, Oxford, 1985–98. Member: Gen. Bd of the Faculties, Oxford, 1980–84; Neurosciences Bd, MRC, 1983–88; Physiol Soc.; Pharmacol Soc. Dir of Pubns, IBRO, 1977–95; Editor: Methods in the Neurosciences (IBRO Handbook Series), 1981–; Neuroscience, 1976–; Mem., editorial bds of various scientific jls. FMedSci 2000. Mem., Norwegian Acad. of Sci. and Letters, 1996; Hon. Mem., Hungarian Acad. of Sci., 1998. Dr *hc* Szeged Univ., 1993; MD *hc* Lund Univ., 1998. (Seventh) Gaddum Meml Prize, British Pharmacol Soc., 1979. *Publications:* (ed) Handbook of Physiology, Section 7 Vol. 6, 1974; (ed) Commentaries in the Neurosciences, 1980; articles on neuropharmacology in jls. *Recreations:* music, travel. *Address:* University Department of Pharmacology, Mansfield Road, Oxford OX1 3QT. *T:* (01865) 271883; *e-mail:* david.smith@pharm.ox.ac.uk.

SMITH, Anthony Glen; Director of Education, Arts and Libraries, Devon County Council, since 1998; *b* 29 July 1955; *s* of Bernard Neil Smith and Jean Margaret Smith; *m* 1978, Anne McLaren; one *s* one *d*. *Educ:* Price's Sch., Fareham; Christ's Coll., Cambridge (BA 1977; MA 1980). Asst Teacher of Geog., Weston Favell Upper Sch., Northampton, 1977–81; Head of Geog., Sir Frank Markham Sch., Milton Keynes, 1981–84; Asst, later Sen. Educn Officer, Wilts CC, 1984–89; Devon County Council: Area Educn Officer, 1989–91; Sen. Educn Officer, 1991–94; Asst Chief Educn Officer, 1994–96; Dep. Chief Educn Officer, 1996–98. *Recreations:* cricket, antique maps, watercolour painting, furniture restoration, gardening, family. *Address:* Trafalgar House, Dawlish Road, Teignmouth, Devon TQ14 8TQ. *T:* (01626) 774289. *Club:* Hawks (Cambridge).

SMITH, Anthony (John Francis); writer, broadcaster; *b* 30 March 1926; 2nd *s* of late Hubert Smith (formerly Chief Agent, National Trust) and Diana Watkin; *m* 1st, 1956, Barbara Dorothy Newman (marr. diss. 1983); one *s* two *d*; 2nd, 1984, Margaret Ann Holloway; one *s*. *Educ:* Dragon School, Oxford; Blundell's School, Devon; Balliol College, Oxford. MA Oxon., 1951. Served with RAF, 1944–48. Oxford University, 1948–51. Manchester Guardian, 1953 and 1956–57; Drum, Africa, 1954–55; Science Correspondent, Daily Telegraph, 1957–63. Founded British Balloon and Airship Club, 1965 (Pres., 1970–); Chm., Airship Heritage Trust, 1997–. Scientific Fellow of Zoological Society. Glaxo Award for Science Writers, 1977; Cherry Kearton Medal and Award, RGS, 1978. TV series include: Balloon Safari, Balloons over the Alps, Great Zoos of the World, Great Parks of the World, Wilderness; radio series include: A Sideways Look, 1977–89; High Street Africa Revisited, 1983–84; Truth to Tell, 1990–93. *Publications:* Blind White Fish in Persia, 1953, repr. 1990; Sea Never Dry, 1958; High Street Africa, 1961; Throw Out Two Hands, 1963; The Body, 1968, new edn 1985; The Seasons, 1970; The Dangerous Sort, 1970; Mato Grosso, 1971; Beside the Seaside, 1972; Good Beach Guide, 1973; The Human Pedigree, 1975; Animals on View, 1977; Wilderness, 1978; A Persian Quarter Century, 1979; A Sideways Look, 1983; The Mind, 1984; Smith & Son, 1984; Which Animal Are You?, 1988; The Great Rift, 1988; Explorers of the Amazon, 1990; Swaps, 1992; The Free Life, 1994; Sex, Genes and All That, 1997; The Human Body, 1998; Survived, 1998; Ballooning, 1998; The Weather, 2000. *Recreations:* travel, lighter-than-air flying. *Address:* 10 Aldbourne Road, W12 0LN. *T:* (020) 8248 9589; St Aidan's, Bamburgh, Northumberland NE69 7BJ. *T:* (01668) 214253.

SMITH, Ven. (Anthony) Michael P.; *see* Percival Smith.

SMITH, Anthony Patrick, CBE 1998; Chief Executive, English National Board for Nursing, Midwifery and Health Visiting, since 1990; *b* 7 Aug. 1939; *s* of Edward Smith and Gladys Smith (*née* Green); *m* 1965, Barbara Marie Johnson; one *d*. *Educ:* Latymer Sch.; Open Univ. (BA Hons); Polytechnic of Central London (MA). RGN, RMN, RNT (Florence Nightingale Scholar, 1971). Asst Dir, Nurse Education, St Bartholomew's Hosp., 1969–75; Dir, Nurse Education, Southampton, 1975–81. Fellow, Florence Nightingale Foundn, 1996. Hon. DSc Southampton, 1998. *Recreations:* countryside pursuits, Staffordshire portrait figures. *Address:* English National Board for Nursing, Midwifery and Health Visiting, Victory House, 170 Tottenham Court Road, W1P 0HA. *T:* (020) 7388 3131.

SMITH, Cdre Anthony Philip M.; *see* Masterton-Smith.

SMITH, Prof. Anthony Terry Hanmer, LLD; Professor of Criminal and Public Laws, University of Cambridge, since 1996 (Chairman, Faculty of Law, 1999–2001); Fellow of Gonville and Caius College, Cambridge, since 1990; *b* 12 Jan. 1947; *s* of William Duncan Hanmer Smith and Rima Patricia Smith (*née* Donnelly); *m* 1968, Gillian Innes (marr. diss. 1981); one *s*. *Educ:* St Bede's Coll., Christchurch, NZ; Univ. of Canterbury (LLB; LLM); PhD 1985, LLD 1999, Cantab. Barrister and solicitor, High Court of NZ, 1979; called to the Bar, Middle Temple, 1992 (Hon. Bencher, 2001). Asst Lectr, Univ. of Canterbury, 1970–72; Lectr in Law, 1973–81, and Tutor, 1974–81, Gonville and Caius Coll., Cambridge; Reader in Law, 1981–85, and Dean of Faculty, 1984, Univ. of Durham; Prof. of Law, 1986–90, and Head of Dept, 1988–90, Univ. of Reading. *Publications:* Offences Against Public Order, 1987; Property Offences, 1994; (ed jtly) Harm and Culpability, 1996; (with Sir David Eady) The Laws of Contempt, 1998. *Recreations:* cookery, travelling, architecture, wine. *Address:* Gonville and Caius College, Cambridge CB2 1TA. *T:* (01223) 332449. *Club:* Athenæum.

SMITH, Anthony Thomas; QC 1977; a Recorder of the Crown Court, since 1977; *b* 21 June 1935; *s* of Sydney Ernest Smith and Winston Victoria Smith; *m* 1959, Letitia Ann Wheldon Griffith; one *s* two *d*. *Educ:* Northampton, Stafford, and Hinckley Grammar Schs; King's Coll., Cambridge (Exhibnr; MA). Called to the Bar, Inner Temple, 1958, Bencher, 1985. Flying Officer, RAF, 1958–60. Founder and Chm., Birmingham Free Representation Scheme. *Recreations:* music, reading, the countryside.

SMITH, Antony Francis; HM Diplomatic Service; High Commissioner to Jamaica, since 1999; *b* 6 May 1942; *s* of Robert Smith and Barbara (*née* Cunningham); *m* 1963, Marion Frances Hickman; two *d*. *Educ:* De La Salle Coll., Manchester. Joined FO, 1960; Cambodia, 1963–64; Vice Consul, Luanda, Angola, 1964–68; Warsaw, 1968–70; Persian lang. studies, SOAS, 1970–71; Tehran, 1971–74; FCO, 1975; First Sec., Accra, 1976–78; UK Delegn, OECD, Paris, 1979–83; Lisbon, 1983–85; Counsellor, FCO, 1985–90; Consul Gen. and Counsellor, Washington, 1990–94; Dep. Hd of Mission, Lisbon, 1994–99. Official, Order of Infante Dom Henriques (Portugal), 1985. *Recreation:* Ski-ing. *Address:* c/o Foreign and Commonwealth Office, King Charles Street, SW1A 2AH; 62 Elm Park Mansions, Park Walk, SW10 0AP. *Club:* Gremio Literario (Lisbon).

SMITH, Arnold Terence, MBE 1963; HM Diplomatic Service, retired; *b* 7 Oct. 1922; *s* of Thomas Smith and Minnie Louisa (*née* Mole); *m* 1st, 1944, Mary James (*d* 1983), Preston, Yorks; one *s* one *d*; 2nd, 1985, Brenda Day (*née* Edwards), Edmonton; one step *s*. *Educ:* Christ Church, Dover; Coll. of Technol., Dover. Enlisted HM Forces, Army, 1939; served War, 1939–45; released, 1947. Joined CRO, 1948; Attaché, Karachi, 1952–56; Second Sec., Madras, 1956–60; CRO, 1960–61; First Sec., Kuala Lumpur, 1961–65; Consul, Oslo, 1965–69; FCO, 1969–73; Head of Chancery, Mbabane, 1973–77; Head of Admin, Nairobi, 1977–78; Counsellor and Consul-Gen., Lagos, Nigeria, 1978–80. *Recreations:* hiking, gardening, golf, swimming. *Address:* Grunters, Cavendish Road, Clare, Suffolk CO10 8PJ. *T:* (01787) 277918.

SMITH, Barney; *see* Smith, L. B.

SMITH, Prof. Barry Edward, PhD; Head of Nitrogen Fixation Laboratory, 1987–2000, and Associate Research Director, 1994–2000, now Emeritus Fellow, John Innes Centre (formerly AFRC Institute of Plant Science Research); *b* 15 Nov. 1939; *s* of late Ernest Smith and Agnes Mary Smith (*née* DeFraine); *m* 1963, Pamela Heather Pullen; one *s* one *d*. *Educ:* Dr Challoner's Grammar Sch., Amersham; Royal Melbourne Tech. Coll., Australia; Hatfield Tech. Coll.; Univ. of Exeter (BSc); Univ. of East Anglia (PhD). Lab. technician, ICIANZ, 1956–59; ICI, 1959–60; res. appts, Univ. of Washington, Seattle, 1966–68, Univ. of Oxford, 1968–69; ARC, subseq. AFRC, Unit of Nitrogen Fixation, 1969–87; Asst Dir, 1986–87. Vis. Prof., Univ. of Essex, 1988–98; Hon. Professorial Fellow, Univ. of Sussex, 1989–95; Hon. Prof., UEA, 1995–. *Publications:* numerous articles in sci. jls and chapters in books on excited state chem., nitrogen fixation and on denitrification. *Address:* Biological Chemistry Department, John Innes Centre, Colney, Norwich NR4 7UH. *T:* (01603) 450720.

SMITH, Bartholomew Evan Eric; Chairman, Amber Foundation, since 1994; *b* 1 Feb. 1955; *s* of Sir John (Lindsay Eric) Smith, *qv*; *m* 1987, Catherine, *d* of Gavin and Mary Rowan Hamilton; three *s* one *d*. *Educ:* Eton Coll.; New Coll., Oxford. Littlemore Scientific Engrg Co., 1976–84; Dir, Lundy Co. Ltd, 1984–; Chairman: Smith Hamilton Ltd, 1989–; Coexis Ltd, 1990– (Dir, 1985–); White Waltham Airfield Ltd, 1992–. Chm., Landmark Trust, 1995–2001. *Recreations:* flying, farming. *Address:* Garden House, Cornwall Gardens, SW7 4BQ. *T:* (020) 7937 7559; Shottesbrooke Farm, White Waltham, Berks SL6 3SD. *T:* (01628) 822559; *e-mail:* b@rtysmith.com. *Clubs:* Pratt's, MCC; West London Aero (White Waltham).

SMITH, Beverley; *see* Smith, Jenkyn B.

SMITH, Sir Brian; *see* Smith, Sir E. B.

SMITH, Sir Brian; *see* Smith, Sir N. B.

SMITH, Brian, CMG 1993; OBE 1975; HM Diplomatic Service, retired; High Commissioner to Trinidad and Tobago, 1991–94; *b* 15 Sept. 1935; *s* of Charles Francis Smith and Grace Amelia (*née* Pope); *m* 1955, Joan Patricia Rivers; one *s* two *d*. *Educ:* Hull Grammar School; BSc Open Univ. 1994. Foreign Office, 1952; HM Forces, 1954–57; Bahrain, 1957; Doha, 1959; Vice-Consul, Luxembourg, 1960, Casablanca, 1962; Tehran, 1964; Berne, 1967; FCO, 1969; Kampala, 1973; Tehran, 1975; FCO, 1977; New York, 1979; Counsellor (Commercial), Bonn, 1982; Overseas Inspector, FCO, 1986; High Comr, Botswana, 1989. *Recreations:* riding, photography, music, handicrafts. *Address:* Bancroft, Castle Walk, Wadhurst, E Sussex TN5 6DB.

SMITH, Brian, CPFA; Chief Executive, Stoke on Trent City Council, since 1992; *b* 16 May 1947; *s* of Albert Frederick and Gladys Smith; *m* 1972, Susan Jane Lund; two *s*. *Educ:* Bristol Univ. (BA Hons). Graduate trainee accountant, Derbyshire CC, 1968; Accountancy Asst, Berkshire CC, 1972; Group Technical Officer, South Yorkshire CC, 1974; Asst County Treasurer, Dorset CC, 1976; Sen. Asst County Treasurer, Avon CC, 1979; Dep. County Treasurer, 1981, County Treasurer, 1983, Staffordshire CC. Hon. Sec., Soc. of County Treasurers, 1990–92; Pres., CIPFA, 1999–2000 (Vice-Pres., 1998–99). *Publications:* various articles in local govt finance jls. *Recreations:* music, gardening, travel. *T:* (office) (01782) 232602.

SMITH, Rt Rev. Brian Arthur; *see* Edinburgh, Bishop of.

SMITH, Brian Stanley, FSA, FRHistS; Secretary, Royal Commission on Historical Manuscripts, 1982–92; *b* 15 May 1932; *s* of late Ernest Stanley Smith and Dorothy (*née* Palmer); *m* 1963, Alison Margaret Hemming; two *d*. *Educ:* Bloxham; Keble College, Oxford (Holroyd Scholar). MA 1957. FSA 1972, FRHistS 1980. Archivist, Worcestershire, 1956–58, Essex, 1958–60, Gloucestershire, 1961–68; County Archivist, Gloucestershire, 1968–79; Asst Sec., Royal Commn on Historical Manuscripts, 1980–81. Part-time Editor, Victoria County History of Gloucestershire, 1968–70; Editor, Bristol and Gloucestershire Archaeological Soc., 1971–79 (Pres., 1986–87). Chm., Soc. of Archivists, 1979–80; Vice Pres., British Records Assoc., 1993–. Lay Mem., Gloucester Diocesan Synod, 1972–76. FRSA 1991. *Publications:* History of Malvern, 1964, 2nd edn 1978; (with Elizabeth Ralph) History of Bristol and Gloucestershire, 1972, 3rd edn 1996; The Cotswolds, 1976, 2nd edn 1992; History of Bloxham School, 1978; Manuscript Sources for the History of St Helena, 1996; articles in learned jls on local history and archives. *Recreations:* mountaineering, gardening, historical research. *Address:* Bryn Farm, Vowchurch Common, Hereford HR2 0RL.

SMITH, Maj.-Gen. Sir Brian W.; *see* Wyldbore-Smith.

SMITH, Brian William, AO 1988; PhD, FIEAust; Chairman of Board, Unisuper Ltd, since 1994; Vice-Chancellor and Professor, University of Western Sydney, 1989–94; *b* 24 June 1938; *s* of William Lyle Smith and Grace Ellen Smith; *m* 1961, Josephine Peden; two *d* (one *s* decd). *Educ:* Univ. of Melbourne (BEng); Univ. of Cambridge (PhD). Australian Paper Manufacturers Ltd, 1964–70; Consolidated Electronic Industries Ltd, 1971–73; Head, School of Electrical Engineering, 1973–77, Dean, Faculty of Engineering, 1977–79, Dir, 1979–89, Royal Melbourne Inst. of Technology. Chm. Bd, Cooperative Res. Centre for Intelligent Manufg Systems and Technologies, 1995–. Hon. LLD Hong Kong Baptist Univ., 1999. *Recreations:* classical guitar, golf, model railway. *Address:* 60 Faraday Street, Carlton, Vic 3053, Australia. *Clubs:* Greenacres Golf, Melbourne Cricket.

SMITH, Dr Bruce Gordon, CBE 1999 (OBE 1992); FREng, FIEE; Chairman, Smith Institute for Industrial Mathematics and System Engineering, since 1993; *b* 4 Oct. 1939; *s* of William Francis Smith and Georgina Lucy May Smith (*née* Tompkins); *m* 1964, Rosemary Jane Martineau; two *s* two *d*. *Educ:* Dulwich Coll.; Christ Church, Oxford (BA 1st cl. Hons Physics 1961; DPhil 1964; MA 1968). FIEE 1978 (MIEE 1971); FREng (FEng 1998). Res. Associate, Univ. of Chicago, 1964–65; mem., tech. staff, Bellcomm Inc., 1965–68; Prin. Engr, Decca Radar Ltd, 1968–71; Man. Dir, 1971–87, Chm., 1987–97, Smith System Engineering Ltd; Chm., Industrial Technology Securities Ltd,

1995– (Dir, 1985–95); Director: Gordon and Co., 1996–; British Maritime Technology Ltd, 1996–99; Southampton Innovations Ltd, 1998–; Esys Ltd, 1999–2001. Domus Fellow, St Catherine's Coll., Oxford, 1991–. Chm., ESRC, 1994–2001; Member: Plenary Bd, RAE, 1987–91; BNSC Earth Observation Prog. Bd, 1986– (Chm., 1998–); Exec. Cttee, Parly Space Cttee, 1989–97; Industrial R&D Adv. Cttee, EC, 1996–99; Chm., UK Industrial Space Cttee, 1992–94. Chm., Eur. Assoc. of Remote Sensing Cos, 1987–91 (Treas., British Assoc., 1985–95); Pres., Assoc. of Indep. Res. and Technol. Orgns, 1991–93; UK Deleg. and Pres., Eur. Assoc. of Contract Res. Orgns, 1995–97; Member: Council, SBAC, 1992–94; Dir's Cttee, British Antarctic Soc., 2001–. Chm., Nat. Space Sci. Centre, 1997–. Vice-Chm., Surrey Br., Prince's Youth Business Trust, 1991–. Mem. Council, Southampton Univ., 2000–; Gov., ICSTM, 1999–. Hon. DSc Leicester, 2001. *Recreations:* mountain walking, dinghy sailing, cycling, music. *Address:* 11 Oxdowne Close, Cobham, Surrey KT11 2SZ. *T:* (01372) 843526. *Club:* Athenæum.

SMITH, Bryan Crossley, CBE 1982; CEng, FIGasE; Member for Marketing, British Gas Corporation, 1977–82; Chairman: C.S.E. (Wendover) Ltd, Business Consultants, since 1981; Sports & Fitness Assessment Ltd, since 1985; Turbine Power Ltd (formerly Power Generation), since 1988; *b* 28 Feb. 1925; *s* of Frank Riley Smith and Fanny Smith; *m* 1948, Patricia Mabbott; one *s* one *d*. *Educ:* Hipperholme Grammar Sch.; Bradford Technical Coll. CEng, FIGasE 1944. Articled pupil to John Corrigan, 1941; Operating Engr, Humphreys & Glasgow, 1944; Works Engr, Middlesbrough Corp. Gas Dept, 1948; N Eastern Gas Board: Asst Works Manager, Huddersfield, 1952; Engr and Man., Dewsbury, 1956; Group Sales Man., Wakefield, 1961; Conversion Man., 1966; Dep. Commercial Man., 1968; Chief Service Man., Gas Council, 1970; Service Dir, British Gas Corp., 1973. Senior Vice-Pres., IGasE, 1980–81. Chm., Wendover Soc., 1985–. *Recreations:* golf, gardening. *Address:* Heron Path House, Wendover, Aylesbury, Bucks HP22 6NN. *T:* (01296) 622742.

SMITH, Catharine Mary S.; *see* Scott-Smith.

SMITH, Sheriff Charles; Sheriff of Tayside, Central and Fife at Cupar and Dundee, 1991–97; a Temporary Sheriff, since 1997; *b* 15 Aug. 1930; *s* of late Charles Smith and Mary Allan Hunter or Smith; *m* 1959, Janet Elizabeth Hurst; one *s* one *d*. *Educ:* Kinnoull Primary Sch.; Perth Academy; St Andrews University. MA, LLB. Solicitor 1956. Practised as principal with Campbell Brooke and Myles, Perth, 1961–82; Interim Depute Procurator Fiscal, 1975–82; Temporary Sheriff, 1977–82; Sheriff (floating appointment): of Glasgow and Strathkelvin, 1982–86; of Tayside, Central and Fife at Perth, 1986–91. Tutor, 1979–82, Hon. Tutor, 1982–86, Dept of Law, Dundee Univ. Member Council: Law Soc. of Scotland, 1977–82 (Convener, various cttees); Sheriffs' Assoc., 1987–90. Mem., Perth Town Council, 1966–68. *Recreations:* tennis, golf, croquet. *Address:* c/o Brodies, WS, 15 Atholl Crescent, Edinburgh EH3 8HA. *T:* (0131) 228 3777. *Clubs:* Western (Glasgow); Kinnoull Lawn Tennis.

SMITH, Sir Charles B.; *see* Bracewell-Smith.

SMITH, Charles M.; *see* Miller Smith.

SMITH, Charles Robert S.; *see* Saumarez Smith.

SMITH, (Charles) Russell, CBE 1984; Chairman, Allied Textile Companies PLC, 1983–91 (Chief Executive, 1963–86); Director, Lloyds Bank plc, 1985–95 (Regional Chairman, Yorkshire and Humberside, 1984–91; Regional Director, 1973–91); *b* 19 Aug. 1925; *m* 1951, Jean Rita Thomas; one *s* three *d*. *Educ:* Rastrick Grammar Sch., Brighouse, W Yorks. Served War, RNVR, 1943–46 (commnd). Armitage and Norton, Chartered Accountants, Huddersfield, 1941–50; Dir, subseq. Man. Dir, R. Beanland and Co. Ltd, 1950–63. Director: Yorkshire Bank PLC, 1978–84; Lloyds Bank UK Management Ltd, 1984–85; Lloyds & Scottish PLC, 1985–86; Lloyds Abbey Life PLC (formerly Abbey Life Gp), 1988–96; Lloyds Merchant Bank (Hldgs) Ltd, 1989–93; Heywood Williams Gp, 1990–96. Pres., British Textile Confedn, 1982 and 1983; Chm., Wakefield Diocesan Bd of Finance, 1974–90; Mem., Yorks and Humberside Regional Develt Bd, 1975–79. *Recreations:* too few. *Address:* Tabara, 12 Wheatcroft Avenue, Scarborough, North Yorks YO11 3BN. *T:* (01723) 376266.

SMITH, Christopher Brian P.; *see* Powell-Smith.

SMITH, Rev. Christopher Hughes; Supernumerary Methodist Minister; President of the Methodist Conference, 1985–86; *b* 30 Nov. 1929; *s* of Rev. Bernard Hughes Smith and Dorothy Lucy Smith; *m* 1956, Margaret Jean Smith; three *s* and one foster *s*. *Educ:* Bolton School; Emmanuel College and Wesley House, Cambridge. MA Cantab. Intercollegiate Sec., SCM, 1955–58; ordained at Methodist Conf., Newcastle upon Tyne, 1958; Leicester South Methodist Circuit, 1958–65; Birmingham South-West Methodist Circuit, 1965–74; Chm., Birmingham Methodist Dist, 1974–87; Lancaster Methodist Circuit, 1987–88; Gen. Sec., Div. of Educn and Youth, Methodist Ch, 1988–95. Pres., Nat. Christian Educn Council, 1995–99. Mem. Court, Univ. of Surrey, Roehampton, 2000. Hon. Fellow: Selly Oak Colls, 1992; Roehampton Inst., 1997. Hon. MA Birmingham, 1985. *Publications:* Music of the Heart—Methodist Spirituality, 1991; (contrib.) A Dictionary of Methodism, 2000; contribs to Methodist Recorder, Epworth Review. *Recreations:* gardening, music, books, walking. *Address:* 12 Spean Court, Wollaton Road, Nottingham NG8 1GL.

SMITH, Rt Hon. Christopher (Robert); PC 1997; PhD; MP (Lab) Islington South and Finsbury, since 1983; *b* 24 July 1951; *s* of Colin Smith and Gladys (*née* Luscombe). *Educ:* Cassiobury Primary Sch., Watford; George Watson's Coll., Edinburgh; Pembroke Coll., Cambridge Univ. (BA 1st Cl. Hons 1972, PhD 1979); Harvard Univ., Mass (Kennedy Scholar, 1975–76). Develt Sec., Shaftesbury Soc. Housing Assoc., 1977–80; Develt Co-ordinator, Soc. for Co-operative Dwellings, 1980–83. Councillor, London Bor. of Islington, 1978–83 (Chief Whip, 1978–79; Chm., Housing Cttee, 1981–83). Opposition spokesman on treasury and economic affairs, 1987–92; principal opposition spokesman on environmental protection, 1992–94, on Nat. Heritage, 1994–95, on social security, 1995–96, on health, 1996–97; Sec. of State for Culture, Media and Sport, and Chm., Millennium Commn, 1997–2001; Chairman: Tribune Gp of MPs, 1988–89 (Sec., 1985–88); Labour Campaign for Criminal Justice, 1985–88; Bd, Tribune Newspaper, 1990–93; Bd, New Century Magazine, 1993–96; Pres., Socialist Envmt and Resources Assoc., 1992–; Mem. Exec., Fabian Soc., 1990–97 (Chm., 1996–97). Pres., Cambridge Union, 1972; Vice-Chm., Young Fabian Gp, 1974–75; Chm., Charing Cross Br., ASTMS, 1980–83; Member: Exec., NCCL, 1986–88; Bd, Shelter, 1986–92; Exec. Cttee, Nat. Trust, 1995–97. Governor, Sadler's Wells Theatre, 1987–97; Trustee, John Muir Trust, 1991–97. Hon. FRIBA 2000. *Publication:* Creative Britain, 1998. *Recreations:* mountaineering, literature, theatre, music. *Address:* House of Commons, SW1A 0AA. *T:* (020) 7219 5119.

SMITH, Sir Christopher Sydney Winwood, 5th Bt *cr* 1809; *b* 20 Sept. 1906; *s* of Sir William Sydney Winwood Smith, 4th Bt, and Caroline, *o d* of James Harris, County Cork; *S* father, 1953; *m* 1932, Phyllis Berenice, *y d* of late Thomas Robert O'Grady, Grafton, New South Wales, and County Waterford, Ireland; six *s* three *d* (and one *s* decd). *Heir: s* Robert Christopher Sydney Winwood Smith [*b* 1939; *m* 1971, Roslyn Nellie, *e d* of late James Keith McKensie; one *s* one *d*]. *Address:* Junction Road, via Grafton, New South Wales 2460, Australia.

SMITH, Clifford Bertram Bruce H.; *see* Heathcote-Smith.

SMITH, Colin Deverell; Chairman, Blue Heath Direct, since 2000; *b* 21 May 1947; *m* 1971, Kathy Morgan; two *s*. *Educ:* All Saints Sch., Bloxham, Banbury; Liverpool Univ. (BCom 1969). FCA 1973. Qualified with Arthur Andersen, Manchester; Argyll Foods: Gp Financial Controller and Co. Sec., 1979–83; Argyll Gp, subseq. Safeway plc: Gp Financial Controller and Co. Sec., 1983–84; Dir, 1984–99; Finance Dir, 1989–93; Gp Chief Exec., 1993–99. Trustee: Nat. Grocers' Benevolent Fund, 2000– (Pres., 1999–2000); SCF, 2001–. *Recreations:* theatre, walking, Rugby, interesting vehicles. *Address:* Pyes, Penn Road, Knotty Green, Beaconsfield, Bucks HP9 2TS. *T:* (01494) 675840.

SMITH, Prof. Colin John, CBE 1997; Professor of Oral Pathology, since 1973, and Deputy Dean, Faculty of Medicine, since 2000, Sheffield University (Dean of Dental Studies, School of Clinical Dentistry, 1978–84 and 1988–2000); *b* 7 June 1938; *s* of Rowland William John Smith and Doris Emily Smith; *m* 1st, 1962, Mary Margaret Kathrine MacMahon (marr. diss. 1995); three *d*; 2nd, 1995, Eunice Turner (*née* Acaster). *Educ:* Purley County Grammar Sch. for Boys; Royal Dental Hosp. Sch. of Dental Surgery, Univ. of London (BDS Hons, PhD). FDSRCS, FRCPath. House Surgeon, Royal Dental Hosp., 1961–62; MRC Scientific Asst, 1962–63, Prophit Cancer Res. Student, 1964–68, Dept of Dental Sci., RCS; Wellcome Travelling Res. Fellow, Dept of Oral Path., Royal Dental Coll., Copenhagen, 1968–69; Nuffield Dental Res. Fellow, Dept of Morbid Anatomy, RPMS, 1969–71; Sen. Lectr and Res. Fellow, Dept of Oral Medicine and Path., Guy's Hosp. Dental Sch., 1971–72; Dir, Charles Clifford Dental Hosp., Central Sheffield Univ. Hosps NHS Trust, 1998–2001. Charles Tomes Lectr, RCS, 1987. Member: GDC, 1979–84, 1994– (Chm., Dental Auxiliaries Cttee, 1999–); Nuffield Foundn Cttee of Inquiry into Dental Educn, 1978–80; Nuffield Foundn Cttee of Inquiry into Educn and Trng of Personnel Auxiliary to Dentistry, 1992–93; MRC Dental Cttee, 1973–84 (Scientific Sec., 1975–84) and Physiological Systems and Disorders Bd, 1988–92; MRC/DHSS/SERC Joint Dental Cttee, 1988–93 (Vice-Chm.); Council, Odontological Sect., RSocMed, 1973–76 and 1989–92 (Pres., 1990–91); Dental Educn Adv. Council, 1978– (Hon. Sec., 1985–90; Chm., 1990–92); British Soc. for Oral Pathology, 1975– (Pres., 1980–81); Internat. Assoc. of Oral Pathologists, 1983– (Mem. Council, 1988–; Pres., 2000–Aug. 2002); Assoc. for Dental Educn in Europe, 1982– (Sec. Gen., 1984–87; Editor, 1989–92); Internat. Assoc. for Dental Res., 1963– (Internat. Relns Cttee, 1982–84; Ethics Cttee, 1992–95); UGC Dental Sub-Cttee, 1985–89; UGC Dental Review Working Party, 1986–88; UFC Medical Cttee, 1989–92; British Council Medical Adv. Cttee, 1985–91; Standing Dental Adv. Cttee, 1992–96; Clinical Standards Adv. Gp, 1995–99; CVCP Task Force on Clin. Acad. Careers, 1996–98; WHO Expert Adv. Panel on Oral Health, 1989–98. Ed.-in-chief, Jl of Oral Pathology and Medicine, 1993–99. Hon. Mem., Hungarian Dental Assoc., 1991. Founder FMedSci 1998. Colgate Prize, British Div., Internat. Assoc. for Dental Res., 1964. *Publications:* (jtly) Oral Cancer: epidemiology, etiology and pathology, 1990; (jtly) Histological typing of cancer and precancer of the oral mucosa, 1997; chapters in books and contribs to professional jls. *Recreations:* lawn tennis, walking, gardening, listening to classical music, theatre. *Address:* Department of Oral Pathology, School of Clinical Dentistry, The University, Claremont Crescent, Sheffield S10 2TA; 138 Townhead Road, Dore, Sheffield S17 3AQ. *T:* (0114) 235 3345. *Club:* Royal Society of Medicine.

SMITH, Colin Milner; QC 1985; **His Honour Judge Colin Smith;** a Circuit Judge, since 1991; *b* 2 Nov. 1936; *s* of Alan Milner Smith and late Vera Ivy Smith; *m* 1979, Moira Soraya, *d* of Reginald Braybrooke; one *s* one *d*. *Educ:* Tonbridge; Brasenose College, Oxford (MA); Univ. of Chicago (JD). Called to the Bar, Gray's Inn, 1962; a Recorder, 1987–91. *Publication:* (jtly) The Law of Betting, Gaming and Lotteries, 1987. *Recreations:* cricket, skiing, reading. *Club:* MCC.

SMITH, Colin Roderick, CVO 1984; CBE 1995; QPM 1987; HM Inspector of Constabulary, 1991–2000; *s* of Humphrey and Marie Smith; *m* 1961, Patricia Joan Coppin. *Educ:* Dorking County and Bexhill Grammar Schools; Univ. of Birmingham (BSocSc, Hons Social Admin.); rcds 1981. Royal Army Service Corps (Lieut), 18 Co. (Amph), 1959–62; East Sussex Constabulary, later Sussex Police, from Constable to Chief Supt, 1962–77; Asst Chief Constable, Thames Valley Police, 1977–82; Dep. Asst Comr, Metropolitan Police, 1982–85 (incl. founder, Royalty and Diplomatic Protection Dept); Chief Constable, Thames Valley Police, 1985–91. *Recreation:* horse riding. *Club:* Royal Automobile.

SMITH, Sir Colin S.; *see* Stansfield Smith.

SMITH, Sir Cyril, Kt 1988; MBE 1966; DL; Managing Director, Smith Springs (Rochdale) Ltd, 1963–87; *b* 28 June 1928; unmarried. *Educ:* Rochdale Grammar Sch. for Boys. Civil Service, 1944–45; Wages Clerk, 1945–48; Liberal Party Agent, Stockport, 1948–50; Labour Party Agent, Ashton-under-Lyne, 1950–53, Heywood and Royton 1953–55; rejoined Liberal Party, 1967; MP Rochdale, Oct. 1972–1992 (L, 1972–88, Lib Dem, 1988–92); Liberal Chief Whip, 1975–76. Newsagent (own account), 1955–58; Production Controller, Spring Manufacturing, 1958–63; founded Smith Springs (Rochdale) Ltd, 1963. Director: Ratcliffe Springs, 1987–90; Robert Riley Springs. Councillor, 1952–66, Alderman, 1966–74, Mayor, 1966–67, Co. Borough of Rochdale (Chm., Education Cttee, 1966–72); Councillor, Rochdale Metropolitan DC, 1973–75. A Dep. Pro-Chancellor, Lancaster Univ., 1978–86. Co. Pres., Greater Manchester N Scouts, 1993–98. Freeman, Borough of Rochdale, 1992. DL Greater Manchester, 1991. Hon. LLD Lancaster, 1993; Hon. DEd Manchester Metropolitan, 1996. OStJ 1976. *Publications:* Big Cyril (autobiog.), 1977; Industrial Participation, 1977. *Recreations:* music (listener), reading, charitable work, local government. *Address:* 14 Emma Street, Rochdale, Lancs OL12 6QW. *T:* (01706) 648840.

SMITH, Cyril Stanley, CBE 1985; MSc, PhD; Secretary to Economic and Social Research Council (formerly Social Science Research Council), 1975–85; *b* 21 July 1925; *s* of Walter and Beatrice May Smith; *m* 1968, Eileen Cameron; two *d* (by first marr.). *Educ:* Plaistow Municipal Secondary Sch.; London Sch. of Economics. HM Forces, Dorset Regt, 1943–47. Univ. of Birmingham, 1950–51; Univ. of Sheffield, 1951–52; Dulwich Coll. Mission, 1952–56; Nat. Coal Board, 1956–61; Univ. of Manchester, 1961–71; Civil Service Coll., 1971–75. Man. Dir, ReStrat, 1985–90. Visiting Prof., Univ. of Virginia, 1965; Academic Visitor, Nuffield Coll., Oxford, 1980–81, 1985–86; Senior Res. Fellow, Wissenschaftszentrum Berlin für Sozialforschung, 1987. British Nat. Expert, European Poverty Prog., 1977–82. Mem., Sec. of State's Cttee on Inequalities in Health, DHSS, 1977–80. Chm., British Sociological Assoc., 1972–74; Pres., Sociol. Sect., British Assoc., 1979. *Publications:* Adolescence, 1968; (sen. author) The Wincroft Youth Project, 1972;

(ed jtly) Society and Leisure in Britain, 1973; numerous articles on youth, leisure and developments in social science.

SMITH, Prof. David; *see* Smith, Prof. A. D.

SMITH, Prof. David; *see* Smith, Prof. N. J. D.

SMITH, David, PhD; FInstPet; consultant; Director, Hampshire Technology Centre, since 1990; formerly Chairman and Managing Director, Esso Chemical Ltd; *b* 18 July 1927; *s* of Walter and Annie Smith; *m* 1951, Nancy Elizabeth (*née* Hawley) (*d* 1999); two *s* three *d*. *Educ:* Burton Grammar School; Univ. of Sheffield. BSc, PhD. Lectr in Fuel Technology and Chemical Engineering, Univ. of Sheffield, 1951–55; Esso Research Ltd, 1955–65; Dir, Products Research Div., Esso Research and Engineering, USA, 1966–68; Marketing Dir and Man. Dir, Esso Chemical Ltd, 1968–71; Vice-Pres., Essochem Europe Inc., Brussels, 1971–73; Vice-Pres., Exxon Chemical Inc., USA, 1973–78. Chm., Assoc. of Hampshire Chambers of Commerce, 1995–97. Chm. Govs, Southampton Inst., 1989–97. *Recreation:* golf. *Address:* Meadowlands, Stockbridge Road, Winchester, Hants SO22 5JH. *T:* (01962) 864880. *Clubs:* MCC; Royal Winchester Golf.

SMITH, Prof. David, FRS 1988; CPhys, FInstP; Chief Scientist, PDZ Europa, since 1999; Professor, Department of Biomedical Engineering and Medical Physics, University of Keele, since 1999 (Visiting Professor, 1995–99); *b* 26 Nov. 1935; *s* of J. and F. L. Smith. *Educ:* Keele Univ. (BA 1959); DSc 1975, PhD 1962, Birmingham Univ. FInstP 1973. Res. Fellow, 1962, Prof. of Chemical Physics, 1984–90, Birmingham Univ.; Prof. of Physics, Institut für Ionenphysik der Universität Innsbruck, Austria, 1991–95. Hon. DSc Keele, 1990. *Publications:* numerous res. pubns and review articles in physics, chemistry and astrophysics, for learned jls incl. British Inst. of Physics jls and Amer. Inst. of Physics jls. *Recreations:* classical music, sport. *Address:* 9 The Elms, Porthill, Newcastle-under-Lyme, Staffs ST5 8RP; Department of Biomedical Engineering and Medical Physics, University of Keele, Thornburrow Drive, Hartshill, Stoke-on-Trent, Staffs ST4 7QB.

SMITH, David Arthur; QC 1982; **His Honour Judge David Smith;** a Circuit Judge, since 1986; *b* 7 May 1938; *s* of late Arthur Heber Smith and Marjorie Edith Pounds Smith; *m* 1967, Clementine Smith, JP (*née* Urquhart); two *s*. *Educ:* Lancing College; Merton Coll., Oxford (MA Hons Jurisprudence). Called to Bar, Middle Temple, 1962; Official Principal of Archdeaconry of Hackney, 1973–; a Recorder, 1978–86. Mem., Parole Bd, 1989–94. Wine Treasurer, Western Circuit, 1980–86; Pres., Council of HM Circuit Judges, 2000 (Treas., 1991–98). *Publications:* John Evelyn's Manuscript on Bees from Elysium Britannicum, 1966; (jtly) Bibliography of British Bee Books, 1979; (with David Frimston) Beekeeping and the Law—Swarms and Neighbours, 1993. *Recreations:* acting (Mem., Old Stagers, 1982–), bees (Sec. of Internat. Bee Research Assoc., 1963–), books, canals, Rossini. *Address:* The Law Courts, Bristol BS1 1DA.

SMITH, David Arthur George, OBE 1996; JP; Headmaster of Bradford Grammar School, 1974–96; *b* 17 Dec. 1934; *o s* of Stanley George and Winifred Smith, Bath, Somerset; *m* 1957, Jennifer, *o d* of John and Rhoda Anning, Launceston, Cornwall; one *s* two *d*. *Educ:* City of Bath Boys' Sch.; Balliol Coll., Oxford. MA, Dip. Ed (Oxon). Assistant Master, Manchester Grammar Sch., 1957–62; Head of History, Rossall School, 1963–70; Headmaster, The King's School, Peterborough, 1970–74. Chm., HMC, 1988. Mem., Parole Bd, 1995–2001. JP West Yorks, 1975. *Publications:* (with John Thorn and Roger Lockyer) A History of England, 1961; Left and Right in Twentieth Century Europe, 1970; Russia of the Tsars, 1971. *Recreations:* writing, walking. *Clubs:* East India; Bradford Athenæum (Bradford).

SMITH, David Buchanan, FSAScot; Sheriff of North Strathclyde at Kilmarnock, since 1975; *b* 31 Oct. 1936; *s* of William Adam Smith and Irene Mary Calderwood Hogarth; *m* 1961, Hazel Mary Sinclair; one *s* one *d* (and one *s* decd). *Educ:* Paisley Grammar Sch.; Glasgow Univ. (MA); Edinburgh Univ. (LLB). Advocate, 1961; Standing Junior Counsel to Scottish Educn Dept, 1968–75. Tutor, Faculty of Law, Univ. of Edinburgh, 1964–72. Member Council: Stair Soc., 1994– (Vice Chm. Council, 1998–); Scottish Nat. Dictionary Assoc., 1994–; Sheriffs' Assoc., 1998–2001 (Treas., 1979–89; archivist, 1989–); Mem., Scottish Records Adv. Council. Trustee, The Scottish Curling Museum Trust, 1980–; Pres., Ayr Curling Club, 1995–96. *Publications:* Curling: an illustrated history, 1981; The Roaring Game: memories of Scottish curling, 1985; George Washington Wilson in Ayrshire, 1991; (contrib.) The Laws of Scotland: Stair Memorial Encyclopedia, vol. 6; (contrib.) Macphail, Sheriff Court Practice, 2nd edn 1999; (contrib.) Sport, Scotland and the Scots, 2000; articles in Scots Law Times, Juridical Rev., Jl of Law Soc. of Scotland, Scottish Book Collector, The Medal, Rev. of Scottish Culture, Scottish Curler, and newspapers. *Recreations:* history of the law and institutions of Scotland, curling, collecting curliana, music, architecture, grandchildren. *Address:* 72 South Beach, Troon, Ayrshire KA10 6EG. *T:* (01292) 312130; Sheriff's Chambers, Sheriff Court House, Kilmarnock KA1 1ED. *T:* (01563) 520211.

SMITH, David C.; *see* Calvert-Smith.

SMITH, Sir David (Cecil), Kt 1986; FRS 1975; FRSE; Principal and Vice-Chancellor, University of Edinburgh, 1987–93; President, Wolfson College, Oxford, 1994–2000; *b* 21 May 1930; *s* of William John Smith and Elva Emily Smith; *m* 1965, Lesley Margaret Mollison Mutch; two *s* one *d*. *Educ:* Colston's Sch., Bristol; St Paul's Sch., London; Queen's Coll., Oxford (Browne Schol., MA, DPhil; Hon. Fellow 2000). Christopher Welch Res. Schol., Oxford, 1951–54; Swedish Inst. Schol., Uppsala Univ., 1951–52; Browne Res. Fellow, Queen's Coll., Oxford, 1956–59; Harkness Fellow, Univ. Calif, Berkeley, 1959–60; Oxford University: Univ. Lectr, Dept Agric., 1960–74; Mem., Linacre Coll., 1962–64, Hon. Fellow, 1988; Royal Soc. Res. Fellow, 1964–71, Tutorial Fellow and Tutor for Admissions, 1971–74, Hon. Fellow, 1987, Wadham Coll.; Melville Wills Prof. of Botany, Bristol Univ., 1974–80; Sibthorpian Prof. of Rural Economy, and Fellow of St John's Coll., Oxford Univ., 1980–87. Vis. Prof., UCLA, 1968. Chairman: NERC Aquatic Life Scis Cttee, 1978–81; Member: AFRC (formerly ARC), 1982–88; Consultative Bd, JCO for Res. in Agric. and Food, 1981–83; SERC Science Board, 1983–85; Co-ordinating Cttee on Marine Sci. and Technology, 1987–91; ABRC, 1989–90; Commn on Scottish Educn, 1994–96. President: British Lichen Soc., 1972–74; British Mycological Soc., 1980; Soc. for Experimental Biol., 1983–85 (Vice-Pres., 1981–83); Internat. Soc. Endocytobiology, 1981–89; Scottish Assoc. for Marine Sci., 1994–2000; Linnean Soc., 2000–. Royal Society: a Vice-Pres., 1978–80, 1983–87; Biological Sec., 1983–87. Bidder Lecture, Soc. for Experimental Biology, 1985; Sir Joseph Banks Lectures, Australian bicentennial, 1988; L. F. Power Meml Lecture, James Cook Univ., 1988. Editor and Trustee, New Phytologist, 1965–. FRSE 1988. Hon. FRCPEd 1993; Hon. FRCSEd 1994. Hon. DSc: Liverpool, Exeter, 1986; Hull, 1987; Aberdeen, 1990; Napier, Heriot-Watt, 1993; Oxford Brookes, 1996; Hon. LLD: Pennsylvania, 1990; Queen's Univ., Ontario, 1991; Dr *hc* Edinburgh, 1994. Linnean Medal, Linnean Soc., 1989. Commendatore dell'Ordine al Merito della Repubblica Italiana, 1991; Comdr, Order of Merit, Republic of Poland, 1994. *Publications:* (with A. Douglas) The Biology of Symbiosis, 1987; various articles on symbiosis, in New Phytol., Proc. Royal Soc., Biol. Rev., etc. *Address:* 13 Abbotsford Park, Edinburgh EH10 5DZ. *Club:* Farmers'.

SMITH, David Douglas R.; *see* Rae Smith.

SMITH, David Grahame G.; *see* Grahame-Smith.

SMITH, Air Marshal Sir David H.; *see* Harcourt-Smith.

SMITH, David Henry; Economics Editor, since 1989, Policy Adviser, since 1995, Assistant Editor, since 1998, The Sunday Times; *b* 3 April 1954; *s* of Charles Henry Smith and Elizabeth Mary Smith (*née* Williams), Walsall; *m* 1980, Jane Howells, Tenby; two *s* two *d*. *Educ:* West Bromwich Grammar Sch.; UC Cardiff (BSc Econ 1st cl. hons; Tassie Medallion, 1975); Worcester Coll., Oxford; Birkbeck Coll., London (MSc Econ). Economic report writer, Lloyds Bank, 1976–77; economist, Henley Centre for Forecasting, 1977–79; economics and business writer, Now! magazine, 1979–81; Asst Editor, Financial Weekly, 1981–84; Economics Corresp., The Times, 1984–89. FRSA 1999. *Publications:* The Rise and Fall of Monetarism, 1987; Mrs Thatcher's Economics, 1988; North and South, 1989, 2nd edn 1994; From Boom to Bust, 1992, 2nd edn 1993; Mrs Thatcher's Economics: her legacy, 1992; UK Current Economic Policy, 1994, 2nd edn 1999; Job Insecurity *vs* Labour Market Flexibility, 1996; Eurofutures, 1997; Will Europe Work?, 1999; (ed) Welfare, Work and Poverty, 2000. *Recreations:* squash, golf, music. *Address:* 1 Pennington Street, E1 9XW. *T:* (020) 7782 5750; *e-mail:* dhsmith@economicsUK.com. *Club:* Bexley Lawn Tennis and Squash.

SMITH, Sir David (Iser), KCVO 1990 (CVO 1977); AO 1986; BA; Director, Winston Churchill Memorial Trust, since 1999; Official Secretary to the Governor-General of Australia, 1973–90; Secretary of the Order of Australia, 1975–90; *b* 9 Aug. 1933; *s* of late W. M. Smith; *m* 1955, June F., *d* of M. A. W. Forestier; three *s*. *Educ:* Scotch Coll., Melbourne; Melbourne Univ.; Australian National Univ., Canberra (BA). Commnd CMF, Melb. Univ. Regt, 1956. Entered Aust. Public Service, 1954; Dept of Customs and Excise, Melb., 1954–57; Trng Officer, Dept of the Interior, Canberra, 1957–58; Private Sec. to Minister for the Interior and Minister for Works, 1958–63; Exec. Asst to Sec., Dept of the Interior, 1963–66; Exec. Officer (Govt), Dept of the Interior, 1966–69; Sen. Adviser, Govt Br., Prime Minister's Dept, 1969–71; Sec., Federal Exec. Council, 1971–73; Asst Sec., Govt Br., Dept of the Prime Minister and Cabinet, 1972–73. Attached to The Queen's Household, Buckingham Palace, June-July 1975. Director: FAI Life Insurance Soc. Ltd, 1991–96; FAI Life Ltd, 1991–96. Australian National University: Vis. Fellow in Pol Sci., Res. Sch. of Social Scis, 1991–92; Vis. Fellow, 1998–99, Vis. Scholar, 2000–01, Faculty of Law. Dir, Canberra Symphony Orch., 1976–96 (Chm., 1991–93). Dir, Nat. Heart Foundn of Aust., 1991–97. Vice-Pres., Scout Assoc. of Australia, 1991–99 (Dist Comr, Capital Hill Dist, 1971–74). KStJ 1991 (CStJ 1974). *Recreations:* music, reading. *Address:* 1/36 Shackleton Circuit, Mawson, ACT 2607, Australia. *T:* (2) 62865094. *Club:* Commonwealth (Canberra).

SMITH, Rt Rev. David James; *see* Bradford, Bishop of.

SMITH, David John Harry, CBE 1998; PhD; FRSC; Chief Executive Officer, since 1996, Board Member, since 1995, and Director, Research and Development, since 1994, Whatman plc; *b* 5 Aug. 1941; *s* of Harry Nelson Smith and Mabel Freda Smith (*née* Stanford); *m* 1963, Dorothy Patricia Evans; one *s* one *d*. *Educ:* Univ. of Aston (BSc Chem. 1963); Univ of Western Ontario (PhD Organic Chem. 1967). FRSC 1982. Univ. Lectr, Chem. Dept, Univ. of Leicester, 1969–80; Res. Dir, Biosynth AG, Zürich, 1978–82; joined BP, 1980; Vice-Pres., R&D, BP America, 1987; Head, BP Gp Res. and Engrg, 1992. Member: Strategic Allocations Cttee, Nat. Sci. and Engrg Council, Canada, 1993–96; Technology Foresight Steering Cttee, 1994–96; EPSRC, 1994–2000; Chm., LINK TCS (formerly LINK) Bd, 1996–. *Publications:* numerous scientific papers and patents. *Recreations:* educating palate, golf. *Address:* Whatman House, St Leonard's Road, 20/20 Maidstone, Kent ME16 0LS. *T:* (01622) 676670.

SMITH, David John Leslie, PhD; CEng, FRAeS; Director of Group Services, Defence Research Agency, 1991–94; *b* 8 Oct. 1938; *s* of Gertrude Mary and late Arthur George Smith; *m* 1962, Wendy Lavinia (*née* Smith); two *d*. *Educ:* Cinderford Tech. Coll.; N Glos Tech. Coll.; Coll. of Aeronautics (MSc); Univ. of London; rcds. Mech. Engrg Apprentice, Rotol Ltd, 1954–59; Nat. Gas Turbine Estabt, Min. of Aviation, 1961, Head of Turbomachinery Dept, 1973; RCDS 1979; Ministry of Defence (PE): Dir, Aircraft Mech. and Elect. Equipment, Controllerate of Aircraft, 1980–81; Head of Aero. Dept, RAE, 1981–84; Dep. Dir (Marine Technology), 1984–85, Dep. Dir (Planning), 1986–87, ARE; Hd, Defence Res. Study Team, MoD, 1988; Asst Under-Sec. of State (Civilian Management) (Specialists), MoD, 1988–91. *Publications:* contribs to learned jls on gas turbine technology and fluid mechanics. *Recreations:* garden (including exhibiting flowers), oil and watercolour painting. *Address:* Michaelchurch Court, St Owens Cross, Hereford, Herefordshire HR2 8LD.

SMITH, David S.; *see* Sands Smith.

SMITH, Dame Dela, DBE 2001; Headteacher, Beaumont Hill Technology College, Primary School and Information, Communication and Technology Centre (formerly Beaumont Hill Special Educational Needs Centre), since 1997; *b* 10 Oct. 1952; *d* of John Henthorne Wood and Norah Wood (*née* Reid); *m* 1976, Colin Smith. *Educ:* schs in York, Bristol and Cambridge; Durham Univ. (AdvDip); Middleton St George Coll. (Cert Ed). Teacher, Dinsdale Park Residential Sch., nr Darlington, 1975–84; Dep. Head Teacher, 1984, Headteacher, 1985–97, Mayfair Special Sch. (Severe Learning Difficulties). *Recreations:* leisure pursuits, caravanning, walking, ski-ing, reading. *Address:* 20 West Green, Heighington, Co. Durham DL5 6RA. *T:* (01325) 314905.

SMITH, Delia, OBE 1995; cookery writer and broadcaster; *m* Michael Wynn Jones. Several BBC TV series; cookery writer, Evening Standard, later the Standard, 1972–85; columnist, Radio Times. Dir, Norwich City FC, 1996–. Hon. Fellow, Liverpool John Moores, 2000; Hon. DLitt: Nottingham, 1996; UEA, 1999. Is a Roman Catholic. *Publications:* How to Cheat at Cooking, 1971; Country Fare, 1973; Recipes from Country Inns and Restaurants, 1973; Family Fare, book 1, 1973, book 2, 1974; Evening Standard Cook Book, 1974; Country recipes from "Look East", 1975; More Country Recipes from "Look East", 1976; Frugal Food, 1976; Book of Cakes, 1977; Recipes from "Look East", 1977; Food for our Times, 1978; Cookery Course, part 1, 1978, part 2, 1979, part 3, 1981, The Complete Cookery Course, 1982; A Feast for Lent, 1983; A Feast for Advent, 1983; One is Fun, 1985; (ed) Food Aid Cookery Book, 1986; A Journey into God, 1988; Delia Smith's Christmas, 1990; Delia Smith's Summer Collection, 1993; Delia Smith's Winter Collection, 1995; Delia's Red Nose Collection, 1997; Delia's How to Cook, Book One, 1998, Book Two, 1999. *Address:* c/o New Crane Publishing, 20 Upper Ground, SE1 9PD.

SMITH, Denis M.; *see* Mack Smith.

SMITH, Derek; Chief Executive, Hammersmith Hospitals NHS Trust, since 2001; *b* 26 Sept. 1948; *s* of Arthur Edmund Smith and Hazel Smith (*née* Proudlove); *m* 1970, Carol Anne Susan Cunio; one *s* one *d*. *Educ:* Univ. of Wales (BSc Hons Econs); Univ. of Strathclyde (Postgrad. Dip. in Russian Lang.). Gen. Manager, Frenchay Hosp., 1982–87; Dist Gen. Manager, S Beds HA, 1987–90; Chief Exec., King's Healthcare NHS Trust, 1990–99; Man. Dir, London Underground Ltd, 1999–2001. Vis. Hon. Prof. in Strategic Mgt, Univ. of N London, 1994–; Vis. Lectr, Sch. of Econs, Univ. of Stockholm, 1995–98. *Recreations:* squash rackets, music, sailing, golf. *Address:* Hammersmith Hospital, Du Cane Road, W12 0HS.

SMITH, Derek B.; *see* Bryce-Smith.

SMITH, Derek Cyril; Under-Secretary, Export Credits Guarantee Department, 1974–87, retired; *b* 29 Jan. 1927; *s* of Albert Cyril and Edith Mary Elizabeth Smith; *m* 1st, 1949, Ursula Kulich (marr. diss. 1967); two *d*; 2nd, 1967, Nina Munday; one *s*. *Educ:* Pinner Grammar Sch.; St Catherine's Soc., Oxford. BA Mod. History 1951. Asst Principal, Min. of Materials, 1952–55; BoT, 1955–57: Asst Private Sec., Minister of State; Private Sec., Parly Sec.; Principal, ECGD, 1958–67; Asst Sec., BoT and DTI, 1967–72: Sec. to Lord Cromer's Survey of Capital Projects Contracting Overseas; Asst Sec., ECGD, 1972–74. *Recreations:* walking, reading, model-building.

SMITH, Derek Edward H.; *see* Hill-Smith.

SMITH, Derek Frank; Alternate Executive Director of the World Bank, and Counsellor (Overseas Develt), Washington, 1979–84; *b* 11 Feb. 1929; *s* of late Frank H. and Rose V. Smith; *m* 1954, Anne Carpenter; one *s* one *d*. *Educ:* Chatham House Sch., Ramsgate. Served RAF, 1947–49. Colonial Office, 1949–66: Sec., Develt and Welfare Org. in WI, 1956–58; transf. to Min. of Overseas Develt, 1966; Financial Adviser, British Develt Div. in the Caribbean, 1966–68; Principal, India Sect., ODA, 1968–72; Asst Sec., 1972; Head of Southern African Develt Div., 1972–75; Establishment Officer, 1976–78, Head of UN Dept B, 1978–79, ODA. Consultant: ODA, 1985; World Bank, 1986–87. Chairman: Sevenoaks Area NT Association, 1992–96; Probus Club, Sevenoaks, 1997–98. *Address:* 3 The Close, Montreal Park, Sevenoaks, Kent TN13 2HE. *T:* (01732) 452534.

SMITH, Desmond; *see* Smith, S. D.

SMITH, Dick K.; *see* King-Smith.

SMITH, Ven. Donald John; Archdeacon of Sudbury, 1984–91, Emeritus, since 1991; Hon. Canon of St Edmundsbury and Ipswich, 1973–91, Emeritus, since 1991; *b* 10 April 1926; *m* 1948, Violet Olive Goss; two *s* (one *d* decd). *Educ:* Clifton Theological Coll.; Cardiff Law Sch., Univ. of Wales (LLM 1996). Deacon, 1953; priest, 1954; Assistant Curate: Edgware, 1953–56; St Margaret's, Ipswich, 1956–58; Vicar of St Mary, Hornsey Rise, Islington, 1958–62; Rector of Whitton, Ipswich, 1962–75; Rector of Redgrave cum Botesdale with The Rickinghalls, 1975–79; Archdeacon of Suffolk, 1975–84. HCF 1964. *Publications:* A Confirmation Course, 1974; (ed) Tourism and the Use of Church Buildings, 1983; Covenanting for Disunity, 1981; Thank you Lord for Alison, 1987; Straightforward and Simple: a guide for churchwardens, 1989. *Recreations:* driving, foreign travel, chess, reading, photography, gardening, good food, dining out. *Address:* St Peter's Cottage, Stretton-on-Fosse, Moreton-in-Marsh, Glos GL56 9SE. *T:* (01608) 662790.

SMITH, Douglas; *see* Smith, I. D.

SMITH, Douglas Armitage; Chief Executive, Child Support Agency, since 2000; *b* 8 April 1947; *s* of James and Joan Smith; *m* 1968, Maureen Buckroyd; one *s* one *d*. *Educ:* Leeds Central High Sch. Board of Inland Revenue: Asst Dir, IT, 1989–93; Director: Change, 1993–95; Self Assessment, 1995–98; Business Ops, 1998–2000. Pres., Assoc. of Inspectors of Taxes, 1986–88. *Recreations:* horse-racing, sport, reading, gym. *Address:* Child Support Agency, Department for Work and Pensions, Benton Park Road, Longbenton, Newcastle upon Tyne NE98 1YX. *T:* (0191) 225 9738. *Club:* Boxmoor Social.

SMITH, Sir Douglas (Boucher), KCB 1992 (CB 1982); Chairman, Advisory, Conciliation and Arbitration Service, 1987–93; *b* 9 June 1932; *m* 1956, Mary Barbara Tarran. *Educ:* Leeds Modern Sch.; Leeds Univ. Entered Ministry of Labour, 1953; successively: Private Sec. to Minister of Labour, 1967–68; to First Sec. of State and Sec. of State for Employment and Productivity, 1968–70; to Sec. of State for Employment, 1970–71; Chief Conciliation Officer, 1971–74, Under Secretary: Dept of Employment, 1974–77; Cabinet Office, 1977–79; Dep. Sec., Dept of Employment, 1979–87. *Address:* 17 Dundas Close, Bracknell, Berkshire RG12 7BX. *T:* (01344) 454573. *Club:* Athenæum.

SMITH, Ven. Douglas Leslie B.; *see* Bartles-Smith.

SMITH, Drew; *see* Smith, F. D.

SMITH, Sir Dudley (Gordon), Kt 1983; DL; management consultant, since 1974; *b* 14 Nov. 1926; *o s* of late Hugh William and Florence Elizabeth Smith, Cambridge; 1st marr. diss.; one *s* two *d*; *m* 2nd, 1976, Catherine Amos, *o d* of late Mr and Mrs Thomas Amos, Liverpool. *Educ:* Chichester High Sch., Sussex. Worked for various provincial and national newspapers, as journalist and senior executive, 1943–66; Asst News Editor, Sunday Express, 1953–59. Vice-Chm. Southgate Conservative Assoc., 1958–59; CC Middlesex, 1958–65; Chief Whip of Majority Group, 1961–63. A Divl Dir, Beecham Group, 1966–70. Contested (C) Camberwell-Peckham, 1955. MP (C) Brentford and Chiswick, 1959–66; Warwick and Leamington, 1968–97; contested (C) Warwick and Leamington, 1997. PPS to Sec. for Tech. Co-operation, 1963–64; an Opposition Whip, 1964–66; an Opposition Spokesman on Employment and Productivity, 1969–70; Parliamentary Under-Secretary of State: Dept of Employment, 1970–74; (Army) MoD, 1974. Vice Chm., Parly Select Cttee on Race Relations and Immigration, 1974–79. UK delegate to Council of Europe and WEU, 1979–97 (Sec.-Gen., European Democratic Group, 1983–96; Chm., WEU Defence Cttee, 1989–93; Pres., WEU Assembly, 1993–97; Hon. Associate, WEU, 1997); a Founder Mem., CSCE Assembly, 1992. Sen. official observer, elecns in Turkey, Russia, Chile, Bulgaria, Slovenia and Azerbaijan for, variously, Council of Europe, CSCE and EDG, 1983–. Promoted Town and Country Planning (Amendment) Act, 1977, as a private member. Governor, Mill Hill Sch., 1958–89; Chm., United & Cecil Club, 1975–80. Freeman, City of London. DL Warwickshire, 1988. Order of the Horseman of Madara, 1st cl. (Bulgaria), 1994; Comdr, Order of Isabella la Católica (Spain), 1994. *Publications:* Harold Wilson: A Critical Biography, 1964; etc. *Recreations:* books, travel, music, wild life and wilderness preservation. *Address:* Church Farm, Weston-under-Wetherley, near Leamington Spa, Warwicks CV33 9BY. *T:* (01926) 632352. *Club:* St Stephen's Constitutional.

SMITH, Dugal N.; *see* Nisbet-Smith.

SMITH, Dr (Edward) Alistair, CBE 1982; Director, University of Aberdeen International Office, since 1989; *b* 16 Jan. 1939; *s* of Archibald Smith and Jean Milne Johnston. *Educ:* Aberdeen Grammar Sch.; Univ. of Aberdeen (MA, PhD); Univ. of Uppsala, Sweden. Lectr, Univ. of Aberdeen, 1963–88. Dir, Univ. of Aberdeen Develt Trust, 1982–90; Mem., Grampian Health Bd, 1983–91. Pres., Scottish Conservative and Unionist Assoc., 1979–81; Dep. Chm., Scottish Conservative Party, 1981–85. Member: Exec., Aberdeen and NE Council on Disability; Exec., Grampian ASH; Scottish Cttee, 1989–91, NE Scotland Regl Bd, 1991–92, NCC; SCOTVEC, 1989–92. *Publications:* (with R. E. H. Mellor) Europe: a geographical survey of the Continent, 1979; articles on Scandinavia, Europe and Scotland. *Recreations:* travel, photography, music. *Address:* 68A Beaconsfield Place, Aberdeen AB15 4AJ. *T:* (01224) 642932; *e-mail:* aberdeensmith@cp.com.

SMITH, Prof. Edwin, PhD; FRS 1996; Consultant and Hon. Fellow, Manchester University-UMIST Materials Science Centre, since 1988; *b* 28 July 1931; *s* of late Albert Edwin Smith and Sarah Ann Smith (*née* Toft); *m* 1958, Patricia Georgina Gale. *Educ:* Chesterfield Grammar Sch.; Nottingham Univ. (BSc); Sheffield Univ. (PhD); MSc Manchester. CEng, FIM. AEI Res. Lab., Aldermaston, 1955–61; CEGB Res. Lab., Leatherhead, 1961–68. Manchester University: Prof. of Metallurgy, UMIST Materials Science Centre, 1968–88; Dean, Faculty of Science, 1983–85; Pro-Vice-Chancellor, 1985–88. Vis. Scientist, Battelle Meml Inst., Columbus, Ohio, 1968. Consultant to industrial organisations in UK, USA, Canada. *Publications:* contribs to learned jls on materials science and engineering. *Recreations:* current interest in various sports; when younger, played cricket for Derbyshire Under 21s, ran 14 marathons (personal best, 2 hrs 47 mins, 1957). *Address:* Manchester University-UMIST Materials Science Centre, Grosvenor Street, Manchester M1 7HS. *T:* (0161) 200 3556.

SMITH, Elaine Agnes; Member (Lab) Coatbridge and Chryston, Scottish Parliament, since 1999; *b* 7 May 1963; *m* 1996, James Vann Smith; one *s*. *Educ:* St Patrick's High Sch., Coatbridge; Glasgow Coll. (BA Hons Social Sci. (Econs and Politics)); St Andrews Teacher Trng Coll. (PGCE); DPSM 1995. Teacher, 1986; work in retail industry, Women's Aid Advice Worker and supply teacher, 1987; Local Authy Homeless Officer and Urban Prog. Asst Co-ordinator, 1988–90; posts in local authy depts, Monklands DC and W Highland Regl Council, 1990–97; Volunteers Manager, 1997–98; Supply Teacher, 1999. *Recreations:* family life, reading, swimming, badminton. *Address:* Scottish Parliament, George IV Bridge, Edinburgh EH99 1SP. *T:* (0131) 348 5824.

SMITH, Elizabeth Jean; Secretary-General, Commonwealth Broadcasting Association, since 1994; *b* 15 Aug. 1936; *d* of Lt-Gen. Sir Robert Hay, KCIE and Mary Carnegie (*née* McAusland); *m* 1960, Geoffrey Smith; one *s* one *d*. *Educ:* St George's Sch., Edinburgh; Univ. of Edinburgh (MA Hons Hist. 1958). BBC Radio: Studio Manager, 1958–61; News Producer, 1961–70; Current Affairs Producer, 1970–78; Producer for BBC Current Affairs TV, 1978–79; Sen. Asst, BBC Secretariat, 1979–81; BBC World Service: Asst Head, Central Talks and Features, 1981–84; Head, Current Affairs, 1984–87; Controller, English Services, 1987–94. Member: Council, RIIA, 1992–97; Bd, Population Communications Internat., 1994–; Bd, Internat. Trng and Res. Consultancies, 1994–98; Bd, Westminster Foundn for Democracy, 1998–2001. Trustee: Oneworld Broadcasting Trust, 1994–2000; Television Trust for the Envmt, 2000–. Consumer columnist, The Listener, 1978–80. Fellow, Radio Acad., 1996 (Mem. Bd, 1990–94). *Publications:* (as Elizabeth Hay) Sambo Sahib: the story of Helen Bannerman, 1981; Sayonara Sanbo, 1993. *Recreations:* gardening, walking, travelling in the developing world. *Address:* Commonwealth Broadcasting Association, 17 Fleet Street, EC4Y 1AA. *T:* (020) 7583 5550, *Fax:* (020) 7583 5549; *e-mail:* elizabeth@cba.org.uk. *Clubs:* Reform, Royal Commonwealth Society.

SMITH, Emma; author; *b* 21 Aug. 1923; *m* 1951, Richard Stewart-Jones (*d* 1957); one *s* one *d*. *Publications:* Maidens' Trip, 1948 (awarded John Llewellyn Rhys Memorial Prize, 1948); The Far Cry, 1949 (awarded James Tait Black Memorial Prize, 1949); Emily, 1959; Out of Hand, 1963; Emily's Voyage, 1966; No Way of Telling, 1972; The Opportunity of a Lifetime, 1978. *Address:* c/o Curtis Brown, 28–29 Haymarket, SW1Y 4SP.

SMITH, Sir (Eric) Brian, Kt 1999; PhD, DSc; FRSC; Vice-Chancellor, Cardiff University (formerly Principal, University of Wales College of Cardiff), 1993–2001; *b* 10 Oct. 1933; *s* of Eric Smith and Dilys Olwen (*née* Hughes); *m* 1st, 1957, Margaret Barr (marr. diss. 1978); two *s* one *d*; 2nd, 1983, Regina Arvidson Ball; two step *d*. *Educ:* Alun Grammar Sch., Mold; Wirral Grammar Sch.; Univ. of Liverpool (BSc; PhD 1957); MA Oxon 1960, DSc Oxon 1988. FRSC 1981. Res. Associate, Univ. of Calif, Berkeley, 1957–59; Oxford University: ICI Fellow, 1959–60; Lectr in Physical Chemistry, 1960–88; Member: Gen. Bd of Faculties, 1980–87 (Chm., 1985–87); Hebdomadal Council, 1985–93; St Catherine's College: Fellow, 1960–88; Vice-Master, 1984–85; Master, 1988–93; Welsh Supernumerary Fellow, Jesus Coll., 1994–95; Dir, Isis Innovation, 1988–97. Vis. Prof., Univ. of Calif, Riverside, 1967; Vis. Lectr, Stanford Univ., 1983, 1984 and 1985; Priestley Lectr, RSC, 1986. Chm., Thermodynamics and Statistical Mechanics Section, RSC, 1979–83; Member: Southern Regional Council for Further Educn, 1965–76; Bd, WDA, 1998–. Pott's Medal, Univ. of Liverpool, 1969. *Publications:* (jtly) Virial Coefficients of Pure Gases and Mixtures, 1969, 2nd edn 1980; Basic Chemical Thermodynamics, 1973, 4th edn 1990; (jtly) Intermolecular Forces: origin and determination, 1981; (jtly) Forces between Molecules, 1986; papers in scientific jls. *Recreation:* mountaineering. *Address:* c/o Cardiff University, Main Building, Park Place, Cardiff CF10 3AT. *Clubs:* Alpine; Gorphwysfa.

SMITH, Eric John R.; *see* Radley-Smith.

SMITH, Eric Norman, CMG 1976; HM Diplomatic Service, retired; British High Commissioner in The Gambia, 1979–81; *b* 28 Jan. 1922; *s* of late Arthur Sidney David Smith; *m* 1955, Mary Gillian Horrocks. *Educ:* Colfe's Sch., London. Served War, Royal Corps of Signals, 1941–46. Foreign Office, 1947–53; HM Embassy, Cairo, 1953–55; UK Delegn to the UN, New York, 1955–57; FO, 1957–60; HM Embassy, Tehran, 1960–64; FO, 1964–68; British Information Services, New York, 1968–71; FCO, 1971–75; Singapore, 1975–79. *Recreations:* music, photography. *Address:* Troodos, Castle Lane, Budleigh Salterton, Devon EX9 7AN.

SMITH, Prof. (Ernest) Alwyn, CBE 1986; PhD; Professor of Epidemiology and Social Oncology, University of Manchester, 1979–90; Chairman, Lancaster Health Authority, 1991–94; *b* 9 Nov. 1925; *s* of Ernest Smith and Constance Barbara Smith; *m* 1950, Doreen Preston; one *s* one *d*. *Educ:* Queen Mary's Sch., Walsall; Birmingham Univ. MB, PhD; FRCP 1970; FRCGP 1973; FFCM 1974. Served War, RM, 1943–46. Res. Fellow in Social Medicine, Birmingham Univ., 1952–55; WHO Vis. Lectr, Univ. of Malaya, 1956–58; Lectr, Univ. of St. Andrews, 1959–61; Sen. Lectr. Univ. of Edinburgh, 1961–66; First Dir, Social Paediatric Res. Gp, Glasgow, 1966–67; Prof. of Community Medicine, Univ. of Manchester, 1967–79. Pres., FCM, 1981–86. *Publications:* Genetics in Medicine, 1966; The Science of Social Medicine, 1968; (ed) Cancer Control, 1979; (ed) Recent Advances in Community Medicine, 1982; papers on epidemiological subjects in Lancet, British Jl of Epidemiol., etc. *Recreations:* music, bird watching, sailing. *Address:* Plum Tree Cottage, Arnside, Cumbria, via Carnforth LA5 0AH. *T:* (01524) 761976.

SMITH, Maj.-Gen. Sir (Francis) Brian W.; *see* Wyldbore-Smith.

SMITH, Sir Francis Graham-, Kt 1986; FRS 1970; Langworthy Professor of Physics, Manchester University, 1987–90, now Emeritus (Professor of Radio Astronomy, 1964–74 and 1981–87); Director, Nuffield Radio Astronomy Laboratories, 1981–88; Astronomer Royal, 1982–90; *b* 25 April 1923; *s* of Claud Henry and Cicely Winifred Smith; *m* 1945, Dorothy Elizabeth (*née* Palmer); three *s* one *d.* *Educ:* Epsom Coll.; Rossall Sch.; Downing Coll., Cambridge. Nat. Sci. Tripos, Downing Coll., 1941–43 and 1946–47; PhD Cantab 1952. Telecommunications Research Estab., Malvern, 1943–46; Cavendish Lab., 1947–64; 1851 Exhibr 1951–52; Warren Research Fellow of Royal Soc., 1959–64; Fellow of Downing Coll., 1953–64, Hon. Fellow 1970; Dir-Designate, 1974–75, Dir, 1976–81, Royal Greenwich Observatory. Vis. Prof. of Astronomy, Univ. of Sussex, 1975. Sec., Royal Astronomical Soc., 1964–71, Pres., 1975–77. Mem. Council and Physical Sec., 1988–94, Vice-Pres., 1990–94, Royal Soc.; For. Associate, RSSAf, 1988. Hon. DSc: QUB, 1986; Keele, 1987; Birmingham, 1989; TCD, 1990; Nottingham, 1990; Manchester, 1993. Royal Medal, Royal Soc., 1987; Glazebrook Medal, Inst. of Physics, 1991. *Publications:* Radio Astronomy, 1960; (with J. H. Thomson) Optics, 1971; Pulsars, 1977; (with Sir Bernard Lovell) Pathways to the Universe, 1988; (with A. G. Lyne) Pulsar Astronomy, 1990, 2nd edn 1998; (with B. F. Burke) Introduction to Radio Astronomy, 1997; (with T. A. King) Optics and Photonics, 2000; papers in Monthly Notices of RAS, Nature and other scientific jls. *Recreations:* beekeeping, walking. *Address:* Jodrell Bank Observatory, Macclesfield, Cheshire SK11 9DL; Old School House, Henbury, Macclesfield, Cheshire SK11 9PH.

SMITH, Prof. Frank Thomas, FRS 1984; Goldsmid Professor of Applied Mathematics in the University of London, at University College London, since 1984; *b* 24 Feb. 1948; *s* of Leslie Maxwell Smith and Catherine Matilda Smith; *m* 1972, Valerie Sheila (*née* Hearn); three *d.* *Educ:* Bournemouth Grammar Sch.; Jesus Coll., Oxford (BA; DPhil); University College London. Research Fellow in Theoretical Aerodynamics Unit, Southampton, 1972–73; Lectr in Maths Dept, Imperial Coll., London, 1973–78; Vis. Scientist, Applied Mathematics Dept, Univ. of Western Ontario, Canada, 1978–79; Reader in Maths Dept, 1979–83, Prof. in Maths, 1983–84, Imperial Coll., London. *Publications:* on applied mathematics, fluid mechanics, computing and natural sciences, in jls. *Recreations:* the family, reading, music, sport. *Address:* Mathematics Department, University College London, Gower Street, WC1E 6BT. *T:* (020) 7679 2837.

SMITH, Frank William G.; *see* Glaves-Smith.

SMITH, (Fraser) Drew; Director, Food By Design (formerly Food Factory), since 1991; senior adviser on food strategy, London Docklands Development Corporation, since 1995; *b* 30 March 1950; *s* of Frank and Beatrice Smith; *m* 1988, Susan Maloney; one *s* one *d.* *Educ:* Westminster School. Worked on Student magazine, 1967; IPC magazines, 1969–72; Westminster Press Newspapers, 1972–81. Editor, Good Food Guide, 1982–89; launched: Good Food Directory, 1985; Budget Good Food Guide, 1986–88; Head of Media Devolt, Dir's Office, Consumers' Assoc., 1988–90; Publishing Dir, Alfresco Leisure Publications, 1990–92. Director: Taste Publishing; West India Co. Columnist, Guardian, 1982–; creator, TV Food File, Channel 4. Chm., Guild of Food Writers, 1990. Trustee, Jane Grigson Liby. Chief Judge, British Cheese Awards, 1995, 1996. Restaurant Writer of the Year, 1981, 1988. *Publications:* Modern Cooking, 1990; Food Watch, 1994; Baby Food Watch, 1995; Good Food, 1995; The Circus (novel), 1997. *Recreations:* walking, music, cooking, people. *Address:* Kins Cottage, Foxley Manor, Foxley, Wilts SN16 0JJ.

SMITH, Prof. Frederick Viggers; Professor of Psychology, University of Durham, 1950–77, now Emeritus; *b* Hamilton, New South Wales, 24 Jan. 1912; *s* of Frederick Thomas Smith and Agnes (*née* Viggers); unmarried. *Educ:* Newcastle (NSW) High School; Sydney and London Universities. BA 1938, MA 1941, Lithgow Schol., Sydney; PhD London 1948. FBPsS, 1950 (Pres., British Psychological Society, 1959–60). Research Office, Dept of Educ., NSW, 1936; Lecturer in Psychology, The Teachers' Coll., Sydney, 1938; Lectr, Birkbeck Coll., Univ. of London, 1946; Lectr, Univ. of Aberdeen, 1948. Visiting Prof., Cornell Univ., USA, 1957, Christchurch and Wellington Univs, NZ, 1960. Consultant, Council of Europe Sub-Cttee on Crime Problems, 1973; Unesco Consultant, Univ. of Riyadh, 1973. Hon. Research Associate, Univ. of Newcastle, NSW, 1980. *Publications:* The Child's Point of View (Sydney), 1946 (under pseudonym Victor Southward); Explanation of Human Behaviour (London), 1951, 1960; Attachment of the Young: Imprinting and Other Developments, 1969; Purpose in Animal Behaviour, 1971; papers to psychological and philosophical jls. *Recreations:* walking, swimming, photography, music, golf. *Address:* 58 Harbourside Haven, Shoal Bay, Port Stephens, NSW 2315, Australia.

SMITH, Rt Hon. Sir Geoffrey J.; *see* Johnson Smith.

SMITH, Geoffrey John; writer and broadcaster; *b* Mich, USA, 23 Aug. 1943; *s* of Earl Willard Smith and Marian Kay Smith (*née* Eisele); *m* 1968, Lenore Ketola (marr. diss. 1985); *m* 1995, Janette Grant; one *s.* *Educ:* Central High Sch., Bay City, Mich; Univ. of Michigan (BA English 1966); Univ. of Wisconsin (Woodrow Wilson Fellow; MA English 1967). Musician, 1959–69; Instr in English, Eastern Michigan Univ., 1967–68; NDEA Title IV Fellow, Univ. of Virginia, 1970–73; freelance writer and lectr, 1973–93; Lectr in English and American Lit., City Univ., 1979–91, City Lit., 1986–92. Music Critic and Consultant, Country Life, 1977–; Arts Corresp., The Economist, 1988–; columnist, BBC Music Mag., 2001–; Presenter, BBC Radio 3, 1988–: documentaries, interviews and concerts; series on Gilbert and Sullivan; CD Review; Jazz Record Requests, 1991–. *Publications:* The Savoy Operas, 1983; Stéphane Grappelli, 1987. *Recreations:* tennis, jogging, family outings, 'gaping and dawdling' (Henry James). *Address:* BBC Radio 3, Broadcasting House, W1A 4WW. *T:* (020) 7765 4327, *Fax:* (020) 7765 4378. *Club:* Cumberland Lawn Tennis.

SMITH, Geoffrey M.; *see* Maitland Smith.

SMITH, Prof. George David William, DPhil; FRS 1996; CEng, FIM; CPhys, FInstP; Professor of Materials Science, since 1996 and Head of Department of Materials, since 2000, University of Oxford; Fellow, Trinity College, Oxford, since 1991; *b* 28 March 1943; *s* of George Alfred William Smith and Grace Violet Hannah Dayton Smith; *m* 1968, Josephine Ann Halford; two *s.* *Educ:* St Benedict's Sch., Aldershot; Salesian Coll., Farnborough; Corpus Christi Coll., Oxford (Scholar; BA Hons Metallurgy 1965; MA, DPhil 1968). CEng 1978; CPhys, FInstP 1996; FIM 1996. SRC Res. Fellow, 1968–70; Jun. Res. Fellow, 1968–72, Res. Fellow, 1972–77, Wolfson Coll., Oxford; Oxford University: Res. Fellow, Dept of Metallurgy, 1970–75; Sen. Res. Fellow, 1975–77; Lectr in Metallurgy, 1977–92; George Kelley Reader in Metallurgy, 1992–96; Fellow, St Cross Coll., Oxford, 1977–91, Emeritus Fellow, 1991–. Man. Dir, Kindbrisk Ltd, 1987–. Councillor (L), W Oxon DC, 1973–76. Co-Chm., UK Materials Congress, 1998. Pres., Internat. Field Emission Soc., 1990–93; Member: Council, Inst. of Materials, 1997–; OST Foresight Panel for Materials, 1999–. Freeman, Armourers' and Brasiers' Co., 1998. FRSA 1997. Sir George Beilby Medal and Prize, SCI, RSC, Inst. Metals, 1985; (jtly) Vanadium Award, 1985, Rosenhain Medal and Prize, 1991, Inst. of Metals. *Publications:* (with M. K. Miller) Atom Probe Microanalysis: principles and applications to materials problems, 1989 (trans. Russian 1993, Chinese 1994); (jtly) Atom Probe Field Ion Microscopy, 1996; numerous contribs to scientific jls. *Recreations:* walking, fishing, bird watching, travel. *Address:* Trinity College, Oxford OX1 3BH. *T:* (01865) 273737.

SMITH, Rt Hon. (George) Iain D.; *see* Duncan Smith.

SMITH, (George) Neil, CMG 1987; HM Diplomatic Service, retired; Secretary General, Society of London Art Dealers, since 1996; Secretary, British Art Market Federation, since 1996; *b* 12 July 1936; *s* of George Smith and Ena (*née* Hill); *m* 1956, Elvi Vappu Hämäläinen; one *s* one *d.* *Educ:* King Edward VII Sch., Sheffield. Joined HM Foreign (subseq. Diplomatic) Service, 1953; served RAF, 1954–56; Foreign Office, 1957; Rangoon, 1958–61; 2nd Sec., Berne, 1961–65; Diplomatic Service Administration, 1965–66; 1st Sec., CO, 1966–68; British Mil. Govt, Berlin, 1969–73; FCO, 1973–77; Counsellor (Commercial), Helsinki, 1977–80; Consul-Gen., Zürich and Principality of Liechtenstein, 1980–85; Head of Trade Relations and Export Dept, FCO, 1985–87; RCDS, 1988; Ambassador to Finland, 1989–95. *Recreations:* music, golf. *Address:* Edgehill, Stonehouse Road, Halstead, Sevenoaks, Kent TN14 7HW.

SMITH, Prof. Gerald Stanton, FBA 2001; Professor of Russian, University of Oxford, and Fellow of New College, since 1986; *b* 17 April 1938; *s* of Thomas Arthur Smith and Ruth Annie Stanton; *m* 1st, 1961, Frances Wetherill (marr. diss. 1981); one *s* one *d*, 2nd, 1982, Barbara Heldt; one step *s* one step *d.* *Educ:* Stretford Grammar Sch.; Sch. of Slavonic and E European Studies, Univ. of London (BA 1964 PhD 1977); DLitt Oxon 1996. Lectr in Russian, Univ. of Nottingham, 1964–71, Univ. of Birmingham, 1971–79; Univ. Research Fellow, Univ. of Liverpool, 1980–82. Visiting Professor: Indiana Univ., 1984; Univ. of California, Berkeley, 1984; Private Scholar, Social Scis and Humanities Res. Council, Canada, 1985; John Simon Guggenheim Meml Fellow, 1986. Pres., MHRA, 2000. *Publications:* (ed) Alexander Galich, Songs and Poems, 1983; Songs to Seven Strings, 1984; Russian Inside and Out, 1989; (ed) D. S. Mirsky, Uncollected Writings on Russian Literature, 1989; Contemporary Russian Poetry: a bilingual anthology, 1993; D. S. Mirsky: Letters to P. P. Suvchinskii, 1995; (co-ed and trans.) M. L. Gasparov, A History of European Versification, 1996; (ed and trans.) Boris Slutsky, Things That Happened, 1999; D. S. Mirsky: a Russian-English life, 2000; Vzglyad izvne: Izbrannye stat'i o russkoi poezii i poetike, 2001; papers in learned jls. *Recreation:* jazz music. *Address:* Taylor Institution, The University, Oxford OX1 3NA. *T:* (01865) 270476.

SMITH, Geraldine; *see* Smith, M. G.

SMITH, Sir Gilbert; *see* Smith, Sir T. G.

SMITH, Gilbert, PhD; writer; Vice-Chancellor and Chief Executive, University of Northumbria at Newcastle, 1996–2001; *Educ:* Brentwood Sch., Essex; Univ. of Leeds (BA Hons 1966); Univ. of Essex (MA 1967); Univ. of Aberdeen (PhD 1973). Research Fellow and Attached Worker, MRC Medical Sociology Unit, Univ. of Aberdeen, 1969–73; Res. Advr, Central Research Unit, Scottish Office, Edinburgh, 1973–75; Sen. Lectr, then Reader, Dept of Social Admin and Social Work, Univ. of Glasgow, 1975–81; University of Hull: Prof. of Social Admin, 1981–96; Head, Dept of Social Admin, 1982–84; Foundn Head, Dept of Social Policy and Professional Studies, 1984–85; Dean, Faculty of Social Scis, 1985–87. Sen. Travelling Scholar in Australia, ACU, 1988. Chm., E Yorks HA, then E Riding Health, 1990–93. Dep. Dir, R&D, DoH and NHS Exec., 1993–96. Numerous board appts, directorships, commns and adv. posts with univs, res. councils, res. funding agencies, publishers, foundns, arts bodies, Govt depts, ACU, UUK and British Council. Editor, Jl of Social Policy, 1991–93. DUniv Moscow State Univ. of Mgt, 1998. *Publications:* Social Work and the Sociology of Organisations, 1970, 2nd rev. edn 1979 (trans. Japanese and Korean); Social Need: policy practice and research, 1980 (trans. Japanese); (with C. Cantley) Assessing Health Care: a study in organisational evaluation, 1985; numerous book chapters; contrib. articles in professional and academic jls of social policy, sociology, social work and healthcare. *Address:* 5 Cragside, Corbridge, Northumberland NE45 5EU. *T:* (01434) 632827.

SMITH, Godfrey, FRSL; writer; *b* 12 May 1926; *s* of Reginald Montague Smith and Ada May Smith (*née* Damen); *m* 1951, Mary (*d* 1997), *d* of Jakub Schoenfeld, formerly of Vienna; three *d.* *Educ:* Surbiton County Sch.; Eggar's Grammar Sch.; Worcester Coll., Oxford (MA; Pres. of Oxford Union Soc. 1950). RAF, 1944–47. Joined Sunday Times as PA to Lord Kemsley, 1951; News Editor, 1956; Asst Editor, 1959; Editor, Magazine, 1965–72, Associate Editor, 1972–91; Editor, Weekly Review, 1972–79; columnist, 1979–; Director, 1968–81. Regent's Lectr, Univ. of California, 1970. FRSL 1995. *Publications: novels:* The Flaw in the Crystal, 1954; The Friends, 1957; The Business of Loving, 1961 (Book Society Choice); The Network, 1965; Caviare, 1976; *non-fiction:* The English Companion, 1984; The English Season, 1987; The English Reader, 1988; *anthologies:* The Best of Nat Gubbins, 1978; A World of Love, 1982; Beyond the Tingle Quotient, 1982; How it Was in the War, 1989; Take the Ball and Run, 1991. *Recreation:* chums. *Address:* Village Farmhouse, Charlton, Malmesbury, Wilts SN16 9DL. *T:* (01666) 822479; 10 Kensington Park Mews, W11 2EY. *T:* (020) 7727 4155. *Clubs:* Garrick, Savile, Royal Air Force, MCC; Leander.

SMITH, Godric William Naylor; Prime Minister's Official Spokesman, since 2001; *b* 29 March 1965; *s* of Eric and Phyl Smith; *m* 1991, Julia Barnes; two *s.* *Educ:* Perse Sch., Cambridge; Worcester Coll., Oxford (MA Lit Hum 1987). Appeals Manager, SANE, 1988–91; Sen. Inf. Officer, 1991–94, Chief Press Officer, 1995, DoH; Prime Minister's Office, 1996–, Dep. Press Sec., 1998–2001. *Recreations:* watching Cambridge United, family. *Address:* 10 Downing Street, SW1A 2AA. *T:* (020) 7930 4433.

SMITH, Gordon E.; *see* Etherington-Smith.

SMITH, Gordon Edward C.; *see* Connell-Smith.

SMITH, Rev. Canon Graham Charles Morell; Rector of Leeds, since 1997; *b* 7 Nov. 1947; *s* of Philip and Helen Smith; *m* 1975, Carys Evans; one *s* two *d.* *Educ:* Whitgift Sch., Croydon; Univ. of Durham (BA Hons Theology 1974); Westcott House, Cambridge. Ordained deacon, 1976, priest, 1977; Asst Curate, All Saints, Tooting Graveney, 1976–80; Team Vicar, St Paul's, Thamesmead, 1980–87; Team Rector, Kidlington with Hampton Poyle, 1987–97; Rural Dean of Oxford, 1988–94. *Recreations:* restoring old houses, theatre and cinema, biography, music. *Address:* Leeds Rectory, 1 Vicarage View, Leeds LS5 3HF. *T:* (0113) 278 6237. *Club:* Leeds (Leeds).

SMITH, Sir Graham (William), Kt 1999; CBE 1990; HM Chief Inspector of Probation, 1992–2001; *b* 15 Aug. 1939; *s* of William George Smith and Edith May Smith; *m* 1958, Jeanne Lilian Ann Goodyear; two *s* one *d.* *Educ:* Univ. of Durham; Univ. of Newcastle upon Tyne (CQSW 1965). Durham: Probation Officer, 1965–69; Sen. Probation Officer, 1969–73; Inner London Probation Service: Asst Chief Probation Officer, 1973–79; Dep. Chief Probation Officer, 1979–80; Chief Probation Officer, 1980–92. Lectr and Examr for Home Office Probation Course, 1972–78; Vis. Prof., UN Asia and FE Inst., Tokyo, 1982. Member: Home Sec.'s Adv. Bd on Restricted Patients, 1986–92; Lord Chancellor's Adv. Cttee on Legal Educn and Conduct, 1991–97. Chairman: Assoc. of Chief Probation Officers, 1988; Penological Cttee, 1995–, Community Sanctions Cttee, 1997, Council of Europe; Centre for Crime and Justice Studies, 2001–. Gov., Nat. Inst. of Social Work, 1992–97. Trustee, Lucy Faithfull Foundn. Freeman, City of London, 1974. Margaret Mead Award, Internat. Assoc. of Residential and Community Alternatives, LA, 1990. *Recreations:* sport, gardening, theatre, grandchildren. *Address:* The Cottage, Swanley Village Road, Swanley Village, Kent BR8 7NG. *T:* (01322) 665427.

SMITH, Prof. Hamilton Othanel; Professor of Molecular Biology and Genetics, Johns Hopkins University School of Medicine, Maryland, USA, since 1981; *b* 23 Aug. 1931; *s* of Bunnie Othanel Smith and Tommie Harkey Smith; *m* 1957, Elizabeth Anne Bolton; four *s* one *d*. *Educ:* Univ. of Illinois; Univ. of California (AB); Johns Hopkins Univ. Sch. of Medicine (MD). Research Associate, Dept of Human Genetics, Univ. of Michigan, 1964–67; Asst Prof. of Microbiology, 1967–69, Associate Prof. of Microbiology, 1969–73, Prof. of Microbiology, 1973–81, Johns Hopkins Univ. Sch. of Medicine. During sabbatical leave in Zürich, worked in collaboration with Prof. Dr M. L. Birnstiel, Inst. für Molekularbiologie II der Univ. Zürich, 1975–76; Vis. Prof., Inst. of Molecular Pathol., Vienna, 1990–91. Nobel Prize in Medicine (jtly), 1978. *Publications:* A restriction enzyme from *Hemophilus influenzae:* I. Purification and general properties (with K. W. Wilcox), in Jl Mol. Biol. *51*, 379, 1970; A restriction enzyme from *Hemophilus influenzae:* II. Base sequence of the recognition site (with T. J. Kelly), in Jl Mol. Biol. *51*, 393, 1970. *Recreations:* piano, classical music. *Address:* Department of Molecular Biology and Genetics, Johns Hopkins University School of Medicine, 720 Rutland Avenue, Baltimore, MD 21205–2109, USA. *T:* (410) 9553650.

SMITH, Prof. Harry, CBE 1993; PhD, DSc; FRCPath; FRS 1979; FIBiol; Professor and Head, Department of Microbiology, University of Birmingham, 1965–88, now Emeritus Professor; *b* 7 Aug. 1921; *s* of Harry and Annie Smith; *m* 1947, Janet Mary Holmes; one *s* one *d*. *Educ:* Northampton Grammar Sch.; University Coll. (of London) at Nottingham. BPharm, BScChem (1st Cl. Hons), PhD, DSc London. Analyst, Boots Pure Drug Co., Nottingham, 1942–45; Asst Lectr, then Lectr, Dept of Chemistry, UCL at Nottingham, 1945–47; Microbiological Research Establishment, Porton: Sen. Scientific Officer, 1947; Principal Sci. Officer, 1951; Sen. Prin. Sci. Officer (Research Merit), 1956; Dep. Chief Sci. Officer (Res. Merit), 1964. Visiting Professor: Dept of Bacteriology, Univ. of Calif, Berkeley, USA, 1964, UCLA, 1972; (summer) Dept of Microbiol., Univ. of Washington, Seattle, USA, 1977, Univ. of Michigan, Ann Arbor, 1981, TCD, 1991. Society for General Microbiology: Mem. Council, 1960–64; Meetings Sec., 1964–68; Treas., 1968–75; Pres., 1975–78; Hon. Mem., 1986; Treas., Fedn of Europ. Microbiol Socs, 1975–82; Pres. and Chm., Organising Cttee, 14th (1986) Internat. Congress of Microbiology, Manchester. Member: Adv. Cttee on Dangerous Pathogens, 1985–88; PHLS Bd, 1985–89; Council, Royal Soc., 1989–91; Assessor, AFRC, 1990–94. Lectures: Amer. Soc. for Microbiol., 1984; Australian Soc. for Microbiol., 1985; Fred Griffith, 1989, Jubilee (50 yrs), 1995, Soc. for Gen. Microbiol.; Leeuvenhoek, Royal Soc., 1991. Hon. MRCP 1986; Hon. ARCVS 1993. Hon. DSc: Leicester, 1992; Nottingham, 2001. Bledisloe Vet. Award, RASE, 1992; Stuart Mudd Award, Internat. Union of Microbiol. Socs, 1994. *Publications:* over 300 papers in jls and books, mainly on mechanisms of microbial (bacterial, viral and fungal) pathogenicity. *Recreation:* interest in farming. *Address:* The Medical School, University of Birmingham, Birmingham B15 2TT. *T:* (0121) 414 6920. *Club:* Athenæum.

SMITH, Prof. Harry, FRS 2000; Special Professor in Photobiology, University of Nottingham, since 2001; *b* 19 Sept. 1935; *s* of Joseph and Alice Smith; *m* 1961, Elinor Anne Chandler; one *s* two *d*. *Educ:* Univ. of Manchester (BSc 1959; DSc 1976); Univ. of Wales (PhD 1962). Theresa Seessel Res. Fellow, Yale Univ., 1962–64; Asst Lectr, Birkbeck Coll., London Univ., 1964–65; Lecturer in Botany: Queen Mary Coll., London Univ., 1965–68; Manchester Univ., 1968–71; Prof. of Plant Physiology, Nottingham Univ., 1971–78; Prof. of botany, Univ. of Leicester, 1978–2001. Miller Foundn Fellow, Univ. of California, Berkeley, 1995. Corresp. Life Mem., Amer. Soc. Plant Physiologists, 1998. Hon. DSc Marseilles, 1978. Chief Ed., Plant, Cell and Envmt, 1975–; Managing Editor: Molecular Ecology, 1990–; Global Change Biology, 1995–. *Publication:* Phytochrome and Photomorphogenesis, 1975. *Recreations:* garden design, classic cars. *Address:* c/o Division of Plant Science, University of Nottingham, Sutton Bonington Campus, Loughborough LE12 5RD.

SMITH, Harvey; *see* Smith, R. H.

SMITH, Hedworth Cunningham, CBE 1972; Chairman: Medical Appeal Tribunals, England and Scotland, 1973–84; Pensions Appeal Tribunals, England, 1973–85; Judge of the Supreme Court of the Bahama Islands, 1965–72, retired; *b* 12 May 1912; *s* of James Smith and Elizabeth (*née* Brown); unmarried. *Educ:* George Watson's Coll., Edinburgh; Edinburgh University. MA 1933; LLB 1936. Solicitor, Scotland, 1937–40; Barrister-at-Law, Gray's Inn, London, 1950. Served War of 1939–45: commnd 1940; Staff Officer, GHQ India Command, 1943–46 (Major). District Magistrate, 1946, Senior District Magistrate, 1950, Gold Coast; Judge of Supreme Court of Ghana, 1957; retd from Ghana Govt service, 1961; Legal Adviser, Unilever Ltd Gp of Cos in Ghana, 1962–64. *Recreation:* golf. *Address:* The Old (Police) House, Main Street, Aberlady, E Lothian. *T:* (01875) 870420. *Clubs:* East India, Devonshire, Sports and Public Schools; Kilspindie Golf.

SMITH, Helen Sylvester, MA; Headmistress, Perse School for Girls, Cambridge, 1989–2001; *b* 7 Jan. 1942; *d* of late S. J. Smith and of K. R. Smith. *Educ:* King Edward VI High Sch. for Girls, Birmingham; St Hilda's College, Oxford (BA 1963, MA 1967 Maths); Hughes Hall, Cambridge (PGCE 1964). Cheltenham Ladies' College, 1964–69; International School of Brussels, 1969–71; Perse Sch. for Girls, 1971– (Dep. Head, 1979–82, 1988–89). FRSA. *Recreations:* music, gardening. *Address:* 6A Cavendish Avenue, Cambridge CB1 7US. *T:* (01223) 249200.

SMITH, Prof. Henry Sidney, FBA 1985; Edwards Professor of Egyptology, 1970–86, Head of Department of Egyptology, 1970–88, University College London, now Professor Emeritus; *b* 14 June 1928; *s* of Prof. Sidney Smith, FBA, and of Mary, *d* of H. W. Parker; *m* 1961, Hazel Flory Leeper (*d* 1991). *Educ:* Merchant Taylors' Sch., Northwood; Christ's Coll., Cambridge (MA); DLit London, 1987. Lectr in Egyptology, Univ. of Cambridge, 1954–63; Budge Fellow in Egyptology, Christ's Coll., Cambridge, 1955–63; Reader in Egyptian Archaeology, University Coll. London, 1963–70. Field Dir for Egypt Exploration Soc. in Nubia, 1961, 1964–65, and at Saqqara and Memphis, Egypt, 1970–88. *Publications:* Preliminary Reports of the Egypt Exploration Society's Nubian Survey, 1962; A Visit to Ancient Egypt, 1974; The Fortress of Buhen: the inscriptions, 1976; The Fortress of Buhen: the archaeological report, 1979; (with W. J. Tait) Saqqara Demotic Papyri I, 1983; The Anubieion at Saqqara, Vol. I (with D. G. Jeffreys), 1988, Vol. II (with L. L. Giddy), 1992; articles in Kush, Jl of Egyptian Arch., Orientalia, Rev. d'Egyptologie, Bull. Inst. Français d'Arch. Or., Z für Äg. Sprache und Altertümskunde, etc.

SMITH, Maj.-Gen. Hugh M.; *see* Macdonald-Smith.

SMITH, Iain William; Member (Lib Dem) North East Fife, Scottish Parliament, since 1999; *b* 1 May 1960; *s* of William Smith and Jane Allison Smith (*née* Farmer). *Educ:* Bell Baxter High Sch., Cupar; Newcastle upon Tyne Univ. (BA Hons Politics and Econs). Fife Regional Council: Mem. (Lib Dem), 1982–96; Sec., Alliance Gp, 1982–86; Leader of Opposition, 1986–96; Mem. (Lib Dem), and Leader of Opposition, Fife Council, 1995–99. Dep. Minister for Parlt, Scottish Exec., 1999–2000. Member: Scottish Lib Dem Appeals and Conf. Cttees, 1988–; Exec., Assoc. of Scottish Lib Dem Councillors, 1988–. *Recreations:* sport (mainly football and cricket), cinema, travel, reading. *Address:* Scottish Parliament, Edinburgh EH99 1SP. *T:* (0131) 348 5817; (office) 16 Millgate, Cupar, Fife KY15 5EG. *T:* (01334) 656361.

SMITH, Iain-Mór L.; *see* Lindsay-Smith.

SMITH, Ian Douglas, GCLM 1979; ID 1970; MP (Cons. Alliance, formerly Republican Front), Zimbabwe, 1980–88; *b* 8 April 1919; *m* Janet Watt (*d* 1994); two *s* one *d*. *Educ:* Selukwe Sch.; Chaplin Sch., Gwelo, S Rhodesia (now Zimbabwe); Rhodes Univ., Grahamstown, S Africa. Served War of 1939–45 in 237 (Rhodesia) Sqdn and 130 Sqdn, RAF. Farmer. Member: Southern Rhodesia Legislative Assembly, 1948–53; Parliament of Fedn of Rhodesia & Nyasaland, 1953–61; former Chief Whip (United Federal Party), 1958; resigned from United Federal Party, 1961; Foundn Mem. and Vice-Pres., Republican Front (formerly Rhodesian Front), 1962, President, 1964–87; Dep. Prime Minister and Minister of the Treasury, S Rhodesia, 1962–64; Prime Minister of Rhodesia, 1964–79; delivered Rhodesia's Unilateral Declaration of Independence, Nov. 1965; Minister Without Portfolio in Bishop Muzorewa's Govt, 1979; Mem., Transitional Exec. Council to prepare for transfer of power in Rhodesia, 1978–79. *Address:* Gwenoro Farm, Shurugwi, Zimbabwe; Box 8198, Causeway, Harare, Zimbabwe. *Clubs:* Harare, Harare Sports (Zimbabwe).

SMITH, Prof. Ian Edward, MD; FRCP, FRCPE; Professor of Cancer Medicine, Institute of Cancer Research, University of London, since 2000; Consultant Cancer Physician, since 1978, and Medical Director, since 2000, Royal Marsden Hospital, London; *b* 16 May 1946; *s* of late David Nicol Smith and Nettie, (Bunty), Thompson Smith (*née* Millar); *m* 1978, Suzanne Dorothy Mackey; three *d*. *Educ:* High Sch. of Dundee; Edinburgh Univ. (BSc Hons 1968; MB ChB 1971; MD 1978). FRCPE 1984; FRCP 1988. House Physician, SHO, then Registrar, Royal Infirmary, Edinburgh, 1971–73; Med. Registrar, Royal Marsden Hosp., London, 1973–75; Res. Fellow, Inst. of Cancer Res., London, 1975–76; UICC Travelling Fellow, Harvard Med. Sch., Boston, 1976–77; Lectr, Royal Marsden Hosp., 1977–78; Head of Section of Medicine, Inst. of Cancer Res., 1994–; Head of Lung Unit, Royal Marsden Hosp., 1994–. Lectures worldwide on breast cancer, lung cancer and new cancer therapies. Chairman: Assoc. of Cancer Physicians, 1995–98; MRC Lung Cancer Wkg Party, 1998–; UKCCCR Lung Gp, 1999–. Member: Amer. Soc. of Clin. Oncology, 1978; British Assoc. for Cancer Res., 1978; Eur. Soc. of Med. Oncology, 1991. *Publications:* (jtly) Autologous Bone Marrow Transplantation, 1984; (jtly) Medical Management of Breast Cancer, 1991; papers, articles and contribs to books. *Recreations:* outdoors, family holidays, reading. *Address:* Royal Marsden Hospital, Fulham Road, SW3 6JJ. *T:* (020) 8661 3280; Royal Marsden Hospital, Downs Road, Sutton, Surrey SM2 5PT.

SMITH, Ian Knight; HM Diplomatic Service, retired; Counsellor and Deputy Head of Mission, Berne, 1993–97; *b* 18 June 1938; *m* 1st, 1964, Glenys Audrey Hayter (*d* 1981); one *s*; 2nd, 1989, Ellen Ragnhild Sweet-Escott; one *s* one *d*. FCO, 1962; Mexico City, 1964; Second Secretary: Calcutta, 1967; Caracas, 1969; First Secretary: FCO, 1972; UKREP Brussels, 1982; FCO, 1987; on secondment as Counsellor to EEC, 1989, to DSS, 1991.

SMITH, Prof. Ian William Murison, PhD; FRS 1995; CChem, FRSC; Mason Professor of Chemistry, University of Birmingham, since 1991; *b* 15 June 1937; *s* of William Murison Smith and Margaret Moir Smith; *m* 1961, Susan Morrish; two *s* two *d*. *Educ:* Giggleswick Sch.; Christ's Coll., Cambridge (BA, MA, PhD). Cambridge University: ICI Res. Fellow, 1964–65; Demonstrator, 1966–71, Lectr, 1971–85, in Physical Chem.; Christ's College: Res. Fellow, 1963–66, Fellow, 1966–85; Tutor, 1968–77; Dir of Studies, 1972–85; University of Birmingham: Prof. of Chemistry, 1985–; Head, Sch. of Chem., 1989–93, 2001. Royal Society of Chemistry: Liversidge Lectr, 2001–Sept 2002; Pres., Faraday Div., 2001–; Special Award for reaction kinetics, 1982; Tilden Medal, 1983; Polanyi Medal, 1990. EU Descartes Prize, 2000. *Publications:* Kinetics and Dynamics of Elementary Gas Reactions, 1980; (ed) Physical Chemistry of Fast Reactions: reaction dynamics, 1980; (ed) Modern Gas Kinetics, 1987; numerous contribs to learned jls. *Recreations:* occasional golf, even more occasional tennis, theatre, walking, gardening under instruction. *Address:* School of Chemistry, The University, Birmingham B15 2TT; 21 St Bernard's Road, Olton, Solihull, West Midlands B92 7AU.

SMITH, Ivor Otterbein, CMG 1963; OBE 1952; Chairman of Public Service and Police Service Commissions and Member of Judicial Service Commission, British Guiana, 1961–66, retired; *b* Georgetown, British Guiana, 13 Dec. 1907; *s* of late Bryce Otterbein Smith and Florette Maud Smith (*née* Chapman); *m* 1936, Leila Muriel Fowler; one *s* two *d*. *Educ:* Queen's Coll., British Guiana; Pitman's Commercial Coll., London. Joined Brit. Guiana CS, as Clerical Asst, Treas., 1925; Sec. Commissioners of Currency, 1933; Asst Dist. Comr, 1941; Private Sec. to Gov., 1943; Dist Comr, 1945; Comr, Cayman Is, 1946–52; Dep. Comr of Local Govt, Brit. Guiana, 1953; Governor's Sec., and Clerk Exec. Coun., 1956; Dep. Chief Sec., 1960; Acted as Chief Sec. on several occasions and was Officer Administering the Govt, Sept.-Oct. 1960. Served with S Caribbean Force, 1941–43; Major, Staff Officer, Brit. Guiana Garrison. Hon. Col, British Guiana Volunteer Force, 1962–66. Chm., Nat. Sports Council, 1962–66. *Recreations:* reading; interested in sports of all kinds; rep. Brit. Guiana at Association and Rugby football, cricket, hockey. *Address:* #109–867 KLO Road, Kelowna, BC V1Y 9G5, Canada.

SMITH, Prof. Ivor Ramsay, FREng; Professor of Electrical Power Engineering, Loughborough University (formerly Loughborough University of Technology), since 1974; *b* 8 Oct. 1929; *s* of Howard Smith and Elsie Emily Smith; *m* 1962, Pamela Mary Voake; three *s*. *Educ:* Univ. of Bristol (BSc, PhD, DSc), CEng, FIEE 1974; FREng (FEng 1988). Design and Develt Engr, GEC, Birmingham, 1956–59; Lectr, Sen. Lectr, Reader, Univ. of Birmingham, 1959–74; Loughborough University of Technology: Hd, Dept of Electronic and Electrical Engrg, 1980–90; Dean of Engrg, 1983–86; Pro-Vice-Chancellor, 1987–91. Director: Loughborough Consultants Ltd, 1980–; E Midlands Regl Technology Network, 1989–. *Publications:* (jtly) Magnetocumulative Generators, 2000; about 300 technical papers and articles on range of power engrg topics, incl. the efficient computation of power supply systems and the prodn and processing of large pulses of energy. *Recreations:* gardening, walking, reading. *Address:* Department of Electronic and Electrical Engineering, Loughborough University, Loughborough, Leics LE11 3TU. *T:* (01509) 222821.

SMITH, Jack, ARCA 1952; artist; *b* 18 June 1928; *s* of John Edward and Laura Smith; *m* 1956, Susan Craigie Halkett. *Educ:* Sheffield College of Art; St Martin's School of Art; Royal College of Art. Exhibitions: Whitechapel Art Gallery, 1959, 1971; Beaux Arts Gallery, 1952–58; Matthiesen Gallery, 1960, 1963; Catherine Viviano Gallery, New York, 1958, 1961; Pittsburgh International, 1955, 1957, 1964; Grosvenor Gallery, 1965; Marlborough Gallery, 1968; Konsthallen, Gothenburg, Sweden, 1968; Hull Univ., 1969; Bear Lane Gallery, Oxford, 1970; Whitechapel Gall., 1970; Redfern Gall., 1973 and 1976; Serpentine Gall., 1978; Fischer Fine Art, London, 1981, 1983; British Painting, Museo Municipal, Madrid, 1983; Flowers East Gall., London, 1990, 1991, 1992, 1994, 1996, 2000. Designer, sets and costumes: Carmen Arcadiae Mechanicae Perpetuum, Ballet Rambert, 1986; Pursuit, Royal Ballet, 1987. Guggenheim Award (Nat.), 1960. Work in permanent collections: Tate Gallery; Arts Council of Great Britain; Contemporary Art Society; British Council. *Address:* 29 Seafield Road, Hove, Sussex BN3 2TP. *T:* (01273) 738312.

SMITH, Jack Stanley, CMG 1970; Professor, and Chairman, Graduate School of Business Administration, University of Melbourne, 1973–77, retired; *b* 13 July 1916; *s* of C. P. T. Smith, Avoca, Victoria; *m* 1940, Nancy, *d* of J. C. Beckley, Melbourne; one *s* two *d. Educ:* Ballarat Grammar Sch.; Melbourne Univ. Construction Engineer, Australasian Petroleum Co., 1938–41. Served in Australian Imperial Forces, 1942–45, Lieut. Project Engineer, Melbourne & Metropolitan Bd of Works, 1946–48. P.A. Management Consultants, UK and Australia, 1949–72, Managing Dir, 1964–72. Hon. LLD Melbourne, 1987. *Recreations:* golf, tennis. *Address:* 15 Glyndebourne Avenue, Toorak, Victoria 3142, Australia. *T:* (3) 98224581. *Clubs:* Melbourne (Melbourne); Lawn Tennis Association of Victoria, Metropolitan Golf (Vic.).

SMITH, Jacqueline Jill, (Jacqui); MP (Lab) Redditch, since 1997; Minister of State, Department of Health, since 2001; *b* 3 Nov. 1962; *d* of Michael and Jill Smith; *m* 1987, Richard James Timney; two *s. Educ:* Hertford Coll., Oxford (BA Hons PPE); Worcester Coll. of Higher Education (PGCE). Res. Asst, Terry Davis, MP, 1984–85; Teacher: Arrow Vale High Sch., Redditch, 1986–88; Worcester Sixth Form Coll., 1988–90; Head of Econs, and GNVQ Co-ordinator, Haybridge High Sch., 1990–97. Mem. (Lab) Redditch BC, 1991–97. Contested (Lab) Mid Worcestershire, 1992. Parly Under-Sec. of State, DfEE, 1999–2001. *Recreations:* family, friends, football, theatre. *Address:* House of Commons, SW1A 0AA.

SMITH, James Andrew Buchan, CBE 1959; DSc; FRSE 1952; retired as Director of the Hannah Dairy Research Institute, Ayr, Scotland, 1951–70 (Acting Director, 1948–51); *b* 26 May 1906; *yr s* of late Dr James Fleming Smith, JP, MB, CM, Whithorn, Wigtownshire; *m* 1933, Elizabeth Marion, *d* of James Kerr, Wallasey, Cheshire; four *d. Educ:* Leamington College, Warwicks; Univ. of Birmingham. PhD (Birmingham) 1929; DSc (London) 1940. Graduate Research Asst: at UCL, 1929–30; at Imperial College, London, 1930–32; Lectr in Biochemistry, Univ. of Liverpool, 1932–36; Biochemist, Hannah Dairy Research Inst., 1936–46; Lectr in Biochemistry, Univ. of Glasgow, 1946–47. President: Society of Dairy Technology, 1951–52; Nutrition Society, 1968–71; Treasurer, Internat. Union of Nutritional Sciences, 1969–75. Hon. LLD Glasgow, 1972. *Publications:* scientific papers in Biochemical Jl, Jl of Dairy Research, Proc. Nutrition Soc., etc. *Recreation:* gardening. *Address:* Flaxton House, 1 St Leonard's Road, Ayr KA7 2PR. *T:* (01292) 264865. *Club:* Farmers'.

SMITH, James Cadzow, CBE 1989; DRC, FREng, FIMechE, FIEE, FIMarE; FRSE; Chairman, Natural Environment Research Council, 1997–2000; *b* 28 Nov. 1927; *s* of James Smith and Margaret Ann Cadzow; *m* 1954, Moira Barrie Hogg; one *s* one *d. Educ:* Bellvue Secondary Sch.; Heriot-Watt Coll.; Strathclyde Univ. FIMechE 1960; FIEE 1960; FIMarE 1960; FREng (FEng 1988); FRSE 1981. Engineer Officer, Mercantile Marine, 1948–53; engineering and managerial appts in fossil and nuclear power generation with SSEB and CEGB, 1953–73; Director of Engineering, N Ireland Electricity Service, 1973–74; Deputy Chairman and Chief Executive, 1975–77; Chairman: E Midlands Electricity Bd, 1977–82; Eastern Electricity Bd, 1982–90; Chief Exec., 1990–93, Chm., 1990–95, Eastern Electricity, later Eastern Gp plc. Pres., IEE, 1989–90. Dir, N. M. Rothschild & Sons Ltd, 1991–97. Freeman, City of London, 1984; Liveryman, 1984, Master, 1997–98, Engineers' Co. Hon. LLD Strathclyde, 1988. *Recreations:* music, drama, mountaineering. *Address:* Wren Wood, Nayland Road, Great Horkesley, Colchester CO6 4HA.

SMITH, Prof. James Cuthbert, PhD; FRS 1993; John Humphrey Plummer Professor of Developmental Biology, Cambridge University, since 2001; Chairman, Wellcome Trust/Cancer Research Campaign Institute of Cancer and Developmental Biology, since 2001; Fellow, Christ's College, Cambridge, since 2001; *b* 31 Dec. 1954; *s* of late Leslie Cuthbert Smith and of Freda Sarah (*née* Wragg); *m* 1979, Fiona Mary Watt; one *s. Educ:* Latymer Upper Sch.; Christ's Coll., Cambridge (BA 1976; MA 1979); London Univ. (PhD 1979). NATO Postdoctoral Fellow, Sidney Farber Cancer Inst. and Harvard Med. Sch., 1979–81; ICRF Postdoctoral Fellow, 1981–84; National Institute for Medical Research: Mem., Scientific Staff, 1984–2000; Head, Div. of Develtl Biol., 1991–2000; Head, Genes and Cellular Controls Gp, 1996–2000. Chm., British Soc. for Developmental Biol., 1994–99; Mem., EMBO, 1992. Howard Hughes Internat. Res. Scholar, 1993–97. Founder FMedSci 1998. Scientific Medal, Zool Soc. of London, 1989; Otto Mangold Prize, Ges. für Entwicklungsbiologie, 1991; EMBO Medal, 1993; Feldberg Foundn Award, 2000. *Publications:* (ed jtly) The Molecular Basis of Positional Signalling, 1989; scientific articles in various jls. *Recreations:* cycling, running, music, conversation, reading biographies. *Address:* Wellcome Trust/CRC Institute, Tennis Court Road, Cambridge CB2 1QR. *T:* (01223) 334132, *Fax:* (01223) 334134; *e-mail:* jim@welc.cam.ac.uk.

SMITH, James Ian, CB 1974; Secretary, Department of Agriculture and Fisheries for Scotland, 1972–84; *b* 22 April 1924; *s* of late James Smith, Ballater, Aberdeenshire, and of Agnes Michie; *m* 1947, Pearl Myra Fraser; one *s. Educ:* Alderman Newton's Sch., Leicester; St Andrews Univ. Served War of 1939–45: India and Burma; RA (attached Indian Mountain Artillery), Lieut, 1943–46. Entered Dept of Agriculture for Scotland, 1949; Private Sec. to Parly Under-Sec. of State, Scottish Office, 1953; Dept of Agriculture for Scotland: Principal, 1953; Asst Sec., 1959; Asst Sec., Scottish Development Dept, 1965–67; Under-Sec., Dept of Agriculture and Fisheries for Scotland, 1967–72. Mem., ARC, 1967–72, 1983–84; Mem., Potato Marketing Bd, 1985–87. Mem., St Andrews Links Trust, 1985–90 (Chm., 1989–90). *Recreation:* golf. *Address:* 7 Hillpark Loan, Edinburgh EH4 7ST. *T:* (0131) 336 4652.

SMITH, Hon. Dame Janet (Hilary), (Dame Janet Mathieson), DBE 1992; **Hon. Mrs Justice Smith;** a Judge of the High Court of Justice, Queen's Bench Division, since 1992; a Judge of the Employment Appeal Tribunal, since 1994; *b* 29 Nov. 1940; *d* of Alexander Roe and Margaret Holt; *m* 1st, 1959, Edward Stuart Smith; two *s* one *d*; 2nd, 1984, Robin Edward Alexander Mathieson. *Educ:* Bolton School. Called to the Bar, Lincoln's Inn, 1972, Bencher, 1992; QC 1986; a Recorder, 1988–92; Presiding Judge, N Eastern Circuit, 1995–98. Shipman Inquiry, 2001–. Mem., Criminal Injuries Compensation Bd, 1988–92; Chm., Security Vetting Appeals Panel, 2000–. Chm., Civil Cttee, Judicial Studies Bd, 2000–. *Recreations:* gardening, music. *Address:* Royal Courts of Justice, Strand, WC2A 2LL.

SMITH, Prof. (Jenkyn) Beverley, FRHistS; Research Professor of Welsh History, University of Wales, Aberystwyth, 1996–98; Commissioner, 1984–99, Chairman, 1991–99, Royal Commission on Ancient and Historical Monuments for Wales; *b* 27 Sept. 1931; *s* of Cecil Nelson Smith and Hannah Jane (*née* Jenkins); *m* 1966, Llinos Olwen Wyn Vaughan; two *s. Educ:* Gowerton Grammar Sch.; UCW, Aberystwyth (BA, MA). FRHistS 1967. National Service, 1954–56. Researcher, Bd of Celtic Studies, Univ. of Wales, 1956–58; Asst Keeper, Dept of MSS and Records, Nat. Library of Wales, 1958–60; Lectr 1960–67, Sen. Lectr 1967–78, Reader 1978–86, Sir John Williams Prof. of Welsh History, 1986–96, Dept of Welsh History, UCW. Sir John Rhys Vis. Fellow, Univ. of Oxford, 1978–79. Member: Court and Council, Nat. Library of Wales, 1974–84; Bd of Celtic Studies, Univ. of Wales, 1965–91 (Sec., History and Law Cttee, 1979–85, Chm 1985–91); Ancient Monuments Bd for Wales, 1992–98. Jt Editor, Bulletin of Bd of Celtic Studies, 1972–93; Editor, Studia Celtica, 1994–98. *Publications:* Llywelyn ap Gruffudd, Tywysog Cymru, 1986; Llywelyn ap Gruffudd, Prince of Wales, 1998; (ed) Medieval Welsh Society, Selected Essays by T. Jones Pierce, 1972; (ed with G. H. Jenkins) Politics and Society in Wales 1840–1922, 1988; articles in English Hist. Review, Welsh Hist. Review, Bulletin Bd of Celtic Studies and other jls. *Recreations:* walking, Welsh terriers. *Address:* Department of History and Welsh History, University of Wales, Aberystwyth, Hugh Owen Building, Penglais, Aberystwyth, Ceredigion SY23 3DY.

SMITH, Jennifer A.; Principal, Harrogate Ladies' College, 1993–95; *b* 11 March 1950; *d* of Geoffrey and Elsie Bird; *m* 1974, Michael Smith; one *d. Educ:* Leeds Univ. (BSc Hons Physics, PGCE); Open Univ. (BA); Liverpool Univ. (MEd). Asst teacher, Physics, 1973–83, Head of Physics, 1983–85, St Richard Gwyn High Sch., Clwyd; Sen. Project Tutor, Science and Electronics, Bodelwyddau TVEI Centre, 1985–88; Dep. Head Teacher, West Kirby Grammar Sch. for Girls, 1988–93. *Recreations:* ski-ing, climbing, music, theatre, electronics.

SMITH, Hon. Jennifer Meredith; JP; MP (Progressive Lab) St George's North, Bermuda, since 1989; Premier of Bermuda, since 1998; *b* 14 Oct. 1947; *d* of late Eugene Wilberforce Smith and Lillian Edith Godet Smith (*née* De Shields). *Educ:* John F. Kennedy Sch. of Govt, Harvard Univ. Formerly newspaper and magazine editor, radio and TV promotions manager and dance instructor. Formerly: Mem., Senate of Bermuda; Shadow Minister of Educn. Progressive Labour Party: Chm., Constitutional Cttee; Dep. Chm.; Leader, 1996–. Member: Bd of Trustees, Bermuda Nat. Gall.; Bermuda Heritage Assoc.; Bermuda Soc. of Arts; Dockyard Arts Cttee; Bermuda Musical and Dramatic Soc; Bd of Trustees, Bermuda Biol Station for Research. Hon. DHumLit: Mount St Vincent, Halifax, Canada, 2000; Morris Brown Coll., Atlanta, USA, 2000. *Address:* Office of the Premier, Cabinet Building, 105 Front Street, Hamilton HM12, Bermuda.

SMITH, Jeremy Fox Eric; DL; Chairman, Smith St Aubyn (Holdings) plc, 1973–86, retired; *b* 17 Nov. 1928; *s* of late Captain E. C. E. Smith, MC, and B. H. Smith (*née* Williams); *m* 1953, Julia Mary Rona, DL, *d* of Sir Walter Burrell, 8th Bt, CBE, TD; two *s* two *d. Educ:* Eton; New College, Oxford. Chairman, Transparent Paper Ltd, 1965–76. Chairman, London Discount Market Assoc., 1978–80. Trustee, Henry Smith's Charity, 1991–97. DL 1988, High Sheriff, 1992–93, West Sussex. *Recreations:* hunting, shooting, stalking, skiing. *Address:* The Old Rectory, Slaugham, Haywards Heath, W Sussex RH17 6AG. *T:* (01444) 400341. *Clubs:* Beefsteak; Leander (Henley on Thames).

See also Duchess of Grafton, Sir J. L. E. Smith, Earl of Verulam.

SMITH, Jeremy James Russell; Director, Local Government International Bureau, since 1996; *b* 12 June 1947; *s* of Horace James Smith and Joan Alistair Russell. *Educ:* Peterhouse, Cambridge (BA Law 1968). Called to the Bar, Lincoln's Inn, 1969; Barrister, 1971–78; Sen. Legal Adviser, Brent Community Law Centre, 1978–83; Legal Services Liaison Officer, GLC, 1983–86; Clerk and Legal Advr, ILEA, 1986–89; Dir of Law and Admin, 1989–90, Chief Exec., 1990–95, London Borough of Camden. *Recreations:* history, current affairs, music, rambling. *Address:* Local Government International Bureau, Local Government House, Smith Square, SW1P 3HZ. *T:* (020) 7664 3100.

SMITH, Jock; *see* Smith, John M. M.

SMITH, Dr John, OBE 1945; TD 1950; Deputy Chief Medical Officer, Scottish Home and Health Department, 1963–75, retired; *b* 13 July 1913; *e s* of late John Smith, DL, JP, Glasgow and Symington, and Agnes Smith; *m* 1942, Elizabeth Fleming (*d* 1981), twin *d* of late A. F. Wylie, Giffnock; three *s* one *d* (and one *s* decd). *Educ:* High Sch., Glasgow; Sedbergh Sch.; Christ's Coll., Cambridge; Glasgow Univ. BA 1935; MA 1943; MB, BChir Cantab 1938; MB, ChB Glasgow 1938; MRCPG 1965; FRCPG 1967; FRCPE 1969; FFPHM (FFCM 1972). TA (RA from 1935, RAMC from 1940); War Service, 1939–46; ADMS Second Army, DDMS (Ops and Plans) 21 Army Group (despatches); OC 155 (Lowland) Fd Amb., 1950–53; ADMS 52 (Lowland) Div., 1953–56; Hon. Col 52 Div. Medical Service, 1961–67. House appts Glasgow Victoria and Western Infirmaries; joined Dept of Health for Scotland, 1947; Medical Supt, Glasgow Victoria Hosps, 1955–58; rejoined Dept of Health for Scotland, 1958; specialised in hospital planning. QHP 1971–74. Officier, Ordre de Leopold I (Belgium), 1947. *Publications:* articles on medical administration and hospital services in various medical jls. *Recreations:* rifle shooting (shot in Scottish and TA representative teams), hill walking, reading. *Address:* 5/10 Oswald Road, Edinburgh EH9 2HE. *T:* (0131) 667 5617. *Clubs:* Naval and Military; New (Edinburgh).

See also Sir R. C. Smith.

SMITH, Sir John (Alfred), Kt 1994; QPM 1986; Deputy Commissioner of the Metropolitan Police, 1991–95; *b* 21 Sept. 1938; *s* of Ruth Alice and Alfred Joseph Smith; *m* 1960, Joan Maria Smith; one *s* one *d. Educ:* St Olave's and St Saviour's Grammar School. Irish Guards, 1959–62. Metropolitan Police, 1962; Head, Scotland Yard drugs squad, 1979; Commander 'P' (Bromley–Lewisham) Dist., 1980; Dep. Chief Constable, Surrey Constabulary, 1981; Metropolitan Police: Dep. Asst Comr, 1984; Inspectorate and Force Reorganisation Team, 1985; Asst Comr, 1987–90; Management Support Dept, 1987–89; Specialist Ops Dept, 1989–90; Inspector of Constabulary for SE England, 1990–91. Mem., Ind. Commn on Policing for NI, 1998–99. Pres., ACPO, 1993–94. Consultant, Football Assoc., 1995–98; non-exec. Dir, Brighton and Hove Albion FC, 1997–2000; Member: Cttee, AA, 1996–99; Govt Football Task Force Wkg Gp, 1997–99; Trustee, English Nat. Stadium Trust, 1997–98. *Recreations:* gardening, sport spectating, horse riding, walking. *Address:* 23 Winterbourne, Horsham, West Sussex RH12 5JW. *T:* (01403) 260935. *Club:* Crystal Palace Football.

SMITH, John Allan Raymond, PhD; FRCS, FRCSE; Consultant General Surgeon, Northern General Hospital NHS Trust (formerly Northern General Hospital, Sheffield), since 1985; a Vice President, Royal College of Surgeons of Edinburgh, 1997–2000; *b* 24 Nov. 1942; *s* of Alexander Macintyre Smith and Evelyn Joyce Smith; *m* Valerie Fullalove; two *s* three *d. Educ:* Boroughmuir Sch., Edinburgh; Edinburgh Univ. (MB ChB 1966);

Aberdeen Univ. (PhD 1979). FRCS 1972; FRCSE 1972. House Officer, Royal Infirmary of Edinburgh, 1966–67; SSC, RAMC, 1967–72; Registrar, Dumfries and Galloway Royal Infirmary, and Royal Infirmary, Aberdeen, 1972–73; Res. Fellow, Lectr in Surgery and Sen. Surgical Registrar, Grampian Health Bd, 1972–78; Sen. Lectr in Surgery and Cons. Surgeon, Royal Hampshire Hosp., Sheffield, 1978–85. Editor, Complications in Surgery series, 1985. *Publications:* (jtly) Wounds and Wound Management, 1992; (ed jtly and contrib.) Pye's Surgical Handicraft. *Recreations:* family, sport. *Address:* 4 Endcliffe Grove Avenue, Sheffield S10 3EJ. *T:* (0114) 268 3094.

SMITH, John Barry, FCCA; Director of Finance and Business Affairs (formerly Director of Finance), BBC, since 1997; *b* 16 Aug. 1957; *s* of Kenneth William Smith and Elsie Smith (*née* Jackson); *m* 1993, Catherine Esther Heywood Hewetson; one *s* one *d. Educ:* South London Coll. (FCCA 1980); Harvard Business Sch. (AMP 1997). Chartered Certified Accountant: Bocock, Bew & Co., Chartered Accountants, 1973–75; BR Gp subsidiaries, 1975–83; BRB, 1983–90; BBC, 1990–. Director: Vickers PLC, 1999–2000; UK Enterprise Adv. Bd, Zurich Financial Services, 2000–. Member: Public Sector and Not for Profit Cttee, Accounting Standards Bd, 1999–2001; 100 Gp of Finance Dirs, 2000–; Public Services Productivity Panel. FRTS 2001. *Address:* BBC, Broadcasting House, W1A 1AA. *T:* (020) 7765 1263.

SMITH, Sir John (Cyril), Kt 1993; CBE 1983; QC 1979; FBA 1973; Professor of Law in the University of Nottingham 1958–87, now Emeritus, and Head of Department of Law 1956–74, and 1977–86; *b* 15 Jan. 1922; 2nd *s* of Bernard and Madeline Smith; *m* 1957, Shirley Ann Walters (*d* 2000); two *s* one *d. Educ:* St Mary's Grammar Sch., Darlington; Downing Coll., Cambridge (Hon. Fellow, 1977). Served Royal Artillery, 1942–47 (Captain). BA 1949, LLB 1950, MA 1954, LLD 1975 Cantab. Called to Bar, Lincoln's Inn, 1950; Hon. Bencher, 1977. Nottingham University: Assistant Lecturer in Law, 1950–52; Lecturer, 1952–56; Reader, 1956–57; Pro-Vice-Chancellor, 1973–77; Hon. Pres. of Convocation, 1978–87. Arthur Goodhart Vis. Prof. in Legal Science, Cambridge, 1989–90. Commonwealth Fund Fellow, Harvard Law Sch., 1952–53. Member: Criminal Law Revision Cttee, 1977– (co-opted, 1960–66 (theft reference) and 1970–77); Policy Adv. Cttee, 1975–85. Pres., Soc. of Public Teachers of Law, 1979–80. Hon. LLD: Sheffield, 1984; Nottingham, 1989; Villanova, 1993; De Montfort, 1995. *Publications:* (with J. A. C. Thomas) A Casebook on Contract, 1957, 11th edn 2000; (with Brian Hogan) Criminal Law, 1965, 9th edn 1999; Law of Theft, 1968, 8th edn 1997; Criminal Law, Cases and Materials, 1975, 7th edn 1999; (with I. H. Dennis and E. J. Griew) Codification of the Criminal Law, 1985; Justification and Excuse in the Criminal Law (Hamlyn Lectures), 1989; Contract, 1989, 3rd edn 1998; Criminal Evidence, 1995. *Recreations:* walking, gardening. *Address:* 445 Derby Road, Lenton, Nottingham NG7 2EB. *T:* (0115) 978 2323.

SMITH, John Derek, MA, PhD; FRS 1976; Member of Scientific Staff, Medical Research Council, Laboratory of Molecular Biology, Cambridge, 1962–88; *b* 8 Dec. 1924; *s* of Richard Ernest Smith and Winifred Strickland Smith (*née* Davis); *m* 1955, Ruth Irwin Aney (marr. diss. 1968). *Educ:* King James's Grammar Sch., Knaresborough; Clare Coll., Cambridge. Mem., Scientific Staff, Agricl Research Council Virus Research Unit, Cambridge, 1945–59; Research Fellow, Clare Coll., 1949–52; with Institut Pasteur, Paris, 1952–53; Rockefeller Foundn Fellow, Univ. of California, Berkeley, 1955–57; California Institute of Technology: Sen. Research Fellow, 1959–62; Sherman Fairchild Scholar, 1974–75. *Publications:* numerous papers in scientific jls on biochemistry and molecular biology. *Recreation:* travel. *Address:* 12 Stansgate Avenue, Cambridge CB2 2QZ. *T:* (01223) 247841.

SMITH, Air Vice-Marshal John Edward, CB 1979; CBE 1972; AFC 1957; Air Officer Administration, Headquarters Strike Command, 1977–81; retired; *b* 8 June 1924; *m* 1944, Roseanne Margurite (*née* Eriksson); four *s* two *d* (and one *s* decd). *Educ:* Tonbridge Sch. Served in Far East, ME, USA and Germany as well as UK Stations since joining the Service in Nov. 1941. *Recreations:* sailing, travel. *Address:* 1 Butlers Grove, Great Linford, Bucks MK14 5DT.

SMITH, (John) Edward (McKenzie) L.; *see* Lucie-Smith.

SMITH, John Francis Jr; Chairman, General Motors Corporation, since 1996; *b* 6 April 1938; *s* of John Francis Smith and Eleanor C. Sullivan; *m* 1st, 1962, Marie Roberta Halloway (marr. diss.); two *s*; 2nd, 1988, Lydia G. Sigrist; one step *d. Educ:* Univ. of Massachusetts (BBA 1960); Boston Univ. (MBA 1965). General Motors Corporation, 1961–: Divisional Manager, 1961–73; Asst Treasurer, NY, 1973–80; Comptroller, Detroit, 1980–81; Dir, Worldwide Planning, 1981–84; Pres. and Gen. Manager, General Motors Canada, 1984–85; Vice-Pres., General Motors Corp. and Pres., General Motors Europe, 1986–88; Exec. Vice-Pres., Internat. Operations, Detroit, 1988–90; Vice-Chm., 1990; Chief Exec. and Pres., 1992–2000. *Address:* c/o General Motors Corporation, 3044 Grand Boulevard, Detroit, MI 48202-3091, USA.

SMITH, John Frederick; DL; Lord Mayor of Cardiff, 1990–91; *b* 28 Sept. 1934; *s* of Charles Frederick Smith and Teresa Smith (*née* O'Brian); *m* 1962, Irene Rice (*d* 1982); one *s. Educ:* St Cuthbert's Jun. Sch.; St Illtyd's Grammar Sch.; Gwent Inst. of Higher Educn, 1981–82 (Dip. Trade Union Studies); University Coll., Cardiff, 1982–85 (BScEcon). Engrg apprenticeship, Edward Curran Engrg, 1951–56; Merchant Navy Engr, Blue Funnel and Andrew Weir, 1956–62; Steel Industry, GKN S Wales, 1964–81; Housing Officer, Adamsdown Housing Assoc. Ltd, 1985–96. Member (Lab), Cardiff City Council, 1972–96, Cardiff County Council, 1995–: Chairman: Housing and Public Works Cttee, 1973–75; Land Cttee, 1987–90; Dep. Lord Mayor, 1988–89; Chief Whip, 1995–99; Chair, Economic Develt, 1996–99; Presiding Officer, 1999–2000; Mem., S Glamorgan CC, 1973–81. Chm., S Wales Film Commn, 1996–99. JP Cardiff, 1977–87; DL S Glam, 1999. *Recreations:* music, spectator of Cardiff RFC and Wales RU, Shakespeare, cooking. *Address:* 128 Corporation Road, Grangetown, Cardiff CF1 7AX. *T:* (029) 2033 3193.

SMITH, John Herbert, CBE 1977; FCA, CPFA, CIGasE; Deputy Chairman and Chief Executive, British Gas Corporation, 1976–83; *b* 30 April 1918; *s* of Thomas Arthur Smith and Pattie Lord; *m* 1945, Phyllis Mary Baxter (*d* 2000); two *s* three *d. Educ:* Salt High Sch., Shipley, Yorks. Articled Clerk, Bradford and Otley, 1934–39. Served War: RAMC, 1940–46. Dep. Clerk and Chief Financial Officer, Littleborough, Lancs, 1946–49; West Midlands Gas Bd, 1949–61 (various posts, finishing as Asst Chief Accountant); Chief Accountant, Southern Gas Bd, 1961–65; Director of Finance and Administration, East Midlands Gas Bd, 1965–68; Mem. (full-time), East Midlands Gas Bd, 1968 (Dep. Chm., 1968–72); Mem. for Finance, Gas Council, June-Dec. 1972; Mem. for Finance, British Gas Corp., 1973–76. Chm., Nationalised Industries Finance Panel, 1978–83. Chairman: Moracrest Investments, 1977–85; United Property Unit Trust (formerly Industrial and Commercial Property Unit Trust), 1986–89 (Mem., 1983–89, Chm., 1986–89, Management Cttee); Member, Management Committee: Pension Funds Property Unit Trust, 1975–89 (Dep. Chm., 1984–89); Lazard American Exempt Fund, 1976–91; British American Property Unit Trust, 1982–93. Member: Council, Inst. of Chartered Accountants, 1977–81; Trilateral Commn, 1976–85. FRSA 1985. *Recreations:* music, piano playing, walking. *Address:* 105 Albany, Manor Road, East Cliff, Bournemouth, Dorset BH1 3EJ. *T:* (01202) 298157.

SMITH, John Hilary, CBE 1970 (OBE 1964); Secretary, Imperial College, London, and Clerk to the Governors, 1979–89 (Fellow, 1992); *b* 20 March 1928; 2nd *s* of late P. R. Smith, OBE and Edith Prince; *m* 1964, Mary Sylvester Head; two *s* one *d. Educ:* Cardinal Vaughan Sch., London; University Coll. London (Fellow, 1987); University Coll., Oxford. BA Hons London 1948; MA Oxon 1991. Mil. service, 1948–50, commnd Queen's Own Royal W Kent Regt. Cadet, Northern Nigerian Administration, 1951; Supervisor, Admin. Service Trng, 1960; Dep. Sec. to Premier, 1963; Dir Staff, Develt Centre, 1964; Perm. Sec., Min. of Finance, Benue Plateau State, 1968; Vis. Lectr, Duke Univ., 1970; Financial Sec., British Solomon Is, 1970; Governor of Gilbert and Ellice Islands, 1973–76, of Gilbert Islands, 1976–78. Procurator, 1990–94, and Fellow, 1991–94, University Coll., Oxford. Public Orator, Univ. of London, 1991–94. Dir, Fleming Ventures, 1985–98. Mem. Council, Scout Assoc., 1980–98 (Chm., Cttee of Council, 1984–88); Pres., Pacific Is Soc. of UK and Ireland, 1981–85. Governor: St Mary's Coll., Strawberry Hill, 1980–88; Cardinal Vaughan School, 1982–88; Heythrop Coll., 1986–93; Member, Board of Management: LSHTM, 1989–98 (Treas., 1993–98; Fellow, 1999); St Mary's Sch., Shaftesbury, 1993–2001 (Chm. Govs, 1994–2001). *Publications:* How to Write Letters that get Results, 1965; Colonial Cadet in Nigeria, 1968; (ed) Administering Empire, 1999; articles in S Atlantic Quarterly, Administration, Jl of Overseas Administration, Nigeria. *Recreations:* walking, writing, music. *Address:* Pound House, Dulverton, Som TA22 9HP. *Club:* Athenæum.

SMITH, Sir John Jonah W.; *see* Walker-Smith.

SMITH, Sir John (Lindsay Eric), Kt 1988; CH 1994; CBE 1975; Director, Coutts & Co., 1950–93; *b* 3 April 1923; *s* of Captain E. C. E. Smith, MC, LLD; *m* 1952, Christian, *d* of late Col U. E. C. Carnegy of Lour, DSO, MC; two *s* two *d* (and one *d* decd). *Educ:* Eton (Fellow, 1974–89); New Coll., Oxford (MA; Hon. Fellow, 1979). Served Fleet Air Arm 1941–45 (Lieut RNVR). MP (C) Cities of London and Westminster, Nov. 1965–1970; Member: Public Accounts Cttee, 1968–69; Exec., 1922 Cttee, 1968–70. National Trust: Mem., Historic Bldgs Cttee, 1952–61; Mem. Exec. Cttee, 1959–85; Mem. Council, 1961–95; Dep. Chm., 1980–85. Member: Standing Commission on Museums and Galleries, 1958–66; Inland Waterways Redevelopment Cttee, 1959–62; Historic Buildings Council, 1971–78; Redundant Churches Fund, 1972–74; Nat. Heritage Memorial Fund, 1980–82. Director: Financial Times Ltd, 1959–68; Rolls Royce Ltd, 1955–75; Dep. Governor, Royal Exchange Assurance, 1961–66. Founder, Manifold and Landmark Charitable Trusts. High Steward of Maidenhead, 1966–75. Freeman of Windsor and Maidenhead, 1975. FSA; Hon. FRIBA 1973; Hon. FRIAS 1983. JP Berks, 1964; DL 1978, Lord-Lieut, 1975–78, Berks. Hon. LLD: Exeter, 1989; Portsmouth, 1994. *Address:* Shottesbrooke Park, Maidenhead, Berks SL6 3SW; 1 Smith Square, SW1P 3PA. *Clubs:* Athenæum, Pratt's, Beefsteak, Brooks's.

See also Duchess of Grafton, B. E. E. Smith, J. F. E. Smith, Hon. A. N. W. Soames.

SMITH, John M.; *see* Maynard Smith.

SMITH, John Mitchell Melvin, (Jock), WS; Partner, Masson & Glennie, Solicitors, Peterhead, 1957–94, retired; *b* 5 July 1930; *s* of John Mitchell Smith and Barbara Edda Smith or Glennie; *m* 1958, Elisabeth Marion Slight; two *s* one *d. Educ:* Fettes College; Edinburgh Univ. (BL). Pres., Law Soc. of Scotland, 1987–88. Mem., Peterhead Burns Club. *Recreations:* golf, theatre. *Address:* 1 Winton Terrace, Edinburgh EH10 7AP. *Clubs:* New (Edinburgh); Bruntsfield Golf; Luffness Golf.

SMITH, John P.; *see* Smith, J. W. P.

SMITH, Sir John Rathborne V.; *see* Vassar-Smith.

SMITH, (John) Stephen; QC 2000; *b* 30 June 1960; *s* of John Slater Smith and Nancy Smith (*née* Clayton); *m* 1982, Lorraine Dunn; four *s* one *d. Educ:* Walton High Sch., Nelson; University Coll., Oxford (BA 1st Cl. Jurisprudence). Called to the Bar: Middle Temple, 1983; Eastern Caribbean, 1994. *Recreations:* family, alpaca farming, deerstalking. *Address:* 12 New Square, Lincoln's Inn, WC2A 3SW. *T:* (020) 7419 1212.

SMITH, (John) Stephen; HM Diplomatic Service; Deputy Head of Mission, Brussels, since 1999; *b* 28 March 1957; *s* of Roy and Ruth Smith; *m* 1984, Wanda Won Min Kim. *Educ:* Clare Coll., Cambridge (MA). Joined FCO, 1979; Third, later Second Sec. (Commercial), Seoul, 1980-85; Second Sec., FCO, 1985-87; Second, later First Sec. (Chancery), UK Mission to UN, NY, 1987-90; First Secretary: FCO, 1990-94; (Political/Internal), Bonn, 1994-98. *Recreations:* ski-ing, sailing, retriever training, opera. *Address:* c/o Foreign and Commonwealth Office, King Charles Street, SW1A 2AH; British Embassy, Rue d'Arlon 85, 1040 Brussels, Belgium.

SMITH, John William Patrick; MP (Lab) Vale of Glamorgan, May 1989–1992 and since 1997; *b* 17 March 1951; *s* of John Henry Smith and Margaret Mary (*née* Collins); *m* 1971, Kathleen Mulvaney; two *s* one *d. Educ:* Penarth County Sch.; Gwent Coll. of Higher Educn (Dip. in Indust. Relations and Trade Union Studies); UCW Cardiff (BSc (Econ) Hons). Building worker, 1966–68; RAF, 1967–71; joiner, 1971–76; mature student, 1976–83; University Tutor, 1983–85; Sen. Lectr in Business Studies, 1985–89; Chief Exec., Gwent Image Partnership, 1992–97. Contested (Lab) Vale of Glamorgan, 1992. PPS to Dep. Leader of the Opposition, 1989–92, to Minister of State for the Armed Forces, 1997–98, to Minister of State (Minister of Transport), DETR, 1998–99. Mem., Select Cttee on Welsh Affairs, 1990–92; formerly Parly spokesperson for Vale of Glam. *Recreations:* reading, boating, walking. *Address:* House of Commons, SW1A 0AA. *T:* (constituency office) (01446) 743769. *Clubs:* West End Labour; Sea View Labour (Barry).

SMITH, Jonathan A.; *see* Ashley-Smith.

SMITH, Jonathan Simon Christopher R.; *see* Riley-Smith.

SMITH, Dr Joseph, FRHistS; Editor, History: Journal of the Historical Association, since 2000; Reader in American Diplomatic History, University of Exeter, since 1995; *b* 2 May 1945; *m* 1971, Marjorie Rachael Eaves. *Educ:* Grey Coll., Univ. of Durham (BA 1966); UCL (PhD 1970). FRHistS 1979. Research Assistant: UCL, 1969–70; Inst. of Latin American Studies, Univ. of London, 1970–71; Lectr in History, Univ. of Exeter, 1971–95. Visiting Professor of History: Coll. of William and Mary, Va, 1976–77; Univ. of Colorado at Denver, 1990–91. Fulbright Schol., 1990–91. Ed., The Annual Bull. of Histl Literature, 1990–99. Rio Branco Prize, Casa do Brasil, London, 1971. *Publications:* Illusions of Conflict, 1979; The Cold War, 1989, 2nd edn 1998; Origins of NATO, 1990; Unequal Giants, 1991; The Spanish-American War, 1994; Historical Dictionary of the Cold War, 2000. *Recreations:* travel, tennis. *Address:* 1 California Close, Exeter, Devon EX4 5ET.

SMITH, Prof. Joseph Victor, FRS 1978; Louis Block Professor of Physical Sciences, since 1977, and Co-ordinator of Scientific Programs, since 1992 (Executive Director, 1988–91), Consortium for Advanced Radiation Sources, University of Chicago (Professor of Mineralogy and Crystallography, 1960–76); *b* 30 July 1928; *s* of Henry Victor Smith and Edith (*née* Robinson); *m* 1951, Brenda Florence Wallis; two *d. Educ:* Cambridge Univ. (MA, PhD). Fellow, Carnegie Instn of Washington, 1951–54; Demonstrator in Mineralogy and Petrology, Cambridge Univ., 1954–56; Asst then Associate Prof., Pennsylvania State Univ., 1956–60. Editor, Power Diffraction File, 1959–69. Visiting Prof., California Inst. of Technology, 1965; Consultant: Union Carbide Corp., 1956–85; UOP, 1985–. Member, US Nat. Acad. of Scis, 1986. Murchison Medal, 1980; Roebling Medal, 1982. *Publications:* Feldspar Minerals, Vols 1 and 2, 1975, 2nd edn 1987; Geometrical and Structural Crystallography, 1982; numerous articles on crystallography, inorganic chemistry, mineralogy, petrology and planetology. *Recreations:* music, art. *Address:* Department of the Geophysical Sciences, University of Chicago, 5734 S Ellis Avenue, Chicago, IL 60637–1434, USA. *T:* (773) 7028110.

SMITH, Sir Joseph (William Grenville), Kt 1991; MD; FRCP; FRCPath; FFPHM; Director, Public Health Laboratory Service, 1985–92; *b* 14 Nov. 1930; *s* of Douglas Ralph and Hannah Letitia Margaret Smith; *m* 1954, Nira Jean (*née* Davies); one *s. Educ:* Cathays High School, Cardiff; Welsh Nat. Sch. of Medicine (MD 1966); Dip. Bact., London Univ.; FRCPath 1975; FFPHM (FFCM 1976); FRCP 1987. FIBiol 1978. Lectr, 1960–63, Sen. Lectr, 1963–65, Dept of Bacteriology and Immunology, LSHTM; Consultant Clinical Bacteriologist, Radcliffe Infirmary, Oxford, 1965–69; Gen. Practitioner, Islington, 1970–71; Consultant Epidemiologist, Dep. Dir, Epidemiological Res. Lab., PHLS, 1971–76; Dir, Nat. Inst. for Biological Standards and Control, 1976–85. Consultant on immunisation to British Army, 1985–96. Member: Cttee on Safety of Medicines, 1978–86 (Chm., Biol Sub-Cttee, 1981–86); Jt Cttee on Vaccination and Immunisation, 1976–93; British Pharmacopoea Commn, 1976–85; MRC, 1989–92; Council, RCPath, 1988–90; Adv. Gp on Rabies Quarantine, MAFF, 1997–98; Chairman: Cttee on Vaccination and Immunization Procedures, MRC, 1976–93; Simian Virus Cttee, MRC, 1982–93; Tropical Medicine Res. Bd, MRC, 1989–90; Expert Adv. Gp on Immunization, 1993–95, Poliomyelitis Commn, 1995–, WHO Eur. Reg.; Chm., WHO Global Polio Commn, 2001– (Co-Chm., 1998–2001). Mem., Ct of Govs and Bd of Management, LSHTM, 1994–97 (Chm. Bd of Mgt, 1995–97). *Publications:* (with E. B. Adams and D. R. Laurence) Tetanus, 1969; papers on tetanus, immunization, and epidemiology of infections in scientific and med. jls. *Recreation:* the arts. *Address:* c/o Public Health Laboratory Service Board, 61 Colindale Avenue, NW9 5DF.

SMITH, Hon. Kenneth George, OJ 1973; Justice of Appeal, Bahamas, 1985–90, retired; *b* 25 July 1920; *s* of Franklin C. Smith; *m* 1942, Hyacinth Whitfield Connell; two *d. Educ:* Primary schs; Cornwall Coll., Jamaica; Inns of Court Sch. of Law, London. Barrister-at-Law, Lincoln's Inn. Asst Clerk of Courts, 1940–48; Dep. Clerk of Courts, 1948–53; Clerk of Courts, 1953–56; Crown Counsel, 1956–62; Asst Attorney-Gen., 1962–65; Supreme Court Judge, 1965–70; Judge of Appeal, Jamaica, 1970–73; Chief Justice of Jamaica, 1973–85. *Recreations:* swimming, gardening. *Address:* 5 Wagner Avenue, Kingston 8, Jamaica.

SMITH, Kingsley Ward; Chief Executive, Durham County Council, since 1988; Clerk to the Lieutenancy, since 1990; *b* 24 Oct. 1946; *s* of Peter and Doris Evelyn Smith; *m* 1968, Kathy Rutherford (marr. diss. 1999); two *s. Educ:* Blue Coat Secondary Sch., Walsall, Staffs; Dame Allan's Boys' Sch., Newcastle upon Tyne. CPFA (IPFA 1970). Trainee Accountant, Gateshead CBC, 1964–67; Durham County Council: Accountant, subseq. Sen. Accountant, 1967–76; Chief Internal Auditor, 1976–79; Sen. Asst County Treasurer, 1979–81; Dep. County Treasurer, 1981–84; County Treasurer, 1984–88. Dir, Durham TEC, 1990–2001; Mem., Learning and Skills Council, Co. Durham, 2001–. Chairman: E Durham Task Force, 1990–; Prince's Trust Regional Council, 1999–. *Recreations:* golfing, fishing, walking his labrador (Sam). *Address:* County Hall, Durham DH1 5UF.

SMITH, Kirstie Louise Stewart-; *see* Hamilton, K. L.

SMITH, Laura; *see* Duncan, A. L. A.

SMITH, Lawrence Edward; yachting consultant, since 1971; *b* 19 Feb. 1956; *s* of Harold and Jean Smith; *m* 1991, Penny Jane Smith (*née* Haydock); two *s* two *d* (of whom one *s* one *d* are twins). *Educ:* Bury Grammar Sch. America's Cup: Skipper, British challenger, Lionheart, 1980, Victory, 1983. Winning skipper: Fastnet Race, 1985; Admiral's Cup, 1989. Whitbread Round the World Race: Skipper, Rothmans, 1990 (4th), Intrum Justitia, 1994 (2nd), Silk Cut, 1997–98 (5th). Skipper, UK crew, Soling class, Olympic Games, 1988, 1992 (Bronze medal). *Publications:* Dinghy Helming, 1985; Dinghy Tuning, 1986; Yacht Tuning, 1987; Science of Speed, 1994. *Recreations:* golf, tennis.

SMITH, Lawrence Joseph, OBE 1976; Assistant General Secretary, Transport and General Workers Union, 1985–88; two *d.* Served in HM Forces, 1941–47; joined London Transport, 1947; District Officer, TGWU, 1961, London District Secretary, 1965, National Officer, 1966, National Secretary, Passenger Services Group, 1971, Exec. Officer, 1979–85. Part-time Mem., London Transport Bd, 1983. Mem., TUC Gen. Council, 1979–88. *Recreations:* gardening, football. *Address:* c/o TGWU, 16 Palace Street, SW1E 5JD.

SMITH, Lawrence Roger Hines, FSA; Keeper of Japanese Antiquities, 1987–97, and Senior Keeper, 1995–97, British Museum, now Keeper Emeritus; *b* 19 Feb. 1941; *s* of Frank Ernest Smith and Eva Lilian Smith (*née* Hines); *m* 1st, 1965, Louise Geraldine Gallini (marr. diss. 1986); one *s* five *d*; 2nd, 1993, Louise Elaine Woodroff; one *d. Educ:* Collyer's Grammar Sch., Horsham; Queens' Coll., Cambridge (Foundn Schol.; BA). British Museum: Asst Keeper, Dept of Manuscripts, 1962; Dept of Oriental Antiquities, 1965; Dep. Keeper, 1976; Keeper, 1977. British Acad. Exchange Fellow, Nihon Gakujutsu Shinkōkai, Kyoto, 1974–75. Academic adviser, Great Japan Exhibn, RA, 1981–82, and contrib. to catalogue. Uchiyama Prize, Ukiyoe Soc. of Japan, 1986. *Publications:* Netsuke: the miniature sculpture of Japan (with R. Barker), 1976; Flowers in Art from East and West (with P. Hulton), 1979; Japanese Prints: 300 years of albums and books (with J. Hillier), 1980; Japanese Decorative Arts 1600–1900 (with V. Harris), 1982; The Japanese Print since 1900, 1983; Contemporary Japanese Prints, 1985; (ed) Ukiyoe: images of unknown Japan, 1988; (ed) Japanese Art: masterpieces in the British Museum, 1990; Nihonga: traditional Japanese painting, 1991; Japanese Prints, 1912–1989: woodblocks and stencils, 1994; contribs to BM multi-cultural catalogues; articles and reviews in learned jls; conference and symposium papers. *Recreations:* walking, sailing, bellringing, music, wine. *Address:* 15 Repton Close, Aylsham, Norfolk NR11 6JE. *T:* (01263) 734499; *e-mail:* lrhsmith@paston.co.uk.

SMITH, Leslie Charles, OBE 1968; Founder Director, Eastway Zinc Alloy Co. Ltd, 1965–82; *b* 6 March 1918; *s* of Edward A. Smith and Elizabeth Smith; *m* 1948, Nancy Smith; two *s* one *d. Educ:* Enfield Central School. Export Buyer, 1938–40; Lieut, RNVR, 1940–46. Founder Dir, Lesney Products, 1947, Jt Man. Dir 1947–73, Man. Dir 1973–80; Chief Exec. Officer, 1980–81, Vice-Chm., 1981–82. FInstM; FIMgt (FBIM 1976); FInstD 1979. Master, Marketors' Co., 1986. *Recreations:* ski-ing, sailing, golf. *Address:* White Timbers, 9a Broad Walk, N21 3DA. *T:* (020) 8886 1656. *Clubs:* Naval; Royal Thames Yacht, Royal Motor Yacht, Parkstone Yacht, Poole Harbour Yacht; Parkstone Golf, Hadley Wood Golf.

SMITH, Sir Leslie (Edward George), Kt 1977; Director, The BOC Group plc (formerly The British Oxygen Co. Ltd), 1966–92 (Chairman, 1972–85); *b* 15 April 1919; *m* 1st, 1943, Lorna Bell Pickworth; two *d*; 2nd, 1964, Cynthia Barbara Holmes; one *s* one *d. Educ:* Christ's Hospital, Horsham, Sussex. Served War, Army (Royal Artillery, Royal Fusiliers), 1940–46. Variety of activities, 1946–55. Joined British Oxygen as Accountant, 1956, Group Man. Dir, 1969–72, Group Chm. and Chief Exec., 1972–79, Chm., 1979–85. Dir, British Gas plc (formerly British Gas Corp.), 1982–90. Mem., Exec. Cttee, King Edward VII Hospital for Officers, 1978–88. FCA. *Recreations:* unremarkable. *Address:* Norton Hall, Mickleton, Chipping Campden, Glos GL55 6PX.

SMITH, Prof. Lewis Lauchlan, PhD; FRCPath; Director, Syngenta (formerly Zeneca) Central Toxicology Laboratory, since 1998; *b* 21 Aug. 1947; *s* of Lewis Smith and Margaret (*née* Wilson); *m* 1972, Susan Lisbeth Baynes; one *s* two *d. Educ:* Hatfield Poly. (BSc, PhD). MRCPath 1990, FRCPath 1997. ICI Central Toxicology Laboratory: Res. Scientist, 1971–80; Sen. Scientist, 1980–85; Hd, Biochem. Toxicology Sect., 1985–91; Dir, Toxicology Unit, 1991–98, and Inst. for Envmt and Health, 1993–98, MRC. *Publications:* numerous in res. jls on mechanisms of toxicity and cellular biochem. *Recreations:* golf, eating, dieting. *Address:* Syngenta Central Toxicology Laboratory, Alderley Park, Macclesfield, Cheshire SK10 4TJ. *T:* (01625) 514848; *e-mail:* lewis.smith@syngenta.com.

SMITH, Llewellyn Thomas; MP (Lab) Blaenau Gwent, since 1992; *b* 16 April 1944; *m* 1969, Pamela Williams; two *s* one *d. Educ:* Cardiff University. Formerly with Pilkington Glass, George Wimpey and Workers' Educational Assoc. MEP (Lab) SE Wales, 1984–94. Mem., CND. *Address:* c/o House of Commons, SW1A 0AA; The Mount, Uplands, Tynewydd, Newbridge, Gwent NP1 4RH.

SMITH, Lloyd Barnaby, (Barney); HM Diplomatic Service; Ambassador to Thailand, since 2000; *b* 21 July 1945; *s* of Arthur and Zena Smith; *m* 1st, 1972, Nicola Mary Whitehead (marr. diss.); 2nd, 1983, Elizabeth Mary Sumner; one *s* one *d. Educ:* Merchant Taylors' Sch., Moor Park; Brasenose Coll., Oxford (MA). Joined Diplomatic Service, 1968; Third, later Second Sec., Bangkok, 1970–74; First Secretary: FCO, 1974–77; Paris, 1977–78; Head of Chancery, Dublin, 1978–81; Ecole Nat. d'Admin, Paris, 1981–82; First Sec., then Counsellor, UK Repn to EEC, Brussels, 1982–86; Counsellor, Bangkok, 1987–90; Dir, Know How Fund for Eastern Europe, 1990–92; Head, S Asia Dept, FCO, 1993–95; Ambassador to Nepal, 1995–99. *Recreation:* sailing. *Address:* c/o Foreign and Commonwealth Office, SW1A 2AH. *Club:* Upper Thames Sailing.

SMITH, Prof. Lorraine Nancy, PhD; Professor of Nursing, University of Glasgow, since 1990 (Head, Nursing and Midwifery School, 1999–2001); *b* 29 June 1949; *d* of Geoffrey Leonard Millington and Ida May (*née* Attfield); *m* 1975, Christopher Murray Smith; one *s* one *d. Educ:* Univ. of Ottawa (BScN); Univ. of Manchester (MEd, PhD). Staff Nurse, Ottawa, 1971–73; Team Leader, Montreal, 1973–76; Sister, Withington Hosp., Manchester, 1976–77; Lectr, Dept of Nursing Studies, Univ. of Manchester, 1977–90. Member: Clin. Standards Adv. Gp (UK); Standards Cttee, Nat. Bd for Scotland, 1997–2000; RCN UK Rep., Work Gp, Eur. Nurse Researchers. Chair, RCN Res. Soc. Scotland. *Publications:* articles in Advanced Jl of Nursing, Nursing Educn Today, Health Bulletin, Jl of Psychiatric Mental Health Nursing. *Recreations:* ski-ing, sailing, reading, bridge. *Address:* Nursing and Midwifery School, University of Glasgow, 68 Oakfield Avenue, Glasgow G12 8LS. *T:* (0141) 330 4051. *Club:* S Caernarvonshire Yacht (Abersoch, N Wales).

SMITH, Dame Maggie, (Dame Margaret Natalie Cross), DBE 1990 (CBE 1970); actress; Director, United British Artists, since 1982; *b* 28 Dec. 1934; *d* of Nathaniel Smith and Margaret Little (*née* Hutton); *m* 1st, 1967, Robert Stephens (later Sir Robert Stephens) (marr. diss. 1975; he *d* 1995); two *s*; 2nd, 1975, Beverley Cross (*d* 1998). *Educ:* Oxford High School for Girls. Studied at Oxford Playhouse School under Isabel van Beers. First appearance, June 1952, as Viola in OUDS Twelfth Night; 1st New York appearance, Ethel Barrymore Theatre, June 1956, as comedienne in New Faces. Played in Share My Lettuce, Lyric, Hammersmith, 1957; The Stepmother, St Martin's, 1958. Old Vic Co., 1959–60 season: The Double Dealer; As You Like It; Richard II; The Merry Wives of Windsor; What Every Woman Knows; Rhinoceros, Strand, 1960; Strip the Willow, Cambridge, 1960; The Rehearsal, Globe, 1961; The Private Ear and The Public Eye (Evening Standard Drama Award, best actress of 1962), Globe, 1962; Mary, Mary, Queen's, 1963 (Variety Club of Gt Britain, best actress of the year); The Country Wife, Chichester, 1969; Design for Living, LA, 1971; Private Lives, Queen's, 1972, Globe, 1973, NY, 1975 (Variety Club of GB Stage Actress Award, 1972); Peter Pan, Coliseum, 1973; Snap, Vaudeville, 1974; Night and Day, Phoenix, 1979; Virginia, Haymarket, 1981 (Standard Best Actress Award, 1982); The Way of the World, Chichester and Haymarket, 1984 (Standard Best Actress Award, 1985); Interpreters, Queen's, 1985; Lettice and Lovage, Globe, 1987, NY, 1990 (Tony Award, best leading actress, 1990); The Importance of Being Earnest, Aldwych, 1993; Three Tall Women, Wyndham's, 1994, 1995; Talking Heads, Chichester, 1996, Comedy Theatre, 1997; A Delicate Balance, Haymarket, 1997; Lady in the Van, Queen's, 1999; *at National Theatre:* The Recruiting Officer, 1963; Othello, The Master Builder, Hay Fever, 1964; Much Ado About Nothing, Miss Julie, 1965; A Bond Honoured, 1966; The Beaux' Stratagem, 1970 (also USA); Hedda Gabler, 1970 (Evening Standard Best Actress award); War Plays, 1985; Coming in to Land, 1986; *at Festival Theatre, Stratford, Ontario:* 1976: Antony and Cleopatra, The Way of the World, Measure for Measure, The Three Sisters; 1977: Midsummer Night's Dream, Richard III, The Guardsman, As You Like It, Hay Fever; 1978: As You Like It, Macbeth, Private Lives; 1980: Virginia; Much Ado About Nothing. *Films:* The VIP's, 1963; The Pumpkin Eater, 1964; Young Cassidy, 1965; Othello, 1966; The Honey Pot, 1967; Hot Millions, 1968 (Variety Club of GB Award); The Prime of Miss Jean Brodie, 1968 (Oscar; SFTA award); Oh! What a Lovely War, 1968; Love and Pain (and the Whole Damned Thing), 1973; Travels with my Aunt, 1973; Murder by Death, 1976; California Suite, 1977 (Oscar); Death on the Nile, 1978; Quartet, 1981; Clash of the Titans, 1981; Evil Under the Sun, 1982; The Missionary, 1982; A Private Function, 1984 (BAFTA award, Best Actress, 1985); The Loves of Lily, 1985; A Room with a View, 1986 (Variety Club of GB Award; BAFTA award, Best Actress, 1986); The Lonely Passion of Judith Hearn, 1989 (Evening Standard British Films Award, 1988, and Best Film Actress BAFTA Award, 1988); Hook, 1992; Sister Act, 1992; The Secret Garden, 1993; Sister Act II, 1994; Richard III, 1996; The First Wives Club, 1996; Washington Square, 1998; Tea with Mussolini, 1999 (Best Supporting Actress, BAFTA, 2000); The Last September, 2000; Harry Potter and the Philosopher's Stone, 2001; Gosford Park, 2001; *television:* Talking Heads: Bed Among the Lentils, 1989 (RTS Award); Memento Mori, 1992; Suddenly Last Summer, 1993; All The King's Men, 1999; David Copperfield, 1999. Fellow: BFI;

BAFTA. Hon. DLitt: St Andrews, 1971; Cambridge, 1995. Hanbury Shakespeare Prize, 1991. *Recreation:* reading. *Address:* c/o Write on Cue, 29 Whitcomb Street, WC2H 7EP. *T:* (020) 7839 3040.

SMITH, Malcolm Andrew F.; *see* Ferguson-Smith.

SMITH, Margaret Elizabeth; JP; Lord Provost and Lord-Lieutenant of Aberdeen City, since 1999; *b* 10 Aug 1931. *Educ:* Twickenham Grammar Sch.; Southport High Sch. for Girls; Lady Mabel Coll., Rotherham (DipPE 1953). Physical Education Teacher: Fleetwood Grammar Sch., 1953–58; Blairgowrie High Sch., 1958–67; Youth Officer, Chichester CC, 1967–73; Neighbourhood Worker, Easterhouse, Glasgow, 1973–78; Housing Worker, Scottish Special Housing Assoc., Glasgow, 1978–81; Community Educn Area Officer, Grampian Regl Council, 1981–91. Aberdeen District, now City, Council: Mem. (Lab), 1988–; Leader of Council, 1996–99; Mem., Drug Strategy Task Gp, 1996–99; Chair, Community Planning Core Gp; COSLA Rep., 1997–99; Convenor, Women's and Equal Opportunities Cttee, 1992–96. Lord High Adm., Northern Seas, 1999–; Vice Adm., Coast of GB and Ireland, 1999–. President: World Energy Cities Partnership, 2000–; Voluntary Service, Aberdeen, 1999–; Aberdeen Br., RNLI, 1999–; Comr, Northern Lighthouse Bd, 1999–; Chair: Froghall Community Project, 1995–99; Aberdeen Alternative Fest. Trust, 1999–; Member: Sunnybank Community Educn Mgt Cttee, 1988–; NE Scotland Econ. Develt Partnership, 1997–99; Aberdeen Gomel Trust, 1999–; Aberdeen Safer Communities Trust, 1999–; Aberdeen Bulawayo Trust, 1999–; Patron: Mental Health, Aberdeen, 1999; Aberdeen Internat. Youth Fest., 1999. JP Aberdeen, 1999. Hon. DL Robert Gordon, Aberdeen, 1999. *Recreations:* walking, theatre and concerts, family and friends, learning Russian, Aberdeen FC. *Address:* (office) Town House, Aberdeen AB10 1LP.

SMITH, Margaret Joy; Member (Lib Dem) Edinburgh West, Scottish Parliament, since 1999; *b* 18 Feb. 1961; *d* of late John Murray and of Anna Murray; *m* 1983, Douglas Robert Smith; one *s* one *d*. *Educ:* Edinburgh Univ. (MA Gen. Arts). Pensions Administrator, Guardian Royal Exchange Assurance, 1982–83; Civil Servant (EO), Registers of Scotland, 1983–88; tour guide and freelance journalist, 1988–90; Scottish Officer, UNA, 1990–96; Political Organiser, Edinburgh W Liberal Democrats, 1996–97. Mem. (Lib Dem) Edinburgh CC, 1995–99. Convenor, Health and Community Care Cttee, Scottish Parlt, 1999–. *Recreations:* golf, reading, caravanning. *Address:* Scottish Parliament, George IV Bridge, Edinburgh EH99 1SP. *T:* (0131) 348 5786. *Club:* Ravelston Golf (Edinburgh).

SMITH, Dame Margôt, DBE 1974; *b* 5 Sept. 1918; *d* of Leonard Graham Brown, MC, FRCS, and Margaret Jane Menzies; *m* 1st, 1938, Bertram Aykroyd (marr. diss. 1947; he *d* 1983), *y s* of Sir Frederic Aykroyd, Bt; one *s* one *d*; 2nd, 1947, Roy Smith, MC, TD (*d* 1983); one *s*. *Educ:* Westonbirt. Chm., Nat. Conservative Women's Adv. Cttee, 1969–72; Chm., Nat. Union of Conservative and Unionist Assocs, 1973–74. Mem., NSPCC Central Exec. Cttee, 1969–86. *Address:* Howden Lodge, Spennithorne, Leyburn, N Yorks DL8 5PR. *T:* (01969) 623621.

See also Sir J. A. F. Aykroyd, Bt.

SMITH, (Maria) Geraldine; MP (Lab) Morecambe and Lunesdale, since 1997; *b* 29 Aug. 1961; *d* of John and Ann Smith. *Educ:* Morecambe Bay Primary Sch.; Morecambe High Sch. Postal Administrator, Royal Mail, 1980–97. *Recreations:* chess, walking. *Address:* 79 West End, Morecambe LA4 4DR. *T:* (01524) 425680.

SMITH, Martin Gregory; Chairman, English National Opera, since 2001; Deputy Chairman, New Star Asset Management, since 2000; *b* 2 Feb. 1943; *s* of late Archibald Gregory Smith, OBE, and Mary Eleanor Smith (*née* Malone); *m* 1971, Elise Barr Becket; one *s* one *d*. *Educ:* St Albans Sch.; St Edmund Hall, Oxford (BA, MA); Stanford Univ., Calif (MBA, AM Econ). Brewer, A. Guinness Son & Co. (Dublin) Ltd, 1964-69; McKinsey & Co. Inc., 1971-73; Dir, Citicorp Internat. Bank Ltd, 1974-80; Chm., Bankers Trust Internat., 1980-83; Co-founder, Phoenix Securities, 1983-97; Chairman: Phoenix Partnership, 1990-97; Phoenix Fund Managers, 1990-97; Eur. Investment Banking, Donaldson, Lufkin & Jenrette, 1997-2000. Director: Amerindo Internet Fund PLC, 2000-; Odgers, Ray & Berndtson, 2001-; Senior Adviser: Bain Capital, 2001-; Phoenix Equity Partners, 2001-. Chairman: Bd of Advrs, Orchestra of Age of Enlightenment, 1985-; Bath Mozartfest, 2000-. Trustee: Science Mus., 1999-; IMS Prussia Cove, 1999-; Becket Collection, 1999-; Wigmore Hall, 2000-. Liveryman, Co. of Musicians, 2000–. St Edmund Fellow, St Edmund Hall, Oxford, 2001. *Recreations:* music, equine pursuits, ski-ing, golf, sailing. *Address:* New Star Asset Management, 1 Knightsbridge Green, SW1X 7NE. *T:* (020) 7225 9200. *Clubs:* Brooks's; Huntercombe Golf; Royal St George Yacht (Dublin); Cape Cod National Golf (USA).

SMITH, Maurice George, OBE 1988; retired; Under-Secretary, Ministry of Overseas Development, 1968–76; *b* 4 Sept. 1915; *s* of Alfred Graham and Laura Maria Smith; *m* 1940, Eva Margaret Vanstone; two *s*. *Educ:* Sir Walter St John's School, Battersea. Examiner, Estate Duty Office, 1939. Flt Lieut RAF, 1942–46. Asst Principal, Min. of Civil Aviation, 1947; Principal, 1948; transferred to Colonial Office, 1950; seconded Commonwealth Office, 1954–55; Asst Secretary, Colonial Office, 1959; transferred to Dept of Technical Co-operation, 1961; Min. of Overseas Development, 1964; Under-Sec. and Principal Finance Officer, ODM, 1968. Chairman, Knights' Assoc. of Christian Youth Clubs, Lambeth, 1970– (Hon. Sec., 1950–70). *Recreations:* voluntary work in youth service, travel. *Address:* 52 Woodfield Avenue, SW16 1LG. *T:* (020) 8769 5356.

SMITH, Melvyn Kenneth; actor, writer, director; *b* 3 Dec. 1952; *s* of Kenneth and Vera Smith; *m* 1988, Pamela Gay-Rees. *Educ:* Latymer Upper Sch., Hammersmith; New Coll., Oxford. Asst Dir, Royal Court Th., 1973; freelance Dir, Bristol Old Vic, 1973, Liverpool Everyman, 1974, Bush Th., 1975; Associate Director: Crucible Th., Sheffield, 1975–78; Young Vic, 1978–79; actor/writer, TV series: Not The Nine O'Clock News, Muck and Brass, Alas Smith and Jones, 1979–81; Smith & Jones, 1982–92, 1995, 1997, 1998; appeared in Small Doses (series of short plays), 1989; Milner, 1994. Films: The Tall Guy, 1989 (Dir); Wilt, 1989; Radioland Murders, 1995 (Dir); Twelfth Night, 1996; Bean, 1997 (Dir); High Heels and Low Lifes, 2001 (Dir). Director: TalkBack Prodns, 1982–; Playback Training Films, 1987–; Smith Jones Campbell (formerly Smith Jones Brown and Cassie Commercials) Ltd, 1988–99; Lola Prodns, 1998–. *Publications:* Not the book, 1981; Not the Nine O'Clock News Diary, 1982; Alas Smith and Jones Coffee Table Book, 1987; Janet Lives with Mel and Griff, 1988. *Address:* TalkBack Management, 20-21 Newman Street, W1P 3HB. *Club:* Groucho.

SMITH, Most Rev. Michael; *see* Meath, Bishop of, (RC).

SMITH, Sir Michael Edward C.; *see* Carleton-Smith.

SMITH, Michael Forbes, FRGS; HM Diplomatic Service; Deputy High Commissioner, Islamabad, since 1999; *b* 4 June 1948; *s* of Forbes Weir Smith and Elizabeth Smith (*née* Mackie); *m* 1st, 1974, Christian Joanna Kersley (marr. diss. 1983, annulled 1986); one *d*; 2nd, 1986, Claire Helen Stubbs; one *s* one *d*. *Educ:* Aberdeen Grammar Sch.; Southampton Univ. (BSc Hons Geog.). BoT, 1966–68; served Army, Capt., Gordon Highlanders, 1971–78. Joined FCO, 1978; Second Sec., FCO, 1978–79; Second, later First, Sec. and Hd of Chancery, Addis Ababa, 1979–83; Pol Advr to Civil Comr, later Gov., Falkland Is, Port Stanley, 1983–85; First Sec., FCO (SE Asia Dept, later FO Spokesman), 1985–89; Consul (Commercial), Zürich, 1990–94; Hd, Press and Public Affairs, Bonn, 1994–99. FRGS 1971; FRSA 1991. Mem., Appeal Cttee and Church Council, Farm St Ch, Mayfair, 1986–90; Vice-Pres., St Thomas More Parish Council, Bonn, 1996–99. Chm., Bonn Caledonian Soc., 1995–99. *Publications:* contrib. various articles to Piping Times. *Recreations:* music (violin, piano, highland bagpipe), sailing, field and winter sports, entertaining and conviviality. *Address:* c/o Foreign and Commonwealth Office, King Charles Street, SW1A 2AH. *T:* (Islamabad) (51) 2822131. *Clubs:* Army and Navy; Royal Northern and University (Aberdeen).

SMITH, Michael Gerard A.; *see* Austin-Smith.

SMITH, Michael John W.; *see* Winkworth-Smith.

SMITH, Michael K.; *see* Kinchin Smith.

SMITH, Prof. (Murdo) Alasdair (Macdonald); DL; DPhil; Vice-Chancellor, University of Sussex, since 1998; *b* 9 Feb. 1949; *s* of late John Smith and of Isabella (*née* Mackenzie); *m* Sherry Ferdman; two *d*. *Educ:* Nicolson Inst., Stornoway; Univ. of Glasgow (MA 1969); London Sch. of Econs (MSc 1970); DPhil Oxford 1973. Lecturer: University Coll., Oxford, 1970–72; LSE, 1972–81; Prof. of Econs, Sussex Univ., 1981–; Research Fellow, Centre for Econ. Policy Res., 1983–. Vis. Prof. of Econs, Coll. of Europe, 1991–98. DL E Sussex, 2001. *Publications:* A Mathematical Introduction to Economics, 1982; (ed with P. Krugman) Empirical Studies of Strategic Trade Policy, 1994; articles on international economics in learned jls. *Recreations:* walking, gardening, cooking. *Address:* Sussex House, University of Sussex, Brighton BN1 9RH. *T:* (01273) 678008; *e-mail:* vc@sussex.ac.uk.

SMITH, Neil; *see* Smith, G. N.

SMITH, Prof. Neilson Voyne, FBA 1999; Professor of Linguistics, University College London, since 1982; *b* 21 June 1939; *s* of Voyne Smith and Lilian Freda Smith (*née* Rose); *m* 1966, Saraswati Keskar; two *s*. *Educ:* Trinity College, Cambridge (BA 1961, MA 1964); UCL (PhD 1964). Lectr in W African Languages, SOAS, 1964–70; Harkness Fellow, MIT and UCLA, 1966–68; Lectr in Linguistics and W African Languages, SOAS, 1970–72; University College London: Reader in Linguistics, 1972–81; Hd, Dept of Phonetics and Linguistics, 1983–90; Vice-Dean, 1992–94. Pres., Assoc. of Heads and Profs of Linguistics, 1993–94. Chm., Linguistics Assoc., 1980–86. Hon. Mem., Linguistic Soc. of America, 1999. *Publications:* An Outline Grammar of Nupe, 1967; The Acquisition of Phonology, 1973; (with Deirdre Wilson) Modern Linguistics, 1979; (ed) Mutual Knowledge, 1982; Speculative Linguistics, 1983; The Twitter Machine, 1989; (with Ianthi Tsimpli) The Mind of a Savant, 1995; Chomsky: ideas and ideals, 1999; articles in learned jls. *Recreations:* music, walking, travel, playing with children. *Address:* 32 Long Buftlers, Harpenden, Herts AL5 1JE; Department of Phonetics and Linguistics, University College London, Gower Street, WC1E 6BT. *T:* (020) 7679 7173; *e-mail:* neil@ling.ucl.ac.uk.

SMITH, Nicholas George Edward L.; *see* Loraine-Smith.

SMITH, Nigel Christopher S.; *see* Starmer-Smith.

SMITH, Sir (Norman) Brian, Kt 1998; CBE 1980; Chairman, Cable and Wireless HKT (formerly Hong Kong Telecommunications) Ltd, 1995–97 and 1998–2000 (non-executive Director, 1997–98); *b* 10 Sept. 1928; *s* of late Vincent and Louise Smith; *m* 1955, Phyllis Crossley; one *s* one *d* (and one *s* decd). *Educ:* Sir John Deane's Grammar Sch., Northwich; Manchester Univ. (PhD Phys. Chemistry, 1954). FTI 1981. Joined ICI Ltd, Terylene Council, 1954; Fibres Division: Textile Develt Dir, 1969; Dep. Chm., 1972; Chm., 1975–78; ICI Main Bd, 1978–85; Director: Fiber Industries Inc., 1972–83; Canadian Industries Ltd, 1981–85; Territorial Dir for the Americas, and Chm., ICI Americas Inc., 1981–85 (Dir, 1980–85); Non-Exec. Dir, Carrington Viyella Ltd, 1979–81. Chairman: Metal Box plc, subseq. MB Group, 1986–89 (Dep. Chm., 1985–86); Lister & Co., 1991–94 (Dir, 1985–94; Dep. Chm., 1990–91); BAA plc, 1991–98; Cable and Wireless, 1995–98 (Dir, 1988–95); Hydron Ltd, 1994–2000; Director: Davy Corp., 1986–91; Yorkshire Chemicals, 1990–91; Mercury Communications, 1990–93; Berisford plc, 1990–96. Pres., British Textile Confedn, 1977–79; Chairman: Man-Made Fibres Producers Cttee, 1976–78; EDC for Wool Textile Industry, 1979–81; Priorities Bd for R&D in Agric. and Food, 1987–92; Heatherwood and Wexham Park Hosps Trust, 1991–97; Dir, John Cabot CTC Bristol Trust, 1997–98; Mem., BOTB, 1980–81, 1983–87 (Chm., N American Adv. Group, 1983–87). Chm., Standing Conf. on Schools' Sci. and Technology, 1992–96. Dir, Oxford Dio. Bd of Finance, 1990–. CIMgt (CBIM 1985); FCIM. Freeman, City of London, 1986; Liveryman, Glovers' Co., 1986. Hon. DBA Buckingham, 1990. *Recreations:* sailing, tennis, gardening. *Club:* Brooks's.

SMITH, Norman Jack, MA, MPhil; FInstPet; Managing Director, Smith Rea Energy Associates Ltd, 1981–99; *b* 14 April 1936; *s* of late Maurice Leslie and Ellen Dorothy Smith; *m* 1967, Valerie Ann, *o d* of late A. E. Frost; one *s* one *d*. *Educ:* Grammar Sch., Henley-on-Thames; Oriel Coll., Oxford (MA); City Univ. (MPhil). FInstPet 1978. Dexion Ltd, 1957; Vickers Ltd, 1960; Baring Brothers & Co. Ltd, 1969; seconded as Industrial Director, 1977, Dir-Gen., 1978–80, Offshore Supplies Office, Dept of Energy; Chairman: British Underwater Engineering Ltd, 1980–83; Mentor Engineering Consultants, 1987–92; Director: Smith Rea Energy Analysts, 1985–2000; Smith Rea Energy Aberdeen, 1990–2000; Gas Transmission, 1989–95; Capcis, 1999–. Mem., Offshore Energy Technology Bd, 1978–80. Fellow, Soc. of Business Economists; FInstD. *Publications:* sundry articles in economic and oil industry jls. *Recreations:* walking, swimming, photography, history. *Club:* Oxford and Cambridge.

SMITH, Prof. (Norman John) David, FRCR; Course Director, Unit of Distance Education, Guy's, King's and St Thomas' (formerly King's) Dental Institute, King's College London, since 1996; Professor of Dental Radiology, University of London, 1978–96; *b* 2 Feb. 1931; *s* of late Norman S. Smith; *m* 1st, 1954, Regina Eileen Lugg (marr. diss.); one *s*; 2nd, 1983, Mary Christine Pocock; one *d*. *Educ:* King's Coll. Sch., Wimbledon; King's Coll., London; KCH Dental Sch. (BDS 1963; MPhil 1969); Royal Free Hosp. Sch. of Medicine (MSc 1966). FRCR 1997. Apprenticed to Pacific Steam Navigation Co., 1948–51; Officer Service, Royal Mail Lines, 1952–58 (Master Mariner, 1957); part-time posts at KCH Dental Sch., Guy's Hosp. Dental Sch. and in gen. dental practice, 1966–69; Sen. Lectr in Dental Surg., KCH Dental Sch., 1969–72; Hd of Dept of Dental Radiol., KCH Dental Sch., later King's Coll. Sch. of Medicine and Dentistry, 1972–96; Reader in Dental Radiol., Univ. of London, 1973–78. Civil Consultant to RAF, 1990–96. Member: Southwark Bor. Council, 1974–78; GLC for Norwood, 1977–86 (Leader of Opposition, ILEA, 1979–86); Thames Water Authority, 1977–83; SE Thames RHA, 1978–86; Council, Open Univ., 1978–81, 1982–91; Court, Univ. of London, 1982–87; Governor, Bethlem Royal and Maudsley Hosps, 1980–82; Mem., Bethlem Royal and Maudsley SHA, 1982–86. Vis. Prof. and lectr worldwide. Gov.,

King's Coll. Sch., Wimbledon, 1998–. Liveryman, Hon. Co. of Master Mariners. DUniv Open, 1993. Sir Charlton Briscoe Res. Prize, KCH Med. Sch., 1969. *Publications:* Simple Navigation by the Sun, 1974; Dental Radiography, 1980; articles in dental jls. *Recreations:* sailing, cooking. *Address:* Beechwood, Old Lane, Tatsfield, Westerham, Kent TN16 2LH. *T:* (01959) 577661. *Club:* Athenæum.

SMITH, Patrick Horace N.; *see* Nowell-Smith.

SMITH, Sir Paul (Brierley), Kt 2000; CBE 1994; RDI 1991; fashion designer; Chairman, Paul Smith Ltd; *b* 5 July 1946; *s* of late Harold and Marjorie Smith; *m* 2000, Pauline Denyer. *Educ:* Beeston Fields Grammar Sch. Opened own shop, 1970 (part-time), 1974 (full time); has shops in London, Nottingham, Manchester, NY, Paris, Hong Kong, Singapore, Taipei, Manila and over 200 in Japan; exporter to numerous other countries; retains Nottingham design room; Queen's Award for Export, 1995. Paul Smith True Brit exhibn, Design Mus., 1995. Freeman, City of Nottingham, 1997. Hon. MDes Nottingham Trent, 1991. *Address:* Paul Smith Ltd, 40–44 Floral Street, WC2E 9DG. *T:* (020) 7836 7828. *Club:* Royal Automobile.

SMITH, Prof. Paul Julian, PhD; Professor of Spanish and Head of Department of Spanish and Portuguese, Cambridge University, since 1991; Fellow, Trinity Hall, Cambridge, since 1991; *b* 11 Nov. 1956; *s* of Albert Charles Smith and Margaret (*née* Tovey). *Educ:* Cambridge Univ. (BA 1980; MA 1982; PhD 1984). Res. Fellow, Trinity Hall, Cambridge, 1983–84; Lectr, QMC, London Univ., 1984–88; Reader, QMW, 1989–91. *Publications:* Quevedo on Parnassus, 1987; Writing in the Margin: Spanish literature of the Golden Age, 1988; The Body Hispanic: gender and sexuality in Spanish and Spanish American literature, 1989; A Critical Guide to El Buscon, 1991; Representing the Other: race, text and gender in Spanish and Spanish American narrative, 1992; Laws of Desire: questions of homosexuality in Spanish writing and film, 1992; Desire Unlimited: the cinema of Pedro Almodóvar, 1994; Vision Machines: cinema, literature and sexuality in Spain and Cuba, 1996; The Theatre of García Lorca: text, performance and psychoanalysis, 1998; The Moderns: time, space and subjectivity in contemporary Spanish culture, 2000. *Address:* Faculty of Modern and Medieval Languages, University of Cambridge, Sidgwick Avenue, Cambridge CB3 9DA. *T:* (01223) 335005.

SMITH, Penelope R.; *see* Russell-Smith.

SMITH, Peter, FSA; Secretary, Royal Commission on Ancient Monuments in Wales, 1973–91, retired; *b* 15 June 1926; *s* of late L. W. Smith, HMI, and Mrs H. Smith (*née* Halsted); *m* 1954, Joyce Evelyn, *d* of late J. W. Abbott and of Alice Abbott (*née* Lloyd); two *s* one *d*. *Educ:* Peter Symonds' Sch., Winchester; Oriel Coll. and Lincoln Coll. (Open Scholar), Oxford (BA, Hons Mod. Hist. 1947); Hammersmith Sch. of Building (Inter ARIBA 1950). Royal Commission on Ancient Monuments in Wales: Jun. Investigator, 1949; Sen. Investigator, 1954; Investigator in Charge of Nat. Monuments Record, 1963. President: Cambrian Archaeological Assoc., 1979; Vernacular Architecture Gp, 1983–86. Hon. DLitt Wales, 1991. G. T. Clark Prize, 1969; Alice Davis Hitchcock Medallion, Soc. of Architectural Historians of GB, 1978. *Publications:* Houses of the Welsh Countryside, 1975; contribs to Agrarian History of England; periodical literature on historic domestic architecture. *Recreations:* reading, drawing, learning Welsh. *Address:* Tŷ-coch, Lluest, Llanbadarn Fawr, Aberystwyth, Ceredigion SY23 3AU. *T:* (01970) 623556.

SMITH, Peter Alan, FCA; Director, NM Rothschild & Sons Ltd, since 2001; *b* 5 Aug. 1946; *s* of Dudley Vaughan Smith and Beatrice Ellen (*née* Sketcher); *m* 1971, Cherry Blandford; two *s*. *Educ:* Mill Hill Sch.; Univ. of Southampton (BSc); Wharton Sch., Univ. of Pennsylvania (AMP). FCA 1970. PricewaterhouseCoopers (formerly Coopers & Lybrand), 1967–2000: Partner, 1975–2000 (Senior Partner, 1998–2000); Chm., 1994–98; Mem., Global Leadership Team, 1998–2000. Dir and Vice Pres., Equitable Life Assce Soc., 2001–. Hon. Treas., UK Housing Trust, 1979–83. Member: Finance Cttee, Nat. Trust, 1991–98, 2001–; Cttee on Corporate Governance, 1996–97; Council, ICAEW, 1997– (Treas., 2001–); POW Business Leaders Forum, 1994–2000; President's Cttee, 1994–98, F and GP Cttee, 1999–, CBI. Liveryman, Chartered Accountants' Co., 1993–. FRSA 1993. *Publication:* Housing Association Accounts and Their Audit, 1980. *Recreations:* golf, gardens. *Address:* The Old Vicarage, Hughenden, High Wycombe, Bucks HP14 4LA. *T:* (01494) 530364. *Clubs:* Carlton; Beaconsfield Golf.

SMITH, Peter Alexander Charles, OBE 1981; Chairman: Securicor Group plc, 1974–95; Security Services plc, 1974–95; *b* 18 Aug. 1920; *s* of Alexander Alfred Smith and Gwendoline Mary (*née* Beer); *m* 1945, Marjorie May Humphrey (*d* 1988); one *s*. *Educ:* St Paul's Sch., London. Admitted solicitor, 1948. Served RA, 1941–46: Captain; Adjt, 17th Medium Regt. Partner, Hextall, Erskine & Co., 1953–79. Chairman: British Security Industry Assoc. Ltd, 1977–81; Metal Closures Gp plc, 1983–87 (Dir, 1972, Dep. Chm., 1981). Mem. Council, Royal Warrant Holders Assoc., 1976–, Vice-Pres., 1981–82, Pres., 1982–83. Vice-Pres., Forest Philharmonic Symphony Orch., 1991–. CIMgt; FRSA. *Recreations:* golf, music, photography. *Address:* c/o Sutton Park House, 15 Carshalton Road, Sutton, Surrey SM1 4LE. *Clubs:* British Racing Drivers (Hon. Life Mem.); Chigwell Golf (Chm., 1990–97).

SMITH, Peter Anthony; General Secretary, Association of Teachers and Lecturers (formerly Assistant Masters and Mistresses Association), since 1988; *b* 25 June 1940; *s* of Charles George and Margaret Patricia Smith; *m* 1961, Anne Elizabeth; one *s* one *d*. *Educ.* Haberdashers' Aske's Boys' Sch., Hatcham; Brasenose Coll., Oxford (MA). Graduate trainee, Midland Bank, 1961–63; teacher: LCC, 1963–66; Whitgift Foundn, 1966–74; Asst Sec., 1974–82, Dep. Gen. Sec., 1982–88, Asst Masters and Mistresses Assoc. Mem., Equal Opportunities Commn, 1994–. FRSA 1991. *Recreations:* cooking, listening to music, living in France, dolls' houses. *Address:* 19 Woodstock Road, Croydon CR0 1JS. *T:* (020) 8686 6726. *Clubs:* Wig and Pen, National Liberal, Royal Commonwealth Society.

SMITH, Peter Bruce; Head Master, Bradfield College, since 1985; *b* 18 March 1944; *s* of Alexander D. Smith and Grace Smith; *m* 1968, Diana Margaret Morgan; two *d*. *Educ:* Magdalen College School, Oxford; Lincoln College, Oxford (Old Members Scholar; MA). Asst Master, Rugby Sch., 1967–85 (Head of Hist. Dept, 1973–77, Housemaster of School Field, 1977–85). Mem. Governing Body, Downe House Sch., 1985–89. Captain Oxfordshire County Cricket Club, 1971–77 (Minor Counties Champions, 1974). *Recreations:* antiquarian, sporting, literary. *Address:* Headmaster's House, Bradfield College, Bradfield, Reading RG7 6AR. *Club:* Vincent's (Oxford).

SMITH, Peter Claudius G.; *see* Gautier-Smith.

SMITH, Most Rev. Peter David; *see* Cardiff, Archbishop of, (RC).

SMITH, Sir Peter Frank Graham N.; *see* Newson-Smith.

SMITH, Prof. Peter George, CBE 2001; Professor of Tropical Epidemiology, since 1989, and Head of Department of Infectious and Tropical Diseases, since 1997, London School of Hygiene and Tropical Medicine; *b* 3 May 1942; *s* of George Henry Smith and Lily Smith (*née* Phillips); *m* 1999, Jill Margaret Routledge; one *s*, and one step *s* one step *d*. *Educ:* City Univ. (BSc Applied Maths 1st Class 1963; DSc Med. Stats 1983). Statistical Res. Unit, MRC, 1965–67; Clinical and Population Cytogenetics Unit, MRC, 1967–69; Makerere Univ. Med. Sch., Uganda, 1970–71; WHO Internat. Agency for Res. on Cancer, Uganda, 1971–72; Cancer Epidemiology and Clinical Trials Unit, ICRF, 1972–79; Dept of Epidemiology, Harvard Sch. of Public Health, 1975; Sen. Lectr, 1979–86, Reader, 1986–89, Hd, Dept of Epidemiol. and Population Scis, 1990–97, LSH&TM. WHO Tropical Diseases Res. Prog., Geneva, 1987–88; Mem., WHO, MRC, and DoH Cttees, incl. Spongiform Encephalopathy Adv. Cttee, 1996– (Actg Chair, 1999–). FMedSci 1999. Hon. MFPHM, 1991. *Publications:* (ed with R. H. Morrow) Methods for field trials of interventions against tropical diseases, 1991, 2nd edn as Field Trials of health interventions in developing countries, 1996; numerous contribs to med. res. literature. *Recreations:* gardening, walking, cycling. *Address:* Department of Infectious and Tropical Diseases, London School of Hygiene and Tropical Medicine, Keppel Street, WC1E 7HT. *T:* (020) 7927 2246.

SMITH, Dr Peter Graham, CB 1988; Director General Guided Weapons and Electronics, Ministry of Defence (Procurement Executive), 1982–88; *b* 12 June 1929; *s* of James A. and Florence L. Smith; *m* 1952, Doreen Millicent (*née* Wyatt); two *d*. *Educ:* Wellington Grammar Sch., Shropshire; Birmingham Univ. (BSc, PhD). Radar Res. Estab., 1953–75: seconded to British Defence Staff, Washington, 1966–68; Supt, Airborne Defensive Radar Div., 1970–75; Dir Defence Science 8, MoD, 1975–78; Dir Surveillance and Instrument Projs, MoD (PE), 1978–82. *Recreations:* gardening, reading, modelling. *Address:* c/o Lloyd's Bank, High Street, Harpenden AL5 2TA.

SMITH, Peter J.; *see* Jefferson Smith.

SMITH, Peter John, CPFA; Chairman, Gateshead Health NHS Trust, since 1998; *b* 31 Dec. 1936; *s* of Frank and Sarah Ann Smith; *m* 1959, Marie Louise Smith; one *s* one *d*. *Educ:* Rastrick Grammar Sch., Brighouse, W Yorkshire. Trainee Accountant, Huddersfield CBC, 1953–59; Accountancy Asst, Bradford CBC, 1959–61; Asst Chief Accountant, Chester CBC, 1961–63; Computer Manager, Keighley BC, 1963–66; Asst City Treasurer, Gloucester CBC, 1966–69; Dep. Borough Treasurer, Gateshead CBC, 1969–73; Asst County Treasurer, Tyne and Wear CC, 1973–74, Dep. County Treasurer, 1974–80, County Treasurer, 1980–86. Gen. Manager, Tyne and Wear Residuary Body, 1985–88. Treasurer: NE Regional Airport Jt Cttee, 1980–86; Northumbria Police Authority, 1980–86; Northumbria Probation and After Care Cttee, 1980–86; Mem., Tyne and Wear Passenger Transport Exec. Bd, 1981–86. Director: N American Property Unit Trust, 1982–93; Northern Investors Co., 1983–86; Westgate Trust, 1990–92; Chm., Gateshead Healthcare and Community NHS Trusts, 1992–98. *Recreation:* fell walking. *Address:* Wheatsheaf House, 19 Station Road, Beamish, Co. Durham DH9 0QU. *T:* (0191) 370 0481.

SMITH, Peter John, CBE 1995; HM Diplomatic Service; Governor, Cayman Islands, since 1999; *b* 15 May 1942; *s* of late John S. Smith and of Irene (*née* Waple); *m* 1964, Suzanne Pauline Duffin; one *s* one *d*. *Educ:* St Dunstan's Coll., London. Joined FO, 1962; Vietnamese lang. student, then 3rd Sec., Saigon, 1964–67; Commercial Attaché, Paris, 1968–69; Commercial Publicity Officer, British Information Services, NY, 1970–73; FCO, 1973–76; 1st Sec., Commercial, Mexico City, 1976–80; Dep. High Comr, Port Louis, Mauritius, 1981–84; FCO, 1984–86; Deputy Consul General: Montreal, 1987–88; Toronto (also Dir, Trade and Investment), 1988–92; RCDS 1992; Ambassador to Madagascar and concurrently Ambassador (non-resident) to The Comoros, 1993–96; High Comr to Lesotho, 1996–99. *Recreations:* golf, cricket, chess, bridge. *Address:* c/o Foreign and Commonwealth Office, King Charles Street, SW1A 2AH. *Club:* MCC.

SMITH, Peter Lincoln Chivers, FRCS, FRCP; Consultant Cardiothoracic Surgeon, Hammersmith Hospitals NHS Trust (formerly Hammersmith Hospital), since 1987; *b* 20 Sept. 1948; *s* of Alfred Stanley Chivers Smith and Cynthia Enid (*née* Anstee); *m* 1976, Susan Margaret Evans; one *s* two *d*. *Educ:* St Bartholomew's Hosp., Univ. of London (MB, BS 1975). MRCP 1978, FRCP 1997; FRCS 1980. General surgical trng, St Bartholomew's Hosp., 1976–79; cardiothoracic surgical trng, St Bartholomew's, Royal Brompton, Middlesex, Harefield and Hammersmith Hosps, 1979–86; Consultant Cardiothoracic Surgeon, Ealing Hosp., 1987–92; Hon. Consultant Cardiothoracic Surgeon, Ealing Hosp. NHS Trust, 1992–. Hunterian Prof., 1986–87, and Mem. Ct of Examiners, 1995–, RCS. *Publications:* (jtly) The Brain and Cardiac Surgery, 1993; numerous scientific pubns on cardiac and thoracic surgical topics. *Recreations:* music, travelling. *Address:* 63 Connaught Gardens, N10 3LG. *T:* (020) 8444 9491. *Clubs:* Royal Automobile, Royal Society of Medicine.

SMITH, Peter Vivian Henworth, CB 1989; Government legal adviser, 1990–99; Legal Adviser, Broadcasting Standards Council, later Broadcasting Standards Commission, 1989–98; *b* 5 Dec. 1928; *s* of Vivian and Dorothea Smith; *m* 1955, Mary Marjorie, *d* of Frank John Willsher and Sybil Marjorie Willsher; five *d*. *Educ:* Clacton County High Sch.; Brasenose Coll., Oxford (MA, BCL). Called to the Bar, Lincoln's Inn, 1953. HM Overseas Civil Service: Resident Magistrate, Nyasaland, 1955–63; Registrar, High Court, Nyasaland, 1963–64; Sen. Resident Magistrate, Malaŵi, 1964–69; Puisne Judge, Malaŵi, 1969–70; HM Customs and Excise: Legal Asst, 1970–72; Sen. Legal Asst, 1972–76; Asst Solicitor, 1976–82; Prin. Asst Solicitor, 1982–85; Solicitor, 1986–89. Legal Advr, Bldg Socs Commn, 1990–92. *Recreations:* classical music, walking on the flat, bridge, computers. *Address:* Likabula, 14 St Albans Road, Clacton-on-Sea CO15 6BA. *T:* (01255) 422053; *e-mail:* pvhsmith@aol.com.

SMITH, Peter William; His Honour Judge Peter Smith; a Circuit Judge, since 1994; *b* 31 Dec. 1945; *s* of late William and Bessie Smith; *m* 1970, Vanessa Mary (*née* Wildash); one *s*. *Educ:* Arnold Sch., Blackpool; Downing Coll., Cambridge (MA). Called to the Bar, Middle Temple, 1969. Practised (as William Smith) on Northern Circuit; a Dep. Judge Advocate, 1983–84; a Recorder, 1991–94. Mem., Mental Health Review Tribunal, 1993–. *Recreation:* weekends in the Lake District. *Address:* c/o The Law Courts, Ring Way, Preston PR1 2LL.

SMITH, Peter William G.; *see* Greig-Smith.

SMITH, Peter Winston; QC 1992; a Recorder, since 1997; *b* 1 May 1952; *s* of George Arthur Smith and Iris Muriel Smith; *m* 1980, Diane Dalgleish; one *s* two *d*. *Educ:* Selwyn Coll., Cambridge (BA 1974; MA 1976); Coll. of Law. Called to the Bar, Lincoln's Inn, 1975, Bencher, 2000. Lectr, Manchester Univ., 1977–83; practice on Northern Circuit, 1979–; Asst Recorder, 1994–97; a Deputy High Court Judge, 1996–. *Recreations:* Titanic Historical Society, British Titanic Society, Jackie Fisher fan, reading military history, football. *Address:* 40 King Street, Manchester M2 6BA. *T:* (0161) 832 9082. *Club:* Athenæum.

SMITH, Rt Rev. Raymond George; Senior Assistant Minister, St Clement Mosman, NSW, since 2002; *b* 7 March 1936; *s* of Gordon William Smith and Alice Mary (*née* Brett); *m* 1960, Shirley Jeanette Gilmore; three *s*. *Educ:* Australian Coll. of Theology (ThSchol); Univ. of New England (BA, Dip Cont. Ed, MEd). Parish priest, dio. of Armidale, 1959–76; Dir of Christian Educn and Archdeacon, Armidale, 1977–86; Dir of Extension Ministries, Trinity Episcopal Sch. for Ministry, Ambridge, Pa, USA, 1986–90; Rector of Wanniassa, 1990–93, and Archdeacon of S Canberra, 1991–93, dio. of Canberra and Goulburn; Bp of Liverpool, NSW, and an Asst Bp of Sydney, 1993–2001. *Publication:* People Caring for People, 1990. *Recreations:* swimming, cycling, photography, stamp collecting, Australian history. *Address:* 144 Raglan Street, Mosman, NSW 2088, Australia.

SMITH, (Raymond) Gordon (Antony) E.; *see* Etherington-Smith.

SMITH, Sir Raymond (Horace), KBE 1967 (CBE 1960); Consultant to Rolls-Royce, 1949–96; Chairman, Hawker Siddeley, 1960–75, and other British companies in Venezuela; *b* 1917; *s* of Horace P. Smith and Mabelle (*née* Osborne-Couzens); *m* 1943, Dorothy, *d* of Robert Cheney Hart. *Educ:* Salesian College, London; Barcelona University. Served War of 1939–45, with British Security Co-ordination, NY, and with Intelligence Corps, in France, India, Burma, Malaya, Indonesia. Civil Attaché British Embassy, Caracas, 1941; Negotiator, sale of British owned railway cos to Venezuelan Govt and other S American govts, 1946–50; Rep., London Reinsurers in Venezuela, 1954–60; Consultant: Cammell Laird; Mirrlees; British Aerospace, 1952–82; Provincial Insurance Co. Ltd, 1960–75; Director: Daily Journal, 1953–95; Anglo-Venezuelan Cultural Inst., 1946–80; British Venezuelan Chamber of Commerce, 1956–86 (Hon. Pres., 1987); Pres. British Commonwealth Assoc. of Venezuela, 1955–57. Companion of Royal Aeronautical Society. Knight Grand Cross, St Lazarus of Jerusalem; Venezuelan Air Force Cross. *Recreations:* tennis, water ski-ing, winter sports (Cresta Run and ski-ing). *Address:* Quinta San Antonio, Calle El Samancito, Avenida El Saman, Caracas Country Club, Caracas 1062, Venezuela; Carlton Lodge, 37 Lowndes Street, SW1X 9JB. *Clubs:* White's, Naval and Military; Caracas Country, Jockey (Caracas); St Moritz Tobogganing (Switzerland).

SMITH, Richard James Crosbie W.; *see* Wilmot-Smith.

SMITH, Richard John, AM 1997; Director-General, Office of National Assessments, Canberra, 1996–98; *b* 14 Dec. 1934; *s* of C. A. Smith and T. A. O'Halloran; *m* 1958, Janet Campbell; two *s* two *d*. *Educ:* Sydney High Sch.; Sydney Univ. (BA, LLB Hons I 1958). Teacher, London, 1958–59; Solicitor, NSW, 1959–61; Foreign Affairs Trainee, 1961; First Sec., Australian Embassy, Washington, 1967–70; Dep. Perm. Rep., Australian Mission to UN, Geneva, 1972–74; Asst Sec., Internat. Legal Branch, 1974–75; Ambassador to Israel, 1975–77; First Assistant Secretary: Legal & Treaties Div., 1977–81; Management & Foreign Service Div., 1981–83; Actg Dep. Sec., Dept of Foreign Affairs, 1983–85; Ambassador to Thailand, 1985–88; Dep. Sec., Dept of Foreign Affairs and Trade, Canberra, 1988–90; High Comr for Australia in the UK, 1991–94; Ambassador to the Philippines, 1994–96. *Recreations:* walking, reading, travel. *Address:* 11 Glebe Street, Edgecliff, NSW 2027, Australia. *T:* (2) 93620504.

SMITH, Richard Lloyd; QC 2001; a Recorder, since 2000; *b* 28 Jan. 1963; *s* of Lloyd and Dorothy Smith; *m* 1990, Anna Sara Webb; one *s* one *d*. *Educ:* King's Coll. London (LLB). Called to the Bar, Middle Temple, 1986. *Recreations:* Rugby, Leeds United Football Club. *Address:* Guildhall Chambers, 23 Broad Street, Bristol BS1 2HG. *T:* (0117) 927 3366.

SMITH, Prof. Richard Lyttleton, PhD; Professor of Statistics, University of North Carolina, 1991–94 and since 1996; *b* 31 March 1953; *s* of Stanley Lyttleton Smith and Hilary Margaret (*née* James). *Educ:* Jesus Coll., Univ. of Oxford (BA Maths 1975; MA 1985); Cornell Univ., USA (PhD Ops Res. 1979). Lectr in Stats, Imperial Coll., London, 1979–85; Prof. of Statistics, Univ. of Surrey, 1985–90; Prof. of Statistical Sci., Univ. of Cambridge, 1994–96. Guy Medal in Silver, Royal Statistical Soc., 1991. *Publications:* (jtly) Statistical Analysis of Reliability Data, 1991; contrib. to Jl Roy. Statistical Soc., Proc. Royal Soc., Biometrika, Annals of Stats, etc. *Recreations:* cross-country and road running, chess, bridge, music. *Address:* 4314 Oak Hill Road, Chapel Hill, NC 27514, USA.

SMITH, Richard Maybury H.; *see* Hastie-Smith.

SMITH, Dr Richard Michael, FRHistS; FBA 1991; Reader in Historical Demography, University of Cambridge, since 1996; Director, Cambridge Group for the History of Population and Social Structure, since 1994; Fellow, Downing College, Cambridge, since 1994; *b* 3 Jan. 1946; *s* of Louis Gordon Smith and Elsie Fanny (*née* Ward); *m* 1971, Margaret Anne McFadden. *Educ:* Earls Colne Grammar Sch.; University Coll. London (BA Hons); St Catharine's Coll., Cambridge (MA 1977; PhD 1974). Lectr in Population Studies, Plymouth Poly., 1973–74; Cambridge University: Asst Lectr in Histl Geography, 1974–76; Sen. Res. Officer, 1976–81, Asst Dir, 1981–83, Cambridge Gp for the Hist. of Population and Social Structure; Fellow, 1977–83, Tutor, 1979–83, Fitzwilliam Coll.; Oxford University: Univ. Lectr in Histl Demography, 1983–89; Fellow, All Souls Coll., 1983–94; Reader in Hist. of Medicine and Dir, Wellcome Unit for Hist. of Medicine, 1990–94. Mem. Council, British Soc. for Population Studies, 1987–91. Sir John Neale Lectr, 1996. Ed., Social Hist. of Medicine, 1986–92. *Publications:* (ed jtly) Bastardy and its Comparative History, 1980; (ed) Land, Kinship and Lifecycle, 1984; (ed jtly) The World We Have Gained: histories of population and social structure, 1986; (ed jtly) Life, Death and the Elderly: historical perspectives, 1991; (ed jtly) Medieval Society and the Manor Court, 1996; contribs to Annales ESC, Jl of Family Hist., Trans RHistS, Ageing and Society, Law and Hist. Rev., Population and Develt Rev. *Recreations:* listening to music, walking in Norfolk. *Address:* Cambridge Group for the History of Population and Social Structure, 27 Trumpington Street, Cambridge CB2 1QA. *T:* (01223) 333181.

SMITH, Sir Richard P.; *see* Prince-Smith, Sir W. R.

SMITH, Richard Philip Morley R.; *see* Reay-Smith.

SMITH, Prof. R(ichard) Selby, OBE 1981; MA (Oxon), MA (Harvard); Professor of Education and Head of Department of Education, University of Tasmania, 1973–79, now Professor Emeritus; *b* 1914; *s* of Selby Smith, Hall Place, Barming, Maidstone, Kent, and Annie Rachel Smith (*née* Rawlins); *m* 1940, Rachel Hebe Philippa Pease, Rounton, Northallerton, Yorks; two *s*. *Educ:* Rugby Sch.; Magdalen Coll., Oxford; Harvard Univ. Asst Master, Milton Acad., Milton, Mass, USA, 1938–39; House Tutor and Sixth Form Master, Sedbergh Sch., 1939–40; War of 1939–45: Royal Navy, 1940–46; final rank of Lt-Comdr, RNVR. Administrative Asst, Kent Education Cttee, 1946–48; Asst Education Officer, Kent, 1948–50; Dep. Chief Education Officer, Warwickshire, 1950–53; Principal, Scotch Coll., Melbourne, 1953–64; Foundation Prof. of Educn, Monash Univ., 1964, Dean of Faculty of Educn, 1965–71; Principal, Tasmanian Coll. of Advanced Education, 1971–73. Chairman: Victorian Univs and Schools Examinations Bd, 1967–71; State Planning and Finance Cttee, Australian Schools Commn, 1974–77, 1980–83; Vice-Pres., Australian Council for Educnl Research, 1976–79. Hon. LLD Monash, 1989. *Publications:* Towards an Australian Philosophy of Education, 1965; (ed jtly) Fundamental Issues in Australian Education, 1971; The Education Policy Process in Tasmania, 1980; Australian Independent Schools: yesterday, today and tomorrow, 1983. *Recreations:* fishing, ornithology. *Address:* Apt 234, Derwent Waters Residential Club, Cadbury Road, Claremont, Tas 7011, Australia.

SMITH, Richard Sydney William, CBE 2000; Editor, British Medical Journal, and Chief Executive, BMJ Publishing Group, since 1991; Visiting Professor, London School of Hygiene and Tropical Medicine, since 1996; *b* 11 March 1952; *s* of Sydney Smith and Hazel Smith (*née* Kirk); *m* 1977, Linda Jean Arnott; two *s* one *d*. *Educ:* Roan Grammar Sch., London; Edinburgh Univ. (BSc 1973; MB ChB 1976); Stanford Univ. (MSc in Management 1990). MFPHM 1992, FFPHM 1997; FRCPE 1992; MRCP 1993, FRCP 1995; FRCGP 1997; FRCSE 2000. Hosp. jobs in Scotland and New Zealand, 1976–79; Asst Editor, 1979, Sen. Asst Editor, 1984, BMJ. BBC Breakfast Time doctor, 1983–87. Founder, 1998, and Vice-Chm., 2001–, Cttee on Publication Ethics; Member: Internat. Cttee of Med. Jl Editors, 1991–; Bd, World Assoc. of Med. Editors, 1994–; Editorial Boards: Nat. Med. Jl of India; Ceylon Med. Jl; Canadian Med. Assoc. Jl; Hong Kong Jl of Family Practice. Mem. Bd, Project HOPE UK, 1996–. Prof. of Med. Journalism, Univ. of Nottingham, 1993–2001. Chm., Foresight Wkg Pty on Inf. and Health, 2000. Founder FMedSci 1998; Fellow, Acad. of Gen. Educn, Karnataka, India, 1993. *Publications:* Alcohol Problems, 1982; Prison Health Care, 1984; The Good Health Kit, 1987; Unemployment and Health, 1987; (ed) Health of the Nation, 1991; (ed) Rationing in Action, 1993; (ed jtly) Management for Doctors, 1995; (ed jtly) Scientific Basis of Health Services, 1996; articles in learned jls. *Recreations:* jazz, cycling, running, wine, talking first and thinking second. *Address:* British Medical Journal, BMA House, Tavistock Square, WC1H 9JR.

SMITH, Robert Carr, CBE 1989; PhD; Vice-Chancellor, Kingston University, 1992–97 (Director, Kingston Polytechnic, 1982–92); *b* 19 Nov. 1935; *s* of late Edward Albert Smith and of Olive Winifred Smith; *m* 1960, Rosalie Mary (*née* Spencer); one *s* one *d*. *Educ:* Queen Elizabeth's School, Barnet; Southampton Univ. (BSc); London Univ. (PhD). Research Asst, Guy's Hosp. Med. Sch., 1957–61; Lectr, Senior Lectr, Reader, Prof. of Electronics, Southampton Univ., 1961–82. Seconded to DoE, 1973–74. Chairman: Engineering Profs' Conf., 1980–82; Polytechnics and Colls Employers' Forum, 1988–90; Vice-Chm., Cttee of Dirs of Polytechnics, 1988–89; Member: Design Council, 1983–88; Council for Industry and Higher Educn, 1985–97; Council, Inst. for Manpower Studies, 1987–95; PCFC, 1988–93; TEC for Kingston, Merton and Wandsworth, 1989–97; Higher Educn Statistics Agency, 1993–97; Univs and Colls Employers' Assoc., 1994–97. Pt-time Chief Exec., SEARCH (careers service for Kingston, Merton and Wandsworth), 1998. Mem., Bd of Govs, Dulwich Coll., 1998–; Chm., Bd of Govs, IoW Further Educn Coll., 1999–. Hon. Fellow, St George's Hosp. Med. Sch., 1998. Freeman, Royal Borough of Kingston upon Thames, 1997. *Publications:* research papers on radiation physics, laser physics, new technology. *Recreations:* visual arts, collecting. *Address:* Maybury House, Church Road, Swanmore, Southampton SO32 2PA. *T:* (01489) 891013.

SMITH, Sir Robert (Courtney), Kt 1987; CBE 1980; FRSE; MA, CA; Chairman, Alliance and Second Alliance Trust, 1984–96; *b* 10 Sept. 1927; 4th *s* of late John Smith, DL, JP, and Agnes Smith, Glasgow and Symington; *m* 1954, Moira Rose, *d* of late Wilfred H. Macdougall, CA, Glasgow; one *s* two *d* (and one *s* decd). *Educ:* Kelvinside Academy, Glasgow; Sedbergh Sch.; Trinity Coll., Cambridge. BA 1950, MA 1957. Served, Royal Marines, 1945–47, and RMFVR, 1951–57; Hon. Col, RM Reserves Scotland, 1992–96. Partner, Arthur Young McClelland Moores & Co., Chartered Accountants, 1957–78. Director: Standard Life Assurance, 1975–94 (Chm., 1982–88); Sidlaw Gp, 1977–97 (Chm., 1980–88); Wm Collins, 1978–89 (Vice-Chm., 1979–89); Trucks (GB), later Volvo Truck and Bus, 1979–98; Edinburgh Investment Trust, 1983–98; British Alcan Aluminium, 1983–99; Bank of Scotland, 1985–97. Mem., Scottish Industrial Develt Adv. Bd, 1972–88 (Chm., 1981–88); Pres., Business Archives Council of Scotland, 1986–97; Chancellor's Assessor, Glasgow Univ., 1984–96. Mem., Horserace Betting Levy Bd, 1977–82; Deacon Convener, Trades House of Glasgow, 1976–78; Dir, Merchants House of Glasgow, 1991–96. Mem. Council, Inst. of Chartered Accountants of Scotland, 1974–79. Trustee, Carnegie Trust for Univs of Scotland. FRSE 1988. Hon. LLD: Glasgow, 1978; Aberdeen, 1991. OStJ. *Recreations:* racing, gardening. *Address:* The Old Rectory, Cathedral Street, Dunkeld, Perthshire PH8 0AW. *T:* (01350) 727574. *Clubs:* East India; Western (Glasgow); Hawks (Cambridge).

See also John Smith.

SMITH, Robert Daglish, CMG 1998; Executive Director, UK Committee for UNICEF, 1980–99; *b* 2 July 1934; *s* of Robert Ramsay Smith and Jessie Smith (*née* Daglish); *m* 1984, Ursula Schmidt-Brümmer (*née* Stollenwerk). *Educ:* Dulwich Coll.; Queens' Coll., Cambridge (MA). Nat. Service, Royal Signals, 1953–55. Master, King's Sch., Canterbury, 1960–65; Lectr, Newland Park Coll. of Education, 1965–67; Consultant, Wells Management Consultants, 1968–70; freelance mgt consultant in fundraising and arts admin, 1970–74; Dir, East Midlands Arts Assoc., 1974–80. Sec., 1976–78, Chair, 1979–80, Standing Cttee of Regl Arts Assocs; Treas., Council, Children's Rights Office, 1992–. Trustee, NSPCC, 1999–; Mem. Internat. Cttee, Shakespeare's Globe, 2000–. FRSA 1990. *Recreations:* music, opera, theatre, travel. *Address:* 37E Westbourne Gardens, W2 5NR. *T:* (020) 7221 0890.

SMITH, Sir Robert (Haldane), Kt 1999; CA; FCIBS; Vice Chairman, Deutsche Asset Management, since 2000; Scottish Governor, BBC, since 1999; *b* 8 Aug. 1944; *s* of Robert Haldane Smith and Jean Smith (*née* Adams); *m* 1969, Alison Marjorie Bell; two *d*. *Educ:* Allan Glen's Sch., Glasgow. CA 1968; FCIBS 1993. With ICFC, 1968–82; Royal Bank of Scotland plc, 1983–85; Man. Dir, Charterhouse Develt Capital Ltd, 1985–89; Chm., Morgan Grenfell Develt Capital Ltd, 1989– (Chief Exec., 1989–98); Chief Exec., Morgan Grenfell Asset Mgt Ltd, 1996–2000. Director: MFI Furniture Gp plc, 1987–2000; Stakis plc, 1997–99 (Chm., 1998–99); Bank of Scotland, 1998–2000. Dir, FSA, 1997–2000. Pres., ICA of Scotland, 1996–97. Chm., Bd of Trustees, Nat. Museums of Scotland, 1993–2001; Mem., Museums and Galls Commn, 1988–98 (Vice Chm., 1996–98). Pres., British Assoc. of Friends of Museums, 1995–. Dr *hc* Edinburgh, 1999; DUniv Glasgow, 2001. *Publication:* (jtly) Managing Your Company's Finances, 1981. *Recreation:* Inchmarnock Island. *Address:* Deutsche Asset Management, 1 Appold Street, EC2A 2UU. *T:* (020) 7545 6000.

SMITH, (Robert) Harvey; show jumper, farmer; *b* 29 Dec. 1938; *m* 1st, Irene Shuttleworth (marr. diss. 1986); two *s*; 2nd, 1987, Susan Dye. First major win with Farmer's Boy. Leading Show Jumper of the Year; other major wins include: King George V Cup, Royal Internat. Horse Show, 1958; has won the John Player Trophy 7 times, King George V Gold Cup once, and the British Jumping Derby 4 times; Grand Prix and Prix des Nations wins in UK, Ireland, Europe and USA; took part in Olympic Games, 1968 and 1972; best-known mounts: Farmer's Boy, Mattie Brown, Olympic Star, O'Malley, Salvador, Harvester. BBC TV Commentator, Los Angeles Olympics, 1984. Assists wife in training of racehorses. *Publications:* Show Jumping with Harvey Smith, 1979; Bedside

Jumping, 1985.
See also R. W. Smith.

SMITH, Prof. Robert Henry Tufrey, AM 1998; PhD; Deputy Chancellor, Southern Cross University, Australia, since 1998; *b* 22 May 1935; *s* of late Robert Davidson Smith and Gladys Smith (*née* Tufrey); *m* 1959, Elisabeth Jones; one *s* one *d*. *Educ:* Farrer Memorial Agricultural High Sch., Tamworth, NSW; Univ. of New England, NSW (BA, 1st Cl. Hons Geography); Northwestern Univ. (MA); ANU (PhD). Lectr in Geography, Univ. of Melbourne, 1961–62; University of Wisconsin: Asst Prof. of Geography, 1962–64; Associate Prof., 1964–67; Prof., 1967–70; Chm., African Studies Programme, 1968–69 (on leave, 1964–66: Associate Res. Fellow, Nigerian Inst. for Social and Econ. Res., and Hon. Vis. Lectr in Geography, Univ. of Ibadan, 1964–65; Vis. Fellow, Dept of Geography, Univ. of Sydney, 1965–66); Prof. of Geography and Head of Dept, Queen's Univ., Kingston, Ontario, 1970–72; Prof. of Geography, Monash Univ., 1972–75 (Chm. of Dept, 1973–75; Associate Dean, Faculty of Arts, 1974–75); University of British Columbia: Prof. of Geography, 1975–85; Head of Dept, 1975–80; Associate Vice-Pres., Academic, 1979–83; Vice-Pres., Academic, 1983–85; Pres. *pro tem*, March–Nov. 1985; Vice-Chancellor, Univ. of WA, 1985–89; Chm., Nat. Bd of Employment, Educn and Trng, Aust., 1989–90; Vice-Chancellor, Univ. of New England, Australia, 1990–93; Exec. Dir, 1994–97, Sen. Consultant, 1997–99, Australian Educn Office, Washington. *Address:* 16 Lakeview Circuit, East Ballina, NSW 2478, Australia.

SMITH, Sir Robert Hill, 3rd Bt *cr* 1945, of Crowmallie, Co. Aberdeen; MP (Lib Dem) Aberdeenshire West and Kincardine, since 1997; *b* 15 April 1958; *s* of Sir (William) Gordon Smith, 2nd Bt, VRD, and of Diana (*née* Goodchild); *S* father, 1983; *m* 1993, Fiona Anne Cormack; three *d*. *Educ:* Merchant Taylors' School; King's Coll., Aberdeen Univ. Contested (SDP/Lib Alliance), Aberdeen North, 1987. Mem. (Lib Dem) Aberdeenshire Unitary Council, 1995–97. Vice Chm., Grampian Jt Police Bd, 1995–97. Gen. Council Assessor, Aberdeen Univ. Court, 1994–98. *Heir: b* Charles Gordon Smith, *b* 21 April 1959. *Address:* Crowmallie House, Pitcaple, Inverurie, Aberdeenshire AB51 5HR. *T:* (01330) 820330; *e-mail:* bobsmith@cix.co.uk.

SMITH, Robert Lee; Director General, Regional Co-ordination Unit, Cabinet Office (formerly at Department of the Environment, Transport and the Regions), since 2000; *b* 9 Feb. 1952; *s* of John Joseph Smith and Joan Margaret Smith (*née* Parry); *m* 1986, Susan Elizabeth Armfield; one *s* one *d*. *Educ:* St Dunstan's Coll., Catford; Magdalene Coll., Cambridge (MA Eng. Lit.). Entered Civil Service as Administrative Trainee, 1974; DES, later DFE, then DFEE, subseq. DfES, 1981–2000: Principal Private Sec. to Sec. of State for Educn and Science, 1985–87; Under Sec., Pupils and Parents Br., 1994; Dir, Pupil Support and Inclusion Gp (formerly Pupils, Parents and Youth), 1995–2000. Public Sector Chm., Inst. of Mgt/CS Network, 1995–2000. Member: Young People and Families Cttee, Joseph Rowntree Foundn, 1997–; Prince's Trust Action Study Support Adv. Gp, 1997–99. *Recreations:* folk dancing and music. *Address:* Regional Co-ordination Unit, 2nd Floor, Riverwalk House, 157–161 Millbank, SW1P 4RR.

SMITH, Robert Walter; showjumper; *b* 12 June 1961; *s* of (Robert) Harvey Smith, *qv*, and Irene Smith; *m* 1988, Leanne Carole Alston; one *s* three *d*. Mem., winning GB junior and senior European events teams, 1977–; Bronze Medal, European Championships, 1997; King George VI Gold Cup winner, 1979, 1989, 1998. *Address:* Brookfurlong Farm, High Cross, Shrewley, Warwickshire CV35 7BD. *T:* (01926) 843886.

SMITH, Robin Anthony, TD 1978; DL; Consultant, DLA (formerly Dibb Lupton Alsop), solicitors, since 1999; *b* 15 Feb. 1943; *s* of late Tom Sumerfield Smith and Mary Smith; *m* 1967, Jennifer Elizabeth Roslington; one *s* one *d*. *Educ:* St Michael's Coll.; Manchester Univ. (LLB). Solicitor, admitted 1966; joined Dibb Lupton & Co., 1966; Partner, 1966–99; Man. Partner, 1988–93; Sen. Partner, Dibb Lupton & Co., later Dibb Lupton Broomhead, then Dibb Lupton Alsop, 1993–98. Mem. Council, Law Society, 1982–91; Pres., Leeds Law Soc., 1993–94. Director: Leeds & Holbeck Bldg Soc., 1998–; Town Centre Securities plc, 1999–; Local Dir, Coutts & Co., 1999–. Gov., Stonyhurst Coll., 1989–98. Commnd 5th Bn LI, TA, 1966; retired 1985, Lt-Col. DL W Yorks, 1991. *Recreations:* tennis, golf. *Address:* DLA, Princes Exchange, Princes Square, Leeds LS1 4BY. *Clubs:* Army and Navy, MCC; Leeds; Alwoodley Golf; York CC (Pres., 2000–).

SMITH, Rt Rev. Robin Jonathan Norman; Suffragan Bishop of Hertford, 1990–2001; *b* 14 Aug. 1936; *s* of Richard Norman and Blanche Spurling Smith; *m* 1961, Hon. Lois Jean, *d* of Baron Pearson, CBE, PC; three *s* one *d*. *Educ:* Bedford Sch.; Worcester Coll., Oxford (MA); Ridley Hall, Cambridge. RAF Regiment Commission, 1955–57. Curate, St Margaret's, Barking, 1962–67; Chaplain, Lee Abbey, 1967–72; Vicar, Chesham St Mary, 1972–80; Rector, Great Chesham, 1980–90. Hon. Canon, Christ Church, Oxford, 1988–90. *Recreations:* gardening, walking. *Address:* 7 Aysgarth Road, Redbourn, Herts AL3 7PJ.

SMITH, Prof. Roderick Arthur, PhD, ScD; FREng, FIMechE, FIM; Professor and Head of Department of Mechanical Engineering, Imperial College of Science, Technology and Medicine, London, since 2000; *b* 26 Dec. 1947; *s* of Eric and Gladys Mary Smith; *m* 1975, Yayoi Yamanoi. *Educ:* Hulme Grammar Sch., Oldham; St John's Coll., Oxford (BA, MA); Queens' Coll., Cambridge (MA; PhD 1975; ScD 1998). CEng 1976; FIMechE 1991; FIM 1992; FREng 1999. Queens' College, Cambridge: Godfrey Mitchell Res. Fellow, 1975–78; Official Fellow, College Lectr and Dir of Studies, 1978–88; Asst Lectr, Engrg Dept, Cambridge Univ., 1977–80, Lectr, 1980–88; Sheffield University: Prof. of Mech. and Process Engrg, 1988–2000; Hd, Dept of Mech. and Process Engrg, 1992–95; Royal Acad. of Engrg/BR Res. Prof., 1995–2000; Chm., Advanced Rly Res. Centre, 1993–; Warden, Stephenson Hall, 1992–2000. Chm., Coll. of Rly Technol., Derby, 1996–97. Consultant to: British Steel plc, 1986–89; BR, 1992– (Mem. Bd, Res. and Tech. Cttee, 1992–96). Mem., Res. and Tech. Cttee, AEA Technology, 1997–. Mem. Council, IMechE, 1999–. *Publications:* Thirty Years of Fatigue Crack Growth, 1986; Innovative Teaching in Engineering, 1991; Engineering for Crowd Safety, 1993; ed books; papers and articles on mech. engrg, design, manufacture, engrg educn and crowd engrg. *Recreations:* mountaineering, reading, history, Japan: its people and technology; conversation, wine. *Address:* Department of Mechanical Engineering, Imperial College of Science, Technology and Medicine, Exhibition Road, SW7 2BX. *T:* (020) 7594 7000. *Clubs:* Royal Over-Seas League; Fell and Rock (Lake District).

SMITH, Rodger H.; *see* Hayward Smith.

SMITH, Roger Bonham; Chairman and Chief Executive Officer, General Motors, 1981–90 (Member, Board of Directors, 1974–92); *b* Columbus, Ohio, 12 July 1925. *Educ:* Detroit University Sch.; Univ. of Michigan (BBA, MBA). Served US Navy, 1944–46. General Motors: Sen. Clerk, subseq. Director, general accounting, Detroit Central Office, 1949–58; Dir, financial analysis sect., NY Central Office, 1960, later Asst Treas.; transf. to Detroit as Gen. Asst Comptroller, then Gen. Asst Treas., 1968; Treasurer, 1970; Vice-Pres. i/c Financial Staff, 1971, also Mem. Admin Cttee, 1971–90; Vice-Pres. and Gp Exec. i/c Nonautomotive and Defense Gp, 1972; Exec. Vice-Pres., Mem. Bd of Dirs and Mem. Finance Cttee, 1974, also Mem. Exec. Cttee, 1974–90; Vice-Chm. Finance Cttee, 1975–80, Chm., 1981–90. Conceived GM Cancer Res. Awards, 1978 (Trustee); Member: Business Council, 1981–; Soc. of Automotive Engrs, 1978–. Hon. degrees from several univs. Hon. Dr DePauw, 1979; Hon. Dr Albion Coll., 1982. *Address:* General Motors Corporation, 31 Judson Street, Pontiac, MI 48342-2230, USA; (home) Bloomfield Hills, MI 48304. *Clubs:* Economic, Detroit, Detroit Athletic (Detroit); Links (NY).

SMITH, Roger John; Chairman: Central Industrial Holdings Ltd, since 1992; European Motor Holdings PLC, since 1994; *b* 20 April 1939; *s* of Horace W. Smith and Marjorie E. Pummery; *m* 1962, Margaret R. Campbell; one *s* two *d*. *Educ:* Bedford School. Nat. Service, Subaltern, RCT, 1958–60. Dir, Family Group business, incl. Lea Heating Merchants (later part of Tricentrol), 1960–70; Man. Dir, Commercial Div., 1971–75, Dir, Special Projects, 1976–78, Tricentrol International; Dir, Group Co-ordination, Tricentrol, 1978–81; Man. Dir, Commercial Div., 1981–83; Dep. Chm., Tricentrol plc, 1983–88. Chm. and Chief Exec., Trimoco plc, 1987–92. Director: Combined Technologies Corp. plc; Brengreen Hldgs plc, and other cos. Pres., Retail Motor Industry Fedn, 1991–93; Pres., Internat. Orgn for Motor Trade and Repair, 1998–2000. Sloan Fellow, Stanford Univ., 1976. Chm., Lord's Taverners, 2000–April 2002. Chm., Central Finance Bd, Methodist Church, 2000–. Liveryman, Coach and Harnessmakers' Co. *Recreations:* sailing, shooting, tennis, reading. *Address:* Gilvers, Markyate, Herts AL3 8AD. *T:* (01582) 840536. *Clubs:* Royal Automobile, Royal Thames Yacht.

SMITH, Roger L.; *see* Lane-Smith.

SMITH, Sir Roland, Kt 1991; a Director, Bank of England, 1991–96; Professor Emeritus of Management Science, University of Manchester, since 1988; *b* 1 Oct. 1928; *s* of late Joshua Smith and of Mrs Hannah Smith; *m* 1954, Joan (*née* Shaw); no *c*. *Educ:* Univs of Birmingham and Manchester. BA, MSc, PhD (Econ). Flying Officer, RAF, 1953. Lectr in Econs, Univ. of Liverpool, 1960; Dir, Univ. of Liverpool Business Sch., 1963; Prof. of Marketing, 1966–88, Hon. Vis. Prof., 1988–, and Chancellor, 1996–, UMIST. Non-Exec. Chm., Senior Engineering Ltd, 1973–92; Chairman: Temple Bar Investment Trust Ltd, 1980–99; House of Fraser, 1981–86; Readicut International, 1984–96; Hepworth plc, 1986–97; British Aerospace, 1987–91; P & P plc, 1988–97; Manchester United Plc, 1991–March 2002; Dir-Consultant to a number of public companies. *Recreation:* walking.

SMITH, Roland Hedley, CMG 1994; HM Diplomatic Service; Ambassador to Ukraine, since 1999; *b* 11 April 1943; *s* of late Alan Hedley Smith and of Elizabeth Louise Smith; *m* 1971, Katherine Jane Lawrence; two *d*. *Educ:* King Edward VII School, Sheffield; Keble College, Oxford (BA 1st cl. hons 1965, MA 1981). Third Sec., Foreign Office, 1967; Second Sec., Moscow, 1969; Second, later First Sec., UK Delegn to NATO, Brussels, 1971; First Sec., FCO, 1974; First Sec. and Cultural Attaché, Moscow, 1978; FCO, 1980; attached to Internat. Inst. for Strategic Studies, 1983; Political Advr and Hd of Chancery, British Mil. Govt, Berlin, 1984–88; Dep. Hd, Sci., Energy and Nuclear Dept, FCO, 1988–90; Hd of Non-Proliferation and Defence Dept, FCO, 1990–92; Minister and Dep. Perm. Rep., UK Delegn to NATO, Brussels, 1992–95; Asst Under-Sec. of State, then Dir, (Internat. Security), FCO, 1995–99. *Publication:* Soviet Policy Towards West Germany, 1985. *Recreations:* music, esp. choral singing, football (Sheffield United), trams. *Address:* c/o Foreign and Commonwealth Office, SW1A 2AH. *Club:* Royal Commonwealth Society.

SMITH, Prof. Roland Ralph Redfern, DPhil; Lincoln Professor of Classical Archaeology and Art, University of Oxford, since 1995; *b* 30 Jan. 1954; *s* of Rupert and Elinor Smith; *m* 1989, Ingrid Gaitet. *Educ:* Fettes Coll., Edinburgh; Pembroke Coll., Oxford (BA 1977; MPhil 1979); Magdalen Coll., Oxford (DPhil 1983). Fellow, Magdalen Coll., Oxford, 1981–86; Asst Prof. of Classical Archaeology, 1986–90, Associate Prof., 1990–95, Inst. of Fine Arts, NY Univ. Harkness Fellow, Princeton, 1983–85; Alexander von Humboldt Fellow, Munich, 1991–92. Dir, Excavations at Aphrodisias, Caria, 1991–. *Publications:* Hellenistic Royal Portraits, 1988; Hellenistic Sculpture, 1991; The Monument of C. Julius Zoilos, 1993; contrib. learned jls. *Address:* Ashmolean Museum, Oxford OX1 2PH.

SMITH, Ronald Alfred D.; *see* Dingwall-Smith.

SMITH, Ronald Angus; General Secretary, Educational Institute of Scotland, since 1995; *b* 9 June 1951; *s* of William Angus and Daisy Smith; *m* 1976, Mary A. Lambie; one *s* one *d*. *Educ:* Anderson Educnl Inst., Lerwick; Univ. of Aberdeen (MA 1972); Aberdeen Coll. of Educn (PGCE 1973). Teacher, later Principal Teacher, Latin and Modern Studies, Broxburn Acad., W Lothian, 1973–88; Asst Sec., Educnl Inst. of Scotland, 1988–95. *Recreation:* Livingston FC. *Address:* (office) 46 Moray Place, Edinburgh EH3 6BH. *T:* (0131) 225 6244.

SMITH, Ronald George; Chief Executive, Defence Secondary Care Agency, Ministry of Defence, since 1995; *b* 12 May 1954; *s* of John Hamilton Smith and Jean Lennox Smith (*née* Graeme); *m* 1st, 1978, Elaine Sheila Murdoch (*née* McClure) (marr. diss. 1988); two *s*; 2nd, 1988, Susan Elizabeth Barstead. *Educ:* George Heriot's Sch., Edinburgh; Edinburgh Univ. (MA Jt Hons Pol. and Mod. Hist., 1976); Queens' Coll., Cambridge (MPhil Internat. Relns, 1988); Kingston Poly. Business Sch. (MBA 1991). Commnd RAF, 1972; RAF Coll., Cranwell, 1976–77 (Queen's Medal); 51 Sqn RAF Regt, 1977–78; 63 Sqn RAF Regt, Gütersloh, 1978–81; HQ RAF Germany, Rheindahlen, 1981–82; RAF Lyneham, 1982–83; Dep. Sqn Ldr II Sqn (Para) RAF Regt, 1983–84; Sqn Ldr, 1984; OC Short Range Air Defence, Belize, 1984–85; OC 1 (Light Armoured) Sqn RAF Regt, RAF Laarbruch, 1985–87; Wing Comdr, 1988; Desk Officer D Air Plans, 1988–92; Dep. Regl Dir, Corporate Planning, Trent RHA, 1992–93; Chief Exec., Lincs HA/FHSA, 1993–95. *Publications:* articles in jls. *Recreations:* downhill ski-ing, hillwalking, tennis, philately, fine wine, English landscape paintings. *Address:* Defence Secondary Care Agency, St Giles Court, 1–13 St Giles Street, WC2H 8LD. *T:* (020) 7305 6190.

SMITH, Ronald Good; Sheriff of North Strathclyde, 1984–99; *b* 24 July 1933; *s* of Adam Smith and Selina Spence Smith; *m* 1962, Joan Robertson Beharrie; two *s*. *Educ:* Glasgow University (BL 1962). Private practice to 1984. *Recreations:* philately, photography, gardening, reading. *Address:* 8 Lomond View, Symington, Ayrshire KA1 5QS. *T:* (01563) 830763.

SMITH, Rosemary Ann, (Mrs G. F. Smith); Headmistress, Wimbledon High School, GPDST, 1982–92; *b* 10 Feb. 1932; *d* of late Harold Edward Wincott, CBE, editor of the Investors Chronicle, and of Joyce Mary Wincott; *m* 1954, Rev. Canon Graham Francis Smith; two *s* two *d*. *Educ:* Brighton and Hove High School, GPDST; Westfield College, Univ. of London (BA Hons); London Univ. Inst. of Education (post grad. Cert. in Education). Assistant Teacher: Central Foundation Girls' School, 1964–69; Rosa Bassett Girls' School, 1970–77; Furzedown Secondary School, 1977–80; Deputy Head, Rowan High School, 1980–82. Mem. Council, GDST (formerly GPDST), 1993–. *Recreations:*

theatre, gardening, reading, walking. *Address:* The Haven, 9 High Street, Syresham, Brackley, Northants NN13 5HL. *T:* (01280) 850421.

SMITH, Air Marshal Sir Roy David A.; *see* Austen-Smith.

SMITH, Gen. Sir Rupert (Anthony), KCB 1996; DSO 1991 (and Bar 1996); OBE 1982; QGM 1978; Deputy Supreme Allied Commander, Europe, 1998–2002; Aide-de-Camp General to the Queen, 2000–02; *b* 13 Dec. 1943; *s* of late Gp Captain Irving Smith, CBE, DFC (and Bar) and Joan Smith (*née* Debenham). Parachute Regt, 1964; Dep. Comdt, Staff Coll., Camberley, 1989–90; Comdr, 1st Armoured Div., BAOR, Gulf, 1990–92; ACDS (Ops), 1992–94; Comdr, UN Protection Force Bosnia-Herzegovina, 1995; GOC and Dir of Military Ops, NI, 1996–98. Lt Col, 1980; Col, 1985; Brig., 1986; Maj.-Gen., 1990; Lt-Gen., 1995. *Address:* c/o RHQ The Parachute Regiment, Aldershot, Hants GU11 2BU.

SMITH, Russell; *see* Smith, C. R.

SMITH, Sidney William; retired; Regional Administrator, East Anglian Regional Health Authority, 1975–83; *b* 17 May 1920; *s* of late Sidney John and Harriet May Smith; *m* 1943, Doreen Kelly; one *s* one *d. Educ:* Wirral Grammar Sch., Cheshire. ACIS. Served RAF, 1940–46. Asst Sec., Bury Infirmary, 1939–48; Dep. Group Sec.: Mansfield Hosp. Management Cttee, 1948–61; Wolverhampton Hosp. Management Cttee, 1961–63; Group Sec., Wakefield Hosp. Management Cttee, 1963–73; Area Administrator, Wakefield Area Health Authority, 1973–75. Member: Management Side, Ancillary Staff, Whitley Council, 1969–83 (Chm., 1982–83); Cttee, Assoc. of Chief Administrators of Health Authorities, 1974–84 (Chm., 1974–76); Health Services Panel, Inst. of Chartered Secretaries and Administrators, 1978–84, 1986–95 (Chm., 1978–83); Council, Soc. of Family Practitioner Cttees, 1989–90; Vice Chm., Cambs FPC, 1985–90; Chm., Pharmaceutical Services Panel, Cambridge and Huntingdon HA (formerly Cambs FHSA), 1991–99. Dir, Sketchley Hosp. Services Ltd, 1983–84. Freeman, City of London, 1985. *Recreations:* gardening, Rugby Union football. *Address:* 77 Gough Way, Cambridge CB3 9LN. *T:* (01223) 362307.

SMITH, Prof. (Stanley) Desmond, OBE 1998; FRS 1976; FRSE 1972; Chairman: Edinburgh Instruments Ltd, since 1971; Edinburgh Sensors Ltd, since 1988; Professor of Physics and Head of Department of Physics, Heriot-Watt University, Edinburgh, 1970–96, now Professor Emeritus (Dean of the Faculty of Science, 1981–84); *b* 3 March 1931; *s* of Henry George Stanley Smith and Sarah Emily Ruth Smith; *m* 1956, Gillian Anne Parish; one *s* one *d. Educ:* Cotham Grammar Sch., Bristol; Bristol Univ. (BSc, DSc); Reading Univ. (PhD). SSO, RAE, Farnborough, 1956–58; Research Asst, Dept of Meteorology, Imperial Coll., London, 1958–59; Lectr, then Reader, Univ. of Reading, 1960–70. Member: ACARD, 1985–87; Defence Scientific Adv. Council, 1985–91; Astronomy, Space & Radio Bd, Engrg Bd, SERC, 1985–88; ACOST, 1987–88. Principal Investigator, Scottish Collaborative Initiative in Optoelectronic Scis, 1991–97. Mem. Council, Inst. of Physics, 1984–87; Chm., Scottish Optoelectronics Assoc., 1996–98. C. V. Boys Prizeman, Inst. of Physics, 1976; Educn in Partnership with Industry or Commerce Prize, DTI, 1982; Technical or Business Innovation in Electronics Prize, Electronics Weekly, 1986; James Scott Prize, RSE, 1987. *Publications:* Infra-red Physics, 1966; Optoelectronic Devices, 1995; numerous papers on semi-conductor and laser physics, satellite meteorology, nonlinear optics and optical computing. *Recreations:* tennis, skiing, mountaineering, golf, raising the temperature. *Address:* Tree Tops, 29D Gillespie Road, Colinton, Edinburgh EH13 0NW. *T:* (0131) 441 7225; (office) (01506) 425300, *Fax:* (01506) 425320; *e-mail:* des.smith@edinst.com, desgillsmith@treetops87.freeserve.co.uk.

SMITH, Stanley Frank, MA; CEng, FIMechE; Vice-President (Technology), Urban Transport Development Company, Kingston, Ontario, 1985–86, retired; *b* 15 Dec. 1924; *s* of Frederick and Edith Maria Smith; *m* 1st, 1946, Margaret (*née* Garrett) (*d* 1984); two *s* three *d*; 2nd, 1987, Catherine Cooke Murphy. *Educ:* Purley Sch.; Hertford Coll., Oxford (MA). Served War, RAF Pilot, 1943–46. Oxford Univ., 1946–49. Rolls-Royce Ltd, 1949–65 (Chief Research Engineer, 1963); British Railways, 1965–71 (Dir of Engineering Research, 1965; Dir of Research, 1966); joined London Transport, 1971: Dir-Gen. of Research and Develt, 1971–72; Chief Mech. Engr, 1972–81, retired; Gen. Manager, Res. Develt, Urban Transport Development Co., 1981–85. *Recreations:* tennis, windsurfing, cycling, walking, ski-ing, sailing. *Address:* Rural Route 1, Bath, ON K0H 1G0, Canada. *T:* (613) 3527429.

SMITH, Stephen; *see* Smith, J. S.

SMITH, Stephen, MA; Headmaster, Bedford Modern School, since 1996; *b* 8 Aug. 1948; *s* of late Joseph Leslie Smith and Audrey May Smith; *m* 1970, Janice Susan Allen; one *s* one *d. Educ:* Loughborough Grammar Sch.; Regent's Park Coll., Oxford (BA Modern History 1969; Cert. Ed. 1970; MA 1974). Loughborough Grammar School: Asst History Master, 1970–87; Junior Housemaster, 1976–79; Head of General Studies, 1983–87; Head of History, 1987–93; Dep. Headmaster, Birkenhead Sch., 1993–96. *Recreations:* piano, organ, singing, oenology, Church and youth work. *Address:* Bedford Modern School, Manton Lane, Bedford MK41 7NT; Bramble Cottage, Chapel Lane, Colmworth, Beds MK44 2JY. *Club:* East India.

SMITH, Stephen, HM Diplomatic Service; Deputy Head of Mission, Brussels, since 1999; b 28 March 1957; s of Roy and Ruth Smith; m 1984, Wanda Won Min Kim. Educ: Univ. of Cambridge (MA). Joined FCO, 1978: Third, later Second Sec. (Commercial), Seoul, 1980-85; Second Sec., FCO, 1985-87; Second, later First Sec. (Chancery), UK Mission to UN, NY, 1987-90; First Secretary: FCO, 1990-94; (Political/Internal), Bonn, 1994-99. Recreations: ski-ing, sailing, retriever training, opera. Address: c/o Foreign and Commonwealth Office, King Charles Street, SW1A 2AH; British Embassy, rue d'Arlon 85, 1040, Brussels, Belgium.

SMITH, Prof. Stephen Kevin, MD; FRCOG; FMedSci; FIBiol; Professor of Obstetrics and Gynaecology, University of Cambridge Clinical School, Addenbrooke's (formerly Rosie Maternity) Hospital, Cambridge, since 1988; Fellow, Fitzwilliam College, Cambridge, since 1991; *b* 8 March 1951; *s* of Albert and Drusilla Smith; *m* 1978, Catriona Maclean Hobkirk Smith; one *s* two *d. Educ:* Birkenhead Sch.; Westminster Med. Sch., Univ. of London (MB BS 1974; MD 1982); FRCOG 1998 (MRCOG 1979); FIBiol 1997. Lecturer: Univ. of Edinburgh, 1979–82; Univ. of Sheffield, 1982–85, Cons. Gynaecologist, MRC Reproductive Biology Unit, Edinburgh, 1985–88. Founder FMedSci 1998. *Publications:* numerous contribs to sci. and med. pubns on the subject of Reproductive Medicine. *Recreations:* flying, football, music, natural history, politics. *Address:* 14 Hertford Street, Cambridge CB4 3AG. *T:* (01223) 357736.

SMITH, Maj.-Gen. Stephen Robert C.; *see* Carr-Smith.

SMITH, Stephen Wynn B.; *see* Boys Smith.

SMITH, Stewart Ranson, CBE 1986; Controller, Europe Division, British Council, 1989–90; *b* 16 Feb. 1931; *s* of John Smith and Elizabeth Smith; *m* 1960, Lee Tjam Mui, (Amy), Singapore. *Educ:* Bedlington Grammar Sch., Northumberland; Nottingham Univ. (BA, MA); Yale Univ., USA (MA). British Council: Asst Rep., Singapore, 1957–59; Reg. Officer, Overseas A, 1959–61; Dir, Curitiba, Brazil, 1961–65; Asst Rep., Sri Lanka, 1965–69; Planning Officer, London, 1969–70; seconded Min. of Overseas Develt, 1970–73; Rep., Kenya, 1973–76; Controller, Overseas B, 1976–80; Rep., Spain, 1980–87; Controller, Higher Educn Div., 1987–89. Chm., Consortium for Madrid Capital City of Culture 1992, 1990–92; Consultant, Internat. Relations, Complutense Univ. of Madrid, 1993–95. Cross, Order of Isabella la Católica (Spain). *Recreations:* music, cricket. *Address:* 7 Rodney Court, 6–8 Maida Vale, W9 1TQ. *Club:* Athenæum.

SMITH, Stuart Brian, FMA; Chief Executive, Trevithick Trust, since 1993; Director, Ironbridge Gorge Museum, 1983–92; *b* 19 Aug. 1944; *s* of Jack Fearnly Smith and Edith Dorothy Turner; *m* 1969, Jacqueline Slater; two *s* one *d. Educ:* Rochdale Grammar Sch.; Univ. of Surrey (BSc); Univ. of Manchester (MSc). Curator of Technology, Sunderland Museum, 1968–72; Curator of Technology, 1972, Dep. Dir, 1977–83, Ironbridge Gorge Museum. Hon. Lectr, Univ. of Birmingham, 1981–92. Vice Pres., Assoc. for Industrial Archaeology, 1992– (Asst Sec., 1975–92); Sec., Internat. Cttee for Conservation of Industrial Heritage, 1986–. Mem., Royal Commn on Ancient and Historical Monuments in Wales, 1991–96; Mem., Industrial Archaeology Panel, English Heritage, 1993–. Pres., Midlands Fedn of Museums and Galls, 1991–92 (Vice-Pres. 1989); Mem. Cttee, Icomos UK, 1987–. Mem. Council, Trevithick Soc., 1993–. Freedom of City of London, 1984. *Publications:* A View from the Ironbridge, 1979; articles in learned jls. *Recreations:* gardening, collecting. *Address:* Chygarth, 5 Beacon Terrace, Camborne, Cornwall TR14 7BU. *T:* and *Fax:* (01209) 612142.

SMITH, Rt Rev. Stuart Meldrum; Assistant Bishop, Diocese of Adelaide, 1992–98; acting Dean, St Peter's Cathedral, Adelaide, 1999–2000; *b* 8 June 1928; *s* of late F. R. and O. E. Smith; *m* 1957, Margaret, *d* of J. L. F. and D. M. Sando; three *s* two *d. Educ:* Univ. of Adelaide (BA Hons English); St Michael's House, SSM (Scholar in Theol. (Hons), ACT). Ordained 1953; Asst Curate, Glenelg, 1954–56; Mission Chaplain, Meadows, 1956–57; Domestic Chaplain, Bishop of Adelaide, and Precentor, St Peter's Cathedral, 1957–58; Priest-in-charge, Kilburn, 1958–61; Editor, Adelaide Church Guardian, 1959–61 and 1965–76; Rector: Clare, 1961–65; Coromandel Valley (with Blackwood, Eden Hills and Belair), 1965–69; Belair, 1969–72; Unley, 1972–84; Canon of Adelaide, 1974–84; Archdeacon: of Sturt, 1976–84; of Adelaide, 1984–92; Dir of Home Mission and Evangelism, 1984–92. Associate in Ministry, St John's, Adelaide, 1999. Visiting Lecturer: St Barnabas Coll., 1966–81; St Michael's House, 1975–77. Hon. Chaplain, Walford C of E Girls' Grammar Sch., 1973–75. Mem., Gen. Synod and Gen. Synod Standing Cttee, 1979–98. Chm., Council of Govs, Pulteney Grammar Sch., 1973–97. *Recreations:* walking, reading, gardening. *Address:* 4B Eleventh Avenue, St Peters, SA 5069, Australia. *T:* (8) 83625847.

SMITH, Thomas C.; *see* Cavalier-Smith.

SMITH, Sir (Thomas) Gilbert, 4th Bt *cr* 1897; Area Manager; *b* 2 July 1937; *er s* of Sir Thomas Turner Smith, 3rd Bt, and Agnes, *o d* of Bernard Page, Wellington, New Zealand; *S* father, 1961; *m* 1962, Patricia Christine Cooper; two *s* one *d. Educ:* Huntley Sch.; Nelson Coll. *Recreation:* skiing. *Heir: s* Andrew Thomas Smith, *b* 17 Oct. 1965.

SMITH, Rt Rev. Timothy D.; *see* Dudley-Smith.

SMITH, Timothy John; Partner, Wm Williams Chartered Accountants, 2001; *b* 5 Oct. 1947; *s* of late Captain Norman Wesley Smith, CBE and Nancy Phyllis Smith; *m* 1980, Jennifer Jane Scott-Hopkins, *d* of Sir James Scott-Hopkins; two *s. Educ:* Harrow Sch.; St Peter's Coll., Oxford (MA). FCA; ATII. Articled with Gibson, Harris & Turnbull, 1969; Audit Sen., Peat, Marwick, Mitchell & Co., 1971; Company Sec., Coubro & Scrutton (Hldgs) Ltd, 1973. Sec., Parly and Law Cttee, ICA, 1979–82. Pres., Oxford Univ. Conservative Assoc., 1968; Chm., Coningsby Club, 1977–78. MP (C): Ashfield, April 1977–1979; Beaconsfield, May 1982–1997. PPS to Chief Sec. HM Treasury, 1983, to Sec. of State for Home Dept, 1983–85; a Vice Chm. and Treas., Conservative Party, 1992–94; Parly Under-Sec. of State, NI Office, 1994. Member: Public Accts Cttee, 1987–92, 1995–97; Select Cttee on NI, 1994–97; Vice-Chm., Cons. Finance Cttee, 1987–92. Mem. Council, ICA, 1992–94. *Recreations:* theatre, gardening. *Address:* Wm Williams Chartered Accountants, Valley House, 53 Valley Road, Plympton, Plymouth, Devon PL7 1RF.

SMITH, Timothy Peter P.; *see* Pigott-Smith.

SMITH, Walter Purvis, CB 1982 OBE 1960 (MBE 1945); Director General, Ordnance Survey, 1977–85, retired; *b* 8 March 1920; *s* of John William Smith and Margaret Jane (*née* Purvis); *m* 1946, Bettie Cox; one *s* one *d. Educ:* Wellfield Grammar Sch., Co. Durham; St Edmund Hall, Oxford (MA). FRICS 1951. Commnd RE (Survey), 1940; served War, UK and Europe, 1940–46; CO 135 Survey Engr Regt (TA), 1957–60. Directorate of Colonial (later Overseas) Surveys: served in Ghana, Tanzania, Malaŵi, 1946–50; Gen. Man., Air Survey Co. of Rhodesia Ltd, 1950–54; Fairey Surveys Ltd, 1954–75 (Man. Dir, 1969–75); Adviser: Surveying and Mapping, UN, NY, 1975–77; Ordnance Survey Review Cttee, 1978–79. Mem., Field Mission, Argentine-Chile Frontier Case, 1965. 15th British Commonwealth Lectr, RAeS, 1968. Dir, Sys Scan (UK) Ltd, 1985–90. President: Photogrammetric Soc., 1972–73; European Council of Heads of National Mapping Agencies, 1982–84; Eur. Orgn for Photogrammetric Res., 1984–85; Guild of Surveyors, 1985–88; Chm., National Cttee for Photogrammetry and Remote Sensing, 1985–88; Dep. Chm., Govt Cttee of Enquiry into Handling of Geographical Information, 1985–87; Mem., Gen. Council, RICS, 1967–70 (Chm., Land Survey Cttee, 1963–64). Patron's Medal, RGS, 1985. *Publications:* papers and technical jls. *Recreations:* music, walking, woodworking. *Address:* 15 Forest Gardens, Lyndhurst, Hants SO43 7AF. *T:* (023) 8028 2566.

SMITH, Wendy Alison K.; *see* Kenway-Smith.

SMITH, Wilbur Addison; author; *b* 9 Jan. 1933; *m* 1971, Danielle Antoinette Thomas (*d* 1999); *m* 2000, Mokhiniso Rakhimova; two *s* one *d* by former marriages. *Educ:* Michaelhouse, Natal; Rhodes Univ. (BCom). Business executive, 1954–58; factory owner, 1958–64; full-time author, 1964–. *Publications:* When the Lion Feeds, 1964; Dark of the Sun, 1965; Sound of Thunder, 1966; Shout at the Devil, 1968; Gold Mine, 1970; Diamond Hunters, 1971; The Sunbird, 1972; Eagle in the Sky, 1974; Eye of the Tiger, 1975; Cry Wolf, 1976; Sparrow Falls, 1977; Hungry as the Sea, 1978; Wild Justice, 1979; A Falcon Flies, 1980; Men of Men, 1981; The Angels Weep, 1982; The Leopard hunts in Darkness, 1984; The Burning Shore, 1985; Power of the Sword, 1986; Rage, 1987; A Time to Die, 1989; Golden Fox, 1990; Elephant Song, 1991; River God, 1993; The Seventh Scroll, 1995; Birds of Prey, 1997; Monsoon, 1999; Warlock, 2001. *Recreations:* fly fishing, big game angling, wing shooting, ski-ing, scuba diving.

SMITH, Sir William Antony John R.; *see* Reardon Smith.

SMITH, William Austin N.; *see* Hon. Lord Nimmo Smith.

SMITH, William Jeffrey, CB 1976; Under-Secretary, Northern Ireland Office, 1972–76; *b* 14 Oct. 1916; 2nd *s* of Frederick Smith, Sheffield, and Ellen Hickinson, Ringinglow, Derbyshire; *m* 1942, Marie Hughes; one *s* one *d*. *Educ:* King Edward VII Sch., Sheffield; University Coll., Oxford (Schol.) (MA). Employed by Calico Printers' Assoc., Manchester, 1938–40 and in 1946. Served War, Army: enlisted Sept. 1939, embodied, 1940; RA and York and Lancaster Regt (Captain), 1940–46. Dominions Office (subseq. CRO), 1946; Principal, 1948; Office of UK High Commissioner in South Africa, 1953–56; Asst Sec., 1959; sundry internat. confs; Dept of Technical Co-operation, 1961–64; Min. of Overseas Development, 1964–70; Overseas Develt Admin., 1970–72; UK Rep. to UNESCO, 1969–72. Sec. to Widgery Tribunal on loss of life in Londonderry, 1972; Northern Ireland Office, 1972. *Recreations:* theatre, scrambling up mountains, walking, bell ringing. *Address:* Lime Tree Cottage, Norris Lane, Chaddleworth, Newbury, Berks RG20 7DZ. *T:* (01488) 638610.

SMITH, (William) Nigel W.; *see* Wenban-Smith.

SMITH, William Peter; *see* Smith, P. W.

SMITH, Zoë Philippa; Her Honour Judge Zoë Smith; a Circuit Judge, since 1999; *b* 16 May 1949; *d* of late Basil Gerrard Smith and of Marjorie Elizabeth Smith (*née* Artz). *Educ:* Queenswood Sch., Hatfield. Called to the Bar, Gray's Inn, 1970; in practice at the Bar, 1970–99; a Recorder, 1991–99. *Recreation:* dining out. *Address:* Hardwicke Building, Lincoln's Inn, WC2A 3SB.

SMITH-BINGHAM, Col Jeremy David; Director General, British Equestrian Federation, 1994–97; *b* 29 July 1939; *s* of Col Oswald Cyril Smith-Bingham and Vera Mabel Smith-Bingham (*née* Johnson); *m* 1969, Priscilla Mary Incledon-Webber; three *s*. *Educ:* Cheam; Eton; RMA, Sandhurst. Commnd Royal Horse Guards (The Blues), 1959; Lt Col, 1981; jssc, 1982; CO, The Blues and Royals, 1982–85; CO, Tactical Sch., RAC, 1985–87; Col, 1987; Chief Exercise Planner, HQ N Army Gp, 1987–90; Comdr, Household Cavalry, and Silver Stick to the Queen, 1990–93; COS, HQ London Dist, 1993–94. *Recreations:* horses, tennis, rackets, ski-ing, water sports. *Address:* St Brannocks House, Braunton, Devon EX33 1HN. *T:* (01271) 812270. *Clubs:* White's, Cavalry and Guards.

SMITH-CAMERON, Rev. Canon Ivor Gill; Chaplain to the Queen, 1995–99; *b* 12 Nov. 1929; *s* of James Smith-Cameron and Cynthia Smith-Cameron (*née* Fitzgerald). *Educ:* Madras Christian Coll., India (MA Eng. Lang. and Lit.); Coll. of Resurrection, Mirfield, Yorks. Ordained deacon, 1954; priest, 1955; Curate, St George's, Rumboldswyke, Chichester, 1954–58; Chaplain, London Univ., 1958–72; Canon Residentiary and Diocesan Missioner, Dio. Southwark, 1972–92; Asst Curate, All Saints, Battersea, 1992–94; retd 1994; Canon Residentiary Emeritus, 1994. *Publications:* Pilgrimage: an exploration into God, 1982; The Church of Many Colours, 1998; New Fire, 2000. *Recreations:* cooking, jam making, reading, walking. *Address:* 100 Prince of Wales Drive, SW11 4BD. *T:* (020) 7622 3809.

SMITH-DODSWORTH, Sir John (Christopher), 8th Bt *cr* 1784; *b* 4 March 1935; *s* of Sir Claude Smith-Dodsworth, 7th Bt, and Cyrilla Marie Louise von Sobbe, (*d* 1984), 3rd *d* of William Ernest Taylor, Linnet Lane, Liverpool; *S* father, 1940; *m* 1st, 1961, Margaret Anne (*née* Jones) (marr. diss. 1971); one *s* one *d*, 2nd, 1972, Margaret Theresa (*d* 1990) (*née* Grey), Auckland, NZ; one *s*; 3rd, 1991, Lolita, *d* of Romeo Pulante; one *s* one *d*. *Educ:* Ampleforth Coll., Yorks. Now resident in Coromandel, New Zealand. *Publications:* (jtly) New Zealand Ferns and Allied Plants, 1989; New Zealand Native Shrubs and Climbers, 1991. *Heir: s* David John Smith-Dodsworth [*b* 23 Oct. 1963; *m* 1996, Elizabeth Anne Brady, Thirsk, N Yorks; one *d*].

SMITH-GORDON, Sir (Lionel) Eldred (Peter), 5th Bt *cr* 1838; engaged in book publishing, since 1960; *b* 7 May 1935; *s* of Sir Lionel Eldred Pottinger Smith-Gordon, 4th Bt, and Eileen Laura (*d* 1979), *d* of late Captain H. G. Adams-Connor, CVO; *S* father, 1976; *m* 1962, Sandra Rosamund Ann, *d* of late Wing Commander Walter Farley, DFC and of Mrs Dennis Poore; one *s* one *d*. *Educ:* Eton College; Trinity College, Oxford. Chm., Smith-Gordon and Co. Ltd; Dir, Dietetic Consultants Ltd. *Heir: s* Lionel George Eldred Smith-Gordon [*b* 1 July 1964; *m* 1993, Kumi, *d* of Masashi Suzuki, Japan; one *s* one *d*]. *Address:* 13 Shalcomb Street, SW10 0HZ. *T:* (020) 7352 8506.

SMITH-LAITTAN, James, CMG 1995; HM Diplomatic Service, retired; *b* 13 May 1939; *s* of James and Etta Smith; *m* 1969, Mary Susan Messer; three *d*. *Educ:* Buckie High Sch.; North West Poly., London. Nat. Service, 1st Queen's Dragoon Guards, 1958–60; Admiralty, 1961–62; joined CRO, 1963; Dacca, 1964–66; FCO, 1966–68; Brussels, 1968; Rabat, 1969–72; Accra, 1972–75; Rome, 1975–79; Asst Overseas Insp., FCO, 1979–82; Trade Comr, Hong Kong, 1982–87; Asst Head, Migration and Visa Dept, FCO, 1987–90; Commercial Mgt and Exports Dept, FCO, 1990–92; Trade Counsellor and Head of China Trade Unit, Hong Kong, 1992–96; Consul-Gen., Auckland, 1996–99. *Recreations:* reading, gardening, travel. *Clubs:* Oriental; Hong Kong (Hong Kong).

SMITH-MARRIOTT, Sir Hugh Cavendish, 11th Bt *cr* 1774, of Sydling St Nicholas, Dorset; Public Relations and Marketing Executive Director, since 1987; Director, H.S.M. Marketing Ltd, Bristol, since 1988; *b* 22 March 1925; *s* of Sir Ralph George Cavendish Smith-Marriott, 10th Bt and Phyllis Elizabeth (*d* 1932), *d* of Richard Kemp; *S* father, 1987; *m* 1953, Pauline Anne (*d* 1985), *d* of F. F. Holt; one *d*. *Educ:* Bristol Cathedral School. Man. Dir, Drawing Office Co., 1956; Group Marketing Executive, Bryan Brothers Group, 1976. *Recreations:* hockey (county level), cricket, painting, theatre. *Heir: b* Peter Francis Smith-Marriott [*b* 14 Feb. 1927; *m* 1961, Jean Graham Martin, *d* of James Sorley Ritchie; five *s* (including twin *s*)]. *Address:* 26 Shipley Road, Westbury-on-Trym, Bristol BS9 3HS. *T:* (0117) 950 2915. *Clubs:* MCC; Gloucestershire CC, Durham CC, Bristol Savages, Bristol RF.

SMITHERS, Prof. Alan George, PhD; CPsychol; Sydney Jones Professor of Education, University of Liverpool, since 1998; *b* 20 May 1938; *s* of late Alfred Edward Smithers and Queenie Lilian Smithers; *m* 1962, Angela Grace Wykes; two *d*. *Educ:* King's Coll., Univ. of London (BSc, PhD 1966); Bradford Univ. (MSc, PhD 1974). CPsychol 1988. Lecturer in: Biol., Coll. of St Mark and St John, Chelsea, 1962–64; Botany, Birkbeck Coll., Univ. of London, 1964–67; Research Fellow, then Sen. Lectr in Educn, Bradford Univ., 1967–76; Prof. of Educn, Univ. of Manchester, 1977–96; seconded to British Petroleum, 1991–92; Prof. of Educn (Policy Res.), Brunel Univ., 1996–98. Member: Nat. Curriculum Council, 1992–93; Beaumont Cttee on Vocational Qualifications, 1995–96; Special Advr, H of C Educn and Employment Cttee, 1997–. Fellow, Soc. for Res. into Higher Educn, 1986. Hon. MEd Manchester, 1981. *Publications:* Sandwich Courses: an integrated education?, 1976; The Progress of Mature Students, 1986; What Employers Want of Higher Education, 1988; The Shortage of Maths and Physics Teachers, 1988; The Growth of Mixed A-Levels, 1988; Increasing Participation in Higher Education, 1989; Teacher Loss, 1990; Trends in Science and Technology Manpower Demands and Mobilities, 1990; Graduates in the Police Service, 1990; Teacher Provision in the Sciences, 1991; Gender, Primary Schools and the National Curriculum, 1991; The Vocational Route into Higher Education, 1991; Teacher Provision: trends and perceptions, 1991; Staffing Secondary Schools in the Nineties, 1991; Every Child in Britain, 1991; Beyond Compulsory Schooling, 1991; Teacher Turnover, 1991; Technology in the National Curriculum, 1992; Technology at A-Level, 1992; Assessing the Value, 1992; General Studies: breadth at A-Level?, 1993; Changing Colleges: further education in the market place, 1993; All Our Futures: Britain's education revolution, 1993; Technology Teachers, 1994; The Impact of Double Science, 1994; Post-18 Education: growth, change, prospect, 1995; Affording Teachers, 1995; Co-educational and Single-Sex Schooling, 1995; Trends in Higher Education, 1996; Technology in Secondary Schools, 1997; Staffing Our Schools, 1997; The New Zealand Qualifications Framework, 1997; Co-educational and Single-Sex Schooling Revisited, 1997; Degrees of Choice, 1998; Assessment in Primary Schools, 1998; Teacher Supply: passing problem or impending crisis?, 1998; Teacher Supply: old story or new chapter?, 1999; Further Education Re-formed, 2000; Coping with Teacher Shortages, 2000; Talking Heads, 2000; Attracting Teachers, 2000; books jtly with Dr Pamela Robinson; numerous papers in jls of biology, psychology and education. *Recreations:* walking, theatre. *Address:* Department of Education, University of Liverpool, 19 Abercromby Square, Liverpool L69 7ZG. *T:* (0151) 794 2568, *Fax:* (0151) 794 3281; *e-mail:* alan.smithers@liv.ac.uk.

SMITHERS, Sir Peter (Henry Berry Otway), Kt 1970; VRD with clasp; DPhil Oxon; Lt-Comdr RNR, retired; *b* 9 Dec. 1913; *o s* of late Lt-Col H. O. Smithers, JP, Hants, and Ethel Berry; *m* 1943, Dojean, *d* of late T. M. Sayman, St Louis, Mo; two *d*. *Educ:* Hawtrey's; Harrow Sch.; Magdalen Coll., Oxford. Demyship in History, 1931; 1st cl. Hons Modern History, 1934. Called to Bar, Inner Temple, 1936; joined Lincoln's Inn, 1937. Commn, London Div. RNVR, 1939; British Staff, Paris, 1940; Naval Intelligence Div., Admiralty; Asst Naval Attaché, British Embassy, Washington; Actg Naval Attaché, Mexico, Central Amer. Republics and Panama. RD Councillor, Winchester, 1946–49. MP (C) Winchester Div. of Hampshire, 1950–64; PPS to Minister of State for Colonies, 1952–56 and to Sec. of State for Colonies, 1956–59; Deleg., Consultative Assembly of Council of Europe, 1952–56 and 1960; UK Deleg. to UN Gen. Assembly, 1960–62; Parly Under-Sec. of State, FO, 1962–64; Sec.-Gen., Council of Europe, 1964–69; Senior Research Fellow, UN Inst. for Trng and Research, 1969–72; General Rapporteur, European Conf. of Parliamentarians and Scientists, 1970–77. Chairman: British-Mexican Soc., 1952–55; Conservative Overseas Bureau, 1956–59; Vice-Chm., Conservative Parly Foreign Affairs Cttee, 1958–62; Vice-Pres., European Assembly of Local Authorities, 1959–62. 22 one-man photographic exhibitions in museums and institutions in England, USA, France and Italy. Master, Turners' Co., 1955; Liveryman, Goldsmiths' Co. Hon. FRHS 1996. Dr of Law *hc* Zürich, 1969. Marzotto Prize, Marzotto Foundn, Italy, 1969; Alexander von Humboldt Gold Medal, 1969; Medal of Honour, Parly Assembly, Council of Europe, 1984; Gold Medal (for photography), RHS, 1981, 1983, 1990, 1991, 1992, Gold Medal and Grenfell Medal, 1985, Veitch Meml Gold Medal, 1993, Lyttel Cup, for breeding lilies, 2001; Herbert Medal, Internat. Bulb Soc., 1997; Gold Medal pro merito, Council of Europe, 1999; Schulthess Prize, best garden in Switzerland, 2001. Hon. Citizen, Commune of Vico Morcote, Switzerland, 1995. Chevalier de la Légion d'Honneur; Orden Mexicana del Aguila Azteca. *Publications:* Life of Joseph Addison, 1954, 2nd edn, 1966; Adventures of a Gardener, 1995. *Recreations:* gardening, computer. *Address:* 6921 Vico Morcote, Switzerland; *e-mail:* ps@vico.to. *Clubs:* Carlton; The Everglades.

SMITHIES, Frederick Albert; General Secretary, National Association of Schoolmasters and Union of Women Teachers, 1983–90; *b* 12 May 1929; *s* of Frederick Albert and Lilian Smithies; *m* 1960, Olga Margaret Yates. *Educ:* St Mary's Coll., Blackburn, Lancs; St Mary's Coll., Twickenham, Mddx. Schoolteacher: Accrington, Lancs, 1948–60; Northampton, 1960–76. NAS/UWT (before 1975, NAS): Nat. Executive Member, 1966–76; Chm. of Education Cttee, 1972–76; Vice-President, 1976; Asst Gen. Secretary, 1976–81; Dep. Gen. Secretary, 1981–82; Gen. Sec. Designate, 1982–83. Member: Exec. Bd, European Trade Union Cttee for Educn, 1982–93; TUC Gen. Council, 1983–89; Exec. Bd, Internat. Fedn of Free Teachers' Unions, 1985–93 (Hon. Treas., 1989–93). *Recreations:* reading, music, theatre. *Address:* High Street, Guilsborough, Northampton NN6 8PY.

SMITHIES, His Honour Kenneth (Charles Lester); a Circuit Judge, 1975–90; *b* 15 Aug. 1927; *s* of late Harold King Smithies and Kathleen Margaret (*née* Walsh); *m* 1st, 1950, Joan Winifred (*née* Ellis) (*d* 1983); one *s* two *d*; 2nd, 1996, Kathleen Mary, (Kitty), Floyd (*née* Stevens). *Educ:* City of London Sch. (Corporation Scholar); University College London (LLB). Volunteered 60th Rifles, 1945, later commnd in Royal Artillery, in India; demobilised, 1948. Called to Bar, Gray's Inn, 1955. *Recreations:* music, bridge, chess, pedantry. *Address:* Flat 3, Minterne Grange, Crichel Mount Road, Poole, Dorset BH14 8LU. *T:* (01202) 707474. *Clubs:* Athenæum; Royal Motor Yacht (Poole).

SMITHSON, Rt Rev. Alan; Bishop Suffragan of Jarrow, 1990–2001; *b* 1 Dec. 1936; *s* of Herbert and Mary Smithson; *m* 1964, Margaret Jean McKenzie; two *s* two *d*. *Educ:* Queen's Coll., Oxford (BA 1962; MA 1968); Queen's Coll., Birmingham (DipTh 1964). Deacon 1964, priest 1965; Curate: Christ Church, Skipton, 1964–68; St Mary the Virgin with St Cross and St Peter, Oxford, 1968–72; Chaplain: Queen's Coll., Oxford, 1969–72; Reading Univ., 1972–77; Vicar of Bracknell, 1977–84; Residentiary Canon, Carlisle Cathedral and Dir of Training and Diocesan Training Inst., 1984–90. *Recreations:* water colour painting, travel, camping, fell walking, 'cello playing. *Address:* St Crispin's House, St Crispin Street, Creetown, Newtown Stewart DG8 7JT.

SMITHSON, Michael; Director, Development Office, University of Oxford, since 1999; Fellow, Magdalen College, Oxford, since 2000; *b* 11 May 1946; *s* of late Arthur Smithson and Doris Smithson (*née* Simpson); *m* 1969, Jacqueline Anne Cowan; one *s* two *d*. *Educ:* Burnage GS, Manchester; London Sch. of Econs (LLB). Thomson Orgn Grad. Trng Scheme, with Newcastle Jl and Evening Chronicle, 1968–71; BBC Radio News: Mem., Editl Staff, 1971–78; Duty Ed., 1978–80; Dep. Hd, BBC TV Licence Campaign, 1980–81; i/c Corporate Publicity Unit, BBC, 1982–84; Dir, Public Relns, RSPCA, 1984–88; Mgt Consultant, 1988–91, Dir, 1990–91, Finite Gp plc; Man. Dir, Pemberley Associates, 1991–94; Dir of Fundraising, LSE, 1994–96; Develt Dir, Univ. of Cambridge, and Fellow of Queens' Coll., Cambridge, 1996–99. Councillor (Lib Dem): Beds CC, 1990–96; Bedford BC, 1996–2000. Contested (Lib Dem) N Beds, 1992. *Recreations:* cycling, bridge, enjoying fine teas, my family. *Address:* University of Oxford Development Office, Oxenford House, Magdalen Street, Oxford OX1 3AB. *T:* (01865) 288083. *Club:* Royal Over-Seas League.

SMITHSON, Peter Denham; architect in private practice since 1950; *b* 18 Sept. 1923; *s* of William Blenkiron Smithson and Elizabeth Smithson; *m* 1949, Alison Margaret (*née* Gill) (*d* 1993); one *s* two *d*. *Educ:* The Grammar School, Stockton-on-Tees; King's College, Univ. of Durham. Served War of 1939–45: Queen Victoria's Own Madras Sappers and Miners, India and Burma, 1942–45. Asst in Schools Div. LCC, 1949–50;

subseq. in private practice with wife. Banister Fletcher Prof. of Architecture, UCL, 1976–77; Vis. Prof. of Architecture: Bath Univ., 1978–90; Univ. of Delft, 1982–83; Univ. of Munich, 1984–85; Univ. of Barcelona, 1985–86. *Buildings:* Hunstanton School, 1950–54; The Economist Building, St James's, 1959–64, Porch 1983; Robin Hood Gardens, Tower Hamlets, 1963–72; Garden Bldg, St Hilda's Coll., Oxford, 1968–70; Ramp at Ansty, Wilts, 1987; for Bath University: Second Arts Bldg, 1978–81; Amenity Bldg, 1979–80, 1984; Arts Barn, 1980–90; Architecture and Building Engrg, 1982–88; Porch, Ansty Plum, Wilts, 1992; Porches at Tecta, Lauenförde, 1992–99; Hexenbesenraum, 1991–96, Hexenhaus Pier, and Tea-Haus, 1997, Lantern Pavilion, 2001, Bad Karlshafen; *furniture:* for Tecta, Germany (with A. Smithson), 1982–; Exhibitions for Tecta, Köln and Berlin, 1993, 1998, 1999, 2000, 2001. *Publications:* (all with A. Smithson) Uppercase 3, 1960; The Heroic Period of Modern Architecture, 1965, rev. edn 1981; Urban Structuring Studies of Alison and Peter Smithson, 1967; Team 10 Primer, 1968; The Euston Arch, 1968; Ordinariness and Light, 1970; Without Rhetoric, 1973; Bath: Walks Within the Walls, 1980; The Shift, 1982; AS in DS, 1983; The 1930s, 1985; Upper Lawn, 1986; Italian Thoughts, 1993 (trans. Italian, 1996); Changing the Art of Inhabitation, 1994; The Charged Void, 2001; Italian Thoughts Followed Further, 2001; theoretical work on town structuring in ILAUD Year Book, Spazio e Società and other periodicals; *relevant publications:* synopsis of professional life in Arch. Assoc.'s Arena, Feb. 1966; selective bibliography in The Shift, 1982; A.+P. Smithson, 1991; Alison & Peter Smithson, 1997. *Address:* Cato Lodge, 24 Gilston Road, SW10 9SR. *T:* (020) 7373 7423.

SMOUT, Prof. (Thomas) Christopher, CBE 1994; PhD; FBA 1988; FRSE; FSAScot; Director, Institute for Environmental History, University of St Andrews, 1992–2001; Historiographer to the Queen in Scotland, since 1993; *b* 19 Dec. 1933; *s* of Sir Arthur and Lady (Hilda) Smout; *m* 1959, Anne-Marie Schøning; one *s* one *d*. *Educ:* The Leys Sch., Cambridge; Clare Coll., Cambridge (MA; PhD 1960). FRSE 1975; FSAScot 1991. Dept of Economic History, Edinburgh University: Asst Lectr, 1959; Lectr, 1962; Reader, 1964; Prof. of Econ. History, 1970; University of St Andrews: Prof. of Scottish History, 1980–91; Dir, St John's House Centre for Advanced Histl Studies, 1992–97. Visiting Professor: Strathclyde Univ., 1991–97; Dundee Univ., 1993–; York Univ., 1998–99. Member: Cttee for Scotland, Nature Conservancy Council, 1986–91; Bd, NCC (Scotland), 1991–92; Bd, Scottish Natural Heritage, 1992–98 (Dep. Chm., 1992–97); Royal Commn on Ancient and Historic Monuments of Scotland, 1987–2000 (Vice-Chm., 2000); Bd of Trustees, Nat. Museums of Scotland, 1991–95; Royal Commn on Historical Manuscripts, 1999–. Hon. Fellow, TCD, 1995. Hon. DSSc QUB, 1995; Hon. DSc (SocSci) Edinburgh, 1996; Hon. DLitt: St Andrews, 1999; Glasgow, 2001. *Publications:* Scottish Trade on the Eve of Union, 1963; A History of the Scottish People, 1969; (with I. Levitt) The State of the Scottish Working Class in 1843, 1979; A Century of the Scottish People, 1986; (with S. Wood) Scottish Voices, 1990; (with A. Gibson) Prices, Food and Wages in Scotland, 1995; Nature Contested, 2000. *Recreations:* birdwatching, butterflies, ferns. *Address:* Chesterhill, Shore Road, Anstruther, Fife KY10 3DZ. *T:* (01333) 310330.

SMYTH, Desmond; *see* Smyth, J. D.

SMYTH, His Honour (James) Robert Staples; a Circuit Judge, 1986–97; *b* 11 July 1926; *s* of late Major Robert Smyth, Gaybrook, Co. Westmeath, and Mabel Anne Georgiana (*née* MacGeough-Bond); *m* 1971, Fenella Joan Mowat; one *s*. *Educ:* St Columba's, Dublin; Merton Coll., Oxford (BA 1948, MA). Served RAF, 1944–46. Called to Bar, Inner Temple, 1949. Resident Magistrate, Northern Rhodesia, 1951–55; a Dep. Circuit Judge, 1974; Stipendiary Magistrate, W Midlands, 1978–86; a Recorder, 1983–86. Dep. Chm., Agricl Land Tribunal, 1974. *Recreations:* shooting, fishing, English literature. *Address:* Leys, Shelsley Beauchamp, Worcs WR6 6RB.

SMYTH, Prof. John Fletcher, MD; FRCPE, FRCP, FRCSE, FRCR; FRSE; Professor of Medical Oncology, since 1979, and Head of Division of Molecular and Clinical Medicine, since 1998, University of Edinburgh; Hon. Director, Imperial Cancer Research Fund Medical Oncology Unit, Edinburgh, since 1980; *b* 26 Oct. 1945; *s* of Henry James Robert Smyth and Doreen Stanger (*née* Fletcher); *m* 1st, 1973, Catherine Ellis; two *d* (marr. diss. 1992); 2nd, 1995, Ann Cull; two step *d*. *Educ:* Bryanston Sch.; Trinity Coll., Cambridge (BA 1967; MA 1971); St Bartholomew's Hosp. (MB BChir 1970); MD Cantab 1976; MSc London 1975. FRCPE 1981; MRCP 1973, FRCP 1983; FRCSE 1994; FRCR 1995; FRSE 1996. House Officer posts: St Bartholomew's Hosp. and RPMS, London, 1970–72; Asst Lectr, Dept of Med. Oncology, St Bartholomew's Hosp., 1972–73; CRC Res. Fellowship, Inst. Cancer Res., 1973–75; MRC Travelling Fellowship, Nat. Cancer Inst., USA, 1975–76; Sen. Lectr, Inst. Cancer Res., 1976–79. Honorary Consultant Physician: Royal Marsden Hosp. and Brompton Hosp., 1977–79; Lothian Health Bd, 1979–; Vis. Prof. of Medicine and Associate Dir for Med. Res., Univ. of Chicago, 1979. Member of Council: EORTC, 1990–97; UICC, 1990–94; Pres., European Soc. of Med. Oncology, 1991–93; Treas., Fedn of European Cancer Socs, 1992–97. Ed.-in-Chief, European Jl of Cancer, 2000–. *Publications:* Basic Principles of Cancer Chemotherapy, 1980; The Management of Lung Cancer, 1984; contrib. various med. and scientific jls on cancer medicine, pharmacology, clinical and exptl cancer therapeutics. *Recreations:* flying and singing (sometimes simultaneously). *Address:* 18 Inverleith Avenue South, Edinburgh EH3 5QA. *T:* (0131) 552 3775. *Club:* Athenæum.

SMYTH, John Jackson; QC 1979; barrister-at-law; Director of Zambesi Ministries, Zimbabwe, since 1986; *b* 27 June 1941; *e s* of Col Edward Hugh Jackson Smyth, FRCSEd, and late Ursula Helen Lucie (*née* Ross); *m* 1968, Josephine Anne, *er d* of late Walter Leggott and Miriam Moss Leggott, Manor Farm, Burtoft, Lincs; one *s* three *d*. *Educ:* Strathcona Sch., Calgary, Alberta; St Lawrence Coll.; Trinity Hall, Cambridge. MA, LLB (Cantab). Called to Bar, Inner Temple (Major Schol.), 1965. A Recorder, 1978–84. *Publications:* Discovering Christianity Today, 1985; Following Christ Today, 1987; Jabulani Bible Reading Notes, 1990–92. *Recreations:* skiing, sailing, trout fishing, real tennis. *Address:* 2 Crown Office Row, Temple, EC4Y 7HJ; PO Box CH 210, Chisipite, Harare, Zimbabwe. *T:* 490561, *Fax:* 494127; *e-mail:* jjsmyth@ecoweb.co.zw. *Club:* Army and Navy.

SMYTH, (Joseph) Desmond, CBE 2000; FCA; Managing Director, Ulster Television, 1983–99; *b* 20 April 1950; *s* of Andrew and Annie Elizabeth Smyth; *m* 1975, Irene Janette (*née* Dale); one *s* one *d*. *Educ:* Limavady Grammar School; Queen's University, Belfast. BSc (Jt Hons Pure Maths and Statistics). Accountancy articles, Coopers and Lybrand, 1971–75; Ulster Television: Chief Accountant, 1975–76; Financial Controller and Company Secretary, 1976–83. Dir, Viridian (formerly NIE) plc, 1996–. Pres., NI Chamber of Commerce and Industry, 1991–92. FRTS 1993. *Recreations:* fishing, gardening. *e-mail:* desmondsmyth@yahoo.co.uk.

SMYTH, Rev. Martin; *see* Smyth, Rev. W. M.

SMYTH, Robert Staples; *see* Smyth, J. R. S.

SMYTH, Sir Thomas Weyland Bowyer-, 15th Bt *cr* 1661; *b* 25 June 1960; *s* of Captain Sir Philip Weyland Bowyer-Smyth, 14th Bt, RN, and of Veronica Mary, *d* of Captain C. W. Bower, DSC, RN; *S* father, 1978; *m* 1992, Sara Louise Breinlinger (marr. diss. 1997); *m* 1998, Mary Rose Helen Giedroyc; one *s*, and one step *s*. *Heir:* *kinsman* John Jeremy Windham [*b* 22 Nov. 1948; *m* 1976, Rachel Mary Finney; one *s* two *d*]. *Address:* c/o Stour House, Fordwich, Canterbury CT2 0DA.

SMYTH, Dr Sir Timothy (John), 2nd Bt *cr* 1956, of Teignmouth, Co. Devon; Health Partner, Phillips Fox Lawyers, since 2000; *b* 16 April 1953; *s* of Julian Smyth (*d* 1974) and of Phyllis, *d* of John Francis Cannon; *S* grandfather, Brig. Rt Hon. Sir John Smyth, 1st Bt, VC, MC, 1983; *m* 1981, Bernadette Mary, *d* of Leo Askew; two *s* two *d*. *Educ:* Univ. of New South Wales. MB, BS 1977; LLB 1987; MBA (AGSM) 1985; FRACMA 1985. Resident Medical Officer, 1977–79; Medical Administrator, Prince Henry Hosp., Prince of Wales Hosp. Gp, Sydney, 1980–86; Chief Exec. Officer, Sydney Health Service, 1986–88; Gen. Man., St George Hosp., Sydney, 1988–91; CEO, Hunter Area Health Service, 1992–97; Dep. Dir-Gen., Policy, DoH, NSW, 1997–2000. *Heir:* *s* Brendan Julian Smyth, *b* 4 Oct. 1981. *Address:* PO Box A2188, Sydney, NSW 1235, Australia.

SMYTH, Rev. (William) Martin; MP (UU) Belfast South, since March 1982 (resigned seat Dec. 1985 in protest against Anglo-Irish Agreement; re-elected Jan. 1986); *b* 15 June 1931; *s* of James Smyth, JP, and Minnie Kane; *m* 1957, Kathleen Jean Johnston, BA; two *d* (and one *d* decd). *Educ:* Methodist Coll., Belfast; Magee University Coll., Londonderry; Trinity Coll., Dublin (BA 1953, BD 1961); Assembly's Coll., Belfast. Assistant Minister, Lowe Memorial, Finaghy, 1953–57; Raffrey Presbyterian Church, Crossgar, 1957–63; Alexandra Presbyterian Church, Belfast, 1963–82. Member, Northern Ireland Convention, 1975; Mem. (UU) Belfast S, NI Assembly, 1982–86 (Chm., Health and Social Services Cttee, 1983–84; Chm., Finance and Personnel Cttee, 1984–86). Chief UU Whip, 1995–2000; Member, Select Committee: for Social Services, 1983–90; on Health, 1990–97; on NI Affairs, 2001–. Member Executive: UK Branch, IPU, 1985–92, 1995–; CPA, 1986–. Ulster Unionist Council: Chm. Exec., 1974–76; Vice-Pres. 1974–2000; Hon. Sec., 2000–01; Pres., 2001–. Governor, Belfast City Mission. Grand Master, Grand Orange Lodge of Ireland, 1972–96; Grand Master of World Orange Council, 1974–82, Pres., 1985–88; Hon. Past Grand Master, Canada, and Hon. Deputy Grand Master, USA, NZ, NSW, of Orange Order. *Publications:* (ed) Faith for Today, 1961; pamphlets: Why Presbyterian?, 1963; Till Death Us Do Part, 1965; In Defence of Ulster, 1970; The Battle for Northern Ireland, 1972; A Federated People, 1988; occasional papers, and articles in Christian Irishman, Evangelical Quarterly, Biblical Theology. *Recreations:* reading, photography; former Rugby player (capped for Magee University College). *Address:* 117 Cregagh Road, Belfast BT6 0LA. *T:* (028) 9045 7009, *Fax:* (028) 9045 0837.

SMYTHE, Clifford Anthony, (Tony); consultant; Director, Medical Action for Global Security (formerly Medical Campaign against Nuclear Weapons), 1989–92; *b* 2 Aug. 1938; *s* of Clifford John and Florence May Smythe; *m*; four *d*. *Educ:* University College School. Conscientious Objector, 1958; General Secretary, War Resisters' International, 1959–64, Treasurer, 1982–86; Council Member, Internat. Confederation for Disarmament and Peace, 1963–71; Gen. Sec., Nat. Council for Civil Liberties, 1966–72; Field Dir, American Civil Liberties Union, 1973; Dir, Mind (Nat. Assoc. for Mental Health), 1973–81. Board Member: Volunteer Centre, 1977–81; Retired Execs Clearing Hse (REACH), 1978–90; Member: Nat. Adv. Council on Employment of Disabled People, 1975–81; Nat. Develt Council for Mentally Handicapped People, 1981; (co-opted), Mddx Area Probation Cttee, 1984–90. Chairman: Campaign for Homeless Single People, 1982–84; National Peace Council, 1982–86; Nat. Assoc. of Voluntary Hostels, 1990–92; Director: Assoc. of Community Health Councils for England and Wales, 1983–86; SHAC, 1986–88. *Publications:* Conscription: a World Survey, 1968; (with D. Madgwick) The Invasion of Privacy, 1974. *Address:* 136 Stapleton Hall Road, N4 4QB.

SMYTHE, Brig. Michael, OBE 1989; Clerk to the Vintners' Company, since 1997; *b* 30 April 1948; *s* of Peter and Kay Smythe; *m* 1976, Sally Paget-Cooke (separated); one *s* one *d*. *Educ:* Ratcliffe Coll. Commnd RA, 1968: Adjt, King's Troop, RHA, 1975–78; psc 1980; CO 94th Regt, RA, 1986–88; MA to C-in-C UKLF, 1988–90; HCSC 1990; COS 2nd Inf. Div., 1990–91; Comdr, RA 1st Armd Div., 1991–93; rcds 1994; Brig., HQ Land, 1995–96. *Recreations:* ski-ing, walking, wine. *Address:* The Vintners' Company, Upper Thames Street, EC4V 3BG. *T:* (020) 7236 1863.

SMYTHE, Tony; *see* Smythe, C. A.

SNAITH, George Robert, FRINA; Partner, Pi-Sigma Technology and Systems Advisers, since 1990; *b* 9 July 1930; *s* of late Robert and Clara Snaith; *m* 1953, Verna Patricia (*née* Codling); one *s* one *d*. *Educ:* University of Durham. BSc Applied Science (Naval Architecture), 1952. A. Kari & Co., Consulting Naval Architects, Newcastle, 1952–57; Northern Aluminium Co. Ltd, Banbury, 1957–59; Burness, Corlett & Partners, Consulting Naval Architects, Basingstoke, 1959–64; British Ship Research Association, 1964–77, Dir of Research, 1976–77; British Shipbuilders: Dir of Research, 1977–81; Technol. and Systems Adviser (formerly Production Systems Adviser), 1981–85; Consultant, Computervision Ltd, 1985–90. Vis. Prof., Dept of Marine Technology (formerly Naval Architecture and Shipbldg), Univ. of Newcastle upon Tyne, 1980–96. FNECInst 1992. Member: Council, RINA, 1977–87; Ship and Marine Technol. Requirements Bd, Dept of Industry, 1978–81; Bd, National Maritime Inst., 1978–82. *Recreations:* ships and shipbuilding, technology, education. *Address:* 10 Fieldhouse Close, Hepscott, Morpeth, Northumberland NE61 6LU. *T:* (01670) 515319.

SNAPE, Peter Charles; *b* 12 Feb. 1942; *s* of late Thomas and of Kathleen Snape; *m* 1963, Winifred Grimshaw (marr. diss. 1980); two *d*. *Educ:* St Joseph's RC Sch., Stockport; St Winifred's Sch., Stockport. Railway signalman, 1957–61; regular soldier, RE and RCT, 1961–67; goods guard, 1967–70; clerical officer BR, 1970–74. Non-exec. Dir, W Midlands Travel, 1992–97; Chm., Travel W Midlands, 1997–2000. MP (Lab) West Bromwich East, Feb. 1974–2001. An Asst Govt Whip, 1975–77; a Lord Comr, HM Treasury, 1977–79; opposition spokesman for Defence, 1979–82, for Home Affairs, 1982–83, for Transport, 1983–92. Mem., Council of Europe and WEU, May-Nov. 1975. Mem., Bredbury and Romiley UDC, 1971–74 (Chm., Finance Cttee). *Address:* Hildercroft, 281 Highfield Road, Hall Green, Birmingham B28 0BU.

SNAPE, Royden Eric; a Recorder of the Crown Court, 1979–92; *b* 20 April 1922; *s* of John Robert and Gwladys Constance Snape; *m* 1949, Unity Frances Money; one *s* one *d*. *Educ:* Bromsgrove Sch. Served War, Royal Regt of Artillery (Field), 1940–46; Adjt, 80th Field Regt, 1945. Admitted Solicitor, 1949; a Deputy Circuit Judge, 1975. Chairman: Med. Appeal Tribunal, 1985–94; Disability Appeal Tribunal, 1992–94. Governor, St John's Sch., Porthcawl, 1971–88 (Chm., 1971–72). *Recreations:* golf, Rugby Union football, cricket, swimming. *Address:* West Winds, Love Lane, Llanblethian, Cowbridge, South Glamorgan, Wales CF71 7JQ. *T:* (01446) 772362. *Club:* Royal Porthcawl Golf.

SNEATH, David Rupert, TD 1991; DL; Regional Chairman, Employment Tribunals, Leeds, since 1998; *b* 7 June 1948; *s* of John and Stella Doreen Sneath; *m* 1st, 1971, Anna

Minding (marr. diss. 1984); two *d*; 2nd, 1986, Carol Parsons. *Educ:* Pembroke Coll., Cambridge (MA). Called to the Bar, Inner Temple, 1970; in practice at the Bar, Nottingham, 1971–92; pt-time Chm., 1983–92, full-time Chm., 1992–98, Industrial Tribunals. Commnd TA, 1969; Comd, 3rd Bn Worcestershire and Sherwood Foresters Regt (V), 1991; Col (TA) 1994; Dep. Hon. Col D (WFR) Co., E of England Regt. Trustee: Worcs and Sherwood Foresters Regt; Sherwood Foresters Mus. DL Notts 1998. *Recreations:* flute playing, choral singing, opera, theatre, ski-ing, scuba diving. *Address:* 7 Kirkby Road, Ravenshead, Nottingham NG15 9HD. *T:* (01623) 456310; 15 Merchant's Quay, East Street, Leeds LS9 8BB. *T:* (0113) 246 5713.

SNEATH, Prof. Peter Henry Andrews, MD; FRS 1995; Professor of Clinical Microbiology, Leicester University, 1975–89, Emeritus Professor, Department of Microbiology and Immunology, since 1989; *b* 17 Nov. 1923; *s* of Rev. Alec Andrews Sneath and Elizabeth Maud Adcock; *m* 1953, Joan Sylvia Thompson; one *s* two *d*. *Educ:* Wycliffe Coll., Stonehouse, Glos; King's Coll., Cambridge (BA 1944; MB BChir 1948, MD 1959); King's Coll. Hosp.; London Sch. of Hygiene and Trop. Med. (Dip. Bact. 1953). MRCS, LRCP 1947. RAMC, Captain and Temp. Major, 1950–52. Mem., Sci. Staff, MRC, 1953–75 and Dir, Microbial Systematics Res. Unit, 1964–75; Hon. Consultant Microbiologist, Leics HA, 1975–89. Hon. mem., microbiol. and bacteriol. socs, UK, France, USA. Hon. DSc Ghent, 1969. *Publications:* (with R. R. Sokal) Principles of Numerical Taxonomy, 1963; Planets and Life, 1970; (with R. R. Sokal) Numerical Taxonomy, 1973; papers in learned jls on microbiology and computing. *Recreations:* reading, gardening, music. *Address:* Sunnyfield, 15 Southmeads Road, Leicester LE2 2LR. *T:* (0116) 271 2206; Department of Microbiology and Immunology, The University, Leicester LE1 7RH. *T:* (0116) 252 2951.

SNEDDEN, David King, CA; Chairman, Trinity International Holdings, 1994–98 (Chief Executive and Managing Director, 1982–93; Deputy Chairman, 1993–94); Chairman, Liverpool Daily Post and Echo, 1985–96; *b* 23 Feb. 1933; *s* of David King Snedden and Isabella (*née* Martin); *m* 1958; two *s* one *d*. *Educ:* Daniel Stewart's College, Edinburgh. CA 1956. Flying Officer, RAF, 1956–57. Investment Adviser, Guinness Mahon, 1958–59; Chief Accountant, Scotsman Publications Ltd, Thomson British Publications Ltd, Thomson Scottish Associates Ltd, 1959–64; Commercial Controller, The Scotsman Publications Ltd, 1964–66; Managing Director: Belfast Telegraph Newspapers Ltd, 1967–70 (Director, 1979–82); The Scotsman Publications Ltd, 1970–78 (Director, 1970–82). Thomson Regional Newspapers Ltd: Dir, 1974–82; Gp Asst Man. Dir, 1979–80; Jt Man. Dir, 1980–82. Chm., Norcor Holdings PLC, 1994–99; Director: Radio Forth Ltd, 1973–77; BSkyB, 1994–97; Scottish Council Research Inst. Ltd, 1975–77; The Press Association Ltd, 1984–94 (Vice-Chm., 1988; Chm., 1989–94); Reuters Holdings PLC, 1988–94. Pres., Scottish Daily Newspaper Soc., 1975–78; Mem., Press Council, 1976–80. *Recreations:* golf, hill walking, fishing. *Address:* 29 Ravelston Heights, Edinburgh EH4 3LX. *Clubs:* Bruntsfield Links Golfing Society; Scarista Golf (Isle of Harris).

SNEDDON, Hutchison Burt, CBE 1983 (OBE 1968); JP; Lord-Lieutenant of Lanarkshire, 1992–99; former Scottish Divisional Director, Nationwide Anglia Building Society (formerly Nationwide Building Society); *b* 17 April 1929; *s* of Robert and Catherine Sneddon; *m* 1960, Elizabeth Jardine; one *s* two *d*. *Educ:* Wishaw High School. Chm., Cumbernauld Develt Corp., 1979–83; Regl Sales Manager (Special Projects), Scottish Gas, 1983–88. Dir, Motherwell Enterprise Develt Co., 1996–. Dir, National Bldg Agency, 1973–82; Vice-Chm., Scottish National Housing and Town Planning Council,1965–71; Member: Bd, Housing Corp., 1977–83; Consultative Cttee, Scottish Develt Agency, 1979–83; Scottish Adv. Commn on Housing Rents, 1973–74; Anderson Cttee on Commercial Rating, 1972–74; Western Regional Hosp. Bd, 1968–70; Scottish Tourist Bd, 1969–83; Chm., Burns Heritage Trail, 1971–83; Sen. Vice Pres., 1988–89, Pres., 1989–90, World Fedn of Burns Clubs (Jun. Vice Pres., 1987–88). Dep. Pres., Convention of Scottish Local Authorities, 1974–76; Chairman: Gas Higher Managers Assoc., Scotland, 1984–88; Gas Higher Managers Assoc., GB, 1987–88. Motherwell and Wishaw Burgh Council: Councillor, 1958–77; Bailie, 1960–64; Chm., Housing Cttee, 1960–71; Chm., Policy and Resources Cttee, 1974–77; Leader, 1960–77; Chm., Motherwell DC, 1974–77; Provost, Burgh of Motherwell and Wishaw, 1971–75. Pres., Lanarks Multiple Sclerosis Assoc., 1998–. Gov., Erskine Hosp., 1993–. Hon. Pres., Royal Marines, Lanarks, 1993–. JP North Motherwell District, 1974 (Mem. JP Adv. Cttee); DL Motherwell, Hamilton, Monklands, E Kilbride and Clydesdale Districts, 1989. Gold Medal of Schweinfurt, Bavaria, 1977 (Internat. Relations). *Recreations:* football (watching), philately. *Address:* 36 Shand Street, Wishaw, Lanarks ML2 8HN.

SNELGROVE, Rt Rev. Donald George, TD 1972; an Assistant Bishop, diocese of Lincoln, since 1995; Bishop Suffragan of Hull, 1981–94; *b* 21 April 1925; *s* of William Henry Snelgrove and Beatrice Snelgrove (*née* Upshell); *m* 1949, Sylvia May Lowe (*d* 1998); one *s* one *d*. *Educ:* Queens' Coll. and Ridley Hall, Cambridge (MA). Served War, commn (Exec. Br.) RNVR, 1943–46. Cambridge, 1946–50; ordained, 1950; Curate: St Thomas, Oakwood, 1950–53; St Anselm's, Hatch End, Dio. London, 1953–56; Vicar of: Dronfield with Unstone, Dio. Derby, 1956–62; Hessle, Dio. York, 1963–70; Archdeacon of the East Riding, 1970–81. Rural Dean of Hull, 1966–70; Canon of York, 1969–81. Chm., Central Church Fund, 1985–2001; Director: Central Bd of Finance, 1975–99; Ecclesiastical Insurance Gp, 1978–94; Church Schools Co., 1981–97; Clergy Stipend Trust, 1985–; Allchurches, 1992–. Chaplain T&AVR, 1960–73. Chm., Linnaeus Centre, 1994–. Director: Cornwall Independence Trust Fund, 1998–; Council, Univ. of Hull, 1988–95. Hon. DD Hull, 1997. *Recreation:* travel. *Address:* Kingston House, 8 Park View, Barton on Humber DN18 6AX. *T:* (01652) 634484.

SNELL, Rt Rev. George Boyd, DD, PhD; *b* Toronto, Ontario, 17 June 1907; *s* of John George Snell and Minnie Alice Boyd (*née* Finnie); *m* 1934, Esther Mary Hartley. *Educ:* Trinity College, Toronto (BA 1929, MA 1930, PhD 1937, Hon. DD 1948). Deacon, Toronto, 1931; Priest, Niagara (for Tor.), 1932; Curate of St Michael and All Angels, Tor., 1931–39; Rector, 1940–48; Private Chaplain to Bp of Tor., 1945–48; Rector of Pro-Cathedral, Calgary, and Dean of Calgary, 1948–51; Exam. Chaplain to Bp of Calgary, 1948–51; Rector of St Clement Eglinton, Tor., 1951–56; Archdeacon of Toronto, 1953–56; Exam. Chaplain to Bp of Toronto, 1953–55. Consecrated Bp Suffragan of Toronto, 1956; elected Bp-Coadjutor of Toronto, 1959; Bishop of Toronto, 1966–72. Hon. DD: Wycliffe Coll., Toronto, 1959; Huron Coll., Ontario, 1968. *Address:* 1210 Glen Road, Mississauga, ON L5H 3K8, Canada. *Clubs:* National, Albany (Toronto).

SNELL, John Nicholas B.; *see* Blashford-Snell.

SNELL, Maeve, (Mrs Gordon Snell); *see* Binchy, M.

SNELL, Paul Stephen; Director of Social Services, Nottingham City Council, since 1997; *b* 29 June 1955; *s* of Bernard Lionel Snell and Irene Gabrielle Snell (*née* Allman). *Educ:* Warwick Univ. (BA Hons Sociology 1976; MA, CQSW 1979). Social Worker, 1977–84, District Manager, 1984–88, Coventry CC; Area Manager, 1988–89, Asst Dir, Social Services, 1989–95, Birmingham CC; Chief Social Services Officer, Bexley LBC, 1995–97. *Recreations:* reading, theatre, French cinema, good food. *Address:* 14 Houndsgate, Nottingham NG1 7BE. *T:* (0115) 915 7000.

SNELL, Philip D.; Member (Lab), Tyne and Wear County Council, 1974–86, Chairman, General Services Committee, 1981–86; *b* 14 Oct. 1915; *s* of Alfred William Snell and Jane Herdman; *m* 1939, Selina Waite; two *d*. *Educ:* Causey Road Council Sch., Gateshead. Miner, Marley Hill Colliery, Gateshead, 1929–57; Industrial Relations Advr, NCB, 1957–61; Education and Welfare Officer: Durham CC, 1961–73; Gateshead MDC, 1973. Chm., Tyne and Wear CC, 1980–81. Trustee, Whickham Glebe Sports Club. *Recreation:* enjoying Northern Federation Brewery Beer. *Address:* School House, Marley Hill, Whickham, Gateshead, Tyne and Wear NE11 9RQ. *T:* (0191) 488 7006. *Club:* Sunniside Social (Gateshead).

SNELLGROVE, David Llewellyn, LittD, PhD; FBA 1969; Professor of Tibetan in the University of London, 1974–82, now Emeritus Professor (Reader, 1960–74, Lecturer, 1950–60); Founder Director of Institute of Tibetan Studies, Tring, 1966–82; *b* Portsmouth, 29 June 1920; *s* of Lt-Comdr Clifford Snellgrove, RN, and Eleanor Maud Snellgrove. *Educ:* Christ's Hospital, Horsham; Southampton Univ.; Queens' Coll., Cambridge. Served War of 1939–45: commissioned in Infantry, 1942; Intell. Officer in India until 1946. Then started seriously on oriental studies at Cambridge, 1946, cont. Rome, 1949–50. BA Cantab 1949, MA Cantab 1953; PhD London 1954; LittD Cantab 1969. Made expedns to India and the Himalayas, 1953–54, 1956, 1960, 1964, 1967, 1974–75, 1978–80, 1982, continued with regular travel in Indonesia, 1987–94, to Cambodia, 1995–; founded with Mr Hugh E. Richardson an Inst. of Tibetan Studies, 1966. Apptd Consultant to Vatican in new Secretariat for non-Christian Religions, 1967. Many professional visits abroad, mainly to W Europe and USA. *Publications:* Buddhist Himalaya, 1957; The Hevajra Tantra, 1959; Himalayan Pilgrimage, 1961, 2nd edn 1981; Four Lamas of Dolpo, 1967; The Nine Ways of Bon, 1967, repr. 1980; (with H. E. Richardson) A Cultural History of Tibet, 1968, 2nd edn 1980; (with T. Skorupski) The Cultural Heritage of Ladakh, vol. I, 1977, vol. II, 1980; (ed) The Image of the Buddha, 1978; Indo-Tibetan Buddhism, 1987; Asian Commitment, 2000; Khmer Civilization & Angker, 2001; articles in Arts Asiatiques (Paris), Bulletin of the Secretariat for non-Christian Religions (Rome), etc. *Address:* Via Matteo Gay 26/7, 10066 Torre Pellice, Italy; Villa Bantay Chah, Krom 11, No 0718, Siem Reap, Cambodia.

SNELSON, Rev. William Thomas; General Secretary, Churches Together in England, since 1997; *b* 10 March 1945; *s* of Samuel and Dorothy Snelson; *m* 1968, Beryl Griffiths; one *s* one *d*. *Educ:* Exeter Coll., Oxford (BA 1967); Fitzwilliam Coll., Cambridge (BA 1969; MA 1975); Westcott House, Cambridge. Ordained deacon, 1969, priest, 1970; Curate: Godalming, 1969–72; Leeds Parish Church, 1972–75; Vicar: Chapel Allerton, Leeds, 1975–81; Bardsey, Leeds, 1981–93; W Yorks County Ecumenical Officer, 1993–97. *Recreations:* bridge, opera, continental holidays. *Address:* Churches Together in England, 27 Tavistock Square, WC1H 9HH. *T:* (020) 7529 8130.

SNODDY, (Matthew) Raymond, OBE 2000; Media Editor, The Times, since 1997; *b* 31 Jan. 1946; *s* of Matthew and Mary Snoddy; *m* 1970, Diana Elizabeth Jaroszek; one *s* one *d*. *Educ:* Larne Grammar Sch., NI; Queen's Univ., Belfast; BA Hons Open Univ. Reporter: Middx Advertiser, 1966–68; Oxford Mail, 1968–71; Parly staff, The Times, 1971–72; Visnews, 1972–74; Dep. Eur. Editor, LA Times and Washington Post News Service, 1974–78; Financial Times, 1978–97. Presenter, Hard News series, Channel 4, 1988–90. Chairman's Award, British Press Awards, 1992. *Publications:* The Good, the Bad and the Unacceptable, 1992; Green Finger: the rise of Michael Green and Carlton Communications, 1996; (with J. Ashworth) It Could be You: the untold story of the UK National Lottery, 2000. *Recreations:* opera, tennis, chess, drinking and eating, supporting Queens Park Rangers. *Address:* 18 Cedars Drive, Hillingdon, Middx UB10 0JT. *T:* (01895) 234589. *Club:* Uxbridge Tennis.

SNODGRASS, Prof. Anthony McElrea, FSA; FBA 1979; Laurence Professor of Classical Archaeology, University of Cambridge, 1976–2001; Fellow of Clare College, Cambridge, since 1977; *b* 7 July 1934; *s* of William McElrea Snodgrass, MC (Major, RAMC), and Kathleen Mabel (*née* Owen); *m* 1st, 1959, Ann Elizabeth Vaughan (marr. diss.); three *d*; 2nd, 1983, Annemarie Künzl; one *s*. *Educ:* Marlborough Coll.; Worcester Coll., Oxford (BA 1959; MA, DPhil 1963; Hon. Fellow, 1999). FSA 1978. Served with RAF in Iraq, 1953–55 (National Service). Student of the British School, Athens, 1959–60; University of Edinburgh: Lectr in Classical Archaeology, 1961; Reader, 1969; Prof., 1975. Sather Classical Vis. Prof., Univ. of California, Berkeley, 1984–85; Geddes-Harrower Vis. Prof., Aberdeen, 1995–96. Myres Meml Lectr, Oxford, 1981. British Academy: Vice-Pres., 1990–92; Mem., Humanities Res. Bd, 1994–95. Corresp. Mem., German Archaeol. Inst., 1977. *Publications:* Early Greek Armour and Weapons, 1964; Arms and Armour of the Greeks, 1967; The Dark Age of Greece, 1971; Archaic Greece, 1980; Narration and Allusion in Early Greek Art, 1982; An Archaeology of Greece, 1987; Homer and the Artists, 1998; contrib. Jl of Hellenic Studies, Proc. of Prehistoric Soc., Gnomon, etc. *Recreations:* mountaineering, skiing. *Address:* Clare College, Cambridge CB2 1TL. *Clubs:* Alpine, Alpine Ski.

See also J. M. O. Snodgrass.

SNODGRASS, John Michael Owen, CMG 1981; HM Diplomatic Service, retired; *b* 12 Aug. 1928; *e s* of Major W. M. Snodgrass, MC, RAMC; *m* 1957, Jennifer James; three *s*. *Educ:* Marlborough Coll.; Trinity Hall, Cambridge (MA, Maths and Moral Scis). Diplomatic Service: 3rd Sec., Rome, 1953–56; FO, 1956–60; 1st Sec., Beirut, 1960–63; S Africa, 1964–67; FCO, 1967–70; Consul-Gen., Jerusalem, 1970–74; Counsellor, South Africa, 1974–77; Hd of South Pacific Dept, FCO, 1977–80; Ambassador: to Zaire, 1980–83 (also to Burundi, Rwanda and Congo); to Bulgaria, 1983–86. CStJ 1975. *Recreations:* golf, travel. *Address:* The Barn House, North Warnborough, Hants RG29 1ET. *T:* (01256) 702816.

See also A. McE. Snodgrass.

SNOW, Adrian John, MA, MEd; Development Officer, Tennis and Rackets Association, since 1994; *b* 20 March 1939; *e s* of Edward Percy John Snow and Marjory Ellen Nicholls; *m* 1963 (marr. diss. 1994); one *s* one *d*. *Educ:* Hurstpierpoint Coll.; Trinity Coll., Dublin (BA, MA, HDipEd); Reading Univ. (MEd). Asst Master, The New Beacon, Sevenoaks, 1958–59; RAF Pilot Officer, 1963; Assistant Master: King's Sch., Sherborne, 1964; High Sch., Dublin, 1964–65 (part-time); Brighton Coll., 1965–66; The Oratory School: Head of Econ. and Pol Studies, 1966–73; Head of Hist., 1967–73; Housemaster, 1967–73; acting Headmaster, Sept. 1972–Mar. 1973; Headmaster, 1973–88. Warden, Oratory Sch. Assoc., 1989–93; Director: Oratory Construction Ltd, 1988–93; Oratory Trading Ltd, 1990–93. Governor: Prior Park Coll., 1981–87 (Mem., Action Cttee, 1980–81); Moreton Hall Prep. Sch., 1984–93; St Mary's Sch., Ascot, 1986–94; St Edward's Sch. and Highlands Sch., Reading, 1987– (Chm., 1990–). Member: Berks Cttee, Prince's Trust, 1989–93 (Vice-Chm., 1990–91); RYA; Tennis Cttee, Tennis and Rackets Assoc., 1990– (Chm., Court Develt Cttee, 1992–). Pres., Old Oratorian CC, 1994–; Chm., Friends of Hardwick Tennis Court, 1996– (Hon. Treas., 1990–97). *Recreations:* athletics (univ. colour), cricket, hockey (Jun. Internat. trialist), Real Tennis, Rugby (Combined Univs).

SNOW, Antony Edmund, MIPA, FIPR; Chairman, Hill and Knowlton, Europe, Middle East and Africa, Ltd, 1994–98; *b* 5 Dec. 1932; 2nd *s* of Thomas Maitland Snow, CMG; *m* 1961, Caroline Wilson; one *s* two *d*. *Educ:* Sherborne Sch.; New College, Oxford. National Service, commnd in 10th Royal Hussars, 1952–53; Royal Wiltshire Yeomanry, TA, 1953–63. W. S. Crawford, 1958; joined Charles Barker & Sons, 1961: Dep. Chm., 1975; Chm. and Chief Exec., 1983–88; Chief Exec. and Dep. Chm., 1991–92, Chm., 1992–98, non-exec. Dir, 1999–, Hill and Knowlton (UK). Non-exec. Dir, Hogg Gp (formerly Hogg Robinson & Gardner Mountain), 1989–94. Vice-Pres., Market Planning, Steuben Glass, 1976; Dep. Dir, Corning Museum of Glass, 1976 (Trustee, 1983–); Dir, Rockwell Museum, 1979. Member: Cttee of Management, Courtauld Institute of Art, 1984–89; Exec. Cttee, Nat. Art-Collections Fund, 1985–; Ancient Monuments Cttee, English Heritage, 1988–91; Design Council, 1989–94. Chm., Fraser Trust, 1996–. Trustee: Monteverdi Choir, 1988–; V & A Mus., 1996–. Council, RCA, 1994–. *Recreation:* English watercolours. *Address:* 16 Rumbold Road, SW6 2JA. *Clubs:* Cavalry and Guards, City of London.
See also Thomas Snow.

SNOW, Jonathan George, (Jon); television journalist; Presenter, Channel Four News, since 1989; *b* 28 Sept. 1947; *s* of late Rt Rev. George Snow and Joan Snow; partner, Madeleine Colvin; two *d*. *Educ:* St Edward's School, Oxford; Liverpool Univ. (no degree; sent down following political disturbances, 1970). VSO, Uganda, 1967–68; Co-ordinator, New Horizon Youth Centre, Covent Garden, 1970–73 (Chm., 1986–); Journalist, Independent Radio News, LBC, 1973–76; Independent Television News: Reporter, 1976–83; Washington Correspondent, 1983–86; Diplomatic Editor, 1986–89; main presenter, Election '92, ITV. Mem., NUJ. Visiting Professor: Broadcast Journalism, Nottingham Trent Univ., 1992–2001; Media Studies, Univ. of Stirling, 2001–. Chairman: Prison Reform Trust, 1992–97; Media Trust, 1995– (Dep. Chm., 1997–); On The Line Steering Gp, 1999–; Trustee: Noel Buxton Trust, 1992–; Chelsea Physic Garden, 1993–; Nat. Gallery, 1999–; Stephen Lawrence Trust, 1999–; Tate Gall., 2000–. Dir, Tricycle Theatre, 1995–. Chancellor, Oxford Brookes Univ., 2001–. Hon. DLitt Nottingham Trent, 1994; DUniv Open, 2001. Monte Carlo Golden Nymph Award, for Eritrea Air Attack reporting, 1979; TV Reporter of the Year, for Afghanistan, Iran and Iraq reporting, RTS, 1980; Valiant for Truth Award, for El Salvador reporting, 1982; Internat. Award, for El Salvador reporting, RTS, 1982; Home News Award, for Kegworth Air Crash reporting, RTS, 1989; RTS Presenter of the Year, 1994. *Publications:* Atlas of Today, 1987; (contrib.) Sons and Mothers, 1996. *Address:* Channel Four News, ITN, 200 Gray's Inn Road, WC1X 8HB. *T:* (020) 7430 4237.

SNOW, Rear-Adm. Kenneth Arthur, CB 1987; Deputy High Bailiff of Westminster, since 1998; *b* 14 April 1934; *s* of Arthur Chandos Pole Snow and Evelyn (*née* Joyce); *m* 1956, Pamela Elizabeth Terry (*née* Sorrell); one *s* two *d*. *Educ:* St Andrews College, Grahamstown; South African Nautical College. Joined RN, 1952; commanded HMS Kirkliston, 1962; qualified navigation specialist, 1963; commanded: HMS Llandaff, 1970; HMS Arethusa, 1979; HMS Hermes, 1983; Dep. Asst Chief of Staff (Ops), SACEUR, 1984–87, retired. Receiver-Gen. and Chapter Clerk, Westminster Abbey, 1987–98. FNI 1992. *Recreations:* gardening, painting. *Address:* Woodlands, Kite Hill, Wootton Bridge, Ryde, Isle of Wight PO33 4LG. *Club:* Army and Navy.
See also Rear-Adm. R. E. Snow.

SNOW, Peter John; television presenter, reporter and author; *b* Dublin, 20 April 1938; *s* of Brig. John F. Snow, CBE and Peggy Mary Pringle; *m* 1st, 1964, Alison Carter (marr. diss. 1975); one *s* one *d*; 2nd, 1976, Ann MacMillan; one *s* two *d*. *Educ:* Wellington College; Balliol College, Oxford (BA Hons Greats 1962). 2nd Lieut, Somerset Light Infantry, 1956–58, served Plymouth and Warminster. Independent Television News: newscaster amd reporter, 1962–66; diplomatic and defence corresp., 1966–79; events covered include: Cyprus, 1964; Vietnam, Laos, Malaysia, 1968–70; China, 1972; Mideast war, 1973; Nigerian civil war, 1969; Oman, 1975; Rhodesia, 1965–79; Britain and EEC, 1970–73; co-presenter, Gen. Elections, Feb. and Oct. 1974, 1979; BBC: presenter, Newsnight, 1979–97; events covered or reported include: Zimbabwe independence, 1980; Falklands war, 1982; S Africa, 1986; co-presenter, Gen. Elections, 1983, 1987, 1992, 1997 and 2001, and US elections; presenter: Tomorrow's World, 1997–; Random Edition, 1997–; Mastermind, R4, 1998–2000; Masterteam, 2001. Judges Award, RTS, 1998. *Publications:* (jtly) Leila's Hijack War, 1970; Hussein: a biography, 1972. *Recreations:* sailing, ski-ing, model railways, photography. *Address:* c/o BBC TV White City, Wood Lane, W12 7TS; *e-mail:* peter.snow@bbc.co.uk.

SNOW, Philip Albert, OBE 1985 (MBE 1979); JP; MA; FRSA; FRAI; author, bibliographer and administrator; *b* 7 Aug. 1915; *s* of William Edward Snow, FRCO and Ada Sophia Robinson; *m* 1940, Anne Harris; one *d*. *Educ:* Newton's Sch., Leicester; Christ's Coll., Cambridge (MA Hons). FRAI 1952. HM Colonial Administrative Service: Provincial Comr, Magistrate, Establishment and Protocol Officer, and Asst Colonial Sec., Fiji and Western Pacific, 1937–52; ADC to Governor and C-in-C, Fiji, 1939; Dep. Sheriff, Fiji, 1940–52; Official Mem., Legislative Council, Fiji, 1951; Fiji Govt Liaison Officer, US and NZ Forces, 1942–44. Bursar, Rugby Sch., 1952–76. Mem., Jt Cttee, Governing Bodies of Schools' Assoc., 1958–65. President: Public Schs Bursars' Assoc., 1962–65; The Worthing Soc., 1983–; Vice-Pres., Fiji Soc., 1944–52; Trustee, Fiji Museum, 1950–52. Founder Member Committee: Union Club, Suva, 1944; Fiji Arts Club, 1945. Founder, Suva Cricket Assoc., Nadi Cricket Assoc. and six other dist cricket assocs, 1939–49; Founder, Fiji Cricket Assoc., 1946, Vice-Patron, 1952–; Captain, Fiji Cricket Team, NZ first-class tour, 1948; Liaison Officer/Manager, first Fiji Cricket Team in England, 1979. International Cricket Conference: Perm. Rep. of Fiji, 1965–90; Mem., first Cricket World Cup Cttee, 1971–75; first Chm., Associate Member Countries, 1982–87; Perm. Rep. of Fiji, Internat. Cricket Council, 1990–94. Organiser, Rugby Sch. 400th anniv. celebrations, 1967; designer, Fiji Govt stamps for centenary of Fiji cricket, 1974. Broadcasts on Fiji radio, BBC and in NZ, 1948–. Literary Executor of Lord Snow. JP Warwicks, 1967–76, and W Sussex, 1976–. FRSA 1984. Foreign Specialist Award, USA Govt, 1964; Independence Silver Jubilee Medal, Fiji, 1995. *Publications:* Air Raids Precautions Services, Lautoka, 1943; (ed with G. K. Roth) Sources Describing Fijian Customs for Fijian Examination Candidates, 1944; (ed) Civil Service Journal, 1945; Cricket in the Fiji Islands, 1949; Rock Carvings in Fiji, 1950; Report on the Visit of Three Bursars to the United States of America and Canada in 1964, 1965; Best Stories of the South Seas, 1967; Bibliography of Fiji, Tonga and Rotuma, vol. 1, 1969; (with Stefanie Snow Waine) The People from the Horizon: an illustrated history of the Europeans among the South Sea Islanders, 1979; Stranger and Brother: a portrait of C. P. Snow, 1982; The Years of Hope: Cambridge, colonial administrator in the South Seas and cricket (autobiog.), 1997; A Time of Renewal: clusters of characters, C. P. Snow and coups (autobiog.), 1998; contrib. TLS, Sunday Times, Daily Telegraph, The Times, Jls of RAI, RGS, Fiji Museum, Pacific History and Polynesian Soc., Jl de la Société des Océanistes, Amer. Anthropologist, Wisden's Almanack, Barclays World of Cricket, Dictionary of Nat. Biog; numerous reviews of, and introductions to, Pacific and general books. *Recreations:* taming robins; formerly cricket (Capt., Leics 2nd XI, 1936–38, Leics, 1946, Cambridge Crusaders, Googlies, MCC (Capt., 1955–65), Authors, Fiji first-class), chess (half-Blue), table-tennis (half-Blue and Cambs), deck-tennis, tennis. *Address:* 46 Bennett Court, Station Road, Letchworth, Herts SG6 3WA. *T:* (01462) 677556. *Clubs:* MCC (Hon. Life Mem. for services to internat. cricket, 1970), Stragglers of Asia (Hon. Mem.); De Flamingos (Hon. Mem.) (Holland); Mastermind; Hawks (Cambridge).

SNOW, Surg. Rear-Adm. Ronald Edward, CB 1991; LVO 1972; OBE 1977; Surgeon Rear Admiral (Operational Medical Services), 1989–91; *b* 17 May 1933; *s* of Arthur Chandos Pole Snow (formerly Soppitt) and Evelyn Dorothea Snow (*née* Joyce); *m* 1959, Valerie Melian French; two *d*. *Educ:* St Andrew's Coll., Grahamstown, S Africa; Trinity Coll., Dublin (MA, MB, BCh, BAO); FFOM, DA, LMCC. HMS Victorious, 1966; HMS Dolphin, 1967; HMY Britannia, 1970; MoD, 1973 and 1977; Inst. of Naval Medicine, 1975 and 1984; Staff of Surg. Rear Adm. (Naval Hosps), 1980; Staff of C-in-C Fleet, 1982; Asst Surg. Gen. (Service Hosps), 1985; Surg. Rear Adm. (Support Med. Services), 1987. QHP 1984–91. OStJ 1986. *Recreation:* National Hunt racing.
See also Rear-Adm. K. A. Snow.

SNOW, Thomas; Director, Oxford University Careers Service (formerly Secretary, Oxford University Appointments Committee), 1970–96; Fellow, New College, Oxford, 1973–96, then Emeritus; *b* 16 June 1929; *e s* of Thomas Maitland Snow, CMG; *m* 1961, Elena Tidmarsh; two *s* one *d*. *Educ:* Winchester Coll.; New Coll., Oxford. Joined Crittall Manufacturing Co. Ltd as Management Trainee, 1952; Dir 1966; Director: Crittall Hope Ltd, Darlington Simpson Rolling Mills, Minex Metals Ltd, 1968. Marriage Counsellor, 1964–70; Chm., Oxfordshire Relate (formerly Oxford Marriage Guidance Council), 1974–90; Member: Cttee of Management, Oxford Univ. Counselling Service, 1992–94 (Chm., 1994–96); Standing Cttee, Assoc. of Graduate Careers Adv. Services, 1973–77, 1985–89. Trustee: Thomas Wall Trust, 1980–99; Ethox, 1998–; Governor: Harpur Trust, 1996–2001; Bedford Sch., 1996–2001. Fellow, Winchester Coll., 1985–98. Mem. (Lab.), Witham UDC, Essex, 1957–61 (Mem., 1957–61, Chm., 1959–61, Finance Cttee); Mem. (Lib Dem), Oxfordshire CC, 1997–2001. JP Braintree, Essex, 1964–69. *Address:* 157 Woodstock Road, Oxford OX2 7NA.
See also A. E. Snow.

SNOWDEN, Prof. Christopher Maxwell, PhD; FREng, FIEEE, FIEE; Professor of Microwave Engineering, University of Leeds, since 1992; Joint Chief Executive Officer, Filtronic plc, since 1999; *b* 5 March 1956; *s* of William and Barbara Snowden; *m* 1993, Irena Lewandowska; two *s*. *Educ:* Univ. of Leeds (BSc Hons, MSc; PhD 1982). FIEE 1993; FIEEE 1996. Applications Engr, Mullard Applications Lab., Surrey, 1977–78; Lectr, Dept of Electronics, Univ. of York, 1982–83; University of Leeds, 1983–: Lectr, then Sen. Lectr, Dept of Electronic and Electrical Engrg, 1983–92; on secondment as Sen. Staff Scientist, M/A-COM Inc., Corporate R&D, Mass, 1990–91; Hd, Sch. of Electronic and Electrical Engrg, 1995–98; Dir, Inst. of Microwaves and Photonics, 1997–98. Exec. Dir of Technol., Filtronic plc, 1998–99. Distinguished Lectr, IEEE (Electron Devices Soc.), 1996–. Mem., Electromagnetics Acad., MIT, 1990–; FREng 2000. FRSA 2000. Microwave Prize, IEEE, 1999. *Publications:* Introduction to Semiconductor Device Modelling, 1986 (trans. Japanese 1988); (ed jtly and contrib.) Semiconductor Device Modelling, 1987; INCA Interactive Circuit Analysis, 1988; Semiconductor Device Modelling, 1988; (ed and contrib.) Semiconductor Device Modelling, 1989; (ed jtly and contrib.) Compound Semiconductor Device Modelling, 1993; (jtly) International Conference on Computational Electronics, 1993; contrib. numerous papers in IEEE, IEE and other learned jls. *Recreations:* photography, painting. *Address:* Filtronic plc, The Waterfront, Salts Mill Road, Saltaire, Shipley BD18 3TT. *T:* (01274) 231452.

SNOWDON, 1st Earl of, *cr* 1961; **Antony Charles Robert Armstrong-Jones,** GCVO 1969; RDI 1978; FCSD; Viscount Linley, 1961; Baron Armstrong-Jones (Life Peer), 1999; Constable of Caernarfon Castle since 1963; Provost, Royal College of Art, since 1995; *b* 7 March 1930; *s* of Ronald Owen Lloyd Armstrong-Jones, MBE, QC, DL (*d* 1966), and Anne (*d* 1992), *o d* of Lt-Col Leonard Messel, OBE (later Countess of Rosse); *m* 1st, 1960, HRH The Princess Margaret (marr. diss. 1978); one *s* one *d*; 2nd, 1978, Lucy Lindsay-Hogg, *d* of Donald Davies; one *d*. *Educ:* Eton; Jesus Coll., Cambridge (coxed winning Univ. crew, 1950). Joined Staff of Council of Industrial Design, 1961, continued on a consultative basis, 1962–87, also an Editorial Adviser of Design Magazine, 1961–87; an Artistic Adviser to the Sunday Times and Sunday Times Publications Ltd, 1962–90; photographer, Telegraph Magazine, 1990–94. Designed: Snowdon Aviary, London Zoo, 1965; Chairmobile, 1972. A Vice President: National Fund for Research for Crippling Diseases; Prince of Wales Adv. Cttee on Disability; Patron, Circle of Guide Dog Owners; Chm., Working Party on Integrating the Disabled (Report 1976); Pres. for England, Cttee, International Year for Disabled People, 1981. Vice Pres., Kensington Soc. Founder, Snowdon Award Scheme, 1980. Hon. Fellow: Institute of British Photographers; Royal Photographic Soc.; Manchester College of Art and Design; Hon. Member: North Wales Society of Architects; South Wales Institute of Architects; Royal Welsh Yacht Club; Patron: Welsh Nat. Rowing Club; Metropolitan Union of YMCAs; British Water Ski Federation. President: Contemp. Art Society for Wales; Welsh Theatre Company; Mem. Council, English Stage Co., 1978–82. Senior Fellow, RCA, 1986. FRSA. Dr *hc* Bradford, 1989; Hon. LLD Bath, 1989; Hon. DLitt Portsmouth, 1994. Silver Progress Medal, RPS, 1985. *Television films:* Don't Count the Candles, 1968 (2 Hollywood Emmy Awards; St George Prize, Venice; awards at Prague and Barcelona film festivals); Love of a Kind, 1969; Born to be Small, 1971 (Chicago Hugo Award); Happy being Happy, 1973; Mary Kingsley, 1975; Burke and Wills, 1975; Peter, Tina and Steve, 1977; Snowdon on Camera, BBC (presenter), 1981. *Exhibitions include:* Photocall, London, 1958; Assignments, Cologne, London, Brussels, USA, 1972, Japan, Canada, Denmark, Holland, 1975, Australia, 1976, France, 1977; Serendipity, Brighton, Bradford, 1989, Bath, 1990; Snowdon on Stage, RNT and Prague, 1997; Photographs by Snowdon: a retrospective, Nat. Portrait Gall., 2000. *Publications:* London, 1958; Malta (in collaboration), 1958; Private View (in collaboration), 1965; A View of Venice, 1972; Assignments, 1972; Inchcape Review, 1977; (jtly) Pride of the Shires, 1979; Personal View, 1979; Sittings, 1983; Israel: a first view, 1986; (with Viscount Tonypandy) My Wales, 1986; Stills 1983–1987, 1987; Public Appearances 1987–1991, 1991; Wild Flowers, 1995; Snowdon on Stage, 1996; Wild Fruit, 1997; London, Sight Unseen, 1999; Photographs by Snowdon 1952–2000, 2000. *Heir: s* Viscount Linley, *qv*. *Address:* 22 Launceston Place, W8 5RL. *Clubs:* Buck's, Oxford and Cambridge; Leander (Henley-on-Thames); Hawks (Cambridge).
See also under Royal Family, and Earl of Rosse.

SNOWLING, (George) Christopher (Edward); Legal Member, Mental Health Review Tribunal, since 1992; *b* 12 Aug. 1934; *s* of George Edward Snowling and Winifred Beryl (*née* Cave); *m* 1961, Flora Skells; one *s* one *d*. *Educ:* The Mercers' Sch.; Fitzwilliam House, Cambridge (MA). Admitted Solicitor, 1961; various local govt posts, 1958–71; Law Society: Legal Aid Admin, 1971–78; Secretary: Educn and Trng, 1978–85, Professional Purposes, 1985–86; Dir, Legal Aid, 1986–89; private practice, 1989–92. Mem., Cuckfield UDC, 1971–74; Mid Sussex District Council: Mem. (C), 1973–; Chm., 1981–82, 1986–87, 1987–88; Chm., Policy and Resources Cttee, 1988–91; Leader majority gp, 1991–95; Leader largest minority gp, 1995–99; Leader majority gp, Leader of Council, and

Chm. Policy and Resources Cttee, 1999–2001; Chm. of Cttees, 2001–. Member: Council, Assoc. of Dist Councils, 1990–97; cttees, LGA, 1996–98. Member: Mid Downs CHC, 1988–96; Crawley & Horsham Local Res. Ethics Cttee; Lindfield Parish Council, 1995– (Vice Chm., 1999–). Pres., Old Mercers' Club, 1998–99. FIMgt (FBIM 1988). *Recreations:* local government, painting. *Address:* Eldon Lodge, Pondcroft Road, Lindfield, West Sussex RH16 2HQ. *T:* (01444) 482172.

SNOWLING, Prof. Margaret Jean, PhD; Professor of Psychology, University of York, since 1994; *b* 15 July 1955; *d* of Walter and Jean Snowling; *m* 1st, 1986, Christopher Parker (marr. diss. 1992); one *s*; 2nd, 1995, Charles Hulme; three step *d. Educ:* Univ. of Bristol (BSc Psychol. 1976); University Coll. London (PhD Psychol. 1979). Dip. Clin. Psychol., BPsS, 1988. College of Speech Sciences, National Hospital, London: Lectr in Psychology, 1979–88; Sen. Lectr, 1988–89; Principal, 1989–92; Prof. of Psychology, Univ. of Newcastle upon Tyne, 1992–94. Vice-Pres., British Dyslexia Assoc., 1997. *Publications:* (ed) Children's Written Language Difficulties, 1985; Dyslexia: a cognitive developmental perspective, 1987, 2nd edn 2000; (ed jtly) Dyslexia: integrating theory and practice, 1991; (ed jtly) Reading Development and Dyslexia, 1994; (ed jtly) Dyslexia, Speech and Language: a practitioner's handbook, 1996; (ed jtly) Dyslexia, Biology and Cognition, 1997. *Recreations:* walking, entertaining, music. *Address:* Department of Psychology, University of York, Heslington, York YO10 5DD. *T:* (01904) 433162.

SNOWMAN, (Michael) Nicholas; Co-Chairman, Wartski, since 1998; *b* 18 March 1944; *s* of Kenneth Snowman and late Sallie Snowman (*née* Moghi-Levkine); *m* 1983, Margo Michelle Rouard; one *s. Educ:* Hall Sch., London; Highgate Sch., London; Magdalene Coll., Cambridge (BA Hons Eng. Lit.). Asst to Hd of Music Staff, Glyndebourne Fest., 1967–69; Co-Founder and Gen. Man., London Sinfonietta, 1968–72; Administrator, Music Th. Ensemble, 1968–71; Artistic Dir, IRCAM, Centre d'Art et de Culture Georges Pompidou, 1972–86; Gen. Dir (Arts), 1986–92, Chief Exec., 1992–98, South Bank Centre, London; Gen. Dir, Glyndebourne, 1998–2000. Co-Founder, 1975, Artistic Advr, 1975–92, Bd Mem., 1992–, Vice-Chm., 1998–, Ensemble InterContemporain, Paris; Mem. Music Cttee, Venice Biennale, 1979–86; Artistic Dir, Projects in 1980 (Stravinsky), 1981 (Webern), 1983 (Boulez), Fest. d'Automne de Paris; Programme Consultant, Cité de la Musique, La Villette, Paris, 1991. Mem. British Sect., Franco-British Council, 1995–. Trustee, New Berlioz Edition, 1996–. Gov., RAM, 1998– (Hon. RAM). Officier de l'Ordre des Arts et des Lettres (France), 1990 (Chevalier, 1985); Order of Cultural Merit (Poland), 1990; Chevalier, l'Ordre National du Mérite (France), 1995. *Publications:* (co-ed) The Best of Granta, 1967; (series ed.) The Contemporary Composers, 1982–; papers and articles on music, architecture, cultural policy. *Recreations:* films, eating, spy novels, France. *Address:* c/o Wartski, 14 Grafton Street, W1X 4DE. *Club:* Garrick.

SNOXELL, David Raymond; HM Diplomatic Service; High Commissioner, Mauritius, since 2000; *b* 18 Nov. 1944; *s* of late Gordon William Snoxell and of Norah Snoxell; *m* 1971, Anne Carter; two *s* one *d. Educ:* Bishop Vesey's Grammar Sch., Sutton Coldfield; Bristol Univ. (BA Hons Hist. 1966); Aston Univ. (Dip. Personnel Mgt 1967). MIPD. UNA Volunteer, Senegal, 1967–68; joined FCO, 1969; Islamabad, 1973–76; UK Mission to Geneva, 1976–81; FCO, 1981–86; Dir, British Information Services, NY, 1986–91; Dep. Head of Drugs and Internat. Crime Dept, FCO, 1991–94; Dep. Head of Southern Africa Dept, FCO, 1994–96; Ambassador to Senegal and concurrently to Mali, Guinea, Guinea Bissau and Cape Verde, 1997–2000. *Recreations:* choral singing, mediaeval churches. *Address:* Old Mill Cottage, Bassetsbury Lane, High Wycombe, Bucks HP11 1QZ. *T:* (01494) 529318; c/o Foreign and Commonwealth Office, King Charles Street, SW1A 2AH.

SNYDER, Prof. Allan Whitenack, FRS 1990; FAA; FTS; Professor of Optical Physics and Visual Sciences, since 1978, Head of Optical Sciences Centre, since 1987, and Peter Karmel Professor of Science and the Mind, since 1998, Australian National University; Director, Centre for the Mind, Australian National University and University of Sydney, since 1999; Anniversary Professor of Science and the Mind, University of Sydney, since 2000; *b* 23 Nov. 1940; *s* of Edward H. Snyder, philanthropist, and Zelda (*née* Cotton), Broadway actress and psychodramatherapist. *Educ:* Central High Sch., Phil. (AB); Pennsylvania State Univ. (BS); MIT (SM); Harvard Univ. (MS); University Coll. London (PhD); DSc London. Greenland Ice Cap Communications Project, 1961; Gen. Telecom. and Elec. Res. Lab., 1963–67; Cons. to Brit. PO and Standard Telecom. Lab., 1968–70; Nat. Sci. Foundn Fellow, Yale Univ., 1970–71; Sen. Res. Fellow, Sen. Fellow, Professorial Fellow, ANU, 1971–79; John Simon Guggenheim Fellow, Yale Univ. Med. Sch., 1977–78; Hd, Dept of Applied Maths, Inst. for Advanced Studies, ANU, 1980–83; Royal Soc. Quest Res. Fellow, Cambridge Univ., 1987. Foundn Dir, Aust. Photonics Cooperative Res. Centre, 1992–95. Associate Editor, Jl of Optical Soc. of America, 1981–83. Fellow, Optical Soc. of Amer., 1980; Foundn Fellow, Nat. Vision Res. Inst. of Aust., 1983. A. E. Mills Meml Orator, RACP, 1996; Harrie Massey Prize and Lect., Inst. of Phys, 1996; Clifford Paterson Lectr, Royal Soc., 2001. Research Medal, Royal Soc. Vic, 1974; Edgeworth David Medal, Royal Soc. NSW, 1974; Thomas Rankin Lyle Medal, Aust. Acad. of Sci., 1985; Stuart Sutherland Meml Medal, Aust. Acad. of Technological Sci. and Engrg, 1991; CSIRO External Medal for Research, 1995; Australia Prize, 1997. *Publications:* Photoreceptor Optics, 1975; Optical Waveguide Theory, 1983; Optical Waveguide Sciences, 1983; articles on the mind, the visual system of animals and on the physics of light propagation in internat sci. jls. *Recreations:* art, culture, language and thought. *Address:* Centre for the Mind, Institute of Advanced Studies, Australian National University, Canberra, ACT 2601, Australia. *T:* (2) 62492626, *Fax:* (2) 62495184; *e-mail:* a.snyder@anu.edu.au; Main Quadrangle, University of Sydney, NSW 2006, Australia. *T:* (2) 9351 8533.

SOAKIMORI, Sir Frederick Pa'Nukuanga, KBE 1996 (OBE 1982); CPM 1976; Commissioner, Royal Solomon Islands Police Force, 1982–96, retired; livestock farmer, since 1996; *b* 7 Jan. 1939; *s* of Alick Rakeitino and Lily Makonavai, Tikopia Is; *m* 1965, Ethel Maesiufia, Malaita Is; six *s* two *d. Educ:* Anglican Sen. Primary Sch., Pawa. Joined Solomon Is Police Force, 1960: driver, 1960–64; detective constable, 1964–67; officer i/c station, 1967–70; Chief Instructor, Police Acad., 1970–75; Dist Police Comdr, 1975–79; Dep. Police Comr, 1979–82. OStJ 1984. *Recreations:* walking, swimming, jogging, canoeing, reading, table tennis. *Address:* Mbumbura Ridge, Honiara, PO Box 595, Solomon Islands. *T:* 23838/26789.

SOAME, Sir Charles (John) Buckworth-Herne-, 12th Bt *cr* 1697; *b* 28 May 1932; *s* of Sir Charles Burnett Buckworth-Herne-Soame, 11th Bt, and Elsie May (*d* 1972), *d* of Walter Alfred Lloyd; *S* father, 1977; *m* 1958, Eileen Margaret Mary, *d* of Leonard Minton; one *s. Heir: s* Richard John Buckworth-Herne-Soame, *b* 17 Aug. 1970. *Address:* Sheen Cottage, Coalbrookdale, Telford, Salop TF8 7EQ.

SOAMES, Lady; Mary Soames, DBE 1980 (MBE (mil.) 1945); Member of Council, 1978–97, and Chairman of Trustees, 1991–June 2002, Winston Churchill Memorial Trust; Chairman, Royal National Theatre Board, 1989–95; *b* 15 Sept. 1922; *y d* of late Rt Hon. Sir Winston Churchill, KG, OM, CH, FRS, and late Baroness Spencer-Churchill, GBE; *m* 1947, Captain Christopher Soames, Coldstream Guards, later Baron Soames, PC, GCMG, GCVO, CH, CBE (*d* 1987); three *s* two *d. Educ:* privately. Served War: Red Cross and WVS, 1939–41; ATS, 1941–46, with mixed anti-aircraft batteries in UK and Europe (Jun. Comdr). Accompanied father on various journeys; campaigned with husband through six elections whilst he was Conservative MP for Bedford, 1950–66; accompanied husband to Paris where he was Ambassador, 1968–72, and to Brussels where he was first British Vice Pres. of Eur. Commn, 1973–76; accompanied husband when he was appointed last British Governor of Southern Rhodesia, Dec. 1979–April 1980. Chm., UK Assoc. for Internat. Year of the Child, 1979. Governor, Harrow Sch., 1980–95. Freeman, City of London, 1994; Hon. Freewoman, Skinners' Co., 1994. JP E Sussex, 1960–74. FRSL 2000. Hon. Fellow, Churchill Coll., Cambridge, 1983. Hon. DLitt: Sussex, 1989; Kent, 1997. Chevalier de la Légion d'Honneur (France), 1995. *Publications:* Clementine Churchill by Her Daughter Mary Soames, 1979 (a Wolfson Prize for History, and Yorkshire Post Prize for Best First Work, 1979); A Churchill Family Album—A Personal Anthology Selected by Mary Soames, 1982; The Profligate Duke: George Spencer-Churchill 5th Duke of Marlborough and his Duchess, 1987; Winston Churchill: his Life as a Painter: a memoir by his daughter Mary Soames, 1990; Speaking for Themselves—The Personal Letters of Winston & Clementine Churchill: edited by their daughter Mary Soames, 1998. *Recreations:* reading, sight-seeing, gardening.

See also Earl Peel, Hon. A. N. W. Soames, Hon. E. M. Soames.

SOAMES, Hon. (Arthur) Nicholas (Winston); MP (C) Mid Sussex, since 1997 (Crawley, 1983–97); *b* 12 Feb. 1948; *s* of Baron Soames, PC, GCMG, GCVO, CH, CBE and of Lady Soames, *qv*; *m* 1st, 1981, Catherine Weatherall (marr. diss. 1990); one *s*; 2nd, 1993, Serena, *d* of Sir John L. E. Smith, *qv*; one *s* one *d. Educ:* Eton. Served 11th Hussars (PAO), 1967–70 (2nd Lieut); Equerry to the Prince of Wales, 1970–72; Asst Dir, Sedgwick Group, 1976–82. PPS to Minister of State for Employment, 1984–85, to Sec. of State, DoE, 1987–89, to Sec. of State, DTI, 1989–90; Parly Sec., MAFF, 1992–94; Minister of State for the Armed Forces, MoD, 1994–97. *Recreation:* country pursuits. *Address:* House of Commons, SW1A 0AA. *T:* (020) 7219 3000. *Clubs:* White's, Turf, Pratt's.

See also Hon. E. M. Soames.

SOAMES, Hon. Emma (Mary); Editor, Telegraph magazine, since 1994; *b* 6 Sept. 1949; *d* of Baron Soames, GCMG, GCVO, CH, CBE, PC and of Lady Soames, *qv*; *m* 1981, James MacManus (marr. diss. 1989); one *d. Educ:* Hamilton House Sch. for Girls; Queen's Coll., London; Sorbonne, Univ. of Paris; Ecole des Sciences Politiques. Journalist, Evening Standard, 1974–81; Editor, Literary Review, 1984–86; Features Editor, Vogue, 1986–88; Editor: Tatler, 1988–90; Evening Standard mag., 1992–94. *Recreations:* travel, gardening. *Address:* 26 Eland Road, SW11 5JY.

See also Hon. A. N. W. Soames.

SOAMES, Hon. Nicholas; *see* Soames, Hon. A. N. W.

SOARES, Dr Mário Alberto Nobre Lopes; President of Portugal, 1986–96; *b* 7 Dec. 1924; *s* of João Lopes Soares and Elisa Nobre Soares; *m* 1949, Maria Barroso Soares; one *s* one *d. Educ:* Univ. of Lisbon (BA 1951; JD 1957); Faculty of Law, Faculty of History and Philosophy, Sorbonne. LèsL, LenD. Leader, United Democratic Youth Movement and Mem., Central Cttee, 1946–48; Mem. Exec., Social Democratic Action, 1952–60; Democratic Opposition candidate, Lisbon, legis. elections, 1965, 1969; deported to São Tomé, March–Nov. 1968; Rep., Internat. League of Human Rights; imprisoned 12 times; exile, Paris, 1970–74; Founder, Portuguese Socialist Party, 1973, Sec. Gen., 1973–86; elected to Legis. Assembly as Mem. (Socialist Party) for Lisbon, 1974; Minister of Foreign Affairs, 1974–75; Minister without Portfolio, 1975; Deputy, Constituent Assembly, 1975, Legis. Assembly, 1976; Mem., Council of State; Prime Minister of Portugal 3 times, 1976–85. Pres., Mário Soares Foundn, 1991–. Joseph Lemaire Prize, 1975; Internat. Prize of Human Rights, 1977; Robert Schuman Prize, 1987; numerous hon. degrees, decorations and orders. *Publications:* A Juventude Não Está com o Estado Novo, 1946; As ideias político-sociais de Teófilo Braga, 1950; A Justificação Jurídica da Restauração e a Teoria da Origem Popular do Poder Político, 1954; Escritos Políticos, 1969; Le Portugal Baillonné, 1972 (Portuguese edn, Portugal Amordaçado, 1947; also trans. English, Italian, German and Spanish); Destruir o Sistema, Construir uma Vida Nova, 1973; Caminho Difícil, do Salazarismo ao Caetanismo, 1973; Escritos do Exílio, 1975; (with Willy Brandt and Bruno Kreisky) Liberdade para Portugal, 1975; Democratização e Descolonização, 1975; Portugal, que Revolução? (interviews with Dominique Pouchin), 1976 (also French, German, Italian and Spanish edns); Relatório as II Congresso do Partida Socialista, 1976; A Europa Connosco, 1976; Na Posse do I Governo Constitucional, 1976; Na Hora da Verdade, 1976; Na Reestruturação do I Governo Constitucional, 1977; Medidas Económicas de Emergência, 1978; Na Posse do II Governo Constitucional, 1978; Em Defesa do Estado Democrático, 1978; Encarar o Futuro com Esperança, 1978; Existe o Eurocomunismo?, 1978; O Futuro será o Socialismo Democrático, 1979; Partida Socialista, Fronteira da Liberdade, 1979; Confiar no Partida Socialista, Apostar em Portugal, 1979; Soares Responde a Artur Portela, 1980; Apelo Irrecusável, 1981; Resposta Socialista para o Mundo em Crise, 1983; Persistir, 1984; A Árvore e a Floresta, 1985; Intervenções (collected speeches): Vol. I, 1987; Vol. II, 1988; Vol. III, 1989; Vol. IV, 1990; Vol. V, 1991; Vol. VI, 1992; Vol. VII, 1993; Vol. VIII, 1994; Vol. IX, 1995; Vol. X, 1996; Moderador e Árbitro, 1995. *Recreations:* bibliophile; collector of contemporary Portuguese paintings. *Address:* Rua Dr João Soares, 2-3°, 1600 Lisboa, Portugal.

SOBER, Phillip, FCA; non-executive Director: Liberty International (formerly Transatlantic Holdings, then Liberty International Holdings), since 1983; Capital and Counties, since 1993; Capital Shopping Centres, since 1994; *b* 1 April 1931; *s* of Abraham and Sandra Sober; *m* 1957, Vivien Louise Oppenheimer; two *d* (and one *d* decd). *Educ:* Haberdashers' Aske's. Qual. as Chartered Accountant, 1953; FCA 1963. Stoy Hayward, Chartered Accountants: Partner, 1958; Internat. Partner, 1975–90; Sen. Partner, 1985–90. Eur. Regl Dir, Horwath Internat., 1990–94. Crown Estate Comr, 1983–94. Mem. Council, UK Central Council for Nursing, Midwifery and Health Visiting, 1980–83. Pres., Norwood Child Care, 1990–94. Trustee, Royal Opera House Trust, 1985–91. Gov., London Inst. Higher Educn Corp., 1994–; Mem. Council, London Univ., 1999–. *Publications:* articles in prof. press on various subjects but primarily on property co. accounting. *Recreations:* interested in all the arts, partic. music; golf main sporting activity. *Address:* 4 Horbury Mews, W11 3NL. *T:* (020) 7727 2427; Amberley Place, Amberley, West Sussex BN18 9NG. *Clubs:* Savile, Royal Automobile, Hurlingham.

SOBERS, Sir Garfield St Auburn, (Sir Garry), Kt 1975; OCC; former cricketer; Consultant, Barbados Tourism Authority; *b* Bridgetown, Barbados, 28 July 1936; *m* 1969, Prudence Kirby; two *s* one *d. Educ:* Bay Street Sch., Barbados. First major match, 1953, for Barbados; played in 93 Test Matches for West Indies, 39 as Captain, 1953–74 (made world record Test Match score, Kingston, 1958); captained West Indies and Barbados teams, 1965–74; Captain of Nottinghamshire CCC, 1968–74. On retirement from Test cricket held the following world records in Test Matches: 365 not out; 26 centuries; 235

wickets; 110 catches. *Publications:* Cricket Advance, 1965; Cricket Crusader, 1966; King Cricket, 1967; (with J. S. Barker) Cricket in the Sun, 1967; Bonaventure and the Flashing Blade, 1967; (with Brian Scovell) Sobers: Twenty Years At The Top (autobiog.), 1988; (jtly) The Changing Face of Cricket, 1995. *Address:* Barbados Tourism Authority, Redman Drive, Harbour Road, St Michael, Barbados, West Indies. *Fax:* 4264080.

SOBHI, Mohamed Ibrahim; Order of Merit, 1st Class, Egypt, 1974; Director General, International Bureau of Universal Postal Union, Berne, 1975–84, retired; *b* Alexandria, 28 March 1925; *s* of Gen. Ibrahim Sobhi and Mrs Zenab Affifi; *m* 1950, Laila Ahmed Sobhi; two *s* one *d*. *Educ:* Cairo Univ. (BE 1949). Construction of roads and airports, Engr Corps, 1950; Technical Sec., Communications Commn, Permanent Council for Develt and National Prodn, Cairo, 1954; Fellow, Vanderbilt Univ., Nashville, Tenn (studying transport and communications services in USA), 1955–56; Tech. Dir, Office of Minister of Communications for Posts, Railways and Coordination between means of transp. and communications, Cairo, 1956–61; Dir-Gen., Sea Transp. Authority (remaining Mem. Tech. Cttees, Postal Org.), 1961–64; Under Sec. of State for Communications and Mem. Bd, Postal Org., Cairo, 1964–68; Chm. Bd, Postal Org., and Sec.-Gen., African Postal Union, Cairo, 1968–74. Universal Postal Union: attended Congress, Ottawa, 1957; attended Cons. Council for Postal Studies session, Brussels, 1958; Head of Egyptian Delegn, Tokyo and Lausanne Congresses, and sessions of CCPS (set up by Tokyo Congress), 1969–74; Dir, Exec. Bureau i/c Egyptian projects in Africa, incl. construction of Hôtel de l'Amitié, Bamako, Mali, and roads, Republic of Mali, 1963–74; as Director-General of UPU, acted as Sec.-Gen. of the Congress, Exec. Council, and Cons. Council for Postal Studies; acted as intermediary between UPU and Restricted Unions, UN and internat. orgns; visited member countries and attended many meetings and congresses, inc. those of Restricted Unions, in all continents. Chm., Communications Cttee, Nat. Dem. Party of Egypt, 1985; Mem., Nat. Council of Production and Econ. Affairs of Egypt, 1985. Mem., Acad. of Scientific Res., 1990. Heinrich von Stephan Medal (Germany), 1979; Order of Postal Merit (Gran Placa) (Spain), 1979. *Recreations:* croquet, philately, music. *Address:* 4 Sheik Zakaria El-Ansary Street, Heliopolis, Cairo, Egypt; 18 Burgstrasse, 3700 Spiez, Switzerland.

SODANO, His Eminence Cardinal Angelo, STD, JCD; Secretary of State to His Holiness the Pope, since 1990; *b* Asti, Italy, 23 Nov. 1927; *s* of Giovanni Sodano and Delfina (*née* Brignolo). *Educ:* Seminario di Asti; Pontifical Università Gregoriana (STD); Pontifical Università Lateranense (JCD). Ordained priest, 1950; Titular Archbishop, 1978; Apostolic Nuncio, Chile, 1978–88; Sec., Council for Public Affairs of Church, later Section for Relns of Holy See with States, 1988–90. Several hon. distinctions. *Address:* Secretariat of State, 00120 Vatican City State.

SODOR AND MAN, Bishop of, since 1989; **Rt Rev. Noël Debroy Jones,** CB 1986; Episcopal Visitor, diocese of Carlisle, since 1994; *b* 25 Dec. 1932; *s* of Brinley and Gwendoline Jones; *m* 1969, Joyce Barbara Leelavathy Arulanandam; one *s* one *d*. *Educ:* Haberdasher's West Monmouth, 1955–59; Vicar of Kano, N Nigeria, 1960–62; Chaplain, RN, 1962; GSM Brunei 1962, Borneo 1963; RM Commando Course prior to service in Aden with 42 Cdo, 1967; GSM S Arabia, 1967; Mid Service Clergy Course at St George's House, Windsor Castle, 1974; Staff Chaplain, MoD, 1974–77; Chaplain of the Fleet and Archdeacon for the Royal Navy, 1984–89. QHC 1983–89. OStJ 1995. *Recreations:* squash, swimming, music, family; formerly Rugby. *Address:* Bishop's House, Quarterbridge Road, Douglas, Isle of Man IM2 3RF. *Club:* Army and Navy.

SOEHARTO, General Mohamed, Hon. GCB 1974; President of Indonesia, 1968–98; *b* 8 June 1921; *s* of Kertosudiro and Sukirah; *m* 1947, Siti Hartinah (*d* 1996); three *s* three *d*. *Educ:* Elementary Sch., Puluhan Village; Junior High Sch., Wonogiri and Yogyakarta; Senior High Sch., Semarang. Military Basic Training Course and Non Commissioned Officers' Sch., 1940; Asst Police Chief, Yogyakarta (Japanese Police Unit Keibuho), 1941; Platoon Leader, Volunteer Corps, Wates, 1943; Co. Comdrs Sch., 1944; Mem., People's Security Army during Physical Revolution's counter insurgency ops against Indonesian Communist Party, 1945–50; crushed rebellion of Andi Aziz, Ujung Pandang, 1950; ops against Moslem rebels, Central Java, 1951–59; Comdg Gen., Liberation of W Irian (Western New Guinea), 1962; ops against Indonesian Communist Party, 1965; took measures to control the country, 1966; Acting President, 1967–68. Holds numerous decorations. *Address:* c/o Office of the President, Jakarta, Indonesia.

SOFER, Mrs Anne Hallowell; Chief Education Officer, London Borough of Tower Hamlets, 1989–97; *b* 19 April 1937; *d* of Geoffrey Crowther (later Baron Crowther) and Margaret Worth; *m* 1958, Jonathan Sofer; two *s* one *d*. *Educ:* St Paul's Sch.; Swarthmore Coll., USA; Somerville Coll., Oxford (MA); DipEd London. Secretary, National Assoc. of Governors and Managers, 1972–75; Additional Member, ILEA Education Cttee, 1974–77; Chairman, ILEA Schools Sub-Cttee, 1978–81; Mem. (SDP), GLC/ILEA for St Pancras N, Oct. 1981–86 (by-election) (Labour, 1977–81). Dir, Channel Four Television Co. Ltd, 1981–83; Columnist, The Times, 1983–87. Mem., SDP Nat. Cttee, 1982–87. Contested Hampstead and Highgate (SDP) 1983, (SDP/Alliance) 1987. Trustee, Nuffield Foundn, 1990–. Chm., Nat. Children's Bureau, 2000–. Dir, London Accord, 1997–98. *Publications:* (with Tyrrell Burgess) The School Governors and Managers Handbook and Training Guide, 1978; The London Left Takeover, 1987. *Address:* 46 Regent's Park Road, NW1 7SX. *T:* (020) 7722 8970.

SOHLMAN, (Per) Michael (Sverre Rolfsson); Executive Director, Nobel Foundation, since 1992; *b* 24 May 1944; *s* of Rolf Rolfsson Sohlman and Zinaida Sohlman (*née* Yarotskaya); *m* 1965, Margareta Borg-Sohlman (marr. diss. 1980); one *s* two *d*. *Educ:* Univ. of Uppsala (BA 1964). Asst Sec., Commn on Environmental Problems, 1969–70; Min. of Industry, 1972–74; Internat. Div., 1974–76, Budget Dept, 1976, Min. of Finance; Financial Counsellor, Permt Swedish Delegn to OECD, Paris, 1977–80; Res. Dept, Social-Democratic Parly Gp, 1981–82; Head of Planning, Econ. Dept, 1982–84, Dir of Budget, 1985–87, Min. of Finance; Under-Sec. of State, Min. of Agriculture, 1987–89; Under-Sec. of State for Foreign Trade, Min. for Foreign Affairs, 1989–91. Member: Stockholm Inst. of Transition Econs, 1990–; Bd, Internat. Crisis Gp, 1995; Swedish Internat. Develt Agency, 1995–98; Chm., Bd of Dirs, Royal Dramatic Theatre, Stockholm, 1993–96. Member: Royal Swedish Acad. of Scis, 1996; Acad. of Engineering Scis, 1995. Hon. DHL Gustavus Adolphus Coll., 1992. *Address:* Nobel Foundation, PO Box 5232, 102 45 Stockholm, Sweden. *T:* (8) 6630920.

SOKOLOV, Dr Avril, FBA 1996; Reader in Russian, University of Durham, 1989–96, Emeritus since 1996; *b* 4 May 1930; *d* of Frederick Cresswell Pyman and Frances Gwenneth Pyman (*née* Holman), MBE; *m* 1963, Kirill Konstantinovich Sokolov; one *d*. *Educ:* Newnham Coll., Cambridge (BA Mod. Langs 1951; PhD 1958). FIL 1949. British Council post-grad. scholarship to Leningrad, 1959–61; freelance writer on and translator of Russian lit., 1962–75; lived in Moscow, 1963–74; University of Durham: part-time Lectr in Russian Lit., 1975–77; Lectr, 1977–86; Sen. Lectr, 1986–89. Mem., Soc. of Authors (Translators' Section), 1974–. Cert. of Merit, Moscow Patriarchate, 1973. *Publications:* as Avril Pyman: The Distant Thunder: a life of Aleksandr Blok, Vol. I, 1979; The Release of Harmony: a life of Aleksandr Blok, Vol. II, 1980; Aleksandr Blok's The Twelve, 1989; A History of Russian Symbolism, 1994 (trans. Russian, 1998); ed and trans. works by Blok, Bulgakov, Shvarts; trans. poetry, prose, art books; numerous articles on Russian Symbolism and later 20th century literature. *Recreations:* travelling, art, theatre, cinema. *Address:* 213 Gilesgate, Durham DH1 1QN. *T:* (0191) 384 2482.

SOLA, Maggie; *see* Koumi, M.

SOLANA MADARIAGA, Javier, Hon. KCMG 1999; Secretary-General, and High Representative for Common Foreign and Security Policy, European Union, since 1999; Secretary-General, Western European Union, since 1999; *b* 14 July 1942; *s* of Luis Solana and Obulia Madariaga; *m* 1972, Concepción Giménez; two *c*. *Educ:* Colegio del Pilar; Univ. Complutense de Madrid (PhD Physics). Fulbright Schol., USA, 1968. Asst to Prof., Univ. of Valencia, 1968–71, then Univ. Autónoma de Madrid; Mem. Exec., Federación Socialista Madrileña and Federación de Trabajadores de la Enseñanza, Unión General de Trabajadores; Prof. of Physical Scis, Univ. Complutense de Madrid. Mem., Congress of Deputies for Madrid; Mem., Fed. Exec. Cttee, PSOE (Press Sec. and Sec. for Res. and Programmes); Minister of: Culture, and Govt Spokesman, 1982–88; Educn and Sci., 1988–92; Foreign Affairs, 1992–95; Sec.-Gen., NATO, 1995–99. *Publications:* several on physics and solid state physics. *Recreations:* swimming, jogging, tennis, paddle tennis. *Address:* Council of the European Union, Rue de la Loi 175, 1048 Brussels, Belgium.

SOLANDT, Jean Bernard; Chairman: Schroder France SA, 1992–97; J. Henry Schroder & Co. Ltd, 1994–97; Director, Woolwich Building Society, 1993–98; *b* 23 Dec. 1936; *s* of Alfred Solandt and Mathilde Braun Solandt; *m* 1966, Sheila Hammill; one *s* one *d*. *Educ:* Lycée Pasteur, Strasbourg; Collège Technique Commercial, Strasbourg. Société Générale, Strasbourg, Paris, London, 1954–68; Schroder Gp, 1968–97: Director: J. Henry Schroder & Co., 1973; Schroders plc, 1982; IBJ Schroder Bank & Trust Co. Inc., 1984–86; Schroders Japan Ltd, 1984–95; Schroder & Co. Inc., 1986–96; Schroder Wertheim Hldgs Inc., 1986–97; Schroder Wertheim & Co. Inc., 1986–97; Schroders Asia, 1991; Schroders AG, 1992; Chairman: Schroder Securities Ltd, 1985–89; Schroder Structured Investments Inc., 1995–97. Director: Royal Trust Co. of Canada (London) Ltd, 1978–82; Banca Woolwich SpA, 1996–98; Banque Woolwich SA, 1996–98. Mem. Exec. Cttee, BBA, 1990–94. Advr, Royal Trustees Investment Cttee, 1991–96. Hon. FCIB. *Recreations:* ski-ing, walking, driving, music. *Address:* 27 Heathgate, NW11 7AP. *T:* (020) 8458 2950; La Clapière, 84190 Vacqueyras, France.

SOLANKI, Ramniklal Chhaganlal, OBE 1999; author; Editor: Garavi Gujarat, newsweekly, since 1968; Asian Trader, trade journal, with controlled circulation in English, Gujarati and Urdu, since 1985; GG2, since 1990; Pharmacy Business, since 1998; Correspondent, Janmabhoomi Group, Bombay, since 1968; *b* 12 July 1931; *s* of Chhaganlal Kalidas and Mrs Ichchhaben Solanki, Surat, Gujarat, India; *m* 1955, Mrs Parvatiben, *d* of Makanji Dullabhji Chavda, Nani Pethan, India; two *s* two *d*. *Educ:* Irish Presbyterian Mission Sch., Surat (Matriculation Gold Medal, 1949); MTB Coll., Gujarat Univ. (BA(Econ)); Sarvajanik Law Coll., Surat, Gujarat (LLB). Pres., Rander Student Union, 1950–54; Sec., Surat Dist Students' Assoc., 1954–55. Sub-Editor, Nutan Bharat and Lok Vani, Surat, 1954–56; freelance columnist for several newspapers, while serving State Govt in India, 1956–63; London correspondent, Gujarat Mitra Surat, 1964–68; European Correspondent, Janmabhoomi Gp of Newspapers, 1968–; Managing Director: Garavi Gujarat Publications Ltd, Garavi Gujarat Property Ltd and Garavi Gujarat Publications (USA) Inc. (columnist of thought of the week on Indian philosophy, Garavi Gujarat, newsweekly); Asian Trade Publications Ltd. Member: Guild of British Newspaper Editors, 1976–; Asian Adv. Cttee, BBC, 1976–80; Nat. Centre for Ind. Language Trng Steering Gp, 1976–; Exec. Cttee, Gujarati Arya Kshtriya Maha Sabha UK, 1979–84; Exec. Cttee, Gujarati Arya Assoc., 1974–84 (Vice-Pres., 1980–81, 1982–83); CPU, 1964–; Foreign Press Assoc., 1984–; Parly Press Gallery, House of Commons; Sec., Indian Journalists Assoc. of Europe, 1978–79. Founder, and Mem. Judging Panel, annual GG2 Leadership and Diversity Awards. Chm., Asian Forum, 1999–. Trustee, Gandhi Bapu Meml Trust, 1993–. Best Reporter of the Year in Gujarati, 1970. *Publications:* contrib. many articles. *Recreations:* reading, writing. *Address:* 74 Harrowdene Road, N Wembley, Middx HA0 2JF. *T:* (020) 8902 2879; (office) Garavi Gujarat House, 1/2 Silex Street, SE1 0DW. *T:* (020) 7928 1234, *Fax:* (020) 7261 0055; *e-mail:* garavi@gujarat.co.uk.

SOLBES MIRA, Pedro; Member, European Commission, since 1999; *b* 31 Aug. 1942; *m* 1973, Pilar Castro; one *s* two *d*. *Educ:* Univ. of Madrid (BL, Dr Pol Scis); Univ. Libre de Bruxelles (Dip. in European Econs). Entered Min. of Foreign Trade, Spain, 1968; Commercial Counsellor, Spanish Mission to EC, 1973–78; Special Advr to Minister for Relns with EC, 1978–79; Dir Gen. of Commercial Policy, Min. of Econs and Trade, 1979–82; Gen. Sec., Min. of Econs and Finance, 1982–85; Sec. of State for Relns with EC, 1985–91; Minister of Agriculture, Food and Fisheries, 1991–93; Minister of Econs and Finance, 1993–96; Deputy (Socialist Party), Cortes, 1996–99. Chm., EBRD, 1994. *Address:* European Commission, rue de la Loi 200, 1049 Brussels, Belgium.

SOLESBURY, William Booth; Associate Director, UK Centre for Evidence-based Policy and Practice, Queen Mary, University of London, since 2000; *b* 10 April 1940; *s* of William and Hannah Solesbury; *m* 1966, Felicity Andrew; one *s* two *d*. *Educ:* Hertford Grammar Sch.; Univ. of Cambridge (BA Hons Geography); Univ. of Liverpool (MCD Town Planning). London County Council, 1961–65; London Borough of Camden, 1965–66; City of Munich, 1966–67; Min. of Housing, 1967–72; NATO Res. Fellow, Univ. of California, Berkeley, 1973; Dept of Environment, 1974–89; Gwilym Gibbon Res. Fellow, Nuffield Coll., Oxford, 1989–90; Sec., ESRC, 1990–95; res. mgt consultant, 1995–2000. *Publications:* Policy in Urban Planning, 1974; articles in Public Administration, Policy and Politics. *Recreations:* home life, films, reading, travel. *Address:* 1 Dolby Road, SW6 3NE. *T:* (020) 7736 2155.

SOLESBY, Tessa Audrey Hilda, CMG 1986; HM Diplomatic Service, retired; Leader, UK Delegation to Conference on Disarmament, Geneva (with personal rank of Ambassador), 1987–92; *b* 5 April 1932; *d* of Charles Solesby and Hilda Solesby (*née* Willis). *Educ:* Clifton High School; St Hugh's College, Oxford. MA; Hon. Fellow, 1988. Min. of Labour and Nat. Service, 1954–55; joined Diplomatic Service, 1956; FO, 1956; Manila, 1957–59; Lisbon, 1959–62; FO, 1962–64; First Sec., UK Mission to UN, Geneva, 1964–68; FO, 1968–70; First Sec., UK Mission to UN, NY, 1970–72; FCO, 1972–75, Counsellor, 1975; on secondment to NATO Internat. Staff, Brussels, 1975–78; Counsellor, East Berlin, 1978–81; temp. Minister, UK Mission to UN, NY, 1981–82; Head of Central African Dept, FCO, 1982–86; Minister, Pretoria, 1986–87. *Recreations:* hill-walking, music. *Address:* c/o Foreign and Commonwealth Office, SW1A 2AH.

SOLEY, Clive Stafford; MP (Lab) Ealing, Acton and Shepherd's Bush, since 1997 (Hammersmith North, 1979–83; Hammersmith, 1983–97); *b* 7 May 1939. *Educ:* Downshall Sec. Modern School; Newbattle Abbey Coll.; Strathclyde Univ. (BA Hons); Southampton Univ. (Dip. in Applied Social Studies). Various appointments; Probation Officer, 1970–75; Senior Probation Officer, 1975–79. Chm., Alcohol Educn Centre, 1977–83. Opposition front bench spokesman on N Ireland, 1981–84, on Home Affairs,

1984–87, on Housing, 1987–92. Chairman: Select Cttee on NI, 1995–97; All Party Parly Gp on Parenting, 1994–96. Chm., PLP, 1997–2001; Mem., NEC, Lab. Pty, 1998–2001. *Publication:* (jtly) Regulating the Press, 2000. *Address:* House of Commons, SW1A 0AA.

SOLLEY, Stephen Malcolm; QC 1989; a Recorder, since 1989; *b* 5 Nov. 1946; *s* of late Leslie Solley, sometime MP, and José Solley; *m* 1971, Helen Olivia Cox; four *s*. *Educ:* University College London (LLB 1968). Called to the Bar, Inner Temple, 1969, Bencher, 1998. The Recorder, South Eastern Circuit, 1984–87. Chm., Bar Human Rights Cttee, 1999–. Dir, Hackney Empire Theatre. *Recreations:* jazz, opera, classic cars, wine, football, cooking. *Address:* Charter Chambers, 2 Dr Johnson's Buildings, Temple, EC4Y 7AY. *T:* (020) 7832 0300. *Club:* Les Six.

SOLOMON, David Joseph; Senior Partner, D. J. Freeman, solicitors, 1992–96; *b* 31 Dec. 1930; *s* of Sydney and Rosie Harriet Solomon; *m* 1959, Hazel Boam; one *s* two *d*. *Educ:* Torquay Grammar Sch.; Univ. of Manchester (LLB). Admitted as Solicitor, 1955. Partner, Nabarro Nathanson, 1961–1968; Head of Property Dept, 1976–90, Chief Exec., 1990–93, D. J. Freeman. Chm., Oriental Art Fund plc (formerly Carter Asian Arts PLC), 1996–. Trustee: Highgate Literary and Scientific Instn, 1999– (Pres., 1993–98); Public Art Develt Trust, 1996– (Chm., Public Art Develt Trust, 1998–2001). Mem. Council, Oriental Ceramic Soc., 1988–91, 1994–97, 1998–. *Recreations:* Chinese ceramics, music, architecture, art, wine. *Address:* Russell House, 9 South Grove, N6 6BS. *T:* (020) 8341 6454; Longecourt les Culetre, 21230 Arnay le Duc, Côte d'Or, France. *T:* 380900555. *Club:* Athenæum.

SOLOMON, Sir Harry, Kt 1991; Chairman, Harveys Holdings, 1994–2000; *b* 20 March 1937; *s* of Jacob and Belle Solomon; *m* 1962, Judith Diana Manuel; one *s* two *d*. *Educ:* St Albans School; Law Society School of Law. Qualified solicitor, 1960; in private practice, 1960–75; Hillsdown Holdings: Man. Dir, 1975–84; Jt Chm., 1984–87; Chm., 1987–93; Dir, 1993–97. Dir, US Industries Inc., 1995–. Pres., Help Medicine, RCP, 1990–; Trustee, CORDA, 1990–. Hon. FRCP 1992. *Recreations:* jogging, tennis, theatre, collector of historical autographed letters. *Address:* Hillsdown House, 32 Hampstead High Street, NW3 1QD.

SOLOMON, Rabbi Dr Norman; Fellow, Oxford Centre for Hebrew and Jewish Studies, 1995–2000; Lecturer, Faculty of Theology, University of Oxford, 1995–2001; *b* Cardiff, 31 May 1933; *s* of late Phillip Solomon and Esther Solomon (*née* Lewis); *m* 1st, 1955, Devora, (Doris), Strauss (*d* 1998); three *s* one *d*; 2nd, 2000, Dr Hilary Nissenbaum. *Educ:* Cardiff High Sch.; St John's Coll., Cambridge (BA 1954); Univ. of Manchester (PhD 1966). London Univ (BMus 1958); ARCM 1956. Rabbi: Whitefield Synagogue, Manchester, 1961–66; Greenbank Drive Synagogue, Liverpool, 1966–74; Hampstead Synagogue, 1974–83; Central Synagogue, Birmingham, 1994; Lectr in Judaism, 1983–89, Dir, Centre for Study of Judaism and Jewish/Christian Relations, 1989–94, Selly Oak Colls, Birmingham. Vis. Lectr, Oxford Centre for Postgraduate Hebrew Studies, 1985–94; Koerner Vis. Fellow, Oxford Centre for Hebrew and Jewish Studies, 1994–95. Adviser, Internat. CCJ, 1988–; Specialist Adviser, CNAA, 1989–92. Vice-Pres., World Congress of Faiths, 1998– (Vice-Chm., 1992–98); President: Birmingham Inter-Faiths Council, 1984–85; British Assoc. for Jewish Studies, 1994. FBIS 1986. 15th Annual Sir Sigmund Sternberg Award, CCJ, 1993. Editor, Jewish Christian Relations, 1985–91. *Publications:* Judaism and World Religion, 1991; The Analytic Movement, 1993; Judaism: a very short introduction, 1996; Historical Dictionary of the Jewish Religion, 1998; articles in learned jls. *Recreation:* playing chamber music. *Address:* 5 Phoebe Court, Bainton Road, Oxford OX2 7AQ. *T:* (01865) 437952.

SOLOMONS, Anthony Nathan, FCA; Chairman: Singer & Friedlander Ltd, 1976–99 (Chief Executive, 1973–90); Singer & Friedlander Group plc, 1987–99; *b* 26 Jan. 1930; *s* of Leslie Emanuel Solomons and Susie Schneiders; *m* 1957, Jean Golding; two *d*. Qual. as chartered accountant, 1953; FCA 1963. National Service, 1953–54: commnd Dorset Regt. Articled 1952; Accountant, Kennedy & Fox Oldfield & Co., 1955; Asst Accountant, then Chief Accountant, Lobitos Oilfields Ltd, 1955–58; Singer & Friedlander 1958–99: successively Exec. Dir, Man. Dir, and Jt Chief Exec.

SOLOW, Prof. Robert Merton; Professor of Economics, Massachusetts Institute of Technology, 1949–95, then Emeritus; *b* 23 Aug. 1924; *s* of Milton H. Solow and Hannah Solow (*née* Sarney); *m* 1945, Barbara Lewis; two *s* one *d*. *Educ:* New York City schools; Harvard College (BA 1947); Harvard University (MA 1949, PhD 1951). Served US forces, 1942–45 (Bronze Star, 1944). Joined MIT Faculty as Asst Prof. of Statistics, 1949, Inst. Prof. of Economics, 1974–95. Senior Economist, Council of Economic Advisers, 1961–62. Eastman Prof. and Fellow of Balliol Coll., Oxford, 1968–69; Overseas Fellow, Churchill Coll., Cambridge, 1984, 1991. President: Econometric Soc., 1965; Amer. Econ. Assoc., 1976; Member: Amer. Acad. of Arts and Scis, 1963; Nat. Acad. of Sciences, USA, 1972; Accademia dei Lincei, 1984; Corr. Mem., British Acad., 1975; Mem., Amer. Philosophical Soc., 1974–. Hon. degrees: Chicago, 1967; Brown, 1972; Williams, 1974; Paris I, 1975; Warwick, 1976; Lehigh, 1977; Geneva, Wesleyan, 1982; Tulane, 1983; Yale, 1986; Bryant, 1987; Massachusetts at Boston, Boston Coll., 1989; Colgate, Dartmouth, Helsinki, 1990; New York at Albany, 1991; Harvard, Glasgow, Chile, 1992; Conservatoire Nat. des Arts et Métiers, Paris, 1995; Colorado Sch. of Mines, 1996; New York, 2000. Nobel Prize for Economics, 1987. Order of Merit (Germany), 1995. *Publications:* Linear Programming and Economic Analysis (with P. Samuelson and R. Dorfman), 1958; Capital Theory and the Rate of Return, 1964; The Sources of Unemployment in the US, 1964; Growth Theory: an exposition, 1970, 2nd edn 1999; The Labor Market as a Social Institution, 1990; (with F. Hahn) A Critical Essay on Modern Macroeconomic Theory, 1995; Learning from Learning by Doing, 1996; (with J. Taylor) Inflation, Unemployment and Monetary Policy, 1998; Monopolistic Competition and Macroeconomic Theory, 1998; Work and Welfare, 1998; articles in learned jls. *Recreation:* sailing. *Address:* 528 Lewis Wharf, Boston, MA 02110, USA. *T:* (617) 2274436.

SOLYMAR, Prof. Laszlo, FRS 1995; PhD; Professor of Applied Electromagnetism, University of Oxford, 1992–97, now Emeritus Professor; Professorial Fellow of Hertford College, Oxford, 1986–97, now Emeritus Fellow; *b* 24 Jan. 1930; *s* of Pál and Aranka Solymar; *m* 1955, Marianne Klopfer; two *d*. *Educ:* Technical University, Budapest (Hungarian equivalents of BSc and PhD in Engineering). Lectr, Technical Univ., Budapest, 1952–53; Research Engineer, Res. Inst. for Telecommunications, Budapest, 1953–56; Res. Engineer, Standard Telecom Labs, Harlow, 1956–65; Oxford University: Fellow in Engineering, Brasenose Coll., 1966–86; Lectr, 1971–86, Donald Pollock Reader in Engrg Sci., 1986–92. Visiting Professor: Ecole Normale Supérieure, Paris, 1965–66; Tech. Univ. of Denmark, 1972–73; Univ. Osnabrück, 1987; Tech. Univ., Berlin, 1990; Univ. Autónoma, Madrid, 1993, 1995; Tech. Univ., Budapest, 1994; ICSTM, 2000–. Consultant: Tech. Univ. of Denmark, 1973–76; Thomson-CSF, Orsay, 1984; British Telecom, 1986–88; GEC Wembley, 1986–88; Pilkington Technol. Centre, 1989–90. Faraday Medal, IEE, 1992. Anaxagoras, Archimedes, Hypatia (radio plays with John Wain), 1991. *Publications:* Lectures on the Electrical Properties of Materials (with D. Walsh), 1970, 6th edn 1998; Superconductive Tunnelling and Applications, 1972; (ed) A Review of the Principles of Electrical and Electronic Engineering, 1974; Lectures on Electromagnetic Theory, 1976, 2nd edn 1984; (with D. J. Cooke) Volume Holography and Volume Gratings, 1981; Lectures on Fourier Series, 1988; (jtly) The Physics and Applications of Photorefractive Materials, 1996; Getting the Message: a history of communications, 1999; articles. *Recreations:* history, languages, chess, swimming. *Address:* Department of Engineering Science, University of Oxford OX1 3PJ. *T:* (01865) 273110.

SOLZHENITSYN, Alexander Isayevitch; author; Hon. Fellow, Hoover Institution on War, Revolution and Peace, 1975; *b* 11 Dec. 1918; *m*; three *s*. *Educ:* Univ. of Rostov (degree in maths and physics); Moscow Inst. of History, Philosophy and Literature (correspondence course). Joined Army, 1941; grad. from Artillery School, 1942; in comd artillery battery and served at front until 1945 (twice decorated); sentenced to eight years' imprisonment, 1945, released, 1953; exile in Siberia, 1953–56; officially rehabilitated, 1957; taught and wrote in Ryazan and Moscow; expelled from Soviet Union, 1974; Soviet citizenship restored, 1990. Member Union of Soviet writers, 1962, expelled 1969; Member: Amer. Acad. of Arts and Sciences, 1969; Russian Acad. of Scis, 1997. Awarded Nobel Prize for Literature, 1970; Templeton Prize for Progress in Religion, 1983; Russian State Literature Prize, 1990. *Publications* in English: One Day in the Life of Ivan Denisovich, 1962, new edn 1991, filmed 1971; An Incident at Krechetovka Station, and Matryona's House (publ. US as We Never Make Mistakes, 1969), 1963; For the Good of the Cause, 1964; The First Circle, 1968; Cancer Ward, part 1, 1968, part 2, 1969 (Prix du Meilleur Livre Etranger, Paris); Stories and Prose Poems, 1970; August 1914, 1972; One Word of Truth: the Nobel speech on literature, 1972; The Gulag Archipelago: an experiment in literary investigation, vol. 1, 1973, vol. 2, 1974, vol. 3, 1976 (first Russian edn, 1989); The Oak and the Calf (autobiog.), 1975; Lenin in Zurich, 1975; Prussian Nights (poem), 1977; The Red Wheel: August 1914, 1983 (revd edn of 1972 publication); October 1916, 1985; March 1917 (4 vols); April 1917 (2 vols); How to Reconstruct Russia, 1991; The Russian Question at the End of the Twentieth Century, 1995; Invisible Allies, 1997; Russia in Collapse, 1998; November 1916: the Red Wheel/Knot II, 1999; Two Hundred Years Together, vol. 1, 2001; *plays:* trilogy: The Love Girl and the Innocent, 1969, Victory Celebrations, Prisoners, 1983. *Address:* c/o Claude Durand, Editions Fayard, 75 rue des Saints-Pères, 75006 Paris, France.

SOMARE, Rt Hon. Sir Michael (Thomas), GCMG 1990; CH 1978; PC 1977; MP; Governor, East Sepik Province, Papua New Guinea, since 1995; *b* 9 April 1936; *m* 1965, Veronica Bula Kaiap; three *s* two *d*. *Educ:* Sogeri Secondary Sch.; Admin. Coll. Teaching, 1956–62; Asst Area Educn Officer, Madang, 1962–63; Broadcasts Officer, Dept of Information and Extension Services, Wewack, 1963–66; Journalism, 1966–68. Member for E Sepik Region (Nat. Parl.), PNG House of Assembly, 1968–; Parly Leader, Pangu Pati, 1968–93; First Chief Minister, 1972–75; first Prime Minister, 1975–80, 1982–85; Leader of Opposition in House of Assembly, 1980–82; Minister for Foreign Affairs, 1988–94; National Alliance Leader. Dep. Chm., Exec. Council, 1972–73, Chm., 1973–75. Mem., Second Select Cttee on Constitutional Develt, 1968–72; Mem. Adv. Cttee, Australian Broadcasting Commission. *Publication:* Sana: an autobiography. *Recreations:* golf, fishing, reading. *Address:* Parliament House, Waigani, NCD, Papua New Guinea; (home) Karan, Murik Lakes, East Sepik, Papua New Guinea.

SOMAVIA, Juan O.; Director General, International Labour Organisation, since 1999; *m*; two *c*. *Educ:* Catholic Univ. of Chile; Univ. of Paris. Joined Min. of Foreign Relations, Chile; Mem. Bd. of Dirs and Vice Pres. for Latin America, Inter-Press Service, 1976–87; Sec. Gen., S American Peace Commn, 1987; Perm. Rep. of Chile to UN, NY, 1990–98; former consultant to GATT and UNDP. Founder and Dir, Latin American Inst. for Transnational Studies. Leonidas Proaño Prize, Latin American Human Rights Assoc. *Address:* International Labour Organisation, 4 route des Morillons, 1211 Geneva 22, Switzerland.

SOMERLEYTON, 3rd Baron *cr* 1916; **Savile William Francis Crossley,** GCVO 1999 (KCVO 1994); DL; Bt 1863; farmer; Master of the Horse, 1991–98; *b* 17 Sept. 1928; *er s* of 2nd Baron Somerleyton, MC; *S* father, 1959; *m* 1963, Belinda Maris Loyd (OBE 1997), *d* of late Vivian Loyd and of Mrs Gerald Critchley; one *s* four *d*. *Educ:* Eton Coll. Captain Coldstream Guards, 1948; retired, 1956. Royal Agricultural Coll., Cirencester, 1958–59; farming, 1959–. A Lord in Waiting to the Queen, 1978–91. Dir, Essex & Suffolk Water plc, 1994–97. DL Suffolk, 1964. *Heir:* *s* Hon. Hugh Francis Savile Crossley, *b* 27 Sept. 1971. *Address:* Somerleyton Hall, Lowestoft, Suffolk NR32 5QQ. *T:* (01502) 730308. *Club:* White's.

SOMERS, 9th Baron *cr* 1784; **Philip Sebastian Somers Cocks;** Bt 1772; *b* 4 Jan. 1948; *o s* of John Sebastian Somers Cocks, CVO, CBE (*d* 1964), and of Marjorie Olive (*née* Weller); *S* cousin, 1995. *Educ:* abroad; Elston Hall, Newark; Craig-y-Parc, Cardiff. *Recreations:* opera, music generally, foreign travel. *Heir:* *cousin* Alan Bromley Cocks [*b* 1930; *m* 1955, Pamela Fay, *d* of A, H. Gourlay, Christchurch, NZ; one *s* three *d*]. *Address:* 19 Kempson Road, SW6 4PX.

See also Hon. A. G. Somers Cocks.

SOMERS, Rt Hon. Sir Edward (Jonathan), Kt 1989; PC 1981; Judge of the Court of Appeal, New Zealand, 1981–90; *b* 9 Sept. 1928; *s* of Ewart Somers and Muriel Ann Crossley; *m* 1953, Mollie Louise Morison; one *s* two *d*. *Educ:* Christ's Coll., Christchurch; Canterbury University Coll., Christchurch, NZ (BA, LLB). Practised as barrister and solicitor, 1952–71; practised as barrister, 1971; QC (NZ) 1973; Judge of Supreme Court of New Zealand, 1974. LLD *hc* Univ. of Canterbury, 1992. *Recreation:* gardening. *Address:* Waverley, Kaiapoi, RD2, New Zealand. *T:* (3) 3277094. *Club:* Christchurch (New Zealand).

SOMERS COCKS, Hon. Anna Gwenllian, (Hon. Mrs Allemandi), FSA; Editor, The Art Newspaper, 1990–94, and since 1996; *b* 18 April 1950; *d* of John Sebastian Somers Cocks, CVO, CBE and Marjorie Olive Weller; *m* 1st, 1971, Martin Walker (marr. diss.); 2nd, 1978, John Hardy (marr. diss.); one *s* one *d*; 3rd, 1991, Umberto Allemandi. *Educ:* abroad; Convent of the Sacred Heart, Woldingham; St Anne's College, Oxford (MA); Courtauld Inst., Univ. of London (MA). Asst Keeper, Dept of Metalwork, 1973–85, Dept of Ceramics, 1985–87, Victoria and Albert Museum; Ed., Apollo Magazine, 1987–90. Chm., Umberto Allemandi Publishing, 1995–98. Mem., Mus., New Buildings and Refurbishment Panel, Heritage Lottery Fund, 1996–97; Trustee, Gilbert Collection, 1998–. Chm., Venice in Peril, 1999–. Mem. Bd, Attingham Summer Sch., 1998–. Annual Prize, Nat. Art Collections Fund, 1992. *Publications:* The Victoria and Albert Museum: the making of the collection, 1980; (ed and jt author) Princely Magnificence: court jewels of the Renaissance, 1980; (with C. Truman) Renaissance Jewels, Gold Boxes and Objets de Vertu in the Thyssen Collection, 1985; journalism in The Telegraph etc, articles in magazines. *Recreations:* ski-ing, entertaining, travelling, walking. *Address:* c/o Umberto Allemandi & Co., via Mancini 8, Turin 10131, Italy.

See also Baron Somers.

SOMERSET, family name of **Duke of Beaufort** and of **Baron Raglan**.

SOMERSET, 19th Duke of, *cr* 1547; **John Michael Edward Seymour;** DL; FRICS; Baron Seymour 1547; Bt 1611; *b* 30 Dec. 1952; *s* of 18th Duke of Somerset and of Gwendoline Collette (Jane), 2nd *d* of Major J. C. C. Thomas; *S* father, 1984; *m* 1978, Judith-Rose, *d* of J. F. C. Hull, *qv*; two *s* two *d*. *Educ:* Eton. DL Wilts, 1993. *Heir: s* Lord Seymour, *qv*. *Address:* Berry Pomeroy, Totnes, Devon TQ9 6NJ.

SOMERSET, David Henry Fitzroy, FCIB; Chief of Banking Department and Chief Cashier, Bank of England, 1980–88; *b* 19 June 1930; *s* of late Brig. Hon. Nigel Somerset, CBE, DSO, MC and Phyllis Marion Offley (*née* Irwin); *m* 1955, Ruth Ivy, *d* of late W. R. Wildbur; one *s* one *d*. *Educ:* Wellington Coll.; Peterhouse, Cambridge (MA). Entered Bank of England, 1952; Personal Asst to Managing Director, International Monetary Fund, Washington DC, 1959–62; Private Secretary to Governor of Bank of England, 1962–63; Asst Chief Cashier, 1968–69; Asst Chief of Establishments, 1969–73; Dep. Chief Cashier, 1973–80; Fellow and Financial Advr, Peterhouse, Cambridge, 1988–97, Emeritus Fellow, 1997–. Dir, Yamaichi Bank (UK) PLC, 1988–95; Consultant, Bank Julius Baer, 1997–2000 (Chm. London Adv. Bd, 1991–97). Comr, English Heritage, 1988–91. Mem. Council, Friends of Peterhouse, 1982–; Vice-Pres., Old Wellingtonian Soc., 1997– (Chm., 1988–97); Gov., Wellington Coll., 1989–2000. *Recreations:* gardening, racing, shooting. *Address:* White Wickets, Boars Head, Crowborough, Sussex TN6 3HE. *T:* (01892) 661111, *Fax:* (01892) 667281. *Club:* Boodle's.

SOMERSET JONES, Eric; QC 1978; a Recorder of the Crown Court, 1975–98; *s* of late Daniel and Florence Somerset Jones; *m* 1966, Brenda Marion, *yr d* of late Hedley Shimmin and Doris (*née* Beacroft) two *d*. *Educ:* Birkenhead Institute; Lincoln College, Oxford. MA Oxon. RAF, 1944–47. Called to Bar, Middle Temple, 1952, Bencher, 1988; Mem., Northern Circuit. Member: Lord Chancellor's County Courts Rule Cttee, 1975–78; Gen. Council of the Bar, 1990–94. *Address:* (home) Southmead, Mill Lane, Willaston, Wirral, Cheshire CH64 1RL. *T:* (0151) 327 5138, *Fax:* (0151) 327 9985; 12 Marryat Square, SW6 6UA. *T:* (020) 7381 5360; (chambers) Goldsmith Building, Temple, EC4Y 7BL. *T:* (020) 7353 7881. *Club:* Royal Chester Rowing (Chester).

SOMERTON, Viscount; James Shaun Christian Welbore Ellis Agar; *b* 7 Sept. 1982; *s* and *heir* of 6th Earl of Normanton, *qv*. *Educ:* Harrow Sch. *Address:* Somerley, Ringwood, Hants BH24 3PL.

SOMERVILLE, Prof. Christopher Roland, PhD; FRS 1991; Director, Department of Plant Biology, Carnegie Institution of Washington, USA and Professor of Biology, Stanford University, since 1994; *b* 11 Oct. 1947; *s* of Hubert Roland Somerville and Teresa Marie (*née* Bond); *m* 1976, Shauna Christine Phimester. *Educ:* Univ. of Alberta, Canada (PhD, BS). Asst Prof. of Genetics, Univ. of Alberta, Canada, 1980–82; Associate Prof. of Botany and Genetics, Michigan State Univ., Mich, 1982–86; Prof. of Botany and Genetics, Michigan State Univ., 1982–93. *Publications:* numerous research articles on genetics, physiology and biochemistry of plants. *Recreation:* sailing. *Address:* 5 Valley Oak, Portola Valley, CA 94305, USA; Carnegie Institution of Washington, 260 Panama Street, Stanford, CA 94305, USA. *T:* (650) 3251521.

SOMERVILLE, David, CB 1971; Under-Secretary, Department of Health and Social Security, 1968–77; *b* 27 Feb. 1917; *e s* of late Rev. David Somerville and Euphemia Somerville; *m* 1950, Patricia Amy Johnston; two *s* two *d*. *Educ:* George Watson's Coll.; Fettes Coll.; Edinburgh Univ.; Christ Church, Oxford. Served with Army, 1940–45; Major, Royal Artillery. Entered Civil Service as Asst Principal, Ministry of Health, 1946; Under-Secretary, Min. of Health, 1963–67. *Recreations:* gardening, University of the Third Age. *Address:* 5 Glebe Road, Dorking, Surrey RH4 3DS. *T:* (01306) 885102. *Club:* Boat of Garten Golf.

SOMERVILLE, Prof. Jane, MD; FRCP; Consultant Cardiologist, Grown-Up Congenital Heart Disease Clinic, Middlesex Hospital, University College London, since 1997; Professor of Cardiology, Imperial College School of Medicine, since 1998; *b* 24 Jan. 1933; *d* of Joseph Bertram Platnauer and Pearl Ashton; *m* 1957, Dr Walter Somerville, *qv*; three *s* one *d*. *Educ:* Queen's Coll., London; Guy's Hosp., London Univ. MB, BS (Treasurer's Gold Medal for Clin. Surg.) 1955; MD 1966. MRCS 1955; FRCP 1973 (LRCP 1955, MRCP 1957). FACC 1972. Med. Registrar, Guy's Hosp., 1956–58; Registrar, Nat. Heart Hosp., 1958–59; First Asst to Dr Paul Wood, 1959–63, Sen. Lectr 1964–74, Inst. of Cardiol.; Hon. Cons. Phys., Nat. Heart Hosp., 1967–74, Hosp. for Sick Children, Gt Ormond St, 1968–88; Consultant Physician: Nat. Heart Hosp., then Royal Brompton & Nat. Heart Hosp., 1974–99, now Emeritus; Cardiac Dept, Grown-Up Congenital Heart Disease Clinic, St Bartholomew's Hosp., 1988–92. Lectr in Cardiovascular Disease, Turin Univ., 1973. Vis. Prof. and Guest Lectr, Europe, ME, USA, Mexico, S America, USSR, China; Lectures: St Cyres, Imperial Coll., London, 1976; 6th Mahboubian, NY, 1981; World Congress Gold Medal, Bombay, 1982; Edgar Mannheimer, Hamburg, 1987; John Keith, Montreal, 1988; Tudor Edwards, RCP, 1991; Paul Wood, British Cardiac Soc., 1995; McCue, Washington, 1997; Henry Neufeld, Israel, 1999. Chm., Staff Cttee, 1988–89, Jt Adv. Cttee, 1989–90, Nat. Heart Hosp.; Chm., Cardiol. Cttee, Royal Brompton & Nat. Heart Hosp., 1990–. Sci. Sec., World Congress, Paed. Cardiol., 1980; Advr on congenital heart disease, Sec. of State's Hon. Med. Adv. Panel on driving and disorders of cardiovascular system, 1986–. Member: Assoc. Europ. Pæd. Cardiol.; British Cardiac Soc. (Mem., Paediatric Cardiol. Services Sub-cttee, 1987–); RSocMed; Harveian Soc.; French Cardiac Soc.; 300 Gp; Sci. Council, Monaco Cardiothoracic Centre. Hon. Member: Argentine Pæd. Soc.; Chilean Cardiac Soc.; Argentine Soc. of Cardiol.; Brazilian Cardiac Soc.; Argentine Cardiac Soc. Founding Fellow, Europ. Soc. of Cardiol. Mem. Council, Stonham Housing Assoc. Governor: Queen's Coll., London, 1970– (Chm., 2000–); Nat. Heart and Chest Hosps, 1977–82, 1988–90. Woman of the Year, 1968. *Publications:* numerous contribs to med. lit. on heart disease in children, adolescents and adults, congenital heart disease and results of cardiac surgery; chapters in Paul Wood's Diseases of Heart and Circulation (3rd edn), Oxford Textbook of Medicine, and Perspectives in Pediatric Cardiology, Vols I and II. *Recreations:* collecting antiques, pictures, porcelain soldiers; chess, roof gardening, orchid culture. *Address:* 30 York House, Upper Montagu Street, W1G 8PP. *T:* (020) 7262 2144, (020) 7724 2238; 81 Harley Street, W1G 8PP. *T:* (020) 7637 3442, *Fax:* (020) 7580 3225.

SOMERVILLE, John Arthur Fownes, CB 1977; CBE 1964; DL; an Under-Secretary, Government Communications Headquarters, 1969–78; *b* 5 Dec. 1917; *s* of late Admiral of the Fleet Sir James Fownes Somerville, GCB, GBE, DSO; *m* 1945, Julia Elizabeth Payne; one *s* two *d*. *Educ:* RNC Dartmouth. Lieut-Comdr 1945; retd 1950. Govt Communications Headquarters, 1950–78. DL Somerset, 1985. *Recreation:* walking. *Address:* The Old Rectory, Dinder, Wells, Som BA5 3PL. *T:* (01749) 674900. *Club:* Army and Navy.

See also J. M. F. Somerville.

SOMERVILLE, Brig. Sir (John) Nicholas, Kt 1985; CBE 1975; self employed consultant, personnel selection, since 1984; *b* 16 Jan. 1924; *s* of Brig. Desmond Henry Sykes Somerville and Moira Burke Somerville; *m* 1951, Jenifer Dorothea Nash; one *s* two *d*. *Educ:* Winchester College. Commissioned, The South Wales Borderers, 24th Regt, 1943; served: France and Germany, D-day—VE day, 1944–45 (despatches 1945); BAOR, War Office, FARELF, Aden, 1967–68 (despatches 1968); Directing Staff, JSSC, 1967–69; Comdt, Junior Div., Staff Coll., 1969–72; Dir of Army Recruiting, 1973–75; retired, 1978. Managing Director, Saladin Security Ltd, 1981–84; voluntary consultant responsible for designing Cons. Party Parly selection board procedure, 1980–. *Recreations:* sailing, gardening, house designing. *Address:* Deptford Cottage, Deptford Lane, Greywell, Hook, Hants RG29 1BS. *T:* (01256) 702796.

SOMERVILLE, Very Rev. Dr John Spenser, ONZ 1991; CMG 1978; MC 1945; Master, Knox College, Dunedin, 1963–78, retired; *b* 7 July 1910; *s* of James Cleland Hall Somerville and Grace Isabella (*née* Isherwood); *m* 1951, Janet Christina Macky (*d* 1988); four *s*. *Educ:* Univ. of Otago (MA 1934); Theol Hall, Knox Coll., Dunedin. Ordained Tapanui, 1938; Chaplain, 2 NZEF, 1942–45; Minister, St Andrews, Wellington, 1947–63. Moderator, Gen. Assembly of Presbyterian Church of NZ, 1960. Mem. Council, 1969–85, Chancellor, 1976–82, Univ. of Otago. Pres., Otago Early Settlers' Assoc., 1979–91. Hon. DD St Andrews, 1969; Hon. LLD Otago, 1979. *Publication:* Jack in the Pulpit (autobiog.), 1987. *Recreations:* cricket, bowls, reading, gardening. *Address:* 19 Constitution Street, Dunedin 9001, New Zealand. *T:* (3) 4779876. *Clubs:* Dunedin, University (Dunedin).

SOMERVILLE, Julia Mary Fownes; Newscaster with ITN, 1987–2001; *b* 14 July 1947; *d* of John Arthur Fownes Somerville, *qv* and Julia Elizabeth (*née* Payne); *m* 1st, 1970, Stephen Band (marr. diss. 1975); 2nd, 1984, Ray Gowdridge (separated, 1992); one *s* one *d*; partner, Sir Jeremy Dixon, *qv*. *Educ:* Headington Sch., Oxford; Sussex Univ. (BA Hons English 1969). IPC Magazines, 1969–70; ed., company newspaper, ITT Creed, 1970–72; BBC Radio News: journalist, 1972–79; news reporter, 1979–81; labour/industrial correspondent, 1981–84; Newscaster: Nine o'clock News, BBC TV, 1984–87; Lunchtime News, News at Ten, ITN, 1987–2000. Mem., Marshall Aid Commn, 1998–2000. Supporter, Advance Housing & Support Ltd, 1995–; Patron: British Brain and Spine Foundn, 1993; Children of Chernobyl Fund, 1993; Friends United Network, 1993; Samantha Dickson Res. Trust, 1997; Barnet Cancer Care, 1998; Vice Patron, Apex Trust, 1995; Companion, Headway. *Recreations:* music, reading, wining, dining, walking. *Club:* Peg's.

SOMERVILLE, Brig. Sir Nicholas; *see* Somerville, Sir J. N.

SOMERVILLE, Sir Quentin Charles Somerville A.; *see* Agnew-Somerville.

SOMERVILLE, Most Rev. Thomas David; Archbishop of New Westminster and Metropolitan of Ecclesiastical Province of British Columbia, 1975–80, retired; Anglican Chaplain, Vancouver School of Theology, 1981–84; *b* 11 Nov. 1915; *s* of Thomas Alexander Somerville and Martha Stephenson Scott; *m* 1985, Frances Best. *Educ:* King George High Sch., Vancouver; Univ. of British Columbia (BA 1937); Anglican Theological Coll. of BC (LTh 1939, BD 1951). Deacon, 1939; priest, 1940; Incumbent of: Princeton, 1940–44; Sardis with Rosedale, 1944–49; Curate of St James, Vancouver, 1949–52, Rector, 1952–60; Chapter Canon, Dio. of New Westminster, 1957; Dean of Residence, Anglican Theological Coll. of BC, 1960–65; Gen. Sec., Gen. Bd of Religious Education, Anglican Church of Canada, 1965–66; Director of Planning and Research, Anglican Church of Canada, 1966–69; Coadjutor Bishop of New Westminster, 1969–71; Bishop of New Westminster, 1971. Hon. DD: Anglican Theol. Coll. of BC, 1969; Vancouver Sch. of Theology, 1981. *Recreations:* music, botany. *Address:* 3485 Capilano Road, North Vancouver, BC V7R 4H9, Canada.

SOMERVILLE, Walter, CBE 1979; MD, FRCP; Hon. Physician to Department of Cardiology, Middlesex Hospital, since 1979 (Physician, 1954–79); to Cardiac Surgical Unit, Harefield Hospital, 1952–78; Lecturer in Cardiology, Middlesex Hospital Medical School, 1954–79; Consultant in Cardiology: to Royal Hospital Chelsea, 1963–79; to the Army, 1963–79, Hon. Consultant, 1980–85, Emeritus Consultant, 1985; Hon. Civil Consultant in Cardiology: to Royal Air Force, since 1963; to Association of Naval Officers, since 1960; to King Edward VII Convalescent Home for Officers, Osborne, since 1970; *b* 2 Oct. 1913; *s* of late Patrick and Catherine Somerville, Dublin; *m* 1957, Jane Platnauer (*see* Jane Somerville); three *s* one *d*. *Educ:* Belvedere Coll., Dublin; University College, Dublin. House appts, Mater Hosp., Dublin, 1937; out-patients Assistant, Brompton Hosp. and Chelsea Chest Clinic, 1938–39. Served in War 1939–45; attached: Canadian Dept of Defense, 1942; US Army, 1943; Lt-Col RAMC 1944. Fellow in Med., Mass General Hosp., Boston, 1946; Registrar, British Postgraduate Med. School, Hammersmith, 1947; studied in Paris, Stockholm and Univ. of Michigan, 1948; Fellow in Medicine, Peter Bent Brigham Hosp. Boston and Harvard Med. Sch., 1949; Med. Registrar, Nat. Heart Hosp. and Inst. of Cardiology, 1951; Sen. Med. Registrar, Middlesex Hosp., 1951–54. Vis. Prof., Cleveland Clinic, Cleveland, Ohio, 1980. Lectures: Carey Coombs, Bristol Univ., 1977; St Cyres, Nat. Heart Hosp., 1978; William Stokes, Irish Cardiac Soc., Belfast, 1983. Editor, British Heart Journal, 1973–80; Editorial Board: American Heart Journal, 1975–; Revista Portuguesa de cardiologia, 1982–. Mem., Med. Adv. Gp, Brewers' Soc., 1988–92. Pres., British Cardiac Soc., 1976–80; former Pres., British Acad. of Forensic Sciences; Mem., Assoc. of Physicians of Great Britain and Ireland and other socs; Corr. Member: Colombian Soc. of Cardiology; Chilean Soc. of Cardiology; Fellow, Amer. Coll. of Cardiology. Trustee, British Assoc. of Performing Arts Medicine, 1986–. Purkyne Medal, Czechoslovakian Cardiac Soc., 1981. Officer, Legion of Merit, USA, 1945. *Publications:* (ed) Paul Wood's Diseases of the Heart and Circulation (3rd edn), 1968; various articles on cardiovascular subjects in British, continental European and American journals. *Address:* 30 York House, Upper Montagu Street, W1H 1FR. *T:* (020) 7262 2144.

SOMJEE, Shamoon; a District Judge (Magistrates' Courts) (formerly Metropolitan Stipendiary Magistrate), since 1995 (Stipendiary Magistrate, Middlesex, 1991–95); *b* 13 Nov. 1943; *s* of Rahim Somjee, former Sessions Judge, Pakistan, and Khairunissah Somjee; *m* 1970, Isabel Fonfria Fernandez; one *s*. *Educ:* St. Lawrence's Sch., Karachi; Univ. of Karachi (BA 1963; LLB 1965). Came to UK, 1965. Called to the Bar, Lincoln's Inn, 1967. Mem., editl team, Halsbury's Statutes of England, and Annotated Legislation Service, Butterworths, 1967–68; Magistrates' Clerk, Inner London, 1968–91: Dep. Chief Clerk: Bow Street, 1968–75; Juvenile Courts, 1976–77; Horseferry Road, 1977–80; Chief Clerk: Wells Street, 1980–84; Old Street, 1984–90; Horseferry Road, 1990–91; Sen. Chief Clerk, S Westminster PSD, 1990–91. Chm., London Magistrates' Clerks Assoc., 1985–87. Member: Home Office Working Party on Magistrates' Courts, 1983–87; Home Office sub-group on Procedure at Substantive Hearings, 1990–91 and Appeals, Warrants and Forms, 1991. *Recreations:* cricket, music, reading. *Address:* c/o Tower Bridge Magistrates' Court, 211 Tooley Street, SE1 2JY. *T:* (020) 7805 6706.

SOMMARUGA, Cornelio; Chairman, J. P. Morgan (Suisse) SA, since 2000; *b* 29 Dec. 1932; *s* of Carlo Sommaruga and Anna-Maria Valagussa; *m* 1957, Ornella Marzorati; two *s* four *d*. *Educ:* schs in Rome and Lugano; Univs of Zürich (LLD 1957), Paris and Rome. Bank trainee, Zürich, 1957–59; joined Swiss Diplomatic Service, 1960: Attaché, Swiss Embassy, The Hague, 1961; Sec., Bonn, 1962–64; Rome, 1965–68; Dep. Hd of Delegn to EFTA, GATT, UNCTAD and ECE/UN, Geneva, 1969–73; Dep. Sec. Gen., EFTA, 1973–75; Minister plenipotentiary, Div. of Commerce, Fed. Dept of Public Economy, Berne, 1976; Amb., 1977; Delegate, Fed. Council for Trade Agreements, 1980–83; State Sec. for External Econ. Affairs, 1984–86. President: Internat. Cttee of the Red Cross, 1987–99 (Hon. Mem., 2000); Moral Rearmament Foundn, 2000–; Chairman: Geneva Internat. Centre for Humanitarian De-mining, 2000–; Bd, Karl Popper Foundn, 2000–. Member: Panel on UN Peace Questions, 2000; Internat. Commn on Intervention and State Sovereignty, 2001. Hon. Dr: (Political Affairs) Fribourg, 1985; (Internat. Relns) Minho, Braga, 1990; (Medicine) Bologna, 1991; Nice-Sophia Antipolis, 1992; (Law) Seoul Nat. Univ., 1992; (Law) Geneva, 1997. Presidential Award, Tel Aviv Univ., 1995. *Publications:* La posizione costituzionale del Capo dello Stato nelle Costituzioni francese ed italiana del dopoguerra, 1957; numerous articles in jls and periodicals. *Address:* 16 chemin des Crêts-de-Champel, 1206 Geneva, Switzerland. *T:* (22) 3474552; *e-mail:* cornelio.sommaruga@bluewin.ch.

SONDHEIM, Stephen Joshua; composer-lyricist; *b* 22 March 1930; *s* of Herbert Sondheim and Janet (*née* Fox). *Educ:* Williams Coll. (BA 1950). Lyrics: West Side Story, 1957; Gypsy, 1959; Do I Hear a Waltz?, 1965; (additional lyrics) Candide, 1973; music and lyrics: A Funny Thing Happened on the Way to the Forum, 1962; Anyone Can Whistle, 1964; Company, 1970; Follies, 1971; A Little Night Music, 1973 (filmed, 1976); The Frogs, 1974; Pacific Overtures, 1976; Sweeney Todd, 1979; Merrily We Roll Along, 1981; Sunday in the Park with George, 1984 (Pulitzer Prize, 1985); Into The Woods, 1987; Assassins, 1991; Passion, 1994; incidental music: The Girls of Summer, 1956; Invitation to a March, 1961; Twigs, 1971; film scores: Stavisky, 1974; Reds, 1981; Dick Tracy, 1990; co-author, The Last of Sheila (film), 1973; songs for Evening Primrose (TV), 1966; *play:* co-author, Getting Away with Murder, 1996; anthologies: Side By Side By Sondheim, 1976; Marry Me A Little, 1981; You're Gonna Love Tomorrow, 1983; Putting It Together, 1992. Vis. Prof. of Drama, and Fellow of St Catherine's Coll., Oxford, Jan.–June 1990. Mem. Council, Dramatists Guild, 1963 (Pres., 1973–81); Mem., AAIL, 1983. Hon. Doctorate, Williams Coll., 1971. Tony Awards and New York Drama Critics' Circle Award for Company, Follies, A Little Night Music, Sweeney Todd, Into the Woods, and Passion; London Evening Standard Best Musical Award for Into the Woods; New York Drama Critics' Circle Award for Pacific Overtures and Sunday in the Park with George; London Evening Standard Best Musical Award, 1987, and SWET Laurence Olivier Award, 1988, for Follies. *Publications:* (book and vocal score): West Side Story, 1958; Gypsy, 1960; A Funny Thing Happened on the Way to the Forum, 1963; Anyone Can Whistle, 1965; Do I Hear a Waltz?, 1966; Company, 1971; Follies, 1972; A Little Night Music, 1974; Pacific Overtures, 1977; Sweeney Todd, 1979; Sunday in the Park with George, 1986; Into the Woods, 1989; Assassins, 1991; Passion, 1996. *Address:* c/o Flora Roberts, 157 West 57th Street, New York, NY 10019, USA.

SONDHEIMER, Prof. Ernst Helmut, MA, ScD; Professor Emeritus of Mathematics, University of London; *b* Stuttgart, 8 Sept. 1923; *er s* of late Max and Ida Sondheimer; *m* 1950, Janet Harrington Matthews, PhD; one *s* one *d*. *Educ:* University College School; Trinity Coll., Cambridge. Smith's Prize, 1947; Fellow of Trinity Coll., 1948–52; Research Fellow, H. H. Wills Physical Lab., University of Bristol, 1948–49; Research Associate, Massachusetts Inst. of Technology, 1949–50; London University: Lecturer in Mathematics, Imperial College of Science and Technology, 1951–54; Reader in Applied Mathematics, Queen Mary Coll., 1954–60; Prof. of Mathematics, Westfield Coll., 1960–82. Vis. Research Asst Prof. of Physics, Univ. of Illinois, USA, 1958–59; Vis. Prof. of Theoretical Physics, University of Cologne, 1967. FKC 1985; Fellow, Queen Mary and Westfield Coll., London, 1989. Editor, Alpine Journal, 1986–91. *Publications:* (with S. Doniach) Green's Functions for Solid State Physicists, 1974, repr. 1998; (with A. Rogerson) Numbers and Infinity, 1981; papers on the electron theory of metals. *Recreations:* gardening, travel, good art, good food, history, the company of friends. *Address:* 51 Cholmeley Crescent, Highgate, N6 5EX. *T:* (020) 8340 6607. *Clubs:* Alpine, Arts.

SONDHI, Ranjit, CBE 1999; Senior Lecturer, Westhill College, Birmingham, since 1985; a Governor, BBC, since 1998; *b* 22 Oct. 1950; *s* of Prem Lal Sondhi and Kanta Sondhi; *m* 1979, Anita Kumari Bhalla; one *s* one *d*. *Educ:* Bedford Sch.; Univ. of Birmingham (BSc Hons Physics). Handsworth Action Centre, Birmingham, 1972–76; Dir, Asian Resource Centre, Birmingham, 1976–85. Freelance lectr and researcher, 1975–. Member: IBA, 1987–90; Radio Authority, 1991–94; Chairman: Jt Council of Welfare for Immigrants, West Midlands, 1987–90; Refugee Employment, Trng and Educn Forum, 1990–93; Dep. Chm., CRE, 1993–95 (Mem., 1991–93); Member: Digbeth Trust, 1986–90; Prince's Youth Business Trust, Birmingham, 1986–91; Royal Jubilee and Prince's Trust, Birmingham, 1986–88; Admin. Council, Prince's Trust, 1986–88; Council for Educn and Trng in Youth and Community Work, 1987–90; Ethnic Minorities Adv. Cttee, Judicial Studies Bd, 1991–95; John Feeney Charitable Trust, 1991–; Glidewell Panel of Enquiry into Immigration and Asylum Bill, 1996; Lord Chancellor's Adv. Cttee on Legal Educn and Conduct, 1997–99; DFEE Task Force on Disability Rights, 1997–99. Trustee: Nat. Primary Centre, 1993–; Nat. Gall., 2000–. Director: Birmingham TEC, 1990–93; Birmingham HA, 1998–. FRSA 1988. *Publications:* (jtly) Race in the Provincial Press, 1977; Divided Families, 1987; contribs to: Ethnicity and Social Work, 1982; Community Work and Racism, 1982; Minorities: community and identity, 1983; Analysing Inter-cultural Communication, 1987; Community Work in the Nineties, 1994; (ed jtly) 20 Years After the RRA76, 1999. (contrib.) Intercultural Europe, 2000. *Recreations:* Indian classical music, yoga, travel, antiquarian books. *Address:* 89 Hamstead Hall Avenue, Handsworth Wood, Birmingham B20 1JU.

SONNABEND, Yolanda; painter and theatre designer; *b* 26 March 1935; *d* of Dr Henry Sonnabend and Dr Fira Sonnabend (*née* Sandler). *Educ:* Eveline High Sch., Bulawayo; Slade Sch. of Fine Art (Dip.). Lectr in Theatre Design, Slade Sch. of Fine Art, 1989–2001. *Painting: exhibitions* include: Whitechapel Art Gall. (solo), 1975; Serpentine Gall. (solo), 1986; portraits of Stephen Hawking and others, Nat. Portrait Gall.; *theatre design: installations:* Japan, Denmark, Poland; *ballet* productions: for Royal Ballet, incl. Swan Lake and works for Kenneth Macmillan (Requiem, My Brother My Sister); for La Scala, Milan; Strasbourg; Lisbon; Stuttgart; Hong Kong; Nice; Chicago; Boston; *opera* productions: Aldeburgh; Sadler's Wells; Italy; *theatre* includes: Oxford Playhouse; RSC; Old Vic; *film:* The Tempest, 1980. Garrick Milne Prize for Theatrical Portraiture, 2000. *Recreations:* usual diversions. *Address:* 30 Hamilton Terrace, NW8 9UG. *T:* (020) 7286 9616.

SONTAG, Susan; writer; *b* 16 Jan. 1933; one *s*. *Educ:* Univ. of Chicago (BA 1952); Harvard Univ. (MA 1955). MacArthur Foundn Fellow, 1990–95. Member: American Acad.-Inst. of Arts and Letters, 1979; Amer. Acad. of Arts and Scis, 1993; Pres., PEN Amer. Center, 1987–89. Nat. Book Award for Fiction, 2000; Jerusalem Prize, 2001. Commandeur de l'Ordre des Arts et des Lettres (France), 1999. *Films:* Duet for Cannibals, 1969; Brother Carl, 1971; Promised Lands, 1974; Unguided Tour, 1983. *Publications: novels:* The Benefactor, 1963; Death Kit, 1967; The Volcano Lover, 1992; In America, 2000; *stories:* I, etcetera, 1978; The Way We Live Now, 1991; *essays:* Against Interpretation, 1966; Styles of Radical Will, 1969; On Photography, 1977; Illness as Metaphor, 1978; Under the Sign of Saturn, 1980; AIDS and its Metaphors, 1989; Where the Stress Falls, 2001; *filmscripts:* Duet for Cannibals, 1970; Brother Carl, 1974; *play:* Alice in Bed, 1993. *Address:* c/o The Wylie Agency, 250 West 57th Street, Suite 2114, New York, NY 10107, USA.

SOPER, Rt Rev. (Andrew) Laurence, OSB; STD; Abbot of Ealing, 1991–2000; *b* 17 Sept. 1943; *s* of Alan and Anne Soper. *Educ:* St Benedict's Sch., Ealing; Blackfriars, Oxford; Sant Anselmo, Rome (STD); Strawberry Hill (PGCE; Hon. Fellow, 1996). Banking until 1964; entered Novitiate at Ealing, 1964; St Benedict's School: Teacher, 1973–83; Bursar, 1975–91; Prior, 1984–91; Asst Chaplain, Harrow Sch., 1981–91. Substitute Prison Chaplain, 1988–2001. Mem. Council, Union of Monastic Superiors, 1994–99 (Chm., 1995–99). Episcopal Vicar for Religious for Westminster (Western Area), 1995–2001. Titular Abbot of St Alban's, 2000–. FRSA. *Publications:* (ed with Rev. Peter Elliott) Thoughts of Jesus Christ, 1970; articles and thesis on T. H. Green and 19th century English theology. *Recreations:* pastoral activities, reading, hill walking. *Address:* Ealing Abbey, W5 2DY. *T:* (020) 8862 2100.

SORABJI, Prof. Richard Rustom Kharsedji, CBE 1999; FBA 1989; Professor of Ancient Philosophy, King's College London, 1981–2000, now Emeritus; Supernumerary Fellow, Wolfson College, Oxford, since 1996; *b* 8 Nov. 1934; *s* of Richard Kaikushru Sorabji and late Mary Katherine (*née* Monkhouse); *m* 1958, Margaret Anne Catherine Taster; one *s* two *d*. *Educ:* Dragon Sch.; Charterhouse; Pembroke Coll., Oxford (BA Greats; MA; BPhil). CS Commn in Russian Lang. Cornell University: joined Sage Sch. of Philosophy, 1962; Associate Prof., 1968; Sen. Res. Fellow, Soc. of Humanities, 1979; King's College, London, 1970–: Designer and Dir, King's Coll. Centre for Philosophical Studies, 1989–91; FKC 1990; British Acad./Wolfson Res. Prof., 1996–99; Chm., Bd of Philosophical Studies, London Univ., 1979–82; Dir, Inst. of Classical Studies, London, 1991–96. Sen. Fellow, Council of Humanities, Princeton Univ., 1985; Adjunct Prof., Philosophy Dept, Univ. of Texas at Austin, 2000–; Ranieri Vis. Scholar, New York Univ., 2000–. Member: Common Room, Wolfson Coll., Oxford, 1991–96; Sen. Common Room, Pembroke Coll., Oxford, 1992–. Gresham Prof. of Rhetoric, 2000–. Lectures: Read-Tuckwell, Bristol, 1985; Simon, Toronto, 1990; Gray, Cambridge, 1991; Townsend, Cornell, 1991–92; Gaisford, Oxford, 1993; Webster, Stanford, 1994; Donnellan, Dublin, 1995; Radhakrishnan Meml, Indian Inst. of Advanced Study, Simla, 1996; Gifford, St Andrews, 1997, Edinburgh, 1997; Prentice, Princeton, 1998. Pres., Aristotelian Soc., 1985–86. Founder and organiser of internat. project for translating the Ancient Commentators on Aristotle, 1985–. For. Hon. Mem., Amer. Acad. of Arts and Scis, 1997. *Publications:* Aristotle on Memory, 1973; (ed jtly) Articles on Aristotle, 4 vols, 1975–79; Necessity, Cause and Blame, 1980; Time, Creation and the Continuum, 1983; (ed) Philoponus and the Rejection of Aristotelian Science, 1987; (ed) The Ancient Commentators on Aristotle, first 29 of 60 vols, 1987–; Matter, Space and Motion, 1988 (Choice Award for Outstanding Academic Book, 1989–90); (ed) Aristotle Transformed, 1990; Animal Minds and Human Morals: the origins of the western debate, 1993; Emotion and Peace of Mind: from Stoic agitation to Christian temptation, 2000. *Recreations:* architecture, archaeology, occasional verses. *Address:* Wolfson College, Oxford OX2 6UD.

SORBIE, Prof. Kenneth Stuart, DPhil; FRSE; Professor of Petroleum Engineering, Heriot-Watt University, since 1992; *b* Prestwick, 15 Jan. 1950; *s* of late Kenneth Sorbie and of Lucy (*née* Ferguson); *m* 1976, Prof. Sheila Riddell; two *d*. *Educ:* Strathclyde Univ. (BSc 1st cl. Hons, 1972); Sussex Univ. (DPhil 1975). Res. Fellow, Cambridge Univ., 1975–76; teaching and lecturing, 1976–80; Group leader, oil res. and enhanced oil recovery, AEE Winfrith, 1980–88; Lectr, 1988–90, Reader, 1990–92, Heriot-Watt Univ. Mem., Soc. of Petroleum Engrs, 1985. FRSE 2001. *Publications:* Polymer Improved Oil Recovery, 1991; over 180 technical papers on petroleum-related research. *Recreations:* listening to and collecting classical music, particularly Renaissance masses and lute music, guitar and chamber music; hill walking, running, weight training—but also fond of good food and wine, alas! *Address:* Department of Petroleum Engineering, Heriot-Watt University, Edinburgh EH14 4AS. *T:* (0131) 451 3139, *Fax:* (0131) 451 3127; *e-mail:* ken.sorbie@pet.hw.ac.uk.

SORENSEN, (Kenneth) Eric (Correll); Chief Executive, London Development Partnership, 1998; *b* 15 Oct. 1942; *m* Susan; two *s* one *d*. *Educ:* Bedford Sch.; Keele Univ. (BA(Hons) Econs and History). Voluntary work, India; joined DoE, 1967; Private Sec. to Sec. of State for Envmt, 1977; NW Regl Dir, Depts of the Envmt and Transport, 1980–81; Dir, Merseyside Task Force, DoE, 1981–84; Dir, Inner Cities Directorate, DoE, 1984–87; Head of Urban Policy Unit, Cabinet Office, 1987–88; Dir of Personnel Management and Trng, Depts of Envmt and Transport, 1988–90; Dep. Sec., Housing and Construction Comd, DoE, 1990–91; Chief Executive: LDDC, 1991–97; Millennium Commn, 1997–98. Civil Service Comr (part-time), 1992–95.

SORINJ, Dr Lujo T.; *see* Tončić-Sorinj.

SORKIN, (Alexander) Michael; Managing Director, SG Hambros, since 1998; *b* 2 March 1943; *s* of Jose Sorkin and Hildegard Ruth Sorkin; *m* 1977, Angela Lucille Berman; one *s* two *d*. *Educ:* St Paul's Sch.; Manchester Univ. (BA (Hons) Econs). Chartered accountant. Joined Hambros, 1968; Dir, 1973–, Vice Chm., 1987–, SG Hambros (formerly Hambros Bank Ltd); Dep. Chm., Hambros Bank Ltd, 1995–98; Dir, Hambros plc, 1986–98. *Recreations:* golf, tennis, football, opera. *Address:* SG Hambros, 41 Tower Hill, EC3N 4SG.

SORLEY WALKER, Kathrine; freelance writer; *d* of James Sorley Walker and Edith Jane Sorley Walker (*née* Robertson). *Educ:* St Margaret's Sch. for Girls, Aberdeen; Crouch End Coll., London; King's Coll. London; Univ. of Besançon; Trinity Coll. of Music. Geographical Magazine, 1951–56; Helga Greene Literary Agency, 1961–86; freelance critic and historian; dance critic, Daily Telegraph, 1969–94. *Publications:* (ed) Raymond Chandler Speaking, 1962; Eyes on the Ballet, 1963; Eyes on Mime, 1969; Saladin, Sultan of the Holy Sword, 1971; Dance and its Creators, 1972; (ed) Writings on Dance, by A. V. Coton, 1975; Emotion and Atmosphere (verse), 1975; Ballet for Boys and Girls, 1979; The Royal Ballet: a picture history, 1981; De Basil's Ballets Russes, 1982; Ninette de Valois: idealist without illusions, 1987; Late Century Poems (verse), 1999; contribs to Dancing Times, Dance Chronicle, Dance Now, Dance International, DanceView, Encyclopedia Britannica, International Encyclopedia of Dance, Enciclopedia dello Spettacolo, Encyclopedia of Dance and Ballet, Dance Expression, International Dictionary of Ballet, New DNB. *Recreations:* travel, art exhibitions, theatre-going. *Address:* 1D Sloane Square, SW1W 8EE.

SOROKOS, Lt-Gen. John A.; Greek Gold Medal for Gallantry (3 times); Greek Military Cross (twice); Medal for Distinguished Services (3 times); Silver and Gold Cross (with swords) of Order of George I; Comdr, Order of George I and Order of Phoenix; Military Medal of Merit (1st Class); Ambassador of Greece to the United States of America, 1972–74; *b* 1917; *s* of A. and P. Sorokos; *m* 1954, Pia Madaros; one *s*. *Educ:* Mil. Acad. of Greece; Staff and Nat. Defence Colls, Greece; British Staff Coll., Camberley; US Mil.

Schools. Company Comdr: in Second World War in Greece, 1940–41; in El Alamein Campaign, N Africa, 1942–43; Div. Staff Officer and Bn Comdr, 1947–49; served as Staff Officer: in Mil. Units in Army HQ and Armed Forces HQ, 1952–63; in NATO Allied Forces Southern Europe, 1957–59; Instructor, Nat. Defence Coll., Greece, 1963–64; Regt Comdr, 1965; Mil. Attaché to Greek Embassies in Washington and Ottawa, 1966–68; Div. Comdr, 1968–69; Dep. Comdr, Greek Armed Forces, 1969; Ambassador to UK, 1969–72. Officer, Legion of Merit (US). *Recreations:* horses, boating, fishing. *Address:* Mimnermou 2, Athens 10674, Greece.

SOROS, George; President, Soros Fund Management, since 1973; *b* Budapest, 12 Aug. 1930; *s* of Tivadar Soros and Elisabeth Soros (*née* Szucs); *m* 1960, Annaliese Witschak (marr. diss. 1983); two *s* one *d*; *m* 1983, Susan Weber; two *s*. *Educ:* LSE, London Univ. (BS 1952). Arbitrage trader, F. M. Mayer, NYC, 1956–59; Economic Analyst, Wertheim & Co., NYC, 1959–63; Vice Pres., Arnhold and S. Bleichroeder, NYC, 1963–73. Member: Exec. Cttee, Helsinki Watch, 1982–; Cttee, Americas Watch, 1982–; Council on Foreign Relations, 1988–. Chm. and Founding Pres., Central European Univ., Prague, Budapest, 1991. Mem., RIIA, 1990. Hon. DCL Oxford, 1990; Hon. DHL Yale, 1991. *Publications:* The Alchemy of Finance, 1987, 2nd edn 1994; Opening the Soviet System, 1990; Underwriting Democracy, 1991; (jtly) Soros on Soros: staying ahead of the curve, 1995; The Crisis of Global Capitalism (Open Society Endangered), 1998; Open Society: reforming global capitalism, 2000. *Address:* Soros Fund Management, 888 7th Avenue, Suite 3300, New York, NY 10106–0001, USA. *Clubs:* Brooks's; Queen's; NY Athletic, Town Tennis.

SORRELL, John William, CBE 1996; FCSD; Chairman, Interbrand Newell & Sorrell (formerly Newell & Sorrell), 1983–2000; *b* 28 Feb. 1945; *s* of late John William Sorrell and Elizabeth Jane Sorrell (*née* Taylor); *m* 1974, Frances Mary Newell; two *s* one *d*. *Educ:* Hornsey Coll. of Art (NDD 1964). Designer, Maine Wolff & Partners, 1964; Partner, Goodwin Sorrell, 1964–71; Design Manager, Wolff Olins, 1971–76; Founder, Newell & Sorrell, 1976. Chm., Design Council, 1994–2000. A Vice-Pres., CSD, 1989–92; Chm., Design Business Assoc., 1990–92. Member: BR Architecture and Design Panel, 1991–93; RSA Design Adv. Gp, 1991–93; Encouraging Innovation Competitiveness Wkg Pty, DTI, 1997–98; Creative Rev. Gp, New Millennium Experience Co., 1997–; Panel 2000, 1998–. Gov., Design Dimension, 1991–93. Hon. Mem., Romanian Design Foundn, 1996. Hon. DDes De Montfort, 1997; Hon. Dr London Inst., 1999. Bicentenary Medal, RSA, 1998. *Recreations:* arboriculture, Arsenal, art, film. *Clubs:* Arts, Groucho, Bluebird.

SORRELL, Sir Martin (Stuart), Kt 2000; Group Chief Executive, WPP Group, since 1986; *b* 14 Feb. 1945; *s* of late Jack and of Sally Sorrell; *m* 1971, Sandra Carol Ann Finestone; three *s*. *Educ:* Haberdashers' Aske's School; Christ's College, Cambridge (MA); Harvard Graduate School of Business (MBA 1968). Consultant, Glendinning Associates, Conn, 1968–69; Vice-Pres., Mark McCormack Orgn, London, 1970–74; Dir, James Gulliver Associates, 1975–77; Gp Financial Dir, Saatchi & Saatchi, 1977–86. Non-exec. Dir, Colefax & Fowler Gp plc, 1997–. Mem. Bd, NASDAQ, 2001–. Member: Adv. Bd, Internat. Graduate Sch. of Mgt, Univ. of Navarra, Spain, 1989–; Adv. Bd, Judge Inst. for Management Studies, Cambridge, 1990–; Deans Adv. Council, Boston Univ. Sch. of Mgt, 1998–; Bd of Dirs of Associates, Harvard Business Sch., 1998–; Bd, Indian Sch. of Business, 1998–. Mem., Panel 2000, 1998–99. Mem., Council for Excellence in Mgt and Leadership, 1999–. Ambassador for British Business, 1997–. Member: Bd and Cttee, Special Olympics, 2000–; Corporate Adv. Gp, Tate Gall., 2000–. Gov., London Business Sch., 1990– (Dep. Chm., 1998–). Trustee: Cambridge Foundn, 1990–; Princess Royal Trust for Carers, 1993–; RCA Foundn, 1999–. Patron, Queen Charlotte's Appeal, Hammersmith Hosp., 1999–. *Recreations:* ski-ing, cricket. *Address:* WPP Group, 27 Farm Street, W1J 5RJ. *T:* (020) 7408 2204. *Clubs:* Reform; Harvard (NY).

SORRIE, George Strath, CB 1993; Medical Adviser and Director, Civil Service Occupational Health Service, 1987–93; *b* 19 May 1933; *s* of Alexander James Sorrie and Florence Edith Sorrie (*née* Strath); *m* 1959, Gabrielle Ann Baird; three *d*. *Educ:* Woodside Sch., Aberdeen; Robert Gordon's Coll., Aberdeen; Univ. of Aberdeen (MB ChB); Univs of London and Dundee. FFOM, DPH, DIH. Medical Branch, RAF, 1958–61; Lectr in Epidemiology, London Sch. of Hygiene and Tropical Medicine, 1965–67; GP, Rhynie, Aberdeenshire, 1967–72; Health and Safety Exec., 1972, Dep. Dir of Med. Services, 1980–87. *Address:* 30 Irvine Crescent, St Andrews, Fife KY16 8LG. *T:* (01334) 474510.

SOUHAMI, Mark; Deputy Chairman, Dixons Group plc, since 1992 (Group Managing Director, 1986–92); *b* 25 Sept. 1935; *s* of late John Souhami and of Freda Souhami (*née* Harris); *m* 1964, Margaret Austin; two *d*. *Educ:* St Marylebone Grammar School. Lieut RA, 1954–56; early career in City and timber industry; joined Dixons 1970: Group Marketing Dir, 1970; Man. Dir, 1973. Dir, Thomson Travel Group plc, 1998–2000. Chm., British Retail Consortium, 1994–98. Mem. Econ. Affairs Cttee, CBI, 1978–94 (Mem. Council, 1978–91 and 1996–2000). Mem., Metropolitan Police Cttee, 1995–99. Trustee, Photographers' Gall., 1978–90. CIMgt; FCIM. Founder Mem., Marketors' Co., 1975. *Recreations:* gardening, fishing, shooting. *Address:* (office) 29 Farm Street, W1X 7RD. *Clubs:* Savile, Royal Automobile.
See also R. L. Souhami.

SOUHAMI, Prof. Robert Leon, MD; FRCP, FRCR; Principal, Royal Free and University College Medical School, University College London, since 1999; *b* 26 April 1938; *s* of John Souhami and Freda Harris; *m* 1966. *Educ:* St Marylebone Grammar Sch.; University Coll. Hosp. Med. Sch. (BSc, MB BS). MD 1975; FRCP 1979; FRCR 1992. Hon. Lectr, St Mary's Hosp. Med. Sch., 1969–71; Sen. Registrar, UCH, 1971–73; Consultant Physician, Poole Gen. Hosp., 1973–75; Consultant Physician and Sen. Lectr, UCH, 1975–87; Kathleen Ferrier Prof. of Clinical Oncology, UCMSM, subseq. UCL Med. Sch., 1987–97; Dean, Faculty of Clinical Scis, 1997–99, and Prof. of Medicine, 1997–, UCL Med. Sch., subseq. Royal Free and UC Med. Sch., UCL; Hon. Consultant Physician, Whittington Hosp. and Royal Nat. Orthopaedic Hosp., 1976–. Chairman: Cancer Therapy Cttee, MRC, 1987–93; Assoc. of Cancer Physicians, 1989–92; Protocol Review Cttee, EORTC, 1994–97; Member, Science Council: Celltech, 1992–; Institut Goustave-Roussy, 1996–; Institut Curie, 1999–. Fellow, UCL, 1990. FMedSci 1998. *Publications:* Tutorials in Differential Diagnosis, 1974, 3rd edn 1992; Cancer and its Management, 1986, 3rd edn 1997; Textbook of Medicine, 1990, 3rd edn 1997; (ed) Oxford Textbook of Oncology, 2001; clinical and scientific articles on aspects of cancer medicine.
See also M. Souhami.

SOULAS, Alain; Chairman, Greenfield Holdings NV, since 1999; *b* 3 May 1943; *s* of Raymond Soulas and Denise Noyer; *m* Simone Gallian; two *d*. *Educ:* Stanford Univ. (MSc 1967); Ingénieur du Génie Maritime, Paris, 1966. Cerci, 1969–74; Cellulose du Pin, 1975–81; Socar, 1981–82; Chief Exec., Condat, 1983–85; Chief Exec., Paper Div., Saint Gobain and Chm., Cellulose du Pin, 1985–92; Chief Executive: Arjo Wiggins Appleton, 1992–96; ASW Hldgs plc, 1996–99. French National Order of Merit. *Recreations:* opera, theatre. *Address:* 16 rue de Fourcy, 75004 Paris, France; 3 South House, Rosemoor Street, SW3 2LP. *Club:* Racing Club de France (Paris).

SOULBURY, 2nd Viscount *cr* 1954, of Soulbury; **James Herwald Ramsbotham;** Baron 1941; *b* 21 March 1915; *s* of 1st Viscount Soulbury, PC, GCMG, GCVO, OBE, MC, and Doris Violet (*d* 1954), *d* of late S. de Stein; *S* father, 1971; *m* 1949, Anthea Margaret (*d* 1950), *d* of late David Wilton. *Educ:* Eton; Magdalen College, Oxford. *Heir:* *b* Hon. Sir Peter Edward Ramsbotham, *qv*.

SOULSBY, family name of **Baron Soulsby of Swaffham Prior**.

SOULSBY OF SWAFFHAM PRIOR, Baron *cr* 1990 (Life Peer), of Swaffham Prior in the County of Cambridgeshire; **Ernest Jackson Lawson Soulsby;** Professor of Animal Pathology, University of Cambridge, 1978–93, now Emeritus; Fellow, Wolfson College, Cambridge, 1978–93; *b* 23 June 1926; *s* of William George Lawson Soulsby and Agnes Soulsby; *m* 1st, 1950, Margaret Macdonald; one *s* one *d*; 2nd, 1962, Georgina Elizabeth Annette Williams. *Educ:* Queen Elizabeth Grammar Sch., Penrith; Univ. of Edinburgh. MRCVS; DVSM; PhD; MA (Cantab). CBiol; FIBiol 1998. Veterinary Officer, City of Edinburgh, 1949–52; Lectr in Clinical Parasitology, Univ. of Bristol, 1952–54; Univ. Lectr in Animal Pathology, Univ. of Cambridge, 1954–63; Prof. of Parasitology, Univ. of Pennsylvania, 1964–78. Ian McMaster Fellow, CSIRO, 1958; Sen. Vis. Fellow, EEC, Poland, 1961; WHO Vis. Worker, USSR, 1962; UN Special Fund Expert, IAEA, Vienna and Zemun, Yugoslavia, 1964; Ford Foundn Visiting Prof., Univ. of Ibadan, 1964; Richard Merton Guest Prof., Justus Liebig Univ., 1974–75; Vis. Prof. Univ. of Qld, 1992. Lectures: Hume Meml, Univ. Fedn Animal Welfare, 1985; Wooldridge Meml, BVA, 1986; Sir Frederick Hobday Meml, British Equine Vet. Assoc., 1986; Richard Turk Meml, Texas A & M Univ., 1991; Harben, RIPH&H, 1991; Stoll Meml, NJ, 1995; Clive Behrens, Leeds Univ., 1996; Stoll-Stunkard, Amer. Soc. Parasitol., 1997. Member: AFRC, 1984–89 (Chm., Animal Res. Grants Bd, 1986–89); Vet. Adv. Cttee, Horserace Betting Levy Bd, 1984–97 (Chm., 1985–97); EEC Adv. Cttee on Vet. Trng, 1981–86; Animal Procedure Cttee, Home Office, 1986–95. Royal College of Veterinary Surgeons: Mem. Council, 1978–93; Jun. Vice-Pres., 1983; Pres., 1984; Sen. Vice-Pres., 1985; Hon. Fellow, 1997. President: World Assoc. Adv. Vet. Parasit., 1963–67 (Hon. Mem., 1985); Helminthol. Soc., Washington, 1970–71 (Hon. Mem., 1990); Cambridge Soc. for Comp. Medicine, 1984–85; Vet. Res. Club, 1985–86; Pet Adv. Cttee, 1997–. Pres., RSocMed, 1998–2000 (Pres., Comp. Medicine Section, 1993–95; Hon. Fellow, 1996). Council Mem., Amer. Soc. Parasitologists, 1974–78. Corresponding Member: German Parasitology Soc.; Acad. Royale de Médecine de Belgique; Hon. Member: Mexican Parasitology Soc.; Argentinian Parasitological Soc.; BVA; British Soc. for Parasitology; World Innovation Foundn; Hon. Life Mem., British Small Animal Vet. Assoc.; Expert Advisor and Consultant, and Member, Scientific Groups: various internat. agencies and govts. Chm., Companion Animal Welfare Council, 1999–; Member: Council, Internat. League for Protection of Horses, 1997–; Soc. for Protection of Animals Abroad, 1997–. Patron: Vet. Benevolent Fund, 1996; Fund for Replacement of Animals in Med. Experiments, 1997–. Founder FMedSci 1998. Hon. AM 1972, Hon. DSc 1984, Univ. of Pennsylvania; Hon. DVMS: Edinburgh, 1991; Glasgow, 2001; Hon. DVM León, 1993; Hon. DSc Univ. of Peradeniya, Sri Lanka, 1994. R. N. Chaudhury Gold Medal, Calcutta Sch. of Tropical Med., Calcutta, 1976; Behring-Bilharz Prize, Cairo, 1977; Ludwig-Schunk Prize, Justus-Liebig Universität, Giessen, 1979; Diploma and Medal, XXI World Vet. Congress, Moscow, 1979; Distinguished Parasitologist Award, Amer. Assoc. of Vet. Parasitologists, 1987; Friedrich Mussenmeier Medal, Humboldt Univ., 1990; World Assoc. for Advancement of Vet. Parasitology/Pfizer Excellence in Teaching Award, 1993; Chiron Award, BVA, 1998. *Publications:* Textbook of Veterinary Clinical Parasitology, 1965; Biology of Parasites, 1966; Reaction of the Host to Parasitism, 1968; Helminths, Arthropods and Protozoa of Domesticated Animals, 6th edn 1968, 7th edn 1982; Immunity to Animal Parasites, 1972; Parasitic Zoonoses, 1974; Pathophysiology of Parasitic Infections, 1976; Epidemiology and Control of Nematodiasis in Cattle, 1981; Immunology, Immunopathology and Immunoprophylaxis of Parasitic Infections, Vols I, II, III & IV, 1986; Zoonoses, 1998; articles in jls of parasitology, immunology and pathology. *Recreations:* travel, gardening, photography. *Address:* House of Lords, SW1A 0PW. *Clubs:* Farmers', Oxford and Cambridge.

SOULSBY, Sir Peter (Alfred), Kt 1999; *b* 27 Dec. 1948; *s* of late Robert and of Mary Soulsby; *m* 1969, Alison Prime; three *d*. *Educ:* Minchenden Sch., Southgate; City of Leicester Coll. (BEd Leicester Univ.). Teacher of children with special educational needs, 1973–90. Mem. (Lab), Leicester City Council, 1973– (Leader, 1981–94 and 1995–99). Member: Audit Commission, 1994–2000; Bd, British Waterways, 1998– (Vice-Chm., 2000–). Vice-Chm., Waterways Trust, 1999–. *Address:* 288 Evington Road, Leicester LE2 1HN. *T:* (0116) 221 7418.

SOUNDY, Andrew John; Senior Partner, Ashurst Morris Crisp (Solicitors), 1992–98; *b* 29 March 1940; *s* of Harold Cecil Soundy and Adele Monica Templeton (*née* Westley); *m* 1963, Jill Marion Steiner; one *s* two *d*. *Educ:* Boxgrove Sch.; Shrewsbury Sch.; Trinity Coll., Cambridge (BA, MA). Ashurst Morris Crisp: articled clerk, 1963–66; qualified as solicitor, 1966; Partner, 1969. Non-exec. Dir, EWFact plc, 1994–98 (Chm., 1997–98). Vice Pres., The Lord Slynn of Hadley Eur. Law Foundn. Dir, St Michael's Hospice, Basingstoke, 1996–. FRSA 1993. *Recreations:* farming, opera, tennis. *Address:* Bartletts Farm, Mattingley, Hook, Hants RG27 8JU. *T:* (0118) 932 6279. *Clubs:* Cavalry and Guards, City Law, Bishopsgate Ward.

SOUROZH, Metropolitan of; *see* Anthony, Archbishop.

SOUTAR, Air Marshal Sir Charles (John Williamson), KBE 1978 (MBE 1958); Director-General, Medical Services (RAF), 1978–81; *b* 12 June 1920; *s* of Charles Alexander Soutar and Mary Helen (*née* Watson); *m* 1944, Joy Dorée Upton; one *s* two *d*. *Educ:* Brentwood Sch.; London Hosp. MB, BS, LMSSA, FFCM, DPH, DIH. Commissioned RAF, 1946. Various appts, then PMO, Middle East Command, 1967–68; Dep. Dir, Med. Organisation, RAF, 1968–70; OC, PMRAF Hosp., Halton, 1970–73; Comdt, RAF Inst. of Aviation Medicine, 1973–75; PMO, Strike Command, 1975–78. QHS 1974–81. CStJ 1972. *Recreations:* sport, gardening, ornithology, music. *Address:* Oak Cottage, High Street, Aldeburgh, Suffolk IP15 5AU. *T:* (01728) 452201. *Club:* Royal Air Force.

SOUTAR, (Samuel) Ian; HM Diplomatic Service; Ambassador to Bulgaria, since 2001; *b* 2 June 1945; *s* of James Soutar and Maud Soutar (*née* McNinch); *m* 1968, Mary Isabella Boyle; one *s* one *d*. *Educ:* Ballymena Acad.; Trinity Coll. Dublin (BA Mod. Langs and Lit.). FCO, 1968–70; UK Delegn to EC, 1970–72; Saigon, 1972–74; First Sec., FCO, 1974–76; Private Sec. to Parly Under-Sec. of State, 1976–77; Washington, 1977–81; FCO, 1981–86; Dep. High Comr, Wellington, 1986–91; RCDS 1991; Head, Inf. Systems Div. (Ops), FCO, 1991–95; Head, Library and Records Dept, FCO, 1995–97; UK Perm. Rep. to Conf. on Disarmament, Geneva, 1997–2001. *Recreations:* walking, listening to music. *Address:* c/o Foreign and Commonwealth Office, SW1A 2AH.

SOUTER, Brian; Chairman, Stagecoach Holdings plc, since 1980; *b* 1954; *s* of Iain and Catherine Souter; *m* 1988, Elizabeth McGoldrick; three *s* one *d*. *Educ:* Dundee Univ.; Univ. of Strathclyde (BA Accountancy). CA; MCIT. *Address:* Stagecoach Holdings plc,

10 Dunkeld Road, Perth PH1 5TW.
See also A. H. Gloag.

SOUTER, David Hackett; Associate Justice of the Supreme Court of the United States, since 1990; *b* 17 Sept. 1939. *Educ:* Harvard Univ. (LLB); Oxford Univ. (Rhodes Scholar; MA). Admitted to NH Bar; Associate, Orr & Reno, Concord, NH, 1966–68; Asst Attorney-Gen., 1968–71, Dep. Attorney-Gen., 1976, Attorney-Gen., 1976–78, New Hampshire; Associate Justice: NH Superior Court, 1978–83; NH Supreme Court, 1983–90. *Address:* Supreme Court Building, 1 First Street NE, Washington, DC 20543, USA.

SOUTH, Sir Arthur, Kt 1974; JP; Partner, Norwich Fur Company, since 1947; *b* 29 Oct. 1914; *s* of Arthur and Violet South, Norwich; *m* 1st, 1937, May Adamson (marr. diss. 1976); two *s*; 2nd, 1976, Mary June (*d* 1982), *widow* of Robert Edward Carter, JP, DL. *Educ:* City of Norwich Sch. RAF and MAP, 1941–46. Mem., Norwich, Lowestoft, Gt Yarmouth Hosp. Management Cttee, 1948–74 (Vice-Chm., 1954–66, Chm., 1966–74); Chairman: Norfolk Area Health Authority, 1974–78; E Anglian RHA, 1978–87; Mem., E Anglia Regional Hosp. Bd, 1969–74. Member: Assoc. of Educn Cttees, 1963–74; Assoc. of Municipal Corporations, 1965–74; E Anglia Econ. Planning Council, 1966–80; E Anglia Rent Assessment Panel, 1967–74; E Anglia Adv. Cttee to BBC, 1970–74; Univ. of E Anglia Council, 1964–80 (Life Mem., Court, 1964); Chairman: E Anglia Roads to Prosperity, 1987–; Norfolk Energy Forum, 1988–. Norwich: City Councillor, 1935–41 and 1946–61; Alderman, 1961–74; Sheriff, 1953–54; Lord Mayor, 1956–57, Dep. Lord Mayor, 1959–60; JP 1949; Dep. Leader, Norwich City Council, 1959–60; Chm., Labour Party Gp and Leader Norwich City Council, 1960–78. Norwich City Football Club: Vice-Pres., 1957–66; Dir, 1966–73; Chm., 1973–85; Member: FA Council, 1981–86; Football League: Mem., Management Cttee, 1981–85; Life Vice-Pres., 1985. Hon. DCL East Anglia, 1989. *Recreations:* football, bowls, cricket. *Address:* 23 Hall Lane, Drayton, Norfolk NR8 6DR. *T:* (01603) 868907. *Clubs:* MCC; Mitre Bowls, Norfolk Cricket, Norwich City Football.

SOUTH, William Lawrence, CBE 1988; FIEE; management consultant, since 1991; *b* 3 May 1933; *s* of Laurence and Anne South; *m* 1960, Lesley (*née* Donaldson); one *s* two *d*. *Educ:* Purley County Grammar Sch. FIEE 1992. RAF, 1951–55 (Pilot, 511 and 220 Sqdns). Director: Pye of Cambridge, 1977–81; Philips Electronics, 1982–94; Origin Holdings, 1990–92; Greenwich Healthcare NHS Trust, 1995–. Member: NPL Supervisory Bd, 1988–96; ITAB, 1988–93; SERC Engrg Bd, 1992–94. Freeman, City of London, 1991; Liveryman, Co. of Information Technologists, 1992–. *Recreations:* sailing, music. *Address:* 22 Meadowbank, Blackheath SE3 9XD. *T:* (020) 8852 3831. *Clubs:* Blackheath Football; Chichester Yacht.

SOUTH EAST ASIA, Archbishop of, since 2000; **Most Rev. Datuk Ping Chung Yong;** Bishop of Sabah, since 1990; *b* 20 Feb. 1941; parents decd; *m* 1969, Julia Yong; two *d*. *Educ:* Meml Univ., Newfoundland (BA 1968); Queen's Coll., Newfoundland (LTh 1969). Ordained, Sabah, 1970; Canon, 1974–90, Archdeacon, 1976–90, Sabah. Chairman: ACC, 1984–90; Council of Churches of E Asia, 1996–99; President: Christian Fedn of Malaysia, 1997–2001; Council of Churches of Malaysia, 1997–2001; Sabah Council of Churches, 1997–. *Address:* PO Box 10811, 88809 Kota Kinabalu, Sabah, Malaysia. *T:* (88) 245846, 247008.

SOUTHALL, Anna Catherine, (Mrs C. Serle); Director, National Museums and Galleries of Wales, since 1998; *b* 9 June 1948; *d* of Stephen Readhead Southall and Philippa (Cadbury) Southall; *m* 1st, 1975, Neil Burton (marr. diss. 1978); 2nd, 1983, Christopher Serle; two *s*. *Educ:* Univ. of E Anglia (BA Hons 1970); Gateshead Tech. Coll. (Post Grad. Dip. 1974). Ecclesiastical Insce Office, 1970; Adv. Bd for Redundant Churches, Church Comrs, 1970–71; teacher, Shoreditch Secondary Sch., ILEA (full and part-time), 1971–74; Conservator, Polychrome Monuments (freelance), 1974–75; Senior Conservator: S Eastern Museums' Service, 1975–81; Tate Gall., London, 1981–96; Asst Dir, Nat. Museums and Galls of Wales, 1996–98. Chm., Barrow Cadbury Trust, 1996–. *Publications:* numerous contribs on 18th and 19th century British artists' materials and techniques in conf. papers, exhibn catalogues and professional jls. *Recreations:* being a daughter, a wife and a mother, and sharing in my family's interests. *Address:* National Museums and Galleries of Wales, Cathays Park, Cardiff CF10 3NP. *T:* (029) 2057 3200, *Fax:* (029) 2037 3214.

SOUTHALL, Kenneth Charles; Under-Secretary, Inland Revenue, 1975–82; *b* 3 Aug. 1922; *s* of Arthur and Margarette Jane Southall; *m* 1947, Audrey Kathleen Skeels; one *s*. *Educ:* Queen Elizabeth's Grammar Sch., Hartlebury, Worcs. Inland Revenue, 1939; RAF, 1942–46; Administrative Staff College, 1962. *Address:* The Green, Brill, Bucks HP18 9RU.

SOUTHAMPTON, 6th Baron *cr* 1780; **Charles James FitzRoy;** *b* 12 Aug. 1928; *o s* of Charles FitzRoy (5th Baron, disclaimed peerage for life, 1964) and Margaret (*d* 1931), *d* of Rev. Preb. Herbert Mackworth Drake; *S* father, 1989; *m* 1st, 1951, Pamela Anne (*d* 1997), *d* of Edward Percy Henniker; one *s* one *d* (and one *s* decd); 2nd, 1997, Alma (*née* Pascual); one *s* one *d*. *Educ:* Stowe. Master: Easton Harriers, 1968–71; Blaikney Foxhounds, 1971–72. *Recreations:* shooting, fishing, golf. *Heir:* *s* Hon. Edward Charles FitzRoy [*b* 8 July 1955; *m* 1978, Rachel Caroline Vincent, 2nd *d* of Peter John Curnow Millett; one *s* three *d*]. *Address:* Stone Cross, Stone Lane, Chagford, Newton Abbot, Devon TQ13 8JU.

SOUTHAMPTON, Bishop Suffragan of, since 1996; **Rt Rev. Jonathan Michael Gledhill;** *b* 15 Feb. 1949; *s* of A. Gavan Gledhill and Susan M. (*née* Roberts); *m* 1971, S. Jane Street, PhD; one *s* one *d*. *Educ:* Keele Univ. (BA Hons 1972); Bristol Univ. (MA 1975); Trinity Coll., Bristol (BCTS 1975). Ordained deacon, 1975, priest, 1976; Curate, All Saints, Marple, Gtr Manchester, 1975–78; Priest-in-charge, St George's, Folkestone, 1978–83; Vicar, St Mary Bredin, Canterbury, 1983–96. RD, Canterbury, 1988–94; Hon. Canon, Canterbury Cathedral, 1992–96. Tutor, Canterbury Sch. of Ministry, then SE Inst. for Theol Studies, 1983–96. Member: Gen. Synod, 1995–96; Meissen Commn, 1993–97. Chm., Nat. Coll. of Evangelists, 1998–. Link Bishop, Old Catholic Churches of Union of Utrecht, 1998–. *Recreations:* sailing, ski-ing. *Address:* 9 The Close, Winchester SO23 9LS.

SOUTHAN, His Honour Robert Joseph; a Circuit Judge, 1986–2001; *b* 13 July 1928; *s* of late Thomas Southan and of Kathleen Southan; *m* 1960, Elizabeth Andreas Evatt, *qv*; one *d* (one *s* decd). *Educ:* Rugby; St Edmund Hall, Oxford (MA); University Coll., London (LLM). Called to the Bar, Inner Temple, 1953; called to the Bar of NSW, 1976; a Recorder, 1983–86. *Recreations:* theatre, opera, sailing, ski-ing, squash, tennis. *Clubs:* Royal Corinthian Yacht, Bar Yacht; Cumberland Lawn Tennis.

SOUTHBY, Sir John (Richard Bilbe), 3rd Bt *cr* 1937, of Burford, Co. Oxford; non-executive Director, Milton Keynes General NHS Trust, since 2001; *b* 2 April 1948; *s* of Sir Archibald Richard Charles Southby, 2nd Bt, OBE and Olive Marion (*d* 1991), *d* of late Sir Thomas Bilbe-Robinson; *S* father, 1988; *m* 1971, Victoria Jane, *d* of John Wilfred Sturrock; two *s* one *d*. *Educ:* Peterhouse, Marandellas, Rhodesia; Loughborough Univ. of Technology (BSc Elec. Eng). CEng, MIEE. East Midlands Electricity: Graduate Trainee, 1971; Asst Engineer 1973, O & M Engineer 1976, Shepshed, Leics; Senior Asst Engineer 1979, O & M Engineer 1981, Boston, Lincs; District Engineer, Grantham, 1986; Dist Manager, then Gen. Manager, Milton Keynes, 1991; Network Gen. Manager Northampton, 1996–99. Chairman: Milton Keynes Large Employers Assoc., 1994–98; Milton Keynes Police Area Adv. Cttee, 1995–99; Mem. Bd, Milton Keynes Economic Partnership, 1994–99; Dir, Milton Keynes Theatre and Gallery Mgt Co., 1996–2000. Pres., Milton Keynes Rotary Club, 1997–98 (Sen. Vice Pres., 1996–97; Sec., 1999–); Asst Sec., 1998–99, Sec., 1999–, Rotary Dist 1260. FIMgt. *Recreations:* ski-ing, gardening, tennis, music, DIY. *Heir:* *s* Peter John Southby [*b* 20 Aug. 1973; *m* 1995, Katherine Margaret, *d* of Dr R. N. Priestland]. *Address:* Lomagundi, High Street, Nash, Bucks MK17 0EP.

SOUTHEND, Archdeacon of; *see* Lowman, Ven. D. W.

SOUTHERN, Dr Peter Campbell David; Head Master, Christ's Hospital, since 1996; *b* 28 Feb. 1947; *s* of Sir Richard Southern, FBA; *m* 1972, Dinah Mitchell; two *s*. *Educ:* Dragon Sch., Oxford; Magdalen College Sch., Oxford; Merton Coll., Oxford (MA); Edinburgh Univ. (PhD). Malosa Secondary Sch., Malawi, 1964–65; Tutorial Asst, Edinburgh Univ., 1970–71; Asst Master, Dulwich Coll., 1973–78; Head of History Dept, Westminster Sch., 1978–85; Head Master, Bancroft's Sch., 1985–96. History Awarder and Reviser, Oxford and Cambridge Examn Bd, 1980–90; Sec., Nat. Centre for Cued Speech, 1990–92. Vice-Chm., Redbridge and Waltham Forest Dist HA, 1993–96. *Publications:* articles on P. G. Wodehouse. *Recreations:* sailing, golf. *Address:* Christ's Hospital, Horsham, West Sussex RH13 7LS. *T:* (01403) 247432.

SOUTHERTON, Thomas Henry, BSc (Eng); CEng, MIEE; Senior Director, Data Processing, Post Office, 1975–78, retired; *b* 1 July 1917; *s* of C. H. Southerton, Birmingham; *m* 1st, 1945, Marjorie Elizabeth Sheen (*d* 1979); one *s*; 2nd, 1981, Joyce Try. *Educ:* Bemrose Sch., Derby; Northampton Coll., London (BSc(Eng)). PO Apprentice, Derby, 1933–36; Engineering Workman, Derby and Nottingham, 1936–40; Inspector, Engineer-in-Chief's Office, 1940–45; Engineer, 1945–50; Sen. Exec. Engr, 1950–53; Factory Manager, PO Provinces, 1953–56; Dep. Controller, Factories Dept, 1956–64; Controller, Factories Dept, 1964–67; Dir, Telecommunications Management Services, 1967–73; Sen. Dir Telecommunications Personnel, 1973–75. Mem., Industrial Tribunals, 1978–86. *Recreations:* art, architecture, music.

SOUTHESK, Earl of; David Charles Carnegie; *b* 3 March 1961; *s* and *heir* of 3rd Duke of Fife, *qv*; held courtesy title Earl of Macduff until 1992; *m* 1987, Caroline, *d* of Martin Bunting, *qv*; three *s*. *Educ:* Eton; Pembroke Coll., Cambridge (BA Law 1982; MA 1986); Royal Agricultural College, Cirencester; Edinburgh Univ. (MBA 1990). Cazenove & Co., 1982–85; Bell Lawrie & Co., 1988–89; chartered accountant, Reeves & Neylan, to 1997. Partner, Southesk Farms; Dir, Scottish Quality Trout. Mem. Council, HHA for Scotland; Gov., Unicorn Preservation Soc.; Chm., Farnell Br., Angus Cons. and Unionist Assoc. Hon. President: Montrose and Dist Angling Club; Angus Show; Hon. Patron, Edinburgh Angus Club. *Heir:* *s* Lord Carnegie, *qv*.

SOUTHGATE, Sir Colin (Grieve), Kt 1992; Chairman: Royal Opera House, Covent Garden, since 1998; EMI Group plc (formerly THORN EMI), 1989–99 (Director, 1984–99); Director, Bank of England, 1991–99; *b* 24 July 1938; *s* of Cyril Alfred and Edith Isabelle Southgate; *m* 1962, Sally Patricia Mead; two *s* two *d*. *Educ:* City of London Sch. ICT, later ICL, 1960–70; formed Software Sciences, 1970; apptd Chief Exec., BOC Computer Services Div. on sale of Software Sciences to BOC, 1980–82; Chief Exec., THORN EMI Information Technology, 1983; Dir, 1990–96, Chm., 1993–96, PowerGen; Chm., Terence Chapman Gp plc, 1999– (non-exec. Dir, 1997–99); non-exec. Dir, Whitehead Mann Gp plc, 1997–. Trustee: Nat. Gall., 1998–; Music Sound Foundn, 1998–. Vice Patron, Home Farm Develt Trust, 1991– (Trustee, 1988–91). *Recreation:* gardening.

SOUTHGATE, Air Vice-Marshal Harry Charles, CB 1976; CBE 1973 (MBE 1950); Director General of Engineering and Supply Policy and Planning, Ministry of Defence (Air), 1973–76, retired; *b* 30 Oct. 1921; *s* of George Harry Southgate and Lily Maud (*née* Clarke); *m* 1945, Violet Louise Davies (*d* 1991); one *s*. *Educ:* St Saviour's Sch., Walthamstow. Entered RAF, 1941; India, 1942–45; HQ 90 Gp, 1946–50; RAF Stafford, 1950–52; Air Min., 1952–53; transf. to Equipment Br., 1953; RAF Tangmere, 1953–55; Singapore, 1955–57; psc 1957; Air Min., 1958–60; jssc 1961; Dirg Staff, RAF Staff Coll., Bracknell, 1961–64; CO 35 MU RAF Heywood, 1965–66; SESO, RAF Germany, 1967–68; idc 1969; Dir Supply Management, MoD Air, 1970–73. Pres., Ripon Arts; Patron, Yorkshire Air Mus., 1990–. *Recreations:* travel, golf, painting, bird-watching. *Address:* The Rushings, Winksley, near Ripon, North Yorkshire HG4 3NR. *T:* (01765) 658582. *Club:* Royal Air Force.

SOUTHGATE, Dame Lesley (Jill), DBE 1999; FRCP, FRCGP; Professor of Primary Care and Medical Education, Royal Free and University College Medical School (formerly at University College London), since 1995; *b* 25 Sept. 1943; *m* Richard Boyd Bennet, GP; three *c*. *Educ:* Liverpool Univ. (MB ChB 1967); Univ. of Western Ontario (MClinSci 1980). MRCGP 1974, FRCGP 1985; FRCP 1997. House surgeon and phys., St Helen's Hosp.; W. K. Kellog Fellow, Univ. of Western Ontario; former GP, Hoddesdon; Sen. Lectr, then Prof. of Gen. Practice, 1992–95, St Bartholomew's Hosp. Med. Coll.; founder Mem., Centre for Health Informatics and Multiprofessional Educn, UCL. Convenor, Panel of MRCGP Examnrs, 1994–99; Chm., Perf. Assessment Implementation Gp, GMC, 1994–. Pres., RCGP, 2000–. Founder FMedSci, 1998. *Publications:* (contrib.) The Certification and Recertification of Doctors, 1993; (jtly) Infection, 1997; (contrib.) Teaching Medicine in the Community, 1997; contrib. to learned jls. *Address:* Centre for Health Informatics and Multiprofessional Education, Holborn Union Building, Archway Campus, Highgate Hill, N19 3UA. *T:* (020) 7288 5209.

SOUTHGATE, Malcolm John; Deputy Managing Director, Eurostar UK (formerly European Passenger Services Ltd), 1990–2000, now non-executive Director; *b* 11 Nov. 1933; *s* of Harold Edwin Southgate and Mary (*née* Kelleher); *m* 1959, Anne Margaret Yeoman; two *s*. *Educ:* Royal Grammar Sch., Colchester; Corpus Christi Coll., Cambridge (BA). British Railways: Divl Manager, S Eastern Div., 1972; Chief Operating Manager, 1975, Dep. Gen. Man., 1977, Southern Region; Dir of Ops, 1980, Dir of Policy Unit, 1983, BRB; Gen. Man., LMR, 1983; Dir, Channel Tunnel, BRB, 1986. *Recreations:* Rugby, education administration, transport affairs. *Address:* 4 Langdale Rise, Maidstone, Kent ME16 0EU. *T:* (01622) 753792.

SOUTHGATE, Robert; Chairman, Birmingham Royal Ballet, since 2000 (Vice-Chairman, 1994–99); *b* 20 Jan. 1934; *s* of Robert Bevis Southgate and Ann Southgate (*née* Boyes); *m* 1957, Elizabeth Benson; four *s*. *Educ:* Morecambe Grammar Sch. Work on national newspapers, 1954–64; Dep. Northern Editor, The Sun, 1964–68; Reporter and Presenter, ITN, 1969–78; Presenter, Thames TV, 1978–80; Controller, News and Current Affairs: TVS, 1980–84; Central TV, 1984–92; non-executive Director: Meridian TV, 1995–97; Central Broadcasting, 1994–97 (former Dep. Man. Dir and Man. Dir). Mem., Arts Council, 1993–97; Chairman: W Midlands Regl Arts Bd, 1992–97; City of Birmingham Touring Opera, 1992–97; Dir, Birmingham Rep. Th., 1996–. *Recreations:* Lyric Theatre, travel, food, wine.

SOUTHGATE, Sir William (David), Kt 1995; conductor, composer and arranger; *b* Waipukurau, NZ, 4 Aug. 1941; *s* of Alfred John Southgate and Phyllis (*née* Maden); *m* 1967, (Alison) Rosemary Martin, *d* of (Alexander James) Lloyd Martin. *Educ:* Otago Boys High Sch.; Otago Univ. (MA Hons First Cl.; BMus Hons First Cl.); Guildhall Sch. of Music and Drama (Ricordi Conducting Prize). Worked in UK with variety of musical orgns incl. Phoenix Opera Co., RSC and BBC TV, 1969–74; worked in NZ, 1974–; Musical Dir, then Principal Guest Conductor, Christchurch Symphony Orch., 1986–97, Conductor Laureate, 1997; Guest Conductor, NZ Symphony Orch., 1975–, and all main NZ orchs and opera cos; Musical Dir, Royal NZ Ballet, 1976–93; Musical Dir, Wellington Youth Orch., 1978–90. Has conducted orchs in Europe, NZ and Australia, incl. Essen Philharmonic, Hallé, Royal Scottish Nat., Royal Philharmonic and Sydney, Melbourne, Queensland, Adelaide, Tasmanian and W Australian Symphony Orchs. Own arts and music progs on TV and radio in NZ. Chm., Adv. Bd, Wellington Poly. Vice Pres., Wellington Youth Orch.; Patron: NZ SO Foundn; Performing Arts Comp. Assoc. of NZ; New Plymouth Orch. Hon. DMus Otago, 1994. Kirk-Burnnand and Brown Citation, Composers' Assoc. of NZ, 1993. *Compositions include:* Aftermath (for brass band), 1975; Cantata 1, 1979; Trombone Concerto, 1980; Trio Sonata (for percussion ensemble), 1982; Cantata 2, 1983; Symphony No 1, 1984; Canzone (for four trombones), 1988; Symphony No 2, 1988; Erewhon (for wind quintet), 1989; Cello Concerto, 1991; Symphony No 3, 1997. *Recreations:* sports of all kinds (Otago University Blue), dining with friends, gardening. *Address:* Box 10229, The Terrace, Wellington, New Zealand.

SOUTHWARD, Sir Leonard (Bingley), (Sir Len), Kt 1986; OBE 1978; Founder (with Lady Southward) of Southward Museum Trust Inc., Paraparaumu, New Zealand, 1972; *b* 20 Sept. 1905; *s* of Philip Edmund Southward and Elizabeth Sarah Southward; *m* 2nd, 1954, Vera Thelma Bellamore; two *s* of former marriage. *Educ:* Te Aro Sch., Wellington, NZ. Started motorcycle repair business, 1926; changed to car repairs, 1935; started prodn engrg and manufacture of steel tubing, 1939; Governing Dir, Southward Engrg Co. Ltd, 1957–. The Southward Museum, which was opened to the public in 1979, contains one of the largest and most varied privately owned collection of veteran and vintage cars in the Southern Hemisphere. *Recreations:* veteran and vintage cars, rallies, etc; formerly speed boat racing, Australasia (first man in region to travel at over 100 mph on water). *Address:* 203 State Highway 1, Paraparaumu, New Zealand. *T:* (4) 2984627.

SOUTHWARD, Dr Nigel Ralph, CVO 1995 (LVO 1985); Apothecary to the Queen, Apothecary to the Household and to the Households of Princess Margaret Countess of Snowdon, Princess Alice Duchess of Gloucester and the Duke and Duchess of Gloucester, since 1975, and of Queen Elizabeth the Queen Mother, since 1986; *b* 8 Feb. 1941; *s* of Sir Ralph Southward, KCVO; *m* 1965, Annette, *d* of J. H. Hoffmann; one *s* two *d*. *Educ:* Rugby Sch.; Trinity Hall, Cambridge; Middlesex Hosp. Med. Sch. MA, MB, BChir, 1965; MRCP 1969. Ho. Surg., Mddx Hosp., 1965; Ho. Phys., Royal Berkshire Hosp., Reading, 1966; Ho. Phys., Central Mddx Hosp., 1966; Casualty MO, Mddx Hosp., 1967; Vis. MO, King Edward VII Hosp. for Officers, 1972–. *Recreations:* sailing, golf, ski-ing. *Address:* 9 Devonshire Place, W1N 1PB. *T:* (020) 7935 8425; Drokesfield, Bucklers Hard, Beaulieu, Hants SO42 7XE. *Clubs:* Royal Yacht Squadron, Royal Cruising.

SOUTHWARK, Archbishop and Metropolitan of, (RC), since 1977; **Most Rev. Michael George Bowen;** *b* 23 April 1930; *s* of late Major C. L. J. Bowen and Maisie Bowen (who *m* 1945, Sir Paul Makins, 4th Bt). *Educ:* Downside; Trinity Coll., Cambridge; Gregorian Univ., Rome. Army, 1948–49, 2nd Lieut Irish Guards; Wine Trade, 1951–52; English Coll., Rome, 1952–59; ordained 1958; Curate at Earlsfield and at Walworth, South London, 1959–63; taught theology, Beda Coll., Rome, 1963–66; Chancellor of Diocese of Arundel and Brighton, 1966–70; Coadjutor Bishop with right of succession to See of Arundel and Brighton, 1970–71; Bishop of Arundel and Brighton, 1971–77. Pres., Bishops' Conf. of England and Wales, 1999–2000 (Vice-Pres., 1996–98). *Recreations:* golf, tennis. *Address:* Archbishop's House, St George's Road, SE1 6HX. *T:* (020) 7928 2495.

SOUTHWARK, Bishop of, since 1998; **Rt Rev. Thomas Frederick Butler;** *b* 5 March 1940; *s* of Thomas John Butler and Elsie Butler (*née* Bainbridge); *m* 1964, Barbara Joan Clark; one *s* one *d*. *Educ:* Univ. of Leeds (BSc 1st Cl. Hons, MSc, PhD). CEng; MIEE. College of the Resurrection, Mirfield, 1962–64; Curate: St Augustine's, Wisbech, 1964–66; St Saviour's, Folkestone, 1966–68; Lecturer and Chaplain, Univ. of Zambia, 1968–73; Acting Dean of Holy Cross Cathedral, Lusaka, Zambia, 1973; Chaplain to Univ. of Kent at Canterbury, 1973–80; Archdeacon of Northolt, 1980–85; Area Bishop of Willesden, 1985–91; Bishop of Leicester, 1991–98. Chairman: Bd of Mission, Gen. Synod of C of E, 1995–2001; C of E Bd for Social Responsibility, 2001–. Six Preacher, Canterbury Cathedral, 1979–84. Hon. LLD: Leicester, 1995; De Montfort, 1998; Hon. DSc Loughborough, 1997. *Publications:* (with B. J. Butler) Just Mission, 1993; (with B. J. Butler) Just Spirituality in a World of Faiths, 1996. *Recreations:* reading, mountain walking. *Address:* Bishop's House, 38 Tooting Bec Gardens, SW16 1QZ. *T:* (020) 8769 3256.

SOUTHWARK, Auxiliary Bishops in, (RC); *see* Henderson, Rt Rev. C. J.; Tripp, Rt Rev. H. G.

SOUTHWARK, Dean of; *see* Slee, Very Rev. C. B.

SOUTHWARK, Archdeacon of; *see* Bartles-Smith, Ven. D. L.

SOUTHWELL, family name of **Viscount Southwell**.

SOUTHWELL, 7th Viscount *cr* 1776; **Pyers Anthony Joseph Southwell;** Bt 1662; Baron Southwell, 1717; International Management and Marketing Consultant; *b* 14 Sept. 1930; *s* of Hon. Francis Joseph Southwell (2nd *s* of 5th Viscount) and Agnes Mary Annette Southwell (*née* Clifford); *S* uncle, 1960; *m* 1955, Barbara Jacqueline Raynes; two *s*. *Educ:* Beaumont Coll., Old Windsor, Berks; Royal Military Academy, Sandhurst. Commissioned into 8th King's Royal Irish Hussars, 1951; resigned commission, 1955. *Recreation:* golf. *Heir:* *s* Hon. Richard Andrew Pyers Southwell, *b* 15 June 1956. *Address:* PO Box 2211, 8062 Paphos, Cyprus. *T:* 6250227. *Clubs:* Army and Navy, MCC.

SOUTHWELL, Bishop of, since 1999; **Rt Rev. George Henry Cassidy;** *b* 17 Oct. 1942; *s* of Joseph Abram Cassidy and Ethel McDonald; *m* 1966, Jane Barling Stevens; two *d*. *Educ:* Belfast High School; Queen's Univ., Belfast (BSc 1965; Cert. Bib. Studies 1968); University Coll. London (MPhil 1967); Oak Hill Theological College. MRTPI 1969. Civil Servant: N Ireland, 1967–68; Govt of Kenya, 1968–70. Curate, Christ Church, Clifton, Bristol, 1972–75; Vicar: St Edyth, Sea Mills, Bristol, 1975–82; St Paul's, Portman Square, W1, 1982–87; Archdeacon of London and Canon Residentiary, St Paul's Cathedral, 1987–99. Member: C of E Pensions Bd, 2001; Cathedrals Fabric Commn for England, 2001. Freeman, Tylers' & Bricklayers' Co., 1988; Hon. Chaplain, Chartered Accountants' Co., 1990; Hon. Liveryman, Founders' Co., 1994. *Recreations:* Rugby football, art, chamber music, walking in the Quantocks. *Address:* Bishop's Manor, Southwell, Notts NG25 0JR. *Club:* National.

SOUTHWELL, Dean of; *see* Leaning, Very Rev. D.

SOUTHWELL, Richard Charles; QC 1977; Judge of the Courts of Appeal of Jersey and Guernsey; Deputy High Court Judge; Recorder; *s* of late Sir Philip Southwell, CBE, MC and Mary Burnett; *m* Belinda Mary, *d* of late Col F. H. Pownall, MC; two *s* one *d*. Commercial Bar. Reader, Inner Temple, 2001. Pres., Lloyd's Appeal Tribunal. *Address:* Serle Court, 6 New Square, Lincoln's Inn, WC2A 3QS. *T:* (020) 7242 6105, *Fax:* (020) 7405 4004; *e-mail:* clerks@serlecourt.co.uk.

SOUTHWELL, (Richard Charles) Edward; His Honour Judge Southwell; a Circuit Judge, since 2000; *b* 31 March 1946; *s* of Dr Neville Southwell and Elizabeth Southwell; *m* 1974, Judith Mary Bowdage; one *s* two *d* (and one *s* decd). *Educ:* Charterhouse Sch. Called to the Bar, Inner Temple, 1970. *Recreations:* golf, sailing, ski-ing, tennis, motoring. *Address:* c/o Croydon Crown Court, Altyre Road, Croydon, Surrey CR0 3NE. *Clubs:* MCC; West Surrey Golf; Bosham Sailing; Brook Tennis.

SOUTHWELL, Ven. Roy; Archdeacon of Northolt, 1970–80, Archdeacon Emeritus, since 1980; Warden of the Community of All Hallows, Ditchingham, Norfolk, 1983–89; *b* 3 Dec. 1914; *s* of William Thomas and Lilian Southwell; *m* 1948, Nancy Elizabeth Lindsay Sharp; two *d*. *Educ:* Sudbury Grammar Sch.; King's Coll., London (AKC 1942). Curate: St Michael's, Wigan, 1942–44; St John the Divine, Kennington, 1944–48; Vicar of Ixworth, 1948–51; Vicar of St John's, Bury St Edmunds, 1951–56; Rector of Bucklesham with Brightwell and Foxhall, 1956–59; Asst Director of Religious Education, Diocese of St Edmundsbury and Ipswich, 1956–58, Director, 1959–67. Hon. Canon of St Edmundsbury, 1959–68; Vicar of Hendon, 1968–71. *Recreations:* reading, singing, watching TV. *Address:* 397 Sprowston Road, Norwich NR3 4HY. *T:* (01603) 405977.

SOUTHWOOD, Prof. David John, PhD; Director of Science, European Space Agency, since 2001; Professor of Physics, Imperial College, London University, since 1986; *b* 30 June 1945; *s* of H. H. J. Southwood and H. M. Southwood; *m* 1967, Susan Elizabeth Fricker; two *s* one *d*. *Educ:* Torquay Boys' Grammar Sch.; Queen Mary Coll., London (BA); Imperial Coll., London (PhD, DIC). UCLA 1970; Lectr, 1971–86, Head of Physics Dept, 1994–97, Imperial Coll., London; on leave of absence as Hd, Earth Observation Strategy, ESA, Paris, 1997–2000. Vis. Prof., 1976, Regents' Prof., 2000–, UCLA. Mem., SERC Boards, 1989–94; Chairman: Commn D, COSPAR, 1986–92; Space Sci. Adv. Cttee, ESA, 1990–93; Sci. Prog. Cttee, ESA, 1993–96; British Nat. Cttee for Space Res.; Sci. Adv. Cttee, Internat. Space Sci. Inst., 1995–. Fellow, Amer. Geophys. Union (James B. Macelwane Award, 1981); Corresp. Mem., Internat. Acad. of Astronautics. *Publications:* numerous contribs in solar terrestrial physics and planetary science to learned jls. *Recreations:* reading, theatre, cinema. *Address:* European Space Agency, 6-8 rue Mario-Nikis, 75738 cedex 15 Paris, France. *T:* (1) 53697107, *Fax:* (1) 53697236; *e-mail:* david.southwood@esa.int.

SOUTHWOOD, Prof. Sir (Thomas) Richard (Edmund), Kt 1984; DL; FMedSci; FRS 1977; Professor of Zoology, University of Oxford and Fellow of Merton College, Oxford, 1979–98, now Emeritus Professor and Emeritus Fellow (Linacre Professor of Zoology, 1979–93); Vice-Chancellor, 1989–93, Pro Vice-Chancellor, 1987–89 and 1993–98, University of Oxford; Director, Glaxo Wellcome (formerly Glaxo Holdings) plc, 1992–99; *b* 20 June 1931; *s* of late Edmund W. Southwood and A. Mary, *d* of Archdeacon T. R. Regg, and *g s* of W. E. W. Southwood; *m* 1955, Alison Langley, *d* of late A. L. Harden, Harpenden, Herts; two *s*. *Educ:* Gravesend Grammar Sch.; Imperial Coll., London. BSc, ARCS 1952; PhD London 1955; DSc London 1963; MA Oxon 1979; DSc Oxon 1987. FIBiol 1968. ARC Research Schol., Rothamsted Experimental Station, 1952–55; Res. Asst and Lecturer, Zoology Dept, Imperial Coll., London, 1955–64; Vis. Prof., Dept of Entomology, University of California, Berkeley, 1964–65; Reader in Insect Ecology, University of London, 1964–67; Prof. of Zoology and Applied Entomology, London Univ., Head of Dept of Zoology and Applied Entomol., and Dir of Field Station, Imperial Coll., 1967–79; Dean, Royal Coll. of Science, 1971–72; Chm., Division of Life Sciences, Imperial Coll., 1974–77. A. D. White Prof.-at-Large, Cornell Univ., 1985–91. Member: ARC Adv. Cttee on Plants and Soils, 1970–72; ARC Res. Grants Bd, 1972–78; JCO Arable and Forage Crops Bd, 1972–79; NERC Terrestrial Life Sciences (formerly Nature Conservancy) Grants Cttee, 1971–76 (Chm., 1972–76); Council, St George's House, Windsor, 1974–80; Adv. Bd Research Councils, 1977–80; Trop. Medicine Panel, Wellcome Trust, 1977–79; Chairman: Royal Commn on Envmtl Pollution, 1981–86 (Mem., 1974–86); Management Cttee, Royal Soc., Royal Swedish Acad. and Norwegian Acad. Surface Water Acidification Prog., 1984–90; NRPB, 1985–94 (Mem., 1980–94); Dept of Health and MAFF Working Party on Bovine Spongiform Encephalopathy, 1988–89; UGC Working Party on Biology in Univs, 1988–89; Inter-Agency Cttee on Global Envmtl Change, 1997–2000; UK Round Table on Sustainable Devlt, 1995–99. Vice-Pres., Royal Soc., 1982–84; President: British Ecological Soc., 1976–78 (Hon. Treas., 1960–64 and 1967–68; Hon. Mem., 1988); Royal Entomological Soc., 1983 (Vice-Pres., 1963–64); Hon. Vice-President: Inst. of Envmtl Health, 1984–2001; Game Conservancy, 1986–. Governor, Glasshouse Crops Research Inst., 1969–81; Trustee: British Museum (Natural History), 1974–83 (Chm., 1980–83); East Malling Trust, 1984–99; Rhodes Trust, 1986– (Chm., 1999–); Lawes Trust, 1987– (Chm., 1991–); Rank Prize Funds Trust, 1993–; Delegate, OUP, 1980–94; Mem., Hebdomadal Council, 1981–94. Lectures: Spencer, Univ. of British Columbia, 1978; Bawden, British Crop Protection Conf., 1979; Le Conte, Georgia, 1989; F. E. Williams, RCP, 1990; Crookshank, RCR, 1993; Croonian, Royal Soc., 1995. Founder FMedSci 1998; Member: Academia Europaea, 1989; Pontifical Acad. of Scis, 1992; Foreign Member: Amer. Acad. of Arts and Sciences, 1981; Norwegian Acad. of Sci. and Letters, 1987; US Nat. Acad. of Science, 1988; Royal Netherlands Acad., 1996; Hungarian Acad. of Scis, 1998; Hon. Mem., Ecol Soc. of America, 1986. Fellow, Eton Coll., 1993–2001; Hon. Fellow: Imperial Coll., 1984; Kellogg Coll., 2000; Mansfield Coll., Oxford, 2000; Entomological Soc. of Amer., 1986. Hon. FRCP 1991; Hon. FRCR 1995. Hon. DSc: Griffith, 1983; McGill, 1988; Warwick, 1989; Liverpool, 1992; Durham, 1994; Sussex, 1994; Victoria, 1994; Hon. LLD: London, 1991; Oxford Brookes, 1993; Bristol, 1994; Fil. Doc. *hc* Lund, 1986; Hon. ScD E Anglia, 1987. Scientific Medal, Zool. Soc., London, 1969; Linnean Medal, Linnean Soc. of London, 1988. DL Oxfordshire, 1993. Cavaliere Ufficiale, Order of Merit, Republic of Italy, 1991; Ordem de Merito (cl. II), Republic of Portugal, 1993. *Publications:* (with D. Leston) Land and Water Bugs of the British Isles, 1959; Life of the Wayside and Woodland, 1963; Ecological Methods, 1966, 3rd edn 2000; (jtly) Insects on Plants, 1984; (ed with B. J. Juniper) Insects and the Plant Surface, 1986; (ed with R. R. Jones) Radiation and Health: the biological effects of low-level exposure to ionizing radiation, 1987; (ed jtly) The Treatment and Handling of Wastes, 1992; many papers in entomological and ecological jls. *Recreations:* natural history, reading, gardening, conversation. *Address:* Merton College, Oxford OX1 4JD. *Clubs:* Athenæum, Oxford and Cambridge.

See also W. F. W. Southwood.

SOUTHWOOD, William Frederick Walter, MD; MChir; FRCS; Consultant Surgeon, Bath Health District, 1966–90; *b* 8 June 1925; *s* of late Stuart W. Southwood, MC, and of Mildred M. Southwood, and *g s* of W. E. W. Southwood; *m* 1965, Margaret Carleton Holderness, *d* of late Sir Ernest Holderness, Bt, CBE, and Lady Holderness; two *s*. *Educ:* Charterhouse; Trinity Coll., Cambridge (MA 1951, MD 1964, MChir 1956); Guy's Hosp. FRCS 1954. Captain, RAMC, 1949–51. Surg. Registrar, West London Hosp. and St Mark's Hosp. for Diseases of the Rectum, 1954–60; Sen. Surg. Registrar, Royal Infirmary, Bristol, 1960–66. Hunterian Prof., RCS, 1961. Vis. Prof. of Surgery, Univ. of Cape Town, 1987. Chm., Professional and Linguistic Assessment Bd, 1984–87 (Mem., 1976–87; Vice-Chm., 1983–84). Mem., Court of Assts, Worshipful Soc. of Apothecaries of London, 1975– (Chm., Exams Cttee, 1981–85; Jun. Warden, 1984–85; Sen. Warden, 1985–86; Master, 1986–87; Hon. Treas., 1989–99; Hon. Freeman, 2000). Mem. Cttee, Non-Univ. Medical Licencing Bodies, 1979–90. Examr in Anatomy and Surgery to GNC, 1957–72. *Publications:* articles in surgical jls. *Recreations:* fishing, snooker. *Address:* 1 Aldwick Avenue, Bognor Regis, W Sussex PO21 3AQ. *T:* (01243) 823073. *Club:* East India.

SOUTHWORTH, Helen Mary; MP (Lab) Warrington South, since 1997; *b* 13 Nov. 1956; *m* Edmund Southworth; one *s*. *Educ:* Larkhill Convent Sch., Preston; Univ. of Lancaster (BA Hons). Director: Age Concern, St Helens; Grosvenor Housing Assoc.; St Helens and Knowsley HA. Mem. (Lab) St Helens MBC, 1994–98 (Chm., Leisure Cttee, 1994–96). Contested (Lab) Wirral South, 1992. *Address:* House of Commons, SW1A 0AA.

SOUTHWORTH, Jean May; QC 1973; a Recorder of the Crown Court, 1972–93; *b* 20 April 1926; *o c* of late Edgar and Jane Southworth, Clitheroe. *Educ:* Queen Ethelburga's Sch., Harrogate; St Anne's Coll., Oxford (MA). Served in WRNS, 1944–45. Called to Bar, Gray's Inn, 1954; Bencher, 1980. Standing Counsel to Dept of Trade and Industry for Central Criminal Court and Inner London Sessions, 1969–73. Fellow, Woodard Corporation (Northern Div.), 1974–90. *Recreations:* music, travel. *Address:* 21 Caroline Place, W2 4AN.

SOUYAVE, Sir (Louis) Georges, Kt 1971; District Judge, Hong Kong, 1980–89; *b* 29 May 1926; *m* 1953, Mona de Chermont; two *s* four *d*. *Educ:* St Louis Coll., Seychelles; Gray's Inn, London. Barrister-at-Law, Gray's Inn, 1949. In private practice, Seychelles, 1949–56; Asst Attorney-Gen., Seychelles, 1956–62; Supreme Court, Seychelles: Additional Judge, 1962–64; Puisne Judge, 1964–70; Chief Justice, 1970–76; New Hebrides: Resident Judge of the High Court (British jurisdiction) and British Judge of the Supreme Ct of the Condominium, 1976–80. *Recreations:* walking, swimming. *Address:* 1 Flinders Court, Mount Ommaney, Brisbane, Qld 4074, Australia.

SOUZAY, Gérard; Chevalier, Légion d'Honneur; Chevalier de l'Ordre des Arts et des Lettres; French baritone; *b* 8 Dec. 1921; *né* Gérard Marcel Tisserand. *Educ:* Paris Conservatoire Musique. World Première, Stravinsky's Canticum Sacrum, Venice Festival, 1956; Bach B Minor Mass at Salzburg Festival; Pelléas et Mélisande, Rome Opera, Opera Comique, 1962, Scala, Milan, 1973; Don Giovanni, Paris Opera, 1963; second tour of Australia and New Zealand, 1964. Also tours in US, South America, Japan, Africa, Europe. Annual Lieder recitals, Salzburg Festival. Has made recordings; Grand Prix du Disque, for Ravel Recital, etc. *Recreations:* tennis, painting.

SOWARD, Prof. Andrew Michael, FRS 1991; Professor of Applied Mathematics, University of Exeter, since 1996; *b* 20 Oct. 1943; *s* of Arthur Layton Soward and Sybil Jessica Lilian Soward (*née* Greathurst); *m* 1968, Elaine Celia McCaully; one *s* one *d*. *Educ:* St Edward's Sch., Oxford; Queen's College, Cambridge (BA 1st cl. Hons Maths 1965; PhD 1969; ScD 1984). University of Newcastle upon Tyne: Lectr, 1971, Reader, 1981–86, Dept of Maths and Stats; Head, Div. of Applied Maths, 1985–95; Prof. of Fluid Dynamics, 1986–95. Visiting appointments: Courant Inst. of Mathematical Scis, NY, 1969–70; CIRES, Boulder, Colorado, 1970–71; IGPP, UCLA, 1977–78. Editor, Jl of Geophysical and Astrophysical Fluid Dynamics, 1991–. *Publications:* contribs to learned jls. *Recreations:* rock-climbing, running. *Address:* 2 Springfield, Western Road, Crediton, Devon EX17 3NG.

SOWDEN, Susan, (Mrs Philip Sowden); Headmistress, St Mary's School, Wantage, since 1994; *b* 10 June 1951; *d* of Albert Henry Letley and Ethel May Letley; *m* 1st, 1973, Michael Geoffrey Bodinham (marr. diss. 1990); one *s* two *d*; 2nd, 2000, Philip Sowden. *Educ:* Clarendon House Grammar Sch. for Girls, Ramsgate; King's Coll., London (BSc 2nd Cl. Hons; AKC; PGCE); Open Univ. (Adv. Dip Ed Man). Geography teacher, Peers Upper Comprehensive, Oxford, 1973–77 and 1984–85; Headington School, Oxford: Geog. teacher, 1985–87; Head of Dept, 1987; Housemistress, 1988; Head of Lower Sixth, 1991–93; Dep. Head, 1993–94. Sen. examng posts with EMREB, Southern Examng Gp and Northern Exams and Assessment Bd. Reader, Church of England, 1993–. *Publications:* articles in Britain and the British (pubd in Poland). *Recreations:* walking, reading, theatre, canoeing, camping, music. *Address:* 57 Alfredston Place, Wantage, Oxon OX12 8DL. *T:* (01235) 763571.

SOWDEN, Terence Cubitt; QC 1989; Relief Stipendiary Magistrate for Jersey, since 2000; HM's Solicitor General for Jersey, 1986–93; *b* 30 July 1929; *s* of George Henry Sowden, RNR, Master Mariner and Margaret Duncan Cubitt; *m* 1955, Doreen Mary Lucas (*d* 1983); one *s* two *d*. *Educ:* Victoria Coll. Prep. Sch.; Victoria Coll.; Hendon Tech. Coll., London. Called to the Bar, Middle Temple, 1951; Advocate, Royal Court of Jersey, 1951; in private practice in Jersey, 1951–85; Deputy for St Helier, States of Jersey, 1960–63; Sen. Partner, Crill Cubitt Sowden & Tomes, Advocates and Solicitors, 1962–83. Juge d'Instruction, 1994–99. *Publication:* (with Paul Matthews) The Jersey Law of Trusts, 1988, 3rd edn 1994. *Recreations:* writing, walking the low tide.

SOWREY, Air Marshal Sir Frederick (Beresford), KCB 1978 (CB 1968); CBE 1965; AFC 1954; *b* 14 Sept. 1922; *s* of late Group Captain Frederick Sowrey, DSO, MC, AFC; *m* 1946, Anne Margaret, *d* of late Captain C. T. A. Bunbury, OBE, RN; one *s* one *d*. *Educ:* Charterhouse. Joined RAF 1940; flying training in Canada, 1941; Fighter-reconnaissance Squadron, European theatre, 1942–44; Flying Instructors Sch., 1944; Airborne Forces, 1945; No 615 (Co. of Surrey) Squadron, RAuxAF ('Winston Churchill's Own'), 1946–48; Fighter Gunnery Sch., 1949–50, comdg 615 Sqdn, 1951–54; RAF Staff Coll., Bracknell, 1954; Chiefs of Staff Secretariat, 1955–58; comdg No 46 Sqdn, 1958–60; Personal Staff Officer to CAS, 1960–62; comdg RAF Abingdon, 1962–64; IDC 1965; SASO, Middle East Comd (Aden), 1966–67; Dir Defence Policy, MoD, 1968–70; SASO, RAF Trng Comd, 1970–72; Comdt, Nat. Defence Coll., 1972–75; Dir-Gen. RAF Training, 1975–77; UK Representative, Permanent Military Deputies Group CENTO, 1977–79. Research Fellow, IISS, 1980–81. Pres., Sussex Indust. Archaeology Soc., 1993– (Chm., 1981–93); Mem., Bd of Conservators, Ashdown Forest, 1984–99; Vice-Pres., Victory Services Assoc., 1994– (Pres., 1989–93; Chm., 1985–89); Life Vice-Pres., RAF Historical Soc., 1996 (Founder Chm., 1986–96); Trustee, Guild of Aviation Artists, 1990–. *Publications:* (contrib.) D-Day Encyclopaedia, 1994; contribs, articles and book reviews for defence jls. *Recreations:* motoring sport (world class records 1956), veteran cars, mechanical devices of any kind and age, working in the Sussex countryside. *Club:* Royal Air Force.

SOYINKA, Wole; Nigerian writer; *b* 13 July 1934; *s* of Ayo and Eniola Soyinka; *m*; *c*. *Educ:* Univ. of Ibadan, Nigeria; Univ. of Leeds. Res. Fellow in Drama, Univ. of Ibadan, 1960–61; Lectr in English, Univ. of Ife, 1962–63; Sen. Lectr in English, Univ. of Lagos, 1965–67; political prisoner, 1967–69; Artistic Dir and Head of Dept of Theatre Arts, Univ. of Ibadan, 1969–72; Res. Prof. in Dramatic Literature, 1972, Prof. of Comparative Literature, 1976–85, Univ. of Ife; Goldwin Smith Prof. of Africana Studies and Theatre, Cornell Univ., 1988–92. Fellow, Churchill Coll., Cambridge, 1973–74. Hon. DLitt: Leeds, 1973; Yale, 1981; Paul Valéry, 1984; Morehouse Coll., 1988. Nobel Prize for Literature, 1986; AGIP/Enrico Mattei Award for the Humanities, 1986. *Publications: plays:* The Lion and the Jewel, 1959; The Swamp Dwellers, 1959; A Dance of the Forests, 1960; The Trials of Brother Jero, 1961; The Strong Breed, 1962; The Road, 1964; Kongi's Harvest, 1965; Madmen and Specialists, 1971; Before the Blackout, 1971; Jero's Metamorphosis, 1973; Camwood on the Leaves, 1973; The Bacchae of Euripides, 1974; Death and the King's Horsemen, 1975; Opera Wonyosi, 1978; A Play of Giants, 1984; From Zia with Love, 1992; A Scourge of Hyacinths, 1992; The Beatification of Area Boy, 1995; *novels:* The Interpreters, 1964; The Forest of a Thousand Daemons (trans.), Season of Anomy, 1973; *poetry:* Idanre and other poems, 1967; A Shuttle in the Crypt, 1972; (ed) Poems of Black Africa, 1975; Ogun Abibman, 1977; Mandela's Earth and other Poems, 1989; *non-fiction:* The Man Died (prison memoirs), 1972; Myth, Literature and the African World (lectures), 1972; Ake, the Years of Childhood (autobiog.), 1982; Art, Dialogue and Outrage (essays), 1988; Isara: a voyage around "Essay" (biog.), 1989; Ibadan (memoir), 1995; The Open Sore of a Continent, 1996; The Burden of Memory, the Muse of Forgiveness (essays), 1999.

SPACIE, Maj.-Gen. Keith, CB 1987; OBE 1974; Chairman, Sudbury Consultants Ltd, 1989–2000; *b* 21 June 1935; *s* of Frederick and Kathleen Spacie; *m* 1961, Valerie Rich; one *s*. Commnd Royal Lincolns, 1955; transf. Parachute Regt, 1959; Staff Coll., Camberley, 1966; DAA&QMG 16 Parachute Bde, 1968–70; Staff, RMA, Sandhurst, 1970–72; Comd, 3rd Bn Parachute Regt, 1973–75; SHAPE, 1976–78; Comdr 7 Field Force, 1979–81; RCDS, 1982; Mil. Comr and Comdr, British Forces Falkland Is, 1983–84; Dir of Army Training, 1984–87. *Recreations:* cross-country running, athletics, walking, battlefield touring. *Clubs:* Army and Navy; Thames Hare and Hounds.

SPACKMAN, Christopher John, FCIOB; Chairman, Bovis Construction Ltd, 1989–96 (Managing Director, 1985–93); Director, Bovis Ltd, 1997–99; *b* 21 May 1934; *s* of Eric Dickens Spackman, MB and Kathleen (*née* Crisp); *m* 1967, Marilyn Ann Rowland; one *s* two *d*. *Educ:* Sherborne Sch., Dorset; Brixton Sch. of Building (HND Building 1959); London Business Sch. FCIOB 1980. Commnd RA, 1952–54. Joined Bovis as trainee, 1955; Asst Contract Manager, then Contract Manager, 1959–64; Regl Dir, 1964; i/c Bovis Bristol Office, 1964–69; Harrow Office, 1969–73; Dir, Bovis Construction Ltd, 1973–99; Asst Man. Dir, 1983–85; Man. Dir, Bovis Europe, 1994–96; Vice-Chm., Bovis Construction Gp, 1996–97. Chm., Deregulation Task Force for Construction, 1993. FRSA 1996. *Recreations:* squash, tennis. *Clubs:* Beaconsfield Squash; Knotty Green Cricket.

SPACKMAN, Brig. John William Charles, PhD; Director: KFKI (CSC), Hungary, since 1993; Eurotelecom Inc., since 1997; LOI Associates BV, since 2000; *b* 12 May 1932; *s* of Lt-Col Robert Thomas Spackman, MBE and Ann (*née* Rees); *m* 1955, Jeanette Vera; two *s* one *d*. *Educ:* Cyfarthfa Castle Grammar School, Merthyr Tydfil; Wellington Grammar School; RMCS. BSc 1st cl. Hons London (external) 1960, PhD 1964; MSc (Management Sci.) UMIST, 1968. Nat. Service, 1950–52; Regular Commission, RAOC, 1952; Regtl appts, 1952–72; Project Wavell, 1969–72; RARDE, 1972–75; Senior Mil. Officer, Chem. Defence and Microbiological Defence Estab., Porton Down, 1975–78; Branch Chief, Inf. Systems Div., SHAPE, 1978–80; Dir, Supply Computer Services, 1980–83; retired from Army, 1983 (Brig.); Under Sec., and Dir, Social Security Operational Strategy, DHSS, 1983–87; Director: Computing and Information Services, BT, 1987–90; Europ. Telecommunications Informatics Services, 1991–93; Management Systems Unit, Govt of Malta, 1993–96; Intelligent Networks Ltd, 1997–98. FBCS 1987 (MBCS 1970); CEng 1990; MIMgt (MBIM 1970); MInstD 1983. Liveryman, Information Technologists' Co., 1989 (Mem., 1987). Freeman, City of London, 1987. *Recreations:* gardening, tennis, hill walking, opera. *Address:* Perrymead, Dilwyn, Hereford HR4 8HN. *T:* (01544) 319085. *Club:* Naval and Military.

SPACKMAN, Michael John; special adviser, National Economic Research Associates, since 1996; Visiting Fellow, Centre for Analysis of Risk and Regulation, London School of Economics, since 2001; *b* 8 Oct. 1936; *s* of late Geoffrey Spackman and Audrey (*née* Morecombe); *m* 1965, Judith Ann Leathem; two *s* two *d*. *Educ:* Malvern Coll.; Clare Coll., Cambridge (MA); Queen Mary Coll., London (MScEcon). Served RA (2nd Lieut), 1955–57; Physicist, UKAEA, Capenhurst, 1960–69; Sen. Physicist/Engr, Nuclear Power Gp Ltd, 1969–71; PSO, then Economic Advr, Dept of Energy, 1971–77; Economic Advr, HM Treasury, 1977–79; Dir of Econs and Accountancy, CS Coll., 1979–80; Hd of Public Services Econs Div., HM Treasury, 1980–85; Under Sec., 1985; Hd of Public Expenditure Econs Gp, HM Treasury, 1985–91 and 1993–95; Chief Economic Advr, Dept of Transport, 1991–93. Vis. Res. Associate, Dept of Govt, LSE, 1996. Gwilym Gibbon Res. Fellow, Nuffield Coll., Oxford, 1995–96. *Recreation:* climbing. *Address:* 44 Gibson Square, Islington, N1 0RA. *T:* (020) 7359 1053.

SPAFFORD, Rev. Christopher Garnett Howsin; Provost and Vicar of Newcastle, 1976–89, retired; *b* 10 Sept. 1924; *s* of late Rev. Canon Douglas Norman Spafford and Frances Alison Spafford; *m* 1953, Stephanie Peel; three *s*. *Educ:* Marlborough Coll.; St John's Coll., Oxford (MA 2nd Cl. Hons Modern History); Wells Theological Coll. Curate of Brighouse, 1950–53; Curate of Huddersfield Parish Church, 1953–55; Vicar of Hebden Bridge, 1955–61; Rector of Thornhill, Dewsbury, 1961–69; Vicar of St Chad's, Shrewsbury, 1969–76. *Recreations:* reading, gardening, walking. *Address:* Low Moor, Elm Close, Leominster, Herefordshire HR6 8JX. *T:* (01568) 614395.

SPAFFORD, George Christopher Howsin; Chancellor, Manchester Diocese, 1976–96; a Recorder of the Crown Court, 1975–88; *b* 1 Sept. 1921; *s* of Christopher Howsin Spafford and Clara Margaret Spafford; *m* 1959, Iola Margaret, 3rd *d* of Bertrand Leslie Hallward, *qv*; one *s* one *d*. *Educ:* Rugby; Brasenose Coll., Oxford (MA, BCL Hons); Univ. of Wales Coll. of Cardiff (LLM 1994). Served RA, 1939–46 (Captain). Called to Bar, Middle Temple, 1948. Mem., Legal Adv. Commn of Gen. Synod, 1981–96. Treasurer, Friends of the Manchester City Art Gall., 1986–92; Hon. Legal Advr, RCA, 2001– (Hon. Treas., 1995–2001); former Treasurer: Parish and People; Red Rose Guild of Designer Craftsmen. RCA 1989 (ARCamA 1986). Hon. LLM Manchester, 1992. *Recreation:* painting pictures. *Address:* 57 Hawthorn Lane, Wilmslow, Cheshire SK9 5DQ.

SPALDING, Prof. (Dudley) Brian, MA, ScD; FRS 1983; FREng, FIMechE, FInstF; Professor of Heat Transfer, London University, 1958–88, now Emeritus, and Head, Computational Fluid Dynamics Unit, Imperial College of Science, Technology and Medicine, 1981–88; Managing Director, Concentration, Heat & Momentum Ltd, since 1975; *b* New Malden, Surrey, 9 Jan. 1923; *s* of H. A. Spalding; *m* 1st, Eda Ilse-Lotte (*née* Goericke); two *s* two *d*; 2nd, Colleen (*née* King); two *s*. *Educ:* King's College Sch., Wimbledon; The Queen's Coll., Oxford (BA 1944); Pembroke Coll., Cambridge (MA 1948; PhD 1951). Bataafsche Petroleum Matschapij, 1944–45; Ministry of Supply, 1945–47; National Physical Laboratory, 1947–48; ICI Research Fellow at Cambridge Univ., 1948–50; Cambridge University Demonstrator in Engineering, 1950–54; Reader in Applied Heat, Imperial College of Science and Technology, 1954–58. Man. Dir, Combustion, Heat and Mass Transfer Ltd, 1970–75; Chm., CHAM of N America Inc., 1977–91. FREng (FEng 1989). *Publications:* Some Fundamentals of Combustion, 1955; (with E. H. Cole) Engineering Thermodynamics, 1958; Convective Mass Transfer, 1963; (with S. V. Patankar) Heat and Mass Transfer in Boundary Layers, 1967, rev. edn 1970; (co-author) Heat and Mass Transfer in Recirculating Flows, 1969; (with B. E. Launder) Mathematical Models of Turbulence, 1972; GENMIX: a general computer program for two-dimensional parabolic phenomena, 1978; Combustion and Mass Transfer, 1979; (jtly) Heat Exchanger Design Handbook, 1982; Numerical Prediction of Flow, Heat Transfer, Turbulence and Combustion (selected works), 1983; numerous scientific papers. *Recreations:* music, poetry. *Address:* Concentration, Heat & Momentum Ltd, Bakery House, 40 High Street, Wimbledon, SW19 5AU.

SPALDING, Frances, PhD; *b* 16 July 1950; *d* of Hedley Stinston Crabtree and Margaret (*née* Holiday); *m* 1974, Julian Spalding, *qv* (marr. diss. 1991); one *s*. *Educ:* Farringtons Sch.; Univ. of Nottingham (BA Hons 1972); PhD CNAA 1988. Lectr in Art Hist., Sheffield City Poly., 1978–88; ind. scholar, 1989–99; Lectr in Art Hist., Univ. of Newcastle upon Tyne, 2000–. Res. co-ordinator, Writers-in-Prison Cttee, 1991–93, Mem. Exec. Cttee, English Centre of Internat. PEN, 1997– (Vice-Chm., 2000). Mem. Council, Charleston Trust, 1990–; Editor, Charleston Mag., 1992–2000. Ashby Lectr, 1997, Vis. Fellow, 1998, Clare Hall, Cambridge. Hon. Sec., Royal Orchestral Soc. for Amateur Musicians, 1992–94. Trustee, Hampstead Church Music Trust, 1999–. FRSL 1984; Hon. FRCA 1998. *Publications:* Magnificent Dreams: Burne-Jones and the late Victorians, 1978; Whistler, 1979, rev. edn 1994; Roger Fry: art and life, 1980; Vanessa Bell, 1983; British Art since 1900, 1986; Stevie Smith: a critical biography, 1988; A Dictionary of 20th Century British Painters and Sculptors, 1990; Paper Darts: selected letters of Virginia Woolf, 1991; Dance Till the Stars Come Down: a biography of John Minton, 1991; Duncan Grant, 1997; The Tate: a history, 1998; The Bloomsbury Group, 1998; Gwen Raverat: friends, family and affections, 2001; contrib. TLS, Sunday Times, Burlington Mag., etc. *Recreation:* music. *Address:* c/o Coleridge & Rogers, 20 Powis Mews, W11 1JN. *T:* (020) 7221 3717; The Flat, 70 Gloucester Crescent, NW1 7EG. *Club:* PEN.

SPALDING, John Oliver, CBE 1988; Vice President, National House-Building Council, since 1992 (Member, 1985–92; Chairman, 1988–92); *b* 4 Aug. 1924; *m* 1952, Mary Whitworth Hull; one *d* one *s*. *Educ:* William Hulme's Grammar School, Manchester; Jesus College, Cambridge (MA). Served War: Capt. RA, attached IA; served India, Burma, Singapore, Java. Admitted a Solicitor, 1952; service with Manchester Corporation and Hampshire CC, 1952–62; Halifax Building Society: Assistant Solicitor, 1962–64; Head Office Solicitor, 1964–74; General Manager, 1970; Director, 1975–88; Deputy Chief General Manager, 1981; Chief Exec., 1982–88. Member: BSA Legal Adv. Panel, 1965–80; Council of BSA, 1981–88; Chairman: Future Constitution and Powers of Bldg Socs Working Party (Spalding Cttee), 1981–83; Calderdale Small Business Advice Centre, 1983–88; Mem., Farrand Cttee investigating Conveyancing, 1984. Dir, NMW Computers Plc, 1989–92. *Recreations:* boats and bird-watching. *Address:* Water's Edge, Springe Lane, Swanley, Nantwich, Cheshire CW5 8NR.

SPALDING, Julian, FMA; Master, Guild of St George (John Ruskin's Guild), since 1996 (Director, since 1983; Companion, 1978); *b* 15 June 1947; *s* of Eric Peter Spalding and Margaret Grace Savager; *m* 1st, 1974, Frances (*née* Crabtree) (*see* F. Spalding) (marr. diss. 1991); one *s*; 2nd, 1991, Gillian (*née* Tait), conservation advisor. *Educ:* Chislehurst and Sidcup Grammar Sch. for Boys; Univ. of Nottingham (BA Hons Fine Art). Dip. Museums Assoc., 1973; FMA 1983. Art Assistant: Leicester Museum and Art Gall., 1970; Durham Light Infantry Mus. and Arts Centre, 1971; Sheffield City Art Galleries: Keeper, Mappin Art Gall., 1972–76; Dep. Dir, 1976–82; Dir of Arts, Sheffield City Council, 1982–85; Dir, Manchester City Art Galls, 1985–89; Acting Dir, Nat. Mus. of Labour History, 1987–88; Dir, Glasgow Museums and Art Galls, 1989–98. Res. Fellow, Nat. Mus. of Denmark, Copenhagen, 1999–2000. Dir, museumuse.com, 2000–. Art Panel Mem., Arts Council of GB, 1978–82 (Chm., Exhibns Sub-Cttee, 1981–82 and 1986–); Founder: Art Galleries Assoc., 1976 (Mem. Cttee, 1976–, Chm., 1987–); Campaign for Drawing, 2000. Member: Crafts Council, 1986– (Member: Projects and Orgn Cttee, 1985–87; Purchasing Cttee, 1986–; Exhibns Cttee, 1986–90); British Council, 1987– (Mem., Fine Arts Adv. Cttee, 1987–). Dir, Niki de Saint Phalle Foundn, 1994. BBC broadcaster (talks and reviews); Third Ear, BBC Radio Three, 1988. *Publications:* L. S. Lowry, 1979; Three Little Books on Painting, 1984; Is There Life in Museums?, 1990; Glasgow Gallery of Modern Art, 1996; pamphlets and exhibition catalogues, including: Modern British Painting 1900–1960, 1975; Fragments against Ruin, 1981; Francis Davison, 1983; George Fullard Drawings, 1984; The Forgotten Fifties, 1984; Modern Art in Manchester, 1986; The Art of Watercolour, 1987; L. S. Lowry, 1987; Ken Currie, 1988; Funfair or Church?, RSA, 1989; Glasgow's Great British Art Exhibition, 1990; Clouds and Tigers: the art of Hock Aun Teh, 1996; contrib. Art Newspaper. *Recreations:* cycling, gardening. *Address:* 90 Grassmarket, Edinburgh EH1 2JR; *e-mail:* JulianSpalding@museumuse.com.

SPALL, Timothy Leonard, OBE 2000; actor, since 1978; *b* 27 Feb. 1957; *s* of Joseph and Sylvia Spall; *m* 1981, Shane Baker; one *s* two *d*. *Educ:* Battersea Co. Comprehensive Sch.; Kingsway and Princeton Coll.; RADA. Birmingham Rep., 1978–79; *theatre* includes: Royal Shakespeare Co., 1978–80: Merry Wives of Windsor; Nicholas Nickleby; The Three Sisters; National Theatre: Saint Joan, 1985; Mandragola, 1985; Le Bourgeois Gentilhomme, 1993; A Midsummer Night's Dream, 1994; This is a Chair, Royal Court, 1996; *television* includes: The Brylcream Boys, 1978; Auf Weidersehen Pet (two series), 1983; Roots, 1993; Frank Stubbs Promotes, 1994–95; Outside Edge, 1994–96; Neville's Island, 1997; Our Mutual Friend, 1997; Shooting the Past, 1999; The Thing About Vince, 2000; Vacuuming Completely Nude in Paradise, 2001; Perfect Strangers, 2001; *films* include: Quadrophenia, 1978; Gothic, 1986; The Sheltering Sky, 1989; Life is Sweet, 1990; Secrets and Lies, 1996; Hamlet, 1996; The Wisdom of Crocodiles, 1998; Still Crazy, 1998; Topsy Turvy, 1999; Clandestine Marriage, 1999; Love's Labours Lost, 2000; Vatel, 2000; Lucky Break, 2001; Intimacy, 2001; Rock Star, 2001; Vanilla Skies, 2001. FRSA 2000. *Recreations:* boating, strolling. *Address:* c/o Markham & Froggatt, 4 Windmill Street, W1P 1HF. *T:* (020) 7636 4412. *Club:* Colony.

SPALVINS, Janis Gunars, (John); Chairman: Galufo Pty Ltd, since 1991; Westall Pty Ltd, since 1981; *b* 26 May 1936; *s* of Peter Spalvins and Hilda Blumentals; *m* 1961, Cecily Westall Rymill (*d* 1991); two *s*. *Educ:* Concordia College, Adelaide; Univ. of Adelaide (BEc). FCIS 1961; FASA 1967. Camelec Group of Cos, 1955–73 (Group Sec./Dir, subsidiary cos); Adelaide Steamship Co.: Asst Gen. Manager, 1973; Gen. Manager, 1977; Chief Gen. Manager and Dir, 1979; Man. Dir, 1981–91. Dir and Chief Exec., David Jones Ltd, 1980–91. Mem., Business Council of Australia, 1986–91. FAIM; MInstD Australia, 1981. *Recreations:* snow ski-ing, water ski-ing, tennis, sailing. *Address:* Galufo Pty, 2 Brookside Road, Springfield, SA 5062, Australia. *T:* (8) 83792965. *Clubs:* Cruising Yacht Club of SA (Adelaide); Mt Osmond Golf.

SPANIER, Suzy Peta, (Mrs D. G. Spanier); *see* Menkes, S. P.

SPANKIE, Hugh Oliver; HM Diplomatic Service, retired; *b* 11 Dec. 1936; *s* of late Col Hugh Vernon Spankie and Elizabeth Ursula (*née* Hills); *m* 1st, 1963, Anne Bridget Colville (marr. diss. 1981); one *s* one *d*; 2nd, 1988, Leena Marjatta Paloheimo. *Educ:* Tonbridge Sch. RM Officer, 1955–66; HM Diplomatic Service, 1967–86: Helsinki, 1968–71; FCO, 1971–74; Helsinki, 1974–77; FCO and CSD, 1977–81; Counsellor, Copenhagen, 1981–85. *Address:* c/o Barclays Bank plc, 1–3 Broad Street, Hereford HR4 8BH.

SPANTON, (Harry) Merrik, OBE 1975; CEng; Chairman, British Coal Enterprise Ltd (formerly NCB (Enterprise) Ltd), 1984–91; *b* 27 Nov. 1924; *s* of late Henry Broadley Spanton and Edith Jane Spanton; *m* 1945, Mary Margaret Hawkins; one *s*. *Educ:* Eastbourne Coll.; Royal Sch. of Mines (BSc (Min) (Eng) 1945; ARSM). CEng, FIMinE 1957 (Hon. FIMinE 1986); CIMgt (CBIM 1979). Colliery Manager, 1950; Agent, 1954; Gp Man., 1956; Dep. Prodn Man., 1958; Dep. Prodn Dir, 1960; Asst Gen. Man., 1962; Gen. Man., 1964; Area Dir, 1967–80; Mem., NCB, 1980–85. Chairman: J. H. Sankey & Son, 1982–83; Coal Industry (Patents) Ltd, 1982–85; Director: British Mining Consultants Ltd, 1980–87 (Chm., 1981–83); Overseas Coal Develts Ltd, 1980–83; Compower, 1981–85 (Chm., 1984–85); NCB (Coal Products) Ltd, 1981–83; Coal Processing Consultants, 1981–83; Staveley Chemicals Ltd, 1981–83; NCB (Ancillaries) Ltd, 1982–85; British Fuel Co., 1983–87; Berry Hill Investments Ltd, 1984–85; CIBT Insurance Services Ltd, 1984–85; CIBT Developments Ltd, 1984–85; Coal Industry Social Welfare Orgn, 1983–85. Member: W European Coal Producers Assoc., 1980–85; CBI Overseas Cttee, 1981–85. Vice-Pres., Coal Trade Benevolent Assoc., 1979– (Chm., 1978). *Publications:* articles in prof. jls. *Recreations:* travel, shooting, genealogy. *Address:* 4 Roselands Gardens, Canterbury, Kent CT2 7LP. *T:* (01227) 769356.

SPÄRCK JONES, Prof. Karen Ida Boalth, PhD; FBA 1995; Professor of Computers and Information, Computer Laboratory, University of Cambridge, since 1999; Fellow, Wolfson College, Cambridge, since 2000; *b* 26 Aug. 1935; *d* of A. Owen Jones and Ida Spärck; *m* 1958, Prof. Roger Michael Needham, *qv*. *Educ:* Girton Coll., Cambridge (BA, PhD). Cambridge University: Research Fellow, Newnham Coll., 1965 68; Royal Society Res. Fellow, 1968–73; Sen. Res. Associate, 1974–88; GEC Fellow, 1983–88; Asst Dir of Res., 1988–94; Reader in Computers and Information, Computer Lab., 1994–99. Vice-Pres., British Acad., 2000–. Fellow: Amer. Assoc. for Artificial Intelligence, 1993; Eur. Co-ordinating Cttee for Artificial Intelligence, 1999. Hon. DSc City, 1997. *Publications:* Automatic Keyword Classification for Information Retrieval, 1971; (jtly) Linguistics and Information Science, 1973; (ed) Information Retrieval Experiment, 1981; (ed jtly) Automatic Natural Language Parsing, 1983; Synonymy and Semantic Classification, 1986; (ed jtly) Readings in Natural Language Processing, 1986; (jtly) Evaluating Natural Language Processing Systems, 1996; (ed jtly) Readings in Information Retrieval, 1997; numerous papers. *Recreation:* art. *Address:* Computer Laboratory, University of Cambridge, New Museums Site, Pembroke Street, Cambridge CB2 3QG. *T:* (01223) 334600.

SPARK, Dame Muriel (Sarah), DBE 1993 (OBE 1967); CLit 1991; writer; *b* Edinburgh; *d* of Bernard Camberg and Sarah Elizabeth Maud (*née* Uezzell); *m* 1937 (marr. diss.); one *s*. *Educ:* James Gillespie's School for Girls, Edinburgh; Heriot Watt Coll., Edinburgh. FO, 1944; General Secretary, The Poetry Society, Editor, The Poetry Review, 1947–49. FRSL 1963; FRSE 1995. Hon. Mem., Amer. Acad. of Arts and Letters, 1978. Hon. DLitt: Strathclyde, 1971; Edinburgh, 1989; Aberdeen, 1995; St Andrews, 1998; Oxford, 1999; DUniv Heriot-Watt, 1995. David Cohen British Literature Prize, 1997; Gold Pen Award, Internat. PEN, 1998. Commandeur de l'Ordre des Arts et des Lettres, France, 1996. *Publications: critical and biographical:* (ed) Selected Poems of Emily Brontë, 1952; Child of Light: a Reassessment of Mary Shelley, 1951, rev. edn, Mary Shelley, 1988; John Masefield, 1953, repr. 1992; (joint) Emily Brontë: her Life and Work, 1953; (ed) The Brontë Letters, 1954; (ed jointly) Letters of John Henry Newman, 1957; The Essence of the Brontës, 1993; *poems:* The Fanfarlo and Other Verse, 1952; Collected Poems I, 1967; Going Up to Sotheby's and other poems, 1982; *fiction:* The Comforters, 1957; Robinson, 1958; The Go-Away Bird, 1958; Memento Mori, 1959 (adapted for stage, 1964; televised, BBC, 1992); The Ballad of Peckham Rye, 1960 (Italia prize, for dramatic radio, 1962); The Bachelors, 1960; Voices at Play, 1961; The Prime of Miss Jean Brodie, 1961 (adapted for stage, 1966, filmed 1969, and BBC TV, 1978); Doctors of Philosophy (play), 1963; The Girls of Slender Means, 1963 (adapted for radio, 1964, and BBC TV, 1975); The Mandelbaum Gate, 1965 (James Tait Black Memorial Prize); Collected Stories I, 1967; The Public Image, 1968; The Very Fine Clock (for children), 1969; The Driver's Seat, 1970 (filmed 1974); Not to Disturb, 1971; The Hothouse by the East River, 1973; The Abbess of Crewe, 1974 (filmed 1977); The Takeover, 1976; Territorial Rights, 1979; Loitering with Intent, 1981; Bang-Bang You're Dead and other stories, 1982; The Only Problem, 1984; The Stories of Muriel Spark, 1987 (Scottish Book of Year Award); A Far Cry from Kensington, 1988; Symposium, 1990; Curriculum Vitae (autobiog.), 1992; The French Window and The Small Telephone (for children), 1993; Omnibus I, 1993; Omnibus II, 1994; Reality and Dreams, 1996; Omnibus III, 1996; Omnibus IV, 1997; Aiding and Abetting, 2000; The Complete Short Stories, 2001. *Recreations:* reading, travel. *Address:* c/o David Higham Associates Ltd, 5–8 Lower John Street, Golden Square, W1R 4HA.

SPARKE, Andrew Philip; Chief Executive, Dudley Metropolitan Borough Council, and Clerk to West Midlands Police Authority, since 1999; *b* 22 July 1956; *s* of Philip Aubrey Sparke and Sheila Myrtle Sparke; *m* 1980, Laura Emma Simmons; one *s* one *d*; partner, Elizabeth Mary Bennett; one *s* (and one *s* decd). *Educ:* Manchester Univ. (LLB Hons 1977). Technician and Surveying Asst, S Hams BC, 1974; admitted Solicitor, 1980. Articled Clerk, Derby CC, 1978–80; Printing Asst, BP, 1981; Solicitor, Kingston upon Hull CC, 1981–85; Asst Town Clerk, 1985–90, Dep. Dir of Corporate Services, 1990–94, Enfield LBC; Chief Exec., Lincoln CC, 1994–99. *Publications:* The Compulsory Competitive Tendering Guide, 1993, rev. edn 1995; The Practical Guide to Externalising Local Authority Services, 1994; The Butterworths Best Value Manual, 1999. *Recreations:* record collecting, Chelsea FC. *Address:* (office) Council House, Priory Road, Dudley DY1 1HF. *T:* (01384) 815201; 4 Oakleigh Road, Old Swinford, Stourbridge DY8 2JX. *T:* (01384) 390401.

SPARKES, Andrew James; HM Diplomatic Service; Deputy High Commissioner, South Africa, since 2001; *b* 4 July 1959; *s* of Rev. James Reginald Sparkes and Brenda

Mary Sparkes (*née* Brown); *m* 1985, Jean Mary Meakin; one *s* one *d*. *Educ:* King Edward's Sch., Edgbaston; Manchester Grammar Sch.; Trinity Hall, Cambridge (MA Hons). MCIPD 1999. English teacher, Japan, 1981–82; joined HM Diplomatic Service, 1983; Second Sec., Political, Ankara, 1985–88; Hd, Political Section, Bangkok, 1992–95; Asst Dir, Personnel Mgt, FCO, 1996–97; on secondment as Dir, Service Exports, DTI, 1997–99; Dep. Hd of Mission, Jakarta, 1999–2001. *Recreations:* music, writing poetry, sailing, golf. *Address:* c/o Foreign and Commonwealth Office, King Charles Street, SW1A 2AH. *T:* (020) 7270 3000. *Clubs:* Oakland Park Golf (Chalfont St Giles); Tanjung Lesung Sailing (W Java, Indonesia).

SPARKES, Sir Robert Lyndley, Kt 1979; State President, National Party of Australia (formerly Country Party), Queensland, 1970–90; Managing Partner, Lyndley Pastoral Co., since 1974; *b* 30 May 1929; *s* of late Sir James Sparkes, Jandowae, Queensland; *m* 1953, June, *d* of M. Morgan; two *s*. *Educ:* Southport Sch., Queensland. Chairman: National Party (formerly Country Party) Lands Cttee, Queensland, 1966–90; NPA Nominees Pty Ltd. Mayor (formerly Chm.), Wambo Shire Council, 1967– (Mem., 1952–55 and 1964–). *Recreation:* reading. *Address:* Dundonald, PO Box 117, Jandowae, Queensland 4410, Australia. *T:* (7) 46685196.

SPARKS, Arthur Charles, BSc (Econ); Under-Secretary, Ministry of Agriculture, Fisheries and Food, 1959–74; *b* 1914; *s* of late Charles Herbert and Kate Dorothy Sparks; *m* 1939, Betty Joan (*d* 1978), *d* of late Harry Oswald and Lilian Mary Simmons; three *d*. *Educ:* Selhurst Grammar Sch.; London School of Economics. Clerk, Ministry of Agriculture and Fisheries, 1931; Administrative Grade, 1936; National Fire Service, 1942–44; Principal Private Secretary to Minister of Agriculture and Fisheries, 1946–47; Asst Secretary, Ministry of Agriculture and Fisheries, 1947–49 and 1951–59; Asst Secretary, Treasury, 1949–51. Chm., Internat. Wheat Council, 1968–69. *Recreations:* reading, walking. *Address:* 2 Stratton Close, Merton Park, SW19 3JF. *T:* (020) 8542 4827.

SPARKS, Ian Leslie, OBE 1999; Chief Executive, The Children's Society, 1986–March 2002; *b* 26 May 1943; *s* of Ronald Leslie and Hilda Sparks; *m* 1967, Eunice Jean; one *d*. *Educ:* Whitefield Road Primary School, Liverpool; Holt High School, Liverpool; Brunel Univ. (MA); Kingston Univ. (DMS). AIB. Bank clerk, 1959–68; social worker, Liverpool, 1971–75; Asst Divl Dir, Barnardo's, 1975–80; Social Work Dir, The Children's Soc., 1981–86. Trustee: NCVCCO, 1995–; Frontier Youth Trust, 2000–; Chairman: British Agencies for Adoption and Fostering, 1996–2000; Internat. Anglican Family Network. *Recreations:* piano playing, gardening in miniature. *Address:* (until April 2002) Edward Rudolf House, Margery Street, WC1X 0JL. *T:* (020) 7837 4299; 16 Frating Crescent, Woodford Green, Essex IG8 0DW.

SPARKS, Prof. (Robert) Stephen (John), FRS 1988; Chaning Wills Professor of Geology, Bristol University, since 1990 (Professor of Geology, since 1989); Natural Environment Research Council Professor of Earth Sciences, since 1998; *b* 15 May 1949; *s* of Kenneth Grenfell Sparks and Ruth Joan Rugman; *m* 1971, Ann Elizabeth Talbot; two *s*. *Educ:* Imperial College London (BSc Hons 1971, PhD 1974). Postdoctoral fellowships, Lancaster Univ., 1974–76, Univ. of Rhode Island, 1976–78, studying physics of volcanic eruptions; Cambridge University: Demonstrator, 1978–82; Lectr in Geology, 1982–89; Fellow, Trinity Hall, 1981–89; Chief Scientist, Monserrat Volcano Observatory, 1997–99. Sherman Fairchild Dist. Scholar, Calif Inst. of Technology, 1987; studies of volcanic eruptions: Heimaey, Iceland, 1973; Etna, 1975; Soufriere, St Vincent, WI, 1979; Mount St Helens, 1980; Soufriere Hills, Montserrat, WI, 1996–. President: Geol Soc. of London, 1994–96; Internat. Assoc. of Volcanology and Chemistry of Earth's Interior, 1999–. Bakerian Lectr, Royal Soc., 2000. Fellow, Amer. Geophys. Union, 1998. Hon. degree: Université Blaise Pascal, Clermont-Ferrand, 1999; Lancaster Univ., 2000. Wager Prize for Volcanology, Internat. Assoc. of Volcanology and Chemistry of Earth's Interior, 1983; Bigsby Medal, 1985, Murchison Medal, 1998, Geol Soc.; Arthur L. Day Medal, Geol Soc. of America, 2000. *Publications:* Volcanic Plumes, 1997; numerous papers on physics of volcanic eruptions, geology of young volcanoes and origins of volcanism. *Recreations:* music, soccer, squash, travel, cooking. *Address:* Walnut Cottage, 19 Brinsea Road, Congresbury, Bristol BS49 5JF.

SPARROW, (Albert) Charles; QC 1966; DL; barrister; *b* Kasauli, India, 16 Sept. 1925; *e s* of Captain Charles Thomas Sparrow, sometime Essex Regt, and Antonia Sparrow; *m* 1949, Edith Rosalie Taylor (*d* 1985); two *s* one *d*. *Educ:* Royal Grammar Sch., Colchester; LLB London Univ., 1951. Served Civil Defence, 1939–43; joined Army, 1943; posted as cadet to India, commnd into Royal Signals and served in Far East, 1944–47; OC, GHQ Signals, Simla, 1947. Admitted to Gray's Inn, 1947 (Holker Senior Scholar, Atkin Scholar, Lee Prizeman and Richards Prizeman); called to Bar, Gray's Inn, 1950 (Bencher, 1976; Master of Pictures and Silver, 1985–2001; Treas., 1994; Barnard's Inn Reader, 1996; Staple Inn Reader, 1998); admitted to Lincoln's Inn, 1967; in practice in Chancery and before Parliament, 1950–99. Member: General Council of the Bar, 1969–73; Senate of the Four Inns of Court, 1970–73; Incorp. Council of Law Reporting, 1977–83. Hon. Legal Adviser to Council for British Archæology (concerned notably with legal protection of antiquities and reform of treasure trove; draftsman of Abinger Bill), 1966–. Chairman: independent Panel of Inquiry for affairs of RSPCA, 1973–74; independent Cttee of Inquiry for Girl Guides Rally at Crystal Palace, 1985. FSA 1972; Pres., Essex Archaeological Soc., 1975–78. Chm., Stock Branch, British Legion, 1970–75 (Pres., 1999–). Mem., Court, Univ. of Essex, 1985–. Advr to assocs of customary freemen, 1972–; Hon. Counsellor to Freemen of England, 1978–; Freeman, City of London; Hon. Life Member: Gild of Freemen of City of York; Freemen of England and Wales; Burgess Freeman, Altrincham. KStJ 1993 (OStJ 1982; CStJ 1987); Mem. St John Council for Essex, 1977–; Comr for Essex, St John Ambulance Bde, 1983–90; Comdr, St John for Essex, 1989–93. DL Essex, 1985. *Recreation:* Romano-British archæology. *Address:* Serle Court Chambers, 6 New Square, Lincoln's Inn, WC2A 3QS. *T:* (020) 7242 6105; Croyde Lodge, Stock, Essex CM4 9QB. *Clubs:* Arts; Essex.

SPARROW, Bryan, CMG 1992; HM Diplomatic Service, retired; Ambassador to Croatia, 1992–94; *b* 8 June 1933; *m* 1958, Fiona Mary Mylechreest; one *s* one *d*. *Educ:* Hemel Hempstead Grammar Sch.; Pembroke Coll., Oxford (BA Hons). Served Army, 1951–53. Belgrade, 1958–61; FO, 1961–64; Moscow, 1964–66; Tunis, 1967–68; Casablanca, 1968–70; FO, 1970–72; Kinshasa, 1972–76; Prague, 1976–78; Counsellor (Commercial), Belgrade, 1978–81; Ambassador, United Republic of Cameroon, 1981–84, and concurrently to Republic of Equatorial Guinea and Central African Republic, 1982–84; Canadian Nat. Defence Coll., 1984–85; Consul-General: Toronto, 1985–89; Lyon, 1989–92. *Recreations:* gardening, travel. *Address:* c/o HSBC, 15 Crescent Road, Windermere, Cumbria LA23 1EF.

SPARROW, Charles; *see* Sparrow, A. C.

SPARROW, Sir John, Kt 1984; Chairman, Horserace Betting Levy Board, 1991–98; *b* 4 June 1933; *s* of Richard A. and Winifred R. Sparrow; *m* 1967, Cynthia Whitehouse. *Educ:* Stationers' Company's School; London School of Economics (BSc Econ 1954; Hon. Fellow, 1994). FCA 1957–97. With Rawlinson & Hunter, Chartered Accountants, 1954–59; Ford Motor Co. Ltd, 1960; AEI-Hotpoint Ltd, 1960–63; United Leasing Corporation, 1963–64; Morgan Grenfell Group (formerly Morgan Grenfell & Co.), 1964–88; Dir, Morgan Grenfell Gp (formerly Morgan Grenfell Hldgs), 1971–88; Chairman: Morgan Grenfell Asset Management, 1985–88; Morgan Grenfell Laurie Hldgs, 1985–88. National & Provincial Building Society: Mem., London Adv. Bd, 1986–89; Dir, 1989–96; Dep. Chm., 1994–96; Chm., Universities Superannuation Scheme Ltd, 1988–96. Chm., Mather & Platt, 1979–81; Director: Federated Chemicals, 1969–78 (Chm., 1974–78); Harris Lebus, 1973–79; United Gas Industries, 1974–82 (Dep. Chm., 1981–82); Coalite Group plc, 1974–82, 1984–89; Gas and Oil Acreage, 1975–78; Tioxide Gp, 1977–78; Peterborough Develt Corp., 1981–88; Short Brothers plc, 1984–89 (Dep. Chm., 1985–89); ASW Holdings Plc, 1987–93; Regalian Properties PLC, 1990–93. Seconded as Head of Central Policy Review Staff, Cabinet Office, 1982–83. Chm., EDC for Process Plant Industry, 1984–85; Chairman: National Stud, 1988–91; Horseracing Forensic Lab., 1991–98. Gov., LSE, 1984– (Vice-Chm. Govs, 1984–93; Actg Chm., 1987–88); Pres., Old Stationers' Assoc., 1995–96. Hon. Fellow, Wolfson Coll., Cambridge, 1987. *Recreations:* cricket, crosswords, horse-racing. *Address:* Padbury Lodge, Padbury, Bucks MK18 2AJ. *Club:* MCC.

SPAWFORTH, David Meredith, MA; Headmaster, Merchiston Castle School, Edinburgh, 1981–98; *b* 2 Jan. 1938; *s* of Lawrence and Gwen Spawforth, Wakefield, Yorks; *m* 1963, Yvonne Mary Gude; one *s* one *d*. *Educ:* Silcoates School; Hertford Coll., Oxford (Heath Harrison Travelling Schol.; MA ModLang). Assistant Master: Winchester Coll., 1961–64; Wellington Coll., 1964–80; Housemaster, Wellington Coll., 1968–80. British Petroleum Education Fellow, Keble Coll., Oxford, 1977. FRSA 1994. *Recreations:* gardening, France, history, theatre, walking. *Address:* Kimberley, Netherbarns, Galashiels, Selkirkshire TD1 3NW.

SPEAIGHT, Anthony Hugh; QC 1995; *b* 31 July 1948; *s* of George Victor Speaight and Mary Olive Speaight (*née* Mudd); *m* 1991, Gabrielle Anne Kooy-Lister; two *s* one *d*. *Educ:* St Benedict's Sch., Ealing; Lincoln Coll., Oxford (MA; Sec., Oxford Union Soc., 1970). Called to the Bar, Middle Temple, 1973. Member: Bar Council, 1986–92, 1998–2000; Bar Working Party on Televising Courts, 1990; Chm., Bar Council Wkg Pty on Modernising Civil Courts, 2001. Chm., Editl Bd, Counsel, jl of Bar of England and Wales, 1990–94. Schuman Silver Medal, FVS Foundn, Germany, 1976. *Publications:* (with G. Stone) The Law of Defective Premises, 1982; (ed jtly) Architects Legal Handbook, 3rd edn 1982 to 7th edn 2000; (ed jtly) Butterworths Professional Negligence Service, 2 vols, 2000. *Recreations:* theatre, cricket, foxhunting. *Address:* 4 Pump Court, Temple, EC4Y 7AN. *T:* (020) 7842 5555. *Clubs:* Carlton, Hurlingham.

SPEAKMAN-PITT, William, VC 1951; *b* 21 Sept. 1927; *m* 1st, 1956, Rachel Snitch; one *s*; 2nd, Jill; one *d*. *Educ:* Wellington Road Senior Boys' Sch., Altrincham. Entered Army as Private. Served Korean War, 1950–53 (VC), King's Own Scottish Borderers. *Recreations:* swimming, and ski-ing.

SPEAR, Prof. Walter Eric, PhD, DSc; FRS 1980; FRSE; Harris Professor of Physics, University of Dundee, 1968–90, now Emeritus Professor; *b* 20 Jan. 1921; *s* of David and Eva Spear; *m* 1952, Hilda Doris King; two *d*. *Educ:* Musterschule, Frankfurt/Main; Univ. of London (BSc 1947, PhD 1950, DSc 1967). Lecturer, 1953, Reader, 1967, in Physics, Univ. of Leicester; Vis. Professor, Purdue Univ., 1957–58. FRSE 1972; FInstP 1962. Max Born Prize and Medal, 1977; Europhysics Prize, 1977; Makdougal-Brisbane Medal, RSE, 1981; Rank Prize, 1988; Mott Award, Jl of Non-crystalline Solids, 1989; Rumford Medal, Royal Soc., 1990. *Publications:* numerous research papers on electronic and transport properties in crystalline solids, liquids and amorphous semiconductors. *Recreations:* literature, music (particularly chamber music), languages. *Address:* 20 Kelso Place, Dundee DD2 1SL. *T:* (01382) 667649.

SPEARING, Prof. Anthony Colin; William R. Kenan Professor of English, University of Virginia, since 1989 (Professor of English, since 1987); *b* 31 Jan. 1936; *s* of Frederick Spearing and Gertrude Spearing (*née* Calnin); *m* 1961, Elizabeth; one *s* one *d*. *Educ:* Alleyn's Sch., Dulwich; Jesus Coll., Cambridge (BA 1957; MA 1960). University of Cambridge: W. M. Tapp Res. Fellow, Gonville and Caius Coll., 1959–60; Univ. Asst Lectr in English, 1960–64; Supernumerary Fellow, Gonville and Caius Coll., 1960; Official Fellow, Queens' Coll., 1960–87; Univ. Lectr in English, 1964–85; Dir of Studies in English, Queens' Coll., 1967–85; Reader in Medieval English Literature, 1985–87; Life Fellow, Queens' Coll., 1987. Vis. Prof. of English, Univ. of Virginia, 1979–80, 1984. *Publications:* Criticism and Medieval Poetry, 1964, 2nd edn 1972; The Gawain-Poet: a critical study, 1970; Chaucer: Troilus and Criseyde, 1976; Medieval Dream-Poetry, 1976; Medieval to Renaissance in English Poetry, 1985; Readings in Medieval Poetry, 1987; The Medieval Poet as Voyeur, 1993; (trans.) The Cloud of Unknowing, 2001; texts, articles in learned jls. *Address:* Department of English, 219 Bryan Hall, University of Virginia, PO Box 400121, Charlottesville, VA 22904-4121, USA.

SPEARING, George David; Technical Adviser, Institution of Highways and Transportation, 1984–86, retired; *b* 16 Dec. 1927; *s* of late George Thomas and Edith Lydia Anna Spearing; *m* 1951, Josephine Mary Newbould; two *s* one *d*. *Educ:* Rotherham Grammar Sch.; Sheffield Univ. BEng; MICE, FIHE. RAF, Airfield Construction Br., 1948. Asst Divl Surveyor, Somerset CC, 1951; Asst Civil Engr, W Riding of Yorks CC, 1953; Asst Engr, MoT, 1957; Supt. Engr, Midland Road Construction Unit, 1967; Asst Chief Engr, MoT, 1969; Regional Controller (Roads and Transportation), West Midlands, 1972; Dep. Chief Engr, DoE, 1973; Under Sec., DoE, 1974; Under Sec., Dept of Transport, and Dir Highways Planning and Management, 1974–78; Regional Dir, Eastern Reg., Depts of the Environment and Transport, and Chm., E Anglia Regional Bd, 1978–83. *Publications:* papers in Proc. Instn CE and Jl Instn HE. *Address:* 23 Colburn Avenue, Caterham, Surrey CR3 6HW. *T:* (01883) 347472.

SPEARING, Nigel John; *b* 8 Oct. 1930; *s* of late Austen and of May Spearing; *m* 1956, Wendy, *d* of Percy and Molly Newman, Newport, Mon; one *s* two *d*. *Educ:* Latymer Upper School, Hammersmith. Ranks and commission, Royal Signals, 1950–52; St Catharine's Coll., Cambridge, 1953–56. Mem., NUT, 1955–. Tutor, Wandsworth School, 1956–68 (Sen. Geography Master, 1967–68); Director, Thameside Research and Development Group, Inst. of Community Studies, 1968–69; Housemaster, Elliott School, Putney, 1969–70. Chairman: Barons Court Labour Party, 1961–63; Hammersmith Local Govt Cttee of the Labour Party, 1966–68. Co-opted Mem. GLC Planning and Transport Cttees, 1966–73. Contested (Lab) Warwick and Leamington, 1964. MP (Lab): Acton, 1970–74; Newham S, May 1974–1997. Introd Private Members Bill, which became Industrial Diseases (Notification) Act 1981. Secretary: Parly Lab. Party Educn Gp, 1971–74; Parly Inland Waterways Gp, 1970–74; Member Select Cttee: Overseas Develt, 1973–74, 1977–79; Members' Interests, 1974–75; Procedure, 1975–79; Sound Broadcasting, 1978–83; European (formerly EEC) Legislation, 1979–97 (Chm., 1983–92); Foreign and Commonwealth Affairs, 1980–87; Chair, Parly Affairs Cttee, PLP, 1989–97. Jt Pres., London Dockland Forum, 1998–; Vice-Pres., River Thames Soc., 1975–; Pres., Socialist Envt and Resources Assoc., 1977–86; Chm., British Anti-Common Market Campaign, 1977–83; a Vice-Pres., Campaign for Indep. Britain, 1997–. Mem. Bd,

Christian Aid, 1987–91. Mem., Congregational Church and URC, 1947–. *Publication:* The Thames Barrier-Barrage Controversy (Inst. of Community Studies), 1969. *Recreations:* rowing, cycling, reading. *Address:* 17 Cambridge Grove, Hammersmith, W6 0LA. *T:* (020) 8748 9266.

SPEARMAN, Sir Alexander Young Richard Mainwaring, 5th Bt *cr* 1840; *b* 3 Feb. 1969; *s* of Sir Alexander Bowyer Spearman, 4th Bt, and Martha, *d* of John Green, Naauwpoort, S Africa; *S* father, 1977; *m* 1994, Anne Stine, *d* of K. Munch. *Heir: uncle* Dr Richard Ian Campbell Spearman, FLS, FZS, *b* 14 Aug. 1926. *Address:* Zorguliet, 3 Sir George Grey Street, Oranjezicht 8001, Cape, S Africa.

SPEARMAN, John L.; Advisory Partner, Electra Partners Europe Ltd; Chairman: Playback Ltd, since 1987; FrameStore Group, since 2001; *b* 25 Nov. 1941; *s* of Thomas Spearman and Elizabeth Alexandra Spearman (*née* Leadbetter); *m* 1st, 1966, Susan Elizabeth Henderson Elms (marr. diss. 1986); one *s* one *d*; 2nd, 1988, Angela Josephine van Praag; one *d*. *Educ:* Trinity Coll., Dublin (MA). Unilever Grad. Trng Scheme; Lintas Ltd; London Press Exchange; Collett Dickenson Pearce, 1972–89: Man. Dir, 1982–83; Chm. and Chief Exec., 1983–89; Chief Exec., 1992–97, Dep. Chm., 1996–97, Classic FM. Chm., Laser Sales (LWT), 1990–93. Member: Government Lead Body for Design, 1991–; Arts Council of England, 1996–. Patron Dir, RIBA. Trustee, World Monuments Fund. FRSA 1996. *Recreations:* music, sailing, ski-ing, walking, gardening. *Address:* c/o Electra Partners Europe Ltd, 65 Kingsway, WC2B 6QT. *Clubs:* Hurlingham; Royal Irish Yacht (Dublin).

See also T. D. Spearman.

SPEARMAN, Richard; QC 1996; a Recorder, since 2000; *b* 19 Jan. 1953; *s* of late Clement Spearman, CBE and of Olwen Regina Spearman (*née* Morgan); *m* 1983, Sandra Elizabeth Harris; three *d*. *Educ:* Bedales; King's Coll., Cambridge. Called to the Bar, Middle Temple, 1977. An Asst Recorder, 1998–2000. *Publication:* (with F. A. Philpott) Sale of Goods Litigation, 1983, 2nd edn 1994. *Recreations:* racquet sports, ski-ing, family. *Address:* 4–5 Gray's Inn Square, Gray's Inn, WC1R 5AY. *T:* (020) 7404 5252. *Clubs:* Brooks's, Hurlingham, MCC.

SPEARMAN, Prof. Thomas David, PhD; President, Royal Irish Academy, since 1999; *b* 25 March 1937; *s* of Thomas Spearman and Elizabeth Alexandra Spearman (*née* Leadbeater); *m* 1961, Juanita Smale; one *s* two *d*. *Educ:* Greenlanes Sch., Dublin; Mountjoy Sch., Dublin; Trinity Coll., Dublin (BA, MA); St John's Coll., Cambridge (PhD 1961). Res. Fellow, UCL and CERN, Geneva, 1961–62; Res. Associate, Univ. of Ill, 1962–64; Lectr in Theoretical Physics, Univ. of Durham, 1964–66; Univ. Prof. of Natural Philosophy, Univ. of Dublin, 1966–97; Trinity College, Dublin: Fellow, 1969, Sen. Fellow, 1994–97; Vice-Provost, 1991–97. Chm., Trustee Savings Bank, Dublin, 1989–92. Mem. Council, Dublin Inst. for Advanced Studies, 1999–. MAE 1988 (Treas., 1989–2000); Member: Governing Council, ESF, 1999– (Vice-Pres., 1983–89); ESTA, 1994–98. Mem., Rep. Body, C of I, 1968–. Gov. and Guardian, Nat. Gall. of Ireland, 1999–. *Publications:* (with A. D. Martin) Elementary Particle Theory, 1970; contrib. papers in elementary particle theory, inverse problems and history of science. *Recreations:* walking, reading, gardening, looking at pictures, listening to music. *Address:* St Elmo, Marlborough Road, Glenageary, Co. Dublin, Ireland; Trinity College, Dublin 2, Ireland. *Club:* Kildare Street and University (Dublin).

See also J. L. Spearman.

SPECTOR, Prof. Roy Geoffrey, MD, PhD; FRCP, FRCPath; Professor of Applied Pharmacology, Guy's Hospital Medical School, 1972–89, now Emeritus; Hon. Physician, Guy's Hospital, since 1967; *b* 27 Aug. 1931; *s* of Paul Spector and Esther Cohen; *m* 1st, 1960, Evie Joan Freeman (marr. diss. 1979); two *s* one *d*; 2nd, 1986, Annette Skinner. *Educ:* Roundhay Sch., Leeds; Sch. of Medicine, Leeds Univ. (MB, ChB, MD); PhD Lond. 1964, Dip. in Biochem. 1966. FRCP 1971; FRCPath 1976. Lectr in Paediatric Res. Unit, Guy's Hosp., 1961–67; Guy's Hosp. Medical School, subseq. United Medical and Dental Schools of Guy's and St Thomas's Hosps: Reader in Pharmacology, 1968–71; Sub Dean for Admissions, 1975–89; Chm., Div. of Pharmacology, 1985–88. Vis. Prof. in Clin. Pharmacology, West China Med. Univ., Chengdu, 1986–87. External Examiner, Hong Kong Univ., 1994–95 and 1996–97. Vice Chm., British Univs' Film Council, 1976–87. FRSocMed. *Publications:* (jtly) The Nerve Cell, 1964, 2nd edn 1986; (jtly) Clinical Pharmacology in Dentistry, 1975, 6th edn 1995; (jtly) Mechanisms in Pharmacology and Therapeutics, 1976; (jtly) Aids to Pharmacology, 1980, 3rd edn 1993; (jtly) Textbook of Clinical Pharmacology, 1981, 2nd edn 1986; (jtly) Aids to Clinical Pharmacology and Therapeutics, 1984, 3rd edn 1993; (jtly) Common Drug Treatments in Psychiatry, 1984; Catechism in Clinical Pharmacology Therapeutics, 1986; (jtly) Drugs and Medicines, 1989; contributor: Textbook of Clinical Pharmacology, 1994; Handbook of Clinical Research, 1994; contribs to jls on pathology, medicine, gen. science, and applied pharmacology. *Recreation:* cookery. *Address:* 3 St Kilda Road, Orpington, Kent BR6 0ES. *T:* (01689) 810069.

SPEDDING, Sir Colin (Raymond William), Kt 1994; CBE 1988; Professor of Agricultural Systems, 1975–90, and Pro-Vice-Chancellor, 1986–90, University of Reading, now Professor Emeritus; *b* 22 March 1925; *s* of Robert Kewley Spedding and Ilynn Spedding; *m* 1952, Betty Noreen George (*d* 1988); one *s* (and one *s* decd). *Educ:* London Univ. (External) (BSc 1951; MSc 1953; PhD 1955; DSc 1967). FZS 1962; FIBiol 1967, CBiol 1984; FRASE 1984; FIHort 1986; FRAgS 1986; FLS 1995. Ilford Ltd, 1940–43; RNVR, 1943–46; Allen & Hanbury, 1948–49; Grassland Research Institute: joined 1949; Head of Ecology Div., 1967–75; Asst Dir, 1969–72; Dep. Dir, 1972–75; University of Reading: Visiting, then part-time Prof. of Agric. Systems, 1970–75; Head of Dept of Agric. and Horticl., 1975–83; Dean, Faculty of Agriculture and Food, 1983–86; Dir, Centre for Agricl Strategy, 1981–90, Consultant Dir, 1990–99. Commonwealth Prestige Fellow, NZ, 1977; Vis. Prof., Univ. of Guelph, Canada, 1978. Editor, Agricultural Systems, 1976–88. Mem., Programme Cttee, Internat. Livestock Centre for Africa, Addis Ababa, 1976–80, Vice Chm., 1980–83; Special Advr, H of C Select Cttee on Agric., 1980–83; Chairman: UK Register of Organic Food Standards Bd, 1987–99; Farm Animal Welfare Council, 1988–98; Apple and Pear Res. Council, 1989–97; Science Council (formerly CSTI), 1994–2000; Assured Chicken Production Ltd, 2000–. Dir, Lands Improvement Hldgs PLC (formerly Gp Ltd), 1986–99 (Dep. Chm., 1990–99). Adv. Dir, WSPA, 1998–; Advr, Companion Animal Welfare Council, 1999–; Specialist Advr, H of L Select Cttee on EC, Sub-Cttee D (Agric., Fisheries and Food), 1999; Hd, UK Delegn to Internat. Whaling Commn, Grenada, 1999. President: European Assoc. of Animal Production Study Commn for Sheep and Goat Production, 1970–76; British Soc. for Animal Production, 1979–80; Vice-Pres., Inst. of Biology, 1997–99 (Pres., 1992–94). Governor: Royal Agricl Coll., 1982–88; Inst. of Grassland and Envmtl Res. (formerly Inst. for Grassland and Animal Production), 1987–91; Mem., Council of Management, PDSA, 1988– (Dep. Chm., 1996–). Mem., Inst. of Dirs, 1992–98. FRSA 1988. Hon. Life Mem., BSAS, 1990; Hon. FIBiol 1994; Hon. Associate, RCVS, 1994; Hon. MRSocMed, 1998. Hon. DSc Reading, 1995. George Hedley Award, 1971; Canadian Inst. of Agric. Recognition Award, 1971; Wooldridge Meml Medal, BVA, 1982; Hawkesbury Centenary Medal of Honour, Univ. of Western Sydney, 1991; Massey Ferguson Nat. Agricl Award, 1991; Victory Medal, Central Vet. Soc., 2000. *Publications:* Sheep Production and Grazing Management, 1965, 2nd edn 1970; Grassland Ecology, 1971; (ed with E. C. Diekmahns) Grasses and Legumes in British Agriculture, 1972; The Biology of Agricultural Systems, 1975; An Introduction to Agricultural Systems, 1979, 2nd edn 1988; (ed) Vegetable Productivity, 1981; (with J. M. Walsingham and A. M. Hoxey) Biological Efficiency in Agriculture, 1981; (ed) Fream's Agriculture, 1983; (ed) Fream's Principles of Food and Agriculture, 1992; Agriculture and the Citizen, 1996; Animal Welfare, 2000; over 250 sci papers in learned jls. *Address:* Vine Cottage, Orchard Road, Hurst, Berks RG10 0SD. *Clubs:* Athenæum, Farmers'.

SPEED, Anthony James, CBE 1999; QPM 1991; DL; Police Adviser on public order, City of London Police Committee, since 1999; non-executive Director, Reliance Project Security Ltd, since 1999; *b* 23 Feb. 1941; *m* 1961, Patricia Elizabeth Boyle; one *s* three *d*. *Educ:* Thomas Calton Technical Sch., Dulwich. Metropolitan Police, 1957–99: Personal Protection Officer to the Prince of Wales, 1969; Scarman Inquiries into Red Lion Square Disorders, 1974, Brixton Disorders, 1981; Divl Comdr, Brixton, 1981–83; posts in Westminster, 1983–99, Asst Comr, Central Area, 1994–99. Div. Pres., St John Ambulance, 2001. DL Greater London, 1999. *Recreation:* horse riding.

SPEED, Sir (Herbert) Keith, Kt 1992; RD 1967; DL; Director, Folkestone & Dover Water Services (formerly Folkestone and District Water Co.), since 1986; *b* 11 March 1934; *s* of late Herbert Victor Speed and Dorothy Barbara (*née* Mumford); *m* 1961, Peggy Voss Clarke; two *s* one *d* (and one *s* decd). *Educ:* Greenhill Sch., Evesham; Bedford Modern Sch.; RNC, Dartmouth and Greenwich. Officer, RN, 1947–56; Lt-Comdr RNR, 1964–79. Sales Man., Amos (Electronics) Ltd, 1957–60; Marketing Man., Plysu Products Ltd, 1960–65; Officer, Conservative Res. Dept, 1965–68. MP (C): Meriden, March 1968–Feb. 1974; Ashford, Oct. 1974–1997. An Asst Govt Whip, 1970–71; a Lord Comr of HM Treasury, 1971–72; Parly Under-Sec. of State, DoE, 1972–74; Opposition spokesman on local govt, 1976–77, on home affairs, 1977–79; Parly Under Sec. of State for Defence for RN, 1979–81; Mem., Parly Select Cttee on Defence, 1983–87; UK Rep. to Parly Assembly of Council of Europe and WEU, 1987–97. Parliamentary Consultant: Professional Assoc. of Teachers, 1982–97; Assoc. for Instrumentation, Control and Automation Industry in UK, 1983–87. DL Kent, 1996. *Publications:* Blue Print for Britain, 1965; Sea Change, 1982; contribs to various political and defence jls. *Recreations:* classical music, reading. *Address:* Strood House, Rolvenden, Cranbrook, Kent TN17 4JJ. *Clubs:* Garrick; Hurst Castle Sailing.

See also J. J. Speed.

SPEED, Jeffery John, CBE 1991; Director of Fundraising and Treasurer's Department, Conservative Central Office, 1995–96; *b* 3 Oct. 1936; *s* of late Herbert Victor Speed and Dorothy Barbara Speed (*née* Mumford); *m* 1985, Hilary Anne Busfield, *d* of late Haley Busfield, Mayfield, Sussex. *Educ:* Bedford Modern Sch. General Motors (Vauxhall), 1955–58; Sales Manager, later Sales Dir, Tompkins Moss Gp, 1959–65; Conservative Party Agent, 1965–78; Dep. Central Office Agent, S Eastern Area, 1978–82; Central Office Agent: E Midlands Area, 1982–88; Greater London Area, 1988–93; Dir, Constituency Services, Cons. Central Office, 1993–95. FISM 1995 (MISM 1993). FRSA 1993. *Publication:* Tudor Townscapes, 2000. *Recreations:* antique maps (especially those by John Speed, 1552–1629), oenology, travel, musical theatre and film. *Club:* Royal Over-Seas League.

See also Sir H. K. Speed.

SPEELMAN, Sir Cornelis Jacob, 8th Bt *cr* 1686; BA; *b* 17 March 1917; *s* of Sir Cornelis Jacob Speelman, 7th Bt and Maria Catharina Helena, Castendijk; *S* father, 1949; *m* 1972, Julia Mona Le Besque (*d* 1978); *m* 1986, Irene Agnes van Leeuwen; two step *c*. Education Dept, Royal Dutch Army, 1947–49; with The Shell Company (Marketing Service Dept), 1950. Student, Univ. of Western Australia, 1952; formerly Master of Modern Languages at Clifton Coll., Geelong Grammar Sch.; Exeter Tutorial Coll.

SPEIGHT, Hon. Sir Graham (Davies), Kt 1983; Judge of the High Court of New Zealand, 1966–98; *b* 21 July 1921; *s* of Henry Baxter and Anna May Speight; *m* 1947, Elisabeth Muriel Booth; one *s* one *d*. *Educ:* Auckland Grammar Sch.; Univ. of Auckland (LLB). Qualified barrister and solicitor, 1942; served 2nd NZ Expeditionary Force, Middle East and Italy, 1943–46: Lieut Royal NZ Artillery, 1943–46; Aide-de-Camp, General B. C. Freyberg, VC (later 1st Baron Freyberg), 1944–45; practising barrister, 1946–66. Justice of Appeal, Fiji, 1980–87; Chief Justice, Cook Is, 1982–87. Chairman: Eden Park Bd, 1988–94; Rothman Foundn, 1988–95; NZ Sports Drug Agency, 1990–2000. Chancellor, Univ. of Auckland, 1973–79; Hon. LLD Auckland, 1983. *Publication:* (ed jtly) Adams: criminal law in New Zealand, 1986. *Recreations:* golf, yachting. *Address:* 5/163 Victoria Avenue, Remuera, Auckland 5, New Zealand. *T:* (9) 5244464. *Clubs:* Auckland Golf, Royal New Zealand Yacht Squadron (Auckland) (Cdre 1961–63).

SPEIRS, Graham Hamilton; *b* 9 Jan. 1927; *s* of Graham Mushet Speirs and Jane (*née* McChesney); *m* 1954, Myra Reid (*née* Mills); one *s* one *d*. *Educ:* High Sch. of Glasgow; Glasgow Univ. (MA 1950, LLB 1952). Anderson, Young and Dickson, Writers, Glasgow, 1950–52; Legal Asst, Dunbarton CC, 1952–54; Sen. Legal Asst, Stirling CC, 1954–59; Depute Sec., then Sec., Assoc. of County Councils in Scotland, 1959–75; Sec., Convention of Scottish Local Authorities, 1975–86, retd. Sec. Gen., Council of European Municipalities (British Section), 1980–84. Member: Scottish Legal Aid Bd, 1986; Bd, Bield Housing Assoc., 1986. *Recreation:* golf. *Address:* 3 Dirleton Avenue, North Berwick EH39 4AX. *T:* (01620) 892801. *Club:* North Berwick Golf (North Berwick).

SPEIRS, William MacLeod; General Secretary, Scottish Trades Union Congress, since 1998; *b* 8 March 1952; *s* of late Ronald Speirs and of Mary Speirs (*née* MacKenzie); *m* 1975, Lynda Speirs (marr. diss. 1990); one *s* one *d*. *Educ:* Univ. of Strathclyde (BA 1st Cl. Hons Politics). Univ. researcher, Strathclyde, 1974–76; Lectr, Cardonald Coll., Glasgow, 1977; bar steward, Paisley, 1977–78; researcher, Paisley Coll. of Technol., 1978–79; Asst Sec., 1979–88, Dep. Gen. Sec., 1988–98, Scottish TUC. FRSA 1993. DUniv Paisley, 1999. *Publications:* (contrib.) The Manpower Services Commission in Scotland, ed Brown and Fairley, 1989; contrib. to Scottish Trade Union Rev. *Recreations:* folk music, reading, watching St Mirren FC, cricket, losing money on horses. *Address:* Scottish Trades Union Congress, 333 Woodlands Road, Glasgow G3 6NG. *T:* (0141) 337 8100. *Club:* Daft Watty's Ramblers (Paisley).

SPELLAR, Rt Hon. John (Francis); PC 2001; MP (Lab) Warley, since 1997 (Warley West, 1992–97); Minister of State (Minister of Transport), Department for Transport, Local Government and the Regions, since 2001; *b* 5 Aug. 1947; *s* of William David and Phyllis Kathleen Spellar; *m* 1981, Anne Rosalind Wilmot; one *d*. *Educ:* Bromley Parish Primary Sch.; Dulwich Coll.; St Edmund's Hall, Oxford (BA PPE). Electrical, Electronic, Telecommunication and Plumbing Union: Res. Officer, 1969–76; Nat. Officer, 1976–92. Contested (Lab) Bromley, 1970. MP (Lab) Birmingham Northfield, 1982–83; contested (Lab) same seat, 1983, 1987. Parly Under-Sec. of State, 1997–99, Minister of State,

1999–2001, MoD. *Recreation:* gardening. *Address:* House of Commons, SW1A 0AA. *T:* (020) 7219 5800. *Clubs:* Bromley Labour; Brandhall Labour.

SPELLER, Antony; Senior Associate (Europe), Resource Planning and Management Systems Ltd, since 1992; Co-founder, and Director, The Farm Villages Ltd, since 1992; *b* 12 June 1929; *s* of late John and Ethel Speller; *m* 1st, Margaret Lloyd-Jones (marr. diss.); two *s* one *d*; 2nd, 1960, Maureen R. McLellan; one *s* one *d*. *Educ:* Loreto; Calcutta; Exeter Sch., Devon; Univ. of London (BScEcon); Univ. of Exeter (BA Social Studies). FHCIMA. Nat. Service, Subaltern, Devonshire Regt, 1951; Major, Devonshire Regt TA, 1965. Nigerian Produce Marketing Boards, 1952–54; Dir, Atlas Ltd, Nigeria, 1955–61. Chairman: Exeter Photo-Copying, 1963–93; EuroSpeedy Printing Centres UK, 1988–93; Copyshops of SW England, 1989–93. Vice Chairman: E Devon Water Bd, 1965–73; Devon River Authority, 1970–73. Councillor, Exeter CC, 1963–74 (Chairman: Public Works Cttee, 1965–69; Education Cttee, 1971–72). MP (C) N Devon, 1979–92; contested (C) N Devon, 1992. Mem., Select Cttee on Energy, 1982–88; Chairman: All-Party Alternative Energy Gp, 1984–92; W Africa Cttee, 1987–92. Chm., W Country Cons. MPs, 1983–87; Pres., 1996–99, Vice-Pres., 2000–, N Devon Cons. Assoc.; Vice-Chm., Tiverton and Honiton Cons. Assoc., 1997–99. Hon. Pres., Nat. Outdoor Events Assoc., 1992–98; Vice-Pres., Railway Develt Soc., 1992–. Mem. Cttee, Duke of Edinburgh Award Scheme, Devon, 2000–. *Address:* 11 Newton House, Newton St Cyres, Exeter, Devon EX5 5BL. *Clubs:* Royal Over-Seas League; Lagos Motor Boat (Nigeria).

SPELLER, John Christopher, MA (Ed); Headteacher, Norton Knatchbull School, since 1997; *b* 10 May 1949; *s* of Sydney and Doris Speller, Woodford Green, Essex; *m* 1981, Jennifer Edgar; twin *s* one *d*. *Educ:* Forest Sch., London; Hatfield Coll., Univ. of Durham (BA Hons French; PGCE); Open Univ. (MA Educn). Asst Teacher, Davenant Foundn Sch., Essex, 1972–76; Head of Languages, Grahame Park Comp. Sch., Barnet, 1977–80; Head of Upper Sch., Nicholas Comp. Sch., Basildon, 1981–83; Dep. Head, Ilford County High Sch. for Boys, 1983–89; Headteacher, Liverpool Blue Coat Sch., 1989–97. FRSA 1994. *Recreations:* cricket, walking, travel (UK and abroad), DIY, gardening. *Address:* The Norton Knatchbull School, Ashford, Kent TN24 0QJ. *T:* (01233) 620045.

SPELLER, Maj.-Gen. Norman Henry, CB 1976; Government Relations Adviser, ICL, 1976–86, retired; *b* 5 March 1921; *s* of late Col Norman Speller and Emily Florence Speller (*née* Lambert); *m* 1950, Barbara Eleanor (*née* Earle); two *s*. *Educ:* Wallingford Grammar School. Commnd RA, 1940; War Service N Africa; transf. to RAOC, 1945; psc 1952; DAA&QMG 39 Inf. Bde, 1953–55; Dirg Staff, Staff Coll., 1955–58; OC 20 Ordnance Field Park, 1958–60; Admin. Staff Coll., 1961; AA&QMG N Ireland, 1961–63; D/SPO COD Donnington, 1964–65; Col AQ 54 (EA) Div./District, 1965–66; AAG AG9, MoD, 1967; DDOS 1 British Corps, 1968–69; idc 1970; Dir of Systems Coordination, MoD, 1971–73; Dir of Ordnance Services, MoD, 1973–76, retired. Col Comdt, RAOC, 1978–83. Chm. Management Cttee, The Royal Homes for Officers' Widows and Daughters (SSAFA), 1987–94. *Recreations:* sailing, golf. *Address:* 1 Steeple Close, SW6 3LE. *Club:* Roehampton.

SPELMAN, Caroline Alice; MP (C) Meriden, since 1997; *b* 4 May 1958; *d* of Marshall Cormack and Helen Margaret Greenfield; *m* 1987, Mark Gerald Spelman; two *s* one *d*. *Educ:* Herts and Essex Grammar Sch. for Girls; Queen Mary Coll., London (BA 1st cl. Hons European Studies). Sugar Beet Advr, NFU, 1981–84; Dep. Dir, European Confedn of Sugar Beet Growers, Paris, 1984–89; Dir, Spelman, Cormack and Associates (food and biotechnology consultancy), 1989–. Contested (C) Bassetlaw, 1992. *Publication:* The Non-Food Uses of Agricultural Raw Materials, 1994. *Recreations:* tennis, ski-ing, hockey. *Address:* 2 Manor Road, Solihull, West Midlands B91 2BH. *T:* (0121) 711 2955.

SPENCE, Prof. Alastair Andrew, CBE 1993; MD; FRCA, FRCSE, FRCPG, FRCPE, FRCS; Professor of Anaesthetics, University of Edinburgh, 1984–98, now Emeritus; *b* 18 Sept. 1936; *s* of James Glendinning Spence and Margaret Macdonald; *m* 1963, Maureen Isobel Aitchison; two *s*. *Educ:* Ayr Acad.; Glasgow Univ. FRCA (FFARCS 1964); FRCPG 1980; FRCSE 1991; FRCPE 1994; FRCS 1994. Western Infirmary, Glasgow, 1961–65; MRC Res. Fellow, Univ. of Glasgow Dept of Surgery, 1965–66; Steinberg Res. Fellow and Clinical Asst to Prof. of Anaesthesia, Univ. of Leeds, 1966–69; Sen. Lectr and Head of Dept of Anaesthesia, later Reader and Prof., Western Infirmary, Glasgow, 1969–84. Hon. Consultant Anaesthetist, Lothian Health Bd, then Royal Infirmary of Edinburgh Trust, 1984–98. Member: Clinical Standards Adv. Gp, 1994–99; Adv. Cttee on Distinction Awards, 1992–2000 (Dir and Med. Vice-Chm., Scottish Sub-Cttee, 1995–98); Scottish Adv. Cttee on Distinction Awards, 1998–2000. Pres., Royal Coll. of Anaesthetists, 1991–94 (Vice-Pres., 1988–91). Hon. FDS 1994; Hon. FFAEM 1997. Editor, British Jl of Anaesthesia, 1973–83 (Chm. Bd, 1983–91). *Publications:* books, chapters and papers on anaesthesia and respiratory care. *Recreations:* golf, gardening. *Address:* Harewood, Kilmacolm, Renfrewshire PA13 4HX. *T:* (01505) 872962.

SPENCE, Christopher Alexander, MBE 1992; Chief Executive, National Centre for Volunteering, since 1998; Hon. President, London Lighthouse, 1996–2000; *b* 24 April 1944; *s* of late Robert Donald Spence and Margaret Summerford Spence; *m* 1990, Nancy Corbin Meadors Kline. *Educ:* Bromsgrove Sch.; South West London Coll. (Dip. in Counselling Skills). Dir, Task Force, 1968–70; Private Sec. to Speaker of House of Commons, 1970–76; freelance organisational develt consultant, 1976–86; Founder and Dir, London Lighthouse, 1986–96. Dir, Oxfordshire Learning Disability NHS Trust, 1996– (Vice-Chm., 1998–). Founding Chair, Pan London HIV/AIDS Providers Consortium, 1992–96; Chair, HIV Project, 1997– (Dir, 1995–97). Chm., Diana, Princess of Wales Meml Fund, 1999– (Trustee, 1998–; Chair, Grants Cttee, 1998–). FRSA 1998. Hon. Fellow, Univ. of Wales, Lampeter, 1999. *Publications:* (with Nancy Kline) At Least a Hundred Principles of Love, 1985, revd edn 1994; AIDS: time to reclaim our power, 1986; On Watch: views from the Lighthouse, 1996. *Recreations:* gardening, reading, writing, walking, vegetarian cooking, cats with challenging behaviour. *Address:* Lower Farm Orchard, Preston Crowmarsh, Wallingford, Oxon OX10 6SL. *T:* (01491) 835266.

SPENCE, Christopher John; Chairman, English Trust Co. Ltd, since 1991 (Managing Director, 1978–91); *b* 4 June 1937; *s* of late Brig. Ian Fleming Morris Spence, OBE, MC, TD, ADC and Ruth Spence (*née* Peacock); *m* 1st, 1960, Merle Aurelia (marr. diss. 1968), *er d* of Sir Leonard Ropner, Bt; one *d* (one *s* decd); 2nd, 1970, Susan, *d* of late Brig. Michael Morley, MBE; one *s* one *d*. *Educ:* Marlborough. 2nd Lieut, 10 Royal Hussars (PWO), 1955–57; Royal Wilts Yeomanry, 1957–66. Mem., London Stock Exchange, 1959–78. Sen. Steward, Jockey Club, 1998–. High Sheriff, Berks, 1996–97. *Recreations:* racing, shooting, golf. *Address:* Chieveley Manor, Newbury, Berks RG20 8UT. *T:* (01635) 248208. *Clubs:* Jockey, Pratt's, Cavalry and Guards; Swinley Forest Golf.

SPENCE, David Lane, CA; London Senior Partner, Grant Thornton, since 1998; *b* 5 Oct. 1943; *s* of Dr Alex S. Spence and Edith F. Spence; *m* 1966, Beverley Esther Cardale; one *s* two *d*. *Educ:* Fettes Coll., Edinburgh. CA 1967. C. F. Middleton & Co., 1962–67; Grant Thornton (formerly Thornton Baker), 1967–: Partner, 1970; Europ. Practice Partner, 1974–80; Exec. Partner, 1983–89. DTI Inspector, 1989 and 1992. Chm., Chartered Accountants Jt Ethics Cttee, 1995–97. Pres., Inst. Chartered Accountants of Scotland, 1998–99 (Vice-Pres., 1996–98). *Recreations:* golf, occasional cycling, tinkering with old MGs. *Address:* c/o Grant Thornton, Grant Thornton House, Melton Street, NW1 2EP. *T:* (020) 7383 5100. *Clubs:* Caledonian; Sunningdale, Royal and Ancient Golf.

SPENCE, Rt Rev. (David) Ralph; *see* Niagara, Bishop of.

SPENCE, Most Rev. Francis John; *see* Kingston (Ontario), Archbishop of.

SPENCE, Captain (Frederick) Michael (Alexander) T.; *see* Torrens-Spence.

SPENCE, Gabriel John; Under Secretary, Department of Education and Science, retired; *b* 5 April 1924; *s* of G. S. and D. A. Spence, Hope, Flints; *m* 1950, Averil Kingston (*née* Beresford) (*d* 1998); (one *s* decd). *Educ:* Arnold House; King's Sch., Chester (King's Schol., Head of School); Wadham Coll., Oxon (Schol.). MA 1949; Stanhope Prize and Proxime, Gibbs Schol., Oxon, 1947; Haldane Essay Prize, Inst. Public Admin, 1959. Joined Civil Service 1949 (Min. of Works, Science Office, Min. of Housing and Local Govt, DES); Jt Sec., Adv. Council on Scientific Policy, 1959–62; Asst Sec., DES, 1964–73; Sec., Council for Scientific Policy, 1964–67; Under Sec., DES, 1973–81; Dep. Sec., UGC, 1978–81. Admin. Staff Coll., Henley, 1957. Trustee, The Oates Meml and Gilbert White Library and Museum, 1982–. *Recreations:* natural history, photography, golf. *Address:* Old Heath, Hillbrow Road, Liss, Hants GU33 7QD. *T:* (01730) 893235.

SPENCE, Ian Richard; international tax consultant and adviser to developing countries, since 1998; *b* 15 Oct. 1938; *s* of John Jack Spence and Floretta Spence (*née* Bate); *m* 1971, Anne Kiggell; two *d*. *Educ:* Dulwich Coll.; Jesus Coll., Cambridge (BA Hist.). Joined Inland Revenue, 1962; seconded to DEA, 1966; Principal, 1967; seconded to CSSB, 1972; Asst Sec., 1975; Under Sec., and Dir, Internat. Div., Bd of Inland Revenue, 1991–98. Mem., Permanent Scientific Cttee, Internat. Fiscal Assoc., 1993–99. Sen. Res. Fellow, Internat. Tax and Investment Centre, 1999–. *Recreations:* theatre, opera, tennis, sailing, golf. *Address:* 98 Burbage Road, SE24 9HE. *T:* and *Fax:* (020) 7274 6198; *e-mail:* Ian_Spence@btinternet.com. *Clubs:* Athenæum; Dulwich Sports; Old Fogeys Golfing Soc.

SPENCE, Prof. Jonathan Dermot, CMG 2001; PhD; Sterling Professor of History, Yale University, since 1993; *b* 11 Aug. 1936; *s* of Dermot Gordon Chesson Spence and Muriel Evelyn Crailsham; *m* 1st, 1962, Helen Alexander (marr. diss. 1993); two *s*; 2nd, 1993, Annping Chin; one step *s* one step *d*. *Educ:* Winchester Coll; Clare Coll., Cambridge (BA 1959); Yale Univ. (MA 1961; PhD 1965). Yale University: Asst Prof., then Prof., 1966–, Chm., 1984–86, History Dept; George Burton Prof., 1976; Dir, Div. of Humanities, 1981–83; Mem. Bd of Govs, Yale Univ. Press, 1994–. Hon. Prof., Univ. of Nanjing, 1994–; Guggenheim Fellow, 1979–80; MacArthur Fellow, 1988–92. Council of Scholars, Library of Congress, 1988–96. Fellow: Amer. Acad. of Arts and Scis, 1985; Amer. Philosophical Soc., 1993; Corresp. FBA 1997. Hon. degrees from 8 American colls, and Chinese Univ. of Hong Kong, 1996. *Publications:* Ts'ao Yin and the K'ang-hsi Emperor: bondservant and master, 1966, 2nd edn 1988; To Change China: Western advisers in China 1620–1960, 1969, 2nd edn 1980; Emperor of China: self-portrait of K'ang-hsi, 1974; The Death of Woman Wang, 1978; (ed with John E. Wills) From Ming to Ch'ing: conquest, region and continuity in seventeenth-century China, 1979; The Gate of Heavenly Peace: the Chinese and their revolution 1895–1980, 1981; The Memory Palace of Matteo Ricci, 1984; The Question of Hu, 1988; The Search for Modern China, 1990, 2nd edn 1999; Chinese Roundabout: essays in history and culture, 1992; God's Chinese Son: the Taiping heavenly kingdom of Hong Xiuquan, 1996; (with Annping Chin) The Chinese Century: a photographic history of the last hundred years, 1996; The Chan's Great Continent: China in Western minds, 1998; Mao Zedong, 1999; Treason by the Book, 2001. *Recreation:* gardening. *Address:* 691 Forest Road, West Haven, CT 06516, USA. *Clubs:* Athenæum; Yale (New York City).

SPENCE, Malcolm Hugh; QC 1979; a Recorder, 1985–99; a Deputy High Court Judge, 1988–99; barrister-at-law, since 1958; *b* 23 March 1934; *s* of late Dr Allan William and Martha Lena Spence; *m* 1967, Jennifer Jane, *d* of Lt-Gen. Sir George Cole, KCB, CBE; one *s* one *d*. *Educ:* Summer Fields, Oxford; Stowe Sch.; Gonville and Caius Coll., Cambridge (MA, LLM). Gray's Inn: James Mould Schol., Holker Sen. Exhibnr, Lee Prizeman; called to the Bar, 1958; Bencher, 1988. Worcester Regt, First Lieut, 1954. Marshal to Mr Justice McNair, 1957; Pupil to Mr Nigel Bridge (now Lord Bridge of Harwich), 1958; entered chambers of Mr John Widgery, QC, 1958; practises mainly in Town and Country Planning and Compensation for Compulsory Purchase. Chm., Planning and Envmt (formerly Local Govt Planning and Envmtl) Bar Assoc., 1994–98. FCIArb 1999. Freeman: Arbitrators' Co., 2001; City of London, 2001. *Publication:* (jtly) Rating Law and Valuation, 1961. *Recreations:* trout fishing, forestry and golf (Captain: Cambridge University Stymies, 1957; Old Stoic Golfing Soc., 1972; Semi-finalist, Scandinavian Amateur Championship, 1964). *Address:* (chambers) 2 Gray's Inn Square, WC1R 5JH. *T:* (020) 7242 4986; 1 Gray's Inn Square, WC1R 5AA. *T:* (020) 7405 4379; Scamadale, Arisaig, Inverness-shire PH39 4NS. *T:* (01687) 450698. *Clubs:* Caledonian; Hawks (Cambridge); Leander (Henley).

SPENCE, Rt Rev. Ralph; *see* Spence, Rt Rev. D. R.

SPENCE, Prof. Robert, FREng; Professor of Information Engineering, Imperial College of Science, Technology and Medicine, 1984–2000, now Emeritus; *b* 11 July 1933; *s* of Robert Whitehair Spence and Minnie Grace Spence (*née* Wood); *m* 1960, Kathleen Potts; one *s* one *d*. *Educ:* Hymers Coll., Hull; Hull Coll. of Technology (BScEng Hons London External 1954); Imperial College, London (DIC 1955; PhDEng 1959; DScEng 1983; Dr RCA 1997). FIEE, FIEEE, FCGI; FREng (FEng 1990). Hull Corp. Telephones, 1950–51; General Dynamics/Electronics, Rochester, NY, 1959–62; Department of Electrical Engineering, Imperial College: Lectr, 1962–68; Reader, 1968–84. Chm. and Founding Dir, Interactive Solutions Ltd, 1985–90. Officier de l'Ordre des Palmes Académiques (France), 1995 (Chevalier, 1985). *Publications:* Linear Active Networks, 1970; Tellegen's Theorem and Electrical Networks, 1970 (trans. Russian and Chinese); Resistive Circuit Theory, 1974; Modern Network Theory, 1978; Sensitivity and Optimization, 1980; Circuit Analysis by Computer, 1986; Tolerance Design of Electronic Circuits, 1988 (trans. Japanese); Information Visualisation, 2001; numerous papers in learned jls. *Recreations:* steel band (bass player), concrete aspects of gardening. *Address:* 1 Regent's Close, Whyteleafe, Surrey CR3 0AH. *T:* (020) 8668 3649.

SPENCE, Ronald Blackwood, CB 1997; Permanent Secretary, Department for Regional Development, for Northern Ireland, since 1999; *b* 13 July 1941; *s* of Harold Spence and Margaret Spence (*née* McClure); *m* 1st, 1964, Julia Fitton (marr. diss. 1989); one *s* one *d*; 2nd, 1989, Sarah McKnight. *Educ:* Methodist Coll., Belfast; Queen's Univ., Belfast (BA Hons). Entered NICS as Asst Principal, 1963; Principal, Min. of Develt, 1967–74; Asst Sec., DoE, 1974–80; Head, Econ. and Social Div., NI Office, 1980–82; Under Sec., Dept of Finance and Personnel, 1982–85; Head, Central Secretariat, 1985–90; Under Sec., Dept of Econ. Develt, 1990–94; Permanent Sec., DoE (NI), 1994–99. Chairman: NI Partnership Bd, 1996–; NI Events Co., 1997–. *Recreation:* golf. *Address:*

Department for Regional Development, Clarence Court, 10–18 Adelaide Street, Belfast BT2 8GB. *T:* (028) 9054 1175.

SPENCE, Stanley Brian; His Honour Judge Spence; a Circuit Judge, since 1991; Resident Judge, Reading Crown Court, since 1999; *b* 3 May 1937; *s* of George Henry Spence and Sarah Spence (*née* Hoad); *m* 1961, Victoria Rosaleen Tapper; one *s* one *d*. *Educ:* Portsmouth Grammar Sch.; Britannia Royal Naval College, Dartmouth. Commissioned Supply and Secretariat Specialisation, RN, 1958; served: HMS Eagle; Staff of FO2 FEF; Portsmouth; 3rd Frigate Sqdn; HMS St Vincent; legal training, 1966–68; called to the Bar, Middle Temple, 1968; served: HMS Terror, Singapore; Staff of Commander FEF; 8th Frigate Sqdn; Legal Advr to C-in-C Naval Home Command and Flag Officer Spithead; retired from RN, 1975; Office of Judge Advocate General of the Forces (Army and RAF), 1975–90; Recorder of the Crown Court, 1987–91. *Recreations:* maintaining a cottage in France, wine. *Address:* The Crown Court, Reading RG1 3EH.

SPENCER, family name of **Viscount Churchill** and of **Earl Spencer**.

SPENCER, 9th Earl *cr* 1765; **Charles Edward Maurice Spencer;** Baron and Viscount Spencer 1761; Viscount Althorp 1765; Viscount Althorp (UK) 1905; writer; *b* 20 May 1964; *s* of 8th Earl Spencer, LVO and of Hon. Frances Ruth Burke Roche, *yr d* of 4th Baron Fermoy; *S* father, 1992; *m* 1989, Victoria (marr. diss. 1997), *d* of John Lockwood; one *s* three *d* (incl. twin *d*). *Educ:* Maidwell Hall; Eton College; Magdalen Coll., Oxford. Page of Honour to HM the Queen, 1977–79; contributing correspondent, NBC News, 1987–91 and 1993–95; reporter, Granada Television, 1991–93; presenter, NBC Super Channel, 1995–96; writer, Planet Wild, 1998–2000. *Publications:* Althorp: the story of an English home, 1998; The Spencer Family, 1999. *Heir: s* Viscount Althorp, *qv*. *Address:* Althorp, Northampton NN7 4HG.

SPENCER, Raine, Countess; *b* 9 Sept. 1929; *d* of late Alexander George McCorquodale and Dame Barbara Cartland, DBE; *m* 1st, 1948, 9th Earl of Dartmouth (marr. diss. 1976); three *s* one *d*; 2nd, 1976, 8th Earl Spencer, LVO; 3rd, 1993, Comte Jean-François de Chambrun (marr. diss. 1996). Westminster City Councillor, 1954–65 (served on various cttees); Member: for Lewisham West, LCC, 1958–65 (served on Town Planning, Parks, Staff Appeals Cttees); for Richmond upon Thames, GLC, 1967–73; GLC Gen. Purposes Cttee, 1971–73; Chm., GLC Historic Buildings Bd, 1968–71; Mem., Environmental Planning Cttee, 1967–71; Chm., Covent Garden Develt Cttee, 1971–72; Chm., Govt working party on Human Habitat in connection with UN Conf. on Environment, Stockholm (June 1972), 1971–72 (report: How Do You Want to Live?); Chm., UK Exec., European Architectural Heritage Year, 1975. British Tourist Authority: Member: Infrastructure Cttee, 1972–86; Board, 1982–93; Chairman: Spas Cttee, 1982–83; Accommodation Cttee (formerly Hotels and Restaurants Cttee), 1983–93; Develt Cttee, 1986–93; Commended Hotels Panel, 1986–90; Cttee, Britain Welcomes Japan, 1990–93; Come to Britain Awards, 1990–93; Member: English Tourist Bd, 1971–75; Adv. Council, V&A Museum, 1980–83; Cttee of Honour, Business Sponsorship of the Arts, 1980–; Tourism Deptl Adv. Cttee, Surrey Univ.; Commn de Tourisme Prestige, Nice, 1993–95. Mem. Jury, improvement of Promenade des Anglais, Nice, 1993–95. Formerly LCC Voluntary Care Cttee Worker, Wandsworth and Vauxhall. Director: Harrods International Ltd, 1996–; Harrods (Management) Ltd, 2001–. Hon. Dr Laws, Dartmouth Coll., USA. *Publications:* What Is Our Heritage?, 1975; The Spencers on Spas (with photographs by Earl Spencer), 1983; Japan and the East (with photographs by Earl Spencer), 1986. *Address:* Flat 22, 35–37 Grosvenor Square, W1X 9AE. *T:* (020) 7495 4525, *Fax:* (020) 7495 4524.

SPENCER, Comdt Anne Christine, CBE 1994; Director, Women's Royal Naval Service, 1991–93; *b* 15 Dec. 1938; *d* of late Ernest Spencer and Dora Harrie (*née* Hauxwell). *Educ:* Newlands High Sch.; Yorks Coll. of Housecraft (HCIMA 1959). Direct Entry Officer, WRNS, 1962; commnd 1963; HMS Victory, 1963–64; HMS Dauntless, 1964–66; HMS Terror, Singapore, 1966–68; HMS St Vincent, 1968–69; HMS Nelson, 1969–70; Officer i/c WRNS, HMS Excellent, 1970–73; HMS Pembroke, 1973–74; Mess Manager, RNC, Greenwich, 1974–76; Defence Intelligence Staff, MoD, 1976–78; RNSC, 1978; Directorate of Naval Service Conditions, MoD, 1978–79; Terminology Co-ordinator, NATO HQ Brussels, 1979–81; WRNS Officers Appointer, MoD, 1981–83; Dep. Dir, WRNS, MoD, 1984–86; Naval Dir, NAAFI Bd of Management, 1986–88; Chief Staff Officer (Admin) to Flag Officer, Plymouth, 1988–91. ADC to HM Queen, 1991–93. *Recreations:* theatre, art, food, friends, Yorkshire. *Address:* 6 Wilkinson House, Gunners Row, Marine Gate, Southsea, Hants PO4 9XQ.

SPENCER, Prof. Anthony James Merrill, FRS 1987; Professor of Theoretical Mechanics, University of Nottingham, 1965–94, now Emeritus; *b* 23 Aug. 1929; *s* of James Lawrence Spencer and Gladys Spencer; *m* 1955, Margaret Bosker; three *s*. *Educ:* Queen Mary's Grammar Sch., Walsall; Queens' Coll., Cambridge (MA, PhD, ScD). Research Associate, Brown Univ., USA, 1955–57; Senior Scientific Officer, UKAEA, 1957–60; Lectr, Reader, Prof., Univ. of Nottingham, 1960–94. Visiting Professor: Brown Univ., 1966 and 1971; Lehigh Univ., 1978; Univ. of Queensland, 1982; Erskine Fellow, Univ. of Canterbury, 1995; Leverhulme Emeritus Fellow, 1995–97. *Publications:* Deformations of Fibre-reinforced Materials, 1972; (jtly) Engineering Mathematics, Vols I and II, 1977; Continuum Mechanics, 1980; Continuum Theory of the Mechanics of Fibre-reinforced composites, 1984; numerous articles in math. and eng. jls. *Address:* 43 Stanton Lane, Stanton-on-the-Wolds, Keyworth, Nottingham NG12 5BE. *T:* (0115) 937 3134; School of Mathematical Sciences, The University, Nottingham NG7 2RD. *T:* (0115) 951 3838.

SPENCER, Charles Easdale; theatre critic, Daily Telegraph, since 1991; *b* 4 March 1955; *s* of Graham Easdale Spencer and Dorothy Aileen Spencer (*née* Brundan); *m* 1983, Nicola Katrak; one *s*. *Educ:* Charterhouse; Balliol Coll., Oxford (BA Hons Eng. Lang. and Lit.). Surrey Daily Advertiser, 1976–79; Arts Reporter, Evening Standard, 1979–84; Chief Sub-editor, The Stage, 1984–86; Dep. Theatre Critic, London Daily News, 1986–87; Asst Arts Editor and Dep. Theatre Critic, Daily Telegraph, 1987–91. Critic of the Year, British Press Awards, 1999. *Publications:* I Nearly Died, 1994; Full Personal Service, 1996; Under the Influence, 2000. *Recreations:* food, tobacco, pop music. *Address:* 16 Derwent Close, Claygate, Esher, Surrey KT10 0RF. *T:* (01372) 465591; (work) (020) 7538 6413. *Club:* Garrick.

SPENCER, Cyril Charles, CMG 1951; First Deputy Executive Director, International Coffee Organisation, London, 1964–68; *b* 1 Feb. 1912; *s* of late Albert Edward Spencer, CBE, and Elsie Maud Spencer; *m* 1st, 1938; (one *d* decd); 2nd, 1949, Catherine Dewar Robertson (*d* 1995); 3rd, 1998, Phyllis Steele (*née* Rees) (*d* 1999); 4th, 2001, Penny Adames (*née* Salvidge). *Educ:* Royal Grammar Sch., Worcester; St John's Coll., Cambridge (BA 1934). Uganda: Asst Treas., 1935; Asst District Officer, 1937; Asst Financial Sec., 1946; Economic Sec., E Africa High Commission, 1948; Financial Sec., 1948; Acting Chief Sec. at various dates; Acting Governor, July 1951; Chairman: Uganda Lint Marketing Bd; Uganda Coffee Marketing Board; Member: Uganda Electricity Board; Uganda Development Corp.; Comr on Special Duty, Uganda, 1953–61; Sec.-Gen., Inter-African Coffee Organisation, Paris, 1961–64. *Recreations:* golf, fishing.

SPENCER, Sir Derek (Harold), Kt 1992; QC 1980; a Recorder, 1979–92 and since 1998; *b* 31 March 1936; *s* of Thomas Harold Spencer and Gladys Spencer (*née* Heslop); *m* 1st, 1960, Joan (*née* Nutter) (marr. diss.); two *s* one *d*; 2nd, 1988, Caroline Alexandra, *yr d* of Dr Franziskus Pärn, Hamburg; one *s*. *Educ:* Clitheroe Royal Grammar Sch.; Keble Coll., Oxford (MA, BCL). 2nd Lieut, then Lieut King's Own Royal Regt, 1954–56; served in Nigeria. Part-time Law Tutor, Keble Coll., Oxford, 1960–64; called to the Bar, Gray's Inn, 1961 (Holt Scholar; Arden Scholar; Bencher, 1991); in practice SE Circuit. Councillor, London Borough of Camden, 1978–83; Dep. Leader, Conservative Party, London Borough of Camden, 1979–81. Contested (C) Leicester South, 1987. MP (C): Leicester South, 1983–87; Brighton Pavilion, 1992–97; contested (C) same seat, 1997. PPS: to Home Office Ministers, 1986; to the Attorney General, 1986–87; Solicitor-Gen., 1992–97. Joint Sec. Cons. Parly Legal Affairs Cttee, 1985–87. Vice-Chm., St Pancras North Cons. Assoc., 1977–78; Treas., City of London and Westminster Cons. Assoc., 1990–91. *Recreations:* reading, swimming, walking. *Address:* 18 Red Lion Court, EC4A 3EB.

SPENCER, Prof. Harrison Clark, MD; President and Chief Executive Officer, Association of Schools of Public Health, Washington, since 2000; *b* 22 Sept. 1944; *s* of Harrison C. and Dorothy M. Spencer; *m* 1977, Christine Michel; two *s*. *Educ:* Haverford Coll. (BA 1965); Johns Hopkins Univ. (MD 1969); Univ. of Calif at Berkeley (MPH 1972); DTM&H London 1972. FACP 1986; FACPM. Intern in Medicine, Vanderbilt Univ., 1969–70; Med. Resident, USPHS Hosp., San Francisco, 1970–71; Epidemic Intelligence Service Officer, CDC Atlanta, 1972–74; Sen. Med. Resident, Univ. of Calif at San Francisco, 1974–75; Med. Res. Officer, Central American Res. Station, El Salvador, 1975–77; MO, Bureau of Tropical Diseases, CDC, 1977–79; SMO and Malaria Res. Co-ordinator, Clin. Res. Center, Kenya Med. Res. Inst., Nairobi, 1979–84; MO, Malaria Action Prog., WHO, Geneva, 1984–87; Chief, Parasitic Diseases Br., CDC, Atlanta, 1987–91; Dean: Sch. of Public Health and Tropical Medicine, Tulane Univ., 1991–95; LSHTM, London Univ., 1996–2000. *Publications:* over 100 articles on epidemiology, malaria, community-based health, internat. health and tropical medicine. *Recreations:* music, ballet, tennis. *Address:* Association of Schools of Public Health, 1101 15th Street NW, Washington, DC 20005, USA.

SPENCER, Herbert, RDI 1965; DrRCA; Professor of Graphic Arts, Royal College of Art, 1978–85; *b* 22 June 1924; *m* 1954, Marianne Möls, Dordrecht; one *d*. DrRCA 1970; FCSD (FSIA 1947). Sen. Res. Fellow, RCA, 1966–78, Hon. Fellow, 1985. Internat. Pres., Alliance Graphique Internat., 1971–74; Mem., PO Stamp Adv. Cttee, 1968–93; External advr to Design Cttee, British Telecom, 1981–83. Dir, Lund Humphries Publishers Ltd, 1970–88. Consultant: W. H. Smith Ltd (formerly W. H. Smith & Son Ltd), 1973–96; Tate Gall., 1981–89; British Rail, 1984–86. Master, Faculty of Royal Designers for Industry, 1979–81; Vice-Pres., RSA, 1979–81. Governor, Bath Acad. of Art, Corsham, 1982–83. One-man exhibitions of paintings: Bleddfa Trust, 1986; Gallery 202, London, 1988–89 and 1990; Eva Jekel Gall., London, 1992; exhibition of photographs, Zelda Cheatle Gall., London, 1991; photographs in perm. collection of V&A Museum. Editor: Typographica, 1949–67; Penrose Annual, 1964–73. *Publications:* Design in Business Printing, 1952; London's Canal, 1961, 2nd edn 1976; Traces of Man, 1967; The Visible Word, 1968, 2nd edn 1969; Pioneers of Modern Typography, 1969, 2nd edn 1982, German edn 1970, Dutch edn 1983, Spanish edn 1995; (with Colin Forbes) New Alphabets A-Z, 1973, French edn 1974; (with Mafalda Spencer) The Book of Numbers, 1975; The Liberated Page, 1987, 2nd edn 1990; Without Words: photographs by Herbert Spencer, 1999. *Address:* 75 Deodar Road, Putney, SW15 2NU. *T:* and *Fax:* (020) 8874 6352. *Club:* Chelsea Arts.

SPENCER, Isobel; *see* Johnstone, I. T.

SPENCER, Ivor; DL; professional toastmaster, since 1956; Chairman and Managing Director, Ivor Spencer Enterprises Ltd, since 1965; *b* 20 Nov. 1924; *s* of Barnet and Dora Isaacs; *m* 1948, Estella Spencer; one *s* one *d*. *Educ:* Rochells Sch., London. Principal: Ivor Spencer Sch. for Professional Toastmasters, 1975–; Ivor Spencer Internat. Sch. for Butler Administrators/Personal Assistants, UK and USA, 1981–. Founder and Life President: Guild of Professional Toastmakers, 1967–98; Guild of Internat. Professional Toastmasters, 1990– (Lifetime Achievement Award, 1998; Toastmaster of the Year 2000); President: Toastmasters for Royal Occasions, 1975–; Toastmasters of GB, 1976–; Toastmasters of England, 1978–. Dir, Guild of British Butlers, 1980–; Chief Executive: British Professional Toastmasters Authority, 1995–; Ivor Spencer Professional Toastmasters Authority, 1998–. AMInstD 1997. DL Greater London, 1985. *Publications:* A Toastmaster's Story, 1975; Speeches and Toasts, 1980. *Recreations:* after-dinner speaking, organising special events worldwide. *Address:* 12 and 14 Little Bornes, Dulwich, SE21 8SE. *T:* (020) 8670 5585, 8424, *Fax:* (020) 8670 0055; *e-mail:* ivor@ivorspencer.com.

SPENCER, James; QC 1991; **His Honour Judge Spencer;** a Circuit Judge, since 2001; *b* 27 May 1947; *s* of James Henry Spencer and Irene Dulcie (*née* Wilson). *Educ:* The King's Sch., Pontefract; Univ. of Newcastle upon Tyne (LLB). Admitted solicitor, 1971; called to the Bar, Gray's Inn, 1975. A Recorder, 1990–2001. *Recreations:* watching Rugby League, playing golf. *Address:* Combined Court Centre, 1 Oxford Row, Leeds LS1 3BG.

SPENCER, Mrs Joanna Miriam, CB 1971; CBE 1961; CompIGasE; *b* 26 July 1910; *d* of late Rev. R. S. Franks; *m* 1954, Frank Woolley Sim Spencer (*d* 1975). *Educ:* Redland High School for Girls, Bristol; Girton College, Cambridge (MA). Asst, Lancs County Library, 1934–35; Asst Librarian: Hull Univ. Coll., 1936–37; Regent Street Polytechnic, 1938; Librarian, Selly Oak Colls, 1938–42. Temp. Civil Servant, Min. of Aircraft Production, 1942–45. Principal, Min. of Supply, 1946; Assistant Secretary, Min. of Supply, 1949–55, Board of Trade, 1955–56, Min. of Power, 1957–64; Under-Secretary: Min. of Power, 1964–69; Min. of Technology, 1969–70; DTI, 1970–72. *Address:* Galsworthy House, 177 Kingston Hill, Kingston on Thames, Surrey KT2 7LX.

SPENCER, John Loraine, TD; Headmaster, Berkhamsted School, 1972–83; Assistant Director, GAP Activity Projects Ltd, 1985–94; *b* 19 Jan. 1923; *s* of late Arthur Loraine Spencer, OBE, and Emily Maude Spencer, OBE, Woodford Green; *m* 1954, Brenda Elizabeth (*née* Loft); two *s* one *d*. *Educ:* Bancroft's Sch.; Gonville and Caius Coll., Cambridge (MA). 1st cl. hons Class. Tripos Pts I and II. War Service in Essex Regt, 1942–45 (Captain, despatches). Asst Master, Housemaster and Sixth Form Classics Master, Haileybury Coll., 1947–61; Headmaster, Lancaster Royal Grammar Sch., 1961–72. Mem. Chairman's Panel, Civil Service Selection Bds, 1985–90. Pres., Soc. of Schoolmasters, 1985–97. Mem. Council, Lancaster Univ., 1968–72. *Address:* Crofts Close, 7 Aston Road, Haddenham, Bucks HP17 8AF. *T:* (01844) 291235.

SPENCER, Prof. John Rason; Professor of Law, University of Cambridge, since 1995; Fellow, Selwyn College, Cambridge, since 1970; *b* 19 March 1946; *s* of Donald Edward Spencer and Catherine Mary Spencer (*née* Cozens); *m* 1972, Rosemary Stewartson; one *s* two *d*. *Educ:* Blandford Grammar Sch.; Selwyn Coll., Cambridge (MA, LLB). Cambridge University: Asst Lectr, Law Faculty, 1973–76; Lectr, 1976–91; Reader, 1991–95; Chm., Law Faculty, 1995–97. Mem., Calcutt Cttee on Privacy and Related Matters, 1990; Consultant, Criminal Courts Review, 2000. Chevalier, Ordre des Palmes Académiques (France), 2000. *Publications:* Jackson's Machinery of Justice, 8th edn 1989; (with Rhona Flin) The Evidence of Children: the law and the psychology, 1990, 2nd edn 1993; La procédure pénale anglaise (Que sais-je?), 1998. *Address:* Selwyn College, Cambridge CB3 9DQ.

SPENCER, Dr Jonathan Page; Director General, Business Competitiveness, Department of Trade and Industry, since 2000; *b* 24 April 1949; *s* of John Spencer and Doreen (*née* Page); *m* 1976, Caroline Sarah Armitage; one *s* two *d*. *Educ:* Bournemouth Sch.; Downing Coll., Cambridge (BA); Oxford Univ. (DPhil). ICI Res. Fellow, Oxford, 1973–74; joined Department of Trade and Industry, 1974: Principal, 1977; Principal Private Sec. to successive Secs of State, 1982–83; Asst Sec., 1983; Cabinet Office, 1987–89; DTI, 1989–91; Under Sec., 1991; Dir, Insurance Div., then Directorate, 1991–97; Dir Gen., Resources and Services, 1997–2000. *Recreations:* music, keeping the house up and the garden down. *Address:* Department of Trade and Industry, 151 Buckingham Palace Road, SW1W 9SS. *T:* (020) 7215 4178.

SPENCER, Michael Gerald; QC 1989; a Recorder, since 1987; *b* 1 Dec. 1947; *s* of Dr Seymour J. G. Spencer and late Margaret (*née* Behn); *m* 1969, Catherine Helen (*née* Dickinson); three *s*. *Educ:* Ampleforth Coll.; Hertford Coll., Oxford (MA Hons). Called to the Bar, Inner Temple, 1970, Bencher, 1996; Mem., Oxford Circuit, 1971, Midland and Oxford Circuit, 1972–. Dir, Yattendon Investment Trust, 1992–. Member: Hertford Coll. Boat Club Soc.; Ampleforth Soc. *Publications:* (contrib.) Medical Negligence, 1990; (contrib.) Doctors, Patients and the Law, 1992. *Recreations:* golf, reading, classical music, paragliding, ski-ing. *Address:* Crown Office Chambers, Temple, EC4Y 7EP. *T:* (020) 7797 8100. *Clubs:* Pegasus, Bar Yacht, Royal Thames Yacht; Chiltern Rugby Football; Beaconsfield Golf, Inner Temple Golf, Bar Golf.

SPENCER, Robin Godfrey; QC 1999; a Recorder, since 1998; *b* 8 July 1955; *s* of late Eric Spencer and of Audrey Elaine Spencer (*née* Brown); *m* 1978, Julia Margaret Eileen Burley; three *d*. *Educ:* King's Sch., Chester; Emmanuel Coll., Cambridge (MA). Called to the Bar, Gray's Inn, 1978 (Holker Sen. Award; Colyer Prize); in practice, Wales and Chester Circuit, 1978–; an Asst Recorder, 1993–98. *Recreations:* music, cricket, football, Methodist history. *Address:* 9–12 Bell Yard, WC2A 2JR. *T:* (020) 7400 1800; Sedan House, Stanley Place, Chester CH1 2LU. *T:* (01244) 348282.

SPENCER, Dame Rosemary (Jane), DCMG 1999 (CMG 1991); HM Diplomatic Service, retired; Ambassador to the Netherlands, 1996–2001; *b* 1 April 1941; *d* of Air Vice-Marshal Geoffrey Roger Cole Spencer, CB, CBE, and late Juliet Mary Spencer (*née* Warwick). *Educ:* Upper Chine Sch., Shanklin, IoW; St Hilda's Coll., Oxford (BA Hons Modern Langs). Joined Foreign Office, 1962; FO, 1962–65; Third Secretary, Nairobi, 1965–67; Second Sec., FCO, 1967–70; Second Sec., UK Delegn to EEC, and Private Sec. to Hon. Sir Con O'Neill, Official Leader of UK negotiating team, 1970–71; First Sec., Office of UK Permanent Representative to EEC, Brussels, 1972–73; First Sec. (Economic), Lagos, 1974–77; First Sec., Asst Head of Rhodesia Dept, FCO, 1977–80; RCDS 1980; Counsellor (Agric. and Economic Affairs), Paris, 1980–84; Counsellor (External Relations), Office of UK Perm. Rep. to EEC, 1984–87; Hd of European Community Dept (External), FCO, 1987–89; Asst Under-Sec. of State, FCO, 1989–92; Minister and Hd of British Embassy Berlin Office, 1993–96. Member Council: Britain in Europe, 2001–; Anglo-Netherlands Soc., 2001–. Member: Governing Bd, Imperial Coll., London Univ., 2001–; Council, St Swithun's Sch., 2001; Gov., Internat. Coll., Sherborne Sch., 2001–. *Recreations:* country walking, travel, domestic arts. *Address:* c/o FCO Association, Old Admiralty Building, SW1A 2AA. *Clubs:* Oxford and Cambridge, Royal Commonwealth Society; International (Berlin).

SPENCER, Sarah Ann; Director, Citizenship and Governance (formerly Human Rights) Programme, Institute for Public Policy Research, since 1994 (Research Fellow, since 1990); *b* 11 Dec. 1952; *d* of late Dr I. O. B. Spencer and of Dr Elspeth Wilkinson; *m* 1978, Brian Hackland; two *s*. *Educ:* Nottingham Univ. (BA Hons); University Coll. London (MPhil). Researcher, Law Faculty, UCL, 1977–79; Res. Officer, Cobden Trust (Civil Liberties Charity), 1979–84, Dir 1984–85; Gen. Sec., NCCL, 1985–89. Member: Home Office Task Force on Implementation of the Human Rights Act, 1998–; Commn on Future of Multi-Ethnic Britain, 1999–2000. Trustee, Cobden Trust, 1985–89. Editor, Rights Jl, 1979–84. FRSA. *Publications:* Called to Account: police accountability in England and Wales, 1985; (jtly) The New Prevention of Terrorism Act, 1985; The Role of Police Authorities during the Miners' Strike, 1985; (jtly) A British Bill of Rights, 1990; (jtly) Accountable Policing: effectiveness, empowerment and equity, 1993; (ed) Strangers and Citizens: a positive approach to migrants and refugees, 1994; (ed) Immigration as an Economic Asset: the German experience, 1994; Migrants, Refugees and the Boundaries of Citizenship, 1995; (jtly) A UK Human Rights Commission, 1998; (jtly) Mainstreaming Human Rights in Whitehall and Westminster, 1999. *Address:* 30–32 Southampton Street, WC2E 7RA.

SPENCER, Shaun Michael; QC 1988; a Recorder, since 1985; a Deputy High Court Judge, since 1999; *b* 4 Feb. 1944; *s* of Edward Michael Spencer, Leeds and Barbara Spencer (*née* Williams); *m* 1971, Nicola, *e d* of F. G. Greenwood, Tockwith, York; three *s* two *d*. *Educ:* Middleton Boys' Sch., Leeds; Cockburn High Sch., Leeds; King's Coll., Newcastle (Univ. of Durham). LLB 1st cl. Hons 1965. Asst Lectr and Lectr in Law, Univ. of Sheffield, 1965–68; called to the Bar, Lincoln's Inn, 1968, Bencher, 1997. *Recreations:* singing, cookery, books. *Address:* 34A Rutland Drive, Harrogate, N Yorks HG1 2NX.

SPENCER, Thomas Newnham Bayley, (Tom); Executive Director, European Centre for Public Affairs, Templeton College, Oxford, 1987–89 and since 1999; *b* 10 April 1948; *s* of Thomas Henry Newnham Spencer and Anne Hester (*née* Readett-Bayley); *m* 1979, Elizabeth Nan Maltby, *er d* of late Captain Ronald Edgar Bath and of Doreen Lester (*née* Bush); two *d* and one step *d*. *Educ:* Nautical Coll., Pangbourne; Southampton Univ. (BSc Social Sciences). Peat, Marwick, Mitchell & Co., 1972–75; Asst to Dir, Britain-in-Europe Campaign, 1975; J. Walter Thompson & Co., 1975–79. Associate Dean, Templeton Coll., Oxford, 1984–89. MEP (C) Derbyshire, 1979–84, contested same seat, 1984; MEP (C) Surrey West, 1989–94, Surrey, 1994–99. European Democratic Group: Dep. Chief Whip, 1989–91; spokesman on: Social Affairs and Employment, 1979–81; External Econ. Relations, 1982–84; Social Affairs, 1993–94; Chm., British Section, EPP Gp, 1994–95; European Parliament: Member: Envmt, Public Health and Consumer Affairs Cttee, 1991–99; Institutional Affairs Cttee, 1991–94; Foreign Affairs Cttee, 1993–99; Chairman: Cttee on Foreign Affairs, Security and Defence Policy, 1997–99; delegn to Czech, Slovene and Slovak Republics, 1993–99; Jt Parly Cttee with Czech Republic, 1995–97. Chm., European Union Cons. and Christian-Democratic Students, 1971–73; Mem. Council, Cons. Gp for Europe, 1999–. Mem., Global Legislators for a Balanced Environment, 1989–99. Chm., Counterpart Europe, 2000–. Vis. Prof., Univ. of Surrey, 2000–. Senior Advisor: Inst. for Global Envmtl Strategies, Japan, 1997–; Inst. of Educn, NY, 1998–. Patron, Global Commons Inst. Trust, 1997–. Mem., Bd of Trustees, Friends of Europe, 2000–. Mem. Court, Univ. of Surrey, 1992–; Mem. Adv. Bd, Centre for Corporate and Public Affairs, Manchester Metropolitan Univ., 2000–. Member Editorial Board: Eur. Business Jl, 1991–; Jl of Public Affairs, 2000–. Robert Schuman Silver Medal, 1974; Green Ribbon Award for most envmtl MEP, 1999. Great Golden Medal for Merit (Republic of Austria), 1995. *Recreations:* gardening, opera, Conservative Party. *Address:* Barford Court, Lampard Lane, Churt, Surrey GU10 2HJ. *Clubs:* Carlton, Brass Monkey.

SPENCER, Timothy John; QC 2001; a Recorder, since 2000; *b* 6 Nov. 1958; *s* of John Spencer and Muriel Spencer (*née* Rowe); *m* 1983, Ann Fiona Rigg; two *s* one *d* (of whom one *s* one *d* are twins). *Educ:* Baines Grammar Sch.; Downing Coll., Cambridge (MA Hons Law). 1st Lieut, 1st RTR, 1978. Called to the Bar, Middle Temple, 1982; Asst Recorder, 1998–2000. *Recreations:* Preston North End, Lancashire County Cricket Club, gardening. *Address:* 7 Bedford Row, WC1R 4BU. *T:* (020) 7242 3555.

SPENCER-CHURCHILL, family name of **Duke of Marlborough**.

SPENCER-NAIRN, Sir Robert (Arnold), 3rd Bt *cr* 1933; Vice Lord-Lieutenant of Fife, since 1996; *b* 11 Oct. 1933; *s* of Sir Douglas Spencer-Nairn, 2nd Bt, TD, and Elizabeth Livingston (*d* 1985), *d* of late Arnold J. Henderson; *S* father, 1970; *m* 1963, Joanna Elizabeth, *d* of late Lt-Comdr G. S. Salt, RN; two *s* one *d*. *Educ:* Eton College; Trinity Hall, Cambridge (MA). Fellow, Game Conservancy, 1993. Mem. Council, Macmillan Cancer Relief, 1997–. DL Fife, 1995. *Heir: s* James Robert Spencer-Nairn [*b* 7 Dec. 1966; *m* 1994, Dominique Jane, *o d* of Michael Williamson and Mrs Charles Newman; two *s*]. *Address:* Barham, Cupar, Fife KY15 5RG. *Clubs:* Royal and Ancient Golf (St Andrews); Falkland Palace Royal Tennis.

SPENCER PATERSON, Arthur; *see* Paterson.

SPENCER-SILVER, Prof. Peter Hele; S. A. Courtauld Professor of Anatomy in the University of London, at the Middlesex Hospital Medical School, 1974–82, now Emeritus; *b* 29 Oct. 1922; 2nd *s* of late Lt-Col J. H. Spencer Silver; *m* 1948, Patricia Anne, *e d* of late Col J. A. F. Cuffe, CMG, DSO, Wyke Mark, Winchester; two *s* one *d*. *Educ:* Harrow School; Middlesex Hosp. Med. School, Univ. of London. MRCS, LRCP; MB, BS London 1945; PhD London 1952. Res., Middlesex Hosp., 1945–46. RAF, 1946–48. Demonstrator in Anatomy, Middlesex Hosp. Med. Sch., 1948–57; Mem. 2nd Internat. Team in Embryology, Hübrecht Laboratory, Utrecht, Netherlands Govt Fellowship, 1956; Reader in Anatomy, Univ. of London, 1957; US Nat. Inst. of Health Post-doctoral Travelling Fellowship, 1961; Carnegie Inst. of Washington, Dept of Embryology, Baltimore, 1961–62; Prof. of Embryology, Mddx Hosp. Medical Sch., 1964–74, Sub-Dean, 1976–81. WHO Vis. Prof., 1976, 1979, 1981; Chm., Dept of Anatomy, King Saud Univ. (Abha Br.), Saudi Arabia, 1984–86. *Publications:* An Introduction to Human Anatomy, 1981; contribs to Jl Embryology and Experimental Morphology, Jl Physiol., Jl Anat., Lancet, etc. *Recreations:* music, George Myers. *Address:* c/o Barclays Bank, Jewry Street, Winchester, Hants SO23 8RG.

SPENCER SMITH, Prof. David, PhD, DPhil; Hope Professor of Zoology/Entomology, University of Oxford, 1980–95; Senior Research Fellow, Jesus College, Oxford, 1995–99, now Emeritus (Fellow, 1980–95); *b* 10 April 1934; *s* of Rev. Harry Chadwick Smith and Mary Edith (*née* Lupton); *m* 1st, 1964, Una Scully; one *d*; 2nd, 1974, Sylvia Hyder. *Educ:* Kingswood Sch.; Cambridge Univ. (BA, MA, PhD); DPhil Oxon 1980. Research Fellow: Rockefeller Univ., NY, 1958–61; St Catharine's Coll., Cambridge, 1961–63 (Res. Fellow); Asst Prof., Univ. of Virginia, 1963–66; Associate Prof. of Medicine and Biology, Univ. of Miami, Fla, 1966–70; Prof. of Medicine, Pharmacology and Biology, Univ. of Miami, 1970–80; engaged in res. on distbn and ecology of butterflies at high altitude in Karakoram, Hunza and Sino-Pakistan border reg., 1994–. Trustee, BM (Natural Hist.), 1984–88. Editor, Tissue & Cell, 1969–94. *Publications:* Insect Cells: their structure and function, 1968; Muscle: a monograph, 1972; The Butterflies of the West Indies and South Florida, 1994; contrib. Standard Catalog of World Coins, annually, 1983–95; papers and chapters in books and jls. *Recreations:* the coinage of China, early coinage of the Indian subcontinent. *Address:* Jesus College, Oxford OX1 3DW.

SPENCER-SMITH, Sir John Hamilton, 7th Bt *cr* 1804; *b* 18 March 1947; *s* of Sir Thomas Cospatric Hamilton-Spencer-Smith, 6th Bt, and Lucy Ashton, *o d* of late Thomas Ashton Ingram, Hopes, Norton-sub-Hamdon, Somerset; *S* father, 1959; *m* 1980, Christine (marr. diss. 1990), *d* of late John Theodore Charles Osborne, Durrington, Worthing, Sussex; one *d*. *Educ:* Milton Abbey; Lackham College of Agriculture, Wilts. *Recreations:* polo, ski-ing. *Heir: cousin* Michael Philip Spencer-Smith, *b* 2 April 1952. *Address:* Dairy Cottage, Elsted Marsh, Midhurst, West Sussex GU29 0JT.

SPENCER WILLS; *see* Wills.

SPENDLOVE, Peter Roy, CVO 1981; HM Diplomatic Service, retired; consultant in development and public administration; Chairman, East Anglia Regional Ambulance Service NHS Trust, 1993–95; *b* 11 Nov. 1925; *s* of H. A. Spendlove and Florence (*née* Jackson); *m* 1952, Wendy Margaret Valentine; two *s* three *d*. *Educ:* Chichester High Sch.; London Sch. of Economics; Edinburgh and Cambridge Univs. BScEcon Hons 1951. Called to Bar, Middle Temple, 1964. Served HM Forces, 1943–47: commnd, Indian Army/Royal Indian Artillery. LSE, 1948–51; Internat. Law Scholar at The Hague, 1951; Univ. of Cambridge, 1951–52. Apptd District Officer, Kenya, 1952; retired after serving in Provincial Admin and Central Govt, 1964. First Secretary, FCO, 1964; served in E Malaysia, Washington, Manila, FO, Jamaica; Counsellor, Economic, Commercial and Aid, Jakarta, 1977–80; Deputy High Comr, Sri Lanka, 1981–82; Dep. Chief Administrator, Broads Authority (E Anglia), 1983–86. Chm., Norfolk Ambulance Service NHS Trust, 1990–94. *Recreation:* riding. *Address:* 7 Wrenshaw Court, The Downs, Wimbledon, SW20 8HR. *T:* (020) 8946 2767.

SPENS, family name of **Baron Spens**.

SPENS, 4th Baron *cr* 1959, of Blairsanquar, Fife; **Patrick Nathaniel George Spens;** Director, Schroder Salomon Smith Barney, since 1999; *b* 14 Oct. 1968; *s* of 3rd Baron Spens and of Barbara Janet Lindsay Spens; *S* father, 2001; *m* 1998, Hon. Philippa Patricia Lennox-Boyd, *yr d* of Viscount Boyd of Merton, *qv*; one *s*. *Educ:* Rugby. Strauss Turnbull, 1987–93; Merrill Lynch International, 1993–99. *Recreations:* racing, shooting, fishing, claret. *Heir: s* Hon. Peter Lathallan Spens, *b* 3 March 2000. *Address:* 33A Pembroke Road, W8 6DP. *Clubs:* Bluebird, Twelve.

SPENS, Colin Hope, CB 1962; FICE, FCIWEM; *b* 22 May 1906; *er s* of late Archibald Hope Spens, Lathallan, Fife and Hilda Constance Hooper; *m* 1941, Josephine, *d* of late Septimus Simond; two *s* one *d*. *Educ:* Lancing Coll.; Imperial College of Science and Technology. Consulting engineering experience, 1928–39. Served War of 1939–45 with Royal Signals, 1939–41; PA to Director of Works in Ministry of Works, 1941–44; Engineering Inspectorate of Min. of Health, 1944–51, Min. of Housing and Local Govt,

1951–60; Chief Engineer, Min. of Housing and Local Govt, 1960–67. Senior Consultant, Rofe, Kennard and Lapworth, 1967–76; Dep. Chm., Sutton District Water Co., 1971–83. Pres., IWES, 1974–75. Hon. FInstPHE. *Address:* Residential Care Home, 20 Saffrons Road, Eastbourne BN21 1DU. *T:* (01323) 638742.

SPENS, David Patrick; QC 1995; a Recorder of the Crown Court, since 1994; *b* 2 May 1950; *s* of Hugh Stuart Spens and Mary Jean Drake (*née* Reinhold); *m* 1979, Danièle Irving; two *d. Educ:* Rugby Sch.; Univ. of Kent at Canterbury (BA). Called to the Bar, Inner Temple, 1973; Junior Treasury Counsel, CCC, 1988–95. *Address:* 6 King's Bench Walk, Temple, EC4Y 7DR. *T:* (020) 7583 0410, *Fax:* (020) 7353 8791.

SPENS, John Alexander, RD 1970; WS; Consultant, Maclay, Murray & Spens, Solicitors, Glasgow and Edinburgh (Partner, 1960–91); *b* 7 June 1933; *s* of Thomas Patrick Spens and Nancy F. Spens (*née* Anderson); *m* 1961, Finella Jane, *d* of Donald Duff Gilroy; two *s* one *d* (and one *s* decd). *Educ:* Cargilfield; Rugby School; Corpus Christi College, Cambridge (BA); Glasgow Univ. (LLB). WS 1977. Director: Scottish Amicable Life Assurance Soc., 1963–97 (Chairman, 1978–81); Standard Property Investment PLC, 1977–87. Carrick Pursuivant, 1974–85; Albany Herald, 1985–. *Recreations:* sailing, countryside and opera. *Address:* The Old Manse, Gartocharn, Dunbartonshire G83 8RX. *T:* (01389) 830456. *Clubs:* Naval; Western (Glasgow).

SPENS, Michael Colin Barkley, MA; Headmaster, Fettes College, since 1998; *b* 22 Sept. 1950; *s* of Richard Vernon Spens and (Theodora) Margaret Yuille Spens (*née* Barkley); *m* 1989, Deborah Susan Lane; one *s* two *d. Educ:* Marlborough Coll.; Selwyn Coll., Cambridge (BA 1972; MA Natural Scis 1976). Asst Master, Rathkeale Coll., NZ, 1968–69; Mktg Dept, United Biscuits plc, 1973–74; Asst Master, 1974–93, Housemaster, 1984–93, Radley Coll.; Headmaster, Caldicott Sch., 1993–98. Liveryman, Grocers' Co., 1981–. *Recreations:* mountaineering, golf, bridge, crosswords, geology, electronics, wood turning, gardening. *Address:* Headmaster's Lodge, Fettes College, Edinburgh EH4 1QX. *T:* (0131) 311 6701. *Clubs:* Hawks (Cambridge); New (Edinburgh); Denham Golf, Trevose Golf.

SPERRY, Rt Rev. John Reginald, CD 1987; Bishop of The Arctic, 1974–90; National President, Canadian Bible Society, since 1990; Vice President, United Bible Societies (Americas Region), since 1992; *b* 2 May 1924; *s* of William Reginald Sperry and Elsie Agnes (*née* Priest); *m* 1952, Elizabeth Maclaren; one *s* one *d* (and one *d* decd). *Educ:* St Augustine's Coll., Canterbury; King's Coll., Halifax (STh). Deacon, 1950; priest, 1951; St Andrew's Mission, Coppermine, NWT, 1950–69; Canon of All Saints' Cathedral, Aklavik, 1957–59; Archdeacon of Coppermine, 1959–69; Rector of St John's, Fort Smith, NWT, 1969–73; Rector of Holy Trinity, Yellowknife, NWT, 1974. Hon. DD: Coll. of Emmanuel, St Chad, 1974; Wycliffe Coll., Toronto, 1979. *Publications:* translations into Copper Eskimo: Canadian Book of Common Prayer (1962), 1969; Four Gospels and Acts of the Apostles, 1972. *Address:* 1 Dakota Court, Yellowknife, NT X1A 2A4, Canada. *T:* (867) 8736163.

SPERRYN, Simon George; Chief Executive, Lloyd's Market Association, since 2001; *b* 7 April 1946; *s* of George Roland Neville Sperryn and Wendy Sperryn (*née* King); *m* 1993, Jessica Alice Hayes; two *s* one *d. Educ:* Rydal School; Pembroke College, Cambridge (MA); Cranfield School of Management (MBA). Birmingham Chamber of Commerce and Industry, 1967–77; Chief Executive: Northants Chamber of Commerce and Industry, 1979–85; Manchester Chamber of Commerce and Industry, 1986–92; London Chamber of Commerce and Industry, 1992–2000. Director: Manchester Phoenix Initiative, 1988–92; Manchester TEC, 1989–92; Manchester Camerata, 1989–92 (Chm.); Business Link London, 1995–2000; Business Link London Central, 1995–2000. British Chambers of Commerce: Mem. Nat. Council, 1986–97; Dir, 1998–2000; Pres., Executives, 1993–95 (Vice Pres., 1991–93); Regl Sec., Southern Reg. Chambers of Commerce, 1995–99; Administrator, London Chamber of Commerce and Industry Commercial Educn Trust, 1992–2000. Vice Pres., World Chambers Fedn, 2000. Mem., Metropolitan Police Service Jt Steering Gp for Community Safety in London, 1998–2000; Chm., City of London Early Years Develt and Childcare Partnership, 1998–2000. Mem., London Regl Cttee, FEFC, 1996–2000. Gov., UC Salford, 1988–92. Freeman, City of London, 1998. FIMgt; FRSA; MIEx. *Address:* Deynes House, Deynes Road, Debden, Saffron Walden, Essex CB11 3LG.

SPICELEY, Peter Joseph, MBE 1976; HM Diplomatic Service, retired; Ambassador to Costa Rica, 1999–Feb. 2002; *b* 5 March 1942; *s* of late Robert Joseph Spiceley and Lucy Violet Spiceley; *m* 1965, Cecilia Orozco-Lemus; two *d. Educ:* Trinity Sch. of John Whitgift, Croydon. Entered Diplomatic Service, 1961; FCO, 1961–64; Bogotá, 1964–66; DSAO, 1966–69; Lima, 1969–72; Second Sec., Yaoundé, 1972–74; Consul, Douala, 1974–76; Second, later First, Sec., Quito, 1976–81; FCO, 1982–86; Consul, Miami, 1986–90; Asst Head of Aviation Dept, FCO, 1991–94; Dep. Consul-Gen. and Dir of Trade Promotion, Sydney, 1994–98. *Recreations:* sailing, reading. *Address:* (until April 2002) c/o Foreign and Commonwealth Office, King Charles Street, SW1A 2AH; (from April 2002) 15 Fitzjames Avenue, Croydon, Surrey CR0 5DL.

SPICER, Clive Colquhoun; retired; Honorary Research Fellow, Exeter University, 1979–91; Director, Medical Research Council Computer Unit, 1967–79; *b* 5 Nov. 1917; *s* of John Bishop Spicer and Marion Isobel Spicer; *m* 1st, 1941, Faith Haughton James, MB; one *s* two *d*; 2nd, 1979, Anne Nolan. *Educ:* Charterhouse Sch.; Guy's Hospital. Operational research on war casualties, 1941–46; Hon. Sqdn Leader, RAF; Staff, Imperial Cancer Research Fund, 1946–49; Dept of Biometry, University Coll., London, 1946–47; Public Health Laboratory Service, 1949–59; WHO Fellow, Univ. of Wisconsin, 1952–53; Vis. Scientist, US Nat. Insts of Health, 1959–60; Statistician, Imperial Cancer Research Fund, 1960–62; Chief Medical Statistician, General Register Office, 1962–66. Main interest has been in application of mathematical methods to medical problems. *Publications:* papers in scientific journals on epidemiology and medical statistics. *Recreations:* sailing, reading. *Address:* Churchtown, Michaelstow, St Tudy, Bodmin PL30 3PD.

SPICER, Sir James (Wilton), Kt 1988; company director; *b* 4 Oct. 1925; *s* of James and Florence Clara Spicer; *m* 1954, Winifred Douglas Shanks; two *d. Educ:* Latymer. Regular army, 1943–57, retd (Major); commnd Royal Fusiliers, 1944; Para. Regt, 1951–57. Nat. Chm., CPC, 1968–71. Mem. (C) European Parlt, 1975–84 (elected Mem. for Wessex, 1979–84); Chief Whip, European Democratic Gp, 1975–79; Chairman: Cons. Group for Europe, 1975–78 (Dir, 1972–74); Conservatives Abroad, 1986–93. MP (C) Dorset West, Feb. 1974–1997. Mem., Select Cttee on Agriculture, 1984–85. A Vice Chm., Cons. Party Orgn, and Chm., Internat. Office, 1985–92. Chairman: Westminster Foundn for Democracy, 1992–97; Agricl and Rural Parlt Trust, 1998–. Chm., Inglewood Health Hydro, 1999–. Patron, Dorset/Somerset, Marie Curie Cancer Care, 2000– (Chm., Dorset Br., 1998–2000); Chm., Dorset Br., Action Res., 1999–2000. *Recreations:* swimming, tennis. *Address:* Whatley, Beaminster, Dorset DT8 3SB. *T:* (01308) 862337.

SPICER, Sir Michael; *see* Spicer, Sir W. M. H.

SPICER, Sir Nicholas (Adrian Albert), 5th Bt *cr* 1906, of Lancaster Gate, Paddington; general medical practitioner, since 1982; *b* 28 Oct. 1953; *o s* of (Sir) Peter James Spicer (4th Bt, but did not use the title) and of Margaret (*née* Wilson); *S* father, 1993; *m* 1992, Patricia Carol Dye; two *s. Educ:* Eton; Birmingham Univ. (MB ChB 1977). *Recreation:* amateur singing. *Heir: s* James Peter Warwick Spicer, *b* 12 June 1993. *Address:* The Old Rectory, Stanford Bishop, Bringsty, Worcs WR6 5TT; Lagafater, New Luce, Newton Stewart, Wigtownshire DG8 0BA.

SPICER, Sir (William) Michael (Hardy), Kt 1996; MP (C) West Worcestershire, since 1997 (South Worcestershire, Feb. 1974–1997); *b* 22 Jan. 1943; *s* of late Brig. L. H. Spicer; *m* 1967, Patricia Ann Hunter; one *s* two *d. Educ:* Wellington Coll.; Emmanuel Coll., Cambridge (MA Econs). Asst to Editor, The Statist, 1964–66; Conservative Research Dept, 1966–68; Dir, Conservative Systems Research Centre, 1968–70; Man. Dir, Economic Models Ltd, 1970–80. PPS, Dept of Trade, 1979–81; Parly Under Sec. of State, 1984–87, and Minister for Aviation, 1985–87, Dept of Transport; Parly Under Sec. of State (Minister for Coal and Power), Dept of Energy, 1987–90; Minister of State (Minister for Housing and Planning), DoE, 1990. Mem., Treasury Select Cttee, 1997–2001. Chm. Exec., 1922 Cttee, 2001– (Mem. Exec., 1997–99). A Vice-Chm., 1981–83, Dep. Chm., 1983–84, Conservative Party. Chairman: Parly OST, 1990; Parly and Scientific Cttee, 1996–99; European Res. Gp, 1994–. Pres., Assoc. of Electricity (formerly Indep. Power) Producers, 1996– (Chm., 1991–96). Gov., Wellington Coll., 1992–. Chm. and Captain, Lords and Commons Tennis Club, 1997–. *Publications:* A Treaty Too Far, 1992; The Challenge from the East, 1996; *novels:* Final Act, 1981; Prime Minister Spy, 1986; Cotswold Manners, 1989; Cotswold Murders, 1990; Cotswold Mistress, 1992; Cotswold Moles, 1993; contrib. Jl Royal Inst. Public Admin. *Recreations:* painting, tennis, writing, bridge. *Address:* House of Commons, SW1A 0AA. *T:* (020) 7219 3000. *Clubs:* Garrick, Pratt's.

SPICKERNELL, Rear-Adm. Derek Garland, CB 1974; CEng, FIMechE, FIEE, CIMgt, FIMarE; Chairman, Ritec Ltd, since 1987; Director General, British Standards Institution, 1981–86 (Technical Director, 1976–81); *b* 1 June 1921; *s* of late Comdr Sidney Garland Spickernell, RN, and Florence Elizabeth (*née* March); *m* 1st, 1946, Ursula Rosemary Sheila Money (*d* 1997); one *s* one *d* (and one *s* decd); 2nd, 1998, Carolyn Mary Jenkins. *Educ:* RNEC, Keyham. Served War, HM Ships Abdiel, Wayland, and Engr Officer HM Submarine Statesman, 1943–45. Engr Officer HM Submarines Telemachus, Tudor and Alcide, 1945–50; Submarine Trials Officer, 1950–51; Engrg Dept, HM Dockyard, Portsmouth, 1951–53; SEO: Portsmouth Frigate Sqdn, 1954–55; 2nd Submarine Sqdn, 1956–57; Supt, ULE, Bournemouth, 1958–59; Dep. Captain Supt, AUWE, Portland, 1959–62; Dep. Manager, Engrg Dept, HM Dockyard, Portsmouth, 1962–64; in command, HMS Fisgard, 1965–66; Dep. Dir, Naval Ship Production, 1967–70; Dep. Chief Exec., Defence Quality Assurance Bd, 1970–71; Dir-Gen., Quality Assurance, MoD (PE), 1972–75. Dir, James Martin Associates PLC, 1986–90; Bd Mem., Southern Water, 1987–89; Chm., Jeniva Landfill, 1987–92. Chm., Nat. Council for Quality and Reliability, 1973–75; A Vice-President: Inst. of Quality Assurance, 1974– (Hon. FIQA); Inst. of Trading Standards Admin, 1986–; Vice-Pres., Internat. Orgn for Standardisation, 1985–87; Bd Mem. for Internat. Affairs, BSI, 1986–87; Dir, Turkish Standards Inst., 1987–90; Member: Internat. Acad. of Quality Assurance, 1977–; Design Council, 1984–87; Council, Cranfield Inst. of Technol. FRSA. *Publications:* papers on Quality Assurance. *Recreation:* golf. *Clubs:* Hockley Golf; Chilworth Golf; Royal Fowey Yacht.

SPIEGL, Fritz; musician, writer, broadcaster; *b* 27 Jan. 1926; *s* of Rudolf Spiegl and Josefine Spiegl (*née* Geiringer); *m* 1st, 1952, Bridget Fry; three *d*; 2nd, 1976, Ingrid Frances Romnes. *Educ:* Magdalen College Sch.; Royal Academy of Music (ARAM, FRAM 1986). Designer/typographer, Colman Prentis & Varley, 1941–46; Principal Flautist, Royal Liverpool Philharmonic, 1948–63 (Hon. Life Mem., 1988); sometime flautist: RPO; CBSO; Hallé; BBC NSO; Founder/Conductor, Liverpool Music Group, Liverpool Wind Ensemble, 1949–; Director, The Spieglers, 1975–. Founder, Scouse Press, 1965. Columnist: Liverpool Daily Post, 1970–; Classical Music, 1979–81; Classic CD, 1990–92; Wordplay/Usage and Abusage columns, Daily Telegraph, 1989–97; contributor to: Guardian; Oldie; Independent; BBC Music Magazine, 1994–. Broadcaster in various capacities for BBC: Start the Week, 1972–80; Up to the Hour, 1977–78; Words, 1978; A–Z of Musical Curios, 1978–79; Fritz on Friday, 1978–80; Mainly for Pleasure, 1982–92; Wives of the Great Composers, 1985–86; Loves of the Great Composers, 1986–87; Inflight music programmes, Swissair, Cathay Pacific, 1988–98; Lectr, Swan Hellenic and Noble Caledonia cruises. *Quondam* question-setter, University Challenge. Mem., Local Radio Adv. Council, 1997–2000. Pres., Merseyside Music Teachers' Assoc., 1991–. *Publications:* various edns of music; What the Papers Didn't Mean to Say, 1964; Lern Yerself Scouse, 1965; The Black-on-White Misprint Show, 1966; ABZ of Scouse, 1967; The Growth of a City, 1967; Liverpool Ballads, 1967; The Liverpool Manchester Railway, 1970; Slavers and Privateers, 1970; A Small Book of Grave Humour, 1971; Dead Funny, 1982; Keep Taking the Tabloids, 1983; Music Through the Looking-Glass, 1984; The Joy of Words, 1986; Fritz Spiegl's In-words & Out-words, 1987; Mediaspeak/Mediawrite, 1989; Scally Scouse, 1989; Sing the Titanic, 1993; Sick Notes: a hypochondriacs' dictionary, 1995; Lives, Wives and Loves of the Composers, 1995; Robson Book of Musical Blunders, 1996; A Game of Two Halves, Brian: the language of soccer, 1996; Scouse International, 2001; MuSick Notes: a medical songbook, 2001; contrib. Grove's Dictionary of Music, New Grove Dictionary of Opera. *Recreations:* printing, cooking, inventing and several deadly sins. *Address:* 4 Windermere Terrace, Liverpool L8 3SB. *T:* (0151) 727 2727, *Fax:* (0151) 727 7272; *e-mail:* fritz@scousepress.demon.co.uk. *Clubs:* Garrick; Athenæum (Liverpool).

SPIELBERG, Steven, Hon. KBE 2001; American film director and producer; *b* 18 Dec. 1947; *s* of Arnold Spielberg and Leah (*née* Posner); *m* 1985, Amy Irving (marr. diss. 1989); one *s*; *m* Kate Capshaw; one *s* two *d*, and one adopted *s* one adopted *d. Educ:* Calif State Coll. TV Director, Universal Pictures, 1968. Founder: Amblin Entertainment; Dreamworks SKG. Fellow, BAFTA, 1986. *Films include: directed:* Sugarland Express, 1974; Jaws, 1975; Close Encounters of the Third Kind, 1977; 1941, 1979; Raiders of the Lost Ark, 1981; (also produced) E.T., 1982; (also produced) Twilight Zone—the movie, 1983; Indiana Jones and the Temple of Doom, 1984; The Color Purple, 1985; Empire of the Sun, 1988; Indiana Jones and the Last Crusade, 1989; Hook, 1991; Jurassic Park, 1992; Schindler's List, 1994; The Lost World: Jurassic Park, 1997; Amistad, 1998; Saving Private Ryan, 1998; A. I. Artificial Intelligence, 2001; *produced:* I Wanna Hold Your Hand, 1978; (also co-wrote) Poltergeist, 1982; Gremlins, 1984; Goonies, 1985; Young Sherlock Holmes, 1985; Back to the Future, 1986; Who Framed Roger Rabbit, 1988; Always, 1990; The Flintstones, 1994; Casper, 1995; Men in Black, 1997; The Last Days, 1999. Co-prod., TV series, Band of Brothers, 2001. *Publication:* (jtly) Close Encounters of the Third Kind. *Address:* Amblin Entertainment, 100 Universal City Plaza, Universal City, CA 91608, USA.

SPIERS, Sir Donald (Maurice), Kt 1993; CB 1987; TD 1966; FREng; Chairman, Computing Devices Co. Ltd, since 1997 (Director, since 1994); *b* 27 Jan. 1934; *s* of Harold

Herbert Spiers and Emma (*née* Foster); *m* 1958, Sylvia Mary Lowman; two *s*. *Educ:* Raynes Park County Grammar Sch.; Trinity Coll., Cambridge (MA). CEng, FRAeS. Commnd RE, 1952–54. de Havilland Engine Co., Hatfield, 1957–60; joined Air Min. as SSO, 1960; operational res. on deterrence, 1960–63; trials and analysis, Aden and Radfan, 1964; Kestrel evaluation trial, 1965; Scientific Adviser to FEAF, Singapore, 1967–70; Asst Chief Scientist (RAF), MoD, 1972–77; Asst Dir, Mil. Aircraft Projs, MoD (PE), 1978; Dir of Aircraft Post Design Services, MoD (PE), 1979–81; Dir Gen. Aircraft 1, MoD (PE), 1981–84; Dep. Controller Aircraft, MoD (PE), 1984–86; Controller of R&D Estabts, later of Estabts, Res. and Nuclear Programmes, and Hd of Profession Defence Engrg Service, MoD, 1986–89; Controller Aircraft, and Head of Profession Defence Sci. and Engrg, MoD, 1989–94. Chm., European Helicopter Industries Ltd, 1998–; Director: Meggitt plc, 1995– (Chm., 1998–2001); Messier-Dowty Internat. Ltd, 1998–; TAG Aviation (UK) Ltd, 1999–. Vice Pres., 1993–95, Pres., 1995–96, RAeS. Pres., Popular Flying Assoc., 1997–2000. Gold Medal, RAeS, 1989. *Recreations:* flying aeroplanes, mending cars. *Address:* 20 Paddock Close, Camberley, Surrey GU15 2BN. *Club:* Royal Air Force.

SPIERS, Prof. Edward Michael, PhD; Professor of Strategic Studies, since 1993, and Dean of Research (Arts), since 1999, University of Leeds; *b* 18 Oct. 1947; *s* of Ronald Arthur Spiers, DSC and Margaret Carlisle Laing Spiers (*née* Manson); *m* 1971, Fiona Elizabeth McLeod; one *s* one *d*. *Educ:* Royal High Sch., Edinburgh; Edinburgh Univ. (MA, PhD). University of Leeds: Defence Lectr, 1975–85; Lectr in History, 1985–87; Reader in Strategic Studies, 1987–93; Chm., School of History, 1994–97. Vis. Lectr, Univ. of Alberta, 1987; Leverhulme Res. Fellow, 1991–92. Mem. (C), Edinburgh DC, 1974. *Publications:* Haldane: an army reformer, 1980; The Army and Society 1815–1914, 1980; Radical General: Sir George de Lacy Evans 1787–1870, 1983; Chemical Warfare, 1986; Chemical Weaponry: a continuing challenge, 1989; The Late Victorian Army 1868–1902, 1992; Chemical and Biological Weapons: a study of proliferation, 1994; (ed) Sudan: the reconquest reappraised, 1998; Weapons of Mass Destruction, 2000. *Address:* 170 Alwoodley Lane, Leeds LS17 7PF. *T:* (0113) 268 5493.

SPIERS, Ven. Graeme Hendry Gordon; Archdeacon of Liverpool, 1979–91, Archdeacon Emeritus, since 1991; *b* 15 Jan. 1925; *s* of Gordon and Mary Spiers; *m* 1958, Ann Chadwick; two *s*. *Educ:* Mercers Sch.; London College of Divinity. Westminster Bank, 1941–49; served RNVR, 1943–47. Deacon 1952, Priest 1953; Curate of Addiscombe, 1952–56; Succentor of Bradford Cathedral, 1956–58; Vicar of Speke, 1958–66; Vicar of Aigburth, 1966–80 and Rural Dean of Childwall, 1975–79. Hon. Canon, Liverpool Cathedral, 1977. *Recreation:* gardening. *Address:* 19 Barkfield Lane, Formby, Merseyside L37 1LY. *T:* (01704) 872902.

SPIERS, John Raymond; Chairman, John Spiers Publishing Ltd, since 1988; External Professor, School of Humanities and Social Studies, University of Glamorgan, since 2001 (External Professor, Business School, 1998–2001); independent health policy commentator and consultant; *b* 30 Sept. 1941; *s* of Horace Henry Spiers and Kate Dawson (*née* Root); *m* 1967, Prof. Margaret Ann Boden, *qv* (marr. diss. 1981); one *s* one *d*; partner, 1994, Leigh Richardson (*née* Radford). *Educ:* Redhill Sch., E Sutton, Kent; Catford Coll. of Commerce; Univ. of Sussex (BA 1st Cl. Hons Hist. 1968). Writer and publisher, 1960–; Founder: Harvester Press Ltd (Chm., 1970–88); Harvester Press Microform Pubns Ltd (Chm., 1973–87) (Queen's Award for Export Achievement, 1986); Wheatsheaf Books Ltd (Chm., 1980–88). Special Advr to Dep. Chm., Cons. Party, 1989–90; Consultant Dir, Special Services Dept, Cons. Central Office, 1990–94; Mem., Citizens' Charter Adv. Panel to PM, 1994; Dep. Treas., Cons. Party SE England Area, 1990–92 (Mem., SE Area Council, 1990–92); Pres., Brighton Kemp Town Cons. Assoc., 1991–95. Founder and Chm., Brighton Business Gp, 1989–95. Health Policy Advr, Social Market Foundn, 1994–99; Chairman: Brighton HA, 1991–92; Brighton Health Care NHS Trust, 1992–94; National Association of Health Authorities and Trusts: Mem., Nat. Council and Exec. Cttee, 1993–94; Chm., Nat. Conf. Cttee, 1993–94; Co-Chm., S Thames Network, 1994; Vice-Chm., Provider Cttee, 1993–94; Member: NHS Mgt Exec. Adv. Gps, 1991–98; Bd, Nat. Care Standards Commn, 2001–. Chairman: Patients Assoc., 1995–97 (Actg Chief Exec., 1995–96); Health Policy Cttee, Centre for Policy Studies, 1997–99; Founding Chm., Inst. for Study of Civil Soc., 1999–2000; Member: Exec. Bd, Internat. Health Policy and Management Inst., 1994–98; Adv. Council, Health and Welfare Unit, IEA, 1989–92, 1997–99; (co-opted), Nat. Exec., Voluntary Euthanasia Soc., 1997–99. Co-Chm., The Radical Soc., 1991–2000. Vice-Chm., Grant Maintained Schools Foundn, 1992–98 (Trustee, 1992–98). Trustee: Choice in Educn, 1990–92; Trident Trust, 1992–99 (Vice Chm., 1993–94; Chm., 1994–97); Brighton Internat. Arts Fest., 1989–96; English Nat. Schs Orch., 1998–; League of Mercy, 1999–; Shakespeare Authorship Trust, 2001–. Chm., Alumni Soc., 1983– (Hon. Fellow, 1998), and Mem. Court, 1989–, Univ. of Sussex. Visiting Fellow: NHS Staff Coll., Wales, 1995–; King's Fund Mgt Coll., 1996–; Res. Fellow, 1997–98, Sen. Res. Fellow, Health and Welfare Unit, 1998–99, Head of Health Care Studies, 1999–2000, IEA; Adjunct Schol., Cascade Policy Inst., Portland, Oregon, 1999. Librarian and Mem. Nat. Council, Francis Bacon Soc., 1998–. Companion, Guild of St George, 1971 (Founding Editor, The Companion, 2000–). Freeman, City of London, 2000. FRSA 1994. DUniv Sussex, 1994. JP E Sussex, 1988–90. Kt Grand Cross, Order of St Stanislaus (Poland), 1998. *Publications:* (with P. Coustillas) The Re-discovery of George Gissing, Novelist, 1971; The Invisible Hospital and the Secret Garden: an insider's commentary on the NHS reforms, 1995; Who Owns Our Bodies?: making moral choices in health care, 1997; (ed) Dilemmas in Modern Health Care, 1997; The Realities of Rationing: priority setting in the National Health Service, 1999; contrib. Health Service Jl, British Jl of Health Management, Health Summary, Healthcare Today, Health Director, Sunday Telegraph, Guardian, Daily Express. *Recreations:* collecting 19th century novels (and reading them), writing, walking, supporting The Arsenal, exploring inland waterways on narrow boat Harvester. *Address:* The Gate Cottage, Twyford, Birch Grove, Haywards Heath, W Sussex RH17 7DJ; *e-mail:* 106247.215@compuserve.com. *Club:* Carlton.

SPIERS, Air Cdre Reginald James, OBE 1972; FRAeS; *b* 8 Nov. 1928; *s* of Alfred James Oscar and Rose Emma Alice Spiers; *m* 1956, Cynthia Jeanette Williams; two *d*. *Educ:* Haberdashers' Aske's Sch.; RAF Coll., Cranwell. FRAeS 1975. Commissioned 1949; 247 and 64 Fighter Sqdns, 1950–54; Graduate, Empire Test Pilots' Sch., 1955; Fighter Test Sqdn, A&AEE, 1955–58; CO 4 Fighter Sqdn, 1958–61; PSO to C-in-C RAF Germany, 1961–63; RAF Staff Coll., 1964; FCO, 1965–67; CO RAF Masirah, 1967–68; Chief Test Flying Instructor, ETPS, 1968–71; Air Warfare Course, 1972; Air Secretary's Dept, MoD, 1972–73; MA to Governor of Gibraltar, 1973–75; CO Experimental Flying Dept, RAE Farnborough, 1975–78; Director, Defence Operational Requirements Staff, MoD, 1978–79; Comdt, A&AEE, Boscombe Down, 1979–83, retd. Marketing Exec., Marconi, later GEC, Avionics, 1984–91. *Recreations:* shooting, aviation. *Address:* Barnside, Penton Mewsey, near Andover, Hants SP11 0RQ. *T:* (01264) 772376. *Club:* Royal Air Force.

SPIERS, Ronald Ian; consultant on international affairs, since 1992; Under-Secretary-General, Department of Political and General Assembly Affairs and Secretariat Services, United Nations, 1989–92; *b* 9 July 1925; *s* of Tomas H. and Blanca De P. Spiers; *m* 1949, Patience Baker; one *s* three *d*. *Educ:* Dartmouth Coll., New Hampshire (BA); Princeton Univ. (Master in Public Affairs, PhD). Mem., US Delegn to UN, 1956–60; US Department of State: Dir, Office of Disarmament and Arms Control, 1960–62; Dir, Office of NATO Affairs, 1962–66; Political Counsellor, London, 1966–69; Asst Sec. of State, Politico-Military Affairs, 1969–73; Ambassador to the Bahamas, 1973–74; Minister, London, 1974–77; Ambassador to Turkey, 1977–80; Asst Sec. of State, Bureau of Intelligence and Research, Dept of State, 1980–81; Ambassador to Pakistan, 1981–83; Under Sec. of State for Management, 1983–89. *Recreations:* swimming, music, theatre-going, gardening. *Address:* Middletown Road, South Londonderry, VT 05155, USA.

SPIERS, Shaun Mark; Chief Executive, Association of British Credit Unions, since 1999; *b* 23 April 1962; *s* of Charles Gordon Spiers and Ann Kathleen Spiers (*née* Hutton). *Educ:* St John's Coll., Oxford (BA Hons PPE); King's Coll. London (MA War Studies). Political Officer, SE Co-op, 1987–94. MEP (Lab Co-op) London SE, 1994–99; contested (Lab) London Region, 1999. *Recreations:* music, sport. *Address:* (office) Holyoake House, Hanover Street, Manchester M60 0AS; *e-mail:* shaun.spiers@abcul.org.

SPIGELMAN, Hon. James Jacob, AC 2000; Lieutenant-Governor and Chief Justice, New South Wales, since 1998; *b* 1 Jan. 1946; *s* of Majloch and Gucia Spigelman; *m* 1979, Alice Kalmar; one *s* two *d*. *Educ:* Maroubra Bay Public Sch.; Sydney Boys' High Sch.; Univ. of Sydney (BA, LLB). Sen. Advr and Principal Private Sec. to Prime Minister, 1972–75; Sec., Dept of Media, 1975; called to the Bar, NSW, 1980; in practice at NSW Bar, 1980–98; QC (NSW) 1986; Actg Solicitor Gen., NSW, 1997. *Publications:* Secrecy: political censorship in Australia, 1972; (jtly) The Nuclear Barons, 1981. *Recreations:* tennis, swimming, recumbency. *Address:* Chief Justice's Chambers, Supreme Court of New South Wales, GPO Box 3, Sydney, NSW 2001, Australia. *T:* (2) 92308218.

SPIKINGS, Barry Peter; Partner, Spikings Entertainment (formerly Pleskow/Spikings Partnership), international production and distribution of feature films, since 1992; *b* Boston, Lincs, 23 Nov. 1939; *m* 1st, 1962, Judith Anne Spikings; one *s* one *d*; 2nd, 1978, Dorothy Spikings; two step *d*. *Educ:* Boston Grammar School. Joint Managing Director: British Lion Films Ltd, 1973–75; EMI Films Ltd, 1975–78; Director, EMI Films Inc., 1975–78; Chm. and Chief Exec. Officer, EMI Film and Theatre Corp., 1978–80; Chm., Elstree Studios, 1978–82; Chm. and Chief Exec., Thorn EMI Films Worldwide, 1980–82; Pres. and Chief Operating Officer, Nelson Entertainment Inc., 1986–91. Oscar award as Producer of Best Picture of the Year, for The Deer Hunter, 1979; elected one of America's Greatest Hundred Movies by Amer. Film Inst., 1999; other films include: as producer: Conduct Unbecoming; The Man Who Fell to Earth; Convoy; Texasville; Beyond Rangoon; as distributor: Close Encounters of the Third Kind; The Deep; City Slickers; When Harry Met Sally; The Last Emperor. *Recreation:* making films. *Address:* 19016 Pacific Coast Highway, Malibu, CA 90265, USA. *Club:* Mark's.

SPILLER, John Anthony Walsh, MBE 1979; Technical Adviser to Organisation for Security and Co-operation in Europe/Office for Democratic Institutions and Human Rights Mission, Montenegro, on secondment to Foreign and Commonwealth Office, 1998; *b* 29 Dec. 1942; *s* of C. H. Spiller and Sarah (*née* Walsh), Moycullen, Co. Galway, Eire; *m* 1972, Angela, *d* of Surtees Gleghorn; one *s* one *d*. *Educ:* County Secondary Sch., Bideford; North Devon College. Member Executive, Nat. League of Young Liberals, 1960–61; Organiser, Torrington Constituency Liberal Assoc., 1962–64; Divl Liberal Agent, Cornwall (Northern) Parly Constituency, 1965–71; Northern Regional Organiser (Election Agent, Rochdale By-Elec. 1972 and Berwick-upon-Tweed By-Elec. 1973), 1972–74; Nat. Agent, Liberal Central Assoc., 1974–76; Mem., Liberal Party Gen. Elec. Campaign Cttee, and Press Officer, Gen. Elections Feb. and Oct. 1974; Western Area Agent, 1977–80; Advisor, African Peoples Union, Independence Elections, Zimbabwe, 1980; By-Elec. and Marginal Seats Agent, Liberal Party Org. Headquarters, 1981–82; Sec. Gen., Liberal Party, 1983–85; Co. Liaison Officer, Devonshire PHAB Organisation UK, 1990–92; Sen. Consultant, Western Approaches PR Ltd, 1993–96. Chm., Lib Dem Campaign, Cornwall (Northern), Gen. Election 1992; Advr, Electoral Reform Soc., Democracy Conf., Lithuania, 1992, Estonia, 1995, Croatia, 1997. Conf. Deleg., Moscow, 1995, Armenia, 1995; Observer, Elections: Republic of Georgia, 1995; Bosnia Herzegovina, 1996, Estonia, 1999, on behalf of OSCE. Mem. Bd of Management, Gladstone Benevolent Fund, 1980–98 (Sec. 1980, Hon. Sec., 1993). *Recreations:* golf, walking in Connemara. *Address:* 5 Royston Road, Bideford, Devonshire EX39 3AN.

SPINDLER, Susan Mary; Controller, Innovation and Factual Drama, Drama, Entertainment and Children's Division, BBC, since 2000; *b* 1 March 1955; *d* of Kenneth Spindler and Elsie Spindler (*née* Knapper); *m* 1980, Peter Guy Brown, two *s* one *d*. *Educ:* Wycombe High Sch; Newnham Coll., Cambridge (BA Hons English 1977). Grad. trainee, Thomson Newspapers, 1978–80; BBC 1980–: prodn trainee, 1980–82; Asst Producer and Producer, 1983–88; Producer, Doctors to Be, 1988–92; Ed., QED, 1992–94; Dep. Hd, Sci. Dept, 1994–96; Chief Advr, Editl Policy, 1997; Hd of Strategy, Drama, 1998–99. *Publications:* The Tomorrow's World Book of Food, 1984; Doctors to Be, 1992. *Recreations:* travel, cooking, writing. *Address:* BBC, Centre House, 56 Wood Lane, W12 7SB.

SPINK, Air Marshal Clifford Rodney, CBE 1992 (OBE 1989); FRAeS; Director General, Saudi Armed Forces Project, since 1998; *b* 17 May 1946; *s* of Ronald Charles Spink and Beryl Spink (*née* Phillips); *m* 1977, Caroline Anne Smith; one *s* one *d*. *Educ:* Sheerness Sch.; Halton Apprentice, RAF Coll., Cranwell. FRAeS 1997. Commissioned RAF 1968; Sqn Pilot, 111/56 Sqn, 1970–76; Instructor, RMA Sandhurst, 1976–78; Flight Comdr, 111 Sqn, 1979–82; NDC, 1982–83; HQ RAF Germany, 1983–86; OC No 74 (Fighter) Sqn, 1986–89; Stn Comdr and Dep. Comdr British Forces, Falkland Islands, 1989–90; Detachment Comdr, Dhahran, Gulf conflict, 1990–91; Stn Comdr, RAF Coningsby, 1990–93; rcds, 1993; SASO, No 11 Group, 1993–95; COS No 18 Group, 1995–96; AOC No 11/18 Gp, 1996–98. Pres., ROC Assoc.; Chm., Historic Aviation Assoc. *Recreations:* vintage aircraft flying, winter sports, golf. *Address:* Castlewood House, 77–91 New Oxford Street, WC1A 1DS. *T:* (020) 7829 8505; PO Box 1003, Riyadh 11431, Saudi Arabia. *Club:* Royal Air Force.

SPINK, Prof. Ian Walter Alfred; Professor of Music, London University at Royal Holloway College, then Royal Holloway and Bedford New College, 1974–97, now Emeritus; *b* 29 March 1932; *s* of William James Spink and Margaret Hamilton (*née* Anderson); *m* 1960, Margaret Storry Walton; three *s* four *d*. *Educ:* Mercers' Sch.; Trinity Coll. of Music (BMus 1952); Barber Inst. of Fine Arts, Univ. of Birmingham (MA 1957). Nat. Service, 1953–55, 2nd Lieut, RA. Overseas Examiner for Trinity Coll. of Music in Canada, NZ and Australia, 1958–59; Dir of Music, Westlain GS, Brighton, Sussex, 1960–62; Lectr, then Sen. Lectr, Univ. of Sydney, NSW, 1962–69; RHC, later RHBNC, University of London: Head of Music Dept., 1969–92; Sen. Lectr, 1969–72; Reader, 1972–74; Dean, Fac. of Arts, 1973–75 and 1983–85; Dean, Fac. of Music, and Mem. Senate, Univ. of London, 1974–78. Leverhulme Res. Fellowship, 1996. *Publications:* English Song: Dowland to Purcell, 1974, 2nd edn 1986; The Seventeenth Century, Blackwell History of Music in Britain, vol. 3, 1992; Restoration Cathedral Music 1660–1714, 1995; Henry Lawes: Cavalier songwriter, 2000; editions of music in: The

English Lute-songs, 2nd series, vol. 17, 1961, 2nd edn 1974, vol. 18, 1962, vol. 19, 1966; Musica Britannica, vol. 33, 1971, 2nd edn 1977, vol. 42, 1978; The Works of Henry Purcell, vol. 2, 1990, vol. 4, 1994, vol. 20, 1998, vol. 22a, 2000, vol. 22b, 2001; (contrib.) The New Grove, 1980, 2nd edn 2001; (contrib.) The New Oxford History of Music, vol. 6, 1986; (contrib.) Purcell Studies, 1995; articles in Acta Musicologica, Music and Letters, Proc. Royal Musical Assoc., etc. *Address:* Bridge House, Trumps Green Road, Virginia Water, Surrey GU25 4JA. *T:* (01344) 843039.

SPINK, Dr Robert Michael; MP (C) Castle Point, 1992–97 and since 2001; Director, Harold Whitehead and Partners, Management Consultants, since 1997; *b* 1 Aug. 1948; *s* of George and Brenda Spink; *m* 1968, Janet Mary Barham; three *s* one *d*. *Educ:* Manchester Univ. (research and academic prizes; BSc 1st Cl. Hons Eng 1971); Cranfield Inst. of Technology (MSc Indust Eng 1974; PhD, Sch. of Management, 1989). CEng, MIProdE, MIIM, MIMgt, MIMC, CDipAF. Mill labourer, 1962–64; RAF, 1964–66; EMI Electronics, 1966–77 (Engrg Apprentice; EMI Graduate Apprentice of the Year, 1971); Management consultant, 1977–; Dir and Co-Owner, Seafarer Navigation International, 1980–84; industrial engr, 1984–; Dir, Bournemouth Internat. Airport, 1989–93. Dorset County Councillor, 1985–93 (Chm., Educn Policy Cttee, 1989–91); Mem., Dorset Police Authy, 1985–93. Contested (C) Castle Point, 1997. PPS to Minister of State, Dept of Employment, then Home Office, 1994–97. Mem., Educn Select Cttee, 1992–97; Vice Chm., Backbench Employment Cttee, 1993–94; Chm., All Party Parly Gp for Prisoners Abroad, 1995–97. Dep. Chm., Poole Cons. Assoc., 1984–92; Mem. Nat. Exec., Baby Life Support Systems Charity, 1985–92. *Recreations:* occasional marathons, gardening, potter. *Address:* c/o House of Commons, SW1A 0AA.

SPINKS, Mary Cecilia, RGN; health services consultant, specialising in risk management, audit and expert opinion on malpractice, since 1993; *b* 20 Sept. 1940; *d* of Francis and Mary Clark; *m* 1st, 1961, Robert Donn (marr. diss. 1975); 2nd, 1992, Leslie Oswald Spinks. *Educ:* St Vincent's Convent, Cork; Student Nurse, Whipps Cross Hosp. (RGN 1962); DipN London; William Rathbone Coll.; Thames Polytechnic (DMS). Post-graduate Staff Nurse, Charing Cross Hosp., 1962; Theatre Sister, St Mary's Hosp., Paddington, 1963–64; Theatre Sister, Nursing Officer, Sen. Nursing Officer, Bromley AHA, 1964–83; Dir, Nursing Services, Lewisham and N Southwark HA, 1983–84; Chief Nursing Officer and Dir, Consumer Affairs, Brighton HA, 1984–90; Regl Nursing Officer, NE Thames RHA, 1990–93. Former chm. and mem., nursing, health, editorial and advisory cttees; Chm., Nat. Assoc. of Theatre Nurses, 1975–78; Member: Maidstone HA, 1985–90; NHS Training Authy, 1988–91. Chm., E Berks Community Trust, 1998–. Dir, Florence Nightingale Foundn, 1996–. MRSM 1992. *Publications:* numerous contribs to professional jls. *Recreations:* horse-racing, cricket, gardening. *Address:* 2 Somerford Close, Maidenhead, Berks SL6 8EJ. *T:* (01628) 675526.

SPINNER, Bruno; Ambassador of Switzerland to the Court of St James's, since 2000; *b* 9 Jan. 1948; *s* of Max Spinner and Ruth Spinner-Schaffner; *m* 1976, Madelon Blaser-Giroud; two *s*. *Educ:* Univ. of Zurich (LLM); Univ. of Geneva. Entered Swiss Diplomatic Service, 1976: Attaché, Ankara, 1977; Diplomatic Sec., Mission to EC, Brussels, 1978–82; Dep. Hd of Mission, Ottawa, 1982–85; Hd, Div. of Internat. Law, Federal Dept of Foreign Affairs, Berne, 1985–89 (Legal Advr to Swiss chief negotiator at GATT negotiations (Uruguay Round), 1987–89; Pres., EFTA Cttee of Legal Experts, 1988–89); Minister, Dep. Hd of Mission to EC, Brussels, 1989–91; Mem., Delegn to EEA negotiations, and Vice-Pres., edtl cttee, 1990–92; Ambassador and Hd, Integration Office, Federal Dept of Foreign Affairs and Federal Dept of the Economy, Berne, 1992–99. Hon. Prof. of European Law, Zurich Univ., 1993–2000. Mem., Royal Philatelic Soc., London, 2000. *Recreations:* sports, philately, art. *Address:* Embassy of Switzerland, 16–18 Montagu Place, W1H 2BQ. T: (020) 7616 6030. *Club:* Garrick.

SPINNEY, Ronald Richard, FRICS; Chairman, Hammerson plc, since 1999 (Chief Executive, 1993–99); *b* 1 April 1941; *m* 1st, Julia (*d* 1996); two *d*; 2nd, 1999, Lu; two step *s* two step *d*. *Educ:* Clayesmore Sch.; Coll. of Estate Mgt. Jt Founder, Greycoat plc, 1976, Jt Man. Dir and Dep. Chm., 1983–92. A Crown Estate Comr, 1996–. Non-executive Director: LDDC, 1992–98; Unicorn Children's Theatre, 1992–; Rentokil Initial, 1997–; London First Centre, 1998– (Chm., 2001–); Fuller Smith & Turner, 2000–; Homestyle Gp plc, 2001. Pres., British Property Fedn, 1999–2000. Patron, Nat. Youth Ballet, 1996–. Chm. Govs, Clayesmore Sch., 1997–. *Address:* Hammerson plc, 100 Park Lane, W1Y 4AR.

SPIRO, Prof. Stephen George, MD; FRCP; Professor of Respiratory Medicine, University College London, since 1997; Consultant Physician, since 1977, Head of Department of Thoracic Medicine, since 1993, and Medical Director, since 2001, University College London Hospitals NHS Trust (Clinical Director of Medical Services, 1994–2000); *b* 24 Aug. 1942; *s* of Ludwig Spiro and late Anna Spiro (*née* Freidmann); *m* 1971, Alison Mary Brown; three *s*. *Educ:* Manchester Univ. (BSc Anatomy 1964; MB ChB 1967; MD 1975). FRCP 1981. Consultant Physician, Royal Brompton Hosp., 1977–93. Res. Fellow, Hammersmith Hosp., 1971–73; Sen. Registrar, Royal Brompton Hosp., 1973–77; Fulbright-Hayes Travelling Scholarship, Seattle, 1975–76. Visiting Professor: South African Respiratory Soc., 1993; Univ. of Queensland, Australia, 1994. Pres., European Respiratory Soc., 1996–97. Exec. Ed., Thorax, 1991–95. *Publications:* Drug Treatment of Respiratory Disease, 1994; (jtly) New Perspectives on Lung Cancer, 1994; Carcinoma of the Lung, 1995; Self-Assessment Colour Review of Respiratory Medicine, 1997; The Lung in Auto-Immune Disease, 1997; Comprehensive Respiratory Medicine, 1999. *Recreations:* tennis, flyfishing, worrying about Arsenal, home handyman. *Address:* 66 Grange Gardens, Pinner, Middx HA5 5QF. *Clubs:* Croxley Hall Fly Fishery; Eastcote Tennis.

SPITTLE, Leslie; His Honour Judge Spittle; a Circuit Judge, since 1996; *b* 14 Nov. 1940; *s* of Samuel and Irene Spittle; *m* 1963, Brenda Clayton; three *s*. *Educ:* Teesside Poly. (ACIS); Hull Univ. (LLB). Mgt trainee, Head Wrightson & Co., 1956–62; Lectr in Law, Econs and Accountancy, Bradford Tech. Coll., 1965–66; Sen. Lectr in Law, Teesside Poly., 1966–70. Called to the Bar, Gray's Inn, 1970; in private practice, 1970–96. *Recreations:* family, friends. *Address:* Teesside Crown Court, Middlesbrough, Cleveland TS1 2AE. *T:* (01642) 340000.

SPITTLE, Dr Margaret Flora, (Mrs David Hare), FRCP, FRCR; Consultant Clinical Oncologist: Middlesex Hospital, since 1971; St John's Centre for Diseases of the Skin, St Thomas' Hospital, since 1971; *b* 10 Nov. 1939; *d* of Edwin William Spittle and Ada Florence Spittle (*née* Axam); *m* 1st, 1965, Dr Clive Lucas Harmer (marr. diss. 1977); two *d*; 2nd, 1986, David John Hare. *Educ:* King's Coll., London (AKC 1963; MSc 1969); Westminster Hosp. Med. Sch. (MB BS 1963). MRCS 1963; LRCP 1963, MRCP 1993, FRCP 1995; DMRT 1966; FRCR (Rohan Williams Gold Medal) 1968. Sen. Registrar, Radiotherapy Dept, Westminster Hosp., 1969; Instr., Radiation Div., Stanford Univ. Med. Centre, 1970; Hon. Consultant Clinical Oncologist: W Middx Univ. Hosp., 1971–; Hammersmith Hosp., 1975–; Royal Nat. Throat, Nose and Ear Hosp., 1986–; St Luke's Hosp. for the Clergy, 1993–. Member: Nat. Radiation Protection Bd, 1991– (Chm., Audit Cttee, 1995–); Govt Adv. Cttee on Breast Screening, 1986–; Govt Cttee on Medicine and Radiation in the Envmt, 1993–; Govt Adv. Gp on Ionizing Radiation, 1995–; DoH Commng Gp for Health of the Nation Projects, 1996. Chairman: Multicentre Cancer Chemotherapy Gp, 1985–; UK AIDS Oncology Gp, 1988–. Vice-President: RSocMed, 1994–96 (Sen. Hon. Treas., 1988–94; Pres., Oncology Sect., 1987, Radiology Sect., 1989); Royal Coll. of Radiologists, 1995 (Dean, Faculty of Clin. Oncology, 1994–96); Pres., Assoc. of Head and Neck Oncologists of GB, 1990–92. *Publications:* chapters and articles on cancer of breast, head and neck, skin, and AIDS-related malignancy. *Recreations:* family, golf, ski-ing, gardening, flying. *Address:* Department of Oncology, Middlesex Hospital, Mortimer Street, W1N 8AA. *T:* (020) 7380 9090. *Clubs:* Royal Automobile, Royal Society of Medicine.

SPITZ, Kathleen Emily, (Mrs Heinz Spitz); *see* Gales, K. E.

SPITZ, Prof. Lewis, PhD; FRCS, FRCSE, FRCPCH; Nuffield Professor of Paediatric Surgery, since 1979, and Head of Surgical Unit, since 1992, Institute of Child Health, London; Consultant Surgeon, Great Ormond Street Hospital for Children Trust (formerly Hospital for Sick Children, Great Ormond Street), since 1979; *b* 25 Aug. 1939; *s* of Woolf and Selma Spitz; *m* 1972, Louise Ruth Dyzenhaus; one *s* one *d*. *Educ:* Univ. of Pretoria (MB, ChB); Univ. of the Witwatersrand (PhD). FRCS (*ad eundem*) 1980; FRCSE 1969; Hon. FAAP 1987; FRCPCH 1997. Smith and Nephew Fellow, Liverpool and London, 1971; Paediatric Surgeon, Johannesburg, 1971–74; Consultant Paediatric Surgeon, Sheffield Children's Hosp., 1974–79. Hon. Consultant in Paediatric Surgery to the Army, 1983–. Windermere Vis. Prof., Univ. of Melbourne, 1988; Chafin-Snyder Vis. Prof., Children's Hosp., UCLA, 1992; Santuli Vis. Prof., Babies Hosp., Columbia Univ., NY, 1992; Penman Vis. Prof., Red Cross Meml Hosp. and Univ. of Cape Town, 2000; Suttman Vis. Prof., Montreal, 2000; Visiting Professor: Toronto, 1991; Seattle, 1992; Univ. of Hong Kong, 1993; Indianapolis, Pittsburgh, Washington, 1995; Royal Coll. of Surgeons, Thailand, 1995; Ann Arbor, 1997; Royal Coll. of Surgeons, Korea, 1997; Japanese Surgical Soc., 1998; Albert Einstein Coll. of Medicine, NY, 1999. Lectures: Sulamaa, Children's Hosp., Univ. of Helsinki, 1993; Amer. Pediatric Surgical Assoc., 1995. Member: British Assoc. of Paediatric Surgeons (Pres., 1996–98); Assoc. of Surgeons of GB and Ireland; BPA (Mem. Acad. Bd, 1991–93); British Soc. of Gastroenterology; Med. Bd, Tracheo-oesophogeal Support Soc., 1982–; Invited Mem., RCS, 1997–; Chm., Specialist Adv. Cttee in Paediatric Surgery, 1994–(RCS Rep., 1991–96); RCS Rep on Intercollegiate Bd of Paediatric Surgery, 1994–97. Patron: Children's Wish, 1998; Global Oesophogeal League, 1999–. MRSocMed. Hon. Mem., Paediatric Surgical Assocs of Switzerland, Austria, Greece, Asia, America and S Africa. Bronze Medal, Nordik Soc. of Paediatric Surgeons, 1990. Exec. Editor, Progress in Paediatric Surgery, 1982; Member, Editorial Board: Jl of Paediatric Surgery, 1980–; Archives of Diseases in Childhood, 1984–89; Turkish Jl of Paediatric Surgery, 1987–; Jl of RCSE, 1992–97; Associate Editor, Pediatric Surgery International, 1986–; Editorial Consultant: Surgery in Childhood International, 1996–; Annals of College of Surgery of Hong Kong, 1996–. *Publications:* A Colour Atlas of Paediatric Surgical Diagnosis, 1981; A Colour Atlas of Surgery for Undescended Testes, 1984; Paediatric Surgery, 4th edn 1988 (Rob and Smith Operative Surgery series), 5th edn 1995; chapters in books on paediatrics and surgery; articles on oesophageal atresia, oesophageal replacement, gastro-oesophageal reflux, neonatal surgical conditions, and paediatric oncology. *Recreation:* tennis. *Address:* Institute of Child Health, 30 Guilford Street, WC1N 1EH. *T:* (020) 7242 9789, (020) 7829 8691; (020) 7405 9200.

SPOKES, Ann; *see* Spokes Symonds, A. H.

SPOKES, John Arthur Clayton; QC 1973; *b* 6 Feb. 1931; 2nd *s* of late Peter Spencer Spokes and Lilla Jane Spokes (*née* Clayton), Oxford; *m* 1961, Jean, *yr d* of late Dr Robert McLean and Jean Symington McLean (*née* Barr), Carluke; one *s* one *d*. *Educ:* Westminster Sch.; Brasenose Coll., Oxford. BA 1954; MA 1959. Nat. Service, Royal Artillery, 1949–51 (commnd 1950). Called to Bar, Gray's Inn, 1955, Bencher, 1985; a Recorder, 1972–93. Chm., Data Protection Tribunal, 1985–. Chancellor, Dio. of Winchester, 1985–93. *Recreation:* local history. *Address:* 31 Southgate Street, Winchester, Hants SO23 9EE. *Club:* Leander (Henley-on-Thames).

See also A. H. Spokes Symonds.

SPOKES SYMONDS, Ann (Hazel); Patron, Age Concern England, since 1994 (Chairman, 1983–86; Vice-President, 1987–94); *b* 10 Nov. 1925; *d* of Peter Spencer Spokes and Lilla Jane Spokes (*née* Clayton); *m* 1980, (John) Richard (Charters) Symonds, *qv*. *Educ:* Wychwood Sch., Oxford; Masters Sch., Dobbs Ferry, NY, USA; St Anne's Coll., Oxford (BA 1947; MA). Organising Secretary: Oxford Council of Social Service, 1959–74; Age Concern Oxford, 1958–80. Dir, ATV, 1978–81; Mem. W Midlands Bd, Central Indep. Television plc, 1981–92. Mem., Thames Valley Police Authy, 1973–85; Chm., No 5 Police Dist. Authy Cttee, 1982–85; Vice-Chm., Personal Social Services Council, 1978–80; Chm., Social Services Cttee, ACC, 1978–82; Mem. Bd, Anchor Housing Assoc., 1976–83, 1985–94; Member: Prince of Wales' Adv. Gp on Disability, 1983–90; Oftel Adv. Cttee for Disabled and Elderly People, 1985–91; Hearing Aid Council, 1986–89; Trustee, CERT, 1986–89. Member: Oxford City Council, 1957–95 (Lord Mayor, 1976–77; Hon. Alderman, 1995–); Oxfordshire CC, 1974–85 (Chm., 1981–83). Contested (C) NE Leicester, 1959, Brigg, 1966 and 1970. Mem., Soc. of Authors, 1992–. FRSA 1991. *Publications:* Celebrating Age: an anthology, 1987; Havens Across the Sea, 1990; The Great Grosvenor Hotel Scandal, 1993; Storks, Black Bags and Gooseberry Bushes, 1993; The Changing Faces of Wolvercote, Wytham and Godstow, 1997; The Changing Faces of North Oxford, Books One and Two, 1998; The Changing Faces of Iffley, 1999; The Changing Faces of Rose Hill, 2000. *Recreations:* lawn tennis, golf, photography, enjoying cats. *Address:* 43 Davenant Road, Oxford OX2 8BU. *T:* (01865) 515661.

See also J. A. C. Spokes.

SPOONER, Prof. Frank Clyffurde, MA, PhD, LittD; Professor of Economic History, University of Durham, 1966–85, now Emeritus; *b* 5 March 1924; *s* of Harry Gordon Morrison Spooner. *Educ:* Bromley Grammar Sch.; Christ's Coll., Cambridge. Hist. Tripos, 1st cl., Pt I 1947 and Pt II 1948; MA 1949; PhD 1953; LittD 1985. War Service, Sub-Lt (S) RNVR, 1943–46; Bachelor Research Scholar, 1948; Chargé de Recherches, CNRS, Paris, 1949–50; Allen Scholar, 1951; Fellow, Christ's Coll., Cambridge, 1951–57; Commonwealth Fund Fellow, 1955–57 at Chicago, Columbia, New York, and Harvard Univs; Ecole Pratique des Hautes Etudes, VI Section, Sorbonne, 1957–61; Lectr, Univ. of Oxford, 1958–59; Vis. Lectr in Econs, Harvard Univ., 1961–62; Irving Fisher Research Prof. of Econs, Yale Univ., 1962–63; Univ. of Durham: Lectr, 1963; Reader, 1964; Resident Tutor-in-charge, Lumley Castle, 1965–70; Dir, Inst. of European Studies, 1969–76; Leverhulme Fellow, 1976–78; Leverhulme Emeritus Fellow, 1985–86. FRHistS 1970; FSA 1983. Prix Limantour de l'Académie des Sciences Morales et Politiques, 1957; West European Award, British Academy, 1979; Ernst Meyer Award, 1983. *Publications:* L'économie mondiale et les frappes monétaires en France, 1493–1680, 1956, revised edn The International Economy and Monetary Movements in France, 1493–1725, 1972; Risks at Sea: Amsterdam insurance and maritime Europe 1766–1780, 1983; contribs to joint works and to jls. *Recreations:* music, photography, walking. *Club:* Oxford and Cambridge.

SPOONER, Sir James (Douglas), Kt 1981; Director, John Swire & Sons, since 1970; *b* 11 July 1932; *s* of late Vice-Adm. E. J. Spooner, DSO, and Megan Spooner (*née* Megan Foster, the singer); *m* 1958, Jane Alyson, *d* of late Sir Gerald Glover; two *s* one *d*. *Educ:* Eton Coll. (Fellow, 1990); Christ Church, Oxford. Chartered Accountant 1962; Partner, Dixon Wilson & Co., Chartered Accountants, 1963–72; Chm., Vantona Viyella, subseq. Coats Viyella, 1969–89. Chm., NAAFI, 1973–86 (Dir, 1968–86); Director: Abingworth, 1973–91; Morgan Crucible, 1978–97 (Chm., 1983–97); J. Sainsbury, 1981–94; Barclays Bank, 1983–94; Hogg Robinson Gp, 1971–85 (Dep. Chm., 1971–85); Dep. Chm., Royal Opera House, Covent Garden, 1992–97 (Dir, 1987–97); Chm. of Trustees, British Telecom Pension Scheme, 1992–98. Chm. Council, King's College London, 1986–98; Gov., RAM, 1997–. *Recreations:* music, history. *Address:* Swire House, 59 Buckingham Gate, SW1E 6AJ. *Clubs:* Beefsteak, Brooks's.

SPORBORG, Christopher Henry, CBE 2001; Chairman, Countrywide Assured Group plc (formerly Hambro Countrywide), since 1986; *b* 17 April 1939; *s* of late H. N. Sporborg and of Mary (*née* Rowlands); *m* 1961, Lucinda Jane (*née* Hanbury); two *s* two *d*. *Educ:* Rugby School; Emmanuel College, Cambridge (BA Hons). Nat. Service, Coldstream Guards, 1957–59 (Lieut). Hambros Bank, 1962–95: Dir, 1970; Dep. Chm., 1983–95; Hambros PLC: Vice-Chm., 1986–90; Dep. Chm., 1990–98. Chairman: United Racecourses (Hldgs), 1994–96; Racecourse Hldgs Trust, 1998– (Dir, 1994–); Dep. Chm., C. E. Heath PLC, 1994–97; Director: Getty Images Inc., 1997–; Lindsay Morden Ltd, 1999–. Mem., Jockey Club, 1982–; Dir, Jockey Club Estates, 1985–; Mem., Horserace Totalisator Bd, 1993–. Trustee: Develt Trust (for the Mentally Handicapped); Sir Jules Thorn Charitable Trust; Fitzwilliam Family Trusts. *Recreations:* hunting (Joint Master, Puckeridge Foxhounds), racing (owner and permit holder), bridge. *Address:* Brooms Farm, Upwick Green, Albury, Ware, Herts SG11 2JX. *T:* (01279) 771444. *Club:* Boodle's.

SPOTSWOOD, Marshal of the Royal Air Force Sir Denis (Frank), GCB 1971 (KCB 1966; CB 1961); CBE 1946; DSO 1943; DFC 1942; *b* 26 Sept. 1916; *s* of late F. H. Spotswood and M. C. Spotswood; *m* 1942, Ann (*née* Child); one *s*. Commissioned in RAF, 1936; UK Service in Squadrons, 1937–41; No 209 Squadron, 1939–41. Served War of 1939–45 (despatches twice, DSO). Chief Instructor, Operation Training Unit, 1941–42; Officer Commanding No 500 (County of Kent) Squadron, RAuxAF, 1942–43; Director of Plans, HQ Supreme Allied Commander, South-East Asia, 1944–46; Directing Staff, RAF Staff Coll., 1946–48; Officer Commanding RAF (Fighter) Stations, Horsham St Faith and Coltishall, 1948–50; Directing Staff, Imperial Defence Coll., 1950–52; Exchange Duties, HQUSAF in USA, 1952–54; Officer Commanding RAF (Fighter) Station, Linton-on-Ouse, 1954–56; Deputy Director of Plans, Air Ministry, 1956–58; AOC and Commandant, RAF Coll., Cranwell, 1958–61; Assistant Chief of Staff (Air Defence), SHAPE, 1961–63; AOC No 3 Group, RAF Bomber Command, 1964–65; C-in-C RAF Germany, 1965–68; Commander, 2nd Allied Tactical Air Force, 1966–68; AOC-in-C, RAF Strike Command, 1968–71; Comdr, UK Air Defence Region, 1968–71; Chief of the Air Staff, 1971–74. Group Captain, 1954; Air Commodore, 1958; Air Vice-Marshal, 1961; Air Marshal, 1965; Air Chief Marshal, 1968; Marshal of the RAF, 1974. ADC to the Queen, 1957–61, Air ADC to the Queen, 1970–74. Vice-Chm. and Dir, Rolls Royce Ltd, 1974–80; Chm., Turbo Union Ltd, 1975–80; Director: RR/Turbomeca Ltd; Dowty Gp, 1980–87; Smiths Industries ADS, 1980–91 (Chm., 1980–82). Pres., SBAC, 1978–79. Chm. of Governors, Royal Star and Garter Home, 1981–85 (Gov., 1974–80); Vice-Patron, RAF Museum (Chm. of Trustees, 1974–80). FRAeS 1975. Officer of the Legion of Merit (USA). *Recreations:* golf, sailing, bridge. *Address:* Coombe Cottage, Hambleden, Henley-on-Thames, Oxon RG9 6SD. *Clubs:* Royal Air Force; Phyllis Court (Henley); Huntercombe Golf.

SPOTTISWOOD, Air Vice-Marshal James Donald, CB 1988; CVO 1977; AFC 1971; Military Advisor to Airwork Ltd, Bournemouth International Airport, since 1997 (Managing Director, 1989–97); *b* 27 May 1934; *s* of James Thomas Spottiswood and Caroline Margaret Spottiswood; *m* 1957, Margaret Maxwell (*née* Harrison); two *s* one *d*. *Educ:* West Hartlepool Grammar School; Boston Univ., USA (MA). Enlisted RAF, 1951, commissioned, 1952; 617 Sqn, 1962–64; Royal Naval Staff Coll., 1965; PSO to C-in-C Middle East, 1966–67; Commanded 53 Sqn, 1968–70; JSSC, 1970; Commanded: RAF Thorney Island, 1972–75; RAF Benson, 1975–76; Dep. Captain, the Queen's Flight, 1975–76; RCDS, 1978; Secretary to IMS, HQ NATO, 1980–83; DG of Trng, RAF, 1983–85; Air Officer Trng, RAF Support Comd, 1985–89, retired. Vice Pres., Support Services Div., Short's, 1994–97. Chm., British Gliding Assoc., 1989–97. FIMgt (FBIM 1983). *Recreations:* gliding, sailing, golf. *Address:* Royal Bank of Scotland, 49–51 Old Christchurch Road, Bournemouth BH1 1EG. *Club:* Royal Air Force.

SPOTTISWOODE, Clare Mary Joan, CBE 1999; Member, Management Group, PA Consulting Group, since 1999; *b* 20 March 1953; *d* of Charlotte and Tony Spottiswoode; *m* 1977, Oliver Richards; one *s* three *d*. *Educ:* Cheltenham Ladies' Coll.; Clare Coll., Cambridge (MA Maths Pt 1, Economics Pt 2); Yale Univ. (MPhil). HM Treasury, 1977–80; Spottiswoode Trading, 1980–84 (wholesale importing business); Chm. and Chief Exec., Spottiswoode and Spottiswoode (micro computer software), 1984–90; Dir Gen. of Gas Supply, 1993–98; Sen. Vice Pres. of Regulatory Affairs, Europe, Azurix, Enron, 1998–99. Hon. DSc Brunel, 1997. *Publications:* Quill, 1984; Abacus, 1984. *Recreations:* children, gardening, theatre.

SPRACKLING, Maj.-Gen. Ian Oliver John, OBE 1977; Master of Signals, since 1997; *b* 3 Oct. 1936; *m* 1959, Ann Vonda (*née* Coote); two *s*. *Educ:* Bristol Grammar School; RMCS (BSc Eng); psc, RCDS. RMA Sandhurst, 1955; 2nd Lieut, Royal Corps of Signals, 1957; RMCS, 1958–61; served Far East, UK, BAOR, 1961–75; Staff Officer, Sultan of Oman's Armed Forces, 1975–77; CO, Electronic Warfare Regt, BAOR, 1977–79; Col, Cabinet Office, 1979–81; Comdr, Catterick Garrison, 1982–84; RCDS 1984; Dir, Mil. Assistance Overseas, 1985–86; Dir Gen., Management and Support of Intelligence, MoD, 1986–89, retired. Defence Advr, 1989–92, Hd of Russian practice, Moscow, 1993–96, Andersen Consulting. Non-exec. Dir, i Ventures Capital, 2000–. *Recreations:* bridge, socialising, keep fit, watching Rugby. *Address:* 2 Arundel Street, WC2R 3LT. *Clubs:* Army and Navy; Fadeaways.

SPRAGGS, Rear-Adm. Trevor Owen Keith, CB 1983; CEng, FIEE; Chief of Staff to Commander-in-Chief, Naval Home Command, 1981–83; *b* 17 June 1926; *s* of Cecil James Spraggs and Gladys Maude (*née* Morey); *m* 1st, 1955, Mary Patricia Light (*d* 1983); two *s*; 2nd, 1986, Gwynedd Kate (*née* Adams) *widow* of Reginald A. W. Green, CEng, MIMechE. *Educ:* Portsmouth Grammar Sch.; St John's Coll., Southsea; Imperial College of Science and Technology, London (BScEng, ACGI). Joined Royal Navy, 1945; courses: HM Ships: King Alfred, Leander, Harrier, 1945–47; Admiralty Compass Obs., Slough, 1948; BRNC, Dartmouth, 1948–50; HM Ships: Dryad, Vanguard, Vernon, Collingwood, Ariel, Falcon, 1950–61; AEI, Manchester, 1962; RNEC, 1962–66; HMS Collingwood, 1966–69 and 1972–75; RNEC, 1969–72, and, as Dean, 1979–80; Dean, RNC, Greenwich, 1975–77; Dir of Naval Trng Support, Dir of Naval Educn and Trng Support, 1977–79; Chief Naval Instr Officer, 1981–83. ADC to the Queen, 1979. Member: Nautical Studies Bd of CNAA, 1975–80; Maritime Studies Adv. Cttee of Plymouth Polytech., 1979–80; Cttee of Management, Royal Hosp. Sch., Holbrook, 1981–83; Governor: Fareham Technical Coll., 1972–75; RN Sch. for Officers' Daughters, Haslemere, 1975–77. Pres., Combined Services and RN Amateur Athletic Assocs, 1981–83. *Recreations:* golf, boating, gardening. *Address:* 46 Sinah Lane, Hayling Island, Hants PO11 0HH. *Clubs:* Royal Naval Sailing Association; Hayling Golf.

SPRAGUE, David Keith, MVO 1972; HM Diplomatic Service, retired; High Commissioner, Sierra Leone, 1991–93; *b* 20 Feb. 1935; *m* 1958, Audrey Mellon; two *s* one *d*. *Educ:* King Edward VI Grammar Sch., Camp Hill, Birmingham. Foreign Office, 1953; Nat. Service, 1953–55; FO, 1955, served Addis Ababa, Paris, Belgrade, Budapest, Kuala Lumpur, Abidjan, Sofia, and FCO; Dep. High Comr, Madras, 1986–89; Ambassador to Mongolia, 1989–91. *Recreations:* bridge, golf. *Address:* 5 Deepdene Drive, Dorking, Surrey RH5 4AD.

SPRAKE, Anthony Douglas; HM Diplomatic Service; Consul-General, Melbourne, since 2001; *b* 16 July 1944; *s* of Douglas Alfred Sprake and Doris Elizabeth Sprake (*née* Grindley); *m* 1977, Jane Bonner McNeill; one *s* (and one *s* decd). *Educ:* City of Bath Boys' Sch.; Univ. of Keele (BA Hons Maths and Physics). Asst Principal, Min. of Labour, 1968–72; Private Sec. to Parly Under-Sec. of State for Employment, 1972–73; Principal, Dept of Employment, 1973–77; Labour Attaché, British Embassy, Brussels, 1977–79; joined Diplomatic Service, 1980: FCO, 1980–82; Dep. High Comr, Freetown, Sierra Leone, 1982–85; Defence Dept, FCO, 1986–88; MoD (on secondment), 1989; Counsellor (Commercial), The Hague, 1990–94; Head, Cultural Relns Dept, FCO, 1994–96; Minister and Consul Gen., Peking, 1996–2000; Hd, China and Hong Kong Dept, FCO, 2000. *Recreations:* sailing, theatre, bridge. *Address:* c/o Foreign and Commonwealth Office, King Charles Street, SW1A 2AH; 160 Rosendale Road, West Dulwich, SE21 8LG. *T:* (020) 8670 5793.

SPRATT, Prof. Brian Geoffrey, PhD; FMedSci; FRS 1993; Professor of Molecular Microbiology, Imperial College School of Medicine, since 2001; Wellcome Trust Principal Research Fellow, since 1989; *b* 21 March 1947; *s* of Clarence Albert Spratt and Marjory Alice (*née* Jeffreys); *m* 1st; one *s*; 2nd, 1995, Jiaji Zhou; one *s*. *Educ:* Tonbridge Sch.; University Coll. London (BSc, PhD). Research Fellow: Princeton Univ., 1973–75; Leicester Univ., 1975–80; Sussex University: Lectr in Biochem., 1980–87; Reader in Molecular Genetics, 1987–89; Prof., 1989–98; Prof. of Biology, Oxford Univ., 1998–2001. Founder FMedSci 1998. *Publications:* numerous pubns on microbiol. and genetics in learned jls. *Address:* Department of Infectious Disease Epidemiology, Imperial College School of Medicine, St Mary's Hospital, W2 1PG. *T:* (020) 7594 3629, *Fax:* (020) 7262 8140.

SPRATT, Sir Greville (Douglas), GBE 1987; TD 1962, Bar 1968; DL; JP; Underwriting Member of Lloyd's, 1950–98; Lord Mayor of London, 1987–88; *b* 1 May 1927; *e s* of Hugh Douglas Spratt and Sheelah Ivy (*née* Stace); *m* 1954, Sheila Farrow Wade; three *d*. *Educ:* Leighton Park; Charterhouse; Sandhurst. Served Coldstream Guards, 1945–46; commnd Oxfordshire and Bucks LI, 1946; seconded to Arab Legion; served Palestine, Trans Jordan and Egypt, 1946–48; GSO III (Ops and Intell.), 1948. Lloyd's, 1948–61; joined J. & N. Wade Gp of Electrical Distributors, 1961; Dir, 1969–76 and Man. Dir, 1972–76. Dir, 1989–92, Chm., 1991–92, City and West End Regl Adv. Bd, National Westminster Bank; Chairman: Forest Mere Ltd, 1993–96 (Dir, 1991–96); Claremount Underwriting Agency, 1994–97; Kingsmead Underwriting Agency, 1997–99; Director: Williams Lea Gp, 1989–96; Charterhouse Enterprises Ltd, 1991–95; Craigie Taylor Internat., 1995–96. Lieut of the City of London, 1972; Life Mem., Guild of Freemen, 1977 (Mem. Court, 1982–90); Liveryman, Ironmongers' Co., 1977– (Mem. Ct, 1982–; Master, 1995–96); Alderman, Castle Baynard Ward, 1978–95; JP 1978; Sheriff of the City of London, 1984–85; DL Greater London, 1986; Mem., Police Cttee, 1989–91, Planning and Communications Cttee, 1990–91, Corp. of City of London. Joined HAC Infantry Bn as private, 1950; re-commnd 1950; CO, 1962–65; Regtl Col, 1966–70; Mem., Ct of Assts, HAC, 1960–70 and 1978–95; ADC to the Queen, 1973–78; Mem., City TA&VRA, 1960– (Vice Chm., 1973–77, Chm., 1977–82); Vice Pres., TA&VRA for Greater London, 1994 (Chm., 1991–94; Mem., Exec. and Finance Cttee, 1977–94); Hon. Colonel: City and NE sector, London ACF, 1983–99; 8th Bn, The Queen's Fusiliers (City of London), 1988–92; The London Regt, 1992–95. Church Comr, 1993–96. Chm., Action Res. for the Crippled Child, 1989–99 (Mem. Council, 1982–; Mem. Haslemere Cttee, 1971–82); President: Alzheimer's Soc., Haslemere, 1995–; Royal British Legion, Haslemere (St James Vice Pres., 1991–); London Fedn of Old Comrades Assocs, 1983–; Vice President: Not Forgotten Assoc., 1990–; British Red Cross, 1993– (Dep. Pres., London, 1983–91); Mem. Council, Reserve Forces Assoc., 1981–84. Chm., Anglo Jordanian Soc., 1990–97; Member: Cttee, Guildhall Sch. of Music and Drama, 1978–80 (Hon. Mem., 1988–); Court, City Univ., 1981–88 (Chancellor, 1987–88); Governing Bodies of Girls' Schs Assoc., 1982–90; Governor: St Ives Sch., 1976– (Vice Chm., 1977–86; Chm., 1986–90); King Edward's Sch., Witley, 1978–96 (Vice-Pres., 1989–96); Christ's Hosp., 1978–95; Bridewell Royal Hosp., 1978–96; City of London Sch. for Girls, 1981–82; Malvern Girls' Coll., 1982–90; St Paul's Cathedral Choir Sch., 1985–99; Charterhouse, 1985–99 (Chm. Governing Body, 1989–95); City of London Freemen's Sch., 1992–95; Life Governor, Corp. of the Sons of the Clergy, 1985–; Patron: Internat. Centre for Child Studies, 1985–; Surrey Charity Gp, 1989–; Emily Appeal, 1992–98; Vice Patron, Almshouse Assoc., 1997–; Chm., David Shepherd Conservation Foundn, 1996–, Mem., St Paul's Cathedral Court of Advisers, 1993–99. Mem., Surrey Scout Council, 1990–. Blackdown Cttee, Nat. Trust, 1977–87. Trustee: Chichester Theatre; Chichester Cathedral; Endowment of St Paul's Cathedral; Childrens' Research Internat. Carthusian Trust; Charterhouse Soc.; Castle Baynard Educnl Trust; Special Trustee, St Bartholomew's Hosp., 1989–96. FRSA; FRGS. Hon. DLitt City Univ., 1988. KStJ 1987 (OStJ 1985). Chevalier de la Légion d'Honneur, 1961; Commandeur de l'Ordre National du Mérite, 1984; Commander, Order of the Lion, Malaŵi, 1985; Mem., Nat. Order of Aztec Eagle, Mexico, 1985; Order of St Olav, Norway, 1988; Order of Merit, Senegal, 1988. *Recreations:* tennis, music, military history. *Address:* West Kingsley Place, Kingsley Green, West Sussex GU27 3LR. *T:* (01428) 644367, *Fax:* (01428) 641405. *Clubs:* City Livery, Guildhall, United Wards; Cowdray Park Golf.

SPRENT, Prof. Janet Irene, OBE 1996; DSc; FRSE; Professor of Plant Biology, University of Dundee, 1989–98, now Emeritus (Deputy Principal, 1995–98); *b* 10 Jan. 1934; *d* of James William and Dorothy May Findlater; *m* 1955, Peter Sprent. *Educ:* Slough High Sch. for Girls; Imperial Coll. of Science and Technol., London (BSc; ARCS 1954); Univ. of Tasmania (PhD 1958); Univ. of London (DSc 1988). FRSE 1990. Scientific Officer, Rothamsted Expmtl Stn, 1954–55; ICIANZ Res. Fellow, Univ. of Tasmania, 1955–58; Botany Mistress, Rochester Girls' Grammar Sch., 1959–61; Lectr, subseq. Sen. Lectr, Goldsmiths' Coll., London, 1960–67; University of Dundee: successively Res. Fellow, Lectr, Sen. Lectr and Reader, 1967–89; Dean, Faculty of Science and Engrg, 1987–89; Hd, Dept of Biol Scis, 1992–95. Hon. Res. Prof., Scottish Crop Res. Inst., 1991–. Extensive overseas collaboration, eg Australia, Brazil, Kenya, in nitrogen fixing crop and tree research. Member: Council, NERC, 1991–95; SHEFC, 1992–96; (indep.) JNCC, 1994–2000; Bd, Scottish Natural Heritage, 2001–. Mem. Governing Body and Trustee, MacAuley Land Use Res. Inst., 1990– (Chm., 1995–2001). *Publications:* The Biology of Nitrogen Fixing Organisms, 1979; The Ecology of the Nitrogen Cycle, 1987; (with P. Sprent) Nitrogen Fixing Organisms: pure and applied aspects, 1990; (with P. Sprent) Suilven's World, 1995; papers in scientific jls and chapters in books and symposium vols. *Recreations:* flying (St John's Air Wing), hill-walking, gardening, music. *Address:* 32 Birkhill Avenue, Wormit, Newport on Tay, Fife DD6 8PW. *T:* (01382) 541706. *Club:* Farmers'.

SPRIDDELL, Peter Henry; Director: Capital & Counties plc, 1988–94; Capital Shopping Centres plc, 1994–2000; Royal Artillery Museums Ltd, 1990–94; *b* 18 Aug. 1928; *s* of Thomas Henry Spriddell and Eva Florence Spriddell; *m* 1952, Joyce Patricia (*née* Haycock); two *s* one *d. Educ:* Plymouth Coll.; Exeter Coll., Oxford (MA); Harvard Business Sch. Marks & Spencer: store management, 1951–68; Sen. Exec. Store Operations, 1968–70; Dir, 1970–88; Alternate Exec. Dir, 1970–72; Exec. Dir Personnel, 1972–75; Exec. Dir Store Operations, Transport, Building and Store Develt, Real Estate, 1975–88; Dir, NFC, 1978–82; non-exec. Mem., British Rail Property Bd, 1986–2001. Mem. Bd, British Council of Shopping Centres, 1983–95 (Pres., 1988–89). Mem. Council, Templeton Coll., Oxford (formerly Oxford Centre for Management Studies), 1978–. Mem. Cttee, Wine Soc., 1998–2000. FRSA. Freeman, City of London; Liveryman, Worshipful Co. of Paviors, 1984. *Recreations:* music, golf. *Address:* 2 Chorleywood House, Rickmansworth Road, Chorleywood, Herts WD3 5SL. *T:* (01923) 286180. *Club:* Moor Park Golf.

SPRIGGE, Prof. Timothy Lauro Squire, PhD; FRSE; Professor Emeritus, University of Edinburgh, since 1989; *b* 14 Jan. 1932; *s* of Cecil and Katriona Sprigge; *m* 1959, Giglia Gordon; one *s* twin *d. Educ:* Gonville and Caius Coll., Cambridge (MA, PhD). FRSE 1993. Lecturer in Philosophy, University Coll. London, 1961–63; Lectr in Philosophy, 1963–70, Reader in Philosophy, 1970–79, Univ. of Sussex; Prof. of Logic and Metaphysics, 1979–89, Endowment Fellow, 1989–98, Univ. of Edinburgh (Hon. Fellow, 1998). Visiting Associate Professor, Univ. of Cincinnati, 1968–69. Member: Aristotelian Soc., 1960– (Pres., 1991–92); Mind Assoc., 1955–; Assoc. for the Advancement of Amer. Philosophy, 1978–; Scots Philosophical Club, 1979–. Chm., St Andrew Animal Fund, 1991–. *Publications:* ed, Correspondence of Jeremy Bentham, vols 1 and 2, 1968; Facts, Words and Beliefs, 1970; Santayana: an examination of his philosophy, 1974; The Vindication of Absolute Idealism, 1983; Theories of Existence, 1985; The Rational Foundations of Ethics, 1988; James and Bradley: American truth and British reality, 1993; contribs to various vols of philosophical essays and to periodicals, incl. Mind, Philosophy, Inquiry, Nous. *Recreation:* backgammon. *Address:* 31a Raeburn Place, Edinburgh EH4 1HX. *T:* (0131) 315 2443; *e-mail:* sprigge@holyrood.ed.ac.uk.

SPRIGGS, Elizabeth; actress; *b* 18 Sept. 1929; *m* Murry Manson; one *d. Educ:* Royal Sch. of Music. Early repertory experience with Bristol Old Vic and Birmingham Rep.; joined RSC, 1962; *stage* includes: Royal Shakespeare Company: Hamlet; Romeo and Juliet; Julius Caesar, The Merry Wives of Windsor, 1968; A Delicate Balance, 1969; Twelfth Night, Major Barbara, and London Assurance, 1970; Much Ado about Nothing, 1971; Othello, 1971; Misalliance, 1986; National Theatre: Blithe Spirit, 1976; Volpone, and The Country Wife, 1977; Macbeth, and Love Letters on Blue Paper (SWET Award for best supporting actress), 1978; When We Are Married, Whitehall, 1986; Arsenic and Old Lace, Chichester, 1991; *television* includes: series: The Glittering Prizes, 1976; Shine on Harvey Moon, 1982–85, 1995; Simon and the Witch; Watching; Lovejoy; Sherlock Holmes; Jeeves and Wooster; Boon; Heartbeat; Ruth Rendel Mysteries; Inspector Alleyn, 1993; Midsomer Murders; Playing the Field, 1997–99; serials: Strangers and Brothers, 1986; Oranges are not the only fruit, 1990; The Old Devils, 1991; Anglo-Saxon Attitudes, 1991; Middlemarch, 1994; Taking Over the Asylum, 1994; Martin Chuzzlewit, 1994; Wives and Daughters, 1999; plays: Able's Will, 1977; Afternoon Off, 1979; We, the Accused, 1980; The Merry Wives of Windsor, 1983; Henry IV, 1996; *films* include: Impromptu, 1992; Sense and Sensibility, 1996; The Secret Agent; Paradise Road; Alice in Wonderland, 1998; A Christmas Carol, 1999. *Address:* c/o Fionna McCullock, ICM, Oxford House, 76 Oxford Street, W1N 0AX.

SPRING, Sir Dryden (Thomas), Kt 1994; dairy farmer and company director; Director, since 1983, Chairman, 1989–99, New Zealand Dairy Board; *b* 6 Oct. 1939; *s* of Maurice Spring and Violet Grace Spring; *m* 1960, Christine Margaret McCarthy; three *s* three *d. Educ:* Walton Primary Sch.; Matamata Coll. NZ Co-operative Dairy Co. Ltd: Dir, 1973–98; Dep. Chm., 1979–82; Chm., 1982–89. Director: Rural Banking and Finance Corp., 1974–88; Maramarua Coalfields Ltd, 1978–84; Nufarm (formerly Fernz Corp.) Ltd, 1982–; Goodman Fielder Ltd, 1989– (Dep. Chm., 2000–); Nat. Bank of NZ, 1994–; Maersk New Zealand Ltd; Fletcher Building Ltd, and other cos; Chairman: WEL Networks Ltd; Ericsson Communications NZ Ltd; Fletcher Challenge Forests Ltd; Dep. Chm., Ports of Auckland Ltd, 1988–94. Member: Prime Minister's Enterprise Council, 1991–94; Asian Pacific Econ. Co-operation Eminent Persons Gp, 1994–96; Trustee, Asia 2000 Foundn of NZ, 1996–. Hon. Chm., NZ/Philippines Business Council, 1992–98. Chm., ASEAN/NZ Combined Business Council, 1998–99; NZ Chm., APEC Business Adv. Council; Patron, NZ/Thailand Business Council, 1995–98. Fellow, 1993, Dist. Fellow, 2000, Inst. of Dirs in NZ. Life Mem., Federated Farmers of NZ (Waikato), 1987. Dist. Fellow, Massey Univ. of Agric., 1999. Hon. DSc Massey, 2000. NZ Commemoration Medal, 1990. *Recreations:* sport, reading. *Address:* 124 Burwood Road, Matamata, New Zealand. *Clubs:* Wellington; Te Aroha; College Old Boys Rugby.

SPRING, Richard, (Dick); Member of the Dáil (TD) (Lab), North Kerry, since 1981; Deputy Prime Minister, 1982–87 and 1993–97; *b* 29 Aug. 1950; *s* of late Daniel and Anne Spring; *m* 1977, Kristi Lee Hutcheson; two *s* one *d. Educ:* Mt St Joseph Coll., Roscrea; Trinity Coll., Dublin (BA 1972). Called to the Bar, King's Inns, Dublin, 1975; in practice on Munster Circuit, 1977–81. Leader of Irish Labour Party, 1982–97; Minister of State, Dept of Justice, 1981–82; Minister for the Environment, 1982–83; Minister for Energy, 1983–87; Minister for Foreign Affairs, 1993–97. Associate Fellow, Kennedy Sch. of Govt, Harvard, 1998–; Fellow, Salzburg Seminar, 1998–. *Recreations:* swimming, reading, golf. *Address:* Dunroamin, Cloonanorig, Tralee, Co. Kerry, Ireland. *T:* (66) 7125337, (1) 6183957.

SPRING, Richard John Grenville; MP (C) West Suffolk, since 1997 (Bury St Edmunds, 1992–97); *b* 24 Sept. 1946; *s* of late H. J. A. Spring and Marjorie (*née* Watson-Morris); *m* 1979, Hon. Jane (marr. diss. 1993), *o d* of Baron Henniker, *qv*; one *s* one *d. Educ:* Rondebosch, Cape; Univ. of Cape Town; Magdalene Coll., Cambridge (MA Econs). Vice-Pres., Merrill Lynch Ltd, 1976–86; Dep. Man. Dir, E. F. Hutton Internat. Associates, 1986–88; Exec. Dir, Shearson Lehman Hutton, 1988–89; Man. Director, Xerox Furman Selz, 1989–92. Contested (C) Ashton-under-Lyne, 1983. PPS to Min. of State, DTI, 1996, to Ministers for the armed forces and for defence procurement, 1996–97; Opposition front bench spokesman on culture, media and sport, 1997–2000, on foreign and Commonwealth affairs, 2000–. Member: Employment Select Cttee, 1992–94; NI Select Cttee, 1994–97; Health Select Cttee, 1995–97; Vice Chm., All Party Racing and Bloodstock Cttee, 1997–98. Pres., Arts and Heritage Cttee, Bow Gp, 1992–97. European Elections Campaign Co-ordinator, 1989; Chm., Westminster CPC, 1990; Dep.-Chm., Small Business Bureau, 1997– (Chm., Parly Adv. Gp, 1992–). *Recreations:* country pursuits, English watercolours. *Address:* c/o House of Commons, SW1A 0AA. *Club:* Boodle's.

SPRING RICE, family name of **Baron Monteagle of Brandon**.

SPRINGFORD, John Frederick Charles, CBE 1980 (OBE 1970); retired British Council Officer; *b* 6 June 1919; *s* of Frederick Charles Springford and Bertha Agnes Springford (*née* Trenery); *m* 1945, Phyllis Wharton; one *s* two *d. Educ:* Latymer Upper Sch.; Christ's College, Cambridge (MA). Served War 1940–46, RAC; seconded Indian Armoured Corps, 1942; Asst Political Agent II in Mekran, 1945. British Council Service, Baghdad and Mosul, Iraq, 1947–51, Isfahan, Iran, 1951–52; British Council Representative: Tanzania, 1952–57; Sudan, 1957–62; Dir, Overseas Students Dept, 1962–66; Representative: Jordan, 1966–69; Iraq, 1969–74; Canada, 1974–79, and Counsellor, Cultural Affairs, British High Commission, Ottawa. Mem. Council, British Sch. of Archaeology in Iraq, 1980–86. Hon. Sec., Sussex Heritage Trust, 1980–83; Chm., Sussex Eastern Sub-Area, 1981–85, Sussex Area, 1985–92, RSCM. Organist, St Mary's Church, Battle, 1986–99. *Recreations:* archaeology, music. *Address:* Precinct, Crowhurst, Battle, East Sussex TN33 9AA. *T:* (01424) 830200.

SPRINGFORD, Prof. Michael, PhD; FInstP; H. O. Wills Professor of Physics, 1996–2001, and Director, Physics Laboratory, 1994–2001, University of Bristol, now Emeritus Professor of Physics; *b* 10 Jan. 1936; *s* of Stanley Walter Springford and Lillian Springford (*née* Tyler); *m* 1st, 1958, Kathleen Elizabeth Wyatt (marr. diss. 1983); two *s* one *d*; 2nd, 1991, Maria Sergeevna (*née* Morosova). *Educ:* Durham Univ. (BSc); Hull Univ. (PhD). Nat. Res. Council of Canada, 1962–64; Univ. of Sussex, 1964–89; Prof. of Experimental Physics, Univ. of Bristol, 1989–2001. Mott Prize Lectr, and Charles Vernon Boys Prize, Inst. of Physics, 1995. *Publications:* (ed) Electrons at the Fermi Surface, 1980; (ed) Electron: a centenary volume, 1997; papers on the quantum properties of condensed matter in learned jls. *Recreations:* music, sailing, walking, cooking, pursuit of quietness. *Address:* c/o H. H. Wills Physics Laboratory, University of Bristol, Tyndall Avenue, Bristol BS8 1TL. *T:* (0117) 928 8731.

SPRINGMAN, Prof. Sarah Marcella, OBE 1997; PhD; CEng; Professor of Geotechnical Engineering, Eidgenössische Technische Hochschule (Swiss Federal Institute of Technology), Zurich, since 1997; *b* 26 Dec. 1956; *d* of (Paul) Michael Eyre Springman and late Dame Ann Marcella Springman, DBE. *Educ:* Wycombe Abbey Sch.; Girton Coll., Cambridge (MA; Roscoe Meml Prize 1978); St Catharine's Coll., Cambridge (MPhil); Magdalene Coll., Cambridge (PhD 1989). 13 blues/half blues in lacrosse, tennis, squash, cross country, swimming, athletics. MICE; CEng 1993. Engr, Sir Alexander Gibb & Partners, UK, Australia and Fiji, 1979–83; Cambridge University: Soil Mechanics Group, Engineering Department: Res. Asst, 1984–88; Res. Associate, 1989–90; Asst Lectr, 1990–93; Lectr, 1993–96; Res. Fellow, 1988–90, Lectr and Fellow, 1991–96, Magdalene Coll. Member: Swisscode Commn Geodesign, 1998–; Swiss Natural Hazards Competence Centre, 1998–; Swiss Council for Sci. and Technol., 2000–. Member: Women's Engrg Soc., 1983–; Instn of RE, 1990–; Swiss Soc. of Engrs and Architects, 1999–. Mem., British Triathlon Team, 1984–93 (Nat. Champion 11 times, European Champion 3 times, European Team Champion 5 times); Mem., GB World Cup Rowing team, 1997; Vice Pres., Internat. Triathlon Union, 1992–96; Gov., World Masters Games, 1993–; Mem., UK (formerly GB) Sports Council, 1993–2001. Governor: Marlborough Coll., 1991–94; Wycombe Abbey Sch., 1993–96. *Publications:* contrib. geotechnical jls. *Recreations:* sculling/rowing, triathlon. *Address:* Institut für Geotechnik, Eidgenössische Technische Hochschule, Hönggerberg, 8093 Zürich, Switzerland. *T:* (1) 6333805, *Fax:* (1) 6331079. *Clubs:* Rob Roy, Cambridge Triathlon (Cambridge); Belvoir (Zurich).

SPROAT, Iain Mac Donald; *b* Dollar, Clackmannanshire, 8 Nov. 1938; *s* of late William Bigham Sproat and Lydia Bain Sproat (*née* Mac Donald); *m* 1979, Judith Mary Kernot (*née* King); one step *s. Educ:* St Mary's Sch., Melrose; Winchester Coll.; Univ. of Aix-en-Provence; Magdalen Coll., Oxford. Served RGJ (4th Bn), 1972–76. Chairman: Milner and Co., 1981, 1983–93, and 1997–; Cricketers' Who's Who Ltd, 1980–81, 1983–93, 1997–. Contested (C) Roxburgh and Berwickshire, 1983. MP (C): Aberdeen South, 1970–83; Harwich, 1992–97; contested (C) Harwich, 1997, 2001. PPS to Sec. of State for Scotland, 1973–74; Parly Under-Sec. of State, Dept of Trade, 1981–83 (Minister: of Aviation and Shipping; of Tourism; responsible for: Govt Statistics; Retail Trade; Distributive Trades; Video, Cinema and Film Industry); Parly Under-Sec. of State, 1993–95, Minister of State, 1995–97, DNH (Minister for Sport, 1993–97). Special Advr to Prime Minister, Gen. Election, 1987. Leader, Cons. Gp, Scottish Select Cttee, 1979–81; Chm., Scottish Cons. Cttee, 1979–81; Chm., Soviet and E European Gp, Cons. Foreign Affairs Cttee, 1975–81. Member: British Parly Delegn to oversee S Vietnamese Elections, 1973; British Parly Delegn to Soviet Union, 1974; Leader, British Parly Delegn to Austria, 1980. Dist. Vis. Prof., Texas Univ., 1992. Lecturer: on guerilla warfare, RCDS, 1973; on Kurdish guerilla warfare in Iran/Iraq, RUSI, 1975. Trustee: African Med. and Res. Foundn (Flying Doctors), 1986–91; Scottish Self-Governing Schools Trust, 1989–. Chairman, Editorial Board: Oxford Univ. Press Hist. of the British Empire, 1987–92; Complete Works of Pushkin, 1987–93, 1997–. Cricket Writer of the Year, Wombwell Cricket Lovers' Soc., 1983. *Publications:* (ed) Cricketers' Who's Who, annually 1980–93; Wodehouse at War, 1981; (contrib.) The British Prime Ministers. *Recreations:* collecting books, Rugby football, cricket. *Address:* c/o Coutts & Co., 2 Lower Sloane Street, SW1W 8BJ. *Clubs:* Cavalry and Guards, Oxford and Cambridge.

SPROT, Lt-Col Aidan Mark, MC 1944; JP; landed proprietor and farmer (Haystoun Estate); Lord-Lieutenant of Tweeddale, 1980–94; *b* 17 June 1919; *s* of Major Mark Sprot of Riddell. *Educ:* Stowe. Commissioned Royal Scots Greys, 1940; served: Middle East, 1941–43; Italy, 1943–44; NW Europe, 1944–45, and after the war in Germany, Libya, Egypt, Jordan and UK; Adjt 1945–46; CO, 1959–62, retired. Councillor, Peeblesshire CC, 1963–75; JP 1966, DL 1966–80, Peeblesshire. Member, Royal Company of Archers (Queen's Body Guard for Scotland), 1950–; Pres., Lowlands of Scotland, TAVRA, 1986–89. Vice-Pres., RHASS, 1986; Trustee, Royal Scottish Agricl Benevolent Instn, 1989–98. British Red Cross Society: County Dir, 1966–74, Patron, 1983–98, Tweeddale Br.; Patron, Borders Br., 1998–; County Comr, 1968–73, Chm., 1975–80, Pres., 1980–94, Tweeddale Scout Assoc.; President: Borders Area Scout Assoc., 1994–99; Lothian Fedn of Boys' Clubs, 1988–96. Hon. President: Tweeddale Soc., 1995–; Peebles Br., RBL, Scotland, 1990–; Hon. Mem., Rotary Club, Peebles, 1986–. Hon. Sec., Royal Caledonian Hunt, 1964–74. Mem., Service Chaplains Cttee, Church of Scotland, 1974–82 and 1985–92. Freeman, Tweeddale Dist, 1994. Scout Medal of Merit, 1994; Badge of Honour, BRCS, 1998. *Publication:* Swifter than Eagles—War Memoirs 1939–1945, 1998. *Recreations:* country pursuits, motor cycle touring. *Address:* Crookston, Peebles EH45 9JQ. *T:* (01721) 740209. *Club:* New (Edinburgh).

SPRY, Christopher John; Director, OD Partnerships Network, since 2001; *b* 29 Aug. 1946; *s* of late Reginald Charles Spry and Kathleen Edith Spry (*née* Hobart); *m* 1st, Jean Banks (marr. diss. 1989); two *s*; 2nd, 1989, Judith Christina (*née* Ryder). *Educ:* Sir Roger Manwood's Sch., Sandwich; Exeter Univ. (BA 1967). AHSM. Dep. Hosp. Sec., Lewisham Hosp., 1970; Hosp. Sec., Nottingham Gen. Hosp., 1973; Asst. Dist Administrator, S Nottingham, 1975, Dist Administrator, 1978; Dist Administrator, 1981, Dist Gen. Manager, 1984, Newcastle HA.; Regl Gen. Manager, SW Thames RHA, 1989–94; Regl Dir, NHS Exec., S Thames, 1994–96; Chief Exec., Gtr Glasgow Health Bd, 1996. Member: ACARD Working Gp on UK Med. Equipment Industry, 1986; Working Party on Alternative Delivery and Funding of Health Services, 1988. *Recreations:* keeping fit, photography, books, enjoying townscapes. *Address:* c/o OD Partnerships Network, 55 St John Street, EC1M 4AN.

SPUFFORD, Prof. (Honor) Margaret, OBE 1996; PhD, LittD; FRHistS; FBA 1995; Research Professor in Social and Local History, University of Surrey, Roehampton (formerly Roehampton Institute), 1994, Emeritus, 2001; *b* 10 Dec. 1935; *d* of Leslie Marshall Clark and Mary (*née* Johnson); *m* 1962, Peter Spufford, *qv*; one *s* (one *d* decd). *Educ:* Univ. of Leicester (MA with Dist. 1963; PhD 1970); LittD Cantab 1986. FRHistS 1974. Calouste Gulbenkian Res. Fellow, Lucy Cavendish Coll., Cambridge, 1968–72; University of Keele: Hon. Lectr, 1974–79; Sen. Res. Fellow, 1978–79; Sen. Res. Associate, Faculty of Hist., Univ. of Cambridge, 1979–81; Fellow, Newnham Coll., Cambridge, 1980–92. Vis. Res. Fellow, Netherlands Inst. for Advanced Study, 1992–93; Vis. Prof., Rikkyo Univ., Tokyo, 1994. Earl Lectr, Univ. of Keele, 1993; James Ford Special Lectr, Univ. of Oxford, 1994. Res. Dir, Roehampton Hearth Tax Centre, 2001– (Dir, 1996–2001). Founder, Bridget's Hostel for Disabled and Chronically Sick Students, Cambridge, 1987 (Chm., Bridget's Trustees, 1999–2000). A Woman of the Year, Women of the Year Assembly and Lunch, 1998. *Publications:* (with P. Spufford) Eccleshall: the story of a Staffordshire market town, 1964; A Cambridgeshire Community: Chippenham from settlement to enclosure, 1966; Contrasting Communities: the English villager in the sixteenth and seventeenth centuries, 1974, 2nd edn 2000; Small Books and Pleasant Histories: popular fiction and its readership in seventeenth century England, 1981; The Great Reclothing of Rural England: petty chapmen and their wares in the seventeenth century, 1984; Celebration, 1989 (trans. Dutch, 1994, French, 1995, Slovene, 2001; USA edn, 1996); (ed) The World of Rural Dissenters, 1995; Poverty Portrayed: Gregory King and Eccleshall, Staffordshire, 1995; Figures in the Landscape: rural society in England, 1500–1700, 1999; contrib. chapters in edited books, including: Literacy and Social Development in the West, 1981; Order and Disorder in Early Modern England, 1985; English Rural Society 1500–1800, 1990; A Miracle Mirror'd: the Dutch Republic in European Perspective, 1995; Spiritual Classics of the late Twentieth Century, 1995; Opening the Nursery Door, 1997; The English Rural Landscape, 2000; contrib. articles in learned jls incl. Albion, Econ. Hist. Review, Proc. Cambridge Antiquarian Soc., Agricl Hist. Rev., Studies in Church Hist., Jl Eccl Hist., Theology. *Recreations:* Benedictine Anglican oblate, exploring countryside, vernacular architecture, listening to people. *Address:* The Guildhall, Whittlesford, Cambridge CB2 4NZ.

SPUFFORD, Prof. Peter, PhD, LittD; FSA; FRHistS; FBA 1994; Professor of European History, University of Cambridge, 2000–01, now Emeritus; Fellow, Queens' College, Cambridge, since 1979; *b* 18 Aug. 1934; *s* of late Douglas Henry Spufford and Nancy Gwendoline Spufford (*née* Battagel); *m* 1962, Honor Margaret Clark (*see* H. M. Spufford); one *s* (one *d* decd). *Educ:* Kingswood Sch.; Jesus Coll., Cambridge (BA 1956; MA 1960; PhD 1963; LittD 1990). FRNS 1955; FRHistS 1968; FSG 1969; FSA 1990. Res. Fellow, Jesus Coll., Cambridge, 1958–60; Asst Lectr, Lectr, Sen. Lectr and Reader, Univ. of Keele, 1960–79; University of Cambridge: Lectr, 1979–90; Reader in Econ. History, 1990–2000. Visiting Fellow: Clare Hall, Cambridge, 1969–70; Netherlands Inst. for Advanced Study, 1992–93; Vis. Prof. of Burgundian Studies, 1972–73, Vis. Prof., Econ. Studies, 1993, Leuven. Vice-Pres., Soc. of Genealogists, 1997–; Chm., British Records Soc., 1985–; Mem. Council, Soc. of Antiquaries, 1996–99. Hon. Mem., Koninklijk Genootschap voor Munt-en Penningkunde, 1992–. *Publications:* Origins of the English Parliament, 1967; Monetary Problems and Policies in the Burgundian Netherlands 1433–1496, 1970; Handbook of Medieval Exchange, 1986; (ed with N. J. Mayhew) Later Medieval Mints, 1988; Money and Its Use in Medieval Europe, 1988; (ed with G. H. Martin) Records of the Nation, 1990; (ed) Index to the Probate Accounts of England and Wales, 2 vols, 1999; chapters in: Cambridge Economic History of Europe, vol. 3, 1965, vol. 2, 2nd edn, 1987; New Cambridge Medieval History, vi, 1999. *Address:* Queens' College, Cambridge CB3 9ET. *T:* (01223) 335511.

SPURGEON, Maj.-Gen. Peter Lester, CB 1980; Chief Executive, Royal Agricultural Benevolent Institution, 1982–91; *b* 27 Aug. 1927; *s* of Harold Sidney Spurgeon and Emily Anne (*née* Bolton); *m* 1959, Susan Ann (*née* Aylward); one *s* one *d*. *Educ:* Merchant Taylors' Sch., Northwood. Commnd, 1946; 1949–66: HMS Glory; Depot, RM Deal; 40 Commando RM; ADC to Maj.-Gen. Plymouth Gp RM; DS Officers' Sch., RM; RAF Staff Coll., Bracknell; Staff of Comdt Gen. RM; 40 Commando RM; Jt Warfare Estab.; GS02 HQ: ME Comd, Aden, 1967; Army Strategic Comd, 1968–69; Second-in-Comd, 41 Commando RM, 1969–71; DS National Defence Coll., Latimer, 1971–73; CO RM Poole, 1973–75; Dir of Drafting and Records, RM, 1975–76; Comdr, Training Gp, RM, 1977–79 and Training and Reserve Forces, RM, 1979–80; retd 1980. Col Comdt, RM, 1987–90. Pres., RM Assoc., 1986–90. *Recreations:* golf, gardening. *Address:* c/o Lloyds TSB, 1 High Street, Oxford OX1 4AA. *Club:* Army and Navy.

SPURLING, (Susan) Hilary; biographer; *b* 25 Dec. 1940; *d* of Gilbert Alexander Forrest and Emily Maureen Forrest; *m* 1961, John Spurling; two *s* one *d*. *Educ:* Somerville Coll., Oxford (BA). Theatre Critic of the Spectator, 1964–70, Literary Editor, 1966–70. *Publications:* Ivy When Young: the early life of I. Compton-Burnett 1884–1919, 1974; Handbook to Anthony Powell's Music of Time, 1977; Secrets of a Woman's Heart: the later life of I. Compton-Burnett 1920–1969, 1984 (Duff Cooper Meml Prize, 1984; Heinemann Literary Award (jtly), 1985); Elinor Fettiplace's Receipt Book, 1986; Paul Scott, A Life, 1990; Paper Spirits, 1992; The Unknown Matisse 1869–1908, vol. i, 1998; La Grande Thérèse, 1999. *Recreations:* reading, ratting, country walks. *Address:* c/o David Higham Associates, 5–8 Lower John Street, Golden Square, W1R 4HA.

SPURR, Margaret Anne, OBE 1994; DL; Headmistress, Bolton School, Girls' Division, 1979–94; Governor, BBC, 1993–98; *b* 7 Oct. 1933; *m* 1953, John Spurr; one *s* one *d*. *Educ:* Abbeydale Girls' Grammar Sch., Sheffield; Univ. of Keele. BA (Hons); PGCE. Tutor: Eng. Lit., Univ. of Glasgow, 1971; Eng. Lit. Dept, Adult Educn, Univ. of Keele, 1972–73. Chairman: Scholaservices, 1990–; Speirhead Education, 1997–. Sen. Examiner, Univ. of London, 1971–80. Pres., GSA, 1985–86. Chairman: Nat. ISIS Cttee, 1987–90; BBC English Nat. Forum, 1994–98; Member: Adv. Cttee, American Studies Resources Centre, Polytechnic of Central London, 1977–90; Scholarship Selection Cttee, ESU, 1983–94; CBI Schools Panel, 1985–89; Exec. Cttee, GBGSA, 1994–99. Vice-Provost, Woodard Corp., 1994–98. Governor: Kent Coll., Tunbridge Wells, 1993–99; John Moores Univ., Liverpool, 1994–98; Colfe's Sch., 1995–; Stafford Coll. of Further Educn, 1996–2000; Mem. Governing Council, Keele Univ., 1996–. Trustee, School Fees Trust Fund, 1994–. Dir, SFS Gp, 1999–; Mid-Atlantic Club, 2000–. Pres., Staffs Soc., 1999–2001. FRSA 1991. DL Staffs, 1998. Hon. DLitt Keele, 1995. *Publications:* (ed) A Curriculum for Capability, 1986; (ed) Girls First, 1987. *Recreations:* gardening, theatre, poetry, music. *Address:* The Old Vicarage, Croxden, Uttoxeter, Staffs ST14 5JQ. *T:* (01889) 507214, *Fax:* (01889) 507424. *Club:* Reform.

SPURRIER, Peter Brotherton; design consultant; Design Director, Maritime Insignia Ltd, since 1995; *b* 9 Aug. 1942; *s* of Eric Jack Spurrier, MBE and late Frances Mary (*née* Brotherton); *m* 1973, Hon. Elizabeth Jane Maude, *d* of Baron Maude of Stratford-upon-Avon, TD, PC; two *s* one *d*. *Educ:* Chetham's Hosp. Sch., Manchester; Manchester Coll. of Art and Design (NDD 1965). MSIAD 1980. Designer for Wade Heath Pottery, Burslem, 1965–66; Asst Design Officer, DoE, 1966–71 (on design team for Investiture of HRH Prince of Wales, 1969); Dir, Dromas Design Ltd, 1971–79; Principal Designer, Idiom Design Ltd, 1979–81; Portcullis Pursuivant of Arms, 1981–93; York Herald of Arms, 1993. Packaging co-ordn and planning advr, human fungal foodstuffs div., The French Garden Ltd, 1995–; Dep. Sen. Asst wall-furniture presentation consultant, Wall Game Ltd, 1996–; heraldic adviser, Burke's Peerage, 1996–. Hon. Asst Curator, Heralds' Mus. at Tower of London, 1981–83. Mem. Council, Heraldry Soc., 1981–90; Chm., Soc. of Heraldic Arts, 1991–. FRSA. Freeman, City of London, 1980; Freeman and Liveryman, Painter Stainers' Co., 1985. OStJ 1990. *Publication:* The Heraldic Art Source Book, 1997. *Recreations:* painting, music, fishing. *Address:* 6 Wroughton Road, SW11 6BG.

SPY, James; Sheriff of North Strathclyde at Paisley, since 1988; *b* 1 Dec. 1952; *s* of James Spy and Jean Learmond; *m* 1980, Jennifer Margaret Malcolm; three *d*. *Educ:* Hermitage Acad., Helensburgh; Glasgow Univ. (LLB Hons). Admitted Solicitor, 1976; passed Advocate, 1979. *Recreations:* music, clocks, model ships, model trains. *Address:* St Ann's, 171 Nithsdale Road, Glasgow G41 5QS.

SPYER, Prof. (Kenneth) Michael, PhD, DSc; Sophia Jex-Blake Professor of Physiology, since 1980, and Dean, Royal Free Campus, since 1998, Royal Free and University College Medical School, University College London; *b* 15 Sept. 1943; *s* of late Harris Spyer and Rebecca Spyer (*née* Jacobs); *m* 1971, Christine Spalton; two *s*. *Educ:* Coopers' Co. Sch.; Univ. of Sheffield (BSc); Univ. of Birmingham (PhD 1969; DSc 1979). Res. Fellow, Univ. of Birmingham Med. Sch., 1969–72; Royal Soc. European Prog. Fellow, Instituto de Fisologia, Pisa, 1972–73; Res. Fellow, 1973–78, Sen. Res. Fellow, 1978–80, Dept of Physiology, Univ. of Birmingham; joined Royal Free Hosp. Sch. of Medicine, 1980; Dir, Neural Control Gp, BHF, 1985–; Head, Jt Depts of Physiology, UCL and Royal Free Hosp. Sch. of Medicine, 1994–99; Dir, Autonomic Neurosci. Inst., 1997–. Founder FMedSci 1998. Hon. MD Lisbon, 1991. *Publications:* (ed jtly) Central Regulation of Autonomic Functions, 1990; papers in Jl of Physiology, Neurosci., Brain Res., Amer. Jl of Physiology, Jl of Autonomic Nervous System, Exptl Physiology. *Recreations:* fly fishing, travelling (particularly in Italy), gardening, books, fine arts. *Address:* Royal Free and University College Medical School, Royal Free Campus, Rowland Hill Street, NW3 2PF. *T:* (020) 7830 2764.

SQUAIR, George Alexander; non-executive Chairman, British Approvals Service for Cables, since 1993; *b* 26 July 1929; *s* of Alexander Squair and Elizabeth (*née* Macdonald); *m* 1953, Joy Honeybone; two *s* one *d*. *Educ:* Woolwich Polytechnic; Oxford Technical Coll.; Southampton Univ. CEng, FIEE 1986; CIMgt (CBIM 1984). Gen. distribution engrg posts, 1950–68; Southern, later South Eastern, Electricity Board, subseq. SEEBOARD: 1st Asst Dist Engr, 1968–69; Dist Engr, Swindon, 1969–70; Area Engr, Newbury, 1970–73; Dist Manager, Oxford, 1973–74; Area Manager, Newbury, 1974–78; Mem., Exec. Bd, 1976–78; Dep. Chm., 1978–83; Chm. and Chief Exec., 1983–92. *Recreations:* reading, golf. *Address:* Swallow Grove Farmhouse, Mangrove Lane, Hertford SG13 8QG.

SQUIRE, Dr (Clifford) William, CMG 1978; LVO 1972; HM Diplomatic Service, retired; Chairman, Grenzebach Glier Europe, since 1996; *b* 7 Oct. 1928; *s* of Clifford John Squire and Eleanor Eliza Harpley; *m* 1st, 1959, Marie José Carlier (*d* 1973); one *s* two *d* (and one *s* decd); 2nd, 1976, Sarah Laetitia Hutchison (*see* S. L. Squire); one *s* one *d*. *Educ:* Royal Masonic Sch., Bushey; St John's Coll., Oxford; Coll. of Europe, Bruges. PhD London 1979. British Army, 1947–49. Nigerian Admin. Service, 1953–59; FO, 1959–60; British Legation, Bucharest, 1961–63; FO, 1963–65; UK Mission to UN, New York, 1965–69; Head of Chancery, Bangkok, 1969–72; Head of SE Asian Dept, FCO, 1972–75; Extramural Fellow, Sch. of Oriental and African Studies, London Univ., 1975–76; Counsellor, later Head of Chancery, Washington, 1976–79; Ambassador to Senegal, 1979–82, concurrently to Cape Verde Is, Guinea (Bissau), Guinea (Conakry), Mali and Mauritania; Asst Under-Sec. of State, FCO, 1982–84; Ambassador to Israel, 1984–88. Develt Dir, Univ. of Cambridge, 1988–96; Fellow of Wolfson Coll., Cambridge, 1988–96. *Address:* 11A Chaucer Road, Cambridge CB2 2EB. *Clubs:* Travellers; Cosmos (Washington, DC).

SQUIRE, Peter John; Headmaster, Bedford Modern School, 1977–96; *b* 15 Feb. 1937; *s* of Leslie Ernest Squire and Doris Eileen Squire; *m* 1965, Susan Elizabeth (*née* Edwards); one *s* one *d*. *Educ:* King Edward's Sch., Birmingham; Jesus Coll., Oxford (BA 1960, MA 1964); Pembroke Coll. and Dept of Educn, Cambridge (Cert. in Educn 1961). Asst Master, Monkton Combe Sch., Bath, 1961–65; Haberdashers' Aske's Sch., Elstree, 1965–77: Sen. Boarding Housemaster, 1968–77; Sen. History Master, 1970–77. Reporting Inspector, HMC/ISI Inspections, 1994–. Chm., Bedfordshire Victim Support, 1997–. Mem., Whitgift Council, 1997–. *Recreations:* foreign travel, gardening, antique collecting. *Address:* 98 Bromham Road, Biddenham, Bedford MK40 4AH. *T:* (01234) 342373.

SQUIRE, Air Chief Marshal Sir Peter (Ted), GCB 2001 (KCB 1997); DFC 1982; AFC 1979; Chief of the Air Staff, since 2000; Air Aide-de-Camp to the Queen, since 1999; *b* 7 Oct. 1945; *s* of late Wing Comdr Frank Squire and Margaret Pascoe Squire (*née* Trump); *m* 1970, Carolyn Joynson; three *s*. *Educ:* King's Sch., Bruton. psc(n). Flying and Staff appts include: commnd 1966; 20 Sqn, Singapore, 1968–70; 4 FTS, Anglesey, 1970–73; 3 (F) Sqn, Germany, 1975–78; OC1 (F) Sqn, 1981–83; Personal Staff Officer to AOC-in-C Strike Comd, 1984–86; Station Comdr, RAF Cottesmore, 1986–88; Dir Air Offensive, 1989–91; SASO, RAF Strike Comd, 1991–93; AOC No 1 Gp, 1993–94; ACAS, 1994–96; DCDS (Progs and Personnel), MoD, 1996–99; AOC-in-C, Strike Comd and Comdr Allied Air Forces NW Europe, 1999–2000. Mem., GAPAN. FRAeS 1995. Gov., King's Sch., Bruton, 1990–. *Recreations:* cricket, golf. *Address:* c/o National Westminster Bank, 5 South Street, Wincanton BA9 9DJ. *Club:* Royal Air Force.

SQUIRE, Rachel Anne; MP (Lab) Dunfermline West, since 1992; *b* 13 July 1954; *d* of Louise Anne Squire (*née* Binder) and step *d* of Percy Garfield Squire; *m* 1984, Allan Lee Mason. *Educ:* Godolphin and Latymer Girls' Sch.; Durham Univ. (BA Hons); Birmingham Univ. (CQSW). Social worker, Birmingham, 1975–81; trade union officer, 1981–92. *Recreations:* reading, cooking, archaeology. *Address:* (office) 10–14 Douglas Street, Dunfermline, Fife KY12 7EB. *T:* (01383) 622889, *Fax:* (01383) 623500.

SQUIRE, Raglan, FRIBA, MSIA; Consultant, Raglan Squire & Partners, Architects, Engineers and Town Planners, since 1981 (Senior Partner, 1948–81); *b* 30 Jan. 1912; *e s* of late Sir John Squire, Kt; *m* 1st, 1938, Rachel, (*d* 1968), *d* of James Atkey, Oxshott, Surrey; two *s*; 2nd, 1968, Bridget Lawless (*d* 1997). *Educ:* Blundell's; St John's Coll., Cambridge. Private practice in London, 1935–. War service with Royal Engineers, 1942–45. Founded firm of Raglan Squire & Partners, 1948. Principal projects: housing, educational and industrial work, 1935–41; pre-fabricated bldgs and industrial design, 1945–48; Eaton Sq. Conversion Scheme, 1945–56; Rangoon Univ. Engineering Coll., 1953–56; Associated Architect, Transport Pavilion, Festival of Britain Exhib., 1951; Town Planning Scheme for Mosul, Iraq, 1955; Bagdad airport report, 1955; factories at Weybridge, Huddersfield, etc; office buildings London, Eastbourne, Bournemouth, etc; gen. practice at home and over-seas incl. major hotels at Teheran, Tunis, Nicosia, Malta and Singapore, Gibraltar, Caribbean and Middle East, 1955–81, retired from active practice. Sec. RIBA Reconstruction Cttee, 1941–42; Council of Architectural Assoc., 1951–52; Guest Editor Architects' Journal, 1947. *Publications:* Portrait of an Architect (autobiog.), 1985; articles in technical press on organisation of Building Industry, Architectural Education, etc. *Recreations:* gardening, chess, ocean racing and designing small yachts. *Address:* 1 Chester Row, SW1W 9JF. *T:* (020) 7730 7275. *Clubs:* Royal Thames Yacht, Royal Ocean Racing; Royal Southern Yacht.

SQUIRE, Robin Clifford; Director, Daruel Ltd, since 1998; *b* 12 July 1944; *s* of late Sidney John Squire and Mabel Alice Squire (*née* Gilmore); *m* 1981, Susan Margaret Fey, *d* of late Arthur Frederick Branch and of Mahala Branch (*née* Parker); one step *s* one step *d*. *Educ:* Tiffin School, Kingston-upon-Thames. FCA. Qualified as Chartered Accountant, 1966; joined Lombard Banking Ltd (subsequently Lombard North Central Ltd) as Accountant, 1968, becoming Dep. Chief Accountant, 1972–79. Dir Advocacy Ltd, 1997–2000. Councillor, London Borough of Sutton, 1968–82; Chm., Finance Cttee, 1972–76; Leader of Council, 1976–79. Chm., Greater London Young Conservatives, 1973; Vice-Chm., Nat. Young Conservatives, 1974–75. Personal Asst to Rt Hon. Robert Carr, Gen. Election, Feb. 1974; contested (C) Havering, Hornchurch, Oct. 1974. MP (C) Hornchurch, 1979–97; contested (C) same seat, 1997, 2001. PPS to Minister of State for Transport, 1983–85, to Rt Hon. Chris Patten, Chm. of Cons. Party, 1991–92; Parliamentary Under-Secretary of State: DoE, 1992–93; DFE, later DFEE, 1993–97. Mem., Commons Select Cttee on Environment, 1979–83 and 1987–91, on European Legislation, 1985–88; Sec., Cons. Parly European Affairs Cttee, 1979–80; Vice-Chm., Cons. Parly Trade Cttee, 1980–83; Chm., Cons. Parly Environment Cttee, 1990–91 (Jt Vice-Chm., 1985–89); Originator of Local Govt (Access to Information) Act, 1985. Chm., Cons. Action for Electoral Reform, 1983–86 (Vice-Chm., 1982–83); Dep. Chm., Anglo-Asian Cons. Soc., 1982–83. Comr, Nat. Lottery Commn, 1999; Adjudicator for Schs Orgns and Admissions, 1999. Mem. Bd, Shelter, 1982–91; Dir, Link Assured Homes series of cos, 1988–92. *Publication:* (jtly) Set the Party Free, 1969. *Recreations:* films, bridge, Rugby. *Address:* Flat 3, 63 Millbank, SW1P 4RW.

SQUIRE, Sara Laetitia, (Sarah); HM Diplomatic Service; Ambassador to Estonia, since 2000; *b* 18 July 1949; *d* of Michael Duncan Hutchison and Margery Betty Hutchison (*née* Martin); *m* 1976, (Clifford) William Squire, *qv*; one *s* one *d*. *Educ:* St Paul's Girls' Sch.; Newnham Coll., Cambridge (BA Hons Hist.). Entered HM Diplomatic Service, 1971: FCO, 1971–72; Tel Aviv, 1972–75; SE Asian Dept, FCO, 1975–76; Washington, 1977–79; Falkland Is Dept, FCO, 1972–84; Tel Aviv, 1986–88; Policy Officer, Cambridge CC, 1989–90; Sen. Inf. Officer, COI, 1990–95; Dep. Dir, Know How Fund, FCO, 1995–96; Dep. Hd, Central Eur. Dept, FCO, 1996–99. *Address:* c/o Foreign and Commonwealth Office, King Charles Street, SW1A 2AH; 11a Chaucer Road, Cambridge CB2 2EB. *T:* (01223) 329547. *Club:* Reform.

SQUIRE, William; *see* Squire, C. W.

SQUIRES, (Charles) Ian; Managing Director: Carlton Studios, since 1994; Central Broadcasting, since 1996; *b* 22 April 1951; *s* of Charles Ian Squires and Mary Squires; *m* 1993, Vanessa Marie Sweet; two *d*. *Educ:* Bede Grammar Sch., Sunderland; University Coll. London (BA Hons English). Westminster Press, 1973–75; Current Affairs and Editor, Omnibus, BBC TV, 1975–86; freelance producer, 1986–88; Head of Network TV, North West, BBC, 1988–90; Man. Dir, Zenith North, 1990–94. Chm., EMMedia, 2001–; Director: London News Network, 1996–; West Midlands Life, 1999–; Birmingham Marketing Partnership, 1999–. Chm., Birmingham City Pride, 2001–. BAFTA Award, Best Arts Prog., for A Simple Man (TV ballet on life of L. S. Lowry), 1987. *Recreations:* riding, shooting, running. *Address:* The Old Rectory, Main Street, Burrough-on-the-Hill, Leics LE14 2JQ. *T:* (01664) 454321.

SRINIVASAN, Krishnan; Deputy Secretary-General, Commonwealth Secretariat, since 1995; *b* 15 Feb. 1937; *s* of late Captain C. Srinivasan, Indian Navy, and of Mrs Rukmani Chari; *m* 1975, Brinda Mukerjea; one *s*. *Educ:* Bedford Sch.; Christ Church, Oxford (MA; Boxing Blue, 1956; Hon. Mem., SCR). Joined Indian Foreign Service, 1959; Chargé d'Affaires, Tripoli, 1968–71; High Comr to Zambia and Botswana, 1974–77; Consul-Gen., NY, 1977–80; High Comr to Nigeria, and Ambassador to Benin and Cameroon, 1980–83; Ambassador, Netherlands, 1986–89; High Comr, Bangladesh, 1989–92; Perm. Sec., Min. of External Affairs, 1992–94; Foreign Secretary, 1994–95. Hind Ratna, 2001. *Publications:* Selections in Two Keys, 1974; The Water's Edge, 1975; The Eccentricity Factor, 1980; The Fourth Profile, 1991; A Fizzle Yield, 1992; Tricks of the Trade, 2000; The Eccentric Effect, 2001. *Recreations:* reading, writing, squash, jazz, watching sports. *Address:* Commonwealth Secretariat, Marlborough House, Pall Mall, SW1Y 5HX. *Clubs:* Oxford and Cambridge; Vincent's (Oxford); Bengal (Calcutta); International Centre (New Delhi).

SRINIVASAN, Prof. Mandyam Veerambudi, PhD; FRS 2001; FAA; Professor of Visual Science, Research School of Biological Sciences, since 1994, and Director, Centre for Visual Science, 1994–96 and since 2000, Australian National University; *b* 15 Sept. 1948; *s* of Mandyam Veerambudi Sundararajan and Mandyam Veerambudi Vedavalli Ammal. *Educ:* Bangalore Univ. (BSc 1st Cl. Electrical Engrg 1968); Indian Inst. of Sci., Bangalore (Masters in Applied Electronics and Servomechanisms 1970); Yale Univ. (MPhil 1973, PhD 1976, Engrg and Applied Sci.). Res. Scientist, Dept of Ophthalmol. and Visual Sci., Yale Univ. Sch. of Medicine, 1977–78; Res. Fellow, Depts of Neurobiol. and Applied Maths, ANU, 1978–82; Asst Prof. of Biophysics, Dept of Neurobiol., Univ. of Zurich, 1982–85; Fellow, Visual Sciences, 1985–91, Sen. Fellow, 1992–93, Res. Sch. of Biol Scis, ANU. Daimler-Benz Fellow, Inst. Advanced Studies, Berlin, 1996–97. FAA 1995. Hon. DSc Neuroethol., ANU, 1994. *Publications:* (ed with S. Venkatesh) From Living Eyes to Seeing Machines, 1997; contrib. numerous res. articles and rev. chapters, one internat. patent. *Recreations:* reading, music, bicycling, jogging. *Address:* (office) Visual Sciences, Research School of Biological Sciences, Australian National University, PO Box 475, Canberra, ACT 2601, Australia; (home) 36 Challinor Crescent, Florey, ACT 2615, Australia.

SRISKANDAN, Kanagaretnam, CEng, FICE, FIStructE, FIHT; consultant in highway and bridge engineering, 1993–2000; *b* 12 Aug. 1930; *s* of Kanagaretnam Kathiravelu and Kanmanyammal Kumaraswamy; *m* 1956, Dorothy (*née* Harley); two *s* one *d*. *Educ:* Royal College, Colombo; Univ. of Ceylon. BSc Hons London 1952. Junior Asst Engineer, PWD, Ceylon, 1953; Asst Engr, Sir William Halcrow and Partners, Cons. Engrs, London, 1956; Section Engr, Tarmac Civil Engineering Ltd, 1958; Asst Engr, West Riding of Yorkshire CC, 1959, left as Principal Engr; Department of Transport: Superintending Engr, Midland Road Construction Unit, 1968; Asst Chief Engr, 1971; Deputy Chief Highway Engr, 1976; Chief Highway Engr, 1980–87; Divl Dir, Mott, Hay and Anderson, subseq. Mott, MacDonald Gp, Consulting Engrs, 1988–93. *Publications:* papers on various engrg topics. *Recreation:* golf.

SRIVASTAVA, Chandrika Prasad, Padma Bhushan 1972; Hon. KCMG 1990; Secretary-General, International Maritime Organization (formerly IMCO), 1974–89, now Emeritus; Founding Chancellor, World Maritime University, 1983–91, now Emeritus; *b* 8 July 1920; *s* of B. B. Srivastava; *m* 1947, Nirmala Salve; two *d*. *Educ:* Lucknow, India. 1st cl. BA 1940, 1st cl. BA Hons 1941, 1st cl. MA 1942, 1st cl. LLB 1944; gold medals for proficiency in Eng. Lit. and Polit. Science. Under-Sec., Min. of Commerce, India, 1948–49; City Magistrate, Lucknow, 1950; Addtl Dist. Magistrate, Meerut, 1951–52; Directorate-Gen. of Shipping, 1953; Dep. Dir-Gen. of Shipping, 1954–57; Dep. Sec., Min. of Transport, and Pvte Sec. to Minister of Transport and Communications, 1958; Sen. Dep. Dir-Gen. of Shipping, 1959–60; Man. Dir, Shipping Corp. of India, 1961–64; Jt Sec. to Prime Minister, 1964–66; Chm. and Man. Dir, Shipping Corp. of India, 1966–73; Director: Central Inland Water Transport Corp., 1967; Central Bd, Reserve Bank of India, 1972–73; Chm., Mogul Line Ltd, 1967–73. Chm., Cttee on Maritime Educn and Trng, Govt of India, 1992. Vice-Pres., Sea Cadet Council, 1970–73. President: Indian Nat. Shipowners' Assoc., 1971–73; Inst. of Marine Technologists, India, 1972–89 (Hon. Mem., 1981); UN Conf. on Code of Conduct for Liner Confs, 1973–74; Internat. Maritime Lectrs' Assoc., 1980–91; Chm., Cttee of Invisibles, 3rd UN Conf. on Trade and Develt, 1972; Member: Nat. Shipping Bd, 1959–73; Merchant Navy Trng Bd, 1959–73; Nat. Welfare Bd for Seafarers, 1966–73; Amer. Bureau of Shipping, 1969; Governing Body, Indian Inst. of Foreign Trade, 1970; State Bd of Tourism, 1970; Nat. Harbour Bd, 1970–73; Gen. Cttee, Bombay Chamber of Commerce and Ind., 1971; Governing Body Indian Inst. of Management, 1972–73; Adv. Bd, Seatrade Acad., 1978–89 (Chm. Awarding Body, Seatrade Annual Awards for Achievement, 1988); Europort Internat. Cttee of Honour, 1980–89; Bd, Internat. Maritime Bureau, ICC, 1981–89; Bd of Dirs, ICC Centre for Maritime Co-operation, 1985–89; Hon. Adv. Cttee, Internat. Congress on The Port—an Ecological Challenge, Hamburg, 1989–90; Chm., Nat. Maritime Day Awards Cttee, India, 2000. Life Gov., Marine Soc., 1984. Vice Pres., Welsh Centre for Internat. Affairs, 1989. FRSA 1981; Fellow: Inst. Marine Engrs, India, 1998; Co. of Master Mariners, India, 1998. Hon. Member: Master Mariners' Co., UK, 1978–89; Royal Inst. of Navigation, 1984; Internat. Fedn of Shipmasters' Assocs, 1985; The Warsash Assoc., 1988; Internat. Maritime Pilots' Assoc., 1988; Hon. Fellow: Plymouth Polytech., 1979; Nautical Inst., 1985. Hon. LLD: Bhopal, 1984; Wales, 1987; Malta, 1988. Admiral Padilla Award, Colombia, 1978; Gran Amigo del Mar Award, Colombia, 1978; Gold Mercury Internat. Award Ad Personam, 1984; Award, Seatrade Acad., 1988. Commandeur du Mérite Maritime, France, 1982; Comdr, Order of St Olav, Norway, 1982; Grande Ufficiale dell'Ordine al Merito, Italy, 1983; Comdr, Order of Prince Henry the Navigator, Portugal, 1983; Gold Order of Distinguished Seafarers, Poland, 1983; Nautical Medal, 1st cl., Greece, 1983; Gran Cruz Distintivo Blanco, Orden Cruz Peruana al Mérito Naval, Peru, 1984; Gran Cruz, Orden de Manuel Amador Guerrero, Panama, 1985; Grande-Oficial, Ordem do Mérito Naval, Brazil, 1986; Commander's Cross, Order of Merit, Poland, 1986; Silver Medal of Honour, Malmö, Sweden, 1988; Kt Great Band, Order of Humane African Redemption, Liberia, 1989; Comdr's Cross of Order of Merit, FRG, 1989; Comdr Grand Cross, Royal Order of the Star of the North, Sweden, 1989; Order of Merit, First Grade, Egypt, 1990; Encomienda de Numero de la Orden de Isabel la Católica, Spain, 1994. *Publications:* Lal Bahadur Shastri: Prime Minister of India 1964–1966—a life of truth in politics, 1995; Corruption: India's Enemy Within, 2001; articles on shipping in newspapers and jls. *Recreations:* music, tennis, reading. *Address:* Palazzo Doria, Cabella Ligure, 15060 (AL), Italy. *Clubs:* Royal Anglo-Belgian; Willingdon (Bombay).

STABB, His Honour Sir William (Walter), Kt 1981; QC 1968; FCIArb; retired; a Circuit Judge (formerly Official Referee, Supreme Court of Judicature), 1969–78; Senior Official Referee, 1978–85; *b* 6 Oct. 1913; 2nd *s* of late Sir Newton Stabb, OBE and late Lady E. M. Stabb; *m* 1940, Dorothy Margaret Leckie (*d* 1999); four *d*. *Educ:* Rugby; University Coll., Oxford. Called to the Bar, 1936; Master of the Bench, Inner Temple, 1964, Treasurer, 1985. Served with RAF, 1940–46, attaining rank of Sqdn Ldr. Junior Counsel to Ministry of Labour, 1960; Prosecuting Counsel to BoT, 1962–68. Dep. Chm. 1961–69, Chm. 1969–71, Bedfordshire QS. *Recreations:* fishing, golf.

STABLE, His Honour (Rondle) Owen (Charles); QC 1963; a Circuit Judge, 1979–95; Senior Circuit Judge, Snaresbrook Crown Court, 1982–95; *b* 28 Jan. 1923; *yr s* of late Rt Hon. Sir Wintringham Norton Stable, MC, and Lucie Haden (*née* Freeman); *m* 1949, Yvonne Brook, *y d* of late Maj. L. B. Holliday, OBE; two *d*. *Educ:* Winchester. Served with Rifle Bde, 1940–46 (Captain). Barrister, Middle Temple, 1948; Bencher, 1969. Dep. Chm., QS, Herts, 1963–71; a Recorder of the Crown Court, 1972–79. Board of Trade Inspector: Cadco Group of Cos, 1963–64; H. S. Whiteside & Co Ltd, 1965–67; International Learning Systems Corp. Ltd, 1969–71; Pergamon Press, 1969–73. Sec. National Reference Tribunal for the Coal Mining Industry, 1953–64; Chancellor of Diocese of Bangor, 1959–88; Member, Governing Body of the Church in Wales, 1960–88; Licensed Parochial Lay Reader, Diocese of St Albans, 1961–; Member: General Council of the Bar, 1962–66; Senate of 4 Inns of Court, 1971–74; Senate of the Inns of Court and the Bar, 1974–75. Chm., Horserace Betting Levy Appeal Tribunal, 1969–74. Mem. Council, Benslow Music Trust, 1995–2001; Chm., Benslow Devélt Appeal, 1995–2000. JP Hertfordshire, 1963–71. *Publication:* (with R. M. Stuttard) A Review of Coursing, 1971. *Recreations:* listening to music, playing the flute. *Address:* Buckler's Hall, Much Hadham, Herts SG10 6EB. *T:* (01279) 842604. *Club:* Boodle's.

STACEY, Air Vice-Marshal John Nichol, CBE 1971; DSO 1945; DFC 1942; *b* 14 Sept. 1920; *s* of Captain Herbert Chambers Stacey and Mrs May Stacey; *m* 1950, Veronica, *d* of late Sinclair Sutherland Rudd-Clarke; two *d*. *Educ:* Whitgift Middle Sch., Croydon. Merchant Marine Apprentice, 1937–38; joined RAF, 1938; flying throughout War of 1939–45 (despatches thrice); comd No 160 Sqdn, 1944–45; Asst Air Attaché, Washington, 1947–48; psc 1949; on staff at Staff Coll., 1958–60; Chief of Air Staff, Royal Malayan Air Force, 1960–63 (JMN); comd RAF Laarbruch, Germany, 1963–66; AOC, Air Cadets, 1968–71; Dir, Orgn and Admin. Planning (RAF), MoD, 1971–74; AOA, Support Comd, 1974–75, retired. Dir, Stonham Housing Assoc., 1976–81; Member: Tunbridge Wells HA, 1981–86; RAFA Housing Assoc., 1982–86; High Weald Housing Assoc., 1990– (Chm., 1992–96; Pres., 1998–). President: Royal British Legion Gondhurst Br., 1991–; Headcorn Br., RAFA; Trustee: Housing Assoc. Charitable Trust, 1978–86; Bedgebury Sch., 1983– (Vice Pres., 1999–). *Recreations:* sailing, golf. *Address:* Riseden Cottage, Riseden, Goudhurst, Cranbrook, Kent TN17 1HJ. *T:* (01580) 211239. *Clubs:* Royal Air Force; Dale Hill Golf.

STACEY, Prof. Margaret; Professor of Sociology, University of Warwick, 1974–89, Emeritus Professor, 1989; *b* 27 March 1922; *d* of Conrad Eugene Petrie and Grace Priscilla Boyce; *m* 1945, Frank Arthur Stacey (*d* 1977); three *s* two *d. Educ:* City of London Sch. for Girls; London Sch. of Econs (BScEcon, 1st Cl. Hons Sociology). Labour Officer, Royal Ordnance Factory, 1943–44; Tutor, Oxford Univ., 1944–51; University Coll. of Swansea: Res. Officer and Fellow, 1961–63; Lectr in Sociol., 1963–70; Sen. Lectr in Sociol., 1970–74; Dir, Medical Sociol. Res. Centre, 1972–74. Lucille Petry Loene Vis. Prof. Univ. of Calif., San Francisco, 1988. British Sociological Association: Mem. Exec. Cttee, 1965–70, 1975–79; Hon. Gen. Sec., 1968–70; Chairperson, 1977–79; Pres., 1981–83; Mem. Women's Caucus, 1974–. Pres., Section N, BAAS, 1990. Scientific Advr to DHSS; Temp. Advr to Reg. Dir, WHO EURO. Pres., Assoc. for Welfare of Children in Hosp. (Wales), 1974–; Member: Assoc. for Welfare of Children in Hosp., 1960–; Welsh Hosp. Bd, 1970–74; Davies Cttee on Hosp. Complaints Procedure, 1971–73; GMC, 1976–84; Sociol. Cttee, SSRC, 1969–71; Health and Health Policy Cttee, SSRC, 1976–77. FRSocMed. Hon. Fellow, UC of Swansea, 1987. Hon. LLD Keele, 1998. *Publications:* Tradition and Change: a study of Banbury, 1960, paperback 1970; (ed) Comparability in Social Research, 1969; (ed and jt author) Hospitals, Children and their Families: a study of the welfare of children in hospital, 1970; Methods of Social Research, 1970; (jtly) Power, Persistence and Change: a second study of Banbury, 1975; (ed) The Sociology of the NHS, 1976; (ed jtly and contrib.) Beyond Separation: further studies of children in hospital, 1979; (jtly) Women, Power and Politics, 1981 (Fawcett Book Prize, 1982); (ed jtly) Concepts of Health, Illness and Disease: a comparative perspective, 1986; Sociology of Health and Healing: a textbook, 1988; Regulating British Medicine: the General Medical Council, 1992; (ed) Changing Human Reproduction: social science perspectives, 1992; contrib. to Feminist Rev., Sociol Rev., Sociol., Brit. Jl of Sociol., Social Science and Med., Jl of Med. Ethics, and Sociol. of Health and Illness. *Recreations:* walking, gardening. *Address:* 8 Lansdowne Circus, Leamington Spa, Warwicks CV32 4SW. *T:* (01926) 312094.

STACEY, Rear-Adm. Michael Lawrence, CB 1979; private consultant in marine pollution; Member, Advisory Committee on Protection of the Sea, since 1988; Life Vice President, Royal National Lifeboat Institution, since 1997; *b* 6 July 1924; *s* of Maurice Stacey and Dorice Evelyn (*née* Bulling); *m* 1955, Penelope Leana (*née* Riddoch); two *s. Educ:* Epsom Coll. Entered RN as Cadet, 1942; Normandy landings, HMS Hawkins, 1944; served in HM Ships Rotherham, Cambrian, Shoreham, Hornet, Vernon, Euryalus, Bermuda, Vigilant; Comdr 1958; staff of RN Staff Coll.; in comd HMS Blackpool, 1960–62; JSSC; Captain 1966; Chief Staff Officer to Admiral Commanding Reserves, 1966–68; in comd HMS Andromeda and Captain (F) Sixth Frigate Sqdn, 1968–70; Dep. Dir of Naval Warfare, 1970–73; in comd HMS Tiger, 1973–75; Asst Chief of Naval Staff (Policy), 1975–76; Flag Officer, Gibraltar, 1976–78. ADC to the Queen, 1975. Dir, Marine Emergency Ops, Marine Div., Dept of Trade, later Dept of Transport, 1979–87. FNI; FIMgt. Younger Brother, Trinity House, 1979. Liveryman, Shipwrights' Co., 1991; Mem., Master Mariners' Co., 1999. *Recreations:* fishing, yachting. *Address:* Little Hintock, 40 Lynch Road, Farnham, Surrey GU9 8BY. *T:* (01252) 713032. *Clubs:* Army and Navy, Royal Navy of 1765 and 1785, Royal Naval Sailing Association.

STACEY, Morna Dorothy, (Mrs W. D. Stacey); *see* Hooker, Prof. M. D.

STACEY, Rev. Nicolas David; Chairman, East Thames Housing Group (formerly East London Housing Association), 1993–98; *b* 27 Nov. 1927; *s* of late David and Gwen Stacey; *m* 1955, Hon. Anne Bridgeman, *er d* of 2nd Viscount Bridgeman, KBE, CB, DSO, MC; one *s* two *d. Educ:* RNC, Dartmouth; St Edmund Hall, Oxford (hons degree Mod. Hist.); Cuddesdon Theol Coll., Oxford. Midshipman, HMS Anson, 1945–46; Sub-Lt, 1946–48. Asst Curate, St Mark's, Portsea, 1953–58; Domestic Chap. to Bp of Birmingham, 1958–60; Rector of Woolwich, 1960–68; Dean of London Borough of Greenwich, 1965–68; Dep. Dir of Oxfam, 1968–70; Director of Social Services: London Borough of Ealing, 1971–74; Kent County Council, 1974–85; Dir, AIDS Policy Unit, sponsored by Citizen Action, 1988–89. Vice-Chm., TV South Charitable Trust, 1988–92. Six Preacher, Canterbury Cathedral, 1984–89. Sporting career: internat. sprinter, 1948–52, incl. British Empire Games, 1949, and Olympic Games, 1952 (semi-finalist 200 metres and finalist 4×400 metres relay); Pres., OUAC, 1951; winner, Oxf. v Cambridge 220 yds, 1948–51; Captain, Combined Oxf. and Camb. Athletic Team, 1951. *Publication:* Who Cares (autobiog.), 1971. *Address:* The Old Vicarage, Selling, Faversham, Kent ME13 9RD. *T:* (01227) 752833, *Fax:* (01227) 752889. *Clubs:* Beefsteak; Royal St George's Golf (Sandwich, Kent).

STACK, (Ann) Prunella, (Mrs Brian St Quentin Power), OBE 1980; President, The Fitness League (formerly Women's League of Health and Beauty), since 1982 (Member of Council, since 1950); *b* 28 July 1914; *d* of Capt. Hugh Bagot Stack, 8th Ghurka Rifles, and Mary Meta Bagot Stack, Founder of The Women's League of Health and Beauty; *m* 1st, 1938, Lord David Douglas-Hamilton (*d* 1944); two *s*; 2nd, 1950, Alfred G. Albers, FRCS (*d* 1951), Cape Town, S Africa; 3rd, 1964, Brian St Quentin Power. *Educ:* The Abbey, Malvern Wells. Mem. of the National Fitness Council, 1937–39. Vice-Pres., Outward Bound Trust, 1980–. *Publications:* The Way to Health and Beauty, 1938; Movement is Life, 1973; Island Quest, 1979; Zest for Life, 1988; Style for Life, 1990. *Recreations:* poetry, music, travel. *Address:* 14 Gertrude Street, SW10 0JN.

STACK, Rt Rev. George; Auxiliary Bishop of Westminster, (RC), and Titular Bishop of Gemellae in Numidia, since 2001; *b* 9 May 1946; *s* of Gerald Stack and Elizabeth (*née* McKenzie). *Educ:* St Aloysius Coll., Highgate; St Edmund's Coll., Ware; St Mary's Coll., Strawberry Hill. BEd (Hons). Ordained priest, 1972; Curate, St Joseph's, Hanwell 1972–75; Diocesan Catechetical Office, 1975–77; Curate, St Paul's, Wood Green, 1977–83; Parish Priest, Our Lady Help of Christians, Kentish Town, 1983–90; VG, Archdiocese of Westminster, 1990–93; Administrator, Westminster Cathedral, 1993–2001. Hon. Canon Emeritus, St Paul's Cathedral, 2001. Prelate of Honour to HH The Pope, 1993; KHS 2000. *Address:* Archbishop's House, Ambrosden Avenue, SW1P 1QJ. *T:* (020) 7798 9033.

STACK, Neville; international editorial consultant and syndicated political columnist, in South and South East Asia, Africa and the Caribbean, since 1989; *b* 2 Sept. 1933; *m* 1953, Molly Rowe; one *s* one *d. Educ:* Arnold School. Reporter: Ashton-under-Lyne Reporter, 1948; Express & Star, 1950; Sheffield Telegraph, and Kemsley National Papers, 1955; Northern News Editor, IPC national papers, 1971; Sub-editor, Daily Express, 1973; Editor, Stockport Advertiser, 1974; Editor, Leicester Mercury, 1974–87; Dir, F. Hewitt and Co. (1927) Ltd (Mercury Publishers), 1982–88; Editorial Consultant, Straits Times, Singapore, 1988–89; Consultant: New Paper, Singapore, 1990–; Trinidad Daily Express, 1990–; Independent Newspapers Gp, SA, 1998–99; Columnist: The Hindu, Madras, 1990–; Today, Singapore; Indian Business Leaders mag., Bombay; political commentator, Singapore Straits Times, 1990–99. Press Fellow, Wolfson Coll., Cambridge, 1987–88. Evaluator, RSA journalism qualification, 1992–; Co-organiser and Mem., Wolfson Coll. Regl Seminar for Editors, 1992–. Mem. Council, Leicester Univ., 1999. Hon. MA Leicester, 1988. *Publications:* The Empty Palace, 1976; Editing for the Nineties, 1988. *Recreations:* writing, computers, travel. *Address:* Cois Farraige, The Glebe, Donegal Town, Co. Donegal, Ireland. *T:* (73) 22241; *e-mail:* nstack@esatclear.ie.

STACK, Prunella; *see* Stack, A. P.

STACPOOLE, John Wentworth; Deputy Secretary, Department of Health and Social Security, 1979–82; *b* 16 June 1926; *s* of late G. W. Stacpoole and of Mrs M. G. Butt; *m* 1954, Charmian, *d* of late J. P. Bishop and Mrs E. M. Bishop; one *s* one *d. Educ:* Sedbergh; Magdalen Coll., Oxford (Demy; MA). Army, 1944–47 (Lieut, Assam Regt). Colonial Office, 1951–68, Private Sec. to Sec. of State, 1964–65; transf. to Min. of Social Security, 1968; Under-Sec., DHSS, 1973. Mem., Maidstone HA, 1982–91. Chm., Maidstone Hospice Appeal, 1987–92. *Recreations:* reading, walking, sketching. *Address:* Fairseat Lodge, Fairseat, near Sevenoaks, Kent TN15 7LU. *T:* (01732) 822201.

STACY, Graham Henry, CBE 1993; FCA; Member, Competition (formerly Monopolies and Mergers) Commission, since 1995; *b* 23 May 1933; *s* of Norman Winny Stacy and Winifred Frances Stacy (*née* Wood); *m* 1958, Mary Fereday; one *s* three *d. Educ:* Stationers' Co.'s Sch. FCA 1955. Articled to Walter Smee Will & Co., 1950–55; Nat. Service, RN (Sub-Lieut), 1955–57; joined Price Waterhouse, 1957: Partner, 1968–93; Dir of Technical Services, 1976–88; Dir of Professional Standards (UK and Europe), 1988–93; Mem., Policy Cttee, 1987–93. Member: Auditing Practices Cttee, 1976–84; Accounting Standards Cttee, 1986–90; Accounting Standards Bd, 1990–94. Hon. Treasurer: URC in UK, 1995–; Sanctuary Housing Assoc., 1995–. *Recreations:* golf, bridge. *Address:* 31 Fordington Road, N6 4TD. *T:* (020) 8444 9314.

STADLEN, Nicholas Felix; QC 1991; a Recorder, since 2000; *b* 3 May 1950; *s* of late Peter Stadlen and of Hedi (*née* Simon); *m* 1972, Frances Edith Howarth, *d* of T. E. B. and Margaret Howarth; three *s. Educ:* St Paul's School (Scholar); Trinity Coll., Cambridge (Open Scholarship and McGill Exhibition; BA Hons Classics Part 1, History Part 2). Pres., Cambridge Union Soc., 1970. First in order of merit, Part 1 Bar Exams, 1975; called to the Bar, Inner Temple, 1976. An Asst Recorder, 1997–2000. Mem., Bar Council Public Affairs Cttee, 1987; Chm., Bar Caribbean pro bono Cttee, 1999–. First Sec., British-Irish Assoc., 1972–74. *Publications:* (with Michael Barnes) Gulbenkian Foundation Reports on National Music and Drama Education, 1974–75; (contrib.) Convention: an account of the 1976 US Democratic Party Presidential Nominating Convention, 1976. *Recreation:* listening to classical music. *Address:* Fountain Court, Temple, EC4Y 9DH. *T:* (020) 7583 3335.

STAFFORD, Marquis of; James Granville Egerton; *b* 12 Aug. 1975; *s* and *heir* of Duke of Sutherland, *qv. Educ:* Eton Coll., Windsor; Univ. of Edinburgh. *Address:* Ley Farm, Stetchworth, Newmarket, Suffolk CB8 9TX.

STAFFORD, 15th Baron *cr* 1640; **Francis Melfort William Fitzherbert;** DL; *b* 13 March 1954; *s* of 14th Baron Stafford and of Morag Nada, *yr d* of late Lt-Col Alastair Campbell; *S* father, 1986; *m* 1980, Katharine Mary Codrington; two *s* two *d. Educ:* Ampleforth College; Reading Univ.; RAC, Cirencester. Director (non-executive): Tarmac Industrial Products Div., 1987–93; Mid Staffs Mental Health Foundn, 1990–99; Hanley Economic BS, 1992–. Pro-Chancellor, Keele Univ., 1993–. Pres., Staffs CCC, 1999; Pres. and Patron various orgns in North Staffs. Governor, Harper Adams Agricl Coll., 1990– (Vice Chm. Govs, 1999–). DL Stafford, 1994. *Recreations:* shooting, cricket, golf. *Heir: s* Hon. Benjamin John Basil Fitzherbert, *b* 8 Nov. 1983. *Address:* Swynnerton Park, Stone, Staffordshire ST15 0QE. *T:* (01782) 796228. *Clubs:* Army and Navy, Lord's Taverners.

STAFFORD, Bishop Suffragan of, since 1996; **Rt Rev. Christopher John Hill;** *b* 10 Oct. 1945; *s* of Leonard and Frances V. Hill; *m* 1976, Hilary Ann Whitehouse; three *s* one *d. Educ:* Sebright Sch., Worcs; King's Coll., London (BD Hons; Relton Prize for Theology, 1967; MTh 1968; AKC 1967). Deacon 1969, priest 1970. Asst Curate, Dio. of Lichfield: St Michael's, Tividale, 1969–73; St Nicholas, Codsall, 1973–74; Asst Chaplain to Archbp of Canterbury for Foreign Relations, 1974–81; Archbp's Sec. for Ecumenical Affairs, 1982–89; Hon. Canon of Canterbury Cathedral, 1982–89; Canon Residentiary, 1989–96, Precentor, 1990–96, St Paul's Cathedral; Chaplain to the Queen, 1987–96. Anglican Secretary: Anglican-RC Internat. Commn (I), 1974–81, Internat. Commn (II), 1983–90 (Mem., 1990–91); Anglican-Lutheran Eur. Commn, 1981–82; Consultant: C of E—German Churches Commn, 1987–90; C of E—Nordic–Baltic Churches Commn, 1989–92; Co-Chairman: C of E—French Lutheran and Reformed Conversations, 1994–98; Meissen Theol Conf., 1998–. Member: C of E Council for Christian Unity, 1989–96; Legal Adv. Commn, Gen. Synod of C of E, 1991–; Faith and Order Adv. Gp, 1996– (Vice-Chm., 1998–); House of Bishops and Gen. Synod of C of E, 1999–; Wkg Pty on Women in the Episcopate, 2001–. Guestmaster, Nikaean Club, 1982–89. Co-Chm., London Soc. of Jews and Christians, 1991–96; Vice-Chm., Ecclesiastical Law Soc., 1993–. *Publications:* (ed jtly) Anglicans and Roman Catholics: the search for unity, 1995; (ed jtly) Documents in the Debate: papers on Anglican orders, 1997; miscellaneous ecumenical articles. *Recreations:* Radio 3, mountain walking, detective stories, Italian food, GWR, unaffordable wine. *Address:* Ash Garth, 6 Broughton Crescent, Barlaston, Stoke-on-Trent ST12 9DD. *T:* (01782) 373308, *Fax:* (01782) 373705. *Club:* Athenæum.

STAFFORD, Archdeaconry of; *see* Lichfield.

STAFFORD, Andrew Bruce; QC 2000; *b* 30 March 1957; *s* of Cyril Henry Stafford and Audrey Estelle Stafford; *m* 1982, Catherine Anne, *d* of Derek and Kathleen Johnson; one *s* four *d. Educ:* Royal Grammar Sch., Newcastle upon Tyne; Trinity Hall, Cambridge (BA Law, MA). Called to the Bar, Middle Temple, 1980. *Address:* Littleton Chambers, 3 King's Bench Walk North, Temple, EC4Y 7HR.

STAFFORD, David Valentine; Secretary, Economic and Social Research Council, 1988–90; *b* 14 Feb. 1930; *s* of Augustus Everard and Emily Blanche Stafford; *m* 1953, Aileen Patricia Wood; one *s* one *d. Educ:* Rutlish School, Merton. Dept of Educn and Science, 1951–88; Sec., Open Univ. Planning Cttee, 1967–69. Acting Chm., ESRC, Feb.–Sept. 1988. *Recreations:* reading, gardening. *Address:* Vallis, Lyncombe Vale Road, Bath, Avon BA2 4LS. *T:* (01225) 312563.

See also N. D. Stafford.

STAFFORD, Godfrey Harry, CBE 1976; PhD; FRS 1979; FInstP; Master of St Cross College, Oxford, 1979–87; *b* 15 April 1920; *s* of Henry and Sarah Stafford; *m* 1950, Helen Goldthorp (*née* Clark); one *s* twin *d. Educ:* Rondebosch Boys High Sch., S Africa; Univ. of Cape Town; Gonville and Caius Coll., Cambridge. MSc Cape Town, 1941; Ebden Scholar, PhD Cantab 1950; MA Oxon 1971. South African Naval Forces, 1941–46. Harwell, 1949–51; Head of Biophysics Subdiv., CSIR, Pretoria, 1951–54; Cyclotron Gp, AERE, 1954–57; Rutherford Laboratory: Head of Proton Linear Accelerator Gp, 1957; Head of High Energy Physics Div., 1963; Dep. Dir, 1966; Dir, Rutherford Lab., Chilton, 1969–79; Dir Gen., 1979–81, Hon. Scientist, 1987–, Rutherford Appleton Laboratory; Fellow, St Cross Coll., Oxford, 1971–79 (Hon. Fellow, 1987). CERN appointments: UK deleg. to Council, 1973; Vice-Pres., Council, 1973; Scientific Policy Cttee, 1973, Vice-

Chm., 1976, Chm., 1978. Vice-Pres. for meetings, Inst. of Physics, 1976; President: European Physical Soc., 1984–86 (Vice-Pres., 1982–84); Inst. of Physics, 1986–88. Governor: Oxford Centre for Post-Graduate Hebrew Studies, 1983–93; Westminster Coll., 1987–93. Glazebrook Prize and Medal, Inst. of Physics, 1981. Hon. DSc Birmingham, 1980. *Publications:* papers and articles in learned jls on: biophysics, nuclear physics, high energy physics. *Recreations:* walking, foreign travel, music. *Address:* Ferry Cottage, North Hinksey Village, Oxford OX2 0NA. *T:* (01865) 247621.

STAFFORD, Prof. Nicholas David, FRCS; Professor of Head and Neck Surgery and Otolaryngology, since 1995, and Head, School of Medicine, since 1997, University of Hull; *b* 13 Aug. 1954; *s* of David Valentine Stafford, *qv*; *m* 1977, Heather Gay Sims; four *d*. *Educ:* Farnborough Grammar Sch.; Univ. of Leeds (MB ChB 1977). FRCS 1983. Various SHO posts, 1978–82; Registrar in ENT Surgery, RNTNEH, 1982–84; Sen. Registrar in ENT/Head and Neck Surgery, Royal Marsden Hosp. and St Mary's Hosp., London, 1985–89; Consultant Head and Neck/ENT Surgeon, St Mary's, Ealing and Charing Cross Hosps, 1989–95. Résident Etranger, Inst. Gustave-Roussy, Paris, 1987–88. *Publications:* (with R. Youngs) Colour Aids: ENT, 1988, 2nd edn 1999; (ed with J. Waldron) Management of Oral Cancer, 1989; contribs mainly in field of head and neck oncology. *Recreation:* classic cars. *Address:* 10 New Walk, Beverley HU17 7AD. *T:* (01482) 871541. *Club:* Alpine Renault (UK).

STAFFORD, Peter Moore, FCA; Member, Board of Partners, Deloitte & Touche (formerly Touche Ross & Co.), 1990–2000 (Chairman, 1992–95); *b* 24 April 1942; *s* of late Harry Shaw Stafford and May Alexandra (*née* Moore); *m* 1973, Elspeth Ann, *d* of James Steel Harvey; one *s* one *d*. *Educ:* Charterhouse. FCA 1976 (ACA 1965). Articled Clerk, Garnett Crewdson & Co., Manchester, 1960–64; Arthur Andersen, 1966–68; Partner, 1968–71, Garnett Crewdson & Co., merged with Spicer & Oppenheim: Partner, 1971–90; Managing Partner, 1990; merged with Touche Ross & Co. Member: Council for Industry and Higher Educn, 1993–97; Professional Standards Office, ICAEW, 1998–. Governor, Terra Nova Sch., 1976–. *Recreations:* travel, gardening, restoring antique launches. *Address:* Holmes Chapel, Cheshire. *T:* (01477) 533339. *Clubs:* Royal Over-Seas League; St James's (Manchester).

STAFFORD-CLARK, Maxwell Robert Guthrie Stewart, (Max); artistic director and founder, Out of Joint Theatre Company, since 1993; *b* 17 March 1941; *s* of late Dr David Stafford-Clark, FRCP, FRCPsych and of Dorothy Stewart (*née* Oldfield); *m* 1st, 1971, Carole Hayman; 2nd, 1981, Ann Pennington; one *d*. *Educ:* Felstead School; Riverdale Country Day School, NY; Trinity College, Dublin. Associate dir, Traverse, 1966, artistic dir, 1968–70; dir, Traverse Workshop Co., 1970–74; founder, Joint Stock Theatre Group, 1974; Artistic Dir, English Stage Company at Royal Court Theatre, 1979–93. Productions include: Cloud 9, 1980; Top Girls, 1982; Falkland Sound, 1983; Tom and Viv, 1984; Rat in the Skull, 1984; Serious Money, 1987; Our Country's Good, 1988; King Lear, 1993; The Steward of Christendom, 1995; Shopping and Fucking, 1996; Blue Heart, 1997. *Publication:* Letters to George, 1989. *Address:* 7 Gloucester Crescent, NW1 7DS. *Clubs:* Groucho; Classic Car.

STAGG, (Charles) Richard (Vernon), CMG 2001; HM Diplomatic Service; Director, Foreign and Commonwealth Office, since 2001; *b* 27 Sept. 1955; *s* of Walter and Elise Patricia Stagg; *m* 1982, Arabella Clare Faber; three *s* two *d*. *Educ:* Winchester; Oriel Coll., Oxford. Joined Diplomatic Service, 1977; FCO, 1977–79; Sofia, 1979–82; The Hague, 1982–85; FCO, 1985–86; UK Repn to EC, Brussels, 1987–88; FCO, 1988–91; Mem., UK Representation to EC, Brussels, 1991–93; Private Sec. to Foreign Sec., 1993–96; Head, EU (Ext.) Dept, FCO, 1996–98; Ambassador to Bulgaria, 1998–2001. *Recreations:* racing, gardening. *Address:* c/o Foreign and Commonwealth Office, King Charles Street, SW1A 2AH. *Clubs:* Turf; Millennium.

STAGG, Prof. Geoffrey Leonard, MBE 1945; Professor Emeritus, Department of Spanish and Portuguese, University of Toronto; *b* 10 May 1913; *s* of Henry Percy Stagg and Maude Emily Bradbury; *m* 1948, Amy Southwell, Wellesley Hills, Mass, USA; two *s* one *d*. *Educ:* King Edward's School, Birmingham (Scholar); Trinity Hall, Cambridge (Scholar). BA 1st cl. Hons Modern and Medieval Languages Tripos, 1934; MA 1946; Joseph Hodges Choate Mem. Fellow, Harvard Univ., 1934–36; AM (Harvard), 1935; Modern Languages Master, King Edward's School, Birmingham, 1938–40, 1946–47; served in Intelligence Corps, 1940–46; Lecturer in Spanish and Italian, Nottingham Univ., 1947–53, and Head of Dept of Spanish, 1954–56; Dept of Italian and Hispanic Studies, Toronto Univ.: Prof., 1956–78; Chm., 1956–66, 1969–78. Vice-Pres., Assoc. of Teachers of Spanish and Portuguese of GB and Ireland, 1948–; Pres., Canadian Assoc. of Hispanists, 1964–66, 1972–74; Vice-Pres., Internat. Assoc. of Hispanists, 1977–83; Chm., Local Organising Cttee, Sixth Congress of Internat. Assoc. of Hispanists, Toronto, 1977. Fellow, New Coll., Univ. of Toronto, 1962–; Senior Fellow, Massey Coll., Univ. of Toronto, 1965–70; Canada Council Senior Fellowship, 1967–68. *Publications:* articles on Spanish literature in learned jls; *festschrift:* Ingeniosa Invención: essays on Golden Age Spanish literature, ed E. M. Anderson and A. R. Williamsen. *Address:* 30 Old Bridle Path, Toronto, ON M4T 1A7, Canada.

STAGG, Richard; *see* Stagg, C. R. V.

STAINTON, Sir (John) Ross, Kt 1981; CBE 1971; retired; *b* 27 May 1914; *s* of late George Stainton and Helen Ross; *m* 1939, Doreen Werner (*d* 2001); three *d*. *Educ:* Glengorse, Eastbourne; Malvern Coll., Worcestershire. Joined Imperial Airways as Trainee, 1933; served in Italy, Egypt, Sudan. Served with RAF in England, West Indies and USA, 1940–46. Man. N America, BOAC, 1949–53; General Sales Man. BOAC, and other Head Office posts, 1954–68; Dep. Man. Dir, 1968–71; Man. Dir, 1971–72; Mem., BOAC Bd, 1968, Chm. and Chief Exec., 1972, until merged into British Airways, 1974; Mem., 1971–, Dep. Chm. and Chief Exec., 1977–79, Chairman, 1979–80, British Airways Bd. Vice Pres., Private Patients Plan, 1986– (Dir, 1979–86). Hon. Treasurer, Air League Council, 1986–91. FCIT (Pres., 1970–71); CRAeS 1978. *Clubs:* Royal Air Force; Royal and Ancient Golf (St Andrews); Sunningdale Golf.

STAINTON, Keith; *b* 8 Nov. 1921; *m* 1946, Vanessa Ann Heald (marr. diss.); three *s* three *d*; *m* 1980, Frances Easton. *Educ:* Kendal Sch.; Manchester Univ. (BA (Com.) Dist. in Economics). Insurance clerk, 1936–39. Served War of 1939–45: Lieut, RNVR, Submarines and with French Resistance, 1940–46. Manchester Univ., 1946–49; Leader Writer, Financial Times, 1949–52; Industrial Consultant, 1952–57; joined Burton, Son & Sanders, Ltd, 1957, Man. Dir 1961–69, Chm. 1962–69; Chm. Scotia Investments Ltd, 1969–72. MP (C) Sudbury and Woodbridge, Dec. 1963–1983; Mem., House of Commons Select Cttees on Expenditure and Science and Technology. Mem. Council of Europe and WEU, 1979–83. Légion d'Honneur, Croix de Guerre avec Palmes, Ordre de l'Armée, 1943. *Address:* Little Bealings House, near Woodbridge, Suffolk IP13 6LX. *T:* (01473) 624205.

STAINTON, Sir Ross; *see* Stainton, Sir J. R.

STAIR, 14th Earl of, *cr* 1703; **John David James Dalrymple;** Bt 1664 and 1698 (Scot); Viscount Stair, Lord Glenluce and Stranraer, 1690; Viscount Dalrymple, Lord Newliston, 1703; Baron Oxenfoord (UK), 1841; *b* 4 Sept. 1961; *s* of 13th Earl of Stair, KCVO, MBE and of Davina Katharine, *d* of late Hon. Sir David Bowes-Lyon, KCVO; *S* father, 1996. Commnd Scots Guards, 1982. *Heir: b* Hon. David Hew Dalrymple, *b* 30 March 1963.

STALLARD, family name of **Baron Stallard**.

STALLARD, Baron *cr* 1983 (Life Peer), of St Pancras in the London Borough of Camden; **Albert William Stallard;** *b* 5 Nov. 1921; *m* 1944, Sheila, *d* of W. C. Murphy; one *s* one *d*. *Educ:* Low Waters Public School; Hamilton Academy, Scotland. Engineer, 1937–65; Technical Training Officer, 1965–70. Councillor, St Pancras, 1953–59, Alderman, 1962–65; Councillor, Camden, 1965–70, Alderman, 1971–78. MP (Lab) St Pancras N, 1970–83; PPS to: Minister of State, Agriculture, Fisheries and Food, 1974; Minister of State for Housing and Construction, 1974–76; an Asst Govt Whip, 1976–78; a Lord Comr, HM Treasury, 1978–79. Chairman: Camden Town Disablement Cttee (Mem., 1951); Camden Assoc. for Mental Health. Mem., Inst. of Training Officers, 1971. AEU Order of Merit, 1968. *Address:* Flat 2, 2 Belmont Street, NW1 8HH.

STALLWORTHY, Prof. Jon Howie, FBA 1990; Professor of English Literature, Oxford University, 1992–2000, now Emeritus; Senior Research Fellow, Wolfson College, Oxford, since 2000 (Fellow, since 1986); *b* 18 Jan. 1935; *s* of Sir John (Arthur) Stallworthy; *m* 1960, Gillian Meredith (*née* Waldock); two *s* one *d*. *Educ:* The Dragon Sch., Oxford; Rugby Sch.; Magdalen Coll., Oxford (MA, BLitt). Served RWAFF (pre-Oxford). At Oxford won Newdigate Prize, 1958 (runner-up, 1957). Joined Oxford Univ. Press, 1959, Dep. Head, Academic Div., 1975–77; John Wendell Anderson Prof. of English Lit., Cornell Univ., 1977–86; Reader in English Lit., Oxford Univ., 1986–92. Chatterton Lectr on an English Poet, British Academy, 1970; during a sabbatical year, 1971–72, was a Visiting Fellow at All Souls Coll., Oxford. FRSL, 1971. *Publications: poems* (collections): The Astronomy of Love, 1961; Out of Bounds, 1963; Root and Branch, 1969; Positives, 1969; The Apple Barrel: selected poems, 1955–63, 1974; Hand in Hand, 1974; A Familiar Tree, 1978; The Anzac Sonata: new and selected poems, 1986; The Guest From the Future, 1995; Rounding the Horn: collected poems, 1998; *criticism:* Between the Lines, W. B. Yeats's Poetry in the Making, 1963; Vision and Revision in Yeats's Last Poems, 1969; *biography:* Wilfred Owen, 1974 (winner of Duff Cooper Meml Prize, W. H. Smith Literary Award and E. M. Forster Award); Louis MacNeice (Southern Arts Lit. Prize), 1995; *autobiography:* Singing School: the making of a poet, 1998; *translations:* (with Peter France) Alexander Blok: The Twelve and other poems, 1970; (with Jerzy Peterkiewicz) poems for 2nd edn of Five Centuries of Polish Poetry, 1970; (with Peter France) Boris Pasternak: Selected Poems, 1983; *edited:* The Penguin Book of Love Poetry, 1973; Wilfred Owen: Complete Poems and Fragments, 1983; The Oxford Book of War Poetry, 1984; The Poems of Wilfred Owen, 1985; First Lines: poems written in youth, from Herbert to Heaney, 1987; Henry Reed: Collected Poems, 1991; The War Poems of Wilfred Owen, 1994; (jtly) The Norton Anthology of Poetry, 4th edn, 1996; (jtly) The Norton Anthology of English Literature, 7th edn, 2000. *Address:* Wolfson College, Oxford OX2 6UD; Long Farm, Elsfield Road, Old Marston, Oxford OX3 0PR. *Club:* Vincent's (Oxford).

STAMER, Sir (Lovelace) Anthony, 5th Bt *cr* 1809; MA; AMIMI; *b* 28 Feb. 1917; *s* of Sir Lovelace Stamer, 4th Bt, and Eva Mary (*d* 1974), *e d* of R. C. Otter; *S* father, 1941; *m* 1st, 1948, Stella Huguette (marr. diss., 1953), *d* of late Paul Burnell Binnie, Brussels; one *s* one *d*; 2nd, 1955, Margaret Lucy (marr. diss., 1959), *d* of late Major Belben; 3rd, 1960, Marjorie June (marr. diss. 1968), *d* of late T. C. Noakes, St James, Cape; 4th, 1983, Elizabeth Graham Smith (*d* 1992), *widow* of G. P. H. Smith, Colyton, Devon; 5th, 1997, Pamela Grace (*née* Hawkins), *widow* of P. B. Cheston. *Educ:* Harrow; Trinity Coll., Cambridge; Royal Agricultural Coll., Cirencester. BA 1947; MA 1963; AMIMI 1963. Served RAF 1939–41; Officer in ATA 1941–45. Executive Director: Bentley Drivers Club Ltd, 1969–73; Bugatti & Ferrari Owners Club, 1973–75; Hon. Treasurer, Ferrari Owners' Club, 1975–81. *Heir: s* Peter Tomlinson Stamer, Sqn Leader, RAF, retd [*b* 19 Nov. 1951; *m* 1979, Dinah Louise Berry (marr. diss. 1989); one *s* one *d*; *m* 1999, Věra Řeháková]. *Address:* 5 Windrush Court, 175 The Hill, Burford, Oxon OX18 4RE.

STAMM, Temple Theodore, FRCS; Orthopædic Surgeon Emeritus, Guy's Hospital; *b* 22 Dec. 1905; *s* of Dr Louis Edward Stamm, Streatham, and Louisa Ethel (*née* Perry), Caterham, Surrey; *m* 1945, Pamela (*d* 1998), *d* of Charles Russell, Chislehurst, Kent. *Educ:* Rose Hill Sch., Surrey; Haileybury Coll.; Guy's Hospital Medical School. MB, BS (London), 1930, MRCS, LRCP 1928, FRCS 1934. Fellow Royal Society of Medicine; Fellow British Orthopædic Assoc.; Member British Med. Assoc. Formerly: Orthopædic Surgeon, Bromley Hospital, 1941–66; Asst Orthopædic Surgeon and Orthopædic Registrar, Royal Nat. Orthopædic Hospital; Asst Orthopædic Surgeon, Orthopædic Registrar, Asst Anæsthetist and Demonstrator of Anatomy, Guy's Hospital. Major RAMC. *Publications:* Foot Troubles, 1957; Guide to Orthopædics, 1958; Surgery of the Foot, British Surgical Practice, Vol. 4; contributions to Blackburn and Lawrie's Textbook of Surgery, 1958; articles in: Lancet, Guy's Hospital Reports, Journal of Bone and Joint Surgery, Medical Press, etc. *Recreations:* farming, sailing, music. *Address:* Little Badgers, 6 The Spinney, Itchenor, W Sussex PO20 7DF.

STAMMERS, Michael Kingsley; Keeper of Merseyside Maritime Museum, since 1986; *b* 30 Aug. 1943; *s* of John Kingsley Stammers and Thelma Marjorie Stammers (*née* Gooch); *m* 1971, Pauline Birch; one *s* one *d*. *Educ:* Norwich Sch.; Univ. of Bristol (BA Hons History). AMA. Curator of Folk Life, Warwick County Museum, 1966–69; Keeper of Shipping, Liverpool City Museum, 1969–74; Curator of Maritime History, Merseyside County Museums, 1974–86. Member: Internat. Commn for Maritime History, 1990–; Nat. Historic Ships Cttee, 1990–. Hon. Mem., Internat. Cape Horners' Assoc., 1971. FRHistS 2000. *Publications:* West Coast Shipping, 1976, 2nd edn 1989; The Passage Makers, 1978; Liverpool: the port and its ships, 1991; (with J. Kearon) The Jhelum: a Victorian merchant ship, 1992; Mersey Flats and Flatmen, 1993; (with J. G. Read) A Guide to the Records of Merseyside Maritime Museum, 1995; A Maritime Fortress, 2001; contribs to learned jls. *Recreations:* going to sea, gardening, music. *Address:* Merseyside Maritime Museum, Albert Dock, Liverpool L3 4AQ. *T:* (0151) 478 4402. *Clubs:* Naval; Athenæum (Liverpool).

STAMP, family name of **Baron Stamp**.

STAMP, 4th Baron *cr* 1938, of Shortlands; **Trevor Charles Bosworth Stamp,** MD; FRCP; Hon. Consultant Physician, Royal National Orthopaedic Hospital, since 1999; Consultant Physician and Director, Department of Bone and Mineral Metabolism, Institute of Orthopaedics, Royal National Orthopaedic Hospital, 1974–99; *b* 18 Sept. 1935; *s* of 3rd Baron Stamp, MD, FRCPath and Frances Hammond (*d* 1998), *d* of late Charles Henry Bosworth, Evanston, Illinois, USA; *S* father, 1987; *m* 1st, 1963, Anne Carolynn Churchill (marr. diss. 1971); two *d*; 2nd, 1975, Carol Anne, *d* of Robert Keith Russell; one *s* one *d*. *Educ:* The Leys School; Gonville and Caius Coll., Cambridge; Yale Univ.; St Mary's Hosp. Medical School. MSc (Yale) 1957; MD (Cantab) 1972; FRCP

1978. Qualified in medicine, 1960; Med. Registrar, Professorial Medical Unit, St Mary's Hosp., 1964–66; Hon. Senior Registrar 1968–73, and Hon. Sen. Lecturer 1972–73, Dept of Human Metabolism, University College Hosp. and Medical School; Hon. Consultant Physician and Sen. Lectr, Middlesex Hosp. and UCL School of Medicine, 1974–99, now Emeritus Consultant, UCL Hosps. Mem., Scientific Adv. Bd, Nat. Osteoporosis Soc. Patron, Nat. Assoc. for Relief of Paget's Disease. Hon. Life Member: Soc. for Bone and Mineral Res.; Internat. Skeletal Soc. Prix André Lichtwitz, France, 1973. *Publications:* numerous papers on disorders of mineral metabolism. *Recreations:* music, golf, contract bridge. *Heir: s* Hon. Nicholas Charles Trevor Stamp, *b* 27 Feb. 1978. *Address:* 15 Ceylon Road, W14 0PY. *T:* (020) 7603 0487.

STAMP, Gavin Mark, MA, PhD; FSA; architectural historian and writer; Senior Lecturer, Mackintosh School of Architecture, Glasgow School of Art, since 1999 (Lecturer, 1990–99); *b* 15 March 1948; *s* of Barry Hartnell Stamp and Norah Clare (*née* Rich); *m* 1982, Alexandra Frances Artley; two *d. Educ:* Dulwich Coll.; Gonville & Caius Coll., Cambridge (MA, PhD). Contributor to The Spectator, The Independent, Daily Telegraph, Private Eye, Architects' Jl, etc. Chm., Twentieth Century (formerly Thirties) Soc., 1983–; Founder and Chm., Alexander Thomson Soc., 1991–. FSA 1998. Hon. FRIAS 1994; Hon. FRIBA 1998. *Publications:* The Architect's Calendar, 1973; Silent Cities, 1977; (text only) Temples of Power, 1979; (jtly) The Victorian Buildings of London 1837–1887, 1980; Robert Weir Schultz and his work for the Marquesses of Bute, 1981; The Great Perspectivists, 1982; The Changing Metropolis, 1984; The English House 1860–1914, 1986; (jtly) The Church in Crisis, 1986; The Telephone Boxes, 1989; (ed jtly) Greek Thomson, 1994; (ed) Recollections of Sir Gilbert Scott, 1995; Alexander 'Greek' Thomson, 1999; Edwin Lutyens Country Houses, 2001; articles in Arch. History, Arch. Design, Jl of RSA, etc. *Address:* 1 Moray Place, Strathbungo, Glasgow G41 2AQ. *T:* (0141) 423 3747.

STAMP, Terence Henry; actor and author; *b* 22 July 1938; *s* of Thomas Stamp and Ethel Esther Perrott. *Educ:* Plaistow County Grammar School; Webber-Douglas Dramatic Acad. (Amehurst Webber Meml Schol., 1958). *Films include:* Billy Budd, 1962; The Collector, 1964; Far from the Madding Crowd, 1966; Blue, 1967; Spirits of the Dead (Fellini sect.), 1967; Theorem, 1968; Superman, 1977; Meetings with Remarkable Men, 1977; Superman 2, 1978; The Hit, 1984; Legal Eagles, 1985; Wall Street, 1987; Young Guns, 1988; The Sicilian, 1988; Alien Nation, 1989; Prince of Shadows, or Beltenebros, 1993; The Real McCoy, 1994; The Adventures of Priscilla the Queen of the Desert, 1994; Bliss, 1995; Limited Edition, 1995; Kiss the Sky, 1998; Love Walked In, 1998; The Limey, 1999; Red Planet, 2000; *stage:* Alfie, Morosco, NY, 1965; Dracula, Shaftesbury, 1978; Lady from the Sea, Roundhouse, 1979. Launched, with Elizabeth Buxton, Stamp Collection range of organic food, 1994. Hon. DArts East London, 1993. *Publications:* autobiography: Stamp Album, 1987; Coming Attractions, 1988; Double Feature, 1989; The Night (novel), 1992; (with Elizabeth Buxton) The Stamp Collection Cookbook, 1997. *Address:* c/o Markham & Froggatt, 4 Windmill Street, W1P 1HF. *Club:* New York Athletic (New York).

STAMPER, John Trevor, MA; FREng, Hon. FRAeS, CIMgt; Corporate Technical Director, British Aerospace, 1977–85, retired; *b* 12 Oct. 1926; *s* of late Col Horace John Stamper and Clara Jane (*née* Collin); *m* 1950, Cynthia Joan Parsons; two *s* one *d. Educ:* Loughborough Grammar Sch.; Jesus Coll., Cambridge (MA 1951). FRAeS 1965 (Hon. FRAeS 1984); CEng 1966; FREng (FEng 1977); CIMgt (CBIM 1983). Blackburn Aircraft Ltd: Post-grad. apprenticeship, 1947; Dep. Head of Aerodynamics, 1955; Head of Structures, 1956; Flight Test Manager, 1960; Chief Designer (Buccaneer), 1961; Dir and Chief Designer, 1963; Hawker Siddeley Aviation Ltd (following merger): Exec. Dir Design (Military), 1966; Exec. Dir and Dep. Chief Engr (Civil), 1968; Tech. Dir, 1968–77. Member: Council, RAeS, 1971–77, 1978–88 (Pres., 1981–82); Tech. Bd, SBAC, 1966–85 (Chm., 1972–74); Council, SBAC, 1981–84; Council, Aircraft Res. Assoc., 1966–85 (Chm., 1976–78); Aeronautical Res. Council, 1971–74; Air Warfare Adv. Bd, Defence Scientific Adv. Council, 1973–84; Noise Adv. Council, 1975–78; Comité Technique et Industriel, Assoc. Européenne des Constructeurs de Matériel Aerospatial, 1971–81 (Chm., 1974–81); Airworthiness Requirements Bd, CAA, 1976–78, 1987–88. Hon. DSc Loughborough, 1986. Hodgeson Prize, RAeS, 1975 and 1986; British Gold Medal for Aeronautics, RAeS, 1976. *Publications:* (contrib.) The Future of Aeronautics, 1970; Air Power in the Next Generation, 1979; papers in Jl RAeS. *Recreations:* sailing, photography. *Address:* 7 Sycamore Close, The Mount, Fetcham, Surrey KT22 9EX. *T:* (01372) 370336.

STANAGE, Rt Rev. Thomas Shaun; Warden, Community of St Michael and All Angels, Bloemfontein, since 1998; Bishop of Bloemfontein, 1982–97; *b* 6 April 1932; *s* of late Robert and Edith Clarice Stanage. *Educ:* King James I Grammar Sch., Bishop Auckland; Univ. of Oxford (MA, Hons Theology, 1956). Curate, St Faith, Great Crosby, 1958–61; Minister of Conventional District of St Andrews, Orford, 1961–63; Vicar, St Andrew, Orford, 1963–70; Rector, All Saints, Somerset West, 1970–75; Dean of Kimberley, 1975–78; Bishop Suffragan of Johannesburg, 1978–82. Liaison Bishop to Missions to Seamen, Southern Africa. Lectr in Systematic Theol., Biblical Studies and Religious Educn, Univ. of Orange Free State, 1998–2001. Hon. DD Nashotah Theol Sem., Wisconsin, 1986. *Recreations:* flying (private pilot); music (organ, violin and piano). *Address:* Walden Lodge, 24 Hippocrene Street, Helicon Heights, Bloemfontein 9301, S Africa. *Clubs:* Bloemfontein; Good Hope Flying, Cape Aero (Cape Town).

STANBRIDGE, Air Vice-Marshal Sir Brian (Gerald Tivy), KCVO 1979 (MVO 1958); CBE 1974; AFC 1952; Director-General, Air Transport Users' Committee, 1979–85; *b* 6 July 1924; *s* of late Gerald Edward and Violet Georgina Stanbridge; *m* 1st, 1949, Kathleen Diana Hayes (marr. diss. 1983); two *d*; 2nd, 1984, Jennifer Anne Jenkins. *Educ:* Thurlestone Coll., Dartmouth. Served War: RAFVR, 1942; commnd, 1944; No 31 Sqdn (SE Asia), 1944–46; No 47 Sqdn, 1947–49; 2FTS/CFS, 1950–52; British Services Mission to Burma, 1952–54; The Queen's Flight (personal pilot and flying instructor to Duke of Edinburgh), 1954–58; Naval Staff Coll., 1958; PSO to AOC-in-C Coastal Comd, 1958–59; W/Cdr, Flying, RAF St Mawgan, 1960–62; jssc, 1962; RAFDS, Army Staff Coll., Camberley, 1962–63; Gp Captain on staff of NATO Standing Gp, Washington, DC, 1963–66; RAF Dir, Jt Anti-Submarine Sch., Londonderry, and Sen. RAF Officer, NI, 1966–68; Gp Captain Ops, HQ Coastal Comd, 1968–70; IDC, 1970; Air Cdre, 1970; Sec., Chiefs of Staff Cttee, MoD, 1971–73; Dep. Comdt, RAF Staff Coll., Bracknell, 1973–75; ADC to the Queen, 1973–75; Air Vice-Marshal, 1975; Defence Services Sec. to the Queen, 1975–79; retired 1979. Pres., No 31 Sqdn Assoc., 1992–. *Address:* 20 Durrant Way, Sway, Lymington, Hants SO41 6DQ. *Club:* Royal Air Force.

STANBRIDGE, Ven. Leslie Cyril; Archdeacon of York, 1972–88, Archdeacon Emeritus since 1988; *b* 19 May 1920. *Educ:* Bromley County Grammar Sch., Kent; St John's Coll., Durham Univ. (MA, DipTheol). Asst Curate of Erith Parish Church, Kent, 1949–51; Tutor and Chaplain, St John's Coll., Durham, 1951–55; Vicar of St Martin's, Hull, 1955–64; Examining Chaplain to the Archbishop of York, 1962–74; Rector of Cottingham, Yorks, 1964–72; Canon of York, 1968–2000, now Emeritus; Succentor Canonicorum, 1988–2000; Rural Dean of Kingston-upon-Hull, 1970–72; Warden, York Diocesan Readers' Assoc., 1988–95. *Recreations:* fell walking, cycling. *Address:* 39 Lucombe Way, New Earswick, York YO32 4DS. *T:* (01904) 750812.

STANBROOK, Clive St George Clement, OBE 1987; QC 1989; Partner, Stanbrook & Hooper, since 1980; *b* 10 April 1948; *s* of Ivor Robert Stanbrook, *qv*; *m* 1971, Julia Suzanne Hillary; one *s* three *d. Educ:* Dragon Sch.; Westminster; University Coll. London. Called to the Bar, Inner Temple, 1972; called to Turks and Caicos Bar, 1986, New York Bar, 1988. Founded Stanbrook & Hooper, 1980. Pres., British Chamber of Commerce for Belgium and Luxembourg, 1985–87. *Publications:* Extradition: the law and practice, 1979, 2nd edn 2000; Dumping: manual of EEC rules, 1980; Dumping and Subsidies, 1982, 3rd edn 1996. *Recreations:* tennis, travel. *Address:* Stanbrook & Hooper, 42 Rue du Taciturne, Brussels 1000, Belgium.

STANBROOK, Ivor Robert; *b* 13 Jan. 1924; *y s* of Arthur William and Lilian Stanbrook; *m* 1946, Joan (*née* Clement) (*d* 2000); two *s. Educ:* state schools; Univs of London (BSc (Econ) 1948), Oxford and East Anglia (PhD 1995). Served RAF, 1942–46. Colonial Administrative Service, Nigeria, 1950–60: Asst Sec., Council of Ministers, Lagos, 1956; Dist Officer, N Region, 1957–60. Called to the Bar, Inner Temple, 1960; practising barrister, 1960–90. Contested (C) East Ham, South, 1966. MP (C) Orpington, 1970–92. Chairman: All Party gps on Nigeria, 1979–92, Zambia, 1985–92, Southern Africa, 1987–92; Cons. parly cttees on constitutional affairs, 1985–92, on Northern Ireland, 1989–92; Mem., Select Cttee on Home Affairs, 1983–91. Founded Britain-Nigeria Assoc., 1961. *Publications:* Extradition—the Law and Practice, 1979, 2nd edn 1999; British Nationality—the New Law, 1981; A Year in Politics, 1988; How to be an MP, 1993. *Recreations:* music, books. *Club:* Royal Commonwealth Society.

See also C. St G. C. Stanbrook.

STANBURY, Richard Vivian Macaulay; HM Diplomatic Service, retired; *b* 5 Feb. 1916; *s* of late Gilbert Vivian Stanbury and Doris Marguerite (*née* Smythe); *m* 1953, Geraldine Anne, *d* of late R. F. W. Grant and of Winifred Helen Grant; one *s* one *d. Educ:* Shrewsbury Sch. (exhibnr); Magdalene Coll., Cambridge (exhibnr, 1st cl. Hons in Classical Tripos). Sudan Political Service, 1937–50 (District Comr in 12 districts, and Magistrate); HM Foreign (subseq. Diplomatic) Service, 1951–71: 2nd Sec., Cairo, 1951; FO 1954; Bahrain, Persian Gulf, 1956; FO 1959; Counsellor, Buenos Aires, 1968. Peach farm in Portugal, 1971–80. *Recreations:* golf, writing, watching cricket (played for Somerset). *Address:* Shepherds House, Peasmarsh, near Rye, East Sussex TN31 6TF. *Clubs:* Royal Over-Seas League; Hawks (Cambridge); Rye Golf; Hurlingham (Buenos Aires).

STANCIOFF, Ivan; Ambassador-at-Large for Bulgaria, since 1994; *b* 1 April 1929; *s* of late Ivan Robert Stancioff and Marion (*née* Mitchell); *m* 1st, 1957, Deirdre O'Donnell (marr. diss.); two *s* two *d*; 2nd, Alexandra Lawrence. *Educ:* Georgetown Univ., Washington (BA); New York Univ. Sch. of Business. Economist, Amer. and Foreign Power Corp., 1957–60; Dir Marketing, IBM World Trade Corp., São Paulo, 1961–63; Rio, 1963–65; Paris, 1965–70; Manager, ITT, Athens, 1970; Vice-Pres., ITEL Corp., London, 1971–74; Dir, Safestore Ltd, London, 1975–77; Vice-Pres., Storage Technol. Corp., London, 1977–81; Dir, Cresta Marketing SA, Geneva, 1981–90; Advr to UDF, Sofia, 1990–91; Ambassador to UK, 1991–94; Minister of Foreign Affairs, Bulgaria, 1994–95; Dir, Cresta Marketing, 1995–. Foreign Policy Advr to Pres. of Bulgaria, 1999–. Dir, Inst. for Intercultural Relations, Sofia, 1992; Chm., Kagin Dom Foundn, 1995–. Mem., Sustrans, Bristol, 1989–. FLS; FRGS. Good Conduct Medal, US Army, 1956; Commander, Legion of Honour (France), 1994. *Recreations:* history, gardening, travel, painting. *Address:* 28 Cresswell Place, SW10 9RB. *Club:* Annabel's.

STANCLIFFE, Rt Rev. David Staffurth; *see* Salisbury, Bishop of.

STANCLIFFE, Martin John, FSA; RIBA; Surveyor to the Fabric, St Paul's Cathedral, since 1990; *b* 28 Dec. 1944; *s* of Very Rev. Michael Staffurth Stancliffe and Barbara Elizabeth Tatlow; *m* 1979, Sara Judith Sanders; two *d. Educ:* Westminster Sch.; Magdalene Coll., Cambridge (MA, DipArch). Private architectural practice, 1975–; Architect to: Lichfield Cath., 1983–; Southwell Minster, 1989–; Christ Church Cath., Oxford, 1990–95. Member: Exec. Cttee, Council for the Care of Churches, 1980–91; Cathedrals' Fabric Commn for England, 1991–2001; Archbishops' Commn on Cathedrals, 1992–94; Historic Bldgs and Areas Adv. Cttee, English Heritage, 1995–2001; Expert Adv. Panel on Bldgs and Land, Heritage Lottery Fund, 1997–99. Chm., Cathedral Architects Assoc., 1999–. Marvin Breckinridge Patterson Lectr, Univ. of Maryland, 2000. FSA 1995. *Recreations:* the baroque oboe, old buildings, sailing. *Address:* 29 Marygate, York YO30 7WH. *T:* (01904) 644001.

See also Bishop of Salisbury.

STANDAGE, Simon Andrew Thomas; violinist; *b* 8 Nov. 1941; *s* of Thomas Ralph Standage and Henrietta Florence Sugg; *m* 1964, Jennifer Ward; three *s. Educ:* Bryanston Sch.; King's Coll., Cambridge (MA). Harkness Fellow, 1967–69; Sub-leader, English Chamber Orch., 1974–78; leader and soloist, English Concert, 1973–91; Founder and Leader, Salomon String Quartet, 1981–; founded Collegium Musicum 90, 1990; Associate Dir, Acad. of Ancient Music, 1991–95. Professor of Baroque Violin: Royal Acad. of Music, 1983–; Dresdner Akademie für Alte Musik, 1993–. Has made numerous recordings. *Recreation:* crosswords. *Address:* 106 Hervey Road, Blackheath, SE3 8BX. *T:* (020) 8319 3372.

STANDARD, Prof. Sir Kenneth (Livingstone), Kt 1982; CD 1976; MD, MPH; FFPHM; Professor, 1968, and Head of Department of Social and Preventive Medicine, 1966–89, University of the West Indies at Mona; Emeritus Professor, University of the West Indies, 1990; *b* 8 Dec. 1920; *m* 1955, Evelyn Francis; one *d. Educ:* UC of West Indies (MB BS); Univ. of Pittsburgh (MPH); Univ. of London (MD). FFPHM (FFCM 1972). Schoolmaster, Lynch's Secondary Sch., Barbados, 1940–48 (Headmaster, 1948); Med. House Officer, UCH of WI, 1956; MO, Nutrition Res., Jamaica, 1957–58; MOH, Barbados, 1958–61; MO, MRC Epidemiol. Res. Unit, Jamaica, 1961–66; Lectr, 1961–65, Sen. Lectr, 1965–68, Dept of Social and Preventive Medicine, Univ. of WI, Jamaica. Adjunct Prof. of Public Health, Grad. Sch. Public Health, Univ. of Pittsburgh, 1972–75; Stubenbord Vis. Prof., Cornell Univ. Med. Coll., USA, 1975–. Thomas Parran Lecture, Grad. Sch. of Public Health, Univ. of Pittsburgh, 1984. Member: WHO Adv. Cttee on Med. Res., 1969–72; WHO Expert Adv. Panel on Public Health Admin, 1969–. Foundn Pres., Caribbean Public Health Assoc., 1988–92. Fellow, Caribbean Coll. of Family Physicians, 1988. Fellowship, 1980, Medal, 1981, Jacques Parisot Foundn, WHO; Abraham Horwitz Award, Pan American Health and Educn Foundn, 1988; Health for All Medal, WHO, 1988; Medical Alumni Pioneer Award, Univ. of WI, 1988. *Publications:* (ed jtly) Manual for Community Health Workers, 1974, rev. edn 1983; Epidemiology and Community Health in Warm Climate Countries, 1976; Alternatives in the Delivery of Health Services, 1976; Four Decades of Advances in Health in the Commonwealth Caribbean, 1979. *Recreations:* reading, poetry, gardening. *Address:* Department of Social and Preventive Medicine, University of the West Indies, Mona, Kingston 7, Jamaica. *T:* 9272476. *Club:* Royal Commonwealth Society.

STANDING, John; *see* Leon, Sir J. R.

STANES, Ven. Ian Thomas; Archdeacon of Loughborough, since 1992; *b* 29 Jan. 1939; *s* of Sydney Stanes and Iris Stanes (*née* Hulme); *m* 1962, Sylvia Alice (*née* Drew); one *d* (one *s* decd). *Educ:* Sheffield Univ. (BSc 1962); Linacre Coll., Oxford (BA 1965; MA 1969); Wycliffe Hall, Oxford. Ordained: deacon, 1965; priest, 1966; Curate, Holy Apostles, Leicester, 1965–69; Vicar, Broom Leys, Coalville, Leicester, 1969–76; Priest Warden, Marrick Priory, Ripon, 1976–82; Willesden Area Officer for Mission, Ministry and Evangelism, London, 1982–92. Prebendary, St Paul's Cathedral, 1989–92. *Recreations:* hockey, rock climbing, walking, photography, music, drama, art appreciation. *Address:* The Archdeaconry, 21 Church Road, Glenfield, Leicester LE3 8DP. *T:* (0116) 231 1632, *Fax:* (0116) 232 1593; *e-mail:* stanes@leicester.anglican.org.

STANESBY, Rev. Canon Derek Malcolm, PhD; SOSc; Canon of St George's Chapel, Windsor, 1985–97 (Steward, 1987–94; Treasurer, 1994–97); *b* 28 March 1931; *s* of Laurence J. C. Stanesby and late Elsie L. Stanesby (*née* Stean); *m* 1958, Christine A. Payne; three *s* one *d.* *Educ:* Orange Hill Central School, London; Northampton Polytechnic, London; Leeds Univ. (BA Hons); Manchester Univ. (MEd, PhD); College of the Resurrection, Mirfield. GPO Radio Research Station, Dollis Hill, 1947–51; RAF (Navigator), 1951–53. Ordained, 1958; Curate: Old Lakenham, Norwich, 1958–61; St Mary, Welling, Dio. Southwark, 1961–63; Vicar, St Mark, Bury, Dio. Manchester, 1963–67; Rector, St Chad, Ladybarn, Manchester, 1967–85. Mem., Archbishop's Commn on Christian Doctrine, 1986–91. FRSA 1993. *Publications:* Science, Reason and Religion, 1985; various articles. *Recreations:* hill walking, sailing, woodwork, idling. *Address:* 32 Elizabeth Way, Uppingham, Rutland LE15 9PQ. *T:* (01572) 821298.

STANFIELD, Rt Hon. Robert Lorne; PC (Canada) 1967; QC; Chairman, Institute for Research on Public Policy, 1981–86; *b* Truro, NS, 11 April 1914; *s* of late Frank Stanfield, sometime MLA and Lieutenant-Governor of NS, and Sarah (*née* Thomas); *m* 1st, 1940, N. Joyce (*d* 1954), *d* of C. W. Frazee, Vancouver; one *s* three *d*; 2nd, 1957, Mary Margaret (*d* 1977), *d* of late Hon. W. L. Hall, Judge of Supreme Court and formerly Attorney-Gen. of NS; 3rd, 1978, Anne Margaret Austin, *d* of Dr D. Nelson, Henderson, Toronto. *Educ:* Colchester County Academy, Truro; Ashbury Coll., Ottawa; Dalhousie Univ.; Harvard Law Sch. Southam Cup, Ashbury Coll.; BA Political Science and Economics 1936, Governor-General's Gold Medal, Dalhousie Univ.; LLB Harvard, 1939. War of 1939–45: attached Halifax Office of Wartime Prices and Trade Bd as Regional Rentals Officer, later as Enforcement Counsel. Admitted Bar of NS, 1940. Practised law, McInnes and Stanfield, Halifax, 1945–56; KC 1950. President, Nova Scotia Progressive Cons. Assoc., 1947–48; Leader, Nova Scotia Progressive Cons. Party, 1948–67; elected to Legislature of NS, 1949, Mem. for Colchester Co.; re-elected Mem., 1953, 1960, 1963, 1967; Premier and Minister of Education, NS, 1956; resigned as Premier of NS, 1967; MP (Progressive C): Colchester-Hants, NS, 1967–68; Halifax, NS, 1968–79; Leader, Progressive Cons. Party of Canada, and of Opposition in House of Commons, 1967–74. Ambassador at Large and special representative of Govt of Canada in Middle East, 1979–80. Dir, Canada Life. Chm., Commonwealth Foundn. Hon. LLD: University of New Brunswick, 1958; St Dunstan's Univ., PEI, 1964; McGill Univ., PQ, 1967; St Mary's Univ., NS, 1969; Dalhousie, 1982; Université Sainte-Anne, NS, Acadia Univ., NS, and Univ. of Toronto, 1987; Mount Allison Univ., 1990. Anglican. *Address:* 136 Acacia Avenue, Rockcliffe Park, Ottawa, ON K1M 0R1, Canada.

STANFORD, Rear Adm. Christopher David; Chief of Staff to Surgeon General, Ministry of Defence, since 1999; *b* 15 Feb. 1950; *s* of late Joseph Gerald Stanford and Elspeth Stanford (*née* Harrison); *m* 1972, Angela Mary, *d* of Commander Derek G. M. Gardner, VRD, RSMA; one *s* three *d.* *Educ:* St Paul's Sch.; Britannia RN Coll., Dartmouth; Merton Coll., Oxford (MA History and French). Joined RN 1967; served HM Ships Puma, Jupiter, Hubberston, Exmouth, Newcastle, Antrim, Brilliant, Fife; commanded: HMS Boxer, 1988–89; HMS Coventry and First Frigate Sqdn, 1993–94; Asst Dir (Ships), Directorate of Operational Requirements, 1990–93; rcds 1995; Dir, Naval Staff Duties, 1995–97; Dir, Operational Capability, 1997–98. FNI (Vice Pres., 1999–). Freeman: City of London, 2000; Master Mariners' Co., 2000. Chm., Combined Services Rugby Union; Vice Pres., RN Rugby Union. Pres., Royal Naval Lay Readers Soc. OStJ 2001. *Publications:* contribs to learned and professional jls on maritime and envtl issues. *Recreations:* art, Rugby, golf, travel, maritime affairs. *Address:* c/o Naval Secretary, Victory Building, HM Naval Base, Portsmouth PO1 3LS. *Clubs:* Naval, Anchorites.

STANFORD, James Keith Edward, OBE 1999; Director General, Leonard Cheshire Foundation, 1991–98; Vice President, Leonard Cheshire, since 2000; *b* 12 April 1937; *s* of late Lt-Col J. K. Stanford, OBE, MC, author and naturalist, and Eleanor Stanford; *m* 1964, Carol Susan Harbord; one *s* one *d.* *Educ:* Rugby Sch.; RMA Sandhurst. 17th/21st Lancers, 1955–64; IBM Corp., 1965–72; industry and City, 1973–90; Chm., David Brown Corp., 1987–90. Dir, Aerospace Engrg, 1990–94. Vice-Chm., Holiday Care Service, 1991–99; Mem. Bd, Signpost Housing Gp, 2000–. Gov., Milton Abbey Sch., 1998–. *Recreations:* country activities. *Address:* Manor Farm, Droop, Hazelbury Bryan, Sturminster Newton, Dorset DT10 2ED.

See also Viscount Folkestone.

STANFORD, Peter James; writer and broadcaster; *b* 23 Nov. 1961; *s* of Reginald James Hughes Stanford and late Mary Catherine (*née* Fleming); *m* 1995, Siobhan, *d* of James and Celine Cross; one *s* one *d.* *Educ:* St Anselm's Coll., Birkenhead; Merton Coll., Oxford (BA Hons 1983). Reporter, The Tablet, 1983–84; News Editor, 1984–88, Editor, 1988–92, The Catholic Herald. Chm., ASPIRE (Assoc. for Spinal Res., Reintegration and Rehabilitation), 1992–. Dir, CandoCo Dance Co., 1994–98 (Patron, 1998–). Panellist: FutureWatch, TV, 1996; radio: The Moral Maze, 1996; Vice or Virtue, 1997; Presenter: The Mission, TV, 1997; various Radio 4 documentaries, 1999–. *Publications:* (ed) Hidden Hands: child workers around the world, 1988; (with Simon Lee) Believing Bishops, 1990; (ed) The Seven Deadly Sins, 1990; (with Kate Saunders) Catholics and Sex, 1992 (televised, 1992; Bronze Medal, NY TV Fest., 1993); Cardinal Hume and the changing face of English Catholicism, 1993; Lord Longford: an authorised life, 1994; (jtly) The Anatomy of the Catholic Church, 1994; (with Leanda de Lisle) The Catholics and their Houses, 1995; The Devil: a biography, 1996 (televised 1998); The She-Pope: a quest for the truth behind the mystery of Pope Joan, 1998 (televised 1998); Bronwen Astor: her life and times, 2000; Heaven: a travellers' guide, 2001. *Recreations:* soap operas, credit cards. *Address:* c/o A. P. Watt, 20 John Street, WC1N 2DR.

STANGER, David Harry, OBE 1987; IEng; FIQA; Chairman and Managing Director, David H. Stanger sprl, 1997–2000; *b* 14 Feb. 1939; *s* of Charles Harry Stanger, CBE and Florence Bessie Hepworth Stanger; *m* 1963, Jill Patricia (*née* Barnes); one *s* two *d.* *Educ:* Oundle Sch.; Millfield Sch. IEng (TEng 1971); FFB 1977; FIQA 1982; MSocIS 1982. Served Corps of RE, 1960–66; joined R. H. Harry Stanger, 1966; Partner, Al Hoty-Stanger Ltd, Saudi Arabia, 1975–; Chm. and Man. Dir, Harry Stanger Ltd, 1975–90 (Sen. Partner, 1972–85); non-exec. Chm., Stanger Consultants Ltd, 1990–93. Chm., Adv. Cttee, NAMAS, 1985–87. Secretary General: Union Internationale des Laboratoires Indépendants, 1983–93 and 2001– (Mem. Governing Bd, 1997–); Eur. Orgn for Testing and Certification, 1993–97. Member: Steering Cttee, NATLAS, 1981–87; Adv. Council for Calibration and Measurement, 1982–87; Council, EUROLAB, 1990–93; Chairman: Standards, Quality and Measurement Adv. Cttee, 1988–92; British Measurement and Testing Assoc., 1990–93; Inst. of Quality Assurance, 1990–93 (a Vice-Pres., 1986–); Adv. Bd, Brunel Centre for Manufacturing Metrology, 1991–93; ILAC Lab. Liaison Cttee, 1998–. Pingat Peringatan, Malaysia, 1966. *Recreation:* collecting vintage wines. *Address:* Avenue Louis Lepoutre 116, 1050 Brussels, Belgium. *T:* (2) 3451242; *e-mail:* dhs@dhs.be.

STANHOPE, family name of **Earl of Harrington**.

STANHOPE, Janet Anne; Director of Resources, Devon County Council, since 2000; *b* 3 Oct. 1952; *d* of Thomas Flynn and Anne Flynn (*née* Atkinson); *m* 1975, Rear-Adm. Mark Stanhope, *qv*; one *d.* *Educ:* Nottingham High Sch. for Girls; Somerville Coll., Oxford (MA Hons Physics). CIPFA 1978. Trainee stockbroker, Montagu, Loebl, Stanley & Co., 1974–75; trainee accountant, W Sussex CC, 1975–77; Devon County Council: various accountancy posts, 1977–93; Dep. Co. Treas., 1993–98; Dep. Dir of Resources, 1998–2000. Mem., Exeter Southernhay Rotary Club, 1994–. *Recreations:* reading, spending time with the family. *Address:* Devon County Council, County Hall, Topsham Road, Exeter EX2 4QJ. *T:* (01392) 383309.

STANHOPE, Rear Adm. Mark, OBE 1988; Director, Operational Management, NATO Regional Command North, since 2000; *b* 26 March 1952; *s* of late Frederick William Stanhope and of Sheila Mary Hattemore (*née* Cutler); *m* 1975, Janet Anne Flynn (*see* J. A. Stanhope); one *d.* *Educ:* London Nautical Sch.; Worthing High Sch.; St Peter's Coll., Oxford (MA Hons Physics). Joined Royal Navy, 1970: Commanding Officer: HMS Orpheus, 1982–84; HMS Splendid, 1987–88; Submarine Comd Course (Teacher), 1989–90; HMS London, 1991–92; Capt., Submarine Sea Trng, 1993–94; Dep. Principal Staff Officer to CDS, MoD, 1994–96; rcds 1997; CO and ADC, HMS Illustrious, 1998–2000. Mem., RNSA. Freeman, City of London, 1993; Liveryman, Upholders' Co., 1996–. *Publications:* contribs to Naval Rev. *Recreations:* family life, reading, sailing. *Address:* NATO Regional Headquarters, AFNORTH, BFPO 28.

STANIER, Sir Beville (Douglas), 3rd Bt *cr* 1917, of Peplow Hall, Hodnet, Salop; farmer, since 1976; *b* 20 April 1934; *o s* of Brig. Sir Alexander Stanier, 2nd Bt, DSO, MC and Dorothy Gladys Miller (*d* 1973); *S* father, 1995; *m* 1963, Shelagh Sinnott; one *s* two *d.* *Educ:* Eton Coll. Joined Welsh Guards, 1952; commnd 2nd Lieut, 1953; Lieut, 1955; Captain, 1958; ADC to Governor-General of Australia, 1959–60. Stockbroker with Kitcat & Aitken, 1960–76 (Partner, 1968–76). *Recreations:* shooting, cricket. *Heir:* *s* Alexander James Sinnott Stanier, *b* 10 April 1970. *Address:* Kings Close House, Whaddon, Buckinghamshire MK17 0NG. *T:* (01908) 501738. *Club:* MCC.

STANIER, Field Marshal Sir John (Wilfred), GCB 1982 (KCB 1978); MBE 1961; DL; Constable, HM Tower of London, 1990–96; *b* 6 Oct. 1925; *s* of late Harold Allan Stanier and Penelope Rose Stanier (*née* Price); *m* 1955, Cicely Constance Lambert; four *d.* *Educ:* Marlborough Coll.; Merton Coll., Oxford. FRGS. Commd in 7th Queen's Own Hussars, 1946; served in N Italy, Germany and Hong Kong; comd Royal Scots Greys, 1966–68; comd 20th Armd Bde, 1969–70; GOC 1st Div., 1973–75; Comdt, Staff Coll., Camberley, 1975–78; Vice Chief of the General Staff, 1978–80; C-in-C, UKLF, 1981–82; CGS, 1982–85. ADC General to the Queen, 1981–85. Col, The Royal Scots Dragoon Guards, 1979–84; Col Comdt, RAC, 1982–85. Chm., RUSI, 1986–89. Pres., Hampshire Br., British Red Cross Soc., 1986–94. Mem. Council, Marlborough Coll., 1984–96. DL Hampshire, 1987. *Publication:* (jtly) War and the Media, 1997. *Recreations:* fishing, sailing, talking. *Address:* The Old Farmhouse, Hazeley Bottom, Hartley Wintney, Hook, Hants RG27 8LU; *e-mail:* john.stanier@amserve.net. *Club:* Cavalry and Guards.

STANIFORTH, Martin John; Deputy Director of Human Resources (NHS), Department of Health, since 1999; *b* 11 Feb. 1953; *s* of late Trevor Staniforth and Doris Nellie Staniforth (*née* Quaife). *Educ:* Kingston Grammar Sch., Kingston upon Thames; Univ. of Newcastle upon Tyne (BA Hons Eng. Lang. and Lit.). Joined DHSS as Admin Trainee, 1975, Principal, 1985–91; Asst Sec., DoH, 1991–96; Hd of Corp. Affairs, NHS Exec., DoH, 1996–99. *Recreations:* hill walking, opera going, cricket watching. *Address:* (office) Quarry House, Quarry Hill, Leeds LS2 7UE. *T:* (0113) 254 6365.

STANIFORTH, Sarah Elizabeth, (Hon. Lady Porritt); Adviser on Paintings Conservation and Environmental Control, National Trust, since 1985; *b* 14 Jan. 1953; *d* of Malcolm Arthur Staniforth and Bridget Christian Salkeld Hall; *m* 1986, Hon. Sir Jonathon Porritt, *qv*; two *d.* *Educ:* St Hilda's Coll., Oxford (BA Hons); Courtauld Inst. of Art, London Univ. (Dip Conservation of Paintings). Higher Scientific Officer, Scientific Dept, Nat. Gall., 1980–85. Trustee, Hunterian Collection, RCS, 1997–; Westminster Abbey Fabric Comr, 1998–. Vice-Pres., Internat. Inst. for Conservation of Historic and Artistic Works, 1998–. *Publications:* (ed jtly) Durability and Change, 1994; (ed with C. Sitwell) Studies in the History of Painting Restoration, 1998; papers in mus. and conservation jls and conf. proc. *Recreations:* swimming, walking. *Address:* 9 Lypiatt Terrace, Lypiatt Road, Cheltenham, Glos GL50 2SX. *T:* (01242) 518218.

STANISZEWSKI, Stefan; Commander's Cross, Order of Polonia Restituta, and other orders; Ambassador of Poland to Libya, 1990–95; *b* 11 Feb. 1931; *s* of Andrzej and Katarzyna Staniszewski; *m* 1953, Wanda Szuszkiewicz; one *d.* *Educ:* Warsaw Univ. (BA Philosophy); Jagiellonian Univ. (BA Pol. Sciences). Active in students' and social organizations, 1951–58; Head of Editorial Dept, ISKRY state publishing firm, 1958–60; entered foreign service, 1960; Minister's Cabinet, Min. of Foreign Affairs, 1960–63; successively 2nd Sec., 1st Sec. and Counsellor, Polish Embassy, Paris, 1963–69; Head of West European Dept and Mem. of Minister's Council, Min. of Foreign Affairs, 1969–72; Ambassador to Sweden, 1972–77; Head of Press, Cultural and Scientific Co-operation Dept, Min. of Foreign Affairs, 1977–81; Ambassador to UK, 1981–86, and to Ireland, 1984–86; Head of Press and Information Dept, 1986–90, and spokesman, 1988–90, Polish Min. of Foreign Affairs. Commander, Légion d'Honneur, 1972; Order of the Star of the North, Sweden, 1977; Commander, Order of the Aztec Eagle, Mexico, 1979. *Recreation:* swimming. *Address:* ul. Okrąg 1 m. 51, 00415 Warsaw, Poland.

STANLEY, family name of **Earl of Derby** and **Baron Stanley of Alderley**.

STANLEY OF ALDERLEY, 8th Baron *cr* 1839 (UK); **Thomas Henry Oliver Stanley;** Bt 1660; Baron Sheffield (Ire), 1783; Baron Eddisbury, 1848; DL; Captain (retired), Coldstream Guards; Tenant Farmer of New College, Oxford, since 1954; *b* 28 Sept. 1927; *s* of Lt-Col The Hon. Oliver Hugh Stanley, DSO, JP (3rd *s* of 4th Baron) (*d* 1952), and Lady Kathleen Stanley (*d* 1977), *e d* of 5th Marquess of Bath; *S* cousin (known as Baron Sheffield), 1971; *m* 1955, Jane Barrett, *d* of Ernest George Hartley; three *s* one *d.* *Educ:* Wellington College, Berks. Coldstream Guards, 1945–52; Guards Parachute Battalion and Independent Company, 1947–50; Northamptonshire Institute of Agriculture, 1952–53.

Mem., Cttee of Management, RNLI, 1981–; Chm., Fund Raising Cttee, RNLI, 1985–94. Governor, St Edward's Sch., Oxford, 1979–98. ARAgS. DL Gwynedd, 1985. *Recreations:* sailing, skiing, fishing. *Heir: e s* Hon. Richard Oliver Stanley, BSc [*b* 24 April 1956; *m* 1983, Carla, *er d* of Dr K. T. C. McKenzie, Solihull; three *d* (one *s* decd)]. *Address:* Trysglwyn Fawr, Amlwch, Anglesey LL68 9RF. *T:* (01407) 830364; Rectory Farm, Stanton St John, Oxford OX9 1HF. *T:* (01865) 351214. *Club:* Farmers'.

STANLEY, Lord; Edward John Robin Stanley; *b* 21 April 1998; *s* and *heir* of Earl of Derby, *qv*.

STANLEY, Colin; *see* Stanley, G. C.

STANLEY, Derek Peter; His Honour Judge Stanley; a Circuit Judge, since 1994; *b* 7 Aug. 1947; *s* of Peter Stanley and Vera Stanley (*née* Sterry-Cooper); *m* 1971, Gabrielle Mary Tully; one *s* two *d*. *Educ:* Solihull Sch.; Inns of Court Sch. of Law. Called to the Bar, Gray's Inn, 1968; practised on Midland and Oxford Circuit, 1969–94; a Recorder, 1988–94. Mem., Bar Council, 1989–91. *Recreations:* squash, tennis, sailing, church music. *Address:* Birmingham Crown Court, Newton Street, Birmingham B4 7NA. *T:* (0121) 681 3300.

STANLEY, Prof. Eric Gerald, MA (Oxford and Yale); PhD (Birmingham); FBA 1985; Rawlinson and Bosworth Professor of Anglo-Saxon in the University of Oxford, and Fellow of Pembroke College, Oxford, 1977–91; Emeritus Professor and Fellow, since 1991; *b* 19 Oct. 1923; *m* 1959, Mary Bateman, MD, FRCP; one *d*. *Educ:* Queen Elizabeth's Grammar Sch., Blackburn; University Coll., Oxford. Lectr in Eng. Lang. and Lit., Birmingham Univ., 1951–62; Reader in Eng. Lang. and Lit., 1962–64, Prof. of English, 1964–75, Univ. of London at QMC; Prof. of English, Yale Univ., 1975–76. Mem., Mediaeval Acad. of America, 1975–; Corresponding Member: Fryske Akad., Netherlands, 1991–; Bavarian Acad. of Scis, 1994–. Sir Israel Gollancz Meml Lectr, British Acad., 1984. Co-Editor, Notes and Queries, 1963–. *Publications:* (ed) The Owl and the Nightingale, 1960, 2nd edn 1972; The Search for Anglo-Saxon Paganism, 1975; A Collection of Papers with Emphasis on Old English Literature, 1987; In the Foreground: Beowulf, 1994; Die altenglische Rechtspflege, 1999; Imagining the Anglo-Saxon Past, 2000; academic articles. *Address:* Pembroke College, Oxford OX1 1DW. *Club:* Athenæum.

STANLEY, Prof. Fiona Juliet, AC 1996; MD; Director, TVW Telethon Institute for Child Health Research, since 1990; Professor of Paediatrics, University of Western Australia, since 1990; *b* 1 Aug. 1946; *d* of Prof. Neville Stanley and Muriel MacDonald Stanley; *m* 1973, Prof. Geoffrey Shellam; two *d*. *Educ:* Univ. of Western Australia (MB BS 1970; MD 1986); LSHTM, Univ. of London (MSc 1976). FFPHM 1989; FAFPHM 1991; FRACP 1994; FRACOG 1995; FASSA 1996. Doctor, Princess Margaret Hosp. Aboriginal Clinic, Perth, 1972; Scientific Staff, MRC Social Medicine Unit, 1972–73, NH & MRC Fellow in Clin. Scis, 1974–75, LSHTM; vis. appt, Nat. Inst. Child Health and Human Develt, NIH, 1976; University of Western Australia: NH & MRC Clin. Scis Res. Fellow, Unit of Clin. Epidemiology, Dept of Medicine, 1977; SMO (Child Health), Community and Child Health Services, Public Health Dept, 1978–79; Dep. Dir, 1980–88, Dir, 1988–90, NH & MRC Res. Unit in Epidemiology and Preventive Medicine. Hon. DSc Murdoch, 1998. *Publications:* (ed jtly) The Epidemiology of Prematurity, 1977; (ed jtly) The Epidemiology of the Cerebral Palsies, 1984; (ed) The Role of Epidemiology and Perinatal Databases for both Research and Care, 1997; (jtly) The Cerebral Palsies: epidemiology and causal pathways, 2000; papers in learned jls, reports, and chapters in books. *Recreations:* bushwalking, swimming. *Address:* TVW Telethon Institute for Child Health Research, PO Box 855, West Perth, WA 6872, Australia. *T:* (8) 9489 7968.

STANLEY, (Geoffrey) Colin; Director General, British Printing Industries Federation, 1988–95; *b* 3 May 1937; *s* of Harold Bertram Smerdon Stanley and Ruth Mary (*née* Dunn); *m* 1962, Lesley Shadrach McWilliam; one *s* one *d*. *Educ:* Wallasey Grammar Sch. Joined Wiggins Teape, 1957: Director and General Manager: Wiggins Teape Toys & Crafts, 1976–78; Wiggins Teape Stationery Ltd, 1979–82; Dir and Manager, Wiggins Teape Paper Ltd, 1982–87; Dir, Wiggins Teape (UK) plc, 1983–85. Dir, John Howitt Gp, 1995–99. Man. Dir, Wessex Childcare Ltd, 1996–98; Chm., Wessex Children's Hospice Trust, 1997–99. Pres., Nat. Assoc. of Paper Merchants, 1986–88. Mem., Council, CBI, 1988–95 (Chm., Industrial Relns, Wages and Conditions Cttee, 1992–95; Mem., Employment Affairs Cttee, 1992–95). FRSA 1991. Freeman, City of London, 1985; Liveryman, Co. of Stationers & Newspaper Makers, 1987–. *Recreations:* golf, weekend gardening, music, reading. *Address:* 2 Abbey Hill Close, Winchester, Hants SO23 7AZ. *Club:* National Liberal.

STANLEY, Rev. Canon John Alexander, OBE 1999; Vicar of Huyton, since 1974; Chaplain to the Queen, 1993–2001; *b* 20 May 1931; *s* of Edward Alexander Stanley and Lucy Vida Stanley; *m* 1956, (Flora) Elaine Wilkes; three *s* two *d*. *Educ:* Birkenhead Sch.; Tyndale Hall Theol Coll., Bristol. Assistant Curate: All Saints', Preston, 1956; St Mark's, St Helens, 1960; Vicar, St Cuthbert's, Everton, Liverpool, 1963; Priest in Charge, St Saviour, Everton, 1969; Vicar, St Saviour with St Cuthbert, Everton, 1970; Area Dean of Huyton, 1989–; Hon. Canon of Liverpool Cathedral, 1987–. Mem., Gen. Synod, and Proctor in Convocation, 1973–2000; Chm., Diocesan House of Clergy, 1979–85; Prolocutor, York Convocation, 1990–2000. A Church Comr, 1983–99 (Mem., Bd of Govs, 1989–99); Member: Crown Appointments Commn, 1992–2000; Archbishops' Council, 1999–2000. Mem., BCC, 1984–87; Trustee, Church Urban Fund, 1987–. *Recreations:* golf, bees, photography. *Address:* The Vicarage, Huyton, Merseyside L36 7SA. *T:* (0151) 449 3900, *Fax:* (0151) 480 6002; *e-mail:* John.Stanley@btinternet.com.

STANLEY, John Mallalieu; Director of Legal Services A, Department of Trade and Industry, 1996–2001; *b* 30 Sept. 1941; *s* of William and Rose Margaret Stanley; *m* 1968, Christine Mary Cunningham; two *s* one *d*. *Educ:* Welwyn Garden City Grammar Sch.; Clare College, Cambridge (MA). Solicitor. Church, Adams, Tatham & Co., 1965–68; Jaques & Co., 1968–75; Department of Industry, later of Trade and Industry, 1975–2001: Under Sec. (Legal), 1989–96. *Address:* 12 Westcombe Park Road, SE3 7RB.

STANLEY, Rt Hon. Sir John (Paul), Kt 1988; PC 1984; MP (C) Tonbridge and Malling, since Feb. 1974; *b* 19 Jan. 1942; *s* of late Mr and Mrs H. Stanley; *m* 1968, Susan Elizabeth Giles; one *s* one *d* (and one *s* decd). *Educ:* Repton Sch.; Lincoln Coll., Oxford (MA). Conservative Research Dept with responsibility for Housing, 1967–68; Research Associate, Internat. Inst. for Strategic Studies, 1968–69; Rio Tinto-Zinc Corp. Ltd, 1969–79. PPS to Rt Hon. Margaret Thatcher, 1976–79; Minister of State (Minister for Housing and Construction), DoE, 1979–83; Minister of State: for the Armed Forces, MoD, 1983–87; Northern Ireland Office, 1987–88. Mem., Parly Select Cttee on Nationalised Industries, 1974, on Foreign Affairs, 1992–. Director: Henderson Highland Trust plc, 1990–; Fidelity Japanese Values plc, 1994–. Trustee, ActionAid, 1989–. *Publication:* (jtly) The International Trade in Arms, 1972. *Recreations:* music, photography, sailing. *Address:* House of Commons, SW1A 0AA.

STANLEY, Martin Edward; Chief Executive, Postal Services Commission, since 2000; *b* 1 Nov. 1948; *s* of Edward Alan and Dorothy Stanley; *m* 1971, Marilyn Joan Lewis (marr. diss. 1992); one *s*; lives with Janice Munday; one *s* (and one *s* decd). *Educ:* Royal GS, Newcastle upon Tyne; Magdalen Coll., Oxford (BA Hons). Inland Revenue, 1971–80; Department of Trade and Industry, 1980–98: various posts, 1980–87; Head, Industry/Educn Unit, 1987–90; Principal Private Sec., 1990–92; Hd of Vehicles, Metals and Minerals Div., later Engrg Automotive and Metals Div., 1992–96; Chief Exec., Oil and Gas Projects and Supplies Office, then Infrastructure and Energy Projects Directorate, 1996–98; Dir, Better Regulation, then Regulatory Impact, Unit, Cabinet Office, 1998–2000. *Publication:* How to be a Civil Servant, 2000. *Recreations:* walking, sailing. *Address:* Postal Services Commission, Hercules House, 6 Hercules Road, SE1 7DB. *T:* (020) 7593 2110.

STANLEY, Oliver Duncan; Chairman, 1972–97 and Director, 1972–2000, Rathbone Brothers (formerly Comprehensive Financial Services) PLC; *b* 5 June 1925; *s* of Bernard Stanley and Mabel Best; *m* 1954, Ruth Brenner, JP, BA; one *s* three *d*. *Educ:* Christ Church, Oxford (MA); Harvard Univ., USA. Called to the Bar, Middle Temple, 1963. Served War, 8 Hussars, 1943–47. HM Inspector of Taxes, 1952–65; Dir, Gray Dawes Bank, 1966–72; founded Comprehensive Financial Services Gp of Cos, 1971. Chief Taxation Adviser, CLA, 1975–83 (Mem., Tax Cttee, 1983–). Chm., Profile Books Ltd, 1996–; Dir, Axa Equity and Law, 1992–97. Member: Soc. of Authors, 1967–; Council of Legal Educn, 1992–96. Gov., Inns of Court Sch. of Law, 1996–99. *Publications:* A Guide to Taxation, 1967; Taxology, 1971; Creation and Protection of Capital, 1974; Taxation of Farmers and Landowners, 1981, 12th edn 2001; Offshore Tax Planning, 1986; contrib. The Times and The Sunday Times, 1966–83; numerous articles in legal and agricultural periodicals. *Recreations:* music, tennis, French civilisation. *Club:* Travellers.

STANLEY, Peter Ian, CBE 2001; PhD; consultant on food, agriculture and environment; Chief Executive, Central Science Laboratory Agency, 1992–2001; *b* 25 June 1946. *Educ:* University College London (PhD 1972). MAF, subseq. MAFF, 1970–2001. *Address:* Century House, Settrington, N Yorks YO17 8NP.

STANNARD, Ven. Colin Percy, TD 1966; Archdeacon of Carlisle and Residentiary Canon of Carlisle Cathedral, 1984–93, now Archdeacon and Canon Emeritus; *b* 8 Feb. 1924; *s* of Percy and Grace Adelaide Stannard; *m* 1950, Joan Callow; one *s* two *d*. *Educ:* Woodbridge School; Selwyn Coll., Cambridge (BA 1947, MA 1949); Lincoln Theological Coll. Deacon 1949, priest 1950; Curate, St James Cathedral, Bury St Edmunds, 1949–52; Priest-in-charge, St Martin's, Grimsby, 1952–55; CF (TA), 1953–67; Vicar: St James's, Barrow-in-Furness, 1955–64; St John the Baptist's, Upperby, 1964–70; Rector of Gosforth, 1970–75; RD of Calder, 1970–75; Hon. Canon of Carlisle, 1975–84; Priest-in-charge of Natland, 1975–76, Vicar, 1976–84; RD of Kendal, 1975–84. *Recreations:* walking, bringing order out of chaos—especially in gardens. *Address:* 51 Longlands Road, Carlisle, Cumbria CA3 9AE. *T:* (01228) 538584.

STANSBY, John; Chairman, UIE (UK) Ltd, 1974–2000 (UK parent company of UIE Scotland Ltd and subsidiary of Offshore Bouygues Group); Director, Bouygues UK, since 1998; *b* 2 July 1930; *s* of late Dumon Stansby and Vera Margaret Main; *m* 1966, Anna Maria Kruschewsky; one *d* and one step *s* one step *d*. *Educ:* Oundle; Jesus Coll., Cambridge (Schol., MA). FInstPet, FCIT, FRSA. Commissioned, Queen's Royal Regt, 1949; Service, 1949–50, Somaliland Scouts. Shell Mex & BP Ltd, 1955–62; AIC Ltd, 1962–66; Dir, Rank Leisure Services, Rank Organisation, 1966–70; Dir, P&O Energy, P&OSN Co., 1970–74; Chm., Dumon Stansby & Co. Ltd, 1974–; Dep. Chm., London Transport Exec., 1978–80; Chairman: SAUR (UK) Ltd, 1986–89; Cementation–SAUR Water Services Ltd, 1986–88; Bouygues (UK) Ltd, 1987–89; SAUR UK Development PLC, 1989–91; Dep. Chm., Energy Resources Ltd, 1990–92. Mem. Council, Franco-British Soc., 1982–. Mem. Council, Almeida Theatre, 1996–. European Bobsleigh Champion, 1952. Chevalier de l'Ordre Nat. du Mérite (France), 1997. *Address:* 13 Phillimore Gardens, W8 7QG. *T:* (020) 7937 3003, *Fax:* (020) 7937 4420. *Club:* Travellers.

STANSFIELD, George Norman, CBE 1985 (OBE 1980); HM Diplomatic Service, retired; *b* 28 Feb. 1926; *s* of George Stansfield and Martha Alice (*née* Leadbetter); *m* 1947, Elizabeth Margaret Williams. *Educ:* Liscard High Sch. Served War, RAF, 1944–47. Ministries of Food and Supply, 1948–58; Private Sec. to Dir-Gen. of Armament Prodn, 1958–61; CRO, 1961; Second Secretary: Calcutta, 1962–66; Port of Spain, 1966–68; First Secretary: FCO, 1968–71; Singapore, 1971–74; Consul, Durban, 1974–78; FCO, 1978; Counsellor, and Head of Overseas Estate Dept, 1980–82; High Comr, Solomon Islands, 1982–86. Training consultant, FCO, 1986–. *Recreations:* sailing, cine-photography, wildlife. *Address:* Deryn's Wood, 80 Westfield Road, Woking, Surrey GU22 9QA. *Club:* Royal Southampton Yacht.

STANSFIELD SMITH, Sir Colin, Kt 1993; CBE 1988; County Architect, 1973–92, Consultant County Architect, since 1992, Hampshire County Council; Professor of Architectural Design, University of Portsmouth (formerly Portsmouth Polytechnic), since 1990; *b* 1 Oct. 1932; *s* of Stansfield Smith and Mary (*née* Simpson); *m* 1961, Angela Jean Earnshaw; one *s* one *d*. *Educ:* William Hulme's Grammar Sch., Manchester; Cambridge Univ. Sch. of Architecture (MA, DipArch). ARIBA. Schools Div., LCC, 1958–60; Sen. Asst then Associate Partner, Emberton Frank & Tardrew, Architects, 1960–65; Partner, Emberton Tardrew & Partners, 1965–71; Dep. County Architect, Cheshire CC, 1971–73. Mem., Royal Fine Art Commn, 1997–99. RIBA Royal Gold Medal, 1991. *Publications:* Hampshire Architecture (1974–1984), 1985; Schools of Thought, Hampshire Architecture (1974–1991), 1991; articles in Architects' Jl and Architectural Review. *Recreations:* golf, painting. *Address:* 8 Christchurch Road, Winchester, Hants SO23 9SR. *T:* (01962) 851970. *Club:* Hockley Golf (Twyford, Hants).

STANSGATE, Viscountcy of (*cr* 1942, of Stansgate); title disclaimed by 2nd Viscount (*see* Benn, Rt Hon. Tony).

STANTON, David, CB 2000; Director (Grade 3), Analytical Services Division, Department for Work and Pensions (formerly Department of Social Security), since 1992; *b* 5 Nov. 1942; *s* of Frederick Charles Patrick Stanton and Ethel (*née* Cout); *m* 1967, Isobel Joan Blair; one *s* one *d*. *Educ:* Bishops Stortford Coll.; Worcester Coll., Oxford (BA PPE 1965); LSE (MSc(Econ) 1970). ODI/Nuffield Fellow, Govt of Uganda, 1965–67; Lectr, Brunel Univ., 1967–70; Economic Adviser: Min. of Transport, 1970; Min. of Housing, then DoE, 1971–74; HM Treasury, 1974–75; Senior Economic Adviser: seconded to Hong Kong Govt, 1975–77; also Head of Unit for Manpower Studies, Dept of Employment, 1977–81; Econs Br., Dept of Employment, 1981–83; also Dir, Employment Market Res. Unit, 1983–87; Chief Economist (Grade 3), Dept of Employment, 1988–92. *Recreations:* people, dogs and other animals, singing. *Address:* Department for Work and Pensions, The Adelphi, 1–11 John Adam Street, WC2N 6HT. *T:* (020) 7962 8611; *e-mail:* davidstanton@dwp.gsi.gov.uk; (home) 5 Durrell Road, Richmond, Surrey TW9 4LF.

STANTON, David Leslie; United Kingdom Permanent Delegate to UNESCO with personal rank of Ambassador, since 1997; *b* 29 April 1943; *s* of Leslie Stanton and C. Mary

Stanton (*née* Staynes); *m* 1989, Rosemary Jane Brown; one *d*. *Educ:* Bootham Sch., York; Balliol Coll., Oxford (BA Hons). Asst Principal, ODM, 1965–69; SSRC Sen. Scholarship, Oxford Univ., 1969–71; Principal, ODA, 1971–75; First Sec., Office of UK Permanent Rep. to EC, 1975–77; Mem., Bd of Dirs, Asian Develt Bank, 1979–82; Head of Dept, ODA, 1982–92; Advr, Finance and Admin, EBRD, 1990–91 (on secondment); Mem. Bd of Dirs, World Bank Gp, 1992–97. Mem., Exec. Bd, 1997–, Chm., Finance and Admin. Commn, 2001, UNESCO. *Recreations:* mountaineering, ski-ing, painting. *Address:* UK Delegation to UNESCO, 1 rue Miollis, 75732 Paris Cedex 15, France.

STANTON, Prof. Graham Norman, PhD; Lady Margaret's Professor of Divinity, since 1998, and Chairman, Faculty Board of Divinity, since 2001, University of Cambridge; Fellow of Fitzwilliam College, Cambridge, since 1998; *b* 9 July 1940; *s* of Norman Schofield Stanton and Gladys Jean Stanton (*née* McGregor); *m* 1965, (Valerie) Esther Douglas, MA; two *s* one *d*. *Educ:* Univ. of Otago, NZ (BA 1960; MA 1961; BD 1964); Fitzwilliam Coll., Cambridge (PhD 1969). Temp. Lectr, Princeton Theological Seminary, 1969; Naden Res. Student, St John's Coll., Cambridge, 1969–70; King's College, London: Lectr in New Testament Studies, 1970–77; Prof. of New Testament Studies, 1977–98; Head of Department: Biblical Studies, 1982–88; Theology and Religious Studies, 1996–98. Humboldt Stiftung Res. Fellow, Tübingen, 1974; lectures on NT and Early Christianity, in Australia, NZ, Ireland, Canada, Finland, Netherlands, Switzerland, Belgium, Israel, US and UK. Chm., British SNTS, 1989–92; Pres., SNTS, 1996–97 (Sec., 1976–82). FKC 1996. Hon. DD Otago, 2000. Editor, New Testament Studies, 1982–90; Gen. Editor, International Critical Commentaries, 1984–. *Publications:* Jesus of Nazareth in New Testament Preaching, 1974; (ed) The Interpretation of Matthew, 1983, 2nd edn 1994; The Gospels and Jesus, 1989 (trans. Japanese and Korean), 2nd edn 2001; A Gospel for a New People: studies in Matthew, 1992; (ed jtly) Resurrection, 1994; Gospel Truth? new light on Jesus and the Gospels, 1995 (trans. French, Dutch, Italian and Spanish); (ed jtly) Tolerance and Intolerance in Early Judaism and Christianity, 1998; Jesus and Gospel, 2000; contrib. learned jls and symposia in UK, Europe and USA. *Recreations:* walking, music, cricket, gardening. *Address:* Faculty of Divinity, West Road, Cambridge CB3 9BS. *T:* (01223) 763042; *e-mail:* gns23@cam.ac.uk.

STANTON, Rev. John Maurice, MA; Rector of Chesham Bois, 1973–83; *b* 29 Aug. 1918; *s* of Frederick William Stanton, MInstCE and Maude Lozel (*née* Cole); *m* 1947, Helen Winifred (*née* Bowden); one *s* two *d*. *Educ:* King's School, Rochester; University College, Oxford (Gunsley Exhibnr; 2nd Class Hons, Final Hon. Sch. of Nat. Science, 1947; MA 1947). Commissioned Royal Artillery, 1940, 92nd Field Regt, RA, 1940–43. ISLD, CMF, 1943–46. Assistant Master, Tonbridge School, 1947–59; Headmaster, Blundell's School, 1959–71; Curate, St Matthew's, Exeter, 1972. Ordained Deacon, 1952; Priest, 1953. Sec., Oxford Diocesan Bd of Patronage, 1984–90. *Recreations:* water colour painting, gardening. *Address:* 16 Emden House, Barton Lane, Headington, Oxford OX3 9JU. *T:* (01865) 765206.

STANTON, Prof. Stuart Lawrence Richard, FRCS, FRCSE, FRCOG; Professor of Pelvic Surgery and Urogynaecology, St George's Hospital Medical School, since 1997; Consultant Gynaecologist and Director of Urogynaecology Unit, St George's Hospital, since 1984; *b* 24 Oct. 1938; *s* of Michael Arthur Stanton and Sarah (*née* Joseph); *m* 1965, Anne Frances Goldsmith (marr. diss. 1991); three *d*; *m* 1991, Julia Heller; one *s* one *d*. *Educ:* City of London Sch.; London Hosp. Med. Sch. (MB BS 1961). FRCS 1966; FRCSE 1966; FRCOG 1987. Surgical Registrar, Royal Masonic Hosp., 1964–65; SHO, Queen Charlotte's Hosp., 1967; Res. Registrar, Inst. of Urology, London, 1971–72; Sen. Registrar, Dept of Obstetrics and Gynaecology, St George's Hosp., London, 1972–74; Consultant Obstetrician and Gynaecologist, St Helier Hosp., 1974–84. Lectures: William Blair Bell Meml, 1974, William Meredith Fletcher Shaw, 1996, RCOG; Victor Bonney, RCS, 1984; J. Marion Sims, Amer. Urogynecologic Soc., 1995. FRSocMed 1975. *Publications:* (ed jtly) Surgery of Female Incontinence, 1980, 2nd edn 1986; (ed) The Principles of Gynaecological Surgery, 1992; (ed jtly) Gynaecology, 2nd edn 1997; (ed jtly) Clinical Urogynaecology, 1999. *Recreations:* family, photography, modern ceramics, biographies, music. *Address:* Flat 10, 43 Wimpole Street, W1G 8EA. *T:* (020) 7486 0677; 1 Church Hill, SW19 7BN.

STANYER, Maj.-Gen. John Turner, CBE 1971 (OBE 1967); *b* 28 July 1920; *s* of late Charles T. Stanyer and late Mrs R. H. Stanyer; *m* 1942, Mary Patricia Pattie; three *s* four *d*. *Educ:* Latymer Upper Sch., Hammersmith. Served War, 2/Lieut The Middlesex Regt, 1941; Lieut to Captain, The Middlesex Regt, 1941–47: Iceland, France, Germany, Palestine. Captain, Royal Army Ordnance Corps, 1947; Student, Staff Coll., Camberley, 1951; AA&QMG, UN Force in Cyprus, 1966; Dir of Ordnance Services, BAOR, 1968–71; Commandant, Central Ordnance Depot, Bicester, 1971–73; Comdr, Base Orgn, RAOC, 1973–75, retired. Col Comdt, RAOC, 1977–82. Dir Gen., Supply Co-ordination, MoD, 1975–80. Mem., Oxford City Council, 1983–87. *Recreation:* sailing. *Address:* Sandy House, Manor Close, Walberswick, Southwold, Suffolk IP18 6UQ. *T:* (01502) 724533.

STAPLE, Rev. David, OBE 1995; General Secretary, Free Church Federal Council, 1986–96, now General Secretary Emeritus; *b* 30 March 1930; *s* of William Hill Staple and Elsie Staple; *m* 1955, Margaret Lilian Berrington; one *s* three *d*. *Educ:* Watford Boys' Grammar Sch.; Christ's Coll., Cambridge (MA); Regent's Park Coll., Oxford; Wadham Coll., Oxford (MA); BD London (external). Baptist Minister: West Ham Central Mission, 1955–58; Llanishen, Cardiff, 1958–74; College Road, Harrow, 1974–86. Chm., Baptist Missionary Soc., 1981–82; Mem. Council, Baptist Union of GB, 1970–96 (Ecumenical Rep. to Gen. Synod of C of E, 1995–2001). Co-Pres., CCBI, 1995–99; Mem. Exec., CCJ, 1986–98. Governor: Regent's Park Coll., Oxford, 1965–March 2002; Westhill Coll., Birmingham, 1986–96. *Recreations:* fell walking, music. *Address:* 1 Althorp Road, St Albans, Herts AL1 3PH. *T:* (01727) 810009, *Fax:* (01727) 867888.

STAPLE, George Warren, CB 1996; Consultant, Clifford Chance (Partner, 1987–92 and 1997–2001); *b* 13 Sept. 1940; *s* of late Kenneth Harry Staple and Betty Mary Staple; *m* 1968, Olivia Deirdre Lowry; two *s* two *d*. *Educ:* Haileybury. Solicitor, admitted 1964. Associate with Condon and Forsyth, NY, 1963; Asst Solicitor, 1964–67, Partner, 1967–87, Clifford-Turner & Co.; Dir, Serious Fraud Office, 1992–97. Legal Assessor, Disciplinary Cttee, Stock Exchange, 1978–92; DTI Inspector, Consolidated Gold Fields, 1986, Aldermanbury Trust, 1988; a Chairman, Authorisation and Disciplinary Tribunals: of The Securities Assoc., 1987–91; of Securities and Futures Authy, 1991–92; Member: Commercial Court Cttee, 1977–92; City Disputes Panel, 1998 ; Law Adv. Cttee, British Council, 1998–; Sen. Salaries Review Body, 2000–. Mem. Council, Law Soc., 1986–2000 (Treas., 1989–92). Gov., City of London Polytechnic, subseq. London Guildhall Univ., 1982–94; Chm. Govs, Haileybury, 2001. FCIArb 1986. Hon. QC 1997; Hon. Bencher, Inner Temple, 2000. *Recreations:* cricket, walking, gardening. *Address:* Clifford Chance, 200 Aldersgate Street, EC1A 4JJ. *Clubs:* Brooks's, City of London, MCC.

See also W. P. Staple.

STAPLE, William Philip; Director, Corporate Finance, Brown, Shipley & Co. Ltd, since 2001; *b* 28 Sept. 1947; *s* of late Kenneth Harry Staple and Betty Mary Staple (*née* Lemon); *m* 1977, Jennifer Frances Walker (marr. diss. 1986); one *s* one *d*. *Educ:* Haileybury; Law Soc. Coll. of Law. Called to the Bar, Inner Temple, 1971; Executive at Cazenove, 1972–81; N. M. Rothschild and Sons Ltd: Asst Dir, 1981–86; Dir, 1986–94 and 1996–99; Dir Gen., Takeover Panel, 1994–96; Man. Dir, Benfield Advisory, 1999–2001. *Recreations:* various sports, theatre, reading. *Address:* (office) Founders Court, Lothbury, EC2R 7HE. *T:* (020) 7282 3380. *Clubs:* White's, City of London.

See also G. W. Staple.

STAPLEFORD, Sally Anne, OBE 1999; President, National Ice Skating Association of UK Ltd, since 1995; *b* 7 July 1945; *d* of Richard Harvey Stapleford and Alice Elizabeth Stapleford. *Educ:* Streatham Hill High Sch.; Clapham High Sch.; private tutor. British Jun. Ice Skating Champion, 1961; Southern Regl Sen. Ice Skating Champion, 1961–63; Gold Medal: Britain, and Canada, 1961; America, 1962; British Sen. Ice Skating Champion, 1963–67; competed in: European Championships, 1963–68 (Silver Medal, 1965); World Championships, 1964–68; Winter Olympics, 1964, 1968; Edinburgh Internat. Trophy, 1968. Nat. judge and referee, 1968–; internat. judge and referee, 1972–; National Ice Skating Association (formerly National Skating Association): Mem., Governing Body, 1970–; Chm., Ice Figure Cttee, 1989–94; Vice-Chm., Fedn of Ice Skating, 1990; Technical Orgnr, internat. figure skating events in UK; Mem., 1988–, Chm., 1992–, Figure Skating Technical Cttee, Internat. Skating Union. *Address:* Flat 3, St Valery's, 54 Beulah Hill, Upper Norwood, SE19 3ER. *T:* (020) 8771 0778.

STAPLES, Brian Lynn; Chief Executive, Amey PLC, since 1997; *b* 6 April 1945; *s* of Stanley Holt Staples and Catherine Emma Annie Staples (*née* Walding); *m* 1st, 1965; one *d*; 2nd, 1973; one *s* two *d*; 3rd, 1999, Anne-Marie Smith; two *s*. *Educ:* Sweyne Grammar Sch., Rayleigh. Joined Tarmac Group, 1964; Chief Executive: Tarmac Construction, 1991–94; United Utilities Plc (formerly North West Water Gp), 1994–97. Non-executive Director: RJB Mining, 1999–; IMI plc, 2000–. *Recreations:* Rugby, music, theatre, hill walking. *Address:* Pendle House, Castle Hill, Prestbury, Cheshire SK10 4AR.

STAPLES, Rev. Canon Edward Eric, CBE 1977 (OBE 1973); Chaplain to The Queen, 1973–80; Chaplain to the Anglican congregations in Helsinki and throughout Finland, in Moscow, Leningrad and elsewhere in the Soviet Union, and in Outer Mongolia, 1964–80; Hon. Chaplain, British Embassy: Helsinki, 1967–80, Moscow, 1968–80, Ulan Bator, 1970–81; Hon. Lecturer, English History, University of Helsinki, 1972–80; Hon. Canon of Gibraltar Cathedral, since 1974; *b* 15 Nov. 1910; *yr s* of Christopher Walter Staples and Esther Jane Staples; *m* 1962, Kate Ethel Thusberg (*née* Rönngren); two step *d*. *Educ:* Chichester Theol Coll. (earlier opportunities so misused that it is unwise to name the establishments concerned!). MA, PhD. Niger Company, 1932. Served with RNVR, 1939–46. Ordained 1948. Assistant of Court of Russia Company, 1977–89, Consul, 1978–88. Life Mem., Finnish-British Soc.; Mem., Anglo-Mongolian Soc. Medal of Univ. of Helsinki, 1980. Kt, Order of the Lion (Finland), 1976; Order of St Vladimir (Russian Orthodox Church), 1977. *Recreations:* climbing, cricket, fishing, gardening (no longer actively), historical research. *Address:* The Old Farmhouse, Ramsbury, Marlborough, Wilts SN8 2PG. *T:* (01672) 521118. *Clubs:* MCC; Helsinki Cricket (Founder Mem.); Moscow Cricket (Founder Mem.); Ulan Bator Golf (Hon. Life Mem.).

STAPLES, (Hubert Anthony) Justin, CMG 1981; HM Diplomatic Service, retired; Ambassador to Finland, 1986–89; *b* 14 Nov. 1929; *s* of late Francis Hammond Staples, formerly ICS, and Catherine Margaret Mary Pownall; *m* 1962, Susan Angela Collingwood Carter; one *s* one *d*. *Educ:* Downside; Oriel Coll., Oxford. Served in RAF 1952–54 (Pilot Officer). Entered Foreign (later Diplomatic) Service, 1954; 3rd Sec., Bangkok, 1955; Foreign Office, 1959; 1st Sec., Berlin (Dep. Political Adviser), 1962; Vientiane, 1965 (acted as Chargé d'Affaires in 1966 and 1967); transf. to FO and seconded to Cabinet Office, 1968; Counsellor, UK Delegn to NATO, Brussels, 1971; Counsellor and Consul-General, Bangkok, 1974 (acted as Chargé d'affaires, 1975 and 1977); Counsellor, Dublin, 1978–81; Ambassador to Thailand, 1981–86 and concurrently to Laos, 1985–86. Pres., Anglo-Finnish Soc., 1993–. *Recreation:* golf. *Address:* 48 Crescent Road, Kingston, Surrey KT2 7RF. *Clubs:* Travellers; Roehampton; Royal Bangkok Sports (Bangkok).

STAPLES, Justin; *see* Staples, H. A. J.

STAPLES, Sir Richard Molesworth, 17th Bt *cr* 1628, of Lissan, co. Tyrone; *b* 11 June 1914; 3rd *s* of Thomas Staples and Mary Ussher Staples (*née* Greer); *S* brother, 1999; *m* 1954, Marjory Charlotte (*née* Jefcoate) (*d* 1998). *Educ:* St Andrew's Coll., Dublin. RAF, 1940–52 (Burma Star, 1943); RNZAF, 1952–59. Teachers' Trng Coll., Christchurch, NZ, 1959–74. *Publication:* John Cain Mole, Airman, WW2, 1998. *Recreations:* travel, reading, gardening, writing, watching tennis on TV. *Club:* Union Jack.

STAPLETON, Air Vice-Marshal Deryck Cameron, CB 1960; CBE 1948; DFC; AFC; psa; *b* 15 Jan. 1918; *s* of John Rouse Stapleton, OBE, Sarnia, Natal; *m* 1942, Ethleen Joan Clifford, *d* of late Sir Cuthbert William Whiteside. *Educ:* King Edward VI Sch., Totnes. Joined RAF, 1936; served Transjordan and Palestine (AFC), 1937–39; War of 1939–45 (DFC). Middle East, N Africa, Italy. Asst Sec. (Air), War Cabinet Offices, 1945–46; Secretary, Chiefs of Staff Cttee, Ministry of Defence, 1947–49; OC RAF, Odiham, 1949–51; subsequently, Plans, Fighter Comd HQ and Ops at AFCENT Fontainebleu; then OC, RAF, Oldenburg (Germany); Plans, Bomber Comd HQ, 1957–60; Air Ministry, 1960–62; Dir, Defence Plans, Min. of Defence, 1963–64; AOC No 1 Group, RAF Bomber Command, 1964–66; Comdt, RAF Staff Coll., Bracknell, 1966–68. BAC Area Manager, Libya, 1969–70; BAC Rep. CENTO Area, Tehran, later BAe Chief Exec. Iran, and Man. Dir, Irano-British Dynamics Co. Iran, 1970–79; Rep. BAe, Peking, China, and Chm., British Cos Assoc., Peking, 1979–83. Associate Fellow, British Interplanetary Soc., 1960. *Publication:* (jtly) Winged Promises, 1996. *Recreations:* most sports.

STAPLETON, Guy, CB 1995; Chief Executive, Intervention Board Executive Agency (formerly Intervention Board for Agricultural Produce), 1986–95; *b* 10 Nov. 1935; *s* of William Algernon Swann Stapleton and Joan Denise Stapleton (*née* Wilson). *Educ:* Malvern Coll. Clerical Officer, Min. of Transport and Civil Aviation, 1954–58; Exec. Officer, 1958; transf. to Min. of Aviation, 1959; Civil Aviation Asst, British Embassy, Rome, 1960–63; Private Sec. to Controller of National Air Traffic Control Services, 1963–65; Asst Principal, MAFF, 1965; Private Sec. to Jt Parly Sec., 1967–68; Principal, 1968; Asst Sec., 1973; Dept of Prices and Consumer Protection, 1974–76; Under Sec., 1981; European Secretariat, Cabinet Office, 1982–85; Dir of Establishments, MAFF, 1985–86. *Publications:* A Walk of Verse, 1961; (compiled) Poet's England: 2, Gloucestershire, 1977, 2nd edn 1982; 4, Avon and Somerset, 1981; 7, Devon, 1986; 9, Hertfordshire, 1988; 12, Leicestershire and Rutland, 1992; 13, Nottinghamshire, 1993; 19, Dorset, 1996; Vale of Moreton Churches, 1989; (ed) Memories of Moreton, 1989; Four Shire Memories, 1992; Moreton & Batsford Roll of Honour, 2000; History of Moreton-in-Marsh Hospital, 2001. *Recreations:* local and family history, topographical verse. *Club:* Royal Over-Seas League.

STAPLETON, Very Rev. Henry Edward Champneys; Dean of Carlisle, 1988–98; *b* 17 June 1932; *s* of Edward Parker Stapleton and Frances Mary Champneys; *m* 1964, Mary Deborah Sapwell; two *d*. *Educ:* Lancing College; Pembroke Coll., Cambridge (BA 1954, MA 1958); Ely Theological Coll. Deacon 1956, priest 1957, York; Assistant Curate: St Olave with St Giles, 1956–59; Pocklington, 1959–61; Vicar of Seaton Ross with Everingham, Harswell and Bielby, 1961–67; RD of Weighton, 1966–67; Rector of Skelton, 1967–75; Vicar of Wroxham with Hoveton, 1975–81; Priest in Charge of Belaugh, 1976–81, with Hoveton St Peter, 1979–81; Canon Residentiary and Precentor of Rochester Cathedral, 1981–88; Warden of Readers, 1981–88. Church Comr, 1993–98; Member: Council for the Care of Churches, 1965–91; Churches Conservation Trust (formerly Redundant Churches Fund), 1976–98; Royal Commn on Historical Manuscripts, 1992–. Trustee, Historic Churches Preservation Trust, 1983–. Fellow, Woodard Corp., 1990–. FSA 1974. Editor, Cathedral, 1976–82. Hon. Fellow, Univ. of Northumbria, Newcastle, 1995. *Publications:* Skelton Village, 1971; Heirs without Title, 1974; The Skilful Master Builder, 1975; The Model Working Parson, 1976; (ed and contrib.) Churchyards Handbook, 2nd edn 1976, 3rd edn 1988; articles in Churchscape and other ecclesiastical jls. *Recreations:* the writings of R. H. Benson, genealogy, visiting churches, second-hand bookshops. *Address:* Rockland House, 20 Marsh Gardens, Honley, Holmfirth, W Yorks HD9 6AF. *T:* (01484) 666629.

STAPLETON, Nigel John; Chairman: Veronis, Suhler International Ltd, since 1999; Uniq plc, since 2001; *b* 1 Nov. 1946; *s* of Frederick Ernest John Stapleton and Katie Margaret Stapleton (*née* Tyson); *m* 1982, Johanna Augusta Molhoek; one *s* one *d*. *Educ:* City of London Sch.; Fitzwilliam Coll., Cambridge (MA; Hon. Fellow 1998).Planning, finance and gen. mgt positions, incl. Vice Pres., Finance, Unilever United States Inc., Unilever plc, 1968–86; Reed International plc: Dir, 1986–99; Finance Dir, 1986–96; Dep. Chm., 1994–97; Chm., 1997–99; Co-Chm., 1996–98, Co-Chief Exec., 1998–99, Reed Elsevier plc. Non-executive Director: Allied Domecq plc, 1992–99; Marconi plc (formerly GEC), 1997–; Axa UK (formerly Sun Life and Provincial Hldgs) plc, 1999–. Dir, London Stock Exchange, 2001–. Trustee, Royal Opera House Trust, 1999. *Recreations:* theatre, opera, travel, tennis. *Address:* c/o Veronis, Suhler International Ltd, Buchanan House, 3 St James's Square, SW1Y 4JU. *T:* (020) 7484 1400, *Fax:* (020) 7484 1410; c/o Uniq plc, 60 Wood Lane, W12 7RP. *Club:* Oxford and Cambridge.

STAPLETON, Prof. Richard Christopher, PhD; Professor of Finance, Strathclyde University, since 1998; *b* 11 Oct. 1942; *s* of Leonard Stapleton and Rosamund Kathleen May Stapleton; *m* 1968, Linda Cairns; one *s* one *d*. *Educ:* Univ. of Sheffield (BAEcon, PhD Business Studies); Open Univ. (BA Maths). Lectr in Business Finance, Sheffield Univ., 1965–73; Asst Prof. of Finance, New York Univ., 1973–76; Sen. Res. Fellow, 1976–77, Nat. West. Bank Prof. of Business Finance, 1977–86, Manchester Business Sch., Univ. of Manchester; Fellow, Churchill Coll., Cambridge, 1986–89; Wolfson Prof. of Finance, Lancaster Univ., 1989–98. Hon. MBA Manchester, 1980. *Publications:* The Theory of Corporate Finance, 1970; International Tax Systems and Financing Policy, 1978; Capital Markets and Corporate Financial Decisions, 1980; contrib. Econ. Jl, Jl of Finance, Jl of Financial Econs, Qly Jl of Econs. *Recreations:* running, golf, reading, travel. *Address:* Department of Accounting and Finance, Strathclyde University, 100 Cathedral Street, Glasgow G4 0LD.

STAPLETON-COTTON, family name of **Viscount Combermere**.

STARK, Sir Andrew (Alexander Steel), KCMG 1975 (CMG 1964); CVO 1965; DL; HM Diplomatic Service, retired; Director, The Maersk Co., 1978–90 (Chairman, 1978–87); Adviser on European Affairs, Society of Motor Manufacturers and Traders, 1977–89; *b* 30 Dec. 1916; *yr s* of late Thomas Bow Stark and Barbara Black Stark (*née* Steel), Fauldhouse, West Lothian; *m* 1944, Helen Rosemary, *er d* Lt-Col J. Oxley Parker, TD, and Mary Monica (*née* Hills); two *s* (and one *s* decd). *Educ:* Bathgate Acad.; Edinburgh Univ. MA (Hons), Eng. Lit, Edinburgh, 1938. Served War of 1939–45, Green Howards and Staff appts. Major 1945. Entered Foreign Service, 1948, and served in Foreign Office until 1950; 1st Secretary, Vienna, 1951–53; Asst Private Sec. to Foreign Secretary, 1953–55; Head of Chancery: Belgrade, 1956–58; Rome, 1958–60; Counsellor: FO, 1960–64; Bonn, 1964–68; attached to Mission to UN with rank of Ambassador, Jan. 1968; British Mem., Seven Nation Cttee on Reorganisation of UN Secretariat; seconded to UN, NY, as Under-Secretary-General, Oct. 1968–1971; HM Ambassador to Denmark, 1971–76; Dep. Under-Sec. of State, FCO, 1976–78. Director: Scandinavian Bank Ltd, 1978–88; Carlsberg Brewery Ltd, 1980–87. Mem., CBI Europe Cttee, 1980–85. Chairman: Anglo-Danish Soc., 1983–95 (Hon. Pres., 1995–); Anglo-Danish Trade Adv. Bd, 1983–93. President: British Assoc. of Former UN Civil Servants, 1989–94; Essex Disabled People's (formerly Essex Physically Handicapped) Assoc., 1979–99; Chm., Rural Community Council of Essex, 1990–93. University of Essex: Mem. Council, 1978– (Chm. Council, 1983–89); Pro-Chancellor, 1983–95; DU 1990. DL Essex, 1981. Grosses Verdienstkreuz, German Federal Republic, 1965; Grand Cross, Order of the Dannebrog, Denmark, 1974. *Recreation:* shooting. *Address:* Fambridge Hall, White Notley, Witham, Essex CM8 1RN. *T:* (01376) 583117. *Clubs:* Travellers (Chairman 1978–81), MCC.

STARK, David; *see* Stark, J. D. S.

STARK, George Robert, PhD; FRS 1990; Chairman, Lerner Research Institute, Cleveland Clinic Foundation, since 1992; *b* 4 July 1933; *s* of Jack and Florence Stark; *m* 1956, Mary Beck; one *s* one *d*. *Educ:* Columbia College, NY (BA 1955); Columbia Univ., NY (Chemistry; PhD 1959). Asst Prof., Rockefeller Univ., 1961; Stanford University: Asst Prof., 1963; Associate Prof., 1966; Prof. of Biochemistry, 1971; ICRF, 1983–92 (Associate Dir of Res., 1989–92). Member: Nat. Acad. of Scis, USA, 1987; European Molecular Biol. Orgn, 1985. *Publications:* contribs to scientific jls. *Recreations:* sports, stamps, books, records. *Address:* Cleveland Clinic Foundation, 9500 Euclid Avenue, Cleveland, OH 44195, USA. *T:* (216) 4443900, *Fax:* (216) 4443279.

STARK, (John) David (Sinclair), CEng; Chairman, Glentay Ltd, since 1997; Member, Competition (formerly Monopolies and Mergers) Commission, since 1998; *b* 16 April 1939; *s* of John and Bertha Stark; *m* 1964, Pamela Margaret Reed; one *s* one *d*. *Educ:* St Bees Sch., Cumberland; Leeds Univ. (BSc). CEng, MIEE 1966. GEC plc, 1960–62; Morgan Crucible plc, 1962–76; Bestobell plc, 1976–81; Man. Dir, Bestobell Australia Ltd, 1981–84; Divl Chief Exec., Unitech plc, 1984–85; Divl Dir, 1985–86, Dir, 1986–97, Tomkins plc; Dir, Norcros plc, 1997–99. Non-exec. Dir, Royal Mint, 2000–. Gov., Esher Church Sch., 1998–. *Recreations:* inland waterways, opera, amateur dramatics. *Address:* Tara, 15 Copsem Drive, Esher, Surrey KT10 9HD. *T:* (01372) 466781.

STARKER, Janos; concert cellist, recording artist; Distinguished Professor of Cello, Indiana University, since 1958; *b* Budapest, 5 July 1924; *s* of F. Sandor and M. Margit; *m* 1944, Eva Uranyi; one *d*; *m* 1960, Rae D. Busch; one *d*. *Educ:* Franz Liszt Academy of Music, Budapest; Zrinyi Gymnasium, Budapest. Professional solo cellist, 1939–; Budapest Opera and Philh., 1945–46; Dallas Symphony, 1948–49; Metropolitan Opera, 1949–53; Chicago Symphony, 1953–58; concert tours on all continents in recitals and as soloist with orchestras; numerous recordings (Grand Prix du Disque, 1948; Grammy Award, 1998). Member: Amer. Fedn Musicians; Indiana Acad. of Arts and Scis; Amer. Acad. of Arts and Scis, 1999; Hon. RAM, 1981. Invented the Starker Bridge. Hon. DMus: Chicago Conservatory Coll., 1961; Cornell, 1978; East-West Univ., 1982; Williams Coll., 1983; Lawrence Univ., 1990. George Washington Award, 1972; Sanford Fellowship Award, Yale, 1974; Herzl Award, Israel, 1978; Ed Press Award, 1983; Kodály Commemorative Medallion, NY, 1983; Arturo Toscanini Award, Toscanini Foundn, 1986; Tracy Sonneborn Award, Indiana Univ., 1986; Pro Cultura Hungarica, 1992; Indiana Governors Award, 1995; La Médaille de la ville de Paris, 1995; Pres's Medal for Excellence, Indiana Univ., 1999; Pres. of Hungary's Gold Medal, 1999. Chevalier, l'Ordre des Arts et des Lettres (France), 1997. *Publications:* Cello Method: an organised method of string playing, 1963; Bach Suites, 1971; Concerto Cadenzas, 1976; Beethoven Sonatas, 1978; Beethoven Variations, 1979; Bach Sonatas, 1979; Schubert-Starker Sonatina, 1980; Dvorak Concerto, 1981; Bottermund-Starker Variations, 1982; Encores, 1985; many articles and essays. *Recreations:* writing, swimming, staying alive. *Address:* Indiana University Music Department, Bloomington, IN 47405, USA; c/o Colbert Artists, 111 West 57th Street, New York, NY 10019, USA.

STARKEY, Dr David, FSA; FRHistS; historian and broadcaster; *b* 3 Jan. 1945; *s* of Robert Starkey and Elsie Starkey (*née* Lyon). *Educ:* Kendal GS; Fitzwilliam Coll., Cambridge (Open Schol.). FRHistS 1984; FSA 1994. Res. Fellow, 1970–72, Vis. Fellow, 1998–2001, Bye-Fellow, 2001–, Fitzwilliam Coll., Cambridge; Lectr in History, Dept of Internat. History, LSE, 1972–98. Vis. Vernon Prof. of Biography, Dartmouth Coll., New Hampshire, 1987, 1989; British Council Specialist Visitor, Australia, 1989. Presenter and writer of television series: This Land of England, 1985; Henry VIII, 1998; Elizabeth I, 2000; Six Wives of Henry VIII, 2001; panellist, Moral Maze, BBC Radio 4, 1992–; Presenter, Starkey on Saturday, then Starkey on Sunday, Talk Radio, 1995–98. Mem., Commemorative Plaques Wkg Gp, English Heritage, 1993–; Pres., Soc. for Court Studies, 1996–. Patron, Tory Campaign for Homosexual Equality, 1994–. Liveryman, Co. of Barbers, 1999– (Freeman, 1992). Mem. Editl Bd, History Today, 1980–; Hon. Associate: Rationalist Press Assoc., 1995–; Nat. Secular Soc., 1999–. Norton Medlicott Medal, for services to history, Historical Assoc., 2001. *Publications:* (jtly) This Land of England, 1985; The Reign of Henry VIII: personalities and politics, 1985, 2nd edn 1991; (ed jtly) Revolution Reassessed: revisions in the history of Tudor government and administration, 1986; (ed) The English Court from the Wars of the Roses to the Civil War, 1987; (ed) Rivals in Power: the lives and letters of the great Tudor dynasties, 1990; Henry VIII: a European court in England, 1991; (ed jtly) The Inventory of Henry VIII, vol. I, 1998; Elizabeth: apprenticeship, 2000 (W H Smith Award for Biog./Autobiog., 2001); Six Wives of Henry VIII, 2001; contribs to newspapers, numerous articles in learned jls. *Recreations:* decorating, gardening, treading on toes. *Address:* Fitzwilliam College, Cambridge CB3 0DG.

STARKEY, Sir John (Philip), 3rd Bt *cr* 1935; DL; *b* 8 May 1938; *s* of Sir William Randle Starkey, 2nd Bt, and Irene Myrtle Starkey (*née* Francklin) (*d* 1965); *S* father, 1977; *m* 1966, Victoria Henrietta Fleetwood, *y d* of Lt-Col Christopher Fuller, TD; one *s* three *d*. *Educ:* Eton College; Christ Church, Oxford. Sloan Fellow, London Business School. A Church Commissioner and Mem. Commissioners' Assets Cttee, 1985–91; Mem., Archbishop's Commn on Rural Areas, 1988–90. Chairman: Notts Br., CLA, 1977–80; E Midlands Regional Cttee, Nat. Trust, 1986–97. UK Vice Pres., Confedn of European Agriculture, 1989–2000; Pres., Newark Chamber of Commerce, 1980–82. Notts: DL, 1981; High Sheriff, 1987–88; JP Newark, 1981–88. FRSA 1990. *Recreations:* cricket, painting, golf. *Heir: s* Henry John Starkey, *b* 13 Oct. 1973. *Address:* Norwood Park, Southwell, Notts NG25 0PF. *T:* (01636) 812762; *e-mail:* starkey@farmline.com. *Club:* MCC.

STARKEY, Dr Phyllis Margaret; MP (Lab) Milton Keynes South West, since 1997; *b* 4 Jan. 1947; *d* of Dr John Williams and Catherine Hooson Williams (*née* Owen); *m* 1969, Hugh Walton Starkey; two *d*. *Educ:* Perse Sch. for Girls, Cambridge; Lady Margaret Hall, Oxford (BA Biochem.); Clare Hall, Cambridge (PhD). Research posts: Strangeways Lab., Cambridge, 1970–81; Sir Wm Dunn Sch. of Pathology, Oxford, 1981–84; Lectr in Obstetrics and Gynaecology, 1984–93, and Fellow of Somerville Coll., 1987–93, Univ. of Oxford; Head of Assessment, BBSRC, 1993–97. Mem. (Lab), Oxford City Council, 1983–97 (Leader, 1990–93); Chm., Local Govt Inf. Unit, 1992–97. PPS to FCO Ministers, 2001–. Mem., Foreign Affairs Select Cttee, 1999–2001. *Publications:* numerous scientific articles in learned jls. *Recreations:* gardening, cinema, walking. *Address:* Labour Hall, Newport Road, New Bradwell, Milton Keynes MK13 0AA. *T:* (01908) 225522.

STARLING, Keith Andrew; Headmaster, The Judd School, since 1986; *b* 12 June 1944; *s* of Stanley Ernest Starling and Gladys Joyce Starling; *m* 1968, Jacqueline Eagers; two *s*. *Educ:* The Perse Sch; Fitzwilliam Coll., Cambridge (MA, CertEd). Asst Master, Lancaster Royal Grammar Sch., 1968–71; Head of Geography, Sedbergh Sch., 1971–80; Dep. Headmaster, Portsmouth Grammar Sch., 1980–86. *Recreations:* music, walking. *Address:* The Judd School, Tonbridge, Kent TN9 2PN. *T:* (01732) 770880.

STARMER-SMITH, Nigel Christopher; BBC TV Sports Commentator, since 1973; *b* 25 Dec. 1944; *s* of Harry Starmer-Smith and Joan Mary Starmer-Smith (*née* Keep); *m* 1973, Rosamund Mary Bartlett; one *s* (and one *s* one *d* decd). *Educ:* Magdalen Coll. Sch., Oxford; University Coll., Oxford (MA). Schoolmaster, Epsom Coll., 1967; Producer and Reporter, BBC Radio Outside Broadcasts, 1971; BBC TV, 1973–; Presenter and Commentator, Rugby Special; commentator, hockey and other sports. Publisher and Editor, Rugby World and Post magazine, 1984–93. Former Rugby Union international: Harlequins, Oxford Univ., Barbarians, England. *Publications* include: The Barbarians, 1977; Rugby: a way of life, 1986. *Recreations:* family, tennis, piano playing, horse racing, gardening. *Address:* North Barn, Sandpit Lane, Dunsden, Oxon RG4 9PQ. *T:* (0118) 948 4285. *Clubs:* Vincent's (Oxford); Leander (Henley); Harlequins FC.

STATHAM, Sir Norman, KCMG 1977 (CMG 1967); CVO 1968; HM Diplomatic Service, retired; *b* Stretford, Lancs, 15 Aug. 1922; *s* of Frederick William and Maud Statham; *m* 1948, Hedwig Gerlich; one *s* one *d* (and one *s* decd). *Educ:* Seymour Park Council School, Stretford; Manchester Grammar School; Gonville and Caius College, Cambridge (MA). Intelligence Corps, 1943–47; Manchester Oil Refinery Ltd and Petrochemicals Ltd, 1948–50; Foreign Service, 1951: Foreign Office, 1951; Consul (Commercial), New York, 1954; First Secretary (Commercial), Bonn, 1958; Administrative Staff College, Henley, 1963; Foreign Office, 1964; Counsellor, Head of European Economic Integration Dept, 1965–68, 1970–71; Consul-General, São Paulo, 1968–70; Minister (Economic), Bonn, 1971; Asst Under Sec. of State, FCO, 1975; Dep. Under Sec. of State, FCO, 1975; Ambassador to Brazil, 1977–79. FCO Special Rep. for British-German Co-operation, 1984–86. Vice-Pres., British Chamber of Commerce in Germany, 1981–85; Pres., Council of British Chambers of Commerce in Continental Europe, 1982–84. *Recreations:* reading, birdwatching, calligraphy. *Address:* 11 Underhill Park Road, Reigate, Surrey RH2 9LU.

STATHATOS, Stephanos; Commander, Order of Phoenix; Officer, Order of George I; *b* 30 Sept. 1922; *s* of Gerassimo and Eugenia Stathatos; *m* 1947, Thalia Mouzina. *Educ:*

Law School, Athens Univ.; post graduate studies: Ecole des Sciences Politiques, Paris; LSE. Entered Greek Diplomatic Service, 1953; served Cairo, NATO, Paris, Athens, Washington; Dep. Perm. Rep. to UN, NY, 1968–72; Dir, Middle East Political Affairs, Min. of Foreign Affairs, 1972–74; Ambassador, Perm. Rep. to EEC, 1974–79; Ambassador, Paris, 1979–82; non-resident Ambassador to Holy See, 1981–82; Dep. Political Dir, 1982–84, Political Dir, 1984–85, Min. of Foreign Affairs; Ambassador to UK, 1986–89, and non-resident Ambassador to Iceland; Head of Prime Minister's Diplomatic Office, 1989–90. Pres., EU *ad hoc* Gp on Stability Pact, 1994; Nat. Rep. to Reflexion Gp for revision of Maastricht Treaty, 1995. Vice-Pres., Hellenic Foundn for Defence and Foreign Policy, 1994– (Mem. Bd, 1992–). Holds numerous foreign orders and decorations. *Address:* 24 Raviné Street, Athens 11521, Greece. *T:* (1) 7222004. *Club:* Athenæum.

STAUGHTON, Rt Hon. Sir Christopher (Stephen Thomas Jonathan Thayer), Kt 1981; PC 1988; FCIArb; arbitrator, part-time judge and lecturer; a Lord Justice of Appeal, 1987–97; Judge of the Court of Appeal, Gibraltar, since 2000; *b* 24 May 1933; *yr s* of late Simon Thomas Samuel Staughton of Melbourne, Australia and Edith Madeline Jones of Halifax, Canada; *m* 1960, Joanna Susan Elizabeth, DL, *er d* of late George Frederick Arthur Burgess; two *d*. *Educ:* Eton Coll. (Scholar); Magdalene Coll., Cambridge (Scholar; Hon. Fellow 1988). 2nd Lieut, 11th Hussars PAO, 1952–53; Lieut, Derbyshire Yeomanry TA, 1954–56. George Long Prize for Roman Law, Cambridge, 1955; BA 1956; MA 1961. Called to Bar, Inner Temple, 1957, Bencher, 1978, Reader, 1996, Treasurer, 1997; QC 1970; a Recorder of the Crown Court, 1972–81; a Judge of the High Court of Justice, QBD, 1981–87. Appeal Adjudicator, enemy property claims, 2001–. Mem., Senate of the Inns of Court and the Bar, 1974–81; Chm., Code of Conduct sub-cttee, 1979–80. Member: Adv. Bd, British Library, 1999–; Police Surveillance Commn, 1999–2000. Chm., St Peter's Eaton Square Church of England Sch., 1974–83. Hon. LLD Hertfordshire, 1996. *Publications:* (Jt Editor) The Law of General Average (British Shipping Laws vol. 7), 1964, new edn, 1975; (jtly) Profits of Crime and their Recovery, 1984; articles on plain English in the law. *Recreations:* bridge, growing dahlias. *Address:* 20 Essex Street, WC2R 3AL. *T:* (020) 7583 9294, *Fax:* (020) 7583 1341; *e-mail:* cstaughton@20essexst.com.

STAUNTON, Imelda Mary Philomena Bernadette; actress, since 1976; *b* 9 Jan. 1956; *d* of Joseph Staunton and Bridie McNicholas; *m* 1983, Jim Carter, actor; one *d*. *Educ:* La Sainte Union Convent, Highgate; RADA. *Theatre* includes: rep., 1976–81; The Corn is Green, Old Vic, 1985; *National Theatre:* Guys and Dolls, 1982, 1996; Beggar's Opera, Chorus of Disapproval (Olivier Award, best supporting actress), 1985; Life × 3, 2000, transf. Old Vic; *Royal Shakespeare Company:* Fair Maid of the West, Wizard of Oz, 1986; Uncle Vanya, Vaudeville, 1988; Into the Woods, Phoenix, 1990 (Olivier Award, best actress in a musical, 1991); *television* includes: The Singing Detective, 1986; Yellowbacks, 1990; Sleeping Life; Roots; Up the Garden Path, 1990; Antonia & Jane; Is it Legal?; *films* include: Peter's Friends, 1992; Much Ado About Nothing, 1993; Deadly Advice, 1994; Sense and Sensibility, Twelfth Night, Remember Me, 1996; Shakespeare in Love, 1999; Crush, 2001. *Address:* c/o Peters Fraser & Dunlop, Drury House, 34–43 Russell Street, WC2B 5HA.

STAUNTON, Prof. James, PhD; FRS 1998; Professor of Chemical Biology, 1999–Oct. 2002, and Fellow of St John's College, since 1969, University of Cambridge; *b* 18 March 1935; *s* of James and Elizabeth Staunton; *m* 1961, Dr Ruth Mary Berry, MB, ChB. *Educ:* St Edward's Coll., Liverpool; Univ. of Liverpool (BSc 1956; PhD 1959); MA Cantab 1969. Postdoctoral Fellow, Stanford Univ., 1959–60; Fellow, 1960–62, Lectr in Organic Chemistry, 1962–69, Liverpool Univ.; Lectr in Organic Chemistry, 1969–78, Reader, 1978–99, Cambridge Univ. Dir, Biotica Technology Ltd, 1996–. Natural Products Award, 1987, Tilden Medal, 1989, Robert Robinson Award, 2001, RSC. *Publications:* Primary Metabolism: a mechanistic approach, 1978; articles in chemical and biochemical jls. *Recreations:* walking, cycling, gardening, travel, DIY. *Address:* (until Oct. 2002) University Chemical Laboratories, Lensfield Road, Cambridge CB2 1EW. *T:* (01223) 336406; St John's College, Cambridge CB2 1TP.

STAUNTON, Marie; Chief Executive, Plan International UK, since 2000; *b* 28 May 1952; *d* of Ann and Austin Staunton; *m* 1986, James Albert Provan; two *d*. *Educ:* Lancaster Univ.; College of Law (BA). Solicitor. Head of casework for Simon Community Hostels for Addicts, Alcoholics and Homeless Families (England, NI and Eire), 1970–72; Articled Clerk and Solicitor in private practice and Law Centres, 1976–83; Legal Officer, NCCL, 1983–87; Dir, British Section, Amnesty Internat., 1987–90 (Vice-Chm., Internat. Exec. Cttee, 1993–95); Publishing Dir, Longman Law Tax & Finance, then Financial Times Law & Tax, 1990–96; Ed., Solicitors' Jl, 1990–95; Dep. Dir, UK Cttee for UNICEF, 1997–2000. *Publications:* Data Protection: putting the record straight, 1987; contribs to NCCL works; chapters in books on allied subjects. *Address:* (office) 5–6 Underhill Street, NW1 7HS. *T:* (020) 7485 6612.

STAVELEY, Sir John (Malfroy), KBE 1980 (OBE 1972); MC 1941; FRCP; FRACPath; Haematologist, Auckland Hospital Board, 1950–64; Director, Auckland Blood Transfusion Service, 1965–76; *b* 30 Aug. 1914; *s* of William Staveley and Annie May Staveley (*née* Malfroy); *m* 1940, Elvira Cliafe Wycherley; one *s* one *d*. *Educ:* Univ. of Dunedin (MB ChB); Univ. of Edinburgh. FRCP 1958; FRACPath 1965. House Surgeon, Auckland Hosp., 1939; war service with 2NZEF, Middle East, 1940–45; post graduate educn, UK, 1946–47; Pathologist, Auckland Hosp., 1948–50. Landsteiner Award, USA, for medical research, 1980. *Publications:* papers in medical and scientific jls (British, American and NZ). *Recreations:* mountaineering, fishing, music. *Address:* 11 Matanui Street, Northcote, Auckland 9, New Zealand.

STAVELEY, Maj.-Gen. Robert; *b* 3 June 1928; *s* of Brig. Robin Staveley, DSO, and Ilys (*née* Sutherland); *m* 1958, Airlie, *d* of Maj.-Gen. W. H. Lambert, CB, CBE; one *s* one *d*. *Educ:* Wellington. RMA Sandhurst, 1947; Staff Colls India and Camberley; commissioned RA, 1948; served BAOR, 1949–51; ADC to GOC Malta, 1951–53; Air OP pilot, Malaya, 1954–57 (despatches); ADC to GOC-in-C Northern Command, 1957–58; Indian Staff Coll., 1959; Staff Officer and Missile Battery Comdr, BAOR, 1960–65; Instructor, Staff Coll., 1966–68; commanded 47 Lt Regt RA, UK and Hong Kong, 1969–71; MoD, 1972; CRA 2nd Div., BAOR, 1973–74; RCDS 1975; Director of Operational Requirements, MoD, 1976–79; C of S, Logistic Exec. (Army), 1979–82. Admin. Controller, Norton Rose, solicitors, 1983–91. Col Comdt, RA, 1982–87. Chm., Bd of Govs, Royal Sch., Hampstead, 1993–98. FIMgt (FBIM 1983). *Recreations:* good food, sailing, skiing, music. *Address:* c/o Lloyds TSB (Cox's & King's Branch), 7 Pall Mall, SW1Y 5NA. *Clubs:* Army and Navy, Royal Ocean Racing; Royal Artillery Yacht (Commodore, 1980–83; Admiral, 1991–97).

STAVERT, Rt Rev. Alexander Bruce; *see* Quebec, Bishop of.

STEAD, Prof. Christian Karlson, CBE 1985; PhD, DLitt; FRSL; writer; Professor of English, University of Auckland, 1968–87, now Emeritus; *b* 17 Oct. 1932; *s* of James Walter Ambrose Stead and Olive Ethel Stead; *m* 1955, Kathleen Elizabeth Roberts; one *s* two *d*. *Educ:* Univ. of NZ (MA 1955); Univ. of Bristol (PhD 1962); Univ. of Auckland (DLitt 1981). Lectr in English, Univ. of New England, NSW, 1956–57; Michael Hiatt Baker Schol., Univ. of Bristol, 1957–59; Lectr, then Sen. Lectr in English, 1960–64, Associate Prof., 1964–68, Univ. of Auckland. Sen. Vis. Fellow, St John's Coll., Oxford, 1996–97. FRSL 1995. Hon. DLitt Bristol, 2001. *Publications: poetry:* Whether the Will is Free, 1964; Crossing the Bar, 1972; Quesada, 1975; Walking Westward, 1978; Geographies, 1981; Paris, 1984; Poems of a Decade, 1985; Between, 1987; Voices, 1990; Straw into Gold: poems new and selected, 1997; The Right Thing, 2000; *fiction:* Smith's Dream, 1971; Five for the Symbol (stories), 1981; All Visitors Ashore, 1984; The Death of the Body, 1986; Sister Hollywood, 1988; The End of the Century at the End of the World, 1991; The Singing Whakapapa, 1994; Villa Vittoria, 1996; Talking about O'Dwyer, 1999; *literary criticism:* The New Poetic, 1964; In the Glass Case: essays on New Zealand literature, 1981; Pound, Yeats, Eliot and the Modernist Movement, 1986; Answering to the Language, 1989; The Writer at Work, 2000; *edited:* New Zealand Short Stories, 2nd series, 1966; Measure for Measure: a casebook, 1971; Letters and Journals of Katherine Mansfield, 1977; Collected Stories of Maurice Duggan, 1981; Faber Book of Contemporary South Pacific Stories, 1993; Werner Forman's New Zealand (photographs), 1995. *Recreations:* music, walking. *Address:* 37 Tohunga Crescent, Auckland 1001, New Zealand.

STEAD, Rev. Canon (George) Christopher, LittD; FBA 1980; Fellow, King's College, Cambridge, 1938–49 and 1971–85 (Professorial Fellow, 1971–80); Emeritus Fellow, Keble College, Oxford, since 1981; *b* 9 April 1913; *s* of Francis Bernard Stead, CBE, and Rachel Elizabeth, *d* of Rev. Canon G. C. Bell; *m* 1958, Doris Elizabeth Odom; two *s* one *d*. *Educ:* Marlborough Coll.; King's Coll., Cambridge (scholar). 1st cl. Classical Tripos Pt I, 1933; Pitt Scholar, 1934; 1st cl. Moral Science Tripos Pt II, 1935; BA 1935, MA 1938, LittD Cantab 1978; New Coll., Oxford (BA 1935); Cuddesdon Coll., Oxford, 1938. Ordained, 1938; Curate, St John's, Newcastle upon Tyne, 1939; Lectr in Divinity, King's Coll., Cambridge, 1938–49; Asst Master, Eton Coll., 1940–44; Fellow and Chaplain, Keble Coll., Oxford, 1949–71 (MA Oxon 1949); Ely Professor of Divinity, Cambridge, and Canon Residentiary of Ely Cathedral, 1971–80, Canon Emeritus, 1981. *Publications:* Divine Substance, 1977; Substance and Illusion in the Christian Fathers, 1985; Philosophie und Theologie I, 1990; Philosophy in Christian Antiquity, 1994 (trans. Portuguese, 1999); Doctrine and Philosophy in Early Christianity: Arius, Athanasius, Augustine, 2000; contributor to: Faith and Logic, 1957; New Testament Apocrypha, 1965; A New Dictionary of Christian Theology, 1983; Dizionario di Patristica, 1983; Theologische Realenzyklopädie, vol. 13 1985, vol. 21 1991; Augustinus-Lexikon, 1986–93; Reallexikon für Antike und Christentum, 1992; Dictionnaire Critique de Théologie, 1998; Routledge Encyclopedia of Philosophy, 1998; about 30 major articles in Jl of Theol Studies, Vigiliae Christianae, and various Festschriften; *festschrift:* Christian Faith and Greek Philosophy in Late Antiquity, 1993. *Recreations:* walking, sailing, music. *Address:* 13 Station Road, Haddenham, Ely, Cambs CB6 3XD.

STEAD, Ian Mathieson, PhD; FSA; FBA 1991; Deputy Keeper, Department of Prehistoric and Romano-British Antiquities, British Museum, 1977–96 (Assistant Keeper, 1974–77); *b* 9 Jan. 1936; *er s* of Sidney William Stead and Edith Johann (*née* Mathieson); *m* 1962, Sheelagh Mary Johnson; one *s* one *d*. *Educ:* Nunthorpe Grammar Sch., York; Fitzwilliam House, Cambridge Univ. (MA; PhD 1965). FSA 1966. Asst Inspector of Ancient Monuments, 1962, Inspector, 1964–74, Min. of Works. Chairman: Herts Archaeol Council, 1970–75; Humberside Jt Archaeol Cttee, 1974–81; Sec., Prehistoric Soc., 1974–76. Hon. Life Mem., Yorks Philosophical Soc., 1982; Corresp. Mem., Deutsches Archäologisches Institut, 1976. *Publications:* La Tène Cultures of Eastern Yorkshire, 1965; Winterton Roman Villa, 1976; Arras Culture, 1979; (with J.-L. Flouest) Iron Age Cemeteries in Champagne, 1979; Rudston Roman Villa, 1980; The Gauls, 1981; Celtic Art in Britain, 1985, 2nd edn 1996; Battersea Shield, 1985; (with J. B. Bourke and D. Brothwell) Lindow Man, the Body in the Bog, 1986; (with V. Rigby) Baldock, 1986; (with V. Rigby) Verulamium, the King Harry Lane Site, 1989; Iron Age Cemeteries in East Yorkshire, 1991; (with Karen Hughes) Early Celtic Designs, 1997; The Salisbury Hoard, 1998 (British Archaeol Awards Book Award, 2000); (with V. Rigby) The Morel Collection, 1999; papers in learned jls. *Address:* Ratcliffe House, Ashwell, Herts SG7 5NP. *T:* (01462) 742396.

STEAD, Ralph Edmund, FCA, FCMA; retired; Chairman, Eastern Region, British Gas Corporation, 1977–81; *b* 7 Jan. 1917; *s* of Albert Stead and Mabel Stead; *m* 1946, Evelyn Annie Ness (*d* 1997); two *s* two *d*. *Educ:* Manchester Grammar Sch.; Ilford County High Sch. FCA 1949; FCMA 1952. Served War, RASC, 1940–46. Asst Divl Accountant, Cambridge Div., Eastern Gas Bd, 1949–50; N Eastern Gas Board: Asst Chief Accountant, 1950–53; Group Accountant, Bradford Gp, 1953–57; N Western Gas Board: Gp Accountant, Manchester Gp, 1957–61; Gen. Man., West Lancs Gp, 1961–65; Head of Management Services, 1966–71; Dir of Finance, 1971–73; Dep. Chm., Eastern Reg., British Gas Corp., 1973–77. Member: Financial Instns Gp, DoE, 1981–82; Management Cttee, Lazards Property Unit Trust, 1979–92; Rent Assessment Panel for Scotland, 1983–87. *Recreations:* golf, gardening, reading. *Address:* 12 Abbotsford Court, Colinton Road, Edinburgh EH10 5EH.

STEADMAN, Alison, OBE 2000; actress; *b* Liverpool, 26 Aug. 1946; *m* 1973, Mike Leigh, *qv*; two *s*. *Theatre includes:* Abigail's Party, Hampstead (Best Actress, Evening Standard Awards), 1977; Joking Apart, Globe, 1979; Uncle Vanya, Hampstead, 1979; Cinderella and her Naughty Sisters, Lyric, Hammersmith, 1980; A Handful of Dust, Lyric, Hammersmith, 1982; Tartuffe, Maydays, RSC, 1985; Kafka's Dick, Royal Court, 1986; Cat on a Hot Tin Roof, NT, 1988; The Rise and Fall of Little Voice, Aldwych (Olivier Best Actress Award), 1992; Marvin's Room, Hampstead, transf. Comedy, 1993; When We Are Married, Chichester, transf. Savoy, 1996; The Provok'd Wife, Old Vic, 1997; The Memory of Water, Vaudeville, 1999; Entertaining Mr Sloane, Arts, 2001; *television includes:* Nuts in May, 1976; Through the Night, 1976; Abigail's Party, 1977; Our Flesh and Blood, 1978; Pasmore, 1980; P'tang Yang Kipperbang, 1982; The Singing Detective, 1986; Virtuoso, 1989; A Small Mourning, 1989; News Hounds, Gone to the Dogs, 1990; Gone to Seed, 1991; Selling Hitler, 1992; Pride and Prejudice, 1995; Wimbledon Poisoner, 1995; Karaoke, 1996; No Bananas, 1996; The Missing Postman, 1997; Let Them Eat Cake, 1999; Fat Friends, 2000; Adrian Mole: The Capuccino Years, 2001; *films include:* Champions, 1983; A Private Function, 1984; Number One, 1985; Clockwise, 1986; The Adventures of Baron Münchhausen, 1989; Shirley Valentine, Wilt, 1989; Life is Sweet, Blame it on the Bellboy, 1991; Topsy-Turvy, 1999. Hon. MA Univ. of East London, 1996. *Address:* c/o Peters, Fraser & Dunlop, Drury House, 34–43 Russell Street, WC2B 5HA.

STEADMAN, Dr John Hubert; consultant in regulatory and environmental toxicology and environmental health, since 1996; *b* 10 Aug. 1938; *s* of late Dr Harry Hubert Steadman and Janet Gilchrist Steadman (*née* MacDonald); *m* 1972, Dr Anthea Howell; one *s* one *d*. *Educ:* Wimbledon Coll.; Guy's Hosp. (MB, BS); University Coll. London (MSc). University College Hospital, London: Beit Meml Fellowship, 1968–72; Sen. Registrar, Dept of Haematology, 1972–78, with secondments to Ahmadu Bello Univ. Hosp.,

Nigeria, 1973, and Royal Perth Hosp., WA, 1974; Cons. Haematologist, King George Hosp., Ilford, 1978–81; MO 1981, SMO 1982, PMO 1984, DHSS; SPMO, Head of Div. of Toxicology and Envmtl Health, subseq. Health Aspects of Envmt and Food, DoH, 1988–93; Hd of Safety and Envmtl Assce, Unilever, 1993–96. Expert Advr on food safety, WHO, 1988–93. *Publications:* articles in learned jls on regulatory toxicology, haematology and biochemistry. *Recreations:* cooking, languages, political philosophy. *Address:* c/o Messrs C. Hoare & Co., 37 Fleet Street, EC4P 4DQ.

See also J. M. M. Curtis-Raleigh.

STEADMAN, Ralph Idris; freelance cartoonist, illustrator and writer; *b* 15 May 1936; *s* of Lionel Raphael Steadman (English), and Gwendoline (Welsh); *m* 1st, 1959, Sheila Thwaite (marr. diss. 1971); two *s* two *d*; 2nd, 1972, Anna Deverson; one *d*. *Educ:* Abergele Grammar Sch.; London Coll. of Printing and Graphic Arts. Apprentice, de Havilland Aircraft Co., 1952; Cartoonist, Kemsley (Thomson) Newspapers, 1956–59; freelance for Punch, Private Eye, Telegraph, during 1960s; Political Cartoonist, New Statesman, 1978–80; retired to work on book about Leonardo da Vinci; as a positive political statement, refuses to draw another politician; 15 Save the Children originals auctioned in aid of Ethiopia Fund, 1990. Retrospective exhibitions: Nat. Theatre, 1977; Royal Festival Hall, 1984; exhibitions: Wilhelm Busch Mus., Hannover, 1988; October Gall. (sculptures and silk screen prints), 1990, Gulf war collages, 1991; Peacock Gall., Aberdeen, 1993; Aberdeen City Art Gall., 1994; The Lord is an Animal, One on One Gall., Denver, USA, 1997; Contemporary Satirists, RA, 1997; Les Sixties, Les Invalides, Paris, transf. Brighton, 1997; centenary Lewis Carroll exhibn, Warrington Mus., 1998; Making a Mark, William Havu Gall., Denver, 2000. Designed set of stamps of Halley's Comet, 1986; opera libretto and concept, Plague and the Moonflower, Exeter Cathedral and Festival, 1989 (artist-in-residence), St Paul's Cathedral, 1989, Canterbury Cathedral and Festival, 1990, performed as Hearts Betrayed, St Martin-in-the-Fields, 1993, televised 1995, recorded 1999; libretto and concept, Love Underground, Norwich Fest., 1997; artist-in-residence, Cheltenham Fest., 1994; designer, Gulliver's Travels, Theatr Clwyd, 1995; artist-in-residence, Leviathan series of films, BBC2, 1999; designer of set and costumes, The Crucible, Royal Ballet, 2000. Writer, dir and performer, TV film, Hanging Garden Centres of Kent, 1992. Hon. Fellow, Kent Inst. of Art and Design, 1993. Hon. DLitt Kent, 1995. D & AD Gold Award (for outstanding contribution to illustration), 1977, and Silver Award (for outstanding editorial illustration), 1977; Black Humour Award, France, 1986; W. H. Smith Illustration Award for best illustrated book for last five years, 1987; BBC Design Award for postage stamps, 1987; Empire Award (for involvement with film Withnail and I), Empire Magazine, 1996. *Publications:* Jelly Book, 1968; Still Life with Raspberry: collected drawings, 1969; The Little Red Computer, 1970; Dogs Bodies, 1971; Bumper to Bumper Book, 1973; Two Donkeys and the Bridge, 1974; Flowers for the Moon, 1974; America: drawings, 1975; America: collected drawings, 1977 (rev. edn, Scar Strangled Banger, 1987); Between the Eyes, 1984; Paranoids, 1986; The Grapes of Ralph, 1992; Teddy! Where are you?, 1994; *written and illustrated:* Sigmund Freud, 1979 (as The Penguin Sigmund Freud, 1982); A Leg in the Wind and other Canine Curses, 1982; I, Leonardo, 1983; That's My Dad, 1986 (Critici in Erba Prize, 1987); The Big I Am, 1988; No Room to Swing a Cat, 1989; Near the Bone, 1990; Tales of the Weirrd, 1990; Still Life with Bottle, Whisky According to Ralph Steadman, 1994; Jones of Colorado, 1995; Gonzo: the art, 1998; little.com, 2000; designed and printed, Steam Press Broadsheets; *illustrated:* Frank Dickens, Fly Away Peter, 1961; Mischa Damjan: The Big Squirrel and the Little Rhinoceros, 1962; The False Flamingoes, 1963; The Little Prince and the Tiger Cat, 1964; Two Cats in America, 1968; Richard Ingrams, The Tale of Driver Grope, 1964; Love and Marriage, 1964; Daisy Ashford, Where Love Lies Deepest, 1964; Fiona Saint, The Yellow Flowers, 1965; Alice in Wonderland, 1967; Midnight, 1967; Tariq Ali, The Thoughts of Chairman Harold, 1968; Dr Hunter S. Thompson: Fear and Loathing in Las Vegas, 1972, 25th anniv. edn, 1997; The Curse of Lono, 1984; Kurt Baumann, The Watchdog and the Lazy Dog, 1974; Contemporary Poets set to Music series, 1972; Through the Looking Glass, 1972; Night Edge: poems, 1973; The Poor Mouth, 1973; John Letts Limericks, 1974; The Hunting of the Snark, 1975; Dmitri Sidjanski, Cherrywood Cannon, 1978; Bernard Stone: Emergency Mouse, 1978; Inspector Mouse, 1980; Quasimodo Mouse, 1984; Ted Hughes, The Threshold (limited edn), 1979; Adrian Mitchell, For Beauty Douglas, 1982; Flann O'Brien, More of Myles, 1982; Wolf Mankowitz, The Devil in Texas, 1984; Treasure Island, 1985; The Complete Alice and The Hunting of the Snark, 1986; Friendship (short stories), 1990 (in aid of John McCarthy); Animal Farm, 50th anniv. edn, 1995; Adrian Mitchell, Heart on the Left, Poems 1953–1984, 1997; Roald Dahl, The Mildenhall Treasure, 1999; Doodaa: the balletic art of Gavin Twinge, 2002. *Recreations:* gardening (planted vineyard), collecting, writing, sheep husbandry, fishing, guitar, trumpet. *Club:* Chelsea Arts.

STEAR, Air Chief Marshal Sir Michael (James Douglas), KCB 1990; CBE 1982; QCVSA 1969; DL; FRAeS; Deputy Commander-in-Chief, Allied Forces Central Europe, 1992–96; *b* 11 Oct. 1938; *s* of late Melbourne Douglas Stear and Barbara Jane Stear (*née* Fletcher); *m* 1966, Elizabeth Jane, *d* of late Donald Edward Macrae, FRCS and of Janet Wallace Macpherson Simpson; two *s* one *d*. *Educ:* Monkton Combe Sch.; Emmanuel Coll., Cambridge (MA; CU Air Sqn (RAFVR), 1959–62). Nat. Service, 1957–59. Joined RAF, 1962; served on 1 Sqn, 1964–67, on 208 Sqn, Persian Gulf, 1967–69; exchange tour with USAF, 1969–71; Air Sec.'s Br., MoD, 1972–74; OC 17 Sqn, Germany, 1974–76; OC 56 Sqn, RAF Wattisham, 1976; PSO to CAS, MoD, 1976–79; OC RAF Gutersloh, 1980–82; Asst C of S (Ops), HQ 2 ATAF, 1982; Air Cdre Plans, HQ Strike Command, 1982–85; AOC No 11 Gp, 1985–87; ACDS (Nato/UK), 1987–89; AOC No 18 Gp, and Comdr Maritime Air Eastern Atlantic and Channel, 1989–92. Mem., Commonwealth War Graves Commn, 1998–. Member: RUSI, 1989–99; Council, Malcolm Clubs, 1988–; RFU Cttee, 1987–98 (Mgt Bd Jt Vice-Chm. (admin), 1997–98); Air League, 1999–; Pres., RAF RU, 1992–97 (Chm., 1983–86). Nat. Pres., RAFA, 1998– (Vice-Pres., 1997–98; Service Vice-Pres., Europe Area, 1992–96). FRAeS 1997. DL Devon, 2000. *Recreations:* Rugby football, keeping sheep, gardening, fishing, shooting. *Club:* Royal Air Force (Vice-Pres., 1990–98).

STEBBING, Nowell, PhD; Chairman, Pharmagene plc (formerly Pharmagene Laboratories Ltd), since 1996; *b* 5 Sept. 1941; *s* of Lionel Charles Stebbing and Margarita (*née* Behrenz); *m* 1st, 1963, Nancy Lynah (marr. diss.); two *d* (one *s* decd); 2nd, 1973, Birgit Griffiths (*née* Evjen); one *s*. *Educ:* Michael Hall Sch., Sussex; Univ. of Edinburgh (BSc Hons 1964; PhD 1968). Demonstrator, Univ. of Edinburgh, 1967–69; Director of Biology: G. D. Searle & Co., 1969–79; Genentech Inc., San Francisco, 1979–82; Vice-Pres., Scientific Affairs, Amgen Inc., Thousand Oaks, Calif, 1982–86; Gen. Manager, Res., ICI Pharmaceuticals, UK, 1986–93; Chief Exec. and Dep. Chm., Chiroscience Gp PLC, 1993–95. Chm., Axis Genetics, 1995–99. *Publications:* numerous papers and articles in scientific and med. jls and books. *Recreations:* theatre, old cars, gardens.

STEDMAN JONES, Prof. Gareth, DPhil; Professor of Political Science, University of Cambridge, since 1997; Co Director, Centre for History and Economics, Cambridge, since 1991; Fellow of King's College, Cambridge, since 1974; *b* 17 Dec. 1942; *s* of Lewis and Joan Olive Stedman Jones; one *s* by Prof. Sally Alexander; one *s* by Prof. Miri Rubin. *Educ:* St Paul's Sch.; Lincoln Coll., Oxford (BA 1964); Nuffield Coll., Oxford (DPhil 1970). Res. Fellow, Nuffield Coll., Oxford, 1967–70; Sen. Associate Mem., St Antony's Coll., Oxford, 1971–72; Humboldt Stiftung Fellow, Dept of Philosophy, Goethe Univ., Frankfurt, 1973–74; University of Cambridge: Lectr in History, 1979–86; Reader in History of Social Thought, 1986–97. Mem., Editl Bd, New Left Review, 1974–81; Jt Founder and Jt Ed., History Workshop Jl, 1976–. *Publications:* Outcast London, 1971, 2nd edn 1976; Languages of Class, 1983; Klassen, Politik, Sprache, 1988; (ed) Charles Fourier, The Theory of the Four Movements, trans. I. Patterson, 1994. *Recreations:* country walks, collecting old books, cricket. *Address:* King's College, Cambridge CB2 1ST. *T:* (01223) 331197.

STEEDMAN, Martha, (Mrs R. R. Steedman); *see* Hamilton, M.

STEEDMAN, Robert Russell, OBE 1997; RSA 1979 (ARSA 1973); RIBA; FRIAS; MLI; Partner, Morris and Steedman, Architects and Landscape Architects, Edinburgh, since 1959; *b* 3 Jan. 1929; *s* of late Robert Smith Steedman and Helen Hope Brazier; *m* 1st, 1956, Susan Elizabeth (marr. diss. 1974), *d* of Sir Robert Scott, GCMG, CBE; one *s* two *d*; 2nd, 1977, Martha Hamilton, *qv*. *Educ:* Loretto Sch.; School of Architecture, Edinburgh College of Art (DA); Univ. of Pennsylvania (MLA). RIBA 1955; ALI 1979. Lieut, RWAFF, 1947–48. Worked in office, Alfred Roth, Zürich, 1953. Architectural works include: Principal's House, Univ. of Stirling; Head Offices for Christian Salvesen, Edinburgh; Administration Building for Shell UK Exploration and Production; Moss Morran Fife; Restoration of Old Waterworks, Perth, to form Tourist Information Centre and Offices; Nat. Lighthouse Mus., Fraserburgh. Ten Civic Trust Awards, 1963–88; British Steel Award, 1971; Saltire Award, 1971, 1999; RIBA Award for Scotland, 1974 and 1989; European Architectural Heritage Medal, 1975; Assoc. for Preservation of Rural Scotland Award, 1977 and 1989. Chm., Central Scotland Woodlands Project, 1984–87; Member: Countryside Commn for Scotland, 1980–88; Adv. Panel on Management of Popular Mountain Areas in Scotland, 1989; Royal Fine Art Commn for Scotland, 1984–96; Council, Nat. Trust for Scotland, 1999–; Sec., Royal Scottish Acad., 1983–90 (Mem. Council 1981–, Dep. Pres. 1982–83, 2000–01); Mem. Bd, Friends of Royal Scottish Acad., 1984–92; Governor, Edinburgh College of Art, 1974–88; Mem., Edinburgh Festival Soc., 1978–; past Mem. Council, RIAS and Soc. of Scottish Artists. Member Panel: Saltire Patrick Geddes Award, 1995–; Assoc. for Protection of Rural Scotland Annual Awards, 1995–99. Hon. Senior, St Leonards Sch., 1987–. FRSA 1995. *Recreations:* ski-ing, sketching. *Address:* 11B Belford Mews, Edinburgh EH4 3BT; (office) 38 Young Street North Lane, Edinburgh EH2 4JD. *T:* (0131) 226 6563. *Clubs:* New (Edinburgh); Royal & Ancient Golf (St Andrews).

STEEDS, Prof. John Wickham, FRS 1988; FInstP; Research Professor in Physics, since 1985, Head of Physics Department, since 2001, and Director, Interface Analysis Centre, since 1990, Bristol University; *b* 9 Feb. 1940; *s* of John Henry William Steeds and Ethel Amelia Tyler; *m* 1969, Diana Mary Kettlewell; two *d*. *Educ:* University College London (BSc 1961); PhD Cantab 1965. FInstP 1991. Research Fellow, Selwyn Coll., Cambridge, 1964–67; IBM Res. Fellow, 1966–67; Fellow, Selwyn Coll., Cambridge, 1967; Lectr in Physics, 1967–77, Reader, 1977–85, Hd of Microstructural Gp, 1985–2001, Bristol Univ. Visiting Professor: Univ. of Santiago, Chile, 1971; Univ. of California, Berkeley, 1981. Chairman: Science Res. Foundn, Emersons Green, 1989–99; Commn on Electron Diffraction, Internat. Union of Crystallography, 1993–99; Emersons Innovations Ltd, 1999; Mem., Council, European Pole Univ., Lille, 1993–. Holweck Medal and Prize, French Physical Soc., 1996. *Publications:* Introduction to Anistropic Elasticity Theory of Dislocations, 1973; (with J. F. Mansfield) Electron Diffraction of Phases in Alloys, 1984; (ed jtly) Thin Film Diamond, 1994; papers on electron diffraction, materials science and solid state physics. *Recreations:* tennis, cycling, overseas travel. *Address:* 21 Canynge Square, Clifton, Bristol BS8 3LA. *T:* (0117) 973 2183.

STEEL, family name of **Baron Steel of Aikwood**.

STEEL OF AIKWOOD, Baron *cr* 1997 (Life Peer), of Ettrick Forest in the Scottish Borders; **David Martin Scott Steel,** KBE 1990; PC 1977; DL; journalist and broadcaster; Member (Lib Dem) Lothians, Scottish Parliament, since 1999; Presiding Officer, since 1999; *b* Scotland, 31 March 1938; *s* of Very Rev. Dr David Steel, *qv*; *m* 1962, Judith Mary, *d* of W. D. MacGregor, CBE, Dunblane; two *s* one *d*. *Educ:* Prince of Wales School, Nairobi, Kenya; George Watson's Coll.; Edinburgh Univ. (MA 1960; LLB 1962). President: Edinburgh University Liberals, 1959; Students' Representative Council, 1960. Asst Secretary, Scottish Liberal Party, 1962–64. MP (L 1965–88, Lib Dem 1988–97) Roxburgh, Selkirk and Peebles, 1965–83, Tweeddale, Ettrick and Lauderdale, 1983–97; youngest member of 1964–66 Parliament, of Privy Council, 1977. Liberal Chief Whip, 1970–75; Mem. Parly Delegn to UN Gen. Assembly, 1967; Sponsor, Private Member's Bill to reform law on abortion, 1966–67. Leader of Liberal Party, 1976–88; Co-Founder, Social and Liberal Democrats, 1988. Pres., Liberal International, 1994–96. Pres., Anti-Apartheid Movement of GB, 1966–69; Chairman: Shelter, Scotland, 1969–73; Countryside Movement, 1995–. Member: British Council of Churches, 1971–75; Council of Management, Centre for Studies in Social Policy, 1971–76; Adv. Council, European Discussion Centre, 1971–76; Chubb Fellow, Yale Univ., 1987. BBC television interviewer in Scotland, 1964–65; Presenter of STV weekly religious programme, 1966–67, and for Granada, 1969, and BBC, 1971–76. Rector, Edinburgh Univ., 1982–85. DL Roxburgh, Ettrick and Lauderdale, 1990. Awarded Freedom of Tweeddale, 1988, of Ettrick and Lauderdale, 1990. DUniv: Stirling, 1991; Heriot-Watt, 1996; Open, 2001; Hon. DLitt Buckingham; Hon. LLD: Edinburgh, 1997; Strathclyde, 2000; Aberdeen, 2001. Commander's Cross, Order of Merit (Germany), 1992. *Publications:* Boost for the Borders, 1964; Out of Control, 1968; No Entry, 1969; The Liberal Way Forward, 1975; A New Political Agenda, 1976; Militant for the Reasonable Man, 1977; New Majority for a New Parliament, 1978; High Ground of Politics, 1979; A House Divided, 1980; (with Judy Steel) Border Country, 1985; (presenter) Partners in One Nation: a new vision of Britain 2000, 1985; (with Judy Steel) Mary Stuart's Scotland, 1987; Against Goliath: David Steel's story, 1989; contrib. to The Times, The Guardian, The Scotsman, other newspapers and political weeklies. *Recreations:* angling, classic car rallying (bronze medallion in London - Capetown, 1998). *Address:* House of Lords, SW1A 0PW; Scottish Parliament, George IV Bridge, Edinburgh EH99 1SP; Aikwood Tower, by Selkirk. *Club:* National Liberal.

See also C. M. Steel.

STEEL, Dame (Anne) Heather, (Dame Heather Beattie), DBE 1993; a Judge of the High Court of Justice, Queen's Bench Division, 1993–2001; *b* 3 July 1940; *d* of late His Honour Edward Steel and Mary Evelyn Griffith Steel; *m* 1967, David Kerr-Muir Beattie; one *s* one *d*. *Educ:* Howell's School, Denbigh; Liverpool University (LLB). Called to the Bar, Gray's Inn, 1963, Bencher, 1993; practice on N Circuit; Prosecuting Counsel to DHSS on N Circuit, 1984–86; a Recorder, 1984–86; a Circuit Judge, 1986–93. Mem., Criminal Cttee, Judicial Studies Bd, 1992–95. President: Merseyside Medico Legal Soc., 1992–94; Law Faculty Assoc., Liverpool Univ., 1994–. Mem. Council, Rossall Sch., 1990–. Mem., Guild of Freeman, City of London, 1996–. Freeman, City of London, 1993; Liveryman, Pattenmakers' Co., 1993. *Recreations:* theatre, gardening, art, antiques.

STEEL, Prof. Christopher Michael, PhD, DSc; Professor in Medical Science, University of St Andrews, since 1994; *b* 25 Jan. 1940; *s* of Very Rev. David Steel, *qv*; *m* 1962, Dr Judith Margaret Spratt, MBE; two *s* one *d*. *Educ:* Prince of Wales Sch., Nairobi; George Watson's Coll., Edinburgh; Univ. of Edinburgh (Bsc Hons, MB, ChB Hons, PhD, DSc). FRCPE; FRCSE (*ad hominem*) 1994; FRCPath; FRSE. Jun. hosp. posts in Edinburgh teaching hosps, 1965–68; Graduate Res. Fellow, Univ. of Edinburgh Faculty of Medicine, 1968–71; Mem. of Clin. Sci. Staff, MRC Human Genetics Unit, Edinburgh, 1971–93 (Asst Dir, 1979–93); MRC Travelling Res. Fellow, Univ. of Nairobi Med. Sch., 1972–73. Hon. Cons., Lothian Health Bd, 1976–. Mem., Adv. Cttee, UK Gene Therapy, 1995–2000. Founder FMedSci 1998. *Publications:* (with D. K. Apps and B. B. Cohen) Biochemistry: a concise text for medical students, 1992; papers on molecular biology of cancer in learned jls. *Recreations:* golf, ski-ing. *Address:* Breakers, 3a The Scores, St Andrews, Fife KY16 9AR. *T:* (01334) 472877. *Club:* Royal Society of Medicine.
See also Baron Steel of Aikwood.

STEEL, Danielle; *see* Schüelein-Steel, D. F.

STEEL, Very Rev. David; Minister of St Michael's, Linlithgow, 1959–76, now Minister Emeritus; Moderator of the General Assembly of the Church of Scotland, 1974–75; *b* 5 Oct. 1910; *s* of John S. G. Steel and Jane Scott, Hamilton; *m* 1937, Sheila Martin, Aberdeen; three *s* two *d*. *Educ:* Peterhead Academy; Robert Gordon's Coll., Aberdeen; Aberdeen Univ. MA 1932, BD 1935. Minister of Church of Scotland: Denbeath, Fife, 1936–41; Bridgend, Dumbarton, 1941–46; Home Organisation Foreign Mission Secretary, 1946–49; Minister of Parish of East Africa and of St Andrew's, Nairobi, 1949–57; Associate Minister, St Cuthbert's, Edinburgh, 1957–59. Vis. Prof., Columbia Theol Seminary, Atlanta, 1979–85. Chm. of Governors, Callendar Park Coll. of Educn, 1974–79; Vice-Pres., Boys' Brigade, 1974–79. Hon. Vice-President: Nat. Bible Soc. of Scotland; W Lothian History and Amenity Soc.; Boys' Brigade. Hon. DD Aberdeen 1964; Hon. LLD Dundee, 1977. *Publications:* History of St Michael's, Linlithgow, 1961; Preaching Through the Year, 1980, 2nd edn 1998; contrib. theological and church jls. *Recreation:* trout fishing. *Address:* 39 Newbattle Terrace, Edinburgh EH10 4SF. *T:* (0131) 447 2180. *Club:* Aberdeen University Senior Common Room.
See also Baron Steel of Aikwood, C. M. Steel.

STEEL, Sir David (Edward Charles), Kt 1977; DSO 1940; MC 1945; TD; Chairman, The Wellcome Trust, 1982–89; *b* 29 Nov. 1916; *s* of late Gerald Arthur Steel, CB; *m* 1956, Ann Wynne (*d* 1997), *d* of Maj.-Gen. C. B. Price, CB, DSO, DCM, VD, CD; one *s* two *d*. *Educ:* Rugby School; University Coll., Oxford (BA; Hon. Fellow, 1981). Inns of Court Regt, 1938; Commissioned 9 QR Lancers, 1940; served 1940–45 France, Middle East, North Africa, Italy (DSO, MC, despatches thrice). Admitted a Solicitor, June 1948; Linklaters and Paines, 1948–50; Legal Dept of The British Petroleum Co. Ltd, 1950–56; Pres. BP (N Amer.) Ltd, 1959–61; Man. Dir, Kuwait Oil Co. Ltd, 1962–65; Man. Dir, 1965–75, a Dep. Chm., 1972–75 and Chm., 1975–81, BP. A Dir, Bank of England, 1978–85; Dir, Kleinwort Benson Gp (formerly Kleinwort, Benson, Lonsdale), 1985–92. Pres., London Chamber of Commerce and Industry, 1982–85. Trustee, The Economist, 1979–95; Chairman: Lenta Educn Trust, 1986–90; London Educn Business Partnership, 1986–89; Governors, Rugby Sch., 1984–88. Hon. Freeman, Tallow Chandlers' Co., 1980. Hon. DCL City Univ., 1983. Order of Taj III, Iran, 1974; Comdr, Order of Leopold, Belgium, 1980. *Recreations:* gardening, golf. *Clubs:* Cavalry and Guards, MCC, Hurlingham; Royal and Ancient (St Andrews).

STEEL, Hon. Sir David (William), Kt 1998; **Hon. Mr Justice Steel;** a Judge of the High Court of Justice, Queen's Bench Division, since 1998; *b* 7 May 1943; *s* of Sir Lincoln Steel and late Barbara (*née* Goldschmidt); *m* 1970, Charlotte Elizabeth Ramsay; two *s*. *Educ:* Eton Coll.; Keble Coll., Oxford (MA Hons Jurisprudence). Called to the Bar, Inner Temple, 1966, Bencher, 1991; with Coudert Bros (Attorneys), New York, 1967–68; commenced practice in England, 1969; Junior Counsel to the Treasury (Common Law) 1978–81; Junior Counsel to the Treasury (Admiralty), 1978–81; QC 1981; a Recorder, 1991–98; a Dep. High Court Judge, 1993–98; Judge, Admiralty Ct, 1998–; Judge, Commercial Ct, 1998–. Wreck Commissioner for England and Wales, 1982–98; Mem., panel of Lloyd's Salvage Arbitrators, 1982–98. Chm., Commercial Bar Assoc., 1990–91; Mem., Lord Chancellor's Adv. Cttee on Legal Educn and Conduct, 1994–98. Chm., OUBC Trust Fund Cttee, 1990–93. *Publications:* Editor: Temperley: Merchant Shipping Acts, 1976–98; Forms and Precedents: British Shipping Laws, 1977–98; Kennedy: Salvage, 1981–98. *Recreations:* golf, shooting, fishing. *Address:* Royal Courts of Justice, Strand, WC2A 2LL. *Club:* Turf.

STEEL, Donald MacLennan Arklay; golf correspondent and golf course architect; *b* 23 Aug. 1937; *s* of William Arklay Steel and Catherine Fanny (*née* Jacobs), internat. golfer; *m* 1988, Rachel Ellen. *Educ:* Fettes Coll; Christ's Coll., Cambridge (MA). Golf correspondent: Sunday Telegraph, 1961–90; Country Life, 1983–93; golf course architect, 1965–: with C. K. Cotton, Pennink, Lawrie and Partners; with C. K. Cotton, Pennink, Steel & Co.; with Donald Steel & Co. President: British Inst. of Golf Course Architects, 1989–91 (Hon. Sec., 1971–83; Chm., 1983–86); Assoc. of Golf Writers, 1993–98 (Treas., 1977–90). *Publications:* (ed jtly) Shell World Encyclopaedia of Golf, 1975; (ed) Guinness Book of Golf Facts and Feats, 1980; Bedside Books of Golf, 1965, 1971; The Classic Links, 1992; (ed) 14 edns, The Golf Course Guide of the British Isles (Daily Telegraph). *Recreations:* cricket, wine. *Address:* 1 March Square, Chichester, West Sussex PO19 4AN. *T:* (01243) 528506. *Clubs:* MCC; Hawks (Cambridge); Royal and Ancient Golf.

STEEL, Elizabeth Mary, (Mrs Stuart Christie); Her Honour Judge Steel; DL; a Circuit Judge, since 1991; *b* 28 Nov. 1936; *d* of His Honour Edward Steel and Mary Evelyn Griffith Steel (*née* Roberts); *m* 1972, Stuart Christie; one *s* one *d*. *Educ:* Howells Sch., Denbigh; Liverpool Univ. (LLB). Admitted solicitor, 1960; Partner, John A. Behn Twyford & Co., 1968–80; Partner, Cuff Roberts, 1980–91; a Recorder, 1989. Member: Cripps Cttee, 1967–69; Race Relations Bd, 1970–78; Council, Radio Merseyside, 1974–78; Gen. Adv. Council, BBC, 1979–82 (Chm., NW Adv. Council). Member: Law Soc., 1960; Liverpool Law Soc., 1960 (Pres., 1989–90); Chm., Steering Cttee, Hillsborough Solicitors' Gp, 1989–91. Member: Royal Liverpool Univ. Hosp. NHS Trust, 1991; Liverpool Playhouse Bd, 1968–95 (Vice-Pres., 1995–99). Nat. Vice-Chm., YCs, 1965–67. DL Merseyside, 1991. *Recreations:* theatre (amateur and professional), music, needlework, cooking. *Address:* Liverpool Crown Court, Queen Elizabeth II Law Courts, Denby Square, Liverpool L2 1XA. *T:* (0151) 473 7373. *Clubs:* University Women's; Athenæum (Vice Pres., 2001–July 2002) (Liverpool).

STEEL, Henry, CMG 1976; OBE 1965; Principal Legal Adviser: Government of British Antarctic Territory, since 1989; Government of British Indian Ocean Territory, since 1991; special consultant to Foreign and Commonwealth Office on human rights reporting, since 1992; consultant on international and commonwealth law; *b* 13 Jan. 1926; *yr s* of late Raphael Steel; *m* 1960, Jennifer Isobel Margaret, *d* of late Brig. M. M. Simpson, MBE; two *s* two *d*. *Educ:* Christ's Coll., Finchley; New Coll., Oxford. BA Oxon 1950. Military Service, RASC and Intell. Corps, 1944–47. Called to Bar, Lincoln's Inn, 1951; Legal Asst, Colonial Office, 1955; Senior Legal Asst, CO, 1960; Asst Legal Adviser, CRO, 1965; Legal Counsellor, FCO, 1967–73; Legal Adviser, UK Mission to UN, NY, 1973–76; Legal Counsellor, FCO, 1976–79; Asst Under-Sec. of State (on loan to Law Officers' Dept), 1979; Legal Adviser to Governor of Southern Rhodesia, 1979–80; Asst Legal Secretary (Under-Secretary), Law Officers' Dept, 1980–83, Legal Sec. (Dep. Sec.), 1983–86; Dir, Commonwealth Legal Adv. Service, British Inst. of Internat. and Comparative Law, 1986–87; Leader, UK Delegn to UN Human Rights Commn, 1987–92 and 1994–97. *Address:* College Place, Chapel Lane, Bledington, Oxon OX7 6UZ.

STEEL, John Brychan; QC 1993; a Recorder, since 2000; *b* 4 June 1954; *s* of John Exton Steel and late Valentine Brychan-Rees; *m* 1981, Susan Rebecca Fraser; two *s* one *d*. *Educ:* Harrow Sch.; Durham Univ. (BSc Hons Chem.). Pres., Durham Univ. Athletic Union, 1975–76. Lieut, Inns of Court and City Yeomanry, 1977–81; called to the Bar, Gray's Inn, 1978; Attorney-General's Suppl. Panel (Common Law), 1989–93; an Asst Recorder, 1998–2000. Dir, Busoga Trust, 1983. Chm., K Racing, 1998–2000. *Recreations:* ski-ing, flying, walking. *Address:* 4–5 Gray's Inn Square, WC1R 5AY. *T:* (020) 7404 5252; Great Rollright Manor, Chipping Norton, Oxon OX7 5RH. *T:* (01608) 730131. *Clubs:* Boodle's; Kandahar (Chm., 1992–96), Ski of GB (Dep. Chm., 1989–91).

STEEL, Patricia Ann, OBE 1990; consultant public affairs adviser, since 1992; *b* 30 Oct. 1941; *d* of Thomas Norman Steel and Winifred Steel. *Educ:* Hunmanby Hall, near Filey, Yorks; Exeter Univ. (BA). Parly Liaison, Chamber of Shipping of UK and British Shipping Fedn, 1968–71; Sec., Highway and Traffic Technicians Assoc., 1972–73; Sec., Instn of Highways and Transportation, 1973–90. Director: LRT, 1984–91; Docklands Light Railway, 1984–91 (Chm., 1988–89); Victoria Coach Station Ltd, 1988–91. Non-executive Director: TRL, 1992–96; Richmond, Twickenham and Roehampton Healthcare NHS Trust, 1992–99. Mem., Occupational Pensions Bd, 1979–84; Lay Mem., Transport Tribunal, 1999–. *Recreations:* music, travel, politics. *Address:* 7 The Strathmore, 27 Petersham Road, Richmond, Surrey TW9 3DQ.

STEEL, Robert, CBE 1979; Secretary-General, Royal Institution of Chartered Surveyors, 1968–85 (Fellow, 1961; Hon. Mem., 1985); *b* 7 April 1920; *e s* of late John Thomas Steel and Jane (*née* Gordon), Wooler, Northumberland; *m* 1943, Averal Frances, *d* of Arthur Pettitt; one *s* one *d*. *Educ:* Duke's Sch., Alnwick, Northumb.; Univ. of London (BSc 1945); Gray's Inn (Barrister, 1956). Surveyor, 1937–46; Asst Sec., Under Sec., RICS, 1946–61; Dir of Town Development, Basingstoke, 1962–67. Hon. Sec.-Gen., Internat. Fedn of Surveyors, 1967–69, Vice-Pres., 1970–72, Hon. Mem., 1983; Hon. Sec., Commonwealth Assoc. of Surveying and Land Economy, 1969–90; Sec., Aubrey Barker Trust, 1970–96; Member: South East Economic Planning Council, 1974–76; Council, British Consultants Bureau, 1977–85. Chm., Geometers Liaison Cttee, EEC, 1972–86. Hon. Editor, Commonwealth Surveying and Land Economy, 1975–90. Founder Mem., 1977, Mem. Ct of Assts, 1977–94, Master, 1988–89, Worshipful Co. of Chartered Surveyors. Organised national networks of beacons for Queen's Silver Jubilee celebrations, 1977, and for the Wedding of Prince Charles and Lady Diana Spencer, 1981. Raised: £71,210 for RICS Benev. Fund by sponsored walk of 1000 miles, John O'Groats to Land's End, 1979 (world record for largest sum raised by a single walker); £66,333 for RICS Benev. Fund and The Prince's Trust by walk of 1100 miles, Cape Wrath to Dover and London, 1985; £113,739 for Lord Mayor of London's Charity Appeal for Children, 1988, by walk of 1,200 miles from Strathy Point, Sutherland, to Portland Bill, Dorset, and London; £133,500 for National Trust Enterprise Neptune, 1990, by walk of 2,000 miles around the perimeter of England; £116,820 for Nat. Trust Centenary 1995 by walk of 4,444 miles around the perimeter of mainland Britain; £80,015 for RICS Benev. Fund and Marie Curie Cancer Care, by walk of 2,000 kms, Iona to Canterbury, 2000. Hon. Member: Bulgarian Mountain Rescue Service, 1964; Union Belge des Geomètres Experts, 1976; Hon. Fellow, Inst. of Surveyors, Malaysia, 1983. Hon. LLD Aberdeen, 1985. Distinguished Service Award, Surveyors Inst. of Sri Lanka, 1986; Help the Aged Tunstall Golden Award for Outstanding Achievement, 1995. Silver Jubilee Medal, 1977. *Publications:* on Property Law; contrib. professional jls and internat. conferences. *Recreations:* mountain walking, travel, music, family genealogy. *Address:* 2 Oaklands Close, Winchester SO22 5PP.

STEEL, Rupert Oliver; *b* 30 April 1922; *s* of Joseph Steel and Beatrice Elizabeth Courage; *m* 1st, Marigold Katharine, *d* of Percy Lowe; two *s*; 2nd, Lucinda Evelyn Tennant, *d* of Arthur James; one *s* one *d*. *Educ:* Eton. Served War of 1939–45 (despatches), Pilot, RNVR, Fleet Air Arm, 1941–46. Courage & Co. Ltd, 1946–78; Imperial Group Ltd, 1975–78; Chm., Everards Brewery Ltd, 1978–84; Director: Lloyds Bank UK Management, 1970–85; Lloyds Bank Ltd, 1977–79; Umeco plc, 1979–95; South Uist Estates Ltd, 1980–94. High Sheriff, Berks, 1985–86. *Recreation:* country. *Address:* Winterbourne Holt, Newbury, Berks RG20 8AP. *T:* (01635) 248220. *Club:* Brooks's.

STEELE, Prof. Alan John; Professor of French, University of Edinburgh, 1972–80, retired; *b* Bellshill, Lanark, 11 April 1916; *s* of John Steele, MA, BD, and Anne (*née* Lawson); *m* 1947, Claire Alice Louise Belet; one *d* (one *s* decd). *Educ:* Royal Grammar School, Newcastle upon Tyne; Blyth Secondary School, Northumberland; Universities of Edinburgh, Grenoble and Paris. MA 1st Cl. Hons in French Language and Literature, Vans Dunlop Schol., Univ. of Edinburgh, 1938. Served War of 1939–45, at sea with 4th Maritime AA Regt, RA, 1941–42; commissioned, 1942, with 64th LAA Regt RA in Algeria, Italy and Greece. Lecturer in French, University of Edinburgh, 1946, Prof. of French Literature, 1961–72. Chairman: Scottish Central Cttee for Modern Languages, 1972–81; Assoc. of Univ. Profs of French, 1974–75; Consultative Cttee, Institut Français d'Ecosse, 1981–88; Vice-Pres., Franco-Scottish Soc., 1961–92. Mem., Church of Scotland Panel on Doctrine, 1978–86. Editor, Modern Language Review (French Section), 1971–79. Chevalier, Légion d'Honneur, 1973; Commandeur, Palmes Académiques, 1988. *Publications:* (with R. A. Leigh) Contemporary French Translation Passages, 1956; Three Centuries of French Verse, 1956, new edn, 1961; contrib. to collective volumes, Cahiers de l'Assoc. Internat. des Etudes françaises, Modern Language Review. *Recreation:* music. *Address:* 17 Polwarth Grove, Edinburgh EH11 1LY. *T:* (0131) 337 5092.

STEELE, Prof. Anthony, FCA; Professor of Accounting, University of Warwick, since 1985; *b* 25 April 1951; *s* of Charles and Brenda Steele; *m* 1977, Judith; one *s* three *d*. *Educ:* Fitzwilliam Coll., Cambridge (BA); Lancaster (MA 1979). FCA 1977. Programmer, Tube Investments, 1970–71; Chartered Accountant, Price Waterhouse, 1974–77; Lectr in Accounting, Lancaster Univ., 1979–85. Vis. Prof.,Univ. of Leuven, 1992–93. Director: Warwick Univ. Training Ltd, 1995–; Warwick Univ. Services Ltd, 1995–. Mem., Competition (formerly Monopolies and Mergers) Commn, 1997–. *Publications:* The Implementation of Current Cost Accounting, 1984; Audit Risk and Audit Evidence, 1992 (trans. Japanese 1997); articles on accounting and finance in learned jls. *Recreation:* theatre. *Address:* Warwick Business School, University of Warwick, Coventry CV4 7AL. *T:* (024) 7652 3523.

STEELE, Dr Bernard Robert; Development and Property Director (formerly Property Secretary), Methodist Homes for the Aged, 1987–91; *b* 21 July 1929; *s* of late Robert

Walter and Phyllis Mabel Steele; *m* 1953, Dorothy Anne Newman; one *s* two *d*. *Educ:* Oakham Sch.; Selwyn Coll., Cambridge (MA, PhD). Scientific Officer, Min. of Supply, 1953–55; Section Leader, UKAEA, Springfields, 1955–66; Building Research Station: Head, Materials Div., 1966–69; Asst Dir, 1969–72; Dep. Dir, Building Res. Estabt, 1972–75; Borough Housing Officer, Haringey, 1975–78; Dir, Science and Research Policy, DoE, 1978–82; Head, Housing Services, GLC, 1982–86. Vis. Prof., Bartlett Sch. of Architecture and Planning, UCL, 1987–89. Chm., Environment Cttee, SRC, later SERC, 1978–81. Pres., RILEM (Internat. Union of Testing and Res. Labs for Materials and Structures), 1974–75. Chm., Watford Churches Housing Assoc., 1975–78. *Publications:* contrib. numerous scientific publications on chemistry, materials science and building. *Recreations:* travelling, photography. *Address:* 1 Broom Grove, Watford WD17 4RY. *T:* (01923) 447584.

STEELE, John Ernest, FCIPS; consultant to shipbuilding and allied industries, 1989–94; Director, Morganite Special Carbons Ltd, 1990–97; *b* 4 June 1935; *s* of William Steele and Amelia Steele (*née* Graham); *m* 1958, Lucy Wilkinson; one *s* three *d*. *Educ:* Rutherford College of Technology, Newcastle upon Tyne. MNECInst. Swan Hunter and Wigham Richardson Ltd: apprentice shipbuilder, 1951–56; Management Progression, 1956–68; Swan Hunter Shipbuilders Ltd: Local Dir, 1968–71; Purchasing Dir, 1971–74; Dep. Chm. and Dep. Chief Exec., 1974–78; Chief Exec., 1977–82; Chm. and Chief Exec., 1978–82; British Shipbuilders: Div. Man. Dir, Composite Yards, 1981–83; part time Bd Mem., 1979–82; Exec. Bd Mem., Offshore, 1982–84; a Corp. Man. Dir, Offshore, 1982–84; Exec. Bd Mem., Procurement, 1984–85; Corporate Man. Dir, Procurement and Special Projects, 1985–89; North East Shipbuilders Ltd: Commercial Dir, 1986–88; Man. Dir, 1988–89. Chairman: Cammell Laird Shipbuilders Ltd, 1981–84; V. O. Offshore Ltd, 1982–84; Scott Lithgow Ltd, 1983–84; Lyon Street Railway Ltd, 1977–84; Vosper Thorneycroft (UK) Ltd, 1984–86; Sunderland Forge Services, 1987–89; Exec. Cttee, Rigby Metal Components Ltd, 1990–91. British Cttee Mem., Det Norske Veritas, 1981–91. Director: Euroroute Construction Ltd, 1985–89; Sunderland Shipbuilders Ltd, 1988–89; Non-Exec. Dir, Gibraltar Shiprepair Ltd, 1987–90. Freeman, Shipwrights' Co. *Recreations:* Rugby football, golf, reading.

STEELE, John Hamilton; Vice President, Esso Norge AS, since 1997; *b* 13 March 1941. *Educ:* North Carolina State Univ. (BS Civil Engr, MS Engr). MInstPet. Exxon Corp., USA: joined 1965; Oil & Gas Production; Calif. Dist Manager, 1976–78; Production Manager, Esso Production Malaysia Inc., Malaysia, 1978–82; Dir, Esso Exploration, Stavanger, 1982–85; Exxon Company, USA: Div. Manager, New Orleans, 1985–92; Production Ops Manager, Houston, 1992–93; Vice-Pres., Production, Houston, 1993–94; Man. Dir, Esso Exploration and Prodn UK, 1995–97. Mem., Soc. of Petroleum Engineers. *Recreations:* golf, ballet, opera. *Address:* Esso Norge AS, PO Box 60, 4033 Forus, Norway.

STEELE, Dr John Hyslop, FRS 1978; FRSE; President, Woods Hole Oceanographic Institution, Mass, 1986–92, now President Emeritus (Director, 1977–89); *b* 15 Nov. 1926; *s* of Adam Steele and Annie Hyslop Steele; *m* 1956, Margaret Evelyn Travis; one *s*. *Educ:* George Watson's Boys' Coll., Edinburgh (Higher Cert. of Educn); University Coll., London Univ. (BSc, DSc). FRSE 1968. Marine Lab., Aberdeen, Scotland: Marine Scientist, 1951–66; Sen. Principal Scientific Officer, 1966–73; Dep. Dir, 1973–77. Dir, Exxon Corp., 1989–97. Mem., Cttee for Res. and Exploration, Nat. Geographic Soc., 1987–2000. Trustee, Robert Wood Johnson Foundn. Fellow, Amer. Acad. of Arts and Sciences, 1980; FAAAS 1985. Hon. Prof., Aberdeen Univ., 1993–. Agassiz Medal, Nat. Acad. of Sciences, USA, 1973. *Publications:* Structure of Marine Ecosystems, 1974; over 100 pubns in oceanographic and ecological jls. *Recreation:* sailing. *Address:* Woods Hole Oceanographic Institution, Woods Hole, MA 02543, USA. *T:* (508) 2892220.

STEELE, John Martin, CB 1995; OBE 1986 (MBE 1979); TD 1970; DL; a Civil Service Commissioner for Northern Ireland, since 1999;; *b* 20 May 1938; *s* of John and Margaret Steele; *m* 1st, 1961, Molly Fulton (*d* 1988); one *s* two *d*; 2nd, 1992, Margaret Norma Armstrong, ISO. *Educ:* Belfast High Sch.; Queen's Univ., Belfast. Various posts, NI Civil Service, 1962–66; staff of NI Parlt, 1966–72; Dept of Community Relations, 1972–73; Second Clerk Asst, NI Assembly, 1973–74; Co-Sec., Gardiner Cttee on measures to deal with terrorism in NI, 1974; Second Clerk Asst, NI Constitutional Convention, 1975–76; DoE, NI, 1976–78; DHSS, NI, 1978–82; Dir, NI Court Service, 1982–87; Northern Ireland Office: Controller of Prisons, 1987–92; Dir, Security, 1992–96; Sen. Dir (Belfast), and Dir, Policing and Security, 1996–98. Mem., TA, 1958–85; formerly Dep. Comd 23 Artillery Bde and CO 102 Air Defence Regt, RA(V); Hon. Colonel: 102 AD Regt, 1987–93; 105 AD Regt, 1998–; Chm., RA Council of NI; Pres., NI Area, RAA. DL Belfast, 1992. *Recreations:* gardening, fly-fishing, reading, cooking. *Club:* Army and Navy.

STEELE, John Roderic, CB 1979; Member, Prisma Consulting Group (formerly Prisma Transport Consultants), since 1987; *b* 22 Feb. 1929; *s* of late Harold Graham Steele and Doris Steele (*née* Hall); *m* 1956, Margaret Marie, *d* of late Joseph and Alice Stevens; two *s* two *d*. *Educ:* Queen Elizabeth Grammar Sch., Wakefield; Queen's Coll., Oxford (MA). Asst Principal, Min. Civil Aviation, 1951; Private Sec. to Parly Sec., MTCA, 1954; Principal, Road Trans. Div., 1957; Sea Transport, 1960; Shipping Policy, 1962; Asst Sec., Shipping Policy, BoT, 1964; Counsellor (Shipping), British Embassy, Washington, 1967; Asst Sec., Civil Aviation Div., DTI, 1971, Under-Sec., Space Div., 1973, Shipping Policy Div., 1974, Gen. Div., 1975, Dept of Trade; Dep. Sec., Dept of Trade, 1976–80, Dept of Industry, 1980–81; Dir-Gen. for Transport, EEC, 1981–86. Chm., P & O European Transport Service, 1989–95; Director: P & O Containers Ltd, 1987–96; P&OSN Co., 1992–99. Mem., Dover Harbour Bd, 1990–92. Dir, Business Aircraft Users Assoc., 1999–. *Recreations:* normal. *Address:* 4 Wickham Court, Wickham Hill, Stapleton, Bristol, BS16 1DQ; Square Ambiorix 30, Bte 30, 1000 Bruxelles, Belgium. *Clubs:* Oxford and Cambridge; Philippics.

STEELE, Kenneth Walter Lawrence, CBE 1980 (OBE 1967); KPM 1936; Chief Constable, Avon and Somerset Constabulary, 1974–79; *b* 28 July 1914; *s* of Walter and Susan Steele, Godalming, Surrey; *m* 1987, Irene Koh, Malaysia. *Educ:* Wellington Sch., Wellington, Somerset. Served War: with Somerset LI and Royal Northumberland Fusiliers, 1942–45. Asst Chief Constable, Buckinghamshire, 1953–55; Chief Constable: Somerset, 1955–66; Somerset and Bath, 1966–74. *Address:* Lloyds TSB, 31 Fore Street, Taunton, Somerset TA1 1HN.

STEELE, Maj.-Gen. Michael Chandos Merrett, MBE 1972; DL; Chief of Joint Services Liaison Organization, Bonn, 1983–86; Regimental Comptroller, Royal Artillery, 1989–2001; *b* 1 Dec. 1931; *s* of late William Chandos Steele and Daisy Rhoda Steele (*née* Merrett); *m* 1961, Judith Ann Huxford; two *s* one *d*. *Educ:* Westminster School; RMA Sandhurst. Commissioned RA, 1952; Staff Coll., Camberley, 1962; BM RA, 53rd Welsh Div., 1965–67; BM, 8th Inf. Brigade, 1970–72; CO 22nd Light Air Defence Regt, RA, 1972–74; GSO1, HQ DRA, 1974–76; Comdr, 7th Artillery Brigade, 1976–78; Nat. Defence Coll., Canada, 1978–79; BGS, Defence Sales Organization, 1979–82. Col Comdt, RA, 1988–94. Hon. Col 104 Air Defence Regt, RA(V), 1987–96. Chm., Tree Council, 1994–96. DL Surrey, 1996. *Recreations:* lawn tennis, gardening. *Address:* Elders, Masons Bridge Road, Redhill, Surrey RH1 5LE. *T:* (01737) 763982.

STEELE, Sir (Philip John) Rupert, Kt 1980; Director, Trust Company of Australia Ltd (formerly Union Fidelity Trustee Co. of Australia), 1984–91; *b* 3 Nov. 1920; *s* of late C. Steele; *m* 1946, Judith, *d* of Dr Clifford Sharp; one *s* two *d*. *Educ:* Melbourne C of E Grammar School. Served RAAF and 115 Sqdn (Lancaster), RAF; POW 1944. Director: Steele & Co. Ltd, 1949–59; Carlton Brewery Ltd, 1964–73; Carlton and United Breweries, 1973–84. Mem. Council, Royal Agr. Soc. of Victoria, 1961–74. Pres., Prahan Football Club, 1980–85; Mem. Cttee, Victoria Racing Club, 1958–85, Hon. Treasurer, 1971–73, Vice-Chm., 1973–77, Chm., 1977–82; Mem., Racecourses Licensing Board, 1975–81. *Recreation:* racing thoroughbred horses. *Address:* 2/64 Irving Road, Toorak, Victoria 3142, Australia.

STEELE, Richard Charles, FIBiol, FICFor; Director General, Nature Conservancy Council, 1980–88; *b* 26 May 1928; *s* of Richard Orson Steele and Helen Curtis Steele (*née* Robertson); *m* 1956, Anne Freda Nelson; two *s* one *d*. *Educ:* Univ. of Wales (BSc Forestry and Botany); Univ. of Oxford. National Service, 1946–48. Assistant Conservator of Forests, Colonial Forest Service (later HMOCS), Tanganyika (later Tanzania), 1951–63; Head: Woodland Management Section, Nature Conservancy, Monks Wood, 1963–73; Terrestrial Life Sciences Section, Natural Environment Research Council, London, 1973–78; Division of Scientific Services, NERC Inst. of Terrestrial Ecology, Cambridge, 1978–80. Past Pres., Inst. of Foresters of Gt Britain. *Publications:* Wildlife Conservation in Woodlands, 1972; ed, Monks Wood: a nature reserve record, 1974; numerous papers on nature conservation, ecology and forestry in professional and scientific jls. *Recreations:* hill-walking, gardening, collecting books on natural history and E African travel. *Address:* 1 Birdhaven, Wrecclesham, Farnham, Surrey GU10 4PB. *T:* (01252) 726219.

STEELE, Sir Rupert; *see* Steele, Sir P. J. R.

STEELE, Tommy, (Thomas Hicks), OBE 1979; actor; *b* Bermondsey, London, 17 Dec. 1936; *s* of late Thomas Walter Hicks and Elizabeth Ellen (*née* Bennett); *m* 1960, Ann Donoghue; one *d*. *Educ:* Bacon's Sch. for Boys, Bermondsey. First appearance on stage in variety, Empire Theatre, Sunderland, Nov. 1956; first London appearance, variety, Dominion Theatre, 1957; Buttons in Rodgers and Hammerstein's Cinderella, Coliseum, 1958; Tony Lumpkin in She Stoops to Conquer, Old Vic, 1960; Arthur Kipps in Half a Sixpence, Cambridge Theatre, London, 1963–64 and Broadhurst Theatre (first NY appearance), 1965; Truffaldino in The Servant of Two Masters, Queen's, 1969; Dick Whittington, London Palladium, 1969; Meet Me In London, Adelphi, 1971; Jack Point, in The Yeomen of the Guard, City of London Fest., 1978; London Palladium: The Tommy Steele Show, 1973; Hans Andersen, 1974 and 1977; one-man show, Prince of Wales, 1979; Singin' in the Rain (also dir.), 1983; Some Like It Hot, Prince Edward, (also dir.), 1992; What a Show!, Prince of Wales, 1995; *films:* Kill Me Tomorrow, 1956; The Tommy Steele Story; The Duke Wore Jeans; Tommy the Toreador; Touch It Light; It's All Happening; The Happiest Millionaire; Half a Sixpence; Finian's Rainbow; Where's Jack?; *television:* wrote and acted in Quincy's Quest, 1979. Composed and recorded, My Life, My Song, 1974; composed: A Portrait of Pablo, 1985; Rock Suite—an Elderly Person's Guide to Rock, 1987. Hon. DLitt South Bank, 1998. *Publications:* Quincy, 1981; The Final Run, 1983. *Recreations:* squash, sculpture. *Address:* c/o International Artistes, 235 Regent Street, W1R 8AX. *T:* (020) 7439 8401.

STEELE-BODGER, Prof. Alasdair, CBE 1980; FRCVS; FRAgS, FRASE; freelance consultant in forensic veterinary medicine; Professor of Veterinary Clinical Studies, University of Cambridge, 1979–90; *b* 1 Jan. 1924; *s* of late Harry Steele-Bodger, MRCVS, and Mrs K. Steele-Bodger (*née* MacDonald); *m* 1948, Anne, 2nd *d* of late Captain A. W. J. Finlayson, RN, and Mrs Nancy Finlayson; three *d*. *Educ:* Shrewsbury Sch.; Caius Coll., Cambridge (BA 1945, MA); Royal 'Dick' Veterinary Coll., Edinburgh Univ. (BSc, MRCVS 1948). Hon. FRCVS 1975; Scientific FZS 1989. Gen. vet. practice, Lichfield, Staffs, 1948–77; consultant practice, Fordingbridge, Hants, 1977–79. Hon. Vet. Consultant to British Agricl Export Council, 1967–88. Vis. Prof., Univ. of Toronto, 1973. Pres., British Small Animal Vet. Assoc., 1962; Member: Horserace Scientific Adv. Cttee (formerly Jockey Club's Horserace Anti-Doping Cttee), 1973–92; UGC's Agricl and Vet. Sub-Cttee, 1973–81; Council: BVA, 1957–85 (Pres., 1966; Hon. Mem., 1985); RCVS, 1960–90 (Pres., 1972); Jt RCVS/BVA Cttee on Eur. Vet. Affairs, 1967–90; Eur. Liaison Gp for Agriculture, 1972–90; Cttee of Inquiry on Experiments on Animals, 1963–65; Council, RASE, 1967–98 (Hon. Fellow, 1993; Hon. Vice-Pres., 1996); Animal Feedingstuffs Industry/BVA/ADAS HQ Liaison Cttee, 1967–85. UK Deleg. to Fedn of Veterinarians of EEC, 1967–90; EEC Official Vet. Expert, 1974–98; Member: EEC Adv. Cttee on Vet. Trng, 1981–90; Home Office Panel of Assessors under Animals (Scientific Procedures) Act, 1986–98. Vice-Pres., Inst. of Animal Technology, 1988–2000. Dir, B & K Universal Ltd (formerly Bantin & Kingman Ltd), 1980–2000. Hon. Vet. Consultant, Nat. Cattle Breeders' Assoc., 1979–99. Mem. Bd of Advisers, Univ. of London, 1984–98. Gov., Cambs Coll. of Agric. and Hortic., 1989–90. Gen. Comr to Bd of Inland Revenue, 1969–81. Chairman: Editorial Bd, Veterinary Times (formerly Veterinary Drug), 1978–88; Adv. Bd, British Veterinary Formulary, 1987–96. Ehrenbürger, Tierärztlich Hochschule, Hannover, 1992. ARAgS 1996, FRAgS 1998. Crookes' Prize, 1970; Dalrymple-Champneys Cup and Medal, 1972. Cambridge Triple Blue. *Publications:* Society of Practising Veterinary Surgeons Economics Report, 1961, and papers in vet. jls on clinical subjects and vet. econs. *Recreations:* swimming, fishing, travel, golf. *Address:* The Little Rectory, Grosmont, Monmouth, Wales NP7 8LW. *Clubs:* Farmers'; Hawks (Cambridge).

See also M. R. Steele-Bodger.

STEELE-BODGER, Michael Roland, CBE 1990; veterinary surgeon in private practice, retired; *b* 4 Sept. 1925; *s* of late Henry William Steele-Bodger and Kathrine Macdonald; *m* 1955, Violet Mary St Clair Murray; two *s* one *d*. *Educ:* Rugby Sch.; Gonville and Caius Coll., Cambridge. MRCVS. Mem., Sports Council, 1976–82. England Rugby Selector, 1954–70; Pres., RFU, 1973–74; Mem., Internat. Rugby Football Bd, 1974–84; Chm., Four Home Rugby Unions' Tours Cttee, 1976–88; Pres., Barbarians FC, 1987–. Cambridge Univ. Rugby Blue, Captain 1946; England Rugby Internat., 1947–48. *Recreation:* interest in all sport. *Address:* Laxford Lodge, Bonehill, Tamworth, Staffs B78 3HY. *T:* (01827) 251001. *Clubs:* East India, Devonshire, Sports and Public Schools (Life Pres.); Hawks (Cambridge).

See also A. Steele-Bodger.

STEELE-PERKINS, Crispian G.; trumpet soloist; *b* 18 Dec. 1944; *s* of Dr Guy Steele-Perkins and Sylvia de Courcey Steele-Perkins; *m* 1st, 1967, Angela Helen Hall (*d* 1991); one *s* two *d*; 2nd, 1995, Jane Elizabeth Mary (*née* Steele-Perkins). *Educ:* Marlborough Coll.; Guildhall Sch. of Music (LGSM, AGSM; Alumni 1995). Has performed with: Sadlers Wells (later ENO), 1966–73; London Gabrieli Brass Ensemble, 1974–84; RPO, 1976–80; English Baroque Soloists, 1980–91; The King's Consort, 1985–. *Fax:* (01306) 730013; *e-mail:* crispiansp@trumpet1.co.uk.

STEEN, Anthony David; MP (C) Totnes, since 1997 (Liverpool Wavertree, Feb. 1974–1983, South Hams, 1983–97); barrister; youth leader; social worker; underwriter; *b* 22 July 1939; *s* of late Stephen Nicholas Steen; *m* 1965, Carolyn Padfield, educational psychologist; one *s* one *d*. *Educ:* Westminster Sch.; occasional student University Coll., London. Called to Bar, Gray's Inn, 1962; practising Barrister, 1962–74; Defence Counsel, MoD (Court Martials), 1964–68. Lectr in Law, Council of Legal Educn, 1964–67; Adv. Tutor, Sch. of Environment, Central London Poly, 1982–83. Youth Club Leader, E London Settlement, 1959–64; Founder, 1964, and First Director, 1964–68, Task Force to help London's old and lonely, with Govt support; Govt Foundn YVFF, tackling urban deprivation, 1968–74; Consultant to Canadian Govt on student and employment matters, 1970–71. PPS to Sec. of State for Nat. Heritage, 1992–94. Member, Select Committee: on Race Relations, 1975–79; on the Envmt, 1991–94; on Europ. Legislation, 1997–; on Deregulation, 1997–; on Public Admin, 2001–. Chairman: Cons. Mems Parly Gp, 1974; Backbench gps on Youth and Young Children, 1976–79; Cons. Cttee on Cities, Urban and New Town Affairs, 1979–83; Parly Urban and Inner City Cttee, 1987–90; All Party Friends of Cycling, 1979–88; Vice-Chairman: Health and Social Services Cttee, 1979–80; All-Party Fisheries Cttee, 1997–; Secretary: Parly Caribbean Gp, 1979– (Vice-Chm.); Cons. back bench Trade and Industry Cttee, 1997–99; 1992 Cttee, 2001–. Chm., Chm.'s Unit Marginal Seats, 1982–84, Minority Parties Unit, 1999–2000, Cons. Central Office. Vice-Chm., Envmt Cttee, 1983–85; Chairman: Deregulation Cttee, 1993–; Parly PNG Gp, 1991–; Sane Planning Gp, 1989–; West Country Mems, 1992–94; Mem., All-Party Child Abuse Cttee; Member: Parly Population and Develt Gp; Commons and Lord's Cycle Gp; Services Cttee; Chm., Cons. Friends of English Wine; Jt Nat. Chm., Impact 80's Campaign. Member: Exec. Council, NPFA; Board, Community Transport; Council of Reference, Internat. Christian Relief; Council Mem., Anglo-Jewish Assoc.; Founder Mem., CSA Monitoring Gp; Chm., Outlandos Charitable Trust; Vice-Chm., Task Force Trust; Vice-President: Ecology Bldg Soc.; Internat. Centre for Child Studies; Bentley Operatic Soc.; S Hams Young Farmers; Assoc. of District Councils; Marlborough with S Huish Horticultural Soc.; Devon CPRE; Dartmoor Preservation Assoc.; Trustee: Educn Extra; Dartington Summer Arts Foundn; Patron: Liverpool's Open Circle for Detached Youth Work; St Luke's Hospice, Plymouth; Kidscape; Sustrans. Pres., Devon Youth Assoc. *Publications:* New Life for Old Cities, 1981; Tested Ideas for Political Success, 1983, 2nd edn 1991; Plums, 1988. *Recreations:* piano, fell-walking, mountain climbing, cycling, wine-tasting. *Address:* House of Commons, SW1A 0AA; Totnes Conservative Association, Station Road, Totnes, Devon TQ9 5HW. *T:* (01803) 866069. *Clubs:* Royal Automobile; Churchill (Liverpool); Brixham; Totnes Conservative (South Hams).

STEER, David; QC 1993; a Recorder, since 1991; *b* 15 June 1951; *s* of Alcombe Steer and Nancy Steer; *m* 1974, Elizabeth May Hide; one *s*. *Educ:* Rainford High Sch.; Manchester Poly. (BA Hons Law). Called to the Bar, Middle Temple, 1974. Mem., Bar Council, 1995–97. *Recreations:* Rugby League, gardening. *Address:* 7 Harrington Street, Liverpool L2 9YH. *T:* (0151) 242 0707.

STEER, Deirdre V.; *see* Clancy, D. V.

STEER, Prof. John Richardson, FSA 1981; Emeritus Professor of the History of Art, University of London; art-historian and director; *b* 14 Oct. 1928; *s* of Walter Wallis Steer and Elsie Gertrude (*née* Colman). *Educ:* Clayesmore Sch., Dorset; Keble Coll., Oxford (MA); Courtauld Inst. of Art, Univ. of London (BA). Gen. Asst, City Art Gall., Birmingham, 1953–56; Asst Lectr, Dept of Fine Art, Univ. of Glasgow, 1956–59; Lectr in Hist. of European Art, Univ. of Bristol, 1959–67; Prof. of Fine Arts, Univ. of St Andrews, 1967–80; Prof. of Hist. of Art, Birkbeck Coll., Univ. of London, 1980–84. Chm., Adv. Cttee on Validation, Heriot-Watt Univ./Edinburgh Coll. of Art, 1978–91; Chm., Art Historians Assoc. of GB, 1980–83; Vice-Chm., Scottish Theatre Ballet, 1969–71; Mem., Cttee for Art and Design, CNAA, 1977–82 (Chm., Hist. of Art/Design and Complementary Studies Bd, 1977–79); Member: Theatre Museum Adv. Council, 1981–83; Theatre Museum Cttee, V&A Mus., 1984–; Exec., Genius of Venice Exhibn, RA, 1983–84; Royal Fine Art Commn, 1992–99. Chm., Theatre Manoeuvres Ltd, 1991–. Trustee, V&A Mus., 1991–99. Adjudicator, National Student Drama Festival, 1977. Theatrical prodns include: The Seagull, St Andrews, 1971; And When Love Speaks, Edinburgh, 1975; The Privacy of the Patients, Edinburgh Fringe, 1977, ICA, 1978; Waiting for Godot, St Andrews, 1978; Minna von Barnhelm, plc, Theatre Co., Young Vic Studio, 1987. Hon. FRCA 1996. Hon. DLitt: St Andrews, 1990; Heriot-Watt, 1991. *Publications:* A Concise History of Venetian Painting, 1967; Mr Bacon's Titian (Selwyn Brinton Lecture, RSA), 1977; Alvise Vivarini, 1982; (with A. White) Atlas of Western Art History, 1994; contribs to Burlington Magazine, Art History. *Recreation:* travel. *Address:* 1 Cheriton Square, SW17 8AE.

STEER, Kenneth Arthur, CBE 1978; MA, PhD, FSA, FSAScot; Secretary, Royal Commission on the Ancient and Historical Monuments of Scotland, 1957–78; *b* 12 Nov. 1913; *o s* of Harold Steer and Emily Florence Thompson; *m* 1st, 1941, Rona Mary Mitchell (*d* 1983); one *d*; 2nd, 1985, Eileen Alice Nelson (*d* 1999). *Educ:* Wath Grammar School; Durham University. Research Fellowship, 1936–38. Joined staff of Royal Commission on Ancient and Historical Monuments of Scotland, 1938. Intelligence Officer in Army, 1941–45 (despatches twice). Monuments, Fine Arts and Archives Officer, North Rhine Region, 1945–46. Corresponding Member, German Archæological Inst.; Horsley Memorial Lectr, Durham University, 1963; Rhind Lectr, Edinburgh, 1968. Pres., Soc. of Antiquaries of Scotland, 1972–75. Arts Council Literary Award, 1978. *Publications:* Late Medieval Monumental Sculpture in the West Highlands (with J. W. M. Bannerman), 1976; numerous articles in archæological journals. *Address:* 2 Morningside Courtyard, Idsall Drive, Prestbury, Cheltenham, Glos GL52 3BU.

STEER, Wilfred Reed; QC 1972; *b* 23 Aug. 1926; *s* of George William and Dorothy Steer; *m* 1953, Jill Park; one *s* one *d*, and two step *s*. *Educ:* Bede Collegiate Sch., Sunderland, Co. Durham; London Sch. of Economics. LLB (Lond.) 1949. Called to the Bar, Gray's Inn, 1950. *Address:* Park Court Chambers, 16 Park Place, Leeds LS1 1SJ. *T:* (0113) 243 3277.

STEERE; *see* Lee-Steere.

STEFF-LANGSTON, Group Captain John Antony, MBE 1959; Executive Secretary, Royal Astronomical Society, 1980–91; *b* 5 Nov. 1926; *s* of William Austen Paul Steff-Langston, organist and composer, and Ethel Maude (*née* Fletcher); *m* 1959, Joyce Marian Brown. *Educ:* Cathedral Choir Sch., Canterbury; King's Sch., Canterbury; Pembroke Coll., Cambridge. RAF Coll., 1945–46; 45 Sqn, Ceylon, 1948; 61 Gp, Kenley, 1949; 34 Sqn, 1950–51; 80 Sqn, Hong Kong, 1951–54; 540, 58 and 82 Sqns, Wyton and Singapore, 1955–57; HQ 3 Gp, 1957–59; 80 Sqn, Germany, 1959–62; Staff Coll., Andover, 1962–63; Air Sec.'s Dept, 1963–65; OC 114 Sqn, Benson, 1966–68; aws 1968; CO Northolt, 1969–71; Defence Advr to High Comrs to NZ and Fiji, 1971–74; sowc Greenwich, 1974–75; AMPs Dept, 1975–78; retd 1978. FIMgt (FBIM 1978); ARAeS 1987; FRAS 1992. Freeman, City of London, 1994; Liveryman, Fletchers' Co., 1994–. *Recreations:* ornithology, photography, travel, music, cricket. *Address:* 6 Beech Wood, Church Hill, Caterham, Surrey CR3 6SB. *T:* (01883) 344348. *Club:* Royal Air Force.

STEGGLE, Terence Harry, CMG 1990; HM Diplomatic Service, retired; Ambassador to Paraguay, 1989–91; *b* 4 March 1932; *s* of Henry Richard Steggle and Jane Steggle; *m* 1st, 1954, Odette Marie (*née* Audisio) (*d* 1988); two *d*; 2nd, 1989, Annemarie Klara Johanne (*née* Wohle). *Educ:* Chislehurst and Sidcup County Grammar School. Crown Agents, 1950–57; Lieut RA (TA), 1951–53; seconded to Govt of E Nigeria, 1957–58, 1960–62; FO 1963; served Laos, 1963, France, 1964, Zaire, 1970, Bolivia, 1978–82; Ambassador to Panama, 1983–86; Consul-Gen., São Paulo, 1986–87; Counsellor, FCO, 1987–89. *Recreations:* swimming, golf, bridge. *Address:* c/o Foreign and Commonwealth Office, SW1A 2AH. *Club:* Rotary (Benahavis, Spain).

STEICHEN, René; Senior Partner, Arendt & Medernach, Luxembourg and Brussels, since 1995; *b* Luxembourg, 27 Nov. 1942; *s* of Félix Steichen and Hélène Rausch; *m* 1975, Marianne Belche; two *s* one *d*. *Educ:* Lycée Classique, Diekirch; Cours Supérieurs, Luxembourg; Univ. of Aix-en-Provence; Univ. of Paris (LLD); Institut d'Etudes Politiques, Paris (Dip. Econs and Finance 1966). Qualified as notary, then solicitor, 1969; practised in Diekirch, 1969–84. Mem., Diekirch DC, 1969–84, Mayor, 1974–84. MP (Social Christian) North constituency, Luxembourg, 1979–93; Sec. of State for Agric. and Viticulture, 1984–89; Minister for Agric., Viticulture and Rural Develt and Minister for Cultural Affairs and Scientific Res., 1989–93; Mem., Commn of the European Communities, 1993–95. Chm. Bd, Soc. Européene des Satellites, 1996–. *Address:* 36 rue Clairefontaine, 9201 Diekirch, Luxembourg.

STEIN, Christopher Richard, (Rick); broadcaster; Chef, The Seafood Restaurant, Padstow, since 1975; *b* 4 Jan. 1947; *s* of late Eric and Dorothy Stein; *m* 1975, Jill Newstead; three *s*. *Educ:* Uppingham; New Coll., Oxford (BA English Lit. 1971). Presenter, BBC TV series: Rick Stein's Taste of the Sea, 1995; Rick Stein's Fruits of the Sea, 1997; Rick Stein's Seafood Odyssey, 1999; Fresh Food, 1999; Rick Stein's Seafood Lovers' Guide, 2000. Glenfiddich Food and Drink Award, for best TV prog., 2001. *Publications:* English Seafood Cookery, 1988 (Glenfiddich Cook Book of the Year, 1989); Taste of the Sea, 1995 (André Simon Cook Book of the Year, 1996); Fish, 1996; Fruits of the Sea, 1997; Rick Stein's Seafood Odyssey, 1999; Rick Stein's Seafood Lovers' Guide, 2000. *Address:* The Seafood Restaurant, Riverside, Padstow, Cornwall PL28 8BY. *T:* (01841) 532632. *Club:* Groucho.

STEIN, Sheriff Colin Norman Ralph; Sheriff of Tayside Central and Fife at Arbroath, since 1991; *b* 14 June 1948; *s* of late Colin Hunter Stein and of Margaret Lindsay Stein; *m* 1979, Dr Linda McNaught; one *s*. *Educ:* Glenalmond Coll.; Durham Univ. (BA Hons Modern History); Edinburgh Univ. (LLB). Admitted Member of Faculty of Advocates, 1975. Standing Jun. Counsel to MoD (RAF), Scotland, 1983–91; Temp. Sheriff, 1987–91. *Recreations:* angling, gardening. *Address:* c/o Sheriff Court, High Street, Arbroath DD11 1HC.

STEIN, Cyril; Chairman, St James's Club Ltd, since 1995; Ladbroke Group PLC, 1966–93; *b* 20 Feb. 1928; *s* of late Jack Stein and Rebecca Stein (*née* Selner); *m* 1949, Betty Young; two *s* one *d*.

STEIN, Prof. Peter Gonville, FBA 1974; JP; Regius Professor of Civil Law in the University of Cambridge, 1968–93, now Emeritus; Fellow of Queens' College, Cambridge, since 1968; *b* 29 May 1926; *o s* of late Walter Stein, MA, Solicitor, and Effie Drummond Stein (*née* Walker); *m* 1st, 1953, Janet Chamberlain; three *d*; 2nd, 1978, Anne M. Howard (*née* Sayer); one step *s*. *Educ:* Liverpool Coll. (Life Gov., 1976); Gonville and Caius Coll., Camb. (Hon. Fellow, 1999); University of Pavia. Served in RN, Sub-lieut (Sp) RNVR, 1944–47. Admitted a Solicitor, 1951; Italian Govt Scholar, 1951–52; Asst Lecturer in Law, Nottingham Univ., 1952–53; Lecturer in Jurisprudence, 1953–56, Prof. of Jurisprudence, 1956–68, Dean of Faculty of Law, 1961–64, Aberdeen Univ.; Chm., Faculty Bd of Law, Cambridge, 1973–76; Vice Pres., Queens' Coll., 1974–81 (Acting Pres., 1976 and 1980–81). Visiting Prof. of Law: Univ. of Virginia, 1965–66, 1978–79; Colorado, 1966; Witwatersrand, 1970; Louisiana State, 1974, 1977, 1983, 1985; Chicago, 1985, 1988, 1990, 1992, 1995; Padua and Palermo, 1991; Tulane, New Orleans, 1992, 1996 and 1998; Salerno, 1994; Lateran, Rome, 1997; Lectures: R. M. Jones, QUB, 1978; Irvine, Cornell, 1979; Sherman, Boston, 1979; Tucker, Louisiana State, 1985; David Murray, Glasgow, 1987; Maccabaean, British Acad., 1995. Fellow, Winchester Coll., 1976–91. Member: Council, Max Planck Inst. for European Legal History, Frankfurt, 1966–88; Council, Internat. Assoc. of Legal History, 1970– (Vice-Pres, 1985–); Internat. Acad. of Comparative Law, 1987–; Sec. of State for Scotland's Working Party on Hospital Endowments, 1966–69; Bd of Management, Royal Cornhill and Assoc. (Mental) Hospitals, Aberdeen, 1963–68 (Chm. 1967–68); UGC, 1971–75; US–UK Educnl (Fulbright) Commn, 1985–91; Council, British Acad., 1988–90. Chm., Ely Diocesan Trust Cttee, 1987–94. Pres., Soc. of Public Teachers of Law, 1980–81; Vice-Pres., Selden Soc., 1984–87. Foreign Fellow: Accad. di Scienze morali e politiche, Naples, 1982; Accademia Nazionale dei Lincei, Rome, 1987; Corres. Fellow, Accademia degli Intronati, Siena, 1988; Fellow, Academia Europaea, 1989; Foreign Fellow, Koninklijke Academie voor Wetenschappen, Belgium, 1991. JP Cambridge, 1970 (Supplementary List, 1988). Hon. QC 1993. Hon. Dr jur Göttingen, 1980; Hon. Dott. Giur. Ferrara, 1991; Hon. LLD Aberdeen, 2000; Hon. Dr: Perugia, 2001; Paris II, 2001. *Publications:* Fault in the formation of Contract in Roman Law and Scots Law, 1958; editor, Buckland's Textbook of Roman Law, 3rd edn, 1963; Regulae Iuris: from juristic rules to legal maxims, 1966; Roman Law in Scotland in Ius Romanum Medii Aevi, 1968; Roman Law and English Jurisprudence (inaugural lect.), 1969; (with J. Shand) Legal Values in Western Society, 1974, Italian edn 1981; (ed jtly) Adam Smith's Lectures on Jurisprudence, 1978; Legal Evolution, 1980, Japanese edn 1987; (ed jtly) Studies in Justinian's Institutes, 1983; Legal Institutions: the development of dispute settlement, 1984, Italian edn 1987; The Character and Influence of the Roman Civil Law: historical essays, 1988; (with F. de Zulueta) The Teaching of Roman Law in England around 1200, 1990; (ed and contrib.) Notaries Public in England since the Reformation (English and Italian edns), 1991; Roman Law in European History, 1999 (German trans., 1996, Spanish and Italian trans, 2001); articles in legal periodicals mainly on Roman Law and legal history. *Recreations:* hill walking, gardening. *Address:* Wimpole Cottage, 36 Wimpole Road, Great Eversden, Cambridge CB3 7HR. *T:* (01223) 262349.

See also Lord Howard of Effingham.

STEIN, Rick; *see* Stein, C. R.

STEINBERG, Gerald Neil, (Gerry); MP (Lab) City of Durham, since 1987; *b* 20 April 1945; *s* of Harry and Esther Steinberg; *m* 1969, Margaret Cruddace Thornton; one *s* one *d*. *Educ:* St Margaret's Primary Sch.; Whinney Hill Secondary Sch.; Durham Johnston Sch.; Sheffield Coll. of Education; Newcastle Polytechnic. Cert. of Educn for Backward Children. Teacher, Dukeshouse Wood Camp Sch., Hexham, 1966–69; Teacher, Elemore Hall, 1969–75, Dep. Head, 1975–79; Head Teacher, Whitworth House Special Sch., 1979–87. Mem., Durham City Council, 1975–87 (Sec., Labour Gp, 1981–87). Member, Select Committee: on Education, 1987–96; on Educn and Employment, 1996–98; on Public Accounts, 1998–; on Catering, 1998–2001; Vice Chm., Labour Educn Cttee, 1997–98 (Chm., 1990–96). *Recreations:* Sunderland AFC supporter; cricket, squash, loves all sport (Pres., Bearpark Cricket Club; Vice Pres., Brandon AFC). *Address:* House of Commons, SW1A 0AA. *Clubs:* Sherburn Workman's, Sherburn Hill Workman's, Brandon Workman's, Crossgate Workman's, Nevilles Cross Workman's.

STEINBERG, Prof. Hannah; Hon. Research Professor in Psychology, School of Social Science, Middlesex University, since 1992; *b* 16 March; *d* of late Michael Steinberg, doctor of law, and Marie (*née* Wein). *Educ:* Schwarzwaldschule, Vienna; Putney High School; Queen Anne's School, Caversham; Univ. of Reading (Cert. Comm.); Denton Secretarial Coll., London; University College London (BA 1st cl. Hons Psychology, PhD; Troughton Schol., 1948–50). FBPsS, CPsychol 1990. Pres., Univ. of London Union, 1947–48; Univ. of London Postgrad. Studentship in Psychol., 1948–50. Sec. to Man. Dir, Omes Ltd, 1943–44. Part-time teacher, LSE, 1951; University College London: Asst Lectr in Pharmacology, 1954–55; Lectr, 1955–62; Reader in Psychopharmacology, 1962–70; Prof. of Psychopharmacology (first in W Europe and USA), 1970–92; Head of Psychopharmacology Gp, Dept of Psychology, 1979–92; Hon. Res. Fellow, Dept of Psychology, 1992–; Prof. Emeritus, Univ. of London, 1989. Hon. Consulting Clinical Psychologist, Dept of Psychological Medicine, Royal Free Hosp., 1970. Member MRC working parties on: Biochemistry and Pharmacology of Drug Dependence, 1968–73; Biological Aspects of Drug Dependence, 1971–75. Vice-President: Collegium Internationale Neuro-Psychopharmacologicum (CINP), 1968–74 (Emeritus Fellow, 1996); Brit. Assoc. for Psychopharmacology, 1974–76 (Hon. Mem., 1989); Mem., Biological Council, 1977–80. Distinguished Affiliate of Amer. Psychol Assoc., Psychopharmacology Div., 1978; Member: British Pharmacol Soc.; Experimental Psychol. Soc.; Soc. for Study of Addiction; European Coll. of Neuropsychopharmacology; European Behavioural Pharmacol Soc.; European Health Psychol Soc.; Soc. for Medicines Res., etc. Convener, Academic Women's Achievement Gp, 1979–92. Accredited Sport Psychologist, British Assoc. of Sport and Exercise Scis, 1992. Special Trustee, Middx Hosp., 1989–92. Initiator, Steinberg Doctrine, Town and Country Planning Act, Listed Buildings Act 1990. British Assoc. for Psychopharmacology/AstraZeneca Lifetime Achievement Award, 2001. Past ed. of scientific jls. *Publications:* (trans. and ed jtly) Animals and Men, 1951; organiser of symposia, workshops and editor: (jtly) Animal Behaviour and Drug Action, 1963; Scientific Basis of Drug Dependence, 1968; (jtly) Psychopharmacology, Sexual Disorders and Drug Abuse, 1972; Joint Editor, Occasional Publications of British Psychological Society: Exercise Addiction, 1995; Quality and Quantity, 1996; Teams and Teamwork, 1996; Cognitive Enhancement, 1997; What Sport Psychologists Do, 1998; Sport Psychology in Practice: the early stages, 2000; articles and reviews on psychopharmacology, psychological benefits of physical exercise, exercise addiction, creativity and writer's block. *Address:* c/o School of Social Science, Middlesex University, Queensway, Enfield, Middx EN3 4SF. *T:* (020) 7267 4783, *Fax:* (020) 7267 4780; *e-mail:* hannah3@mdx.ac.uk.

STEINBERG, Saul Phillip; Founder, 1961, and Chairman, since 1961, Reliance Group Holdings Inc. (Chief Executive Officer, 1961–2000); *b* 13 Aug. 1939; *m* 3rd, 1984, Gayfryd McNabb; one *d* and one step *s*; and three *s* one *d* by previous marriages. *Educ:* Wharton School of Univ. of Pennsylvania (BScEcon). Director: Zenith National Insurance Corp.; Symbol Technologies Inc. Dir, Long Island Jewish Medical Center. Mem., Bd of Overseers, Cornell Univ. Medical Coll.; Chm., Wharton Bd of Overseers; Trustee: Univ. of Pennsylvania; NY Public Library. *Address:* (office) Park Avenue Plaza, 55 E 52 Street, New York, NY 10055-0002, USA. *T:* (212) 9091110.

STEINBERGER, Prof. Jack; Professor of Physics, Scuola Normale Superiore, Pisa, since 1986; *b* 25 May 1921; *s* of Ludwig and Bertha Steinberger; *m* 1st, 1943, Joan Beauregard; two *s*; 2nd, 1962, Cynthia Eve Alff; one *s* one *d*. *Educ:* New Trier Township High Sch.; Armour Inst. of Technology; Univ. of Chicago (BS Chem 1942; PhD Phys 1948). Mem., Inst. of Advanced Study, Princeton, 1948–49; Asst, Univ. of California, Berkeley, 1949–50; Prof., Columbia Univ., 1950–68 (Higgins Prof., 1965–68); Physicist, CERN, Geneva, 1968–86. Member: Nat. Acad. of Sciences; Amer. Acad. of Arts and Sciences; Heidelberg Acad. of Science; Accad. Nationale dei Lincei. (Jtly) President's Science Award, USA, 1988; (jtly) Nobel Prize for Physics, 1988; Mateuzzi Medal, Soc. Italiana della Scienze, 1991. *Publications:* papers in learned jls on discoveries leading to better understanding of elementary particles. *Recreations:* flute; formerly mountaineering, tennis, yachting. *Address:* CERN, 1211 Geneva 23, Switzerland; 25 Ch. des Merles, 1213 Onex, Switzerland.

STEINBY, Prof. Eva Margareta, FSA; Professor of Archaeology of the Roman Empire, and Fellow of All Souls College, University of Oxford, since 1994; *b* 21 Nov. 1938; *d* of Kaarlo Erkki Wilén and Doris Margareta Steinby. *Educ:* Univ. of Helsinki (Hum. Kand. 1963; Fil. Kand. 1964; Fil. Lic. 1970; Fil. Dr 1976); MA Oxon 1995. FSA 1997. Institutum Romanum Finlandiae, Rome: Asst, 1973–77; Dir, 1979–82 and 1992–94; Sen. Res. Fellow, Finnish Acad., Helsinki, 1985–92. Docent in History, Univ. of Helsinki, 1977–; Vis. Fellow, All Souls Coll., Oxford, 1990–91. Fellow, Suomen Historiallinen Seura, 1978; Corresp. Fellow, Pontificia Accademia Romana di Archeologia, 1982, Fellow, 1993; Fellow: Societas Scientiarum Fennica, 1983; Academia Scientiarum Fennica, 2000; Corresp. Fellow, Deutsches Archaologisches Institut, 1984; For. Hon. Mem., Archaeol Inst. of America, 1998. Medaglia d'Oro per Benemeriti Culturali (Italy), 1983. Officer, 1st Cl., Order of White Rose (Finland), 1991. *Publications:* La cronologia delle figlinae doliari urbane, 1976; Lateres signati Ostienses, Vol. I 1977, Vol. II 1978; Indici complementari ai bolli doliari urbani (CIL, XV, 1), 1987; (ed) Lacus Iuturnae I, 1989; (ed) Lexicon Topographicum Urbis Romae, 6 vols, 1993–2000; (ed) Ianiculum-Gianicolo, 1997; articles in Italian, German and Finnish learned jls. *Address:* University of Oxford Institute of Archaeology, 36 Beaumont Street, Oxford OX1 2PG. *T:* (01865) 278248; All Souls College, Oxford OX1 4AL. *T:* (01865) 279379.

STEINER, Prof. (Francis) George, MA, DPhil; FBA 1998; FRSL; Fellow, Churchill College, Cambridge, since 1961; Weidenfeld Professor of Comparative Literature, and Fellow of St Anne's College, Oxford, 1994–95; *b* 23 April 1929; *s* of Dr F. G. and Mrs E. Steiner; *m* 1955, Zara Steiner (*née* Shakow); one *s* one *d*. *Educ:* Paris (BèsL); Univ. of Chicago (BA); Harvard (MA); Oxford (DPhil). Member, staff of the Economist, in London, 1952–56; Inst. for Advanced Study, Princeton, 1956–58; Gauss Lectr, Princeton Univ., 1959–60; Prof. of English and Comparative Literature, Univ. of Geneva, 1974–94, Prof. Emeritus, 1994–. Lectures: Massey, 1974; Leslie Stephen, Cambridge, 1986; W. P. Ker, 1986, Gifford, 1990, Univ. of Glasgow; Page-Barbour, Univ. of Virginia, 1987; Paul Tillich, Harvard, 1999. Fulbright Professorship, 1958–69; Vis. Prof., Collège de France, 1992; Charles Eliot Norton Prof., Harvard, 2001–02. Pres., English Assoc., 1975; Corresp. Mem., (Federal) German Acad. of Literature, 1981; Hon. Mem., Amer. Acad. of Arts and Scis, 1989; Hon. FRA 1999. FRSL 1964. Hon. Fellow: Balliol Coll., Oxford, 1995; St Anne's Coll., Oxford, 1998. Hon. DLitt: East Anglia, 1976; Louvain, 1980; Mount Holyoke Coll., USA, 1983; Bristol, 1989; Glasgow, 1990; Liège, 1990; Ulster, 1993; Durham, 1995; Kenyan Coll., USA, 1996; Trinity Coll., Dublin, 1996; Rome, 1998; Sorbonne, 1998. O. Henry Short Story Award, 1958; Guggenheim Fellowship, 1971–72; Zabel Award of Nat. Inst. of Arts and Letters of the US, 1970; Faulkner Stipend for Fiction, PEN, 1983; PEN Macmillan Fiction Prize, 1993; Truman Capote Lifetime Award for Lit., 1999; Prince of Asturias Prize, Spain, 2001. Chevalier de la Légion d'Honneur, 1984. *Publications:* Tolstoy or Dostoevsky, 1958; The Death of Tragedy, 1960; Anno Domini, 1964; Language and Silence, 1967; Extraterritorial, 1971; In Bluebeard's Castle, 1971; The Sporting Scene: White Knights in Reykjavik, 1973; After Babel, 1975 (adapted for TV as The Tongues of Men, 1977); Heidegger, 1978; On Difficulty and Other Essays, 1978; The Portage to San Cristobal of A. H., 1981; Antigones, 1984; George Steiner: a reader, 1984; Real Presences: is there anything in what we say?, 1989; Proofs and Three Parables, 1992; The Deeps of the Sea (fiction), 1996; No Passion Spent, 1996; Errata: an examined life, 1997; Grammars of Creation, 2001. *Recreations:* music, chess, mountain walking. *Address:* 32 Barrow Road, Cambridge CB2 2AS. *T:* (01223) 61200. *Clubs:* Athenæum, Savile; Harvard (New York).

STEINER, Prof. Hillel Isaac, PhD; FBA 1999; Professor of Political Philosophy, University of Manchester; *b* 1942; *m* 1966. *Educ:* Univ. of Toronto (BA); Carleton Univ. (MA); Univ. of Manchester (PhD). Lectr in Politics and Public Admin, Univ. of Saskatchewan, 1966–67; Res. Associate, 1967–71, Lectr, then Sen. Lectr, in Pol Philosophy, 1971, Dept of Govt, Univ. of Manchester. *Publications:* Essay on Rights, 1994; contrib. to learned jls. *Address:* Department of Government, University of Manchester, Oxford Road, Manchester M13 9PL.

STEINER, Prof. Robert Emil, CBE 1979; Professor of Diagnostic Radiology, University of London, Royal Postgraduate Medical School, 1961–83, now Emeritus; *b* 1 Feb. 1918; *s* of Rudolf Steiner and Clary (*née* Nordlinger); *m* 1945, Gertrude Margaret Konirsch; two *d*. *Educ:* University of Vienna; University College, Dublin. Dep. Director, Dept of Radiology, Hammersmith Hosp.; Lecturer Diagnostic Radiology, Postgraduate Med. School of London, 1950, Sen. Lecturer, 1955, Director, 1955–. Vice-Chm., Nat. Radiological Protection Bd, 1972–83. Past Consultant Adviser in Radiology to DHSS; Past Civil Consultant in Radiology to Med. Dir-Gen., Navy. Warden of Fellowship, Faculty of Radiologists. Former Mem. Council, RCS; Past Pres., British Inst. Radiology; Pres., RCR, 1977–80. Hon. Fellow: Amer. Coll. of Radiology; Australian Coll. of Radiology; Faculty of Radiologists, RCSI. Hon. Mem., Radiological Socs of Finland, N America, Switzerland and Austria; Amer. Roentgen Ray Soc.; Germany Roentgen Soc. Barclay Medal British Inst. of Radiology; Gold Medal, RCR, 1986. Former Editor, British Jl of Radiology. *Publications:* Clinical Disorders of the Pulmonary Circulation, 1960; Recent Advances of Radiology, vols 4–8, 1979–85; contrib. to British Journal of Radiology, Clinical Radiology, British Heart Jl, Lancet, BMJ, etc. *Address:* 12 Stonehill Road, East Sheen, SW14 8RW. *T:* (020) 8876 4038. *Club:* Hurlingham.

STEINFELD, Alan Geoffrey; QC 1987; *b* 13 July 1946; *s* of Henry Chaim Steinfeld and Deborah Steinfeld; *m* 1976, Josephine Nicole (*née* Gros); two *s*. *Educ:* City of London Sch.; Downing Coll., Cambridge (BA Hons, LLB). Arnold McNair Schol. in Internat. Law, 1967; Whewell Schol. in Internat. Law, 1968. Called to the Bar, Lincoln's Inn, 1968, Bencher, 1996; commenced pupillage at the Bar, 1968, practice at the Bar, 1969; a Dep. High Court Judge, 1995–. *Recreations:* tennis, ski-ing, sailing, opera. *Address:* (chambers) 24 Old Buildings, Lincoln's Inn, WC2A 3UJ. *T:* (020) 7404 0946. *Clubs:* Royal Automobile; Cumberland Lawn Tennis.

STELL, Prof. Philip Michael, FRCS, FRCSE; Professor of Oto-rhino-laryngology, University of Liverpool, 1979–92, now Emeritus; Research Associate, Centre for Medieval Studies, York, since 1996; *b* 14 Aug. 1934; *s* of Frank Law Stell and Ada Stell; *m* 1959, Shirley Kathleen Mills; four *s* one *d*. *Educ:* Archbishop Holgate's Grammar Sch., York; Edinburgh Univ. (MB, ChB 1958); York Univ. (MA with distinction, 1995). ChM Liverpool, 1976. FRCS 1966; FRCSE 1962. Jun. hosp. appts, Edinburgh and Liverpool, 1958–63; Fellow, Washington Univ., St Louis, USA, 1964–65; Sen. Lectr, Univ. of Liverpool, 1965–78. Hunterian Prof., RCS, 1976. President: Otorhinolaryngological Res. Soc., 1983–86; Assoc. of Head and Neck Oncologists of GB, 1986–89; Liverpool Med. Inst., 1986–87 and 1987–88; Sect. of Laryngology, RSM, 1990–91. Mem., Deutsche Akademie der Naturforscher Leopoldina, 1990. Hon. Life Member: Netherlands ENT Soc., 1992; N of England ENT Soc., 1993. Yearsley Gold Medal, 1980; Harrison Prize, RSM, 1982; Semon Medal, Univ. of London, 1986; George Davey Meml Prize, Univ. of London, 1987; Centenary Medal, Dudley Road Hosp., Birmingham, Gold Medal, Irish ENT Soc., 1988; Leegaard Medal, Norwegian ENT Soc., Gold Medal, Marie Curie Inst., Warsaw, Swedish Med. Assoc. Medal, Jobson Horne Prize, BMA, 1989; Gold Medal, German ENT Soc., 1991. *Publications:* approx. 20 books and over 300 articles in learned jls on surgery for cancer of head and neck. *Recreations:* history, gardening. *Address:* 69 The Village, Haxby, York YO32 2JE. *T:* (01904) 761469.

STELLINI, Salv. John; Permanent Secretary, Ministry of Foreign Affairs, Malta, since 1996; *b* 19 July 1939; *s* of Joseph and Victoria Stellini; *m* 1969, Lucinda Flannery; one *s* one *d*. *Educ:* Royal Univ. of Malta (BA Hons); Univ. of Alberta (MA); LSE (Dip. Int. Rel.). Teacher, 1959–65; Maltese Diplomatic Service, 1966–80: 2nd Sec., New York, 1968–71; 1st Sec., London, 1974–79; Dir for Internat. Marketing, 1981–87; Ambassador to USA, 1988–91; High Comr for Malta in London, 1991–96. *Recreations:* reading, visiting historical sites, museums, theatre. *Address:* Ministry of Foreign Affairs, Palazzo Parisio, Merchant's Street, Valletta CMR 02, Malta.

STELZER, Irwin Mark, PhD; Director, Regulatory Studies, and Senior Fellow, Hudson Institute, since 1998; President, Irwin M. Stelzer Associates, since 1981; Columnist, Sunday Times, since 1985; *b* 22 May 1932; *s* of Abraham Stelzer and Fanny Dolgins Stelzer; *m* 1981, Marian Faris Stuntz; one *s*. *Educ:* New York Univ. (BA 1951; MA 1952); Cornell Univ. (PhD 1954). Researcher and consultant, 1951–61; Lectr, New York Univ., and City Coll., NY, 1951–61; Teaching Asst, Cornell Univ., 1953–54; Instr, Univ. of Connecticut, 1954–55; Pres., Nat. Economic Res. Associates, 1961–81; Dir, Energy and Envmtl Policy Center, Harvard Univ., 1985–88; Resident Schol., American Enterprise Inst., 1990–98. Mem. Bd of Dirs, Regulatory Policy Inst., Oxford. Mem., Editl Bd, Public Interest. *Publications:* Selected Antitrust Cases: landmark decisions, 1955; The Antitrust Laws: a primer, 1996, 3rd edn 1998; contrib. to Public Interest, Commentary and other jls. *Recreation:* photography. *Address:* (office) 18b Charles Street, W1J 5DU. *Clubs:* Reform, Royal Automobile; Cosmos, Metropolitan (Washington).

STEMBRIDGE, David Harry; QC 1990; a Recorder of the Crown Court, 1977–97; *b* 23 Dec. 1932; *s* of Percy G. Stembridge and Emily W. Stembridge; *m* 1956, Therese C. Furer; three *s* one *d*. *Educ:* St Chad's Cathedral Choir Sch., Lichfield; Bromsgrove Sch.; Birmingham Univ. (LLB Hons). Called to the Bar, Gray's Inn, 1955; practising barrister, 1956–. *Recreations:* organ playing, sailing. *Address:* 5 Fountain Court, Steelhouse Lane, Birmingham B4 6DR; 199 Strand, WC2R 1DR. *Club:* Bar Yacht.

STEMPLOWSKI, Dr Ryszard; Director, Polish Institute of International Affairs, Warsaw, since 1999; Editor, Polish Diplomatic Review, since 2000; *b* 25 March 1939; *s* of Kazimierz Stemplowski and Eugenia Białecka; *m* 1st, 1964, Anita Zajaczkowska; 2nd, 1975, Irena Zasłona; two *d*. *Educ:* Tech. Lycée (Civil Build.), Bydgoszcz; Tech. Univ., Wrocław; Univ. of Wrocław (LLM 1968); Inst. of History, Polish Acad. of Scis (PhD 1973); Dr Habilitatus Warsaw Univ., 1999. Res. Fellow, Inst. of History, 1973–90; Chief of Chancellery of Sejm (Chamber of Deputies), Poland, 1990–93; Polish Ambassador to UK, 1994–99. Vis. Fellow, St Antony's Coll., Oxford, 1974; Vis. Prof., Oakland Univ., USA, 1976; Vis. Scholar and Alexander von Humboldt Fellow, Univ. of Cologne, 1981–82. Interfaith Golden Medallion, Peace Through Dialogue, UK, 1999. Kt Cross, Order of Polonia Restituta (Poland), 2000; Grand Cross of Merit, Constantinian Order of St George (House of Bourbon Two Sicilies), 1996. *Publications:* Dependence and Defiance: Argentina and rivalries among USA, UK and Germany 1930–46, 1975; (jtly) History of Latin America 1850–1980, 3 vols, 1978–80; (jtly) Economic Nationalism in East Central Europe and South America 1918–39, 1990; (jtly) The Slavic Settlers in Misiones 1897–1947, 1992; State-Socialism in Real Capitalism: Chile 1932, 1996; numerous other works and translations in Polish, German, Spanish, English. *Recreations:* music, astrophysics. *Address:* Polski Instytut Spraw Miedzynarodowych, ul. Warecka 1a, 00–950 Warszawa, Poland. *T:* (22) 8268939, *Fax:* (22) 8268882; *e-mail:* pism@pism.pl.

STENHAM, Anthony William Paul, (Cob); Chairman, Telewest Communications plc, since 1999 (Deputy Chairman, 1994–99); *b* 28 Jan. 1932; *s* of Bernard Basil Stenham and Annie Josephine (*née* Naylor); *m* 1st, 1966, Hon. Sheila Marion Poole (marr. diss.); 2nd, 1983, Anne Martha Mary O'Rawe; two *d. Educ:* Eton Coll.; Trinity Coll., Cambridge (MA). Qualified Accountant FCA 1958–98. Mem., Inner Temple, 1955. Price Waterhouse, 1955–61; Philip Hill Higginson Erlanger, 1962–64; William Baird & Co., 1964–69: Finance Dir and Jt Man. Dir; Unilever, 1969–86: Financial Dir, 1970–86, Corporate Develt Dir, 1984–86, Unilever PLC and Unilever NV; Chm., Unilever United States Inc., 1978–79; a Man. Dir, Bankers Trust Co. of NY, 1986–90 (Chm., Bankers Trust UK and Europe); Chm., Wiggins Teape Appleton, subseq. Arjo Wiggins Appleton plc, 1990–97. Director: Equity Capital for Industry, 1976–81; Capital Radio, 1982–94; Virgin Gp, 1986–89; Rank Organisation, 1987–96; Rank Gp, 1996–2000; VSEL plc, 1987–95 (Dep. Chm., 1989–); Rothmans Internat., 1988–99; Unigate, 1989–98; STC, 1990–91; Arjomari Prioux, 1990–93; Colonial Mutual Gp (UK Hldgs), 1987–92; Standard Chartered, 1991–; Worms et Cie, 1991–96; Trafalgar House, 1993–96; Jarrold & Sons Ltd, 1997–; Hawkpoint Partners, 1999–; Altanamara Shipping, 1999–; Proudfoot Consulting, 2000–; Chairman: Darfield Investments Ltd, 1997–; Whatsonwhen, 2000–; IFonline, 2000–. Sen. Industrialist Advr to DG of Water Services, 1998–. Institute of Contemporary Arts: Chm. Council, 1977–87; Chm., Adv. Bd, 1987–89; Mem. Council, Architectural Assoc., 1982–84; Royal Coll. of Art: Mem. Court, 1978–; Mem. Council, 1978–81; Chm. Council and Pro-Provost, 1979–81; Hon. Fellow, 1980. Governor: Museum of London, 1986–92; Theatres Trust, 1989–96. Trustee, Design Mus., 1992–96. FRSA. *Recreations:* cinema, opera, painting. *Address:* Telewest Communications plc, 160 Great Portland Street, W1N 5TB. *T:* (020) 7299 5562, *Fax:* (020) 7299 6560; *e-mail:* cob_stenham@flextech.co.uk; 4 The Grove, Highgate, N6 6JU. *T:* (020) 8340 2266, (020) 7839 7771; *e-mail:* awps@compuserve.com. *Clubs:* White's, Beefsteak.

STEPAN, Prof. Alfred, PhD; FBA 1997; Wallace S. Sayre Professor of Government, Columbia University, New York, since 1999; *b* 22 July 1936; *s* of Alfred C. Stepan, Jr and Mary Louise Quinn; *m* 1964, Nancy Leys; one *s* one *d. Educ:* Univ. of Notre Dame (BA 1958); Balliol Coll., Oxford (BA PPE 1960; MA 1963); Columbia Univ. (PhD Comparative Politics 1969). Special Corresp., Economist, 1964; Staff Mem., Social Sci. Dept, Rand Corp., 1966–69; Yale University: Asst Prof., Associate Prof., and Prof. of Political Science, 1970–83; Dir, Concilium on Internat. and Area Studies, 1982–83; Columbia University: Dean, Sch. of Internat. and Public Affairs, 1983–91, Prof. of Political Sci., 1983–87; Burgess Prof. of Political Sci., 1987–93; first Rector and Pres., Central European Univ., Budapest, Prague and Warsaw, 1993–96; Gladstone Prof. of Govt, and Fellow of All Souls Coll., Oxford Univ., 1996–99. Guggenheim Fellow, 1974–75; Vis Prof. and Lectr to numerous acad. bodies and confs, USA, Europe, S America and Asia. Former Member: Bd of Govs, Foreign Policy Assoc.; NEC, Americas Watch. Former Chm., Richard Tucker Music Foundn. Fellow, Amer. Acad. of Arts and Scis. Member, Editorial Board: Jl of Democracy, 1989–; Government and Opposition, 1996–. *Publications:* The Military in Politics: changing patterns in Brazil, 1971; The State and Society: Peru in comparative perspective, 1978; Rethinking Military Politics: Brazil and the southern cone, 1988; (with Juan J. Linz) Problems of Democratic Transition and Consolidation: Southern Europe, South America and post-Communist Europe, 1996; editor, jt editor and contrib. to numerous other works and learned jls. *Recreations:* opera, gardening, walking. *Address:* 210 Riverside Drive, New York, NY 10025, USA; 8 Frognal Gardens, NW3 6UX.

STEPHANOPOULOS, Konstantinos; President of Greece, since 1995; *b* Patras, 1926; *s* of Demetrius and Vrisiis Stephanopoulos; *m* 1959, Eugenia El Stounopoulou; two *s* one *d. Educ:* Univ. of Athens. Private law practice, 1954–74. MP for Achaia: (Nat. Radical Union), 1964; (New Democracy Party), 1974–89; (Party of Democratic Renewal), 1989–93; Under-Sec. of Commerce, 1974; Minister of the Interior, 1974–76; Minister of Social Services, 1976–77; Prime Minister's Office, 1977–81; Parly Rep., New Democracy Party, 1981–85; Leader, Party of Democratic Renewal, 1985–94. *Publications:* (jtly) The National Interest and Security Policy, 1995; (jtly) Nouvelles Etudes d'Histoire, vol. XI, 1995. *Address:* Presidential Palace, Herodou Atticou Street, Athens, Greece.

STEPHEN, Alexander, FCCA; Chief Executive, Dundee City Unitary Council, 1995–2000; *b* 17 Sept. 1948; *m* Joyce Robertson; one *s* one *d.* FCCA 1977. Local govt posts, 1970–; Chief Exec., Dundee City DC, 1991–95, Dundee CC, 1995–96. Treas., Revival, 1991–. *Address:* (office) c/o 21 City Square, Dundee DD1 3BY. *T:* (01382) 434201.

STEPHEN, Barrie Michael Lace; *see* Stephen, M.

STEPHEN, David; *see* Stephen, J. D.

STEPHEN, Derek Ronald James, CB 1975; Deputy Under-Secretary of State, Ministry of Defence, 1973–82; *b* 22 June 1922; *s* of late Ronald James Stephen; *m* 1948, Gwendolen Margaret, *d* of late William James Heasman, CBE; two *s* one *d* (and one *s* decd). *Educ:* Bec Sch.; Christ's Coll., Cambridge (1st cl. Hons Classics). Served War, 1941–45; 11th Hussars and HQ 7th Armoured Div., N Africa, Italy, NW Europe; Captain. Entered Admin. Class, Home Civil Service: Asst Principal, War Office, 1946; Asst Private Sec. to Sec. of State for War, 1949–50; Principal, 1951; Private Sec. to Sec. of Cabinet, 1958–60; Asst Sec., WO (later MoD), 1960; IDC 1966; HM Treasury, 1968; Civil Service Dept (on its formation), 1968; Under-Sec., 1969–71; Asst Under-Sec. of State, MoD, 1972–73; Dep. Under-Sec. of State (Navy), MoD, and Mem. Admiralty Bd, 1973–78; Dep. Under-Sec. of State (Army), MoD, and Mem., Army Bd, 1978–82; Asst Sec., Royal Hosp., Chelsea, 1982–88. Army Benevolent Fund: Member: Grants Cttee, 1984–99; Finance Cttee, 1988–99; Mem. Council, Royal Cambridge Home for Soldiers' Widows, 1987–2000. Trustee, Tank Museum, 1982–97. Gov., Royal Sch., Hampstead, 1984–99. *Recreations:* choral singing, listening to music, opera, golf. *Club:* Naval and Military.

STEPHEN, Dr (George) Martin; High Master, Manchester Grammar School, since 1994; *b* 18 July 1949; *s* of Sir Andrew Stephen, MB, ChB and late Lady Stephen (*née* Frances Barker); *m* 1971, Jennifer Elaine Fisher, JP; three *s. Educ:* Uppingham Sch.; Univ. of Leeds (BA); Univ. of Sheffield (Dip Ed, Dist., PhD; Hallam Prize for Educn, 1971). Child supervisor, Leeds and Oxford Remand Homes, 1966–67; Teacher of English, Uppingham, 1971–72, Haileybury, 1972–83 (and Housemaster); Second Master, Sedbergh, 1983–87; Headmaster, Perse Sch. for Boys, Cambridge, 1987–94. Vis. Lectr, Manchester Univ., 2001–02. Member: ESRC, 1990–; Naval Review, 1992–; Community Service Volunteers' Educnl Adv. Council, 1994–; HMC/GSA Univ. Admissions Working Gp, 1994–; British Assoc. for Sport and Law, 1995–; Chm., HMC Community Service Cttee, 1992–95. Associate Mem., Combination Room, GCCC, 1988–94. Member: Portico Library, Manchester, 1995–; Bd, Royal Exchange Theatre, Manchester, 1999–. Trustee, Project Trust, 1994–. Mem. Court, Univ. of Salford, 2000–; Governor: Withington Sch., Manchester, 1994–; Pownall Hall Sch., Wilmslow, 1994–; Ducie High Sch., Moss Side, 1995–. FRSA 1996. Hon. DEd De Montfort, 1997. *Publications:* An Introductory Guide to English Literature, 1984; Studying Shakespeare, 1984; British Warship Designs since 1906, 1985; English Literature, 1986, 4th edn 1999; (ed) Never Such Innocence, 1988, 3rd edn 1993; Sea Battles in Close Up, 1988, 2nd edn 1996; The Fighting Admirals, 1991; (ed) The Best of Saki, 1993, 2nd edn 1996; The Price of Pity: poetry, history and myth in the Great War, 1996; (contrib.) Machiavelli, Marketing and Management, 2000; Machiavelli's Choice, 2002; contrib. York Notes series; articles and reviews for various jls. *Recreations:* writing, directing plays, pen and ink drawing, field and water sports, music. *Address:* Manchester Grammar School, Manchester M13 0XT. *Club:* East India (Hon. Mem.).

STEPHEN, Henrietta Hamilton, (Rita), MBE 1973; National Officer, GMB, 1989–91; *b* 9 Dec. 1925; *d* of late James Pithie Stephen, engine driver, Montrose and late Mary Hamilton Morton, South Queensferry. *Educ:* Wolseley Street and King's Park Elem. Schs, Glasgow; Queen's Park Sen. Secondary, Glasgow; Glasgow Univ. (extra-mural); LSE (TUC Schol.). McGill Univ. and Canada/US Travel, 1958–59. Law office junior, 1941; Clerk, Labour Exchange (Mem. MLSA), 1941–42; Post Office Telephonist, 1942–60; Officer and delegate, Union of Post Office Workers, Glasgow Br., 1942–60; Member: UPW Parly Panel, 1957; London and Home Counties Area Organiser, CAWU, 1960–65; Nat. Sec., CAWU, subseq. APEX, 1965–89. Negotiator in public and private sectors of industry, 1960–91; Editor, The Clerk, 1965–71; Union Educn Officer, 1965–72; Delegate: TUC; Labour Party Annual Confs; Member: EDC for Food and Drink Manufacturing, 1976–90; Food Standards Cttee, 1968–80; Mary Macarthur Educnl Trust, 1965–; Distributive Industry Trng Bd, 1968–73; Monopolies and Mergers Commn, 1973–83; British Wool Marketing Bd, 1973–88; LSE Court, 1976–; Hon. Treas., Low Pay Unit, 1990–; Trustee, Mary Macarthur Holiday Trust, 1993– (Hon. Treas., 1991–). Mem., TUC Women's Adv. Cttee, 1983; Chair, Nat. Jt Cttee of Working Women's Organisations, 1983–84; Jt Sec., British Coal Nat. Jt Council (Clerical), 1988–90. Life Mem., Industrial Soc., 1992 (former Mem. Council and Exec.). *Publications:* (jtly) Training Shop Stewards, 1968; (with Roy Moore) Statistics for Negotiators, 1973; contrib. Clerk, Industrial Soc. Jl, Target, etc. *Recreations:* food, walking, conversation, travel, theatre, reading. *Address:* 3 Pond Road, SE3 9JL. *T:* (020) 8852 7797; *e-mail:* ritas@britishlibrary.net.

STEPHEN, (John) David; Representative of the UN Secretary-General, and Director, UN Office for Somalia, since 1997; *b* 3 April 1942; *s* of late John Stephen and Anne Eileen Stephen; *m* 1968, Susan Dorothy (*née* Harris); three *s* one *d. Educ:* Denbigh Road Primary Sch., Luton; Luton Grammar Sch.; King's Coll., Cambridge (BA Mod. Langs, 1964); Univ. of San Marcos, Lima, Peru; Univ. of Essex (MA Govt, 1968). Educn Officer, CRC, 1969–70; with Runnymede Trust, 1970–75 (Dir, 1973–75); Latin American Regional Rep., Internat. Univ. Exchange Fund, 1975–77; Special Adviser to Sec. of State for Foreign and Commonwealth Affairs, 1977–79; Editor, International Affairs, 1979–83; Dir, UK Immigrants Advisory Service, 1983–84; Commonwealth Development Corporation: Mem., Management Bd, 1985–92; Head of External Relations, 1985–89; Dir of Corporate Relns, 1989–92; Principal Officer, Exec. Office of Sec.-Gen., UN, 1992–96 and March–Sept 1997; Dir, UN Verification Mission, Guatemala, June 1996–Feb. 1997. Trustee, Action Aid, 1981–92. Contested (SDP-Liberal Alliance), N Luton, 1983, 1987. *Address:* 69 Shelley House, Churchill Gardens, SW1V 3JE.

STEPHEN, His Honour Lessel Bruce; a Circuit Judge, 1972–89; *b* 15 Feb. 1920; *s* of L. P. Stephen, FRCS(E); *m* 1949, Brenda (*née* Tinkler). *Educ:* Marlborough; Sydney Sussex Coll., Cambridge (BA). Called to the Bar, Inner Temple, 1948; subsequently practised NE Circuit; Recorder, 1972. *Recreations:* golf, wine. *Address:* 2 Harcourt Buildings, Temple, EC4Y 9DB. *T:* (020) 7353 2548.

STEPHEN, Martin; *see* Stephen, G. M.

STEPHEN, Mhairi Margaret; Sheriff of Lothian and Borders at Edinburgh (Floating), since 1997; *b* 22 Jan. 1954; *d* of William Strachan Stephen and Alexandrina Wood Stephen (*née* Grassam). *Educ:* George Watson's Ladies' Coll.; Univ. of Edinburgh (BA 1974; LLB 1976). With Allan McDougall & Co., SSC, Edinburgh, 1976–97, Partner, 1981–97. *Recreations:* curling, hill-walking, golf, music. *Address:* Edinburgh Sheriff Court, 27 Chambers Street, Edinburgh EH1 1LB. *T:* (0131) 225 2525. *Clubs:* Murrayfield Golf, Murrayfield Curling.

STEPHEN, Michael; international lawyer; *b* 25 Sept. 1942; *s* of late Harry Lace Stephen and of Edna Florence Stephen; *m* 1989, Virginia Mary (*née* de Trensé). *Educ:* King Henry VIII Sch., Coventry; Stanford Univ. (LLM 1971); Harvard Univ. Admitted Solicitor, 1964 (Dist. Company Law); called to the Bar, Inner Temple, 1966 (Hons); commissioned, The Life Guards, 1966–70; Harkness Fellowship in Internat. Law, 1970–72; Asst Legal Adviser, UK Delegn to UN, 1971; London Bar practice, 1973–87; Internat. Trade and Public Affairs Consultant, 1988–91. Member: RIIA, 1984–; IISS, 1994–. County Councillor, Dunmow, Essex, 1985–91; Mem., Nat. Exec., ACC, 1989–91; contested (C) Doncaster North, 1983. MP (C) Shoreham, 1992–97. Member: Select Cttee on the Environment, 1994–97; Trade and Industry Select Cttee, 1996–97; European Standing Cttee, 1994–97. Vice Chm., Cons. Parly Home Affairs and Legal Cttees, 1994–97. Author, Bail (Amendment) Act, 1993. *Publications:* The Cyprus Question, 1997, revd edn 2001; numerous political pamphlets. *Recreations:* tennis, sailing, history, theatre; *e-mail:* ms2@vizzavi.net. *Club:* Royal Automobile.

STEPHEN, Nicol Ross; Member (Lib Dem) Aberdeen South, Scottish Parliament, since 1999; *b* 23 March 1960; *s* of R. A. Nicol Stephen and Sheila G. Stephen; *m* Caris Doig; one *s* one *d. Educ:* Robert Gordon's Coll., Aberdeen; Aberdeen Univ. (LLB 1980); Edinburgh Univ. (DipLP 1981). Admitted Solicitor, 1983; C&PH Chalmers, 1981–83; Milne & Mackinnon, 1983–88; Sen. Corporate Finance Manager, Touche Ross & Co., 1988–90. Dir, Glassbox Ltd, 1992–99. Mem. (Lib Dem) Grampian Regl Council, 1982–92 (Chm., Econ. Develt and Planning Cttee, 1986–91). MP (Lib Dem) Kincardine and Deeside, Nov. 1991–1992. Dep. Minister for Enterprise and Lifelong Learning, 1999–2000; for Educn, Europe and Ext. Affairs, 2000–, Scottish Exec. Contested: Kincardine and Deeside, (L/All) 1987, (Lib Dem) 1992; (Lib Dem) Aberdeen S, 1997. *Recreations:* golf, swimming. *Address:* Scottish Parliament, Edinburgh EH99 1SP.

STEPHEN, Rt Hon. Sir Ninian (Martin), KG 1994; AK 1982; GCMG 1982; GCVO 1982; KBE 1972; PC 1979; Governor-General of Australia, 1982–89; *b* 15 June 1923; *o s* of late Frederick Stephen and Barbara Stephen (*née* Cruickshank); *m* 1949, Valery Mary, *d* of late A. Q. Sinclair and of Mrs G. M. Sinclair; five *d. Educ:* George Watson's Sch., Edinburgh; Edinburgh Acad.; St Paul's Sch., London; Chillon Coll., Switzerland; Scotch Coll., Melbourne; Melbourne Univ. (LLB). Served War, HM Forces (Australian Army), 1941–46. Admitted as Barrister and Solicitor, in State of Victoria, 1949; signed Roll of Victorian Bar, 1951; QC 1966. Appointed Judge of Supreme Court of Victoria, 1970; Justice of High Court of Australia, 1972–82; Australian Ambassador for the Envmt, 1989–92; Chm., Anglo-Irish Talks (2nd strand), 1992; Judge, Internat. War Crimes Tribunal for Yugoslavia, 1993–97; Chm., UN Expert Gp on Cambodia, 1998–99. Mem., Ethics Commn, IOC, 2000–. Hon. Bencher Gray's Inn, 1981. Chm., Nat. Liby of Aust., 1989–94. Hon. Liveryman, Clothworkers' Co., 1991. Hon. LLD: Sydney, 1984; Melbourne, 1985; Griffith, 1988; Hon. DLitt WA, 1993. KStJ 1982. Comdr, Legion of Honour (France), 1993. *Address:* Flat 13/1, 193 Domain Road, South Yarra, Vic 3141, Australia.

STEPHEN, Rita; *see* Stephen, H. H.

STEPHENS, Anthony William, CB 1989; CMG 1976; Deputy Under Secretary of State, Northern Ireland Office, 1985–90; *b* 9 Jan. 1930; *s* of late Donald Martyn Stephens and Norah Stephens (*née* Smith-Cleburne); *m* 1954, Mytyl Joy, *d* of late William Gay Burdett; four *d. Educ:* Bradfield Coll.; Bristol Univ. (LLB); Corpus Christi Coll., Cambridge. RM (commnd), 1948–50. Colonial Administrative Service, 1953; District Officer, Kenya, 1954–63; Home Civil Service, 1964; Principal, MoD, 1964–70; Asst Private Sec. to successive Secretaries of State for Defence, 1970–71; Asst Sec., 1971; Chief Officer, Sovereign Base Areas, Cyprus, 1974–76; Under Sec., NI Office, 1976–79; Asst Under Sec. of State, General Staff, 1979–83, Ordnance, 1983–84, MoD. Trustee and Sec., Sherborne House Trust, 1995–. *Recreations:* travel and the outdoor life, music, theatre. *Club:* Royal Over-Seas League.

STEPHENS, Barbara Marion, (Mrs T. J. Stephens); Chief Executive, Local Government Commission for England, since 1998; *b* 25 Aug. 1951; *d* of late Sydney and of Edna Webb; *m* 1970, Trevor James Stephens. *Educ:* Mid-Essex Technical Coll. (HNC Engrg); NE London Poly. (DMS); City Univ. (MBA Engrg Mgt). IEng; MIEE (MIProdE 1976); MIIE (MIET 1992). Mechanical technician apprentice, Marconi Co., 1969–73; various technical and managerial posts, Marconi Communication Systems Ltd, 1973–88; Industrial Advr, Electronic Applications, NEDO, 1988–92; Dir of Ops, then Chief Exec., W Cumbria Develt Agency, 1993–98. Member: Engineering Council, 1990–96; HEFCE, 1995–; Adv. Forum (formerly Council) for Develt of RN Personnel, 1995– (Chm., 2001–); Dir, Assoc. of MBAs, 2001–. Non-exec. Dir, Cumbria Ambulance Service NHS Trust, 1996–98. Lay Mem., Professional Conduct and Complaints Cttee, Gen. Council of Bar, 2000–. FIMgt 1994 (MBIM 1978); FRSA 1992. *Recreations:* embroidery, reading, letter-writing, encouraging women to pursue engineering careers. *Address:* Crook Hall, 28 High Seaton, Workington, Cumbria, CA14 1PD. *T:* (01900) 871095.

STEPHENS, Sir Barrie; *see* Stephens, Sir E. B.

STEPHENS, Prof. Christopher David, OBE 1999; FDSRCS, FDSRCSE; Professor of Child Dental Health, University of Bristol, since 1984; *b* 29 May 1942; *s* of late Wilfred Ernest Donnington Stephens, OBE, PhD, and of Phyllis Margaret Stephens (*née* Lecroissette); *m* 1966, Marion Kay Prest; two *s. Educ:* Dulwich Coll.; Guy's Hosp. Dental Sch. (BDS); MDS Bristol. DOrthRCS 1968, MOrthRCS 1988; FDSRCSE 1970; FDSRCS 1986. Hse Surgeon, 1965, Registrar in Children's Dentistry, 1966–69, Guy's Hosp. Dental Sch.; Registrar in Orthodontics, Royal Dental Hosp., 1969–71; Lectr in Orthodontics, 1971–76, Consultant Sen. Lectr in Orthodontics, 1976–84, Univ. of Bristol. Civil Consultant in Orthodontics to RAF, 1988–. Pres., British Orthodontic Soc., 2001–Sept. 2002. *Publications:* (jtly) Functional Orthodontic Appliances, 1990; (with K. G. Isaacson) Practical Orthodontic Assessment, 1990; (jtly) A Textbook of Orthodontics, 2nd edn 1992; contrib. numerous papers to refereed jls. *Recreations:* amateur radio, dry stone-walling, woodland management, walking. *Address:* University of Bristol Dental School, Lower Maudlin Street, Bristol BS1 2LY. *T:* (0117) 928 4355.

STEPHENS, Christopher Wilson Treeve; *see* Stephens, W. T.

STEPHENS, Sir (Edwin) Barrie, Kt 1998; CEng; Chairman, 1990–98, Hon. President, since 1998, Siebe plc. *Educ:* Christ Coll., Brecon; Manchester Univ. (Dip. Chem. Engrg). CEng 1962. Industrial Engr, General Dynamics, USA, 1954; Production Manager, Barden Corp., Conn, USA, 1962; Dir. of Manufg, Barden Corp. Ltd, UK, 1962–63; Man. Dir, Siebe Gorman and Co. Ltd, 1963–75; Gp Man. Dir and CEO, Siebe Gorman Hldgs Ltd, 1975–86; Vice-Chm., 1987–90, CEO, 1987–93, Siebe plc. Hon. DSc Plymouth, 1993. *Club:* Carlton.

STEPHENS, Jonathan Andrew de Sievrac; a Superintending Director, Joint Entry Clearance Unit, since 2001; *b* 8 Feb. 1960; *s* of Prescot and Peggy Stephens; *m* 1983, Rev. Penny; one *s* one *d. Educ:* Sevenoaks Sch.; Christ Church, Oxford (MA). NI Office, 1983–89; HM Treasury, 1989–92; Northern Ireland Office, 1992–2000: Principal Private Sec., 1993–94; Associate Pol Dir, 1996–2000; Dir, Modernising Public Services, Cabinet Office, 2000–01. *Address:* Joint Entry Clearance Unit, 89 Albert Embankment, SE1 7TP.

STEPHENS, Prof. Kenneth Gilbert, CEng, FIEE; CPhys, FInstP; Professor of Electronic and Electrical Engineering, 1978–96, now Emeritus, and Dean of the Faculty of Engineering, 1992–96, University of Surrey; *b* 3 May 1931; *s* of George Harry Stephens and Christiana Stephens; *m* 1980, Elizabeth Carolynn (*née* Jones); one *s* one *d*, and two step *s. Educ:* Bablake Sch., Coventry; Birmingham Univ. (BSc, PhD). Nuclear Reactor Res. Physicist, AEI Ltd, Aldermaston, 1955–62; Sen. Res. Engr, Pye Ltd, Cambridge, 1963–66; University of Surrey: Lectr 1966; Reader 1967; Head, Dept of Electronic and Electrical Engrg, 1983–91. *Publications:* (ed jtly) Low Energy Ion Beams (conf. procs), 1978, 1980; (ed jtly) Ion Implantation Technology (conf. procs), 1991; articles on ion beam effects on semiconductors in learned jls. *Recreations:* reading, music, gardening, watching sport, especially cricket. *Address:* 10 Brockway Close, Merrow, Guildford, Surrey GU1 2LW. *T:* (01483) 575087. *Clubs:* MCC; Blackheath Cricket, Surrey County Cricket.

STEPHENS, Malcolm George, CB 1991; Chairman: International Financial Consulting, since 1998; IFC Training, since 2001; *b* 14 July 1937; *s* of Frank Ernest Stephens and Janet (*née* McQueen); *m* 1975, Lynette Marie Caffery, Brisbane, Australia. *Educ:* St Michael's and All Angels; Shooter's Hill Grammar Sch.; St John's Coll., Oxford (Casberd Scholar; BA 1st Cl. Hons PPE; MA 1995). National Service, RAOC, 1956–58. CRO, 1953; British High Commission: Ghana, 1959–62; Kenya, 1963–65; Export Credits Guarantee Dept, 1965–82: Principal, 1970; seconded to Civil Service Coll., 1971–72; Asst Sec., 1974; Estab. Officer, 1977; Under Sec., 1978; Head of Proj. Gp B, 1978–79; Principal Finance Officer, 1979–82; Internat. Finance Dir, Barclays Bank Internat. Ltd, 1982–84; Dir, Barclays Export Services, 1984–87; Export Finance Dir, Barclays Bank PLC, 1985–87; Chief Executive: ECGD, 1987–91; London Chamber of Commerce and Industry, 1991–92; Pres., 1989–91, Sec.-Gen., 1992–98, Internat. Union of Credit and Investment Insurers (Berne Union); Man. Dir and Dep. Chm., Commonwealth Investment Guarantee Agency, 1998–99; Exec. Dir, IPCIS, 1999–2001. Chm., Del Credere Insurance Services Ltd, 1999–; Director: European Capital, 1992–2000; Arab-British Chamber of Commerce, 1992–95; Major Projects Assoc., 1995–99; Berry, Palmer & Lyle, 1997–; EULER Internat., 1998–2000. Consultant: to EU PHARE Prog., 1997–99; to World Bank, 1997–2001; Eur. Commn, 1999–2000; OECD (Russia), 1999–2000; Govt of Chile, 1999, of Bangladesh, 1999, of Iran, 2000–01, of Sri Lanka, 2000, of S Africa, 2000–01, of Australia, 2000–01, of NZ, 2001, of Turkey, 2001. Advr, CDR Internat., 1998–2000; Exec. Vice-Pres., SGA Internat., Florida, 1998–2000. Member: Overseas Projects Bd, 1985–87; BOTB, 1987–91. Vis. Schol., IMF, 1998–99. FCIB (FIB 1984); FIEx 1987; MICM 1990. *Publication:* The Changing Role of Export Credit Agencies, 1999. *Recreations:* gardening, reading, swimming, tapestry, watching cricket and football (Charlton Athletic). *Address:* 111 Woolwich Road, Bexleyheath, Kent DA7 4LP. *T:* (020) 8303 6782. *Club:* Travellers.

STEPHENS, Martin; *see* Stephens, S. M.

STEPHENS, Rev. Peter; *see* Stephens, Rev. W. P.

STEPHENS, Peter Norman Stuart; Director, News Group Newspapers, 1978–87, Editorial Director, 1981–87; *b* 19 Dec. 1927; *s* of J. G. Stephens; *m* 1950, Constance Mary Ratheram; two *s* one *d. Educ:* Mundella Grammar Sch., Nottingham. Newark Advertiser, 1945–48; Northern Echo, 1948–50; Daily Dispatch, 1950–55; Daily Mirror, Manchester, 1955–57; Asst Editor, Newcastle Journal, 1957–60; Asst Editor, Evening Chronicle, Newcastle, 1960–62, Editor 1962–66; Editor, Newcastle Journal, 1966–70; Asst Editor, The Sun, 1970–72, Dep. Editor 1972; Associate Editor, News of the World, 1973, Editor, 1974–75; Associate Editor, The Sun, 1975–81. *Publications:* Newark: the magic of malt, 1993; Grey Sanctuary: the story of the Newark Friary, 1996. *Recreations:* the printed word, supporting Derby County Football Club. *Address:* The Friary, Newark on Trent, Notts NG24 1JY.

STEPHENS, (Stephen) Martin; QC 1982; **His Honour Judge Stephens;** a Circuit Judge, since 1986; a Judge of the Central Criminal Court, since 1999; *b* 26 June 1939; *s* of late Abraham Stephens and Freda Stephens, Swansea; *m* 1965, Patricia Alison, *d* of late Joseph and Anne Morris, Mapperley, Nottingham; one *s* one *d* (and one *s* decd). *Educ:* Swansea Grammar Sch.; Wadham Coll., Oxford (MA). Called to the Bar, Middle Temple, 1963; Wales and Chester Circuit; a Recorder, 1979–86. Mem., Parole Bd, 1995–. Mem., Criminal Cttee, 1995–2000, Main Bd, 1997–2000, Judicial Studies Bd. *Recreations:* cricket, theatre. *Address:* c/o Central Criminal Court, Old Bailey, EC4M 7EH.

STEPHENS, Rev. Prof. (William) Peter; Minister of the Mint Church, Exeter, and Methodist Chaplain, University of Exeter, since 2000; Professor of Church History, University of Aberdeen, 1986–99; *b* 16 May 1934; *s* of Alfred Cyril William Joseph Stephens and Jennie Eudora Stephens (*née* Trewavas). *Educ:* Lescudjack Sch., Penzance; Truro Sch.; Clare Coll., Cambridge (MA, BD); Wesley House, Cambridge; Univs of Lund, Strasbourg (Docteur ès Sciences Religieuses) and Münster. Asst Tutor, Hartley Victoria Coll., Manchester, 1958–61; ordained, Methodist Ministry, 1960; Minister in Nottingham and Methodist Chaplain to Univ. of Nottingham, 1961–65; Minister, Shirley, Croydon, 1967–71; Ranmoor Prof. of Church History, Hartley Victoria Coll., Manchester, 1971–73; Randles Prof. of Historical and Systematic Theology, Wesley Coll., Bristol, 1973–80; Res. Fellow, 1980–81, Lectr in Church History, 1981–86, Queen's Coll., Birmingham; Dean, 1987–89, Provost 1989–90, Faculty of Divinity, Univ. of Aberdeen. Pres., Methodist Conf., 1998–99; Superintendent Minister, Plymouth Methodist Mission, 1999–2000. Mem., Bristol City Council, 1976–83. Mem. Central Cttee, Conf. of European Churches, 1974–92. Max Geilinger Prize, Switzerland, 1997. *Publications:* (trans. jtly) Luther's Works, Vol. 41, 1966; The Holy Spirit in the Theology of Martin Bucer, 1970; Faith and Love, 1971; The Theology of Huldrych Zwingli, 1986; Zwingli: An Introduction to His Thought, 1992; Methodism in Europe, 1993; (ed) The Bible, the Reformation and the Church, 1995; Zwingli: Einführung in sein Denken, 1997; Zwingli le théologien, 1999; contributions to religious works; articles and reviews in learned jls and other pubns. *Recreations:* squash, swimming, tennis, gardening, hill-walking, theatre, opera. *Address:* 70 Sweetbrier Lane, Exeter EX1 3AQ.

STEPHENS, Wilson (Treeve); Editor of The Field, 1950–77, Consultant 1987–90; Consultant, Country Illustrated (formerly Countryweek), since 1991; *b* 2 June 1912; *s* of Rev. Arthur Treeve Stephens, Shepton Beauchamp, Somerset, and Margaret Wilson; *m* 1st, 1934, Nina, *d* of Arthur Frederick Curzon, Derby; two *d*; 2nd, 1960, Marygold Anne, *o d* of Major-General G. O. Crawford, CB, CBE; two *d. Educ:* Christ's Hosp. Formerly on editorial staffs of several provincial newspapers, and of The Daily Express. Served War of 1939–45, Royal Artillery. *Publications:* The Guinness Guide to Field Sports, 1979; Gundog Sense and Sensibility, 1982, 3rd edn 2001; Pigeon Racing, 1983; A Year Observed, 1984; Rivers of Britain (series) 1985–; contribs to numerous publications. *Recreations:* fly-fishing, shooting. *Address:* c/o Blake, Friedmann, 122 Arlington Road, NW1 7HP.

STEPHENSON, Ashley; *see* Stephenson, R. A. S.

STEPHENSON, Darryl Leslie; Chief Executive, East Riding of Yorkshire Unitary Council, since 1995; *b* 4 Sept. 1950; *s* of late Lawrence Stephenson and of Olga Mary Stephenson; *m* 1984, Susan Marialuisa Lockwood; one *s* one *d. Educ:* Warwick Sch.; Trent Poly. (BA Hons); Coll. of Law, Chester; Univ. of Birmingham (Advanced Mgt Develt Prog., 1986). Admitted Solicitor, 1980. Articled Clerk, W Bromwich CBC, 1972–74; Solicitor, Warwick DC, 1974–80; Principal Asst Chief Exec., Leicester CC, 1980–89; Dep. Town Clerk, subseq. Town Clerk and Chief Exec., Hull CC, 1989–95. Co. Sec., Humber Forum Ltd, 1992–. Clerk to: Humber Bridge Bd, 1993–96; Humberside Police Authy, 1996–97; Lord Lieut, E Riding of Yorks, 1996–; Sec., N Eastern Sea Fisheries Cttee, 1996–. Chm., E Riding Drug Action Team, 1995–; Mem. Council, Hull and E Riding Chamber of Commerce, Industry and Shipping, 1995–. Mem. of Court, Univ. of Hull, 1993–; Gov., Beverley Coll., 1998–. *Recreations:* motor boating, music, painting, food and wine. *Address:* County Hall, Beverley, ER Yorks HU17 9BA. *T:* (01482) 884830. *Club:* Portcullis (Warwick).

STEPHENSON, George Anthony C.; *see* Carter-Stephenson.

STEPHENSON, Sir Henry Upton, 3rd Bt *cr* 1936; TD; Director: Stephenson Blake & Co. Ltd, 1952–75; Stephenson, Blake (Holdings) Ltd, 1972–99; *b* 26 Nov. 1926; *s* of Lt-Col Sir Henry Francis Blake Stephenson, 2nd Bt, OBE, TD, and Joan, *d* of Major John Herbert Upton (formerly Upton Cottrell-Dormer); *S* father, 1982; *m* 1962, Susan, *o d* of Major J. E. Clowes, Ashbourne, Derbyshire; four *d. Educ:* Eton. Formerly Major, QO Yorkshire Dragoons. High Sheriff of Derbyshire, 1975. *Heir: cousin* Timothy Hugh

Stephenson [*b* 5 Jan. 1930; *m* 1959, Susan Lesley, *yr d* of late George Arthur Harris; two *s*]. *Address:* Tissington Cottage, Rowland, Bakewell, Derbyshire DE45 1NR.

STEPHENSON, Prof. Hugh; writer and journalist; Professor of Journalism, City University, since 1986; *b* 18 July 1938; *s* of late Sir Hugh Stephenson; *m* 1st, 1962, Auriol Stevens, *qv* (marr. diss. 1987); two *s* one *d*; 2nd, 1990, Diana Eden. *Educ:* Winchester Coll.; New Coll., Oxford (BA); Univ. of Calif, Berkeley. Pres., Oxford Union, 1962. HM Diplomatic Service, 1964–68; joined The Times, 1968; Editor, The Times Business News, 1972–81; Editor, The New Statesman, 1982–86. Mem., Cttee to Review Functioning of Financial Instns, 1977–80. Councillor, London Bor. of Wandsworth, 1971–78. Dir, History Today Ltd, 1981–. FRSA 1987. *Publications:* The Coming Clash, 1972; Mrs Thatcher's First Year, 1980; Claret and Chips, 1982; (jtly) Libel and the Media, 1997. *Address:* Department of Journalism, City University, Northampton Square, EC1V 0HB.

STEPHENSON, His Honour Jim; a Circuit Judge, 1983–98; *b* 17 July 1932; *s* of late Alex and Norah Stephenson, Heworth, Co. Durham; *m* 1964, Jill Christine, *d* of late Dr Lindeck, Fairwarp, Sussex; three *s*. *Educ:* Royal Grammar Sch. and Dame Allan's Sch., Newcastle; Exeter Coll., Oxford (Exhibnr, BA). Pres., Oxford Univ. Law Society, Michaelmas, 1955. Called to Bar, Gray's Inn, 1957. Mem., General Council of the Bar, 1961–64; Junior, NE Circuit, 1961; a Recorder of the Crown Court, 1974–83. Pres., NE Br., Magistrates' Assoc., 1988–92. Additional Mem. of Bd, Faculty of Law, Newcastle Univ., 1984–90. Gov., Newcastle Prep. Sch., 1985–92. *Recreations:* reading, travel, history. *Address:* Garth House, Wetheral, Carlisle CA4 8JN. *T:* (01228) 560986.

STEPHENSON, Maj.-Gen. John Aubrey, CB 1982; OBE 1971; defence consultant, 1991–93; Managing Director, Weapon Systems Ltd, 1982–91; Deputy Master General of the Ordnance, 1980–81; *b* 15 May 1929; *s* of Reginald Jack Stephenson and Florence Stephenson; *m* 1953, Sheila Colbeck; two *s* one *d*. *Educ:* Dorchester Grammar School. Commnd RA, 1948; served Malaya (despatches, 1951), Libya, Canal Zone and Germany, 1949–58 (student pilot, 1953–54); student, RMCS, 1958–60; 39 Missile Regt, 1960–61; student, RMCS and Staff Coll., 1961–62; served UK and Germany, 1962–67; Staff, RMCS, 1967–69; CO 16 Light Air Defence Regt RA, 1969–71; Project Manager, 155mm Systems, Woolwich, 1971–73; student, RCDS, 1974; Comdr, 1st Artillery Bde, Germany, 1975–77; Sen. Mil. Officer, RARDE, 1977–78; Dir Gen. Weapons (Army), 1978–80. Dir, ATX Ltd, 1984–91. Col Comdt, RA, 1984–89; Hon. Regtl Col, 16 Regt (formerly 16 Light Air Defence Regt), RA, 1989–95. Governor, The Dorchester Thomas Hardye Sch. (formerly Hardye's Sch.), 1984–96. FIMgt. *Recreations:* fishing, sailing, gardening, bridge, golf, military history. *Address:* Collingwood, 27 Trafalgar Way, Stockbridge, Hants SO20 6ET. *T:* (01264) 810458. *Club:* Royal Over-Seas League.

STEPHENSON, Lt-Col John Robin, CBE 1994 (OBE (mil.) 1976); Secretary: Marylebone Cricket Club, 1987–93; International Cricket Council (formerly International Cricket Conference), 1987–93; *b* 25 Feb. 1931; *s* of John Stewart Stephenson and Edith Gerda Greenwell Stephenson; *m* 1962, Karen Margrethe Koppang; one *s* two *d*. *Educ:* Christ's Hospital; RMA Sandhurst. Commissioned Royal Sussex Regt, 1951; served Egypt, Korea, Gibraltar, Libya, Germany, N Ireland; Instructor, Mons Officer Cadet Sch., 1958–60; Infantry Rep., Sch. of Signals, 1968–70; SOWC, 1972–73; Comdg Officer, 5 (V) Queen's Regt, 1973–75; Dep. Pres., Regular Commissions Bd, 1976; Staff Officer, Cs-in-C Cttee, 1977–79. Asst Sec. (Cricket), MCC, 1979–86; managed MCC tours, Bangladesh, 1979–80, 2000, E Africa, 1980–81, Canada, 1985, Kenya, 1993. President: Forty Club, 1994–96; Stragglers of Asia CC, 1994–. Governor: St Bede's Sch., Eastbourne, 1989–94; Clayesmore Sch., Dorset, 1989–2000; Chm. Governors, Leaden Hall Sch., Salisbury, 1995–. Order of Orange-Nassau, 1972. *Recreations:* Rugby football (RMA Sandhurst (Capt.), Richmond, Army, Sussex), cricket (RMA Sandhurst, Army), golf, boating, gardening. *Address:* Plum Tree Cottage, Barford St Martin, Salisbury, Wilts SP3 4BL. *T:* (01722) 743443. *Clubs:* East India, Farmers', MCC (Mem. Cttee, 2000–); IZ, Free Foresters, Stragglers of Asia.

STEPHENSON, Lynne, (Mrs Chaim Stephenson); *see* Banks, L. R.

STEPHENSON, Margaret Maud; *see* Tyzack, M. M.

STEPHENSON, Prof. Patrick Hay, MA, CEng, FIMechE; retired consultant Mechanical Engineer; *b* 31 March 1916; *e s* of late Stanley George Stephenson and Florence (*née* Atkinson); *m* 1947, Pauline Roberts (decd); two *s* one *d*. *Educ:* Wyggeston Sch., Leicester; Cambridge Univ. (MA). Apprenticeship and Research Engr, Brit. United Shoe Machinery Co., 1932–39. War Service as Ordnance Mechanical Engr and REME, India and Far East, 1939–45; held as POW by Japanese, 1942–45. Chief Mechanical Engr, Pye Ltd, 1949–67; Prof. of Mech. Engrg, Univ. of Strathclyde, 1967–79; Dir, Inst. of Advanced Machine Tool and Control Technology, Min. of Technology, 1967–70; Dir, Birniehill Inst. and Manufacturing Systems Group, DTI, 1970–72; Head of Research Requirements Branch 2, DoI, 1972–77. Research advisor to Institution of Mechanical Engineers; senior industrial advisor to the Design Council. Mem. Council, IMechE, 1960–68; Member: Bd, UKAC, 1964–73; Engrg Bd, SRC, 1973–. *Publications:* papers and articles in technical press. *Recreations:* music, vintage motoring. *Address:* Toft Lane, Great Wilbraham, Cambridge CB1 5JH. *T:* (01223) 880405.

STEPHENSON, Paul; Regional Director, Wales and the West, Focus Consultancy Ltd, since 1992; *b* 6 May 1937; *s* of Olive Stephenson; *m* 1965, Joyce Annikie; one *s* one *d*. *Educ:* Westhill Coll. of Educn, Selly Oak, Birmingham. MIPR 1978. Youth Tutor, St Paul's, Bristol, 1962–68; Sen. Community Relations Officer, Coventry, 1968–72; National Youth Trng Officer, Community Relations Commn, 1972–77; Sen. Liaison Officer, CRE, 1980–92. Chm., Muhammad Ali Sports Develt Assoc., Brixton and Lambeth, 1974–; Member: British Sports Council, 1976–82; Press Council, 1984–90. *Recreations:* travel, cinema, reading, international politics. *Address:* 12 Downs Park East, Westbury Park, Bristol BS6 7QD. *T:* (0117) 962 3638; Focus Consultancy Ltd, Elmsgate House, Steeple Aston, Wilts BA14 6HP.

STEPHENSON, (Robert) Ashley (Shute), LVO 1990 (MVO 1979); FIHort; Bailiff of the Royal Parks, 1980–90; *b* 1 Sept. 1927; *s* of late James Stephenson and Agnes Maud Stephenson; *m* 1955, Isabel Dunn; one *s* one *d*. *Educ:* Walbottle Secondary Sch. Diploma in Horticulture, RHS, Wisley, 1954; MIHort 1987, FIHort 1998. Apprenticeship, Newcastle upon Tyne Parks Dept, 1942; served RASC, Palestine and Cyprus, 1946; Landscape Gardener, Donald Ireland Ltd, 1949; Student, RHS's gardens, Wisley, 1952; Royal Parks, 1954–: Supt, Regent's Park, 1969; Supt, Central Royal Parks, 1972. Gardening Correspondent, The Times, 1982–87. President: British Pelargonium and Geranium Soc., 1983–95; South East in Bloom, 2001– (Chm., 1990–2001); Member: Cttee, RHS, 1981–; London in Bloom Cttee, English Tourism Council (formerly English Tourist Bd), 1980– (Vice-Chm., 1983); Chm., Floral Jersey, 1990–; Nat. Chm., Britain in Bloom, 1991–; Mem., The Queen's Anniversary Cttee 1952–92, 1992– (Chm., Horticl Cttee, 1992–). Contributor to television and radio programmes; regularly on BBC Radio Sussex gardening programmes; gardening correspondent to professional and amateur papers. *Publications:* The Garden Planner, 1981; contribs to nat. press. *Recreations:* sport, judging horticultural shows, natural history, walking, golf. *Address:* 17 Sandore Road, Seaford, E Sussex BN25 3PZ.

STEPHENSON, Stanley, CMG 1987; HM Diplomatic Service, retired; *b* 30 Sept. 1926; *s* of George Stephenson and Margaret Jane (*née* Nicholson); *m* 1957, Grace Claire Lyons (*d* 1987); one *s* one *d*. *Educ:* Bede Sch., Sunderland. Inland Revenue, 1942; Royal Navy, 1944–48; Foreign (later Diplomatic) Service, 1948–: Cairo, Jedda, Damascus, Curaçao, Ciudad Trujillo (now Santo Domingo), San José, Seoul, Santiago de Cuba, Bogotá (twice), Asunción, San Francisco, FCO; Diplomatic Service Inspector, 1978–80; Ambassador to Panama, 1981–83; Consul-Gen., Vancouver, 1983–86. *Recreations:* tennis, cricket, Rugby, theatre, gardening. *Address:* Marymount, Raggleswood, Chislehurst, Kent BR7 5NH. *T:* (020) 8467 6066. *Clubs:* Civil Service; Crescent Lawn Tennis (Sidcup).

STEPHENSON, Air Vice-Marshal Tom Birkett, CB 1982; Assistant Chief of Defence Staff (Signals), 1980–82, retired; *b* 18 Aug. 1926; *s* of Richard and Isabel Stephenson; *m* 1951, Rosemary Patricia (*née* Kaye) (*d* 1984); one *s* three *d*. *Educ:* Workington Secondary Sch.; Manchester Univ.; Southampton Univ. (DipEl). Commissioned in RAF Engrg Branch, 1945; Staff Coll., 1962; Wing Comdr, Station and Staff appointments, until 1967; Command Electrical Engr, HQASC, 1967–69; Dep. Director Op. Requirements, 1969–72; AOEng, HQ NEAF, 1972–74; RCDS 1975; Director of Signals (Air), 1976–79. *Recreations:* sport, walking, reading. *Address:* c/o National Westminster Bank, High Street, Maidenhead SL6 1PY. *Club:* Royal Air Force.

STEPNEY, Area Bishop of, since 1996; **Rt Rev. John Mugabi Tucker Sentamu,** PhD; *b* 10 June 1949; *s* of John Walakira and Ruth; *m* 1973, Margaret (*née* Wanambwa); one *s* one *d*. *Educ:* Masooli, Kyambogo and Kitante Hill and Old Kampala Sch., Uganda; Makere Univ.(LLB 1971); Selwyn Coll., Cambridge (Pattison Student; BA 1976; MPhil 1979; MA, PhD 1984); Ridley Hall, Cambridge; Dip. in Legal Practice, Uganda, 1972. Advocate, Uganda High Ct, 1971–74. Ordained deacon and priest, 1979; Asst Chaplain, Selwyn Coll., Cambridge, 1979; Asst Curate, St Andrew, Ham, and Chaplain, HM Remand Centre, Latchmere House, 1979–82; Asst Curate, St Paul, Herne Hill, 1982–83; Priest-in-charge, Holy Trinity, and Vicar, St Matthias, Tulse Hill, 1983–84, Vicar of jt parish, 1985–96; Priest-in-charge, St Saviour, Brixton Hill, 1987–89. Hon. Canon, Southwark Cathedral, 1993–96. Mem., Gen. Synod of C of E, 1985–96; Chm., Cttee for Minority Ethnic Anglican Concerns, 1990–99. Member: Young Offenders Cttee, NACRO, 1986–95; Council, Family Welfare Assoc., 1989–; Stephen Lawrence Judicial Inquiry, 1997–99; Chm., London Marriage Guidance Council, 2000–. Freeman, City of London, 2000. Fellow: Canterbury Christ Church UC; QMW. DUniv Open. *Recreations:* music, cooking, reading. *Address:* 63 Coborn Road, Bow, E3 2DB. *T:* (020) 8981 2323.

STERLING, family name of **Baron Sterling of Plaistow**.

STERLING OF PLAISTOW, Baron *cr* 1991 (Life Peer), of Pall Mall in the City of Westminster; **Jeffrey Maurice Sterling,** Kt 1985; CBE 1977; Chairman: The Peninsular and Oriental Steam Navigation Company, since 1983; P&O Princess Cruises, 2000–Oct. 2002; *b* 27 Dec. 1934; *s* of late Harry and of Alice Sterling; *m* 1985, Dorothy Ann Smith; one *d*. *Educ:* Reigate Grammar Sch.; Preston Manor County Sch.; Guildhall School of Music. Paul Schweder & Co. (Stock Exchange), 1955–57; G. Eberstadt & Co., 1957–62; Fin. Dir, General Guarantee Corp., 1962–64; Man. Dir, Gula Investments Ltd, 1964–69; Chm., Sterling Guarantee Trust plc, 1969–85, when it merged with P&O Steam Navigation Co. Mem., British Airways Bd, 1979–82. Special Advr to Sec. of State for Industry, later for Trade and Industry, 1982–90. Mem. Exec., 1966–, Chm. Organisation Cttee, 1969–73, World ORT Union; Chm., ORT Technical Services, 1974–; Vice-Pres., British ORT, 1978–; President: Gen. Council of British Shipping, 1990–91; EC Shipowners' Assocs, 1992–94. Dep. Chm. and Hon. Treasurer, London Celebrations Cttee, Queen's Silver Jubilee, 1975–83. Chm., Young Vic Co., 1975–83; Chm., of the Governors, Royal Ballet Sch., 1983–99; Gov., Royal Ballet, 1986–99; Chm., Motability, 1994– (Chm. Exec., 1977–). Freeman, City of London. Hon. Captain, RNR, 1991. Elder Brother, Trinity House, 1991. Hon. FIMarE 1991; Hon. FICS 1992; Hon. MRICS 1993; FSVA 1995; Hon. FRINA 1997. Hon. DBA Nottingham Trent, 1995; Hon. DCL Durham, 1996. KStJ 1998. *Recreations:* music, swimming, tennis. *Address:* The Peninsular and Oriental Steam Navigation Company, 79 Pall Mall, SW1Y 5EJ. *Clubs:* Garrick, Carlton, Hurlingham.

STERLING, Dr (Isobel Jane) Nuala, CBE 1993; FRCP; Consultant Physician in Geriatric Medicine, Southampton University Hospitals NHS Trust (formerly Royal South Hants Hospital), since 1979; *b* 12 Feb. 1937; *d* of Prof. F. Bradbury and Mrs J. Bradbury; *m* 1961, Dr G. M. Sterling; five *s* (one *d* decd). *Educ:* Friends' Sch., Saffron Walden; King's Coll. and St George's Hosp., London (MB BS 1960). MRCS LRCP 1960; MRCP 1971, FRCP 1981. House Officer and Registrar posts, St George's Hosp., 1960–67; in general practice: London, 1963–64; Oxford, 1968; Lectr in Medicine, Univ. of Calif., San Francisco, 1969–70; Sen. House Officer then Registrar, Oxford, 1970–71; Sen. Registrar and Lectr in Geriatric Medicine, Southampton Univ. Hosps, 1972–79. Member: Standing Med. Adv. Cttee to Sec. of State for Health, 1986–96 (Chm., 1990–94); Clinical Standards Adv. Gp, 1990–94; Indep. Review Panel on Advertising of Medicines, 2000–; Vice-Chairman: Wessex Regl Adv. Cttee on Distinction Awards, 1998–99; Southern Regl Adv. Cttee on Distinction Awards, 2000–Oct. 2002. Royal College of Physicians: Chm., Standing Cttee of Mems, 1978–79; Mem., Jt Consultants Cttee, 1986–92; Pres., Medical Women's Fedn, 1989–90. *Publications:* research publications on immunology and cancer, endocrine and respiratory disorders in the elderly, provision of medical services and training. *Recreations:* music, modern art, growing orchids, watching cricket. *Address:* Southampton General Hospital, Southampton SO16 6YD.

STERLING, Michael John Howard, FREng, FIEE; FInstMC; Vice-Chancellor, Birmingham University, since 2001; *b* 9 Feb. 1946; *s* of Richard Howard Sterling and Joan Valeria Sterling (*née* Skinner); *m* 1969, Wendy Karla Anstead; two *s*. *Educ:* Hampton Grammar Sch., Middx; Univ. of Sheffield (BEng 1968; PhD 1971; DEng 1988). CEng 1975. Student apprentice, AEI, 1964–68; research engineer, GEC-Eliott Process Automation, 1968–71; Sheffield University: Lectr in Control Engineering, 1971–78; Industrial Liaison Officer, 1976–80; Sen. Lectr in Control Engineering, 1978–80; Prof. of Engineering, Univ. of Durham, 1980–90 (Dir, Microprocessor Centre, 1980–85); Vice-Chancellor and Princ., Brunel Univ., 1990–2001. Chairman: OCEPS Ltd, 1990–; WASMACS Ltd, 1994–. Member: UUK (formerly CVCP), 1990– (Mem. Council, 1994–95); Cttee for Internat. Co-op. in Higher Educn, British Council, 1991–96. Chairman: Univs Statistical Record, 1992–95; Higher Educn Stats Agency, 1992–; Jt Performance Indicators Wkg Gp, Higher Educn Councils for England, Scotland and Wales, 1992–95; Member: Quality Assessment Cttee, 1992–95, Additional Student Numbers and Funds Adv. Gp, 1997–99, HEFCE; Mech. Aeronautical and Prodn Engrg Assessment Panel, RAE, 1992, 1996. Member: Electricity Supply Res. Council, 1987–89; ESRC, 1987–89; Engrg Bd, SERC, 1989–92; Engrg Council, 1994–96. FREng (FEng 1991; Mem., Standing Cttee for Educn, Trng and Competence to Practise, 1993–97); FInstMC 1983 (Mem. Cttee, 1975–80, Chm., 1979–80, S Yorks Sect.; Mem. Council,

1983–91; Vice Pres., 1985–88; Nat. Pres., 1988); FIEE 1985 (Mem. Council, 1991–93 and 1997–; Vice-Pres., 1997–; Chm., Qualifications Bd, 1997–). FRSA 1984. Dir, W London TEC, 1999– (Dir, Charitable Trust, 1999–). Governor: Hampton Sch., 1991– (Chm., 1997–); Burnham Grammar Sch., 1991–. Trustee, Hillingdon Partnership Trust, 1993–98. Freeman, City of London, 1996; Liveryman, Engineers' Co., 1998–. Hon. DEng Sheffield, 1995. *Publications:* Power Systems Control, 1978; contribs to: Large Scale Systems Engineering Applications, 1980; Computer Control of Industrial Processes, 1982; Real Time Computer Control, 1984; Comparative Models for Electrical Load Forecasting, 1985; over 120 papers in learned jls. *Recreations:* gardening, DIY, computers, model engineering. *Address:* Birmingham University, Birmingham B15 2TT.

STERLING, Nuala; *see* Sterling, I. J. N.

STERN, Baroness *cr* 1999 (Life Peer), of Vauxhall, in the London Borough of Lambeth; **Vivien Helen Stern,** CBE 1992; Secretary-General, Penal Reform International, since 1989; Senior Research Fellow, International Centre for Prison Studies, King's College, London, since 1997; *b* 25 Sept. 1941; *d* of Frederick Stern and Renate Mills. *Educ:* Kent Coll., Pembury, Kent; Bristol Univ. (BA, MLitt, CertEd). Lectr in Further Educn until 1970; Community Relations Commn, 1970–77; Dir, NACRO, 1977–96. Vis. Fellow, Nuffield Coll., Oxford, 1984–91. Member: Special Programmes Bd, Manpower Services Commn, 1980–82; Youth Training Bd, 1982–88; Gen. Adv. Council, IBA, 1982–87; Cttee on the Prison Disciplinary System, 1984–85; Adv. Council, PSI, 1993–96; Bd, Assoc. for Prevention of Torture, Geneva, 1993–99; Bd, Eisenhower Foundn, Washington, 1993–; Law Adv. Council, British Council, 1995–. Mem., Select Cttee on EU, H of L. Pres., New Bridge, 2000–. Hon. Fellow, LSE, 1997. Hon. LLD: Bristol, 1990; Oxford Brookes, 1996. Margaret Mead Award for contribution to social justice, Internat. Assoc. for Residential & Community Alternatives, 1995. *Publications:* Bricks of Shame, 1987; Imprisoned by Our Prisons, 1989; Deprived of their Liberty, a report for Caribbean Rights, 1990; A Sin Against the Future: imprisonment in the world, 1998; Alternatives to Prison in Developing Countries, 1999; (ed) Sentenced to Die?: the problem of TB in prisons in Eastern Europe and Central Asia, 1999. *Address:* International Centre for Prison Studies, School of Law, King's College, 75–79 York Road, SE1 7AW.

STERN, Linda Joy; QC 1991; **Her Honour Judge Stern;** a Circuit Judge, since 2001; *b* 21 Dec. 1941; *d* of late Mrs L. R. Saville; *m* 1st, 1961, Michael Brian Rose (decd); two *s*; 2nd, 1978, Nigel Maurice Stern. *Educ:* St Paul's Girls' Sch. Called to the Bar, Gray's Inn, 1971; Mem., S Eastern Circuit. A Recorder, 1990–2001. FRSA 1993. *Recreations:* music, theatre, reading, travel. *Address:* The Law Courts, Lordship Lane, Wood Green, N22 5LF.

STERN, Michael Charles, FCA; Proprietor, Michael Stern & Co., since 1998; *b* 3 Aug. 1942; *s* of late Maurice Leonard Stern and of Rose Stern; *m* 1976, Jillian Denise Aldridge; one *d*. *Educ:* Christ's College Grammar School, Finchley. Mem. ICA 1964; FCA 1969. Partner, Percy Phillips & Co., Accountants, 1964–80; Partner, Halpern & Woolf, Chartered Accountants, 1980–92; Consultant, Cohen Arnold & Co., 1992–98. Chm., The Bow Group, 1977–78; co-opted Mem., Educn Cttee, Borough of Ealing, 1980–83. Contested (C) Derby S, 1979. MP (C) Bristol NW, 1983–97; contested (C) same seat, 1997. PPS to Minister of State, HM Treasury, 1986–87, to Paymaster General, 1987–89, to Minister for Corporate Affairs, DTI, 1991. Chief Finance Officer, 1990–91, Vice-Chm., 1991–92, Cons. party. *Publications:* papers for The Bow Group. *Recreations:* fell walking, bridge, chess. *Address:* 61 Shalimar Gardens, Acton, W3 9JG. *Clubs:* Royal Automobile, United and Cecil, London Mountaineering.

STERN, Prof. Nicholas Herbert, FBA 1993; Chief Economist and Senior Vice-President, World Bank, since 2000; *b* 22 April 1946; *s* of Adalbert Stern and Marion Fatima Stern; *m* 1968, Susan Ruth (*née* Chesterton); two *s* one *d*. *Educ:* Peterhouse, Cambridge (BA Mathematics); Nuffield Coll., Oxford (DPhilEcon). Jun. Res. Fellow, The Queen's Coll., Oxford, 1969–70; Fellow/Tutor in Econs, St Catherine's Coll., and Univ. Lectr, Oxford, 1970–77; Prof. of Econs, Univ. of Warwick, 1978–85; Sir John Hicks Prof. of Econs, LSE, 1986–97; Chief Economist, 1994–99, and Special Counsellor to Pres., 1997, EBRD; Jt Chm., London Economics, 1999–2000. Research Associate/Visiting Professor: MIT, 1972; Ecole Polytech., 1977; Indian Statistical Inst. (Overseas Vis. Fellow of British Acad., 1974–75, and Ford Foundn Vis. Prof., 1981–82); People's Univ. of China, Beijing, 1988; LSE, 1997–; Hon. Prof., People's Univ. of China, 2001. For. Hon. Mem., Amer. Acad. of Arts and Scis, 1998. Fellow, Econometric Soc., 1978. Hon. Fellow, St Catherine's Coll., Oxford, 2000. Editor, Journal of Public Economics, 1980–98. *Publications:* An Appraisal of Tea Production on Smallholdings in Kenya, 1972; (ed jtly) Theories of Economic Growth, 1973; (jtly) Crime, the Police and Criminal Statistics, 1979; (jtly) Palanpur: the economy of an Indian village, 1982; (jtly) The Theory of Taxation for Developing Countries, 1987; (with P. Lanjouw) Economic Development in Palanpur over Five Decades, 1998; articles in Econ. Jl, Rev. of Econ. Studies, Jl of Public Econs, Jl of Develt Econs, and others. *Recreations:* reading novels, walking, watching sport, food. *Address:* World Bank, 1818 H Street NW, Washington, DC 20433, USA.

STERNBERG, Sir Sigmund, Kt 1976; JP; Chairman, Martin Slowe Estates Ltd, since 1971; *b* Budapest, 2 June 1921; *s* of late Abraham and Elizabeth Sternberg; *m* 1970, Hazel (*née* Everett Jones); one *s* one *d*, and one *s* one *d* from a previous marriage. Vice Pres., Labour Finance and Industry Gp, 2001– (Dep. Chm., 1972–93). Chm., St Charles Gp, HMC, 1974; Sen. Vice-Pres., Royal Coll. of Speech and Language Therapists, 1995–; Chm., Inst. for Archaeo-Metallurgical Studies. Pres., Reform Synagogues of GB, 1998–; Patron, Internat. Council of Christians and Jews; Mem., Board of Deputies of British Jews; Governor, Hebrew Univ. of Jerusalem; Life Pres., Sternberg Centre for Judaism, 1996; Founder: Three Faiths Forum (Christians, Muslims & Jews Dialogue Gp), 1997; Human Business Partnership, 1998. Life Mem., Magistrates' Assoc., 1965. Mem., John Templeton Foundn, 1998– (Templeton Prize for Progress in Religion, 1998). Mem., Court, Essex Univ.; Vis. Prof., Moderna Univ., Lisbon, 1998. Freeman, City of London, 1970; Liveryman, Co. of Horners. JP Middlesex, 1965. FRSA 1979. Hon. FCST 1989; Hon. Fellow, UCL, 2001. DU: Essex, 1996; Hebrew Union Coll., Cincinnati, 2000; DUniv Open, 1998. Paul Harris Fellow, Rotary Foundn of Rotary Internat., 1989 (Rotary Internat. Award of Honour, 1998); Medal of Merit, Warsaw Univ., 1995; Wilhelm Leuschner Medal, Wiesbaden, 1998. Order of the Orthodox Hospitallers, First Class with Star and Badge of Religion, 1986; OStJ 1988. KCSG 1985; Order of Merit (Poland), 1989, Comdr's Cross, 1992, Comdr's Cross with Star, 1999; Order of the Gold Star (Hungary), 1990; Commander's Cross, 1st cl. (Austria), 1992; Comdr of the Order of Civil Merit (Spain), 1993; Commander's Cross, Order of Merit (Germany), 1993; Comdr, Order of Honour (Greece), 1996; Comdr, Royal Order of Polar Star (Sweden), 1997; Order of Commandatore (Italy), 1999; Citizen of Honour (Uruguay), 1999; Gran Oficial, Orden de Mayo al Merito (Argentina), 1999; Grand Cross, Order of Bernado O'Higgins (Chile), 2000. *Recreations:* golf, swimming. *Address:* 80 East End Road, N3 2SY. *Fax:* (020) 7485 4512. *Clubs:* Reform, City Livery.

STEVAS; *see* St John-Stevas, family name of Baron St John of Fawsley.

STEVELY, Prof. William Stewart, DPhil; FIBiol; Principal and Vice-Chancellor, Robert Gordon University, since 1997; *b* 6 April 1943; *s* of Robert Reid Stevely and Catherine Callow Stevely; *m* 1968, Sheila Anne Stalker; three *s* two *d*. *Educ:* Ardrossan Acad.; Glasgow Univ. (BSc 1965; DipEd 1973); St Catherine's Coll., Oxford (DPhil 1968). FIBiol 1988. Asst Lectr, 1968–70, Lectr, 1970–83, Sen. Lectr, 1983–88, in Biochemistry, Univ. of Glasgow; Prof. and Head of Dept of Biology, 1988–92, Vice Principal, 1992–97, Paisley Coll. of Tech., then Univ. of Paisley. Chm., Scottish Council, Inst. of Biology, 1993–95; Member: Nat. Bd for Nursing, Midwifery and Health Visiting for Scotland, 1992–; SHEFC, 1993–96; Bd, QAA, 1998–; Bd, Scottish Enterprise Grampian (formerly Grampian Enterprise) Ltd, 1998–. Mem. Council, Inst. for Learning and Teaching in Higher Educn, 1998–. *Publications:* papers on herpes viruses. *Address:* Robert Gordon University, Schoolhill, Aberdeen AB10 1FR. *T:* (01224) 262001.

STEVEN, Stewart; Chairman, National Campaign for the Arts, since 1996; *b* 30 Sept. 1935; *s* of Rudolph and Trude Steven; *m* 1965, Inka Sobieniewska; one *s*. *Educ:* Mayfield Coll., Sussex. Political Reporter, Central Press Features, 1961–63; Political Correspondent, Western Daily Press, 1963–64; Daily Express: Political Reporter, 1964–65; Diplomatic Correspondent, 1965–67; Foreign Editor, 1967–72; Daily Mail: Asst Editor, 1972–74; Associate Editor, 1974–82; Editor: The Mail on Sunday, 1982–92 (Columnist, 1996–); Evening Standard, 1992–95; Chairman: Liberty Publishing & Media Ltd, 1996–98; Punch, 1996–98. Dir, Prospect. Chm., Equity Theatre Commn, 1995–97; Member: Thames Adv. Gp, 1995–98; Better English Campaign, 1995–98; Dir, London Film Commn, 1996–2000. *Publications:* Operation Splinter-Factor, 1974; The Spymasters of Israel, 1976; The Poles, 1982. *Recreation:* the arts. *Address:* 20 Woodstock Road, W4 1UE. *Clubs:* Garrick, Groucho.

STEVENS, family name of **Baron Stevens of Ludgate**.

STEVENS OF LUDGATE, Baron *cr* 1987 (Life Peer), of Ludgate in the City of London; **David Robert Stevens;** Chairman: United News & Media (formerly United Newspapers plc), 1981–99 (Director, 1974–99); Express Newspapers, 1985–99; *b* 26 May 1936; *s* of late (Arthur) Edwin Stevens, CBE; *m* 1st Patricia Rose (marr. diss. 1971); one *s* one *d*; 2nd, 1977, Melissa Milicevich (*d* 1989); 3rd, 1990, Meriza Giori. *Educ:* Stowe Sch.; Sidney Sussex Coll., Cambridge (MA Hons Econ). Management Trainee, Elliott Automation, 1959; Director: Hill Samuel Securities, 1959–68; Drayton Group, 1968–74. Chairman: Alexander Proudfoot Hldgs (formerly City & Foreign), 1976–95; Drayton Far East, 1976–93; English & International, 1976–79; Consolidated Venture (formerly Montagu Boston), 1979–93; Drayton Consolidated, 1980–92; Drayton Japan, 1980–88; Oak Industries, 1989–96; Mid States, 1989–95; Premier Asset Mgt plc, 1997–2001; PNC Tele.Com (formerly Personal Number Co.), 1998–; Chief Exec., 1980–87, Chm., 1980–93, Montagu Investment Management, subseq. INVESCO MIM Management; Dep. Chm., 1987–89, Chm., 1989–93, Britannia Arrow Hldgs, subseq. INVESCO MIM. Chm., EDC for Civil Engrg, 1984–86. *Recreations:* golf, gardening. *Address:* House of Lords, SW1A 0PW. *Clubs:* White's; Sunningdale Golf.

STEVENS, Prof. Anne Frances, PhD; Professor of European Studies and Head of School of Languages and European Studies, Aston University, since 1998; *b* 28 Dec. 1942; *d* of Robert Ross, *qv* and Margaret Helen Ross (*née* Steadman); *m* 1966, Handley Michael Gambrell Stevens, *qv*; three *d*. *Educ:* Blackheath High Sch. for Girls; Newnham Coll., Cambridge (BA 1964; MA 1975); LSE, Univ. of London (MSc Econ (with distinction) 1975; PhD 1980). Asst Principal, Dept of Technical Co-operation, ODM, 1964–66; part-time Lectr, Univ. of Malaya, 1966–68; HEO, British High Commn, Kuala Lumpur, 1968–69; School of European Studies, University of Sussex: Lectr in Politics, 1978–90; Dean, 1988–90; Prof. of European Studies, Univ. of Kent at Canterbury, 1991-98. *Publications:* (jtly) Hostile Brothers: competition and closure in the European electronics industry, 1990; The Government and Politics of France, 1992, 2nd edn 1996; Brussels Bureaucrats: the administration of the European Union, 2000; articles on comparative admin. *Recreations:* walking, English dancing, needlework. *Address:* School of Languages and European Studies, Aston University, Aston Triangle, Birmingham B4 7ET. *T:* (0121) 359 3611.

STEVENS, Anthony John; Post Graduate Veterinary Dean for London and South East England, Royal College of Veterinary Surgeons/British Veterinary Association, 1986–97; engaged in consultancy and literary work; *b* 29 July 1926; *s* of John Walker Stevens and Hilda Stevens; *m* 1954, Patricia Frances, *d* of Robert Gill, Ponteland; one *s* two *d*. *Educ:* Liverpool and Manchester Univs; Magdalene Coll., Cambridge. MA, BVSc, MRCVS, DipBact. Veterinary Investigation Officer, Cambridge, 1956–65; Animal Health Expert for UNO, 1959–63; Suptg Veterinary Investigation Officer, Leeds, 1965–68; Ministry of Agriculture, Fisheries and Food: Dep. Dir, Central Vet. Lab., 1968–71; Asst Chief Vet. Officer, 1971–73; Dep. Chief Vet. Officer, 1973–78; Dir, Vet. Labs, MAFF, 1979–86. External Examr, Dublin, Liverpool and Edinburgh Univs., 1964–70. Past Pres., Veterinary Research Club. Vice Pres., Zoological Soc., 1989–90 and 1995–98 (Mem. Council, 1987–91, 1994–98). Vice Chm., Surrey Industrial History Gp, 1990–. FRSA. *Publications:* UN/FAO Manual of Diagnostic Techniques; regular contributor to Veterinary Record, etc. *Recreations:* industrial archaeology particularly canals, all forms of livestock. *Address:* Marigold Cottage, Great Halfpenny Farm, Guildford, Surrey GU4 8PY. *T:* (01483) 565375.

STEVENS, Auriol; Editor, Times Higher Education Supplement, since 1992; *d* of Capt. E. B. K. Stevens and Ruth M. Howard (*née* Pugh); *m* 1st, 1962, Prof. Hugh Stephenson, *qv* (marr. diss. 1987); 2nd, 1988, Dr J. M. Ashworth, *qv*. *Educ:* Somerville Coll., Oxford (BA Hons); London Univ. (Dip. (Ext.)). Freelance journalist, 1962–72; TES, 1972–78; educn corresp., Observer, 1978–83; reporter, A Week in Politics, TV, 1983–86; Dir, Univs Inf. Unit, Cttee of Vice-Chancellors, 1986–92. Chm. Govs, Elliot Sch., Putney, 1981–85; Council: PSI, 1985-91; RCA, 1998–. Member: Exec. Cttee, Forum UK, 1999–; Inst. of Cancer Res., 2000–. FRSA. *Publication:* Clever Children in Comprehensive Schools, 1978. *Recreations:* walking, sailing, gardening, domestic arts. *Address:* Garden House, Wivenhoe, Essex CO7 9BD. *T:* (01206) 822256. *Clubs:* Forum UK; Wivenhoe Sailing.

STEVENS, Clifford David, CB 1997; Civil Service Commissioner, since 1997; *b* 11 June 1941; *s* of late Robert Stevens and of Ivy (*née* White); *m* 1964, Mary Olive (*née* Bradford); one *s* two *d*. *Educ:* Stationers' Company's Sch., London. FO, 1959–63; BoT, 1963–64; DEA, 1964–70 (Private Sec. to successive Ministers, 1967–70); CSD, 1970–76; Cabinet Office, 1976–78; CSD, 1978–81; Management and Personnel Office, 1981–86; Welsh Office, 1986–97: Dir, Industry Dept, 1987–94; Principal Establishment Officer, 1994–97. *Recreations:* gardening, bowls, golf. *Address:* c/o Office of the Civil Service Commissioners, 35 Great Smith Street, SW1P 3BQ. *T:* (020) 7276 2615.

STEVENS, Prof. Denis William, CBE 1984; President and Artistic Director, Accademia Monteverdiana, since 1961; *b* 2 March 1922; *s* of William J. Stevens and Edith Driver; *m* 1st, 1949, Sheila Elizabeth Holloway; two *s* one *d*; 2nd, 1975, Leocadia Elzbieta Kwasny. *Educ:* Royal Grammar Sch., High Wycombe; Jesus College, Oxford. Served War of

1939–45, RAF Intelligence, India and Burma, 1942–46. Producer, BBC Music Div., 1949–54; Assoc. Founder and Conductor, Ambrosian Singers, 1952; Vis. Professor of Musicology, Cornell Univ., 1955, Columbia Univ., 1956; Secretary, Plainsong and Mediaeval Music Soc., 1958–63; Editor, Grove's Dictionary of Music and Musicians, 1959–63. Professor, Royal Acad. of Music, 1960. Vis. Prof. Univ. of California (Berkeley), 1962; Dist. Vis. Prof., Pennsylvania State Univ., 1962–63; Prof. of Musicology, Columbia Univ., 1964–76; Vis. Prof. Univ. of California (Santa Barbara), 1974–75; Brechemin Dist. Vis. Prof., Univ. of Washington, Seattle, 1976; Visiting Professor: Univ. of Michigan, Ann Arbor, 1977; San Diego State Univ., 1978; Goldsmiths Coll., London Univ., 1995–; Acad. Musicale de Villecroze, 1996. Lectures on music, especially British, and contrib. musicolog. confs, in England, France, Germany, Italy, USA and Russia; Organizer and Leader, Rockefeller Congress on Music, Bellagio, 1974; concerts, conducting own and ancillary ensembles at internat. festivals in GB (incl. 5 proms, the first introducing Monteverdi 1967), Europe and USA; TV and radio programmes in Europe and N America; first broadcast perfs of unknown works by Dufay, Dunstable and Telemann, of Charpentier's Medée and Monteverdi's Orfeo; cons. for films. FSA; Mem., Co. of Musicians. Hon. RAM, 1960. Hon.D, Humane Letters, Fairfield Univ., Connecticut, 1967. *Publications:* The Mulliner Book, 1952; Thomas Tomkins, 1957, rev. edn 1966; A History of Song, 1960, rev. edn, 1971; Tudor Church Music, 1966; A Treasury of English Church Music (I), 1965; (ed) First and Second Penguin Book of English Madrigals, 1967, 1971; Early Tudor Organ Music (II), 1969; Music in Honour of St Thomas of Canterbury, 1970; Monteverdi: sacred, secular and occasional music, 1978; Musicology: a practical guide, 1980; The Letters of Monteverdi, 1980, 2nd edn 1995; Renaissance Dialogues, 1981; The Worcester Fragments, 1981; Musicology in Practice, 1987; Early Music, 1997; Monteverdi: songs & madrigals, 1999; Monteverdi in Venice, 2001; many edns of early music, including Monteverdi Vespers, 1961, 2nd edn 1994, and Orfeo; choral works by Gabrieli, Gesualdo, Lassus, Machaut, Tallis, Tomkins; contrib. Encyclopaedia Britannica, Amer. Acad. Encyclopedia, Grove's Dictionary, Die Musik in Geschichte und Gegenwart, Enciclopedia della Musica; reviews and articles in English and foreign journals; also many stereo recordings with Ambrosian Singers and Accademia Monteverdiana, ranging from plainsong to Beethoven. *Recreations:* travel, photography. *Address:* The Quadrangle, Morden College, SE3 0PW. *Club:* Garrick.

STEVENS, Handley Michael Gambrell; Research Associate, European Institute, London School of Economics and Political Science, since 1994; *b* 29 June 1941; *s* of Ernest Norman Stevens and Kathleen Emily Gambrell; *m* 1966, Anne Frances Ross (*see* A. F. Stevens); three *d. Educ:* The Leys Sch., Cambridge; Phillips Acad., Andover, Mass (E-SU schol.); King's Coll., Cambridge (BA). Joined Foreign Office, 1964; Third, later Second, Sec., Kuala Lumpur, 1966; Asst Private Sec. to the Lord Privy Seal, 1970; Principal: CSD, 1971; DTI, 1973; Asst Sec., Dept of Trade, 1976; Under Sec., Dept of Transport, 1983–94. *Publications:* Transport Policy in Britain, 1998; Brussels Bureaucrats?, 2000. *Recreations:* music, hill walking, travel. *Address:* 18a Belsize Lane, NW3 5AB.

STEVENS, Sir Jocelyn (Edward Greville), Kt 1996; CVO 1993; Chairman: English Heritage, 1992–2000; Royal Commission on Historical Monuments of England, 1999–2000; *b* 14 Feb. 1932; *s* of late Major C. G. B. Stewart-Stevens and Mrs Greville Stevens; *m* 1956, Jane Armyne Sheffield (marr. diss. 1979); one *s* two *d* (and one *s* decd). *Educ:* Eton; Cambridge. Military service in Rifle Bde, 1950–52; Journalist, Hulton Press Ltd, 1955–56; Chairman and Managing Dir, Stevens Press Ltd, and Editor of Queen Magazine, 1957–68; Personal Asst to Chairman of Beaverbrook Newspapers, May-Dec. 1968; Director, 1971–81; Managing Director: Evening Standard Co. Ltd, 1969–72; Daily Express, 1972–74; Beaverbrook Newspapers, 1974–77; Express Newspapers, 1977–81 (Dep. Chm. and Man. Dir); Editor and Publisher, The Magazine, 1982–84; Dir, Centaur Communications, 1982–84; Rector and Vice Provost, RCA, 1984–92; Dep. Chm., ITC, 1991–96; Dir, TV Corp., 1996–. Personal Special Advr on Stonehenge to Sec. of State for Culture, Media and Sport, 2000–. Chairman: Silver Trust, 1990–93; Phoenix Trust, 2000–; Trustee: Mental Health Foundn, 1972–94; Eureka! The Museum for Children, 1986–; Butrint Foundn, 2000–; Prince's Foundn, 2000–; Pres., Cheyne Walk Trust, 1989–93. Governor: Imperial Coll. of Science, Technology and Medicine, 1985–92; Winchester Sch. of Art, 1986–89. FRSA 1984; Senior Fellow RCA, 1990. Hon. FCSD 1990. Hon. DLitt: Loughborough, 1989; Buckingham, 1998. *Address:* 14 Cheyne Walk, SW3 5RA. *Clubs:* Buck's, Beefsteak, White's.

STEVENS, Sir John (Arthur), Kt 2000; QPM 1992; DL; Commissioner, Metropolitan Police, since 2000; *b* 21 Oct. 1942; *s* of C. J. and S. Stevens; *m*; two *s* one *d. Educ:* St Lawrence Coll., Ramsgate; Leicester Univ. (LLB Hons); Southampton Univ. (MPhil). Joined Metropolitan Police, 1963; DS, Police Staff Coll., 1983–84; Asst Chief Constable, Hampshire Constabulary, 1986–89; Dep. Chief Constable, Cambridgeshire Constab., 1989–91; Chief Constable, Northumbria, 1991–96; HM Inspector of Constabulary, 1996–98; Dep. Comr, Metropolitan Police, 1998–99. Chairman: Jt Cttee on Offender Profiling, 1991; ACPO Crime Prevention Sub-Cttee, 1994. Chm., NI Enquiry into alleged collusion between paramil. and security forces (Stevens Enquiry), 1989–92; headed Enquiry into alleged malpractice at Nat. Criminal Intelligence Service, 1995–96; 'Stevens 3' NI Enquiry into Collusion, 1999. Advr, Forensic Sci. Service. Vis. Prof., City Univ., NY, 1984–85; Vis. Lectr, Internat. Crime Prevention Centre, Canada, 1998–; Sen. Mem., 1996–, Hon. Fellow, 2000, Wolfson Coll., Cambridge. DL Greater London, 2001. Hon. LLD Leicester, 2000; Hon. DCL Northumbria, 2001. *Recreations:* walking, cricket, squash, Rugby, flying (qualified pilot). *Address:* New Scotland Yard, Broadway, SW1H 0BG. *Clubs:* East India; Northern Counties.

STEVENS, John Christopher Courtenay; *b* 23 May 1955; *s* of Sir John Melior Stevens, KCMG, DSO, OBE and of Anne Hely-Hutchinson. *Educ:* Winchester Coll.; Magdalen Coll., Oxford (BA Jurisprudence). Foreign exchange and Bond trader, Banque Indosuez, Paris, 1976–77; Bayerische Hypotheken und Wechselbank, Munich, 1977–78; Morgan Grenfell, London, 1979–89, Internat. Dir, 1986–89; Advr, St James's Place Capital plc, 1989. MEP (C) Thames Valley, 1989–99. *Recreations:* riding, ski-ing. *Address:* 39 St James's Place, SW1A 1NS. *Club:* Carlton.

STEVENS, Prof. John Edgar, CBE 1980; PhD; FBA 1975; President of Magdalene College, Cambridge, 1983–88, Fellow, 1950–88, now Emeritus; Professor of Medieval and Renaissance English, University of Cambridge, 1978–88, now Emeritus; *b* 8 Oct. 1921; *s* of William Charles James and Fanny Stevens; *m* 1946, Charlotte Ethel Mary (*née* Somner); two *s* two *d. Educ:* Christ's Hospital, Horsham; Magdalene College, Cambridge (Schol.; MA, PhD). Served Royal Navy; Temp. Lieut RNVR. Cambridge University: Bye-Fellow 1948, Research Fellow 1950, Fellow 1953 and Tutor 1958–74, Magdalene Coll.; Univ. Lectr in English, 1954–74; Reader in English and Musical History, 1974–78. Vis. Dist. Prof. of Medieval Studies, Univ. of California, Berkeley, 1989. Chm., Plainsong and Medieval Music Soc., 1988–95. Hon. MusD Exeter, 1989. *Publications:* Medieval Carols (Musica Britannica vol. 4), 1952, 2nd edn 1958; Music and Poetry in the Early Tudor Court, 1961; Music at the Court of Henry VIII (Musica Britannica vol. 18), 1962, 2nd edn 1969; (with Richard Axton) Medieval French Plays, 1971; Medieval Romance, 1973; Early Tudor Songs & Carols (Musica Britannica vol. 36), 1975; Words and Music in the Middle Ages, 1986. *Recreation:* viol-playing. *Address:* 4 & 5 Bell's Court, Castle Street, Cambridge CB3 0AH.

STEVENS, Hon. John Paul; Associate Justice, Supreme Court of the United States, since 1975; *b* 20 April 1920; *s* of Ernest James Stevens and Elizabeth Stevens (*née* Street); *m* 1st, 1942, Elizabeth Jane Sheeren; one *s* three *d*; 2nd, 1979, Maryan Mulholland. *Educ:* Univ. of Chicago (AB 1941); Northwestern Univ. (JD 1947). Served War, USNR, 1942–45 (Bronze Star). Law Clerk to US Supreme Ct Justice Wiley Rutledge, 1947–48; Associate, Poppenhusen, Johnston, Thompson & Raymond, 1948–50; Associate Counsel, sub-cttee on Study Monopoly Power, Cttee on Judiciary, US House of Reps, 1951; Partner, Rothschild, Hart, Stevens & Barry, 1952–70; US Circuit Judge, 1970–75. Lectr, anti-trust law, Northwestern Univ. Sch. of Law, 1953; Univ. of Chicago Law Sch., 1954–55; Mem., Attorney-Gen.'s Nat. Cttee to study Anti-Trust Laws, 1953–55. Mem., Chicago Bar Assoc. (2nd Vice-Pres. 1970). Order of Coif, Phi Beta Kappa, Psi Upsilon, Phi Delta Phi. *Publications:* chap. in book, Mr Justice (ed Dunham and Kurland); contrib. to Antitrust Developments: a supp. to Report of Attorney-Gen.'s Nat. Cttee to Study the Anti-trust Laws, 1955–68; various articles etc, in Ill. Law Rev., Proc. confs, and reports. *Recreations:* flying, tennis, bridge, reading, travel. *Address:* Supreme Court of the United States, Washington, DC 20543, USA.

STEVENS, John Williams, CB 1988; Member, 1989–90, Deputy Chairman, 1991–94, Civil Service Appeal Board; *b* 27 Feb. 1929; *s* of John Williams and Kathleen Stevens; *m* 1949, Grace Stevens; one *s* one *d. Educ:* St Ives School. Min. of Supply, 1952; UK Defence Res. and Supply Staff, Australia, 1958–61; HM Treasury, 1966; Civil Service Dept, 1969–73; Price Commn, 1973–74; Head of Personnel, Stock Exchange, 1975–76; Principal Private Sec. to Lord Pres. of the Council and Leader of the House of Commons, 1977–79, to Chancellor of Duchy of Lancaster and Leader of the House, 1979–80; Principal Estabts and Finance Officer, Cabinet Office, 1980–89; Under Sec. 1984. *Recreations:* Cornwall, reading, theatre. *Address:* 14 Highbury Crescent, Portsmouth Road, Camberley, Surrey GU15 1JZ. *Club:* Athenæum.

STEVENS, Kenneth Henry, CBE 1983; DL; Chief Executive Commissioner, The Scout Association, 1970–87; *b* 8 Oct. 1922; *s* of late Horace J. Stevens, CBE, sometime Senior Principal Inspector of Taxes, and late Nora Stevens (*née* Kauntze); *m* 1947, Yvonne Grace Ruth (*née* Mitchell); one *s* one *d. Educ:* Brighton Coll.; Brighton Technical Coll. South Coast Civil Defence, 1941–44. Alliance Assurance Co., 1944–47; Asst Dir of Adult Leader Training, Internat. Scout Training Centre, Gilwell Park, Chingford, 1947–56; Organising Comr, World Scout Jamboree, Indaba and Rover Moot, Sutton Coldfield, 1956–58; Dep. Dir of Adult Leader Training, Internat. Scout Training Centre, 1958–61; Asst Chief Exec. Comr, The Scout Assoc., 1961–63; Dep. Chief Exec. Comr, 1963–70. DL Surrey, 1989. *Publication:* Ceremonies of The Scout Movement, 1958. *Recreations:* motoring, gardening. *Address:* Drovers, Crampshaw Lane, Ashtead, Surrey KT21 2UF. *T:* (01372) 277841. *Club:* MCC.

STEVENS, Prof. Kenneth William Harry; Professor of Theoretical Physics, 1958–87, now Emeritus, and Senior Research Fellow, 1987–88, University of Nottingham; *b* 17 Sept. 1922; *s* of Harry and Rose Stevens; *m* 1949, Audrey A. Gawthrop; one *s* one *d. Educ:* Magdalen College School, Oxford; Jesus and Merton Colleges, Oxford. MA 1947, DPhil 1949. Pressed Steel Company Ltd Research Fellow, Oxford University, 1949–53; Research Fellow, Harvard University, 1953–54; Reader in Theoretical Physics, University of Nottingham, 1953–58. Leverhulme Emeritus Fellow, 1990. Mem., IUPAP Commn on Magnetism, 1984–87. (Jointly) Maxwell Medal and Prize, 1968. *Publications:* Magnetic Ions in Crystals, 1997; contrib. to learned journals. *Recreations:* music, tennis, walking. *Address:* The University, Nottingham NG7 2RD.

STEVENS, Sir Laurence (Houghton), Kt 1983; CBE 1979; company director and business consultant; Chairman, Sir George Elliot Charitable Trust, since 1993; *b* 9 Jan. 1920; *s* of Laurence Stevens and Annie (*née* Houghton); *m* 1943, Beryl J. Dickson; one *s* two *d. Educ:* Auckland Boys' Grammar Sch.; Auckland Univ. (BCom). FCA NZ 1969; CMA 1966. Served War, Pacific (Tonga Defence Force) and ME (2NZEF). Joined Auckland Knitting Mills Ltd, 1946; Man. Dir, 1952; retd 1980. Chairman: Thorn EMI Gp of Cos, NZ, 1980–93; Chambard Property Develt (formerly Les Mills Corporation) Ltd, 1985–91; Fay Richwhite & Co. (formerly Capital Markets Ltd), 1986–96; Ascent Corp. Ltd, 1986–88; Auckland Internat. Airport Ltd, 1988–96 (Dir, 1988–98); Marker Ltd, 1990; CMI Screws & Fasteners Ltd, 1992–97; Hawk Packaging Ltd, 1993–98 (Dir, 1998–2000); Director: Guardian Royal Exchange, 1983–90; Wormald International NZ Ltd, 1983–90; Reserve Bank of New Zealand, 1978–86; Petroleum Corp. of New Zealand Ltd, 1984–88; R. W. Saunders Ltd, 1984–87; Petralgas Chemicals NZ Ltd, 1986–87; Wormald Pacific Ltd, 1987–90. Past President and Life Member: NZ Knitting Industries Fedn; Textile and Garment Fedn of NZ; Auckland Manufrs' Assoc.; Pres., NZ Manufrs' Fedn, 1970–71 and 1980–81; Chm., Auckland Agricl, Pastoral and Indust. Shows Bd, 1976–86; Mem., Melanesian Trust Bd, 1977–93. Laureate, NZ Business Hall of Fame, 1999. *Recreation:* tennis (Pres., Auckland Lawn Tennis Assoc., 1983–84). *Address:* 1/1 Watene Crescent, Orakei, Auckland 5, New Zealand. *T:* (9) 5210476. *Club:* Northern (Auckland).

STEVENS, Lewis David, MBE 1982; management and industrial engineering consultant (self-employed), since 1979; *b* 13 April 1936; *s* of Richard and Winnifred Stevens; *m* 1959, Margaret Eileen Gibson; two *s* one *d. Educ:* Oldbury Grammar Sch.; Liverpool Univ.; Lanchester Coll. RAF 1956–58. Various engrg cos, mainly in industrial engrg and production management positions, 1958–79. Mem., Nuneaton Borough Council, 1966–72. MP (C) Nuneaton, 1983–92; contested (C) Nuneaton, 1992. *Address:* 151 Sherbourne Avenue, Nuneaton, Warwicks CV10 9JN. *T:* (024) 7674 4541.

STEVENS, Dr Robert Bocking; Of Counsel, Covington & Burling, Washington and London, since 1992; Senior Research Fellow, Constitution Unit, University College London; *b* 8 June 1933; *s* of John Skevington Stevens and Enid Dorothy Stevens; *m* 1st, 1961, Rosemary Anne Wallace (marr. diss., 1982); one *s* one *d*; 2nd, 1985, Katherine Booth; one *d. Educ:* Oakham Sch.; Keble Coll., Oxford (BA 1956; BCL 1956; MA 1959; DCL 1984); Yale Univ. (LLM 1958). Called to the Bar, Gray's Inn, 1956, Bencher, 1999. Yale University: Asst Prof. of Law, 1959–61; Associate Prof., 1961–65; Prof., 1965–76; Provost, Tulane Univ., 1976–78; Pres., Haverford Coll., 1978–87; Chancellor, Univ. of Calif., Santa Cruz, 1987–91; Master, Pembroke Coll., Oxford, 1993–2001. Chm., Marshall Aid Commemoration Commn, 1995–2000. Gov., Abingdon Sch., 1993–2000. Hon. LLD: NY Law Sch., 1984; Villanova, 1985; Pennsylvania, 1987; Hon. DLitt Haverford Coll., 1991. *Publications:* (with B. S. Yamey) The Restrictive Practices Court, 1965; (with B. Abel-Smith) Lawyers and the Courts, 1967; (with B. Abel-Smith) In Search of Justice, 1968; Income Security, 1970; (with R. A. Stevens) Welfare Medicine in America, 1974; Law and Politics, 1978; The American Law School, 1983; The Independence of the Judiciary, 1993. *Recreations:* walking, tennis, nineteenth century, politics. *Address:* Mill Bank, Northleach, Cheltenham, Glos GL54 3HJ. *T:* (01451) 860060; 53 Coniston Court, Kendal Street, W2 2AN; Covington & Burling, Leconfield House, Curzon Street, W1Y 8AS. *T:* (020) 7495 5655. *Club:* Reform.

STEVENS, Rear Adm. Robert Patrick, CB 2000; Chief of Staff to Commander Allied Naval Forces Southern Europe, and Senior British Officer Southern Region, since 2002; *b* 14 March 1948; *s* of late Major Philip Joseph Stevens, RMP, and of Peggy Stevens (*née* Marshall); *m* 1973, Vivien Roberts; one *s* one *d*. *Educ:* Prince Rupert Sch., Wilhelmshaven; BRNC, Dartmouth. Commanding Officer: HMS Odin, 1979–81; comdg officers qualifying course, HMS Dolphin, 1983–85; HMS Torbay, 1985–88; USN War Coll., 1988–89; Asst Dir, Strategic Systems, MoD, 1989–91; Captain: 7th Frigate Sqdn and CO, HMS Argonaut, 1992–93; Navy Presentation team, 1993–94; Dir, Jt Warfare, MoD, 1994–98; FO, Submarines, Comdr Submarines (NATO), Eastern Atlantic and NW, and COS (Ops) to C-in-C Fleet, 1998–2001. Pres., RN Football Assoc., 1998–. Mem., RNSA. *Recreations:* hockey, tennis, ski-ing, sailing, cricket (RNCC). *Address:* Eastbury Park, Northwood, Middx HA6 3HP. *T:* (01923) 837358. *Clubs:* Royal Navy of 1765 and 1785; Eastcote Hockey; South West Shingles Yacht.

STEVENS, Timothy John, OBE 2000; Executive Director, Hermitage Rooms, and Deputy Director, Gilbert Collection, Somerset House; *b* 17 Jan. 1940; *s* of Seymour Stevens and Joan Rudgard; *m* 1969, Caroline Sankey; twin *s*. *Educ:* King's Sch., Canterbury; Hertford Coll., Oxford (MA); Courtauld Inst., Univ. of London (Academic Diploma, History of Art). Walker Art Gallery: Asst Keeper of British Art, 1964–65; Keeper of Foreign Art, 1965–67; Dep. Dir, 1967–70; Dir, 1971–74; Dir, Merseyside CC Art Galls, 1974–86; Dep. Dir, Nat. Museums and Galleries on Merseyside, 1986–87; Keeper of Art, Nat. Mus. of Wales, 1987–94; Asst Dir (Collections), V&A Mus., 1994–2000. Hon. LittD Liverpool, 1985. Chevalier de l'Ordre des Arts et des Lettres (France), 1988. *Recreation:* gardening. *Address:* Hunybeach, Hunworth, Melton Constable, Norfolk NR24 2EQ.

STEVENS, Rt Rev. Timothy John; *see* Leicester, Bishop of.

STEVENS, William David; President and Chief Operating Officer, Mitchell Energy & Development Corp., Houston, since 1994; *b* USA, 18 Sept. 1934; *s* of Walter Gerald and Amy Grace Stevens; *m* 1st, 1954, Barbara Ann Duncan (marr. diss. 1994); one *s* three *d*; 2nd, 1994, Virginia L. Wilkinson. *Educ:* Texas A&I Univ. (BScEng). Joined Humble Oil, 1958: various assignments, US Gulf Coast, 1958–73; Exxon Corporation: Executive Asst to President, 1974; various assignments, New York, 1974–77; Vice Pres., Gas, 1977–78; Man. Dir, Esso UK Ltd, London, and Vice Pres. Upstream, Esso Europe, Inc., 1978–85; Executive Vice President: Esso Europe, 1985–86; Exxon Co., USA, Houston, 1986–87; Pres., Exxon Co., 1988–92, retired. *Recreations:* golf, shooting, hiking. *Address:* Mitchell Energy & Development Corp., PO Box 4000, The Woodlands, Houston, TX 77387–4000, USA. *T:* (713) 377 5500.

STEVENSON, family name of **Baron Stevenson of Coddenham**.

STEVENSON OF CODDENHAM, Baron *cr* 1999 (Life Peer), of Coddenham, in the county of Suffolk; **Henry Dennistoun Stevenson, (Dennis),** Kt 1998; CBE 1981; Chairman: Pearson plc, since 1997 (Director, 1986–97); Halifax plc, since 1999; *b* 19 July 1945; *s* of Alexander James Stevenson and Sylvia Florence Stevenson (*née* Ingleby); *m* 1972, Charlotte Susan, *d* of Hon. Sir Peter Vanneck, GBE, CB, AFC, AE; four *s*. *Educ:* Glenalmond; King's Coll., Cambridge (MA). Chairman: SRU Gp of cos, 1972–96; GPA, then AerFi, Gp, 1993–2000; Director: British Technology Gp, 1979–89; Tyne Tees Television, 1982–87; Manpower Inc. (formerly Blue Arrow), 1988–; Thames Television plc, 1991–93; J. Rothschild Assurance plc, 1991–97; J. Rothschild Assurance Hldgs plc, 1991–97; English Partnerships, 1993–99; BSkyB Gp plc, 1994–2000; Lazard Bros, 1997–2000; Whitehall Trust Ltd, 1997–; St James's Place Capital, 1997–; Economist Newspapers, 1998–. Chm., Trustees, Tate Gall., 1988–98. Chairman: Newton Aycliffe and Peterlee New Town Develt Corp., 1971–80; Intermediate Technology Develt Gp, 1983–90; Director: Nat. Building Agency, 1977–81; LDDC, 1981–88. Chairman: govt working party on role of voluntary movements and youth in the envmt, 1971, '50 Million Volunteers' (HMSO); Indep. Adv. Cttee on Pop Fests, 1972–76, 'Pop Festivals, Report and Code of Practice' (HMSO); Advr on Agricl Marketing to Minister of Agric., 1979–83; Special Advr to PM and Sec. of State for Educn on use of IT in Educn, 1997–2000; Chm., H of L Appts Commn, 2000–; Member: Panel on Takeovers and Mergers, 1992–2000; Bd, British Council, 1996–. Chairman: NAYC, 1973–81; Sinfonia 21 (formerly Docklands Sinfonietta), 1989–99; Tate Gall. Foundn, 1998–; Aldeburgh Productions, 2000–. Mem. Admin. Council, Royal Jubilee Trusts, 1978–80. Chancellor, London Institute, 2000–. *Recreation:* home. *Clubs:* Brooks's, MCC.

STEVENSON, (Arthur) William, TD 1980; QC 1996; a Recorder, since 1992; *b* 17 Oct. 1943; *s* of late Arthur John Stevenson, TD, MA and Olivia Diana Stevenson (*née* Serocold); *m* 1969, Bridget Laura York; two *s* one *d*. *Educ:* Marlborough Coll.; Trinity Coll., Oxford (MA). Called to the Bar, Lincoln's Inn, 1968, Bencher, 2001; in practice, 1968–. *Recreations:* country sports, ski-ing, sailing. *Address:* Crown Office Chambers, 1 Paper Buildings, Temple, EC4Y 7EP. *T:* (020) 7797 8100, *Fax:* (020) 7797 8101; *e-mail:* awsqc@crownofficechambers.com. *Clubs:* Boodle's, Royal Thames Yacht, Bar Yacht.

STEVENSON, Christopher Terence S.; *see* Sinclair Stevenson.

STEVENSON, Prof. David John, PhD; FRS 1993; George Van Osdol Professor of Planetary Science, California Institute of Technology, since 1995; *b* 2 Sept. 1948; *s* of Ian McIvor Stevenson and Gwenyth (*née* Carroll). *Educ:* Rongotai Coll.; Victoria Univ., Wellington, NZ (BSc, BSc Hons, MSc); Cornell Univ., NY (PhD). Res. Fellow, ANU, 1976–78; Asst Prof., UCLA, 1978–80; California Institute of Technology: Associate Prof., 1980–84; Prof. of Planetary Science, 1984–95; Chm., Div. of Geol and Planetary Scis, 1989–94. Fellow, Amer. Geophysical Union, 1986 (Whipple Award, 1994; Hess Medal, 1998). Urey Prize, Amer. Astronomical Soc., 1984. *Publications:* numerous papers in learned jls, principally in earth and planetary scis. *Recreations:* hiking, biking. *Address:* Division of Geological and Planetary Sciences, California Institute of Technology, Pasadena, CA 91125, USA. *T:* (626) 3956534.

STEVENSON, Prof. George Telford; Professor of Immunochemistry, Faculty of Medicine, University of Southampton, 1974–97, now Visiting Professor; *b* 18 April 1932; *s* of Ernest George Stevenson and Mary Josephine Madden; *m* 1963, Freda Kathryn Hartley; three *s*. *Educ:* North Sydney High Sch.; Univ. of Sydney (MB, BS; MD); Univ. of Oxford (DPhil). Resident MO, 1955–56, Resident Pathologist, 1957, Sydney Hosp.; Research Fellow, Dept of Medicine, Univ. of Sydney, 1958–61; Nuffield Dominions Demonstrator, Dept of Biochemistry, Univ. of Oxford, 1962–64; Sen. Research Fellow, Dept of Biochemistry, Univ. of Sydney, 1965–66; Scientific Staff, MRC Immunochemistry Unit, Univ. of Oxford, 1967–70; Dir, Tenovus Research Lab., Southampton Gen. Hosp., 1970–97; Consultant Immunologist, Southampton Univ. Hosps, 1976–97, now Hon. Consultant Immunologist. Hammer Prize for Cancer Research (jtly) (Armand Hammer Foundn, LA), 1982. *Publications:* Immunological Investigation of Lymphoid Neoplasms (with J. L. Smith and T. J. Hamblin), 1983; research papers on immunology and cancer, considered mainly at molecular level. *Address:* 9 Meadowhead Road, Bassett, Southampton SO16 7AD. *T:* (023) 8076 9092.

STEVENSON, George William; MP (Lab) Stoke-on-Trent South, since 1992; *b* 30 Aug. 1938; *s* of Harold and Elsie May Stevenson; *m* 1st, 1958, Doreen June (decd); two *s* one *d*; 2nd, 1991, Pauline Brookes. *Educ:* Uttoxeter Road Primary School; Queensberry Road Secondary School, Stoke-on-Trent. Pottery caster, 1953–57; coal miner, 1957–66; transport driver, 1966–84; shop steward, TGWU 5/24 Branch, 1968–84 (Mem., 1964–; Chm., 1975–81). Deputy Leader: Stoke-on-Trent City Council, 1972–83; Staffs County Council, 1981–85. MEP (Lab) Staffs East, 1984–94; Pres., Eur. Parlt Delegn for Relations with S Asia, 1989–92 (Vice-Pres., 1984–89). Member, Select Committee: on European Legislation, 1995–, on Environment, Transport and the Regions, 1997–; Mem., Speaker's Panel of Chairmen. Chairman: All-Party Tibet Gp, 1995–; PLP Agric. Cttee, 1993–2001. *Recreations:* walking, cinema, travel, reading. *Address:* (home) 823 Lightwood Road, Lightwood, Stoke-on-Trent ST3 7HA; (office) Stoke South Constituency Office, 2A Stanton Road, Meir, Stoke-on-Trent, Staffs ST3 6DD. *T:* (01782) 593393.

STEVENSON, Hugh Alexander; Chairman, Equitas Ltd, since 1998; *b* 7 Sept. 1942; *s* of William Hugh Stevenson and Elizabeth Margaret (*née* Wallace); *m* 1965, Catherine May Peacock; two *s* two *d*. *Educ:* Harrow Sch.; University Coll., Oxford (BA 1964; Hon. Fellow 1999); Harvard Business School (AMP 103). Admitted as Solicitor, 1967; with Linklaters & Paines, 1964–70; with S. G. Warburg & Co., 1970–92; Dir, S. G. Warburg Gp plc, 1986–95; Chairman: Mercury Asset Management Gp plc, 1992–98 (Dir, 1986–98); The Merchants Trust plc, 2000– (Dir, 1999–). Chm., Instnl Fund Managers Assoc., 1998–99; Director: British Museum Co., 1984–; Securities Inst., 1994–98 (Hon. FSI 1998); IMRO, 1995–2000; Standard Life Assurance Co., 1999–. Hon. Treas., Inst. of Child Health, 1991–96 (Hon. Fellow 1996); Chairman: The Sick Children's Trust, 1982–99; Gt Ormond St Hosp. Develt Trust, 1999–; Special Trustee, Gt Ormond St Hosp., 1996–. Hon. Fellow, UCL, 2000. *Address:* Equitas Ltd, 33 St Mary Axe, EC3A 8LL. *T:* (020) 7342 2000.

STEVENSON, (James Alexander) Stewart; Member (SNP) Banff and Buchan, Scottish Parliament, since June 2001; *b* 15 Oct. 1946; *s* of late James Thomas Middleton Stevenson, MB ChB and Helen Mary Berry MacGregor, MA; *m* 1969, Sandra Isabel Pirie, MA. *Educ:* Bell Baxter Sch., Cupar; Univ. of Aberdeen (MA 1969). Various technology posts, later Dir of Technology Innovation, Bank of Scotland, 1969–99; pt-time Lectr, Sch. of Mgt, Heriot-Watt Univ., 2001–. Scottish Parliament: contested (SNP) Linlithgow, 1999; Member: Rural Develt Cttee, 2001–; Justice Cttee, 2001–. Mem., SNP, 1961–. *Recreations:* private pilot, computing, travel, public speaking. *Address:* Scottish Parliament, Edinburgh EH99 1SP. *Clubs:* Edinburgh Flying; Moray Flying.

STEVENSON, Dr Jim; Chief Executive, Educational Broadcasting Services Trust, since 1988; *b* 9 May 1937; *s* of George Stevenson and Frances Mildred Groat; *m* 1963, Brenda Cooley; one *s* one *d*. *Educ:* Kirkham Grammar Sch.; Univ. of Liverpool (BSc, PhD). NATO Res. Fellow, Univ. of Trondheim, 1963–65; Lectr in Biochemistry, Univ. of Warwick, 1965–69; BBC Open Univ. Production Centre: Producer, 1969–75; Exec. Producer, 1975–76; Editor (Science), 1976–79; Head of Programmes, 1979–82; Dep. Sec., BBC, 1982–83; Head of Educnl Broadcasting Services and Educn Sec., BBC, 1983–89. *Publications:* contribs to sci. jls and communications jls. *Recreations:* television, history. *Address:* 34 Vallance Road, N22 7UB. *T:* (020) 8889 6261.

STEVENSON, John, CBE 1987; Deputy Licensing Authority: South East Traffic Area, 1987–95; Metropolitan Traffic Area, 1989–95; Eastern Traffic Area, 1990–95; Western Traffic Area, 1991–95; *b* 15 June 1927; *s* of John and Harriet Esther Stevenson; *m* 1956, Kathleen Petch; one *s* one *d*. *Educ:* Durham Univ. (LLB); MA Oxon 1982. Solicitor. Legal Asst, Borough of Hartlepool, 1951; Junior Solicitor, County Borough of Sunderland, 1952; Solicitor, Hertfordshire CC, 1953, Asst Clerk, 1964; Clerk of the Peace and County Solicitor, Gloucestershire CC, 1969; Chief Executive, Buckinghamshire CC, 1974; Sec., ACC, 1980–87. Hon. Fellow, Inst. Local Govt Studies, Birmingham Univ., 1981–; Vis. Fellow, Nuffield Coll., Oxford, 1982–90. Vice President, Inst. of Trading Standards Administration, 1988. *Address:* Mark Two, Abbots Worthy, Winchester, Hants SO21 1DR. *T:* (01962) 886766.

STEVENSON, Dr John, FRHistS; Reader in History, University of Oxford, since 1995; Fellow and Tutor, Worcester College, Oxford, since 1990; *b* 26 Sept. 1946; *s* of John Stevenson and Bridget Stevenson; *m* 1971, Jacqueline Patricia Johns. *Educ:* Boteler GS, Warrington; Worcester Coll., Oxford (MA 1968; DPhil 1975). Lectr in Hist., Oriel Coll., Oxford, 1971–76; Lectr, 1976, Sen. Lectr, 1979, Reader in History, 1986–90, Univ. of Sheffield. Editor, English Historical Rev., 1996–2000. *Publications:* (with R. E. Quinault) Popular Protest and Public Order, 1974; Social Conditions in Britain between the Wars, 1977; London in the Age of Reform, 1977; (jtly) Crime and Law in Nineteenth Century Britain, 1978; Popular Disturbances in 1700–1870, 1979, 2nd edn 1992; (with M. Bentley) High and Low Politics in Modern Britain, 1983; British Society 1914–45, 1984; (with A. J. Fletcher) Order and Disorder in early modern England, 1985; (with S. Salter), The Working Class and Politics in Europe and America 1929–1945, 1990; The Macmillan Dictionary of British and European History since 1914, 1991; (with A. O'Day) Irish Historical Documents since 1800, 1992; Third Party Politics since 1945, 1993; (with J. C. Binfield) Sport, Culture and Politics, 1993; (with J. Gregory) The Longman Companion to the Eighteenth Century, 1999; with C. P. Cook: The Slump: society and politics during the Depression, 1977, 2nd edn 1993; The Longman Atlas of Modern British History, 1978; British Historical Facts 1760–1830, 1980; The Longman Handbook of Modern British History 1714–1980, 1983, 2nd edn 1996; The Longman Handbook to Modern European History 1760–1985, 1987, 2nd edn 1998; British Historical Facts 1688–1760, 1988; The Longman Handbook of World History since 1914, 1991; The Longman Companion to Britain since 1945, 1996, 2nd edn 2000; The Longman Handbook of the Modern World, 1998. *Recreations:* book-collecting, gardening. *Address:* Worcester College, Oxford OX1 2HB. *T:* (01865) 278348.

STEVENSON, Joseph Aidan; non-executive Director, Johnson Matthey plc, 1991–95; Chairman, Young Group plc, 1992–95; *b* 19 April 1931; *s* of Robert and Bridget Stevenson; *m* 1956, Marjorie Skinner; one *s* two *d*. *Educ:* Birmingham Univ. (BSc Hons Metallurgy). Instr Lieut, RN, 1955–58. Joined Johnson Matthey, 1958, as development metallurgist; held a number of sen. management, operating and div. dirships within the Johnson Matthey Gp; Gp Exec. Dir, 1982–91; Chief Exec. Officer, 1989–91. Chm. of Govs, Combe Bank Indep. Girls' Sch., Kent, 1985–91. Royal London Society for the Blind: Mem. Council, 1990–98 (Vice-Chm., 1995–98); Special Advr, Workbridge Scheme for employment of blind people, 1998–; Chm. Govs, RLSB Coll. of Further Educn (Dorton House), 1995–98. FIM 1990 (Mem. Council, 1991–). Liveryman: Goldsmiths' Co.; Clockmakers' Co. Distinguished Achievement Award, Inst. of Precious Metals, 1989. *Recreations:* golf, sailing. *Club:* Knole Park Golf (Sevenoaks).

STEVENSON, Juliet Anne Virginia, CBE 1999; actress; Associate Artist, Royal Shakespeare Company; *b* 30 Oct. 1956; partner, Hugh Brody; one *s* one *d*. *Educ:* RADA (Bancroft Gold Medal). With Royal Shakespeare Company, 1978–86: Les Liaisons Dangereuses; As You Like It; Troilus and Cressida; Measure for Measure; A Midsummer Night's Dream; The Witch of Edmonton; Money; Henry IV parts I and II; Once in a

Lifetime; The White Guard; Hippolytus; Antony and Cleopatra; The Churchill Play; Breaking the Silence; *other plays* include: Yerma, NT, 1987; Hedda Gabler, NT, 1989; Burn This, Hampstead, transf. Lyric, 1990; Death and the Maiden, Royal Court, transf. Duke of York's, 1991; The Duchess of Malfi, Greenwich, transf. Wyndhams, 1995; Caucasian Chalk Circle, RNT, 1997; Not I, and Footfalls, RSC and European tour, 1998; Private Lives, RNT, 1999; Country, Royal Court, 2000; *films* include: Drowning by Numbers, 1988; Ladder of Swords, 1990; Truly, Madly, Deeply, 1991; The Trial, 1993; The Secret Rapture, 1994; Emma, 1996; several television rôles. *Publication:* (jtly) Clamorous Voices, 1988. *Address:* c/o Markham and Froggatt Ltd, Julian House, 4 Windmill Street, W1P 1HF.

STEVENSON, Rt Rev. Kenneth William; *see* Portsmouth, Bishop of.

STEVENSON, Michael Charles; Joint Director, Factual and Learning, BBC, since 2000; *b* 14 Aug. 1960; *s* of Michael Anthony and Ena Elizabeth Stevenson; *m* 1987, Deborah Frances Taylor; one *s* two *d. Educ:* Doncaster Grammar Sch.; Christ Church, Oxford (LitHum). British Broadcasting Corporation: trainee, 1983; Producer, Talks and Documentaries, Radio, 1984; Producer, News and Current Affairs, TV, 1988; Chief Assistant, Policy and Planning Unit, 1990; Dep. Editor, On The Record, 1991; Secretary, 1992–96; Dep. Dir, Regl Broadcasting, 1996–99; Dir of Educn, 1999–2000. Mem. Bd, Re:source, 2000–. Mem. Council, Nat. Coll. for Sch. Leadership, 2000–. Sir Huw Wheldon Fellow, Univ. of Wales, 1989. *Recreations:* music, tennis. *Address:* BBC Broadcasting House, W1A 1AA. *T:* (020) 7580 4468. *Club:* Vanderbilt Racquet.

STEVENSON, Prof. Olive, CBE 1994; DLitt; Professor of Social Work Studies, University of Nottingham, 1984–94 (Head, School of Social Studies, 1987–91), now Professor Emeritus; Fellow, St Anne's College, University of Oxford, since 1970; *b* 13 Dec. 1930; *d* of John and Evelyn Stevenson. *Educ:* Purley County Grammar Sch. for Girls; Lady Margaret Hall, Oxford (BA EngLitt, MA 1955); London Sch. of Economics (Dip. in Social Studies, Dip. in Child Care); DLitt Nottingham, 1992. Tavistock Clinic; Child Care Officer, Devon CC, 1954–58; Lecturer in Applied Social Studies: Univ. of Bristol, 1959–61; Univ. of Oxford, 1961–68; Social Work Adviser, Supplementary Benefits Commn, 1968–70; Reader in Applied Social Studies, Univ. of Oxford, 1970–76; Prof. of Social Policy and Social Work: Univ. of Keele, 1976–82; Univ. of Liverpool, 1983–84. Member: Royal Commn on Civil Liability, 1973–78; Social Security Adv. Cttee, 1982–; Registered Homes Tribunal, 1985–90; Chairman: Adv. Cttee, Rent Rebates and Rent Allowances, 1977–83; Age Concern England, 1980–83; Councils of Voluntary Service Nat. Assoc., 1985–88; Care and Repair, 1993–97; Peterborough, Cambridge, Leicester City, Leics and Rutland County Area Child Protection Cttees, 1997–2000. Series Ed., Working Together for Children, Young People and Families, 1996–99. Hon. LittD East Anglia, 1996. *Publications:* Someone Else's Child, 1965, rev. edn 1977; Claimant or Client?, 1970; Social Service Teams: the practitioner's view, 1978; Child Abuse: interprofessional communication, 1979; Specialisation in Social Service Teams, 1981; (with Fuller) Policies, Programmes and Disadvantage, 1983; Age and Vulnerability, a guide to better care, 1988; (ed) Child Abuse: public policy and professional practice, 1989; (jtly) Community Care and Empowerment, 1993; Neglected Children: issues and dilemmas, 1998; (jtly) Child Welfare in the UK, 1998. *Recreations:* music, cookery, conversation. *Address:* c/o Centre for Social Work, University of Nottingham, Nottingham NG7 2RD.

STEVENSON, Maj.-Gen. Paul Timothy, OBE 1985 (MBE 1975); Clerk to Carpenters' Co., since 1992; *b* 9 March 1940; *s* of Ernest Stevenson and Dorothy Stevenson (*née* Trehearn); *m* 1965, Ann Douglas Drysdale; one *s* one *d. Educ:* Bloxham Sch. Commissioned Royal Marines 1958; 41 Commando, 1960; 45 Commando, Aden, 1962; HMS Mohawk, Gulf and W Indies, 1965–68; Army Staff Coll., 1972; 45 Commando, 1973–75; HMS Bulwark, 1975; Instructor, RN Staff Coll., 1978; SO Plans, HQ Land Forces, Falklands Campaign, 1982; CO 42 Commando, 1983; NATO Defence Coll., 1986; Dir, RM Personnel, 1987–88; RCDS 1989; Comdr, British Forces, Falkland Is, 1989–90. Pres., RMA, 1997–. Modern Pentathlon British Team, 1962–69 (Olympic Team Manager, 1964); Biathlon British Team, 1965. *Recreations:* field sports, golf, gardening, ski-ing. *Address:* Lacys, Wortley, Wotton-under-Edge, Glos GL12 7QP. *Club:* Army and Navy.

STEVENSON, Robert Bryce; General President, National Union of Footwear Leather and Allied Trades, 1980–90, retired; *b* 26 June 1926; *s* of Daniel Liddle Stevenson and Christina Stevenson; *m* 1947, Margaret Eugenia; two *d. Educ:* Caldercruix Advanced Sch., Airdrie, Lanarks. Full-time Officer NUFLAT, Street, Som. Branch, 1961–80. Member, 1980–: Internat. Textile, Garment and Leather Workers Fedn Exec. Council and Cttee (Brussels); Jt Cttee, Footwear Industry in Europe (Brussels); Footwear Econ. Devlt Cttee, 1980–88; TUC Textile, Clothing and Footwear Industries Cttee; Council, Shoe and Allied Trades Res. Assoc.; Boot and Shoe Repairing Wages Council for GB; Bd of Management, Boot Trade Benevolent Soc.; Mem., Footwear Leather and Fur Skin Industry Trng Bd, 1980–82; Mem., TUC Gen. Council, 1984–90. JP Wells and Glastonbury 1970 (on Supplementary List, Northants, 1981). *Recreations:* listening to and playing music, all sports.

STEVENSON, Robert Wilfrid, (Wilf); Director, Smith Institute, since 1997; *b* 19 April 1947; *s* of James Alexander Stevenson and Elizabeth Anne Stevenson (*née* Macrae); *m* 1st, 1972, Jennifer Grace Antonio (marr. diss. 1979); 2nd, 1991, Elizabeth Ann Minogue; one *s* two *d. Educ:* Edinburgh Academy; University College, Oxford (MA Natural Sciences, Chemistry); Napier Polytechnic. FCCA. Research Officer, Edinburgh Univ. Students' Assoc., 1970–74; Sec., Napier Coll., Edinburgh, 1974–87; Dep. Dir, 1987–88, Dir, 1988–97, BFI. *Recreations:* cinema, hill walking, bridge. *Address:* Missenden House, Little Missenden, Amersham, Bucks HP7 0RD. *T:* (01494) 890689, *Fax:* (01494) 868127; *e-mail:* wilfstevenson@msn.com.

STEVENSON, Sir Simpson, Kt 1976; DL; *b* 18 Aug. 1921; *s* of T. H. Stevenson, Greenock; *m* 1945, Jean Holmes Henry, JP, Port Glasgow. *Educ:* Greenock High Sch. Member: Greenock Town Council, 1949–67 and 1971– (Provost of Greenock, 1962–65); Inverclyde DC, 1974– (Provost, 1984–88); Vice-Chm., Clyde Port Authority, 1966–69; Chm., Greater Glasgow Health Bd, 1973–83; Chm., Scottish Health Services Common Service Agency, 1973–77, 1983–87. Member: Western Regional Hosp. Bd (Scotland), 1959–; Scottish Hosp. Administrative Staffs Cttee, 1965–74 (Chm., 1972 74); Chm., W Regional Hosp. Bd (Scotland), Glasgow, 1967–74; Member: Scottish Hosp. Endowments Commn, 1969–70; Scottish Health Services Planning Council; Royal Commn on the NHS, 1976–79. Chm., Consortium of Local Authorities Special Programme (CLASP), 1974. DL Renfrewshire, 1990. Hon. LLD Glasgow, 1982. *Recreations:* football, reading, choral singing. *Address:* 3F Cragburngate, Albert Road, Gourock PA19 1NZ.

STEVENSON, Stewart; *see* Stevenson, J. A. S.

STEVENSON, Struan John Stirton; farmer; Member (C) Scotland, European Parliament, since 1999; *b* 4 April 1948; *s* of late Robert Harvey Ure Stevenson and Elizabeth Robertson (*née* Stirton); *m* 1974, Patricia Anne Taylor; two *s. Educ:* Strathallan Sch.; West of Scotland Agricl Coll. (DipAgr 1970). Member (C): Girvan DC, 1970–74; Kyle and Carrick DC, 1974–92 (Leader, 1986–88); Conservative Gp Leader, COSLA, 1986–88; Scottish agriculture spokesman, 1992–97, Scottish spokesman on envmt, transport, media, arts, heritage and tourism, 1997–98, Conservative Party; UK spokesman on fisheries, and dep. UK spokesman on agric., EP, 1999–. Contested (C): Carrick, Cumnock and Doon Valley, 1987; Edinburgh S, 1992; Dumfries, 1997; NE Scotland, EP elecn, Nov. 1998. Chm., Tuesday Club, 1998–. Hon. DSc State Med. Acad. of Semipalatinsk, Kazakstan, 2000. *Recreations:* contemporary art, music, opera, poetry, theatre, cinema, photography. *Address:* European Parliament, Rue Wiertz, 1047 Brussels, Belgium. *T:* (2) 2847710. *Club:* New (Edinburgh).

STEVENSON, Timothy Edwin Paul; Chairman, Travis Perkins plc, since 2001; *b* 14 May 1948; *s* of late Derek Paul Stevenson, CBE; *m* 1973, Marion Emma Lander Johnston; three *d. Educ:* Canford Sch., Dorset; Worcester Coll., Oxford (BA Jurisp.). Burmah Castrol: Asst Gp Legal Advr, 1975–77; Gp Planning Manager, 1977–81; Chief Exec., Castrol España, 1981–85; Marketing Manager, Develt, 1985–86; Manager, Corporate Develt, 1986–88; Chief Exec., Expandite Gp, 1988–90; Chief Exec., Fuels Gp, 1990–93; Dir, Lubricants, 1993–98; Chief Exec., 1998–2000. Non-exec. Dir, DfEE, 1997–; Sen. Ind. Dir, and Chm. Audit Cttee, National Express, 2001–. Mem. Council, MOMA, Oxford, 1998–. Vice-Chm., Open Democracy. Sloan Fellow, London Business Sch. *Recreations:* hill walking, reading, music. *Address:* Travis Perkins plc, Ryehill House, Rye Hill Close, Lodge Farm Industrial Estate, Northampton NN5 7UA.

STEVENSON, Wilf; *see* Stevenson, R. W.

STEVENSON, William; *see* Stevenson, A. W.

STEVENSON, William Trevor, CBE 1985; DL; *b* 21 March 1921; *o s* of late William Houston Stevenson and Mabel Rose Stevenson (*née* Hunt); *m* Alison Wilson (*née* Roy). *Educ:* Edinburgh Acad. Apprentice mechanical engineer, 1937–41; engineer, 1941–45; entered family food manufacturing business, Cottage Rusks, 1945; Man. Dir, 1948–54; Chm., 1954–59; Chief Executive, Cottage Rusks Associates, (following merger with Joseph Rank Ltd), 1959–69; Reg. Dir, Ranks Hovis McDougall, 1969–74; Dir, various cos in food, engrg, medical, hotel and aviation industries, 1974–; Chairman: Gleneagles Hotels, 1981–83; Scottish Transport Gp, 1981–86; Hodgson Martin Ventures, 1982–88; Alexander Wilkie, 1977–90. Master, Co. of Merchants of City of Edinburgh, 1978–80. DL City of Edinburgh, 1984. *Recreations:* flying, sailing, curling. *Club:* Caledonian.

STEWARD, Rear Adm. Cedric John, CB 1984; Director, Antric Park, since 1986; Horse Stud Owner, Antric Park, Auckland; Chief of Naval Staff, New Zealand, 1983–86, retired; *b* 31 Jan. 1931; *s* of Ethelbert Harold Steward and Anne Isabelle Steward; *m* 1952, Marie Antoinette Gurr; three *s. Educ:* Northcote College, Auckland, NZ; RNC Dartmouth; RNC Greenwich. Served: HMS Devonshire, 1950; HMS Illustrious, 1950; HMS Glory, 1951 (Korean Campaign and UN Medals, 1951); HMAS Australia, HMAS Barcoo, 1952; HM NZ Ships Hawea, 1953, Kaniere, 1954 (Korea), Tamaki, 1955–58, Stawell, 1958–59; HMAS Creswell (RAN College), 1959–62; HM NZ Ships Rotoiti, 1962–63 (Antarctic support), Tamaki, 1963–64, Royalist, 1965–66 (Confrontation), Philomel, 1966, Inverell (in Command), 1966–67; JSSC Latimer, 1960, RNZN Liaison Officer Australia and Dep. Head, NZ Defence Liaison Staff, Canberra, 1969–73; in Command, HMNZS Otago, 1973–74; in Command and Captain F11, HMNZS Canterbury, 1974–75; Defence HQ, 1976–77; RCDS, 1978; Dep. Chief of Naval Staff, NZ, 1979–81; Commodore, Auckland, and NZ Maritime Comdr, 1981–83. Member: US Naval Inst., 1983; Australian Naval Inst., 1993. *Recreations:* rugby, golf, tennis, equestrian events, fishing, boating, philately, farming. *Clubs:* Helensville Golf (Kaukapakapa), Auckland Racing (Ellerslie).

STEWART, family name of **Earl of Galloway** and **Baron Stewartby**.

STEWART; *see* Vane-Tempest-Stewart, family name of Marquess of Londonderry.

STEWART, Sir Alan, KBE 1981 (CBE 1972); Vice-Chancellor of Massey University, 1964–83; *b* 8 Dec. 1917; *s* of Kenneth and Vera Mary Stewart; *m* 1950, Joan Cecily Sisam; one *s* three *d. Educ:* Massey Agricultural College; University College, Oxford. Sen. Lectr, Massey Agric. Coll., 1950–54; Chief Consulting Officer, Milk Marketing Board, England and Wales, 1954–58; Principal, Massey Agric. Coll., 1959–63. Hon. DSc Massey, 1984. *Address:* PO Box 3, Whakatane, New Zealand. *T:* (7) 3086619.

STEWART, Sir Alan (d'Arcy), 13th Bt *cr* 1623; yachtbuilder; *b* 29 Nov. 1932; *s* of Sir Jocelyn Harry Stewart, 12th Bt, and Constance Mary (*d* 1940), *d* of D'Arcy Shillaber; *S* father, 1982; *m* 1952, Patricia, *d* of Lawrence Turner; two *s* two *d. Educ:* All Saints College, Bathurst, NSW. *Heir: s* Nicholas Courtney d'Arcy Stewart, BSc, HDipEd, *b* 4 Aug. 1953. *Address:* One Acre, Ramelton, Co. Donegal.

STEWART, Alastair James; presenter: London Tonight, since 1993; The Sunday Programme with Alastair Stewart, GMTV, since 1994; *b* 22 June 1952; *s* of Group Captain James F. Stewart and Joan Mary Stewart (*née* Lord); *m* 1978, Sally Ann Jung; three *s* one *d. Educ:* St Augustine's Abbey Sch., Ramsgate; Univ. of Bristol. Dep. Pres., Nat. Union of Students, 1974–76. Reporter and presenter, Southern ITV, 1976–80; industrial corresp., ITN, 1980; presenter, ITN: News at Ten, 1981; Channel 4 News, 1983; News at One, 1985; News at 5.45, 1986; Parliament Programme, 1988; News at Ten, 1989, 1991–92; Washington corresp., 1990–91; presenter: BBC Radio, 1994; Missing, LWT, 1992–96; The Carlton Debates, 1993–; Police, Camera, Action, Carlton TV, 1994–. Commentator and presenter, numerous parly programmes and State occasions, UK and overseas, incl. first live transmission from House of Lords, 1985, House of Commons, 1989, Gulf War and liberation of Kuwait, 1991; ITV General Election, 1992, 1997; Who Wants to be a London Mayor?, 2000; King of the Castle, 2001. Vice President: Homestart UK, 1997–; NCH Action for Children, 1998–. Patron: Lord Mayor Treloar Coll.; Hope Medical; Vice Patron: Missing Person's Helpline, 1993–; Zito Trust, 1995–; SANE, 1999–. Annual Award, RBL, 1996. *Recreations:* travel, cartography, a catholic taste in music. *Address:* London News Network, London Television Centre, Upper Ground, SE1 9LT. *T:* (020) 7827 7700.

STEWART, Alastair Lindsay; QC (Scot.) 1995, Sheriff of Tayside, Central and Fife at Dundee, since 1990; Temporary Judge in Supreme Courts, Scotland, since 1996; *b* 28 Nov. 1938; *s* of Alexander Lindsay Stewart and Anna Stewart; *m* 1st, 1968, Annabel Claire Stewart (marr. diss. 1991), *yr d* of late Prof. W. McC. Stewart; two *s*; 2nd, 1991, Sheila Anne Mackinnon (*née* Flockhart), *o d* of late David H. Flockhart. *Educ:* Edinburgh Academy; St Edmund Hall, Oxford (BA); Univ. of Edinburgh (LLB). Admitted to Faculty of Advocates, 1963; Tutor, Faculty of Law, Univ. of Edinburgh, 1963–73; Standing Junior Counsel to Registrar of Restrictive Trading Agreements, 1968–70; Advocate Depute, 1970–73; Sheriff of South Strathclyde, Dumfries and Galloway, at Airdrie, 1973–79, of Grampian, Highland and Islands, at Aberdeen and Stonehaven, 1979–90. Chairman: Grampian Family Conciliation Service, 1984–87 (Hon. Pres., 1987–90); Scottish Assoc.

of Family Conciliation Services, 1986–89. Mem., Judicial Studies Cttee, 2000–. Governor, Robert Gordon's Inst. of Technology, 1982–90 (Vice-Chm. of Governors, 1985–90). Editor, Scottish Civil Law Reports, 1992–95. *Publications:* (contrib.) Sheriff Court Practice, by I. D. Macphail, 1988, jt gen. editor, 2nd edn 1998; The Scottish Criminal Courts in Action, 1990, 2nd edn 1997; various articles in legal jls. *Recreations:* reading, music, walking. *Address:* Sheriffs' Chambers, Sheriff Court House, 6 West Bell Street, Dundee DD1 9AD. *T:* (01382) 318218. *Club:* New (Edinburgh).

STEWART, Sir Alastair (Robin), 3rd Bt *cr* 1960, of Strathgarry, Perth; *b* 26 Sept. 1925; 2nd *s* of Sir Kenneth Dugald Stewart, 1st Bt, GBE and Noel (*d* 1946), *yr d* of Kenric Brodribb, Melbourne; *S* brother, 1992; *m* 1953, Patricia Helen, MBE, ARIBA, *d* of late J. A. Merrett; one *s* three *d. Educ:* Marlborough Coll. Lieut, 1st Royal Gloucestershire Hussars, 1945–47. Dir, Neale & Wilkinson Ltd, 1947–71; Man. Dir, Stewart & Harvey Ltd, 1971–90. *Recreation:* gardening. *Heir: s* John Kenneth Alexander Stewart, *b* 15 Dec. 1961. *Address:* Walters Cottage, North Hill, Little Baddow, Chelmsford, Essex CM3 4TQ. *T:* (01245) 222445.

STEWART, Alec James, MBE 1998; Member: Surrey County Cricket team; England cricket team (Captain, 1998–99); *b* 8 April 1963; *s* of Michael James, (Micky), Stewart and Sheila Marie Macdonald Stewart; *m* 1991, Lynn Blades; one *s* one *d. Educ:* Tiffin Boys' Sch. Joined Surrey County Cricket Club, 1981, capped 1985, Captain, 1992–97; Test début, 1989; overseas tours with England team: W Indies, 1989–90, 1993–94 (Vice Capt.), 1997–98; Australia and NZ, 1990–91; India and Sri Lanka, 1992–93; Australia, 1994–95, 1998–99; S Africa, 1995–96, 1999–2000; Zimbabwe and NZ, 1996–97. *Publication:* (with Brian Murgatroyd) Alec Stewart: a Captain's Diary, 1999. *Address:* c/o Surrey County Cricket Club, The Oval, SE11 5SS.

STEWART, Alexandra Joy, (Mrs M. McBride); Director, Museums, Galleries, Libraries and Heritage, Department for Culture, Media and Sport, since 1999; *b* 11 April 1953; *d* of Charles Stewart and Myrtle Stewart (*née* Sheppard); *m* 1st, 1976, Andrew Smyth (marr. diss. 1990); one *d*; 2nd, 1991, Michael McBride. *Educ:* Bexhill Grammar Sch. for Girls; Durham Univ. (BA Hons). Joined DES, 1975; admin trainee, 1975–79; Private Sec. to Minister for Educn, 1979–81; Principal, 1981–88; Assistant Secretary: Hd of City Technol. Unit, 1988–92; joined DNH, subseq. DCMS, 1992; Hd of Sports Div., then Finance Dir, 1992–99. *Recreations:* my family, gardening, the South Downs, horses. *Address:* Department for Culture, Media and Sport, 2–4 Cockspur Street, SW1Y 5DH. *T:* (020) 7211 6122.

STEWART, Allan; *see* Stewart, J. A.

STEWART, Andrew Struthers, (Andy); farmer; Chairman, Agricultural Training Board, 1992–98; *b* 27 May 1937; *s* of late James Stewart and of Elizabeth Stewart; *m* 1961, Louise Melvin (*née* Skimming); one *s* one *d. Educ:* Strathaven Acad., Scotland; West of Scotland Agricl Coll. Farming Beesthorpe Manor Farm, 1961–. Mem., Caunton Parish Council, 1973–83; Conservative Mem., Notts CC, 1975–83; Cons. spokesman on leisure services, 1981–83. MP (C) Sherwood, 1983–92; contested (C) Sherwood, 1992. PPS to Minister of Agriculture, Fisheries and Food, 1987–89, to Sec. of State for Educn and Science, 1989–90, to Lord Pres. of Council and Leader of H of C, 1990–92. Comr, Rural Develt Commn, 1993–99. Chairman: Strathaven Br., Young Conservatives, 1957 and 1958; Caunton, Maplebeck and Kersall Cons. Br., 1970–73 (Founder Mem.). Chairman: Lantra, NTO for land based industries, 1998–2000; Lantra Trust, 2000–; Member: Newark Br., NFU, 1961– (Mem., County Exec. Cttee, 1966–); Newark and Notts Agricl Soc.; Adv. Mem., Nottingham University Coll. of Agriculture, 1977–82 (formerly Chm., Notts Coll. of Agriculture Brackenhurst); formerly Chm., Governing Bd, Rufford Comprehensive Sch. Youth Club Leader, 1965–76; Life Vice President: Southwell Rugby Club; Caunton Cricket Club; Trustee, Southwell Recreation Centre, 1979–83. *Address:* Beesthorpe Manor Farm, Caunton, Newark, Notts NG23 6AT. *T:* (01636) 636270. *Clubs:* Farmers'; Bentinck Conservative (Hucknall, Notts).

STEWART, Angus; QC (Scot.); *b* 14 Dec. 1946; *s* of Archibald Ian Balfour Stewart, CBE, BL, FSAScot and Ailsa Rosamund Mary Massey; *m* 1975, Jennifer Margaret Stewart; one *d. Educ:* Edinburgh Acad.; Balliol Coll., Oxford (BA); Edinburgh Univ. (LLB). Called to the Scottish Bar, 1975. Keeper, Advocates' Liby, 1994–. Chm., Scottish Council of Law Reporting, 1997–. Trustee: Nat. Liby of Scotland, 1994–; Stewart Heritage Trust, 1994–; Internat. E Boat Class Assoc., 1993–. Chm., Abbotsford Liby Project, 1996–. *Address:* 8 Ann Street, Edinburgh EH4 1PJ. *T:* (0131) 332 4083.

STEWART, Annie; Editor, The Voice, 1995–99; *b* 24 Dec. 1959; *d* of Charles Alanzo Stewart and Madge Petrona Stewart; one *d. Educ:* Stratford Grammar Sch. Reporter: Walthamstow Express, 1986–87; The Voice, 1987–95; Editor-in-Chief, The Weekly Jl, 1997–99. Dir, M&M Media, 1997–. *Recreations:* stocks and shares, travel. *Address:* 7 Capstan Court, 24 Wapping Wall, E1 9TE. *T:* (020) 7737 7377. *Club:* Royal Commonwealth Society.

STEWART, Brian John, CBE 1996; Chairman, Scottish & Newcastle plc, since 2000; *b* 9 April 1945; *m* 1971, Seonaid Duncan; two *s* one *d. Educ:* Edinburgh Univ. (MSc). Mem., Scottish Inst. of Chartered Accountants. Scottish and Newcastle Breweries, subseq. Scottish and Newcastle plc: joined 1976; Finance Dir, 1988–91; Gp Chief Exec., 1991–2000; Dep. Chm., 1997–2000. Director: Booker, 1993–99; Standard Life Assurance Co., 1993–. *Recreations:* golf, ski-ing. *Address:* 33 Ellersley Road, Edinburgh EH12 6HX.

STEWART, Brian Thomas Webster, CMG 1969; Business Development Adviser (China), since 1996; Hon. Lecturer, Hong Kong University, 1986–98; *b* 27 April 1922; *s* of late Redvers Buller Stewart and Mabel Banks Sparks, Broich, Crieff; *m* 1946, Millicent Peggy Pollock (marr. diss. 1970); two *d*; *m* 1972, Sally Nugent; one *s* one *d. Educ:* Trinity Coll., Glenalmond; Worcester Coll., Oxford (MA). Commnd The Black Watch (RHR), 1942; served Europe and Far East (Capt.). Joined Malayan Civil Service, 1946; studying Chinese Macau, 1947; Asst Sec., Chinese Affairs, Singapore, 1949; Devonshire Course, Oxford, 1950; Asst Comr for Labour, Kuala Lumpur, 1951; Sec. for Chinese Affairs, Supt of Chinese Schs, Malacca and Penang, 1952–57; joined HM Diplomatic Service, 1957; served Rangoon, Peking, Shanghai, Manila, Kuala Lumpur, Hanoi; Asst Sec., Cabinet Office, 1968–72; Counsellor, Hong Kong, 1972–74; FCO, 1974–78. Special Rep., Rubber Growers Assoc., Malaysia, 1979–82; Dir of Ops (China), Racal Electronics, 1982–96. *Publication:* All Men's Wisdom (anthology of Chinese Proverbs), 1957. *Recreations:* climbing, sailing, ski-ing, chamber music, orientalia particularly chinoiserie. *Address:* c/o Royal Bank of Scotland, Crieff, Perthshire PH7 3RX. *Clubs:* Athenæum, Special Forces; Hong Kong.

STEWART, Rev. Dr Charles Edward; Chaplain, Royal Hospital School, since 2000; *b* 10 June 1946; *s* of Charles Stewart and Mary Stewart (*née* McDougall); *m* 1970, Margaret Marion Smith; two *s* one *d. Educ:* Strathclyde Univ. (BSc; PhD); Glasgow Univ. (BD); Edinburgh Univ. (MTh). Ordained, C of S, 1976; Chaplain: HMS Sea Hawk, RNAS Culdrose, 1976–78; Clyde Submarine Base, 1978–80; Staff of Flag Officer 3rd Flotilla, 1980; Chaplain: HMS Hermes, Falklands Conflict, 1981; HMS Neptune, 1982–85; HMS Drake and Staff of Flag Officer Plymouth, 1985–87; HMS Raleigh, 1987–90; BRNC, Dartmouth, 1990–92; Asst Dir Naval Chaplaincy Service, 1992–94; HMS Invincible, Bosnia, 1994–96; Dir Naval Chaplaincy Service, 1996–97; Dir Gen. Naval Chaplaincy Service, 1997–2000; Chaplain of the Fleet, 1998–2000. QHC 1996–2000. South Atlantic Medal, 1982; NATO Medal, 1995. *Recreations:* gardening, water colours (painting), music, hill walking, model ship construction. *Address:* 48 Royal Hospital School, Holbrook, Ipswich, Suffolk IP9 2RX.

STEWART, Colin MacDonald, CB 1983; FIA; Directing Actuary, Government Actuary's Department, 1974–84; *b* 26 Dec. 1922; *s* of John Stewart and Lillias Cecilia MacDonald Fraser; *m* 1948, Gladys Edith Thwaites; three *d. Educ:* Queen's Park Secondary Sch., Glasgow. Clerical Officer, Rosyth Dockyard, 1939–42. Served War: Fleet Air Arm (Lieut (A) RNVR), 1942–46. Govt Actuary's Dept, London, 1946–84. Head of Actuarial Res., Godwins Ltd, 1985–88. FIA 1953. *Publications:* The Students' Society Log 1960–85, 1985; (contrib.) Life, Death and Money, 1998; numerous articles on actuarial and demographic subjects in British and internat. jls. *Recreations:* genealogical research, foreign travel, grandchilding. *Address:* 8 The Chase, Coulsdon, Surrey CR5 2EG. *T:* (020) 8660 3966.

STEWART, Sir David James H.; *see* Henderson-Stewart.

STEWART, David John; MP (Lab) Inverness East, Nairn and Lochaber, since 1997; *b* 5 May 1956; *s* of John and Alice Stewart; *m* 1982, Linda MacDonald; one *s* one *d. Educ:* Paisley Coll. (BA Hons); Stirling Univ. (Dip. Social Wk, CQSW); Open Univ. (Professional Dip. Mgt). Social work manager. Member (Lab): Nithsdale DC, 1984–86; Inverness DC, 1988–96 (Dep. Leader, Labour Gp). Contested (Lab) Inverness, Nairn and Lochaber, 1987 and 1992. *Address:* House of Commons, SW1A 0AA.

STEWART, Captain Sir David (John Christopher), 7th Bt *cr* 1803, of Athenree, Tyrone; *b* 19 June 1935; *s* of Sir Hugh Charlie Godfray Stewart, 6th Bt and his 1st wife, Rosemary Elinor Dorothy, *d* of Maj. George Peacocke; *S* father, 1994; *m* 1959, Bridget Anne, *er d* of late Patrick W. Sim; three *d. Educ:* Bradfield Coll.; RMA Sandhurst. Commnd Royal Inniskilling Fusiliers, 1956; seconded to Trucial Oman Scouts, 1957–58 (Jebel Akhdar Campaign, 1957); Adjt 1958; served in Trucial States, Oman and Muscat, 1957–58, Germany, 1958–59, Kenya, 1960–62 (Kuwait Operation, 1961), UN Peacekeeping Force, Cyprus, 1964; retd as Captain, 1965. Representative for E. S. & A. Robinson, Bristol, 1965–69; Director: Maurice James Holdings, Coventry, 1969–77; Papropak UK, 1977–79; self-employed, 1979–; owner, George Inn, Middlezoy, Somerset, 1982–85. Hon. Organiser, RBL Poppy Appeal, Wiveliscombe, 1996–; Hon. Treas., Friends of Somerset SSAFA-Forces Help, 1998–. *Recreations:* golf, cricket, picture restoration and framing. *Heir:* half *b* Hugh Nicholas Stewart [*b* 20 April 1955; *m* 1976, Anna Leeke; one *s* three *d*]. *Address:* Tower View, 8 Silver Street, Wiveliscombe, Taunton, Somerset TA4 2PA. *Clubs:* MCC; Oake Manor Golf.

STEWART, Sir Edward (Jackson), Kt 1980; Chairman, Stewarts Hotels Pty Ltd, 1956–96; *b* 10 Dec. 1923; *s* of Charles Jackson Stewart and Jessie Stewart (*née* Dobbie); *m* 1956, Shirley Patricia Holmes; four *s. Educ:* St Joseph's College, Brisbane. Fellow Catering Inst. of Australia (FCIA); FAIM. Served with Australian Army, RAA, 1942–44. Chairman: Castlemaine Perkins Ltd, 1977–80 (Dir, 1970); Castlemaine Tooheys Ltd, 1980–85; Director: Birch Carroll & Coyle Ltd, 1967–92; Roadshow (Qld) Pty Ltd, 1970–92; Darwin Cinemas Pty Ltd, 1972–92; G. R. E. (Australia) Ltd, 1980–92; Besser (Qld) Ltd, 1981–87; Bank of Queensland Ltd, 1986–96; QUF Industries Ltd, 1986–95. President: Queensland Hotels Assoc., 1963–69; Aust. Hotels Assoc., 1966–69. Mem. Totalisator Administration Bd of Queensland, 1977–81. Chm., Queensland Inst. of Medical Research Trust, 1980–88. *Recreations:* reading, fishing and thoroughbred breeding. *Address:* 33 Eckersley Avenue, Buderim, Qld 4556, Australia. *Clubs:* Australian (Sydney); Brisbane, Tattersall's (Past Pres.) (Brisbane); Queensland Turf.

STEWART, Prof. Sir Frederick (Henry), Kt 1974; FRS 1964; PhD Cantab; FRSE; FGS; Regius Professor of Geology, 1956–82, now Emeritus, Dean of Science Faculty, 1966–68, and Member, University Court, 1969–70, Edinburgh University; *b* 16 Jan. 1916; *o s* of Frederick Robert Stewart and Hester Alexander, Aberdeen; *m* 1945, Mary Florence Elinor Rainbow (*see* Mary Stewart); no *c. Educ:* Fettes Coll.; Univ. of Aberdeen (BSc); Emmanuel Coll., Cambridge. Mineralogist in Research Dept of ICI Ltd (Billingham Div.), 1941–43; Lectr in Geology, Durham Colls in the Univ. of Durham, 1943–56. Vice-Pres., Geological Soc. of London, 1965–66; Member: Council for Scientific Policy, 1967–71; Adv. Council for Applied R&D, 1976–79; Chairman: NERC, 1971–73 (Mem., Geol. Geophysics Cttee, 1967–70); Adv. Bd for Res. Councils, 1973–79 (Mem., 1972–73); Mem. Council, Royal Soc., 1969–70; Trustee, BM (Nat. Hist.), 1983–87; Mem. Council, Scottish Marine Biol Assoc., 1983–89. Lyell Fund Award, 1951, J. B. Tyrrell Fund, 1952, Geological Soc. of London; Mineralogical Soc. of America Award, 1952; Lyell Medal, Geological Soc. of London, 1970; Clough Medal, Edinburgh Geol. Soc., 1971; Sorby Medal, Yorks Geol. Soc., 1975. Hon. DSc: Aberdeen, 1975; Leicester, 1977; Heriot-Watt, 1978; Durham, 1983; Glasgow, 1988. *Publications:* The British Caledonides (ed with M. R. W. Johnson), 1963; Marine Evaporites, 1963; papers in Mineralogical Magazine, Jl of Geol. Soc. of London, etc., dealing with igneous and metamorphic petrology and salt deposits. *Recreation:* fishing. *Address:* House of Letterawe, Lochawe, Dalmally, Argyll PA33 1AH. *T:* (01838) 200329. *Club:* New (Edinburgh).

STEWART, George Girdwood, CB 1979; MC 1945; TD 1954; Associate Director, Oakwood Environmental, since 1990; *b* 12 Dec. 1919; *o s* of late Herbert A. Stewart, BSc, and of Janetta Dunlop Girdwood; *m* 1950, Shelagh Jean Morven Murray; one *s* one *d. Educ:* Kelvinside Academy, Glasgow; Glasgow Univ.; Edinburgh Univ. (BSc). Served RA, 1940–46 (MC, despatches); CO 278 (Lowland) Field Regt RA (TA), 1957–60. Dist Officer, Forestry Commn, 1949–61; Asst Conservator, 1961–67; Conservator, West Scotland, 1967–69; Comr for Forest and Estate Management, 1969–79; National Trust for Scotland: Mem., Council, 1975–79; Rep., Branklyn Garden, Perth, 1980–84; Regional Rep., Central and Tayside, 1984–88; Forestry Consultant, 1989–93. Specialist advr, Select Cttee on EEC Forestry Policy, 1986; Cairngorm Estate Advr, Highlands and Islands Enterprise, 1988–98. Member: BR Bd Envt Panel, 1980–90; Countryside Commn for Scotland, 1981–88; Chm., Scottish Wildlife Trust, 1981–87; Cairngorm Recreation Trust, 1986–. Pres., Scottish Nat. Ski Council, 1988–94 (Hon. Vice-Pres., 1998–). Pres., Scottish Ski Club, 1971–75; Vice-Pres., Nat. Ski Fedn of GB; Chm., Alpine Racing Cttee, 1975–78. Mem., British Team, Veterans World Team Tennis Championships, 1999, 2001. FRSA; FICFor; Hon. FLI. Nat. Service to Sport Award, Scottish Sports Council, 1995. *Recreations:* ski-ing, tennis, studying Scottish painting. *Address:* 11 Mansfield Road, Scone, Perth PH2 6SA. *T:* (01738) 551815. *Club:* Ski Club of Great Britain.

STEWART, (George Robert) Gordon, OBE 1984; Secretary, 1976–83, Legal Adviser 1983–89, Institute of Chartered Accountants of Scotland; *b* 13 Oct. 1924; *s* of David Gordon Stewart and Mary Grant Thompson or Stewart; *m* 1952, Rachel Jean Morrison;

two *s* one *d.* *Educ:* George Watson's Coll., Edinburgh; Edinburgh Univ. (MA 1947, LLB 1949). WS. Mem., Law Soc. of Scotland, 1949–92. Served War, 1943–46: Captain, Royal Signals; Burma and SEAC. In practice as WS, Melville & Lindesay, WS, Edinburgh, 1950–59; Asst Sec., subseq. Sec., and Dir, Ideal-Standard Ltd, Hull, 1959–75. *Recreations:* aerobics, gardening. *Address:* 15 Hillpark Loan, Edinburgh EH4 7BH. *T:* (0131) 312 7079.

STEWART, Prof. George Russell, PhD, DSc; Executive Dean, Faculty of Science, University of Western Australia, since 1998; *b* 25 Feb. 1944; *s* of George and Isobella Stewart; *m* 1978, Janice Anne Grimes; three *d.* *Educ:* Pinner County Grammar Sch.; Univ. of Bristol (BSc 1965; PhD 1968); DSc London 1991. Lectr in Botany, Univ. of Manchester, 1968–81; London University: Prof. of Botany and Head of Dept, Birkbeck Coll., 1981–85; Quain Prof. of Botany, 1985–91 and Head of Dept of Biology, 1987–91, UCL; Dean of Faculty of Sci., 1990–91; Prof. of Botany, Univ. of Queensland, 1992–98. Vis. Lectr, Dept of Biology, Univ. of Lagos, Nigeria; Visiting Professor: Dept of Botany, Univ. of Queensland, Aust.; Dept of Biology, Univ. of Campinas, Brazil; Dept of Biology, Univ. of WA. Member: Plants and Envmt Cttee, AFRC, 1989–91; Plants and Envmt Res. Bd, AFRC (Chm., 1989–91); Agriculture Cttee, Long Ashton Res. Station, 1990–91; Inter-Agency Cttee on Res. into Global Envmtl Change (Working Gp 2), 1990–91; Inst. of Zoology Cttee, 1989–91. Mem., Bd of Dirs, SciTech Discovery Centre, 1999–. *Publications:* (ed jtly) The Genetic Manipulation of Plants and its Application to Agriculture, 1984; numerous scientific papers on plant physiology and metabolism and chapters in books and conf. proc. *Recreations:* cycling, cooking. *Address:* Faculty of Science, University of Western Australia, Nedlands, WA 6907, Australia. *T:* (8) 93803159; *e-mail:* gstewart@science.uwa.edu.au.

STEWART, Gillian Mary; Head of Children and Young People's Group, Scottish Executive Education Department, since 1999; *b* 2 June 1945; *d* of John Knott and Nora Elizabeth Knott; marr. diss.; two *s.* *Educ:* Blyth Grammar Sch.; Univ. of Durham (BA Hons Class 1 German). Joined Scottish Office, 1970; posts in educn and social work; Asst Sec., 1984; posts in historic buildings and local govt; Under-Sec., 1992; Hd of Criminal Justice Gp, 1992–97; Hd of Social Work Services Gp, Home Dept, 1997–99. *Recreations:* swimming, walking, music, theatre. *Address:* (office) Victoria Quay, Edinburgh EH6 6QQ.

STEWART, Prof. Gordon Thallon, MD; Mechan Professor of Public Health, University of Glasgow, 1972–84, now Emeritus Professor; Hon. Consultant in Epidemiology and Preventive Medicine, Glasgow Area Health Board; *b* 5 Feb. 1919; *s* of John Stewart and Mary L. Thallon; *m* 1946, Joan Kego; two *s* two *d;* *m* 1975, Neena Walker. *Educ:* Paisley Grammar Sch.; Univs of Glasgow and Liverpool. BSc 1939; MB, ChB 1942; DTM&H 1947; MD (High Commendation) 1949; FRCPath 1964; FFCM 1972; MRCPGlas 1972; FRCPGlas 1975. House Phys. and House Surg., 1942–43; Surg. Lieut RNVR, 1943–46; Res. Fellow (MRC), Univ. of Liverpool, 1946–48; Sen. Registrar and Tutor, Wright-Fleming Inst., St Mary's Hosp., London, 1948–52; Cons. Pathologist, SW Metrop. Regional Hosp. Bd, 1954–63; Res. Worker at MRC Labs Carshalton, 1955–63; Prof. of Epidem. and Path., Univ. of N Carolina, 1964–68; Watkins Prof. of Epidem., Tulane Univ. Med. Center, New Orleans, 1968–72. Vis. Prof., Dow Med. Coll., Karachi, 1952–53 and Cornell Univ. Med. Coll., 1970–71; Cons. to WHO, and to NYC Dept of Health; Vis. Lectr and Examr, various univs in UK and overseas. Sen. Fellow, Nat. Science Foundn, Washington, 1964; Delta omega, 1969. *Publications:* (ed) Trends in Epidemiology, 1972; (ed jtly) Penicillin Allergy, 1970; Penicillin Group of Drugs, 1965; papers on chemotherapy of infectious diseases, drug allergy and epidemiology in various med. and sci. jls. *Recreations:* gardening, drawing, music. *Address:* 3 Leyden Terrace, Tenby, Pembrokeshire SA70 7BJ.

STEWART, Prof. Harold Charles, CBE 1975; FRCP; FRSE; DL; Head of Pharmacology Department, St Mary's Hospital Medical School, 1950–74; Professor of Pharmacology in the University of London 1965–74, now Emeritus Professor (Reader, 1949–64); Consultant in Pharmacology to: St Mary's Hospital, 1946; Ministry of Defence (Army), since 1961; *b* 23 Nov. 1906; *s* of Bernard Halley Stewart, MA, MD, FRSE, FKC, Pres. of Sir Halley Stewart Trust, and Mabel Florence Wyatt; *m* 1st, 1929, Dorothy Irene Lowen (*d* 1969); one *s* one *d;* 2nd, 1970, Audrey Patricia Nicolle. *Educ:* Mill Hill Sch.; University Coll. London; Jesus Coll., Cambridge (BA 1928, MA 1934; MB, BCh 1931, MD 1935); University Coll. Hosp.; PhD London 1941; MRCP 1949. Gen. practice, Barnet, Herts, 1932–36. Sub-Dean, St Mary's Hospital Med. Sch., 1950–52; Gresham Prof. in Physic, City Univ., 1968–70. Examr now or formerly, Univs of London, Cambridge, Birmingham, Bristol and Wales, RCS, Soc. of Apothecaries. Research work, mainly on fat absorption and transport in the human subject, and on problems of pain and analgesia. Cons. in Pharmacology to Army; Med. Adviser and Mem. Commonwealth Council, Brit. Commonwealth Ex-Services League; Pres., Sir Halley Stewart Trust for Research, 1986– (Chm., 1979–86); Mem. Asthma Research Council; Dir-Gen., St John Ambulance Assoc., 1976–78 (Dep Dir-Gen., 1973–76; Dist Surg. for London, SJAB, 1950–64); Mem. Chapter-Gen., Order of St John (KStJ); Mem. Council, Stewart Soc.; Chm., Buttle Trust for Children, 1979–; Vice-Chairman: Med. Council of Alcoholism, 1986–87 (now Patron); St Christopher's Hospice for terminal cases, 1963–87 (Vice Pres., 1987); Sen. Vice-Pres. and British Rep., Assoc. Internat. de Sauvetage et de Premiers Secours en Cas d'Accidents, 1974–. Hon. Vice Pres., Stewart Soc., 1988. Liveryman, Soc. of Apothecaries of London; Freeman, City of London. Mem. Physiolog., Brit. Pharmacolog., Socs. FRCA (FFARCS 1969). FRSE 1974. RAMC, T, 1935; Mem. LDV, later Major and Med. Adviser, HG; comd and reformed Med. Unit, Univ. of London STC as Major RAMC, 1942–46. Defence Medal; Gen. Serv. Medal, 1939–46; Coronation Medal, 1953; Guthrie Meml Medal, 1974. DL Greater London, 1967–82. *Publications:* Drugs in Anæsthetic Practice (with F. G. Wood-Smith), 1962; (with W. H. Hughes) Concise Antibiotic Treatment, 2nd edn 1973; contribs to jls. *Recreations:* voluntary service; sport (lacrosse: Cambridge Half-Blue 1928; lawn tennis); genealogy and heraldry. *Address:* 41 The Glen, Green Lane, Northwood, Mddx HA6 2UR. *T:* (01923) 824893. *Club:* Athenæum.

See also Baron Stewartby.

STEWART, Sir Houston Mark S.; *see* Shaw-Stewart.

STEWART, Hugh Parker, FCA; Chairman: Demaglass Ltd, 1994–99; Image Precision International Ltd, 1997–99; *b* 23 May 1934; *s* of George and Barbara Stewart; *m* 1960, Marion Gordon Cairns; one *s* one *d.* *Educ:* Sullivan Upper Sch., Holywood, Co. Down; Queen's Univ., Belfast (LLB Hons). Audit Manager, Hill Vellacott & Bailey, Belfast, 1959–62; Financial Comptroller, STC (NI) Ltd, Monkstown, 1962–67; Admin Manager, AMF Beaird, Belfast, 1967–70; Gp Financial Controller, Brightside Engrg Hldgs, Sheffield, 1970–71; SMM Ltd, Greenwich: Financial Dir., 1971–74; Overseas Dir, 1974–78; Man. Dir, SMM Foundries Ltd, Greenwich, 1978–79; Finance Dir, Westland plc, 1979–81; Finance Dir, Westland plc, and Exec. Dir, Westland Technologies Ltd, 1981–84; Man. Dir, Westland Technologies Ltd, 1984–85; Chief Exec., Westland Gp plc, 1985–88. Chm., Scheduling Technology Gp Ltd, 1989–90; Practice Chm., Aaron & Partners, Solicitors, 1989–91; Chairman: Programming Research Ltd, 1990–91; Wootton Jeffreys Consultants Ltd, 1991–94; Aerospace Systems & Technologies, 1993–95; Western Computer Gp, 1993–95; Wellmann plc, 1995–98 (Dir, 1992–98); Director: DSK Systems Ltd, 1989–91; Cityflyer Express Ltd, 1991–99; Chessington Computer Centre, 1995–96 (Mem., Ministerial Adv. Bd, 1995–96). Governor, Sherborne Sch., 1982–. *Recreations:* golf, gardening. *Address:* Ferncroft House, Walton Elm, Marnhull, Dorset DT10 1QG.

STEWART, Ian; MP (Lab) Eccles, since 1997; *b* 28 Aug. 1950; *s* of John and Helen Stewart; *m* 1968, Merilyn Holding; two *s* one *d.* *Educ:* David Livingstone Primary Meml Sch., Blantyre; Calder Street Secondary, Blantyre; Alfred Turner Secondary Modern Sch., Salford; Stretford Technical Coll.; Manchester Metropolitan Univ. Regl Officer, TGWU, 1978–97. PPS to Minister of State for Industry and Energy, DTI, 2001–. Member: Deregulation Select Cttee, 1997–2001; Information Select Cttee, 1998–2001; PLP Employment and Trng Cttee, 1997–; PLP Trade and Industry Cttee, 1997–; PLP Foreign Affairs Cttee, 1997–; PITCOM, 1997–; Vice Chm., All Party China Gp, 1997– (Mem., GB China Centre Exec., 1997–); Chm., Parly Gp for Vaccine Damaged Children, 1998–2001. A Founder, Eur. Foundn for Social Partnership and Continuing Trng Initiatives, 1993. Member: UK Soc. of Industrial Tutors, 1980–; Manchester Industrial Relations Soc., 1994–; Member: Internat. Soc. of Indust. Relns, 1996–; Council, European Informatics Market, 1998–. Fellow, Industry and Parlt Trust, 1997; Vis. Fellow, Salford Univ., 1998. *Address:* House of Commons, SW1A 0AA.

STEWART, Prof. Ian George; Professor of Economics, University of Edinburgh, 1967–84; *b* 24 June 1923; *s* of David Tweedie Stewart, MA and Ada Doris Montgomery Haldane; *m* 1949, Mary Katharine Oddie; one *s* two *d.* *Educ:* Fettes Coll.; Univ. of St Andrews (MA 1st Class Hons); MA Cantab 1954. Pilot, RAF, 1942–46. Commonwealth Fund Fellow, 1948–50. Research Officer, Dept of Applied Economics, Univ. of Cambridge, 1950–57; University of Edinburgh: Lectr in Economics, 1957–58; Sen. Lectr, 1958–61; Reader, 1961–67; Curator of Patronage, 1979–84. Vis. Associate Prof., Univ. of Michigan, 1962; Vis. Prof., Univ. of S Carolina, 1975. Dir, Scottish Provident Instn, 1980–90, Dep. Chm., 1983–85. Mem., British Library Bd, 1980–87. Governor, Fettes Coll., 1976–89. *Publications:* National Income of Nigeria (with A. R. Prest), 1953; (ed) Economic Development and Structural Change, 1969; articles in jls and bank reviews. *Recreations:* golf, fishing, gardening. *Address:* 571 Lanark Road West, Edinburgh EH14 7BL. *Club:* New (Edinburgh).

STEWART, Ian James, CB 1997; Chief Executive, Bradford City Council, since 1999; *b* 30 Aug. 1946; *m* 1967, Morag Gardiner Duncan; two *d.* *Educ:* Perth Acad. Area Dir, Newcastle Benefits Directorate, 1990–92; Mem. Bd of Mgt and Dir, Benefits Agency, DSS, 1993–95; Project Dir, Jobseekers' Allowance, DfEE, 1995–97; Dir Gen., Benefit Fraud Inspectorate, DSS, 1997–99. *Address:* City of Bradford Metropolitan District Council, City Hall, Bradford BD1 1HY.

STEWART, Prof. Ian Nicholas, PhD; FRS 2001; CMath, FIMA; Professor of Mathematics, University of Warwick, since 1990; *b* 24 Sept. 1945; *s* of Arthur Reginald Stewart and Marjorie Kathleen Stewart (*née* Diwell); *m* 1970, Avril Bernice Montgomery; two *s.* *Educ:* Cambridge Univ. (MA); Warwick Univ. (PhD). FIMA 1993; CMath 1993. University of Warwick: Lectr, 1969–84; Reader, 1984–90. Humboldt Fellow, Tübingen, 1974; Vis. Fellow, Auckland, 1976; Associate Prof., Storrs, Conn, 1977–78; Professor: Carbondale, Ill, 1978; Houston, Texas, 1983–84; Gresham Prof. of Geometry, 1994. Hon DSc: Westminster, 1999; Louvain, 2000. Michael Faraday Medal, Royal Soc., 1995; IMA Gold Medal, 2000; Ferran Sunyer i Balaguer Prize, 2001. *Publications* include: Galois Theory, 1973; Concepts of Modern Mathematics, 1975; Catastrophe Theory and its Applications, 1978; The Problems of Mathematics, 1987; Does God Play Dice?, 1989; Game Set & Math, 1991; Another Fine Math You've Got Me Into, 1992; Fearful Symmetry, 1992; The Collapse of Chaos, 1994; Nature's Numbers, 1995; From Here to Infinity, 1996; Figments of Reality, 1997; The Magical Maze, 1997; Life's Other Secret, 1998; (jtly) The Science of Discworld, 1999; (jtly) Wheelers, 2000; Flatterland, 2001. *Recreations:* science fiction, painting, guitar, keeping fish. *Address:* Mathematics Institute, University of Warwick, Coventry CV4 7AL. *T:* (024) 7652 3740.

STEWART, Sir Jackie; *see* Stewart, Sir John Young.

STEWART, James Cecil Campbell, CBE 1960; consultant; *b* 25 July 1916; *s* of late James Stewart and Mary Campbell Stewart; *m* 1946, Pamela Rouselle, *d* of William King-Smith; one *d.* *Educ:* Armstrong College and King's College, Durham University (BSc Physics). Telecommunications Research Establishment, 1939–46; Atomic Energy Research Establishment, Harwell, 1946–49; Industrial Group, UKAEA, 1949–63; Dep. Chm., British Nuclear Design and Construction, 1969–75; Member: UKAEA, 1963–69; Central Electricity Generating Bd, 1965–69; Dep. Chm., Nuclear Power Co. Ltd, 1975–80; Dir, National Nuclear Corp. Ltd, 1980–82. Chairman: British Nuclear Forum, 1974–92; Nuclear Power Co. Pension Trustee Ltd, 1979–92. Consultant, Internat. Adv. Cttee Concord, Denver, 1986–94. *Recreation:* tending a garden. *Address:* White Thorns, Higher Whitley, Cheshire WA4 4QJ. *T:* (01925) 730377. *Clubs:* East India, Devonshire, Sports and Public Schools; Les Ambassadeurs.

STEWART, Sir James (Douglas), Kt 1983; agricultural consultant; Principal, Lincoln University College of Agriculture, 1974–84, retired; *b* 11 Aug. 1925; *s* of Charles Edward Stewart and Edith May Stewart (*née* Caldwell); *m* 1953, Nancy Elizabeth Dunbar; one *s* three *d.* *Educ:* Lincoln UC (Dip. Valuation and Farm Management); Canterbury Univ. (MA); Reading Univ. (DPhil). Lectr in Farm Management, Lincoln Coll., NZ, 1951–59; Research Fellow, Reading Univ., 1959–61; Sen. Lectr, Lincoln Coll., 1962–64; Prof. of Farm Management, Lincoln Coll., 1964–74. Chairman: NZ Vice-Chancellors Cttee, 1981–82; NZ Wheat Bd, 1986–87 (Dep. Chm., 1984–86); NZ Nat. Educn Qualifications Authority, 1989–95. Chm., Pyne Gould Guinness Internat. Ltd, 1987–95; Director: Pyne Gould Corp., 1982–95; Alpine Dairy Products Ltd, 1985–91. Chairman: Canterbury Develt Corp., 1983–89 (Dir, 1983–); Christchurch Sch. of Medicine, 1987–88; NZ Crown Res. Insts Implementation Cttee, 1991–. Silver Jubilee Medal, 1977. *Publications:* contrib. Jl Agricl Econs, Jl Farm Econs, Econ. Record, etc. *Recreations:* swimming, part-time farming. *Address:* 16 Cedar Place, Amberley, New Zealand.

STEWART, James Harvey; consultant in healthcare management; Chief Executive (formerly District General Manager), Barking and Havering (formerly Barking, Havering and Brentwood) Health Authority, 1985–95; *b* 15 Aug. 1939; *s* of Harvey Stewart and Annie (*née* Gray); *m* 1965, Fiona Maria Maclay Reid; three *s* one *d.* *Educ:* Peterhead Acad.; Aberdeen Univ. (MA 1962); Manchester Univ. (DSA 1964). Pres., Jun. Common Room, Crombie Hall, Aberdeen Univ., 1961–62. Hosp. Sec., Princess Margaret Rose Orthopaedic Hosp., Edinburgh, 1965–67; Principal Admin. Asst, 1967–68, and Dep. Gp Sec. and sometime Acting Gp Sec., 1968–73, York A HMC; Area Administrator, 1973–82, and Dist Administrator, 1982–83, Northumberland AHA; Regional Administrator, East Anglian RHA, 1983–85. Mem., Cambridge CHC, 1999–. Hon. Treasurer, Assoc. of Chief Administrators of Health Authorities in England and Wales, 1982–85 (Mem. Council, 1975–82). Mem., London Hosp. Officers Club, 1985–. Member: (LibDem) S Cambs DC, 1998–; Hardwick Parish Council, 1999–. Mem.,

Cambridge Rotary Club, 1983–. Hon. Pres., Cambs Rehab. Club for Visually Handicapped, 1999–. *Recreations:* music, reading, walking, sport. *Address:* White Cottage, Hardwick, Cambridge CB3 7QU. *T:* (01954) 210961. *Club:* Cambridge Univ. Rugby Union Football.

STEWART, Sir (James) Moray, KCB 1995 (CB 1990); Chairman, Civil Service Healthcare, 1993–2000; *b* 21 June 1938; third *s* of James and Evelyn Stewart; *m* 1963, Dorothy May Batey, *o d* of Alan and Maud Batey; three *s. Educ:* Marlborough Coll.; Univ. of Keele (BA First Cl. Hons History and Econs). Sec., Univ. of Keele Union, 1960–61. Breakdown and Information Service Operator, AA, 1956–57; Asst Master, Northcliffe Sch., Bognor Regis, 1957–58; Asst Principal, Air Min., 1962–65; Private Sec. to 2nd Permanent Under Sec. of State (RAF), MoD, 1965–66; Principal, MoD, 1966–70; First Sec. (Defence), UK Delegn to NATO, 1970–73; Asst Sec., MoD, 1974–75; Private Sec. to successive Secs of State for NI, 1975–77; Dir, Naval Manpower Requirements, MoD, 1977; Dir, Defence Policy Staff, MoD, 1978–80; Asst Under Sec. of State, MoD, 1980–84; Asst Sec. Gen. for Defence Planning and Policy, NATO, 1984–86; Dep. Under Sec. of State, Personnel and Logistics, 1986–88, Defence Procurement, 1988–90, MoD; Second Permanent Under Sec. of State, MoD, 1990–96. Commissioner: Royal Hosp. Chelsea, 1986–88; Queen Victoria Sch., Dunblane, 1996–; Mem. Bd of Mgt, N Glasgow Coll., 1996–; Trustee, Imperial War Museum, 1986–88; Mem. Council, RUSI, 1988–92. Vice Pres., Civil Service RFU, 1993–. Chm., Arvon Foundn in Scotland, 1998–; Trustee, Pegasus Trust, 1993–. Hon. DLitt Keele, 1995. *Recreations:* reading, listening to music, walking. *Address:* c/o Drummonds, Royal Bank of Scotland, 49 Charing Cross, SW1A 2DX. *Clubs:* Farmers'; New (Edinburgh); Golf House (Elie).

STEWART, James Robertson, CBE 1971 (OBE 1964); Principal, University of London, 1978–83; *b* 1917; *s* of James and Isabella Stewart; *m* 1941, Grace Margaret Kirsop (*d* 1992); two *s* one *d. Educ:* Perth Acad.; Whitley and Monkseaton High Sch.; Armstrong Coll. (later King's Coll.), Newcastle, Univ. of Durham. BA Dunelm (1st cl. hons Mod. History) 1937; DThPT (1st cl.) 1938; research in Canada (Canada Co.), 1938–39; awarded Holland Rose Studentship, Cambridge, and William Black Noble Fellowship, Durham, 1939; admitted to Christ's Coll., Cambridge, 1939; MA Dunelm 1941. Served Army, 1939–46: Royal Artillery (BEF); Combined Ops HQ; Directorate of Combined Ops, India and SE Asia; Major (Actg Lt-Col); Certif. of Good Service. Dep. Clerk of Court, Univ. of London, 1946–49, Clerk of Court, 1950–82. Dir, Charterhouse Venture Fund Management, 1984–94. Mem., Sec. of State's Adv. Gp on London Health Services, 1980–81. Member, governing bodies: RPMS, 1983–89; Sch. of Pharmacy, London Univ., 1983–99 (Hon. Treas., 1984–99); Wye Coll., 1983–91; Inst. of Educn, 1983–93; RVC, 1983– (Hon. Treas., 1984–96); LSE, 1984–89; Brunel Univ., 1984–89; Inst. of Germanic Studies, 1984–92 (Chm.); Roedean Sch., 1984–99; Sussex Univ., 1985–97; Westfield Coll., London, 1985–89. Hon. Fellow: KCL, 1982; Sch. of Pharmacy, London Univ., 1982; Birkbeck Coll., London, 1982; LSE, 1982; UCL, 1982; Wye Coll., 1987; Queen Mary and Westfield Coll., London, 1989 (Westfield Coll., 1981); Inst. of Germanic Studies, 1993. Hon. LLD: London, 1983; Western Ontario, 1984. Symons Medal, ACU, 1983; Betts Prize, RVC, 1994. *Recreations:* military history, gardening, watching soccer and cricket. *Address:* 2 Hilltop, Dyke Road Avenue, Brighton, Sussex BN1 5LY. *T:* (01273) 551039. *Club:* Athenæum.

See also N. A. Stewart.

STEWART, James Simeon Hamilton; QC 1982; barrister; a Recorder of the Crown Court, since 1982; *b* 2 May 1943; *s* of late Henry Hamilton Stewart, MD, FRCS and of Edna Mary Hamilton Stewart; *m* 1972, Helen Margaret Whiteley (*d* 1998); two *d. Educ:* Cheltenham Coll.; Univ. of Leeds (LLB Hons). Called to the Bar, Inner Temple, 1966, Bencher, 1992; a Dep. High Court Judge, 1993–. *Recreations:* cricket, golf, gardening. *Address:* Park Court Chambers, 16 Park Place, Leeds LS1 1SJ. *Clubs:* Sloane; Bradford (Bradford); Leeds Taverners (Leeds).

STEWART, (John) Allan; *b* 1 June 1942; *s* of Edward MacPherson Stewart and Eadie Barrie Stewart; *m* 1973, Marjorie Sally (Susie); one *s* one *d. Educ:* Bell Baxter High Sch., Cupar; St Andrews Univ. (1st Cl. Hons MA 1964); Harvard Univ. (Rotary Internat. Foundn Fellow, 1964–65). Lectr in Polit. Economy, St Andrews Univ., 1965–70 (Warden, John Burnet Hall, 1968–70); Confederation of British Industry: Head of Regional Develt Dept, 1971–73; Dep. Dir (Econs), 1973–76; Scottish Sec., 1976–78; Scottish Dir, 1978–79. Councillor, London Bor. of Bromley, 1975–76. Contested (C) Dundee E, 1970. MP (C): E Renfrewshire, 1979–83; Eastwood, 1983–97. PPS to Minister of State for Energy, 1981; Parly Under-Sec. of State, Scottish Office, 1981–86 and 1990–95. Mem., Select Cttee on Scottish Affairs, 1979–81 and 1995–97. Mem., Chairman's Panel, H of C, 1996–97. *Publications:* (with Harry Conroy) The Long March of the Market Men, 1996; articles in academic and gen. pubns on econ. and polit. affairs. *Recreations:* bridge, hedgehogs. *Address:* Crofthead House, Neilston, E Renfrewshire G78 3LE.

STEWART, Rt Rev. John Craig; Rector, Parish of Woodend, Victoria, since 2001; *b* 10 Aug. 1940; *s* of J. J. Stewart; *m* 1967, Janine (*née* Schahinger); two *s. Educ:* Newington Coll., Sydney; Wesley Coll., Melbourne; Ridley Theol Coll., Melbourne. Ordained: deacon, 1965; priest, 1966; Curate, S Australia, 1965–68; Associate Priest, St John's, Crawley, 1968–70; Vicar: St Aidan's, Parkdale, 1970–74; St Luke's, Frankston, 1974–79; Gen. Sec., Church Missionary Soc., Victoria, 1979–84; Asst Bishop, Dio. Melbourne, 1984–2001. *Publications:* From London to Dartmoor, 1996; From Bolton to Ballarat, 1996. *Recreations:* family history, geology, music. *Address:* St Mary's Church, PO Box 699, Woodend, Vic 3442, Australia.

STEWART, Prof. John David, DPhil; Professor of Local Government and Administration, Birmingham University, 1971–96, Hon. Professor, 1996–99, Emeritus Professor, since 1999; *b* 19 March 1929; *s* of Dr David Stewart and Phyllis Stewart (*née* Crossley); *m* 1953, Theresa Stewart, *qv*; two *s* two *d. Educ:* Stockport Grammar Sch.; Balliol Coll., Oxford (MA 1966); Nuffield Coll., Oxford (DPhil 1966). Industrial Relns Dept, NCB, 1954–66; Birmingham University: Sen. Lectr, 1966–71, Dir, 1976–83, Inst. of Local Govt Studies; Hd of Sch. of Public Policy, 1990–93. Member: Layfield Cttee on Local Govt Finance, 1974–76; Acad. Adv. Panel on local govt, DETR, 1997–98. *Publications:* British Pressure Groups, 1958; Management in Local Government, 1971; The Responsive Local Authority, 1974; (jtly) Corporate Management in English Local Government, 1974; Local Government: the conditions of local choice, 1983; (jtly) The Case for Local Government, 1983; Understanding the Management of Local Government, 1988; (jtly) The Politics of Hung Authorities, 1992; Management for the Public Domain, 1994; (jtly) The Changing Organisation and Management of Local Government, 1994; (ed jtly) Local Government in the 1990s, 1995; The Nature of British Local Government, 2000. *Recreations:* gardening, walking. *Address:* 15 Selly Wick Road, Birmingham B29 7JJ. *T:* (0121) 472 1512.

STEWART, John Hall; Sheriff of South Strathclyde, Dumfries and Galloway at Hamilton (formerly at Airdrie), since 1985; *b* 15 March 1944; *s* of Cecil Francis Wilson Stewart and Mary Fyfe Hall or Stewart; *m* 1968, Marion MacCalman; one *s* two *d. Educ:* Airdrie Acad.; St Andrews Univ. (LLB). Advocate. Enrolled solicitor, 1970–77; Mem. Faculty of Advocates, 1978–. *Recreations:* scuba diving, golf, spectator sports, his children. *Address:* 3 Fife Crescent, Bothwell, Glasgow G71 8DG. *T:* (01698) 853854. *Club:* Uddingston Rugby (Past Pres.), Uddingston Cricket and Sports (Past Pres.).

STEWART, John Morrison, FCIB; Deputy Group Chief Executive, Barclays Bank, since 2000; *b* 31 May 1949; *s* of Peter and Jane Stewart; *m* 1971, Sylvia Jameson; one *s* one *d. Educ:* Boroughmuir Sch., Edinburgh; Open Univ. (BA 1975). ACII 1979; FCIB 1989. Posts with Legal & General; Woolwich Building Society: joined 1977, as Br. Manager; Asst Gen. Manager, Insurance Services, 1988–91; General Manager: Financial Services, 1991–92; Retail Ops, 1992–95; Group Ops Dir, 1995–96; Gp Chief Exec., Woolwich Bldg Soc., subseq. Woolwich plc, 1996–2000. Chm., Woolwich Indep. Financial Adv. Services (Dir, 1989–95); Director: Banca Woolwich, Italy, 1996–2000; Banque Woolwich, France, 1996–2000. CIMgt 1996. Hon. DLitt Heriot-Watt, 1997. *Recreation:* sailing. *Address:* Barclays Bank, 54 Lombard Street, EC3P 3AH.

STEWART, Sir (John) Simon (Watson), 6th Bt *cr* 1920, of Balgownie; MD, FRCP, FRCR; Consultant in Clinical Oncology at St Mary's Hospital and Imperial College School of Medicine (formerly Royal Postgraduate Medical School), since 1989; *b* 5 July 1955; *s* of Sir John Keith Watson Stewart, 5th Bt and of Mary Elizabeth, *d* of John Francis Moxon; *S* father, 1990; *m* 1978, Dr Catherine Stewart, *d* of H. Gordon Bond; one *s* one *d. Educ:* Uppingham Sch.; Charing Cross Hosp. Med. Sch. BSc (1st cl. Hons) 1977; MB BS Lond. 1980; MRCP 1983, FRCP 1994; FRCR 1986; MD 1989. Mem., Cavalhead Soc., 1978–. *Heir: s* John Hamish Watson Stewart, *b* 12 Dec. 1983. *Address:* 38 Dukes Avenue, Chiswick, W4 2AE. *T:* (020) 8995 2213. *Club:* Oriental.

STEWART, Sir John Young, (Sir Jackie), Kt 2001; OBE 1972; racing driver, retired 1973; developed Gleneagles Jackie Stewart Shooting School; Chairman, Stewart Grand Prix Ltd, 1996–2000; *b* 11 June 1939; *s* of late Robert Paul Stewart and of Jean Clark Young; *m* 1962, Helen McGregor; two *s. Educ:* Dumbarton Academy. First raced, 1961; competed in 4 meetings, 1961–62, driving for Barry Filer, Glasgow; drove for Ecurie Ecosse and Barry Filer, winning 14 out of 23 starts, 1963; 28 wins out of 53 starts, 1964; drove Formula 1 for BRM, 1965–67 and for Ken Tyrrell, 1968–73; has won Australian, New Zealand, Swedish, Mediterranean, Japanese and many other non-championship, major internat. Motor Races; set up new world record by winning his 26th World Championship Grand Prix (Zandvoort), July 1973, and 27th (Nurburgring), Aug. 1973; 3rd in World Championship, 1965; 2nd in 1968 and 1972; World Champion, 1969, 1971, 1973. BARC Gold Medal, 1971, 1973. Daily Express Sportsman of the Year, 1971, 1973; BBC Sports Personality of the Year, 1973; Scottish Sportsman of the Year, 1973; US Sportsman of the Year, 1973; Segrave Trophy, 1973. Hon. Dr Automotive Engrg, Lawrence Inst. of Technology, Mich, USA, 1986; Hon. Dr Engrg Glasgow Caledonian, 1993; Hon. DEng Heriot-Watt, 1996. *Film:* Weekend of a Champion, 1972. *Publications:* World Champion, 1970 (with Eric Dymock); Faster!, 1972 (with Peter Manso); On the Road, 1983; Jackie Stewart's Principles of Performance Driving, 1986; The Jackie Stewart Book of Shooting, 1991. *Recreations:* golf, fishing, tennis, shooting (Mem. Scottish and British Teams for Clay Pigeon shooting; former Scottish, English, Irish, Welsh and British Champion; won Coupe des Nations, 1959 and 1960; reserve for two-man team, 1960 Olympics). *Address:* Jaguar Racing, Bradbourne Drive, Tilbrook, Milton Keynes MK7 8BJ. *T:* (01908) 656600, *Fax:* (01908) 656610. *Clubs:* (Hon.) Royal Automobile, British Racing Drivers' (Vice-Pres.); (Hon.) Royal Scottish Automobile; (Pres.) Scottish Motor Racing (Duns); Royal and Ancient (St Andrews); Prestwick Golf; (Hon.) Gleneagles; Sunningdale; Loch Lomond Golf; Wentworth; Geneva Golf.

STEWART, Joseph Martin, OBE 1994; JP; Secretary and Chief Executive, Police Authority for Northern Ireland, since 1995; *b* 5 Nov. 1955; *s* of late Joseph Aloysius Stewart and of Annie Margaret Mary Stewart (*née* Friel); *m* 1978, Deirdre Ann Ritchie. *Educ:* Queen's Univ., Belfast (LLB Hons 1978); Univ. of Ulster (Post Grad. Dip. in Mgt Studies 1980). Engineering Employers Federation (NI) Association: Asst Indust. Relns Officer, 1978–80; Indust. Relns Officer, 1980–85; Dir, 1985–90; Personnel Dir, Harland & Wolff Shipbuilding and Heavy Industries Ltd, 1990–95. JP Ards Circuit, 1990. *Recreations:* game shooting, pedigree sheep breeding, motorcycle touring. *Address:* (office) River House, 48 High Street, Belfast BT1 2DR. *T:* (028) 9023 0111. *Club:* Ulster Reform (Belfast).

STEWART, Kenneth Hope, PhD; Director of Research, Meteorological Office, 1976–82; *b* 29 March 1922; *s* of Harry Sinclair Stewart and Nora Hassan Parry; *m* 1950, Hilary Guest (*d* 1993); four *s* four *d. Educ:* Trinity Coll., Cambridge (MA, PhD). Entered Meteorol Office, 1949; Dep. Dir, Physical Res., 1974. *Publications:* Ferromagnetic Domains, 1951; contrib. physical and meteorol jls. *Address:* 19 Harston Road, Newton, Cambridge CB2 5PA.

STEWART, Hon. Kevin James, AO 1989; *b* 20 Sept. 1928; *m* 1952, Jean, *d* of late F. I. Keating; two *s* five *d. Educ:* Christian Brothers School, Lewisham, NSW; De La Salle College, NSW. Officer, NSW Govt Rlys, 1944–62 (Regional Pres., Aust. Transport Officers' Assoc. and Fedn, 1959–62). MLA for Canterbury, NSW, 1962–85; Exec., NSW Parly Labor Party and Spokesman on Health Matters, 1967; NSW State Exec., Aust. Labor Party, 1968; Minister, NSW: for Health, 1976–81; for Youth and Community Services, 1981–83; for Mineral Resources, 1983–84; for Local Govt, 1984–85. Mem., Labor Transport Cttee, 1965–76; Chm., Labor Health Cttee, 1968–76; Mem., Jt Cttee, Legislative Council upon Drugs. Agent General for NSW in UK, 1986–88. Vice-Chm., Federal Govt Sydney Area Consultant Cttee, 1993–. Life Mem., British-Australia Soc., 1988. Chm., Bd of Canterbury Hosp., 1955–76 (Dir, 1954). FRSA 1988. Freeman, City of London, 1987. Hon. Citizen of Tokyo, Japan, 1985. *Recreations:* supporter of community services, Rugby Football League, swimming, bowls. *Address:* 44 Chalmers Street, Belmore, NSW 2192, Australia. *T:* (2) 97597777. *Club:* Canterbury Bankstown League (Patron) (Sydney).

STEWART, Mary (Florence Elinor), (Lady Stewart); *b* 17 Sept. 1916; *d* of Rev. Frederick A. Rainbow, Durham Diocese, and Mary Edith (*née* Matthews), NZ; *m* 1945, Sir Frederick Henry Stewart, *qv*; no *c. Educ:* Eden Hall, Penrith, Cumberland; Skellfield School, Ripon, Yorks; St Hild's Coll., Durham Univ. BA 1938; MA 1941. Asst Lectr in English, Durham Univ., 1941–45; Part-time Lectr in English, St Hild's Training Coll., Durham, and Durham Univ., 1948–56. Hon. Fellow, Newnham Coll., Cambridge, 1986. *Publications: novels:* Madam, Will You Talk?, 1954; Wildfire at Midnight, 1956; Thunder on the Right, 1957; Nine Coaches Waiting, 1958; My Brother Michael, 1959; The Ivy Tree, 1961; The Moonspinners, 1962; This Rough Magic, 1964; Airs Above the Ground, 1965; The Gabriel Hounds, 1967; The Wind Off The Small Isles, 1968; The Crystal Cave, 1970 (Frederick Niven Award); The Little Broomstick, 1971; The Hollow Hills, 1973; Ludo and the Star Horse, 1974 (Scottish Arts Council Award); Touch Not the Cat, 1976; The Last Enchantment, 1979; A Walk in Wolf Wood, 1980; The Wicked Day, 1983; Thornyhold, 1988; Frost on the Window and Other Poems, 1990; Stormy Petrel, 1991; The Prince and the Pilgrim, 1995; Rose Cottage, 1997; also articles, radio plays.

Recreations: gardening, music, painting. *Address:* House of Letterawe, Loch Awe, Dalmally, Argyll PA33 1AH.

STEWART, Very Rev. Maurice Evan; Dean of St Patrick's Cathedral, Dublin, 1991–99; *b* 8 Jan. 1929; *s* of Robert Carlisle and Annie Stewart; *m* 1965, Wendy Margaret McConnell; two *d*. *Educ:* Royal Belfast Academical Instn; Trinity Coll., Dublin (MA 1953; BD 1967); Queen's Univ., Belfast (PhD 1975). Ordained: deacon, 1952; priest, 1953; Curate, St James, Belfast, 1952–55; Chaplain, Bishop's Coll., Cheshunt, 1955–58; Head of TCD Mission in Belfast, 1958–61; Rector of Newcastle, Co. Down, 1961–69; Lectr, C of I Theol Coll., 1969–91; Lectr in Divinity, TCD, 1973–91; St Patrick's Cathedral, Dublin: Chancellor, 1980–89; Precentor, 1989–91. *Recreations:* Anglican theology, Swiftiana. *Address:* 12 Mounthaven, New Road, Greystones, Co. Wicklow, Ireland. *Club:* Kildare Street and University (Dublin).

STEWART, Michael James; Reader in Political Economy, University College, London University, 1969–94, now Emeritus; *b* 6 Feb. 1933; *s* of late John Innes Mackintosh Stewart; *m* 1962, Frances Kaldor, *d* of Baron Kaldor, FBA; one *s* two *d* (and one *d* decd). *Educ:* Campbell Coll., Belfast; St Edward's Sch., Oxford; Magdalen Coll., Oxford. 1st cl. PPE (Oxon), 1955. Asst Res. Officer, Oxford Univ. Inst. of Statistics, 1955–56; Barnett Fellow, Cornell Univ., 1956–57; Econ. Asst, HM Treasury, 1957–60; Sec. to Council on Prices, Productivity and Incomes, 1960–61; Econ. Adviser, HM Treasury, 1961–62, Cabinet Office, 1964–67 (Senior Econ. Advr, 1967), Kenya Treasury, 1967–69; Special Adviser to Sec. of State for Trade, Apr.-Oct. 1974; Economic Adviser to Malta Labour Party, 1970–73; Special Econ. Advr to Foreign Sec., 1977–78. Guest Scholar, Brookings Instn, Washington, DC, 1978–79. Mem., Acad. Adv. Panel, Bank of England, 1977–83. Contested (Lab): Folkestone and Hythe, 1964; Croydon North-West, 1966. Asst Editor, Nat. Inst. Econ. Review, 1962–64. Consultant to various UN agencies, 1971–. *Publications:* Keynes and After, 1967; The Jekyll and Hyde Years: politics and economic policy since 1964, 1977; Controlling the Economic Future: policy dilemmas in a shrinking world, 1983; (with Peter Jay) Apocalypse 2000: economic breakdown and the suicide of democracy 1989–2000, 1987; Keynes in the 1990s: a return to economic sanity, 1993. *Recreations:* looking at paintings, eating at restaurants in France. *Address:* 79 South Hill Park, NW3 2SS. *T:* (020) 7435 3686. *Club:* Oxford and Cambridge.

STEWART, Sir Moray; *see* Stewart, Sir J. M.

STEWART, Neill Alastair; His Honour Judge Stewart; a Circuit Judge, since 1999; *b* 8 June 1947; *yr s* of James Robertson Stewart, *qv*; *m* 2001, Tiffany, *d* of His Honour William Llewellyn Monro Davies, *qv*. *Educ:* Whitgift Sch.; Clare Coll., Cambridge (BA Mech. Scis Tripos). Engr, Sir Alexander Gibb & Partners, 1968–70; called to the Bar, Middle Temple, 1973; in practice at the Bar, 1975–99. *Recreation:* sports. *Address:* c/o Hollis Whiteman Chambers, Queen Elizabeth Building, Temple, EC4Y 9BS. *Club:* Royal St George's Golf.

STEWART, Nicholas John Cameron; QC 1987; *b* 16 April 1947; *s* of John Cameron Stewart and Margaret Mary (*née* Botsford); *m* 1974, Pamela Jean Windham; one *s* two *d*. *Educ:* Bedford Modern Sch.; Worcester Coll., Oxford (BA). CDipAF. Called to the Bar, Inner Temple, 1971, Bencher, 1999; a Dep. High Ct Judge, Chancery Div., 1991–. Chm., Bar Human Rights Cttee, 1994–98. Narrator, No Further Questions, BBC Radio series, 1993 and 1995. *Recreations:* walking, Spain, photography. *Address:* Hardwicke Building, New Square, Lincoln's Inn, WC2A 3SB. *T:* (020) 7242 2523, *Fax:* (020) 7831 1234; *e-mail:* nstewart@dial.pipex.com.

STEWART, Norman MacLeod; Senior Partner, 1984–97, Consultant, 1997–99, Allan, Black & McCaskie; President, The Law Society of Scotland, 1985–86; *b* 2 Dec. 1934; *s* of George and Elspeth Stewart; *m* 1959, Mary Slater Campbell; four *d*. *Educ:* Elgin Acad.; Univ. of Edinburgh (BL); SSC. Alex. Morison & Co., WS, Edinburgh, 1954–58; Allan, Black & McCaskie, Solicitors, Elgin, 1959–99, Partner, 1961–97. Law Society of Scotland: Mem. Council, 1976–87; Convener: Public Relations Cttee, 1979–81; Professional Practice Cttee, 1981–84; Vice-Pres., 1984–85. Chm., Elgin and Lossiemouth Harbour Bd, 1993–. Hon. Mem., American Bar Assoc., 1985–. *Recreations:* walking, golf, music, Spanish culture. *Address:* Argyll Lodge, Lossiemouth, Moray IV31 6QT. *T:* (01343) 813150; *e-mail:* nms@argyll-co.demon.co.uk. *Club:* New (Edinburgh).

STEWART, Col Robert Alexander, DSO 1993; independent business consultant; *b* 7 July 1949; *s* of late Sqdn Leader A. A. Stewart, MC and Marguerita Joan Stewart; *m* 1st (marr. diss. 1993); one *s* one *d*; 2nd, 1994, Claire Podbielski; three *d*. *Educ:* Chigwell Sch.; RMA Sandhurst; Univ. of Wales, Aberystwyth (BSc 1st Cl. Hons Internat. Politics). Commnd, Cheshire Regt, 1969; Instructor, RMA, 1979–80; Army Staff Coll., 1981; Company Comdr, N Ireland, 1982–83; Staff Officer, MoD, 1984–85; 2 i/c 1st Bn Cheshire Regt, 1986–87; JSSC 1988; MA to Chm., NATO Mil. Cttee, HQ NATO, Brussels, 1989–91; Bosnia, 1991–92; CO, 1st Bn Cheshire Regt, 1991–93; Chief of Policy, SHAPE, 1994–95; resigned Regular Army, 1996. Sen. Consultant, Public Affairs, Hill & Knowlton (UK) Ltd, 1996–98; Sen. Vice Pres., WorldSpace UK, 1998–2001. *Publication:* Broken Lives, 1993. *Recreations:* cycling, writing, history, helping to convict war criminals. *Address:* 35 Crescent Road, Kingston upon Thames, Surrey KT2 7RD. *T:* (020) 8546 5205. *Club:* Army and Navy.

STEWART, Lt-Col Robert Christie, CBE 1983; TD 1962; Lord-Lieutenant of Clackmannan, 1994–2001; *b* 3 Aug. 1926; *m* 1953, Ann Grizel Cochrane; three *s* two *d*. *Educ:* Eton; University College, Oxford. Lt Scots Guards, 1945–49. Oxford Univ., 1949–51 (BA Agric.). TA, 7 Argyll and Sutherland Highlanders, 1948–66; Lt-Col Comdg 7 A & SH, 1963–66. Hon. Col, 1/51 Highland Volunteers, 1972–75. Chm. and Pres., Bd of Governors, E of Scotland Coll. of Agric., 1970–83. Chm., Kinross CC, 1963–73. DL Kinross, 1956, Vice Lieut, 1958; Lord-Lieutenant, Kinross-shire, 1966–74. *Address:* Arndean, by Dollar, Clackmannanshire FK14 7NH. *T:* (01259) 742527. *Club:* Royal Perth Golfing Society.

STEWART, Dr Robert William, OC 1979; FRS 1970; FRSC 1967; Adjunct Professor, School of Earth and Ocean Sciences, University of Victoria, since 1989; Hon. Professor of Physics and Oceanography, University of British Columbia, since 1971; Hon. Professor of Science, University of Alberta, since 1985; *b* 21 Aug. 1923; *m* 1st, 1948, V. Brande (marr. diss. 1972); two *s* one *d*; 2nd, 1973, Anne-Marie Robert; one *s*. *Educ:* Queen's Univ., Ontario. BSc 1945, MSc 1947, Queen's; PhD Cantab 1952. Canadian Defence Research Bd, 1950–61; Prof. of Physics and Oceanography, Univ. of British Columbia, 1961–70; Dir, Marine Scis Br., Pacific Reg., Environment Canada, 1970–74; Dir-Gen., Ocean and Aquatic Scis, Pacific Reg., Fisheries and Marine Service, Dept of Fisheries and Oceans, Canada, 1974–79; Dep. Minister, Ministry of Univs, Science and Communications, BC, Canada, 1979–84; Pres., Alberta Res. Council, 1984–87; Dir, Centre for Earth and Ocean Res., Univ. of Victoria, 1987–89. Vis. Professor: Dalhousie Univ., 1960–61; Harvard Univ., 1964; Pennsylvania State Univ., 1964; Commonwealth Vis. Prof., Cambridge Univ., 1967–68. Vice-Chm., 1968–72, Chm., 1972–76, Jt Organizing Cttee, Global Atmospheric Res. Program; Pres., Internat. Assoc. of Physical Scis of Ocean, 1975–79; Mem., Cttee on Climatic Changes and the Ocean, 1980–92 (Chm., 1983–87); Vice Chm., Sci. Cttee for Internat. Geosphere-Biosphere Prog., 1991–94. *Publications:* numerous, on turbulence, oceanography and meteorology. *Address:* School of Earth and Ocean Studies, University of Victoria, PO Box 1700, Victoria, British Columbia V8W 2Y2, Canada.

STEWART, Sir Robertson (Huntly), Kt 1979; CBE 1970; CEng, FIProdE, FPRI, FNZIM, FInstD; Founder President: PDL Holdings Ltd (manufacturers of electrical and plastic products), since 1995 (Chairman and Managing Director, 1957–82; Executive Chairman, 1982–95); PDL (Asia), since 1995 (Executive Chairman, 1975–95); *b* 21 Sept. 1913; *s* of Robert McGregor Stewart and Ivy Emily (*née* Grigg); *m* 1st, 1937, Ada Gladys Gunter; two *s* one *d*; 2nd, 1970, Ellen Adrienne Cansdale; two *s*. *Educ:* Christchurch Boys' High Sch.; Christchurch Technical Inst. CEng, FIEE (FIProdE 1967); FPRI 1960; FNZIM 1962; FInstD 1970. Introd plastics industry to NZ, 1936; commenced manuf. of electrical products in NZ, 1937; estabd PDL Gp of Cos, 1947. Led NZ Trade Missions, 1962, 1964, 1966, 1967, 1970 and 1972. Pres., NZ Manufrs Fedn, 1963–64. Hon. DEng Canterbury, 1999. Hon. Malaysian Consul. Hon. JSM 1998. *Recreations:* motor racing, tennis, fishing. *Address:* 127 Scarborough Road, Sumner, Christchurch, New Zealand. *T:* (3) 3265213. *Club:* Canterbury (Christchurch).

STEWART, Robin Milton; QC 1978; a Recorder of the Crown Court, 1978–99; *b* 5 Aug. 1938; *s* of late Brig. Guy Milton Stewart and of Dr Elaine Oenone Stewart, MD, BS; *m* 1962, Lynda Grace Medhurst; three *s*. *Educ:* Winchester; New Coll., Oxford (MA). Called to the Bar, Middle Temple, 1963, Bencher, 1988; called to the Irish Bar, King's Inns, Dublin, 1975. Prosecuting Counsel to Inland Revenue, NE Circuit, 1976–78. Dir, Bar Mutual Indemnity Fund, 1988–93. Mem., Professional Conduct Cttee, Bar Council, 1991–93; (first) Chm., Professional Negligence Bar Assoc., 1991–93. Contested (C) Newcastle upon Tyne West, Feb. and Oct. 1974. Freeman, City of London, 1966; Liveryman, Co. of Glaziers, 1966–98. Trustee, Parkinson's Disease Soc., 1999–. *Recreations:* pictures, gardening, Scottish family history. *Address:* 199 Strand, WC2R 1DR. *T:* (020) 7379 9779; Kilburn House, 96 Front Street, Sowerby, Thirsk, N Yorks YO7 1JJ. *T:* (01845) 522922. *Club:* Oriental.

STEWART, Roger Paul Davidson; QC 2001; *b* 17 Aug. 1963; *s* of late Martin Neil Davidson Stewart and of Elizabeth Janet Stewart (*née* Porter); *m* 1988, Georgina Louise Smith; two *s* one *d*. *Educ:* Oundle Sch.; Jesus Coll., Cambridge (MA, LLM). Called to the Bar, Inner Temple, 1986; barrister, Lincoln's Inn, 2000–. *Publication:* (gen. ed.) Jackson and Powell on Professional Negligence, 3rd edn 1992 and 5th edn 2001. *Recreations:* sailing, ski-ing, skiving. *Address:* 57 Rectory Grove, SW4 0DS; The Old Free Church Manse, Isle of Raasay, by Kyle, Inverness IV40 8NT; (chambers) 4 New Square, Lincoln's Inn, WC2A 3RJ. *Clubs:* National Liberal; Lost Valley Mountaineering (Glencoe).

STEWART, Rosemary Gordon, (Mrs I. M. James), PhD; author of management books; *d* of William George Stewart and Sylvia Gordon Stewart (*née* Sulley); *m* 1961, Ioan Mackenzie James, *qv*. *Educ:* Univ. of British Columbia (BSc); London School of Economics, Univ. of London (MSc, PhD). Dir, Acton Soc. Trust, 1956–61; Res. Fellow, London Sch. of Economics, 1964–66; Fellow in Organizational Behaviour, Templeton Coll. (formerly Oxford Centre for Mgt Studies), 1967–93; Dir, Centre for Develt and Population Activities, Washington, 1988–; Co-Dir, Oxford Health Care Mgt Inst., Templeton Coll., Oxford, 1993–. Gov., Headington Sch., Oxford, 1991–. Hon. Fellow, Templeton Coll., Oxford, 2000. Hon. DPhil Uppsala, 1998. *Publications:* (jtly) The Boss: the life and times of the British businessman, 1958; The Reality of Management, 1963, 3rd edn 1997; Managers and their Jobs, 1967, 2nd edn 1988; The Reality of Organizations, 1970, 3rd edn 1993; How Computers Affect Management, 1971; Contrasts in Management, 1976 (John Player Award for best British mgt book); (contrib.) The District Administrator in the NHS, 1982; Leading in the NHS, 1989, 2nd edn 1995; Managing Today and Tomorrow, 1994; (jtly) The Diversity of Management, 1994; (contrib.) Managing in Britain and Germany, 1994; (ed) Managerial Work, 1998; (ed) Management of Health Care, 1998; Evidence-based Management, 2001. *Recreations:* travel, painting, art appreciation, golf, gardening, theatre. *Address:* Templeton College, Oxford OX1 5NY. *T:* (01865) 422500.

STEWART, Sir Simon; *see* Stewart, Sir J. S. W.

STEWART, Stephen Paul; QC 1996; a Recorder, since 1999; Deputy Judge, Technology and Construction Court, since 2000; *b* 9 Oct. 1953; *s* of Cyril Stewart and Phyllis Mary Stewart; *m* 1980, Dr (Mary) Felicity Dyer; one *s* one *d*. *Educ:* Stand GS, Whitefield, Manchester; St Peter's Coll., Oxford (MA; half blue for badminton). Called to the Bar, Middle Temple, 1975 (Harmsworth Major Exhibnr, 1973; Harmsworth Schol., 1975); in practice on Northern Circuit; Asst Recorder, 1995–99. *Recreations:* running, music. *Address:* 12 Byrom Street, Manchester M3 4PP. *T:* (0161) 829 2100. *Club:* Alderley Edge Cricket.

STEWART, Suzanne Freda; *see* Norwood, S. F.

STEWART, Theresa; Member (Lab), Birmingham City Council, since 1970 (Leader, 1993–99); Lord Mayor of Birmingham, 2000–01; *b* 24 Aug. 1930; *d* of John Raisman and Ray Raisman (*née* Baker); *m* 1953, John David Stewart, *qv*; two *s* two *d*. *Educ:* Cowper Street Sch., Leeds; Allerton High Sch., Leeds; Somerville Coll., Oxford (MA; Hon. Fellow, 2001). Member: Birmingham Regl Hosp. Bd, 1968–71; W Midland CC, 1974–77; Birmingham City Council: Chair: Birmingham Community Develt Project, 1973–76; Social Services Cttee, 1981–82 and 1984–87; Direct Labour Contract Services Cttee, 1989–93; Policy and Resources Cttee, 1997–; W Midlands Jt Cttee, 1998–. Vice-Chm., AMA Social Services Cttee, 1985–87; Chair, W Midlands LGA, 1999– (Sen. Vice Chair, 1998–99). Chm., Assoc. of Direct Labour Orgns, 1994–95. Hon. LLD Birmingham, 2000. *Recreations:* relaxing in a hot bath with a good book, walking, cooking. *Address:* 15 Selly Wick Road, Birmingham B29 7JJ. *T:* (0121) 472 1512.

STEWART, Victor Colvin, FCA; Registrar General for Scotland, 1978–82; *b* 12 April 1921; *s* of Victor Stewart and Jean Cameron; *m* 1949, Aileen Laurie; one *s*. *Educ:* Selkirk High Sch.; Edinburgh Univ. (BCom). FCA 1954. Served War in RAF, Africa and ME, 1942–46. Joined Dept of Health for Scotland, 1938; Chief Exec. Officer, 1959; Principal, SHHD, 1963, Asst Sec. 1971; Dep. Registrar Gen. for Scotland, 1976. *Recreations:* golf, walking, bridge. *Address:* Tynet, Lodgehill Road, Nairn IV12 4QL. *T:* (01667) 452050. *Club:* Royal Commonwealth Society.

STEWART, Dr William, CB 1977; DSc; aerospace consultant, 1983–94; *b* Hamilton, 29 Aug. 1921; *m* 1955, Helen Cairney; two *d*. *Educ:* St John's Grammar Sch.; Hamilton Acad.; Glasgow Univ. BSc Hons (engin.); DSc 1958. RAE, Farnborough, 1942–53; British Jt Services Mission, Washington, 1953–56; Dep. Head of Naval Air Dept, RAE, Bedford, 1956–63; Imperial Defence College, 1964; Asst Dir, Project Time and Cost Analysis, 1965–66; Dir, Anglo-French Combat Trainer Aircraft Projects, 1966–70; Dir-Gen., Multi-Role Combat Aircraft, 1970–73; Dep. Controller, Aircraft A, 1973–78,

Aircraft, 1978–81, MoD (PE). Silver Medal, RAeS, 1981. *Address:* 25 Brickhill Drive, Bedford MK41 7QA.

STEWART, Sir William (Duncan Paterson), Kt 1994; PhD, DSc; FRS 1977; FRSE; President, Royal Society of Edinburgh, since 1999; Chairman, Tayside University Hospitals NHS Trust, since 1999; Chief Scientific Adviser, Cabinet Office, 1990–95, and Head of Office of Science and Technology, 1992–95; *b* 7 June 1935; *s* of John Stewart and Margaret (*née* Paterson); *m* 1958, Catherine MacLeod (*d* 1998); one *s*. *Educ:* Bowmore Junior Secondary Sch., Isle-of-Islay; Dunoon Grammar Sch.; Glasgow Univ. (BSc, PhD, DSc). FRSE 1973. Asst Lectr, Univ. of Nottingham, 1961–63; Lectr, Westfield Coll., Univ. of London, 1963–68; University of Dundee: Hd of Dept of Biol Scis, 1968–83; Boyd Baxter Prof. of Biology, 1968–94; Vice-Principal, 1985–87; Sec. and Chief Exec., AFRC, 1988–90. Vis. Res. Worker, Univ. of Wisconsin, 1966 and 1968; Vis. Professor: Univ. of Kuwait, 1980; Univ. of Otago, 1984. Chairman: Royal Soc. Biological Educn Cttee, 1977–80; Sci. Adv. Cttee, Freshwater Biol. Assoc., 1974–85; Royal Soc. Study Group on Nitrogen Cycle, 1979–84; Internat. Cttee on Microbial Ecology, 1983–86 (Sec., 1980–83); Royal Soc. Biotechnology and Educn Wkg Gp, 1980–81; Independent Adv. Gp on Gruinard Is., 1985–87; Vice-Pres., 1973–75, Pres., 1975–77, British Phycological Soc.; President: Section K, BAAS, 1984; Council, Scottish Marine Biol. Assoc., 1985–87 (Mem., 1969–74, 1982–); Bioindustry Assoc., 1995–99; Vice-Pres., Freshwater Biol. Assoc., 1984–. Trustee, Estuarine and Brackish-Water Sciences Assoc., 1978–88. Member: Council, RSE, 1976–79; Council, Marine Biol. Assoc., 1973–76, 1977–80, 1981–84; Plants and Soils Res. Grants Bd, ARC, 1978–84; British Nat. Cttee for problems of environment, Royal Soc., 1979–85; UNESCO Panel on Microbiology, 1975–81; Council, NERC, 1979–85 (Chm., Aquatic Life Scis Grants Cttee, 1973–78, Marine Life Scis Preparatory Gp, 1982–85); Internat. Cell Res. Org., 1979–84; Royal Soc. Study Gp on Science Educn, 1981–82; Royal Soc. Study Gp on Pollution Control Priorities, 1987–88; Council, Royal Soc., 1984–86 (Vice-Pres., 1995–); Royal Commn on Environmental Pollution, 1986–88; Biol Sciences Sub-Cttee, UGC, 1988; DSAC, 1990–95. Chairman: Govt Technol. Foresight Steering Gp, 1993–95; Govt Sci. and Engrg Base Co-ordinating Cttee, 1993–; Mem., DTI Link Steering Gp, 1990–94; Dep. Chm., Council for Sci. and Technology, 1993–95. Royal Soc. Assessor, AFRC, 1985–87; Assessor: ABRC, 1990–93 (Mem., 1988–90); ACOST, 1990–93. Dir (non-exec.), Water Research Centre plc, 1995–. Member, Governing Body: Scottish Hort. Res. Inst., 1971–80; Scottish Crop Res. Inst., 1980–88; Macaulay Land Use Res. Inst., 1987–88. Chm., Dundee Teaching Hosps NHS Trust, 1997–99. Lectures: Phycological Soc. of America Dist., 1977; Barton-Wright, Inst. Biol., 1977; Sir David Martin Royal Soc.-BAYS, 1979; Plenary, 2nd Internat. Symp. on Microbial Ecology, 1980; Holden, Nottingham Univ., 1983; Leeuwenhoek, Royal Soc., 1984; Plenary, 2nd Internat. Phycological Congress, Copenhagen, 1985; Diamond Jubilee, Hannah Res. Inst., 1989; Napier, 1992; Macaulay, 1992; British Geol Survey, 1993; Dainton, 1995; Bernal, Royal Soc., 1995. Fellow: QMW, 1993; Hebrew Univ., Jerusalem, 1996. Hon. DSc: Edinburgh, 1990; UEA, Glasgow, Nottingham, and Sheffield, 1991; Loughborough, Surrey and Westminster, 1992; Cranfield, Keele, 1993; Aberdeen, Buckingham, Birmingham, Sunderland, West of England, Glamorgan, 1994; Napier, Dundee, 1995; Paisley, 1996; DUniv Stirling, 1991. President's Medal, Royal Acad. Engrg, 1995. *Publications:* Nitrogen Fixation in Plants, 1966; (jtly) The Blue-Green Algae, 1973; Algal Physiology and Biochemistry, 1974; (ed) Nitrogen Fixation by Free-living Organisms, 1975; (ed jtly) Nitrogen Fixation, 1980; (ed jtly) The Nitrogen Cycle of the United Kingdom, 1984; papers in learned jls of repute. *Recreations:* watching soccer, playing the bagpipes (occasionally). *Address:* 45 Fairfield Road, Broughty Ferry, Dundee DD5 1PL. *Clubs:* Farmers; Dundee United.

STEWART, William Ian; *see* Allanbridge, Hon. Lord.

STEWART-CLARK, Sir John, (Sir Jack), 3rd Bt *cr* 1918; Member (C) European Parliament, East Sussex and Kent South, 1994–99 (Sussex East, 1979–94); a Vice-President, 1992–97; *b* 17 Sept. 1929; *e s* of Sir Stewart Stewart-Clark, 2nd Bt, and Jane Pamela (*d* 1993), *d* of late Major Arundell Clarke; *S* father, 1971; *m* 1958, Lydia Frederike, *d* of J. W. Loudon, Holland; one *s* four *d*. *Educ:* Eton; Balliol College, Oxford; Harvard Business School. Commissioned with HM Coldstream Guards, 1948–49. Oxford, 1949–52. With J. & P. Coats Ltd, 1952–69; Managing Director: J. & P. Coats, Pakistan, Ltd, 1961–67; J. A. Carp's Garenfabrieken, Holland, 1967–69; Philips Industries, 1971–79: Managing Director: Philips Electrical Ltd, London, 1971–75; Pye of Cambridge Ltd, 1975–79. Director: A. T. Kearney Ltd, 1979–92; Low and Bonar plc, 1980–95; Pioneer Concrete plc, 1986–99; TSB Scotland, 1986–89. Pres. Supervisory Bd, Eur. Inst. for Security, 1984–86; Mem. Council, RUSI, 1979–83. Dir and Trustee, Eur. Centre for Work and Society, 1982–; Mem., Bd of Govs, Eur. Inst. for Media, 1995–; Chairman: Conf. of Regions of North Western Europe, 1986–92; Eur. Parliamentarians and Industrialists Council, 1990–99. Treas., Eur. Democratic Group, 1979–92. Member Royal Company of Archers, Queen's Body Guard for Scotland. Contested (U) North Aberdeen, Gen. Election, 1959. *Publications:* Competition Law in the European Community, 1990; It's My Problem As Well: drugs prevention and education, 1993. *Recreations:* golf, tennis, photography, vintage cars. *Heir:* *s* Alexander Dudley Stewart-Clark, *b* 21 Nov. 1960. *Address:* Dundas Castle, South Queensferry, near Edinburgh EH30 9SP. *T:* (0131) 331 1114. *Clubs:* White's; Royal Ashdown Golf, Dalmahoy Golf.

STEWART COX, Maj.-Gen. Arthur George Ernest, DFC 1952; General Officer Commanding Wales, 1978–80; *b* 11 April 1925; *s* of Lt-Col Arthur Stewart Cox and Mrs Dorothea Stewart Cox, *d* of Maj.-Gen. Sir Edward May; *m* 1953, Mary Pamela, *d* of Hon. George Lyttelton; two *s* one *d* (and one *s* decd). *Educ:* Marlborough Coll.; Aberdeen Univ. Commissioned RA, 1944; parachutist, RA regts, 1945–50; army pilot, Far East and Korea, 1950–52; ADC to Comdt, RMA Sandhurst, 1954–56; Staff Coll., 1956; SO 99 Gurkha Inf. Bde, 1957–58; SO MoD, Malaya, 1963–65; CO 29 Commando Light Regt, RA, 1965–68; SO Sch. of Artillery, 1968–69; Comdr RA 4th Div., 1969–72; RCDS, 1973; Dep. Dir of Manning (Army), MoD, 1974–76. Col Comdt, RA, 1980–90; Hon. Colonel: 3rd Bn RWF, TAVR, 1980–85; 289 Commando Battery, RA, TAVR, 1983–91. *Recreations:* shooting, fishing, lepidoptery, gardening. *Address:* Long Mead, Brixton Deverill, Warminster, Wilts BA12 7EJ. *T:* (01985) 840877.

STEWART-JONES, Mrs Richard; *see* Smith, Emma.

STEWART-MOORE, Alexander Wyndham Hume; DL; Chairman, Gallaher Ltd, 1975–79 (Managing Director, 1966–75); Director, American Brands Inc., 1975–79; *b* 14 Feb. 1915; 2nd *s* of late James Stewart-Moore, DL, Ballydivity, Dervock, Co. Antrim, and of Katherine Marion (*née* Jackson); *m* 1948, Magdalene Clare (*d* 1999), *y d* of Sir David Richard Llewellyn, 1st Bt, LLD, JP; three *s* one *d*. *Educ:* Shrewsbury. Joined Gallaher Ltd, Nov. 1934. Served War, Royal Artillery (Middle East and Italy), 1939–46. DL Co. Antrim, 1982. *Recreations:* farming, fishing, gardening. *Address:* Moyarget Farm, 98 Moyarget Road, Ballycastle, Co. Antrim, NI BT54 6HL. *T:* (028) 2076 2287.

STEWART-RICHARDSON, Sir Simon (Alaisdair), 17th Bt *cr* 1630; *b* 9 June 1947; *er s* of Sir Ian Rorie Hay Stewart-Richardson, 16th Bt, and of Audrey Meryl (who *m* 1975, P. A. P. Robertson, *qv*), *e d* of late Claude Odlum; *S* father, 1969; *m* 1990, Marilene Cabal do Nascimento (marr. diss.); one *s* one *d*. *Educ:* Trinity College, Glenalmond. *Heir:* *s* Jason Rorie Stewart-Richardson, *b* 5 Oct. 1990. *Address:* Lynedale, Longcross, near Chertsey, Surrey KT16 0DP. *T:* (01932) 872329.

STEWART-ROBERTS, Phyllida Katharine, OBE 1995; Lord-Lieutenant, East Sussex, since 2000 (Vice Lord-Lieutenant, 1996–2000); Superintendent-in-Chief, St John Ambulance Brigade, 1990–93; *b* 19 Aug. 1933; *d* of Lt-Col Walter Harold Bamfield, Royal Welch Fusiliers and Veronica Grissell; *m* 1955, Andrew Kerr Stewart-Roberts; one *s* one *d*. *Educ:* Tormead Sch.; RAM (Diploma). Primary sch. teacher, LCC, 1954–57; Love Walk Hostel for Disabled Workers: Mem., Management Cttee, 1972–94; Vice Chm., 1980–83; Chm., 1983–89; Pres., 1994–. Trustee: Community Service Volunteers, 1984–; Orders of St John Trust, 1994–; Member: Management Cttee, Habinteg Housing Assoc., 1988–96 (Chm., Southern Cttee, 1994–96); St John Ambulance Brigade, Sussex, 1962–89, 1994–; Jt Pres., Council of Order of St John, Sussex, 2000– (County Pres., 1984–89; Chm., 1995–2000); Chm., Jt Cttee, Order of St John of Jerusalem and BRCS, 1991– (Mem., 1990–); Mem., Florence Nightingale Foundn, 1990–; Vice-Pres., VAD Assoc., 1991–. Mem. Council, Sussex Univ., 1995–2001 (Vice-Chm., 1999–2001). JP Inner London, 1980–95. DL E Sussex, 1991. DStJ 1993. *Recreations:* needlework, the gentler country pursuits. *Address:* Mount Harry Lodge, Offham, Lewes, E Sussex BN7 3QW.

STEWART-SMITH, Christopher Dudley, CBE 1995; Chairman, Cautley Ltd, since 1997; Vice-President, Eurochambres, since 1994; *b* 21 Jan. 1941; *s* of late Ean Stewart-Smith and Edmee von Wallerstain und Marnegg; *m* 1964, Olivia Barstow (marr. diss. 1989); one *s* two *d*. *Educ:* Winchester; King's Coll., Cambridge (MA Mod Langs); MIT (SM Management). Courtaulds, 1962–65; McKinsey & Co. Management Consultants, 1966–71; joined Sterling Guarantee Trust, 1971, Dir, 1973; served on main bd after merger with Town & City Properties and later with P&OSNCo., until 1986; Chairman: Earls Court and Olympia Exhibns Gp, 1974–85; Sutcliffe Catering Gp, 1975–85; Butlers Warehousing & Distribution, 1971–85; Sterling Guards, 1974–85; P&O Cruises, Swan Hellenic, and Princess Cruises, 1985–86; Conder Group plc, 1987–92; Collett Dickenson Pearce Internat., 1990–91; Producer Responsibility Gp and V-Wrag, 1994–96; London & Henley Ltd, 1995–98; Healthcall Gp plc, 1991–98. Director: Outer London Reg. Bd, 1984–88, Southern Adv. Bd, 1988–92, Nat. Westminster Bank; Williamson Tea Holdings, 1986–94; Life Sciences Internat., 1987–97; Erith plc, 1992–95; Strategic Partnership, 1997–2000; Gartmore SNT plc, 1998–; Brompton Bicycle Ltd, 2000–. Chm., London Chamber of Commerce and Industry, 1988–90; Pres., ABCC, 1992–94. Member: Council, Worldaware, 1988–2000 (Trustee, 2000–); Council of Management, Acad. of St Martin-in-the-Fields, 1990–93; Cttee, Royal Tournament, 1976–85; Vice-Pres., Olympia Internat. Showjumping, 1977–85; Hon. Mem., Royal Smithfield Club, 1985–. Mem. Ct of Assts, Grocers' Co., 1990. FRSA. *Recreations:* design of gardens and buildings, tennis, shooting, ski-ing. *Address:* 52 Westbourne Terrace, W2 3UJ. *T:* (020) 7262 0514. *Club:* Travellers.

STEWART-SMITH, (Dudley) Geoffrey; *b* 28 Dec. 1933; *s* of Dudley Cautley Stewart-Smith; *m* 1956, Kay Mary (marr. diss. 1990); three *s*. *Educ:* Winchester; RMA Sandhurst. Regular Officer, The Black Watch, 1952–60. Dir, Foreign Affairs Res. Inst., 1976–86. Director: Foreign Affairs Circle; Freedom Communications Internat. News Agency; Editor, East-West Digest; Dir, Foreign Affairs Publishing Co.; Financial Times, 1968. MP (C) Derbyshire, Belper, 1970–Feb 1974. Liveryman, Grocers' Co., 1962. *Publications:* The Defeat of Communism, 1964; No Vision Here: Non-Military Warfare in Britain, 1966; (ed) Brandt and the Destruction of NATO, 1973; The Struggle for Freedom, 1980. *Recreations:* study of religious and esp. inter-faith matters, gardening.

STEWART-SMITH, Kirstie Louise; *see* Hamilton, K. L.

STEWART-WILSON, Lt-Col Sir Blair (Aubyn), KCVO 1994 (CVO 1989 LVO 1983); Deputy Master of the Household and Equerry to Her Majesty, 1976–94, an Extra Equerry, since 1994; *b* 17 July 1929; *s* of late Aubyn Wilson and late Muriel Stewart Stevens; *m* 1962, Helen Mary Fox; three *d*. *Educ:* Eton; Sandhurst. Commnd Scots Guards, 1949, Atholl Highlanders, 1952 (Major, 1996); served with Regt in UK, Germany and Far East; Adjutant 2nd Bn, 1955–57; ADC to Viscount Cobham, Governor General and C-in-C, New Zealand, 1957–59; Equerry to late Duke of Gloucester, 1960–62; Regtl Adjutant, 1966–68; GSO1, Foreign Liaison Sect. (Army), MoD, 1970–73; Defence, Military and Air Attaché, British Embassy, Vienna, 1975–76. HM's Rep. Trustee, Bd of Royal Armouries, 1995–. Somerset County Patron, Cancer Res. Campaign, 1999–; Trustee, Wells Cathedral Trust, 1997–. *Address:* c/o Royal Bank of Scotland, 84 Atholl Road, Pitlochry PH16 5BJ. *T:* (home) (01823) 490111. *Club:* Pratt's.

STEWARTBY, Baron *cr* 1992 (Life Peer), of Portmoak in the District of Perth and Kinross; **Bernard Harold Ian Halley Stewart,** Kt 1991; PC 1989; RD 1972; FBA 1981; FRSE 1986; *b* 10 Aug. 1935; *s* of Prof. H. C. Stewart, *qv*; *m* 1966, Hon. Deborah Charlotte Buchan, JP, *d* of Baron Tweedsmuir, *qv*; one *s* two *d*. *Educ:* Haileybury; Jesus Coll., Cambridge (MA; LittD 1978; Hon. Fellow, 1994). 1st cl. hons Class. Tripos Cantab. Nat. Service, RNVR, 1954–56; subseq. Lt-Cmdr RNR. Seccombe, Marshall & Campion Ltd, bill brokers, 1959–60; joined Brown, Shipley & Co. Ltd, 1960, Dir 1971–83; Director: Seccombe Marshall & Campion Hldgs Ltd, 1989–98; Diploma plc, 1990–; Standard Chartered plc, 1990– (Dep. Chm., 1993–); Portman Building Soc., 1995–; Chm., Throgmorton Trust, 1990–; Dep. Chm., Amlin (formerly Angerstein Underwriting Trust), 1995–. Mem., SIB, later FSA, 1993–97. MP (C) Hitchin, Feb. 1974–1983, N Herts, 1983–92. PPS to Chancellor of the Exchequer, 1979–83; Parly Under-Sec. of State for Defence Procurement, MoD, Jan.-Oct. 1983; Economic Sec. to HM Treasury, 1983–87; Minister of State: for the Armed Forces, MoD, 1987–88; NI Office, 1988–89. Jt Sec., Cons. Parly Finance Cttee, 1975–76, 1977–79; Member: Public Expenditure Cttee, 1977–79; Public Accounts Cttee, 1991–92. UK rep., Europ. Budget Council, 1983–85; responsible for: Trustee Savings Banks Act, 1985; Building Socs Act, 1986; Banking Act, 1987. Mem. British Academy Cttee for Sylloge of Coins of British Isles, 1967– (Chm., 1993–); Numismatic advr, NACF, 1988–; Chm., Treasure Valuation Cttee, 1996–2001. Hon. Treas., Westminster Cttee for Protection of Children, 1960–70, Vice-Chm., 1975–92. FSA (Mem. Council 1974–76); FSAScot; Dir, British Numismatic Soc., 1965–75 (Sanford Saltus Gold Medal 1971); FRNS (medallist 1996). Mem. Council, British Museum Soc., 1975–76. Life Governor, 1977, Mem. Council, 1980–95, Haileybury; Trustee, Sir Halley Stewart Trust, 1978–. Hon. Vice-Pres., Stewart Soc. 1989–. County Vice-Pres., St John Ambulance for Herts, 1978–; KStJ 1992. *Publications:* The Scottish Coinage, 1955 (2nd edn 1967); Scottish Mints, 1971; (ed with C. N. L. Brooke and others) Studies in Numismatic Method, 1983; (with C. E. Blunt and C. S. S. Lyon) Coinage in Tenth-Century England, 1989; (with C. E. Challis and others) New History of the Royal Mint, 1992; many papers in Proc. Soc. Antiquaries of Scotland, Numismatic Chronicle, British Numismatic Jl, etc. *Recreations:* history; tennis (Captain CU Tennis Club, 1958–59; 1st string v Oxford, 1958 and 1959; winner Coupe de Bordeaux 1959; led 1st Oxford and Cambridge Tennis and Rackets team to USA, 1958);

Homer. *Address:* House of Lords, SW1A 0PW. *Clubs:* Beefsteak, Royal Automobile, MCC; New (Edinburgh); Hawks, Pitt (Cambridge).

STEYN, family name of **Baron Steyn.**

STEYN, Baron *cr* 1995 (Life Peer), of Swafield in the county of Norfolk; **Johan Steyn,** Kt 1985; PC 1992; a Lord of Appeal in Ordinary, since 1995; *b* 15 Aug. 1932; *m* Susan Leonore (*née* Lewis); two *s* two *d* by previous *m*, and one step *s* one step *d*. *Educ:* Jan van Riebeeck Sch., Cape Town, S Africa; Univ. of Stellenbosch, S Africa (BA, LLB); University Coll., Oxford (MA; Hon. Fellow, 1995). Cape Province Rhodes Scholar, 1955; commenced practice at S African Bar, 1958; Sen. Counsel of Supreme Court of SA, 1970; settled in UK; commenced practice at English Bar, 1973 (Bencher, Lincoln's Inn, 1985); QC 1979; a Presiding Judge, Northern Circuit, 1989–91; Judge of the High Court, QBD, 1985–91; a Lord Justice of Appeal, 1992–95. Member: Supreme Court Rule Cttee, 1985–89; Deptl Adv. Cttee on Arbitration Law, 1986–89 (Chm., 1990–94); Chairman: Race Relations Cttee of the Bar, 1987–88; Lord Chancellor's Adv. Cttee on Legal Educn and Conduct, 1993–96. Chm., Adv. Council, Centre for Commercial Law Studies, QMW, 1993–94. Pres., British Insce Law Assoc., 1992–94. Hon. Mem., Amer. Law Inst., 1999. Hon. LLD: QMW, 1997; UEA, 1998. *Address:* House of Lords, SW1A 0PW.

STIBBARD, Peter Jack, CStat; Head, Labour Market Statistics Group, Central Statistical Office, 1995–96; international consultancies, 1996–99; *b* 15 May 1936; *s* of late Frederick Stibbard and Gladys Stibbard (*née* Daines); *m* 1964, Christine Fuller; two *d*. *Educ:* City of Norwich Grammar School; Hull Univ. (BSc Econ). Served RAF, 1954–56. Kodak Ltd, 1959–64; Thos Potterton Ltd, 1964–66; Greater London Council, 1966–68; Central Statistical Office, 1968–82; HM Treasury, 1982–85; Under Sec., Statistics Div. 2, DTI, 1985–89; Dir of Statistics, Dept of Employment, 1989–95. *Publications:* articles in official and trade jls. *Address:* 62 Allington Drive, Tonbridge, Kent TN10 4HH.

STIBBON, Gen. Sir John (James), KCB 1988; OBE 1979; CEng, FICE; Chief Royal Engineer, 1993–99; *b* 5 Jan. 1935; *s* of Jack Stibbon and Elizabeth Matilda Stibbon (*née* Dixon); *m* 1957, Jean Fergusson Skeggs, *d* of John Robert Skeggs and Florence Skeggs (*née* Hayes); two *d*. *Educ:* Portsmouth Southern Grammar School; Royal Military Academy; Royal Military College of Science. BSc (Eng). CEng 1989; FICE 1989. Commissioned RE, 1954; CO 28 Amphibious Engineer Regt, 1975–77; Asst Military Secretary, 1977–79; Comd 20 Armoured Brigade, 1979–81; Comdt, RMCS, 1983–85; ACDS Operational Requirements (Land Systems), 1985–87; Master Gen. of the Ordnance, 1987–91. Director: Chemring Gp plc, 1993–; ITT Defence, 1993–. Colonel Commandant: RAPC, 1985–92; RPC, 1986–91; RE, 1987–99. Vice Pres., Royal Star & Garter Home, 1996–; Chm., Gordon Foundn, 1992–; Comr, Duke of York's Royal Mil. Sch., 1993–99. Hon DSc: Cranfield Inst. of Technology, 1989; Greenwich, 2001. *Recreations:* Association football, athletics, painting, palaeontology. *Club:* Army and Navy.

STIBBS, Prof. Douglas Walter Noble, MSc Sydney, DPhil Oxon; FRAS; FRSE; Visiting Fellow, Australian National University Research School of Astronomy and Astrophysics, Mount Stromlo and Siding Spring Observatories, since 1990; Visiting Professor, School of Mathematical Sciences, and Hon. Librarian to the School, since 1996, Australian National University (Hon. Fellow, Centre for Theoretical Astrophysics, 1994–2000); *b* 17 Feb. 1919; 2nd *s* of Edward John Stibbs, Sydney, NSW; *m* 1949, Margaret Lilian Calvert, BSc, DipEd (Sydney), *er d* of Rev. John Calvert, Sydney, NSW; two *d*. *Educ:* Sydney High Sch.; Univ. of Sydney; New College, Oxford. Deas Thomson Scholar, Sch. of Physics, Univ. of Sydney, 1940; BSc (Sydney), 1st Class Hons, Univ. Medal in Physics, 1942; MSc (Sydney), 1943; DPhil (Oxon), 1954. Johnson Memorial Prize and Gold Medal for Advancement of Astronomy and Meteorology, Oxford Univ., 1956. Res. Asst, Commonwealth Solar Observatory, Canberra, ACT, 1940–42; Asst Lectr, Dept of Mathematics and Physics, New England University Coll., Armidale, NSW (now the Univ. of New England), 1942–45; Scientific Officer and Sen. Scientific Officer, Commonwealth Observatory, Canberra, ACT, 1945–51; Radcliffe Travelling Fellow in Astronomy, Radcliffe Observatory, Pretoria, S Africa, and Univ. Observatory, Oxford, 1951–54; PSO, UKAEA, 1955–59; University of St Andrews: Napier Prof. of Astronomy, and Dir, Univ. Observatory, 1959–89; Sen. Prof. Senatus Academicus, 1987–89; Prof. Emeritus, 1990–. Vis. Prof. of Astrophysics, Yale Univ. Observatory, 1966–67; British Council Vis. Prof., Univ. of Utrecht, 1968; Prof., Collège de France, 1975–76 (Médaille du Collège, 1976). University College, London: External Expert (appts and promotions), 1970–74 and 1976–80; External Examr (BSc Astronomy), 1977–81. Member: Internat. Astronomical Union, 1951– (Chm. Finance Cttee, 1964–67, 1973–76, 1976–79); Amer. Astronomical Soc., 1956–73; Adv. Cttee on Meteorology for Scotland, 1960–69, 1972–75, 1978–80; Board of Visitors, Royal Greenwich Observatory, 1963–65; Council RAS, 1964–67, 1970–73 (Vice-Pres., 1972–73), Editorial Board, 1970–73; Council, RSE, 1970–72; National Cttee for Astronomy, 1964–76; SRC Cttees for Royal Greenwich Observatory, 1966–70, and Royal Observatory, Edinburgh, 1966–76, Chm., 1970–76; SRC Astronomy, Space and Radio Bd, 1970–76; SRC, 1972–76; S African Astron. Obs. Adv. Cttee, 1972–76; Chairman: Astronomy Policy and Grants Cttee, 1972–74; Northern Hemisphere Observatory Planning Cttee, 1972–75; Astronomy II Cttee, 1974–75; Mem., Centre National de la Recherche Scientifique Cttee, Obs. de Haute Provence, 1973–82. Life Member: Sydney Univ. Union, 1942; New Coll. Soc., 1953; New England Univ. Union, NSW, 1957. Mem., Western Province Masters Athletics Assoc., Cape Town, 1983–. Marathon Medals: Paris, Caithness, Edinburgh (3hrs 59mins), Flying Fox (British Veterans Championships), Honolulu, 1983; London, Loch Rannoch, and Aberdeen (Veterans Trophy Winner), 1984; Stoke-on-Trent (Potteries), Athens, Honolulu, 1985; London, Edinburgh (Commonwealth Games Peoples Marathon), Stoke-on-Trent (Potteries), Berlin, Honolulu, 1986; Boston, 1987; Half-marathons: 13 events incl. Windsor Great Park, Dundee, Dunfermline, Wagga (Australian Veterans Games, 1991, Gold Medallist), Canberra. *Publications:* The Outer Layers of a Star (with Sir Richard Woolley), 1953; contrib. Theoretical Astrophysics and Astronomy in Monthly Notices of RAS and other jls. *Recreations:* music, ornithology, photography, golf, coaching (long-distance running). *Address:* Mount Stromlo Observatory, Australian National University, Canberra, ACT 0200, Australia. *T:* (2) 62901773. *Club:* Royal and Ancient (St Andrews).

STIGLITZ, Prof. Joseph Eugene, PhD; Professor of Economics, Columbia Business School, Columbia University, since 2001; Chairman, Brookdale Group, since 2000; *b* 9 Feb. 1943; *m*; two *s* two *d*. *Educ:* Amherst Coll. (BA 1964); MIT (PhD 1966); Cambridge Univ. (MA 1970). Professor of Economics: Yale Univ. 1970–74; Stanford Univ., 1974–76; Drummond Prof. of Political Economy, Oxford Univ. and All Souls Coll., 1976–79; Prof. of Economics, Princeton Univ., 1979–88; Prof. of Econs, 1988–2001, Joan Kenney Prof. of Econs, 1992–2001, Stanford Univ. Mem., 1993–97, Chm., 1995–97, Council of Econ. Advrs to Pres. of USA; Chief Economist, World Bank, 1997–99. Fellowships: Nat. Sci. Foundn, 1964–65; Fulbright, 1965–66; SSRC Faculty, 1969–70; Guggenheim, 1969–70; Oskar Morgenstern Distinguished Fellowship, Mathematica and Inst. for Advanced Study, Princeton, 1978–79. Consultant: Nat. Sci. Foundn, 1972–75; Ford Foundn Energy Policy Study, 1973; Dept of Labor (Pensions and Labor Turnover), 1974; Dept of Interior (Offshore Oil Leasing Programs), 1975; Federal Energy Admin (Intertemporal Biases in Market Allocation of Natural Resources), 1975–79; World Bank (Cost Benefit Analysis; Urban Rural Migration; Natural Resources), 1975–; Electric Power Res. Inst., 1976–; OECD; Office of Fair Trading; Treasury (Office of Tax Analysis), 1980; US AID (commodity price stabilization), 1977; Inter-American Development Bank; Bell Laboratories; Bell Communications Research; State of Alaska; Seneca Indian Nation. Internat. Prize, Academia Lincei, 1988; Union des Assurances de Paris Scientific Prize, 1989. Gen. Editor, Econometric Soc. Reprint Series; Associate Editor: Jl of Economic Theory, 1968–73; American Economic Rev., 1972–75; Jl of Economic Perspectives, 1988–; Co-editor, Jl of Public Economics, 1968–83; American Editor, Rev. of Economic Studies, 1968–76; Editorial Bd, World Bank Economic Review, The Geneva Papers, Revista de Econometrica, Assicurazioni. Vice-Pres., American Econ. Assoc. 1985. Fellow: Econometric Soc., 1972 (Sec./Treasurer, 1972–75); Amer. Acad. of Arts and Scis; Inst. for Policy Reform, 1990–; Senior Fellow: Hoover Instn, 1988–; Brookings Instn, Washington, 2001–. Corresp. FBA 1993. Hon. MA Yale, 1970; Hon. DHL Amherst, 1974. John Bates Clark Medal, Amer. Econ. Assoc; (jtly) Nobel Prize for Economics, 2001. *Publications:* (ed) Collected Scientific Papers of P. A. Samuelson, 1965; (ed with H. Uzawa) Readings in Modern Theory of Economic Growth, 1969; (with A. B. Atkinson) Lectures in Public Finance, 1980; (with D. Newbery) The Economic Impact of Price Stabilization, 1980; Economics of the Public Sector, 1986; contribs on economics of growth, development, natural resources, information, uncertainty, imperfect competition, corporate finance and public finance in Amer. Econ. Rev., Qly Jl of Econs, Jl of Pol. Econ., Econometrica, Internat. Econ. Rev., Econ. Jl, Rev. of Econ. Studies, Jl of Public Econs, Jl of Econ. Theory, Oxford Econ. Papers. *Address:* Room 814, Uris Hall, Columbia Business School, New York, NY 10027, USA. *T:* (212) 8540671.

STIHLER, Catherine Dalling; Member (Lab) Scotland, European Parliament, since 1999; *b* 30 July 1973; *d* of Gordon McLeish Taylor and Catherine Doreen Taylor; *m* 2000, David Stihler. *Educ:* Coltness High Sch., Wishaw; Univ. of St Andrews (MA Hons Geography and Internat. Relns 1996; MLitt Internat. Security Studies 1998). Pres., Univ. of St Andrews Students' Assoc., 1994–95. Young Labour Representative: Exec. Cttee, SLP, 1993–95; Lab Party NEC, 1995–97; Women's Rep. and Local Orgns Rep., SLP Exec., 1997–99. Researcher and facilitator to Anne Begg, MP, 1997–99. Contested (Lab) Angust), 1997. *Publication:* (contrib.) Women and the Military, 2000. *Recreations:* going to the gym, watching films, singing, playing backgammon. *Address:* European Parliament, Rue Wiertz, 1047 Brussels, Belgium.

STILGOE, Richard Henry Simpson, OBE 1998; DL; songwriter, lyricist, entertainer and broadcaster, since 1962; *b* 28 March 1943; *s* of late John Henry Tweedie Stilgoe and Joan Lucy Strutt Stilgoe; *m* 1st, 1964, Elizabeth Caroline Gross; one *s* one *d*; 2nd, 1975, Annabel Margaret Hunt; two *s* one *d*. *Educ:* Liverpool Coll.; Monkton Combe Sch.; Clare Coll., Cambridge (choral exhibnr). One-man show worldwide, incl. Windsor Castle, 1982 and British Embassy, Washington, 1986; Two-man show with Peter Skellern, 1985–99. Author and composer: Bodywork (children's musical), 1987; Brilliant the Dinosaur, 1991. Word-processor for Andrew Lloyd Webber on Cats, Starlight Express and Phantom of the Opera. Stilgoe Saturday Concerts, RFH, 1999–. Founder and Dir, Orpheus Trust (music and disabled people), 1985–; Pres., Surrey Care Trust, 1986–2000; Trustee, Nat. Foundn for Youth Music, 1999–. Hon. DLitt Greenwich, 1999. Monaco Radio Prize, 1984, 1991, 1996; NY Radio Fest. Gold Award, 1989; Prix Italia, 1991. DL, 1996, High Sheriff, 1998, Surrey. *Publications:* The Richard Stilgoe Letters, 1981; Brilliant The Dinosaur, 1994. *Recreations:* sailing, cricket, architecture, building, demolition, children. *Address:* c/o The Orpheus Trust, Trevereux Manor, Limpsfield Chart, Oxted, Surrey RH8 0TL. *Clubs:* MCC, Lord's Taverners; Surrey CC.

STILLMAN, Dr Bruce William, AO 1999; FRS 1993; Director, since 1994, and Chief Executive Officer, Cold Spring Harbor Laboratory, New York; *b* Melbourne, Australia, 16 Oct. 1953; *s* of Graham Leslie Stillman and Jessie May (*née* England); *m* 1981, Grace Angela Begley; one *s* one *d*. *Educ:* Glen Waverley High Sch.; Sydney Boys' High Sch.; Univ. of Sydney (BSc Hons); ANU (PhD). Cold Spring Harbor Laboratory, New York: Damon Runyon-Walter Winchell Postdoctoral Res. Fellow, 1979–80; Staff Investigator, 1981–82; Sen. Staff Investigator, 1983–85; Sen. Scientist, 1985–90; Asst Dir, 1990–93; Adjunct Prof. of Microbiology, SUNY, 1982–. Damon Runyon-Walter Winchell Cancer Fund Fellow, 1979–80; Rita Allen Foundn Scholar, 1982–87; Charter Fellow, Molecular Medicine Soc., 1995. Lectures: Harvey Soc., 1993; Nieuwland, Univ. of Notre Dame, 1993; Doty, Harvard Univ., 1998. For. Associate, NAS, USA, 2000; Fellow, Amer. Acad. of Microbiol., 2000. Hon. DHL Hofstra, 2001; Hon. DSc NY Inst. Tech. Commonwealth Postgrad. Award, 1976–80; Merit Award, NIH, 1986. *Publications:* numerous scientific pubns. *Address:* Cold Spring Harbor Laboratory, One Bungtown Road, Cold Spring Harbor, NY 11724, USA. *T:* (516) 3678383.

STIMSON, Prof. Gerald Vivian, PhD; Imperial College of Science, Technology and Medicine: Director, Centre for Research on Drugs and Health Behaviour, since 1990; Professor of Sociology of Health Behaviour, since 1991; Head, Department of Social Science and Medicine, since 1997; *b* 10 April 1945; *s* of late Geoffrey Edward Vivian Stimson and Maud Ellen Stimson; *m* 1st, 1971, Carol Anne Fowler (marr. diss. 1992, she *d* 1997); two *s*; 2nd, 1993, Elizabeth Louise Tacey; one *s*. *Educ:* City of London Sch.; London Sch. of Econs (BSc 1966; MSc 1967); Inst. of Psychiatry, Univ. of London (PhD 1971). Res. worker, Addiction Res. Unit, Inst. of Psychiatry, Univ. of London, 1967–71; Res. Fellow, Med. Sociology Res. Centre, UC of Swansea, 1971–75; London University: Lectr, then Sen. Lectr, Addiction Res. Unit, Inst. Psychiatry, 1975–78; Goldsmiths' College: Sen. Lectr in Sociology, 1978–89; Head, Sociology Dept, 1980–83; Dir, Monitoring Res. Gp, Sociology Dept, 1987–89. Fulbright Schol., NY Univ., 1983; Vis. Prof., Thames Valley Univ., 1995–. Advisory Council on Misuse of Drugs: Mem., 1984–99; Mem., Wkg Gp on AIDS and Drug Misuse, 1987–92; Chm., Stats Inf. and Res. Cttee, 1990–99; Member: Council, Inst. for Study of Drug Dependence, 1985–90 (Vice-Chm., 1987); Scientific Cttee, Eur. Monitoring Centre for Drugs and Drug Addiction, 1994–97; Consultant, WHO Global Prog. on AIDS, 1988–95, and Prog. on Substance Abuse, 1990. Pres., Action on Hepatitis C; Chm., UK Harm Reduction Alliance. Member, Editorial Board: Brit. Jl Addiction, 1982–; Addiction Res., 1991–; AIDS, 1993–96; Ed., Internat. Jl Drug Policy, 2000–. Trustee, AIDS Educnl and Res. Trust, 1995–. Hon. MFPHM 1998. *Publications:* Heroin and Behaviour: diversity among addicts attending London clinics, 1973; (with B. Webb) Going to See the Doctor: the consultation process in general practice, 1975; (with E. Oppenheimer) Heroin Addiction: treatment and control in Britain, 1982; (ed jtly) AIDS and Drug Misuse: the challenge for policy and practice in the 1990's, 1990; (ed jtly) Drug Injecting and HIV Infection: global issues and local responses, 1998; (ed jtly) Drug Use in London, 1998. *Recreations:* walking, the countryside, travel. *Address:* Reynolds Building, Imperial College, St Dunstan's Road, W6 8RP. *T:* (020) 7594 0776. *Club:* Athenæum.

STIMSON, Robert Frederick, CBE 1992; Governor and Commander-in-Chief of St Helena and its Dependencies, 1987–91; *b* 16 May 1939; *s* of Frederick Henry Stimson and Gladys Alma Stimson (*née* Joel); *m* 1961, Margaret Faith Kerry; two *s* one *d*. *Educ:*

Rendcomb Coll.; Queen Mary Coll., London (BSc First Cl. Hons; MSc (by thesis) mathematical physics). HM Diplomatic Service: FO, 1966–67; Saigon, 1967–68; Singapore, 1968–70; Cabinet Office, 1970–73; Mexico City, 1973–75; FCO, 1975–80; Counsellor, East Berlin, 1980–81; Head of Home Inspectorate, 1982–83; Counsellor and Hd of Chancery, Dublin, 1984–87. Order of Aztec Eagle, Mexico, 1975. *Publications:* contrib. Jl Physics and Chemistry of Solids.

STINCHCOMBE, Paul David; MP (Lab) Wellingborough, since 1997; *b* 25 April 1962; *s* of Lionel Walter Stinchcombe and Pauline Sylvia Ann (*née* Hawkins); *m* 1990, Suzanne Jean Gardiner; two *s* one *d. Educ:* Royal Grammar Sch., High Wycombe; Trinity Coll., Cambridge (Sen. Schol.; BA Law double 1st cl. Hons 1983); Harvard Law Sch. (Frank Knox Fellow; LLM 1984). Called to the Bar, Lincoln's Inn, 1985; in practice at the Bar, 1985–. Mem. (Lab), Camden Council, 1990–94 (Chm., Labour Gp, 1992–94). *Recreations:* football, cricket, golf. *Address:* House of Commons, SW1A 0AA; 4/5 Gray's Inn Square, WC1R 5AY.

STINSON, His Honour David John; a Circuit Judge (formerly County Court Judge), 1969–86; *b* 22 Feb. 1921; *s* of late Henry John Edwin Stinson, MC, MA, LLB, Beckenham, Kent (sometime Chief Commoner of City of London, solicitor), and late Margaret Stinson (*née* Little); *m* 1950, Eleanor Judith (*née* Chance); two *s* two *d* (and one *s* decd). *Educ:* Eastbourne Coll.; Emmanuel Coll., Cambridge. MA 1946; Jesters Club, 1949 (Rugby Fives). Served War of 1939–45: Essex Yeomanry, Captain, RA, and Air OP, 1941–46 (despatches). Called to Bar, Middle Temple, 1947 (Harmsworth Schol., 1948); Dep. Chm., Herts QS, 1965–71; Suffolk and Essex County Court Circuit, 1973–86. Chancellor, dio. of Carlisle, 1971–90. Chm., Ipswich Family Conciliation Service, 1982–88; Pres., Parents' Conciliation Trust, 1988–99. *Recreations:* bird-watching, gardening. *Address:* Barrack Row, Waldringfield, Woodbridge, Suffolk IP12 4QX. *T:* (01473) 736280.

STIRLING, Sir Alexander (John Dickson), KBE 1981; CMG 1976; HM Diplomatic Service, retired; Council Member, SOS Sahel International—UK, since 1987 (Chairman, 1993–97); *b* 20 Oct. 1926; *e s* of late Brig. A. Dickson Stirling, DSO, MB, ChB, DPH, and Isobel Stirling, MA, DipEd, DipPsych, *d* of late Rev. J. C. Matthew (former senior Presidency Chaplain, Bombay); *m* 1955, Alison Mary, *y d* of Gp Capt. A. P. Campbell, CBE; two *s* two *d. Educ:* Edinburgh Academy; Lincoln Coll., Oxford (MA). RAFVR, 1945–48 (Egypt, 1945–47). Entered Foreign Office, 1951; Lebanon, 1952; British Embassy, Cairo, 1952–56 (Oriental Sec., 1955–56); FO, 1956–59; First Sec., British Embassy, Baghdad, 1959–62; First Sec. and Consul, Amman, 1962–64; First Sec., British Embassy, Santiago, 1965–67 (led UK Delegn to Fourth Antarctic Treaty Consultative Meeting, 1966); FO, 1967–69; British Political Agent, Bahrain, 1969–71, Ambassador, 1971–72; Counsellor, Beirut, 1972–75; RCDS 1976; Ambassador to Iraq, 1977–80, to the Tunisian Republic, 1981–84, to the Sudan, 1984–86. Chm., 1989–92, Mem. Council, 1994–2000, Soc. for Protection of Animals Abroad (formerly Soc. for Protection of Animals in N Africa).

See also C. J. M. Stirling.

STIRLING, Sir Angus (Duncan Æneas), Kt 1994; Chairman: Greenwich Foundation for the Royal Naval College, since 1996; Joint Nature Conservation Committee, since 1997; *b* 10 Dec. 1933; *s* of late Duncan Alexander Stirling and Lady Marjorie Murray, *e d* of 8th Earl of Dunmore, VC, DSO, MVO; *m* 1959, Armyne Morar Helen Schofield, *e d* of late W. G. B. Schofield and Hon. Armyne Astley, *d* of 21st Baron Hastings; one *s* two *d. Educ:* Eton Coll.; Trinity Coll., Cambridge; London Univ. (Extra Mural) (Dip. History of Art). Christie, Manson and Woods Ltd, 1954–57; Lazard Bros and Co. Ltd, 1957–66; Asst Dir, Paul Mellon Foundn for British Art, 1966–69 (Jt Dir, 1969–70); Dep. Sec.-General, Arts Council of GB, 1971–79; Dep. Dir-Gen., 1979–83, Dir-Gen., 1983–95, Nat. Trust; Sen. Policy Advr, Nat. Heritage Meml Fund, 1996–97. Mem., Govt Task Force on Tourism and the Envmt, 1991. Mem. Bd, Royal Opera House, Covent Garden, 1979–96 (Chm., 1991–96); Chm., Friends of Covent Garden, 1981–91; Dep. Chm., Royal Ballet Bd, 1988–91; a Gov., Royal Ballet, 1988–96; Member: Crafts Council, 1980–85; Council of Management, Byam Shaw Sch. of Art, 1965–89; Management Cttee, Courtauld Inst. of Art, 1981–83; Adv. Council, London Symphony Orchestra, 1979–; Bd of Governors, Live Music Now, 1982–89; Bd of Trustees, The Theatres Trust, 1983–91; Bd of Trustees, Heritage of London Trust, 1983–95; Tourism Cttee, ICOMOS UK, 1993–; Council, RSCM, 1996–98; Fabric Adv. Cttee, Wells Cathedral, 2001–. Chairman: Policy Cttee, CPRE, 1996–; Adv. Panel for Local Heritage Initiative, Countryside Commn, 1998–99; Mem. Adv. Cttee, Stowe Landscape Gardens, 1996–; Trustee: Stowe House Preservation Trust, 1998–; Samuel Courtauld Trust (formerly Home House (Courtauld Collection)), 1983–; World Monuments Fund in Britain, 1996–. Mem. Bd of Govs, Gresham Sch., 1999–. CIMgt; FRSA. Mem., Court, Fishmongers' Co., 1991–. Hon. DLitt Leicester, 1995. *Recreations:* music, travel, walking, landscape photography. *Address:* 25 Ladbroke Grove, W11 3AY. *Clubs:* Garrick, Brooks's.

STIRLING, Prof. Charles James Matthew, FRS 1986; CChem, FRSC; Professor of Organic Chemistry, University of Sheffield, 1990–98, now Emeritus; *b* 8 Dec. 1930; *s* of Brig. Alexander Dickson Stirling, DSO, MB, ChB, DPH, RAMC, and Isobel Millicent Stirling, MA, DipPsych; *m* 1956, Eileen Gibson Powell, BA, MEd, *yr d* of William Leslie and Elsie May Powell; two *d* (and one *d* decd). *Educ:* Edinburgh Acad.; Univ. of St Andrews (Harkness Exhibn; BSc; Biochem. Medal 1951); Univ. of London (PhD, DSc). FRSC, CChem 1967. Civil Service Jun. Res. Fellowship, Porton, 1955, Sen. Fellowship, 1956; ICI Fellowship, Univ. of Edinburgh, 1957; Lectr, QUB, 1959; Reader in Org. Chem., KCL, 1965; University of Wales, Bangor: Prof. of Organic Chemistry, 1969–81; Dean of Faculty of Science, 1977–79; Hd of Dept of Chemistry, 1981–90; Sheffield University: Hd, Dept of Chemistry, 1991–94; Dir, Engrg and Physical Scis Div., Grad. Sch., 1994–97; Public Orator, 1995–. Vis. Prof., Hebrew Univ. of Jerusalem, 1981; Vis. Fellow, ANU, Canberra, 1999. Royal Instn Christmas Lects, BBC TV, 1992. Mem., IUPAC Commn on Physical Organic Chemistry, 1992–95. Mem., Perkin Council, RSC, 1971–93 (Vice-Pres., 1985–88 and 1991–93, Pres., 1989–91); Pres., Section B (Chemistry), BAAS, 1990; Pres., Yorks and Humberside Sect., ASE, 1993–95. Hon. DSc: St Andrews, 1994; Aix-Marseille, 1999. Award for Organic Reaction Mechanisms, RSC, 1988; Millennium Commn Award, 1999. *Publications:* Radicals in Organic Chemistry, 1965; (ed) Organic Sulphur Chemistry, 1975; (ed) The Chemistry of the Sulphonium Group, 1981; (ed) The Chemistry of Sulphones and Sulphoxides, 1988; numerous res. papers mainly in Jls of RSC. *Recreations:* choral music, the collection of chiral objects, furniture restoration. *Address:* Department of Chemistry, University of Sheffield, Sheffield S3 7HF. *T:* (0114) 222 9453; 114 Westbourne Road, Sheffield S10 2QT.

See also Sir A. J. D. Stirling.

STIRLING of Garden, Col James, CBE 1987; TD; FRICS; Lord-Lieutenant of Stirling and Falkirk, since 1983; *b* 8 Sept. 1930; *s* of Col Archibald Stirling of Garden, OBE; *m* 1958, Fiona Janetta Sophia Wood Parker; two *s* two *d. Educ:* Rugby; Trinity Coll., Cambridge. BA; Dip. Estate Management. Chartered Surveyor in private practice. Partner, K. Ryden and Partners, Chartered Surveyors, 1962–89. Director: Local Bd, Scotland and N Ireland, Woolwich Building Soc., 1973–97; Scottish Widows and Life Insurance Fund, 1975–96. Hon. Sheriff, Stirling, 1998. DL 1970, Vice-Lieutenant 1979–83, Stirling. Chm., Highland TAVR Assoc., 1982–87 (Pres., 1992). Hon. Col, 3/51st Highland Volunteers, TA, 1979–86. KStJ 1987 (Prior, Order of St John, Scotland, 1995–). *Address:* Garden, Buchlyvie, Stirlingshire FK8 3NR. *T:* (01360) 850212. *Club:* New (Edinburgh).

STIRLING, John Fullarton; JP; Librarian, University of Exeter, 1972–94; *b* 12 April 1931; *s* of Reginald Stirling and Jeanette Sybil (*née* Fullarton); *m* 1960, Sheila Mary Fane; two *d. Educ:* Waterloo Grammar sch.; Univ. of Liverpool (BA 1st Cl. Hons 1953; MA 1962). Asst, Liverpool Public Libraries, 1953–56; Asst Librarian, UCL, 1956–62; Sub-librarian, 1962–64, Dep. Librarian, 1964–66, Univ. of York; Librarian, Univ. of Stirling, 1966–71; Librarian designate, Univ. of Exeter, 1971–72. Member: various cttees, SCONUL, 1977–; UGC Working Gp on Liby Automation, 1986; British Liby Cttee for Bibliographic Services, 1987. JP Exeter, 1976. *Publications:* (ed) University Librarianship, 1981; contrib. various professional jls. *Address:* c/o Devon and Exeter Institution, 7 Cathedral Close, EX1 1EZ. *T:* (01392) 257413. *Club:* Devon and Exeter Institution (Exeter).

STIRLING, Rear-Adm. Michael Grote; Agent-General for British Columbia in the United Kingdom and Europe, 1968–75; *b* 29 June 1915; *s* of late Hon. Grote Stirling and late Mabel Katherine (*née* Brigstocke), Kelowna, British Columbia; *m* 1942, Sheelagh Kathleen Russell; two *s* one *d. Educ:* Shawnigan Lake School, BC; RNC Greenwich. Cadet, RCN, 1933; HMS Frobisher for training till 1934, then as Midshipman and Sub-Lt in RN, returning Canada Jan. 1938; Ships of RCN until 1941; specialized in Signals at HM Signal School, Portsmouth, then Home Fleet; Deputy Director, Signal Div., Naval Service HQ, Ottawa, 1942–43; SSO to C-in-C, Canadian North-West Atlantic, 1943–44; Commanded destroyers, 1944–46; Director Naval Communications, rank of Commander, 1949–51; promoted Captain and staff of Supreme Allied Commander Atlantic, Norfolk, Va, 1953–55; Commanded HMCS Cornwallis, 1955–57; 2nd Cdn Escort Sqdn, 1957–58; Naval Member of Directing Staff, Nat. Defence College as Commodore, 1958–61; Senior Canadian Officer Afloat, 1961–62; Chief of Naval Personnel, 1962–64; Maritime Comdr, Pacific, 1964–66. Rear-Adm. 1962. Dir, Univ. of Victoria Foundation, 1967–68. *Recreations:* golf, ski-ing. *Address:* 302–1280 Newport Avenue, Victoria, BC V8S 5E7, Canada. *Club:* Victoria Golf (Victoria, BC).

STIRLING of Fairburn, Captain Roderick William Kenneth, TD 1965; JP; Lord Lieutenant of Ross and Cromarty and Skye and Lochalsh, since 1988; *b* 17 June 1932; *s* of late Major Sir John Stirling, KT, MBE and Lady Marjory Kythé, *d* of Sir Kenneth Mackenzie, 7th Bt of Gairloch; *m* 1963, Penelope Jane Wright; four *d. Educ:* Wellesley House; Harrow. National Service, Scots Guards, 1950–52; commissioned 1951; TA Seaforth Highlanders and Queen's Own Highlanders (Seaforth and Cameron), 1953–69. Member: Ross and Cromarty County Council, 1970–74 (Chm. of Highways, 1973–74); Ross and Cromarty District Council, 1984–96. Mem., Red Deer Commn, 1964–89 (Vice-Chm., 1975–89); Chm., S Ross Deer Mgt Gp, 1997–; Director: Moray Firth Salmon Fishing Co., 1973–91; Scottish Salmon and Whitefish Co., 1972–91 (Chm., 1980–). Mem., Scottish Council, NPFA, 1971–91 (Chm., Highland Cttee); President: Ross and Cromarty CVS, 1990–95; Ross and Sutherland Scout Council, 1990–; Highlands, Islands and Moray Br., Scots Guards Assoc., 1994–; Jun. Vice-Pres., Scottish Accident Prevention Council, 1991–92. JP Ross and Cromarty, 1975. *Recreations:* stalking, shooting, fishing, gardening, curling. *Address:* Arcan, Muir of Ord, Ross and Cromarty IV6 7UL. *T:* (01997) 433207. *Club:* New (Edinburgh).

STIRLING, Prof. (William) James, PhD; FRS 1999; Professor of Mathematical Sciences and Physics, since 1992, and Director, Institute for Particle Physics Phenomenology, since 2000, University of Durham; *b* 4 Feb. 1953; *s* of late John Easton Stirling and of Margaret Eleanor Stirling (*née* Norris); *m* 1975, Paula Helene Close; one *s* one *d. Educ:* Belfast Royal Acad.; Peterhouse, Cambridge (MA, PhD 1979). CPhys, FInstP 1992. Res. Associate, Univ. of Washington, 1979–81; Res. Fellow, Peterhouse, 1981–83; Fellow and Staff Mem., CERN, Geneva, 1983–86; Lectr, 1986–89, Sen. Lectr, 1989–90, Reader, 1990–92, Depts of Math. Scis and Physics, Univ. of Durham. SERC and PPARC Sen. Fellow, 1993–98. Chm., Sci. Cttee, PPARC, 2001–. Gov., Royal Grammar Sch., Newcastle, 1996–. Humboldt Res. Award, 1997. *Publications:* (jtly) QCD and Collider Physics, 1996; numerous articles on elementary particle theory in learned jls. *Recreations:* playing and listening to Irish music, outdoor activities, travelling. *Address:* Department of Physics, University of Durham, South Road, Durham DH1 3LE. *T:* (0191) 374 2169; *e-mail:* w.j.stirling@durham.ac.uk; (home) 52 South Street, Durham DH1 4QP. *T:* (0191) 384 4431.

STIRLING-HAMILTON, Sir Malcolm William Bruce, 14th Bt *cr* 1673 (NS), of Preston, Haddingtonshire; *b* 6 Aug. 1979; *s* of Sir Bruce Stirling-Hamilton, 13th Bt and of Stephanie (who *m* 1990, Anthony Tinsley), *d* of Dr William Campbell, LRCP, LRCS; S father, 1989. *Educ:* Stowe. *Heir: cousin* Rev. Andrew Robert Hamilton [*b* 5 Sept. 1937; *m* 1972, Josephine Mary, *d* of Reginald Sargant]. *Address:* Narborough Hall, King's Lynn, Norfolk PE32 1TE.

STIRRAT, Prof. Gordon Macmillan, MA, MD; FRCOG; Vice-Provost, Institute for Advanced Studies, University of Bristol, since 1999; Senior Research Fellow, Centre for Ethics in Medicine, since 2000; Professor of Obstetrics and Gynaecology, University of Bristol, 1982–2000, now Emeritus; *b* 12 March 1940; *s* of Alexander and Caroline Mary Stirrat; *m* 1965, Janeen Mary (*née* Brown); three *d. Educ:* Hutcheson's Boys' Grammar Sch., Glasgow; Glasgow Univ. (MB, ChB). MA Oxon, MD London. FRCOG 1981. Jun. hosp. doctor appts, Glasgow and environs, and London, 1964–71; Lectr, St Mary's Hosp. Med. Sch., London, 1971–75; Clinical Reader, Univ. of Oxford, 1975–81; Dean, Faculty of Medicine, 1990–93, Pro-Vice-Chancellor, 1993–97, Univ. of Bristol. Dep. Chm., Bristol and Dist HA, 1991–96. Member: Acad. of Experts, 1996–; Expert Witness Inst., 1997–. *Publications:* Legalised Abortion: the continuing dilemma, 1979; Obstetrics Pocket Consultant, 1981, 2nd edn 1986; Aids to Reproductive Biology, 1982; (jtly) You and Your Baby—a Mother's Guide to Health, 1982; Aids to Obstetrics and Gynaecology, 1983, 4th edn 1996; (jtly) The Immune System in Disease, 1992; (jtly) Handbook of Obstetric Management, 1996. *Recreations:* fly-fishing, walking, photography. *Address:* Malpas Lodge, 24 Henbury Road, Westbury-on-Trym, Bristol BS9 3HJ. *T:* (0117) 950 5310.

STIRRUP, Air Marshal Graham Eric, CB 2000; AFC 1983; FRAeS; Deputy Commander-in-Chief, Strike Command, Commander NATO Combined Air Operations Centre 9, and Director European Air Group, since 2000; *b* 4 Dec. 1949; *s* of William Hamilton Stirrup and Jacqueline Brenda Stirrup (*née* Coulson); *m* 1976, Mary Alexandra Elliott; one *s. Educ:* Merchant Taylors' Sch., Northwood; Royal Air Force Coll., Cranwell. Qualified Flying Instr, 1971–73; Loan Service, Sultan of Oman's Air Force, 1973–75; Fighter Reconnaissance Pilot, 1976–78; Exchange Pilot, USAF, 1978–81; Flt Comdr, 1982–84; OC No II (Army Co-operation) Sqn, 1985–87; PSO to CAS, 1987–90; OC RAF Marham, 1990–92; rcds, 1993; Dir, Air Force Plans and Progs, MoD, 1994–97;

AOC No 1 Gp, 1997–98; ACAS, 1998–2000. FIMgt 1983; FRAeS 1991. *Recreations:* golf, music, theatre, history. *Clubs:* Royal Air Force, Royal Commonwealth Society.

STIRTON, Prof. Charles Howard, PhD; CBiol; FLS; Director, National Botanic Garden of Wales, since 1996; *b* 25 Nov. 1946; *s* of Charles Aubrey and Elizabeth Maud Stirton; *m* 1979, Jana Žantovská; one *d.* *Educ:* Univ. of Natal (BSc, BSc Hons, MSc); Univ. of Cape Town (PhD 1989). CBiol 1993. Botanist, Botanical Res. Inst., Pretoria, 1975–82; S African Liaison Botanist, 1979–82, B. A. Krukoff Botanist for Neotropical Legumes, 1982–87, Royal Botanic Gardens, Kew; Associate Prof., Univ. of Natal, Pietermaritzburg, 1988–90; self-employed, 1990; economic botanist, 1990–92, Dep. Dir, and Dir, Sci. and Horticulture, 1992–96, Royal Botanic Gardens, Kew. Vis. Prof., Univ. of Reading, 1993–96; Hon. Prof., Univ. of Wales, 1997–. FLS 1975; FIMgt 1999; MInstD 1995. *Publications:* (ed) Plant Invaders: beautiful but dangerous, 1978; (ed with J. Zarucchi) Advances in Legume Biology, 1990; (ed) Advances in Legume Systematics 3, 1987; (ed) The Changing World of Weeds, 1995; contrib. numerous scientific papers. *Recreations:* gardening, reading, postal history, postcards, cinema. *Address:* National Botanic Garden of Wales, Llanarthne, Carmarthenshire SA32 8HG. *T:* (01558) 668768.

STITT, (Thomas) Clive Somerville; HM Diplomatic Service; Director, Export Services Section, Central Services Group, British Trade International, since 1999; *b* 1 Jan. 1948; *m* 1977, Margaret Ann Milward; two *d.* FCO, 1970; Kabul, 1972; Third, then Second, Sec., New Delhi, 1974; First Sec., FCO, 1977; UK Mission to UN, Geneva, 1982; First Sec., then Counsellor, FCO, 1986; Counsellor, UK Mission to UN, NY, 1992–95; Overseas Inspector, Mgt Consultancy and Inspection Dept, FCO, 1996–99. *Address:* British Trade International, Kingsgate House, 66–74 Victoria Street, SW1E 6SW.

STOATE, Dr Howard Geoffrey Alvan, FRCGP; MP (Lab) Dartford, since 1997; *b* 14 April 1954; *s* of Alvan Stoate and Maisie Stoate (*née* Russell); *m* 1979, Deborah Jane Dunkerley; two *s.* *Educ:* Kingston Grammar Sch.; King's Coll., London (MB BS 1977; MSc 1989). DRCOG 1981; FRCGP 1994. GP training, Joyce Green Hosp., Dartford, 1978–81; gen. med. practice, Albion Surgery, Bexleyheath, 1982–; GP Tutor, Queen Mary's Hosp., Sidcup, 1989–; Chm., Local Res. Ethics Cttee, Bexley HA, 1995–97; Vice-Chm., Regl Graduate Educn Bd, South Thames, 1997–99. Mem. (Lab) Dartford BC, 1990–99 (Chm., Finance and Corporate Business Cttee, 1996–99); Vice Pres., Dartford Racial Equality Council. PPS to Minister of State for Crime Reduction, Policy and Community Safety, Home Office, 2001–. Mem., Health Select Cttee, 1997–2001; Co-Chm., All Party Parly Gp on Primary Care and Public Health, 1998–; Chairman: All Party Pharmacy Gp, 2000–; All Party Gp on Men's Health, 2001–. Mem. Assembly, Univ. of Greenwich, 1997–. *Recreations:* running, sailing, travelling, reading. *Address:* 36 Heathclose Road, Dartford, Kent DA1 2PU. *Club:* Emsworth Sailing.

STOATE, Isabel Dorothy; HM Diplomatic Service, retired; Counsellor, Foreign and Commonwealth Office, 1980–82; *b* 31 May 1927; *d* of late William Maurice Stoate and Dorothy Evelyn Stoate (*née* French). *Educ:* Talbot Heath Sch., Bournemouth; St Andrews Univ. Athlone Press, London Univ., 1950–52; joined HM Diplomatic Service, 1952; served Cyprus, Vienna, Buenos Aires, Tokyo, Athens, Rio de Janeiro and FCO, 1952–80. *Recreations:* travel, tapestry. *Address:* 177 Gloucester Street, Cirencester, Glos GL7 2DP.

STOATE, Jane Elizabeth; *see* Davidson, J. E.

STOCK, Rt Rev. (William) Nigel; *see* Stockport, Bishop Suffragan of.

STOCK-NORMAN, Gailene Patricia, AM 1997; Director, Royal Ballet School, since 1999; *b* 28 Jan. 1946; *d* of Roy Keith Stock and Sylvia May Stock; *m* 1976, Gary William Norman; one *d.* *Educ:* Convent of Mercy, Melbourne; RMIT (Grad. DipEd Visual and Performing Arts); Royal Acad. Dancing (Overseas Schol. at Royal Ballet Sch.; ARAD). Soloist and Principal Artist, Australian Ballet, 1962–74; Principal Artist: Nat. Ballet Canada, 1974–76; Royal Winnipeg Ballet, 1976–77; Australian Ballet, 1977–78; Dir, Nat. Ballet Sch., Vic, Australia, 1979–85; Lectr in Classical Dance, Vic Coll. of Arts, 1985–88; Administrator, Nat. Ballet Sch., Vic, 1988–90; Dir, Australian Ballet Sch., 1990–98. *Recreations:* reading, gardening, travelling, welfare of animals. *Address:* Royal Ballet School, 155 Talgarth Road, W14 9DE. *T:* (020) 8748 6335.

STOCKDALE, Sir (Arthur) Noel, Kt 1986; DFM 1942; Life President, ASDA (formerly ASDA–MFI), 1986 (Chairman, 1969–86); *b* 25 Dec. 1920; *s* of Arthur and Florence Stockdale; *m* 1944, Betty Monica Shaw; two *s.* *Educ:* Woodhouse Grove School; Reading University. Joined Hindells Dairy Farmers, 1939; RAF, 1940–46; rejoined Hindells Dairy Farmers, 1946, subseq. Associated Dairies & Farm Stores (Leeds) Ltd, 1949, Associated Dairies Group PLC, 1977 and ASDA–MFI Group PLC, 1985. Hon. LLD Leeds, 1986. *Recreations:* fishing, garden. *Address:* 20 The Old Mill, Scott Lane, Wetherby, Yorks LS22 6NB. *T:* (01937) 582970.

STOCKDALE, David Andrew; QC 1995; a Recorder, since 1993; *b* 9 May 1951; 2nd *s* of late John Ramsden Stockdale and of Jean Stewart Stockdale (*née* Shelley), Austwick, N Yorks; *m* 1985, Melanie Jane, *e d* of Anthony Newis Benson and Barbara Lewis Benson, Adlington, Cheshire; one *s* three *d.* *Educ:* Giggleswick Sch.; Pembroke Coll., Oxford (MA Lit. Hum.). Called to the Bar, Middle Temple, 1975; in practice, Northern Circuit, 1976–; Jun., Northern Circuit, 1978; Asst Recorder, 1990–93. Governor: Giggleswick Sch., 1982– (Chm. of Govs, 1997–); Terra Nova Sch., 2000–. *Recreations:* family, the outdoors, remote Scotland. *Address:* Deans Court Chambers, 24 St John Street, Manchester M3 4DF. *T:* (0161) 214 6000. *Club:* Sloane.

STOCKDALE, His Honour Eric; a Circuit Judge, 1972–94; *b* 8 Feb. 1929; *m* 1952, Joan (*née* Berry); two *s.* *Educ:* Collyers Sch., Horsham; London Sch. of Economics. LLB, BSc(Econ.), LLM, PhD (Lond.); MSc (Cranfield). 2nd Lieut, RA, 1947–49. Called to the Bar, Middle Temple, 1950; practised in London and on Midland Circuit until 1972; admitted to State Bar, Calif, 1983. Mem., Supreme Court Procedure Cttee, 1982–94. Tech. Advr, Central Council of Probation Cttees, 1979–84; Vice-Pres., NACRO, 1980–94 (Mem. Council, 1970–80); President: British Soc. of Criminology, 1978–81; Soc. of English and Amer. Lawyers, 1986–89 (Chm., 1984–86). Member: Central Council for Educn and Trng in Social Work, 1984–89; Parole Board, 1985–89; Criminal Injuries Compensation Bd, 1995–2000; Criminal Injuries Compensation Appeals Panel, 1997–. Vis. Prof., Queen Mary and Westfield Coll., London Univ., 1989–93. Governor, 1977–89, Vis. Fellow, 1986–94, Vis. Prof., 1994–, Univ. of Hertfordshire (formerly Hatfield Poly.). Consultant Ed., Blackstone's Criminal Practice, 1991–. Hon. LLD Hertfordshire, 1995. *Publications:* The Court and the Offender, 1967; A Study of Bedford Prison 1660–1877, 1977; Law and Order in Georgian Bedfordshire, 1982; The Probation Volunteer, 1985; (with Keith Devlin) Sentencing, 1987; (with Silvia Casale) Criminal Justice Under Stress, 1992. *Address:* 20 Lyonsdown Road, New Barnet, Herts EN5 1JE. *T:* (020) 8449 7181. *Club:* Athenæum.

STOCKDALE, Sir Noel; *see* Stockdale, Sir A. N.

STOCKDALE, Sir Thomas (Minshull), 2nd Bt *cr* 1960, of Hoddington, Co. Southampton; barrister; *b* 7 Jan. 1940; *s* of Sir Edmund Villiers Minshull Stockdale, 1st Bt and Hon. Louise Fermor-Hesketh (*d* 1994), *er d* of 1st Lord Hesketh; *S* father, 1989; *m* 1965, Jacqueline Ha-Van-Vuong; one *s* one *d.* *Educ:* Eton; Worcester Coll., Oxford (MA). Called to Bar, Inner Temple, 1966; Bencher, Lincoln's Inn, 1994. *Recreations:* shooting, travel. *Heir:* *s* John Minshull Stockdale, *b* 13 Dec. 1967. *Address:* Manor Farm, Weston Patrick, Basingstoke, Hants RG25 2NT; 73 Alderney Street, SW1V 4HH. *Clubs:* Turf, MCC.

STOCKEN, Oliver Henry James, FCA; Chairman: Rutland Trust, since 1999; Lupus Capital plc, since 1999; Stanhope plc, since 2000; *b* 22 Dec. 1941; *s* of late Henry Edmund West Stocken and Sheila Guiscard Stocken (*née* Steele); *m* 1967, Sally Forbes Dishon; two *s* one *d.* *Educ:* Felsted Sch.; University Coll., Oxford (BA). FCA 1978. Director: N M Rothschild & Sons Limited, 1968–77; Esperanza Trade & Transport, 1977–79; Barclays Merchant Bank, 1979–81; Man. Dir, Barclays Australia, 1982–84; Finance Director: BZW, 1985–93; Barclays plc, 1993–99. Non-executive Director: Steel Burrill Jones Group plc, 1992–96; MEPC plc, 1995–2000; Pilkington plc, 1998–; Rank plc, 1998–; Bunzl plc, 1998–2000; 3i Group plc, 1999–; Novar plc, 2000–; Great Universal Stores plc, 2000–. Trustee, Natural Hist. Mus., 1999–. Mem. Council, RCA, 1998–. Chairman, Trustees: Children's Leukaemia Trust, 1993–; Devas Club, 1997–. *Recreations:* running, Rugby, cricket. *Address:* 25c Marryat Road, Wimbledon, SW19 5BB. *Clubs:* Brooks's, MCC (Mem. Cttee, 1998–, Chm. Finance, 2000–); Australian (Sydney).

STOCKER, Prof. Bruce Arnold Dunbar, FRS 1966; MD; Professor of Microbiology and Immunology in Stanford University, 1966–87, now Emeritus Active; *b* 26 May 1917. *Educ:* King's College, London; Westminster Hosp. Med. Sch. MB, BS, 1940; MRCS, LRCP, 1940; MD 1947. Guinness Prof. of Microbiology, Univ. of London, and Dir of Guinness-Lister Microbiological Research Unit, Lister Inst. of Preventive Med., until Dec. 1965. *Publications:* articles in scientific jls. *Address:* Department of Microbiology and Immunology, Stanford University School of Medicine, Stanford, CA 94305–5124, USA. *T:* (650) 7232006, *Fax:* (650) 7256757; *e-mail:* bstocker@stanford.edu.

STOCKER, John Wilcox, AO 1999; PhD; FRACP; Principal, Foursight Associates Pty Ltd, since 1996; Chairman, Sigma Co. Ltd, since 1999; *b* 23 April 1945; *s* of W. R. Stocker and Gladys Noelle Davies; *m* 1973, Joanne Elizabeth Gross; two *d.* *Educ:* Wesley Coll., Univ. of Melbourne (MB BS BMedSc). FTS. RMO, Royal Melbourne Hosp., 1970–72; Res. Scientist, Walter & Eliza Hall Inst. of Med. Res., 1974–76; Mem., Basel Inst. of Immunology, 1976–78; Central Res. Unit, 1979–84; Dir, Pharm. Res., Hoffman-La Roche & Co., Basel, 1986–87; Dir, Vic. Govt Strategic Res. Foundn, 1988–93; Chief Exec., CSIRO, 1990–95; Govt Chief Scientist, Australia, 1996–99. Founding Man. Dir, AMRAD, 1987–90; Director: Gene Shears Pty, 1992–96; Cambridge Antibody Technology Ltd, 1995–; Telstra Corp., 1996–; Circadian Technologies Pty Ltd, 1996–; Rothschild Bioscience Managers Ltd, 1996–98; Nufarm Ltd, 1998–. Chairman: Australian Sci. Technol. and Engrg Council, 1997–98; Grape and Wine R&D Corp., 1997–; Mem., numerous Industry and Govt sci. orgns. *Publications:* scientific papers, contribs to learned jls. *Recreations:* tennis, tiling, viticulture, reading. *Address:* Foursight Associates Pty Ltd, Level 2, Richard Allen Building, 164 Flinders Lane, Melbourne, Vic 3000, Australia. *Club:* Winzergenossenschaft zur Landskron (Switzerland).

STOCKHAUSEN, Karlheinz; composer and conductor; *b* 22 Aug. 1928; *s* of late Simon and Gertrud Stockhausen; *m* 1st, 1951, Doris Andreae; one *s* three *d;* 2nd, 1967, Mary Bauermeister; one *s* one *d.* *Educ:* Hochschule für Musik, and Univ., Cologne, 1947–51; studied with: Messiaen, 1952–53; Prof. Werner Meyer-Eppler, Bonn Univ., 1954–56. With Westdeutscher Rundfunk Electronic Music Studio, 1953–, Artistic Dir, 1963–77. Lectr, Internat. Summer Sch. for New Music, Darmstadt, 1953–74; Dir, Interpretation Group for live electronic music, 1964–; Founder, and Artistic Dir, Kölner Kurse für Neue Musik, 1963–68; Visiting Professor: Univ. of Pa, 1965; Univ. of Calif, 1966–67; Prof. of Composition, Cologne State Conservatory, 1971–77. Co-Editor, Die Reihe, 1954–59. First annual tour of 30 concerts and lectures, 1958, USA and Canada, since then throughout world. Has composed over 280 individually performable works and made more than 100 records of his own works; since 1991 has been involved with production of complete issue of his works on CD. Member or Foreign Member: Akad. der Künste, Hamburg, 1968; Kungl. Musikaliska Akad., Sweden, 1970; Akad. der Künste, Berlin, 1973; Amer. Acad. and Inst. of Arts and Letters, 1977; Acad. Filarmonica Romana, 1979; Acad. Européenne des Sciences, des Arts et des Lettres, 1980; Hon. RAM 1987. Awards and Prizes from France, Germany, Italy and USA; Prix Ars Electronica, Cluiz, Austria, 1990; Picasso Medal, UNESCO, 1992; Edison Prize, Holland, 1996; Polar Prize, Swedish Royal Acad. of Arts, 2001. Bundesverdienstkreuz 1st class, 1974; Verdienstorden des Landes Nordrhein-Westfalen, 1992. *Publications:* Texte, 10 vols, 1963–91; Stockhausen on Music, 1989; *compositions:* Chöre für Doris, Drei Lieder, Choral, 1950–51; Sonatine, Kreuzspiel, Formel, 1951; Schlagtrio, Spiel für Orchester, Etude, 1952; Punkte, 1952, rev. 1962, Klavierstücke I-XI, 1952–56; Kontra-Punkte, 1953; Elektronische Studien I and II, 1953–54; Zeitmasze, Gesang der Jünglinge, 1956; Gruppen, 1957; Zyklus, Refrain, 1959; Carré, Kontakte für elektronische Klänge, Kontakte für elektronische Klänge, Klavier und Schlagzeug, 1960; Originale (musical play with Kontakte), 1961; Plus Minus, 1963; Momente, 1962–64, completed, 1969; Mixtur (new arr. 1967), Mikrophonie I, 1964; Mikrophonie II, Stop (new arr. 1969), 1965; Telemusik, Solo, Adieu, 1966; Hymnen, Prozession, Ensemble, 1967; Kurzwellen, Stimmung, Aus den sieben Tagen, Spiral, Musik für ein Haus, 1968; Für Kommende Zeiten, 1968–70; Hymnen mit Orchester, Fresco, Dr K-Sextett, 1969; Pole, Expo, Mantra, 1970; Sternklang, Trans, 1971; Alphabet für Liège, Am Himmel wandre ich, (Indianerlieder), Ylem, 1972; Inori, 1973–74; Vortrag über Hu, Herbstmusik, Atmen gibt das Leben…, 1974; Musik im Bauch, Harlekin, Der Kleine Harlekin, 1975; Tierkreis, 1975–76; Sirius, 1975–77; Amour, 1976; Jubiläum, In Freundschaft, 1977; Licht, die sieben Tage der Woche (an operatic cycle for solo voices, solo instruments, solo dancers/choirs, orchestras, ballet and mimes/electronic and concrete music), 1977–: Donnerstag 1978–80 (Donnerstags-Gruss, or Michaels-Gruss, 1978; Unsichtbare Chöre, 1978–79; Michaels Jugend, 1979; Michaels Reise um die Erde, 1978; Michaels Heimkehr, 1980; Donnerstags-Abschied, 1980); Samstag, 1981–84 (Samstags-Gruss or Luzifers-Gruss, 1983; Luzifers Traum or Klavierstück XIII, 1981; Kathinkas Gesang als Luzifers Requiem, 1982–83; Luzifers Tanz, 1983; Luzifers Abschied, 1982); Montag, 1984–88 (Montags-Gruss, or Eva-Gruss, 1984/88; Evas Erstgeburt, 1987; Evas Zweitgeburt, 1984/87; Evas Zauber, 1986; Montags-Abschied, or Eva-Abschied, 1988); Dienstag, 1977/1990–91 (Dienstags-Gruss, 1987–88; Jahreslauf, 1977–91; Invasion-Explosion mit Abschied, 1990–91); Freitag, 1991–94 (Freitags-Gruss, 1991; Freitag-Versuchung, 1991; Freitags-Abschied, 1994); Mittwoch, 1993–98 (Mittwochs-Gruss, 1998; Welt-Parlament, 1995; Orchester-Finalisten, 1995; Helikopter-Streichquartett, 1993; Michaelion, 1997–98; Mittwochs-Abschied, 1996); Sonntag, 1999– (Lichter - Wasser, 1999). *Address:* Stockhausen-Verlag, Kettenberg 15, 51515 Kürten, Germany.

STOCKING, Barbara Mary, (Mrs R. J. MacInnes), CBE 2000; Director, Oxfam, since 2001; *b* 28 July 1951; *d* of Percy Frederick Stocking and Mary Stocking; *m* 1981, Dr R. John MacInnes; two *s.* *Educ:* New Hall, Cambridge (BA); Univ. of Wisconsin (MS).

Teaching Asst, Dept of Physiology and Biophysics, Univ. of Illinois, 1972–73; Staff Associate, Nat. Acad. of Scis, Washington, 1974–76; Jt Research Fellow, Nuffield Provincial Hosps Trust and Centre for Med. Res., Univ. of Sussex, 1977–79; Sec., WHO Independent Commn on Long Term Prospects of Onchocerciasis Control Programme, LSHTM, 1979–91; Fellow in Health Policy, Innovation and Evaluation, King's Fund Coll., 1983–86; Dir, King's Fund Centre for Health Services Develt, 1987–93; Chief Executive: Oxford RHA, 1993–94; Anglia and Oxford RHA, 1994–96; Regl Dir, Anglia and Oxford, 1994–98, South East, 1999–2000, NHS Exec., DoH; Dir, NHS Modernisation Agency, 2000–01(on secondment). Chair: NHS Patient Partnership Steering Gp, 1993–98; NHS Resource Allocation Gp, 1995–97. Member: UK Harkness Fellowships Adv. and Selection Cttee, 1989–95; NHS Central R&D Cttee, 1992–96. Hon. DSc: Luton, 1998; Oxford Brookes, 1999. *Publications:* (jtly) The Image and the Reality: a case study of the impacts of medical technology, 1978; Initiative and Inertia: case studies in the health services, 1985; (ed) Expensive Medical Technologies, 1988; (Series Editor) A Study of the Diffusion of Medical Technology in Europe, 3 vols, 1991; (jtly) Criteria for Change, 1991; Medical Advances: the future shape of acute services, 1991. *Recreations:* music, family. *Address:* 7 Dunstan Road, Oxford OX3 9BY. *T:* (work) (020) 7725 2547.

STOCKPORT, Bishop Suffragan of, since 2000; **Rt Rev. (William) Nigel Stock;** *b* 29 Jan. 1950; *s* of Ian Heath Stock and Elizabeth Mary Stock; *m* 1973, Carolyne Grace (*née* Greswell); three *s*. *Educ:* Durham Sch.; Durham Univ. (BA Hons Law and Politics); Ripon Coll., Cuddesdon (Oxford Univ. DipTh). Ordained deacon, 1976, priest, 1977; Asst Curate, Stockton St Peter, Durham, 1976–79; Priest-in-charge, Taraka St Peter, Aipo Rongo, PNG, 1979–84; Vicar, St Mark, Shiremoor, Newcastle, 1985–91; Team Rector, North Shields Team Ministry, 1991–98; RD, Tynemouth, 1992–98; Hon. Canon, Newcastle Cathedral, 1997–98; Residentiary Canon, Durham Cathedral, 1998–2000. Commissary for Archbp of PNG, 1986–. *Recreations:* walking, photography, travel. *Address:* Bishop's Lodge, Back Lane, Dunham Town, Altrincham, Cheshire WA14 4SG. *T:* (0161) 928 5611.

STOCKTON, 2nd Earl of, *cr* 1984; **Alexander Daniel Alan Macmillan;** Viscount Macmillan of Ovenden, 1984; Member (C) South West Region, England, European Parliament, since 1999; President, Macmillan Ltd, since 1990; *b* Oswestry, Shropshire, 10 Oct. 1943; *s* of Viscount Macmillan of Ovenden, PC, MP (*d* 1984) and of Katharine Viscountess Macmillan of Ovenden, DBE; *S* grandfather, 1986; *m* 1st, 1970, Hélène Birgitte Hamilton (marr. diss. 1991); one *s* two *d*; 2nd, 1995, Miranda Elizabeth Louise, Lady Nuttall, *d* of Richard Quarry and Diana, Lady Mancroft. *Educ:* Eton; Université de Paris, Strathclyde Univ. FRICS 1999. Contested (C) Bristol, Eur. Parly elecns, 1994. MIMgt (MBIM 1981); FRSA 1987. Liveryman: Worshipful Co. of Merchant Taylors, 1972 (Mem., Ct of Assts, 1987–; Master, 1992–93); Worshipful Co. of Stationers and Newspaper Makers, 1973 (Mem., Ct of Assts, 1996–). DUniv Strathclyde, 1993; Hon. DLitt: De Montfort, 1993; Westminster, 1995. *Heir: s* Viscount Macmillan of Ovenden, *qv*. *Address:* (office) Porters South, 4–6 Crinan Street, N1 9XW. *T:* (020) 7833 4000; *e-mail:* estockton@europarl.eu.int. *Clubs:* Beefsteak, Buck's, Garrick, Pratt's, White's.

STOCKWIN, Prof. James Arthur Ainscow; Nissan Professor of Modern Japanese Studies, Director of Nissan Institute of Japanese Studies, University of Oxford, since 1982; Fellow, St Antony's College, Oxford, since 1982 (Sub-Warden, 1999–2001); *b* 28 Nov. 1935; *s* of Wilfred Arthur Stockwin and Edith Mary Stockwin; *m* 1960, Audrey Lucretia Hobson Stockwin (*née* Wood); one *s* two *d* (and one *s* decd). *Educ:* Exeter Coll., Oxford Univ. (MA); Australian Nat. Univ. (PhD). Australian National University: Lectr, Dept of Political Science, 1964–66; Sen. Lectr, 1966–72; Reader, 1972–81. Pres., British Assoc. of Japanese Studies, 1994–95. Gen. Ed., Nissan Inst.—Routledge Japanese Studies Series, 1984–. *Publications:* The Japanese Socialist Party and Neutralism, 1968; (ed) Japan and Australia in the Seventies, 1972; Japan, Divided Politics in a Growth Economy, 1975, 2nd edn 1982; Why Japan Matters, 1983; (jtly, also ed) Dynamic and Immobilist Politics in Japan, 1988; (trans.) Junji Banno, The Establishment of the Japanese Constitutional System, 1992; The Story of Tim, 1993; (ed jtly) The Vitality of Japan: sources of national strength and weakness, 1997; Governing Japan, 1999; articles, largely on Japanese politics and foreign policy, in Pacific Affairs, Aust. Outlook, Aust. Jl Politics and History, Asian Survey, Japan Forum, etc. *Recreations:* languages, exercise. *Address:* Nissan Institute of Japanese Studies, 27 Winchester Road, Oxford OX2 6NA. *T:* (01865) 274570, *Fax:* (01865) 274574.

STODART, family name of **Baron Stodart of Leaston**.

STODART OF LEASTON, Baron *cr* 1981 (Life Peer), of Humbie in the District of East Lothian; **James Anthony Stodart;** PC 1974; *b* 6 June 1916; *yr s* of late Col Thomas Stodart, CIE, IMS, and of Mary Alice Coullie; *m* 1940, Hazel Jean Usher (*d* 1995). *Educ:* Wellington. Farming at Kingston, North Berwick, 1934–58, and at Leaston, Humbie, East Lothian, 1959–2001. Hon. Pres., Edinburgh Univ. Agricultural Soc., 1952; Pres. East Lothian Boy Scouts' Assoc., 1960–63. Contested: (L) Berwick and East Lothian, 1950; (C) Midlothian and Peebles, 1951; Midlothian, 1955; MP (C) Edinburgh West, 1959–Oct. 1974; Jt Under-Sec. of State, Scottish Office, Sept. 1963–Oct. 1964; An Opposition spokesman on Agriculture and on Scottish Affairs, 1966–69; Parly Sec., MAFF, 1970–72; Minister of State, MAFF, 1972–74; Vice-Chm., Conservative Agric. Cttee, House of Commons, 1962–63, 1964–65, 1966–70. Led Parly Delegns to Canada, 1974, 1983. Dir, FMC, 1980–82; Chm., Agricultural Credit Corp. Ltd, 1975–87. Chairman: Cttee of Inquiry into Local Govt in Scotland, 1980; Manpower Review of Vet. Profession in UK, 1984–85. *Publications:* (jt author) Land of Abundance, a study of Scottish Agriculture in the 20th Century, 1962; contrib. on farming topics to agricultural journals and newspapers. *Recreations:* music, collecting and looking at vintage films, preserving a sense of humour. *Address:* Lorimers, North Berwick, East Lothian EH39 4NG. *T:* (01620) 892457. *Clubs:* Cavalry and Guards; New (Edinburgh); Hon. Company of Edinburgh Golfers.

STODDART, family name of **Baron Stoddart of Swindon**.

STODDART OF SWINDON, Baron *cr* 1983 (Life Peer), of Reading in the Royal County of Berkshire; **David Leonard Stoddart;** *b* 4 May 1926; *s* of Arthur Leonard Stoddart, coal miner, and Queenie Victoria Stoddart (*née* Price); *m* 1961, Jennifer Percival-Alwyn; two *s* (one *d* by previous marr.). *Educ:* elementary; St Clement Danes and Henley Grammar Schools. Youth in training, PO Telephones, 1942–44; business on own account, 1944–46; Railway Clerk, 1947–49; Hospital Clerk, 1949–51; Power Station Clerical Worker, 1951–70. Joined Labour Party, 1947; Reading County Borough Council: Member, 1954–72; served at various times as Chairman of Housing, Transport and Finance Cttees; Leader, Labour Group of Councillors, 1962–70; Leader of Council, 1967–72. Contested (Lab) Newbury, 1959 and 1964, Swindon, 1969, 1983. MP (Lab) Swindon, 1970–83; PPS to Minister for Housing and Construction, 1974–75; an Asst Govt Whip, 1975; a Lord Comr, HM Treasury, 1976–77; an opposition whip, and opposition spokesman on energy, House of Lords, 1983–88. Chairman: Campaign for an Indep. Britain, 1985–; Anti-Maastricht Alliance, 1992–; Global Britain, 1998–. *Recreations:* gardening, music. *Address:* Sintra, 37A Bath Road, Reading, Berks RG1 6HL. *T:* (0118) 957 6726.

STODDART, Anne Elizabeth, CMG 1996; HM Diplomatic Service, retired; Deputy Permanent Representative (Economic Affairs), UK Mission to the United Nations, Geneva, 1991–96; *b* 29 March 1937; *d* of late James Stoddart and Ann Jack Stoddart (*née* Inglis). *Educ:* Kirby Grammar School, Middlesbrough; Somerville College, Oxford. MA. Entered Foreign Office, 1960; British Military Govt, Berlin, 1963–67; FCO, 1967–70; First Secretary (Economic), Ankara, 1970–73; Head of Chancery, Colombo, 1974–76; FCO, 1977–81; Dep. Permanent UK Rep. to Council of Europe, Strasbourg, 1981–87; seconded to External Eur. Policy Div., DTI, 1987–91. *Address:* Flat 1, 63 The Avenue, Richmond, Surrey TW9 2AH.

STODDART, Caroline Ann Tuke; *see* Malone, C. A. T.

STODDART, Charles Norman, PhD; Sheriff of Lothian and Borders at Edinburgh, since 1995; *b* 4 April 1948; *s* of Robert Stoddart and Margaret (*née* Allenby); *m* 1981, Anne Lees; one *d*. *Educ:* Edinburgh Univ. (LLB, PhD); McGill Univ. (LLM). Admitted Solicitor, 1972, practised, 1972–73, 1980–88; Lectr in Scots Law, Edinburgh Univ., 1973–80; Sheriff of N Strathclyde at Paisley, 1988–95. Dir, Judicial Studies in Scotland, 1997–2000. Editor, Green's Criminal Law Bulletin, 1992–. *Publications:* (with H. Neilson) The Law and Practice of Legal Aid in Scotland, 1979, 4th edn 1994; (with C. H. W. Gane) A Casebook on Scottish Criminal Law, 1980, 3rd edn 2001; Bible John (crime documentary), 1980; (with C. H. W. Gane) Cases and Materials on Scottish Criminal Procedure, 1983, 2nd edn 1994; Criminal Warrants, 1991, 2nd edn 1999; contribs to professional jls. *Recreations:* music, foreign travel. *Address:* Sheriff's Chambers, Sheriff Court House, 27 Chambers Street, Edinburgh EH1 1LB. *T:* (0131) 225 2525.

STODDART, Christopher West; Chief Executive Officer, Go Racing, since 2001; *b* 10 April 1950; *s* of Dr Ian West Stoddart and Bridget Stoddart (*née* Pilditch); *m* 1st, 1972, Deborah Ounsted (marr. diss. 1984); 2nd, 1985, Dr Hazel Grasmere, *d* of Hon. Robert and Evelyn Grasmere, USA. *Educ:* Winchester Coll.; Churchill Coll., Cambridge (BA Hons 1971). Joined CS, 1971; DoE, 1971–75; Research Sec., Centre for Envmtl Studies, 1976–80; Regl Companies Sec., 1980–81, Sec. 1981–82, ITCA; Tyne Tees Television: Gen. Manager, 1982–83; Dir of Resources, 1983–88; Man. Dir and Chief Exec., Satellite Information Services Ltd, 1988–92; Man. Dir, GMTV, 1992–2001. Non-exec. Dir, Sterling Publishing Gp, 1999–2001. Chm., Trustees, Changing Faces, 1999–. *Publication:* The Inner City as Testing Ground for Government-funded Research, 1980. *Recreations:* mountaineering, wind-surfing, bad weather. *Address:* 7 Lyndhurst Terrace, NW3 5QA.

STODDART, Prof. (James) Fraser, FRS 1994; CChem, FRSC; Winstein Professor of Organic Chemistry, University of California at Los Angeles, since 1997; *b* 24 May 1942; *s* of Thomas Fraser Stoddart and Jane Spalding Hislop Stoddart; *m* 1968, Norma Agnes Scholan; two *d*. *Educ:* Melville Coll., Edinburgh; Univ. of Edinburgh (BSc 1964; PhD 1966; DSc 1980). CChem, FRSC 1978. Nat. Res. Council of Canada Post-doctoral Fellow, Queen's Univ., Canada, 1967–69; University of Sheffield: ICI Res. Fellow, subseq. Lectr in Chemistry, 1970–82; seconded to Catalysis Gp, ICI Corporate Lab., Runcorn, 1978–81; Reader in Chemistry, 1982–91; Prof. of Organic Chem., 1990–97, Hd, Sch. of Chem., 1993–97, Univ. of Birmingham. Vis. Lectr, Univ. of Parana, Brazil, 1972; SRC Sen. Vis. Fellow, UCLA, 1978; Visiting Professor: Texas A&M Univ., 1980; Univ. of Messina, Italy, 1986–88; Mulhouse, France, 1987. Awards include: Internat. Izatt-Christensen in macrocyclic chem., 1993; Chair Bruylants, Univ. of Louvain-La-Neuve, 1994; Adolf Steinhofer, Univ. of Kaiserslautern, 1995; Arthur C. Cope Schol. Award, ACS, 1999. Mem., various editl bds in Europe and USA. *Publications:* over 600 papers, reviews and monographs in Angewandte Chemie, Chemistry—A Europ. Jl, Jl of the American Chemical Soc. on nanoscale science and self-assembly processes. *Address:* Department of Chemistry and Biochemistry, University of California at Los Angeles, 405 Hilgard Avenue, Los Angeles, CA 90095, USA.

STODDART, Prof. John Little, CBE 1994; PhD, DSc; FIBiol; FRAgS; Director of Research, Institute of Grassland and Environmental Research, Agricultural and Food Research Council, 1988–93; *b* 1 Oct. 1933; *s* of John Little Stoddart and Margaret Pickering Dye; *m* 1957, Wendy Dalton Leardie; one *d* (one *s* decd). *Educ:* South Shields High Sch. for Boys; University Coll., Durham (BSc Botany 1954); University of Wales, Aberystwyth (PhD 1961); Durham Univ. (DSc 1973). FIBiol 1984; ARPS 1985; FRAgS 1993. Nat. Service, RA, UK, Hong Kong and Malaya, 1954–56. Fulbright-Hays Sen. Fellow, 1966–67; Res. Associate, Mich. State Univ./Atomic Energy Commn Plant Res. Lab., 1966–67; Welsh Plant Breeding Station: Dep. Dir, 1985–87; Dir, 1987–88; Head of Plants and Soils Div., 1985–88. Hon. Prof., Sch. of Agric. and Biol Scis, Univ. of Wales, 1988–. Chm., Plant Sci. Prog. Adv. Cttee, ODA, 1995–98. Mem. Council, NIAB, 1988–93. Non-executive Director: Derwen NHS Trust (W Wales), 1994–97; Pembrokeshire & Derwen NHS Trust, 1997–; IGER Technologies, 2000–. Trustee, Stapledon Meml Trust, 1996– (Mem., 1988–). *Publications:* scientific articles, reviews and contribs to scientific books. *Recreations:* photography (pictorial), golf. *Address:* Institute of Biological Sciences, University of Wales, Aberystwyth, Ceredigion SY23 3DA.

STODDART, John Maurice, CBE 1995; Principal and Vice-Chancellor, Sheffield Hallam University, 1992–98 (Principal, Sheffield City Polytechnic, 1983–92); *b* 18 Sept. 1938; *s* of Gordon Stoddart and May (*née* Ledder). *Educ:* Wallasey Grammar Sch.; Univ. of Reading (BA Pol Econ.). FBIM 1977. Teacher, Wallasey GS, 1960–62; Lectr, Mid Cheshire Coll. of Further Educn, 1962–64; Lectr, Enfield Coll., 1964–70; Head, Dept of Econs and Business Studies, Sheffield Polytechnic, 1970–72; Asst Dir, NE London Polytechnic, 1972–76; Dir, Hull Coll. of Higher Educn (now Univ. of Humberside), 1976–83. Dir, Sheffield Science Park Co. Ltd, 1988–96; Deputy Chairman: Northern Gen. Hosp. NHS Trust, 1999–2001; Sheffield Teaching Hosps NHS Trust, 2001–. Chm., CNAA Cttee for Business and Management, 1985–88 (Chm., Undergrad. Courses Bd, 1976–83); Mem., CNAA, 1982–88, 1991–93; Chm., Cttee of Dirs of Polys, 1990–93 (Vice-Chm., 1988–90). Member: Sea Fisheries Trng Council, 1976–80; Architects Registration Council, UK, 1979–85; Council for Management Educn and Develt, 1988–; Council for Industry and Educn, 1989–94; Council for Educn and Trng in Social Work, 1989–94; BTEC, 1991–95; Chm., Higher Educn Quality Council, 1992–97. Member: Court, Univ. of Hull, 1976–83; Council, Univ. of Sheffield, 1983–92. Companion, British Business Graduates Soc., 1983; Hon. Fellow, Humberside Coll., 1983; FRSA 1977. CIMgt (CBIM 1990). Hon. DEd CNAA, 1992; Hon. DLitt Coventry, 1993; DUniv: Middlesex, 1993; Sheffield Hallam, 1998; Hon. LLD Sheffield, 1998. *Publications:* articles on business and management educn. *Address:* 58 Riverdale Road, Sheffield S10 3FB. *T:* (0114) 268 3636. *Clubs:* Reform; Leander (Henley-on-Thames).

STODDART, Sir Kenneth (Maxwell), KCVO 1989; AE 1942; JP; DL; Lord-Lieutenant, Metropolitan County of Merseyside, 1979–89; *b* 26 May 1914; *s* of late Wilfrid Bowring Stoddart and Mary Hyslop Stoddart (*née* Maxwell); *m* 1940, Jean Roberta Benson Young, DL; two *d*. *Educ:* Sedbergh; Clare Coll., Cambridge. Chairman: Cearns and Brown Ltd, 1973–84; United Mersey Supply Co. Ltd, 1978–81. Commissioned No

611 (West Lancashire) Sqdn, Auxiliary Air Force, 1936; served War, UK and Europe; comd W Lancashire Wing, Air Trng Corps, 1946–54; Vice-Chm. (Air) W Lancashire T&AFA, 1954–64. Pres., Merseyside Wing, ATC, 1991–99. Chairman, Liverpool Child Welfare Assoc., 1965–81. DL Lancashire 1958 (transf. to Metropolitan County of Merseyside, 1974); JP Liverpool 1952; High Sheriff of Merseyside, 1974. Hon. Fellow, Liverpool John Moores Univ. (formerly Liverpool Poly.), 1989. Hon. LLD Liverpool, 1986. KStJ 1979. *Recreations:* gardening, walking. *Address:* Dunlins, 8 Hadlow Lane, Willaston, Neston CH64 2UH. *T:* (0151) 327 5183. *Club:* Liverpool Racquet.

STODDART, Michael Craig, FCA; Chairman, Electra Investment Trust, 1986–2000; Senior Business Advisor, Fleming Family and Partners, since 2001; *b* 27 March 1932; *s* of late Frank Ogle Boyd Stoddart and Barbara (*née* Craig); *m* 1961, (Susan) Brigid (*née* O'Halloran); two *s* two *d*. *Educ:* Abberley Hall, Worcs; Marlborough Coll. Chartered Accountant 1955; joined Singer & Friedlander, 1955: resp. for opening provincial network; retired as Jt Chief Exec., 1973; Dep. Chm. and Chief Exec., Electra Investment Trust, 1974–86; pioneered into substantial unlisted investments, incl. developing venture capital arm; Chm., Electra Kingsway Gp, 1989–95. Non-executive Chairman: Britax (formerly BSC) plc, 1994–2000; Elderstreet Millenium (formerly Gartmore) Venture Capital Trust plc, 1996–; non-executive Director: Bullough, 1968–; Chesterfield Properties plc, 1997–99; Private Investors Capital Ltd, 1997–, and other UK cos. Underwriting Mem. of Lloyd's, 1972–96. Chm., Foundn for Entrepreneurial Mgt, London Business Sch. (Mem., Develt Bd); Mem. Bd, Britech Foundn Ltd, 1999–. *Recreations:* country pursuits, shooting, tennis, golf, theatre. *Address:* Fleming Family and Partners, Ely House, 37 Dover Street, W1S 4NJ; Compton House, Kinver, Worcs DY7 5LY; 27 Crown Reach, 145 Grosvenor Road, SW1V 3JU. *Clubs:* Boodle's, Pratt's.

STODDART, Dr Simon Kenneth Fladgate, FSA; Fellow, Magdalene College, Cambridge, since 1998; Senior Lecturer, University of Cambridge, since 2000; Editor, Antiquity, since 2001; *b* 8 Nov. 1958; *s* of Kenneth Bowring Stoddart and Daphne Elizabeth Fladgate (*née* Hughes); *m* 1983, Dr Caroline Ann Tuke Malone, *qv*; two *d*. *Educ:* Winchester Coll.; Magdalene Coll., Cambridge (BA 1980; PhD 1987); Univ. of Michigan (MA 1983). FSA 1994. Rome Schol. in Archaeol., British Sch. at Rome, 1980–81; Power Schol., Univ. of Michigan, 1981–83; Res. Fellow, Magdalene Coll., Cambridge, 1986–89; Lecturer: Univ. of York, 1988–90; Univ. of Bristol, 1990–94 (Sen. Lectr, 1994–96); Univ. of Cambridge, 1996–2000. Charter Fellow, Wolfson Coll., Oxford, 1992–93. MIFA 1987. *Publications:* (ed with C. Malone) Papers in Italian Archaeology, Vols 1–4, 1985; (with N. Spivey) Etruscan Italy, 1990; (ed with C. Mathers) Development and Decline in the Mediterranean Bronze Age, 1994; (ed with C. Malone) Territory, Time and State: the archaeological development of the Gubbio Basin, 1994; (ed) Landscapes from Antiquity, 2000; contrib. acad. articles. *Recreations:* walking, travel. *Address:* Magdalene College, Cambridge CB3 0AG. *T:* (01223) 332168.

STOICHEFF, Prof. Boris Peter, OC 1982; FRS 1975; FRSC 1965; Professor of Physics, 1964–89, now Emeritus, and University Professor, 1977–89, now Emeritus, University of Toronto; *b* 1 June 1924; *s* of Peter and Vasilka Stoicheff; *m* 1954, Lillian Joan Ambridge; one *s*. *Educ:* Univ. of Toronto, Faculty of Applied Science and Engineering (BASc), Dept of Physics (MA, PhD). McKee-Gilchrist Fellowship, Univ. of Toronto, 1950–51; National Research Council of Canada: Fellowship, Ottawa, 1952–53; Res. Officer in Div. of Pure Physics, 1953–64; Mem. Council, 1978–83. Exec. Dir, Ontario Laser and Lightwave Res. Centre, 1988–91. Visiting Scientist, Mass Inst. of Technology, 1963–64. Chm., Engrg Science, Univ. of Toronto, 1972–77. Izaak Walton Killam Meml Scholarship, 1977–79; Senior Fellow, Massey Coll., Univ. of Toronto, 1979–. Dist. Vis. Prof., Univ. of Central Florida, 2000. H. L. Welsh Lecture, Univ. of Toronto, 1984; Elizabeth Laird Meml Lecture, Univ. Western Ontario, 1985; UK/Canada Rutherford Lectr, 1989. Pres., Canadian Assoc. of Physicists, 1983–84; Council Mem., Assoc. of Professional Engrs of Ontario, 1985–91; Vice-Pres., IUPAP, 1994–96. For. Co-Sec., RSC, 1995–2000. Fellow, Optical Soc. of America, 1965 (Pres. 1976); Fellow, Amer. Phys. Soc., 1969; Geoffrey Frew Fellow, Australian Acad. of Science, 1980. Hon. Fellow: Indian Acad. of Scis, 1971; Macedonian Acad. of Sci. and Arts, 1981; Foreign Hon. Fellow, Amer. Acad. of Arts and Scis, 1989. Hon. DSc: York, Canada, 1982; Skopje, Yugoslavia, 1982; Windsor, Canada, 1989; Toronto, 1994. Gold Medal for Achievement in Physics of Canadian Assoc. of Physicists, 1974; William F. Meggers Award, Optical Soc. of America, 1981; Frederic Ives Medal, Optical Soc. of America, 1983; Henry Marshall Tory Medal, RSC, 1989. Centennial Medal of Canada, 1967. *Publications:* numerous scientific contribs to phys. and chem. jls. *Address:* Department of Physics, University of Toronto, Toronto, ON M5S 1A7, Canada. *T:* (416) 9782948.

STOKE-UPON-TRENT, Archdeacon of; *no new appointment at time of going to press.*

STOKER, Dr Dennis James, FRCP, FRCS, FRCR; Consultant Radiologist: Royal National Orthopaedic Hospital, 1972–93, and since 1997; St George's Hospital, 1972–87; London Clinic, 1976–93; King Edward VII Hospital for Officers, 1985–98; Senior Lecturer and Director of Radiological Studies, Institute of Orthopaedics, 1977–93; *b* 22 March 1928; *yr s* of Dr George Morris Stoker and Elsie Margaret Stoker (*née* Macqueen); *m* 1st, 1951, Anne Sylvia Nelson Forster (*d* 1997); two *s* two *d*; 2nd, 1999, Sheila Mary Mercer. *Educ:* Oundle Sch.; Guy's Hosp. Med. Sch. MB BS; DMRD; FRCP 1976; FRCS 1992. Guy's Hosp. appts, 1951–52; RAF Med. Branch, 1951–68; served Cyprus and Aden; Wing Cdr (retd). Consultant Physician, RAF, 1964–68; Registrar and Sen. Registrar, Diagnostic Radiology, St George's Hosp., London, 1968–72; Dean, Inst. of Orthopaedics, 1987–91. Royal Society of Medicine: Fellow, 1958; Mem. Council, Section of Radiol., 1975–77; Vice-Pres., 1978–80; Royal College of Radiologists: Fellow, 1976; Examr, 1981–84 and 1985–88; George Simon Lectr, 1988; Dean and Vice-Pres., 1989–91; Robert Knox Lectr, 1992. Fellow, British Orth. Assoc.; Mem., Internat. Skeletal Soc., 1974– (Medal, 1993). Special Trustee, Royal Nat. Orthopaedic Hosp., 1984–2000 (Chm., 1992–98). Editor, Skeletal Radiology, 1984–96; Mem., Editl Bd, Clinical Radiology, 1974–84. *Publications:* Knee Arthrography, 1980; (jtly) Self Assessment in Orthopaedic Radiology, 1988; The Radiology of Skeletal Disorders, 1990; chapters in textbooks; papers on metabolic medicine, tropical disease and skeletal radiology. *Recreations:* philology, medical history, genealogy. *Address:* 3 Pearce's Orchard, Henley-on-Thames, Oxon RG9 2LF. *T:* (01491) 575756. *Clubs:* Royal Air Force; Phyllis Court (Henley).

STOKER, John Francis; Chief Charity Commissioner, since 1999; *b* 11 Sept. 1950; *s* of Francis Charles Stoker and Joyce Stoker (*née* Barnwell); *m* 1982, Julie Puddicombe. *Educ:* King Edward's Sch., Birmingham; Brasenose Coll., Oxford (BA Lit.Hum.). Department of the Environment: Admin Trainee, 1973–78; Principal, 1978; Tenant's Right to Buy, 1979–81; Alternatives to Rates, 1981–83; Cabinet Office, 1983–85; Grade 5, 1985; Envmt White Paper Div., 1990–92; Grade 3, 1992; Dir, Merseyside Task Force, 1992–94; Regl Dir, Govt Office for Merseyside, 1994–96; Dep. Dir Gen., 1997–98, Dir Gen., 1998–99, Nat. Lottery. *Recreations:* books, music, gardening. *Address:* Charity Commission, Harmsworth House, 13–15 Bouverie Street, EC4Y 8DP. *Clubs:* Travellers; Middlesex CC.

STOKER, Sir Michael (George Parke), Kt 1980; CBE 1974; FRCP 1979; FRS 1968; FRSE 1960; President of Clare Hall, Cambridge, 1980–87 (Fellow, 1978); *b* 4 July 1918; *e s* of Dr S. P. Stoker, Maypole, Monmouth; *m* 1942, Veronica Mary English; three *s* two *d*. *Educ:* Oakham Sch.; Sidney Sussex Coll., Cambridge (Hon. Fellow 1981); St Thomas' Hosp., London. MRCS, LRCP 1942; MB, BChir 1943; MD 1947. RAMC, 1942–47; Demonstrator in Pathology, Cambridge Univ., 1947–48; Univ. Lecturer in Pathology, 1948–50; Huddersfield Lecturer in Special Pathology, 1950–58; Asst Tutor and Dir of Medical Studies, Clare Coll., 1949–58; Fellow of Clare College, 1948–58, Hon. Fellow, 1976; Prof. of Virology, Glasgow Univ., and Hon. Dir, MRC Experimental Virus Research Unit, 1959–68; Dir, Imperial Cancer Res. Fund Laboratories, 1968–79. Hon. Consultant, ICRF Cell Interactions Lab., Cambridge Univ. Med. Sch., 1980–. WHO Travel Fellow, 1951; Rockefeller Foundn Travel Fellow, 1958; Vis. Prof., UCL, 1968–79. Royal Society: For. Sec., 1977–81; a Vice-Pres., 1977–81; Leeuwenhoek Lecture, 1971, Blackett Meml Lecture, 1980; Mendel Gold Medal, 1978. Dir, Celltech Ltd, 1980–86. Member: European Molecular Biology Organisation; Council for Scientific Policy, DES, 1970–73; Gen. Cttee, Internat. Council of Scientific Unions, 1977–81; Eur. Acad. of Arts, Scis and Humanities, 1980; Med. Res. Council, 1982–86; Chairman: UK Co-ordinating Cttee, Cancer Res., 1983–86; Scientific Cttee, Ludwig Inst. Cancer Res., 1985–. Foreign Hon. Member: Amer. Acad. of Arts and Scis, 1973; Czech Acad. of Scis, 1980. Chm. of Trustees, Strangeways Res. Lab., Cambridge, 1981–93. Hon. DSc Glasgow, 1982. *Publications:* various articles on cell biology and virology. *Recreation:* painting. *Address:* 3 Barrington House, South Acre Drive, Cambridge CB2 2TY.

STOKES, family name of **Baron Stokes**.

STOKES, Baron *cr* 1969 (Life Peer), of Leyland; **Donald Gresham Stokes,** Kt 1965; TD; DL; FREng, FIMechE; MSAE; FIMI; FCIT; FICE; Chairman, KBH Communications, 1987–95; Chairman and Managing Director, 1968–75, Chief Executive, 1973–75, British Leyland Motor Corporation Ltd; President, BL Ltd, 1975–79; Consultant to Leyland Vehicles, 1979–81; *b* 22 March 1914; *o s* of Harry Potts Stokes; *m* 1939, Laura Elizabeth Courteney Lamb (*d* 1995); one *s*; *m* 2000, Patricia June Pascall. *Educ:* Blundell's School; Harris Institute of Technology, Preston. Started Student Apprenticeship, Leyland Motors Ltd, 1930. Served War of 1939–45: REME (Lt-Col). Re-joined Leyland as Exports Manager, 1946; General Sales and Service Manager, 1950; Director, 1954; Managing Director, and Deputy Chairman, Leyland Motor Corp., 1963, Chm. 1967; Chm. and Man. Dir, British Leyland Ltd, 1973. Director: National Westminster Bank, 1969–81; London Weekend Television Ltd, 1967–71; Opus Public Relations Ltd, 1979–84; Scottish & Universal Investments Ltd, 1980–92; Dovercourt Motor Co. Ltd, 1982–90; Beherman Auto-Transport SA, 1983–89; GWR Gp, 1990–94. Vice-President, Empresa Nacional de Autocamiones SA, Spain, 1959–73. Chairman: British Arabian Adv. Co. Ltd, 1977–85; Two Counties Radio Ltd, 1978–84, 1990–94 (Pres., 1984–90); Jack Barclay Ltd, 1980–90; British Arabian Technical Co-operation Ltd, 1981–85; Reliant Group, 1990; Dutton Forshaw Motor Gp, 1980–90. Vice-Pres., Engineering Employers Fedn, 1967–75; President: SMMT, 1961–62; Motor Industry Res. Assoc., 1965–66; Manchester Univ. Inst. of Science and Technology, 1972–76 (Vice-Pres., 1967–71); IMechE, 1972 (Vice-Pres., 1971); Chm., EDC for Electronics Industry, 1966–67; Member: NW Economic Planning Council, 1965–70; IRC, 1966–71 (Dep. Chm. 1969); EDC for the Motor Manufacturing Industry, 1967–; Council, Public Transport Assoc.; Worshipful Co. of Carmen. Fellow, IRTE (Pres., 1983–84), Hon. FIRTE. DL Lancs 1968. Hon. Fellow, Keble Coll., Oxford, 1968. Hon. LLD Lancaster, 1967, Hon. DTech Loughborough, 1968; Hon. DSc: Southampton, 1969; Salford, 1971. Officier de l'Ordre de la Couronne (Belgium), 1964; Commandeur de l'ordre de Leopold II (Belgium), 1972. *Recreation:* sailing. *Address:* 2 Branksome Cliff, Westminster Road, Poole, Dorset BH13 6JW. *Clubs:* Army and Navy; Royal Motor Yacht (Commodore, 1979–81).

STOKES, Dr Adrian Victor, OBE 1983; CChem; CEng; FBCS; Chief Executive, CAT Ltd, since 2000; *b* 25 June 1945; *s* of Alfred Samuel and Edna Stokes; *m* (marr. diss.). *Educ:* Orange Hill Grammar School, Edgware; University College London (BSc (1st cl. Hons) 1966; PhD 1970. CChem 1976; MRSC 1976; FBCS 1978; CEng 1990. Research Programmer, GEC-Computers Ltd, 1969–71; Research Asst, Inst. of Computer Science, 1971–73; Research Fellow, UCL, 1973–77; Sen. Research Fellow and Sen. Lectr, Hatfield Polytechnic, 1977–81; Dir of Computing, St Thomas' Hosp., 1981–88 (King's Fund Fellow, 1981–84); Consultant, 1986–88 (on secondment), Principal Consultant, 1989–97, NHS Centre for IT, then Inf. Mgt Centre; Asst Dir, NHS Inf. Mgt Centre, 1997–99; Jt Dir, NHS Inf. Authy (Standards), 1999–2000. Chm., European Workshop for Open Systems Expert Gp on Healthcare, 1991–97. Vis. Prof., Nene Coll., 1994–96 (Hon. Vis. Prof., 1996–99). Non-exec. Dir, Barnet Primary Care Trust, 2000–. Member: Silver Jubilee Cttee on Improving Access for Disabled People, 1977–78; Cttee on Restrictions Against Disabled People, 1979–81; Social Security Adv. Cttee, 1980–; Dept of Transport Panel of Advisers on Disability, 1983–85; Disabled Persons' Transport Adv. Cttee, 1986–89. Chm., Disabled Drivers' Motor Club, 1972–82, 1991–94, 1997–2000, Vice-Pres., 1982–; Chm., Exec. Cttee, RADAR, 1985–92. Governor, Motability, 1978–; Trustee: PHAB, 1982–90; Indep. Living (1993) Fund, 1993–; Independent Living (Extension) Fund, 1993–; Mobility Choice, 1998–. MIMgt (MBIM 1986); FInstD 1986; FRSA 1997. Freeman, City of London, 1988; Freeman, Co. of Information Technologists, 1988. Hon. DSc Hertfordshire, 1994. *Publications:* An Introduction to Data Processing Networks, 1978; Viewdata: a public information utility, 1979, 2nd edn 1980; The Concise Encyclopaedia of Computer Terminology, 1981; Networks, 1981; (with C. Saiady) What to Read in Microcomputing, 1982; Concise Encyclopaedia of Information Technology, 1982, 3rd edn 1986, USA edn 1983; Integrated Office Systems, 1982; (with M. D. Bacon and J. M. Bacon) Computer Networks: fundamentals and practice, 1984; Overview of Data Communications, 1985; The A to Z of Business Computing, 1986; Communications Standards, 1986; OSI Standards and Acronyms, 1987, 3rd edn 1991; (with H. de Glanville) The BJHC Abbreviary, 1995; numerous papers and articles, mainly concerned with computer technology. *Recreations:* philately, science fiction, collecting Elvis Presley records, computer programming. *Address:* 97 Millway, Mill Hill, NW7 3JL. *T:* (020) 8959 6665; (mobile) 07785 502766, *Fax:* (020) 8906 4137.

STOKES, Dr Alistair Michael; Chief Executive Officer, Ipsen Ltd (formerly Speywood Pharmaceuticals), since 1995; *b* 22 July 1948; *s* of Alan Philip and Janet Ross Stokes; *m* 1970, Stephanie Mary Garland; two *d*. *Educ:* University College, Cardiff (BSc, PhD). With Pharmacia AB (Sweden), 1974–76; Monsanto Co., St Louis, USA, 1976–82; Glaxo Pharmaceuticals, 1982–85; Regional Gen. Manager, Yorkshire RHA, 1985–87; Dir, Glaxo Pharmaceuticals, 1987–90; Dir and Chief Operating Officer, Porton Internat., 1990–95. Chairman: Stowic PLC, 1998–99; Quadrant Healthcare PLC, 1999–2000. Chm., E Berks Community Health NHS Trust, 1993–98. *Publications:* Plasma Proteins, 1977; biochemical and scientific papers. *Recreations:* music, cricket, travel. *Address:* Ipsen Ltd, 1 Bath Road, Maidenhead SL6 4UH. *Club:* Naval and Military.

STOKES, David Mayhew Allen; QC 1989; **His Honour Judge Stokes;** a Permanent Judge, Central Criminal Court, since 1999; *b* 12 Feb. 1944; *s* of Henry Pauntley Allen Stokes and Marjorie Joan Stokes; *m* 1970, Ruth Elizabeth, *d* of late Charles Tunstall Evans,

CMG, Haywards Heath; one *s* one *d*. *Educ:* Radley College; Inst. de Touraine (Tours); Churchill College, Cambridge (MA History/Law). Admitted Student, Gray's Inn, 1964; Holt Scholar, 1966; called to the Bar, 1968, Bencher, 1998. A Recorder, 1985–99. Dep. Chancellor, dio. of Norwich, 2001–. Mem., Gen. Council of the Bar, 1989–91, Additional Mem., 1992–98, Chm., Professional Conduct Cttee, 1997–98 (Vice-Chm., 1994–96); Chm., SE Circuit Liaison Cttee, 1991–99. Vis. Instructor/Team Leader, Nat. Inst. Trial Advocacy Workshop, Osgoode Hall Law Sch., York Univ., Toronto, 1986–. Trustee/Dir, London Suzuki Gp, 1988–94. Chairman: Cambridge Bar Mess, 1991–99; E Anglian Bar Mess, 1999. *Recreations:* amateur dramatics, madrigals. *Address:* c/o Central Criminal Court, Old Bailey, EC4M 7EH. *Club:* Norfolk (Norwich).

See also M. A. Evans.

STOKES, Harry Michael; HM Diplomatic Service, retired; Counsellor, Foreign and Commonwealth Office, 1979–81; *b* 22 July 1926; *s* of late Wing Comdr Henry Alban Stokes, RAF, and Lilian Frances (*née* Ede); *m* 1951, Prudence Mary Watling; two *s* one *d*. *Educ:* Rossall Sch.; Worcester Coll., Oxford (BA, Dip. Slavonic Studies). Served RAF, 1944–47. Joined Foreign Service, 1951; attached Control Commission, Germany, 1952–55; Foreign Office, 1955; Singapore, 1958; FO, 1959; Washington, 1961; Copenhagen, 1963; FO 1965; New Delhi, 1976; FO, 1977. Chm., British Assoc. for Cemeteries in S Asia, 1985–92. Dir, Indo-British Review, 1988–92. *Recreations:* walking, racquet games, photography, music. *Club:* Royal Commonwealth Society.

STOKES, John Fisher, MA, MD, FRCP; Physician, University College Hospital, since 1947; *b* 19 Sept. 1912; *e s* of late Dr Kenneth Stokes and Mary (*née* Fisher); *m* 1940, Elizabeth Joan, *d* of Thomas Rooke and Elizabeth Frances (*née* Pearce); one *s* one *d*. *Educ:* Haileybury (exhibitioner); Gonville and Caius Coll., Cambridge (exhibitioner); University Coll. Hosp. (Fellowes Silver Medal for clinical medicine). MB BChir (Cambridge) 1937; MRCP 1939; MD (Cambridge) 1947 (proxime accessit, Horton Smith prize); FRCP 1947; FRCPE 1975; Thruston Medal, Gonville and Caius Coll., 1948. Appointments on junior staff University Coll. Hosp. and Victoria Hosp. for Children, Tite St, 1937–42; RAMC 1942–46; served in Far East, 1943–46, Lt-Col (despatches). Examiner in Medicine, various Univs, 1949–70. Member of Council, Royal Soc. of Med., 1951–54, 1967–69. Vice-Pres., RCP, 1968–69; Harveian Orator, RCP, 1981. Trustee, Leeds Castle Foundn, 1984–. Amateur Squash Rackets Champion of Surrey, 1935, of East of England, 1936, Runner-up of British Isles, 1937; English International, 1938; Technical Adviser to Squash Rackets Assoc., 1948–52; Chm. Jesters Club, 1953–59. *Publications:* Examinations in Medicine (jtly), 1976; contrib. on liver disease and general medicine in medical journals. *Recreations:* music, tennis, painting. *Address:* Ossicles, Newnham Hill, near Henley-on-Thames, Oxon RG9 5TL. *Club:* Savile.

STOKES, Sir John (Heydon Romaine), Kt 1988; *b* 23 July 1917; *o surv. s* of late Victor Romaine Stokes, Hitchin; *m* 1st, 1939, Barbara Esmée (*d* 1988), *y d* of late R. E. Yorke, Wellingborough; one *s* two *d*; 2nd, 1989, Elsie Frances (*d* 1990), *widow* of John Plowman; 3rd, 1991, Ruth (marr. diss. 1996), *widow* of Sir Timothy Bligh, KBE, DSO, DSC; 4th, 1996, Frances Jean Stirling, *widow* of Lt Comdr Donald Packham, RN. *Educ:* Temple Grove; Haileybury Coll.; Queen's Coll., Oxford. BA 1938; MA 1946. Hon. Agent and Treas., Oxford Univ. Conservative Assoc., 1937; Pres., Monarchist Soc., 1937; Pres., Mermaid Club, 1937. Asst Master, Prep. Sch., 1938–39. Served War, 1939–46: Dakar Expedn, 1940; wounded in N Africa, 1943; Mil. Asst to HM Minister Beirut and Damascus, 1944–46; Major, Royal Fusiliers. Personnel Officer, Imperial Chemical Industries, 1946–51; Personnel Manager, British Celanese, 1951–59; Dep. Personnel Manager, Courtaulds, 1957–59; Dir, Clive & Stokes, Personnel Consultants, 1959–80. Mem., Gen. Synod of C of E, 1985–90. Contested (C): Gloucester, 1964; Hitchin, 1966; MP (C) Oldbury and Halesowen, 1970–74, Halesowen and Stourbridge, 1974–92. Mem., Select Cttee on Parly Commn for Admin (Ombudsman), 1979–83. Leader, Parly delegations: to Portugal, 1980; to Falkland Islands, 1985; to Malta, 1988; to Trinidad and Tobago, 1991. Mem., Delegn to Council of Europe and WEU, 1983–92; Leader, Delegn from Council of Europe to observe elections in Albania, March 1992. Pres., W Midlands Cons. Clubs, 1971–84. Chm., Gen. Purposes Cttee, Primrose League, 1971–85; Vice-Pres., Royal Stuart Soc.; Member: Oxford Soc., 1946–; Prayer Book Soc., 1970–; Trustee, Battlefields Trust, 1998–. Evelyn Wrench Speaker, ESU (USA), 1992. *Publications:* articles on political and historical subjects. *Recreations:* gardening, travel, English history, church affairs, writing to The Times. *Address:* 4 The Bradburys, Stratton Audley, near Bicester, Oxon OX6 9BW. *T:* (01869) 277875.

STOKES, Michael George Thomas; QC 1994; **His Honour Judge Michael Stokes;** a Circuit Judge, since 2001; *b* 30 May 1948; *e s* of late M. P. Stokes, Leyland, Lancs; *m* 1994, Alison Hamilton Pollock; one *s* one *d*. *Educ:* Preston Catholic Coll.; Univ. of Leeds (LLB Hons 1970). Asst Lectr, Univ. of Nottingham, 1970–72; called to the Bar, Gray's Inn, 1971; in practice on Midland and Oxford Circuit, 1973–2001; Asst Recorder, 1986–90, Recorder, 1990–2001. Pres., Mental Health Review Tribunals, 1999–. Circuit Rep., Remuneration and Terms of Work (formerly Fees & Legal Aid) Cttee, Bar Council, 1996–2000; Mem., Northants Criminal Justice Strategy Cttee, 2000–01. *Recreations:* racing, ski-ing, trying to breed a Group 1 winner! *Address:* c/o Nottingham Crown Court, 60 Canal Street, Nottingham NG1 7EL. *Club:* Northampton and County (Northampton).

STOKOE, Maj. Gen. John Douglas, CB 1999 CBE 1991 (MBE 1981); Managing Director, Amey Defence; *b* 30 Dec. 1947; *s* of late Major John Alexander Gordon Stokoe and Elsie Mary Stokoe; *m* 1972, Jenny (*née* Beach); one *s* two *d*. *Educ:* Richmond Grammar Sch.; Army Apprentices Coll., Harrogate; RMA, Sandhurst. Commnd Royal Signals, 1968; served Far East, UK and BAOR; Comdr Communications, Germany, 1991–93; Higher Comd and Staff Course, 1992; DCS, Germany, 1993–94; rcds 1994; Dir, Army Staff Duties, 1994–97; DCS, HQ Land Comd, 1997–98; Dep. C-in-C, HQ Land Comd and Insp. Gen., TA, 1998–99. Defence Business Develt Dir, Amey Gp, 1999. Col Comdt, RCS, 1998–. *Recreations:* sailing, long distance running, fell walking, water colour artist.

STOLLER, Anthony David; Chief Executive, Radio Authority, since 1995; *b* 14 May 1947; *s* of Louis and Pearl Stoller; *m* 1969, Andrea Lewisohn; one *s* one *d*. *Educ:* Hendon County Grammar Sch.; Gonville and Caius Coll., Cambridge (MA, LLB). Head of Radio Programming, IBA, 1974–79; Dir, Assoc. of Indep. Radio Contractors, 1979–81; Man. Dir, Thames Valley Broadcasting, 1981–85; John Lewis Partnership, 1985–95: Man. Dir, Tyrrell and Green, 1987–95. Mem., Cttee of Reference, Friends Provident Stewardship Fund, 1999–. *Publication:* Wrestling with The Angel, 2001. *Recreations:* cricket, sailing, music. *Address:* Radio Authority, Holbrook House, 14 Great Queen Street, WC2B 5DG. *T:* (020) 7430 2724.

STOLLERY, Prof. John Leslie, CBE 1994; DScEng; FREng; FCGI; FAIAA; Professor of Aerodynamics, 1973–95, now Emeritus, and Head, College of Aeronautics, 1976–86, and 1992–95, Cranfield University (formerly Cranfield Institute of Technology); *b* 21 April 1930; *s* of George and Emma Stollery; *m* 1956, Jane Elizabeth, *d* of Walter and Mildred Reynolds; four *s*. *Educ:* East Barnet Grammar Sch.; Imperial Coll. of Science and Technol., London Univ. (BScEng 1951, MScEng 1953, DScEng 1973). DIC; CEng, FREng (FEng 1992); FCGI 1984; FAIAA 1988. Aerodynamics Dept, De Havilland Aircraft Co., 1952–56; Lectr, 1956, Reader, 1962, Aeronautics Dept, Imperial Coll., London; Dean, Faculty of Engrg, 1976–79, Pro Vice-Chancellor, 1982–85, Cranfield Inst. of Technol. Chairman: Aerospace Technology Bd, MoD, 1986–89; Aviation Cttee, DTI, 1986–94; Mem., Airworthiness Requirements Bd, 1990–2000. Pres., RAeS, 1987–88. Visiting Professor: Cornell Aeronautical Labs, Buffalo, USA, 1964; Aeronaut. Res. Lab., Wright Patterson Air Force Base, 1971; Nat. Aeronaut. Lab., Bangalore, India, 1977; Peking Inst. of Aeronautics and Astronautics, 1979; Univ. of Queensland, 1983. Hon. FRAeS (FRAeS 1975). *Publications:* (Chief Editor) Shock Tube Research, 1971; papers in Jl of Fluid Mechanics, and various other aeronautical jls. *Recreations:* playing tennis, watching football, travelling. *Address:* 28 The Embankment, Bedford MK40 3PE. *T:* (01234) 406773.

STOLTENBERG, Gerhard, DrPhil; Member of the Bundestag, 1957–71 and 1982–98; Minister of Defence, Federal Republic of Germany, 1989–92; *b* 29 Sept. 1928; *m* 1958, Margot Rann; one *s* one *d*. *Educ:* Bad Oldesloe; Kiel Univ. (DrPhil 1954). Military service, 1944–45; local govt, 1945–46; Asst Lectr, 1954–60, Lectr, 1960–65, Kiel Univ. Mem., CDU, 1947–: Dep. Chm., 1955–71, Chm., 1971–82, Schleswig-Holstein CDU; Nat. Dep. Chm., 1969–. Nat. Chm., Young Union, 1955–61. Schleswig-Holstein Parliament: Mem., 1954–57, 1971–82; Prime Minister, 1971–82. Bundestag: Minister of Scientific Research, 1965–69; Dep. Chm., CDU/CSU, 1969–71; Minister of Finance, 1982–89. *Publications:* The German Reichstag 1871–1873, 1954; Political Currents in Rural Schleswig-Holstein 1919–1933, 1960; State and Science, 1969; Schleswig-Holstein: present and future, 1978.

STOLTENBERG, Thorvald; President, Norwegian Red Cross, since 1999; *b* 8 July 1931; *s* of Emil and Ingeborg Stoltenberg; *m* 1957, Karin Heiberg; one *s* two *d*. *Educ:* Oslo Univ. (law degree). Joined Foreign Service, Norway, 1958; served: San Francisco, 1959–61; Belgrade, 1961–64; Press Secretary, Foreign Min., 1964–65; Executive Officer: Foreign Minister's Secretariat, 1965–70; Lagos, 1970; State Secretary: Foreign Min., 1971–72; MoD, 1973–74; Min. of Commerce and Shipping, 1974–76; Min. of Foreign Affairs, 1976–79; Defence Minister, 1979–81; Minister for Foreign Affairs, Norway, 1987–89; Ambassador to UN, NY, 1989–90; UN High Comr for Refugees, Jan.–Nov. 1990; Minister for Foreign Affairs, 1990–93; Special Rep. of UN Sec.-Gen. for Former Yugoslavia, 1993–94; UN peace negotiator, Former Yugoslavia, 1993–96; Ambassador of Norway to Denmark, 1996–99. Internat. Sec., Norwegian Fedn of Trade Unions, 1970–71, 1972–73 and 1981–83; active in local politics in Oslo, 1983–87; Dep. Mayor of Oslo, 1985–87. *Address:* Norwegian Red Cross, POBox 1 Grønland, 0133 Oslo, Norway. *T:* 22054000, *Fax:* 22054040.

STOMBERG, Dr Rolf Wilhelm Heinrich; non-executive Chairman: John Mowlem & Co. PLC, since 1999; Unipoly SA, Luxembourg, since 1999; Management Consulting Group (formerly Proudfoot Consulting), since 2000; *b* Emden, Germany, 10 April 1940; *s* of Friedrich Stomberg and Johanna (*née* Meiners). *Educ:* Univ. of Hamburg (Dipl. Kfm. 1966; Dr. rer. pol. 1969). Apprenticeship in shipping; Asst Prof., Univ. of Hamburg, 1966–69; joined BP Group, 1970; Finance Dir and Mem., Bd of Mgt, Deutsche BP, 1981–83; Oilstream Dir, 1983–86; Dep. Chm., Deutsche BP, 1986–89; Chm., Europe-Continental Div., BP Oil Internat., 1988; Chm., Bd of Mgt, Deutsche BP, 1989–91; CEO, BP Oil Europe, 1990; Chm., BP Europe, 1994; Man. Dir, BP plc and CEO, BP Oil Internat., 1995–97. Non-executive Director: Smith & Nephew, 1998–; Cordiant Communications plc, 1998–; Scania AB, 1998–; Stinnes AG, 1998–; TPG Gp, 1998–; Reed Elsevier plc, 1999–. Member, Advisory Board: Dresdner Bank AG, 1991–; Gerling-Konzern, Cologne, 1990–. Vis. Prof., Imperial Coll., London. *Address:* John Mowlem & Co. PLC, 25 Ely Place, EC1N 6TD.

STONE, family name of **Baron Stone of Blackheath**.

STONE OF BLACKHEATH, Baron *cr* 1997 (Life Peer), of Blackheath in the London Borough of Greenwich; **Andrew Zelig Stone;** *b* 7 Sept. 1942; *s* of Sydney Stone and Louise Sophia Stone (*née* Gould); *m* 1973, Vivienne Wendy Lee; one *s* two *d*. *Educ:* Cardiff High School. Marks & Spencer: Mgt Trainee, 1966; Israel 1967; Merchandise Manager, 1973; PA to Chm., 1978–80; Divl Dir, 1986; Menswear, 1986; Dir, 1990–99; Jt Man. Dir, 1994–99. Non-exec. Director: Thorn plc, 1996–98; Design Ville Ltd; Dipex. Mem., Nat. Adv. Cttee on Culture and Creativity in Educn, 1998–. Pres., BOTB Gp for Israel, 1991–. Gov., Weizmann Inst. of Sci., 1996–; Mem. Council, Royal Instn. Trustee, Jewish Assoc. of Business Ethics. Hon. Vice Pres., Reform Synagogues of GB, 2000–. Patron, Interalia Inst. of Arts and Science. FRSA. Hon. LLD Oxford Brookes, 1998; Hon. DDes Kingston, 1999. *Recreations:* reading, walking, thinking. *Address:* House of Lords, SW1A 0PW.

STONE, Maj.-Gen. Anthony Charles Peter, CB 1994; Chairman and Managing Director, The Nash Partnership Ltd, international defence advisers, since 1996; Defence Adviser, since 1997, and Partner, since 1998, Gracemoor Consultants (UK) Ltd; *b* 25 March 1939; *s* of Major (retd) Charles C. Stone and Kathleen M. Stone (*née* Grogan); *m* 1967, (Elizabeth) Mary, *d* of Rev. Canon Gideon Davies; two *s*. *Educ:* St Joseph's Coll.; RMA, Sandhurst; Staff Coll., Camberley. Commnd RA, 1960; served in light, field, medium, heavy, locating and air defence artillery in BAOR, FE and ME and in various general and weapons staff appts in MoD; commanded 5th Regt, RA, 1980–83; founded Special OP Troop, 1982; Col, Defence Progs Staff, MoD, 1983–84; Mil. Dir of Studies, RMCS, 1985–86; Ministry of Defence: Dir of Operational Requirements (Land), 1986–89; Dir of Light Weapons Projects, 1989–90; Dir Gen. Policy and Special Projects, 1990–92; Dir Gen. Land Fighting Systems, MoD (PE), 1992–95. Hon. Col, 5th Regt, RA, 1990–; Col Comdt, 1993–2001, Rep. Col Comdt, 1998, Royal Regt of Artillery. Vis. Res. Fellow, Dept of Defence Studies, Univ. of York, 1996–; Army Mem., Steering Cttee, UK Defence Forum, 1997–. FRUSI 1997. *Recreations:* shooting (game), family, ski-ing. *Club:* Army and Navy.

STONE, David Radcliffe, OBE 1997; CEng, FIM; Chairman, Sheffield Teaching Hospitals NHS Trust, since 2001; *b* 19 Sept. 1935; *s* of Arthur Thomas Stone and Esther Stone; *m* 1959, Janet Clarke (*d* 1996); two *d*. *Educ:* Barking Abbey Sch., Essex; Univ. of Manchester (BSc Hons 1957). CEng 1983; FIM 1994. Manager, United Steel Cos Ltd, 1957–68; Consultant, PA Mgt Consultants, 1968–73; Works Dir, Firth Brown Ltd, 1973–78; Managing Director: Doncaster Sheffield Ltd, 1978–85; Stocksbridge Engrg Steels Ltd, 1985–89; UES Steels 1989–94; United Engrg Steels Ltd, 1994–96. Pres., British Iron and Steel Producers Assoc., 1993–94. Chairman: Weston Park Hosp. NHS Trust, 1997–99; Central Sheffield Univ. Hosps NHS Trust, 1999–2001; S Yorks Forum, 1997–2001; Trustee: Freshgate Foundn, 1996–; Sheffield Botanical Gardens, 1997–. Guardian, Sheffield Assay Office, 1998–. Freeman, City of London, 1995; Liveryman, Co. of Blacksmiths, 1997–; Master Cutler, Co. of Cutlers in Hallamshire, 1995–96. Hon. Consul, Finland, 1996–. *Recreations:* golf, gardening, fishing, shooting, music. *Address:* 98 Graham Road, Sheffield S10 3GQ. *T:* (0114) 263 0334. *Clubs:* Royal Automobile; Hallamshire Golf; Cressbrook and Litton Flyfishers'.

STONE, Evan David Robert; QC 1979; a Recorder of the Crown Court, 1979–98; *b* 26 Aug. 1928; *s* of Laurence George and Lillian Stone; *m* 1959, Gisela Bridget Mann; one *s*. *Educ:* Berkhamsted; Worcester Coll., Oxford (MA). National Service (commnd, Army), 1947–49; served Middle East and UK. Called to Bar, Inner Temple, 1954, Bencher, 1985; sometime HM Deputy Coroner: Inner West London; West Middlesex; City of London. Mem. Senate of Inns of Court and the Bar, 1985–86. Formerly Associate Editor, Medico-Legal Journal. Councillor, later Alderman, London Borough of Islington, 1969–74 (Dep. Leader, later Leader of Opposition). Chm., City and Hackney HA, 1984–92. Mem., Criminal Injuries Compensation Bd, 1989–. Governor: Moorfields Eye Hosp., 1970–79; Highbury Grove Sch., 1971–86 (Chm. of Governors, 1978–83). *Publications:* Forensic Medicine, 1987 (with Prof. H. Johnson); contrib. Social Welfare and the Citizen (paperback), 1957; contribs to Medico-Legal Jl and other professional jls. *Recreations:* reading, writing, sport, listening to music. *Address:* 60 Canonbury Park South, N1 2JG. *T:* (020) 7226 6820; The Mill House, Ridgewell, Halstead, Essex CO9 4SR. *T:* (01440) 785338; (chambers) 29 Bedford Row, WC1R 4HE. *T:* (020) 7831 2626. *Clubs:* Garrick, MCC; Norfolk (Norwich), Western (Glasgow).

STONE, Prof. (Francis) Gordon (Albert), CBE 1990; FRS 1976; Head of Department of Inorganic Chemistry, and Professor, Bristol University, 1963–90, now Professor Emeritus; Robert A. Welch and University Distinguished Professor of Chemistry, Baylor University, Texas, since 1990; *b* 19 May 1925; *s* of Sidney Charles and Florence Stone; *m* 1956, Judith M. Hislop, Sydney, Australia; three *s*. *Educ:* Exeter Sch.; Christ's Coll., Cambridge. BA 1948, MA and PhD 1952, ScD 1963, Cambridge. Fulbright Schol., Univ. of Southern Calif., 1952–54; Instructor and Asst Prof., Harvard Univ., 1954–62; Reader, Queen Mary Coll., London, 1962–63. Vis. Professor: Monash Univ., 1966; Princeton Univ., 1967; Univ. of Arizona, 1970; Carnegie-Mellon Univ., 1972; Texas A&M Univ., 1980; ANU, 1982; Guggenheim Fellow, 1961; Sen. Vis. Fellow, Australian Acad. of Sciences, 1966; A. R. Gordon Distinguished Lectr, Univ. of Toronto, 1977; Misha Strassberg Vis. Lectr, Univ. of WA, 1982. Lectures: Boomer, Univ. of Alberta, 1965; Firestone, Univ. of Wisconsin, 1970; Tilden, Chem. Soc., 1971; Ludwig Mond, RSC, 1982; Reilly, Univ. of Notre Dame, 1983; Waddington, Univ. of Durham, 1984; Sir Edward Frankland Prize, RSC, 1987; G. W. Watt, Univ. of Texas (Austin), 1988. Member: Council, Royal Soc. of Chemistry (formerly Chemical Soc.), 1968–70, 1981–83; Dalton Div. Council, 1971–74, 1981–85 (Vice-Pres. 1973 and 1984–85; Pres., 1981–83); Chemistry Cttee, SERC, 1982–85 (Mem., Chem. Cttee, SRC, 1971–74); Council, Royal Soc., 1986–88 (Vice-Pres., 1987–88). Hon. DSc: Exeter, and Waterloo, Canada, 1992; Durham, Salford, 1993; Zaragoza, 1994. Organometallic Chemistry Medal, 1972, Transition Metal Chemistry Medal, 1979, RSC; Chugaev Medal, Inst. of Inorganic Chem., USSR Acad. of Sciences, 1978; Amer. Chem. Soc. Award in Inorg. Chem., 1985; Davy Medal, Royal Soc., 1989; Longstaff Medal, RSC, 1990. *Publications:* Leaving no Stone Unturned (autobiog.), 1993; (Editor) Advances in Organometallic Chemistry, vols 1–47, 1964–2000; (ed) Comprehensive Organometallic Chemistry, 1985–1995 (14 vols), 1995; numerous papers in Jl Chem. Soc., Jl Amer. Chem. Soc., etc. *Recreation:* world travel. *Address:* 60 Coombe Lane, Bristol BS9 2AY. *T:* (0117) 968 6107; 88 Hackberry Avenue, Waco, TX 76706, USA. *T:* (254) 7523617.

STONE, Frederick Alistair, CBE 1988; DL; solicitor, now retired; Clerk and Chief Executive, Surrey County Council, 1973–88; *b* 13 Sept. 1927; *s* of Cyril Jackson and Elsie May Stone; *m* 1963, Anne Teresa Connor; one *s* one *d*. *Educ:* William Hulme's Grammar Sch.; Dulwich Coll.; Brasenose Coll., Oxford (BCL, MA). Asst Solicitor: Norwich City Council, 1954–58; Hampshire CC, 1958–60; Sen. Solicitor, CC of Lincoln (Parts of Lindsey), 1960–63; Asst Clerk, Hampshire CC, 1963–65; Dep. Clerk, Cheshire CC, 1965–73. Chairman: RIPA, 1979–81; Assoc. of County Chief Executives, 1986–87. Chm., Surrey Bd, Prince's Youth Business Trust, 1989–96; Dep. Chm., Anchor Housing Assoc. and Trust, 1990–97. Chm. of Govs, Worth Sch., 1990–99. DL Surrey, 1988. *Recreations:* music, walking, gardening. *Address:* Stables Cottage, Kiln Lane, Brockham, Betchworth RH3 7LZ. *T:* (01737) 842178.

STONE, Gerald Charles, PhD; FBA 1992; University Lecturer in non-Russian Slavonic Languages, Oxford University, and Fellow of Hertford College, Oxford, 1972–99; *b* 22 Aug. 1932; *s* of Albert Leslie Stone and Grace Madeline Stone (*née* Varndell); *m* 1st, 1953, Charlotte Johanna Steinbach (marr. diss. 1973); two *s* one *d*; 2nd, 1974, Vera Fedorovna Konnova; one *d*. *Educ:* Windsor Grammar Sch.; School of Slavonic Studies, London Univ. (BA 1964; PhD 1969). Nat. service, Army, Trieste, 1951–53. Metropolitan Police, 1953–64; Asst Master, Bexhill Grammar Sch., 1964–65; Asst Lectr, 1966–67, Lectr, 1967–71, Nottingham Univ.; Asst Dir of Res., Cambridge Univ., 1971–72. General Editor, Oxford Slavonic Papers, 1983–94. *Publications:* The Smallest Slavonic Nation: the Sorbs of Lusatia, 1972; (with B. Comrie) The Russian Language since the Revolution, 1978; An Introduction to Polish, 1980, 2nd edn 1992; (ed with D. Worth) The Formation of the Slavonic Literary Languages, 1985; (ed) Kěrluše, 1995; (with B. Comrie and M. Polinsky) The Russian Language in the Twentieth Century, 1996; (ed) Kjarliže, 1996; (ed) A Dictionarie of the Vulgar Russe Tongue Attributed to Mark Ridley, 1996. *Recreations:* gardening, walking, visiting pubs. *Address:* 6 Lathbury Road, Oxford OX2 7AU. *T:* (01865) 558227.

STONE, Gordon; *see* Stone, F. G. A.

STONE, Gregory; QC 1994; **His Honour Judge Stone;** a Circuit Judge, since 2001; *b* 12 Dec. 1946; *s* of Frederick Albert Leslie Stone and Marion Gerda Stone (*née* Heller); *m* (separated); three *d*. *Educ:* Chislehurst and Sidcup Grammar Sch.; St Joseph's Coll., London; Université de Rennes; Queen's Coll., Oxford (MA); Univ. of Manchester (Dip. Econ. Develt (distinction) 1971; MA (Econ.) 1972). Sen. Economist, Morgan Grenfell, 1974–76; called to the Bar, Inner Temple, 1976; Standing Counsel to DTI for Criminal Matters on South Eastern Circuit, 1989–90; a Recorder, 2000–01. *Publications:* The Law of Defective Premises, 1982; The Architect's Legal Handbook, 2nd edn, 1978, to 7th edn 1999. *Recreations:* travel, music, walking, cinema, theatre, opera, architecture, landscape.

STONE, James Hume Walter Miéville; Member (Lib Dem) Caithness, Sutherland and Easter Ross, Scottish Parliament, since 1999; *b* 16 June 1954; *s* of Edward Reginald Stone and Susannah Gladys Hume (*née* Waddell-Dudley); *m* 1981, Flora Kathleen Margaret Armstrong; one *s* two *d*. *Educ:* Tain Royal Acad.; Gordonstoun Sch.; St Andrew's Univ. (MA 1977). Cleaner, Loch Kishorn, fish-gutter, Faroe Is, English teacher, Sicily, 1977–79; stores clerk, Wimpey Internat., 1979–81; Asst Site Administrator, then Site Administrator, subseq. Project Co-ordinator, Bechtel GB Ltd, 1981–84; Admin Manager, Odfjell Drilling and Consulting Co. Ltd, 1984–86; Dir, Highland Fine Cheeses Ltd, 1986–94; Mem., Cromarty Firth Port Authy, 1998–2000; freelance newspaper columnist and broadcaster, 1990–. Chm., Tain Community Council, 1984; Member: (Ind, 1986–88, Lib Dem, 1988–96) Ross and Cromarty DC, 1986–96 (Vice Chm., Policy and Resources); (Lib Dem) Highland Council, 1995–99 (Vice-Chm., Finance); Scottish Constitutional Convention, 1988–96; Scottish Lib Dem agriculture spokesman, 1998–99; Scottish Parliament: Lib Dem spokesman on educn and children, 1999–2000, on Highlands and Fisheries, 2000–01; Mem., Holyrood Progress Gp, 2000–. Chm., Dornoch Firth Fest., 1990–92; Director: Highland Fest., 1994–2000; Grey Coast Theatre, 2000–. Trustee: Highland Building Preservation Trust; Tain Guildry Trust, 1987–; Tain Mus. Trust, 1992–. Gov., Eden Court Th., Inverness, 1995–99. FRSA. *Recreations:* shooting, reading, music, gardening, funghi, steam engines, the identification of butterflies. *Address:* Scottish Parliament, Edinburgh EH99 1SP; Sloibcoyle, Edderton, Tain IV19 1LQ. *T:* (01862) 821500. *Clubs:* New (Edinburgh); Armagh (N Ireland).

STONE, Lucille Madeline, (Lucy), (Mrs C. Coleman); QC 2001; *b* 16 Oct. 1959; *d* of late Alexander Stone and of Rene Stone; *m* 1994, Charles Coleman; one *s*. *Educ:* Newnham Coll., Cambridge (MA 1984); Inns of Court Sch. of Law. Called to the Bar, Middle Temple, 1983; specialist in divorce law. *Recreations:* family, entertaining, reading. *Address:* Queen Elizabeth Building, Temple, EC4Y 9BS. *T:* (020) 7797 7837.

STONE, Marcus; Sheriff of Lothian and Borders, 1984–93; Advocate; *b* 22 March 1921; *s* of Morris and Reva Stone; *m* 1956, Jacqueline Barnoin; three *s* two *d*. *Educ:* High Sch. of Glasgow; Univ. of Glasgow (MA 1940, LLB 1948). Served War of 1939–45, RASC: overseas service, West Africa, att. RWAFF. Admitted Solicitor, 1949; Post Grad. Dip., Psychology, Univ. of Glasgow, 1953; admitted Faculty of Advocates, 1965; apptd Hon. Sheriff Substitute, 1967, Sheriff, 1971–76, of Stirling, Dunbarton and Clackmannan, later N Strathclyde at Dumbarton; Sheriff of Glasgow and Strathkelvin, 1976–84. Accredited Mediator, Centre for Dispute Resolution, London, 1993; Principal, Dispute Resolution Bureau; Chm., The Mediation Bureau; practising mediator, 1994–; Hon. Pres., Assoc. of Mediators, 1997–. *Publications:* Proof of Fact in Criminal Trials, 1984; Cross-examination in Criminal Trials, 1988, 2nd edn 1995; Fact-finding for Magistrates, 1990; Representing Clients in Mediation, 1998. *Recreations:* swimming, music. *Address:* Advocates' Library, Parliament House, Edinburgh EH1 1RF.

STONE, Prof. Norman; Professor of International Relations, Bilkent University, Ankara, since 1997; *b* 8 March 1941; *s* of late Norman Stone and Mary Stone (*née* Pettigrew); *m* 1st, 1966, Nicole Aubry (marr. diss. 1977); two *s*; 2nd, 1982, Christine Margaret Booker (*née* Verity); one *s*. *Educ:* Glasgow Acad.; Gonville and Caius Coll., Cambridge (MA). Research student in Austria and Hungary, 1962–65; University of Cambridge: Research Fellow, Gonville and Caius Coll., 1965–67; Univ. Lectr in Russian History, 1967–84; Fellow and Dir of Studies in History, Jesus Coll., 1971–79; Fellow of Trinity Coll., 1979–84; Prof. of Modern History, and Fellow, Worcester Coll., Univ. of Oxford, 1984–97. Vis. Lectr, Sydney Univ., 1978. Trustee, Margaret Thatcher Foundn, 1991–. Order of Merit (Polish Republic), 1993. *Publications:* The Eastern Front 1914–1917, 1975, 3rd edn 1978 (Wolfson Prize for History, 1976); Hitler, 1980; Europe Transformed 1878–1919 (Fontana History of Europe), 1983; (ed jtly) Czechoslovakia, 1989; (jtly) The Other Russia, 1990; The Russian Chronicles, 1990. *Recreations:* Eastern Europe, music, languages, Turkey. *Address:* 22 St Margaret's Road, Oxford OX2 6RX. *T:* (01865) 439481, *Fax:* (Turkey) (312) 2667835. *Clubs:* Beefsteak, Garrick, Polish.

STONE, Oliver William; screenwriter; director; *b* NYC, 15 Sept. 1946; *s* of Louis Stone and Jacqueline Stone (*née* Goddet). *Educ:* Yale Univ.; NY Univ. (BFA). Film Sch. Teacher, Cholon, Vietnam, 1965–66; wiper, US Merchant Marine, 1966; served US Army, Vietnam, 1967–68 (Purple Heart with oak leaf cluster, Bronze Star); taxi driver, NYC, 1971. *Screenwriter:* Seizure, 1973; Midnight Express, 1978 (Acad. Award, Writers' Guild of Amer. Award); The Hand, 1981; (with J. Milius) Conan the Barbarian, 1982; Scarface, 1983; (with M. Cimino) Year of the Dragon, 1985; (with D. L. Henry) 8 Million Ways to Die, 1986; (with R. Boyle) Salvador, 1986; (also Dir) Platoon, 1986 (Acad. Award, Dirs Guild of Amer. Award, BAFTA Award); *co-writer:* Evita, 1996; *co-writer and director:* Wall Street, 1987; Talk Radio, 1988; The Doors, 1991; *screenwriter, producer and director:* Born on the Fourth of July, 1989 (Acad. Award, 1990); JFK, 1991; Heaven & Earth, 1993; Natural Born Killers, 1994; Nixon, 1995; *director:* U-Turn, 1997; *producer:* South Central, 1992; Zebrahead, 1992; The Joy Luck Club, 1993; New Age, 1994; Wild Palms (TV mini-series), 1993; Freeway, 1995; The People vs Larry Flynt, 1996; Saviour, 1998; *executive producer:* Killer: A Journal of Murder, 1995; (HBO) Indictment: The McMartin Preschool, 1995. Member: Writers' Guild of America; Directors' Guild of America; Acad. of Motion Picture Arts and Scis. *Publication:* A Child's Night Dream, 1997. *Address:* Ixtlan, 201 Santa Monica Boulevard, 6th Floor, Santa Monica, CA 90401, USA.

STONE, Maj.-Gen. Patrick Philip Dennant, CB 1992; CBE 1984 (OBE 1981 MBE 1975); Director General, Personal Services (Army), 1988–91; *b* 7 Feb. 1939; *s* of Philip Hartley Stone and Elsie Maude Stone (*née* Dennant); *m* 1967, Christine Iredale Trent; two *s* one *d*. *Educ:* Christ's Hospital; psc 1972. Nat. Service, 1959; commissioned East Anglian Regt, 1959; seconded 6 KAR, 1960–62 (Tanganyika); served British Guyana and Aden, 1962–65; ADC to Governor of W Australia, 1965–67; RAF Staff Coll., 1972; Comd 2nd Bn, Royal Anglian Regt, 1977–80 (UK and Berlin); Chief of Staff, 1st Armoured Div., 1981–84; Comdr, Berlin Inf. Bde, 1985–86; Dep. Mil. Sec. (B), 1987. Dep. Col, Royal Anglian Regt, 1986–91, Col, 1991–97; Col Comdt, Mil. Provost Staff Corps, 1988–92; Dep. Col Comdt, AGC, 1992–93. *Recreations:* country interests, travel, conservation. *Address:* c/o Lloyds TSB, 90A Mill Road, Cambridge. *Club:* Army and Navy.

STONE, Richard Frederick; QC 1968; *b* 11 March 1928; *s* of Sir Leonard Stone, OBE, QC, and Madeleine Marie (*née* Scheffler); *m* 1st, 1957, Georgina Maxwell Morris (decd); two *d*; 2nd, 1964, Susan van Heel; two *d*. *Educ:* Lakefield College Sch., Canada; Rugby; Trinity Hall, Cambridge (MA). Lt, Worcs Regt, 1946–48. Called to Bar, Gray's Inn, 1952, Bencher, 1974, Treasurer, 1992. Member: Panel of Lloyd's Arbitrators in Salvage Cases, 1968–99; Panel of Wreck Comrs, 1968–98. *Recreation:* sailing. *Address:* The Cleve, Woodgreen, near Fordingbridge, Hants SP6 2AX. *T:* (01725) 512324; Flat N, Rectory Chambers, Old Church Street, Chelsea, SW3 5DA. *T:* (020) 7351 1719.

STONE, Prof. Richard Thomas Horner; Principal, Inns of Court School of Law, 1997–2001; *b* 7 March 1951; *s* of late Rev. Ross Stone and of Bettine Stone (*née* Horner); *m* 1973, Margaret Peerman; one *s* three *d*. *Educ:* Reading Sch.; Southampton Univ. (LLB); Hull Univ. (LLM 1978). Called to the Bar, Gray's Inn, 1998. Leicester University: Lectr in Law, 1975–89; Sen. Lectr in Law, 1989–93; Dean, Faculty of Law, 1987–90; Resident Dir, Sunway Coll., Malaysia, 1989; Prof., 1993–97, Dean, 1996–97, Nottingham Law Sch., Nottingham Trent Univ. Vis. Lectr, Loughborough Univ., 1978–91; Vis. Prof., City Univ., 1997–. FRSA 1998; FICPD 1998. *Publications:* Entry, Search and Seizure, 1985, 3rd edn 1997; Textbook on Civil Liberties, 1994, 3rd edn 2000; Principles of Contract Law, 1994, 4th edn 2000; Law of Agency, 1996; Offences Against the Person, 1999; articles in legal jls. *Recreations:* books, music. *Address:* c/o Department of Law, City University, Northampton Square, EC1V 0HB.

STONE, Rt Rev. Ronald Francis; *see* Rockhampton, Bishop of.

STONE, Prof. Trevor William, PhD, DSc; Professor of Pharmacology, University of Glasgow, since 1989; *b* 7 Oct. 1947; *s* of Thomas William Stone and Alice Stone (*née* Reynolds); *m* 1971, Anne Corina. *Educ:* Sch. of Pharmacy, London Univ. (BPharm 1969; DSc 1983); Aberdeen Univ. (PhD 1972). Lectr in Physiology, Univ. of Aberdeen, 1970–77; Sen. Lectr, 1977–83, Reader, 1983–86, Prof., 1986–88, in Neuroscis, St

George's Hosp. Sch. of Medicine, Univ. of London. Res. Fellow, Nat. Inst. of Mental Health, Washington, 1974, 1977; Vis. Prof. of Pharmacology, Univ. of Auckland, 1988. FRSocMed. Hon. Mem., Portuguese Pharmacol Soc., 1989. *Publications:* Microiontophoresis and Pressure Ejection, 1985; Purines: basic and clinical aspects, 1989; Quinolinic Acid and Kynurenines, 1989; Adenosine in the Nervous System, 1991; CNS Transmitters and Neuromodulators, I 1994, II and III 1995, IV 1996; Neuropharmacology, 1995; Pills, Potions & Poisons, 2000; over 400 sci. papers and abstracts. *Recreations:* piano, photography, snooker, music, work. *Address:* West Medical Building, University of Glasgow, Glasgow G12 8QQ. *T:* (0141) 330 4481.

STONEFROST, Maurice Frank, CBE 1983; DL; Director General and Clerk, Greater London Council, 1984–85; *b* 1 Sept. 1927; *s* of Arthur and Anne Stonefrost, Bristol; *m* 1953, Audrey Jean Fishlock; one *s* one *d*. *Educ:* Merrywood Grammar Sch., Bristol (DPA). IPFA. Nat. Service, RAF, 1948–51; local govt finance: Bristol County Borough, 1951–54; Slough Borough, 1954–56; Coventry County Borough, 1956–61; W Sussex CC, 1961–64; Sec., Inst. of Municipal Treasurers and Accountants, 1964–73; Comptroller of Financial Services, GLC, 1973–84; Chief Exec., BR Pension Fund, 1986–90; Chairman: Municipal Mutual Insce, 1990–93; CLF Municipal Bank, 1993–98. Dep. Pro Chancellor, and Vice-Chm. Council, City Univ., 1992–99. President: Soc. of County Treasurers, 1982–83; CIPFA, 1984–85. Chm., Commn on Citizenship, 1989–90; Member: Marre Cttee on Future of Legal Profession, 1989–90; Review Cttee of Finances of C of E, 1993. Member: Architectural Heritage Fund, 1990–96 (Vice Chm., 1996–98); Foundn for Accountancy and Financial Management, Eastern Europe, 1993–2000; London Pensions Fund Authority, 1996–. Chm., Dolphin Sq. Trust, 1993–. DL Greater London, 1986. Hon. DSc City Univ., 1987. *Recreation:* gardening.

See also W. J. G. Keegan.

STONEHAM, Prof. Arthur Marshall, PhD; FRS 1989; Massey Professor of Physics, and Director, Centre for Materials Research, University College London, since 1995; *b* 18 May 1940; *s* of Garth Rivers Stoneham and Nancy Wooler Stoneham (*née* Leslie); *m* 1962, Doreen Montgomery; two *d*. *Educ:* Univ. of Bristol (BSc 1961; PhD 1964). CPhys, FInstP 1981; FIM 1996. Harwell Laboratory, UKAEA, 1964–95: Group Leader, 1974; Individual Merit promotions to Band level, 1974, and Sen. level, 1979; Hd of Materials Physics and Metallurgy Div., 1989–90; Hd of Technical Area, Core and Fuel Studies, UKAEA, 1988–90; Dir of Res., AEA Industrial Technology, 1990–93; Chief Scientist, UKAEA, 1993–97 (pt-time based at UCL, 1995–97). Wolfson Industrial Fellow, Oxford Univ., 1985–89; Fellow, Wolfson Coll., Oxford, 1989–95; Sen. Fellow, BT Labs, subseq. Corning Res. Centre, 1998–2000. Visiting Professor: Univ. of Illinois, 1969; Univ. of Connecticut, 1973; Univ. of Keele, 1988–; Univ. of Salford, 1992–; visiting scientist: Gen. Electric, Schenectady, 1969; Centre d'Etudes Nucléaires Grenoble, 1970; KFA Julich, 1973; IBM Yorktown Heights, 1982; PTB Braunschweig, 1985, etc. Member, Council: Royal Soc., 1994–96; Inst. of Physics, 1994– (Vice Pres., 1997–). Dir, Oxford Authentication, 1997–. Fellow, APS, 1997. Dir, Inst. of Physics Publications; Editor, Jl of Physics C: Solid State Physics, 1983–88; Divl Associate Ed., Physical Review Letters, 1992–96; mem. editl bds of other learned jls. *Publications:* Theory of Defects in Solids, 1975, new edn 1985, repr. as Oxford Classic, 2001 (Russian edn 1978); (with W. Hayes) Defects and Defect Processes in Non-Metallic Solids, 1985; (with M. G. Silk and J. A. G. Temple) Current Issues in Semiconductor Science, 1986; Current Issues in Condensed Matter Structure, 1987; Reliability of Non-Destructive Inspection, 1987; Ionic Solids at High Temperatures, 1989; Current Issues in Condensed Matter Spectroscopy, 1990; Materials Modelling: from theory to technology, 1992; (with S. C. Jain) GeSi Strained Layers and their Applications, 1995; (with J. A. Gillaspie and D. L. Clark) Wind Ensemble Sourcebook, 1997 (C. B. Oldman Prize, IAML, 1999); (with J. A. Gillaspie and D. L. Clark) The Wind Ensemble Catalog, 1998; (with N. Itoh) Materials Modification by Electronic Excitation, 2000; research papers on defect properties of the solid state, quantum diffusion, and ordered structures in Jl Phys C: Solid State Phys, Phys Rev., Phys Rev. Lett., Procs of Royal Soc., etc. *Recreations:* music, esp. horn playing in orchestral and chamber music, musical scholarship, reading. *Address:* 14 Bridge End, Dorchester-on-Thames, Wallingford, Oxon OX10 7JP. *T:* (01865) 340066; *e-mail:* ucapams@ucl.ac.uk.

STONES, (Elsie) Margaret, AM 1988; MBE 1977; botanical artist; *b* 28 Aug. 1920; *d* of Frederick Stones and Agnes Kirkwood (*née* Fleming). *Educ:* Swinburne Technical Coll., Melbourne; Melbourne National Gall. Art Sch. Came to England, 1951; working independently as botanical artist, 1951–: at Royal Botanic Gardens, Kew; Nat. Hist. Museum; Royal Horticultural Soc., and at other botanical instns; Contrib. Artist to Curtis's Botanical Magazine, 1957–82. Drawings (water-colour): 20, Aust. plants, National Library, Canberra, 1962–63; 250, Tasmanian endemic plants, 1962–77; Basalt Plains flora, Melbourne Univ., 1975–76; Vis. Botanical Artist, Louisiana State Univ., 1977–86 (200 drawings of Louisiana flora, exhibited: Fitzwilliam, Cambridge, Royal Botanic Garden, Edinburgh, Ashmolean Mus., Oxford, 1991). Exhibitions: Colnaghi's, London, 1967–; retrospective, Melbourne Univ., 1976; Louisiana Drawings, Smithsonian, USA, 1980, Louisiana State Mus., 1985, Univ. of Virginia, 1993; Baskett & Day, 1984, 1989; Boston Athenæum, 1993; 50 year retrospective, Nat. Gall. of Victoria, Melbourne, 1996. Workshop, Cornell Univ., USA, 1990. Hon. DSc: Louisiana State Univ. Bâton Rouge, 1986; Melbourne Univ., 1989. Eloise Payne Luquer Medal, Garden Club of Amer., 1987; Gold Veitch Meml Medal, RHS, 1989. *Publications:* The Endemic Flora of Tasmania (text by W. M. Curtis), 6 Parts, 1967–78; Flora of Louisiana: water-colour drawings, 1991; illus. various books. *Recreations:* gardening, reading. *Address:* 1 Bushwood Road, Kew, Richmond, Surrey TW9 3BG. *T:* (020) 8940 6183.

STONES, Sir William (Frederick), Kt 1990; OBE 1980; Managing Director, China Light & Power Co., Hong Kong, 1984–92 (Director, 1975–93); Chairman, Hong Kong Nuclear Investment Co., 1985–93; *b* 3 March 1923; *s* of Ralph William Stones and Ada Stones (*née* Armstrong); *m* 1st, 1946, Irene Mary Punter (marr. diss.); one *s* one *d*; 2nd, 1968, Margaret Joy Catton. *Educ:* Rutherford Coll., Newcastle upon Tyne. Chief Chemist, Michie & Davidson, 1948–51; Regional Res. Dir, CEGB NE Region, 1951–63; Supt, Ferrybridge Power Station, 1963–66; CEGB NE Region: Group Manager, 1966–68; Dir, Operational Planning, 1968–71; Dir, Generation, and Dep. Dir-Gen., 1971–75; Gen. Manager, China Light & Power Co., 1975–83. Dep. Chm., Guandong Nuclear Power Joint Venture Co., 1985–93; Sen. Advr, West Merchant Bank, 1993–2000. Commander, Order of Leopold II (Belgium), 1986. *Recreations:* fishing, country life. *Address:* Pirnie House, Kelso, Roxburghshire TD5 8NS. *T:* (01835) 823854. *Clubs:* Caledonian; New (Edinburgh); Hong Kong.

STONEY, Brigadier Ralph Francis Ewart, CBE 1952 (OBE, 1943); Director-General, The Royal Society for the Prevention of Accidents, 1959–68; *b* 28 June 1903; *o s* of late Col R. D. S. Stoney, The Downs, Delgany, Co. Wicklow and Mrs E. M. M. Stoney; *m* 1st, 1939, Kathleen Nina (*née* Kirkland) (*d* 1973); one *d*; 2nd, 1979, Bridget Mary St John Browne. *Educ:* Royal Naval Colleges, Osborne and Dartmouth; Royal Military Academy, Woolwich. Commissioned Royal Engineers, 1923; Staff College, Camberley, 1937–38. Served War of 1939–45 as GSO, 1939–43 (OBE) and as CRE, 82 Div., 1943–46, in Burma (despatches twice). CRE 5th Div. and 2nd Div., 1947–48; Col GS (Intelligence), War Office, 1949–51; Brig. GS (Intelligence), Middle East, 1952–54. Retired, 1954. *Address:* Kinsale, Hook Heath Avenue, Woking, Surrey GU22 0HN.

STONHOUSE, Rev. Sir Michael Philip, 19th Bt *cr* 1628 and 15th Bt *cr* 1670, of Radley, Berkshire; Rector and Incumbent, St James, Saskatoon, Saskatchewan, since 1992; *b* 4 Sept. 1948; *er s* of Sir Philip Allan Stonhouse, 18th Bt and 14th Bt, and Winnifred Emily (*d* 1989), *e d* of J. M. Shield; *S* father, 1993; *m* 1977, Colleen Coucill; three *s*. *Educ:* Medicine Hat Coll., Univ. of Alberta (BA); Wycliffe Coll. (MDiv). Ordained deacon, 1977, priest, 1978, dio. Calgary, Canada. Asst Curate, St Peter's, Calgary, 1977–80; Rector and Incumbent: Parkland Parish, Alberta, 1980–87; St Mark's Innisfail and St Matthew's Bowden, Alberta, 1987–92. *Heir:* *s* Allan James Stonhouse, *b* 20 March 1981. *Address:* 3413 Balfour Street, Saskatoon, SK S7H 3Z3, Canada.

STONIER, Prof. Peter David, PhD; consultant in pharmaceutical medicine, since 2000; *b* 29 April 1945; *s* of Frederick Stonier and Phyllis Maud Stonier; *m* 1989, Elizabeth Margaret Thomas; one *s* one *d*. *Educ:* Cheadle Hulme Sch.; Univ. of Birmingham (BSc 1st cl. Hons 1966); Univ. of Sheffield (PhD 1969); Univ. of Manchester (MB ChB Hons 1974); Open Univ. (BA 1990). FFPM 1989; FRCPE 1993; MRCPsych 1994; FRCP 1998. House Officer, Manchester Royal Infirmary, 1974–75; Senior House Officer: Univ. Hosp. S Manchester, 1975–76; Leicester Royal Infirmary, 1976–77; Med. Advr, 1977–80, Head of Med. Services, 1980–81, Med. Dir, 1982–2000, and Bd Mem., 1994–2000, Hoechst UK Ltd, later Hoechst Roussel Ltd, then Hoechst Marion Roussel Ltd. Visiting Professor: Univ. of Surrey, 1992– (Course Dir, MSc in Pharmaceutical Medicine, 1993–2001); KCL, 1998–. Member: Pharm. Industry Trng Council, 1998–; Appeal Panel, NICE, 2000–. Chm., British Assoc. of Pharmaceut. Physicians, 1988–90; Mem. Council, British Assoc. of Psychopharmacology, 1993–97; Council, RCP, 1997–2001; Faculty of Pharmaceutical Medicine, Royal Colleges of Physicians of UK: Vice Pres., 1992–96, Pres., 1997–2001; Mem., Bd of Examrs, 1994–; Chm., Fellowship Cttee, 1997–; Convenor and Chair, Task Force for Specialist Trng in Pharmaceut. Medicine, 1995–99. Pres., Internat. Fedn of Assocs of Pharmaceut. Physicians, 1996–98. FRSocMed 1982 (Pres., Sect. of Pharmaceut. Medicine and Res., 1994–96); FMS 1999; FRSA 2000; AMInstD 1995. Founder Ed., Pharmaceutical Physician, 1989–98; Associate Editor, Human Psychopharmacology, 1990–; Internat. Jl of Pharmaceut. Medicine, 1997–. *Publications:* (ed jtly) Perspectives in Psychiatry, 1988; (ed with I. Hindmarch) Human Psychopharmacology: methods and measures, vol. 1 1988, vol. 2 1989, vol. 3 1991, vol. 4 1993, vol. 5 1996, vol. 6 1997; (ed) Discovering New Medicines: careers in pharmaceutical research and development, 1994; (ed jtly) Clinical Research Manual, 1994–; (ed jtly) Medical Marketing Manual, 2001; articles on psychopharmacology and pharmaceut. medicine. *Recreations:* opera, writing, cooking, spending time with young family, collecting prints, powerboat cruising in the Mediterranean. *Address:* 5 Branstone Road, Kew, Richmond-on-Thames, Surrey TW9 3LB. *T:* (020) 8940 2025.

STONOR, family name of **Baron Camoys**.

STONOR, Air Marshal Sir Thomas (Henry), KCB 1989; Group Director and Controller, National Air Traffic Services, 1988–91; *b* 5 March 1936; *s* of Alphonsus and Ann Stonor; *m* 1964, Robin Antoinette, *er d* of late Wilfrid and Rita Budd; two *s* one *d*. *Educ:* St Cuthbert's High Sch., Newcastle upon Tyne; King's Coll., Univ. of Durham (BSc (Mech Eng) 1957). Commissioned, RAF, 1959; served No 3 Sqn, 2ATAF, 1961–64; CFS, 6 FTS and RAF Coll., Cranwell, 1964–67; No 231 Operational Conversion Unit, 1967–69; RAF Staff Coll., Bracknell, 1970; HQ, RAF Germany, 1971–73; OC 31 Sqn, 1974–76; Mil. Asst to VCDS, MoD, 1976–78; OC RAF Coltishall, 1978–80; RCDS, 1981; Inspector of Flight Safety, RAF, 1982–84; Dir of Control (Airspace Policy), NATS, 1985–86; Dep. Controller, NATS, 1986–88. Sen. Consultant, Siemens Plessey Systems, 1991–98; Defence Advr, BT Defence Sales Sector, 1991–; non-exec. Dir, Parity PLC (formerly COMAC Gp), 1994–. *Recreations:* gardening, music. *Address:* 213 Woodstock Road, Oxford OX2 7AD; 82190 Lacourde Visa, France; *e-mail:* thomas.stonor@virgin.net. *Club:* Royal Air Force.

STOPFORD, family name of **Earl of Courtown**.

STOPFORD, Viscount; James Richard Ian Montagu Stopford; *b* 30 March 1988; *s* and *heir* of Earl of Courtown, *qv*.

STOPFORD, Prof. John Morton, DBA; Professor of International Business, London Business School, since 1974; *b* 16 Sept. 1939; *s* of Rt Rev. and Rt Hon. Robert Wright Stopford, KCVO, CBE, DD and Winifred Sophia Stopford (*née* Morton); *m* 1966, Sarah Woodman; two *s*. *Educ:* Sherborne Sch.; Hertford Coll., Oxford (BA); MIT (SM); Harvard Univ. (DBA). Apprentice fitter, Baker Perkins, 1958; Engineer, Shell Chemicals, 1962–64; Acting Man. Dir, Guyana Stockfeeds, 1965; Sen. Lectr, Manchester Business Sch., 1968–70; Vis. Prof., Harvard Business Sch., 1970–71; Reader, London Business Sch., 1971–74. Non-exec. Dir, Shell UK, 1973–77; Dir, InterMatrix, 1977–; Chm., The Learning Partnership Internat. Inc., 1997–; Dep. Chm., Strategic Partnership, 1994–. Pres., Eur. Internat. Business Assoc., 1978–79; Vice-Pres., Acad. of Internat. Business, 1994–96; Sen. Staff Officer, UN Centre on Transitional Corps, NY, 1977–78. Visiting Professor: MIT, 1993; Stockholm Sch. of Econs, 1994–95; Aoyama Gakuin Univ., Tokyo, 1994–95; Harry Reynolds Vis. Prof., Wharton Sch., Univ. of Penn., 1999–2000. US Acad. of Management Book Prize, 1992. *Publications:* (with L. T. Wells) Managing the Multinational Enterprise, 1972; (with B. Garratt) Breaking down Barriers, 1980; Growth and Organisational Change, 1980; The Directory of Multinationals, 1980, 2nd edn, 1992; (with J. H. Dunning) Multinationals, 1983; (with L. Turner) Britain and the Multinationals, 1985; (with S. Strange) Rival States, Rival Firms, 1991; (with C. Baden-Fuller) Rejuvenating the Mature Business, 1992, rev. edn 1994; (ed jtly) Handbook of Organizational Learning, 2000; contribs to learned jls. *Recreations:* hill-walking, tennis, reading. *Address:* London Business School, Sussex Place, Regent's Park, NW1 4SA; 6 Chalcot Square, NW1 8YB.

STOPFORD, Maj.-Gen. Stephen Robert Anthony, CB 1988; MBE 1971; Director General Fighting Vehicles and Engineer Equipment, Ministry of Defence (Procurement Executive), 1985–89; *b* 1 April 1934; *s* of Comdr Robert Stopford, RN, and Elsie Stopford; *m* 1963, Vanessa (*née* Baron). *Educ:* Downside; Millfield. Graduate MIERE. Commissioned Royal Scots Greys, 1954; regimental service and various staff appts until 1977; Project Manager, MBT80, 1977–80; Military Attaché, Washington, 1983–85. Dir, David Brown Vehicle Transmissions Ltd, 1990–99. *Recreations:* sailing, scuba diving, shooting. *Address:* 18 Thornton Avenue, SW2 4HG. *T:* (020) 8674 1416.

STOPPARD, Miriam, (Lady Hogg), MD; FRCP; writer and broadcaster; *b* 12 May 1937; *d* of Sydney and Jenny Stern; *m* 1st, 1972, Sir Tom Stoppard, *qv* (marr. diss. 1992); two *s* and two step *s*; 2nd, 1997, Sir Christopher Hogg, *qv*. *Educ:* Newcastle upon Tyne Central High Sch. (State Scholar, 1955); Royal Free Hosp. Sch. of Medicine, Univ. of London (Prize for Experimental Physiol., 1958); King's Coll. Med. Sch. (Univ. of Durham), Newcastle upon Tyne (MB, BS Durham, 1961; MD Newcastle, 1966). FRCP 1998 (MRCP 1964). Royal Victoria Infirmary, King's Coll. Hosp., Newcastle upon

Tyne: House Surg., 1961; House Phys., 1962; Sen. House Officer in Medicine, 1962–63; Univ. of Bristol: Res. Fellow, Dept of Chem. Pathol., 1963–65 (MRC Scholar in Chem. Pathol.); Registrar in Dermatol., 1965–66 (MRC Scholar in Dermatol.); Sen. Registrar in Dermatol., 1966–68; Syntex Pharmaceuticals Ltd: Associate Med. Dir, 1968; Dep. Med. Dir, 1971; Med. Dir, 1974; Dep. Man. Dir, 1976; Man. Dir, 1977–81. TV series: Where There's Life (5 series), 1981; Baby & Co. (2 series), 1984; Woman to Woman, 1985; Miriam Stoppard's Health and Beauty Show, 1988; Dear Miriam, 1989. MRSocMed (Mem. Dermatol. Sect., Endocrinol. Sect.); Member: Heberden Soc.; Brit. Assoc. of Rheumatology and Rehabilitation. *Publications:* Miriam Stoppard's Book of Baby Care, 1977; (contrib.) My Medical School, 1978; Miriam Stoppard's Book of Health Care, 1979; The Face and Body Book, 1980; Everywoman's Lifeguide, 1982; Your Baby, 1982; Fifty Plus Lifeguide, 1982; Your Growing Child, 1983; Baby Care Book, 1983; Pregnancy and Birth Book, 1984; Baby and Child Medical Handbook, 1986; Everygirl's Lifeguide, 1987; Feeding Your Family, 1987; Miriam Stoppard's Health and Beauty Book, 1988; Every Woman's Medical Handbook, 1988; Lose 7 lb in 7 Days, 1990; Test Your Child, 1991; The Magic of Sex, 1991; Conception, Pregnancy and Birth, 1993; The Menopause, 1994; Questions Children Ask and How to Answer Them, 1997; Sex Ed—Growing up, Relationships and Sex, 1997; Baby's Play and Learn Pack, 2000; over 40 pubns in med. jls. *Recreations:* my family, gardening. *Address:* c/o Dorling Kindersley, 80 Strand, WC2R 0RL.

STOPPARD, Sir Tom, OM 2000; Kt 1997; CBE 1978; FRSL; playwright and novelist; *b* 3 July 1937; *yr s* of late Eugene Straussler and of Mrs Martha Stoppard; *m* 1st, 1965, Jose (marr. diss. 1972), *yr d* of John and Alice Ingle; two *s*; 2nd, 1972, Dr Miriam Moore-Robinson (*see* Miriam Stoppard) (marr. diss. 1992); two *s*. *Educ:* abroad; Dolphin Sch., Notts; Pocklington, Yorks. Journalist: Western Daily Press, Bristol, 1954–58; Bristol Evening World, 1958–60; freelance, 1960–63. Mem., Royal Nat. Theatre Bd, 1989–. Hon. degrees: Bristol, 1976; Brunel, 1979; Leeds, 1980; Sussex, 1980; London, 1982; Kenyon Coll., 1984; York, 1984. Shakespeare Prize, 1979. *Plays:* Enter a Free Man, London, 1968 (TV play, A Walk on the Water, 1963); Rosencrantz and Guildenstern are Dead, Nat. Theatre, 1967, subseq. NY, etc (Tony Award, NY, 1968; NY Drama Critics Circle Award, 1968); The Real Inspector Hound, London, 1968; After Magritte, Ambiance Theatre, 1970; Dogg's Our Pet, Ambiance Theatre, 1972; Jumpers, National Theatre, 1972 (Evening Standard Award); Travesties, Aldwych, 1974 (Evening Standard Award; Tony Award, NY, 1976); Dirty Linen, Newfoundland, Ambiance Theatre, 1976; Every Good Boy Deserves Favour (music-theatre), 1977; Night and Day, Phoenix, 1978 (Evening Standard Award); Dogg's Hamlet and Cahoot's Macbeth, Collegiate, 1979; Undiscovered Country (adaptation), NT, 1979; On the Razzle, NT, 1981; The Real Thing, Strand, 1982 (Standard Award), subseq. NY (Tony Award, 1984); Rough Crossing (adaptation), NT, 1984; Dalliance (adaptation), NT, 1986; Hapgood, Aldwych, 1988; Arcadia, NT, 1993 (Evening Standard Award; Olivier Award); Indian Ink, Aldwych, 1995; The Seagull (trans.), Old Vic, 1997; The Invention of Love, NT, 1997 (Evening Standard Award); *radio:* The Dissolution of Dominic Boot, 1964; M is for Moon Among Other Things, 1964; If You're Glad I'll Be Frank, 1965; Albert's Bridge, 1967 (Prix Italia); Where Are They Now?, 1970; Artist Descending a Staircase, 1972; The Dog it was That Died, 1982 (Giles Cooper Award; televised 1988); In the Native State, 1991; *television:* A Separate Peace, 1966; Teeth, 1967; Another Moon Called Earth, 1967; Neutral Ground, 1968; (with Clive Exton) Boundaries, 1975; (adapted) Three Men in a Boat, 1976; Professional Foul, 1977; Squaring the Circle, 1984; *screenplays:* (with T. Wiseman) The Romantic Englishwoman, 1975; Despair, 1978; The Human Factor, 1979; (with Terry Gilliam and Charles McKeown) Brazil, 1985; Empire of the Sun, 1987; Rosencrantz and Guildenstern are Dead, 1990 (also dir); The Russian House, 1991; Billy Bathgate, 1991; (with Marc Norman) Shakespeare in Love (Oscar Award for Best Screenplay), 1999; Enigma, 2001. John Whiting Award, Arts Council, 1967; Evening Standard Award for Most Promising Playwright, 1968. *Publications:* (short stories) Introduction 2, 1964; (novel) Lord Malquist and Mr Moon, 1965; *plays:* Rosencrantz and Guildenstern are Dead, 1967; The Real Inspector Hound, 1968; Albert's Bridge, 1968; Enter a Free Man, 1968; After Magritte, 1971; Jumpers, 1972; Artists Descending a Staircase, and, Where Are They Now?, 1973; Travesties, 1975; Dirty Linen, and New-Found-Land, 1976; Every Good Boy Deserves Favour, 1978; Professional Foul, 1978; Night and Day, 1978; Undiscovered Country, 1980; Dogg's Hamlet, Cahoot's Macbeth, 1980; On the Razzle, 1982; The Real Thing, 1983; The Dog it was that Died, 1983; Squaring the Circle, 1984; Four plays for radio, 1984; Rough Crossing, 1985; Dalliance and Undiscovered Country, 1986; (trans.) Largo Desolato, by Vaclav Havel, 1987; Hapgood, 1988; In the Native State, 1991; Arcadia, 1993; The Television Plays 1965–1984, 1993; The Invention of Love, 1997. *Address:* c/o Peters, Fraser & Dunlop, Drury House, 34–43 Russell Street, WC2B 5HA.

STOPS, Timothy William Ashcroft J.; *see* Jackson-Stops.

STORAR, John Robert Allan Montague, CA; Chairman, Mitchell Cotts PLC, 1985–87 (Director, 1973–87; Deputy Chairman, 1978); *b* 6 Nov. 1925; *s* of James and Leonore Storar; *m* 1952, Catherine Swanson Henderson; two *s* one *d*. *Educ:* Dollar Academy. Dir 1960–74, Dep. Chief Exec. 1972–74, Drayton Corporation Ltd; Dir 1974–85, Dep. Chm. 1974–81, Man. Dir 1981–82, Samuel Montagu & Co. Ltd; Dir, Consolidated Gold Fields PLC, 1969–89. Chm., Assoc. of Investment Trust Cos, 1979–81. *Recreation:* fly fishing. *Address:* 2 Oxford House, Wimbledon, SW19 5NE. *Club:* Caledonian.

STORER, David George; Under Secretary, Department of Social Security (formerly of Health and Social Security), 1984–89; *b* 27 June 1929; *s* of Herbert Edwards Storer; *m* 1960, Jean Mary Isobel Jenkin; one *s* two *d*. *Educ:* Monmouth School; St John's Coll., Cambridge (MA). Assistant Principal, Min. of Labour, 1952; Principal, 1957; Cabinet Office, 1963–66; Asst Secretary, Dept of Employment, 1966–73; Director, Training Opportunities Scheme, 1973–77; Dir of Corporate Services, MSC, 1977–84. *Recreations:* reading, walking. *Address:* 5a Carlton Road, Redhill, Surrey RH1 2BY.

STORER, James Donald, CEng, MRAeS; author and museum consultant; Keeper, Department of Science, Technology and Working Life, Royal Museum of Scotland, Edinburgh, 1985–88; *b* 11 Jan. 1928; *s* of James Arthur Storer and Elizabeth May Gartshore (*née* Pirie); *m* 1955, Shirley Anne (*née* Kent); one *s* one *d*. *Educ:* Hemsworth Grammar Sch., Yorks; Imperial Coll., London (BSc Hons, ACGI). Design Office, Vickers Armstrongs (Aircraft) Ltd, and British Aircraft Corporation, Weybridge, 1948–66; Dept of Technology, Royal Scottish Museum, 1966–85. Hon. Secretary: British Aviation Preservation Council, 1990–95 (Vice-Pres., 1996); Sheringham Mus. Trust; Chm., Friends of Ironbridge Gorge Museum, 1994–98. MRAeS (AFRAeS 1958). *Publications:* Steel and Engineering, 1959; Behind the Scenes in an Aircraft Factory, 1965; It's Made Like This: Cars, 1967; The World We Are Making: Aviation, 1968; A Simple History of the Steam Engine, 1969; How to Run An Airport, 1971; How We Find Out About Flight, 1973; Flying Feats, 1977; Book of the Air, 1979; Great Inventions, 1980; (jtly) Encyclopedia of Transport, 1983; (jtly) East Fortune: Museum of Flight and history of the airfield, 1983; The Silver Burdett Encyclopedia of Transport: Air, 1984; Ship Models in the Royal Scottish Museum, 1986; The Conservation of Industrial Collections, 1989; (jtly) Fly Past, Fly Present, 1995; (contrib.) Biographical Dictionary of the History of Technology, 1996; (jtly) Industry and Transport in Scottish Museums, 1997; Liverpool on Wheels, 1998. *Recreations:* aircraft preservation, industrial archaeology, gardening. *Address:* 41 Campion Way, Sheringham, Norfolk NR26 8UN. *T:* (01263) 825086.

STORER, Prof. Roy; Professor of Prosthodontics, 1968–92 and Dean of Dentistry, 1977–92 (Clinical Sub-Dean, 1970–77), The Dental School, University of Newcastle upon Tyne, Professor Emeritus, since 1992; *b* 21 Feb. 1928; *s* of late Harry and Jessie Storer; *m* 1953, Kathleen Mary Frances Pitman; one *s* two *d*. *Educ:* Wallasey Grammar Sch.; Univ. of Liverpool. LDS (Liverpool) 1950; FDSRCS 1954; MSc (Liverpool) 1960; DRD RCS Ed, 1978. House Surg., 1950, and Registrar, 1952–54, United Liverpool Hosps; Lieut (later Captain) Royal Army Dental Corps, 1950–52; Lectr in Dental Prosthetics, Univ. of Liverpool, 1954–61; Visiting Associate Prof., Northwestern Univ., Chicago, 1961–62; Sen. Lectr in Dental Prosthetics, Univ. of Liverpool, 1962–67; Hon. Cons. Dental Surgeon: United Liverpool Hosps, 1962–67; United Newcastle Hosps (later Newcastle Health Authority), 1968–92. Chm., Div. of Dentistry, Newcastle Univ. Hosps, 1972–75. Mem. Council and Sec., British Soc. for the Study of Prosthetic Dentistry, 1960–69 (Pres., 1968–69); Member: GDC, 1977–92 (Chm. Educn Cttee, 1986–91); Bd of Faculty, RCS, 1982–90; Dental Sub-Cttee, UGC, 1982–89; EC Dental Cttee for trng of dental practitioners, 1986–93; Med. Cttee, UFC, 1989–92. Pres., Med. Rugby Football Club (Newcastle), 1968–82; Mem. Bd of Dirs, Durham CCC, 1994–98. Mem., Northern Sports Council, 1973–88; External Examiner in Dental Subjects: Univs of Belfast, Birmingham, Bristol, Dublin, Dundee, Leeds, London, Newcastle upon Tyne, RCS, and RCPSGlas. *Publications:* A Laboratory Course in Dental Materials for Dental Hygienists (with D. C. Smith), 1963; Immediate and Replacement Dentures (with J. N. Anderson), 3rd edn, 1981; papers on sci. and clin. subjects in dental and med. jls. *Recreations:* cricket, Rugby football, gardening, vexillology. *Address:* 164 Eastern Way, Darras Hall, Ponteland, Newcastle upon Tyne NE20 9RH. *T:* (01661) 823286. *Clubs:* MCC, East India.

STOREY, Christopher Thomas; QC 1995; a Recorder, since 2000; *b* 13 Feb. 1945; *s* of Leslie Hall Storey and Joan Storey; *m* 1968, Hilary Johnston; two *s*. *Educ:* Rugby Sch. Chartered Accountant, 1967; Glass & Edwards, Liverpool, 1964–68; Price Waterhouse & Co., 1968–70; A. E. Smith Coggins Group, 1970–72; Stacey's, 1972–74; private practice as Chartered Accountant, 1974–82; called to the Bar, Lincoln's Inn, 1979; practising Barrister, NE Circuit, 1982–. *Recreations:* music, cricket, classic cars, flying light aircraft (instructor). *Address:* Park Lane House, Westgate, Leeds LS1 2RA. *T:* (0113) 228 5000.

STOREY, David Malcolm; writer and dramatist; *b* 13 July 1933; *s* of Frank Richmond Storey and Lily (*née* Cartwright); *m* 1956, Barbara Rudd Hamilton; two *s* two *d*. *Educ:* Queen Elizabeth Grammar Sch., Wakefield, Yorks; Slade School of Fine Art, London; Fellow, UCL, 1974. *Plays:* The Restoration of Arnold Middleton, 1967 (Evening Standard Award); In Celebration, 1969 (Los Angeles Critics' Award); The Contractor, 1969 (Writer of the Year Award, Variety Club of GB, NY Critics' Award) (televised, 1989); Home, 1970 (Evening Standard Award, Critics' Award, NY); The Changing Room, 1971 (Critics' Award, NY); Cromwell, 1973; The Farm, 1973; Life Class, 1974; Mother's Day, 1976; Sisters, 1978; Early Days, 1980; The March on Russia, 1989; Stages, 1992. *Publications:* This Sporting Life, 1960 (Macmillan Fiction Award, US); Flight into Camden, 1960 (John Llewellyn Meml Prize); Radcliffe Somerset Maugham award, 1963; Pasmore, 1972 (Geoffrey Faber Meml Prize, 1973); A Temporary Life, 1973; Edward, 1973; Saville, 1976 (Booker Prize, 1976); A Prodigal Child, 1982; Present Times, 1984; Storey's Lives: poems 1951–1991, 1992; A Serious Man, 1998. *Address:* c/o Jonathan Cape, Random House, 20 Vauxhall Bridge Road, SW1V 2SA.

STOREY, Graham, OBE 1997; LittD; Emeritus Reader in English, and Emeritus Fellow of Trinity Hall, Cambridge University, since 1988 (Hon. Fellow, Trinity Hall, 1995); *b* 8 Nov. 1920; *o surv. s* of late Stanley Runton Storey, LDS RCS and Winifred Storey (*née* Graham). *Educ:* St Edward's Sch., Oxford; Trinity Hall, Cambridge (MA 1944); LittD Cantab 1997. Served War, RA, 1941–45; Lieut 1942; mentioned in despatches. Called to the Bar, Middle Temple, 1950, but did not practise. Cambridge University: Fellow, 1949–88, Sen. Tutor, 1958–68, Vice-Master, 1970–74, Trinity Hall; Univ. Lectr in English, 1965–81; Reader, 1981–88; Chm., Faculty Bd of English, 1972–74. Vis. Fellow, All Souls Coll., Oxford, 1968. Leverhulme Emeritus Res. Fellowship, 1988. Warton Lectr, British Acad., 1984; Lecture tours for British Council overseas. Syndic, CUP, 1983. Vice-Pres., G. M. Hopkins Soc., 1971; Pres., Dickens Soc. of America, 1983–84. Governor: St Edward's, Oxford, 1959–69; Eastbourne Coll., 1965–69. Jt Gen. Editor, Letters of Dickens, Pilgrim edn, 1965–; General Editor: Cambridge Renaissance and Restoration Dramatists, 1975–89; Cambridge English Prose Texts, 1980–. *Publications:* Reuters' Century, 1951; Journals and Papers of G. M. Hopkins, 1959 (completed edn on death of Humphry House); (ed) A. P. Rossiter, Angel with Horns, 1961; (ed) Selected Verse and Prose of G. M. Hopkins, 1966; (ed jtly) Letters of Charles Dickens, vol. I, 1965, vol. II, 1969, vol. III, 1974, vol. V, 1981, vol. VI, 1988, vol. VII, 1993, vol. VIII, 1995, vol. IX, 1997, vol. X, 1998; A Preface to Hopkins, 1981; (ed with Howard Erskine-Hill) Revolutionary Prose of the English Civil War, 1983; Bleak House (critical study), 1987; David Copperfield (critical study), 1991; contributions to: New Cambridge Bibliography, 1967; Writers and their Work, 1982; Dickens and Other Victorians, 1988; periodicals. *Recreations:* theatre, gardening, travel. *Address:* Trinity Hall, Cambridge CB2 1TJ. *T:* (01223) 332500; Crown House, Caxton, Cambs CB3 8PQ. *T:* (01954) 719316.

STOREY, Dr Hugo Henry; a Vice-President, Immigration Appeal Tribunal, since 2000; *b* 30 Sept. 1945; *s* of Harry MacIntosh Storey and Barbara Storey; *m* 1983, Sehba Haroon; three *s*. *Educ:* N Sydney Boys' High Sch.; Univ. of Sydney (BA Hons 1967; Medal in Govt); Balliol Coll., Oxford (BPhil Politics); Nuffield Coll., Oxford; Univ. of Leeds (PhD 1988). Adult educn teaching, legal res., and journalism, 1971–76; Organiser, Tribunal Assistance Unit, Chapeltown CAB, 1976–78; Sen. Legal Worker, Chapeltown and Harehills Law Centre, 1978–88; Human Rights Fellow, Council of Europe, 1983–88; legal worker, John Howell & Co., 1989–90; Sen. Lectr, Law Dept, Leeds Poly., 1990–91; Lectr and Dep. Dir for Study of Law in Europe, Law Dept, 1991–95, Hon. Res. Fellow, 1995–98, Univ. of Leeds. Adjudicator, Immigration Appellate Authy, 1995–2000. Mem. Council, Internat. Assoc. Refugee Law Judges, 1998–. *Publications:* (jtly) I Want to Appeal: a guide to Supplementary Benefit Appeal Tribunals, 1978; (jtly) Social Security Appeals: a guide to National Insurance Local Tribunals and Medical Appeal Tribunals, 1980; (with G. Crawford) Sacked? Made Redundant? Your Rights if You Lose Your Job: a guide to Industrial Tribunals and the Employment Appeal Tribunal, 1981; (with W. Collins) Immigrants and the Welfare State, 1985; (ed jtly) Asylum Law, 1995; (ed jtly) Butterworth's Immigration Law Handbook, 2001; contribs to various legal jls in UK, Europe and internat. *Recreations:* family, travel, golf, writing poetry (esp. haiku), music, chess. *Address:* Fairfield, The Avenue, Whyteleafe, Surrey CR3 0AQ. *T:* (020) 8660 6088.

STOREY, Jeremy Brian; QC 1994; a Recorder, since 1995; Deputy Judge of the Technology and Construction Court (formerly Official Referee), since 1996; Acting Deemster, Isle of Man Courts, since 1999; *b* 21 Oct. 1952; *s* of late Captain James Mackie Storey and Veronica Walmsley; *m* 1981, Carolyn Margaret Ansell; two *d*. *Educ:*

Uppingham Sch.; Downing Coll., Cambridge (Scholar; BA Law 1st Class, MA). MCIArb 1999 (ACIArb 1997). Called to the Bar, Inner Temple, 1974; Asst Recorder, 1991–95. Asst Boundary Comr for Eng. and Wales, 2000–. Member: Western Circuit; Technology and Construction Bar Assoc. (approved Adjudicator, 1999–); Cttee, London Common Law and Commercial Bar Assoc.; Commercial Bar Assoc.; Personal Injuries Bar Assoc.; Professional Negligence Bar Assoc.; Soc. for Computers and Law; Chm., Barristers' Overseas Advocacy Cttee. *Recreations:* travel, cricket, theatre. *Address:* 4 Pump Court, Temple, EC4Y 7AN. *T:* (020) 7842 5555. *Clubs:* MCC; Glamorgan CC.

STOREY, Maude, CBE 1987; President, Royal College of Nursing, 1986–90; *b* 24 March 1930; *d* of late Henry Storey and of Sarah Farrimond Storey. *Educ:* Wigan and District Mining and Techn. Coll.; St Mary's Hosp., Manchester; Lancaster Royal Infirmary; Paddington Gen. Hosp.; Royal Coll. of Nursing, Edinburgh; Queen Elizabeth Coll., London. SRN 1952; SCM 1953; RCI (Edin.) 1962; RNT 1965. Domiciliary Midwife, Wigan County Borough, 1953–56; Midwifery Sister, St Mary's Hosp., Manchester, 1956–57; Charge Nurse, Intensive Therapy, Mayo Clinic, USA, 1957–59; Theatre Sister, Clinical Instructor, 1959–63, subseq. Nurse Tutor, 1965–68, Royal Albert Edward Infirmary, Wigan; Lectr in Community Nursing, Manchester Univ., 1968–71; Asst, subseq. Principal Regional Nursing Officer, Liverpool Regional Hosp. Bd, 1971–73; Regional Nursing Officer, Mersey RHA, 1973–77; Registrar, GNC for England and Wales, 1977–81; Registrar and Chief Exec., UKCC, 1981–87. Member: Standing Nursing and Midwifery Adv. Cttee, 1977–90; Wigan and Leigh HA, 1974–77; West Berks HA, 1982–93; Non-exec. Dir, Berks HA, 1993–96; Chm., W Berks Res. Ethics Cttee, 1992–96. Mem. Council, 1988–2000, Mem. Court, 2001–, Reading Univ. FRCN 1996. Hon. Fellow, Univ. of Central Lancashire, 1998. CStJ 1987. *Recreations:* travel, theatre. *Address:* 14 Conifer Drive, Long Lane, Tilehurst, Berks RG31 6YU. *T:* (0118) 941 2082.

STOREY, Paul Mark; QC 2001; a Recorder, since 2000; *b* 12 March 1957; *s* of George Daniel Storey and Denise Edna Storey (*née* Baker); *m* 1st, 1977, Margaret Jane Aucott (marr. diss. 1994); two *d*; 2nd, 1994, Alexa Roseann Rea; two *s*. *Educ:* Notre Dame Sch., Lingfield; John Fisher Sch., Purley; N London Poly.; Newcastle Poly.; UCL; Inns of Court Law Sch.; BA Hons; CPE. Called to the Bar, Lincoln's Inn, 1982; in practice as barrister, 1983–; Asst Recorder, 1999–2000. *Publications:* contrib. various articles to Family Law. *Recreations:* football, cycling, Rugby, cricket, my family. *Address:* (chambers) 29 Bedford Row, WC1R 4HE.

STOREY, Hon. Sir Richard, 2nd Bt *cr* 1960; CBE 1996; DL; Chairman of Portsmouth and Sunderland Newspapers plc, 1973–98 (Director, 1962–99); *b* 23 Jan. 1937; *s* of Baron Buckton (Life Peer) and Elisabeth (*d* 1951), *d* of late Brig.-Gen. W. J. Woodcock, DSO; *S* to baronetcy of father, 1978; *m* 1961, Virginia Anne, 3rd *d* of Sir Kenelm Cayley, 10th Bt; one *s* two *d*. *Educ:* Winchester; Trinity Coll., Cambridge (BA, LLB). National service commission, RNVR, 1956. Called to the Bar, Inner Temple, 1962. Administers agricultural land and woodland in Yorkshire. Director: One Stop Community Stores Ltd, 1971–98; Reuters Hldgs PLC, 1986–92; Press Association Ltd, 1986–95 (Chm., 1991–95); Fleming Enterprise Investment Trust PLC, 1989– (Chm., 1996–); Foreign & Colonial Smaller Cos PLC, 1993–; Sunderland PLC, 1996–; eFinancialNews Ltd, 2000–. Chm., York Health Services Trust, 1991–97. Member: Nat. Council and Exec., CLA, 1980–84, Yorks Exec., CLA (Chm., 1974–76); Employment Policy Cttee, CBI, 1984–88, CBI Regl Council, Yorks and Humberside, 1974–76; Press Council, 1980–86; Pres., Newspaper Soc., 1990–91 (Mem. Council, 1980–98). Chm., Sir Harold Hillier Arboretum Management Cttee, 1989–; Dir, Castle Howard Arboretum Trust, 1997–; Trustee, Royal Botanic Gardens Kew Foundn, 1990–. Mem. Council: INCA-FIEJ Res. Assoc., 1983–88; European Newspaper Publishers' Assoc., 1991–96. Contested (C): Don Valley, 1966; Huddersfield W, 1970. High Sheriff, 1992–93, DL 1998, N Yorks. Hon. Fellow, Univ. of Portsmouth, 1989. Hon. DLitt Sunderland Poly., 1992. *Recreations:* sport, dendrology. *Heir: s* Kenelm Storey [*b* 4 Jan. 1963; *m* 2001, Karen, *d* of Keith Prothero]. *Address:* Settrington House, Malton, Yorks YO17 8NP. *T:* (01944) 768200; 11 Zetland House, Marloes Road, W8 5LB. *T:* (020) 7937 8823; 18 Lexham Mews, W8 5LB. *T:* (020) 7937 2888.

STORIE-PUGH, Col Peter David, CBE 1981 (MBE 1945); MC 1940; TD 1945 and 3 clasps; DL; Lecturer, University of Cambridge, 1953–82; Fellow of Wolfson College, Cambridge, since 1967; *b* 1 Nov. 1919; *s* of late Prof. Leslie Pugh, CBE, BSc, MA, FRCVS and Paula Storie; *m* 1st, 1946, Alison (marr. diss. 1971), *d* of late Sir Oliver Lyle, OBE; one *s* two *d*; 2nd, 1971, Leslie Helen, *d* of Earl Striegel; three *s* one *d*. *Educ:* Malvern; Queens' Coll., Cambridge (Hon. Foundn Scholar; MA, PhD); Royal Veterinary Coll., Univ. of London (FRCVS). CChem, FRSC. Served War of 1939–45, Queen's Own Royal W Kent Regt (escaped from Spangenberg and Colditz); comd 1st Bn, Cambs Regt, comd 1st Bn Suffolk and Cambs Regt; Col, Dep. Comdr, 161 Inf. Bde, ACF County Comdt. Wellcome Res. Fellow, Cambridge, 1950–52. Mem. Council, RCVS, 1956–84 (Chm. Parly Cttee, 1962–67; Pres., 1977–78); President: Cambridge Soc. for Study of Comparative Medicine, 1966–67; Internat. Pig Vet. Soc., 1967–69 (Life Pres., 1969); British Veterinary Assoc., 1968–69 and 1970–71 (Hon. Life Mem., 1984; Dalrymple-Champneys Cup and Medal, 1986); Mem. Exec. Cttee, Cambridgeshire Farmers Union, 1960–65; UK delegate, EEC Vet. Liaison Cttee, 1962–75 (Pres., 1973–75); UK Rep., Fedn of Veterinarians of EEC, 1975–83 (Pres. of Fedn, 1975–79); Chm., Eurovet, 1971–73; Mem. Jt RCVS/BVA Cttee on European Vet. Affairs, 1971–92; Observer, European Liaison Gp for Agric., 1972–80; Jt Pres., 1st European Vet. Congress, Wiesbaden, 1972; Permanent Mem. EEC Adv. Vet. Cttee, 1976–82; Mem. Council, Secrétariat Européen des Professions Libérales, 1976–80; Mem. Permanent Cttee, World Vet. Assoc., 1964–75. Member: Parly and Sci. Cttee, 1962–67; Home Sec.'s Adv. Cttee (Cruelty to Animals Act, 1876), 1963–80; Nat. Agric. Centre Adv. Bd, 1966–69; Production Cttee, Meat and Livestock Commn, 1967–70; Min. of Agriculture's Farm Animal Adv. Cttee, 1970–73; Econ. and Social Cttee, EEC, 1982–90. Chm., Nat. Sheep Breeders' Assoc., 1964–68; Vice-Pres., Agric. Section, British Assoc., 1970–71. Corresp. Mem., Bund Deutscher Veterinäroffiziere, 1979–. Robert von Ostertag Medal, German Vet. Assoc., 1972. DL Cambs, 1963. *Publications:* (and ed jtly) Eurovet: an Anatomy of Veterinary Europe, 1972; Eurovet-2, 1975. *Address:* Fort Mahon, 81630 Salvagnac, France. *T:* 563335427.

STORKEY, Elaine; President, Tear Fund, since 1997; *b* 1 Oct. 1943; *d* of James and Anne Lively; *m* 1968, Alan James Storkey; three *s*. *Educ:* UCW, Aberystwyth (BA); McMaster Univ., Ontario (MA); York Univ. Tutor, Manchester Coll., Oxford, 1967–68; Res. Fellow, Univ. of Stirling, 1968–69; Tutor, then Lectr, Open Univ., 1976–90; Exec. Dir, Inst. for Contemporary Christianity, 1990–98. Visiting Professor: Calvin Coll., USA, 1980–81; Covenant Coll., Chatanooga, USA, 1981–82; Vis. Scholar, KCL, 1996–; New Coll. Schol., Univ. of NSW, 1997. Associate Ed., Third Way, 1988–. Member: Cathedrals Commn, 1992–96; Gen. Synod of C of E, 1987–; Forum for the Future, 1994–. Vice-Pres., Cheltenham & Gloucester Coll., 1995–. DD Lambeth 1998. *Publications:* What's Right with Feminism, 1986; Mary's Story, Mary's Song, 1993; The Search for Intimacy, 1995; Magnify the Lord, 1998; (with Margaret Hebblethwaite) Conversations on Christian Feminism, 1999; Men and Women: created or constructed, 2000; contrib. to Scottish Jl Theol., Gospel and Culture, The Independent. *Recreations:* broadcasting, making film documentaries. *Address:* (home) The Old School, Coton, Cambs CB3 7PL. *T:* (020) 8449 3034.

STORMER, Prof. Horst Ludwig, PhD; physicist; Professor of Physics and Applied Physics, Columbia University, since 1998; Adjunct Physics Director, Lucent Technologies (formerly AT&T Bell Laboratories), since 1997; *b* Frankfurt am Main, 6 April 1949; *s* of Karl Ludwig Stormer and Marie Stormer (*née* Ihrig); *m* 1982, Dominique A. Parchet. *Educ:* Univ. of Stuttgart (PhD 1977). AT&T Bell Laboratories: Mem., Technical Staff, 1978–83; Dept Head, 1983–92; Dir, Physical Res. Lab., 1992–97. Bell Labs Fellow, 1983. Mem., US Nat. Acad. of Scis, 1999. Buckley Prize, 1984; Otto Klung Prize, Free Univ., Berlin, 1985; Benjamin Franklin Medal, 1998; (jtly) Nobel Prize for Physics, 1998; NYC Mayor's Award for Excellence in Sci. and Technol., 2000. Officier de la Légion d'Honneur (France), 1999; Grosse Verdienstkreuz mit Stern (Germany), 1999. *Address:* Department of Physics and Department of Applied Physics, Columbia University, 704 Pupin Hall, New York, NY 10027, USA.

STORMONT, Viscount; Alexander David Mungo Murray; *b* 17 Oct. 1956; *s* and *heir* of 8th Earl of Mansfield and Mansfield, *qv*; *m* 1985, Sophia Mary Veronica, *o d* of Biden Ashbrooke, St John, Jersey; one *s* three *d*. *Educ:* Eton. *Heir: s* Master of Stormont, *qv*. *Address:* Scone Palace, Perthshire PH2 6BD.

STORMONT, Master of; Hon. William Philip David Mungo Murray; *b* 1 Nov. 1988; *s* and *heir* of Viscount Stormont, *qv*.

STORMONTH DARLING, Peter; Director, since 1967, and Chairman, since 1995, Deltec International SA (formerly Deltec Panamerica SA); *b* 29 Sept. 1932; *s* of Patrick Stormonth Darling and Edith Mary Ormston Lamb; *m* 1st, 1958, Candis Hitzig; three *d*; 2nd, 1971, Maureen O'Leary. *Educ:* Winchester; New Coll., Oxford (MA). 2nd Lieut, Black Watch, 1950–53, served Korean War; RAFVR, 1953–56. Director: S. G. Warburg & Co. Ltd, 1967–85 (Vice-Chm., 1977–85); S. G. Warburg Group plc, 1974–94; Europe Fund, 1990–2000; Scottish Equitable plc, 1992–99; Merrill Lynch UK (formerly Mercury Keystone) Investment Co., 1992–; Greenwich Associates, 1993–; Scottish and Southern Energy (formerly Scottish Hydro-Electric) plc, 1994–2000; Sagitta Asset Mgt Ltd, 1996–; Guardian Capital Gp Ltd (Canada), 1998–; Aegon (UK) plc, 1999–; Howard de Walden Estates Ltd, 2001–; Chairman: Mercury Asset Mgt Gp, 1979–92 (Dir, 1969–98); Mercury International Investment Trust, 1990–98; Mercury European Investment (formerly Mercury Europe Privatisation) Trust, 1994–; Welbeck Land Ltd, 2001–. Dir, The UK Fund Inc., 1994–2000. Member: UN Pension Fund Investments Cttee, 1990–; Exec. (formerly Finance and Investments) Cttee, IISS, 1994–. *Publication:* City Cinderella, 1999. *Address:* Brettenham House, 1 Lancaster Place, WC2E 7EN.

See also R. A. Stormonth Darling.

STORMONTH DARLING, Robin Andrew; Chairman: Capital Opportunities (formerly Voyageur European Smaller Companies) Trust, since 1994; Dumyat Investment Trust, since 1995; Intrinsic Portfolio Fund PCC Ltd, since 2000; *b* 1 Oct. 1926; *s* of Patrick Stormonth Darling and Edith Mary Ormston Lamb; *m* 1st, 1956, Susan Marion Clifford-Turner (marr. diss. 1970); three *s* one *d*; 2nd, 1974, Harriet Heathcoat-Amory (*née* Nye) (marr. diss. 1978); 3rd, 1981, Carola Marion Brooke, *er d* of Sir Robert Erskine-Hill, 2nd Bt. *Educ:* Abberley Hall; Winchester Coll. Served Fleet Air Arm (Pilot), 1945; 9th Queen's Royal Lancers, 1946–54: ADC to GOC-in-C Scotland, 1950–52; Officer Cadet Instr, 1952–54. Alexanders Laing & Cruickshank (formerly Laing & Cruickshank), 1954–87, Chm., 1980–87; Director: Austin Motor Co., 1959; British Motor Corp., 1960–68; British Leyland, 1968–75. Chm., Tranwood Gp, subseq. Tranwood, 1987–91. Director: London Scottish Bank (formerly London Scottish Finance Corp.), 1984–92; Mercantile House Holdings, 1984–87 (non-exec. Dep. Chm., 1987); GPI Leisure Corp. (Australia), 1986–90; Ptarmigan Internat. Capital Trust, 1993–. Stock Exchange: Mem., 1956–87; Mem. Council, 1978–86; Chairman: Quotations Cttee, 1981–85; Disciplinary Appeals Cttee, 1985–90. Dep. Chm., Panel on Take-Overs and Mergers, 1985–87; Mem., Securities and Investments Bd, 1985–87. Hon. Consul of Mexico at Edinburgh, 1993–. *Recreations:* shooting, ski-ing, flying, swimming. *Address:* Balvarran, Enochdhu, Blairgowrie, Perthshire PH10 7PA. *T:* (01250) 881248. *Clubs:* White's, MCC, Hurlingham; Perth Hunt.

See also P. Stormonth Darling.

STOTHARD, Peter Michael; Editor of The Times, since 1992; *b* 28 Feb. 1951; *s* of late Wilfred Max Stothard and of Patricia J. Stothard (*née* Savage); *m* 1980, Sally Ceris Emerson; one *s* one *d*. *Educ:* Brentwood Sch., Essex; Trinity Coll., Oxford (BA Lit. Hum.; MA; Hon. Fellow, 2000). BBC journalist, 1974–77; with Shell Internat. Petroleum, 1977–79; business and political writer, Sunday Times, 1979–80; The Times: Features Ed. and Leader writer, 1980–86; Dep. Ed., 1986–92; US Ed., 1989–92. *Recreation:* ancient and modern literature. *Address:* c/o The Times, 1 Pennington Street, E98 1TT. *T:* (020) 7782 5000. *Clubs:* Garrick, Reform.

STOTT, Sir Adrian, 4th Bt *cr* 1920; management consultant, since 1989; *b* 7 Oct. 1948; *s* of Sir Philip Sidney Stott, 3rd Bt, and Cicely Florence (*d* 1996), *o d* of Bertram Ellingham; *S* father, 1979. *Educ:* Univ. of British Columbia (BSc (Maths) 1968, MSc (Town Planning) 1974); Univ. of Waterloo, Ont (MMaths (Computer Science) 1971). Dir of Planning for a rural region of BC, 1974; formed own consulting practice, 1977; property develt, gen. management and town planning consultant, 1977–85; Manager: BC Govt Real Estate Portfolio, 1980; Islands Trust (coastal conservation and property develt control agency), 1985; Man. Dir, direct sales marketing company, 1986–88. Member: Cdn Inst. of Planners (MCIP); Assoc. for Computing Machinery. *Recreations:* music, inland waterways, computers, politics. *Heir: b* Vyvyan Philip Stott, *b* 5 Aug. 1952. *Address:* The Downs, Little Amwell, Herts SG13 7SA.

STOTT, (Charlotte) Mary, OBE 1975; journalist, retired; *b* 1907; *d* of Robert Guy Waddington and Amalie Waddington (*née* Bates); *m* 1937, Kenneth Stott (*d* 1967); one *d*. *Educ:* Wyggeston Grammar Sch., Leicester. Leicester Mail, 1925–31; Bolton Evening News, 1931–33; Co-operative Press, Manchester, editing women's and children's publications, 1933–45; News sub-editor, Manchester Evening News, 1945–50; Women's Editor, The Guardian, 1957–72. Last Pres., Women's Press Club, 1970; Chm., Fawcett Soc., 1980–82; Pres., Nat. Assoc. of Widows, 1993–95. Hon. Fellow, Manchester Polytechnic, 1972. Hon. MA: Open, 1991; Leicester, 1995; Hon. DLitt De Montfort, 1996. *Publications:* Forgetting's No Excuse, 1973, rev. edn 1989; Organization Woman, 1978; Ageing for Beginners, 1981; Before I Go …, 1985; Women Talking, 1987. *Recreations:* committees, music (especially choir singing), painting (water colours), gardening. *Address:* 4/11 Morden Road, Blackheath, SE3 0AA. *T:* (020) 8852 2901.

STOTT, Rev. John Robert Walmsley, MA Cantab; DD Lambeth; Director, London Institute for Contemporary Christianity, 1982–86, now President; Chaplain to the Queen, 1959–91, Extra Chaplain, since 1991; *b* 27 April 1921; *s* of late Sir Arnold W. Stott, KBE, physician, and late Emily Caroline Holland. *Educ:* Rugby Sch.; Trinity Coll., Cambridge; Ridley Hall, Cambridge. Curate of All Souls, Langham Place, 1945; Rector of All Souls, 1950–75 (with St Peter's, Vere Street, 1952), now Rector Emeritus. Hon. DD: Trinity Evangelical Divinity Sch., Deerfield, USA, 1971; Wycliffe Coll., Toronto, 1993; Brunel, 1997. *Publications:* Men with a Message, 1954, revd edn with Stephen Motyer, 1994; What Christ Thinks of the Church, 1958; Basic Christianity, 1958; Your Confirmation, 1958, 2nd edn 1991; Fundamentalism and Evangelism, 1959; The Preacher's Portrait, 1961; Confess Your Sins, 1964; The Epistles of John, 1964; Canticles and Selected Psalms, 1966; Men Made New, 1966; Our Guilty Silence, 1967; The Message of Galatians, 1968; One People, 1969; Christ the Controversialist, 1970; Understanding the Bible, 1972; Guard the Gospel, 1973; Balanced Christianity, 1975; Christian Mission in the Modern World, 1975; Baptism and Fullness, 1975; The Lausanne Covenant, 1975; Christian Counter-Culture, 1978; Focus on Christ, 1979, 2nd edn as Life in Christ, 1991; God's New Society, 1979; I Believe in Preaching, 1982; The Bible Book for Today, 1982; Issues Facing Christians Today, 1984, 3rd edn 1999; The Authentic Jesus, 1985; The Cross of Christ, 1986; (with David Edwards) Essentials, 1988; The Message of Acts, 1990; The Message of I and II Thessalonians, 1991; The Contemporary Christian, 1992; The Message of Romans, 1994; The Message of Timothy and Titus, 1996; Evangelical Truth, 1999; The Birds Our Teachers: Biblical lessons from a lifelong bird-watcher, 1999. *Recreations:* bird watching and photography. *Address:* 13 Bridford Mews, Devonshire Street, W1W 5BJ.

STOTT, Kathryn Linda; pianist; *b* 10 Dec. 1958; *d* of Desmond Stott and Elsie Stott (*née* Cheetham); *m* 1st, 1979, Michael Ardron (marr. diss. 1983); 2nd, 1983, John Elliott (marr. diss. 1997); one *d. Educ:* Yehudi Menuhin Sch.; Royal Coll. of Music, London (ARCM). Regular duo partner of Yo-Yo Ma; has worked with all major British orchs; recitals throughout UK; tours of Europe, USA and Far East; world premières of concertos by George Lloyd, Michael Nyman and Sir Peter Maxwell Davies. Artistic Director: Fauré and the French Connection, 1995; Piano 2000, Manchester, 2000. Numerous recordings. Chevalier de l'Ordre des Arts et des Lettres (France), 1996. *Recreations:* horse riding, travel, Spanish language. *Address:* c/o Jane Ward, 38 Townfield, Rickmansworth, Herts WD3 2DD. *T:* and *Fax:* (01923) 493903.

STOTT, Mary; *see* Stott, C. M.

STOTT, Richard Keith; journalist; Political and Current Affairs Columnist, Sunday Mirror, since 2001; *b* 17 Aug. 1943; *s* of late Fred B. Stott and Bertha Stott; *m* 1970, Penny, *yr d* of Air Vice-Marshal Sir Colin Scragg, KBE, CB, AFC; one *s* two *d. Educ:* Clifton College, Bristol. Bucks Herald, 1963–65; Ferrari Press Agency, 1965–68; Daily Mirror: Reporter, 1968–79; Features Editor, 1979–81; Asst Editor, 1981; Editor: Sunday People, 1984; Daily Mirror, 1985–89; The People, 1990–91; Daily Mirror, 1991–92; Today, 1993–95; columnist: News of the World, 1997–2001; Microsoft Network, 1997–2001. Dir, People Publishing Co., 1990–91. Reporter of the Year, British Press Awards, 1977; Editor of the Year, What the Papers Say Awards, 1993. *Recreations:* theatre, reading. *Address:* 20 Albany Park Road, Kingston-upon-Thames, Surrey KT2 5SW.

STOUGHTON-HARRIS, Anthony Geoffrey, CBE 1989; DL; FCA; Deputy Chairman, Nationwide Building Society, 1990–95; *b* 5 June 1932; *s* of Geoffrey Stoughton-Harris and Kathleen Mary (*née* Baker Brown); *m* 1959, Elizabeth Thackery (*née* White); one *s* two *d. Educ:* Sherborne Sch., Dorset. FCA 1956. Partner, Norton Keen & Co., chartered accountants, 1958–74; Man. Dir, London & South of England Building Soc., 1975; Chief Gen. Manager, Anglia Building Soc., 1983–87; Vice-Chm., Nationwide Anglia Building Soc., 1987–90. Chm., Electronic Funds Transfer Ltd, 1984–89; Director: Southern Electric, 1981–98 (Dep. Chm., 1993–98); Guardian Royal Exchange, 1990–95. Gen. Comr, Inland Revenue, 1982–2000. Part-time Treasurer, W Herts Main Drainage Authority, 1964–70. Chairman: BSA, 1987–89; Northants TEC, 1990–95; Northants Chamber of Commerce, Trng and Enterprise, 1995–96. FCBSI. DL 1994, High Sheriff, 2000, Northants. *Recreations:* sport, gardening, DIY. *Address:* Old Farm House, Blackmile Lane, Grendon, Northants NN7 1JR. *T:* (01933) 664235.

STOURTON, family name of **Baron Mowbray, Segrave and Stourton**.

STOURTON, Edward John Ivo; Presenter, BBC News and Current Affairs programmes, since 1993; *b* 24 Nov. 1957; *s* of Nigel John Ivo Stourton, OBE, and Rosemary Jennifer Rushworth Stourton (*née* Abbott), JP; *m* 1980, Margaret, *e d* of Sir James Napier Finnie McEwen, 2nd Bt; two *s* one *d. Educ:* Ampleforth; Trinity Coll., Cambridge (MA; Pres., Cambridge Union, Lent, 1979). Joined ITN, 1979; founder mem., Channel 4 News, 1982, Washington Corresp., 1986–88; Paris Corresp., BBC TV, 1988–90; Diplomatic Ed., ITN, 1990–93; BBC Television: Presenter: One O'Clock News, 1993–99; Call Ed Stourton, 1997–98; Reporter: Panorama; former Reporter, Correspondent; Presenter, Today, BBC Radio 4, 1999–; has written and presented series for BBC2 and Radio 4, incl. Asia Gold (Sony Gold Award for Current Affairs, 1997). KM 1984. *Publication:* Absolute Truth: the Catholic Church in the world today, 1998. *Recreations:* conversation, buying books, croquet, racing demon. *Address:* BBC Television Centre, Wood Lane, W12 7RJ. *T:* (020) 8743 8000. *Clubs:* Hurlingham, Travellers.

STOUT, Prof. David Ker; Director, Centre for Business Strategy, London Business School, 1992–98; *b* Bangor, N Wales, 27 Jan. 1932; *s* of late Prof. Alan Ker Stout, FAHA, FASSA and of Evelyn Roberts; *m* 1956, Margaret Sugden; two *s* two *d. Educ:* Sydney High Sch.; Sydney Univ., NSW (BA 1st Cl. English Lit, Econs, and University Medal in Econs, 1953); NSW Rhodes Scholar 1954; Magdalen Coll., Oxford; George Webb Medley Jun. Scholar 1955, Sen. Scholar 1956; PPE 1st Cl. 1956; Nuffield Coll., Oxford (Studentship 1956); Magdalen Prize Fellow by Examination, 1958–59. Fellow and Lectr in Econs, University Coll., Oxford, 1959–76; Economic Dir, NEDO, 1971–72 and 1976–80; Tyler Prof. of Econs, Leicester Univ., 1980–82; Head of Econs, Unilever, 1982–92. Adviser on tax structure to Syrian Govt, 1965, and New Hebrides Condominium, 1966; Sen. Econ. Adviser to Monopolies Commn, 1969; Consultant on VAT, Nat. Bureau of Econ. Res., NY, 1970; Adviser to Australian Govt on Prices Justification, 1973, and on Wage Indexation, 1975–76. Member: Exec. Cttee, NIESR, 1974–82, 1992–98; EEC Expert Gp on Community Planning, 1976–78, and on Adjustment Policy, 1979–80; ESRC, 1989–92 (Mem., Econ. Affairs Cttee, 1980–86; Chm., Industry, Economics and Envmt Cttee, 1989–92); Manufacturing Foresight Panel, OST, 1994–98; Technology Interaction Bd, BBSRC, 1994–96; Bd of Trustees, Strategic Planning Inst., Cambridge, Mass, 1983–87. Editor, Business Strategy Review, 1994–98. *Publications:* papers on taxation policy, VAT, investment, incomes policy, trade performance, indust. policy, de-industrialisation, and European planning. *Recreations:* music, chess, bivalves. *T:* (01732) 780904; *e-mail:* davidkerstout@aol.com.

STOUT, Prof. Robert William, MD, DSc; FRCP, FRCPE, FRCPI, FRCPGlas, FMedSci; Professor of Geriatric Medicine, Queen's University, Belfast, since 1976; *b* 6 March 1942; *s* of William Ferguson Stout, *qv* and Muriel Stout (*née* Kilner); *m* 1969, Helena Patricia Willis; two *s* one *d. Educ:* Campbell Coll., Belfast (schol.); Queen's Univ., Belfast (MD, DSc). FRCP 1979; FRCPE 1988; FRCPI 1989; FRCPSGlas 1994. MRC Eli Lilly Foreign Educnl Fellow, Univ. of Washington Sch. of Medicine, Seattle, 1971–73; Queen's University, Belfast: BHF Sen. Res. Fellow, 1974; Sen. Lectr in Medicine, 1975; Dean, Faculty of Medicine, 1991–96; Provost for Medicine and Health Scis., 1993–98; Dean, Faculty of Medicine and Health Scis, 1998–2001. Mem., GMC, 1991– (Member: Standards Cttee, 1994–95; Educn Cttee, 1995–98, 1999–). Member, Health & Social Services Boards: Southern, 1982–91; Eastern, 1993–; Chm. Specialty Adv. Cttee on Geriatric Medicine, Jt Cttee on Higher Medical Trng, 1986–92; Mem., Royal Commn on Long-Term Care for the Elderly, 1997–99. Vice-Pres., Age Concern Northern Ireland, 1988– (Chm., 1985–88). NI Regl Advr, RCP, 1984–90. Mem., Bd of Govs, Methodist Coll., Belfast, 1983– (Chm., 1994–97); Governor, Research in Ageing, 1989 (Mem., Med. Adv. Cttee, 1982–89). Visiting Professor: Univ. of Auckland, NZ, 1990; Hong Kong Geriatric Soc., 1993. Founder FMedSci 1998. *Publications:* Hormones and Atherosclerosis, 1982; Arterial Disease in the Elderly, 1984; Diabetes and Atherosclerosis, 1992; articles in scientific jls on geriatric medicine and related topics. *Recreations:* golf, gardening, reading. *Address:* 3 Larch Hill Drive, Craigavad, Co. Down BT18 0JS. *T:* (028) 9042 2253. *Clubs:* Royal Society of Medicine; Royal Belfast Golf.

STOUT, William Ferguson, CB 1964; Security Adviser to Government of Northern Ireland, 1971–72, retired; *b* Holywood, Co. Down, 22 Feb. 1907; *s* of late Robert and Amelia Stout; *m* 1938, Muriel Kilner; one *s* one *d. Educ:* Sullivan Upper Sch., Holywood; Queen's Univ., Belfast. Ministry of Home Affairs: Principal, 1943; Asst Sec., 1954; Senior Asst Sec., 1959; Permanent Sec., 1961–64; Permanent Secretary: Min. of Health and Local Govt, 1964; Min. of Development, 1965–71. *Recreation:* golf.
See also R. W. Stout.

STOUTE, Sir Michael (Ronald), Kt 1998; race horse trainer, since 1972; *b* 22 Oct. 1945; *m*; one *s* one *d. Educ:* Harrison College, Barbados. Leading flat racing trainer, 1981, 1986, 1989, 1994, 1997 and 2000; leading international trainer, 1986, 1996 and 1997; trained: Derby winners, Shergar, 1981, Shahrastani, 1986; Irish Derby winners, Shergar, 1981, Shareef Dancer, 1983, Shahrastani, 1986; 1000 Guineas winner, Musical Bliss, 1989; Irish 1000 Guineas winner, Sonic Lady, 1986; 2000 Guineas Winners, Shadeed, 1985, Doyoun, 1988, Entrepreneur, 1997, King's Best, 2000, Golan, 2001; Irish 2000 Guineas winner, Shaadi, 1989; Oaks winners, Fair Salinia, 1978, Unite, 1987; Irish Oaks winners, Fair Salinia, 1978, Colorspin, 1986, Unite, 1987, Melodist, 1988, Pure Grain, 1995, Petrushka, 2000; Breeders Cup Turf winners, Pilsudski, 1996, Kalanisi, 2000; Japan Cup winner, Singspiel, 1996, Pilsudski, 1997; Dubai World Cup winner, Singspiel, 1997. *Recreations:* cricket, golf. *Address:* Freemason Lodge, Bury Road, Newmarket, Suffolk CB8 7BT. *T:* (01638) 663801.

STOW, Archdeacon of; *see* Ellis, Ven. T. W.

STOW, Sir Christopher P.; *see* Philipson-Stow.

STOW, Graham Harold; Group Chief Executive, Britannia Building Society, since 1999; *b* 29 April 1944; *s* of Joseph Stow and Carrie Stow (*née* Meakin); *m* 1st, 1966, Susan Goldingay (marr. diss. 1983); three *s*; 2nd, 1984, Christine Probert. *Educ:* Liverpool Collegiate Sch. Retail Ops, then Divl Dir, Personnel, Littlewoods Orgn, 1962–82; Dir, Marlar Internat., 1982–84; ASDA Group plc: Personnel Dir, ASDA Stores, 1984–87; Gp Human Resources Dir, 1987–88; Man. Dir, 1988–89, Chief Exec., 1989–91, ASDA Stores; Director: George Davies Corp., 1991–92; Sandpiper Consultants, 1992; Exec. Vice Pres., Minet Gp, 1992–96; Retail Ops Dir, 1996–98, Dep. Gp Chief Exec., 1998–99, Britannia Building Soc. Non-exec. Dir, Northern Racing, 2001–. Dep. Chm., Building Socs Assoc., 2001–. Chm., Staffordshire Moorlands Local Agenda 21 Cttee, 1999–2001; Ind. Bd Mem., DSS, 2000–01. Chm. of Trustees, Second World War Experience Centre, 1998–. Pres., Inst. of Home Econs, 1990–91; Mem., Council and Court, Leeds Univ., 1991–94; Vice Chm. of Govs, Harrogate GS, 1989–91; Governor: Leeds GS, 1989–94; Staffordshire Univ., 1999–; Denstone Coll., 1999–2001. Mem., HAC. FCIPD (FIPD 1986); FRSA 1990. Liveryman, Co. of Curriers, 1994–. *Recreation:* military history. *Address:* (office) Britannia House, Leek, Staffs ST13 5RG. *T:* (01538) 399399. *Club:* Special Forces.

STOW, (Julian) Randolph; writer; *b* Geraldton, W Australia, 28 Nov. 1935; *s* of Cedric Ernest Stow, barrister and Mary Stow (*née* Sewell). *Educ:* Guildford Grammar Sch., W Australia; Univ. of Western Australia. Lecturer in English Literature: Univ. of Leeds, 1962; Univ. of Western Australia, 1963–64; Harkness Fellow, United States, 1964–66; Lectr in English and Commonwealth Lit., Univ. of Leeds, 1968–69. Miles Franklin Award, 1958; Britannica Australia Award, 1966; Patrick White Award, 1979. *Publications: poems:* Outrider, 1962; A Counterfeit Silence, 1969; *novels:* To The Islands, 1958, rev. edn 1981; Tourmaline, 1963; The Merry-go-round in the Sea, 1965; Visitants, 1979; The Girl Green as Elderflower, 1980; The Suburbs of Hell, 1984; *music theatre* (with Peter Maxwell Davies): Eight Songs for a Mad King, 1969; Miss Donnithorne's Maggot, 1974; *for children:* Midnite, 1967. *Address:* c/o Sheil Land Associates Ltd, 43 Doughty Street, WC1N 2LF.

STOW, Ralph Conyers, CBE 1981; FCIS, FCIB; President and Chairman, Cheltenham & Gloucester Building Society, 1982–87 (Managing Director, 1973–82); *b* 19 Dec. 1916; *s* of Albert Conyers Stow and Mabel Louise Bourlet; *m* 1943, Eleanor Joyce Appleby; one *s* one *d. Educ:* Woodhouse Sch., Finchley. FCIS 1959; FBS 1952. Supt of Branches, Temperance Permanent Bldg Soc., 1950, Asst Manager 1958; Gen. Man. and Sec., Cheltenham & Gloucester Bldg Soc., 1962, Dir 1967. Pres., Bldg Socs Inst., 1971–72; Chm., Midland Assoc. of Bldg Socs, 1973–74; Chm., Bldg Socs Assoc., 1977–79. Mem., Glos AHA, 1973–81; Chm., Cheltenham DHA, 1981–88. *Recreations:* photography, oil painting. *Club:* Rotary (Cheltenham).

STOW, Randolph; *see* Stow, J. R.

STOW, Timothy Montague Fenwick; QC 1989; **His Honour Judge Stow;** a Circuit Judge, since 2000; *b* 31 Jan. 1943; *s* of late Geoffrey Montague Fenwick Stow and Joan Fortescue Stow (*née* Flannery); *m* 1965, Alisoun Mary Francis Homberger; one *s* one *d. Educ:* Eton Coll. Called to the Bar, Gray's Inn, 1965, Bencher, 1998; became a tenant in common law chambers of David Croom-Johnson, QC (later Lord Justice Croom-Johnson), 1966; Hd of Chambers, 1998; a Recorder, 1989–2000. *Recreations:* swimming, squash, tennis, foreign travel, music, looking after their country property. *Address:* c/o 12 King's Bench Walk, Temple, EC4Y 7EL. *T:* (020) 7583 0811.

STOW, William Llewelyn; UK Deputy Permanent Representative to the European Union, since 1999; *b* 11 Jan. 1948; *s* of Alfred Frank and Elizabeth Mary Stow; *m* 1976, Rosemary Ellen Burrows; two *s. Educ:* Eastbourne Grammar Sch.; Churchill Coll., Cambridge (MA). Joined DTI, 1971; seconded to FCO, 1980–83 (UK Delegn to OECD) and 1985–88 (UK Perm. Repn to EC, Brussels); Internal European Policy, 1988–91; Financial and Resource Management, 1991–94; Hd, EC and Trade Policy Div., 1994–96; Dep. Dir-Gen., Trade Policy and Europe, 1996–98; Dir, Employment Relns, 1998. *Recreations:* hill and coastal walking, bird-watching, cricket, reading. *Address:* UK Permanent Representation to the European Union, 10 Avenue d'Auderghem, 1040 Brussels, Belgium. *Club:* Mandarins Cricket.

STOWE, Sir Kenneth (Ronald), GCB 1986 (KCB 1980; CB 1977); CVO 1979; Chairman, Working Group of voluntary-community sector on compact with Labour Goverment, since 1997; *b* 17 July 1927; *er s* of Arthur and Emily Stowe; *m* 1949, Joan Frances Cullen (*d* 1995); two *s* one *d*. *Educ:* County High Sch., Dagenham; Exeter Coll., Oxford (MA; Hon. Fellow, 1989). Asst Principal, Nat. Assistance Board, 1951; Principal, 1956; seconded UN Secretariat, New York, 1958; Asst Sec., 1964; Asst Under-Sec. of State, DHSS, 1970–73; Under Sec., Cabinet Office, 1973–75, Dep. Sec., 1976; Principal Private Sec. to the Prime Minister, 1975–79; Permanent Under Sec. of State, NI Office, 1979–81; Perm. Sec., DHSS, 1981–87. Member: President's Commn to review Public Service, Zimbabwe, 1987–89; Pres. Mandela's Commn on Public Service of SA, 1996–98. Mem., Bd of Dirs, Commonwealth Assoc. for Public Admin and Management, 1994–98, now Emeritus Dir (Chm., Founding Conf., PEI, 1994); Advr on admin. reform to HM Govt, UN Develt Prog., and Commonwealth Secretariat. Chairman: Inst. of Cancer Res., 1987–97; Thrombosis Res. Inst., 1998–2000; Dir, Royal Marsden Hosp. NHS Trust, 1994–97; Mem. Council, CRC, 1987–. Trustee: CHASE Children's Hospice, 1999–; Carnegie UK Trust, 1988–99; Chairman: Carnegie Inquiry into The Third Age, 1989–93; Carnegie Young People Project, 1996–99. *Recreations:* listening and thinking. *Club:* Athenæum.

STOWELL, Dr Michael James, FRS 1984; Research Director, Alcan International Ltd, 1990–94 (Principal Consulting Scientist, 1989–90); *b* 10 July 1935; *s* of Albert James Stowell and Kathleen Maud (*née* Poole); *m* 1st, 1962, Rosemary Allen (marr. diss. 1990); one *s* one *d*; 2nd, 1995, Kerry June Brice (*née* Kern) (*d* 1998). *Educ:* St Julian's High Sch., Newport; Bristol Univ. (BSc 1957, PhD 1961). Res. Scientist and Gp Leader, Tube Investments Research Labs, 1960–78; Research Manager, Materials Dept, TI Research, 1978–88. Post-doctoral Res. Fellow, Ohio State Univ., 1962–63; Res. Fellow, Univ. of Minnesota, 1970. L. B. Pfeil Medal, Metals Soc., 1976; Sir Robert Hadfield Medal, Metals Soc., 1981. *Publications:* papers on electron microscopy, epitaxy, nucleation theory, superplasticity and physical metallurgy, in various jls. *Recreation:* music. *Address:* 1 Chalklands, Saffron Walden, Essex CB10 2ER. *T:* and *Fax:* (01799) 526486; *e-mail:* mjs@mezzo.demon.co.uk.

STOYLE, Roger John B.; *see* Blin-Stoyle.

STRABOLGI, 11th Baron *cr* 1318, of England; **David Montague de Burgh Kenworthy;** a Deputy Speaker and Deputy Chairman of Committees, House of Lords, since 1986; an Extra Lord in Waiting to the Queen, since 1998; *b* 1 Nov. 1914; *e s* of 10th Baron Strabolgi and Doris Whitley (*d* 1988), *o c* of late Sir Frederick Whitley-Thomson, MP; *S* father, 1953; a co-heir to Baronies of Cobham and Burgh; *m* 1961, Doreen Margaret, *e d* of late Alexander Morgan, Ashton-under-Lyne, and Emma Morgan (*née* Mellor). *Educ:* Gresham's School; Chelsea Sch. of Art; Académie Scandinave, Paris. Served with HM Forces, BEF, 1939–40; MEF, 1940–45, as Lt-Col RAOC. Mem. Parly Delegations to USSR, 1954, SHAPE, 1955, and France, 1981, 1983 and 1985; PPS to Minister of State, Home Office, 1968–69; PPS to Leader of the House of Lords and Lord Privy Seal, 1969–70; Asst Opposition Whip, and spokesman on the Arts, House of Lords, 1970–74; Captain of the Queen's Bodyguard of the Yeomen of the Guard (Dep. Govt Chief Whip), and Govt spokesman on Energy and Agriculture, 1974–79; Opposition spokesman on arts and libraries, 1979–85. Member: Jt Cttee on Consolidation Bills, 1986–; Select Cttee for Privileges, 1987–; Private Bills Cttee, 1987–96; Ecclesiastical Jt Cttee, 1991–; Select Cttee on Procedure, 1993–96, 1998–2001; Franco-British Parly Relations Cttee (Hon. Treas., 1991–96); Vice Pres., All-Pty Arts and Amenities Gp; elected Mem., H of L, 1999. Pres., Franco-British Soc.; Member: British Sect., Franco-British Council, 1981–98; Council, Alliance Française in GB, 1972–97. Dir, Bolton Building Soc., 1958–74, 1979–87 (Dep. Chm., 1983, Chm., 1986–87). Hon. Life Mem., RPO, 1977. Freeman, City of London, 1960. Officier de la Légion d'Honneur, 1981. *Recreation:* the arts. *Heir-pres: nephew* Andrew David Whitley Kenworthy; *b* 11 Feb. 1967. *Address:* House of Lords, SW1A 0PW. *Club:* Reform.

See also Sir Harold Hood, Bt.

STRACEY, Sir John (Simon), 9th Bt *cr* 1818; *b* 30 Nov. 1938; *s* of Captain Algernon Augustus Henry Stracey (2nd *s* of 6th Bt) (*d* 1940) and Olive Beryl (*d* 1972), *d* of late Major Charles Robert Eustace Radclyffe; *S* cousin, 1971; *m* 1968, Martha Maria, *d* of late Johann Egger; two *d*. *Heir: cousin* Henry Mounteney Stracey [*b* 24 April 1920; *m* 1st, 1943, Susanna, *d* of Adair Tracey; one *d*; 2nd, 1950, Lysbeth, *o d* of Charles Ashford, NZ; one *s* one *d*; 3rd, 1961, Jeltje, *y d* of Scholte de Boer]. *Address:* Holbeam Wood Cottage, Wallcrouch, Wadhurst, East Sussex TN5 7JT. *T:* and *Fax:* (01580) 201061.

STRACHAN, Alan Lockhart Thomson; theatre director; *b* 3 Sept. 1946; *s* of Roualeyn Robert Scott Strachan and Ellen Strachan (*née* Graham); *m* 1977, Jennifer Piercey-Thompson. *Educ:* Morgan Acad., Dundee; St Andrews Univ. (MA); Merton Coll., Oxford (B.Litt). Associate Dir, Mermaid Theatre, 1970–75; Artistic Director: Greenwich Th., 1978–88; Theatre of Comedy Co., 1991–97; Churchill Theatre, Bromley, 1995–97. *Productions directed include: Mermaid:* The Watched Pot, 1970; John Bull's Other Island, The Old Boys, 1971; (co-deviser) Cowardy Custard, 1972; Misalliance, 1973; Children, (co-deviser and dir) Cole, 1974; *Greenwich:* An Audience Called Edouard, 1978; The Play's the Thing, I Sent a Letter to my Love, 1979; Private Lives (transf. Duchess), Time and the Conways, 1980; Present Laughter (transf. Vaudeville), The Golden Age, The Doctor's Dilemma, 1981; Design for Living (transf. Globe), The Paranormalist, French Without Tears, 1982; The Dining Room, An Inspector Calls, A Streetcar Named Desire, 1983 (transf. Mermaid, 1984); The Glass Menagerie, Biography, 1985; One of Us, Relatively Speaking, For King and Country, 1986; The Viewing, The Perfect Party, 1987; How the Other Half Loves (transf. Duke of York's), 1988; *freelance:* Family and a Fortune, Apollo, 1975; (deviser and dir) Shakespeare's People, world tours, 1975–78; Confusions, Apollo, 1976; (also jt author) Yahoo, Queen's, 1976; Just Between Ourselves, Queen's, 1977; The Immortal Haydon, Mermaid, 1977 (transf. Greenwich, 1978); Bedroom Farce, Amsterdam, 1978; Noël and Gertie, King's Head, 1983, Comedy, 1989; (replacement cast) Woman in Mind, Vaudeville, 1987; The Deep Blue Sea, Haymarket, 1988; Re: Joyce!, Fortune, 1988 (transf. Vaudeville, 1989; USA, 1990), Vaudeville, 1991; (replacement cast) Henceforward …, Vaudeville, 1989; June Moon, Scarborough, 1989, Hampstead, transf. Vaudeville, 1992; Toekomstmuziek, Amsterdam, 1989; Alphabetical Order, Scarborough, 1990; (replacement cast) Man of the Moment, Globe, 1990; Other People's Money, Lyric, 1990; Taking Steps, NY, 1991; London Assurance, Dublin, 1993; Make Way for Lucia, Bromley and tour, 1995; Switchback, Bromley and tour, 1996; Høfeber, Copenhagen, 1996; All Things Considered, Scarborough, 1996, Hampstead, 1997; Loot, W Yorks Playhouse, 1996; Live and Kidding, Duchess, 1997; Mrs Warren's Profession, Guildford and tour, 1997; Hooikoorts, Amsterdam, 1997; New Edna—The Spectacle!, Haymarket, 1998; Troilus and Cressida, Regent's Park, 1998; How the Other Half Loves, Oxford Playhouse and tour, 1998; The Merry Wives of Windsor, Regent's Park, 1999; Private Lives, Far East tour, 1999; Hobson's Choice, and Larkin with Women, Scarborough, 1999; A Midsummer Night's Dream, Regent's Park, 2000, 2001; Harvey, Singapore, 2000; The Real Thing, Bristol Old Vic and tour, 2001. *Producer/co-Producer:* Out of Order, tour, 1991; The Pocket Dream, Albery, 1992; Six Degrees of Separation, Royal Court, transf. Comedy, 1992; Hay Fever (also dir), Albery, 1992; Happy Families, tour, 1993; Hysteria, Royal Court, 1993; Under Their Hats (also devised), King's Head, 1994; The Prime of Miss Jean Brodie (also dir.), Strand, 1994; (exec. prod.) Love on a Branch Line, BBC1, 1994. Frequent broadcasts. *Publications:* contribs to periodicals and newspapers. *Recreations:* music, tennis, travelling. *Address:* c/o MLR Ltd, Douglas House, 16–18 Douglas Street, SW1P 4PB. *T:* (020) 7834 4646. *Club:* Garrick.

STRACHAN, Alexander William Bruce, OBE 1971; HM Diplomatic Service, retired; *b* 2 July 1917; *s* of William Fyfe and Winifred Orchar Strachan; *m* 1940, Rebecca Prince MacFarlane; one *s* one *d*. *Educ:* Daniel Stewart's Coll., Edinburgh; Allen Glen's High Sch., Glasgow. Served Army, 1939–46 (dispatches). GPO, 1935; Asst Postal Controller, 1949–64; Postal Adviser to Iraq Govt, 1964–66; First Sec., FCO, 1967–68; Jordan, 1968–72; Addis Ababa, 1972–73; Consul General, Lahore, 1973–74; Counsellor (Economic and Commercial) and Consul General, Islamabad, 1975–77. Order of Istiqlal, Hashemite Kingdom of Jordan, 1971.

STRACHAN, Major Benjamin Leckie, CMG 1978; HM Diplomatic Service, retired; Special Adviser (Middle East), Foreign and Commonwealth Office, 1990–91; *b* 4 Jan. 1924; *e s* of late Dr C. G. Strachan, MC FRCPE and Annie Primrose (*née* Leckie); *m* 1958, Lize Lund; three *s* and one step *s* one step *d*. *Educ:* Rossall Sch. (Scholar); RMCS. Royal Dragoons, 1944; France and Germany Campaign, 1944–45 (despatches); 4th QO Hussars, Malayan Campaign, 1948–51; Middle East Centre for Arab Studies, 1952–53; GSO2, HQ British Troops Egypt, 1954–55; Technical Staff Course, RMCS, 1956–58; 10th Royal Hussars, 1959–61; GSO2, WO, 1961; retd from Army and joined Foreign (subseq. Diplomatic) Service, 1961; 1st Sec., FO, 1961–62; Information Adviser to Governor of Aden, 1962–63; FO, 1964–66; Commercial Sec., Kuwait, 1966–69; Counsellor, Amman, 1969–71; Trade Comr, Toronto, 1971–74; Consul General, Vancouver, 1974–76; Ambassador to Yemen Arab Republic, 1977–78, and to Republic of Jibuti (non-resident), 1978, to the Lebanon, 1978–81, to Algeria, 1981–84. Principal, Mill of Strachan Language Inst., 1984–89. Vice Chm., Kincardine and Deeside Lib Dems, 1993–95; Chm., W Aberdeenshire and Kincardine Lib Dems, 1995; Mem. Policy Cttee, Scottish Lib Dems, 1998–. *Recreations:* crofting, writing. *Address:* Mill of Strachan, Strachan, Kincardineshire AB31 6NS. *T:* (01330) 850663. *Club:* Lansdowne.

STRACHAN, Crispian; *see* Strachan, J. C.

STRACHAN, Hon. Sir Curtis (Victor), Kt 1996; CVO 1985; MP; Speaker, House of Representatives, Grenada, West Indies; *b* 29 May 1926; *s* of Walter and Rosanna Strachan; *m* 1959; one *s*. *Educ:* Constantine Methodist Sch.; Grenada Boys' Secondary Sch.; Univ. of W Indies. Public Officer, then Permt Sec., later Clerk of Parlt, Grenada. *Publications:* Mainly for Parliamentary Freshmen; Assisting the New Member. *Recreations:* tennis, swimming. *Address:* Bloomsbury, PO Box 681, 5 Tanteen Terrace, Grenada, West Indies. *T:* (home) 4402687; (office) 4402684.

STRACHAN, Douglas Frederick; Vice-Chairman, Cheltenham & Gloucester plc, since 1995 (Director, since 1995); *b* 26 July 1933; *s* of Hon. Lord Strachan and Lady (Irene Louise) Strachan (*née* Warren); *m* 1st, 1956, Mary Scott Hardie (*d* 1976); four *s* one *d*; 2nd, 1980, Jane, *widow* of Lt-Col I. D. Corden-Lloyd, OBE, MC; three step *s*. *Educ:* Rugby Sch.; Corpus Christi Coll., Oxford (MA). Brewer, Arthur Guinness Son & Co. (Dublin) Ltd, 1956–67; Man. Dir, Cantrell & Cochrane Gp Ltd, Dublin, 1967–72; Dir, Showerings, Vine Products & Whiteways Ltd, 1972–77; Man. Dir, Allied Breweries Ltd, 1977–85; Dir, Allied-Lyons Plc, 1976–85; Dir (Chief Executive), PRO NED, 1985–89; Dir, Cheltenham & Gloucester BS, 1991–95 (Vice-Chm., 1994–95).Chm., Somerset FHSA, 1989–93; Mem., South Western RHA, 1990–93. *Recreations:* gardening, music, golf. *Address:* North Hill Farm, West Camel, Yeovil, Somerset BA22 7RF. *T:* (01935) 850404.

STRACHAN, (Douglas) Mark (Arthur); QC 1987; a Recorder, since 1990; a Deputy High Court Judge, Queen's Bench Division, since 1993; *b* 25 Sept. 1946; *s* of late William Arthur Watkin Strachan and Joyce Olive Strachan; *m* 1995, Elizabeth Vickery; one *s*. *Educ:* Orange Hill Grammar Sch., Edgware, Middx; St Catherine's Coll., Oxford (Open Exhibnr in Eng. Lit.; BCL, MA); Nancy Univ. (French Govt Schol.). Called to the Bar, Inner Temple, 1969 (Major Schol. 1969–71); Asst Recorder, 1987–90. *Publications:* contributor to Modern Law Rev. *Recreations:* son Charlie, France, Far East, antiques, paintings, food.

STRACHAN, Prof. Hew Francis Anthony, PhD; Chichele Professor of The History of War, and Fellow of All Souls College, Oxford, since 2002; *b* 1 Sept. 1949; *s* of late Michael Francis Strachan, CBE and of Iris Strachan; *m* 1st, 1971, Catherine Margaret Blackburn (marr. diss. 1980); two *d*; 2nd, 1982, Pamela Dorothy Tennant (*née* Symes); one *s*, and one step *s* one step *d*. *Educ:* Rugby; Corpus Christi Coll., Cambridge (MA, PhD 1977). Res. Fellow, Corpus Christi Coll., Cambridge, 1975–78; Sen. Lectr in War Studies, RMA, Sandhurst, 1978–79; Corpus Christi College, Cambridge: Fellow, 1979–92, Life Fellow, 1992; Admissions Tutor, 1981–88, Sen. Tutor, 1989–92; Dean of Coll., 1981–86; Prof. of Modern Hist., 1992–2001, and Dir, Scottish Centre for War Studies, 1996–2001, Glasgow Univ. Vis. Prof., Royal Norwegian Air Force Acad., 2000–. Lees Knowles Lectr, Cambridge, 1995; Thank Offering to Britain Fellow, British Acad., 1998–99. Member of Council: Lancing Coll., 1982–90; Nat. Army Mus., 1994–; Governor: Rugby Sch., 1985–; Stowe Sch., 1990–. Mem., Royal Co. of Archers, Queen's Bodyguard for Scotland, 1996–. *Publications:* British Military Uniforms 1768–1796, 1975; History of Cambridge University Officers' Training Corps, 1976; European Armies and the Conduct of War, 1983; Wellington's Legacy: the reform of the British Army, 1984; From Waterloo to Balaclava: tactics, technology and the British Army 1815–1854, 1985 (Templer Medal, Soc. for Army Histl Res.); The Politics of the British Army, 1997 (Westminster Medal, RUSI); (ed) Oxford Illustrated History of the First World War, 1998; (ed) The British Army, Manpower and Society, 2000; The First World War: vol. 1, To Arms, 2001. *Recreations:* shooting, Rugby football (now spectating). *Address:* All Souls College, Oxford OX1 4AL. *Club:* Hawks (Cambridge).

STRACHAN, James Murray; Chief Executive, Royal National Institute for Deaf People, since 1997; *b* 10 Nov. 1953; *s* of Eric Alexander Howieson Strachan and Jacqueline Georgina Strachan. *Educ:* King's Sch., Canterbury; Christ's Coll., Cambridge (MA); London Coll. of Printing; London Business Sch. Chase Manhattan Bank, 1976–77; joined Merrill Lynch, 1977, Man. Dir, 1986–89; writer and photographer, 1989–97. Rotating Chair, Disability Charities Consortium, 1997–; Co-Chair: Task Force on Social Services Provision for Deaf and Hard of Hearing People, 1998–; NHS Modernising Hearing Aid Services Gp, 1999–; Chm., Task Force on Audiology Services, 2000–; Member: Trustee and Finance Cttee, RNID, 1994–96; Ministerial Disability Rights Task Force, 1997–99; Ministerial Disability Benefits Forum, 1998–99; Bd and Audit Cttee, Ofgem; Bd, Community Fund, 2001–; Comr for Communications, Disability Rights Commn, 2000–. Mem., Adv. Gp on Diversity, NCVO; Pres., Midland Regl Assoc. for Deaf, 2001–. Trustee, SCF, 1999–. *Publications:* Madrid, 1991; numerous illustrated travel books as photographer; contrib. Sunday Times. *Recreations:* photography, film, reading, swimming. *Address:* 10B Wedderburn Road, NW3 5QG. *T:* (020) 7794 9687, *Fax:* (020) 7794 4593; *e-mail:* james_strachan@hotmail.com. *Club:* Groucho.

STRACHAN, Jeremy Alan Watkin; Secretary, British Medical Association, since 2001; *b* 14 Dec. 1944; *s* of William Arthur Watkin Strachan and Joyce Olive Strachan; *m* 1976, Margaret Elizabeth McVay; two step *d*. *Educ:* Haberdashers' Aske's Sch., Elstree; St Catharine's Coll., Cambridge (MA, LLM). Called to the Bar, Inner Temple, 1969 (Paul Methven Entrance Schol.); Legal Asst, Law Commn, 1967–72; Legal Advr, BSC, 1972–78; Principal Legal Advr and Hd, Legal and Patent Services, ICL, 1978–84; Gp Legal Advr, Standard Telephones and Cables, 1984–85; Dir, Gp Legal Services, and Corporate Affairs, Glaxo Hldgs, 1986–91; Exec. Dir, responsible for legal services, corporate policy and public affairs, and business develt, Glaxo Wellcome, 1992–2000. *Recreations:* France, food, controversy. *Address:* British Medical Association, BMA House, Tavistock Square, WC1H 9JP.

STRACHAN, John Charles Haggart, FRCS, FRCSE; Orthopaedic Consultant, Chelsea and Westminster Hospital, since 1993; *b* 2 Oct. 1936; *s* of late Charles George Strachan, MBE and Elsie Strachan; *m* 1966, Caroline Mary Parks; one *s* three *d*. *Educ:* St Mary's Hosp., Univ. of London (MB BS 1961). Consultant Orthopaedic Surgeon, Charing Cross Hosp., 1971–95; Consultant Surgeon, Royal Ballet, 1971–. *Publications:* contribs to professional jls. *Recreations:* sailing, fishing. *Address:* 28 Chalcot Square, NW1 8YA. *T:* (020) 7586 1278. *Clubs:* Garrick, Flyfishers', Royal Thames Yacht; Royal Southern Yacht.

STRACHAN, (John) Crispian, QPM 1996; Chief Constable, Northumbria Police, since 1998; *b* 5 July 1949; *s* of Dr (Mark) Noel Strachan and Barbara Joan Strachan; *m* 1974, Denise Anne Farmer; one *s* three *d*. *Educ:* Jesus Coll., Oxford (BA Jurisp 1971; MA 1989); Sheffield Univ. (MA Criminology 1972). Joined Metropolitan Police, 1972; Inspector, 1977–83; Chief Inspector, 1983–87; Superintendent, 1987–90; Chief Superintendent, 1990–93; Asst Chief Constable, Strathclyde Police, 1993–98. *Publications:* (with A. Comben) A Short Guide to Policing in the UK, 1992; (contrib.) Clinical Forensic Medicine, 2nd edn 1996. *Recreations:* woodworking, photography, the countryside, family above all. *Address:* Northumbria Police Headquarters, Ponteland, Newcastle upon Tyne NE20 0BL. *T:* (01661) 868011, *Fax:* (01661) 868024.

STRACHAN, Dame Valerie (Patricia Marie), DCB 1998 (CB 1991); Deputy Chair, Community Fund (formerly National Lottery Charities Board), since 2000; *b* 10 Jan. 1940; *d* of John Jonas Nicholls and Louise Nicholls; *m* 1965, John Strachan; one *s* one *d*. *Educ:* Newland High Sch., Hull; Manchester Univ. (BA). Joined HM Customs and Excise, 1961; Dept of Economic Affairs, 1964; Home Office, 1966; Principal, HM Customs and Excise, 1966; Treasury, 1972; Asst Secretary, HM Customs and Excise, 1974, Comr, 1980; Head, Joint Management Unit, HM Treasury/Cabinet Office, 1985–87; a Dep. Chm., 1987–93, Chm., 1993–2000, Bd of Customs and Excise. Chm., CS, PO and BT Lifeboat Fund, 1998–. CIMgt. Hon. LLD Manchester, 1995. *Club:* Reform.

STRACHAN, Walter, CBE 1967; CEng, FRAeS; Consulting Engineer since 1971; *b* 14 Oct. 1910; *s* of William John Strachan, Rothes, Morayshire, and Eva Hitchins, Bristol; *m* 1937, Elizabeth Dora Bradshaw, Aldershot; two *s*. *Educ:* Newfoundland Road Sch., Bristol; Merchant Venturers Technical Coll., Bristol. Bristol Aeroplane Co.: Apprentice, 1925; Aircraft Ground Engr, 1932; RAE, Farnborough, 1934; Inspector: Bristol Aeroplane Co., 1937. BAC Service Engr, RAF Martlesham Heath, 1938; BAC: Asst Service Manager, 1940; Asst Works Manager, 1942; Manager, Banwell, building Beaufort and Tempest aircraft, 1943; Gen.-Manager, Banwell and Weston Factories, manufrg Aluminium Houses, 1945; Gen. Manager, Banwell and Weston Factories, building helicopters and aircraft components, 1951; Managing Dir, Bristol Aerojet, Banwell, Rocket Motor Develt and Prod., 1958. Liveryman, Coachmakers' & Coach Harness Makers' Co., 1961. *Recreations:* golf, music, ornithology. *Address:* 18 Clarence Road East, Weston-super-Mare, Somerset BS23 4BW. *T:* (01934) 623878. *Clubs:* Naval and Military; Royal Automobile.

STRACHEY, family name of **Baron O'Hagan**.

STRACHEY, Charles; local government officer, retired; *b* 20 June 1934; *s* of Rt Hon. Evelyn John St Loe Strachey (*d* 1963) and Celia (*d* 1980), 3rd *d* of late Rev. Arthur Hume Simpson; *S* to baronetcy of cousin, 2nd Baron Strachie, 1973 as 6th Bt *cr* 1801, but does not use the title; *m* 1973, Janet Megan, *d* of Alexander Miller; one *d*. *Heir: kinsman* Henry Leofric Benvenuto Strachey, *b* 17 April 1947. *Address:* 31 Northchurch Terrace, N1 4EB. *T:* (020) 7684 5479.

[His name does not appear on the Official Roll of the Baronetage.]

STRADBROKE, 6th Earl of, *cr* 1821; **Robert Keith Rous;** Bt 1660; Baron Rous 1796; Viscount Dunwich 1821; *b* 25 March 1937; *s* of 5th Earl of Stradbroke and Pamela Catherine Mabell (*d* 1972), *d* of Captain Hon. Edward James Kay-Shuttleworth; *S* father, 1983; *m* 1960, Dawn Antoinette (marr. diss. 1977), *d* of Thomas Edward Beverley, Brisbane; two *s* five *d*; 2nd, 1977, Roseanna Mary Blanche, *d* of late Francis Reitman, MD; six *s* two *d*. *Educ:* Harrow. *Recreation:* making babies. *Heir: s* Viscount Dunwich, *qv*. *Address:* Mount Fyans, RSD Darlington, Vic 3271, Australia. *T:* (3) 55901294, *Fax:* (3) 55901298.

STRADLING, Donald George; Group Personnel Director, John Laing & Son Ltd, then John Laing plc, 1969–89; Director, Quantum Care, since 2000; *b* 7 Sept. 1929; *s* of George Frederic and Olive Emily Stradling; *m* 1955, Mary Anne Hartridge (*d* 2000); two *d*. *Educ:* Clifton Coll.; Magdalen Coll., Oxford (Open Exhibnr; MA). CIPM. School Master, St Albans Sch., 1954–55; Group Trng and Educn Officer, John Laing & Son Ltd, Building and Civil Engrg Contractors, 1955. Vis. Prof., Univ. of Salford, 1989–94. Comr, Manpower Services Commn, 1980–82; Mem. Council, Inst. of Manpower Studies, 1975–81; Member: Employment Policy Cttee, CBI, 1978–84, 1986–91; Council, CBI, 1982–86; FCEC Wages and Industrial Cttee, 1978–95; Council, FCEC, 1985–95; National Steering Gp, New Technical and Vocational Educn Initiative, 1983–88; NHS Trng Authy, 1985–89. Director: Building and Civil Engrg Benefits Scheme (Trustee, 1984–); Building and Civil Engrg Holidays Scheme Management, 1984–; Construction ITB, 1985–90. Vice-Pres., Inst. of Personnel Management, 1974–76. Vice-Chm. of Governors, St Albans High Sch., 1977–95; Mem. Council, Tyndale House, 1977–96. Liveryman, Glaziers' and Painters of Glass Co., 1983–95. Hon. PhD Internat. Management Centre, Buckingham, 1987; Hon. DSc Salford, 1995. *Publications:* contribs on music and musical instruments, et al. to New Bible Dictionary, 1962. *Recreations:* singing (St Albans Bach Choir), listening to music (espec. opera), walking. *Address:* Courts Edge, 12 The Warren, Harpenden, Herts AL5 2NH. *Club:* Institute of Directors.

STRAFFORD, 8th Earl of, *cr* 1847; **Thomas Edmund Byng;** Baron Strafford, 1835; Viscount Enfield, 1847; nurseryman, riverkeeper and artist's companion; *b* 26 Sept. 1936; *s* of 7th Earl of Strafford, and Maria Magdalena Elizabeth, *d* of late Henry Cloete, CMG, Alphen, S Africa; *S* father, 1984; *m* 1963, Jennifer Mary (marr. diss. 1981), *er d* of late Rt Hon. W. M. May, FCA, PC, MP, and of Mrs May, Mertoun Hall, Holywood, Co. Down; two *s* two *d*; 2nd, 1981, Mrs Julia Mary Howard, (Judy), *d* of Sir Dennis Pilcher, CBE. *Educ:* Eton; Clare Coll., Cambridge. Lieut, Royal Sussex Regt (National Service). Councillor, Winchester and District, 1983–87. *Recreations:* gardening, travelling. *Heir: s* Viscount Enfield, *qv*. *Address:* Apple Tree Cottage, Easton, Winchester, Hants SO21 1EF. *T:* (01962) 779467.

STRAKER, Anita, CB 2001; OBE 1990; Director, Key Stage 3 National Strategy, Department for Education and Skills (formerly Department for Education and Employment), since 2000; *b* 22 June 1938; *d* of David William Barham and Laura Barham; *m* 1961, Patrick Vincent Straker; four *s*. *Educ:* Weston-super-Mare Grammar Sch. for Girls; University Coll. London (BSc Hons); Royal Holloway Coll., Univ. of London (MSc); Univ. of Cambridge Inst. of Educn (PGCE). Teacher, 1961–62 and 1968–74; Inspector for maths, Surrey LEA, 1974–78; Gen. Advr, Wilts LEA, 1978–83; Dir, Microelectronics Educn Prog. Primary Project, DES, 1983–86; Dist Inspector, ILEA, 1986–89; Principal Advr, Berks LEA, 1989–93; Dep. Dir of Educn, Camden LEA, 1993–96; Dir, Nat. Numeracy Strategy, DFE, then DfEE, 1996–2000. *Publications:* Mathematics for Gifted Pupils, 1980; Children Using Computers, 1988; Mathematics from China, 1990; Primary Maths Extension Activities, 1991; Talking Points in Mathematics, 1993; Mental Maths (series), 1994; Home Maths (series), 1998. *Recreations:* holidays abroad, cooking, reading, swimming. *Address:* Mundays, St Mary Bourne, Andover, Hants SP11 6AY. *T:* (01264) 738474.

STRAKER, Rear-Adm. Bryan John, CB 1980; OBE 1966; Area Appeal Manager, Cancer Relief Macmillan Fund, 1993–94; *b* 26 May 1929; *s* of late George and Marjorie Straker; *m* 1954, Elizabeth Rosemary, *d* of Maj.-Gen. C. W. Greenway, CB, CBE, and Mrs C. W. Greenway; two *d*. *Educ:* St Albans Sch. FIMgt (FBIM 1978). Cadet, RNC Dartmouth, 1946; Flag Lieut to Flag Officer, Malayan Area, 1952–53; qual. in communications, 1955; CO: HMS Malcolm, 1962–63; HMS Defender, 1966–67; Asst Dir, Naval Operational Requirements, MoD, 1968–70; CO HMS Fearless, 1970–72; Dir of Naval Plans, MoD, 1972–74; Comdr British Forces Caribbean Area and Island Comdr, Bermuda, 1974–76; Asst Chief of Naval Staff (Policy), 1976–78; Sen. Naval Mem., DS, RCDS, 1978–80; RN retd, 1981. Hd of Personnel Services, ICRF, 1981–89; Appeal Dir, Macmillan (Cancer Relief) Service, Midhurst, 1990–93. Freeman, City of London. *Recreations:* tennis, gardening. *Address:* The Cottage, Durford Court, Petersfield, Hants GU31 5AR. *Club:* Steep Lawn Tennis.

STRAKER, Major Ivan Charles; Chairman, Seagram Distillers plc, 1984–93 (Chief Executive, 1983–90); *b* 17 June 1928; *s* of Arthur Coppin Straker and Cicely Longueville Straker; *m* 1st, 1954, Gillian Elizabeth Grant (marr. diss. 1971); one *s* one *d* (and one *s* decd); 2nd, 1976, Sally Jane Hastings (marr. diss. 1986); one *s*; 3rd, 1998, Rosemary Ann Whitaker. *Educ:* Harrow; RMA, Sandhurst. Commissioned 11th Hussars (PAO), 1948; served Germany, N Ireland, Middle East and Mil. Intell. Staff, War Office; left HM Armed Forces, 1962. Man. Dir, D. Rintoul & Co., 1964; Man. Dir, The Glenlivet and Glen Grant Agencies, 1964–71; apptd Main Board, The Glenlivet and Glen Grant Distillers, 1967; Chief Exec., The Glenlivet Distillers Ltd, 1971. Dir, Lothians Racing Syndicate Ltd, 1986–. Council Mem., Scotch Whisky Assoc., 1978–90 (Chm., Public Affairs Cttee, 1986–90). *Recreations:* fishing, shooting, racing. *Address:* Oaktree Cottage, Acomb, Hexham, Northumberland NE46 4PL. *T:* (01434) 604509. *Clubs:* Jockey, Cavalry and Guards, White's.

STRAKER, Timothy Derrick; QC 1996; a Recorder, since 2000; *b* 25 May 1955; *s* of late Derrick Straker, solicitor, and Dorothy Elizabeth, *o d* of late Brig. T. L. Rogers, CBE; *m* 1982, Ann Horton Baylis; two *d*. *Educ:* Malvern Coll.; Downing Coll., Cambridge (BA 1st Cl. Hons Law, MA). Called to the Bar: Gray's Inn, 1977 (Holt Schol.); Lincoln's Inn, *ad eundem*, 1979; NI, 2001; Trinidad and Tobago, 2001; in practice at the Bar, 1977–; an Asst Recorder, 1998–2000. Member: Admin. Law Bar Assoc., 1986–; Local Govt, Planning and Envmtl Bar Assoc., 1986–; Crown Office Users' Cttee, 1993–2000; Administrative Court Users' Assoc., 2000–. *Publications:* Annotated Current Law Statutes, 1994; (Consultant Ed.) Registration of Political Parties: a guide to Returning Officers, 1999; Public Health and Environmental Protection, in Halsbury's Laws of England, 2000; contrib. Rights of Way Law Review, Judicial Review. *Recreations:* cricket, history. *Address:* 4–5 Gray's Inn Square, Gray's Inn, WC1R 5JP. *T:* (020) 7404 5252. *Club:* Highgate Irregular Cricket.

STRAND, Prof. Kenneth T.; Professor, Department of Economics, Simon Fraser University, 1968–86, now Emeritus; *b* Yakima, Wash, 30 June 1931; Canadian citizen since 1974; *m* 1960, Elna K. Tomaske; no *c*. *Educ:* Washington State Coll. (BA); Univ. of Wisconsin (PhD, MS). Woodrow Wilson Fellow, 1955–56; Ford Foundn Fellow, 1957–58; Herfurth Award, Univ. of Wisconsin, 1961 (for PhD thesis). Asst Exec. Sec., Hanford Contractors Negotiation Cttee, Richland, Wash, 1953–55; Asst Prof., Washington State Univ., 1959–60; Asst Prof., Oberlin Coll., 1960–65 (on leave, 1963–65); Economist, Manpower and Social Affairs Div., OECD, Paris, 1964–66; Assoc. Prof., Dept of Econs, Simon Fraser Univ., 1966–68; Pres., Simon Fraser Univ., 1969–74 (Acting Pres., 1968–69). Member: Industrial Relations Research Assoc.; Internat. Industrial Relations Assoc.; Canadian Industrial Relations Assoc. (Pres., 1983). Hon. LLD Simon Fraser Univ., 1983. FRSA 1972. *Publications:* Jurisdictional Disputes in Construction: The Causes, The Joint Board and the NLRB, 1961; contribs to Review of Econs and Statistics, Amer. Econ. Review, Industrial Relations, Sociaal Mannblad Arbeid. *Recreations:* fishing, ski-ing. *Address:* 2212 Aspen Drive, Whistler, BC V0N 1B2, Canada.

STRANG, family name of **Baron Strang**.

STRANG, 2nd Baron *cr* 1954, of Stonesfield; **Colin Strang;** Professor of Philosophy, University of Newcastle upon Tyne, 1975–82; Dean of the Faculty of Arts, 1976–79; retired 1982; *b* 12 June 1922; *s* of 1st Baron Strang, GCB, GCMG, MBE, and Elsie Wynne (*d* 1974), *d* of late J. E. Jones; *S* father, 1978; *m* 1st, 1948, Patricia Marie, *d* of Meiert C. Avis, Johannesburg; 2nd, 1955, Barbara Mary Hope Carr (*d* 1982); one *d*; 3rd, 1984, Mary Shewell. *Educ:* Merchant Taylors' School; St John's Coll., Oxford (MA, BPhil). *Heir:* none. *Address:* Broombank, Lochranza, Isle of Arran KA27 8JF.

STRANG, Rt Hon. Gavin (Steel); PC 1997; MP (Lab) Edinburgh East and Musselburgh, since 1997 (Edinburgh East, 1970–97); *b* 10 July 1943; *s* of James Steel Strang and Marie Strang (*née* Finkle); *m*. *Educ:* Univs of Edinburgh and Cambridge. BSc Hons Edinburgh, 1964; DipAgricSci Cambridge, 1965; PhD Edinburgh, 1968. Mem., Tayside Econ. Planning Consultative Group, 1966–68; Scientist with ARC, 1968–70. Opposition front bench spokesman on Scottish affairs, 1972–73, on energy, 1973–74; Parly Under-Sec. of State, Dept of Energy, March-Oct. 1974; Parly Sec., MAFF, 1974–79; Opposition front bench spokesman on agriculture, 1979–82, on employment, 1987–89, on food, agriculture and rural affairs, 1992–97; Mem., Shadow Cabinet, 1994–97; Minister for Transport, 1997–98. Chm., PLP Defence Group, 1984–87. *Publications:* articles in Animal Production. *Recreations:* golf, swimming, watching football.

Address: House of Commons, SW1A 0AA. *Clubs:* Jewel Miners' Welfare, Newcraighall Miners' Welfare (Edinburgh).

STRANG, Prof. John Stanley, MD; FRCPsych; Professor of the Addictions, Institute of Psychiatry, London University, and Director, National Addiction Centre, since 1995; *b* 12 May 1950; *s* of late William John Strang, CBE, FRS, and of Margaret Nicholas Strang (*née* Howells); *m* 1984, Jennifer Abbey; two *s* (one *d* decd). *Educ:* Bryanston Sch., Dorset; Guy's Hosp. Med. Sch. (MB BS; MD 1995). FRCPsych 1994. Consultant psychiatrist in drug dependence: Manchester, 1982–86; Maudsley Hosp., London, 1986–; Getty Sen. Lectr in the Addictions, Nat. Addiction Centre, Inst. of Psychiatry, 1991–95. Consultant Advr (drugs), DoH, 1986–. Mem., Adv. Council on Misuse of Drugs, 1989–. *Publications:* (with G. Stimson) AIDS and Drug Misuse: the challenge for policy and practice in the 1990's, 1990; (jtly) Drugs, Alcohol and Tobacco: making the science and policy connections, 1993; (with M. Gossop) Heroin Addiction and Drug Policy: the British system, 1994. *Address:* National Addiction Centre, Addiction Sciences Building, 4 Windsor Walk, SE5 8AF. *T:* (020) 7919 3438. *Club:* Athenæum.

STRANG STEEL, Major Sir (Fiennes) Michael, 3rd Bt *cr* 1938, of Philiphaugh, Selkirk; CBE 1999; DL; *b* 22 Feb. 1943; *s* of Sir (Fiennes) William Strang Steel, 2nd Bt and Joan Strang Steel (*d* 1982), *d* of Brig-Gen. Sir Brodie Haldane Henderson, KCMG, CB; *S* father, 1992; *m* 1977, Sarah Jane Russell; two *s* one *d*. *Educ:* Eton. Major, 17/21 Lancers, 1962–80, retd. Forestry Comr, 1988–99. DL Borders Region (Districts of Roxburgh, Ettrick & Lauderdale), 1990. *Heir: s* (Fiennes) Edward Strang Steel, *b* 8 Nov. 1978. *Address:* Philiphaugh, Selkirk TD7 5LX. *Club:* Cavalry and Guards.

STRANGE, Baroness (16th in line), *cr* 1628; **Jean Cherry Drummond;** *b* 17 Dec. 1928; *e c* of 15th Baron Strange (*d* 1982) and Violet Margaret Florence (*d* 1975), *d* of Sir Robert William Buchanan-Jardine, 2nd Bt; *S* (after termination of abeyance), 1986; *m* 1952, Captain Humphrey ap Evans, MC, who assumed name of Drummond of Megginch by decree of Lord Lyon, 1965; three *s* three *d*. *Educ:* St Andrews Univ. (MA 1951); Cambridge Univ. Pres., War Widows' Assoc. of GB, 1990–. Elected Mem., H of L, 1999. FSAScot 1989. Hon. FIMarE 1996. *Publications:* Love from Belinda, 1960; Lalage in Love, 1962; Creatures Great and Small, 1968; Love is For Ever, 1988; The Remarkable Life of Victoria Drummond, Marine Engineer, 1994. *Heir: s* Hon. Adam Humphrey Drummond, Major Grenadier Guards [*b* 20 April 1953; *m* 1988, Mary Emma Dewar; one *s* one *d*]. *Address:* Megginch Castle, Errol, Perthshire PH2 7SW. *T:* (01821) 642222; Tresco, 160 Kennington Road, SE11 6QR. *T:* (020) 7735 3681.

STRANGWAYS; *see* Fox-Strangways, family name of Earl of Ilchester.

STRANRAER-MULL, Very Rev. Gerald; Dean of Aberdeen and Orkney, since 1988; Rector of Ellon and Cruden Bay, since 1972; *b* 24 Nov. 1942; *s* of Gerald and Lena Stranraer-Mull; *m* 1967, Glynis Mary Kempe; one *s* one *d* (and one *s* decd). *Educ:* Woodhouse Grove School, Apperley Bridge; King's College, London (AKC 1969); Saint Augustine's College, Canterbury. Journalist, 1960–66. Curate: Hexham Abbey, 1970–72; Corbridge, 1972; Editor of Aberdeen and Buchan Churchman, 1976–84, 1991–94; Director of Training for Ministry, Diocese of Aberdeen and Orkney, 1982–90; Canon of Saint Andrew's Cathedral, Aberdeen, 1981–. Director: Oil Chaplaincy Trust, 1993–; Iona Cornerstone Foundn, 1995–. *Address:* The Rectory, Ellon, Aberdeenshire AB41 9NP. *T:* (01358) 720366.

STRATFORD, Prof. Neil Martin; Professor of History of Medieval Art, Ecole Nationale des Chartes, Paris, since 2000; Keeper of Medieval and Later Antiquities, British Museum, 1975–98, now Keeper Emeritus; *b* 26 April 1938; *s* of late Dr Martin Gould Stratford and Dr Mavis Stratford (*née* Beddall); *m* 1966, Anita Jennifer Lewis; two *d*. *Educ:* Marlborough Coll.; Magdalene Coll., Cambridge (BA Hons English 1961, MA); Courtauld Inst., London Univ. (BA Hons History of Art 1966). 2nd Lieut Coldstream Guards, 1956–58; Trainee Kleinwort, Benson, Lonsdale Ltd, 1961–63; Lecturer, Westfield Coll., London Univ., 1969–75. British Academy/Leverhulme Sen. Res. Fellow, 1991; Mem., Inst. for Advanced Study, Princeton, 1998–99; Appleton Vis. Prof., Florida State Univ., 2000. Chm., St Albans Cathedral Fabric Cttee, 1995–; Conseil Scientifique, Société Française d'Archéologie, 1994–. Liveryman, Haberdashers' Company 1959–. Hon. Mem., Académie de Dijon, 1975; For. Mem., Société Nationale des Antiquaires de France, 1985. FSA 1976. *Publications:* La Sculpture Oubliée de Vézelay, 1984; Catalogue of Medieval Enamels in the British Museum, vol. II, Northern Romanesque Enamel, 1993; Westminster Kings and the medieval Palace of Westminster, 1995; The Lewis Chessmen and the enigma of the hoard, 1997; Studies in Burgundian Romanesque Sculpture, 1998; articles in French and English periodicals. *Recreations:* opera, food and wine, cricket and football. *Address:* 17 Church Row, NW3 6UP. *T:* (020) 7794 5688. *Clubs:* Beefsteak, Garrick, MCC, I Zingari; University Pitt, Hawks (Cambridge).

STRATHALLAN, Viscount; John Eric Drummond; *b* 7 July 1935; *e s* of 17th Earl of Perth, *qv*; *m* 1963, Margaret Ann (marr. diss. 1972), *o d* of Robin Gordon; two *s*; *m* 1988, Mrs Marion Elliot. *Educ:* Trinity Coll., Cambridge; Harvard Univ. (MBA). *Heir: s* Hon. James David Drummond, *b* 24 Oct. 1965.

STRATHALMOND, 3rd Baron *cr* 1955; **William Roberton Fraser,** CA; Finance Director, Owen & Wilby Underwriting Agency Ltd, since 1995; *b* 22 July 1947; *s* of 2nd Baron Strathalmond, CMG, OBE, TD, and of Letitia, *d* of late Walter Krementz, New Jersey, USA; *S* father, 1976; *m* 1973, Amanda Rose, *yr d* of Rev. Gordon Clifford Taylor; two *s* one *d*. *Educ:* Loretto. Man. Dir, London Wall Members Agency Ltd, 1986–91 (Dir, 1985–91); Director: London Wall Hldgs plc, 1986–91; Owen and Wilby Underwriting Agency, later Gerling at Lloyd's, Ltd, 1995–; Chm., R. W. Sturge Ltd, 1991–94. Chm. Trustees, RSAS Agecare, 1984–. Liveryman, Girdlers' Co., 1979–. *Heir: s* Hon. William Gordon Fraser, *b* 24 Sept. 1976.

STRATHCARRON, 2nd Baron, *cr* 1936, of Banchor; **David William Anthony Blyth Macpherson;** Bt, *cr* 1933; Partner, Strathcarron & Co.; Director: Kirchhoff (London) Ltd; Seabourne World Express Group plc; Kent International Airport PLC; *b* 23 Jan. 1924; *s* of 1st Baron and Jill (*d* 1956), *o d* of Sir George Rhodes, 1st Bt; *S* father, 1937; *m* 1st, 1947, Valerie Cole (marr. annulled on his petition, 1947); 2nd, 1948, Mrs Diana Hawtrey Curle (*d* 1973), *o d* of Comdr R. H. Deane; two *s*; 3rd 1974, Mrs Eve Samuel (*d* 1999), *o d* of late J. C. Higgins, CIE; 4th, 1999, Diana, *widow* of Hugo Nicholson. *Educ:* Eton; Jesus College, Cambridge. Served War of 1939–45, RAFVR, 1942–47. Motoring Correspondent of The Field, 1954–. Member, British Parly Delegn to Austria, 1964. President: Inst. of Freight Forwarders, 1974–75; Guild of Motoring Writers, 1971–; Guild of Experienced Motorists, 1980–86; National Breakdown Recovery Club, 1982–96; Driving Instructors' Assoc., 1982–; Vehicle Builders' and Repairers' Assoc., 1983–; IRTE, 1990–2000; Order of the Road, 1994– (Chm., 1974–94); Fellowship of the Motor Industry, 1994–. FIMI 1989; FCIT 1991; Fellow, Inst. of Advanced Motorists, 1993; Fellow, Motor Industry, 1995. *Publication:* Motoring for Pleasure, 1963. *Recreations:* motor-racing, sailing, motorcycling. *Heir: s* Hon. Ian David Patrick Macpherson, *b* 31 March 1949. *Address:* 3 Elizabeth Court, Milmans Street, SW10 0DA. *T:* (020) 7351 3224; Otterwood, Beaulieu, Hants SO42 7YS. *T:* (01590) 612334. *Clubs:* Boodle's, Royal Air Force.

STRATHCLYDE, 2nd Baron *cr* 1955, of Barskimming; **Thomas Galloway Dunlop du Roy de Blicquy Galbraith;** PC 1995; Leader of the Opposition, House of Lords, since 1998; *b* 22 Feb. 1960; *s* of Hon. Sir Thomas Galloway Dunlop Galbraith, KBE, MP (*d* 1982) (*e s* of 1st Baron) and Simone Clothilde Fernande Marie Ghislaine (*d* 1991), *e d* of late Jean du Roy de Blicquy; *S* grandfather, 1985; *m* 1992, Jane, *er d* of John Skinner; three *d*. *Educ:* Wellington College; Univ. of East Anglia (BA 1982); Université d'Aix-en-Provence. Insurance Broker, Bain Dawes, subseq. Bain Clarkson Ltd, 1982–88. Contested (C) Merseyside East, European Parly Election, 1984. Spokesman for DTI, Treasury and Scotland, H of L, 1988–89; Govt Whip, 1988–89; Parly Under-Sec. of State, Dept of Employment, 1989–90, DoE, 1990, 1992–93, Scottish Office (Minister for Agric. and Fisheries), 1990–92, DTI, 1993–94; Minister of State, DTI, 1994; Captain of the Hon. Corps of Gentlemen at Arms (Govt Chief Whip in H of L), 1994–97; Opposition Chief Whip, House of Lords, 1997–98; elected Mem., H of L, 1999. *Heir: b* Hon. Charles William du Roy de Blicquy Galbraith [*b* 20 May 1962; *m* 1992, Bridget, *d* of Brian Reeve; two *s* one *d*]. *Address:* House of Lords, SW1A 0AA. *T:* (020) 7219 5353.

STRATHCONA AND MOUNT ROYAL, 4th Baron *cr* 1900; **Donald Euan Palmer Howard;** *b* 26 Nov. 1923; *s* of 3rd Baron Strathcona and Mount Royal and Diana Evelyn (*d* 1985), twin *d* of 1st Baron Wakehurst; *S* father, 1959; *m* 1st, 1954, Lady Jane Mary Waldegrave (marr. diss. 1977), 2nd *d* of 12th Earl Waldegrave, KG, GCVO; two *s* four *d* (incl. twin *s* and *d*); 2nd, 1978, Patricia (*née* Thomas), *widow* of John Middleton. *Educ:* King's Mead, Seaford; Eton; Trinity Coll., Cambridge; McGill University, Montreal (1947–50). Served War of 1939–45: RN, 1942–47: Midshipman, RNVR, 1943; Lieutenant, 1945. With Urwick, Orr and Partners (Industrial Consultants), 1950–56. Lord in Waiting (Govt Whip), 1973–74; Parly Under-Sec. of State for Defence (RAF), MoD, 1974; Jt Dep. Leader of the Opposition, House of Lords, 1976–79; Minister of State, MoD, 1979–81. Dir, Computing Devices, Hastings, 1981–92. Chairman, Bath Festival Society, 1966–70. Dep. Chm., SS Great Britain Project, 1970–73; Founder Chm., Coastal Forces Heritage Trust, 1995–; President: Falkland Is Trust, 1982–; Steamboat Assoc. of GB, 1972–; Mem. Council, RN Mus., 1982–95. *Recreations:* gardening, sailing. *Heir: s* Hon. Donald Alexander Smith Howard [*b* 24 June 1961; *m* 1992, Jane Maree, *d* of Shaun Gibb; one *s*]. *Address:* Townsend Barn, Poulshot, Devizes, Wilts SN10 1SD. *T:* (01380) 228329; Kiloran, Isle of Colonsay, Argyll PA61 7YU. *T:* (01951) 200301. *Clubs:* Brooks's, Pratt's; Royal Yacht Squadron.

STRATHEDEN, 6th Baron *cr* 1836, **AND CAMPBELL,** 6th Baron *cr* 1841; **Donald Campbell;** *b* 4 April 1934; *s* of 5th Baron Stratheden and Campbell and of Evelyn Mary Austen, *d* of late Col Herbert Austen Smith, CIE; *S* father, 1987; *m* 1957, Hilary Ann Holland (*d* 1991), *d* of Lt-Col William D. Turner; one *s* three *d*. *Educ:* Eton. *Heir: s* Hon. David Anthony Campbell [*b* 13 Feb. 1963; *m* 1993, Jennifer Margaret Owens; one *d*]. *Address:* Yalara, Ridgewood, MS 401, Cooroy, Queensland 4563, Australia.

STRATHERN, Prof. Andrew Jamieson, PhD; Andrew Mellon Professor of Anthropology, University of Pittsburgh, since 1987; Emeritus Professor of Anthropology, University of London; Hon. Research Fellow, Institute of Papua New Guinea Studies, Port Moresby, since 1977 (Director, 1981–86); *b* 19 Jan. 1939; *s* of Robert Strathern and Mary Strathern (*née* Sharp); *m* 1963, Ann Marilyn Evans (marr. diss. 1986); two *s* one *d*; *m* 1997, Pamela J. Stewart. *Educ:* Colchester Royal Grammar Sch.; Trinity Coll., Cambridge (BA, PhD). Research Fellow, Trinity Coll., Cambridge, 1965–68; Research Fellow, then Fellow, Australian National Univ., 1969–72; Professor, later Vis. Professor, Dept of Anthropology and Sociology, Univ. of Papua New Guinea, 1973–77; Prof. of Anthropology and Hd of Dept of Anthropology, UCL, 1976–83. Hon. Mem., Phi Beta Kappa, 1993. Rivers Memorial Medal, RAI, 1976. 10th Independence Anniv. Medal (PNG), 1987. *Publications:* The Rope of Moka, 1971; One Father, One Blood, 1972; (with M. Strathern) Self-decoration in Mount Hagen, 1972; Melpa Amb Kenan, 1974; Myths and Legends from Mt Hagen, 1977; Beneath the Andaiya Tree, 1977; Ongka, 1979; (with Malcolm Kirk) Man as Art, 1981; Inequality in New Guinea Highlands Societies, 1982; Wiru Laa, 1983; A line of power, 1984; (ed jtly) Strauss, The Mi Culture of the Mount Hagen People, 1990; (with P. Birnbaum) Faces of Papua New Guinea, 1991; Landmarks: reflections on anthropology, 1993; Voices of Conflict, 1993; Ru, 1993; Body Thoughts, 1996; (ed jtly) Millennial Markers, 1997; (ed jtly) Bodies and Persons, 1998; (ed jtly) Identity Work, 2000; with P. J. Stewart: A Death to Pay For: individual voices, 1998; Curing and Healing, 1999; Collaborations and Conflicts: a leader through time, 1999; Arrow Talk, 2000; The Python's Back: pathways of comparison between Indonesia and Melanesia, 2000; articles in Man, Oceania, Ethnology, Jl Polyn Soc., Amer. Anthropology, Amer. Ethnology, Mankind, Bijdragen, Jl de la Soc. des Océanistes, Oral History, Bikmaus, Pacific Studies, Ethos, Jl of Ethnomusicology, Canberra Anthropology, Historische Anthropologie, Aust. Jl of Anthropology, Ethnohistory. *Address:* Department of Anthropology, University of Pittsburgh, Pittsburgh, PA 15260, USA. *T:* (office) (412) 6487519.

STRATHERN, Dame (Ann) Marilyn, DBE 2001; FBA 1987; Mistress of Girton College, Cambridge, since 1998; William Wyse Professor of Social Anthropology, University of Cambridge, since 1993; *b* 6 March 1941; *d* of Eric Charles Evans and Joyce Florence Evans; *m* 1963, Andrew Jamieson Strathern, *qv* (marr. diss. 1986); twin *s* one *d*. *Educ:* Bromley High Sch (GPDST); Girton Coll., Cambridge (MA, PhD). Asst Curator, Mus. of Ethnology, Cambridge, 1966–68; Res. Fellow, ANU, 1970–72 and 1974–75; Bye-Fellow, Sen. Res. Fellow, then Official Fellow, Girton Coll., 1976–83; Fellow and Lectr, Trinity Coll., Cambridge, 1984–85 (Hon. Fellow, 1999); Prof. and Hd of Dept of Social Anthropology, Manchester Univ., 1985–93; Fellow, Girton Coll., Cambridge, 1993–98. Sen. Res. Fellow, ANU, 1983–84; Vis. Prof., Univ. of California, Berkeley, 1984. Hon. Foreign Mem., Amer. Acad. Arts and Scis, 1996. Hon. DSc (Soc Sci): Edinburgh, 1993; Copenhagen, 1994. Rivers Meml Medal, RAI, 1976. *Publications:* Self-Decoration in Mt Hagen (jtly), 1971; Women In Between, 1972; (co-ed) Nature, Culture and Gender, 1980; Kinship at the Core: an anthropology of Elmdon, Essex, 1981; (ed) Dealing With Inequality, 1987; The Gender of the Gift, 1988; Partial Connections, 1991; (ed) Big Men and Great Men in Melanesia, 1991; After Nature, 1992; Reproducing the Future, 1992; (jtly) Technologies of Procreation, 1993; (ed) Shifting Contexts, 1995; Property, Substance and Effect, 1999. *Address:* Girton College, Cambridge CB3 0JG.

STRATHMORE AND KINGHORNE, 18th Earl of, *cr* 1677 (Scot.); Earl (UK) *cr* 1937; **Michael Fergus Bowes Lyon;** Lord Glamis, 1445; Earl of Kinghorne, Lord Lyon and Glamis, 1606; Viscount Lyon, Lord Glamis, Tannadyce, Sidlaw and Strathdichtie, 1677; Baron Bowes (UK), 1887; DL; Captain, Scots Guards; *b* 7 June 1957; *s* of 17th Earl of Strathmore and Kinghorne and of Mary Pamela, DL, *d* of Brig. Norman Duncan McCorquodale, MC; *S* father, 1987; *m* 1984, Isobel, *yr d* of Capt. A. E. Weatherall, Cowhill, Dumfries; three *s*. *Educ:* Univ. of Aberdeen (BLE 1979). Page of Honour to HM Queen Elizabeth The Queen Mother, 1971–73; commissioned, Scots Guards, 1980. A Lord in Waiting (Govt Whip), 1989–91; Captain of the Yeomen of the Guard (Dep. Govt

Chief Whip), 1991–94. Director: Polypipe PLC, 1994–99; Lancaster PLC, 1994–99. Pres., Boys' Brigade, 1994–99. DL Angus, 1993. *Heir: s* Lord Glamis, *qv*. *Address:* Glamis Castle, Forfar, Angus DD8 1QJ. *Clubs:* Turf, White's, Pratt's, Mark's; Third Guards'; Perth (Perth).

STRATHNAVER, Lord; Alistair Charles St Clair Sutherland; DL; Master of Sutherland; with Sutherland Estates, since 1978; Vice Lord-Lieutenant of Sutherland, since 1993; *b* 7 Jan. 1947; *e s* of Charles Noel Janson, and the Countess of Sutherland, *qv*; *heir* to mother's titles; *m* 1st, 1968, Eileen Elizabeth, *o d* of Richard Wheeler Baker, Jr, Princeton, NJ; two *d*; 2nd, 1980, Gillian, *er d* of Robert Murray, Gourock, Renfrewshire; one *s* one *d*. *Educ:* Eton; Christ Church, Oxford. BA. Metropolitan Police, 1969–74; with IBM UK Ltd, 1975–78. DL Sutherland, 1991. *Heir: s* Hon. Alexander Charles Robert Sutherland, *b* 1 Oct. 1981. *Address:* Sutherland Estates Office, Golspie, Sutherland KW10 6RP. *T:* (01408) 633268.

STRATHSPEY, 6th Baron *cr* 1884; **James Patrick Trevor Grant of Grant;** Bt (NS) 1625; Chief of Clan Grant; *b* 9 Sept. 1943; *s* of 5th Baron and of his 1st wife, Alice, *o c* of late Francis Bowe; *S* father, 1992; *m* 1st, 1966, Linda (marr. diss. 1984), *d* of David Piggott; three *d*; 2nd, 1985, Margaret (marr. diss. 1993), *d* of Robert Drummond. *Heir:* half *b* Hon. Michael Patrick Francis Grant of Grant; *b* 22 April 1953.

STRATHTAY AND STRATHARDLE, Earl of; Michael Bruce John Murray; *b* 5 March 1985; *s* and *heir* of Marquess of Tullibardine, *qv*.

STRATTON, Prof. Michael Rudolf, PhD; Professor of Cancer Genetics, Institute of Cancer Research, since 1997; Head, Cancer Genome Project, Sanger Centre, since 2000; *b* 22 June 1957; *s* of Henry Stratton and Nita Stratton; *m* 1981, Dr Judith Breuer; one *s* one *d*. *Educ:* Brasenose Coll., Oxford (BA Physiol Scis); Guy's Hosp. Med. Sch., London (MB BS 1982); Inst. Cancer Res., London (PhD 1989). MRCPath 1991. House and res. posts at Guy's Hosp., Beckenham Hosp., Inst. Psychiatry and Westminster Hosp., 1982–84; Registrar in Histopathol., RPMS, Hammersmith Hosp., 1984–86; MRC Trng Fellow, Inst. Cancer Res., 1986–89; Sen. Registrar, Dept Neuropathol., Inst. Psychiatry, 1989–91; Institute of Cancer Research: Team Leader, 1991–; Reader in Molecular Genetics of Cancer, 1996–97. Hon. Consultant, Royal Marsden Hosp., 1992–. FMedSci 1999. *Publications:* contrib. papers on genetic basis of cancer. *Address:* Sanger Centre, Wellcome Trust Genome Campus, Hinxton, Cambridge CB10 1SA.

STRATTON, Air Vice-Marshal William Hector, CB 1970; CBE 1963; DFC 1939 and Bar 1944; Chief of the Air Staff, RNZAF, 1969–71, retired 1971; *b* 22 July 1916; *s* of V. J. Stratton; *m* 1954, Dorothy M., *d* of J. D. Whyte; one *s* two *d*. *Educ:* Hawera Tech. High School, and privately. RAF, 1937–44: No 1 Sqn, France, 1939–40; CO Advanced Trng Sqn, Rhodesia, 1940–43; CO 134 Sqn, ME and India, 1943–44; RNZAF appointments include: CO, Ohakea; Air Member for Personnel; ACAS; Head NZ Defence Staff, Canberra; Head NZ Defence Staff, London. *Address:* 41 Goldsworthy Road, Claremont, Perth, WA 6010, Australia.

STRAUSS, Claude L.; *see* Levi-Strauss.

STRAUSS, Nicholas Albert; QC 1984; a Recorder, since 2000; *b* 29 July 1942; *s* of late Walter Strauss and Ilse Strauss (*née* Leon); *m* 1972, Christine M. MacColl; two *d*. *Educ:* Highgate School; Jesus College, Cambridge (BA 1964; LLB 1965). Called to the Bar, Middle Temple, 1965 (Harmsworth Scholar). *Address:* 1 Essex Court, Temple, EC4Y 9AR. *T:* (020) 7583 2000.

STRAUSS-KAHN, Dominique Gaston André; Deputy, Assemblée National, France, since 2001; Minister of the Economy and of Finance, France, 1997–99; *b* 25 April 1949; *s* of Gilbert Strauss-Kahn and Jacqueline (*née* Fellus); *m* 1991, Anne Sinclair; four *c* by previous marriages. *Educ:* Lycée de Monaco; Lycée Carnot à Paris; Univ. de Paris X-Nanterre (DEconSc). Lectr, Univ. de Nancy II, 1977–80; Scientific Advr, l'Institut national de la statistique et des études économiques, 1978–80; Dir, Cerepi, CNRS, 1980–; Prof., Univ. de Paris X-Nanterre, 1981; Hd, Dept of Finance, Gen. Commn of the Nat. Plan, 1982–84, Asst Comr, 1984–86. Mem., Exec. Cttee, Socialist Party, 1983– (Nat. Sec., 1984–89). Deputy (Soc.) from Haute-Savoie, 1986–88, from Val-d'Oise, 1988–91, 2001–; Pres., Commn of Finance, Nat. Assembly, 1988; Minister in Dept of Finance, 1991–92; Minister for Industry and Foreign Trade, 1992–93. Mayor, 1995–97, Dep. Mayor, 1997–2001, Sarcelles. *Publications:* Economie de la famille et Accumulation patrimoniale, 1977; (jtly) La Richesse des Français, 1977; (jtly) L'Epargne et la Retraite, 1982. *Address:* BP26, 95203 Sarcelles, France.

STRAW, Alice Elizabeth, (Mrs J. W. Straw); *see* Perkins, A. E.

STRAW, Rt Hon. John Whitaker, (Rt Hon. Jack); PC 1997; MP (Lab) Blackburn, since 1979; Secretary of State for Foreign and Commonwealth Affairs, since 2001; barrister; *b* 3 Aug. 1946; *s* of Walter Arthur Whitaker Straw and of Joan Sylvia Straw; *m* 1st, 1968, Anthea Lilian Weston (marr. diss. 1978); (one *d* decd); 2nd, 1978, Alice Elizabeth Perkins, *qv*; one *s* one *d*. *Educ:* Brentwood Sch., Essex; Univ. of Leeds. LLB 1967. Called to Bar, Inner Temple, 1972, Bencher, 1997. Political Advr to Sec. of State for Social Services, 1974–76; Special Advr to Sec. of State for Environment, 1976–77; on staff of Granada TV (World in Action), 1977–79. Pres., Leeds Univ. Union, 1967–68; Pres., Nat. Union of Students, 1969–71; Mem., Islington Borough Council, 1971–78; Dep. Leader, Inner London Educn Authority, 1973–74; Mem., Labour Party's Nat. Exec. Sub-Cttee on Educn and Science, 1970–82; Chm., Jt Adv. Cttee on Polytechnic of N London, 1973–75. Vice-Pres., Assoc. of District Councils, 1984–. Contested (Lab) Tonbridge and Malling, Feb. 1974. Opposition spokesman on the Treasury, 1980–83, on the environment, 1983–87; Principal Opposition Spokesman on educn, 1987–92, on the envmt (local govt), 1992–94, on home affairs, 1994–97; Sec. of State for the Home Office, 1997–2001. Mem., Shadow Cabinet, 1987–97; Mem., NEC, Labour Pty, 1994–95. Vis. Fellow, Nuffield Coll., Oxford, 1990–98. Member Council: Inst. for Fiscal Studies, 1983–; Lancaster Univ., 1988–91; Governor: Blackburn Coll., 1990–; Pimlico Sch., 1994– (Chm., 1995–98). FSS 1995. *Publications:* Granada Guildhall Lecture, 1969; University of Leeds Convocation Lecture, 1978; Policy and Ideology, 1993; contrib. pamphlets, articles. *Recreations:* walking, cycling, cooking puddings, music. *Address:* House of Commons, SW1A 0AA.

STRAWSON, Maj.-Gen. John Michael, CB 1975; OBE 1964; idc, jssc, psc; Senior Military Adviser, Westland Aircraft Ltd, 1978–85 (Head of Cairo Office, 1976–78); *b* 1 Jan. 1921; *s* of late Cyril Walter and Nellie Dora Strawson; *m* 1960, Baroness Wilfried von Schellersheim; two *d*. *Educ:* Christ's Coll., Finchley. Joined Army, 1940; commnd, 1942; served with 4th QO Hussars in Middle East, Italy, Germany, Malaya, 1942–50, 1953–54, 1956–58; Staff Coll., Camberley, 1950; Bde Major, 1951–53; Instructor, Staff Coll. and Master of Drag Hounds, 1958–60; GSO1 and Col GS in WO and MoD, 1961–62 and 1965–66; comd QR Irish Hussars, Malaysia and BAOR, 1963–65; comd Inf. Bde, 1967–68; idc 1969; COS, Live Oak, SHAPE, 1970–72; COS, HQ UKLF, 1972–76. Col, Queen's Royal Irish Hussars, 1975–85. US Bronze Star, 1945. *Publications:* The Battle for North Africa, 1969; Hitler as Military Commander, 1971; The Battle for the Ardennes, 1972; The Battle for Berlin, 1974; (jtly) The Third World War, 1978; El Alamein, 1981; (jtly) The Third World War: the untold story, 1982; A History of the SAS Regiment, 1984; The Italian Campaign, 1987; Gentlemen in Khaki: the British Army 1890–1990, 1989; Beggars in Red: the British Army 1789–1889, 1991; The Duke and the Emperor, 1994; Churchill and Hitler: in victory and defeat, 1997; On Drag-hunting, 1999. *Recreations:* equitation, shooting, reading. *Club:* Cavalry and Guards.

See also Sir P. F. Strawson.

STRAWSON, Sir Peter (Frederick), Kt 1977; FBA 1960; Fellow of Magdalen College, Oxford, 1968–87, Hon. Fellow, 1989; Waynflete Professor of Metaphysical Philosophy in the University of Oxford, 1968–87 (Reader, 1966–68); Fellow of University College, Oxford, 1948–68, Honorary Fellow since 1979; *b* 23 November 1919; *s* of late Cyril Walter and Nellie Dora Strawson; *m* 1945, Grace Hall Martin; two *s* two *d*. *Educ:* Christ's College, Finchley; St John's College, Oxford (scholar; Hon. Fellow, 1973). Served War of 1939–45, RA, REME, Capt. Asst Lecturer in Philosophy, University Coll. of N. Wales, 1946; John Locke Schol., Univ. of Oxford, 1946; Lecturer in Philosophy, 1947, Fellow and Praelector, 1948, University Coll., Oxford. Vis. Prof., Duke Univ., N Carolina, 1955–56; Fellow of Humanities Council and Vis. Associate Prof., Princeton Univ., 1960–61, Vis. Prof., 1972; Woodbridge Lectr, Columbia Univ., NY, 1983; Immanuel Kant Lectr, Munich, 1985; Vis. Prof., Collège de France, 1985. MAE 1990; For. Hon. Mem., Amer. Acad. Arts and Scis, 1971. Hon. Dr Munich, 1998. Internat. Kant Prize, Berlin, 2000. *Publications:* Introduction to Logical Theory, 1952; Individuals, 1959; The Bounds of Sense, 1966; (ed) Philosophical Logic, 1967; (ed) Studies in the Philosophy of Thought and Action, 1968; Logico-Linguistic Papers, 1971; Freedom and Resentment, 1974; Subject and Predicate in Logic and Grammar, 1974; Scepticism and Naturalism: some varieties, 1985; Analyse et Métaphysique, 1985; Analysis and Metaphysics, 1992; Entity and Identity, 1997; The Philosophy of P. F. Strawson (autobiog. and replies to critics), 1998; contrib. to Mind, Philosophy, Proc. Aristotelian Soc., Philosophical Review, etc. *Address:* 25 Farndon Road, Oxford OX2 6RT. *T:* (01865) 515026. *Club:* Athenæum.

See also J. M. Strawson.

STREAMS, Peter John, CMG 1986; HM Diplomatic Service, retired; Ambassador to Sudan, 1991–94; *b* 8 March 1935; *s* of Horace Stanley Streams and Isabel Esther (*née* Ellaway); *m* 1956, Margareta Decker; two *s* one *d*. *Educ:* Wallington County Grammar Sch. BoT, 1953; Bombay, 1960, Calcutta, 1962, Oslo, 1966; FCO, 1970; Mexico, 1973; FCO, 1977, Counsellor, 1979; Consul-Gen., Karachi, 1982; Counsellor, Stockholm, 1985; Ambassador to Honduras and concurrently to El Salvador, 1989. Head, EU Monitoring Mission to former Yugoslavia, 1998. *Recreations:* walking, golf. *Address:* c/o Foreign and Commonwealth Office, SW1A 2AH.

STREATFEILD, Maj.-Gen. Timothy Stuart Champion, CB 1980; MBE 1960; Director, Royal Artillery, 1978–81; *b* 9 Sept. 1926; *s* of Henry Grey Champion and Edythe Streatfeild; *m* 1951, Annette Catherine, *d* of Sir John Clague, CMG, CIE, and Lady Clague; two *s* one *d*. *Educ:* Eton; Christ Church, Oxford (MA). FIMgt. Commnd into RA, 1946; Instructor, Staff Coll., Camberley, 1963–65; Chief Instructor, Sudan Armed Forces Staff Coll., 1965–67; Commander, 7th Parachute Regt, RHA, 1967–69; Col Adjt and QMG, 4 Div., 1969–70; Commander, RA 2 Div., 1971–72; RCDS, 1973; Brigadier Adjt and QMG, 1st Corps, 1974–75; COS, Logistic Exec., MoD, 1976–78. Regtl Comptroller, RA, 1986–89. Col. Commandant: RA, 1980–91; RHA, 1981–91. *Recreations:* fishing, sporting, the countryside, music. *Address:* Toatley Farm, Chawleigh, Chulmleigh, N Devon EX18 7HW. *T:* (01363) 83363. *Club:* Army and Navy.

STREATFEILD-JAMES, David Stewart; QC 2001; *b* 22 Oct. 1963; *e s* of Capt. John Jocelyn Streatfeild-James, *qv*; *m* 1991, Alison; two *s* two *d*. *Educ:* Charterhouse; University Coll., Oxford. Called to the Bar, Inner Temple, 1986. *Recreations:* family, sport, gardening, cookery. *Address:* The Manor, Queen Charlton, Bristol BS32 2SH. *T:* (0117) 986 2025.

STREATFEILD-JAMES, Captain John Jocelyn; RN retired; *b* 14 April 1929; *s* of late Comdr Rev. Eric Cardew Streatfeild-James, OBE, and Elizabeth Ann (*née* Kirby); *m* 1962, Sally Madeline (*née* Stewart); three *s* (one *d* decd). *Educ:* RNC, Dartmouth. Specialist in Undersea Warfare. Naval Cadet, 1943–47; Midshipman, 1947–49; Sub-Lt, 1949–51; Lieutenant: Minesweeping, Diving and Anti-Bandit Ops, Far East Stn, 1951; Officer and Rating Trng, Home Stn, 1952–53; specialised in Undersea Warfare, 1954–55; Ship and Staff Duties, Far East Stn, 1955–57; Exchange Service, RAN, 1957–59; Lieutenant-Commander: instructed Officers specialising in Undersea Warfare, 1960–61; Sea Duty, Staff Home Stn, 1962–63; Sen. Instr, Jt Anti-Submarine Sch., HMS Sea Eagle, 1964–65; Commander: Staff of C-in-C Western Fleet and C-in-C Eastern Atlantic Area, 1965–67; Jt Services Staff Coll., 1968; Staff of Comdr Allied Naval Forces, Southern Europe, Malta, 1968–71; HMS Dryad, 1971–73; Captain: Sen. Officers' War Course, RNC, Greenwich, 1974; Dir, OPCON Proj., 1974–77; HMS Howard (i/c), Head of British Defence Liaison Staff, Ottawa, and Defence Advr to British High Comr in Canada, 1978–80 (as Cdre); HMS Excellent (i/c), 1981–82; ADC to the Queen, 1982–83. *Recreations:* sailing, carpentry, painting. *Address:* South Lodge, Tower Road, Hindhead, Surrey GU26 6SP. *T:* (01428) 606064.

See also D. S. Streatfeild-James.

STREATOR, Edward; consultant; *b* 12 Dec. 1930; *s* of Edward J. and Ella S. Streator; *m* 1957, Priscilla Craig Kenney; one *s* two *d*. *Educ:* Princeton Univ. (AB). US Naval Reserve, served to Lieut (jg), 1952–56; entered Foreign Service, 1956; Third Sec., US Embassy, Addis Ababa, 1958–60; Second Sec., Lome, 1960–62; Office of Intelligence and Research, Dept of State, 1962–64; Staff Asst to Sec. of State, 1964–66; First Sec., US Mission to NATO, 1966–69; Dep. Director, then Director, Office of NATO Affairs, Dept of State, 1969–75; Dep. US Permanent Representative to NATO, Brussels, 1975–77; Minister, US Embassy, London, 1977–84; US Ambassador to OECD, 1984–87. Mem., South Bank Bd, 1990–99. Member: Council, RUSI, 1988–92; Exec. Cttee, IISS, 1988–99; Bd, British Amer. Arts Assoc., 1989–99; Develt Cttee, Nat. Gallery, 1991–95; Adv. Bd, Fulbright Commn, 1995–; Chm., New Atlantic Initiative, 1996–. President: American Chamber of Commerce (UK), 1989–94; European Council, American Chambers of Commerce, 1992–95. Mem. Exec. Cttee, The Pilgrims, 1984–; Governor: Ditchley Foundn, 1984–; ESU, 1989–95. Hon. FRSA 1992. Benjamin Franklin Medal, RSA, 1992. *Recreation:* swimming. *Address:* 16 Eaton Place, SW1X 8AE. *T:* (020) 7823 1444; Château de St Aignan, 32480 La Romieu, France. *T:* 562288035. *Clubs:* White's, Beefsteak, Garrick; Metropolitan (Washington); Mill Reef (Antigua).

STREEP, Mary Louise, (Meryl); American actress; *b* 22 June 1949; *d* of Harry and Mary Streep; *m* 1978, Donald Gummer; one *s* three *d*. *Educ:* Vassar Coll. (BA 1971); Yale (MA 1975). *Stage appearances include:* New York Shakespeare Fest., 1976; Alice in Concert, NY Public Theater, 1981; The Seagull, NY, 2001; *television appearances include:* The Deadliest Season (film), 1977; Holocaust, 1978; *films include:* The Deer Hunter, 1978; Manhattan, 1979; The Seduction of Joe Tynan, 1979; Kramer versus Kramer, 1979 (Academy Award, 1980); The French Lieutenant's Woman (BAFTA Award), 1981; Sophie's Choice

(Academy Award), 1982; Still of the Night, 1982; Silkwood, 1983; Falling in Love, 1984; Plenty, 1985; Out of Africa, 1985; Heartburn, 1986; Ironweed, 1987; A Cry in the Dark, 1989; She-Devil, 1990; Postcards from the Edge, 1991; Defending your Life, 1991; Death Becomes Her, 1992; The House of the Spirits, 1994; The River Wild, 1995; The Bridges of Madison County, 1995; Before and After, 1996; Marvin's Room, 1997; Dancing at Lughnasa, 1998; One True Thing, 1999; Music of the Heart, 2000. Hon. DFA: Dartmouth Coll., 1981; Yale, 1983. *Address:* c/o Creative Artists Agency, 9830 Wilshire Boulevard, Beverly Hills, CA 90212, USA.

STREET, Hon. Anthony Austin; manager and company director; *b* 8 Feb. 1926; *s* of late Brig. the Hon. G. A. Street, MC, MHR; *m* 1951, Valerie Erica, *d* of J. A. Rickard; three *s*. *Educ:* Melbourne C of E Grammar Sch. RAN, 1945–46. MP (L) Corangamite, Vic, 1966–84 (resigned); Mem., various Govt Mems Cttees, 1967–71; Mem., Fed. Exec. Council, 1971–; Asst Minister for Labour and Nat. Service, 1971–72; Mem., Opposition Exec., 1973–75 (Special Asst to Leader of Opposition and Shadow Minister for Labour and Immigration, March-Nov. 1975); Minister for Labour and Immigration, Caretaker Ministry after dissolution of Parliament, Nov. 1975; Minister for Employment and Industrial Relations and Minister Assisting Prime Minister in Public Service Matters, 1975–78; Minister for: Industrial Relations, 1978–80; Foreign Affairs, 1980–83. Chm., Fed. Rural Cttee, Liberal Party, 1970–74. *Recreations:* cricket, golf, tennis, flying. *Address:* 153 The Terrace, Ocean Grove, Vic 3226, Australia. *Clubs:* MCC; Melbourne; Royal Melbourne Golf, Barwon Heads Golf.

STREET, John Edmund Dudley, CMG 1966; retired; *b* 21 April 1918; *er s* of late Philip Edmund Wells Street and of Elinor Gladys Whittington-Ince; *m* 1st, 1940, Noreen Mary (*d* 1981), *o d* of Edward John Griffin Comerford and Mary Elizabeth Winstone; three *s* one *d*; 2nd, 1983, Mrs Patricia Curzon. *Educ:* Tonbridge School; Exeter College, Oxford. Served War of 1939–45, HM Forces, 1940–46. Entered Foreign Service, 1947; First Secretary: British Embassy, Oslo, 1950; British Embassy, Lisbon, 1952; Foreign Office, 1954; First Secretary and Head of Chancery, British Legation, Budapest, 1957–60; HM Ambassador to Malagasy Republic, 1961–62, also Consul-General for the Island of Réunion and the Comoro Islands, 1961–62; Counsellor, FO, 1963–67; Asst Sec., MoD, 1967–76; Asst Under-Sec. of State, MoD, 1976–78. *Recreation:* reading. *Address:* Cornerways, High Street, Old Woking, Surrey GU22 9JH. *T:* (01483) 764371.

STREET, Hon. Sir Laurence (Whistler), AC 1989; KCMG 1976; Lieutenant-Governor of New South Wales, 1974–89; Chief Justice of New South Wales, 1974–88; *b* Sydney, 3 July 1926; *s* of Hon. Sir Kenneth Street, KCMG; *m* 1st, 1952, Susan Gai, AM, *d* of E. A. S. Watt; two *s* two *d*; 2nd, Penelope Patricia, *d* of G. Ferguson; one *d*. *Educ:* Cranbrook Sch., Sydney; Univ. of Sydney (LLB Hons). RANVR, incl. war service in Pacific, 1943–47; Comdr, Sen. Officer RANR Legal Br., 1964–65. Admitted to NSW Bar, 1951; QC 1963; Judge, Supreme Court of NSW, 1965–74; Judge of Appeal, 1972–74; Chief Judge in Equity, 1972–74. Dir, John Fairfax Holdings Ltd, 1991–97 (Chm., 1994–97); Dir, Monte Paschi Aust. Ltd, 1992–97. Lectr in Procedure, Univ. of Sydney, 1962–63, Lectr in Bankruptcy, 1964–65; Member: Public Accountants Regn Bd, 1962–65; Companies Auditors Bd, 1962–65; Pres., Courts-Martial Appeal Tribunal, 1971–74; Chairman: Aust. Commercial Disputes Centre Planning Cttee, 1985–86; Aust. Govt Internat. Legal Services Adv. Council, 1990–; Aust. Mem., WIPO Arbitration Consultative Commn, Geneva, 1994–; Aust. Govt Designated Conciliator, ICSID, Washington, 1995–. Mem. Court, London Court of Internat. Arbitration, 1988– (Pres., Asia-Pacific Council, 1989–). Pres., Aust. Br., 1990–94, World Pres., 1990–92, Life Vice-Pres., 1992, Internat. Law Assoc.; Chm., Judiciary Appeals Bd, NSW Rugby League, 1989–. Chm., Sydney Univ. Law Sch. Foundn, 1990–; President: Sydney Univ. Law Grads Assoc., 1963–65; Cranbrook Sch. Council, 1966–74; St John Amb. Aust. (NSW), 1974–. Hon. Col, 1st/15th Royal NSW Lancers, 1986–96. FCIArb 1992. Hon. FIArbA 1989. Hon. LLD: Sydney, 1984; Macquarie, 1989; Univ. of Technol., Sydney, 1998 (Fellow, 1990); Hon. DEc New England, 1996. KStJ 1976. Grand Officer of Merit, SMO Malta, 1977. *Address:* 121 Macquarie Street, Sydney, NSW 2000, Australia. *T:* (2) 92580801, *Fax:* (2) 92580833. *Clubs:* Union (Sydney); Royal Sydney Golf.

STREET, Prof. Peter Ronald, PhD; Development Director, Genus International Consultancy, since 1999; Director, Produce Studies Ltd, since 1992; *b* 4 May 1944; *s* of Leslie Arthur John and Winifred Marjorie Street; *m* 1969, Christine Hill; two *d*. *Educ:* Univ. of Reading (BScAgr, PhD Management and Econs). Lectr in Management and Econs, Faculty of Agricl Sci., Univ. of Nottingham, 1971–74; Tropical Products Institute: Principal Res. Officer, 1974–82; Sen. Principal Res. Officer and Head, Mkting and Industrial Econs Dept, 1982–85; Mem., Directorate Bd, 1982–85; Dir and Chief Economist, Produce Studies Ltd, 1985–89; Prof. of Agricl Systems and Head, Dept of Agriculture, Univ. of Reading, 1989–92. Visiting Professor: ICSTM, 1998–; Imperial Coll., London, 1998–; RAC, 2000–. Chm., Selskya Zhign Consultants, Moscow, 1994–; Mem. Bd, British Consultants Bureau, 1999–; Man. Dir, GFA-RACE Partners Ltd, 2000–; Vice Pres., Online Global Commodities Exchange, 2000–. Numerous internat. consultancy assignments. MIMgt (MBIM 1972). *Publication:* (ed with J. G. W. Jones) Systems Theory Applied to Agriculture and the Food Chain, 1990. *Recreations:* gardening, fly fishing. *Address:* Rockford Green Cottage, Rockford, Ringwood, Hants BH24 3NA. *T:* (01425) 475222.

STREET, Prof. Robert, AO 1985; DSc; Vice-Chancellor, University of Western Australia, 1978–86, Hon. Research Fellow, since 1986; *b* 16 Dec. 1920; *s* of late J. Street, Allerton Bywater, Yorkshire, UK; *m* 1943, Joan Marjorie Bere; one *s* one *d*. *Educ:* Hanley High Sch.; King's Coll., London. BSc, MSc, PhD, DSc (London). MIEE, FInstP, FAIP, FAA. Scientific Officer, Dept of Supply, UK, 1942–45; Lectr, Dept of Physics, Univ. of Nottingham, 1945–54; Sen. Lectr, Dept of Physics, Univ. of Sheffield, 1954–60; Foundn Prof. of Physics, Monash Univ., Melbourne, Vic., 1960–74; Dir, Research Sch. of Physical Sciences, Aust. Nat. Univ., 1974–78. Former President: Aust. Inst. of Nuclear Science and Engrg; Aust. Inst. of Physics; Mem. and Chm., Aust. Research Grants Cttee, 1970–76; Chm., Nat. Standards Commn, 1967–78; Member: State Energy Adv. Council, WA, 1981–86; Australian Science and Technology Council, 1977–80; Council, Univ. of Technology, Lae, Papua New Guinea, 1982–84; Bd of Management, Royal Perth Hosp., 1978–85. Fellow, Aust. Acad. of Science, 1973 (Treas., 1976–77). Hon. DSc: Sheffield, 1986; Western Australia, 1988. *Publications:* research papers in scientific jls. *Recreation:* swimming. *Address:* Department of Physics, University of Western Australia, 35 Stirling Highway, Crawley, WA 6009, Australia. *Club:* Weld (Perth).

STREET, Susan Ruth; Permanent Secretary, Department for Culture, Media and Sport, since 2001; *b* 11 Aug. 1949; *d* of late Dr Stefan Galeski and of Anna Galeski; *m* 1972, Richard Street; one *s* one *d*. *Educ:* St Andrews Univ. (MA Philosophy). Home Office, 1974–2001: Course Dir, Top Mgt Prog., Cabinet Office, 1989–91 (on secondment); Supervising Consultant, Price Waterhouse, 1991–94; Director: Central Drugs Co-ordination Unit, Cabinet Office, 1994–96 (on secondment); Fire and Emergency Planning, 1996–99; Sentencing and Correctional Policy, 1999–2000; Criminal Policy, 2000–01. FRSA 1992. *Recreations:* family, ballet, theatre, remedial tennis. *Address:* Department for Culture, Media and Sport, 2-4 Cockspur Street, SW1Y 5DH.

STREET-PORTER, Janet; journalist and broadcaster, since 1967; Editor-at-large, The Independent on Sunday, 2001 (Editor, 1999–2001); *b* 27 Dec. 1946; *m* 1st, 1967, Tim Street-Porter (marr. diss. 1975); 2nd, 1976, A. M. M. Elliott, *qv* (marr. diss. 1978); 3rd, 1978, Frank Cvitanovich (marr. diss. 1988; he *d* 1995). *Educ:* Lady Margaret Grammar Sch., Fulham; Architectural Assoc. TV presenter, 1975–; TV producer, 1981–; Exec., BBC TV, 1988–94; Man. Dir, Live TV, 1994–95. Pres., Ramblers Assoc., 1994–97. FRTS 1994. Hon. FRIBA 2001. Award for originality, BAFTA, 1988; Prix Italia, 1993. *Publications:* The British Teapot, 1977; Scandal, 1981; Coast to Coast, 1998; As the Crow Flies, 1999. *Recreations:* walking, talking, modern art. *Address:* c/o Bob Storer, Harbottle & Lewis, 14 Hanover Square, W1R 0BE. *T:* (020) 7667 5000.

STREETEN, Paul Patrick, DLitt; Professor, Boston University, 1980–93, now Emeritus (Director: Center for Asian Development Studies, 1980–84; World Development Institute, 1984–90); *b* 18 July 1917; *e s* of Wilhelm Hornig, Vienna; changed name to Streeten under Army Council Instruction, 1943; *m* 1951, Ann Hilary Palmer, *d* of Edgar Higgins, Woodstock, Vermont; two *d* (and one step *s*). *Educ:* Vienna; Aberdeen Univ.; Balliol Coll., Oxford (Hon. Schol.); 1st cl. PPE, 1947; Student, Nuffield Coll., Oxford, 1947–48. DLitt Oxon, 1976. Mil. service in Commandos, 1941–43; wounded in Sicily, 1943. Fellow, Balliol Coll., Oxford, 1948–66 (Hon. Fellow, 1986); Associate, Oxford Univ. Inst. of Econs and Statistics, 1960–64; Dep. Dir-Gen., Econ. Planning Staff, Min. of Overseas Develt, 1964–66; Prof. of Econs, Fellow, Acting and Dep. Dir of Inst. of Develt Studies, Sussex Univ., 1966–68; Warden of Queen Elizabeth House, Dir, Inst. of Commonwealth Studies, Univ. of Oxford, and Fellow of Balliol Coll., 1968–78; Special Adviser, World Bank, 1976–79; Dir of Studies, Overseas Develt Council, 1979–80. Rockefeller Fellow, USA, 1950–51; Fellow, Johns Hopkins Univ., Baltimore, 1955–56; Fellow, Center for Advanced Studies, Wesleyan Univ., Conn.; Vis. Prof., Econ. Develt Inst. of World Bank, 1984–86; Jean Monnet Prof., European Univ. Inst., Florence, 1991. Sec., Oxford Econ. Papers, until 1961, Mem. Edit. Bd, 1971–78; Editor, Bulletin of Oxford Univ. Inst. of Econs and Statistics, 1961–64; Chm. Editorial Bd, World Develt, 1972–. Member: UK Nat. Commn of Unesco, 1966; Provisional Council of Univ. of Mauritius, 1966–72; Commonwealth Develt Corp., 1967–72; Statutory Commn, Royal Univ. of Malta, 1972–; Royal Commn on Environmental Pollution, 1974–76. Mem., Internat. Adv. Panel, Canadian Univ. Service Overseas. Vice-Chm., Social Sciences Adv. Cttee, 1971; Member, Governing Body: Queen Elizabeth House, Oxford, 1966–68; Inst. of Develt Studies, Univ. of Sussex, 1968–80 (Vice-Chm.); Dominion Students' Hall Trust, London House; Mem. Council, Overseas Develt Institute, until 1979. Pres., UK Chapter, Soc. for Internat. Develt until 1976. Mem., Phi Beta Delta. Hon. Fellow, Inst. of Develt Studies, Sussex, 1980. Raffaele Mattioli Lectr, Milan, 1991. Hon. LLD Aberdeen, 1980; Hon. DLitt Malta, 1992. Development Prize, Justus Liebig Univ., Giessen. Silver Sign of Honour (Vienna). *Publications:* (ed) Value in Social Theory, 1958; Economic Integration, 1961, 2nd edn 1964; (contrib.) Economic Growth in Britain, 1966; The Teaching of Development Economics, 1967; (ed with M. Lipton) Crisis in Indian Planning, 1968; (contrib. to) Gunnar Myrdal, Asian Drama, 1968; (ed) Unfashionable Economics, 1970; (ed, with Hugh Corbet) Commonwealth Policy in a Global Context, 1971; Frontiers of Development Studies, 1972; (ed) Trade Strategies for Development, 1973; The Limits of Development Research, 1975; (with S. Lall) Foreign Investment, Transnationals and Developing Countries, 1977; Development Perspectives, 1981; First Things First, 1981; (ed with Richard Jolly) Recent Issues in World Development, 1981; (ed with H. Maier) Human Resources, Employment and Development, 1983; What Price Food?, 1987; (ed) Beyond Adjustment, 1988; Mobilizing Human Potential, 1989; Paul Streeten in South Africa, 1992; Strategies for Human Development, 1994; (co-ed) The UN and the Bretton Woods Institutions, 1995; Thinking About Development, 1995; Globalisation: threat or opportunity, 2001; contribs to learned journals; *festschrift:* (ed S. Lall and F. Stewart) Theory and Reality in Development, 1986. *Address:* PO Box 92, Spencertown, NY 12165, USA. *Club:* Oxford and Cambridge.

STREETER, Gary Nicholas; MP (C) Devon South West, since 1997 (Plymouth Sutton, 1992–97); *b* 2 Oct. 1955; *s* of Kenneth Victor Streeter and Shirley Nellie (*née* Keable); *m* 1978, Janet Stevens; one *s* one *d*. *Educ:* Tiverton Grammar Sch.; King's Coll., London (LLB 1st cl. Hons). Articled at Coward Chance, London, 1978–80; admitted solicitor, 1980; joined Foot & Bowden, solicitors, Plymouth, 1980, Partner, 1984–99. Plymouth City Council: Mem., 1986–92; Chm., Housing Cttee, 1989–91. PPS to Solicitor-General, 1993–95, and to Attorney-General, 1994–95; an Asst Govt Whip, 1995–96; Parly Sec., Lord Chancellor's Dept, 1996–97; Opposition front bench spokesman on European affairs, 1997–98; Shadow Sec. of State for Internat. Develt, 1998–2001. *Recreations:* lover of cricket and Rugby. *Address:* House of Commons, SW1A 0AA. *T:* (020) 7219 4070.

STREETON, Sir Terence (George), KBE 1989 (MBE 1969); CMG 1981; HM Diplomatic Service, retired; Chairman: Healthco Pvt Ltd, Harare, since 1994; Director, Contact International Ltd, Harare, since 1992; *b* 12 Jan. 1930; *er s* of late Alfred Victor Streeton and Edith Streeton (*née* Deiton); *m* 1962, Molly Horsburgh; two *s* two *d*. *Educ:* Wellingborough Grammar School. Inland Revenue, 1946; Prison Commission, 1947; Government Communications Headquarters, 1952; Foreign Office (Diplomatic Wireless Service), 1953; Diplomatic Service, 1965–89: First Secretary, Bonn, 1966; FCO, 1970; First Secretary and Head of Chancery, Bombay, 1972; Counsellor and Head of Joint Admin Office, Brussels, 1975; Head of Finance Dept, FCO, 1979; Asst Under-Sec. of State and Prin. Finance Officer, FCO, 1982–83; High Comr to Bangladesh, 1983–89. Pres., Bangladesh-British Chamber of Commerce, 1993–97. *Recreations:* walking, golf. *Address:* 189 Billing Road, Northampton NN1 5RS. *T:* (01604) 473510. *Club:* Oriental.

STREISAND, Barbra Joan; singer, actress, director, producer, writer, composer, philanthropist; *b* Brooklyn, NY, 24 April 1942; *d* of Emanuel and Diana Streisand; *m* 1963, Elliott Gould (marr. diss. 1971); one *s*; *m* 1998, James Brolin. *Educ:* Erasmus Hall High Sch. Nightclub début, Bon Soir, Greenwich Village, 1961; NY theatre début, Another Evening with Harry Stoones, 1961; musical comedy, I Can Get It For You Wholesale, 1962 (NY Critics' Best Supporting Actress Award, 1962); musical, Funny Girl, NY, 1964, London, 1966 (Best Foreign Actress, Variety Poll Award, 1966). Special Tony Award, 1970. *Films:* Funny Girl, 1968 (Golden Globe Award, Acad. Award, 1968); Hello Dolly, 1969; On a Clear Day You Can See Forever, 1970; The Owl and the Pussycat, 1971; What's Up Doc?, 1972; Up the Sandbox, 1972; The Way We Were, 1973; For Pete's Sake, 1974; Funny Lady, 1975; A Star is Born (also prod), 1976; The Main Event (also prod), 1979; All Night Long, 1981; Yentl (also co-wrote, dir. and prod), 1984 (Golden Globe Award for Best Picture and Best Dir); Nuts (also prod), 1987; The Prince of Tides (also dir. and prod), 1990; The Mirror Has Two Faces (also dir. and co-prod), 1997. *Television specials:* My Name is Barbra, 1965 (5 Emmy Awards, Peabody Award); Color Me Barbra, 1966; Belle of 14th Street, 1967; A Happening in Central Park, 1968; Musical Instrument, 1973; One Voice, 1986; Barbra Streisand, the Concert (also prod and co-dir.),

1994 (Peabody Award, 3 Cable Ace Awards, 5 Emmy Awards); Serving in Silence: the Margarethe Cammermeyer story (exec. prod.), 1995. Began recording career, 1962; Grammy Awards for best female pop vocalist, 1963, 1964, 1965, 1977, 1986, for best songwriter (with Paul Williams), 1977; (jtly) Acad. Award for composing best song (Evergreen), 1976; awarded: 37 Gold Albums (exceeded only by Elvis Presley and The Beatles); 22 Platinum Albums; 12 Multi-Platinum Albums (most for any female artist). *Albums include:* People, 1965; My Name is Barbra, 1965; The Way We Were, 1974; Guilty, 1980; The Broadway Album, 1986; Just for the Record (retrospective album), 1991; Back to Broadway, 1993; Barbra Streisand, the Concert (double album and video), 1994; The Mirror Has Two Faces (soundtrack), 1996. *Address:* Barwood Productions, 433 N Camden Drive, Suite 500, Beverley Hills, CA 90210, USA.

STRETTON, Eric Hugh Alexander, CB 1972; Deputy Chief Executive in Property Services Agency, Department of the Environment, 1972–76, Deputy Chairman, 1973–76; *b* 22 June 1916; *y s* of Major S. G. Stretton, Wigston, Leicester; *m* 1946, Sheila Woodroffe Anderson, MB, BS (*d* 1997), *d* of Dr A. W. Anderson, Cardiff (formerly of Ogmore Vale); one *s* one *d. Educ:* Wyggeston Sch; Pembroke Coll., Oxford. BA 1939, MA 1942. Leics Regt and 2/4 PWO Gurkha Rifles (Major), 1939–46. Asst Sec., Birmingham Univ. Appointments Board, 1946. Entered Ministry of Works, 1947; Prin. Private Sec. to Minister of Works, 1952–54; Asst Sec., 1954; Under-Secretary: MPBW, 1962–70; DoE, 1970–72; Dep. Sec., 1972. Chm., Structure Plan Examns in Public, Salop, 1979, Lincs, 1980, Central and N Lancs, 1981. *Publication:* Dacre Castle, 1994.

STRETTON, James, FFA; Chief Executive, UK Operations, Standard Life Assurance Co., 1994–2001; Director, Bank of England, since 1998; *b* 16 Dec. 1943; *s* of Donald and Muriel Stretton; *m* 1968, Isobel Robertson; two *d. Educ:* Laxton Grammar Sch., Oundle; Worcester Coll., Oxford (BA Maths). FFA 1970. Standard Life Assurance Company, 1965–2001: Asst Pensions Manager, 1974–77; Asst Investment Manager, 1977–84; General Manager (Ops), 1984–88; Dep. Man. Dir, 1988–94. Member: Scottish New Deal Adv. Task Force, 1997–99; Scottish Business Forum, 1998–99. Pres., YouthLink Scotland, 1994–2000. Director: PIA, 1992–94; Scottish Community Educn Council, 1996–99. Chm., Foresight Ageing Population Panel, 1999–2000. Dir, Edinburgh Internat. Fest. Ltd, 1997–. Mem. Court, Univ. of Edinburgh, 1996–. *Recreations:* music, reading, gardening. *Address:* 15 Letham Mains, Haddington EH41 4NW.

STRETTON, Peter John; His Honour Judge Stretton; a Circuit Judge, since 1986; *b* 14 June 1938; *s* of Frank and Ella Stretton; *m* 1973, Eleanor Anne Wait; three *s* one *d. Educ:* Bedford Modern Sch. Called to the Bar, Middle Temple, 1962; Head of Chambers, 1985. A Recorder, 1982–86. *Recreations:* squash, gardening. *Address:* Derby Crown Court, Morledge, Derby DE1 2XE.

STRETTON, Ross; Director, Royal Ballet, since 2001; *m* Valmai. Trained at Australian Ballet Sch., Melbourne. Dancer: Australian Ballet, 1972–79 (Prin. Artist); Joffrey Ballet; American Ballet Theatre, NY, 1981–91; Asst Artistic Dir, American Ballet Theatre, 1993–97; Dir, Australian Ballet, 1997–2001. *Address:* Royal Ballet, Royal Opera House, Covent Garden, WC2E 9DD.

STRICK, Robert Charles Gordon; Clerk to the Drapers' Company, 1980–93 (Liveryman, Court of Assistants, 1994); *b* 23 March 1931; *m* 1960, Jennifer Mary Hathway; one *s* one *d. Educ:* Royal Grammar Sch., Guildford; Sidney Sussex Coll., Cambridge (MA). Served RA, 1949–51; TA, 1951–55. Spicers Ltd, 1954–55; joined HMOCS, 1955; Dist Officer, Fiji, 1955–59; Sec., Burns Commn into Natural Resources and Population Trends, 1959–60; Asst Sec., Suva, 1960–61; Sec. to Govt, Tonga, 1961–63; Develt Officer and Divl Comr, 1963–67, Sec. for Natural Resources, 1967–71, Fiji; retired 1971; Under Sec., ICA, 1971–72; Asst Sec.-Gen., RICS, 1972–80; Clerk, Chartered Surveyors' Co., 1977–80. Hon. Member: CGLI, 1991; Old Students' Assoc., Aberystwyth, 1993–; Shrewsbury Co. of Drapers, 1992 (Court of Assts, 1993). Governor, Royal GS, Guildford, 1994–. Hon. Fellow, QMW, 1993. Hon. DLitt Coll. of William and Mary, Virginia, USA, 1993. *Recreations:* the countryside, walking, golf, gardening. *Address:* Lane End, Sheep Lane, Midhurst GU29 9NT. *T:* (01730) 813151.

STRICKLAND, Benjamin Vincent Michael, FCA; Chairman, Iron Trades Insurance Group, since 1996; *b* 20 Sept. 1939; *s* of Maj.-Gen. Eugene Vincent Michael Strickland, CMG, DSO, OBE, MM, and of Barbara Mary Farquharson Meares Lamb, *d* of Major Benjamin Lamb, RFA; *m* 1965, Tessa Mary Edwina, *d* of Rear-Adm. John Grant, CB, DSO; one *s* one *d. Educ:* Mayfield Coll.; University Coll., Oxford, 1960–63 (MA PPE); Harvard Business Sch. (AMPDip 1978). FCA 1967. Lieutenant: 17/21 Lancers, BAOR, 1959–60; Inns of Court and City Yeomanry, 1963–67. Jun. Man., Price Waterhouse & Co., 1963–68; joined J. Henry Schroder Wagg & Co. in Corp. Finance, 1968: Dir, Schroder Wagg, 1974–91; Chm., G. D. Peters Engineering, 1972–74; Dir, Property Hldgs Internat. (USA), 1974–75; Chm. and Chief Exec., Schroders Australia, 1978–82; Gp Man. Dir (Gp Strategy and Finances) and Dir, Schroders PLC, 1983–91. Adviser: on strategy to leading City law firm, 1992–93, 1994–95, to leading media gp, 1993; on mission and finances, Westminster Cathedral, 1991 (Chm., Planning and Finance Cttee, 1991–96); on private banking, 1994; *inter alia*, to two investment banks, 1996–97. Mem. steering gp, Vision for London, 1991–2000. Mem. Council, St George's Med. Sch., 1984–87. FRSA. *Publications:* Bow Group pamphlet on Resources of the Sea (with Laurance Reed), 1965; (contrib.) Financial Services Handbook, 1986. *Recreations:* travel, military and general history, shooting, theatre, film. *Address:* 23 Juer Street, SW11 4RE. *T:* (020) 7585 2970. *Clubs:* Boodle's, Hurlingham.

STRICKLAND, Frank, OBE 1986; Vice-President, The Building Societies Association, since 1992 (Deputy Chairman, 1987–89; Chairman, 1989–91); *b* 4 Feb. 1928; *s* of Robert and Esther Strickland; *m* 1953, Marian Holt; one *d. Educ:* Harris Inst., Preston, Lancs. Asst Sec., Chorley and District Building Soc., 1952; Branch Manager, Hastings and Thanet Building Soc., 1955; Asst Sec., later Jt Sec., Corporation and Eligible Building Soc., 1965; Sunderland and Shields Building Society, later North of England Building Society: Gen. Manager, 1969; Chief Exec., 1975–89; Dir, 1982–92; Exec. Dep. Chm., 1989–91. Pres., European Fedn of Bldg Socs, 1989–91. *Recreations:* bowls, cricket. *Address:* 43 Kewhurst Avenue, Cooden, Bexhill-on-Sea, East Sussex TN39 3BH. *T:* (01424) 846795. *Club:* MCC.

STRICKLAND-CONSTABLE, Sir Frederic, 12th Bt *cr* 1641, of Boynton, Yorkshire; *b* 21 Oct. 1944; *er s* of Sir Robert Frederick Strickland-Constable, 11th Bt and Lettice, *yr d* of Major Frederick Strickland; *S* father, 1994; *m* 1981, Pauline Margaret Harding, one *s* one *d. Educ:* Westminster; Corpus Christi Coll., Cambridge (BA); London Business Sch. (MSc). *Heir: s* Charles Strickland-Constable, *b* 10 Oct. 1985. *Address:* Estate Office, Old Maltongate, Malton YO17 0EG.

STRIKER, Prof. Gisela, DPhil; Professor of Classical Philosophy, Harvard University, since 2000; *b* 26 Nov. 1943. *Educ:* Univ. of Göttingen (DPhil 1969). Asst. Prof., 1970–83, Prof., 1983–86, Univ. of Göttingen; Prof., Dept of Philosophy, Columbia Univ., NY, 1986–89; Prof. of Classical Philosophy, 1989–90, George Martin Lane Prof. of Philosophy and Classics, 1990–97, Harvard Univ.; Laurence Prof. of Ancient Philosophy, Univ. of Cambridge, and Fellow, Trinity Coll., Cambridge, 1997–2000. *Publications:* Essays on Hellenistic Epistemology and Ethics, 1996; articles in learned jls. *Address:* Department of Philosophy, Emerson Hall, Harvard University, Cambridge, MA 02138, USA.

STRINGER, Sir Donald (Edgar), Kt 1993; CBE 1987; *b* 21 Aug. 1930; *o s* of late Donald Bertram Frederick and Marjorie Stringer, Croydon; *m* 1957, Pamela Irene Totty; three *s. Educ:* Whitgift Sch., Croydon. Served Army, RMP, 1951–53. Conservative Party Agent, Fulham, Harrow and Honiton, 1954–65; Conservative Central Office: Dep. Area Agent, W Midlands, 1965–71; Central Office Agent: Northern Area, 1971–73; Greater London Area, 1973–88; Wessex Area, 1988–93. Member: Cons. Agents Exam. Bd, 1987–93; Agents Employment Adv. Cttee, 1988–93. Chm., Salisbury Abbeyfield Soc., 1996–. Mem., Guild of Freemen, City of London, 1988. *Recreations:* golf, walking, military history, philately. *Address:* Beech Cottage, Barford St Martin, Salisbury, Wilts SP3 4AS.

STRINGER, Graham Eric; MP (Lab) Manchester Blackley, since 1997, a Lord Commissioner of HM Treasury (Government Whip), since 2001; *b* 17 Feb. 1950; *s* of late Albert Stringer and of Brenda Stringer. *Educ:* Moston Brook High Sch.; Sheffield Univ. (BSc Hons Chemistry). Analytical chemist. Mem., (Lab) Manchester City Council, 1979–98 (Leader, 1984–96; Chm., Policy and Resources Cttee). Chm., Manchester Airport, 1996–97. *Address:* House of Commons, SW1A 0AA.

STRINGER, Sir Howard, Kt 2000; Chairman and Chief Executive Officer, Sony Corporation of America, since 1998; *b* Cardiff, 19 Feb. 1942; naturalised US citizen, 1985 (dual nationality); *s* of Harry and Marjorie Mary Stringer; *m* 1978, Jennifer Kinmond Patterson; one *s* one *d. Educ:* Oundle Sch.; Merton Coll., Oxford (BA Modern History 1964; MA; Hon. Fellow, 1999). Served US Army, Vietnam, 1965–67. Joined CBS Inc., 1967; Executive Producer: CBS Reports, 1976–81; CBS Evening News, 1981–84; Exec. Vice Pres., 1984–86, Pres., 1986–88, CBS News; Pres., CBS Broadcast Gp, 1988–95; Chm. and CEO, Tele-TV, 1995–97. Chairman: Sony Canada, 1997–; Sony Electronics Inc., 1998–; Mem. Bd, Sony Corp., 1999–. Board Member: Nature Conservancy; United Cerebral Palsy; Amer. Theater Wing; Amer. Friends of BM; NY Presbyterian Hosp. Chm., Bd of Trustees, Amer. Film Inst., 1999–. Foundn Award, Internat. Radio and TV Soc., 1994; Steven J. Ross Humanitarian Award, UJA-Fedn of NY, 1999. *Address:* Sony Corporation of America, 550 Madison Avenue, New York, NY 10022, USA. *T:* (212) 833 6777.

STRINGER, Prof. Joan Kathleen, CBE 2001; PhD; FRSE; Principal and Vice Patron, since 1996, Professor (personal chair), since 1999, Queen Margaret University College (formerly Queen Margaret College), Edinburgh; *b* 12 May 1948; *d* of Francis James and Doris Joan Bourne; *m* 1993, Roelof Marinus Mali. *Educ:* Portland House High Sch., Stoke-on-Trent; Stoke-on-Trent Coll. of Art; Keele Univ. (BA, CertEd, PhD Politics 1986). Graphic designer, ICL, 1966–70; Local Govt Officer, Staffs, 1970–74; teacher, Sudbury Open Prison, Derbys, 1978–80; Robert Gordon University: Lectr, 1980–88; Head, Sch. of Public Admin and Law, 1988–91; Asst Principal, 1991–96. Comr (Scotland), EOC, 1995–2001; Chm. Wkg Gp, NI Equality Commn, 1999. Mem., Scottish Parlt Consultative Steering Gp and Financial Issues Adv. Gp, 1998–99; Comr, Scottish Election Commn, 1999–. Mem., HFEA, 1996–99. Vice-Convener, Univs in Scotland, 1998–; Member: CVCP Commn on Univ. Career Opportunities, 1996–2001; Scottish Cttee, Cttee of Inquiry into Higher Educn (Dearing Cttee), 1996–97; Scottish Council for Postgrad. Med. and Dental Educn, 1999–; Scottish Health Minister's Learning Together Strategy Implementation Gp, 2000–; Exec. Cttee, Scottish Council Develt and Industry, 1998–; Scottish Cttee, British Council, 2000–; DoH Wkg Gp on modernisation of SHO, 2001–; Adv. Gp, Scottish Nursing and Midwifery Educn Council, 2001–; UUK Equality Challenge Steering Gp, 2001–. Non-exec. Dir, Grampian Health Bd, 1994–96. Convenor, Product Standards Cttee, Scottish Quality Salmon, 2001–. Mem., Develt Adv. Bd, Scottish Opera and Ballet, 2001–. Mem., Bd of Mgt, Aberdeen Coll., 1992–96. Member Council: World Assoc. for Co-op. Educn, 1998–; Edinburgh Internat. Festival Soc., 1999–. CIMgt 1999 (MIMgt 1990); FRSA 1994; FRSE 2001. *Publications:* contrib. articles in field of politics with particular ref. to British Public Admin and employment and trng policy. *Recreations:* music (especially opera), gardening, cats. *Address:* Queen Margaret University College, Clerwood Terrace, Edinburgh EH12 8TS. *T:* (0131) 317 3200.

STRINGER, Pamela Mary; Headmistress, Clifton High School for Girls, 1965–85; *b* 30 Aug. 1928; *e d* of late E. Allen Stringer. *Educ:* Worcester Grammar Sch. for Girls; St Hugh's Coll., Oxford. MA (Hons Lit Hum). Asst Classics Mistress, Sherborne Sch. for Girls, 1950–59; Head of Classics Dept, Pate's Grammar Sch. for Girls, Cheltenham, 1959–64 (Dep. Head, 1963–64). Member: Exec. Cttee, Assoc. of Headmistresses, 1975–; Exec. Cttee, Girls Schools Assoc., 1975– (Pres., 1978–79; Chm., Educn Cttee, 1981 84); Council, Secondary Heads Assoc., 1978–79 (Pres. Area 7, 1978–79). *Recreations:* travel in Tuscany and Umbria, reading, arctophily, cooking. *Address:* 36 Henleaze Gardens, Bristol BS9 4HJ.

STROHM, Prof. Paul Holzworth, PhD; J. R. R. Tolkien Professor of Medieval Language and Literature, and Fellow of St Anne's College, University of Oxford, since 1998; *b* 30 July 1938; *s* of Paul H. Strohm and Catherine Poole Strohm; *m* 1960, Jean Sprowl (marr. diss. 1977); two *s. Educ:* Amherst Coll. (BA 1960); Univ. of California, Berkeley (PhD 1965). Indiana University: Asst Prof., 1965–68; Associate Prof., 1968–73; Full Prof. of English, 1973–98. Guggenheim Fellow, 1994–95; Vis. Fellow, Clare Hall, Cambridge, 1994–95; Henry R. Luce Fellow, Nat. Humanities Center, 1996–97. First Vice Pres., Amer. Assoc. of Univ. Profs, 1985–86, Ed., Academe: Bull. of AAUP, 1986–92; Pres., New Chaucer Soc., 1998–2000. *Publications:* Social Chaucer, 1989; Hochon's Arrow: the social imagination of medieval texts, 1992; England's Empty Throne: usurpation and the language of legitimation, 1998; Theory and the Premodern Text, 2000. *Address:* St Anne's College, Woodstock Road, Oxford OX2 6HS.

STROHM, Prof. Reinhard, PhD; FBA 1993; Heather Professor of Music, and Fellow of Wadham College, Oxford University, since 1996; *b* 4 Aug. 1942. *Educ:* Tech. Univ., Berlin (PhD 1971). Lectr, then Reader, in Music, KCL, 1975–83; Prof. of Music Hist., Yale Univ., 1983–89; Reader, 1990–91, Prof. of Histl Musicology, 1991–96, KCL. Edward J. Dent Medal, Royal Musical Assoc., 1977. *Publications:* Italienische Opernarien des frühen Settecento, 1976; Die italienische Oper im 18 Jahrhundert, 1979, 2nd edn 1991; Music in Late Medieval Bruges, 1985, 2nd edn 1990; Essays on Handel and Italian Opera, 1985; The Rise of European Music 1380–1500, 1993; Dramma per Musica: Italian opera seria of the 18th century, 1997; many contribs to books and learned jls. *Recreations:* travel, mountaineering. *Address:* Faculty of Music, St Aldate's, Oxford OX1 1DB; 19 Hunt Close, Bicester, Oxon OX26 6HX.

STRONACH, David Brian, OBE 1975; FSA; Professor of Near Eastern Studies, University of California, Berkeley, since 1981 (Chair of Department, 1994–97); Curator of Near Eastern Archaeology, Lowie Museum of Anthropology, Berkeley, since 1982; *b* 10 June 1931; *s* of Ian David Stronach, MB, FRCSE, and Marjorie Jessie Duncan (*née*

Minto); *m* 1966, Ruth Vaadia; two *d*. *Educ:* Gordonstoun; St John's Coll., Cambridge (MA). Pres., Cambridge Univ. Archaeological Field Club, 1954. British Inst. of Archaeology at Ankara: Scholar, 1955–56; Fellow, 1957–58; Fellow, British Sch. of Archaeology in Iraq, 1957–60; Brit. Acad. Archaeological Attaché in Iran, 1960–61; Dir, British Inst. of Persian Studies, 1961–80, Hon. Vice Pres., 1981–. Asst on excavations at: Istanbul, 1954; Tell Rifa'at, 1956; Beycesultan, 1956–57; Hacilar, 1957–59; Nimrud, 1957–60; Charsada, 1958. Director, excavations at: Ras al'Amiya, 1960; Yarim Tepe, 1960–62; Pasargadae, 1961–63; Tepe Nush-i Jan, 1967–77; Nineveh, 1987–90; Co-director, excavations at: Shahr-i Qumis, 1967–78; Horom, 1992–93; Velikent, 1994–97. Mem., Internat. Cttee of Internat. Congresses of Iranian Art and Archaeology, 1968–80. Hagop Kevorkian Visiting Lectr in Iranian Art and Archaeology, Univ. of Pennsylvania, 1967; Lectures: Rhind, Edin., 1973; Norton, Amer. Inst. of Archaeology, 1980; Columbia in Iranian Studies, Columbia Univ., 1986; Leventritt, Harvard Univ., 1991; Cohodas, Hebrew Union Coll., Jerusalem, 1992; McNicoll, Univ. of Sydney, 1994. Vis. Prof. of Archaeology, Hebrew Univ., Jerusalem, 1977; Vis. Prof. of Archaeology and Iranian Studies, Univ. of Arizona, Tucson, 1980–81; Vis. Prof., Collège de France, Paris, 1999. Mem., German Archaeological Inst., 1973 (Corr. Mem., 1966); Associate Mem., Royal Belgian Acad., 1988–. Ghirshman Prize, Académie des Inscriptions et Belles-Lettres, Paris, 1979; Sir Percy Sykes Meml Medal, Royal Soc. for Asian Affairs, 1980. Adv. Editor: Jl of Mithraic Studies, 1976–79; Iran, 1980–; Iranica Antiqua, 1984–; Bulletin of Asia Inst., 1986–; Amer. Jl of Archaeol., 1989–97. *Publications:* Pasargadae, a Report on the Excavations conducted by the British Institute of Persian Studies, 1978; archaeological articles in: Jl of Near Eastern Studies; Iran; Iraq; Anatolian Studies, etc. *Recreations:* fly fishing, mediaeval architecture, tribal carpets; repr. Cambridge in athletics, 1953. *Address:* Department of Near Eastern Studies, University of California, Berkeley, CA 94720, USA. *Clubs:* Achilles; Hawks (Cambridge); Explorers' (New York).

STRONG, Air Cdre David Malcolm, CB 1964; AFC 1941; *b* 30 Sept. 1913; *s* of Theo Strong; *m* 1941, Daphne Irene Warren-Brown; two *s* one *d*. *Educ:* Cardiff High School. Pilot, under trng, 1936; Bomber Sqdn, 1937–41; POW, 1941–45. Station Commander, RAF Jurby, RAF Driffield, 1946–48; Staff Coll. (psa), 1949; Staff Officer, Rhodesian Air Trng Grp, 1949–51; Directing Staff, Staff Coll., 1952–55; Air Warfare Coll. (pfc), 1956; Station Comdr, RAF Coningsby, 1957–59; Dir of Personnel, Air Min., 1959–61; Senior Air Staff Officer, RAF Germany, 1962–63; Officer Commanding, RAF Halton, 1964–66. Retired, 1966. Chairman: RAF Rugby Union, 1954–56; RAF Golf Soc., 1964–66. *Recreation:* golf. *Clubs:* Royal Air Force; Ashridge Golf.

STRONG, Hilary Jane Veronica; Executive Director, Greenwich Theatre, since 1999; Member, Arts Council of England, since 1998; *b* 3 June 1957; *d* of Robert Hedley Strong and Estelle Flora Strong (*née* Morris). *Educ:* Chichester High Sch. for Girls; Lombard Sch. of Dancing. Freelance stage-manager and actress, 1979–83; Administrator: Merlin Theatre, Frome, 1986–88; Natural Theatre Co., Bath, 1989–94; Dir, Edinburgh Festival Fringe, 1994–99. Member Board: Nat. Campaign for Arts, 1990–92; Dance Base, Edinburgh, 1995–99. *Recreations:* singing, dancing, reading, travelling on buses abroad. *Address:* c/o Greenwich Theatre, Crooms Hill, SE10 8ES.

STRONG, Jaqueline Ann Mary; Director of Education, Leicestershire County Council, since 1995; *b* 2 Oct. 1944; *d* of Donald Cameron McKeand and Gwendoline Mary Ann McKeand (*née* Graham); *m* 1966, Roger Francis Strong. *Educ:* Sexey's Grammar Sch.; Chipping Sodbury Grammar Sch.; Univ. of Wales (BSc, DipEd 1st cl.); Univ. of Bristol (MEd). Teacher, St Julian's Jun. High Sch., Newport, 1966–69; Lectr, Rhydyfelin Coll. of FE, 1967–70; teacher: Belfast, 1970–73; St Peter's Comp. Sch., Huntingdon, 1974, Dep. Head Teacher, 1974–81; Warden, The Village Coll., Bassingbourn, 1981–88; Asst Dir of Educn, Cambs CC, 1988–93; Dir of Educn, Leeds MDC, 1993–95. Mem., Exec. Bd, Encounter, 1984–. *Publications:* articles in educational magazines. *Recreations:* singing, exotic foreign travel, photography, walking, reading, concert and theatre going, taking in unwanted Great Danes. *Address:* County Hall, Glenfield, Leicester LE3 8RF; *e-mail:* education@leics.gov.uk.

STRONG, Dr John Anderson, CBE 1978 (MBE (mil.) 1942); MD; FRCP; FRCPE; FRSE; President, Royal College of Physicians of Edinburgh, 1979–82; *b* 18 Feb. 1915; *s* of Charles James Strong and Mabel Emma Strong (*née* Anderson); *m* 1939, Anne Frances Moira Heaney (*d* 1997); one *s* two *d*. *Educ:* Monkton Combe Sch., Bath; Trinity Coll., Dublin (MB 1937, MA, MD). Served RAMC, UK, India and Burma, 1939–46 (despatches, Burma, 1945); Hon. Lt-Col RAMC, 1946. Senior Lecturer, Dept of Medicine, Univ. of Edinburgh, 1949; Hon. Cons. Phys., Western General Hosp., Edinburgh, 1949; Hon. Physician, MRC Clinical and Population Cytogenetics Unit, 1959–80; Professor of Medicine, Univ. of Edinburgh, 1966–80, Professor Emeritus, 1981. Mem., Medicines Commn, 1976–83; Chm., Scottish Health Educn Co-ordinating Cttee, 1986–88. Hon. FACP 1980; Hon. FRCPI 1980; Hon. Fellow: Coll. of Physicians of Philadelphia, 1981; TCD, 1982; Coll. of Physicians of S Africa, 1982; Fellow *ad eundem*, RCGP, 1982; Mem., Acad. of Medicine, Singapore, 1982. *Publications:* chapter on Endocrinology in Principles and Practice of Medicine, ed L. S. P. Davidson, 1952, 12th edn 1977; articles in general medical and endocrinological jls. *Recreations:* fishing, golf, stalking, natural history. *Address:* 12 Lomond Road, Edinburgh EH5 3JR. *T:* (0131) 552 2865. *Clubs:* New (Edinburgh); Hon. Company of Edinburgh Golfers (Muirfield).

STRONG, John Clifford, CBE 1980; HM Diplomatic Service, retired; Governor, Turks and Caicos Islands, 1978–82; *b* 14 Jan. 1922; *m* 1942, Janet Browning (*d* 1992); three *d*. *Educ:* Beckenham Grammar Sch.; London Sch. of Economics and Political Science. LLB 1953. Served RN, 1942–46; HMOCS Tanzania, 1946–63; CRO, 1963; First Sec., Nairobi, 1964–68; FCO, 1968–73; Counsellor and Head of Chancery, Dar es Salaam, 1973–78. *Address:* Oakover, 24 Crescent Road, Beckenham BR3 6NE. *Club:* Royal Over-Seas League.

STRONG, Julia Trevelyan; *see* Oman, J. T.

STRONG, Liam; Chief Executive, *WORLDCOM* International, since 1997; *b* 6 Jan. 1945; *s* of Gerald Strong and Geraldine Strong (*née* Crozier); *m* 1970, Jacqueline Gray; one *s* one *d*. *Educ:* Trinity Coll., Dublin. Procter & Gamble, 1967–71; Reckitt & Colman, 1971–88; Dir of Mktg and Ops, British Airways, 1988–91; Chief Exec., Sears plc, 1991–97. Dir, Skystream Inc., USA, 2000–. *Recreations:* film, walking, sailing.

STRONG, Hon. Maurice Frederick, PC (Can.) 1993; OC 1976; FRSC 1987; Senior Advisor to the President, World Bank, since 1995; Special Advisor to Secretary-General of the United Nations, since 1998; *b* 29 April 1929; *s* of Frederick Milton Strong and late Mary Fyfe Strong; *m* 1st, 1950 (marr. diss. 1980); two *s* two *d*; 2nd, 1981, Hanne Marstrand; one foster *d*. *Educ:* Public and High Sch., Oak Lake, Manitoba, Canada. Served in UN Secretariat, 1947; worked in industry and Pres. or Dir, various Canadian and internat. corporations, 1948–66; Dir-Gen., External Aid Office (later Canadian Internat. Develt Agency), Canadian Govt, 1966–71; Under-Sec.-Gen. with responsibility for envmtl affairs, and Sec.-Gen. of 1972 Conf. on the Human Environment, Stockholm, 1971–72; Exec. Dir, UN Envmtl Programme, 1972–75; Pres., Chm. of Bd and Chm. of Exec. Cttee, Petro-Canada, 1976–78; Chm. of Bd, AZL Resources Inc., USA, 1978–83; Under-Sec.-Gen., UN, 1985–87 and 1989–92; Exec. Co-ordinator, UN Office for Emergency Ops in Africa, NY, 1985–87; Sec.-Gen., UN 1992 Conf. on Envmt and Develt, 1990–92; Under-Sec. Gen. and Exec. Co-ordinator for UN Reform, 1997. Chm. and CEO, Ontario Hydro, 1992–95; Chairman: Quantum Energy Technologies Corp.; Technology Development Corp.; Strovest Hldgs Inc.; formerly: Dir, Massey Ferguson, Canada; Dir, Mem. Exec. Cttee and Vice Chm., Canada Develt Corp., Toronto; Chm., Canada Develt Investment Corp., Vancouver. Chairman: Centre for Internat. Management Studies, Geneva, 1971–78; American Water Development, Denver, 1986; Internat. Energy Develt Corp., Geneva (also Special Advr); Bd of Govs, Internat. Develt Res. Centre, 1977–78; Co-Chm., Interaction Policy Bd, Vienna; Vice-Chm. and Dir, Soc. Gén. pour l'Energie et les Ressources, Geneva, 1980–86; Foundn Dir, World Economic Forum. Chm., Internat. Adv. Gp, CH2M Hill Cos Ltd; Member: Internat. Adv. Bd, Toyota Motor Corp.; Internat. Adv. Council, Fedn of Korean Industries; Bd of Dirs, TOTAL Foundn; Adv. Bd, Lamont-Doherty Observatory; Bd, Bretton Woods Cttee, Washington; World Commn on Envmt and Develt; Alt. Gov., IBRD, ADB, Caribbean Develt Bank. President: World Fedn of UN Assocs, 1987; Better World Soc., 1988; Chairman: North South Energy Roundtable, Washington; North South Energy Roundtable, Rome; World Resources Inst.; Earth Council; Stockholm Envmt Inst.; Adv. Cttee, UN Univ., Tokyo, Japan; Pres. Council and Rector, UN Univ. for Peace; Mem., and Chm. Exec. Cttee, UN Foundn. Director: Leadership for Envmt and Develt; Lindisfarne Assoc.; Mem., Internat. Asia Soc., NY. Trustee: Rockefeller Foundn, 1971–78; Aspen Inst., 1971–; Internat. Foundn for Develt Alternatives. FRSA. Holds numerous hon. degrees from univs and colls in Canada, USA and UK. First UN Internat. Envmt Prize. Order of the Star of the North (Sweden); Comdr, Order of the Golden Ark (Netherlands). *Publications:* articles in various jls, including Foreign Affairs Magazine, Natural History Magazine. *Recreations:* swimming, skin-diving, farming, reading. *Address:* The Earth Council Institute, 255 Consumers Road, Suite 401, Toronto, ON M2J 5B6, Canada. *Clubs:* Yale (New York); University (Toronto).

STRONG, Sir Roy (Colin), Kt 1982; PhD; FSA; FRSL; writer and historian, diarist, lecturer, critic, columnist, contributor to radio and television and organiser of exhibitions; Director, Oman Productions Ltd; *b* 23 Aug. 1935; *s* of G. E. C. Strong; *m* 1971, Julia Trevelyan Oman, *qv*. *Educ:* Edmonton Co. Grammar Sch.; Queen Mary Coll., London (Fellow, 1976); Warburg Inst., London. Asst Keeper, 1959, Director, Keeper and Secretary 1967–73, Nat. Portrait Gallery; Dir, Victoria and Albert Museum, 1974–87. Ferens Prof. of Fine Art, Univ. of Hull, 1972. Walls Lectures, Pierpont Morgan Library, 1974; Andrew Carnduff Ritchie Lectr, Yale Univ., 1999. Member: Fine Arts Adv. Cttee, British Council, 1974–87; Westminster Abbey Architectl Panel, 1975–89; Council, RCA, 1979–87; Arts Council of GB, 1983–87 (Chm., Arts Panel, 1983–87); Vice-Chm., South Bank Centre (formerly South Bank Bd), 1985–90. High Baliff and Searcher of the Sanctuary, Westminster Abbey, 2000–. Pres., Garden History Soc., 2001–. Trustee: Arundel Castle, 1974–86; Chevening, 1974–87; Sutton Place, 1982–84; Patron, Pallant House, Chichester, 1986– (Trustee, 1980–86). Writer and presenter, TV series incl. Royal Gardens 1992. Sen. Fellow, RCA, 1983; FRSL. Hon. DLitt: Leeds, 1983; Keele, 1984. Shakespeare Prize, FVS Foundn, Hamburg, 1980. *Publications:* Portraits of Queen Elizabeth I, 1963; (with J. A. van Dorsten) Leicester's Triumph, 1964; Holbein and Henry VIII, 1967; Tudor and Jacobean Portraits, 1969; The English Icon: Elizabethan and Jacobean Portraiture, 1969; (with Julia Trevelyan Oman) Elizabeth R, 1971; Van Dyck: Charles I on Horseback, 1972; (with Julia Trevelyan Oman) Mary Queen of Scots, 1972; (with Stephen Orgel) Inigo Jones: the theatre of the Stuart court, 1973; contrib. Burke's Guide to the Royal Family, 1973; Splendour at Court: Renaissance Spectacle and the Theatre of Power, 1973; (with Colin Ford) An Early Victorian Album: the Hill-Adamson collection, 1974; Nicholas Hilliard, 1975; (contrib.) Spirit of the Age, 1975; The Cult of Elizabeth: Elizabethan Portraiture and Pageantry, 1977; And When Did You Last See Your Father?, 1978; The Renaissance Garden in England, 1979; (contrib.) The Garden, 1979; Britannia Triumphans: Inigo Jones, Rubens and Whitehall Palace, 1980; (introd.) Holbein, 1980; (contrib.) Designing for the Dancer, 1981; (jtly) The English Miniature, 1981; (with Julia Trevelyan Oman) The English Year, 1982; (contrib.) Pelican Guide to English Literature vol. 3, 1982; (with J. Murrell) Artists of the Tudor Court, 1983; The English Renaissance Miniature, 1983; (contrib.) Glyndebourne: a celebration, 1984; Art & Power, 1984; Strong Points, 1985; Henry, Prince of Wales and England's Lost Renaissance, 1986; (contrib.) For Veronica Wedgwood These, 1986; Creating Small Gardens, 1986; Gloriana, Portraits of Queen Elizabeth I, 1987; A Small Garden Designer's Handbook, 1987; Cecil Beaton: the Royal portraits, 1988; Creating Small Formal Gardens, 1989; (contrib.) British Theatre Design, 1989; Lost Treasures of Britain, 1990; (contrib.) Sir Philip Sidney's Achievements, 1990; (contrib.) England and the Continental Renaissance, 1990; (ed) A Celebration of Gardens, 1991; The Garden Trellis, 1991; Small Period Gardens, 1992; Royal Gardens, 1992; A Country Life, 1994; Successful Small Gardens, 1994; William Larkin, 1995; The Tudor and Stuart Monarchy, vol. I, Tudor, 1995, vol. II, Elizabethan, 1996; The Story of Britain, 1996; Country Life 1897–1997: the English Arcardia, 1996; The Roy Strong Diaries 1967–1987, 1997; (with Julia Trevelyan Oman) On Happiness, 1998; The Spirit of Britain, 1999; Garden Party, 2000; The Artist and the Garden, 2000; Ornament in the Small Garden, 2001. *Recreations:* gardening, cooking, keeping fit. *Address:* The Laskett, Much Birch, Herefords HR2 8HZ. *Club:* Garrick.

STRONG, Prof. Russell Walker, AC 2001; CMG 1987; RFD 1995; FRCS, FRACS, FACS; FRACDS; Professor of Surgery, University of Queensland, since 1992; Director of Surgery, Princess Alexandra Hospital, Brisbane, since 1981; *b* 4 April 1938; *s* of Aubrey and Anne Strong; *m* 1960, Judith Bardsley; two *d*. *Educ:* Lismore High Sch.; Univ. of Sydney (BDS); Charing Cross Hosp. Med. Sch., Univ. of London (MB BS). LRCP 1965; MRCS 1965, FRCS 1970; FRACDS 1966; FRACS 1974; FACS 1984. Intern, Bromley Hosp., Kent, 1965–66; Tutor in Anatomy, Charing Cross Hosp. Med. Sch., 1966–67; SHO, Birmingham Accident Hosp., 1968; Surgical Registrar: Charing Cross Hosp., 1969; St Helier Hosp., 1970–71; Sen. Surgical Registrar, Whittington Hosp., 1972–73; Surgical Supervisor, Princess Alexandra Hosp., Brisbane, 1973–80. Vis. Prof. and Guest Lectr on numerous occasions worldwide. James IV Surgical Traveller, 1987; Vis. Schol., Pembroke Coll., Cambridge, 2001. Hon. Fellow: Assoc. of Surgeons of GB and Ireland, 1996; Surgical Res. Soc. of SA, 1996; Hon. FRCSE 2001; Distinguished Academician, Acad. of Medicine, Singapore, 1998; Hon. Mem., Internat. Coll. of Surgeons, 1989. Inaugural Award for Excellence in Surgery, RACS, 1993; Prize, Internat. Soc. of Surgeons, 2001. *Publications:* contrib. book chapters and numerous articles in scientific jls. *Recreations:* golf, tennis. *Address:* 7 Wills Court, Mt Ommaney, Brisbane, Qld 4074, Australia. *T:* (7) 33762357.

STRONGE, Christopher James; Partner, Coopers & Lybrand Deloitte, 1967–92; *b* 16 Aug. 1933; *s* of Reginald Herbert James Stronge and Doreen Marjorie Stronge; *m* 1964, Gabrielle; one *s* one *d*. *Educ:* Chigwell Sch.; Magdalene Coll., Cambridge (MA Math.). FCA. Deloitte Haskins & Sells: joined 1957; Partner 1967; Dep. Sen. Partner, 1985.

Member: Accounting Standards Cttee, 1980–83; Internat. Accounting Standards Cttee, 1985–90; Treasurer, RIIA, 1981–91. *Recreations:* opera, golf, sailing. *Club:* Little Ship.

STRONGE, Sir James Anselan Maxwell, 10th Bt *cr* 1803; *b* 17 July 1946; *s* of Maxwell Du Pré James Stronge (*d* 1973) (*g g s* of 2nd Bt) and Eileen Mary (*d* 1976), *d* of Rt Hon. Maurice Marcus McCausland, PC, Drenagh, Limavady, Co. Londonderry; *S* cousin, 1981. *Heir:* none. *Address:* Camphill Community Clanabogan, 15 Drudgeon Road, Clanabogan, Omagh, Co. Tyrone BT78 1TJ.

STROUD, Sir (Charles) Eric, Kt 1989; FRCP; Professor of Child Health, King's College School of Medicine and Dentistry (formerly King's College Hospital Medical School), and Director, Department of Child Health, 1968–88; Paediatric Consultant to RAF, since 1976; *b* 15 May 1924; *s* of Frank Edmund and Lavinia May Stroud; *m* 1950, June, *d* of Harold Neep; one *s* two *d*. *Educ:* Cardiff High Sch. for Boys; Welsh National Sch. of Medicine. BSc 1945, MB, BCh 1948 (Wales); MRCP 1955, DCH 1955, FRCP 1968 (London). Sqdn Ldr, RAF, 1950–52. Med. Qual., 1948; Paediatric Registrar, Welsh Nat. Sch. of Med.; Sen. Registrar, Great Ormond Street Children's Hosp., 1957–61; Paediatrician, Uganda Govt, 1958–60; Asst to Dir, Dept of Child Health, Guy's Hosp., 1961–62; Cons. Paediatrician, King's Coll. Hosp., 1962–68. Med. Advr, Eastern Hemisphere, Variety Clubs Internat., 1985–; Hon. Med. Dir, Children Nationwide Med. Res. Fund. FKC 1989. *Publications:* chapters in Textbook of Obstetrics, 1958; Childhealth in the Tropics, 1961; various articles in med. jls, mainly on sickle cell anaemia, nutrition and health of ethnic minorities. *Recreations:* bad golf, good fishing, cheap antiques, planning for retirement. *Address:* 84 Copse Hill, Wimbledon, SW20 0EF. *T:* (020) 8947 1336.

STROUD, Derek H.; *see* Hammond-Stroud.

STROUD, Sir Eric; *see* Stroud, Sir C. E.

STROUD, Ven. Ernest Charles Frederick; Archdeacon of Colchester, 1983–97, now Emeritus; *b* 20 May 1931; *s* of Charles Henry and Irene Doris Stroud; *m* 1959, Jeanne Marguerite Evans; two *d*. *Educ:* Merrywood Grammar School; Merchant Venturers' Technical College; St Chad's Coll., Univ. of Durham. BA (Hons Theology), Diploma in Theology, Diploma in Rural Ministry and Mission. Esso Petroleum Co. Ltd, 1947–55. Deacon 1960, priest 1961, dio. Wakefield; Asst Curate, All Saints, S Kirkby, Yorks, 1960–63; Priest-in-Charge, St Ninian, Whitby, 1963–66; Minister of Conventional District, and first Vicar, All Saints, Chelmsford, 1966–75; Vicar of St Margaret of Antioch, Leigh on Sea, 1975–83; Asst RD of Southend, 1976–79; RD of Hadleigh, 1979–83; Hon. Canon of Chelmsford, 1982–. Member: General Synod, 1981–96; C of E Pensions Bd, 1984– (Vice-Chm., 1990–94, Chm., 1994–96, Finance and Investment Cttee). Chairman: Additional Curates Soc., 1988–98; Church Union, 1989–96; Dr George Richard's Charity, 1990–97. *Publication:* contrib. on ministry of healing to Christian. *Recreations:* travel, music, theatre. *Address:* St Thérèse, 67 London Road, Hadleigh, Benfleet, Essex SS7 2QL.

STROUD, Dr Michael Adrian, OBE 1993; FRCP, FRCPE; Senior Lecturer and Consultant in Medicine, Gastroenterology and Nutrition, Southampton General Hospital, since 1998 (Research Fellow in Nutrition and Gastroenterology, 1995–98); *b* 17 April 1955; *s* of Victor and Vivienne Stroud; *m* 1987, Thea de Moel; one *s* one *d*. *Educ:* University Coll. London (BSc); St George's Hosp. Med. Sch. (MB, BS, MD); FRCP 1994; FRCPE 1994. Med. trng, St George's Hosp., London, 1973–79; postgrad. trng and work in various NHS hosps, 1979–89; govt res. in survival and endurance physiology, 1989–95. Has taken part in many expeditions to Polar regions, incl. the first unassisted crossing of Antartica on foot, with Sir Ranulph Fiennes, 1992–93. Polar Medal, 1995. *Publications:* Shadows on the Wasteland: crossing Antarctica with Ranulph Fiennes, 1993; Survival of the Fittest, 1998; articles on thermal and survival physiology, endurance exercise, and nutrition in med. jls. *Recreations:* climbing, multi-sport endurance events. *Address:* Institute of Human Nutrition, Southampton General Hospital, Tremona Road, Southampton SO16 6YD. *T:* (023) 8079 6317.

STROWGER, (Gaston) Jack, CBE 1976; Managing Director, Thorn Electrical Industries, 1970–79; *b* 8 Feb. 1916; *s* of Alfred Henry Strowger, Lowestoft boat-owner, and Lily Ellen Tripp; *m* 1939, Katherine Ellen Gilbert; two *s* one *d*. *Educ:* Lowestoft Grammar School. Joined London Electrical Supply Co., 1934; HM Forces, 1939–43. Joined TEI, as an Accountant, 1943; Group Chief Accountant, 1952; joined Tricity Finance Corp. as Dir, 1959; Exec. Dir, TEI, 1961; full Dir 1966; Financial Dir 1967; Dep. Chm., Tricity Finance Corp., 1968; Chm., Thorn-Ericsson, 1974–81. Dir (non-exec.), Hornby Hobbies (Chm., 1981–93). FIMgt. *Recreations:* gardening, bowling. *Address:* 43 Blake Court, 1 Newsholme Drive, Winchmore Hill, N21 1SQ.

STROYAN, His Honour Ronald Angus Ropner; QC 1972; a Circuit Judge, 1975–96; a Senior Circuit Judge, 1993–96; Hon. Recorder of Newcastle upon Tyne, 1993–96; *b* 27 Nov. 1924; *e s* of Ronald S. Stroyan of Boreland, Killin; *m* 1st, 1952, Elisabeth Anna Grant (marr. diss. 1965), *y d* of Col J. P. Grant of Rothiemurchus; one *s* two *d*; 2nd, 1967, Jill Annette Johnston, *d* of late Sir Douglas Marshall; one *s* (and two step *s* two step *d*). *Educ:* Harrow School; Trinity College, Cambridge; BA(Hons). Served 1943–45 with The Black Watch (NW Europe); attd Argyll and Sutherland Highlanders, Palestine, 1945–47 (despatches); Captain; later with Black Watch TA. Barrister-at-Law, 1950, Inner Temple. Dep. Chm., North Riding QS, 1962–70, Chm., 1970–71; a Recorder of the Crown Court, 1972–75. Member: Gen. Council of the Bar, 1963–67, 1969–73 and 1975; Parole Bd, 1996–. Chm., West Rannoch Deer Management Gp, 1989–. *Recreation:* country sports. *Address:* Boreland, Killin, Perthshire FK21 8TT. *T:* (01567) 820252. *Club:* Caledonian.

STRUDWICK, Air Cdre Arthur Sidney Ronald, CB 1976; DFC 1945; *b* 16 April 1921; *s* of Percival and Mary Strudwick; *m* 1941, Cissily (*d* 1983); two *s* one *d*. *Educ:* Guildford Tech. Coll.; RAF Colls. Joined RAF 1940; War Service as Fighter Pilot, 1941–43; POW Germany, 1944; Test Flying, Canada, 1948–50; CO No 98 Sqdn, 1951–53; Staff Coll., Camberley, 1954; Commanded Jt Services Trials Unit, Woomera, 1956–59; JSSC, 1959–60; MoD Planning Staff, 1960–62; Dir of Plans, Far East, 1962–64; Commanded RAF Leuchars, 1965–67; Air Cdre Plans, Strategic Comd, 1967–69; IDC 1969; Dir of Flying (R&D), MoD PE, 1970–73; AOC Central Tactics and Trials Orgn, 1973–76, retired 1976. Defence Liaison Officer, Singer Co., Link-Miles Div., 1976–86. *Recreations:* golf, gardening. *Club:* Royal Air Force.

STRUDWICK, Maj. Gen. Mark Jeremy, CBE 1990; Chief Executive, The Prince's Scottish Youth Business Trust; *b* 19 April 1945; *s* of late Ronald Strudwick and Mary Strudwick (*née* Beresford); *m* 1970, Janet Elizabeth Coleridge Vivers; one *s* one *d*. *Educ:* St Edmund's Sch., Canterbury; RMA Sandhurst. Commnd Royal Scots (The Royal Regt), 1966; served UK, BAOR, Cyprus, Canada, India, NI (despatches twice); Comd, 1st Bn Royal Scots, 1984–87; Instr, Staff Coll., 1987–88; ACOS HQ NI, 1988–90; Higher Comd and Staff Course, 1989; Comd 3 Inf. Bde, 1990–91; NDC New Delhi, 1992; Dep. Mil. Sec., MoD, 1993–95; Dir of Infantry, 1996–97; ADC to the Queen, 1996–97; GOC Scotland and Gov. of Edinburgh Castle, 1997–2000. Col, Royal Scots, 1995–; Col Comdt, Scottish Div., 1997–2000. Mem., Queen's Body Guard for Scotland, 1994 (Royal Company of Archers). Cdre, Infantry Sailing Assoc., 1997–2000. Governor: Royal Sch., Bath, 1993–2000; Gordonstoun Sch., 1999–. *Recreations:* golf, shooting, sailing. *Address:* Regimental HQ, The Royal Scots, The Castle, Edinburgh EH1 2YT. *T:* (0131) 310 5014, *Fax:* (0131) 310 5019. *Clubs:* Army and Navy, Royal Scots (Trustee, 1995–) (Edinburgh).

STRUNIN, Prof. Leo, MD; FRCA; BOC Professor of Anaesthesia, St Bartholomew's and Royal London School of Medicine and Dentistry, Queen Mary and Westfield College (formerly London Hospital Medical College), University of London, since 1990; President, Association of Anaesthetists of Great Britain and Ireland, 2000–Sept. 2002; *b* 19 Nov. 1937; *m* 1968, Jane Smith. *Educ:* Univ. of Durham (MB BS 1960); Univ. of Newcastle upon Tyne (MD 1974). FRCA (FFARCS 1964); FRCP(C) 1980. Training posts, Newcastle upon Tyne, Sunderland, Manchester and London, 1960–67; Lectr, 1967–69, Sen. Lectr, 1969–72, Anaesthetics Unit, London Hosp. Med. Coll.; Sen. Lectr, 1972–74, Prof., 1975–79, Anaesthetic Dept, King's Coll. Hosp. and Med. Sch.; Prof. and Head, Dept of Anaesthesia, Univ. of Calgary, Canada, 1980–90. Pres., RCAnaes, 1997–2000. *Publications:* Anaesthesia and the Liver, 1977; (with S. Thomson) Anaesthesia and the Liver, 1992; (with J. A. Stamford) Neuroprotection, 1996. *Recreation:* whippet and greyhound racing. *Address:* Anaesthetics Unit, Royal London Hospital, E1 1BB. *T:* (020) 7377 7119. *Club:* Athenæum.

STRUTHERS, Alastair James, OBE 1995; *b* 25 July 1929; *s* of Alexander Struthers and Elizabeth Struthers (*née* Hutchison); *m* 1967, Elizabeth Henderson; three *d*. *Educ:* Stowe; Trinity Coll., Cambridge (MA). Chairman: J. & A. Gardner & Co. Ltd, 1962–; Scottish National Trust plc, 1983–98; Caledonian MacBrayne Ltd, 1990–94. Chairman: Steamship Mutual Underwriting Assoc., 1988–95; Steamship Mutual Trustees (Bermuda) Ltd, 2000–. Chm., Racing and Thoroughbred Breeding Trng Bd, 1992–98. Comr, Northern Lighthouse Bd, 1980–99. Dep. Sen. Steward, Jockey Club, 1990–94. *Recreations:* racing, shooting, golf. *Address:* Craigmaddie, Milngavie, by Glasgow G62 8LB. *T:* (0141) 956 1262. *Club:* Western (Glasgow).

STRUTT, family name of **Barons Belper** and **Rayleigh**.

STRUTT, Sir Nigel (Edward), Kt 1972; TD; DL; formerly Managing Director: Lord Rayleigh's Farms; Strutt & Parker (Farms); *b* 18 Jan. 1916; *yr s* of late Edward Jolliffe Strutt and Amélie, *d* of Frederic Devas. *Educ:* Winchester; Wye Agricultural College (Fellow, 1970). Essex Yeomanry (Major), 1937–56. Member: Eastern Electricity Bd, 1964–76; Agricultural Advisory Council, 1963– (Chm. 1969–73; Chm., Adv. Council for Agriculture and Horticulture, 1973–80); NEDC for Agriculture, 1967–82. President: Country Landowners' Association, 1967–69; British Friesian Cattle Soc., 1974–75; Royal Agricultural Soc. of England, 1982–83. Master, Farmers' Co., 1976–77. DL Essex 1954; High Sheriff of Essex, 1966. Hon. FRASE, 1971. Hon. DSc Cranfield, 1979; DU Essex, 1981; Hon. DPhil Anglia Polytech. Univ., 1993. Massey Ferguson Award, 1976. Von Thünen Gold Medal, Kiel Univ., 1974. *Recreations:* shooting, travelling. *Address:* Sparrows, Terling, Essex CM3 2QY. *T:* (01245) 233213. *Clubs:* Brooks's, Farmers'.

STUART, family name of **Earl Castle Stewart, Earl of Moray** and **Viscount Stuart of Findhorn**.

STUART; *see* Crichton-Stuart, family name of Marquess of Bute.

STUART, Viscount; Andrew Richard Charles Stuart; *b* 7 Oct. 1953; *s* and *heir* of 8th Earl Castle Stewart, *qv*; *m* 1973, Annie Le Poulain, St Malo, France; one *d*. *Educ:* Wynstones, Glos; Millfield, Som.; Univ. of Exeter. *Recreations:* running, hiking. *Address:* Combe Hayes Farm, Buckerell, near Honiton, Devon EX14 0ET.

STUART OF FINDHORN, 3rd Viscount *cr* 1959, of Findhorn co. Moray; **James Dominic Stuart;** *b* 25 March 1948; *s* of 2nd Viscount Stuart of Findhorn and his 1st wife, Grizel Mary Wilfreda, *d* of D. T. Fyfe and *widow* of Michael Gillilan; *S* father, 1999; *m* 1979, Yvonne Lucienne, *d* of Edgar Després. *Educ:* Eton. *Heir: half-b* Hon. Andrew Moray Stuart, *b* 20 Oct. 1957. *Address:* 15 Stowe Road, W12 8BQ.

STUART, Andrew Christopher, CMG 1979; CPM 1961; HM Diplomatic Service, retired; Chairman, Centre for British Teachers, since 1991; *b* 30 Nov. 1928; *s* of late Rt Rev. Cyril Edgar Stuart and Mary Summerhayes; *m* 1959, Patricia Kelly; two *s* one *d*. *Educ:* Bryanston; Clare Coll., Cambridge (MA). Royal Navy, 1947–49. Colonial Admin. Service, Uganda, 1953; retd from HMOCS as Judicial Adviser, 1965. Called to Bar, Middle Temple, 1965. Entered HM Diplomatic Service, 1965; 1st Sec. and Head of Chancery, Helsinki, 1968; Asst, S Asian Dept, FCO, 1971; Head of Hong Kong and Indian Ocean Dept, FCO, 1972–75; Counsellor, Jakarta, 1975–78; British Resident Comr, New Hebrides, 1978–80; Ambassador to Finland, 1980–83. Principal, United World Coll. of the Atlantic, 1983–90. Consultant, VSO, 1990–96. Order of the Lion (Finland), 1990. *Recreations:* sailing, gliding. *Address:* Long Hall, North Street, Wareham, Dorset BH20 4AG. *T:* (01929) 551658, *Fax:* (01929) 551712; *e-mail:* astuart@cfbt-hq.org.uk. *Clubs:* Oxford and Cambridge, Royal Commonwealth Society, Alpine; Jesters; Royal Naval Sailing Association.

STUART, Antony James Cobham E.; *see* Edwards-Stuart.

STUART, (Charles) Murray, CBE 1995; Chairman, Scottish Power, 1992–2000 (Director, 1990–2000); *b* 28 July 1933; *s* of Charles Maitland Stuart and Grace Forrester Stuart (*née* Kerr); *m* 1963, Netta Caroline; one *s* one *d*. *Educ:* Glasgow Acad.; Glasgow Univ. (MA, LLB). Scottish Chartered Accountant; CA. With P. & W. McLellan, Ford Motor Co., Sheffield Twist Drill & Steel Co., and Unicorn Industries, 1961–73; Finance Dir, Hepworths, 1973–74; Finance Dir and Dep. Man. Dir, ICL, 1974–81; Metal Box, subseq. MB Group: Finance Dir, Dir—Finance, Planning and Admin, 1981–86; Man. Dir, Dec. 1986–Dec. 1987; Gp Chief Exec., 1988–89; Chm., 1989–90; Finance Dir, 1990–91, Chief Exec., 1991, Berisford International. Vice Chm., CMB Packaging SA, 1989–90; Vice-Chm. and Dir, Hill Samuel, 1992–93; Chairman: Hill Samuel Scotland, 1993–94; Intermediate Capital Group PLC, 1993–2001; Hammersmith Hospitals NHS Trust, 1996–2000; non-executive Director: Save & Prosper Insurance, 1987–91; Save & Prosper Securities, 1988–91; Hunter Saphir, 1991–92; Clerical Medical & General Life Assurance Soc., 1993–96; Royal Bank of Scotland Gp, 1996–; Royal Bank of Scotland, 1996–; Willis Corroon Gp plc, 1996–97; CMG plc, 1998–; Old Mutual PLC, 1999–; Nat. Westminster Bank, 2000–; Member: Supervisory Bd, Vivendi Environnement, 2000–; European Adv. Bd, Credit Lyonnais, 2000–. Dep. Chm., Audit Commn, 1991–95 (Mem., 1986–95); Mem., Private Finance Initiative Panel, 1995–97. Mem., W Surrey and NE Hants HA, 1990–93. Mem., Meteorological Office, 1994–98. Non-exec. Dir, Royal Scottish Nat. Orch., 1998–2000. DUniv: Paisley, 1999; Glasgow, 2001. *Recreations:* theatre, gardening, travel. *Address:* Longacre, Guildford Road, Chobham, Woking, Surrey GU24 8EA. *T:* (01276) 857144. *Club:* Caledonian.

STUART, Prof. David Ian, PhD; FRS 1996; MRC Professor of Structural Biology, since 1996, and Fellow of Hertford College, since 1985, University of Oxford. *Educ:* London Univ. (BSc); PhD Bristol; MA Oxon. Lectr in Structural Molecular Biology, Oxford Univ., 1985–96. *Address:* Department of Structural Biology, Henry Wellcome Building for Genomic Medicine, Roosevelt Drive, Oxford OX3 7BN.

STUART, Duncan, CMG 1989; HM Diplomatic Service, retired; Special Operations Executive Adviser, Foreign and Commonwealth Office, since 1996; *b* 1 July 1934; *s* of late Ian Cameron Stuart and Patricia Forbes; *m* 1961, Leonore Luise Liederwald; one *s* one *d*. *Educ:* Rugby Sch.; Brasenose Coll., Oxford (MA). Served 1st Bn Oxfordshire and Bucks LI, 1955–57 (2nd Lieut). Joined Foreign, later Diplomatic, Service, 1959; Office of Political Advr, Berlin, 1960–61; FO, 1961–64; Helsinki, 1964–66; Head of Chancery, Dar-es-Salaam, 1966–69; FCO, 1969–70; Helsinki, 1970–74; FCO, 1974–80; Counsellor, Bonn, 1980–83; FCO, 1983–86; Counsellor, Washington, 1986–88; FCO, 1988–92; Advr, MoD, 1992–94. Chm. and Chief Exec., Cyrus Internat., 1994–95. Gov., St Clare's, Oxford, 1991–. *Address:* c/o C. Hoare & Co., 37 Fleet Street, EC4P 4DQ. *Clubs:* Boodle's, Oxford and Cambridge, Special Forces, MCC.

STUART, Gisela Gschaider; MP (Lab) Birmingham Edgbaston, since 1997; *b* 26 Nov. 1955; *d* of late Martin and of Liane Gschaider; *m* 1980, Robert Scott Stuart (marr. diss. 2000); two *s*. *Educ:* Staatliche Realschule, Vilsbiburg; Manchester Poly.; London Univ. (LLB 1991). Dep. Dir, London Book Fair, 1982; Law Lectr, Worcester Coll. of Technol., 1992–97; res. in pension law, Birmingham Univ., 1995–97. PPS to Minister of State, Home Office, 1998–99; Parly Under-Sec. of State, DoH, 1999–2001. Member: Social Security Select Cttee, 1997–98; Foreign Affairs Select Cttee, 2001–. *Address:* House of Commons, SW1A 0AA. *T:* (020) 7219 3000.

STUART, Rev. Canon Herbert James, CB 1983; Canon Emeritus of Lincoln Cathedral, since 1983 (Canon, 1980–83); *b* 16 Nov. 1926; *s* of Joseph and Jane Stuart; *m* 1955, Adrienne Le Fanu; two *s* one *d*. *Educ:* Mountjoy School, Dublin; Trinity Coll., Dublin (BA Hons, MA). Priest, 1950; served in Church of Ireland, 1950–55; Chaplain, RAF, 1955; Asst Chaplain-in-Chief, RAF, 1973; Chaplain-in-Chief and Archdeacon, RAF, 1980–83; QHC, 1978–83; Rector of Cherbury, 1983–87. *Recreations:* gardening, travel, books. *Address:* Abbots Walk, Lechlade Park, Lechlade, Glos GL7 3DB. *Club:* Royal Air Force.

STUART, Rt Rev. Ian Campbell; Assistant Bishop, Diocese of Liverpool, since 1999; Provost, Liverpool Hope University, since 2001; *b* 17 Nov. 1942; *s* of Campbell Stuart and Ruth Estelle Stuart (*née* Butcher); *m* 1976, Megan Helen Williams; one *s* two *d*. *Educ:* Univ. of New England (BA, Cert Ed); Univ. of Melbourne (MA, DipEdAdmin). Headmaster, Christchurch Grammar Sch., Melbourne, 1977–84; ordained deacon and priest, 1985; Principal, Trinity Anglican Sch., Queensland, 1984–93; Warden, St Mark's Coll., James Cook Univ., 1993–96; Principal, All Souls' and St Gabriel's Sch., 1993–98; Diocese of North Queensland: Archdeacon, 1989–92; Asst Bishop, and Bishop Administrator, 1992–98. *Recreations:* reading, travel, my laptop computer. *Address:* 55 Woolacombe Road, Liverpool L16 9JG. *T:* (0151) 291 3547.

STUART, Sir (James) Keith, Kt 1986; Chairman, Associated British Ports Holdings PLC, 1983–April 2002; *b* 4 March 1940; *s* of James and Marjorie Stuart; *m* 1966, Kathleen Anne Pinder (*née* Woodman); three *s* one *d*. *Educ:* King George V School, Southport; Gonville and Caius College, Cambridge (MA). FCIT, CIMgt, FRSA. District Manager, South Western Electricity Bd, 1970–72; British Transport Docks Board: Sec., 1972–75; Gen. Manager, 1976–77; Man. Dir, 1977–82; Dep. Chm., 1980–82; Chm., 1982–83. Dir, Internat. Assoc. of Ports and Harbors, 1983–2000 (Vice-Pres., 1985–87); Pres., Inst. of Freight Forwarders, 1983–84. Director: Royal Ordnance Factories, 1983–85; BAA Plc, 1986–92; Seeboard plc, 1989–96 (Chm., 1992–96); City of London Investment Trust plc, 1999–; RMC Group plc, 1999–. Mem., Gas and Electricity Markets Authy, 2000–. Chm., UK-S Africa Trade Assoc., 1988–93; Vice-Chairman: UK-Southern Africa Business Assoc., 1994–95; Southern Africa Business Assoc., 1995–. Chartered Inst. of Transport: Mem. Council, 1979–88; Vice-Pres., 1982–83; Pres., 1985–86. Pres. and Chm. Bd, British Quality Foundn, 1997–2001. Liveryman, Clockmakers' Co., 1987 (Mem. Ct of Assts, 1998–). Governor: Trinity Coll. of Music, 1991–; NYO of GB, 1997–; Dir, Trinity Coll. London, 1992–. Hon. FTCL 1998. *Recreation:* music. *Address:* Weir Cottage, 33 Mill Road, Marlow, Bucks SL7 1QB. *Clubs:* Brooks's, Oxford and Cambridge (Trustee, 1989–94).

STUART, Prof. (John) Trevor, FRS 1974; Professor of Theoretical Fluid Mechanics, Imperial College of Science, Technology and Medicine, University of London, 1966–94, now Emeritus; Dean, Royal College of Science, 1990–93; *b* 28 Jan. 1929; *s* of Horace Stuart and Phyllis Emily Stuart (*née* Potter); *m* 1957, Christine Mary (*née* Tracy); two *s* one *d*. *Educ:* Gateway Sch., Leicester; Imperial Coll., London. BSc 1949, PhD 1951; FIC 1998. Aerodynamics Div., Nat. Physical Lab., Teddington, 1951–66; Sen. Principal Scientific Officer (Special Merit), 1961; Hd, Maths Dept, Imperial Coll., London, 1974–79, 1983–86. Vis. Lectr, Dept of Maths, MIT, 1956–57; Vis. Prof. of Maths, MIT, 1965–66; Vis. Prof. of Theoretical Fluid Mechanics, Brown Univ., 1978–; Hon. Prof., Tianjin Univ., China, 1983–. Member: Council, Royal Soc., 1982–84; SERC, 1989–94 (Chm., Mathematics Cttee, 1985–88). Pres., London Mathematical Soc., 2000–Nov. 2002 (Vice-Pres., 1999–2000). 1st Stewartson Meml Lectr, Long Beach, Calif., 1985; 1st DiPrima Meml Lectr, Troy, NY, 1985; Ludwig Prandtl Meml Lectr, Dortmund, 1986. Hon. ScD: Brown Univ., 1986; East Anglia, 1987. Senior Whitehead Prize, London Mathematical Soc., 1984; Otto Laporte Award, Amer. Physical Soc., 1987. *Publications:* (contrib.) Laminar Boundary Layers, ed L. Rosenhead, 1963; articles in Proc. Royal Soc., Phil. Trans Royal Soc., Jl Fluid Mech., Proc. 10th Int. Cong. Appl. Mech., Jl Lub. Tech. (ASME). *Recreations:* theatre, music, gardening, reading, ornithology. *Address:* Mathematics Department, Imperial College, SW7 2AZ. *T:* (020) 7594 8535; 3 Steeple Close, Wimbledon, SW19 5AD. *T:* (020) 8946 7019; *e-mail:* t.stuart@ic.ac.uk.

STUART, Joseph B.; *see* Burnett-Stuart.

STUART, Sir Keith; *see* Stuart, Sir J. K.

STUART, Prof. Sir Kenneth (Lamonte), Kt 1977; MD, FRCP, FRCPE, FACP, FFPM, FFPHM, DTM&H; Hon. Medical and Scientific Adviser, Barbados High Commission, since 1991; *b* 16 June 1920; *s* of Egbert and Louise Stuart; *m* 1958, Barbara Cecille Ashby; one *s* two *d*. *Educ:* Harrison Coll., Barbados; Queen's Univ., Belfast (MB, BCh, BAO 1948). Consultant Physician, University Coll. Hospital of the West Indies, 1954–76; University of the West Indies: Prof. of Medicine, 1966–76; Dean, Medical Faculty, 1969–71; Head, Dept of Medicine, 1972–76; Mem. Council, 1971–76; Medical Adviser, Commonwealth Secretariat, 1976–84. Rockefeller Foundation Fellow in Cardiology, Massachusetts Gen. Hosp., Boston, 1956–57; Wellcome Foundation Research Fellow, Harvard Univ., Boston, 1960–61; Gresham Prof. of Physic, 1988–92. Consultant to WHO on Cardiovascular Disorders, 1969–89. Chairman: Commonwealth Caribbean MRC, 1989–96; Adv. Council, Centre for Caribbean Medicine, UK, 1998; Commonwealth Health Res. Inter-regional Consultation, 1998–. Chm., Court of Governors, LSHTM, 1982–86; Member: Council, Liverpool Sch. of Tropical Medicine, 1980–97; Council, UMDS Guy's and St Thomas's Hosps, 1994–98; Council, KCL, 1998–; Court of Governors, Internat. Develt Res. Centre of Canada, 1985–90; Council, London Lighthouse, 1994–2000; Central Council, Royal Over-Seas League, 1994–. Trustee, Schools Partnership Worldwide, 1986–; Chm., Errol Barrow Meml Trust, 1989–2000. Freeman, City of London, 1994. Hon. DSc QUB, 1986. *Publications:* articles on hepatic and cardiovascular disorders in medical journals. *Recreations:* tennis, music. *Address:* 3 The Garth, Cobham, Surrey, KT11 2DZ.

STUART, Marian Elizabeth; consultant on social issues, particularly child care projects; *b* 17 July 1944; *d* of William and Greta Stuart; one *s* one *d*. *Educ:* Eye Grammar School, Suffolk; Mount Grace Comprehensive School, Potters Bar; Leicester Univ. (MA). Joined Min. of Health as Asst Principal, 1967; Principal, DHSS, 1971; Asst Sec., 1979; Dep. Chief Inspector of Social Services, 1988; Under Sec., Finance Div., DoH, 1989–93; Resident Chm., CSSB, 1993–99 (on secondment); pt-time consultant on child care projects, DoH, 1993–99. *Recreations:* reading, bridge, ski-ing. *Address:* 15 Connaught Avenue, SW14 7RH. *T:* (020) 8878 1173.

STUART, Sir Mark M.; *see* Moody-Stuart.

STUART, Michael Francis Harvey; Treasury Adviser, UK Mission to the United Nations, 1974–82, retired; *b* 3 Oct. 1926; *s* of late Willoughby Stuart and Ethel Candy; *m* 1961, Ruth Tennyson-d'Eyncourt; one *s* one *d*. *Educ:* Harrow; Magdalen Coll., Oxford (Demy). Air Min., 1950–65; DEA, 1965–69; HM Treasury, 1969–74. Mem., UN Adv. Cttee on Administrative and Budgetary Questions, 1975–80. *Recreations:* music, golf. *Address:* Bourne House, Chertsey Road, Chobham, Woking, Surrey GU24 8NB. *T:* (01276) 857954.

STUART, Murray; *see* Stuart, C. M.

STUART, Nicholas Willoughby, CB 1990; Director General for Lifelong Learning, Department for Education and Skills (formerly Department for Education and Employment), 2000–01; *b* 2 Oct. 1942; *s* of Douglas Willoughby Stuart and Margaret Eileen Stuart; *m* 1st, 1963, Sarah Mustard (marr. diss. 1974); one *d* (one *s* decd); 2nd, 1975, Susan Jane Fletcher; one *s* one *d*. *Educ:* Harrow Sch.; Christ Church Coll., Oxford (MA). Asst Principal, DES, 1964–68; Private Sec. to Minister for the Arts, 1968–69; Principal, DES, 1969–73; Private Secretary to: Head of the Civil Service, 1973; Prime Minister, 1973–76; Asst Sec., DES, 1976–78; Advr, Cabinet of Pres. of EEC, 1978–80; Under Sec., 1981–87, Dep. Sec., 1987–92, DES; Dir of Resources and Strategy, Dept of Employment, 1992–95; Dir Gen. for Employment and Lifelong Learning, later for Employment, Lifelong Learning and Internat. Directorate, DFEE, 1995–2000. Bd Mem., Investors in People (UK), 1995–2001. Governor: Harrow Sch., 1996–; South Hampstead High Sch., 1997–. *Recreation:* collecting Tunbridgeware.

STUART, Sir Phillip (Luttrell), 9th Bt *cr* 1660; late F/O RCAF; President, Agassiz Industries Ltd; *b* 7 September 1937; *s* of late Luttrell Hamilton Stuart and late Irene Ethel Jackman; *S* uncle, Sir Houlton John Stuart, 8th Bt, 1959; *m* 1st, 1962, Marlene Rose Muth (marr. diss. 1968); two *d*; 2nd, 1969, Beverley Clare Pieri; one *s* one *d*. *Educ:* Vancouver. Enlisted RCAF, Nov. 1955; commnd FO (1957–62). *Heir:* *s* Geoffrey Phillip Stuart, *b* 5 July 1973. *Address:* Apt 50, 10980 Westdowne Road, RR2 Ladysmith, BC V0R 2E0, Canada.

[*His name does not appear on the official Roll of Baronets.*]

STUART, Trevor; *see* Stuart, J. T.

STUART-FORBES, Sir Charles Edward; *see* Forbes.

STUART-MENTETH, Sir James; *see* Menteth.

STUART-MOORE, Michael; QC 1990; **Hon. Mr Justice Stuart-Moore;** Vice-President of the Court of Appeal of Hong Kong, since 1999; a Recorder of the Crown Court, since 1985; *b* 7 July 1944; *s* of (Kenneth) Basil Moore and Marjorie (Elizabeth) Moore; *m* 1973, Katherine Ann, *d* of William and Ruth Scott; one *s* one *d*. *Educ:* Cranleigh School. Called to the Bar, Middle Temple, 1966. A Judge of the High Court, later of the Court of First Instance of the High Court, Hong Kong, 1993–98; a Judge of the Court of Appeal of the High Court, Hong Kong, 1998–99. *Recreations:* photography, travel, music, tennis. *Address:* 2 Hare Court, Temple, EC4Y 7BH. *T:* (020) 7353 5324; Court of Appeal, High Court, 38 Queensway, Hong Kong.

STUART-PAUL, Air Marshal Sir Ronald (Ian), KBE 1990 (MBE 1967); RAF, retired; Chief Executive, British Aerospace, Saudi Arabia, since 1997; *b* 7 Nov. 1934; *s* of Dr J. G. Stuart-Paul and Mary (*née* McDonald); *m* 1963, Priscilla Frances (*née* Kay); one *s* one *d*. *Educ:* Dollar Acad.; RAF Coll., Cranwell. Served 14, 19, 56 and 92 Sqns and 11 and 12 Groups, 1957–73; Defence Attaché, Saudi Arabia, 1974–75; Stn Comdr, RAF Lossiemouth, 1976–78; RCDS, 1979; Dep. Comdr, NAEW Force, SHAPE, 1980–82; Dir of Ops Air Defence, RAF, 1982–83; AO Training, RAF Support Command, 1984–85; Dir Gen., Saudi Air Force Project, 1985–92. *Recreations:* golf, campanology, sailing, rug-making. *Address:* Sycamore House, Gaunts Common, Wimborne, Dorset BH21 4JP. *T:* (01258) 840430; PO Box 1732, Riyadh 11441, Saudi Arabia. *Club:* Royal Air Force.

STUART-SHAW, Max, CBE 1963; Executive Director, Olympic Airways, 1969–71; *b* 20 Dec. 1912; *e s* of Herman and Anne Louise Stuart-Shaw; *m* 1967, Janna Job, *d* of C. W. Howard. *Educ:* Belmont School, Sussex; St Paul's, London. Imperial Airways/BOAC, 1931–46; Aer Lingus Irish Airlines; Traffic Manager, Commercial Manager, Asst Gen. Manager, 1947–57; Chief Exec. and Gen. Manager Central African Airways, Salisbury, Rhodesia, 1958–65; Man. Dir, BUA, 1966–67; Vice-Chairman, British United Airways, 1967–68. FCIT. *Recreation:* air transport.

STUART-SMITH, James, CB 1986; QC 1988; Judge Advocate General, 1984–91 (Vice Judge Advocate General, 1979–84); a Recorder, 1985–91; *b* 13 Sept. 1919; *s* of James Stuart-Smith and Florence Emma (*née* Armfield); *m* 1957, Jean Marie Therese Young Groundsell, *d* of Hubert Young Groundsell, Newport, IoW; one *s* one *d*. *Educ:* Brighton Coll.; London Hospital. Medical student, 1938. Served War of 1939–45: commnd KRRC, 1940; served ME and Italy, and staff appointments in UK; demobilised 1947. Called to Bar, Middle Temple, 1948; practised in London, 1948–55; Legal Asst, JAG's Office, 1955; Dep. Judge Advocate, 1957; Asst Judge Advocate General, 1968; Dep. Judge Advocate, Middle East Comd (Aden), 1964–65; Dep. Judge Advocate General, British Forces Germany, 1976–79. Hon. Pres., Internat. Soc. for Military Law and the Law of War, 1991– (Vice-Pres., 1979–85; Pres., 1985–91). *Publications:* contribs to Internat. Soc. for Military Law and Law of War Rev. and Law Qly Rev., on history and practice of British military law. *Recreations:* composing letters, inexpert carpentry. *Address:* 3 Marine Parade, Bognor Regis PO21 2LT. *T:* (01243) 842255. *Club:* Royal Air Force.

STUART-SMITH, Rt Hon. Sir Murray, Kt 1981; PC 1988; a Lord Justice of Appeal, 1988–2000; *b* 18 Nov. 1927; *s* of Edward Stuart-Smith and Doris Mary Laughland; *m* 1953, Joan Elizabeth Mary Motion, BA, JP, DL (High Sheriff of Herts, 1983); three *s* three *d*. *Educ:* Radley; Corpus Christi Coll., Cambridge (Foundn Scholar; 1st Cl. Hons Law Tripos, Pts I and II; 1st Cl. Hons LLM; MA; Hon. Fellow 1994). 2nd Lieut, 5th Royal Inniskilling Dragoon Guards, 1947. Called to the Bar, Gray's Inn, 1952 (Atkin Scholar), Bencher 1977; Vice-Treas., 1997; Treas., 1998; QC 1970; a Recorder of the Crown Court, 1972–81; a Judge of the High Court of Justice, QBD, 1981–88; Presiding Judge, Western Circuit, 1983–87. Judge of Court of Appeal, Gibraltar, 2001–. Jt Inspector into Grays Bldg Soc., 1979. Mem., Criminal Injuries Compensation Bd, 1980–81. Commissioner: for the Security Service, 1989–2000; for the Intelligence Services, 1994–2000. Chm., Proscribed Orgns Appeal Commn, 2001–. Pres., Dacorum SO, 1994–. *Recreations:* playing 'cello, shooting, building, playing bridge. *Address:* Serge Hill, Abbots Langley, Herts WD5 0RY.

STUART TAYLOR, Sir Nicholas (Richard), 4th Bt *cr* 1917; *b* 14 Jan. 1952; *s* of Sir Richard Laurence Stuart Taylor, 3rd Bt, and of Iris Mary, *d* of Rev. Edwin John Gargery; *S* father, 1978; *m* 1984, Malvena Elizabeth Sullivan, (marr. diss. 1999); two *d*. *Educ:* Bradfield. Admitted Solicitor, 1977. *Recreations:* ski-ing and other sports. *Heir:* none. *Address:* 30 Siskin Close, Bishop's Waltham, Hants SO32 1RQ. *Club:* Ski Club of Great Britain.

STUART-WHITE, Sir Christopher (Stuart), Kt 1993; a Judge of the High Court of Justice, Family Division, 1993–99; *b* 18 Dec. 1933; *s* of Reginald Stuart-White and Catherine Mary Wigmore Stuart-White (*née* Higginson); *m* 1957, Pamela (*née* Grant); one *s* two *d*. *Educ:* Winchester; Trinity Coll., Oxford (BA). Called to Bar, Inner Temple, 1957, Bencher 1993. Barrister on the Midland and Oxford Circuit, 1958–78; a Recorder of the Crown Court, 1974–78; a Circuit Judge, 1978–93; Liaison Judge, Family Div., Midland and Oxford Circuit, 1994–98. Chairman: Magisterial Cttee, Judicial Studies Bd, 1985–90; County Court Rule Cttee, 1988–92. Contributing Editor: County Court Practice, 1991–99; Civil Court Practice, 1999–2000. *Recreation:* gardening.

STUBBS, Imogen Mary; actress; *b* 20 Feb. 1961; *d* of late Robin Desmond Scrivener Stubbs and Heather Mary Stubbs (*née* McCracken); *m* 1994, Trevor Robert Nunn, *qv*; one *s* one *d*. *Educ:* St Paul's Girls' Sch.; Westminster Sch.; Exeter Coll., Oxford (BA 1st cl. Hons); RADA. *Theatre:* Cabaret, Ipswich, 1985; The Rover, 1986, The Two Noble Kinsmen, 1987, Desdemona in Othello, 1989, RSC; Heartbreak House, Theatre Royal, Haymarket, 1992; title rôle, St Joan, Strand, 1994; Uncle Vanya, Chichester Fest., then Albery, 1996; A Streetcar Named Desire, Theatre Royal, Haymarket, 1996; Closer, Lyric, 1998; Betrayal, RNT, 1998; The Relapse, RNT, 2001; *television:* The Rainbow, 1988; Othello, 1990; After the Dance, 1992; Anna Lee, 1994; *films:* Nanou, 1985; Erik the Viking, 1988; Fellow Traveller, 1990; True Colors, 1990; Sandra, c'est la vie; Lucy in Sense and Sensibility, 1995; Viola in Twelfth Night, 1996. *Address:* c/o ICM Ltd, Oxford House, 76 Oxford Street, W1N 0AX. *T:* (020) 7636 6565.

STUBBS, John Francis Alexander H.; *see* Heath-Stubbs.

STUBBS, Prof. Michael Wesley, PhD; Professor of English Linguistics, University of Trier, Germany, since 1990; *b* 23 Dec. 1947; *s* of late Leonard Garforth Stubbs and Isabella Wardrop (*née* McGavin). *Educ:* Glasgow High Sch. for Boys; King's Coll., Cambridge (MA); Univ. of Edinburgh (PhD 1975). Res. Associate, Univ. of Birmingham, 1973–74; Lectr in Linguistics, Univ. of Nottingham, 1974–85; Prof. of English in Educn, Inst. of Educn, Univ. of London, 1985–90. Vis. Prof. of Linguistics, Univ. of Tübingen, Germany, 1985; Hon. Sen. Res. Fellow, Univ. of Birmingham, 1994–. Chm., BAAL, 1988–91. Mem., Nat. Curriculum English Working Gp (Cox Cttee), 1988–89. *Publications:* Language, Schools and Classrooms, 1976, 2nd edn 1983; Language and Literacy, 1980; Discourse Analysis, 1983; Educational Linguistics, 1986; Text and Corpus Analysis, 1996; articles in Lang. and Educn, Applied Linguistics, Jl of Pragmatics, Functions of Lang., Text. *Recreation:* walking. *Address:* FB2 Anglistik, University of Trier, 54286 Trier, Germany. *T:* (651) 2012278.

STUBBS, Sukhvinder Kaur; Chair, European Network Against Racism, since 1998; non-executive Director, Crown Prosecution Service, since 2000; *b* Punjab, India, 25 Oct. 1962; *d* of S. Inderjit Singh Thethy and Charanjit Kaur; *m* 1985, David Brian Stubbs. *Educ:* Hertford Coll., Oxford (MA Geography; Henry Oliver Becket Meml Prize). MCIM 1992. Lectr, Orpington Coll., 1984–85; Graduate Manager, British Telecom, 1985–86; Mkting Exec., Prisoners Abroad, 1986–87; Appeals Dir, British Dyslexia Assoc., 1987–90; Dir of Corporate Affairs, Community Develt Foundn, 1990–94; Community Develt Manager, English Partnerships, 1994–96; Chief Exec., Runnymede Trust, 1996–2000. Non-exec. Dir, W Midlands Regl Develt Agency (Advantage W Midlands), 1998–. Chm., Birmingham Secondary Educn Commn, 1998; Mem., Birmingham Democracy Commn, 2000–01. Trustee, Demos, 1998–. Mem., Lunar Soc., 1999. FRSA 1996. *Publications:* (contrib.) Renewing Citizenship and Democracy, 1997; (contrib.) Mindfields, 1998; papers, articles in jls. *Recreations:* adventure travel, mountain hiking, gardening. *Address:* (office) 629 Kings Road, Birmingham B44 9HW. *Club:* Royal Commonwealth Society.

STUBBS, Thomas, OBE 1980; HM Diplomatic Service, retired; *b* 12 July 1926; *s* of Thomas Stubbs and Lillian Marguerite (*née* Rumball, formerly Bell); *m* 1951, Dorothy Miller (*d* 1997); one *s* one *d*. *Educ:* Heaton Tech. Sch., Newcastle upon Tyne. Served in Army, 1944–48. Joined Min. of Nat. Insce, later Min. of Pensions and Nat. Insce, 1948; transf. to CRO, 1960; New Delhi, 1962; CRO, 1964; Wellington, NZ, 1965; Vice-Consul, Düsseldorf, 1970; seconded to BOTB, 1974; First Sec. (Commercial) and Consul, Addis Ababa, 1977; Consul, Hannover, 1980; Dep. High Comr, Madras, 1983–86. Mayor, Borough of Spelthorne, 1992–93 (Mem. (C) Council, 1987–; Vice-Chairman: Leisure and Amenities Cttee, 1987–89; Planning Cttee, 1999–; Chairman: Personnel Cttee, 1989–91; Resources Cttee, 1995–96; Finance Sub-Cttee, 1996–98; Dep. Mayor, 1991–92). Hon. Pres., County of Middlesex Trust, 1992–. *Recreations:* reading, golf. *Address:* 17 Chester Close, Ashford Common, Middlesex TW15 1PH.

STUBBS, William Frederick; QC 1978; *b* 27 Nov. 1934; *s* of William John Stubbs and Winifred Hilda (*née* Johnson); *m* 1961, Anne Katharine (*d* 1966), *d* of late Prof. W. K. C. Guthrie, FBA; one *s* one *d*. *Educ:* The High Sch., Newcastle-under-Lyme, Staffs; Gonville and Caius Coll., Cambridge; Harvard Law Sch. Open Minor Scholar in Nat. Sci., Gonville and Caius Coll., 1951; Student, Gray's Inn, 1953; 1st Cl. Hons Law Tripos Pt I, and George Long Prize for Roman Law, Cambridge, 1954; Major Scholar, Gonville and Caius Coll., 1954; 1st Cl. Hons with Distinction Law Tripos Pt II, Cambridge, 1955; LLB 1st Cl. Hons with Dist., and Chancellor's Medal for English Law, Cambridge, 1956; Tapp Post-Grad. Law Scholar, Gonville and Caius Coll., 1956 (also awarded Schuldham Plate); Joseph Hodges Choate Meml Fellow, Harvard Coll., 1957; Bar Final Exam., 2nd Cl. Hons Div. 1, 1957; Holker Sen. Scholar and Macaskie Scholar, Gray's Inn, 1957; called to the Bar, Gray's Inn, 1957, Bencher, 1987. Has practised in Courts of Malaysia, Singapore, Hong Kong, Cayman Is and IOM. *Recreations:* reading, walking, natural history. *Address:* Erskine Chambers, 30 Lincoln's Inn Fields, WC2A 3PF. *T:* (020) 7242 5532; 3 Atherton Drive, SW19 5LB. *T:* (020) 8947 3986. *Club:* MCC.

STUBBS, Sir William (Hamilton), Kt 1994; Rector, The London Institute, 1996–2001; *b* 5 Nov. 1937; *s* of Joseph Stubbs and Mary Stubbs (*née* McNicol); *m* 1963, Marie Margaret Pierce; three *d*. *Educ:* Workington Grammar Sch.; St Aloysius Coll., Glasgow; Glasgow Univ. (BSc, PhD). Res. Associate, Univ. of Arizona, 1963–64; with Shell Oil Co., San Francisco, 1964–67; teaching, 1967–72; Asst Dir of Educn, Carlisle, 1972–74; Asst Dir of Educn, 1974–76, Second Dep. Dir of Educn, 1976–77, Cumbria; Second Dep. Educn Officer, 1977–79, Dir of Educn (Schools), 1979–82, Educn Officer and Chief Exec., 1982–88, ILEA; Chief Exec., PCFC, 1988–93; Chief Exec., FEFC, 1992–96. Member: Council, CRAC, 1993–; Nat. Cttee of Inquiry into Higher Educn, 1996–97; Bd, NACETT, 1997–; Council, Inst. of Employment Studies, 1997–; Design Council, 1999–; Chairman: CBI Educn Foundn, 1996–99; Qualifications and Curriculum Authority, 1997–. Hon. Prof., Dept of Continuing Educn, Univ. of Warwick, 1993. Trustee, Geffrye Mus., 1999–. Gov., Birkbeck Coll., London, 1998–. CIMgt; FRSA. DUniv: Open, 1995; Sheffield Hallam, 1996; Hon. DLitt Exeter, 1996; Hon. DSc UWE, 1997. *Address:* Lockes Cottage, Manor Road, West Adderbury, near Banbury, Oxon OX17 3EL.

STÜCKLEN, Richard; Grosskreuz des Verdienstordens der Bundesrepublik Deutschland, 1963; Bayerischer Verdienstorden; President of the Bundestag, Federal Republic of Germany, 1979–83 (Vice-President, 1976–79 and 1983–90); *b* 20 Aug. 1916; *s* of Georg Stücklen and Mathilde (*née* Bach); *m* 1943, Ruth Stücklen (*née* Geissler); one *s* one *d*. *Educ:* primary sch.; technical sch.; engineering sch. Industrial Dept Manager and Manager in family business, 1945–49. Mem. of Bundestag, 1949–90; Dep. Chm., CDU/Christian Social Union and Party Leader, Christian Social Union, 1953–57 and 1967–76; Federal Minister of Posts and Telegraphs, 1957–66. *Publications:* Bundestagsreden und Zeitdokumente, 1979; and others. *Recreations:* skating, chess, soccer. *Address:* Eichstätter Strasse 27, 91781 Weissenburg, Germany. *Club:* Lions.

STUCLEY, Sir Hugh (George Coplestone Bampfylde), 6th Bt *cr* 1859; DL; Lieut Royal Horse Guards, retired; *b* 8 Jan. 1945; *s* of Major Sir Dennis Frederic Bankes Stucley, 5th Bt, and Hon. Sheila Bampfylde (*d* 1996), *o d* of 4th Baron Poltimore; *S* father, 1983; *m* 1969, Angela Caroline, *e d* of Richard Charles Robertson Toller, MC, Theale, Berks; two *s* two *d*. *Educ:* Milton Abbey School; Royal Agricultural College, Cirencester. Chm., Badgworthy Land Co., 1999–. Chm., Devon Br., CLA, 1995–97; Pres., Devonshire Assoc., 1997–98. DL Devon, 1998. *Heir:* *s* George Dennis Bampfylde Stucley [*b* 26 Dec. 1970; *m* 1997, Amber, *yr d* of Thomas Gage; two *s*]. *Address:* Affeton Castle, Worlington, Crediton, Devon EX17 4TU. *Club:* Sloane.

STUDD, Sir Edward (Fairfax), 4th Bt *cr* 1929; *b* 3 May 1929; *s* of Sir Eric Studd, 2nd Bt, OBE, and Stephana (*d* 1976), *o d* of L. J. Langmead; *S* brother, 1977; *m* 1960, Prudence Janet, *o d* of Alastair Douglas Fyfe, OBE, Riding Mill, Northumberland; two *s* one *d*. *Educ:* Winchester College. Lieutenant Coldstream Guards, London and Malaya, 1947–49; Macneill & Barry Ltd, Calcutta, 1951–62; Inchcape & Co. Ltd, London, 1962–86 (Dir, 1974–86). Master, Merchant Taylor's Co., 1987–88 and 1993–94. *Recreations:* walking, shooting, fishing. *Heir:* *s* Philip Alastair Fairfax Studd [*b* 27 Oct. 1961; *m* 1987, Georgina (marr. diss. 1999), *d* of Roger Neville; one *s* one *d*].

STUDD, John William Winston, MD, DSc; FRCOG; Director, Fertility and Endocrine Centre, Lister Hospital, Chelsea, since 1987; Consultant Gynaecologist, Chelsea and Westminster Hospital, since 1994; *b* 4 March 1940; *s* of late Eric Dacombe Studd and Elsie Elizabeth (*née* Kirby); *m* 1980, Dr Margaret Ann Johnson, *d* of Drs Frederick Johnson and Rosemary Johnson; one *s* two *d*. *Educ:* Royal Hosp. Sch., Holbrook; Univ. of Birmingham (MB ChB 1962; MD 1969; DSc 1995). MRCOG 1967, FRCOG 1982. Res. Fellow, Queen Elizabeth Hosp., Birmingham, 1967–70; Lectr in Obstetrics and Gynaecol., UC of Rhodesia, 1970–71; Consultant and Sen. Lectr, Univ. of Nottingham, 1974–75; Consultant Obstetrician and Gynaecologist, KCH, 1975–94. Visiting Professor: Yale Univ., 1982; Duke Univ., 1984; Univ. of Singapore, 1989; Harvard Univ., 1995. Mem. Council, 1980–97, and Pres., Sect. of Obstetrics and Gynaecol., 1994–95, RSocMed. Chm., Nat. Osteoporosis Soc., 1992–; Pres., Internat. Soc. Reproductive Medicine. Chm., PMS and Menopause Trust. Ed., Yearbook, 1993–97, Publications Officer, 1994–97, RCOG. Editor: Menopause Digest, 1994–; Obstetric and Gynaecol Reviews, 1994–; The Diplomate, 1995–; Member Editorial Board: Brit. Jl Obstetrics and Gynaecol.; Jl RSocMed; N American Jl of Menopause; Europ. Menopause Jl; Brit. Jl Hosp. Medicine; Osteoporosis Internat. *Publications:* Management of Labour, 1985; Self Assessment in Obstetrics and Gynaecology, 1985; Management of the Menopause, 1988; Progress of Obstetrics and Gynaecology, Vols 1–12, 1982–97; Multiple Choice Questions in Obstetrics and Gynaecology, 1993; The Menopause and Osteoporosis, 1993; Annual Progress in Reproductive Medicine, Vols 1 and 2, 1993–94; contrib. numerous articles on the menopause, osteoporosis, pre-menstrual syndrome, post-natal depression, labour, sickle cell disease and HIV infection in women. *Recreations:* tennis, theatre, opera, history of medicine, collecting antiquarian medical books. *Address:* 27 Blomfield Road, W9 1AA. *T:* (020) 7266 0058, *Fax:* (020) 7266 2663; 120 Harley Street, W1N 1AG. *T:* (020) 7486 0497, *Fax:* (020) 7224 4190; Fertility and Endocrine Centre, Lister Hospital, Chelsea Bridge Road, SW1W 8RH. *T:* (020) 7730 5433, *Fax:* (020) 7823 6108.

STUDD, Sir Peter Malden, GBE 1971; KCVO 1979; Kt 1969; DL; MA, DSc; *b* 15 Sept. 1916; *s* of late Brig. Malden Augustus Studd, DSO, MC and Netta Cramsie; *m* 1943, Angela Mary Hamilton (*née* Garnier) (*d* 1995); two *s*. *Educ:* Harrow; Clare Coll., Cambridge (MA). Captain of cricket, Harrow and Cambridge Univ. Served War of 1939–45, Royal Artillery, ME and European campaigns. De La Rue Co., 1939–81; Dir, Lloyds & Scottish plc, 1973–84. Alderman, Cripplegate Ward, City of London, 1959–76; Sheriff, 1967–68; Lord Mayor of London, 1970–71; Hon. DSc City Univ., 1971. Chm., King George's Jubilee Trust, 1972; Dep. Chm., Queen's Silver Jubilee Trust, 1976–80; Vice-Pres., Britain-Australia Bicentennial Cttee '88, 1985–; Pres., British Chiropractic Advancement Assoc., 1987–90; Vice-President: The Arts Educational Schools, 1984–; Seven Springs Centre, 1998–; Trustee, Royal Jubilee Trusts, 1980–95. Pres., London Bridge Mus. Trust, 2001–. Former Governor: Regent Street Poly.; Lady Eleanor Holles Sch.; Pangbourne Coll.; Harrow Sch. Liveryman, Merchant Taylors' Co., 1959 (Asst, 1959–, Master, 1973–74); Hon. Liveryman, Worshipful Cos of Fruiterers and Plaisterers. DL Wilts, 1983. KStJ 1968 (Pres., Co. of Surrey, 1967–76). *Recreations:* fishing, photographing, saving St Paul's, 'lighting up the Thames'. *Address:* c/o Messrs C. Hoare & Co., 37 Fleet Street, EC4P 4DQ. *Clubs:* MCC, I Zingari; Hawks (Cambridge); Houghton (Stockbridge).

STUDER, Cheryl Lynn; opera singer, freelance since 1986; *b* Midland, USA, 24 Oct. 1955; *m* 1992, Ewald Schwarz; two *d*. *Educ:* Interlochen Arts Acad.; Oberlin Coll. Conservatory, Ohio; Univ. of Tennessee; Hochschule für Musik und Darstellende Kunst, Vienna. First professional recital, Virginia Highlands Fest., 1977; operatic début, Bavarian State Opera, 1980; *débuts:* Royal Opera House, Covent Garden, 1984; Bayreuth Fest., 1985; La Scala, Milan, 1987; NY Met, 1988; Vienna State Opera, 1989; has sung at all major opera houses and festivals in the world; regular appearances at Bayreuth and Salzburg Fests; extensive concert tours with all major orchestras and conductors; world-wide recitals. Many recordings, incl. La Traviata, Faust, Salomé, Lohengrin, Figaro, Strauss' Four Last Songs. Franz Schubert Inst. Award, 1979; Grammy Award, 1991, 1994; Internat. Classical Music Award for best female singer, 1992; Furtwängler Preis, 1992; Vocalist of the Year Award, Musical America Directory of Performing Arts, 1994. *Address:* c/o International Performing Artists Inc, 125 Crowfield Drive, Knoxville, TN 37922, USA. *Fax:* (423) 694 8044.

STUDHOLME, Sir Henry (William), 3rd Bt *cr* 1956, of Perridge, Co. Devon; *b* 31 Jan. 1958; *s* of Sir Paul Henry William Studholme, 2nd Bt and Virginia (*d* 1990), *yr d* of Sir (Herbert) Richmond Palmer, KCMG, CBE; *S* father, 1990; *m* 1988, Sarah Lucy Rosita (*née* Deans-Chrystall); two *s* one *d*. *Educ:* Eton; Trinity Hall, Cambridge (MA). ACA, ATII. Chm., SW Regl Adv. Cttee on Forestry, 2000–. *Heir:* *s* Joshua Henry Paul Studholme, *b* 2 Feb. 1992. *Address:* Halscombe Farm, Ide, near Exeter EX2 9TQ. *Club:* Brooks's.

See also J. G. Studholme.

STUDHOLME, Joseph Gilfred; Chairman and Co-founder, Getmapping (formerly Getmapping.com) plc, since 1998; *b* 14 Jan. 1936; *s* of Sir Henry Gray Studholme, 1st Bt, CVO and of Judith Joan Mary (*née* Whitbread); *m* 1959, Rachel Fellowes, *d* of Sir William Albemarle Fellowes, KCVO; three *s*. *Educ:* Eton; Magdalen Coll., Oxford (MA). Nat. Service, 2nd Lieut, KRRC (60th Rifles), 1954–56. Man. Dir, King & Shaxson Ltd (Billbrokers), 1961–63; Co-founder, Chm. and Man. Dir, Editions Alecto Gp, 1963–. Mem. Council, Byam Shaw Sch. of Art, 1963–94 (Chm., 1988–94). Chm., Wessex Regl Cttee, NT, 1996– (Mem., 1993–). Sen. Fellow, RCA, 1999. *Address:* The Court House, Lower Woodford, Salisbury, Wilts SP4 6NQ. *T:* (01722) 782237. *Clubs:* Garrick, Double Crown, MCC.

STUNELL, (Robert) Andrew, OBE 1995; MP (Lib Dem) Hazel Grove, since 1997; *b* 24 Nov. 1942; *s* of late Robert George and Trixie Stunell; *m* 1967, Gillian (*née* Chorley); two *s* three *d*. *Educ:* Surbiton Grammar Sch.; Manchester Univ.; Liverpool Poly. Architectural asst, CWS Manchester, 1965–67, Runcorn New Town, 1967–81, freelance, 1981–85; various posts incl. Political Sec., Assoc. of Liberal Democrat Councillors, 1985–97. Member: Chester City Council, 1979–90; Cheshire CC, 1981–91 (Leader, Lib Dem Gp); Stockport MBC, 1994–. Vice-Chm., ACC, 1985–90. Contested: (L) 1979, (Lib/Alliance), 1983 and 1987, City of Chester; (Lib Dem) Hazel Grove, 1992. Lib Dem Chief Whip, 2001–. *Address:* House of Commons, SW1A 0AA; 84 Lyme Grove, Romiley, Stockport SK6 4DJ.

STURDEE, Rear-Adm. Arthur Rodney Barry, CB 1971; DSC 1945; *b* 6 Dec. 1919; *s* of Comdr Barry V. Sturdee, RN, and Barbara (*née* Sturdee); *m* 1953, Marie-Claire Amstoutz (*d* 1995), Mulhouse, France; one *s* one *d*; *m* 2001, Joyce (*née* Jeacock), *widow* of Major James Hunter. *Educ:* Canford Sch. Entered Royal Navy as Special Entry Cadet, 1937. Served War of 1939–45: Midshipman in HMS Exeter at Battle of the River Plate, 1939; Lieut, 1941; specialised in Navigation, 1944; minesweeping in Mediterranean, 1944–45 (DSC). Lt-Comdr, 1949; RN Staff Coll., 1950–51; Staff of Navigation Sch., 1951–52; Comdr, 1952; JSSC, 1953; BJSM, Washington, 1953–55; Fleet Navigating Officer, Medit., 1955–57; Exec. Officer, RNAS, Culdrose, 1958–59; Captain 1960; NATO Defence Coll., 1960–63; Queen's Harbour-Master, Singapore, 1963–65; Staff of Chief of Defence Staff, 1965–67; Chief of Staff to C-in-C, Portsmouth (as Cdre), 1967–69; Rear-Adm. 1969; Flag Officer, Gibraltar, 1969–72; retired 1972. ADC to the Queen, 1969. *Address:* Cider Mill Cottage, Hancocks Lane, Castlemorton Common, Malvern, Worcestershire WR13 6LG. *T:* (01684) 573627.

STURDY, Henry William, OBE 1975 (MBE 1968); HM Diplomatic Service, retired; Deputy Consul General and Counsellor Commercial, Chicago, 1976–78; *b* 17 Feb. 1919; *s* of late Henry William Dawson Sturdy and Jemima Aixill; *m* 1945, Anne Jamieson Marr; one *s* one *d*. *Educ:* Woolwich Polytechnic (Mechanical Engineering). Served War in Middle East, 1939–45; Allied Control Commission, Germany, 1946. Executive Branch of Civil Service and Board of Trade, 1951; tour in Trade Commission Service, 1953; appointments: Pakistan, Bangladesh, Sri Lanka, Canada. First Secretary, Diplomatic Service, 1965; Counsellor, Korea, 1976. Defence Medal; 1939–45 Medal; General Service Medal, 1939, with Palestine Clasp, 1945. *Recreations:* bridge, reading, argument, international cuisine. *Address:* 12A Homewood Court, Badgers Walk, Chorleywood, Herts WD3 5GB.

STURDY, Robert William; Member (C) Eastern Region, England, European Parliament, since 1999 (Cambridgeshire, 1994–99); *b* 22 June 1944; *s* of late Gordon Sturdy and of Kathleen Sturdy (*née* Wells); *m* 1969, Elizabeth Hommes; one *s* one *d*. *Educ:* Ashville Coll., Harrogate. Accountant; Partner, G. E. Sturdy & Son, North Deighton Farms, 1965–. European Parliament: Cons. Agric. spokesman; Vice-Pres., Delegn to SE Europe, 1994–; Dep. Leader, Cons. Delegn in Europe; Chm., Canadian Interparly Delegn; Substitute Member: Cttee on Agric. and Rural Develt, 1997– (Mem., 1994–97); Agric. and Envmt Cttee, 1999–. *Recreations:* fishing, tennis, ski-ing, cricket. *Address:* 153 St Neots Road, Hardwick, Cambridge CB3 7QJ. *T:* (01954) 211790.

STURGE, Maj.-Gen. (Henry Arthur) John, CB 1978; *b* 27 April 1925; *s* of Henry George Arthur Sturge and Lilian Beatrice Sturge; *m* 1953, Jean Ailsa Mountain; two *s* one *d*. *Educ:* Wilson's Sch., (formerly) Camberwell, London; Queen Mary Coll., London. Commissioned, Royal Signals, 1946; UK, 1946–50; Egypt, 1950–53; UK, incl. psc, 1953–59; Far East, 1959–62; jssc, 1962; BAOR, 1963–64; RMA, Sandhurst, 1965–66; BAOR, incl. Command, 1966–69; Min. of Defence, 1970–75; Chief Signal Officer, BAOR, 1975–77; ACDS (Signals), 1977–80. Col Comdt, Royal Corps of Signals, 1977–85. Colonel, Queen's Gurkha Signals, 1980–86. Gen. Manager, 1981–84, Dir, 1983–84, Marconi Space and Defence Systems; Man. Dir, 1984–85, Chm., 1985–86, Marconi Secure Radio Systems; Prin. Consultant, Logica Space and Defence Systems, 1986–90; Chm., Logica Defence and Civil Government Ltd, 1991–94. Vice Chm., Governors, Wilson's Sch., 1979–99. *Recreations:* sailing, (formerly) Rugby. *Address:* 18 High Street, Odiham, Hampshire RG29 1LG.

STURGEON, Nicola; Member (SNP) Glasgow, Scottish Parliament, since 1999; *b* 19 July 1970; *d* of Robert and Joan Sturgeon. *Educ:* Univ. of Glasgow (LLB Hons; Dip. Legal Practice). Trainee Solicitor, McClure Naismith, Glasgow, 1993–95; Asst Solicitor, Bell & Craig, Stirling, 1995–97; Associate Solicitor, Drumchapel Law Centre, Glasgow, 1997–99. *Recreations:* theatre, reading. *Address:* Scottish Parliament, Edinburgh EH99 1SP. *T:* (0131) 348 5695; 2/2, 2467 Dumbarton Road, Glasgow G14 0NT. *T:* (0141) 952 0845.

STURKEY, (Robert) Douglas, CVO 1995; AM 1999; Official Secretary to the Governor-General of Australia, 1990–98; Secretary of the Order of Australia, 1990–98; *b* 7 Sept. 1935; *s* of late James Robert Sturkey and Jessie Grace (*née* Meares). *Educ:* Wesley Coll., S Perth; Univ. of WA (BA Hons); ANU (MA 2000). Mem., Australian Diplomatic Service, 1957–90: service abroad at Wellington, Lagos, Suva, Malta, Calcutta; Counsellor, later Dep. Perm. Rep., UN, New York, 1974–77; Ambassador to Saudi Arabia (also concurrently to countries of Arabian peninsula), 1979–84; Head, S Asia, Africa and ME Br., Dept of Foreign Affairs, Canberra, 1984–87; Principal Advr, Asia Div., Dept of Foreign Affairs and Trade, Canberra, 1987–90. CStJ 1992. *Recreations:* opera, music, theatre. *Address:* PO Box 62, Hughes, ACT 2605, Australia. *T:* (2) 62324722.

STURLEY, Air Vice-Marshal Philip Oliver, CB 2000; MBE 1985; FRAeS; Assistant Chief of Air Staff, Ministry of Defence, since 2000; *b* 9 July 1950; *s* of William Percival Sturley and Delia Agnes Sturley (*née* Grogan); *m* 1972, Micheline Leetch; one *d*. *Educ:* St Ignatius Coll., London; Southampton Univ. (BSc 1971). FRAeS 1993. Pilot trng, RAF Coll., Cranwell, 1971–72; 41 Sqn Coningsby, 1973–76; II (Army Co-operation) Sqn Laarbruch, 1977–80, 1982–84, OC, 1987–89; HQ 1 (British) Corps Bielefeld, 1980–82; jsdc, 1984; Comd Briefing Team, 1984–85, Plans, 1985–86, HQ Strike Comd; Air Plans, 1989–90, Dir of Air Staff Briefing and Co-ordination, 1990–92, MoD; OC RAF Cottesmore, 1992–94; Sec. IMS, HQ NATO, 1994–98; SASO HQ Strike Comd and AOC No 38 Gp, 1998–2000. *Recreations:* gliding, golf, ski-ing. *Address:* RAF Innsworth, Glos GL3 1EZ. *Club:* Royal Air Force.

STURROCK, Philip James; Chairman and Group Chief Executive, The Continuum International Publishing Group Ltd, since 1999; *b* 5 Oct. 1947; *s* of James Cars Sturrock and Joyce Sturrock (*née* Knowles); *m* 1972, Susan Haycock (marr. diss. 1995); one *s* two *d*; *m* 2000, Madeleine Frances Robinson. *Educ:* Queen Mary's School, Walsall; Trinity College, Oxford (MA); Manchester Business School (MBA). Managing Director: IBIS Information Services, 1972–80; Pitman Books, 1980–83; Group Man. Dir, Routledge & Kegan Paul, 1983–85; Chm. and Man. Dir, Cassell, 1986–99. Chm., Soc. of Bookmen, 2001–April 2002. Governor, Pusey House, Oxford, 1975–95. Trustee, St Albans Cathedral Educn Trust, 1988–. FRSA 1992. Liveryman, Glaziers' Co., 1983–. *Recreations:* reading, walking, music. *Address:* 20 Somerville Point, Trinity Wharf, 305 Rotherhithe Street, SE16 5EQ. *T:* (020) 7231 7103. *Club:* Athenæum.

STUTTAFORD, Dr (Irving) Thomas, OBE 1996; medical columnist, The Times, since 1991; *b* 4 May 1931; 2nd *s* of late Dr W. J. E. Stuttaford, MC, Horning, Norfolk and Mrs Marjorie Stuttaford (*née* Royden); *m* 1957, Pamela, *d* of late Col Richard Ropner, TD, DL, Tain; three *s*. *Educ:* Gresham's Sch.; Brasenose Coll., Oxford; West London Hosp. 2nd Lieut, 10th Royal Hussars (PWO), 1953–55; Lieut, Scottish Horse (TA), 1955–59. Qualif. MRCS, LRCP, 1959; junior hosp. appts, 1959 and 1960. Gen. Med. practice, 1960–70. Mem. Blofield and Flegg RDC, 1964–66; Mem., Norwich City Council, 1969–71. MP (C) Norwich S, 1970–Feb. 1974; Mem. Select Cttee Science and Technology, 1970–74. Contested (C) Isle of Ely, Oct. 1974, 1979. Physician, BUPA Medical Centre, 1971–96; Clinical Assistant to: The London Hosp., 1975–93; Queen Mary's Hosp. for East End, 1974–79; Moorfields Eye Hosp., 1975–79. Member: Council, Research Defence Soc., 1970–79; Birth Control Campaign Cttee, 1970–79; British Cancer Council, 1970–79. Medical Adviser: Rank Organisation, 1980–85; Barclays Bank, Standard Chartered Bank, Hogg Robinson, Rank Hotels and other cos; Medical Corresp. to The Times, 1982–91. Contributor to: Elle, For Him, Oldie, Options, etc. *Publications:* To Your Good Health: the wise drinker's guide, 1997; (jtly) In Your Right Mind, 1999. *Recreation:* country life. *Address:* 36 Elm Hill, Norwich, Norfolk NR3 1HG. *T:* (01603) 615133; 8 Devonshire Place, W1N 1PB. *T:* (020) 7935 5011. *Clubs:* Athenæum, Reform, Cavalry and Guards, Beefsteak; Norfolk (Norwich).

STYLE, Sir William Frederick, 13th Bt *cr* 1627, of Wateringbury, Kent; *b* 13 May 1945; *s* of Sir William Montague Style, 12th Bt, and of La Verne, *d* of late T. M. Comstock; *S* father, 1981; *m* 1st, 1968, Wendy Gay (marr. diss. 1971), *d* of Gene Wittenberger, Hartford, Wisconsin, USA; two *d*; 2nd, 1986, Linnea Lorna, *d* of Donn Erickson, Sussex, Wisconsin, USA; one *s* two *d*. *Heir:* *s* William Colin Style, *b* 1995.

STYLER, Granville Charles; His Honour Judge Styler; a Circuit Judge, since 1992; *b* 9 Jan. 1947; *s* of Samuel Charles Styler and Frances Joan Styler (*née* Clifford); *m* 1971, Penelope Darbyshire; three *d*. *Educ:* King Edward VI Sch., Stratford-on-Avon. Called to the Bar, Gray's Inn, 1970; a Recorder, 1988–92. *Recreations:* carriage driving, tennis, gardening, horse racing. *Address:* c/o Stoke-on-Trent Crown Court, Bethesda Street, Hanley, Stoke-on-Trent ST1 3BP. *Club:* Outer Hebrides Tennis.

STYLES, (Frank) Showell, FRGS; author; *b* 14 March 1908; *s* of Frank Styles and Edith (*née* Showell); *m* 1954, Kathleen Jane Humphreys; one *s* two *d*. *Educ:* Bishop Vesey's Grammar Sch., Sutton Coldfield. Served Royal Navy, 1939; retd (Comdr), 1946. Professional author, 1946–76, retd. Led two private Arctic expedns, 1952–53; led private Himalayan expedn, 1954. FRGS 1954. *Publications:* 130 books: *travel*, incl. Mountains of the Midnight Sun, 1954; Blue Remembered Hills, 1965; *biography*, incl. Mr Nelson's Ladies, 1954; Mallory of Everest, 1967; *mountain guidebooks*, incl. The Mountains of North Wales, 1973; The Glyder Range, 1973; *instructional books*, incl. Modern Mountaineering, 1964; Introduction to Mountaineering, 1955; *naval historical fiction*, incl. Stella and the Fireships, 1985; The Lee Shore, 1986; Gun-brig Captain, 1987; HMS Cracker, 1988; Nelson's Midshipman, 1990; *children's fiction*, incl. Kami the Sherpa, 1957; The Shop in the Mountain, 1961; *detective fiction* (under *pen-name*, Glyn Carr), incl. Death under Snowdon, 1954; The Corpse in the Crevasse, 1957. *Recreations:* mountaineering, gardening, music. *Address:* Trwyn Cae Iago, Borth-y-Gest, Porthmadog, Gwynedd LL49 9TW. *T:* (01766) 2849. *Club:* Midland Association of Mountaineers (Birmingham).

STYLES, Lt-Col George; *see* Styles, Lt-Col S. G.

STYLES, Showell; *see* Styles, F. S.

STYLES, Lt-Col (Stephen) George, GC 1972; retired; *b* 16 March 1928; *s* of Stephen Styles and Grace Lily Styles (*née* Preston); *m* 1952, Mary Rose Styles (*née* Woolgar); one *s* two *d*. *Educ:* Collyers Sch., Horsham; Royal Military Coll. of Science. Ammunition Technical Officer, commissioned RAOC, Nov. 1947; seconded to 1 Bn KOYLI, 1949–51 (despatches, 1952); RMCS, 1952–56; HQ Ammunition Organisation, 1956–58; OC 28 Commonwealth Bde, Ordnance Field Park, Malaya, 1958–61; 2i/c 16 Bn RAOC, Bicester, 1961–64; OC Eastern Command Ammunition Inspectorate, 1964–67; Sen. Ammo Tech. Officer, 3 BAPD, BAOR, 1967–68; OC 1(BR) Corps Vehicle Company, 1968–69; Sen. Ammo Tech. Officer, Northern Ireland, 1969–72; Chief Ammo Tech. Officer (EOD), HQ DOS (CILSA), 1972–74. Member: Royal Soc. of St George, NRA, NSRA. *Publications:* Bombs Have No Pity, 1975; contrib. Proc. ICE, Jl of Forensic Science Soc. *Recreation:* rifle and game shooting, cartridge collector. *Address:* c/o Barclays Bank, Abingdon.

SUAREZ, Juan L.; *see* Lechin-Suarez.

SUBAK-SHARPE, Prof. John Herbert, CBE 1991; FRSE 1970; Professor Emeritus and Hon. Senior Research Fellow, University of Glasgow, since 1994 (Professor of Virology, 1968–94); Hon. Director, Medical Research Council Virology Unit, 1968–94; *b* 14 Feb. 1924; *s* of late Robert Subak and late Nelly (*née* Bruell), Vienna, Austria; *m* 1953,

Barbara Naomi Morris; two *s* one *d*. *Educ:* Humanistic Gymnasium, Vienna; Univ. of Birmingham. BSc (Genetics) (1st Cl. Hons) 1952; PhD 1956. Refugee from Nazi oppression, 1939; farm pupil, 1939–44; HM Forces (Parachute Regt), 1944–47. Asst Lectr in Genetics, Glasgow Univ., 1954–56; Mem. scientific staff, ARC Animal Virus Research Inst., Pirbright, 1956–60; Nat. Foundn Fellow, California Inst. of Technology, 1961; Mem. Scientific staff of MRC, in Experimental Virus Research Unit, Glasgow, 1961–68. Visiting Professor: US Nat. Insts of Health, Bethesda, Md, 1967; US Univ. of Health Services, Bethesda, Md, 1985; Vis. Fellow, Clare Hall, Cambridge, 1986–87. Sec., Genetical Soc., 1966–72, Vice-Pres. 1972–75, Trustee 1971–99. Member: European Molecular Biology Orgn, 1969– (Chm., Course and Workshops Cttee, 1976–78); Genetic Manipulation Adv. Gp, 1976–80; Biomed. Res. Cttee, SHHD Chief Scientist Orgn, 1979–84; British Nat. Cttee of Biophysics, 1970–76; Governing Body, W of Scotland Oncological Orgn, 1974–; Scientific Adv. Body, W German Cancer Res. Centre, 1977–82; Governing Body, Animal Virus Res. Inst., Pirbright, 1986–87; MRC Training Awards Panel, 1985–89 (Chm., 1986–89); Scientific Adv. Gp of Equine Virology Res. Foundn, 1987–98; MRC Cell and Disorders Bd, 1988–92. CIBA Medal, Biochem. Soc., 1993. *Publications:* articles in scientific jls on genetic studies with viruses and cells. *Recreations:* travel, hill walking, bridge. *Address:* 63 Kelvin Court, Glasgow G12 0AG. *T:* (0141) 334 1863. *Club:* Athenæum.

SUBBA ROW, Raman, CBE 1991; Chairman, Test and County Cricket Board, 1985–90; *b* 29 Jan. 1932; *s* of Panguluri Venkata Subba Row and Doris Mildred Subba Row; *m* 1960, Anne Dorothy (*née* Harrison); two *s* one *d*. *Educ:* Whitgift Sch., Croydon; Trinity Hall, Cambridge (MA Hons). Associate Dir, W. S. Crawford Ltd, 1963–69; Man. Dir, Management Public Relations Ltd, 1969–92. *Recreations:* sport, bridge. *Address:* Leeward, Manor Way, South Croydon, Surrey CR2 7BT. *T:* (020) 8688 2991. *Clubs:* Royal Air Force, Institute of Directors, MCC, Surrey County Cricket; Bloemfontein (South Africa); Cricket of India (Bombay); Kingston Cricket (Jamaica).

SUCH, Frederick Rudolph Charles; Immigration Adjudicator, London Region, since 2000; a Recorder of the Crown Court, since 1979; *b* 19 June 1936; *s* of Frederick Sidney Such and Anne Marie Louise (*née* Martin); *m* 1961, Elizabeth, *d* of late Judge Norman and Mrs Harper, Cloughton, Yorkshire; one *s* one *d*. *Educ:* Mbeya Sch., Tanganyika Territory, E Africa (Tanzania); Taunton Sch.; Keble Coll., Oxford (MA). Called to the Bar, Gray's Inn, 1960; practised: London, 1960–69, then North Eastern Circuit, 1969–2000. FCIArb 1995. *Recreations:* theatre, opera, Real tennis. *Address:* (office) Field House, 15–25 Bream's Buildings, EC4A 1DZ. *Clubs:* Jesters, Queen's; Jesmond Dene Real Tennis.

SUCHET, David; actor; associate artiste, Royal Shakespeare Co.; *b* 2 May 1946; *s* of late Jack and Joan Suchet (*née* Jarché); *m* 1976, Sheila Ferris, actress; one *s* one *d*. *Educ:* Wellington Sch.; LAMDA (Best Drama Student, 1968). *Stage:* repertory theatres, incl. Chester, Birmingham, Exeter, Worthing, Coventry, 1969–73; for Royal Shakespeare Co.: Romeo and Juliet (Mercutio and Tybalt), As You Like It (Orlando), Once in a Lifetime (Glogauer), Measure for Measure (Angelo), The Tempest (Caliban), King Lear (The Fool), King John (Hubert), Merchant of Venice (Shylock), Troilus and Cressida (Achilles), Richard II (Bolingbroke), Every Good Boy Deserves Favour, 1983, Othello (Iago), 1986, Timon of Athens (title rôle), 1991; Separation, Comedy, 1988; Oleanna, Royal Court, 1993 (Variety Club Award for Best Actor, 1994); Who's Afraid of Virginia Woolf?, Aldwych, 1996 (Best Actor Award, Critics' Circle and South Bank Awards); Saturday, Sunday, Monday, Chichester, 1998; Amadeus, Old Vic, 1998 (Variety Club Award for Best Actor, 1999), Los Angeles and NY, 1999–2000 (Drama League Award); *films include:* Tale of Two Cities, 1978; The Missionary, 1982; Red Monarch (Best Actor award, Marseilles Film Fest.), 1983; Falcon and the Snowman, 1985; Thirteen at Dinner, 1985; Song for Europe, 1985; Harry and the Hendersons, 1986; When the Whales came, 1990; Deadly Voyage, 1995; Executive Decision, 1996; Sunday, 1996 (winner, Sundance Film Festival); Wing Commander, 1998; A Perfect Murder, 1998; RKO, 2000; Sabotage, 2000; serials and series for *television:* Oppenheimer, 1978; Reilly, 1981; Saigon, 1982; Freud, 1983; Blott on the Landscape, 1984; Oxbridge Blues, 1984; Playing Shakespeare, 1985; Great Writers, 1988; Agatha Christie's Hercule Poirot, 1989, 1990, 1991, 1992, 1993, 1994, 2000, 2001; The Secret Agent, 1992; Solomon, 1997; Seesaw, 1998; National Crime Squad, 2001; Murder in Mind, 2001; Victoria and Albert, 2001; The Way We Live Now, 2001; *radio:* one-man show, Kreutzer Sonata (Best Radio Actor, Pye Radio Awards, 1979); numerous other parts. Mem. Council, LAMDA, 1985–. Lectr, US univs; Vis. Prof., Univ. of Nebraska, 1975. Numerous awards, incl. Best Actor, RTS, 1986. *Publications:* (contrib.) Players of Shakespeare, 2 vols, 1985 and 1988; essays on interpretation of roles. *Recreations:* clarinet, photography, reading, ornithology, theology, narrow boating. *Address:* c/o Gillie Sanguinetti, Ken McReddie Ltd, 91 Regent Street, W1R 7TB. *Clubs:* Garrick, St James's.

See also J. A. Suchet.

SUCHET, John Aleck; television journalist, Independent Television News, since 1972; *b* 29 March 1944; *s* of late Jack and Joan Suchet; *m* 1st, 1968, Moya Hankinson (marr. diss. 1985); three *s*; 2nd, 1985, Bonnie Simonson. *Educ:* Uppingham; Univ. of St Andrews (MA Hons). Reuters News Agency, 1967–71; BBC TV News, 1971–72; Independent Television News, 1972–: reporter, 1976–86; Washington corresp., 1981–83; newscaster, 1986–. Pres., Friends of RAM, 1998–; Patron, Stamford Literary Fest., 1999–. Hon. FRAM 2001. Hon. LLD Dundee, 2000. TV Journalist of the Year, RTS, 1986; Newscaster of the Year, TRIC, 1996. *Publications:* TV News: the inside story, 1989; The Last Master (fictional biography of Ludwig van Beethoven): vol. 1, Passion and Anger, 1996; vol. 2, Passion and Pain, 1997; vol. 3, Passion and Glory, 1998. *Recreations:* classical music, photography. *Address:* ITN, 200 Gray's Inn Road, WC1X 8XZ. *T:* (020) 7833 3000.

See also D. Suchet.

SUCKLING, Dr Charles Walter, CBE 1989; FRS 1978; FRSC; *b* 24 July 1920; *s* of Edward Ernest and Barbara Suckling (*née* Thomson); *m* 1946, (Eleanor) Margaret Watterson; two *s* one *d*. *Educ:* Oldershaw Grammar Sch., Wallasey; Liverpool Univ. (BSc, PhD). ICI: joined Gen. Chemicals Div., 1942; R&D Director, Mond Div., 1967; Dep. Chairman, Mond Div., 1969; Chairman, Paints Div., 1972; Gen. Man., Res. and Technol., 1977–82; Chm., Bradbury, Suckling and Partners, 1982–93; Dir, Albright and Wilson, 1982–89. Hon. Visiting Professor: Univ. of Stirling, 1968–93; UEA, 1977–83. Member: BBC Science Consultative Gp, 1980–85; Royal Commn on Environmental Pollution, 1982–92; Electricity Supply Res. Council, 1983–90; ABRC/NERC Gp into Geol Surveying, 1985–87; Cttee of Inquiry into Teaching of English Language, 1987–88; Nat. Curriculum English Working Gp, 1988–89; Nat. Curriculum Mod. For. Langs Wkg Gp, 1989–90; Council, RCA, 1981–90 (Treasurer, 1984–90); Chm., Roy. Soc. Study Gp on Pollution Control Priorities, 1988–92; Member: Nat. Adv. Gp on Eco-labelling, 1990–92; Adv. Cttee on Dangerous Pathogens Microbiol Risk Assessment Wkg Gp, 1993–95. Bicentennial Lecture, Washington Coll., Maryland, 1981; Robbins Lecture, Stirling Univ., 1990; Joseph Clover Lecture, Royal Coll. of Anaesthetists, 1994. Senior Fellow, RCA, 1986. Hon. DSc Liverpool, 1980; DUniv Stirling, 1985. Liverpool Univ. Chem. Soc. Medal, 1964; John Scott Medal, City of Philadelphia, 1973; Medal, Royal Coll. of Anaesthetists, 1992. *Publications:* (with A. Baines and F. R. Bradbury) Research in the Chemical Industry, 1969; (with C. J. Suckling and K. E. Suckling) Chemistry through Models, 1978; papers on anaesthetics, industrial research and strategy in journals. *Recreations:* music, gardening, languages, writing. *Address:* 1 Desborough Drive, Tewin, Welwyn, Herts AL6 0HQ. *T:* (01438) 798250.

SUDBOROUGH, Air Vice-Marshal Nigel John, OBE 1989; FRAeS; Deputy Chief of Staff Operations, Strike Command, since 2000; *b* 23 March 1948; *s* of Alexander and Beryl Sudborough; *m* 1971, Anne Brown; one *s* one *d*. *Educ:* Oundle Sch. Commnd as navigator, Royal Air Force, 1967; various flying tours, incl. Vulcan, Phantom and Tornado; PSO to Vice-Chief of Air Staff, MoD, 1983–85; i/c 29 (F) sqdn, 1985–87; RAF Mt Pleasant, Falkland Is, 1987–88; DS, RAF Staff Coll., 1988–90; HQ RAF Germany, 1990–93; i/c RAF Leuchars, 1993–95; rcds 1996; AO Plans, HQ Strike Comd, 1997–2000. FCIPD 2000; FRAeS 2001. Freeman, City of London, 1985; Liveryman, Co. of Pattenmakers, 1985. *Recreations:* fly-fishing, philately. *Address:* RAF High Wycombe, Bucks HP14 4UE. *T:* (01494) 497606. *Club:* Royal Air Force.

SUDBURY, Archdeacon of; see Cox, Ven. J. S.

SUDBURY, Dr Wendy Elizabeth, (Mrs A. J. Bates); Director, Cambridge Management Group, since 1994; *b* 14 June 1946; *d* of Clifford Frank Edwards and Betty Edwards (*née* Foster); one *d*; *m* 1st, 1973, R. M. Sudbury (marr. diss. 1980); 2nd, 1993, Alexander John Bates; one step *s* two step *d*. *Educ:* Finchley Co. Grammar Sch.; Lucy Cavendish Coll., Cambridge (MA); Christ Church, Oxford; Cranfield Sch. of Mgt (PhD 1992). Chief Exec., Mus. Documentation Assoc., 1989–97. Expert Advr, EC, 1996–. Mem., RCHM, 1997–99. Mem. Adv. Bd, Judge Inst. of Mgt Studies, Cambridge Univ., 1992–94. *Publications:* (with A. Fahy) Information: the Hidden Resource, Museums & the Internet, 1995; contrib. to learned jls. *Recreations:* humanities, travel, gardening, hiking, family life. *Address:* 16 Wimbourne House, Blandford Square, Harewood Avenue, NW1 6NU.

SUDDABY, Arthur, CBE 1980; PhD, MSc; CChem, FRSC; CEng, MIChemE; scientific consultant on the carriage of goods by sea, until 1990; Provost, City of London Polytechnic, 1970–81; *b* 26 Feb. 1919; *e s* of George Suddaby, Kingston-upon-Hull, Yorks; *m* 1944, Elizabeth Bullin Vyse (decd), *d* of Charles Vyse; two *s*. *Educ:* Riley High Sch., Kingston-upon-Hull; Hull Technical Coll.; Chelsea Polytechnic; Queen Mary Coll. London. Chemist and Chemical Engr, in industry, 1937–47; Lectr in Physical Chemistry, and later Sen. Lectr in Chem. Engrg, West Ham Coll. of Technology, 1947–50; Sir John Cass Coll.: Sen. Lectr in Physics, 1950–61; Head of Dept of Physics, 1961–66; Principal, 1966–70. Chm., Cttee of Directors of Polytechnics, 1976–78; Member: Chem. Engrg Cttee, 1948–51; London and Home Counties Regional Adv. Council, 1971–; Bd of Examrs and Educn Cttee, Inst. of Chem. Engrs, 1948–51; Oakes Cttee on Management of Public Sector Higher Educn, 1977–78; CNAA: Chem. Engrg Bd, 1969–75; Nautical Studies Bd, 1972–75; Chm., Standing Conf. of Approved Coll. Res. Deg. Cttees, 1979–81; Court of the City University, 1967–81; Vis. Cttee, Cranfield Inst. of Technology, 1979–85; Chm., Assoc. of Navigation Schs, 1972. *Publications:* various original research papers in theoretical physics, in scientific jls; review articles. *Recreations:* country sports, music. *Address:* Flat 3, 16 Elm Park Gardens, Chelsea, SW10 9NY. *T:* (020) 7352 9164; Castle Hill House, Godshill Wood, near Fordingbridge, Hants SP6 2LU. *T:* (01425) 652234. *Club:* Athenæum.

SUDELEY, 7th Baron *cr* 1838; **Merlin Charles Sainthill Hanbury-Tracy,** FSA; *b* 17 June 1939; *o c* of late Captain Michael David Charles Hanbury-Tracy, Scots Guards, and Colline Ammabel (*d* 1985), *d* of late Lt-Col C. G. H. St Hill and *widow* of Lt-Col Frank King, DSO, OBE; *S* cousin, 1941; *m* 1980, Hon. Mrs Elizabeth Villiers (marr. diss. 1988), *d* of late Viscount Bury (*s* of 9th Earl of Albemarle); *m* 1999, Mrs Margarita Kellett. *Educ:* at Eton and in the ranks of the Scots Guards. Chairman: Monday Club; Constitutional Monarchy Assoc.; Vice-Chancellor, Monarchist League. Patron: Assoc. of Bankrupts; Anglican Assoc.; Lay Patron, Prayer Book Soc. *Publications:* (jtly) The Sudeleys—Lords of Toddington, 1987; (contrib.) The House of Lords: a thousand years of British tradition, 1994; contribs to Quarterly Review, Contemporary Review, Family History, Trans of Bristol and Gloucestershire Archaeol. Soc., Montgomeryshire Collections, Bull. of Manorial Soc., Die Waage (Zeitschrift der Chemie Grünenthal), Monday Club Jl, London Miscellany. *Recreations:* ancestor worship; cultivating his sensibility. *Heir: kinsman* Desmond Andrew John Hanbury-Tracy [*b* 30 Nov. 1928; *m* 1st, 1957, Jennifer Lynn (marr. diss. 1966), *d* of Dr R. C. Hodges; one *s*; 2nd, 1967, Lillian, *d* of Nathaniel Laurie; one *s*; 3rd, 1988, Mrs Margaret Cecilia White, *d* of late Alfred Henry Marmaduke Purse]. *Address:* 25 Melcombe Court, Dorset Square, NW1 6EP. *Club:* Brooks's.

SUDJIC, Deyan, OBE 2000; Architecture Critic, The Observer, since 2000; Editor, Domus magazine, since 2000; *b* 6 Sept. 1952; *s* of Milivoj Jovo Sudjic and Miroslava Pavlovic; *m* 1984, Sarah Isabel Miller; one *d*. *Educ:* Latymer Upper Sch.; Edinburgh Univ. (BSc Soc. Sci.; DipArch). Founding Ed., Blueprint mag., 1983–94; Architecture Critic, Guardian, 1991–97; Dir, Glasgow 1999 UK City of Architecture and Design, 1996–2000. Vis. Prof., Acad. for Applied Arts, Vienna, 1993–98. Exhibition Curator: *exhibitions:* Royal Acad., 1986; ICA, 1988; Louisiana Mus., Copenhagen, 1996; McLennan Galls, Glasgow, 1999; BM, 2001. Fellow, Glasgow Sch. of Art, 1999. Hon. FRIAS 2000. *Publications:* Cult Objects, 1983; Foster, Rogers, Stirling: new British architecture, 1986; Rei Kawakubo and Comme des Garçons, 1991; The Hundred Mile City, 1992; The Architecture Pack, 1996; Ron Arad, 1999; John Pawson: Works, 2000. *Recreation:* looking at buildings. *Address:* c/o The Observer, 119 Farringdon Road, EC1R 3ER.

SUENSON-TAYLOR, family name of **Baron Grantchester.**

SUFFIELD, 11th Baron *cr* 1786; **Anthony Philip Harbord-Hamond,** Bt 1745; MC 1950; Major, retired, 1961; *b* 19 June 1922; *o s* of 10th Baron and Nina Annette Mary Crawfuird (*d* 1955), *e d* of John Hutchison of Laurieston and Edingham, Stewartry of Kirkcudbright; *S* father, 1951; *m* 1952, Elizabeth Eve (*d* 1995), *er d* of late Judge Edgedale; three *s* one *d*. *Educ:* Eton. Commission, Coldstream Guards, 1942; served War of 1939–45, in North African and Italian campaigns, 1942–45; Malaya, 1948–50. One of HM Hon. Corps of Gentlemen-at-Arms, 1973–92 (Harbinger, 1990–92). *Recreation:* artist. *Heir: s* Hon. Charles Anthony Assheton Harbord-Hamond [*b* 3 Dec. 1953; *m* 1st, 1983, Lucy (marr. diss. 1990), *yr d* of Comdr A. S. Hutchinson; 2nd, 1999, Mrs Emma Louise Royds, *er d* of Sir Lawrence Williams, Bt, *qv*; one *d*. Commissioned Coldstream Guards, 1972, RARO 1979]. *Address:* Gardeners Cottage, Gunton Park, Hanworth, Norfolk NR11 7HL. *T:* (01263) 768423. *Clubs:* Army and Navy, Pratt's.

SUFFOLK AND BERKSHIRE, 21st Earl of, *cr* 1603; **Michael John James George Robert Howard;** Viscount Andover and Baron Howard, 1622; Earl of Berkshire, 1626; *b* 27 March 1935; *s* of 20th Earl of Suffolk and Berkshire, GC (killed by enemy action, 1941) and Mimi (*d* 1966), *yr d* of late A. G. Forde Pigott; *S* father, 1941; *m* 1st, 1960, Mme Simone Paulmier (marr. diss. 1967), *d* of late Georges Litman, Paris; (one *d* decd); 2nd, 1973, Anita (marr. diss. 1980), *d* of R. R. Fuglesang, Haywards Heath, Sussex; one *s* one *d*; 3rd, 1983, Linda Viscountess Bridport; two *d*. Owns 5,000 acres. *Heir: s* Viscount Andover, *qv*. *Address:* Charlton Park, Malmesbury, Wilts SN16 9DG.

SUFFOLK, Archdeacon of; *see* Arrand, Ven. G. W.

SUGAR, Sir Alan (Michael), Kt 2000; Executive Chairman: Amstrad (formerly Betacom) Plc, since 1997; Viglen, since 1997; *b* 24 March 1947; *s* of Nathan and Fay Sugar; *m* 1968, Ann Simons; two *s* one *d*. *Educ:* Brooke House School, London. Founder Chm., Amstrad, 1968–97; co. divided into Betacom and Viglen, 1997. Chm., 1991–2001, Chief Exec., 1998–2000, Tottenham Hotspur plc. Hon. DSc City, 1988. *Recreation:* tennis. *Address:* 169 King's Road, Brentwood, Essex CM14 4EF. *T:* (01277) 228888.

SUGAR, Vivienne, FCIH; Chief Executive, City and County of Swansea, since 1995; *b* Gorseinon, 23 Feb. 1947; *d* of Jack Hopkins and Phyllis Hopkins (*née* Suter); *m* 1972, Adrian Sugar. *Educ:* Mynydd Cynnfig Comprehensive Sch.; Leeds Univ. (BA). Worked in various private and public sector orgns, Leeds and Teesside, until 1979; Area Improvement Officer, 1979–88, Dir of Housing, 1988–90, Newport BC; Dir of Housing, Cardiff CC, 1990–95. *Publications:* various articles in Municipal Jl, Local Govt Chronicle and Inside Housing. *Recreations:* politics and current affairs, walking, birdwatching, cooking. *Address:* County Hall, Oystermouth Road, Swansea SA1 3SN. *T:* (01792) 636702.

SUGDEN, Sir Arthur, Kt 1978; Chief Executive Officer, Co-operative Wholesale Society Ltd, 1974–80; Chairman: Co-operative Bank Ltd, 1974–80; Co-operative Commercial Bank Ltd, 1974–80; *b* 12 Sept. 1918; *s* of late Arthur and Elizabeth Ann Sugden; *m* 1946, Agnes Grayston; two *s*. *Educ:* Thomas Street, Manchester. Certified Accountant, Chartered Secretary. FIB 1975. Served War of 1939–45, Royal Artillery; CPO 6th Super Heavy Battery; Adjt 12th Medium Regt; Staff Captain 16th Army Group. CWS Ltd: Accountancy Asst, 1946; Office Man., 1950; Factory Man., 1954; Group Man., Edible Oils and Fats Factories, 1964; Controller, Food Div., 1967; Dep. Chief Exec. Officer, 1971. Chairman, 1974–80: FC Finance Ltd; CWS (Longburn) Ltd; CWS (New Zealand) Holdings Ltd; CWS Marketing Ltd; CWS (India) Ltd; Ocean Beach Freezing Co. Ltd; Shaw's Smokers' Products Ltd; Former Director: Co-operative City Investments Ltd; Co-operative Pension Funds Unit Trust Managers' Ltd; Associated Co-operative Creameries Ltd; CWS Svineslagterier A/S Denmark; CWS (Overseas) Ltd; Tukuyu Tea Estates Ltd; Spillers French Holdings Ltd; J. W. French (Milling & Baking Holdings) Ltd; North Eastern Co-operative Soc. Ltd; Manchester Ship Canal Ltd, 1978–87; Manchester Chamber of Commerce. Former Vice-President: Inst. of Bankers; Inst. of Grocery Distribution Ltd. Member: Central Cttee, Internat. Co-operative Alliance; Management Bds, Euro-Coop and Inter-Coop (Pres., 1979–80). Pres., Co-operative Congress, 1978. CIMgt; FIGD. *Recreations:* music, reading, walking. *Address:* 56 Old Wool Lane, Cheadle Hulme, Cheadle, Cheshire SK8 5JA.

SUGDEN, John Goldthorp, MA; ARCM; Headmaster, Wellingborough School, 1965–73; *b* 22 July 1921; *s* of A. G. Sugden, Brighouse, Yorkshire; *m* 1954, Jane Machin; two *s*. *Educ:* Radley; Magdalene College, Cambridge. War Service, Royal Signals, 1941–46. Asst Master, Bilton Grange Prep. School, 1948–52; Asst Master, The King's School, Canterbury, 1952–59; Headmaster, Foster's School, Sherborne, 1959–64. *Publications:* Niccolo Paganini, 1980; Sir Arthur Bliss, 1997. *Recreations:* music, golf. *Address:* Woodlands, 2 Linksview Avenue, Parkstone, Poole, Dorset BH14 9QT. *T:* (01202) 707497.

SUGDEN, Prof. Robert, DLitt; FBA 1996; Leverhulme Personal Research Professor of Economics, University of East Anglia, since 1998 (Professor of Economics, 1985–98); *b* 26 Aug. 1949; *s* of late Frank Gerald Sugden and Kathleen Sugden (*née* Buckley); *m* 1982, Christine Margaret Upton; one *s* one *d*. *Educ:* Eston GS, Cleveland; Univ. of York (BA; DLitt 1988); UC, Cardiff (MSc). Lectr in Econs, Univ. of York, 1971–78; Reader in Econs, Univ. of Newcastle upon Tyne, 1978–85. *Publications:* (with A. Williams) The Principles of Practical Cost-Benefit Analysis, 1978; The Political Economy of Public Choice, 1981; The Economics of Rights, Co-operation and Welfare, 1986; (jtly) The Theory of Choice: a critical guide, 1992; (with D. Gauthier) Rationality, Justice and the Social Contract, 1993. *Recreations:* family, walking, gardening. *Address:* School of Economic and Social Studies, University of East Anglia, Norwich NR4 7TJ. *T:* (01603) 593423.

SUGG, Aldhelm St John, CMG 1963; retired as Provincial Commissioner, Southern Province of Northern Rhodesia, August 1963; *b* 21 Oct. 1909; *s* of H. G. St J. Sugg; *m* 1935, Jessie May Parker (*d* 1994); one *s* one *d*. *Educ:* Colchester Royal Grammar School. Palestine Police, 1930–31; Northern Rhodesia Police, 1932–43; Colonial Administrative Service, in N Rhodesia, 1943–63. Retired to England, 1963. *Recreations:* sailing, field sports. *Address:* Bushbury, Blackboys, Uckfield, East Sussex TN22 5JE. *T:* (01825) 890282. *Club:* Royal Commonwealth Society.

SUHARTO, Gen.; *see* Soeharto.

SUIRDALE, Viscount; John Michael James Hely Hutchinson; company director since 1981; *b* 7 Aug. 1952; *s* and *heir* of 8th Earl of Donoughmore, *qv*; *m* 1976, Marie-Claire Carola Etienne van den Driessche; one *s* two *d*. *Educ:* Harrow. *Recreations:* golf, fishing, etc. *Heir: s* Hon. Richard Gregory Hely Hutchinson, *b* 3 July 1980. *Address:* 38 Thornton Avenue, Chiswick W4 1QG.

See also Hon. T. M. Hely Hutchinson.

SULIVAN, Maj.-Gen. Timothy John, CB 2001; CBE 1991; Vice-President, Customer Relations, CDC Systems UK Ltd; Business Strategist, BCD Modelling Ltd; *b* 19 Feb. 1946; *s* of late Col John Anthony Sulivan, OBE and Elizabeth Joyce Sulivan (*née* Stevens); *m* 1977, Jane Annette Ellwood; one *s* one *d*. *Educ:* Wellington Coll.; RMCS (BSc); Higher Command and Staff course. Commnd RA, 1966; transf. Blues and Royals, 1980; CO, Blues and Royals, 1987–89; attached US Special Plans Team, C-in-C US CENTCOM, 1990–91; Comd 7 Armd Bde, 1991–93; PSO to CDS, 1993–94; Dir-Gen., Develt and Doctrine, MoD, 1994–96 (deployed as Jt Force Comd Op. Driver, Kuwait/Saudi Arabia, 1994); COS, HQ ARRC, 1996–98; GOC Fourth Div., 1998–2001. Pres., Army Hockey, 1996. Bronze Star, USA, 1991. *Recreations:* shooting, ski-ing, squash, cabinet making. *Club:* Army and Navy.

SULLIVAN, David Douglas Hooper; QC 1975; author and historian; *b* 10 April 1926; *s* of Michael and Maude Sullivan; *m* 1st, 1951, Sheila, *d* of Henry and Georgina Bathurst; three *d*; 2nd, 1981, Ann Munro, *d* of Malcolm and Eva Betten. *Educ:* Haileybury (schol.); Christ Church, Oxford (schol.). MA 1949, BCL 1951. Served War, with RNVR (Sub-Lieut), 1944–46. Called to Bar, Inner Temple, 1951, Bencher, 1984, retired 1988. Mem., Central Policy Cttee, Mental Health Act Commn, 1983–86. Chm., Burgh House Trust, 1978–95. Author of various plays and media programmes, including: radio: Shadows are Realities to me; A right-royal Burglary; Straw and Steel; stage: John Constable and Maria. *Publication:* The Westminster Corridor, 1994. *Recreations:* painting, medieval history. *Address:* Well Mount Cottage, Well Road, NW3 1LJ. *T:* (020) 7431 3433.

SULLIVAN, Prof. (Donovan) Michael; Professor of Oriental Art, 1966–85, Christensen Professor, 1975–85, Stanford University, California; Fellow, St Catherine's College, Oxford, 1979–90, now Emeritus Fellow; *b* 29 Oct. 1916; *s* of Alan Sullivan and Elisabeth Hees; *m* 1943, Khoan, *d* of Ngo Eng-lim, Kulangsu, Amoy, China; no *c*. *Educ:* Rugby School; Corpus Christi College, Cambridge (MA); Univ. of London (BA Hons); Harvard Univ. (PhD); LittD Cambridge, 1966; MA, DLitt Oxon, 1973. Chinese Govt Scholarship, Univ. of London, 1947–50; Rockefeller Foundn Travelling Fellowship in USA, 1950–51; Bollingen Foundn Research Fellowship, 1952–54; Curator of Art Museum and Lectr in the History of Art, Univ. of Malaya (now Univ. of Singapore), Singapore, 1954–60; Lectr in Asian Art, Sch. of Oriental and African Studies, Univ. of London, 1960–66. Vis. Prof. of Far Eastern Art, Univ. of Michigan (Spring Semester), 1964; Slade Prof. of Fine Art, Oxford Univ., 1973–74, Cambridge Univ., 1983–84; Guggenheim Foundn Fellowship, 1974; Vis. Fellow, St Antony's Coll., Oxford, 1976–77; Nat. Endowment for the Humanities Fellowship, 1976–77; Professorial Fellow, Corpus Christi Coll., Cambridge, 1983–84; Vis. Fellow, Humanities Centre, ANU, 1987. Mem., Amer. Acad. of Arts and Sciences, 1977. *Publications:* Chinese Art in the Twentieth Century, 1959; An Introduction to Chinese Art, 1961; The Birth of Landscape Painting in China, 1962; Chinese Ceramics, Bronzes and Jades in the Collection of Sir Alan and Lady Barlow, 1963; Chinese and Japanese Art, 1965; A Short History of Chinese Art, 1967, 3rd edn as The Arts of China, 1973, 4th edn 1999; The Cave Temples of Maichishan, 1969; The Meeting of Eastern and Western Art, 1973, rev. and expanded edn 1989; Chinese Art: recent discoveries, 1973; The Three Perfections, 1975, 2nd edn 1999; Chinese Landscape Painting, vol. II, The Sui and T'ang Dynasties, 1979; Symbols of Eternity: the art of landscape painting in China, 1979; Studies in the Art of China and South-East Asia, vol. 1, 1991, vol. 2, 1992; Art and Artists of Twentieth Century China, 1996; contrib. to learned journals, Encyclopedia Britannica, Chambers's Encyclopædia, etc. *Address:* St Catherine's College, Oxford OX1 3UJ. *Club:* Arts.

SULLIVAN, Edmund Wendell, FRCVS; Chief Veterinary Officer, Department of Agriculture for Northern Ireland, 1983–90; *b* 21 March 1925; *s* of Thomas Llewellyn Sullivan and Letitia Sullivan; *m* 1957, Elinor Wilson Melville; two *s* one *d*. *Educ:* Portadown College; Queen's University, Belfast; Royal (Dick) Veterinary College. MRCVS 1947, FRCVS 1991. General Veterinary Practice, Appleby, Westmoreland, 1947; joined staff of State Veterinary Service, Dept. of Agriculture for N Ireland, 1948; Headquarters staff, 1966–90. *Recreations:* hill walking, wood craft, following rugby and cricket. *Address:* Kinfauns, 26 Dillon's Avenue, Newtownabbey, Co. Antrim BT37 0SX. *T:* (028) 9086 2323.

SULLIVAN, Hon. Sir Jeremy (Mirth), Kt 1997; **Hon. Mr Justice Sullivan;** a Judge of the High Court of Justice, Queen's Bench Division, since 1997; *b* 17 Sept. 1945; *s* of late Arthur Brian and of Pamela Jean Sullivan; *m* 1st, 1970, Ursula Klara Marie Hildenbrock (marr. diss. 1993); two *s*; 2nd, 1993, Dr Sandra Jean Farmer; two step *s*. *Educ:* Framlingham Coll.; King's Coll., London. LLB 1967, LLM 1968; LAMTPI 1970, LMRTPI 1976. 2nd Lieut, Suffolk & Cambs Regt (TA), 1963–65. Called to the Bar, Inner Temple, 1968, Bencher, 1993; Lectr in Law, City of London Polytechnic, 1968–71; in practice, Planning and Local Govt Bar, Parly Bar, 1971–97; QC 1982; a Recorder, 1989–97; a Dep. High Court Judge, 1993–97; Attorney Gen. to the Prince of Wales, 1994–97. Hon. Standing Counsel to CPRE, 1994–97. Chm., Tribunals Cttee, Judicial Studies Bd, 1999–. Mem. Council, RTPI, 1984–87. Gov., Highgate Sch., 1991–. *Recreation:* the Wotton Light Railway. *Address:* Royal Courts of Justice, Strand, WC2A 2LL.

SULLIVAN, Linda Elizabeth, (Mrs J. W. Blake-James); QC 1994; a Recorder, since 1990; *b* 1 Jan. 1948; *d* of Donal Sullivan and Esmé Beryl Sullivan (*née* McKenzie); *m* 1972, Dr Justin Wynne Blake-James (marr. diss. 1994); one *s* twin *d*. *Educ:* St Leonard's-Mayfield Sch.; Univ. of Kent (BA Hons Phil. and English 1969); St Hilda's Coll., Oxford (Cert Ed 1970). Called to the Bar, Middle Temple, 1973, Bencher, 1993; Mem., Western Circuit. *Address:* 35 Essex Street, Temple, WC2R 3AR. *T:* (020) 7353 6381.

SULLIVAN, Prof. Michael; *see* Sullivan, D. M.

SULLIVAN, Michael Frederick, MBE 1981; HM Diplomatic Service, retired; Consul-General, Hamburg, 1994–99; *b* 22 June 1940; *s* of late Frederick Franklin Sullivan and Leonora Mary Sullivan; *m* 1967, Jennifer Enid Saunders. *Educ:* King's Sch., Canterbury; Jesus Coll., Oxford (BA). CRO 1962–66; Moscow, 1967; Ulan Bator, Mongolia, 1967–69; Sydney, 1970–74; FCO, 1975–77; First Sec., W Indian and Atlantic Dept, FCO, 1977–79; Consul (Industrial Develt), British Trade Develt Office, NY, 1979–81; Cultural Attaché, Moscow, 1981–85; Assistant Head: Personnel Services Dept, FCO, 1985–86; Energy, Sci. and Space Dept, FCO, 1986–88; Counsellor (Cultural Affairs), Moscow, 1988–89; Counsellor, Export Promotion Policy Unit, DTI, 1989–90; Hd of Nationality, Treaty and Claims Dept, FCO, 1990–93. Res. analyst, FCO, 2000. Mem., Hamburg-Wandsbeck Rotary Club. *Recreations:* piano playing, music and the arts, tennis, jogging, swimming.

SULLIVAN, Richard Arthur, (9th Bt *cr* 1804, but does not use the title); geoenvironmental consultant; *b* 9 Aug. 1931; *s* of Sir Richard Benjamin Magniac Sullivan, 8th Bt, and Muriel Mary Paget (*d* 1988), *d* of late Francis Charles Trayler Pineo; *S* father, 1977; *m* 1962, Elenor Mary, *e d* of late K. M. Thorpe; one *s* three *d*. *Educ:* Univ. of Cape Town (BSc); Massachusetts Inst. of Technology (SM). Chartered Engineer, UK; Professional Engineer, Ontario, Texas and Louisiana. *Publications:* papers and articles to international conferences and technical journals. *Recreation:* tennis. *Heir: s* Charles Merson Sullivan, MA, VetMB Cantab, MRCVS, *b* 15 Dec. 1962. *Address:* 2460 North Park Boulevard, Santa Ana, CA 92706, USA.

SULSTON, Sir John (Edward), Kt 2001; PhD; FRS 1986; Staff Scientist, MRC Laboratory of Molecular Biology, Cambridge, since 1969; Director, The Sanger Centre (for genome research), Hinxton, Cambridge, 1992–2000; *b* 27 March 1942; *s* of late Rev. Canon Arthur Edward Aubrey Sulston and Josephine Muriel Frearson (*née* Blocksidge); *m* 1966, Daphne Edith Bate; one *s* one *d*. *Educ:* Merchant Taylors' School; Pembroke College, Cambridge (BA, PhD; Hon. Fellow, 2000). Postdoctoral Fellow, Salk Inst., San Diego, 1966–69. Hon. ScD TCD, 2000. W. Alden Spencer Award (jtly), Coll. of Physicians and Surgeons, Columbia Univ., 1986; Gairdner Foundn Award (jtly), 1991; Darwin Medal, Royal Soc., 1996; Rosenstiel Award (jtly), Brandeis Univ., 1998; Sir Frederick Gowland Hopkins Medal, Biochemical Soc., 2000; Pfizer Prize for Innovative Sci., 2000. *Publications:* (with Georgina Ferry) The Common Thread: a story of science, politics, ethics and the human genome, 2002; articles on organic chemistry, molecular and developmental biology in sci. jls. *Recreations:* gardening, walking, avoiding people. *Address:* 39 Mingle Lane, Stapleford, Cambridge CB2 5BG. *T:* (01223) 842248; *e-mail:* jes@sanger.ac.uk.

SULZBERGER, Arthur Ochs; Chairman and Chief Executive Officer, New York Times Co., 1992–97, now Chairman Emeritus; Publisher of The New York Times, 1963–92; *b* 5 Feb. 1926; *s* of late Arthur Hays Sulzberger; *m* 1st, 1948, Barbara Grant (marr. diss. 1956); one *s* one *d*; 2nd, 1956, Carol Fox Fuhrman (*d* 1995); one *d* (and one adopted *d*); 3rd, 1996, Allison Stacey Cowles. *Educ:* Browning School, New York City; Loomis School, Windsor, Conn; Columbia University, NYC. Reporter, Milwaukee Journal, 1953–54; Foreign Correspondent, New York Times, 1954–55; Asst to the Publisher, New York Times, 1956–57; Asst Treasurer, New York Times, 1957–63. Chm. Emeritus, Metropolitan Mus. of Art; Trustee Emeritus, Columbia Univ. Hon. LLD: Dartmouth, 1964; Bard, 1967; Hon LHD: Montclair State Coll.; Tufts Univ., 1984. *Recreation:* fishing. *Address:* 229 West 43rd Street, New York, NY 10036, USA. *T:* (212) 5561771. *Clubs:* Overseas Press, Explorers (New York); Metropolitan, Army and Navy (Washington, DC).

SUMBERG, David Anthony Gerald; Member (C) North West Region, England, European Parliament, since 1999; Director, Parliamentary Forum Ltd, since 1998; *b* 2 June 1941; *s* of Joshua and Lorna Sumberg; *m* 1972, Carolyn Ann Rae Franks; one *s* one *d*. *Educ:* Tettenhall Coll., Staffs; Coll. of Law, London. Qualified as a Solicitor, 1964. Mem. (C) Manchester City Council, 1982–84. Contested (C) Manchester, Wythenshawe, 1979. MP (C) Bury South, 1983–97; contested (C) same seat, 1997. PPS to: Solicitor-General, 1986–87; Attorney-General, 1987–90. Member: Home Affairs Select Cttee, 1991–92; Foreign Affairs Select Cttee, 1992–97. Dir, Irwell Insurance Co. Ltd. Dir, Anglo-Israel Assoc., 1997–. Mem., Adv. Council on Public Records, 1993–97. *Recreation:* family. *Address:* 9 Montford Enterprise Centre, Wynford Square, Salford M5 2SN.

SUMMERFIELD, Prof. Arthur, BSc Tech; BSc; CPsychol, FBPsS, FInstD; Chairman, LearnIT Ltd, since 1991; Professor of Psychology, University of London, 1961–88, now Emeritus, and Head of the Department of Psychology at Birkbeck College, 1961–88; *b* 31 March 1923; *s* of late Arthur and Dora Gertrude Summerfield; *m* 1st, 1946, Aline Whalley; one *s* one *d*; 2nd, 1974, Angela Barbara, MA Cantab, PhD London, CPsychol, FBPsS, *d* of late George Frederick and Estelle Steer. *Educ:* Manchester Grammar Sch.; Manchester Univ.; University Coll. London (1st cl. hons Psychology). Served War of 1939–45, Electrical Officer, RNVR, 1943–46: Naval Air Stations, 1943–46; Dept of Sen. Psychologist to the Admiralty, 1946. Lectr in Psychology, University Coll. London, 1949–61, Hon. Research Associate, 1961–70, Hon. Research Fellow, 1970–; first Dean, Fac. of Econs, Birkbeck Coll., 1971–72, Governor, 1982–86; Hon. Lectr in Psychology, Westminster Med. Sch., 1974–76. Member: Univ. of London Acad. Adv. Bd in Medicine, 1974–88; Acad. Council Standing Sub-Cttee on Science and Engrg, 1974–77. Hon. Life Mem., British Psychological Soc., 1993 (Mem. Council, 1953–65, 1967–75, 1977–84; Hon. Gen. Sec., 1954–59; Dep. Pres., 1959–62; Pres., 1963–64; Vice-Pres., 1964–65; first Chm., Scientific Affairs Bd, 1974–75); Member: Cttee on Internat. Relations in Psychology, Amer. Psychological Assoc., 1977–79; Bd of Dirs, European Coordination Centre for Res. and Documentation in Social Scis (Vienna Centre), 1977–81; ICSU Study Gp on biol, med. and physical effects of large scale use of nuclear weapons, 1983–87; Pres., International Union of Psychological Science, 1976–80 (Mem., Exec. Cttee, 1963–84, Assembly, 1957–84; Vice-Pres., 1972–76); Pres., Section J (Psychology) BAAS, 1976–77; Pres., Internat. Soc. Sci. Council, 1977–81 (Mem. Prog. Cttee, 1973–83; Mem. Exec. Cttee, 1977–83); Chm., DES Working Party on Psychologists in Educn Services, 1965–68 (Summerfield report). Member: DSIR Human Sciences Res. Grants Cttee, 1962–65; SSRC, 1979–81; Psychology Cttee, SSRC, 1979–81. Vis. Prof., Univ. of California (at Dept of Psychobiology, Irvine Campus), 1968. Governor, Enfield Coll. of Technology, 1968–72. Dir, British Jl of Educnl Psychology Ltd, 1976–93; Asst Editor, Brit. Jl Psychology (Statistical Section), 1950–54; Editor, British Journal of Psychology, 1964–67; Scientific Editor, British Med. Bulletin issues on Experimental Psychology, 1964, Cognitive Psychology, 1971, (with D. M. Warburton) Psychobiology, 1981. *Publications:* (trans. and ed jtly) Animals and Men, 1951; articles on perception, memory, statistical methods and psycho-pharmacology in scientific periodicals. *Address:* Rose Bank, Sutton-under-Whitestonecliffe, Thirsk, N Yorks YO7 2PR. *T:* (01845) 597395, *T:* (office) (01845) 597097, *Fax:* (01845) 597005; *e-mail:* asummerfield@learnit.co.uk. *Club:* Athenæum.

SUMMERFIELD, Lesley; *see* Regan, L.

SUMMERFIELD, Prof. Rodney John, DSc; CBiol, FIBiol; Professor of Crop Production, since 1995, and Dean, Faculty of Agriculture and Food, since 1998, University of Reading; *b* 15 Nov. 1946; *s* of Ronald John Summerfield and Doris Emily Summerfield (*née* Ellis); *m* 1969, Kathryn Dorothy Olive; one *s* one *d*. *Educ:* Hinckley GS; Univ. of Nottingham (BSc 1st cl. Hons Botany 1968; PhD Eco-Physiol. 1971); Univ. of Reading (DSc 1987); FIBiol 1982. Univ. Demonstr., Univ. of Nottingham, 1969–71; (part-time) Lectr, Trent Poly., 1970–71; University of Reading: Res. Fellow, 1971–73, Lectr in Crop and Plant Physiology, 1973–83, Dept of Agriculture and Horticulture; Dep. Dir, 1979–94, Dir, 1994–99, Plant Envmt Lab.; Reader in Crop Physiology, 1983–90, Prof. of Crop Physiology, 1990–95, Dept of Agriculture; Hd, Dept of Agric., 1992–98. Pres., Eur. Assoc. for Res. in Grain Legumes, 1995–99. EurBiol 1995. Dr *hc* Debrecen Univ., Hungary, 1999. *Publications:* (ed jtly) Advances in Legume Science, 1980; (ed jtly) Grain Legume Crops, 1985; (ed) World Crops: cool season food legumes, 1988; articles in learned jls. *Recreations:* walking, angling. *Address:* Department of Agriculture, University of Reading, Earley Gate, PO Box 236, Reading, Berks RG6 6AR. *T:* (0118) 931 8482.

SUMMERHAYES, Dr Colin Peter; Director, Global Ocean Observing System Project Office, Intergovernmental Oceanographic Commission, Unesco, since 1997; *b* 7 March 1942; *s* of late Leonard Percy Summerhayes and of Jessica Adelaide (*née* Crump); *m* 1st, 1966 (marr. diss. 1977); one *s* one *d*; 2nd, 1981, Diana Ridley (*née* Perry); one step *s* one step *d*. *Educ:* Slough Grammar Sch.; UCL (BSc 1963); Keble Coll., Oxford; Victoria Univ., Wellington, NZ (MSc 1967; DSc 1986); Imperial Coll., London (DIC; PhD 1970). Scientific Officer, DSIR, NZ Oceanographic Inst., 1964–67; Res. Asst, Geol. Dept, Imperial Coll., London, 1967–70; Sen. Scientific Officer, CSIR, Marine Geosci. Unit, Univ. of Cape Town, 1970–72; Asst Scientist, Geol. and Geophys Dept, Woods Hole Oceanographic Instn, 1972–76; Research Associate/Project Leader: Geochem. Br., Exxon Prodn Res. Centre, Houston, 1976–82; Global Paleoreconstruction Sect., Stratigraphy Br., BP Res. Centre, 1982–85; Manager and Sen. Res. Associate, Stratigraphy Br., BP Res. Centre, 1985–88; Dir, NERC Inst. of Oceanographic Scis Deacon Lab., 1988–95; Dep. Dir, and Hd of Seafloor Processes Div., Southampton Oceanographic Centre, 1995–97. Vis. Prof., UCL, 1987–95. Member: Geol Soc.; Challenger Soc. for Marine Sci.; Soc. for Underwater Technology. *Publications:* 100 papers in various geol, geochem., oceanographic jls, 3 on seabirds. *Recreations:* ornithology, jogging, reading, films and theatre. *Address:* Intergovernmental Oceanographic Commission, Unesco, 1 rue Miollis, 75732 Paris Cedex 15, France.

SUMMERHAYES, David Michael, CMG 1975; HM Diplomatic Service, retired; Disarmament Adviser, Foreign and Commonwealth Office, 1983–92; *b* 29 Sept. 1922; *s* of Sir Christopher Summerhayes, KBE, CMG and late Anna (*née* Johnson); *m* 1959, June van der Hardt Aberson; two *s* one *d*. *Educ:* Marlborough; Emmanuel Coll., Cambridge. Served War of 1939–45 in Royal Artillery (Capt.) N Africa and Italy. 3rd Sec., FO, 1948; Baghdad, 1949; Brussels, 1950–53; 2nd Sec., FO, 1953–56; 1st Sec. (Commercial), The Hague, 1956–59; 1st Sec. and Consul, Reykjavik, 1959–61; FO, 1961–65; Consul-General and Counsellor, Buenos Aires, 1965–70; Head of Arms Control and Disarmament Dept, FCO, 1970–74; Minister, Pretoria/Cape Town, 1974–78; Ambassador and Leader, UK Delegn to Cttee on Disarmament, Geneva, 1979–82. Hon. Officer, Order of Orange Nassau. *Recreations:* golf, walking. *Address:* Ivy House, South Harting, Petersfield, Hants GU31 5QQ. *Club:* Oxford and Cambridge.

SUMMERHAYES, Gerald Victor, CMG 1979; OBE 1969; *b* 28 Jan. 1928; *s* of Victor Samuel and Florence A. V. Summerhayes. Administrative Service, Nigeria, 1952–81; Permanent Secretary: Local Govt, North Western State, 1975–76, Sokoto State, 1976–77; Cabinet Office (Political and Trng), 1977–79; Dir of Trng, Cabinet Office, Sokoto, 1979–81. *Address:* Bridge Cottage, Bridge Street, Sidbury, Devon EX10 0RU. *T:* (01395) 597311.

SUMMERS, Andrew William Graham, CMG 2001; Chief Executive, Design Council, since 1995; *b* 19 June 1946; *s* of Basil Summers and Margaret (*née* Hunt); *m* 1971, Frances Halestrap; one *s* two *d*. *Educ:* Mill Hill Sch. (Exhibnr); Fitzwilliam Coll., Cambridge (MA Natural Scis and Econs); Harvard Business Sch. (Internat. SMP). Various mgt rôles, Ranks Hovis McDougall plc, 1968–75; J. A. Sharwood & Co.: Mkting Manager, 1975–78; Mkting Dir, 1978–80; Man. Dir, 1980–85; RHM Foods Ltd: Commercial Dir, 1986; Man. Dir, 1987–90; Chief Exec., Management Charter Initiative, 1991–94; non-exec. Dir, S. Daniels plc, 1991–. Member: Food from Britain Export Council, 1982–86; DTI European Trade Cttee, 1986–2000 (Chm., 1998–2000); BOTB, 1998–99; British Trade Internat., 1999–; Creative Industries Export Promotion Adv. Gp, 1998–; Adv. Council, Design Mgt Inst. USA, 1998–; Small Business Service Steering Bd, 2000–. Stockton Lectr, London Bus, Sch., 2000. CIMgt 1997. FRSA 1991. *Publications:* (contrib.) Future Present, 2000; contribs on design to Design Mgt Jl and Sunday Times. *Recreations:* tennis, fives, theatre. *Address:* Design Council, 34 Bow Street, WC2E 7DL. *T:* (020) 7420 5200.

SUMMERS, Henry Forbes, CB 1961; Under-Secretary, Department of the Environment (formerly Ministry of Housing and Local Government), 1955–71; *b* 18 August 1911; *s* of late Rev. H. H. Summers, Harrogate, Yorks; *m* 1937, Rosemary, *d* of late Robert L. Roberts, CBE; two *s* one *d*. *Educ:* Fettes Coll., Edinburgh; Trinity College, Oxford. *Publications:* Smoke After Flame, 1944; Hinterland, 1947; Tomorrow is my Love, 1978; The Burning Book, 1982. *Address:* Folly Fields, Tunbridge Wells, Kent TN2 5QU. *T:* (01892) 527671.
See also N. Summers.

SUMMERS, Janet Margaret, (Mrs L. J. Summers); *see* Bately, J. M.

SUMMERS, Jonathan; baritone; *b* 2 Oct. 1946; *s* of Andrew James Summers and Joyce Isabel Smith; *m* 1969, Lesley Murphy; three *c*. *Educ:* Macleod High Sch., Melbourne; Prahan Tech. Coll., Melbourne. Professional début, Rigoletto (title rôle), Kent Opera, 1975; performances include: Royal Opera, Covent Garden: début, Der Freischütz, 1977; Samson et Dalila, Don Pasquale, Werther, 1983; Andrea Chénier, A Midsummer Night's Dream, 1984; Die Zauberflöte, Le Nozze di Figaro, 1985; Simon Boccanegra, 1986; Falstaff, 1987; Madama Butterfly, 1988; La Bohème, 1990; Fedora, 1994; English National Opera: début, I Pagliacci, 1976; Rigoletto, 1982; Don Carlos, 1985; La Bohème, 1986; Simon Boccanegra, 1987; Eugene Onegin, 1989; Macbeth, 1990; Peter Grimes, 1991; The Force of Destiny, 1992; The Pearl Fishers, 1994; Tristan and Isolde, 1996; Figaro's Wedding, 1997; Parsifal, 1999; Opera Australia: Il Trovatore, 1983; Otello, 1991; Un Ballo in Maschera, 1993; La Traviata, 1994; Il Tabarro, 1995; Nabucco, Falstaff, 1996; Wozzeck, 1999; has also appeared at Glyndebourne, with Opera North, Welsh National Opera, in Toulouse, Chicago, Lausanne etc, and as concert soloist. Numerous recordings. *Address:* c/o Patricia Greenan, 7 Whitehorse Close, Royal Mile, Edinburgh EH8 8BU. *T:* (0131) 557 5872.

SUMMERS, Hon. Lawrence H.; President, Harvard University, since 2001; *b* 30 Nov. 1954; *s* of Robert and Anita Summers; *m* Victoria (Perry) Summers; one *s* twin *d*. *Educ:* MIT (BS 1975); Harvard Univ. (PhD 1982). Economics Prof., MIT, 1979–82; Domestic Policy Economist, President's Council of Economic Advrs, 1982–83; Prof. of Economics, 1983–93, Nathaniel Ropes Prof., 1987, Harvard Univ.; Vice-Pres., Develt Economics and Chief Economist, World Bank, 1991–93; Under Sec. for Internat. Affairs, 1993–95, Dep. Sec., 1995–99, Sec., 1999–2001, US Treasury; Arthur Okun Dist. Fellow, Brookings Instn, 2001. Alan Waterman Award, 1987; John Bates Clark Medal, 1993. *Publications:* Understanding Unemployment, 1990; (jtly) Reform in Eastern Europe, 1991. *Recreations:* tennis, ski-ing. *Address:* Harvard University, Cambridge, MA 02138, USA.

SUMMERS, Nicholas; Under Secretary, Department for Education and Employment (formerly of Education and Science, then for Education), 1981–96; *b* 11 July 1939; *s* of Henry Forbes Summers, *qv*; *m* 1965, Marian Elizabeth Ottley; four *s*. *Educ:* Tonbridge Sch.; Corpus Christi Coll., Oxford. Min. of Educn, 1961–64; DES, 1964–74; Private Sec. to Minister for the Arts, 1965–66; Cabinet Office, 1974–76; DES, subseq. Dept for Educn, 1976–96. Mem., Stevenson Commn on Information and Communications Technol. in Schs, 1996–97. *Recreations:* family, music. *Address:* c/o Department for Education and Employment, Sanctuary Buildings, Great Smith Street, SW1P 3BT.

SUMMERSCALE, David Michael, MA; Head Master of Westminster School, 1986–98; *b* 22 April 1937; *s* of late Noel Tynwald Summerscale and Beatrice (*née* Wilson); *m* 1975, Pauline, *d* of Prof. Michel Fleury, Président de l'Ecole des Hautes Etudes, Paris, Directeur des Antiquités Historiques de l'Ile-de-France; one *s* one *d*. *Educ:* Northaw; Sherborne Sch.; Trinity Hall, Cambridge. Lectr in English Literature and Tutor, St Stephen's Coll., Univ. of Delhi, 1959–63; Charterhouse, 1963–75 (Head of English, Housemaster); Master of Haileybury, 1976–86. Director: Namdang Tea Co. (India) Ltd, 1991–95; The Education Group Ltd, 1996–98. Oxford and Cambridge Schs Examination Bd Awarder and Reviser in English. Vice-Chm., E-SU Scholarship Cttee, 1982–93; Member: Managing Cttee of Cambridge Mission to Delhi, 1965; C. F. Andrews Centenary Appeal Cttee, 1970; HMC Academic Policy Sub-Cttee, 1982–86; Council, Charing Cross and Westminster Med. Sch., 1986–97. Governor: The Hall Sch., Hampstead, 1986–98; Arnold House Sch., St John's Wood, 1988–98; King's House Sch., Richmond, 1991–98; Hellenic Coll., London, 1996–; Shri Ram Sch., Delhi, 1996–; Gayhurst Sch., Gerrards Cross, 1998–; Solihull Sch., 1998–. Staff Advr, Governing Body, Westminster Abbey Choir Sch., 1989–98; Member, Governing Body: Merchant Taylors' Sch., 1996–2001 (Nominated Mem., Sch. Cttee, Merchant Taylors' Co., 1988–96); Haberdashers' Aske's Schs, 2001–; Consultant and Gov., Assam Valley Sch., India, 1989–; Exec. Advr, British Sch., Colombo, Sri Lanka, 1999–; Member Council: Queen's Coll., London, 1991– (Vice-Chm., 2000–); Book Aid Internat. (formerly Ranfurly Library Service), 1992–98. Trustee, Criterion Theatre Trust, 1992–. Advr, Rajiv Gandhi (UK) Foundn, 1999–; Ext. Advr, Hong Kong Mgt Assoc. Coll., 1999–. Patron, Multi Lang. Acad., Yangon, Myanmar, 1999–. FRSA 1984. *Publications:* articles on English and Indian literature; dramatisations of novels and verse. *Recreations:* music, reading, mountaineering, games (squash (Mem. SRA), cricket, tennis, rackets (Mem. Tennis and Rackets Assoc.), golf).

Address: 4 Ashley Gardens, Ambrosden Avenue, SW1P 1QD. *Clubs:* Athenæum, I Zingari, Free Foresters, Jesters; Club Alpin Suisse.

SUMMERSCALE, Peter Wayne; HM Diplomatic Service, retired; *b* 22 April 1935; *s* of Sir John Summerscale, KBE; *m* 1st, 1964, Valerie Turner (marr. diss. 1983); one *s* two *d*; 2nd, 1985, Cristina Fournier (marr. diss. 1986); 3rd, 1989, Elizabeth Carro. *Educ:* Rugby Sch.; New Coll., Oxford Univ. (Exhibnr; 1st Cl. Hons Modern History); Russian Res. Centre, Harvard Univ. FO, 1960–62; Polit. Residency, Bahrain, 1962–65; 1st Sec., Tokyo, 1965–68; FCO, 1968–69; Cabinet Office, 1969–71; 1st Sec. and Head of Chancery, Santiago, Chile, 1971–75; Head of CSCE Unit, FCO, 1976–77; Dep. Leader, UK Delegn, Belgrade Rev. Conf., 1977–78; Counsellor and Head of Chancery, Brussels, 1978–79; Vis. FCO Res. Fellow, RIIA, Chatham House, 1979–81; Head of Civilian Faculty, Nat. Defence Coll., 1981–82; Ambassador to Costa Rica, 1982–86, and concurrently (non-resident) to Nicaragua; Dep. Leader, UK Delegn to CSCE, 1986–88; Hd, CSCE Unit, FCO, 1989–90. Hd UK Delegn, 1992, Belgrade Regl Centre, 1995, EC Monitoring Mission, Yugoslavia; UK expert, EU Programme for Human Rights in Central America, 1992–; Consultant, UNDP, Honduras, 2000–. *Publications:* (jtly) Soviet—East European Dilemmas, 1981; The East European Predicament, 1982; articles on E Europe and communism. *Recreations:* tennis, ski-ing, walking. *Address:* Flat 3, 11 North Road, N6 4BD.

SUMMERSKILL, Dr the Hon. Shirley Catherine Wynne; Medical Practitioner; Medical Officer in Blood Transfusion Service, 1983–91; *b* London, 9 Sept. 1931; *d* of late Dr E. J. Samuel and Baroness Summerskill, CH, PC. *Educ:* St Paul's Girls' Sch.; Somerville Coll., Oxford; St Thomas' Hospital. MA, BM, BCh., 1958. Treas., Oxford Univ. Labour Club, 1952. Resident House Surgeon, later House Physician, St Helier Hosp., Carshalton, 1959; Partner in Gen. Practice, 1960–68. Contested (Lab): Blackpool North by-election, 1962; Halifax, 1983. MP (Lab) Halifax, 1964–83; opposition spokesman on health, 1970–74; Parly Under-Sec. of State, Home Office, 1974–79; opposition spokesman on home affairs, 1979–83. Vice-Chm., PLP Health Gp, 1964–69, Chm., 1969–70; Mem., Labour Party NEC, 1981–83. UK delegate, UN Status of Women Commn, 1968 and 1969; Mem. British delegn, Council of Europe and WEU, 1968, 1969. *Publications:* A Surgical Affair (novel), 1963; Destined to Love (novel), 1986. *Recreations:* music, reading, attending literature classes.

SUMMERSON, Hugo Hawksley Fitzthomas; Director: Palatine Properties Ltd, since 1983; Speaker Skills Training, since 1994; *b* 21 July 1950; *s* of late Thomas Hawksley Summerson, OBE and of Joan Florence Summerson; *m* 1995, Diana, *d* of late Lt-Col T. J. C. Washington, MC; one *s*. *Educ:* Harrow School; Royal Agricultural College. FRICS; MRAC. Land Agent with Knight, Frank and Rutley, 1973–76; travel in S America, 1977; self-employment, 1978–83. Consultant: Amhurst Properties Ltd, 1992–94; Grandfield Public Affairs Ltd, 1996–98; Butler Kelly Ltd, 2001–; Dir, Meridian Clocks Ltd, 1999–. Contested (C): Barking, 1983; Walthamstow, 1992. MP (C) Walthamstow, 1987–92. Mem., Select Cttee on Envmt, 1991–92; Treas., British Latin-American Parly Gp, 1990; Vice-Chm., All-Party Parly Gp on Child Abduction, 1991–92; Sec., Cons. Back Bench Agriculture Cttee, 1991–92. Chm., Greater London Area Adopted Parly Candidates Assoc., 1986; Vice-Pres., Greater London Area, Nat. Soc. of Cons. and Unionist Agents, 1989; Mem. Council, British Atlantic Gp of Young Politicians, 1989; Parly Advr to Drinking Fountain Assoc., 1989; Treas., Assoc. of Cons. Parly Candidates (formerly Westminster Candidates' Assoc.), 1998–2001. Fellow, Industry and Parlt Trust, 1991. Trustee: Trinity Chapel Site Charity, 1998–; Hyde Park Place Estate Charity, 1998–; St George's Hanover Sq. Sch., 1998–. Churchwarden, St George's, Hanover Sq., 1998–. Sir Anthony Berry Meml Scholar, 1985. *Recreations:* fishing, music. *Address:* 23 Swanage Road, Wandsworth, SW18 2DZ. *T:* (020) 8874 6223. *Club:* Royal Over-Seas League.

SUMMERTON, Dr Neil William, CB 1997; Director, Oxford Centre for the Environment, Ethics and Society, and Fellow, Mansfield College, University of Oxford, since 1997; Director, Oxford Centre for Water Research, since 1998; *b* 5 April 1942; *s* of H. E. W. Summerton and Nancy Summerton; *m* 1965, Pauline Webb; two *s*. *Educ:* Wellington Grammar Sch., Shropshire; King's Coll., London (BA History 1963; PhD War Studies 1970). Min. of Transport, 1966–69; PA to Principal, 1969–71, Asst Sec. (Co-ordination), 1971–74, KCL; DoE, 1974–97; Asst Sec., heading various housing Divs, 1978–85; Under Sec., Planning Land-Use Policy Directorate, 1985–87; Under Sec., Planning and Develt Control Directorate, 1987–88; Under Sec., Local Govt Finance Policy Directorate, 1988–91; Under Sec., Water, 1991–95; Dir, Water and Land, 1996–97. Attended HM Treasury Centre for Admin. Studies, 1968–69; Civil Service Top Management Programme, 1985. Non-executive Director: Redland Bricks Ltd, 1988–91; Folkestone and Dover Water Services Ltd, 1998–; North Surrey Water Co. Ltd, 1998–2000; Three Valleys Water, 2000–; Director: Partnership (UK) Ltd, 1994–; Christian Impact Ltd, 1989–98; London Christian Housing plc, 1990–98; Christian Research Assoc., 1992–98. Member: Cttee of Management, Council on Christian Approaches to Defence and Disarmament, 1983– (Hon. Sec., 1984–91); Council, Evangelical Alliance, 1990–96 and 1997–. *Publications:* A Noble Task: eldership and ministry in the local church, 1987, 2nd edn 1994; articles and essays on historical, theological and ethical matters. *Address:* Mansfield College, Oxford OX1 3TF.

SUMNER, Hon. Sir Christopher (John), Kt 1996; **Hon. Mr Justice Sumner;** a Judge of the High Court of Justice, Family Division, since 1996; *b* 28 Aug. 1939; *s* of His Honour W. D. M. Sumner, OBE, QC and M. K. Sumner; *m* 1970, Carole Ashley Mann; one *s* two *d*. *Educ:* Charterhouse; Sidney Sussex Coll., Cambridge (MA). Called to the Bar, Inner Temple, 1961, Bencher, 1994; Asst Recorder, 1983; Recorder, 1986; a Circuit Judge, 1987–96. Mem., Judicial Studies Bd, 1991–96, 1999– (Jt Dir of Studies, 1995–96). *Club:* Hurlingham.

SUMPTION, Anthony James Chadwick, DSC 1944; *b* 15 May 1919; *s* of late John Chadwick Sumption and late Winifred Fanny Sumption; *m* 1946, Hedy Hedigan (marr. diss. 1979); two *s* two *d*. *Educ:* Cheltenham Coll.; London Sch. of Economics. Served RNVR, 1939–46; HM Submarines, 1941–45: comd Varangian, 1944; Upright, 1945; Flag Lieut to Flag Officer Gibraltar and Mediterranean Approach, 1945–46. Solicitor, 1946; called to the Bar, Lincoln's Inn, 1971; a Recorder of the Crown Court, 1980–85. Member (C): LCC, 1949–52; Westminster City Council, 1953–56. Contested (C): Hayes and Harlington, March 1953; Middlesbrough W, 1964. *Publications:* Taxation of Overseas Income and Gains, 1973, 4th edn 1982; Tax Planning, (with Philip Lawton) 6th edn 1973–8th edn 1979, (with Giles Clarke) 9th edn 1981–10th edn 1982; Capital Gains Tax, 1981. *Recreations:* painting, angling. *Address:* c/o Coutts & Co., 440 Strand, WC2R 0QS. *Club:* Garrick.

See also J. P. C. Sumption.

SUMPTION, Jonathan Philip Chadwick; QC 1986; *b* 9 Dec. 1948; *s* of Anthony James Chadwick Sumption, *qv*; *m* 1971, Teresa Mary (*née* Whelan); one *s* two *d*. *Educ:* Eton; Magdalen College, Oxford (MA). Fellow (in History) of Magdalen College, Oxford, 1971–75; called to the Bar, Inner Temple, 1975, Bencher, 1990. A Recorder, 1993; a Judge of the Courts of Appeal of Jersey and Guernsey, 1995–. *Publications:* Pilgrimage: an image of medieval religion, 1975; The Albigensian Crusade, 1978; The Hundred Years' War, vol. 1, 1990, vol. 2, 1999. *Recreations:* music, history. *Address:* Brick Court Chambers, 7–8 Essex Street, WC2R 3LD.

SUMRAY, Monty, CBE 1989; Chairman, FII Group, 1965–95 (Managing Director, 1965–95); *b* 12 Oct. 1918; *m* 1939, Catherine Beber; one *s* one *d*. *Educ:* Upton House, London. Royal Berkshire Regt, 1939–46; served in Burma (Captain). UK footwear manufacturing, 1934–95; Dir, FII Group. Pres., British Footwear Manufacturers' Fedn, 1976–77, formerly: Member: Footwear Industry Study Steering Gp (Chm., Home Working Cttee); Footwear Economic Develt Cttee (4 years); Pres., London Footwear Manufacturers' Assoc.; Chm., London Branch, British Boot & Shoe Instn. FCFI 1974; FInstD 1981; FRSA 1993. *Recreations:* bowls, reading, social and charitable work. *Address:* 6 Inverforth House, North End Way, NW3 7EU. *T:* (020) 8458 2788.

SUMSION, John Walbridge, OBE 1991; Senior Fellow, Department of Information Science (formerly Information and Library Studies), Loughborough University, since 1996; *b* 16 Aug. 1928; *s* of late Dr Herbert Sumsion, CBE; *m* 1st, 1961, Annette Dorothea Wilson (marr. diss. 1979); two *s* two *d*; 2nd, 1979, Hazel Mary Jones (*née* English). *Educ:* St George's Choir Sch., Windsor Castle; St Thomas' Choir Sch., New York City; Rendcomb Coll., Cirencester; Clare Coll., Cambridge (BA (Hons) History); Yale Univ., USA (MA Economics); Cornell Univ., USA (Teaching Fellow). Somervell Brothers (K Shoemakers) Ltd: Graduate trainee, 1954; Production Manager (Women's Shoes), 1959; Director, 1962–81; Registrar, Public Lending Right, 1981–91; Dir, Library and Inf. Statistics Unit, Loughborough Univ., 1991–96. Dir, TeleOrdering Ltd, 1992–94. Mem., Library and Information Services Council (England), 1992–95; Chm., Stats Section, IFLA, 1995–99. Editor, Library & Information Res. News, 1997–2001. Hon. FLA 1990. *Publications:* Setting Up Public Lending Right, 1984; PLR in Practice, 1988, 2nd edn 1991; Practical Performance Indicators, 1992; (with L. England) Perspectives of Public Library Use, 1995; (jtly) Library Economics in Europe: millennium study, 2000; (jtly) Economic Value of Public Libraries, 2001; various statistical reports. *Recreation:* music (flute, singing). *Address:* The Granary, 29 Main Street, Rotherby, Melton Mowbray, Leics LE14 2LP. *T:* (01664) 434485. *Club:* Oxford and Cambridge.

SUNDERLAND, Earl of; George Spencer-Churchill; *b* 28 July 1992; *s* and *heir* of Marquess of Blandford, *qv*.

SUNDERLAND, (Arthur) John; Commissioner-in-Chief, St John Ambulance Brigade, 1986–90; *b* 24 Feb. 1932; *s* of George Frederick Irvon Sunderland and Mary Katharine Sunderland; *m* 1st, 1958, Audrey Ann Thompson (*d* 1992); three *s*; 2nd, 1995, Mrs Penelope J. R. Hall (*née* Wood). *Educ:* Marlborough Coll. Served Army, RE, 1953–55 (2nd Lieut). Director: James Upton Ltd, 1963–69; Surrey Fine Art Press Ltd, 1963–69; Sunderland Print Ltd, 1969–84; Randall Bros Ltd, 1970–84; Alday Green & Welburn, 1978–84; Foxplan Ltd, 1984–; Rapidflow Ltd, 1985–91; SADC Ltd, 1986–. Chm., Adventure Service Challenge Scheme, 2000–. Dep. County Comr, 1976–78, County Comr, 1978–86, St John Ambulance Bde, W Midlands; KStJ 1986 (CStJ 1982; OStJ 1978). Chm., Ladypool Road Neighbourhood Centre, Balsall Heath, 1970–76. Governor, West House Sch., Birmingham, 1973–91. *Recreations:* walking, sport generally. *Address:* Rowans, Grafton Flyford, Worcs WR7 4PJ. *T:* (01905) 391281.

SUNDERLAND, Prof. Eric, OBE 1999; PhD; FIBiol; Principal, later Vice-Chancellor, University College of North Wales, Bangor, 1984–95, now Emeritus Professor, University of Wales; Lord-Lieutenant of Gwynedd, since 1999; *b* 18 March 1930; *s* of Leonard Sunderland and Mary Agnes (*née* Davies); *m* 1957, Jean Patricia (*née* Watson); two *d*. *Educ:* Amman Valley Grammar Sch.; Univ. of Wales (BA, MA); Univ. of London (PhD). FIBiol 1975. Commnd Officer, RA, 1955–56. Res. Asst, UCL, 1953–54; Res. Scientist, NCB, 1957–58; Univ. of Durham: Lectr, 1958–66; Sen. Lectr, 1966–71; Prof. of Anthropology, 1971–84; Pro Vice-Chancellor, 1979–84; Vice-Chancellor, Univ. of Wales, 1989–91. Welsh Supernumerary Fellow, Jesus Coll., Oxford, 1987–88 and 1992–93. Sec.-Gen., Internat. Union of Anthropol and Ethnol Sciences, 1978–98 (Pres., 1998–); President, Royal Anthropol Inst., 1989–91 (Hon. Sec., 1978–85; Hon. Treasurer, 1985–89); Chm., Biosocial Soc., 1981–85. Member: Welsh Language Bd, 1988–91; Ct of Govs, Nat. Mus. of Wales, 1991–94; Gen. Cttee, ICSU, 1993–99; Bd, British Council, 1996–2001 (Chm., Welsh Cttee, 1996–2001); BBC Broadcasting Council for Wales, 1996–2000; Vice Pres., Internat. Social Sci. Council, 1994; Chairman: Welsh Language Educn Develt Cttee, 1987–94; Local Govt Boundary Commn for Wales, 1994–2001; Adv. Cttee for Wales, Environment Agency, 1996–2001. Pres., Univ. of Wales, Lampeter, 1998–2001. Hon. Mem., The Gorsedd, 1985. High Sheriff, 1998–99, DL 1998, Gwynedd. Hon. Fellow: Univ. of Wales, Lampeter, 1995; Univ. of Wales, Bangor, 1996. Hon. LLD Wales, 1997. *Publications:* Elements of Human and Social Geography: some anthropological perspectives, 1973; (ed jtly) Genetic Variation in Britain, 1973; (ed jtly) The Operation of Intelligence: biological preconditions for the operation of intelligence, 1980; (ed jtly) Genetic and Population Studies in Wales, 1986; contrib. Annals of Human Biol., Human Heredity, Man, Human Biol., Nature, Amer. Jl of Phys. Anthropol., and Trans Royal Soc. *Recreations:* travel, gardening, book collecting, reading. *Address:* University of Wales, Bangor, Gwynedd LL57 2DG. *T:* (01248) 351151; Y Bryn, Ffriddoedd Road, Bangor, Gwynedd LL57 2EH. *T:* (01248) 353265. *Club:* Athenæum.

SUNDERLAND, (Godfrey) Russell, CB 1991; FRAeS; FCIT; Director, Air Miles Travel Promotions Ltd; *b* 28 July 1936; *s* of Allan and Laura Sunderland; *m* 1965, Greta Jones; one *s* one *d*. *Educ:* Heath Grammar Sch., Halifax; The Queen's College, Oxford (MA). FRAeS 1993. Ministry of Aviation: Asst Principal, 1962; Asst Private Sec. to Minister, 1964; Principal, 1965; HM Diplomatic Service: First Sec. (Civil Air), Beirut, and other Middle East posts, 1969; Principal, Board of Trade, 1971; Asst Sec., DTI, 1973; Under Sec., DTI, 1979; Dir of Shipping Policy and Emergency Planning, Dept of Transport, 1984; Dep. Sec., Aviation, Shipping and Internat., Dept of Transport, 1988–94. Chairman: Consultative Shipping Group, 1984–88; Maritime Transport Cttee, OECD, 1992–94. Advr, Maersk Co. Ltd, 1994–. FCIT 1995 (Vice Pres., 1997). FRSA 1991. *Recreations:* garden, piano, amateur theatre. *Address:* Windrush, Silkmore Lane, West Horsley, Leatherhead, Surrey KT24 6JQ. *T:* (01483) 282660.

SUNDERLAND, John; *see* Sunderland, A. J.

SUNDERLAND, John Michael; Chief Executive, Cadbury Schweppes plc, since 1996; *b* 24 Aug. 1945; *s* of Harry Sunderland and Joyce Eileen Sunderland (*née* Farnish); *m* 1966, Jean Margaret Grieve; three *s* one *d*. *Educ:* St Andrews Univ. (MA Hons). Joined Cadbury, 1968. *Address:* (office) 25 Berkeley Square, W1J 6HB. *T:* (020) 7830 5004.

SUNDERLAND, Russell; *see* Sunderland, G. R.

SUNLEY, John Bernard; Chairman, Sunley Holdings plc, since 1979; *b* 31 May 1936; *s* of late Bernard and Mary Sunley; *m* 1st, 1961, Patricia Taylor (marr. diss. 1975); three *s* one *d*; 2nd, 1978, Anne Crosby (marr. diss. 1989); 3rd, 1992, Fiona Bateman; one *s* one *d. Educ:* Elstree Sch.; Harrow Sch.; Columbia Univ. Nat. Service, RM, 1954–56. Trainee Accountant, Allan Charlesworth, Chartered Accountants, 1956–57; Trainee Surveyor, Weatherall Green and Smith, Chartered Surveyors, 1957–58; joined family business as jun. exec., 1960; Director: Bernard Sunley Investment Trust Co. Ltd, 1962–; Blackwood Hodge Ltd, 1962–; Chairman: Bernard Sunley and Sons Ltd, 1964– (Dir, 1962–); Sunley Homes Ltd, 1964– (Dir, 1962–). Chm., Bernard Sunley Charitable Foundn, 1964–. High Sheriff, Kent, 1999. *Recreations:* golf, tennis, squash, thoroughbred horse racing, farming, ski-ing. *Address:* Sunley Holdings, 20 Berkeley Square, W1J 6LH. *T:* (020) 7499 8842. *Clubs:* MCC, Royal Thames Yacht; Royal and Ancient Golf; Royal St George's Golf.

SUPHAMONGKHON, Dr Konthi, Kt Grand Cordon of the White Elephant, Kt Grand Cordon, Order of the Crown of Thailand; Kt Grand Commander, Order of Chula Chom Klao; Hon. GCVO 1972; *b* 3 Aug. 1916; *m* 1951, Dootsdi Atthakravi; two *s* one *d. Educ:* Univ. of Moral and Political Sciences, Bangkok (LLB); Univ. of Paris (Dr-en-Droit). Joined Min. of Foreign Affairs, 1941; Second Sec., Tokyo, 1942–44; Chief of Polit. Div., 1944–48; Dir-Gen., Western Affairs Dept, 1948–50; UN Affairs Dept, 1950–52; Minister to Australia, 1952–56, Ambassador, June 1956–59, and to New Zealand, Oct. 1956–59; Dir-Gen. of Internat. Organizations, 1959–63; Adviser on Foreign Affairs to the Prime Minister, 1962–64; Sec.-Gen., SEATO, 1964–65; Ambassador to Federal Republic of Germany, 1965–70, and to Finland, 1967–70; Ambassador to Court of St James's, 1970–76. Frequent Lecturer, 1944–; notably at Thammasat Univ., 1944–52, at National Defence Coll., 1960–62, and at Army War Coll., Bangkok, 1960–63. Member: Internat. Law Assoc.; IISS; RIIA. Holds foreign decorations, incl. Grosskreuz des Verdienstordens (Germany), 1970. *Publications:* Thailand and her relations with France, 1940 (in French); Account of a return journey from Marseilles to Singapore, 1965 (in French); Thai Foreign Policy, 1984 (in Thai). *Recreations:* tennis, golf, swimming. *Address:* Kanta Mansion, 73 Soi 26, Sukhumvit Road, Bangkok, Thailand; 60 Kensington Court, Kensington, W8 5DG. *Clubs:* Siam Society, Royal Sport of Bangkok, Royal Turf (Bangkok).

SUPPERSTONE, Michael Alan; QC 1991; a Recorder, since 1996 (Assistant Recorder, 1992–96); a Deputy High Court Judge, since 1998; *b* 30 March 1950; *s* of late Harold Bernard Supperstone and Muriel Supperstone; *m* 1985, Dianne Jaffe; one *s* one *d. Educ:* St Paul's School; Lincoln College, Oxford (MA, BCL). Called to the Bar, Middle Temple, 1973, Bencher, 1999; in practice, 1974. Vis. Scholar, Harvard Law Sch., 1979–80; Vis. Lectr, Nat. Univ. of Singapore, 1981, 1982. Chm., Administrative Law Bar Assoc., 1997–99 (Sec., 1986–91; Treas., 1991–94; Vice-Chm., 1995–96). Consulting Ed., Butterworths Local Government Reports, 1999–. *Publications:* Brownlie's Law of Public Order and National Security, 2nd edn 1981; Immigration: the law and practice, 1983, 3rd edn 1994, cons. ed., 4th edn, as Immigration and Asylum, 1996; (contrib.) Halsbury's Laws of England, 4th edn reissue, Administrative Law Title, 1989, Extradition Law Title, 2000; (ed jtly and contrib.) Judicial Review, 1992, 2nd edn 1997; (contrib.) Butterworths Local Government Law, 1998; (jtly) Local Authorities and the Human Rights Act 1998, 1999; articles on public law. *Recreation:* playing tennis. *Address:* 11 King's Bench Walk, Temple, EC4Y 7EQ. *T:* (020) 7583 0610. *Clubs:* Garrick, Roehampton.

SUPPLE, Prof. Barry Emanuel, CBE 2000; FRHistS; FBA 1987; Director, Leverhulme Trust, 1993–2001; Professor of Economic History, University of Cambridge, 1981–93, now Professor Emeritus; *b* 27 Oct. 1930; *s* of Solomon and Rose Supple; *m* 1958, Sonia (*née* Caller); two *s* one *d. Educ:* Hackney Downs Grammar Sch.; London Sch. of Econs and Polit. Science (BScEcon 1952); Christ's Coll., Cambridge (PhD 1955). LittD Cambridge, 1993. FRHistS 1972. Asst Prof. of Business History, Grad. Sch. of Business Admin, Harvard Univ., 1955–60; Associate Prof. of Econ. Hist., McGill Univ., 1960–62; University of Sussex: Lectr, Reader, then Prof. of Econ. and Social Hist., 1962–78; Dean, Sch. of Social Sciences, 1965–68; Pro-Vice-Chancellor (Arts and Social Studies), 1968–72; Pro-Vice-Chancellor, 1978; University of Oxford: Reader in Recent Social and Econ. Hist., 1978–81; Professorial Fellow, Nuffield Coll., 1978–81; Professorial Fellow, 1981–83, Hon. Fellow, 1984, Christ's Coll., Cambridge; Master of St Catharine's Coll., Cambridge, 1984–93 (Hon. Fellow, 1993). Hon. Fellow, Worcester Coll., 1986; Associate Fellow, Trumbull Coll., Yale, 1986. Chm., Consultative Cttee of Assessment of Performance Unit, DES, 1975–80; Member: Council, SSRC, 1972–77; Social Science Fellowship Cttee, Nuffield Foundn, 1974–97. Pres., Econ. Hist. Soc., 1992–95. Foreign Sec., British Acad., 1995–99. Co-editor, Econ. Hist. Rev., 1973–82. Hon. DLitt: London Guildhall, 1993; Sussex, 1998; Leicester, 1999; Warwick, 2000; Bristol, 2001. FRSA 2000. Hon. FRAM 2001. *Publications:* Commercial Crisis and Change in England, 1600–42, 1959; (ed) The Experience of Economic Growth, 1963; Boston Capitalists and Western Railroads, 1967; The Royal Exchange Assurance: a history of British insurance, 1720–1970, 1970; (ed) Essays in Business History, 1977; History of the British Coal Industry: vol. 4, 1914–46, The Political Economy of Decline, 1987; (ed) The State and Economic Knowledge: the American and British experience, 1990; (ed) The Rise of Big Business, 1992; articles and revs in learned jls. *Recreations:* tennis, photography. *Address:* 41 Lensfield Road, Cambridge CB2 1EN. *T:* (01223) 353726.

SURFACE, Richard Charles; Director, Oliver, Wyman & Co., since 2000; *b* 16 June 1948; *s* of James Richard Surface and Mary Ellen Surface (*née* Shaver); *m* 1977, Stephanie Maria Josefa Ruth Hentschel von Gilgenheimb; two *s* one *d. Educ:* Univ. of Minnesota; Univ. of Kansas (BA Maths); Harvard Grad. Sch. of Business Admin (MBA). Actuarial Asst, Nat. Life & Accident Insce Co., Nashville, Tenn, 1970–72; Corporate Treasury Analyst, Mobiloil Corp., NY, 1974–77; Dir, Corporate Planning, Northwest Industries Inc., Chicago, 1977–81; American Express Co., London and Frankfurt, 1981–89: Regl Vice-Pres. (Card Strategic Planning), 1981–82; Divisional Vice-President: Business Develt, 1982–86; Card Mkting, 1986–87; and Gen. Manager, Personal Financial Services, 1987–89; Gen. Manager, Corporate Develt, Sun Life, 1989–91; Managing Director: Sun Life Internat., 1991–95; Pearl Group PLC, 1995–99; AMP (UK) PLC, 1995–99. *Recreations:* antiquarian books, ski-ing, opera, theatre, tennis. *Clubs:* Royal Automobile, Groucho.

SURR, Jeremy Bernard, CB 1993; consultant; Director Operations (South and East), Training Enterprise and Education Directorate, Department of Employment, 1990–92; *b* 23 Jan. 1938; *s* of Thomas Bernard Surr, ISO, and Mabel Edith Moore; *m* 1965, Gillian Mary Lapage. *Educ:* Rutlish Sch., Wimbledon; Bury Grammar Sch., Lancs. National Service, RCS, 1956–58. Min. of Labour, 1959–65; computer systems analyst, 1965–70; Asst Private Sec. to Sec. of State for Employment, 1971–74; Principal, Employment Protection, Incomes Policy and Res. and Planning, 1974–78, on secondment to Australian Dept of Employment and Industrial Relations, 1978–80; joined MSC as Head of Sheltered Employment and Employment Rehabilitation Br., 1980; Head of Special Measures Br., 1982–85; Dir of Special Measures, 1985–86; Chief Exec., Employment and Enterprise Gp, 1986–87; Dir of Adult Programmes, 1987–89, Dir, Operations and Trng and Enterprise Councils Develt, 1989–90, Training Agency (formerly MSC, later Training Commn). Dir, Energy Action Grants Agency, 1993–. Trustee, Drive for Youth, 1993–. FRSA 1993. *Recreations:* golf, walking, gardening, DIY. *Address:* 48 Oak Hill Road, Nether Edge, Sheffield S7 1SH. *T:* (0114) 255 7554. *Clubs:* East India, Devonshire, Sports and Public Schools; Abbeydale Golf (Sheffield).

SURREY, Archdeacon of; *see* Reiss, Ven. R. P.

SURTEES, John, MBE 1961; controls companies in automotive research and development and property development; *b* 11 Feb. 1934; *s* of late John Norman and Dorothy Surtees; *m* 1st, 1962, Patricia Phyllis Burke (marr. diss. 1979); 2nd, 1987, Jane A. Sparrow; one *s* two *d. Educ:* Ashburton School, Croydon. 5 year engineering apprenticeship, Vincent Engrs, Stevenage, Herts. Motorcycle racing, 1952–60; British Champion, 1954, 1955; World 500 cc Motorcycle Champion, 1956; World 350 and 500 cc Motorcycle Champion, 1958, 1959, 1960. At end of 1960 he retd from motorcycling; motor racing, 1961–72; with Ferrari Co., won World Motor Racing title, 1964; 5th in World Championship, 1965 (following accident in Canada due to suspension failure); in 1966 left Ferrari in mid-season and joined Cooper, finishing 2nd in World Championship; in 1967 with Honda Motor Co. as first driver and develt engr (1967–68); 3rd in World Championship; with BRM as No 1 driver, 1969; designed and built own Formula 1 car, 1970. *Publications:* Motorcycle Racing and Preparation, 1958; John Surtees Book of Motorcycling, 1960; Speed, 1963; Six Days in August, 1968; John Surtees—World Champion, 1991; (jtly) The Pirelli Album of Motor Racing Heroes, 1992. *Recreations:* period architecture, mechanical restorations; interested in most sports. *Address:* c/o John Surtees Ltd, Monza House, Fircroft Way, Edenbridge, Kent TN8 6EJ. *T:* (01732) 865496.

SUSMAN, Peter Joseph; QC 1997; a Recorder, since 1993; *b* 20 Feb. 1943; *s* of Albert Leonard Susman and Sybil Rebecca Susman (*née* Joseph); *m* 1966, Peggy Judith Stone (marr. diss. 1996); one *s* one *d*; lives with, Belinda Zoe Schwehr; one *s. Educ:* Dulwich Coll.; Lincoln Coll., Oxford (Oldfield Open Law Schol.; BA 1964; MA 1970); Law Sch., Univ. of Chicago (British Commonwealth Fellow; Fulbright Schol.; JD 1965). Called to the Bar, Middle Temple, 1966; in practice as a barrister, 1966–70 and 1972–; Associate, Debevoise, Plimpton, Lyons & Gates, NYC, 1970–71; Asst Recorder, 1989–93. *Recreations:* playing the clarinet, windsurfing, ski-ing, squash. *Address:* 4 Field Court, Gray's Inn, WC1R 5EF. *T:* (020) 7440 6900.

SUSSKIND, Janis Elizabeth; Director, Composers and Repertoire, Boosey & Hawkes Music Publishers Ltd, London, since 1997; *b* 27 Nov. 1952; *d* of John H. Tomfohrde, Jr, and Ruth Elizabeth Robbins Tomfohrde; *m* 1st, 1973, Walter Susskind (*d* 1980); 2nd, 1993, Antony Fell. *Educ:* Princeton Univ. (BA *cum laude*). Hd of Promotion, Boosey & Hawkes Music Publishers Ltd, 1984–96. Dir, NMC Record Co., 1991–92. Chm., SPNM, 1983–88. Arts Council of England: Mem., Music Panel, 1993–; Mem. and Dep. Chm., Stabilization Adv. Panel, 1996–. Mem. Council, RCM, 1996–. Mem. Bd, Birmingham Contemporary Music Gp, 1991–2000. Trustee, Britten-Pears Foundn, 2001–. *Recreations:* reading, theatre, contemporary art, ski-ing, wind-surfing, tennis, playing chamber music. *Address:* 15 Ravenshaw Street, NW6 1NP.

SUSSKIND, Prof. Richard Eric, OBE 2000; DPhil; FRSE; author and independent consultant, since 1997; Information Technology Adviser to Lord Chief Justice of England, since 1998; *b* 28 March 1961; *s* of Dr Werner and Shirley Susskind; *m* 1985, Michelle Latter; two *s* one *d. Educ:* Hutchesons' Grammar Sch., Glasgow; Univ. of Glasgow (LLB Hons 1st class; Dip. Legal Practice); Balliol Coll., Oxford (Snell Exhibnr; DPhil 1986). Tutor in Law, Univ. of Oxford, 1984–86; Head of Expert Systems, Ernst & Young, 1986–89; Special Advr, 1989–94, Mem. of Mgt Bd, 1994–97, Masons. Vis. Prof., Law Sch., Univ. of Strathclyde, 1990–; Gresham Prof. of Law, 2000–. IT Advr, Lord Woolf's Access to Justice Inquiry, 1995–96. Chm., Soc. for Computers and Law, 1990–92 (Hon. Mem., 1992–). Member: Inf. Technol. and the Courts Cttee, 1990–; Court of Appeal (Civil Div.) Review Team, 1996–97; Modernising Govt Project Bd, 1999–. Expert Consultee: Criminal Courts Rev., 2000–; Tribunals Rev., 2000–. Gen. Editor, Internat. Jl of Law and Information Technology, 1992–; Law columnist, The Times, 1999–. Freeman, City of London, 1992; Freeman, 1992, Liveryman, 1993, Mem. Court, 1994–, Co. of Information Technologists. Mem., Balliol Coll. Campaign Bd, 2000–. Gov., Haberdashers' Aske's Schs, Elstree, 1998–. FRSA 1992; FBCS 1997; FRSE 1997. George & Thomas Hutcheson Award, 2001. *Publications:* Expert Systems in Law, 1987; (with P. Capper) Latent Damage Law: the expert system, 1988; Essays on Law and Artificial Intelligence, 1993; The Future of Law, 1996; Transforming the Law, 2000. *Recreations:* running, reading, golf, cinema, ski-ing. *Address:* 67 Aldenham Avenue, Radlett, Herts WD7 8JA. *T:* (01923) 469655.

SUTCH, Christopher Timothy, (Rev. Dom Antony Sutch); Headmaster, Downside School, since 1995; *b* 19 June 1950; *s* of late Ronald Antony Sutch and of Kathleen Sutch (*née* Roden). *Educ:* Downside Sch.; Exeter Univ.; St Benet's Hall, Oxford. Chartered Accountant, 1971–75; postulant, 1975, novice, 1977, professed Benedictine monk, 1981; priest, 1981; Housemaster, Caverel House, Downside Sch., 1985–95. Member: BBC Ind. Assessment Bd on Religious Broadcasting, 1998; Cttee, Catholic Ind. Schs Conf., 2000–. Mem., Governing Body, Bath Univ., 1995–; Gov., All Hallows Prep. Sch., 1996–; Chm. Govs, Sacred Heart Primary, Chew Magna, 1997–; Guardian, St Mary's Sch., Shaftesbury, 1999–. TV and radio progs. *Publications:* articles in newspapers, magazines and jls. *Recreations:* gardening, cricket, horse racing. *Address:* Downside Abbey, Stratton-on-the-Fosse, Bath BA3 4RJ. *T:* (01761) 235100, 235161. *Clubs:* East India; Emeriti, Ravens Cricket, Stratton Cricket (Pres.).

SUTCH, Peter Dennis Antony, CBE 1995; GBS 2000; FRAeS; Director, John Swire & Sons Ltd, since 1999; Chairman: Aviation Partners Worldwide plc, since 2000; Magtibay Holdings BV, since 2001; *b* 8 April 1945; *s* of Ronald Antony Sutch and Kathleen (*née* Roden); *m* 1st, 1968, Rosemary Aisling Langan (marr. diss. 1996); three *s* one *d*; 2nd, 1996, Gillian Stevens (marr. diss. 2001). *Educ:* Downside Sch., Stratton-on-Fosse; Exeter Coll., Oxford Univ. (MA Hist.). Joined John Swire & Sons Ltd, Hong Kong, 1966: Shipping Division: Hong Kong, 1966–67; Japan, 1967–69; Cathay Pacific Airways: Manager, W Japan, 1970–72; Passenger Sales Manager, Hong Kong, 1972–76; Gen. Manager, Japan, 1976–81; Dep. Dir and Gen. Manager, Hong Kong, 1981–83; Dep. Man. Dir, 1983–84; Man. Dir, 1984–88; Dep. Chm. and Man. Dir, 1988; Dep. Chm., John Swire & Sons (HK) Ltd and Swire Pacific Ltd, 1988–92; Chairman: Hong Kong Aircraft Engrg Co. Ltd, 1987–95; Swire Gp, Hong Kong, 1992–99; Director: Cathay Pacific Airways Ltd, 1983–2001 (Chm., 1992–99); Swire Pacific Ltd, 1984–2001 (Chm., 1992–99); John Swire & Sons (HK) Ltd, 1984–2000 (Chm., 1992–99); GlobalInflight Services Ltd, 2000–; iVenture Investment Mgt (BVI) Ltd, 2000–; National Jet Italia SpA, 2001–. Board Member: Hongkong & Shanghai Banking Corp., 1992–99; Lee Gardens Internat. Hldgs, 1992–96; Community Chest of Hong Kong, 1992–99; Council Mem., Univ. of Hong Kong, 1992–99; Member: Aviation Adv. Bd; Gen. Cttee, Hong Kong Gen. Chamber of Commerce, 1992–99 (Chm., 1998–99); Hong Kong Trade Develt Council, 1992–99; CIT in Hong Kong, 1992–99; Hong Kong Chief Exec's Commn on Strategic Develt, 1998–99; Mem., Barristers Disciplinary Tribunal Panel, Hong Kong, 1993–99. Mem. Adv. Bd., Hong Kong Red Cross, 1996–99. *Recreations:* golf, travel, boating. *Address:* (office) 132 Ebury Street, SW1W 9QQ; (home) 2/33 Cranley Gardens, SW7 3BD. *Clubs:* Royal Automobile; Naunton Downs Golf; Hong Kong, Hong Kong Jockey, Hong Kong Golf, Shek O Country (Hong Kong).

SUTCLIFFE, Allan; a Director, British Gas plc, 1986–91; *b* 30 Jan. 1936; *s* of Bertie and May Sutcliffe; *m* 1983, Pauline, *d* of Mark and Lilian Abrahams; one *s* one *d* by a previous marr. *Educ:* Neath Grammar Sch.; University Coll. London (LLB); FCMA, CIGasE. Graduate trainee, BR, 1957–60; various positions in Finance in Western, Eastern and Southern Regions and at HQ, BR, 1960–70; Wales Gas Board: Chief Accountant, 1970; Dir of Finance, 1972; Deputy Chairman: British Gas W Midlands, 1980; British Gas N Thames, 1983; British Gas plc: Man. Dir, Finance, 1987; Gp Man. Dir, Finance, 1991, retd. Freeman, City of London, 1985. *Recreations:* music, 19th century fiction (esp. Dickens). *Address:* Manor Cottage, 106 Kenilworth Road, Knowle, Solihull, W Midlands B93 0JD. *T:* (01564) 771538. *Club:* Royal Automobile.

SUTCLIFFE, Andrew Harold Wentworth; QC 2001; a Recorder, since 2000; *b* 7 Sept. 1960; *s* of John Harold Vick Sutcliffe, *qv*; *m* 1988, Emma Elisabeth Stirling; three *d* (one *s* decd). *Educ:* Winchester Coll.; Worcester Coll., Oxford (MA). Pres., Oxford Union Soc., 1981. 2nd Lieut, Royal Scots Dragoon Guards, 1978–79. Called to the Bar, Inner Temple, 1983; in practice as barrister, 1983–, specialising in commercial law, esp. banking and entertainment. Mem., Special Project Gp, Duke of Edinburgh's Award, 1986–96. Mem., Cttee, Moorland Assoc., 1996–; Chm., Kildale Agricl and Horticultural Show Cttee, 1988–; Vice Pres., Black Face Sheep Breeders' Assoc., 1989–. Liveryman, Co. of Fishmongers, 1996–. Gov., Fox Primary Sch., Kensington, 1993–. Trustee, Zebra Housing Assoc., 1988–. *Recreations:* walking, trees, opera. *Address:* Kildale Hall, Whitby, Yorks YO21 2RQ; 3 Verulam Buildings, Gray's Inn, WC1R 5NT. *T:* (020) 7831 8441. *Club:* Kildale Cricket (Pres.).

SUTCLIFFE, Anne-Marie Christine Elizabeth; Headmistress, Emanuel School, since 1998; *b* 24 Jan. 1949; *d* of late Dr Norman Mutton and of Mary Mutton (*née* Dobson); *m* 1970, Victor Herbert Sutcliffe; one *s* one *d*. *Educ:* convent schs; Girton Coll., Cambridge (BA 1st cl. Hons History tripos). Teacher, Stroud Girls' High Sch., 1975–79; Head of History Department: Bishop Thomas Grant Sch., 1979–81; Ursuline Convent High Sch., 1981–86; organising confs, servicing cttees, etc, CAFOD, Council on Christian Approaches to Defence and Disarmament, 1986–88; Teacher, 1988–95, Head of History, 1991–95, St Paul's Girls' Sch.; Dep. Head, Channing Sch., 1995–98. *Recreations:* theatre, opera, travel, history. *Address:* 36 Parklands Road, SW16 6TE. *T:* (020) 8769 8345.

SUTCLIFFE, Gerard; MP (Lab) Bradford South, since June 1994; Vice Chamberlain of HM Household, since 2001; *b* 13 May 1953; *s* of Henry and Margaret Sutcliffe; *m* 1972, Maria Holgate; three *s*. *Educ:* Cardinal Hinsley Grammar Sch.; Bradford Coll. Salesperson, Brown Muff dept store, 1969–71; display advertising clerk, Bradford Telegraph and Argus, 1971–75; Field Printers, 1975–80; Dep. Sec., SOGAT, subseq. GPMU, 1980–94. Bradford Metropolitan District Council: Councillor, 1982–88 and 1990–94; Leader, 1992–94. PPS to Chief Sec., HM Treasury, 1998, to Sec. of State for Trade and Industry, 1998–99; an Asst Govt Whip, 1999–2001. Chm., Parly Football Team. *Recreations:* sport, music, politics. *Address:* House of Commons, SW1A 0AA. *T:* (020) 7219 3247; (office) (01274) 400007.

SUTCLIFFE, James Thomas, (Tom); Opera Critic, Evening Standard, since 1996; *b* 4 June 1943; *s* of Lt-Comdr James Denis Sutcliffe, OBE, RN and Rosamund Sutcliffe, *d* of Major T. E. G. Swayne; *m* 1973, Meredith Frances Oakes, playwright, music critic, translator; one *s* one *d*. *Educ:* Prebendal Sch., Chichester; Hurstpierpoint Coll.; Magdalen Coll., Oxford (MA English 1967). English Teacher, Central Tutorial Sch. for Young Musicians, 1964–65; Manager, Musica Reservata, 1965–69; concert perfs with Musica Reservata, Schola Polyphonica, Pro Cantione Antiqua, Concentus Musicus, Vienna, 1965–70; opera début, Ottone in L'incoronazione di Poppea, Landestheater, Darmstadt, 1970; Countertenor Lay Clerk, Westminster Cathedral, 1966–70; Editor, Music and Musicians, 1970–73; Sub-Editor, Features, Dep. Arts Editor, opera & music critic, and feature writer, Dep. Obituaries Editor, The Guardian, 1973–96; opera, theatre and music critic, Vogue, 1975–87. Chm., music sect., Critics' Circle, 1999–. Mem., Gen. Synod, C of E, 1990–; Mem., Exec. Cttee, Affirming Catholicism, 1996–. Leverhulme Fellow, 1991. *Publications:* (contrib.) Theatre 71, 1972, Theatre 72, 1973, and Theatre 74, 1975; (ed) Tracts for our Times, 1983; (ed) In Vitro Veritas, 1984; Believing in Opera, 1996; (ed) The Faber Book of Opera, 2000; articles in Opera News, Musical Times, Classic CD, Opera Now, The Spectator. *Recreations:* conversation, travel, gardening. *Address:* 12 Polworth Road, Streatham, SW16 2EU. *T:* (020) 8677 5849.

SUTCLIFFE, John Harold Vick, CBE 1994; DL; company director; Chairman, Great Fosters (1931) Ltd, since 1958; *b* 30 April 1931; *o s* of late Sir Harold Sutcliffe and Emily Theodora Cochrane; *m* 1st, 1959, Cecilia Mary (*d* 1998), *e d* of Ralph Meredyth Turton; three *s* one *d*; 2nd, 2001, Katherine Fox. *Educ:* Winchester Coll.; New Coll., Oxford (MA). 2nd Lieut RA, 1950–51. Called to Bar, Inner Temple, 1956; practised until 1960, Midland Circuit. Chm., North Housing Association Ltd, 1985–94 (Dir, 1977–86); Director: Allied Investors Trusts Ltd, 1958–69; Norton Junction Sand & Gravel Ltd, 1958–64; Tyne Tees Waste Disposal Ltd, 1964–71. Estate management, Kildale, 1965–. Member: Housing Corp., 1982–88; Bd, Teesside Develt Corp., 1987–98. Mem. Bd, Civic Trust, 1989–93; Chairman: Northern Heritage Trust, 1981–89; NE Civic Trust, 1989–93 (Vice-Chm., 1977–89). Contested (C): Oldham West, 1959; Chorley, Lancs, 1964; Middlesbrough West, 1966. MP (C) Middlesbrough W, 1970–Feb. 1974. Contested (C) Teesside Thornaby, Oct. 1974. Chairman: Country Endeavour, 1983–88; Bow Street Project, Guisborough, 1988–; Pres., N Yorks Youth Clubs, 1984–93 (Chm., 1966–70); Mem., N Yorks Moors Nat. Park Cttee, 1982–88. DL Cleveland, 1983–96, N Yorks, 1996–; High Sheriff, N Yorks, 1987–88. *Recreations:* woodlands, gardening, travel, shooting. *Address:* Chapelgarth, Great Broughton, Middlesbrough, N Yorks TS9 7ET. *T:* (01642) 712228.

See also A. H. W. Sutcliffe.

SUTCLIFFE, Linda, (Mrs P. B. Walker); Her Honour Judge Sutcliffe; a Circuit Judge, since 1993; *b* 2 Dec. 1946; *d* of James Loftus Woodward and Florence Woodward; *m* 1st, 1968 (marr. diss. 1979); 2nd, 1987, Peter Brian Walker. *Educ:* Eccles Grammar Sch.; LSE (LLB Hons 1968). Called to the Bar, Gray's Inn, 1975; Lectr in Law, Univ. of Sheffield, 1968–76, part-time 1976–81; in practice at the Bar, 1976–93; a Recorder, 1991–93. Part-time Chm., Industrial Tribunals, 1983–92. *Recreations:* music, gardening. *Address:* c/o The Court Service, Group Manager's Office, Sheffield Group of Courts, Sovereign House, Queen Street, Sheffield S1 2ES.

SUTCLIFFE, Tom; *see* Sutcliffe, J. T.

SUTER, Helen Anne; *see* Alexander, H. A.

SUTER, Michael; solicitor in private practice, since 1992; Chief Executive, Shropshire County Council, 1987–92; *b* 21 Jan. 1944; *s* of Robert and Rose Suter; *m* 1963, Sandra Harrison; two *s*. *Educ:* Liverpool Collegiate Sch.; Liverpool Univ. (LLB). Solicitor. Dep. Chief Exec., Notts CC, 1980–87. *Recreations:* music, gardening, watching old Hollywood films, visiting Spain. *Address:* (office) 7 Barker Street, Shrewsbury, Shropshire SY1 1QJ. *T:* (01743) 365217, *Fax:* (01743) 355545; Redcliffe House, Weston-under-Redcastle, Shrewsbury, Shropshire SY4 5UX.

SUTHERLAND, family name of **Countess of Sutherland** and **Baron Sutherland of Houndwood**.

SUTHERLAND, 7th Duke of, *cr* 1833; **Francis Ronald Egerton;** Bt 1620; Baron Gower 1703; Earl Gower, Viscount Trentham 1746; Marquess of Stafford 1786; Viscount Brackley and Earl of Ellesmere 1846; *b* 18 Feb. 1940; *o s* of Cyril Reginald Egerton and Mary, *d* of Rt Hon. Sir Ronald Hugh Campbell, GCMG; *S* cousin, 2000; *m* 1974, Victoria Mary, twin *d* of Maj.-Gen. Edward Alexander Wilmot Williams, CB, CBE, MC; two *s*. *Educ:* Eton; RAC Cirencester. *Heir: s* Marquis of Stafford, *qv*. *Address:* Ley Farm, Stetchworth, Newmarket, Suffolk CB8 9TX.

SUTHERLAND, Countess of (24th in line) *cr* (*c*) 1235; **Elizabeth Millicent Sutherland;** Lady Strathnaver (*c*) 1235; Chief of Clan Sutherland; *b* 30 March 1921; *o c* of Lord Alistair St Clair Sutherland-Leveson-Gower, MC (*d* 1921; 2nd *s* of 4th Duke), and Baroness Osten Driesen (*d* 1931); *niece* of 5th Duke of Sutherland, KT, PC; *S* (to uncle's Earldom of Sutherland and Lordship of Strathnaver), 1963; *m* 1946, Charles Noel Janson (DL, 1959–93), late Welsh Guards; two *s* one *d* (and one *s* decd). *Educ:* Queen's College, Harley Street, W1, and abroad. Land Army, 1939–41; Laboratory Technician: Raigmore Hospital, Inverness, 1941–43; St Thomas' Hospital, SE1, 1943–45. Chm., Dunrobin Castle Ltd. *Recreations:* reading, swimming. *Heir: e s* Lord Strathnaver, *qv*. *Address:* Dunrobin Castle, Sutherland; House of Tongue, by Lairg, Sutherland; 39 Edwardes Square, W8 6HJ.

SUTHERLAND OF HOUNDWOOD, Baron *cr* 2001 (Life Peer), of Houndwood in the Scottish Borders; **Stewart Ross Sutherland,** Kt 1995; FBA 1992; FRSE; Principal and Vice-Chancellor, University of Edinburgh, since 1994; *b* 25 Feb. 1941; *s* of late George A. C. Sutherland and of Ethel (*née* Masson); *m* 1964, Sheena Robertson; one *s* two *d*. *Educ:* Woodside Sch.; Robert Gordon's Coll.; Univ. of Aberdeen (MA); Corpus Christi Coll., Cambridge (Hon. Schol.; MA; Hon. Fellow, 1989). FRSE 1995. Asst Lectr in Philosophy, UCNW, 1965; Lectr in Philosophy, 1968, Sen. Lectr, 1972, Reader, 1976, Univ. of Stirling; King's College London: Prof. of Hist. and Philos. of Religion, 1977–85, Titular Prof., 1985–94; Vice-Principal, 1981–85; Principal, 1985–90; FKC 1983.; Vice-Chancellor, London Univ., 1990–94; Chief Inspector of Schools, 1992–94. Vis. Fellow, ANU, 1974; Gillespie Vis. Prof., Wooster Ohio, 1975. Lectures: Hope, Stirling, 1979; Ferguson, Manchester, 1982; Wilde, Oxford, 1981–84; Boutwood, Cambridge, 1990; F. D. Maurice, KCL, 1993; Drummond, Stirling, 1993; St George's, Windsor, 1993; Debrabant, Southampton, 1994; Ballard Matthews, Bangor, 1994; Cook, St Andrews and Oxford, 1995; Sir Robert Menzies, Melbourne, 1995. Chairman: British Acad. Postgrad. Studentships Cttee, 1987–95; Royal Inst. of Philosophy, 1988–; London Conf. on Overseas Students, 1989–94; Cttee on Appeals Criteria and Procedure (Scotland), 1994–96; Vice-Chm., CVCP, 1989–92. Member: C of E Bd of Educn, 1980–84; Arts Sub-Cttee, UGC, 1983–85; City Parochial Foundn, 1988–90; Council for Sci. and Technology, 1993–; Humanities Res. Bd, Brit. Acad., 1994–95; UGC (Hong Kong), 1995–; HEFCE, 1996–. Chm., Royal Commn on Long Term Care of the Elderly, 1997–99; Member: NW Thames RHA, 1992–94; N Thames RHA, 1994. Pres., Soc. for the Study of Theology, 1985, 1986. Chm., Ethiopian Gemini Trust, 1987–92. Editor, Religious Studies, 1984–90; Member, Editorial Board: Scottish Jl of Religious Studies, 1980–; Modern Theology, 1984–91. Associate Fellow, Warwick Univ., 1986–; Hon. Fellow, UCNW, 1990. FCP 1994. Hon. LHD: Wooster, Ohio, 1986; Commonwealth Univ. of Virginia, 1992; New York, 1996; Hon. LLD: Aberdeen, 1990; NUI, 1992; Hon. DLitt: Richmond Coll., 1995; Wales, 1996; Glasgow, 1999; Warwick, 2001; DUniv Stirling, 1993; Dr *hc* Uppsala, 1995. *Publications:* Atheism and the Rejection of God, 1977, 2nd edn 1980; (ed with B. L. Hebblethwaite) The Philosophical Frontiers of Christian Theology, 1983; God, Jesus and Belief, 1984; Faith and Ambiguity, 1984; (ed) The World's Religions, 1988; (ed with T. A. Roberts) Religion, Reason and the Self, 1989; articles in books and learned jls. *Recreations:* Tassie medallions, theatre, jazz. *Address:* University of Edinburgh, Old College, South Bridge, Edinburgh EH8 9YL. *T:* (0131) 650 2150. *Club:* Athenæum.

SUTHERLAND, Rt Hon. Lord; Ranald Iain Sutherland; PC 2000; a Senator of the College of Justice in Scotland, 1985–2001; *b* 23 Jan. 1932; *s* of J. W. and A. K. Sutherland, Edinburgh; *m* 1964, Janice Mary, *d* of W. S. Miller, Edinburgh; two *s*. *Educ:* Edinburgh Academy; Edinburgh University (MA 1951, LLB 1953). Admitted to Faculty of Advocates, 1956; QC (Scot.) 1969. Advocate Depute, 1962–64, 1971–77; Standing Junior Counsel to Min. of Defence (Army Dept), 1964–69. Mem., Criminal Injuries Compensation Bd, 1977–85. *Recreations:* sailing, shooting. *Address:* 38 Lauder Road, Edinburgh EH9 1UE. *T:* (0131) 667 5280. *Clubs:* New (Edinburgh); Hon. Company of Edinburgh Golfers.

SUTHERLAND, Colin John MacLean; *see* Carloway, Hon. Lord.

SUTHERLAND, Euan Ross, CB 1993; Parliamentary Counsel, since 1989; *b* 24 Nov. 1943; *s* of Dr Alister Sutherland and Margaret Sutherland; *m* 1967, Katharine Mary Jenkins (marr. diss. 1995), *qv*; one *s* one *d*. *Educ:* Kingswood Sch., Bath; Balliol Coll., Oxford (BA Hist.). Called to the Bar, Inner Temple, 1969; Office of the Parliamentary Counsel, 1974–; seconded to: Govt of Solomon Is, 1979–81; Law Commn, 1986–88. *Recreations:* music, gardening, hill-walking. *Address:* Office of the Parliamentary Counsel, 36 Whitehall, SW1A 2AY.

SUTHERLAND, Prof. Grant Robert, AC 1998; FRS 1996; FAA; Director, Department of Cytogenetics and Molecular Genetics, Women's and Children's Hospital, Adelaide, since 1990; Affiliate Professor, Department of Paediatrics, since 1991, and Department of Genetics, since 1998, University of Adelaide; *b* 2 June 1945; *s* of John Sutherland and Hazel Wilson Mason McClelland; *m* 1979, Elizabeth Dougan; one *s* one *d*. *Educ:* Numurkah High Sch.; Univ. of Melbourne (BSc 1967; MSc 1971); Univ. of Edinburgh (PhD 1974; DSc 1984). FAA 1997. Cytogeneticist, Mental Health Authy, Melbourne, 1967; Cytogeneticist i/c, Royal Hosp. for Sick Children, Edinburgh, 1971; Chief, Cytogenetics Unit, Adelaide Children's Hosp., 1975. Internat. Res. Scholar, Howard Hughes Med. Inst., Maryland, 1993. President: Human Genetics Soc. of Australasia, 1989–91; Human Genome Orgn, 1996–97. Hon. FRCPA 1994. Australia Prize in Molecular Genetics (jtly), 1998. *Publications:* (with F. Hecht) Fragile Sites on Human Chromosomes, 1985; (with R. J. M. Gardner) Chromosome Abnormalities and Genetic Counselling, 1989, 2nd edn 1996; numerous papers in sci. and med. jls. *Recreation:* beef cattle farming. *Address:* Department of Cytogenetics and Molecular Genetics, Women's and Children's Hospital, Adelaide, SA 5006, Australia. *T:* (8) 82047284; POB 300 Macclesfield, SA 5153, Australia. *T:* (8) 83889524.

SUTHERLAND, Ian, MA; Director of Education and Training to Health Education Council, 1971–86; *b* 7 July 1926; *m* 1951, Virginia Scovil Bliss (marr. diss. 1978); one *s* one *d*. *Educ:* Wyggeston Grammar School, Leicester; Sidney Sussex College, Cambridge.

Assistant Professor of Classics, Univ. of New Brunswick, NB, Canada, 1949–50; Asst Master: Christ's Hospital, 1951–52; Harrow School, 1952–60; Head Master, St John's School, Leatherhead, 1960–70; Dir of Educn, Health Educn Council, 1970–71. Mem., Wandsworth HA, 1986–89. Governor, Reeds Sch., 1980–93. *Publications:* From Pericles to Cleophon, 1954; (ed) Health Education: perspectives and choices, 1979; Health Education, Half a Policy: the rise and fall of the Health Education Council, 1987; Around the World by Train, 1991; Coastal Corners, 1997. *Recreations:* painting, cricket. *Address:* 14 The Green, Great Bowden, Market Harborough, Leics LE16 7EU. *Clubs:* Oxford and Cambridge, MCC, Free Foresters'.

SUTHERLAND, Dr Ian Boyd; Senior Administrative Medical Officer, South Western Regional Hospital Board, 1970–73; Regional Medical Officer, South Western Regional Health Authority, 1973–80; *b* 19 Oct. 1926; *s* of William Sutherland and Grace Alexandra Campbell; *m* 1950, Charlotte Winifred Cordin; two *d*. *Educ:* Bradford Grammar Sch.; Edinburgh Univ. MB, ChB; FRCPE, FFCM, DPH. Medical Officer, RAF, 1950–52; Asst MOH, Counties of Roxburgh and Selkirk, 1953–55; Dep. MOH, County and Borough of Inverness, 1955–59; Dep. County MOH, Oxfordshire CC, 1959–60; Asst SMO, Leeds Regional Hosp. Bd, 1960–63; Dep. Sen. Admin. MO, SW Regl Hosp Bd, 1963–70; Community Medicine Specialist, Lothian Health Bd, 1980–86. Research Fellow, Dept of Clin. Surgery, Univ. of Edinburgh, 1986–88. *Recreations:* reading, art. *Address:* 8 Chesterfield Road, Eastbourne, E Sussex BN20 7NU.

SUTHERLAND, Dame Joan, OM 1991; AC 1975 DBE 1979 (CBE 1961); soprano; *b* 7 Nov. 1926; *d* of McDonald Sutherland, Sydney, NSW, and Muriel Alston Sutherland; *m* 1954, Richard Bonynge, *qv*; one *s*. *Educ:* St Catherine's, Waverley, Sydney. Début as Dido in Purcell's Dido and Aeneas, Sydney, 1947; subsequently concerts, oratorios and broadcasts throughout Australia. Came to London, 1951; joined Covent Garden, 1952, where she remained resident soprano for 7 years; won international fame with début as Lucia di Lammermoor, Covent Garden, 1959, and by early 1960s had sung throughout the Americas and Europe. Has specialised throughout her career in the popular and lesser-known bel canto operatic repertoire of 18th and 19th centuries, and has made many recordings. Hon. DMus: Sydney, 1984; Oxon, 1992. *Publications:* The Joan Sutherland Album (autobiog., with Richard Bonynge), 1986; A Prima Donna's Progress: the autobiography of Joan Sutherland, 1997; *relevant publications:* Joan Sutherland, by R. Braddon, 1962; Joan Sutherland, by E. Greenfield, 1972; La Stupenda, by B. Adams, 1980; Joan Sutherland, by Norma Major, 1987. *Recreations:* reading, gardening, needlepoint. *Address:* c/o Ingpen & Williams, 26 Wadham Road, SW15 2LR.

SUTHERLAND, John Alexander Muir; Chief Executive, Celtic Films Ltd, since 1986; *b* 5 April 1933; *m* 1970, Mercedes Gonzalez; two *s*. *Educ:* India; Trinity Coll., Glenalmond; Hertford Coll., Oxford (MA). 2nd Lieut, HLI, 1952–53. Economist, Fed. Govt of Nigeria, 1957–58; film production, Spain and Portugal, 1958–62; Head of Presentation and Programme Planning, Border TV, 1963–66; Programme Co-Ordinator: ABC TV, 1966–68; Thames TV, 1968–72; Controller of Programme Sales, Thames TV, 1973–74; Man. Dir, 1975–82, Dep Chm., 1982–86, Thames TV Internat.; Dir of Programmes, Thames TV, 1982–86. Dir, Border TV, 1986–. *Productions include:* The Saint (TV), 1989; The Monk (film), 1990; Red Fox (TV), 1991; Sharpe (TV films), 1992–96; Kiszko (TV film), 1998. *Address:* Celtic Films Ltd, Government Buildings, Bromyard Avenue, W3 7XH. *T:* (020) 8740 6880.

SUTHERLAND, Prof. John Andrew, PhD; FRSL; Lord Northcliffe Professor of Modern English Literature, University College London, since 1992; *b* 9 Oct. 1938; *s* of Jack Sutherland and Elizabeth (*née* Salter); *m* 1967, Guilland Watt; one *s*. *Educ:* Colchester Royal Grammar Sch.; Leicester Univ. (BA 1964; MA 1966); Edinburgh Univ. (PhD 1973). FRSL 1991. Nat. Service, 2nd Lieut, Suffolk Regt, 1958–60. Lectr in English, Univ. of Edinburgh, 1965–72; Lectr, then Reader in English, UCL, 1972–84; Prof. of English, CIT, 1984–92. Hon. DLitt Leicester, 1998. *Publications:* Thackeray at Work, 1974; Victorian Novelists and Publishers, 1976; Fiction and the Fiction Industry, 1978; Bestsellers, 1980; Offensive Literature, 1982; The Longman Companion to Victorian Fiction, 1989; Mrs Humphry Ward, 1992; The Life of Walter Scott: a critical biography, 1995; Victorian Fiction: writers, publishers, readers, 1995; (ed) The Oxford Book of English Love Stories, 1996; Is Heathcliff a Murderer?, 1996; Can Jane Eyre Be Happy?, 1997; Who Betrays Elizabeth Bennet?, 1999. *Recreation:* walking. *Address:* Department of English, University College London, Gower Street, WC1E 6BT. *T:* (020) 7387 7050. *Club:* Athenæum.

SUTHERLAND, John Brewer; (3rd Bt *cr* 1921, but does not use the title); *b* 19 Oct. 1931; *s* of Sir (Benjamin) Ivan Sutherland, 2nd Bt, and Marjorie Constance Daniel (*d* 1980), *yr d* of Frederic William Brewer, OBE; *S* father, 1980; *m* 1st, 1958, Alice Muireall (*d* 1984), *d* of late W. Stamford Henderson, Kelso; three *s* one *d*; 2nd, 1988, Heather, *d* of late David A. Gray, Chester-le-Street. *Educ:* Sedbergh; St Catharine's Coll., Cambridge. *Heir: s* Peter William Sutherland [*b* 18 May 1963; *m* 1988, Suzanna Mary, *d* of R. M. Gledson; one *s* two *d*].

SUTHERLAND, John Menzies, Eur Ing, CEng, FICE, FIStructE; Secretary, Joint Board of Moderators, Institution of Civil Engineers, 1985–93; *b* 19 June 1928; *s* of John Menzies and Margaret Rae Sutherland; *m* 1962, Margaret Mary (*née* Collins); one *s* one *d*. *Educ:* Royal Technical Coll., Glasgow. FIStructE 1962; CEng, FICE 1968; Eur Ing 1988. Indentured Civil Engineer, City Engineer, Glasgow, 1945–51; Engineer, Costains Group, 1952–56; Site Agent, Pakistan and Chief Engineer, Middle East, Gammon Group, 1956–61; Engineer Adviser (Colombo Plan), new capital city, Islamabad, Pakistan, 1962–66; Associate Partner, Bullen & Partners, 1966–69; Chief Civil Engineer, overseas plant construction, Union International Co. (Vestey Gp Holding Co.), 1970–74; Board Dir and Dir Engineering Projects, Internat. Military Services Ltd, 1974–83 (2 years Malaysia); Gen. Manager, BTR-Swire Projects, Singapore, 1983–85. *Publication:* Naval Bases and Infrastructure, 1979. *Recreations:* music, collecting Victorian ceramics. *Address:* 13 Ravenshill, Chislehurst, Kent BR7 5PD. *T:* (020) 8467 0037. *Clubs:* Royal Over-Seas League; Chislehurst Golf.

SUTHERLAND, Dr Kathryn; Reader in Bibliography and Textual Criticism, University of Oxford, since 1996; Professorial Fellow, St Anne's College, Oxford, since 1996; *b* 7 July 1950; *d* of Ian Donald Sutherland and Joyce Sutherland (*née* Bartaby). *Educ:* Bedford Coll., Univ. of London (BA 1971); Somerville Coll., Oxford (DPhil 1978; MA 1996). Lectr in English Literature, Univ. of Manchester, 1975–93; Prof. of Modern English Literature, Univ. of Nottingham, 1993–96. *Publications:* Adam Smith: interdisciplinary essays, 1995; Electronic Text: method and theory, 1997; Women Prose Writers 1780–1830, 1998; critical edns; contrib. books and learned jls. *Recreation:* gardening. *Address:* St Anne's College, Oxford OX2 6HS. *T:* (01865) 274893.

SUTHERLAND, Muir; *see* Sutherland, J. A. M.

SUTHERLAND, Peter Denis, SC; Partner and Chairman, Goldman Sachs International, since 1995; non-executive Chairman, BP (formerly BP Amoco), since 1998 (Deputy Chairman, 1995–97, Chairman, 1997–98, The British Petroleum Co. plc); *b* 25 April 1946; *s* of W. G. Sutherland and Barbara Sutherland (*née* Nealon); *m* 1971, Maria Del Pilar Cabria Valcarcel; two *s* one *d*. *Educ:* Gonzaga Coll.; University Coll. Dublin (BCL). Called to Bar: King's Inns, 1968; Middle Temple, 1976; Attorney of New York Bar, 1981; Attorney and Counsellor of Supreme Court of USA, 1986. Tutor in Law, University Coll., Dublin, 1968–71; practising member of Irish Bar, 1968–81, and 1981–82; Senior Counsel 1980; Attorney General of Ireland, June 1981–Feb. 1982 and Dec. 1982–Dec. 1984; Mem. Council of State, 1981–82 and 1982–84; Comr for Competition and Comr for Social Affairs and Educn, EEC, 1985–86, for Competition and Relns with European Parliament, 1986–88; Chm., Allied Irish Banks, 1989–93; Dir Gen., GATT, later WTO, 1993–95. Director: GPA, 1989–93; CRH plc, 1989–93; James Crean plc, 1989–93; Delta Air Lines Inc., 1990–93; Investor, 1995–; Telefonaktiebolaget LM Ericsson, 1996–; ABB Ltd, 1999–; Royal Bank of Scotland, 2001–. Chm. (Europe), Trilateral Commn. Chm., Bd of Govs, Eur. Inst. of Public Admin, 1991–. Hon. LLD: St Louis, 1985; NUI, 1990; Dublin City, 1992; Holy Cross, Mass, 1994; Bath, 1995; Suffolk, USA, 1995; TCD, 1996; Reading, 1997; Nottingham, 1999; Exeter, 2000; DUniv Open, 1995. Gold Medal, Eur. Parlt, 1988; NZ Commemorative Medal, 1990. Grand Cross: King Leopold II (Belgium), 1989; Order of Infante Dom Henrique (Portugal), 1998; Grand Cross of Civil Merit (Spain), 1989; Chevalier, Légion d'Honneur (France), 1993; Comdr, Order of Ouissam Alaouite (Morocco), 1994; Order of Rio Branco (Brazil), 1996. *Publications:* Premier Janvier 1993 ce qui va changer en Europe, 1988; contribs to law jls. *Recreations:* sports generally, reading. *Address:* Goldman Sachs International, Peterborough Court, 133 Fleet Street, EC4A 2BB. *Clubs:* Hibernian United Service, Fitzwilliam Lawn Tennis (Dublin); Lansdowne FC.

SUTHERLAND, Ranald Iain; *see* Sutherland, Rt Hon. Lord.

SUTHERLAND, Prof. Rosamund Jane, PhD; Professor of Education, University of Bristol, since 1996; *b* 19 Jan. 1947; *d* of Percy and Joan Hatfield; *m* 1968, Ian Sutherland; one *s* one *d*. *Educ:* Monmouth Sch. for Girls; Univ. of Bristol (BSc); Hatfield Poly. (Cert Ed); Inst. of Educn, Univ. of London (PhD 1988). Programmer/Analyst, BAC, 1968–69; Res. Asst, Dept of Physiology, Univ. of Bristol, 1969–71; Tutor, Open Univ., 1975–83; Lectr, De Havilland Further Educn Coll., 1979–83; Lectr and Dir of Res. Projects, 1983–93, Sen. Lectr, 1993–96, Inst. of Educn, Univ. of London. Chm., Jt Mathematical Council and Royal Soc. Wkg Gp on Changes to Sch. Algebra, 1997 (report pubd 1997). Mem., Canynge Square Reading Circle. *Publications:* (with C. Hoyles) Logo Mathematics in the Classroom, 1989; (with L. Healy) Exploring Mathematics with Spreadsheets, 1990; (ed with J. Mason) Exploiting Mental Imagery with Computers in Mathematics Education, 1995; (with S. Pozzi) The Changing Mathematical Background of Undergraduate Engineers, 1995; (jtly) A Spreadsheet Approach to Maths for GNVQ Engineering, 1996. *Recreations:* reading, cycling, dining out, relaxing with family. *Address:* 8 Canynge Square, Clifton, Bristol BS8 3LA.

SUTHERLAND, Dame Veronica (Evelyn), DBE 1998; CMG 1988; HM Diplomatic Service, retired; President, Lucy Cavendish College, Cambridge University, since 2001; *b* 25 April 1939; *d* of late Lt-Col Maurice George Beckett, KOYLI, and of Constance Mary Cavenagh-Mainwaring; *m* 1981, Alex James Sutherland. *Educ:* Royal Sch., Bath; London Univ. (BA); Southampton Univ. (MA). Joined HM Diplomatic Service, 1965; Second, later First Sec., Copenhagen, 1967–70; FCO, 1970–75; First Sec., New Delhi, 1975–78; FCO, 1978–80; Counsellor, 1981; Perm. UK Deleg. to UNESCO, 1981–84; Counsellor, FCO, 1984–87; Ambassador to Côte d'Ivoire, 1987–90; Asst Under-Sec. of State (Personnel), FCO, 1990–95; Ambassador to Republic of Ireland, 1995–99; Dep. Sec. Gen. (Econ. and Social Affairs), Commonwealth Secretariat, 1999–2001. Chm., Airey Neave Trust, 2000–. *Recreations:* theatre, painting. *Address:* Lucy Cavendish College, Lady Margaret Road, Cambridge CB3 0BU.

SUTHERLAND, Sir William (George MacKenzie), Kt 1988; QPM 1981; HM Chief Inspector of Constabulary for Scotland, 1996–98; *b* 12 Nov. 1933; *m* 1957, Jennie Abbott; two *d*. *Educ:* Inverness Technical High Sch. Cheshire Police, 1954–73; Surrey Police, 1973–75; Hertfordshire Police, 1975–79; Chief Constable: Bedfordshire, 1979–83; Lothian and Borders Police, 1983–96. Hon. Sec., ACPO in Scotland, 1985–96; Chm., British Police Athletic Assoc., 1991–96 (Chm., Squash Section, 1984–96; Chm., Ski Section, 1992–96). FRSA 1992. *Recreations:* golf, ski-ing, hill walking.

SUTHERS, Martin William, OBE 1988; DL; Senior Partner, 1999–2000, Consultant, since 2000, Hopkins, Solicitors; *b* 27 June 1940; *s* of Rev. Canon George Suthers and Susie Mary Suthers (*née* Jobson); *m* 1st, 1970, Daphne Joan Oxland (marr. diss. 1988); 2nd, 1990, Philippa Leah Melville la Borde. *Educ:* Dulwich Coll.; Christ's Coll., Cambridge (MA). Admitted Solicitor, 1965. Asst Solicitor, Wells, Hind, 1965–66; Conveyancing Asst, Clerk's Dept, Notts CC, 1966–69; Asst Solicitor, Fishers, 1969–70; Partner, 1971–92, Sen. Partner, 1992–2000, J. A. Simpson & Coulby, then Hopkins (following merger). Pres., Notts Law Soc., 1998–99. Chm., Queen's Med. Centre Nottingham Univ. Hosp. NHS Trust, 1993–2000. Mem. (C), Nottingham CC, 1967–69, 1976–95, 2000–; Lord Mayor of Nottingham, 1988–89; Hon. Alderman, 1997. DL Notts 1999. *Recreation:* ornithology. *Address:* The Manor House, Main Street, Flintham, Newark, Notts NG23 5LA. *T:* (01636) 525554.

SUTHIWART-NARUEPUT, Dr Owart, Kt Grand Cordon: Order of Crown of Thailand, 1981; Order of White Elephant, 1985; Hon. CMG 1972; Lecturer, Thammasat University, since 1987; *b* 19 Sept. 1926; *s* of Luang Suthiwart-Narueput and Mrs Khae; *m* 1959, Angkana (*née* Sthapitanond); one *s* one *d*. *Educ:* Thammasat Univ., Thailand (BA Law); Fletcher Sch. of Law and Diplomacy, Tufts Univ., USA (MA, PhD); Nat. Defence Coll. Joined Min. of For. Affairs, 1945; Asst Sec. to Minister, 1958; SEATO Res. Officer, 1959; Protocol Dept, 1963; Econ. Dept, 1964; Counsellor, Thai Embassy, Canberra, 1965; Dir-Gen. of Inf. Dept, 1969; Ambassador to India, Nepal, Sri Lanka, and Minister to Afghanistan, 1972; Ambassador to Poland, E Germany and Bulgaria, 1976; Dir-Gen. of Political Dept, 1977; Under-Sec. of State (Permanent Sec.) for For. Affairs, 1979; Ambassador to France and Perm. Representative to UNESCO, 1980; Ambassador: to Switzerland and to Holy See, 1983; to UK, 1984–86, concurrently to Ireland, 1985–86. Mem., Civil Service Bd, Min. of Foreign Affairs, 1994–. Commander: Order of Phoenix, Greece, 1963; Order of Orange-Nassau, Netherlands, 1963; Bintang Djasa (1st Cl.), Indonesia, 1970; Order of Merit, Poland, 1979; Grand Officier, L'Ordre Nat. du Mérite, France, 1983. *Publication:* The Evolution of Thailand's Foreign Relations since 1855: from extraterritoriality to equality, 1955. *Recreations:* reading, music. *Address:* 193 Lane 4 Navathanee, Serithai Road, Kannayao, Bangkok 10230, Thailand. *Clubs:* Old England Students' Assoc., Amer. Univs Alumni Assoc. (Bangkok).

SUTLIEFF, Barry John; Fellow, Centre for Management and Policy Studies, Cabinet Office, since 2000; *b* 26 Dec. 1942; *s* of Basil Eric and Ruby Ellen Sutlieff; *m* 1967, Linda Valerie Hook; one *s* one *d*. *Educ:* Brooklands Coll., Weybridge; Coll. for Distributive Trades, London (CAM Dip. PR). Trainee advertising exec., 1961–66; gen. publicity roles, Depts of Trade, Transport and the Envmt, and Price Commn, 1966–75; Chief Press Officer: DoE, 1975–79; Dept of Trade, 1979–83; Dep. Hd of Inf., Home Office,

Feb.–July 1985; Dir, Inf. Services, MSC, 1985–87; Director: of Inf., Dept of Employment, 1987–94; of Communication, Cabinet Office, 1994–2000. *Recreations:* travel, reading modern history, lifelong Dickens fanatic, sport, notably football and cricket. *Address:* The Hollies, 26 Hutton Road, Ash Vale, Aldershot, Hants GU12 5HA. *T:* (01252) 654727.

SUTTIE, Sir James (Edward) Grant-, 9th Bt *cr* 1702, of Balgone, Haddingtonshire; farmer; *b* 29 May 1965; *o s* of Sir Philip Grant-Suttie, 8th Bt and of Elspeth Mary Grant-Suttie (*née* Urquhart); *S* father, 1997; *m* 1st, 1989, Emma Jane Craig (marr. diss. 1996); one *s*; 2nd, 1997, Sarah Jane Smale; two *s*. *Educ:* Fettes Coll., Edinburgh; Aberdeen Coll. of Agric. *Recreations:* golf, shooting. *Heir: s* Gregor Grant-Suttie, *b* 29 Oct. 1991.

SUTTON, Alan John; Founder Chairman and Chief Executive, Anglolink Ltd, since 1985; Chief Executive Officer, DigiTec Direct Ltd, since 1998; *b* 16 March 1936; *s* of William Clifford Sutton and Emily Sutton (*née* Batten); *m* 1957, Glenis (*née* Henry); one *s* one *d*. *Educ:* Bristol Univ. BSc (Hons) Elec. Engrg; MIEE. Design, Production and Trials Evaluation of Guided Missiles, English Electric Aviation Ltd, 1957–63; Design, Production, Sales and General Management of Scientific Digital, Analogue and Hybrid Computers, Solartron Electronic Group Ltd, 1963–69; International Sales Manager, Sales Director, of A. B. Electronic Components Ltd, 1969–73; Managing Director, A. B. Connectors, 1973–76; Industrial Dir, Welsh Office, 1976–79; Welsh Development Agency: Exec. Dir (Industry and Investment), 1979–83; Exec. Dir (Marketing), 1983–85; Sen. Vice-Pres., USA W Coast Div., WINvest, 1985–88. Dir, A NOVO UK Ltd, 2001–. *Recreation:* golf. *Address:* 56 Heol-y-Delyn, Lisvane, Cardiff CF14 0SR. *T:* (029) 2075 3194.

SUTTON, Barry Bridge; JP; MA; Headmaster, Taunton School, 1987–97; *b* 21 Jan. 1937; *s* of Albert and Ethel Sutton; *m* 1961, Margaret Helen (*née* Palmer); one *s* two *d*. *Educ:* Eltham Coll.; Peterhouse, Cambridge (MA Hist. Tripos); Bristol Univ. (PGCE). Asst Master and Housemaster, Wycliffe College, 1961–75; Headmaster, Hereford Cathedral School, 1975–87. Chairman: Cttee, Scout Assoc. Council, 1994–96; Som Co. Scout Council, 1994–; Taunton ESU, 1998–. JP Hereford, 1982, Taunton, 1987. *Recreations:* hill-walking, scouting. *Address:* Burt's Barn, Peak Lane, Dundon, Somerton, Somerset TA11 6NZ.

SUTTON, Colin Bertie John, QPM 1985; policing consultant, UK and overseas; Director, Police Scientific Development Branch, Home Office, 1991–93; *b* 6 Dec. 1938; *s* of Bertie Sidney Russell Sutton and Phyllis May; *m* 1960, Anne Margaret Davis. *Educ:* King Edward VI Grammar School, Stratford-upon-Avon; University College London (LLB 1970). Police Constable, 1957, Sergeant, 1964, Inspector, 1966, Warwicks County Police; Chief Inspector, 1970, Supt, 1972, Chief Supt, 1974, Warwicks and Coventry Constabulary; Chief Supt, W Midlands Police, 1974–77; Asst Chief Constable, Leics Constabulary, 1977; Metropolitan Police: Dep. Asst Comr, 1983–84; Asst Comr, 1984–88; Dir, Police Requirements Support Unit, Home Office, 1988–91. Columnist, Police Guardian. Freeman, City of London, 1988; Liveryman, Fletchers' Co., 1989. SBStJ 1990. *Recreations:* golf, angling, squash, music, art, literature.

SUTTON, Sir Frederick (Walter), Kt 1974; OBE 1971; Founder and Chairman of Directors of the Sutton Group of Companies; *b* 1 Feb. 1915; *s* of late William W. Sutton and Daisy Sutton; *m* 1934; three *s*; *m* 1977, Morna Patricia Smyth. *Educ:* Sydney Technical College. Motor Engineer, founder and Chief Executive of the Sutton group of Companies. *Recreations:* flying, going fishing, boating. *Address:* (office) Level 1, 134 William Street, Potts Point, Sydney, NSW 2011, Australia. *T:* (2) 93571777. *Clubs:* Royal Automobile of Victoria; American (Sydney).

SUTTON, Dr (Howard) Michael, CChem, FRSC; Principal Research Fellow, University of Warwick, since 1999; *b* 12 Nov. 1942; *s* of Albert Sutton and Constance Olive Sutton (*née* Topham); *m* 1967, Diane Cash; one *s* one *d*. *Educ:* Univ. of Edinburgh (BSc 1965; PhD 1968). Res. Fellow, Univ. of Kent at Canterbury, 1968–70; Warren Spring Laboratory: Materials Handling Div., 1970–78; Head, Planning and Marketing, 1978–85; Dep. Dir, 1985–88; Department of Trade and Industry: Head, Shipbuilding and Marine Engineering, 1988–91; Head, Single Market Unit, 1991–93; Head, Mech. Engrg Sponsorship, 1993–94; Dir, Trade and Industry, W Midlands, 1994–98; Hd of Secretariat, W Midlands Regl Develt Agency (in preparation), 1998–99; Advr, Advantage W Midlands - the Develt Agency, 1999–2000. *Publications:* contribs to learned jls. *Recreations:* writing, drama, music, walking. *Address:* 161 Moor Green Lane, Birmingham B13 8NT; *e-mail:* h.m.sutton@warwick.ac.uk.

SUTTON, Prof. John, PhD; FBA 1996; Sir John Hicks Professor of Economics, London School of Economics and Political Science, since 1998 (Professor of Economics, 1988–98); *b* 10 Aug. 1948; *s* of John Sutton and Marie (*née* Hammond); *m* 1974, Jean Drechsler; one *s* two *d*. *Educ:* University Coll., Dublin (BSc Physics 1969); Trinity Coll., Dublin (MSc Econ. 1973); PhD Sheffield 1978. Voluntary service, UNA, Turkey, 1969–70; Mgt Services, Herbert-BSA, Coventry, 1970–72; Lectr, Sheffield Univ., 1973–77; Lectr, 1977–84, Reader, 1984–88, LSE. Visiting Professor: Tokyo Univ., 1981; Univ. of Calif, San Diego, 1986; Marvin Bower Fellow, Harvard Business Sch., 1990–91; Gaston Eyskens Prof., Leuven Univ., 1996–97; Vis. Prof. of Econs, Harvard Univ., 1998. Mem., Adv. Council, Japan External Trade Orgn, Tokyo, 1995–. Fellow, Econometric Soc., 1991. Medal of Franqui Foundn, Belgium, 1992. *Publications:* (jtly) Protection and Industrial Policy in Europe, 1986; Sunk Costs and Market Structure, 1991; Technology and Market Structure: theory and history, 1998; Marshall's Tendencies: what can economists know?, 2000. *Address:* London School of Economics, Houghton Street, WC2A 2AE. *T:* (020) 7955 7716.

SUTTON, Air Marshal Sir John (Matthias Dobson), KCB 1986 (CB 1981); Chairman, Arrow Group of Companies, since 1990; *b* 9 July 1932; *s* of late Harry Rowston Sutton and Gertrude Sutton; *m* 1954 (marr. diss. 1968); one *s* one *d*; *m* 1969, Angela Faith Gray; two *s*. *Educ:* Queen Elizabeth's Grammar Sch., Alford, Lincs. Joined RAF, 1950; pilot trng, commnd, 1951; served on Fighter Sqdns, UK and Germany; Staff Coll., 1963; OC 249 Sqdn, 1964–66; Asst Sec., Chiefs of Staff Cttee, 1966–69; OC 14 Sqdn, 1970–71; Asst Chief of Staff (Policy and Plans), HQ 2 ATAF, 1971–73; Staff, Chief of Def. Staff, 1973–74; RCDS, 1975; Comdt Central Flying Sch., 1976–77; Asst Chief of Air Staff (Policy), 1977–79; Dep. Comdr, RAF Germany, 1980–82; ACDS (Commitments), 1982–84; ACDS (Overseas), 1985; C-in-C, RAF Support Comd, 1986–89; Lt-Gov. and C-in-C, Jersey, 1990–95. Pres., RAFA, May 2002–. Chm., Bd of Governors, UC Northampton (formerly Nene Coll.), 1996–2000. KStJ 1990. *Recreations:* golf, ski-ing. *Address:* Pantiles, Stretton, Rutland LE15 7QZ. *Clubs:* Royal Air Force; Colonels; Luffenham Heath Golf.

SUTTON, John Sydney, CBE 1996; Director, International Business Education Co-operation Charitable Trust, since 1998; General Secretary, Secondary Heads Association, 1988–98; *b* 9 June 1936; *s* of late Sydney and of Mabel Sutton; *m* 1961, Carmen Grandoso Martinez; three *s*. *Educ:* King Edward VI Sch., Southampton; Univ. of Keele (BA Hons, MA). Asst Teacher, Christopher Wren Sch., London, 1958–60; Asst Master, later Head of History, Bemrose Sch., Derby, 1960–68; Head, Social Studies Dept, Sir Wilfrid Martineau Sch., Birmingham, 1968–73; Headmaster: Corby Grammar Sch., 1973; Southwood Sch., Corby, 1973–82; Queen Elizabeth Sch., Corby, 1982–88. Mem. Council, Hansard Soc. for Parly Govt, 1973–2000. Trustee, Teaching Awards Trust, 1998–. *Publications:* American Government, 1974; Understanding Politics in Modern Britain, 1977; (with L. Robbins and T. Brennan) People and Politics in Britain, 1985; (jtly) School Management in Practice, 1985; (as Archimedes) TES Management Guide for Heads and Senior Staff, 1996. *Recreations:* wine appreciation, Geddington Volunteer Fire Brigade. *Address:* 24 Bright Trees Road, Geddington, Kettering, Northants NN14 1BS. *T:* (01536) 742559. *Clubs:* Royal Over-Seas League; Rotary (Kettering Huxloe).

SUTTON, Rt Rev. Keith Norman; *see* Lichfield, Bishop of.

SUTTON, Kenneth David; Director of Resettlement, HM Prison Service, since 1999; *b* 17 May 1958; *s* of David Vivien Sutton and Audrey Sutton; *m* 1982, Ruth Hopkin; two *s* one *d*. *Educ:* Cefn Hengoed Comprehensive Sch., Swansea; University Coll., Oxford (BA 1st Cl. Hons PPE 1979). Home Office, 1979–: Private Sec. to Parly Under Sec. of State, 1983–85; Private Sec. to Permanent Under Sec. of State, 1991–92; Asst Sec., Immigration and Nationality Dept, 1992–95; Principal Private Sec. to Home Secretary, 1995–99. *Recreations:* cycling, holidays in France and Wales. *Address:* HM Prison Service, Cleland House, Page Street, SW1P 4LN. *T:* (020) 7217 6203.

SUTTON, Michael; *see* Sutton, H. M.

SUTTON, Rt Rev. Peter (Eves), CBE 1990; Bishop of Nelson, New Zealand, 1965–90; Senior Anglican Bishop, 1979–90; Acting Primate, New Zealand, 1985–86; *b* Wellington, NZ, 7 June 1923; *m* 1956, Pamela Cherrington, *e d* of R. A. Dalley, Patin House, Kidderminster; one *s* one *d*. *Educ:* Wellesley Coll.; Nelson Coll.; University of New Zealand. BA 1945; MA 1947; LTh 1948. Deacon, 1947; Priest, 1948 (Wellington); Curate of Wanganui, New Zealand, 1947–50; St John the Evangelist, Bethnal Green, 1950–51; Bishops Hatfield, Diocese of St Albans (England), 1951–52; Vicar of St Cuthberts, Berhampore (NZ), 1952–58; Whangarei, Diocese of Auckland, New Zealand, 1958–64; Archdeacon of Waimate, 1962–64; Dean of Dunedin and Vicar of St Paul's Cathedral, Dunedin, 1964–65. Chm., Cawthron Inst., 1977–90, 1991–93. Founding Mem., Nelson Civic Trust; Founder: Protect our Heritage, Nelson; Friends of Nelson City; Life Mem., Founder's Mus., Nelson; Rep., Provincial Mus. Cttee, 1989–; Patrons' Rep., Suter Art Gall. Bd, 1990–93; NZ Co-ordinator, All Religions, Amnesty Internat.; NZ Rep., St Deiniol's Library, Hawarden, 1988–; Trustee, Nelson Civic Heritage Protection, 1995–. Governor, St John's Coll., Auckland, 1965–90. ChStJ 1986; Sub-Prelate, Order of St John, NZ, 1987–. Silver Jubilee Medal, 1977; NZ Commemoration Medal, 1990. *Publication:* Freedom for Convictions, 1971. *Recreation:* golf (Canterbury Univ. Blue). *Address:* 3 Ngatiawa Street, Nelson, New Zealand. *Club:* Nelson Golf (New Zealand).

SUTTON, Dr Peter Morgan; Director, Public Health Laboratory Service Centre for Applied Microbiology and Research, Porton Down, 1979–92; *b* 21 June 1932; *s* of Sir Graham Sutton, CBE, FRS and late Lady Sutton (*née* Doris Morgan); *m* 1959, Helen Ersy Economides; two *s* two *d*. *Educ:* Bishop Wordsworth Sch., Salisbury; Wrekin Coll., Wellington; University Coll. (Fellow, 1985) and University Coll. Hosp. Med. Sch., London. House Surgeon and House Physician, UCH, 1956–57; Graham Scholar in Pathology, Univ. of London, 1958–59; on academic staff of UCH Med. Sch., 1960–65; Vis. Asst Prof. of Pathology, Univ. of Pittsburg, USA, 1966–67; Hon. Consultant Pathologist, UCH, 1967–79; Reader in Pathology, Univ. of London, 1971–79; Vice-Dean, UCH Med. Sch., 1973–78. Vis. Prof., Dept of Biochemical Pathology, UCL, 1983–. Sometime Examr in Pathology, Univ. of London and RCS. *Publications:* The Nature of Cancer, 1962; various papers on fibrinolytic enzymes and novel antiviral compounds. *Recreations:* English literature, history of science. *Address:* Manderley, 34 Bower Gardens, Salisbury, Wilts SP1 2RL. *T:* (01722) 323902.

SUTTON, Philip John, RA 1989 (ARA 1977); *b* 20 Oct. 1928; *m* 1954; one *s* three *d*. *Educ:* Slade Sch. of Fine Art, UCL. One-man exhibitions: Roland Browse and Delbanco (now Browse and Darby) Gallery, London, 1958–81; Leeds City Art Gallery, 1960; Newcastle-on-Tyne, 1962; Bradford, 1962; Edinburgh, 1962; Sydney, 1963, 1966, 1970, 1973; Perth, 1963, 1972; Royal Acad. (Diploma Gall.), London, 1977; David Jones Gall., Sydney, 1980; Bonython Art Gall., Adelaide, 1981; Norwich, Bath and New York, 1983; Lichfield Fest., 1985; Beaux Arts Gall., Bath, 1985; Galerie Joël Salaün, Paris, 1988; exhibn of ceramics, Oditte Gilbert Gall., London, 1987; Agnews, London, 1992; touring exhibn, Wales, 1993–94; Shakespeare exhibn, RA, Internat. Shakespeare Globe Centre, RSC Stratford, Royal Armouries Mus., Leeds, Berkeley Square Gall., 1997; Piano Nobile, London 2001; Hay-on-Wye Fest., 2001. Designed Post Office 'Greetings' stamps, 1989. *Recreations:* swimming, running. *Address:* 3 Morfa Terrace, Manorbier, Tenby, Pembrokeshire SA70 7TH.

SUTTON, Dr Richard, DSc (Med); FRCP, FACC, FESC, FAHA; Consultant Cardiologist: Royal Brompton and Harefield Trust (formerly Royal Brompton National Heart and Lung Hospital), since 1993; Chelsea and Westminster Hospital (formerly Westminster Hospital), since 1976; *b* 1 Sept. 1940; *s* of late Dick Brasnett Sutton and Greta Mary (*née* Leadbeter); *m* 1964, Anna Gunilla (*née* Cassö) (marr. diss. 1998); one *s*. *Educ:* Gresham's Sch.; King's Coll., London; King's Coll. Hosp. (MB, BS 1964); DSc (Med) London 1988. FRCP 1983 (MRCP 1967); FACC 1975; FESC 1990; FAHA 2001. Gen. medical trng followed graduation; career in cardiology began at St George's Hosp., London, 1967; Fellow in Cardiol., Univ. of NC, 1968–69; Registrar, Sen. Registrar, then Temp. Consultant, National Heart Hosp., London, 1970–76. Consultant Cardiologist, St Stephen's Hosp., 1976–89; Hon. Consultant Cardiologist: Italian Hosp., London, 1977–89; St Luke's Hosp., London, 1980–. Chm., Eur. Wkg Gp on Cardiac Pacing, 1998–2000. Member: British Medical Assoc.; British Cardiac Soc.; British Pacing and Electrophysiology Group (Co-Founder, Past Pres. and Hon. Sec.). Governors' Award, Amer. Coll. of Cardiol., 1979 (Scientific Exhibit, Physiol Cardiac Pacing), and 1982 (1st Prize; Scientific Exhibit, 5 yrs of Physiol Cardiac Pacing). Editor in Chief: European Jl of Cardiac Pacing and Electrophysiology, 1991–97; Europace, 1998–. *Publications:* Foundations of Cardiac Pacing, pt 1, 1991, pt 2, 1999; articles on many aspects of cardiology incl. cardiac pacing, coronary artery disease, left ventricular function, and assessment of pharm. agents, in Circulation, Jl of Amer. Coll. of Cardiol., Amer. Jl of Cardiol., Amer. Heart Jl, Brit. Heart Jl, Heart, Pace, Lancet, BMJ, and Oxford Textbook of Medicine, 1967–. *Recreations:* opera, foreign travel, tennis. *Address:* 149 Harley Street, W1G 6DE. *T:* (020) 7935 4444.

SUTTON, Richard Lewis; Regional Director, Northern Region, Department of Industry, 1974–81; *b* 3 Feb. 1923; *s* of William Richard Sutton and Marina Susan Sutton (*née* Chudleigh); *m* 1944, Jean Muriel (*née* Turner). *Educ:* Ealing County Grammar Sch. Board of Trade, 1939. Served War: HM Forces (Lieut RA), 1942–47. Asst Trade Comr, Port of Spain, 1950–52; BoT, 1953–62; Trade Comr, Kuala Lumpur, 1962–66; Monopolies Commn, 1966; BoT, 1967–68; Dir, British Industrial Develt Office, New York, 1968–71; Regional Dir, West Midland Region, Dept of Trade and Industry,

1971–74. *Recreations:* music, walking, bridge. *Address:* Barton Toft, Dowlish Wake, Ilminster, Somerset TA19 0QG. *T:* (01460) 57127.

SUTTON, Sir Richard (Lexington), 9th Bt *cr* 1772; farmer; *b* 27 April 1937; *s* of Sir Robert Lexington Sutton, 8th Bt, and of Gwynneth Gwladys, *o d* of Major Arnold Charles Gover, MC; *S* father, 1981; *m* 1959, Fiamma, *o d* of G. M. Ferrari, Rome; one *s* one *d*. *Educ:* Stowe. *Recreations:* ski-ing, sailing, swimming, tennis. *Heir: s* David Robert Sutton [*b* 26 Feb. 1960; *m* 1992, Annette, *o d* of B. David; one *d*]. *Address:* Moorhill, Langham, Gillingham, Dorset SP8 5NY. *T:* (01747) 862665.

SUTTON, Richard Patrick; QC 1993; a Recorder, since 1994 (Assistant Recorder, 1991–94); *b* 13 Nov. 1944; *s* of Jack Doherty Sutton and Beryl Clarisse Scholes Sutton (*née* Folkard); *m* 1978, Jean Folley; one *s* one *d*. *Educ:* Culford Sch.; Wadham Coll., Oxford (BA Hons Jurisprudence). Called to the Bar, Middle Temple, 1969. *Recreations:* playing guitar, meeting people.

SUTTON, Shaun Alfred Graham, OBE 1979; television producer and writer; script consultant, Richard Price Television Associates; Head of Drama Group, BBC Television, 1969–81; *b* 14 Oct. 1919; *s* of Eric Graham Sutton and Beryl Astley-Marsden; *m* 1948, Barbara Leslie; one *s* three *d*. *Educ:* Latymer Upper Sch.; Embassy Sch. of Acting, London. Actor and Stage Manager, Q, Embassy, Aldwych, Adelphi, Arts, Criterion Theatres, 1938–40. Royal Navy, 1940–46, Lieut RNVR. Stage Dir, Embassy and provincial theatres, 1946–48; Producer, Embassy, Buxton, Croydon Theatres, 1948–50; toured S Africa as Producer, 1950; Producer, Embassy, Ipswich, Buxton, 1951–52; entered BBC TV Service, 1952; produced and wrote many children's TV plays and serials; directed many series incl. Z Cars, Softly Softly, Sherlock Holmes, Kipling, etc; Head of BBC Drama Serials Dept, 1966–69; dramatised Rogue Herries and Judith Paris for BBC Radio, 1971; Producer: BBC TV Shakespeare series, 1982–84; Theatre Night series, BBC 2, including Season's Greetings, Make and Break, The Devil's Disciple, What the Butler Saw, Absent Friends, The Master Builder, Strife, The Miser, The Rivals, Journey's End, When We are Married, Once in a Lifetime, Benefactors, The Contractor, The Winslow Boy, Relatively Speaking, Merlin, Re-Joyce, The Spirit of R101, Spy in the Cab. Fellow, Royal TV Soc.; Mem., BAFTA. *Publications:* A Christmas Carol (stage adaptation), 1949; Queen's Champion (children's novel), 1961; The Largest Theatre in the World, 1982. *Recreations:* gardening, walking. *Address:* The Cottage, Brewery Road, Trunch, Norfolk NR28 0PX.

SUVA, Archbishop of, (RC), since 1976; **Most Rev. Petero Mataca;** *b* 28 April 1933; *s* of Gaberiele Daunivucu and Akeneta Taina. *Educ:* Holy Name Seminary, Dunedin, NZ; Propaganda Fidei, Rome. Priest, Rome, 1959; Vicar-Gen. of Archdiocese of Suva, 1966; Rector of Pacific Regional Seminary, 1973; Auxiliary Bishop of Suva, 1974. Pres., Episcopal Conf. of South Pacific, 1981. *Address:* Archbishop's House, Box 393, Suva, Fiji. *T:* 301955.

SUYIN; *see* Han Suyin.

SUZMAN, Mrs Helen, OM (Gold) South Africa, 1997; Hon. DBE 1989; Member, South African Human Rights Commission, 1996–98; *b* 7 Nov. 1917; *d* of late Samuel Gavronsky; *m* 1937, Dr M. M. Suzman, FRCP (*d* 1994); two *d*. *Educ:* Parktown Convent, Johannesburg; Univ. of Witwatersrand (BCom). Lectr in Economic History, Univ. of Witwatersrand, 1944–52. Elected MP for Houghton, RSA, 1953 (United Party, 1953–61; Progressive Party (later Progressive Reform Party and Progressive Federal Party), 1961–89); Inaugural Mem. Progressive Party, 1959; sole rep. of Progressive Party in Parlt, 1961–74; returned unopposed as Progressive Federal party MP, 1977. Mem., Ind. Electoral Commn, 1994. Pres., SA Inst. of Race Relns, 1991–93. Hon. Fellow: St Hugh's Coll., Oxford, 1973; London Sch. of Economics, 1975; New Hall, Cambridge, 1990. Hon. DCL Oxford, 1973; Hon. LLD: Harvard, Witwatersrand, 1976; Columbia, Smith Coll., 1977; Brandeis, 1981; Cape Town, Jewish Theological Seminary, NY, 1986; Ohio, Western Ontario, 1989; Rhodes, S Africa, Cambridge, Glasgow, Nottingham, Warwick, Ulster, 1990; Indiana, Rutgers, 1992; Toronto, 1993; De Montfort, 1994; Wales, 1996; Hon. DHL: Denison, 1982; New Sch. for Social Res., NY, Sacred Heart Univ., USA, 1984; DUniv Brunel, 1991; Hon. Dr Yale, 1999. UN Human Rights Award, 1978; Roger E. Joseph Award, Hebrew Union Coll., NY, 1986; Moses Mendelssohn Prize, Berlin Senate, 1988; B'Nai B'Rith Dor L'Dor Award, 1992; Notre Dame Univ., Indiana, Award, 1995. Freedom of Sandton, 1989. *Publication:* In No Uncertain Terms (autobiog.), 1993. *Recreations:* swimming, fishing, bridge. *Address:* 52 2nd Avenue, Illovo, Sandton, Transvaal 2196, South Africa. *T:* and *Fax:* (11) 7882833. *Clubs:* Lansdowne; Inanda, Wanderers (Johannesburg).
See also Prof. J. L. Jowell.

SUZMAN, Janet; actress and director; *b* 9 Feb. 1939; *d* of Saul Suzman; *m* 1969, Trevor Nunn, *qv* (marr. diss. 1986); one *s*. *Educ:* Kingsmead Coll., Johannesburg; Univ. of the Witwatersrand (BA); London Acad. of Music and Dramatic Art. Hon. Associate Artist, RSC, 1980. Vis. Prof of Drama Studies, Westfield Coll., London, 1983–84. Lectures: Spencer, Harvard Univ., 1988; Tanner, Brasenose Coll., Oxford, 1995; Sixth World Shakespeare Congress, LA, 1996; Judith Wilson, Trinity Coll., Cambridge, 1996; Drapers', QMW, 1997; Morrell Meml Address on Toleration, Univ. of York, 1999. Vice-Chm., LAMDA Council, 1992– (Mem., 1978–). Rôles played for *Royal Shakespeare Co.* incl.: Joan La Pucelle in The Wars of the Roses, 1963–64; Lulu in The Birthday Party, Rosaline, Portia, 1965; Ophelia, 1965–66; Katharina, Celia, and Berinthia in The Relapse, 1967; Beatrice, Rosalind, 1968–69; Cleopatra and Lavinia, 1972–73; Clytemnestra and Helen of Troy in The Greeks, 1980; *other rôles* incl.: Kate Hardcastle, and Carmen in The Balcony, Oxford Playhouse, 1966; Hester in Hello and Goodbye, King's Head Theatre, 1973; Masha in Three Sisters, Cambridge, 1976; Good Woman of Setzuan, Newcastle, 1976, Royal Court, 1977; Hedda Gabler, Duke of York's, 1977; Boo-hoo, Open Space, 1978; The Duchess of Malfi, Birmingham, 1979; Cowardice, Ambassadors, 1983; Boesman and Lena, Hampstead, 1984; Vassa, Greenwich, 1985; Andromache, Old Vic, 1988; Another Time, Wyndham's, 1989; Hippolytus, Almeida, 1991; The Sisters Rosenweig, Greenwich, 1994, Old Vic, 1994–95; The Retreat from Moscow, Chichester, 1999; Cherished Disappointments in Love, Soho, 2001; *director:* Othello, Market Theatre, Johannesburg, 1987 (Best Prodn, Vita Awards, 1988); A Dream of People, The Pit, 1990; The Cruel Grasp, Edinburgh Fest., 1991; No Flies on Mr Hunter, Chelsea Centre, 1992; Death of a Salesman, 1993 (Liverpool Echo and Daily Post Arts Awards, Best Production, 1994), The Deep Blue Sea, 1996, Theatr Clywd; The Good Woman of Sharkville, Market Theatre, Johannesburg, 1996, UK tour, 1998; The Free State, Birmingham, 1997, UK tour, 2000 (Barclays Theatrical Managers' Assoc. Award, Best Dir, 1997); The Snow Palace, tour and Tricycle Theatre, 1998, Warsaw Fest., 1999; The Guardsman, Albery, 2000. *Films:* A Day in the Death of Joe Egg, 1970; Nicholas and Alexandra, 1971; The Priest of Love, 1980; The Draughtsman's Contract, 1981; E la Nave Va, 1983; A Dry White Season, 1990; Nuns on the Run, 1990; Leon the Pig Farmer, 1993; *television:* plays for BBC and ITV incl.: St Joan, 1968; Three Sisters, 1969; Macbeth, 1970; Hedda Gabler, 1972; Twelfth Night, 1973; Antony and Cleopatra, 1974; Miss Nightingale, 1974; Clayhanger, serial, 1975–76; Mountbatten—The Last Viceroy, 1986; The Singing Detective, 1986, The Miser, 1987; dir., Othello, 1988; Cripples, 1989; The Amazon, 1989; master class on Shakespearean comedy, BBC, 1990. Acad. Award Nomination, Best Actress, 1971; Evening Standard Drama Awards, Best Actress, 1973, 1976; Plays and Players Award, Best Actress, 1976. Hon. MA Open, 1984; Hon. DLitt: Warwick, 1990; Leicester, 1992; London, 1997. *Publications:* Acting with Shakespeare, 1996; The Free State, 2000; (commentary) Antony and Cleopatra, 2001. *Address:* c/o Steve Kenis & Co., Royalty House, 72–74 Dean Street, W1D 3SG. *T:* (020) 7534 6001.

SVENSON, Dame Beryl; *see* Grey, Dame Beryl.

SVETLANOV, Yevgeny Fyodorovich; Principal Conductor, Russia (formerly USSR) State Symphony Orchestra, since 1965; Chief Conductor, Residentie Orkest, The Hague, since 1992; composer; *b* 6 Sept. 1928. *Educ:* Moscow Conservatoire. Conductor, 1955–63, Chief Conductor, 1963–65, Bolshoi Theatre. Prin. Guest Conductor, LSO, 1979–. *Compositions* include: Concerto, 1951; Siberian Fantasy, 1953; Rhapsody, 1954; Symphony, 1957; sonatas, sonatinas. *Address:* Apt 41, Stanislavsky Str. 14, 103009 Moscow, Russia; Residentie Orkest, Spuiplein 150, 2511 DG Den Haag, Netherlands.

SVOBODA, Prof. Josef, RDI 1989; stage designer, since 1947, head designer, since 1951, National Theatre, Prague; Professor at Academy of Applied Arts, since 1968; *b* Čáslav, 10 May 1920; *m* 1948, Libuše Svobodová; one *d*. *Educ:* Sch. of Fine and Applied Arts, Prague. EXPO 58, Brussels: success with Laterna Magica; EXPO 67, Montreal: polyvision, polydiaekran. Artistic Dir, Laterna Magika, indep. theatre (formerly experimental studio, Nat. Theatre, Prague), 1973–. Stage designs for numerous theatres including: Metropolitan Opera, New York; Covent Garden; Geneva; Bayreuth; Frankfurt; Hamburg; Stuttgart; Berlin; Zurich; Vienna; Barcelona; Milan; Montreal; Banff. Hon. RA 1969. Hon. DFA: Denison, Ohio, 1978; Western Michigan, 1984. Internat. Theatre Award, Amer. Theater Assoc., 1976; Internat. Prize for scenery and costumes, Teatro de l'Europa, 1984. Laureate of State Prize, 1954; Merited Artist of CSSR, 1966; National Artist of CSSR, 1968; Chevalier, Ordre des Arts et des Lettres (France), 1976; Légion d'honneur (France), 1993. *Publications:* relevant monographs: Josef Svoboda (by Theatre Inst.) 1967 (Prague); Josef Svoboda (by Denis Bablet) 1970 (France); The Scenography of J. Svoboda (by Jarka Burian) 1971, 1974 (USA); Teatr Josefa Svobody (by V. Berjozkin) 1973 (USSR); Josef Svoboda: the secret of the theatrical space, Czech edn 1992, Italian edn 1997. *Recreations:* theatre, photography, creative arts, music, literature. *Address:* Filmařská 535/17, 15200 Prague 5, Czech Republic; Laterna Magika, Liliová 9, 11000 Prague 1, Czech Republic.

SWABY, Peter; County Treasurer, Derbyshire County Council, since 1991; *b* 8 Oct. 1947; *s* of late Arthur Swaby and of Mona Swaby; *m* 1974, Yvette Shann; one *s* one *d*. *Educ:* Longcroft Sch., Beverley. CPFA (CIPFA 1973). E Riding CC, 1967; Humberside CC, 1974, Chief Internal Auditor, 1983; Asst County Treasurer, S Glam CC, 1985. *Recreation:* classical guitarist (ALCM, ALCM(TD)). *Address:* Derbyshire County Council, County Hall, Matlock, Derbys DE4 3AG.

SWADE, Doron David; Assistant Director and Head of Collections, Science Museum, since 1999; *b* 14 Oct. 1946; *s* of Max Jack Swade and Ruth Leah Swade (*née* Rosenberg). *Educ:* Univ. of Cape Town (BSc Hons 1969; MSc 1971). CEng 1994; FBCS 2001. Consultant electronics design engr, UK and USA, 1975–82; Science Museum: Electronics Design Engr, 1982–83; Section Head, audiovisual, electronics and computer-based displays, 1983–85; Sen. Curator, Computing and IT, 1985–99. Consultant to computer industry, 1972–96. *Publications:* Charles Babbage and his Calculating Engines, 1991; (jtly) The Dream Machine: exploring the computer age, 1991; The Cogwheel Brain: Charles Babbage and the quest to build the first computer, 2000; popular and scholarly articles. *Recreations:* writing, restoring woodworking machinery, making things. *Address:* Science Museum, Exhibition Road, South Kensington, SW7 2DD. *T:* (020) 7942 4100.

SWAFFIELD, Sir James (Chesebrough), Kt 1976; CBE 1971; RD 1967; Chairman, British Rail Property Board, 1984–91; solicitor, retired; *b* 16 Feb. 1924; *s* of Frederick and Kate Elizabeth Swaffield, Cheltenham; *m* 1950, Elizabeth Margaret Ellen, 2nd *d* of A. V. and K. E. Maunder, Belfast; two *s* two *d*. *Educ:* Cheltenham Grammar Sch.; Haberdashers' Aske's Hampstead Sch.; London Univ. (LLB); MA Oxon 1974. RNVR, 1942–46. Articled Town Clerk, Lincoln, 1946–49; Asst Solicitor: Norwich Corp., 1949–52; Cheltenham Corp., 1952–53; Southend-on-Sea Corp., 1953–56; Dep. Town Clerk, subseq. Town Clerk and Clerk of Peace, Blackpool, 1956–62; Sec., Assoc. of Municipal Corps, 1962–73; Dir-Gen. and Clerk to GLC, Clerk to ILEA and Clerk of Lieutenancy for Greater London, 1973–84. Chairman: St Paul's Cathedral Ct of Advrs, 1982–99; London Marathon Charitable Trust; Jubilee Walkway Trust; Vice-Pres; Age Concern, London; Patron, Age Resource. Lt Comdr RNR retd. DL Greater London, 1978–99. OStJ. Dist. Service Award (Internat. City Management Assoc.), 1984. *Address:* 10 Kelsey Way, Beckenham, Kent BR3 3LL. *Clubs:* Reform, Naval.

SWAIN, Henry Thornhill, CBE 1971; RIBA; County Architect, Nottinghamshire County Council, 1964–88, retired; *b* 14 Feb. 1924; *s* of Thornhill Madge Swain and Bessie Marion Swain; *m*; three *d*. *Educ:* Bryanston Sch.; Architectural Assoc. (Hons Dipl.). Served with RN, 1943–46. Herts County Architect's Dept, 1949; worked in primary school group; Notts CC, 1955; Group Leader i/c initial develt of CLASP construction; Dep. County Architect, 1958. *Publications:* many articles in architectural jls. *Recreation:* sailing. *Address:* 50 Loughborough Road, West Bridgford, Nottingham NG2 7JJ. *T:* (0115) 981 8059.

SWAINE, Sir John (Joseph), Kt 1995; CBE 1987 (OBE 1980); QC (Hong Kong) 1975; JP; President, Legislative Council, Hong Kong, 1993–95; *b* 22 April 1932; *s* of Henry Edward Swaine, MBE and Gladys Elizabeth Luke Swaine; *m* 1959, Fatima Gwendoline Jorge Cotton; four *s* one *d*. *Educ:* Univ. of Hong Kong (BA). Admin. Officer, Hong Kong Govt, 1952–57; called to the Bar, Lincoln's Inn, 1960, Hong Kong, 1960; in practice, 1960–. Non-exec. Dir, Hong Kong & Shanghai Banking Corp. Ltd, 1986–97. JP Hong Kong, 1975. Hon. LLD: Baptist, HK, 1992; City, HK, 1993; Hon. PhD (Hum) Lingnan Coll., HK, 1994; Hon. DLett Open, HK, 1996. *Recreation:* breeding and racing thoroughbred horses. *Address:* 704D Admiralty Centre, Tower 1, 18 Harcourt Road, Hong Kong. *Clubs:* Hong Kong Jockey (Chm., 1993–96), Country (Hong Kong).

SWAINSON, Eric, CBE 1981; Vice-Chairman, Fairey Group, 1987–97; Director, Lloyds TSB Group plc, 1996–97; *b* 5 Dec. 1926; *m* 1953, Betty Heywood; two *d*. *Educ:* Sheffield Univ. (BMet 1st cl. Hons; W. H. A. Robertson medal, 1959). Joined Imperial Chemical Industries Metals Div. (now IMI), 1946; Technical Officer, Res. Dept, 1946–53; Manager, Titanium Melting Plant, 1953–56; Asst Manager, Technical Dept, 1956–59; Gen. Manager and Man. Dir, Lightning Fasteners, 1961–69; Dir, IMI, 1969–86; Asst Man. Dir, 1972–74; Man. Dir, 1974–86; Dep. Chm., Pegler-Hattersley plc, 1986; Lloyds Bank plc: Dir, 1986–95; Vice-Chm., 1992–95. Director: Birmingham Broadcasting, 1973–92; AMEC, 1987–95; Midlands Radio Hldgs, 1988–92; Lloyds Merchant Bank Hldgs, 1989–93; Cheltenham & Gloucester Bldg Soc., 1995–97; Chm., Birmingham and West Midlands Reg. Bd, Lloyds Bank, 1985–91 (Reg. Dir, 1979–91). Chm., W Midlands

Industrial Develt Bd, 1985–90; Member: Review Bd for Govt Contracts, 1978–93; NEDC Cttee on Finance for Industry, 1978–86; Council, CBI, 1975–86; W Midlands Reg. Council, CBI, 1973–83 (Chm. 1976–78); Industrial Develt Adv. Bd, 1982–88. Pro-Chancellor, Aston Univ., 1981–86. FRSA 1985. Hon. DSc Aston, 1986. *Address:* Paddox Hollow, Norton Lindsey, Warwick CV35 8JA.

SWAINSON, Roy; Executive Director, Merseyside Special Investment Fund, since 1998; Practice Director, Morecroft Urquhart (Solicitors), since 1998; *b* 15 April 1947; *s* of William Swainson and Florence Swainson (*née* Moss); *m* 1973, Irene Ann Shearson; one *s* one *d*. *Educ:* Merchant Taylors' Sch., Crosby; Univ. of Manchester (LLB). Southport County Borough Council: Asst Solicitor, 1969–71; Sen. Asst Solicitor, 1971–74; Asst Borough Solicitor and Sec., Sefton MBC, 1974–82; Dep. City Solicitor and Sec., Liverpool CC, 1982–90; Chief Exec. and Dir Gen., Merseytravel, 1990–98. Chm., Mersey Ferries Ltd, 1990–98; Co. Sec., Liverpool Airport PLC, 1990–99; non-exec. Dir, CAA, 1999–. Chm., N Liverpool Partnership, 1996–99; Member: Mersey Partnership Bd, 1996–98; Liverpool City Partnership Bd, 1998–99. Non-exec. Dir, Sefton Community Foundn, 1998–. Trustee, Merseyside Police and High Sheriff's Charitable Trust, 1998–. *Recreations:* reading, theatre, travel. *Address:* (office) 8 Dale Street, Liverpool L2 4TQ. *T:* (0151) 282 0423; (office) 5th Floor, Cunard Building, Pier Head, Liverpool L3 1DS. *T:* (0151) 236 4040.

SWALES, Prof. Martin William, PhD; FBA 1999; Professor of German, University College London, since 1976; *b* 3 Nov. 1940; *s* of Percy Johns Swales and Doris (*née* Davies); *m* 1966, Erika Marta Meier; one *s* one *d*. *Educ:* King Edward's Sch., Birmingham; Christ's Coll., Cambridge (BA 1961); Univ. of Birmingham (PhD 1963). Lectr in German, Univ. of Birmingham, 1964–70; Associate Prof. of German, Univ. of Toronto, 1970–72; Reader in German, KCL, 1972–75; Prof. of German, Univ. of Toronto, 1975–76. Hon. Fellow, UCL, 1996. Verdienstkreuz (Germany), 1994. *Publications:* Arthur Schnitzler, 1971; The German Novelle, 1977; The German Bildungsroman, 1978; Thomas Mann, 1980; Goethe's Werther, 1987; Thomas Mann's Buddenbrooks, 1991; Epochenbuch Realismus, 1997; Reading Goethe, 2001. *Recreations:* music, theatre (incl. amateur dramatics), incompetent house and car maintenance. *Address:* Department of German, University College London, Gower Street, WC1E 6BT. *T:* (020) 7380 7120.

SWALLOW, Dr Deborah Anne; Director of Collections, Victoria and Albert Museum, since 2001; *b* 27 Aug. 1948; *d* of Arnold Birkett Swallow and Denise Vivienne Swallow (*née* Leighton). *Educ:* Perse Sch. for Girls; New Hall, Cambridge (MA); Darwin Coll., Cambridge (PhD). Cambridge University: Asst Curator, Mus. of Archaeology and Anthropology, 1974–83; Lectr, Girton Coll., 1975–80; Fellow, Darwin Coll., 1975–83; Victoria and Albert Museum: Asst Keeper, Indian Dept, 1983–89; Chief Curator, Indian and SE Asian Dept, 1989–2001. *Address:* c/o Victoria and Albert Museum, SW7 2RL. *T:* (020) 7942 2321.

SWALLOW, Comdt Patricia; *see* Nichol, Comdt D. P.

SWALLOW, Sydney; Senior Director, Procurement, Post Office, 1977–81; Chief Procurement Officer, British Telecommunications, 1981–83; *b* 29 June 1919; *s* of William and Charlotte Lucy Swallow; *m* 1950, Monica Williams; one *s*. *Educ:* Woking County Sch.; St Catharine's Coll., Cambridge (Scholar; BA 1st cl. Hons 1940, MA). Mines Dept, Board of Trade, 1940–42. Served War: Royal Engineers (Survey), 1942–46. Nat. Coal Bd, 1946–59; Central Electricity Generating Bd, 1959–65; Associated Electrical Industries Ltd, 1965–68; General Electric Co. Ltd, 1968; Dir of Supplies, GLC, 1968–77. Chm., Educn Cttee, Inst. of Purchasing and Supply, 1967–77; Visiting Prof., Univ. of Bradford Management Centre, 1972–75; Vis. Fellow, ASC, 1976–80. FCIPS. *Publications:* various articles on purchasing and supply in professional jls. *Recreations:* charity work, gardening. *Address:* 101 Muswell Hill Road, N10 3HT. *T:* (020) 8444 8775.

SWAMINATHAN, Dr Monkombu Sambasivan, FRS 1973; Chairman, M. S. Swaminathan Research Foundation, since 1990; Hon. Director, since 1990, and UNESCO Professor in Ecotechnology, since 1996, Centre for Research on Sustainable Agricultural and Rural Development, Madras; *b* 7 Aug. 1925; *m* Mina Swaminathan; three *d*. *Educ:* Univs of Kerala, Madras and Cambridge. BSc Kerala, 1944; BSc (Agric.) Madras, 1947; Assoc. IARI 1949; PhD Cantab, 1952. Responsible for developing Nat. Demonstration Project, 1964, and for evolving Seed Village concept; actively involved in develt of High Yielding Varieties, Dryland Farming and Multiple Cropping Programmes. Vice-Pres., Internat. Congress of Genetics, The Hague, 1963; Gen. Pres., Indian Science Congress, 1976; Mem. (Agriculture), Planning Commn, 1980–82 (formerly Dir-Gen., Indian Council of Agricultural Research); Dir-Gen., Internat. Rice Res. Inst., Manila, 1982–88; Pres., IUCN, 1984–90. First Zakir Hussain Meml Lectr, 1970; UGC Nat. Lectr, 1971; lectures at many internat. scientific symposia. Foreign Associate, US Nat. Acad. of Scis; For. Mem., All Union Acad. of Agricl Scis, USSR; Hon. Mem., Swedish Seed Assoc.; Hon. Fellow, Indian Nat. Acad. of Sciences. FNA; Fellow, Italian Nat. Sci. Acad. Hon. DSc from thirty-three universities. Shanti Swarup Bhatnagar Award for contribs in Biological Scis, 1961; Mendel Centenary Award, Czechoslovak Acad. of Scis, 1965; Birbal Sahni Award, Indian Bot. Soc., 1965; Ramon Magsaysay Award for Community Leadership, 1971; Silver Jubilee Award, 1973, Meghnath Saha Medal, 1981, Indian Nat. Science Acad.; R. B. Bennett Commonwealth Prize, RSA, 1984; Albert Einstein World Science Award, 1986; World Food Prize, 1987; Tyler Prize for Envmtl Achievement, 1991; Honda Prize for Eco-technology, 1991; Jawaharlal Nehru Centenary Award, 1993; Sasakawa Envmt Prize, UN, 1994; Volvo Internat. Envmt Prize, 1999; UNESCO Gandhi Gold Medal, 1999; Franklin D. Roosevelt Four Freedoms Medal, 2000. Padma Shri, 1967; Padma Bhushan, 1972; Padma Vibhushan, 1989. *Publications:* numerous scientific papers. *Address:* 11 Rathna Nagar, Teynampet, Madras 600018, India.

SWAN, Sir Conrad (Marshall John Fisher), KCVO 1994 (CVO 1986 LVO 1978); PhD; Garter Principal King of Arms, 1992–95; Genealogist: Order of the Bath, 1972–95; Grand Priory, OStJ, 1976–95; First Hon. Genealogist, Order of St Michael and St George, 1989–95; *b* 13 May 1924; *yr s* of late Dr Henry Peter Swan, Major RAMC and RCAMC, of BC, Canada and Colchester, Essex, and of Edna Hanson Magdalen (*née* Green), Cross of Honour Pro Ecclesia et Pontifice; *m* 1957, Lady Hilda Susan Mary Northcote (*d* 1995), Dame of Honour and Devotion, SMO Malta, 1979, and of Justice of SMO of Constantine St George, 1975, *yr d* of 3rd Earl of Iddesleigh; one *s* four *d*. *Educ:* St George's Coll., Weybridge; Sch. of Oriental and African Studies, Univ. of London; Univ. of Western Ontario (BA 1949; MA 1951); Peterhouse, Cambridge (PhD 1955). Served Europe and India (Capt. Madras Regt, IA), 1942–47. Assumption Univ. of Windsor, Ont.: Lectr in History, 1955–57; Asst Prof. of Hist., 1957–60; Univ. Beadle, 1957–60. Rouge Dragon Pursuivant of Arms, 1962–68; York Herald of Arms, 1968–92; Registrar and Sen. Herald-in-Waiting, College of Arms, 1982–92. Inspector of Regimental Colours, 1993–95. On Earl Marshal's staff for State Funeral of Sir Winston Churchill, 1965 and Investiture of HRH Prince of Wales, 1969. In attendance: upon HM The Queen at Installation of HRH Prince of Wales as Great Master of Order of the Bath, 1975; during Silver Jubilee Thanksgiving Service, 1977; on Australasian Tour, 1977; at Commonwealth Heads of Govt Conf., 1987; Gentleman Usher-in-Waiting to HH the Pope, GB visit, 1982. Woodward Lectr, Yale, 1964; Centennial Lectr, St Thomas More Coll., Univ. of Saskatchewan, 1967; Inaugural Sir William Scott Meml Lectr, Ulster-Scot Hist. Foundn, 1968; 60th Anniv. Lectr, St Joseph's Coll., Univ. of Alberta, 1987; first Herald to execute duties across Atlantic (Bermuda, 1969) and in S Hemisphere (Brisbane, Qld, 1977) (both in tabard) and in Canada in attendance upon the Sovereign (Vancouver, 1987), to visit Australia, 1970, S America, 1972, Thailand, Japan, 1973, NZ, 1976, Poland, 1991, 1995, Lithuania, 1994. World lecture tours, 1970, 1973, 1976. Adviser to PM of Canada on establishment of Nat. Flag of Canada and Order of Canada, 1964–67; at invitation of Sec. of State of Canada participated in nat. forum on heraldry in Canada, 1987. Co-founder (with Lady Hilda Swan), Heraldic Garden, Boxford, Suffolk, 1983. Hon. Citizen, State of Texas; Freemanships in USA; Freeman: St George's, Bermuda, 1969; City of London, 1974. Fellow, 1976, Hon. Vice-Pres. and a Founder, Heraldry Soc. of Canada; Fellow, Geneal. Soc. of Victoria (Australia), 1970; FSA 1971; FZS 1986. Master, Gunmakers' Co., 1993 (Liveryman and Freeman, 1974; Mem., Ct of Assts, 1983). KStJ 1976. Kt of Honour and Devotion, SMO of Malta, 1979 (Kt of Grace and Devotion, 1964) (Genealogist Br. Assoc., 1974–95); Cross of Comdr of Order of Merit, SMO of Malta, 1983; Comdr (with Star), Royal Norwegian Order of Merit, 1995; Cross of Comdr, Order of Merit, Poland, 1995. *Publications:* Heraldry: Ulster and North American Connections, 1972; Canada: Symbols of Sovereignty, 1977; (jtly) Blood of the Martyrs, 1993; many articles in learned jls on heraldic, sigillographic and related subjects. *Recreations:* hunting, driving (horse drawn vehicles), rearing ornamental pheasants and waterfowl, marine biology. *Address:* Boxford House, Suffolk CO10 5JT. *T:* (01787) 210208.

SWAN, Dermot Joseph, MVO 1972; HM Diplomatic Service, retired; HM Consul-General, Marseilles, 1971–77; *b* 24 Oct. 1917; *s* of Dr William Swan and Anne Cosgrave; *m* 1947, Jeanne Labat; one *d*. *Educ:* St George's, Weybridge; University Coll., London Univ. BA (Hons) French and German. Served War, HM Forces, 1939–46. HM Foreign (later Diplomatic) Service: Vice-Consul, Marseilles, 1947; Saigon, 1949; Foreign Office, 1951; Brazzaville, 1951; Budapest, 1953; FO 1955; First Sec., 1958; Head of Chancery, Phnom Penh, 1959, and Budapest, 1961; UK Mission, New York, 1963; FO (later FCO), 1967; Counsellor, Special Asst to Sec.-Gen. of CENTO, Ankara, 1969. *Recreations:* swimming, golf, bridge. *Address:* Las Brisas, San Feliu de Guixols, 17220 Spain.

SWAN, Sir John (William David), KBE 1990; JP; MP (United Bermuda Party) Paget East, since 1972; Premier of Bermuda, 1982–95; *b* 3 July 1935; *s* of late John N. Swan and of Margaret E. Swan; *m* 1965, Jacqueline A. D. Roberts; one *s* two *d*. *Educ:* West Virginia Wesleyan Coll. (BA). Salesman, Real Estate, Rego Ltd, 1960–62; Founder, Chairman and Chief Exec., John W. Swan Ltd, 1962–. Minister for: Marine and Air Services; Labour and Immigration, 1977–78; Home Affairs, 1978–82; formerly: Parly Sec. for Finance; Chairman: Bermuda Hosps Bd; Dept of Civil Aviation; Young Presidents' Organization, 1974–86. Member: Chief Execs Orgn; World Business Council, 1986. Mem. and Fellow, Senate, Jun. Chamber Internat., 1992. Hon. Freeman of London, 1985. Hon. LLD: Univ. of Tampa, Fla, 1985; W Virginia Wesleyan Coll., 1987; Atlantic Union Coll., Mass, 1991. Internat. Medal of Excellence (1st recipient), Poor Richard Club of Philadelphia, 1987; Outstanding Learning Disabled Achiever Award, Lab Sch. of Washington, 1992. *Recreations:* sailing, tennis. *Address:* 11 Grape Bay Drive, Paget PG 06, Bermuda. *T:* 361303; Challenger Banks Ltd, PO Box HM 2413, Hamilton HM JX, Bermuda. *T:* 2951785, *Fax:* 2956270; *e-mail:* sirjohn@ibl.bm. *Clubs:* Hamilton Rotary, Royal Bermuda Yacht (Bermuda); Bohemian (San Francisco); Chevy Chase (Maryland).

SWAN, Robert Charles, OBE 1995; FRGS; polar explorer, since 1980; *b* 28 July 1956; *s* of late Robert Douglas Swan and of Margaret Swan; *m* 1993, Nicola Begg; one *s*. *Educ:* Aysgarth Sch.; Sedbergh Sch.; Durham Univ. (BA). With British Antarctic Survey, 1980–81; planning and fund raising, In the Footsteps of Scott, Antarctic Expedn, 1979–84; arrived at South Pole with R. Mear and G. Wood, 11 Jan. 1986; planning and fund raising, Icewalk, North Pole Expedn, 1988–89; Icewalk Internat. Student Expedn (22 participants from 15 nations), 1989; reached North Pole with 8 walkers from 7 nations (first person to have walked to both Poles), 14 May 1989; planning and fund raising, One Step Beyond, South Pole Challenge Expedn, 1994–96; One Step Beyond (35 young explorers from 25 nations), 1996–97; started Mission Antarctica, five year challenge dedicated to preservation of Antarctic wilderness, 1997. Vis. Prof., Sch. of Envmt, Leeds Metropolitan Univ., 1992–. Director: 2nd Nature Ltd; One Step Beyond Expeditions Ltd; Mission Antarctica Ltd. Founded Robert Swan Foundn (for promotion of youth and scientific endeavour in the envmt), 1993. Keynote speaker at first Earth Summit, Rio de Janeiro, 1992. Mem. Council, WWF (UK), 1987; Vice-Pres., Countryside Mgt Assoc., 1995; Pres., Scott Soc., 2000. UN Goodwill Ambassador with special resp. for youth, 1989; Special Envoy to Dir Gen., UNESCO, 1994. Paul Harris Fellow, Rotary Internat., 1991. FRGS 1987. Hon. LittD Robert Gordon, 1993. Polar Medal, 1988. Global 500 Award, UN, 1989; Smithsonian Award, 1998. *Publications:* In the Footsteps of Scott, 1987; A Walk to the Pole, 1987; Antarctic Survival, 1989; Destination South, 1990; Icewalk, 1990. *Recreations:* yachting, running, tree surgery. *Address:* 2nd Nature Ltd, Crown Street Chambers, Darlington, Co. Durham DL1 1RN. *T:* (01325) 462041, *Fax:* (01325) 462601; Bleathgill Edge, South Stainmore, Kirkby Stephen, Cumbria CA17 4ET. *T:* (01768) 341860; *e-mail:* robert@2041.co.uk. *Clubs:* Special Forces; Amstel (Netherlands); Explorers (New York).

SWANN, Benjamin Colin Lewis; Controller, Finance, British Council, 1975–79, retired; *b* 9 May 1922; *s* of Henry Basil Swann and Olivia Ophelia Lewis; *m* 1946, Phyllis Julia Sybil Lewis; three *s* one *d*. *Educ:* Bridgend County School. CA. RAFVR, 1941; Transatlantic Ferry, 1942; Flt Lieut, Transport Command, 1944; Flt Supervisor, BOAC, 1946. Apprentice Chartered Accountant, 1950; Audit Asst, George A. Touche & Co., 1953; Treasury Acct, Malaya, 1954; Financial Adviser, Petaling Jaya, 1956; Partner, Milligan Swann & Co., Chartered Accountants, Exeter, 1957; British Council, 1960; Regional Acct, SE Asia, 1961; Dep. Dir Audit, 1965; Asst Representative, Delhi, 1970; Director, Budget, 1972; Dep. Controller, Finance, 1972. *Recreations:* cuisine, lepidoptery.

SWANN, Julian Dana Nimmo H.; *see* Hartland-Swann.

SWANN, Sir Michael (Christopher), 4th Bt *cr* 1906, of Prince's Gardens, Royal Borough of Kensington; TD 1979; Partner, Smith Swann & Co., since 1992; *b* 23 Sept. 1941; *s* of Sir Anthony Swann, 3rd Bt, CMG, OBE and of Jean Margaret, *d* of late John Herbert Niblock-Stuart; *S* father, 1991; *m* 1st, 1965, Hon. Lydia Hewitt (marr. diss. 1985), *e d* of 8th Viscount Lifford; two *s* one *d*; 2nd, 1988, Marilyn Ann Morse (*née* Tobitt). *Educ:* Eton Coll. APMI 1978. Lt KRRC (The Royal Green Jackets), 1960–63; T&AVR 4th Bn The Royal Green Jackets, 1964–79 (Brevet Lt-Col 1979). Director: Wright Deen (Life and Estate Duty), 1964–74; Richards Longstaff (Holdings) Ltd, 1974–86; Richards Longstaff Ltd, 1974–88; Gerrard Vivian Gray (Life & Pensions), 1988–92 (Man. Dir). Trustee, Gabbitas Truman and Thring, 1978– (Chm., 1998–). General Comr of Income Tax, 1988–. *Recreations:* bridge, golf, ski-ing, gardening, growing orchids, racing. *Heir: s* Jonathan Christopher Swann [*b* 17 Nov. 1966; *m* 1994, Polly, *d* of Comdr David Baston; twin *s*]. *Address:* 38 Hurlingham Road, SW6 3RQ. *T:* (020) 7731 5601. *Clubs:* Turf, Hurlingham, IZ, MCC; Rye Golf.

SWANNELL, Nicola Mary, (Mrs Graham Swannell); *see* Pagett, N. M.

SWANNEY, Rajni; Floating Sheriff, North Strathclyde at Greenock, since 1999; *b* 27 Aug. 1954; *d* of Sat Dev Dhir and Swarn Lata Dhir; *m* 1981, Robert Todd Swanney; two *s*. *Educ:* Glasgow Univ. (LLB). Court Assistant: MacRoberts, Glasgow, 1978–80; various Glasgow firms, 1982–88; Chm. (pt-time), Child Support Tribunal, 1993–96; Immigration Adjudicator (pt-time), 1995–99. *Recreations:* gardening, reading, enjoying all things French! *Address:* Greenock Sheriff Court, Nelson Street, Greenock PA15 1TR. *T:* (01475) 787073.

SWANSEA, 4th Baron *cr* 1893; **John Hussey Hamilton Vivian,** Bt 1882; DL; *b* 1 Jan. 1925; *s* of 3rd Baron Swansea, DSO, MVO, TD and Hon. Winifred Hamilton (*d* 1944), 4th *d* of 1st Baron Holm Patrick; *S* father, 1934; *m* 1st, 1956, Miriam Antoinette (marr. diss. 1973; she *d* 1975), 2nd *d* of A. W. F. Caccia-Birch, MC, of Guernsey Lodge, Marton, NZ; one *s* two *d*; 2nd, 1982, Mrs Lucy Temple-Richards (*née* Gough). *Educ:* Eton; Trinity Coll., Cambridge. DL Powys (formerly Brecknock), 1962. CStJ 1994. *Recreations:* shooting, fishing, rifle shooting. *Heir: s* Hon. Richard Anthony Hussey Vivian [*b* 24 Jan. 1957; *m* 1996, Anna Clementine, *d* of M. Austin]. *Address:* 16 Cheyne Gardens, SW3 5QT.

SWANSEA and BRECON, Bishop of, since 1999; **Rt Rev. Anthony Edward Pierce;** *b* 16 Jan. 1941; *s* of Gwynfor Pierce and Martha Jane Pierce (*née* Owen). *Educ:* Dynevor Sch., Swansea; University Coll., Swansea (BA Hons Hist. 1963); Linacre Coll., Oxford (BA Hons Theol 1965; MA 1971); Ripon Hall, Oxford. Deacon 1965, priest 1966; Curate: St Peter, Swansea, 1965–67; St Mary and Holy Trinity, Swansea, 1967–74; Vicar of Llwynderw, 1974–92; Priest-in-charge, St Barnabas, Swansea, 1992–96; Canon Res., Brecon Cathedral, 1993; Archdeacon of Gower, 1995–99; Vicar, St Mary, Swansea, 1996–99. Sec., Dio. Conf. and Dio. Patronage Bd, 1991–95; Dio. Dir of Educn, 1992–96. Mem., Prov. Selection Panel, 1984–97; Chm., Social Action Sect., 1985–90, Chm. Div. Social Responsibility, 1990–92, Prov. Bd of Mission. Chm., Ecumenical Aids Monitoring Gp (Wales), 1988–95. University College, Swansea: Bp's Chaplain to Anglican Students, 1971–74; Mem. Ct of Govs, 1981–; Chaplain, 1984–88. Mem. Council, Univ. of Wales, Swansea, 1995–. Chaplain, Singleton Hosp., 1980–95; Co-ordinator, Hosp. Chaplains, 1982–95. Hon. Ed., Welsh Churchman, 1972–75. *Recreations:* reading, theatre, music. *Address:* Ely Tower, Brecon, Powys LD3 9DE. *T:* (01874) 622008.

SWANSON, John Alexander; His Honour Judge Swanson; a Circuit Judge, since 1996; *b* 31 May 1944; *s* of Sidney Alexander Swanson and Joan Swanson; *m* 1981, Pauline Ann Hearn (*née* Woodmansey) (marr. diss.); two *d*. *Educ:* Giggleswick Sch., Settle; Univ. of Newcastle upon Tyne (LLB 1966). Solicitor, 1970–75; called to the Bar, Inner Temple, 1975; a Recorder, 1994–96. Asst Comr, Boundary Commn for England, 1992–95. *Recreations:* hill-walking, American West, 19th and 20th century music, history of railways, malt whisky. *Address:* Sheffield Combined Court, West Bar, Sheffield S3 8PH. *T:* (0114) 281 2400. *Clubs:* Bridlington Rugby Union Football; Bridlington Yacht.

SWANSON, Dr Kenneth Macgregor; JP; farmer, since 1991; Vice Lord-Lieutenant for Caithness, since 1996; *b* 14 Feb. 1930; *s* of Magnus Houston Swanson and Margaret Swanson (*née* Macgregor); *m* 1956, Elspeth Janet Will Paton; two *s* one *d*. *Educ:* Wick High Sch.; St Andrews Univ. (BSc 1st cl. Hons Natural Philosophy 1951; PhD 1959). Nat. service, FO (Pilot), RAF, 1952–54; St Andrews Univ. Air Sqn, RAFVR, 1954–58. Lectr in Physics, UCNW, Bangor, 1955–58; United Kingdom Atomic Energy Authority, Dounreay: SSO, Fast Reactor Fuel Develt, 1958–61; PSO, 1961–71; Res. Manager, Fuels, 1971–86; Asst Dir, 1986–91, retired. Chm., European Cttee on Fast Reactor Fuel Develt, 1987–90; Mem. Bd, NW Reg., 1992–97, Northern Areas, 1997–99, Scottish Natural Heritage; Chm., Caithness Jobs Commn, 1988–98; Dir, Caithness and Sutherland Enterprise, 1990–99 (Vice Chm., 1995–99). JP, 1970, DL, 1977, Caithness. *Publications:* papers and patents on develt of plutonium fuels for electricity production. *Recreations:* enjoying the countryside, sailing. *Address:* Knockglass, Westfield, Thurso, Caithness KW14 7QN. *T:* (01847) 871201.

SWANSON, Prof. Sydney Alan Vasey, FREng; Professor of Biomechanics, Imperial College, University of London, 1974–97; *b* 31 Oct. 1931; *s* of Charles Henry William Swanson and Hannah Elizabeth Swanson (*née* Vasey); *m* 1956, Mary Howarth; one *s* one *d*. *Educ:* Scarborough Boys' High Sch.; Imperial Coll., London. DSc (Eng), PhD, DIC, FCGI, FIMechE; FREng (FEng 1987). Engineering Laboratories, Bristol Aircraft Ltd, 1955–58; Imperial College, London: Lectr, Mechanical Engineering, 1958–69; Reader in Biomechanics, 1969–74; Dean, City and Guilds Coll., 1976–79; Head of Mechanical Engineering Dept, 1978–83; Pro Rector, 1983–86; Pro Rector (Educnl Quality), 1994–97; Dep. Rector, 1997. *Publications:* Engineering Dynamics, 1963; Engineering in Medicine (with B. M. Sayers and B. Watson), 1975; (with M. A. R. Freeman) The Scientific Basis of Joint Replacement, 1977; papers on bone, cartilage and joints in learned jls. *Recreations:* photography, cycling, fell-walking. *Address:* 12 Holmwood Gardens, Wallington, Surrey SM6 0HN. *Club:* Lyke Wake (Northallerton).

SWANSTON, Roderick Brian, FRCM, FRCO; Reader in Historical and Interdisciplinary Studies, Royal College of Music, since 1997; *b* 28 Aug. 1948; *s* of Comdr David Swanston and Sheila Anne Swanston (*née* Lang). *Educ:* Stowe Sch.; Royal Coll. of Music (ARCM 1967; GRSM 1969; FRCM 1994); Pembroke Coll., Cambridge (Organ Schol., 1969; BA 1971, MA 1974; MusB 1975). LRAM 1970; FRCO 1975. Asst Organist, Tower of London, 1967–68; Director of Music: Christ Church, Lancaster Gate, 1972–77; St James, Sussex Gardens, 1977–80; Tutor, Faculty of Contg Educn, Birkbeck Coll., London Univ., 1974–; freelance lectr, 1974–, and broadcaster, 1990–; Prof., RCM, 1976–; Lectr in Humanities, Imperial Coll., London Univ., 1996–; Vis. Prof., Dartmouth Coll., NH, 1995, 1999. Artistic Dir, Austro-Hungarian Music Fest., 1994–. *Publications:* A Dictionary of Biblical Interpretation, 1990; Fairest Isle, 1995; Ultimate Encyclopaedia of Instruments, 1996; Collins Encyclopaedia of Music, 2000; contrib. Musical Times, Gramophone, Early Music, Classic CD. *Recreations:* reading, poetry, theatre, thinking. *Address:* Royal College of Music, Prince Consort Road, SW7 2BS. *T:* (020) 7589 3643. *Club:* Athenæum.

SWANSTON, Roy; Chairman, East and North Hertfordshire NHS Trust, since 2001; *b* 31 Oct. 1940; *s* of Robert Trotter Swanston and Margaret Ann Swanston (*née* Paxton); *m* 1963, Doreen Edmundson; one *s* one *d*. *Educ:* Berwick-upon-Tweed Grammar Sch.; FRICS, FIMgt. County Borough of Sunderland, 1958–67; Clasp Develt Gp, Nottingham, 1967–71; Notts CC, 1971–74; Durham CC, 1974–75; Dir of Building Economics, 1975–82, of Dept of Architecture, 1982–87, Cheshire CC; Sen. Management Consultant, Peat Marwick McLintock, 1987–88; Dir of Develt, Bucknall Austin, 1988–90; Dir, Properties in Care, 1990–93, Res. and Professional Services, 1993–95, English Heritage; Chm., Local Govt Residuary Bd (England), 1995–99. Chm., W Herts HA, 1996–2001. Chairman: Jones Lang Wootton Educn Trust, 1995–2000; Jt Contracts Tribunal for Standard Form of Building Contract, 1995–. Pres., RICS, 1994–95 (Pres., QS Div., 1982–83; Hon Treas., 1987–90; Chm., Bldg Conservation Diploma Adv. Bd, 2000–); Sec. Gen., Internat. Fedn of Surveyors, 1995–99. Visiting Professor: Liverpool John Moores Univ., 1995–; Luton Univ., 1996– (Mem. Court, 1999–); Salford Univ., 1999– (Vis. Fellow, 1986–99). Mem., Yorks Dales Nat. Park Authy, 2001–. Trustee, NE Civic Trust, 1998–. Mem., Barnardo's Council, 1989–. Methodist Local Preacher. Hon. DSc Salford, 1994. *Recreations:* supporter of Sunderland AFC, fell walking.

SWANWICK, Sir Graham Russell, Kt 1966; MBE 1944; Judge of the High Court of Justice (Queen's Bench Division), 1966–80; Presiding Judge, Midland and Oxford Circuit, 1975–78; *b* 24 August 1906; *s* of Eric Drayton Swanwick and Margery Eleanor (*née* Norton), Whittington House, Chesterfield; *m* 1st, 1933, Helen Barbara Reid (marr. diss., 1945; she *d* 1970); two *s*; 2nd, 1952, Audrey Celia Parkinson (*d* 1987). *Educ:* Winchester Coll.; University Coll., Oxford (BA). Called to Bar, Inner Temple, 1930, Master of the Bench, 1962; QC 1956; Leader Midland Circuit, 1961–65. Wing Comdr RAFVR, 1940–45 (MBE, despatches). Recorder: City of Lincoln, 1957–59; City of Leicester, 1959–66; Judge of Appeal, Channel Islands, 1964–66; Derbyshire QS: Chm., 1963–66; Dep. Chm., 1966–71. *Recreation:* country pursuits. *Address:* Burnett's Ashurst, Steyning, West Sussex BN44 3AY. *T:* (01403) 710241. *Club:* Royal Air Force.

SWARBRICK, Catherine Marie; Director, National Childbirth Trust, 1995–99; *b* 25 Nov. 1950; *d* of Hubert Joseph Swarbrick and Margaret Swarbrick. *Educ:* Goldsmiths' Coll., Univ. of London (BA Hons, PGCE). Secondary sch. teacher, 1973–79; Sec., Law Dept, LSE, 1980–82; Exams Officer, British Computer Soc., 1982–85; Sen. Manager, RCGP, 1985–95. *Recreations:* fitness, reading, art history. *Address:* c/o National Childbirth Trust, Alexandra House, Oldham Terrace, W3 6NH. *T:* (020) 8896 3136.

SWARBRICK, Prof. James, PhD, DSc; FRSC, CChem; FRPharmS; President, PharmaceuTech Inc., since 2001; Vice President, Scientific Affairs, aaiPharma (formerly Applied Analytical Industries) Inc., since 1999 (Vice-President, Research and Development, 1993–99); *b* 8 May 1934; *s* of George Winston Swarbrick and Edith M. C. Cooper; *m* 1960, Pamela Margaret Oliver. *Educ:* Sloane Grammar Sch.; Chelsea Coll., Univ. of London (BPharm Hons 1960; PhD 1964; DSc 1972). FRSC (FRIC 1970); FRPharmS (FPS 1978; MPS 1961). Asst Lectr, 1962, Lectr, 1964, Chelsea Coll.; Vis. Asst Prof., Purdue Univ., 1964; Associate Prof., 1966, Prof. and Chm. of Dept of Pharmaceutics, 1969, Asst Dean, 1970, Univ. of Conn; Dir of Product Develt, Sterling-Winthrop Res. Inst., NY, 1972; first Prof. of Pharmaceutics, Univ. of Sydney, 1975–76; Dean, Sch. of Pharmacy, Univ. of London, 1976–78; Prof. of Pharmacy and Chm., Res. Council, Univ. of S California, Los Angeles, 1978–81; Prof. of Pharmaceutics and Chm., Div. of Pharmaceutics, Univ. of N Carolina, 1981–93. Vis. Scientist, Astra Labs, Sweden, 1971; Vis. Prof., Shanghai Med. Univ., 1991–92. Indust. Cons., 1965–72, 1975–; Cons., Aust. Dept. of Health, 1975–76; Mem., Cttee on Specifications, National Formulary, 1970–75; Chm., Jt US Pharmacopoeia-Nat. Formulary Panel on Disintegration and Dissolution Testing, 1971–75. Member: Cttee on Grad. Programs, Amer. Assoc. of Colls of Pharmacy, 1969–71; Practice Trng Cttee, Pharm. Soc. of NSW, 1975–76; Academic Bd, Univ. of Sydney, 1975–76; Collegiate Council, 1976–78; Educn Cttee, Pharmaceutical Soc. of GB, 1976–78; Working Party on Pre-Registration Training, 1977–78. Pharmaceutical Manufacturers Assoc. Foundation: Mem., Basic Pharmacology Adv. Cttee, 1982–91; Chm., Pharmaceutics Adv. Cttee, 1986–; Mem., Scientific Adv. Cttee, 1986–; Mem., Generic Drugs Adv. Cttee, Food and Drug Admin, 1992–96 (Chm., 1994–96). FAAAS 1966; Fellow: Acad. of Pharm. Sciences, 1973; Amer. Assoc. of Pharmaceutical Scientists, 1987. Kenan Res. Study Award, 1988. Mem. Editorial Board: Jl of Biopharmaceutics and Pharmacokinetics, 1973–79; Drug Development Communications, 1974–82; Pharmaceutical Technology, 1978–; Biopharmaceutics and Drug Disposition, 1979–; series Editor, Current Concepts in the Pharmaceutical Sciences, Drugs and the Pharmaceutical Sciences. *Publications:* (with A. N. Martin and A. Cammarata) Physical Pharmacy, 2nd edn 1969, 3rd edn 1983; (ed jtly) Encyclopedia of Pharmaceutical Technology; contributed: American Pharmacy, 6th edn 1966 and 7th edn 1974; Remington's Pharmaceutical Sciences, 14th edn 1970 to 20th edn 2001; contrib. Current Concepts in the Pharmaceutical Sciences: Biopharmaceutics, 1970; res. contribs to internat. sci. jls. *Recreation:* woodworking, listening to music, golf. *Address:* PharmaceuTech Inc., 785 Donald Ross Drive, Pinehurst, NC 28374, USA. *T:* (910) 2550104, *Fax:* (910) 2550105; *e-mail:* james.swarbrick@aaiintl.com.

SWARBRICK, William Alfred, CEng; Chief Executive, Cumbria County Council, 1997–2000; *b* 30 Sept. 1940; *s* of William and Agnes Swarbrick; *m* 1963, Catherine Lamey; one *s* one *d*. *Educ:* Manchester Grammar Sch.; Manchester Univ. (BSc Tech.). CEng, MICE 1968; Dip. in Traffic Engrg, IMunE, 1971; FIHT 1991. Cumberland CC, later Cumbria CC, 1963–2000; Gen. Manager, County Contracting, 1987–92; Dir, Cumbria Contract Services, 1992–97. Chm., PAC Ltd. Chairman: Victim Support Cumbria (Mem., Nat. Council); Carlisle RFC. MIMgt 1987. *Recreations:* cooking, gardening, viola and timpani playing. *Address:* 5 St Aidan's Road, Carlisle CA1 1LT.

SWARTZ, Rt Rev. George Alfred; Bishop of Kimberley and Kuruman, 1983–91; *b* 8 Sept. 1928; *s* of Philip and Julia Swartz; *m* 1957, Sylvia Agatha (*née* George); one *s* one *d*. *Educ:* Umbilo Road High Sch., Durban; Univ. of the Witwatersrand, Johannesburg; Coll. of the Resurrection, Mirfield, Yorks; St Augustine's Coll., Canterbury. BA, Primary Lower Teacher's Cert., Central Coll. Dip. (Canterbury). Asst Teacher, Sydenham Primary Sch., 1951–52; Deacon, 1954; Priest, 1955; Asst Curate, St Paul's Church, Cape Town, 1955–56; Priest in Charge, Parochial Dist of St Helena Bay, Cape, 1957–60; St Augustine's Coll., Canterbury, 1960–61; Dir, Cape Town Dio. Mission to Muslims, 1962–63; Dir, Mission to Muslims and Rector St Philip's Church, Cape Town, 1963–70; Regional Dean of Woodstock Deanery, 1966–70; Priest in Charge, Church of the Resurrection, Bonteheuwel, Cape, 1971–72; a Bishop Suffragan of Cape Town, 1972–83; Canon of St George's Cathedral, Cape Town, 1969–72. Dean of the Province, Church of the Province of Southern Africa, 1986–89. *Recreations:* cinema, music (traditional jazz; instruments played are guitar and saxophone). *Address:* 11 Tanglin, Thomas Road, Kenilworth, Cape Town, 7708, Republic of South Africa. *T:* (21) 7979079.

SWARTZ, Col Hon. Sir Reginald (William Colin), KBE 1972 (MBE (mil.) 1948); ED; FAIM, FIMgt, FAICD; retired parliamentarian and company director (director of nine companies, 1973–83); *b* 14 April 1911; *s* of late J. Swartz, Toowoomba, Qld; *m* 1st, 1936, Hilda (*d* 1995), *d* of late G. C. Robinson; two *s* one *d*; 2nd, 1998, Muriel McKinstry. *Educ:* Toowoomba and Brisbane Grammar Schs. Commonwealth Military Forces, 1928–40, Lieut, 1934. Served War of 1939–45: Captain 2–26 Bn, 8 Div., AIF, 1940; Malaya (PoW): Singapore, Malaya, Thailand (Burma-Thailand Rly); CMF, in Darling Downs Regt, Lt-Col, AQMG, CMF, N Comd, Col (RL), 1961. Hon. Col Australian Army Aviation Corps, 1969–75. MHR (L) Darling Downs, Qld, 1949–72; Parly Under-Sec. for Commerce and Agric., 1952–56; Parly Sec. for Trade, 1956–61; Minister: (of State) for Repatriation, Dec. 1961–Dec. 1964; for Health, 1964–66; for Social Services, 1965; for Civil Aviation, 1966–69; for Nat. Develt, 1969–72; Leader, House of Representatives, Canberra, 1971–72. Leader of many delegns overseas incl. Aust. Delegn to India, 1967, and Trade Mission to SE Asia, 1958; Parly Delegn to S and SE Asia, 1966. Patron and/or Vice-Pres. or Mem. of numerous public organizations. Chm. of Trustees, Australian Army Aviation Corps, 1978–91. Past Chm., Inst. of Dirs (Queensland). Member, RSL. *Recreation:* bowls. *Address:* 56 Immanuel Gardens, 10 Magnetic Drive, Buderim, Qld 4556, Australia. *Clubs:* United Service (Brisbane); Twin Towns Services

(Tweed Head); Darling Downs Aero; Probus (Doncaster) (Life Mem., Foundation Pres.); Templestowe Bowling (Life Mem.) (Melbourne).

SWARUP, Prof. Govind, PhD; FRS 1991; INSA Hon. Scientist, Tata Institute of Fundamental Research, Bombay, since 2001; *b* 29 March 1929; *m* Bina Jain; one *s* one *d*. *Educ:* Allahabad Univ. (BSc 1948; MSc 1950); Stanford Univ., USA (PhD 1961). Sec., Radio Res. Cttee, CSIR, Nat. Physical Lab., New Delhi, 1950–53; Colombo-Plan Fellowship, CSIRO, Sydney, 1953–55; Res. Associate, Harvard Univ., 1956–57; Grad. Student, Stanford Univ., USA, 1957–60, Asst Prof. 1961–63; Tata Institute of Fundamental Research, Bombay: Reader, 1963–65; Associate Prof., 1965–70; Prof., 1970–79; Sen. Prof., 1979–90; Dir, Giant Metrewave Radio Telescope Project, 1987–96; Prof. of Eminence, 1990–94; Prof. Emeritus, 1994–99; Homi Bhabha Sen. Fellow, 1999–2001. Visiting Professor: Univ. of Md, USA, 1980; Univ. of Groningen, Netherlands, 1980–81; Univ. of Leiden, Netherlands, 1981. Chm., Indian Nat. Cttee, URSI, 1986–88, 1994–97. Fellow: Indian Nat. Sci. Acad.; Indian Acad. Scis; Nat. Acad. Scis, India; Indian Geophysical Union. Associate, RAS; Member: Astronomical Soc. India (Pres., 1975–77); IAU (Pres., Radio Astronomy Commn, 1979–82); Indian Physics Assoc.; Indian Physical Soc. Member Editorial Board: Indian Jl Radio and Space Physics; Nat. Acad. of Science, India. Numerous awards, incl. Delinger Award, URSI; S. S. Bhatnager Award, India, 1973; Tskolovosky medal, Fedn of Cosmonautics, USSR, 1987; Third World Acad. of Scis Award, Trieste, 1988; R. D. Birla Award, India, 1990; Khwarizmi Award, Iran, 1999. *Publications:* (ed jtly) Quasars, 1986; (ed jtly) History of Oriental Astronomy, 1987. *Address:* National Centre for Radio Astrophysics, Tata Institute of Fundamental Research, Poona University Campus, Post Bag 3, Ganeshkhind, Pune 411007, India. *T:* (office) (20) 5656111; (home) (20) 5899030.

SWAYNE, Desmond Angus, TD; MP (C) New Forest West, since 1997; *b* 20 Aug. 1956; *s* of George Joseph Swayne and Elizabeth McAlister Swayne (*née* Gibson); *m* 1987, Moira Cecily Teek; one *s* two *d*. *Educ:* Bedford Sch.; Univ. of St Andrews (MTh). Schoolmaster: Charterhouse, 1980–81; Wrekin Coll., 1982–87; Systems Manager, Royal Bank of Scotland, 1988–96. Opposition front bench spokesman on defence, 2001–. TA Officer. Prison visitor, 1989–. *Address:* House of Commons, SW1A 0AA. *Clubs:* Cavalry and Guards; Serpentine Swimming.

SWAYNE, Giles Oliver Cairnes; composer; *b* 30 June 1946; *s* of Sir Ronald Oliver Carless Swayne, MC and Charmian Swayne (*née* Cairnes); *m* 1st, 1972, Camilla Rumbold (marr. diss. 1983); one *s*; 2nd, 1984, Naa Otua Codjoe (marr. diss. 2001). *Educ:* Ampleforth Coll.; Trinity Coll., Cambridge; Royal Acad. of Music. *Compositions:* Six love-songs, 1966; La Rivière, 1966; The Kiss, 1967; Sonata for String Quartet, 1968; Three Shakespeare Songs, 1969; Chamber Music for Strings, 1970; Four Lyrical Pieces, 1970; The Good-Morrow, 1971; String Quarter No 1, 1971; Paraphrase, 1971; Trio, 1972; Canto for Guitar, 1972; Canto for Piano, 1973; Canto for Violin, 1973; Orlando's Music, 1974; Synthesis, 1974; Scrapbook, 1974; Canto for Clarinet, 1975; Charades, 1975; Duo, 1975; Suite for Guitar, 1976; Pentecost Music, 1976; Alleluia!, 1976; String Quartet No 2, 1977; A World Within, 1978; Phoenix Variations, 1979; CRY, 1979; The Three Rs, 1980; Freewheeling, 1980; Count-down, 1981; Canto for Cello, 1981; Rhythm Studies, 1982; Magnificat, 1982; Riff-raff, 1983; A Song for Haddi, 1983; Symphony for Small Orchestra, 1984; Le Nozze di Cherubino (opera, after Mozart), 1984; Naaotwa Lala, 1984; Missa Tiburtina, 1985; Into the Light, 1986; Solo, 1986; Godsong, 1986; Nunc Dimittis, 1986; O Magnum Mysterium, 1986; Tonos, 1987; Veni Creator I, 1987; Veni Creator II, 1987; Songlines, 1987; The Coming of Saskia Hawkins, 1987; Harmonies of Hell, 1988; The Song of Leviathan, 1988; A Memory of Sky, 1989; No Quiet Place, 1990; No Man's Land, 1990; Circle of Silence, 1991; Zebra Music, 1992; The Song of the Tortoise, 1992; The Owl and the Pussycat, 1993; String Quartet No 3, 1993; Fiddlesticks, 1994; Goodnight, Sweet Ladies, 1994; Squeezy, 1994; All About Henry, 1995; The Tiger, 1995; Communion Service in D, 1995; A Convocation of Worms, 1995; Two Romantic Songs, 1996; The Silent Land, 1996; Ophelia Drowning, 1996; Tombeau, 1997; Beatus Vir, 1997; Mr Leary's Mechanical Maggot, 1997; Chinese Whispers, 1997; Petite Messe Solitaire, 1997; Echo, 1997; Winter Solstice Carol, 1998; Groundwork, 1998; Merlis Lied, 1998; The Flight of the Swan, 1999; HAVOC, 1999; Perturbèd Spirit, 2000; Canto for flute, 2000; The Akond of Swat, 2000; Mancanza, 2001; The Murder of Gonzago, 2001. *Address:* c/o Performing Arts, 6 Windmill Street, W1P 1HF. *T:* (020) 7255 1362, *Fax:* (020) 7631 4631.

SWAYTHLING, 5th Baron *cr* 1907, of Swaythling, co. Southampton; **Charles Edgar Samuel Montagu;** Bt 1894; Director, The Health Partnership; *b* 20 Feb. 1954; *o s* of 4th Baron Swaythling and of Christine Françoise (*née* Dreyfus); *S* father, 1998; *m* 1996, Hon. Angela, *d* of Baron Rawlinson of Ewell, *qv*; one *d*. Member: Amer. Council of Hypnotist Examiners (Mem. Adv. Bd); British Council of Hypnotist Examiners; Scientific and Medical Network; Adv. Bd, British Council for Complementary Medicine. Patron, Focus Counselling Trust. *Heir: uncle* Hon. Anthony Trevor Samuel Montagu [*b* 3 Aug. 1931; *m* 1962, Deirdre Bridget (*née* Senior); two *s* one *d*]. *Address:* c/o The Health Partnership, 12A Thurloe Street, SW7 2ST.

SWEENEY, Brendan, FRCGP; Principal in general practice, Govan, since 1975; *b* 11 July 1946; *s* of James and Angela Sweeney; *m* 1974, Dr Rosalie T. Dunn; two *s* three *d*. *Educ:* Univ. of Glasgow (MA 1965; MB ChB 1971). DObstRCOG 1973; MRCGP 1975, FRCGP 1985. McKenzie Lectr, RCGP, 1997. Hon. Sen. Lectr, Dept of Postgrad. Med. Educn, Univ. of Glasgow. Royal College of General Practitioners: Vice-Chm., Council, 1994–97; Chairman: Cttee of Med. Ethics, 1992–98; W of Scotland Cttee on Postgrad. Med. Educn, 1997–. *Recreations:* squash, golf, opera, theatre, books. *Address:* 25 Stewarton Drive, Cambuslang, Glasgow G72 8DF. *T:* (0141) 583 1513. *Clubs:* Turnberry Golf, Cathkin Braes Golf; Newlands Squash and Tennis.

SWEENEY, Edward; General Secretary, UNIFI, since 2000 (Joint General Secretary, 1999–2000); *b* 6 Aug. 1954; *s* of William Sweeney and Louise Sweeney; *m* 1987, Janet Roydhouse. *Educ:* Warwick Univ. (BA Hons); London Sch. of Economics (MSc Econ.). Banking, Insurance and Finance Union: Research Officer, 1976–79; Negotiating Officer (TSB), 1979–86; National Officer: Scotland, 1986–89; Insurance, 1989–91; Dep. Gen. Sec., 1991–96; Gen. Sec., 1996–99, when BIFU amalgamated with UNIFI. *Recreations:* sport, reading, Egyptology. *Address:* UNIFI, 1b Amity Grove, Raynes Park, SW20 0LG. *T:* (020) 8946 9151.

SWEENEY, Sir George, Kt 2000; Principal, Knowsley Community College, since 1990; *b* 26 Jan. 1946; *s* of George Sweeney and Margaret, (Peggy), Sweeney (*née* Carlin); *m* 1968, Susan Anne Wilson; two *d*. *Educ:* Prescot Boys' GS; Hull Univ. (BA Hons Hist. and Pols 1967; MA 1973). Teacher: Hull Coll. of Technol., 1967–70; Kirby Coll., Teesside, 1970–73; S Trafford Coll., 1973–75 and 1977–83; S Cheshire Coll., 1975–77; Vice Principal, Grimsby Coll. of Technol., 1983–90; Actg Principal, Sheffield Coll., Jan.–Aug. 2000. *Recreations:* painting, drawing, gardening, political biography. *Address:* 12 Red Lane, Appleton, Cheshire WA4 5AD. *T:* (01925) 265113.

SWEENEY, Nigel Hamilton; QC 2000; a Recorder, since 1997; *b* 18 March 1954; *s* of Alan Vincent Sweeney and Dorothy Sweeney; *m* 1985, Joanna Clair Slater (marr. diss.); one *s* one *d*. *Educ:* Wellington Sch., Som; Nottingham Univ. (LLB 1975). Called to the Bar, Middle Temple, 1976 (Harmsworth Schol. 1976), Bencher, 1997; Central Criminal Court: Jun. Prosecuting Counsel to the Crown, 1987–91; First Jun. Prosecuting Counsel, 1991–92; Sen. Prosecuting Counsel, 1992–97; First Sen. Prosecuting Counsel, 1997–2000. *Recreations:* golf, tennis, the arts. *Address:* 6 King's Bench Walk, Temple, EC4Y 7DR. *T:* (020) 7583 0410. *Clubs:* Garrick; Wisley Golf.

SWEENEY, Thomas Kevin; Senior Medical Officer, Department of Health and Social Security, 1983–88, retired; *b* 10 Aug. 1923; *s* of John Francis and Mildred Sweeney; *m* 1950, Eveleen Moira Ryan; two *s* two *d*. *Educ:* O'Connell Sch., Dublin; University Coll., Dublin (MB, BCh, BAO NUI; DTM&H London; TDD Wales). FFPHM (FFCM 1983). Principal Med. Officer, Colonial Medical Service, 1950–65, retd; Asst Sen. Med. Officer, Welsh Hosp. Bd, 1965–68; Department of Health and Social Security: Med. Officer, 1968–72; Sen. Med. Officer, 1972–79; SPMO, 1979–83. QHP 1984–87. *Publication:* contrib. BMJ. *Recreations:* gardening, golf, cathedrals. *Address:* Tresanton, Wych Hill Way, Woking, Surrey GU22 0AE. *T:* (01483) 828199.

SWEENEY, Timothy Patrick; Director: AIB Group UK; WRAP; Chairman, AMICUS VISION; *b* 2 June 1944; *s* of John Sylvester Sweeney and Olive Bridget (*née* Montgomery-Cunningham); *m* 1965, Carol Ann Wardle; one *s* one *d*. *Educ:* Pierrepont School; Sussex Univ. (MA Philosophy); Surrey Univ. (MSc Econs). With Bank of England, 1967–94; Dir Gen., BBA, 1994–2001. *Recreations:* music, archery, walking. *Address:* Cedar Cottage, Sutton Place, Abinger Hammer, Surrey RH5 6RP.

SWEENEY, Walter Edward; Solicitor, Walter Sweeney & Co., since 1997; *b* Dublin, 23 April 1949; *s* of Patrick Anthony Sweeney, veterinary surgeon and Jane Yerbury Sweeney, retired head teacher; *m* 1992, Dr Nuala Maire Kennan; three *d*. *Educ:* Church Lawford Primary Sch.; Lawrence Sheriff Sch., Rugby; Univ. of Aix-Marseille; Univ. of Hull (BA Hons; MA); Darwin Coll., Cambridge (MPhil); Cert. Ed. TEFL. Admitted Solicitor, 1976. Mem., Vale of Glam CHC, 1991–92. Joined Cons. Party, 1964; Chairman: Rugby Div. YCs, 1965; Church Lawford Cons. Br., 1969; Rugby Cons. Political Centre, 1970. Member: Church Lawford Parish Council, 1971–74; Rugby BC, 1974–77; Beds CC, 1981–89 (Vice-Chm. and Gp spokesman on Police Cttee). Contested (C) Stretford, 1983. MP (C) Vale of Glamorgan, 1992–97; contested (C) same seat, 1997. Member, Select Committee: on Welsh Affairs, 1992–97; on Home Affairs, 1995–97; on Channel Tunnel Rail Link, 1995–96; Vice Chairman: All-Party Penal Affairs Cttee, 1993–97 (Sec., 1992–93); Cons. back bench Legal Affairs Cttee, 1995–97 (Sec., 1994–95); Sec., Cons. back bench Home Affairs Cttee, 1994–97. *Recreations:* walking, swimming, flying, theatre, reading. *Address:* Walter Sweeney & Co., The Old Stables, 5 Westgate, North Cave, Brough HU15 2NG.

SWEET, Prof. Peter Alan, MA, PhD; FRAS; Regius Professor of Astronomy in the University of Glasgow, 1959–82; retired; *b* 15 May 1921; *s* of David Frank Sweet; *m* 1947, Myrtle Vera Parnell; two *s*. *Educ:* Kingsbury County Grammar School, London; Sidney Sussex College, Cambridge. Open Maj. Schol. in Maths, Sidney Sussex Coll., 1940–42, Wrangler, 1942, BA Cantab 1943. Junior Scientific Officer, Min. of Aircraft Prod., 1942–45; BA Scholar, at Sidney Sussex Coll., 1945–47; MA Cantab 1946; Mayhew Prizeman, 1946, PhD Cantab 1950. FRAS 1949. Lectr in Astronomy, Univ. of Glasgow, 1947–52; Lectr in Astronomy and Asst Director of the Observatory, Univ. of London, 1952–59; Dean, Faculty of Science, Univ. of Glasgow, 1973–75. Visiting Asst Professor of Astronomy, Univ. of California, Berkeley, 1957–58; Vis. Sen. Res. Fellow, NASA Inst. for Space Studies, NY, 1965–66. *Publications:* papers on Stellar Evolution, Cosmic Magnetism, and Solar Flares in Monthly Notices of Royal Astronomical Soc., etc. *Recreations:* music, gardening. *Address:* 17 Westbourne Crescent, Glasgow G61 4HB. *T:* (0141) 942 4425.

SWEETBAUM, Henry Alan; Chairman, Huntingdon Securities, since 1973; Managing Director, PS Capital LLC, since 1997; *b* 22 Nov. 1937; *s* of late Irving and Bertha Sweetbaum; *m* 1st, 1960, Suzanne Milberg (decd); three *s*; 2nd, 1971, Anne Betty Leonie de Vigier; one *s*. *Educ:* Wharton School, Univ. of Pennsylvania (BS Econ 1959). Underwood Corp., 1960; Exec. Vice-Pres. and Dir, Reliance Corp., 1962–70; Exec. Dir, Plessey Corp., 1970; Data Recording Instrument Co.: non-exec. Dir, 1973–76; Chm., 1976–82; Chm. and Chief Exec., Wickes plc, 1982–96. University of Pennsylvania Wharton School Board Member: Bd of Overseers; European Adv. Bd; SEI Center for Advanced Management Studies. CIMgt 1993. *Publication:* Restructuring the Management Challenge, 1990. *Recreations:* swimming, shooting, Keep Fit. *Address:* Huntingdon Securities, 105/109 Strand, WC2R 0AA. *T:* (020) 7240 4888. *Clubs:* Reform; University (New York).

SWEETING, Prof. Martin Nicholas, OBE 1996; FRS 2000; FREng, FIEE, FRAeS, FInstP; Professor of Satellite Engineering, since 1990, and Director, Surrey Space Centre (formerly Centre for Satellite Engineering Research), since 1996, University of Surrey; Chief Executive, Surrey Satellite Technology Ltd, since 1994; *b* 12 March 1951; *s* of Frank Morris Sweeting and Dorothy May Sweeting; *m* 1975, Christine Ruth Taplin. *Educ:* Aldenham School, Elstree; University of Surrey (BSc Hons 1974; PhD 1979). Marconi Space & Defence Systems, 1972–73; University of Surrey: Research Fellow, 1978–81; Lectr, 1981–86; Univ. Research Fellow in Satellite Engrg, 1984–87; Dir, Satellite Engrg, 1986–90; Dep. Dir, Centre for Satellite Engrg Res., 1990–96. Res. Dir, Satellites Internat., 1983–84; Surrey Satellite Technology: Technical Dir, 1985–94; Acting Man. Dir, 1989–94. Ext. Examr, Aerospace Engrg, Cranfield Inst. of Technology. Member: Adv. Bd, Space Technology, BNSC; Defence and Aerospace Panel, UK Technology Foresight Cttee. FREng (FEng 1996); FInstP 2001. *Publications:* papers in professional jls. *Recreations:* cycling in Himalaya, photography, languages, music, amateur radio. *Address:* 47 Barnett Close, Wonersh, Surrey GU5 0SD.

SWEETMAN, Jennifer Joan, (Mrs Ronald Andrew); *see* Dickson, J. J.

SWEETMAN, John Francis, CB 1991; TD 1964; Clerk Assistant, 1987–90 and Clerk of Committees, 1990–95 of the House of Commons; *b* 31 Oct. 1930; *s* of late Thomas Nelson Sweetman and Mary Monica (*née* D'Arcy-Reddy); *m* 1st, 1959, Susan Margaret Manley; one *s* one *d*; 2nd, 1983, Celia Elizabeth, *yr d* of Sir William Nield, GCMG, KCB; two *s*. *Educ:* Cardinal Vaughan Sch.; St Catharine's Coll., Cambridge (MA Law). 2nd Lieut, RA, Gibraltar, 1949–51; TA (City of London RA) and AER, 1951–65. A Clerk, House of Commons, 1954–95: Clerk of Select Cttees on Nationalised Industries and on Sci. and Technol., 1962–65, 1970–73; Second Clerk of Select Cttees, 1979–83; Clerk of the Overseas Office, 1983–87; Clerk of Select Cttee on Sittings of the House, 1991–92. Parly Advr, BBC, 1996–98. Parly missions to Armenia, Croatia, Gambia, Kazakhstan, Kyrgyzstan, Moldova, Uganda, Ukraine and Yemen, 1996–2000. Member: Assoc. of Secs-Gen. of Parliaments, IPU, 1987–; Assoc. of Clerks-at-the-Table, Canada, 1996–. Mem., Oxford and Cambridge Catholic Educn Bd, 1964–84. *Publications:* contrib. to: Erskine May's Parliamentary Practice; Halsbury's Laws of England; parly jls; (ed) Council of Europe, Procedure and Practice of the Parliamentary Assembly. *Address:* 41 Creffield Road, W5 3RR. *T:* (020) 8992 2456. *Clubs:* Garrick, MCC.

SWEETMAN, Stuart John, FCA; Group Managing Director, Consignia plc (formerly Post Office), since 1999; *b* 6 Aug. 1948; *s* of Arthur John Sweetman and Joan Sweetman; *m* 1978, Patricia Dean; two *s* one *d*. *Educ:* University Coll. London (BSc Geog.). FCA 1979. Joined Touche Ross & Co., Chartered Accountants, 1969; held various posts from Articled Clerk to Sen. Manager; Dir, Financial Accounts, PO, 1982–86; Royal Mail: Finance Dir, 1986–92; Business Centres Dir, 1992–94; Service Delivery Dir, 1994–95; Asst Man. Dir, 1995–96; Man. Dir, PO Counters Ltd, 1996–99. Chm. and Dir, Consignia (Customer Mgt) Ltd (formerly Subscription Services Ltd), 1999–. Dir, British Quality Foundn, 1998–; Mem. Bd, Inst. of Customer Services, 1998–2001. Mem. Adv. Cttee for Business in the Envmt, DTI/DETR, 1997–2001. *Recreations:* family, infrequent golf, cooking and eating, Internet surfing. *Address:* 1 Chalmers Road, Banstead, Surrey SM7 3HF. *T:* (office) (020) 7250 2129.

SWEETNAM, Sir (David) Rodney, KCVO 1992; CBE 1990; MA; FRCS; Orthopaedic Surgeon to the Queen, 1982–92; President: Royal College of Surgeons of England, 1995–98 (Vice-President, 1992–94); Royal Medical Benevolent Fund, since 1998; *b* 5 Feb. 1927; second *s* of late Dr William Sweetnam and Irene (*née* Black); *m* 1959, Patricia Ann, *er d* of late A. Staveley Gough, OBE, FRCS; one *s* one *d*. *Educ:* Clayesmore; Peterhouse, Cambridge (Titular Scholar; BA 1947, MA 1951); Middlesex Hosp. Med. Sch. (MB, BChir 1950). FRCS 1955. Surg. Lieut RNVR, 1950–52. Jun. appts, Mddx Hosp., London Hosp. and Royal National Orthopaedic Hosp.; Consultant Surgeon to: The Middlesex Hospital, 1960–92; King Edward VII Hospital for Officers, London, 1964–97. Hon. Civil Consultant in Orth. Surgery to the Army, 1974–92; Hon. Consultant Orthopaedic Surgeon, Royal Hosp., Chelsea, 1974–92. Consultant Advisor in Orth. Surgery to DHSS, 1981–90; Hon. Consultant Surgeon, Royal Nat. Orthopaedic Hosp., 1983–92. Dir, Medical Sickness Annuity and Life Assce Soc. Ltd, 1982–97; Dir and Vice-Chm., Permanent Insurance Co., 1989–95. Chairman: DHSS Adv. Gp on Orthopaedic Implants, 1973–81; MRC's Working Party on Bone Sarcoma, 1980–85. Royal College of Surgeons: Mem. Council, 1985–98; Jacksonian Prize, 1966; Hunterian Prof., 1967; Gordon Taylor Meml Lectr, 1982; Stanford Cade Meml Lectr, 1986; Bradshaw Lectr, 1992; Robert Jones Lectr, 1993. President: Combined Services Orthopaedic Soc., 1983–86; British Orthopaedic Assoc., 1984–85 (Hon. Fellow, 1998). Mem. Exec. Cttee, Arthritis and Rheumatism Council, 1985–93; Mem. Council, ICRF, 1995–98. Trustee: Develt Trust, Queen Elizabeth Foundn for the Disabled, 1984–97; Smith & Nephew Charitable Trust 1988–99; Frances and Augustus Newman Foundn, 1989– (Chm., 2000–); Hunterian Collection, 1998–. Fellow, UCL, 1993. Chm., British Editorial Soc. of Bone and Joint Surgery, 1992–95 (Sec. and Treas., 1975–92). Hon. FRCSGlas 1997; Hon. FRCSI 1997; Hon. FCSSA 1998; Hon. FACS 1998; Hon. FDS RCS 1998; Hon. FRCSE 1999. *Publications:* (ed jtly) The Basis and Practice of Orthopaedics, 1980; contrib. med. books and jls in field of gen. orth. surgery, trauma and bone tumours. *Recreation:* gardening. *Address:* 25 Woodlands Road, Bushey, Watford, Herts WD23 2LS. *T:* (01923) 223161.

SWIFT, Caroline Jane, (Mrs C. P. L. Openshaw); QC 1993; a Recorder, since 1995; a Deputy High Court Judge, since 2000; *b* 30 May 1955; *d* of late Vincent Seymour Swift and of Amy Ruth Swift; *m* 1979, Charles Peter Lawford Openshaw, *qv*; one *s* one *d*. *Educ:* Lancaster Girls' Grammar Sch.; Univ. of Durham (BA Hons Law). Pres., Durham Union Soc., 1975. Called to the Bar, Inner Temple, 1977, Bencher, 1997; practised on Northern Circuit, 1978–; Asst Recorder, 1992–95. *Publications:* (jtly) Ribchester: 100 years in photographs, 1994; Ribchester: a millennium record, 2001. *Recreations:* home and family, participating in parish affairs, cooking, theatre, ski-ing. *Address:* 12 Byrom Street, Manchester M3 4PP. *T:* (0161) 829 2100; 22 Old Buildings, Lincoln's Inn, WC2A 3UJ.

SWIFT, Clive Walter; actor, author, teacher; initiator, 1980, now Adviser to the Board, Actor's Centre; *b* 9 Feb. 1936; *s* of Abram Swift and Lillie (*née* Greenman); *m* 1960, Margaret Drabble, *qv* (marr. diss. 1975); two *s* one *d*. *Educ:* Clifton Coll., Bristol; Caius Coll., Cambridge (MA Hons Eng. Lit.). Teaching at LAMDA and RADA, 1967–79; teaching verse-speaking at Actor's Centre, 1980–. *Theatre:* début, Nottingham Playhouse, 1959; RSC, 1960–68; Man and Superman, Arts, Vaudeville, and Garrick, 1965; The Young Churchill, Duchess, 1969; Dirty Linen, Arts, 1976; Inadmissible Evidence, Royal Court, 1978; The Potsdam Quartet, Lyric, Hammersmith, 1980; Messiah, Hampstead, Aldwych, 1982; The Genius, Royal Court, 1983; King Lear, New Vic, 1986; The Sisterhood, New End, 1987; An Enemy of the People, Young Vic, Playhouse, 1988; Othello, Other Place, Young Vic, 1990; Pooter, in Mr and Mrs Nobody, nat. tour, 1993–94; Whittlestaff, in An Old Man's Love, Royal, Northampton, and tour, 1996; Doña Rosita, Almeida, 1997; Higher than Babel, Bridewell, 1999; Hysteria, Minerva Theatre, Chichester, 2000; Chichester Festival theatre seasons, 1965 and 1971; *director:* at LAMDA: The Wild Goose Chase, 1969; The Cherry Orchard, 1973; The Lower Depths, 1969; *television:* Love Story, 1961; Dombey & Son, 1968; Waugh on Crime, 1970; The Exorcism, 1972; South Riding, 1974; Gibbon, 1975; Barchester Chronicles, 1982; Pickwick Papers, 1984; First Among Equals, 1985; Keeping up Appearances, 5 series, 1990–95; Peak Practice, 1997; Aristocrats, 1998; *radio:* reader, Fielding's Tom Jones, 1963; Young Churchill, 1969; Radio Rep, 1973; Sword of Honour, 1974; narrator, Babar, 1986; Getting Stratford (monologue), 1987; Heavy Roller, 1988; From the depths of Waters, 1990 (Sony Award Winner); Madame Bovary, 1992; Black Box, 1993; The Double Dealer, 1995; Happy Days, 1995; Everybody Comes to Schicklgruber's, 1996; A Fine and Private Place, 1997; If You Knew Suzy, 1998; The Rose and the Ring, 1998; Sunnyside Up, 1998, 2000; Altaban the Magnificent, 1999; Poor Pen, 2001; *films:* Catch us if You Can, 1963; Frenzy, 1971; The National Health, 1972; Excalibur, 1980; A Passage to India, 1984; Sir Horace Jones, in Tower Bridge Permanent Exhibn film, 1994; Gaston's War, 1996; Vacuums, 2001. Hon. Fellow, Liverpool John Moores Univ., 1999. Cyprus Medal, 1956. *Publications:* The Job of Acting, 1976, 2nd edn 1985; The Performing World of the Actor, 1981. *Recreations:* playing and listening to music, watching Lancashire CCC and Arsenal, golf. *Address:* c/o Roxane Vacca, Vacca Management, 73 Beak Street, W1R 3LF. *T:* (020) 7734 8085. *Club:* Groucho.

SWIFT, David Rowland; His Honour Judge Swift; a Circuit Judge, since 1997; *b* 21 April 1946; *s* of James Rowland Swift and Iris Julia Swift; *m* 1974, Josephine Elizabeth Williamson; two *s* two *d*. *Educ:* Kingsmead Sch., Hoylake; Ruthin Sch.; Liverpool Coll. of Commerce. Admitted Solicitor, 1970; Partner, Percy Hughes and Roberts, Birkenhead, 1971–97; a Recorder, 1993–97. Pres., Liverpool Law Soc., 1995–96. Chairman: Wirral Adult Literacy Project, 1978–84; Liverpool Bd of Legal Studies, 1985–88. Gov., Ruthin Sch., 1988– (Chm. Govs, 1993–99). FRSA. *Publications:* Proceedings Before the Solicitors Disciplinary Tribunal, 1996; articles in legal jls. *Recreations:* sailing, walking, history. *Club:* North West Venturers Yacht.

SWIFT, Graham Colin, FRSL; author; *b* 4 May 1949; *s* of Sheila Irene Swift and Lionel Allan Stanley Swift. *Educ:* Dulwich Coll.; Queens' Coll., Cambridge (MA); Univ. of York. *Publications: novels:* The Sweet Shop Owner, 1980; Shuttlecock, 1981 (Geoffrey Faber Meml Prize, 1983); Waterland, 1983 (Winifred Holtby Award, RSL, 1983; Guardian Fiction Prize, 1983; Premio Grinzane Cavour, 1987); Out of This World, 1988; Ever After, 1992 (Prix du Meilleur Livre Etranger, 1994); Last Orders (Booker Prize, James Tait Black Meml Prize), 1996; *short stories:* Learning to swim and other stories, 1982; (ed with David Profumo) The Magic Wheel (anthology), 1985. Hon. LittD UEA, 1998; DUniv York, 1998. *Recreation:* fishing. *Address:* c/o A. P. Watt, 20 John Street, WC1N 2DR.

SWIFT, John Anthony; QC 1981; Head of Monckton Chambers, since 1999; *b* 11 July 1940; *s* of late Jack Swift and Clare Medcalf; *m* 1972, Jane Carol Sharples; one *s* one *d*. *Educ:* Birkenhead Sch.; University Coll., Oxford (MA); Johns Hopkins Univ.; Bologna. Called to the Bar, Inner Temple, 1965, Bencher, 1992. Rail Regulator, 1993–98. FCIT 1994. *Recreations:* theatre, walking, gardening, golf. *Address:* Monckton Chambers, Gray's Inn, WC1R 5BP. *Clubs:* Reform; Huntercombe Golf.

SWIFT, Lionel; QC 1975; JD; Barrister, since 1961; a Recorder of the Crown Court, and Deputy High Court Judge, 1979–96; *b* Bristol, 3 Oct. 1931; *s* of late Harris and Bessie Swift, Hampstead; *m* 1966, Elizabeth (*née* Herzig) (Liz E, London fashion writer); one *d*. *Educ:* Whittingehame Coll., Brighton; University Coll., London (LLB 1951); Brasenose Coll., Oxford (BCL 1959); Univ. of Chicago (Juris Doc, 1960). Solicitor, Natal, S Africa, 1954; called to the Bar, Inner Temple, 1959, Bencher, 1984. British Commonwealth Fellow, Univ. of Chicago Law Sch., 1960; Amer. Social Science Res. Council Grant for work on admin of criminal justice, 1960. Jun. Counsel to Treasury in Probate Matters, 1974. Chm., Inst. of Laryngology and Otology, 1985–86. *Publication:* The South African Law of Criminal Procedure (Gen. Editor, A. B. Harcourt, QC), 1957. *Address:* (chambers) 4 Paper Buildings, Temple, EC4Y 7EX.

SWIFT, Malcolm Robin Farquhar; QC 1988; a Recorder, since 1987; *b* 19 Jan. 1948; *s* of late Willie Swift and Heather May Farquhar Swift, OBE (*née* Nield); *m* 1969, Anne Rachael (marr. diss. 1993), *d* of Ernest Rothery Ayre; one *s* two *d*. *Educ:* Colne Valley High Sch., Yorks; King's Coll. London (LLB, AKC). Called to the Bar, Gray's Inn, 1970, Bencher, 1998. Co-opted Mem., Remuneration Cttee of Bar Council, 1978–89 (rep. NE Circuit); Mem., Bar Council, 1995–; Leader, NE Circuit, 1998–. *Recreations:* music ("Count One and the t.i.cs"), theatre, cycling, re-cycling. *Address:* Park Court Chambers, 16 Park Place, Leeds LS1 2SJ. *T:* (0113) 243 3277; 6 Gray's Inn Square, Gray's Inn, WC1R 5EZ. *T:* (020) 7242 1052.

SWINBURN, Lt-Gen. Sir Richard (Hull), KCB 1991; landowner; *b* 30 Oct. 1937; *s* of late Maj.-Gen. H. R. Swinburn, CB, OBE, MC and Naomi Barbara Swinburn, *d* of late Maj.-Gen. Sir Amyatt Hull, KCB, and *sister* of late Field Marshal Sir Richard Hull, KG, GCB, DSO; *m* 1964, Jane Elise Brodie, *d* of late Antony Douglas Brodie and of Juliane (*née* Falk). *Educ:* Wellington Coll.; RMA Sandhurst. Commnd 17th/21st Lancers, 1957; Adjt, Sherwood Rangers Yeomanry and 17th/21st Lancers, 1963–65; sc 1968–69; MA to VCGS, 1971–72; Instructor, Staff Coll., 1975–76; MA to COS AFCENT, 1976–78; Comdr 17th/21st Lancers, UK and BAOR, 1979–81; Col ASD 2, MoD, Falklands Campaign, 1982; Comdr, 7th Armoured Bde, BAOR, 1983–84; rcds 1985; Dir Army Plans, 1986–87; GOC 1st Armoured Div., BAOR, 1987–89; ACGS, MoD, 1989–90; Lt-Gen., 1990; GOC SE Dist, 1990–92; GOC Southern Dist, 1992–94; Dep. C-in-C, UKLF, Comdr, UK Field Army, and Inspector Gen., TA, 1994–95, retd. Chm., Cavalry Cols, 1997–2001; Col, Queen's Royal Lancers, 1995–2001; Hon. Col, Exeter Univ. OTC, 1994–. Dir, Glancal Property Co., 1990–96. Pres., Somerset Army Benevolent Fund, 1999–. Mem. Council, RUSI, 1991–95. Comr, Duke of York's Royal Mil. Sch., 1990–94. Huntsman: RMA Sandhurst Beagles, 1956–57; Dhekelia Draghounds, Cyprus, 1971; (and Master) Staff Coll. Draghounds, 1975–76; Chm., Army Beagling Assoc., 1988–94. *Recreations:* agricultural and country pursuits. *Address:* Stone, Exford, Somerset TA24 7NX. *Club:* Cavalry and Guards.

SWINBURN, Walter Robert John; *b* 7 Aug. 1961; *s* of Walter Swinburn. Joined Frenchie Nicholson, 1977; rode 1st winner, Kempton, 1978; first jockey for Michael Stoute, 1981, for Sheikh Maktoum Al Maktoum, 1993. Won on Shergar, 1981, Chester Vase, Derby and King George VI and Queen Elizabeth Diamond Stakes; Irish Derby, 1983, on Shareef Dancer; Derby and Irish Derby, 1986, on Sharastani; Derby, 1995, on Lammtarra; Irish 1,000 Guineas, 1986, on Sonic Lady, 1992, on Marling; Oaks, 1987, on Unite; 2,000 Guineas, 1988, on Doyoun; 1,000 Guineas, 1989, on Musical Bliss, 1992, on Hatoof, 1993, on Sayyedati; Irish 2,000 Guineas, 1989, on Shaadi; Prix de l'Arc de Triomphe, 1983, on All Along.

SWINBURNE, Prof. Richard Granville, FBA 1992; Nolloth Professor of Philosophy of Christian Religion, University of Oxford, 1985–Sept. 2002; *b* 26 Dec. 1934; *s* of William Henry Swinburne and Gladys Edith Swinburne (*née* Parker); *m* 1960, Monica Holmstrom (separated 1985); two *d*. *Educ:* Exeter College, Oxford (Scholar). BPhil 1959, MA 1961, DipTheol 1960. Fereday Fellow, St John's Coll., Oxford, 1958–61; Leverhulme Res. Fellow in Hist. and Phil. of Science, Univ. of Leeds, 1961–63; Lectr in Philosophy, then Sen. Lectr, Univ. of Hull, 1963–72; Prof. of Philosophy, Univ. of Keele, 1972–84. Vis. Associate Prof. of Philosophy, Univ. of Maryland, 1969–70; Dist. Vis. Schol., Univ. of Adelaide, 1982; Vis. Prof. of Philosophy, Syracuse Univ., 1987; Vis. Lectr, Indian Council for Philosophical Res., 1992; Lectures: Wilde, Oxford Univ., 1975–78; Forwood, Liverpool Univ., 1977; Marrett Meml, Exeter Coll., Oxford, 1980; Gifford, Univ. of Aberdeen, 1982–84; Edward Cadbury, Univ. of Birmingham, 1987; Wade, St Louis Univ., 1990; Dotterer, Pennsylvania State Univ., 1992; Aquinas, Marquette Univ., 1997. *Publications:* Space and Time, 1968, 2nd edn 1981; The Concept of Miracle, 1971; An Introduction to Confirmation Theory, 1973; The Coherence of Theism, 1977, rev. edn 1993; The Existence of God, 1979, rev. edn 1991; Faith and Reason, 1981; (with S. Shoemaker) Personal Identity, 1984; The Evolution of the Soul, 1986, rev. edn 1997; Responsibility and Atonement, 1989; Revelation, 1992; The Christian God, 1994; Is There a God?, 1996; Providence and the Problem of Evil, 1998; Epistemic Justification, 2001; articles and reviews in learned jls. *Address:* Oriel College, Oxford OX1 4EW. *T:* (01865) 276589.

See also D. R. Cope.

SWINBURNE, Prof. Terence Reginald; Professor of Horticultural Development, Wye College, London University, 1994–98, now Emeritus; *b* 17 July 1936; *s* of Reginald and Gladys Swinburne; *m* 1958, Valerie Parkes; two *s*. *Educ:* Imperial Coll., Univ. of London (DSc, ARCS, DIC, PhD); FIHort. Plant Pathology Res. Div., Min., later Dept, of Agriculture for NI, 1960–80; Scientific Officer, 1960–62; Sen. Scientific Officer, 1962–71; PSO, 1971–79; SPSO, 1979–80; Queen's University, Belfast: Asst Lectr, Faculty of Agriculture, 1961–64; Lectr, 1965–77; Reader, 1977–80; Head of Crop Protection Div., E Malling Res. Stn, 1980–85; Dir, Inst. of Hortl Res., AFRC, 1985–90; Sen. Res. Fellow, Wye Coll., London Univ., 1990–94. Kellogg Fellow, Oregon State Univ., 1964–65; Vis. Prof., Dept of Pure and Applied Biology, Imperial Coll., London, 1986–91. Gov., Hadlow Coll., 2000–. *Publication:* Iron Siderophores and Plant Diseases, 1986. *Recreation:* sailing. *Address:* Tan House, 15 Frog Lane, West Malling, Kent ME19 6LN. *T:* (01732) 846090. *Club:* Farmers'.

SWINDELLS, Maj.-Gen. (George) Michael (Geoffrey), CB 1985; Controller, Army Benevolent Fund, 1987–97; *b* 15 Jan. 1930; *s* of late George Martyn Swindells and Marjorie Swindells; *m* 1955, Prudence Bridget Barbara Tully; two *d* (and one *s* decd). *Educ:* Rugby School. Nat. Service Commission, 5th Royal Inniskilling Dragoon Guards, 1949; served in Germany, Korea and Canal Zone; Adjutant, Cheshire Yeomanry, 1955–56; Staff Coll., 1960; transfer to 9th/12th Royal Lancers, to command, 1969–71; Comdr 11th Armd Brigade, 1975–76; RCDS course, 1977; Dir of Op. Requirements (3), MoD, 1978–79; Chief of Jt Services Liaison Organisation, Bonn, 1980–83; Dir of Management and Support of Intelligence, 1983–85. Col, 9th/12th Royal Lancers, 1990–95. Chairman: Royal Soldiers' Daughters Sch., 1985–89; BLESMA, 1991–96; Council, Wilts Wildlife Trust, 1998–; Royal Soc. for Asian Affairs, 1999–. *Recreations:* country life, gardening.

SWINDELLS, Heather Hughson, (Mrs R. Inglis); QC 1995; a Recorder, since 1994; a Deputy High Court Judge, since 2000; *d* of Mrs Debra Hughson Swindells; *m* 1976, Richard Inglis, *qv*; one *s*. *Educ:* Nottingham High Sch. for Girls; St Anne's Coll., Oxford (MA Lit.Hum.). Called to the Bar, Middle Temple, 1974. *Publications:* Family Law and the Human Rights Act 1998; (contrib.) Family Law: essays for the new millennium. *Recreations:* books, music, art, archaeology. *Address:* St Philip's Chambers, 55 Temple Row, Birmingham B2 5LS. *T:* (0121) 246 7000; One King's Bench Walk, Temple, EC4Y 7DB. *T:* (020) 7936 1500; King Charles House, Standard Hill, Nottingham NG1 6FX. *T:* (0115) 941 8851; Zenith Chambers, 10 Park Square, Leeds LS1 2LH. *T:* (0113) 245 5438.

SWINDEN, (Thomas) Alan, CBE 1971; Executive Chairman, Institute of Manpower Studies, 1978–86; *b* 27 Aug. 1915; *s* of Thomas and Ethel Swinden; *m* 1941, Brenda Elise Roe; one *d*. *Educ:* Rydal Sch.; Sheffield Univ. (BEng). With Rolls-Royce, 1937–55; seconded to AFV Div., Min. of Supply, 1941–45; with Engrg Employers Fedn, 1955–65, Dir, 1964–65; Dir, Engrg Industry Trng Bd, 1965–70; Confederation of British Industry: Dep. Dir Gen. (Industrial Relations), 1970–74; Chief Advr, Social Affairs, 1974–78; Consultant, 1978–81; Chm., 1974–85, Dir, 1980–84, Kingston Regional Management Centre. Chm., Derby No 1 HMC, 1953–55. Council Member: British Employers Confedn, 1955–65; ACAS, 1974–84; Inst. for Employment Studies (formerly of Manpower Studies), 1976–96; British Assoc. for Commercial and Industrial Educn, 1982–94; Mem., BBC Consultative Gp on Industrial and Business Affairs, 1977–83. Governor, Box Hill Sch., 1995–99. *Address:* 85 College Road, Epsom, Surrey KT17 4HH. *T:* (01372) 720848. *Club:* Royal Automobile.

SWINDON, Bishop Suffragan of, since 1994; **Rt Rev. Michael David Doe;** *b* Lymington, Hants, 24 Dec. 1947; *s* of late Albert Henry Doe and of Violet Nellie Doe (*née* Curtis). *Educ:* Brockenhurst Grammar Sch.; Durham Univ. (BA 1969); Ripon Hall Theol Coll., Oxford. Ordained deacon, 1972, priest, 1973; Asst Curate, 1972–76, Hon. Curate, 1976–81, St Peter, St Helier, Morden; Youth Sec., BCC, 1976–81; Priest-Missioner, 1981–88, Vicar, 1988–89, Blackbird Leys LEP, Oxford; RD, Cowley, 1986–89; Social Responsibility Advr, dio. of Portsmouth, and Canon Residentiary, Portsmouth Cathedral, 1989–94. Mem., Gen. Synod of C of E, 1990–94. *Publication:* Seeking the Truth in Love, 2000. *Recreations:* travel, radio, television. *Address:* Mark House, Field Rise, Swindon, Wilts SN1 4HP. *T:* (01793) 538654.

SWINFEN, 3rd Baron *cr* 1919; **Roger Mynors Swinfen Eady;** *b* 14 Dec. 1938; *s* of 2nd Baron Swinfen and of Mary Aline (*see* M. A. Siepmann); *S* father, 1977; *m* 1962, Patricia Anne, *o d* of late F. D. Blackmore, Dundrum, Dublin; one *s* three *d*. *Educ:* Westminster; RMA, Sandhurst. ARICS 1970. Mem., Direct Mail Services Standards Bd, 1983–97. Mem., Select Cttee on EC Sub-Cttee C (Envmtl and Social Affairs), 1991–94; elected Mem., H of L, 1999. Chm., Parly Gp, Video Enquiry Working Party, 1983–85. Pres. SE Reg., British Sports Assoc. for the Disabled, 1986–; Patron: Disablement Income Gp, 1995–; 1 in 8 Gp, 1996–; Labrador Rescue SE, 1996–; Hon. Pres., Britain Bangladesh Friendship Soc., 1996–. Fellow, Industry and Parlt Trust. Liveryman, Drapers' Co. JP Kent, 1983–85. *Publication:* (jtly) An Evaluation of the First Year's Experience with a Low-cost Telemedicine Link in Bangladesh, 2001. *Heir:* *s* Hon. Charles Roger Peregrine Swinfen Eady, *b* 8 March 1971. *Address:* House of Lords, SW1A 0PW.

SWINGLAND, Owen Merlin Webb; QC 1974; Barrister-at-Law; *b* 26 Sept. 1919; *er s* of Charles and Maggie Eveline Swingland; *m* 1941, Kathleen Joan Eason (*née* Parry), Newport, Mon; one *s* two *d*. *Educ:* Haberdashers' Aske's Hatcham Sch.; King's Coll., London. LLB 1941, AKC. Called to Bar, Gray's Inn, 1946, Bencher, 1985; practice at Chancery Bar, 1948–88; Barrister of Lincoln's Inn, 1977. A Church Comr, 1982–90. Past Pres., British Insurance Law Assoc. Mem., Court of Assts, Haberdashers' Co. (Master, 1987–88); Freeman of the City of London. *Recreations:* music, theatre, fishing, reading; interested in competitive sports. *Address:* Redwings House, Bayleys Hill, Weald, Sevenoaks, Kent TN14 6HS. *T:* (01732) 451667.

SWINGLER, Raymond John Peter; editorial and information technology consultant, since 1992; *b* 8 Oct. 1933; *s* of Raymond Joseph and Mary Swingler; *m* 1960, Shirley (*d* 1980), *e d* of Frederick and Dorothy Wilkinson, Plymouth; two *d*. *Educ:* St Bede's Coll., Christchurch, NZ; Canterbury Univ. Journalist, The Press, Christchurch, NZ, 1956–57; Marlborough Express, 1957–59; Nelson Mail, 1959–61; freelance Middle East, 1961–62; Cambridge Evening News, 1962–79. Press Council: Mem., 1975–78; Mem., Complaints Cttee, 1976–78; Sec. and conciliator, 1980–91; Asst Dir, 1989–91; Asst Dir, Press Complaints Commn, 1991. Member: Nat. Exec. Council, Nat. Union of Journalists, 1973–75, 1978–79; Provincial Newspapers Industrial Council, 1976–79; Chm., General Purposes Cttee (when journalists' Code of Professional Conduct (revised) introduced), 1974–75. Partner: Haringey Telematics Project, 1995–98; Lee Valley Univ. for Industry, 1997–99; Hon. Sec./Treas., Connexions Project (teaching IT to the disabled), 1994–97. *Recreation:* horses and horsewomen. *Address:* 11A Church Path, E17 9QR.

SWINLEY, Margaret Albinia Joanna, OBE 1980; British Council Service, retired; *b* 30 Sept. 1935; *er* twin *d* of late Captain Casper Silas Balfour Swinley, DSO, DSC, RN and Sylvia Jocosa Swinley, 4th *d* of late Canon W. H. Carnegie. *Educ:* Southover Manor Sch., Lewes; Edinburgh Univ. (MA Hons Hist.). English Teacher/Sec., United Paper Mills, Jämsänkoski, Finland, 1958–60; joined British Council, 1960; Birmingham Area Office, 1960–63; Tel Aviv, 1963; Lagos, 1963–66; seconded to London HQ of VSO, 1966–67; New Delhi, 1967–70; Dep. Rep., Lagos, 1970–73; Dir, Tech. Assistance Trng Dept, 1973–76; Rep., Israel, 1976–80; Asst, then Dep., Controller, Educn, Medicine and Science Div., 1980–82; Controller, Africa and Middle East Div., 1982–86; Controller, Home Div., 1986–89. Trustee, Lloyd Foundn; Mem., Council of Govs, Internat. Students' House, London; Governor: Westbury-on-Severn C of E Primary Sch. (Chm., 1990–96); Hosting for Overseas Students. Mem. Exec. Cttee, S Wales Shire Horse Soc., 1993– (Pres., 1998). Lay Mem., Local Ministry Team, benefice of Westbury-on-Severn with Flaxley and Blaisdon, 1998–. *Recreations:* theatre-going, country life, keeping dogs and Shire horses. *Club:* Royal Commonwealth Society.

SWINNERTON-DYER, Prof. Sir (Henry) Peter (Francis), 16th Bt *cr* 1678; KBE 1987; FRS 1967; Chief Executive, Universities Funding Council, 1989–91; *b* 2 Aug. 1927; *s* of Sir Leonard Schroeder Swinnerton Dyer, 15th Bt, and Barbara (*d* 1990), *d* of Hereward Brackenbury, CBE; *S* father, 1975; *m* 1983, Dr Harriet Crawford, *er d* of Rt Hon. Sir Patrick Browne, OBE, TD, PC. *Educ:* Eton; Trinity College, Cambridge (Hon. Fellow 1981). University of Cambridge: Research Fellow, 1950–54, Fellow, 1955–73, Dean, 1963–73, Trinity Coll.; Master, St Catharine's Coll., 1973–83 (Hon. Fellow, 1983); Univ. Lectr, 1960–71 (at Mathematical Lab., 1960–67); Prof. of Maths, 1971–88; Vice-Chancellor, 1979–81. Commonwealth Fund Fellow, Univ. of Chicago, 1954–55. Vis. Prof., Harvard Univ., 1971. Hon. Fellow, Worcester Coll., Oxford, 1980. Chairman: Cttee on Academic Organisation, Univ. of London, 1980–82; Meteorological Cttee, 1983–94; UGC, 1983–89; CODEST, 1986–91; European Sci. and Technol. Assembly, 1994–. Chm., Sec. of State for Nat. Heritage's Adv. Cttee, Liby and Inf. Services Council, 1992–95; Mem., Library and Information Commn, 1995–98. Hon. DSc: Bath, 1981; Ulster, Wales, 1991; Birmingham, Nottingham, 1992; Warwick, 1993; Hon. LLD Aberdeen, 1991. *Publications:* numerous papers in mathematical journals. *Recreation:* gardening. *Heir:* *kinsman* John Dyer-Bennet [*b* 17 April 1915; *m* 1951, Mary Abby Randall; one *s* one *d*]. *Address:* The Dower House, Thriplow, Royston, Herts SG8 7RJ. *T:* (01763) 208220.

SWINNEY, John Ramsay; Member (SNP) North Tayside, since 1999, and Leader of the Opposition, since 2000, Scottish Parliament; Leader, Scottish National Party, since 2000; *b* 13 April 1964; *s* of Kenneth Swinney and Nancy Swinney (*née* Hunter); *m* 1991, Lorna Ann King (marr. diss. 2000); one *s* one *d*. *Educ:* Univ. of Edinburgh (MA Hons Politics). Sen. Managing Consultant, Developments Options Ltd, 1988–92; Strategic Planning Principal, Scottish Amicable, 1992–97. MP (SNP) Tayside North, 1997–2001. Scottish Parliament: Dep. Leader of Opposition, 1999–2000; Convener, Enterprise and Lifelong Learning Cttee, 1999–2000. Scottish National Party: Nat. Sec., 1986–92; Vice Convenor for Publicity, 1992–97; Treasury Spokesman, 1995–2000; Dep. Leader, 1998–2000. *Recreations:* cycling, hill walking. *Address:* 35 Perth Street, Blairgowrie PH10 6DL. *T:* (01250) 876576.

SWINSON, Christopher, FCA; Senior Partner, BDO Stoy Hayward, since 1997 (Partner, 1993–97); *b* 27 Jan. 1948; *s* of Arthur Montagu Swinson and Jean Swinson; *m* 1972, Christine Margaret Hallam; one *s*. *Educ:* Wadham Coll., Oxford (MA). FCA 1979 (ACA 1974). Price Waterhouse, 1970–77; Hacker Young, 1977–79; with Binder Hamlyn, 1979–92 (Nat. Man. Partner, 1989–92). Institute of Chartered Accountants in England and Wales: Mem. Council, 1985–; Vice-Pres., 1996–97; Dep. Pres., 1997–98; Pres., 1998–99; Chm., Regulation Review Working Party, 1995–2001. Mem., Audit Commn, 2000–. Treasurer: Navy Records Soc., 1987–94; Soc. for Nautical Res., 1991–95; NCVO, 1993–97; Trustee, Greenwich Foundn, RNC, 1997–. FRSA 1992. *Publications:* Companies Act 1989, 1990; Regulation of Auditors, 1990; Delivering a Quality Service, 1992; Group Accounts, 1993. *Recreation:* model railway construction. *Address:* 2 Seymour Close, Hatch End, Pinner, Middx HA5 4SB. *T:* (020) 8421 0951, *Fax:* (020) 8421 3344. *Club:* Athenæum.

SWINSON, Sir John (Henry Alan), Kt 1984; OBE 1974; Commercial Director (Ireland), Forte (formerly Trusthouse Forte) plc, 1965–96; *b* 12 July 1922; *s* of Edward Alexander Stanley Swinson and Mary Margaret McLeod; *m* 1944, Margaret Sturgeon Gallagher; two *s*. *Educ:* Royal Belfast Academical Institution. Founded J. H. A. Swinson and Co. Ltd, 1946; Man. Dir (also of associated cos), until 1959; merged with Lockhart Gp, 1959, which merged with Trust Houses (later Trusthouse Forte plc), 1965. Chairman: Catering Industry Training Board, 1966–75; NI Training Executive, 1975–83; Livestock Marketing Commn (NI), 1970–85; NI Tourist Bd, 1979–88 (Mem., 1970–88); Member: Council, NIHCA, 1961– (Past Pres.); Catering Wages Council, 1965–82; NI Economic Council, 1977–81; Industrial Forum for NI, 1980–83. *Recreation:* sailing. *Address:* 22A Ailsa Road, Cultra, Co. Down BT18 0AS.

SWINTON, 2nd Earl of, *cr* 1955; **David Yarburgh Cunliffe-Lister;** JP; DL; Viscount Swinton, 1935; Baron Masham, 1955; *b* 21 March 1937; *s* of Major Hon. John Yarburgh Cunliffe-Lister (*d* of wounds received in action, 1943) and Anne Irvine (*d* 1961), *yr d* of late Rev. Canon R. S. Medlicott (she *m* 2nd, 1944, Donald Chapple-Gill); *S* grandfather, 1972; *m* 1959, Susan Lilian Primrose Sinclair (*see* Baroness Masham of Ilton); one *s* one *d* (both adopted). *Educ:* Winchester; Royal Agricultural College. Member: N Riding Yorks CC, 1961–74; N Yorks CC, 1973–77. Captain of the Yeoman of the Guard (Dep. Govt Chief Whip), 1982–86. Dir, Leeds Permanent Building Soc., 1987–93. Mem., Countryside Commn, 1987–93. JP North (formerly NR) Yorks, 1971; DL North Yorks, 1978. *Heir:* *b* Hon. Nicholas John Cunliffe-Lister [*b* 4 Sept. 1939; *m* 1966, Hon. Elizabeth Susan (marr. diss.), *e d* of Viscount Whitelaw, KT, CH, MC, PC; two *s* one *d*; *m* 1996, Pamela Sykes]. *Address:* Dykes Hill House, Masham, N Yorks HG4 4NS. *T:* (01765) 689241; 46 Westminster Gardens, SW1P 4JG. *T:* (020) 7834 0700. *Clubs:* White's, Pratt's; Leyburn Market (N Yorks).

SWINTON, Countess of; *see* Masham of Ilton, Baroness.

SWINTON, Maj.-Gen. Sir John, KCVO 1979; OBE 1969; JP; Lord-Lieutenant of Berwickshire, 1989–2000; *b* 21 April 1925; *s* of late Brig. A. H. C. Swinton, MC, Scots Guards; *m* 1954, Judith, *d* of late Harold Killen, Merribee, NSW; three *s* one *d*. *Educ:* Harrow. Enlisted, Scots Guards, 1943, commissioned, 1944; served NW Europe, 1945 (twice wounded); Malaya, 1948–51 (despatches); ADC to Field Marshal Sir William Slim, Governor-General of Australia, 1953–54; Staff College, 1957; DAA&QMG 1st Guards Brigade, 1958–59; Regimental Adjutant Scots Guards, 1960–62; Adjutant, RMA Sandhurst, 1962–64; comd 2nd Bn Scots Guards, 1966–68; AAG PS12 MoD, 1968–70; Lt Col Comdg Scots Guards, 1970–71; Comdr, 4th Guards Armoured Brigade, BAOR, 1972–73; RCDS 1974; Brigadier Lowlands and Comdr Edinburgh and Glasgow Garrisons, 1975–76; GOC London Dist and Maj.-Gen. Comdg Household Divn, 1976–79; retired 1979. Mem., Queen's Body Guard for Scotland (Royal Co. of Archers), 1954– (Lieut, 2001–); Hon. Col 2nd Bn 52nd Lowland Volunteers, 1983–90. Pres., Lowland TA & VRA, 1992–96; Nat. Chm., Royal British Legion Scotland, 1986–89 (Nat. Vice-Chm., 1984–86); Mem. Council, British Commonwealth Ex-Services League, 1984–98. Mem., Central Adv. Cttee on War Pensions, 1986–89. Pres., Borders Area SSAFA, 1993–. Trustee: Army Museums Ogilby Trust, 1978–90; Scottish Nat. War Meml, 1984– (Vice-Chm., 1987–96; Chm., 1996–); Scots at War Trust, 1996–; Berwick Mil. Tattoo, 1996–; Chm., Thirlestane Castle Trust, 1984–90. Patron, Prosthetic and Orthotic Worldwide Educn and Relief, 1995–. Borders Liaison Officer, Duke of Edinburgh's Award Scheme, 1982–84. Chairman: Berwicks Civic Soc., 1982–98 (Pres., 1998–); Roxburgh and Berwickshire Cons. Assoc., 1983–85; Jt Management Cttee, St Abb's Head Nat. Nature Reserve, 1991–98; Berwicks Recreation Sports Trust, 1997–; Scottish Nat. Motorsport Collection, 1998–; Pres., Berwickshire Naturalists Club, 1996–97. Pres., RHAS, 1993–94. DL, 1980–89, JP, 1989, Berwickshire. *Address:* Kimmerghame, Duns, Berwickshire TD11 3LU. *T:* (01361) 883277.

SWIRE, Sir Adrian (Christopher), Kt 1982; DL; Hon. President and Executive Director, John Swire and Sons Ltd, since 1998 (Director, 1961; Deputy Chairman, 1966–87; Chairman, 1987–97); Director: Cathay Pacific Airways, since 1965; Swire

Pacific Ltd, since 1978; HSBC Holdings plc, since 1995; *b* 15 Feb. 1932; *yr s* of late John Kidston Swire and Juliet Richenda, *d* of Theodore Barclay; *m* 1970, Lady Judith Compton, *e d* of 6th Marquess of Northampton, DSO; two *s* one *d*. *Educ:* Eton; University Coll., Oxford (MA). Served Coldstream Guards, 1950–52; RAFVR and RAux AF (AE 1961; Hon. Air Cdre, 1987–2000). Joined Butterfield & Swire in Far East, 1956. Director: Brooke Bond Gp, 1972–82; NAAFI, 1972–87; Mem., Internat. Adv. Council, China Internat. Trust and Investment Corp., Beijing, 1995–. Mem., Gen. Cttee, Lloyd's Register, 1967–99. Pres., General Council of British Shipping, 1980–81; Chm., Internat. Chamber of Shipping, 1982–87. Elder Brother, Trinity House, 1990. Vis. Fellow, Nuffield Coll., Oxford, 1981–89 (Hon. Fellow, 1998). Chm., RAF Benevolent Fund, 1996–2000; Mem. Council, Air League, 2000–. Trustee, RAF Mus., 1983–91. Pres., Spitfire Soc., 1996–. Pro-Chancellor, Southampton Univ., 1995–. Mem. Council, Wycombe Abbey Sch., 1988–95. Hon. CRAeS 1991. Liveryman: Fishmongers' Co., 1962; GAPAN, 1986. DL Oxon, 1989. Hon. DSc Cranfield, 1995. *Address:* Swire House, 59 Buckingham Gate, SW1E 6AJ. *Clubs:* White's, Brooks's, Pratt's; Hong Kong (Hong Kong).

See also Sir J. A. Swire.

SWIRE, Hugo George William; MP (C) Devon East, since 2001; *b* 30 Nov. 1959; *s* of Humphrey Roger Swire and Philippa Sophia Montgomerie; *m* 1996, Alexandra, (Sasha), Petruška Mina, *d* of Rt Hon. Sir John William Frederick Nott, *qv*; two *d*. *Educ:* Eton; Univ. of St Andrews; RMA Sandhurst. Lieut, 1 Bn Grenadier Guards, 1980–83; Head, Develt Office, Nat. Gall., 1988–92; Southeby's, 1992–: Dep. Dir, 1996–97; Dir, 1997–. Contested (Scottish C and Unionist) Greenock and Inverclyde, 1997. FRSA 1993. *Recreations:* field sports, ski-ing, gardening. *Address:* House of Commons, SW1A 0AA. *Clubs:* White's, Pratt's, Beefsteak.

SWIRE, Sir John (Anthony), Kt 1990; CBE 1977; DL; Life President, John Swire & Sons Ltd, since 1997 (Chairman, 1966–87, Executive Director, 1955–92; Hon. President and Director, 1987–97); *b* 28 Feb. 1927; *er s* of late John Kidston Swire and Juliet Richenda, *d* of Theodore Barclay; *m* 1961, Moira Cecilia Ducharne; two *s* one *d*. *Educ:* Eton; University Coll., Oxford (MA). Served Irish Guards, UK and Palestine, 1945–48. Joined Butterfield & Swire, Hong Kong, 1950; Director: Swire Pacific Ltd, 1965–92; Royal Insurance plc, 1975–80; British Bank of the Middle East, 1975–79; James Finlay plc, 1976–92; Ocean Transport & Trading plc, 1977–83; Shell Transport and Trading Co., 1990–95. Chairman: Hong Kong Assoc., 1975–87; Cook Soc., 1984. Member: London Adv. Cttee, Hongkong and Shanghai Banking Corp., 1969–89; Euro-Asia Centre Adv. Bd, 1980–91; Adv. Council, Sch. of Business, Stanford Univ., 1981–90; Council, Univ. of Kent at Canterbury, 1989–99 (Dep. Pro-Chancellor, 1993–99). Hon. Fellow: St Antony's Coll., Oxford, 1987; University Coll., Oxford, 1989. Hon. LLD Hong Kong, 1989; Hon. DCL Kent, 1995. DL Kent, 1996. *Address:* Swire House, 59 Buckingham Gate, SW1E 6AJ. *T:* (020) 7834 7717. *Clubs:* Brooks's, Pratt's, Cavalry and Guards, Flyfishers' (Pres., 1988–89); Union (Sydney); Hong Kong (Hong Kong).

See also Sir A. C. Swire.

SWITZER, Barbara; Assistant General Secretary, Manufacturing Science Finance, 1988–97; *b* 26 Nov. 1940; *d* of Albert and Edith McMinn; *m* 1973, John Michael Switzer. *Educ:* Chorlton Central Sch., Manchester; Stretford Technical Coll. City & Guilds Final Cert. for Electrical Technician. Engrg apprentice, Metropolitan Vickers, 1957–62; Draughtswoman: GEC, Trafford Park, 1962–70; Cableform, Romiley, 1970–71; Mather & Platt, 1972–76; Divisional Organiser 1976–79, National Organiser 1979–83, AUEW (TASS); Dep. Gen. Sec., TASS—The Manufacturing Union, 1983–87. President: CSEU, 1995–97; Nat. Assembly of Women, 1999–; Mem., TUC Gen. Council, 1993–97. Mem., Employment Appeal Tribunal, 1996–. Dir, Women of the Year Lunch and Assembly, 1996–. TUC Women's Gold Badge for services to Trade Unionism, 1976. *Address:* 16 Follett Drive, Abbots Langley, Herts WD5 0LP. *T:* (01923) 674662.

SWORD, Dr Ian Pollock, FRCPE; CChem, FRSC; FRSE; Senior Executive Vice President, Société Générale de Surveillance, since 1993; *b* 6 March 1942; *s* of John Pollock Sword and Agnes McGowan (*née* Fyfe); *m* 1967, Flora Collins; two *s* one *d*. *Educ:* Univ. of Glasgow (BSc; PhD). CChem 1975; FRSC 1975; FRSE 1996; FRCPE 1997. Univ. of Princeton, 1967–69; Res. Associate, Univ. of Oxford, 1969–70; Hd of Metabolism, then Chemistry Dept, Huntingdon Res. Centre, 1970–73; Chm., Inveresk Res., 1973–. Mem., MRC, 1995–98. *Publications:* (ed) Standard Operating Procedures, vol. 3, 1980, vol. 4, 1981. *Recreations:* music, golf. *Address:* Area Management, Inveresk Research, Tranent EH33 2NE. *T:* (01875) 614545. *Club:* New (Edinburgh).

SWORD, John Howe; Director, Oral History Project, University of Toronto, 1981–90; a Vice-President, Associated Medical Services Inc., 1984–92; *b* Saskatoon, Saskatchewan, 22 Jan. 1915; *m* 1947, Constance A. Offen; one *s* one *d*. *Educ:* public and high schs, Winnipeg; Univ. of Manitoba (BA); Univ. of Toronto (MA). Served War, RCAF, Aircrew navigation trg and instr in Western Canada; Armed Services Div., Wartime Inf. Bd, Ottawa, 1945. Taught for six years, before War, in Roland, Teulon and Winnipeg, Manitoba. Secretary, Manitoba Royal Commn on Adult Educn, 1945–46. Univ. of Toronto: Asst Sec. and Sec., Sch. of Grad. Studies, 1947–60; Exec. Asst to the President, 1960–65; Vice-Provost, 1965–67; Actg Pres., 1967–68; Exec. Vice-Pres. (Academic), and Provost, 1968–71; Actg Pres., 1971–72; Vice-Pres., Institutional Relations and Planning, 1972–74; Special Asst to the President, Institutional Relations, 1974–80, retired; Acting Dir, Sch. of Continuing Studies, 1980–81 and 1983–84. Chm., Art Cttee, 1980–83, Finance Cttee, 1983–88, Mem. Bd of Stewards, 1988–94, Hart House, Univ. of Toronto. Chm., Certificate Review Adv. Cttee, Ministry of Educn, 1984–94. Member: Bd, Addiction Res. Foundn of Ont, 1981–88; Council, Royal Canadian Inst., Toronto, 1981–93. Dir, Toronto Dist Heating Corp., 1983–87. Chm., Toronto Round Table, 1991–93; Mem. Management Bd, Geneva Park YMCA, 1972–85; Trustee: Toronto Sch. of Theology, 1978–83; Wychwood Pk Heritage Conservation Dist, 1986–90. Mem., United Church. Hon. LLD: Univ. of Manitoba, 1970; Univ. of Toronto, 1988. Silver Jubilee Medal, 1977. *Recreations:* lawn bowling, swimming. *Address:* #716–602 Melita Crescent, Toronto, ON M6G 3Z5, Canada. *T:* (416) 530 7799. *Clubs:* Faculty (Univ. of Toronto), Arts and Letters, Queen's, Wells Hill Lawn Bowling (Toronto).

SYCAMORE, Phillip; His Honour Judge Sycamore; a Circuit Judge, since 2001; *b* 9 March 1951; *s* of Frank and Evelyn Martin Sycamore; *m* 1974, Sandra, JP, *d* of late Peter Frederick Cooper and of Marjorie Cooper; two *s* one *d*. *Educ:* Lancaster Royal Grammar Sch.; Holborn Coll. of Law (LLB London (ext.) 1972). Admitted Solicitor, 1975; Partner, Lonsdales, solicitors, 1980–2001; Asst Recorder, 1994–99; a Recorder, 1999–2001. Law Society: Mem. Council, 1991–99; Vice-Pres., 1996–97; Pres., 1997–98. Member: Woolf Civil Justice Review (Access to Justice), 1994–96; Criminal Injuries Compensation Panel, 2000–01. Governor: Lancaster Royal Grammar Sch.; Coll. of Law. Hon. LLD: Westminster, 1998; Lancaster, 1999. *Recreations:* family, golf, theatre, travel, ski-ing. *Address:* Preston Law Courts, Ringway, Preston PR1 2LL. *Clubs:* Athenæum; Royal Lytham and St Anne's Golf.

SYDNEY, Archbishop of, since 2001; **Most Rev. Peter Jensen;** *b* 11 July 1943; *s* of Arthur Henry Jensen and Dorothy Lake Jensen (*née* Wilins); *m* 1968, Christine Willis Jensen (*née* O'Donell); three *s* two *d*. *Educ:* Univ. of London (BD 1970); Sydney Univ. (MA 1976); Univ. of Oxford (DPhil 1980). Ordained deacon, 1969, priest, 1970, Anglican Ch of Australia; Curate, Broadway, 1969–76; Moore College: Lectr, 1973–76 and 1980–84; Principal, 1985–2001. *Publications:* The Quest for Power, 1973; At the Heart of the Universe, 1991. *Recreations:* golf, reading. *Address:* Anglican Church Diocese of Sydney, PO Box Q190, QVB Post Office, NSW 1230, Australia. *T:* (2) 92651521.

SYDNEY, Archbishop of, (RC), since 2001; **Most Rev. George Pell,** DD, DPhil; *b* 8 June 1941; *s* of G. A. and M. L. Pell. *Educ:* St Patrick's Coll., Vic; Corpus Christi Coll., Vic; Urban Univ., Rome (STB, STL); Campion Hall, Oxford Univ. (DPhil); Monash Univ. (MEd). FACE. Episcopal Vicar for Educn, dio. Ballarat, 1973–84; Principal, Inst. for Catholic Educn, 1981–84; Rector, Corpus Christi Coll., Clayton, 1985–87; Auxiliary Bishop, archdio. of Melbourne, 1987–96; Archbishop of Melbourne, 1996–2001. Co-Dep. Nat. Chaplain, Order of St Lazarus, 1998–; Grand Prior, Australian Lieutenancy of the Equestrian Order of the Holy Sepulchre of Jerusalem, 1998–. Member: Vatican Council for Justice and Peace, 1990–95; Vatican Congregation for the Doctrine of the Faith, 1990–2000. Consultor, Vatican Council for the Family, 1996–. Chm., Australian Catholic Relief, 1989–97. Foundn Pro-Chancellor, Australian Catholic Univ., 1990–95 (Pres., 1996–). Apostolic Visitor, Seminaries of NZ, 1994, PNG, and Solomon Is, 1995, Pacific, 1996, Irian Jaya, and Sulawesi, 1998. Honour of the Pallium, Rome, 1997, 2001; GCLJ 1998. *Publications:* The Sisters of St Joseph in Swan Hill 1922–72, 1972; Catholicism in Australia, 1988; Rerum Novarum: one hundred years later, 1992; Issues of Faith and Morals, 1996; Catholicism and the Architecture of Freedom, 1999. *Address:* St Mary's Cathedral, Sydney, NSW 2000, Australia. *Clubs:* Melbourne, Australian (Melbourne); Kelvin, Richmond Football (Vic).

SYDNEY, NORTH, Bishop of; *see* Barnett, Rt Rev. P. W.

SYDNEY, WESTERN, Bishop of; *see* King, Rt Rev. B. F. V.

SYDNEY, Assistant Bishops of; *see* Barnett, Rt Rev. P. W.; King, Rt Rev. B. F. V.; Piper, Rt Rev. R. J.

SYKES, Prof. Alfred Geoffrey, PhD, DSc; FRS 1999; CChem, FRSC; Professor of Inorganic Chemistry, University of Newcastle upon Tyne, 1980–99, now Emeritus; *b* 12 Jan. 1934; *s* of Alfred H. Sykes and Edith A. (*née* Wortley); *m* 1963, Elizabeth Blakey; two *s* one *d*. *Educ:* Huddersfield Coll.; Univ. of Manchester (BSc; PhD 1958; DSc 1973). CChem, FRSC 1972. Lectr, 1961–70, Reader, 1970–80, Univ. of Leeds. Vis. Scientist, Argonne Nat. Labs, USA, 1968; Visitor or Visiting Professor: Heidelberg Univ., 1975; Northwestern Univ., 1978; Univ. of Sydney, 1984; Univ. of Kuwait, 1989; Univs of Adelaide and Melbourne, 1992; Univ. of Newfoundland, 1995; Univs of the W Indies, 1997; Univ. of Lausanne, 1998; Univs of Stellenbosch, Cape Town and Bloemfontein, 1999; Univ. La Laguna, Spain, 2000; City Univ., Hong Kong, 2001; Troisième Cycle Lectr, Les Rasses, 1971, Les Diablerets, 1987, Champéry, 2000, French-speaking Swiss Univs. Editor: Advances in Inorganic and Bio-inorganic Mechanisms (vols 1–4), 1982–86; Advances in Inorganic Chem. (vols 32–52), 1988–. Tilden Lectr (Medal and Prize), RSC, 1984. Fellow, Japanese Soc. for Promotion of Sci., 1986. *Publications:* Kinetics of Inorganic Reactions, 1966; contrib. numerous papers and reviews in chemistry jls. *Recreations:* travel, ornithology, classical music, sport. *Address:* Department of Chemistry, University of Newcastle, Newcastle upon Tyne NE1 7RU; 73 Beech Court, Darras Hall, Newcastle upon Tyne NE20 9NE.

SYKES, Sir David Michael, 4th Bt *cr* 1921, of Kingsknowes, Galashiels, co. Selkirk; Senior Partner, Sykes Office Supplies, since 1985; *b* 10 June 1954; *s* of Michael le Gallais Sykes and Joan Sykes (*née* Groome); S uncle, 2001; *m* 1st, 1974, Susan Elizabeth Hall (marr. diss. 1987); one *s*; 2nd, 1987, Margaret Lynne McGreavy; one *d*. *Educ:* Purbrook Park Grammar Sch. Sales Dir, Frank Groome (Nottingham) Ltd, 1974–85. Chm., Libra Office Equipment Ltd, 2000–. Mem., LTA. MInstD. *Recreations:* travel, food and wine, tennis. *Heir: s* Stephen David Sykes, *b* 14 Dec. 1978.

SYKES, Dr Donald Armstrong; Principal of Mansfield College, Oxford, 1977–86, now Hon. Fellow; *b* 13 Feb. 1930; *s* of late Rev. Leonard Sykes and Edith Mary Sykes (*née* Armstrong); *m* 1962, Marta Sproul Whitehouse (*d* 2000); two *s*. *Educ:* The High Sch. of Dundee; Univ. of St Andrews (MA 2nd cl. Classics 1952; Guthrie Scholar); Mansfield Coll., Oxford (BA 1st cl. Theol. 1958; MA 1961; DPhil 1967); Univ. of Glasgow (DipEd). Fellow in Theology, 1959–77, Senior Tutor, 1970–77, and Sen. Res. Fellow, 1986–89, Mansfield Coll., Oxford; retired from tutoring, 2000. Vis. Prof. in Classics and Religion, St Olaf Coll., Northfield, Minn, 1969–70, 1987. Hon. DD St Olaf, 1979. *Publications:* (contrib.) Studies of the Church in History: essays honoring Robert S. Paul, ed Horton Davies, 1983; (introd., trans. and commentary) Gregory of Nazianzus, *Poemata Arcana*, 1997; articles and reviews in Jl Theological Studies, Studia Patristica, Byzantinische Zeitschrift. *Recreations:* miscellaneous reading, recorded music, walking, gardening. *Address:* 23 Weyland Road, Headington, Oxford OX3 8PE. *T:* (01865) 761576.

SYKES, Edwin Leonard, CMG 1966; *b* 1 May 1914; *m* 1st, 1946, Margaret Elizabeth McCulloch (*d* 1973); 2nd, 1976, Dorothy Soderberg (*d* 1996). *Educ:* Leys School, Cambridge (Schol.); Trinity Coll., Cambridge (Senior Schol.). Entered Dominions Office, 1937; Asst Priv. Sec. to Secretary of State, 1939. Served War, 1939–45 (despatches). Served in British High Commissions, Canada, 1945–47, India, 1952–54; idc 1955; Dep. UK High Commissioner in Federation of Rhodesia and Nyasaland, 1956–59; Asst Under-Sec. of State, CRO, 1964–65; Dep. UK High Commissioner in Pakistan, 1965–66; Sec., Office of the Parly Comr for Administration, 1967–74. *Address:* 22 Garth House Nursing Home, Tower Hill Road, Dorking, Surrey RH4 2AY.

SYKES, Eric, OBE 1986; actor, writer, director, producer; *b* 4 May 1923; *s* of Vernon and Harriet Sykes; *m* 1952, Edith Eleanore Milbrandt; one *s* three *d*. Wireless Operator, Mobile Signals Unit, RAF, 1941–49. *Films* include: actor: Orders are Orders; Watch Your Stern; Very Important Person; Heavens Above; Shalako; Those Magnificent Men in their Flying Machines, 1964; Monte Carlo or Bust!, 1969; The Boys in Blue, 1982; Absolute Beginners, 1986; The Others, 2001; *radio* includes: writer: Educating Archie; Variety Bandbox; *television* includes: actor: Sykes and A…, 1960–80 (also writer); Charley's Aunt, 1977; If You Go Down to the Woods Today (also prod. and dir), 1980; The 19th Hole, 1989; *silent films:* (actor, writer and dir): The Plank, 1980 (Press Award, Montreux Fest.); Mr H is Late; It's Your Move, 1984; The Big Freeze; Rhubarb, Rhubarb; *theatre* includes: actor: Big Bad Mouse, tour of Australia, 1977–78; A Hatful of Sykes, tour of Australia, Canada, Rhodesia, UK, 1977–78; Run For Your Wife, Shaftesbury, Criterion, and tour of Canada; The 19th Hole, nat. tour, 1992; Two of a Kind, nat. tour, 1995; Fools Rush In, nat. tour, 1996; The School for Wives, Kafka's Dick, 1998, Piccadilly; Charley's Aunt, nat. tour, 2001; Caught in the Net, Vaudeville, 2001. Freeman, City of London, 1988. Hon. Fellow, Univ. of Lancashire, 1999. Lifetime Achievement Award, Writers' Guild, 1992. *Publications:* Sykes of Sebastopol Terrace; The Great Crime of Grapplemick (novel),

1985; UFOs are coming Wednesday, 1995; Smelling of Roses, 1997. *Address:* c/o Eric Sykes Ltd, 9 Orme Court, W2 4RL. *T:* (020) 7727 1544. *Club:* Royal and Ancient Golf.

SYKES, Sir (Francis) John (Badcock), 10th Bt *cr* 1781, of Basildon, Berkshire; Partner, Thring Townsend, solicitors, Bath, Swindon and Newbury, since 1972; *b* 7 June 1942; *s* of Sir Francis Godfrey Sykes, 9th Bt and Lady Eira Betty Sykes (*née* Badcock) (*d* 1970); *S* father, 1990; *m* 1966, Susan Alexandra, *er d* of Adm. of the Fleet Sir E. B. Ashmore, *qv*; three *s*. *Educ:* Shrewsbury; Worcester Coll., Oxford (MA). Admitted solicitor, 1968; Assistant Solicitor: Gamlens, Lincoln's Inn, 1968–69; Townsends, 1969–71. Hon. Solicitor, 1973–98, Pres., 1981, Swindon Chamber of Commerce. Governor: Swindon Coll., 1982–90; Swindon Enterprise Trust, 1982–89. Trustee: Roman Research Trust, 1990–2001; Merchant's House (Marlborough) Trust, 1991–; Wilts Community Foundn, 1993–2000. Member: HAC; City Barge Club, Oxford. *Recreations:* local and Anglo-Indian history, venetian rowing. *Heir: s* Francis Charles Sykes, *b* 18 June 1968. *Address:* Kingsbury Croft, Kingsbury Street, Marlborough, Wilts SN8 1HU.

SYKES, Sir Hugh (Ridley), Kt 1997; DL; Chairman: Bamford Hall Holdings Ltd, since 1972; Yorkshire Bank plc, since 1999 (Director, since 1990); *b* 12 Sept. 1932; *m* 1st, 1957, Norah Rosemary Dougan; two *s*; 2nd, 1978, Ruby Anderson; two *s*. *Educ:* Bristol Grammar Sch.; Clare Coll., Cambridge (MA, LLB). CA 1960. Articled with Thomson McLintock, Chartered Accountants, 1956–61; Treas., 1961–69, Asst Man. Dir, 1969–72, Man. Dir (Finance), 1972–73, Steetley & Co.; Chm. and Chief Exec., Thermal Scientific plc, 1977–88. Non-exec. Dep. Chm., Harris Queensway plc, 1978–83; non-exec. Chm., Harveys Furnishings, 1988–94; non-executive Director: National Australia Gp (Europe) Ltd, 1997–; Clydesdale Bank plc, 1999–. Chm., Sheffield Develt Corp., 1988–97; Mem. Bd, Sheffield TEC, 1990–95. Chairman: Hugh and Ruby Sykes Charitable Trust, 1988–; Sheffield Galleries and Museums Trust, 1998–; Trustee, Industrial Trust, 1998–. Mem. Council, Univ. of Sheffield, 1997– (Treas., 1998–). DL S Yorks, 1996. Freeman, City of London, 1990. FCIB 2001. Hon. Fellow, Sheffield Hallam Univ., 1991. Hon. LLD Sheffield, 1996. *Publications:* Working for Benefit, 1997; Welfare to Work: the new deal—maximising the benefits, 1998. *Recreations:* walking, travel, golf, Victorian paintings, shooting, helping to find a solution to the problem of unemployment. *Address:* Bamford Hall, The Hollow, Bamford, Hope Valley S33 0AU. *T:* (01433) 651190. *Clubs:* Carlton, Mark's; Lindrick Golf, Sickleholme Golf.

SYKES, (James) Richard; QC 1981; Chairman, Financial Reporting Review Panel, since 2000; *b* 28 May 1934; *s* of late Philip James and Lucy Barbara Sykes; *m* 1959, Susan Ethne Patricia Allen, *d* of late Lt-Col J. M. and Mrs E. M. B. Allen, Morrinsville, NZ; one *s* three *d*. *Educ:* Charterhouse; Pembroke Coll., Cambridge (BA 1957; MA 1971). Nat. Service, 2nd Lieut RASC, 1952–54. Called to the Bar, Lincoln's Inn, 1958, Bencher, 1989; in practice at Bar, 1958–99. CEDR Accredited Mediator, 1999. Member: City Company Law Cttee, 1974–79; City Capital Markets Cttee, 1980–94; Steering Gp, Govt Review of Company Law, 1998–; Chairman: Judging Panel, Accountant and Stock Exchange Annual Awards, 1982–90; Judging Panel, Stock Exchange and Inst. of Chartered Accountants Awards, 1990–99. Mem. Management Cttee, Internat. Exhibn Co-operative Wine Soc. Ltd, 1986–. Mem. Council, VSO, 1987–99 (Mem. Exec., 1987–93). *Publications:* (Consultant Editor) Gore-Browne on Companies, 42nd edn 1972, 43rd edn 1977, 44th edn 1986; (ed jtly) The Conduct of Meetings, 20th edn 1966, 21st edn 1975. *Address:* c/o Erskine Chambers, 30 Lincoln's Inn Fields, WC2A 3PF. *T:* (020) 7242 5532.

SYKES, Sir John; *see* Sykes, Sir F. J. B.

SYKES, Rev. Canon John; Vicar, St Mary with St Peter, Oldham and Team Rector, Parish of Oldham, since 1987; Chaplain to the Queen, since 1995; *b* 20 March 1939; *s* of George Reginald Sykes and Doris Sykes (*née* Briggs); *m* 1967, Anne Shufflebotham; one *s* one *d*. *Educ:* St James C of E Sch., Slaithwaite; Royds Hall Grammar Sch., Huddersfield; W Bridgford Grammar Sch., Nottingham; Manchester Univ. (BA); Ripon Hall, Oxford. Ordained deacon, 1963, priest, 1964; Curate: St Luke's, Heywood, 1963–67; i/c Holy Trinity, Bolton, 1967–71; Lectr, Bolton Inst. of Technol., 1967–71; Chaplain to Bolton Colls of Further Educn, 1967–71; Rector, St Elisabeth, Reddish, 1971–78; Vicar, Saddleworth, 1978–87. Proctor in Convocation and Mem., Gen. Synod of C of E, 1980–90. Council for the Care of Churches: Mem., 1986–90; Vice-Chm., Art and Design Sub-cttee, 1988–90. Mem., various Manchester Diocesan Cttees and Councils, 1968–93. Chaplain to: Coliseum Theatre, Oldham, 1987–; four Mayors of Oldham, 1989–99; High Sheriff of Gtr Manchester, 1993–94, 1996–97; Gtr Manchester Police, Q Div., 1995–99. Hon. Canon, Manchester Cathedral, 1991–. *Recreations:* architecture, fine arts, music, walking. *Address:* Oldham Vicarage, 15 Grotton Hollow, Grotton, Oldham OL4 4LN. *T:* and *Fax:* (0161) 678 6767. *Club:* Manchester Pedestrians.

SYKES, John David; Director, Group Petroleum Retail Division, Shaw Fuels Ltd, since 1981; *b* 24 Aug. 1956; *m* 1981, Jane Aspinall; one *s* two *d*. *Educ:* St David's Prep. Sch., Huddersfield; Giggleswick Sch., N Riding. Joined Shaw Fuels Ltd (family company), 1974: graduated through every company dept, specialising in sales and transport; Dir, 1978–79; also Dir, subsid. cos. MP (C) Scarborough, 1992–97; contested (C) Scarborough and Whitby, 1997, 2001. PPS to Lord Privy Seal and Leader of H of L, 1995–97. Mem., Select Cttee on Deregulation, 1995–97; Vice Chm., Backbench Deregulation Cttee, 1995–97 (Sec., 1993–95). *Recreations:* walking, reading, Rugby Union, playing piano. *Address:* The Old Vicarage, North Street, Scalby, Scarborough, N Yorks YO13 0RP.

SYKES, Joseph Walter, CMG 1962; CVO 1953; Chairman, Fiji Public Service Commission, 1971–80, retired 1981; *b* 10 July 1915; *s* of Samuel Sykes and Lucy M. Womack; *m* 1940, Elima Petrie, *d* of late Sir Hugh Hall Ragg; three *s* two *d*. *Educ:* De La Salle Coll., Sheffield; Rotherham Gram. Sch.; Jesus Coll., Oxford. Colonial Administrative Service, Fiji; Cadet, 1938; Dist Officer, 1940; District Commissioner, 1950; Deputy Secretary for Fijian Affairs, 1952; Assistant Colonial Secretary, 1953; transferred to Cyprus as Dep. Colonial Sec., Nov. 1954; Admin. Sec., Cyprus. 1955–56; Colonial Sec., Bermuda, 1956–68; Chief Sec., Bermuda, 1968–71; retired. *Publication:* The Royal Visit to Fiji 1953, 1954. *Recreations:* gardening, carpentry. *Address:* 8 Dorking Road, City Beach, Perth, WA 6015, Australia.

SYKES, Sir Keith; *see* Sykes, Sir M. K.

SYKES, Sir (Malcolm) Keith, Kt 1991; Nuffield Professor of Anaesthetics, University of Oxford, 1980–91, Emeritus Professor since 1991; Hon. Fellow of Pembroke College, Oxford, since 1996 (Fellow, 1980–91, Supernumary Fellow, 1991–96); *b* 13 Sept. 1925; *s* of Joseph and Phyllis Mary Sykes; *m* 1956, Michelle June (*née* Ratcliffe); one *s* three *d*. *Educ:* Magdalene Coll., Cambridge (MA, MB, BChir); University Coll. Hosp., London (DA; FFARCS). RAMC, 1950–52. House appointments, University Coll. and Norfolk and Norwich Hosps, 1949–50; Sen. House Officer, Registrar and Sen. Registrar in anaesthetics, UCH, 1952–54 and 1955–58; Rickman Godlee Travelling Scholar and Fellow in Anesthesia, Mass. General Hosp., Boston, USA, 1954–55; RPMS and Hammersmith Hosp., 1958–80: Lectr and Sen. Lectr, 1958–67; Reader, 1967–70; Prof. of Clinical Anaesthesia, 1970–80. Vis. Prof., univs in Canada, USA, Australia, NZ, Malaysia, Europe. Eponymous lectures: Holme, 1970; Clover, 1976; Weinbren, 1976; Rowbottom, 1978; Gillespie, 1979; Gillies, 1985; Wesley Bourne, 1986; Husfeldt, 1986; Della Briggs, 1988; E. M. Papper, 1991; BOC Healthcare, 1992; Harold Griffith, 1992; Sir Robert Macintosh, 1992. Mem. Bd, Fac. of Anaesthetists, 1969–85; Pres., Section of Anaesthetics, RSM, 1989–90; Vice Pres., Assoc. of Anaesthetists, 1990–92 (Mem. Council, 1967–70); Senator and Vice Pres., European Acad. of Anaesthesiology, 1978–85. Hon. FANZCA (Hon. FFARACS 1979); Hon. FCA(SA) (Hon. FFA(SA) 1989). Dudley Buxton Prize, Fac. of Anaesthetists, 1980; Fac. of Anaesthetists Medal, 1987; John Snow Medal, Assoc. of Anaesthetists, 1992. *Publications:* Respiratory Failure, 1969, 2nd edn 1976; Principles of Measurement for Anaesthetists, 1970; Principles of Clinical Measurement, 1980; Principles of Measurement and Monitoring in Anaesthesia and Intensive Care, 1991; Respiratory Support, 1995; Respiratory Support in Intensive Care, 1999; chapters and papers on respiratory failure, intensive care, respiratory and cardiovascular physiology applied to anaesthesia, etc. *Recreations:* sailing, walking, birdwatching, gardening, music. *Address:* 10 Fitzherbert Close, Iffley, Oxford OX4 4EN. *T:* (01865) 771152.

SYKES, Richard; *see* Sykes, J. R.

SYKES, Sir Richard (Brook), Kt 1994; FRS 1997; Chairman, GlaxoSmithKline plc, since 2000 (Chairman, Glaxo Wellcome plc, 1997–2000); Rector, Imperial College of Science, Technology and Medicine, since 2001; *b* 7 Aug. 1942; *s* of late Eric Sykes and of Muriel Mary Sykes; *m* 1969, Janet Mary Norman; one *s* one *d*. *Educ:* Queen Elizabeth Coll., London (1st Cl. Hons Microbiol.); Bristol Univ. (PhD Microbial Biochem.); DSc London, 1993. Glaxo Res. UK (Head of Antibiotic Res. Unit), 1972–77; Squibb Inst. for Med. Res., USA, 1977–86 (Vice-Pres., Infectious and Metabolic Diseases, 1983–86); Glaxo Group Research: Dep. Chief Exec., 1986; Chm. and Chief Exec., 1987–93; Glaxo plc: Group R&D Dir, 1987–93; Dep. Chm. and Chief Exec., 1993–97; Dep. Chm. and Chief Exec., Glaxo Wellcome, 1993–97. Dir, British Pharma Gp, 1998–; non-executive Director: Rio Tinto plc, 1997–; Rio Tinto Ltd, 1997–. Member: Council for Sci. and Technol., 1993–; Adv. Council, Save British Science, 1993–; Foundn for Sci. and Technol. Council, 1994–2000; Trade Policy Forum, 1995–2000; Internat. Adv. Council, Economic Develt Bd, 1995–; Council for Industry and Higher Educn, 1995–; Bd, Eur. Fedn of Pharm. Industries and Assocs, 1997–2000; Council, Internat. Fedn of Pharm. Manufrs Assocs, 1998–; Pres., BAAS, 1998–99. Mem., Bd of Trustees, Natural Hist. Mus., 1996–. Chairman: Business Leader Gp, British Lung Foundn, 1993–; Global Business Council on HIV/AIDS, 1997–2000. Vice-Pres., Nat. Soc. for Epilepsy, 1995–. Mem. Bd of Mgt, LSHTM, 1994–. Fleming Fellow, Lincoln Coll., Oxford, 1992; FKC 1997; FIC 1999. Founder FMedSci 1998. Hon. FRCP. Hon. Fellow, Univ. of Wales, 1997. Hon. DPharm Madrid, 1993; Hon. DSc: Brunel, Hull, Hertfordshire, 1994; Bristol, Newcastle, 1995; Huddersfield, Westminster, 1996; Leeds, 1997; Edinburgh, Strathclyde, 1998; London, Cranfield, Leicester, Sheffield, Warwick, 1999; Hon. MD Birmingham, 1995; Hon. LLD Nottingham, 1997. *Recreations:* opera, tennis, swimming. *Address:* GlaxoSmithKline, Berkeley Avenue, Greenford, Middx UB6 0NN. *T:* (020) 8966 8606. *Club:* Athenæum.

SYKES, Robert Hedley; Chief Executive, Worcestershire County Council, since 1997; *b* 21 Aug. 1952; *s* of Hedley Sykes and Edith (*née* Oliver); *m* 1987, Jill Frances Brice; two *d*. *Educ:* Danum Grammar Sch.; Leeds Univ. (BSc, CQSW); Sheffield Poly. (DMS). Social worker, later Principal Officer (Children's Services), Doncaster MBC, 1975–86; Dep. Divl Dir, Social Services, N Yorks CC, 1986–89; Dep. Dir, Social Services, Oxfordshire CC, 1989–92; Dir, Social Services, Hereford and Worcester CC, 1992–97. FRSA 1999. *Recreations:* family, badminton, theatre. *Address:* County Hall, Spetchley Road, Worcester WR5 2NP. *T:* (01905) 766100.

SYKES, Rt Rev. Prof. Stephen Whitefield; Principal, St John's College, and Professor of Theology, University of Durham, since 1999; Assistant Bishop, diocese of Durham, since 1999; *b* 1 Aug. 1939; *m* 1962, Marianne Joy Hinton; one *s* two *d*. *Educ:* St John's Coll., Cambridge (BA 1961; MA 1964). Univ. Asst Lectr in Divinity, Cambridge Univ., 1964–68, Lectr, 1968–74; Fellow and Dean, St John's Coll., Cambridge, 1964–74; Van Mildert Canon Prof. of Divinity, Durham Univ., 1974–85; Regius Prof. of Divinity, and Fellow, St John's College, Cambridge, 1985–90; Bishop of Ely, 1990–99. Mem., Archbishop's Cttee on Religious Educn, 1967. Chairman: Doctrine Commn of C of E, 1997–; InterAnglican Theol and Doctrinal Commn, 1999–. Hon. Canon of Ely Cathedral, 1985–90. Examining Chaplain to Bishop of Chelmsford, 1970–75. Edward Cadbury Lectr, Univ. of Birmingham, 1978; Hensley Henson Lectr, Univ. of Oxford, 1982–83. Chm., North of England Inst. for Christian Educn, 1980–85. Pres., Council of St John's Coll., Durham, 1984–94. *Publications:* Friedrich Schleiermacher, 1971; Christian Theology Today, 1971; (ed) Christ, Faith and History, 1972; The Integrity of Anglicanism, 1978; (ed) Karl Barth: studies in his theological method, 1980; (ed) New Studies in Theology, 1980; (ed) England and Germany, Studies in Theological Diplomacy, 1982; The Identity of Christianity, 1984; (ed) Authority in the Anglican Communion, 1987; (ed) The Study of Anglicanism, 1988; (ed) Karl Barth: Centenary Essays, 1989; (ed) Sacrifice and Redemption, 1991; Unashamed Anglicanism, 1995; The Story of Atonement, 1997. *Recreation:* walking. *Address:* St John's College, 3 South Bailey, Durham DH1 3RJ. *T:* (0191) 374 3500.

SYKES, Sir Tatton (Christopher Mark), 8th Bt *cr* 1783; landowner; *b* 24 Dec. 1943; *s* of Sir (Mark Tatton) Richard Tatton-Sykes, 7th Bt and Virginia (*d* 1970), *d* of late John Francis Grey Gilliat; *S* father, 1978; granted use of additional arms of Tatton, 1980. *Educ:* Eton; Univ. d'Aix-Marseille; Royal Agric. Coll., Cirencester. *Heir: b* Jeremy John Sykes [*b* 8 March 1946; *m* 1982, Pamela June (marr. diss. 1995; she *m* 2nd, Hon. Nicholas Cunliffe-Lister), *o d* of Thomas Wood]. *Address:* Sledmere, Driffield, East Yorkshire YO25 0XG.

SYLVESTER-EVANS, Alun, CB 1975; Deputy Chief Executive, Property Services Agency, Department of the Environment, 1973–78, retired; Member, Chairman's Panel of Assessors, Civil Service Selection Boards, 1980–88; *b* 21 April 1918; *o c* of Daniel Elias Evans and Esther Evans, Rhymney, Mon.; *m* 1945, Joan Maureen (*d* 1998), *o c* of A. J. Sylvester, CBE; two *s*. *Educ:* Lewis' School, Pengam; University of Wales, Aberystwyth. Armed services, 1940–46. Asst Research Officer, Min. of Town and Country Planning, 1946–47; Asst Principal, 1947–48; Principal Private Sec. to Minister of Housing and Local Govt, 1954–57; Asst Secretary, 1957–66, Under-Sec., 1966–73, Min. of Housing and Local Govt, later DoE. *Recreation:* golf. *Address:* Rudloe Cottage, Rudloe, Corsham, Wilts SN13 0PG. *T:* (01225) 810375. *Club:* Royal Commonwealth Society.

SYMES, (Lilian) Mary; Clerk to Justices, 6 Divisions in Suffolk, 1943–74; Chairman, Norfolk and Suffolk Rent Tribunal, 1974–83; *b* 18 Oct. 1912; *d* of Walter Ernest and Lilian May Hollowell; *m* 1953, Thomas Alban Symes (*d* 1984); one *s*. *Educ:* St Mary's Convent, Lowestoft; Great Yarmouth High School. Articled in Solicitor's Office; qualified as Solicitor, 1936. Became first woman Clerk to Justices (Stowmarket), 1942; first woman Deputy Coroner, 1945; Clerk to the Justices, Woodbridge, 1946, Bosmere and

Claydon, 1951; first woman Coroner, 1951; Deputy Coroner, Northern District, Suffolk, 1956–82. *Recreations:* Worcester porcelain, gardening. *Address:* Leiston Old Abbey, Leiston, Suffolk IP16 4RF.

SYMES, Dr Robert Frederick, OBE 1996; FGS; Keeper of Mineralogy, Natural History Museum, 1995–96; *b* 10 Feb. 1939; *s* of Alfred Charles Symes and Mary Emily Symes; *m* 1965, Carol Ann Hobbs; two *d. Educ:* Birkbeck Coll., London Univ. (BSc Hons); Queen Mary Coll., London Univ. (PhD 1981). FGS 1991. Nat. service, RAF, 1959–61. Natural History Museum, 1957–96: Asst Scientific Officer, 1957–59 and 1961–72; SSO, 1972–81; PSO, 1981–92; Dep. Keeper, 1992–95. Pres., GA, 1996–98. *Publications:* (jtly) Minerals of Cornwall and Devon, 1987; Rock and Mineral, 1988; (jtly) Crystal and Gem, 1991. *Recreations:* countryside, industrial archaeology, local history, tennis, Association Football. *Address:* Violet House, Salcombe Road, Sidmouth, Devon EX10 8PU. *T:* (01395) 578114.

SYMINGTON, Prof. Sir Thomas, Kt 1978; MD; FRSE; Director, 1970–77, and Professor of Pathology, 1970–77, Institute of Cancer Research, Royal Cancer Hospital; *b* 1 April 1915; *m* 1943, Esther Margaret Forsyth, MB, ChB; two *s* one *d. Educ:* Cumnock Academy; Glasgow Univ. BSc 1936; MB ChB, 1941; MD 1950. Maj., RAMC (Dep. Asst Dir Pathology, Malaya, 1947–49). St Mungo (Notman) Prof. of Pathology, Univ. of Glasgow, 1954–70. Visiting Prof. of Pathology, Stanford Univ., Calif., 1965–66. Member, Medical Research Council, 1968–72. FRSE, 1956; FRIC, 1958 (ARIC, 1951); FRCP(G), 1963; FRFPS (G), 1958; FRCPath, 1964. Hon. MD Szeged Univ., Hungary, 1971; Hon. DSc McGill Univ., Canada, 1983. *Publications:* Functional Pathology of the Human Adrenal Gland, 1969; Scientific Foundations of Oncology, 1976; numerous papers on problems of adrenal glands in Journals of Endocrinology and Pathology. *Recreation:* golf. *Address:* Greenbriar, 2 Lady Margaret Drive, Troon KA10 7AL. *T:* (01292) 315707.

SYMMONDS, Algernon Washington, GCM 1980; QC (Barbados) 1995; solicitor and attorney-at-law; *b* 19 Nov. 1926; *s* of late Algernon French Symmonds and Olga Ianthe (*née* Harper); *m* 1954, Gladwyn Ward; one *s* one *d. Educ:* Combermere Sch.; Harrison Coll.; Codrington Coll., Barbados. Solicitor, Barbados, 1953, enrolled in UK, 1958; in practice as Solicitor, Barbados, 1953–55; Dep. Registrar, Barbados, 1955–59; Crown Solicitor, Barbados, 1959–66; Permanent Secretary: Min. of Home Affairs, 1966–72; Min. of Educn, 1972–76; Min. of External Affairs and Head of Foreign Service, 1976–79; appointed to rank of Ambassador, 1977; High Comr in UK, 1979–83 and non-resident Ambassador to Denmark, Finland, Iceland, Norway and Sweden, 1981–83, and to the Holy See, 1982–83; Perm. Sec., Prime Minister's Office, Barbados, 1983–86; Head of CS, 1986. President: Barbados CS Assoc., 1958–65; Fedn of British CS Assocs in Caribbean, 1960–64; Dep. Mem. Exec., Public Services Internat., 1964–66. Pres., Barbados Bar Assoc., 2001 (Chm. Disciplinary Cttee, 1991–97); Chm., Barbados Br., WI Cttee, 1992–95; Dep. Chm., Caribbean Examinations Council, 1973–76. Past Pres., Barbados Lawn Tennis Assoc. *Recreations:* tennis, cricket broadcasting (represented Barbados in football, lawn tennis, basketball). *Address:* Melksham, Margaret Terrace, 12 Pine Gardens, St Michael, Barbados, WI; Symmonds, Greene, Reifer, Pinfold Street, Bridgetown, Barbados, WI. *Clubs:* Empire (Cricket and Football) (Life Mem. and Past Vice-Pres.), Summerhayes Tennis (Past Pres.) (Barbados).

See also Dame O. P. Symmonds.

SYMMONDS, Dame (Olga) Patricia, DBE 2000; GCM 1985; Senator, Parliament of Barbados, since 1994; *b* 18 Oct. 1925; *d* of late Algernon French Symmonds and Olga Ianthe Symmonds (*née* Harper). *Educ:* Queen's Coll., Barbados; Univ. of Reading (BA 2nd Cl. Hons); Inst. of Educn, Univ. of London (PGCE). Teacher, 1945–85, Dep. Principal, 1963–76, Principal, 1976–85, St Michael Sch., Barbados; pt-time Lectr and Tutor, Cave Hill Campus, Univ. of WI, 1963–65. PC (Barbados), 1997–2000. *Publications:* On Language and Life Styles, 1989; (jtly) Caribbean Basic English, 1993; Longer Lasting than Bronze, 1993; contrib. to educnl jls. *Recreations:* reading, music. *Address:* Bank Hall Road, St Michael, Barbados. *T:* 4266470. *Clubs:* Barbados Cricket, Barbados Lawn Tennis.

See also A. W. Symmonds.

SYMON, Prof. Lindsay, CBE 1994; TD 1967; FRCS, FRCSE; Professor of Neurological Surgery, Institute of Neurology, London University and the National Hospital, Queen Square, 1978–95, now Emeritus; *b* 4 Nov. 1929; *s* of William Lindsay Symon and Isabel Symon; *m* 1954, Pauline Barbara Rowland; one *s* two *d. Educ:* Aberdeen Grammar Sch.; Aberdeen Univ. (MB, ChB Hons). FRCSE 1957; FRCS 1959. House Physician and Surgeon, Aberdeen Royal Infirmary, 1952–53; Jun. Specialist in Surgery, RAMC, 1953–55; Surgical Registrar, Aberdeen Royal Infirmary, 1956–58; Neurosurgical Registrar, Middlesex and Maida Vale Hosps, 1958–61, Sen. Neurosurgical Registrar, 1962–65; Mem., External Scientific Staff, MRC, 1965–78; Consultant Neurosurgeon: Nat. Hosp. for Nervous Diseases, Queen Square and Maida Vale, 1965–78; St Thomas' Hosp., 1970–78. Hon. Consultant Neurological Surgeon, St Thomas' Hosp., Hammersmith Hosp., Royal Nose, Throat and Ear Hosp., 1978–95; Hon. Consultant Neurosurgeon, Nat. Hosp. for Neurology and Neurosurgery, 1978–95; Civilian Advr in Neurological Surgery to RN, 1979–95. Adjunct Prof., Dept of Surgery, Southwestern Med. Sch., Dallas, 1982–95. Rockefeller Travelling Fellow in Medicine, Wayne State Univ., Detroit, 1961–62. Pres., Harveian Soc., of London, 1998. Hon. Pres., World Fedn Neurosurgical Socs, 1993– (Pres., 1989–93). Freeman, City of London, 1982. Hon. FACS 1994; Hon. FRSocMed 1997. Jamieson Medal, Australasian Neurosurgical Soc., 1982; John Hunter Medal, RCS, 1985; K. J. Zulch Medal, Max Planck Ges., 1993; Otfrid Förster Medal, Deutsche Ges. für Neurochirurgie, 1998. *Publications:* Operative Surgery/Neurosurgery, 1976, 2nd edn 1986; Advances and Technical Standards in Neurosurgery, 1972, 18th edn 1991; numerous papers on cerebral circulation and metabolism, brain tumours, general neurosurgical topics, etc. *Recreation:* golf. *Address:* Maple Lodge, Rivar Road, Shalbourne, near Marlborough, Wilts SN8 3QE. *T:* and *Fax:* (01672) 870501. *Clubs:* Caledonian; Royal & Ancient (St Andrews).

SYMON, Rev. Canon Roger Hugh Crispin; Canon Residentiary, Canterbury Cathedral, since 1994; *b* 25 Oct. 1934; *s* of Rev. Alan Symon and Margaret Sarah Symon (*née* Sharp); *m* 1963, Daphne Mary Roberts; two *d. Educ:* King's Sch., Canterbury; St John's Coll., Cambridge (MA); Coll. of the Resurrection, Mirfield. Curate, St Stephen's, Westminster, 1961–66; Priest-in-Charge, St Peter's, Hascombe, 1966–68; Chaplain, Univ. of Surrey, Guildford, 1966–74; Vicar, Christ Church, Lancaster Gate, 1974–79, with St James, Sussex Gardens, 1977–79; Home Staff, USPG, 1980–86; Actg Sec. for Anglican Communion Affairs to Archbp of Canterbury, 1987–91, Sec., 1991–94. *Address:* 19 The Precincts, Canterbury, Kent CT1 2EP.

SYMONDS, Ann Hazel S.; *see* Spokes Symonds.

SYMONDS, Jane Ursula; *see* Kellock, J. U.

SYMONDS, (John) Richard (Charters); Senior Research Associate, Queen Elizabeth House, Oxford, since 1979; *b* 2 Oct. 1918; *s* of Sir Charles Putnam Symonds, KBE, CB, DM, FRCP, and Janet (*née* Poulton); *m* 1980, Ann Hazel Spokes (*see* A. H. Spokes Symonds); two *s* by a previous marriage. *Educ:* Rugby Sch.; Corpus Christi Coll., Oxford (Scholar in Mod. History, MA); Secretary Elect, Oxford Union, 1939. Friends Amb. Unit, 1939–44; Dep. Dir Relief and Rehab., Govt of Bengal, 1944–45; UNRRA, Austria, 1946–47; Friends Service Unit, Punjab and Kashmir, 1947–48; UN Commn for India and Pakistan (Kashmir), 1948–49; UN Technical Assistance Board: New York, 1950–51; Liaison Officer in Europe, 1952–53; Resident Rep., Ceylon, 1953–55, Yugoslavia, 1955–58; Rep. in Europe, 1959–62; Reg. Rep., E Africa, 1961. Sen. Res. Officer, Oxford Univ. Inst. of Commonwealth Studies, 1962–65; Reg. Rep. in Southern Africa, UNTAB, 1964–65; Professorial Fellow, IDS, Univ. of Sussex, 1966–69, later Vis. Prof.; Consultant, UN Population Div., 1968–69; Rep. in Europe, UNITAR, 1969–71; UNDP Resident Rep. in Greece, 1972–75, and in Tunisia, 1975–78; Sen. Adviser, UNDP and UN Fund for Population Activities, NY, 1978–79; Sen. Associate Mem., St Antony's Coll., Oxford, 1979–92; Hon. Dir, UN Career Records Project, 1989–92; Consultant: Commonwealth Foundn, 1980; WHO, 1981. Mem. Council, Royal Commonwealth Soc., 1983–86. *Publications:* The Making of Pakistan, 1950; The British and their Successors, 1966; (ed) International Targets for Development, 1970; (with M. Carder) The United Nations and the Population Question, 1973; Oxford and Empire—the last lost cause?, 1986; Alternative Saints: the post Reformation British people commemorated by the Church of England, 1988; Far Above Rubies: the women uncommemorated by the Church of England, 1993; Inside the Citadel: men and the emancipation of women 1850–1920, 1999; In the Margins of Independence: a relief worker in India and Pakistan 1942–49, 2001. *Recreations:* walking, travel. *Address:* 43 Davenant Road, Oxford OX2 8BU. *Club:* Royal Over-Seas League.

SYMONDS, Matthew John; Associate Editor, The Economist, since 2001; *b* 20 Dec. 1953; *s* of Lord Ardwick and Anne Symonds; *m* 1981, Alison Mary Brown; one *s* two *d. Educ:* Holland Park, London; Balliol College, Oxford (MA). Graduate trainee, Daily Mirror, 1976–78; Financial Times, 1978–81; economics and defence leader writer, economics columnist, Daily Telegraph, 1981–86; Founding Director, Newspaper Publishing plc, 1986–94; The Independent: Dep. Editor, 1986–94; Exec. Editor, 1989–94; columnist, Sunday Express, 1995; Dir of Strategy, BBC Worldwide Television, 1995–97; Technol. and Communications Ed., The Economist, 1997–2000. Sen. Financial Journalist, Wincott Awards, 1999. *Recreations:* history, looking at churches and pictures, novels, theatre, boating, tennis, Chelsea FC. *Address:* 16 St Peter's Road, St Margarets, Twickenham, Middx TW1 1QX.

SYMONDS, Richard; *see* Symonds, J. R. C.

SYMONS OF VERNHAM DEAN, Baroness *cr* 1996 (Life Peer), of Vernham Dean in the county of Hampshire; **Elizabeth Conway Symons;** PC 2001; Minister of State (Minister for Trade), Foreign and Commonwealth Office and Department of Trade and Industry, since 2001; *b* 14 April 1951; *d* of Ernest Vize Symons, CB and Elizabeth Megan Symons (*née* Jenkins); *m* 2001, Philip Alan Bassett; one *s. Educ:* Putney High Sch. for Girls; Girton Coll., Cambridge (MA; Hon. Fellow, 2001). Research, Girton Coll., Cambridge, 1972–74; Administration Trainee, DoE, 1974–77; Asst Sec. 1977–88, Dep. Gen. Sec., 1988–89, Inland Revenue Staff Fedn; Gen. Sec., Assoc. of First Div. Civil Servants, 1989–96. Parly Under-Sec. of State, FCO, 1997–99; Minister of State, MoD, 1999–2001. Mem., Employment Appeal Tribunal, 1995. Mem., EOC, 1995–97. Member: Gen. Council, TUC, 1989–96; Council, RIPA, 1989–97; Exec. Council, Campaign for Freedom of Information, 1989–97; Hansard Soc. Council, 1992–97; Council, Industrial Soc., 1994–97; Trustee, IPPR, 1993; Exec. Mem., Involvement and Participation Assoc., 1992. Member: Council, Open Univ., 1994–97; Adv. Council, Civil Service Coll., 1992–97; Governor: Polytechnic of North London, 1989–94; London Business Sch., 1993–97. FRSA. Hon. Associate, Nat. Council of Women, 1989. *Recreations:* reading, gardening, friends.

SYMONS, Christopher John Maurice; QC 1989; a Recorder, since 1993 (an Assistant Recorder, 1990–93); a Deputy High Court Judge, since 1998; *b* 5 Feb. 1949; *s* of Clifford Louis Symons and Pamela Constance Symons; *m* 1974, Susan Mary Teichmann; one *s* one *d. Educ:* Sherborne Prep. Sch.; Clifton Coll.; Kent Univ. (BA Hons (Law)). Called to the Bar, Middle Temple, 1972, Bencher, 1998; called to the Bar of Gibraltar, 1985, to the Irish Bar, 1988, to the NI Bar, 1990, to the Brunei Bar, 1999. Jun. Crown Counsel (Common Law), 1985–89. *Recreation:* hitting balls. *Address:* 3 Verulam Buildings, Gray's Inn, WC1R 5NT. *T:* (020) 7831 8441. *Clubs:* Hurlingham; Berkshire Golf, Woking Golf, Royal Tennis Court (Hampton Court), Jesters; Sotogrande Golf (Spain).

SYMONS, Prof. Martyn Christian Raymond, FRS 1985; Visiting Research Professor: De Montfort University, since 1993; Nottingham Trent University, since 1995; London University, since 1995; Essex University, since 1997; Greenwich University, since 1997; *b* 12 Nov. 1925; *s* of Marjorie LeBrasseur and Stephen White Symons; *m* 1950, Joy Lendon (decd); one *s* one *d. Educ:* Battersea Polytechnic (BSc, PhD, DSc London); CChem, FRSC. Army, 1945–48. Lecturer: Battersea Polytechnic, 1948–53; Southampton Univ., 1953–60; Leicester University: Prof. of Physical Chem., 1960–88; Res. Prof. of Chem., CRC Sen. Fellow, and Dir, CRC Electron Spin Resonance Res. Gp, 1988–93. Royal Soc. of Chemistry: Vice Pres., Faraday Div., 1985–87; Bruker Lectr (first), 1986; R. A. Robinson Lectr, 1987. FRSA. *Publications:* The Structure of Inorganic Radicals (with P. W. Atkins), 1967; Chemical and Biochemical Aspects of Electron Spin Resonance Spectroscopy, 1978; (jtly) Techniques in Free Radical Research, 1992; (with J. Gutteridge) Free Radicals and Iron: chemistry, biology and medicine, 1998; over 1000 scientific articles mainly in chem. jls. *Recreations:* watercolour landscape painting, piano playing. *Address:* 33 Castle Road, Hadleigh, Essex SS7 2AU.

SYMONS, Sir Patrick (Jeremy), KBE 1986; Chairman, Sussex Weald and Downs (formerly Chichester Priority Care Services) NHS Trust, 1994–98; *b* 9 June 1933; *s* of Ronald and Joanne Symons; *m* 1961, Elizabeth Lawrence; one *s* one *d. Educ:* Dartmouth Royal Naval College. Commissioned 1951; in command, HMS Torquay, 1968–70, HMS Birmingham, 1976–77, HMS Bulwark, 1980–81; Naval Attaché, Washington, 1982–84; C of S to Comdr, Allied Naval Forces Southern Europe, 1985–88; SACLANT's Rep. in Europe, 1988–92; retired in rank of Vice-Adm. *Recreations:* sailing, skiing, swimming. *Club:* Royal Naval Sailing Association (Portsmouth).

SYMONS, Prof. Robert Henry, FRS 1988; FAA 1983; Professor, Department of Plant Science, University of Adelaide, 1991–99, Emeritus Professor, since 2000; *b* 20 March 1934; *s* of Irene Olivette Symons (*née* Wellington) and Henry Officer Symons; *m* 1958, Verna Helen Lloyd; two *s* two *d. Educ:* Univ. of Melbourne (BAgSc 1956; PhD 1963). Senior Demonstrator, Univ. of Melbourne, 1958–60; Post-Doctoral Fellow, UK, 1961–62; Lectr, Sen. Lectr, Reader, Prof., Dept of Biochemistry, Univ. of Adelaide, 1962–90. Hon. DSc Macquarie, 1992. Lemberg Medal, Aust. Biochem. Soc., 1985. *Publications:* papers to learned jls on nucleic acid biochemistry and allied subjects. *Recreations:* gardening, wine, managing wine grape vineyard. *Address:* Department of Plant

Science, Waite Institute, University of Adelaide, Glen Osmond, SA 5064, Australia. *T:* (8) 83037423, *Fax:* (8) 83037102.

SYMS, John Grenville St George, OBE 1981; QC 1962; Barrister-at-Law; a Recorder of the Crown Court, 1972–80; *b* 6 Jan. 1913; *s* of late Harold St George Syms and Margaret (*née* Wordley); *m* 1st, 1951, Yvonne Yolande Rigby (marr. diss. 1971); one *s*; 2nd, 1971, Anne Jacqueline, *d* of Brig. J. B. P. Willis-Fleming, CBE, TD. *Educ:* Harrow; Magdalen College, Oxford (BA). Called to the Bar, 1936. Dep. Chm., Huntingdon and Peterborough QS, 1965–71. Chm., SE Agricultural Land Tribunal, 1972–83. Served in RAFVR, 1940–45 (despatches); Wing Commander, 1944. *Recreation:* fishing. *Address:* Wesley House, New Park Road, Cranleigh, Surrey GU6 7HL. *T:* (01483) 276017.

SYMS, Robert Andrew Raymond; MP (C) Poole, since 1997; *b* 15 Aug. 1956; *s* of Raymond Syms and Mary Syms (*née* Brain); *m* 1st, 1991, Nicola Guy (marr. diss. 1999); 2nd, 2000, Fiona Mellersh, *d* of late Air Vice-Marshal F. R. L. Mellersh, CB, DFC and bar. *Educ:* Colston's Sch., Bristol. Dir, C. Syms & Sons Ltd, family building and plant hire gp, 1975–. Mem., Wessex RHA, 1988–90. Member (C): N Wilts DC, 1983–87 (Vice Chm., 1984–87; Leader, Cons. Gp, 1984–87); Wilts CC, 1985–97. Contested (C) Walsall N, 1992. PPS to Chm., Conservative Party, 1999; Opposition front bench spokesman on the envmt, 1999–2001. Member: Health Select Cttee, 1997–2000; Procedure Select Cttee, 1998–99; Vice-Chm., Cons. back bench Constitutional Cttee, 1997–2001. N Wiltshire Conservative Association: Treas., 1982–83; Dep. Chm., 1983–84; Chm., 1984–96; Vice Pres., 1986–88. FCIOB 1999. *Recreations:* reading, travel, cycling. *Address:* House of Commons, SW1A 0AA; c/o Poole Conservative Association, 38 Sandbanks Road, Poole BH14 8BX. *T:* (01202) 739922. *Club:* Carlton.

SYNGE, Sir Robert Carson, 8th Bt *cr* 1801; Manager and Owner, Rob's Furniture; *b* 4 May 1922; *s* of late Neale Hutchinson Synge (2nd *s* of 6th Bt) and Edith Elizabeth Thurlow (*d* 1933), Great Parndon, Essex; *S* uncle, 1942; *m* 1944, Dorothy Jean Johnson, *d* of T. Johnson, Cloverdale; two *d*. *Heir: cousin* Neale Francis Synge [*b* 28 Feb. 1917; *m* 1939, Kathleen Caroline Bowes; one *s* one *d*].

SYNNOTT, Hilary Nicholas Hugh, CMG 1997; HM Diplomatic Service; High Commissioner to Pakistan, since 2000; *b* 20 March 1945; *s* of late Commander Jasper Nicholas Netterville Synnott, DSC, RN and Florence England Synnott (*née* Hillary); *m* 1973, Anne Penelope Clarke; one *s* decd. *Educ:* Beaumont College; Dartmouth Naval College (scholar); Peterhouse, Cambridge (MA); RN Engineering College. CEng; MIEE. RN 1962–73 (HM Submarines, 1968–73). Joined HM Diplomatic Service, FCO, 1973; UK Delegn to OECD, Paris, 1975; Bonn, 1978; FCO, 1981; Head of Chancery, Amman, 1985; Head of Western European Dept, FCO, 1989; Head of Security Co-ordination Dept, FCO, 1991; Minister and Dep. High Comr, New Delhi, 1993–96; Dir (S and SE Asia), FCO, 1996–98; Vis. Fellow, Inst. of Developing Studies, Univ. of Sussex, and IISS, 1999–2000. *Publication:* The Causes and Consequences of South Asia's Nuclear Tests, 1999. *Address:* c/o Foreign and Commonwealth Office, King Charles Street, SW1A 2AH. *Club:* Oxford and Cambridge.

SYSONBY, 3rd Baron *cr* 1935, of Wonersh; **John Frederick Ponsonby;** *b* 5 Aug. 1945; *s* of 2nd Baron Sysonby, DSO and Sallie Monkland, *d* of Dr Leonard Sanford, New York; *S* father, 1956. *Address:* c/o Friars, White Friars, Chester CH1 1XS.

SZASZY, Dame Miraka Petricevich, (Dame Mira), DBE 1990 (CBE 1976); QSM 1975; JP; *b* 7 Aug. 1921; *d* of Lovré (Lawrence) Cvitanov Petricevich and Mákeretá Raharuhi; *m* 1956, Albert Szaszy (decd); two *s*. *Educ*, Te Hapua Primary Sch.; Queen Victoria Maori Girls' Sch., Auckland; Auckland Girls' Grammar Sch.; Auckland Teachers' Training Coll. (BCert 1942); Auckland Univ. (BA 1945); Univ. of Hawaii (Dip. Soc. Sci. 1949). Teacher, 1946, 1968–70; social welfare work, 1946–48, Employment Officer, 1951–52, Maori Affairs Dept; Exec. Sec., Maori Women's Welfare League, 1952–57; Lecturer: Teachers' Training Coll., 1972 and 1974–79; Ardmore Trng Coll., 1973; Dir, Community Dept, Ngatapuwae Sec. Sch., 1980–84; returned to tribal home in north of NZ, 1984; helped re-establish Iwi tribal roots of Ngati Kuri through Waananga (study of history, genealogy and lore), 1989. Member: Wellington UN Club; SE Asian and Pacific Women's Assoc.; Board of Trustees, Queen Victoria and St Stephen's Schs; Anglican Church and Soc. Commn, 1970; Bishopric of Aotearoa, 1988–; NZ Anglican Synod, 1989–; NZ Race Relations Council, 1969–70; Bd, NZ Broadcasting Council (Mem., Northern NZ Broadcasting Council, 1969–70; Dep. Chm., Radio NZ); NZ Council, Protection Citizens Rights (Vice-Pres.); Social Welfare Commn, 1988–90; Maori Educn Foundn Trust Board; Maori Fisheries Commn, 1990–; Shellfish Recovery Trust, 1993–; Women's Adv. Cttee on estabt of Ministry of Women's Affairs; Maori Women's Gp which estabd Te Ohu Whakatupu (Maori Women's Secretariat) within Women's Ministry; Maori Women's Develt Trust Fund, 1988–; Muriwhenua Runanga, 1986; Muriwhenua Incorporation, 1991–; Te Orangikaupapa Trust, 1987–; Ngati Kuri Trust Bd, 1993–; Telethon Family Trust Cttee, 1982–85; Managing Trustee, Waiora Papakainga Trust, 1989–; Chm., Waiora Marae Trustees, 1988–; Maori Women's Welfare League: Rep., 1962–70; 1st Vice-Pres., 1971; Pres., 1974–77; Mem., 1st Delegn to Govt on Equal Pay for Women; Delegate: Maori Congress, 1990; Taitokerau Forum, 1990. Pres., Three Combined Tribes, 1988. LLD *hc* Victoria Univ. of Wellington, 1993. Silver Jubilee Medal, 1977. *Recreations:* tennis, basketball (rep. Auckland Univ., rep. North Island), reading, gardening. *Address:* Ngataki, RD4, Kaitaia, New Zealand. *T:* (9) 4098558.

SZÉLL, Patrick John, CMG 2001; Head, International and EC Environmental Law Division, since 1985, and Director (Legal), Department for Environment, Food and Rural Affairs (formerly Department of the Environment, then Department of the Environment, Transport and the Regions), since 1992; *b* Budapest, Hungary, 10 Feb. 1942; *s* of Dr János Széll and Vera Széll (*née* Beckett); *m* 1967, Olivia (*née* Brain), JP; two *s* one *d*. *Educ:* Reading Sch.; Trinity Coll., Dublin (MA, LLB; Julian Prize 1964). Called to the Bar, Inner Temple, 1966. Joined Min. of Housing and Local Govt as Legal Asst, 1969; Department of the Environment: Sen. Legal Asst, 1973–85; Asst Solicitor, 1985–92. Legal Advr to UK Delegns at internat. envmtl negotiations, 1974–, including: UN/ECE Convention on Long-Range Transboundary Air Pollution and its protocols, 1979–; Vienna Convention for Protection of Ozone Layer and Montreal Protocol, 1982–; Basle Convention on Transboundary Movements of Hazardous Wastes, 1988–93; Climate Change Convention and Kyoto Protocol, 1990–; Biodiversity Convention and Biosafety Protocol, 1990–2000. Mem., 1982–2000, Regl Internat. Council of Envmtl Law, Bonn; Mem., Gov., 2000–, IUCN Commn on Envmtl Law, 1994–. Global Ozone Award, UNEP, 1995; Elizabeth Haub Prize, Free Univ. of Brussels, 1995. *Recreations:* travel, hockey, butterflies. *Address:* Department for Environment, Food and Rural Affairs, 55 Whitehall, SW1A 2EY.

SZENTIVÁNYI, Gábor, Hon. GCVO 1999; Ambassador of the Republic of Hungary to the Court of St James's, since 1997; *b* 9 Oct. 1952; *s* of Jozsef Szentiványi and Ilona Fejes; *m* 1976, Gabriella Gönczi; one *s* one *d*. *Educ:* Budapest Univ. of Econmic Scis. Min. of Foreign Affairs, Hungary, 1975; Sec. for Press, Cultural and Educnl Affairs, Baghdad, 1976–81; Protocol Dept, Min. of Foreign Affairs, 1981–86; Counsellor for Press and Media Relations, Washington, 1986–91; Man. Dir, Burson-Marsteller Budapest, 1991–94; Spokesman and Dir Gen., Press and Internat. Information Dept, Min. of Foreign Affairs, 1994–97. Member: PR Assoc., Hungary, 1992–; Foreign Affairs Soc., Hungary, 1993–; Atlantic Council, Hungary, 1997–. Officer, Order of Prince Henry the Navigator (Portugal), 1983. *Recreation:* boating. *Address:* Embassy of the Republic of Hungary, 35 Eaton Place, SW1X 8BY. *T:* (020) 7235 5218. *Club:* Athenæum.

SZWARC, Michael M., FRS 1966; Distinguished Professor of Chemistry of the State University of New York, 1966–79, now Professor Emeritus; *b* 9 June 1909; Polish; *m* 1933, Marja Frenkel; one *s* two *d*. *Educ:* Warsaw Inst. of Technology (Chem. Eng. 1933); Hebrew Univ., Jerusalem (PhD 1942). University of Manchester (Lecturer), 1945–52; PhD (Phys. Chem.) 1947; DSc 1949; State University Coll. of Environmental Scis at Syracuse, NY, 1952–82: Prof. of Physical and Polymer Chemistry; Research Prof.; Distinguished Prof. of Chemistry; Dir, Polymer Research Inst. Baker Lectr, Cornell Univ., 1972. Nobel Guest Prof., Univ. of Uppsala, 1969–72; Visiting Professor: Univ. of Leuven, 1974; Univ. of Calif, San Diego, 1979–80. Foreign Mem., Polish Acad. of Scis, 1988. Hon. Dr: Leuven, Belgium, 1974; Uppsala, Sweden, 1975; Louis Pasteur Univ., France, 1978. Amer. Chem. Soc. Award for Outstanding Achievements in Polymer Chemistry, 1969; Gold Medal, Soc. of Plastic Engrs, 1972; Gold Medal, Benjamin Franklin Inst., 1978; Herman Mark Award, Amer. Chem. Soc., 1990; Kyoto Award, 1991. *Publications:* Carbanions, Living Polymers and Electron Transfer Processes, 1968; Ions and Ion-pairs in Organic Chemistry, Vol. I, 1972, Vol. II, 1974; Ionic Polymerization and Living Polymers, 1993; Ionic Polymerization Fundamentals, 1996; numerous contribs to Jl Chem. Soc., Trans Faraday Soc., Proc. Royal Soc., Jl Am. Chem. Soc., Jl Chem. Phys., Jl Phys. Chem., Jl Polymer Sci., Nature, Chem. Rev., Quarterly Reviews, etc. *Address:* 1176 Santa Luisa Drive, Solana Beach, CA 92075, USA. *T:* (619) 4811863.

SZYMBORSKA, Wisława; Polish poet, translator, literary critic; *b* 2 July 1923; *d* of Wincenty Szymborski and Anna Rottermund; *m* Adam Włodek. *Educ:* Jagiellonian Univ., Cracow. Editorial Staff, Zycie Literackie, 1953–67. Mem., 1952–83, Mem. Gen. Bd, 1978–83, Polish Writers' Assoc. Nobel Prize for Literature, 1996. Gold Cross of Merit (Poland), 1955; Kt Cross, Order of Polonia Restituta (Poland), 1974. *Publications:* Dlatego żyjemy, 1952; Pytania zadawanie sobie, 1954; Wołanie do Yeti, 1957; Sól, 1962; Wiersze wybrane, 1964; Poezje wybrane, 1967; Sto pociech, 1967; Poezje, 1970; Wszelki wypadek, 1972; Wybór wierszy, 1973; Tarsjusz i inne wiersze, 1976; Wielka liczba, 1976; Poezje wybrane II, 1983; Ludzie na moście, 1986; People on a Bridge, 1990; Koniec i początek, 1993; View with a Grain of Sand, 1995; Widok z ziarnkiem piasku, 1996; Poems New and Collected 1957–1997, 1998. *Address:* (office) ul. Kanonicza 7, 31–002 Kraków, Poland. *Fax:* (12) 4224773; c/o Forest Books, 20 Forest View, Chingford, E4 7AY.

T

TABACHNIK, Eldred; QC 1982; a Recorder, since 2000; *b* 5 Nov. 1943; *s* of Solomon Joseph Tabachnik and Esther Tabachnik; *m* 1966, Jennifer Kay Lawson; two *s* one *d*. *Educ:* Univ. of Cape Town (BA, LLB); Univ. of London (LLM). Called to the Bar, Inner Temple, 1970, Bencher, 1988. Lectr, UCL, 1969–72. Pres., Bd of Deputies of British Jews, 1994–2000. *Recreation:* reading. *Address:* 11 King's Bench Walk, Temple, EC4Y 7EQ. *T:* (020) 7632 8500. *Club:* Reform.

TABAKSBLAT, Morris; Chairman, Reed Elsevier plc, since 1999; *b* Rotterdam; *m*; two *s* one *d*. *Educ:* Leiden Univ. (law degree). Joined Unilever, 1964; positions in Spain, Brazil, Holland; Dir, 1984; Personal Products Co-ordinator, 1984; Regl Dir for N America, NY, 1987–90; Chm., Foods Exec., 1990–92; Mem., Unilever Special Cttee, 1992–99; Chm. and CEO, Unilever NV, 1994–99. Chm., Mauritshuis Mus. *Address:* Reed Elsevier plc, Van de Sande Bakhuyzenstraat 4, 1061 AG Amsterdam, Netherlands.

TABBARA, Hani Bahjat, Hon. GCVO 1984; Ambassador, Inspector General, Ministry of Foreign Affairs, Jordan; *b* 10 Feb. 1939; *s* of Bahjat and Nimat Tabbara; *m* 1980, Wafa; three *s*. *Educ:* University of Alexandria. Entered Govt service, 1963; Jordan Embassy, London, 1971–73; Counsellor, Foreign Ministry, Amman, 1973; Minister Plenipotentiary, Jordan Embassy, London, 1973–76; Private Sec. to Prime Minister, Amman, 1976–77; Ambassador: Morocco, 1977–80; Romania, 1980–82; Saudi Arabia, 1982–84; UK, 1984–85; Turkey, 1985–87; Yugoslavia, 1987–92; Australia, 1993–99. Order of El Istiqlal (Jordan), 1988. *Address:* Foreign Ministry, Amman, Jordan.

TABONE, Dr Vincent, (Censu), FRCSE; President of Malta, 1989–94; *b* 30 March 1913; *s* of Elisa Calleja and Nicolo Tabone; *m* 1948, Maria Wirth; four *s* five *d* (and one *c* decd). *Educ:* St Aloysius Coll.; Univ. of Malta. Dip. Opth. Oxford 1946; FRCSE 1948; Dip. RCP; Dip. RCS; Dip. in Med. Jurisp., Soc. of Apothecaries of London, 1963. Surgeon Captain, Royal Malta Artillery (campaign medals), 1939–45 War. WHO Consultant on Trachoma in Taiwan, Indonesia, Iraq; Dep., Internat. Panel of Trachoma Experts, WHO, 1956; Lectr in Clinical Ophthalmology, Dept of Surgery, Univ. of Malta, 1960. MP, 1966–89; Minister of Labour, Employment and Welfare, 1966–71; Minister of Foreign Affairs, 1987–89. Mem., Council of Europe Cttees; Chm., Council of Ministers, 1988. Founded Medical Officers Union of Malta, 1954. Vis. Prof., Univ. of Malta, 1995–. Hon. LLD Univ. of Malta, 1989. Awarded UN Testimonial for service to UN Programme on Aging, 1989. *Recreations:* reading, watch repairing, travel. *Address:* 33 Carmel Street, St Julian's, Malta. *Clubs:* Casino Maltese (1852), Sliema Band.

TABOR, Prof. David, PhD, ScD; FRS 1963; Professor of Physics in the University of Cambridge, 1973–81, now Emeritus; Head of Physics and Chemistry of Solids, Cavendish Laboratory, 1969–81; Fellow of Gonville and Caius College, Cambridge, since 1957; *b* 23 Oct. 1913; *s* of Charles Tabor and Rebecca Weinstein; *m* 1943, Hannalene Stillschweig; two *s*. *Educ:* Regent St Polytechnic; Universities of London and Cambridge. BSc London 1934; PhD Cambridge 1939; ScD Cambridge 1956. Reader in Physics, Cambridge Univ., 1964–73. Vis. Prof., Imperial Coll., London, 1981–. For. Associate, US NAE, 1995. Hon. DSc Bath, 1985. Inaugural Gold Medal of Tribology, Instn of Engrs, 1972; Guthrie Medal, Inst. Physics, 1975. *Publications:* The Hardness of Metals, 1951; Gases, Liquids and Solids, 1969, 3rd edn 1991; (with F. P. Bowden) Friction and Lubrication of Solids, Part I, 1950, rev. edn 1954, repr. 1986; Part II, 1964; contributions to learned jls on friction, adhesion, lubrication and hardness. *Recreation:* Judaica. *Address:* Cavendish Laboratory, Madingley Road, Cambridge CB3 0HE; Gonville and Caius College, Cambridge CB2 1TA; 3 Westberry Court, Grange Road, Cambridge CB3 9BG. *T:* (01223) 304585.

TABOR, Maj.-Gen. David John St Maur, CB 1977; MC 1944; late Royal Horse Guards; GOC Eastern District, 1974–77, retired; *b* 5 Oct. 1922; *y s* of late Harry Tabor, Hitchin, Herts; *m* 1st, 1955, Hon. Pamela Roxane (*d* 1987), 2nd *d* of 2nd Baron Glendyne; two *s*; 2nd, 1989, Marguerite, *widow* of Col Peter Arkwright. *Educ:* Eton; RMA, Sandhurst. Served War: 2nd Lieut, RHG, 1942; NW Europe, 1944–45 (wounded, 1944); Major, 1946. Lt-Col Comdg RHG, 1960; Lt-Col Comdg Household Cavalry, and Silver Stick in Waiting, 1964; Col, 1964; Brig., 1966; Comdr Berlin Inf. Bde, 1966; Comdr, British Army Staff and Mil. Attaché, Washington, 1968; RCDS, 1971; Maj.-Gen., 1972; Defence Attaché, Paris, 1972–74. *Recreations:* shooting, fishing, gardening. *Address:* Lower Farm, Compton Abdale, Cheltenham, Glos GL54 4DS. *T:* (01242) 890234. *Clubs:* Turf, Royal Automobile, MCC.

See also Baron Glendyne.

TACKABERRY, John Antony; QC 1982; FCIArb, FFB; a Recorder, since 1988; *b* 13 Nov. 1939; *s* of late Thomas Raphael Tackaberry and Mary Catherine (*née* Geoghegan); *m* 1st, 1966, Penelope Holt (*d* 1994); two *s*; 2nd, 1996, Kate Jones; one *d*. *Educ:* Downside; Trinity Coll., Dublin; Downing Coll., Cambridge (MA, LLM). Called to the Bar, Gray's Inn, 1967. FCIArb 1973; FFB 1979. Teacher in China, 1964–65 and in London, 1965–67. Adjunct Prof. of Law, Qld Univ. of Technology, 1989. Comr, UN Compensation Commn, 1998–. Chm., CIArb, 1990–91 (Mem. Council, 1985–94); President: Soc. of Construction Law, 1983–85; Eur. Soc. of Construction Law, 1985–87. Registered Arbitrator, 1993; Mem., many panels of internat. arbitrators. *Recreations:* good food, good wine, good company. *Address:* Arbitration Chambers, 22 Willes Road, NW5 3DS. *T:* (020) 7267 2137.

TACON, Air Cdre (Ernest) William, CBE 1958; DSO 1944; LVO 1950; DFC 1940 (Bar 1944); AFC 1942 (Bar 1953); *b* 6 Dec. 1917; *s* of Ernest Richard Tacon, Hastings, New Zealand; *m* 1st, 1949, Clare Keating (*d* 1956), *d* of late Michael Keating, Greymouth, NZ; one *s* two *d*; 2nd, 1960, Bernardine, *d* of Cecil Leamy, Wellington, NZ; three *s*. *Educ:* St Patrick's College, Silverstream, New Zealand. Joined RNZAF, 1938; served with RAF, 1939–46; transferred to RAF, 1946; CO, King's Flight, Benson, 1946–49; served: Canal Zone, 1951–53; Cyprus, 1956–58; Persian Gulf, 1961–63; Commandant, Central Fighter Establishment, 1963–65; Air Cdre, Tactics, HQ Fighter Comd, 1966–67; AOC Military Air Traffic Ops, 1968–71, retired. MIMgt. *Address:* 69 McLeans Road, Bucklands Beach, Auckland, NZ. *T:* (9) 5344757.

TADIÉ, Prof. Jean-Yves; Chevalier de l'Ordre National du Mérite, 1974; Officier des Palmes académiques, 1988; Professor of French Literature, Université de Paris-Sorbonne, since 1991; *b* 7 Sept. 1936; *s* of Henri Tadié and Marie (*née* Férester); *m* 1962, Arlette Khoury; three *s*. *Educ:* St Louis de Gonzague, Paris; Lycée Louis-le-Grand; Ecole Normale Supérieure (Agrégé de lettres); DèsL Sorbonne 1970; MA Oxford 1988. Lectr, Univ. of Alexandria, 1960–62; Asst Prof., Faculté des Lettres de Paris, 1964; Professor: Univ. de Caen, 1968–69; Univ. de Tours, 1969–70; Univ. de la Sorbonne nouvelle, Paris III, 1970; Hd of French Dept, Cairo Univ., 1972–76; Dir, French Inst., London, 1976–81; Marshal Foch Prof. of French Literature, and Fellow, All Souls Coll., Oxford Univ., 1988–91. Corresp. FBA, 1991. Grand Prix de l'Acad. française, 1988. Officier de l'Ordre de la Couronne de Belgique, 1979. *Publications:* Introduction à la vie littéraire du XIXe Siècle, 1970; Lectures de Proust, 1971; Proust et le Roman, 1971; Le Récit poétique, 1978; Le Roman d'aventures, 1982; Proust, 1983; La Critique littéraire au XXe Siècle, 1987; (ed) M. Proust, A la Recherche du Temps perdu, 1987–89; Portrait de l'Artiste, 1990; Le Roman au XXe Siècle, 1990; Marcel Proust (biography), 1996, Eng. edn 2000; (ed) N. Sarraute, Oeuvres Complètes, 1996; Le Sens de la Mémoire, 1999. *Recreations:* tennis, opera, cinema. *Address:* Université de Paris-Sorbonne, 1 rue Victor Cousin, 75005 Paris, France.

TAFROV, Stefan Lubomirov; Ambassador of Bulgaria to France, and Permanent Representative of Bulgaria to UNESCO, since 1998; *b* Sofia, 11 Feb. 1958; *s* of Lubomir Tafrov and Nadezhda Tafrova. *Educ:* Sofia Univ. (MA in Journalism). Foreign News Editor, Democratzia, newspaper, Jan. 1990; Chief, Foreign Affairs Dept, Union of Democratic Forces, Feb.–Aug. 1990; Foreign Affairs Advr to Pres. of Bulgaria, 1990–92; First Dep. Minister of Foreign Affairs, 1992–93; Ambassador to Italy, 1993–95; Ambassador to UK, 1995–98. *Recreation:* music. *Address:* c/o Bulgarian Embassy, 1 avenue Rapp, 75007 Paris, France.

TAFT, William Howard, IV; Partner, Fried, Frank, Harris, Shriver & Jacobson, since 1992; *b* 13 Sept. 1945; *s* of William Howard Taft, III and Barbara Bradfield Taft; *m* 1974, Julia Ann Vadala; one *s* two *d*. *Educ:* St Paul's Sch., Concord, NH; Yale Coll. (BA 1966); Harvard Univ. (JD 1969). Attorney, Winthrop, Stimson, Putnam & Roberts, NY, 1969–70; Attorney Advr to Chm., Federal Trade Commn, 1970; Principal Asst to Dep. Dir, Office of Management and Budget, 1970–72, Exec. Asst to Dir, 1972–73; Exec. Asst to Sec., Health, Educn and Welfare, 1973–76; Gen. Counsel, Dept of Health, Educn and Welfare, 1976–77; Partner, Leva, Hawes, Symington, Martin & Oppenheimer, 1977–81; General Counsel 1981–84, Dep. Sec. of Defense 1984–89, US Dept of Defense; US Perm. Rep. on N Atlantic Council, 1989–92. Mem., DC Bar Assoc., Washington. Bd Mem., Washington Opera, 1977–81, 1992–. Woodrow Wilson Vis. Teaching Fellow, Woodrow Wilson Foundn, 1977–81. Dir, Atlantic Council, 1993–. *Publication:* contrib. Indiana Law Jl. *Recreation:* tennis. *Address:* 1001 Pennsylvania Avenue NW, Washington, DC 20004–2505, USA. *T:* (202) 6397000. *Clubs:* Cosmos, Leo, Literary Society (Washington, DC).

TAFTI, Rt Rev. Hassan Barnaba D.; *see* Dehqani-Tafti.

TAGER, Romie; QC 1995; *b* 19 July 1947; *s* of Osias Tager and Minnie Tager (*née* Mett); *m* 1971, Esther Marianne Sichel; twin *s*. *Educ:* Hasmonean Grammar Sch., Hendon; University Coll. London (Hurst prize; LLB 1st Cl. Hons 1969). Called to the Bar, Middle Temple, 1970. Chm., Greenquest Gp, 1998–. Hon. Sec., Jewish Book Council, 1990–. *Recreations:* opera, theatre, travel. *Address:* Hardwicke Building, New Square, Lincoln's Inn, WC2A 3SB. *T:* (020) 7242 2523.

TAGG, Alan; freelance designer/theatre designer; *b* 13 April 1928; *s* of Thomas Bertram Tagg and Edith Annie Hufton. *Educ:* Mansfield Coll. of Art; Old Vic Theatre Sch. Worked as asst to Cecil Beaton, Oliver Messel, etc; first play, Charles Morgan's The River Line, 1952; worked for H. M. Tennent Ltd; Founder Mem., English Stage Co., 1956: designed first prodn of Look Back in Anger, 1956; designed The Entertainer (with Laurence Olivier), 1957; also 15 other prodns at Royal Court Theatre; designed 4 prodns for RSC, including Graham Greene's The Return of A. J. Raffles, 1975; designed 12 prodns at Chichester Festival Theatre, including: Dear Antoine (with Edith Evans), 1971; Waters of the Moon (with Ingrid Bergman), 1977; 9 plays by Alan Ayckbourn; designed: 10 prodns for NT; 93 West End prodns, including: Billy Liar, 1959; How the Other Half Loves, 1970; The Constant Wife, 1973; Alphabetical Order, 1975; Donkeys Years, 1976; The Kingfisher, 1977; Candida, 1977; The Millionairess, 1978; Peter Shaffer's Lettice and Lovage (with Maggie Smith), 1987; 11 prodns on Broadway, including Peter Shaffer's Black Comedy, 1967, Lettice and Lovage, 1990 (US tour 1992); Look Back in Anger, Moscow Arts Theatre, 1957; Sleuth, Berlin, 1991; directors worked with include Lindsay Anderson, Michael Blakemore, John Dexter, John Gielgud, Tony Richardson and Michael Rudman; exhibitions designed include: Shakespeare, Stratford-upon-Avon, 1964; Hector Berlioz, 1969; 25 Years of Covent Garden, V&A Museum, 1971; Byron, 1974. *Recreation:* living in France. *Address:* 19 Parsons Green, SW6 4UL. *T:* (020) 7731 2787; Chemin de Masmolène, Vallabrix, 30700 Uzès, France. *T:* 466226393. *Club:* Chelsea Arts.

TAHOURDIN, John Gabriel, CMG 1961; HM Diplomatic Service, retired; *b* 15 Nov. 1913; *s* of late John St Clair Tahourdin; *m* 1957, Margaret Michie; one *s* one *d*. *Educ:* Merchant Taylors' School; St John's College, Oxford. Served HM Embassy, Peking,

1936–37; Private Secretary to HM Ambassador at Shanghai, 1937–40; BoT, 1940–41; Vice-Consul, Baltimore, 1941; Foreign Office, 1942; Private Secretary to Parliamentary Under-Secretary of State, 1943, and to Minister of State, 1945; Athens, 1946; returned to Foreign Office, 1949; Counsellor, British Embassy, The Hague, 1955; Foreign Office, 1957; Minister, UK Delegn to 18 Nation Disarmament Conf., Geneva, 1963–66; HM Ambassador to: Senegal, 1966–71, and concurrently to Mauritania, 1968–71, to Mali, 1969–71, and to Guinea, 1970–71; Bolivia, 1971–73. Mem., Internat. Inst. for Strategic Studies. Price Commission, 1975–77; Kleinwort Benson, 1977–79. *Recreations:* music cinematography, foreign languages, travel. *Address:* Diana Lodge, Little Kineton, Warwick CV35 0DL. *T:* (01926) 640276. *Clubs:* Athenæum, Travellers, Beefsteak; Norfolk.

TAIN, Paul Christopher; District Judge (Magistrates' Courts) (formerly Stipendiary Magistrate), East and West Sussex, since 1992; a Recorder, since 2000; *b* 18 Feb. 1950; *s* of Reginald Tain and Kathleen (*née* Hoffland); *m* 1971, Angela Margaret Kirkup; four *s*. *Educ:* London Univ. (BA Hist.); Inst. of Judicial Admin, Birmingham Univ. (MJur). Admitted solicitor, 1975; solicitor, Wolverhampton MBC and N Yorks County Council, 1976–80; private practitioner, 1980–92; Dep. Stipendiary Magistrate, 1989–92; Asst Recorder, 1996–2000. Columnist, Solicitors' Jl, 1998. *Publications:* Local Authority Lawyers and Childcare, 1980; Childcare Law, 1993; Criminal Justice Act, 1994; Public Order Law, 1996. *Recreations:* sailing, sailing and sailing. *Address:* The Law Courts, Edward Street, Brighton, Sussex BN2 2LG.

TAIT, Dr Alan Anderson; Director, International Monetary Fund in Geneva, 1995–98; *b* 1 July 1934; *s* of Stanley Tait and Margaret Ruth (*née* Anderson); *m* 1963, Susan Valerie Somers; one *s*. *Educ:* Heriot's Sch., Edinburgh; Univ. of Edinburgh (MA); Trinity Coll., Dublin (PhD; Hon. Fellow, 1996). Lectr, Trinity Coll., Dublin, 1959–71 (Fellow, 1968, Sen. Tutor, 1970); Visiting Prof., Univ. of Illinois, 1965–66. Economic adviser to Irish Govt on industrial develt and taxation and chief economic adviser to Confedn of Irish Industry, 1967–71; Prof. of Money and Finance, Univ. of Strathclyde, 1971–77; economic consultant to Sec. of State for Scotland, 1972–77; International Monetary Fund: Visiting Scholar, 1972; Consultant, 1973, 1974, 1999, 2001; Chief, Fiscal Analysis Div., 1976–79; Asst Dir, 1979–82; Dep. Dir, Fiscal Affairs Dept, 1982–94. Hon. Prof., Univ. of Kent at Canterbury, 2000–. Co-Chm., Wkg Gp on Financing Health, Commn on Macroeconomics and Health, 2000–01. *Publications:* The Taxation of Personal Wealth, 1967; (with J. Bristow) Economic Policy in Ireland, 1968; (with J. Bristow) Ireland: some problems of a developing economy, 1971; The Value Added Tax, 1972; The Value Added Tax: international practice and problems, 1988; (ed) Value Added Tax: administrative and policy issues, 1991; articles on public finance in Rev. of Economic Studies, Finanzarchiv, Public Finance, Staff Papers, etc. *Recreations:* undemanding mountain walking, painting. *Address:* Cramond House, Harnet Street, Sandwich, Kent CT13 9ES. *T:* (01304) 621038. *Club:* Cosmos (Washington DC).

TAIT, Adm. Sir (Allan) Gordon, KCB 1977; DSC 1943; Chief of Naval Personnel and Second Sea Lord, 1977–79; Chairman, Lion Nathan Ltd (incorporating NZ Breweries Ltd, Lion Breweries Ltd and Lion Corporation), 1984–97; *b* 30 Oct. 1921; *s* of Allan G. Tait and Ann Gordon, Timaru, NZ; *m* 1952, Philippa, *d* of Sir Bryan Todd; two *s* two *d*. *Educ:* Timaru Boys' High Sch.; RNC Dartmouth. War Service, Atlantic and N Russia Convoys, 1939–42; Submarines, Mediterranean and Far East, 1942–45 (despatches); commanded HM Submarines: Teredo, 1947; Solent, 1948; ADC to Governor-General of New Zealand (Lt-Gen. Lord Freyberg, VC), 1949–51; commanded HM Submarines: Ambush, 1951; Aurochs, 1951–53; Tally Ho, 1955; Sanguine, 1955–56; Asst Naval Adviser, UK High Commn, Canada, 1957–59; Dep. Dir Ops, Admiralty, 1963–65; commanded HM Ships: Caprice, 1960–62; Ajax, 1965–67; Maidstone, 1967–68; commanded: 2nd Destroyer Squadron (Far East), 1965–66; 3rd Submarine Sqdn, 1967–69; Chief of Staff, Submarine Comd, 1969–70; commanded, Britannia RNC, 1970–72; Rear-Adm., 1972; Naval Secretary, MoD, 1972–74; Vice-Adm., 1974; Flag Officer, Plymouth, Port Admiral, Devonport, NATO Comdr, Central Sub Area, Eastern Atlantic, 1975–77; Adm., 1978. Naval ADC to the Queen, 1972. Director: NZ Bd, Westpac Banking Corp., 1981–93; Todd Bros Ltd, 1981–87; Todd Corp., 1987–97 (Dep. Chm.); Todd Petroleum Mining, 1994–97 (Dep. Chm.); Owens Gp Ltd, 1984–93; AGC (NZ) Ltd, 1987–93. Pres., and Chm. of Trustees, NZ Sports Foundn, 1981–86; Chairman: NZ Family Trust, 1983–; NZ Internat. Yachting Trust, 1989–94; Trustee, NZ Nat. Maritime Mus., 1990–97; Mem., Spirit of Adventure Trust Board, 1982–91. *Address:* 22 Orakei Road, Auckland 5, New Zealand. *Clubs:* White's; Royal Yacht Squadron; Northern (Auckland).

TAIT, Andrew Wilson, OBE 1967; Deputy Chairman, Barratt plc, 1991–96 (Director, 1988–96); Chairman, National House-Building Council, 1984–87 (Director-General, 1967–84); *b* 25 Sept. 1922; *s* of late Dr Adam and Jenny Tait; *m* 1954, Elizabeth Isobel Maclennan; three *d*. *Educ:* George Watson's Coll., Edinburgh; Edinburgh Univ. (MA 1st Class Hons History). Served Army, 1942–45. Leader writer, The Scotsman, 1947–48; Scottish Office, 1948–64; Chm., Housing Res. Foundn, 1969–85. Chairman: Internat. Housing and Home Warranty Assoc., 1984–87; Jt Land Requirements Cttee, 1981–87; Home Buyers Adv. Service, 1985–; Bridging the Gap, 1986–; New Homes Mktg Bd, 1988–89; Johnson Fry Property, 1988–95; New Homes Envmtl Gp, 1988–91; Cost Reduction Partnership, 1995–. Mem., Lloyd's, 1985–98. *Recreations:* golf, tennis, chess. *Address:* Orchard Croft, Grimmshill, Great Missenden, Bucks HP16 9BA. *T:* (01494) 862061. *Club:* Caledonian.

TAIT, Arthur Gordon; Secretary-General, Institute of Actuaries, 1991–97; *b* 28 July 1934; *s* of George Aidan Drury Tait and Margaret Evelyn Tait (*née* Gray); *m* 1958, Ann Sutcliffe Gilbert; two *s* two *d* (and one *s* decd). *Educ:* Eton Coll.; St John's Coll., Cambridge (BA Hist., MA). FIPD. Commnd KRRC, 1953–54. Imperial Chemical Industries, 1957–91: Personnel Dir, Mond Div., 1976–82; Internat. Personnel Manager, 1983–91. Chm., Friends of Brompton Cemetery, 1998–. FRSA. *Recreations:* family, swimming, travel, friends who visit, following most sports. *Address:* 39 Hollywood Road, SW10 9HT. *T:* (020) 7352 5127.

TAIT, Eric, MBE 1980; Director of European Operations, since 1989 and International Executive Director, since 1992, Pannell Kerr Forster, Chartered Accountants; *b* 10 Jan. 1945; *s* of William Johnston Tait and Sarah Tait (*née* Jones); *m* 1st, 1967, Agnes Jean Boag (*née* Anderson) (marr. diss. 1998); one *s* one *d*; 2nd, 1998, Stacey Jane (*née* Todd). *Educ:* George Heriot's Sch., Edinburgh; RMA Sandhurst; RMCS Shrivenham (BSc Eng); Churchill Coll., Cambridge (MPhil). 2nd Lieut, Royal Engineers, 1965; despatches 1976; 68 advanced staff course, RAF Staff Coll., Bracknell, 1977; OC 7 Field Sqn, RE, 1979–81; Lt-Col 1982; Directing Staff, Staff Coll., Camberley, 1982–83, retired, at own request, 1983; Sec., Inst. of Chartered Accountants of Scotland, 1984–89. Mem. of Exec., Scottish Council (Develt and Industry), 1984–89. Editor in Chief, The Accountant's Magazine, 1984–89. Chm., European Forum, Nottingham Trent Univ., 1993–98. FRSA 1997. *Recreations:* swimming, hill walking, reading. *Address:* PKF International Ltd, New Garden House, 78 Hatton Garden, EC1N 8JA. *T:* (020) 7831 7393.

TAIT, Prof. James Francis, PhD; FRS 1959; engaged in writing reviews of endocrine subjects; Emeritus Professor, University of London, since 1982; *b* 1 December 1925; *s* of Herbert Tait and Constance Levinia Brotherton; *m* 1956, Sylvia Agnes Simpson (*née* Wardropper) (*see* S. A. S. Tait). *Educ:* Darlington Grammar Sch.; Leeds Univ. Lectr in Medical Physics, Middlesex Hospital Medical School, 1948–55; External Scientific Staff, Medical Research Council, Middlesex Hospital Medical School, 1955–58; Senior Scientist, Worcester Foundation for Experimental Biology, USA, 1958–70; Joel Prof. of Physics as Applied to Medicine, Univ. of London, 1970–82; Co-Dir, Biophysical Endocrinology Unit, Physics Dept, Middlesex Hosp. Med. Sch., 1970–85. (With S. A. S. Tait) R. Douglas Wright Lectr and Medallion, Univ. of Melbourne, 1989. Hon. DSc Hull, 1979. Society for Endocrinology: Medal, 1969 and Sir Henry Dale Medal, 1979; Tadeus Reichstein Award, Internat. Soc. of Endocrinology, 1976; CIBA Award, Amer. Heart Assoc. for Hypertension Research, 1977. *Publications:* papers on medical physics, biophysics and endocrinology. *Recreations:* gardening, photography, chess. *Address:* Moorlands, Main Road, East Boldre, near Brockenhurst, Hants SO42 7WT. *T:* and *Fax:* (01590) 626312; *e-mail:* jftait@globalnet.co.uk.

TAIT, Michael Logan, CMG 1987; LVO 1972; HM Diplomatic Service, retired; Chairman, Oxford and Edinburgh Consultants, since 1995; *b* 27 Sept. 1936; *s* of William and Dorothea Tait; *m* 1st, 1968, Margaret Kirsteen Stewart (marr. diss. 1990); two *s* one *d*; *m* 2nd, 1999, Amel Boureghda. *Educ:* Calday Grange Grammar Sch.; New College, Oxford. Nat. service, 2nd Lieut Royal Signals, 1955–57. Foreign Office, 1961; served MECAS, 1961; Bahrain, 1963; Asst Political Agent, Dubai, Trucial States, 1963; FO, 1966; Private Sec. to Minister of State, FO, later FCO, 1968; First Sec. and Hd of Chancery, Belgrade, 1970; First Sec. (Political), Hd of Chancery and Consul, Amman, 1972; FCO, 1975; Counsellor and Hd of Chancery, Baghdad, 1977; Counsellor, FCO, 1978; Dep. Hd of Delegn, CSCE, Madrid, 1980; Dep. Hd of Delegn and Counsellor (Econ. and Finance), OECD, Paris, 1982; Hd of Economic Relns Dept, FCO, 1984; Ambassador to UAE, 1986–89; Asst Under-Sec. of State with responsibility for Soviet Union and Eastern Europe, 1990–92; Ambassador to Tunisia, 1992–95. *Recreations:* languages, mountains, sailing. *Address:* c/o Oxford and Edinburgh Consultants, 8 Chalcot Crescent, NW1 8YD. *Clubs:* Garrick; Vanderbilt.

TAIT, Richard Graham, DPhil; Editor-in-Chief, Independent Television News, since 1995; *b* 22 May 1947; *s* of Dr William Graham Tait and Isabella Dempster Tait (*née* Cumiskey); *m* 1st, 1980, Sandra Janine McKenzie McIntosh (marr. diss. 1984); 2nd, 1995, Kathryn Jane Ellison. *Educ:* Bradfield Coll.; New Coll,, Oxford (BA Mod. Hist.; MA; DPhil 1978). St Edmund Jun. Res. Fellow, St Edmund Hall, Oxford, 1972–74; BBC Television: Researcher, Money Prog., 1974–75; Producer, Nationwide, 1976–82; Editor: People and Power, 1982; Money Prog., 1983–85; Newsnight, 1985–87; General Election Results Prog., 1987; Independent Television News: Editor: Channel Four News, 1987–90; Channel Four progs, 1990–95. Internat. Bd Mem., IPI, 1998–. FRTS 1996. *Recreations:* history, ballet, opera, tennis, ski-ing. *Address:* Independent Television News, 200 Gray's Inn Road, WC1X 8XZ. *T:* (020) 7833 3000.

TAIT, Sylvia Agnes Sophia, (Mrs James F. Tait), FRS 1959; Honorary Research Associate and Co-Director, Biophysical Endocrinology Unit, Physics Department, Middlesex Hospital Medical School, 1982; biochemist; distinguished for her work on the hormones controlling the distribution of salts in the body; *m* 1956, James Francis Tait, *qv*. Research Asst, Courtauld Inst. of Biochemistry, Middlesex Hosp. Med. Sch., 1944–55; External Scientific Staff, MRC, Middlesex Hosp. Med. Sch., 1955–58; Senior Scientist, Worcester Foundn for Experimental Biology, USA, 1958–70; Research Associate and Co-Director, Biophysical Endocrinology Unit, Dept of Physics as Applied to Medicine, Middlesex Hosp. Med. School, 1970–82. (With Prof. J. F. Tait) R. Douglas Wright Lecture and Medallion, Univ. of Melbourne, 1989. Hon. DSc Hull, 1979. Tadeus Reichstein Award, Internat. Endocrine Society, 1976; Gregory Pincus Meml Medal, 1977; CIBA Award, American Heart Assoc. for Hypertension Research, 1977; Sir Henry Dale Medal of Soc. for Endocrinology, 1979. *Address:* Moorlands, Main Road, East Boldre, Brockenhurst, Hants SO42 7WT. *T:* (01590) 626312.

TAK; *see* Drummond, T. A. K.

TALBOT; *see* Chetwynd-Talbot, family name of Earl of Shrewsbury and Waterford.

TALBOT OF MALAHIDE, 10th Baron *cr* 1831 (Ire.); **Reginald John Richard Arundell;** Hereditary Lord Admiral Malahide and Adjacent Seas; Vice Lord-Lieutenant of Wiltshire, since 1996; *b* 9 Jan. 1931; *s* of Reginald John Arthur Arundell (*g g g s* of 1st Baroness) (who assumed by Royal Licence, 1945, names and arms of Arundell in lieu of Talbot, and *d* 1953), and Winifred (*d* 1954), *d* of R. B. S. Castle; *S* cousin, 1987; *m* 1st, 1955, Laura Duff (*d* 1989), *d* of late Group Captain Edward John Tennant, DSO, MC; one *s* four *d*; 2nd, 1992, Patricia Mary Blundell-Brown, *d* of late J. Riddell, OBE. *Educ:* Stonyhurst. DL Wilts. KStJ 1988 (CStJ 1983; OStJ 1978); Chm., St John Council for Wilts, 1976–97. Knight of Malta, 1977. Hon. Citizen, State of Maryland, USA, 1984. *Heir: s* Hon. Richard John Tennant Arundell [*b* 28 March 1957; *m* 1984, Jane Catherine, *d* of Timothy Heathcote Unwin; one *s* four *d*]. *Address:* Park Gate, Donhead, Shaftesbury, Dorset SP7 9EU. *Clubs:* Pratt's, Farmers'.

TALBOT, Sir Hilary Gwynne, Kt 1968; a Judge of the High Court of Justice, Queen's Bench Division, 1968–83; Judge of the Employment Appeals Tribunal, 1978–81; *b* 22 Jan. 1912; *s* of late Rev. Prebendary A. T. S. Talbot, RD, and Mrs Talbot; *m* 1963, Jean Whitworth (JP Wilts), *o d* of late Mr and Mrs Kenneth Fisher. *Educ:* Haileybury Coll.; Worcester Coll., Oxford. MA Oxon. Served War of 1939–45; Captain, RA. Called to Bar, Middle Temple, 1935, Bencher, 1968. Dep. Chm., Northants QS, 1948–62; Chm., Derbyshire QS, 1958–63; Dep. Chm. Hants QS, 1964–71; Judge of County Courts, 1962–68; a Presiding Judge, Wales and Chester Circuit, 1970–74. Mem., Parole Bd, 1980–82. Dep. Chm., Boundary Commn for Wales, 1980–83. Formerly Dep. Chm., Agricultural Land Tribunals; formerly Mem., County Court, Divorce Court and Supreme Court Rules Cttees. *Recreations:* fishing, bird-watching. *Address:* Old Chapel House, Little Ashley, Bradford-on-Avon, Wilts BA15 2PN.

TALBOT, John Andrew, FCA; Director, Talbot Hughes Ltd, since 2001; *b* 2 Aug. 1949; *s* of Robert Talbot and Lucy E. Talbot (*née* Jarvis); *m* 1st, 1969, Susan Hollingbery (marr. diss.); one *s* one *d*; 2nd, 1983, Jennifer Anne Houghton; one *s* two *d*. CA 1971; accountant in manufacturing, 1972–73; Bernard Phillips & Co., Accountants, 1973–75; Spicer & Pegler, 1975–83, Partner, 1979; Partner, Arthur Andersen, 1983–99: Hd, UK Insolvency Practice, 1988; Man. Partner, Worldwide Global Corporate Finance Practice, 1995–2000; Administrator, Maxwell Private Cos, 1991; Receiver: Leyland DAF, 1993; Ferranti, 1994; Transtec plc, 2000. Hon. Treas., 1990–97, Mem. Bd, 2000, English Nat. Ballet; Mem. Bd, Conservatoire for Dance and Drama, 2001. *Recreations:* contemporary art, antiquarian books, modern and classical dance. *Address:* Talbot Hughes Ltd, 18 Bevis Marks, EC3A 7JB. *Club:* Royal Automobile.

TALBOT, Commandant Mary (Irene), CB; Director, Women's Royal Naval Service, 1973–76; *b* 17 Feb. 1922. *Educ:* Bristol Univ. BA Hons, Philosophy and Economics. Joined WRNS as a Naval recruiting asst, Nov. 1943; Officer training course, 1944, and apptd to HMS Eaglet, in Liverpool, as an Educn and Resettlement Officer; served on staffs of C-in-Cs: Mediterranean; the Nore; Portsmouth, 1945–61; First Officer, and apptd to staff of Dir Naval Educn Service, 1952; subseq. served HMS Condor, Dauntless and Raleigh; Chief Officer, and apptd Sen. WRNS Officer, the Nore, 1960; on staff of Dir Naval Manning, 1963–66, and then became Asst Dir, WRNS; Superintendent, and served on staff of C-in-C Naval Home Command, 1969; Supt in charge, WRNS training estabt, HMS Dauntless, near Reading, 1972–73. Hon. ADC, 1973–76. Hon. LLD Bristol, 1993. *Recreations:* bridge, gardening, racing. *Address:* Sonning Cottage, Pound Lane, Sonning-on-Thames RG4 6XE. *T:* (0118) 969 3323.

TALBOT, Prof. Michael Owen, FBA 1990; James and Constance Alsop Professor of Music, University of Liverpool, since 1986; *b* 4 Jan. 1943; *s* of Alan and Annelise Talbot; *m* 1970, Shirley Ellen Mashiane; one *s* one *d. Educ:* Welwyn Garden City Grammar Sch.; Royal Coll. of Music (ARCM); Clare Coll., Cambridge (Open, later Meml Scholar; MusB Hons 1963; MA; PhD 1968). Lectr in Music, 1968, Sen. Lectr, 1979, Reader, 1983–86, Univ. of Liverpool. Corresp. Mem., Ateneo Veneto, Venice, 1986. Order of Merit (Italy), 1980. *Publications:* Vivaldi, 1978 (Italian, German and Polish edns); Vivaldi, 1979 (Japanese, Brazilian and Spanish edns); Albinoni: Leben und Werk, 1980; Antonio Vivaldi: a guide to research, 1988 (Italian edn); Tomaso Albinoni: the Venetian composer and his world, 1990; Benedetto Vinaccesi: a musician in Brescia and Venice in the age of Corelli, 1994; The sacred vocal music of Antonio Vivaldi, 1995; Venetian Music in the Age of Vivaldi, 1999; The Finale in Western Instrumental Music, 2001. *Recreations:* chess, reading novels, travel. *Address:* 36 Montclair Drive, Liverpool L18 0HA. *T:* (0151) 722 3328.

TALBOT, Patrick John; QC 1990; a Recorder, since 1997; *b* 28 July 1946; *s* of John Bentley Talbot, MC, and late Marguerite Maxwell Talbot (*née* Townley); *m* 1st, 1976, Judith Anne Urwin (marr. diss. 1999); one *s* two *d*; 2nd, 2000, Elizabeth Evans; two *s. Educ:* Charterhouse (Foundn Schol.); University Coll., Oxford (MA). Called to Bar, Lincoln's Inn, 1969, Bencher, 1996; in practice at Chancery Bar, 1970–. Member: Senate of Inns of Court and the Bar, 1976–78; Council of Legal Educn, 1977–95 (Vice-Chm., 1992–95). A Judicial Chm., City Disputes Panel, 1997–; a Lieut Bailiff of Guernsey, 2000–. Affiliate British Trustee, British Amer. Educnl Foundn, 1984–. Hon. Life Mem., Nat. Union of Students, 1982. *Recreations:* cricket, ski-ing, collecting toys, bridge. *Address:* Serle Court, 6 New Square, Lincoln's Inn, WC2A 3QS. *T:* (020) 7242 6105. *Clubs:* MCC, Wimbledon Wanderers CC.

TALBOYS, Rt Hon. Sir Brian (Edward), Hon. AC 1982; CH 1981; KCB 1991; PC 1977; *b* Wanganui, 7 June 1921; *s* of Francis Powell Talboys and Katherine Janet (*née* Balfour); *m* 1950, Patricia Floyd Adamson, *d* of Adam Laurence Adamson and Alice Floyd Harrington; two *s. Educ:* Wanganui Collegiate Sch.; Univ. of Manitoba; Victoria Univ., Wellington (BA). Served war of 1939–45, RNZAF. MP for Wallace, NZ, 1957–81; Dep. Leader, National Party, 1974–81; Parly Under-Sec. to Minister of Trade and Industry, 1960; Minister of Agriculture, 1962–69; Minister of Science, 1964–72; Minister of Education, 1969–72; Minister of Overseas Trade and Trade and Industry, 1972; Minister of Nat. Develt, 1975–77; Dep. Prime Minister and Minister of For. Affairs and Overseas Trade, 1975–81. Leader of a number of NZ delegns to overseas confs; NZ Rep., Standing Cttee of Pacific Economic Co-operation Conf., 1983–90. Grand Cross 1st Class, Order of Merit, Fed. Republic of Germany, 1978. Hon. DSc Massey Univ., 1981; Hon. DLitt Chung-Ang Univ., Seoul, 1981. *Address:* 1 Hamilton Avenue, Winton, New Zealand.

TALINTYRE, Douglas George; Director, Office of Manpower Economics, 1989–92; *b* 26 July 1932; *o s* of late Henry Matthew Talintyre and Gladys Talintyre; *m* 1956, Maureen Diana Lyons; one *s* one *d. Educ:* Harrow County Grammar School; London School of Economics. BSc (Econ.) 1956; MSc (Industrial Relns and Personnel Management) 1983. Joined National Coal Board, 1956: Administrative Assistant, 1956–59; Marketing Officer, Durham Div., 1959–61; Head of Manpower Planning and Intelligence, HQ, 1961–62; Dep. Head of Manpower, HQ, 1962–64; Head of Wages and Control, NW Div., 1964–66. Entered Civil Service, 1966: Principal, Naval Personnel (Pay) Div., MoD, 1966–69; Senior Industrial Relations Officer, CIR, 1969–71; Director of Industrial Relations, CIR, 1971–74; Asst Secretary, Training Services Agency, 1974–75; Counsellor (Labour), HM Embassy, Washington DC, 1975–77; Head of Policy and Planning, Manpower Services Commn, 1977–80; Department of Employment: Hd of Health and Safety Liaison, 1980–83; Asst Sec., Industrial Relations Div., 1983–86; Under Sec., 1986; Dir of Finance and Resource Management, and Principal Finance Officer, 1986–89. Freeman, Co. of Cordwainers, Newcastle upon Tyne, 1952. *Recreations:* travel, wine, gardening, short tennis. *Address:* Woodwards, School Lane, Cookham Dean, Berks SL6 9PQ. *Club:* Reform.

See also P. A. Rowan.

TALLBOYS, Richard Gilbert, CMG 1981; OBE 1974; FCA; FCIS; FCPA; international trade consultant; writer and speaker on international affairs; *b* 25 April 1931; *s* of late Harry Tallboys; *m* 1954, Margaret Evelyn, *d* of late Brig. H. W. Strutt, DSO, ED, Hobart; two *s* two *d. Educ:* Palmer's School. LLB (London), BCom (Tasmania). Merchant Navy apprentice, 1947–51; Third/Second Mate, Australian coast, 1952–55; Lt-Comdr, RANR (ASM 1945–75), retd 1991. Accounting profession in Australia, 1955–62; Alderman, Hobart City Council, 1958–62; Australian Govt Trade Commissioner, Johannesburg, Singapore, Jakarta, 1962–68. HM Diplomatic Service, 1968–88: First Secretary i/c Brasilia, 1969; Head of Chancery, Phnom Penh, 1972 (Chargé d'Affaires *ai* 1972, 1973); FO, 1973; Counsellor Commercial, Seoul, 1976–80 (Chargé d'Affaires *ai* 1977, 1978, 1979); Consul-General, Houston, 1980–85; Ambassador to Vietnam, 1985–87; Chief Exec., World Coal Inst., London, 1988–93. Mem., Internat. Trade Cttee, and Mem. Council, London Chamber of Commerce and Industry, 1990–93, 1995–98. Mem. Council, RIIA, 1995–2001. Councillor (C), City of Westminster, 1998–. Freeman, City of London, 1985; Liveryman, Chartered Secretaries and Administrators' Co., 1999–. *Publications:* (ed) Developing Vietnam, 1995; (jtly) 50 Years of Business in Indonesia 1945–1995, 1995. *Recreations:* sailing, ski-ing, cautious adventuring. *Address:* 7 Chapel Side, W2 4LG. *Clubs:* Travellers; Tasmanian (Hobart).

TALLING, John Francis, DSc; FRS 1978; Research Fellow, Freshwater Biological Association, since 1991; *b* 23 March 1929; *s* of Frank and Miriam Talling; *m* 1959, Ida Björnsson; one *s* one *d. Educ:* Sir William Turner's Sch., Coatham; Univ. of Leeds. BSc, PhD, DSc. Lecturer in Botany, Univ. of Khartoum, 1953–56; Visiting Research Fellow, Univ. of California, 1957; Plant Physiologist (SPSO), Freshwater Biological Assoc., 1958–89; Hon. Reader, 1979–84, Vis. Prof., 1992–, Univ. of Lancaster. *Publications:* (jtly) Water Analysis: some revised methods for limnologists, 1978; (jtly) Ecological Dynamics of Tropical Inland Waters, 1998; papers in various learned jls. *Recreation:* country walking. *Address:* 18 Brow Crescent, Windermere, Cumbria LA23 2EZ. *T:* (01539) 442836.

TALLIS, Prof. Raymond Courteney, FRCP; Professor of Geriatric Medicine, University of Manchester, since 1987; Hon. Consultant Physician in Health Care of the Elderly, Salford Royal Hospitals NHS Trust, since 1987; *b* 10 Oct. 1946; *s* of Edward Ernest Tallis and Mary Tallis (*née* Burke); *m* 1972, Theresa Bonneywell; two *s. Educ:* Liverpool Coll.; Keble Coll., Oxford (Open schol., 1964; BA 1967; BM BCh 1970); St Thomas' Hosp. Med. Sch. FRCP 1989. Clinical Res. Fellow, Wessex Neurological Centre, 1977–80; Sen. Lectr in Geriatric Medicine, Univ. of Liverpool, 1982–87. Numerous vis. professorships, named lectures, etc. Mem., various med. socs. FMedSci 2000. Hon. DLitt: Hull, 1997; Manchester, 2002. *Publications:* Not Saussure, 1988, 2nd edn 1995; In Defence of Realism, 1988, 2nd edn 1998; Clinical Neurology of Old Age, 1988; The Explicit Animal, 1991, 2nd edn 1999; (ed jtly) Brocklehurst's Textbook of Geriatric Medicine and Gerontology, 4th edn 1992, 5th edn 1998; Newton's Sleep, 1995; Epilepsy in Elderly People, 1996; Enemies of Hope, 1997, 2nd edn 1999; Theorrhoea and After, 1998; Increasing Longevity: medical, social and political implications, 1998; On the Edge of Certainty: philosophical explorations, 1999; A Raymond Tallis Reader, 2000; A Conversation with Martin Heidegger, 2001; *fiction:* Absence (novel), 1999; short stories; *poetry:* Between the Zones, 1985; Glints of Darkness, 1989; Fathers and Sons, 1993; over 150 scientific papers and articles mainly in the fields of neurology and neurological rehabilitation of older people; numerous articles in literary criticism and theory. *Recreations:* thinking, my family, Stella Artois, music. *Address:* 5 Valley Road, Bramhall, Stockport, Cheshire SK7 2NH. *T:* (0161) 439 2548. *Clubs:* Athenæum, 1942.

TALLON, John Mark; QC 2000; FCA; *b* 19 March 1948; *s* of late Claude Reginald Tallon and Blanche Mary Tallon; *m* 1st, 1974, Josephine Rowntree (marr. diss.); one *s* one *d*; 2nd, 1988, Patricia Steel. *Educ:* Rugby Sch. FCA 1970. Called to the Bar, Middle Temple, 1975; Mem., Pump Court Tax Chambers, 1976–. *Recreations:* golf, tennis, reading. *Address:* 16 Bedford Row, WC1R 4EB. *T:* (020) 7414 8080. *Club:* Walton Heath Golf (Surrey).

TALWAR, Rana Gurvirendra Singh; Chief Executive Officer, Standard Chartered Plc, since 1998; *b* 22 March 1948; *s* of R. S. and Veera Talwar; *m* 1st, 1970, Roop Som Dutt (marr. diss.); one *s* one *d*; 2nd, 1995, Renuka Singh; one *s. Educ:* Lawrence Sch., Sanawar, India; St Stephen's Coll., Delhi (BA Hons Econs). Citibank, 1969–97: exec. trainee for internat. banking, 1969–70; various operational, corporate and institutional banking assignments, India, 1970–76; Gp Hd for Treasury and Financial Instns, 1976; Regl Manager for Eastern India, 1977; Gp Hd, Treasury and Financial Instns Gp, Saudi American Bank (Citibank affiliate), Jeddah, 1978–80; COS, Asia Pacific Div., 1981; Regl Consumer Business Manager, Singapore, Malaysia, Indonesia, Thailand and India, 1982–88; Div. Exec., Asia Pacific, 1988–91; Exec. Vice Pres. and Gp Exec. responsible for Consumer Bank in Asia Pacific, ME and Eastern Europe, 1991–95; Exec. Vice Pres., Citicorp and principal subsid., Citibank, resp. for US and Europe, 1996–97; Gp Exec. Dir, Standard Chartered Plc, 1997–98. Non-exec. Dir, Pearson plc, 2000–. Governor: Indian Business Sch., 1998–; London Business Sch., 1999–. *Recreations:* golf, tennis, bridge, travel. *Address:* Standard Chartered Plc, 1 Aldermanbury Square, EC2V 7SB. *T:* (020) 7280 7088. *Clubs:* Tanglin (Singapore); Bengal (Calcutta); Delhi Golf (New Delhi).

TAMARÓN, 9th Marqués de; **Santiago de Mora-Figueroa;** Spanish Ambassador to the Court of St James's, since 1999; *b* 18 Oct. 1941; *s* of José de Mora-Figueroa, 8th Marqués de Tamarón, and Dagmar Williams; *m* 1966, Isabelle de Yturbe; one *s* one *d. Educ:* Univ. of Madrid; Escuela Diplomática. Lieut, Spanish Marine Corps, 1967; joined Spanish Diplomatic Service, 1968; Secretary: Mauritania, 1968–70; Paris, 1970–73; Banco del Noroeste (on voluntary leave), 1974; Counsellor, Denmark, 1975–80; Minister Counsellor, Ottawa, 1980–81; Private Sec. to Minister of Foreign Affairs, 1981–82; Head of Studies and Dep. Dir, Escuela Diplomática, 1982–88; Dir, Inst. de Cuestiones Internacionales y Política Exterior, 1988–96; Dir, Inst. Cervantes, 1996–99. Comdr, Orden de Carlos III (Spain), 1982; Gran Cruz, Orden del Mérito Naval (Spain), 1999; Commander: Order of Dannebrog (Denmark), 1980; Order of Merit (Germany), 1981; Officier, Ordre Nat. du Mérite (France), 1974. *Publications:* Pólvora con Aguardiente, 1983; El Guirigay Nacional, 1988; Trampantojos, 1990; El Siglo XX y otras Calamidades, 1993; (jtly) El Peso de la Lengua Española en el Mundo, 1995. *Recreations:* mountain walking, gardening, philology. *Address:* Spanish Embassy, 39 Chesham Place, SW1X 8SB. *Club:* Nuevo (Madrid).

TAMBLIN, Air Cdre Pamela Joy, CB 1980; retired; Director, Women's Royal Air Force, 1976–80; *b* 11 Jan. 1926; *d* of late Albert Laing and Olga Victoria Laing; *m* 1970, Douglas Victor Tamblin; one step *s* one step *d. Educ:* James Gillespie's High Sch., Edinburgh; Heaton High Sch., Newcastle upon Tyne; Durham Univ. (BA Hons). ATS, 1943–45. Essex County Council Planning Officer, 1949–51. Joined Royal Air Force, 1951; served Education Branch, 1951–55: RAF Locking; RAF Stanmore Park; RAF Wahn, Germany; Secretarial subseq. Administrative, Branch, 1955–76; Schools Liaison Recruiting, 1955–59; Accountant Officer, RAF St Mawgan and RAF Steamer Point, Aden, 1959–61; Staff College, 1962–63; MoD, Air Secretary's Dept, 1963–66; Sen. Trng Officer, RAF Spitalgate, 1966–68; Admin. Plans Officer, HQ Maintenance Comd, 1968–69; Command WRAF Admin. Officer, HQ Strike Comd, 1969–71; Station Comdr, RAF Spitalgate, 1971–74; Command Accountant, HQ Strike Comd, 1974–76. Chm., Cttee on Women in NATO Forces, 1977–79. Pres., E Cornwall Branch, RAFA, 1984–; Chm., S Western Area Council, RAFA, 1991–93 (Mem., 1986–; Vice-Chm., 1988–91). FIMgt (FBIM 1977, CBIM 1979); FRSA 1979. *Recreations:* various charitable works, tapestry work, handbell ringing. *Address:* Trecairne, 3 Plaidy Park Road, Looe, Cornwall PL13 1LG. *Club:* Royal Air Force.

TAMBLING, Pauline Ann; Executive Director, Research and Development, Arts Council of England, since 1999; *b* 23 April 1955; *d* of James William and Anne Dorling; *m* 1976, Jeremy Tambling; one *s* one *d. Educ:* Ely High Sch. for Girls; Stockwell Coll., Bromley (Cert Ed London); Univ. of Leeds (MA). Teacher, 1976–83; Head of Educn, Royal Opera House, 1983–97; Dir, Educn and Trng, Arts Council of England, 1997–99. Deviser/writer, Top Score, TV series, 1996–97; co-dir/researcher, orchestral educn programmes, NFER, 1997–98. FRSA 1990. *Publications:* Performing Arts in the Primary School, 1990; Lessons in Partnership, 1996; articles in Cultural Trends, British Jl Music Educn. *Recreations:* arts, cinema, travel, current affairs. *Address:* 9 Sumburgh Road, SW12 8AJ. *T:* (020) 7228 8089; Arts Council of England, 14 Great Peter Street, SW1P 3NQ. *T:* (020) 7973 6842.

TAMBUNTING, Jesus Paraiso; Ambassador of the Philippines to the Court of St James's, and concurrently to Ireland, 1993–98; *b* 21 Dec. 1937; *s* of Antonio Tambunting and Aurora Paraiso Tambunting; *m* 1967, Margarita Ansaldo; two *s* two *d. Educ:* Univ. of Maryland (BS, BA Econs). Chairman: Planters Development Bank, 1975–; Planters DB Leasing Corp., 1992–. Perm. Rep. of Philippines to IMO, 1993. Hon. Pres., British–Philippine Soc., 1993. *Recreations:* tennis, golf. *Clubs:* Queen's; Roehampton Golf.

TAMI, Mark Richard; MP (Lab) Alyn and Deeside, since 2001; *b* 3 Oct. 1962; *s* of Michael John Tami and Patricia Tami; *m* 1992, Sally Daniels; two *s. Educ:* Enfield Grammar Sch.; UCW, Swansea (BA Hons). Head of Res. and Communications,

1992–99, Head of Policy, 1999–2001, AEEU. *Publication:* Votes for All: compulsory voting in elections, 2000. *Recreations:* football, cricket, antiques. *Address:* House of Commons, SW1A 0AA.

TAMMADGE, Alan Richard; Headmaster, Sevenoaks School, 1971–81; *b* 9 July 1921; *m* 1950, Rosemary Anne Broadribb; two *s* one *d.* *Educ:* Bromley County Sch.; Dulwich Coll.; Emmanuel Coll., Cambridge. BA (Maths) 1950; MA 1957. Royal Navy Special Entry, 1940; resigned, 1947 (Lt); Cambridge, 1947–50; Lectr, RMA Sandhurst, 1950–55; Asst Master, Dulwich College, 1956–58; Head of Mathematics Dept, Abingdon School, 1958–67; Master, Magdalen College School, Oxford, 1967–71. Royal Instn Mathematics Master Classes, 1982–94. Pres., Mathematical Assoc., 1978–79. FIMA 1965. *Publications:* Complex Numbers, 1965; (jtly) School Mathematics Project Books 1–5, 1965–69; (jtly) General Education, 1969; Parents' Guide to School Mathematics, 1976; articles in Mathemat. Gazette, Mathematics Teacher (USA), Aspects of Education (Hull Univ.). *Recreations:* music, gardens. *Address:* 20 Claverham Way, Battle, East Sussex TN33 0JE.

TAMUNO, Prof. Tekena Nitonye, DLit; Emeritus Professor, University of Ibadan, since 1994; Distinguished Fellow, National Institute for Policy and Strategic Studies, Kuru, Nigeria, 1992–94 (Research Professor in History, 1990–92); *b* 28 Jan. 1932; *s* of late Chief Mark Tamuno Igbiri and Mrs Ransoline I. Tamuno; *m* 1963, Olu Grace Tamuno (*née* Esho); two *s* two *d.* *Educ:* University Coll. Ibadan; Birkbeck Coll., Univ. of London; Columbia Univ., New York City. BA (Hons) History, PhD History, DLit (London). University of Ibadan: Professor of History, 1971; Head, Dept of History, 1972–75; Dean of Arts, 1973–75; Chairman, Cttee of Deans, 1974–75; Vice-Chancellor, 1975–79; Res. Prof. in History, Inst. of African Studies, 1979–90. Principal, University Coll., Ilorin, Oct.–Nov. 1975; Pro-Chancellor and Chm. Council, Rivers State Univ. of Sci. and Technol., Port-Harcourt, 1981–88; Vis. Prof. in History, Nigerian Defence Acad., Kaduna, 1989–90. Chairman: Presidential Panel on Nigeria Since Independence History Project, 1980–; Panel on Policing Nigeria Project, 1992–93. Chm. Bd of Dirs, New Nigerian Newspapers Ltd, 1984–89. Nat. Vice-Pres., Historical Soc. of Nigeria, 1974–78 (Fellow, 1992). Fellow, Nigerian Acad. of Letters, 2000. Gen. Ed., African Leadership Forum Biographical Series, 1991. JP Ibadan, 1976. *Publications:* Nigeria and Elective Representation, 1923–1947, 1966; The Police in Modern Nigeria, 1961–1965, 1970; The Evolution of the Nigerian State: The Southern Phase, 1898–1914, 1972; (ed with Prof. J. F. A. Ajayi) The University of Ibadan, 1948–1973: A History of the First Twenty-Five Years, 1973; History and History-makers in Modern Nigeria, 1973; Herbert Macaulay, Nigerian Patriot, 1975; (ed with E. J. Alagoa) Eminent Nigerians of the Rivers State, 1980; (ed) Ibadan Voices: Ibadan University in Transition, 1981; Songs of an Egg-Head (poems), 1982; (ed) National Conference on Nigeria since Independence: addresses at the formal opening, 1983; (ed) Proceedings of the National Conference on Nigeria since Independence, Zaria, March 1983, Vol. III: The Civil War Years, 1984; Nigeria Since Independence: The First Twenty-Five Years: (ed with J. A. Atanda) Vol. III, Education, 1989; (ed with J. A. Atanda) Vol. IV, Government and Public Policy, 1989; (ed with S. C. Ukpabi) Vol. VI, The Civil War Years, 1989; (ed with E. J. Alagoa) Land and People of Nigeria: Rivers State, 1989; Peace and Violence in Nigeria, 1991; (ed jtly) Policing Nigeria: past, present and future, 1993; Festival of Songs & Drums (poems), 1999. *Recreations:* music, photography, swimming, horse-riding, gardening, domestic pets. *Address:* Institute of African Studies, University of Ibadan, Ibadan, Nigeria. *T:* (22) 410352. *Club:* University Senior Staff (Ibadan).

TAMWORTH, Viscount; Robert William Saswalo Shirley, FCA; Managing Director, Ruffer Investment Management Ltd, since 1999 (Director, since 1994); *b* 29 Dec. 1952; *s* and *heir* of 13th Earl Ferrers, *qv*; *m* 1980, Susannah, *y d* of late C. E. W. Sheepshanks, Arthington Hall, Yorks; two *s* one *d.* *Educ:* Ampleforth. Teaching in Kenya, under CMS's Youth Service Abroad Scheme, 1971–72. Articled to Whinney Murray & Co., CA, 1972–76; employed at Ernst & Whinney, 1976–82, Asst Manager, 1981–82; Gp Auditor, 1982–85, Sen. Treasury Analyst, 1986, BICC plc; Director: Viking Property Gp Ltd, 1987–88 (Financial Controller and Company Sec., 1986–87); Ashby Securities, subseq. Norseman Hldgs, 1987–92. Admitted to Inst. of Chartered Accountants of England and Wales, 1976. *Recreations:* the British countryside and related activities, the garden. *Heir: s* Hon. William Robert Charles Shirley, *b* 10 Dec. 1984. *Address:* The Old Vicarage, Shirley, Ashbourne, Derbyshire DE6 3AZ. *Club:* Boodle's.

TAN, Melvyn; pianist; *b* 13 Oct. 1956; *s* of Keng Hian Tan and Sov Yuen Wong. *Educ:* Anglo-Chinese Sch.; Yehudi Menuhin Sch.; Royal Coll. of Music. Performer of classical piano repertoire on period instruments, 1983–; solo career, 1985–; extended repertoire to include modern piano, 1996–; performs in internat. music festivals, incl. Austria, Germany, Holland, France, Scandinavia, UK, USA, Japan; pioneered interest in keyboard music of 18/19th centuries, incl. tour with Beethoven's own Broadwood piano, 1992; cycle of complete Beethoven sonatas, Japan, 1994–97; numerous recordings. *Recreations:* swimming, wine, travelling to places where free of performing. *Address:* Valerie Barber PR & Personal Management, Suite 2, 9a St John's Wood High Street, NW8 7NG.

TANBURN, Jennifer Jephcott; business historian, since 1997; *b* 6 Oct. 1929; *d* of late Harold Jephcott Tanburn and Elise Noel Tanburn (*née* Armour). *Educ:* St Joseph's Priory, Dorking; Settrington Sch., Hampstead; University Coll. of the South West, Exeter (BSc (Econ)). Market Research Dept, Unilever Ltd, 1951–52; Research and Information, Lintas Ltd, 1952–66, Head of Div., 1962–66, Head of Special Projects, 1966–74; British Airways Board, 1974–76; Head of Res. and Consumer Affairs, 1975–76, a Dir, 1976–83, Booker McConnell Food Distbn Div.; res. consultant, 1984–94. Member: Marketing Policy Cttee, 1977–80, and Potato Product Gp, 1980–82, Central Council for Agricl and Hortl Co-operation; Marketing Gp of GB; Packaging Council, 1978–82; Chm., Consumers' Cttees for GB and England and Wales under Agricl Marketing Act of 1958, 1982–91. Hon. Vis. Academic, Middlesex Univ., 1997–. Hon. Fellow, Durham Univ. (Business Sch.), 1991–94. *Publications:* Food, Women and Shops, 1968; People, Shops and the '70s, 1970; Superstores in the '70s, 1972; Retailing and the Competitive Challenge: a study of retail trends in the Common Market, Sweden and the USA, 1974; Food Distribution: its impact on marketing in the '80s, 1981; articles on retailing and marketing subjects. *Recreations:* travel, golf, television viewing, reading. *Address:* 5 Finch Green, Cedars Village, Dog Kennel Lane, Chorleywood, Herts WD3 5GE. *T:* (01923) 497422.

TANCRED, Sir Henry L.; *see* Lawson-Tancred.

TANDY, Virginia Ann; Director, Manchester City Art Galleries, since 1998; *b* 29 Feb. 1956; *d* of William Arthur Francis Tandy and Lucy Tandy (*née* Saunders); *m* 1984, Brian Stephen Fell; one *s.* *Educ:* Newcastle upon Tyne Poly. (BA Hons); Manchester Univ. (Post-grad. Dip. Mus. Studies). Museums Officer, Tameside MBC, 1980–84; Exhibns Officer, Cornerhouse Arts Centre, 1985–87; Visual Arts Officer and Hd, Visual Arts, NW Arts Bd, 1988–94; Dir, Cornerhouse Arts Centre, 1994–98. *Recreations:* family, gardening. *Address:* Art Galleries Department, Town Hall, Albert Square, Manchester M60 2LA. *Club:* Labour (Glossop).

TANFIELD, Jennifer Bridget; Librarian, House of Commons, 1993–99; *b* 19 July 1941; *d* of Doylah and Phyllis Tanfield. *Educ:* Abbots Bromley; LSE (BSc Econ 1962). House of Commons: Library Clerk, 1963–72; Head, Econ. Affairs Section, later Statistical Section, 1972–87; Head, Parly Div., 1987–91; Dep. Librarian, 1991–93. Chm., IFLA Sect. on Library and Res. Services for Parliaments, 1997–99. *Publication:* In Parliament 1939–1951, 1991. *Recreations:* opera, theatre, travel, squash. *Address:* 23 Hugo Road, N19 5EU. *T:* (020) 7607 5082.

TANGAROA, Hon. Sir Tangaroa, Kt 1987; MBE 1984; Queen's Representative, Cook Islands, 1984–90; *b* 6 May 1921; *s* of Tangaroa and Mihiau; *m* 1941; two *s* seven *d.* *Educ:* Avarua Primary School, Rarotonga. Radio operator, 1939–54; Shipping Clerk, A. B. Donald Ltd and J. & P. Ingram Ltd, 1955–63; MP for Penrhyn, 1958–84; Minister of Educn, Works, Survey, Printing and Electric Power Supply; Minister of Internal Affairs, 1978–80; retired from politics, 1984. Pres., Cook Is Crippled Children's Soc., 1966–; Deacon, Cook Is Christian Church (served 15 years in Penrhyn, 28 years in Avarua); former community positions: Mem., Tereora Coll. Sch. Cttee for 20 years and 10 as Sec./Treasurer; Pres., Cook Is Boys Brigade for 15 years; delegate to Cook Is Sports Assoc. *Address:* PO Box 870, Avarua, Rarotonga, Cook Islands.

TANKERVILLE, 10th Earl of, *cr* 1714; **Peter Grey Bennet;** Baron Ossulston, 1682; *b* 18 Oct. 1956; *s* of 9th Earl of Tankerville, and Georgiana Lilian Maude (*d* 1998), *d* of late Gilbert Wilson, MA, DD, PhD; *S* father, 1980. *Educ:* Oberlin Conservatory, Ohio (Bachelor of Music); San Francisco State Univ. (Master of Music). Working as musician, San Francisco. *Heir: uncle* Rev. the Hon. George Arthur Grey Bennet [*b* 12 March 1925; *m* 1957, Hazel Glyddon, *d* of late E. W. G. Judson; two *s* one *d*]. *Address:* 139 Olympia Way, San Francisco, CA 94131, USA. *T:* (415) 8266639.

TANLAW, Baron *cr* 1971 (Life Peer), of Tanlawhill, Dumfries; **Simon Brooke Mackay;** Chairman and Managing Director, Fandstan Ltd, since 1973; *b* 30 March 1934; *s* of 2nd Earl of Inchcape; *m* 1st, 1959, Joanna Susan, *d* of Major J. S. Hirsch; one *s* two *d* (and one *s* decd); 2nd, 1976, Rina Siew Yong Tan, *d* of late Tiong Cha Tan and Mrs Tan; one *s* one *d.* *Educ:* Eton College; Trinity College, Cambridge (MA 1966). Served as 2nd Lt XII Royal Lancers, Malaya. Inchcape Group of Companies, India and Far East, 1960–66; Managing Director, Inchcape & Co., 1967–71, Dir 1971–92; Chm., Thwaites & Reed Ltd, 1971–74; Chm. and Man. Dir, Fandstan Group of private cos, 1973–. Chm., Building Cttee, Univ. of Buckingham (formerly UC at Buckingham), 1973–78, Mem. Council of Management 1973–, Hon. Fellow, 1981, DUniv 1983; Mem. Ct of Governors, LSE, 1980–96. Mem., Lord Chancellor's Inner London Adv. Cttee on Justices of the Peace, 1972–83. Contested (L) Galloway, by-election and gen. election, 1959, and gen. election, 1964. Mem., EC Cttee Sub-Cttee F (Energy, Transport Technology and Research), H of L, 1980–83; Chairman: Parly Liaison Gp for Alternative Energy Strategies, 1981–83; Parly Astronomy and Space Envmt Gp, 1999–. Joint Treasurer, 1971–72, Dep. Chm., 1972, Scottish Liberal Party. Pres., Sarawak Assoc., 1973–75. Chm., Nat. Appeal, Elizabeth FitzRoy Homes for the mentally handicapped, 1985–. FBHI 1996. *Publications:* articles and papers. *Recreations:* normal. *Address:* Tanlawhill, Eskdalemuir, By Langholm, Dumfriesshire DG13 0PQ. *T:* (01387) 373273; 31 Brompton Square, SW3 2AE. *Clubs:* White's, Oriental; Puffin's (Edinburgh).

TANNER, Brian Michael, CBE 1997; DL; Chairman, Taunton and Somerset NHS Trust, since 1998; *b* 15 Feb. 1941; *s* of Gerald Evelyn Tanner and Mary Tanner; *m* 1963, June Ann Walker; one *s* one *d.* *Educ:* Acklam Hall Grammar Sch., Middlesbrough; Bishop Vesey Grammar Sch., Sutton Coldfield; Bristol Univ. (BA 1st class Hons). CIPFA. Trainee Accountant, Birmingham CBC, 1962–66; Economist, Coventry CBC, 1966–69; Chief Accountant, Teesside CBC, 1969–71; Warwickshire County Council: Asst County Treasurer, 1971–73; Asst Chief Exec., 1973–75; Somerset County Council: County Treasurer, 1975–90; Chief Exec., 1990–97; Treasurer, Avon and Somerset Police Authy, 1975–91. Advr, ACC Cttees on agric., educn, nat. parks, finance, policy, police, 1976–92; Mem., Accounting Standards Cttee, 1982–85; Chief Negotiator with Central Govt on Rate Support Grant, 1985–88; Mem., Investment Cttee, Nat. Assoc. of Pension Funds, 1988–91. Director: Avon Enterprise Fund, 1988–97; Somerset TEC, 1990–97; Jupiter Internat. Green Investment Trust, 1997–2001. Chairman: SW Reg., Nat. Lottery Charities Bd, 1997–; Taunton Town Centre Partnership, 1998–; a Comr, Public Works Loan Bd, 1997–; Member: SW Regl FEFC, 1997–99; Wessex Ofwat, 1998–99. Trustee, Avon and Somerset Police Trust, 1999–. Trustee, Central Bureau for Educnl Visits and Exchanges, 1981–92. Governor: Millfield Sch., 1989–99; Bridgwater Coll., 1994–. Freeman, City of London, 1990. DL Somerset, 1998. *Publication:* Financial Management in the 1990's, 1989. *Recreations:* gardening, golf, philately, antiques. *Address:* 8 Broadlands Road, Taunton, Somerset TA1 4HQ. *T:* (01823) 337826. *Club:* Sloane.

TANNER, Lt-Col Cecil Eustace; Vice Lord-Lieutenant of Bedfordshire, since 1998; *b* 14 Oct. 1934. Commnd 2nd Lieut, RASC, 1955; GSO 2, MoD, 1969–71; DAQMG (Logistics), HQ Land SE, 1973–75; Lt-Col 1976; CO 156 Regt, RCT(V), 1977; retd 1987. Formerly Cadet EO for Beds, ACF, TA. *Address:* c/o Lieutenancy Office, County Hall, Cauldwell Street, Bedford MK42 9AP.

TANNER, David Williamson, DPhil; Under Secretary, Head of Science Branch, Department of Education and Science, 1981–89; *b* 28 Dec. 1930; *s* of late Arthur Bertram Tanner, MBE and of Susan (*née* Williamson); *m* 1960, Glenis Mary (*née* Stringer); one *s* two *d.* *Educ:* Raynes Park County Grammar Sch.; University Coll., Oxford (MA, DPhil); UEA (BA Hons Phil. 1st cl., 1997). Univ. of Minnesota (post-doctoral research), USA, 1954–56; Dept of Scientific and Industrial Research (Fuel Research Station and Warren Spring Lab.), 1957–64; Dept of Educn and Science, 1964–89. *Publications:* papers on physical chem. in Trans Faraday Soc., Jl Applied Chem., Jl Heat and Mass Transfer, etc. *Recreations:* family, philosophy. *Address:* The Old Maltings, 98 Commercial End, Swaffham Bulbeck, Cambs CB5 0NE. *T:* (01223) 811211.

TANNER, Dr John Benedict Ian, CBE 1979; Founding Director: Royal Air Force Museum, 1963–88; Battle of Britain Museum, 1978–88; Cosford Aero-Space Museum, 1978–88; Bomber Command Museum, 1982–88; Hon. Archivist, since 1980, and Senior Research Fellow, 1982–97, now Supernumary Fellow, Pembroke College, Oxford; *b* London, 2 Jan. 1927; *o s* of R. A. and I. D. M. Tanner; *m* 1st, 1953, April Rothery (marr. diss. 1972, and subseq. by RC Tribunal); one *d*; 2nd, 1991, Dr Andrea Isobel Duncan, FSA. *Educ:* City of London Library Sch.; Universities of London, Nottingham (MA, PhD) and Oxford (MA). Reading Public Library, 1950; Archivist-Librarian, Kensington Library, 1950–51; Leighton House Art Gall. and Museum, 1951–53; Curator, Librarian and Tutor, RAF Coll., 1953–63; Hon. Sec., Old Cranwellian Assoc., 1956–64; Extra-mural Lectr in History of Art, Univ. of Nottingham, 1959–63. Walmsley Lectr, City Univ., 1980. Vis. Fellow, Wolfson Coll., Cambridge, 1983–; Prof., The Polish Univ., 1987–94, now Emeritus. Chm., Internat. Air Museum Cttee; Vice-President: Guild of Aviation Artists; Croydon Airport Museum Soc.; Trustee, Manchester Air and Space Museum; Mem. Founding Cttee, All England Lawn Tennis Museum; Mem. Br. Cttee, Caen Memorial Musée pour la Paix; President: Anglo-American Ecumenical Assoc.; USAF European Meml Foundn. Life Vice-Pres., Friends of RAF Mus. FLA, FMA,

FRHistS, FRAeS, FSA. Freeman, City of London, 1966; Liveryman: Worshipful Co. of Gold and Silver Wyre Drawers, 1966; Scriveners' Co., 1978. Freeman, Guild of Air Pilots and Air Navigators, 1979. Hon. Mem. Collegio Araldico of Rome, 1963. Hon. DLitt City, 1982; Hon. LLD The Polish Univ., 1989; Hon. DCL Assumption Coll., Worcester, Mass, 1993. Tissandier Award, Fedn Aeronautique Internat., 1977. KStJ 1978 (OStJ 1964; St John Service Medal, 1985); KCSG 1977; KCSG, with Star, 1985; Cross of Merit, Order of Malta, 1978. Grand Comdr, OM Holy Sepulchre (Vatican); Order of Polonia Restituta (Poland), 1985; Nile Gold Medal (Egypt), 1987. *Publications:* (ed) List of Cranwell Graduates, 2nd edn, 1963; (jtly) Encyclopedic Dictionary of Heraldry, 1968; How to trace your Ancestors, 1971; Man in Flight (limited edn), 1973; The Royal Air Force Museum: one hundred years of aviation history, 1973; (with W. E. May and W. Y. Carman) Badges and Insignia of the British Armed Services, 1974; Charles I, 1974; Who's Famous in Your Family: a Reader's Digest guide to genealogy, 1975, 2nd edn 1979; Wings of the Eagle (exhibition catalogue), 1976; (ed) They Fell in the Battle, 1980 (limited edn, to commemorate 40th anniv. of Battle of Britain); Sir William Rothenstein: an RAF Museum exhibition catalogue, 1985; RAF Museum — a combined guide, 1987; Editor, RAF Museum Air Publication series, 10 vols; General Editor: Museums and Libraries (Internat. Series); Studies in Air History; reviews and articles in professional and other jls. *Recreations:* cricket, opera, reading. *Address:* Flat One, 57 Drayton Gardens, SW10 9RU. *Clubs:* Athenæum, Reform, MCC.

TANNER, John W., CBE 1983; FRIBA, FRTPI; Director, United Nations Relief and Works Agency for Palestine Refugees, Jordan, 1971–83 (accorded rank of Ambassador to Hashemite Kingdom of Jordan, 1973); *b* 15 Nov. 1923; *s* of Walter George Tanner and Elizabeth Wilkes Tanner (*née* Humphreys); *m* 1st, 1948, Hazel Harford Harford-Jones (*d* 1996); one *s* two *d*; 2nd, 1999, Jacqueline Mary Richards (*née* Hands). *Educ:* Clifton Coll.; Liverpool Univ. Sch. of Architecture and Dept of Civic Design. MCD, BArch (Hons). Sen. Planning Officer, Nairobi, 1951; Architect, Nairobi, 1953; Hon. Sec., Kenya Chapter of Architects, 1954; UN Relief and Works Agency: Architect and Planning Officer, Beirut, 1955; Chief Techn. Div., 1957. Past Mem. Cttee, Fedn of Internat. Civil Servants Assoc., 1968–70. *Buildings:* vocational and teacher training centres (Damascus, Syria; Siblin, Lebanon; Ramallah; Wadi Seer; Amman, Jordan); schools; low cost housing and health centres; E African Rugby Union HQ, Nairobi. *Publications:* The Colour Problem in Liverpool: accommodation or assimilation, 1951; Building for the UNRWA/UNESCO Education and Training Programme, 1968. *Recreations:* formerly: Rugby football (Waterloo, Lancs, 1950; Kenya Harlequins, Kenya and E Africa); ski-ing, squash, board sailing. *Address:* 69B La Pleta, Ordino, Andorra.

TANNER, Mary Elizabeth, (Mrs J. B. Tanner), OBE 1999; Secretary, Council for Christian Unity, General Synod of the Church of England, 1991–98; *b* 23 July 1938; *d* of Harold Fussell and Marjorie (*née* Teucher); *m* 1961, John Bryan Tanner; one *s* one *d*. *Educ:* Colston's Girls' Sch., Bristol; Birmingham Univ. (BA Hons). Lecturer in: OT and Hebrew, Hull Univ., 1960–67; OT and Hebrew, Bristol Univ., 1972–75; OT, Westcott House, Cambridge, 1978–82; Theol Sec., Bd for Mission and Unity, C of E, 1982–91. DD Lambeth, 1988; Hon. DD: General Seminary, NY, 1991; Birmingham, 1997; Virginia Seminary, 1999. Plaque of St Erik, Ch of Sweden, 1997. Officer's Cross, Order of Merit (Germany), 1991; Comdr, Royal Order of the Polar Star (Sweden), 2000. *Publications:* essays in: Feminine in the Church, 1984; The Study of Anglicanism, 1988; Runcie by His Friends, 1989; Women and Church, 1991; Encounters for Living, 1995; Living Evangelism, 1996; Festschrift for Jean Tillard, 1996; The Vision of Christian Unity, 1997; A Church for the 21st Century, 1998; Ecumenical Theology in Worship, Doctrine and Life, 1999; articles in Theology, Ecumenical Rev., One in Christ, etc. *Recreations:* music, gardening. *Address:* Highclere, Camp End Road, Weybridge, Surrey KT13 0NW. *T:* (01932) 842786.

TANNER, Meg; *see* Beresford, M.

TANNER, Prof. Roger Ian, PhD; FRS 2001; FAA, FTSE; P. N. Russell Professor of Mechanical Engineering, University of Sydney, since 1975; *b* 25 July 1933; *s* of Reginald Jack Tanner and Ena Maud Tanner (*née* Horsington); *m* 1957, Elizabeth Bogen; two *s*, three *d*. *Educ:* Univ. of Bristol (BSc 1956); Univ. of California (MS 1958); Manchester Univ. (PhD 1961). FAA 1979; FTSE 1977. Lectr, Manchester Univ., 1958–61; Reader, Univ. of Sydney, 1961–66; Prof. Brown Univ., Providence, USA, 1966–75. *Publications:* Engineering Rheology, 1985, 2nd edn 2000; (with K. Walters) Rheology: an historical perspective, 1998; several hundred jl papers. *Recreations:* tennis, golf. *Address:* School of Aerospace, Mechanical and Mechatronic Engineering, University of Sydney, Sydney, NSW 2006, Australia. *T:* (2) 9351 7153.

TANNOCK, Dr (Timothy) Charles Ayrton; Member (C) London, European Parliament, since 1999; *b* 25 Sept. 1957; *s* of Robert Cochrane William Tannock and Anne (*née* England); *m* 1984, Rosa Maria Vega Pizarro (marr. diss. 1988); one *s*. *Educ:* St George's Sch., Rome; St Julian's Sch., Lisbon; Bradfield Coll.; Balliol Coll., Oxford (BA Hons Natural Scis; MA); Middlesex Hosp. Med. Sch. (MB BS). MRCPsych 1988. House surgeon, Middx Hosp., and house physician, Harefield Hosp., 1984–85; W London Psychiatric Registrar Rotation, Charing Cross and Westminster Hosps, 1985–90; Res. Fellow, Charing Cross and Westminster Hosp. Med. Sch., 1988–90; N London Psychiatric Sen. Registrar Rotation, UCH and Middx Hosp., 1990–95; Consultant Psychiatrist and Hon. Sen. Lectr, Camden and Islington NHS Community Trust at UCH and UCL Med. Sch., 1995–99. European Parliament: Mem., Economic and Monetary Affairs Cttee, 1999–; substitute Member: Envmt, Public Health and Consumer Affairs Cttee, 1999–; Develt Cttee, 2000–; financial services spokesman, 1999–, Asst Whip, 2000–, Cons. delegn; Mem., EP-Slovakia Jt Parly Cttee, 1999–. Mem. (C), RBK&C, 1998–2000. Freeman, City of London, 2000. Commendatore, Order of St Maurice and St Lazarus, 2000. *Publications: political:* Community Care: the need for action, 1989; A Marriage of Convenience–or reform of the Community Charge, 1991; *medical:* numerous contribs to med. jls in areas of mood disorders and chronic fatigue syndrome. *Recreations:* ski-ing, travel, surfing the internet. *Address:* (office) Conservative Central Office, 32 Smith Square, SW1P 3HH. *T:* (020) 7984 8235, *Fax:* (020) 7984 8292; *e-mail:* ctannock@europarl.eu.int.

TANNOUDJI, Claude C.; *see* Cohen-Tannoudji, C.

TANSEY, Rock Benedict; QC 1990; a Recorder, since 1995; *m* 1964, Wendy Carver; one *s* two *d*. *Educ:* Bristol Univ. (LLB Hons; Dip. Social Studies). Called to the Bar, Lincoln's Inn, 1966. *Recreations:* politics, theatre, opera, football, tennis, golf. *Address:* 3 Gray's Inn Square, Gray's Inn, WC1R 5AH.

TANSLEY, Anthony James Nicholas; HM Diplomatic Service; Counsellor and Deputy Head of Mission, Muscat, since 1998; *b* 19 July 1962; *er s* of Thomas Anthony Tansley and Marian Tansley (*née* Baron); *m* 1998, Bláithín Mary Curran. *Educ:* Tonbridge Sch.; St John's Coll., Oxford (MA); Sch. of Oriental and African Studies, Univ. of London (MSc). Joined FCO, 1984: lang. trng, 1986; Second Secretary (Chancery): Riyadh, 1988–89; Baghdad, 1989–91; First Secretary: FCO, 1991–94; Dublin, 1994–98. *Recreations:* Islamic architecture, history, cricket. *Address:* c/o Foreign and Commonwealth Office, King Charles Street, SW1A 2AH. *Club:* Oxford and Cambridge.

TANTUM, Geoffrey Alan, CMG 1995; OBE 1981; Middle East consultant; HM Diplomatic Service, retired; *b* 12 Nov. 1940; *s* of George Frederick Tantum and Margaret Amelia Tantum (*née* Goozée); *m* 1977, Caroline Kent; three *d*. *Educ:* Hampton Grammar Sch.; RMA Sandhurst; St John's Coll., Oxford (MA 1st Class Hons Oriental Studies (Arabic)). MIL. HM Forces, 1959–66; joined Diplomatic Service, 1969; Kuwait, 1970–72; Aden, 1972–73; FCO, 1973–76; Amman, 1977–80; FCO, 1980–85; Counsellor, Rome, 1985–88; FCO, 1988–95. Chm., Bd of Dirs, Internat. Community Sch. (Jordan) Ltd, 1978–80. Order of the Star of Jordan, 2nd cl., 1995. *Publication:* Muslim Warfare: Islamic arms and armour, 1979. *Recreations:* sailing, oriental studies. *Club:* Travellers.

TANZANIA, Archbishop of, since 1998; **Most Rev. Donald Leo Mtetemela;** Bishop of Ruaha, since 1990; *b* Nov. 1947; *s* of Weston Mtetemela and Anjendile Mtetemela; *m* 1990, Gladys; three *s* four *d*. *Educ:* Dodoma Secondary Sch.; St Philip's Theol Coll., Kongwa (LTh); Wycliffe Hall, Oxford; DipTh London Univ. Ordained, 1971; Pastor, 1971–82; Asst Bishop, Central Tanganyika, 1982–90. *Address:* c/o Diocese of Ruaha, Box 1028, Iringa, Tanzania. *T:* (64) 2667.

TANZER, John Brian Camille; His Honour Judge Tanzer; a Circuit Judge, since 2001; *b* 27 Dec. 1949; *s* of William and Edith Tanzer; *m* 1980, Suzanne Coates, *qv*; two *s*. *Educ:* Town Sch., NY; St Faith's Sch., Cambridge; The Leys, Cambridge; Keble Coll., Oxford; Sussex Univ. (BA); Inns of Court Sch. of Law. Teacher, Japan, 1968; engr, Southampton, 1973; called to the Bar, Gray's Inn, 1975; in practice, specialising in criminal and common law, Brighton, 1975–91, London, 1991–2001. *Recreations:* sailing, ski-ing, photography, computing, motor-cycling. *Address:* Woodfield House, Isaacs Lane, Burgess Hill, W Sussex RH15 8RA; *e-mail:* john@tanzer.co.uk. *Club:* Bar Yacht.

TAPLIN, Prof. Oliver Paul, DPhil; FBA 1995; Professor of Classical Languages and Literature, University of Oxford, since 1996; Tutorial Fellow in Classics, Magdalen College, Oxford, since 1973; *b* 2 Aug. 1943; *s* of Walter Taplin and Susan (*née* Rosenberg); *m* 1st, 1964, Kim Stampfer (marr. diss. 1996); one *s* one *d*; 2nd, 1998, Beaty Rubens; one *d*. *Educ:* Sevenoaks Sch.; Corpus Christi Coll., Oxford (MA; DPhil 1974). Fellow by Examination, Madgalen Coll., Oxford, 1968–72; Fellow, Center for Hellenic Studies, Washington, 1970–71; Lectr, Bristol Univ., 1972–73; Reader in Greek Lit., Oxford Univ., 1994–96. Visiting Professor: Dartmouth Coll., 1981; UCLA, 1987, 1990. Pres., Classical Assoc., 1999. *Publications:* The Stagecraft of Aeschylus, 1977; Greek Tragedy in Action, 1978; Greek Fire, 1989; (jtly) An Odyssey Round Odysseus, 1990; Homeric Soundings, 1992; Comic Angels, 1993; (ed) Literature in the Greek and Roman Worlds, 2000. *Recreations:* theatre, Greece. *Address:* Madgalen College, Oxford OX1 4AU. *T:* (01865) 276069.

TAPP, David Robert George; District Judge (Magistrates' Courts) (formerly Provincial Stipendiary Magistrate), County of Merseyside, since 1992; *b* 13 Oct. 1948; *s* of Victor George Tapp and May Allen Tapp. *Educ:* Stockport Sch.; Manchester Univ. (LLB Hons). Solicitor. Articled Clerk, Wigan Magistrates' Court, 1971–73; Principal Asst, Eccles Magistrates' Court, 1973–80; Dep. Justices' Clerk, 1980–83, Justices' Clerk, 1983–92, Stoke-on-Trent Magistrates' Court. Mem., British Pottery Manufrs' Fedn Club. *Recreations:* watching sport, waterfowl, music, Manchester City FC, Lancashire CCC. *Address:* 45 East Quay, Wapping Dock, Liverpool L3 4BU. *T:* (0151) 707 1608; Magistrates' Court, 107/111 Dale Street, Liverpool L2 2JQ. *T:* (0151) 236 5871.

TAPPER, Prof. Colin Frederick Herbert; Professor of Law, 1992–Sept. 2002, and Fellow of Magdalen College, since 1965, Oxford University; Special Consultant on Computer Law to Messrs Masons (Solicitors), since 1990; *b* 13 Oct. 1934; *s* of Herbert Frederick Tapper and Florence Gertrude Tapper; *m* 1961, Margaret White; one *d*. *Educ:* Bishopshalt Grammar Sch.; Magdalen Coll., Oxford. Lectr, LSE, 1959–65; All Souls Reader in Law, Oxford Univ., 1979–92. Visiting Professor, Universities of: Alabama, 1970; NY, 1970; Stanford, 1975; Monash, 1984; Northern Kentucky, 1986; Sydney, 1989; Western Australia, 1991. *Publications:* Computers and the Law, 1973; Computer Law, 1978, 4th edn 1990; (ed) Crime Proof and Punishment, 1981; (ed) Cross on Evidence, 6th edn 1985, to 9th edn 1999; (ed) Cross and Wilkins Introduction to Evidence, 6th edn 1986; (ed) Handbook of European Software Law, 1993. *Recreations:* reading, computing, writing. *Address:* Corner Cottage, Stonesfield, Oxon OX29 8QA. *T:* (01993) 891284.

TAPPIN, Michael; Lecturer in Politics, Department of American Studies, University of Keele, since 1974; *b* 22 Dec. 1946; *s* of Thomas and Eileen Tappin; *m* 1971, Angela Florence (*née* Reed); one *s* one *d*. *Educ:* Univ. of Essex; LSE; Strathclyde Univ. Dist Cllr (Lab), Newcastle-under-Lyme BC, 1980–84; Staffordshire County Council: Councillor (Lab), 1981–97; Chairman: Planning Cttee, 1985–89; Enterprise and Econ. Develt Cttee, 1989–94; European Cttee, 1990–94. MEP (Lab) Staffordshire West and Congleton, 1994–99; contested (Lab) W Midlands Reg., 1999. European Parliament: Member: Budget Cttee, 1994–99; Budget Control Cttee, 1994–99; Substitute Mem., Econ. and Monetary Affairs Cttee, 1994–99; Mem., Delegn for relations with USA, 1994–99. Dep. Chm., Staffs Develt Assoc., 1985–94; Chm., N Staffs Steel Partnership Trng, 2000. Chm., W Midlands Regl Forum of Local Authorities, 1993–94. Chm., S Stoke Primary Care Trust, 2001–. Pres., Staffs Ramblers' Assoc., 1998–2000. *Publication:* (jtly) American Politics Today, 1980, 3rd edn 1993. *Recreations:* squash, reading, cinema, theatre. *Address:* 7 Albert Road, Trentham, Stoke-on-Trent, Staffs ST4 8HE. *T:* and *Fax:* (01782) 659554; *e-mail:* michaeltappin@yahoo.com. *Club:* British Pottery Manufacturers Federation (Stoke-on-Trent).

TAPPS GERVIS MEYRICK; *see* Meyrick.

TAPSELL, Sir Peter (Hannay Bailey), Kt 1985; MP (C) Louth and Horncastle, since 1997 (Nottingham West, 1959–64; Horncastle, Lincs, 1966–83; East Lindsey (Lincs), 1983–97); *b* Hove, Sussex, 1 Feb. 1930; *s* of late Eustace Bailey Tapsell (39th Central India Horse) and Jessie Maxwell (*née* Hannay); *m* 1st, 1963, Hon. Cecilia Hawke (marr. diss. 1971), 3rd *d* of 9th Baron Hawke; (one *s* decd); 2nd, 1974, Mlle Gabrielle Mahieu, *e d* of late Jean and Bathelde Mahieu, Normandy, France. *Educ:* Tonbridge Sch.; Merton Coll., Oxford (1st Cl. Hons Mod. Hist., 1953; Hon. Postmaster, 1953; MA 1957; Hon. Fellow, 1989). Nat. Service, Subaltern, Royal Sussex Regt, 1948–50 (Middle East). Librarian of Oxford Union, 1953; Rep. Oxford Union on debating tour of United States, 1954 (Trustee, Oxford Union, 1985–93). Conservative Research Department, 1954–57 (Social Services and Agriculture). Personal Asst to Prime Minister (Anthony Eden) during 1955 General Election Campaign. Contested (C) Wednesbury, bye-election, Feb. 1957. Opposition front bench spokesman on Foreign and Commonwealth affairs, 1976–77, on Treasury and economic affairs, 1977–78. Mem., Trilateral Commn, 1979–98. London Stock Exchange, 1957–90; Partner, James Capel & Co., 1960–90. Internat. investment advr to several central banks, foreign banks and trading cos; Hon. Mem., Brunei Govt Investment Adv. Bd, 1976–83; Hon. Dep. Chm., Mitsubishi Trust Oxford Foundn,

1988–; Member: Council, Inst. for Fiscal Studies; Court, Univ. of Nottingham, 1959–64; Court, Univ. of Hull, 1966–92. Chm., Coningsby Club, 1957–58. Jt Chm., British-Caribbean Assoc., 1963–64. Mem. Organising Cttee, Zaire River Expedn, 1974–75. Vice Pres., Tennyson Soc., 1966–. Hon. Life Mem., 6th Sqdn RAF, 1971. Brunei Dato, 1971. *Recreations:* travel in Third World, walking in mountains, reading history. *Address:* c/o House of Commons, SW1A 0AA. *T:* (020) 7219 3000. *Clubs:* Athenæum, Carlton, Hurlingham.

TAPSELL, Hon. Sir Peter (Wilfred), KNZM 1997; MBE 1968; FRCSE, FRCS; *b* Rotorua, 21 Jan. 1930; *s* of Peter and May Tapsell; *m* 1956, Margaret Diane Bourke; two *s* two *d*. *Educ:* Rotorua High Sch.; Otago Univ. Med. Sch. (MB ChB 1954). FRCSE 1959; FRCS 1961. Hse surgeon, Waikato Hosp., 1955; demonstrator in anatomy, Sch. of Medicine, Dunedin, 1956; Resident Surgical Officer, Dunedin Public Hosp., 1957–58; post-grad. trng, Royal Infirmary, Edinburgh and London, 1958–61; Resident Surgeon, Woolwich, 1959; Orthopaedics Specialist, Orthopaedic Hosp., Oswestry, 1960–61; Orthopaedic Surgeon, Rotorua and Queen Elizabeth Hosps, 1961–81. MP (Lab) Eastern Maori, NZ, 1981–96; Minister of Internal Affairs, Civil Defence, Minister for the Arts and Associate Minister for Local Govt and Tourism, 1984–87; Minister: of Police, 1987–89; of Forestry and Recreation and Sport, 1987–90; of Lands, Survey and Land Inf. and in charge of Valuation Dept, 1987–90; of Science and DSIR, 1989; of Defence, 1990; Speaker, House of Reps, 1994–96. Dep. Mayor, Rotorua City, 1979–83. Chm., NZ Maori Arts and Crafts Inst., 1973–82. Member Council: Univ. of Waikato, 1975; Waikato Teachers' Trng Coll., 1976. Hon. Fellow, Inst. Architects of NZ, 1986. Played Rugby for Otago and NZ Univs; Vice-Capt., Maori All Blacks tour to Fiji, 1954. Hon. LLD Otago, 1996; Hon. Dr Waikato, 1997. *Recreations:* hunting, shooting, fishing. *Address:* 2 Ngahu Street, Rotorua, New Zealand.

TARAR, Muhammad Rafiq; President of Pakistan, 1998–2001; *b* 2 Nov. 1929; *s* of Chaudhry Sardar Tarar; *m* Razia Tarar; three *s* one *d*. *Educ:* Univ. of the Punjab, Lahore (BA, LLB). Pleader, 1951–53; Advocate of the High Court, 1953–66; Additional Dist and Sessions Judge, 1966; Dist and Sessions Judge, 1967–74; Judge, High Court Bench, 1974–89; Chief Justice, Lahore High Court, 1989–91; Judge, Supreme Court of Pakistan, 1991–94. Mem., Senate, 1997–98. *Recreations:* reading, walking. *Club:* Islamabad (Islamabad).

TARASSENKO, Prof. Lionel, DPhil; FREng; FIEE; Professor of Electrical and Electronic Engineering, and Fellow of St John's College, University of Oxford, since 1997; *b* 17 April 1957; *s* of Sergei and Rachel Tarassenko; *m* 1st, 1978, Lady Ann Mary Elizabeth (marr. diss. 2001), *d* of 6th Earl of Craven; two *s* one *d*; 2nd, 2001, Anne Elizabeth Le Grice; two step *s* one step *d*. *Educ:* Keble Coll., Oxford (BA 1978; Edgell Shepee Prize, 1978; MA; DPhil 1985). FIEE 1996. Electronics Engr, Racal Research Ltd, 1978–81; Lectr in Engrg Science, and Fellow of St Hugh's Coll., Oxford Univ., 1988–97. Founder Director: Third Phase Ltd, 2000–; Oxford BioSignals Ltd, 2000–. FREng 2000. BCS Medal, 1996. *Publications:* (with A. F. Murray) Analogue Neural VLSI, 1994; A Guide to Neural Computing Applications, 1998; contribs to jls on electronics, signal processing and artificial intelligence. *Recreations:* family life, football coaching. *Address:* Department of Engineering Science, University of Oxford, Parks Road, Oxford OX1 3PJ. *T:* (01865) 273113.

TARBAT, Viscount; Colin Ruaridh Mackenzie; *b* 7 Sept. 1987; *s* and *heir* of Earl of Cromartie, *qv*.

TARGETT, Prof. Geoffrey Arthur Trevor, PhD, DSc; Professor of Immunology of Protozoal Diseases, London School of Hygiene and Tropical Medicine, since 1983; *b* 10 Dec. 1935; *s* of Trevor and Phyllis Targett; *m* 1st, 1958, Sheila Margaret Gibson (*d* 1988); two *s* three *d*; 2nd, 1997, Julie Ann Thompson. *Educ:* Nottingham Univ. (BSc Hons Zool. 1957); London Univ. (PhD 1961; DSc 1982). Research Scientist: MRC Bilharzia Res. Gp, 1957–62; Nat. Inst. for Med. Res., 1962–64; Lectr, Dept of Natural History, St Andrews Univ., 1964–70; London School of Hygiene and Tropical Medicine: Sen. Lectr, 1970–76; Reader, 1976–83; Hd of Dept of Med. Parasitology, 1988–97; Acting Dean, 2000. *Publications:* Malaria: waiting for the vaccine, 1991; numerous papers in internat. med. and scientific jls. *Recreations:* golf, music, travel. *Address:* London School of Hygiene and Tropical Medicine, 50 Bedford Square, WC1B 3DP. *T:* (020) 7299 4708.

TARJANNE, Pekka; international consultant, since 2000; *b* 19 Sept. 1937; *s* of P. K. Tarjanne and Annu Tarjanne; *m* 1962, Aino Kairamo; two *s* one *d* (and one *d* decd). *Educ:* Helsinki Univ. of Technology (Dr Tech. 1962). Prof. of Theoretical Physics, Univ. of Oulu, 1965–66, Univ. of Helsinki, 1967–77. MP, Finland, 1970–77; Minister of Communications, 1972–75; Dir Gen., Posts and Telecommunications, 1977–89; Sec. Gen., ITU, UN, 1989–99; Vice-Chm., Project Oxygen, 1999–2000. Commander, Order of White Rose of Finland, 1977; Grand Cross, Order of Finnish Lion, 1998; Comdr, Legion of Honour (France), 1999.

TARLO, Christine; *see* McCafferty, C.

TARN, Prof. John Nelson, OBE 1992; DL; Professor of Architecture, 1995–99 (Roscoe Professor, 1974–95), and Pro-Vice-Chancellor, 1988–91 and 1994–99, University of Liverpool; *b* 23 Nov. 1934; *s* of Percival Nelson Tarn and Mary I. Tarn (*née* Purvis); unmarried. *Educ:* Royal Grammar Sch., Newcastle upon Tyne; Univ. of Durham (BArch); Univ. of Cambridge (PhD). 1st cl. hons Dunelm; FRIBA, FRSA, FRHistS, FSA. Lectr in Architecture, Univ. of Sheffield, 1963–70; Prof. of Architecture, Univ. of Nottingham, 1970–73; Actg Vice-Chancellor, 1991–92, Public Orator, 1994–, Liverpool Univ. Member: Professional Literature Cttee, RIBA, 1968–77; RIBA Educn Cttee, 1978–97 (Vice-Chm., 1983–95; Chm., Moderators and Examiners Cttee, 1975–97); Council, RIBA, 1987–93; Council, ARCUK, 1980–90 (Vice-Chm., 1986–87; Chm., 1987–90; Vice-Chm., Bd of Educn, 1981–83, Chm., 1983–86); Technology Sub-Cttee, UGC, 1974–84; Adv. Cttee on Architectural Educn to EEC, Brussels, 1987–; CNAA Built Environment Bd, 1987–90; Ministerial nominee, Peak Park Jt Planning Bd, 1973–82, a rep. of Greater Manchester Council, PPJPB, 1982–86 (Vice-Chm. of Bd, 1981–86; co-opted Mem., Planning Control Cttee and Park Management Cttee, 1986–97; Chm., Planning Control Cttee, 1979–97); Mem., National Parks Review Cttee, 1990. Trustee, Museums and Art Galls in Merseyside, 1996– (Chm., Building and Design Cttee, 1996–). Chm., Art and Architecture Dept, Liturgy Commn, Archdio. of Liverpool, 1978–; Member: Design and Planning Cttee, Central Council for Care of Churches, 1981–86; DAC for Derby, 1979–93; Liverpool Cathedral Adv. Cttee, 1992–; Sub-cttee for Patrimony, Catholic Bishops' Conf. for England and Wales, 1995–. Chm., Riverside Housing Assoc., 1998– (Dep. Chm., 1997–98). DL Merseyside, 1999. DUniv Sheffield Hallam, 1997; Hon. LLD Liverpool, 1999. *Publications:* Working Class Housing in Nineteenth Century Britain, 1971; The Peak District National Park: its architecture, 1971; Five Per Cent Philanthropy, 1974; (adv. ed.) Sir Banister Fletcher's History of Architecture, 19th edn, 1987. *Recreations:* music, cooking. *Address:* 2 Ashmore Close, Barton Hey Drive, Caldy, Wirral CH48 2JX. *Club:* Athenæum.

TARR, Robert James; Principal, The OakVine Consultancy, since 1997; Director, OakVine.net, since 1999; *b* 8 June 1944; *s* of Jack William Tarr; *m* 1966, Linda Andrews. *Educ:* Whytemead and Downsbrook Schools, Worthing; Worthing High Sch. for Boys. CPFA (IPFA 1967); BSc(Econ) Hons London, 1977; BA Open Univ., 1979. FILT (FCIT 1989). W Sussex CC, Worthing BC, Denbighshire CC, Sunderland Met. BC to 1975; Corporate Planning Co-ordinator and Head of Policy Unit, Bradford Met. Council, 1975–81; Chief Exec., Royal Borough of Kingston upon Thames, 1981–83; Chief Exec. and Town Clerk, Coventry City Council, 1983–87; Dir Gen., Centro (W Midlands PTE), 1987–95; Sec. Gen., Light Rail Transit Assoc., 1997–99. *Publications:* contribs to jls and conf. papers. *Recreations:* viticulture and wine-making, soaking up sun and scenery, the Pre-Raphaelites and Victorian architecture, mountains and alpine flowers, canal-boating, photography, computing, amateur radio (call sign G3PUR), keeping fit. *Address: email:* bobtarr@oakvine.net.

TARRANT, Christopher John; radio and television presenter, producer and writer; *b* 10 Oct. 1946; *s* of Major Basil Tarrant, MC, and Joan Ellen Tarrant (*née* Cox); *m* 1st, 1977, Sheila Roberton (marr. diss.); two *d*; 2nd, 1991, Ingrid Dupré; one *s* one *d*. *Educ:* King's Sch., Worcester; Univ. of Birmingham (BA Hons). *Television* includes: presenter and writer, ATV Today, 1972–74; presenter, writer and producer: Tiswas, 1974–82; OTT, 1981–83; presenter: Everybody's Equal, 1989–91; Tarrant on Television, 1989–; Lose a Million, 1993; Pop Quiz, 1994–95; Man o Man, 1996–98; Who Wants to be a Millionaire, 1997–; *radio:* presenter, Breakfast Show, Capital Radio, 1987–. Sony Radio Awards: Radio Personality of the Year, 1990; Best Use of Comedy, 1990; Silver Medal, 1992, 1993; Best Breakfast Show, 1995; Gold Award, 2001; Ind. Radio Personality, Variety Club of GB, 1991; Best Breakfast Show, NY World Awards, 1997; GQ Radio Man of the Year, 1999; Best TV Performer in non-acting role, BPG TV Awards, 1999; Nat. TV Awards Special Recognition, 2000; Lifetime Achievement Award, ITV, 2000. *Publications:* Ken's Furry Friends, 1986; Frishfriar's Hall Revisited, 1987; Ready Steady Go, 1990; Rebel Rebel, 1991; Tarrant off the Record, 1997; The Ultimate Book of Netty Nutters, 1998; Tarrant on Millionaires, 1999. *Recreations:* fishing, cricket. *Address:* c/o Paul Vaughan, PVA Management Ltd, Hallow Park, Worcester WR2 6PG. *T:* (01905) 640663, *Fax:* (01905) 641842; *e-mail:* md@pva.co.uk. *Clubs:* Lord's Taverners, White Swan Piscatorials.

TARRANT, Prof. John Rex, PhD; Vice-Chancellor and Principal, University of Huddersfield, since 1995; *b* 12 Nov. 1941; *s* of Arthur Rex Tarrant and Joan Mary (*née* Brookes); *m* 1991, Biddy Fisher. *Educ:* Marling Grammar Sch., Stroud; Univ. of Hull (BSc; PhD 1966). Asst Lectr, UC, Dublin, 1966–68; University of East Anglia: Sen. Lectr, 1974–82; Dean, Sch. of Envmtl Scis, 1974–77 and 1981–84; Reader, 1982–94; Pro Vice-Chancellor, 1985–88; Dep. Vice-Chancellor, 1989–95; Prof., 1994–95; Hon. Fellow, 1996. Vis. Prof., Dept of Geog., Univ. of Nebraska, 1970; Vis. Lectr, Dept of Geog., Univ. of Canterbury, NZ, 1973; Vis. Res. Associate, Internat. Food Policy Res. Inst., Washington, 1977–78; Vis. Schol., Food Res. Inst., Stanford Univ., USA, 1978; Harris Vis. Prof., Coll. of Geoscis, Texas A&M Univ., 1989. Hon. DSc Hull, 2000. *Publications:* Agricultural Geography, 1974; Food Policies, 1980; Food and Farming, 1991; contrib. chapters in books; numerous articles in professional jls. *Recreations:* gliding, motor-cycling. *Address:* University of Huddersfield, Queensgate, Huddersfield HD1 3DH. *T:* (01484) 472215.

TARUA, Ilinome Frank, CBE 1988 (OBE 1980); Consultant specialising on Papua New Guinea and South Pacific, since 1993; *b* 23 Sept. 1941; *s* of Peni Frank Tarua and Anaiele Tarua; *m* 1970, Susan Christine (*née* Reeves); two *d*. *Educ:* Sydney University; University of Papua New Guinea (BL 1971). Legal Officer, Dept of Law, 1971–72; Legal Constitutional Advisor to Prime Minister, 1972–76; Dep. Perm. Head, Prime Minister's Dept, 1977–78; Secretary to Cabinet, 1978–79; High Commissioner to NZ, 1980; Ambassador to UN, 1980–81; Perm. Head, Dept of Public Service, 1982; Perm. Head, Prime Minister's Dept, 1982–83; High Comr in London, 1983–89, concurrently Ambassador to Greece, Israel and Italy; Consul Gen., Sydney, 1989–91; Consultant Lawyer with Gadens Ridgeway Lawyers, Australia and PNG, 1991–93. *Recreations:* cricket, squash, golf.

TARUSCHIO, Franco Vittorio; chef and restaurateur, Walnut Tree Inn, Abergavenny, since 1963; *b* 29 March 1938; *s* of Giuseppe Taruschio and Apina (*née* Cecati); *m* 1963, Ann Forester; one adopted *d* (and one *d* decd). *Educ:* Hotel Sch., Bellagio, Italy. Trainee Chef: Hotel Splendide, Lugano, 1958; Restaurant La Belle Meunière, Clermont-Ferrand, 1959–60; Head Waiter, Three Horseshoes Hotel, Rugby, 1961–63. *Publications:* Leaves from the Walnut Tree: recipes of a lifetime, 1993; Bruschetta, Crostoni and Crostini, 1995; Franco and Friends: Food from the Walnut Tree, 1997; Ice Creams and Semi Freddi, 1997. *Recreations:* funghi and wild food foraging, swimming, walking. *Address:* The Walnut Tree Inn, Llandewi Skirrid, Abergavenny, Monmouthshire NP7 8AW. *T:* (01873) 852797.

TASKER, Prof. Philip Westerby, PhD; FRSC, FInstP; Vice Chancellor, De Montfort University, since 1999; *b* 6 July 1950; *s* of John Westerby Tasker and Alianore Doris Tasker (*née* Whytlaw-Gray); *m* 1974, Alison Helen Davis; one *s* one *d*. *Educ:* King Alfred's Grammar Sch., Wantage; Univ. of Birmingham (BSc Chem. 1971; PhD 1974). FInstP 1989; FRSC 1990. Research Fellow: Univ. of Bristol, 1974–75; Theoretical Physics Div., Harwell Lab., UKAEA, 1975–90; Divl Manager, AEA Technol., 1990–93; Chief Exec., Safeguard Internat. 1993–96; Pro-Vice Chancellor, De Montfort Univ., 1996–99. *Publications:* contribs to Philosophical Jl, Jl Physics, Faraday Trans, Physical Rev., etc. *Address:* De Montfort University, The Gateway, Leicester LE1 9BH. *T:* (0116) 250 6077.

TASMANIA, Bishop of, since 2000; **Rt Rev. John Douglas Harrower,** OAM 2000; *b* 16 Oct. 1947; *s* of John Lawrence Harrower and Enid Dorothy Harrower (*née* Thomas); *m* 1970, Gayelene Melva Harrower (*née* Robin); two *s*. *Educ:* Melbourne Univ. (BE 1970, BA 1973); Ridley Coll., ACT (ThL 1992); Bible Col. of Vict., ACT (MA (Theol.) 1996, Adv. Dip. Missiol Studies 1996). CEng 1976; MIChemE 1976. Process Engr, Petroleum Refineries (Aust.) P/L, Melbourne, 1970–72; Prject Officer, Tariff Bd, Melbourne, 1972–74; Director: Industy Studies Br., Industries Assistance Commn, 1975; IMPACT Project, Melbourne, 1975–78; Univ. Chaplain, Buenos Aires, 1979–81; Missionary, CMS, Argentina, 1979–88; Exec Chm., CERTEZA-ABUA, Buenos Aires, 1981–87; Gen. Sec., Argentine Univs Bible Assoc., 1981–86; ordained deacon, 1984, priest, 1986, Buenos Aires; Asst Minister, Iglesia Anglicana de San Salvador, Buenos Aires, 1984–88; Vicar: St Paul's, Glen Waverley, Vic, Aust., 1989–95; St Barnabas Anglican Ch, Glen Waverley, 1995–2000; Area Dean, Waverley-Knox, 1992–94; Archdeacon of Kew, Dio. Melbourne, 1994–2000. *Publications:* all in Spanish: Personal Evangelism, 1985, new edn 1996; (with Silvia Chaves) Spiritual Gifts: a body in mission, 1985, new edn 1989; 30 Days with Jeremiah, 1989, new edn 1998. *Recreations:* reading, pottering in the garden. *Address:* Diocese of Tasmania, GPO Box 748, Hobart, Tas 7001, Australia. *T:* (3) 62238811, *Fax:* (3) 62238968; *e-mail:* bishop@anglicantas.org.au. *Club:* Athenæum (Hobart).

TATA, Dr Jamshed Rustom, FRS 1973; Head, Division of Developmental Biochemistry, National Institute for Medical Research, 1973–96; *b* 13 April 1930; *s* of

Rustom and Gool Tata; *m* 1954, Renée Suzanne Zanetto; two *s* one *d*. *Educ:* Univ. of Bombay (BSc); Univ. of Paris, Sorbonne (D-ès-Sc). Post-doctoral Fellow, Sloan-Kettering Inst., New York, 1954–56; Beit Memorial Fellow, Nat. Inst. for Med. Research, 1956–60; Vis. Scientist, Wenner-Gren Inst., Stockholm, 1960–62; Mem., Scientific Staff, MRC, Nat. Inst. for Med. Research, 1962–. Visiting Professor: King's Coll., London, 1968–69, and 1970–77; Univ. of California, Berkeley, 1969–70; Vis. Senior Scientist, Nat. Institutes of Health, USA, 1977, 1997; Fogarty Scholar, NIH, USA, 1983, 1986, 1989. The Wellcome Trust: Chm., Cell and Molecular Panel, 1990–92; Mem., Basic Sci. Gp, 1992–93; Mem., Internat. Interest Gp, 1997–. Chm., Bd of Trustees, Oxford Internat. Biomed. Centre, 1999– (Trustee, 1996–99). Non-exec. Dir, Biotech Analytics, 2000–. Fellow: Indian Nat. Science Acad., 1978; Third World Acad. of Sci., 1986. Van Meter Award, 1954; Colworth Medal, 1966; Medal of Soc. for Endocrinology, 1973; Jubilee Medal, Indian Inst. of Sci., 1985. *Publications:* (jtly): The Thyroid Hormones, 1959; The Chemistry of Thyroid Diseases, 1960; Metamorphosis, 1996; Hormonal Signalling and Postembryonic Development, 1998; papers in jls of: Biochemistry; Developmental Biology. *Address:* 15 Bittacy Park Avenue, Mill Hill, NW7 2HA. *T:* (020) 8346 6291.

TATE, Dr (Edward) Nicholas, CBE 2001; Headmaster, Winchester College, since 2000; *b* 18 Dec. 1943; *s* of Joseph Edwin Tate and Eva Elsie Tate; *m* 1973, Nadya Grove; one *s* two *d*. *Educ:* Huddersfield New Coll.; Balliol Coll., Oxford (Scholar; MA); Univ. of Bristol (PGCE); Univ. of Liverpool (MA; PhD 1985). Teacher, De La Salle Coll., Sheffield, 1966–71; Lectr, City of Birmingham Coll. of Educn, 1972–74; Lectr, then Sen. Lectr, Moray House Coll. of Educn, Edinburgh, 1974–88; Professional Officer, Nat. Curriculum Council, 1989–91; Asst Chief Exec., Sch. Exams and Assessment Council, 1991–93; Asst Chief Exec., 1993–94, Chief Exec., 1994–97, SCAA; Chief Exec., QCA, 1997–2000. Trustee, Nat. Trust, 1996–99. Hon. DCL Huddersfield, 1998. *Publications:* various history books for schools; articles on history and education. *Recreations:* reading, music. *Address:* Winchester College, Winchester, Hants SO23 9NA. *Club:* Reform.

TATE, Sir (Henry) Saxon, 5th Bt *cr* 1898, of Park Hill, Streatham; CBE 1991; Chairman, London Futures and Options Exchange (formerly London Commodity Exchange Co. Ltd), 1985–91; Director, Tate & Lyle Ltd, 1956–99; *b* 28 Nov. 1931; *er s* of Lt-Col Sir Henry Tate, 4th Bt, TD and his 1st wife, Nairne (*d* 1984), *d* of Saxon Gregson-Ellis, JP; *S* father, 1994; *m* 1st, 1953, Sheila Ann (marr. diss. 1975; she *d* 1987), *e d* of Duncan Robertson; four *s* (incl. twin *s*); 2nd, 1975, Virginia Sturm. *Educ:* Eton; Christ Church, Oxford. FIMgt (FBIM 1975). National Service, Life Guards (Lieut), 1949–50. Joined Tate & Lyle Ltd, 1952, Director, 1956; Pres. and Chief Executive Officer, Redpath Industries Ltd, Canada, 1965–72; Tate & Lyle Ltd: Chm., Executive Cttee, 1973–78; Man. Dir, 1978–80; Vice Chm., 1980–82. Chief Executive, Industrial Development Bd of NI, 1982–85. Fellow, Amer. Management Assoc., 1972. *Recreations:* various. *Heir: s* Edward Nicholas Tate, *b* 2 July 1966. *Address:* 26 Cleaver Square, SE11 4EA.

TATE, Dr Jeffrey Philip, CBE 1990; Principal Conductor, English Chamber Orchestra, since 1985; *b* 28 April 1943; *s* of Cyril Henry Tate and Ivy Ellen Naylor (*née* Evans). *Educ:* Farnham Grammar Sch.; Christ's Coll., Cambridge (MA; MB, BChir; Hon. Fellow, 1989); St Thomas' Hosp., London. Trained as doctor of medicine, 1961–67; left medicine for London Opera Centre, 1969; joined Covent Garden Staff, 1970; assisted conductors who included Kempe, Krips, Solti, Davies, Kleiber, for performances and recordings; records made as harpsichordist, 1973–77; Assistant to Boulez for Bayreuth Ring, 1976–81; joined Cologne Opera as assistant to Sir John Pritchard, 1977; conducted Gothenberg Opera, Sweden, 1978–80; NY Metropolitan Opera début, USA, 1979; Covent Garden début, 1982; Salzburg Fest. début (world première Henze/Monteverdi), 1985; Principal Conductor, Royal Opera House, Covent Garden, 1986–91, Principal Guest Conductor, 1991–94; Chief Conductor and Artistic Dir, Rotterdam Phil. Orch., 1991–94; Chief Guest Conductor, Geneva Opera, 1983–95; Principal Guest Conductor: Orchestre National de France, 1989–98; RAI Nazionale Orch., Turin, 1998–; Artistic Dir, Minnesota Orch. Summer Fest., 1997–. Appearances with major symph. orchs in Europe and Amer.; numerous recordings with English Chamber Orch. President: ASBAH, 1989–; Music Space Trust, 1991–. Hon. DMus Leicester, 1993. Officier, Ordre des Arts et des Lettres (France), 1993; Chevalier, Légion d'Honneur (France), 1999. *Recreation:* church-crawling, with gastronomic interludes.

TATE, Nicholas; *see* Tate, E. N.

TATE, Prof. Robert Brian, FBA 1980; FRHistS; Professor and Head of Department of Hispanic Studies, Nottingham University, 1958–83, retired; *b* 27 Dec. 1921; *s* of Robert and Jane Grantie Tate; *m* 1951, Beth Ida Lewis; one *s* one *d*. *Educ:* Royal Belfast Academical Instn; Queen's Univ. Belfast (MA, PhD). FRHistS 1990. Asst Lectr, Manchester Univ., 1949–52; Lectr, QUB, 1952–56; Reader in Hispanic Studies, Nottingham Univ., 1956–58. Vis. Prof., Univs of Harvard, Cornell, SUNY at Buffalo, Texas and Virginia. Corresponding Fellow: Institut d'Estudis Catalans, Barcelona, 1964; Real Academia de Historia, Madrid, 1974; Real Academia de Buenas Letras de Barcelona, 1980. *Publications:* Joan Margarit i Pau, Cardinal Bishop of Gerona: a biographical study, 1954; Ensayos sobre la historiografia peninsular del siglo XV, 1970; The Medieval Kingdoms of the Iberian Peninsula, in P. E. Russell, Spain: a companion to Spanish studies, 1973; El Cardenal Joan Margarit, vida i obra, 1976; (with Marcus Tate) The Pilgrim Route to Santiago, 1987; Pilgrimages to St James of Compostella from the British Isles during the Middle Ages, 1990; *edited:* (with A. Yates) Actes del Colloqui internacional de llengua i literatura catalanes, 1976; Essays on Narrative Fiction in the Iberian Peninsula, 1982; (with T. Turville Petre) Two Pilgrim Itineraries of the Later Middle Ages, 1995; *edited with introduction and notes:* Fernán Pérez de Guzmán, Generaciones y Semblanzas, 1965; Fernando del Pulgar, Claros varones de Castilla, 1971, rev. edn 1985; (with I. R. Macpherson) Don Juan Manuel, Libro de los estados, 1974, rev. edn 1991; Anon, Directorio de príncipes, 1977; Alfonso de Palencia, Epistolario, 1983; (with J. H. N. Lawrance) Alfonso de Palencia, Gesta Hispaniensia, vols 1 and 2, 1998, vol. 3, 2001; contrib. articles in numerous learned jls. *Recreations:* architecture and the history of art, jazz. *Address:* 11 Hope Street, Beeston, Nottingham NG9 1DJ. *T:* (0115) 925 1243.

TATE, Sir Saxon; *see* Tate, Sir H. S.

TATE, William John; Solicitor to Bloody Sunday Inquiry, since 1999; *b* 12 June 1951; *s* of William Kenneth Tate and Dorothy Tate; *m* 1976, Helen Elizabeth Quick; one *s* one *d*. *Educ:* Eastcliffe Grammar Sch., Newcastle upon Tyne; King's Coll., London (LLB 1973). Called to the Bar, Gray's Inn, 1974; Flt Lieut, RAF Directorate of Legal Services, 1976–78; Solicitor's Office, HM Customs and Excise: Legal Asst, 1978–80; Sen. Legal Asst, 1980–86; Sen. Prin. Legal Officer, 1986–88; Asst Dir, Serious Fraud Office, 1988–96; Dep. Parly Comr for Admin, 1996–99. *Publication:* (Delegated Legislation Ed.) Current Law, annually 1975–95. *Recreations:* rowing, reading, music, gardening. *Address:* The Bloody Sunday Inquiry, PO Box 18031, SW1Y 4WG. *T:* (020) 7464 8767. *Clubs:* Royal Air Force; Kingston Grammar School Veterans Rowing.

TATHAM, David Everard, CMG 1991; HM Diplomatic Service, retired; consultant; *b* 28 June 1939; *s* of late Lt-Col Francis Everard Tatham and of Eileen Mary Wilson; *m* 1963, Valerie Ann Mylechreest; three *s*. *Educ:* St Lawrence Coll., Ramsgate; Wadham Coll., Oxford (BA History). Entered HM Diplomatic Service, 1960; 3rd Sec., UK Mission to the UN, New York, 1962–63; Vice-Consul (Commercial), Milan, 1963–67; ME Centre for Arabic Studies, 1967–69; Jeddah, 1969–70; FCO, 1971–74; Muscat, 1974–77; Asst Head of ME Dept, FCO, 1977–80; Counsellor, Dublin, 1981–84; Ambassador to Yemen Arab Republic, also accredited to Republic of Djibouti, 1984–87; Hd of Falkland Is Dept, FCO, 1987–90; Ambassador to Lebanese Republic, 1990–92; Governor, Falkland Is, and Comr for S Georgia and S Sandwich Is, 1992–96; High Comr, Sri Lanka, also accred to Republic of Maldives, 1996–99. Adviser to Palestinian Authy on Diplomatic Trng, 2000; Census Dist Manager, Leabury/Ross, 2000–01. Chm., Shackleton Scholarship Fund, 1999–. *Recreations:* walking uphill, fishing, historical research. *Address:* c/o Foreign and Commonwealth Office, SW1A 2AH. *T:* (01531) 634085. *Club:* Athenæum.

TATHAM, Francis Hugh Currer; Editor of Whitaker's Almanack, 1950–81; *b* 29 May 1916; *s* of late Harold Lewis Tatham, Gravesend, Kent, and late Frances Eva (*née* Crook); *m* 1945, Nancy Margaret, *d* of John Robins, Newton Abbot; two *s*. *Educ:* Charterhouse; Christ Church, Oxford. Missioner, Shrewsbury School Mission, Liverpool, 1939–42; Sub-Warden, Mary Ward Settlement, 1942–45; Army Cadet Force, 1943–45; Editor, Church of England Newspaper, 1945–47. Vice-Pres., Harrow RFC. *Recreations:* watching cricket, travel in England. *Address:* 27 Montacute Road, Lewes, East Sussex BN7 1EN. *T:* (01273) 473585. *Club:* MCC.

TATLOW, John Colin, PhD, DSc (Birmingham); CChem; FRSC; consultant; Professor of Organic Chemistry, University of Birmingham, 1959–82, now Emeritus; *b* 19 Jan. 1923; *s* of Thomas George and Florence Annie Tatlow, Cannock, Staffs; *m* 1946, Clarice Evelyn Mabel, *d* of Eric Millward and Mabel Evelyn Joiner, Sutton Coldfield; two *d*. *Educ:* Rugeley Grammar School, Staffs; University of Birmingham. Scientific Officer, Min. of Supply, 1946–48; University of Birmingham: Lectr in Chemistry, 1948–56; Sen. Lectr, 1956–57; Reader in Organic Chemistry, 1957–59; Head of Dept of Chemistry, 1974–81. Council of Chemical Society, 1957–60. Examiner, Royal Inst. of Chemistry, 1963–67. ACS Award for creative work in fluorine chemistry, 1990. *Publications:* over 300 scientific papers on fluorine chemistry, mainly in Jl of Chem. Soc., Tetrahedron, Nature, and Jl of Fluorine Chem.; Editor, Jl of Fluorine Chemistry. *Address:* 30 Grassmoor Road, King's Norton, Birmingham B38 8BP. *T:* (0121) 458 1260.

TATTEN, Jonathan Altenburger; Partner, Denton Wilde Sapte (formerly Denton Hall), Solicitors, since 1983 (Managing Partner, 1993–99); *b* 17 March 1952; *s* of John Stephenson Tatten and Anna Tatten. *Educ:* Duke of York Sch., Nairobi; Exeter Univ. (LLB); Harvard Business Sch. (AMP). Trainee solicitor, Trower Still & Keeling, 1973–76; solicitor, Holman Fenwick & Willan, Solicitors, 1976–83. *Recreations:* opera, running, eating. *Address:* 105 Arlington Road, NW1 7ET. *T:* (020) 7209 2781.

TATTERSALL, Geoffrey Frank; QC 1992; a Recorder, since 1989; *b* 22 Sept. 1947; *s* of Frank Tattersall and Margaret (*née* Hassall); *m* 1971, Hazel Shaw; one *s* two *d*. *Educ:* Manchester Grammar Sch.; Christ Church, Oxford (MA Jurisprudence). Called to the Bar, Lincoln's Inn, 1970 (Tancred Studentship in Common Law), Bencher, 1997; in practice, Northern Circuit, 1970–; called to the Bar, NSW, 1992; SC 1995; Judge of Appeal, IOM, 1997–. Lay Chm., Bolton Deanery Synod, 1993–; Chm., House of Laity and Vice Pres., Manchester Diocesan Synod, 1994–; Mem., Gen. Synod, 1995– (Chm., Standing Orders Cttee, 1999–). *Recreations:* family, music, travel. *Address:* 12 Byrom Street, Manchester M3 4PP. *T:* (0161) 829 2100.

TATTERSALL, Jane Patricia; *see* Griffiths, J. P.

TATTERSFIELD, Prof. Anne Elizabeth, MD; Professor of Respiratory Medicine, University of Nottingham, since 1984; Hon. Consultant Physician, City Hospital, Nottingham, since 1984; *b* 13 June 1940; *d* of Charles Percival Tattersfield and Bessie Wharton Tattersfield (*née* Walker). *Educ:* Fairfield High Sch., Manchester; Durham Univ. (MB BS 1963); MD Newcastle 1970. MRCP 1966, FRCP 1979. Jun. hosp. posts, Royal Victoria Infirmary, Newcastle, Leicester Royal Infirmary, Central Middx Hosp. and Brompton Hosp., 1963–66; Medical and Research Registrar posts: Central Middx Hosp., 1966–69; Hammersmith Hosp., 1969–71; Sen. Registrar, London Hosp., 1971–74; Sen. Lectr and Reader in Medicine, Southampton Univ., 1974–83. Sir James Wattie Meml Vis. Prof., NZ, 1987. Altounyan Lectr, British Thoracic Soc., 1995; Philip Ellman Lectr, RCP, 1999. Pres., British Thoracic Soc., 2000. *Publications:* (with M. W. McNicol) Respiratory Disease, 1987; contribs to scientific pubns on asthma, airway pharmacol. and lymphangioleiomyomatosis. *Recreations:* travel, opera, gardening. *Address:* Division of Respiratory Medicine, Clinical Sciences Building, City Hospital, Nottingham NG5 1PB. *Club:* Lansdowne.

TAUBE, Prof. Henry, PhD; Professor, Department of Chemistry, Stanford University, 1962–86, now Emeritus; *b* 30 Nov. 1915; *s* of Samuel and Albertina (Tiledetski) Taube; *m* 1952, Mary Alice Wesche; two *s* two *d*. *Educ:* Univ. of Saskatchewan (BS 1935, MS 1937); Univ. of California, Berkeley (PhD 1940). Instructor, Univ. of California, Berkeley, 1940–41; Instructor and Asst Prof., Cornell Univ., 1941–46; Asst Prof., Associate Prof., Prof., Univ. of Chicago, 1946–61; Chm., Dept of Chemistry, Univ. of Chicago, 1956–59; Chm., Dept of Chemistry, Stanford Univ., 1972–74 and 1978–79. Foreign Mem., Royal Soc., 1988; Hon. Member: Canadian Soc. for Chemistry, 1986; Hungarian Acad. of Scis, 1988; Corresponding Member: Brazilian Acad. of Scis, 1991; Australian Acad. of Sci., 1991; Foreign Associate, Engrg Acad. of Japan, 1991. Hon. FRSC 1989; Hon. Fellow, Indian Chem. Soc., 1989; Hon. FRS(Can) 1997. Hon. LLD Saskatchewan, 1973; Hon. PhD Hebrew Univ. of Jerusalem, 1979; Hon. DSc: Chicago, 1983; Polytechnic Inst., NY, 1984; State Univ. of NY, 1985; Guelph Univ., 1987; Seton Hall Univ., 1988; Lajos Kossuth Univ., Debrecen, Hungary, 1988. Guggenheim Fellow, 1949, 1955. ACS Award for Nuclear Applications in Chemistry, 1955; ACS Award for Distinguished Service in the Advancement of Inorganic Chemistry, 1967; Willard Gibbs Medal, Chicago Section, ACS, 1971; Nat. Medal of Science, Washington DC, 1977; T. W. Richards Medal of the Northwestern Section, ACS, 1980; ACS Award in Inorganic Chemistry of the Monsanto Co., 1981; Nat. Acad. of Sciences Award in Chemical Sciences, 1983; Robert A. Welch Foundn Award in Chemistry, 1983; Nobel Prize for Chemistry, 1983; Priestley Medal, ACS, 1985; Dist. Achievement Award, Internat. Precious Metals Inst., 1986. *Publications:* numerous papers in scientific jls on the reactivity of coordination compounds. *Recreations:* gardening, collecting classical vocal records. *Address:* 441 Gerona Road, Stanford, CA 94305, USA. *T:* (415) 3282759.

TAUBE, Simon Axel Robin; QC 2000; *b* 16 June 1957; *s* of Nils Taube and Idonea Taube; *m* 1984, Karen Pilkington; three *d*. *Educ:* Merton Coll., Oxford (BA Hist.). Called to the Bar, Middle Temple, 1980; in practice at Chancery Bar, 1980–. *Recreations:* singing, tennis, hill-walking. *Address:* 10 Old Square, Lincoln's Inn, WC2A 3SU. *T:* (020) 7405 0758.

TAUNTON, Bishop Suffragan of, since 1998; **Rt Rev. Andrew John Radford;** *b* 26 Jan. 1944; *m* 1969, Christine Davis; two *d*. *Educ:* Kingswood Grammar Sch.; Trinity Coll., Bristol. Local govt service; jt founder and manager, building co., 1965–72; ordained deacon, 1974, priest, 1975; Curate: Shirehampton, 1974–78; Henleaze, 1978–80; producer, Religious Progs, BBC Radio Bristol, 1974–80; Vicar, St Barnabas with Englishcombe, Bath, 1980–85; Diocesan Communications Officer, Gloucester, 1985–93; Religious Progs Presenter, Severn Sound, 1985–93; Develt and Trng Officer, C of E Communications Unit, 1993–98; Archbishops' Advr for Bishops' Ministry, 1998. Hon. Canon, Gloucester Cathedral, 1991–98. Local Radio Personality of the Year, SONY Radio Award, 1987. *Address:* Bishop's Lodge, Monkton Heights, W Monkton, Taunton, Som TA2 8LU.

TAUNTON, Archdeacon of; *see* Reed, Ven. J. P. C.

TAUSKY, Vilem, CBE 1981; FGSM 1968; conductor; Director of Opera, Guildhall School of Music, 1966–87; *b* 20 July 1910; *s* of Emil Tausky, MD, Prerov, Czechoslovakia, and Josefine Ascher, opera singer; *m* 1948, Margaret Helen Powell (*d* 1982). *Educ:* Univ. of Brno; Janáček Conservatoire, Brno; Meisterschule, Prague. Military Service in France and England, 1939–45. National Opera House, Brno, Czechoslovakia, 1929–39; Musical Director, Carl Rosa Opera, 1945–49; Artistic Dir, Phoenix Opera Co., 1967. BBC Conductor, 1950. Guest Conductor: Royal Opera House, Covent Garden, 1951; Sadler's Wells Opera, 1953. Freeman, City of London, 1979. Jan Masaryk Gratias Agit Prize, 2000; Gold Medal, Acad. of Performing Arts, Prague Univ., 2000. Czechoslovak Military Cross, 1944; Czechoslovak Order of Merit, 1945. *Publications:* Czechoslovak Christmas Carols, 1942; Oboe Concerto, 1957; Concertino for harmonica and orchestra, 1963; Divertimento for strings, 1966; Soho: Scherzo for orchestra, 1966; Concert Overture for Brass Band, 1969; Cakes and Ale: Overture for Brass Band, 1971; Ballad for Cello and Piano; From Our Village: orchestral suite, 1972; Sonata for Cello and Piano, 1976; Suite for Violin and Piano, 1979; String Quartet, 1981; (book) Vilem Tausky Tells his Story, 1979; Leoš Janáček, Leaves from his Life, 1982; contribs to: Tension in the Performance of Music, 1979; The Spectator, 1979. *Recreation:* country life. *Address:* Ivor Newton House, 10–12 Edward Road, Sundridge Park, Bromley, Kent BR1 3NQ. *T:* (020) 8466 5112.

TAUSSIG, Andrew John, PhD; Research Associate (Media Programme), Centre for Socio-Legal Studies, Wolfson College, University of Oxford; Consultant, Merlin Communications International; *b* 30 March 1944; *s* of Leo Charles Taussig and Magdalene Taussig (*née* Szücs); *m* 1971, Margaret Celia Whines; one *s* two *d*. *Educ:* Bramcote Sch., Scarborough; Winchester Coll. (Schol.); Magdalen Coll., Oxford (MA Hons Modern History 1962); Harvard Univ. (PhD Pol Sci. 1970). British Broadcasting Corporation, 1971-2000: Gen. Trainee, World Service Talks Dept, BBC North Leeds, and Radio Current Affairs, 1971–72; TV Current Affairs, 1973–80; Special Asst to Dir, News and Current Affairs, 1979–80; Dep. Editor, Nationwide, 1980–81; Chief Asst, TV Current Affairs, 1982–86; Head of Central European Service, 1986–88; Controller, European Services, 1988–94; Regl Head, Europe, 1994–96; Dir, World Service Regions (all foreign lang. services), 1996–2000. Member: Commonwealth Partners for Technol. Management; Meetings and Events Cttee, RIIA (Chatham Hse). *Recreations:* photography, travelling. *Address:* 30 Bathgate Road, Wimbledon, SW19 5PJ. *T:* (020) 8946 7652. *Club:* Le Beaujolais.

TAVAIQIA, Ratu Sir Josaia (Nasorowale), KBE 1986; JP; First Vice President, Republic of Fiji, 1993 (Second Vice President, 1992–93); *b* 25 Dec. 1930; *s* of Ratu Josaia Tavaiqia and Adi Lusiana Ratu; *m* 1955, Adi Lady Merewalesi Naqei; three *d*. *Educ:* Queen Victoria Sch.; Natabua Indian Secondary Sch., Fiji (Sen. Cambridge Examination). Custom Officer, Custom Dept, Fiji, 1949–59; Hotel Manager, 1961–75; Minister of State for Forests, 1977–89. Pres., Rural Youth Council of Fiji, 1979–92. Traditional role as Tui (Chief) of Vuda, with tradit. title of Tui Vuda (Chief of Vuda). *Recreation:* Rugby management. *Address:* Viseisei, Vuda, Fiji. *T:* 661273. *Clubs:* Royal Commonwealth Society, Union.

TAVARÉ, Andrew Kenneth; Special Commissioner of Income Tax, 1976–88 (Deputy Special Commissioner, April–Oct. 1988); *b* 10 Jan. 1918; *s* of late L. A. Tavaré, Bromley, Kent; *m* 1950, June Elinor Attwood, Beckenham, Kent; three *s*. *Educ:* Chatham House School, Ramsgate; King's College, London University. LLB (London). Solicitor of the Supreme Court. Served War with 79th HAA Regt (Hertfordshire Yeomanry), RA, 1940–45; N Africa and Italy, rank of Captain. Admitted Solicitor, 1948; Solicitor's Office, Inland Revenue, 1953–; Assistant Solicitor, 1965–75. Consultant Editor of Sergeant on Stamp Duties, 4th edition 1963, to 8th edition 1982. *Publications:* (contrib.) Simon's Taxes, 2nd edn, 1965, and 3rd edn, 1970.
See also Sir J. Tavaré.

TAVARÉ, Sir John, Kt 1989; CBE 1983; CEng; Chairman, Luxonic Lighting plc, 1986–2000; *b* 12 July 1920; *s* of Leon Alfred Tavaré and Grace Tavaré; *m* 1949, Margaret Daphne Wray; three *s* (and one *s* decd). *Educ:* Chatham House, Ramsgate; Bromley Grammar Sch.; King's Coll., London (BScEng 1946). FInstD 1983; FIWEM 1991; FIMechE 1996. Trainee, Thames Board Mills Ltd, 1938–43; Works Manager, Wm C. Jones Ltd, 1946–48; Personnel Administration Ltd, UK, Australia and NZ, 1949–58; Thames Board Mills Ltd (Unilever), 1958–68: Sales and Marketing Dir, 1960–65; Vice-Chm., 1966–68; Paper, Plastics and Packaging Bd, Unilever, 1968–70; Whitecroft plc, 1970–85: Gp Man. Dir, 1973–76; Chm. and Gp Man. Dir, 1976–85. Chm., Mersey Basin Campaign, DoE, 1985–92. Member: Nat. Council, CBI, 1978–85 (Chm., NW Reg., 1980–82); Nat. Rivers Authy Adv. Bd, NW Region, 1989–92. *Recreations:* golf, garden, environment, business. *Address:* The Gables, 4 Macclesfield Road, Prestbury, Macclesfield, Cheshire SK10 4BN. *T:* (01625) 829778.
See also A. K. Tavaré.

TAVENAS, Prof. François Aimé; Rector, and Professor, Department of Civil Engineering, Laval University, since 1997; *b* 12 Sept. 1942; *s* of Adrien Tavenas and Marie-Thérèse Bazin; *m* 1963, Gundula Schlichting; one *s* two *d*. *Educ:* Inst. Nat. des Scis Appliquées, Lyons, France (Diplôme Ingénieur 1963); Univ. of Grenoble (doctorate in soil mech. 1965). Laval University: Lectr, Dept of Civil Engrg, 1968–70; Asst Prof., 1970–73; Associate Prof., 1973–78; Prof., 1978–89; Dean, Faculty of Sci. and Engrg, 1985–89; McGill University: Prof., Dept of Civil Engrg and Applied Mechanics, 1989–97; Vice-Principal, Planning and Computing, 1989–90, Planning and Resources, 1990–97; actg Vice Principal, Macdonald Campus, 1995–97. President: Canadian Geotechnical Soc., 1990–92 (Robert F. Legget Award, 1995); Assoc. Canadienne-Française pour l'Avancement des Sciences, 1997–98; Réseau Interordinateurs Scientifique Québecois, 1998–; Chm., Standing Adv. Cttee on Univ. Res., Assoc. of Univs and Colls of Canada, 1998–; Mem. Council, Natural Scis and Engrg Res. Council, Ottawa, 1989–95. Fellow, Canadian Acad. of Engrg, 1998. Keefer Gold Medal, 1980, Julian C. Smith Medal, 2001, Engrg Inst. of Canada; Telford Premium, ICE, 1986, 1989. Chevalier, Légion d'honneur (France), 2000. *Publications:* Remblais sur argiles molles, 1985; papers in jls, conf. proceedings and other pubns. *Recreations:* tennis, sailing, travelling. *Address:* Rector's Office, Université Laval, Québec, QC G1K 7P4, Canada. *T:* (418) 6562272.

TAVENER, Sir John (Kenneth), Kt 2000; composer; *b* 28 Jan. 1944; *m* 1991, Maryanna (*née* Schaefer); two *d*. *Educ:* Highgate Sch.; Royal Academy of Music (LRAM). Prof. of Composition, Trinity Coll. of Music, London, 1968–. Hon. FRAM, Hon. FTCL, Hon. FRSCM. Russian Orthodox religion. Dr *hc* New Delhi, 1990. Apollo Award, Friends of Greek Nat. Opera, 1993. *Compositions include: orchestral:* Grandma's Footsteps; Theophany; Towards the Son: Ritual Procession; *solo instrument/voice and orchestra:* Eternal Memory; Palintropos; Piano Concerto; The Protecting Veil; The Repentant Thief; Tears of the Angels; *choral and orchestra:* Akhmatova Requiem; Eternity's Sunrise; Agraphon; In Alium; The Immurement of Antigone; Sappho; Lyrical Fragments; 16 Haiku of Seferis; Three Holy Sonnets; Akathist of Thanksgiving; The Apocalypse; Celtic Requiem; Ikon of St Seraphim; Introit for March 27th, the Feast of St John Damascene; Kyklike Kinesis; The Last Discourse; Resurrection; Ultimos Ritos; We Shall See Him As He Is; The Whale; Risen!; Agraphon; Let's Begin Again; Total Eclipse; Fall and Resurrection; *choral:* Annunciation; Canticle of the Mother of God; A Christmas Round; Eonia; The Great Canon of St Andrew of Crete; Ikon of Light; Ikon of St Cuthbert of Lindisfarne; Ikon of the Trinity; The Lamb; Lament of the Mother of God; Let Not the Prince be Silent; Liturgy of St John Chrysostom; O, Do Not Move; Orthodox Vigil Service; Panikhida; Prayer for the World; Psalm 121, I Will Lift Up Mine Eyes Unto The Hills; Song for Athene; Thunder Entered Her; Today the Virgin; Two Hymns to the Mother of God; The Tyger; The Uncreated Eros; A Village Wedding; The World is Burning; Three Antiphons; Innocence; Svyatuiee (O Holy One); Amen; As One Who Has Slept; Hymn of the Unwaning Light; Notre Père; Prayer to the Holy Trinity; Wedding Prayer; *choral and instruments:* The Myrrh-Bearer; Hymns of Paradise; Responsorium in Memory of Annon Lee; Akhmatova Songs; The Child Lived; Lamentation, Last Prayer and Exaltation; Let's Begin Again; Meditation on the Light; Six Abbasid Songs; Three Sections from T. S. Eliot's 'The Four Quartets'; Three Surrealist Songs; Feast of Feasts; *chamber:* Greek Interlude; The Hidden Treasure; In Memoriam Igor Stravinsky; The Last Sleep of the Virgin; Trisagion; Mandelion; Mandoodles; Palin; Thrinos; Lament for Phaedra; Chant for Solo Cello; Akhmatova Songs; Diodia; Vlepondas; Samaveda; *opera:* Cain and Abel (1st Prize, Monaco); The Cappemakers; Eis Thanaton; A Gentle Spirit; Mary of Egypt; Thérèse. *Publications:* (jtly) Ikons: meditations in words and music, 1994; (ed Brian Keeble) The Music of Silence: a composer's testament, 1999. *Address:* c/o Chester Music, 8–9 Frith Street, W1D 3JB.

TAVERNE, family name of **Baron Taverne**.

TAVERNE, Baron, *cr* 1996 (Life Peer), of Pimlico in the City of Westminster; **Dick Taverne;** QC 1965; Chairman, AXA Equity & Law Life Assurance Society plc, since 1997 (Director, since 1972); *b* 18 Oct. 1928; *s* of Dr N. J. M. and Mrs L. V. Taverne; *m* 1955, Janice Hennessey; two *d*. *Educ:* Charterhouse School; Balliol College, Oxford (First in Greats). Oxford Union Debating tour of USA, 1951. Called to Bar, 1954. MP (Lab) Lincoln, March 1962–Oct. 1972, resigned; MP (Democratic Lab) Lincoln, March 1973–Sept. 1974; Parliamentary Under-Secretary of State, Home Office, 1966–68; Minister of State, Treasury, 1968–69; Financial Secretary to the Treasury, 1969–70. Chm., Public Expenditure (General) Sub-Cttee, 1971–72. Institute for Fiscal Studies: First Dir, 1970; Dir-Gen., 1979–81; Chm., 1981–82; Chm., Public Policy Centre, 1984–87. Non-exec. Dir, BOC Gp, 1975–95; Dir, PRIMA Europe Ltd, 1987–98 (Chm., 1991–93; Pres., 1993–98). Mem., Internat. Ind. Review Body to review workings of European Commn, 1979. Chairman: Alcohol and Drug Prevention and Treatment Ltd, 1996–; Adv. Bd, Oxford Centre for Envmt, Ethics and Society, 1997–. Member: Nat. Cttee, SDP, 1981–87; Federal Policy Cttee, Liberal Democrats, 1989–90. Contested (SDP): Southwark, Peckham, Oct. 1982; Dulwich, 1983. *Publication:* The Future of the Left: Lincoln and after, 1973. *Recreation:* sailing. *Address:* 60 Cambridge Street, SW1V 4QQ.
See also S. Taverne.

TAVERNE, Suzanna; Managing Director, British Museum, 1999–Spring 2002; *b* 3 Feb. 1960; *d* of Baron Taverne, *qv* and Janice Taverne (*née* Hennessey); *m* 1993, Marc Vlessing; one *s* one *d*. *Educ:* Balliol Coll., Oxford (BA Hons 1982). S. G. Warburg and Co. Ltd, 1982–90; Head, Strategic Planning, 1990–92, Finance Dir, 1992–94, Newspaper Publishing plc; Consultant, Saatchi and Saatchi, 1994–95; Dir, Strategy and Develt, then Man. Dir FT Finance, Pearson plc, 1995–98. *Address:* c/o British Museum, WC1B 3DG. *T:* (020) 7323 8948.

TAVERNER, Marcus Louis; QC 2000; *b* 24 April 1958; *s* of Geoffrey Clifford Taverner, DFC and Mildred Taverner (née Thomas); *m* 1983, Dr Deborah Mary Hall; one *s* three *d*. *Educ:* Monmouth Sch.; Leicester Univ. (LLB Hons); King's Coll. London (LLM). Called to the Bar, Gray's Inn, 1981. *Recreations:* my 4 children, poetry, trees, guitar, theatre, dramatics, Robin Trower. *Address:* Benington Park, Benington, Stevenage, Herts SG2 7BU. *T:* (01438) 869007.

TAVISTOCK, Marquess of; Henry Robin Ian Russell; DL; Director, London Pacific Group Ltd (formerly Berkeley Govett & Co. Ltd), since 1985; *b* 21 Jan. 1940; *s* and *heir* of 13th Duke of Bedford, *qv*; *m* 1961, Henrietta Joan, *d* of late Henry F. Tiarks; three *s*. *Educ:* Le Rosey, Switzerland; Harvard University. Partner, De Zoete and Bevan, 1970–82; Chairman: Cedar Investment Trust, 1977–82; Berkeley Devclt Capital Ltd, 1984–92; TR Property Investment Trust, 1982–89 (Dir, 1982–91); Director: Touche, Remnant Holdings, 1977–88; Trafalgar House Ltd, 1977–91; United Racecourses, 1977–94. Hon. Trustee, Kennedy Memorial Trust (Chm., 1985–90). Pres., Woburn Golf and Country Club. DL Beds, 1985. *Heir:* *s* Lord Howland, *qv*. *Address:* Woburn Abbey, Woburn, Bedfordshire MK17 9WA. *T:* (01525) 290666. *Clubs:* White's; Jockey Club Rooms; The Brook (New York).

TAVNER, Teresa, (Terry); Editor, Woman's Own, since 1998; *b* 18 Jan. 1952; *d* of Bernard Joseph Hayes and Hanorah Hayes; *m* 1972, Barry Tavner; one *s* one *d*. *Educ:* Notre Dame Grammar Sch., Battersea. Sub Ed. and Fiction Ed., Honey mag., 1981–84; Dep. Chief Sub-Ed., then Chief Sub-Ed., then Asst Ed., She mag., 1984–88; Editor: Chat mag., 1988–96; Eva mag., 1997–98. Editors' Editor, BSME, 1990. *Recreations:* ski-ing, travelling, cinema, reading, socialising. *Address:* Woman's Own, King's Reach Tower, Stamford Street, SE1 9LS. *T:* (020) 7261 5500.

TAYLER, His Honour (Harold) Clive; QC 1979; a Circuit Judge, 1984–99; *b* 4 Nov. 1932; *m* 1959, Catherine Jane (*née* Thomas); two *s* one *d*. *Educ:* Solihull Sch.; Balliol Coll., Oxford (Eldon Schol.); BCL and BA (Jurisprudence); Inner Temple Entrance Schol. Called to the Bar, Inner Temple, 1956; in practice, Birmingham, 1958–84, and London, 1979–84; a Recorder of the Crown Court, 1974–84; Midland and Oxford Circuit.

TAYLOR; *see* Suenson-Taylor, family name of Baron Grantchester.

TAYLOR, family name of **Barons Ingrow, Kilclooney, Taylor of Blackburn,** and **Taylor of Warwick**.

TAYLOR OF BLACKBURN, Baron *cr* 1978 (Life Peer), of Blackburn in the County of Lancashire; **Thomas Taylor,** CBE 1974 (OBE 1969); JP; DL; Consultant, British Aerospace, Shorrock Security Systems Ltd, and other companies; *b* 10 June 1929; *s* of James and Edith Gladys Taylor; *m* 1950, Kathleen Nurton; one *s*. *Educ:* Mill Hill Primary Sch.; Blakey Moor Elementary Sch. Mem., Blackburn Town Council, 1954–76 (Leader, chm. of cttees and rep. on various bodies). Chm., Electricity Cons. Council for NW and Mem. Norweb Bd, 1977–80; Member: NW Econ. Planning Council; NW AHA (Chm. Brockhall HMC, 1972–74, Vice-Chm. Blackburn HMC, 1964–74); Council for Educational Technology in UK; Nat. Foundn for Educn Research in Eng. and Wales; Schools Council; Regional Rent Tribunal. Chairman: Govt Cttee of Enquiry into Management and Govt of Schools; Nat. Foundn for Visual Aids. Former Mem., Public Schools Commn; past Pres., Assoc. of Educn Cttees. Dir, Councils and Education Press. University of Lancaster: Founder Mem. and Mem. Council; author of Taylor Report on problems; former Dep. Pro-Chancellor. Former Dep. Dir, Central Lancs Family and Community Project. Non-executive Director: Canatxx Energy Ventures Ltd, 1995–; Grove (1997) Ltd (formerly Grove Properties Ltd), 1992–; Chameleon Educnl Systems Ltd (formerly Oracle Educnl Systems Ltd), 1996–. Elder, URC; Pres., Free Church Council, 1962–63. Hon. LLD Lancaster, 1996. JP Blackburn, 1960, DL Lancs, 1994; former Chm., Juvenile Bench. Freeman, Blackburn, 1992. *Address:* 9 Woodview, Cherry Tree, Blackburn BB2 5LL. *T:* (01254) 209571.

TAYLOR OF WARWICK, Baron *cr* 1996 (Life Peer), of Warwick in the county of Warwickshire; **John David Beckett Taylor;** barrister-at-law; writer; radio and television presenter; *b* 21 Sept. 1952; *s* of late Derief David Samuel Taylor and of Enid Maud Taylor; *m* 1981, Dr Jean Katherine Taylor (*née* Binysh); one *s* two *d*. *Educ:* Univ. of Keele (BA Hons Law). Called to the Bar, Gray's Inn, 1978; practised on Midland & Oxford Circuit, 1978–90. Special Advr to Home Sec. and Home Office Ministers, 1990–91. Consultant, Lowe Bell Communications Ltd, 1991–92; Producer/Presenter, BBC Radio and Television, 1994–; Chm., Warwick Consulting Internat. Ltd, 1997–; Dir, Warwick Leadership Foundn, 1999–. Member: Solihull FPC, 1986–90; Greater London FEFC Cttee, 1994–96. Non-exec. Dir, NW Thames RHA, 1992–93. Pres., African Caribbean Westminster Initiative, 1997–; Vice-President: Small Business Bureau, 1997–; BBFC, 1998–. Dir, City Technology Colls Trust, 1994–95. Mem. (C), Solihull DC, 1986–90. Contested (C): Birmingham, Perry Barr, 1987; Cheltenham, 1992. MInstD 1997. Barker, Variety Club Children's Charity; Patron: Parents for Children, adoption charity; Kidscape, 1997–; Mem. Exec. Cttee, Sickle Cell Anaemia Relief. Pres., Ilford Town FC, 1998–; Mem., Aston Villa FC. Freeman, City of London, 1999. Hon. LLD Warwick, 1999. *Recreations:* soccer, cricket, singing, spending time with my lovely family. *Address:* House of Lords, SW1A 0PW. *T:* (020) 7219 3000, *Fax:* (020) 7219 5979; *e-mail:* taylorjdb@parliament.uk.

TAYLOR, Alan; *see* Taylor, Robert A.

TAYLOR, Alan Broughton; His Honour Judge Alan Taylor; a Circuit Judge, since 1991; *b* 23 Jan. 1939; *yr s* of Valentine James Broughton Taylor and Gladys Maud Taylor; *m* 1964, Diana Hindmarsh; two *s*. *Educ:* Malvern Coll.; Geneva Univ.; Birmingham Univ. (LLB); Brasenose Coll., Oxford (BLitt, re-designated MLitt 1979). Called to the Bar, Gray's Inn, 1961; barrister on Oxford Circuit, subseq. Midland and Oxford Circuit, 1963–91; a Recorder, 1979–91. Gov., St Matthew's Sch., Sandwell, 1988–92. FCIArb 1994. *Publication:* (contrib.) A Practical Guide to the Care of the Injured, ed P. S. London, 1967. *Recreations:* philately, fell walking. *Address:* c/o Circuit Administrator's Office, The Priory Courts, 33 Bull Street, Birmingham B4 6DW.

TAYLOR, Lt-Gen. Sir Allan (Macnab), KBE 1972; MC 1944; Deputy Commander-in-Chief, United Kingdom Land Forces, 1973–76, retired; *b* 26 March 1919; *s* of Alexander Lawrence Taylor and Winifred Ethel (*née* Nisbet); *m* 1945, Madeleine Turpin (marr. diss. 1963); two *d*. *Educ:* Fyling Hall School, Robin Hood's Bay. Joined TA, 1938; Troop Leader, 10th Royal Tank Regt, 1940; Squadron Leader, 7th Royal Tank Regt, 1942; 6th Royal Tank Regt, 1946; Staff College, 1948; GSO 2, 56 London Armoured Div., 1949; Bde Major 20 Armoured Bde, 1952; Instructor, Staff College, 1954; Squadron Leader, 1st R Tank Regt, 1957; Second in Comd 5th RTR, 1959; Comdg Officer: 5th RTR, 1960 and 3rd, 1961; AA&QMG, 1st Div., 1962; Commandant, RAC Gunnery School, 1963; Comd Berlin Brigade, 1964; Imperial Defence College, 1967; Comdr, 1st Div., 1968; Commandant, Staff College, Camberley, 1969–72; GOC South East District, April-Dec. 1972. Chm., Cttee on Regular Officer Training, 1972–. Col Comdt, RTR, 1973–77. *Recreation:* golf. *Address:* 4 Mill Close, Middle Assendon, Henley-on-Thames, Oxon RG9 6BA. *T:* (01491) 575167.

TAYLOR, Andrew David; Chairman, Richards Butler, Solicitors, since 2000; *b* 6 March 1952; *s* of Vernon Stephen Taylor and Elizabeth Taylor; *m* 1977, Alison Jane Wright; one *s* two *d*. *Educ:* Magdalen Coll. Sch., Oxford; Lincoln Coll., Oxford (MA). With Richards Butler, Solicitors, 1977–, specialising in shipping law. *Publication:* Voyage Charters, 1993, 2nd edn 2001. *Recreations:* hockey, walking, opera. *Address:* Richards Butler, 15 St Botolph Street, EC3A 7EE. *Clubs:* City University; Vincent's (Oxford).

TAYLOR, Rt Hon. Ann; *see* Taylor, Rt Hon. (Winifred) Ann.

TAYLOR, Anthony John N.; *see* Newman Taylor.

TAYLOR, Arnold Joseph, CBE 1971; DLitt, MA; FBA 1972; FSA; Hon. Vice-President, Society of Antiquaries, since 1978 (Vice-President, 1963–64; Secretary, 1964–70; Director, 1970–75; President, 1975–78); *b* 24 July 1911; *y s* of late John George Taylor, Headmaster of Sir Walter St John's School, Battersea; *m* 1940, Patricia Katharine, *d* of late S. A. Guilbride, Victoria, BC; one *s* one *d*. *Educ:* Merchant Taylors' School; St John's College, Oxford (MA). Assistant master, Chard School, Somerset, 1934; Assistant Inspector of Ancient Monuments, HM Office of Works, 1935. Served War of 1939–45, Intelligence Officer, RAF, 1942–46. Inspector of Ancient Monuments for Wales, Min. of Works, 1946–54, Asst Chief Inspector, 1954–61; Chief Inspector of Ancient Monuments and Historic Buildings, MPBW, later DoE, 1961–72. Commissioner: Royal Commissions on Ancient and Historical Monuments (Wales and Monmouthshire), 1956–83; Historical Monuments (England), 1963–78; Mem., Ancient Monuments Board: for England, 1973–82; for Scotland, 1974–79; for Wales, 1974–82. Member: Cathedrals Advisory Cttee, 1964–80; Adv. Bd for Redundant Churches, 1973–82 (Chm., 1975–77); Westminster Abbey Architectural Adv. Panel, 1979–92; Vice-President: English Place-Name Soc., 1986–; British Archaeol Assoc., 1993; Hon. Vice-President: Flintshire Hist. Soc., 1953; Royal Archaeol Inst., 1979– (Vice-Pres., 1968–72); Surrey Archaeol Soc., 1979; President: Oxford Univ. Archaeol Soc., 1932; Cambrian Archaeol Assoc., 1969; London and Middx Archaeol Soc., 1971–74; Soc. for Medieval Archaeology, 1972–75; Friends of Lydiard Tregoze, 1983–86; Sir Walter St John's Old Boys' Assoc., 1969–70 (Hon. Life Patron, 1992); Old Merchant Taylors' Soc., 1985–86. Mem., Sir Walter St John's Schools Trust, 1970. Reckitt Lectr, British Acad., 1977. Hon. Corres. Mem., Société Jersiaise, 1983. Hon. Pres., Colloque Internat. du Château Gaillard, 1992. Hon. DLitt Wales, 1970; Docteur *hc* Caen, 1980. Reginald Taylor Prize, British Archaeol Assoc., 1949; G. T. Clark Prize, Cambrian Archaeol Assoc., 1956; Gold Medal, Soc. of Antiquaries, 1988. Médaille d'Honneur de la Ville de Saint-Georges d'Espéranche, 1988. Silver Jubilee Medal, 1977. *Publications:* Records of the Barony and Honour of the Rape of Lewes, 1940; official guides to various historical monuments in care Ministry of Works (now DoE), 1939–80; chapter on Military Architecture, in vol. Medieval England, 1958; (part author) History of the King's Works, 1963; Four Great Castles, 1983; Studies in Castles and Castle-Building, 1986; contribs on medieval architectural history in Eng. Hist. Rev., Antiquaries Jl, Archaeologia Cambrensis, etc. *Recreations:* reading and using records, resisting iconoclasts. *Address:* Rose Cottage, Lincoln's Hill, Chiddingfold, Surrey GU8 4UN. *T:* (01428) 682069.

TAYLOR, Sir (Arthur) Godfrey, Kt 1980; DL; Chairman, The Shrievalty Association, 1995–98; *b* 3 Aug. 1925; *s* of Fred and Lucy Taylor; *m* 1945, Eileen Dorothy Daniel; one *s* two *d* (and one *d* decd). *Educ:* Stockport Secondary School. Sutton and Cheam Borough Council: Councillor, 1951–62; Alderman, 1962–65; London Bor. of Sutton: Alderman, 1964–78; Councillor, 1978–82; Hon. Freeman, 1978. Managing Trustee, Municipal Mutual Insurance Ltd, 1979–86; Chairman: Southern Water Authority, 1981–85; London Residuary Body, 1985–96. Chm., Assoc. of Metropolitan Authorities, 1978–80. Chm., London Bor. Assoc., 1968–71. High Sheriff, 1984, DL, 1988, Greater London. *Recreation:* golf. *Address:* 23 Somerhill Lodge, Somerhill Road, Hove, E Sussex BN3 1RU. *T:* (01273) 776161.

TAYLOR, Arthur Robert; President, Muhlenberg College, Pennsylvania, since 1992; *b* 6 July 1935; *s* of Arthur Earl Taylor and Marian Hilda Scott; *m* Kathryn Pelgrift; three *d* by previous marriage. *Educ:* Brown Univ., USA (AB, MA). Asst Dir, Admissions, Brown Univ., June 1957–Dec. 1960; Vice-Pres./Dir, The First Boston Co., Jan. 1961–May 1970; Exec. Vice-Pres./Director, Internat. Paper Co., 1970–72; Pres., CBS Inc., 1972–76; Chm., Arthur Taylor & Co. Inc., 1977–. Dean, Grad. Sch. of Business, Fordham Univ., 1985–92. Director: Louisiana Land & Exploration Co.; Pitney Bowes; Nomura Pacific Basin Fund, Inc.; Trustee, Drucker Foundn; Trustee Emeritus, Brown Univ. Hon. degrees: Dr Humane Letters: Simmons Coll., 1975; Rensselaer Polytechnic Inst., 1975; Dr of Humanities, Bucknell Univ., 1975. *Publications:* contrib. chapter to The Other Side of Profit, 1975; articles on US competitiveness and corporate responsibility in jls. *Recreations:* sailing, tennis, riding. *Address:* (office) Muhlenberg College, 2400 Chew Street, Allentown, PA 18104–5586, USA. *Clubs:* Century (New York); Metropolitan (Washington); California (Los Angeles).

TAYLOR, Arthur Ronald, MBE (mil.) 1945; DL; Chairman, Willis Faber plc, 1978–81; Vice-Chairman, Legal and General Group plc, 1984–86 (Director, 1982–86); *b* 13 June 1921; *yr s* of late Arthur Taylor and Kathleen Frances (*née* Constable Curtis); *m* 1949, Elizabeth Josephine Kiek; three *s*. *Educ:* Winchester Coll.; Trinity Coll., Oxford. Served Grenadier Guards, 1940–53 (despatches); sc; Bde Major 32nd Guards Bde. Laurence Philipps & Co. (Insurance) Ltd, 1953–58; Member of Lloyd's, 1955; Director, Willis, Faber and Dumas Ltd, 1959; Dep. Chm., Willis Faber Ltd, 1974. Vice-President: Corporation of Insurance Brokers, 1967–78; British Insurance Brokers Assoc., 1978–81. DL Hants, 1994. *Recreations:* golf, shooting. *Address:* Coutts & Co., 1 Cadogan Place, SW1X 9PX.

TAYLOR, Bernard David, CBE 1993; Chairman, Cambridge Laboratories Ltd, since 1997; *b* 17 Oct. 1935; *s* of Thomas Taylor and Winifred (*née* Smith); *m* 1959, Nadine Barbara; two *s* two *d*. *Educ:* Univ. of Wales, Bangor (BSc Zoology). Science Teacher, Coventry Educn Authority, 1958; Sales and Marketing, SK&F, 1960; Sales and Marketing Manager, Glaxo NZ, 1964; New Products Manager, Glaxo UK, 1967; Man. Dir, Glaxo Australia, 1972; Dir, Glaxo Holdings plc, and Man. Dir, Glaxo Pharmaceuticals UK, 1984; Chief Exec., Glaxo Holdings, 1986–89; Chm., Medeva plc, 1990–96. Councillor and Vice-Pres., Aust. Pharm. Manufrs' Assoc., 1974–79; Councillor, Victorian Coll. of Pharmacy, 1976–82. Member: CBI Europe Cttee, 1987–89; BOTB, 1987–96. Trustee, WWF (UK), 1990–96. CIMgt (CBIM 1986). Fellow, London Business Sch., 1988.

TAYLOR, Prof. Brent William, PhD; FRCP, FRACP, FRCPCH; Professor of Community Child Health, Royal Free and University College Medical School, University of London (formerly Royal Free Hospital School of Medicine), since 1988; *b* 21 Nov. 1941; *s* of Robert Ernest Taylor and Norma Gertrude Taylor; *m* 1970, Moira Elizabeth Hall; one *s* one *d*. *Educ:* Christchurch Boys' High Sch.; Otago Univ. (MB ChB 1966); Bristol Univ. (PhD 1986). FRACP 1977; FRCP 1985; FRCPCH 1997. Jun. hosp. posts, Christchurch, NZ, 1967–71; Res. Fellow and Sen. Registrar, Great Ormond Street Hosp. for Sick Children, 1971–74; Senior Lecturer: in Paediatrics, Christchurch Clin. Sch. of Medicine, 1975–81; in Social Paediatrics and Epidemiology, Bristol Univ., 1981–84; in Child Health, St Mary's Hosp. Med. Sch., 1985–88. Hon. Prof., Inst. of Child Health, 1994–; Vis. Prof., Tongji Med. Univ., Wuhan, China, 1995–. Chm., Nat. Child Health Informatics Consortium, 1995–. *Publications:* chapters and papers on child health, social influences, respiratory problems and informatics. *Recreations:* family, music (Handel), walking, computing. *Address:* Department of Child Health, Royal Free and University College Medical School, Rowland Hill Street, NW3 2QG. *T:* (020) 7830 2288; *e-mail:* b.taylor@rfc.ucl.ac.uk.

TAYLOR, Brian Arthur Edward; Director General, Civilian Personnel (formerly Assistant Under-Secretary of State, Civilian Management), Ministry of Defence, 1996–2001; *b* 10 Jan. 1942; *s* of Arthur Frederick Taylor and Gertrude Maclean Taylor (*née* Campbell); *m* 1967, Carole Ann Smith; three *s* one *d*. *Educ:* St Benedict's Sch., Ealing; Corpus Christi Coll., Oxford (MA Lit.Hum.). Ministry of Defence, 1965–2001: Asst Private Sec. to Sec. of State, 1969–70; Private Sec. to Chief of Air Staff, 1973–75; Head, Management Services Div., 1977–79; Head, Naval Personnel Div., 1979–81; RCDS 1982; Central Policy Review Staff, Cabinet Office, 1983; Head, Civilian Management Div., MoD, 1984–86; Asst Under-Sec. of State (Quartermaster), 1986–88, Air (PE), 1988–91; Head of Personnel Policy Gp (Under Sec.), HM Treasury, 1992–94; Asst Under-Sec. of State (Civilian Mgt (Policy)), MoD, 1994–96. *Recreations:* sport, music, reading, family. *Club:* Richmond Rugby.

TAYLOR, Brian William; Under Secretary, Civil Service Commission, retired; Resident Chairman, Recruitment and Assessment Services, Office of Minister for Civil Service, 1990–93; *b* 29 April 1933; *s* of late Alan Taylor and Betty Taylor; *m* 1959, Mary Evelyn Buckley; two *s* two *d*. *Educ:* Emanuel School. Entered Ministry of Nat. Insurance (subseq. DHSS, then DSS) as Exec. Officer, 1952; Higher Exec. Officer, 1963; Principal, 1968; Asst Sec., 1976; Under Sec., 1982; on loan from DSS, 1990–93. *Recreations:* music, theatre, literature, walking, grandchildren.

TAYLOR, Catherine Dalling; *see* Stihler, C. D.

TAYLOR, Cavan; Senior Partner, Lovell White Durrant, 1991–96; *b* 23 Feb. 1935; *s* of late Albert William Taylor and Constance Muriel (*née* Horncastle); *m* 1962, Helen Tinling; one *s* two *d*. *Educ:* King's Coll. Sch., Wimbledon; Emmanuel Coll., Cambridge (BA 1958; LLM 1959). 2nd Lieut, RASC, 1953–55. Articled with Herbert Smith & Co., 1958–61;

qualified as solicitor, 1961; Legal Dept, Distillers' Co. Ltd, 1962–65; Asst Solicitor, Piesse & Sons, 1965–66, Partner, 1966; by amalgamation, Partner, Durrant Piesse and Lovell White Durrant; Dep. Sen. Partner, Lovell White Durrant, 1990–91. Director: Hampton Gold Mining Areas plc, 1979–86; Ludorum Management Ltd, 1996–2000; Link Plus Corp., 1999–. Adjudicator for Investment Ombudsman, 1996–. Gov., King's Coll. Sch., Wimbledon, 1970– (Chm., 1973–90, 2000–). Trustee, School Fees Charitable Trust, 2000–. Liveryman, Solicitors' Co., 1983–. *Publications:* articles in legal jls. *Recreations:* reading, gardening, conversation with my children. *Address:* Covenham House, 10 Broad Highway, Cobham, Surrey KT11 2RP. *T:* (01932) 864258, *Fax:* (01932) 865705. *Club:* Travellers.

TAYLOR, Prof. Charles Margrave, CC 1996; DPhil; FBA 1979; Professor of Political Science, McGill University, since 1982; *b* 5 Nov. 1931; *s* of Walter Margrave Taylor and Simone Beaubien; *m* 1st, 1956, Alba Romer (*d* 1990); five *d*; 2nd, 1995, Aube Billard. *Educ:* McGill Univ. (BA History); Oxford Univ. (BA PPE, MA, DPhil). Fellow, All Souls Coll., Oxford, 1956–61; McGill University: Asst Prof., later Associate Prof., later Prof. of Polit. Science, Dept of Polit. Science, 1961–76; Prof. of Philosophy, Dept. of Philos., 1973–76; Chichele Prof. of Social and Political Theory, and Fellow of All Souls Coll., Oxford Univ., 1976–81; Mem., Sch. of Social Science, Inst. for Advanced Study, Princeton, 1981–82. Prof. asst, later Prof. agrégé, later Prof. titulaire, Ecole Normale Supérieure, 1962–64, Dept de Philos., 1963–71, Univ. de Montréal. Vis. Prof. in Philos., Princeton Univ., 1965; Mills Vis. Prof. in Philos., Univ. of Calif, Berkeley, 1974. For. Hon. Mem., Amer. Acad. of Arts and Scis, 1986. *Publications:* The Explanation of Behavior, 1964; Pattern of Politics, 1970; Hegel, 1975; Erklarung und Interpretation in den Wissenschaften vom Menschen, 1975; Social Theory as Practice, 1983; Philosophical Papers, 1985; Negative Freiheit, 1988; Sources of the Self, 1989; The Ethics of Authenticity, 1992; Philosophical Arguments, 1995. *Recreations:* skiing, swimming. *Address:* 6603 Jeanne Mance, Montréal, QC H2V 4L1, Canada.

TAYLOR, Christopher Charles, FSA; FBA 1995; Head, Archaeological Survey, Royal Commission on Historical Monuments, 1985–93, retired; *b* 7 Nov. 1935; *s* of Richard Hugh Taylor and Alice Mary Taylor (*née* Davies); *m* 1st, 1961, Angela Ballard (*d* 1983); one *s* one *d*; 2nd, 1985, Stephanie, *d* of Wing Comdr R. J. S. Spooner; one step *d*. *Educ:* King Edward VI Sch., Lichfield; Univ. of Keele (BA 1958); Inst. of Archaeol., Univ. of London (Dip. Archaeol. 1960). FSA 1966; MIFA 1987. Investigator, Sen. Investigator and Principal Investigator, RCHM, 1960–93. Mem., English Heritage Historic Parks and Gardens Adv. Cttee, 1987–2001; Historic Settlement and Landscape Adv. Cttee, 2001–. Pres., Cambridge Antiquarian Soc., 1994–96. Hon. DLitt Keele, 1997. *Publications:* Dorset, 1970; The Making of the Cambridgeshire Landscape, 1973; Fieldwork in Medieval Archaeology, 1974; Fields in the English Landscape, 1975, 3rd edn 1987; Roads and Tracks in Britain, 1979, 2nd edn 1982; The Archaeology of Gardens, 1983; Village and Farmstead, 1983; (ed) W. G. Hoskins, The Making of the English Landscape, rev. edn 1988; Parks and Gardens of Britain, 1998; contrib. to various pubns of RCHM; papers in learned jls on archaeol. and landscape hist. *Recreations:* gardening, garden history. *Address:* 11 High Street, Pampisford, Cambridge CB2 4ES.

See also D. H. C. Taylor.

TAYLOR, Prof. Christopher Malcolm, FREng, FIMechE; Professor of Tribology, since 1990, and Pro-Vice-Chancellor, since 1997, University of Leeds; *b* 15 Jan. 1943; *s* of William Taylor and Esther Hopkinson; *m* 1st, 1968, Gillian Walton (marr. diss. 1986); one *d*; 2nd, 1994, Diane Shorrocks. *Educ:* King's College London (BScEng); Univ. of Leeds (MSc, PhD, DEng). FIMechE 1986. Research Engineer, English Electric Co.; Sen. Engr, Industrial Unit of Tribology, Leeds, 1968–71; University of Leeds: Academic Staff, 1971–; Head of Dept of Mechanical Engrg, 1992–96; Dean of Faculty of Engrg, 1996–97. Vice-Pres., 1997–2001, Dep. Pres., 2001–, IMechE. FREng (FEng 1995); FCGI 1999. Tribology Trust Silver Medal, 1992; Donald Julius Groen Prize, IMechE, 1993. Editor, Part J, Procs IMechE. *Publications:* numerous contribs to learned jls. *Recreations:* walking, cycling. *Address:* School of Mechanical Engineering, The University, Leeds LS2 9JT. *T:* (0113) 233 2156.

TAYLOR, Claire Mavis, RRC 1994 (ARRC 1977); Matron-in-Chief, 1994–97, and Captain (formerly Principal Nursing Officer), Queen Alexandra's Royal Naval Nursing Service, 1990–97; *b* 26 May 1943; *d* of late William Taylor and Sybil (*née* Matthews). *Educ:* George Dixon Grammar Sch., Edgbaston. SRN 1964; SCM 1967; RNT 1977. Served QARNNS, 1967–73; Nursing Sister, Papua New Guinea, 1973–74; rejoined QARNNS 1975; QHNS, 1994–97. OStJ. *Recreations:* travel, reading. *Address:* c/o Lloyds TSB, 20–24 High Street, Gosport, Hants. *Club:* Army and Navy.

TAYLOR, Clifford; management consultant; Director, Resources Television, BBC, 1988–93 (Deputy Director, 1987–88); *b* 6 March 1941; *s* of Fred Taylor and Annie Elisabeth (*née* Hudson); *m* 1962, Catherine Helen (*née* Green); two *d*. *Educ:* Barnsley and District Holgate Grammar Sch.; Barnsley College of Mining and Technology. ACMA. NCB, 1957–65; Midlands Counties Dairies, 1965–68; BBC: Radio Cost Accountant, 1968–71; Television Hd of Costing, 1971–76; Chief Accountant, Corporate Finance, 1976–77 and 1982–84; Chief Acct, Engineering, 1977–82; Dep. Dir, Finance, 1984–86. *Recreations:* sport — plays squash, golf, enjoys horse racing. *Address:* 35 Hare Hill Close, Pyrford, near Woking, Surrey GU22 8UH. *T:* (01932) 348301. *Clubs:* MCC, BBC; Pyrford Golf.

TAYLOR, Sir Cyril (Julian Hebden), Kt 1989; Chairman: Technology Colleges Trust, since 1987; American Institute for Foreign Study, since 1964; *b* 14 May 1935; *s* of Cyril Eustace Taylor and Margaret Victoria (*née* Hebden); *m* 1965, June Judith Denman; one *d*. *Educ:* St Marylebone Grammar Sch.; Trinity Hall, Cambridge (MA); Harvard Business Sch. (MBA). National Service, Officer with KAR in Kenya during Mau Mau Emergency, 1954–56 (seconded from E Surrey Regt). Brand Manager in Advertising Dept, Proctor & Gamble, Cincinnati, Ohio, 1961–64; Founder Chm., American Institute for Foreign Study, 1964–: group cos include: Amer. Inst. for Foreign Study; Amer. Council for Internat. Studies; Camp America; Au Pair in America. Advr to Sec. of State for Educn and Employment, 1987–. Mem. for Ruislip Northwood, GLC, 1977–86: Chm., Professional and Gen. Services Cttee, 1979–81; Opposition spokesperson for employment, 1981–82, transport, 1982–85, policy and resources, 1985–86; Dep. Leader of the Opposition, 1983–86; Mem., Wkg Party reviewing legislation to abolish GLC and MCCs, 1983–86. Pres., Ruislip Northwood Cons. Assoc., 1986–97; contested (C): Huddersfield E, Feb. 1974; Keighley, Oct. 1974. Member: Bd of Dirs, Centre for Policy Studies, 1984–98; Council, Westfield Coll., Univ. of London, 1983–89; Council, RCM, 1988–95; Bd of Governors, Holland Park Comprehensive Sch., 1971–74; Chm., Bd of Trustees, Richmond Coll., American Internat. Univ. in London, 1977–. Chm., Lexham Gdns Residents' Assoc., 1986–. Pres., Harvard Business Sch. Club, London, 1990–93; Vice Pres., Alumni Council, Harvard Business Sch., 1994–96 (Mem., 1993–96). FRSA 1990. High Sheriff, Greater London, 1996. Hon. LLD: New England, 1991; Richmond Coll., American Internat. Univ. in London, 1998. *Publications:* (jtly) The New Guide to Study Abroad, USA 1969, 4th edn 1976; Peace has its Price, 1972; No More Tick, 1974; The Elected Member's Guide to Reducing Public Expenditure, 1980; A Realistic Plan for London Transport, 1982; Reforming London's Government, 1984; Quangoes Just Grow, 1985; London Preserv'd, 1985; Bringing Accountability Back to Local Government, 1985; Employment Examined: the right approach to more jobs, 1986; Raising Educational Standards, 1990; The Future of Higher Education, 1996. *Recreations:* keen tennis player, swimmer, gardener, theatre-goer. *Address:* 1 Lexham Walk, W8 5JD. *T:* (020) 7370 2081; American Institute for Foreign Study, 37 Queen's Gate, SW7 5HR. *T:* (020) 7581 7391, *Fax:* (020) 7581 7388; *e-mail:* ctaylor@aifs.co.uk. *Clubs:* Carlton, Hurlingham, Chelsea Arts; Harvard, Racquet (New York).

TAYLOR, Dr Daniel Brumhall Cochrane; JP; Vice-Chancellor, Victoria University of Wellington, New Zealand, 1968–82; Referee of the Small Claims Tribunal, Wellington, 1985–88; *b* 13 May 1921; *s* of Daniel Brumhall Taylor, Coleraine, NI and Anna Martha Taylor (*née* Rice); *m* 1955, Elizabeth Page, Christchurch, NZ; one *s* one *d*. *Educ:* Coleraine Academical Instn, NI; Queen's Univ., Belfast. BSc (Mech. Engrg) 1942, BSc (Elec. Engrg) 1943, MSc 1946, PhD 1948, QUB; MA Cantab 1956; FIMechE 1968. Lecturer in Engineering: Liverpool Univ., 1948–50; Nottingham Univ., 1950–53; ICI Fellow, Cambridge Univ., 1953–56; Lectr in Mechanical Sciences, Cambridge Univ., 1956–68; Fellow of Peterhouse, 1958–68, Fellow Emeritus, 1968; Tutor of Peterhouse, 1958–65, Senior Tutor, 1965–68. Member: NZ/USA Educnl Foundn, 1970–82; Council, Assoc. of Commonwealth Univs, 1974–77 (Chm., 1975–76); Chm., NZ Vice-Chancellors' Cttee, 1975–77. JP New Zealand, 1985. Hon. LLD Victoria Univ. of Wellington, 1983. *Publications:* numerous engrg and metallurgical papers. *Address:* 361 Fergusson Drive, Heretaunga, New Zealand. *T:* (4) 5280720. *Club:* Leander (Henley-on-Thames).

See also M. J. Kelly.

TAYLOR, Daria Jean, (Dari); MP (Lab) Stockton South, since 1997; *b* 13 Dec. 1944; *d* of Daniel and Phyllis Jones; *m* 1970, David Taylor; one *d*. *Educ:* Nottingham Univ. (BA Hons 1970); Durham Univ. (MA 1990). Lectr in Further Educn, Nottingham, 1970–80; part-time Lectr in Sociology and Social Policy, N Tyneside, 1986–90; Regl Educn Officer, GMB, 1990–97. Mem. (Lab) Sunderland CC, 1986–97. PPS to Parly Under Sec. of State, MoD, 2001–; Member: Defence Select Cttee, 1997–99; All Party Cancer Gp, 1998–; Chm., All Party Gp on Adoption, 2001–; Treasurer: All Party Chemical Industries Gp, 1997–; All Party Opera Gp, 1998–. Vice Chm., Westbridgford Br., NATFHE, 1970–80. *Recreations:* opera, walking, classical music, travelling. *Address:* House of Commons, SW1A 0AA. *T:* (020) 7219 4608; (office) The Old Town Hall, Mandale Road, Thornaby, Stockton-on-Tees TS17 6AW. *T:* (01642) 604546.

TAYLOR, David George Pendleton, CBE 1993; Governor of Montserrat, West Indies, 1990–93; *b* 5 July 1933; *s* of George James Pendleton Taylor and Dorothy May Taylor (*née* Williams). *Educ:* Clifton College; Clare College, Cambridge (MA). Nat. Service as Sub-Lieut (Special) RNVR, 1952–54; Admin. Officer, HMOCS Tanganyika, 1958–63; joined Booker McConnell, 1964; Chm. and Chief Exec., Bookers (Malaŵi) Ltd, 1976–77; Director: Consumer Buying Corp. of Zambia, 1978; National Drug Co., Zambia, 1978; Bookers (Zambia), 1978; Minvielle & Chastanet Ltd, St Lucia, 1979; United Rum Merchants Ltd, 1981; Estate Industries Ltd, Jamaica, 1981; seconded full time to Falkland Is Govt, Dec. 1983; Chief Exec., Falkland Islands Govt and Exec. Vice Chm., FI Devlt Corp., 1983–87 and 1988–89 (sometime acting Governor). Dir, Booker Agric. Internat., 1987–88. Member: Royal African Soc., 1986–; RIIA, 1988–. Mem., Commonwealth Election Observer Mission to Tanzania, 1995. Mem. Council, Book Aid Internat., 1996–2001. Trustee: Falklands Conservation, 1996–; Montserrat Foundn, 1997–. Governor, Clifton Coll., 1987–; Pres., Old Cliftonian Soc., 1993–95. FRGS 1990. *Recreations:* water colour painting, travel, rural France. *Address:* 53 Lillian Road, Barnes, SW13 9JF. *Clubs:* Oxford and Cambridge, Royal Commonwealth Society, MCC.

TAYLOR, David John; writer and editor; *b* 17 March 1947: *s* of John Whitfield Taylor and Alice Elaine Oldacre; *m* 1972, Ann Robinson; two *d*. *Educ:* High Sch., Newcastle-under-Lyme; Magdalene Coll., Cambridge (MA (English)). Reporter, Staffordshire Evening Sentinel, 1966; Editor, Varsity, 1969; BBC TV, Late Night Line-Up, 1969; Asst Editor, 1970–78, Dep. Editor, 1978–87, Editor, 1988, Punch; Editor: Business Life, 1988–93; Business Standards (BSI), 1996–. Columnist, Daily Telegraph. *Recreations:* bell-ringing, golf, personal computers. *Address:* Premier Magazines, Haymarket House, 1 Oxendon Street, SW1Y 4EE.

TAYLOR, David Leslie; MP (Lab and Co-op) Leicestershire North West, since 1997; *b* 22 Aug. 1946; *s* of late Leslie Taylor and of Eileen Mary Taylor; *m* 1969, Pamela (*née* Caunt); four *d* (one *s* decd). *Educ:* Ashby-de-la-Zouch Boys' Grammar Sch.; Leicester Poly.; Lanchester Poly. (CPFA); Open Univ. (BA Maths and Computing). Accountant and computer manager, Leics CC, 1977–97. Mem. (Lab) NW Leics DC, 1981–87, 1992–95. Contested (Lab) Leics NW, 1992. JP Ashby-de-la-Zouch, 1985. *Address:* House of Commons, SW1A 0AA.

TAYLOR, David William; Director of Inspection, Office for Standards in Education, since 1999; *b* 10 July 1945; *s* of Harry William Taylor and Eva Wade Taylor (*née* Day); *m* 1972, Pamela Linda (*née* Taylor); one *s* one *d*. *Educ:* Bancroft's Sch.; Worcester Coll., Oxford (BA Hons 1967; MA 1972); Inst. of Education, Univ. of London (PGCE, Distinction; Story-Miller Prize, 1968). Watford Grammar School: Classics Teacher, 1968–73; Head of Classics, 1973–78; HM Inspector of Schools, 1978–86; Staff Inspector, 1986–92; seconded to Touche Ross Management Consultants, 1991; Office for Standards in Education: Manager, Work Prog., 1992–93; Head, Strategic Planning, 1993–96; Head, Teacher Educn and Training, 1996–99. Exec. Sec., JACT, 1976–78. Schoolteacher Fellowship, Merton Coll., Oxford, 1978. *Publications:* Cicero and Rome, 1973; Work in Ancient Greece and Rome, 1975; Acting and the Stage, 1978; Roman Society, 1980; The Greek and Roman Stage, 1999; numerous articles in professional jls. *Recreations:* chess, classical (esp. choral) music, cricket, classical literature, theatre, poetry, travel, gardening, rookie golf. *Address:* Firgrove, Seal Hollow Road, Sevenoaks, Kent TN13 3SF. *T:* (01732) 455410. *Clubs:* Athenæum; Nizels Golf.

TAYLOR, David Wilson; Chairman, David Taylor Partnerships Ltd, since 2000; *b* 9 May 1950; *s* of Eric and Sybil Taylor; *m* 1980, Brenda Elizabeth Birchall; two *s*. *Educ:* Galashiels Acad.; Dundee Univ. Sch. of Architecture; Architectural Assoc. (DipArch, Dip. Urban and Regl Planning). Research and journalism, 1979–81; Advisor on regl policy to John Prescott, MP, 1981–83; Lancashire Enterprises Ltd: Dep. Man. Dir, 1983–85; Man. Dir, 1985–89; AMEC plc: Man. Dir, AMEC Regeneration, 1989–92; Man. Dir, AMEC Develts, 1992–93; Chief Exec., English Partnerships, 1993–96; Gp Chief Exec., Lancs Enterprises, subseq. Enterprise plc, 1996–2000. Director: INWARD, 1996–99; Preston North End plc, 1996–; non-executive Chairman: Vektor Ltd, 1996–; Angela Campbell Gp, 1996–98; non-exec. Director: John Maunders Gp plc, 1996–98; Central Lancs Develt Agency, 1997–2001; United Waste Services, 1997–2000; Manchester Commonwealth Games Ltd, 1999–; bookameal.com Ltd, 2000–; London and Southern Ltd, 2000–. Special Advr to Dep. Prime Minister, 1997–98. Chm., NW Film Commn, 1996–2001. Chm., Era, 1997–. Chm., Phoenix Trust, 1997–2001; Trustee, Princes Foundn, 2000–. Hon.

Fellow, Univ. of Central Lancashire, 1996. *Recreations:* football (British and American), Rugby (Union and League). *Address:* (office) Chandos House, Hill Road, Penwortham, Preston PR1 9XH. *T:* (01772) 751306. *Club:* Royal Automobile.

TAYLOR, Desmond Philip S.; *see* Shawe-Taylor.

TAYLOR, Douglas Hugh Charles, PhD; FREng; independent consultant on internal combustion engines, since 1992; *b* 4 April 1938; *s* of Richard Hugh Taylor and Alice Mary Davies; *m* 1970, Janet Elizabeth Scott; two *d.* *Educ:* King Edward VI Grammar Sch., Lichfield; Loughborough University of Technology. PhD, BTech; FREng (FEng 1987); FIMechE. Ruston & Hornsby/GEC Ruston Diesels, 1962–72, Chief Research Engineer, 1968; Ricardo Consulting Engineers, 1972–90: Head of Large Engines, 1973; Dir, 1977; Man. Dir, 1984–90; Chm., 1987–90; Gp Man. Dir, Ricardo Internat., 1990–91. Vis. Prof., Loughborough Univ., 1994–. *Recreations:* campanology, flying.
See also C. C. Taylor.

TAYLOR, Sir Edward Macmillan, (Sir Teddy), Kt 1991; MP (C) Rochford and Southend East, since 1997 (Southend East, March 1980–1997); journalist, consultant and company director; *b* 18 April 1937; *s* of late Edward Taylor and of Minnie Hamilton Taylor; *m* 1970, Sheila Duncan; two *s* one *d.* *Educ:* Glasgow High School and University (MA (Hons) Econ. and Politics). Commercial Editorial Staff of Glasgow Herald, 1958–59; Industrial Relations Officer on Staff of Clyde Shipbuilders' Assoc., 1959–64. Director: Shepherds Foods, 1968–; Ansvar (Temperance) Insurance, 1970–98. Advr, Port of London Police Fedn, 1972–. MP (C) Glasgow, Cathcart, 1964–79; Parly Under-Sec. of State, Scottish Office, 1970–71, resigned; Parly Under-Sec. of State, Scottish Office, 1974; Opposition spokesman on Trade, 1977, on Scotland affairs, 1977–79. Vice-Chm., Cons. Parly Party Home Affairs Cttee, 1992–94 (Sec., 1983–92). *Publications:* (novel) Hearts of Stone, 1968; contributions to the press. *Address:* 12 Lynton Road, Thorpe Bay, Southend-on-Sea, Essex SS1 3BE. *T:* (01702) 586282.

TAYLOR, Prof. Edwin William, FRS 1978; Louis Block Professor of Molecular Genetics and Cell Biology, University of Chicago, 1984–99, half-time, since 1999 (Professor, Department of Biophysics, 1975–99); part-time Research Professor, Department of Cell and Molecular Biology, Northwestern University Medical School, since 2000; *b* Toronto, 8 June 1929; *s* of William Taylor and Jean Taylor (*née* Christie); *m* 1956, Jean Heather Logan; two *s* one *d.* *Educ:* Univ. of Toronto (BA 1952); McMaster Univ. (MSc 1955); Univ. of Chicago (PhD 1957). Asst Prof., 1959–63, Associate Prof., 1963–67, Prof., 1967–72, Univ. of Chicago; Prof. of Biology, King's College and MRC Unit, London, 1972–74; Associate Dean, Div. of Biol Sci and Medicine, 1977–79, Prof. and Chm., Dept of Biology, 1979–84, Univ. of Chicago. Rockefeller Foundn Fellow, 1957–58; Nat. Insts of Health Fellow, 1958–59, cons. to NIH, 1970–72, 1976–80. Instructor in Physiology, Marine Biol Lab. summer program, Woods Hole, Ma, 1991–98. Member: Amer. Biochem. Soc.; Biophysical Soc.; Fellow, Amer. Acad. of Arts and Scis, 1991; NAS, USA, 2001. E. B. Wilson Medal, Amer. Soc. for Cell Biology, 1999. *Address:* Cummings Life Sciences Center, University of Chicago, 920 East 58th Street, Chicago, IL 60637, USA. *T:* (773) 7021660; 5805 South Dorchester Avenue, Apt 11C, Chicago, IL 60637, USA. *T:* (773) 9552441.

TAYLOR, Dame Elizabeth (Rosemond), DBE 2000; film actress; *b* London, 27 Feb. 1932; *d* of late Francis Taylor and Sara (*née* Sothern); *m* 1st, 1950, Conrad Nicholas Hilton, Jr (marr. diss.; he *d* 1969); 2nd, 1952, Michael Wilding (marr. diss.; he *d* 1979); two *s*; 3rd, 1957, Mike Todd (*d* 1958); one *d*; 4th, 1959, Eddie Fisher (marr. diss. 1964); 5th, 1964, Richard Burton, CBE (*d* 1984) (marr. diss.; remarried 1975; marr. diss. 1976); 7th, 1976, Senator John Warner (marr. diss. 1982); 8th, 1991, Larry Fortensky (marr. diss.). *Educ:* Byron House, Hampstead; Hawthorne School, Beverly Hills; Metro-Goldwyn-Mayer School; University High School, Hollywood. First film, There's One Born Every Minute, 1942. *Films include:* Lassie Come Home, The White Cliffs of Dover, 1943; Jane Eyre, National Velvet, 1944; Courage of Lassie, Life with Father, 1946; Cynthia, 1947; A Date With Judy, 1948; Julia Misbehaves, 1948; The Big Hangover, 1949; Father's Little Dividend, Little Women, The Conspirator, Father of the Bride, 1950; A Place in the Sun, Love is Better than Ever, 1951; Ivanhoe, 1952; Beau Brummel, Elephant Walk, Rhapsody, 1954; Last Time I Saw Paris, 1955; Giant, 1956; Raintree County, 1957; Cat on a Hot Tin Roof, 1958; Suddenly Last Summer, 1959; Holiday in Spain, Butterfield 8 (Academy Award for Best Actress), 1960; Cleopatra, The VIPs, 1963; The Sandpiper, 1965; Who's Afraid of Virginia Woolf? (Academy Award for Best Actress), 1966; The Taming of the Shrew, Doctor Faustus, 1967; Boom!, The Comedians, Reflections in a Golden Eye, Secret Ceremony, 1968; The Only Game in Town, 1970; Under Milk Wood, Zee and Co., Hammersmith is Out, 1972; Night Watch, 1973; Ash Wednesday, 1974; The Driver's Seat, Blue Bird, 1975; A Little Night Music, 1977; Winter Kills, 1979; The Mirror Crack'd, 1980; Between Friends, 1983; Young Toscanini, 1988; The Flintstones, 1994. Stage debut as Regina in The Little Foxes, NY, 1981, London stage debut, Victoria Palace, 1982; Private Lives, NY, 1983. Fellow, BAFTA, 1999. Initiated Elizabeth Taylor-Ben Gurion Univ. Fund for Children of the Negev, 1982; founded American Foundn for AIDS Res., 1985, Internat. Fund, 1985, Elizabeth Taylor AIDS Foundn, 1991. Aristotle S. Onassis Foundn Award, 1988; Humanitarian Award, American Academy, 1993. Comdr of Arts and Letters (France), 1985; Legion of Honour (France), 1987. *Publications:* (with Richard Burton) World Enough and Time, 1964; Elizabeth Taylor, 1966; Elizabeth Takes Off, 1988. *Address:* PO Box 55995, Sherman Oaks, CA 91413, USA.

TAYLOR, Enid, FRCS, FRCOphth; Consultant Ophthalmic Surgeon, North Middlesex Hospital, 1974–98; *b* 18 June 1933; *d* of Joseph William Wheldon and Jane Wheldon; *m* 1959, Thomas Henry Taylor; two *s.* *Educ:* Girton Coll., Cambridge (MA); London Hosp. Med. Coll. (MB BChir; DO). FRCS 1965; FRCOphth 1988. Consultant Ophthalmic Surgeon, Elizabeth Garrett Anderson Hosp., 1966–73. Chm., NE Thames Ophthalmic Adv. Cttee, DHSS, 1979–86. Member Council: Faculty of Ophthalmologists, 1980-88; Coll. of Ophthalmologists, 1988–90; Sect. Ophthalmol, RSocMed, 1981–85 (Vice-Pres., 1985–88); Mem., Ophthalmic Cttees, BMA, 1982–2000. Liveryman, 1973, Asst, 1989–, Sen. Warden, 2001–Aug. 2002, Soc. of Apothecaries. *Publications:* contrib. papers and presentations on diabetic retinal disease. *Recreations:* cooking, needlework. *Address:* 60 Wood Vale, N10 3DN. *T:* (020) 8883 6146.

TAYLOR, Eric; a Recorder of the Crown Court, 1978–98; *b* 22 Jan. 1931; *s* of Sydney Taylor and Sarah Helen (*née* Lea); *m* 1958, Margaret Jessie Taylor, *qv.* *Educ:* Wigan Grammar Sch.; Manchester Univ. (LLB 1952; Dauntesey Sen. Legal Scholar; LLM 1954). Admitted solicitor, 1955. Partner, Temperley Taylor (formerly Temperley Taylor Chadwick), Middleton, Manchester, 1957–2001, Consultant (full-time), 2001–. Part-time Lectr in Law, Manchester Univ., 1958–80, Hon. Special Lectr in Law, 1980–. Examr, (Old) Law Soc. Final Exams, 1968–81, Chief Examr, (New) Law Soc. Final Exams, 1978–83; External Examiner, Qualified Lawyers' Transfer Test, 1990–; Chief Examr for solicitors qualifying to appear as advocates, 1993–97. President: Oldham Law Assoc., 1970–72; Rochdale Law Assoc., 1998–99. Chairman: Manchester Young Solicitors' Gp, 1963; Manchester Nat. Insurance Appeal Tribunal, 1967–73; Disciplinary Cttee, Architects Registration Council, 1989–95. Member: Council, Law Soc., 1972–91 (Chm., Educn and Trng Cttee, 1980–83; Chm., Criminal Law Cttee, 1984–87); CNAA Legal Studies Bd, 1975–84; Lord Chancellor's Adv. Cttee on Trng of Magistrates, 1974–79. Governor: Coll. of Law, 1984–2000; Bd, Common Professional Examn, 1990–. *Publications:* Modern Conveyancing Precedents, 1964, 2nd edn 1989; Modern Wills Precedents, 1969, 3rd edn 1997; contrib. legal jls. *Recreations:* equestrian sports. *Address:* 10 Mercers Road, Heywood, Lancs OL10 2NP. *T:* (01706) 366630. *Club:* Farmers'.

TAYLOR, Prof. Eric Andrew, FRCP, FRCPsych, FMedSci; Professor of Child and Adolescent Psychiatry, Institute of Psychiatry, King's College Hospital, since 1999; Hon. Consultant, Maudsley Hospital, since 1978; *b* 22 Dec. 1944; *s* of Dr Jack Andrew Taylor and Grace Taylor; *m* 1969, Anne Patricia Roberts (*d* 2000); two *s.* *Educ:* Trinity Hall, Cambridge (MA); Harvard Univ.; Middx Hosp. Med. Sch. (MB). FRCP 1986; FRCPsych 1988. SHO, Middx Hosp., 1969–71; Res. Fellow, Harvard Univ., 1971; Registrar, then Sen. Registrar, Maudsley Hosp., 1973–76; Institute of Psychiatry: Lectr, then Sen. Lectr, 1976–86; Reader, 1986–93; Prof. of Developmental Neuropsychiatry, 1993–99; Clinical Scientist, MRC, 1990–99. Ed., Jl Child Psychol. and Psychiatry, 1984–95. FMedSci 2000. Hon. Mem., child psychiatry assocs in Germany, Chile and UK. *Publications:* The Hyperactive Child: a parents' guide, 1985, 3rd edn 1997; The Overactive Child, 1986 (Spanish and Japanese edns 1991); The Epidemiology of Childhood Hyperactivity, 1991; (ed jtly) Child and Adolescent Psychiatry: modern approaches, 3rd edn 1994, 4th edn 2001; contrib. numerous papers to scientific jls on child neuropsychiatry. *Address:* Department of Child and Adolescent Psychiatry, Institute of Psychiatry, King's College London, De Crespigny Park, SE5 8AF. *T:* (020) 7848 0488. *Club:* Royal Society of Medicine.

TAYLOR, Floella; *see* Benjamin, F.

TAYLOR, Frank Henry; Principal, Frank H. Taylor & Co., City of London, Chartered Accountants; *b* 10 Oct. 1907; 2nd *s* of George Henry Taylor, Cambridgeshire; *m* 1936, Margaret Dora Mackay (*d* 1944), Invernesshire; one *d*; *m* 1948, Mabel Hills (*d* 1974), Hertfordshire; two *s*; *m* 1978, Glenys Mary Edwards, MBE, Bethesda, N Wales. *Educ:* Rutlish School, Merton, Surrey. FCIS 1929; FCA 1930. Commenced in practice as Chartered Accountant, 1930; Ministry of Food Finance Director of Tea, Coffee, Cocoa and Yeast, 1942; Min. of War Transport Finance Rep. overseas, 1944; visited over 40 countries on financial and political missions. Lt-Colonel comdg 1st Caernarvonshire Bn Home Guard, 1943. Contested (C) Newcastle under Lyme, 1955, Chorley, 1959; MP (C) Manchester, Moss Side, Nov. 1961–Feb. 1974. Governor of Rutlish School, 1951–89. Liveryman, City of London; Master, Bakers' Co., 1981–82; Mem. Ct, Worshipful Co. of World Traders (formerly Co. of World Traders), 1982–. Mem., GAPAN. *Publication:* Called to Account (autobiog.), 1993. *Recreations:* numerous including Rugby (for Surrey County), sculling (Thames Championship), punting (several Thames championships), golf (Captain RAC 1962). *Address:* 4 Barrie House, Lancaster Gate, W2 3QJ. *T:* (020) 7262 5684. *Clubs:* City Livery, Royal Automobile, Dinosaurs.

TAYLOR, Dr Frank Henry; Secretary, Charles Wallace India Trust, since 1992; *b* 20 Jan. 1932; *s* of Frank Taylor and Norah (*née* Dunn). *Educ:* Frimley and Camberley Co. Grammar Sch.; King's Coll., London (BSc 1953; PhD 1957). Beit Meml Fellow for Med. Res., Imperial Coll., London and Pasteur Inst., Paris, 1957–60; British Council, 1960–92: Science Officer, 1960–61; Asst Cultural Attaché, Cairo, 1961–64; Asst Regl Rep., Calcutta, 1965–69; Science Officer, Rio de Janeiro, 1970–74; Dir, Science and Technology Dept, 1974–78; Rep., Saudi Arabia, 1978–81; Head Operations, Technical Educn and Trng in Overseas Countries, and Dep. Controller, Science, Technology and Education Div., 1981–84; Counsellor, British Council and Cultural Affairs, Ankara, 1984–87; Dep. Controller, Asia and Pacific Div., then S and W Asia Div., 1987–88; Controller, Africa and ME Div., 1989–90; Dir, Libraries, Books and Inf. Div., 1990–92. *Publications:* articles on surface chemistry and reviews in Proc. Royal Soc., etc. *Recreations:* music, bridge, bookbinding, Middle East. *Address:* 9 Shaftesbury Road, Richmond, Surrey TW9 2TD.

TAYLOR, Prof. Fredric William, DPhil; Halley Professor of Physics, since 1999, Head of Department of Atmospheric, Oceanic and Planetary Physics, 1979–2000, Oxford University; Fellow, Jesus College, Oxford, since 1979; *b* 24 Sept. 1944; *s* of William Taylor and Ena Lloyd (*née* Burns); *m* 1969, Doris Jean Buer. *Educ:* Duke of Northumberland's Sch.; Univ. of Liverpool (BSc 1966); Univ. of Oxford (DPhil 1970; MA 1983). Resident Res. Associate, US Nat. Res. Council, 1970–72; Sen. Scientist, Jet Propulsion Lab., CIT, 1972–79; Oxford University: Reader in Atmospheric Physics, 1983–89; Prof. of Atmospheric Physics, 1990–99. *Publications:* Cambridge Atlas of the Planets, 1982, 2nd edn 1986 (trans. German 1984, Italian 1988); Remote Sounding of Atmospheres, 1984, 2nd edn 1987; contrib. to learned jls. *Recreations:* walking, theatre, poker, literature, history, railways. *Address:* Clarendon Laboratory, Oxford OX1 3PU; Jesus College, Oxford OX1 3DW. *T:* (01865) 272903.

TAYLOR, Geoffrey H.; *see* Handley-Taylor.

TAYLOR, Geoffrey William, FCIB; Chairman, Private and Commercial Finance Group (formerly The Asset Management Corporation) PLC, since 1995; *b* 4 Feb. 1927; *s* of late Joseph William and Doris Taylor; *m* 1951, Joyce (*née* Walker); three *s* one *d.* *Educ:* Heckmondwike Grammar School; Univ. of London. BComm. Joined Midland Bank Ltd, 1943; Gen. Man. and Man. Dir, Midland Bank Finance Corp. Ltd, 1967–76; Asst Chief General Manager, 1974–80, Dep. Group Chief Exec., 1980–82, Group Chief Exec., 1982–86, Dir, 1982–87, Vice-Chm., 1986–87, Midland Bank Plc; Chm., Daiwa Europe Bank, 1987–94. Dir, Y. J. Lovell (Hldgs), 1987–96; Chairman: Fosters Trading Co. (formerly Foster Brother Menswear), 1992–98; Atkins Hldgs, 1994–2000. Mem., Internat. Adv. Council, Wells Fargo & Co., 1987–95. Mem., Banking Law Review, (Jack), Cttee, 1987–90. *Recreations:* golf, reading, music. *Address:* Private and Commercial Finance Group PLC, 15 Great College Street, SW1P 3RX. *Club:* Burhill Golf.

TAYLOR, Sir Godfrey; *see* Taylor, Sir A. G.

TAYLOR, Gordon; Chief Executive, Professional Footballers' Association, since 1981; *b* 28 Dec. 1944; *s* of Alec and Mary Taylor; *m* 1968, Catharine Margaret Johnston; two *s.* *Educ:* Ashton-under-Lyne Grammar Sch.; Bolton Technical Coll.; Univ. of London (BScEcon Hons (ext.)). Professional footballer with: Bolton Wanderers, 1960–70; Birmingham City, 1970–76; Blackburn Rovers, 1976–78; Vancouver Whitecaps (N American Soccer League), 1977; Bury, 1978–80, retd. Professional Footballers Association: Mem., Management Cttee, 1971; Chm., 1978–80; (full-time) Asst Sec., 1980; Sec./Treasurer, 1981; Pres., Internat. Assoc. of Professional Footballers Unions, 1994–. Hon. MA Loughborough Univ. of Technol., 1986 (for services to football); Hon. DArts De Montfort, 1998. *Recreations:* theatre, dining-out, watching football, reading. *Address:* (office) 20 Oxford Court, Bishopsgate, Manchester M2 3WQ. *T:* (0161) 236 0575.

TAYLOR, Dr Gordon William; Managing Director, Firemarket Ltd, since 1988; *b* 26 June 1928; *s* of William and Elizabeth Taylor; *m* 1954, Audrey Catherine Bull; three *s* two *d*. *Educ:* J. H. Burrows Sch., Grays, Essex; Army Apprentice Sch.; London Univ. (BScEng Hons, PhDEng). MICE, MIMechE, AMIEE. Kellogg Internat. Corp., 1954–59; W. R. Grace, 1960–62; Gen. Man., Nalco Ltd, 1962–66; BTR Industries, 1966–68; Managing Director: Kestrel Chemicals, 1968–69; Astral Marketing, 1969–70; Robson Refractories, 1970–87. Greater London Council: Alderman, 1972–77; Mem. for Croydon Central, 1977–80; Chairman: Public Services Cttee, 1977–78; London Transp. Cttee, 1978–79. *Recreations:* theatre, reading, tennis. *Address:* 33 Royal Avenue, Chelsea, SW3 4QE. *Club:* Holland Park Lawn Tennis.

TAYLOR, Graham; Manager, Watford Football Club, 1977–87 and 1996–2001; *b* Worksop, Notts, 15 Sept. 1944; *s* of Tommy Taylor; *m* 1965, Rita Cowling; two *d*. *Educ:* Scunthorpe Grammar Sch. Professional football player: Grimsby Town, 1962–68; Lincoln City, 1968–72; Manager: Lincoln City, 1972–77; Aston Villa, 1987–90; England Football Team, 1990–93; Wolverhampton Wanderers, 1994–95.

TAYLOR, Hamish Wilson; Chief Executive, Sainsbury's Bank, since 2000; *b* Kitwe, N Rhodesia, 18 June 1960; *s* of late Dr Douglas James Wilson Taylor and of Mairi Helen Taylor (*née* Pitt); *m* 1984, Fiona Marion Darroch; three *s*. *Educ:* Skinners' Sch., Tunbridge Wells; Univ. of St Andrews (Pres., Athletic Union, 1981–82; MA Hons Econs 1982); Emory Univ., Atlanta (Robert T. Jones Schol., 1983; Business Sch. Fellow; St Andrews Soc of Washington Schol., 1983–84; MBA 1984). FCIT 1999. Brand Manager, Procter and Gamble Ltd, 1984–90; Mgt Consultant, Price Waterhouse, 1990–93; Gen. Manager, Brands, British Airways, 1993–97; Man. Dir, Eurostar (UK) Ltd, 1997–99; Chief Exec., Eurostar Gp, 1999. FRSA 1999. Freeman, City of Glasgow, 1979. Rail Professional Business Manager of the Year, Rail Professional Magazine, 1998. *Recreations:* athletics (Scottish Junior international, 1979), football, piano. *Address:* c/o Sainsbury's Bank, Keith House, Redheughs Rigg, South Gyle Crescent, Edinburgh EH12 9DQ. *T:* (0131) 442 5000.

TAYLOR, Henry George; DSc(Eng); Director of Electrical Research Association, 1957–69, retired; *b* 4 Nov. 1904; *m* 1931, Gwendolyn Hilda Adams; one *s* two *d*. *Educ:* Taunton School; Battersea Polytechnic Inst., City and Guilds Engineering College. Metropolitan Vickers, 1929–30; Electrical Research Assoc., 1930–38; Copper Development Assoc., 1938–42; Philips Lamps Ltd, 1942–47; British Welding Research Assoc., 1947–57. *Publications:* contribs to: Instn of Electrical Engineers Jl, Jl of Inst. of Physics, etc. *Recreation:* walking.

TAYLOR, Hugh Henderson, CB 2000; Director of External and Corporate Affairs, Department of Health, since 2001; *b* 22 March 1950; *s* of late Leslie Henderson Taylor and of Alison Taylor; *m* 1989, Diane Bacon; two *d*. *Educ:* Brentwood Sch.; Emmanuel Coll., Cambridge (BA). Joined Home Office, 1972; Private Sec. to Minister of State, 1976–77; Principal Private Sec. to Home Sec., 1983–85; Asst Sec., 1984; Prison Service, 1985–88 and 1992–93; seconded to Cabinet Office, 1988–91; Under Sec, 1993–96, and Dir, Top Mgt Prog., 1994–96, Cabinet Office; Dir of Services, Prison Service, 1996–97; Dir of Human Resources, NHS Exec., DoH, 1998–2001. *Recreations:* arts, sport. *Address:* c/o Department of Health, Richmond House, 79 Whitehall, SW1A 2NS. *Club:* MCC.

TAYLOR, Rt Rev. Humphrey Vincent; *see* Selby, Bishop Suffragan of.

TAYLOR, Ian Colin, MBE 1974; MP (C) Esher and Walton, since 1997 (Esher, 1987–97); *b* 18 April 1945; *s* of late Horace Stanley Taylor and Beryl Taylor (*née* Harper); *m* 1974, Hon. Carole Alport, *d* of Baron Alport, PC, TD; two *s*. *Educ:* Whitley Abbey Sch., Coventry; Keele Univ. (BA); London School of Economics (Res. Schol.). Corporate financial adviser; Director: Mathercourt Securities Ltd, 1980–90; Hudson Venture Partners, 1997–2000. Nat. Chm., Fedn of Cons. Students, 1968–69; Chm., Europ. Union of Christian Democratic and Cons. Students, 1969–70; Hon. Sec., Brit. Cons. Assoc. in France, 1976–78; Chairman: Commonwealth Youth Exchange Council, 1980–84; Cons. Foreign and Commonwealth Council, 1990–96; Nat. Chm., Cons. Gp for Europe, 1985–88. Contested (C) Coventry SE, Feb. 1974. Parliamentary Private Secretary: FCO, 1990; to Sec. of State for Health, 1990–92; to Chancellor of Duchy of Lancaster, 1992–94; Parly Under-Sec. of State, DTI, 1994–97 (for Trade and Technol., 1994–95; for Sci. and Technol., 1995–97); opposition front bench spokesman on NI, 1997. Member, Select Committee on: Foreign Affairs, 1987–90; Science and Technol., 1998–. Chm., Cons. Parly European Affairs Cttee, 1988–89. Vice-Chm., Assoc. of Cons. Clubs, 1988–92. Gov., Research into Ageing, 1997–2001. AIIMR 1972; FInstD 1983. Freeman, Co. of Information Technologists, 1998–. *Publications:* various pamphlets; contrib. to various jls, etc, on politics and business. *Recreations:* cricket, opera, cigars, shooting. *Address:* House of Commons, SW1A 0AA. *T:* (020) 7219 5221; *e-mail:* taylori@parliament.uk. *Clubs:* Buck's, Royal Commonwealth Society.

TAYLOR, Prof. Ian Galbraith, CBE 1987; MD; FRCP, FRCPCH; Ellis Llwyd Jones Professor of Audiology and Education of the Deaf, University of Manchester, 1964–88, now Emeritus; *b* 24 April 1924; *s* of David Oswald Taylor, MD, and Margaret Ballantine Taylor; *m* 1954, Audrey Wolstenholme; two *d*. *Educ:* Manchester Grammar Sch.; Univ. of Manchester (MB, ChB, DPH; MD (Gold Medal) 1963). MRCP 1973, FRCP 1977; FRCPCH 1997. Ho. Surg., Manchester Royal Infirm., 1948; DAD, Army Health of N Regional Canal Zone, and OC Army Sch. of Hygiene, ME, 1949–51; Asst MO, City of Manchester, 1951–54. Univ. of Manchester: Hon. Special Lectr and Ewing Foundn Fellow, Dept of Education of the Deaf, 1956–60; Lectr in Clinical Audiology, 1963–64. Consultant in Audiological Medicine, United Manchester Hosps, 1968. Pres., Hearing Concern (formerly British Assoc. of the Hard of Hearing), 1981–. *Publication:* Neurological Mechanisms of Hearing and Speech in Children, 1964. *Recreations:* gardening, fishing. *Address:* Croft Cottage, Cinderhill, Whitegate, Northwich, Cheshire CW8 2BH.

TAYLOR, Prof. Irving, MD; FRCS; Professor of Surgery, University College London, and Chairman, Academic Division of Surgical Specialties and Head of Department, Royal Free and University College Medical School (formerly University College London Medical School), since 1993; *b* 7 Jan. 1945; *s* of Sam and Fay Taylor; *m* 1969, Berenice Penelope Brunner; three *d*. *Educ:* Roundhay Sch., Leeds; Sheffield Univ. Med. Sch. (MB ChB 1968; MD 1973; ChM 1978). FRCS 1972. Royal Infirmary, then Royal Hospital, Sheffield: House Officer, 1968; SHO, 1969–70; Surg. Registrar, 1971–73; Sen. Registrar in Surgery, 1973–77; Sen. Lectr and Consultant Surgeon, Liverpool Univ., 1977–81; Prof. of Surgery, Univ. of Southampton, 1981–93. Hunterian Prof., RCS, 1981 (Jacksonian Award, 1996; Stanford Cade Medal, 2000); Bennett Lectr, TCD, 1990; Gordon Bell Lectr, RACS, 1996. Examnr, RCS, 2000–01. Chm., MRC Colorectal Cancer Cttee, 1990–95; Pres., British Assoc. of Surgical Oncology, 1995–98; Sec., Surgical Res. Soc., 1988–90; Editorial Sec., Assoc. of Surgeons, 1988–91. Ed.-in-Chief, Eur. Jl of Surgical Oncology, 1995–. FRSocMed 1983; FMedSci 2000. *Publications:* Progress in Surgery, 1985, 3rd edn 1989; Complications of Surgery of the Gastrointestinal Tract, 1985; Benign Breast Disease, 1990; Essential General Surgical Oncology, 1995; Surgical Principles, 1996; Recent Advances in Surgery, annually, 1991–; Fast Facts: colorectal cancer, 1999; articles and papers on gen. surgery, surgical educn, surgical oncology, breast, colorectal and liver cancer in med. jls. *Recreations:* bridge, swimming, rambling, watching cricket, travel, supporting Leeds United. *Address:* 43 Ridgeway Gardens, Hornsey Lane, Highgate, N6 5NH. *T:* (020) 7263 8086.

TAYLOR, His Honour Ivor Ralph; QC 1973; a Circuit Judge, 1976–94; *b* 26 Oct. 1927; *s* of late Abraham and Ruth Taylor; *m* 1st, 1954, Ruth Cassel (marr. diss. 1974); one *s* one *d* (and one *d* decd); 3rd, 1984, (Audrey) Joyce Goldman (*née* Wayne). *Educ:* Stand Grammar Sch., Whitefield; Manchester Univ. Served War of 1939–45, AC2 in RAF, 1945. Called to Bar, Gray's Inn, 1951. Standing Counsel to Inland Revenue, N Circuit, 1969–73; a Recorder of the Crown Court, 1972–76. Chm., Inquiry into Death of Baby Brown at Rochdale Infirmary, 1974. Chm., PTA, Dept of Audiology, Manchester Univ., 1966–67. Pres., Manchester and District Medico Legal Soc., 1974, 1975. Gov., Royal Manchester Children's Hosp., 1967–70; Mem. Management Cttee, Salford Hosp., 1967–70.

TAYLOR, Dr James; Geographical Director, Africa, Middle East and South Asia, British Council, since 2000; *b* 22 April 1951; *s* of George Thomson Taylor and Elizabeth Gibson Taylor (*née* Dunsmore); *m* 1986, Dianne Carol Cawthorne; one *s*. *Educ:* Cumnock Acad.; Strathclyde Univ. (BSc 1973; PhD 1977). ACS Petroleum Res. Fellow, Bristol Univ., 1977–78; von Humboldt Fellow, Univ. des Saarlandes, Germany, 1978–79; Res. Chemist, Proctor & Gamble, 1979–80; SSO, Scottish Marine Biol Assoc., 1980–84; British Council: Asst Dir, Kuwait, 1984–86; First Sec. (Sci. and Develt), British High Commn, Calcutta, 1986–88; Head, Tech. Adv. Service, Sci. and Technol. Dept, 1988–90; Asst Registrar, Res. Support Unit, Leeds Univ., 1990–92; Development and Training Services, British Council: Contract Dir, Central and Eastern Europe, 1992–93; Head, Europe Gp, 1993–95; Head, Africa and ME Gp, 1995–97; Dir, Zimbabwe and Head, Africa Gp, 1997–2000. *Publications:* contribs on marine sediment chem. to sci. jls. *Recreations:* gardening, TV soaps, walking. *Address:* British Council, 10 Spring Gardens, SW1A 2BN. *T:* (020) 7389 4705.

TAYLOR, Dame Jean (Elizabeth); *see* Dowling, Dame J. E.

TAYLOR, Jessie; *see* Taylor, M. J.

TAYLOR, Rt Rev. John Bernard, KCVO 1997; Bishop of St Albans, 1980–95; Lord High Almoner to HM the Queen, 1988–97; Hon. Assistant Bishop: diocese of Ely, since 1995; diocese of Europe, since 1998; *b* 6 May 1929; *s* of George Ernest and Gwendoline Irene Taylor; *m* 1956, Linda Courtenay Barnes; one *s* two *d*. *Educ:* Watford Grammar Sch.; Christ's Coll., Cambridge; Jesus Coll., Cambridge. MA Cantab. Vicar of Henham and Elsenham, Essex, 1959–64; Vice-Principal, Oak Hill Theological Coll., 1964–72; Vicar of All Saints', Woodford Wells, 1972–75; Archdeacon of West Ham, 1975–80. Examining Chaplain to Bishop of Chelmsford, 1962–80. Hon. Chaplain, Jesus Coll., Cambridge, 1997–. Chm., Gen. Synod's Cttee for Communications, 1986–93. Member: Churches' Council for Covenanting, 1978–82; Liturgical Commn, 1981–86; Doctrine Commn, 1989–95. Chairman Council: Haileybury Coll., 1980–95; Wycliffe Hall, Oxford, 1985–99; Tyndale House, Cambridge, 1997–. President: Hildenborough Evangelistic Trust, 1985–99; Garden Tomb Assoc., Jerusalem, 1986–; Church's Ministry among Jewish People, 1996–; Bible Soc., 1997–. Took his seat in House of Lords, 1985. Hon. LLD Hertfordshire, 1995. *Publications:* A Christian's Guide to the Old Testament, 1966; Evangelism among Children and Young People, 1967; Tyndale Commentary on Ezekiel, 1969; Preaching through the Prophets, 1983; Preaching on God's Justice, 1994. *Address:* 22 Conduit Head Road, Cambridge CB3 0EY. *T:* (01223) 313783. *Club:* National.

TAYLOR, Rev. John Brian, PhD; Chairman, Liverpool District, Methodist Church, since 1995; *b* 3 July 1937; *s* of Frank and Alice Taylor; *m* 1959, Patricia Margaret Lord; two *s*. *Educ:* Buxton Coll.; Durham Univ. (BA, DipEd); Hartley Victoria Coll. and Manchester Univ. (BD); PhD Open Univ. 1992. Headmaster, Cours Secondaire Protestant de Dabou, Côte d'Ivoire, 1961–64; Methodist Minister, 1964–; Chaplain, Univ. of Sheffield, 1976–79; Tutor, Queen's Coll., Birmingham, 1979–88 (Fellow, 2001); Gen. Sec., Methodist Church Div. of Ministries, 1988–95; Pres., Methodist Conf., 1997–98. Commandeur: l'Ordre National (Côte d'Ivoire), 1997; l'Ordre du Mono (Togo), 2000. *Publications:* various articles in learned jls. *Recreations:* geneaology, gardening, music. *Address:* 49 Queen's Drive, Mossley Hill, Liverpool L18 2DT. *T:* and *Fax:* (0151) 722 1219.

TAYLOR, Prof. John Bryan, FRS 1970; Fondren Professor of Plasma Theory, University of Texas at Austin, 1989–94; *b* 26 Dec. 1928; *s* of Frank and Ada Taylor, Birmingham; *m* 1951, Joan M. Hargest; one *s* one *d*. *Educ:* Oldbury Grammar Sch.; Birmingham Univ., 1947–50 and 1952–55. RAF, 1950–52. Atomic Weapons Research Establishment, Aldermaston, 1955–59 and 1960–62; Harkness Fellow, Commonwealth Fund, Univ. of California (Berkeley), 1959–60; Culham Laboratory (UKAEA), 1962–69 and 1970–89 (Head of Theoretical Physics Div., 1963–81; Chief Physicist, 1981–89); Inst. for Advanced Study, Princeton, 1969. FInstP 1969. Fellow, Amer. Phys. Soc., 1984. Maxwell Medal, IPPS, 1971; Max Born Medal, German Phys. Soc., 1979; Award for Excellence in Plasma Physics Res., 1986, James Clerk Maxwell Prize, 1999, Amer. Phys. Soc.; Dist. Career Award, Fusion Power Associates, 1999. *Publications:* contribs to scientific learned jls. *Recreations:* gliding, model engineering. *Address:* Radwinter, Winterbrook Lane, Wallingford OX10 9EJ. *T:* (01491) 837269.

TAYLOR, John Charles; QC 1983; *b* 22 April 1931; *s* of late Sidney Herbert and Gertrude Florence Taylor, St Ives, Cambs; *m* 1964, Jean Aimée Monteith; one *d*. *Educ:* Palmers Sch., Grays, Essex; Queens' Coll., Cambridge (MA, LLB); Harvard Law School (LLM). Called to the Bar, Middle Temple, 1958. Mem., Stephens Cttee on Minerals Planning Control, 1972–74. Contested (C) Kettering, 1970. *Recreations:* country pursuits, art, boardsailing, motorcycling. *Address:* Clifton Grange, Clifton, Shefford, Beds SG17 5EW. *Clubs:* Athenæum, Travellers.

TAYLOR, John Clayton, PhD; FRS 1981; FInstP; Professor of Mathematical Physics, Cambridge University, and Fellow of Robinson College, Cambridge, 1980–95, now Professor and Fellow Emeritus; *b* 4 Aug. 1930; *s* of Leonard Taylor and Edith (*née* Tytherleigh); *m* 1959, Gillian Mary (*née* Schofield); two *s*. *Educ:* Selhurst Grammar Sch., Croydon; Cambridge Univ. (MA). Lectr, Imperial Coll., London, 1956–60; Lectr, Cambridge Univ., and Fellow of Peterhouse, 1960–64; Reader in Theoretical Physics, Oxford Univ., and Fellow of University Coll., Oxford, 1964–80 (Hon. Fellow, 1989). *Publications:* Gauge Theories of Weak Interactions, 1976; Hidden Unity in Nature's Laws, 2001. *Address:* 9 Bowers Croft, Cambridge CB1 8RP.

TAYLOR, John D.; *see* Debenham Taylor.

TAYLOR, John Derek, CBE 1992; Deputy Chairman, Conservative Party, and Chairman, National Conservative Convention, since 2000; *b* 12 Nov. 1943; *s* of late Percy

Otto Taylor and of Ethel Taylor (*née* Brocklehurst); *m* 1968, Julia Aileen Cunnington, *d* of late Leslie and Evelyn Cunnington, Bedford; two *s*. *Educ:* Holbeach Primary Sch.; St Felix Sch., Felixstowe; Bedford Sch. Dir, family horticultural and farming businesses, 1968–. Dir, 1990–, Chm., 2000–, Springfields Horticl Soc. Ltd, and associated cos. Chairman: EC Working Party on European Bulb Industry, 1982; NFU Bulb Sub-cttee, 1982–87. Governor: Glasshouse Crops Res. Inst., 1984–88; Inst. of Horticl Res., 1987–90; Mem., Horticl Develt Council, 1986–91. Member, Minister of Agriculture's Regional Panel: Eastern Reg., 1990–92; E Midlands Reg., 1992–96. Chm., Holbeach and E Elloe Hosp. Charitable Trust, 1989–; Trustee, Brogdale Horticl Trust, 1998–. Member: Lincoln Diocesan Bd of Finance, 1995–2001; Lincoln Diocesan Synod, 1997–2001. East Midlands Conservative Council: Mem., Exec. Cttee, 1966–98; Hon. Treas., 1984–89; Chm., 1989–94; Mem., Cons. Bd of Finance, 1985–89; Mem., Cons. Bd of Mgt, 1996–98; National Union of Conservative Associations: Member: Exec. Cttee, 1966–68 and 1984–98; Gen. Purposes Cttee, 1988–98; Standing Rev. Cttee, 1988–98; Agents Employment Adv. Cttee, 1988–94; Agents Exam Bd, 1994–98; Vice Pres., 1994–97; Pres. and Cons. Conf. Chm., 1997–98; Chm., Cons. Party Constitutional Review, 1998–2000. Founder Chm., local Young Cons. Br., 1964; Mem., Holland with Boston Cons. Assoc., 1964–95 (formerly Treas., Vice Chm., Chm. and Pres.); Pres., S Holland and The Deepings Cons. Assoc., 1995–2001, now Patron. Contested (C): Chesterfield, Feb. and Oct. 1974; Nottingham, EP elections, 1979. Editor, In Touch with the National Union, 1993–96. FRSA 1994. *Publication:* (ed) Taylor's Bulb Book, 1994. *Recreations:* English landscape and vernacular buildings, travel, particularly in France, literature, arts, music. *Address:* Conservative Party, 32 Smith Square, SW1P 3HH. *Club:* Farmers'.

TAYLOR, John Edward; Chief Executive, Advisory, Conciliation and Arbitration Service, since 2001; *b* 14 Nov. 1949; *s* of Thomas Taylor and Margaret Jane Taylor (*née* Renwick); *m* 1977, Valerie Joan Ticehurst (marr. diss. 1982). *Educ:* Chester-le-Street Grammar Sch.; Durham Univ. (BA Gen. Arts). Department of Employment: various posts as Exec. Officer, 1972–79; Private Sec. to Minister of State, 1979–80; Head: of Personnel, 1980–83; of Res. Br., 1983–84; Regl Employment Manager, Midlands, 1984–86; Hd, Overseas Labour Div., 1986–88; Dep. Chief Exec., Rural Develt Commn, 1988–95; Chief Executive: Develt Bd for Rural Wales, 1995–98; SE Wales TEC, 1998–2001. German Marshall Fellowship Schol., USA, 1986. Vis. Prof. for Employment Relns, Glamorgan Univ., 2001–. Mem., UK Delegn to USSR on SME Develt, 1991. *Recreations:* Sunderland AFC, all sport, CAMRA, travel. *Address:* ACAS, Brandon House, 180 Borough High Street, SE1 1LW; Dol-y-Dderwen, Pont Robert, Meifod, Powys SY21 6JR. *T:* (01938) 500679. *Club:* Durham County Cricket.

TAYLOR, Prof. John Gerald; Professor of Mathematics, King's College, University of London, 1971–96, now Emeritus; *b* 18 Aug. 1931; *s* of William and Elsie Taylor; *m* Pamela Nancy (*née* Cutmore); two *s* three *d*. *Educ:* King Edward VI Grammar Sch., Chelmsford; Mid-Essex Polytechnic, Chelmsford; Christ's Coll., Cambridge. Fellow, Inst. for Advanced Study, Princeton, NJ, USA, 1956–58 (Mem., 1961–63); Fellow, Christ's Coll., Cambridge, 1958–60; Asst Lectr, Faculty of Mathematics, Univ. of Cambridge, 1959–60. Dir, Centre for Neural Networks, KCL, 1990–. Member: Inst. des Hautes Etudes Scient., Paris, 1960; Res. Inst. Advanced Study, Baltimore, Md, USA, 1960. Sen. Res. Fellow, Churchill Coll., Cambridge, 1963–64; Prof. of Physics, Rutgers Univ., New Brunswick, NJ, 1964–66; Fellow, Hertford Coll., Oxford, and Lectr, Math. Inst., Oxford, 1966–67; Reader in Particles and Fields, Queen Mary Coll., London, 1967–69; Prof. of Physics, Univ. of Southampton, 1969–71. Guest Scientist, Inst. of Medicine, Res. Centre, Juelich, Germany, 1996–99. Chm., 1982–87, Vice-Chm., 1988–91, Mathematical Physics Gp, Inst. of Physics. Chm., Jt European Neural Net Initiative, 1990–91; Convener, British Neural Networks Soc., 1989–94; President: European Neural Network Soc., 1993–94 (Vice-Pres., 1991–93); Internat. Neural Network Soc., 1995–96 (Past Pres., 1996–97); Dir, NEURONET, 1994–95. Institute of Physical and Chemical Research, Tokyo: Mem. Adv. Council, Human Sci. Frontiers Program, 1995–97; Mem. Adv. Bd, Brain Scis Inst., 1998–. European Editor-in-Chief, Neural Networks, 1991–. *Publications:* Quantum Mechanics, an Introduction, 1969; The Shape of Minds to Come, 1970; The New Physics, 1972; Black Holes: the end of the Universe?, 1973; Superminds, 1975; Special Relativity, 1975; Science and the Supernatural, 1980; The Horizons of Knowledge, 1982; Finite Superstrings, 1992; The Promise of Neural Networks, 1993; When the Clock Struck Zero, 1994; The Race for Consciousness, 1999; *edited:* Supergravity, 1981; Supersymmetry and Supergravity, 1982; Tributes to Paul Dirac, 1987; Recent Developments in Neural Computation, 1990; Coupled Oscillating Neurons, 1992; Theory and Applications of Neural Networks, 1992; Mathematical Approaches to Neural Networks, 1993; Neural Networks, 1995; Concepts for Neural Networks, 1997; also scientific papers in Proc. Royal Soc., Phys. Rev., Proc. Camb. Phil. Soc., Jl Math. Phys., Neural Networks, Neural Computation, etc. *Recreations:* listening to music, theatre, walking. *Address:* 33 Meredyth Road, Barnes, SW13 0DS. *T:* (020) 8876 3391.

TAYLOR, John H.; *see* Hermon-Taylor.

TAYLOR, John Jeffrey; FIChemE; Chief Executive, Borealis A/S, since 2001; *b* 26 Nov. 1947; *s* of F. John Taylor and M. Joan Taylor; *m* 1971, Julie Anne Oldman; three *d*. *Educ:* Hurstpierpoint Coll., Sussex; Univ. of Wales Coll. of Swansea (BSc Hons ChemEng 1969). FIChemE 1998. Exxon Chemical: London and Belgium, 1969; Product Exec. for Olefins, Connecticut, USA, 1983; European HQ Manager, Elastomers, 1985; Vice-Pres., Polymers Marketing, 1986; European Vice-Pres., Polyolefins, 1990; Chief Exec., British Nuclear Fuels plc, 1996–2000. *Recreations:* Rugby, squash, sailing, ski-ing, travel, theatre. *Address:* Overy Manor, Dorchester-on-Thames, Oxon OX10 7JU. *T:* (01865) 343069. *Club:* Royal Automobile.

TAYLOR, Sir John Lang, (Sir Jock Taylor), KCMG 1979 (CMG 1974); HM Diplomatic Service, retired; *b* 3 Aug. 1924; *y s* of Sir John William Taylor, KBE, CMG; *m* 1952, Molly, *o d* of James Rushworth; five *s* three *d*. *Educ:* Prague; Vienna; Imperial Services Coll., Windsor; Baltimore Polytechnic Inst., Md; Cornell Univ.; Trinity Coll., Cambridge. RAFVR, 1944–47 (Flt-Lt 1946). Joined HM Foreign (now Diplomatic) Service, 1949; served in: FO, 1949–50 and 1957–60; Saigon, 1950–52; Hanoi, 1951; Beirut, 1952–55; Prague, 1955–57; Montevideo, 1960–64; Bonn, 1964–69; Minister (Commercial), Buenos Aires, 1969–71; RCDS, 1972; Head of Industry, Science and Energy Dept, FCO, 1972–73; Asst Under-Sec. of State, FCO, 1973–74; Under-Sec., Dept of Energy, 1974–75; Ambassador to: Venezuela, 1975–79; the Netherlands, 1979–81; FRG, 1981–84. Non executive Chairman: Klöckner INA Ltd, 1984–92; Siemens Ltd, 1985–91; non-exec. Dir, Schering Ltd, 1985–91. Chm., Latin Amer. Trade Adv. Gp, BOTB, 1986–89. Hon. Vice Pres., Hispanic and Luso-Brazilian Councils (Canning House), 1989 (Vice-Chm., 1987; Chm., 1987–89); Trustee, Anglo-German Foundn for the Study of Industrial Soc., 1988. *Address:* 44 Danemere Street, Putney, SW15 1LT.

TAYLOR, John Mark; MP (C) Solihull, since 1983; *b* 19 Aug. 1941; *s* of Wilfred and Eileen Martha Taylor. *Educ:* Eversfield Prep. School; Bromsgrove School and College of Law. Admitted Solicitor, 1966; Senior Partner, John Taylor & Co., 1983–88. Member: Solihull County Borough Council, 1971–74; W Midlands Metropolitan County Council, 1973–86 (Opposition (Conservative) Leader, 1975–77; Leader, 1977–79). Mem., W Midlands Economic Planning Council, 1978–79. Mem. (C) Midlands E, European Parlt, 1979–84; EDG spokesman on Community Budget, 1979–81, Group Dep. Chm., 1981–82. Contested (C) Dudley East, Feb. and Oct. 1974. PPS to Chancellor of Duchy of Lancaster and Minister for Trade and Industry, 1987–88; an Asst Govt Whip, 1988–89; a Lord Comr of HM Treasury (Govt Whip), 1989–90; Vice Chamberlain of HM Household, 1990–92; Parly Sec., Lord Chancellor's Dept, 1992–95; Parly Under-Sec. of State for Competition and Consumer Affairs, DTI, 1995–97; an Opposition Whip, 1997–99; Opposition spokesman on NI, 1999–2001. Mem., Select Cttee on the Environment, 1983–87; Sec., Cons. Back bench Cttee on Eur. Affairs, 1983–86 (Vice-Chm., 1986–87); Vice-Chm., Cons. Back bench Cttee on Sport, 1986–87, on Trade and Industry, 1997, on Legal Affairs, 1997. Mem., Parly Assembly, Council of Europe and WEU, 1997. Vice-Pres., AMA, 1979–86 (Dep. Chm., 1978–79). Governor, Univ. of Birmingham, 1977–81. *Recreations:* fellowship, cricket, golf, reading. *Address:* Northampton House, Poplar Road, Solihull, West Midlands B91 3AW. *T:* (office) (0121) 704 3071. *Clubs:* Carlton, MCC.

TAYLOR, (John) Martin; Chairman, W. H. Smith Group plc, since 1999; *b* 8 June 1952; *m* 1976, Janet Davey; two *d*. *Educ:* Eton; Balliol Coll., Oxford. Reuters, 1974–78; Financial Times, 1978–82; Courtaulds plc, 1982–90 (Dir, 1987–90); Courtaulds Textiles plc, 1990–93 (Chief Exec., 1990–93; Chm., 1993); Chief Exec., Barclays plc, 1994–98. *Address:* W. H. Smith Group plc, Nations House, 103 Wigmore Street, W1H 0WH.

TAYLOR, (John) Maxwell (Percy); Chairman, Lloyd's, 1998–2000; *b* 17 March 1948; *s* of Harold Guy Percy Taylor and Anne Katherine Taylor (*née* Stafford); *m* 1970, Dawn Susan Harling; one *s* one *d*. *Educ:* Haileybury; ISC. Joined Willis Faber & Dumas, 1970; Dir, Willis Faber, then Willis Corroon Gp plc, 1990–97. Chm., Lloyd's Insce Brokers Cttee, 1997. *Recreations:* music, travel. *Club:* Royal Automobile.

TAYLOR, John Michael, OBE 1994; PhD; FRS 1998; FREng; Director General of Research Councils, Office of Science and Technology, Department of Trade and Industry, since 1999; *b* 15 Feb. 1943; *s* of Eric and Dorothy Taylor; *m* 1965, Judith Moyle; two *s* two *d*. *Educ:* Emmanuel Coll., Cambridge (MA; PhD 1969; Hon. Fellow, 2000). FIEE 1985; FBCS 1986; FREng (FEng 1986). Supt, Communication Systems Div., 1977–79, Computer Applications Div., 1979–81; RSRE; Head, Command, Control and Communications Dept, ARE, 1981–84; Dir, Hewlett-Packard Labs, Europe, 1984–98. Pres., IEE, 1998–99. FRSA; FInstP. Hon. DEng: Bristol, 1998; UWE, 1999; Surrey, 1999; Exeter, 2000; Brunel, 2000. *Recreations:* family, photography, sailing, music. *Address:* Office of Science and Technology, Department of Trade and Industry, Albany House, 94-98 Petty France, SW1H 9ST. *T:* (020) 7271 2030.

TAYLOR, Rt Rev. John Mitchell; Bishop of Glasgow and Galloway, 1991–98; Assistant Bishop of Glasgow and Galloway, since 2000; *b* 23 May 1932; *m* 1959, Edna Elizabeth (*née* Maitland); one *s* one *d*. *Educ:* Banff Acad.; Aberdeen Univ. (MA 1954); Edinburgh Theol Coll. Ordained deacon, 1956, priest, 1957; Asst Curate, St Margaret, Aberdeen, 1956–58; Rector: Holy Cross, Glasgow, 1958–64; St Ninian, Glasgow, 1964–73; St John the Evangelist, Dumfries, 1973–91; Chaplain: Crichton Royal Hospital; Dumfries and Galloway Royal Infirmary, 1973–91; Canon, St Mary's Cathedral, 1979–91, Hon. Canon, 1999–. *Recreations:* angling, hill walking, music, ornithology. *Address:* 10 St George's, Castle Douglas DG7 1LN. *T:* and *Fax:* (01556) 502593.

TAYLOR, John Russell; Art Critic, The Times, since 1978; *b* 19 June 1935; *s* of Arthur Russell and Kathleen Mary Taylor (*née* Picker). *Educ:* Dover Grammar Sch.; Jesus Coll., Cambridge (MA); Courtauld Inst. of Art, London. Sub-Editor, Times Educational Supplement, 1959; Editorial Asst, Times Literary Supplement, 1960; Film Critic, The Times, 1962–73. Lectr on Film, Tufts Univ. in London, 1970–71; Prof., Div. of Cinema, Univ. of Southern California, 1972–78. Editor, Films and Filming, 1983–90. *Publications:* Anger and After, 1962; Anatomy of a Television Play, 1962; Cinema Eye, Cinema Ear, 1964; Penguin Dictionary of the Theatre, 1966; The Art Nouveau Book in Britain, 1966; The Rise and Fall of the Well-Made Play, 1967; The Art Dealers, 1969; Harold Pinter, 1969; The Hollywood Musical, 1971; The Second Wave, 1971; David Storey, 1974; Directors and Directions, 1975; Peter Shaffer, 1975; Hitch, 1978; The Revels History of Drama in English, vol. VII, 1978; Impressionism, 1981; Strangers in Paradise, 1983; Ingrid Bergman, 1983; Alec Guinness, 1984; Vivien Leigh, 1984; Portraits of the British Cinema, 1985; Hollywood 1940s, 1985; Orson Welles, 1986; Edward Wolfe, 1986; Great Movie Moments, 1987; Post-war Friends, 1987; Robin Tanner, 1989; Bernard Meninsky, 1990; Impressionist Dreams, 1990; Liz Taylor, 1991; Ricardo Cinalli, 1993; Igor Mitoraj, 1993; Muriel Pemberton, 1993; Claude Monet, 1995; Michael Parke, 1996; Bill Jacklin, 1997; The Sun is God, 1999; Geoffrey Dashwood, 2001; Peter Coker, 2001. *Address:* c/o The Times, 1 Pennington Street, E1 9XN.

TAYLOR, Jonathan Francis; Chairman, Booker plc, 1993–98 (Chief Executive, 1984–93); *b* 12 Aug. 1935; *s* of Sir Reginald Taylor, CMG and Lady Taylor; *m* 1965, Anthea Gail Proctor; three *s*. *Educ:* Winchester College; Corpus Christi College, Oxford (Schol.; BA Mod. Hist.; MA; Hon. Fellow 1996). Joined Booker, 1959; Chm., Agricultural Div., 1976–80; Dir, Booker plc, 1980; Pres., Ibec Inc. (USA), 1980–84; Dir, Arbor Acres Farm Inc., 1980–98 (Dep. Chm., 1985–90; Chm., 1990–95). Director: Sifida Investment Bank, Geneva, 1978–90; Tate & Lyle, 1988–99; MEPC, 1992–2000; Equitable Life Assurance Soc., 1995–2001; Chm., Ellis & Everard, 1993–99. Mem., Adv. Council, UNIDO, 1986–93; Director: Foundn for Develt of Polish Agric., 1991– (Chm., 1992–99); Internat. Agribusiness Management Assoc., 1991– (Pres., 1993–94); Winrock Internat. Inst. for Agricl Develt (US), 1991–. Chm., Marshall Aid Scholarship Commn, 2000–. Chm., Governing Body, SOAS, London Univ., 1999– (Gov., 1988–); Governor: RAC, Cirencester, 1995–; Commonwealth Inst., 1998–. Co-opted Curator, Bodleian Library, 1989–97; Chairman: Bodleian Liby Develt Bd, 1989–2000; Paintings in Hosps, 1996–. *Recreations:* collecting water colours, ski-ing, travel. *Address:* 48 Edwardes Square, W8 6HH. *Club:* Brooks's.

TAYLOR, Jonathan McLeod Grigor; Director, Macroeconomic Policy and International Finance Directorate, HM Treasury, since 1998; *b* 5 March 1955; *s* of John Grigor Taylor and Dorothy Jean Taylor (*née* McLeod); *m* 1984, Stella Schimmel; one *s* one *d*. *Educ:* Bedales Sch.; New Coll., Oxford (BA PPE). HM Treasury, 1977–: Admin. trainee, 1977–79; Private Sec. to Perm. Sec., 1979–81; Principal, 1981; First Sec. (Budget), UK Perm. Rep., Brussels, 1982–84 (on secondment); Private Sec. to Chancellor of Exchequer, 1987–89; Asst Sec., 1990; Counsellor (Econ. and Financial), UK Perm. Rep., Brussels, 1994–98 (on secondment). Gov., Bedales Sch., 1998–. *Recreations:* watching football, reading crime fiction, cooking. *Address:* c/o HM Treasury, Parliament Street, SW1P 3AG.

TAYLOR, Prof. Joseph Hooton, Jr, PhD; James McDonnell Distinguished University Professor of Physics, since 1986, and Dean of the Faculty, since 1997, Princeton University (Professor of Physics, 1980–86); *b* 29 March 1941; *s* of Joseph Taylor and Sylvia Taylor (*née* Evans); *m* 1st, 1963, Alexandra Utgoff (marr. diss. 1975); one *s* one *d*; 2nd, 1976, Marietta Bisson; one *d*. *Educ:* Haverford Coll. (BA Physics 1963); Harvard Univ. (PhD Astronomy 1968). Res. Fellow and Lectr, Harvard Univ., 1968–69; University of Massachusetts, Amherst: Asst Prof. of Astronomy, 1969–72; Associate Prof., 1973–77; Prof., 1977–81. Wolf Prize in Physics, Wolf Foundn, 1982; Einstein Prize, Albert Einstein Soc., 1991; (jtly) Nobel Prize in Physics, 1993. *Publications:* (with R. N. Manchester) Pulsars, 1977; over 150 articles in jls. *Recreations:* sailing, ham radio, golf. *Address:* Department of Physics, Princeton University, PO Box 708, Princeton, NJ 08544, USA.

TAYLOR, Judy, (Julia Marie), (Judy Hough), MBE 1971; writer and publisher; *b* 12 Aug. 1932; adopted *d* of Gladys Spicer Taylor; *m* 1980, Richard Hough, writer (*d* 1999). *Educ:* St Paul's Girls' Sch. Joined The Bodley Head, 1951, specialising in children's books; Director: The Bodley Head Ltd, 1967–84 (Dep. Man. Dir, 1971–80); Chatto, Bodley Head & Jonathan Cape Ltd, 1973–80; Chatto, Bodley Head & Jonathan Cape Australia Pty Ltd, 1977–80. Publishers Association: Chm., Children's Book Gp, 1969–72; Mem. Council, 1972–78; Member: Book Develt Council, 1973–76; Unicef Internat. Art Cttee, 1968–70, 1976, 1982–83; UK Unicef Greeting Card Cttee, 1982–85. Consultant to Penguin (formerly to Frederick Warne) on Beatrix Potter, 1981–87, 1989–92; Associate Dir, Weston Woods Inst., USA, 1984–; Consulting Ed., Reinhardt Books, 1988–93. Chm., Beatrix Potter Soc., 1990–97, 2000–; Volunteer Reading Help: Mem., 1993–99, Chm., 1989–99, London, subseq. Inner London, Cttee; Trustee, 2000–. *Publications: children's:* Sophie and Jack, 1982; Sophie and Jack Help Out, 1983; Sophie and Jack in the Snow, 1984; Dudley and the Monster, 1986; Dudley Goes Flying, 1986; Dudley in a Jam, 1986; Dudley and the Strawberry Shake, 1986; My Dog, 1987; My Cat, 1987; Dudley Bakes a Cake, 1988; Sophie and Jack in the Rain, 1989; *non-fiction:* My First Year: a Beatrix Potter baby book, 1983; Beatrix Potter: artist, storyteller and countrywoman, 1986; That Naughty Rabbit: Beatrix Potter and Peter Rabbit, 1987; Beatrix Potter and Hawkshead, 1988; Beatrix Potter and Hill Top, 1989; (ed) Beatrix Potter's Letters: a selection, 1989; (ed) Letters to Children from Beatrix Potter, 1992; (ed) So I Shall Tell You a Story: encounters with Beatrix Potter, 1993; (ed) The Choyce Letters: Beatrix Potter to Louie Choyce 1916–1943, 1994; (ed) Beatrix Potter: a holiday diary, 1996; (ed) Beatrix Potter's Farming Friendship, 1998; (ed) Sketches for Friends, by Edward Ardizzone, 2000; *play:* (with Patrick Garland) Beatrix, 1996; numerous professional articles. *Recreations:* collecting early children's books, growing things. *Address:* 31 Meadowbank, Primrose Hill Road, NW3 3AY. *T:* (020) 7722 5663, *Fax:* (020) 7722 7750; *e-mail:* taylor.hough@talk21.com.

TAYLOR, Keith Breden, MA, DM; FRCP; Vice-Chancellor for International Development, St George's University (formerly St George's University School of Medicine), since 1998 (Vice-Chancellor, 1989–90 and 1992–98); George de Forest Barnett Professor of Medicine, Stanford University, 1966–81 and 1982–89, now Emeritus; *b* 16 April 1924; *yr s* of Francis Henry Taylor and Florence (*née* Latham); *m* 1st, 1949, Ann Gaynor Hughes Jones (*d* 1971); three *s* one *d* (and one *s* decd); 2nd, 1972, Kym Williams (*d* 1992), Adelaide, Aust. *Educ:* King's College Sch., Wimbledon; Magdalen Coll., Oxford (Exhibnr; BA Hons Physiology 1946, BM BCh 1949). Member, SHAEF Nutrition Survey Team, 1945; RAMC (Major), 1951–53; Dir Gen., Health Educn Council, 1981–82. Late Hon. Consultant, Central Middlesex Hosp.; Mem., MRC Gastroenterology Research Unit; Asst in Nuffield Dept Clin. Med., Oxford. Radcliffe Travelling Fellow, 1953; Rockefeller Foundn Fellow, 1959; Guggenheim Fellow, 1971; Fogarty Sen. Fellow, USPHS, 1978–79. Cons., US National Insts of Health; Mem., USPHS Trng Grants Cttee in Gastroenterology and Nutrition, 1965–70; Chm., Stanford Univ. Cttee on Human Nutrition, 1974–81; Vis. Professorships include: Rochester, NY, 1966; Columbia-Presbyterian, NY, 1969; Univ. of Adelaide, 1971; Academic Medical Unit, Royal Free Hosp., 1978–79. *Publications:* contribs to scientific jls, also texts, espec. in biochemistry and physiology of vitamin B12, immunological and other aspects of gastrointestinal disease and nutrition. *Recreations:* theatre, tennis, walking, gardening. *Address:* St George's International School of Medicine, Grenada, Kingdon's Yard, Parchment Street, Winchester, Hampshire SO23 8AT. *Club:* Athenæum.

TAYLOR, Kenneth, OBE 1981; FREng, FIMechE, FIEE; consultant on railway mechanical and electrical engineering; Director of Mechanical and Electrical Engineering, British Railways Board, 1977–82; *b* 29 Sept. 1921; *s* of Charles Taylor and Amy (*née* Booth); *m* 1945, Elsie Armitt; one *d*. *Educ:* Manchester Coll. of Technol. FIMechE, FIEE 1971; FREng (FEng 1981). Principal appts with British Railways: Electric Traction Engr, Manchester, 1956; Electrical Engr, LMR, 1963; Chief Mech. and Elec. Engr, LMR, 1970; Traction Engr, BR Bd HQ, 1971. *Recreations:* golf, gardening. *Address:* 137 Burley Lane, Quarndon, Derby DE22 5JS. *T:* (01332) 550123.

TAYLOR, Prof. Kenneth MacDonald, MD; FRCSE, FRCSGlas; FSAScot; British Heart Foundation Professor of Cardiac Surgery, University of London, since 1983; Professor and Chief of Cardiac Surgery, Imperial College School of Medicine (formerly Royal Postgraduate Medical School), Hammersmith Hospital, since 1983; Vice-Head, Division of Heart, Lung and Circulation, Imperial College School of Medicine, since 1997; *b* 20 Oct. 1947; *s* of late Hugh Baird Taylor and Mary Taylor; *m* 1971, Christine Elizabeth (*née* Buchanan); one *s* one *d*. *Educ:* Jordanhill College School; Univ. of Glasgow (MB ChB, MD; Cullen Medal, 1968; Gairdner Medal, 1969; Allan Hird Prize, 1969). Univ. of Glasgow: Hall Fellow in Surgery, 1971–72, Lectr and Sen. Lectr in Cardiac Surgery, 1975–83; Consultant Cardiac Surgeon, Royal Infirmary and Western Infirmaries, Glasgow, 1979–83. Vis. Prof., Dept of Bio-engineering, Univ. of Strathclyde, 1997–. Chm., Specialist Adv. Cttee in Cardiothoracic Surgery, 1992–95 (Mem., 1986–92); Dir, UK Heart Valve Registry, 1986–; Clin. Dir, UK Sch. of Perfusion Science, 1987–. Member: Exec. Cttee, Soc. of Cardiothoracic Surgeons of GB and Ire., 1992–95; Wkg Gp on Cardiac Waiting Times, DoH, 1994–95; Central R & D Cttee, Acute Sector Panel, DoH, 1996–; Reference Gp, Nat. Service Framework, Coronary Heart Disease, DoH, 1999–; Chairman: Database Cttee, European Assoc. for Cardiothoracic Surgery, 1994–; UK Cardiac Audit Steering Gp, 1994–. FESC 1995; FECTS 1998 (Mem., 1988); Member: British Cardiac Soc., 1983–; Amer. Soc. of Thoracic Surgeons, 1984–; Hon. Member: Amer. Acad. of Cardiovascular Perfusion, 1993; Amer. Assoc. for Thoracic Surgery, 1998 (Mem., 1988–98; Honoured Guest, 1998); Soc. of Perfusionists of GB and Ire., 1998 (Pres., 1989–93; Hon. Life Mem., 1999). Hon. Alumnus, Cleveland Clinic, USA, 2000. Governor, Drayton Manor High Sch., London, 1989–96. Editor, Perfusion, 1986–; Member, Advisory Editorial Board: Annals of Thoracic Surgery, 1990–; Jl of Cardiovascular Anaesthesia, 1993–; Jl of Heart Valve Disease, 1993–. Peter Allen Prize, Soc. of Thoracic and Cardiovascular Surgeons, 1975; Patey Prize, Surgical Res. Soc., 1977; Fletcher Prize, RCSG, 1977; Watson Prize, RCSG, 1982. *Publications:* Pulsatile Perfusion, 1979, 2nd edn 1982; Handbook of Intensive Care, 1984; Cardiopulmonary Bypass, 1986; Cardiac Surgery, 1987; Principles of Surgical Research, 1989, 2nd edn 1995; The Brain and Cardiac Surgery, 1992; numerous articles on cardiac surgery. *Recreations:* family, church, music. *Address:* 129 Argyle Road, Ealing, W13 0DB.

TAYLOR, Kim; *see* Taylor, L. C.

TAYLOR, Prof. Laurence John, (Laurie); Professor of Sociology, University of York, 1974–93; *s* of Stanley Douglas Taylor and Winifred Agnes (*née* Cooper); marr. diss.; one *s*. *Educ:* St Mary's Coll., Liverpool; Rose Bruford College of Drama, Kent; Birkbeck Coll., Univ. of London (BA); Univ. of Leicester (MA). Librarian, 1952–54; Sales Asst, 1954–56; Professional Actor, 1960–61; English Teacher, 1961–64; Lectr in Sociology, 1965–73, Reader in Sociology, 1973–74, Univ. of York. Vis. Prof., 1994–, Fellow, 1996–, Birkbeck Coll., Univ. of London. *Publications:* Deviance and Society, 1971; (jtly) Psychological Survival, 1972; (jtly) Crime, Deviance and Socio-Legal Control, 1972; (ed jtly) Politics and Deviance, 1973; Man's Experience of the World, 1976; (jtly) Escape Attempts, 1976, 2nd edn 1992; (jtly) Prison Secrets, 1978; (jtly) In Whose Best Interests?, 1980; In the Underworld, 1984; (jtly) Uninvited Guests, 1986; Professor Lapping Sends His Apologies, 1987; The Tuesday Afternoon Time Immemorial Committee, 1989; Laurie Taylor's Guide to Higher Education, 1994; articles, reviews, broadcasts, TV series. *Address:* 42 Witley Court, Coram Street, WC1N 1HD. *T:* (020) 7837 5996.

TAYLOR, Len Clive, (Kim); Director, Calouste Gulbenkian Foundation (UK Branch), 1982–88, retired; *b* 4 Aug. 1922; *s* of late S. R. Taylor, Calcutta, India; *m* 1951, Suzanne Dufault, Spencer, Massachusetts, USA; one *s* two *d*. *Educ:* Sevenoaks School; New College, Oxford; Chicago University. New College, Oxford; 1st Cl. Hons Mod. Hist.; Commonwealth Fund Fellowship. Assistant Master, St Paul's School, Darjeeling, India, 1940–42 and 1945–46; Indian Army Intelligence Corps, 1942–45; New College, Oxford, 1946–49; Chicago University, 1949–50; Senior History Master, Repton School, 1950–54; Headmaster, Sevenoaks School, 1954–68; Dir, Nuffield Foundn 'Resources for Learning' Project, 1966–72; Principal Administrator, Centre for Educnl Res. and Innovation, OECD, Paris, 1972–77; Head of Educnl Prog. Services, IBA, 1977–82. Comdr, Order of Henry the Navigator (Portugal), 1989. *Publications:* Experiments in Education at Sevenoaks, 1965; Resources for Learning, 1971; (ed) Camões, Epic and Lyric, 1990; (ed) They Went to Portugal Too, 1990; (ed) A Centenary Pessoa, 1995; (ed) A Companion History of Portugal, 1997. *Address:* 43 The Drive, Sevenoaks, Kent TN13 3AD. *T:* (01732) 451448.

TAYLOR, Malcolm; *see* McDowell, M.

TAYLOR, (Margaret) Jessie, OBE 1989; Headmistress, Whalley Range High School for Girls, 1976–88; *b* 30 Nov. 1924; *d* of Thomas Brown Gowland and Ann Goldie Gowland; *m* 1958, Eric Taylor, *qv*. *Educ:* Queen Elizabeth's Grammar Sch., Middleton; Manchester Univ. (BA Hons, DipEd). Jun. Classics Teacher, Cheadle Hulme Sch., 1946–49; North Manchester Grammar School for Girls: Sen. Classics Teacher, 1950; Sen. Mistress, 1963; Actg Headmistress, Jan.–July 1967; Dep. Head Teacher, Wright Robinson Comprehensive High Sch., 1967–75. Voluntary worker, UNICEF, 1988–97. Dir, Piccadilly Radio, 1979–2000. Chm., Manchester High Sch. Heads Gp, 1984–88; Member: Council and Exams Cttee, Associated Lancs Schs Examining Bd, 1976–91 (Mem. Classics Panel, 1968–72); Exams Cttee, Northern Exams Assoc., 1988–92; Nursing Educn Cttee, S Manchester Area, 1976–84; Home Office Cttee on Obscenity and Film Censorship, 1977–79; Consultant Course Tutor, NW Educnl Management Centre, Padgate, 1980–82. Mem. Court, Salford Univ., 1982–88; Gov., William Hulme's Grammar Sch., 1989–. FRSA 1980. *Recreations:* music, riding. *Address:* 10 Mercers Road, Hopwood, Heywood, Lancs OL10 2NP. *T:* (01706) 366630.

TAYLOR, Mark Christopher; Director, Museums Association, since 1989; *b* 24 Nov. 1958; *s* of Norman and June Taylor; *m* 1989, Debra Howes; two *s* one *d*. *Educ:* Loughborough Grammar Sch.; Birmingham Univ. (BA Medieval and Modern Hist.); Leeds Poly. (postgrad. Hotel Management qualification). Hotel Management, Norfolk Capital Hotels, 1981–84; Conf. Manager, Museums Assoc., 1984–89. Chairman: Network of Eur. Museum Orgns, 1998–; Campaign for Learning through Museums, 1998–; Dir, Nat. Campaign for Arts, 1999–. *Recreations:* sport, films, food. *Address:* Museums Association, 42 Clerkenwell Close, EC1R 0PA. *T:* (020) 7250 1789.

TAYLOR, Martin; *see* Taylor, J. M.

TAYLOR, Martin Gibbeson, CBE 1993; FCA; Vice Chairman, Hanson plc, 1988–95; *b* 30 Jan. 1935; *s* of late Roy G. Taylor and Vera Constance (*née* Farmer); *m* 1960, Gunilla Chatarina Bryner; two *s*. *Educ:* Haileybury; St Catharine's Coll., Cambridge (MA 1962). Company Sec., Dow Chemical (UK), 1963–69; joined Hanson plc, 1969, Dir 1976–95. Chm., National Westminster Life, 1992–2000; Dep. Chm., Charter plc, 1995–. Non-executive Director: Vickers plc, 1986–99; National Westminster Bank plc, 1990–2000; Securities Assoc., 1987–90; UGI plc, 1979–82; Millennium Chemicals Inc., 1996–. Confederation of British Industry: Mem. Council, 1981–96; Member: Companies Cttee, 1981–94 (Chm., 1990–94); City/Industry Task Force, 1987; President's Cttee, 1990–94; Steering Gp on Long Termism & Corporate Governance, 1990–92; Takeover Panel 1989–95. Mem., Industrial Develt Adv. Bd, 1993–97. Hon. Treas., Snapshot Appeal, Nat. Assoc. for Epilepsy, 1992–95. Governor, Mall Sch. Trust, 1987–2000. *Recreations:* art, books, sport, theatre. *Address:* c/o 150 Brompton Road, SW3 1HX. *T:* (020) 7584 6817. *Club:* MCC.

TAYLOR, Prof. Martin John, PhD; FRS 1996; Professor of Pure Mathematics, University of Manchester Institute of Science and Technology, since 1986; *b* 18 Feb. 1952; *s* of John Maurice Taylor and Sheila Mary Barbara Taylor (*née* Camacho); *m* 1973, Sharon Lynn Marlow; two *s* two *d*. *Educ:* St Clare's Prep. Sch., Leicester; Wyggeston Boys' Sch., Leicester; Pembroke Coll., Oxford (BA 1st Class); King's College, London (PhD). Res. Assistant, KCL, 1976–77; Jun. Lectr, Oxford Univ., 1977–78; Lectr, QMC, 1978–81; Fellow, Trinity Coll., Cambridge, 1981–85; Univ. Asst Lectr, Cambridge, 1984–85. Associate Researcher, CNRS, Besançon, 1979–80; NSF Researcher, Univ. of Illinois, Urbana, 1981; Royal Soc. Leverhulme Sen. Res. Fellowship, 1991–92; CNRS Poste Rouge, Bordeaux, 1996; EPSRC Sen. Res. Fellow, 1999–. Pres., London Mathematical Soc., 1998–2000; Mem. Council, Royal Soc., 2000–01. *Publications:* Class Groups of Group Rings, 1984; (with Ph. Cassou-Noguès) Elliptic Functions and Rings of Integers, 1987; (with J. Coates) L-functions and Arithmetic, 1991; (with A. Fröhlich) Algebraic Number Theory, 1991; (with K. Roggenkamp) Group Rings and Class Groups, 1992. *Recreations:* fly fishing, hill walking. *Address:* Department of Mathematics, UMIST, PO Box 88, Manchester M60 1QD. *T:* (0161) 200 3640.

TAYLOR, Matthew Owen John; MP (Lib Dem) Truro and St Austell, since 1997 (MP Truro, March 1987–1997, L, 1987–88, Lib Dem, 1988–97); *b* 3 Jan. 1963; *s* of Ken Taylor and Jill Taylor (*née* Black). *Educ:* Treliske School, Truro; University College School; Lady Margaret Hall, Oxford (Scholar; BA Hons). Pres., Oxford Univ. Student Union, 1985–86. Economic policy researcher to Parly Liberal Party (attached to David Penhaligon, MP), 1986–87. Parly spokesman on energy, 1987–88, on local govt, 1988–89, on trade and industry, 1989–90, on educn, 1990–92, on citizen's charter, 1992–94, on environment, 1994–99, and transport, 1997–99, on the economy, 1999–. Communications Chm. for Lib Dems, 1989–92; Lib Dem Chm. of Campaigns and Communications, 1992–94. *Address:* House of Commons, SW1A 0AA. *T:* (020) 7219 6686.

TAYLOR, Rt Rev. Maurice; *see* Galloway, Bishop of, (RC).

TAYLOR, Maxwell; *see* Taylor, J. M. P.

TAYLOR, Rev. Prof. Michael Hugh, OBE 1998; Professor of Social Theology, University of Birmingham, since 1999; *b* 8 Sept. 1936; *s* of Albert Ernest and Gwendoline Louisa Taylor; *m* 1960, Adèle May Dixon; two *s* one *d*. *Educ:* Northampton Grammar School; Univ. of Manchester (BA, BD, MA); Union Theological Seminary, NY (STM). Baptist Minister, N Shields, 1961–66, Birmingham Hall Green, 1966–69; Principal, Northern Baptist Coll., Manchester, 1970–85; Lectr, Univ. of Manchester, 1970–85; Dir, Christian Aid, 1985–97; Pres. and Chief Exec., Selly Oak Colls, 1998–99. Mem. Council, ODI, 1989–2000; Chairman: Assoc. of Protestant Develt Agencies in Europe, 1991–94; The Burma Campaign UK, 2000–; Mem., WCC Commn on Sharing and Service, 1991–. Trustee, Mines Adv. Gp, 1998–, Chm., 2000–. JP Manchester, 1980–85. DLitt Lambeth, 1997. *Publications:* Variations on a Theme, 1973; Sermon on the Mount, 1982; (ed) Christians and the Future of Social Democracy, 1982; Learning to Care, 1983; Good for the Poor, 1990; Christianity and the Persistence of Poverty, 1991; Not Angels But Agencies, 1996; NGOs and their Future in Development, 1997; Poverty and Christianity, 2000; contribs to books and jls. *Recreations:* walking, cooking, music, cinema, theatre. *Address:* University of Birmingham, Selly Oak, Bristol Road, Birmingham B29 6LQ.

TAYLOR, Michael John; His Honour Judge Michael Taylor; a Circuit Judge, since 1996; *b* 28 Feb. 1951; *m* 1973, Pamela Ann Taylor. *Educ:* Hull Univ. (LLB). Called to the Bar, Inner Temple, 1974; in practice, 1974–96. *Address:* Teesside Combined Court Centre, Russell Street, Middlesbrough TS1 2AE.

TAYLOR, Miranda; *see* Haines, M.

TAYLOR, Neil; *see* Taylor, R. N.

TAYLOR, Neville, CB 1989; Principal Associate, Defence Public Affairs Consultants Ltd, 1989–99; *b* 17 Nov. 1930; *y s* of late Frederick Taylor and of Lottie Taylor; *m* 1954, Margaret Ann, *y d* of late Thomas Bainbridge Vickers and Gladys Vickers; two *s*. *Educ:* Sir Joseph Williamson's Mathematical Sch., Rochester; Coll. of Commerce, Gillingham, Kent. Junior Reporter, Chatham News Group, 1947; Royal Signals, 1948–50; Journalism, 1950–58; Asst Information Officer, Admiralty, 1958; Information Officer (Press), Admiralty, 1960; Fleet Information Officer, Singapore, 1963; Chief Press Officer, MoD, 1966; Information Adviser to Nat. Economic Develt Office, 1968; Dep. Dir, Public Relns (Royal Navy), 1970; Head of Information, Min. of Agriculture, Fisheries and Food, 1971; Dep. Dir of Information, DoE, 1973–74, Dir of Information, 1974–79; Dir of Information, DHSS, 1979–82; Chief of Public Relations, MOD, 1982–85; Dir-Gen., COI and Hd of Govt Inf. Service, 1985–88. *Recreation:* fishing. *Address:* Crow Lane House, Crow Lane, Rochester, Kent ME1 1RF. *T:* (01634) 842990.

TAYLOR, Sir Nicholas Richard S.; *see* Stuart Taylor.

TAYLOR, Prof. Pamela Jane, (Mrs J. C. Gunn); FRPsych; Professor of Special Hospital Psychiatry, Institute of Psychiatry, London University, since 1995; Hon. Consultant Psychiatrist: Broadmoor Hospital, since 1995; Bethlem Royal and Maudsley Hospital, since 1995; *b* 23 April 1948; *d* of Philip Geoffrey Taylor and Joan Taylor (*née* Alport); *m* 1989, John Charles Gunn, *qv*. *Educ:* Merchant Taylors' Girls' Sch., Liverpool; Guy's Hosp. Med. Sch. and King's Coll. Hosp. Med. Sch. (MB BS 1971). MRCP 1974; MRCPsych 1976, FRCPsych 1989. Gen. prof. trng in psychiatry, Guy's Hosp., 1972–74; Teaching Fellow in Psychiatry, Univ. of Vermont, 1975; clin. res., Guy's Hosp. Trustees, 1976–79; MRC res. scientist, Inst. of Psychiatry, 1979–81; Sen. Lectr in Forensic Psychiatry, and Hon. Cons. Psychiatrist, 1982–89, Dir of Medium Secure Service, 1988–89, Inst. of Psychiatry and Bethlem Royal and Maudsley Hosp.; Hd of Med. Services, Special Hosps' Service Authy, 1990–95. Member: Inner London Probation Bd, 1990–; DoH and Home Office Steering Gp, Review of Health and Social Services for Mentally Disordered Offenders and other requiring similar services, 1990–94 (Chm., Res. Sub Gp, 1990–91); Wkg Party on Genetics of Mental Disorders, Nuffield Council on Bio-Ethics, 1996–. Member: RSocMed, 1972–; British Soc. of Criminology, 1980–; various cttees and wkg parties, RCPsych, 1982–; Mental Health Foundn, 1990–94; Howard League for Penal Reform, 1990–. Jt Founder and Jt Editor, Criminal Behaviour and Mental Health, 1991–. Gaskell Gold Medal and Prize, RCPsych, 1978. *Publications:* (ed jtly) Forensic Psychiatry: clinical, legal and ethical issues, 1993; (ed) Violence in Society, 1993; Couples in Care and Custody, 1999; numerous sci. papers, editorials, reviews and contribs to books. *Recreations:* family, friends, an acre of previously neglected garden and, in every spare moment, a book. *Address:* Department of Forensic Psychiatry, Institute of Psychiatry, SE5 8AF. *T:* (020) 7919 3123, *Fax:* (01344) 754385.

TAYLOR, Paul David; Director, Chemical and Biological Defence, CBD Porton Down, since 1997; *b* 30 Aug. 1962; *s* of Keith Taylor and Ann Taylor; *m* 1989, Jacqueline Green; one *s* one *d*. *Educ:* St Bartholomew's Sch., Newbury; Teesside Poly. (BSc Hons Chem. Engrg). Science fast stream trainee, MoD, 1988; Pvte Sec. to Chief Scientific Advr, MoD, 1993–95. MInstD 1997. *Recreations:* walking, rough and game shooting, reading, pub quiz team. *Address:* CBD Porton Down, Salisbury, Wilts SP4 0JQ. *Club:* Civil Service.

TAYLOR, Ven. Peter Flint; Archdeacon of Harlow, since 1996; *b* 7 March 1944; *s* of late Alan Flint Taylor and of Josephine Overbury Taylor (*née* Dix); *m* 1971, Joy M. Sampson; one *d*. *Educ:* Clifton Coll., Bristol; Queens' Coll., Cambridge (MA); London Coll. of Divinity (BD ext. London Univ.). Ordained deacon, 1970, priest, 1971; Assistant Curate: St Augustine's, Highbury, 1970–73; St Andrew's, Plymouth, 1973–77; Vicar, Christ Church, Ironville, Derbys., 1977–83; Priest-in-charge, St James, Riddings, 1982–83; Rector, Holy Trinity, Rayleigh, Chelmsford, 1983–96. Part-time Chaplain, Bullwood Hall Prison and Youth Custody Centre, 1986–90; Rural Dean of Rochford, 1989–96. *Recreations:* walking, electronics and computing, astronomy, archaeology of Jerusalem. *Address:* Glebe House, Church Lane, Sheering, Bishops Stortford CM22 7NR. *T:* (01279) 734524, *Fax:* (01279) 734426; *e-mail:* a.harlow@chelmsford.anglican.org.

TAYLOR, Peter John Whittaker, OBE 1990; Director, Spain, British Council, 1995–99; *b* 22 April 1939; *s* of late Claud Whittaker Taylor and of Mary Elizabeth Taylor (*née* Garlick); *m* 1987, Carolina Haro; one *d* by previous marriage. *Educ:* Solihull Sch.; St Catharine's Coll., Cambridge (MA Hons English); Reading Univ. (MA Applied Linguistics). Dir, Internat Lang. Centre, Paris, 1970–78; British Council, 1978–99: Eng. Lang. Officer, Mexico, 1979–81; Regl Dir, Valencia, Spain, 1981–85; Dep. Dir, Saudi Arabia, 1985–87; Dir, Morocco, 1987–90; Dep. Dir, Africa and ME Div., 1990–93; Regl Dir, ME and N Africa, 1993–94. *Recreations:* books, classical music. *Address:* Apartado 118, 46117 Betera, Valencia, Spain. *T:* and *Fax:* (96) 1680476.

TAYLOR, Peter William Edward; QC 1981; *b* 27 July 1917; *s* of late Peter and Julia A. Taylor; *m* 1948, Julia Mary Brown (*d* 1997), *d* of Air Cdre Sir Vernon Brown, CB, OBE; two *s*. *Educ:* Peter Symonds' Sch., Winchester; Christ's Coll., Cambridge (MA; Wrangler, Math. Tripos, Part II; 1st Class, Law Tripos, Part II). Served RA, 1939–46: France and Belgium, 1939–40; N Africa, 1942–43; NW Europe, 1944–45 (mentioned in dispatches); Actg Lt-Col 1945; transferred to TARO as Hon. Major, 1946. Called to the Bar, Inner Temple, 1946; Lincoln's Inn, *ad eundem*, 1953 (Bencher, 1976); practice at the Bar, 1947–94; Occasional Lectr, LSE, 1946–56; Lectr in Construction of Documents, Council of Legal Educn, 1952–70; Conveyancing Counsel of the Court, 1974–81. Member: General Council of the Bar, 1971–74; Senate of Inns of Court and the Bar, 1974–75; Inter-Professional Cttee on Retirement Provision, 1974–92; Land Registration Rule Cttee, 1976–81; Standing Cttee on Conveyancing, 1985–87; Incorporated Council of Law Reporting, 1977–91 (Vice-Chm., 1987–91); Council, Selden Soc., 1977–. *Recreations:* sailing, shooting, music. *Address:* 46 Onslow Square, SW7 3NX. *T:* (020) 7589 1301.

TAYLOR, Philippe Arthur; Managing Director, Seatrain Sailing, since 1993; *b* 9 Feb. 1937; *s* of Arthur Peach Taylor and Simone Vacquin; *m* 1973, Margaret Nancy Wilkins; two *s*. *Educ:* Trinity College, Glenalmond; St Andrews University. Procter & Gamble, 1963; Masius International, 1967; British Tourist Authority, 1970; Chief Executive, Scottish Tourist Board, 1975–80; Man. Dir, Taylor and Partners, 1980–82; Chief Exec., Birmingham Convention and Visitor Bureau Ltd, 1982–94. Vice-Chm., Ikon Gall., 1982–92; Chm., British Assoc. of Conf. Towns, 1987–90. *Publications:* childrens' books; various papers and articles on tourism. *Recreations:* sailing, making things, tourism, reading. *Address:* Ore Cottage, Mill Road, Friston, Saxmundham, Suffolk IP17 1PH. *Clubs:* Royal Northumberland Yacht (Blyth); Orford Sailing.

TAYLOR, Phyllis Mary Constance, MA; Honorary Associate, Institute of Education, London, 1983–85; *b* 29 Sept. 1926; *d* of Cecil and Constance Tedder; *m* 1949, Peter Royston Taylor; one *s*. *Educ:* Woodford High Sch.; Sudbury High Sch., Suffolk; Girton Coll., Cambridge (State Scholar; BA Hons History, 1948; MA 1951). Asst Hist. Mistress, Loughton High Sch., 1948–51, Head of Hist., 1951–58; Teacher of Hist. and Religious Educn, Lancaster Royal Grammar Sch. for Boys, 1959; Head of Hist., Casterton Sch. (private boarding), Kirby Lonsdale, 1960; Teacher of Gen. Subjects, Lancaster Girls' Grammar Sch., 1960–61, Head of Hist., 1961–62; Dep. Headmistress, Carlisle Sch., Chelsea, 1962–64; Headmistress: Walthamstow High Sch. for Girls, 1964–68; Walthamstow Sen. High Sch., 1968–75; Wanstead High Sch., London Borough of Redbridge, 1976–82. Consultant Head to NE London Polytechnic (Counselling/Careers sect.), 1974–78; Moderator, Part-time Diploma, Pastoral Care and Counselling, 1979–85. Pres., Essex Sector, Secondary Heads' Assoc., 1978–79. Member: UGC, 1978–83 (Mem., Educn Sub-Cttee, 1978–85, and Wkg Party on Continuing Educn, 1983); Teacher Trng Sub-Cttee, Adv. Cttee on Supply and Educn of Teachers, 1980–85; former Mem., Nat. Exec., Assoc. of Head Mistresses. Mem., RAM Foundn Appeals Cttee, 1985–86. Parish Councillor, High Roding, 1995–. Chm., Dunmow Liberals, 1986–88. Governor, Rodings Primary Sch., 1988–90. *Publications:* (as Julianne Royston) The Penhale Saga: The Penhale Heiress, 1988; The Penhale Fortune, 1989. *Recreations:* music, theatre, bridge, horses, country life, ecology. *Address:* White Horses, High Roding, Great Dunmow, Essex CM6 1NS. *T:* (01371) 873161.

TAYLOR, Prof. Richard Edward, FRS 1997; Professor, Stanford Linear Accelerator Center, Stanford University, since 1968; *b* 2 Nov. 1929; *s* of Clarence Richard Taylor and Delia Alena Taylor (*née* Brunsdale); *m* 1951, Rita Jean Bonneau; one *s*. *Educ:* Univ. of Alberta (BS 1950; MS 1952); Stanford Univ. (PhD 1962). Boursier, Lab. de l'Accelerateur Linéaire, France, 1958–61; physicist, Lawrence Berkeley Lab., Berkeley, Calif., 1961–62; staff mem., 1962–68, Associate Dir, 1982–86, Stanford Linear Accelerator Center. Distinguished Prof., Univ. of Alberta, 1992–. Fellow: Guggenheim Foundn, 1971–72; Amer. Phys. Soc (W. K. H. Panofsky Prize, Div. of Particles and Fields, 1989); FRSC; FRSL; Fellow, Amer. Acad. of Arts and Scis, 1992. Hon DSc: Paris-Sud, 1980; Alberta, 1991; Lethbridge, 1993; Victoria, 1994; Blaise Pascal, 1997; Carleton, Ottawa, 1999; Liverpool, 1999; Queen's, Kingston, Ont., 2000; Hon. LLD Calgary, 1993. Von Humboldt Award, 1982; Nobel Prize in Physics, 1990. *Address:* Stanford Linear Accelerator Center, 2575 Sand Hill Road, M/S 96, Menlo Park, CA 94025, USA. *T:* (650) 9262417.

TAYLOR, Prof. Richard Kenneth Stanley, PhD; Professor and Director of Continuing Education, University of Leeds, since 1991; *b* 18 Nov. 1945; *s* of Jeanne Ann Taylor and Kenneth Charles Taylor; *m* 1967, Jennifer Teresa Frost; one *s* two *d*. *Educ:* Merchant Taylors' Sch., Northwood; Exeter Coll., Oxford (MA 1967); PhD Leeds 1983. Admin. Asst, Univ. of Lancaster, 1967–70; University of Leeds: Admin. Asst, Dept of Adult and Continuing Educn, 1970–73; Warden, Non-Residential Centre for Adult Educn, Bradford, 1973–83; Dir of Extramural Studies, 1985–88; Head, Dept of Adult and Continuing Educn, 1988–91. Sec., Univs Assoc. for Continuing Educn, 1994–98; Chm., Nat. Inst. for Adult Continuing Educn, 1999– (Vice Chm., 1996–99). *Publications:* (with Colin Pritchard) Social Work: reform or revolution?, 1978; (with Colin Pritchard) The Protest Makers, 1980; (jtly) Adult Education in England and the USA, 1985; (with Kevin Ward) Adult Education and the Working Class, 1986; Against the Bomb: the British peace movement 1958–65, 1988; (with Nigel Young) Campaigns for Peace, 1988; (with Tom Steele) Learning Independence, 1995; Beyond the Walls, 1996; (with David Watson) Lifelong Learning and the University: a post-Dearing agenda, 1998. *Recreations:* mountain walking and climbing, cricket, politics, pubs. *Address:* School of Continuing Education, The University, Leeds LS2 9JT. *T:* (0113) 233 3180, *Fax:* (0113)2333233; *e-mail:* r.k.s.taylor@leeds.ac.uk. *Club:* Yorkshire County Cricket.

TAYLOR, Prof. Richard Lawrence, PhD; FRS 1995; Professor of Mathematics, Harvard University, since 1996; *b* 19 May 1962; *s* of John Clayton Taylor and Gillian Mary Taylor (*née* Schofield); *m* 1995, Christine Jiayou Chang; one *s* one *d*. *Educ:* Magdalen Coll. Sch., Oxford; Clare Coll., Cambridge (BA); Princeton Univ. (PhD). Fellow, Clare Coll., Cambridge, 1988–95; Asst Lectr, 1989–92, Lectr, 1992–94, Reader, 1994–95, Cambridge Univ.; Savilian Prof. of Geometry, and Fellow of New Coll., Oxford Univ., 1995–96. *Recreation:* hill walking. *Address:* Department of Mathematics, Harvard University, 1 Oxford Street, Cambridge, MA 02138, USA. *T:* (617) 4955487.

TAYLOR, Prof. R(ichard) Neil, PhD; Professor of Geotechnical Engineering, City University, since 1996; *b* 14 May 1955; *s* of Charles L. Taylor and Mary Taylor; *m* 1995, Chrysanthi Savvidou; one *d*. *Educ:* Emmanuel Coll., Cambridge (BA 1976; MPhil 1979; MA 1980; PhD 1984). MICE 1990. Lectr in Geotechnical Engrg, 1984–91, Sen. Lectr, 1991–96, City Univ. Associate, Geotechnical Consulting Gp, 1990–. Sec. Gen., Internat. Soc. for Soil Mechanics and Geotechnical Engrg, 1999–. *Publications:* (ed) Geotechnical Centrifuge Technology, 1995; contrib. papers to jls and confs mainly associated with ground movements caused by tunnels and excavations incl. geotechnical centrifuge modelling and analysis. *Recreation:* walking. *Address:* 26 High Street, Little Shelford, Cambs CB2 5ES. *T:* (01223) 842942.

TAYLOR, Richard Thomas, FRCP; MP (Ind.) Wyre Forest, since 2001; *b* 7 July 1934; *s* of Thomas Taylor and Mabel (*née* Hickley); *m* 1st, 1962, Ann Brett (marr. diss.); one *s* two *d*; 2nd, 1990, Christine Miller; one *d*. *Educ:* Leys Sch.; Clare Coll., Cambridge (BA); Westminster Med. Sch. (MB, BChir). FRCP 1979. Jun. hosp. doctor trng posts,

Westminster Hosp. and other London hosps, 1959–72; MO, RAF, 1961–64; Consultant Physician, Kidderminster Gen. Hosp., 1972–95 (Chm., Hosp. Med. Staff Cttee, 1975–77 and 1986–90). Consultant Rep., Kidderminster DHA, 1982–86. Chairman: Kidderminster Hosp. League of Friends, 1996–2001; Save Kidderminster Hosp. Campaign Cttee, 1997–2001. Pres., Kidderminster Med. Soc., 1993. *Publications:* articles on drug treatment and rheumatic diseases in med. jls. *Recreations:* family, ornithology, gardening, classic cars. *Address:* House of Commons, SW1A 0AA; 11 Church Walk, Kidderminster, Worcs DY11 6XY. *T:* (01562) 60010. *Club:* Royal Society of Medicine.

TAYLOR, (Robert) Alan; Chief Executive and Town Clerk, Royal Borough of Kensington and Chelsea, 1990–2000; *b* 13 Sept. 1944; *s* of Alfred Taylor and Hilda Mary (*née* Weekley); *m* 1st, 1965, Dorothy Joan Walker (*d* 1986); two *s*; 2nd, 1987, Margaret Susanne Barnes. *Educ:* Thornbury Grammar Sch., Thornbury, Glos.; King's Coll., Univ. of London (LLB). Solicitor. Asst Solicitor, Plymouth CBC, 1970–74; Plymouth City Council: Dep. City Solicitor and Sec., 1974–76; Asst Town Clerk, 1976–81; Chief Exec., London Borough of Sutton, 1981–90. Pres., SOLACE, 1998–99 (Hon. Sec., 1992–95; Sen. Vice-Pres., 1997–98). *Recreations:* theatre, books, walking. *Address:* Old Venn, Bridford, Devon EX6 7LF. *T:* (01647) 252611.

TAYLOR, Robert Carruthers; His Honour Judge Robert Taylor; a Circuit Judge, since 1984; *b* 6 Jan. 1939; *o s* of late John Taylor, CBE and Barbara Taylor; *m* 1968, Jacqueline Marjorie, JP, *er d* of Nigel and Marjorie Chambers; one *s* one *d*. *Educ:* Wycliffe Coll.; St John's Coll., Oxford. MA 1967. Called to Bar, Middle Temple, 1961; practised NE Circuit, 1961–84; a Recorder, 1976–84. Chm., Agricl Land Tribunal, Yorks and Humberside Areas, 1979–. *Recreations:* reading, music, spectating, gardening, domestic life. *Address:* The Courthouse, 1 Oxford Row, Leeds LS1 3BE. *T:* (0113) 283 0040. *Club:* Royal Commonwealth Society.

TAYLOR, Prof. Robert Henry, PhD; Vice-Chancellor, University of Buckingham, 1997–2001; *b* 15 March 1943; *s* of Robert E. Taylor and Mabelle L. Taylor (*née* Warren), Greenville, Ohio; *m* 1st (marr. diss.); one *s* one *d*; 2nd, 2000, Ingrid Porteous. *Educ:* Ohio Univ. (BA 1965); Antioch Coll. (MA 1967); Cornell Univ. (PhD 1974). Social Studies Teacher, Cardozo High Sch., Washington DC, 1965–67; Instructor in Pol. Sci., Wilberforce Univ., Ohio, 1967–69; Lectr in Govt, Univ. of Sydney, 1974–79; School of Oriental and African Studies, University of London: Lectr, 1980–88, Sen. Lectr, 1988–89, in Politics (with ref. to SE Asia); Prof. of Politics, 1989–96; Pro-Dir, 1991–96. *Publications:* Marxism and Resistance in Burma, 1985; The State in Burma, 1987; (contrib.) In Search of Southeast Asia: a modern history, 1987; (ed) Handbooks of the Modern World: Asia and the Pacific, 2 vols, 1991; (ed) The Politics of Elections in Southeast Asia, 1996; (ed) Burma: political economy under military rule, 2001; numerous articles in books and learned jls. *Address:* 13 Baron Close, N11 3PS. *Club:* Travellers.

TAYLOR, Robert Richard, OBE 1989 (MBE (mil.) 1972); JP; Lord Lieutenant, County of West Midlands, since 1993; *b* 14 June 1932; *s* of Sydney Arthur Taylor and Edith Alice Taylor; *m* 1957, Sheila Welch. *Educ:* Yardley Grammar Sch., Birmingham. Pilot then Sqdn Leader, RAF, 1950–73. Progressive Properties, Birmingham, 1973–74; Asst Dir, 1974–76, Airport Dir, 1976–86, Man. Dir, 1986–94, Birmingham Airport plc. Freeman, City of London, 1998. JP W Midlands, 1994. DUniv Central England, 1993. KStJ 1994. QCVSA 1966; Hon. LLD Birmingham, 1998. *Recreations:* literature, people. *Address:* Lieutenancy Office, The Coach House, Barston, Solihull B92 0JL. *Club:* Royal Air Force.

TAYLOR, Dr Robert Thomas, CBE 1990; Chairman, Management Interviewing and Research Institute, since 1993; *b* 21 March 1933; *s* of George Taylor and Marie Louise Fidler; *m* 1965, Rosemary Janet Boileau; three *s* one *d*. *Educ:* Boteler Grammar Sch., Warrington; University Coll., Oxford (Open Exhbnr; BA 1954, MA 1957; DPhil 1957). Fulbright Scholar. Research Associate, Randall Lab. of Physics, Univ. of Michigan, USA, 1957–58; ICI Research Fellow, 1958–59, Lectr, Physics Dept, 1959–61, Univ. of Liverpool; Chief Examr for NUJMB, GCE Physics (Scholarship Level), 1961; British Council: Asst Regional Rep., Madras, 1961–64; Science Officer, Madrid, 1964–69; Dir, Staff Recruitment Dept, 1969–73; Regional Educn Advr, Bombay, 1973–77; Rep., Mexico, 1977–81; Controller, Personnel, 1981–86; Rep., Greece, 1986–90; Asst Dir-Gen., British Council, 1990–93. Vis. Sen. Fellow, Manchester Business Sch., 1993–99. *Publications:* contrib. to Chambers Encyclopaedia, 1967 edn; papers in scientific jls. *Recreations:* computers, war and war gaming. *Address:* Mark Haven, Ashford Road, High Halden, Kent TN26 3LY. *T:* (01233) 850994.

TAYLOR, Roger Miles Whitworth; Chairman, Newchurch and Company, since 1997 (Director, since 1994); *b* 18 May 1944; *s* of Richard and Joan Taylor; *m* 1969, Georgina Lucy Tonks (separated 1995); two *s* two *d*. *Educ:* Repton School; Birmingham University (LLB). Solicitor, admitted 1968; Asst Sol., Cheshire CC, 1969–71; Asst County Clerk, Lincs parts of Lindsey, 1971–73; Dep. County Secretary, Northants CC, 1973–79; Dep. Town Clerk, 1979–85, Town Clerk and Chief Exec., 1985–88, City of Manchester; Chief Exec., Birmingham CC, 1988–94. Mem., Farrand Cttee on Conveyancing, 1983–84; Clerk, Greater Manchester Passenger Transport Authy, 1986–88. Sec., W Midlands Jt Cttee, 1988–94. Chairman: Birmingham Marketing Partnership, 1993–94; Birmingham Common Purpose, 1994; Local Govt Television Adv. Bd, 1994–95; Dir, Birmingham TEC, 1990–93. Dir, Ex Cathedra Chamber Choir, 1996–98. Mancunian of the Year, Manchester Jun. Chamber of Commerce, 1988. *Publications:* contribs to Local Govt Chronicle, Municipal Review, Municipal Jl. *Recreations:* sailing, walking. *Address:* Newchurch and Company, 25 Christopher Street, EC2A 2BS.

TAYLOR, Ronald George, CBE 1988; Director-General, British Chambers of Commerce (formerly Association of British Chambers of Commerce), 1984–98; *b* 12 Dec. 1935; *s* of Ernest and May Taylor; *m* 1960, Patricia Stoker; one *s* two *d*. *Educ:* Jesus College, Oxford (BA Modern Langs). Commnd Royal Signals, 1957–59. Leeds Chamber of Commerce and Industry: joined, 1959; Asst Sec., 1964–74; Director, 1974–84. Reg. Sec., Assoc. of Yorks and Humberside Chambers of Commerce, 1974–84. *Recreations:* Rugby Union, bridge. *Address:* 2 Holly Bush Lane, Harpenden, Herts AL5 4AP. *T:* (01582) 712139.

TAYLOR, Prof. Ronald Wentworth, MD; FRCOG; Professor Emeritus of Obstetrics and Gynaecology, United Medical and Dental Schools of Guy's and St Thomas' Hospitals, since 1989; *b* 28 Oct. 1932; *s* of George Richard and Winifred Taylor; *m* 1962, Mary Patricia O'Neill; three *s* one *d*. *Educ:* St Mary's Coll., Crosby; Liverpool Univ. (MB ChB 1958; MD 1972). MRCOG 1965, FRCOG 1975. Jun. House Officer posts, Liverpool, 1958–59; Sen. House Officer posts, Preston, 1960, Manchester, 1962; GP, Ormskirk, Lancs, 1962–63; Registrar, Whittington Hosp., London, 1963–64; St Thomas' Hospital: Lectr, 1965–67; Sen. Lectr, 1968–76; Prof., 1977–89, subseq. at UMDS of Guy's and St Thomas' Hosps. Founder Mem., Expert Witness Inst., 1995–. *Publications:* Gynaecological Cancer, 1975; "Ten Teachers" Obstetrics and Gynaecology, 14th edn 1985; (ed) Confidential Enquiry into Perinatal Deaths, 1988; Endometrial Cancer, 1988. *Recreations:* fell walking, sailing, silversmithing, restoration of furniture, photography. *Address:* Keld Head, Keld Shap, Penrith, Cumbria CA10 3QF. *T:* (01931) 716553. *Club:* Royal Society of Medicine.

TAYLOR, Rupert Maurice T.; *see* Thornely-Taylor.

TAYLOR, Russell Philip; writer and cartoonist; *b* 8 July 1960; *s* of Captain Hal Taylor and Iona Taylor (*née* Mackenzie); *m* 1990, Anne-Frederique Dujon. *Educ:* St Anne's Coll., Oxford (BA Russian and Philosophy). Freelance writer and journalist, 1984–87; writer of Alex cartoon (with Charles Peattie) in: London Daily News, 1987; The Independent, 1987–91; Daily Telegraph, 1992–; writer of Celeb cartoon (with Charles Peattie and Mark Warren), Private Eye, 1987–; composer of film and TV music, 1991–. *Publications:* (with Marc Polonsky) USSR from an original idea by Karl Marx, 1986; The Looniness of the Long Distance Runner, 2001; with Charles Peattie: Alex, 1987; The Unabashed Alex, 1988; Alex II: Magnum Force, 1989; Alex III: Son of Alex, 1990; Alex IV: The Man with the Golden Handshake, 1991; Celeb, 1991; Alex V: For the Love of Alex, 1992; Alex Calls the Shots, 1993; Alex Plays the Game, 1994; Alex Knows the Score, 1995; Alex Sweeps the Board, 1996; Alex Feels the Pinch, 1997; The Full Alex, 1998; The Alex Technique, 1999. *Recreations:* playing piano, running, perudo, time-wasting. *Address:* c/o Andrew Mann, 1 Old Compton Street, W1V 5PH. *T:* (020) 7734 4751. *Clubs:* Groucho, Soho House.

TAYLOR, Sandra Anne; Director of Social Services, Birmingham City Council, since 1999; *b* 5 Sept. 1953; *d* of Harold E. Taylor and May Taylor (*née* Draper). *Educ:* Portsmouth Poly. (BA Hons); Essex Univ. (MA). Lectr and Tutor, Hull Univ., 1977–80; Res. Fellow and Lectr, UCL, 1981–82; Nottinghamshire County Council: Community Develt Officer, 1982–86; Principal Officer, 1986–88, Principal Asst, 1988–89, Asst Dir, 1990–96, Social Services Dept; Dir, Social Services, Leics City Council, 1996–99. *Publication:* (ed) Nottinghamshire Labour Movement, 1986. *Recreations:* swimming, gardening, walking. *Address:* Social Services Department, Louisa Ryland House, 44 Newhall Street, Birmingham B3 3PL.

TAYLOR, Sir Teddy; *see* Taylor, Sir E. M.

TAYLOR, Wendy Ann, CBE 1988; FRBS 1995; sculptor; Member, Royal Fine Art Commission, 1981–99; *b* 29 July 1945; *d* of Edward Philip Taylor and Lilian Maude Wright; *m* 1982, Bruce Robertson; one *s*. *Educ:* St Martin's School of Art. LDAD (Hons). One-man exhibitions: Axiom Gall., London, 1970; Angela Flowers Gall., London, 1972; 24th King's Lynn Fest., Norfolk, and World Trade Centre, London, 1974; Annely Juda Fine Art, London, 1975; Oxford Gall., Oxford, 1976; Oliver Dowling Gall., Dublin, 1976 and 1979; Building Art—the process, Building Centre Gall., 1986; Austin, Desmond and Phipps, 1992; Nature and Engineering, Osborne Gp, London, 1998. Shown in over 100 group exhibitions, 1964–82. Represented in collections in GB, USA, NI, Eire, NZ, Germany, Sweden, Qatar, Switzerland, Seychelles. Major commissions: The Travellers 1970, London; Gazebo (edn of 4) 1970–71, London, New York, Suffolk, Oxford; Triad 1971, Oxford; Timepiece 1973, London; Calthae 1978, Leicestershire; Octo 1980, Milton Keynes; Counterpoise 1980, Birmingham; Compass Bowl 1980, Basildon; Sentinel 1981, Reigate; Bronze Relief 1981, Canterbury; Equatorial Sundial 1982, Bletchley; Essence 1982, Milton Keynes; Opus 1983, Morley Coll., London; Gazebo 1983, Golder's Hill Park, London; Network, 1985, London; Roundacre Improvement Scheme Phase I, 1985–88, Phase II, 1989–90, Basildon; Geo I & Geo II 1986, Stratford-Upon-Avon; Landscape, and Tree of the Wood 1986, Fernhurst, Surrey; Pharos 1986, Peel Park, E Kilbride; Ceres 1986, Fernhurst, Surrey; Nexus 1986, Corby, Northants; Globe Sundial 1987, Swansea Maritime Quarter; Spirit of Enterprise 1987, Isle of Dogs, London; Silver Fountain 1988, Continuum 1990, Guildford, Surrey; The Whirlies 1988, Pharos II 1989, Phoenix 1989–90, E Kilbride; Pilot Kites 1988, Norwich Airport; Fireflow 1988, Strathclyde Fire Brigade HQ, Hamilton; Armillary Sundial 1989, The New Towns, Essex; Globe Sundial II 1990, London Zool Gdns; Butterfly Mosaic 1990, Barking and Dagenham Council; Square Piece 1991, Plano, Ill; Sundial Meml 1991, Sheffield; Anchorage 1991, Salford Quays, Manchester; Wyvern 1992, Leics; stained glass window, St George's Church, Sheffield Univ., 1994; The Jester, Emmanuel Coll., Cambridge, 1994; Challenge, Stockley Park, Middx, 1995; Equilibrium, Coopers & Lybrand, London, 1995; Spirit, Vann, Guildford, 1996; Rope Circle, Hermitage Waterside, London, 1997; Waves, Berners Mews, London, 1998; Dancer, Chelsea and Westminster Hosp., 1998; Dung Beetles, Millennium Conservation Bldg, Zool Soc., Regent's Park, 1999; Mariner's Astrolabe, Virginia Settlers Meml, Brunswick Quay, 1999; Globe View, Blackfriars, 2000; Millennium Fountain, Chase Gardens, Enfield, 2000; Voyager, Cinnibar Wharf, London. Mem., CNAA, 1980–85 (Specialist Advr, 1985–93; Mem., Cttee for Art and Design, 1987–91); Consultant, New Town Commn (Basildon) (formerly Basildon Develt Corp.), 1985–; Design Consultant, London Borough of Barking and Dagenham, 1989–93 and 1997–; LDDC Mem., Design Adv. Panel, 1989–98. Mem., Adv. Gp, PCFC, 1989–90. Examiner, Univ. of London, 1982–83; Mem. Court, RCA, 1982–; Mem. Council, Morley Coll., 1984–88. Trustee, Leicestershire's Appeal for Music and the Arts, 1993–. FZS 1989; Fellow, QMW, 1993. Awards: Walter Neurath, 1964; Pratt, 1965; Sainsbury, 1966; Arts Council, 1977; Duais na Riochta (Kingdom Prize), 1977; Gold Medal, Eire, 1977; 1st Prize Silk Screen, Barcham Green Print Comp., 1978. *Recreation:* gardening. *Address:* 73 Bow Road, Bow E3 2AN. *T:* (020) 8981 2037, *Fax:* (020) 8980 3153.

TAYLOR, Sir William, Kt 1990; CBE 1982; President, Society for Research in Higher Education, since 1996; *b* 31 May 1930; *s* of Herbert and Maud E. Taylor, Crayford, Kent; *m* 1954, Rita, *d* of Ronald and Marjorie Hague, Sheffield; one *s* two *d*. *Educ:* Erith Grammar Sch.; London Sch. of Economics; Westminster Coll., Oxford (Hon. Fellow, 1990); Univ. of London Inst. of Educn. BSc Econ 1952, PhD 1960. Teaching in Kent, 1953–56; Deputy Head, Slade Green Secondary Sch., 1956–59; Sen. Lectr, St Luke's Coll., Exeter, 1959–61; Head of Educn Dept, Bede Coll., Durham, 1961–64; Tutor and Lectr in Educn, Univ. of Oxford, 1964–66; Prof. of Educn and Dir of Sch. of Educn, Univ. of Bristol, 1966–73; Dir, Univ. of London Inst. of Educn, 1973–83; Principal, Univ. of London, 1983–85; Vice-Chancellor: Univ. of Hull, 1985–91; Univ. of Huddersfield, 1994–95; Thames Valley Univ., 1998–99. Visiting Professor of Education: Oxford Univ., 1991–97; Southampton Univ., 1998–; Commonwealth Vis. Fellow, Australian States, 1975; NZ UGC Prestige Fellowship, 1977; Hon. Vis. Fellow, Green Coll., Oxford, 1991–97. Research Consultant, Dept of Educn and Science (part-time), 1968–73; Chairman: European Cttee for Educnl Research, 1969–71; UK Nat. Commn for UNESCO, 1975–83 (Mem., 1973–83); Educnl Adv. Council, IBA, 1974–82; UCET, 1976–79; Cttee on Training of Univ. Teachers, 1981–88; NFER, 1983–88; CATE, 1984–93; Univs Council for Adult and Continuing Educn, 1986–90; N of England Univs Management and Leadership Prog., 1987–91; Studies in Education, 1991–; UUK Higher Educn Funding Review Gp, 2000–01. Member: UGC Educn Cttee, 1971–80; British Library Res. and Develt Cttee, 1975–79; Open Univ. Academic Adv. Cttee, 1975–82; SSRC Educnl Research Board, 1976–80 (Vice-Chm., 1978–80); Adv. Cttee on Supply and Training of Teachers, 1976–79; Working Gp on Management of Higher Educn, 1977–78; Steering Cttee on Future of Examinations at 16+, 1977–78; Cttee of Vice-Chancellors and Principals, 1980–91; Adv. Cttee on Supply and Educn of Teachers (Sec.

of State's nominee), 1980–83. UK Rep., Permanent Educn Steering Cttee, Council of Europe, 1971–73; Rapporteur, OECD Review of Educn in NZ, 1982–83. Chm. of Convocation, Univ. of London, 1994–97; Member: Senate, Univ. of London, 1977–85; Cttee of Management, Inst. of Advanced Legal Studies, 1980–83; Council, Open Univ., 1984–88; Council, Coll of Preceptors, 1987–89; Editl Adv. Bd, World Book Internat., 1989–; CBI Educn Foundn, 1993–98. President: Council for Educn in World Citizenship, 1979–90; English New Educn Fellowship, 1979–86; Comparative Educn Soc. of GB, 1981–84; Assoc. of Colls of Further and Higher Educn, 1984–88; European Assoc. for Institnl Res., 1990–92; Univs of N of England Consortium for Internat. Develt, 1991–94; N of England Educn Conference, 1992; Inst. of Educn Soc., 1990–93; Vice President: British Educnl Admin, and Management Soc., 1985–; Council for Internat. Educn, 1992–. Chm., NFER/Nelson Publishing Co., 1985–86, 1987–99; Dir, Fenner plc, 1988–93. Trustee, Forbes Trust, 1987–88. Governor: Wye Coll., 1981–83; Hymers Coll., Hull, 1985–91; Westminster Coll., Oxford, 1991–96; Univ. of Glamorgan (formerly Poly. of Wales), 1991–; Sevenoaks Sch., 1994–97; Christ Church UC, Canterbury, 1996–; Mem. Council, Hong Kong Inst. of Educn, 1998–. Freeman, City of London, 1985. Yeoman, 1982–87, Liveryman, 1988–, Worshipful Soc. of Apothecaries of London. Hon. FCP 1977; Hon. FCCEA 1980. Hon. Fellow: Thames Polytechnic, 1991; Inst. of Educn, Univ. of London, 1995. Hon. DSc Aston (Birmingham), 1977; Hon. LittD Leeds, 1979; Hon. DCL Kent, 1981; DUniv: Open, 1983; Ulster, 2000; Hon. DLitt: Loughborough, 1984; Southampton, 1998; London, 1999; Hon. LLD: Hull, 1992; Bristol, 2001; Hon. DEd: Kingston, 1993; Oxford Brookes, 1993; Plymouth, 1993; UWE, 1994; Hon. DSc (Educ) QUB, 1997. *Publications:* The Secondary Modern School, 1963; Society and the Education of Teachers, 1969; (ed with G. Baron) Educational Administration and the Social Sciences, 1969; Heading for Change, 1969; Planning and Policy in Post Secondary Education, 1972; Theory into Practice, 1972; Research Perspectives in Education, 1973; (ed with R. Farquhar and R. Thomas) Educational Administration in Australia and Abroad, 1975; Research and Reform in Teacher Education, 1978; (ed with B. Simon) Education in the Eighties: the central issues, 1981; (ed) Metaphors of Education, 1984; Universities Under Scrutiny, 1987; Policy and Strategy for Higher Education: collaboration between business and higher eduction, 1989; articles and papers in professional jls. *Recreations:* writing, walking. *Address:* University of London, Institute of Education, 20 Bedford Way, WC1H 0AL. *T:* and *Fax:* (01962) 883485; *e-mail:* william.taylor@btinternet.com.

TAYLOR, William, CBE 2001; QPM 1991; HM Chief Inspector of Constabulary for Scotland, 1999–2001; *b* 25 March 1947; *s* of late William Taylor and Margaret Taylor; *m* 1978, Denise Lloyd; two step *s*. *Educ:* Blairgowrie High Sch.; Nat. Police Coll. (8th Special Course and 16th Sen. Command Course). Joined Metropolitan Police Service, 1966; served Central London locations as Det. Constable, Sergeant and Inspector, and Chief Inspector, 1966–76; New Scotland Yard: Community Relations Branch, 1976–78; Det. Supt, Central Drugs Squad, 1978–79; Staff Officer to Comr of Police, 1980–82 (Det. Chief Supt); Comdr CID NE London, then Uniform Comdr, Hackney; Comdr Robbery Squad (Flying Squad) and Regional Crime Squad, 1982–85; Asst Comr, City of London Police, 1985–89; Dep. Chief Constable, Thames Valley Police, 1989–90; Asst Comr, Specialist Ops, Metropolitan Police, 1990–94; Comr, City of London Police, 1994–98; HM Inspector of Constabulary, 1998. Chm., Crime Cttee, ACPO, 1994–98; Mem. Exec. Cttee, Interpol, 1995–98; Dir, Police Extended Interviews, 1996–98. Police Long Service and Good Conduct Medal, 1988. *Recreations:* reading (travel, management and historical), hill walking, horse riding, collecting some Dalton ware.

TAYLOR, William Edward Michael; His Honour Judge William Taylor; a Circuit Judge, Western Circuit, since 1989; Resident Judge for Plymouth, since 1990; *b* 27 July 1944; *s* of William Henry Taylor and Winifred Mary (*née* Day); *m* 1969, Caroline Joyce Gillies; two *d*. *Educ:* Denstone Coll., Uttoxeter, Staffs; Council of Legal Educn. Called to the Bar, Inner Temple, 1968. Practised from 2 Harcourt Bldgs, Temple; a Recorder, 1987–89; Liaison Judge for Devon and Cornwall, 1999–. Lectr, Council of Legal Educn, 1976–89. Chm., Criminal Justice Strategy Cttee for Devon and Cornwall, 2000–; Mem., Probation Cttees for Devon and Cornwall. Hon. Pres., Univ. of Plymouth Law Soc. *Recreations:* music, opera, fishing, vintage cars, wine. *Address:* c/o Court Administrator, The Castle, Exeter, Devon EX4 3TH. *T:* (01392) 74876. *Clubs:* Royal Western Yacht (Plymouth); English XX.

TAYLOR, Very Rev. William Henry, PhD; Dean (formerly Provost) of Portsmouth, since 2000; *b* 23 Dec. 1956; *s* of Thomas Mather Taylor and Barbara Taylor (*née* Pitt). *Educ:* Westcott House, Cambridge. MA, MTh, PhD. Ordained deacon, 1983, priest, 1984; Asst Curate, All Saints and St Philip with Tovil, Canterbury, 1983–86; Archbp's Advisor on Orthodox Affairs, Lambeth Palace, 1986–88; Curate, All Saints, Margaret St, London, 1986–88; Chaplain, Guy's Hosp., 1988; CMS 1988–91; Chaplain, Jordan Chaplaincy, 1988–91; Vicar, St Peter, Ealing, 1991–2000; Area Dean, Ealing, 1993–98. FRAS 1982. Freeman, City of London, 1997. *Publication:* (ed) Christians in the Holy Land, 1994. *Recreations:* good wine, challenging travel. *Address:* The Deanery, Pembroke Road, Portsmouth PO1 2NS. *Club:* Nikaean.

TAYLOR, William James; QC (Scot) 1986; QC 1998; *b* 13 Sept. 1944; *s* of Cecil Taylor and Ellen Taylor (*née* Daubney). *Educ:* Robert Gordon's College, Aberdeen; Aberdeen Univ. (MA Hons 1966; LLB 1969); Glasgow Univ. (Cert. in European Law (French) 1990). Admitted Faculty of Advocates, 1971; called to the Bar, Inner Temple, 1990. Standing Junior Counsel to DHSS, 1978–79, to FCO, 1979–86; Temp. Sheriff, 1997–. Member: Criminal Injuries Compensation Bd, 1997–; Scottish Criminal Cases Review Commn, 1999–. Contested (Lab) Edinburgh W, Feb. and Oct. 1974; Regional Councillor (Lab), 1973–82. FRSA. *Recreations:* the arts, ski-ing, sailing, Scottish mountains, swimming, travel, restoring a garden, cooking. *Address:* 3 Northumberland Street, Edinburgh EH3 6LL. *T:* (0131) 556 0101; (office) Parliament House, Parliament Square, Edinburgh EH1 1RF. *T:* (0131) 226 2881, *Fax:* (0131) 225 3642; 3 Gray's Inn Square, WC1R 5AH. *T:* (020) 7831 2311, *Fax:* (020) 7404 4939; *e-mail:* qc@wjt.org.uk. *Clubs:* Scottish Arts, Traverse Theatre (Edinburgh).

TAYLOR, William McCaughey; Chairman, Northern Ireland Coal Importers Association, 1986–91, retired; *b* 10 May 1926; *s* of William and Georgina Lindsay Taylor; *m* 1955, June Louise Macartney; two *s* two *d*. *Educ:* Campbell College, Belfast; Trinity College, Oxford (MA 1950). Lieut, Royal Inniskilling Fusiliers, 1944–47. International Computers Ltd, 1950–58; Lobitos Oilfields Ltd, 1958–60; HM Vice Consul, New York, 1960–63, HM Consul, 1963–65; NI Dept of Commerce, 1965–79; Sec. and Chief Exec., NI Police Authy, 1979–86. *Recreations:* golf, bridge, gardening, piano. *Club:* Royal Belfast Golf.

TAYLOR, William Rodney E.; *see* Eatock Taylor.

TAYLOR, Rt Hon. (Winifred) Ann; PC 1997; MP (Lab) Dewsbury, since 1987; *b* Motherwell, 2 July 1947; *m* 1966, David Taylor; one *s* one *d*. *Educ:* Bolton Sch.; Bradford Univ.; Sheffield Univ. Formerly teaching. Past part-time Tutor, Open Univ.; interested in housing, regional policy, and education. Monitoring Officer, Housing Corp., 1985–87. Member: Association of Univ. Teachers; APEX; Holmfirth Urban District Council, 1972–74. Contested (Lab): Bolton W, Feb. 1974; Bolton NE, 1983. MP (Lab) Bolton W, Oct. 1974–1983. PPS to Sec. of State for Educn and Science, 1975–76; PPS to Sec. of State for Defence, 1976–77; an Asst Govt Whip, 1977–79; Opposition front bench spokesman on education, 1979–81, on housing, 1981–83, on home affairs, 1987–90 (Shadow Water Minister, 1988), on environment, 1990–92, on education, 1992–94; Shadow Chancellor of Duchy of Lancaster, 1994–95; Shadow Leader of H of C, 1994–97; Pres. of Council and Leader of H of C, 1997–98; Parly Sec. to HM Treasury (Govt Chief Whip), 1998–2001. Mem., Select Cttee on Standards and Privileges, 1995–97; Chm., Select Cttee on Modernisation, 1997–98. Hon. Fellow, Birkbeck Coll. *Address:* House of Commons, SW1A 0AA.

TAYLOR BRADFORD, Barbara; *see* Bradford.

TAYLOR THOMPSON, (John) Derek, CB 1985; Commissioner of Inland Revenue, 1973–87; Secretary, Churches' Main Committee, since 1990; *b* 6 Aug. 1927; *o s* of late John Taylor Thompson and Marjorie (*née* Westcott); *m* 1954, Helen Laurie Walker; two *d*. *Educ:* St Peter's Sch., York; Balliol Coll., Oxford. MA. Asst Principal, Inland Revenue, 1951; Private Sec. to Chm., 1954; Private Sec. to Minister without Portfolio (Rt Hon. William Deedes), 1962; Asst Sec., Inland Revenue, 1965. Chm., Fiscal Affairs Cttee, OECD, 1984–89. Chm., Legislation-Monitoring Service for Charities, 1991–. *Recreations:* rural pursuits, reading, historical writing. *Address:* Jessops, Nutley, Sussex TN22 3PD. *Club:* Oxford and Cambridge.

TAYLORSON, John Brown; Managing Director: John Taylorson Associates, since 1990; Inflight Marketing Services, since 1990; *b* 5 March 1931; *s* of John Brown Taylorson and Edith Maria Taylorson; *m* 1st, 1960, Barbara June (*née* Hagg) (marr. diss.); one *s* one *d*; 2nd, 1985, Helen Anne (*née* Parkinson); one *s*. *Educ:* Forest School, Snaresbrook; Hotel School, Westminster. Sales Director, Gardner Merchant Food Services Ltd, 1970–73; Managing Director: International Division, Gardner Merchant Food Services, 1973–77; Fedics Food Services, 1977–80; Chief Executive, Civil Service Catering Organisation, 1980–81; Hd of Catering Servs, British Airways, 1981–89. Chm., 1990–96, Dir, 1990–97, Internat. Service Industry Search. Corporate Appeals Dir, DEBRA, 1993–. Pres., Internat. Flight Catering Assoc., 1983–85; Chm., Inflight Services Gp, Assoc. of European Airlines, 1983–85. *Recreations:* golf, theatre, crossword puzzles. *Address:* Deer Pond Cottage, Highfields, East Horsley, Surrey KT24 5AA. *Clubs:* Old Foresters; Burhill Golf.

TAYLOUR, family name of **Marquess of Headfort**.

TCHALENKO, Janice Anne, FRCA; potter, since 1964; Chief Designer, Dartington Pottery, since 1984; *b* 5 April 1942; *d* of late Eric Cooper and Marjorie Cooper (*née* Dodd); *m* 1964, Dr John Stephen Tchalenko; one *s*. *Educ:* Barr's Hill Grammar Sch., Coventry. FRCA 1987. Clerical Officer, PO Telephones, Coventry and FO, London, 1958–60; Art Therapist, The Priory, Roehampton, 1965–69; studio pottery course, Harrow Sch. of Art, 1969–71; travelled extensively in Soviet Union and Middle East, 1965–77; set up workshop, London, 1971; pt-time Tutor, Camberwell Sch. of Art and Crafts, 1972–86; Tutor, RCA, 1981–96; Curator: Colours of the Earth exhibn, British Council, 1989–92 (toured India, 1991–92); British Ceramics for Brazil, British Council, 2000 (touring). Mem., Crafts Council, 1994–2000. Consultant: Goa You Porcelain Factory, China, 1991; Blue Factory, China, 1991–92. *Works* include: (with Spitting Image Workshop) Seven Deadly Sins, 1993, Modern Antiques, 1996; pottery designs for Dartington range, 1984–, Designers Guild, 1985, Next Interiors, 1986, and Poole Pottery, 1994–95; exhibits in major public collections, including: Helsinki Mus. of Decorative Art; Los Angeles County Mus. of Art; Mus. für Kunst und Gewerbe, Hamburg; Nat. Mus. of Modern Art, Kyoto; Stockholm Nat. Mus.; V&A Mus.; *solo exhibitions* include: Sideshow, ICA, 1980; Craftshop, V&A Mus., 1981; Scottish Gall., Edinburgh, 1989, 2001; Stockholm Nat. Mus., 1990; retrospective, Ruskin Gall., Sheffield, and tour, 1992; Beaux Arts, Bath, 1997. *Recreations:* gardening, reading. *Address:* 30 Therapia Road, East Dulwich, SE22 0SE.

TCHURUK, Serge; Chairman and Chief Executive Officer, Alcatel (formerly Alcatel Alsthom), since 1995; *b* 13 Nov. 1937; *s* of Georges Tchuruk and Mathilde (*née* Dondikian); *m* 1960, Héléna Kalfus; one *d*. *Educ:* Ecole Nationale Supérieure de l'Armement; Ecole Polytechnique. With Mobil Oil in France, USA and Netherlands, 1968–80; Head, Mobil Oil BV, Rotterdam, 1979–80; with Rhône-Poulenc, 1980–86: Gen. Manager, Fertilizer Div., 1980–82; Mem., Exec. Cttee, 1981; Dep. Man. Dir, 1982–83; Man. Dir, 1983–86; Chm. Mgt Bd, 1986–87, Chm. and CEO, 1987–90, CDF Chimie, later ORKEM; Chm. and CEO, Total SA, Paris, 1990–95. Officier de la Légion d'Honneur, 1998. *Recreations:* music, ski-ing, tennis. *Address:* Alcatel, 54 rue La Boétie, 75008 Paris, France. *T:* 40761010, *Fax:* 40761400.

TEACHER, Michael John, FCA; Chief Executive, Unipoly, since 2001; *b* 2 June 1947; *s* of Charles and Ida Teacher; *m* 1972, Sandra Posner; three *s*. *Educ:* City Univ. (MSc Financial Mgt 1972). FCA 1969. Articled Clerk, Abey, Lish & Co., 1964–69; Audit Senior, Deloitte & Co., 1969–71; Corporate Finance Exec., Corinthian Holdings, then Welbeck Investment, 1973–76; Man. Dir, Holding Co. Ltd, Welbeck Investment Plc, 1976–82; Exec. Dir, Sir Joseph Causton Plc, 1983–84; Man. Dir, Pointon York Ltd, Venture Capital Co., 1984–87; Hillsdown Holdings PLC: Man. Dir, HIT Plc (Venture Capital subsid.), 1987–93; Exec. Dir, 1993–98; Chief Exec., 1998–99. Non-executive Chairman: Princedale Gp plc; e Techonology VCT plc; Presentation Services Gp Ltd; Wireless Lans Holdings Ltd. *Recreations:* tennis, soccer, running, charitable work. *Address:* 18 Valencia Road, Stanmore, Middx HA7 4JH. *T:* (020) 8954 2637.

TEAGLE, Vice-Adm. Sir Somerford (Francis), KBE 1994; Chief of Defence Force, New Zealand, 1991–95; *b* 9 June 1938; *s* of Leonard Herbert Teagle and Muriel Frances Teagle; *m* 1961, Leonie Marie Maire; one *s* one *d*. *Educ:* Christ's Coll., Christchurch, NZ; Royal Naval Coll., Dartmouth. Royal New Zealand Navy: Sea and Staff appts, 1958–85: Commanding Officer HMNZS: Manga, 1962–64; Taranaki, 1977; jssc, Canberra, 1977; HMNZS Canterbury, 1978–79; Captain, Naval Trng, 1981–84; ndc, Canada, 1983; Cdre, Auckland, 1986–87; Dep. Chief of Naval Staff, 1988–89; Chief of Naval Staff, 1989–91. *Recreations:* wine growing, flying. *Address:* Omarere, Ponatahi Road, PO Box 84, Martinborough, New Zealand. *Club:* Wellington (Wellington).

TEAGUE, (Edward) Thomas (Henry); QC 2000; a Recorder, since 1997; *b* Weymouth, 21 May 1954; *s* of Harry John Teague and Anne Elizabeth Teague (*née* Hunt); *m* 1980, Helen Mary Howard; two *s*. *Educ:* St Francis Xavier's Coll., Liverpool; Christ's Coll., Cambridge (MA). Called to the Bar, Inner Temple, 1977; in practice on Wales and Chester Circuit, 1978–; Asst Recorder, 1993–97. FRAS 1991. *Recreations:* music, fly-fishing, astronomy. *Address:* 22 Nicholas Street, Chester CH1 2NX. *T:* (01244) 323886; 3 Paper Buildings, Temple, EC4Y 7EU. *Club:* Lansdowne.

TEAR, Robert, CBE 1984; concert and operatic tenor; first Professor of International Singing, Royal Academy of Music, since 1985; *b* 8 March 1939; *s* of Thomas Arthur and Edith Tear; *m* 1961, Hilary Thomas; two *d*. *Educ:* Barry Grammar Sch.; King's Coll.,

Cambridge (MA; Hon. Fellow 1989). Hon. RCM, RAM. Mem., King's Coll. Choir, 1957–60; subseq. St Paul's Cathedral and solo career; joined English Opera Group, 1964. By 1968 worked with world's leading conductors, notably Karajan, Giulini, Bernstein and Solti; during this period created many rôles in operas by Benjamin Britten. Has appeared in all major festivals; close association with compositions of Sir Michael Tippett, 1970–; Covent Garden: début, The Knot Garden, 1970, closely followed by Lensky in Eugène Onégin; Fledermaus, 1977; Peter Grimes, 1978; Rake's Progress, 1979; Thérèse, 1979; Loge in Rheingold, 1980; Admetus in Alceste, 1981; David in Die Meistersinger, 1982; Captain Vere in Billy Budd, 1982; appears regularly with Royal Opera. Glyndebourne: début, Aschenbach in Death in Venice, 1989; Marriage of Figaro, and Rake's Progress, 1994; The Makropoulos Case, 1997. Started relationship with Scottish Opera (singing in La Traviata, Alceste, Don Giovanni), 1974. Paris Opera: début, 1976; Lulu 1979. Début as conductor with Thames Chamber Orchestra, QEH, 1980. Has conducted Minneapolis Orch., ECO, LSO, Philharmonia, London Mozart Players. Has worked with every major recording co. and made numerous recordings (incl. solo recital discs). Sermon, King's Coll. Chapel, Cambridge Univ., 1990. *Publications:* Victorian Songs and Duets, 1980; Tear Here (autobiog.), 1990; Singer Beware, 1995. *Recreations:* any sport; interested in 18th and 19th century English water colours. *Club:* Arts.

TEARE, Andrew Hubert; Chief Executive, Rank Group (formerly Rank Organisation) plc, 1996–98; *b* 8 Sept. 1942; *s* of Arthur Hubert Teare and Rosalind Margaret Baker; *m* 1964, Janet Nina Skidmore; three *s*. *Educ:* Kingswood School, Bath; University College London (BA Hons Classics 1964). Turner & Newall, 1964–72; CRH, 1972–83 (Gen. Manager Europe, 1978–83); Rugby Group, 1983–90 (Asst Man. Dir, 1983–84; Man. Dir, 1984–90); Gp Chief Exec., English China Clays plc, 1990–95. Non-executive Director: Heiton Holdings, 1984–90; NFC, 1989–96; Prudential Corp., 1992–98. Pres., Nat. Council of Building Material Producers, 1990–92. CIMgt. *Recreations:* ski-ing, mountain walking, reading. *Address:* Flat 2, 34 Craven Street, WC2N 5PB. *Club:* Hibernian United Service (Dublin).

TEARE, Jonathan James; His Honour Judge Teare; a Circuit Judge, since 1998; Deputy Senior Judge, Sovereign Base Areas, Cyprus, since 2001; *b* 13 Dec. 1946; *y s* of Prof. Donald Teare, MD, FRCP, FRCPath, DMJ and Kathleen Teare; *m* 1972, Nicola Jill, 2nd *d* of Lt-Col Peter Spittall, RM, CP and Peggy Spittall; two *d*. *Educ:* Pinewood Sch.; Rugby Sch. Called to the Bar, Middle Temple, 1970; practised, Midland and Oxford Circuit, 1971–98; Asst Recorder, 1985–90; Recorder, 1990–98. Served TA, HAC, 1965–69, RRF, 1970–72. Freeman, City of London, 1981; Liveryman, Soc. of Apothecaries, 1980–. *Recreations:* countryside, the kitchen garden. *Address:* The Castle, Castle Square, Lincoln LN1 5DA. *T:* (01522) 525222. *Club:* Nottingham and Notts United Services.

TEARE, Nigel John Martin; QC 1991; a Recorder, since 1997; *b* 8 Jan. 1952; *s* of Eric John Teare and Mary Rackham Teare; *m* 1975, Elizabeth Jane Pentecost; two *s* one *d*. *Educ:* King William's Coll., Isle of Man; St Peter's Coll., Oxford (BA 1973; MA 1975). Called to the Bar, Lincoln's Inn, 1974; practising barrister, 1975–; Jun. Counsel to Treasury in Admiralty matters, 1989–91; Asst Recorder, 1993–97. Lloyd's Salvage Arbitrator, 1994–2000, Lloyd's Salvage Appeal Arbitrator, 2000–. *Recreations:* collecting Manx paintings, squash, tennis. *Address:* 4 Essex Court, Temple, EC4Y 9AJ. *T:* (020) 7583 8381. *Club:* Royal Automobile.

TEASDALE, Prof. Graham Michael; FRCP, FRCSE, FRCSGlas; Professor and Head of Department of Neurosurgery, University of Glasgow, since 1981; *b* 20 Sept. 1940; *s* of Thomas Teasdale and Eva Teasdale (*née* Elgey); *m* 1971, Dr Evelyn Muriel Arnott; three *s* one *d*. *Educ:* Johnston Grammar Sch., Durham; Durham Univ. Med. Sch. (MB BS 1963). MRCP 1966, FRCP 1988; FRCSE 1970; FRCSGlas 1981. Trng in medicine, surgery and specialisation in neurosurgery, 1963–75; University of Glasgow: Sen. Lectr in Neurosurgery, 1975–79; Reader in Neurosurgery, 1979–81; Associate Dean for Med. Res., 1999–. President: Internat. Neurotrauma Soc., 1994–98; Eur. Brain Injury Consortium, 1993–; Soc. of British Neurological Surgeons, 2000–. FMedSci 1999. *Publications:* (jtly) Management of Head Injuries, 1982; (jtly) Current Neurosurgery, 1992; articles and papers on med. res., particularly on head injuries, in med. jls. *Recreations:* water sports, hill walking and midge dodging in the West of Scotland. *Address:* University Department of Neurosurgery, Institute of Neurological Sciences, Southern General Hospital, Govan Road, Glasgow G51 4TF. *T:* (0141) 201 2019.

TEASDALE, John Douglas, PhD; FBA 2000; Special Scientific Appointment, MRC Cognition and Brain Sciences (formerly Applied Psychology) Unit, since 1991; *b* 1 Sept. 1944; *s* of George Eric Teasdale and Vera Joan Teasdale; *m* 1969, Jacqueline Blackburn; two *s*. *Educ:* Emmanuel Coll., Cambridge (BA 1965, MA); Inst. of Psychiatry, Univ. of London (Dip. Psych. 1966; PhD 1971). Lectr, Psychology Dept, Inst. of Psychiatry, Univ. of London, 1967–71; Principal Clin. Psychologist, University Hosp. of Wales, Cardiff, 1971–74; Sen. Res. Worker, Dept of Psychiatry, Univ. of Oxford, 1974–85; Sen. Scientist, MRC Applied Psychol. Unit, 1985–91. Vis. Prof., Inst. of Psychiatry, Univ. of London, 1995–. FMedSci 2000. *Publications:* (with P. J. Barnard) Affect, Cognition and Change, 1993; (with Z. V. Segal and J. M. G. Williams) Mindfulness-Based Cognitive Therapy for Depression, 2001; approx. 100 articles in books and learned jls. *Recreation:* sitting quietly, doing nothing. *Address:* MRC Cognition and Brain Sciences Unit, 15 Chaucer Road, Cambridge CB2 2EF. *T:* (01223) 355294.

TE ATAIRANGIKAAHU, Arikinui, ONZ 1987; DBE 1970; Arikinui and Head of Maori Kingship, since 1966; *b* 23 July 1931; *o d* of King Koroki V; *m* 1952, Whatumoana; two *s* five *d*. *Educ:* Waikato Diocesan School, Hamilton, NZ. Elected by the Maori people as Head of the Maori Kingship on the death of King Koroki, the fifth Maori King, with title of Arikinui (Queen), in 1966. Hon. Dr Waikato, 1979; Hon. LLD Victoria Univ., Wellington, 1999. OStJ 1986. Gold and Silver Star, Order of Sacred Treasure (Japan), 1996. *Recreation:* the fostering of all aspects of Maori culture and traditions. *Address:* Turongo House, Turangawaewae Marae, PO Box 63, Ngaruawahia 2171, New Zealand.

TEBALDI, Renata; Italian soprano; *b* Pesaro, Italy, 1 Feb. 1922; *o c* of Teobaldo and Giuseppina (Barbieri) Tebaldi. Studied at Arrigo Boito Conservatory, Parma; Gioacchino Rossini Conservatory, Pesaro; subsequently a pupil of Carmen Melis and later of Giuseppe Pais. Made professional début as Elena in Mefistofele, Rovigo, 1944; first sang at La Scala, Milan, at post-war reopening concert (conductor Toscanini), 1946; has sung at Covent Garden and in opera houses of Naples, Rome, Venice, Pompeii, Turin, Cesana, Modena, Bologna and Florence; toured England, France, Spain and South America; American début in title rôle Aïda, San Francisco, 1950; Metropolitan Opera House Season, New York, 1955, and regularly until retirement from public perf., 1976; subseq. teaching. Recordings of complete operas include: Otello; Adriana Lecouvreur; Il Trittico; Don Carlo; La Gioconda; Un Ballo in Maschera; Madame Butterfly; Mefistofele; La Fanciulla Del West; La Forza Del Destino; Andrea Chenier; Manon Lescaut; La Tosca; Il Trovatore; Aida, La Bohème. *Address:* 1 Piazzetta della Guastalla, 20122 Milan, Italy. *T:* (02) 5512273.

TEBBIT, family name of **Baron Tebbit**.

TEBBIT, Baron *cr* 1992 (Life Peer), of Chingford, in the London Borough of Waltham Forest; **Norman Beresford Tebbit,** CH 1987; PC 1981; Director: Sears (Holdings) PLC, 1987–99; British Telecommunications plc, 1987–96; BET, 1987–96; Spectator (1828) Ltd, since 1989; journalist; *b* 29 March 1931; 2nd *s* of Leonard and Edith Tebbit, Enfield; *m* 1956, Margaret Elizabeth Daines; two *s* one *d*. *Educ:* Edmonton County Grammar Sch. Embarked on career in journalism, 1947. Served RAF: commissioned GD Branch; qualif. Pilot, 1949–51; Reserve service RAuxAF, No 604 City of Mddx Sqdn, 1952–55. Entered and left publishing and advertising, 1951–53. Civil Airline Pilot, 1953–70 (Mem. BALPA; former holder various offices in that Assoc.). Active mem. and holder various offices, Conservative Party, 1946–. MP (C) Epping, 1970–74, Chingford, 1974–92; PPS to Minister of State, Dept of Employment, 1972–73; Parly Under Sec. of State, Dept of Trade, 1979–81; Minister of State, Dept of Industry, 1981; Secretary of State for: Employment, 1981–83; Trade and Industry, 1983–85; Chancellor of the Duchy of Lancaster, 1985–87; Chm., Conservative Party, 1985–87. Former Chm., Cons. Members Aviation Cttee; former Vice-Chm. and Sec., Cons. Members Housing and Construction Cttee; Sec. House of Commons New Town Members Cttee. Dir, J. C. Bamford Excavators, 1987–91. Co-presenter, Target, Sky TV, 1989–98; columnist: The Sun, 1995–97; The Mail on Sunday, 1997–. *Publications:* Upwardly Mobile (autobiog.), 1988; Unfinished Business, 1991. *Address:* c/o House of Lords, SW1A 0PW.

TEBBIT, Sir Donald (Claude), GCMG 1980 (KCMG 1975; CMG 1965); HM Diplomatic Service, retired; *b* 4 May 1920; *m* 1947, Barbara Margaret Olson Matheson; one *s* three *d*. *Educ:* Perse School; Trinity Hall, Cambridge (MA). Served War of 1939–45, RNVR. Joined Foreign (now Diplomatic) Service, 1946; Second Secretary, Washington, 1948; transferred to Foreign Office, 1951; First Secretary, 1952; transferred to Bonn, 1954; Private Secretary to Minister of State, Foreign Office, 1958; Counsellor, 1962; transferred to Copenhagen, 1964; Commonwealth Office, 1967; Asst Under-Sec. of State, FCO, 1968–70; Minister, British Embassy, Washington, 1970–72; Chief Clerk, FCO, 1972–76; High Comr in Australia, 1976–80. Chairman: Diplomatic Service Appeals Bd, 1980–87; E-SU, 1983–87; Mem., Appeals Bd, Council of Europe, 1981–90. Dir, RTZ Corp., 1980–90. Dir Gen., British Property Fedn, 1980–85. Pres. (UK), Australian-British Chamber of Commerce, 1980–90; Chairman: Zimbabwe Tech. Management Training Trust, 1983–91; Marshall Aid Commemoration Commn, 1985–95; Jt Commonwealth Socs Council, 1987–93. Governor, Nuffield Hospitals, 1980–90, Dep. Chm., 1985–90. President: Old Persean Soc., 1981–82; Trinity Hall Assoc., 1984–85. *Address:* Priory Cottage, Toft, Cambridge CB3 7RH.

TEBBIT, Kevin Reginald, CMG 1997; Permanent Secretary, Ministry of Defence, since 1998; *b* 18 Oct. 1946; *s* of R. F. J. Tebbit and N. M. Tebbit (*née* Nichols); *m* 1969, Elizabeth Alison, *d* of John and Elizabeth Tinley; one *s* one *d*. *Educ:* Cambridgeshire High Sch.; St John's Coll., Cambridge (Schol.; BA Hons 1969). Asst Principal, MoD, 1969–72; Asst Private Sec. to Sec. of State for Defence, 1973–74; Principal, MoD, 1974–79; First Sec., UK Delegn to NATO, 1979–82; transferred to FCO, 1982; E European and Soviet Dept, 1982–84; Hd of Chancery, Ankara, 1984–87; Dir, Cabinet of Sec. Gen. of NATO, 1987–88; Counsellor (Politico-Mil.), Washington, 1988–91; Hd, Econ. Relns Dept, FCO, 1992–94; Dir (Resources) and Chief Inspector, FCO, 1994–97; Dep. Under-Sec. of State, FCO, 1997; Dir, GCHQ, 1998. *Recreations:* music, countryside, archaeology, West Ham Utd. *Address:* Ministry of Defence, Old War Office Building, Whitehall, SW1A 2EU. *Club:* Savile.

TECKMAN, Jonathan Simon Paul; Director, British Film Institute, since 1999; *b* 27 May 1963; *s* of Sidney Teckman and Stephanie Audrey Teckman (*née* Tresman); *m* 1997, Anne Caroline Fletcher. *Educ:* Weston Favell Upper Sch., Northampton; Univ. of Warwick (BSc Hons Mgt Scis). Admin trainee, 1984–86, HEO (Develt), 1986–90, DoE; Gp Finance Manager, Historic Royal Palaces Agency, 1990–93; Department of National Heritage, subsequently Department for Culture, Media and Sport: Principal, Nat. Lottery Div., 1993–95; Films Div., 1995–98 (Sec. to Adv. Cttee on Film Finance); Dep. Dir, BFI, 1998. *Recreations:* cinema, reading, cricket, golf. *Address:* British Film Institute, 21 Stephen Street, W1P 2LN. *T:* (020) 7957 8903. *Club:* Bold Dragoon Cricket (Northampton).

TEDDER, family name of **Baron Tedder**.

TEDDER, 3rd Baron *cr* 1946, of Glenguin, Co. Stirling; **Robin John Tedder;** investor and vigneron; Director, Glenguin Wine Co., since 1996; *b* 6 April 1955; *er s* of 2nd Baron Tedder and of Peggy Eileen Growcott; *S* father, 1994; *m* 1st, 1977, Jennifer Peggy (*d* 1978), *d* of John Mangan, NZ; 2nd, 1980, Rita Aristeia, *yr d* of John Frangidis, Sydney, NSW; two *s* one *d*. MW; Associate, Securities Inst. of Australia, 1981. *Heir:* *s* Hon. Benjamin John Tedder, *b* 23 April 1985. *Address:* 11 Kardinia Road, Clifton Gardens, Sydney, NSW 2088, Australia.

TEDFORD, Prof. David John, OBE 1997; ScD; CEng, FIEE; CPhys, FInstP; Professor of Electrical Engineering, University of Strathclyde, 1972–97, now Emeritus; Fellow, University of Strathclyde, 1999; *b* 12 July 1931; *s* of Thomas Tedford and Eliza Jane (*née* Yates); *m* 1956, Mary White Gardner; three *s* one *d*. *Educ:* Coatbridge High Sch.; Royal Tech. Coll. (ARCST 1952); Glasgow Univ. (BSc 1952; PhD 1955). CEng, FIEE 1970; CPhys, FInstP 1970. Res. Engr, Ferranti Ltd, Edinburgh, 1955–57; Strathclyde University: Lectr, 1957–64; Sen. Lectr, 1964–69; Reader, 1969–72; Dep. Principal, 1982–84; Vice-Principal, 1984–88; Dep. Principal (Internat. Affairs), 1988–91; Special Advr to Principal, 1991–92. Scientific Advr to Scottish Office Industry Dept, 1992–94; Chief Scientific Advr to Sec. of State for Scotland, 1994–96. Non-exec. Dir, Startech Partners Ltd, 1997–; Dir, Scottish Academic Consultants, 1996–. Chm., Technol. Educn Adv. Gp, Scottish Consultative Council on Curriculum, 1996–2001. Member: Scottish Univ. Council on Entrance, 1982–94 (Chm., 1989–94); Brit. Nat. Cttee and Exec. Cttee, CIGRE 1985–96; Standing Conf. on Univ. Entrance, 1989–93; Scottish Exam. Bd, 1986–93; Mgt Bd, SCOTVEC, 1993–97; Scottish Science Trust, 1997–(Chm., Scientific Adv. Cttee, 2001–); Steering Gp, Skills Strategy for Electronics Industry, Scotland, 1996–; Dundee Science Trust, 1998–; Business Services Steering Gp, Glasgow Sci. Centre, 1998–; Planning Cttee and Council, Hong Kong Univ. of Sci. and Technol., 1987–91; Mgt Bd, Bell Coll. of Technol., Hamilton, 1990– (Chm. College Council, 1990–93); Chm. Court, Univ. of Abertay Dundee, 1997–. Member: Educn Cttee and Internat. Relns Cttee, Royal Soc., 1991–93; Council, IEE, 1992–95; Vice-Pres., RSE, 1992–95; SMIEE, 1982. FRSE 1978; FRSA 1983. FUniv Strathclyde, 1999. Hon. ScD Lodz, 1988; Hon. DTech Abertay Dundee, 1995; Hon. DSc Robert Gordon, 1997; DUniv Strathclyde, 1997. Achievement Medal, IEE, 1997; Distinguished Mem., CIGRE, 1998. Civil Defence Medal, 1982. Commander's Cross, Order of Merit (Poland), 2001. *Publications:* numerous in scientific and engrg jls. *Recreations:* hill-walking, music, amateur astronomy, current affairs. *Address:* 76 Woodlands Drive, Coatbridge, Lanarkshire ML5 1LB. *T:* and *Fax:* (01236) 422016.

TEELOCK, Dr Boodhun; High Commissioner for Mauritius in London, 1989–91; *b* 20 July 1922; *s* of Ramessur Teelock and Sadny Teelock; *m* 1956, Riziya; three *d*. *Educ:* Edinburgh Univ. (MB ChB 1950); Liverpool Univ. (DTM&H 1951). DPH. Ministry of Health, Mauritius: School MO, 1952–58; Senior School MO, 1958–59; Principal MO,

1960–68; World Health Organisation: Regional Adviser, Public Health Administration, Brazzaville, 1968–71; Chief of Mission, Tanzania, 1971–74, Kenya and Seychelles, 1974–79; Immunisation MO, Air Mauritius, 1980–88. *Recreation:* reading. *Address:* 12 Labourdonnais Avenue, Quatre Bornes, Mauritius.

TEGNER, Ian Nicol, CA; Chairman, Children of the Andes, since 2001; *b* 11 July 1933; *s* of Sven Stuart Tegner, OBE, and Edith Margaret Tegner (*née* Nicol):; *m* 1961, Meriel Helen, *d* of Brig. M. S. Lush, CB, CBE, MC; one *s* one *d*. *Educ:* Rugby School. CA. Clarkson Gordon & Co., Toronto, 1958–59; Manager 1959–65, Partner 1965–71, Barton Mayhew & Co., Chartered Accts; Finance Dir, Bowater Industries, 1971–86; Chm., Cayzer Steel Bowater, 1981–86; Dir, Gp Finance, Midland Bank, 1987–89. Chairman: Control Risks Gp, 1992–2000; Crest Packaging, 1993–99; Director: Wiggins Teape Appleton, subseq. Arjo Wiggins Appleton, 1990–2000; Opera 80, subseq. English Touring Opera, 1991–99; TIP Europe plc, 1992–93; Teesside Power Ltd, 1993–2001; Coutts & Co., 1996–98. Institute of Chartered Accountants of Scotland: Mem. Council 1981–86; Pres., 1991–92; Mem., Accounting Standards Cttee of CCAB, 1984–86; Chm., Hundred Gp of Finance Dirs, 1988–90. *Publications:* articles on accountancy in various jls and pubns. *Recreations:* book collecting, travel, hill-walking, choral singing, family life. *Address:* 44 Norland Square, W11 4PZ.

TEJAN-JALLOH, Sulaiman; High Commissioner for Sierra Leone in London, since 2000; also Ambassador to Scandinavia, Spain, Greece, Portugal and Ireland, since 2000; *b* 21 July 1949; *s* of late Alihaj A. B. Tejan-Jalloh and Hajja Isatu Tejan-Jalloh; *m* 1989, Marima Tejan-Jalloh (*née* Jabbie); two *s* two *d*. *Educ:* American Univ., Washington (BSc Admin of Justice); SOAS, London (LLB Hons). Called to the Bar, Gray's Inn, 1980; enrolled Sierra Leone Bar, 1981, in practice as barrister and solicitor, 1981–96. MP (People's Party) Sierra Leone, 1996–98; Minister of Transport, Communications and Envmt, 1996–98; Dep. High Comr to UK, 1999–2000. *Recreations:* music, walking, gardening. *Address:* 3 Ingram Avenue, NW11 6TG. *T:* (020) 8731 7250.

TE KANAWA, Dame Kiri (Jeanette), ONZ 1995; DBE 1982 (OBE 1973); opera singer; *b* Gisborne, New Zealand, 6 March 1944; *m* 1967, Desmond Stephen Park (marr. diss. 1997); one *s* one *d*. *Educ:* St Mary's Coll., Auckland, NZ; London Opera Centre. Major rôles at Royal Opera House, Covent Garden, include: the Countess, in Marriage of Figaro; Elvira, in Don Giovanni; Mimi, in La Bohème; Desdemona, in Otello; Marguerite, in Faust; Amelia, in Simon Boccanegra; Fiordiligi, in Così Fan Tutte; Tatiana, in Eugene Onegin; title rôle in Arabella; Rosalinde, in Die Fledermaus; Violetta, in La Traviata; Manon, in Manon Lescaut. Has sung leading rôles at Metropolitan Opera, New York, notably, Desdemona, Elvira, and Countess; also at the Paris Opera, Elvira, Fiordiligi, and Pamina in Magic Flute, title rôle in Tosca; at San Francisco Opera, Amelia and Pamina; at Sydney Opera House, Mimi, Amelia, and Violetta in La Traviata; Elvira, with Cologne Opera; Amelia at La Scala, Milan; Countess in Le Nozze di Figaro at Salzburg Fest. Many recordings, incl. Maori songs. Hon. DMus: Oxford, 1983; Cambridge, 1997. *Publications:* Land of the Long White Cloud, 1989; Opera for Lovers, 1997. *Recreations:* golf, swimming, tennis. *Address:* c/o Jules Haefliger, Impresario AG, Postfach 3320, 6002 Lucerne, Switzerland.

TELFER, Robert Gilmour Jamieson, (Rab), CBE 1985; PhD; Executive Chairman, BSI Standards, 1989–92; Director, Manchester Business School, 1984–88; *b* 22 April 1928; *s* of late James Telfer and Helen Lambie Jamieson; *m* 1953, Joan Audrey Gunning; three *s*. *Educ:* Bathgate Academy (Dawson Trust Bursary); Univ. of Edinburgh (Mackay-Smith Prize; Blandfield Prize; BSc (Hons 1st cl.) 1950, PhD 1953). Shift Chemist, AEA, 1953–54; Imperial Chemical Industries Ltd: Res. Chemist, Billingham Div., 1954–58; Heavy Organic Chemicals Div., 1958–71; Fibre Intermediates Dir and R & D Dir, 1971–75; Div. Dep. Chm., 1975–76, Div. Chm., 1976–81, Petrochemicals Div.; Chm. and Man. Dir, 1981–84, Dir, 1984, Mather & Platt Ltd; Chm., European Industrial Services Ltd, 1988–89. Mem. Bd, Philips-Imperial Petroleum Ltd, 1975–81; Director: Renold PLC, 1984–98 (Chm., Audit Cttee, 1993–98); Volex PLC, 1986–98 (Chm., Audit Cttee, 1993–98); Teesside Hldgs Ltd, 1993–95. Sen. Vis. Fellow, Manchester Business Sch., 1988–. Group Chm., Duke of Edinburgh's Study Conf., 1974; Mem., ACORD for Fuel and Power, 1981–87; Chm., Adv. Council on Energy Conservation, 1982–84. Personal Adviser to Sec. of State for Energy, 1984–87. British Standards Institution: Mem. Main Bd, and Mem. Finance Cttee, 1988–92; non-exec. Chm., Standards Bd and Testing Bd, 1988–89. Member: Civil Service Coll. Adv. Council, 1986–89; HEFCE, 1992–97 (Chairman: Audit Cttee, 1993–97; Quality Assessment Cttee, 1996–98); Dir, Quality Assurance Agency for Higher Educn, 1997–98. Governor, Univ. of Teesside (formerly Teesside Polytechnic), 1989–97 (Chm., Govs, 1992–97; Chm., Resources Cttee, 1989–92). CIMgt. Hon. MBA Manchester, 1989; Hon. LLD Teesside, 1998. *Publications:* papers in Jl Chem. Soc. and Chemistry and Industry. *Recreations:* walking, swimming, poetry, decorative egg collecting, supporting Middlesbrough FC. *Address:* Downings, Upleatham Village, Redcar, Cleveland TS11 8AG.

TELFORD, Sir Robert, Kt 1978; CBE 1967; DL; FREng, FIEE; Life President, The Marconi Company Ltd, 1984 (Managing Director, 1965–81; Chairman, 1981–84, retired); *b* 1 Oct. 1915; *s* of Robert and Sarah Annie Telford; *m* 1st, 1941 (marr. diss. 1950); one *s*; 2nd, 1958, Elizabeth Mary (*née* Shelley); three *d*. *Educ:* Quarry Bank Sch., Liverpool; Queen Elizabeth's Grammar Sch., Tamworth; Christ's Coll., Cambridge (MA). FREng (FEng 1978). Manager, Hackbridge Works, The Marconi Co. Ltd, 1940–46; Man. Dir, Companhia Marconi Brasileira, 1946–50; The Marconi Company Ltd: Asst to Gen. Manager, 1950–53; Gen. Works Manager, 1953–61; Gen. Manager, 1961–65; Man. Dir, GEC-Marconi Electronics Ltd, 1968–84; Chm., GEC Avionics Ltd, 1982–86; Director: The General Electric Co., 1973–84; Canadian Marconi Co., Montreal, 1968–84; Ericsson Radio Systems AB (formerly SRA Communications, AB), Stockholm, 1969–85. Chairman: DRI Hldgs Ltd, 1984–88; Prelude Technology Investments, 1985–91; CTP Investments, 1987–90; Diametric, 1988–89; Dir, BAJ Hldgs, 1985–87. Visitor, Hatfield Polytech., 1986–91. President: Electronic Engrg Assoc., 1963–64; IProdE, 1982–83; Chairman: Electronics and Avionics Requirement Bd, DTI, 1980–85; Alvey Steering Cttee, 1983–88; SERC Teaching Company Management Cttee, 1984–87; Commonwealth Engineers' Council, 1989–93; Member: Electronics EDC, 1964–67, 1981–85; Engrg Industry Trng Bd, 1968–82; Council, Industrial Soc., 1982–86; Council, Fellowship of Engrg, 1983–86; BTEC, 1984–86; SERC Engrg Bd, 1985–88; Engrg Council, 1985–89; IT Adv. Gp, DTI, 1985–88. Advr to Comett Programme of European Community, 1987–95; Mem., Industrial R & D Adv. Cttee to European Community, 1988–92. Mem., Council of Sen. Advrs to Internat. Assoc. of Univ. Presidents, 1992. Mem., Council, 1981–88, and Court, 1981–, Univ. of Essex. DL Essex, 1981. Freeman, City of London, 1984. CIMgt; FRSA. Hon. FIMechE, 1983; Hon. FIEE, 1987; Hon. FICE 1992. Hon. Fellow, Hatfield Poly., 1991. Hon. DSc: Salford, 1981; Cranfield, 1983; Bath, 1984; Aston, 1985; Hon. DEng: Bradford, 1986; Birmingham, 1986; Hon. DTech Anglia Inst., 1989. Leonardo da Vinci Medal, SEFI, 1992. *Address:* Rettendon House, Rettendon, Chelmsford, Essex CM3 8DW. *T:* (01268) 733131. *Club:* Royal Air Force.

TELLER, Prof. Edward; Senior Research Fellow, Hoover Institution, since 1975; University Professor, University of California, Berkeley, 1971–75, now Emeritus (Professor of Physics, 1960–71); Chairman, Department of Applied Science, University of California, 1963–66; Associate Director, Lawrence Radiation Laboratory, University of California, 1954–75, now Emeritus; *b* Budapest, Hungary, 15 Jan. 1908; *s* of a lawyer; became US citizen, 1941; *m* 1934, Augusta Harkanyi; one *s* one *d*. *Educ:* Karlsruhe Technical Inst., Germany; Univ. of Munich; Leipzig (PhD). Research Associate, Leipzig, 1929–31; Research Associate, Göttingen, 1931–33; Rockefeller Fellow, Copenhagen, 1934; Lectr, Univ. of London, 1934–35; Prof. of Physics, George Washington Univ., Washington, DC, 1935–41; Prof. of Physics, Columbia Univ., 1941–42; Physicist, Manhattan, Engineer District, 1942–46, Univ. of Chicago, 1942–43; Los Alamos Scientific Laboratory, 1943–46; Prof. of Physics, Univ. of Chicago, 1946–52; Asst Dir, Los Alamos (on leave, Chicago), 1949–52; Consultant, Livermore Br., Univ. of Calif, Radiation Laboratory, 1952–53; Prof. of Physics, Univ. of Calif, 1953–60; Dir, Livermore Br., Lawrence Livermore Lab., Univ. of Calif, 1958–60, now Dir Emeritus. Mem. Nat. Acad. of Sciences, etc. Holds several hon. degrees, 1954–. Has gained awards, 1957–, incl. Enrico Fermi Award, 1962; Harvey Prize, Israel, 1975; Gold Medal, Amer. Coll. of Nuclear Med., 1980; Man of the Year, Achievement Rewards for College Scientists, 1980; Nat. Medal of Science, 1983. *Publications:* The Structure of Matter, 1949; Our Nuclear Future, 1958; The Legacy of Hiroshima, 1962; The Reluctant Revolutionary, 1964; The Constructive Uses of Nuclear Explosives, 1968; Great Men of Physics, 1969; Nuclear Energy in a Developing World, 1977; Energy from Heaven and Earth, 1979; Pursuit of Simplicity, 1980; Better a Shield than a Sword, 1987; Conversations on the Dark Secrets of Physics, 1991. *Address:* Stanford, CA 94305, USA.

TELLO, Manuel, CMG (Hon.) 1975; Permanent Representative of Mexico to the United Nations, 1993–94 and since 1995; *b* 15 March 1935; *s* of late Manuel Tello and Guadalupe M. de Tello; *m* 1983, Rhonda M. de Tello. *Educ:* schools in Mexico City; Georgetown Univ.; Sch. for Foreign Service, Washington, DC; Escuela Libre de Derecho; Institut de Hautes Etudes Internationales, Geneva. Equivalent of BA in Foreign Service Studies; post-grad. studies in Internat. Law. Joined Mexican Foreign Service, 1957; Asst Dir Gen. for Internat. Organizations, 1967–70, Dir Gen., 1970–72; Dir for Multilateral Affairs, 1972–74; Dir for Political Affairs, 1975–76; Ambassador to UK, 1977–79; Under Sec., Dept of Foreign Affairs, Mexico, 1979–82; Perm. Rep. of Mexico to Internat. Orgns, Geneva, 1983–89; Ambassador to France, 1989–92; Minister of Foreign Affairs, 1994–95. Alternate Rep. of Mexico to: OAS, 1959–63; Internat. Orgs, Geneva, 1963–65; Conf. of Cttee on Disarmament, Geneva, 1963–66; Rep. of Mexico to: Org. for Proscription of Nuclear Weapons in Latin America, 1970–73; 3rd UN Conf. on Law of the Sea, 1971–76 and 1982. Has attended several Sessions of UN Gen. Assembly. Holds decorations from Chile, Ecuador, Egypt, France, Italy, Jordan, Panama, Senegal, Sweden, Venezuela, Yugoslavia. *Publications:* contribs to learned jls in the field of international relations. *Recreations:* tennis, theatre, music. *Address:* 2 UN Plaza, 28th Floor, New York, NY 10017, USA.

TEMIRKANOV, Yuri; Music Director and Principal Conductor, St Petersburg (formerly Leningrad) Philharmonic Orchestra, since 1988; Music Director, Baltimore Symphony Orchestra, since 2000; *b* 10 Dec. 1938. *Educ:* Leningrad Conservatory (graduated violinist, 1962, conductor, 1965). Musical Dir, Leningrad Symphony Orch., 1969–77; Artistic Dir and Chief Conductor, Kirov Opera, Leningrad, 1977–88; Principal Conductor, Royal Philharmonic Orch., 1978–98, now Conductor Laureate. Principal Guest Conductor, Dresden Philharmonic Orch., 1994–98. Has conducted: Boston Symphony; Dresden Philharmonic; Danish Nat. Radio Symphony; Orch. of Santa Cecilia, Rome; Orch. Nat. de France; La Scala, Milan; Philadelphia Orch.; San Francisco Symphony; New York Philharmonic, etc. Recordings of major orchestral works of Tchaikovsky, Stravinsky, Prokofiev, Mussorgsky and Shostakovich. *Address:* c/o IMG Artists Europe, 616 Chiswick High Road, W4 5RX. *T:* (020) 8233 5800.

TEMKIN, Prof. Jennifer, (Mrs G. J. Zellick); Professor of Law, University of Sussex, since 1992; *b* 6 June 1948; *d* of late Michael Temkin and Minnie Temkin (*née* Levy); *m* 1975, Prof. Graham Zellick, *qv*; one *s* one *d*. *Educ:* S Hampstead High Sch. for Girls; LSE (LLB, LLM (Dist.)); Inns of Court Sch. of Law. Called to the Bar, Middle Temple, 1971; Lectr in Law, LSE, 1971–89; Prof. of Law and Dean, Sch. of Law, Univ. of Buckingham, 1989–92; Dir, Centre for Legal Studies, Univ. of Sussex, 1994–96. Vis. Prof., Univ. of Toronto, 1978–79. Mem., Cttee of Heads of Univ. Law Schs, 1989–92, 1994–96. Member: Scrutiny Cttee on Draft Criminal Code, CCC, 1985–86; Home Sec's Adv. Gp on Use of Video Recordings in Criminal Proceedings, 1988–89; NCH Cttee on Children Who Abuse Other Children, 1990–92; External Reference Gp, Home Office Sex Offences Review, 1999–2000. Patron, Standing Cttee on Sexually Abused Children, 1993–96. Gov., S Hampstead High Sch. for Girls, 1991–99. FRSA 1989. Member: Editl Adv. Gp, Howard Jl of Criminal Justice, 1984–; Editl Bd, Jl of Criminal Law, 1986–. *Publications:* Rape and the Legal Process, 1987; Rape and Criminal Justice, 1995; articles in Mod. Law Rev., Criminal Law Rev., Cambridge Law Jl, Law Qly Rev., Internat. and Comparative Law Qly and other learned and professional jls. *Address:* School of Legal Studies, University of Sussex, Falmer, Brighton, Sussex BN1 9QN. *T:* (01273) 606755.

TEMKO, Edward James, (Ned); Editor, Jewish Chronicle, since 1990; *b* 5 Nov. 1952; *s* of Stanley L. Temko and Francine (*née* Salzman); *m* 1st, 1980, Noa Weiss (marr. diss. 1984); 2nd, 1986, Astra Bergson Kook; one *s*. *Educ:* Williams Coll., USA (BA Hons Pol Sci. and Econs). Reporter, Associated Press, Lisbon, 1976; United Press International: Europe, ME and Africa Editl Desk, Brussels, 1977; Correspondent, ME Office, Beirut, 1977–78; Christian Science Monitor: Chief ME Correspondent, Beirut, 1978–80; Moscow Correspondent, 1981–83; ME Correspondent, Jerusalem, 1984–85; SA Correspondent, Johannesburg, 1986–87; Sen. TV Correspondent for Europe, ME and Africa in London, World Monitor TV, 1989–90. *Publications:* To Win or To Die: a biography of Menachem Begin, 1987. *Recreations:* tennis, reading, computers, travel. *Address:* 25 Furnival Street, EC4A 1JT. *T:* (020) 7405 9252.

TEMPANY, Myles McDermott, OBE 1984; Vice-Principal (External Affairs), King's College London, 1986–88; *b* 31 March 1924; *m* 1951, Pamela Allan; one *s* one *d*. *Educ:* St Muredach's College, Ballina, Co. Mayo; Intermediate and University College, Dublin. Military service, 1944–47. King's College London: Asst Acct, 1948–70; Acct, 1970–73; Finance Officer and Acct, 1973–77; FKC 1975; Bursar, 1977–81; Head of Admin and Bursar, 1981–83; Secretary, 1983–85; Mem. Council, 1986–89. Mem. Delegacy, King's Coll. Sch. of Medicine and Dentistry, 1986–88; Founder Chm., St Raphael's Training Centre Develt Trust, 1978–83; Mem., Governing Body, Univ. of Hertfordshire (formerly Hatfield Polytechnic), 1985–96; Chm., Bd of Governors, Pope Paul Sch., Potters Bar, 1986–96. KHS 1972, KCHS 1978; KSG 1983, KCSG 1996. President's Award, Develt Bd, Univ. of Texas Health Science Center, Houston, 1986. *Recreations:* golf, watching Association Football. *Address:* 18 Tiverton Road, Potters Bar, Herts EN6 5HY. *T:* (01707) 656860. *Clubs:* Institute of Directors; Brookman's Park Golf.

TEMPLE OF STOWE, 8th Earl *cr* 1822; **Walter Grenville Algernon Temple-Gore-Langton;** *b* 2 Oct. 1924; *s* of Comdr Hon. Evelyn Arthur Temple-Gore-Langton, DSO, RN (*d* 1972) (*y s* of 4th Earl) and Irene (*d* 1967), *d* of Brig.-Gen. Cavendish Walter Gartside-Spaight; *S* cousin, 1988; *m* 1st, 1954, Zillah Ray (*d* 1966), *d* of James Boxall; two *s* one *d*; 2nd, 1968, Margaret Elizabeth Graham, *o d* of late Col H. W. Scarth of Breckness. *Heir: s* Lord Langton, *qv*.

TEMPLE, Anthony Dominic Afamado; QC 1986; a Recorder, since 1989; *b* 21 Sept. 1945; *s* of Sir Rawden John Afamado Temple, CBE, QC and late Margaret Jessie Temple; *m* 1st, 1975 (marr. diss.); 2nd, 1983, Suzie Bodansky; two *d*. *Educ:* Haileybury and ISC; Worcester College, Oxford (Hon. Sec., OU Modern Pentathlon Assoc.). Called to the Bar, Inner Temple, 1968, Bencher, 1995; Crown Law Office, Western Australia, 1969; Assistant Recorder, 1982; a Dep. High Ct Judge, 1994–. *Recreations:* modern pentathlon, travel, history. *Address:* 4 Pump Court, EC4Y 7AN.
See also V. B. A. Temple.

TEMPLE, Ven. George Frederick; Archdeacon of Bodmin, 1981–89, Archdeacon Emeritus since 1989; *b* 16 March 1933; *s* of George Frederick and Lilian Rose Temple; *m* 1961, Jacqueline Rose Urwin; one *s* one *d*. *Educ:* St Paul's, Jersey; Wells Theological College. Deacon 1968, priest 1969, Guildford; Curate: St Nicholas, Great Bookham, 1968–70; St Mary the Virgin, Penzance, 1970–72; Vicar of St Just in Penwith with Sancreed, 1972–74; Vicar of St Gluvias, Penryn, 1974–81; Vicar of Saltash, 1982–85. Mem., General Synod of C of E, 1981–85; Chm., House of Clergy, Truro Diocesan Synod, 1982–85; Diocesan Dir of Ordinands, 1985–87. Hon. Canon of Truro, 1981–89. *Recreations:* poetry, history, walking. *Address:* 3 Sycamore Close, Bodmin, Cornwall PL31 1QB.

TEMPLE, Prof. John Graham, FRCSE, FRCS, FRCPE, FRCP; Professor of Surgery, University of Birmingham, since 1995; President, Royal College of Surgeons of Edinburgh, since 2000; *b* 14 March 1942; *s* of Joseph Henry Temple and Norah Temple; *m* 1966, Margaret Jillian Leighton Hartley; two *s* one *d*. *Educ:* William Hulme's Grammar Sch., Manchester; Liverpool Univ. Med. Sch. (MB ChB Hons; ChM). FRCSE 1969; FRCS 1970; FRCP, FRCPE 1999. Consultant Surgeon, Queen Elizabeth Hosp., Birmingham, 1979–98; Regl Postgrad. Dean, W Midlands, 1991–2000. Chm., Conf. Postgrad. Med. Deans UK, 1995–. Mem. Council, RCSE, 1997–. Mem., Specialist Trng Authy, 1996–. FMedSci 1999; Fellow, Polish Soc. Surgeons, 1997. *Publications:* papers on postgraduate education and training. *Recreations:* off-shore sailing and racing, ski-ing. *Address:* Wharncliffe, 24 Westfield Road, Edgbaston, Birmingham B15 3QG.

TEMPLE, Nicholas John; Chairman, Cyber-CV.com, since 2000; non-executive Director: Electrocomponents PLC, since 1997; Blick PLC, since 1999; auxinet, since 2000; *b* 2 Oct. 1947; *s* of late Leonard Temple and of Lilly Irene Temple (*née* Thornton); *m* 1975, Janet Perry (marr. diss. 2001); one *s* two *d*. *Educ:* King's Sch., Glos. Joined IBM, 1965; Chief Exec., 1992–94, Chm., 1994–96, IBM UK; Vice Pres., Industries, IBM Europe, 1995–96; mgt consultant, N. M. Rothschild & Sons, 1996. Council Mem., Foundn for Mfg and Ind., 1993–. Chm., Action: Employees in the Community, 1993–. Mem., President's Adv. Gp, Spastics' Soc., 1993–. *Recreations:* rowing, ski-ing, opera. *Address:* 10 Markham Square, SW3 4UY. *T:* (020) 7581 2181.

TEMPLE, Reginald Robert, CMG 1979; HM Diplomatic Service, retired; *b* 12 Feb. 1922; *s* of Lt-Gen. R. C. Temple, CB, OBE, RM, and Z. E. Temple (*née* Hunt); *m* 1st, 1952, Julia Jasmine Anthony (marr. diss. 1979); one *s* one *d*; 2nd, 1979, Susan McCorquodale (*née* Pick); one *d* (one step *s* one step *d*). *Educ:* Wellington College; Peterhouse, Cambridge. HM Forces, 1940–46, RE and Para Regt; Stockbroking, 1947–51; entered HM Foreign Service, 1951; Office of HM Comr Gen. for SE Asia, 1952–56; 2nd Sec., Beirut, 1958–62; 1st Sec., Algiers, 1964–66, Paris, 1967–69; FCO, 1969–79; Counsellor 1975; Sultanate of Oman Govt Service, 1979–85. Director: Shearwater Securities Ltd, I of M, 1989–92; City and International Securities Ltd, I of M, 1993–96; Consultant, Capital International Securities Ltd, I of M, 1997–2000. American Silver Star, 1944; Order of Oman, 3rd Class, 1985. *Recreations:* sailing, fishing. *Address:* Scarlett House, near Castletown, Isle of Man IM9 1TB. *Clubs:* Army and Navy, Royal Cruising, Royal Ocean Racing.

TEMPLE, Sir Richard Anthony Purbeck, 4th Bt, *cr* 1876; MC 1941; *b* 19 Jan. 1913; *s* of Sir Richard Durand Temple, 3rd Bt, DSO; *S* father, 1962; *m* 1st, 1936, Lucy Geils (marr. diss., 1946), 2nd *d* of late Alain Joly de Lotbinière, Montreal; two *s*; 2nd, 1950, Jean, *d* of late James T. Finnie, and *widow* of Oliver P. Croom-Johnson; one *d*. *Educ:* Stowe; Trinity Hall, Cambridge; Lausanne University. Served War of 1939–45 (wounded, MC). Sometime Major, KRRC. *Recreation:* sailing. *Heir: s* Richard Temple [*b* 17 Aug. 1937; *m* 1964, Emma Rose, 2nd *d* of late Maj.-Gen. Sir Robert Laycock, KCMG, CB, DSO; three *d*]. *Address:* c/o National Westminster Bank, 55 Kensington High Street, W8 5ZG.

TEMPLE, Victor Bevis Afoumado; QC 1993; a Recorder of the Crown Court, since 1989; *b* 23 Feb. 1941; *s* of Sir Rawden John Afamado Temple, CBE, QC and late Margaret Jessie Temple; *m* 1974, Richenda Penn-Bull; two *s*. *Educ:* Shrewsbury Sch.; Inns of Court Sch. of Law. TA, Westminster Dragoons, 1960–61. Marketing Exec., 1960–68. Called to the Bar, Inner Temple, 1971, Bencher, 1996; Jun. Prosecuting Counsel to the Crown, 1985–91, Sen. Treasury Counsel, 1991–93, CCC. DTI Inspector into Nat. Westminster Bank Ltd, 1992. Mem. Panel of Chairmen, Police Discipline Tribunals, 1993–. *Recreations:* rowing, carpentry. *Address:* 6 King's Bench Walk, Temple, EC4Y 7DR. *T:* (020) 7583 0410. *Club:* Thames Rowing.
See also A. D. A. Temple.

TEMPLE-GORE-LANGTON, family name of **Earl Temple of Stowe**.

TEMPLE-MORRIS, family name of **Baron Temple-Morris**.

TEMPLE-MORRIS, Baron *cr* 2001 (Life Peer), of Llandaff in the County of South Glamorgan and of Leominster in the County of Herefordshire; **Peter Temple-Morris;** Consultant Solicitor, Moon Beever, Solicitors; *b* 12 Feb. 1938; *o s* of His Honour Sir Owen Temple-Morris, QC and Lady (Vera) Temple-Morris (*née* Thompson); *m* 1964, Taheré, *e d* of HE Senator Khozeimé Alam, Teheran; two *s* two *d*. *Educ:* Hillstone Sch., Malvern; Malvern Coll.; St Catharine's Coll., Cambridge (MA). Chm., Cambridge Univ. Conservative Assoc., 1961; Mem. Cambridge Afro-Asian Expedn, 1961. Called to Bar, Inner Temple, 1962. Judge's Marshal, Midland Circuit, 1958; Mem., Young Barristers' Cttee, Bar Council, 1962–63; in practice on Wales and Chester Circuit, 1963–66; London and SE Circuit, 1966–76; 2nd Prosecuting Counsel to Inland Revenue, SE Circuit, 1971–74; admitted a solicitor, 1989. Contested (C): Newport (Mon), 1964 and 1966; Norwood (Lambeth), 1970; MP Leominster, Feb. 1974–2001 (C, Feb. 1974–1997, Ind., 1997–98, Lab, 1998–2001). PPS to Minister of Transport, 1979. Member: Select Cttee on Agriculture, 1982–83; Select Cttee on Foreign Affairs, 1987–90. Chairman: British-Lebanese Parly Gp, 1983–94 (Vice-Chm., 1994–97); British-Netherlands Parly Gp, 1988–; British-Iranian Parly Gp, 1989– (Sec., 1974–89); British-South Africa (formerly British-Southern Africa) All-Party Gp, 1992–95 (Vice-Chm., 1995–2001); British-Russian All-Party Gp, 1992–94; British-Spanish All-Party Gp, 1994–2001; House of Lords and Commons Solicitors Gp, 1992–97; Co-Chm., Working Party to establish British-Irish Inter-Parly Body, 1988–90, first British Co-Chm., 1990–97, Mem., 1997–; Secretary: Conservative Parly Transport Cttee, 1976–79; Cons. Parly Legal Cttee, 1977–78; Vice-Chairman: Cons. Parly Foreign and Commonwealth Affairs Cttee, 1982–90 (Sec., 1979–82); Cons. Parly NI Cttee, 1989–92; British-Argentina Parly Gp, 1990–94; European-Atlantic Gp, 1991–97. Member: Exec. British Branch, IPU, 1977–97 (Chm., 1982–85; British delegate, fact-finding mission on Namibia, 1977); Exec. Cttee, UK Br., CPA, 1993–98; Mem., 1980, Leader, 1984, Parly Delegation to UN Gen. Assembly; Mem., Argentine-British Conf., 1991. Chm., Hampstead Conservative Political Centre, 1971–73; Society of Conservative Lawyers: Mem. Exec., 1968–71, 1990–97 (Chm., 1995–97); Vice-Chm., Standing Cttee on Criminal Law, 1976–79; Chm., F&GP Cttee, 1992–95. Chm., Bow Gp Standing Cttee on Home Affairs, 1975–79. Chm., Afghanistan Support Cttee, 1981–82; Vice-Chm., GB-Russian Centre (formerly GB-USSR Assoc.), 1993–98 (Mem. Council, 1982–92); Pres., Iran Soc., 1995– (Mem. Council, 1968–80); Hon. Pres., British-Iranian Business Assoc.; Bd of Dirs, British Iranian Chamber of Commerce; Adv. Council, British Inst. of Persian Studies. Mem., RIIA. Nat. Treas., UNA, 1987–97 (Hon. Vice Pres., 1997–). Freeman, City of London; Liveryman, Barbers' Co., 1993. Gov., Malvern Coll., 1975– (Council Mem., 1978–); Mem. Council, Wilton Park Conf. Centre, (FCO), 1990–97. Fellow, Industry and Parlt Trust, Barclays Bank, 1988. Hon. Associate, BVA, 1976. Hon Citizen: New Orleans; Havana, Cuba. Chevalier du Tastevin, 1991; Jurade de St Emilion, 1999. *Recreations:* travel, wine and food, family relaxation. *Address:* House of Lords, SW1A 0PW. *Clubs:* Reform; Cardiff and County.

TEMPLEMAN, family name of **Baron Templeman**.

TEMPLEMAN, Baron *cr* 1982 (Life Peer), of White Lackington in the County of Somerset; **Sydney William Templeman,** Kt 1972; MBE 1946; PC 1978; a Lord of Appeal in Ordinary, 1982–94; *b* 3 March 1920; *s* of late Herbert William and Lilian Templeman; *m* 1st, 1946, Margaret Joan (*née* Rowles) (*d* 1988); two *s*; 2nd, 1996, Mrs Sheila Barton Edworthy. *Educ:* Southall Grammar School; St John's College, Cambridge (Schol.; MA 1944; Hon. Fellow 1982). Served War of 1939–45: commnd 4/1st Gurkha Rifles, 1941; NW Frontier, 1942; Arakan, 1943; Imphal, 1944; Burma with 7 Ind. and 17 Ind. Divisions, 1945 (despatches; Hon. Major). Called to the Bar, 1947; Harmsworth and MacMahon schols; Mem., Middle Temple and Lincoln's Inn; Mem., Bar Council, 1961–65, 1970–72; QC 1964; Bencher, Middle Temple, 1969 (Treasurer, 1987). Attorney Gen. of the Duchy of Lancaster, 1970–72; a Judge of the High Court of Justice, Chancery Div., 1972–78; a Lord Justice of Appeal, 1978–82. Member: Tribunal to inquire into matters relating to the Vehicle and General Insurance Co., 1971; Adv. Cttee on Legal Education, 1972–74; Royal Commn on Legal Services, 1976–79; Chm., Bishop of London's Commn on City Churches, 1992–94. Treasurer, Senate of the Four Inns, 1972–74; Pres., Senate of the Inns of Court and the Bar, 1974–76. President: Bar Assoc. for Commerce, Finance and Industry, 1982–85; Bar European Gp, 1987–95; Assoc. of Law Teachers, 1997–. Pres., Holdsworth Club, 1983–84. Hon. Member: Canadian Bar Assoc., 1976; Amer. Bar Assoc., 1976; Newfoundland Law Soc., 1984. Hon. DLitt Reading, 1980; Hon. LLD: Birmingham, 1986; CNAA, 1990; Exeter, 1991; W of England, 1993; Nat. Law Sch. of India, 1994. *Address:* Mellowstone, 1 Rosebank Crescent, Exeter EX4 6EJ. *T:* (01392) 275428.

TEMPLEMAN, Michael; Group Tax Director, Schroders PLC; *b* 6 May 1943; *s* of late Geoffrey Templeman and Dorothy May Templeman (*née* Heathcote); *m* 1970, Jane Margaret Willmer Lee; four *d*. *Educ:* King Edward's Sch., Birmingham; Selwyn Coll., Cambridge (MA). Inland Revenue, 1965–93: Inspector of Taxes, 1965; Dist Inspector, Cannock, 1971–72; Head Office Specialist, Oil Taxation, 1972–78; Dist. Inspector, Luton, 1978–81; Head Office Specialist, Financial Concerns, 1981–89; Controller, Oil Taxation Office, 1989–92; Dir, Financial Institutions Div., 1992–93; J. Henry Schroder Wagg, then J. Henry Schroder, & Co., now Schroders PLC: Gp Tax Dir, 1994–. *Recreations:* distance running, cricket, classical music, cooking. *Address:* (office) 31 Gresham Street, EC2V 7QA. *T:* (020) 7658 6450.

TEMPLER, Maj.-Gen. James Robert, CB 1989; OBE 1978 (MBE 1973); Managing Director, Templers Flowers, since 1990; *b* 8 Jan. 1936; *s* of Brig. Cecil Robert Templer, DSO and Angela Mary Templer (*née* Henderson); *m* 1963 (marr. diss. 1979); two *s* one *d*; 2nd, 1981, Sarah Ann Evans (*née* Rogers). *Educ:* Charterhouse; RMA Sandhurst. RCDS, psc. Commissioned Royal Artillery, 1955; Instructor, Staff Coll., 1974–75; Comd 42nd Regt, 1975–77; Comd 5th Regt, 1977–78; CRA 2nd Armd Div., 1978–82; RCDS 1983; ACOS Training, HQ UKLF, 1983–86; ACDS (Concepts), MoD, 1986–89. Mem., British Cross Country Ski Team, 1958; European 3 Day Event Champion, 1962; Mem., British Olympic 3 Day Event Team, 1964. FIMgt (FBIM 1988). *Recreations:* sailing, ski-ing, riding, gardening, fishing, beekeeping, DIY. *Address:* c/o Lloyds TSB, Crediton, Devon EX17 3AH.

TEMPLETON, Prof. (Alexander) Allan, FRCOG; Professor of Obstetrics and Gynaecology, University of Aberdeen, since 1985; *b* 28 June 1946; *s* of Richard and Minnie Templeton; *m* 1980, Gillian Constance Penney; three *s* one *d*. *Educ:* Aberdeen Grammar School; Univ. of Aberdeen (MB ChB 1969; MD Hons 1982); MRCOG 1974, FRCOG 1987. Resident and Registrar, Aberdeen Hosps, 1969–75; Lectr and Sen. Lectr, Dept of Obst. and Gyn., Univ. of Edinburgh, 1976–85. Chm., Soc. for the Study of Fertility, 1996–99; Mem., HFEA, 1995–2000. Hon. Sec., RCOG, 1998–. *Publications:* clinical and sci. articles on human infertility and *in vitro* fertilisation. *Recreation:* mountaineering. *Address:* Knapperna House, Udny, Aberdeenshire AB41 6SA. *T:* (01651) 842481.

TEMPLETON, Darwin Herbert, CBE 1975; Senior Partner, Price Waterhouse Northern Ireland (formerly Ashworth Rowan Craig Gardner), 1967–82; *b* 14 July 1922; *s* of Malcolm and Mary Templeton; *m* 1950; two *s* one *d*. *Educ:* Rocavan Sch.; Ballymena Academy. FICAI. Qualified as Chartered Accountant, 1945. Partner, Ashworth Rowan, 1947. Chm., Ulster Soc. of Chartered Accountants, 1961–62; Pres., ICAI, 1970–71. Mem., Royal Commn on Legal Services, 1976–79. Chm. and Dir, several cos. *Recreations:* music, golf, motor racing. *Address:* 4 Cashel Road, Broughshane, Ballymena, Co. Antrim, Northern Ireland BT42 4PL. *T:* (028) 2586 1017. *Club:* Royal Scottish Automobile.

TEMPLETON, Mrs Edith; author, since 1950; *b* 7 April 1916; *m* Edmund Ronald, MD (*d* 1984); one *s*. *Educ:* Prague and Paris; Prague Medical University. During War of 1939–45 worked in American War Office, in office of Surgeon General. Conference Interpreter for British Forces in Germany, 1945–46, rank of Capt. *Publications:* Summer in the Country, 1950 (USA 1951), repr. 1985; Living on Yesterday, 1951, repr. 1986; The Island of Desire, 1952, repr. 1985; The Surprise of Cremona, 1954 (USA 1957), repr. 1985; This Charming Pastime, 1955; (as Louise Walbrook) Gordon, 1966 (US edn as The Demon's Feast, 1968); Three (USA 1971); Murder in Estoril, 1992; contributor to The

New Yorker, Holiday, Atlantic Monthly, Vogue, Harper's Magazine. *Recreation:* travel, with the greatest comfort possible. *Address:* 76 Corso Europa, 18012 Bordighera, Italy.

TEMPLETON, Ian Godfrey; Warden, Glenalmond College, Perth, since 1992; *b* 1 Feb. 1944; *s* of late Anthony Godard Templeton and Mary Gibson Templeton (*née* Carrick Anderson); *m* 1970, Elisabeth Aline Robin; one *s* one *d*. *Educ:* Gordonstoun Sch.; Edinburgh Univ. (MA); Bedford Coll., London Univ. (BA 1st cl. Hons Philosophy). Asst Master, 1969–71, Housemaster, 1971–73, Melville Coll.; Housemaster, Daniel Stewart's and Melville Coll., 1973–78; Asst Headmaster, Robert Gordon's Coll., Aberdeen, 1978–85; Headmaster, Oswestry Sch., 1985–92. FRSA. *Recreations:* golf, choral singing, travel. *Address:* Warden's House, Glenalmond College, Glenalmond, Perth PH1 3RY. *T:* (01738) 880227. *Clubs:* East India, Lansdowne, Royal & Ancient.

TEMPLETON, Sir John (Marks), Kt 1987; Secretary, John Templeton Foundation, since 1985; Chairman, Templeton, Galbraith and Hansberger Ltd, 1986–92; Chairman Emeritus, Templeton International, Inc.; chartered financial analyst, 1965–92; *b* 29 Nov. 1912; *s* of Harvey Maxwell Templeton and Vella Templeton (*née* Handly); *m* 1st, 1937, Judith Dudley Folk (*d* 1950); two *s* one *d*; 2nd, 1958, Irene Reynolds Butler; one step *s* one step *d*. *Educ:* Yale Univ. (BA *summa cum laude*); Balliol Coll., Oxford (MA; Rhodes Scholar). Vice Pres., Nat. Geophysical Co., 1937–40; President: Templeton Dobbrow and Vance Inc., 1940–60; Templeton Growth Fund Ltd, 1954–85; Templeton Investment Counsel Ltd of Edinburgh, 1976–92; Templeton World Fund Inc., 1978–87; Founder: Templeton Prizes for Progress in Religion, 1972; Templeton UK Project Trust, 1984; Trustee, Templeton Educn and Charity Trust, 1991–; Pres., Bd of Trustees, Princeton Theol Seminary, 1967–73 and 1979–85; Mem., Bd of Trustees, Westminster Abbey Trust, 1991–96. Mem. Council, Templeton College (formerly Oxford Centre for Management Studies), 1983–95 (Hon. Fellow, 1991). Hon. LLD: Beaver Coll., 1968; Marquette Univ., 1980; Jamestown Coll., 1983; Maryville Coll., 1984; Moravian Coll., 1994; Stone Hill Coll., 1995; Hon. LHD: Wilson Coll., 1974; Brigham Young Univ., 1998; Hon. DD Buena Vista Coll., 1979; Hon. DCL Univ. of the South, 1984; Hon. DLitt Manhattan Coll., 1990; Hon. DHL Campbell Univ., 1993; Hon. DH Furman Univ., 1995; Hon. PhD: Rhodes Coll., Babson Coll., Florida Southern Coll., Univ. of Dubuque, and Univ. of Rochester, 1992; Notre Dame Univ., 1995. Benjamin Franklin Award, RSA, 1993; Lifetime Achievement Award, Laymans Nat. Bible Assoc., 1995; Nat. Business Hall of Fame Award, Jun. Achievement Assoc., 1996; Interfaith Gold Medallion, Internat. Council of Christians and Jews, 1997; Abraham Lincoln Award, Union League of Philadelphia, 1997; Indep. Award, Brown Univ., 1998. KStJ 1995. *Publications:* The Humble Approach, 1982; Riches for the Mind and Spirit, 1990; (jtly) The God Who Would Be Known, 1990; Is God the Only Reality, 1993; (ed) Evidence of Purpose, 1994; Future Agenda, 1995; Discovering the Laws of Life, 1994; Worldwide Laws of Life, 1998; Possibilities, 2000; (ed) Worldwide Worship, 2001; articles in professional jls. *Recreations:* swimming, gardening. *Address:* Box N7776, Lyford Cay, Nassau, Bahamas. *T:* 3624295. *Clubs:* Athenæum, White's, Oxford and Cambridge; University (NY); Lyford Cay (Bahamas).

TEMPLETON-COTILL, Rear-Adm. John Atrill, CB 1972; retired; *b* 4 June 1920; *s* of late Captain Jack Lionel Cottle, Tank Corps. *Educ:* Canford Sch.; New Coll., Oxford. Joined RNVR, 1939; served war 1939–45; HMS Crocus, 1940–41; British Naval Liaison Officer, French warship Chevreuil, 1941–42; staff, GOC New Caledonia (US), 1942; US Embassy, London, 1943; Flag Lieutenant to Vice-Adm., Malta, 1943–44; 1st Lieut, MTB 421, 1944–45; ADC to Governor of Victoria, 1945–46; served in HMS London, Loch Quoich, Whirlwind, Jutland, Barrosa and Sparrow, 1946–55; Comdr 1955; comd HMS Sefton and 108th Minesweeping Sqdn, 1955–56; jssc 1956; Comdr-in-Charge, RN School of Work Study, 1957–59; HMS Tiger, 1959–61; Captain 1961; British Naval Attaché, Moscow, 1962–64; comd HMS Rhyl and Captain (D), 23rd Escort Sqdn, 1964–66; Senior Naval Mem., Defence Operational Analysis Estabt, 1966–68; comd HMS Bulwark, 1968–69; Rear-Adm. Jan. 1970; Chief of Staff to Comdr Far East Fleet, 1970–71; Flag Officer, Malta, and NATO Comdr, SE Area Mediterranean, 1971–73; Comdr, British Forces Malta, 1972–73. Director: Sotheby Parke Bernet (France), 1974–81; Sotheby Parke Bernet (Monaco), 1975–81. *Recreations:* gardening, riding, shooting, travel, skiing. *Address:* Moulin de Fontvive, Ribas, par 30290 Laudun, France. *T:* 66794737.

TENBY, 3rd Viscount *cr* 1957, of Bulford; **William Lloyd-George;** *b* 7 Nov. 1927; 2nd *s* of 1st Viscount Tenby, TD, PC, and Edna Gwenfron (*d* 1971), *d* of David Jones, Gwynfa, Denbigh; *S* brother, 1983; *m* 1955, Ursula Diana Ethel, *y d* of late Lt-Col Henry Edward Medlicott, DSO; one *s* two *d*. *Educ:* Eastbourne College; St Catharine's Coll., Cambridge (Exhibnr; BA 1949). Captain, Royal Welch Fusiliers, TA. Dir, Williams Lea & Co., 1988–93; Chm., St James Public Relations, 1990–93; non-exec. Dir, Ugland Internat. plc, 1993–96. House of Lords: Member: Cttee on Procedure, 1995–98; Cttee of Selection, 1998–; Sub-Cttee on Admin and Works, 1992–95; All Party Media Gp; elected Mem., H of L, 1999. Pres., Hants Br., CPRE. JP Hants (Chm., NE Hants (formerly Odiham) Bench, 1990–94). *Heir:* *s* Hon. Timothy Henry Gwilym Lloyd-George, *b* 19 Oct. 1962. *Address:* The White House, Dippenhall Street, Crondall, Farnham, Surrey GU10 5PE.

TENCH, David Edward, OBE 1987; Head of Legal Department, 1988–94, Director of Legal Affairs, 1991–94, Consumers' Association (publishers of Which?); consultant on public policy and consumer law, since 1994; *b* 14 June 1929; *s* of late Henry George Tench and Emma Rose (*née* Orsborn); *m* 1st, 1957, Judith April Seaton Gurney (*d* 1986); two *s* one *d*; 2nd, 1988, Elizabeth Ann Irvine Macdonald. *Educ:* Merchant Taylors' Sch., Northwood, Mddx. Solicitor, 1952. Private practice, 1954–58; Office of Solicitor of Inland Revenue, 1958–69. Chm., Domestic Coal Consumers' Council, 1976–87; Energy Comr, 1977–79. Broadcaster on consumer affairs, 1964–. *Publications:* The Law for Consumers, 1962; The Legal Side of Buying a House, 1965 (2nd edn 1974); Wills and Probate, 1967 (6th edn 1977); How to Sue in the County Court, 1973; Towards a Middle System of Law, 1981. *Recreations:* music, bland gardening. *Address:* Pleasant View, The Platt, Amersham, Bucks HP7 0HX. *T:* (01494) 724974.

TENET, George J.; Director, Central Intelligence Agency, since 1997; *b* 5 Jan. 1953; *m* A. Stephanie Glakas; one *c*. *Educ:* Georgetown Univ., Washington; Columbia Univ., NY (MIA 1978). Legislative Asst specialising in nat. security and energy issues, then Legislative Dir to Senator H. John Heinz, III; Designee to Vice Chm., Senator Patrick J. Leahy, 1985–86; Dir, Oversight of Arms Control Negotiations between Soviet Union and US, then Staff Dir, Senate Select Cttee on Intelligence, 1986–93; National Security Council: Mem., Presidential Transition Team, 1993; Special Asst to Pres. and Sen. Dir for Intelligence Programs, 1993–95; Dep. Dir, CIA, 1995–97. *Publication:* The Ability of US Intelligence to Monitor the Intermediate Nuclear Force Treaty. *Address:* c/o Central Intelligence Agency, Washington, DC 20505, USA. *T:* (703) 4827558, *Fax:* (703) 4826790.

TENISON; *see* Hanbury-Tenison.

TENISON; *see* King-Tenison.

TENNANT, family name of **Baron Glenconner**.

TENNANT, Sir Anthony (John), Kt 1992; Senior Adviser, Morgan Stanley UK Group, 1993–2000; Deputy Chairman, Arjo Wiggins Appleton plc, 1996–2000; *b* 5 Nov. 1930; *s* of late Major John Tennant, TD and Hon. Antonia, *d* of 1st Baron Charnwood and later Viscountess Radcliffe; *m* 1954, Rosemary Violet Stockdale; two *s*. *Educ:* Eton; Trinity College, Cambridge (BA). National Service, Scots Guards (Malaya). Mather & Crowther, 1953–66 (Dir, 1959); Marketing Consultancy, 1966–70; Dir, 1970, then Dep. Man. Dir, Truman Ltd; Dir, Watney Mann & Truman Brewers, 1972–76; Man. Dir, 1976–82, Chm., 1983–87, International Distillers & Vintners Ltd; Gp Chief Exec., 1987–89, Chm., 1989–92, Guinness plc; Deputy Chairman: Forte plc, 1992–96; Wellcome plc, 1994–95; Chm., Christie's Internat. plc, 1993–96 (Dir, 1993–98); Director: Exploration Co. plc, 1967–89; El Oro Mining and Exploration Co. plc, 1967–89; Grand Metropolitan PLC, 1977–87; Close Brothers Group plc, 1980–90; Guardian Royal Exchange, 1989–99; Guardian Assurance, 1989–94; BNP Paribas UK Hldgs Ltd, 1990–; Mem., Supervisory Bd, LVMH Moet Hennessy Louis Vuitton, Paris, 1988–92. Dir (non-exec.), Internat. Stock Exchange of UK and Republic of Ireland Ltd, 1991–94. Chm., Priorities Bd for R & D in Agric. and Food, 1992–93; Mem. Council, Food From Britain, 1983–86. Chairman: RA Trust, 1996– (Trustee, 1994–); Southampton Univ. Develt Trust, 1996– (Trustee, 1992–); Trustee, Cambridge Foundn., 1992–2000. Hon. DBA Nottingham Trent, 1996; DUniv Southampton, 2000. Médaille, Ville de Paris, 1989. Chevalier, Légion d'Honneur (France), 1991. *Address:* 18 Hamilton House, Vicarage Gate, W8 4HL. *T:* (020) 7937 6203. *Club:* Boodle's.

See also M. I. Tennant of Balfluig.

TENNANT, Bernard; Director of Retail, British Chambers of Commerce, 1993–95; *b* 14 Oct. 1930; *s* of Richard and Phyllis Tennant; *m* 1956, Marie (*née* Tonge); two *s* one *d*. *Educ:* Farnworth Grammar Sch.; Open Univ. (BA Govt and Modern European Hist.). Nat. Service, RAF, 1949. Local authority admin, Worsley and Bolton, 1950; Secretary: Bolton Chamber of Trade, 1960–74; Bolton Chamber of Commerce and Industry, and numerous trade associations, 1968–74; National Chamber of Trade, 1975–92, Dir Gen., 1987–92. Member: British Retail Consortium Council, 1986–95; Home Office Standing Cttee on Crime Prevention, 1986–92; Dept of Employment Retail Price Index Adv. Cttee, 1988–92. Magistrate, Bolton, 1968–75; Reading, 1975–78. Founder Sec., Moorside Housing Gp of charitable housing assocs, 1964–75. Editor, NCT News, 1986–92. *Publications:* articles in professional and trade jls, historical and lifestyle magazines. *Recreations:* music, photography, collating historical chronology.

TENNANT, Lady Emma; Chairman, National Trust Gardens Advisory Panel, since 1984; Member, Council, National Trust, since 1990; *b* 26 March 1943; *d* of Duke of Devonshire, *qv* and of Duchess of Devonshire, *qv*; *m* 1963, Hon. Tobias William Tennant, *y s* of 2nd Baron Glenconner; one *s* two *d*. *Educ:* St Elphins' Sch., Darley Dale; St Anne's Coll., Oxford (BA History 1963). *Publication:* Rag Rugs, 1992. *Recreations:* gardening, painting. *Address:* Shaws, Newcastleton, Roxburghshire TD9 0SH. *T:* (01387) 376241.

TENNANT, Emma Christina, FRSL 1982; writer; *b* 20 Oct. 1937; *d* of 2nd Baron Glenconner and Elizabeth Lady Glenconner; one *s* two *d*. *Educ:* St Paul's Girls' School. Freelance journalist to 1973; became full time novelist, 1973; founder Editor, Bananas, 1975–78; general editor: In Verse, 1982–; Lives of Modern Women, 1985–. TV film script, Frankenstein's Baby, 1990. Hon. DLitt Aberdeen, 1996. *Publications:* The Colour of Rain (pseud. Catherine Aydy), 1963; The Time of the Crack, 1973; The Last of the Country House Murders, 1975; Hotel de Dream, 1976; (ed) Bananas Anthology, 1977; (ed) Saturday Night Reader, 1978; The Bad Sister, 1978; Wild Nights, 1979; Alice Fell, 1980; Queen of Stones, 1982; Woman Beware Woman, 1983; Black Marina, 1985; Adventures of Robina by Herself, ed Emma Tennant, 1986; Cycle of the Sun: The House of Hospitalities, 1987, A Wedding of Cousins, 1988; The Magic Drum, 1989; Two Women of London, 1989; Sisters and Strangers, 1990; Faustine, 1991; Tess, 1993; Pemberley, 1993; An Unequal Marriage, 1994; Elinor and Marianne, 1996; Emma in Love, 1996; Strangers: a family romance, 1998; Girlitude: a memoir of the 50s and 60s, 1999; Burnt Diaries, 1999; The Ballad of Sylvia and Ted, 2001; (contrib.) Novelists in Interview (ed John Haffenden), 1985; (contrib.) Women's Writing: a challenge to theory (ed Maria Monteith), 1986; *for children:* The Boggart (with Mary Rayner), 1979; The Search for Treasure Island, 1981; The Ghost Child, 1984. *Recreation:* walking about. *Address:* c/o Jonathan Cape, Random House, 20 Vauxhall Bridge Road, SW1V 2SA.

TENNANT, Harry; Commissioner of Customs and Excise, 1975–78; *b* 10 Dec. 1917; *s* of late Robert and Mary Tennant; *m* 1944, Bernice Baker; one *s*. *Educ:* Oldham High School. Appointed Officer of Customs and Excise, 1938; Inspector, 1960; Principal Inspector, 1970; Asst Sec., 1971; Dep. Chief Inspector, 1973; Mem., CS Appeal Bd, 1980–87. *Publications:* Back to the Bible, 1962, repr. 1984; Moses My Servant, 1966, repr. 1990; The Man David, 1968, repr. 1996; The Christadelphians: what they believe and preach, 1986; Steps to True Marriage, 1999. *Recreations:* walking, travel. *Address:* Strathtay, Alexandra Road, Watford, Herts WD1 3QY. *T:* (01923) 222079.

TENNANT, Helen Anne, (Lena); Lecturer, Faculty of Education, St Andrew's Campus, University of Glasgow (formerly St Andrew's College, Glasgow), since 1989; *b* 15 Dec. 1943; *d* of late Joseph Dawson and Anna Dawson (*née* Giavarini); *m* 1975, Gerard E. Tennant; three *s* one *d*. *Educ:* St Mary's Acad., Bathgate; Notre Dame Coll. of Education, Glasgow (DipCE); RSAMD (Dip. Speech and Drama). Lectr in Speech and Drama, Notre Dame Coll. of Educn, Glasgow, 1969–75; extra-mural Lectr, St Peter's Seminary, Cardross, subseq. Glasgow, 1972–92; part-time Lectr, Coatbridge Coll., 1983–89. Member: Viewer's Consultative Council (Scotland), 1989–94; Radio Authy, 1995–2000. *Recreations:* theatre-going, playing church organ. *Address:* 75 Fernleigh Road, Glasgow G43 2TY. *T:* (0141) 637 0921.

TENNANT, Sir Iain (Mark), KT 1986; JP; Lord-Lieutenant of Morayshire, 1963–94; Crown Estate Commissioner, 1970–90; Lord High Commissioner to General Assembly, Church of Scotland, 1988–89; *b* 11 March 1919; *e s* of late Col Edward Tennant, Innes, Elgin and Mrs Georgina Tennant; *m* 1946, Lady Margaret Helen Isla Marion Ogilvy, 2nd *d* of 12th Earl of Airlie, Kt, GCVO, MC; two *s* one *d*. *Educ:* Eton College; Magdalene College, Cambridge. Scots Guards, 1939–46. Caledonian Cinemas, 1947; Chm., Grampian Television Ltd, 1968–89; Director: Times Publishing Co. Ltd, 1962–66; Clydesdale Bank Ltd, 1968–89; The Seagram Co. Ltd, Montreal, 1978–81; Moray Enterprise Trust Ltd, 1986–94; Chairman: The Glenlivet Distillers Ltd, 1964–84; Seagram Distillers, 1979–84. Mem. Newspaper Panel, Monopolies and Mergers Commn, 1981–86. Chm. Bd of Governors, Gordonstoun School, 1954–71. Lieut, Queen's Body Guard for Scotland (Royal Company of Archers), 1981–. FRSA 1971; CIMgt (CBIM 1983). DL Moray, 1954; JP Moray, 1961. Freeman, Dist of Moray, 1994. Hon. LLD Aberdeen, 1990. *Recreations:* shooting, fishing; formerly rowing (rowed for Eton, 1937). *Address:* Lochnabo, Lhanbryde, Moray IV30 3QY. *T:* (01343) 842228, *Fax:* (01343) 842696.

TENNANT, Lena; *see* Tennant, H. A.

TENNANT of Balfluig, Mark Iain; Master of the Supreme Court, Queen's Bench Division, since 1988; Baron of Balfluig; *b* 4 Dec. 1932; *s* of late Major John Tennant, TD, KStJ and Hon. Antonia Mary Roby Benson, *d* of 1st Baron Charnwood and later Viscountess Radcliffe; *m* 1965, Lady Harriot Pleydell-Bouverie, *y d* of 7th Earl of Radnor; one *s* one *d*. *Educ:* Eton College; New College, Oxford (MA 1959). Lieut, The Rifle Brigade (SRO). Called to the Bar, Inner Temple, 1958, Bencher, 1984; Recorder, 1987–96. Restored Balfluig Castle (barony of Balfluig *cr* of Charles II, 1650), dated 1556 in 1967 (the first to obtain a grant from Historic Bldgs Council for Scotland for bldg not inhabited or inhabitable). Chm., Royal Orchestral Soc. for Amateur Musicians, 1989–. *Recreations:* music, architecture, books, shooting. *Address:* Royal Courts of Justice, Strand, WC2A 2LL; Balfluig Castle, Aberdeenshire AB33 8EJ; 30 Abbey Gardens, NW8 9AT. *Club:* Brooks's.
See also Sir A. J. Tennant.

TENNANT, Maj.-Gen. Michael Trenchard, CB 1994; Army Adviser, British Aerospace, 1998–2001; *b* 3 Sept. 1941; *s* of Lt-Col Hugh Trenchard Tennant, MC and Mary Isobel Tennant (*née* Wilkie); *m* 1st, 1964, Susan Daphne (*d* 1993), *d* of Lt-Col Frank Beale, LVO; three *s*; 2nd, 1996, Jacqueline Mary Parish (*née* ap Ellis), *widow* of David Parish; two step *d*. *Educ:* Wellington College. psc†. Commissioned RA 1961; served Bahrain, Aden, BAOR, Hong Kong, UK, 1962–71; Staff College, 1972–73; MoD, 1974–75; Bty Comdr, 127 (Dragon) Bty, BAOR, 1976–78; Directing Staff, Staff Coll., 1978–80; CO, 1 RHA, UK and BAOR, 1980–83; Comdr British Training Team, Nigeria, 1983–85; CRA 3 Armd Div., BAOR, 1985–87; CRA UKLF, 1988–91; Dir, RA, 1991–94. Hd of External Commns, Royal Ordnance Div., BAe, 1994–98. Col Comdt, RA, 1994–; Hon. Col, 1 RHA, 1994–99. Chm., CCF Assoc., 1996–. President: Army Cricket, 1992–93; RA Golf Soc., 1998–. *Recreations:* bridge, golf, tennis. *Clubs:* Army and Navy; Fadeaways; Denham Golf, Rye Golf, Senior Golfers.

TENNYSON, family name of **Baron Tennyson**.

TENNYSON, 5th Baron *cr* 1884; **Comdr Mark Aubrey Tennyson,** DSC 1943; RN retd; *b* 28 March 1920; *s* of 3rd Baron and Hon. Clarissa Tennant (*d* 1960), *o d* of 1st Baron Glenconner; *S* brother, 1991; *m* 1964, Deline Celeste Budler (*d* 1995). *Educ:* RNC Dartmouth. RN, 1937–60; served war 1939–45 on destroyers in action in Atlantic and Mediterranean (despatches 1945). Production Manager, Rowntree-Mackintosh (S Africa), 1960–67; Export Sales Dir, Joseph Terry & Sons (UK), 1968–82. Skied for RN, 1947–51; Captain, RN Cresta Run team, 1951–54. *Heir: cousin* David Harold Alexander Tennyson, *b* 4 June 1960. *Address:* 304 Grosvenor Square, Duke Road, Rondebosch, Cape Town 7700, South Africa. *Clubs:* White's, Royal Automobile.

TENNYSON-d'EYNCOURT, Sir Mark (Gervais), 5th Bt *cr* 1930, of Carter's Corner Farm, Herstmonceux; *b* 12 March 1967; *o s* of Sir Giles Gervais Tennyson-d'Eyncourt, 4th Bt and of Juanita, *d* of late Fortunato Borromeo; *S* father, 1989. *Heir:* none. *Educ:* Charterhouse; Kingston Polytechnic (BA Hons Fashion). Freeman, City of London, 1989.

TENZIN GYATSO; The Dalai Lama XIV; spiritual and temporal leader of Tibet, since 1940; *b* 6 July 1935; named Lhamo Thondup; *s* of Chokyong Tsering and Diki Tsering. *Educ:* Monasteries of Sera, Drepung and Gaden, Lhasa; traditional Tibetan degree equivalent to Dr in Buddhist philosophy, 1959. Enthroned Dalai Lama, Lhasa, 1940; given name Jetsun Jampel Ngawang Losang Yeshi Tenzin Gyatso Sisum Wang-gyur Tsungpa Mepai De Pel Sangpo. Fled to Chumbi, South Tibet, on Chinese invasion, 1950; negotiated with China, 1951; fled to India after abortive revolt of Tibetan people against Communist Chinese, 1959, and established govt-in-exile in Dharamsala. Awards include: Magsaysay, Philippines, 1959; Lincoln, USA, 1960; Albert Schweizer Humanitarian, USA, 1987; numerous other awards, hon. doctorates, hon. citizenships from France, Germany, India, Mongolia, Norway, USA; Nobel Peace Prize, 1989. *Publications:* My Land and My People (autobiog.), 1962; The Opening of the Wisdom Eye, 1963; An Introduction to Buddhism, 1965; Key to the Middle Way, 1971; Universal Responsibility and Good Heart, 1977; Four Essential Buddhist Commentaries, 1982; A Human Approach to World Peace, 1984; Kindness, Clarity and Insight, 1987; Freedom in Exile (autobiog.), 1990; The Good Heart, 1996; Ethics for the New Millennium, 1998; Ancient Wisdom, Modern World, 1999; A Simple Path, 2000. *Address:* Thekchen Choeling, Mcleod Ganj 176219, Dharamsala, HP, India.

TERESHKOVA, Valentina Vladimirovna; Russian cosmonaut; Chairman, Russian Association of International Co-operation, since 1992; Head, Russian Centre for International Scientific and Cultural Co-operation, Russian Federation, since 1994; *b* Maslennikovo, 6 March 1937; *d* of late Vladimir Aksyonovich Tereshkov and of Elena Fyodorovna Tereshkova; *m*; one *d*. Formerly textile worker, Krasny Perekop mill, Yaroslavl; served on cttees; Sec. of local branch, Young Communist league, 1960; Member: CPSU, 1962–91; Central Cttee, CPSU, 1971–90; Deputy, 1966–90, Mem. of Presidium, 1970–90, USSR Supreme Soviet; Chairperson: Soviet Women's Cttee, 1968–87; Union of Soviet Societies for Friendship and Cultural Relns with Foreign Countries, 1987–92. Joined Yaroslavl Air Sports Club, 1959, and started parachute jumping; joined Cosmonaut Training Unit, 1962; became first woman in the world to enter space when she made 48 orbital flights of the earth in spaceship Vostok VI, 16–19 June 1963. Hero of the Soviet Union; Order of Lenin; Gold Star Medal; Order of October Revolution; Joliot-Curie Peace Medal; Nile Collar (Egypt), 1971; holds honours and citations from other countries. *Address:* 14 Vozdvizhenka Street, 103885 Moscow, Russia.

TERFEL, Bryn; *see* Jones, B. T.

ter HAAR, Roger Eduard Lound; QC 1992; *b* 14 June 1952; *s* of Dirk ter Haar and Christine Janet ter Haar; *m* 1977, Sarah Anne Martyn; two *s* one *d*. *Educ:* Felsted Sch.; Magdalen Coll., Oxford (BA 1973). Called to the Bar, Inner Temple, 1974, Bencher, 1993. *Recreations:* gardening, reading. *Address:* Crown Office Chambers, Temple, EC4Y 7EP. *T:* (020) 7797 8100. *Club:* Brooks's.

TERLEZKI, Stefan, CBE 1992; *b* Ukraine, 29 Oct. 1927; *s* of late Oleksa Terlezki and Olena Terlezki; *m* 1955, Mary; two *d*. *Educ:* Cardiff Coll. of Food Technol. and Commerce. Member: Hotel and Catering Inst., 1965–80; Chamber of Trade, 1975–80. Member: Cardiff CC, 1968–83 (Press Officer, 1970–83; Chairman: Licensing Cttee, 1975–78; Environment Services Cttee, 1978–80; Housing Liaison Cttee, 1978–80); S Glam CC, 1973–85; S Wales Police Auth., 1975–80; Welsh Jt Educn Cttee, 1975–85; Chm., Jt Consultative Cttee, S Glam Health Auth., 1978–79; Member: Educn Authority for Cardiff CC and S Glam CC, 1969–85; Planning, Finance and Policy Cttee, 1965–83. Member: Welsh Tourist Council, 1965–80; Welsh Games Council, 1974–80; Cardiff Wales Airport Authy, 1979–83; Adv. Bd of Internat. Politics, Univ. of Wales, Aberystwyth, 1993–. Contested (C): Cardiff South East, Feb. and Oct. 1974; Cardiff West, 1987; South Wales, European Parly elecn, 1979. MP (C) Cardiff West, 1983–87. Mem., Parly Select Cttee on Welsh Affairs, 1983–87. Chairman: Keep Britain in Europe Campaign, 1973–75; Cons. Gp for European Movement, 1973–75; Foreign Affairs Forum, 1974–; European Freedom Council, 1986–91. Vice-Pres., Wales Area Young Conservatives, 1975–80; Member: Central Council, CPC, 1979–83; Official Nat. Speaking Panels of Cons. Party, European Movement, and Eur. Parlt; British delegn, Council of Europe, 1985–87 (UK Rep. Mem., Convention Cttee for the Prevention of Torture and In-Human or Degradation Treatment and Punishment, 1989–); WEU, 1985–87; Industry and Parlt Trust; IPU, 1987– (Life Mem., British Parly Gp); UN Temple of Peace, Cardiff, 1979–87; Rapporteur, Assembly of Western European Community for Parly and Public Relns, 1986–87. Vice Pres., Cardiff Business Club, 1993–. Life Mem., CPA; Mem., Primrose League. Mem. Gen. Council, Ukrainian Assoc. in GB, 1949–. Consultant on econ. and public affairs to Embassy of Ukraine in the UK. Chairman: Cardiff City Football Club, 1975–77; Cardiff High Sch. Bd of Governors, 1975–83; Mem. Ct of Governors, Univs of Swansea and Aberystwyth, 1975–83. Liveryman, Welsh Livery Guild, 1996. Languages: Ukrainian, Polish, Russian, German (basic). Radio and television broadcasts; occasional journalism. Silver Jubilee Medal, 1977. *Recreations:* sport, travel, music, theatre, documentaries, historical and Hollywood musical films. *Address:* 16 Bryngwyn Road, Cyncoed, Cardiff CF23 6PQ. *T:* (029) 2075 9524. *Club:* Dinosaurs.

TERRAINE, John Alfred; FRHistS; author; *b* 15 Jan. 1921; *s* of Charles William Terraine and Eveline Holmes; *m* 1945, Joyce Eileen Waite; one *d*. *Educ:* Stamford Sch.; Keble Coll., Oxford (Hon. Fellow, 1986). Joined BBC, 1944; Pacific and S African Programme Organiser, 1953–63; resigned from BBC, 1964. Associate producer and chief scriptwriter of The Great War, BBC TV, 1963–64; part-scriptwriter The Lost Peace, BBC TV, 1965; scriptwriter, The Life and Times of Lord Mountbatten, Rediffusion/Thames TV, 1966–68; scriptwriter, The Mighty Continent, BBC TV, 1974–75. Founder Pres., Western Front Assoc., 1980–97, Patron, 1997–. Mem. Council, RUSI, 1976–84. FRHistS 1987. Chesney Gold Medal, RUSI, 1982. C. P. Robertson Meml Trophy, Air Public Relations Assoc., 1985. *Publications:* Mons: The Retreat to Victory, 1960; Douglas Haig: The Educated Soldier, 1963; The Western Front, 1964; General Jack's Diary, 1964; The Great War: An Illustrated History, 1965 (NY), unillustrated reprint, The First World War, 1983; The Life and Times of Lord Mountbatten, 1968; Impacts of War 1914 and 1918, 1970; The Mighty Continent, 1974; Trafalgar, 1976; The Road to Passchendaele, 1977; To Win a War: 1918 The Year of Victory, 1978; The Smoke and the Fire, 1980; White Heat: The New Warfare 1914–1918, 1982; The Right of the Line: the Royal Air Force in the European War 1939–45, 1985 (Yorkshire Post Book of the Year Award, 1985); Business in Great Waters: the U-Boat Wars 1916–1945, 1989. *Recreation:* convivial and congenial conversation. *Address:* 77 Sirdar Road, W11 4EQ. *T:* (020) 7229 8152.

TERRELL, Prof. (Richard) Deane, PhD; Vice-Chancellor, 1994–2000, now Emeritus Professor, National Graduate School of Management, Australian National University; *b* 22 April 1936; *s* of Norman Walter Terrell and Dorothy Ismay Terrell; *m* 1961, Jennifer Anne Kathleen, *d* of Leonard Spencer and Margaret Rose Doman; two *s* one *d*. *Educ:* St Peter's Coll., Adelaide; Adelaide Univ. (Rhodes Scholar; BEc Hons); Oxford Univ.; ANU (PhD). Teaching appts, Univ. of Adelaide and MIT, 1959–64; Australian National University: Lectr, 1964–70; Sen. Lectr, Stats, 1970; Prof. of Econometrics, 1971–89; Dean, Faculty of Econs and Commerce, 1975–77, 1982–89; Head, Dept of Stats, 1979–82, 1989–91; Chm., Bd of Faculties, 1989–92; Acting Dep. Vice-Chancellor, and Dep. Vice-Chancellor, 1991–93. Vis. Prof., Princeton and LSE, 1972–73. Chm., Bd of Mgt, AARNet; Vice-Pres., IDP Educn Australia. *Publications:* numerous articles in professional jls. *Recreations:* farming, football, cricket. *Address:* c/o Australia Asia Management Centre, APSEM, Sir Roland Wilson Building No 120, Australian National University, Canberra, ACT 0200, Australia. *Club:* Commonwealth (Canberra).

TERRELL, Colonel Stephen, OBE 1952; TD; QC 1965; DL. Called to the Bar, Gray's Inn, 1946; Bencher, Gray's Inn, 1970. South Eastern Circuit. Pres., Liberal Party, 1972. Contested (L) Eastbourne, Feb. 1974. DL Middlesex, 1961.

TERRINGTON, 6th Baron *cr* 1918, of Huddersfield, co. York; **Christopher Richard James Woodhouse,** FRCS; Reader in Adolescent Urology, University College London, since 1997; Clinical Director of Urology, University College London Hospitals, since 2001; Consultant Urologist, Royal Marsden Hospital, since 1981; *b* 20 Sept. 1946; *s* of 5th Baron Terrington, DSO, OBE and Lady Davina Woodhouse (*née* Lytton), *widow* of 5th Earl of Erne; *S* father, 2001; *m* 1975, Hon. Anna Philipps, *d* of 3rd Baron Milford; one *s* one *d*. *Educ:* Winchester; Guy's Hosp. Med. Sch. (MB, BS 1970). FRCS 1975. Sen. Registrar in Urology, Inst. of Urology and St Peter's Hosps, 1977–81; Sen. Lectr in Urology, Insts of Urology, 1981–97. Consultant Urologist, St George's Hosp., 1985–95. Hon. Consultant Urologist: Inst. of Urology, University Coll. London Hosps, 1981–; Hosp. for Sick Children, Great Ormond Street, 1981–. Vis. Professorships in Europe, USA and Australasia. Fellow, European Bd of Urology, 1993. Pres., Genito-Urinary Reconstructive Surgeons, USA, 2001. Corresp. Mem., Amer. Urological Assoc., 1985; Hon. Mem., Australasian Urological Assoc., 1999. *Publications:* (with F. D. Thompson) Physiological Basis of Medicine: disorders of the kidney and urinary tract, 1987; Long Term Paediatric Urology, 1991; contrib. to learned jls. *Recreations:* gardening, walking. *Heir: s* Hon. Jack Henry Lehmann Woodhouse, *b* 7 Dec. 1978. *Address:* Lister House, Lister Hospital, Chelsea Bridge Road, SW1W 8RH. *T:* (020) 7730 6204; *e-mail:* cwoodhouse2@compuserve.com. *Club:* Leander (Henley-on-Thames).

TERRY, Air Marshal Sir Colin George, KBE 1998 (OBE 1983); CB 1995; FREng; Group Managing Director, Inflite Engineering Services Ltd, London Stansted Airport, since 1999; *b* 8 Aug. 1943; *e s* of George Albert Terry and Edna Joan Terry (*née* Purslow); *m* 1966, Gillian, *d* of late Conrad Glendor Grindley and Muriel Grace Grindley (*née* Duffield); two *s* one *d*. *Educ:* Bridgnorth Grammar Sch.; RAF Coll.; Imperial Coll., London. CEng, BScEng, FCGI, FRAeS; FREng 2001. Commnd, Engr Br., RAF, 1962; served Abingdon, RAF Coll., Church Fenton, Leeming, Oakington, Finningley, RNAY Belfast, Laarbruch, Wildenrath, HQ Strike Comd; Student, RAF Coll., 1978; OC Eng Wing, RAF Coltishall, 1979–82; Eng Authy Staff, HQ Strike Comd, 1982–84; OC Eng Wing, RAF Stanley, 1982–83; Dep. Comd Engr, HQ Strike Comd, 1985–86; Station Comdr, RAF Abingdon, 1986–88; RCDS 1989; Dir, Support Management and Sen. Dir, MoD Harrogate, 1990–92; Dir Gen., Support Management, RAF, 1993–95; COS and Dep. C-in-C, Logistics Comd, RAF, 1995–97; AOC-in-C, Logistics Comd and Air Mem. for Logistics, RAF, 1997–99; Chief Engr (RAF), 1996–99. Member: Council, RAeS, 1999–; Senate, Engrg Council, 1999–. FRSA; FILog. Commodore, RAF Sailing Assoc., 1994–99; Pres., Assoc. of Service Yacht Clubs, 1997–99; Flag Officer, RAFVR(T), 1999. *Recreations:* sailing, flying, ski-ing, modern languages, music. *Address:* Inflite Engineering Services Ltd, Inflite House, London Stansted Airport, Stansted, Essex CM24 1RY. *Club:* Royal Air Force.

TERRY, Ian Keith; Managing Partner, Freshfields Bruckhaus Deringer (formerly Freshfields), since 1996; *b* 26 July 1955; *s* of late Keith Harold Terry and of Shirley Margaret Terry; *m* 1993, Dr Elizabeth Ann Fischl; one *d*. *Educ:* Leeds Grammar Sch.; Keble Coll., Oxford (BA, BCL). Freshfields: trainee solicitor, 1978–80; admitted solicitor,

1980; Partner (Commercial Litigation), 1986–96. *Recreations:* tennis, golf, ski-ing, opera, family. *Address:* (office) 65 Fleet Street, EC4Y 1HS. *T:* (020) 7936 4000.

TERRY, (John) Quinlan, FRIBA 1962; architect in private practice, since 1967; *b* 24 July 1937; *s* of Philip and Phyllis Terry; *m* 1961, Christine de Ruttié; one *s* four *d*. *Educ:* Bryanston School; Architectural Association; Rome Scholar. Assistant to Raymond Erith, RA, FRIBA, 1962, Partner 1967–, Erith & Terry; work includes: new private houses in classical style, UK, America and Germany; Ionic, Veneto, Gothick, Corinthian and Regency Villas, Regent's Park for Crown Estate Comrs; offices, shops, flats and public gardens at Richmond Riverside; offices and shops in Baker Street; new Library, Lecture Theatre, and Residential Bldg, Downing Coll., Cambridge; new Brentwood Cathedral; restoration of the three State Drawing Rooms, 10 Downing Street; restoration of St Helen's, Bishopsgate, and Castletown Cox, Co. Kilkenny. Mem., Royal Fine Art Commn, 1994–97. *Publication:* Architects Anonymous, 1994. *Recreation:* the Pauline epistles. *Address:* Old Exchange, High Street, Dedham, Colchester, Essex CO7 6HA. *T:* (01206) 323186.

TERRY, Sir Michael Edward Stanley I.; *see* Imbert-Terry.

TERRY, Air Chief Marshal Sir Peter (David George), GCB 1983 (KCB 1978; CB 1975); AFC 1968; QCVSA 1959 and 1962; *b* 18 Oct. 1926; *s* of James George Terry and Laura Chilton Terry (*née* Powell); *m* 1946, Betty Martha Louisa Thompson; one *s* one *d* (and one *s* decd). *Educ:* Chatham House Sch., Ramsgate. Joined RAF, 1945; commnd in RAF Regt, 1946; Pilot, 1953. Staff Coll., 1962; OC, No 51 Sqdn, 1966–68; OC, RAF El Adem, 1968–70; Dir, Air Staff Briefing, MoD, 1970–71; Dir of Forward Policy for RAF, 1971–74; ACOS (Policy and Plans), SHAPE, 1975–77; VCAS, 1977–79; C-in-C RAF Germany and Comdr Second Allied Tactical Air Force, 1979–81; Dep. C-in-C, Allied Forces Central Europe, Feb.–April 1981; Dep. Supreme Allied Commander, Europe, 1981–84; Governor and C-in-C, Gibraltar, 1985–89. Vice-Pres., Re-Solv, 1985–. KStJ 1986. *Recreation:* golf. *Club:* Royal Air Force.

TERRY, Quinlan; *see* Terry, J. Q.

TESH, Robert Mathieson, CMG 1968; HM Diplomatic Service, retired; Ambassador to Ethiopia, 1979–82; *b* 15 Sept. 1922; *s* of late E. Tesh, Hurst Green, Surrey; *m* 1950, Jean Bowker; two *s* one *d*. *Educ:* Queen Elizabeth's, Wakefield; Queen's College, Oxford (MA). Oxford, 1940–42 and 1945–47; Rifle Brigade, 1942–45; HM Foreign Service, 1947: New Delhi, 1948–50; FO, 1950–53 and 1957–60; Delegation to NATO, Paris, 1953–55; Beirut, 1955–57; Bangkok, 1960–64; Dep. High Comr, Ghana, 1965–66; Lusaka, 1966; Consul-General British Interests Section, Canadian Embassy, Cairo, 1966–67; Counsellor, British Embassy, Cairo, 1968; IDC, 1969; Head of Defence Dept, FCO, 1970–72; Ambassador to Bahrain, 1972–75; Ambassador to: the Democratic Republic of Vietnam, 1976; the Socialist Republic of Vietnam, 1976–78; FCO, 1978–79. *Recreations:* music, theatre. *Address:* 2 Belvedere House, 115 High Street, Esher, Surrey KT10 9LG. *T:* (01372) 464192. *Club:* Travellers.

TESLER, Brian, CBE 1986; Deputy Chairman, LWT (Holdings) plc, 1990–94; Chairman: London Weekend Television Ltd, 1984–92 (Managing Director, 1976–90; Deputy Chairman, 1982–84; Deputy Chief Executive, 1974–76); The London Studios Ltd (formerly LWT Production Facilities Ltd), 1989–92; LWT International Ltd, 1990–92; LWT Programmes Ltd, 1990–92; *b* 19 Feb. 1929; *s* of late David Tesler and of Stella Tesler; *m* 1959, Audrey Mary Maclean; one *s*. *Educ:* Chiswick County School for Boys; Exeter Coll., Oxford (State Schol.; MA). Theatre Editor, The Isis, 1950–51; Pres., Oxford Univ. Experimental Theatre Club, 1951–52. British Forces Broadcasting Service, 1947–49; Producer/Director: BBC Television, 1952; ATV, 1957; ABC Television: Head of Features and Light Entertainment, 1960; Programme Controller, 1961; Dir of Programmes, 1962; Dir of Programmes, Thames Television, 1968. Chairman: ITV Superchannel Ltd, 1986–88; ITCA, 1980–82; Indep. TV Network Prog. Cttee, 1976–78, 1986–88; LWT Programme Adv. Bd, 1990–92; ITCA Cable and Satellite Television Wkg Party, 1981–88; ITV Film Purchase Cttee, 1989–90; The Magazine Business Ltd, 1992–96. Director: ITN Ltd, 1979–90; Channel Four Television Ltd, 1980–85; Oracle Teletext Ltd, 1980–92; Services Sound and Vision Corp. (formerly Services Kinema Corp.), 1981–. Chm., Lord Chancellor's Adv. Cttee on JPs, 1993–96 (Mem., 1991–96); Lay Interviewer for Judicial Appts, 1994–99; Ind. Assessor, 2001–. Member: British Screen Adv. Council, 1985–94 (Wkg Party on Future of British Film Industry, 1975–77; Interim Action Cttee on Film Industry, 1977–85); TRIC, 1979– (Pres., 1979–80; Companion, 1986); Vice-Pres., RTS, 1984–94 (FRTS 1992). Governor: Nat. Film and TV Sch. (formerly Nat. Film Sch.), 1977–95; BFI, 1986–95 (Dep. Chm., 1993–95). Daily Mail Nat. TV Award, 1954; Guild of Television Producers and Directors Award, 1957; Lord Willis Trophy for Outstanding Services to Television, Pye Television Award, 1986; Presidential Award, TRIC, 1991. *Recreations:* books, theatre, cinema, music.

TESORIÈRE, Harcourt Andrew Pretorius, FRGS; HM Diplomatic Service; Ambassador to Latvia, from March 2002; *b* 2 Nov. 1950; *s* of Pieter Ivan Tesorière and Joyce Margaret Tesorière (*née* Baxter); *m* 1987, Dr Alma Gloria Vasquez. *Educ:* Nautical Coll., Pangbourne; Britannia Royal Naval Coll., Dartmouth; University Coll. of Wales, Aberystwyth (BScEcon Hons); Ecole Nat. d'Admin, Paris. RNR, 1964–68; RN Officer, 1969–73; joined FCO, 1974; Persian lang. student, SOAS and Iran, 1975–76; Oriental Sec., Kabul, 1976–79; Third Sec., Nairobi, 1980–81; Second Sec., Abidjan (also accredited to Ouagadougou and Niamey), 1981–84; First Sec. and Hd of Chancery, later Chargé d'Affaires, Damascus, 1987–91; Hd, Field Ops, UN Office for Co-ordination of Humanitarian Assistance to Afghanistan, Afghanistan, 1994–95; Ambassador to Albania, 1996–98; Actg Hd of Mission and Sen. Pol Advr, UN Special Mission to Afghanistan, 1998–2000 (on secondment). FRGS 1993. *Recreations:* travel, sport, foreign languages, art, countryside. *Address:* c/o Foreign and Commonwealth Office, King Charles Street, SW1A 2AH.

TESSIER-LAVIGNE, Prof. Marc, PhD; FRS 2001; FRSC 1999; Professor of Biological Sciences, Stanford University, since 2001; Investigator, Howard Hughes Medical Institute, since 1997; *b* 18 Dec. 1959; *s* of Sheila and Jacques Tessier-Lavigne; *m* 1989, Mary Alanna Hynes; two *s* one *d*. *Educ:* McGill Univ., Montreal (BSc 1st Cl. Hons Physics 1980); New Coll., Oxford (BA 1st Cl. Hons Phil. and Physiol., 1982); University Coll. London (PhD 1987; Schaffer Prize). University of California, San Francisco: Asst Prof., Dept of Anatomy, 1991–95; Associate Prof., 1995–97; Prof., Depts of Anatomy and Biochem. and Biophysics, 1997–2001; Asst Investigator, Howard Hughes Med. Inst., 1994–97. McKnight Investigator Award, 1994; Charles Judson Herrick Award in Comparative Neurol., Amer. Assoc. Anatomists, 1995; Ameritec Foundn Prize, 1995; (jtly) Fondation IPSEN Prize for Neuronal Plasticity, 1996; Viktor Hamburger Award, Internat. Soc. for Develtl Neurosci., 1997; Young Investigator Award, Soc. for Neurosci., USA, 1997; (jtly) Wakeman Foundn Award for contribs in field of neuronal regeneration, 1998. *Publications:* contribs in physiol. and develtl neurobiol. to scientific jls. *Recreations:* family, history. *Address:* Stanford University, Department of Biological Sciences, Gilbert, Herrin Laboratory and Hall, 371 Serra Mall, Stanford, CA 94305–5020, USA.

TETLEY, Glen; choreographer, since 1948; *b* 3 Feb. 1926; *s* of Glenford Andrew Tetley and Mary Eleanor (*née* Byrne). *Educ:* Franklyn and Marshal Coll., Lancaster, USA (pre-med); New York Univ. (BSc). Studied medicine, then dance with Hanya Holm, Antony Tudor, Martha Graham. Danced with Holm's Co., 1946–51; New York City Opera, 1952–54; John Butler Dance Theatre, 1955; Joffrey Ballet, 1956–57; Martha Graham Co., 1958; American Ballet Theatre, 1960; Robbins Ballets USA, 1961. Joined Netherlands Dance Theatre as dancer and choreographer, 1962, eventually becoming artistic co-director; directed own company, 1969; Dir, Stuttgart Ballet, 1974–76. *Choreography:* Pierrot Lunaire, own company, 1962, Ballet Rambert, 1985; Netherlands Dance Theatre: The Anatomy Lesson, 1964; Circles, 1968; Imaginary Film, 1970; Mutations, 1970; Summer's End, 1980; American Ballet Theatre (formerly Company): Ricercare, 1966; Nocturne, 1977; Sphinx, 1977; Contredances, 1979; Ballet Rambert: Freefall, 1967; Ziggurat, 1967; Embrace Tiger and Return to Mountain, 1968; Rag Dances, 1971; Praeludium, 1978; The Tempest, first full-length work, 1979; Murderer, Hope of Women, 1983; Royal Ballet: Field Figures, 1970; Laborintus, 1972; Dances of Albion, 1980; Amores, 1997; Stuttgart Ballet: Voluntaries, 1973; Daphnis and Chloe, 1975; Greening, 1975; National Ballet of Canada: Alice, 1986; La Ronde, 1987; Tagore, 1989; Oracle, 1994; also: Le Sacre du Printemps, Munich State Opera Ballet, 1974; Tristan, Paris Opera, 1974; Firebird, Royal Danish Ballet, 1981; Revelation and Fall, Australian Dance Theatre, 1984; Pulcinella, Festival Ballet, 1984; Dream Walk of the Shaman, Aterballetto, 1985; Orpheus, Australian Ballet, 1987; Dialogues, Dance Theatre of Harlem, 1991; Lux in Tenebris, Houston Ballet, 1999. Hon DFA Franklin and Marshall Coll., Penn, 2001. Queen Elizabeth Coronation Award, Royal Acad. of Dancing, 1980; Prix Italia, 1982; Ohioana Career Medal, 1986; NY Univ. Achievement Award, 1988. Kt, Order of Merit (Norway), 1997. *Address:* 860 United Nations Plaza, Apt 106, New York, NY 10017, USA. *T:* (212) 3711835.

TETLEY, Air Vice-Marshal John Francis Humphrey, CB 1987; CVO 1978; *b* 5 Feb. 1932; *s* of Humphrey and Evelyn Tetley; *m* 1960, Elizabeth, *d* of Wing Comdr Arthur Stevens; two *s*. *Educ:* Malvern College. RAF Coll., Cranwell, 1950–53; served No 249 Sqn, No 204 Sqn and HQ Coastal Command, 1955–64; RAF Staff Coll., 1964; HQ Middle East Command, 1965–67; OC No 24 Sqn, 1968–70; JSSC 1970; MoD (Air), 1971–72; RAF Germany, 1973–75; Dir Air Staff Briefing, MoD (Air), 1975–76; Silver Jubilee Project Officer, 1977; RCDS, 1978; SASO HQ 38 Group, 1979–82; Dir of Ops (Air Support), RAF, 1982–83; AO Scotland and NI, 1983–86; Sen. Directing Staff (Air), RCDS, 1986–87; retired 1987. Mem. Exec. Cttee, RNLI, 1993– (Vice-Pres., 1996; Dep Chm., 2000). *Recreations:* gardening, photography, boating. *Club:* Royal Air Force.

TETLEY, Ven. Joy Dawn, PhD; Archdeacon of Worcester and Canon Residentiary of Worcester Cathedral, since 1999; *b* 9 Nov. 1946; *d* of Frederick and Mary Payne; *m* 1980, Rev. Brian Tetley, BA, FCA. *Educ:* Durham Univ. (BA 1968; PhD 1988); Leeds Univ. (CertEd 1969); St Hugh's Coll., Oxford (BA 1975; MA 1980); NW Ordination Course. Ordained deaconess 1977, deacon 1987, priest 1994; Deaconess: Bentley, 1977–79; St Aidan, Buttershaw, 1979–80; Durham Cathedral, 1980–83; Lectr, Trinity Coll., Bristol, and Deaconess, Chipping Sodbury and Old Sodbury, 1983–86; Deacon, 1987–89, Hon. Canon, 1990–93 (Canon Emeritus, 1993–), Rochester Cathedral, and Dio. Dir, Post-Ordination Trng, 1988–93; Principal, E Anglian Ministerial Trng Course, 1993–99. Former Columnist, Church Times. *Publications:* Encounter with God in Hebrews, 1995; Sunday by Sunday, 1995; A Way into Hebrews, 1998. *Address:* 15b College Green, Worcester WR1 2LH. *T:* and *Fax:* (01905) 724157; *e-mail:* jtetley@cofe-worcester.org.uk.

TETLOW, Christopher Bruce; His Honour Judge Tetlow; a Circuit Judge, since 1992; *b* 27 Feb. 1943; *s* of George Wilfred Tetlow and Betty Tetlow; *m* 1981, Rosalind Jane Cope; two *s* one *d*. *Educ:* Stowe Sch.; Magdalene Coll., Cambridge (MA). Called to the Bar, Middle Temple, 1969. *Club:* St James's (Manchester).

TETTENBORN, Richard Garstin, OBE 1993; Treasurer: Staffordshire County Council, since 1992; Staffordshire Police Authority, since 1995; Stoke on Trent and Staffordshire Combined Fire Authority, since 1997; *b* 23 Sept. 1940; *s* of Philip Arthur de Gleichen Tettenborn and Helena Louise Tettenborn (*née* Sharpe); *m* 1983, Susan Margaret Wrigley (*née* Crew); one *s*. *Educ:* Herbert Strutt Sch., Belper; Brasenose Coll., Oxford (MA). IPFA 1967. Trainee accountant, Derbyshire CC, 1963–67; Sen. Accountant, London Borough of Sutton, 1967–70; Asst Treas., W Sussex CC, 1970–76; Dep. Treas., Mid Glamorgan CC, 1976–79; Treas., S Glamorgan CC, 1980–92. Financial Advr, Welsh Counties Cttee, 1984–91; Comr, Public Works Loan Bd, 1991–95. Mem. Bd, Police IT Orgn, 1998–2000. President: Soc. of Co. Treasurers, 1992–93; CIPFA, 1994–95. *Recreations:* family, golf, watching sport, theatre. *Address:* County Buildings, Eastgate Street, Stafford ST16 2NF. *T:* (01785) 276300; Sweetbriar, 68 Weeping Cross, Stafford ST17 0DL. *T:* (01785) 604613. *Club:* Oxford and Cambridge.

TEVERSON, Robin; Chairman, Finance South West Ltd, since 1999; *b* 31 March 1952; *s* of Dr Crofton Teverson and Joan Teverson; *m* 1975, Rosemary Anne Young; two *d*. *Educ:* Exeter Univ. (BA Hons Econs). Managing Director: SPD Ltd and Dir, Exel Logistics, 1987–89; Supply Chain Consultancy (Rationale Ltd), 1989–94. MEP (Lib Dem) Cornwall and West Plymouth, 1994–99; contested (Lib Dem) SW Reg., 1999. *Recreations:* history, riding, astronomy, travel, music. *Address:* c/o Rationale Ltd, 3 Charles Street, Truro, Cornwall TR1 2PQ. *T:* (01872) 275755.

TEVIOT, 2nd Baron *cr* 1940, of Burghclere; **Charles John Kerr;** genealogist; *b* 16 Dec. 1934; *s* of 1st Baron Teviot, DSO, MC, and Florence Angela (*d* 1979), *d* of late Lt-Col Charles Walter Villiers, CBE, DSO; *S* father, 1968; *m* 1965, Patricia Mary Harris; one *s* one *d*. *Educ:* Eton. Bus Conductor and Driver; genealogical and historical record agent. Director: Debrett's Peerage Ltd, 1977–83; Burke's Peerage Research, 1983–85; Burke's Peerage Ltd, 1984–85. Mem., Adv. Council on Public Records, 1974–83. Pres., Assoc. of Genealogists and Record Agents, 1997–. Fellow, Soc. of Genealogists, 1975. *Recreations:* reading, walking. *Heir:* *s* Hon. Charles Robert Kerr [*b* 19 Sept. 1971; *m* 2000, Yamaleth Molina Guillen; one *d*]. *Address:* 28 Hazel Grove, Burgess Hill, West Sussex RH15 0BY. *T:* (01444) 242605.

TEW, Prof. John Hedley Brian, OBE 1988; PhD; External Professor, Economics Department, University of Loughborough, 1982–99; Midland Bank Professor of Money and Banking, University of Nottingham, 1967–82; *b* 1 Feb. 1917; *s* of Herbert and Catherine Mary Tew; *m* 1944, Marjorie Hoey Craigie; one *s* one *d*. *Educ:* Mill Hill School, Leicester; University College, Leicester; Peterhouse, Cambridge. BSc (Econ.) London; PhD Cantab. Iron and Steel Control, 1940–42; Ministry of Aircraft Production, 1942–45; Industrial and Commercial Finance Corp., 1946; Professor of Economics, Univ. of Adelaide (Australia), 1947–49; Professor of Economics, University of Nottingham, 1950–67. Part-time Member: Iron and Steel Board, 1964–67; East Midlands Electricity Board, 1965–76; Tubes Div., BSC, 1969–73; Mem., Cttee of Enquiry on Small Firms, Dept of Trade and Industry, 1969–71. *Publications:* Wealth and Income, 1950; International Monetary Co-operation 1952; (jt editor) Studies in Company Finance, 1959;

Monetary Theory, 1969; The Evolution of the International Monetary System, 1977. *Address:* 121 Bramcote Lane, Wollaton, Notts NG8 2NJ.

TEWKESBURY, Bishop Suffragan of, since 1996; **Rt Rev. John Stewart Went;** *b* 11 March 1944; *s* of Douglas and Barbara Went; *m* 1968, Rosemary Evelyn Amy (*née* Dunn); three *s*. *Educ:* Corpus Christi Coll., Cambridge (1st Cl Classics Pt I, starred 1st Theology Pt II; MA). Curate, Emmanuel, Northwood, Mddx, 1969–75; Vicar, Holy Trinity, Margate, 1975–83; Vice-Principal, Wycliffe Hall, Oxford, 1983–89; Archdeacon of Surrey, 1989–95. Warden of Readers, Gloucester dio., 1996–2000. Chm., Diocesan Council for Unity and Mission, Guildford, 1990–95; Member Council: Bible Reading Fellowship, 1989–; World Vision, 1996–. *Publication:* contrib. One in Christ. *Recreations:* music, photography, crosswords. *Address:* Green Acre, 166 Hempsted Lane, Gloucester GL2 5LG. *T:* (01452) 521824, *Fax:* (01452) 505554; *e-mail:* bshptewk@star.co.uk.

TEWSON, Jane, (Mrs C. Lane), CBE 1999; Founder and Director, Pilotlight Australia, since 2000; *b* 9 Jan. 1958; *d* of Dr Tim Tewson, Oxford, and Dr Blue Tewson (*née* Johnston); *m* 1992, Dr Charles Lane; two *s*. *Educ:* Headington Sch., Oxford; Lord William's Sch., Thame. Project Co-ordinator, MENCAP, 1979–83; Founder: and Chief Exec., Charity Projects and Comic Relief, 1984–96; Pilotlight UK, 1996–99; TimeBank, 1999. Trustee: Media Trust, 1986–; Oxfam, 1987–; Camelot Foundn, 1987–. *Recreations:* travel, walking, gardening, reading. *Address:* 35 Cressy Street, Malvern, Melbourne, Vic 3144, Australia. *T:* (3) 98248331.

TEYNHAM, 20th Baron *cr* 1616; **John Christopher Ingham Roper-Curzon;** *b* 25 Dec. 1928; *s* of 19th Baron Teynham, DSO, DSC, and Elspeth Grace (who *m* 2nd, 1958, 6th Marquess of Northampton, DSO, and *d* 1976), *e d* of late William Ingham Whitaker; *S* father, 1972; *m* 1964, Elizabeth, *yr d* of Lt-Col the Hon. David Scrymgeour-Wedderburn, DSO, Scots Guards (killed on active service 1944), and of Patricia, Countess of Dundee; five *s* five *d* (of whom one *s* one *d* are twins). *Educ:* Eton. A Land Agent. Late Captain, The Buffs (TA), formerly Coldstream Guards; active service in Palestine, 1948. ADC to Governor of Bermuda, 1953 and 1955; ADC to Governor of Leeward Islands, 1955; Private Secretary and ADC, 1956; ADC to Governor of Jamaica, 1962. Pres., Inst. of Commerce, 1972–; Vice Pres., Inst. of Export. Member of Council, Sail Training Association, 1964–69. OStJ. Lord of the Manors of South Baddesley and Sharpricks. *Recreations:* shooting and fishing. *Heir:* *s* Hon. David John Henry Ingham Roper-Curzon [*b* 5 Oct. 1965; *m* 1985, Lydia Lucinda, *d* of Maj.-Gen. Sir Christopher Airy, *qv*; two *s* one *d*]. *Address:* Pylewell Park, Lymington, Hants SO41 5SJ. *Clubs:* Carlton, Turf; House of Lords Yacht; Ocean Cruising; Puffin's (Edinburgh).

THACKER, David Thomas; theatre, film and television director; *b* 21 Dec. 1950; *s* of Thomas Richard Thacker and Alice May (*née* Beaumont); *m* 1983, Margot Elizabeth Leicester; three *s* one *d*. *Educ:* Wellingborough Grammar Sch.; Univ. of York (BA English and Related Lit.; MA Shakespeare). Theatre Royal, York: Asst Stage Manager, Dep. Stage Manager and Stage Manager, 1974–75; Asst Dir, 1975–76; Gateway Theatre, Chester: Arts Council Asst Dir, 1975–76; Associate Dir, 1977–78; Duke's Playhouse, Lancaster: Arts Council Associate Dir, 1978–79; Dir, 1980–84; Dir, Young Vic Theatre, 1984–93; Dir-in-Residence, RSC, 1993–95. *Theatre productions* include: Young Vic: Ghosts, 1987; Who's Afraid of Virginia Woolf?, 1987; A Touch of the Poet, An Enemy of the People, 1989; The Winter's Tale, 1991; The Last Yankee, 1993; RSC: Pericles, The Two Gentlemen of Verona, 1991; As You Like It, 1992; The Merchant of Venice, 1993; Julius Caesar, Coriolanus, 1995; Bingo, The Tempest, 1995; Broken Glass, RNT, 1994, transf. Duke of York's, 1995; A View from the Bridge, Bristol Old Vic, 1994, transf. Strand, 1995; Death of a Salesman, RNT, 1996. *Television:* A Doll's House, Measure for Measure, Death of a Salesman, Broken Glass, The Scold's Bridle, Kavanagh QC, The Vice, Grafters; Blue Dove; The Mayor of Casterbridge. Trustee, Hoghton Tower Shakespeare Centre. Dir of the Year, Laurence Olivier Awards, 1991. *Recreations:* sport, family, film and television, reading, politics. *Address:* 55 Onslow Gardens, Muswell Hill, N10 3JY. *T:* and *Fax:* (020) 8444 8436; *e-mail:* DavidTThacker@aol.com.

THAIN, Eric Malcolm, PhD; FRSC; Director, Tropical Development and Research Institute (formerly Tropical Products Institute), Overseas Development Administration, 1981–86; Hon. Research Fellow, Chemistry Department, University College London, since 1986; *b* 29 Nov. 1925; *s* of late Arthur Robert Thain and Olive Grace (*née* Parsons); *m* 1954, Nancy Garbutt Key, *d* of late Mr and Mrs T. G. Key; one *s* one *d*. *Educ:* St Dunstan's Coll., Catford; Univ. of London (BSc, PhD). Lister Institute of Preventive Medicine, 1949: ICI Research Fellow, 1953–54; Royal Society/National Academy of Science Research Fellow, Univ. of California, Berkeley, 1954–55; ICI Research Fellow, University Coll. London, 1955–57; Tropical Products Institute: Member, Scientific Staff, 1957; Asst Director, 1963; Dep. Director, 1969. Member: WHO and FAO Expert Committees on Pesticides, 1961–; Executive Cttee, Essex Bird Watching and Preservation Soc., 1950–85 (Chm. 1970–73); Queckett Microscopical Club (Pres., 1980–81). Mem. Council, Norfolk and Norwich Naturalists' Soc., 1994–97. *Publications:* research papers on organic chemistry and pesticides in jls of various learned societies. *Recreations:* natural history, visiting museums, painting. *Address:* 36 Friars Quay, Norwich, Norfolk NR3 1ES. *T:* (01603) 625017.

THAKKER, Prof. Rajesh Vasantlal, MD; FRCP, FRCPE, FRCPath, FMedSci; May Professor of Medicine, and Fellow of Somerville College, University of Oxford, since 1999; *b* 27 Aug. 1954; *s* of late Vasantlal Gordhandas Thakker and of Indira Vasantlal Thakker; *m* 1980, Julie Clare Magee; one *d*. *Educ:* Pembroke Coll., Cambridge (MA, MB BChir, MD); Middlesex Hosp. Med. Sch. MRCP 1983, FRCP 1993; FRCPE 1997; FRCPath 1998. Middlesex Hospital: House Physician, 1980–81; Registrar, 1983–85; MRC Trng Fellow and Hon. Sen. Registrar, 1985–88; Sen. House Physician, Northwick Park Hosp. and Hammersmith Hosp., 1981–83; MRC Clin. Scientist and Consultant Physician, Northwick Park Hosp., 1988–92; Sen. Lectr and Consultant Physician, 1988–94, Reader of Medicine, 1994–95, RPMS; Hd of MRC Molecular Endocrinology Gp, 1994–99, and Prof. of Medicine, 1995–99, RPMS, then ICSM, Univ. of London. FMedSci 1999. *Publications:* (ed) Genetic and Molecular Biological Aspects of Endocrine Disease, 1995; (ed) Molecular Genetics of Endocrine Disorders, 1997; articles in jls. *Recreations:* running, rambling, reading. *Address:* Somerville College, Oxford OX2 6HD.

THANKI, (Frances) Jane; *see* McIvor, F. J.

THARP, Twyla; American dancer and choreographer; *b* 1 July 1941; *m* Peter Young (marr. diss.); *m* Robert Huot (marr. diss.); one *s*. *Educ:* Pomona Coll.; American Ballet Theatre Sch.; Barnard Coll. (BA Art History 1963). With Paul Taylor Dance Co., 1963–65; Founder, 1965, choreographer, 1965–87, Twyla Tharp Dance Foundn; Artistic Associate Choreographer, American Ballet Theatre, 1988–91; *modern dances/ballets* choreographed include: Tank Dive, 1965; Re-Moves, 1966; Generation, 1968; Medley, 1969; Shout, The One Hundreds, 1970; Eight Jelly Rolls, 1971; Deuce Coupe, Joffrey Ballet, 1973; As Time Goes By, Joffrey Ballet, 1973; Sue's Leg, 1975; Push Comes to Shove, American Ballet Theatre, 1976; Mud, 1977; Baker's Dozen, 1979; The Catherine Wheel, 1981; The Little Ballet, American Ballet Theatre, 1984; In the Upper Room, 1987 (Olivier Award, 1991); Everlast, 1989; The Rules of the Game, 1990; (with Mikhail Baryshnikov) Cutting Up, 1993; Demeter and Persephone, 1994; Mr Wordly Wise, Royal Ballet, Covent Garden, 1995; Heroes, Sweet Fields, 66, 1997; Known By Heart, 1998; The Beethoven Seventh, 2000; *films* choreographed: Hair, 1979; Ragtime, 1981; Amadeus, 1984; White Nights, 1985; I'll Do Anything, 1992. Hon. Mem., Amer. Acad. Arts and Letters, 1997. Creative Arts Award, Brandeis Univ., 1972. *Publication:* Push Comes to Shove (autobiog.), 1992.

THATCHER, family name of **Baroness Thatcher**.

THATCHER, Baroness *cr* 1992 (Life Peer), of Kesteven in the County of Lincolnshire; **Margaret Hilda Thatcher,** LG 1995; OM 1990; PC 1970; FRS 1983; *b* 13 Oct. 1925; *d* of late Alfred Roberts, Grantham, Lincs; *m* 1951, Denis Thatcher (*see* Sir Denis Thatcher, Bt); one *s* one *d* (twins). *Educ:* Kesteven and Grantham Girls' School; Somerville College, Oxford (MA, BSc). Research Chemist, 1947–51; called to the Bar, Lincoln's Inn, 1954, Hon. Bencher, 1975. MP (C) Finchley, 1959–92; Joint Parly Sec., Min. of Pensions and National Insurance, Oct. 1961–64; Sec. of State for Educn and Sci., 1970–74; Leader of the Opposition, 1975–79; Prime Minister and First Lord of the Treasury, 1979–90. Co-Chm., Women's Nat. Commn, 1970–74. Chancellor: Univ. of Buckingham, 1992–98; William and Mary Coll., Virginia, 1993–2000. Chm. Bd, Inst. of US Studies, London Univ., 1994–. Hon. Fellow, Somerville Coll., Oxford, 1970. Freedom of Borough of Barnet, 1980, of City of London, 1989. Donovan Award, USA, 1981. *Publications:* In Defence of Freedom, 1986; The Collected Speeches of Margaret Thatcher, 1997; *memoirs:* The Downing Street Years 1979–90, 1993; The Path to Power, 1995. *Recreations:* music, reading. *Address:* House of Lords, SW1A 0PW. *Club:* Carlton.

THATCHER, Anthony Neville, CEng, FIMechE; Vice Chairman, Thyssen-Bornemisza SAM, since 1993 (President and Chief Executive Officer, Thyssen-Bornemisza Group, 1991–92); *b* 10 Sept. 1939; *s* of Edwin Neville Thatcher and Elsie May Webster; *m* 1968, Sally Margaret Clark. *Educ:* Sir John Lawes Sch., Harpenden; Luton Tech. Coll.; Manchester Univ. (MSc). Student apprentice, Haywards Tyler & Co., Luton, 1956–64; Project Engineer, Smiths Industries, 1964–67; Ultra Electronics: Operations Res. Asst, Acton, 1967–69; Vice-Pres., Sales, USA, 1970–73; Marketing Dir, Acton, 1973–77; Managing Dir, Ultra Electronic Controls, 1977; Managing Director: Dowty Electronic Controls, 1978–82; Electronics Div., Dowty Gp, 1982; Dir, 1983–91, Chief Exec., 1986–91, Dowty Gp. Member: Avionics Cttee, Electronics and Avionics Requirements Bd, DTI, 1981–85; Council, Electronics Engineering Assoc., 1983–91 (Pres., 1986–87); RARDE Management Bd (Indust.), 1986–91; Council, SBAC, 1986–91; Innovation Adv. Bd, DTI, 1988–91; Engrg Markets Adv. Bd, DTI, 1988–90; Engrg Council, 1989–91. Council Mem., Cheltenham Ladies' Coll., 1988–91. Freeman, City of London; Liveryman, Glass Sellers' Co. *Recreations:* art, jazz piano, opera, fishing, gardening, bird watching. *Address:* 12 Gayfere Street, SW1P 3HP. *Clubs:* Athenæum; Georgetown (Washington).

THATCHER, Arthur Roger, CB 1974; Director, Office of Population Censuses and Surveys, and Registrar General for England and Wales, 1978–86; *b* 22 Oct. 1926; *s* of Arthur Thatcher and Edith Mary Ruth (*née* Dobson); *m* 1950, Mary Audrey Betty (*née* Street); two *d*. *Educ:* The Leys Sch.; St John's Coll., Cambridge (MA). Instr Lieut, Royal Navy, 1947–49. North Western Gas Board, 1949–52; Admiralty, 1952–61; Cabinet Office, 1961–63; Ministry of Labour, 1963–68; Director of Statistics, Dept of Employment, 1968–78, Dep. Sec., 1972–78. *Publications:* (jtly) The Force of Mortality at Ages 80 to 120, 1998; official publications; articles in jls. *Address:* 129 Thetford Road, New Malden, Surrey KT3 5DS. *Club:* Army and Navy.

THATCHER, Sir Denis, 1st Bt *cr* 1991, of Scotney in the County of Kent; MBE (mil.) 1944; TD 1946; company director; *b* 10 May 1915; *m* 1951, Margaret Hilda Roberts (*see* Baroness Thatcher); one *s* one *d* (twins). *Educ:* Mill Hill Sch. Major, RA, 1938–46. Man. Dir, Atlas Preservative Co., 1949; Director: Castrol, 1963; Burmah Oil Trading Ltd, 1969–; non-exec. Dir, various cos, 1975–. *Recreation:* golf. *Heir:* *s* Hon. Mark Thatcher [*b* 15 Aug. 1953; *m* 1987, Diane Bergdorf, Dallas, Texas; one *s* one *d*]. *Address:* 73 Chester Square, SW1W 9DU. *Clubs:* Carlton, East India, Buck's, Pratt's.

THAW, John Edward, CBE 1993; actor; *b* 3 Jan. 1942; *s* of John Edward Thaw and Dorothy (*née* Abblott); *m* 1st (marr. diss.); one *d*; 2nd, 1973, Sheila Hancock, *qv*; one *d* one step *d*. *Educ:* Ducie Technical High Sch., Manchester; RADA (Vanbrugh Award; Liverpool Playhouse Award). *Theatre* appearances include: A Shred of Evidence, Liverpool Playhouse, 1960; The Fire Raisers, Royal Court, 1961; Women Beware Women, Arts, 1962; Semi-Detached, Saville, 1962; So What About Love?, Criterion, 1969; Random Happenings in the Hebrides, Edinburgh Fest., 1970; The Lady from the Sea, Greenwich, 1971; Collaborators, Duchess, 1973; Absurd Person Singular (tour), 1976; Night and Day, Phoenix, 1978; Sergeant Musgrave's Dance, NT, 1982; Twelfth Night, The Time of Your Life, Henry VIII, RSC, 1983; Pygmalion, Shaftesbury, 1984; All My Sons, Royal Exchange, Manchester, 1988; The Absence of War, Royal NT, 1993 (televised, 1995); *television* appearances include: Redcap, 1965–66; Thick As Thieves, 1973; The Sweeney, 1974–78; Sir Francis Drake, 1981; Mitch, 1983; The Life and Death of King John, 1984; Home to Roost, 1985–89; Inspector Morse, 1986–2000; Stanley and the Women, 1991; A Year in Provence, 1993; Kavanagh QC, 1994–99; Plastic Man, 1999; The Waiting Time, 1999; Monsignor Renard, 2000; The Glass, 2001; Buried Treasure, 2001; films include: The Bofors Gun, 1968; The Sweeney, 1976; The Sweeney II, 1977; The Grass is Singing, 1982; Cry Freedom, 1987; Charlie, 1992. *Address:* c/o John Redway Associates, Nederlander House, 7 Great Russell Street, WC1B 3NH.

THAW, Sheila, (Mrs John Thaw); *see* Hancock, S.

THEAKSTON, John Andrew; Chief Executive, Swan Hill Group plc (formerly Higgs & Hill plc), since 1991;; *b* 23 May 1952; *s* of Robert Francis Theakston and Jane Hawley (*née* Boyle); *m* 1977, Elizabeth Jane Morgan; one *s* one *d*. *Educ:* Sedbergh Sch., Yorks; Worcester Coll., Oxford (MA Mod. History); Durham Univ. (MSc). Trainee, T. & R. Theakston, Brewers, 1975–77; Donald Macpherson Group: Corporate Planning Manager, 1977–81; Overseas Div. Manager, 1981–84; Higgs & Hill plc: Business Develt Manager, 1985–87; Gp Finance Dir, 1987–89; Jt Gp Man. Dir. 1989–90. Dir, Black Sheep Brewery, 1992–. *Recreations:* sailing, walking, trout fishing. *Address:* (office) Swan Court, Waterman's Business Park, Kingsbury Crescent, Staines, Middx TW18 3BA. *T:* (01784) 464351.

THELLUSSON, family name of **Baron Rendlesham**.

THELWELL, Norman; freelance artist-cartoonist since 1957; *b* Birkenhead, 3 May 1923; *s* of Christopher Thelwell and Emily (*née* Vick); *m* 1949, Rhona Evelyn Ladbury; one *s* one *d*. *Educ:* Rock Ferry High Sch., Birkenhead; Liverpool Coll. of Art. Nat. Diploma of Art; ATD. Teacher of Art, Wolverhampton Coll. of Art, 1950–57. Regular contributor to Punch, 1952–; cartoonist for: News Chronicle, 1956–60; Sunday Dispatch, 1960–61; Sunday Express, 1962–. Drawings for general publications, advertising, book jackets, illustrations, etc. *Publications:* Angels on Horseback, 1957; Thelwell Country, 1959; A Place of Your Own, 1960; Thelwell in Orbit, 1961; A Leg at Each Corner, 1962; The Penguin Thelwell, 1963; Top Dog, 1964; Thelwell's Riding Academy, 1965; Drawing Ponies, 1966; Up the Garden Path, 1967; Thelwell's Compleat Tangler, 1967; Thelwell's Book of Leisure, 1968; This Desirable Plot, 1970; The Effluent Society, 1971; Penelope, 1972; Three Sheets in the Wind, 1973; Belt Up, 1974; Thelwell Goes West, 1975; Thelwell's Brat Race, 1977; A Plank Bridge by a Pool, 1978; Thelwell's Gymkhana, 1979; Thelwell Annual, 1980; A Millstone Round My Neck, 1981; Thelwell Annual, 1981; Pony Cavalcade, 1981; How to Draw Ponies, 1982; Some Damn Fool's Signed the Rubens Again, 1982; Thelwell's Magnificat, 1983; Thelwell's Sporting Prints, 1984; Wrestling with a Pencil: the life of a freelance artist, 1986; Play It As It Lies: Thelwell's golfing manual, 1987; Penelope Rides Again, 1988; The Cat's Pyjamas, 1992. *Recreations:* trout and salmon angling, painting. *Address:* Herons Mead, Timsbury, Romsey, Hants SO51 0NE. *T:* (01794) 368238.

THEOBALD, George Peter; JP; company director, since 1958; *b* 5 Aug. 1931; *s* of late George Oswald Theobald and Helen (*née* Moore); *m* 1955, Josephine Mary (*née* Boodle); two *s* three *d*. *Educ:* Betteshanger Sch.; Harrow. National Service commission, 5 Regt RHA, 1950–52; 290 (City of London) RA (TA), 1953–59. Robert Warner Ltd, 1953–74: Director, 1958; Man. Dir, Chm. Gp subsidiaries, 1965; private company director, 1974–; Tea Clearing House, 1959–72 (Chm., 1970–72); Moran Holdings (formerly Moran Tea Holdings) plc, 1980– (Chm., 1992–); Moran Tea Co. (India) plc, 1981– (Chm., 1992–). City of London (Queenhithe Ward): Chm., Ward Club, 1966–68; Common Councilman, 1968–74; Alderman, 1974–79. Member: Transport Users' Consultative Cttee for London, 1969–84 (Dep. Chm. 1978); London Regional Passengers Cttee, 1984–90. Governor: Bridewell Royal Hosp., 1974–93; King Edward's Sch., Witley, 1974–93 (Trustee, Educational Trust, 1977–95); Donation Governor, Christ's Hosp., 1976–91; Governor, St Leonards-Mayfield Sch., 1982–88; Chm., St John's Sch., Northwood, 1989–97; Mem. Cttee, Langford Cross Children's Home, 1976–90; Trustee: National Flood and Tempest Distress Fund, 1977–; Harrow Mission, 1978–. Church Commissioner for England, 1978–79. Master, Merchant Taylors' Co., 1989–90, 1991–92. JP City of London, 1974. *Recreations:* gardening, transport, walking. *Address:* Towerhill Manor, Gomshall, Guildford, Surrey GU5 9LP. *T:* (01483) 202381. *Clubs:* Oriental, City Livery, Guildhall, MCC.

THEOCHAROUS, Archbishop Gregorios; His Eminence The Most Rev. Gregorios; Greek Orthodox Archbishop of Thyateira and Great Britain, since 1988; *b* 2 Jan. 1929. *Educ:* High Sch., Lefkoniko, Famagusta; Pan Cyprian Gymnasium, Nicosia; Theol Faculty, Univ. of Athens. Monk in the Sacred Monastery, Stavrovouni, Cyprus; ordained: deacon, 1953; presbyter, 1959; asst parish priest and later parish priest, All Saints, Camden Town, 1959–69; Archdiocese of Thyateira: Chancellor, 1965–79; Asst Bishop of Tropaeou, 1970–88; locum tenens on death of Archbishop Athenagoras, 1979; spiritual oversight of Community of St Barnabas, Wood Green, 1970–88. Dr *hc* North London, 1993. *Address:* Thyateira House, 5 Craven Hill, W2 3EN. *T:* (020) 7723 4787, *Fax:* (020) 7224 9301.

THÉODORE, Jean-François; Chief Executive Officer and Chairman, Paris Bourse, since 1999; Chairman, SICOVAM, since 1993; *b* 5 Dec. 1946; *m* 1976, Claudine Lefebvre; one *s* two *d*. *Educ:* Univ. of Paris (Licencé); Institut d'Etudes Politiques; Ecole Nationale d'Administration. Asst Hd, State Holdings Bureau, French Treasury, 1974–78, seconded to Credit National, as Mem., Exec. Bd, 1978–80; Treasury: Hd, African States-Franc Zone Bureau, 1980–82; Hd, Foreign Investment Bureau, 1982–84; Dep. Dir i/c, Banking Dept, 1984–86; Dep. Dir, Investments, State Participations and Public Corps Dept, 1986–93; CEO, 1990–99, Chm., 1991–99, SBF-Paris Bourse; Chm., MATIF, 1998–99. President: Internat. Fedn of Stock Exchanges, 1993–94; Fedn European Stock Exchanges, 1998–2000. Chm. Steering Cttee, Paris Europlace. Chevalier, Légion d'Honneur, 1994. *Address:* 39 rue Cambon, 75001 Paris, France. *T:* 49271102. *Clubs:* Paris-Europlace, Bourse (Paris).

THÉRIAULT, Hon. Camille Henri; MLA (L) Kent South, 1987–2001; Premier of New Brunswick, 1998–99; *b* 25 Feb. 1955; *m* Gisèle; two *c*. *Educ:* Baie-Sainte-Anne High Sch.; Université de Moncton (BSocSc Political Sci.). Formerly: Vice-Pres., Corporate Affairs, United Maritime Fisherman's Co-operative; Manager, Kent Industrial Commn. Minister of: Fisheries and Aquaculture, 1991–94; Advanced Educn and Labour, 1994–95; Economic Develt and Tourism, 1995–98. Chair: Public Accounts Cttee, 1987; Select Cttee on Representation and Electoral Boundaries; Jt Chair, Ministerial Cttee on Creating New Options; Member: Standing Cttee on Estimates, 1987; Cabinet Cttee on Policy and Priorities, 1994. Leader, NB Liberal Party, 1998–2001. *Address:* c/o Centennial Building, 670 King Street, PO Box 6000, Fredericton, NB E3B 5H1, Canada. *T:* (506) 4532506, *Fax:* (506) 4537154.

THEROUX, Paul Edward, FRSL; FRGS; writer; *b* 10 April 1941; *s* of Albert Eugene Theroux and Anne Dittami Theroux; *m* 1st, 1967, Anne Castle (marr. diss. 1993); two *s*; 2nd, 1995, Sheila M. L. Donnelly. *Educ:* Univ. of Massachusetts (BA). Lecturer: Univ. of Urbino, 1963; Soche Hill Coll., Malawi, 1963–65; Makerere Univ., Kampala, Uganda, 1965–68; Univ. of Singapore, 1968–71; Writer-in-Residence, Univ. of Virginia, 1972. Mem., AAAL (formerly AAIL), 1984. Hon. DLitt: Trinity Coll., Washington DC, 1980; Tufts Univ., Mass, 1980; Univ. of Mass, 1988. *Publications: novels:* Waldo, 1967; Fong and the Indians, 1968; Girls at Play, 1969; Murder in Mount Holly, 1969; Jungle Lovers, 1971; Sinning with Annie, 1972; Saint Jack, 1973 (filmed, 1979); The Black House, 1974; The Family Arsenal, 1976; Picture Palace, 1978 (Whitbread Award, 1978); A Christmas Card, 1978; London Snow, 1980; The Mosquito Coast, 1981 (James Tait Black Prize, 1982; filmed, 1987); Doctor Slaughter, 1984 (filmed as Half Moon Street, 1987); O-Zone, 1986; My Secret History, 1989; Chicago Loop, 1990; Doctor de Marr, 1990; Millroy the Magician, 1993; My Other Life, 1996; Kowloon Tong, 1997; The Collected Short Novels, 1998; Hotel Honolulu, 2001; *short stories:* The Consul's File, 1977; World's End, 1980; The London Embassy, 1982 (televised, 1987); The Collected Stories, 1997; *play:* The White Man's Burden, 1987; *criticism:* V. S. Naipaul, 1972; *memoir:* Sir Vidia's Shadow, 1998; *travel:* The Great Railway Bazaar, 1975; The Old Patagonian Express, 1979; The Kingdom by the Sea, 1983; Sailing through China, illus. Patrick Procktor, 1983; Sunrise with Seamonsters: travels and discoveries 1964–84, 1985; The Imperial Way, 1985; Riding the Iron Rooster, 1988; Travelling The World, 1990; The Happy Isles of Oceania, 1992; The Pillars of Hercules, 1995; Fresh-Air Fiend, 2000; *screenplay:* Saint Jack, 1979; reviews in New York Times, etc. *Recreation:* paddling. *Address:* c/o Hamish Hamilton Ltd, 27 Wrights Lane, W8 5TZ.

THESIGER, family name of **Viscount Chelmsford**.

THESIGER, Roderic Miles Doughty; Director, P. & D. Colnaghi and Co. Ltd, 1955–71; *b* 8 Nov. 1915; *y s* of late Hon. Wilfred Thesiger, DSO, and Mrs Reginald Astley, CBE; *m* 1st, 1940, Mary Rose (marr. diss. 1946; she *d* 1962), *d* of Hon. Guy Charteris; 2nd, 1946, Ursula, *d* of A. W. Whitworth, Woollas Hall, Pershore; one *s* one *d*. *Educ:* Eton; Christ Church, Oxford; Courtauld Institute. Served War of 1939–45, Welsh Guards, 1939–41; 1st Parachute Bde, 1941–44 (twice wounded, POW). Assistant, Tate Gallery, 1945–46; afterwards worked with Messrs Sotheby and privately until 1954. *Recreations:* visiting Italy and France. *Address:* The Paddocks, Lucton, Leominster, Herefordshire HR6 9PG. *T:* (01568) 780327.

See also Sir W. P. Thesiger.

THESIGER, Sir Wilfred (Patrick), KBE 1995 (CBE 1968); DSO 1941; MA Oxon; *b* 3 June 1910; *e s* of late Hon. Wilfred Thesiger, DSO, and Mrs Reginald Astley, CBE. *Educ:* Eton; Magdalen College, Oxford (MA; Hon. Fellow, 1982). Repres. Oxford at boxing, 1930–33; Captain Oxford Boxing Team, 1933; Hon. Attaché Duke of Gloucester's Mission to Abyssinia, for Haile Selassie's coronation, 1930; served Middle East, 1941 (DSO); explored Danakil country of Abyssinia and the Aussa Sultanate, 1933–34 (awarded Back Grant by RGS, 1935); Sudan Political Service, Darfur-Upper Nile, 1935–40; served in Ethiopian, Syrian and Western Desert campaigns with SDF and SAS regiment with rank of Major; explored in Southern Arabia, 1945–49; twice crossed the Empty Quarter. Hon. Vice-Pres., RSAA, 1990–. FRSL 1966; Hon. FBA 1982; Hon. DLitt: Leicester, 1967; Bath, 1992. Founder's Medal, RGS, 1948; Lawrence of Arabia Medal, RCAS, 1955; Livingstone Medal, RSGS, 1962; W. H. Heinemann Award (for 1964), RSL, 1965; Burton Memorial Medal, Roy. Asiatic Soc., 1966. 3rd Class Star of Ethiopia, 1930; Order of Independence (UAE), 2000. *Publications:* Arabian Sands, 1959; The Marsh Arabs, 1964; Desert, Marsh and Mountain: the world of a nomad, 1979; The Life of my Choice (autobiog.), 1987; Visions of a Nomad, 1987; My Kenya Days, 1994; The Danakil Diary: journeys through Abyssinia 1930–34, 1996; Among the Mountains: travels in Asia, 1998; Crossing the Sands, 1999. *Recreations:* travelling, photography. *Address:* Woodcote Grove House, Meadow Hill, Coulsdon, Surrey CR5 2XL. *T:* (020) 8668 5309. *Clubs:* Travellers' (Special Mem.), Beefsteak (Hon. Life Mem.).

See also R. M. D. Thesiger.

THETFORD, Bishop Suffragan of, since 2001; **Rt Rev. David John Atkinson;** *b* 5 Sept. 1943; *s* of Thomas John Collins and Adèle Mary Atkinson; *m* 1969, Suzan Elizabeth; one *s* one *d*. *Educ:* King's Coll., London (BSc, PhD, AKC); Bristol Univ. (MLitt); Oxford Univ. (MA). Ordained deacon, 1972, priest, 1973; Assistant Curate: St Peter Halliwell, Bolton, 1972–74; Harborne Heath, Birmingham, 1974–77; Librarian, Latimer House, Oxford, 1977–80; Chaplain, 1980–93, Fellow, 1984–93, Corpus Christi Coll., Oxford; Canon Chancellor and Missioner, Southwark Cathedral, 1993–96; Archdeacon of Lewisham, 1996–2001. Co-Founder, Oxford Christian Inst. for Counselling, 1985. Mem., SOSc, 1987. *Publications:* To Have and To Hold, 1979; The Bible Speaks Today (series): Ruth, 1983; Genesis 1–11, 1990; Job, 1991; Proverbs, 1996; Peace in Our Time?, 1985; Pastoral Ethics, 1989, 2nd edn 1994; (jtly) Counselling in Context, 1994, 2nd edn 1998; (ed jtly) New Dictionary of Christian Ethics and Pastoral Theology, 1995; Jesus, Lamb of God, 1996; God So Loved the World, 1999; articles and reviews in jls. *Recreations:* music, walking, painting. *Address:* Rectory Meadow, Bramerton, Norwich NR14 7DW. *T:* (01508) 528251.

THIAN, Robert Peter; Chairman: Astron Group Ltd, since 2001; Orion Group Ltd, since 2001; *b* 1 Aug. 1943; *s* of Clifford Peter Thian and Frances Elizabeth (*née* Stafford-Bird); *m* 1964, Liselotte von Borges; two *d*. *Educ:* Geneva Univ. (Lic. en Droit 1967). Called to the Bar, Gray's Inn, 1971. Glaxo Group plc: Legal Advr, 1967–71; Man. Dir, Portugal, 1972–80; Abbott Laboratories (USA): European Business Develt Dir, 1981–84; Regional Dir, Europe, 1985–87; Vice Pres., Internat. Operations, Novo Industri A/S (Denmark), 1987–89; Gp Chief Exec., North West Water Group, 1990–93; Chief Exec., The Stationery Office Gp, 1996–99; Chm., IMO Gp, 1999; Pres., Conseil de Surveillance, Expand Santé Groupe, 1999–2001; Chm., e-doc Gp Ltd, 2000–01. Non-executive Director: Celltech Gp, 1991–99; Medeval Ltd, 1995–98; Tactica Solutions Ltd, 1999–2000. *Recreations:* horses, golf, reading. *Clubs:* Lansdowne; Chantilly Golf.

THICKETT, Michael Godfrey, CMG 1995; HM Diplomatic Service; Counsellor, Foreign and Commonwealth Office, since 1986; *b* 22 Oct. 1940; *s* of Stanley Thickett and Margery Louvain Thickett (*née* Fletcher); *m* 1970, Heather Caroline Fraser; two *s* one *d*. *Educ:* Univ. of Birmingham (BSocSc); Faculté de Droit and Sorbonne, Univ. of Paris (Dip. Droit Internat. Publique). NUS, 1962–63; Programme Manager, Internat. Student Conf., Leiden, Netherlands, 1964–66; Dir, Internat. Dept, NUS, 1967–69; Joined FCO, 1970; Lusaka, 1971–75; Hamburg, 1978–80; Bonn, 1980–83; Pretoria, 1986–90. *Recreations:* fishing, gardening, reading, watching football, Rugby and cricket, writing, DIY—woodworking.

THICKNESSE, John Dacres; Cricket Correspondent, Evening Standard, 1967–96; *b* 30 July 1931; *s* of late Very Rev. Cuthbert Carroll Thicknesse, Dean of St Albans, and Rhoda Thicknesse (*née* Pratt); *m* 1957, Anne Margaret Hardie; two *s* one *d*. *Educ:* Summer Fields, Oxford; Harrow; Trinity Coll., Oxford. News and sports reporter, sports sub-editor, sports diarist, cricket writer: Daily Express, 1957–58; Daily Telegraph, 1958–61 and 1965–66; Sunday Telegraph, 1961–65; The Times, 1996–2001. *Recreations:* bridge, golf, racing, fantasising that one day England will win back the Ashes. *Address:* 17 Silver Street, Warminster, Wilts BA12 8PS. *T:* (01985) 213443. *Clubs:* Somerset Stragglers, IZ, Arabs; West Wilts Golf.

THIESSEN, Gordon, PhD; Governor, Bank of Canada, 1994–2001; *b* 14 Aug. 1938; *m* 1964, Annette Hillyar; two *d*. *Educ:* Univ. of Saskatchewan (BA 1960; MA 1961); London School of Economics (PhD 1972). Lectr in Economics, Univ. of Saskatchewan, 1962; joined Bank of Canada, 1963; Res., and Monetary and Financial Analysis Depts, 1963–79; Advr to Gov., 1979–84; Dep. Gov. (Econ. Res. and Financial Analysis), 1984–87; Sen. Dep. Gov., 1987–94; Mem., Exec. Cttee, 1987–2001; Mem., 1987–2001, Chm., 1994–2001, Bd of Dirs. Vis. Economist, Reserve Bank of Australia, 1973–75. *Address:* c/o Bank of Canada, 234 Wellington Street, Ottawa, ON K1A 0G9, Canada.

THIMONT, Bernard Maurice, CB 1979; Secretary, Churches' Main Committee, 1981–90; *b* 1 July 1920; *s* of Georges André Thimont; *m* 1949, Joy Rowe; one *s* one *d*. *Educ:* St Ignatius Coll., London. Served War of 1939–45, in Army (Major), 1939–48. Foreign Office, 1948–50; HM Treasury, 1950–65; IDC, 1966; Cabinet Office, 1967; HM Treasury, 1967–68; Civil Service Dept, 1968–77; Controller, HM Stationery Office and Queen's Printer of Acts of Parlt, 1977–80. MA Lambeth, 1990. *Recreations:* music, building. *Address:* Trusham, Kingsnorth Close, Bridport, Dorset DT6 4BZ. *T:* (01308) 425426.

THIRD, Rt Rev. Richard Henry McPhail; Assistant Bishop, Diocese of Bath and Wells, since 1992; *b* 29 Sept. 1927; *s* of Henry McPhail and Marjorie Caroline Third; *m* 1966, Helen Illingworth; two *d*. *Educ:* Alleyn's Sch.; Reigate Grammar Sch.; Emmanuel Coll., Cambridge (BA 1950, MA 1955); Lincoln Theological Coll. Deacon 1952, priest 1953; Southwark; Curate: S Andrew, Mottingham, 1952–55; Sanderstead (in charge of St Edmund, Riddlesdown), 1955–59; Vicar of Sheerness, 1959–67; Vicar of Orpington, 1967–76; RD of Orpington, 1973–76; Hon. Canon of Rochester, 1974–76; Proctor in Convocation, 1975–76 and 1980–85; Bishop Suffragan: of Maidstone, 1976–80; of Dover,

1980–92. Hon. DCL Kent, 1990. *Recreations:* music, walking, reading, gardening. *Address:* 25 Church Close, Martock, Somerset TA12 6DS. *T:* (01935) 825519.

THIRLWALL, Prof. Anthony Philip, PhD; Professor of Applied Economics, University of Kent, since 1976; *b* 21 April 1941; *s* of Isaac Thirlwall and Ivy Florence Ticehurst; *m* 1966, Gianna Paoletti (separated 1986); one *s* one *d* (and one *s* decd). *Educ:* Harrow Weald County Grammar Sch.; Univ. of Leeds (BA 1962; PhD 1967); Clark Univ. (MA 1963). Teaching Fellow, Clark Univ., 1962–63; Tutor, Cambridge Univ., 1963–64; Asst Lectr, Univ. of Leeds, 1964–66; Lectr and Reader, Univ. of Kent, 1966–76. Economic Adviser: ODM, 1966; Dept of Employment, 1968–70. Res. Associate, Princeton Univ., 1971–72; Visiting Professor: West Virginia Univ., 1967; Melbourne Univ., 1981, 1988; Vis. Scholar, King's Coll., Cambridge, 1979; Bye-Fellow, Robinson Coll., Cambridge, 1985–86; Dist. Vis. Fellow, La Trobe Univ., 1994. Consultant: Pacific Islands Develt Program, 1989–90, 1996; African Develt Bank, 1993–94 and 1999. Member: Council and Exec. Cttee, Royal Econ. Soc., 1979–89; Council, Business for Sterling, 1999–. Governor, NIESR, 1979–. Trustee, New Europe Res. Trust, 1999–. Member, Editorial Board: Jl of Develt Studies, 1979–; Jl of Post Keynesian Econs, 1998–; African Develt Review, 1999–; Portuguese Econ. Review, 1999–. *Publications:* Growth and Development, 1972, 6th edn 1999 (trans. Chinese and Greek 2002); Inflation, Saving and Growth in Developing Economies, 1974 (trans. Spanish 1978); (with R. Dixon) Regional Growth and Unemployment in the UK, 1975; Financing Economic Development, 1976 (trans. Greek 1977, Spanish 1978, Turkish 1980); (with H. Gibson) Balance of Payments Theory and the UK Experience, 1980, 4th edn 1992; Nicholas Kaldor, 1987; (with S. Bazen) Deindustrialisation, 1989, 3rd edn 1997; Performance and Prospects of the Pacific Island Economies in the World Economy, 1991; (with J. McCombie) Economic Growth and the Balance of Payments Constraint, 1994; Economics of Growth and Development: selected essays, vol. 1, 1995; Macroeconomic Issues from a Keynesian Perspective: selected essays, vol. 2, 1997; The Euro and Regional Divergence in Europe, 2000; The Nature of Economic Growth: an alternative framework for understanding the performance of nations, 2002; numerous edited books, esp. on Lord Keynes and Lord Kaldor; articles in professional jls. *Recreations:* athletics (rep. GB, European Veterans Athletics Champs (400 m, 800 m), 1982), tennis, gardening, travel. *Address:* 14 Moorfield, Canterbury, Kent CT2 7AN. *T:* (01227) 769904; *e-mail:* at4@ukc.ac.uk. *Club:* Royal Over-Seas League.

THIRLWALL, Kathryn Mary; QC 1999; a Recorder, since 2000; *b* 21 Nov. 1957; *d* of Brian Edward Thirlwall and Margaret Thirlwall (*née* Earl); *m* 1984, Charles Kelly; one *s* one *d*. *Educ:* St Anthony's Sch., Sunderland; Bristol Univ. (BA Hons 1980); Newcastle Poly. (CPE 1981). Called to the Bar, Middle Temple, 1982. *Address:* (chambers) 7 Bedford Row, WC1R 4BU.

THIRSK, Dr (Irene) Joan, CBE 1994; FBA 1974; Reader in Economic History in the University of Oxford, and Fellow of St Hilda's College, Oxford, 1965–83 (Hon. Fellow, 1983); *b* 19 June 1922; *d* of William Henry Watkins and Daisy (*née* Frayer); *m* 1945, James Wood Thirsk; one *s* one *d*. *Educ:* Camden School for Girls, NW5; Westfield Coll., Univ. of London (Hon. Fellow, QMW, 1997). BA, PhD London; MA Oxford. Subaltern, ATS, Intelligence Corps, 1942–45. Asst Lectr in Sociology, LSE, 1950–51; Sen. Res. Fellow in Agrarian History, Dept of English Local History, Leicester Univ., 1951–65. Ford Lectr in English History, Oxford, 1975. Sen. Mellon Fellow, Nat. Humanities Centre, 1986–87. Member: Royal Commn on Historical Monuments (England), 1977–86; Econ. and Social Hist. Cttee, SSRC, 1978–82; Royal Commn on Historical Manuscripts, 1989–96. Mem. Council, Economic Hist. Soc., 1955–83; Vice-Chm., Standing Conf. for Local Hist., 1965–82; President: British Agricl Hist. Soc., 1983–86, 1995–98 (Mem. Exec. Cttee, 1953–83, Chm. Exec. Cttee, 1974–77); Edmonton Hundred Historical Soc., 1978–96; Oxfordshire Local Hist. Assoc., 1981–86 (Vice-Pres., 1980–81); Conf. of Teachers of Regional and Local Hist. in Tertiary Educn, 1981–82; British Assoc. for Local Hist., 1986–92; Kent Hist. Fedn, 1990–99; Vice-Pres., Soc. for Lincs Hist. and Archaeol., 1979–; Foreign Mem., Amer. Philos. Soc., 1982–; Corresp. Mem., Colonial Soc. of Massachusetts, 1983–. Editor, Agricultural History Review, 1964–72; Gen. Editor, The Agrarian History of England and Wales, 1974–2000 (Dep. Gen. Ed., 1966–74); Mem. Editorial Bd, Past and Present, 1956–92. Hon. DLitt: Leicester, 1985; East Anglia, 1990; Kent, 1993; Sussex, 1994; Greenwich, 2001; DUniv Open, 1991; Hon. DAgric. Wageningen Agricl Univ., Netherlands, 1993. *Publications:* English Peasant Farming, 1957; Suffolk Farming in the Nineteenth Century, 1958; Tudor Enclosures, 1959; The Agrarian History of England and Wales: vol. IV, 1500–1640, 1967; vol. V, 1640–1750, 1984; (with J. P. Cooper) Seventeenth-Century Economic Documents, 1972; The Restoration, 1976; Economic Policy and Projects, 1978; The Rural Economy of England (collected essays), 1985; England's Agricultural Regions and Agrarian History 1500–1750, 1987; Alternative Agriculture: a history from the Black Death to the present day, 1997; The English Rural Landscape, 2000; articles in Economic History Rev., Agric. History Rev., Past and Present, History, Jl Modern History, etc. *Recreations:* gardening, sewing, machine-knitting. *Address:* 1 Hadlow Castle, Hadlow, Tonbridge, Kent TN11 0EG.

THISELTON, Prof. Rev. Canon Anthony Charles, PhD, DD; Professor of Christian Theology and Head of Department of Theology, University of Nottingham, 1992–2001, now Professor Emeritus; Canon Theologian: Leicester Cathedral, since 1994; Southwell Minster, since 2000; *b* 13 July 1937; *s* of Eric Charles Thiselton and Hilda Winifred (*née* Kevan); *m* 1963, Rosemary Stella Harman; two *s* one *d*. *Educ:* City of London School; King's Coll., London. BD 1959; MTh 1964 (London); PhD (Sheffield) 1977; DD (Durham) 1993. Curate, Holy Trinity, Sydenham, 1960–63; Lectr and Chaplain, Tyndale Hall, Bristol, 1963–67, Sen. Tutor, 1967–70; Recognised Teacher in Theology, Univ. of Bristol, 1965–71; University of Sheffield: Sir Henry Stephenson Fellow, 1970–71; Lectr in Biblical Studies, 1971–79; Sen. Lectr, 1979–86; Principal, St John's Coll., Nottingham and Special Lectr in Theology, Univ. of Nottingham, 1986–88; Principal, St John's Coll. with Cranmer Hall, Univ. of Durham, 1988–92; Public Orator, Nottingham Univ., 1999–2001. British Acad. Res. Leave Award, 1995–96. Visiting Professor: Calvin Coll., Grand Rapids, USA, 1982–83; Regent Coll., Vancouver, 1983; Fuller Theolog. Seminary, Pasadena, Calif, 1984; North Park Coll. and Seminary, Chicago, 1984; Scottish Jl of Theol. Lectures, 1994. Exam. Chaplain to Bishop of Sheffield, 1977–80, to Bishop of Leicester, 1979–89 and 1993–. Member: C of E Faith and Order Adv. Group, 1971–81, 1987–90; Doctrine Commn, 1977–90, 1996– (Vice-Chm., 1987–90); Wkg Pty on Revised Catechism, 1988–89; Gen. Synod of C of E, 1995– (Mem., Theol. Educn and Trng Cttee, 1999–2000; Chm., Evangelical Gp, 1999–2000); Crown Appts Commn, 2000–; Wkg Pty on Women in the Episcopate, 2001–; C of E Evangelical Council, 2001–. Consultant, Clergy Discipline (Doctrine) Gp, 2000–. Mem., HFEA, 1995–99. Council for National Academic Awards: Vice-Chm., Bd of Theol and Religious Studies, 1984–87; Mem., Cttee for Humanities, 1987–89. Pres., Soc. for the Study of Theology, 1998–2000. Adv. Editor, Jl for Study of NT, 1981–91; Editl Consultant, Ex Auditu (Princeton and Chicago), 1985–; Mem. Editl Bd, Biblical Interpretation (Brill, Leiden), 1992–, Internat. Jl Systematic Theol, 1999–. *Publications:* The Two Horizons: New Testament Hermeneutics and Philosophical Description, 1980; (with C. Walhout and R. Lundin) The Responsibility of Hermeneutics, 1985; New Horizons in Hermeneutics: theory and practice of transforming biblical reading, 1992; Interpreting God and the Postmodern Self, 1995; (with C. Walhout and R. Lundin) The Promise of Hermenentics, 1999; First Corinthians: a commentary on the Greek text, 2000; contribs to learned jls and other books on New Testament, doctrine, and philosophical hermeneutics. *Recreation:* choral and organ music. *Address:* Department of Theology, University of Nottingham, University Park, Nottingham NG7 2RD. *T:* (0115) 951 5852, *Fax:* (0115) 951 5887; *e-mail:* anthony.thiselton@ntlworld.com.

THISTLETHWAITE, Prof. Frank, CBE 1979; founding Vice-Chancellor, 1961–80, and Emeritus Professor, University of East Anglia; *b* 24 July 1915; *s* of late Lee and Florence Nightingale Thistlethwaite; *m* 1940, Jane (*d* 1992), *d* of H. Lindley Hosford, Lyme, Connecticut, USA; one *s* three *d* (and one *s* decd). *Educ:* Bootham School; St John's College, Cambridge (Exhibitioner and Scholar). BA 1938, MA 1941. FRHistS. Editor, The Cambridge Review, 1937. Commonwealth Fund Fellow, University of Minnesota, 1938–40; British Press Service, New York, 1940–41. RAF, 1941–45; seconded to Office of War Cabinet (Joint-Amer. Secretariat), 1942–45. Fellow, St John's College, Cambridge, 1945–61; at various times, Tutor, Praelector, Steward; University Lecturer in Faculty of Economics and Politics, 1949–61. Visiting Prof. of American Civilization, Univ. of Pennsylvania, 1956; Vis. Fellow, Henry E. Huntington Library, Calif, 1973; Leverhulme Emeritus Fellow, 1981; Hill Vis. Prof., Univ. of Minnesota, 1986. Chairman: British Assoc. for Amer. Studies, 1955–59; Cttee of Management, Inst. of US Studies, Univ. of London, 1966–80; IUPC (formerly IUC), 1977–81 (Mem., 1962–81); Member: Inst. for Advanced Study, Princeton, 1954; Academic Adv. Cttee, Open Univ., 1969–74; Provisional Council, Univ. of Zambia, 1965–69; Univ. of Malaŵi, 1971–75; Univ. of Mauritius, 1974–84; Marshall Aid Commemoration Commn, 1964–80; US-UK Educnl (Fulbright) Commn, 1964–79; European Adv. Council, Salzburg Seminar in Amer. Studies, 1969–74; Bd, British Council, 1971–82; British Cttee of Award, Harkness Fellowships, 1974–80; Adviser to Nat. Council of Higher Educn, Ceylon, 1967. Governor, Sedbergh Sch., 1958–73. Pres., Friends of Cambridge Univ. Library, 1983–95. Hon. Fellow, St John's Coll., Cambridge, 1974. Hon. Prof. of History, Univ. of Mauritius, 1981. Hon. FRIBA 1985. Hon. LHD Colorado, 1972; Hon. DCL East Anglia, 1980; Hon. DSc Minnesota, 1994. *Publications:* The Great Experiment: An Introduction to the History of the American People, 1955 (trans. 14 languages); The Anglo-American Connection in the Early Nineteenth Century, 1958; Dorset Pilgrims: the story of West Country pilgrims who went to New England in the 17th century, 1989; Migration from Europe Overseas in the Nineteenth and Twentieth Centuries, in, A Century of European Migrations 1830–1930, 1991; A Lancashire Family Inheritance, 1996; Our War 1938–45, 1997; Cambridge Years 1945–61, 1999; Origins, 2000; contrib. New Cambridge Modern History and other historical works and journals; New Universities in the Modern World (ed M. G. Ross). *Recreation:* music. *Address:* 15 Park Parade, Cambridge CB5 8AL. *Club:* Athenæum.

See also J. H. Pellew.

THODAY, Prof. John Marion, BSc Wales, PhD, ScD Cantab; FRS 1965; Arthur Balfour Professor of Genetics, Cambridge University, 1959–83, now Emeritus; Life Fellow of Emmanuel College, 1983 (Fellow, 1959); *b* 30 Aug. 1916; *s* of Professor D. Thoday, FRS; *m* 1950, Doris Joan Rich, PhD (Emeritus Fellow, Lucy Cavendish College); one *s* one *d*. *Educ:* Bootham School, York; University Coll. of N Wales, Bangor; Trinity College, Cambridge. Photographic Intelligence, Royal Air Force, 1941–46; Cytologist, Mount Vernon Hospital, 1946–47; Asst Lectr, then Lectr for Cytogenetics, Departments of Botany and Zoology, University of Sheffield, 1947–54; Head of Department of Genetics: Sheffield, 1954–59; Cambridge, 1959–82. Leverhulme Emeritus Res. Fellow, 1984–86. Director, OECD Project for reform of secondary school Biology teaching 1962, 1963. Chm., UK Nat. Cttee for Biology, 1982–88. Pres., Genetical Soc., 1975–78. *Publications:* (with J. N. Thompson) Quantitive Genetics, 1979; articles on radiation cytology, experimental evolution, the genetics of continuous variables, biological progress and on genetics and society. *Address:* 7 Clarkson Road, Cambridge CB3 0EH; *e-mail:* thoday@waitrose.com.

THOM, Dr Gordon; International Managing Director, Dyson Ltd, since 2001; *b* 18 May 1953; *m* 1977, Margaret Pringle; one *s* one *d*. DoE, 1978; joined FCO, 1979; Second, subseq. First Sec., Tokyo, 1981; FCO, 1985; First Sec., New Delhi, 1989; Economic Counsellor, Tokyo, 1994; Man. Dir, Dyson Japan, 1998. *Address:* Dyson Ltd, Tetbury Hill, Malmesbury, Wilts SN16 0RP.

THOM, Kenneth Cadwallader; HM Diplomatic Service, retired; *b* 4 Dec. 1922; *m* 1948, Patience Myra (*née* Collingridge); three *s* one *d*. *Educ:* University College School, London; St Andrews Univ.; MA(Hons). Army Service, 1942–47; Assistant District Officer, then District Officer, Northern Nigerian Administration, 1950–59; 1st Secretary: FO, 1959; UK Mission to UN, NY, 1960–63; FO, 1963–66; Budapest, 1966–68; FCO, 1968–72; Counsellor, Dublin, 1972–74; Counsellor, FCO, 1974–78; Consul-General: Hanover, 1978–79; Hamburg, 1979–81; retired, and re-employed, FCO, 1981–85. FIL 1981. *Address:* Heybrook, Lower Backway, Bruton, Somerset BA10 0EA.

THOMAS; *see* Elis-Thomas.

THOMAS, family name of **Barons Thomas of Gresford, Thomas of Gwydir, Thomas of Macclesfield, Thomas of Swynnerton** and **Baroness Thomas of Walliswood.**

THOMAS OF GRESFORD, Baron *cr* 1996 (Life Peer), of Gresford in the co. borough of Wrexham; **Donald Martin Thomas,** OBE 1982; QC 1979; a Recorder of the Crown Court, since 1976; *b* 13 March 1937; *s* of Hywel and Olwen Thomas; *m* 1961, Nan Thomas (*née* Kerr) (*d* 2000); three *s* one *d*. *Educ:* Grove Park Grammar Sch., Wrexham; Peterhouse, Cambridge (MA, LLB). Solicitor at Wrexham, 1961–66; Lectr in Law, 1966–68; called to the Bar, Gray's Inn, 1967, Bencher, 1989; Barrister, Wales and Chester Circuit, 1968–; Dep. Circuit Judge, 1974–76; Dep. High Court Judge, 1985–. Mem., Criminal Injury Compensation Bd, 1985–93. Contested (L): W Flints, 1964, 1966, 1970; Wrexham, Feb. and Oct. 1974, 1979, 1983, 1987; Vice Chm., Welsh Liberal Party, 1967–69, Chm. 1969–74; President: Wrexham Liberal Assoc., 1975–; Welsh Liberal Party, 1977, 1978, 1979; Welsh Liberal Democrats, 1993–97 (Vice-Pres., 1991–93). Chm., Marcher Sound, 1991– (ind. local radio for NE Wales and Cheshire) (Vice Chm., 1983–91). *Recreations:* Rugby football, rowing, golf, music-making, fishing. *Address:* Glasfryn, Gresford, Wrexham, Clwyd LL12 8RG. *T:* (01978) 852205. *Clubs:* Reform; Western (Glasgow); Wrexham Rugby Football.

THOMAS OF GWYDIR, Baron *cr* 1987 (Life Peer), of Llanrwst in the county of Gwynedd; **Peter John Mitchell Thomas;** PC 1964; QC 1965; a Recorder of the Crown Court, 1974–88; *b* 31 July 1920; *o s* of late David Thomas, Solicitor, Llanrwst, Denbighshire, and Anne Gwendoline Mitchell; *m* 1947, Frances Elizabeth Tessa (*d* 1985), *o d* of late Basil Dean, CBE and Lady Mercy Greville; two *s* two *d*. *Educ:* Epworth College, Rhyl; Jesus College, Oxford (MA; Hon. Fellow, 2001). Served War of 1939–45, in RAF (Bomber Comd); Prisoner of War (Germany), 1941–45. Called to Bar, Middle Temple, 1947 (Master of the Bench 1971, Emeritus 1991); Member of Wales and Chester Circuit;

Deputy Chairman: Cheshire QS, 1966–70; Denbighshire QS, 1968–70. Arbitrator, Court of Arbitration, Internat. Chamber of Commerce, Paris, 1974–88. MP (C): Conway Div. of Caernarvonshire, 1951–66; Hendon South, 1970–87; PPS to the Solicitor-General, 1954–59; Parly Secretary, Min. of Labour, 1959–61; Parly Under-Sec. of State, Foreign Office, 1961–63; Minister of State for Foreign Affairs, 1963–64; Opp. Front Bench Spokesman on Foreign Affairs and Law, 1964–66; Sec. of State for Wales, 1970–74. Member: Select Cttee on Conduct of Members, 1976–77; Select Cttee on Procedure (Supply), 1981–83 (Chm.); Select Cttee on Foreign Affairs, 1983–87 (Dep. Chm.); Select Cttee on Privileges, 1984–87; Chairman: Select Cttee on Members' Salaries, 1981–82; Select Cttee on Revision of Standing Orders, 1982–83. Chm., Cons. Party Organisation, 1970–72. Pres., Nat. Union of Conservative and Unionist Assocs, 1974 and 1975. Mem., Council of Europe and WEU, 1957–59. Member, Historic Buildings Council for Wales, 1965–67. *Address:* 37 Chester Way, SE11 4UR. *T:* (020) 7735 6047; Millicent Cottage, Elstead, Surrey GU8 6HD. *T:* (01252) 702052. *Club:* Carlton.

THOMAS OF MACCLESFIELD, Baron *cr* 1997 (Life Peer), of Prestbury in the co. of Cheshire; **Terence James Thomas,** CBE 1997; Managing Director, The Co-operative Bank, 1988–97; Chairman, Northwest Development Agency, since 1998; *b* 19 Oct. 1937; *s* of late William Emrys Thomas and Mildred Evelyn Thomas; *m* 1963, Lynda, *d* of late William John Stevens; three *s*. *Educ:* Queen Elizabeth Grammar Sch., Carmarthen; Univ. of Bath (Postgrad. Dip. Business Admin); INSEAD (AMP). FCIB. Nat. Provincial, later Nat. Westminster Bank, 1962–71; Joint Credit Card Co., 1971–73; The Co-operative Bank: Mkting Manager, 1973–77; Asst Gen. Manager, then Jt Gen. Manager, 1977–83; Dir, 1984; Exec. Dir, Gp Develt, 1987. Director: Stanley Leisure Organisation plc, 1994–98; Capita Gp, 1998–99; Rathbone CI, 1998. Chm., Venture Technic (Cheshire) Ltd, 1984–97. Director: English Partnerships (Central), 1998–99; Commn for the New Towns, 1998–99; CDA; Chm., NW Partnership, 1994–97. Mem., Regl Economic Develt Commn. Mem., Gen. Council, CIB, until 1997; Pres., Internat. Co-operative Banking Assoc., 1988–95. Chm., NW Media Charitable Trust, 1998–99. Vis. Prof., Univ. of Stirling, 1988–91. Mem., Ct of Governors, UMIST, 1996–. Mem. Bd Trustees, UNICEF, 1998–99. FRSA; CIMgt. Hon. Fellow, Univ. of Central Lancs, 2000. Hon. DLitt Salford, 1996; Hon. DBA Manchester Metropolitan, 1998; DUniv: Manchester, 1999; UMIST, 1999. Mancunian of the Year, 1998. *Address:* 51 Willowmead Drive, Prestbury, Cheshire SK10 4DD. *T:* (01625) 828092.

THOMAS OF SWYNNERTON, Baron *cr* 1981 (Life Peer), of Notting Hill in Greater London; **Hugh Swynnerton Thomas;** historian; *b* 21 Oct. 1931; *s* of Hugh Whitelegge Thomas, CMG, Colonial Service, Gold Coast (Ghana) and late Margery Swynnerton; *m* 1962, Vanessa Jebb, *d* of 1st Baron Gladwyn, GCMG, GCVO, CB; two *s* one *d*. *Educ:* Sherborne; Queens' Coll., Cambridge (Scholar); Sorbonne, Paris. Pres. Cambridge Union, 1953. Foreign Office, 1954–57; Sec. to UK delegn to UN Disarmament Sub-Cttee, 1955–56; Lectr at RMA Sandhurst, 1957; Prof. of History, 1966–76, and Chm., Grad. Sch. of Contemp. European Studies, 1973–76, Univ. of Reading. Anshen Lectr, Frick Mus., NY, 1991; Yaseen Lectr, Met. Mus. of Art, NY, 1995. King Juan Carlos I (Vis.) Prof., New York Univ., 1995; Vis. Prof. of History, Univ. of Boston, 1996; Univ. Prof., Boston Univ., 1997–. Chm., Centre for Policy Studies, 1979–90. Trustee, Fundación Medinaceli, 1996–. Corresp. Mem., Real Acad. de la Historia, Madrid, 1994. Somerset Maugham Prize, 1962; Arts Council prize for History (1st Nat. Book Awards), 1980. Order of Aztec Eagle (Mexico), 1994; Knight Grand Cross, Order of Isabel la Católica (Spain), 2001. *Publications:* (as Hugh Thomas) The World's Game, 1957; The Spanish Civil War, 1961, rev. edn 1977, rev. illustrated edn, Spain, 1979; The Suez Affair, 1967; Cuba, or the Pursuit of Freedom, 1971; (ed) The selected writings of José Antonio Primo de Rivera, 1972; Goya and The Third of May 1808, 1972; Europe, the Radical Challenge, 1973; John Strachey, 1973; The Cuban Revolution, 1977; An Unfinished History of the World, 1979, rev. edn 1982 (US 1979, A History of the World); The Case for the Round Reading Room, 1983; Havannah (novel), 1984; Armed Truce, 1986; A Traveller's Companion to Madrid, 1988; Klara (novel), 1988; Ever Closer Union: Britain's destiny in Europe, 1991; The Conquest of Mexico, 1993; The Slave Trade: the history of the Atlantic slave trade 1440–1870, 1997; The Future of Europe, 1997; Who's Who of the Conquistadors, 2000. *Address:* 29 Ladbroke Grove, W11 3BB.

THOMAS OF WALLISWOOD, Baroness *cr* 1994 (Life Peer), of Dorking in the County of Surrey; **Susan Petronella Thomas,** OBE 1989; DL; Chairman, Surrey County Council, 1996–97 (Member (Lib Dem), 1985–97; Vice Chairman, 1993–96); *b* 20 Dec. 1935; *m* 1958, David Churchill Thomas, *qv* (separated); one *s* two *d*. *Educ:* Cranborne Chase Sch.; Lady Margaret Hall, Oxford. NEDO, 1971–74; Chief Exec., British Clothing Industries Council for Europe, 1974–78. Chm. and Treas., Richmond Liberal Assoc., 1974–77; former Pres., Women Lib Dems. Chm., Highways and Transport Cttee, Surrey CC, 1993–96; Mem., Surrey Probation Cttee, 1997–. Contested: (Lib Alliance) Mole Valley, 1983 and 1987; (Lib Dem) Surrey, Eur. Parly elecns, 1994. Lib Dem spokesman on transport, H of L, 1994–; Chm. Associate (formerly All-Party) Parly Gp on Sex Equality, 1998–. DL Surrey, 1996. *Address:* House of Lords, SW1A 0PW. *T:* (020) 7219 3599, *Fax:* (020) 7219 2082.

See also Hon. D. W. P. Thomas.

THOMAS, Prof. Adrian Tregerthen; Professor of Music, University of Wales, Cardiff, since 1996; *b* 11 June 1947; *s* of Owen George Thomas and Jean Tregerthen. *Educ:* Univ. of Nottingham (BMus 1969); University Coll., Cardiff (MA 1971). Lectr in Music, 1973–82, Sen. Lectr, 1982–85, Hamilton Harty Prof. of Music, 1985–96, QUB. Hd of Music, BBC Radio 3, 1990–93. Medal of Polish Composers' Union, for Distinguished Service to Contemporary Polish Music, 1989; Order of Merit for Polish Culture, 1996. *Publications:* Grazyna Bacewicz: chamber and orchestral music, USA 1985; (contrib.) Cambridge Companion to Chopin, 1992; (contrib.) New Grove Dictionary of Opera, 1993; (contrib.) New Grove Dictionary of Women Composers, 1994; Górecki, 1997; (contrib.) New Grove Dictionary of Music and Musicians, 2nd edn 2000; contrib. Music Rev., THES, Contemp. Music Rev., Music and Letters. *Recreations:* poetry, oriental arts, hill-walking. *Address:* Department of Music, University of Wales, Cardiff, Cardiff CF10 3EB.

THOMAS, Sir Alan; *see* Thomas Sir J. A.

THOMAS, Aneurin Morgan; Director, Welsh Arts Council, 1967–84; *b* 3 April 1921; *s* of Philip Thomas and Olwen Amy Thomas (*née* Davies); *m* 1947, Mary Dineen; one *s* one *d*. *Educ:* Ystalyfera Intermediate Sch., Glamorgan; Swansea School of Art and Crafts. British and Indian Armies, 1941–46 (Major). Lecturer, later Vice-Principal, Somerset College of Art, 1947–60; Vice-Principal, Hornsey College of Art, 1960–67. Member, Board of Governors: Loughborough Coll. of Art and Design, 1980–89; S Glamorgan Inst. of Higher Educn, 1985–89 (Chm., Faculty of Art and Design Adv. Cttee, 1985–90); Carmarthenshire Coll. of Tech. and Art, 1985– (Chm., Faculty of Art and Design Adv. Cttee, 1985–); Vice-President: Nat. Soc. for Art Educn, 1967–68; Llangollen Internat. Music Eisteddfod, 1970–. Chm., Assoc. of Art Instns, 1977–78. *Publications:* periodic contribs to books and professional jls. *Recreation:* observing with interest and humour but also with increasing bewilderment. *Address:* Netherwood, 8 Lower Cwrt-y-vil Road, Penarth, Vale of Glamorgan CF64 3HQ. *T:* (029) 2070 2239.

THOMAS, (Anthony) Richard, CMG 1995; HM Diplomatic Service, retired; High Commissioner, Jamaica, and non-resident Ambassador to Haiti, 1995–99; *b* 11 July 1939; *s* of Frederick James Thomas and Winifred Kate Apthorpe Webb; *m* 1976, Ricky Parks Prado, London and Lima; one *s* one *d*. *Educ:* Ampleforth; Peterhouse, Cambridge (MA). FO 1962; served Caracas, Budapest, Washington, Madrid and FCO; Counsellor, Dep. Consul-Gen., Johannesburg, 1981; Minister Counsellor and Consul-Gen., Brasilia, 1985; FCO 1989; Ambassador to Angola, São Tomé and Principe, 1993. *Recreations:* listening to music, reading, theatre, visual arts, cooking. *Address:* c/o 83 Broxash Road, SW11 6AD.

THOMAS, Prof. (Antony) Charles, CBE 1991; DL; DLitt; FSA; FRHistS; FBA 1989; Professor of Cornish Studies, University of Exeter, 1971–91, Professor Emeritus, 1993; Director, Institute of Cornish Studies, 1971–91; *b* 24 April 1928; *s* of late Donald Woodroffe Thomas and Viva Warrington Thomas; *m* 1959, Jessica Dorothea Esther, *d* of late F. A. Mann, CBE, FBA, Hon. QC; two *s* two *d*. *Educ:* Winchester; Corpus Christi Coll., Oxon (BA Hons Jurisp.); Univ. of London (Dipl. Prehist. Archaeol.; Fellow, UCL, 1993); DLitt Oxon, 1983. FSA 1960; FRHistS 1983. Lectr in Archaeology, Univ. of Edinburgh, 1957–67; Prof. of Archaeology, Univ. of Leicester, 1967–71. Leverhulme Fellowship, 1965–67; Sir John Rhys Fellow, Univ. of Oxford, and Vis. Sen. Res. Fellow, Jesus Coll., 1985–86; Emeritus Leverhulme Fellowship, 1993–95. Lectures: Dalrymple, Univ. of Glasgow, 1991; (first) Whithorn Trust, 1992; (first) John Jamieson, Scottish Church History Soc., 1997; Rhind, Edinburgh, 1999. President: Council for British Archaeology, 1970–73; Royal Instn of Cornwall, 1970–72; Cornwall Archaeol. Soc., 1984–88; Soc. for Medieval Archaeology, 1986–89; Soc. for Landscape Studies, 1993–. Chairman: BBC SW Reg. Adv. Council, 1975–80; DoE Area Archaeol Cttee, Cornwall and Devon, 1975–79; Cornwall Cttee Rescue Archaeol., 1976–88; Soc. for Church Archaeol., 1995–98; Mem., Royal Commn on Historical Monuments (England), 1983–97 (Acting Chm., 1988–89; Vice Chm., 1991–97). Hon. Mem., Royal Irish Acad., 1973; Hon. Fellow: RSAI, 1975, St David's Univ. Coll. Lampeter, 1992; Hon. FSAScot 2000. Hon. DLitt NUI, 1996. DL Cornwall, 1988. William Frend Medal, Soc. of Antiquaries, 1982. *Publications:* Christian Antiquities of Camborne, 1967; The Early Christian Archaeology of North Britain, 1971; Britain and Ireland in Early Christian Times, 1971; (with A. Small and D. Wilson) St Ninian's Isle and its Treasure, 1973; (with D. Ivall) Military Insignia of Cornwall, 1974; Christianity in Roman Britain to AD 500, 1981; Exploration of a Drowned Landscape, 1985; Celtic Britain, 1986; Views and Likenesses: photographers in Cornwall and Scilly 1839–70, 1988; Tintagel, Arthur and Archaeology, 1993; And Shall These Mute Stones Speak?: post-Roman inscriptions in Western Britain, 1994; Christian Celts, Messages and Images, 1998; Silent in the Shroud, 1999; The Penzance Market Cross, 1999. *Recreations:* military history, archaeological fieldwork. *Address:* Lambessow, St Clement, Truro, Cornwall TR1 1TB.

THOMAS, Cedric Marshall, CBE 1991 (OBE 1983); consultant on business, health and safety; Director, Jesse Shirley Ltd, since 1999; Deputy Chairman, Thomas William Lench Ltd, since 1993 (Director, since 1991); *b* 26 May 1930; *s* of David J. Thomas and Evis (*née* Field); *m* 1st, 1954, Dora Ann Pritchard (*d* 1975); one *s* one *d*; 2nd, 1976, Margaret Elizabeth (*née* Crawley); one step *s* three step *d*. *Educ:* King Edward's Sch., Birmingham; Univ. of Birmingham (BSc Hons, PhD). CEng, FIMM; FMES (Pres., 1969–71); CIMgt. NCB, 1954–60; Johnson Progress Group, 1961–77 (Chief Exec., 1970–77); Business Consultant, 1977–80; Benjamin Priest Group, 1980–84 (Chief Exec., 1983); Dir and Chief Exec., Engrg Employers' W Midlands Assoc., 1984–91; Chm., Jesse Shirley & Son, then Jesse Shirley, Ltd, 1991–99; Dir, Poplars Resource Management Co. Ltd, 1992–99. Member: Management Bd, Engrg Employers' Fedn, 1974–80, 1983–84; HSC, 1980–90; Engrg Employers' Fedn Council, 1992–95. Non-exec. Director: Staffs Ambulance Service NHS Trust, 1995– (Vice Chm., 1999–); Staffordshire Environmental Funding Ltd, 1997– (Chm., 2000–). Chairman: Special Programmes Area Bd, 1978–83; Area Manpower Bd, 1986–88. Pres., Engineering Employers' W Midlands Assoc., 1976–78. Governor, N Staffs Polytechnic, 1973–80. Hon. FFOM 1992. FRSA. *Recreations:* Rugby football (spectator), tennis, theatre, walking. *Address:* Parkfields House, Tittensor, Staffs ST12 9HQ. *T:* (01782) 373677.

THOMAS, Charles; *see* Thomas, A. C.

THOMAS, Ven. Charles Edward; Archdeacon of Wells, 1983–93; *b* 1927. *Educ:* St David's College, Lampeter (BA 1951); College of the Resurrection, Mirfield. Deacon 1953, priest 1954; Curate of Ilminster, 1953–56; Chaplain and Asst Master, St Michael's Coll., Tenbury, 1956–57; Curate of St Stephen's, St Albans, 1957–58; Vicar, St Michael and All Angels, Boreham Wood, 1958–66; Rector, Monksilver with Elworthy, 1966–74, with Brompton Ralph and Nettlecombe, 1969–74 (Curate-in-charge of Nettlecombe, 1968–69); Vicar of South Petherton with the Seavingtons, 1974–83. RD of Crewkerne, 1977–82. *Address:* Geryfelin, Pentre, Tregaron, Ceredigion SY25 6ND. *T:* (01974) 298102.

THOMAS, (Christopher) Paul; Deputy Chief Executive, Manchester Training and Enterprise Council, since 1998; *b* 9 Feb. 1951; *s* of Donald Thomas and Rita Thomas (*née* Kershaw); *m* 1981, Colleen Doey. *Educ:* Hutton Grammar Sch.; Bridlington Sch.; Keble Coll., Oxford (MA PPE). Civil Service, 1973–97: served in Customs & Excise, HM Treasury, Cabinet Office, Dept of Employment, and DfEE; Regl Policy Advr, Yorks and Humberside TECs, 1997–98. *Recreations:* squash, cricket, golf, walking, sailing, jazz. *Address:* Croft Head, Aston Lane, Hope Valley, Derbys S33 6RA. *T:* (01433) 621764.

THOMAS, Christopher Sydney, PhD; FCIArb; QC 1989; a Recorder, since 2000; *b* 17 March 1950; *s* of late John Raymond Thomas and of Daphne May Thomas; *m* 1979, Patricia Jane Heath; one *s* one *d*. *Educ:* King's Sch., Worcester; Univ. of Kent at Canterbury (BA Hons, 1st Cl.); Faculté International de Droit Comparé, Paris (Diplôme de Droit Comparé (avec mérite), 1972); King's Coll., London (PhD 1994). FCIArb 1994. Hardwick Scholar and Jenkins Scholar, Lincoln's Inn; called to the Bar, Lincoln's Inn, 1973; Asst Recorder, 1994–2000. Called to Gibraltar Bar, 1989. CEDR accredited Mediator, 1999. *Recreation:* farming. *Address:* Keating Chambers, 10 Essex Street, WC2R 3AA. *T:* (020) 7544 2600.

THOMAS, Claire C.; *see* Curtis-Thomas.

THOMAS, Clarence; Associate Justice of the Supreme Court of the United States, since 1991; *b* 23 June 1948. *Educ:* Yale Univ. (JD). Asst to Attorney Gen., State of Missouri, 1974–77; attorney in private practice, 1977–79; Legislative Asst, US Senate, 1979–81; Asst Sec. for Civil Rights, Dept of Educn, Washington, 1981–82; Chm., Equal Employment Opportunity Commn, Washington, 1982–90; Judge, US Court of Appeals, 1990–91. *Address:* United States Supreme Court, 1 First Street NE, Washington, DC 20543, USA.

THOMAS, Colin Agnew; chartered accountant; *b* 14 Feb. 1921; *s* of Harold Alfred Thomas and Nora (*née* Williams); *m* 1947, Jane Jardine Barnish, *d* of Leonard Barnish,

FRIBA; one *s* one *d*. *Educ:* Oundle School. Lieut, RNVR, 1941–46. Finance Comptroller, Lloyd's, 1964–75, Sec.-Gen., 1976–79. Member: Cirencester Art Soc.; South Cerney Art Club. *Recreations:* gardening, sketching. *Address:* Spinet Cottage, 35 Cheltenham Road, Cirencester GL7 2HU. *T:* (01285) 653978; 15 Ravenspoint, Trearddur Bay, Anglesey LL65 2AJ. *T:* Trearddur Bay (01407) 860091. *Club:* Trearddur Bay Sailing.

THOMAS, David; *see* Thomas, W. D.

THOMAS, Rt Rev. David; Provincial Assistant Bishop, Church in Wales, since 1996; *b* 22 July 1942; *s* of late Rt Rev. John James Absalom Thomas; *m* 1967, Rosemary Christine Calton; one *s* one *d*. *Educ:* Christ College, Brecon; Keble College, Oxford; St Stephen's House, Oxford. MA Oxon. Curate of Hawarden, 1967–69; Tutor, St Michael's College, Llandaff, Cardiff, 1969–70, Chaplain 1970–75; Secretary, Church in Wales Liturgical Commn, 1970–75; Vice-Principal, St Stephen's House, Oxford, 1975–79; Vicar of Chepstow, 1979–82; Principal, St Stephen's House, Oxford, 1982–87; Vicar of St Peter's, Newton, Swansea, 1987–96; Residentiary Canon, Brecon Cathedral, 1994–96. Mem., Standing Doctrinal Commn, 1975–93, Standing Liturgical Adv. Commn, 1987–, Church in Wales. *Publication:* (contrib.) The Ministry of the Word (ed G. J. Cuming), 1979. *Recreations:* music, walking. *Address:* Bodfair, 3 White's Close, Belmont Road, Abergavenny NP7 5HZ. *T:* (01873) 858780, *Fax:* (01873) 858269.

THOMAS, Prof. David; Professor of Geography, University of Birmingham, 1978–95, now Professor Emeritus; *b* 16 Feb. 1931; *s* of William and Florence Grace Thomas; *m* 1955, Daphne Elizabeth Berry; one *s* one *d*. *Educ:* Bridgend Grammar School; University College of Wales, Aberystwyth (BA, MA); PhD London. Asst Lectr, Lectr, Reader, University College London, 1957–70; Prof. and Head of Dept, St David's University College, Lampeter, 1970–78; Birmingham University: Head of Dept of Geography, 1978–86; Head of Sch. of Geog., 1991–93; Pro Vice-Chancellor, 1984–89. Pres., IBG, 1988 (Hon. Sec., 1976–78); Mem., Council, RGS, 1988–91. *Publications:* Agriculture in Wales during the Napoleonic Wars, 1963; London's Green Belt, 1970; (ed) An Advanced Geography of the British Isles, 1974; (with J. A. Dawson) Man and his world, 1975; (ed) Wales: a new study, 1977; (with P. T. J. Morgan) Wales: the shaping of a nation, 1984; articles in learned jls. *Recreations:* music, wine, spectating. *Address:* 3 Is-y-Coed, Wenvoe, Cardiff CF5 6DL. *T:* (029) 2059 2861.

THOMAS, David; Principal Ombudsman (Banking and Loans), Financial Ombudsman Service, since 2000; *b* 7 Nov. 1945; *s* of late Harold Bushell Thomas and Margaret Thomas; *m* (marr. diss.); three *s* one *d*; partner, Jane Bibby. *Educ:* St Anselm's Coll., Birkenhead; Liverpool Univ. (LLB Hons 1966). Admitted Solicitor, England and Wales, 1969, Ireland, 1991; with F. S. Moore & Price, subseq. Lees Moore & Price, Birkenhead, then Lees Lloyd Whitley, Liverpool and London: Solicitor, 1969–71; Partner, 1971–84; Managing Partner, 1984–93; Chm., 1993–96; Banking Ombudsman, 1997–2000. Mem., Investigation and Discipline Bd, Accountancy Foundn, 2001–. Sec., 1981–86, Vice-Pres., 1986–87, Pres., 1987–88, Liverpool Law Soc.; Council Mem., Law Soc., 1987–96. *Recreations:* modern history, theatre, naval aviation, walking. *Address:* Financial Ombudsman Service, South Quay Plaza, 183 Marsh Wall, E14 9SR. *T:* (020) 7964 1000.

THOMAS, David Bowen, PhD; Keeper, Department of Physical Sciences, Science Museum, 1984–87 (Keeper, Department of Physics, 1978–84); *b* 28 Dec. 1931; *s* of Evan Thomas and Florence Annie Bowen. *Educ:* Tredegar Grammar Sch.; Manchester Univ. (BSc). Research Fellow, Wayne Univ., Detroit, USA, 1955–57; Research Scientist, Min. of Agriculture, Fisheries and Food, Aberdeen, 1957–61; Asst Keeper, Science Museum, Dept of Chemistry, 1961–73; Keeper, Dept of Museum Services, 1973–78. Hon. FRPS 1985. *Publications:* The First Negatives, 1964; The Science Museum Photography Collection, 1969; The First Colour Motion Pictures, 1969. *Recreation:* country walking. *Address:* Tanglewood, Moushill Lane, Milford, Godalming, Surrey GU8 5BQ.

THOMAS, David Churchill, CMG 1982; HM Diplomatic Service, retired; Assistant Under Secretary of State, Foreign and Commonwealth Office, 1984–86; *b* 21 Oct. 1933; *o s* of late David Bernard Thomas and Violet Churchill Thomas (*née* Quicke); *m* 1958, Susan Petronella Arrow (*see* Baroness Thomas of Walliswood) (separated); one *s* two *d*. *Educ:* Eton Coll.; New Coll., Oxford (Exhibnr). Mod. Hist. 1st Cl., 1957. Army, 2nd Lieut, Rifle Brigade, 1952–54. Foreign Office, 1958; 3rd Sec., Moscow, 1959–61; 2nd Sec., Lisbon, 1961–64; FCO, 1964–68; 1st Sec. (Commercial), Lima, 1968–70; FCO, 1970–73; Head of South West European Dept, 1974; Asst Sec., Cabinet Office, 1973–78; Counsellor (Internal Affairs), Washington, 1978–81; Ambassador to Cuba, 1981–84. Advr on Overseas Scholarships Funding, FCO, 1989–2000. Mem., Marshall Aid Commemoration Commn, 1999–. Mem. Council, RIIA, 1988–94. Mem. Bd, Inst. of Latin American Studies, Univ. of London, 1988–93. Associate Fellow, Centre for Caribbean Studies, Warwick Univ., 1990–96. *Publications:* essays and review articles on Latin American affairs. *Recreations:* photography, listening to music. *Address:* 11 Crookham Road, SW6 4EG. *T:* (020) 7736 9096.

See also Hon. D. W. P. Thomas.

THOMAS, David (Edward); *b* 12 Jan. 1955; *m* 1975, Janet Elizabeth Whatrup; one *s* one *d*. *Educ:* Univ. of East Anglia (BA). Served RN, 1972–80; Suffolk Constabulary, 1980–88. Mem. (Lab) Suffolk CC, 1993. Mem., Police Authy. MEP (Lab) Suffolk and SW Norfolk, 1994–99; contested (Lab) Eastern Reg., 1999.

THOMAS, David Emrys, OBE 1998; management and personnel consultant, since 1991; Member, Local Government Commission for England, 1992–98; *b* Ewell, 9 July 1935; *s* of Emrys and Elsie Florence Thomas; *m* 1957, Rosemary, *d* of Alexander and Kathleen De'Ath of Hampton, Middx; two *s* one *d*. *Educ:* Tiffin Grammar Sch., Kingston upon Thames. Dip. Mun. Admin; FIPD. Local Govt Administrator, 1951–63; Indust. Relations Officer, LACSAB, 1963–68; Chief Admin. Officer, LGTB, 1968–69; Dep. Estab. Officer, Surrey CC, 1969–70; County Personnel Officer, Surrey, 1970–77; Under-Sec. (Manpower), AMA, 1977–81; Dep. Sec., 1981–87, Sec., 1987–91, LACSAB; Employers' Sec. to nat. jt negotiating councils in local govt, 1987–91; Official Side Sec., Police Negotiating Bd, 1987–91; Sec., UK Steering Cttee on Local Govt Superannuation, 1987–91. Founder Pres., Soc. of Chief Personnel Officers in Local Govt, 1975. *Recreations:* unskilled gardening, the musical theatre (Mem., Olivier Awards panel, 1998; Sec., Stage Musical Appreciation Soc.). *Address:* The White House, Three Pears Road, Merrow, Guildford, Surrey GU1 2XU. *T:* (01483) 569588; *e-mail:* DEThomas41@aol.com.

THOMAS, Prof. David Glyndor Treharne, FRCSE, FRCP, FRCPG, FRCS; Professor of Neurological Surgery and Head of University Department of Neurological Surgery, Institute of Neurology, National Hospital, Queen Square, since 1995; *b* 14 May 1941; *s* of Dr John Glyndor Treharne Thomas, MC and Ellen Thomas (*née* Geldart); *m* 1970, Dr Hazel Agnes Christina Cockburn, FFARCS; one *s*. *Educ:* Perse Sch., Cambridge; Gonville and Caius Coll., Cambridge (BA, MA); St Mary's Hosp. Med. Sch.; MB BChir Cantab. Hosp. appts at St Mary's to 1969 and Asst Lectr in Anatomy, 1967–68; Sen. House Officer in Surgery, 1970, Registrar in Cardio-Thoracic Surgery, 1970–71, RPMS; Registrar, Sen. Registrar and Lectr in Neurosurgery, Inst. of Neur. Scis, Glasgow, 1972–76; Sen. Lectr, 1976–92, Prof. of Neurosurgery, 1992–95, Inst. of Neurology; Consultant Neurosurgeon: Nat. Hosp. for Neurology and Neurosurgery and Northwick Park Hosp., Harrow, 1976–; St Mary's Hosp., 1994–. Vice-President: Eur. Assoc. of Neurosurgical Socs, 1991–95; Eur. Soc. for Stereotactic and Functional Neurosurgery, 1994–. *Publications:* (ed with D. I. Graham) Brain Tumours, 1980; (ed with M. D. Walker) Biology of Brain Tumour, 1986; (ed) Neuro-oncology: primary brain tumours, 1989; (ed) Stereotactic and Image Directed Surgery of Brain Tumours, 1993; (ed with D. I. Graham) Malignant Brain Tumours, 1995. *Recreation:* military and naval history. *Address:* The National Hospital, Queen Square, WC1N 3BG. *T:* (020) 7829 8755; Flat 1, 14 Montagu Square, W1H 1RD. *T:* (020) 7486 8566. *Clubs:* Athenæum, Royal Society of Medicine.

THOMAS, David Hamilton Pryce, CBE 1977; solicitor, retired; Chairman, Land Authority for Wales, 1980–86 (Deputy Chairman, 1975–80); President, Rent Assessment Panel for Wales, 1971–89 (Member, 1966); *b* 3 July 1922; *s* of Trevor John Thomas and Eleanor Maud Thomas; *m* 1948, Eluned Mair Morgan; two *s* one *d*. *Educ:* Barry County Sch.; University College, Cardiff. Served War of 1939–45; British and Indian Armies, terminal rank T/Captain (GSO III), 1941–46. Qualified as Solicitor, 1948, with hons; Partner in J. A. Hughes & Co., Solicitors, Barry, 1950–75; Notary Public, 1953. Director 1962–67, Vice-Chm. 1967–71, Chm. 1971–78, Barry Mutual Building Society; Vice Chm., 1978, Chm., 1982–84, Glam. Building Soc.; Chm., Wales Area Bd, Bradford and Bingley Bldg Soc., 1984–87; Vice-Chm., Building Socs Assoc. for Wales, 1983; Mem., Adv. Cttee on Fair Rents, 1973; Chm., E Glam. Rent Tribunal, 1967–71; District Comr of Scouts, Barry and District, 1963–70; Chm., Barry District Scout Assoc. 1971–81; Vice-Chm., S Glam. Scout Council, 1975–81. *Recreations:* books, music. *Address:* 34 Camden Road, Brecon, Powys LD3 7RT.

See also M. C. P. Thomas, R. L. Thomas.

THOMAS, David Hugh; Chief Executive: Morgan Grenfell & Co. Ltd, since 1997; Bankers Trust International, since 1999; *b* 6 Dec. 1951; *s* of John William Hugh Thomas and late Joyce Thomas (*née* Fox); *m* 1978, Frances Mary Brown; one *s* one *d*. *Educ:* Hertford GS; Corpus Christi Coll., Oxford (BA 1st cl. Hons Lit. Hum. 1974; Sec., then Librarian, Oxford Union Soc., 1973); St John's Coll., Oxford (MA; DPhil 1978). Joined Morgan Grenfell & Co. Ltd, 1978; Italian Export Credits, 1978–83; Eurobonds, 1983–84; Interest Rate and Currency Swaps, 1984–87; Dir, 1988–; Market and Credit Risk Mgt, 1988–97; Global Head of Risk, Investment Banking Activities, Deutsche Bank Gp, 1995–98. *Recreations:* classical studies, playing the piano (very badly). *Address:* (office) 23 Great Winchester Street, EC2P 2AX. *T:* (020) 7545 7596, *Fax:* (020) 7545 6133.

THOMAS, David (John), MD; FRCP; Senior Consultant Neurologist, St Mary's Hospital, London, since 1978; *b* 7 Dec. 1943; *s* of Jack and Rachel Lloyd Thomas, Cwmgorse; *m* 1966, Celia Margaret Barratt, *d* of Sir Charles and Lady Barratt; two *s* three *d*. *Educ:* Alleyn's Sch.; Clare Coll., Cambridge (BA Nat. Sci. 1966; BChir 1969; MA, MB 1970); Univ. of Birmingham Med. Sch. (MD 1977). MRCP 1972, FRCP 1985. Consultant Neurologist: King Edward VII Hosp., Windsor, Heatherwood Hosp., Ascot, Wexham Park Hosp., Slough and St Mark's Hosp., Maidenhead, 1978–2000; Sen. Lectr in Neurology, Inst. of Neurology and Hon. Consultant Neurologist, Nat. Hosp. for Neurology and Neurosurgery, 1979–, and Chalfont Centre for Epilepsy, 1995–. Sec. and Chm., Special Adv. Cttee on Neurology to RCP, 1985–91. Member: Council, Stroke Assoc., 1992–; Stroke Council, Amer. Heart Assoc., 1992–; European Stroke Council, 1993–. Chm., Charitable Assoc. Supplying Hosps, 1984–99. *Publications:* Strokes and their Prevention, 1988; The Eye and Systemic Disease, 1989; Neurology: what shall I do?, 1990, 2nd edn 1997; papers on cerebrovascular disease and other neurological subjects. *Recreations:* photography, lecturing. *Address:* Woolletts, Fulmer, Bucks SL3 6JE. *T:* (01753) 662147. *Clubs:* Athenæum, Royal Society of Medicine.

THOMAS, David Owen; QC 1972; a Recorder of the Crown Court, 1972–98; *b* 22 Aug. 1926; *s* of late Emrys Aeron Thomas and Dorothy May Thomas; *m* 1967, Mary Susan Atkinson; three *d* (and one *d* decd). *Educ:* Queen Elizabeth's, Barnet; John Bright Sch., Llandudno; Queen's Univ., Belfast. Served War, HM Forces, 1943–45 and to 1948. Called to the Bar, Middle Temple, 1952, Bencher, 1980; Dep. Chairman, Devon QS, 1971. Mem., Criminal Injuries Compensation Bd, 1987. Freeman, City of London; Liveryman, Needlemakers' Co. *Recreations:* acting, cricket, Rugby football. *Address:* 2 King's Bench Walk, Temple, EC4Y 7DE. *Clubs:* Garrick, MCC; Western (Glasgow).

THOMAS, (David) Roger, CMG 2000; HM Diplomatic Service; Consul-General, San Francisco, since 2001; *b* 1 Jan. 1945; *s* of Alun Beynon Thomas, FRCS, and Doreen Thomas (*née* James); *m* 1st, 1968 (marr. diss. 1977); two *d*; 2nd, 1978, Fiona Tyndall. *Educ:* Leys Sch., Cambridge; Sch. of Oriental and African Studies, London Univ. (BA Hons Turkish). Entered Foreign Office, 1968: FO, 1968–71; Third Sec. (Chancery), Cairo, 1971–74; Second Sec. (Envmt), UK Repn to EEC, Brussels, 1974–78; Consul, Ankara, 1979–82; UN and EC Dept, FCO, 1982–86; Consul (Commercial), Frankfurt, 1986–90; Consul-Gen., Stuttgart, 1990–93; Non-Proliferation, then Far Eastern and Pacific Dept, FCO, 1993–97; Ambassador to Azerbaijan, 1997–2000. *Recreations:* gardening, ski-ing, sailing, photography. *Address:* c/o Foreign and Commonwealth Office, King Charles Street, SW1A 2AH.

THOMAS, Prof. David Stephen Garfield, DPhil; Professor of Geography, University of Sheffield, since 1994; *b* Dover, 2 Oct. 1958; *s* of Frederick Garfield Thomas and Ruth Muriel Thomas; *m* 1st, 1987, (Helen) Elizabeth Martin (*d* 1990); 2nd, 1992, Lucy Marie Heath; two *d*. *Educ:* Dover Grammar Sch. for Boys; Hertford Coll., Oxford (BA Hons 1980; PGCE 1981; DPhil 1984). Department of Geography, University of Sheffield: Lectr, 1984–93; Sen. Lectr, 1993–94; Chm., 1997–2000; Dir, Sheffield Centre of Internat. Drylands Res., 1994–. Occasional Consultant, UNEP, 1990–. Mem. Council, RGS, 2001–; Chm., British Geomorphological Res. Gp, 2002–. Res. into long and short term envmtl change in drylands, dry land geomorphology, human-envmt interactions in drylands, esp. in Southern Africa. *Publications:* Arid Zone Geomorphology, 1989, 2nd edn 1997; (with P. Shaw) The Kalahari Environment, 1991; (with N. Middleton) World Atlas of Desertification, 1992, 2nd edn 1997; (ed with R. Allison) Landscape Sensitivity, 1993; (with N. Middleton) Desertification: exploding the myth, 1995; (ed with A. Goudie) Dictionary of Physical Geography, 3rd edn 2000; (with D. Sporton) Sustainable Livelihoods in Kalahari Environments, 2002. *Recreations:* Africa, Dover Athletic FC, Cabernet Sauvignon, gardening. *Address:* Department of Geography, University of Sheffield, Sheffield S10 2TN. *T:* (0114) 222 7909.

THOMAS, Hon. David (William Penrose); author, journalist; *b* 17 Jan. 1959; *s* of David Churchill Thomas, *qv* and Baroness Thomas of Walliswood, *qv*; *m* 1986, Clare Jeremy; one *s* two *d*. *Educ:* Eton; King's College, Cambridge (BA History of Art). Freelance journalist, 1980–84; Editor, The Magazine, 1984–85; Editor, Extra Magazine, Sunday Today, 1986; Asst Editor and Chief Feature Writer, You Magazine, Mail on Sunday, 1986–89; Ed., Punch, 1989–92; TV Critic, Sunday Express, 1991–96. Young Journalist of the Year (British Press Awards), 1983; Columnist of the Year (Magazine Publishing Awards), 1989. *Publications:* Not Guilty: in defence of the modern man, 1993;

Great Sporting Moments, 1990; Girl (novel), 1995; with Ian Irvine: Bilko: the Fort Baxter Story, 1985; Fame and Fortune, 1988; Sex and Shopping, 1988. *Recreations:* if only …. *Address:* c/o Lucas Alexander Whitley Literary Agency, Elsinore House, 77 Fulham Palace Road, W6 8JA. *T:* (020) 8600 3800. *Club:* Groucho.

THOMAS, Derek John, CBE 1996; DL; CPFA; Chief Executive, Surrey County Council, 1988–95; *b* 3 Dec. 1934; *s* of late James Llewellyn Thomas and Winifred Mary Thomas; *m* 1st (marr. diss.); three *d*; 2nd, 1978, Christine (*née* Brewer); one *s*. *Educ:* Hele's Sch., Exeter. Formerly: Treasurer's Depts: Devon CC; Corby Development Corporation; Bath CC; Taunton Bor. Council; Sen. Asst Bor. Treasurer, Poole Bor. Council; Asst County Treasurer, Gloucestershire CC; Principal Asst County Treasurer, Avon CC; County Treasurer, Surrey CC. Mem. Council, CIPFA, 1977–78, 1985–87; Mem. Cttee of Mgt, Schroder Exempt Property Unit Trust, 1981–. Chm., Local Management in Schools Initiative, 1988–93. Mem. Bd, Surrey TEC, 1990–95; Chm., Surrey First, 1996–. Chm., Disability Initiative, 1996–. Surrey University: Mem. Council, 1994–; Chm., F and GP Cttee, 1995–; Treas., 1997–. CIMgt. DL Surrey, 1996. *Publication:* (ed jtly) A Fresh Start for Local Government, 1997. *Address:* Squirrels Leap, 14 Lime Avenue, Camberley, Surrey GU15 2BS. *T:* (01276) 684433.

THOMAS, Sir Derek (Morison David), KCMG 1987 (CMG 1977); consultant; *b* 31 Oct. 1929; *s* of K. P. D. Thomas and Mali McL. Thomas; *m* 1956, Lineke van der Mast; two *c*. *Educ:* Radley Coll., Abingdon; Trinity Hall, Cambridge (Mod. Langs Tripos; MA; Hon. Fellow, 1997). Articled apprentice, Dolphin Industrial Developments Ltd, 1947. Entered HM Foreign Service, 1953; Midshipman 1953, Sub-Lt 1955, RNVR; FO, 1955; 3rd, later 2nd, Sec., Moscow, 1956–59; 2nd Sec., Manila, 1959–61; UK Delegn to Brussels Conf., 1961–62; 1st Sec., FO, 1962; Sofia, 1964–67; Ottawa, 1967–69; seconded to Treasury, 1969–70; Financial Counsellor, Paris, 1971–75; Head of N American Dept, FCO, 1975–76; Asst Under Sec. of State, FCO, 1976–79; Minister Commercial and later Minister, Washington, 1979–84; Dep. Under Sec. of State for Europe and Political Dir, FCO, 1984–87; Amb. to Italy, 1987–89. European Advr to N M Rothschild & Sons, 1990–; Director: Rothschild Italia, 1990–97; Christow Consultants, 1990–99; N. M. Rothschild & Sons, 1991–99; Nexus Marketing Consultancy, 1991–92; Associate, CDP Nexus, 1990–92. Chm., Liberalisation of Trade in Services Cttee, BI, 1992–96; Mem., Export Guarantees Adv. Cttee, 1992–97. Member, Council: RIIA, 1994–97; Reading Univ., 1991–99. Chm., British Inst. of Florence, 1987–89 and 1997–. *Recreations:* listening to people and music; being by, in or on water; grandfathering, gardening. *Address:* Flat 1, 12 Lower Sloane Street, SW1W 8BJ; Ferme l'Epine, 14490 Planquery, France. *Clubs:* Oxford and Cambridge; Leander.

See also Sir E. W. Gladstone, Bt.

THOMAS, Donald Michael; poet and novelist; *b* Redruth, Cornwall, 27 Jan. 1935; *s* of Harold Redvers Thomas and Amy (*née* Moyle); two *s* one *d*. *Educ:* Redruth Grammar Sch.; Univ. High Sch., Melbourne; New Coll., Oxford (BA 1st cl. Hons in English; MA). School teacher, Teignmouth Grammar Sch., 1959 63; Lectr, Hereford Coll. of Educn, 1964–78; full-time author, 1978–. *Publications: poetry:* Penguin Modern Poets 11, 1968; Two Voices, 1968; Logan Stone, 1971; Love and Other Deaths, 1975; The Honeymoon Voyage, 1978; Dreaming in Bronze, 1981; Selected Poems, 1983; *novels:* The Flute-Player, 1979; Birthstone, 1980; The White Hotel, 1981; Russian Nights, a quintet (Ararat, 1983; Swallow, 1984; Sphinx, 1986; Summit, 1987; Lying Together, 1990); Flying in to Love, 1992; Pictures at an Exhibition, 1993; Eating Pavlova, 1994; Lady with a Laptop, 1996; Charlotte, 2000; *translations:* Requiem and Poem without a Hero, Akhmatova, 1976; Way of All the Earth, Akhmatova, 1979; Bronze Horseman, Pushkin, 1982; *memoirs:* Memories and Hallucinations, 1988; *biography:* Alexander Solzhenitsyn: a century in his life, 1998. *Recreations:* travel, Russia and other myths, the culture and history of Cornwall, the life of the imagination. *Address:* The Coach House, Rashleigh Vale, Truro, Cornwall TR1 1TJ.

THOMAS, Donnall; *see* Thomas, Edward D.

THOMAS, Dudley Lloyd; a District Judge (Magistrates' Courts) (formerly Stipendiary Magistrate), Somerset and Avon, since 1999; Member: Family Proceedings Court Panel, since 1991; Youth Court Panel, since 1994; *b* 11 Jan. 1946; *s* of late Myrddin Lloyd Thomas and Marjorie Emily (*née* Morgan); *m* 1970, Dr Margaret Susan Early; two *s* (and one *s* decd). *Educ:* King Edward's Sch., Bath; Coll. of Law, London. Justices Clerk's Asst, 1966–71; admitted as solicitor, 1971; Partner, Trump & Partners, Bristol, 1973–88; called to the Bar, Gray's Inn, 1988; Metropolitan Stipendiary Magistrate, 1990–99. Mem., Western Circuit. Member: Bristol Medico-Legal Soc.; Heritage in Wales. Friend: Royal Acad. of Arts; V&A. *Recreations:* Rugby football, cricket, music, theatre, travel, classic motor cars, dogs and walking. *Address:* c/o Bristol Magistrates' Court, PO Box 107, Nelson Street, Bristol BS99 7BJ. *T:* (0117) 943 5100. *Club:* Royal Over-Seas League.

THOMAS, Prof. (Edward) Donnall, MD; Member, Fred Hutchinson Cancer Research Center, Seattle, since 1974 (Director, Medical Oncology, 1974–89; Associate Director, Clinical Research Programs, 1982–89); Professor Emeritus of Medicine, University of Washington School of Medicine, Seattle, since 1990; *b* Mart, Texas, 15 March 1920; *m* 1942, Dorothy Martin; two *s* one *d*. *Educ:* Univ. of Texas, Austin (BA 1941; MA 1943); Harvard Medical Sch. (MD 1946). Assignments in internal medicine, US Army, 1948–50; Nat. Res. Council Postdoctoral Fellow in Medicine, Dept of Biol., MIT, 1950–51; Chief Med. Resident and Sen. Asst Resident, Peter Bent Brigham Hosp., Seattle, 1951–53, Hematologist, 1953–55; Instructor in Medicine, Harvard Med. Sch. and Res. Associate, Cancer Res. Foundn, Children's Med. Center, Boston, 1953–55; Physician-in-Chief, Mary Imogene Bassett Hosp., Cooperstown, NY and Associate Clinical Prof. of Medicine, Coll. of Physicians and Surgeons, Columbia Univ., NY, 1955–63; Prof. of Medicine, Univ. of Washington Sch. of Medicine, Seattle, 1963–90, Hd, Div. of Oncology, 1963–85. Consulting Physician, Children's Orthopedic Hosp. and Med. Center, Seattle, 1963–90; Attending Physician, Seattle: Univ. of Washington Hosp., 1963–90; Harborview Med. Center, 1963–90; Veterans Admin Hosp., 1963–90; Providence Med. Center, 1973–90; Swedish Hosp., 1975–90. Member Editorial Board: Blood, 1962–75, 1977–82; Transplantation, 1970–76; Procs Soc. Exptl Biol. and Medicine, 1974–81; Leukemia Res., 1977–87; Hematological Oncology, 1982–87; Jl Clinical Immunology, 1982–87; Amer. Jl Hematology, 1985–; Bone Marrow Transplantation, 1986–. Member: Amer. Assoc. Cancer Res.; Amer. Assoc. Physicians; Amer. Fedn Clinical Res.; Amer. Soc. Clinical Oncology; Amer. Soc. Clinical Investigation; Amer. Soc. Hematology (Pres., 1987–88); Nat. Acad. Scis and other foreign socs on related subjects. Lectures in US and UK on hematology and cancer res. Numerous awards from instns in N America and abroad incl. Nobel Prize for Physiology or Medicine, 1990; Presidential Medal of Science, 1990. *Recreations:* hunting, fishing, hiking. *Address:* c/o Fred Hutchinson Cancer Research Center, 1100 Fairview Avenue N, D5–100, PO Box 19024, Seattle, WA 98109–1024, USA.

THOMAS, Edward Stanley, FIA; National Secretary, National Council of YMCAs, since 1998; *b* 19 Dec. 1945; *s* of Stanley Frederick Thomas and Kate Dickason Thomas (*née* Bates); *m* 1974, Elizabeth Mary Helen Casson; three *s* one *d*. *Educ:* King Edward VI Grammar Sch., Stourbridge; Slough Grammar Sch.; Clare Coll., Cambridge (MA). FIA 1974; ACII. Teacher, Sherwood Coll., Naini Tal, India, 1965; Actuarial trainee, Prudential, 1968–70; joined Bacon & Woodrow, 1970, Partner, 1978–98. Liveryman, Actuaries' Co. *Recreations:* climbing Munroes, travelling rough, swimming, golf, piano, reading (especially John Masters and Patrick White). *Address:* National Council of YMCAs, 640 Forest Road, E17 3DZ. *Club:* Royal Automobile.

THOMAS, Elizabeth; *see* Thomas, M.E.

THOMAS, Elizabeth Marjorie; Secretary General, 1979–83, Literary Consultant, 1984–85, The Authors' Lending and Copyright Society; *b* 10 Aug. 1919; *d* of Frank Porter and Marjorie Porter (*née* Pascall); *m* 1941, George Thomas; one *s* one *d*. *Educ:* St George's Sch., Harpenden; Girton Coll., Cambridge (BA 1st Cl.; MA 1998). Journalist, 1951–59 and Literary Editor, 1959–71, Tribune; Asst Literary Editor, New Statesman, 1971–76; Political Adviser to Rt Hon. Michael Foot, MP, Lord Pres. of the Council and Leader of the House of Commons, 1976–79. Mem., Arts Council, 1974–77 (Mem., Literature Panel, 1971–77); Chm., Literature Panel, Eastern Arts Assoc., 1978–84; Member: Ethnic Minority Arts Cttee, Commission for Racial Equality, 1979–82; British Council Bd, 1982–88. *Publication:* (ed) Tribune 21, 1959. *Address:* 27 Delavale Road, Winchcombe, Glos GL54 5YL. *T:* (01242) 602788.

THOMAS, Emyr, CBE 1980; LLB, LMTPI; DL; General Manager, Telford New Town Development Corporation, 1969–80; Chairman, Telford Community Council, 1980–84; *b* 25 April 1920; *s* of late Brinley Thomas, MA, Aldershot; *m* 1947, Barbara J. May; one *d*. *Educ:* Aldershot County High School. Served War of 1939–45, RASC. Admitted Solicitor, 1947. Asst Solicitor, Exeter City Council, 1947–50; Sen. Asst Solicitor, Reading County Borough Council, 1950–53; Dep. Town Clerk, West Bromwich County Borough Council, 1953–64; Sec. and Solicitor, Dawley (later Telford) Development Corp., 1964–69. First Hon. Sec., 1968–89, Hon. Curator and Vice-Pres., 1989–, Ironbridge Gorge Museum Trust. DL Salop, 1979. *Publications:* Coalbrookdale and the Darby Family, 1999; Coalbrookdale in the 18th Century, 2001. *Recreation:* industrial archaeology. *Address:* 8 Vixen Walk, New Milton, Hampshire BH25 5RU. *T:* (01425) 628826.

THOMAS, Prof. Eric Jackson, MD; Vice-Chancellor, University of Bristol, since 2001; *b* 24 March 1953; *s* of Eric Jackson Thomas and Margaret Mary Thomas (*née* Murray); *m* 1976, Narell Marie Rennard; one *s* one *d*. *Educ:* Ampleforth Coll.; Univ. of Newcastle upon Tyne (MB BS 1976; MD 1987). MRCOG 1983. Jun. hosp. posts, 1976–84; Res. Fellow, and Lectr, Univ. of Sheffield, 1984–87; Sen. Lectr, Univ. of Newcastle upon Tyne, 1987–90; Consultant Obstetrician and Gynaecologist: Newcastle Gen. Hosp., 1987–90; Princess Anne Hosp., Southampton, 1991–2001; Southampton University: Prof. of Obstetrics and Gynaecol., 1991–2001; Hd of Sch. of Medicine, 1995–98; Dean, Faculty of Medicine, Health and Biol Scis, 1998–2000. Chm., 7th World Congress of Endometriosis, 2000. Mem. Council, RCOG, 1995–2001 (Chm. Scientific Adv. Cttee, 1998–2000). Non-executive Director: Southampton Univ. Hosps NHS Trust, 1998–2000; Southampton and SW Hampshire HA, 2000–01. Trustee, Nat. Endometriosis Soc., 1998–2000. William Blair Bell Meml Lectr, RCOG, 1987. Founder FMedSci 1998. FRSA 1998. *Publications:* (ed jtly) Modern Approaches to Endometriosis, 1991; articles on endometriosis and reproductive biology. *Recreations:* Newcastle United, fiction, golf. *Address:* Senate House, Tyndall Avenue, Bristol BS8 1TH. *Club:* Athenæum.

THOMAS, Rt Rev. Eryl Stephen; Hon. Assistant Bishop of Swansea and Brecon, since 1988; *b* 20 Oct. 1910; *s* of Edward Stephen and Margaret Susannah Thomas; *m* 1939, Jean Mary Alice Wilson; three *s* one *d*. *Educ:* Rossall Sch.; St John's Coll., Oxford (BA 2nd Class Hon. Theology, 1932; MA 1935); Wells Theological Coll. Curate of Colwyn Bay, 1933–38, of Hawarden, 1938–43; Vicar of Risca, Mon, 1943–48; Warden of St Michael's Theological Coll., Llandaff, 1948–54; Dean of Llandaff, 1954–68; Bishop of Monmouth, 1968–71, of Llandaff, 1971–75. Chm., Church in Wales Liturgical Commn for revision of Prayer Book, 1954–68. Chaplain and Sub-Prelate, Order of St John of Jerusalem, 1969. *Address:* 17 Orchard Close, Gilwern, Abergavenny NP7 0EN. *T:* (01873) 831050.

THOMAS, Franklin Augustine; lawyer, consultant; *b* 27 May 1934; *s* of James Thomas and Viola Thomas (*née* Atherley); *m* (marr. diss.); two *s* two *d*. *Educ:* Columbia College, New York (BA 1956); Columbia Univ. (LLB 1963). Admitted to NY State Bar, 1964; Attorney, Fed. Housing and Home Finance Agency, NYC, 1963–64; Asst US Attorney for Southern District, NY, 1964–65; Dep. Police Comr, charge legal matters, NYC, 1965–67; Pres., Chief Exec. Officer, Bedford Stuyvesant Restoration Corp., Brooklyn, 1967–77; Pres., Ford Foundn, 1979–96. Hon. LLD: Yale, 1970; Fordham, 1972; Pratt Institute, 1974; Pace, 1977; Columbia, 1979. *Address:* 595 Madison Avenue, New York, NY 10022, USA. *T:* (212) 7533200.

THOMAS, Gareth; MP (Lab) Clwyd West, since 1997; *b* 25 Sept. 1954; *s* of William and Megan Thomas; *m* 1989, Sioned Wyn; one *s* one *d*. *Educ:* Rockferry High Sch., Birkenhead; UCW, Aberystwyth (LLB). ACII. Worked in insurance industry. Called to the Bar, Gray's Inn, 1977. Member (Lab): Flints CC, 1995–97; Mold Town Council, 1995–97. PPS to Sec. of State for Wales, 2001–. Member: Social Security Select Cttee, 1999–2001; Jt Human Rights Cttee, 2000–01. Mem., Bethesda, Mold, Presbyterian Church of Wales. *Recreations:* walking, theatre, music. *Address:* House of Commons, SW1A 0AA. *T:* (020) 7219 3516.

THOMAS, Gareth Richard; MP (Lab) Harrow West, since 1997; *b* 15 July 1967; *s* of Howard and Susan Thomas. *Educ:* UCW, Aberystwyth (BScEcons Hons Politics 1988); Univ. of Greenwich (PGCE 1991); KCL (MA Imperial and Commonwealth Hist. 1997). Teacher, 1992–97. Mem. (Lab) Harrow BC, 1990–97. PPS to Minister Without Portfolio and Party Chairman, 2001–. Vice Chair, Social Services Cttee, Assoc. of Local Govt, 1996–97. Chm., Co-op Party, 2000–. *Publication:* At the Energy Crossroads, 2001. *Recreations:* white water and sea canoeing, road running, supporting Swansea City FC and Harrow Borough FC, watching Welsh RU team. *Address:* House of Commons, SWA 0AA.

THOMAS, Dr Geoffrey Price; Director, University of Oxford Department for Continuing Education, since 1986; President, Kellogg College (formerly Rewley House), since 1990; *b* 3 July 1941; *s* of Richard Lewis Thomas and Aerona (*née* Price); *m* 1965, Judith Vaughan, *d* of Arsul John Williams; two *d*. *Educ:* Maesteg Grammar Sch.; UC of Swansea (BSc 1st Cl. Hons Physics); Churchill Coll., Cambridge (PhD 1966); Univ. of Oxford (MA). Post-doctoral res., Cavendish Lab., Univ. of Cambridge, 1966–67; Staff Tutor, UC of Swansea, 1967–78; Dep. Dir, Dept of Ext. Studies, Univ. of Oxford, 1978–86; Fellow, Linacre Coll., Oxford, 1978–90, Hon. Fellow, 1990. Co-Chm., Council on Scientific Literacy, Chicago Acad. of Sci., 1993–. Mem., HEFCW, 2000–. Visiting Scholar: Smithsonian Instn, 1986; Northern Illinois Univ., 1986; Univ. of Calif, Berkeley, 1993; Univ. of Washington, 1993; Harvard Univ., 1993; Univ. of Georgia, 1999. *Publications:* (ed jtly) The Nuclear Arms Race, 1982; (ed jtly) Science and Sporting Performance, 1982; numerous articles on public understanding of science, and on continuing educn policy. *Address:* Kellogg College, 1 Wellington Square, Oxford OX1 2JA. *T:* (01865) 270376, *Fax:* (01865) 270296. *Club:* Oxford and Cambridge.

THOMAS, Sir (Godfrey) Michael (David), 11th Bt *cr* 1694; Member of Stock Exchange, London, 1959–88; *b* 10 Oct. 1925; *o s* of Rt Hon. Sir Godfrey Thomas, PC, GCVO, KCB, CSI, 10th Bt, and Diana, *d* of late Ven. B. G. Hoskyns (*d* 1985); *S* father, 1968; *m* 1956, Margaret Greta Cleland, *yr d* of John Cleland, Stormont Court, Godden Green, Kent; one *s* two *d* (of whom one *s* one *d* are twins). *Educ:* Harrow. The Rifle Brigade, 1944–56. *Heir: s* David John Godfrey Thomas, *b* 11 June 1961. *Address:* 81 Rivermead Court, Ranelagh Gardens, SW6 3SA. *T:* (020) 7736 6896. *Clubs:* MCC, Hurlingham.

See also Sir R. Hutchison, Bt.

THOMAS, Graham Stuart, OBE 1975; VMH 1968; Gardens Consultant to National Trust, since 1974; *b* 3 April 1909; *s* of W. R. Thomas and L. Thomas. *Educ:* horticultural and botanical training, Cambridge Univ. Botanic Garden, 1926–29. Six Hills Nursery, Stevenage, 1930; Foreman, later Manager, T. Hilling & Co., Chobham, 1931–55; Manager, Sunningdale Nurseries, Windlesham, 1956, Associate Dir, 1968–71; Gardens Adviser, National Trust, 1955–74. Vice-President: RHS; Garden History Soc.; British Hosta and Hemerocallis Soc.; Vice-Patron, Royal Nat. Rose Soc. (Dean Hole Medal, 1976); Hon. Mem., Irish Garden Plant Soc. Veitch Meml Medal, RHS, 1966; Nat. Trust Founders' Award, 1996; Lifetime Achievement Award, Garden Writers' Guild, 1996. *Publications:* The Old Shrub Roses, 1955, 5th edn 1978; Colour in the Winter Garden, 1957, 3rd edn 1984; Shrub Roses of Today, 1962, rev. edn 1980; Climbing Roses Old and New, 1965, new edn 1983; Plants for Ground Cover, 1970, rev. edn 1989; Perennial Garden Plants, 1976, rev. and enlarged edn 1990; Gardens of the National Trust, 1979; Three Gardens, 1983; Trees in the Landscape, 1983; The Art of Planting, 1984; A Garden of Roses, 1987; The Complete Flower Paintings and Drawings of Graham Stuart Thomas, 1987; The Rock Garden and its Plants, 1989; An English Rose Garden, 1991; Ornamental Shrubs, Climbers and Bamboos, 1992; The Graham Stuart Thomas Rose Book, 1994; Cuttings from my Garden Notebooks, 1997; Treasured Perennials, 1999; Thoughts from a Garden Seat, 2000; The Garden Through the Year, 2001. *Recreations:* horticulture, music, painting and drawing plants. *Address:* 21 Kettlewell Close, Horsell, Woking, Surrey GU21 4HY.

THOMAS, Gwenda; Member (Lab) Neath, National Assembly for Wales, since 1999; *b* 22 Jan. 1942; *d* of Hermas and Menai Evans (*née* Parry); *m* 1963, Morgan Thomas; one *s*. *Educ:* Pontardawe Grammar Sch. Clerical Officer, County Courts Br., LCD; Exec. Officer, Benefits Agency. Member: Gwaun Cae Gurwen Community Council, 1986–99 (Chm., 1988–89); Llanguicke Community Council, 1981–86; W Glamorgan CC, 1989–96 (Chm., Social Services Cttee); Neath Port Talbot CBC, 1996–99 (Chm., Social Services Cttee). Mem., CPSA (Br. Chm., 1974–84). *Address:* National Assembly for Wales, Cardiff Bay, Cardiff CF99 1NA.

THOMAS, Gwyn Edward Ward, CBE 1973; DFC; Chairman and Chief Executive, Yorkshire–Tyne Tees Television Holdings plc; *b* 1 Aug. 1923; *o s* of William J. and Constance Thomas; *m* 1st, 1945, Patricia Cornelius (marr. diss. 1989); one *d*; 2nd, 1991, Janice Thomas; one *s*. *Educ:* Bloxham Sch.; The Lycée, Rouen. Served RAF, 1 Group Bomber Command and 229 Group Transport Command, 1941–46. Swissair, 1947–53; Granada Television, 1955–61; Man. Dir, Grampian Television, 1961–67; Man. Dir, 1967–73, Dep. Chm., 1973–81, Yorkshire Television; Man. Dir, 1970–84, Chm., 1976–84, Trident Television. Chairman: Castlewood Investments Ltd, 1969–83; Don Robinson Holdings Ltd, 1969–83; Watts & Corry Ltd, 1969–83; Trident Casinos, 1982–84. British Bureau of Television Advertising: Dir, 1966; Chm., 1968–70; Mem. Council, Independent Television Companies Assoc., 1961–76 (Chairman: Labour Relations Cttee, 1967; Network Programme Cttee, 1971). Croix de Guerre, 1945. *Recreations:* ski-ing, boats, photography. *Address:* Pipers Lodge, Pipers End, Wentworth, Surrey GU25 4AW; La Gamberge, Les Hauts de St Paul 06570, France. *Club:* British Racing Drivers'.

THOMAS, Harvey; *see* Thomas, J. H. N.

THOMAS, Helen Frances Octavia; Director, Social Policy Group, National Assembly for Wales, since 1999; *b* 21 Sept. 1950; *d* of George Longmate Proctor and Anne Innes Louie Angus; *m* 1976, Peter Humphrey Robert Thomas (marr. diss. 1992); two *d*. *Educ:* Red Maids' Sch., Bristol; Newnham Coll., Cambridge (BA 1973); UWCC (MSc Econ 1992). Joined Welsh Office as Admin. Trainee, 1975; Principal, Schs Curriculum Div., 1987–90; Asst Sec., Central Mgt Services, 1991–97; Grade 5, Social Services and Children, 1997–99. *Recreations:* patchwork, singing, modern Welsh history, women's history. *Address:* c/o National Assembly for Wales, Cathays Park, Cardiff CF10 3NQ. *T:* (029) 2082 3060.

THOMAS, Prof. Howard Christopher, PhD; FRCP, FRCPath, FMedSci; Professor of Medicine, since 1987, Head of Department of Medicine A, and Vice Chairman, Division of Medicine, since 1997, Imperial College School of Medicine (formerly St Mary's Hospital Medical School), London University; *b* 31 July 1945; *s* of Harold Thomas and Hilda Thomas; *m* 1975, Dilys Ferguson; two *s* one *d*. *Educ:* Univ. of Newcastle (BSc Physiol; MB, BS); PhD Glasgow. MRCPath 1983, FRCPath 1992; MRCP 1969, FRCP 1983; FRCPGlas 1984. Lectr in Immunology, Glasgow Univ., 1971–74; Royal Free Hospital Medical School, London: Lectr in Medicine, 1974–78; Sen. Wellcome Fellow in Clin. Sci., 1978–83; Reader in Medicine, 1983–84; Titular Prof. of Medicine, 1984–87. Mem., DoH Adv. Gp on Infected Health Care Personnel; Chairman: DoH Adv. Gp on Hepatitis, 1999–; DoH Strategy Cttee on Hepatitis C, 2001. Trustee, British Liver Trust; Pres., British and Eur. Assocs for Study of the Liver, 1996–97. Editor, Jl of Viral Hepatitis. Humphry Davy Rolleston Lectr, RCP, 1986. FMedSci 1999. British Soc. of Gastroenterology Res. Medal, 1984; Hans Popper Internat. Prize for Distinction in Hepatology, 1989. *Publications:* Clinical Gastrointestinal Immunology, 1979; (ed jtly) Recent Advances in Hepatology, vol. 1, 1983, vol. 2, 1986; (ed jtly) Viral Hepatitis, 1996, 2nd edn 1998; pubns in Hepatology. *Recreations:* fishing, golf. *Address:* Department of Medicine, Imperial College School of Medicine, St Mary's Hospital, Praed Street, W2 1PG. *T:* (020) 7725 6454. *Club:* Athenæum.

THOMAS, Hugh; *see* Thomas of Swynnerton, Baron.

THOMAS, Rev. (Hywel) Rhodri Glyn; Member (Plaid Cymru) Carmarthen East and Dinefwr, National Assembly for Wales, since 1999; *b* 11 April 1953; *s* of late Thomas Glyn Thomas and Eleanor Glyn Thomas; *m* 1975, Marian Gwenfair Davies; two *s* one *d*. *Educ:* Ysgol Morgan Llwyd, Wrexham; UCW, Aberystwyth, Bangor and Lampeter. Minister of Religion, St Clears Area, 1978–89 and 1992–; Man. Dir, Cwmni'r Gannwyll Cyf, 1989–95; Welsh Spokesman, Forum of Private Business, 1992–99; Dir, "Sgript" Cyf, 1992–. Plaid Cymru spokesperson: on transport and communication, 1992–; on agriculture and rural develt. *Address:* National Assembly for Wales, Cardiff Bay, Cardiff CF99 1NA; Llanddwyn, Llangynin, St Clears, Carmarthenshire SA33 4JY; (office) 37 Wind Street, Ammanford, Carmarthenshire SA18 3DN.

THOMAS, Prof. Hywel Rhys, PhD; Professor and Head of School of Education, since 1993, and Director of Lifelong Learning, since 2001, University of Birmingham; *b* 11 Jan. 1947; *s* of John Howard Thomas and Eva Beryl Thomas (*née* James); *m* 1st, 1968, Patricia Anne Beard (marr. diss.); 2nd, 1980, Christine MacArthur; one *s* two *d*. *Educ:* Llanelli Boys' Grammar Sch.; Univ. of Manchester (BA, MEd, PGCE); Univ. of Birmingham (PhD 1988). Parkinson Cowan Ltd, 1968–69; teacher: New Mills Sch., Derbys, 1970–73; Kersal High Sch., Salford, 1974–79; University of Birmingham: Lectr, 1979–89; Sen. Lectr, 1989–91; Reader, 1991–93. Sen. Educn Advr, British Council, 1997–. *Publications:* Managing Education: the system and the institution, 1985; Economics and Education Management, 1986; Education Costs and Performance, 1990; Financial Delegation and Local Management of Schools, 1990; Managing Resources for School Improvement, 1996; Schools at the Centre?, 1997. *Address:* School of Education, University of Birmingham, Edgbaston, Birmingham B15 2TT. *T:* (0121) 414 4841; 30 Linden Road, Bournville, Birmingham B30 1JU.

THOMAS, Prof. Jean Olwen, CBE 1993; ScD; FRS 1986; Professor of Macromolecular Biochemistry, University of Cambridge, since 1991; Fellow, New Hall, Cambridge, since 1969; *b* 1 Oct. 1942; *o c* of John Robert Thomas and Lorna Prunella Thomas (*née* Harris). *Educ:* Llwyn-y-Bryn High School for Girls, Swansea; University Coll., Swansea, Univ. of Wales (BSc and Ayling Prize, 1964; PhD and Hinkel Research Prize, 1967 (Chem.)); MA Cantab 1969; ScD Cantab 1985. Beit Meml Fellow, MRC Lab. of Molecular Biology, Cambridge, 1967–69; Demonstrator in Biochemistry, 1969–73, Lectr, 1973–87, Reader in the Biochemistry of Macromolecules, 1987–91, Univ. of Cambridge; Tutor, 1970–76, Vice-Pres., 1983–87, Coll. Lectr, 1969–91, New Hall, Cambridge. Chm., Cambridge Centre for Molecular Recognition, 1993–. Member: SERC, 1990–94; Council, Royal Soc., 1990–92; EPSRC, 1994–97; Council and Scientific Adv. Cttee, ICRF, 1994–; Scientific Adv. Cttee, Lister Inst., 1994–2000. Trustee, BM, 1994–. Gov., Wellcome Trust, 2000–. Member: EMBO, 1982; Academia Europaea, 1991. Hon. Fellow: UCW, Swansea, 1987; Univ. of Wales, Cardiff, 1998. Hon. DSc Wales, 1992. K. M. Stott Research Prize, Newnham Coll., Cambridge, 1976. *Publications:* Companion to Biochemistry: selected topics for further study, vol. 1, 1974, vol. 2, 1979 (ed jtly and contrib.); papers in sci. jls, esp. on histones and chromatin structure. *Recreations:* reading, music, walking. *Address:* Department of Biochemistry, 80 Tennis Court Road, Cambridge CB2 1GA. *T:* (01223) 333670; 26 Eachard Road, Cambridge CB3 0HY. *T:* (01223) 362620.

THOMAS, Jenkin; HM Diplomatic Service, retired; Deputy UK Permanent Representative and Counsellor (Economic and Financial), OECD, Paris, 1990–94; *b* 2 Jan. 1938; *s* of late William John Thomas and of Annie Muriel (*née* Thomas). *Educ:* Maesydderwen Sch.; University Coll. London (BA Hons); Univ. of Michigan, Ann Arbor (MA). Joined HM Foreign (subseq. Diplomatic) Service, 1960; Foreign Office, 1960–63; Pretoria/Cape Town, 1963–66; Saigon, 1966–68; FCO, 1968–73; Washington, 1973–77; FCO, 1977–79; Cabinet Office, 1979–80; Tokyo, 1980–82; Athens, 1982–87; FCO, 1987–90. Mem., Council, Cymmrodorion Soc. *Recreations:* reading, music, amateur musical comedies. *Address:* 43 Charleville Mansions, Charleville Road, W14 9JA.

THOMAS, Sir Jeremy (Cashel), KCMG 1987 (CMG 1980); HM Diplomatic Service, retired; Member, Chichester Harbour Conservancy Advisory Committee, since 1990; *b* 1 June 1931; *s* of Rev. H. C. Thomas and Margaret Betty (*née* Humby); *m* 1957, Diana Mary Summerhayes; three *s*. *Educ:* Eton; Merton Coll., Oxford. 16th/5th Lancers, 1949–51. Entered FO, 1954; served Singapore, Rome and Belgrade; Dep. Head, Personnel Ops Dept, FCO, 1970–74; Counsellor and Head of Chancery, UK Mission to UN, NY, 1974–76; Head of Perm. Under-Sec.'s Dept, FCO, 1977–79; Ambassador to Luxembourg, 1979–82; Asst Under-Sec. of State, FCO, 1982–85; Ambassador to Greece, 1985–89. *Publication:* The Rhythm of the Tide: tales through the ages of Chichester Harbour, 1999. *Recreations:* sailing, fishing. *Address:* East Manor Farm, Pook Lane, East Lavant, near Chichester, West Sussex PO18 0AH. *T:* (01243) 531661. *Clubs:* Oxford and Cambridge; Itchenor Sailing, Bosham Sailing.

THOMAS, Jeremy Jack; film producer; Chairman, British Film Institute, 1993–97; *b* 26 July 1949; *s* of late Ralph Philip Thomas, MC and of Joy Thomas; *m* 1st, 1977, Claudia Frolich (marr. diss. 1981); one *d*; 2nd, 1982, Vivien Coughman; two *s*. *Educ:* Millfield. Has worked in most aspects of film prodn, esp. in editing dept before becoming a producer. Producer: Mad Dog Morgan, 1974; The Shout, 1977; The Great Rock 'n Roll Swindle, 1979; Bad Timing, 1980; Merry Christmas, Mr Lawrence, 1982; Eureka, 1982; The Hit, 1984; Insignificance, 1985; The Last Emperor, 1987 (Acad. Award for Best Film); Everybody Wins, 1990; The Sheltering Sky, 1990; The Naked Lunch, 1991; Let Him Have It, 1991; Little Buddha, 1992; Stealing Beauty, 1996; The Brave, 1996; Blood and Wine, 1997; Sexy Beast, 1999; Brother, 1999; Executive Producer: Crash, 1995; The Cup, 1999; Gohatto, 1999; Prod./Dir, All The Little Animals, 1998. Special Award for Outstanding Contribn to Cinema, Evening Standard, 1990; Michael Balcon Award for Outstanding Contribn to Cinema, BAFTA, 1991. *Address:* Recorded Picture Co. Ltd, 24 Hanway Street, W1T 1UH. *T:* (020) 7636 2251. *Club:* Royal Automobile.

THOMAS, Sir (John) Alan, Kt 1993; *b* 4 Jan. 1943; *s* of Idris Thomas and Ellen Constance Thomas (*née* Noakes); *m* 1966, Angela Taylor; two *s*. *Educ:* Dynevor Sch.; Nottingham Univ. (Richard Thomas & Baldwin's Industrial Schol.; BSc Mech. Engrg). FCMA (First Prizewinner); CEng; FIEE. Chief Exec., Data Logic, 1973–85; Vice Pres., Raytheon Co. (US), 1985–89; Pres. and Chief Exec. Officer, Raytheon Europe, 1985–89; Chm., Tag Semi-Conductors (US), 1985–89; Dir, Eur. subsids, 1978–89; seconded to MoD as Head of Defence Export Services Orgn, 1989–94. Chairman: Firth Hldgs, 1994–; Micro Quoted Growth Trust plc, 1998–; Chelverton Asset Management, 1998–; Three Valleys Water plc, 2000–; Dir, Powergen plc, 1996–99; Sen. Industrial Advr, OFWAT, 1998–2000. Member: Defence Industries Council, 1990–94; Engrg Council, 1994–96. Dir, Centre for Policy Studies, 1996–. Polytechnic of Central London, now University of Westminster: Vis. Prof., 1981–; Gov., 1989–, Chm., Ct of Govs, 1999–. Dir, London Welsh RFC, 1997–. Pres., Computing Services Assoc., 1980–81. Liveryman, Co. of Information Technologists, 1988–. CIMgt 1997. *Recreations:* music, sport. *Address:* (office) 40 Catherine Place, SW1E 6HL. *T:* (020) 7828 9989; *e-mail:* siralanthomas@aol.com. *Club:* Athenæum.

THOMAS, Dr John Anthony Griffiths; counsellor; publishing consultant; Managing Director, BBC Worldwide Learning, 1995–97; Deputy Chairman, BBC Worldwide Publishing, 1994–97; *b* 28 Aug. 1943; *s* of late William and Bernice Thomas; *m* 1965, Sylvia Jean Norman; two *d*. *Educ:* Leeds Univ. (BSc Chem. 1965); Univ. of Keele (PhD 1968). Teacher of Chemistry, Leeds Grammar Sch., 1968–69; Reed Business Publishing Ltd: Editor, 1969–75; Editorial Dir, 1975–77; Publishing Dir, 1977–84; Divisional Man. Dir, Med. Div., 1984–86; BBC Enterprises Ltd: Dir, BBC Magazines and Electronic Publishing Gp, 1986–93; Man. Dir, 1993–94; Man. Dir, BBC Worldwide Television Ltd, 1994–95; Dir, BBC Worldwide Ltd, 1994–97. Chairman: Redwood Publishing Ltd,

1988–93; Frontline Ltd, 1990–94; BBC Haymarket Exhibns Ltd, 1992–94; Galleon Ltd, 1993–94; Dir, Periodicals Publishing Assoc., 1989–94. Stanford Univ. Alumni, 1991. *Publications:* (ed) Energy Modelling, 1974; Energy Today, 1977; (ed) Energy Analysis, 1977; The Quest for Fuel, 1978. *Recreations:* psychology, reading, music, walking.

THOMAS, Prof. John David, PhD; FBA 1989; Professorial Fellow in Papyrology, University of Durham, 1990–92, now Emeritus Professor; *b* 23 June 1931; *s* of Henry Thomas and Elsie Thomas (*née* Bruin); *m* 1956, Marion Amy Peach; two *s*. *Educ:* Wyggeston Grammar Sch., Leicester; Worcester Coll., Oxford (MA); PhD Wales. Lectr in Classics, UCW, Aberystwyth, 1955–66; University of Durham: Lectr, then Sen. Lectr in Palaeography, 1966–77; Reader in Papyrology, 1977–90. Vis. Fellow, Wolfson Coll., Oxford, 1981. Member: Inst. for Advanced Study, Princeton, 1972; Comité Internat. de Papyrologie, 1983–95. *Publications:* Greek Papyri in the Collection of W. Merton III, 1967; The Epistrategos in Ptolemaic and Roman Egypt, Pt I 1975, Pt II 1982; (with A. K. Bowman) Vindolanda: the Latin writing tablets, 1983; (with A. K. Bowman) The Vindolanda writing-tablets: Tabulae Vindolandenses II, 1994; contribs to the Oxyrhynchus Papyri XXXVIII, XLIV, XLVII, L, LVII, LXV–LXVII; articles and reviews in learned jls. *Recreations:* music, bird watching, walking. *Address:* 39 Wearside Drive, Durham DH1 1LE. *T:* (0191) 3861723.

THOMAS, (John) Harvey (Noake), CBE 1990; international public relations consultant, since 1976; Consultant Director of Presentation, Conservative Party, 1986–91; *b* 10 April 1939; *s* of John Humphrey Kenneth Thomas and Olga Rosina Thomas (*née* Noake); *m* 1978, Marlies (*née* Kram); two *d*. *Educ:* Westminster School; Northwestern Bible College, Minneapolis; Univs of Minnesota and Hawaii. Billy Graham Evangelistic Assoc., 1960–75; Dir of Press and Communications, Conservative Party, 1985–86. Mem., Bd of Dirs, London Cremation Co., 1984–. FIPR, FCIJ, FRSA. *Publications:* In the Face of Fear, 1985; Making an Impact, 1989; If they haven't heard it—you haven't said it, 1995. *Recreations:* travel, family, trains. *Address:* 23 The Service Road, Potters Bar, Herts EN6 1QA. *T:* (01707) 649910, *Fax:* (01707) 662653; *e-mail:* harvey@hthomas.net. *Club:* Institute of Directors.

THOMAS, Sir (John) Maldwyn, Kt 1984; President, Welsh Liberal Party, 1985–86; *b* 17 June 1918; *s* of Daniel and Gwladys Thomas; *m* 1975, Maureen Elizabeth (Dame Maureen Thomas, DBE 1999). *Educ:* Porth Rhondda Grammar Sch. FCIS. Called to Bar, Gray's Inn, 1953; Solicitor, 1965; readmitted to Gray's Inn, 1987. Lewis & Tylor Ltd, Cardiff, 1940–56; Signode Ltd, Swansea, 1956–59; Commercial Agreements Manager, UKAEA, 1959–63; Rank Xerox Ltd: Sec., 1964–70; Man. Dir, 1970–72; Chm., 1972–79; Dir, Xerox Corp., USA, 1974–79; non-executive Director: Internat. Military Services, 1978–84; Thos Cook Inc. (USA), 1978–84; Westland PLC, 1985–94; non-exec. Dep. Chm., John Brown plc, 1984–86. Chm., European Govt Business Relations Council, 1978–79. Contested (L) Aberavon, 1950. Pres., London Welsh Assoc. and Trust. Trustee, London Welsh Sch. *Address:* 9 Chester Terrace, Regent's Park, NW1 4ND. *Clubs:* Reform, National Liberal.

THOMAS, Sir John Meurig, Kt 1991; MA, PhD, DSc, ScD; FRS 1977; Master of Peterhouse, Cambridge, since 1993; *b* Llanelli, Wales, 15 Dec. 1932; *s* of David John and Edyth Thomas; *m* 1959, Margaret (*née* Edwards); two *d*. *Educ:* Gwendraeth Grammar Sch. (State Scholar); University College of Swansea (Hon. Fellow, 1985); Queen Mary Coll., London; DSc Wales, 1964; ScD Cantab, 1994. Scientific Officer, UKAEA, 1957–58; Asst Lectr 1958–59, Lectr 1959–65, Reader 1965–69, in Chemistry, UCNW, Bangor; Prof. and Head of Dept of Chemistry, UCW, Aberystwyth, 1969–78 (Hon. Fellow, 1996); Prof. and Head of Dept of Physical Chemistry, and Fellow of King's Coll., Univ. of Cambridge, 1978–86; Dir, Royal Instn of GB, and Davy Faraday Res. Lab., 1986–91; Resident Prof. of Chemistry, 1986–88, Fullerian Prof. of Chemistry, 1988–94, Prof. of Chemistry, 1994–, Royal Instn of GB; Dep. Pro-Chancellor, Univ. of Wales, 1991–94. Visiting appointments: Tech. Univ. Eindhoven, Holland, 1962; Penna State Univ., USA, 1963, 1967; Tech. Univ. Karlsruhe, Germany, 1966; Weizmann Inst., Israel, 1969; Univ. of Florence, Italy, 1972; Amer. Univ. in Cairo, Egypt, 1973; IBM Res. Center, San José, 1977; Harvard, 1983; Ecole Nat. Sup. de Chimie de Paris, 1991. Ind. Mem., Radioactive Waste Management Cttee, 1978–80; Member: Chem. SRC, 1976–78; SERC, 1986–90; Adv. Cttee, Davy-Faraday Labs, Royal Instn, 1978–80; Scientific Adv. Cttee, Sci. Center, Alexandria, 1979–; ACARD (Cabinet Office), 1982–85; COPUS, 1986–92; Bd of Governors, Weizmann Inst., 1982–; Academia Europaea, 1989. Mem., Royal Commn for Exhibn of 1851, 1995– (Chm., Scientific Res. Cttee, 1996–). Chm., Chemrawn (Chem. Res. Applied to World Needs), IUPAC, 1987–93; Member, International Advisory Board: NSF Lab. of Molecular Scis, CIT, 1999–; Nat. Inst. of Informatics, Tokyo, 2000–; President: Chem. Section, BAAS, 1988–89; London Internat. Youth Sci. Fortnight, 1989–93. Trustee: BM (Natural Hist.), 1987–92; Science Mus., 1990–95. Vice-President: Cambridge Univ. Musical Soc., 1994–; Cambridge Philosophical Soc., 1994–. Hon. Visiting Professor: in Physical Chem., QMC, 1986–; of Chem., Imperial Coll., London, 1986–91; Academia Sinica, Beijing; Inst. of Ceramic Sci., Shanghai, 1986–. New mineral, meurigite, named in his honour, 1995. Lectures: BBC Welsh Radio Annual, 1978; Gerhardt Schmidt Meml, Weizmann Inst., 1979; Baker, Cornell Univ., 1982–83; Hund-Klemm, Max Planck Ges., Stuttgart, 1987; Christmas Lectures, Royal Instn, 1987 (televised, 1988); First Kenneth Pitzer, Coll. of Chem., Univ. of Calif, Berkeley, 1988; Van't Hoff, Royal Dutch Acad. of Arts and Scis, 1988; Bakerian, Royal Soc., 1990; Bruce Preller Prize, RSE, 1990; Sir Krishnan Meml, Delhi, 1991; Watson Centennial, CIT, 1991; Birch, ANU Canberra, 1992; Liversidge, Univ. of Sydney, 1992; Sir Joseph Larmor, Cambridge Philos. Soc., 1992; Patten, Indiana Univ., 1993; François Gault, Eur. Fedn of Catalyst Socs, 1995; Prettre, Lyons, 1996; Rutherford Meml, Royal Soc., 1997; Tetelman, Yale Univ., 1997; Pollack, Technion Haifa, 1998; Ziegler Centenary, Max Planck Inst., Mülheim, 1998; Linus Pauling, CIT, 1999; Taylor, Penn State, 1999; Major, Univ. of Connecticut, 2000; Miller, Univ. of Calif., Berkeley, 2000; Linus Pauling, Oregon State, 2000; John C. Polanyi Nobel Laureate Series Speaker, Univ. Toronto, 2000; Griffiths Meml (250th anniv.), Hon. Soc. of Cymmrodorian, London, 2001; Debye, Univ. of Utrecht, 2001; Plenary Speaker, World Congress of Chemistry, Brisbane, 2001. Hon. FRSE 1993; Hon. FInstP 1999; Hon. FREng 1999. Hon. Fellow: Indian Acad. of Science, 1980; UMIST, 1984; UCNW, Bangor, 1988; RMS, 1989; Queen Mary and Westfield Coll., London, 1990; Foreign Fellow, INA, 1985; Hon. Foreign Member: Amer. Acad. of Arts and Scis, 1990; Venezuelan Acad. of Scis, 1994; Hon. For. Assoc., Engrg Acad. of Japan, 1991; For. Mem., Amer. Philosophical Soc., 1993; Hon. Foreign Fellow: Russian Acad. of Scis, 1994; Hungarian Acad. of Sci., 1998; Polish Acad. of Arts and Scis, 1999; Amer. Carbon Soc., 1999. Hon. Bencher, Gray's Inn, 1987. Hon. LLD Wales, 1984; Hon. DLitt CNAA, 1987; Hon. DSc: Heriot-Watt, 1989; Birmingham, 1991; Complutense, Madrid, 1994; Western Ontario, Glamorgan, 1995; Hull, 1996; Aberdeen, 1997; DUniv: Open, 1991; Surrey, 1997; Dr *hc*: Lyon, 1994; Eindhoven, 1996. Corday Morgan Silver Medal, Chem. Soc., 1967; first Pettinos Prize, American Carbon Soc., 1969; Tilden Medal and Lectr, Chem. Soc., 1973; Chem. Soc. Prizewinner in Solid State Chem., 1978; Hugo Müller Medal, RSC, 1983; Faraday Medal and Lectr, RSC, 1989; Messel Medal, SCI, 1992; Davy Medal, Royal Soc., 1994; Gibbs Gold Medal, ACS, 1995; Longstaff Medal, RSC, 1996; Hon. Medal, Polish Acad. of Scis, Warsaw, 1996; Semenov Centenary Medal, Russian Acad. of Sci., 1996 (first recipient) ACS Award for creative res. in homogeneous or heterogeneous catalysis, 1999. Crystals and Lasers, TV series, 1987; Dylanwadau, radio series, 1990. Founding Editor: (jtly), Catalysis Letters, 1988; (jtly) Topics in Catalysis, 1992; (jtly) Current Opinion in Solid State and Materials Sci., 1996. *Publications:* (with W. J. Thomas) Introduction to the Principles of Heterogeneous Catalysis, 1967 (trans. Russian, 1970); Pan edrychwyf ar y nefoedd, 1978; Michael Faraday and the Royal Institution: the genius of man and place, 1991 (trans. Japanese, 1994); (with K. I. Zamaraev) Perspectives in Catalysis, 1992; Heterogeneous Catalysis: theory and practice, 1997; numerous articles on solid state and surface chemistry, catalysis and influence of crystalline imperfections, in Proc. Royal Soc., Jl Chem. Soc., etc. *Recreations:* ancient civilizations, bird watching, hill walking, Welsh literature, reading other people's recreations in Who's Who. *Address:* Master's Lodge, Peterhouse, Cambridge CB2 1QY. *T:* (01223) 338200, *Fax:* (01223) 337578.

THOMAS, Kathrin Elizabeth, (Mrs E. V. Thomas); JP; Vice Lord-Lieutenant, Mid Glamorgan, since 1994; *b* 20 May 1944; *d* of Dillwyn Evans and Dorothy Nelle (*née* Bullock); *m* 1967, Edward Vaughan Thomas; two *s*. *Educ:* Cheltenham Ladies' Coll. Chairman: Mid Glamorgan FHSA, 1990–94; Mid Glamorgan HA, 1994–96; Bro Taf HA, 1996–99; Prince's Trust, Cymru, 1999–; Mem., Prince's Trust Council, 1996–. Hon. Col 203 (Welsh) Field Hosp. RAMC (V), 1998. Mid Glamorgan: JP 1983; High Sheriff 1986–87; DL 1989. *Recreations:* farming, talking, reading. *Address:* Gelli Hir, Nelson, Treharris, Mid Glamorgan CF46 6PL. *Club:* Army and Navy.

THOMAS, Keith Henry Westcott, CB 1982; OBE 1962; FREng, FRINA; RCNC; Chief Executive, Royal Dockyards, and Head of Royal Corps of Naval Constructors, 1979–83; *b* 20 May 1923; *s* of Henry and Norah Thomas; *m* 1946, Brenda Jeanette Crofton; two *s*. *Educ:* Portsmouth Southern Secondary Sch.; HM Dockyard Sch., Portsmouth; RNC, Greenwich. Asst Constructor, Admiralty Experiment Works, Haslar, 1947–49; Constructor: Admty, London, 1949–56; Large Carrier Design Section, Admty, Bath, 1956–60; Submarines and New Construction, HM Dockyard, Portsmouth, 1960–63; Project Leader, Special Refit HMS Hermes, Devonport, 1963–66; Dep. Planning Manager, HM Dockyard, Devonport, 1966–68; Project Man., Ikara Leanders, MoD(N), 1968–70; Dir-Gen. of Naval Design, Dept of Navy, Canberra, Aust. (on secondment), 1970–73; Planning Man., 1973–75, Gen. Man., 1975–77, HM Dockyard, Rosyth; Gen. Manager, HM Dockyard, Devonport, 1977–79. Chm., Portsmouth Royal Dockyard Historical Trust, 1995– (Pres., Portsmouth Royal Dockyard Historical Soc., 1988–95); Mem., Nat. Historic Ships Cttee, 1996–2000. FIMgt. *Recreations:* music, lapidary, painting. *Address:* 6 Wyborn Close, Hayling Island, Hants PO11 9HY. *T:* (023) 9246 3435.

THOMAS, Sir Keith (Vivian), Kt 1988; FBA 1979; Fellow of All Souls College, Oxford, 1955–57 and since 2001; President of Corpus Christi College, Oxford, 1986–2000 (Hon. Fellow, 2000); *b* 2 Jan. 1933; *s* of late Vivian Jones Thomas and Hilda Janet Eirene Thomas (*née* Davies); *m* 1961, Valerie Little; one *s* one *d*. *Educ:* Barry County Grammar Sch.; Balliol Coll., Oxford (Brackenbury Schol.; 1st Cl. Hons Mod. History, 1955; Hon. Fellow 1984). Oxford University: Senior Scholar, St Antony's Coll., 1955; Fellow of St John's Coll., 1957–86 (Tutor, 1957–85; Hon. Fellow, 1986); Reader in Modern Hist., 1978–85; Prof. of Modern Hist., Jan.–Sept. 1986; Pro-Vice-Chancellor, 1988–2000; Mem., Hebdomadal Council, 1988–2000. Vis. Professor, Louisiana State Univ., 1970; Vis. Fellow, 1970, Lawrence Stone Vis. Prof., 2001, Princeton Univ. Joint Literary Director, Royal Historical Soc., 1970–74, Mem. Council, 1975–78, Vice-Pres., 1980–84; Pres., British Acad., 1993–97. Member: ESRC, 1985–90; Reviewing Cttee on Export of Works of Art, 1989–92; Royal Commn on Historical Manuscripts, 1992–; Trustee: Nat. Gall., 1991–98; British Museum, 1999–; Chairman: British Liby Adv. Cttee for Arts, Humanities and Social Scis, 1997–; Adv. Council, Warburg Inst., Univ. of London, 2000–. Delegate, OUP, 1980–2000 (Chm., Finance Cttee, 1988–2000). Lectures: Stenton, Univ. of Reading, 1975; Raleigh, British Acad., 1976; Neale, University Coll. London, 1976; G. M. Trevelyan, Univ. of Cambridge, 1978–79; Sir D. Owen Evans, University Coll. of Wales, Aberystwyth, 1980; Kaplan, Univ. of Pennsylvania, 1983; Creighton, Univ. of London, 1983; Ena H. Thompson, Pomona Coll., 1986; Prothero, RHistS, 1986; Merle Curti, Univ. of Wisconsin-Madison, 1989; Spinoza, Univ. of Amsterdam, 1992; Ford's in British History, Univ. of Oxford, 2000. MAE 1993 (Trustee, 1997–); For. Hon. Mem., Amer. Acad. of Arts and Scis, 1983. Hon. Fellow, Univ. of Wales Coll. of Cardiff, 1995. Hon. DLitt: Kent, 1983; Wales, 1987; Hull, 1995; Leicester, 1996; Sussex, 1996; Warwick, 1998; Hon. LLD: Williams Coll., Mass, 1988; Oglethorpe Univ., Ga, 1996; Hon. LittD: Sheffield, 1992; Cantab, 1995. Cavaliere Ufficiale, Ordine al Merito della Repubblica Italiana, 1991. Gen. Editor, Past Masters Series, OUP, 1979–. *Publications:* Religion and the Decline of Magic, 1971 (Wolfson Lit. Award for History, 1972); Rule and Misrule in the Schools of Early Modern England, 1976; Age and Authority in Early Modern England, 1977; ed (with Donald Pennington), Puritans and Revolutionaries, 1978; Man and the Natural World, 1983; (ed) The Oxford Book of Work, 1999; contribs to historical books and jls. *Recreation:* visiting secondhand bookshops. *Address:* All Souls College, Oxford OX1 4AL; The Broad Gate, Broad Street, Ludlow, Shropshire SY8 1NJ.

See also W. T. Gowers.

THOMAS, Kenneth Rowland, OBE 1995; General Secretary, Civil and Public Services Association, 1976–82; *b* 7 Feb. 1927; *s* of William Rowland Thomas and Anne Thomas; *m* 1955, Nora (*née* Hughes); four *s*. *Educ:* St Joseph's Elementary Sch., Penarth; Penarth Grammar Sch. Trainee Reporter, South Wales Echo and Western Mail, 1943–44; Civil Servant, 1944–54; Asst Sec., Civil and Public Services Assoc., 1955, Dep. Gen. Sec., 1967. Mem., TUC Gen. Council, 1977–82. Member: Occupational Pensions Bd, 1981–97; CSAB, 1984–91; Law Soc. Professional Purposes Cttee, 1984–86; Solicitors Complaints Bureau, 1986–92; Trustee: Post Office Pension Fund, 1969–84; London Develt Capital Fund, 1984–99; British Telecommunications Fund, 1983–97; Charity Aid Foundn, 1982–92; Director: Postel, 1982–95; W Midlands Enterprise Bd, 1982–; Univ. of Warwick Sci. Park, 1986–, Sci. Park Foundn, 1998–, and Sci. Park Innovation Centre, 1998–; Warwickshire Venture Capital Fund, 1988–91; Coventry Venture Capital Fund, 1988–91; W Midlands Growth Fund, 1990–; W Midlands Technol. Transfer Co., 1997–99. Governor and Chm. Audit Cttee, Coleg Harlech, 1997–. *Recreations:* music, anything Welsh. *Address:* Pen-y-Bryn, Penlon, Bangor, Gwynedd LL57 1PX. *T:* (01248) 353289.

THOMAS, Prof. Lancelot; FInstP; Professor of Physics, University of Wales, Aberystwyth, 1981–95, Research Professor, 1995–97, now Emeritus Professor (Head of Department, 1981–94); *b* 4 Aug. 1930; *s* of Evan Lancelot Redvers Thomas and Olive Margaretta Thomas; *m* 1955, Helen McGraith Reilly; two *s* one *d*. *Educ:* Port Talbot Secondary Grammar Sch.; University College of Swansea (BSc, PhD, DSc). Flying Officer, RAF, 1954–56; Royal Soc. post-doctoral appt, UC of Swansea, 1956–58; SSO, PSO, then Individual Merit SPSO, SERC Appleton Lab., 1959–65, 1966–81; Guest Worker, Envmtl Res. Labs, Nat. Oceanic and Atmospheric Admin, Boulder, Colorado, 1965–66; Principal Investigator, SERC/NERC VHF Radar Facility, 1981–97. Chm.,

British Nat. Cttee for Solar Terrestrial Physics, Royal Soc., 1982–87; Member: Adv. Cttee on Solar Systems, ESA, 1973–76; Royal Soc. Study Gp on Pollution in the Atmosphere, 1975–77; Solar System Cttee, Astronomy, Space and Radio Bd, SERC, 1975–79; Scientific Adv. Cttee, British Antarctic Survey, 1983–86; Earth Observation Prog. Bd, BNSC, 1987–88; Astronomy and Planetary Sci. Bd, SERC, 1989–93; Royal Soc. Interdisciplinary Sci. Cttee on Space Res., 1990–93; Astronomy Cttee, PPARC, 1994–97; Council, Inst. of Physics, 1994–98. Hon. Fellow, Univ. of Wales, Swansea, 1998. Charles Chree Medal and Prize, Inst. of Physics, 1991. *Publications:* (ed jtly) Space Research X, 1970; numerous papers in learned jls on atmospheric and ionospheric physics. *Recreations:* music, modern history, golf. *Address:* Branas, Lôn Tyllwyd, Llanfarian, Aberystwyth, Dyfed SY23 4UH. *T:* (01970) 617223.

THOMAS, Leslie John; author; *b* 22 March 1931; *s* of late David James Thomas and late Dorothy Hilda Court Thomas, Newport (Mon); *m* 1st, 1956, Maureen Crane (marr. diss.); two *s* one *d*; 2nd, 1970, Diana Miles; one *s*. *Educ:* Dr Barnardo's, Kingston-upon-Thames; Kingston Technical Sch.; SW Essex Technical Coll., Walthamstow. Local Newspapers, London area, 1948–49 and 1951–53; Army, 1949–51 (rose to Lance-Corporal); Exchange Telegraph News Agency, 1953–55; Special Writer, London Evening News, 1955–66; subseq. author. Vice Pres., Barnardo's, 1998–. Hon. MA Wales, 1995; Hon. DLitt Nottingham, 1998. *Publications: autobiography:* This Time Next Week, 1964; In My Wildest Dreams, 1984; *novels:* The Virgin Soldiers, 1966; Orange Wednesday, 1967; The Love Beach, 1968; Come to the War, 1969; His Lordship, 1970; Onward Virgin Soldiers, 1971; Arthur McCann and All His Women, 1972; The Man with Power, 1973; Tropic of Ruislip, 1974; Stand up Virgin Soldiers, 1975; Dangerous Davies, 1976; Bare Nell, 1977; Ormerod's Landing, 1978; That Old Gang of Mine, 1979; The Magic Army, 1981; The Dearest and the Best, 1984; The Adventures of Goodnight and Loving, 1986; Dangerous in Love, 1987; Orders For New York, 1989; The Loves and Journeys of Revolving Jones, 1991; Arrivals and Departures, 1992; Dangerous by Moonlight, 1993; Running Away, 1994; Kensington Heights, 1996; Chloë's Song, 1997; Dangerous Davies and the Lonely Heart, 1998; Other Times, 1999; *non-fiction:* Some Lovely Islands, 1968; The Hidden Places of Britain, 1981; A World of Islands, 1983; Short Singles, 1986; TV Plays and Documentaries, etc, incl. Channel Four series, Great British Isles (also presented), 1989; also short stories. *Recreations:* islands, antiques, cricket. *Address:* St Mary's Lodge, Captains' Row, Lymington, Hants SO41 9RR. *Clubs:* MCC, Saints and Sinners, Lord's Taverners.

THOMAS, Sir Maldwyn; *see* Thomas, Sir J. M.

THOMAS, Margaret, Women's International Art Club, 1940; RBA 1947; NEAC 1950; Contemporary Portrait Society, 1970; RWA 1971; Practising Artist (Painter); *b* 26 Sept. 1916; *d* of late Francis Stewart Thomas and Grace Whetherly. *Educ:* privately; Slade Sch.; RA Schools. Slade Scholar, 1936. Hon. Sec. Artists International Assoc., 1944–45; FRSA 1971. Group exhibitions, Wildensteins, 1946, 1949 and 1962; First one-man show at Leicester Galls, 1949, and subsequently at same gallery, 1950; one-man shows in Edinburgh (Aitken Dotts), 1952, 1955, 1966, and at Outlook Tower, Edinburgh, during Internat. Fest., 1961; RBA Galleries, London, 1953; at Canaletto Gall. (a barge, at Little Venice), 1961; Exhibition of Women Artists, Wakefield Art Gall., 1961; Howard Roberts Gallery Cardiff, 1963, The Minories, Colchester, 1964, QUB, 1967, Mall Galls, London, 1972; Octagon Gall., Belfast, 1973; Court Lodge Gallery, Kent, 1974; Gallery Paton, Edinburgh, 1977; Scottish Gall., Edinburgh (major retrospective), 1982; Sally Hunter, London, 1988, 1991, 1995 and 1998; RWA, 1992; Messum Gall., London, 2001; regular exhibitor Royal Academy and Royal Scottish Academy. Official purchases: Prince Philip, Duke of Edinburgh; Chantrey Bequest; Arts Council; Exeter College, Oxford; Min. of Education; Min. of Works; Wakefield, Hull, Paisley and Carlisle Art Galleries; Edinburgh City Corporation; Nuffield Foundation Trust; Steel Co. of Wales; Financial Times; Mitsukoshi Ltd, Tokyo; Scottish Nat. Orchestra; Robert Flemming collection; Lloyd's of London; Sock Shop Internat.; Mercury Asset Mgt; Nat. Library of Wales; GLC and county education authorities in Yorks, Bucks, Monmouth, Derbyshire, Hampshire and Wales. Coronation painting purchased by Min. of Works for British Embassy in Santiago. Winner, Hunting Gp Award for best oil painting of the year, 1981. *Publications:* work reproduced in: Daily Telegraph, News Chronicle, Listener, Studio, Scottish Field, Music and Musicians, The Lady, Arts Review, Western Mail; Illustrated London News, The Artist, The Spectator, Eastern Daily Press. *Recreations:* antique collecting, gardening, vintage cars. *Address:* Ellingham Mill, near Bungay, Suffolk NR35 2EP. *T:* (01508) 518656; 13A North Road, Highgate Village, N6 4BD. *T:* (020) 8340 2527.

THOMAS, (Mary) Elizabeth; with Shropshire Music Service (part-time), 1993–98; Director, West Midlands Board, Central Television plc, 1982–92 (Member, Regional Advisory Council, 1993); *b* 22 March 1935; *d* of Kathleen Mary Thomas (*née* Dodd) and David John Thomas; *m* 1962, Brian Haydn Thomas; two *d*. *Educ:* Dr Williams' School, Dolgellau; Talbot Heath School, Bournemouth; Royal Acad. of Music. ARCM, GRSM. Head of Music, High Sch., Totnes, 1958–61; Music Lectr, Ingestre Hall, Stafford, 1962; Berkshire Music Schs, 1964–66; Adult Educn Lectr, Bridgnorth Coll. of Further Educn, 1966–69. Chm., Pentabus Arts Ltd, 1983–87. Arts Council of Great Britain: Member, 1984–88; Chm., Regl Adv. Cttee, 1984–86; Chm., Planning and Develt Bd, 1986–88. Chairman: W Midlands Arts, 1980–84; Council, Regional Arts Assocs, 1982–85; Nat. Assoc. of Local Arts Councils, 1980–82 (Vice-Pres., 1982); City of Birmingham Touring Opera, 1987–92. Mem., Much Wenlock Town Council, 1999– (Mayor, 2000–01). *Recreations:* collecting antique glass, gardening. *Address:* Cutters House, 48 Sheinton Street, Much Wenlock, Shropshire TF13 6HU.

THOMAS, Rt Rev. Maxwell McNee; ThD; Warden of St Paul's College, University of Sydney, 1985–94; Lecturer in History and Thought of Christianity, University of Sydney, 1986–94; *b* 23 Aug. 1926; *s* of Rev. Charles Elliot Thomas, ThL, and Elsie Frances Thomas (*née* McNee); *m* 1952, Elaine Joy Walker; two *s* one *d*. *Educ:* St Paul's Coll., Univ. of Sydney (MA, BD); General Theological Seminary, New York (ThD). Lectr in Theology and Greek, St John's Coll, Morpeth, NSW, 1950; deacon, 1950; priest, 1952; Curate: St Peter's, E. Maitland, 1951–52; St Mary Magdalene, Richmond, Surrey, 1952–54; All Saints', Singleton, NSW, 1955. Priest-in-Charge and Rector, The Entrance, NSW, 1955–59; Fellow and Tutor, General Theol. Seminary, NY, 1959–63; Hon. Chaplain to Bishop of New York, 1959–63, Chaplain, 1963–64; Chaplain, Univ. of Melbourne and of Canterbury Fellowship, 1964–68; Consultant Theologian to Archbishop of Melbourne, Stewart Lectr in Divinity, Trinity Coll. and Chaplain of Canterbury Fellowship, 1968–75; Bishop of Wangaratta, 1975–85. Member: Gen. Synod's Commn on Doctrine, 1970–92 (Chm., 1976–92); Faith and Order Commn, WCC, 1977–79; Internat. Commn for Anglican-Orthodox Theol Dialogue (formerly Anglican-Orthodox Jt Doctrinal Discussion Gp), 1978–. *Address:* 1 Butler Avenue, Mornington, Vic 3931, Australia. *Fax:* (3) 59770936. *Clubs:* Melbourne, Royal Automobile of Victoria; Australian (Sydney).

THOMAS, Prof. (Meurig) Wynn, FBA 1996; Professor of English, since 1994, and Director, Centre for Research into the English Literature and Language of Wales, since 1998, University of Wales, Swansea (formerly University College of Swansea); *b* 12 Sept. 1944; *s* of William John Thomas and Tydfil Thomas (*née* Rees); *m* 1975, Karen Elizabeth Manahan; one *d*. *Educ:* Gowerton Boys' Grammar Sch.; UCW, Swansea (BA 1965). University College of Swansea: Asst Lectr, 1966–69; Lectr in English, 1969–88; Sen. Lectr, 1988–94. Mem., British Library Adv. Cttee, Arts, Humanities and Social Scis, 2000–. Visiting Professor: Harvard, 1991–92; Univ. of Tübingen, 1994–95; Obermann Fellow, Univ. of Iowa, 1992. Mem., Welsh Arts Council and Chm., Literature Cttee, 1985–91; Vice-Chm., Welsh Language Section, Welsh Acad., 1996–97; Sec., Univ. of Wales Assoc. for Study of Welsh Writing in English, 1983–96; Adjudicator, David Cohen Prize, 1996–97. Hon. Mem., Nat. Eisteddfod Gorsedd of Bards, 2000. *Publications:* Morgan Llwyd, 1984; The Lunar Light of Whitman's Poetry, 1987; (ed) Morgan Llwyd, Llyfr y Tri Aderyn, 1988; Emyr Humphreys, 1989; (ed) Emyr Humphreys, A Toy Epic, 1989; (ed) R. S. Thomas: y cawr awenydd, 1990; (ed) Wrenching Times: Whitman's Civil War poetry, 1991; Morgan Llwyd: ei gyfeillion a'i gyfnod, 1991 (Welsh Arts Council Prize, Vernam Hull Meml Prize, Ellis Griffith Meml Prize); Internal Difference: literature in twentieth-century Wales, 1992; (ed) The Page's Drift: R. S. Thomas at eighty, 1993; (ed) DiFfinio Dwy Lenyddiaeth Cymru (essays), 1995; (trans.) Dail Glaswellt, 1995; John Ormond, 1997; Corresponding Cultures: the two literatures of Wales, 1999; (ed) Gweld Sêr: Cymru a chanrif America, 2001; contrib. to jls and books. *Recreations:* reading, music, televiewing sport. *Address:* Department of English, University of Wales, Swansea, Singleton Park, Swansea SA2 8PP. *T:* (01792) 295926.

THOMAS, Meyric Leslie, OBE 1987; Vice Lord-Lieutenant of West Glamorgan, 1997–2001; Consultant, Hutchinson Morris & L. C. Thomas (formerly L. C. Thomas and Son), Solicitors, since 1990 (Partner, 1956–90); *b* 17 Nov. 1928; *s* of Charles Leslie Thomas and Edith Annie Thomas; *m* 1956, Jillian Hamilton Armstrong; two *s* one *d*. *Educ:* Beaudesert Park; Clifton Coll.; Jesus Coll., Oxford (Mem., Univ. Boat Race crew, 1952, 1953; Pres., OUBC, 1953; MA Jurisprudence). Admitted Solicitor, 1956. Nat. Service, Glos Regt, 1947–49 (Belt of Honour, Eaton Hall, 1948). Mem. (Ind.), Neath BC, 1957–74 (Mayor, 1967). Pres., Neath RFC, 1973–78. DL W Glamorgan, 1993. *Recreations:* Rugby Union (spectator), bowls. *Address:* Braye Lea, Val Reuters, Alderney, Channel Islands GY9 3XE. *T:* (01481) 823465. *Clubs:* Constitutional (Neath); Alderney Bowls.

THOMAS, Sir Michael, 3rd Bt; *see* Thomas, Sir W. M. M.

THOMAS, Sir Michael, 11th Bt; *see* Thomas, Sir G. M. D.

THOMAS, Michael Christopher Pryce; Legal Adviser, Cabinet Office (European Secretariat), since 1997; *b* 31 Oct. 1949; *s* of David Hamilton Pryce Thomas, *qv* and Eluned Mair Thomas (*née* Morgan); *m* 1978, Pauline Marie Buckman. *Educ:* St John's Coll., Oxford (BA); Univ. of Sussex (MA). Admitted solicitor, 1976; in private practice as asst solicitor, 1976–79; Legal Dept, MAFF, 1980–86; Law Officers' Dept, 1986–88; Grade 5, Legal Dept, MAFF, 1988–92; Legal Advr, Dept of Transport, later DETR, 1993–97. *Recreations:* music, theatre, ski-ing. *Address:* Treasury Solicitor's Department, Queen Anne's Chambers, 28 Broadway, SW1H 9JS. *T:* (020) 7210 3202.

THOMAS, Michael David, CMG 1985; QC 1973; barrister in private practice; Attorney-General of Hong Kong, 1983–88; Member, Executive and Legislative Councils, Hong Kong, 1983–88; Chairman, Law Reform Commission, Hong Kong, 1983–88; *b* 8 Sept. 1933; *s* of late D. Cardigan Thomas and Kathleen Thomas; *m* 1st, 1958, Jane Lena Mary (marr. diss. 1978), *e d* of late Francis Neate; two *s* two *d*; 2nd, 1981, Mrs Gabrielle Blakemore (marr. diss. 1986); 3rd, 1988, Hon. Lydia Dunn (*see* Baroness Dunn). *Educ:* Chigwell Sch., Essex; London Sch. of Economics. LLB (Hons) 1954. Called to Bar, Middle Temple, 1955 (Blackstone Entrance Schol., 1952; Harmsworth Schol., 1957); Bencher, 1981. Nat. Service with RN, Sub-Lt RNVR, 1955–57. In practice at Bar from 1958. Junior Counsel to Minister of Defence (RN) and to Treasury in Admty matters, 1966–73. Wreck Commissioner under Merchant Shipping Act 1970; one of Lloyd's salvage arbitrators, 1974. Governor: Chigwell Sch., 1971–83; LSE, 2001–. *Publications:* (ed jtly) Temperley: Merchant Shipping Acts, 6th edn 1963 and 7th edn 1974. *Recreations:* music, travel. *Address:* Essex Court Chambers, 24 Lincoln's Inn Fields, WC2A 3ED; Temple Chambers, 16F One Pacific Place, 88 Queensway, Hong Kong. *Clubs:* Garrick; Hong Kong (Hong Kong).

THOMAS, Col Michael John Glyn; private consultant in transfusion medicine, since 1995; Clinical Director, Blood Care Foundation, since 1995; Director, MG & SJ Enterprises, since 1995; *b* 14 Feb. 1938; *s* of Glyn Pritchard Thomas and Mary Thomas (*née* Moseley); *m* 1969, Sheelagh Thorpe; one *d*. *Educ:* Haileybury and ISC; Trinity College, Cambridge; St Bartholomew's Hosp. MA, MB, BChir, LMSSA, DTM&H. FRCPE 1997. Qualified 1962; House Surgeon, Essex County Hosp. and House Physician, St James, Balham, 1963; Regtl MO, 2nd Bn The Parachute Regt, 1965; Trainee Pathologist, BMH Singapore, 1968; Specialist in Pathology, Colchester Mil. Hosp., 1971; Senior Specialist in Pathology, Army Blood Supply Depot, 1977; Exchange Pathologist, Walter Reed Army Inst. of Research, 1982–84; Officer in Charge of Leishman Lab., Cambridge Mil. Hosp., 1985–87; CO, Army Blood Supply Depot, 1987–95. Hon. Consultant Haematologist, UCH/Middlesex Hosp., 1987. Member: Council, BMA, 1974–82 (Chm., Junior Mems Forum, 1974–75; Chm., Central Ethical Cttee, 1978–82; Mem., expert panel on AIDS, 1986–; Mem., Bd of Sci. and Educn, 1987–93; Fellow, 1995); Cttee on Transfusion Equipment, BSI; Economic and Social Cttee, EEC, 1989–; Council, British Blood Transfusion Soc., 1998– (Founder Chm., 1992–98, Sec., 1998–, Autologous Transfusion Special Interest Gp). *Publications:* contribs to ref. books, reports and jls on Medical Ethics, Haematology and Blood Banking, Malariology and subjects of general medical interest. *Recreations:* sailing, travel, photography, philately. *Address:* 12 Winchfield Court, Winchfield, Hook, Hants RG27 8SP. *Club:* Tanglin (Singapore).

THOMAS, Rear-Adm. Michael Richard, BSc (Eng); CEng, FIEE; RN, 1960–96: served HMS Lincoln, Dido, and Andromeda; subseq. HM Dockyards Devonport and Portsmouth; Naval Sec's Dept, MoD; Naval Asst to Chief of Fleet Support; Supt Ships, Devonport; comd HMS Drake, 1992; Pres., Ordnance Bd, and DG Technical Services, 1994–96. Comdr 1977; Capt. 1985; Cdre 1993. Dir, Electrical Contractors' Assoc., 1996; Man. Dir, Penzance Drydock Co. Ltd, 1997–. Life Vice-President: Plymouth Scouts; Sea Cadet Corps. Gov., Plymouth Univ. FIMgt; MInstD. *Recreation:* Rugby administration. *Address:* Millstone, Links Lane, Yelverton, Devon PL20 6BZ.

THOMAS, Michael Stuart, (Mike); Chairman: Corporate Communications Strategy, since 1988; Atalink Ltd, since 1998; SMF Displays Ltd, since 2000; Music Choice Group, since 2000; 422 Ltd, since 2001; Director, Metal Bulletin plc, since 1999; *b* 24 May 1944; *s* of Arthur Edward Thomas. *Educ:* Latymer Upper Sch.; King's Sch., Macclesfield; Liverpool Univ. (BA). Pres., Liverpool Univ. Guild of Undergraduates, 1965–66; Past Mem. Nat. Exec., NUS. Head of Research Dept, Co-operative Party, 1966–68; Sen. Res. Officer, Political and Economic Planning (now PSI), 1968–73; Dir, Volunteer Centre, 1973–74; Dir of Public Relations and Public Affairs, Dewe Rogerson, 1984–88; Mem.,

BR Western Reg. Bd, 1985–92; Chairman: Media Audits, 1990–2001; Fotorama (Holdings) Ltd, 1995–2000; Dir, Lopex plc, 1998–2000. MP (Lab and Co-op 1974–81, SDP 1981–83) Newcastle upon Tyne E, Oct. 1974–1983. Mem., Select Cttee on Nationalised Industries, 1975–79; Chm., PLP Trade Gp, 1979–81; SDP spokesman on health and social services, 1981–83; Member: SDP Nat. Cttee, 1981–90; SDP Policy Cttee, 1981–90; Chairman: Organisation Cttee of SDP, 1981–88; By-election Cttee, SDP, 1984–88; SDP Finance Working Gp, 1988–90; a Vice-Pres., SDP, 1988–90; Mem., Alliance Strategy Cttee, 1983–87. Contested: (SDP) Newcastle upon Tyne East, 1983; (SDP/Alliance) Exeter, 1987. Mem., USDAW; founder of parly jl The House Magazine. *Publications:* Participation and the Redcliffe Maud Report, 1970; (ed) The BBC Guide to Parliament, 1979, 1983; various PEP pamphlets, contribs, etc, 1971–; various articles, reviews, etc. *Recreations:* collecting pottery and medals relating to elections; theatre, music, cooking. *Address:* Milton Lodge, Iver, Bucks SL0 0AA. *T:* (01753) 772572. *Club:* Reform.

THOMAS, Michael T.; *see* Tilson Thomas.

THOMAS, Neville; *see* Thomas, R. N.

THOMAS, Norman, CBE 1980; HM Chief Inspector of Schools (Primary Education), 1973–81; Specialist Professor in Primary Education, University of Nottingham, 1987–88; *b* 1 June 1921; *s* of Bowen Thomas and Ada Thomas (*née* Redding); *m* 1942, Rose Henshaw; two *d*. *Educ:* Latymer's Sch., Edmonton; Camden Coll. Qual. Teacher. Commerce and Industry, then primary schs in London and Herts, 1948–56; Head, Longmeadow Sch., Stevenage, 1956–61; HM Inspector of Schools, Lincs and SE England, 1962–68; HMI, Staff Inspector for Primary (Junior and Middle) Schs, 1969–73. Chm., Cttee of Enquiry on Primary Educn in ILEA, 1983–84. Adviser to Parly Cttee on Educn, Science and Art, 1984–86, on Educn, 1994–97. Visiting Professor: NE London Polytechnic, 1984–86; Univ. of Herts (formerly Hatfield Poly.), 1991–; Hon. Prof., Univ. of Warwick, 1986–94. Hon. FCP 1988. Hon. DLitt Hertfordshire, 1998. *Publications:* Primary Education from Plowden to the 1990s, 1990; chapters in books and articles in professional jls. *Recreations:* photography, reading. *Address:* 19 Langley Way, Watford, Herts WD17 3EJ. *T:* (01923) 223766.

THOMAS, Owen John; Member (Plaid Cymru) Central South Wales, National Assembly for Wales, since 1999; *b* 3 Oct. 1939; *s* of late John Owen Thomas and Evelyn Jane Thomas; *m* 1985, Siân Wyn Evans; twin *s*; three *s* one *d* by a previous marriage. *Educ:* Glamorgan Coll. of Educn (Cert Ed 1971); UC, Cardiff (MA 1990). Tax Officer, Inland Revenue, 1956–61; Chemical Analyst, 1961–68; Primary Sch. Teacher, 1971–78; Dep. Headteacher, 1979–99. Shadow Minister for Culture, Sport and Welsh Lang., Nat. Assembly for Wales, 2001–. *Recreations:* reading, socialising. *Address:* 4 Llwyn y Grant Place, Penylan, Cardiff CF23 9EX. *T:* (home) (029) 2049 9868; (office) (029) 2089 8295. *Club:* Ifor Bach (Cardiff).

THOMAS, Patricia Anne; Commissioner for Local Administration in England, since 1985; Vice-Chairman, Commission for Local Administration in England, since 1994; *b* 3 April 1940; *d* of Frederick S. Lofts and Ann Elizabeth Lofts; *m* 1968, Joseph Glyn Thomas; one *s* two *d*. *Educ:* King's College London. LLB, LLM. Lectr in Law, Univ. of Leeds, 1962–63, 1964–68; Teaching Fellow, Univ. of Illinois, 1963–64; Sen. Lectr, then Principal Lectr, Head of Sch. of Law and Prof., Lancashire Polytechnic, 1973–85. Mem., 1976–84, Vice-Pres., 1984, Pres., 1985, Greater Manchester and Lancashire Rent Assessment Panel; Chm., Blackpool Supplementary Benefit Appeal Tribunal, 1980–85. Hon. Fellow, Lancashire Polytech., 1991. *Publication:* Law of Evidence, 1972. *Recreations:* farming, family. *Address:* Commission for Local Administration in England, Beverley House, Shipton Road, York YO30 5FZ. *T:* (01904) 663200.

THOMAS, Patrick Anthony; QC 1999; a Recorder, since 1992; *b* 30 Oct. 1948; *s* of Basil and Marjorie Thomas; *m* 1978, Sheila Jones; two *d*. *Educ:* Rugby Sch.; Lincoln Coll., Oxford (BA). Called to the Bar, Gray's Inn, 1973. *Recreations:* reading, theatre, walking. *Address:* 4 Fountain Court, Steelhouse Lane, Birmingham B4 6DR. *T:* (0121) 236 3476.

THOMAS, Paul; *see* Thomas, C. P.

THOMAS, Rear Adm. Paul Anthony Moseley, CB 1998; FREng, FIMechE; Director, Strategic Development, AEA Technology Nuclear Engineering, since 2000; *b* 27 Oct. 1944; *s* of Glyn Pritchard Thomas and Mary (*née* Moseley); *m* 1972, Rosalyn Patricia Lee; one *s* two *d*. *Educ:* Haileybury; London Univ. (BSc(Eng) 1969); MSc CNAA 1971. CEng 1985, FREng (FEng 1998); FIMechE 1993; MCGI 1995. Joined RN, 1963; Asst Marine Engr Officer, HMS Renown, 1971–77; Sen. Engr Officer, HMS Revenge, 1977–82 (mentioned in despatches, 1979); Asst Dir, Reactor Safety, 1982–84; Naval Superintendent, Vulcan Naval Reactor Test Estabt, Dounreay, 1984–87; Chm., Naval Nuclear Technical Safety Panel, 1987–90; Dir, Nuclear Propulsion, 1990–94; Captain, RNEC Manadon, 1994–95; Chief Strategic Systems Exec., MoD (PE), 1995–98. *Recreations:* cycling, sailing, ballooning, railways. *Address:* Byway, Chapel Lane, Box, Corsham, Wilts SN13 8NU.

THOMAS, Philip Lloyd, CMG 2001; HM Diplomatic Service; High Commissioner, Nigeria, since 2001; *b* 10 June 1948; *s* of Gwyn Thomas and Eileen Thomas (*née* Jenkins); one *s*. *Educ:* Dulwich Coll.; St John's Coll., Cambridge (MA). Joined HM Diplomatic Service, 1972; Third Sec., FCO, 1972–74; Second Sec., Belgrade, 1974–77, FCO, 1977–80; First Secretary: (Commercial), Madrid, 1981–87; UK Perm. Representation to EU, Brussels, 1987–89; Cabinet Office, 1989–91; Counsellor (Politico-Military), Washington, 1991–96; Head, Eastern Dept, FCO, 1996–98; Consul Gen., Düsseldorf, and Dir-Gen. for Trade and Investment Promotion in Germany, 1999–2000. *Address:* c/o Foreign and Commonwealth Office, King Charles Street, SW1A 2AH.

THOMAS, Prof. Phillip Charles, FRSE; FIBiol; FRAgS; Managing Director, Artilus Ltd, since 1999; Chairman, Animal Medicines Training Regulatory Authority, since 1999; Professor of Agriculture, University of Glasgow, 1987–99, now Emeritus; *b* 17 June 1942; *s* of William Charles Thomas and Gwendolen (*née* Emery); *m* 1967, Pamela Mary Hirst; one *s* one *d*. *Educ:* University College of North Wales, Bangor (BSc, PhD). FIBiol 1983; FRSE 1993; FRAgS 1997. Lectr in animal nutrition and physiology, Univ. of Leeds, 1966–71; progressively, SSO to SPSO, Hannah Research Inst., 1971–87; Principal: West of Scotland Coll., 1987–90; Scottish Agricl Coll., 1990–99. Hon. Prof., Edinburgh Univ., 1990–; Vis. Prof., Univ. of Glasgow, 1999–. Chm., Govt Adv. Cttee on Animal Feedingstuffs, 1999–2001; Mem., Scottish Food Adv. Cttee, 2000–. Chm., Central Scotland Countryside Trust, 2001–. *Publications:* (with J. A. F. Rook) Silage for Milk Production, 1982; (with J. A. F. Rook) Nutritional Physiology of Farm Animals, 1983. *Address:* 33 Cherry Tree Park, Balerno, Midlothian EH14 5AJ. *Club:* Farmers'.

THOMAS, Sir Quentin (Jeremy), Kt 1999; CB 1994; Head of Constitution Secretariat, Cabinet Office, 1998–99; *b* 1 Aug. 1944; *s* of late Arthur Albert Thomas and Edith Kathleen Thomas (*née* Bigg); *m* 1969, Anabel Jane, *d* of late J. H. Humphreys; one *s* two *d*. *Educ:* Perse School, Cambridge; Gonville and Caius College, Cambridge. Home Office, 1966; Private Sec. to Perm. Under-Sec. of State, 1970; Crime Policy Planning Unit, 1974–76; Sec. to Royal Commn on Gambling, 1976–78; Civil Service (Nuffield and Leverhulme) Travelling Fellowship, 1980–81; Head, Broadcasting Dept, Home Office, 1984–88; Under Sec., 1988–91, Dep. Sec., then Political Dir, 1991–98, NI Office. *Address:* 19 Claremont Road, Highgate, N6 5DA.

See also R. C. Thomas.

THOMAS, Dr Raymond Tudor, OBE 1994; Director, Turkey, British Council, since 2000; *b* 19 May 1946; *s* of Edgar William Thomas and Lilian Phylis Thomas; *m* 1973, Gloria Forsyth; two *s*. *Educ:* King's Sch., Macclesfield; Jesus Coll., Oxford (BA Modern Hist. 1968); Inst. of Internat. Relns, Univ. of WI (Dip. 1970); Univ. of Sussex (DPhil 1976). Tutor, Davies's Ltd, 1969–70; Lectr, Inst. of Internat. Relns, Trinidad, 1970–71; British Council: Assistant Representative: Morocco, 1974–77; Pakistan, 1977–80; Malaysia, 1980–82; Regl Rep., Sabah, Malaysia, 1982–84; Projects Officer, London, 1984–85; Dep. Dir 1985–88, Dir 1988–90, Educnl Contracts Dept; Dir, EC Relns, Brussels, 1990–95; Regl Dir, subseq. Policy Dir, Middle East and N Africa, 1995–2000. *Publication:* Britain and Vichy: the dilemma of Anglo-French relations 1940–42, 1979. *Recreations:* family life, travel, reading, fly-fishing. *Address:* British Council, PK 34, Ankara, Turkey.

THOMAS, Dr Reginald; Ambassador, retired; Lecturer on protocol, etiquette and diplomatic correspondence, Diplomatic Academy, Vienna, and in other foreign institutions, 1994–2001; *b* 28 Feb. 1928; *s* of Dr Leopold Thomas and Irma Thomas (*née* von Smekal); *m* 1960, Ingrid Renate Leitner; three *s* one *d*. *Educ:* Univ. of Vienna (Dr jur 1950). Entered Austrian Foreign Service, 1951; Austrian Legation, Bern, 1952–56; Dep. Legal Adviser on Internat. Law, Min. of Foreign Affairs, Vienna, 1956–59; Austrian Embassy, Tokyo, 1959–62; Head of Office of Sec. Gen. for Foreign Affairs, Vienna, 1962–68; Ambassador to Pakistan and concurrently accredited to Union of Burma, 1968–71; Ambassador to Japan and concurrently accredited to Republic of Korea, 1971–75; Head of Dept of Administration, Min. of Foreign Affairs, Vienna, 1975–82; concurrently Dep. Sec. Gen. for Foreign Affairs, Vienna, 1978–82; Austrian Ambassador to UK, 1982–87; Inspector Gen. in Min. of Foreign Affairs, Vienna, 1988–93. Mem., Austrian Assoc. for Foreign Policy and Internat. Relations, Vienna. Knight Comdr's Cross (Austria), 1993; Foreign orders include: Grand Cross: Order of the Rising Sun (Japan); Order of Diplomatic Service (Korea); Independence Order (Jordan); Order of F. de Miranda (Venezuela); Hilal-i-Qaid-i-Azam (Pakistan). *Recreation:* sports. *Address:* Schwarzenbergstrasse 8, 1010 Wien, Austria. *Club:* Queen's (Life Mem.).

THOMAS, Rev. Rhodri Glyn; *see* Thomas, Rev. H. R. G.

THOMAS, Richard; *see* Thomas, A. R.

THOMAS, Richard, CMG 1990; HM Diplomatic Service, retired; International Chairman, since 2000, and Trustee, since 1999, Leonard Cheshire; *b* 18 Feb. 1938; *s* of late Anthony Hugh Thomas, JP and of Molly Thomas, MBE; *m* 1966, Catherine Jane Hayes, Sydney, NSW; one *s* two *d*. *Educ:* Leighton Park; Merton Coll., Oxford (MA). Nat. Service, 2nd Lt, RASC, 1959–61. Entered CRO, later FCO, 1961; Accra, 1963–65; Lomé, 1965–66; UK Delegn NATO, Paris and Brussels, 1966–69; FCO, 1969–72; New Delhi, 1972–75; FCO, 1976–78; FCO Visiting Res. Fellow, RIIA, 1978–79; Counsellor, Prague, 1979–83; Ambassador, Iceland, 1983–86; Overseas Inspector, 1986–89; Ambassador to Bulgaria, 1989–94; High Comr, Eastern Caribbean, 1994–98. *Publication:* India's Emergence as an Industrial Power: Middle Eastern Contracts, 1982. *Recreations:* foreign parts, gardening, sketching. *Address:* Whole Farm Cottage, Stone-in-Oxney, Tenterden, Kent TN30 7JG.

THOMAS, Richard James, LLB; Director, Public Policy, Clifford Chance, since 1992; *b* 18 June 1949; *s* of Daniel Lewis Thomas, JP, and Norah Mary Thomas; *m* 1974, Julia Delicia, *d* of Dr E. G. W. Clarke; two *s* one *d*. *Educ:* Bishop's Stortford Coll.; Univ. of Southampton (LLB Hons); College of Law. Admitted Solicitor, 1973. Articled clerk and Asst Solicitor, Freshfields, 1971–74; Solicitor, CAB Legal Service, 1974–79; Legal Officer and Hd of Resources Gp, Nat. Consumer Council, 1979–86; Under Sec. and Dir of Consumer Affairs, OFT, 1986–92. Chm., British Univs N America Club, 1970–71; Trustee, W London Fair Housing Gp, 1976–79; Member: Management Cttee, Gtr London CAB Service, 1977–79; Legal Services Gp, Nat. Assoc. of CABx, 1978–86; Management Cttee, Royal Courts of Justice CAB, 1992–; London Electricity Cons. Council, 1979–84; European Consumer Law Gp, 1981–86; European Commn Working Party on Access to Justice, 1981–82; Cttee of City of Westminster Law Soc., 1984–86; Lord Chancellor's Adv. Cttee on Civil Justice Rev., 1985–88; Council, Office of Banking Ombudsman, 1992–; Adv. Cttee, Oftel, 1995–; Advertising Adv. Cttee, ITC, 1996–; Bd, Financial Ombudsman Service, 1999–. FRSA 1992. *Publications:* reports, articles and broadcasts on range of legal and consumer issues. *Recreations:* family, maintenance of home and garden, travel. *Address:* Clifford Chance, 200 Aldersgate Street, EC1A 4JJ.

THOMAS, Rita Margaret Easen-; *see* Donaghy, R. M.

THOMAS, Sir Robert (Evan), Kt 1967; DL, JP; Leader, Greater Manchester Metropolitan County Council, 1973–77; Deputy Chairman, Manchester Ship Canal, 1971–74; *b* 8 Oct. 1901; *s* of Jesse and Anne Thomas; *m* 1924, Edna Isherwood (*d* 1992); one *s* one *d*. *Educ:* St Peter's, Leigh, Lancs. Miner, 1914; served Army, 1919–21; Bus Driver, 1924–37; Trade Union Official, 1937–66; Member, Manchester City Council, 1944–74; Lord Mayor of Manchester, 1962–63. Chairman: Assoc. of Municipal Corps, 1973–74; Assoc. of Metropolitan Authorities, 1974–77; British Sector, Internat. Union of Local Authorities, 1974–77. JP Manchester, 1948; DL: County Palatine of Lancaster, 1967–73, County Palatine of Greater Manchester, 1974. Hon. MA Manchester, 1974. *Publication:* Sir Bob (autobiog.), 1984. *Recreations:* gardening, golf. *Address:* Gorton Parks, 121 Taylor Street, Gorton, Manchester M18 8DF.

THOMAS, Dr Robert Kemeys, FRS 1998; Lecturer in Physical Chemistry, University of Oxford, since 1978; Fellow, University College, Oxford, since 1978; *b* 25 Sept. 1941; *s* of Preb. H. S. G. Thomas and Dr A. P. Thomas; *m* 1968, Pamela Woods; one *s* two *d*. *Educ:* Radley Coll., Abingdon; St John's Coll., Oxford (MA, DPhil 1968). Royal Soc. Pickering Fellow, 1970–75; Fellow, Merton Coll., Oxford, 1975–78. Hon. Prof., Inst. of Chemistry, Chinese Acad. of Scis, Beijing, 1999–. *Publications:* contribs to chemical jls. *Recreations:* flora, funghi, music, Chinese language. *Address:* University College, High Street, Oxford OX1 4BH. *T:* (01865) 276602.

THOMAS, (Robert) Neville; QC 1975; barrister-at-law; a Recorder of the Crown Court, 1975–82; *b* 31 March 1936; *s* of Robert Derfel Thomas and Enid Anne Thomas; *m* 1970, Jennifer Anne Brownrigg; one *s* one *d*. *Educ:* Ruthin Sch.; University Coll., Oxford (MA, BCL). Called to Bar, Inner Temple, 1962, Bencher, 1985. *Recreations:* fishing, walking, gardening, reading. *Address:* Glansevern, Berriew, Welshpool, Powys SY21 8AH. *Club:* Garrick.

THOMAS, Roger; *see* Thomas, D. R.

THOMAS, Prof. Roger Christopher, FRS 1989; Professor and Head of Department of Physiology, University of Cambridge, since 1996; Fellow, Downing College, Cambridge, since 1996; *b* 2 June 1939; *e s* of late Arthur Albert Thomas and Edith Kathleen (*née* Bigg); *m* 1964, Monica Mary, *d* of late Lt-Comdr William Peter Querstret, RN; two *s*. *Educ:* Perse Sch., Cambridge; Univ. of Southampton (BSc, PhD). Res. Associate, Rockefeller Univ., NY, 1964–66; Hon. Res. Asst, Biophysics, UCL, 1966–69; Bristol University: Lectr, 1969–77; Reader in Physiology, 1977–86; Prof. of Physiol., 1986–96; Hd of Dept of Physiol., 1985–90; Dean, Faculty of Science, 1990–93. Vis. Prof., Yale Univ., 1979–80. *Publications:* Ion-Sensitive Intracellular Microelectrodes, 1978; many papers on ion transport in learned jls. *Recreation:* cooking. *Address:* Department of Physiology, Downing Street, Cambridge CB2 3EG. *T:* (01223) 333869, *Fax:* (01223) 333840; *e-mail:* rct26@cam.ac.uk.
See also Sir Q. J. Thomas.

THOMAS, Roger Humphrey; strategy consultant; Chairman, Abbeystone Construction Ltd, since 1997; Chairman and Managing Director, Black & Decker, 1983–96; *b* 12 April 1942; *s* of Cyril Lewis Thomas and Phyllis Amy Thomas; *m* 1962, Myfanwy Ruth, (Nikki), Nicholas; three *s*. *Educ:* Slough Grammar School. FCCA. Black & Decker, 1970–96. Non-exec. Dir, Scholl plc, 1997–. *Recreations:* theatre, DIY, golf. *Address:* Hartley Grange, Parsonage Lane, Farnham Common, Bucks SL2 3PA. *T:* (01753) 647291.

THOMAS, Hon. Sir (Roger) John Laugharne, Kt 1996; **Hon. Mr Justice Thomas;** a Judge of the High Court of Justice, Queen's Bench Division, since 1996; Presiding Judge, Wales and Chester Circuit, 1998–2001; *b* 22 Oct. 1947; *s* of Roger Edward Laugharne Thomas and Dinah Agnes Thomas, Cwmgiedd; *m* 1973, Elizabeth Ann, *d* of S. J. Buchanan, Ohio, USA; one *s* one *d*. *Educ:* Rugby School; Trinity Hall, Cambridge (BA); Univ. of Chicago (Commonwealth Fellow; JD). Called to Bar, Gray's Inn, 1969, Bencher, 1992; QC 1984; a Recorder, 1987–96; Judge of the Commercial Court, 1996–. Asst Teacher, Mayo College, Ajmer, India, 1965–66; Lord Morris of Borth-y-Gest Lectr, Univ. of Wales, 2000. Faculty Fellow, Law Sch., Univ. of Southampton, 1990. DTI Inspector, Mirror Gp Newspapers plc, 1992. *Publications:* papers and articles on commercial, maritime and insurance law, the Welsh courts and devolution. *Recreations:* gardens, walking, travel. *Address:* Royal Courts of Justice, Strand, WC2A 2LL. *T:* (020) 7947 6399; *e-mail:* jthomas@lix.compulink.co.uk.

THOMAS, Roger Lloyd; Senior Clerk (Acting), Committee Office, House of Commons, 1979–84 and Clerk, Select Committee on Welsh Affairs, 1982–84, retired; *b* 7 Feb. 1919; *er s* of Trevor John Thomas and Eleanor Maud (*née* Jones), Abercarn, Mon; *m* 1945, Stella Mary, *d* of Reginald Ernest Willmett, Newport, Mon; three *s* one *d*. *Educ:* Barry County Sch.; Magdalen Coll., Oxford (Doncaster Schol.; Heath Harrison Trav. Schol.). BA 2nd Mod. Langs, 1939; MA 1946. Pres., OU Italian Soc., 1938–39. Served 1939–46, RA and Gen. Staff (Major GSO2) in India, Middle East, N Africa, Italy and Germany. Civil Servant, 1948–70: Min. of Fuel and Power, Home Office, Treasury, Welsh Office and Min. of Housing and Local Govt; Private Sec. to Perm. Under-Sec. of State, Home Office, 1950 and to successive Parly Under-Secs of State, 1951–53; Sec., Interdeptl Cttee on powers of Subpoena, 1960; Asst Sec., 1963; Sec., Aberfan Inquiry Tribunal, 1966–67; Chm., Working Party on Building by Direct Labour Organisations, 1968–69; Gen. Manager, The Housing Corporation, 1970–73; Asst Sec., DoE, 1974–79. *Publications:* sundry reports. *Recreation:* growing flowers. *Address:* 5 Park Avenue, Caterham, Surrey CR3 6AH. *T:* (01883) 342080. *Club:* Union (Oxford).
See also D. H. P. Thomas.

THOMAS, Roger Lloyd; QC 1994; a Recorder, since 1987; *b* 7 Feb. 1947; *s* of David Eyron Thomas, CBE and Marie Lloyd Thomas; *m* 1974, Susan Nicola Orchard; one *s* one *d*. *Educ:* Cathays High Sch., Cardiff; University Coll. of Wales Aberystwyth (LLB). Called to the Bar, Gray's Inn, 1969. *Recreations:* tennis, music, reading. *Address:* 9 Park Place, Cardiff CF1 3DP. *T:* (029) 2038 2731. *Club:* Cardiff Lawn Tennis.

THOMAS, Roger Martin; QC 2000; *b* 18 Aug. 1954; *s* of Donald Thomas and Jessie Thomas (*née* Attwood); *m* 1981, Vanessa Julia Valentine Stirum; one *s* two *d*. *Educ:* Worksop Coll., Notts; Univ. of Hull (LLB). Called to the Bar, Inner Temple, 1976. *Recreation:* sport. *Address:* Croft House, 35 Westgate, Almondbury, Huddersfield, Yorks HD5 8XF.

THOMAS, Roger R.; *see* Ridley-Thomas.

THOMAS, Ronald Richard; *b* March 1929. *Educ:* Ruskin Coll. and Balliol Coll., Oxford (MA). Sen. Lectr, Econ. and Indust. Studies, Univ. of Bristol. Contested (Lab): Bristol North-West, Feb. 1974; Bristol East, 1987; MP (Lab) Bristol NW, Oct. 1974–1979. Former Mem., Bristol DC. Mem. ASTMS. *Address:* 64 Morris Road, Lockleaze, Bristol BS7 9TA.

THOMAS, Roydon Urquhart; QC 1985; a Recorder, since 1986; *b* 17 May 1936; *s* of Rowland Daniel Thomas and Jean Milne Thomas; *m* (marr. diss.); one *s* one *d* (and one *s* decd). *Educ:* Fettes College; Sidney Sussex College, Cambridge (BA). Called to the Bar, Middle Temple, 1960, Bencher, 1993; South Eastern Circuit. *Publication:* (Asst Editor) Tolstoy on Divorce, 1964. *Recreations:* golf, fishing, erratic ski-ing. *Address:* 1 Essex Court, Temple, EC4Y 9AR. *T:* (020) 7583 2000. *Clubs:* Hurlingham; High Post Golf.

THOMAS, Simon; MP (Plaid Cymru) Ceredigion, since Feb. 2000; *b* Aberdare, 28 Dec. 1963; *m* 1997, Gwen Lloyd Davies; one *s* one *d*. *Educ:* UCW, Aberystwyth (BA Hons Welsh 1985); Coll. of Librarianship, Aberystwyth (Post-grad. DipLib 1988). Asst Curator, Nat. Liby of Wales, Aberystwyth, 1986–92; Policy and Res. Officer, Taff-Ely BC, 1992–94; Develt Officer, 1994–97, Manager, Jigso, 1997–2000, Wales Council for Voluntary Action. Mem. (Plaid Cymru) Ceredigion CC, 1999–2000. Vice Chm., Parly Envmt Gp, 2000–; Mem., Envmtl Audit Cttee, 2000–. Plaid Cymru: Member: Nat. Exec., 1995–98; Nat. Assembly Policy Gp, 1997–99; Policy Forum, 1999– (Policy Co-ordinator for the Envmt). *Publications:* As Good as Our Words: guidelines for the use of Welsh by voluntary organisations, 1996; Plaid Cymru election manifestos, 1997, 1999; contrib. numerous articles in Welsh and English lang. jls. *Recreations:* culture and literature, cycling, family life. *Address:* House of Commons, SW1A 0AA. *T:* (020) 7219 5021; *e-mail:* thomassi@parliament.uk; (office) 8 Heol y Dwr, Aberaeron, Ceredigion SA46 0DG. *T:* (01545) 571688, *Fax:* (01545) 571567.

THOMAS, Rt Hon. Sir Swinton (Barclay), Kt 1985; PC 1994; a Lord Justice of Appeal, 1994–2000; *b* 12 Jan. 1931; *s* of late Brig. William Bain Thomas, CBE, DSO, and Mary Georgina Thomas; *m* 1967, Angela, Lady Cope; one *s* one *d*. *Educ:* Ampleforth Coll.; Lincoln Coll., Oxford (Scholar) (MA). Served with Cameronians (Scottish Rifles), 1950–51, Lieut. Called to Bar, Inner Temple, 1955 (Bencher, 1983; Reader, 2000; Treas., 2001); QC 1975; a Recorder of the Crown Court, 1975–85; a Judge of the High Court of Justice, Family Div., 1985–90, QBD, 1990–94. A Presiding Judge, Western Circuit, 1987–90. Member: General Council of the Bar, 1970–74; Criminal Injuries Compensation Bd, 1984–85; Vice-Chm., Parole Bd, 1994 (Mem., 1992–95). *Recreations:* reading, travel. *Club:* Garrick.

THOMAS, Trevor Anthony, FRCA; Consultant Anaesthetist, United Bristol Healthcare NHS Trust (formerly United Bristol Hospitals), since 1972; *b* 16 March 1939; *s* of Arthur William Thomas and Gladys Mary Gwendoline Thomas (*née* Hulin); *m* 1965, Yvonne Louise Mary Branch; one *s*. *Educ:* Bristol Grammar Sch.; Univ. of St Andrews (MB ChB 1964). FRCA (FFARCS 1969). Chm., Dept of Anaesthesia, United Bristol Hosps, 1977–80; Hon. Clin. Sen. Lectr, Bristol Univ., 1980–. SW Regl Assessor in Anaesthesia, 1978–2000, Central Assessor, 1999–, Confidential Enquiries into Maternal Deaths in UK (formerly Confidential Enquiry into Maternal Deaths in England and Wales). Chm., Med. Cttee, Bristol and Weston DHA, 1988–90. Mem. Council, 1989–96, Hon. Sec., 1994, Sect. of Anaesthetists, RSocMed; Obstetric Anaesthetists Association: Mem. Cttee, 1978–85; Minute Sec., 1980–81; Hon. Sec., 1981–85; Mem. Cttee and Pres. Elect, 1994–95; Pres., 1995–99; Society of Anaesthetists, SW Region: Mem. Cttee, 1975–85; Hon. Sec., 1985–88; Pres., 1997–98. Examr, Fellowship Exams, RCAnaes, 1985–96. Trustee and Mem. Council, St Peter's Hospice, 1996–. Asst Ed., 1975–76, Ed., 1976–80, Anaesthesia Points West. *Publications:* (with A. Holdcroft) Principles and Practice of Obstetric Anaesthesia and Analgesia, 2000; contrib. chapters to textbooks; contribs to learned jls, mainly on matters related to obstetric anaesthesia. *Recreations:* music, theatre, scuba diving, shooting. *Address:* 14 Cleeve Lawns, Downend, Bristol BS16 6HJ. *Club:* Royal Society of Medicine.

THOMAS, Victor Gerald B.; *see* Bulmer-Thomas.

THOMAS, Vivian Elliott Sgrifan, CBE 1998 (OBE 1992); Chairman, British Standards Institution, since 1992; *b* 13 March 1932; *s* of William Edward Thomas and Cicely (*née* Elliott); *m* 1962, Valerie Slade Thomas; one *s* one *d*. *Educ:* Swindon High Sch.; Southampton Univ. (1st Class Marine Engrg). Engr Officer, Union Castle Line, 1953–58; with British Petroleum plc, 1959–92; Chief Exec. Officer, BP Oil UK Ltd, 1989–92. Director: Southern Water plc, 1992–96; Jaguar Ltd, 1993–; Gowrings Plc, 1992–. *Recreations:* golf, music, theatre. *Address:* Camelot, Bennett Way, West Clandon, Guildford, Surrey GU4 7TN. *T:* (01483) 222665. *Club:* Royal Automobile.

THOMAS, Maj.-Gen. Walter Babington, CB 1971; DSO 1943; MC and Bar, 1942; Commander, HQ Far East Land Forces, Nov. 1970–Nov. 1971 (Chief of Staff, April-Oct. 1970); retired Jan. 1972; *b* Nelson, NZ, 29 June 1919; *s* of Walter Harington Thomas, Farmer; *m* 1947, Iredale Edith Lauchlan (*née* Trent); three *d*. *Educ:* Motueka Dist High Sch., Nelson, NZ. Clerk, Bank of New Zealand, 1936–39. Served War of 1939–45 (despatches, MC and Bar, DSO): 2nd NZEF, 1940–46, in Greece, Crete, Western Desert, Tunis and Italy; Comd 23 (NZ) Bn, 1944–45; Comd 22 (NZ) Bn, in Japan, 1946; transf. to Brit. Army, Royal Hampshire Regt, 1947; Bde Major, 39 Inf. Bde Gp, 1953–55 (despatches); GSO2, UK JSLS, Aust., 1958–60; AA&QMG, HQ 1 Div. BAOR, 1962–64; Comd 12 Inf. Bde Gp, 1964–66; IDC, 1967; GOC 5th Div., 1968–70. Silver Star, Medal, 1945 (USA). *Publications:* Dare to be Free, 1951; Touch of Pitch, 1956. *Recreation:* riding. *Address:* Kerry Road, M/S 413, Beaudesert, Qld 4285, Australia.

THOMAS, (William) David; a District Judge (Magistrates' Courts) (formerly Stipendiary Magistrate), South Yorkshire, since 1989; *b* 10 Oct. 1941; *s* of Arnold and Ada Thomas; *m* 1st, 1966, Cynthia Janice Jackson (marr. diss. 2000); one *s* two *d*; 2nd, 2000, Mrs Muriel Hainsworth. *Educ:* Whitcliffe Mount Grammar Sch., Cleckheaton; LSE (LLB Hons 1963); Part II, Law Society Finals, 1964. Admitted Solicitor, 1966. Asst Solicitor 1966, Partner, 1967–89, Finn Gledhill & Co., Halifax. *Publications:* contribs to Yorkshire Ridings Magazine and Pennine Radio, Bradford. *Recreations:* Rugby, theatre, ballet, gardening. *Address:* Bradford Magistrates' Court, PO Box 187, The Tyrls, Bradford BD1 1JL. *T:* (01274) 390111. *Club:* Halifax Rugby Union Football.

THOMAS, William Fremlyn Cotter; His Honour Judge Thomas; a Circuit Judge, since 1990; *b* 18 March 1935; *s* of Stephen Kerr Thomas and Nâdine Dieudonnée Thomas (*née* March); *m* 1st, 1960, Mary Alanna Mudie (decd); one *d*; 2nd, 1968, Thalia Mary Edith Myers (marr. diss. 1975); 3rd, 1978, Hon. Ursula Nancy Eden, *d* of 7th Baron Henley and of Nancy, Lady Henley; one *s* one *d*. *Educ:* Bryanston Sch., Dorset; University Coll., Oxford. National Service, 2nd Lieut, 1954–56. Called to the Bar, Inner Temple, 1961; SE Circuit; a Recorder, 1986. *Recreations:* music, architecture. *Address:* The Crown Court, 6–8 Penrhyn Road, Kingston upon Thames, Surrey KT1 2BB. *Club:* Reform.

THOMAS, Sir William James Cooper, 2nd Bt *cr* 1919; TD; JP; DL; Captain RA; *b* 7 May 1919; *er s* of Sir William James Thomas, 1st Bt, and Maud Mary Cooper, Bexhill-on-Sea; *S* father, 1945; *m* 1947, Freida Dunbar (*d* 1990), *yr d* of late F. A. Whyte; two *s* one *d*. *Educ:* Harrow; Downing Coll., Cambridge. Barrister, Inner Temple, 1948. Member TA, 1938. Served War of 1939–45. Monmouthshire: JP 1958; DL 1973; High Sheriff, 1973. *Heir: s* William Michael Thomas, *b* 5 Dec. 1948. *Address:* Tump House, Llanrothal, Monmouth, Gwent NP5 3QL. *T:* (01600) 712757.

THOMAS, Ven. William Jordison; Archdeacon of Northumberland, 1983–92, Archdeacon Emeritus 1993; *b* 16 Dec. 1927; *s* of Henry William and Dorothy Newton Thomas; *m* 1954, Kathleen Jeffrey Robson, *d* of William Robson, Reaveley, Powburn, Alnwick. *Educ:* Holmwood Prep. School, Middlesbrough; Acklam Hall Grammar School, Middlesbrough; Giggleswick School; King's Coll., Cambridge (BA 1951, MA 1955); Cuddesdon College. National Service, RN, 1946–48. Assistant Curate: St Anthony of Egypt, Newcastle upon Tyne, 1953–56; Berwick Parish Church, 1956–59; Vicar: Alwinton with Holystone and Alnham and the Lordship of Kidland, 1959–70; Alston with Garrigill, Nenthead and Kirkhaugh, 1970–80, i/c Knaresdale, 1973–80; Industrial Chaplain, 1972–80; Team Rector of Glendale, 1980–82; RD of Bamburgh and Glendale, 1980–82. Travel leader, chaplain and lectr, 1992–. Hon. Chaplain: Actors' Church Union, 1953–56; Northumberland County NFU, 1978–2000. Harbour Comr, N Sunderland, 1990–92. *Recreations:* sailing own dinghy and other people's yachts, making pictures, travelling and making magic. *Address:* Wark Cottage, Whittingham, Alnwick, Northumberland NE66 4RB. *T:* (01665) 574300. *Clubs:* Victory Services; Northern Constitutional (Newcastle upon Tyne).

THOMAS, Sir (William) Michael (Marsh), 3rd Bt *cr* 1918; *b* 4 Dec. 1930; *s* of Sir William Eustace Rhyddlad Thomas, 2nd Bt, and Enid Helena Marsh; *S* father 1957; *m* 1957, Geraldine Mary, *d* of Robert Drysdale, Anglesey; three *d*. *Educ:* Oundle School, Northants. Formerly Man. Dir, Gors Nurseries Ltd. *Address:* Belan, Rhosneigr, Gwynedd LL64 5JE.

THOMAS, Wyndham, CBE 1982; Chairman, Cambridge New Town Corporation PLC, since 1999; *b* 1 Feb. 1924; *s* of Robert John Thomas and Hannah Mary; *m* 1947, Elizabeth Terry Hopkin; one *s* three *d*. *Educ:* Maesteg Grammar School. Served Army (Lieut, Royal Welch Fusiliers), 1943–47. Schoolmaster, 1950–53; Director, Town and Country Planning Association, 1955–67; Gen. Manager, Peterborough New Town Develt Corp., 1968–83; Chm., Inner City Enterprises, 1983–92. Member: Land

Commission, 1967–68; Commission for the New Towns, 1964–68; Property Adv. Gp, DoE, 1978–90; London Docklands Develt Corp., 1981–88. Chm., House Builders' Fedn Commn of Inquiry into Housebuilding and the Inner Cities, 1986–87 (report published 1987). Mayor of Hemel Hempstead, 1958–59. Contested (Lab) SW Herts, 1955. Hon. MRTPI 1979 (Mem. Council, 1989–98). Officer of the Order of Orange-Nassau (Netherlands), 1982. *Publications:* many articles on town planning, housing, etc, in learned jls. *Recreations:* collecting/restoring old furniture, work, golf. *Address:* 8 Westwood Park Road, Peterborough PE3 6JL. *T:* (01733) 564399.

THOMAS, Wynn; *see* Thomas, M. W.

THOMASON, Prof. George Frederick, CBE 1983; Montague Burton Professor of Industrial Relations, University College, Cardiff, 1969–85, now Emeritus; *b* 27 Nov. 1927; *s* of George Frederick Thomason and Eva Elizabeth (*née* Walker); *m* 1953, Jean Elizabeth Horsley; one *s* one *d*. *Educ:* Kelsick Grammar Sch.; Univ. of Sheffield (BA); Univ. of Toronto (MA); PhD (Wales). CIPM, FIMgt. University College, Cardiff: Research Asst, 1953; Asst Lectr, 1954; Research Associate, 1956; Lectr, 1959; Asst Man. Dir, Flex Fasteners Ltd, Rhondda, 1960; University College, Cardiff: Lectr, 1962; Sen. Lectr, 1963; Reader, 1969; Dean, Faculty of Economics, 1971–73; Dep. Principal (Humanities), 1974–77. Member: Doctors' and Dentists' Pay Review Body, 1979–95; Pay Rev. Body for Nurses, Midwives, Health Service Visitors and Professions allied to Medicine, 1983–95. Chm., Prosthetic and Orthotic Worldwide Educn and Relief, 1995–. *Publications:* Welsh Society in Transition, 1963; Personnel Manager's Guide to Job Evaluation, 1968; Professional Approach to Community Work, 1969; The Management of Research and Development, 1970; Improving the Quality of Organization, 1973; Textbook of Personnel Management, 1975, 5th edn as Textbook of Human Resource Management, 1988; Job Evaluation: Objectives and Methods, 1980; Textbook of Industrial Relations Management, 1984. *Recreation:* gardening. *Address:* Ty Gwyn, 149 Lake Road West, Cardiff CF23 5PJ. *T:* (029) 2075 4236.

THOMASON, (Kenneth) Roy, OBE 1986; Chairman, Charminster Estates Ltd, since 1998; director of property companies; solicitor; *b* 14 Dec. 1944; *s* of Thomas Roger and Constance Dora Thomason; *m* 1969, Christine Ann (*née* Parsons); two *s* two *d*. *Educ:* Cheney Sch., Oxford; London Univ. (LLB). Admitted Solicitor, 1969; Partner, 1970–91, Sen. Partner, 1979–91, Horden & George, Bournemouth. Mem., Bournemouth Council, 1970–92 (Leader, 1974–82; past Chm. Policy, Ways and Means, and Finance Cttees). Association of District Councils: Mem. Council, 1979–91; Leader, 1981–87; Chm., 1987–91; Chm., Housing and Environmental Health Cttee, 1983–87. Mem., Cons. Nat. Local Govt Adv. Cttee, 1981–97; various Cons. Party positions at constituency and area level, 1966–97 (Constituency Chm., 1981–82); contested (C) Newport E, 1983. MP (C) Bromsgrove, 1992–97. Member: Envmt Select Cttee, 1992–97; Jt Statutory Instrument Cttee, 1992–97; Chm., All-Party Export Gp, 1996–97 (Sec., 1993–96); Vice Chm., Cons. Parly Envmt Cttee, 1993–97. Fellow, Industry and Parlt Trust, 1996. FRSA. *Recreations:* walking, reading, architectural history, involvment with vilaage church (Treas.) and other local activities. *Address:* Fockbury House, Fockbury, Dodford, Bromsgrove, Worcs B61 9AP.

THOMPSON; *see* Pullein-Thompson.

THOMPSON, Alan, CB 1978; Chairman, Review Group on the Youth Service 1981–82; *b* 16 July 1920; *s* of Herbert and Esther Thompson; *m* 1944, Joyce Nora Banks (*d* 2000); two *s* one *d*. *Educ:* Carlisle Grammar Sch.; Queen's Coll., Oxford. Joined Min. of Education, 1946; Private Sec. to Minister of Education, 1954–56; Asst Sec., Further Education Br., 1956–64; Under Sec., UGC, 1964–71; Under Sec., Science Br., DES, 1971–75; Dep. Sec., DES, 1975–80. *Address:* 1 Haven Close, Wimbledon, SW19 5JW.

THOMPSON, Prof. Alan Eric; A. J. Balfour Professor of the Economics of Government, 1972–87, Professor Emeritus, since 1987, Heriot-Watt University; *b* 16 Sept. 1924; *o c* of late Eric Joseph Thompson and of Florence Thompson; *m* 1960, Mary Heather Long; three *s* one *d*. *Educ:* University of Edinburgh (MA 1949, MA (Hons Class I, Economic Science), 1951, PhD 1953, Carnegie Research Scholar, 1951–52). FSAScot 1995. Served army (including service with Central Mediterranean Forces), World War II. Asst in Political Economy, 1952–53, Lectr in Economics (formerly Political Economy), 1953–59, and 1964–71, Univ. of Edinburgh. Parly Adviser to Scottish Television, 1966–76; Scottish Governor, BBC, 1976–79. Visiting Professor, Graduate School of Business, Stanford Univ., USA, 1966, 1968. Contested (Lab) Galloway, 1950 and 1951; MP (Lab) Dunfermline, 1959–64. Mem., Speaker's Parly Delegn to USA, 1962. Chm., Adv. Bd on Economics Educn (Esmée Fairbairn Research Project), 1970–76; Jt Chm., Scottish-Soviet Co-ordinating Cttee for Trade and Industry, 1985–90; Member: Scottish Cttee, Public Schools Commn, 1969–70; Cttee enquiring into conditions of service life for young servicemen, 1969; Scottish Council for Adult Educn in HM Forces, 1973–; Jt Mil. Educn Cttee, Edinburgh and Heriot-Watt Univs, 1975–; Local Govt Boundary Commn for Scotland, 1975–82; Royal Fine Art Commn for Scotland, 1975–80; Adv. Bd, Defence Finance Unit, Heriot-Watt Univ., 1987–90; Chm., Northern Offshore (Maritime) Resources Study, 1974–77; Chm., Edinburgh Cttee, Peace Through NATO, 1984–. Parly Adviser, Pharmaceutical Gen. Council (Scotland), 1984–2000. Hon. Vice-Pres., Assoc. of Nazi War Camp Survivors, 1960–; Pres., Edinburgh Amenity and Transport Assoc., 1970–75; Dir, Scottish AIDS Res. Foundn, 1988–. Chm. of Governors, Newbattle Abbey Coll., 1980–82 (Governor, 1975–82); Governor, Leith Nautical Coll., 1981–;85 Trustee, Bell's Nautical Trust, 1981–85. Has broadcast and appeared on TV (economic and political talks and discussions) in Britain and USA. FRSA 1972. *Publications:* Development of Economic Doctrine (jtly), 1980; contribs to learned journals. *Recreations:* writing children's stories and plays, bridge, croquet. *Address:* 11 Upper Gray Street, Edinburgh EH9 1SN. *T:* (0131) 667 2140; Ardtrostan Cottage, St Fillans, Perthshire PH6 2NL. *T:* (01764) 685275. *Clubs:* New (Edinburgh); Loch Earn Sailing.

THOMPSON, Anthony Arthur Richard; QC 1980; **His Honour Judge Anthony Thompson;** a Circuit Judge, since 1992; Designated Civil Judge for Hampshire and Dorset, since 1999; *b* 4 July 1932; *s* of late William Frank McGregor Thompson and Doris Louise Thompson (*née* Hill); *m* 1958, Françoise Alix Marie Reynier; two *s* one *d* (and one *s* decd). *Educ:* Latymer Upper Sch.; University Coll., Oxford; La Sorbonne. FCIArb 1991. Called to the Bar, Inner Temple, 1957, Bencher, 1986; admitted to Paris Bar, 1988; a Recorder, 1985–92; Liaison Judge for Cornwall, 1993–99; Resident Judge for Cornwall, 1995–99. Chm., Bar European Gp, 1984–86 (Vice-Chm., 1982–84); Mem., Internat. Relations Cttee, Bar Council, 1984–86. QC, St Vincent and the Grenadines, 1986. Vice Pres., Cornwall Magistrates' Assoc., 1995–. Contested (Lab) Arundel and Shoreham, Oct. 1964. *Recreations:* food and wine, lawn tennis, theatre, cinema, 19th century music, 20th century painting. *Address:* Law Courts, Winchester, Hants SO23 9EL. *Club:* Roehampton.

THOMPSON, Aubrey Gordon D.; *see* Denton-Thompson.

THOMPSON, Bruce Kevin, MA; Head, Strathallan School, since 2000; *b* 14 Nov. 1959; *s* of Keith Bruce Thompson, *qv*; *m* 1993, Fabienne Goddet; two *d*. *Educ:* Newcastle High Sch., Newcastle-under-Lyme; New Coll., Oxford (MA Lit.Hum.). Asst Master, 1983–86, Head of Classics, 1986–94, Cheltenham Coll.; Dep. Rector, Dollar Acad., 1994–2000. *Recreations:* coaching Rugby, weight training, rowing, literature, music. *Address:* c/o Strathallan School, Forgandenny, Perth PH2 9EG. *T:* (01738) 815000. *Club:* Leander (Henley-on-Thames).

THOMPSON, Charles Allister; HM Diplomatic Service, retired; *b* 21 July 1922; *yr s* of late Herbert Ivie and Margaret (*née* Browne-Webber) Thompson, Managua, Nicaragua; *m* 1950, Jean Margaret, *er d* of late Alexander Bruce Dickson; one *s* two *d* (and one *s* decd). *Educ:* Haileybury; Hertford Coll., Oxford (MA, BLitt). War Service, 1942–46, 1st King's Dragoon Guards. Joined Foreign Service (now Diplomatic Service), 1947, and served in FO until 1949; 3rd Sec., Prague, 1949–50; 2nd Sec. (Commercial), Mexico City, 1950–53; FO 1953–56; 1st Sec., Karachi, 1956–59; Head of Chancery, Luxembourg, 1959–62; FO, 1962–65; Counsellor, 1965; Dep. Consul-Gen., New York, 1965–67; Dep. High Comr, Port of Spain, 1967–70; HM Consul-Gen., Philadelphia, 1970–74; Vis. Fellow, Centre for Internat. Studies, LSE, 1974–75; Head of Training Dept, FCO, and Dir, Diplomatic Service Language Centre, 1975–76. Founding Chm., HELP Jávea, 1978. *Recreations:* gardening, golf, gerontology. *Address:* Calle San Joaquín 9–4° 25, Jávea 03730, Alicante, Spain. *T:* (96) 5792283.

THOMPSON, Charles Norman, CBE 1978; CChem; FRSC; Head of Research and Development Liaison, and Health, Safety and Environment Administration, Shell UK Ltd, 1978–82, retired; Consultant to Shell UK Ltd, since 1982; *b* 23 Oct. 1922; *s* of Robert Norman Thompson and Evelyn Tivendale Thompson (*née* Wood); *m* 1946, Pamela Margaret Wicks; one *d*. *Educ:* Birkenhead Institute; Liverpool Univ. (BSc). Research Chemist, Thornton Research Centre (Shell Refining & Marketing Co. Ltd), 1943; Lectr, Petroleum Chemistry and Technology, Liverpool Coll. of Technology, 1947–51; Personnel Supt and Dep. Associate Manager, Thornton Research Centre, Shell Research Ltd, 1959–61; Dir (Res. Admin), Shell Research Ltd, 1961–78. Mem. Council, 1976–82, Vice Pres., 1977–80, 1981–82, Inst. of Petroleum (Chm., Res. Adv. Cttee, 1973–82). Pres., RIC, 1976–78. Chairman: Professional Affairs Bd, 1980–84, Water Chemistry Forum, 1987–90, RSC; Council of Science and Technology Insts, 1981–83 (Chm., Health Care Scientific Adv. Cttee, 1986–94); Bd Mem., Thames Water Authority, 1980–87; Member: Technician Educn Council, 1980–83; Ct, Univ. of Surrey, 1980–; Parly and Scientific Cttee, 1976–. *Publications:* Reviews of Petroleum Technology, vol. 13: insulating and hydraulic oils, 1953; numerous papers in Jl Inst. Petroleum, Chem. and Ind., Chem. in Brit., on hydrocarbon dielectrics, insulating oils, diffusion as rate-limiting factor in oxidation, antioxidants in the oil industry, mechanism of copper catalysis in insulating oil oxidation, scientific manpower, etc. *Recreations:* golf, bowls. *Address:* Delamere, Horsell Park, Woking, Surrey GU21 4LW. *T:* (01483) 714939.

THOMPSON, Maj.-Gen. Christopher Noel, CB 1988; *b* 25 Dec. 1932; *s* of late Brig. William Gordon Starkey Thompson and Kathleen Elizabeth (*née* Craven); *m* 1964, Margaret (*née* Longsworth); one *s* twin *d*. *Educ:* Wellington College; RMA Sandhurst; Sidney Sussex College, Cambridge (BA); University College London. Commissioned RE, 1953; served BAOR, 1957–59; Bomb Disposal, UK, 1959–62; Aden, 1963–66; Canada, 1966–68; OC 13 Field Survey Sqn, 1969–70; USA, 1971–75; CO 42 Survey Engr Regt, 1975–77; Dep. Dir, Planning and Develt, Ordnance Survey, 1978–79; Dir, Surveys and Production, Ordnance Survey, 1980–83; Dir of Mil. Survey, MoD, 1984–87. Col Comdt, RE, 1987–92. Pres., Commission D, European Organisation for Experimental Photogrammetric Research, 1980–87. *Publications:* articles on surveying and mapping in Chartered Surveyor, Photogrammetric Record. *Recreations:* sailing, tennis, gardening, house restoration. *Address:* Burgh House, Burgh-by-Sands, Carlisle CA5 6AN.

THOMPSON, Lt-Col Sir Christopher (Peile), 6th Bt *cr* 1890; non-executive Chairman, Nuclear Decommissioning Ltd, 1995–2000 (Director, since 1994); *b* 21 Dec. 1944; *s* of Lt-Col Sir Peile Thompson, 5th Bt, OBE, and Barbara Johnson (*d* 1993), *d* of late H. J. Rampling; *S* father, 1985; *m* 1969, Anna Elizabeth (marr. diss. 1997), *d* of Major Arthur Callander; one *s* one *d*; *m* 2001, Penelope (*née* Allin), widow of 9th Viscount Portman. *Educ:* Marlborough; RMA Sandhurst. Commnd 11th Hussars (PAO), 1965; Tank Troop Leader and Reconnaissance Troop Leader, 11th Hussars, 1965–69; Gunnery Instructor, RAC Gunnery Sch., 1970–72; Sqdn Second i/c, A Sqdn, Royal Hussars, 1972–75; GSO 3 Intelligence, Allied Staff, Berlin, 1975–76; RMCS Shrivenham, 1977; Staff Coll., Camberley, 1978; DAAG (a) M2 (A) (Officer Manning), MoD, 1978–81; C Sqdn Ldr, Royal Hussars, 1981–83; GSO 2 (Operational Requirements), HQ DRAC, 1983–85; CO, Royal Hussars (PWO), 1985–87; SO1, Sen. Officers Tactics Div., 1987–90, retd. Equerry to HRH Prince Michael of Kent, 1989– (Private Sec., 1990–92). Director: Logical Security Ltd, 1996–98; Falcon Security Control (Overseas) Ltd, 2000–. Dir, Hyde Park Appeal, 1990–; Trustee: Bike Aid, 1990–; Queen Elizabeth Gate Appeal, 1990–; Tusk, 1994–; Antigua Heritage Trust (UK), 1997–2000. Mem., Standing Council of the Baronetage, 2001–. Patron, Earth 2000, 1997–. *Recreations:* fishing, shooting, reading, golf, tennis, squash. *Heir: s* Peile Richard Thompson, *b* 3 March 1975. *Clubs:* Cavalry and Guards, Woodroffe's; Mill Reef (Antigua).

THOMPSON, Christopher Ronald; Senior Partner, Aldenham Business Services Ltd, since 1984; *b* 14 Dec. 1927; *s* of late Col S. J. Thompson, DSO, DL and Margaret Thompson (née Green); *m* 1949, Rachael Meynell; one *s* one *d* (and one *s* decd). *Educ:* Shrewsbury School; Trinity College, Cambridge. 1st Bn KSLI (Lieut), 1946–48. Dir, John Thompson Ltd, 1954–68, Chm., 1969; Dir, Rockwell-Thompson Ltd, 1973–74; Vice-Pres., Rockwell Europe, 1974–78. Chairman: NEI Internat., 1979–84; Wynn Electronics, 1983–87; Filtermist Internat. plc, 1985–97; John Sutcliffe Shipping Ltd, 1986–89; Director: Saraswati Syndicate pte India, 1954–; Barclays Bank Birmingham Bd, 1974–87; G. T. Japan Investment Trust, 1983–; Isotron plc, 1984–; Craven Grain Storage Ltd, 1984–95; Plessey Co. plc, 1988–89. Member: Overseas Projects Bd, BOTB, 1981–84; Sino-British Trade Council, 1983–85.; Indo-British Industrial Forum, 1987–93. Pres., BEAMA, 1984–85. Chm., CLA Cttee for Shropshire, 1996–. Mem. Council, HHA, 1992–. Chm., Anglo-Venezuelan Soc., 1981–85. Trustee: Hereford Cathedral Trust, 1984–; Mappa Mundi Trust, 1990–98. High Sheriff, Shropshire, 1984–85. *Recreations:* flyfishing, shooting, forestry. *Address:* Aldenham Park, near Bridgnorth, Shropshire WV16 4RN. *T:* (01746) 714218. *Club:* Boodle's.

THOMPSON, Clive Hepworth, CBE 1998; independent consultant, since 1996; Director, AB Biomonitoring Ltd, since 2000; *b* 7 July 1937; *s* of late Sidney Hepworth Thompson and Vera Wynne; *m* 1962, Joan Mary Kershaw; two *s*. *Educ:* Holywell Grammar Sch.; Manchester Univ. (BTech, MSc); Harvard Business Sch. BP Chemicals: Technical and Management appts; Works Gen. Manager, Barry Plant, 1975–78, Baglan Bay Plant, 1978–82; Gen. Manager, later Dir, Worldwide Petrochemicals, Production and Human Resources, 1982–90; Vice-Pres., Ops and Supply, Arco Chemical Europe, 1990–95. Mem., Audit Commn, 1990–97 (Dep. Chm., 1995–97). Member: Welsh Water Authy, 1980–82; Chem. Industries Assoc. Cttees, 1985–; Chm., Inter-Company Productivity Group, 1987–90 (Mem., 1983–90). Non-exec. Dir, Frimley Park Hosp. NHS Trust, 1999–. Liveryman, Horners' Co. (Mem., Ct of Assts, 1995–). *Publications:*

contribs to newspapers and learned jls on petrochemicals, environment policy and costs, quality management. *Recreations:* hill walking, opera, music, golf, reading history. *Address:* Dwr Golau, 13 Heronscourt, Lightwater, Surrey GU18 5SW. *T:* and *Fax:* (01276) 476410. *Clubs:* Harvard Business School; Windlesham Golf.

THOMPSON, Sir Clive (Malcolm), Kt 1996; Group Chief Executive, Rentokil Initial plc (formerly Rentokil Group), since 1983; *b* 4 April 1943; *s* of Harry Louis Thompson and Phyllis Dora Thompson; *m* 1968, Judith Howard; two *s*. *Educ:* Clifton Coll.; Univ. of Birmingham (BSc). Marketing Executive: Royal Dutch Shell Gp, 1964–67; Boots Co. plc, 1967–70; Gen. Manager, Jeyes Gp Ltd, 1970–73; Managing Director: Aerosols Internat. Ltd, 1973–75; Jeyes Ltd, 1975–78; Health and Hygiene Div., Cadbury Schweppes, 1978–82; Gp Chief Exec. Designate, Rentokil Gp plc, 1982. Director: Caradon plc, 1986–96; Kleeneze plc (formerly Farepak plc), 1988–; Wellcome plc, 1993–95; Sainsbury plc, 1995–2001; BAT Industries plc, 1995–98; Seeboard plc, 1995–96. Member: BOTB, 1997–99; Cttee on Corporate Governance, 1996–98; Dep. Chm., Financial Reporting Council, 1999–2001. Vice Pres., Chartered Inst. of Marketing, 1996–; Pres., CBI, 1998–2000 (Dep. Pres., 1997–98 and 2000–01). Hon. DSc Birmingham, 1999. *Recreations:* current affairs, stockmarket, golf, walking. *Address:* Rentokil Initial plc, Felcourt, East Grinstead, W Sussex RH19 2JY. *T:* (01342) 833022. *Club:* Wildernesse (Sevenoaks).

THOMPSON, Colin Edward, CBE 1983; FRSE 1978; Director, National Galleries of Scotland, 1977–84; *b* 2 Nov. 1919; *s* of late Edward Vincent Thompson, CB, and Jessie Forbes Cameron; *m* 1950, Jean Agnes Jardine O'Connell; one *s* one *d*. *Educ:* Sedbergh Sch.; King's College, Cambridge; Chelsea Polytechnic Sch. of Art. MA (Cantab). FMA. FS Wing CMP, 1940–41; Foreign Office (Bletchley Park), 1941–45. Lectr, Bath Acad. of Art, Corsham, 1948–54; Asst Keeper, 1954, Keeper, 1967, National Gall. of Scotland. Sen. Adviser, Res. Centre in Art Educn, Bath Acad. of Art, 1962–65; Chm., Scottish Museums Council, 1984–87; Member: Scottish Arts Council, 1976–83; Edinburgh Fest. Council, 1979–82; Bd of Governors, Edinburgh Coll. of Art, 1985–91 (Chm., 1989–91); Scottish Mining Museum Trust, 1987– (Chm., 1992–97); Expert Panel on Museums, Nat. Heritage Lottery Fund, 1995–98. DUniv Edinburgh, 1985. *Publications:* (with Lorne Campbell) Hugo van der Goes and the Trinity Panels in Edinburgh, 1974; Exploring Museums: Scotland, 1990; guide books, catalogues and a history of the National Gallery of Scotland; articles in Burlington Magazine, Museums Jl, etc. *Address:* Edenkerry, Lasswade, Midlothian EH18 1LW. *T:* (0131) 663 7927.

See also D. C. Thompson.

THOMPSON, Collingwood Forster James; QC 1998; a Recorder, since 1997; *b* 19 Dec. 1952; *s* of Collingwood Forster James Thompson and Lillian Thompson; *m* 1985, Valerie Joyce Britchford. *Educ:* Merchiston Castle Sch., Edinburgh; University Coll. London (LLB Hons 1974). Called to the Bar, Gray's Inn, 1975; in practice at the Bar, 1977–. *Recreations:* fly-fishing (badly), hill walking (slowly), wine tasting (frequently), music, reading. *Address:* 7 Bedford Row, WC1R 4BU. *T:* (020) 7242 3555.

THOMPSON, David; Head of Films and Single Drama, BBC, since 1997; *b* London, 1950. *Educ:* Cambridge Univ. (BA Hons English). English and Gen. Studies teacher; joined BBC, 1975: Documentary Producer, Open Univ. Prodns, 1975–79; Producer, Everyman, 1979–85 (incl. first drama, Shadowlands (BAFTA and Emmy Awards)); BBC Drama, 1985–94 (created Screenplay series focusing on new talent); Exec. Producer, Single Drama, 1994–97. Exec. producer of films for cinema and TV incl. Woman in White, A Rather English Marriage, Shadowlands, Safe, The Firm, Perfect Strangers, Madam Bovary, Nice Girls, When I Was 12, Captives, Face, Billy Elliot, Wonderland, Mansfield Park, Maybe Baby, Born Romantic, Last Resort, Liam. *Address:* BBC Films and Single Drama, First Floor, 1 Mortimer Street, W1T 3JA.

THOMPSON, David Anthony Roland, FCA; Finance Director, since 1990, and Deputy Chief Executive, since 2000, Boots Co. plc; *b* 4 Sept. 1942; *s* of Harold Alfred Thompson and Olive Edna (*née* Marlow); *m* 1966, Stella Eunice Durow; two *s*. *Educ:* Burton Grammar Sch. FCA 1964. Joined Boots Co. plc, 1966: Gp Mgt Accountant, 1973–77; Vice-Pres. Finance, Boots Drug Stores, Canada, 1977–80; Finance Dir, Retail Div., 1980–89; Gp Financial Controller, 1989–90; Jt Gp Man. Dir, 1997–2000. Non-executive Director: E Midlands Electricity, 1996–97; Cadbury Schweppes, 1998–. *Recreations:* all sports (especially football), gardening, music. *Address:* Boots Company plc, Nottingham NG2 3AA. *T:* (0115) 968 7005.

THOMPSON, David Brian; Director, Cheveley Park Stud Ltd, since 1975; Chairman, Union Square plc, 1987–91; *b* 3 April 1936; *s* of Bernard Thompson and Rosamund Dee; *m* 1962, Patricia Henchley; one *s* two *d*. *Educ:* Haileybury and ISC. Jt Man. Dir, B. Thompson Ltd, 1960–70; Chm. and co-founder, 1974–84, Jt Chm., 1984–87, Dir, 1987–89, Hillsdown Holdings plc. *Recreations:* family, business, breeding and racing of bloodstock, swimming.

THOMPSON, David George Fossett; Chairman, Wolverhampton & Dudley Breweries plc, since 2001 (Managing Director, 1986–2001); *b* 4 July 1954; *s* of Edwin John and Helen Wilson Thompson; *m* 1980, Marika Ann Moran Davies; one *s* three *d*. *Educ:* Winchester Coll.; Magdalene Coll., Cambridge (Exhibnr; Schol.; BA 1975). Cons. research dept, 1975–76; Whitbread plc, 1976–77; various posts with Wolverhampton & Dudley Breweries plc, 1977–. Chm., Wolverhampton TEC, 1990–95; Dir, W Midlands Regl Develt Agency, 1999–. Non-executive Director: The Income & Growth Trust plc; Persimmon plc; El Oro Mining & Exploration plc; Exploration Co. plc. *Address:* The Wolverhampton & Dudley Breweries plc, Park Brewery, Wolverhampton WV1 4NY. *T:* (01902) 372036.

THOMPSON, David John; Director, Economics and Statistics, Department for Environment, Food and Rural Affairs, since 2001; *b* 22 Nov. 1951; *s* of Cyril Thompson and Doris (*née* Savage). *Educ:* Beverley Grammar Sch.; Manchester Univ. (BA Econs 1973); London Sch. of Economics (MSc Econs 1977). Economist: DoE and Dept of Transport, 1973–83; Monopolies and Mergers Commn, 1984; Dept of Transport, 1987–88; HM Treasury, 1989–91; Dir of Res. on Regulation, Inst. for Fiscal Studies, 1985–86; Sen. Economic Advr, DfEE, 1992–98; Hd of Econs and Stats, MAFF, 1998–2001. Sen. Res. Fellow, London Business Sch., 1989–91. Dir, Economics Plus, 1996–98. *Publications:* contribs to books, articles in learned jls. *Recreations:* watching soccer, Rugby League and the Tour de France, rock and roll. *Address:* Department for Environment, Food and Rural Afairs, Whitehall Place (West), SW1A 2HH. *T:* (020) 7270 8539.

THOMPSON, (David) Robin (Bibby), CBE 1997; TD 1987; Director, Bibby Line Ltd, 1974–87; Deputy Chairman, Rural Development Commission, 1992–96 (Member, 1986–96); *b* 23 July 1946; *s* of Noel Denis Thompson and Cynthia Joan (*née* Bibby); *m* 1971, Caroline Ann Foster (marr. diss. 1998); one *s* one *d*; *m* 1999, Jane Craddock; one *d*. *Educ:* Uppingham Sch.; Mons Officer Cadet Sch. Short service commn, QRIH, 1965; comd Queen's Own Yeomanry (TA), 1984–87; Hon. ADC to the Queen, 1987–90. Member: Council, Royal Agricl Soc. of England, 1985–91; Bd, Housing Corp., 1989–98; Chm., S Shropshire Housing Assoc., 1991–2000. High Sheriff, Shropshire, 1989. *Recreations:* ski-ing, horses, conservation. *Address:* Sansaw Hall, Clive, Shrewsbury, Shropshire SY4 3JR. *Club:* Cavalry and Guards.

THOMPSON, Dennis Cameron; Founder, Journal of World Trade (formerly Journal of World Trade Law), 1967 (Editor, 1977–86); *b* 25 Oct. 1914; *s* of late Edward Vincent Thompson, CB, and late Jessie Forbes; *m* 1959, Maria von Skramlik; one *d*. *Educ:* Oundle; King's Coll., Cambridge. Nat. Sci. Tripos Pt I, Law Pt II; MA 1949. RAF, 1940–45: Sqdn-Ldr, personnel staff, Desert Air Force, and Germany. Called to Bar, Inner Temple, 1939; practised London and Midland Circuit, 1946–63; Asst Dir (European Law), British Inst. of Internat. and Comparative Law, 1963–66; Legal Adviser, Secretariat of EFTA, Geneva, 1967–73; participated in negotiations for European Patent Convention, 1969–73; Dir, Restrictive Practices and Dominant Positions, EEC, 1973–76; Consultant to UNCTAD on Restrictive Business Practices and Transfer of Technol., 1977–82. Convenor, Geneva Conf., Antarctica, the Environment and the Future, 1992; Pres., Internat. Cttee for Cryosphere Ecosystems, Geneva, 1993–. Vis. Prof., Georgia Univ. Sch. of Law, Athens, GA, 1978. Trustee, Federal Trust, 1962–71. *Publications:* (ed) Kennedy, CIF Contracts, 3rd edn 1959; (with Alan Campbell) Common Market Law, 1962; The Proposal for a European Company, 1969; articles in Internat. and Compar. Law Quarterly; (ed jtly) Common Market Law Review, 1963–67. *Recreations:* walking, Antarctic studies. *Address:* 8 rue des Belles Filles, 1299 Crans, Switzerland. *T:* (22) 7761687, *Fax:* (22) 7767303. *Club:* Oxford and Cambridge.

See also C. E. Thompson.

THOMPSON, Dianne; *see* Thompson, I. D.

THOMPSON, Sir Donald, Kt 1992; *b* 13 Nov. 1931; *s* of Geoffrey and Rachel Thompson; *m* 1957, Patricia Ann Hopkins; two *s*. Formerly Dir, Halifax Farmers' Trading Assoc.; Man. Dir, Armadillo Plastics (Glass Fibre Manufacturers), 1974–79. Member: WR CC, 1967–74; W Yorks CC, 1974–75; Calderdale Dist Council, 1975–79. Contested (C): Batley and Morley, 1970; Sowerby, Feb. and Oct. 1974. MP (C) Sowerby, 1979–83, Calder Valley, 1983–97; contested (C) Calder Valley, 1997. An Asst Govt Whip, then a Lord Comr of HM Treasury, 1981–86; Parly Sec., MAFF, 1986–89. A Govt Whip, Council of Europe and WEU, 1990–94. Chm., Cons. Candidates' Assoc., 1972–74. Chm. Appeal Fund, Animal Health Trust, 1989–. Dir-Gen., Friends of War Memls, 1997–. *Recreations:* Rugby football, poor golf, conversation. *Address:* Moravian House, Lightcliffe, Halifax HX3 8AL. *Clubs:* Beefsteak, Pratt's, St Stephen's Constitutional; Brodleians (Hipperholme); Octave (Elland).

THOMPSON, Donald Henry, MA Oxon; Headmaster, Chigwell School, Essex, 1947–71; *b* 29 Aug. 1911; *s* of H. R. Thompson, solicitor, Swansea; *m* 1942, Helen Mary Wray; four *s*. *Educ:* Shrewsbury School; Merton College, Oxford (Postmaster in Classics, 1930; 1st Class Hon. Mod., 1932; 1st Class Literae Humaniores, 1934). Asst Master Haileybury Coll., Hertford, 1934–46. Served War of 1939–45, RA, 1940–45. JP Essex, 1955–81. *Recreations:* cricket, bird-watching, conservation. *Address:* Glasses Farm, Holcombe Bath, Somerset BA3 5EQ. *T:* (01761) 232322.

THOMPSON, Dr Dorothy Joan, FBA 1996; Fellow and Lecturer in Classics and History, Girton College, Cambridge, since 1968; Isaac Newton Trust Lecturer in Classics, University of Cambridge, since 1992; *b* 31 May 1939; *d* of Frank William Walbank, *qv* and late Mary (*née* Woodward); *m* 1st, 1966, Michael Hewson Crawford, *qv* (marr. diss. 1979); 2nd, 1982, John Alexander Thompson. *Educ:* Birkenhead High Sch.; Girton Coll., Cambridge (BA 1961; MA 1965; PhD 1966); Bristol Univ. (CertEd 1962). Girton College, Cambridge: Research Fellow, 1965–68; Grad. Tutor (Arts), 1971–81 and 1995–96; Sen. Tutor, 1981–92; Dir of Studies in Classics, 1983–; Lectr in Classics, Clare Coll., Cambridge, 1973–. Vis. Mem., IAS, Princeton, 1982–83; Vis. Prof., Princeton Univ., 1986; Fellow, Nat. Humanities Center, N Carolina, 1993–94. James H. Breasted Prize, American Historical Assoc., 1989. *Publications:* Kerkeosiris: an Egyptian village in the Ptolemaic period, 1971; (jtly) Studies on Ptolemaic Memphis, 1980; Memphis under the Ptolemies, 1988; numerous articles and reviews in learned jls. *Recreations:* reading, walking. *Address:* Girton College, Cambridge CB3 0JG. *T:* (01223) 338999.

THOMPSON, Emma; actor; *b* 15 April 1959; *d* of late Eric Norman Thompson and of Phyllida Ann Law; partner, Greg Wise; one *d*. *Educ:* Newnham College, Cambridge (MA; Hon. Fellow, 1996). *Stage:* Footlights, Australia, 1982; Me and My Girl, Adelphi, 1984; Look Back in Anger, Lyric, 1989; King Lear, and A Midsummer Night's Dream, Renaissance Th. Co. world tour, 1989; *films:* Henry V, 1988; The Tall Guy, 1988; Impromptu, 1989; Dead Again, 1990; Howards End, 1992 (BAFTA Best Actress, Academy Award, Golden Globe Award, 1993); Peter's Friends, 1992; Much Ado About Nothing, 1993; The Remains of the Day, 1993; In the Name of the Father, 1993; Junior, 1994; Carrington, 1995; Sense and Sensibility (also wrote screenplay; BAFTA Best Actress; awards for screenplay incl. Academy Award), 1996; The Winter Guest, 1997; Judas Kiss, 1997; Primary Colors, 1998; Wit, 2001; *television series and serials:* Alfresco, 1983; Tutti Frutti, 1986 (BAFTA Best Actress); Fortunes of War, 1986 (BAFTA Best Actress); Thompson, 1987. *Recreations:* reading, walking, cooking, acting. *Address:* c/o Hamilton Asper Ltd, Ground Floor, 24 Hanway Street, W1P 9DD. *T:* (020) 7636 1221.

THOMPSON, Prof. Francis Michael Longstreth, CBE 1992; FBA 1979; Director, Institute of Historical Research, and Professor of History in the University of London, 1977–90, now Emeritus Professor; *b* 13 Aug. 1925; *s* of late Francis Longstreth-Thompson, OBE; *m* 1951, Anne Challoner; two *s* one *d*. *Educ:* Bootham Sch., York; Queen's Coll., Oxford (Hastings Schol.; MA, DPhil). ARICS 1968. War service, with Indian Artillery, 1943–47; James Bryce Sen. Schol., Oxford, 1949–50; Harmsworth Sen. Schol., Merton Coll., Oxford, 1949–51; Lectr in History, UCL, 1951–63; Reader in Economic History, UCL, 1963–68; Prof. of Modern Hist., Univ. of London, and Head of Dept of Hist., Bedford Coll., London, 1968–77. Joint Editor, Economic History Review, 1968–80. Sec., British Nat. Cttee of Historical Scis, 1978–94; British Mem., Standing Cttee for Humanities, European Sci. Foundn, 1983–93; President: Economic Hist. Soc., 1983–86; RHistS, 1988–92 (Fellow, 1964); British Agricl Hist. Soc., 1989–92; Hon. Treas., Internat. Econ. History Assoc., 1986–94. Member: Senate and Academic Council, Univ. of London, 1970–78; Senate and Collegiate Council, 1981–89. Ford's Lectr, Oxford Univ., 1994. Fellow, RHBNC, 1992–. DUniv York, 1995. *Publications:* English Landed Society in the Nineteenth Century, 1963; Chartered Surveyors: the growth of a profession, 1968; Victorian England: the horse-drawn society, 1970; Countrysides, in The Nineteenth Century, ed Asa Briggs, 1970; Hampstead: building a borough, 1650–1964, 1974; introd. to General Report on Gosford Estates in County Armagh 1821, by William Greig, 1976; Britain, in European Landed Elites in the Nineteenth Century, ed David Spring, 1977; Landowners and Farmers, in The Faces of Europe, ed Alan Bullock, 1980; 2 chapters in The Victorian Countryside, ed G. E. Mingay, 1981; (ed) The Rise of Suburbia, 1982; (ed) Horses in European Economic History, 1983; Towns, Industry and the Victorian Landscape, in The English Landscape, ed S. R. J. Woodell, 1985; Private Property and Public Policy, in Salisbury: The Man and his Policies, ed Lord Blake and Hugh Cecil, 1987; Rise of Respectable Society: a social history of Victorian Britain, 1988; (ed) The Cambridge Social History of Britain 1750–1950, vol. 1 Regions and Communities, vol. 2 People and their Environment, vol. 3 Social Agencies and Social Institutions, 1990; (ed) The University of London and the World of Learning 1836–1986, 1990; (ed) Landowners, Capitalists, and Entrepreneurs: essays for Sir John Habakkuk, 1994; Gentrification and the Enterprise Culture: Britain 1780–1980, 2000; numerous articles in Economic History Review, History, English Historical Review, etc. *Recreations:* gardening, walking, carpentry. *Address:* Holly Cottage, Sheepcote Lane, Wheathampstead, Herts AL4 8NJ. *T:* (01582) 833129.

THOMPSON, Dr Frank Derek, FRCP; Senior Consultant Nephrologist, St Peter's Hospital, since 1981; Dean, Institute of Urology and Nephrology, London University, since 1985, at Royal Free and University College Medical School; *b* 18 May 1939; *s* of Frank and Irene Thompson; *m* 1964, Elizabeth Ann Sherwood; two *s* one *d*. *Educ:* St Catharine's College, Cambridge (MA, MB BChir); St Mary's Hosp., London. FRCP 1983. Sen. Lectr, Inst. of Urology, 1974; Consultant Nephrologist to Harefield and Mount Vernon Hosps, 1979–; Hon. Consultant Nephrologist to Nat. Heart Hosp., 1980–; Vice-Dean, Faculty of Clinical Science, University College and Middx Sch. of Medicine, 1990. *Publications:* Disorders of the Kidney and Urinary Tract, 1987; contribs to BMJ, Clinical Nephrology. *Recreations:* golf, gardening, ornithology. *Address:* 27 Moor Park Road, Northwood, Middx HA6 2DL. *T:* (01923) 827361. *Club:* Moor Park Golf.

THOMPSON, Rt Rev. (Geoffrey) Hewlett; Bishop of Exeter, 1985–99; *b* 14 Aug. 1929; *o s* of late Lt-Col R. R. Thompson, MC, RAMC; *m* 1954, Elisabeth Joy Fausitt, MA (Oxon), *d* of late Col G. F. Taylor, MBE and Dr Frances Taylor; two *s* two *d*. *Educ:* Aldenham Sch.; Trinity Hall, Cambridge (MA); Cuddesdon Theol College. 2nd Lieut, Queen's Own Royal West Kent Regt, 1948–49 (Nat. Service). Ordained 1954. Curate, St Matthew, Northampton, 1954; Vicar: St Augustine, Wisbech, 1959; St Saviour, Folkestone, 1966; Bishop Suffragan of Willesden, 1974. Chairman: Community and Race Relations Unit, BCC, 1980–84 (Vice-Chm., 1976–80); Hospital Chaplaincies Council, 1991–97. Introduced into House of Lords, 1990. *Recreations:* fell walking, reading, gardening, music. *Address:* Low Broomrigg, Warcop, Appleby, Cumbria CA16 6PT. *T:* (017683) 41281. *Club:* Oxford and Cambridge.

THOMPSON, Rev. George H.; Parish Priest, St Peter's, Dalbeattie, since 1995; *b* 11 Sept. 1928. *Educ:* Dalry Sch.; Kirkcudbright Acad.; Edinburgh Univ. Teacher, modern languages, Kirkcudbright Academy; Principal Teacher of French, 1979–85, Principal Teacher of Modern Languages, 1985–86, Annan Acad., Dumfriesshire. Contested (SNP): Galloway, Feb. 1974, 1979; Galloway and Upper Nithsdale, 1983. Former SNP Asst Nat. Sec.; MP (SNP) Galloway, Oct. 1974–1979; SNP Spokesman: on health, Oct. 1974–79; on forestry, 1975. Deacon, RC dio. of Galloway, 1989, priest 1989; Asst Priest, St Teresa's, Dumfries, 1989–93; Administrator, St Margaret of Scotland's, Irvine, 1993–95. *Address:* St Peter's, Craignair Street, Dalbeattie DG5 4AX. *T:* (01556) 610358).

THOMPSON, Sir Gilbert (Williamson), Kt 1993; OBE 1985; Chairman: British Airports Group, since 1995; Alltram, since 1997; Chief Executive, 1981–93, and Board Member, 1986–93, Manchester Airport plc; *b* 1 March 1930; *s* of Henry Gordon Thompson and Isabella Thompson; *m* 1954, Dorothy Millar; two *d*. *Educ:* London Business Sch.; Manchester Business Sch. British European Airways, later British Airways: mgt trainee, Belfast, 1950; Regl Manager, Los Angeles, 1965–67; Manager, Irish Republic, 1967–69; General Manager: USA, 1969–72; Scotland, 1972–74; N of England, 1974–81. Dep. Chm., Campbell & Armstrong, 1996–. Pres., British Amer. Business Gp, 1995–; Member: British Amer. Business Council, 1995–; Bd, Nimtech, 1996–; BOTB, 1997–. Hon. DLitt Salford, 1993. *Recreations:* golf, bridge, soccer, jogging, keep fit. *Address:* Longridge, 29 Hilltop Hale, Cheshire WA15 0NN. *T:* (0161) 980 1429.

THOMPSON, Godfrey; *see* Thompson, W. G.

THOMPSON, Sir Godfrey James M.; see Milton-Thompson.

THOMPSON, (Henry) Antony Cardew W.; *see* Worrall Thompson.

THOMPSON, Rt Rev. Hewlett; *see* Thompson, Rt Rev. G. H.

THOMPSON, Howard; *see* Thompson, James H.

THOMPSON, Hugh Glenn, CB 2001; business consultant; Under Secretary, Civil Service, 1996–2001; *b* 11 Nov. 1949; *s* of Hugh Glenn Thompson and Sarah (*née* McMaster); *m* 1971, Elizabeth McClements; two *d*. *Educ:* Regent House Grammar Sch., Newtownards. Clerk to Principal, NICS, 1967–86; Asst Sec., Industrial Develt Bd for NI, 1986–89; Regl Manager, 1989–92, Exec. Dir, 1992–96, Crestacare plc. *Recreations:* travel, Rugby, Formula 1 motor racing.

THOMPSON, (Hugh) Patrick; *b* 21 Oct. 1935; *s* of late Gerald Leopold Thompson and of Kathleen Mary Landsdown Thompson; *m* 1962, Kathleen Howson. *Educ:* Felsted Sch., Essex; Emmanuel Coll., Cambridge (MA). Nat. Service, 2nd Lieut, KOYLI, 1957–59; TA, Manchester, 1960–65; Gresham's Sch., CCF, 1965–82 (CFM 1980); Major, retd. Engr, English Electric Valve Co., Chelmsford, 1959–60; Sixth Form Physics Master: Manchester Grammar Sch., 1960–65; Gresham's Sch., Holt, 1965–83. MP (C) Norwich North, 1983–97. Parliamentary Private Secretary: to Minister of State for Transport, 1987–88; to Minister of State, Dept of Social Security, 1988–89; to Minister for Health, 1992–94. Member: Parly and Scientific Cttee, 1983–97; Select Cttee, Educn, Science and the Arts, 1991–92; Select Cttee, Sci. and Technol., 1995–97; Speaker's Panel of Chairmen, 1994–97; Founder Mem., All Party Gp for Engrg Develt, 1985–97; Secretary: Cons. Back Bench Energy Cttee, 1986–87; Cons. Back Bench European Cttee, 1991–92. *Publication:* Elementary Calculations in Physics, 1963. *Recreations:* travel, music, gardening. *Club:* Norfolk (Norwich).

THOMPSON, Sir (Humphrey) Simon M.; *see* Meysey-Thompson.

THOMPSON, Ian; Director of Finance and Property (formerly Chief Finance and Property Officer), Swindon Borough Council, since 1997; *b* 20 May 1951; *s* of Eber Edward Thompson and Edith (*née* Gilchrist); *m* 1st, 1972, Anne Rosalind Clouston (marr. diss. 1995); one *d*; 2nd, 1998, Karin Bell. *Educ:* Workington Grammar Sch.; Univ. of Hull (BSc). IPFA. With Humberside CC, 1974–80; Northamptonshire County Council, 1980–89: Chief Acctnt, 1986–88; Sen. Asst Educn Officer, 1988–89; Berkshire County Council: Sen. Asst Co. Treas., 1989–93; Co. Treas., 1993–96. *Recreations:* fell-walking, playing squash, playing trains. *Address:* Civic Offices, Euclid Street, Swindon SN1 2JH. *T:* (01793) 464588.

THOMPSON, Dr (Ian) McKim; Vice President, British Medical Association, since 1998; *b* 19 Aug. 1938; *s* of late J. W. Thompson and Dr E. M. Thompson; *m* 1962, Dr Veronica Jane Richards (marr. diss. 1988); two *s* one *d*. *Educ:* Epsom Coll.; Birmingham Univ. (MB, ChB 1961). Lectr in Pathology, Univ. of Birmingham, 1964–67; Sen. Registrar, Birmingham RHB, 1967–69; Sen. Under Sec., 1969–85, Dep. Sec., 1985–96, BMA. Consulting Forensic Pathologist to HM Coroner, City of Birmingham, 1966–97. Part time Tutor, Dept of Adult and Continuing Educn, Keele Univ., 1985–; Tutor, Wedgwood Meml Coll., Barlaston, 1990–. Man. Dir, RN Diesel Engine Co. Ltd, 1997–. Member: GMC, 1979–94; Cttee, Birmingham Med. Inst. FRSocMed 1987. Hon. Collegian, Med. Colls of Spain, 1975. *Publications:* (ed) The Hospital Gazeteer, 1972; (ed) BMA Handbook for Hospital Junior Doctors, 1977, 5th edn 1990; (ed) BMA Handbook for Trainee Doctors in General Practice, 1982, 3rd edn 1985; various medical scientific papers. *Recreations:* inland waterways, rambling. *Address:* Canal Cottage, Hinksford Lane, Kingswinford DY6 0BH. *T:* (01384) 294131.

THOMPSON, (Ila) Dianne; Chief Executive, Camelot Group plc, since 2000 (Commercial Director, 1997–2000); *b* 31 Dec. 1950; *d* of Ronald Wood and Joan Wood (*née* Pinder); *m* 1972, Roger Thompson (marr. diss. 1992); one *d*. *Educ:* Batley Girls' Grammar Sch.; Manchester Poly. (BA Hons ext. London). FCIM 2000. Product Manager, CWS, 1972–74; Mktg Manager, ICI, 1974–79; Lectr, Manchester Poly., 1979–86; Mktg Dir, Sterling Roncraft, 1986–88; Man. Dir, Sandvik Saws & Tools, 1988–92; Marketing Director: Woolworths plc, 1992–94; Signet Gp, 1994–97. FRSA 1999. Member: Mktg Soc., 1990; Mktg Gp of GB, 1993. Veuve Cliquot Businesswoman of the Year, 2000. *Recreations:* theatre, cinema, entertaining, travel. *Address:* Adam Cottage, Hammersley Lane, Penn, Bucks HP10 8HB.

THOMPSON, James, FLA; University Librarian, University of Birmingham, 1987–95; *b* 11 Jan. 1932; *s* of James Thompson and Mary Margaret Thompson (*née* Harland); *m* 1st, 1958, Mary Josephine McAndrew (marr. diss. 1987); one *s* one *d*; 2nd, 1988, Susan Lesley Challans. *Educ:* St Cuthbert's Grammar Sch.; Univ. of Durham (BA 1st Cl. Hons English). FLA 1963. Newcastle City Libraries, 1948–59; Nottingham Univ. Liby, 1959–63; Sen. Asst Librarian, UEA, 1963–65; Dep. Librarian, Univ. of Glasgow, 1965–67; Univ. Librarian, Univ. of Reading, 1967–87. Member: Council, LA, 1972–74; Berks Co. Liby Sub-cttee, 1973–87; SCONUL Council, 1983–86. Pres., Reading AUT, 1981–83. Project Hd, Location Register of Twentieth Century English Literary MSS and Letters, 1982–87. *Publications:* The Librarian and English Literature, 1968, 2nd edn as English Studies, 1971; Books: an anthology, 1968; An Introduction to University Library Administration, 1970, 4th edn 1987 (Spanish edn 1989); Library Power, 1974; A History of the Principles of Librarianship, 1977; (ed) University Library History, 1980; The End of Libraries, 1982; Redirection of Academic Library Management, 1991; A Centennial History of the Library of the University of Birmingham, 2000; contribs to books, conf. proceedings and jls. *Recreation:* gardening. *Address:* 35 Meadow Rise, Bournville, Birmingham B30 1UZ. *T:* (0121) 472 1735.

THOMPSON, James Craig; Director of Policy: Maidstone and Mid Kent Chamber of Commerce and Industry Ltd, since 1994; Kent Gateway Chamber of Commerce, since 2001; *b* 27 Oct. 1933; *s* of Alfred Thompson and Eleanor (*née* Craig); *m* 1957, Catherine (*née* Warburton); one *s* one *d*. *Educ:* Heaton Grammar Sch., Newcastle upon Tyne; Rutherford Coll., Newcastle upon Tyne. Commercial Exec., Belfast Telegraph, Newcastle Chronicle and Journal, Scotsman Publications, Liverpool Post and Echo, 1960–76; Advertising and Marketing Manager, Kent Messenger Gp, 1976–79, Dir, 1972–79; Man. Dir, South Eastern Newspapers, 1975–79; Chm. and Man. Dir, 1973–89, Consultant Dir, 1989–92, Adverkit Internat. Ltd; Chm. and Man. Dir, Harvest Publications Ltd, 1983–95. Dir, Weekly Newspaper Advtg Bureau, 1977. Director: Ad Builder Ltd, 1971–89; MLO Ltd, 2000–; Business Point Maidstone Ltd, 1996–; Maidstone Enterprise Agency Ltd, 1998–; Associated Kent Chambers, 2001–; Chm., Presscom Ltd, 1997–. Life Governor, Kent County Agricl Soc., 1974. Hon. Life Mem., Kent CCC, 1978; Mem., Catenian Assoc. (Pres., Maidstone Circle, 1974–75). Chm., Maidstone United Football Club, 1970–92; Chm., Southern Football League, 1977–79 (Life Mem., 1985); Pres., The Football Conf. Ltd, 1989–; Mem. Council, Football Assoc., 1982–92. FInstD; MInstM; MIMgt. Freeman, City of London; Liveryman, Co. of Stationers and Newspaper Makers. Distinguished Service Award, Internat. Classified Advertising Assoc., Baltimore, 1968. *Publications:* numerous articles on commercial aspects of newspaper publishing and Association football. *Recreations:* walking, Northumbrian history. *Address:* Prescott House, Otham, Kent ME15 8RL. *T:* (01622) 861606. *Clubs:* Wig and Pen (Life Mem.), MCC; Maidstone (Maidstone) (Life Mem., Pres., 1997).

THOMPSON, (James) Howard, OBE 1984; British Council Director in Brazil, 1997–March 2002; *b* 26 March 1942; *s* of James Alan Thompson and Edna (*née* Perkins); *m* 1965, Claire Marguerite Dockrell; one *s* one *d*. *Educ:* Northampton Grammar Sch.; Magdalene Coll., Cambridge (BA); Stanford Univ. (MA). English Language Officer, British Council, Yugoslavia, 1966–69; Associate Prof., Punjab Univ., 1970–73; Dep. Representative, British Council, Kenya, 1974–78; Advr, Schs and Further Educn Dept, 1978–80; Educn Attaché, British Embassy, Washington, 1980–84; Dep. Controller, 1984–87, Controller, 1987–89, Science, Technology and Educn Div., British Council; Chm., Educn and Trng Export Cttee, 1988–89; British Council Director: Indonesia, 1989–92; Egypt, 1993–96. *Publication:* Teaching English, 1972. *Recreations:* photography, travel, golf. *Address:* 1 Homefield Road, W4 2LN; (until March 2002) c/o British Council, 10 Spring Gardens, SW1A 2BN.

THOMPSON, Rt Rev. James Lawton; Bishop of Bath and Wells, 1991–2001; *b* 11 Aug. 1936; *s* of Bernard Isaac and Marjorie May Thompson; *m* 1965, Sally Patricia Stallworthy; one *s* one *d*. *Educ:* Dean Close School, Cheltenham; Emmanuel Coll., Cambridge (MA 1964; Hon. Fellow, 1992). FCA 1959. 2nd Lt, 3rd Royal Tank Regt, 1959–61. Deacon, 1966; Curate, East Ham, 1966–68; Chaplain, Cuddesdon Coll., Oxford, 1968–71; Rector of Thamesmead and Ecumenical Team Leader, 1971–78; Suffragan, then Area, Bishop of Stepney, 1978–91. Mem., House of Bishops, Gen. Synod of C of E, 1988–2001. Chairman: Cttee for Relations with People of Other Faiths, BCC, 1983–89; Urban Studies Centre, then Urban Learning Foundn, 1985–91; Interfaith Network (UK), 1987–92; Church at Work, London, 1989–91; Social Policy Cttee, 1990–95, Social, Economic and Industrial Affairs Cttee, 1996–97, Bd for Social Responsibility; London Churches Broadcasting Gp, 1987–91; Children's Soc., 1997–2001; Jt Pres., English Churches Housing Trust, 1995–2000. Pres., Royal Bath and West Soc., 1997–98. Visitor, Wadham Coll., Oxford, 1992. Entered House of Lords, 1997. Hon. Fellow, QMC, 1986. Hon. DLitt E London Poly., 1989; Bath, 1998; Hon. DD Exeter, 1995. (Jointly) Sir Sigmund Sternberg Award for Christian-Jewish Relations, 1987. *Publications:* Halfway: reflections in midlife, 1986; (contrib.) Trevor Huddleston, ed D. D. Honoré, 1989; The Lord's Song, 1990; Stepney Calling, 1991; Why God?, 1996. *Recreations:* riding, painting, a horse, sport.

THOMPSON, Janet, CB 2000; DPhil; CPhys, FInstP; Chief Executive, Forensic Science Service, 1988–2001; *b* 23 Oct. 1941; *d* of late Arthur Hugh Denison Fairbarns and Eleanor Mary Fairbarns (*née* Cattel); *m* 1999, Elliot Grant; one *s* one *d*, and one *s* from a former marriage. *Educ:* North London Collegiate Sch.; Brighton Coll. of Technol. (BSc 1963); Univ. of Oxford (DPhil 1968). CPhys, FInstP 1999. Chm., Science, Technol. and Mathematics Council, 1999–. Chm., European Network of Forensic Insts, 1997–99.

Address: Science, Technology and Mathematics Council, 20–22 Queensberry Place, SW7 2DZ.

THOMPSON, Jeff; *see* Thompson, John J.

THOMPSON, John; DL; *b* 27 Aug. 1928; *s* of Nicholas and Lilian Thompson; *m* 1952, Margaret Clarke; one *s* one *d. Educ:* Bothal Sch.; Ashington Mining Coll. Electrical Engr, 1966–83. Councillor: Wansbeck DC, 1974–79; Northumberland CC, 1974–85 (Leader, and Chm., Policy and Resources, and Employment Cttees, 1981–83). MP (Lab) Wansbeck, 1983–97. An Opposition Whip, 1990–97. Mem., Select Cttee on Educn, Science and Arts, 1985–87; Chm., Northern Labour MPs, 1991–92 (Sec., 1985–90). Member: Council of Europe (Chm., Fisheries Sub Cttee, 1995–97); WEU (Chm., Rules and Privileges Cttee, 1992–97). DL Northumberland, 1996. *Address:* 20 Falstone Crescent, Ashington, Northumberland NE63 0TY. *T:* (01670) 817830.

THOMPSON, John, MBE 1975; HM Diplomatic Service; Head of Information Management Group, FCO Services, Foreign and Commonwealth Office, since 1999; *b* 28 May 1945; *s* of late Arthur Thompson and Josephine (*née* Brooke); *m* 1966, Barbara Hopper; one *d. Educ:* Whiteheath County Primary Sch., Ruislip, Mddx; St Nicholas Grammar Sch., Northwood, Mddx; Polytechnic of Central London (DMS). Joined FO, 1964; Vice-Consul, Düsseldorf, 1966–69; Consular Officer, later Vice-Consul, Abu Dhabi, 1969–72; Vice-Consul, Phnom Penh, 1972–74; seconded to DTI, 1975–77; First Sec., FCO, 1977–79; First Sec., Hd of Chancery and Consul, Luanda, 1979–81; Consul (Commercial), São Paulo, 1981–85; Assistant Head: S Pacific Dept, FCO, 1985–87; Aid Policy Dept, FCO, 1987–88; High Comr to Vanuatu, 1988–92; Dep. Consul-Gen. and Dir of Trade, NY, 1992–97; Hd of Inf. Systems Dept and Library and Records Dept, FCO, 1997–99. *Recreations:* philately, walking, reading, bridge. *Address:* c/o Foreign and Commonwealth Office, King Charles Street, SW1A 2AH.

THOMPSON, Sir John; *see* Thompson, Sir T. d'E. J.

THOMPSON, John Brian, CBE 1980; Director of Radio, Independent Broadcasting Authority, 1973–87; *b* 8 June 1928; *y s* of late John and Lilian Thompson; *m* 1957, Sylvia, *d* of late Thomas Waterhouse, CBE, and of Doris Waterhouse (*née* Gough); two *s* one *d. Educ:* St Paul's; Pembroke College, Oxford (BA; MA). Eileen Power Studentship, LSE, 1950; Glaxo Laboratories Ltd, 1950–54; Masius & Fergusson Ltd, 1955; Asst Editor, Truth, 1956–57; Daily Express, 1957–59 (New York Correspondent; Drama Critic); ITN, 1959–60 (Newscaster/Reporter); Editor, Time and Tide, 1960–62; News Editor, The Observer, 1962–66; Editor, Observer Colour Magazine, 1966–70; Publisher and Editorial Dir, BPC Publishing Ltd, 1971; Editor, The Viewer, 1988–90. Vis. Prof., Sch. of Media, Lancashire Poly., 1987–90. Sen. Advr on Radio to Minister of Posts and Telecommunications, 1972; Mem., MoD Study Group on Censorship, 1983. Director: Worlds End Productions Ltd, 1987–91; The Observer, 1989–93; Dep. Chm., Zabaxe Gp, 1988–90. Vice-Chm. (radio), EBU, 1986–88. Mem. Delegacy, Goldsmiths' Coll., London, 1986–96. Associate Mem., Nuffield Coll., Oxford, 1988–90. Judge, Booker Fiction Prize, 1987; Panel of Selection Bd Chairmen, CS Commn/RAS, 1988–93. Sony Radio special award, 1983. *Address:* 1 Bedwyn Common, Great Bedwyn, Marlborough, Wilts SN8 3HZ. *T:* (01672) 870641. *Clubs:* Garrick, Groucho.
See also Hon. Sir R. G. Waterhouse.

THOMPSON, (John) Derek T.; *see* Taylor Thompson.

THOMPSON, Prof. John Griggs, PhD; FRS 1979; Rouse Ball Professor of Mathematics, University of Cambridge, 1971–93; Fellow of Churchill College, Cambridge, since 1968; *b* Kansas, 13 Oct. 1932; *s* of John and Eleanor Thompson; *m* 1960, Diane Oenning; one *s* one *d. Educ:* Yale (BA 1955); Chicago (PhD 1959); MA Cantab 1972. Prof. of Mathematics, Chicago Univ., 1962–68; Vis. Prof. of Mathematics, Cambridge Univ., 1968–70. Hon. DSc Oxon, 1987. Cole Prize, 1966; Field Medal, 1970; Berwick Prize, London Math. Soc., 1982; Sylvester Medal, Royal Soc., 1985; Wolf Prize, 1992; Poincaré Medal, 1992. *Address:* 16 Millington Road, Cambridge CB3 9HP.

THOMPSON, John Handby, CB 1988; CVO 1994; Ceremonial Officer, Cabinet Office, and Secretary, Political Honours Scrutiny Committee, 1988–94; *b* 21 Feb. 1929; *s* of late Rev. John Thomas Thompson and Clara Handby. *Educ:* Silcoates Sch., Wakefield; St John's Coll., Oxford (MA); Sheffield Univ. (PhD 1991). Served Intell. Corps, 1947–49. HM Inspector of Taxes, 1953–63; Dept of Educn and Science, 1964–88: Schs Council, 1971–73; Asst Sec., 1973; Mem., Prep. Cttee of European Univ. Inst., 1973–75; Dep. Accountant-Gen., 1976–78; Under Sec., 1978; Head of Schs Br. 1, 1978–80; Head of Further and Higher Educn Br. 1, 1980–84; Dir of Estabts and Orgn, 1985–88. Gov., Univ. (formerly Poly.) of N London, 1989–98 (Hon. Fellow, 1999). Pres., Chapels Soc., 1998–2001. *Publications:* A History of the Coward Trust 1738–1988, 1998; Highgate Dissenters: their history since 1660, 2001. *Recreations:* reading about Albania, Nonconformist history. *Address:* 2 Alwyne Villas, N1 2HQ. *Club:* Reform.

THOMPSON, Air Vice-Marshal John Hugh, CB 2000; Defence Attaché and Head of British Defence Staff, Washington, since 2000; *b* 18 Sept. 1947; *m* 1969, Mary Emerson; two *s* one *d. Educ:* Fielding High Sch., NZ; RAF Coll., Cranwell. Hunter pilot, Bahrain, 1970–71; Harrier pilot, weapons instructor and Sqdn Comdr; Army Staff Coll., 1982; Station Comdr, Wittering, 1988–90; RCDS, 1991; Higher Comd and Staff Course, 1992; SASO, Rheindahlen, 1993–96; Office of the High Rep., Sarajevo, 1996; AOC and Comdt, RAF Coll., Cranwell, 1997–98; AOC No 1 Gp, 1998–2000. *Recreations:* golf, reading. *Address:* HBDS (W), BFPO 2. *Club:* Royal Air Force.

THOMPSON, Prof. John Jeffrey, (Jeff), CBE 1989; PhD; CChem, FRSC; Professor of Education, since 1979, and Director, Centre for the Study of Education in an International Context, since 1992, University of Bath; *b* 13 July 1938; *s* of John Thompson and Elsie May Thompson (*née* Wright); *m* 1963, Kathleen Audrey Gough; three *d. Educ:* King George V Sch., Southport; St John's Coll., Cambridge (MA); Balliol Coll., Oxford (MA); PhD (CNAA); DipEd (Oxon). Asst Master, Blundell's Sch., 1961–65; Head of Chemistry, Watford Grammar Sch., 1965–69; Lectr in Educn, KCL, 1968–69; Shell Fellow, UCL, 1969–70; Lectr and Tutor, Dept of Educnl Studies, Oxford Univ., 1970–79; Lectr in Chemistry, Keble Coll., Oxford, 1970–76; Pro-Vice-Chancellor, Univ. of Bath, 1986–89. Chief Examnr, Internat. Baccalaureate, 1970– (Chm., Bd of Chief Examnrs, 1985–89); Chm. Res. Cttee, 1998–, Dir for Internat. Educn, 2000–, Internat. Baccalaureate Orgn; Dep. Chm., Examination Appeals Bd, 1999–. Chairman: Assoc. for Science Educn, 1981; Nat. Curriculum Science Working Gp, 1987–88. Mem., Council, 1988–92, Dep. Chm., 1989–92, School Exams and Assessment Council; Member: Nat. Commn on Educn, 1991–93; English Nat. Bd for Nursing, Midwifery and Health Visiting, 1993–April 2002. Pres., Educn Div., Royal Soc. of Chemistry, 1983–85; Dep. Chm., Educn Cttee, Royal Soc., 1995–98; British Association for the Advancement of Science: Vice Pres., 1996–2001; Vice Pres. and Gen. Sec., 1985–91; Chm. Council, 1991–96. Governor and Mem. Council, United World Coll. of the Atlantic, 1992–. Hon. Mem., ASE, 1994. Mem. Council, Wildfowl Trust, 1981–91. FRSA 1983. Freeman, 1992, Liveryman, 1995, Goldsmiths' Co., 1992; Freeman, City of London, 1992. Gen. Editor, Bath Science series, age gps 16–19 (12 titles), and 5–16 (78 titles), 1990–. Hon DLitt Hertfordshire, 2001. *Publications:* Introduction to Chemical Energetics, 1967; European Curriculum Studies; Chemistry, 1972; (ed) Practical Work in Sixthform Science, 1976; Foundation Course in Chemistry, 1982; Modern Physical Chemistry, 1982; (ed) Dimensions of Science (9 titles), 1986; The Chemistry Dimension, 1987; International Education: Principles and Practice, 1998; (ed) International Schools and International Education, 2000. *Recreations:* music (brass bands and blue grass), North Country art, collecting sugar wrappers. *Address:* University of Bath, Claverton Down, Bath BA2 7AY.

THOMPSON, John Keith Lumley, CMG 1982; MBE (mil.) 1965; TD 1961; President, Lumley Associates, since 1983; *b* 31 March 1923; *s* of late John V. V. and Gertrude Thompson; *m* 1950, Audrey Olley; one *s. Educ:* Wallsend Grammar Sch.; King's Coll., Durham Univ. (BSc). FIMgt (FBIM; MBIM 1975); MSAE 1983. Served War of 1939–45: Officer in REME, 1942–47, NW Europe; BEME 44 Para Bde (V), 1948–70. Dep. Inspector, REME (V) Southern Comd, 1970–72 (Lt-Col); Dep. Comdr, 44 Para Bde (V), 1972–75 (Col). Road Research Lab., DSIR, 1948–55; AWRE, Aldermaston, 1955–64; Staff of Chief Scientific Adviser, MoD, 1964–65; Head of E Midlands Regional Office, Min. Tech., 1965–70; Head, Internat. Affairs, Atomic Energy Div., Dept of Energy, 1972–74; Regional Dir, W Midlands and Northern Regional Offices, DoI, 1970–72 and 1974–78; Counseller (Sci. and Tech.), Washington, 1978–83. ADC to the Queen (TAVR), 1974–78. *Publications:* papers on vehicle behaviour, crash helmets and implosion systems; numerous articles on American science and technology. *Recreations:* outdoor activities, reading. *Address:* c/o Lumley Associates, 7 School Lane, Baston, Peterborough PE6 9PD. *T:* (01778) 560374.

THOMPSON, John Leonard C.; *see* Cloudsley-Thompson.

THOMPSON, John Michael Anthony, FMA; museums and heritage consultant, since 1991; Senior Consultant, Prince Research Consultants Ltd, since 1995; *b* 3 Feb. 1941; *s* of George Thompson and Joan Smith; *m* 1965, Alison Sara Bowers; two *d. Educ:* William Hulme's Grammar Sch., Manchester; Univ. of Manchester. BA, MA; FMA 1980. Research Asst, Whitworth Art Gall., 1964–66; Keeper, Rutherston Collection, City Art Gall., Manchester, 1966–68; Director: North Western Museum and Art Gall. Service, 1968–70; Arts and Museums, Bradford City Council, 1970–74; Chief Arts and Museums Officer, Bradford Metropolitan Council, 1974–75; Dir, Art Galls and Museums, Tyne and Wear County Museums, 1975–91. Councillor, Museums Assoc., 1977–80, 1984–87 (Chm., Accreditation Cttee, 1978–80); Advisor to Arts and Recreation Cttee, AMA, 1981–91; Pres., Museums North, 1977, and 1991–92; Chm., Soc. of County Museum Dirs, 1982–86; Founder Mem. and Hon. Sec., Gp of Dirs of Museums in the British Isles, 1985–91. Dir, Museums and Galleries Consultancy Ltd, 1992–95; Mem. Bd, Jarrow 700 AD Ltd, 1992–. External Verifier: Museum Trng Inst., 1996–99; Qualifications for Industry, 1999–. Chm., Gosforth Adult Educn Assoc., 1994–. Vice Chm. Governors, Gosforth High Sch., 1997–99. *Publications:* (ed) The Manual of Curatorship: a guide to museum practice, 1984, 2nd edn 1993; Contracting Culture: museums and local government, 1994; articles in Museums Jl, Penrose Annual, Connoisseur. *Recreations:* classical guitar, running, walking. *Address:* 21 Linden Road, Gosforth, Newcastle upon Tyne NE3 4EY. *T:* and *Fax:* (0191) 284 7304; *e-mail:* jma@thompsonjma.fsnet.co.uk; Prince Research Consultants, 3 Homer Street, W1H 1HN. *T:* (020) 7706 0365, *Fax:* (020) 7724 5856; *e-mail:* prcltd@compuserve.com.

THOMPSON, Prof. John Michael Tutill, FRS 1985; Professor of Nonlinear Dynamics, Department of Civil Engineering, and Director, Centre for Nonlinear Dynamics and Its Applications, University College London, since 1991; Chairman, ES-Consult (Consulting Engineers), Copenhagen, since 1995; *b* 7 June 1937; *s* of John Hornsey Thompson and Kathleen Rita Thompson (*née* Tutill); *m* 1959, Margaret Cecilia Chapman; one *s* one *d. Educ:* Hull Grammar Sch.; Clare Coll., Cambridge (MA, PhD, ScD). FIMA; CMath. Research Fellow, Peterhouse, 1961–64; Vis. Res. Associate, Stanford (Fulbright grant), 1962–63; Lectr, 1964–68, Reader, 1968–77, Prof. of Structural Mechanics, 1977–91, UCL; Chm., Bd of Studies in Civil and Mech. Eng., Univ. of London, 1984–86. Vis. Prof., Faculté des Sciences, Univ. Libre de Bruxelles, 1976–78; Vis. Mathematician, Brookhaven Nat. Lab., 1984; Vis. Res. Fellow, Centre for Nonlinear Studies, Univ. of Leeds, 1987–; Sen. Fellow, SERC, 1988–93. Mem. Council, IMA, 1989–92 (Organizer, Conf. on Chaos, UCL, 1990). Cambridge University Prizes: Rex Moir, 1957; Archibald Denny, 1958; John Winbolt, 1960; OMAE Award, ASME, 1985; James Alfred Ewing Medal, ICE, 1992. Organizer and Editor, IUTAM Symposium: on Collapse: the buckling of structures in theory and practice, 1982; on non-linearity and chaos in engrg dynamics, 1993; Ed., Phil. Trans Roy. Soc., Series A, 1998– (Actg Ed., 1990; Ed. and Organizer, first Theme Issue, 1990 and three Millennium Issues, 2000); sci. contribs to radio and TV, 1975–. *Publications:* (with G. W. Hunt) A general theory of elastic stability, 1973; Instabilities and catastrophes in science and engineering, 1982; (with G. W. Hunt) Elastic instability phenomena, 1984; (with H. B. Stewart) Nonlinear dynamics and chaos, 1986; (ed) Localisation and solitary waves in solid mechanics, 1999; Visions of the Future, vol. I, Astronomy and Earth Science, vol. II, Physics and Electronics, vol. III, Chemistry and Life Science, 2001; 160 articles in learned jls (and mem., editl bds). *Recreations:* walking, music, tennis, astronomy with grandchildren. *Address:* 33 West Hill Road, Foxton, Cambs CB2 6SZ. *T:* (01223) 704354.

THOMPSON, (John) Peter (Stuart); Director, Solicitors' Complaints Bureau, 1986–90; *b* 6 July 1925; *s* of Frederick Charles Victor Thompson and Hilda Mary (*née* Hampton); *m* 1956, Valerie Merriel (*née* Harman). *Educ:* Burton Grammar Sch.; Royal Naval Coll., Dartmouth; Royal Naval Engineering Coll., Devonport; Univ. of Birmingham, 1952–55 (LLB). Admitted Solicitor, 1966. Served Royal Navy, 1943–47. Arts Council Drama Dept and associated theatres: Actor/Stage Dir, 1947–52. Asst Company Sec., Saunders-Roe Ltd, Aircraft Manufrs, 1955–61; articled clerk, Helder Roberts & Co., Solicitors, London, 1961–66, Partner 1966–70; Law Soc. Professional Purposes Dept, 1971–86. *Recreations:* gardening, marine technology, 18th Century music, flora and fauna of tropical islands. *Address:* Parkhurst Lodge, Abinger Common, Dorking, Surrey RH5 6LL. *T:* (01306) 730522.

THOMPSON, John William McWean, CBE 1986; Editor, Sunday Telegraph, 1976–86; *b* 12 June 1920; *s* of Charles and Charlotte Thompson; *m* 1947, Cynthia Ledsham; one *s* one *d. Educ:* Roundhay Sch., Leeds. Previously on staffs of Yorkshire Evening News, Evening Standard, London, and The Spectator (Dep. Editor); joined Sunday Telegraph, 1970; Asst Editor, 1975. *Publications:* (as Peter Quince) Country Life, 1975; articles and reviews in many jls. *Address:* Corner Cottage, Burnham Norton, Norfolk PE31 8DS. *T:* (01328) 738396. *Club:* Travellers.
See also D. B. Johnson.

THOMPSON, Julian; *see* Thompson, R. J. de la M.

THOMPSON, Maj.-Gen. Julian Howard Atherden, CB 1982; OBE 1978; Visiting Professor, Department of War Studies, King's College London, since 1997; *b* 7 Oct. 1934; *s* of late Major A. J. Thompson, DSO, MC and Mary Stearns Thompson (*née* Krause); *m* 1960, Janet Avery, *d* of late Richard Robinson Rodd; one *s* one *d*. *Educ:* Sherborne School. 2nd Lieut RM, 1952; served 40, 42, 43, 45 Commandos RM, 1954–69; Asst Sec., Chiefs of Staff Cttee, 1970–71; BM, 3 Cdo Brigade, 1972–73; Directing Staff, Staff Coll., Camberley, 1974–75; CO 40 Cdo RM, 1975–78; Comdr 3 Cdo Brigade, 1981–83, incl. Falklands campaign (CB); Maj.-Gen. Comdg Trng Reserve Forces and Special Forces RM, 1983–86, retired. Sen. Res. Fellow in Logistics and Armed Conflict in the Modern Age, KCL, 1987–97. Life Vice-Pres., British Assoc. for Physical Training, 1998 (Pres., 1988–98). *Publications:* No Picnic: 3 Commando Brigade in the South Atlantic 1982, 1985; Ready for Anything: The Parachute Regiment at War 1940–1982, 1989; (contrib.) Military Strategy in a Changing Europe, 1991; (contrib.) Fallen Stars, 1991; The Lifeblood of War, 1991; (contrib.) The Observer at 200, 1992; The Imperial War Museum Book of Victory in Europe: North West Europe 1944–45, 1994; The Imperial War Museum Book of the War at Sea: the Royal Navy in the Second World War, 1996; (contrib.) Leadership and Command, 1997; The Imperial War Museum Book of War Behind Enemy Lines, 1998; (contrib.) Dimensions of Sea Power, 1998; The Royal Marines: from Sea Soldiers to a Special Force, 2000; (contrib.) Lightning Strikes Twice: the Great World War 1914–1945, 2000. *Recreations:* sailing, shooting, history, cross-country ski-ing, ballet, opera, jazz. *Address:* c/o Lloyds TSB, Royal Parade, Plymouth, Devon PL1 1HB. *Clubs:* Army and Navy; Royal Marines Sailing.

THOMPSON, Julian O.; *see* Ogilvie Thompson.

THOMPSON, Keith Bruce; Vice-Chancellor, Staffordshire University, 1992–95; *b* 13 Sept. 1932; *m* 1956, Kathleen Reeves; one *s* one *d*. *Educ:* Bishopshalt School, Hillingdon; New College, Oxford (Sec./Librarian, Oxford Union). PPE 1955, Dip Educn (distn), 1956, MA 1959; MEd Bristol, 1968. Schoolmaster, City of Bath Boys' School, 1956–62; Lectr, Newton Park Coll., Bath, 1962–67; Head of Dept, Philippa Fawcett Coll., Streatham, 1967–72; Principal, Madeley Coll. of Educn, 1972–78; Dep. Dir, 1978–86, Dir, 1987–92, N Staffs, later Staffs Poly. Chairman: Standing Conf. on Studies in Educn, 1980–82; Undergraduate Initial Training Bd (Educn), CNAA, 1981–85; Chm., Polytechnics Central Admissions System, 1989–93; Dep. Chm., UCAS, 1993–95; Member: Bd, Nat. Adv. Body for Public Sector Higher Educn, 1983–88 (Chm., Teacher Educn Gp, 1983–85). Editor, Educn for Teaching, 1968–74. *Publications:* Education and Philosophy, 1972; (jtly) Curriculum Development, 1974; articles on educn, philosophy, physical educn. *Recreations:* sport, music, books. *Address:* 3 Swindon Manor, Swindon Village, Cheltenham GL51 9RQ. *T:* (01242) 698554.
See also B. K. Thompson.

THOMPSON, Hon. Lindsay Hamilton Simpson, AO 1990; CMG 1975; Premier of Victoria, 1981–82; Leader of the Opposition, Victoria, 1982; *b* 15 Oct. 1923; *s* of Arthur K. Thompson and Ethel M. Thompson; *m* 1950, Joan Margaret Poynder; two *s* one *d*. *Educ:* Caulfield Grammar Sch., Victoria (Captain and Dux 1941); Melbourne Univ. (BA Hons, BEd). MACE. AIF, New Guinea, 1942–45. MP (Lib.) in Victorian Legislative Council: Higinbotham Prov., 1955–67; Monash Prov., 1967–70; MLA Malvern, 1970–82; Member of Cabinet, 1956–82; Parly Sec. of Cabinet 1956–58; Asst Chief Sec. and Asst Attorney Gen., 1958–61, Asst Minister of Transport, 1960–61; Minister of Housing and Forests, 1961–67; Dep. Leader of Govt in Legislative Council, 1962–70; Minister in charge of Aboriginal Welfare, 1965–67; Minister of Educn, 1967–79 (longest term ever in this portfolio); Leader of Legislative Assembly, 1972–79; Dep. Premier of Victoria, 1972–81; Minister for Police and Emergency Services, 1979–81; Treasurer, 1979–82; served longest period as Cabinet Minister in history of Victoria. Director: Mutual Friendly Soc., 1986–; Composite Benefits Soc., 1986–92. State Govt Rep., Melbourne Univ. Council, 1955–59. Dep. Chm., Aust. Advertising Standards Council, 1990–97 (Mem., 1988–90). Pres., Royal Life Saving Soc., 1970–96. Trustee: Melb. Cricket Ground, 1967–2000 (Chm., 1987–99); Nat. Tennis Centre Trust, 1986–96 (Chm., 1994–96); Patron: Victorian Cricket Assoc., 1978–92; Prahran CC; Aust. Quadriplegic Assoc.; Richmond FC; Australian Children's Choir. Bronze Medal, Royal Humane Soc., 1974. *Publications:* Australian Housing Today and Tomorrow, 1965; Looking Ahead in Education, 1969; A Fair Deal for Victoria, 1981; I Remember, 1989. *Recreations:* cricket, golf, tennis. *Address:* 19 Allenby Avenue, Glen Iris, Victoria 3146, Australia. *T:* (3) 98856191. *Clubs:* Melbourne (Melbourne), Kingston Heath Golf, Sorrento Golf.

THOMPSON, McKim; *see* Thompson, I. McK.

THOMPSON, Marjorie Ellis; Director, Cause Related Marketing, Octagon Marketing, since 2001; *b* St Louis, Mo, 8 June 1957; *d* of John William Thompson, III and Janet Ann (*née* Neubeiser); *m* 1982, Kevin Mark Williams (marr. diss. 2000); partner 1984–92, Dafydd Elis Thomas (now Baron Elis-Thomas). *Educ:* Woodrow Wilson High Sch., Long Beach, California; Colorado Coll., Colorado Springs (BSc Hons 1978); LSE (MSc Econ 1979). Campaign for Nuclear Disarmament: Parly Officer, 1983–86; Hd of Press and Public Relns, 1986–87; Vice-Chair, 1987–90; Chair, 1990–93; Researcher for Ann Clwyd, MP, 1987; Royal College of Nursing: Parly Officer, 1988–91; Advr, Dept of Nursing Policy and Practice, 1991–93; Head of Communications, CRE, 1993–97; Dir, Cause Connection, Saatchi & Saatchi, 1997–2000. Co-Chair, Cttee to Stop War in the Gulf, 1990–91; Hon. Pres., Cttee for Just Peace in ME, 1991; Hon. Vice-Pres., Scottish CND, 1994–. Mem., IISS, 1992–94. Fellow: British–American Project, 1990–; Davos World Econ. Forum, 2000; Chair, Bd Dirs, Catalyst, 1997–2000. Mem. Editl Bd and contrib., Jl of Nonprofit and Voluntary Sector Marketing, 1998–. *Publications:* (contrib.) Nursing: the hidden agenda, 1993; (with Hamish Pringle) Brand Spirit: how cause-related marketing builds brands, 1999; contrib. New Statesman & Society, Tribune, AdMap, Harpers & Queen, Market Leader. *Recreations:* travel, contemporary fiction, cinema. *Address:* c/o Octagon Marketing, Octagon House, 81/83 Fulham High Street, SW6 3JW. *T:* (020) 7862 0000.

THOMPSON, Mark; *see* Thompson, O. M.

THOMPSON, Mark John Thompson; Director of Television, BBC, since 2000; *b* 31 July 1957; *s* of Duncan John Thompson and Sydney Columba Corduff; *m* 1987, Jane Emilie Blumberg; two *s* one *d*. *Educ:* Stonyhurst Coll.; Merton Coll., Oxford (BA; Violet Vaughan Morgan English Prize). BBC Television: Research Asst Trainee, 1979–80; Asst Producer, Nationwide, 1980–82; Producer, Breakfast Time, 1982–84; Output Editor: London Plus, 1984–85; Newsnight, 1985–87; Editor: Nine O'Clock News, 1988–90; Panorama, 1990–92; Head of Features, 1992–94; Head of Factual Progs, 1994–96; Controller, BBC2, 1996–98; Dir of Nat. and Regl Broadcasting, 1998–2000. Chm., Edinburgh Internat. TV Fest., 1996. FRTS 1998; FRSA 2000. *Recreations:* walking, cooking. *Address:* c/o BBC, Broadcasting House, Portland Place, W1A 1AA. *T:* (020) 7580 4468.

THOMPSON, Michael, FRAM; Professor of Horn, Royal Academy of Music, since 1985; Principal Horn, London Sinfonietta, since 1986; *b* 4 Jan. 1954; *s* of Ronald and Joan Thompson; *m* 1975, Valerie Botwright; two *s* one *d*. *Educ:* Royal Acad. of Music. FRAM 1988. Principal Horn: BBC Scottish SO, 1972–75; Philharmonia Orch., 1975–85; internat. soloist and recording artist, 1985–. *Publications:* Warm-up Exercises, 1986; Schumann, Konzertstuck: performing edition, 1988; Cadenzas for Haydn and Mozart Horn Concerti, 1990. *Recreations:* reading, walking, cooking. *Address:* 26 Presburg Road, New Malden, Surrey KT3 5AH. *T:* (020) 8942 0768.

THOMPSON, Michael Harry Rex, OBE 1992; FCIB; Director: Wellington Underwriting plc, 1996–2001; Wellington Underwriting Agencies Ltd, 1995–2001; Deputy Chairman, Lloyds Bank Plc, 1991–95 (Director, 1986–95); *b* 14 Jan. 1931; *s* of late William Henry Thompson and Beatrice Hylda Thompson (*née* Heard); *m* 1958, Joyce (*née* Redpath); one *s* one *d*. *Educ:* St John's Sch., Leatherhead, Surrey. Joined Lloyds Bank, 1948; Dep. Chief Exec., 1987–91; Director: National Bank of New Zealand, 1978–82, 1991–95; Lloyds Abbey Life 1991–95; Chm., German Investment Trust, 1990–95. Financial Advr to Dean and Chapter, 1995–, Lay Canon, 1996–2001, Salisbury Cathedral. Trustee, Bankers Club, 1995–2001. *Recreation:* Rugby football.

THOMPSON, Michael Jacques, CMG 1989; OBE 1977; HM Diplomatic Service, retired; *b* 31 Jan. 1936; *s* of late Christopher Thompson and of Colette Jeanne-Marie Thompson; *m* 1967, Mary Susan (*née* Everard); one *s* one *d*. *Educ:* Uppingham; Christ's Coll., Cambridge (Law Tripos, 1956–60; MA). National Service, Kenya, Aden and Cyprus, 1954–56. HMOCS, Kenya, 1960–63; FCO, 1964; served Kuala Lumpur, Saigon, Lusaka and FCO, 1965–79; Counsellor, Kuala Lumpur, 1979–82; seconded to Comdr, British Land Forces, Hong Kong, 1982–85; Counsellor, FCO, 1985. Mem., Royal Asia Soc. Mem., Co. of Barbers. *Recreations:* tennis, golf, gardening. *Address:* Bodgers Wood, Hill Top Lane, Chinnor, Oxfordshire OX9 4BH. *Clubs:* Oxford and Cambridge; Huntercombe Golf.

THOMPSON, Sir Michael (Warwick), Kt 1991; DSc; FInstP; Deputy Chairman, Alliance & Leicester PLC, 1997–2000 (Deputy Chairman, Alliance & Leicester Building Society, 1995–97); Vice-Chancellor and Principal, University of Birmingham, 1987–96, Emeritus Professor, since 1996; *b* 1 June 1931; *s* of Kelvin Warwick Thompson and Madeleine Thompson; *m* 1st, Sybil (*née* Spooner) (*d* 1999); two *s*; 2nd, 2000, Jenny (*née* Mitchell). *Educ:* Rydal Sch.; Univ. of Liverpool (BSc, DSc). Research scientist, AERE, Harwell, 1953–65; Sussex University: Prof. of Experimental Physics, 1965–80; Pro-Vice-Chancellor, 1973–77, actg Vice-Chancellor, 1976; Vis. Prof., 1980–86; Vice-Chancellor, UEA, 1980–86. Chairman: Physics Cttee, SRC, 1975–79; British Council Cttee for Academic Res. Collaboration with Germany, 1989–; Review of ISIS Neutron Source for Central Labs Res. Council, 1997–98. Member: E Sussex AHA, 1974–79; E Sussex Educn Cttee, 1973–78; non-exec. Dir, W Midlands RHA, 1987–96; Chm., Review of London SHAs, 1993. Member: Council, Birmingham Chamber of Industry and Commerce, 1987–96; Council, CNAA, 1989–91; Council for Internat. Co-operation in Higher Educn, 1989–91; Council, CVCP, 1990–93, 1994–96 (Chm. Med. Cttee, 1994–96); Council for Industry and Higher Educn, 1991–96; Council, ACU, 1991–95. Director: Alliance & Leicester PLC (formerly Alliance Bldg Soc., then Alliance & Leicester Bldg Soc.), 1979–2000; Cabuild Ltd, 1987–96. Member Council: Eastbourne Coll., 1977–2000; QMW, 1996–2000. Trustee: Barber Inst. of Fine Arts, 1987–; St Bartholomew's Hosp. Med. Coll., 1998–2000. Mem., Lunar Soc., 1991–96. Hon. LLD Birmingham, 1997; Hon. DSc Sussex, 1998. Oliver Lodge Prizewinner, Univ. of Liverpool, 1953; Prizewinner, Materials Science Club, 1970; C. V. Boys Prizewinner, Inst. of Physics, 1972. Officer's Cross, Order of Merit (Germany), 1997. *Publications:* Defects and Radiation Damage in Metals, 1969; (jtly) Channelling, 1973; over 90 papers in sci. jls. *Recreations:* the arts, navigation in small ships. *Address:* Stoneacre, The Warren, Polperro, Cornwall PL13 2RD. *Clubs:* Athenæum, Royal Over-Seas League; Royal Fowey Yacht.
See also P. Warwick Thompson.

THOMPSON, Sir Nicholas (Annesley Marler), 2nd Bt *cr* 1963, of Reculver, co. Kent; solicitor with CMS Cameron McKenna (formerly Cameron McKenna), since 1997; *b* 19 March 1947; *s* of Sir Richard Hilton Marler Thompson, 1st Bt and of Anne Christabel de Vere Marler Thompson (*née* Annesley); *S* father, 1999; *m* 1982, Venetia Catherine, *yr d* of Mr and Mrs John Heathcote; three *s* one *d*. *Educ:* King's Sch., Canterbury; Univ. of Kent at Canterbury (BA Law 1969). Admitted a solicitor, 1973. Mem. (C) Westminster City Council, 1978–86; Dep. Lord Mayor of Westminster, 1983–84. Contested (C) Newham South, 1983. *Recreations:* foreign travel, cycling, walking, theatre, reading. *Heir:* *s* Simon William Thompson, *b* 10 June 1985. *Address:* Maxgate, George Road, Kingston-upon-Thames, Surrey KT2 7NR. *T:* (020) 8942 7251. *Club:* Carlton.

THOMPSON, Nicolas de la Mare; Chairman, Heinemann Educational Books, 1985–91; *b* 4 June 1928; *s* of Rupert Spens Thompson and Florence Elizabeth Thompson (*née* de la Mare); *m* 1st, 1956, Erica Pennell (*d* 1993); two *s* one *d*; 2nd, 1997, Caroline Graham (*née* Middleton). *Educ:* Eton; Christ Church, Oxford (MA). Managing Director, George Weidenfeld and Nicolson, 1956–70; Publishing Dir, Pitman, 1970–85; Managing Dir, Heinemann Gp of Publishers, 1985–87; Director: Octopus Publishing Gp, 1985–92; Reed Internat. Books, 1990–93; Internat. Book Develt Ltd, 1991–; Chairman: Ginn & Co., 1985–91; Heinemann Professional Publishing, 1986–90; George Philip & Son, 1988–90; Mitchell Beazley, 1988–90; Copyright Licensing Agency Ltd, 1994–96. Chairman: Book Development Council, 1984–86; Publishers Licensing Soc., 1992–96; Treas., Publishers Assoc., 1986–88. Dir, Almeida Theatre Co. Ltd, 1993–2001. *Address:* 8 Ennismore Gardens, SW7 1NL. *Club:* Garrick.

THOMPSON, Dr Noel Brentnall Watson, CEng; education and training consultant; Councillor (Lab), London Borough of Brent, since 1999; *b* 11 Dec. 1932; *s* of George Watson Thompson and Mary Henrietta Gibson; *m* 1957, Margaret Angela Elizabeth Baston; one *s*. *Educ:* Manchester Grammar School; Cambridge Univ. (MA); Imperial College, London (MSc Eng, PhD). National Service, RN (Sub-Lieut), 1951–53. Research, Imperial Coll., 1958–61; Lectr in Physical Metallurgy, Univ. of Birmingham, 1961–65; Dept of Education and Science, 1966–67, 1969–77 and 1979–88 (Under Sec., 1980–88; Head of Higher and Further Educn III Br., 1980–86; Head of Schools 2 Br. and Internat. Relations, 1986–88); Secretary, National Libraries Cttee, 1967–69; Cabinet Office, 1977–79; Chief Exec., Nat. Council for Educnl Technol., 1988–92. Consultant and Vis. Prof. of Educnl Develt, Luton Univ., 1993–98. Chief Exec., English Folk Dance and Song Soc., 1995–97. *Publications:* papers in professional journals. *Recreations:* railways of all sizes, mechanics, music, traditional dance, modern history, photography, walking. *Address:* 101 Woodcock Hill, Kenton, Harrow HA3 0JJ. *T:* (020) 8907 1716; *e-mail:* nbwt@cwcom.net.

THOMPSON, Norman Sinclair, CBE 1980; *b* 7 July 1920; *s* of Norman Whitfield Thompson and Jane Thompson (*née* Robinson); *m* 1945, Peggy Sivil; two *s* (one *d* decd). *Educ:* Middlesbrough High Sch. Qual. Chartered Accountant, 1947 (FCA); Cost and Management Accountant (ACMA), 1949. Served War, Merchant Seaman, 1940–45. Asst

Sec., Paton's and Baldwin's Ltd, 1947; Commercial Manager, Cowan's Sheldon & Co. Ltd, 1955; Group Secretary, Richardson's Westgarth & Co. Ltd, 1957; Financial Dir, David Brown & Sons (Huddersfield) Ltd, 1961; Gen. Manager, Malta Drydocks, Swan Hunter Group Ltd, 1963; apptd Swan Hunter Bd, 1964; Overseas Dir, 1967; Dep. Managing Dir, 1969; The Cunard Steam-Ship Co. Ltd: Man. Dir, Cargo Shipping, 1970; Man. Dir, 1971–74; Chairman: Mass Transit Railway Corp., Hong Kong, 1975–83; Poole Harbour Comrs, 1984–86; Dep. Chm., New Hong Kong Tunnel Co., 1986–92; Director: Hong Kong and Shanghai Banking Corp., 1978–86; British Shipbuilders, 1983–86; Portland Port Ltd, 1995–96. Chm., Burton Bradstock Parish Council, 1999. *Recreations:* dogs, music. *Address:* Shadrach House, Burton Bradstock, Bridport, Dorset DT6 4QG. *Clubs:* Oriental; Hong Kong, Royal Hong Kong Yacht, Hong Kong Jockey.

THOMPSON, (Owen) Mark; theatre designer; *b* 12 April 1957; *s* of late Owen Edgar Thompson and of Barbara Adele (*née* Lister). *Educ:* Radley Coll.; Birmingham Univ. (BA Hons Drama and Theatre Arts). Worked in rep. at Worcester, Exeter, Sheffield and Leeds; designs for: The Scarlet Pimpernel, Chichester, 1985 (transf. Her Majesty's); Cabaret, Strand, 1986; The Sneeze, Aldwych, 1988; Ivanov, and Much Ado About Nothing, Strand, 1989; A Little Night Music, Piccadilly, 1989; Shadowlands, Queen's, 1989 (transf. NY); Joseph and the Amazing Technicolor Dreamcoat, Palladium and Canadian, Australian and American tours, 1991 (Set Design Olivier Award, 1992); Company, Albery, 1996; Art, Wyndhams and NY, 1997; The Blue Room, Donmar Warehouse and NY, Dr Dolittle, Apollo Labbatts, 1998; Mamma Mia, Prince Edward, 1999, Toronto, 2000, US tour, Australia; Blast!, Apollo, 1999, NY, 2001; Lady in the Van, Queen's, 1999; Follies, NY, 2001; *for Royal Exchange Manchester:* Jumpers, 1984; The Country Wife, Mumbo Jumbo, 1986; The School for Scandal, 1990; *for RSC:* Measure for Measure, 1987; The Wizard of Oz, Much Ado About Nothing, 1988; The Comedy of Errors, 1990 (Set Design and Costume Design Olivier Awards, 1992); The Unexpected Man, 1998; *for Almeida:* Volpone, 1990; Betrayal, Party Time, 1991; Butterfly Kiss, 1992; *for Royal National Theatre:* The Wind in the Willows, 1990 (Olivier Award, Plays and Players Award, Critics Circle Award, 1991); The Madness of George III, 1991 (costume design for film, 1994); Arcadia, 1993; Pericles, 1994; What the Butler Saw, 1997; The Day I Stood Still, 1998; Life x 3, 2000; *for Royal Court:* Six Degrees of Separation, 1992 (transf. Comedy); Hysteria, 1994 (Olivier Award for Set Design); The Kitchen, 1995 (Critics' Circle Award); Mouth to Mouth, 2001; *opera:* Montag aus Licht, La Scala, 1989 (costume design only); Falstaff, Scottish Opera, 1991; Peter Grimes, Opera North, 1989; Ariadne auf Naxos, Saltzburg, 1991; Il Viaggio a Reims, Royal Opera, 1992; Hansel and Gretel, Sydney, 1992; The Two Widows, ENO, 1993; Queen of Spades, Metropolitan Opera, New York, 1995; *ballet:* Don Quixote, Royal Ballet, 1993. *Recreations:* cooking, gardening. *Address:* c/o Simpson Fox Associates, 52 Shaftesbury Avenue, W1V 7DE. *T:* (020) 7434 9167.

THOMPSON, Patrick; *see* Thompson, H. P.

THOMPSON, Sir Paul (Anthony), 2nd Bt *cr* 1963; company director; *b* 6 Oct. 1939; *s* of Sir Kenneth Pugh Thompson, 1st Bt, and Nanne (*d* 1994), *yr d* of Charles Broome, Walton, Liverpool; *S* father, 1984; *m* 1971, Pauline Dorothy, *d* of Robert O. Spencer, Bolton, Lancs; two *s* two *d*. *Educ:* Aldenham School, Herts. *Heir: s* Richard Kenneth Spencer Thompson, *b* 27 Jan. 1976. *Address:* Woodlands Farmhouse, Ruff Lane, Ormskirk, Lancs L39 4UL.

THOMPSON, Prof. Paul Richard, DPhil; social historian; Research Professor in Social History, University of Essex, since 1988; Founder, National Life Story Collection, 1987; *b* 1935; *m* 1st, Thea Vigne; one *s* one *d*; 2nd, Natasha Burchardt; one *d*. *Educ:* Bishop's Stortford Coll., Corpus Christi Coll., Oxford; The Queen's Coll., Oxford (Junior Research Fellow, 1961–64). MA, DPhil 1964. University of Essex: Lectr in Sociology, 1964–69; Sen. Lectr, 1969–71; Reader, 1971–88; Sen. Res. Fellow, Nuffield Coll., Oxford, 1968–69; Vis. Prof. of Art History, Johns Hopkins Univ., 1972; Hoffman Wood Prof. of Architecture, Univ. of Leeds, 1977–78; Benjamin Meaker Prof., Univ. of Bristol, 1987. Dir, Qualidara, 1994–2001. Editor: Victorian Soc. Conf. Reports, 1965–67; Oral History, 1970–; Life Stories, 1985–89; International Yearbook of Oral History and Life Stories, 1992–96; Memory and Narrative, 1996–. *Publications:* History of English Architecture (with Peter Kidson and Peter Murray), 1965, 2nd edn 1979; The Work of William Morris, 1967, 3rd edn 1991; Socialists, Liberals and Labour: the struggle for London 1880–1914, 1967; The Edwardians: the remaking of British Society, 1975, 2nd edn 1992; The Voice of the Past: Oral History, 1978, 3rd edn 2000; Living the Fishing, 1983; I Don't Feel Old: the experience of later life, 1990; (with Raphael Samuel) The Myths We Live By, 1990; (with Gloria Wood) The Nineties, 1993; (with Hugo Slim) Listening for a Change, 1993; (with Cathy Courtney) City Lives, 1996; (with Daniel Bertaux) Pathways to Social Class, 1997; (jtly) Growing Up in Stepfamilies, 1997. *Recreations:* cycling, drawing, music, friendship, travel. *Address:* 5 West Street, Wivenhoe, Essex CO7 9DE. *T:* (01206) 824644.

THOMPSON, Paul W.; *see* Warwick Thompson.

THOMPSON, Peter; *see* Thompson, J. P. S.

THOMPSON, Sir Peter (Anthony), Kt 1984; FCIT; Chairman: Child Base Ltd, since 1989; Douglas Stewart Ltd, since 1992; MK Theatre and Gallery Co., since 1996; Goldcrest Homes plc, since 1998; Phoenix Asset Management Ltd, since 1998; Green Energy plc, since 2001; *b* 14 April 1928; *s* of late Herbert Thompson and Sarah Jane Thompson; *m* 1st, 1958, Patricia Anne Norcott (*d* 1983); one *s* two *d*; 2nd, 1986, Lydia Mary Kite (*née* Hodding); two *d*. *Educ:* Royal Drapers Sch.; Bradford Grammar Sch.; Leeds Univ. (BA Econ). Unilever, 1952–62; GKN, 1962–64; Transport Controller, Rank Organisation, 1964–67; Head of Transport, BSC, 1967–72; Group Co-ordinator, BRS Ltd, 1972–75; Exec. Vice-Chm. (Operations), Nat. Freight Corp., 1975–77; Chief Exec., Nat. Freight Corp., later Nat. Freight Co., 1977–80; Dep. Chm. and Chief Exec., 1980–82, Chm. and Chief Exec., 1982–84, Exec. Chm., 1984–90, Pres., 1991–93, NFC. Dir, 1989–90, Dep. Chm., 1989–90, Chm., March–July 1990, British & Commonwealth Hldgs; Chairman: Community Hospitals plc, 1981–96; FI Group plc, 1990–99; Stocktrade, 2000–01; Dep. Chm., Wembley plc, 1991–95; Director: Granville & Co. Ltd, 1984–90; Pilkington plc, 1985–93; Kenning Motor Group, 1985–86; Smiths Industries PLC, 1986–98; Meyer International, 1988–92; Aegis plc, 1993–99; Brewin Dolphin Gp, 1994–2000; Legal Document Co., 2001–; Pres., ProShare, 1994–99 (Chm., 1992–94). Mem., Nat. Trng Task Force, 1989–93. President: Inst. of Freight Forwarders, 1982–83; Inst. of Logistics and Distribn Management (formerly Inst. of Physical Distribn Management), 1988–93 (Chm., 1985–88); Vice-Pres., CIT, 1982–85; Chm., CBI Wider Share Ownership Task Force, 1990. CIMgt. Hon. LLD: Leeds, 1991; Nottingham, 1991; Hon. DTech Bradford, 1991; Hon. DSc Cranfield Inst. of Technol., 1992. Hambro Businessman of the Year, 1983; BIM Gold Medal, 1991. *Publication:* Sharing the Success: the story of the NFC, 1990. *Recreations:* golf, walking, music. *Address:* The Mill House, Mill Street, Newport Pagnell, Bucks MK16 8ER. *Club:* Royal Automobile.

THOMPSON, Peter John; education and training consultant; *b* 17 April 1937; *s* of late George Kenneth Thompson and Gladys Pamela (*née* Partington), W Midlands; *m* 1961, Dorothy Ann Smith; one *s* three *d*. *Educ:* Aston Univ. (BSc 1st Cl. Hons MechEngrg; MSc); CNAA (DTech). Whitworth Soc. Prize. CEng, FIEE; FIPD. With Tube Investments, 1952–61; Lectr 1961, Sen. Lectr 1968–70, Harris Coll., Preston; Sen. Sci. Officer, UKAEA, Preston, 1965–68; Prin. Lectr, Sheffield City Poly., 1970–77; Hd of Dept and Dean of Engrg, Trent Poly., Nottingham, 1977–83; Pro Rector, then Dep. Rector, Poly. of Central London, 1983–86; Professor: Trent Poly., 1980–83; Poly. of Central London, 1983–86; Chief Exec., NCVQ, 1986–91; Vis. Prof., Sch. of Mgt, Open Univ., 1991–94. Consultant, HR Services, 1997–. Mem., then Chm., Manufacturing Bd, CNAA, 1978–86; Mem., Cttee for Sci. and Technology, CNAA, 1982–86; Mem. then Chm., Cttee for Engrg in Polytechnics, 1981–86; Member: Engrg Adv. Cttee, NAB, 1980–84; Engrg Scis Divl Bd of IMechE, 1984–86; Chm., Materials Tech. Activities Cttee, IMechE, 1984–86; Mem., Council, Open Coll., 1987–90. Sen. Awards Consultant, C&G, 1992–95. Hon. Mem., C&G, 1991. FRSA. *Publications:* numerous papers on engrg manufacture and vocational educn and trng, 1968–, incl. papers on hydrostatic extension, lubrication, cutting tool wear and mechanics and metal forming; patents. *Recreations:* genealogy, numismatics, golf. *Address:* Berkhamsted, Herts HP4 3JJ. *T:* (01442) 865127.

THOMPSON, Peter John; His Honour Judge Peter Thompson; a Circuit Judge, since 1998; *b* 30 Dec. 1943; *s* of late Eric Thompson and Olive Ethel Thompson (*née* Miskin); *m* 1969, Elizabeth Anne Granger Rees; one *s* two *d*. *Educ:* Glyn Grammar Sch., Epsom; St Catherine's Coll., Oxford (MA Jurisp.). Admitted Solicitor, 1970; Solicitor and Barrister, Supreme Court of Vic., Australia, 1972; Partner: Turner Martin & Symes, Solicitors, Ipswich, 1976–91; Eversheds, Solicitors, Ipswich, 1991–98. *Recreations:* jazz, playing and listening, soccer, playing and watching, jogging and walking in English and French countryside, family, literature, travel. *Address:* Ipswich Crown Court, Civic Drive, Ipswich, Suffolk IP1 2DX. *T:* (01473) 220750.

THOMPSON, Peter Kenneth James; Solicitor to Departments of Health and of Social Security, 1989–97; *b* 30 July 1937; *s* of Kenneth George Thompson and Doreen May Thompson; *m* 1970, Sandy Lynne Harper; two *d*. *Educ:* Worksop Coll.; Christ's Coll., Cambridge (MA, LLB). Called to the Bar, Lincoln's Inn, 1961; practised at Common Law Bar, 1961–73; Lawyer in Govt Service: Law Commission, 1973–78; Lord Chancellor's Dept, 1978–83; Under Sec., DHSS, 1983. General Editor: The County Court Practice, 1991–98; The Civil Court Practice, 1999–. Hon. QC 1997. *Publications:* The Unfair Contract Terms Act 1977, 1978; The Recovery of Interest, 1985; *radio plays:* A Matter of Form, 1977; Dormer and Grand-Daughter, 1978. *Recreation:* writing.

THOMPSON, Pratt; *see* Thompson, W. P.

THOMPSON, Raymond, CBE 1988; PhD; FRSC; FREng; Deputy Chairman, Borax Research Ltd, 1986–90 (Managing Director, 1980–86); Director: RTZ Chemicals (formerly Borax Consolidated) (Borides) Ltd, 1986–89; Boride Ceramics and Composites Ltd, 1990–92; Azmat Ltd, since 1993; *b* 4 April 1925; *s* of late William Edward Thompson and Hilda Thompson (*née* Rowley). *Educ:* Longton High Sch.; Univ. of Nottingham (MSc 1950, PhD 1952); Imperial Coll., Univ. of London (DIC 1953). Research Manager, Borax Consolidated, 1961; Res. Dir, 1969–86, Business Develt Dir, 1986–87, Scientific Advr, 1987–95, Borax Hldgs Ltd, later RTZ Borax and Minerals Ltd. Consultant: RTZ Chemicals Ltd, 1988–89; CRA Ltd, 1988–91; Rhône-Poulenc, 1989–92. Special Professor of Inorganic Chemistry, Univ. of Nottingham, 1975–96; Hon. Prof., Molecular Sciences, Univ. of Warwick, 1975–94. Member Council: Royal Inst. of Chemistry, 1969–72; Chemical Soc., 1977–80 (Chm., Inorganic Chemicals Gp, 1972–83); RSC, 1983–88 (Vice-Pres., Industrial Div., 1981–83, Pres., 1983–85 and 1988–89). Governor, Kingston-upon-Thames Polytechnic, 1978–88. Hon. Associate, RHC, London Univ., 1984. Freeman, City of London. FREng (FEng 1985). Industrial Chemistry Award, Chem. Soc., 1976. *Publications:* (ed) The Modern Inorganic Chemicals Industry, 1977; (ed) Mellors Comprehensive Treatise, Boron Supplement, Part A, 1979, Part BI, 1981; (ed) Speciality Inorganic Chemicals, 1981; (ed) Energy and Chemistry, 1981; (ed) Trace Metal Removal From Aqueous Solution, 1986; (ed) The Chemistry of Wood Preservation, 1991; Industrial Inorganic Chemicals: production and uses, 1995; various papers on inorganic boron and nitrogen chemistry. *Recreation:* gardening. *Address:* 10 Waldorf Heights, Hawley Hill, Camberley, Surrey GU17 9JH. *T:* (01276) 32900.

THOMPSON, Richard Paul Hepworth, DM; FRCP; Physician to the Queen and Head of HM Medical Household, since 1993 (Physician to the Royal Household, 1982–93); Consultant Physician, St Thomas' Hospital, since 1972; Physician, King Edward VII Hospital for Officers, since 1982; *b* 14 April 1940; *s* of Stanley Henry and Winifred Lilian Thompson; *m* 1974, Eleanor Mary Hughes. *Educ:* Epsom Coll.; Worcester Coll., Oxford (MA, DM); St Thomas's Hosp. Med. Sch. MRC Clinical Res. Fellow, Liver Unit, KCH, 1967–69; Fellow, Gastroenterology Unit, Mayo Clinic, USA, 1969–71; Lectr, Liver Unit, KCH, 1971–72. Mem., Lambeth, Southwark and Lewisham AHA, 1979–82. Examiner in Medicine: Soc. of Apothecaries, 1976–80; Faculty of Dental Surgery, RCS, 1980–86; Examr, 1991–, Censor, 1998–2000, RCP. Governor, Guy's Hosp. Med. Sch., 1980–82; Member Cttee of Management: Inst. of Psychiatry, 1981–95; King Edward VII Hosp. Fund, 1985–89, 1992–96 (Mem., Gen. Council, 1985–). Vice-Chm., Council, BHF, 2001–; Trustee, Thrive, 2001–. *Publications:* Physical Signs in Medicine, 1980; Lecture Notes on the Liver, 1986; papers and reviews in med. jls. *Address:* 36 Dealtry Road, SW15 6NL. *T:* (020) 8789 3839.

THOMPSON, Robin; *see* Thompson, D. R. B.

THOMPSON, (Rupert) Julian (de la Mare); non-executive Chairman, Sotheby's Asia, since 1992; *b* 23 July 1941; *s* of Rupert Spens Thompson and Florence Elizabeth (*née* de la Mare); *m* 1965, Jacqueline Mary Ivimy; three *d*. *Educ:* Eton Coll.; King's Coll., Cambridge (MA). Joined Sotheby's, 1963: appointed a Director, 1969; Chm., 1982–86; Dep. Chm., 1987–92; Chm., Sotheby's International, 1982–85, 1987–88. *Address:* 47 Warrington Crescent, W9 1EJ. *T:* (020) 7289 3145.
See also N. de la M. Thompson.

THOMPSON, Ruth; Director of Finance, Department for Education and Skills (formerly Department for Education and Employment), since 2000; *b* 4 July 1953; *d* of Arthur Frederick (Pat) Thompson and Mary Thompson (*née* Barritt). *Educ:* Somerville Coll., Oxford (MA Modern Hist.); St Antony's Coll., Oxford and Instituto di Tella, Buenos Aires (DPhil Econ. Hist. 1978). Depts of Industry, Trade and Prices and Consumer Protection, 1978–90; Private Sec. to Parly Under-Sec., Dept of Trade and successive Secs of State for Trade and Industry, 1982–84; Cabinet Office, 1987; Asst Sec., DTI, 1990–92; HM Treasury, 1992–98; DSS, 1999–2000. *Recreations:* walking, swimming. *Address:* Department for Education and Skills, Sanctuary Buildings, Great Smith Street, SW1P 3BT. *T:* (020) 7925 7402.

THOMPSON, Tanni Carys Davina G.; *see* Grey-Thompson.

THOMPSON, Sir (Thomas d'Eyncourt) John, 6th Bt *cr* 1806, of Hartsbourne Manor, Hertfordshire; Investment Director, King Sturge, Spain; *b* 22 Dec. 1956; *o s* of Sir (Thomas) Lionel Tennyson Thompson, 5th Bt and of Margaret Thompson (*née* Browne); *S* father, 1999. *Educ:* Eton; King's Coll., London (BA; MSc). ARICS 1993. *Address:* Ventura Rodriguez 20, 5°, 28008 Madrid, Spain. *T:* (91) 5483606.

THOMPSON, (William) Godfrey, MA; FSA, FLA; library planning consultant, since 1983; *b* 28 June 1921; *s* of late A. and E. M. Thompson, Coventry; *m* 1946, Doreen Mary Cattell; one *s. Educ:* King Henry VIII Sch., Coventry. MA Loughborough, 1977. Served with Royal Signals and Indian Signal Corps, 1941–46. Entered Library Service, Coventry, 1937; Dep. Borough Librarian, Chatham, 1946; Dep. City Librarian: Kingston-upon-Hull, 1952; Manchester, 1958; City Librarian, Leeds, 1963; Guildhall Librarian, Director of Libraries and Art Galleries, City of London, 1966–83; Cultural Consultant, UAE, Abu Dhabi, 1983–86. Organiser, City Treasures exhibns in Brussels, 1967, Vienna, 1968, San Francisco, 1970–71, etc. Hon. Librarian to Clockmakers' Co., Gardeners' Co., Charles Lamb Soc.; Pres., Assoc. of Assistant Librarians, 1962. Member: Council, Library Assoc., 1968–81 (Hon. Treasurer, 1974–77; Pres., 1978); Council, Aslib, 1968–71; Liby Adv. Bd, British Council, 1974–83; Adv. Panel to Sec. of State on allocation of books received under Capital Transfer Tax; Adv. Panel to Sec. of State on Export of Works of Art. Mem. Exec. Cttee, Friends of the Nat. Libraries; Founding Hon. Sec. Internat. Assoc. Metropolitan Libraries, 1968–70. Governor, St Bride Foundn. Mem. Adv. Bd, New Library World; Libraries Specialist, Architects' Jl, 1968–74; consultant on libraries to more than 20 overseas governments and nat. bodies, including the planning of twelve nat. libraries; Advr, Botswana Nat. Liby project, 1994, 1996. FRSA. *Recreation:* reading — at last. *Publications:* London's Statues, 1971; Planning and Design of Library Buildings, 1972, 3rd edn 1989; (ed) London for Everyman, 1969; (ed) Encyclopædia of London, 1969. *Address:* Southdown, Down Lane, Compton, Surrey GU3 1DN.

THOMPSON, William John; *b* 26 Oct. 1939; *s* of William H. Thompson and Catherine Thompson; *m* 1962, Violet Joyce Armstrong; one *s* two *d. Educ:* Edenderry Primary Sch.; Deverney Primary Sch.; Omagh Acad. With Tyrone CC, 1957–66; radio and TV retailer, 1966–97. Member: NI Assembly, 1973–74 and 1982–85; NI Convention, 1975–76; Omagh DC, 1981–93. MP (UU) Tyrone West, 1997–2001; contested same seat, 2001. *Recreations:* reading, occasional round of golf. *Address:* 129 Donaghanie Road, Beragh, Co. Tyrone, N Ireland BT79 0XE.

THOMPSON, (William) Pratt; consultant and director, various companies; *b* 9 Feb. 1933; *s* of Philip Amos Thompson and Regina Beatrice (*née* Kirby); *m* 1963, Jenny Frances Styles; two *d. Educ:* Princeton Univ.; Columbia Univ. (BA Econ *magna cum laude*, Phi Beta Kappa); Centre d'Etudes Industrielles, Geneva (MBA). AMF Incorporated, 1959–73: executive assignments in NYC, Geneva, Tokyo, Hong Kong and London; Vice Pres., 1968; Dep. Managing Director, Bowthorpe Holdings Ltd, 1973–78; BL Limited, 1978–81: Man. Dir, Jaguar Rover Triumph Ltd, 1978–79; Chm., BL Internat. Ltd, 1979–81; Dir, Metalurgica de Santa Ana SA (Madrid), 1978–81; Vice-Chm., Colbert Gp (Geneva), 1981–84; Chairman: AIDCOM International plc, 1983–86 (Dir, 1982–); AIDCOM Technology Ltd, 1982–86; Husky Computers Ltd, 1982–86; Gallex Ltd, 1989–91; Dir, 1987–93, Man. Dir, 1989–93, Unitech plc. Member: Council, SMM&T, 1978–81; Council on Foreign Relations (USA), 1980–89. *Recreations:* various. *Address:* Trinity Hall, Castle Hedingham, Essex CO9 3EY. *Clubs:* Brooks's; Hong Kong (Hong Kong).

THOMPSON, Willoughby Harry, CMG 1974; CBE 1968 (MBE 1954); *b* 3 Dec. 1919; *m* 1963, Sheelah O'Grady; no *c*. Served War: RA, and E African Artillery, 1939–47. Kenya Govt Service, 1947–48; Colonial Administrative Service, Kenya, 1948–63; Colonial Sec., Falkland Islands, 1963–69 (Actg Governor, 1964 and 1967); Actg Judge, Falkland Islands and Dependencies Supreme Court, 1965–69; Actg Administrator, British Virgin Islands, May-July 1969; HM Comr in Anguilla, July 1969–1971; Governor of Montserrat, 1971–74.

THOMPSON HANCOCK, P(ercy) E(llis); *see* Hancock.

THOMPSON-McCAUSLAND, Benedict Maurice Perronet, FCA; Partner, Temax Associates, since 1991; Group Managing Director, National & Provincial Building Society, 1987–90; *b* 5 Feb. 1938; *s* of late Lucius P. Thompson-McCausland, CMG and Helen Laura McCausland; *m* 1964, Frances Catherine Fothergill Smith; three *d. Educ:* Eton Coll.; Trinity Coll., Cambridge (MA; Rowing Blue). FCA 1974. Articled to Coopers & Lybrand, Chartered Accountants, 1961–64; Arbuthnot Latham & Co. Ltd, 1964–80: Asst to Dirs, 1964; Banking Manager, 1967; Dir, 1968; Dep. Chm., 1978; London Life Association Ltd: Dir, 1976–81; Vice-Pres., 1979–87; Chief Exec., 1981–87. Dir, Advanced Personnel Technology, 1993–2001; formerly Director: Western Trust & Savings Ltd; Concord Internat.; First National Finance Corp. plc. Chm., Lombard Assoc., 1979–81. Director: British Sch. of Osteopathy, 1991– (Chm., 1996–2000); Harefield Hosp. NHS Trust, 1992–98. Mem. Council, 1987–2000, and Mem. Exec. Cttee, 1988–91, Industrial Soc. Mem., Council of Management, Arnolfini Gall., 1983–86. John Loxham Lectr, Inst. of Quality Assurance, 1997. *Publications:* (with Derek Biddle) Change, Business Performance and Values, 1985; (with J. Bergwerk) Leading to Success: how leaders unlock energy, 1994; articles in business jls. *Recreations:* windsurfing, ski-ing, walking. *Address:* 91 Blenheim Crescent, W11 2EQ. *T:* (020) 7727 1266. *Clubs:* Leander (Henley-on-Thames); Hawks (Cambridge).

THOMSON, family name of **Barons Thomson of Fleet** and **Thomson of Monifieth**.

THOMSON OF FLEET, 2nd Baron *cr* 1964; **Kenneth Roy Thomson;** publishing executive; Chairman of the Board and Director, The Thomson Corporation; *b* Toronto, Ont., 1 Sept. 1923; *s* of 1st Baron Thomson of Fleet, GBE, founder of Thomson Newspapers, and Edna Annis (*d* 1951), *d* of John Irvine, Drayton, Ont.; *S* father, 1976; *m* 1956, Nora Marilyn, *d* of A. V. Lavis; two *s* one *d. Educ:* Upper Canada Coll.; Univ. of Cambridge, England (MA). Served War of 1942–45 with RCAF. Began in editorial dept of Timmins Daily Press, Timmins, Ont., 1947; Advertising Dept, Galt Reporter, Cambridge, Ont, 1948–50, General Manager, 1950–53; returned to Toronto Head Office of Thomson Newspapers to take over direction of Company's Canadian and American operations. Pres., Thomson Works of Art Ltd; Dep. Chm., 1966–67, Chm., 1968–70, Co-Pres., 1971–81, Times Newspapers Ltd; Chm., The Woodbridge Co. Ltd. *Recreations:* collecting paintings and works of art, walking, golf. *Heir: s* Hon. David Kenneth Roy Thomson, *b* 12 June 1957. *Address:* (home) 8 Castle Frank Road, Toronto, ON M4W 2Z4, Canada; 8 Kensington Palace Gardens, W8 4QP; (office) The Thomson Corporation, 65 Queen Street West, Toronto, ON M5H 2M8, Canada; The Thomson Corporation plc, The Quadrangle, PO Box 4YG, 180 Wardour Street, W1A 4YG. *Clubs:* Granite, Hunt, Toronto, York, York Downs (Toronto).

THOMSON OF MONIFIETH, Baron *cr* 1977 (Life Peer), of Monifieth, Dundee; **George Morgan Thomson,** KT 1981; PC 1966; Chairman, Independent Broadcasting Authority, 1981–88 (Deputy Chairman, 1980); Chancellor, Heriot Watt University, 1977–91; *b* 16 Jan. 1921; *s* of late James Thomson, Monifieth; *m* 1948, Grace Jenkins; two *d. Educ:* Grove Academy, Dundee. Served War of 1939–45, in Royal Air Force, 1940–46. Assistant Editor, Forward, 1946, Editor, 1948–53. Contested (Lab) Glasgow, Hillhead, 1950; MP (Lab) Dundee East, July 1952–72. Joint Chm., Council for Education in the Commonwealth, 1959–64; Adviser to Educational Institute of Scotland, 1960–64. Minister of State, Foreign Office, 1964–66; Chancellor of the Duchy of Lancaster, 1966–67; Joint Minister of State, Foreign Office, 1967; Secretary of State for Commonwealth Affairs, Aug. 1967–Oct. 1968; Minister Without Portfolio, 1968–69; Chancellor of the Duchy of Lancaster, 1969–70; Shadow Defence Minister, 1970–72. Chm., Labour Cttee for Europe, 1972–73; Commissioner, EEC, 1973–Jan. 1977. Mem., Lib Dems, 1989– (spokesman on foreign affairs and broadcasting, H of L, 1990–98). Chairman: European Movement in Britain, 1977–80; Advertising Standards Authority, 1977–80; European TV and Film Forum, 1989–91. First Crown Estate Comr, 1978–80. Director: Royal Bank of Scotland Gp, 1977–90; ICI plc, 1977–89; Woolwich Equitable Building Soc., 1979–91 (Dep. Chm., 1988–91); Chairman: Value and Income Trust, 1988–2000; Grant Leisure, 1990–94; Woolwich Europe, 1990–92. President: Hist. of Advertising Trust, 1985–99; Prix Italia, 1989–91; Dir, ENO, 1987–93. Chm., Suzy Lamplugh Trust, 1990–93; Dep. Chm., Ditchley Foundn, 1983–87; Pilgrims Trustee, 1977–97; Trustee: Thomson Foundn, 1977–; Leeds Castle Foundn, 1978– (Chm., 1994–). FRSE 1985; FRTS 1990 (Vice-Pres., 1982–89). Hon. LLD Dundee, 1967; Hon. DLitt: Heriot-Watt, 1973; New Univ. of Ulster, 1984; Hon. DSc Aston, 1976. *Address:* House of Lords, SW1A 0PW.

See also C. Thomson.

THOMSON, Adam McClure; HM Diplomatic Service; Counsellor, Foreign and Commonwealth Office, since 1998; *b* 1 July 1955; *e s* of Sir John Thomson, *qv*; *m* 1984, Fariba Shirazi; one *s* two *d. Educ:* Westminster Sch.; Trinity Coll., Cambridge (MA); Harvard Univ. (MPP). Joined FCO, 1978; Third, later Second Sec., Moscow, 1981–83; Second, later First Sec., UK delegn to NATO, Brussels, 1983–86; First Sec., FCO, 1986–89; Cabinet Office, 1989–91; First Sec. (Political), Washington, 1991–95; Counsellor (Political), New Delhi, 1995–98. *Address:* c/o Foreign and Commonwealth Office, King Charles Street, SW1A 2AH. *Club:* Athenæum.

THOMSON, Prof. Andrew James, DPhil; FRS 1993; CChem, FRSC; Norwich Research Park Professor, since 1995, and Dean, School of Chemical Sciences, since 1999, University of East Anglia (Professor of Chemistry, since 1985); *b* 31 July 1940; *s* of late Andrew Henderson Thomson and Eva Frances Annie (*née* Moss); *m* 1966, Anne Marsden; two *s. Educ:* Steyning Grammar Sch.; Wadham Coll., Oxford (MA, DPhil). FRSC 1990. Res. Asst Prof., Dept of Biophysics, Michigan State Univ., 1967; School of Chemical Sciences, University of East Anglia: Demonstrator, 1967–68; Lectr, 1968–77; Sen. Lectr, 1977–83; Reader, 1983–85; Hd of Inorganic Chem. Sector, 1984–97. Royal Society of Chemistry: Silver Medal for analytical chemistry, 1991; Hugo Muller Lectureship, 1997; Interdisciplinary Award, 2000. *Publications:* papers in scientific jls. *Recreation:* walking. *Address:* 12 Armitage Close, Cringleford, Norwich NR4 6XZ. *T:* (01603) 504623; *e-mail:* a.thomson@uea.ac.uk.

THOMSON, Prof. Andrew William John, PhD; OBE 1993; Professor, School of Management, Open University, 1988–2001; *b* 26 Jan. 1936; *s* of Andrew Edward Thomson and Helen Thomson; *m* 1st, 1966, Joan Marjorie Hughes (marr. diss. 1980); two *s*; 2nd, 1992, Rosemary Joy Hetherington Smith (*d* 1998). *Educ:* St Bees Sch.; St Edmund Hall, Oxford (BA Hons PPE 1959); Cornell Univ. (MS 1961; PhD 1968). 2nd Lieut, RA, 1954–56; Lieut, Parachute Regt TA, 1958–63; Brand Manager, Lever Brothers, 1961–65; University of Glasgow: Lectr, Sen. Lectr and Reader, 1968–78; Prof. of Business Policy, 1978–87; Dean: Scottish Business Sch., 1983–87; Sch. of Management, Open Univ., 1988–93. Prof., Univ. of Chicago, 1973, 1977. Dir, Scottish Transport Gp, 1977–84; Mem., Scottish Agricl Wages Bd, 1985–99; Vice-Chairman: Mgt and Industrial Relations Cttee, SSRC, 1982–85; Industry and Employment Cttee, ESRC, 1985–88; Chm., Jt Cttee, ESRC-SERC, 1987–90. Chairman: Council of Univ. Mgt Schs, 1985–87; British Acad. of Mgt, 1990–93. *Publications:* (with L. C. Hunter) The Nationalised Transport Industries, 1973; (with S. R. Engleman) The Industrial Relations Act, 1975; (with V. V. Murray) Grievance Procedures, 1976; (with P. B. Beaumont) Collective Bargaining in the Public Sector, 1978; (ed with M. Warner) The Behavioural Sciences and Industrial Relations, 1981; (ed with M. B. Gregory) A Portrait of Pay, 1990; (jtly) Changing Patterns of Management Development, 2001. *Recreations:* golf, walking. *Address:* The Willow House, Daventry Road, Norton, Northants NN11 5ND. *T:* (01327) 879147. *Club:* Waitangi Golf.

THOMSON, Brian Harold, TD 1947; DL; Chairman, since 1974, Joint Managing Director, since 1948, D. C. Thomson & Co. Ltd; *b* 21 Nov. 1918; *e s* of late William Harold Thomson of Kemback and Helen Irene, *d* of Sir Charles Ballance; *m* 1947, Agnes Jane Patricia Cunninghame (*d* 1991); one *s* four *d. Educ:* Charterhouse. Served War of 1939–45: 1st Fife and Forfar Yeomanry, and on Staff, DAQMG 1st Armoured Div., N Africa and Italy, 1943–44. GSO2 Instructor, Staff Coll., Haifa, 1944–46; Lt-Col Comdg Fife and Forfar Yeomanry TA, 1953–56. Entered D. C. Thomson & Co. Ltd, 1937. Director: John Leng & Co. Ltd, 1948–; Southern Television, 1959–88; Alliance Trust and Second Alliance Trust, 1961–89. DL Fife, 1988. *Recreations:* golf, shooting. *Club:* Royal and Ancient Golf (St Andrews).

THOMSON, Caroline, (Mrs R. Liddle); Director, Public Policy, BBC, since 2000; *b* 15 May 1954; *d* of Lord Thomson of Monifieth, *qv*; *m* 1st, 1977, Ian Bradley (marr. diss. 1980); 2nd, 1983, Roger Liddle; one *s. Educ:* Mary Datchelor Grammar Sch.; Univ. of York (BA Hons). BBC trainee, 1975–77; producer: Analysis, BBC Radio, 1978–81; Panorama, 1982; Political Advr to Rt Hon. Roy Jenkins, 1983; Commng Ed., Business and Sci., 1984-90, Hd, Corporate Affairs, 1991-95, Channel 4; Dep. Chief Exec., BBC World Service, 1995-2000. *Recreations:* domesticity, music. *Address:* BBC, Broadcasting House, W1A 1AA. *T:* (020) 7765 4974.

THOMSON, Sir David; *see* Thomson, Sir F. D. D.

THOMSON, David Paget, RD 1969; Chairman, Dresdner RCM (formerly Kleinwort) Emerging Markets Trust, since 1993; Director, Foreign & Colonial European Investment Trust, since 1998; *b* 19 March 1931; *s* of Sir George Paget Thomson, FRS, Nobel Laureate, and Kathleen Buchanan Smith; *m* 1959, Patience Mary, *d* of Sir William Lawrence Bragg, CH, OBE, MC, FRS, Nobel Laureate; two *s* two *d. Educ:* Rugby Sch.; Grenoble Univ.; Trinity Coll., Cambridge (scholar; BA 1953, MA 1957). Nat. Service, RN (Sub-Lieut), 1953–55; subseq. Lieut-Comdr RNR. Lazard Bros & Co., 1956, Director, 1965–86; seconded to HM Diplomatic Service, 1971–73, as Counsellor (Economic), Bonn. Dir Gen., BIEC, 1987–90; Dep. Chm., City Communications Centre, 1987–89. Chairman: Jufcrest, 1984–89; Medical Sickness Annuity and Life Assce Soc. Ltd, 1995–97; Dep. Chm., Permanent Insce Co., 1995–97; Director: Finance Co. Viking, Zurich, 1969–87; Richard Daus & Co., bankers, Frankfurt, 1974–81; Applied Photophysics, 1976–87; Wesleyan Assce Soc. Ltd, 1997–2000. Mem., Monopolies and Mergers Commn, 1984–94. Member: Council, Brunel Univ., 1974–85; Court of

Governors, Henley Management Coll., 1979–94; Dir, Henley Distance Learning Ltd, 1985–95. Hon. Treasurer, British Dyslexia Assoc., 1984–86. Chairman: Fitzwilliam Mus. Trust, 1988–93; Portsmouth Naval Base Property Trust, 1992–98; Royal Institution: Treasurer, 1976–81; Chm. Council, 1985. CC Oxon 1985–89. Master, Plumbers' Co., 1980–81. *Recreations:* hill-walking, gardening, real tennis. *Address:* Little Stoke House, Wallingford, Oxon OX10 6AX. *T:* (01491) 837161. *Club:* Athenæum (Chm., 1995–98).
See also S. L. Bragg, Sir J. A. Thomson.

THOMSON, Maj.-Gen. David Phillips, CB 1993; CBE 1989; MC 1965; Senior Army Member, Royal College of Defence Studies, 1992–95; *b* 30 Jan. 1942; *s* of Cyril Robert William Thomson and Louise Mary Thomson (*née* Phillips). *Educ:* Eastbourne Coll.; RMA Sandhurst. Commnd, Argyll and Sutherland Highlanders, 1962; despatches, 1968; Bde Major, 6th Armd Bde, 1975; Instr, Staff Coll., 1980; CO, 1st Bn, A and SH, 1982; Chief of Staff: RMCS, 1985; 1st Armd Div., 1986; Comdr, 1st Inf. Bde/UK Mobile Force, 1987; despatches, 1992. Col, Argyll and Sutherland Highlanders, 1992–2000. Captain, Royal Castle of Tarbert, 1992–2000. Chm., Sussex Combined Services Museum Trust, 1995–. FRGS 1993. *Recreations:* golf, historical research. *Address:* Regimental HQ, Argyll and Sutherland Highlanders, The Castle, Stirling FK8 1EH. *T:* (01786) 475165. *Club:* Caledonian.

THOMSON, Prof. Derick Smith, FBA 1992; FRSE; Professor of Celtic, University of Glasgow, 1963–91, now Emeritus; *b* 5 Aug. 1921; *s* of James and Christina Thomson; *m* 1952, Carol Mac Michael Galbraith; five *s* one *d*. *Educ:* Nicolson Inst., Stornoway; Univ. of Aberdeen (MA); University College of North Wales, Bangor; Emmanuel Coll., Cambridge (BA 1948). Asst in Celtic, Univ. of Edinburgh, 1948–49; Lectr in Welsh, Univ. of Glasgow, 1949–56; Reader in Celtic, Univ. of Aberdeen, 1956–63. Chm., Gaelic Books Council, 1968–91; Pres., Scottish Gaelic Texts Soc., 1964–96. Editor: Scottish Gaelic Studies, 1962–76; Gairm, 1952–. Hon. DLitt: Wales, 1987; Aberdeen, 1994. First recipient, Ossian Prize, FVS Foundn, Hamburg, 1974. *Publications:* The Gaelic Sources of Macpherson's Ossian, 1952; Branwen Verch Lyr, 1961, 2nd edn 1968; An Introduction to Gaelic Poetry, 1974, 2nd edn 1990; The Companion to Gaelic Scotland, 1983, 3rd edn 1994; The MacDiarmid MS Anthology, 1992; Gaelic Poetry in the Eighteenth Century, 1993; Alasdair Mac Mhaighstir Alasdair, Selected Poems, 1996; *poetry:* Creachadh Na Clàrsaich (Plundering the Harp), Collected Poems, 1982; Smeur an Dòchais (Bramble of Hope), 1992; Meall Garbh (The Rugged Mountain), 1995. *Recreations:* writing, travel, politics, gardening. *Address:* 15 Struan Road, Cathcart, Glasgow G44 3AT. *T:* (0141) 637 3704. *Clubs:* Glasgow Art, Town and Gown (Glasgow).

THOMSON, Dick; HM Diplomatic Service; Consul General, Barcelona, since 1999; *b* 18 Dec. 1942; *s* of Adam and Janet Alexander Thomson; *m* 1972, Jacqueline Margaret Dunn; one *s* one *d*. *Educ:* Port Glasgow High Sch.; Greenock High Sch. With Ministry of Transport, 1961–66; entered FCO, 1966; served: Havana, 1969–70; Athens, 1970–71; Rome, 1971–72; Warsaw, 1972–73; Personnel Dept, FCO, 1973–76; San Francisco, 1976–80; Consul, Algiers, 1980–83; Near East and N Africa Dept, FCO, 1984–87; First Sec., Copenhagen, 1988–92; Head of Parly Relns Unit, FCO, 1992–95; Ambassador to Dominican Republic, 1995–98. *Recreations:* mainly sport—soccer, tennis, swimming. *Address:* c/o Foreign and Commonwealth Office, SW1A 2AH.

THOMSON, Duncan, PhD; Keeper, Scottish National Portrait Gallery, 1982–97; *b* 2 Oct. 1934; *s* of Duncan Murdoch Thomson and Jane McFarlane Wilson; *m* 1964, Julia Jane Macphail; one *d*. *Educ:* Airdrie Acad.; Univ. of Edinburgh (MA 1956, PhD 1970); Edinburgh Coll. of Art (Cert. of Coll.; Post-Dip. Scholarship); Moray House Coll. of Educn. Teacher of Art, 1959–67; Asst Keeper, Scottish National Portrait Gall., 1967–82. Scottish Arts Council: Mem., Art Cttee, 1983–89; Chm., Exhibn Panel, 1985–89. Chm., Mansfield Traquair Trust, 1996–. Mem., Editl Bd, Scottish Cultural Resources Access Network, 1998–. Hon. Fellow, Faculty of Arts, Univ. of Edinburgh, 1998. *Publications:* The Life and Art of George Jamesone, 1974; Sir Henry Raeburn, 1994; Arikha, 1994; *exhibition catalogues:* A Virtuous and Noble Education, 1971; Painting in Scotland 1570–1650, 1975; Eye to Eye, 1980; (jtly) John Michael Wright, 1982; (jtly) The Queen's Image, 1987; Raeburn: the art of Sir Henry Raeburn 1756–1823, 1997. *Recreation:* reading poetry (and thinking about writing it). *Address:* 3 Eglinton Crescent, Edinburgh EH12 5DH. *T:* (0131) 225 6430.

THOMSON, Elaine Margaret; Member (Lab) Aberdeen North, Scottish Parliament, since 1999; *b* 10 Aug. 1957; *d* of Dr Charles Thomson and Moira Thomson; partner, Archie Flockhart. *Educ:* Aberdeen Univ. (BSc Pure Sci.). Analyst/Programmer, ABB Vetco Gray UK Ltd, 1982–94; IT Consultant, Absoft Ltd, 1995–99. *Recreations:* ski-ing, walking, reading. *Address:* Scottish Parliament, Edinburgh EH99 1SP. *T:* (0131) 348 5917.

THOMSON, Sir (Frederick Douglas) David, 3rd Bt *cr* 1929; Chairman: Britannia Steam Ship Insurance Association Ltd, since 1986 (Director, since 1965); Through Transport Mutual Insurance Ltd, since 1983 (Director, since 1973); Laurence J. Smith, since 1994 (Director, since 1993); *b* 14 Feb. 1940; *s* of Sir James Douglas Wishart Thomson, 2nd Bt, and of Evelyn Margaret Isabel, (Bettina), *d* of Lt-Comdr D. W. S. Douglas, RN; *S* father, 1972; *m* 1967, Caroline Anne (marr. diss. 1994), *d* of Major Timothy Stuart Lewis; two *s* one *d*. *Educ:* Eton; University College, Oxford (BA Agric). Worked for Ben Line, 1961–89. Director: Danae Investment Trust, 1979–; Martin Currie Pacific Trust, 1985–; Asset Management Investment Trust, 1994–(Chm., 2001); Ionian Gp, 1994–; Bolero International Ltd, 1998–; Chairman: Jove Investment Trust, 1983–; Ptarmigan Internat. Capital Trust (formerly Castle Cairn Investment Trust Co.), 1990–; S. A. Meacock, 1996–. Member: Queen's Body Guard for Scotland, Royal Company of Archers. *Recreations:* shooting, ski-ing, music. *Heir:* *s* Simon Douglas Charles Thomson, *b* 16 June 1969. *Address:* Holylee, Walkerburn, Peeblesshire EH43 6BD. *T:* (01896) 870673. *Club:* Boodle's.

THOMSON, Garry, CBE 1983; Scientific Adviser to the Trustees and Head of the Scientific Department, National Gallery, London, 1960–85; *b* 13 Sept. 1925; *s* of late Robert Thomson and Mona Spence; *m* 1954, M. R. Saisvadi Svasti; four *s*. *Educ:* Charterhouse; Magdalene College, Cambridge (MA). Editorial Staff of A History of Technology, 1951; Research Chemist, National Gallery, 1955; Hon. Editor, Studies in Conservation, 1959–67; Pres., Internat. Inst. for Conservation of Historic and Artistic Works, 1983–86. Vice-Pres., Buddhist Soc., London, 1978–88. Trustee, Nat. Museums and Galls on Merseyside, 1986–91. (First) Plowden Gold Medal, Royal Warrant Holders Assoc., 1999 (for achievement in field of conservation). *Publications:* Recent Advances in Conservation (ed), 1963; Museum Climatology (ed), 1967; The Museum Environment, 1978; Reflections on the Life of the Buddha, 1982; The Sceptical Buddhist, 1995. *Address:* Squire's Hill, Tilford, Surrey GU10 2AD. *T:* (01252) 782206.

THOMSON, Sir Ian; *see* Thomson, Sir J. S.

THOMSON, James Phillips Spalding; Consultant Surgeon, St Mark's Hospital, 1974–99, now Emeritus (Clinical Director, 1990–97); Administrator, Priory Church of St Bartholomew the Great, since 2000; Master, Sutton's Hospital in Charterhouse, since 2001; *b* 2 Oct. 1939; *s* of Peggy Marion Thomson (*née* Phillips) and James Laing Spalding Thomson, MB ChB; *m* 1968, Dr Anne Katharine (*née* Richards), MB BS, MRCP; one *s* three *d*. *Educ:* Haileybury and Imperial Service Coll.; Middlesex Hosp. Med. Sch., Univ. of London (MB BS 1962; MS 1974); LRCP, MRCS, 1962, FRCS 1969; DObst RCOG 1964. Jun. med. and surgical appts, 1962–71; Demonstrator, Dept of Anatomy, Middlesex Hosp. Med. Sch., 1964–66; Consultant Surgeon: Royal Northern Hosp., 1975–77; Hackney Hosp., 1977–86; Homerton Hosp., 1986–90. Hon. Consultant Surgeon: St John's Hosp. for Diseases of the Skin, 1973–75; St Mary's Hosp., 1982–99; St Luke's Hosp. for the Clergy, 1976–99; Civil Cons. in Surgery, RAF, 1984–99, now Hon. Civil Cons.; Civilian Cons. in Colorectal Surgery, RN, 1986–99, now Emeritus Cons. in Surgery; Hon. Lectr in Surgery, Bart's Hosp. Med. Coll., 1977–94; Hon. Clin. Sen. Lectr in Surgery, Imperial Coll. Sch. of Medicine at St Mary's (formerly St Mary's Hosp. Med. Sch., Imperial Coll.), London, 1994–99. Hon. Cons. Advr in Surgery, Ileostomy Assoc., 1986–99. Examr in Surgery, Univs of Cambridge, Liverpool and London; Mem., Court of Examrs, RCS, 1986–92. Vice-Chm. of Council and Trustee, St Luke's Hosp. for the Clergy, 1992–; Governor, Corp. of Sons of the Clergy, 1988–. Liveryman: Apothecaries' Soc., 1980–; Barbers' Co., 1992–. Frederick Salmon Medal, RSocMed, 1996. DM Lambeth, 1987. *Publications:* (jtly) Colorectal Disease, 1981; (jtly) Frontiers in Colorectal Disease, 1986; (jtly) Updates in Coloproctology, 1992; contribs to books and learned jls. *Recreations:* church music, railways, canals. *Address:* Master's Lodge, Charterhouse, Charterhouse Square, EC1M 6AN. *T:* (020) 7253 0272; St Martin's House, The Street, Hindringham, Norfolk NR21 0PR. *T:* (01328) 822093; St Luke's Hospital, 14 Fitzroy Square, W1P 6AH, *T:* (020) 7388 4954. *Club:* Royal Society of Medicine.

THOMSON, Sir John (Adam), GCMG 1985 (KCMG 1978; CMG 1972); MA; HM Diplomatic Service, retired; Chairman, Minority Rights Group International, since 1991; *b* 27 April 1927; *s* of late Sir George Thomson, FRS, Master of Corpus Christi Coll., Cambridge, 1952–62 (*s* of Sir J. J. Thomson, OM, FRS, Master of Trinity Coll., Cambridge, 1919–40), and late Kathleen, *d* of Very Rev. Sir George Adam Smith, DD, LLD, Principal of Aberdeen Univ., 1909–35; *m* 1st, 1953, Elizabeth Anne McClure (*d* 1988), *d* of late Norman McClure, Pres. of Ursinus Coll., Penn, USA; three *s* one *d*; 2nd, 1992, Judith Ogden Bullitt, *d* of late John Stanley Ogden, NY, and Olga Geddes Bradshaw, Melbourne. *Educ:* Phillips Exeter Acad., USA; Univ. of Aberdeen; Trinity Coll., Cambridge. Foreign Office, 1950; Third Sec., Jedda, 1951; Damascus, 1954; FO, 1955; Private Sec. to Permanent Under-Secretary, 1958–60; First Sec., Washington, 1960–64; FO, 1964; Acting Head of Planning Staff, 1966; Counsellor, 1967; Head of Planning Staff, FO, 1967; seconded to Cabinet Office as Chief of Assessments Staff, 1968–71; Minister and Dep. Permanent Rep. to N Atlantic Council, 1972–73; Head of UK Delegn to MBFR Exploratory Talks, Vienna, 1973; Asst Under-Sec. of State, FCO, 1973–76; High Comr to India, 1977–82; UK Perm. Rep. to UN, 1982–87. Chm., Fleming Emerging Markets Investment Trust, 1991–98; Internat. Advr, ANZ Grindlays Bank, 1996–97 (Dir, 1987–96). Mem., Howie Cttee on Scottish Secondary Educn, 1990–93. Trustee, Nat. Museums of Scotland, 1991–99. Principal Dir, 21st Century Trust, 1987–90; Dir, Minority Rights Gp, USA, 1993–. Member: Council, IISS, 1987–96; Council, ODI, 1987–; Governing Body, IDS, 1987–. Director's Visitor, IAS, Princeton, 1995–96. Trustee, Indian Nat. Trust, 1989–. Associate Mem., Nuffield Coll., Oxford, 1987–91. Hon. LLD: Ursinus Coll., Penn, 1984; Aberdeen, 1986; Hon. DHL Allegheny Coll., Penn, 1985. *Publication:* Crusader Castles (with R. Fedden), 1956. *Recreations:* carpets, castles, walking. *Clubs:* Athenæum; Century (New York).
See also A. McC. Thomson, Janet Adam Smith (Mrs John Carleton), D. P. Thomson.

THOMSON, Sir John Sutherland, (Sir Ian), KBE 1985 (MBE (mil.) 1944); CMG 1968; retired, 1987; *b* 8 Jan. 1920; *s* of late William Sutherland Thomson and of Jessie McCaig Malloch; *m* 1st, 1945, Nancy Marguerite Kearsley (*d* 1988), Suva, Fiji; seven *s* one *d*; 2nd, 1989, Nancy Caldwell (*née* McColl). *Educ:* High Sch. of Glasgow; Univ. of Glasgow (MA Hons). Served War of 1939–45: Black Watch, 1940; Fiji Military Forces, 1941–45 (Captain). Appointed Cadet, Colonial Administrative Service, Fiji and Western Pacific, 1941; District Administration and Secretariat, Fiji, 1946–54; Seconded to Colonial Office, 1954–56; Dep. Comr, Native Lands and Fisheries, Fiji, 1957–58; Comr of Native Reserves and Chairman, Native Lands and Fisheries Commission, Fiji, 1958–62; Divisional Commissioner, Fiji, 1963–66; Administrator, British Virgin Islands, 1967–71; Acting Governor-Gen., Fiji, 1980–83 on occasions. Indep. Chm., Fiji Sugar Industry, 1971–84; Chairman: Fiji Coconut Bd, 1973–83; Economic Develt Bd, Fiji, 1980–86; Fiji Liquor Laws Review Cttee, 1985; Fiji Nat. Tourism Assoc., 1984–87; Chairman: Sedgwick (Fiji) Ltd, 1984–87; Air Pacific Ltd, 1984–87; Thomson Pacific Resources Ltd, 1988–92. *Publication:* Fiji in the Forties and Fifties, 1994. *Recreations:* golf, gardening. *Address:* 1/4 Fettes Rise, Edinburgh EH4 1QH. *T:* (0131) 552 6421.

THOMSON, Prof. Joseph McGeachy, FRSE; Regius Professor of Law, University of Glasgow, since 1991; Commissioner, Scottish Law Commission, since 2000; *b* 6 May 1948; *s* of James Thomson and Catherine (*née* McGeachy); *m* 1999, Marilyn Ann Iverson. *Educ:* Keil Sch., Dumbarton; Univ. of Edinburgh (LLB 1970). FRSE 1996. Lectr in Law, Univ. of Birmingham, 1970–74; Lectr in Laws, King's Coll., London, 1974–84; Prof. of Law, Univ. of Strathclyde, 1984–90. Dep. General Editor, Stair Meml Encyclopaedia of Laws of Scotland, 1984–96. *Publications:* Family Law in Scotland, 1987, 3rd edn 1996; Delictual Liability, 1994, 2nd edn 1999; (with H. McQueen) Contract Law in Scotland, 2000; contribs to Law Qly Review, Modern Law Review, Juridical Review, Scots Law Times, etc. *Recreations:* opera, ballet, wine and food. *Address:* Scottish Law Commission, 140 Causewayside, Edinburgh EH9 1PR. *T:* (0131) 668 2131; 2 Kew Terrace, Glasgow G12 0TD. *Club:* Glasgow Art.

THOMSON, Malcolm George; QC (Scot.) 1987; *b* 6 April 1950; *s* of late George Robert Thomson, OBE, and of Daphne Ethel Thomson; *m* 1978, Susan Gordon Aitken; two *d*. *Educ:* Edinburgh Acad.; Edinburgh Univ. (LLB). Advocate 1974; called to the Bar, Lincoln's Inn, 1991. Standing Junior Counsel to Dept of Agriculture and Fisheries for Scotland and Forestry Commn in Scotland, 1982–87. Chm., NHS Tribunal (Scotland), 1995–; Mem., Scottish Legal Aid Bd, 1998–. Trustee, Nat. Liby of Scotland, 1995–. *Recreations:* sailing, ski-ing. *Address:* 12 Succoth Avenue, Edinburgh EH12 6BT. *T:* (0131) 337 4911. *Club:* New (Edinburgh).

THOMSON, Sir Mark (Wilfrid Home), 3rd Bt *cr* 1925, of Old Nunthorpe, Co. York; *b* 29 Dec. 1939; *s* of Sir Ivo Wilfrid Home Thomson, 2nd Bt and Sybil Marguerite, *yr d* of C. W. Thompson; *S* father, 1991; *m* 1976, Lady Jacqueline Rufus Isaacs (marr. diss. 1997), *o d* of 3rd Marquess of Reading, MBE, MC; three *s* one *d* (incl. twin *s*). *Heir:* *s* Albert Mark Home Thomson, *b* 3 Aug. 1979. *Address:* 148 Oakwood Court, Abbotsbury Road, W14 8JS.

THOMSON, Nigel Ernest Drummond, CBE 1993; Sheriff of Lothian and Borders, at Edinburgh and Peebles, 1976–96; *b* 19 June 1926; *y s* of late Rev. James Kyd Thomson and Joan Drummond; *m* 1964, Snjólaug Magnússon, *yr d* of late Consul-General Sigursteinn Magnússon; one *s* one *d*. *Educ:* George Watson's College, Edinburgh; Univs of St Andrews and Edinburgh. Served with Scots Guards and Indian Grenadiers, 1944–47.

MA (St Andrews) 1950; LLB (Edin.) 1953. Called to Scottish Bar, 1953. Standing Counsel to Scottish Educn Dept, 1961–66; Sheriff of Lanarkshire, later S Strathclyde, Dumfries and Galloway, at Hamilton, 1966–76. Chm., Music Cttee, Scottish Arts Council, 1978–83; Chm., Edinburgh Youth Orchestra, 1986–92. Convenor, Council for Music in Hosps in Scotland, 1992–2001. Pres., Speculative Soc., Edinburgh, 1960; Vice President: Tenovus-Scotland, 1985–; British Assoc. for Counselling, 1992–. Hon. Texas Ranger, 1994. *Recreations:* music, woodwork, golf. *Address:* 50 Grange Road, Edinburgh. *T:* (0131) 667 2166. *Clubs:* New (Edinburgh); Bruntsfield Golf (Edinburgh).

THOMSON, Peter Alexander Bremner, CVO 1986; HM Diplomatic Service, retired; *b* 16 Jan. 1938; *s* of Alexander Thomson, financial journalist, and Dorothy (*née* Scurr); *m* 1965, Lucinda Sellar; three *s*. *Educ:* Canford School; RN College, Dartmouth; Sch. of African and Oriental Studies, London (BA 1970; MPhil 1975; MA 1991). Sub Lieut and Lieut RN in HM Ships Albion, Plover, Tiger, Ark Royal, Eagle; Lt Comdr ashore in Taiwan and Hong Kong; joined Diplomatic Service, 1975; First Sec., FCO, Lagos, Hong Kong, 1975–84; Counsellor, Peking, 1984–87; High Comr, Belize, 1987–90; Counsellor, FCO, 1991–95; High Comr, Seychelles, 1995–97. *Recreations:* sailing, walking, 19th century fiction. *Address:* The Red House, Charlton Horethorne, near Sherborne DT9 4NL.

THOMSON, Robert Howard Garry; *see* Thomson, Garry.

THOMSON, Robert John Stewart, CMG 1969; MBE 1955; Ministry of Defence, 1969–81; *b* 5 May 1922; *s* of late John Stewart Thomson, FRIBA, and late Nellie Thomson (*née* Morris). *Educ:* Bromsgrove Sch.; Worcester Coll., Oxford. Service with Sudan Defence Force, 1943–45. Sudan Political Service, 1943–54 (District Commissioner, 1950–54). Attached Ministry of Defence, 1955–56; First Sec., British High Commission, Accra, 1956–60, 1962–64, Counsellor, 1966–69. *Recreations:* gardening, singing. *Address:* Ardgowan, 119 Lenthay Road, Sherborne, Dorset DT9 6AQ.

THOMSON, Prof. Robert William, PhD; FBA 1995; Calouste Gulbenkian Professor of Armenian Studies, University of Oxford, 1992–2001, now Professor Emeritus; Fellow of Pembroke College, Oxford, 1992–2001; *b* 24 March 1934; *s* of late David William Thomson and Lilian (*née* Cramphorn); *m* 1963, Judith Ailsa Cawdry; two *s*. *Educ:* George Watson's Boys' Coll., Edinburgh; Sidney Sussex Coll., Cambridge (BA 1955); Trinity Coll., Cambridge (PhD 1962). Halki Theol Coll., Istanbul, 1955–56; Jun. Fellow, Dumbarton Oaks, Washington, 1960–61; Louvain Univ., 1961–62; Harvard University: Instructor, then Asst Prof. of Classical Armenian, Dept of Near Eastern Langs, 1963–69; Mashtots Prof. of Armenian Studies, 1969–92; Chm., Dept of Near Eastern Langs, 1973–78, 1980–81. Dir, Dumbarton Oaks, Washington DC, 1984–89. *Publications:* (ed with J. N. Birdsall) Biblical and Patristic Studies in Memory of Robert Pierce Casey, 1963; Athanasiana Syriaca, 4 parts, 1965–77; Athanasius: Contra Gentes and De Incarnatione, 1971; The Teaching of Saint Gregory, 1971, 2nd edn 2001; Introduction to Classical Armenian, 1975; Agathangelos: history of the Armenians, 1977; (with K. B. Bardakjian) Textbook of Modern Western Armenian, 1977; Moses Khorenatsi: history of the Armenians, 1978; Elishe: history of Vardan, 1982; (ed with N. G. Garsoian and T. J. Mathews) East of Byzantium, 1982; (with B. Kendall) David the Invincible Philosopher, 1983; Thomas Artsruni: history of the Artsruni House, 1985; The Armenian Version of Dionysius the Areopagite, 2 vols, 1987; Lazar Parpetsi: history of the Armenians, 1991; Studies in Armenian Literature and Christianity, 1994; The Syriac Version of the Hexaemeron by Basil of Caesarea, 1995; A Bibliography of Classical Armenian Literature, 1995; Rewriting Caucasian History: the Armenian version of the Georgian Chronicles, 1996; (ed with J.-P. Mahé) From Byzantium to Iran: Armenian studies in honour of Nina G. Garsoian, 1997; (with J. Howard-Johnston) The Armenian History of Sebeos, 1999; The Lawcode of Mxit'ar Gosh, 2000; The Armenian Adaptation of the Ecclesiastical History of Socrates Scholasticus, 2001; contribs to Jl Theol Studies, Le Muséon, Revue des études arméniennes, Dumbarton Oaks Papers, Oxford Dictionary of Byzantium, Encyclopedia Iranica. *Address:* Oriental Institute, Pusey Lane, Oxford OX1 2LE.

THOMSON, Rosemary Edith Robertson, CBE 1997 (OBE 1992); JP; DL; Vice-President, Magistrates' Association, since 1996 (Chairman of Council, 1993–96); *b* 3 Oct. 1934; *d* of James Heggie and Cecilia (*née* Walker); *m* 1958, Peter Thomson; one *s* one *d*. *Educ:* Watford Grammar Sch. for Girls; Girton Coll., Cambridge (MA); McGill Univ., Montreal. Open University: Tutor-counsellor, 1974–96; counsellor to students in Broadmoor Hosp., 1974–84. Feltham Young Offenders' Institution: Mem., 1980–86; Chm., Bd of Visitors, 1984–86. Mem., Berks Probation Cttee, 1987–96. Magistrates' Association: Mem. Council, 1975–96; Chm., Trng Cttee, 1981–87; Chm., Berks Br., 1987–92; Dep. Chm., Council, 1987–93. Member: Lord Chancellor's Adv. Cttee on Trng of Magistrates, 1981–84; Judicial Studies Bd, 1985–88; Criminal Justice Consultative Council, 1992–99; Magistrates' Courts Consultative Council, 1992–96; Berkshire and Oxfordshire Magistrates' Courts Cttee, 1997–99; Council, Commonwealth Magistrates and Judges Assoc., 1991–95 (Mem., Trng Cttee, 1987–95); Criminal Injuries Compensation Appeal Panel, 1996–; Lord Chancellor's Adv. Cttee on Legal Educn and Conduct, 1997–99; Home Office Strategy Bd for Correctional Services, 2000–; Vice Chm., Thames Valley Magistrates' Courts Cttee, 1999–. Non-executive Director: Prison Service, 1997–; Nat. Probation Service, 2000–; Expert Consultee, Criminal Justice Rev., 1999–2001. JP Maidenhead, 1971; DL Berks, 2000. Hon. Dr Central England, 1995. *Publications:* numerous articles on magisterial matters mostly in The Magistrate. *Recreations:* sedentary and literary pursuits, looking at pictures, family life. *Address:* Little Lodge, Lower Cookham Road, Maidenhead, Berks SL6 8JT. *T:* (01628) 626816.

THOMSON, Sir Thomas (James), Kt 1991; CBE 1984 (OBE 1978); FRCPGlas, FRCP, FRCPEd, FRCPI; retired; Chairman, Greater Glasgow Health Board, 1987–93; Consultant Physician and Gastroenterologist, Stobhill General Hospital, Glasgow, 1961–87; Hon. Lecturer, Department of Materia Medica, University of Glasgow, 1961–87; *b* 8 April 1923; *s* of Thomas Thomson and Annie Jane Grant; *m* 1948, Jessie Smith Shotbolt; two *s* one *d*. *Educ:* Airdrie Acad.; Univ. of Glasgow (MB, ChB 1945). FRCPGlas 1964 (FRFPSG 1949); FRCP 1969 (MRCP 1950); FRCPEd 1982; FRCPI 1983. Lectr, Dept of Materia Medica, Univ. of Glasgow, 1953–61; Postgrad. Adviser to Glasgow Northern Hosps, 1961–80. Sec., Specialist Adv. Cttee for Gen. Internal Medicine for UK, 1970–74; Chairman: Medico-Pharmaceutical Forum, 1978–80 (Chm., Educn Adv. Bd, 1979–84); National Med. Consultative Cttee for Scotland, 1982–87; Conf. of Royal Colls and Faculties in Scotland, 1982–84; Hon. Sec., 1965–73, Pres., 1982–84, RCPSGlas. Active participation in postgrad. med. educnl cttees, locally, nationally and in EEC. Mem. Ct, Strathclyde Univ., 1993–97. Hon. FACP 1983. Hon. LLD Glasgow, 1988; DUniv Strathclyde, 1997. *Publications:* (ed jtly) Dilling's Pharmacology, 1969; Gastroenterology—an integrated course, 1972, 3rd edn 1983; pubns related to gen. medicine, gastroent. and therapeutics. *Recreations:* swimming, golfing. *Address:* 1 Varna Road, Glasgow G14 9NE. *T:* (0141) 959 5930. *Club:* Royal Air Force.

THOMSON, Dr Wendy; Head, Office of Public Services Reform, Cabinet Office, since 2001; *b* Montreal, 28 Oct. 1953; *d* of Shirley and Grace Thomson; *m* David Dorne (*d* 1999); two step *s*. *Educ:* McGill Univ. (BSW; Masters of Social Work); Univ. of Bristol (PhD). Asst Chief Exec., Islington BC, 1987–93; Chief Executive: Turning Point, 1993–96; Newham BC, 1996–99; Dir of Inspection, Audit Commn, 1999–2001. *Recreations:* yoga, gardening, theatre, travel, shopping. *Address:* 10 Downing Street, SW1A 2AA. *T:* (020) 7930 4433.

THOMSON, William Oliver, MD, DPH, DIH; Chief Administrative Medical Officer, Lanarkshire Health Board, 1973–88; *b* 23 March 1925; *s* of William Crosbie Thomson and Mary Jolie Johnston; *m* 1956, Isobel Lauder Glendinning Brady; two *s*. *Educ:* Allan Glen's Sch., Glasgow; Univ. of Glasgow (MB ChB, MD). DPA; FFCM; FRCPGlas 1988 (MRCPGlas 1986). Chronic student of Gray's Inn, London. Captain, RAMC, 1948–50. Hospital appointments, 1951–53; appointments in Public Health, Glasgow, 1953–60; Admin. MO, Western Regional Hospital Bd, 1960–70; Group Medical Superintendent, Glasgow Maternity and Women's Hospitals, 1970–73; Mem., Health Services Ind. Adv. Cttee, 1980–86. Visiting Lecturer: Univ. of Michigan, Ann Arbor; Ministry of Health, Ontario; Hon. Lectr, Univ. of Glasgow. Med. Advr, Scottish TV, 1992–98. Diploma of Scottish Council for Health Educn (for services to health educn), 1979. *Publications:* (jtly) In England Now, 1989; articles on clinical medicine, community medicine, general practice, occupational health and health education, in various medical jls; humorous pieces in The Lancet, BMJ, etc. *Recreations:* walking, talking, writing. *Address:* Flat 7, Silverwells Court, Silverwells Crescent, Bothwell, Glasgow G71 8LT. *T:* (01698) 852586.

THONEMANN, Peter Clive, MSc, DPhil; Professor Emeritus, University of Wales, Swansea; *b* 3 June 1917. *Educ:* Melbourne Church of England Grammar Sch., Melbourne; Sydney and Oxford Univs. BSc Melbourne, 1940; MSc Sydney, 1945; DPhil Oxford, 1949. Munition Supply Laboratories, Victoria, Australia, 1940; Amalgamated Wireless, Australia, 1942; University of Sydney, Commonwealth Research Fellow, 1944; Trinity Coll. and Clarendon Laboratory, Oxford, ICI Research Fellow, 1946; initiated research for controlled fusion power, 1947–49; United Kingdom Atomic Energy Authority: Head of Controlled Fusion Res., 1949–60; designed and built prototype fusion reactor, ZETA, 1954–57; with Res. Unit, 1960–64, Head of B Div., 1964–67, Dep. Dir, 1967–68, Culham Laboratory; Prof. and Hd of Dept of Physics, UC, Swansea, 1968–84. *Publications:* many contributions to learned journals. *Address:* Department of Physics, University of Wales, Swansea, Singleton Park, Swansea, Wales SA2 8PP; 130 Bishopston Road, Swansea SA3 3EU. *T:* (01792) 232669.

't HOOFT, Prof. Gerardus; Professor of Theoretical Physics, Utrecht University, since 1977; *b* 5 July 1946; *s* of H. 't Hooft and M. A. van Kampen; *m* 1972, Albertha A. Schik, MD; two *d*. *Educ:* Dalton Lyceum Gymnasium beta, The Hague; Utrecht Univ. Fellow, Theoretical Physics Div., CERN, Geneva, 1972–74; Asst Prof., Univ. of Utrecht, 1974–77. Heineman Prize, NY, 1979; Wolf Prize, Wolf Foundn, Israel, 1982; Franklin Medal, Franklin Inst., Philadelphia, 1995; (jtly) Nobel Prize for Physics, 1999; High Energy Physics Prize, Eur. Physical Soc., 1999. Commandeur de Orde van de Nederlandse Leeuw, 1999. *Publications:* De bouwstenen van de Schepping, 1992 (In Search of the Ultimate Building Blocks, 1996); (contrib.) Under the Spell of the Gauge Principle, 1994. *Address:* Spinoza Institute, Leuvenlaan 4, PO Box 80.195, 3508 TD Utrecht, Netherlands. *T:* 302531863.

THORBURN, Andrew, BSc; FRTPI; FTS; Chairman, Thorburns, since 1990; Bow Street Partners, since 1999; Principal, Andrew Thorburn Associates, since 1985; *b* 20 March 1934; *s* of James Beresford Thorburn and Marjorie Clara Burford; *m* Margaret Anne Crack; one *s* two *d*. *Educ:* Bridport Grammar Sch.; Univ. of Southampton (BSc). MRTPI 1959, FRTPI 1969. National Service, RN, 1954–56. Planning Asst, Kent CC, 1957–59; Planning Officer, Devon CC, 1959–63; Asst County Planning Officer, Hampshire CC, 1963–68; Dir, Notts and Derbyshire Sub-Region Study, 1968–70; Dep. County Planning Dir, Cheshire CC, 1970–73; County Planning Officer, E Sussex CC, 1973–83; Chief Exec., English Tourist Bd, 1983–85; Head of Tourism and Leisure Div., Grant Thornton, 1986–90. Pres., RTPI, 1982; Mem. Exec., Town and Country Planning Assoc., 1969–81; Founder Trustee, Sussex Heritage Trust, 1978–99. Fellow, Tourism Soc., 1983–. *Publication:* Planning Villages, 1971. *Recreations:* sailing, countryside appreciation. *Address:* 1 Mill House, Lower Quay, Fareham, Hants PO16 0RH.

THORLEY, Charles Graham; *b* 4 Jan. 1914; *s* of Charles Lord Thorley; *m* 1958, Peggy Percival Ellis (*née* Boor); one step *s* one step *d*. *Educ:* Manchester Grammar Sch.; King's Coll., Cambridge (Mod. Lang. Scholar). Served War of 1939–45, Eritrea and Cyrenaica (Lt-Col). Entered Civil Service as Economist, Bd of Trade, 1936; attached to British Embassy, China, 1936–38; Mem. British Economic Mission to Belgian Congo, 1940–41; HM Treasury, 1940–57; served on UK financial delegns and missions in Japan, US, Egypt, France, Switzerland, W Germany, etc; Min. of Power, 1957; Under-Secretary and Head of Coal Div., 1965–69; Acct-Gen. and Dir of Finance, 1969. Chm., NATO Petroleum Planning Cttee, 1962–65; Under-Sec., Min. of Technology and DTI, 1969–74. Specialist Advr, House of Lords, 1975–79. *Address:* 6 Greenacres Drive, Wantage, Oxon OX12 9NR. *T:* (01235) 770176.

THORLEY, Giles Alexander; Executive Chairman, Punch Pub Co., since 2001; *b* 29 June 1967; *s* of Hugh A. Thorley and Jillian E. Thorley; *m* 1993, Michelle Britt; three *s*. *Educ:* Hereford Cathedral Sch.; QMC, Univ. of London (LLB); Inns of Court Sch. of Law. Called to the Bar, Inner Temple, 1990. Director: Nomura Internat. plc, 1990–98; Inntrepreneur Pub Co., 1998–99; Chief Exec., Unique Pub Co. plc, 1999–2001. Dir and Supervisory Bd Mem., Brewers and Licenced Retailers Assoc. Mem. Editl Bd, Licensee and Morning Advertiser. *Recreations:* ski-ing, water sports, the family. *Address:* Punch Pub Co., 107 Station Street, Burton upon Trent DE14 1BZ.

THORLEY, Simon Joe; QC 1989; *b* 22 May 1950; *s* of Sir Gerald Bowers Thorley, TD and of Beryl, *d* of G. Preston Rhodes; *m* 1983, Jane Elizabeth Cockcroft; two *s* one *d*. *Educ:* Rugby Sch.; Keble Coll., Oxford (MA Jurisprudence). Called to the Bar, Inner Temple, 1972, Bencher, 1999; pupilled to William Aldous; in practice at Patent Bar; apptd by Lord Chancellor to hear Trade Mark Appeals, 1996–; Dep. High Court Judge, 1998–. Dep. Chm., Copyright Tribunal, 1998–. Chm., IP Bar (formerly Patent Bar) Assoc., 1995–99; Member: Gen. Council of the Bar, 1995–99; Council, British Gp, Internat. Assoc. for Protection of Industrial Property, 1993–95. *Publication:* (co-ed) Terrell on The Law of Patents, 13th edn 1982 to 15th edn 2000. *Recreations:* family, shooting, opera. *Address:* 3 New Square, Lincoln's Inn, WC2A 3RS. *T:* (020) 7405 1111.

THORN, E. Gaston; Politician, Luxembourg; President: Banque Internationale, Luxembourg, since 1985; Mouvement Européen International, since 1985; President—Director General, RTL Luxembourg, since 1987; *b* 3 Sept. 1928; *s* of Edouard Thorn and Suzanne Weber; *m* 1957, Liliane Petit; one *s*. *Educ:* Univs of Montpellier, Lausanne, and Paris. DenD. Admitted to Luxembourg Bar; Pres., Nat. Union of Students, Luxembourg, 1959; Member, European Parlt, 1959–69, Vice-Pres., Liberal Group; Pres., Democratic Party, Luxembourg, 1969; Minister of Foreign Affairs and of Foreign Trade, also Minister of Physical Educn and Sport, 1974–77; Prime Minister and Minister of State, 1974–79; Minister of Nat. Econ. and Middle Classes, 1977; of Justice, 1979; Dep. Prime Minister, and Minister of Foreign Affairs, July 1979–1980; Pres., EEC, 1981–85. Pres., 30th Session of UN Gen. Assembly, 1975–76. President: Liberal International, 1970–82; Fedn of Liberal and Democratic Parties of European Community, 1976–80. Mem., Public Review Board, Arthur Andersen & Co. Decorations include Grand Cross of Orders of Adolphe de Nassau, Couronne de Chêne, and Mérite (Luxembourg), Grand Cross of Légion d'Honneur (France), GCVO and GCMG (GB) and other Grand Crosses. *Recreations:* tennis, reading. *Address:* 1 rue de la Forge, Luxembourg.

THORN, John Leonard, MA; writer and educational consultant; Headmaster of Winchester College, 1968–85; *b* 28 April 1925; *s* of late Stanley and Winifred Thorn; *m* 1955, Veronica Laura (*d* 1999), *d* of late Sir Robert Maconochie, OBE, QC; one *s* one *d*. *Educ:* St Paul's School; Corpus Christi College, Cambridge. Served War of 1939–45, Sub-Lieutenant, RNVR, 1943–46. Asst Master, Clifton Coll., 1949–61; Headmaster, Repton School, 1961–68. Dir, Winchester Cathedral Trust, 1986–89. Dir, Royal Opera House, Covent Garden, 1971–76. Chm., Headmasters' Conference, 1981. Member: Bd, Securities Assoc., 1987–91; Exec. Cttee, Cancer Res. Campaign, 1987–90; Chm., Hants Bldgs Preservation Trust, 1992–96 (Vice-Chm., 1989–92); Trustee: British Museum, 1980–85; Oakham Sch., 1985–89. Governor, Stowe Sch., 1985–90; Chm. of Governors, Abingdon Sch., 1991–94. *Publications:* (joint) A History of England, 1961; The Road to Winchester (autobiog.), 1989; various articles. *Address:* 6 Chilbolton Avenue, Winchester SO22 5HD. *T:* (01962) 855990. *Club:* Garrick.

THORN, Sir John (Samuel), Kt 1984; OBE 1977; Mayor, Port Chalmers Borough Council, 1956–89 (Member, 1938–41, 1947–50 and 1950–53); *b* 19 March 1911; *s* of J. S. Thorn; *m* 1936, Constance Maud (*d* 1997), *d* of W. T. Haines; one *s*. *Educ:* Port Chalmers School; King Edward Technical College. Served 1939–45 war, 3rd Div. Apprentice plumber, later plumbing contractor and land agent; Manager, Thorn's Bookshop, 1950–80. Chairman: Municipal Insce Co.; Coastal N Otago United Council. Pres., Municipal Assoc., 1974–; Dep. Chm., Nat. Roads Board, 1974–83. *Address:* 94C Stevenson Avenue, Sawyers Bay, Dunedin, New Zealand.

THORN, Roger Eric; QC 1990; a Recorder, and Deputy High Court Judge, since 1999; *b* 23 March 1948; twin *s* of James Douglas 'Pat' Thorn and Daphne Elizabeth (*née* Robinson). *Educ:* Mill Hill Sch.; Newcastle Univ. (LLB Hons). Called to the Bar, Middle Temple, 1970 (Harmsworth Schol. and Major Exhibn; Bencher, 1999); NE Circuit, 1970–; Asst Recorder, 1995–99. Member: Bd of Faculty of Law, Newcastle Univ., 1990–94; Advocacy Studies Bd, Bar Council, 1996–; Panel of Arbitrators, Bar Council, 1999–; Restricted Patients Panel, Mental Health Rev. Tribunal, 2000–. Hd of Mission to Kosovo, Bar Human Rights Cttee, 2000. Life Gov., Mill Hill Sch., 1994. *Publications:* A Practical Guide to Road Traffic Accident Claims, 1987, 2nd edn 1991; legal contributor to Negotiating Better Deals, by J. G. Thorn (twin *b*), 1988; (jtly) Kosovo 2000: justice not revenge, 2000. *Recreations:* theatre, music, walking, local Amenity Society (Chairman, 1986–99). *Address:* 11 King's Bench Walk, Temple, EC4Y 7EQ; New Court Chambers, 3 Broad Chare, Quayside, Newcastle upon Tyne NE1 3DQ. *T:* (0191) 232 1980; Whitton Grange, Rothbury, via Morpeth, Northumberland NE65 7RL. *Clubs:* National Liberal; Old Mill Hillians; Durham County.

THORNBURGH, Richard Lewis; Partner, Kirkpatrick & Lockhart LLP, 1987–88, 1991–92 and since 1994; *b* 16 July 1932; *s* of Charles G. and Alice S. Thornburgh; *m* 1955, Virginia Hooton (decd); *m* 1963, Virginia Judson; four *s*. *Educ:* Yale Univ. (BEng 1954); Univ. of Pittsburgh Sch. of Law (LLB 1957). Staff Counsel, Aluminum Co. of America, 1957–59; Associate, Kirkpatrick, Pomeroy, Lockhart & Johnson, 1959–69; US Attorney, Western District, Pennsylvania, 1969–75; Asst Attorney General, Criminal Div., US Dept of Justice, 1975–77; Partner, Kirkpatrick Lockhart, Johnson & Hutchison, 1977–79; Governor, Commonwealth of Pennsylvania, 1979–87; Attorney Gen. of the USA, 1988–91; Under-Sec.-Gen. for Admin and Management, UN, 1992–93. Dir, Inst. of Politics, John F. Kennedy Sch. of Govt, 1987–88. Numerous hon. degrees. *Publications:* articles in professional jls. *Address:* 2540 Massachusetts Avenue NW, Washington, DC 20008, USA; Kirkpatrick & Lockhart LLP, 1800 Massachusetts Avenue NW, 2nd Floor, Washington, DC 20036–1800, USA.

THORNE, Benjamin, CMG 1979; MBE 1966; consultant on Far East trade; *b* 19 June 1922; *m* 1949, Sylvia Una (*née* Graves); one *s* two *d*. *Educ:* St Marylebone Grammar Sch.; Regent Street Polytechnic. Served War, RAF, 1940–46. Joined Civil Service, 1946; British Trade Commission: India, 1950–54; Ghana, 1954–58; Nigeria, 1958–61; Hong Kong, 1964–68; Dir, British Week in Tokyo, 1968–69; Commercial Counsellor, Tokyo, 1973–79, retd. Life Vice Pres., Japan Soc., 1998. Japanese Order of the Sacred Treasure, 3rd cl., 1975. *Recreations:* cricket, travel, gardening, reading. *Address:* 34 Quarry Hill Road, Borough Green, Sevenoaks, Kent TN15 8RH. *T:* (01732) 882547. *Clubs:* Civil Service; Hong Kong (Hong Kong); Foreign Correspondents' (Tokyo); Yokohama Country and Athletic.

THORNE, Rear-Adm. (retd) Edward Courtney, CB 1975; CBE 1971; Chairman, New Zealand Fire Service Commission, 1976–86; Chief of Naval Staff, New Zealand, 1972–75; *b* 29 Oct. 1923; *s* of Ernest Alexander Thorne and Ethel Violet Thorne; *m* 1949, Fay Bradburn (*née* Kerr); three *s*. *Educ:* Rongotai Coll.; Nelson Coll., NZ. IDC 1966. Chm., Nat. Council, United World Colls, 1982–94; Mem., Nat. Council, Duke of Edinburgh Award Scheme, 1976–89; Pres., Sea Cadet Assoc. of NZ, 1990–98. Hon. FIFireE 1983. *Recreations:* gardening, walking. *Address:* 75 Hatton Street, Karori, Wellington 6005, New Zealand.

THORNE, Sir Neil (Gordon), Kt 1992; OBE 1980; TD 1969; DL; *b* 8 Aug. 1932; *s* of late Henry Frederick Thorne and Ivy Gladys Thorne. *Educ:* City of London Sch.; Coll. of Estate Mgt (BSc London Univ.). FCGI; FRICS. Asst Adjt, 58 Med. Regt, RA, BAOR, 1957–59. Sen. Partner, Hull & Co., Chartered Surveyors, 1962–76. Councillor, London Borough of Redbridge, 1965–68, Alderman, 1975–78; Mem., GLC and Chm., Central Area Bd, 1967–73. MP (C) Ilford South, 1979–92; contested (C) same seat, 1992, 1997. Founder and first Chm., Unpaired Members Gp, 1982–85; Chairman: British Nepalese Parly Gp, 1983–92; British Korean Parly Gp, 1988–92; Vice Chm., UK Br., IPU, 1987–90; Member: Defence Select Cttee, 1983–92; Court of Referees, 1987–92. Chm., H of C Motor Club, 1985–91; Founder and Chairman: Armed Forces Parly Scheme, 1988–; Police Service Parly Scheme, 1994–. Chm., Britain-Nepal Soc., 1992–98. Fellow, Industry and Parliament Trust, 1980 and 1990; Pres., Inst. of Civil Defence and Disaster Studies, 1996–; Chairman: Nat. Council for Civil Defence, 1982–86; St Edward's Housing Assoc., 1986–93; Ilford Age Concern, 1984–87, 1990–93; President: Redbridge Parkinson's Disease Soc., 1982–; Ilford Arthritis Care, 1986–; Gtr London Dist, St John Ambulance, 1992–; Redbridge Age Concern, 1993–; Vice Pres., Ilford Tuberculosis and Chest Care Assoc., 1987–2000; Patron, Jubilee Club for Visually Handicapped, 1986–2000; Trustee: Children In Distress, 1986–; Meml Gates Trust, 1999–. Chm., Lord Mayor's Appeal for St Paul's Cathedral, 1993–94. Mem., Mil. Educn Cttee, 1994–, and Court, 1995–2001, Univ. of Leeds. Jun. Grand Warden, United Grand Lodge of England, 1994–95; Prov. Grand Master for Essex, 1995–; Master, Grand Stewards, 2001–02. Prime Warden, Blacksmiths' Co., 2000–01. Member: TA, 1952–82; Metropolitan Special Constab. (HAC), 1983–92; CO, London Univ. OTC, 1976–80; Hon. Col, Leeds Univ. OTC, 1999–. DL Greater London, 1991; Rep. DL London Bor. of Brent, 2001–. KStJ 1995 (Mem., Chapter Gen., 1989–97; Almoner, 1995–97). Silver Jubilee Medal, 1977. HQA (Pakistan), 1991; GDB (Nepal), 1991. *Publications:* Pedestrianised Streets: a study of Europe and America, 1973; Highway Robbery in the Twentieth Century: policy reform for compulsory purchase, 1990. *Address:* 13 Cowley Street, Westminster, SW1P 3LZ. *T:* (020) 7222 0480. *Club:* Honourable Artillery Company.

THORNE, Sir Peter (Francis), KCVO 1981; CBE 1966; ERD; Serjeant at Arms, House of Commons, 1976–82; *b* 1914; *y s* of late Gen. Sir Andrew Thorne, KCB, CMG, DSO; *m* 1959, Lady Anne Pery, MA, DPhil (Senior Res. Fellow, Imperial College, London), *d* of 5th Earl of Limerick, GBE, CH, KCB, DSO, TD; one *s* three *d*. *Educ:* Eton; Trinity Coll., Oxford. Served War of 1939–45: with 3rd Bn Grenadier Guards (wounded), 1939–41; HQ 2nd Div., 1941–42; Staff College, Quetta, 1942; on staff of India Command and HQ, SACSEA, 1943–45; demobilised with rank of Hon. Lieut-Col, 1946. With Imperial Chemical Industries Ltd, 1946–48. Assistant Serjeant at Arms, House of Commons, 1948–57, Dep. Serjeant at Arms, 1957–76. *Publications:* The Royal Mace in the House of Commons, 1990; various HMSO pamphlets and articles in parly and historical pubns. *Address:* Chiddinglye Farmhouse, West Hoathly, East Grinstead, West Sussex RH19 4QS. *T:* (01342) 810338. *Clubs:* Cavalry and Guards; Royal Yacht Squadron.

THORNE, Robin Horton John, CMG 1966; OBE 1963; HM Overseas Service, retired; *b* 13 July 1917; *s* of late Sir John Anderson Thorne; *m* 1946, Joan Helen Wadman (*d* 2000); one *s*. *Educ:* Dragon Sch., Oxford; Rugby (open scholar); Exeter College, Oxford (open scholar; MA). War Service, Devonshire Regiment and King's African Rifles, 1939–46. Colonial Administrative Service (now HM Overseas Civil Service), 1946–67; Tanganyika Administration, 1946–58; Aden, 1958–67; Asst Chief Sec. (Colony), MLC and Mem. of Governor's Exec. Coun., 1959–63; Ministerial Sec. to Chief Minister, 1963–65; Assistant High Commissioner, 1966–67. With Vice-Chancellors' Cttee, 1967–77; part-time admin. work, Univ. of Sussex, 1978–81. Trustee of Aden Port Trust, 1959–66; Chm., Staines Trust, 1979–85; Mem., Management Cttee, Sussex Housing Assoc. for the Aged, 1983–87. *Recreations:* various. *Address:* Care Village, Winsley Road, Limpley Stoke, Bath BA2 7FF. *T:* (01255) 722447. *Club:* Royal Commonwealth Society.

THORNE, Stanley George; *b* 22 July 1918; *s* of postman and dressmaker; *m* Catherine Mary Rand; two *s* three *d*. *Educ:* Ruskin Coll., Oxford; Univ. of Liverpool. Dip. Social Studies Oxon 1968; BA Hons Liverpool 1970. 30 yrs in industry and commerce: coal-miner, semi-skilled fitter, chartered accountant's clerk, rly signalman, office manager, auditor, commercial manager, etc; lectr in govt and industrial sociology. MP (Lab): Preston South, Feb. 1974–1983; Preston 1983–87. *Recreations:* chess, bridge, golf. *Address:* 26 Station Road, Gateacre, Liverpool L25 3PZ.

THORNELY, Gervase Michael Cobham; Headmaster of Sedbergh School, 1954–75; *b* 21 Oct. 1918; *er s* of late Major J. E. B. Thornely, OBE, and late Hon. Mrs M. H. Thornely; *m* 1954, Jennifer Margery, *d* of late Sir Hilary Scott, Knowle House, Addington, Surrey; two *s* two *d*. *Educ:* Rugby Sch.; Trinity Hall, Cambridge. Organ Scholar; 2nd Cl. Hons, Modern and Mediæval Languages Tripos; BA, 1940; MA, 1944. FRSA 1968. Assistant Master, Sedbergh School, 1940. *Recreations:* music, fly-fishing. *Address:* High Stangerthwaite, Killington, Sedbergh, Cumbria LA10 5EP. *T:* (01539) 620444.

THORNELY-TAYLOR, Rupert Maurice; Consultant in Noise, Vibration and Acoustics, since 1968; Director, Rupert Taylor Ltd, since 1993; farmer; *b* Whalton, Northumberland, 21 May 1946; *s* of late Maurice Humphrey Taylor and Mary Patricia Stuart Taylor (*née* Wood); surname changed to Thornely-Taylor by Deed Poll, 1988; *m* 1st, 1964, Alison Grant, *d* of late Alistair Grant Saunders (marr. diss. 1987, she *d* 1999); 2nd, 1988, Frances Marion, *d* of late William John Lindberg. *Educ:* Harrow Sch. Acoustical engr, Burgess Products Co. Ltd, 1964–68; Dir, Rupert Taylor and Partners Ltd, 1970–81; Consultant to: London Underground, 1984–; LDDC, 1984–98; Railtrack, 1999–; res. contract, DoE, 1996. Consultant, New Victoria Th., N Staffs, 1984–86. Breeder, Rumsden Herd of Pedigree Charolais Cattle. Conservator, Ashdown Forest, 1997–. Mem., Noise Adv. Council, 1970–80 (Chm., Wkg Gp on Noise Monitoring). Mem. Council, British Acoustical Soc., 1968–71; Founder Member and Hon. Treasurer: Assoc. Noise Consultants, 1970–74 (Vice Chm., 2001–); Inst. Acoustics, 1971–74 (Fellow, 1981). Mem. (C) Wealden DC, 1995– (Leader, 1999–). Member: E Sussex Econ. Partnership, 1999–; Inter-reg. Jt Monitoring Cttee, 1999–; SE England Regl Assembly, 1999–; Mem., Exec. Cttee, Wealden Constituency Cons. Assoc., 1993–. Churchill Fellow, USA, 1972. Hon. Treas., Nat. Pony Soc., 1991–97. *Publications:* Noise, 1970, 4th edn 2001; Le Bruit et ses Méfaits, 1972; (ed) Noise Control Data, 1976; (jtly) Handbook of Noise Assessment, 1978; Electricity, 1979; contrib. papers to Proc. Inst. Acoustics, Internat. Inst. Acoustics and Vibration, Internat. Inst. Noise Control Engrg. *Recreations:* painting, music, gardening, Tibetan Spaniels. *Address:* Spring Garden, Fairwarp, Uckfield, E Sussex TN22 3BG. *T:* (01825) 712435.

See also Bishop Suffragan of Selby.

THORNEYCROFT, Lady; Carla Thorneycroft, DBE 1995; Founder Member, Trustee and Vice-Chairman, 1971–96, President, since 1996, Venice in Peril Fund; *b* 12 Feb. 1914; *e d* of late Count Malagola Cappi and Alexandra Dunbar-Marshall; *m* 1st, 1934, Count Giorgio Roberti (marr. annulled 1946); one *s* one *d*; 2nd, 1949, Major George Edward Peter Thorneycroft, MP, later Baron Thorneycroft of Dunston, CH, PC (*d* 1994); one *d*. *Educ:* privately. Fashion Editor, Vogue, 1946–51; political campaign with husband, 1949–66. Pres. and Founder, League of Friends of Italian Hosp., 1956–89; Vice-Pres., British-Italian Soc., 1957–; Founder Mem., Trustee and Patron, Rosehill Arts Theatre, 1959–77; Founder Mem. and Trustee, Chichester Fest. Theatre Trust, 1962–88; Trustee, Royal Sch. of Needlework, 1964–76; Vice-Chm., Italian Art and Archives Rescue Fund, 1966–69; Vice-Pres., Council of Friends of Westminster Cathedral, 1993– (Mem. Council, 1976–); Trustee, Conservative Winter Ball (Pres., 1984–94). Order of Merit (Italy), 1967. *Recreations:* arts, politics, travel, charity work.

THORNEYCROFT, Rev. Prebendary Pippa Hazel Jeanetta; Priest-in-Charge, Shareshill, since 1996; Chaplain to HM the Queen, since 2001; *b* 18 Feb. 1944; *d* of Philip Fitzgerald Mander and Priscilla Patricia (*née* Waller); *m* 1965, John Patrick Thorneycroft; two *s* two *d*. *Educ:* Cheltenham Ladies' Coll.; Exeter Univ. (BA Hons French 1965); Queen's Coll., Birmingham (GOE 1988); W Midlands Ministerial Trng Course. Ordained deacon, 1988, priest, 1994; Curate (non-stipendiary), St Mary Magdalene, Albrighton, 1988–90; asst deacon/priest (non-stipendiary), Badger, Beckbury, Kemberton, Ryton, Stockton and Sutton Maddock, 1990–96; Advr for Women in Ministry, Lichfield Dio., 1993–99; Rural Dean of Penkridge, 2001–. Mem., Skinners' Co. *Recreations:* walking, cycling, bee-keeping. *Address:* The Vicarage, 11 Brookhouse Lane, Featherstone, Wolverhampton WV10 7AW. *T:* (01902) 727579; Poole's Yard, Kemberton, Shifnal, Shropshire TF11 9LL.

THORNHILL, Andrew Robert; QC 1985; a Recorder, since 1997; *b* 4 Aug. 1943; *s* of Edward Percy Thornhill and Amelia Joy Thornhill; *m* 1971, Helen Mary Livingston; two *s* two *d*. *Educ:* Clifton Coll. Prep. Sch.; Clifton Coll.; Corpus Christi Coll., Oxford. Called to the Bar, Middle Temple, 1969, Bencher, 1995; entered chambers of H. H. Monroe, QC, 1969. Chm. Council, Clifton Coll., 1994–. *Publications:* (ed) Potter & Monroe: Tax Planning with Precedents, 7th edn 1974, to 9th edn 1982; (jtly) Tax Planning Through Wills, 1981, 1984; (jtly) Passing Down the Family Farm, 1982; (jtly) Passing Down the Family Business, 1984. *Recreations:* dinghy sailing, squash, Real tennis, rackets, walking. *Address:* 37 Canynge Road, Clifton, Bristol BS8 3LD. *T:* (0117) 974 4015. *Clubs:* Oxford and Cambridge; Tamesis (Teddington); Bristol Avon Sailing.

THORNING-PETERSEN, Rudolph; Knight Commander, Order of the Dannebrog, 1994; Ambassador; Chamberlain to the Queen of Denmark, since 1998; *b* 17 July 1927; *s* of Erik Thorning-Petersen, FRDanAA, architect, and Helga (*née* Westergaard); *m* 1949, Britta Leyssac; one *s* one *d*. *Educ:* Copenhagen Univ. (LLM 1952). Entered Royal Danish Foreign Service, 1952; alternating service, Min. of Foreign Affairs and at Danish Embassies in Cairo, Moscow and Stockholm, 1952–75; Ambassador: to Lebanon, Syria, Jordan, Iraq and Cyprus (resident Beirut), 1975; to People's Republic of China, 1980; to USSR, 1983–89; to UK, 1989–96; Ambassador at large, 1996–97 (missions on behalf of Chm., OSCE, to Minsk and Belgrade; Hd, OSCE Assistance Gp to Chechnya, May–Dec. 1997). Knight Grand Cross, Order of Cedar (Lebanon); Order of Independence (Jordan); Comdr, Order of Polar Star (Sweden); Kt Comdr, Order of White Rose (Finland). *Recreations:* modern history, genealogy, history of art. *Address:* Jaegersborg Alle 23,2, 2920 Charlottenlund, Denmark.

THORNTON, Baroness *cr* 1998 (Life Peer), of Manningham in the co. of West Yorkshire; **Dorothea Glenys Thornton;** independent public affairs consultant, since 1992; *b* 16 Oct. 1952; *e c* of Peter and Jean Thornton; *m* 1977, John Carr; one *s* one *d*. *Educ:* Thornton Secondary Sch., Bradford; LSE (BSc Econ 1976). Nat. Organiser, Gingerbread, 1976–78; N London Area Officer, Greater London CABx, 1978–79; Projects Dir, Inst. of Community Studies, 1979–81; Political Sec., Royal Arsenal Co-op. Soc., 1981–86; Public and Political Affairs Advr, CWS, 1986–92. Fabian Society: Gen. Sec., 1993–94; Develt Dir, 1994–96; Mem., Nat. Exec. Cttee, 1997–. Chm., Greater London Labour Party, 1986–91. Director: Labour Women's Network, 1990–; EMILY's List UK, 1993–. FRSA. *Recreations:* canoeing, hill-walking, Star Trek. *Address:* House of Lords, SW1A 0PW.

THORNTON, Allan Charles; Chairman, Environmental Investigation Agency, since 1988 (Co-Founder and Director, 1984–86); *b* 17 Nov. 1949; *s* of Robert Charles Thornton and Jessie (Waldram) Thornton; *m* 1995, Polly Ghazi, journalist and author. *Educ:* Banff Centre of Fine Art, Banff, Canada. Co-ordinator of Banff Centre Creative Writing Programme, 1976, 1977; established Greenpeace UK, 1977; Exec. Dir, 1977–81 and 1986–88; co-founder of Greenpeace vessel, Rainbow Warrior, 1978; Internat. Project Co-ordinator with Greenpeace International, 1981. *Publication:* To Save an Elephant, 1990. *Recreation:* viewing elephants and other wildlife in their natural habitat. *Address:* c/o Environmental Investigation Agency, 69 85 Old Street, EC1V 9HX. *T:* (020) 7490 7040.

THORNTON, Anthony Christopher Lawrence; QC 1988; **His Honour Judge Thornton;** a Judge of the Technology and Construction Court of the High Court, since 1998; *b* 18 Aug. 1947; *s* of Richard Thornton and Margery Alice (*née* Clerk); *m* 1983, Lyn Christine Thurlby (marr. diss. 1998); one *s*. *Educ:* Eton Coll.; Keble Coll., Oxford (BCL, MA). FCIArb. Called to the Bar, Middle Temple, 1970, Bencher, 1992. A Recorder, 1992–94; a Circuit Judge, 1994 . Chairman: Fulham Legal Advice Centre, 1973–78; Hammersmith and Fulham Law Centre, 1975–78. External Moderator, Centre of Construction and Project Management, KCL, 1987–; Hon. Sen. Vis. Fellow, Centre for Commercial Law Studies, QMC, 1987–. Mem., Gen. Council of the Bar, 1988–94 (Treas., 1990–92; Chm., Professional Standards Cttee, 1992–93). Dir, Apex Trust, 1991–94. Liveryman, Leathersellers' Co., 1976–. Jt Editor, Construction Law Jl, 1984–94. *Publications:* (ed jtly) Building Contracts, in Halsbury's Laws of England, vol. 4, 1972; (contrib.) Construction Disputes: liability and the expert witness, 1989; contribs to Construction Law Jl. *Recreations:* football, opera, ski-ing, legal history. *Address:* St Dunstan's House, 133–137 Fetter Lane, EC4A 1HD. *T:* (020) 7947 6022. *Club:* Royal Automobile.

THORNTON, Air Vice-Marshal Barry Michael, CEng, FIMechE; Controller Aircraft RAF, and Executive Director, Defence Procurement Agency, Ministry of Defence, since 2000; *b* 19 Nov. 1952; *s* of Ronald Thornton and Enid Margaret Thornton (*née* Baxendale); *m* 1977, Delia Brown, barrister; two *s*. *Educ:* Baines Grammar Sch.; Nottingham Univ. (BSc); RMCS, Cranfield Univ. (MSc). CEng 1981; FIMechE 1994. Joined RAF, 1971; initial and professional trng, 1974–75; aircraft and weapon systems appts at RAF Waddington, RAF Lyneham, RAF Abingdon and HQ RAF Germany, 1975–87; Advanced Staff Trng, 1988; OC Engrg and Supply Wing, RAF Honington, 1988–90; OC Engrg Wing, RAF Detachment Tabuk, Gulf War; Weapons Support Authy and Standardization, MoD, 1991–93; Combat Aircraft Test and Evaluation, DERA, MoD, 1994–96; rcds 1997; Dir Maritime Projects, MoD PE, 1998; Nimrod MRA4 Integrated Project Team Leader, Defence Procurement Agency, MoD, 1998–2000. FIMgt 1995. *Recreations:* hill-walking, golf, gardening, classic cars. *Address:* Ministry of Defence, Main Building, Whitehall, SW1A 2HB. *Club:* Royal Air Force.

THORNTON, Clive Edward Ian, CBE 1983; FInstLEx, FCBSI; Chairman: Melton Mowbray Building Society, since 1991 (Director, since 1988); Armstrong Capital Holdings Ltd, since 1988; *b* 12 Dec. 1929; *s* of Albert and Margaret Thornton; *m* 1956, Maureen Carmine (*née* Crane); one *s* one *d*. *Educ:* St Anthony's Sch., Newcastle upon Tyne; Coll. of Commerce, Newcastle upon Tyne; College of Law, London; LLB 1977, BA Hons 1996, MA 1999, London Univ. (ext.); BSc Hons 1998, Dip. Geog. 1998, Open Univ. FInstLEx 1958; FCBSI 1970. Solicitor. Associate, Pensions Management Inst., 1978. Articled to Kenneth Hudson, solicitor, London, 1959; admitted solicitor of Supreme Court, 1963. Asst Solicitor, Nationwide Building Soc., 1963; Solicitor, Cassel Arenz Ltd, Merchant Bankers, 1964–67; Abbey National Building Society: Chief Solicitor, 1967; Dep. Chief Gen. Man., 1978; Chief Gen. Manager, 1979–83; Dir, 1980–83; Partner, Stoneham Langton and Passmore, Solicitors, 1985–88. Chm., Metropolitan Assoc. of Building Socs, 1981–82. Chairman: Mirror Group Newspapers, 1984; Financial Weekly, 1985–87; Thamesmead Town Ltd, 1986–90; Gabriel Communications (formerly Universe Publications) Ltd, 1986–96; Dir, Investment Data Services Ltd, 1986–90. Proprietor, Thorndale Devon Cattle, 1983–; Pres., Devon Cattle Breeders Soc., 1997–98. Member: Law Soc. (Chm., Commerce and Industry Gp, 1974); Council, Chartered Bldg Socs Inst., 1973–81; Council, Building Socs Assoc., 1979–83; Bd, Housing Corp., 1980–86. Chairman: SHAC, 1983–86; Belford Hall Management Co. Ltd, 1990–93. Member: Council, St Mary's Hosp. Med. Sch., 1984–96; St Mary's Develt Trust, 1984–98. Freeman, City of London; Liveryman, Worshipful Co. of Bakers. *Publications:* Building Society Law, Cases and Materials, 1969 (3rd edn 1988); History of Devon Cattle, 1994. *Recreations:* antique collecting, music, reading, farming. *Address:* Keythorpe Grange, East Norton, Leics LE7 9XL.

THORNTON, Sir (George) Malcolm, Kt 1992; Chairman, Keene Public Affairs Consultants Ltd, since 1997; *b* 3 April 1939; *s* of George Edmund and Ethel Thornton; *m* 1st, 1962; one *s*; 2nd, 1972, Shirley Ann, (Sue) (*née* Banton) (*d* 1989); 3rd, 1990, Rosemary (*née* Hewitt). *Educ:* Wallasey Grammar Sch.; Liverpool Nautical Coll. Liverpool Pilot Service, 1955–79 (Sen. 1st cl. Licence holder). Chm., River City Hldgs Ltd, 1998–. Member: Wallasey County Borough Council, 1965–74 (Chm., Transport Cttee, 1968–69); Wirral Metropolitan Council, 1973–79 (Council Leader, 1974–77); Chairman: Merseyside Metropolitan Districts Liaison Cttee, 1975–77; Educn Cttee, AMA, 1978–79 (Mem., 1974–79); Council of Local Educn Authorities, 1978. Mem., Burnham (Primary and Secondary) Cttee, 1975–79. MP (C) Liverpool, Garston, 1979–83, Crosby, 1983–97; contested Crosby, 1997. PPS to Sec. of State for Industry, 1981–83, for the Environment, 1983–84. Chairman: Select Cttee on Educn, Sci. and the Arts, 1989–96 (Mem., 1985–96); Select Cttee on Educn and Employment, 1996–97. Hon. Col 156 (NW) Transport Regt, RLC (V), 2000–. FRSA. Hon. DEd De Montfort, 1994. *Recreations:* fishing, walking, cooking. *Address:* Meadow Brook, 79 Barnston Road, Heswall, Wirral CH60 1UE. *Club:* Wirral Game Fishing.

THORNTON, Helen Ann Elizabeth, (Mrs J. E. C. Thornton); *see* Meixner, H. A. E.

THORNTON, Prof. Janet M., CBE 2000; PhD; FRS 1999; Professor of Biomolecular Structure, University College London, since 1990; Bernal Professor of Crystallography, Birkbeck College, London University, since 1996; *b* 23 May 1949; *d* of Stanley James McLoughlin and Kathleen McLoughlin (*née* Barlow); *m* 1970, Alan D. Thornton; one *s* one *d*. *Educ:* Nottingham Univ. (BSc 1st Cl. Hons Physics); King's Coll. London and NIMR (PhD 1973). Research Assistant: Lab. of Molecular Biophysics, Oxford, 1973–78; Molecular Pharmacol., NIMR, 1978; Crystallography Department, Birkbeck College, London: SERC Advanced Fellow, 1979–83; Lectr, 1983–89; Sen. Lectr, 1989–90; Tutor, Open Univ., 1976–83; Dir, Biomolecular Structure and Modelling Unit, UCL, 1990–; Hd, Jt Res. Sch. in Molecular Scis, UCL and Birkbeck Coll., 1996–. Consultant, Eur. Bioinformatics Inst., EMBL, 1994–. *Publications:* contrib. numerous articles to jls incl. Jl Molecular Biol., Structure, Nature, Trends in Biochemical Scis, Proc. Nat. Acad. Sci., Protein Science. *Recreations:* reading, music, gardens, home. *Address:* Department of Biochemistry and Molecular Biology, University College London, Gower Street, WC1E 6BT. *T:* (020) 7679 7048.

THORNTON, John Henry, OBE 1987; QPM 1980; Deputy Assistant Commissioner, Metropolitan Police, 1981–86; *b* 24 Dec. 1930; *s* of late Sidney Thornton and Ethel Thornton (*née* Grinnell); *m* 1st, 1952, Norma Lucille (marr. diss. 1972; decd), *d* of late Alfred and Kate Scrivenor; two *s*; 2nd, 1972, Hazel Ann (marr. diss. 1996), *d* of late William and Edna Butler; one *s* one *d* (and one *s* decd); 3rd, 1996, Mary Elizabeth, *d* of John Patrick and late Elizabeth Unity Jackson. *Educ:* Prince Henry's Grammar School. Evesham. RN 1949–50. Metropolitan Police, 1950, Comdr, 1976; Head of Community Relations, 1977–80; RCDS, 1981; Dep. Asst Commissioner, 1981; Dir of Information, 1982–83; Hd of Training, 1983–85; NW Area, 1985–86. Vice-Pres., British Section, Internat. Police Assoc., 1969–79. Chm., Breakaway Theatre Co., St Albans, 1987–94; Chm., St Albans Internat. Organ Fest., 1988–91. Chm. of Govs, Townsend C of E Sch., St Albans, 1990–96. Lay Canon and Cathedral Warden, St Albans, 1988–94. Liveryman, Glaziers' Co., 1983. CStJ 1984. *Recreations:* music, gardening, homes. *Address:* c/o Barclays Bank, PO Box 300, St Albans, Herts AL1 3EQ.

THORNTON, John Lawson; President and co-Chief Operating Officer, Goldman Sachs Group, Inc., since 1999; *b* 2 Jan. 1954; *s* of John and Edna Thornton; *m* 1990, Margaret Bradham; two *s* one *d*. *Educ:* Hotchkiss Sch.; Harvard Coll. (AB); Oxford Univ. (MA); Yale Sch. of Mgt. Joined Goldman Sachs, 1980: Gen. Partner, 1988; Co-CEO, Goldman Sachs Internat. (Europe, ME and Africa), 1995–96; Chm., Goldman Sachs-Asia, 1996–98; Dir, Mem. Mgt Cttee, and Co-Chm., Partnership Cttee. Director: Ford Motor Co.; BSkyB Gp plc; Pacific Century Gp, Inc.; Laura Ashley plc. Mem., Council on Foreign Relns. Dir, Goldman Sachs Foundn. Member, Board of Trustees: Hotchkiss Sch.; Asia Soc.; Morehouse Coll.; Member: Bd of Dirs, Brookings Instn; Investment Cttee, Yale Univ.; Adv. Bd, Yale Sch. of Mgt. *Address:* Goldman Sachs, Peterborough Court, 133 Fleet Street, EC4A 2BB. *T:* (020) 7774 4351.

THORNTON, Sir Malcolm; *see* Thornton, Sir G. M.

THORNTON, Neil Ross; Director, Animal Health, Department for Environment, Food and Rural Affairs (formerly Head of Animal Health Group, Ministry of Agriculture, Fisheries and Food), since 2000; *b* 11 Feb. 1950; *s* of late George and Kay Thornton; *m* 1977, Christine Anne Boyes; two *d*. *Educ:* Sedbergh Sch.; Pembroke Coll., Cambridge (BA Eng. 1971). Private Sec. to Perm. Sec., DoI, 1975; HM Treasury, 1979; Asst Sec., DTI, 1984; Principal Private Sec. to Sec. of State for Trade and Industry, 1988–90; Under Sec., 1990, Head, Europe Div., 1990–93, Exports to Europe and the Americas Div., 1993–96, DTI; Hd of Food, Drink and Marketing Policy Gp, 1996–99, Hd of Food Industry Competitiveness and Consumers, 1999–2000, MAFF. *Recreations:* literature, choral singing, golf. *Address:* Department for Environment, Food and Rural Affairs, 1A Page Street, SW1P 4PQ.

THORNTON, Peter Anthony, FRICS; FICE; Chief Executive, Greycoat Estates Ltd (formerly Greycoat Plc), since 1994; *b* 8 May 1944; *s* of Robert and Freda Thornton; *m* 1st, 1969, Patricia Greenwood (marr. diss. 1987); one *s* two *d*; 2nd, 1997, Susan Harris. *Educ:* Bradford Grammar Sch.; Manchester Univ. (BSc). FRICS 1984; FICE 1990. Engineer, Binnie & Partners (Consulting Engrs), 1967–71; self-employed, 1972–75; Commercial Manager, Sears Hldgs plc, 1975–79; Greycoat Plc, 1979–99: Dir, 1981–99; Jt Man. Dir, 1986–94. *Recreations:* cars, tennis, water ski-ing. *Address:* Van Buren Cottage, Queen's Ride, Barnes Common, SW13 0JF. *T:* (020) 8788 1969. *Clubs:* Royal Automobile, Harbour.

THORNTON, Sir Peter (Eustace), KCB 1974 (CB 1971); Permanent Secretary, Department of Trade, 1974–77; *b* 28 Aug. 1917; *s* of Douglas Oscar Thornton and Dorothy (*née* Shepherd); *m* 1946, Rosamond Hobart Myers, US Medal of Freedom, Sewanee, Tennessee; two *s* one *d*. *Educ:* Charterhouse; Gonville and Caius Coll., Cambridge. Served with RA, mainly in Middle East and Italy, 1940–46. Joined Board of Trade, 1946. Secretary, Company Law Cttee (Jenkins Cttee), 1959–62; Assistant Under-Secretary of State, Department of Economic Affairs, 1964–67; Under-Sec., 1967–70, Dep. Sec., 1970–72, Cabinet Office, with central co-ordinating role during British negotiations for membership of EEC; Dep. Sec., DTI, March-July 1972; Sec. (Aerospace and Shipping), DTI, 1972–74; Second Permanent Sec., Dept of Trade, 1974. Director: Hill Samuel Gp, 1977–83; Rolls Royce, 1977–85; Courtaulds, 1977–87; Laird Gp, 1978–92; Superior Oil, 1980–84. Mem., Megaw Cttee of Inquiry into Civil Service Pay, 1981–82. Pro-Chancellor, Open Univ., 1979–83 (DUniv 1984). Governor, Sutton's Hosp., Charterhouse, 1980–89.

THORNTON, Peter Kai, CBE 1996; FSA 1976; Curator of Sir John Soane's Museum, 1984–95; *b* 8 April 1925; *s* of Sir Gerard Thornton, FRS, and of Gerda, *d* of Kai Nørregaard, Copenhagen; *m* 1950, Mary Ann Rosamund (marr. diss. 2001), *d* of E. A. P. Helps, Cregane, Rosscarbery, Co. Cork; three *d*. *Educ:* Bryanston Sch.; De Havilland

Aeronautical Technical Sch.; Trinity Hall, Cambridge. Served with Army, Intelligence Corps, Austria, 1945–48; Cambridge, 1948–50; Voluntary Asst Keeper, Fitzwilliam Museum, Cambridge, 1950–52; Joint Secretary, National Art-Collections Fund, London, 1952–54; entered Victoria and Albert Museum as Asst Keeper, Dept of Textiles, 1954; transf. to Dept of Woodwork, 1962; Keeper, Dept of Furniture and Woodwork, 1966–84. Sen. Vis. Res. Fellow, St John's Coll., Oxford, 1985–86; Leverhulme Emeritus Res. Fellow, 1988–89. Chm., Furniture History Soc., 1974–84; Member: Council, Nat. Trust, 1983–85; London Adv. Cttee, English Heritage, 1986–88. Iris Foundn award, Bard Center, NY, 1999. *Publications:* Baroque and Rococo Silks, 1965; Seventeenth Century Interior Decoration in England, France and Holland, 1978 (Alice Davis Hitchcock Medallion, Soc. of Architectural Historians of GB, 1982); (jtly) The Furnishing and Decoration of Ham House, 1981; Musical Instruments as Works of Art, 1982; Authentic Decor: the domestic interior 1620–1920, 1984, rev. edn 2000 (Sir Bannister Fletcher Prize, RIBA, 1985); The Italian Renaissance Interior 1400–1600, 1992 (Prix Vasari International du Livre d'Art for French edn, 1992); (jtly) A Miscellany of Objects from Sir John Soane's Museum, 1992; Form and Decoration: innovation in the decorative arts 1470–1870, 1998. *Address:* 10 Grove Park Road, W4 3SE.
See also Hon. P. Jay.

THORNTON, Peter Ribblesdale; QC 1992; a Recorder, since 1997; *b* 17 Oct. 1946; *s* of Robert Ribblesdale Thornton, *qv*; *m* 1981, Susan Margaret Dalal; one *s* one *d*. *Educ:* Clifton Coll.; St John's Coll., Cambridge (BA). Called to the Bar, Middle Temple, 1969; an Asst Recorder, 1994–97. Chairman: NCCL, 1981–83; Civil Liberties Trust, 1991–95. *Publications:* (contrib.) Civil Liberties 1984, 1984; We Protest: Public Order Debate, 1985; The Civil Liberties of the Zircon Affair, 1987; Public Order Law, 1987; (contrib.) The Polygraph Test, 1988; Decade of Decline: Civil Liberties in the Thatcher Years, 1989; (ed jtly) Penguin Civil Liberty Guide, 1989; (jtly) Justice on Trial, 1992; (ed jtly) Archbold's Criminal Pleadings, Evidence and Practice, 1992–; (contrib.) Analysing Witness Testimony, 1999. *Address:* Doughty Street Chambers, 11 Doughty Street, WC1N 2PL. *T:* (020) 7404 1313.

THORNTON, Sir Richard (Eustace), KCVO 1997; OBE 1980; JP; HM Lord Lieutenant of Surrey, 1986–97; *b* 10 Oct. 1922; *m* 1954, Gabrielle Elizabeth Sharpe; four *d*. *Educ:* Eton Coll.; Trinity Coll., Cambridge (MA). Member: Thames Conservancy, 1968–74; TWA, 1974–80; Royal Commission on Environmental Pollution, 1977–84. Chm., Mount Alvernia Management Trust, 1992–. Chm. Govs, Bishop Reindorp Sch., 1985–98; Mem. Governing Body, Charterhouse Sch. (Chm., 1981–89). Surrey: DL; High Sheriff 1978–79; JP. KStJ 1986. *Address:* Hampton, Seale, near Farnham, Surrey GU10 1JE. *T:* (01483) 810208.

THORNTON, Robert John, CB 1980; Assistant Under Secretary of State and Director General of Supplies and Transport (Naval), Ministry of Defence, 1977–81; *b* 23 Dec. 1919; *s* of Herbert John Thornton and Ethel Mary Thornton (*née* Dunning); *m* 1944, Joan Elizabeth Roberts; three *s*. *Educ:* Queen Elizabeth Grammar School, Atherstone. MBIM 1970. Joined Naval Store Dept, Admiralty, as Asst Naval Store Officer, 1938; Singapore, 1941; Dep. Naval Store Officer, Colombo, 1942; Support Ship Hong Siang, 1943; Naval Store Officer, Admiralty, 1945; Gibraltar, 1951; Asst Dir of Stores, 1955; Superintending Naval Store Officer, Portsmouth, 1960; Dep. Dir of Stores, 1964; Dir of Victualling, 1971; Dir of Supplies and Transport (General Stores and Victualling), 1971. *Recreations:* bowls, fly fishing, gardening.

THORNTON, Robert Ribblesdale, CBE 1973; DL; solicitor; Deputy Chairman, Local Government Boundary Commission for England, 1982 (Member, 1976–82); *b* 2 April 1913; *s* of Thomas Thornton and Florence Thornton (*née* Gatenby); *m* 1940, Ruth Eleonore Tuckson; one *s* one *d*. *Educ:* Leeds Grammar Sch.; St John's Coll., Cambridge (MA, LLM). Asst Solicitor, Leeds, 1938–40 and 1946–47. Served War, 1940–46. Asst Solicitor, Bristol, 1947–53; Dep. Town Clerk, Southampton, 1953–54; Town Clerk: Salford, 1954–66; Leicester, 1966–73; Chief Exec., Leicestershire CC, 1973–76. Pres., Soc. of Town Clerks, 1971. Treasurer, Leicester Univ., 1980–85. Hon. LLD Leicester, 1987. DL Leicestershire, 1974–85. French Croix de Guerre, 1946. *Recreations:* music, sport. *Address:* 16 St Mary's Close, Winterborne Whitechurch, Blandford Forum, Dorset DT11 0DJ. *T:* (01258) 880980.
See also P. R. Thornton.

THORNTON, Sally; *see* Burgess, Sally.

THORNTON, Stephen; Chief Executive, National Health Service Confederation, since 1997; *b* 23 Jan. 1954; *s* of Harry Thornton and Alice Thornton (*née* Ainsworth); *m* 1976, Lorraine Anne Cassells; one *s* one *d*. *Educ:* Paston Sch., N Walsham, Norfolk; Manchester Univ. (BA Hons Politics and Mod. Hist.). MHSM, DipHSM. NHS Nat. Mgt Trng scheme, 1979; Administrator: Prestwich Hosp., Manchester, 1980–82; Salford Royal Hosp., 1982–83; Fulbourn Hosp., Cambridge, 1983–85; Gen. Manager, Community Health Services, Cambs, 1985–89; Dir of Planning, E Anglia RHA, 1989–93; Chief Exec., Cambridge and Huntingdon HA, 1993–96; Cabinet Office Top Mgt Programme, 1996. Mem., NHS Modernisation Bd, 2000. FRSocMed 1998. Sec., Girton Baptist Church. *Publications:* articles in Health Service Jl. *Recreations:* gardening, trying to keep up with my teenage children. *Address:* 100 High Street, Girton, Cambridge CB3 0QL. *T:* (01223) 267237.

THORNTON, Rt Rev. Timothy Martin; *see* Sherborne, Area Bishop of.

THORNTON, Dr William Dickson, CB 1990; Deputy Chief Medical Officer, Department of Health and Social Services, Northern Ireland, 1978–90, retired; *b* 9 July 1930; *s* of late William J. Thornton and of Elfreda Thornton (*née* Dickson); *m* 1957, Dr Maureen Gilpin; one *s* three *d*. *Educ:* Portora Royal School; Trinity College Dublin (BA, MD). FFPHM. General medical practitioner, 1955–65; NI Hospitals Authy, 1966–72; Dept of Health and Social Services (NI), 1973–90. Civil QHP, 1990–92. Chm., Age Concern (NI), 1993–97. *Recreations:* yachting, reading, gardening. *Address:* 54 Deramore Park South, Belfast BT9 5JY. *T:* (028) 9066 0186.

THOROGOOD, Alfreda, (Mrs D. R. Wall); ARAD (PDTC); Artistic Director of Dance, Elmhurst Ballet School, since 1994 (Senior Teacher, 1992–94); Artistic Advisor, Royal Academy of Dancing, since 1989; *b* 17 Aug. 1942; *d* of Alfreda and Edward Thorogood; *m* 1967, David Wall, *qv*; one *s* one *d*. *Educ:* Lady Eden's Sch.; Royal Ballet Sch., Jun. and Sen. Royal Ballet Company, 1960–80: Soloist, Aug. 1965; Principal Dancer, 1968; Bush Davies School: Sen. Teacher, 1982–84; Dep. Ballet Principal, 1984–89; Dir, 1988–89. *Recreations:* listening to music, cooking, interior design, art, painting. *Address:* 34 Croham Manor Road, S Croydon CR2 7BE.

THOROGOOD, Rev. Bernard George, OBE 1992; General Secretary, United Reformed Church, 1980–92; *b* 21 July 1927; *s* of Frederick and Winifred Thorogood; *m* 1952, Jannett Lindsay Paton (*née* Cameron) (*d* 1988); two *s*; *m* 1991, Joan Tierney. *Educ:* Glasgow Univ. (MA); Scottish Congregational College. Ordained in Congregational Church, 1952; missionary appointment under London Missionary Society in South Pacific Islands, 1953–70; Gen. Sec., Council for World Mission, 1971–80. Moderator, Exec. Cttee, BCC, 1984–90; Mem., Central Cttee, WCC, 1984–91. DD Lambeth 1992. *Publications:* Not Quite Paradise, 1960; Guide to the Book of Amos, 1971; Our Father's House, 1983; Risen Today, 1987; The Flag and The Cross, 1988; No Abiding City, 1989; On Judging Caesar, 1990; One Wind Many Flames, 1991; Looking at Leisure: a European view, 1991; (ed) Gales of Change, 1994; Letters to Paul, 1999. *Recreation:* sketching. *Address:* 2 Ashmore Avenue, Pymble, NSW 2073, Australia. *T:* (2) 91441822.

THOROGOOD, Kenneth Alfred Charles; *b* 1924; *s* of Albert Jesse and Alice Lucy Thorogood; *m* 1st, 1947, José Patricia Smith; two *d*; 2nd, 1979, Mrs Gaye Lambourne. *Educ:* Highbury County Grammar School. Pilot, RAF, 1941–46. Chm., Tozer Kemsley & Millbourn (Holdings) plc, 1972–82; Dep. Chm. and Dir, Felixstowe Dock and Railway Co., 1976–81; Director: Alexanders Discount Co. Ltd, to 1983; Royal Insurance Co. Ltd; Abelson Plant (Holdings) Ltd; Spicer-Firgos Ltd; Welbeck Finance plc, 1984–88. Chairman, Brit. Export Houses Assoc., 1968–70; Mem., Cttee of Invisibles, 1968–70. *Recreations:* aviation, music. *Address:* Flat 1, 18 Lowndes Square, SW1X 9HB. *Clubs:* Travellers, City of London, Royal Air Force, MCC; Wanderers (Johannesburg).

THOROLD, Sir (Anthony) Oliver, 16th Bt *cr* 1642, of Marston, Lincolnshire; *b* 15 April 1945; *o s* of Captain Sir Anthony Thorold, 15th Bt, OBE, DSC and Jocelyn Elaine Laura Thorold (*née* Heathcote-Smith); *S* father, 1999; *m* 1977, Genevra Mercy Richardson, *qv*; one *s* one *d*. *Educ:* Winchester; Lincoln Coll., Oxford. Called to the Bar, Inner Temple, 1971. *Heir:* *s* Henry Lowry Thorold, *b* 6 Aug. 1981. *Address:* (chambers) 11 Doughty Street, WC1N 2PG; 8 Richmond Crescent, N1 0LZ.

THORP, David; Managing Director, Friends Ivory & Sime Private Equity (formerly Ivory & Sime Baronsmead) plc, since 1997 (Director, since 1995); *b* 22 July 1945; *s* of late John and Kathleen Mary Thorp; *m* 1969, Christine Janice Kenyon; three *s*. *Educ:* Portsmouth Grammar Sch.; Queens' College, Cambridge (MA Natural Scis); London Business School (MBA). Alcan (UK), 1967–69; ICFC, then FFI, subseq. 3i plc, 1971–91, Dir, 1985–91; Dir-Gen, ESU, 1991–94. Chairman: Unipalm Ltd, 1992–94; Unipalm Gp plc, 1994–95; non-exec. Dir, Patientline plc (formerly Patientline Ltd), 1998– (Chm., Patientline Ltd, 1994–98). Mem. Council, 1997–June 2002, Chm., 2000–01, BVCA (formerly British Venture Capital Assoc.). Non-exec. Director: Royal Surrey County Hosp., 1990–97; Baronsmead VCT plc, 1995–. *Recreations:* cricket, tennis, singing. *Address:* Larks Hill, 16 Longdown, Guildford, Surrey GU4 8PP. *T:* (01483) 561016.

THORP, Jeremy Walter, CMG 2001; HM Diplomatic Service, retired; Ambassador to Colombia, 1998–2001; *b* 12 Dec. 1941; *s* of Walter and Dorothy Bliss Thorp; *m* 1973, Estela Lessa Guyer. *Educ:* King Edward VII Sch., Sheffield; Corpus Christi Coll., Oxford (MA). HM Treasury, 1963–67; DEA, 1967–69; HM Treasury, 1969–71; First Sec. (Financial), HM Embassy, Washington, 1971–73; HM Treasury, 1973–78; FCO, 1978–82; Head of Chancery, Lima, 1982–86; FCO, 1986–88; Dep. Hd of Mission, Dublin, 1988–92; Head of Resource and Finance, then Resource Planning, Dept, FCO, 1993–97; with Unilever PLC, 1997–98. *Recreations:* music, travel, 20th century history, walking. *Address:* c/o Foreign and Commonwealth Office, King Charles Street, SW1A 2AH.

THORPE, Adrian Charles, CMG 1994; MA; HM Diplomatic Service; Ambassador to Mexico, since 1999; *b* 29 July 1942; *o s* of late Prof. Lewis Thorpe and of Dr Barbara Reynolds, *qv*; *m* 1968, Miyoko Kosugi. *Educ:* The Leys Sch., Cambridge; Christ's Coll., Cambridge (MA). HM Diplomatic Service, 1965–: Tokyo, 1965–70; FCO, 1970–73; Beirut, 1973–76 (Head of Chancery, 1975–76); FCO, 1976; Tokyo, 1976–81; FCO, 1981–85, Hd of IT Dept, 1982–85; Counsellor (Econ.), Bonn, 1985–89; Dep. High Comr, Kuala Lumpur, 1989–91; Minister, Tokyo, 1991–95; Ambassador to the Philippines, 1995–98. FRSA. *Publications:* articles in journals. *Recreations:* opera, travel, bookshops, comfort. *Address:* c/o Foreign and Commonwealth Office, SW1A 2AH. *Clubs:* Tokyo, Foreign Correspondents' (Tokyo).

THORPE, Anthony Geoffrey Younghusband; His Honour Judge Thorpe; a Circuit Judge, since 1990; Resident Judge, Chichester Crown Court, since 2000; *b* 21 Aug. 1941; *s* of G. J. Y. Thorpe, MBE; *m* 1966, Janet Patricia; one *s* one *d*. *Educ:* Highgate School; Britannia Royal Naval College (scholarship); King's College London. Royal Navy: served HM Ships Hermes, Ark Royal, Vidal, Blake; Captain 1983; Chief Naval Judge Advocate, 1983–86; retired from RN 1990. Called to the Bar, Inner Temple, 1972 (Treasurer's Prize); Asst Recorder, 1984–89, Recorder, 1989–90. Pres., Indep. Tribunal Service, 1992–94 (Social Security, Medical, Disability, and Vaccine Damage Appeals, Child Support Appeals). *Publications:* articles in learned jls. *Recreations:* sailing. *Address:* The Crown Court, Southgate, Chichester, W Sussex PO19 1SX; c/o Lloyds TSB, Cox's and King's, 6 Pall Mall, SW1Y 5NH. *Club:* Naval.

THORPE, Brian Russell, CBE 1987; Deputy Chairman, Southern Water PLC (formerly Southern Water Authority), 1983–93 (Chief Executive, 1973–88); *b* 12 July 1929; *s* of late Robert and Florrie Thorpe; *m* 1955, Ann Sinclair Raby; three *d*. *Educ:* Rastrick Grammar Sch. LLB London, LLM Leeds. Solicitor, 1952. Asst Prosecuting Solicitor, Bradford CC, 1954–55; Asst Solicitor, later Asst Town Clerk, Southampton CC, 1955–61; Dep. Town Clerk, Blackpool, 1961–65; Gen. Man., Sussex River Authority, 1965–73. Churchill Fellow, 1972. *Recreations:* golf, gardening, foreign travel. *Address:* First Avenue, Worthing. *Club:* Worthing Golf.

THORPE, Rt Hon. (John) Jeremy; PC 1967; Chairman, Jeremy Thorpe Associates (Development Consultants in the Third World), since 1984; *b* 29 April 1929; *s* of late J. H. Thorpe, OBE, KC, MP (C) Rusholme, and Ursula, *d* of Sir John Norton-Griffiths, 1st Bt, KCB, DSO, sometime MP (C); *m* 1st, 1968, Caroline (*d* 1970), *d* of Warwick Allpass, Kingswood, Surrey; one *s*; 2nd, 1973, Marion, *d* of late Erwin Stein. *Educ:* Rectory Sch., Connecticut, USA; Eton Coll.; Trinity Coll., Oxford, Hon. Fellow, 1972. President, Oxford Union Society, Hilary, 1951; Barrister, Inner Temple, 1954. Member Devon Sessions. Contested (L) N Devon, 1955; MP (L) Devon N, 1959–79. Hon. Treasurer, Liberal Party Organisation, 1965–67; Leader, Liberal Party, 1967–76; Pres., N Devon Liberal Democrats (formerly N Devon Liberal Assoc.), 1987–. United Nations Association: Chm., Exec., 1976–80; Chm., Political Cttee, 1977–85. FRSA. Hon. LLD Exeter, 1974. *Publications:* (jtly) To all who are interested in Democracy, 1951; Europe: the case for going in, 1971; In My Own Time, 1999; contrib. to newspapers and periodicals. *Recreations:* music; collecting Chinese ceramics. *Address:* 2 Orme Square, W2 4RS. *Clubs:* National Liberal; N Devon Liberal.

THORPE, Rt Hon. Sir Mathew Alexander, Kt 1988; PC 1995; **Rt Hon. Lord Justice Thorpe;** a Lord Justice of Appeal, since 1995; *b* 30 July 1938; *s* of late Michael Alexander Thorpe and Dorothea Margaret Lambert; *m* 1st, 1966, Lavinia Hermione Buxton (marr. diss. 1989); three *s*; 2nd, 1989, Mrs Carola Millar. *Educ:* Stowe; Balliol Coll., Oxford. Called to the Bar, Inner Temple, 1961, Bencher, 1985; QC 1980; a

Recorder, 1982–88; a Judge of the High Court, Family Div., 1988–95. *Address:* Royal Courts of Justice, Strand, WC2A 2LL.

THORPE, Nigel James, CVO 1991; HM Diplomatic Service; Ambassador to Hungary, since 1998; *b* 3 Oct. 1945; *s* of Ronald Thorpe and Glenys (*née* Robilliard); *m* 1969 (marr. diss. 1976); two *s*; *m* 1978 (marr. diss. 2001); three *d*. *Educ:* East Grinstead Grammar Sch.; University Coll. of S Wales and Monmouthshire (BA Hons). Joined HM Diplomatic Service, 1969; Warsaw, 1970–72; Dacca, 1973–74; FCO, 1975–79; Ottawa, 1979–81; seconded to Dept of Energy, 1981–82; Asst Hd of Southern Africa Dept, FCO, 1982–85; Counsellor, Warsaw, 1985–88; Dep. High Comr, Harare, 1989–92; Head, Central European Dept, FCO, 1992–96; Sen. Directing Staff, RCDS (on secondment), 1996–97. Founder, Adam Clark Foundn. Trustee, Liszt Acad. Network. *Publications:* Harmincad Utca 6, a 20th Century History of Budapest, 1999. *Recreations:* my children, reading, history. *Address:* c/o Foreign and Commonwealth Office, King Charles Street, SW1A 2AH.

THORPE, Phillip Andrew; President, Futures Industry Institute, Washington, since 2001; *b* 26 Aug. 1954; *s* of Reginald Thorpe, OBE and Fay Eglantine Thorpe; *m* 1st, 1976, Isabell Hanna Henkel (marr. diss. 1989); one *s* two *d*; 2nd, 1990, Melinda Kilgour Lowis (marr. diss. 1997); one *s* one *d*; 3rd, 1998, Jane Chunhae Kang. *Educ:* Victoria Univ., Wellington, NZ (BA Pol Sci., LLB); Univ. of Hong Kong (MSocSc Dist.). Admitted Barrister and Solicitor of Supreme Court of NZ and as Solicitor and Notary Public, Republic of Nauru. Solicitor, Beyer Christie O'Regan & Partners, Wellington, NZ, 1976–79; Legal Officer and Public Prosecutor, Govt of Republic of Nauru, 1979–81; Solicitor, Registrar-General's Dept, Hong Kong Govt, 1981–83; Hong Kong Securities Commission: Sen. Legal Advr, 1983–86; Asst Comr, 1986–88; Dep. Comr, 1988–89; Exec. Vice-Chm. and Chief Exec., Hong Kong Futures Exchange, 1987–89; Chief Exec., Assoc. of Futures Brokers and Dealers Ltd, 1989–91; Exec. Dir and Dep. Chief Exec., SFA Ltd, 1991–93; Exec. Dir and Chief Exec., London Commodity Exchange (1986) Ltd, 1991–92; Chief Exec., IMRO, 1993–98; Man. Dir, Authorisations, Enforcement, and Consumer Relns, FSA, 1998–2001. *Publication:* (Country Editor for Hong Kong) International Securities Regulation, 1986. *Recreations:* viticulture, bricolage, long distance driving. *Address:* 2001 Pennsylvania Avenue, NW, Washington, DC 20006, USA. *Club:* Hong Kong Cricket.

THORPE, Prof. Stephen Austen, PhD; FRS 1991; Professor of Oceanography, University of Southampton, since 1986. *Educ:* Rutherford Coll., Newcastle (BSc); Trinity Coll., Cambridge (BA 1961; PhD 1966). SPSO, Inst. of Oceanographic Scis, NERC, until 1986. Mem., NERC, 1991–94 (Mem., Marine Scis Cttee). Hon. Prof., Sch. of Ocean Scis, Univ. of Wales, Bangor, 2001–. Pres., RMetS, 1990–92; Vice-Pres., Scottish Assoc. for Marine Sci., 1993–. Walter Munk Medal, US Office of Naval Res. and Oceanography Soc., 1998; Fridtjof Nansen Medal, Eur. Geophysical Soc., 2000. *Publications:* (ed) Oceanography, 1996; contribs to learned jls. *Address:* School of Ocean and Earth Sciences, Southampton Oceanography Centre, Southampton SO14 3ZH. *T:* (023) 8059 3755; Bodfryn, Llangoed, Beaumaris, Anglesey LL58 8PH.

THORPE-TRACEY, Stephen Frederick; Controller, Newcastle Central Office, Department of Social Security (formerly of Health and Social Security), 1986–89, retired; *b* 27 Dec. 1929; *s* of Rev. and Mrs J. S. V. Thorpe-Tracey; *m* 1955, Shirley Byles; one *s* two *d*. *Educ:* Plymouth Coll. Emergency Commn, 1948; Short Service Commn, 1950; Regular Commn, DLI, 1952; Staff Coll., Camberley, 1960 (psc); GS02, Defence Operational Res. Estabt, 1961–64; Training Major, 8 DLI (TA), 1964–65; Major, 1 DLI, 1965–66; GSO2, MoD, 1966–70; direct entry, Home Civil Service, 1970; Principal, DHSS, 1970; Asst Sec., 1977; Under Sec., 1986. Chm., Northern Gp, RIPA, 1988–90. Mem., Prescription Pricing Authy, 1990–93. Vice Chm., Carr-Gomm (Tyneside) Housing Assoc. Ltd, 1990–91. Hon. Secretary: Mid Devon Div., SSAFA Forces Help (formerly SSAFA and FHS), 1992–99; Uffculme Br., RBL, 1995–. Mem., Uffculme Parish Council, 1995–. Chm., Uffculme Soc., 1994–. Chairman: Trustees, Coldharbour Mill, 1996– (Hon. Sec., 1994–96); Coldharbour Mill Ltd, 1998–. Hon. Sec., Civil Service Chess Assoc., 1974–77; Chm., Tiverton Chess Club, 1994–; Cdre, Goring Thames Sailing Club, 1981–82. *Publications:* T^2 series of articles in military jls. *Recreations:* chess, golf, fell-walking. *Address:* 9 Grantlands, Uffculme, Cullompton, Devon EX15 3ED. *T:* (01884) 841864.

THOULESS, Prof. David James, FRS 1979; Professor of Physics, University of Washington, since 1980; *b* 21 Sept. 1934; *s* of late Robert Henry Thouless; *m* 1958, Margaret Elizabeth Scrase; two *s* one *d*. *Educ:* Winchester Coll.; Trinity Hall, Cambridge (BA); Cornell Univ. (PhD). Physicist, Lawrence Radiation Laboratory, Berkeley, Calif, 1958–59; ICI Research Fellow, Birmingham Univ., 1959–61; Lecturer, Cambridge Univ., and Fellow of Churchill Coll., 1961–65; Prof. of Mathematical Physics, Birmingham Univ., 1965–78; Prof. of Applied Science, Yale Univ., 1979–80; Royal Soc. Res. Prof., and Fellow of Clare Hall, Cambridge Univ., 1983–86. Mem., US Nat. Acad. Scis, 1995. Wolf Prize for Physics, Wolf Foundn, Israel, 1990; Dirac Prize, Inst. of Physics, 1993. *Publications:* Quantum Mechanics of Many-Body Systems, 1961, 2nd edn 1972; Topological Quantum Numbers in Non-Relativistic Physics, 1998. *Address:* Department of Physics, Box 351560, University of Washington, Seattle, WA 98195, USA.

THOURON, Sir John (Rupert Hunt), KBE 1976 (CBE 1967); *b* 10 May 1908; *m* 1st, 1930, Lorna Ellett (marr. diss. 1939; she *d* 2000); one *s*; 2nd, 1953, Esther duPont (*d* 1984). *Educ:* Sherborne School, Dorset. Served War of 1939–45; Major, Black Watch. With Lady Thouron, Founder of the Thouron University of Pennsylvania Fund for British-American Student Exchange, 1960. *Recreations:* shooting, fishing, golf, gardening. *Address:* Unionville, Chester County, PA 19375, USA. *T:* (610) 3845542; (winter) 416 South Beach Road, Hobe Sound, FL 33455, USA. *T:* (561) 5463577. *Clubs:* White's; Brook (NY); Sunningdale Golf; Royal St George Golf; Wilmington, Wilmington Country, Vicmead (all Delaware); Pine Valley, British Officers Club of Philadelphia (Pennsylvania); Seminole Golf, Island Club of Hobe Sound (Florida).

THRELFALL, David; actor; *b* 12 Oct. 1953. *Educ:* Wilbraham Comprehensive Sch.; Sheffield Art Coll.; Manchester Polytechnic Sch. of Theatre. Associate Artistic Dir, Royal Exchange Theatre, Manchester, 1998–. *Stage:* Bed of Roses, Royal Court; 3 years with RSC, incl. Savage Amusement, Nicholas Nickleby, 1980 (Clarence Derwent Award, British Theatre Assoc., SWET Award); Not Quite Jerusalem, Royal Court, 1982; Hamlet, Edinburgh Fest., 1986; Bussy D'Ambois, Old Vic, 1988; Wild Duck, Phoenix, 1990; Count of Monte Cristo, Royal Exchange, 1994; Richard II, Cottesloe, RNT, 1995; Hedda Gabler, Chichester, 1996; Present Laughter, Royal Exchange, 1997; The Rehearsal, NY, 1997; Peer Gynt, Royal Exchange, 1999; *television:* The Kiss of Death, 1976; Jumping the Queue, 1989; Clothes in the Wardrobe, 1993; Mary and Jesus, 1999; In the Beginning, 2000; series: Nicholas Nickleby, 1984; Paradise Postponed, 1985; The Marksman, 1988; Nightingales, 1990; Titmuss Regained, 1991; Statement of Affairs, Diana: Her True Story, 1993; Men of the World, 1994; Sex & Chips & Rock-'n'-Roll, 1999; Dinner of Herbs, 2000; *films:* When the Whales Came, 1989; The Russia House, 1990; Patriot Games, 1992. Plays and Players Promising Newcomer, 1978. *Recreations:* motor bike, gym, friends. *Address:* c/o Chatto & Linnit Ltd, 123A Kings Road, SW3 4PL.

THRIFT, Prof. Nigel John, PhD, DSc; Professor of Geography, University of Bristol, since 1990; *b* 12 Oct. 1949; *s* of Leonard John Thrift and Joyce Mary Wakeley; *m* 1979, Lynda Jean Sharples; two *d*. *Educ:* UCW, Aberystwyth (BA Hons); Univ. of Bristol (PhD 1979; DSc 1992). Research Fellow: Dept of Architecture, Univ. of Cambridge, 1975–76; Dept of Geog., Univ. of Leeds, 1976–78; Dept of Human Geog., ANU, 1979–81 (Sen. Res. Fellow, 1981–83); Lectr, 1984–86, Reader, 1986–87, St David's UC, Lampeter; Bristol University: Lectr, 1987–88; Reader, 1988–90; Head, Dept of Geog., 1995–99; Chm., Res. Assessment Panel, 1997–. Visiting Professor: Macquarie Univ., 1989; UCLA, 1992; Univ. of Vienna, 1998. Fellow: Netherlands Inst. Advanced Study, 1993; Swedish Collegium for Advanced Study in Social Scis, 1999. AcSS 2001. Heath Award, RGS, 1988; Medal, Univ. of Helsinki, 1999. *Publications:* (with D. N. Parkes) Times, Spaces, Places, 1980; (with D. K. Forbes) The Price of War, 1986; Spatial Formations, 1996; (with A. Leyshon) Money/Space, 1997; (jtly) Shopping, Place and Identity, 1998; (with P. Glennie) The Measured Heart, 2002; (with A. Amin) Cities, 2002; numerous ed volumes; contrib. chapters in ed vols, and papers in learned jls. *Recreations:* reading, writing. *Address:* School of Geographical Sciences, University of Bristol, University Road, Bristol BS8 1SS. *T:* (0117) 928 8306, *Fax:* (0117) 928 7878; *e-mail:* N.J.Thrift@bristol.ac.uk.

THRING, Rear-Adm. George Arthur, CB 1958; DSO 1940 and Bar 1952; DL; *b* 13 Sept. 1903; *s* of late Sir Arthur Thring, KCB; *m* 1929, Betty Mary (*d* 1983), *er d* of Colonel Stewart William Ward Blacker, DSO; two *s* two *d*. *Educ:* Royal Naval Colleges, Osborne and Dartmouth. Commander, 1941; Captain, 1946; Rear-Admiral, 1956; retired, 1958. Commanded: HMS Deptford, 1940–41; 42nd and 20th Escort Groups, Atlantic, 1943–45; HMS Ceylon, 1951–52; Flag Officer, Malayan Area, 1956–58. Officer, Legion of Merit (USA), 1945. DL Somerset, 1968. *Recreations:* golf, fishing. *Address:* Alford House, Castle Cary, Somerset BA7 7PN. *T:* (01963) 240329.

THRING, Prof. Meredith Wooldridge, ScD; FREng; Professor of Mechanical Engineering, Queen Mary College, London University, 1964–81; *b* 17 Dec. 1915; *s* of Captain W. H. C. S. Thring, CBE, RN, and Dorothy (*née* Wooldridge); *m* 1940, Alice Margaret Hooley (*d* 1986); two *s* one *d*. *Educ:* Malvern Coll., Worcs; Trinity Coll., Cambridge (Senior Scholar, 1937; BA Hons Maths and Physics, 1937; ScD 1964). Student's Medal, Inst. of Fuel, for work on producer gas mains, 1938; British Coal Utilisation Research Assoc.: Asst Scientific Officer, 1937; Senior Scientific Officer and Head of Combustion Research Laboratory, 1944; British Iron and Steel Research Assoc.: Head of Physics Dept, 1946; Superintendent, 1950; Assistant Director, 1953; Prof. of Fuel Technology and Chemical Engineering, Sheffield Univ., 1953–64. General Superintendent International Flame Radiation Research Foundn, 1951–76. Visitor: Production Engineering Research Assoc., 1967; Machine Tool Industry Research Assoc., 1967. Member Clean Air Council, 1957–62; Fuel Research Board, 1957–58; Fire Research Board, 1961–64; BISRA Council, 1958–60; President, Inst. of Fuel, 1962–63 (Vice-President, 1959–62); Member: Adv. Council on Research and Development, Ministry of Power, 1960–66; Acad. Adv. Council, University of Strathclyde, 1962–67; Education Cttee, RAF, 1968–76; Unesco Commn to Bangladesh, 1979. FInstP 1944; FInstF 1951; FIChemE 1972 (MIChemE 1956); FIMechE 1968 (MIMechE 1964); FIEE 1968 (MIEE 1964); FREng (a Founder Fellow, 1976); FRSA 1964; MRI 1965; FRAeS 1969. Elected Mem., Royal Norwegian Scientific Soc., 1974; Mem., NY Acad. of Scis; Corresp. Mem., Nat. Acad. of Engineering of Mexico, 1977. Lectures: Parsons Meml on Magnetohydrodynamics, 1961; First Wenca, Lagos, 1989. DUniv Open, 1982. Sir Robert Hadfield medal of Iron and Steel Inst. for studies on open hearth furnaces, 1949. *Publications:* The Science of Flames and Furnaces, 1952, 2nd edn, 1960; (with J. H. Chesters) The Influence of Port Design on Open Hearth Furnace Flames (Iron and Steel Institute Special Report 37), 1946; (with R. Edgeworth Johnstone) Pilot Plants, Models and Scale-up Methods in Chemical Engineering, 1957; (ed.) Air Pollution, 1957; Nuclear Propulsion, 1961; Man, Machines and Tomorrow, 1973; Machines—Masters or Slaves of Man?, 1973; (ed with R. J. Crookes) Energy and Humanity, 1974; (with E. R. Laithwaite) How to Invent, 1977; The Engineer's Conscience, 1980; Robots and Telechirs, 1983; Quotations from G. I. Gurdjieff's Teachings, 1998. *Recreations:* arboriculture, wood-carving. *Address:* Bell Farm, Brundish, Suffolk IP13 8BL. *Club:* Athenæum.

THROCKMORTON, Clare McLaren, (Mrs Andrew McLaren); *see* Tritton, E. C.

THRUSH, Prof. Brian Arthur, FRS 1976; Professor of Physical Chemistry, University of Cambridge, 1978–95, now Emeritus; Fellow, Emmanuel College, Cambridge, since 1960; *b* Hampstead Garden Suburb, 23 July 1928; *s* of late Arthur Albert Thrush and late Dorothy Charlotte Thrush (*née* Money); *m* 1958, Rosemary Catherine Terry, *d* of late George and Gertrude Terry, Ottawa; one *s* one *d*. *Educ:* Haberdashers' Aske's Sch.; Emmanuel Coll., Cambridge (Schol. 1946–50). BA 1949, MA, PhD 1953, ScD 1965. University of Cambridge: Demonstrator in Physical Chemistry, 1953; Asst Dir of Research, 1959; Lectr in Physical Chemistry, 1964, Reader, 1969; Hd of Dept of Physical Chemistry, 1986–88; Head of Dept of Chemistry, 1988–93; Tutor, 1963–67, Dir of Studies in Chemistry, 1963–78, Vice-Master, 1986–90 and Acting Master, 1986–87, Emmanuel Coll. Consultant Physicist, US Nat. Bureau of Standards, Washington, 1957–58; Sen. Vis. Scientist, Nat. Res. Council, Ottawa, 1961, 1971, 1980. Tilden Lectr, Chem. Soc., 1965; Vis. Prof., Chinese Acad. of Science, 1980–; Member: Faraday Council, Chem. Soc., 1976–79; US Nat. Acad. of Scis Panel on Atmospheric Chemistry, 1975–80; Lawes Agric. Trust Cttee, 1979–89; NERC, 1985–90; Council, Royal Soc., 1989–91; NATO Panel on Global Change, 1989–92. Pres., Chemistry Sect., BAAS, 1986. Mem., Academia Europaea, 1990 (Mem., Council, 1992–98). M. Polanyi Medal, RSC, 1980; Rank Prize for Opto-Electronics, 1992. *Publications:* papers on gas kinetics and spectroscopy in Proc. Royal Soc., Trans Faraday Soc., etc. *Recreations:* wine, walking. *Address:* Brook Cottage, Pemberton Terrace, Cambridge CB2 1JA. *T:* (01223) 357637.

THUBRON, Colin Gerald Dryden; travel writer and novelist, since 1966; *b* 14 June 1939; *s* of late Brig. Gerald Ernest Thubron, DSO, OBE, and of Evelyn (*née* Dryden). *Educ:* Eton Coll. Editorial staff, Hutchinson & Co., 1959–62; freelance television film maker, Turkey, Japan, Morocco, 1962–64; Editorial staff, Macmillan Co., New York, 1964–65. FRSL 1969. Mungo Park Medal, RSGS, 2000; Lawrence of Arabia Meml Medal, RSAA, 2001. *Publications:* non-fiction: Mirror to Damascus, 1967; The Hills of Adonis, 1968, 2nd edn 1987; Jerusalem, 1969, 2nd edn 1986; Journey into Cyprus, 1975; The Royal Opera House, 1982; Among the Russians, 1983; Behind the Wall, 1987 (Thomas Cook Award, Hawthorden Prize, 1988); The Lost Heart of Asia, 1994; In Siberia, 1999; novels: The God in the Mountain, 1977; Emperor, 1978; A Cruel Madness, 1984 (Silver Pen Award, 1985); Falling, 1989; Turning Back the Sun, 1991; Distance, 1996; contribs The Times, TLS, The Independent, Sunday Telegraph. *Address:* Garden Cottage, 27 St Ann's Villas, W11 4RT. *T:* (020) 7602 2522.

THURLEY, Dr Simon John; Director, Museum of London, since 1997; *b* 29 Aug. 1962; *s* of late Thomas Manley Thurley and of Rachel Thurley (*née* House). *Educ:* Kimbolton Sch., Cambs; Bedford Coll., London (BA Hist.); Courtauld Inst., London (MA, PhD Art

Hist.). Inspector of Ancient Monuments, Crown Buildings and Monuments Gp, English Heritage, 1988–90; Curator, Historic Royal Palaces, 1990–97. Vis. Prof. of Medieval London History, Royal Holloway, Univ. of London, 2000. Member: Cttee, Soc. for Court Studies, 1996–; Adv. Council, Royal Collection Studies, 1996–; Adv. Cttee, Lambeth Palace Chapel, 1999–; Metropolitan History Adv. Cttee, 2000–; Council, St Paul's Cathedral, 2001. Pres., City of London Archaeol Soc., 1997–; Vice-Pres., NADFAS, 2000. Trustee, Dickens House Museum, 1998–; Patron, London Parks and Gardens Trust, 2001. MIFA 1998. Editorial Adviser: London Jl, 1997–; Jl of British Art, 2000–; BBC History Mag., 2000–. *Publications:* (jtly) Henry VIII: images of a Tudor King, 1989; The Royal Palaces of Tudor England, 1993; Whitehall Palace, 1999; contribs to books and jls inc. Architectural Hist., London Topographical Soc. Record, Apollo, Country Life. *Recreation:* ruins. *Address:* Museum of London, London Wall, EC2Y 5HN. *T:* (020) 7814 5700; *e-mail:* director@museumoflondon.org.uk.

THURLOW, 8th Baron *cr* 1792; **Francis Edward Hovell-Thurlow-Cumming-Bruce,** KCMG 1961 (CMG 1957); Governor and C-in-C of the Bahamas, 1968–72; *b* 9 March 1912; *s* of 6th Baron Thurlow and Grace Catherine, *d* of Rev. Henry Trotter; *S* brother, 1971; *m* 1949, Yvonne Diana Aubyn Wilson, CStJ 1969 (*d* 1990); one *s* two *d* (and one *s* decd). *Educ:* Shrewsbury Sch.; Trinity Coll., Cambridge. Asst Principal, Dept of Agriculture for Scotland, 1935; transferred to Dominions Office, 1937; Asst Private Sec. to Sec. of State, 1939; Asst Sec., Office of UK High Comr in NZ, 1939; Asst Sec., Office of UK High Comr in Canada, 1944; Secretariat, Meeting of Commonwealth Prime Ministers in London, 1946; served with UK Delegn at Paris Peace Conf., 1946, and at UN Gen. Assemblies, 1946 and 1948; Principal Private Sec. to Sec. of State, 1946; Asst Sec., CRO, 1948; Head of Political Div., Office of UK High Comr in New Delhi, 1949; Establishment Officer, CRO, 1952; Head of Commodities Dept, CRO, 1954; Adviser on External Affairs to Governor of Gold Coast, 1955; Deputy High Comr for the UK in Ghana, 1957; Asst Under-Sec. of State, CRO, April 1958; Deputy High Comr for the UK in Canada, 1958; High Comr for UK: in New Zealand, 1959–63; in Nigeria, 1964–67; Dep. Under-Sec. of State, FCO, 1964. KStJ 1969. *Heir: s* Hon. Roualeyn Robert Hovell-Thurlow-Cumming-Bruce [*b* 13 April 1952; *m* 1980, Bridget Anne, *o d* of H. B. Ismay Cheape, Fossoway Lodge, Kinross; two *s* two *d*]. *Address:* 102 Leith Mansions, Grantully Road, W9 1LJ. *T:* (020) 7289 9664; Philham Water, Hartland, Bideford EX39 6EZ. *T:* (01237) 441433. *Club:* Travellers.

THURLOW, Alan John; Organist and Master of the Choristers, Chichester Cathedral, since 1980; *b* 18 May 1947; *s* of John Edward Thurlow and Mary Bruce Thurlow (*née* Bennallack); *m* 1974, Christina Mary Perren. *Educ:* Bancroft's Sch., Woodford; Sheffield Univ. (BA 1st cl. Hons 1968); Emmanuel Coll., Cambridge. Sub Organist, Durham Cathedral, 1973–80. Chairman: Friends of Cathedral Music, 1990–; Organs Adv. Cttee, Council for the Care of Churches, 1997–; Pres., Cathedral Organists Assoc., 1995–96. *Recreations:* walking, cycling. *Address:* 2 St Richard's Walk, Chichester, W Sussex PO19 1QA. *T:* (01243) 784790. *Club:* Chichester City.

THURNHAM, Peter Giles; Chairman, WR Group Holdings Ltd (formerly First and Third Securities Ltd, then Wathes Group of Cos), since 1972; *b* 21 Aug. 1938; *s* of late Giles Rymer Thurnham and Marjorie May (*née* Preston); *m* 1963, Sarah Janet Stroude (separated 1998); one *s* three *d* and one adopted *s*. *Educ:* Oundle Sch.; Peterhouse, Cambridge (MA 1967); Cranfield Inst. of Technol. (Dip. in Advanced Engrg, 1967); SRC/NATO Scholarship, Harvard Business Sch., Harvard Univ. (MBA 1969). CEng 1967; FIMechE 1985. Design Engr, NEI Parsons Ltd, 1957–66; Divl Dir, British Steam Specialties Ltd, 1967–72. MP Bolton North East, 1983–97 (C, 1983–96, Ind, 1996, Lib Dem, 1996–97). Parliamentary Private Secretary: to Sec. of State for Employment, 1987–90; to Eric Forth, MP and Robert Jackson, MP, 1991–92; to Sec. of State for the Envmt, 1992–93. Lib Dem spokesman on social services, 1996–97. Member: Select Cttee on Employment, 1983–87; Public Accounts Cttee, 1995–97. Treas., All-Party Parly Gp, Chemical Industry, 1985–87; Vice Chairman: All-Party Parly Gp for Children, 1986–97; All Party Disability Gp, 1992–97. Conservative Back Bench 1922 Committees: Vice-Chairman: Smaller Business Cttee, 1985–87; Home Improvement Sub-Cttee, 1986–87; Secretary: Employment Cttee, 1986–87; Social Security Cttee, 1990–91; Founder and Chm., Cons. Disability Gp, 1989–96. Mem. Council, PSI, 1985–89. Dir, Rathbone, 1997–. Founder Mem., 1985 and Mem. Cttee, 1985–, Progress, Campaign for Res. into Reproduction; Founder and Vice Pres., Campaign for Inter Country Adoption, 1991 (Pres., 1995); President: Croft Care Home, 1995–2001; Adoption Forum, 1997–. Patron, Stork, Assoc. of Families who have Adopted from Abroad, 1991–. *Publications:* discussion papers; contrib. technical jls. *Recreations:* country life, restoring classic British engineering. *Address:* Crane Farm, South Cerney, Cirencester, Glos GL7 5TN. *T:* (01285) 869132, *Fax:* (01285) 869134; *e-mail:* peter@southcerney.com.

THURSBY, Peter Lionel, FRBS; sculptor; President, Royal West of England Academy, 1995–2000; *b* 23 Dec. 1930; *s* of Lionel Albert Thursby and Florence Bessie Thursby (*née* Macey); *m* 1956, Maureen Suzanne Aspden. *Educ:* Bishop Wordsworth Sch., Salisbury; Mons Officer Cadet Sch.; St Paul's Coll., Cheltenham; West of England Coll. of Art, Bristol; Exeter Coll. of Art (NDD Sculpture); Bristol Univ. (ATD). FRBS 1983 (ARBS 1973); RWA 1971. Nat. Service, 1949–51, RARO, 1951–57. Head of Art, Heles Grammar Sch., Exeter, 1960–71; Head of Sch. of Art and Design, Exeter Coll., 1971–89. Invited Sculptor, Chichester Fest., 1994–96. *Solo exhibitions* include: Arnolfini, Bristol, 1963; AIA Gall., London, 1963; Marjorie Parr Gall., London, 1964, 1965, 1971; Sheviock Gall., Cornwall, 1969; Royal Albert Mus. and Art Gall., Exeter, 1969, Millennium Retrospective, 2000; Univ. of Exeter, 1974; Alwin Gall., London, 1976; RWA, 1981; Bruton Street Gall., London 1994, 1995, 1998; *public commissions:* Plymstock School, 1965; Raeburn House, Harrow, 1966; Randolph House, Croydon, 1966; Guildhall Square, Exeter, 1977 (to commemorate Silver Jubilee of HM Queen Elizabeth II); Bronze Fountain, Dallas, 1980; Bronze fountain and relief, Mazda head office, 1982; External bronze relief, City of Westminster, 1986 (Silver Medal, RBS); Bronze fountain, McDonald's Restaurants head office, 1988; Uxbridge, Coca-Cola Schweppes Beverages Ltd, 1988; Bath, NY State, 1996. Hon. DArt UWE, 1995. *Publication:* (illustrated) Roger Iredale, Turning Bronzes: an anthology of poetry, 1974. *Recreations:* genealogy, music, cinema, ornithology, swimming. *Address:* Oakley House, 28 Oakley Close, Pinhoe, Exeter, Devon EX1 3SB. *T:* and *Fax:* (01392) 467931; *e-mail:* thursby.sculpture@virgin.net. *Clubs:* Chelsea Arts; Exeter Golf and Country.

THURSO, 3rd Viscount *cr* 1952, of Ulbster; **John Archibald Sinclair;** Bt 1786; MP (Lib Dem) Caithness, Sutherland and Easter Ross, since 2001; *b* 10 Sept. 1953; *er s* of 2nd Viscount Thurso and of Margaret Beaumont Sinclair (*née* Robertson); *S* father, 1995; *m* 1976, Marion Ticknor (*née* Sage); two *s* one *d*. *Educ:* Summerfields; Eton Coll. FHCIMA 1991; Master Innholder 1991. Savoy Hotel plc: Trainee, 1972; Gen. Manager and Dir, Lancaster Hotel, Paris, 1981–85; Gen. Manager and Dir, Cliveden, 1985–92; Chief Executive Officer: Granfel Hldgs, 1992–95; Champneys Gp Ltd, 1995–2001; Chm., Scrabster Harbour, 1997–; non-executive Director: Savoy Hotel plc, 1993–98; Lochdhu Hotels Ltd, 1975– (Chm., 1995–); Sinclair Family Trust Ltd, 1976– (Chm., 1995–); Thurso Fisheries Ltd, 1979– (Chm., 1995–); Ulbster Hldgs Ltd, 1994– (Chm., 1994–); Profile Selection and Recruitment Ltd, 1995–; Walker Greenbank PLC, 1997– (Chm., 1999–); Royal Olympic Cruise Lines Inc. (USA), 1997–99; Mossimanns Ltd, 1998–. President: Licensed Victuallers Schs, 1997–98; Acad. of Food and Wine Service, 1998–. Patron: HCIMA, 1998–; IMS, 1998–. Lib Dem Spokesman on Tourism, 1997–99, on Food, 1998–99, H of L. FInstD 1997. *Recreations:* shooting, fishing, food and wine. *Heir: s* Hon. James Alexander Robin Sinclair, *b* 14 Jan. 1984. *Address:* Thurso East Mains, Thurso, Caithness KW14 8HW. *Clubs:* Brooks's; New (Edinburgh).

THURSTON, Dame Thea; *see* King, Dame T.

THUYSBAERT, Jonkheer Prosper; Ambassador of Belgium to the Court of St James's, 1994–97; *b* 7 Dec. 1931; *s* of Prosper Thuysbaert and Marguerite Levie; *m* 1957, Marie-Claire Vuylsteke; two *s*. *Educ:* Leuven Univ. (grad. in Law and Notarial Scis; BA Thomistic Philosophy). Entered Belgian Diplomatic Service, 1957: Attaché, Luxembourg, 1960–61; Economic Attaché, Paris, 1961–62; 1st Sec., Tel Aviv, 1963–64; Advr to Minister for Foreign Trade, 1964–65; Counsellor, Perm. Repn to EC, 1965–70; European Adviser to: Minister for Foreign Affairs, 1970–77; Prime Minister, 1977–80; Dir, European Orgns, Ministry for Foreign Affairs, 1980–81; Chef de Cabinet to Minister for External Relns, 1981–83; Political Dir, Ministry for Foreign Affairs, 1983–85; Ambassador: Perm. Repn to UN, Geneva, 1985–87; Perm. Repn to NATO, Brussels, 1987–93; EC Consultant for European Stability Pact, 1993–94. Prof., Univ. of Leuven, Belgium, 1992–. Officer 1978, Comdr 1987, Order of Leopold (Belgium); Comdr 1987, Grand Officer, 1995, Order of Crown (Belgium). Grand Officer, Order of Leopold II (Belgium), 1991. *Publications:* La Diplomatie Multilatérale, 1991; Multilateraal Kunst en Vliegwerk, 1991; Het Belgisch Buitenlandse Beleid, 1995. *Recreations:* art, tennis, ski-ing, swimming. *Address:* Clos d'Orleans 12, 1150 Brussels, Belgium. *Club:* Anglo-Belgian.

THWAITE, Ann Barbara, DLitt; FRSL; writer; *b* London, 4 Oct. 1932; *d* of A. J. Harrop, LittD, PhD and H. M. Valentine of New Zealand; *m* 1955, Anthony Simon Thwaite, *qv*; four *d*. *Educ:* Marsden School, Wellington, NZ; Queen Elizabeth's Girls' Grammar Sch., Barnet; St Hilda's Coll., Oxford (MA 1959); DLitt Oxford 1998. FRSL 1987. Vis. Prof., Tokyo Women's Univ., 1985–86; Helen Stubbs Meml Lectr, Toronto Public Library, 1990; Ezra Jack Keats Meml Lectr, Univ. of Southern Mississippi, 1992. Churchill Travelling Fellowship, 1993; Gladys Krieble Delmas Fellowship, British Library, 1998–99. Hon. Fellow, Univ. of Surrey Roehampton (Nat. Centre for Res. in Children's Literature), 2001. Regular reviewer of children's books: TLS, 1963–85; Guardian; TES. Governor: St Mary's Middle Sch., Long Stratton, Norfolk, 1990–; Hapton VC Primary Sch., Norfolk, 1995–. *Publications:* Waiting for the Party: the life of Frances Hodgson Burnett, 1974; (ed) My Oxford, 1977; Edmund Gosse: a literary landscape, 1984 (Duff Cooper Meml Prize, 1985); A. A. Milne: his life, 1990 (Whitbread Biography Award); (ed) Portraits from Life: essays by Edmund Gosse, 1991; The Brilliant Career of Winnie-the-Pooh, 1992; Emily Tennyson: the poet's wife, 1996; *children's books include:* The Camelthorn Papers, 1969; Tracks, 1978; (ed) Allsorts 1–7, 1968–75; (ed) Allsorts of Poems, 1978; The Ashton Affair, 1995; The Horse at Hilly Fields, 1996. *Recreations:* other people's lives, messing about on the river. *Address:* The Mill House, Low Tharston, Norfolk NR15 2YN. *T:* (01508) 489569. *Clubs:* Society of Authors, Royal Over-Seas League.

THWAITE, Anthony Simon, OBE 1990; FRSL; FSA; poet; Editorial Consultant, André Deutsch Ltd, 1992–95 (Director, 1986–92); *b* 23 June 1930; *s* of late Hartley Thwaite, JP, FSA, and Alice Evelyn Mallinson; *m* 1955, Ann Barbara Harrop (*see* A. B. Thwaite); four *d*. *Educ:* Kingswood Sch.; Christ Church, Oxford (MA). Vis. Lectr in English, Tokyo Univ., 1955–57; Producer, BBC, 1957–62; Literary Editor, The Listener, 1962–65; Asst Prof. of English, Univ. of Libya, 1965–67; Literary Editor, New Statesman, 1968–72; co-editor, Encounter, 1973–85. Henfield Writing Fellow, Univ. of East Anglia, 1972; Vis. Prof., Kuwait Univ., 1974; Japan Foundn Fellow, Tokyo Univ., 1985–86; Poet-in-Residence, Vanderbilt Univ., 1992. Chm. of Judges, Booker Prize, 1986. FRSL 1978; FSA 2000. Hon. Fellow, Westminster Coll., Oxford, 1990. Hon. DLitt Hull, 1989. Cholmondeley Poetry Award, 1983. *Publications: poetry:* Home Truths, 1957; The Owl in the Tree, 1963; The Stones of Emptiness, 1967 (Richard Hillary Memorial Prize, 1968); Penguin Modern Poets 18, 1970; Inscriptions, 1973; New Confessions, 1974; A Portion for Foxes, 1977; Victorian Voices, 1980; Poems 1953–1983, 1984; Letter from Tokyo, 1987; Poems 1953–1988, 1989; The Dust of the World, 1994; Selected Poems 1956–1996, 1997; A Different Country, 2000; *criticism:* Contemporary English Poetry, 1959; Poetry Today, 1973, rev. and expanded, 1985, 1996; Twentieth Century English Poetry, 1978; Six Centuries of Verse, 1984 (companion to Thames TV/Channel 4 series); Anthony Thwaite in Conversation with Peter Dale and Ian Hamilton, 1999; *travel:* (with Roloff Beny) Japan, 1968; The Deserts of Hesperides, 1969; (with Roloff Beny and Peter Porter) In Italy, 1974; (with Roloff Beny) Odyssey: Mirror of the Mediterranean, 1981; *editor:* (with Geoffrey Bownas) Penguin Book of Japanese Verse, 1964, rev and expanded, 1998; (with Peter Porter) The English Poets, 1974; (with Fleur Adcock) New Poetry 4, 1978; Larkin at Sixty, 1982; (with John Mole) Poetry 1945 to 1980, 1983; Collected Poems of Philip Larkin, 1988; Selected Letters of Philip Larkin, 1992; Further Requirements: Philip Larkin, 2001; *for children:* Beyond the Inhabited World, 1976. *Recreations:* archaeology, travel. *Address:* The Mill House, Low Tharston, Norfolk NR15 2YN. *T:* (01508) 489569.

THWAITES, Prof. Sir Bryan, Kt 1986; MA, PhD; CMath, FIMA; Hon. Professor, Southampton University, since 1983; *b* London, 6 December 1923; *e s* of late Ernest James and Dorothy Marguerite Thwaites; *m* 1948, Katharine Mary (*d* 1991), 4th *c* of late H. R. Harries and late Mrs L. Harries, Longhope, Glos; four *s* two *d*. *Educ:* Dulwich College; Winchester College; Clare College, Cambridge (Wrangler, 1944). Scientific Officer, National Physical Laboratory, 1944–47; Lecturer, Imperial College, London, 1947–51; Assistant Master, Winchester College, 1951–59; Professor of Theoretical Mechanics, Southampton Univ., 1959–66; Principal, Westfield Coll., London, 1966–83 (Hon. Fellow, 1983; Hon. Fellow, QMW, 1990). Gresham Prof. in Geometry, City Univ., 1969–72. Co-founder and Co-Chm., Education 2000, 1982–86. Hon. Sec. and Treas., Dulwich College Mission, 1946–57; inventor of the Thwaites Flap, 1947. Chm. and Mem. ARC Cttees, 1948–69. Special Lecturer, Imperial College, 1951–58. Chm., Southampton Mathematical Conf., 1961. Founding Director of the School Mathematics Project, 1961–75, Chm. of Trustees, 1966–83, Life Pres., 1984; Chm. of Internat. Mathematical Olympiad, first in UK, 1979; Chm. Adv. Council, ICL/CES, 1968–84. Member: Approved Sch. Cttee, Hampshire CC, 1954–58, 1961–66; US/UK (Fulbright) Commn, 1966–76; Davies Cttee on CSSB, 1969–70; Council, Kennedy Inst. of Rheumatology, 1969–71; Ct of London Univ., 1975–81; Council, Middlesex Hosp. Med. Sch., 1975–83; Court, Southampton Univ., 1981–94. Chairman: Collegiate Council, London Univ., 1973–76; Delegacy, Goldsmiths' Coll., 1975–80. Mem. Acad. Advisory Committee: Univ. of Bath, 1964–71; Open Univ., 1969–75. Chairman of: Council of C of E Colleges of Education, 1969–71; Church of England Higher Educn Cttee, 1974–76; Northwick Park Hosp. Management Cttee, 1970–74; Brent and Harrow AHA, 1973–82; Wessex RHA, 1982–88; King's Fund Enquiry into Sen. Management Trng in NHS, 1975–76; Nat. Staff Cttee for Admin. and Clerical Staff, NHS, 1983–86;

Enquiry into Radiotherapy Incident, Exeter Hosp., 1988. Founding Chm., British False Memory Soc., 1993. Chairman: Govs, Heythrop Coll., 1978–82; Friends of Winchester Coll., 1989–91; Govs, More House, 1993–96; Trustee: Westfield Coll. Develt Trust, 1979–83; Southampton Med. Sch. Trust, 1982–88; Richmond Coll., 1987–93 (Academic Gov., 1992–2000); City Tech. Colls Trust, 1987–97; Forbes Trust, 1987–; Patron, Winchester Detached Youth Project, 1990–96. Mercier Lectr, Whitelands Coll., 1973; Foundn Lectr, Inst. of Health Policy Studies, Southampton Univ., 1987; 25th Anniv. Lectr, Nuffield Inst., Leeds Univ., 1988. Shadow Vice-Chancellor, Independent Univ., July–Nov. 1971. Hon. Life Mem., Math. Assoc., 1962. JP, Winchester City Bench, 1963–66. A Vice-Pres., Friends of GPDST, 1975–95. Mem. Council, 1964–94, Pres., 1966–67, Institute of Mathematics and its Applications. Sponsor, Family and Youth Concern (formerly The Responsible Society), 1979–98 (Trustee, 1992–98). *Publications:* (ed) Incompressible Aerodynamics, 1960; (ed) On Teaching Mathematics, 1961; The SMP: the first ten years, 1973; (ed) Hypotheses for Education in AD 2000, 1983; numerous contributions to Proc. Royal Soc., Reports and Memoranda of Aeronautical Research Council, Quart. Jl of Applied Mech., Jl of Royal Aeronautical Soc., etc. *Recreations:* music, sailing. *Address:* Albany, Piccadilly, W1J 0AL. *T:* and *Fax:* (020) 7439 7600; *e-mail:* bthwaites@dial.pipex.com. *Clubs:* Athenæum, Royal Over-Seas League.

THWAITES, Jacqueline Ann; *see* Duncan, J. A.

THWAITES, Ronald; QC 1987; *b* 21 Jan. 1946; *e s* of Stanley Thwaites and Aviva Thwaites; *m* 1972, Judith Myers; three *s* one *d*. *Educ:* Richard Hind Secondary Tech. Sch.; Grangefield Grammar Sch., Stockton-on-Tees; Kingston Coll. of Technol. (subseq. Polytechnic, now Univ.); LLB London (external) 1968. Called to the Bar, Gray's Inn, 1970. *Recreations:* squash, swimming, lighting bonfires. *Address:* (chambers) Ely Place Chambers, 30 Ely Place, EC1N 6TD. *T:* (020) 7400 9600.

THWAITES, Roy; Deputy Director, South Yorkshire Branch, British Red Cross Society, 1990–96; *b* 13 Aug. 1931; *s* of Walter and Emily Alice Thwaites; *m* 1st, 1954, Margaret Anne (*née* Noble) (marr. diss.); one *s*; 2nd, 1991, Mary (*née* Appleby). *Educ:* Southey Green Secondary Sch.; Sheffield Central Technical Sch. City Councillor, Sheffield, 1965–74, Chief Whip and Chm. of Transport Cttee, 1969–74; South Yorkshire County Council: Councillor, 1973–86; Chief Whip and Chm. Passenger Transport Authority, 1973–78; Dep. Leader, 1978–79; Leader, and Chm. of Policy Cttee, 1979–86. Dep. Chm. and Dir, SYT Ltd, 1986–93. Member: E Midlands Airport Consultative Gp, 1982–86; Industrial Tribunals, 1987–. Vice-Chm., 1979–84, Dep. Chm., 1984–86, AMA; Member: Local Authorities' Conditions of Service Adv. Bd, 1979–86; Yorks and Humberside County Councils Assoc., 1983–86; Vice-Chm., 1982–85, Chm., 1985–86, NJC Local Govt Manual Workers Employers. Mem., Special Employment Measures Adv. Gp, MSC, 1983–86. Director: Yorks Mining Museum Trust, 1986–92; Northern Racing Sch. Trust, 1986–. Hon. Fellow, Sheffield City Poly., 1982. *Recreations:* walking, reading, photography. *Address:* 2 Borough Road, Sheffield S6 2AY.

THYATEIRA AND GREAT BRITAIN, Archbishop of; *see* Theocharous, Archbishop Gregorios.

THYNE, Malcolm Tod, MA; FRSE; Chairman, Scotland and North of England Committee, Cancer and Leukaemia in Childhood, since 2001 (Member, since 1990); *b* 6 Nov. 1942; *s* of late Andrew Tod and Margaret Melrose Thyne; *m* 1969, Eleanor Christine Scott; two *s*. *Educ:* The Leys Sch., Cambridge; Clare Coll., Cambridge (MA Nat. Scis with Pt II in Chem.; Cert. of Educn). FRSE 1994. Asst Master, Edinburgh Acad., 1965–69; Asst Master, Oundle Sch., 1969–72, Housemaster, 1972–80; Headmaster: St Bees School, 1980–88; Fettes Coll., Edinburgh, 1988–98. Develt Dir, Arkwright Scholarship Trust, 1999–2000. Trustee, CLIC, 2000–. Governor: Hunter Hall Sch., Penrith, 1998–; Newcastle Prep. Sch., 1998–; St Bees Sch., Cumbria, 2000–; Dir, Edinburgh Acad., 2000–. *Publications:* Periodicity, Atomic Structure and Bonding (Revised Nuffield Chemistry), 1976; contrib: Revised Nuffield Chemistry Handbook for Pupils, 1978; Revised Nuffield Chemistry Teachers' Guides, Vols II and III, 1978. *Recreations:* hillwalking, ski-ing, organic gardening. *Address:* Howbeck House, Hesket Newmarket, Wigton, Cumbria CA7 8JN. *T:* (01697) 478216. *Club:* New (Edinburgh).

THYNN, family name of **Marquess of Bath**.

THYNN, Alexander; *see* Bath, Marquess of.

THYNNE, John Corelli James, CB 1990; PhD, DSc; FIEE; Vice Chairman, Newport Networks Corporation Ltd, since 2000; *b* 27 Nov. 1931; *s* of Corelli James Thynne and Isabel Ann (*née* Griffiths). *Educ:* Milford Haven Grammar Sch.; Nottingham Univ. (BSc, PhD); Edinburgh Univ. (DSc). FIEE 1997. Res. Chemist, English Electric Co. (Guided Missile Div.), 1956–58; Fellow: Nat. Res. Council, Ottawa, 1958–59; UCLA, 1959–60; Univ. of Leeds, 1960–63; Lectr in Chemistry and Dir of Studies, Univ. of Edinburgh, 1963–70; Principal, DTI, 1970–73; Counsellor (Scientific), British Embassy, Moscow, 1974–78; Asst Sec., IT Div., DoI, 1978–83; Department of Trade and Industry: Under Sec., 1983; Regl Dir, NW Reg., 1983–86; Electronic Applications Div., 1986–87; IT Div., 1987–89; Dir, Information Engrg Directorate, 1989–90. Dir Gen., Electronic Components Industry Fedn, 1991–94. Chm., ComCare Systems Ltd, 1992–94; Dep. Chm., nCipher Corp. Ltd, 1996–99; Dir, Camrose Consultancy Services, 1991–99; Sen. Advr, InterMatrix Gp, 1991–98; Director: Newbridge Networks Corp., 1992–2000; LTW Ltd, 1993–95; Celtic House Investment Partners Ltd, 1993–; Nolton Consultancy Services Ltd, 1995–; Spikes Cavell Ltd, 1996–99; UWS Ventures, 1998–2000; Lanergy Ltd, 2001–. Member: Exec. Cttee, Nat. Electronics Council, 1986–90; NEDO Electronics Industries Sector Gp, 1986–90; Welsh Funding Councils Res. Gp, 1992–94; Radiocommunications Agency Bd, 1994–99. Mem. Council, Salford Univ., 1984–87; Gov., Univ. of Glamorgan (formerly Poly. of Wales), 1991–95. Vice Chm. Trustees, Mus. of Sci. and Industry, 1991–97. Hon. Fellow, Univ. of Wales Swansea, 1998. Hon. DSc Glamorgan, 1996. *Publications:* contribs on physical chemistry to scientific journals. *Recreation:* cricket. *Address:* Couvignac, 46800 Montcuq, France. *T:* (5) 65243910, *Fax:* (5) 65249952; 5 Eldon Grove, NW3 5PS. *T:* (020) 7794 4841; *e-mail:* john.thynne@wanadoo.fr. *Clubs:* Athenæum, MCC.

THYSSEN BORNEMISZA de KASZON, Baron Hans Heinrich; industrialist and art collector; *b* The Hague, 13 April 1921; Swiss citizen; *s* of Baron Dr Heinrich Thyssen Bornemisza and Baroness Margit Bornemisza de Kaszon; *m* 1st, Theresa zur Lippe; 2nd, Nina Dyer; 3rd, Fiona Campbell-Walter; 4th, Denise Shorto; 5th, 1985, Carmen Cervera; one adopted *s*, and three *s* one *d* by former marriages. *Educ:* Realgymnasium, The Hague; Fribourg Univ. Chm., and Hon. Pres. Supervisory Bd, TBG Holdings NV (formerly Thyssen-Bornemisza Gp NV). Hon. Chairman: Fundación Colección Thyssen-Bornemisza, Madrid; Thyssen-Bornemisza Foundation, Lugano; Foundation Friends of Mauritshuis, The Hague. Emeritus Mem., Trustees' Council, Nat. Gallery of Art, Washington; Mem., Sotheby's Holdings Adv. Bd. Corresp. Mem., Acad. of Fine Arts, San Fernando, Madrid. Art collection housed and exhibited in Museum Thyssen-Bornemisza, Madrid and partially in Villa Favorita, Castagnola-Lugano. Johann Wolfgang von Goethe Gold Medal, Hamburg, 1992; Royal Museum Medal, Netherlands, 1993. OStJ. Gran Cruz, Orden Carlos III (Spain), 1988; Order of the Banner (Hungary), 1990; Grande Ufficiale, Order of Merit of the Republic (Italy), 1991; Commander, Order of Orange Nassau (Netherlands), 1995; Middle Cross of Merit (Hungary), 1996. *Address:* Villa Favorita, 6976 Castagnola, Lugano, Switzerland. *Clubs:* Corviglia (St Moritz); Eagle Ski (Gstaad); Knickerbocker (NY).

TIBBER, His Honour Anthony Harris; a Circuit Judge, 1977–99; *b* 23 June 1926; *s* of Maurice and Priscilla Tibber; *m* 1954, Rhona Ann Salter; three *s*. *Educ:* University College School, London; Magdelen College School, Brackley. Served in Royal Signals, 1945–48; called to the Bar, Gray's Inn, 1950; a Recorder of the Crown Court, 1976. Member: Matrimonial Causes Rule Cttee, 1980–84; Matrimonial Causes Procedure Cttee (Booth Cttee), 1983–85. *Recreations:* cultivating, idling, pottering. *Address:* 22 Holmwood Gardens, N3 3NS. *T:* (020) 8349 1287.

See also P. H. Tibber.

TIBBER, Peter Harris, DPhil; HM Diplomatic Service; Director, International Management Directorate, British Trade International, since 2001; *b* 7 Sept. 1956; *s* of His Honour Anthony Harris Tibber, *qv*; *m* 1983, Eve Levy-Huet, MSc (Oxon); three *s*. *Educ:* Haberdashers' Aske's Sch.; University Coll., Oxford (MA; DPhil 1983). FCO, 1984–86; Paris, 1986–88; First Sec., FCO, 1988–90; Private Sec. to Minister of State, FCO, 1990–92; Ankara, 1993–96; Dep. Hd of Mission, Mexico City, 1996–2000; Dir, Africa and ME, Trade Partners UK, 2000–01. *Recreations:* choral singing, piano, tennis, swimming, fiction. *Address:* c/o British Trade International, Kingsgate House, 66–74 Victoria Street, SW1E 6SW.

TIBBITS, Captain Sir David (Stanley), Kt 1976; DSC 1942; FNI; RN retired; Deputy Master and Chairman of Board, Trinity House, 1972–76; *b* 11 April 1911; *s* of late Hubert Tibbits, MB, BCh, Warwick, and Edith Lucy (*née* Harman) Tibbits; *m* 1938, Mary Florence Butterfield, Hamilton, Bermuda; two *d*. *Educ:* Wells House, Malvern Wells; RNC, Dartmouth. RN Cadet 1925; navigation specialist, 1934; served War, 1939–45, HMS York, Devonshire and Anson; Comdr 1946; Captain 1953; Dir, Radio Equipment Dept, Admty, 1953–56; in comd, HM Ships Manxman, Dryad and Hermes, 1956–61; retd. Trinity House: Elder Brother, 1961; Warden, 1969. Hon. Sec., King George's Fund for Sailors, 1974–80; Lay Vice-Pres., Missions to Seamen, 1972–. Engaged in various voluntary activities in Bermuda including: Mem., Marine Board and Port Authy, 1978–92; Chm., Pilotage Commn, 1978–92; Pres., Sea Cadet and Sail Trng Assoc., 1978–87; Chm. and Pres., Bermuda Soc. for Blind, 1982– (Mem. Cttee, 1977–). Mem. Court, Worshipful Co. of Shipwrights, 1976–. Trustee, National Maritime Museum, 1974–77. Governor, Pangbourne Coll., 1973–78. Founder Mem., 1972, Fellow 1979–, Nautical Inst. CStJ 1993 (Mem. Council for Bermuda, 1978–). *Recreations:* sailing, colour photography, classical music. *Address:* Harting Hill, PO Box HM 1419, Hamilton, Bermuda HM FX; c/o Trinity House, Tower Hill, EC3N 4DH. *Clubs:* Army and Navy, Hurlingham; Royal Bermuda Yacht (Bermuda).

TIBBS, Craigie John, FRICS; Head of Estates and Planning Department, BBC, 1980; *b* 17 Feb. 1935; *s* of Arthur and Gladys Tibbs; *m* 1959, Carol Ann (*née* Linsell); two *d*. *Educ:* King George V School, Southport; Heaton Grammar School, Newcastle upon Tyne; RMA Sandhurst; London University. BSc; FRICS. Trainee Estates Officer, London Transport, 1959–62; Valuer and Senior Valuer, Luton Corp., 1962–67; Chief Valuer and Surveyor, London Borough of Newham, 1967–71; Development Officer, City of Birmingham, 1971–73; County Estates Officer, Hants County Council, 1973–76; Under Sec. (Dir of Land Economy), Depts of Environment and Transport, 1976–80. *Recreations:* music, reading, writing, walking, swimming, golf, the Well Game.

TIBBS, (Geoffrey) Michael (Graydon), OBE 1987; Secretary of the Royal College of Physicians, 1968–86 (Secretary of Joint Faculty of Community Medicine, 1971–72 and of Faculty of Occupational Medicine, 1978–86); *b* 21 Nov. 1921; *s* of Rev. Geoffrey Wilberforce Tibbs, sometime Chaplain RN and Vicar of Lynchmere, Sussex, and Margaret Florence Tibbs (*née* Skinner); *m* 1951, Anne Rosemary Wortley; two *s*. *Educ:* Berkhamsted Sch.; St Peter's Hall, Oxford. BA Hons Geography, 1948; MA 1952. FInstAM; MIPM; FRGS. Served RNVR, Ordinary Seaman/Lieut, 1940–46 (despatches), HMS Cottesmore, HMS Sheffield, HM S/M Tantalus, HM S/M Varne. Sudan Political Service, Kordofan Province, 1949–55: seconded to MECAS, 1950; Dist Comr, Dar Messeria District, 1953. Various appointments in personnel, organisation and overseas services depts, Automobile Assoc., 1955–68. Hon. Mem., Soc. of Occupational Medicine, 1983; Hon. FRCP 1986; Hon. FFOM 1986; Hon. FFCM 1987. Freeman, City of London, 1986. *Publications:* (with Anne Tibbs): A Look at Lynchmere, 1990; A Sudan Sunset, 2000. *Recreations:* producing pantomimes, parish affairs, preserving lowland heath, making bonfires. *Address:* Welkin, Lynchmere Ridge, Haslemere, Surrey GU27 3PP. *T:* (01428) 643120, 642176. *Club:* Naval.

TICEHURST, Maj.-Gen. Arthur Christopher; Medical Officer, Army Medical Directorate (Medico-Legal), 1994–95; *b* 22 April 1933; *s* of late Arthur William Ticehurst and Edith Violet Ticehurst (*née* Adams); *m* 1959, Valerie Jean Hughes; four *s*. *Educ:* Chichester High Sch.; King's Coll. London; Westminster Hosp. (MB BS 1955). MFCM 1977; FFPHM 1990. House appointments, Westminster Hosp., 1955–56; National Service, RAMC, 1958–60; Regular Commn, 1961; Medical Officer: Kent, Cyprus, 1958–61; Singapore, Brunei, Thailand, 1962–65; CO, 11 Field Dressing Station, BAOR, 1965–67; Instructor, RAMC Trng Centre, 1967–68; Army Staff Coll., 1968–69; MoD, 1970–72; CO, 4 Armoured Field Ambulance, 1972–74; ndc, 1974–75; Army Med. Directorate, MoD, 1976–80; Chief Instructor, RAMC Trng Centre, 1980–83; Comdr, Med. HQ, NE Dist, 1983–84; Dep. Comdr, Med. HQ, BAOR, 1984–87; Asst Surgeon Gen., MoD, 1987–90; Dir, Med. Ops and Plans, MoD, 1990; Comdr Med., HQ UKLF, 1990–93. QHS 1991–93. FIMgt (FBIM 1992). OStJ 1972. *Publications:* (ed jtly) Royal Army Medical Corps 1898–1998: reflections of one hundred years of service, 1997; articles on use of medical services in disaster relief to professional jls. *Recreations:* tennis, military history, maps, water colours. *Address:* c/o Lloyds TSB, 19 Obelisk Street, Camberley, Surrey GU15 3SE.

TICEHURST, David Keith; His Honour Judge Ticehurst; a Circuit Judge, since 1998; *b* 1 May 1950; *s* of Frederick John and Barbara Elisabeth Ticehurst; *m* 1972, Gillian Shepherd; two *s* one *d*. *Educ:* Taunton's Grammar Sch., Southampton; Keynsham Grammar Sch., Bristol; Kingston Poly. (BA). Admitted solicitor, 1975; articled clerk, 1971–73, Solicitor, 1975–78, Lawrence & Co., Bristol; Solicitor, Osborne Clarke, Bristol, 1978–98 (Partner, 1980–98); Asst Recorder, 1991–94; Recorder, 1994–98. Founder Mem., Employment Lawyers' Assoc., 1992. *Recreations:* cricket, watching Rugby, painting, reading. *Address:* The Law Courts, Small Street, Bristol BS1 1DA. *Clubs:* Winscombe Rugby Football (Pres.), Bristol Rugby Football; Gloucestershire County Cricket (Life Mem.), Old Herpesians Cricket.

TICKELL, Sir Crispin (Charles Cervantes), GCMG 1989 KCVO 1983 (MVO 1958); HM Diplomatic Service, retired; Warden, Green College, Oxford, 1990–97 (Hon.

Fellow, 1997); Chancellor, University of Kent at Canterbury, since 1996; *b* 25 Aug. 1930; *s* of late Jerrard Tickell and Renée (*née* Haynes); *m* 1st, 1954, Chloë (marr. diss. 1976), *d* of late Sir James Gunn, RA, PRP; two *s* one *d*; 2nd, 1977, Penelope, *d* of late Dr Vernon Thorne Thorne. *Educ:* Westminster (King's Schol.; Hon. Fellow, 1993); Christ Church, Oxford (Hinchliffe and Hon. Schol.; 1st Cl. Hons Mod. Hist. 1952). Served with Coldstream Guards, 1952–54; entered HM Diplomatic Service, 1954. Served at: Foreign Office, 1954–55; The Hague, 1955–58; Mexico, 1958–61; FO (Planning Staff), 1961–64; Paris, 1964–70; Private Sec. to successive Ministers responsible for British entry into the European Community, 1970–72; FCO, 1972–75; Fellow, Center for Internat. Affairs, Harvard Univ., 1975–76; Chef de Cabinet to Pres. of Commn of European Community, 1977–81; Vis. Fellow, All Souls Coll., Oxford, 1981; Ambassador to Mexico, 1981–83; Dep. Under-Sec. of State, FCO, 1983–84; Perm. Sec., ODA, 1984–87; British Perm. Rep. to UN, 1987–90. Director: IBM (UK), 1990–95 (Mem. IBM Adv. Bd, 1995–2000); BOC Envmtl Foundn, 1990–; Govett Mexican Horizons, 1991–96; Govett American Smaller Cos Trust, 1996–98; Govett Enhanced Income Investment Trust, 1999–. Chairman: Internat. Inst. for Envmt and Develt, 1990–94; Climate Inst. of Washington, 1990–; Earthwatch (Europe), 1990–97; Adv. Cttee on the Darwin Initiative for the Survival of Species, 1992–99. Trustee: Baring Foundn, 1992–; Natural Hist. Mus., 1992–2001; WWF (UK), 1993–99; Royal Botanic Garden, Edinburgh, 1997–2001; Reuters Foundn, 2000–. President: Marine Biol. Assoc., 1990–2001; RGS, 1990–93; Earth Centre, 1996–; Nat. Soc. for Clean Air and Envmtl Protection, 1997–99; Gaia Soc., 1998–2001. Convenor, Govt Panel on Sustainable Develt, 1994–2000; Member, Government Task Force: on Urban Regeneration, 1998–99; on Near Earth Objects, 2000. Mem., Global 500 (UN Roll of Honour for Envmtl Achievement), 1991. Hon. Fellow, St Edmund's Coll., Cambridge, 1995. Hon. FRIBA 2000. Mem. (Dr *hc*), Mexican Acad. of Internat. Law, 1983 (Orden Academico del Derecho, de la Cultura y de la Paz, 1989). Hon. LLD: Massachusetts, 1990; Bristol, 1991; Birmingham, 1991; Kent, 1996; Hon. DSc: UEA, 1990; Sussex, 1991; Cranfield, 1992; Loughborough, 1995; Exeter, 1999; Hull, 2001; Plymouth, 2001; Dr *hc*: Central London Poly., 1990; Stirling, 1990; Sheffield Hallam, 1996; E London, 1998. Global Envmtl Leadership Award, Climate Inst., 1996; Patron's Medal, RGS, 2000. Officer, Order of Orange Nassau (Netherlands), 1958; Order of Aztec Eagle with sash (Mexico), 1994. *Publications:* (contrib.) The Evacuees, 1968; (contrib.) Life After Death, 1976; Climatic Change and World Affairs, 1977, 1986 (contrib.) The United Kingdom/The United Nations, 1990; (contrib.) Sustaining Earth, 1990; (contrib.) Sir Francis Galton, 1991; (contrib.) Monitoring the Environment, 1992; (contrib.) Threats Without Enemies, 1993; (contrib.) Science for the Earth, 1995; (contrib.) The Changing World, 1996; Mary Anning of Lyme Regis, 1996. *Recreations:* climatology; palæohistory; art, especially pre-Columbiana; mountains. *Address:* Ablington Old Barn, Ablington, Cirencester, Glos GL7 5NU. *Clubs:* Brooks's, Garrick.

TICKELL, Maj.-Gen. Marston Eustace, CBE 1973 (MBE 1955); MC 1945; CEng, FICE; Commandant Royal Military College of Science, 1975–78, retired; *b* 18 Nov. 1923; *er s* of late Maj.-Gen. Sir Eustace Tickell, KBE, CB, MC; *m* 1961, Pamela Vere, *d* of Vice-Adm. A. D. Read, CB; no *c*. *Educ:* Wellington Coll.; Peterhouse, Cambridge (MA). Commnd in RE, 1944; NW Europe Campaign and Middle East, 1944–45; psc 1954; Mil. Ops, MoD, 1955–57; served in Libya, Cyprus and Jordan, 1958–59; US Armed Forces Staff Coll. and Instructor RMCS and Staff Coll., 1959–62; Defence Planning Staff, MoD, 1962–64; CRE 4th Div., 1964–66; comd 12 Engr Bde, 1967–69; Indian Nat. Defence Coll., 1970; COS Northern Ireland, 1971–72; E-in-C, MoD, 1972–75. Col Comdt, RE, 1978–83. Hon. Col, Engr and Transport Staff Corps, 1983–88. Lord Chancellor's Panel of Independent Inspectors, 1979–93. Pres., Instn of Royal Engrs, 1979–82. FICE 1974. *Recreation:* sailing. *Address:* The Old Vicarage, Branscombe, Seaton, Devon EX12 3DW. *Clubs:* Army and Navy; Royal Ocean Racing.

TICKLE, Brian Percival, CB 1985; Senior Registrar of the Family Division, High Court of Justice, 1982–88 (Registrar, 1970–88); *b* 31 Oct. 1921; *s* of late William Tickle and Lucy (*née* Percival); *m* 1945, Margaret Alice Pendrey (*d* 1994); one *s* one *d*. *Educ:* The Judd Sch., Tonbridge. Entered Civil Service, 1938. Served War, Royal Signals, 1941–46. Civil Service, 1946–70. Member: Matrimonial Causes Rules Cttee, 1982–88; Independent Schs Tribunal, 1988–93. Vice Pres., Nevill Golf Club, 1997–. *Publications:* Rees Divorce Handbook, 1963; Atkin's Court Forms and Precedents (Probate), 2nd edn 1974, rev. edn 1984. *Recreations:* golf, watching cricket and Rugby. *Address:* Hillbrow Court, 1A Royal Chase, Tunbridge Wells, Kent TN4 8AX.

TICKLE, Prof. Cheryll Anne, PhD; FRS 1998; FRSE; Professor of Developmental Biology, University of Dundee, since 1998; *b* 18 Jan. 1945; *d* of Lewis Sidney Tickle and Gwendoline Muriel Tickle; *m* 1979, John Gray. *Educ:* Girton Coll., Cambridge (MA); Glasgow Univ. (PhD 1970). NATO Fellowship, Yale Univ., 1970–72; Middlesex Hospital Medical School, subseq. University College London Medical School: Research Fellow, Lectr, Sen. Lectr, 1972–87; Reader, 1987–91; Prof. of Developmental Biology, 1991–98. Mem., BBSRC. FRSE 2000. *Address:* Wellcome Trust Biocentre, University of Dundee, Dow Street, Dundee DD1 5EH.

TIDBURY, Sir Charles (Henderson), Kt 1989; DL; Chairman, Whitbread PLC, 1978–84; Deputy Chairman, Inspec PLC, 1994–98; *b* 26 Jan. 1926; *s* of late Brig. O. H. Tidbury, MC, and Beryl (*née* Pearce); *m* Anne, *d* of late Brig. H. E. Russell, DSO, and of Lady O'Connor; two *s* three *d*. *Educ:* Eton Coll. Served KRRC, 1944–52: Palestine, 1946–48 (despatches); Queen's Westminsters TA, 1952–60. Joined Whitbread & Co. Ltd, 1952; a Man. Dir, 1959; Chief Exec., 1974; Dep. Chm., 1977; Dir, 1984–88. Chm., Brickwoods Brewery Ltd, 1966–71. Director: Whitbread Investment Co. PLC, 1975–93; Barclays Bank PLC, 1978–91; Mercantile Gp plc, 1985–91; Nabisco Gp Ltd, 1985–88; Vaux Gp plc, 1985–91; ICL (Europe, formerly UK), 1985–93; Pearl Assurance PLC, 1985–94; Gales Brewery, Horndean, 1989–96. Dir, Centre for Policy Studies, 1988–93. Pres., Inst. of Brewing, 1976–78; Chm., 1982–84, Vice-Pres., 1985–, Brewers' Soc.; President: Shire Horse Soc., 1985–87; British Inst. of Innkeeping, 1985–92 (Vice-Pres., 1992–); Brewing Res. Foundn Internat. (formerly Brewing Res. Foundn), 1993– (Chm., 1985–93). Chairman: Mary Rose Development Trust, 1980–86; William and Mary Tercentenary Trust, 1986–93; Hampshire Enterprise Partnership (formerly Business Liaison Exec. Bd), 1993–; Mem., Portsmouth and SE Hants Health Commn, 1992–96; Trustee, Nat. Maritime Museum, 1984–96. Governor: Nat. Heart and Chest Hosps, 1988–90; Portsmouth Univ. (formerly Polytechnic), 1988–96; Chm. Govs, Portsmouth High Sch., 1992–96. Master, Brewers' Co., 1988–89. DL Hampshire, 1989. Hon. LLD Portsmouth, 1997. *Recreations:* my family, messing about in boats, rough shooting, the countryside. *Address:* Crocker Hill Farm, Forest Lane, Wickham, Hants PO17 5DW. *Clubs:* Royal Yacht Squadron, Bembridge Sailing.

TIDMARSH, James Napier, MBE 1989; Lord-Lieutenant, County of Bristol, since 1996; Keeper of the Rolls, Avon Commission of the Peace, since 1997; *b* 15 Sept. 1932; *yr s* of late Edward and Madeline Tidmarsh; *m* 1967, Virginia, *y d* of late Robin Warren; two *s*. *Educ:* Taunton Sch. National Service: commnd 1st Bn Duke of Cornwall's LI; served Germany, Jamaica and British Honduras, 1952–54; TA 4/5 Bn Somerset LI, 1955–60. Involved in footwear industry, UK and Australasia, 1955–72; Man. Dir, Dycem Ltd, 1972–96; Founder Dir, GWR plc, 1985–89. Director: Bristol Chamber of Commerce and Initiative, 1992–; Learning Partnership West (formerly Western Educn and Trng Partnership), 1995–99. Vice-Chm., Nat. Assoc. Prison Visitors, 1966–69. Trustee: Bristol Benevolent Instn, 1974–; Bristol Archdeaconry Charities, 1996–; Founder Trustee, Gtr Bristol Foundn, 1987; Chm., John Cabot's Matthew Trust, 1996–. Pres., Avon & Bristol Fedn of Clubs for Young People, 1994–98 (Chm., 1982–94); Patron, Avon Youth Assoc., 1998–. Mem. Council, Bristol Univ., 1994–2000. Governor, Colston's Collegiate Sch., 1986–94. Hon. Col, RM Reserve, Bristol, 1998–. Master, Soc. of Merchant Venturers, 1994–95. JP Bristol, 1977; High Sheriff, Avon, 1995–96. FRSA 2000. KStJ 1997. *Address:* 8 Prince's Buildings, Clifton, Bristol BS8 4LB. *T:* (0117) 973 0462. *Clubs:* Army and Navy, Royal Commonwealth Society, Saintsbury; Clifton (Bristol).

TIDY, Morley David; Assistant Under-Secretary of State (Personnel) (Air), Ministry of Defence, 1990–92; *b* 23 April 1933; *s* of James Morley and Winnie Tidy; *m* 1957, Wendy Ann Bennett; one *s* two *d*. *Educ:* Hove County Grammar School; Magdalene College, Cambridge (MA). National Service, RAF, 1951–53. Dept of Employment, 1956–57; HM Inspector of Taxes, Inland Revenue, 1957–66; MoD, 1966; Manchester Business School, 1967; First Sec. (Defence), UK Delegn to NATO, 1969–72; MoD, 1973; RCDS, 1977; Chief Officer, SBAA, Cyprus, 1980–83; Asst Under-Sec., Air Staff, MoD, 1984; Asst Under Sec. (Ordnance), MoD, 1985; Asst Under Sec., Defence Export Services, Administration, MoD, 1988. *Recreations:* tennis, cricket, golf, jigsaws.

TIDY, William Edward, (Bill), MBE 2001; freelance cartoonist, since 1958; writer, playwright, television and radio presenter; *b* 9 Oct. 1933; *s* of William Edward Tidy and Catherine Price; *m* 1960, Rosa Colotti; two *s* one *d*. *Educ:* Anfield Road Jun. Sch., Liverpool; St Margaret's Sen. Sch., Anfield, Liverpool. Shipping office boy, R. P. Houston, Liverpool, 1950–51. Served RE, 1952–55. Layout artist, Pagan Smith Advertising Agency, 1956–58. Presented for BBC TV: Tidy Up Walsall; Tidy Up Naples; My City; Draw Me; radio broadcasting includes: The News Quiz (also Guest Presenter); Midweek (also Guest Presenter); I'm Sorry I Haven't a Clue; Back to Square One; The Law Game; Trivia Test Match; Down Your Way; radio adaptation, The Fosdyke Saga (with John Junkin). After dinner speaker for many major cos. *Publications: (written and illustrated):* Sporting Chance, 1961; O Cleo, 1962; Laugh with Bill Tidy, 1966; Up the Reds, Up the Blues, 1968; Tidy's World, 1969; The Cloggies, 1969; Tidy Again, 1970; The Fosdyke Saga (14 vols), 1972–85; The Cloggies Dance Back, 1973; The Great Eric Ackroyd Disaster, 1976; The Cloggies Are Back, 1977; Mine's a Pint, What's Yours (The Kegbuster Story), 1981; Robbie and the Blobbies, 1982; Bill Tidy's Little Rude Book, 1984; A Day at Cringemound School, 1985; Bill Tidy's Book of Classic Cockups, 1985; The World's Worst Golf Club, 1987; The Incredible Bed, 1990; Draw me 387 Baked Beans in 10 seconds, 1991; Save Daring Waring with a pencil, 1993; Is there any news of the Iceberg? (autobiog.), 1995; (with P. Bahn) Disgraceful Archaeology, 1999; Bill Tidy's Book of Quotations, 1999; has also illustrated over seventy other books; contrib. to What's Brewing?, Classic FM Magazine, British Archaeology, Archaeology (USA). *Recreation:* cricket (Lord's Taverners). *Address:* Terry Meadow Farm, Boylestone, Derbyshire DE6 5AB. *T:* (01509) 600616; *e-mail:* bill@tidystudio.freeserve.co.uk. *Clubs:* Cartoonist of Great Britain; Nottinghamshire County Cricket.

TIERNEY, John; Member (SDLP) Foyle, Northern Ireland Assembly, since 1998; *b* 9 Dec. 1951; *s* of Paddy and Catherine Tierney; *m* 1972, Bernie Harkin; two *s* one *d*. *Educ:* St Joseph's, Derry. Mem. (SDLP) Derry CC, 1981–; Mayor of Derry, 1984–85. *Address:* 1st Floor, 5 Bayview Terrace, Derry BT48 7EE. *T:* (028) 7136 2631, *Fax:* (028) 7136 2632.

TIERNEY, Sydney; JP; President, 1977–81, and 1983–91, and National Officer, 1979–91, Union of Shop, Distributive and Allied Workers; Chairman, Labour Party, 1986–87 (Vice-Chairman, 1985–86); *b* 16 Sept. 1923; *m* 1985, Margaret Olive (*née* Hannah); two *d*. *Educ:* Secondary Modern Sch., Dearne; Plater Coll., Oxford. Mem., Co-operative Party; an Official and Member, USDAW. Vice-Chm., W Midlands Labour Gp of MPs, 1974–79; Mem., Labour Party NEC, to 1990. MP (Lab) Birmingham, Yardley, Feb. 1974–1979; PPS to Min. of State for Agriculture, 1976–79. JP Leicester, 1966. *Address:* Rocklands, 56 Priory Lane, Kents Bank, Grange Over Sands, Cumbria LA11 7BJ.

TIETJEN, Tina, (Mrs G. R. Robertson); Chairman, Women's Royal Voluntary Service, since 1999; *b* 10 June 1947; *d* of Arthur Tietjen and Mary Alice (*née* Storey); *m* 1972, Gordon R. Robertson. *Educ:* Coloma Convent Grammar Sch. Jt Man. Dir, Video Arts Gp Ltd; Dir, MediaKey Gp, 1996–. Non-exec. Director: Phoenix Business Consultants; PPIAB. Mem. Bd, 1992–97, Mem., Human Resources Leadership Team, 1997–, BITC. Gov., Thames Valley Univ. *Recreations:* travel, theatre, opera, gardening. *Address:* WRVS, Milton Hill House, Milton Hill, Steventon, Abingdon, Oxon OX13 6AD.

TIETMEYER, Dr Hans; President, Deutsche Bundesbank, 1993–99 (Vice-Governor, 1991–93); *b* 18 Aug. 1931; *s* of Bernhard and Helene Tietmeyer; *m* 1st, Marie-Luise Floßdorf (*d* 1978); one *s* one *d*; 2nd, 1980, Maria-Therese Kalff. *Educ:* Univs of Münster, Bonn and Cologne (Dr Rer Pol). Sec., Bischöfliche Studienförderung Cusanuswerk, 1959–62; Fed. Min. of Economics, 1962–82, Head of Div. of Gen. Economic Policy, 1973–82; Mem., Econ. Policy Cttee of EC and OECD, 1972–82; Sec. of State, Min. of Finance, 1982–89; Mem., Bd of Dirs, Deutsche Bundesbank, 1990–99. Chm. Bd, German Fed. Foundn for the Envmt, 1990–; Chm. of Govs, G–10 Central Bank, 1994–99. Hon. Prof., Faculty of Econ. Scis, Martin Luther Univ., Halle-Wittenberg, 1996–. *Publications:* numerous articles on economics. *Recreation:* sport. *Address:* c/o Deutsche Bundesbank, Wilhelm Epstein Strasse 14, 60431 Frankfurt, Germany.

TIKARAM, Sir Moti, KBE 1980; CF 1996; **Hon. Justice Sir Moti Tikaram;** Justice of the Court of Appeal, Fiji, since 1988; Judge of Supreme Court, Fiji, 2000–March 2002; *b* 18 March 1925; *s* of Tikaram and Singari; *m* 1944, Satyawati (*d* 1981); two *s* one *d*. *Educ:* Marist Brothers High Sch., Suva; Victoria Univ., Wellington, NZ (LLB 1954). Started law practice, 1954; Stipendiary Magistrate, 1960; Puisne Judge, 1968; acted as Chief Justice, 1971 and thereafter on several occasions; Pres., Fiji Court of Appeal, 1994–2000. Ombudsman, Fiji, 1972–87. Patron, Fiji Lawn Tennis Assoc. Scouting Medal of Merit, 1986. *Publications:* articles in The Pacific Way and in Recent Law 131. *Recreation:* tennis. *Address:* (home) 65 Knolly Street, PO Box 514, Suva, Fiji. *T:* 308415, *Fax:* 308619; (office) PO Box 2215, Government Buildings, Suva. *T:* 211489. *Clubs:* Fiji, Fiji Golf (Suva).

TILBY, Rev. Angela Clare Wyatt; Tutor, since 1997 and Vice Principal, since 2001, Westcott House, Cambridge; Lecturer in Spirituality and Early Church History in the Cambridge Theological Federation, since 1997; *b* 6 March 1950; *d* of Julian George Wyatt Tilby and Constance Mary (*née* Collier). *Educ:* North London Collegiate Sch.; Girton Coll., Cambridge (MA). Producer, Religious Programmes, BBC Radio, 1973–79, BBC TV 1979–94; Sen. Producer, Religious Programmes, BBC North, 1994–97. Ordained deacon, 1997, priest, 1998. Mem., C of E Liturgical Commn, 1998–. *Publications:*

Teaching God, 1978; Won't You Join the Dance, 1984; Let There be Light, 1989; Science and the Soul, 1992; The Little Office Book, 1997; Son of God, 2001. *Recreations:* science and crime fiction, history, psychology, cooking, wine. *Address:* Westcott House, Cambridge CB5 8BP. *T:* (01223) 741014.

TILEY, Prof. John, LLD; Professor of the Law of Taxation, University of Cambridge, since 1990; Fellow, Queens' College, Cambridge, since 1967 (Vice-President, 1988–96); *b* 25 Feb. 1941; *s* of William Arthur Tiley, OBE and Audrey Ellen (*née* Burton); *m* 1964, Jillinda Millicent Draper; two *s* one *d. Educ:* Winchester Coll.; Lincoln Coll., Oxford (BA 1962; BCL 1963; MA 1967); LLD Cantab 1995. Called to the Bar, Inner Temple, 1964, Hon. Bencher, 1993; a Recorder, 1989–99. Lecturer: Lincoln Coll., Oxford, 1963–64; Univ. of Birmingham, 1964–67; University of Cambridge: Asst Lectr, 1967–72; Lectr, 1972–87; Reader in Law of Taxation, 1987–90. Visiting Professor: Dalhousie Univ., 1972–73; Univ. of W Ontario, 1978–79; Univ. of Melbourne, 1979; Case Western Reserve Univ., 1985–86, 1996. Gen. Editor, Butterworth's Tax Guide, subseq. Tiley and Collison's UK Tax Guide, 1982–. *Publications:* A Casebook on Equity and Succession, 1968; Revenue Law, 1976, 4th edn 2000; contrib. to legal jls. *Recreations:* walking, cricket, music. *Address:* Queens' College, Cambridge CB3 9ET. *T:* (01223) 335546.

TILGHMAN, Prof. Shirley Marie, PhD; FRS 1995; Howard A. Prior Professor of the Life Sciences, Princeton University, since 1986; Investigator, Howard Hughes Medical Institute, Princeton University, since 1988; *b* 17 Sept. 1946; *d* of Henry W. Caldwell and Shirley P. Carre; *m*; one *s* one *d. Educ:* Queen's Univ., Kingston, Canada (BSc Hons 1968); Temple Univ., Philadelphia (PhD Biochem. 1975). Fogarty Internat. Fellow, NIH, Bethesda, 1975–78; Asst Prof., Temple Univ., 1978–79; Mem., Inst. for Cancer Res., Pa, 1979–86; Adjunct Associate Prof. of Human Genetics, Biochem. and Biophysics, Univ. of Pa, 1980–86; Adjunct Prof., Dept of Biochem., Univ. of Medicine and Dentistry of New Jersey-Robert Wood Johnson Med. Sch., NJ, 1988–. Ed. and Mem., Editl Bd, Molecular and Cell Biol., 1985–94; Member, Editorial Board: Jl Cell Biol., 1988–91; Genes and Develt, 1990–. Fellow, Inst. of Medicine, USA, 1995; Foreign Associate, Nat. Acad. of Scis, USA, 1996. Hon. DSc City Coll. of NY, 1994. *Publications:* (ed with K. E. Davies) Genome Analysis: Vol. I 1990, Vols II and III 1991, Vol. IV 1992, Vols V and VI 1993; contrib. chapters in books; contrib. numerous articles and papers in Proc. Nat. Acad. Scis, USA, Jl Biol. Chem., Science, Nature, Genes Develt, Jl Cell Biol., Molecular Cell Biol. and others. *Recreations:* ski-ing, tennis, gardening, reading. *Address:* Department of Molecular Biology, Princeton University, Princeton, NJ 08544, USA. *T:* (609) 2582900.

TILL, Barry Dorn; Principal of Morley College, London, 1965–86; Adviser, 1973–86, Director, 1986–92, Baring Foundation; *b* 1 June 1923; *s* of John Johnson and Hilda Lucy Till; *m* 1st, 1954, Shirley Philipson (marr. diss. 1965); two *s*; 2nd, 1966, Antonia, *d* of Sir Michael Clapham, *qv*; two *d. Educ:* Harrow; Jesus College and Westcott House, Cambridge. 1st Class Theology Pt III, 1949; Lightfoot Scholar, 1949. Served War, Coldstream Guards, 1942–46; Italian campaign. Deacon, 1950; Priest, 1951; Asst Curate, Bury Parish Church, Lancs, 1950–53; Fellow of Jesus Coll., Cambridge, 1953–60, Chaplain, 1953–56, Dean, 1956–60, Tutor, 1957–60; Univ. Preacher, Cambridge, 1955; Examining Chaplain to Bishop of Lichfield, 1957–60; Dean of Hong Kong, 1960–64. Chm., Asia Christian Colleges Assoc., 1968–76, Vice-Pres., 1976–. Governor, British Inst. of Recorded Sound, 1967–72; Mem., Adv. Council, V&A Museum, 1977–83. Chairman: Greater London AACE, 1976–82; Work-Out, 1986–89; Mary Ward Settlement, 1987–98. Founder Mem., Exec. Cttee, Assoc. of Charitable Foundns, 1989–91. Governor, St Olaf's Grammar Sch., 1973–82 (Chm., 1980–82); Member: Cultural Cttee, European Culture Foundn, 1976–78; Council, London Sinfonietta, 1992–. Trustee: Thomas Cubitt Trust, 1978–99; LentA Educnl Trust, 1987–92 (Chm., 1990–92); Open Coll. of the Arts, 1992–; Charity House, 1992–98; Transport 2000, 1992–; London Educn Business Partnership, 1992–99; Fitzwilliam Mus. Trust, 1993–. *Publications:* contrib. to The Historic Episcopate, 1954; Change and Exchange, 1964; Changing Frontiers in the Mission of the Church, 1965; contrib. to A Holy Week Manual, 1967; The Churches Search for Unity, 1972; contrib. New DNB. *Recreations:* travel, gardening, opera. *Address:* 44 Canonbury Square, N1 2AW. *T:* (020) 7359 0708. *Club:* Brooks's.

TILL, Prof. James Edgar, OC 1994; PhD; FRS 2000; FRSC; University Professor, University of Toronto, 1984–97, now Professor Emeritus; Senior Scientist, Ontario Cancer Institute, 1957–96, Emeritus, since 1997; Senior Fellow, Massey College, Toronto, since 1990; *b* 25 Aug. 1931; *s* of William Till and Gertrude Ruth Till (*née* Isaac); *m* 1959, Marion Joyce Sinclair; one *s* two *d. Educ:* Univ. of Saskatchewan (BA Arts and Sci. 1952; MA Physics 1954); Yale Univ. (PhD Biophysics 1957). Postdoctoral Fellow, Connaught Med. Res. Labs, 1956–57; University of Toronto: Asst Prof., 1958–62, Associate Prof., 1962–65, Dept of Med. Biophysics; Prof., 1965–97; Associate Dean, Life Scis, Sch. of Grad. Studies, 1981–84; Hd, Div. of Biol Res., Ont. Cancer Inst., 1969–82. FRSC 1969. Internat. Award, Gairdner Foundn, 1969; Thomas W. Eadie Medal, RSC, 1991; Robert L. Noble Prize, Nat. Cancer Inst. of Canada, 1993. *Publications:* contrib. chapters in books and conf. proceedings; numerous contribs to refereed jls. *Address:* Ontario Cancer Institute, University Health Network, 610 University Avenue, Room 9-416, Toronto, ON M5G 2M9, Canada. *T:* (416) 9462948; 182 Briar Hill Avenue, Toronto, ON M4R 1H9, Canada.

TILL, Very Rev. Michael Stanley; Dean of Winchester, since 1996; *b* 19 Nov. 1935; *s* of Stanley Brierley Till and Mary Till; *m* 1965, Tessa, *d* of Capt. Stephen Roskill; one *s* one *d. Educ:* Brighton, Hove and Sussex Grammar School; Lincoln Coll., Oxford (BA, History 1960, Theology 1962; MA 1967); Westcott House, Cambridge. Curate, St John's, St John's Wood, NW8, 1964–67; Chaplain 1967–70, Dean and Fellow 1970–81, King's College, Cambridge; Vicar of All Saints', Fulham, 1981–86; Area Dean, Hammersmith and Fulham, 1984–86; Archdeacon of Canterbury, 1986–96. *Address:* The Deanery, The Close, Winchester, Hants SO23 9LS. *T:* (01962) 853738.

TILL, Stewart Myles, CBE 2000; Deputy Chairman, Film Council, since 1999; *b* 24 April 1951; *s* of Ronald Leslie and Olive Till; *m* 1986, Lynda Helen Jones; one *s* one *d. Educ:* Univ. of Bath (BSc Hons Business Studies); Essex Univ. (MA American Politics). Account Exec., Saatchi & Saatchi, 1976–78; Marketing Dir, WEA Records, 1978–83; Vice-Pres., N Europe CBS/Fox Video, 1983–88; Dep. Managing Dir, Sky TV, 1988–92; President: International Polygram Filmed Entertainment, 1992–99; Universal Pictures Internat., 1999–2000. Non-exec. Dir, Tiger Aspect, 2000–. FRSA 2001. *Recreations:* most sports, particularly football; family. *Address:* Remenham Place, Remenham Hill, Henley-on-Thames, Oxon RG9 3EU.

TILLER, Rev. Canon John; Chancellor and Canon Residentiary of Hereford Cathedral, since 1984; Diocesan Director of Training, Hereford, 1991–2000; *b* 22 June 1938; *s* of Harry Maurice Tiller and Lucille Maisie Tiller; *m* 1961, Ruth Alison (*née* Watson); two *s* one *d. Educ:* St Albans Sch.; Christ Church, Oxford (MA, 2nd Cl. Mod. Hist.); Bristol Univ. (MLitt). Ordained deacon 1962, priest 1963, St Albans. Asst Curate: St Cuthbert, Bedford, 1962–65; Widcombe, Bath, 1965–67; Chaplain and Tutor, Tyndale Hall, Bristol, 1967–71; Lectr in Church History and Worship, Trinity Coll., Bristol, 1971–73; Priest-in-Charge, Christ Church, Bedford, 1973–78; Chief Sec., ACCM, 1978–84. Hon. Canon of St Albans Cathedral, 1979–84. *Publications:* The Service of Holy Communion and its Revision (with R. T. Beckwith), 1972; A Modern Liturgical Bibliography, 1974; The Great Acquittal, 1980; Puritan, Pietist, Pentecostalist, 1982; A Strategy for the Church's Ministry, 1983; The Gospel Community, 1987; contribs to: The New International Dictionary of the Christian Church, 1974; Anglican Worship Today, 1980; New Dictionary of Christian Theology, 1988; The Parish Church?, 1988; (with G. E. Aylmer) Hereford Cathedral: a history, 2000. *Recreations:* walking, bird-watching, spuddling. *Address:* Canon's House, 3 St John Street, Hereford HR1 2NB. *T:* (01432) 265659.

TILLETT, Michael Burn; QC 1996; a Recorder, since 1989; *b* 3 Sept. 1942; *s* of late Cyril Vernon Tillett and Norah Phyllis Tillett; *m* 1977, Kathryn Ann Samuel; two *d. Educ:* Marlborough Coll.; Queens' Coll., Cambridge (MA (Hons) Law). Called to the Bar, Inner Temple, 1965; in practice, 1966–; Asst Recorder, 1984–89. Legal Mem., Mental Health Rev. Tribunal, 2000–. *Recreations:* mountaineering, ski-ing, riding, sailing. *Address:* 39 Essex Street, WC2R 3AT. *T:* (020) 7832 1142. *Clubs:* Royal Automobile, Hurlingham; Downhill Only; Seaview Yacht.

TILLEY, John Vincent; Head, Parliamentary Office, Co-operative Group, since 2000; *b* June 1941; *m* Kathryn Riley; two *d.* Mem., Wandsworth Borough Council, 1971–78. Mem., Co-operative Party. MP (Lab) Lambeth Central, Apr. 1978–83. Contested (Lab): Kensington Div. of Kensington and Chelsea, Feb. and Oct. 1974; Southwark and Bermondsey, 1983. Chief Economic Advisor, London Borough of Hackney, 1983–88; Parly Sec., Co-operative Union, 1988–99. *Address:* 35 Point Hill, SE10 8QW.

TILLEY, Olwen Mary, (Mrs A. Tilley); *see* Rice, O. M.

TILLING, George Henry Garfield; Chairman, Scottish Postal Board, 1977–84, retired; *b* 24 Jan. 1924; *s* of late Thomas and Anne Tilling; *m* 1956, Margaret Meriel, SSStJ, *d* of late Rear-Adm. Sir Alexander McGlashan, KBE, CB, DSO; two *s* two *d. Educ:* Hardye's Sch., Dorchester; University Coll., Oxford (Open Exhibnr, Kitchener Schol., Farquharson Prizeman, MA). Served War of 1939–45, NW Europe: Captain, Dorset Regt, 1943–46. Post Office: Asst Principal, 1948; Principal, 1953; Private Sec. to Postmaster General, 1964; Dep. Dir of Finance, 1965; Dir, Eastern Postal Region, 1967; Sec. of the Post Office, 1973–75; Dir of Postal Ops, 1975–77. Mem. Council, Lord Kitchener Nat. Meml Fund, 1979–90. Order of St John: Mem. Council, London, 1975–77; Mem. Cttee of the Order for Edinburgh, 1978–87; Mem., Scottish Priory Chapter, 1993–99. Trustee, Bield Retirement Housing Trust, 1988–98. Hon. Mem., St Andrew's Ambulance Assoc., 1980. KStJ. FSAScot; FCIT. *Recreations:* orders and medals, heraldry, uniforms. *Address:* 1 Standpretty, Gorebridge, Midlothian EH23 4QG. *T:* (01875) 822409.

TILLOTSON, Maj.-Gen. (Henry) Michael, CB 1983; CBE 1976 (OBE 1970, MBE 1956); author; European Union consultant, since 1989; *b* 12 May 1928; *er s* of late Henry and May Elizabeth Tillotson; *m* 1956, Angela, *d* of late Bertram Wadsworth Shaw; two *s* one *d. Educ:* Chesterfield Sch.; RMA Sandhurst. Professional soldier, 1948–83: commnd E Yorks Regt, 1948; served: Austria, 1948–50; Germany and Berlin, 1951–52; Indo China (attached French Union Forces), 1953 (Croix de Guerre with Palm); Malayan Emergency, 1953–55; Indonesian Confrontation, 1964–65; S Arabia, 1965–67 (despatches); MoD Intelligence, 1967–69; Inf. Bn Comdr, Cyprus, 1969–71; Col GS, Hong Kong, 1974–76; Chief of Staff UN Force, Cyprus, and Comdr British Contingent, 1976–78; research mission for UN Sec.-Gen. to UN Forces, Israel, Lebanon, Syria and Sinai, 1978; Dep. Dir, Army Staff Duties, and MoD rep., Cabinet Civil Contingencies Unit, 1978–79; Chief of Staff (Maj.-Gen.) to C-in-C UKLF, 1980–83. Regl Dir SE Asia, Internat. Mil. Services Ltd, 1983–86. Col, PWO Regt of Yorks, 1979–86. Hon. Life Fellow, RSPB, 1993. *Publications:* Finland at Peace and War 1918–1993, 1993, 2nd edn 1996 (Finnish Gold Medal of Merit, 1996); With the Prince of Wales's Own, 1995; articles in Eur., mil. and other jls, 1954–. *Recreations:* abroad, birds, listening to music. *Address:* PO Box 13, Romsey, Hants SO51 0BA. *Clubs:* Army and Navy; Prince Albert (Brussels).

TILLOTSON, Maj.-Gen. Michael; *see* Tillotson, Maj.-Gen. H. M.

TILLSLEY, Gen. Bramwell Harold; General of the Salvation Army, 1993–94; *b* 18 Aug. 1931; *s* of Harold Tillsley and Doris Tillsley (*née* Lawrence); *m* 1953, Maude Pitcher; two *s* one *d. Educ:* Kitchener-Waterloo Collegiate; Univ. of Western Ontario (BA); Wycliffe Coll., Toronto; Salvation Army Trng Coll., Toronto. Social worker, Children's Aid Soc., Kitchener, Ont., 1952–55; Salvation Army: Windsor, Nova Scotia, 1956–58; Oakville, Ont., 1958–59; on staff, Salvation Army Coll., Toronto, 1959–65; Divl Youth Sec., Saskatchewan, 1965–66; N Toronto Congregation, 1966–71; Training Principal: Newfoundland, 1971–74; NY, 1974–77; Provincial Comdr, Newfoundland, 1977–79; Divl Comdr, Metro-Toronto, 1979–81; Trng Principal, London, 1981–85; Chief Sec., USA, South, 1985–89; Territorial Comdr, Australian Southern Territory, 1989–91; COS, Internat. HQ, London, 1991–93. Mem., Rotary Club, Toronto, Melbourne and London. Queen's Medal (Canada), 1978. *Publications:* Life in the Spirit, 1966; Life More Abundant, 1968; Manpower for the Master, 1970; This Mind in You, 1989. *Recreations:* music, golf, sports (ice hockey in youth). *Address:* 65 Spring Garden Avenue, Unit 604, North York, ON M2N 6H9, Canada.

TILNEY, Charles Edward, CMG 1956; Minister for Finance and Economics, Tanganyika, 1957–60; *b* 13 April 1909; *yr s* of late Lt-Col N. E. Tilney, CBE, DSO, and Mrs Tilney; *m* 1952, Rosalind Hull (*d* 1993), *e d* of late Lt-Col E. C. de Renzy-Martin, CMG, DSO, MC, and Mrs de Renzy-Martin; two *s. Educ:* Rugby School; Oriel College, Oxford. Ceylon Civil Service, 1932; Tanganyika: Asst Chief Secretary (Finance), 1948; Dep. Financial Secretary, 1948; Secretary for Finance, 1950; Member for Finance and Economics, 1953. Retd from E Africa, 1960. *Address:* 8 Butts Close, Biddestone, Chippenham, Wilts SN14 7DZ. *T:* (01249) 714770.

TILSON, Joseph Charles, (Joe), RA 1991 (ARA 1985); painter, sculptor and printmaker; *b* 24 Aug. 1928; *s* of Frederick Albert Edward Tilson and Ethel Stapley Louise Saunders; *m* 1956, Joslyn Morton; one *s* two *d. Educ:* St Martin's School of Art; Royal Coll. of Art (ARCA); British School at Rome (Rome Scholar). RAF, 1946–49. Worked in Italy and Spain, 1955–59; Vis. Lectr, Slade Sch., Univ. of London and King's Coll., Univ. of Durham, 1962–63; taught at Sch. of Visual Arts, NY, 1966; Vis. Lectr, Staatliche Hochschule für Bildende Kunste, Hamburg, 1971–72. Mem., Arts Panel, Arts Council, 1966–71. Exhib. Venice Biennale, 1964; work at Marlborough Gall., 1961–77, later at Waddington Galls; retrospective exhibitions: Boymans Van Beuningen Mus., Rotterdam, 1973; Vancouver Art Gall., 1979; Volterra, 1983. Biennale Prizes: Krakow, 1974; Ljubljana, 1985, 1995. Subject of TV films, 1963, 1968, 1974. *Recreation:* planting trees.

TILSON THOMAS, Michael; Music Director, San Francisco Symphony Orchestra, since 1995; Principal Guest Conductor, London Symphony Orchestra, since 1995 (Principal Conductor, 1988–95); Artistic Director (formerly Artistic Adviser), New World Symphony, since 1988; concert pianist; *b* 21 Dec. 1944; *s* of Theodor and Roberta

Thomas; *g s* of Boris and Bessie Thomashefsky, founders of Yiddish Theater, United States. *Educ:* Univ. of Southern California (Master of Music). Conductor, Young Musicians' Foundn Orchestra, LA, and conductor and pianist, Monday Evening Concerts, 1963–68; musical asst, Bayreuth, 1966–67; Koussevitzky Prize, Tanglewood, 1968; Asst then Principal Guest Conductor, Boston Symphony, 1969–74; NY début, 1969; London début, with LSO, 1970; Music Director: Buffalo Philharmonic, 1971–79; televised NY Philharmonic Young Peoples' Concerts, 1971–77; Principal Guest Conductor, LA Philharmonic, 1981–85; Music Dir, Great Woods Festival, 1985; Co-Artistic Dir, Pacific Music Fest., Sapporo, Japan, 1990–; guest conductor with orchestras and opera houses in US and Europe; numerous recordings. Grammy Award: best orchestral recording, 1997, for Prokofiev's Romeo and Juliet with San Francisco SO; best classical album of the year, 1999, for Stravinsky's Firebird and Rite of Spring with San Francisco SO. *Address:* MTT Inc., 888 7th Avenue, 35th Floor, New York, NY 10106, USA. *Club:* St Botolph (Boston).

TILT, Sir (Robin) Richard, Kt 1999; Chairman, Northamptonshire Health Authority, since 2000; Director General, HM Prison Service, 1995–99; *b* 11 March 1944; *s* of Francis Arthur Tilt and Mary Elizabeth (*née* Ashworth); *m* 1966, Kate Busby; two *s* one *d*. *Educ:* King's Sch., Worcester; Univ. of Nottingham (BA Hons); Open Univ. (Dip). HM Prison Service: Asst Governor, HM Borstal, Wellingborough, 1968–71; Tutor, Prison Service Staff Coll., 1971–74; Governor, HM Borstal, Pollington, 1974–75; Deputy Governor: Ranby, 1975–78; Gartree, 1978–80; Governor, Bedford, 1980–82; Hd, Manpower Section, HQ, 1982–84; Governor, Gartree, 1984–88; Dep. Regl Dir, Midlands, 1988–89; Hd, Industrial Relns, HQ, 1989–92; Hd of Finance, Police Dept, 1992–94; Dir of Services, 1994; Dir of Security and Progs, 1995. Chm., Kettering Gen. Hosp. NHS Trust, 1999–2000. Mem., Sentencing Adv. Panel, 1999–. Social Fund Comr for UK, 2000–. Churchill Fellow, 1991. Friend of RA. *Recreations:* walking, reading, theatre, art. *Address:* Northamptonshire Health Authority, Highfield House, Cliftonville Road, Northampton NN1 5DN.

TILTMAN, John H.; *see* Hessell Tiltman.

TIMBERLAKE, Herman Leslie Patterson, (Tim); Director, Abbey National Building Society, 1972–84 (Chief General Manager, 1971–79; Deputy Chairman, 1976–79); *b* 3 Feb. 1914; *s* of William Walter and Mabel Timberlake; *m* 1940, Betty (*née* Curtis); two *s*. *Educ:* Watford Grammar Sch. FCIS; FCIB. Served War of 1939–45. Joined Abbey Road Building Soc., 1930; Asst Branch Manager, Watford, 1936; became Abbey National Building Soc., 1944; Branch Manager appts, 1946–59; Manager: Branches Admin. Dept, 1959; Investments Admin. Dept, 1964; Branches and Agencies, 1966; Jt General Manager, 1968. Mem. Council, Building Societies Assoc., 1975–79; Pres., Building Societies Institute, 1977–78. *Address:* 1 Rochester Drive, Pinner, Middx HA5 1DA. *T:* (020) 8866 1554.

TIMBURY, Morag Crichton, MD, PhD; FRSE; FRCP, FRCPGlas, FRCPath; Director, Central Public Health Laboratory, Public Health Laboratory Service, 1988–95; *b* 29 Sept. 1930; *d* of William McCulloch and Dr Esther Sinclair McCulloch (*née* Hood); *m* 1954, Dr Gerald Charles Timbury, FRCPE, FRCPGlas, FRCPsych (decd); one *d*. *Educ:* St Bride's Sch.; Univ. of Glasgow (MB ChB; MD; PhD). MRCPath 1964, FRCPath 1976; MRCPGlas 1972, FRCPGlas 1974; FRCP 1994; FRSE 1979. University of Glasgow: Maurice Bloch Res. Fellow in Virology, 1960–63; Lectr in Bacteriology, 1963–65; Sen. Lectr in Virology, 1966–76; Reader, 1976–78; Prof. of Bacteriology and William Teacher Lectr, 1978–88. Hon. Cons. in Bacteriology and Virology, 1966–88. Member Council: RCPSG, 1985–88; RCPath, 1987–90. External examiner in med. microbiol., 1973–88, variously at QUB, Univs of Aberdeen, Cambridge, Dundee, Edinburgh, London, Newcastle. Vis. Associate Prof. in Virology, Baylor College of Medicine, Houston, Texas, 1975; Vis. Mayne Guest Prof., Univ. of Queensland, Brisbane, 1990; Hon. Vis. Prof. of Virology, ICSM, 1997–99. Chm., Ind. Rev. Gp, Rev. of Food-Related Scientific Services in Scotland, 1998. Mem., RSM, 1986–. *Publications:* Notes on Medical Virology, 1967, 11th edn 1997; (with J. D. Sleigh) Notes on Medical Bacteriology, 1981, 5th edn 1998; (co-ed) vol. 4, Virology, Topley and Wilson's Principles of Bacteriology, Virology and Immunity, 1929, 8th edn 1990; sci. papers on bacterial and viral infections, genetics of herpes simplex virus type 2. *Recreations:* military history, theatre. *Address:* 22 Monckton Court, Strangways Terrace, W14 8NF. *T:* (020) 7602 3345.

TIMMINS, Col John Bradford, OBE (mil.) 1973; TD 1968 (1st Clasp 1974); JP; Lord Lieutenant of Greater Manchester, since 1987; Chairman, Warburton Properties Ltd, since 1973; *b* 23 June 1932; *s* of John James Timmins and Janet Gwendoline (*née* Legg); *m* 1956, Jean Edwards; five *s* one *d*. *Educ:* Dudley Grammar Sch.; Wolverhampton Technical Coll.; Univ. of Aston-in-Birmingham (MSc). Building and Civil Engrg Industry, 1949–80; NW Regional Pres., Nat. Fedn of Building Trade Employers, 1974–75. Commnd RE, 1954; National Service, 1954–56; TA, 1956–80; comd 75 Eng. Regt(V), 1971–73, Hon. Col of the Regt, 1980–90; Hon. Colonel: Manchester and Salford Univ. OTC, 1990–98; Gtr Manchester ACF, 1991–. Pres., TA&VRA for NW England, 1994–99 (Vice-Chm., 1983–87; Vice-Pres., 1987–94, 1999–). ADC to the Queen, 1975–80. High Sheriff of Gtr Manchester, 1986–87. JP Trafford, 1987. President, Greater Manchester: Order of St John, 1987–; Royal Soc. of St George, 1988–. FRSA 1996. Hon. RNCM 1994. Hon. DSc Salford, 1990; Hon. LLD Manchester, 2001. KStJ 1988; KLJ 1990. *Recreations:* sailing, gardening. *Address:* The Old Rectory, Warburton, Lymm WA13 9SS. *Club:* Army and Navy.

TIMMS, Kate; *see* Timms, V. K.

TIMMS, Prof. Noel Walter; Professor of Social Work and Director, School of Social Work, University of Leicester, 1984–89, now Emeritus Professor; *b* 25 Dec. 1927; *s* of Harold John Timms and Josephine Mary Cecilia Timms; *m* 1956, Rita Caldwell; three *s* three *d*. *Educ:* Cardinal Vaughan School; Univ. of London (BA Hons History; MA Sociology); Univ. of Oxford. Social Worker, Family Service Units, 1952–54; Psychiatric social worker, 1955–57; Lectr, Dept of Social Science, Cardiff University Coll., 1957–61; Lectr, LSE, 1963–69; Prof. of Applied Social Studies, Bradford Univ., 1969–75; Prof. of Social Studies, Newcastle upon Tyne Univ., 1975–84. *Publications:* Social Casework, Principles and Practice, 1964; Language of Social Casework, 1968; (with John Mayer) The Client Speaks, 1970; (with Rita Timms) Dictionary of Social Welfare, 1982; Social Work Values: an enquiry, 1983; Family and Citizenship, 1992; (jtly) Secure Accommodation in Child Care, 1993; (jtly) Mediation: the making and remaking of co-operative relationships, 1994; In Pursuit of Quality, 1995; Authority in the Catholic Priesthood, 2001; (jtly) Diocesan Dispositions and Parish Voices in the Roman Catholic Church, 2001. *Recreations:* Evensong, looking at old furniture and at performances of Don Giovanni. *Address:* 157 Kingsway, Orpington, Kent, BR5 1PP. *T:* (01689) 877982.

TIMMS, Stephen Creswell; MP (Lab) East Ham, since 1997 (Newham North East, June 1994–1997); Minister of State (Minister for School Standards), Department for Education and Skills, since 2001; *b* 29 July 1955; *s* of late Ronald James Timms and of Margaret Joyce Timms (*née* Johnson); *m* 1986, Hui-Leng Lim. *Educ:* Farnborough Grammar Sch.; Emmanuel Coll., Cambridge (MA, MPhil). Consultant, Logica, 1978–86; Ovum: Principal Consultant, 1986–94; Manager, Telecommunications Reports, 1994. Sec., Newham NE Labour Party, 1981–84. Newham Borough Council: Councillor (Lab), 1984–97; Chm., Planning Cttee, 1987–90; Leader, 1990–94. PPS to Minister of State, DFEE, 1997–98, to Sec. of State for NI, 1998; Parly Under-Sec. of State, DSS, 1998–99; Minister of State (Minister for Pensions), DSS, 1999; Financial Sec., HM Treasury, 1999–2001. Mem., H of C Treasury Select Cttee, 1996–97; Mem. Council, 1996, Hon. Treas., 1997–98, Parly IT Cttee. Mem., Plaistow Christian Fellowship; Vice-Chm., Christian Socialist Movement, 1996–99. Mem., Ramblers' Assoc. Hon. Pres., Telecommunications Users' Assoc., 1995–99. *Publications:* Broadband Communications: the commercial impact, 1986; ISDN: customer premises equipment, 1988; Broadband Communications: market strategies, 1992. *Address:* House of Commons, SW1A 0AA. *T:* (020) 7219 4000; 94 Katherine Road, E6 1EN. *T:* (020) 8471 7090.

TIMMS, (Vera) Kate, (Mrs E. W. Gordon), CB 1999; Policy Director, Health and Safety Executive, since 2001; *b* 8 Oct. 1944; *d* of late Kenneth Timms and Elsie Timms (*née* Cussans); *m* 1977, Ernest William Gordon; one step *d*. *Educ:* Queen Anne Grammar School, York; St Hilda's College, Oxford (PPE hons). Economic Asst, NEDO, 1966–70; Ministry of Agriculture, Fisheries and Food, 1970; Asst Private Sec. to Minister of Agric., 1974–75; seconded to European Secretariat of Cabinet Office, 1976–79; Principal Private Sec. to Minister of Agric. 1980–82; Asst Sec. responsible for marketing policy, MAFF, 1982–84; Counsellor, Paris, seconded to HM Diplomatic Service, 1984–88; Asst Sec. and Head of Sugar and Oilseeds Div., MAFF, 1988–89; Under Sec., Arable Crops Gp, MAFF, 1989–90; Minister (Agriculture), Office of the UK Perm. Rep., Brussels, 1990–95; Principal Finance Officer, MAFF, 1995–96; Dep. Sec., Agriculture, Crops and Commodities, later Agriculture and Food Industry, MAFF, 1996–2001. Ordre du Mérite Agricole (France), 1988. *Address:* Holly House, 62A London Street, Swaffham, Norfolk PE37 7DJ. *T:* (01760) 723034; 42 The Foreshore, SE8 3AG. *T:* (020) 8691 0823.

TIMNEY, Jacqueline Jill; *see* Smith, J. J.

TIMPERLEY, Prof. Stuart Read; Chairman, Slatter Timperley Associates, since 1990; Senior Associate, Judge Institute, University of Cambridge, since 1998; Professor, Istituto Studi Direzionali, University of Milan, since 1998; *b* 30 July 1943; *s* of Kenneth Read Timperley and Florence Timperley (*née* Burgess); *m* 1967, Veronica Parke; two *d*. *Educ:* Birkenhead Sch.; Univ. of Strathclyde (BA 1967; MBA 1968); Univ. of London (BSc 1967); Univ. of Liverpool (Shell Mex Res. Fellow, 1968; PhD 1971). Lectr, Univ. of Liverpool, 1970–72; London Business School: Lectr, 1972–80; Sen. Lectr, 1980–89; Dir, Sloan Fellows Prog., 1976–80; Dir, Centre for Mgt Develt, 1984–91; Associate Prof., 1989–95. Vis. Prof., European Inst. for Advanced Studies in Mgt, Brussels, 1973–85. Chm., Freightliner Ltd, 1988–91 (Dir, 1979); Director: Jermyn Hldgs Ltd, 1978–80; Intasun Ltd, 1983–87; ILG Ltd, 1986–89; Communisis plc, 2000–; Pres., Consulteque. comS.p.A., 2000–. Chairman: Eastern Arts Bd, 1998–; English Regl Arts Bds, 2000–01. Chm., Watford FC, 1993–97 (Dir, 1990). Gov., London Business Sch., 1991–94. *Publications:* Personnel Planning and Occupational Choice, 1974; Humanisation of Work, 1982. *Recreations:* performing arts, football. *Address:* Slatter Timperley Associates, 50 Harley Street, W1N 1AD. *T:* (020) 7637 4499.

TIMPSON, John Harry Robert, OBE 1987; writer and broadcaster; *b* 2 July 1928; *s* of late John Hubert Victor Timpson and Caroline (*née* Willson); *m* 1951, (Muriel) Patricia Whale; two *s*. *Educ:* Merchant Taylors' Sch. National Service, RASC, 1946–49. Reporter: Wembley News, 1945–46 and 1949–51; Eastern Daily Press, 1951–59; BBC News Staff, 1959–87; BBC Dep. Court Correspondent, 1962–67 (reporting Australian, Ethiopian and other Royal tours); Presenter: Newsroom, BBC2, 1968–70; Tonight, BBC1, 1976–78; Today, BBC Radio 4, 1970–76, 1978–86; Chm., Any Questions, BBC Radio 4, 1984–87, Presenter, Timpson's Country Churches, ITV, 1995–98. Hon. MA UEA, 1991. Sony Gold Award for outstanding services to radio, 1986. *Publications:* Today and Yesterday (autobiog.), 1976; The Lighter Side of Today, 1983; The Early Morning Book, 1986; Timpson's England—A Look beyond the Obvious, 1987; Paper Trail (novel), 1989; Timpson's Towns, 1989; Timpson's Travels in East Anglia, 1990; Sound Track (novel), 1991; Timpson's English Eccentrics, 1991; Little Trains of Britain, 1992; Timpson's English Villages, 1992; Timpson's Other England, 1993; Timpson's Timepaths, 1994; Timpson's English Country Inns, 1995; Timpson's Book of Days, 1996; Timpson's Adaptables, 1997; Timpson's Country Churches, 1998; Timpson's Leylines, 2000; Timpson's Norfolk Notebook, 2001. *Recreation:* enjoying Norfolk. *Address:* Kennel House, The Green, Weasenham St Peter, King's Lynn, Norfolk PE32 2TD.

TIMS, Sir Michael (David), KCVO 1992 (CVO 1984; LVO 1973 MVO 1963); Serjeant-at-Arms to HM The Queen, 1987–92, retired; *b* 14 Sept. 1931; *s* of late William Edward Tims and Eva Ida Tims; *m* 1959, Jacqueline Lily Clark; one *s*. *Educ:* Christ's Hosp. Nat. Service Commn, ACC, 1950–52. The Queen's Household: Dep. Comptroller of Supply, 1953–68; Asst to the Master of the Household, 1968–92. Mem., Bd of Green Cloth, 1988–. FRSA 1992. JP Inner London, 1984–91. Freeman, City of London, 1986; Liveryman, Co. of Cooks, 1993–. Various hon. foreign awards. *Publications:* articles on fishing in national magazines. *Recreations:* battling with and painting big game fish. *Address:* Clock Tower House, The Royal Paddocks, Hampton Court Road, E Molesey, Surrey KT8 9DA.

TIMSON, Penelope Anne Constance; *see* Keith, P. A. C.

TINDALE, Gordon Anthony, OBE 1983; Director of Government and Public Affairs, WH Smith (USA) Inc., 1995–99; *b* 17 March 1938; *s* of George Augustus Tindale and Olive Sarah Collier; *m* 1960, Sonia Mary Soper; one *s* one *d*. *Educ:* Highgate Sch.; Trinity Coll., Oxford (BA (Mod. Hist)); Birkbeck Coll., London (MA (Int. Relations)). Nat. Service, 1956–58. Joined British Council, 1961; postings in Iraq, Jordan, London and Egypt; Representative: Lesotho, Botswana and Swaziland, 1975–78; Zambia, 1979–83; Controller, Management Div., 1984–87; Representative, Egypt, 1987–89; Cultural Counsellor (formerly Cultural Attaché), Washington, 1989–94. *Recreations:* music, golf. *Address:* 26 Oppidans Road, Primrose Hill, NW3 3AG. *T:* (020) 7722 9343. *Club:* Hendon Golf.

TINDALE, Patricia Randall; architect; Chief Architect, Department of the Environment, 1982–86; *b* 11 March 1926; *d* of Thomas John Tindale and May Tindale (*née* Uttin). *Educ:* Blatchington Court, Seaford, Sussex; Architectural Assoc. Sch. of Architecture (AADip.). ARIBA. Architect, Welsh Dept, Min. of Educn, 1949–50; Min. of Educn Develt Gp, 1951–60; Min. of Housing and Local Govt R&D Gp, 1960–70; DoE Housing Develt Gp, 1970–72; Head, Building Regulations Professional Div., DoE, 1972–74; Dir, Housing Develt Directorate, DoE, 1974–81; Dir, Central Unit of Built Environment, DoE, 1981–82. Member: Building Regulations Adv. Cttee, 1993; British Bd of Agrement, 1993–99; Anchor Housing Assoc., 1993–98. Mem., AA Council, 1965–68. *Publication:* Housebuilding in the USA, 1966. *Recreations:* weaving, travelling. *Club:* Reform.

TINDALL, Gillian Elizabeth, FRSL; novelist, biographer, historian; *b* 4 May 1938; *d* of D. H. Tindall and U. M. D. Orange; *m* 1963, Richard G. Lansdown; one *s. Educ:* Univ. of Oxford (BA 1st cl., MA). Freelance journalism: occasional articles and reviews for Observer, Guardian, London Evening Standard, The Times, Independent, Daily Telegraph and New York Times. Occasional broadcasts, BBC. JP (as Gillian Lansdown), Inner London, 1980–98. FRSA. Chevalier de l'Ordre des Arts et des Lettres (France), 2001. *Publications: novels:* No Name in the Street, 1959; The Water and the Sound, 1961; The Edge of the Paper, 1963; The Youngest, 1967; Someone Else, 1969, 2nd edn 1975; Fly Away Home, 1971 (Somerset Maugham Award, 1972); The Traveller and His Child, 1975; The Intruder, 1979; Looking Forward, 1983; To the City, 1987; Give Them All My Love, 1989; Spirit Weddings, 1992; *short stories:* Dances of Death, 1973; The China Egg and Other Stories, 1981; Journey of a Lifetime and Other Stories, 1990; *biography:* The Born Exile (George Gissing), 1974; *other non-fiction:* A Handbook on Witchcraft, 1965; The Fields Beneath, 1977; City of Gold: the biography of Bombay, 1981, 2nd edn 1992; Rosamond Lehmann: an Appreciation, 1985; (contrib.) Architecture of the British Empire, 1986; Countries of the Mind: the meaning of place to writers, 1991; Célestine: voices from a French village, 1995 (Franco-British Soc. Award, 1996); The Journey of Martin Nadaud, 1999. *Recreations:* keeping house, foreign travel. *Address:* c/o Curtis Brown Ltd, 28/29 Haymarket, SW1Y 4SP.

TINDALL, Prof. Victor Ronald, CBE 1992; MD; FRCS, FRCOG; Professor of Obstetrics and Gynaecology, University of Manchester at St Mary's Hospital, 1972–93, now Emeritus; *b* 1 Aug. 1928; *m* 1955, Brenda Fay; one *s* one *d. Educ:* Wallasey Grammar Sch.; Liverpool Univ. (MB ChB; MD); Manchester Univ. (MSc). Sen. Lectr and Consultant, Welsh Nat. Sch. of Medicine, Cardiff, 1965–70; Consultant Obstetrician and Gynaecologist, Univ. Hosp. of Wales, 1970–72. Sen. Vice-Pres., RCOG, 1990–93. FRCS by election, 1991. *Publications:* MCQ Tutor, MRCOG Part I, 1977, 2nd edn 1985, combined edn 1987; (jtly) Practical Student Obstetrics, 1980; Colour Atlas of Clinical Gynaecology, 1981; Essential Sciences for Clinicians, 1981; Clinical Gynaecology, 1986; (ed) Jeffcoates' Principles of Gynaecology, 5th edn 1987; Diagnostic Picture Tests in Obstetrics and Gynaecology, 1986; (ed jtly) Current Approaches to Endometrial Carcinoma, 1988; (jtly) Preparations and Advice for the Members of the Royal College of Obstetricians and Gynaecologists, 1989; Illustrated Textbook of Gynaecology, 1991; (ed jtly) Self Assessment Picture Tests: obstetrics and gynaecology, 1996; reports for DHSS on maternal deaths in the UK. *Recreations:* ex England Rugby international, international sporting activities. *Address:* 4 Planetree Road, Hale, Altrincham, Cheshire WA15 9JJ. *T:* (0161) 980 2680; (office) (0161) 904 8222.

TINDEMANS, Leo; Member (EPP) European Parliament, 1979–81, and 1989–99; Member (Christian Democratic Party), House of Representatives, Belgium, 1961–89; *b* Zwijndrecht, 16 April 1922; *m* 1960, Rosa Naesens; two *s* two *d. Educ:* State Univ., Ghent; Catholic Univ., Louvain. Minister: for Community Relations, 1968–71; of Agriculture and Middle Class Affairs, 1972–73; Dep. Prime Minister and Minister for the Budget, 1973–74; Prime Minister of Belgium, 1974–78; Minister of Foreign Relations, 1981–89. Mayor of Edegem, 1965–76. President: Christian Democratic Party, 1979–81; European People's Party, 1976–85; Gp of Eur. People's Party, EP, 1992–94. Prof., Faculty of Social Scis, Catholic Univ., Louvain, 1975–87, now Emeritus; first holder, Jacques Delors Chair, Maastricht, 1993. Pres., Internat. Commn on the Balkans, 1996–. Hon. DLitt: City Univ., 1976; Heriot-Watt Univ., 1978; Georgetown Univ., Washington, 1984; Univ. de Deusto, Bilbao, 1991. Charlemagne Prize, 1976; St Liborius Medaille für Einheit und Frieden, 1977; Stresemann Medaille, 1979; Schuman Prize, 1980; Médaille d'Or du Cercle Chateaubriand, 1992; Heinrich Brauns Prize, 1994. *Publications:* L'autonomie culturelle, 1971; Een handvest voor woelig België, 1972; Dagboek van de werkgroep Eyskens, 1973; European Union, 1975; Europe, Ideal of our Generation, 1976; Atlantisch Europa, 1981; Europa zonder Kompas, 1987; L'Europe de l'Est vue de Bruxelles, 1989; Duel met de Minister, 1991; De toekomst van een idee, 1993; Kaïn in de Balkan, 1996. *Recreations:* reading, writing, walking. *Address:* Jan Verbertlei 24, 2650 Edegem, Belgium.

TINDLE, David, RA 1979 (ARA 1973); painter; *b* 29 April 1932; *m* 1969, Janet Trollope (marr. diss. 1992); one *s* two *d. Educ:* Coventry Sch. of Art. MA Oxon 1985. Worked as scene painter and commercial artist, 1946–51; subseq. taught at Hornsey Coll. of Art; Vis. Tutor, Royal Coll. of Art, 1972–83, Fellow, 1981, Hon. FRCA, 1984; Ruskin Master of Drawing, Oxford Univ., and Professorial Fellow, St Edmund Hall, Oxford, 1985–87 (Hon. Fellow, 1988). RE, 1988–91. Hon. RBSA 1989. First showed work, Archer Gall., 1952 and 1953; regular one-man exhibns, Piccadilly Gall., from 1954; one-man exhibns at many public and private galleries in Gt Britain incl. Fischer Fine Art, 1985, 1989, 1992; Redfern Gall., London, 1994, 1996, 1998, 2000, 2001; Galerie du Tours, San Francisco and Los Angeles, 1964; Gallerie Vinciana, Milan, 1968; Galleria Carbonesi, Bologna, 1968; Gallery XX, Hamburg, 1974, 1977, 1980; rep. in exhibns at: Piccadilly Gall., 1954–; Royal Acad.; Internat. Biennale of Realist Art, Bruges, 1958 and Bologna, 1967; British Exhibn Art, Basel, 1958; John Moores, 1959 and 1961; Arts Council Shows: British Self-Portraits; Painters in East Anglia; Thames in Art; The British Art Show, 1979–80; Salon de la Jeune Peinture, Paris, 1967; Mostra Mercato d'Arte Contemporanea, Florence, 1967; British Painting 1974, Hayward Gall.; British Painting 1952–77, RA; Six English Painters—Eros in Albion, Arezzo, Italy, 1989; Portrait of the Artist, Tate Gall., 1989. Set of 3 Mural decorations for Open Univ., Milton Keynes, 1977–78. Designed sets for Iolanta, Aldeburgh Fest., 1988. Work rep. in numerous public and private collections, incl. Nat. Portrait Gall.; Chantrey Bequest purchases, 1974 and 1975, now in Tate Gall. Critic Prize, 1962; Europe Prize for Painting, 1969; Critics' Choice, Tooths, 1974; Waddington Prize, Chichester Nat. Art Exhibn, 1975; Johnson Wax Award, RA, 1983. *Address:* Redfern Gallery, 20 Cork Street, W1X 2HL; Via Giovanni Pacchini 118B, S. Maria del Giudice, 55058 Lucca, Italy.

TINDLE, Sir Ray (Stanley), Kt 1994; CBE 1987 (OBE 1973); DL; Chairman: Tindle Newspapers Ltd, since 1972; Tindle Radio Ltd, since 1998; *b* 8 Oct. 1926; *s* of late John Robert Tindle and Maud Tindle; *m* 1949, Beryl Julia (*née* Ellis), MA, DipEd; one *s. Educ:* Torquay Grammar Sch.; Strand Sch. FCIS; FCIArb. War service, Devonshire Regt (Captain), 1944–47. Asst to Dir, Newspaper Soc., 1952–58; Managing Director: Surrey Mirror Newspapers, 1959–63; Surrey Advertiser Newspapers, 1963–78 (Chm., 1978–97). Pres., Newspaper Soc., 1971–72; Vice Pres. and Chm. of Appeal, Newspaper Press Fund, 1990; Member: Newspaper Panel, Monopolies and Mergers Commn, 1987–93; Council, CPU, 1987–; Press Bd of Finance, 1990–. Founder, Tindle Enterprise Centres for the Unemployed, 1984–. Master, Stationers' and Newspaper Makers' Co., 1985–86. DL Surrey, 1989. Hon. DLitt Buckingham, 1999. *Publication:* The Press Today and Tomorrow, 1975. *Recreations:* veteran cars, newspapers, boating. *Address:* 114 West Street, Farnham, Surrey GU9 7HL. *Clubs:* Royal Automobile, Veteran Car, City Livery Yacht.

TING, Prof. Samuel Chao Chung; Thomas D. Cabot Institute Professor, Massachusetts Institute of Technology, since 1977; *b* 27 Jan. 1936; *s* of K. H. Ting and late T. S. Wang; *m*; two *d*; *m* 1985, Susan Carol Marks; one *s. Educ:* Univ. of Michigan (PhD). Ford Fellow, CERN, Geneva, 1963; Asst Prof. of Physics, Columbia Univ., 1965; Prof. of Physics, MIT, 1969–. Assoc. Editor, Nuclear Physics B, 1970; Mem. Editorial Board: Nuclear Instruments and Methods, 1977; Mathematical Modeling, 1980. Hon. Professor: Beijing Normal Coll., 1984; Jiatong Univ., Shanghai, 1987. Member: US Nat. Acad. of Science, 1976; European Physical Soc.; Italian Physical Soc.; Foreign Member: Pakistan Acad. of Science, 1984; Academia Sinica (Republic of China), 1975; Soviet Acad. of Science, 1988; Russian Acad. of Sci.; Hungarian Acad. of Sci.; Deutsche Akad. Naturforscher Leopoldina. Fellow, Amer. Acad. of Arts and Science, 1975. Hon. ScD: Michigan, 1978; Chinese Univ. of Hong Kong, 1987; Bologna, 1988; Columbia, 1990; Univ. of Sci. and Technol. of China, 1990; Moscow State Univ., 1991; Bucharest, 1993. Nobel Prize for Physics (jt), 1976; Ernest Orlando Lawrence Award, US Govt, 1976; A. E. Eringen Medal, Soc. of Engineering Science, USA, 1977; Gold Medal in Science, City of Brescia, Italy, 1988; De Gasperi Prize, Italian Republic, 1988; Forum Engelberg Prize, 1996. *Publications:* articles in Physical Review and Physical Review Letters. *Address:* Department of Physics, Massachusetts Institute of Technology, 51 Vassar Street, Cambridge, MA 02139–4308, USA. *Club:* Explorers' (NY).

TINKER, Prof. Anthea Margaret, CBE 2000; PhD; AcSS; Professor of Social Gerontology, since 1988, Director, Age Concern Institute of Gerontology, 1988–98, King's College London; *b* 24 Oct. 1932; *d* of Lt-Comdr James Collins and Margaret Collins (*née* Herring); *m* 1956, Rev. Preb. Dr Eric Tinker, OBE; two *s* one *d. Educ:* Univ. of Birmingham (BCom Econs, Pol., Sociol. 1953); City Univ. (PhD 1976). Asst Buyer, then Buyer, Boxfoldia Ltd, 1953–54; Res. Officer, BoT, 1954; HM Insp. of Factories, Min. of Labour, 1954–58; (pt-time) Res. Asst to Dir, Inst. of Local Govt Studies, and Lectr in Public Admin, Univ. of Birmingham, 1958–65; (pt-time) Lectr in Public Admin, Birmingham Sch. of Planning, 1958–65; (pt-time) Lectr in Social Policy, Extra-Mural Dept, Univ. of London, 1965–75; engaged in res., Royal Commn on Local Govt, 1967; Res. Fellow, City Univ., 1975–77; Sen., then Principal Res. Officer, DoE, 1977–88. Consultant: OECD, 1989–90; EU, 1991–. Exec. Mem., British Soc. of Gerontology, 1987–93; Member: Cttee on Ageing, C of E Bd of Social Responsibility, 1988–89; Cttee on Long Term Care, Joseph Rowntree Foundn, 1995–96. Gov., Centre for Policy on Ageing, 1988–94. FRSocMed 1995 (Pres., Sect. of Geriatrics and Gerontology, 1998–2000); FKC 1998; Founder AcSS 1999. *Publications:* The Elderly in Modern Society, 1981, 4th edn as Older People in Modern Society, 1997; Staying at Home: helping elderly people, 1984; The Telecommunication Needs of Disabled and Elderly People, 1989; An Evaluation of Very Sheltered Housing, 1989; *jointly:* Women in Housing: access and influence, 1980; Families in Flats, 1981; A Review of Research on Falls among Elderly People, 1990; Falls and Elderly People: a study of current professional practice in England and innovations abroad, 1991; Life After Sixty: a profile of Britain's older population, 1992; Caring: the importance of third age carers, 1992; Homes and Travel: local life in the third age, 1992; The Information Needs of Elderly People, 1993; The Care of Frail Elderly People in the UK, 1994; Difficult to Let Sheltered Housing, 1995; Alternative Models of Care for Older People, Research Vol. 2, Royal Commn on Long Term Care, 1999; Home Ownership in Old Age, 1999; To Have and to Hold: the bond between older people and the homes they own, 1999; Eighty-five Not Out, 2001; pamphlets and booklets; contrib. to learned and other jls. *Recreations:* family, France, houses. *Address:* 35 Theberton Street, N1 0QY. *T:* (020) 7359 4750.

TINKER, Dr Jack; FRCP, FRCSGlas; Emeritus Consultant, University College Hospitals, since 1996; Dean, Royal Society of Medicine, since 1998; *b* 20 Jan. 1936; *s* of Lawrence and Jessie Tinker; *m* 1961, Maureen Ann Crawford; two *s. Educ:* Manchester Univ. (BSc (Hons), MB ChB); DIC. Dir, Intensive Therapy Unit, Middlesex Hosp., 1974–88; Hon. Cons. Physician, Middlesex Hosp., 1988–96; Hon. Sen. Clin. Lectr, UCL Med. Sch. (formerly UCMSM), 1988–96; Hon. Sen. Lectr, St Bartholomew's Hosp. Med. Coll., 1991–96; Dean of Postgrad. Medicine, Univ. of London and N Thames RHA, 1988–96. Sen. Med. Consultant, Sun Life of Canada, 1983–2000; Med. Advr, Rio Tinto plc (formerly RTZ Gp), 1986–; Med. Dir, Health Screening Unit, London Clinic, 1994–. FRSocMed 1989 (Hon. Sub-Dean, 1996–98). FRSA 1997. Editor in Chief, British Jl of Hospital Medicine, 1985–; Man. Editor, Intensive Care Medicine, 1973–88. *Publications:* A Course in Intensive Therapy Nursing, 1980; Care of the Critically Ill Patient, 1982, 2nd edn 1991; A Pocket Book for Intensive Care, 1986, 2nd edn 1990; Critical Care, Standards, Audit and Ethics, 1996; contribs to intensive care and cardiological jls. *Recreations:* road running, cricket. *Address:* 1 Rectory Road, Barnes, SW13 0DU. *T:* (020) 8878 0159. *Clubs:* Royal Automobile, MCC; Scarborough.

TINKER, Dr Philip Bernard Hague, OBE 2000; FIBiol, FRSC; Director of Terrestrial and Freshwater Science, Natural Environment Research Council, 1985–92; *b* 1 Feb. 1930; *s* of Philip and Gertrude Tinker; *m* 1955, Maureen Ellis; one *s* one *d. Educ:* Rochdale High Sch.; Sheffield Univ. (BSc); PhD 1955; MA, DSc 1984, Oxon. FIBiol 1974; FRSC 1985. Overseas Res. Service, 1955–62; Sen. Scientific Officer, Rothamsted Experimental Stn, 1962–65; Lectr, Oxford Univ., 1965–71; Prof. of Agricultural Botany, Leeds Univ., 1971–77; Head of Soils Div., 1977–85, and Dep. Dir, 1981–85, Rothamsted Experimental Stn; Fellow, 1969–72, Sen. Res. Fellow, 1988–96, St Cross Coll., Oxford. Hon. Vis. Prof., Imperial Coll., 1992–95; Sen. Vis. Fellow, Plant Scis Dept, Oxford Univ., 1995–. Lectures: Regents, Univ. of California, 1979; Hannaford Meml, Adelaide, 1990; Francis New Meml and Medal, Fertilizer Soc., 1991. Chairman: UK Man and Biosphere Cttee, 1990–93; UK Cttee for Internat. Geosphere-Biosphere Prog., 1992–98; Biology Cttee, Palm Oil Res. Inst., Malaysia, 1995–98 (Mem., 1987–98). Member: UNESCO Adv. Cttee for Biosphere Reserves, 1992–96; IGBP Scientific Cttee, 1992–98. Pres., British Soil Sci. Soc., 1983–84; Gov., Macaulay Land Use Res. Inst., Aberdeen, 1990–2001. Fellow, Norwegian Acad. of Science and Letters, 1987; Hon. FRASE, 1990. Busk Medal, RGS, 1994. *Publications:* (with F. E. Sanders and B. Mosse) Endomycorrhizas, 1975; (with P. H. Nye) Solute Movement in the Soil-root System, 1977; Soil and Agriculture—Critical Reviews, 1980; (with L. Fowden and R. M. Barrer) Clay Minerals, 1984; (with A. Läuchli) Advances in Plant Nutrition, vol. I, 1984, vol. II, 1986, vol. III, 1988; (with P. H. Nye) Solute Movement in the Rhizosphere, 2000; Shades of Green: a review of UK farming systems, 2000; *c* 175 papers. *Recreations:* reading, gardening, map collecting. *Address:* The Glebe House, Broadwell, Lechlade, Glos GL7 3QS. *T:* (01367) 860436. *Club:* Farmers'.

TINNISWOOD, Maurice Owen; *b* 26 March 1919; *y s* of late Robert Tinniswood, OBE; *m* 1946, Anne Katharine, *yr d* of late Rev. J. Trevor Matchett; one *s* one *d. Educ:* Merchant Taylors' School. Served with Royal Hampshire Regt, 1939–46 (Major). Joined PO, 1938 as Executive Officer, Principal, 1949; Asst Secretary, 1958; Imperial Defence College, 1963; Director of Establishments and Organisation, 1965; Director of Reorganization, 1966; Secretary to the Post Office, 1969–70; Dir of Personnel, BBC, 1970–77. Chm., Kingston, Richmond and Esher Community Health Council, 1980–81; Mem., Kingston and Esher HA, 1982–85. CIMgt. *Address:* Little Croft, Weston Green Road, Thames Ditton, Surrey KT7 0HY. *T:* (020) 8398 4561.

See also P. M. Tinniswood.

TINNISWOOD, Peter Maurice; Head Master, Lancing College, since 1998; *b* 30 May 1951; *s* of Maurice Owen Tinniswood, *qv*; *m* 1975, Catharina Elizabeth Oeschger. *Educ:*

Charterhouse; Magdalen Coll., Oxford (MA); INSEAD (MBA 1981). Assistant Master: Repton Sch., 1974–76; Marlborough Coll., 1976–80; Sec. Gen., Franco-British Chamber of Commerce and Industry, Paris, 1981–83; Marlborough College: Asst Master, 1983–91; Head of Dept, 1983–86; Housemaster, 1985–91; Master, Magdalen Coll. Sch., Oxford, 1991–98. *Publications:* Marketing Decisions, 1981; Marketing and Production Decisions, 1991. *Address:* The Old Farmhouse, Lancing College, West Sussex BN15 0RN.

TINSON, Dame Susan (Myfanwy), DBE 1990; Associate Editor, Independent Television News, since 1989; *b* 15 Jan. 1943; *d* of John and Kathleen Thomas; *m* 1968, Trevor James Tinson (marr. diss. 1979). *Educ:* South Hampstead High Sch.; Hull Univ. (BA Hons Social Studies). Independent Television News: trainee, 1964; Chief Sub Editor, News at Ten, 1975; Senior Editor, News at Ten and Asst Editor, ITN, 1982; Head of Special Events, ITN, 1989–. Non-executive Director: Freeserve plc, 1999–; Yorkshire Building Soc., 1999–. Comr, Commonwealth War Graves Commn, 1999–. Trustee, Nat. Heritage Meml Fund, 1995–. FRTS 1996. *Address:* c/o ITN, 200 Gray's Inn Road, WC1X 8XZ. *T:* (020) 7430 4546.

TINSTON, Robert Sydney, CBE 2001; Regional Director, NHS Executive North West, since 1996; *b* 29 March 1951; *s* of Sydney Tinston and Rita (*née* Jardine); *m* 1975, Catherine Mary Somers; one *s* one *d*. *Educ:* Stockport Sch.; Edinburgh Univ. (BSc). DipHSM 1979; MHSM 1979. Assistant Sector Administrator: Withington Hosp., Manchester, 1976–78; King's Coll. Hosp., London, 1978–79; Hosp. Sec., Cookridge Hosp., Leeds, 1979–83; Commissioning Officer, Clarendon Wing, Leeds, 1983–86; Gen. Manager, Leeds General Infirmary, 1986–89; Chief Exec., Royal Liverpool Hosp., 1989–91; Dep. Chief Exec., then Chief Exec., Mersey RHA, 1991–94; Chief Exec., NW RHA, 1994–96. FRSA 1994. Hon. Vis. Prof., Univ. of Manchester, 1996–. CIMgt 1997. *Recreations:* astronomy, genealogy, Stockport County Football Club. *Address:* The Thatched Cottage, Utkinton, Tarporley, Cheshire CW6 0LL.

TIPLER, Laura; *see* Drysdale, L.

TIPPET, Vice-Adm. Sir Anthony (Sanders), KCB 1984; Chairman, Bradford Education Policy Partnership, since 2001; *b* 2 Oct. 1928; *s* of W. K. R. Tippet and H. W. P. Kitley (*née* Sanders); *m* 1950, Lola Bassett; two *s* one *d* (and one *s* decd). *Educ:* West Buckland Sch., Devon. Called to the Bar, Gray's Inn, 1959. Entered RN, 1946; Lieut 1950; HM Ships Ceres, Superb, Staff C-in-C Mediterranean; Lt Comdr 1958; HMS Trafalgar, Britannia RNC; Comdr 1963; Secretary: to Director of Naval Intelligence; to Flag Officer Middle East; CO HMS Jufair, Supply Officer, HMS Eagle; Captain 1970: Asst Director Naval Plans (Warfare), 1970–72; CSO (Administration) to Flag Officer Plymouth, 1972–74; Director of Naval Officers' Appointments (Supply and WRNS Officers), 1974–76; Captain HMS Pembroke and Flag Captain to Flag Officer Medway, 1976–79; Rear-Adm. 1979; Asst Chief of Fleet Support, MoD, 1979–81; Flag Officer and Port Admiral, Portsmouth, and Chief Naval Supply and Secretariat Officer, 1981–83; Chief of Fleet Support and Mem., Admiralty Bd, 1983–86. Gen. Manager, Hospitals for Sick Children, London, 1987–94; Chief Exec., Gt Ormond Street Hosp. for Children NHS Trust, 1994–95. Chm., Funding Agency for Schs, 1997–99. Chairman: RN Benevolent Soc. for Officers, 1995–98; Children in Hospital, 1990–98; Write Away, 1990–97; Nat. Appeal for Music Therapy, 1995–97; Halifax Educn Action Zone, 1998–. Trustee, Sea Cadet Assoc., 1999–. Pres., West Buckland Sch., 2000– (Gov., 1979–2001; Chm., 1989–96). CIMgt. Hon. Fellow, Inst. of Child Health, 1995; Hon. Fellow, S Bank Univ., 1995. *Recreations:* sailing, hill walking. *Clubs:* Royal Naval Sailing Association; Anchorites.

TIPPETTS, Rutherford Berriman; *b* 8 Feb. 1913; *s* of late Percy William Berriman Tippetts and Katherine Brown Rutherford; *m* 1948, Audrey Helen Wilson Cameron; one *s* one *d*. *Educ:* Rugby; Trinity Coll., Oxford (MA). Asst Principal, BoT, 1936; Principal Private Sec. to Ministers of Supply and Presidents of BoT, 1941–45; idc 1954; Chief Exec., Dollar Exports Council, 1959–61; served in Commercial Relations and Exports, Industry and Tourism Divs of BoT; Under-Sec., Export Services Div., DTI, 1970–73. Mem., Council, CGLI. Master, Worshipful Co. of Armourers and Brasiers, 1975–76. *Address:* 74 Ebury Mews East, SW1W 9QA. *T:* (020) 7730 6464; Linden Lodge, Linden Hill Lane, Kiln Green, Berks RG10 9XP. *T:* (0118) 4091621. *Clubs:* Carlton, Royal Wimbledon.

TIPPING, Rt Hon. Andrew (Patrick Charles), PC 1998; **Rt Hon. Justice Tipping;** a Judge of the Court of Appeal, New Zealand, since 1997; *b* 22 Aug. 1942; *s* of Wing Comdr Patrick Alexander Tipping, RAF retd and Elizabeth Ayliffe Tipping; *m* 1967, Judith Ann Oliver; two *s* one *d*. *Educ:* Christ's Coll., Christchurch; Univ. of Canterbury (BA, LLB 1965; LLM 1st Cl. Hons 1966). Canterbury Dist Law Soc. Gold Medal, 1966; Sir Timothy Cleary Meml Prize, NZ Law Soc., 1967. Partner, Wynn Williams & Co., Barristers and Solicitors, 1967–86; Judge, High Court of NZ, 1986–97. Member of Council: Canterbury Dist Law Soc., 1976–84 (Pres., 1984); NZ Law Soc., 1982–84 (Mem., 1979–86, Chm., 1985–86, Courts and Tribunals Cttee). *Recreations:* gardening, fishing, tramping. *Address:* 14 Cluny Avenue, Kelburn, Wellington 5, New Zealand. *T:* (4) 4753755. *Clubs:* Christchurch (Christchurch); Wellington (Wellington).

TIPPING, Sir David Gwynne E.; *see* Evans-Tipping.

TIPPING, Simon Patrick, (Paddy); MP (Lab) Sherwood, since 1992; *b* 24 Oct. 1949; *m* 1970, Irene Margaret Quinn; two *d*. *Educ:* Hipperholme Grammar Sch.; Nottingham Univ. (BA 1972; MA 1978). Social Worker, Notts, 1972–79; Project Leader, C of E Children's Soc., Nottingham, 1979–83. Mem. (Lab) Notts CC, 1981–93 (Chm., Economic Develt and Finance Cttees); Director: Notts Co-op. Develt Agency, 1983–92; Nottingham Develt Enterprise, 1987–93. Contested (Lab) Rushcliffe, 1987. *Recreations:* running, walking, gardening. *Address:* House of Commons, SW1A 0AA.

TIPPLER, John; Director, Network, British Telecom, UK Communications Division, 1986–89, retired; *b* 9 Aug. 1929; *s* of George Herbert and Sarah Tippler, Spalding, Lincs; *m* 1st, 1952, Pauline Taylor (marr. diss. 1983); two *s*; 2nd, 1992, Martha Elisabet Berg, psychoanalyst, Stockholm. *Educ:* Spalding Grammar School. Architect's Dept, Spalding RDC, 1945; Post Office Telephone Service, 1947; Royal Signals, 1949–50; Staff Mem., PO Central Engineering Sch., 1954–59; PO Engineering Develt, 1960–80; Dir, Exchange and Data Systems Op. and Develt, 1980; Dir of Engrg, BT, 1982–86. Dir, IT Inst., 1986–88. *Recreations:* music, country walking, travel, cinema, theatre, support to Birzeit Univ. *Address:* 44 Pinchbeck Road, Spalding, Lincs PE11 1QF.

TIRVENGADUM, Sir Harry (Krishnan), Kt 1987; Chevalier, Ordre National de la Légion d'Honneur 1986; Chairman and Managing Director, Air Mauritius, since 1981; Managing Director, Air Afrique, since 1997; *b* 2 Sept. 1933; *s* of late Govinden Tirvengadum and Meenatchee Sangeelee; *m* 1970, Elahe Amin Amin; three *d*. *Educ:* Royal College, Mauritius; Oxford Univ. Asst Sec., Min. of Works, 1952–67; Principal Assistant Secretary: Min. of Communications, in charge of Depts of Civil Aviation, Telecommunications, Marine Services, Posts & Telegraphs and Meteorological Services, 1968–72; Min. of Commerce and Industry, 1970; Air Mauritius: Gen. Manager, 1972–78; Dep. Chm. and Dep. Man. Dir, 1978–81. Chairman: Rodrigues Hotel, 1981–; New Airport Catering Services, 1988–; Mauritius Shopping Paradise Ltd, 1984–93; Director: Mauritius Hotels Gp, 1973–81; Plaisance Airlift Catering Unit, 1980–92; Mauritius Telecom, 1984–; Mauritius Estate Development & Co., 1986–; Mauritius Commercial Bank, 1989–; State Bank Internat., 1990–. Chm., Municipal Commn, Quatre-Bornes, 1974–77. Chief delegate of Mauritius, Triennial Assemblies, ICAO, 1971–; Rep. of Employers on Employment of Disabled Persons Bd, 1988–. Member: Exec. Cttee, IATA, 1988–91 (Chm., 1992–93); Nat. Educn Award Panel, 1988. Pres., African Airlines Assoc., 1995–96. FCIT; FInstD. Citoyen d'Honneur, Town of Beau Bassin/Rose Hill, Mauritius, 1986. Chevalier, Légion d'Honneur (France), 1986. *Recreations:* bridge, swimming, walking. *Address:* Dr Arthur De Chazal Lane, Floréal, Mauritius. *T:* 6966003. *Club:* Mauritius Gymkhana.

TISHLER, Gillian, (Mrs Richard Wood); Chief Executive, Young Women's Christian Association of Great Britain, since 1993; *b* 27 March 1958; *d* of Harry and Joyce Tishler; *m* 1991, Richard Wood. *Educ:* King Edward VI Sch., Morpeth; St Anne's Coll., Oxford (BA Hons Mod. Langs). Ministry of Agriculture, Fisheries and Food: fast stream trainee, 1979; Private Office (Private Sec. to Parly Sec.), 1986–87; Royal National Institute for the Blind: Parly Officer, 1987–89; Head of Public Affairs, 1989–93. *Recreations:* theatre, singing, walking. *Address:* Young Women's Christian Association of Great Britain, Clarendon House, 52 Cornmarket Street, Oxford OX1 3EJ. *T:* (01865) 304209.

TITCHENER, Alan Ronald, CB 1993; Managing Director, Resource (Science and Technology Expertise) Ltd, 1993–96; *b* 18 June 1934; *s* of Edmund Hickman Ronald Titchener and Minnie Ellen Titchener; *m* 1959, Joyce Blakesley; two *s*. *Educ:* Harrow County Grammar Sch.; London School of Economics. BSc(Econ) 1962. RAF, 1952. Colonial Office, 1954; Min. of Transport, 1962; Board of Trade, 1964; HM Consul New York, 1969; Dept of Trade, 1973; HM Consul-Gen., Johannesburg, 1978; Under Secretary, Department of Trade and Industry, 1982–93: Overseas Trade Div., 1982; Enterprise Initiative Div., 1987; Head of Personnel, 1991. FRSA 1993. *Club:* Royal Air Force.

TITCHMARSH, Alan Fred, MBE 2000; DL; writer and broadcaster; *b* 2 May 1949; *s* of Alan Titchmarsh and Bessie Titchmarsh (*née* Hardisty); *m* 1975, Alison Margaret Needs; two *d*. *Educ:* Ilkley County Secondary Sch.; Shipley Art and Tech. Inst.; Herts Coll. of Agric. and Hortic. (Nat. Cert. Hort.); Royal Botanic Gardens, Kew (DipHort). FIHort 1998. Apprentice gardener, Parks Dept, Ilkley UDC, 1964–68; Supervisor, Staff Trng, Royal Botanic Gardens, 1972–74; Asst Editor, gardening books, Hamlyn Publishing, 1974–76; Asst Editor and Dep. Editor, Amateur Gardening, 1976–79; freelance writer and broadcaster, 1979–; gardening correspondent: Woman's Own, 1980–85; Daily Mail, 1985–99; Daily Express, and Sunday Express, 1999–; Radio Times, 1996–2001; gardening editor, Homes & Gardens, 1985–89; contrib. to BBC Gardeners' World Magazine, 1992–. *BBC radio series include:* You and Yours, Down to Earth, A House in a Garden, Alan Titchmarsh Show; numerous other progs; *BBC TV:* Nationwide, Breakfast Time, Open Air, Daytime Live; Chelsea Flower Show, 1983–97, 2001–; Songs of Praise, 1989–94; Pebble Mill, 1991–96; Sweet Inspiration, 1993–94; Gardeners' World, 1995–; Ground Force, 1997–; How to be a Gardener, 2002–. Founder, Alan Titchmarsh's Gardens for Schools, 2001–. Vice-President: Wessex Cancer Trust, 1988–; Butterfly Conservation, 2000–; Arboricultural Assoc., 2000–; Patron: Rainbow Trust, 1993–; Kaleidoscope Theatre, 1995–; Cowes Inshore Lifeboat, 2000–; Vice Patron, Jubilee Sailing Trust, 2000–; President: Gardening for Disabled Trust, 1989–; Telephones for the Blind, 1993–; London Children's Flower Soc., 2001–. Mem., Consultative Cttee, Nat. Pinetum, 1996–. Freeman, City of London; Liveryman, Gardeners' Co. DL Hants, 2001. Hon. FCGI 2000. Hon. DSc Bradford, 1999; DUniv Essex, 1999. Gardening Writer of the Year, 1980, 1983; RHS Gold Medal, Chelsea Flower Show, 1985; Television Broadcaster of the Year, Garden Writer's Guild, 1997, 1998, 1999, 2000; Yorks Man of the Year, 1997. *Publications:* Starting With House Plants, 1976; Gardening Under Cover, 1979, 2nd edn 1985; Guide to Greenhouse Gardening, 1980; Climbers and Wall Plants, 1980; Everyone's Book of House Plants, 1981; (with R. C. M. Wright) Complete Book of Plant Propagation, 1981; Gardening Techniques, 1981; Pocket Indoor Gardener, 1982; Hamlyn Guide to House Plants, 1982; Pest-Free Plants, 1982; The Allotment Gardener's Handbook, 1982, 2nd edn 1993; The Rock Gardener's Handbook, 1983; How to be a Supergardener, 1983, 3rd edn 1999; (ed) 1,000 Handy Gardening Hints, 1983; Alan Titchmarsh's Avant Gardening, 1984, 2nd edn 1994; Alan Titchmarsh's Gardening Guides, 1984; The Gardener's Logbook, 1985; (ed) A–Z of Popular Garden Plants, 1985; Pocket Guide to Gardening, 1987; (cons. ed.) All Your Gardening Questions Answered, 1988; Daytime Live Gardening Book, 1990; The English River, 1993; Alan Titchmarsh's Favourite Gardens, 1995; Mr MacGregor (novel), 1998; (cons. ed) Ground Force Weekend Workbook, 1999; Gardeners' World Complete Book of Gardening, 1999; The Last Lighthouse Keeper (novel), 1999; Animal Instincts (novel), 2000; Only Dad (novel), 2001; How to be a Gardener, 2001. *Recreation:* boating. *Address:* c/o Arlington Enterprises, 1–3 Charlotte Street, W1P 1HD. *T:* (020) 7580 0702. *Clubs:* Lord's Taverners; Royal London Yacht (Cowes).

TITCHMARSH, Prof. John, DPhil; Royal Academy of Engineering/AEA Technology/INSS Research Professor in Microanalytical Techniques for Structural Integrity Problems, University of Oxford, since 1998; Fellow, St Anne's College, Oxford, since 1998. *Educ:* Christ's Coll., Cambridge (BA Nat. Sci. 1966; MA 1970); Wadham Coll., Oxford (DPhil 1969). Res. Asst, Univ. of Oxford, 1969–73; UKAEA, 1975–94; Philips Prof. in Materials Analysis, Sheffield Hallam Univ., 1994–98. Member of Committee: Inst. of Physics; RMS. Birks Award, Microbeam Analysis Soc., USA, 1995. *Publications:* papers in learned jls on electron microscopy. *Address:* St Anne's College, Oxford OX2 6JF.

TITE, Prof. Michael Stanley, DPhil; FSA; Edward Hall Professor of Archaeological Science, Director of Research Laboratory for Archaeology and History of Art, and Fellow of Linacre College, University of Oxford, since 1989; *b* 9 Nov. 1938; *s* of late Arthur Robert Tite and Evelyn Frances Violet Tite (*née* Endersby); *m* 1967, Virginia Byng Noel; two *d*. *Educ:* Trinity Sch. of John Whitgift, Croydon; Christ Church, Oxford (MA, DPhil). FSA 1977. Research Fellow in Ceramics, Univ. of Leeds, 1964–67; Lectr in Physics, Univ. of Essex, 1967–75; Keeper, Dept of Scientific Res. (formerly Res. Lab.), British Museum, 1975–89. *Publications:* Methods of Physical Examination in Archaeology, 1972; papers on scientific methods applied to archaeology in various jls. *Recreations:* travelling with "The Buildings of England", gardening. *Address:* 7 Kings Cross Road, Oxford OX2 7EU. *T:* (01865) 558422; Research Laboratory for Archaeology and History of Art, 6 Keble Road, Oxford OX1 3QJ.

TITFORD, Jeffrey William; Member (UK Ind) Eastern Region, England, European Parliament, since 1999; *b* 24 Oct. 1933; *s* of Guy Frederick Titford and Queta Mehalah (*née* D'Wit); *m* 1956, Margaret Cheeld; one *s* three *d*. *Educ:* state schools, Essex. Dip. Funeral Directing. With family funeral dirs, Titford Funeral Service Ltd, 1954–89, Man. Dir, 1970–89. Pres., Nat. Assoc. Funeral Dirs, 1975–76. Ldr, UK Independence Party,

2000. Contested (Referendum) Harwich, 1997. *Recreations:* fishing, walking, golf. *Address:* St Beda, Second Avenue, Frinton-on-Sea, Essex CO13 9LY. *T:* (01255) 676577. *Clubs:* East India; Frinton Golf.

TITHERIDGE, Roger Noel; QC 1973; a Recorder of the Crown Court 1972–99; Barrister-at-Law; *b* 21 Dec. 1928; *s* of Jack George Ralph Titheridge and Mabel Titheridge (*née* Steains); *m* 1963, Annabel Maureen (*née* Scott-Fisher); two *d. Educ:* Midhurst Grammar Sch.; Merton Coll., Oxford (Exhibnr). MA (History and Jurisprudence). Called to the Bar, Gray's Inn, 1954; Holker Sen. Scholar, Gray's Inn, 1954; Bencher, Gray's Inn, 1985; Dep. High Court Judge, QBD, 1984–98; Leader, Western Circuit, 1989–92. *Recreations:* tennis, sailing. *Address:* 1 Paper Buildings, Temple, EC4Y 7EP. *T:* (020) 7353 3728; 13 The Moat, Traps Lane, New Malden, Surrey KT3 4SB. *T:* (020) 8942 2747.

TITLEY, Gary; Member (Lab) North West Region, England, European Parliament, since 1999 (Greater Manchester West, 1989–99); *b* 19 Jan. 1950; *s* of Wilfred James and Joyce Lillian Titley; *m* 1975, Maria, (Charo), Rosario; one *s* one *d. Educ:* York Univ. (BA Hons Hist./Educn, 1973; PGCE 1974). TEFL, Bilbao, 1973–75; taught History, Earls High Sch., Halesowen, 1976–84; Personal Assistant to MEP, 1984–89. Mem., W Midlands CC, 1981–86 (Vice-Chair: EDC, 1981–84; Consumer Services Cttee, 1984–86). Dir, W Midlands Enterprise Bd, 1982–89; Chairman: W Midlands Co-op Finance Co., 1982–89; Black Country Co-op Develt Agency, 1982–88. Contested (Lab): Bromsgrove, 1983; Dudley W, 1987. Pres., Eur. Parlt delegn for relations with Finland, 1992–94; rapporteur, accession of Finland to EU. President: European Economic Area Jt Parly Assembly, 1994–95; Jt Parly Cttee for relns with Lithuania. Commander, White Rose (Finland), 1995; Golden Cross (Austria), 1996. *Recreations:* family, reading, sport. *Address:* (office) 16 Spring Lane, Radcliffe, Manchester M26 2TQ. *T:* (0161) 724 4008. *Club:* Little Lever (Bolton).

TITLEY, Commandant Nursing Officer Jane, CBE 1995; RRC 1990 (ARRC 1986); Director of Defence Nursing Services, 1992–95; *b* 22 April 1940; *d* of Louis and Phyllis Myra (Josephine) Titley. *Educ:* St Catherine's Convent, Nottingham; St Bartholomew's Hosp.; Sussex Maternity Hosp. SRN 1962; SCM 1963. Joined QARNNS, 1965; served in Naval hosps and estabts in UK, Malta, Singapore, Naples and Gibraltar; Matron, 1986; Dep. Matron-in-Chief, 1988; Matron-in-Chief, 1990–94; QHNS, 1990–94. OStJ 1990. *Recreations:* 'to stand and stare', personal correspondence, gardening, dress-making. *Address:* Flat 10, 28 Pembridge Square, W2 4DS.

TITMAN, Sir John (Edward Powis), KCVO 1991 (CVO 1982; LVO 1966; MVO 1957); JP; DL; Secretary of the Lord Chamberlain's Office, 1978–91; Serjeant-at-Arms to the Queen, 1982–91; *b* 23 May 1926; *s* of late Sir George Titman, CBE, MVO, sometime Secretary, Lord Chamberlain's Office, and Lady Titman; *m* 1953, Annabel Clare (*née* Naylor); two *s. Educ:* City of London School. Entered Lord Chamberlain's Office, 1947; State Invitations Asst, 1956; Asst Sec., 1976; retired 1991. Master, Wax Chandlers' Co., 1984. JP Surrey, 1971, DL Surrey, 1991. *Address:* Friars Garth, The Parade, Epsom, Surrey KT18 5DH. *T:* (01372) 722302. *Clubs:* Royal Automobile, MCC.

TIWARI, Narayan Datt; MP (Congress), Nainital, Lok Sabha, since 1999; Chief Minister, Uttar Pradesh, 1976–77, 1984–85, March–Sept. 1985 and 1988–89; Member, National Working Committee, Indian National Congress; *b* Balyuti, UP, 18 Oct. 1925; *s* of Poorna Nand Tiwari and Chandrawati Devi Tiwari; *m* 1954, Dr Sushila Tiwari (*d* 1993). *Educ:* Allahabad Univ., UP (Golden Jubilee Schol. 1948; MA Diplomacy and Internat. Affairs; LLB; Pres., Students' Union). Studied Scandinavian Econ. and Budgetary Systems in Sweden, 1959; Congressional Practices and Procedures in USA, 1964; Whitley Council System, UK, and Co-op. Banking System in Germany, Dairy Develt in Denmark. Joined Freedom Movement, 1938, and Quit India Movement, 1942, resulting in 15 months in jail, 1942. MLA (Socialist) UP, 1952, re-elected nine times. State Govt appts, 1969–77: Chm., Public Accts Cttee; Minister for Finance, Heavy Industry, Sugar Cane Develt; Dep. Chm., State Planning Commn, 1980. Leader of Opposition in UP, 1977–79, 1991. MP: Nainital, Lok Sabha, 1980–84 and 1995–98; Rajya Sabha, 1985–88; Union Minister for Planning and Labour and Dep. Chm., Planning Commn, India, 1980; Union Minister: for Industry and Steel and Mines, 1981–84; of Industry, Petroleum and Natural Gas, Ext. Affairs, Finance and Commerce, 1985–87; of Finance and Commerce, India, 1987–88; Leader of House, Rajya Sabha, 1986–88. Editor, Prabhat (a Hindi Monthly magazine). *Publications:* European Miscellany, 1964; hundreds of articles as a journalist. *Recreations:* playing cricket, hockey, chess; reading. *Address:* Village Padampuri, PO Padampuri, Dist Nainital, UP, India; B 315, Sector B, Dr Sushila Tiwari Marg, Mahanagar, Lucknow, UP. *T:* (522) 384859, (522) 239398, (11) 3382259, (11) 3382218.

TIZARD, Prof. Barbara, PhD; FBA 1997; FBPsS; Professor of Education, Institute of Education, University of London, 1982–90, now Emeritus; Director, Thomas Coram Research Unit, Institute of Education, 1980–90; *b* 16 April 1926; *d* of late Herbert Parker and Elsie Parker (*née* Kirk); *m* 1947, Jack Tizard (*d* 1979); one *s* two *d* (and two *s* decd). *Educ:* St Paul's Girls' School; Somerville College, Oxford. BA Oxon, PhD London. Lectr, Dept of Experimental Neurology, Inst. of Psychiatry, 1963–67; Res. Officer then Senior Res. Fellow, Inst. of Education, 1967–77, Reader in Education, 1978–80. Chm., Assoc. of Child Psychology and Psychiatry, 1976–77. Co-editor, British Jl of Psychology, 1975–79; Member Editorial Board: Jl of Child Psychology and Psychiatry, 1979–90; Social Development, 1992–. *Publications:* Early Childhood Education, 1975; Adoption: a second chance, 1977; (with J. Mortimore and B. Burchell) Involving Parents in Nursery and Infant Schools, 1981; (with M. Hughes) Young Children Learning, 1984; (jtly) Young Children at School in the Inner City, 1988; (with A. Phoenix) Black, White or Mixed Race? Race and racism in the lives of young people of mixed parentage, 1993; articles on transracial and intercountry adoption, children in care, child development and early education. *Address:* Thomas Coram Research Unit, 27 Woburn Square, WC1H 0AA.

See also M.C. Parker.

TIZARD, Dame Catherine (Anne), GCMG 1990; GCVO 1995; DBE 1985; QSO 1996; Governor-General of New Zealand, 1990–96; *b* 4 April 1931; *d* of Neil Maclean and Helen Montgomery Maclean; *m* 1951, Rt Hon. Robert James Tizard, *qv* (marr. diss. 1983); one *s* three *d. Educ:* Matamata College; Auckland University (BA). Tutor in Zoology, Univ. of Auckland, 1967–84. Member: Auckland City Council, 1971–83 (Mayor of Auckland, 1983–90); Auckland Regional Authy, 1980–83. Chair: NZ Historic Places Trust, 1996–; Sky City Charitable Trust, 1996–; Trustee, NZ SO, 1996–. *Recreations:* music, reading, drama, cryptic crosswords. *Address:* 12A Wallace Street, Herne Bay, Auckland 1002, New Zealand.

TIZARD, Rt Hon. Robert James; PC (NZ) 1985; MP for Tamaki, Otahuhu, Pakuranga, and Panmure, New Zealand, 1957–90; Minister of Defence, Science and Technology, 1987–90; retired; *b* 7 June 1924; *s* of Henry James and Jessie May Tizard; *m* 1951, Catherine Anne Maclean (*see* Dame Catherine Tizard) (marr. diss. 1983); one *s* three *d*; *m* 1983, Mary Christina Nacey; one *s. Educ:* Auckland Grammar Sch.; Auckland Univ. MA, Hons Hist., 1949. Served War: RNZAF, 1943–46, incl. service in Canada and Britain; (commnd as a Navigator, 1944). Pres., Students' Assoc., Auckland Univ., 1948; Lectr in History, Auckland Univ., 1949–53; teaching, 1954–57 and 1961–62. MP 1957–60 and 1963–90; Minister of Health and State Services, 1972–74; Dep. Prime Minister and Minister of Finance, 1974–75; Dep. Leader of the Opposition, 1975–79; Minister of Energy, Science and Technol., and Statistics, and Minister i/c Audit Dept, 1984–87. *Recreation:* golf. *Address:* 8 Glendowie Road, Auckland 5, New Zealand.

TJANDRA, Sir Soekandar, KBE 2001 (MBE 1994); Owner and Managing Director, Papindo Group of Companies, since 1974; *b* Pontianak, Indonesia, 14 Nov. 1947; *s* of Kusuma Tjandra and late Ho Youw Hiang; *m* 1975, Tjan Soe Lan; one *d*. Dip. Electrical Engrg. Arrived in PNG, 1974; established: Papindo Trading Co., 1974; Amalgamated Knitwear Industries, 1976; established or acquired nineteen other cos, 1976–; Papindo branches throughout PNG, 1985–. Mem., Prime Minister's Business Delegn to Qld, 1994, to China, 2001. Member: Food Mktg Inst., USA; Chamber of Commerce and Industries, PNG. Member: Bd of Govs, Lake Provincial High Sch., 1995–; Lae Tech. Coll., 1995–; Adv. Bd, Business Studies Dept, PNG Univ. of Technol., 1999–; Governing Council, Angau Meml Hosp., 1997. Mem., PNG Nat. Shooting Team to NZ, 1989. Hon. Consul-Gen. for Romania in PNG, 1997–. *Recreations:* listening to music, travelling, swimming, recreation fishing, competition pistol and rifle shooting. *Address:* PO Box 1, Lae, Morobe Province, Papua New Guinea 411. *Clubs:* Lae Pistol (Vice-Pres.), Lae Rifle (Vice-Pres.).

TOBIAS, Dr Jeffrey Stewart, FRCP, FRCR; Consultant in Radiotherapy and Oncology, University College and Middlesex Hospitals, since 1981; *b* 4 Dec. 1946; *s* of late Gerald Joseph Tobias and of Sylvia Tobias (*née* Pearlberg); *m* 1973, Dr Gabriela Jill Jaecker; two *s* one *d. Educ:* Hendon Grammar Sch.; Gonville and Caius Coll., Cambridge (MA, MD, BChir); St Bartholomew's Hosp. Med. Sch. Junior hosp. posts, St Bartholomew's, Whittington, UCH and Hammersmith Hosps, 1971–74; Research Fellow in Oncology, Harvard Med. Sch., 1975–76; Fellow in Oncology, St Bartholomew's and Royal Marsden Hosps, 1976–80; Clinical Dir, Meyerstein Inst. of Oncology, Middlesex Hosp., 1992–97. Chairman: CRC New Studies Breast Cancer Working Party, 1990–2000; UK Co-ordinating Cttee for Cancer Research Head and Neck Working Party, 1990–2000; CRC Educn Cttee, 2000–; Member: Nat. Adv. Gp for Screening in Oral Cancer, 1994–97; various MRC Adv. Gps. Advr, Audit Commn for Nat. Cancer Services, 2000. Founder Sec., British Oncological Assoc., 1986; Member Council: RCR, 1992–94; CRC, UK, 2000–; Pres., British Assoc. of Head and Neck Oncologists, 1996–98. *Publications:* (with M. J. Peckham) Primary Management of Breast Cancer, 1985; (with R. L. Souhami) Cancer and its Management, 1986, 4th edn 2002; (with C. J. Williams) Cancer, a Colour Atlas, 1993; (with P. R. Thomas) Current Radiation Oncology, 3 vols, 1994, 1995, 1997; Cancer: what every patient needs to know, 1995, rev. edn 1999; (with A. C. Silverstone) Gynecologic Oncology, 1997; (with J. Houghton) Breast Cancer—New Horizons in Research and Treatment, 2000; (with L. Doyal) Informed Consent in Medical Research, 2001; (with K. Eaton) Living with Cancer, 2001; many contribs to newspapers and learned jls about cancer management and medical ethics. *Recreations:* nothing too strenuous: music, cycling, ski-ing, reading, writing, theatre, food and drink. *Address:* Meyerstein Institute of Oncology, Middlesex Hospital, Mortimer Street, W1T 3AA. *T:* (020) 7380 9214, (020) 7637 1214, *Fax:* (020) 7637 1201; 48 Northchurch Road, N1 4EJ; *e-mail:* j.tobias@uclh.org. *Clubs:* Garrick, Royal Society of Medicine, Les Six; Albatross Wind and Water.

TOBIAS, Prof. Phillip Vallentine, PhD, DSc; FRCP; FRS 1996; Professor Emeritus and Hon. Professorial Research Fellow, University of the Witwatersrand, since 1993 (Director, Palaeo-anthropology Research Unit, 1966–96); Director, Sterkfontein Research Unit, since 1999; *b* 14 Oct. 1925; *s* of Joseph Newman Tobias and Fanny Rosendorff. *Educ:* Univ. of the Witwatersrand, Johannesburg (BSc 1946; BSc Hons 1947; PhD 1953; MB BCh 1950; DSc 1967). FRCP 1992. University of the Witwatersrand Medical School: Lectr in Anatomy, 1951–52; Sen. Lectr, 1953–58; Prof., 1959–93; Hd, Dept of Anatomy, 1959–90; Dean, Faculty of Medicine, 1980–82. Visiting Professor: Univ. of Penn, 1992–94; Univ. of Florence, 1996; Andrew White Prof.-at-Large, Cornell Univ., 1996–Dec. 2002. For. Associate, NAS of USA, 1987; Mem., Amer. Philosophical Soc., 1996. Hon. FRSSAf 1987; Hon. Fellow, Coll. of Medicine, S Africa, 1998; Hon. Member: Amer. Assoc. of Anatomists, 1987; Canadian Assoc. of Anatomists, 1989; Anatomical Soc. of GB and Ireland, 1994; Geol Soc. of S Africa, 1999. Hon. DSc: Natal, 1980; Western Ont, 1986; Alberta, 1987; Cape Town, 1988; Guelph, 1990; S Africa, 1990; Durban-Westville, 1993; Witwatersrand, 1994; Musée Nat. d'Histoire Naturelle, Paris, 1996; Barcelona, 1997; Charles Univ., Prague, 1999; Stellenbosch, 1999; Hon. ScD: Cambridge, 1988; Penn, 1994; Hon. DMedChir Turin, 1998. Anisfield-Wolf Award in Race Relns, Cleveland Foundn, USA, 1978; Cert. of Honour, Univ. of Calif, Berkeley, 1983; Balzan Internat. Prize for Physical Anthropology, 1987; First L. S. B. Leakey Prize, 1991; Huxley Meml Medal, RAI, 1996; Charles R. Darwin Lifetime Achievement Award, Amer. Assoc. of Physical Anthropologists, 1997; Wood Jones Medal, RCS, 1997. Order of Meritorious Service, Gold Class (S Africa), 1992; Order of Southern Cross, Silver Class (S Africa), 1999; Commander: Nat. Order of Merit (France), 1998; Order of Merit (Italy), 1998. *Publications:* Chromosomes, Sex-cells and Evolution in a Mammal, 1956; (jtly) Man's Anatomy, 1963, 4th edn 1988; Olduvai Gorge, Vol. 2, 1967, Vols 4A and 4B, 1991; The Brain in Hominid Evolution, 1971; (ed) The Bushmen, 1978; Dart, Taung and the Missing Link, 1984; (ed) Hominid Evolution, Past, Present and Future, 1985; Images of Humanity, 1991; (ed) The Origins and Past of Modern Humans—towards Reconciliation, 1998; (ed) Humanity from African Naissance to Coming Millennia, 2001. *Recreations:* people, music, books, philately, art, writing. *Address:* Department of Anatomical Sciences, University of the Witwatersrand Medical School, 7 York Road, Parktown, Johannesburg 2193, South Africa. *T:* (2711) 7172516. *Club:* Explorers (New York).

TOBIN, Hon. Brian Vincent; PC (Can.) 1993; MP (L) Bonavista–Trinity–Conception, Canada, since 2000; Minister of Industry, Canada, since 2000; *b* 21 Oct. 1954; *s* of Patrick Vincent Tobin and Florence Mary Tobin (*née* Frye); *m* 1977, Jodean Smith; two *s* one *d. Educ:* Meml Univ. of Newfoundland. MP (L) Humber–St Barbe–Baie Verte, 1980–96; Parly Sec. to Minister of Fisheries and Oceans, 1981; Minister of Fisheries and Oceans, 1993–96; MHA (L) Bay of Islands, 1996–99, Straits and White Bay North, 1999–2000; Premier of Newfoundland and Labrador, 1996–2000. Leader, Liberal Party of NF, 1996–2000; Chair, Nat. Liberal Caucus, 1989. *Recreations:* reading, music, sports. *Address:* Ministry of Industry, 235 Queen Street, Ottawa, ON K1A 0H5, Canada.

TOBIN, Prof. James, PhD; Sterling Professor of Economics, Yale University, 1957–88, now Emeritus; *b* 5 March 1918; *s* of Louis Michael and Margaret Edgerton Tobin; *m* 1946, Elizabeth Fay Ringo; three *s* one *d. Educ:* Harvard Univ. AB 1939 (*summa cum laude*); MA 1940; PhD 1947. Economist, Office of Price Admin, and Civilian Supply and War Production Bd, Washington, 1941–42; line officer, destroyer, USN, 1942–46. Teaching Fellow in Econs, 1946–47, Jun. Fellow, Soc. of Fellows, 1947–50, Harvard Univ.; Yale University: Associate Prof. of Econs, 1950–55; Prof. of Econs, 1955–57; Mem., 1955–, Dir, 1955–61, Cowles Foundn for Res. in Econs; Chm., Dept of Econs, 1968–69, 1974–78. Vis. Prof., Univ. of Nairobi, 1972–73; Ford Vis. Res. Prof. of Econs, Univ. of

Calif, Berkeley, 1983; P. K. Seidman Vis. Dist. Prof. of Internat. Studies, Rhodes Coll., 1992. Mem., Pres.'s Council of Econ. Advrs, 1961–62. Corresp. FBA 1984. LLD *hc* Syracuse Univ., 1967; Univ. of Illinois, 1969; Dartmouth Coll., 1970; Swarthmore Coll., 1980; New Sch. for Social Res., and New York Univ., 1982; Univ. of Hartford, 1984; Colgate Univ., 1984; Western Maryland Coll., 1984; Univ. of New Haven, 1986; Harvard, 1995; Univ. of Wisconsin-Madison, 1996; DEcon *hc* New Univ. of Lisbon, 1980; Hon. DHL: Bates Coll., 1982; Hofstra Univ., 1983; Gustavus Adolphus Coll., 1986; Sacred Heart Univ., 1990; Bard Coll., 1995; Beloit Coll., 1996; Quinnipiac Univ., 2001; DSocSc *hc* Helsinki, 1986; DEcon and Bus *hc* Athens, 1992. Foreign Associate, Acad. of Sciences, Portugal, 1980. Nobel Prize in Economics, 1981; Centennial Medal, Harvard Univ. Graduate Sch., 1989. Grand Cordon, Order of the Sacred Treasure (Japan), 1988. *Publications:* (jtly) The American Business Creed, 1956; National Economic Policy, 1966; Essays in Economics: vol. 1, Macroeconomics, 1971; vol. 2, Consumption and Econometrics, 1975; vol. 3, Theory and Policy, 1982; vol. 4, National and International, 1996; The New Economics One Decade Older, 1974; Asset Accumulation and Economic Activity, Reflections on Contemporary Macroeconomic Theory, 1980; Policies for Prosperity, 1987; Two Revolutions in Economic Theory, 1988; Full Employment and Growth, 1996; Money Credit and Capital, 1997; contribs to professional jls. *Recreations:* tennis, ski-ing, sailing, canoeing, fishing, chess. *Address:* Cowles Foundation for Research in Economics, Yale University, Box 208281, New Haven, CT 06520–8281, USA. *T:* (203) 4323720. *Clubs:* Yale (New York); Mory's Association, The Club (New Haven).

TOBIN, Patrick Francis John; Principal, Mary Erskine School and Daniel Stewart's and Melville College, Edinburgh, 1989–2000; *b* 4 Oct. 1941; *s* of Denis George and Una Eileen Tobin; *m* 1970, Margery Ann Sluce; one *s* three *d*. *Educ.* St Benedict's Sch., Ealing; Christ Church, Oxford (MA in Modern Hist.); London Univ. (PGCE). Head: of Econs, St Benedict's Sch., Ealing, 1963–71; of History, Christ Coll., Brecon, 1971–75; of History, Tonbridge Sch., 1975–81; Headmaster, Prior Park Coll., Bath, 1981–89. Chm., HMC, 1998. Governor: Bryanston Sch.; Portsmouth Grammar Sch.; Ryde Sch.; Advisory Governor: Ampleforth Coll.; St Benedict's Ealing (Chm.). *Recreations:* reading, travelling, canal boats. *Address:* Glentruim, Ashlake Copse Lane, Kite Hill, Wootton, Isle of Wight P033 4LG. *Club:* East India.

TOD, John Mackenzie, OBE 1987; Director, France, British Council, since 1998; *b* 24 Oct. 1944; *s* of John Alexander Tod and Eleanor May Tod (*née* Darrah); *m* 1970, Christiane Teytaud; two *s* one *d*. *Educ:* Calday Grange GS; King's Coll., Cambridge (BA); Leeds Univ. (postgrad. Dip. TESL 1969); Inst. of Educn, London Univ. (MA Ed 1983). VSO, Malaita, Solomon Is, 1963–64; teacher, Ruffwood Comp. Sch., Kirby, 1965; joined British Council, 1968: Ghana, 1969–72; Brazil, 1972–74; Asst Dir (Educn), Kano, Nigeria, 1975–78; Asst Dir, Overseas Educnl Appts Dept, 1978–82; Rep., Senegal, 1983–88; Regl Dir and Supt Gen., Sociedade Brasileira de Cultura Inglesa, São Paulo, 1988–93; Dir of Arts, 1993–98. *Recreations:* choral music, literature, theatre, sailing. *Address:* British Council, 10 Spring Gardens, SW1A 2BN. *T:* (020) 7930 8466.

TOD, Vice-Adm. Sir Jonathan (James Richard), KCB 1996; CBE 1982; Chairman, Sea Cadets Association, since 1998; *b* 26 March 1939; *e s* of late Col Richard Logan Tod and Elizabeth Allan Tod; *m* 1962, Claire Elizabeth Russell Dixon; two *s*. *Educ:* Gordonstoun Sch. BRNC, Dartmouth, 1957–59; Flying trng, 1961; Hal Far (Malta), 1963; HM Ships: Ark Royal, Hermes, Eagle, RNAS, Lossiemouth, 1962–70; BRNC, Dartmouth, 1970–72; Exec. Officer, HMS Devonshire, 1972–74; Naval Staff, 1975–77; Comd HMS Brighton, 1978–80; Cabinet Office, 1980–82; RCDS 1983; Comd HMS Fife, 1984–85; Dir, Defence Programme, 1986–88; Comd HMS Illustrious, 1988–89; Flag Officer Portsmouth and Naval Base Comdr Portsmouth, 1989–90; ACDS (Policy and Nuclear), MoD, 1990–94; Dep. Comdr Fleet, 1994–97. *Recreations:* sailing, driving pony and trap. *Address:* c/o Naval Secretary, Victory Building, HM Naval Base, Portsmouth PO1 3LS.

TODD, Rev. Alastair, CMG 1971; *b* 21 Dec. 1920; *s* of late Prof. James Eadie Todd, MA, FRHistS (formerly Prof. of History, Queen's University, Belfast) and Margaret Simpson Johnstone Maybin; *m* 1952, Nancy Hazel Buyers; two *s* two *d*. *Educ:* Royal Belfast Academical Institution; Fettes Coll., Edinburgh; Corpus Christi Coll., Oxford; London Univ. (External); Salisbury and Wells Theological Coll. BA (Oxon), DipTheol (London). Served War, Army, 1940–46, Capt. RHA. Apptd Colonial Administrative Service, Hong Kong, 1946; Joint Services Staff Coll., 1950; Defence Sec., Hong Kong, 1957–60; Dep. Colonial Sec., Hong Kong, 1963–64; Dir of Social Welfare, also MLC, 1966–68; and, again, Defence Sec., 1968–71, retd. Ordained Deacon by Bishop of Chichester, 1973 and Priest, 1974; Asst Curate, Willingdon, 1973–77; Vicar, St Augustine's, Brighton, 1978–86. *Recreations:* reading, embroidery, gardening. *Address:* 59 Park Avenue, Eastbourne BN21 2XH. *T:* (01323) 505843.

TODD, Rev. Andrew Stewart; Minister of St Machar's Cathedral, Old Aberdeen, 1967–93; Extra Chaplain to the Queen in Scotland, since 1996 (Chaplain, 1991–96); *b* 26 May 1926; *s* of late William Stewart Todd and Robina Victoria Fraser; *m* 1953, Janet Agnes Brown Smith, *d* of late John Smith, JP, DL, Glasgow and Symington; two *s* two *d*. *Educ:* High Sch. of Stirling; Edinburgh Univ. (MA Hons, Classics 1947); New Coll., Edinburgh (BD 1950); Basel Univ. Asst Minister, St Cuthbert's, Edinburgh, 1951–52; ordained, 1952; Minister: Symington, Lanarkshire, 1952–60; North Leith, 1960–67. Convener, Gen. Assembly's Cttee on Public Worship and Aids to Devotion, 1974–78; Moderator, Aberdeen Presbytery, 1980–81; Convener, Panel on Doctrine, 1990–95; Member: Church Hymnary Cttee, 1963–73; Church Hymnary Trust. Hon. President: Church Service Soc.; Scottish Church Soc. Hon. DD Aberdeen, 1982. *Publications:* jt translator, Oscar Cullmann, Early Christian Worship, 1953; translator: Ludwig Koehler, Old Testament Theology, 1957; Ernst Lohmeyer, Lord of the Temple, 1961; contributions to liturgical jls. *Recreations:* music, gardening. *Address:* Culearn, Balquhidder, Lochearnhead, Perthshire FK19 8PB. *Club:* Royal Over-Seas League.

TODD, Damian Roderic; HM Diplomatic Service; Ambassador to the Slovak Republic, since 2001; *b* 29 Aug. 1959; *s* of George Todd and Annette Todd (*née* Goodchild); *m* 1987, Alison Digby; one *s* two *d*. *Educ:* Lawrence Sheriff Grammar Sch., Rugby; Worcester Coll., Oxford (BA Hons History). Joined HM Diplomatic Service, 1980; Third Sec., then Second Sec., Pretoria and Cape Town, 1981–84; FCO, 1984–87; HM Consul and First Sec., Prague, 1987–89; FCO, 1989–91; First Sec. (Econ.), Bonn, 1991–95; on secondment to HM Treasury, 1995–97, Hd of Agric. Team, 1996–97; FCO, 1997; on loan to HM Treasury as Hd of EU Co-ordination and Strategy Team, 1998–2001. *Recreations:* history, family life, looking at buildings. *Address:* c/o Foreign and Commonwealth Office, King Charles Street, SW1A 2AH.

TODD, Daphne Jane, (Mrs P. R. T. Driscoll), RP 1985; NEAC; artist; President, Royal Society of Portrait Painters, 1994–2000; *b* 27 March 1947; *d* of Frank Todd and Annie Mary Todd (*née* Lord); *m* 1984, Lt-Col (Patrick Robert) Terence Driscoll; one *d*. *Educ:* Simon Langton Grammar Sch. for Girls, Canterbury; Slade Sch. of Fine Art, UCL (DFA 1969; HDFA 1971). Vis. Lectr, Byam Shaw Sch. of Art, 1971–75 and 1978–80; Dir of Studies, Heatherley Sch. of Fine Art, 1980–86. NEAC 1984; Royal Society of Portrait Painters: Mem. Council, 1986–90; Hon. Sec., 1990–91. Hon. Mem., Soc. of Women Artists, 1995. Work in exhibitions, including: Royal Acad. Summer Exhibns, 1969–; Critic's Choice, Tooth's, 1972; Slade Centenary, 1972; Slade Ladies, Mall Gall., 1991; President's Exhibn, Birmingham, 1995; solo retrospective exhibn, Morley Gall., London, 1989. Work in private and public collections including: Royal Acad. (Chantrey Bequest); Lady Margaret Hall and UC, Oxford; Pembroke Coll. and St Catharine's Coll., Cambridge; UCL; St David's Univ., Lampeter; De Montfort Univ.; Royal Holloway Mus. and Art Gall.; Bishop's Palace, Hereford; Wellington Barracks; BMA; ICE; NUMAST; Science Mus.; Nat. Portrait Gall. Portrait commissions include: Grand Duke of Luxembourg; Lord Adrian; Dame Janet Baker; Spike Milligan; Sir Neil Cossons; Baron Klingspor; Sir Kirby and Lady Laing; Christopher Ondaatje; Dame Anne Mueller; Lord Sainsbury of Preston Candover; Lord Sharman; Prof. Marilyn Strathern; Lord Morris of Castle Morris. Governor: Thomas Heatherley Educnl Trust, 1987–; FBA, 1994–. Freeman, Painter Stainers' Co., 1997. FRSA 1996. Hon. DArts De Montfort, 1998. 2nd Prize, John Player Award, Nat. Portrait Gall., 1983 (Special Commendation, 1984); First Prize, Oil Painting of Year, Hunting Gp Nat. Art Prize, 1984; GLC Prize, Spirit of London, RFH, 1985; Ondaatje Prize for Portraiture, and RP Gold Medal, 2001. *Publications:* contribs to The Artist. *Recreation:* gardening. *Address:* Salters Green Farm, Mayfield, E Sussex TN20 6NP. *T:* and *Fax:* (01892) 852472. *Clubs:* Arts, Chelsea Arts.

TODD, Prof. Sir David, Kt 1995; CBE 1990 (OBE 1982); FRCP, FRCPE, FRCPGlas, FRACP, FRCPath; Professor of Medicine, University of Hong Kong, 1972–96; *b* 17 Nov. 1928; *s* of Paul J. Todd and Margaret S. Todd. *Educ:* Univ. of Hong Kong (MB BS, MD). FRCPE 1966; FRACP 1974; FRCP 1976; FRCPGlas 1979; FRCPath 1992. University of Hong Kong: Lectr, Sen. Lectr and Reader, 1958–72; Head of Dept, 1974–89; Sub-Dean of Medicine, 1976–78; Pro-Vice-Chancellor, 1978–80. Hong Kong Government: Consultant in Medicine, 1974–89; Chm., Research Grants Council, Hong Kong, 1991–93. President: Hong Kong Coll. of Physicians, 1986–92; Hong Kong Acad. of Medicine, 1992–96; Chm., Council for Aids Trust Fund, Hong Kong, 1993–96. Hon. FAMS Singapore, 1986. Hon DSc Chinese Univ. of Hong Kong, 1990; Hon DSc Univ. of Hong Kong, 1992. *Publications:* articles on: haematological disorders in liver disease and splenomegaly; thalassaemia; G6PD deficiency; lymphoma; leukaemia; med. educn and physician training. *Recreations:* swimming, travelling, classical music. *Address:* D12 Breezy Court, 2A Park Road, Mid-levels, Hong Kong. *Clubs:* Hong Kong Golf, Hong Kong Country.

TODD, Hon. Sir Garfield; *see* Todd, Hon. Sir R. S. G.

TODD, Sir Ian (Pelham), KBE 1989; FRCS; Consulting Surgeon: King Edward VII Hospital for Officers, since 1989 (Consultant Surgeon, 1972–89); St Bartholomew's Hospital, since 1981 (Consultant Surgeon, 1958–81); St Mark's Hospital, since 1986 (Consultant Surgeon, 1954–86); *b* 23 March 1921; *s* of Alan Herepath and Constance Todd; *m* 1946, Jean Audrey Ann Noble; two *s* three *d*. *Educ:* Sherborne Sch.; St Bartholomew's Hosp. Med. Coll.; Toronto Univ. (Rockefeller studentship, 1941–43; MD 1945; MS 1956). MRCS, LRCP 1944; DCH 1947; FRCS 1949. Served RAMC, Captain (AER Major). Wellcome Res. Fellow, 1955–56. Lectures: Wilson-Hay Meml, Perth, 1978; Howard H. Frykman Meml, Minneapolis, 1979; Patrick Hanley Meml, New Orleans, 1982; Gordon Watson, St Bart's Hosp., 1982; Purdue Frederick, New Orleans, 1984; Zachary Cope Meml, RCS, 1985; Henry Floyd Meml, Stoke Mandeville, 1986; John Clive Meml, Calif., 1986; Pybus Meml, Durham, 1988; Chesledon, St Thomas' Hosp., 1988; Cutait Oration, São Paulo, 1991. Visiting Professorships incl.: Montevideo; Ribeirao Preto; La Paz; Vellore; New Orleans; Minneapolis; Madras; Detroit. Examiner in Surgery: Univ. of London, 1958–64; Cambridge Univ., 1988; Dhaka, 1990; Ex-civilian Cons. (Proctology), RN, 1970–86. President: Sect. Colo-proctology, RSM, 1970–71; Med. Soc. of London, 1984–85; RCS, 1986–89 (Mem. Council, 1975–89; Hunterian Prof., 1953; Arris and Gale Lectr, 1957–58); British Colostomy Assoc., 1991–95; Vice-President: Imperial Cancer Res. Fund, 1986–89; Internat. Fedn of Surgical Colls, 1990–93. Founder, Leeds Castle Polyposis Gp, 1983. Fellow, Assoc. of Surgeons of GB and Ire., 1960; Founder Mem., Surgical Sixty Club; Hon. Member: Amer. Soc. of Colon and Rectal Surgs, 1974; RACS, 1974; Soc. Gastroent. Belge, 1964; Ileostomy Soc. of GB and Ire.; Surgical Res. Soc. of SA; Hellenic Surgical Assoc.; Assoc. of Surgs of India; Acad. of Medicine of Malaysia; NY State Surgical Soc., and S Amer. socs. Hon. FCSSA 1987; Hon. FRACS 1988; Hon. FACS 1988; Hon. FRCSCan 1989; Hon. FRCPSGlas 1989; FCPS (Bangladesh) 1990; Hon. Fellow, Colo-rectal Soc. of Sydney. Lister Prize in Surgery, Toronto, 1956. Star of Jordan, 1973. *Publications:* Intestinal Stomas, 1978; (ed) Rob and Smith, Operative Surgery, vol. 3, 1982; many articles on surgery of colon and rectum in Brit. and Amer. jls. *Recreations:* travel, music. *Address:* 4 Longmead Close, Farleigh Road, Norton St Philip, Bath BA2 7NS.

TODD, Prof. Janet Margaret, PhD; Francis Hutcheson Professor of English Literature, University of Glasgow, since 2000; *b* 10 Sept. 1942; *d* of George and Elizabeth Dakin; *m* 1966 (marr. diss.); one *s* one *d*. *Educ:* Newnham Coll., Cambridge (BA 1964); Univ. of Leeds; Univ. of Florida (PhD). Lectr, Univ. of Cape Coast, Ghana, 1966–67; Asst Prof. of English, Univ. of Puerto Rico, 1972–74; Asst, Associate, Full Prof. of English, Rutgers Univ., NJ, 1974–83; Fellow in English, Sidney Sussex Coll., Cambridge, 1983–89; Prof. of English Lit., UEA, 1990–2000. Vis. Prof. Univ. of Southampton, 1982–83. Bye-Fellow, Newnham Coll., Cambridge, 1998. Numerous awards. *Publications:* In Adam's Garden: a study of John Clare, 1973; Mary Wollstonecraft: an annotated bibliography, 1976; Women's Friendship in Literature, 1980; (jtly) English Congregational Hymns in the 18th Century, 1983; Sensibility, 1986; Feminist Literary History, 1988; The Sign of Angellica: women writing and fiction 1660–1800, 1989; (ed jtly) The Complete Works of Mary Wollstonecraft, 1989; (ed) A Dictionary of British Women Writers, 1989; (ed) The Works of Aphra Behn, 7 vols, 1992–96; (ed) Aphra Behn's Oroonoko, The Rover and Other Works, 1993; Gender, Art and Death, 1993; (ed) Aphra Behn Studies, 1996; The Secret Life of Aphra Behn, 1996; (ed) Female Education, 6 vols, 1996; The Critical Fortunes of Aphra Behn, 1998; Mary Wollstonecraft: a revolutionary life, 2000. *Address:* 38 Victoria Park, Cambridge CB4 3EL.

TODD, Prof. John Andrew, PhD; Professor of Medical Genetics, and Fellow of Gonville and Caius College, University of Cambridge, since 1998; *b* 23 June 1958; *s* of William and Elizabeth Todd; *m* 1988, Anne Nicola Roberts; two *s* one *d*. *Educ:* Coleraine Academical Instn; Edinburgh Univ. (BSc 1st cl. Hons 1980); Gonville and Caius Coll., Cambridge (PhD Biochemistry 1983). Research Fellow: Dept of Biochemistry, Cambridge Univ., 1983–85; MRC Molecular Biology Lab., Cambridge, 1984; SERC/NATO Res. Fellow, Dept of Microbiology and Immunology, Stanford Univ., Calif, 1985–88; Career Develt Award Fellow, Juvenile Diabetes Foundn Internat., 1988–90 (Grodzy Prize, 1998); University of Oxford: Sen. Scientist, Nuffield Dept of Surgery, 1988–98; Mem., Faculty of Medicine, 1989–98; Wellcome Trust Sen. Fellow in Basic Biomed. Sci., 1990–93; Univ. Res. Lectr, 1992–98; Wellcome Trust Prin. Res. Fellow, 1993–98; Prof. of Human Genetics, 1996–98. Wellcome Vis. Prof., Louisiana State Univ., 1997. Lectures: Balfour, Genetical Soc., 1994; Lilly, QUB, 1995; Dorothy Hodgkin, Diabetes UK, 2001. Hon. MRCP 2000. Minkowski Prize, Eur. Assoc. for Study of Diabetes, 1995; Res. Prize,

Boehringer Mannheim and Juvenile Diabetes Res. Foundn Internat., 1995; Biennial Biochem. Soc. Medal, Wellcome Trust, 1998; R. and B. Sackler Res. Award, 1998; Carter Medal and Lecture, Clin. Genetics Soc., 1999. *Publications:* articles in learned jls. *Recreations:* lateral thinking, study of natural selection and evolution, fishing, ski-ing, swimming, child minding. *Address:* JDRF/WT Diabetes Inflammation Laboratory, Cambridge Institute for Medical Research, Wellcome Trust/MRC Building, Hills Road, Cambridge CB2 2XY. *T:* (01223) 762101.

TODD, Prof. John Francis James, PhD; CEng, FInstMC; CChem, FRSC; Professor of Mass Spectroscopy, University of Kent at Canterbury, 1991–2000, now Emeritus; *b* 20 May 1937; *o s* of late Eric Todd and Annie Lewin Todd (*née* Tinkler); *m* 1963, Mavis Georgina Lee; three *s*. *Educ:* Leeds Grammar Sch.; Leeds Univ. (BSc, Cl. I Hons Chem.). Research Fellow: Leeds Univ., 1962–63; Yale Univ., USA, 1963–65; University of Kent at Canterbury: Asst Lectr in Chemistry, 1965–66; Lectr in Chemistry, 1966–73; Sen. Lectr, 1973–89; Reader in Physical Chemistry, Faculty of Natural Scis, 1990; Dir, Univ. Chemical Lab., 1991–94; Dep. Head, Chemistry Dept (Finance), 1996–97; Master of Rutherford Coll., 1975–85. CIL Distinguished Vis. Lectr, Trent Univ., Canada, 1988. J. B. Cohen Prizeman, Leeds Univ., 1963; Fulbright Research Scholar, 1963–65. Chm., Canterbury and Thanet HA, 1982–86. Chairman: Kent Section of Chem. Soc., 1975; British Mass Spectroscopy Soc., 1980–81 (Treas., 1990–93); Titular Mem., IUPAC Commn on Molecular Structures and Spectroscopy, 1979–91; Nat. Mem. Council, RSC, 1993–95. Mem., Kent Educn Cttee, 1983–88. Member: Clergy Orphan Corp., 1985–96; Council, Strode Park Foundn for the Disabled, 1986–90. Governor: S Kent Coll. of Technology, 1977–89; Canterbury Christ Church UC (formerly Canterbury Christ Church Coll.), 1994–; Chm. of Govs, St Edmund's Sch., Canterbury, 1996–. Mem., Amer. Soc. of Sigma Xi, Yale Chapter. Jt Editor, Internat. Jl of Mass Spectrometry and Ion Processes, 1985–98. Thomson Gold Medal, Internat. Mass Spectrometry Soc., 1997. *Publications:* Dynamic Mass Spectrometry, vol. 4, 1975, vol. 5, 1978, vol. 6, 1981; Advances in Mass Spectrometry 1985, 1986; Practical Aspects of Ion Trap Mass Spectrometry, vols 1–3, 1995; reviews and papers, mainly on mass spectrometry, in Jl of Chem. Soc. and Jl of Physics, etc. *Recreations:* music, travel, genealogy. *Address:* University Chemical Laboratory, School of Physical Sciences, University of Kent at Canterbury, CT2 7NH. *T:* (01227) 823518; West Bank, 122 Whitstable Road, Canterbury, Kent CT2 8EG. *T:* (01227) 769552.

TODD, John Rawling, CVO 1972; OBE 1985; Secretary for Housing, Hong Kong Government, 1986–88; *b* 15 Feb. 1929; *s* of William Rawling Todd and Isabella May Todd; *m* 1960, Ingrid von Rothermann; one *s* one *d*. *Educ:* Durham Univ. (BSc). Nat. Service, RA, 1952. Joined HMOCS; Admin. Officer, Gambia, 1955; New Hebrides, 1962; Administrator, British Indian Ocean Territory, 1966; Dep. Governor, Seychelles, 1970; seconded to FCO, 1974; Hong Kong: Dep. Sec., 1976; Dir of Lands, 1982. Sen. British Rep., Sino-British Land Commn, 1984–88; Chm., Special Cttee on Compensation and Betterment, Hong Kong, 1991. *Recreations:* reading, gardening, walking, croquet. *Address:* Longridge, Crudwell, Malmesbury, Wilts SN16 9ER. *Club:* Royal Commonwealth Society.

TODD, Keith; *see* Todd, T. K.

TODD, Prof. Malcolm, FSA 1970; Principal, Trevelyan College, Durham, 1996–2000; *b* 27 Nov. 1939; *s* of Wilfrid and Rose Evelyn Todd; *m* 1964, Molly Tanner; one *s* one *d*. *Educ:* Univ. of Wales (BA, DLitt); Brasenose Coll., Oxford (Dip. Class. Archaeol (Dist.)). Res. Assistant, Rheinisches Landesmus., Bonn, 1963–65; Lectr 1965–74, Sen. Lectr 1974–77, Reader in Archaeology 1977–79, Univ. of Nottingham; Prof. of Archaeology, Univ. of Exeter, 1979–96. Vis. Prof., New York Univ., 1979; Visiting Fellow: All Souls Coll., Oxford, 1984; Brasenose Coll., Oxford, 1990–91; Sen. Res. Fellow, British Acad./Leverhulme Trust, 1990–91. Vice-Pres., Roman Soc., 1985–; Member: RCHM, 1986–92; Council, National Trust, 1987–91. Trustee: Roman Res. Trust, 1994–; Trevelyan Trust, 1996–. Archaeological Consultant, Durham Cathedral, 1996–. Corr. Mem., German Arch. Inst., 1977–. Editor, Britannia, 1984–89. *Publications:* The Northern Barbarians, 1975, 2nd edn 1987; The Walls of Rome, 1978; Roman Britain, 1981, 3rd edn 1999; The South-West to AD 1000, 1987; (ed) Research on Roman Britain 1960–89, 1989; Les Germains: aux frontières romaines, 1990 (trans. Italian and German); The Early Germans, 1992; papers in Germania, Britannia, Antiquaries Jl, Antiquity, Amer. Jl of Arch. *Recreations:* reading, writing, travel on foot. *Address:* 58 Polsloe Road, Exeter, Devon EX1 2EA.

TODD, Mark James, CBE 1995 (MBE 1984); equestrian rider; *b* 1 March 1956; *s* of Norman Edward Todd and Lenore Adele Todd; *m* 1986, Carolyn Faye Berry; one *s* one *d*. *Educ:* Cambridge High Sch., NZ; Hamilton Tech. Inst. (Dip. Agric.). Three-day event wins: Badminton, 1980 (Southern Comfort), 1994 (Horton Point), 1996 (Bertie Blunt); Burghley, 1987 (Wilton Fair, also runner up, on Charisma), 1990 (Welton Greylag), 1991 (Face the Music), 1997 (Broadcast News), 1999 (Diamond Hall Red); Olympic Games: Individual Gold Medal, 1984 (Charisma), 1988 (Charisma); Individual Bronze Medal, 2000 (Eye Spy II); World Championships: NZ Team Gold Medal, 1990; Silver Medal, 1998 (Broadcast News). New Zealand Sportsman of the Year, 1988; Event Rider of the Century, Internat. Equestrian Fedn, 1999; Equestrian Personality of the Century, Horse & Hound; Sportsman of the Century, Waikato, NZ. *Publications:* Charisma; Mark Todd's Cross-Country Handbook, 1991; One Day Eventing, 1996; So Far, So Good, 1998. *Recreations:* ski-ing, swimming, tennis, squash, horse racing, music. *Address:* Rivermonte Farms Ltd, Kaipaiki Road, RD3, Cambridge, New Zealand.

TODD, Mark Wainwright; MP (Lab) Derbyshire South, since 1997; *b* 29 Dec. 1954; *s* of Matthew and Viv Todd; *m* 1979, Sarah Margaret (*née* Dawson); one *s*. *Educ:* Sherborne Sch.; Emmanuel Coll., Cambridge (BA History 1976; MA). Longman Group, later Addison Wesley Longman, 1977–96: Man. Dir, Longman Industry and Public Service Mgt, 1988–92, Longman Cartermill, 1990–92; Dir, IT, 1992–94, Ops, 1994–96. *Address:* House of Commons, SW1A 0AA.

TODD, Mary Williamson Spottiswoode, MA; Headmistress of Harrogate College, 1952–73; *b* 11 June 1909; *d* of John and Mary Todd, Oxford. *Educ:* Oxford High School; Lady Margaret Hall, Oxford (MA Hons Oxon; Final Hon. Sch.: Mathematics, 1932, Nat. Science, 1933); London Diploma in Theology, 1941. Various teaching posts: St Felix School, Southwold, 1933–37; Clifton High School, Bristol, 1937–39; Westonbirt School, Glos, 1939–46; Headmistress of Durham, 1946–52. Lay Reader, 1975–. *Address:* 93 Oakdale, Harrogate, North Yorks HG1 2LT. *T:* (01423) 566411.

TODD, Michael Alan; QC 1997; *b* 16 Feb. 1953; *y s* of Charles Edward Alan Todd and late Betty Todd (*née* Bromwich); *m* 1976, Deborah Collett. *Educ:* Kenilworth Grammar Sch.; Keele Univ. (BA 1976). Called to the Bar, Lincoln's Inn, 1977; Jun. Counsel to the Crown, Chancery Div., 1992–97. *Recreation:* equestrianism. *Address:* Erskine Chambers, Lincoln's Inn, WC2A 3PD. *T:* (020) 7242 5532.

TODD, Hon. Sir (Reginald Stephen) Garfield, Kt 1986; *b* 13 July 1908; *s* of late Thomas and Edith C. Todd; *m* 1932, Jean Grace Wilson; three *d*. *Educ:* Otago Univ.; Glen Leith Theol Coll., NZ; University of Witwatersrand. Superintendent Dadaya Mission, 1934–53, Chm. Governing Bd 1963–85. MP for Shabani, 1946–58; Prime Minister of S Rhodesia, 1953–58; Mem. Senate, Parlt of Zimbabwe, 1980–85. First Vice-President, World Convention of Churches of Christ, 1955–60; awarded Citation for Christian Leadership in Politics and Race Relations; former Member Executive: United Coll. of Educn, Bulawayo; Rhodesian Christian Council. Arrested by Smith regime in 1965 and confined to Hokonui Ranch for one year; arrested by Smith regime in 1972 and imprisoned, then detained, Jan 1972–June 1976. Received medal acknowledging efforts for peace and justice in Rhodesia, from Pope Paul, 1973. Holds hon. doctorates, NZ and USA. Knighted for services to NZ and Africa. *Address:* Box FM 693, Famona, Bulawayo, Zimbabwe. *Club:* Bulawayo.

See also Baron Acton.

TODD, Richard, (Richard Andrew Palethorpe-Todd), OBE 1993; actor; *b* 11 June 1919; *s* of Major A. W. Palethorpe-Todd, MC, Castlederg, Co. Tyrone, and Marvil Agar-Daly, Ballymalis Castle, Kerry; *m* 1st, 1949, Catherine Stewart Crawford Grant-Bogle (marr. diss. 1970); one *s* one *d*; 2nd, 1970, Virginia Anne Rollo Mailer (marr. diss. 1992); one *s* (and one *s* decd). *Educ:* Shrewsbury; privately. Entered the theatre in 1937. Served in King's Own Yorkshire Light Infantry and The Parachute Regt, 1940–46; GSO iii (Ops), 6 Airborne Div., 1944–45. *Films* since War of 1939–45 include: The Hasty Heart, 1949; Stage Fright, 1950; Robin Hood, 1952; Rob Roy, 1953; A Man Called Peter, 1954; The Dambusters, 1954; The Virgin Queen, 1955; Yangtse Incident, 1957; Chase a Crooked Shadow, 1957; The Long and the Short and the Tall, 1960; The Hellions, 1961; The Longest Day, 1962; Operation Crossbow, 1964; Coast of Skeletons, 1964; The Love-Ins (USA), 1967; Subterfuge, 1968; Dorian Grey, 1969; Asylum, 1972; Secret Agent 008, 1976; The House of the Long Shadows, 1982; The Olympus Force, 1988. *Stage* appearances include: An Ideal Husband, Strand, 1965–66; Dear Octopus, Haymarket, 1967; USA tour, The Marquise, 1972; Australia tour, Sleuth, 1973; led RSC N American tour, 1974; Equus, Australian Nat. Theatre Co., 1975; On Approval (S Africa), 1976; nat. tour of Quadrille, and The Heat of the Moment, 1977; Nightfall (S Africa), 1979; This Happy Breed (nat. tour), 1980; The Business of Murder, Duchess, 1981, Mayfair, 1982–88; The Woman in Black, Sydney Opera House, Liverpool Playhouse, 1991; nat. tour of Sweet Revenge, 1993; nat. tour of Brideshead Revisited, 1995; An Ideal Husband, Old Vic and tour, 1997, Gielgud and Albery, 1998, Theatre Royal, Haymarket and Lyric, 1999. *Television:* Heathcliffe, in Wuthering Heights, 1960; Carrington VC, 1964; H. G. Wells, in Beautiful Lies, 1991; series, Virtual Murder, 1992; Dr Newman, in Silent Witness, 2000. Formed Triumph Theatre Productions, 1970. Pres., Age Concern, Birmingham, 1990–. Past Grand Steward, Past Master, Lodge of Emulation No 21. *Publications:* Caught in the Act (autobiog.), 1986; In Camera (autobiog.), 1989. *Recreations:* shooting, gardening. *Address:* Chinham Farm, Faringdon, Oxon SN7 8EZ; Little Ponton House, near Grantham, Lincs NG33 5BS. *Club:* Army and Navy.

TODD, Ronald; General Secretary, Transport and General Workers' Union, 1985–92; *b* 11 March 1927; *s* of late George Thomas Todd and of Emily Todd; *m* 1945, Josephine Tarrant; one *s* two *d*. *Educ:* St Patrick's Sch., Walthamstow, E17. Served with Royal Marine Commandos; spent considerable time in China. Joined TGWU: worked at Ford Motor Co., 1954–62, latterly Dep. Convener; full-time officer of TGWU, 1962; Regional Officer, 1969; Reg. Sec., 1976; Nat. Organiser, 1978. Mem., TUC Gen. Council, 1984–92; Chm., TUC Internat. Cttee, 1985–92. Chm. (TU side), Ford Nat. Jt Council, 1978–85; Jt Sec., Nat. Jt Council for Stable Staff (Workpeople's side), 1978–85. Member: NEDC, 1985–92; MSC, 1986–88; former Mem., Employment Appeal Tribunal. Member: Unity Trust, 1986– (Pres., 1986–89); Council for Charitable Support, 1988–. Hon. Vice-President: CND; BDA. Patron, Margaret Centre Macmillan Appeal. *Recreations:* collecting Victorian music covers, archaeology. *Address:* 65 Surrey Road, Dagenham, Essex RM10 8ET.

TODD, (Thomas) Keith, FCMA; Chairman and Chief Executive Officer, Dexterus Ltd, since 2001; Chairman, Knotty Green Consulting Ltd, since 2000; *b* 22 June 1953; *s* of Thomas William Todd and Cecilie Olive Todd; *m* 1979, Anne Elizabeth Hendrie; two *s* two *d*. FCMA 1985. Chief Accountant, Marconi Co. Ltd, 1978–81; Chief Financial Officer, Cincinnati Electronics, USA, 1981–86; Financial Dir, Marconi Co. Ltd, 1986–87; Dir, Finance and Business Strategy, 1987–96, Chief Exec., 1996–2000, ICL plc. Mem. Board, Camelot Gp plc, 1994–2000; non-exec. Dir, Ecsoft plc. Mem. Council, Open Univ., 1992–2000 (Hon. Treas., 1992–97). FRSA 1996. DUniv Open, 1999. *Recreation:* sports. *Address:* The Hill, Penn Road, Knotty Green, Bucks HP9 2TS. *Clubs:* Royal Automobile; Wisley Golf, Beaconsfield Golf.

TOFFOLO, Rt Rev. Mgr Adrian Titian; Episcopal Vicar for Formation, diocese of Plymouth, and Parish Priest, Church of the Holy Spirit, Bovey Tracey, since 1999; *b* 22 Sept. 1944; *s* of Sante Battista Toffolo and Ethel Elizabeth (*née* Hannaford-Hill). *Educ:* St Boniface's Coll., Plymouth; Gregorian Univ., Rome (PhL, STL). Asst Priest, Penzance, 1969–72; Prof. of Theology, Oscott Coll., 1972–76; Assistant Priest: Torquay, 1976–80; Plymouth, 1980–84; Parish Priest: St Austell, 1984–85; Truro, 1985–91; Rector, Venerable English College, Rome, 1991–99. Prelate of Honour, 1992. *Recreations:* mountain walking, music, DIY. *Address:* The Presbytery, Church of the Holy Spirit, Ashburton Road, Bovey Tracey, Devon TQ13 9BY. *T:* (01626) 833432.

TOFT, Dr Anthony Douglas, CBE 1995; FRCPE; Consultant Physician, Royal Infirmary, Edinburgh, since 1978; Physician to the Queen in Scotland, since 1996; *b* 29 Oct. 1944; *s* of William Vincent Toft and Anne Laing; *m* 1968, Maureen Margaret Darling; one *s* one *d*. *Educ:* Perth Academy; Univ. of Edinburgh (BSc Hons, MD). FRCPE 1980; FRCP 1992; FRCPI 1993; FRCPGlas 1993; FRCSE (*ad hominem*), 1994. House Physician and House Surgeon, 1969–70, jun. med. posts, 1970–78, Royal Infirmary, Edinburgh. Chief Medical Adviser, Scottish Equitable Life Assurance Soc., 1989–. Mem., Health Appointments Adv. Cttee, 1994–2000. Royal Coll. of Physicians of Edinburgh: Chm., Collegiate Members' Cttee, 1977; Mem. Council, 1986–88; Vice-Pres., 1990–91; Pres., 1991–94; Chm. Trustees, 1999–. Chairman: Scottish Royal Colls, 1993–94; Jt Cttee on Higher Med. Trng, 1994–96; Vice-Chm., UK Conf. of Med. Royal Colls, 1993–94. General Medical Council: Mem., 1999–; Occasional Chm., Professional Conduct Cttee, 1999–; Chm., Prof. and Linguistic Assessments Bd, 1999–. Pres., British Thyroid Assoc., 1997–99; Mem., Assoc. of Physicians of GB and Ireland, 1983–; Sec., Harveian Soc., 1980–94. Hon. Mem., Acad. of Medicine of Malaysia, 1993. Hon. FCPS (Pak) 1990; Hon. FACP 1993; Hon. FRACP 1993; Hon. FRCPC 1994; Hon. FRCGP 1994; Hon. FFPM 1994; Hon. Fellow, Acad. of Medicine of Singapore, 1994; Hon. FCPS (Bangladesh) 1995; Hon. FFAEM 1997. *Publications:* Diagnosis and Management of Endocrine Diseases, 1982; papers on thyroid disease. *Recreations:* golf, gardening, hill-walking. *Address:* 41 Hermitage Gardens, Edinburgh EH10 6AZ. *T:* (0131) 447 2221.

TOGANIVALU, Ratu Josua Brown, CBE 1980; JP; Chairman, Fiji Meat Industry Board, since 1997; *b* Fiji, 2 May 1930; *m*; two *s* one *d*. *Educ:* Levuka Public Sch.; Marist

Brothers Sch., Suva; Queensland Agricultural Coll.; Royal Agricultural Coll., Cirencester. With Native Lands Trust Board, 1953–71; MP Fiji, 1966–77: Minister for Lands, Mines and Mineral Resources, 1972–73; Minister for Agriculture, Fisheries and Forests, 1974–77; High Commissioner for Fiji: to New Zealand, 1978–81; in London, 1981–85. Chairman: Fiji Public Service Commn, 1989–92; Fiji Broadcasting Commn, 1988–94; Mem., Fiji Electoral Commn, 1997–. Represented Fiji at ACP Meeting, Guyana, 1975, ACP Meeting, Malawi, 1976, ACP/EEC Sugar Meetings, Brussels, 1976. Chm., Fiji Care Insurance Ltd, 1995–99; Director: Hunts Travel Service, 1994–; Hunts Investment, 1994–; Treasure Island Resort Ltd, 1996–. JP (Fiji) 1968. *Recreations:* cricket, Rugby, boxing. *Address:* Box 13326, Suva, Fiji. *Clubs:* United, Defence (Fiji).

TOH CHIN CHYE; Nila Utama, 1st class, 1990; BSc, PhD, DipSc; *b* 10 Dec. 1921; *m. Educ:* Raffles Coll., Singapore; University College, London; Nat. Inst. for Medical Research, London. Reader in Physiology, 1958–64, Research Associate 1964, Vice-Chancellor, 1968–75, Univ. of Singapore. Chm., People's Action Party, 1954–81 (a Founder Mem.); MP, Singapore, 1959–88; Dep. Prime Minister of Singapore, 1959–68; Minister for Science and Technology, 1968–75; Minister for Health, 1975–81. Chm., Applied Res. Corp., 1973–75. Chairman, Board of Governors: Singapore Polytechnic, 1959–75; Regional Inst. of Higher Educn and Devel, 1970–75; Mem. Admin. Bd, Assoc. of SE Asian Insts of Higher Learning, 1968–75. DLitt (*hc*) Singapore, 1976. *Publications:* papers in Jl of Physiology and other relevant jls. *Address:* 23 Greenview Crescent, Singapore 1128.

TOKATY, Prof. Grigori Alexandrovich; aerospace adviser; Professor Emeritus, City University; *b* North Caucasus, Russia; Ossetian by mother tongue. *Educ:* Leningrad Rabfak, 1929–30; Rykov Rabfak of Moscow Higher Technical Coll. MVTU, 1930–32; Zhukovsky Air Force Academy of Aeronautics, Moscow, 1932–37. DEng, PhD, DAeSc, CEng, CanTechSc. Lt Col, Air Force. Zhukovsky Academy: Aeronautical Research Engineer, 1937–38; Head of Aeronautics Laboratory, 1938–41; Dep. Head of Res. Dept, 1941; Lectr in Aerodynamics and Aircraft Design, 1941–45; Acting Prof. of Aviation, Moscow Engrg Inst, 1939–45; Rocket research and development, 1944–45; Rocket scientist, Berlin, 1945–47. Varied work for HM Govt, London, 1948–52; Imperial Coll., and Coll. of Aeronautics, Cranfield, 1953–56; work on theoretical rocket dynamics and orbital flight mechanics associated with Apollo programme, 1956–68; Reader in Aeronautics and Astronautics, Northampton Coll. of Advanced Technology, 1960–61; Head, 1961–75, and Prof., 1967–75, Dept of Aeronautics and Space Technology, Northampton Coll. of Advanced Technology and City Univ. Chief Scientific Adviser, WTI, 1976–78. Visiting Professor: Univs of the US, Jordan, Nigeria, Iran, Turkey, Holland. FRAeS, FAIAA, FIMA. *Publications:* numerous, including seven books: Rocketdynamics, 1961; The History of Rocket Technology (jt), 1964; A History and Philosophy of Fluid Mechanics, 1971; Cosmonautics-Astronautics, 1976; Higher Education, 1982; Scientific Technological Education for the shape of things to come, 1988; Theoretic Principles of Spaceship Design, 1989; articles and booklets (alone or jointly) in the fields of fluid mechanics, gasdynamics, rocketdynamics, theory and philosophy of educn, and non-scientific subjects. *Recreations:* writing, broadcasting, travelling. *Address:* Centre for Aeronautics, City University, Northampton Square, EC1V 0HB. *Club:* National Liberal.

TOKSVIG, Sandra Birgitte, (Sandi); writer and comedian; *b* 3 May 1958; *d* of late Claus Bertel Toksvig and of Julie Anne Toksvig; one *s* two *d*. *Educ:* Mamaroneck High Sch., NY; Tormead, Guildford; Girton Coll., Cambridge (MA Hons). *Television* includes: No 73, 1980–86; Whose Line Is It Anyway?; Behind the Headlines, 1993; Great Journeys, 1993; The Big One, 1993; Island Race, 1995; Call My Bluff, 1996–; *stage* includes: (performer) Nottingham Playhouse Rep., 1980; Open Air Theatre, Regent's Park, 1980; (jt writer) The Pocket Dream, 1993; (performer and writer) Big Night Out at the Little Sands Picture Palace, 1995; *radio* includes: Loose Ends, 1994–; I'm Sorry I Haven't a Clue, 1998–; Presenter, Midweek, 1996. *Publications: for children:* Tales from the Norse's Mouth, 1994; Unusual Day, 1997; If I Didn't Have Elbows, 1998; Super-saver Mouse, 1999; Super-saver Mouse to the Rescue, 2000; The Troublesome Tooth Fairy, 2001; *play:* The Pocket Dream, 1994; *travel books:* Great Journeys of the World, 1994; (with John McCarthy) Island Race, 1995; *novels:* Whistling for the Elephants, 1999; Flying Under Bridges, 2001. *Recreations:* golf, ski-ing, scuba diving, sewing. *Club:* Two Brydges.

TOLAND, Prof. John Francis, FRS 1999; Professor of Mathematics, University of Bath, since 1982; *b* 28 April 1949; *s* of Joseph Toland and Catherine Toland (*née* McGarvey); *m* 1977, Susan Frances Beck. *Educ:* St Columb's Coll., Derry; Queen's Univ., Belfast (BSc 1970, DSc 1993); Univ. of Sussex (MSc 1971, DPhil 1973). Batelle Advanced Studies Centre, Geneva, 1973; Lectr in Maths and Fellow of Fluid Mechanics Res. Inst., Univ. of Essex, 1973–79; Lectr in Maths, UCL, 1979–82; EPSRC Sen. Res. Fellow, 1997–Sept. 2002. Vis. lectr, Europe, Australia, USA. Hon. DSc QUB, 2000. Sen. Berwick Prize, LMS, 2000. *Publications:* mathematical research papers, mainly in nonlinear analysis. *Recreations:* archery, horses. *Address:* Department of Mathematical Sciences, University of Bath, Claverton Down, Bath BA2 7AY. *T:* (01225) 826188; *e-mail:* jft@maths.bath.ac.uk. *Club:* Bath Archers.

TOLER; *see* Graham-Toler, family name of Earl of Norbury.

TOLER, Maj.-Gen. David Arthur Hodges, OBE 1963; MC 1945; DL; *b* 13 Sept. 1920; *s* of Major Thomas Clayton Toler, DL, JP, Swettenham Hall, Congleton; *m* 1951, Judith Mary (*d* 2000), *d* of James William Garden, DSO, Aberdeen; one *s* one *d*. *Educ:* Stowe; Christ Church, Oxford (MA). 2nd Lieut Coldstream Guards, 1940; served War of 1939–45, N Africa and Italy; Regimental Adjt, Coldstream Guards, 1952–54; Bde Major, 4th Gds Bde, 1956–57; Adjt, RMA Sandhurst, 1958–60; Bt Lt-Col 1959; Br Liaison Officer, US Continental Army Comd (Col), 1960–62; comd 2nd Bn Coldstream Guards, 1962–64; comd Coldstream Guards, 1964–65; comd 4th Guards Bde, 1965–68; Dep. Comdt, Staff Coll., Camberley, 1968–69; GOC E Midland Dist, 1970–73; retired 1973. Dep. Hon. Col, Royal Anglian Regt (Lincolnshire) TAVR, 1979–84. Emergency Planning Officer, Lincolnshire CC, 1974–77. Chm., Lincoln Dio. Adv. Cttee, 1981–86. Pres., SSAFA, Lincs, 1978–98. DL Lincs, 1982. *Recreation:* gardening. *Address:* Rutland Farm, Fulbeck, Grantham, Lincs NG32 3LG. *Club:* Army and Navy.

TOLHURST, Rear Adm. John Gordon, CB 1995; Military Deputy to Head of Defence Export Services, Ministry of Defence, since 1997; *b* 22 April 1943; *s* of Cdre Virgil George Tolhurst, VRD, RNR, and Elizabeth Mary Tolhurst; *m* 1975, Susan Jayne Spencer; one *s* one *d*. *Educ:* Sevenoaks Sch. Joined RN 1961; Commanding Officer: HMS Berwick, 1977; HMS Exeter, 1984; Asst Dir, Naval Warfare, 1986; Commodore, HMS Nelson, 1988; CO HMS Invincible, 1990; ADC to the Queen, 1990; Flag Officer: Sea Trng, 1992–96; Scotland, Northern England and NI, 1996–97. Mem., Search and Rescue Cttee, and Mgt Cttee, RNLI, 1997–. Younger Brother, Trinity House. *Recreations:* classic cars, shooting, gardening. *Address:* Ministry of Defence, St Christopher House SE1 0TD.

TOLLEMACHE, family name of **Baron Tollemache**.

TOLLEMACHE, 5th Baron *cr* 1876; **Timothy John Edward Tollemache;** Vice Lord-Lieutenant of Suffolk, since 1994; Director, Fortis (UK), and other companies; farmer and landowner; *b* 13 Dec. 1939; *s* of 4th Baron Tollemache, MC, DL, and Dinah Susan (*d* 1998), *d* of late Sir Archibald Auldjo Jamieson, KBE, MC; *S* father, 1975; *m* 1970, Alexandra Dorothy Jean, *d* of late Col Hugo Meynell, MC; two *s* one *d*. *Educ:* Eton. Commissioned into Coldstream Guards, 1959; served Kenya, Persian Gulf and Zanzibar, 1960–62; Course of Estate Management at Sandringham, Norfolk, 1962–64. President: NW Agronomy, 1983–; E Anglian Productivity Assoc., 1984–88; Suffolk Agricl Assoc., 1988; The Milk Gp, 1994–; Chm., CLA, Suffolk, 1990–93; Vice Pres., Suffolk Assoc. of Local Councils, 1996– (Pres., 1978–96). Mem., Firearms Consultative Cttee, 1995–98. Vice Pres., Cheshire Red Cross, 1980–; Chm., St John's Council for Suffolk, 1982–89. President: Friends of Ipswich Museums, 1980–96; Suffolk Family History Soc., 1988–; SSAFA, Suffolk, 1996–; CAB, Ipswich & dist, 1998–; Chairman: HHA (E Anglia), 1979–83; Bury St Edmunds Cathedral Appeal, 1986–90; Trustees, Suffolk Historic Churches Trust, 1996–; Vice Patron, Suffolk Preservation Soc., 1992–. Patron: Suffolk Accident Rescue Service, 1983–; E Suffolk Assoc. for the Blind, 1992–. DL Suffolk, 1984. CStJ 1988. *Recreations:* shooting, fishing, natural history. *Heir:* *s* Hon. Edward John Hugo Tollemache, *b* 12 May 1976. *Address:* Helmingham Hall, Stowmarket, Suffolk IP14 6EF. *Clubs:* White's, Pratt's, Special Forces.

TOLLEMACHE, Sir Lyonel (Humphry John), 7th Bt *cr* 1793, of Hanby Hall; JP; DL; *b* 10 July 1931; *s* of Maj.-Gen. Sir Humphry Tollemache, 6th Bt, CB, CBE, DL and Nora Priscilla (*d* 1990), *d* of John Taylor; *S* father, 1990; *m* 1960, Mary Joscelyne, *d* of late William Henry Whitbread, TD; one *s* two *d* (and one *s* decd). *Educ:* Uppingham Sch.; RMA Sandhurst; RAC Cirencester. FRICS. Major, Coldstream Guards, retd 1963. Member: Melton and Belvoir RDC, 1969–74, Melton BC, 1974–87 (Mayor, 1981–82); Leics CC, 1985–97. Gov., Royal Star and Garter Home, Richmond, 1985–2001. High Sheriff 1978–79, JP 1978, DL 1980, Leics. *Heir:* *s* Richard John Tollemache, JP [*b* 4 May 1966; *m* 1992, Amanda, *er d* of Gordon Phillips; one *s* one *d*]. *Address:* Buckminster Park, Grantham NG33 5RU.

TOLLETT, Lorna Ann; *see* Casselton, L. A.

TOLLEY, Rev. Canon George; SOSc; Hon. Canon, 1976–98, now Canon Emeritus, and Hon. Assistant, since 1990, Sheffield Cathedral; *b* 24 May 1925; *s* of George and Elsie Tolley, Old Hill, Staffordshire; *m* 1947, Joan Amelia Grosvenor; two *s* one *d*. *Educ:* Halesowen Grammar Sch.; Birmingham Central Tech. Coll. (part-time); Princeton Univ., USA; Lincoln Theol Coll., 1965–67; Sheffield Univ. (MA). BSc, MSc, PhD (London); FRSC; FIM; CIMgt. Rotary Foundation Fellow, Princeton Univ., 1949–50. Head, Department of Chemistry, College of Advanced Technology, Birmingham, 1954–58; Head of Research and Experimental Dept, Allied Ironfounders Ltd, 1958–61; Principal, Worcester Tech. College, 1961–65; Senior Director of Studies, Royal Air Force Coll., Cranwell, 1965–66; Principal, Sheffield Coll. of Technology, 1966–69, Sheffield City Polytechnic, 1969–82; Manpower Services Commission: Dir, Open Tech Unit, 1983–84; Head, Quality Branch, 1984–85; Chief Officer, Review of Vocational Qualifications, 1985–86; Advr, NCVQ, 1986–88; Advr, Trng Commn, then Trng Agency, 1988–90. Ordained deacon, 1967, priest, 1968; Curate, St Andrew's, Sharrow, 1967–90. Chairman: Council, Plastics Inst., 1959–61; Further Educn Adv. Cttee, Food, Drink and Tobacco Ind. Trng Bd, 1974–78; Bd, Further Educn Curriculum Unit, 1978–82; BTec Continuing Educn Cttee, 1983–85; Council of the Selly Oak Colls, Birmingham, 1984–92; Adv. Bd, Pitman Exams Inst., 1987–92; Central Sheffield Univ. Hosps NHS Trust, 1992–95; Pres., Inst. of Home Economics, 1987–90; Vice-Pres., Educn 2000, 1990–92; Hon. Sec., Assoc. of Colleges of Further and Higher Educn, 1975–82; Member: CNAA (Chm., Cttee for Business and Management Studies, 1972–83); Yorks and Humberside Economic Planning Council, 1976–79; RAF Trng and Educn Cttee, 1975–80; Governing Body, Derbyshire Coll. of Higher Educn, 1984–87. Member Council: PSI, 1981–89; RSA, 1983–92. Dep. Chm., S Yorks Foundn, 1986–90. Hon. Treas., SOSc, 1995–. Sheffield Church Burgess. Hon. FCP; Hon. Fellow: Sheffield City Polytechnic, 1982; Columbia—Pacific Univ., 1983; CGLI, 1984; Inst. of Trng and Develt, 1989. Hon. DSc: Sheffield, 1984; CNAA, 1986; DUniv Open, 1984. *Publications:* Meaning and Purpose in Higher Education, 1976; A History of the Sheffield Church Burgesses, 1998; Bringing Prayer to Life, 2001; many papers relating to plastics and education in British and foreign journals. *Recreation:* savouring remembered sounds. *Address:* 74 Furniss Avenue, Dore, Sheffield S17 3QP.

TOLOLO, Sir Alkan, KBE 1985 (CBE); High Commissioner for Papua New Guinea in Malaysia, 1986; *m* Nerrie Tololo, MBE; two *s* two *d*. Teaching, 1957–61; supervisory teacher, 1963–65; Superintendent of Schools, 1967–69; Mem., Public Service Board, 1969–70; First Comr, PNG Teaching Service, 1971–73; Dir of Education, 1973–79; Chm., Public Services Commn, 1979–80; Consul-General Sydney, 1981; High Comr in Australia, 1983–86. Former Mem. or Chm. of numerous Boards and Cttees on education, culture and employment, PNG. Hon. LLD 1982, Hon. DTech 1982, Univ. of Papua New Guinea. *Address:* PO Box 3014, Boroko NCD, Papua New Guinea.

TOLPUTT, John Nigel, MA; Head, The Purcell School, since 1999; *b* 1 May 1947; *s* of Basil Tolputt and Betty Durrant; *m* 1971, Patta Davis; one *s* one *d*. *Educ:* St John's Coll., Cambridge (MA); Bristol Univ. (Cert Ed 1969). Teacher, Bromsgrove Sch., 1969–74; Head of English and Drama, Cranleigh Sch., 1974–87; Head, Rendcomb Coll., 1987–99. FRSA 1994. *Recreation:* theatre. *Address:* Headmaster's House, The Purcell School, Aldenham Road, Bushey, Herts WD23 2TS.

TOLSON, Robin Stewart; QC 2001; a Recorder, since 2000; *b* 21 June 1958; *s* of Trevor and Vivian Tolson; *m* 1987, Carol Atkinson; two *d*. *Educ:* Hull Grammar Sch.; Jesus Coll., Cambridge (MA). Called to the Bar, Inner Temple, 1980; in practice as barrister, 1980–, specialising in family law and local govt admin. law; Asst Recorder, 1998–2000. *Publications:* (contrib.) Encyclopedia of Financial Provision in Family Matters. *Recreation:* triathlon. *Address:* (chambers) 35 Essex Street, Temple, WC2R 3AR. *T:* (020) 7353 6381.

TOM, Peter William Gregory; Chief Executive, Aggregate Industries plc, since 1997; *b* 26 July 1940; *s* of late John Gregory Tom and of Barbara Tom (*née* Lambden); two *d* (and one *s* decd). *Educ:* Hinckley Grammar Sch. Joined Bardon Hill Quarries Ltd, 1956: Man. Dir, 1977; Chm. and Chief Exec., 1985; merged with: Evered plc, 1991, to form Evered Bardon; CAMAS, 1997, to form Aggregate Industries plc. Chm., Quarry Products Assoc., 1997. Chm., Leicester FC, 1992–. *Address:* Aggregate Industries plc, Bardon Hall, Copt Oak Road, Markfield, Leics LE67 9PJ. *T:* (01530) 816600.

TOMALIN, Claire; writer; *b* 20 June 1933; *d* of Emile Delavenay and Muriel Herbert; *m* 1st, 1955, Nicholas Osborne Tomalin (*d* 1973); one *s* two *d* (and one *s* one *d* decd); 2nd, 1993, Michael Frayn, *qv*. *Educ:* Hitchin Girls' Grammar Sch.; Dartington Hall Sch.; Newnham Coll., Cambridge (MA). Publishers' reader and editor, Messrs Heinemann, Hutchinson, Cape, 1955–67; Evening Standard, 1967–68; New Statesman: Asst Literary Editor, 1968–70; Literary Editor, 1974–77; Literary Editor, Sunday Times, 1979–86. Stage play, The Winter Wife, Nuffield, Southampton, 1991. Trustee, Nat. Portrait Gallery, 1992–. Registrar, Royal Literary Fund, 1984– (Mem. Cttee, 1974–99; Vice-

Pres., 2000). Vice-Pres., English PEN, 1997–. FRSL (Mem. Council, 1993–2000). *Publications:* The Life and Death of Mary Wollstonecraft, 1974; Shelley and his World, 1980; Parents and Children, 1981; Katherine Mansfield: a secret life, 1987; The Invisible Woman: the story of Nelly Ternan and Charles Dickens, 1990 (NCR, Hawthornden, and James Tait Black Prizes, 1991); Mrs Jordan's Profession, 1994; Jane Austen: a life, 1997; (ed) Mary Shelley, Maurice, 1998; Several Strangers: writing from three decades, 1999; literary journalism. *Recreations:* travelling in Europe, walking in Regent's Park. *Address:* c/o David Godwin, 14 Goodwins Court, WC2N 4LL.

TOMBS, family name of **Baron Tombs**.

TOMBS, Baron *cr* 1990 (Life Peer), of Brailes in the county of Warwickshire; **Francis Leonard Tombs,** Kt 1978; FREng; Chairman: Rolls-Royce, 1985–92 (Director, 1982–92); Old Mutual South Africa Trust, 1994–98; *b* 17 May 1924; *s* of Joseph and Jane Tombs; *m* 1949, Marjorie Evans; three *d. Educ:* Elmore Green Sch., Walsall; Birmingham Coll. of Technology; BSc (Econ) Hons, London. GEC, 1939–45; Birmingham Corp., 1946–47; British Electricity Authority, Midlands, then Central Electricity Authority, Merseyside and N Wales, 1948–57; Gen. Man., GEC, Erith, 1958–67; Dir and Gen. Man., James Howden & Co., Glasgow, 1967–68; successively Dir of Engrg, Dep. Chm., Chm., South of Scotland Electricity Bd, 1969–77; Chm., Electricity Council, 1977–80. Chairman: Weir Group, 1981–83; Turner & Newall, 1982–89; subseq. T & N, 1982–89; Director: N. M. Rothschild & Sons, 1981–94; Shell-UK, 1983–94. Pres., Molecule Theatre Ltd, 1993–96 (Chm., 1985–92). Member: Nature Conservancy Council, 1978–82; Standing Commn on Energy and the Environment, 1978–; SERC, 1982–85; Chairman: Engrg Council, 1985–88; ACARD, 1985–87 (Mem., 1984–87); ACOST, 1987–90. Chm., H of L Select Cttee on Sustainable Develt, 1994–95; Mem., H of L Select Cttee on Sci. and Technol., 1997–. Pres., IEE, 1981–82; formerly Vice-Pres., Fellowship of Engrg; Vice-Pres., Engineers for Disaster Relief, 1985–94. Chm., Assoc. of British Orchestras, 1982–86. FREng (FEng 1977); FRAeS 1994, Hon. FRAeS 1995; Hon. FIChemE 1985; Hon. FICE 1986; Hon. FIProdE 1986; Hon. FIMechE 1989; Hon. FIEE 1991; Hon. FRSE 1996; Hon. Mem., British Nuclear Energy Soc. Pro-Chancellor and Chm. Council, Cranfield Inst. of Technol., 1985–91; Chancellor, Strathclyde Univ., 1991–97 (Hon. LLD 1976; DUniv 1991). Freeman, City of London, 1980; Liveryman, 1981–, and Prime Warden, 1994–95, Goldsmiths' Co. Hon. DTech Loughborough, 1979; Hon. DSc: Aston, 1979; Lodz, Poland, 1980; Cranfield, 1985; Bradford, 1986; City, 1986; Surrey, 1988; Nottingham, 1989; Warwick, 1990; Cambridge, 1990; DSc(Eng) QUB, 1986; DEd CNAA, 1989. *Recreations:* music, golf. *Address:* Honington Lodge, Honington, Shipston-upon-Stour, Warwickshire CV36 5AA.

TOMBS, Sebastian Martineau, FRIAS; Secretary, Royal Incorporation of Architects in Scotland, since 1995; *b* 11 Oct. 1949; *s* of late Dr David M. Tombs and Joan (*née* Parley); *m* 1988, Eva Heirman; four *s* two *d. Educ:* Bryanston; Corpus Christi Coll., Cambridge (BArch, DipArch). ACIArb 1977; FRIAS 1992. RMJM, Edinburgh, 1975–76; Roland Wedgwood, Edinburgh, 1976–77; Fountainbridge Housing Assoc., Edinburgh, 1977–78; Housing Corp., 1978–81; Housing Dept, Edinburgh DC, 1982–86; Depute Sec., RIAS, 1986–94. Founder and first Sec., Scottish Ecological Design Assoc., 1991–94 (Chm., 1994–97); Founder and first Chm., Assoc. Planning Supervisors, 1995–97. Contested (Lib Dem): Edinburgh N and Leith, Scottish Parlt, 1999; Edinburgh N and Leith, 2001. *Recreations:* choral music, doggerel, sketching. *Address:* Royal Incorporation of Architects in Scotland, 15 Rutland Square, Edinburgh EH1 2BE. *T:* (0131) 229 7545, *Fax:* (0131) 228 2188; *e-mail:* stombs@rias.org.uk.

TOMEI, Anthony Laurence; Director, Nuffield Foundation, since 1995; *b* 1 June 1949; *s* of late Laurence Stephen Tomei and Dora Tomei (*née* Myring); *m* 1977, Nicola Bourn; one *s* two *d. Educ:* St Joseph's Coll., London; Univ. of Sussex (BSc); Univ. of Manchester (MSc). Physics teacher, VSO, Johore, Malaysia, 1970–72; teacher, William Ellis Sch., London, 1972–74; Nuffield Foundation: Research Grants Officer, 1977–82; Asst Dir, 1982–95. Trustee: Bristol Exploratory, 1983–86; Rutherford Trust, 1992–96; Integrated Educn Fund (NI), 1992–97. Gov., Nuffield Chelsea Curriculum Trust, 1980–98. Gov., Parliament Hill Sch., London, 1992–2000. *Recreations:* tennis, family life. *Address:* c/o Nuffield Foundation, 28 Bedford Square, WC1B 3JS. *T:* (020) 7631 0566.

TOMKINS, Sir Edward Emile, GCMG 1975 (KCMG 1969; CMG 1960); CVO 1957; Grand Officiér, Légion d'Honneur, 1984; HM Diplomatic Service, retired; HM Ambassador to France, 1972–75; *b* 16 Nov. 1915; *s* of late Lt-Col E. L. Tomkins; *m* 1955, Gillian Benson; one *s* two *d. Educ:* Ampleforth Coll.; Trinity Coll., Cambridge. Foreign Office, 1939. Military service, 1940–43. HM Embassy, Moscow, 1944–46; Foreign Office, 1946–51; HM Embassy, Washington, 1951–54; HM Embassy, Paris, 1954–59; Foreign Office, 1959–63; HM Embassy, Bonn, 1963–67; HM Embassy, Washington, 1967–69; Ambassador to the Netherlands, 1970–72. Mem., Bucks CC, 1977–85. *Address:* Winslow Hall, Winslow, Bucks MK18 3HL. *T:* (01296) 712323.

TOMKYS, Sir (William) Roger, KCMG 1991 (CMG 1984); DL; HM Diplomatic Service, retired; Master of Pembroke College, Cambridge, since 1992; *b* 15 March 1937; *s* of late William Arthur and Edith Tomkys; *m* 1963, Margaret Jean Abbey; one *s* one *d. Educ:* Bradford Grammar Sch.; Balliol Coll., Oxford (Domus Scholar; 1st cl. Hons Lit. Hum.). Entered Foreign Service, 1960; MECAS, 1960; 3rd Sec., Amman, 1962; 2nd Sec., FCO, 1964; 1st Sec., Head of Chancery, Benghazi, 1967; Planning Staff, FCO, 1969; Head of Chancery, Athens, 1972; Counsellor, seconded to Cabinet Office, 1975; Head of Near East and North Africa Dept, FCO, 1977–80; Counsellor, Rome, 1980–81; Ambassador: to Bahrain, 1981–84; to Syria, 1984–86; Asst Under Sec. of State and Principal Finance Officer, FCO, 1987–89; Dep. Under Sec. of State, FCO, 1989–90; High Comr, Kenya, 1990–92. DL Cambridgeshire, 1996. Commendatore dell'Ordine al Merito, 1980; Order of Bahrain, 1st cl., 1984. *Address:* The Master's Lodge, Pembroke College, Cambridge CB2 1RF. *Club:* Royal & Ancient Golf (St Andrews).

TOMLINSON, Baron *cr* 1998 (Life Peer), of Walsall in the co. of West Midlands; **John Edward Tomlinson;** *b* 1 Aug. 1939; *s* of Frederick Edwin Tomlinson, headmaster, and Doris Mary Tomlinson. *Educ:* Westminster City Sch.; Co-operative Coll., Loughborough; Nottingham Univ. (Dip. Polit. Econ. Social Studies); MA (Industrial Relations) Warwick, 1982. Sec., Sheffield Co-operative Party, 1961–68; Head of Research Dept, AUEW, 1968–70; Lectr in Industrial Relations, 1970–74. MP (Lab) Meriden, Feb. 1974–1979; PPS to Prime Minister, 1975–76; Parly Under-Sec. of State, FCO, 1976–79, and ODM, 1977–79. Sen. Lectr in Industrial Relations and Management, later Hd of Social Studies, Solihull Coll. of Tech., 1979–84. MEP (Lab) Birmingham W, 1984–99; Eur. PLP spokesman on budgetary control, 1989–99. Vice Chm., Hansard Soc., 1993–. Trustee, Industry and Parlt Trust, 1988–. Pres., British Fluoridation Soc., 1998–. Contested (Lab) Warwicks N, 1983. *Publication:* Left, Right: the march of political extremism in Britain, 1981. *Address:* House of Lords, SW1A 0PW. *Club:* West Bromwich Labour.

TOMLINSON, Prof. (Alfred) Charles, CBE 2001; Professor of English, University of Bristol, 1982–92, now Emeritus, Senior Research Fellow, since 1996; *b* 8 Jan. 1927; *s* of Alfred Tomlinson and May Lucas; *m* 1948, Brenda Raybould; two *d. Educ:* Longton High School; Queens' Coll., Cambridge (MA; Hon. Fellow, 1974); Royal Holloway and Bedford Colls, Univ. of London (MA; Hon. Fellow RHBNC, 1991). Lecturer, 1957–68, Reader in English poetry, 1968–82, Bristol Univ. Visiting Prof., Univ. of New Mexico, 1962–63; O'Connor Prof., Colgate Univ., NY, 1967–68 and 1989; Vis. Fellow, Princeton Univ., 1981; Lamont Prof., Union Coll., NY, 1987; Vis. Prof., McMaster Univ., Canada, 1987; Hon. Prof. of English, Keele Univ., 1989. Arts Council Poetry Panel, 1964–66. Lectures: Witter Bynner, Univ. of New Mexico, 1976; Clark, Cambridge, 1982; Edmund Blunden, Hong Kong, 1987; Stubbs, Toronto, 1992; St Jerome, London, 1995. Exhibition of Graphics: Ely House, OUP, London, 1972; Clare Coll., Cambridge, 1975; Arts Council touring exhibn, 1978–80; Poetry Soc., 1983; Regent's Coll. Gall., 1986; in Surrealism in English Art, touring exhibn, 1986–87; Colby Coll., Maine, USA, 1987; McMaster Univ. Gall., Canada, 1987. FRSL 1974. Hon. DLitt: Keele, 1981; Colgate, 1981; New Mexico, 1986. Cholmondeley Award, 1979; Wilbur Award, 1982; Citadella Premio Europeo, 1991; Bennett Award, NY, 1993; Il Premio Internazionale di Poesia Ennio Flaiano, 2001. *Publications: poetry:* Relations and Contraries, 1951; The Necklace, 1955, repr. 1966; Seeing is Believing, 1960 (US 1958); A Peopled Landscape, 1963; Poems, 1964; American Scenes, 1966; The Poem as Initiation, 1968; The Way of a World, 1969; Poems, in Penguin Modern Poets, 1969; Renga, 1970, 1972, 1979; Written on Water, 1972; The Way In, 1974; Selected Poems, 1978; The Shaft, 1978; (with Octavio Paz) Air Born, 1981 (Mexico 1979); The Flood, 1981; Notes from New York and other Poems, 1984; Collected Poems, 1985, expanded repr., 1987; The Return, 1987; Nella pienezza del tempo, 1987; Annunciations, 1989; Selected Poems, 1989; The Door in the Wall, 1992; Poemas, 1992; Charles Tomlinson: sette poesie, 1993; Gedichte, 1994; La insistencia de las cosas, 1994; La huella del cievo, 1994; En la plenitud del tiempo, 1994; Jubilation, 1995; In Italia, 1996; Portuguese Pieces, 1996; The Fox Gallery, 1996; Selected Poems 1955–97, 1997; The Vineyard Above the Sea, 1999; Luoghi Italiani, 2000; *prose:* Some Americans: a personal record, 1980 (US); Poetry and Metamorphosis, 1983; The Letters of William Carlos Williams and Charles Tomlinson, 1992, expanded edn, 1999; American Essays: making it new, 2001; *graphics:* Words and Images, 1972; In Black and White, 1975; Eden, 1985; *translations:* (with Henry Gifford): Versions from Fyodor Tyutchev, 1960; Castilian Ilexes: Versions from Antonio Machado, 1963; Ten Versions from Trilce by César Vallejo, (US) 1970; Translations, 1983; Attilio Bertolucci: selected poems, 1993; *edited:* Marianne Moore: A Collection of Critical Essays, (US) 1969; William Carlos Williams: A Collection of Critical Essays, 1972; William Carlos Williams: Selected Poems, 1976, rev. edn (US) 1985; Octavio Paz: Selected Poems, 1979; The Oxford Book of Verse in English Translation, 1980; George Oppen: selected poems, 1990; Eros Englished: erotic poems from the Greek and Latin, 1992; contribs to: Essays in Criticism, Hudson Review, Modern Painters, Poetry (Chicago), Poetry Nation Review, Sewanee Review, Times Lit. Supp., Vuelta. *Recreations:* music, walking. *Address:* Ozleworth, Glos GL12 7QB.

TOMLINSON, Sir Bernard (Evans), Kt 1988; CBE 1981; DL; MD; FRCP, FRCPath; Chairman, Northern Regional Health Authority, 1982–90; Emeritus Professor of Pathology, University of Newcastle upon Tyne, since 1985; Consultant Neuropathologist, Newcastle Health Authority (formerly Area Health Authority), since 1976; *b* 13 July 1920; *s* of James Arthur Tomlinson and Doris Mary (*née* Evans); *m* 1944, Betty Oxley; one *s* one *d. Educ:* Brunts Sch., Mansfield; University Coll. and University Coll. Hosp., London (BS 1943, MD 1962). FRCP 1965; FRCPath 1964. Trainee Pathologist, EMS, 1943–47; served RAMC as Specialist Pathologist, 1947–49 (Major). Newcastle upon Tyne General Hospital: Sen. Registrar, Pathology, 1949–50; Consultant Pathologist, 1950–53; Sen. Consultant Pathologist, 1953–82; Hon. Lectr in Path., Univ. of Newcastle upon Tyne, 1960–71, Hon. Prof., 1972–85. Hon. Mem. Scientific Staff, MRC Neurochemical Pathology Unit, 1987–; Founding Chm., Res. Gp on Dementia, World Fedn of Neurology, 1984–87. Chm., Jt Planning Appts Cttee, DHSS, 1986–90; Mem., Disablement Services Authority, 1987–91. Leader of indep. enquiry into London's health services, 1991–92; non-exec. Dir, Newcastle City Health Trust, 1994–95. Mem. Council, Assoc. of Clinical Pathologists, 1965–68; Privy Council Mem., RPharmS, 1990–95 (Hon. Mem., 1997). President: British Neuropathological Soc., 1979–81; NE Alzheimer Disease Soc., 1985–. Hon. Mem., Amer. Neurol Assoc., 1997. Hon. MD Newcastle upon Tyne, 1993. Chm., Friends of Durham Cathedral, 1991–94. DL Tyne and Wear 1988. Dorothy Russell Lectr and Medallist, British Neuropath. Soc., 1989; Gold Medal Sci. Award, 3rd Internat. Conf. on Alzheimer's Disease, Padua, 1992. *Publications:* articles and book chapters on neuropath., partic. on path. of brain injury, brain changes in old age and on dementia. *Recreations:* gardening, golf, music, walking. *Address:* Greyholme, Wynbury Road, Low Fell, Gateshead, Tyne and Wear NE9 6TS.

TOMLINSON, Charles; *see* Tomlinson, A. C.

TOMLINSON, Heather Ann; Director of Education, Nottingham City Council, since 2001; *b* 23 June 1953; *d* of Kenneth and Joan Veneear; partner, Charles George Sisum; two *d. Educ:* Cheshunt Grammar Sch.; Univ. of Sheffield (BEd Hons; MEd; DPSE). Teacher, Rotherham LEA, 1976–80; Teacher, 1981–88, Educn Advr, 1988–98, Sheffield LEA; Regl Advisory Teacher, S Yorks and Humberside LEAs, 1988–90; Asst Dir of Educn, Nottingham City LEA, 1998–2001. *Recreations:* sailing, coastal walks, wines. *Address:* Nottingham City Council, Sandfield Centre, Sandfield Road, Lenton, Nottingham NG7 1QH. *T:* (0115) 915 0601. *Club:* St Mawes Sailing (Cornwall).

TOMLINSON, Prof. John Race Godfrey, CBE 1983; MA; Professor of Education, 1985–97 and Director, 1985–96, Institute of Education, University of Warwick, now Professor Emeritus; Deputy Chairman, General Teaching Council for England, since 2000; *b* 24 April 1932; *s* of John Angell Tomlinson and Beatrice Elizabeth Race Godfrey; *m* 1954, Audrey Mavis Barrett; two *s* two *d. Educ:* Stretford Grammar Sch.; Manchester Univ. (MA); London Inst. of Historical Research. Flt Lt, RAF, 1955–58. Teaching, 1958–60; Admin. Asst, Salop LEA, 1960–63; Asst Educn Officer, Lancs LEA, 1963–67; Dep. Dir of Educn, Cheshire LEA, 1967–72; Dir of Educn, Cheshire CC, 1972–84. Chairman: Schools Council, 1978–81; NICEC, 1985–89; Arts in Education Project, SCDC, 1985–90; Academic Sec., UCET, 1997–2000. Member: Court Cttee on Child Health Services, 1973–76; Gulbenkian enquiries into Drama, Music and Dance, 1974–78; Founder Chm., Further Educn Curriculum Review and Develt Unit, 1976; Member: Special Programmes Bd, MSC, 1977–82; Delegacy for Continuing Educn, Open Univ., 1978–81; Study Commn on the Family, 1978–83; Adv. Cttee on Supply and Trng of Teachers, 1979–82; Council, Foundn for Educn Business Partnerships, 1990–91; Educn Advr, RNCM, 1972–85. Chm., Exec. Cttee and Trustees, 1982–95, Patron, 1995–, Nat. Schs Curriculum Award; Chairman: MSC TVEI Quality and Standards Gp, 1986–88; Enquiry into Freedom of Information, ILEA, 1986–87; Gen. Teaching Council initiative, 1991–2000; FEFC Enquiry, Disability and Learning Difficulties, 1993–96; Gulbenkian Enquiry into Personal and Social Education, 1998–2000. Royal Society of Arts: Vice-Pres., 1986; Chm., Exams Bd, 1986–89; Chm. Council, 1989–91 (Mem. Council, 1982–99); FRSA 1976. Pres., Soc. of Educn Officers, 1982; Trustee, Community Service Volunteers, 1981–89; Edward Boyle Trust, 1988–98; Chm., Comino Foundn, 2001–. Governor: Chetham's Sch., Manchester, 1984–92; Menuhin Sch., 1987–89. Hon. Prof.,

Dept of Educn, Keele Univ., 1981–84; Distinguished Vis. Academic, QUB, 1996. Lectures: Wilfred Fish Meml, GDC, 1978; Charles Gittens Meml, Univ. of Wales, 1980; Lockyer, RCP, 1980; Schools Council, BAAS, 1981; Standing Conf. on Schools' Science and Technology Annual, 1987; Barry and Tye Meml, Manchester Univ., 1987; Internat. Schs Distinguished, Internat. Schs Assoc. Conf., Hamburg, 1994. FIMgt (MBIM 1976); FCP 1980. Hon. RNCM 1980. Freeman, City of London, 1989; Liveryman, Goldsmiths' Co., 1991– (Mem., Educn Cttee, 1982–89, 1994–99). DUniv: Open, 1999; Surrey, 1999; Hon. EdD UWE, 1999. *Publications:* Additional Grenville Papers 1763–65, 1962; (ed) The Changing Government of Education, 1986; Teacher Appraisal: a nationwide approach, 1989; The Control of Education, 1993; School Co-operation: new forms of governance, 1994; articles in various jls. *Recreations:* family and garden, music and walking, a relentless search for good bitter. *Address:* General Teaching Council for England, 344–354 Gray's Inn Road, WC1X 8BP; The Barn House, 76 Birmingham Road, Allesley, Coventry CV5 9GX. *Clubs:* Athenæum, Army and Navy.

TOMLINSON, John Rowland, CBE 1997; operatic bass; *b* 22 Sept. 1946; *s* of Rowland and Ellen Tomlinson; *m* 1969, Moya (*née* Joel); one *s* two *d*. *Educ:* Accrington GS; Manchester Univ. (BSc Civil Engrg); Royal Manchester Coll. of Music. Since beginning career with Glyndebourne in 1970, has sung over 100 operatic bass roles with ENO, Royal Opera, Covent Garden, Opera North, Scottish Opera, and in Geneva, Lisbon, Bologna, Florence, Milan, Copenhagen, Amsterdam, Stuttgart, Bayreuth, Berlin, Dresden, Madrid, Santiago, Tokyo, Vienna, Paris, Bordeaux, Avignon, Aix-en-Provence, Orange, San Diego, San Francisco, Pittsburgh, Vancouver, NY, Munich, Chicago and Salzburg; also broadcasts and recordings; best known for interpretations of Wagner bass and bass-baritone rôles, incl. Hans Sachs, Wotan (Bayreuth, 1988–98), Wanderer, Hagen and Gurnemanz; other rôles include: Boris, four villains in Hoffman, Méphistophélès, Zaccharia, Claggart, Bluebeard, Baron Ochs, Rocco, Golaud, Moses, Philip II, Attila, Oberto, Green Knight and Borromeo. Hon. FRNCM 1996. Hon. Dr: Sussex, 1997; Manchester, 1998. Singer of the Year, Royal Philharmonic Soc., 1991, 1998; Grammy Award (for Bartok, Cantata Profana), 1993; Reginald Goodall Award, Wagner Soc., 1996; Evening Standard Opera Award, 1998. *Address:* c/o Music International, 13 Ardilaun Road, Highbury, N5 2QR. *T:* (020) 7359 5183.

TOMLINSON, Michael John, CBE 1997; HM Chief Inspector of Schools, since 2000; *b* 17 Oct. 1942; *s* of Edith Cresswell and Jack Tomlinson; *m* 1965, Maureen Janet; one *s* one *d*. *Educ:* Oakwood Technical High Sch., Rotherham; Bournemouth Boys' Sch.; Durham Univ. (BSc Hons Chem.); Nottingham Univ. (post-grad. Cert Ed (First Div.)). Chemistry teacher, Henry Mellish GS, Nottingham, 1965–69; Head of Chemistry, Ashby-de-la-Zouch GS, 1969–77; School/Industry Liaison Officer, ICI (secondment), 1977; Chief Inspector (Schools), HM Inspectorate of Schs, 1989–92; Dep. Dir, 1992–95, Dir of Inspection, 1995–2000, Office for Standards in Education. Chem. Soc. Award in Chem. Educn (Bronze Medal), 1975. Silver Jubilee Medal, 1977. *Publications:* New Movements in the Study and Teaching of Chemistry, 1975; Organic Chemistry: a problem-solving approach, 1977; Mechanisms in Organic Chemistry: case studies, 1978; BP educn service contribs, 1974–78; articles in professional jls. *Recreations:* gardening, food and wine, reading. *Address:* Brooksby, Mayhall Lane, Chesham Bois, Amersham, Bucks HP6 5NR. *T:* (01494) 726967.

TOMLINSON, Prof. Richard Allan, FSA; Director, British School at Athens, 1995–96; *b* 25 April 1932; *s* of James Edward Tomlinson and Dorothea Mary (*née* Grellier); *m* 1957, Heather Margaret Murphy; three *s* one *d*. *Educ:* King Edward's Sch., Birmingham; St John's Coll., Cambridge (BA, MA). FSA 1970. Asst, Dept of Greek, Univ. of Edinburgh, 1957; University of Birmingham: Asst Lectr 1958, Lectr 1961, Sen. Lectr 1969, Prof., 1971–95, now Emeritus, Dept of Ancient History and Archaeology; Head of Sch. of Antiquity, 1988–91. British School at Athens: Editor, Annual, 1978–91; Chm. Managing Cttee, 1991–95; Vice-Pres., 2001–. *Publications:* Argos and the Argolid, 1972; Greek Sanctuaries, 1976; Epidaurus, 1983; (ed) Greek Architecture, by A. W. Lawrence, 5th edn 1996; (contrib.) Sir Banister Fletcher, A History of Architecture, 20th edn, 1996; Greek Architecture, 1989; The Athens of Alma-Tadema, 1991; From Mycenae to Constantinople, 1992; Greek and Roman Architecture, 1995; articles in Annual of British Sch. at Athens, Jl of Hellenic Studies, Amer. Jl of Archaeology, etc. *Recreations:* architecture, walking. *Address:* 15 Eymore Close, Birmingham B29 4LB.

TOMLINSON, Prof. Sally, PhD; Goldsmiths Professor of Policy and Management in Education, Goldsmiths College, London University, 1992–98, now Emeritus; Research Associate, Department of Education, University of Oxford, since 1998; *b* 22 Aug. 1936; *d* of Clifford Gilmore Entwistle and Alice Nora Stubbs; *m* 1957, Brian Joseph Tomlinson, Sqdn Ldr, RAF (retd); one *s* two *d*. *Educ:* Macclesfield Grammar Sch.; Liverpool Univ. (BA Hons); Birmingham Univ. (MSocSci); Warwick Univ. (PhD); Manchester Univ. (PGCE). Lectr and Sen. Lectr, West Midlands Coll. of Educn, 1970–74; Sen. Res. Fellow, Warwick Univ., 1974–78; Lectr, then Sen. Lectr, later Prof. of Educn, Lancaster Univ., 1978–91; Prof. of Educn, UC Swansea, 1991–92; Dean, Faculty of Educn, 1992–95, Pro Warden, 1994–97, Goldsmiths' Coll., London Univ. Sen. Associate Mem., St Antony's Coll., Oxford, 1984–85. Member: Court, Univ. of Bradford, 2001–; Council, Cheltenham and Gloucester Coll. of Higher Educn, 2001–. Mem., Commn on Future of Multi-ethnic Britain, 1998–2000. Trustee: Africa Educational Trust; Learning from Experience Trust, 1992–99; Educn Extra. FRSA 1996. *Publications:* (with John Rex) Colonial Immigrants in a British City, 1979; Educational Subnormality, 1981; A Sociology of Special Education, 1982; Ethnic Minorities in British Schools, 1983; Home and School in Multicultural Britain, 1984; (ed with Len Barton) Special Education and Social Interests, 1984; (with David Smith) The School Effect, 1989; Multicultural Education in White Schools, 1990; Educational Reform and its consequences, 1994; (jtly) The Assessment of Special Educational Needs: whose problem?, 1994; (ed with Maurice Craft) Ethnic Relations and Schooling, 1995; Education 14–19: critical perspectives, 1997; (ed jtly) School Effectiveness for Whom?, 1998; (jtly) Hackney Downs: the school that dared to fight, 1999; Education in a Post-Welfare Society, 2001; many contribs to books and learned jls. *Recreations:* walking, politics. *Address:* Department of Educational Studies, University of Oxford, 15 Norham Gardens, Oxford OX2 9PY. *T:* (01865) 274024.

TOMLINSON, Prof. Stephen, MD; FRCP; FMedSci; Vice-Chancellor, University of Wales College of Medicine, since 2001; Hon. Consultant Physician, Cardiff and Vale NHS Trust, since 2001; *b* 20 Dec. 1944; *s* of Frank Tomlinson and Elsie Tomlinson (*née* Towler); *m* 1970, Christine Margaret Hope; two *d*. *Educ:* Hayward GS, Bolton; Univ. of Sheffield (MB ChB 1968; MD 1976). FRCP 1982. SHO and Registrar, Sheffield Royal Infirmary, 1969–72; Registrar, Middlesex Hosp., 1972–73; MRC Clin. Res. Fellow, 1973–75, Hon. Lectr, 1974–76, Middlesex Hosp. Med. Sch.; Sen. Registrar, Middlesex Hosp., 1975–76; Sir Henry Wellcome Travelling Fellow, MIT, 1976–77; Sheffield University: Wellcome Trust Sen. Res. Fellow in Clin. Sci., 1977–80; Wellcome Sen. Lectr, 1980–85; Hon. Reader in Medicine, 1982–85; Hon. Cons. Physician, Sheffield HA, 1977–85; Manchester University: Prof. of Medicine, 1985–2001; Dean of Med. Sch. and Faculty of Medicine, 1993–97, of Faculty of Medicine, Dentistry and Nursing, 1997–99; Hon. Consultant Physician, Manchester Royal Infirmary, 1985–2001. Chairman: Assoc. of Clin. Profs of Med., 1996–99; Fedn of Assocs of Clin. Profs, 1997–2000; Pres., Assoc. of Physicians, April 2002– (Hon. Sec. and Treas., 1988–98); Exec. Sec., Council of Heads of Med. Schs, 1997–99; Mem., GMC Educn Cttee, 1999. Founder FMedSci, 1998. *Publications:* papers on stimulus-response coupling and intracellular signalling in endocrine tissues; the orgn of health services for people with diabetes. *Recreations:* quotations, history of medicine, good food and wine (mine and others!). *Address:* Office of the Vice-Chancellor, University of Wales College of Medicine, Heath Park, Cardiff CF4 4XN. *T:* (029) 2074 2029. *Clubs:* Athenæum; Medical Pilgrims (Hon. Sec.).

TOMLINSON, Hon. Sir Stephen (Miles), Kt 2000; **Hon. Mr Justice Tomlinson;** a Judge of the High Court of Justice, Queen's Bench Division, since 2000; *b* 29 March 1952; *s* of Enoch Tomlinson and Mary Marjorie Cecilia Tomlinson (*née* Miles); *m* 1980, Joanna Kathleen Greig; one *s* one *d*. *Educ:* King's Sch., Worcester (schol.); Worcester Coll., Oxford (schol.; Eldon Law Schol.; MA). Called to the Bar, Inner Temple, 1974, Bencher, 1990. Lectr in Law, Worcester Coll., Oxford, 1974–76. QC 1988; a Recorder, 1995–2000; a Dep. High Court Judge, 1996–2000. *Recreations:* gardening, family, cricket. *Address:* Royal Courts of Justice, Strand, WC2A 2LL. *Club:* MCC.

TOMPKINS, Hon. Sir David (Lance), KNZM 1999; Judge of the High Court of New Zealand, 1983–97, Acting Judge, since 1997; Judge of the Privy Council and Court of Appeal of Tonga, since 1995; Justice of Appeal, Court of Appeal of Fiji, since 1997; Judge, Supreme Court of Vanuatu, since 1998; *b* 26 July 1929; *s* of Arthur Lance Tompkins, Judge, Supreme Court of NZ, and Marjorie Rees Tompkins (*née* Manning); *m* 1956, Erica Lya Felicity Ann Faris; two *s* one *d*. *Educ:* Whitiora Primary Sch.; Southwell Sch., Hamilton; King's Coll., Auckland; Auckland University Coll. (LLB 1951). Served 1st Field Regt, RNZA, TA, 1949–59 (Capt. 1958). Partner, Tompkins & Wake, Hamilton, 1953–71; Barrister, 1971; QC (NZ) 1974; Courts Martial Appeal Court Judge, 1982–83; Exec. Judge, Auckland High Court, 1989–92; Judge, Criminal Appeal Div., Court of Appeal of NZ, 1996–97. Chairman: Council of Legal Educn, 1992–97; Nat. Case Mgt Cttee, 1994–97; Electricity Mkt Appeal, 1998–. Pres., Hamilton Dist Law Soc., 1969–71; Mem. Council, 1969–71, Vice Pres., 1979–81, NZ Law Soc.; Mem. Council, 1976–83, Life Mem., 1987, Law Asia; Pres., Auckland Medico-Legal Soc., 1994–95. Associate, Arbitrators' and Mediators' Inst., 1997; Mem., LEADR, 1997–. Pro-Chancellor, 1979–80, Chancellor, 1980–85, Waikato Univ. Outward Bound Trust: Vice-Pres., 1981–83; Pres., 1983–84; Guardian, 1992–. Hon. Dr Waikato Univ., 1986. Silver Jubilee Medal, 1977; Commemoration Medal (NZ), 1990. *Recreations:* sailing, croquet, ski-ing, computers, trout fishing, cooking. *Address:* PO Box 25 153, St Heliers, Auckland, New Zealand. *Clubs:* Hamilton (Life Mem.), Northern, Royal New Zealand Yacht Squadron (Auckland).

TOMS, Edward Ernest; Director, Porcelain & Pictures Ltd, since 1983; *b* 10 Dec. 1920; *s* of Alfred William and Julia Harrington Toms; *m* 1946, Veronica Rose, Dovercourt, Essex; three *s* one *d*. *Educ:* St Boniface's Coll.; Staff Coll., Camberley (psc), Nat. Defence Coll. (jssc). War service 1939–45; Captain Seaforth Highlanders; Special Forces, W Desert, Italy, Balkans, NW Europe; Regular Army, 1946, Seaforth Highlanders and QO Highlanders; Brigade Major, Berlin, 1959–61; Col GS (UK Cs-in-C Cttee), 1967–69. Principal, Home Civil Service, 1969; Asst Sec., Dept of Employment, 1973; seconded to Diplomatic Service as Counsellor, Bonn and Vienna, 1977–81; Internat. Labour Advr, FCO, 1981–83. *Recreation:* hill-walking (founder Mem., Aberdeen Mountain Rescue Assoc., 1964). *Address:* c/o Clydesdale Bank, Principal Branch Piccadilly, 35 Regent Street, SW1Y 4ND. *Club:* Special Forces.

TOMSETT, Alan Jeffrey, OBE 1974; Director, Associated British Ports Holdings PLC, 1983–92 (Finance Director, 1983–87); chartered accountant; *b* 3 May 1922; *s* of Maurice Jeffrey Tomsett and Edith Sarah (*née* Mackelworth); *m* 1948, Joyce May Hill; one *s* one *d*. *Educ:* Trinity School of John Whitgift, Croydon; Univ. of London (BCom). JDipMA. Hodgson Harris & Co., Chartered Accountants, London, 1938. Served War, with RAF, 1941–46 (Middle East, 1942–45). Smallfield Rawlins & Co., Chartered Accountants, London, 1951; Northern Mercantile & Investment Corp. Ltd, 1955; William Baird & Co. Ltd, 1962–63. British Transport Docks Board, later Associated British Ports: Dep. Chief Accountant, 1963; Chief Accountant, 1964; Financial Controller, 1970; Bd Mem., 1974–87 (Finance Dir, 1974–85). Churchwarden, St John's, Shirley, 1988–92. FCA, FCMA, CPFA, FCIS, FCIT (Vice-Pres., 1981–82; Hon. Treasurer, 1982–88); FRSA 1969. *Address:* 102 Ballards Way, Croydon, Surrey CR0 5RG. *T:* (020) 8657 5069.

TONBRIDGE, Bishop Suffragan of, since 2002; **Rt Rev. Dr Brian Colin Castle;** *b* 7 Sept. 1949; *s* of Ernest and Sarah Castle; *m* 1979, Jane Richmond; one *s* two *d*. *Educ:* UCL (BA (Hons) Classics 1972); Cuddesdon Theol Coll. (MA Theol. Oxford 1980); Birmingham Univ. (PhD Theol. 1989). Social worker, 1972–74; teacher, Lesotho, Southern Africa, 1974. Ordained deacon, 1977, priest, 1978; Assistant Curate: St Nicholas, Sutton, 1977; Limpsfield, Surrey, 1977–81; Priest i/c, Chingola, Chililabombwe and Solwezi, Zambia, 1981–84; Vis Lectr, Ecumenical Inst., Geneva, 1984–85; Vicar, N Petherton and Northmoor Green, Somerset, 1985–92; Vice-Principal and Dir of Pastoral Studies, Ripon Coll., Cuddesdon, Oxford, 1992–2001. *Publications:* Hymns: the making and shaping of a theology for the whole people of God, 1990; Sing a New Song to the Lord, 1994; articles in various theol jls. *Recreations:* fly fishing, cross country ski-ing. *Address:* 48 St Botolph's Road, Sevenoaks, Kent TN13 3AG. *T:* (01732) 456070.

TONBRIDGE, Archdeacon of; *see* Rose, Ven. K. J.

TONČIĆ-SORINJ, Dr Lujo; Secretary-General, Council of Europe, 1969–74; *b* Vienna, 12 April 1915; *s* of Dušan Tončić-Sorinj (formerly Consul-Gen. in service of Imperial Ministry for Foreign Affairs), and Mabel (*née* Plason de la Woesthyne); *m* 1956, Renate Trenker; one *s* four *d*. *Educ:* Secondary sch. (Gymnasium), Salzburg. Studied law and philosophy at Univs of Vienna and Agram (Zagreb), 1934–41, also medicine and psychology (LLD Vienna); political science, Institut d'Etudes Politiques, Paris. Head of Polit. Dept of Austrian Research Inst. for Economics and Politics in Salzburg and Editor of Berichte und Informationen (political periodical published by Austrian Research Inst. for Economics and Politics), 1946–49. MP for Land Salzburg, 1949–66; Chairman: Legal Cttee of Austrian Parl., 1953–56; For. Affairs Cttee, 1956–59; in charge of For. Affairs questions, Austrian People's Party, 1959–66. Austrian Parly Observer to Consultative Assembly of Council of Europe, 1953–56; Austrian Mem., Consultative Assembly, 1956–66; Vice-Pres., Council of Europe; Vice-Pres., Political Commn, 1961–62; Minister for Foreign Affairs, Austria, 1966–68. Permanent Rep. of Austrian People's Party to Christian-Democratic Gp, European Parlt, 1980–95; Permanent Rep. of Croatian Democratic Union to European Union of Christian Democrats, 1991–. Chm., Austrian Assoc. of UN, 1978–92; Pres., Union Internationale de la Propriété Immobilière, 1987–99. Grand Cross of several orders including Order of St Michael and St George, Great Britain (Hon. GCMG). *Publications:* Erfüllte Träume (autobiog.), 1982; Am Abgrund vorbei, 1992; Usamljena borba Hrvatske, 1998 (trans. German); over 350 articles and essays on politics, economics, internat. law and history. *Recreations:* swimming, diving, history, geography. *Address:* Schloss Fürberg, Pausingerstrasse 11, 5020 Salzburg, Austria. *T:* (662) 642886.

TONEGAWA, Prof. Susumu; Professor of Biology and Neuroscience, Center for Cancer Research, since 1981, and Director, Centre for Learning and Memory, Department of Biology, since 1994, Massachusetts Institute of Technology; *b* Nagoya, 5 Sept. 1939; *s* of Tsutomo and Miyoko Tonegawa; *m* 1985, Mayumi Yoshinari; two *s* one *d. Educ:* Kyoto Univ. (BS); Univ. of San Diego (PhD). Postgraduate work: Univ. of California, San Diego, 1968–69; Salk Inst., San Diego, 1969–70; Mem., Basel Inst. of Immunology, 1971–81. Investigator, Howard Hughes Med. Inst., 1988–. Avery Landsteiner Prize, Ges. für Immunologie, 1981; Gairdner Foundn Internat. Award, 1983; Nobel Prize for Physiology or Medicine, 1987. *Address:* Massachusetts Institute of Technology, 77 Massachusetts Avenue, Cambridge, MA 02139–4307, USA.

TONEY, Terence; Director, British Council, Japan, since 1999; *b* 23 Aug. 1952; *s* of Norman Toney and Margaret Toney (*née* Taglione); *m* 1977, Young Hae Kim; one *s. Educ:* Cardinal Hinsley Grammar Sch.; King's Coll. London (BA Hons German and Philosophy); Inst. of Educn, Univ. of London (PGCE); Univ. of Lancaster (MA). Lectr in English, British Centre, Sweden, 1975–76; English teacher, Dortmund, 1976–78; Lectr in English, Hokkaido Univ., Japan, 1980–82; British Council, 1983–: Asst Consultant, English Lang., London, 1983–85; Asst English Lang. Officer, Tokyo, 1985–87; English Lang. Officer, Colombia, 1987–90; Acad. Dir, Cultura Inglesa, São Paulo, 1990–94; Dir, Korea, 1994–99. Pres., English Sch. Bd, Bogotá, 1989–90; Trustee, British Sch. in Tokyo, 1999–. *Recreations:* travelling, reading, foreign languages, walking. *Address:* Easter Cottage, Stretton-on-Fosse, Moreton-in-Marsh GL56 9SB; British Council, 2 Kagurazaka I-chome, Shinjuku-ku, Tokyo 162–0825, Japan.

TONGA, HM the King of; **King Taufa'ahau Tupou IV,** Hon. GCMG 1977 (Hon. KCMG 1968); Hon. GCVO 1970; Hon. KBE 1958 (Hon. CBE 1951); *b* 4 July 1918; *s* of Prince Uiliami Tupoulahi Tungi and Queen Salote Tupou of Tonga; *S* mother, 1965; *m* 1947, Halaevalu Mata'aho 'Ahome'e; three *s* one *d. Educ:* Tupou College, Tonga; Newington College, Sydney; Wesley College, Sydney University. Minister for Health and Education, Tonga, 1943–50; Prime Minister, 1950–65. *Heir: s* HRH Prince Tupouto'a, *b* 4 May 1948. *Address:* The Palace, Nukualofa, Tonga. *T:* 21000.

TONGE, Brian Lawrence, PhD; Director, Oxford Polytechnic, 1981–85; *b* 19 April 1933; *s* of Lawrence and Louisa Tonge; *m* 1955, Anne Billcliff; one *d. Educ:* Bury High Sch.; London Univ. (BSc 1st Cl. Chemistry); Manchester Univ. (PhD). FRIC 1964. Scientific Officer, Hirst Research Centre, GEC Ltd, 1956–59; Chemist, Medical Research Council Carcinogenic Substances Research Unit, Exeter Univ., 1959; Lectr in Chemistry, Plymouth Coll. of Technology, 1960–63; Research Manager, Pure Chemicals Ltd, 1963–65; Principal Lectr in Chemistry, West Ham Coll. of Technology, 1965–67; Head of Dept of Applied Science and Dean of Faculty of Science, Wolverhampton Polytechnic, 1967–71; Dep. Director, Oxford Polytechnic, 1971–81. Member, Wolfson Coll., Oxford, 1975–85. *Publications:* numerous contribs to learned jls and articles in scientific and educnl press. *Recreations:* gardening, reading, music. *Address:* The Hollies, Welshampton, Ellesmere, Shropshire SY12 0QA.

TONGE, Jennifer Louise, FRIPHH; MP (Lib Dem) Richmond Park, since 1997; *b* 19 Feb. 1941; *d* of late Sidney Smith and Violet Smith (*née* Williams); *m* 1964, Dr Keith Angus Tonge; two *s* one *d. Educ:* Dudley Girls' High Sch.; University Coll. London (MB BS 1964). Mem. Faculty of Family Planning, RCOG, 1994; FRIPHH 1997. GP and family planning doctor, Ealing, 1964–96; Hd, Womens' Services, Ealing HA, 1983–89. Mem. (Lib Dem), Richmond on Thames LBC, 1981–90 (Chm., Social Services, 1983–89). Contested (Lib Dem) Richmond and Barnes, 1992. Lib Dem spokesman on internat. develt, 1999–. *Address:* House of Commons, SW1A 0AA; 5 Bush Road, Kew Green, Richmond, Surrey TW9 3AN. *T:* (020) 8948 1649. *Club:* National Liberal.

TONGUE, Carole; adviser and lecturer on the media, broadcasting, culture and European affairs, since 1999; artistic producer; Consultant Citigate Public Affairs, since 2001; *b* 14 Oct. 1955; *d* of Muriel Esther Lambert and Walter Archer Tongue; *m* 1990, Chris Pond (marr. diss. 1999), *qv*; one *d. Educ:* Brentwood County High School; Loughborough University of Technology (BA Govt (Hons) and French). Asst Editor, Laboratory Practice, 1977–78; courier/guide in France with Sunsites Ltd, 1978–79; Robert Schuman scholarship for research in social affairs with European Parlt, Dec. 1979–March 1980; sec./admin. asst, Socialist Group of European Parlt, 1980–84. MEP (Lab) London E, 1984–99; contested (Lab) London Reg., 1999. Dep. Leader, Eur. PLP, 1989–91. Bd Mem., Westminster Foundn for Democracy, 1990–93. Sen. Vis. Lectr, Dept European Studies, Loughborough Univ., 1995–; Vis. Lectr, Media Sch., London Coll. of Printing, 2000–. Member: Adv. Bd, Eur. Media Forum, 1996–; Bd, London Film and Video Develt Agency, 1999–. Pres., Cities and Cinemas Assoc., 1997–. Patron, Couper Art Collection. Member: Fabian Soc.; GMB; MSF. Trustee, CSV, 1995–. FRSA. *Publications:* chapters in books on European media; EP reports; articles on culture, film, citizenship, European affairs. *Recreations:* piano, cello, tennis, squash, horse riding, cinema, theatre, opera. *Address:* 409 Liverpool Road, N7 8PR. *T:* (020) 7609 0878, *Fax:* (020) 7607 4648; *e-mail:* carole.tongue@poptel.net.

TONKIN, Boyd Miles; Literary Editor, The Independent, since 1996; *b* 7 April 1955; *s* of Douglas George Marcus Tonkin and Joan Yvonne Tonkin (*née* Collis). *Educ:* Haberdashers' Aske's Sch., Elstree; Trinity Coll., Cambridge (MA English). Res. Student and pt-time Tutor, Univ. of Cambridge, 1978–81; Adult Educn Lectr, City Univ., 1981–83; Lecturer in English: Manchester Poly., 1983–84; West Sussex Inst., 1984–85; Staff Writer and Features Editor, Community Care mag., 1986–89; Social Affairs Editor, 1989–91, Literary Editor, 1991–96, New Statesman. Broadcaster, BBC Radio arts progs, 1995–. Judge: Whitbread Biography award, 1997; Booker Prize, 1999; Foreign Fiction Award, Independent, 2000– (also Convenor). *Publications:* (contrib.) Oxford Readers' Guide to Fiction, 2000; contribs to lit. guides and ref. works; essays in lit. jls in UK, US, France and Germany; articles in jls. *Recreations:* music, cinema, cricket, walking. *Address:* 104 Islington High Street, N1 8EG. *T:* (020) 7005 2656.

TONKIN, Derek, CMG 1982; HM Diplomatic Service, retired; *b* 30 Dec. 1929; *s* of Henry James Tonkin and Norah Wearing; *m* 1953, Doreen Rooke; one *s* two *d* (and one *s* decd). *Educ:* High Pavement Grammar Sch., Nottingham; St Catherine's Society, Oxford (MA). HM Forces, 1948–49; FO, 1952; Warsaw, 1955; Bangkok, 1957; Phnom Penh, 1961; FO, 1963; Warsaw, 1966; Wellington, 1968; FCO, 1972; East Berlin, 1976; Ambassador to Vietnam, 1980–82; Minister, Pretoria, 1983–86; Ambassador to Thailand, and concurrently to Laos, 1986–89. Chairman: Beta Viet Nam Fund Ltd, 1993–99; Beta Mekong Fund Ltd, 1994–2000. Dir, Ockenden Internat. Bd of Trustees, 1990–; Chairman: Adv. Bd, Centre for SE Asia Studies, SOAS, 1990–93; Thai-British Business Assoc., 1991–93; Vietnam-Britain Business Assoc., 1993–94. *Recreations:* tennis, music. *Address:* Heathfields, Berry Lane, Worplesdon, Guildford, Surrey GU3 3PU. *Club:* Royal Over-Seas League.

TONKING, (Russel) Simon (William Ferguson); His Honour Judge Tonking; a Circuit Judge, since 1997; *b* 25 March 1952; *s* of John Wilson Tonking and Mary Oldham Tonking (*née* Ferguson); *m* 1976, (Sylvia) Mithra McIntyre; one *s* one *d. Educ:* King's Sch., Canterbury; Emmanuel Coll., Cambridge (MA). Called to the Bar, Inner Temple, 1975; barrister, Midland and Oxford Circuit, 1976–97. Lichfield Cathedral: Steward, 1978– (Head Steward, 1985–87); Mem. Council, 2000– (Mem. Transitional Council, 1998–2000); Dep. Chancellor, Diocese of Southwell, 1997–. *Recreations:* many! *Address:* c/o The Court Service, Combined Court Centre, Victoria Square, Stafford ST16 2QQ. *T:* (01785) 610730. *Club:* Vintage Sports Car.

TONKS, Julian Matthew John; Senior Partner, Pinsent Curtis Biddle Solicitors, since 2001; *b* 19 April 1953; *s* of John and Irene Tonks, Comhampton, Worcs; *m* 1980, Ann Miles Henderson; one *s. Educ:* Dudley GS; Trinity Coll., Oxford (MA, MLitt). Admitted solicitor, 1982; Asst Solicitor, Freshfields, 1982–86; Tax Partner, 1987–94, Sen. Partner, 1994–95, Pinsent & Co.; Sen. Partner, Pinsent Curtis, 1995–2001. Mem. Regl Council, W Midlands, CBI, 1998–. Chairman: Common Purpose, Birmingham, 1994–2001; W Midlands NSPCC Full Stop Appeal, 1999–2001. Trustee, Birmingham Royal Ballet Trust, 1996–. *Recreations:* visiting castles, swimming, country sports, wine, reading modern novels and medieval history. *Address:* 17 Ampton Road, Edgbaston, Birmingham B15 2UJ. *T:* (0121) 454 0053.

TONRY, Prof. Michael; Professor of Law and Public Policy, and Director, Institute of Criminology, University of Cambridge, since 1999; Sonosky Professor of Law and Public Policy, University of Minnesota, since 1990; *b* 9 June 1945; *s* of J. Richard Tonry and Frances Zimmerman Tonry (*née* Keedy); *m* 1966, Penelope Tyson; two *s* two *d. Educ:* Univ. of N Carolina (AB Hist. 1966); Yale Univ. (LLB). Admitted to legal practice: Illinois, 1970; Pennsylvania, 1975; Maine, 1982. Lecturer in Law: Univ. of Chicago, 1971–73; Univ. of Birmingham, 1973–74; Dechert Price & Rhodes, Esqs, 1974–76; Prof. of Law, Univ. of Md, 1976–83; Pres., Castine Res. Corp., 1983–; Ed. and Publisher, The Castine Patriot, 1987–90. *Publications:* Sentencing Reform Impacts, 1987; Malign Neglect: race, crime and punishment in America, 1994; Sentencing Matters, 1996; Ethnicity, Crime and Immigration, 1997; Intermediate Sanctions in Sentencing Guidelines, 1997; Handbook of Crime and Punishment, 1998; Penal Reform in Overcrowded Times, 2001; *jointly*: Reform and Punishment: essays on criminal sentencing, 1983; Hypnotically Refreshed Testimony, 1985; Communities and Crime, 1986; The Sentencing Commission: guidelines for criminal sanctions, 1987; Prediction and Classification, 1987; Managing Appeals in Federal Courts, 1988; Family Violence, 1990; Between Prison and Probation, 1990; Drugs and Crime, 1990; Human Development and Criminal Behavior, 1991; Modern Policing, 1992; Beyond the Law: crime in complex organisations, 1993; Intermediate Sanctions in Overcrowded Times, 1995; Building a Safer Society, 1995; Sentencing Reform in Overcrowded Times, 1997; Youth Violence, 1998; Prisons, 1999; Sentencing and Sanctions in Western Countries, 2001. *Address:* Institute of Criminology, 7 West Road, Cambridge CB3 9DT.

TOOBY, Michael Bowen; Director, National Museum & Gallery, Cardiff, since 2000; *b* 20 Dec. 1956; *s* of Leslie and Jill Tooby; *m* 1980, Jane Pare; one *s* one *d. Educ:* King Henry VIII Sch., Coventry; Magdalene Coll., Cambridge. Asst Curator, Kettle's Yard, Cambridge, 1978–80; Exhibns Orgnr, Third Eye Centre, Glasgow, 1980–84; Keeper, Mappin Art Gall., Sheffield, 1984–92; Founding Curator, Tate Gall. St Ives, and Curator, Barbara Hepworth Mus. and Sculpture Gdn, 1992–99. Chm., engage, (nat. assoc. for visual arts educn), 1999–. *Publications:* The True North: Canadian painting 1896–1939, 1988; monograph studies of: Lois Williams, 1996; Iwan Bala, 1999; David Nash, 2000. *Address:* c/o National Museum & Gallery, Cathays Park, Cardiff CF10 3NP.

TOOHEY, Hon. John Leslie, AC 1988 (AO 1986); Member, Bloody Sunday Inquiry Tribunal, since 2000; *b* 4 March 1930; *s* of Albert Leslie and Sylvia Josephine Toohey; *m* 1953, Loma Jean Buckenara; two *s* five *d. Educ:* Univ. of WA (BA, LLB 1st Cl. Hons). Admitted as Legal Practitioner, WA, 1952; QC (Aust.) 1968; Judge: Federal Court of Australia, 1977–87; Supreme Court of NT, 1977–87; Justice of High Court of Australia, 1987–98. Comr, Aboriginal Land, NT, 1977–87. Hon. LLD Murdoch, 1998. *Recreations:* music, tennis. *Address:* 13A Rosser Street, Cottesloe, WA 6011, Australia. *T:* (8) 93851783.

TOOHEY, Mrs Joyce, CB 1977; Under-Secretary, Department of the Environment, 1970–76; *b* 20 Sept. 1917; *o d* of Louis Zinkin and Lena Zinkin (*née* Daiches); *m* 1947, Monty I. Toohey, MD, MRCP, DCH (*d* 1960); two *d. Educ:* Brondesbury and Kilburn High Sch.; Girton Coll., Cambridge; London Sch. of Economics. BA 1938, MA 1945, Cambridge. Asst Principal, Min. of Supply, 1941; transferred to Min. of Works, 1946; Principal, 1948; Asst Secretary, MPBW, 1956; Under-Secretary, 1964. Harvard Business Sch., 1970. *Recreations:* reading, walking. *Address:* 11 Kensington Court Gardens, W8 5QE. *T:* (020) 7937 1559.

TOOK, Barry; freelance writer and broadcaster; *b* 19 June 1928; *s* of Charles William Took and Kate Louie Rose Took (*née* Cox); *m* 1st, 1950, Dorothy Bird (marr. diss.); two *s* one *d*; 2nd, 1964, Lynden Leonard; one *d. Educ:* Stationers' Co. Sch. First broadcast (radio), 1951; *West End Revues:* performer: For Amusement Only, 1956–58; For Adults Only, 1958–59; *Scriptwriter:* radio series: Beyond Our Ken, 1959–60; Round the Horne, 1965–68; television series: Bootsie and Snudge, 1960–64; Marty, 1968–69; On the Move, 1974–79; writer and presenter, Points of View (TV series), 1979–86; Chair, The News Quiz (radio series), 1979–96. *Publications:* The Max Miller Blue Book, 1975; Laughter in the Air, 1976; Tooks Eye View (essays), 1983; Comedy Greats, 1989; A Point of View (autobiog.), 1990; Star Turns, 1992; Round the Horne: the complete and utter history, 1998; (with Mat Coward) The Best of Round the Horne, 2000. *Recreations:* golf, gossip. *Address:* c/o Jules Bennett, PO Box 25, Moreton in Marsh, Glos GL56 9YJ.

TOOK, John Michael Exton, MBE 1964; Controller, Europe and North Asia Division, British Council, 1983–86, retired; Chairman, Romney Marsh Historic Churches Trust, 2001; *b* 15 Sept. 1926; *s* of late George Took, Dover, and Ailsa Clowes (*née* Turner); *m* 1964, Judith Margaret, *d* of late Brig. and Mrs W. J. Birkle; two *d. Educ:* Dover Coll.; Jesus Coll., Cambridge. Served Indian Army, 1944–47. HM Colonial Admin. Service (later HMOCS), N Rhodesia, 1950–57; Min. of External Affairs, Fedn of Rhodesia & Nyasaland, 1957–63; Min. of External Affairs, Republic of Zambia, 1964–65; joined British Council, 1965; Asst Reg. Dir, Frankfurt, 1965–67; Reg. Dir, Cape Coast, 1967–69; Rep., Cyprus, 1971–74; Cultural Attaché, British Embassy, Budapest, 1974–77; Dep. Controller, European Div., 1977–80; Rep., Greece, 1980–83. Dir, UK Cttee, Eur. Cultural Foundn, 1992–94. *Publications:* Common Birds of Cyprus, 1973, 4th edn 1986; Birds of Cyprus, 1992; contribs to ornithological jls. *Recreations:* ornithology, fishing, natural history. *Address:* Pilgrims, Appledore, near Ashford, Kent TN26 2AE. *T:* (01233) 758215. *Club:* Oxford and Cambridge.

TOOKE, Prof. John Edward, DM, DSc; FRCP; Dean, Peninsula Medical School, Universities of Exeter and Plymouth, since 2000; *b* 4 March 1949; *s* of Thomas Edward Tooke and Edna (*née* Wilgose); *m* 1972, Elizabeth Moore; one *s* one *d. Educ:* St John's

Coll., Oxford (MA 1970; MSc 1972; BM BCh 1974; DM 1982; DSc 1998); King's Coll. Hosp. Med. Sch. FRCP 1993. Lectr in Medicine, Leeds Univ., 1979–82; BHF Res. Fellow, Karolinska Inst. Dept of Medicine, Sweden, 1982–83; Wellcome Trust Sen. Lectr in Medicine and Physiol., Charing Cross and Westminster Med. Sch., 1984–87; Sen. Lectr, then Prof. of Vascular Medicine and Consultant Diabetologist, Univ. of Exeter, 1987–2000. FMedSci 2000. Camillo Golgi Award, Eur. Assoc. for Study of Diabetes, 1994. *Publications:* (ed with G. D. Lowe) A Textbook of Vascular Medicine, 1996; (ed) Diabetic Angiopathy, 1999. *Recreations:* angling, golf, le bricolage. *Address:* Peninsula Medical School, ITC Building, Tamar Science Park, Derriford, Plymouth PL6 8BX.

TOOKEY, Richard William, CBE 1984; Director and Group Public Affairs Co-ordinator, Shell International Petroleum Co. Ltd, 1984–93; *b* 11 July 1934; *s* of Geoffrey William Tookey, QC and Rosemary Sherwell Tookey (*née* Clogg); *m* 1st, 1956, Jill (*née* Ransford) (marr. diss. 1994); one *s* one *d* (and one *s* decd); 2nd, 1994, Colleen (*née* Channon). *Educ:* Charterhouse. National Service, 2nd Lieut, 1st King's Dragoon Guards, 1952–54; Lanarkshire Yeomanry (TA), 1954–56; Inns of Court Regt/Inns of Court and City Yeomanry (TA), 1957–64. Joined Royal Dutch/Shell Group, 1954; posts in internat. oil supply and trading, 1954–73; Head of Supply Operations, 1973–75; Vice-Pres., Shell Internat. Trading Co., 1975–77; Man. Dir, Shell Tankers (UK) Ltd, 1978–79, Chm., 1980–84; Man. Dir, Shell Internat. Marine Ltd, 1980–84; Marine Co-ordinator, Shell Internat. Petroleum Co. Ltd, 1980–84. Part-time Mem., BRB, 1985–90; Mem., Gen. Cttee, Lloyd's Register of Shipping, 1978–85; Pres., Gen. Council of British Shipping, 1983–84. Liveryman, Shipwrights' Co., 1983–, Mem. Ct of Assts, 1987–96. *Recreation:* home. *Address:* PO Box 15849, Emerald Hill, Port Elizabeth, 6011, South Africa. *T:* (41) 3791643, *Fax:* (41) 3794900; *e-mail:* rwtookey@iafrica.com.

TOOLEY, Prof. James Nicholas, PhD; Professor of Education Policy, University of Newcastle upon Tyne, since 1998; Director, Education Programme, Institute of Economic Affairs, London, since 1995; *b* 21 July 1959; *s* of Arthur Henry Tooley and Barbara May Tooley (*née* Tubby). *Educ:* Kingsfield Sch., Bristol; Univ. of Sussex (BSc 1983; MSc 1986); PhD London 1994. Mathematics Teacher, Zimbabwe, 1983–86; Sen. Res. Officer, NFER, 1988–91; Res. Fellow, Univ. of Oxford, 1994–95; Sen. Res. Fellow, Univ. of Manchester, 1995–98. *Publications:* Disestablishing the School, 1995; Education without the State, 1996; Educational Research: a critique, 1998; The Global Education Industry, 1999; The Seven Habits of Highly Effective Schools, 1999; Reclaiming Education, 2000; The Miseducation of Women, 2001; The Enterprise of Education, 2001. *Recreation:* walking in the foothills of the Simonside hills. *Address:* Daisy Cottage, Fontburn Halt, Northumberland NE61 4PR. *T:* (01669) 621009. *Club:* Athenæum.

TOOLEY, Sir John, Kt 1979; Arts consultant, since 1988; General Director, Royal Opera House, Covent Garden, 1980–88; *b* 1 June 1924; *yr s* of late H. R. Tooley; *m* 1st, 1951, Judith Craig Morris (marr. diss., 1965); three *d*; 2nd, 1968, Patricia Janet Norah Bagshawe (marr. diss. 1990), 2nd *d* of late G. W. S. Bagshawe; one *s*; 3rd, 1995, Jennifer-Anne Shannon. *Educ:* Repton; Magdalene Coll., Cambridge. Served The Rifle Brigade, 1943–47. Sec., Guildhall School of Music and Drama, 1952–55; Royal Opera House, Covent Garden: Asst to Gen. Administrator, 1955–60; Asst Gen. Administrator, 1960–70; Gen. Administrator, 1970–80. Chairman: Nat. Music Council Executive, 1970–72; HEFCE Music Conservatories Adv. Gp, 1993–97. Director: Britten Estate Ltd, 1989–97; South Bank Bd, 1991–97; Compton Verney Opera Project, 1991–97; WNO, 1992–2000; David Gyngell & Co. Ltd, 1995–97; Almeida Th., 1997– (Chm., 1990–97); LPO, 1998–; Chm., Monument Insurance Brokers Ltd, 1997–; Consultant: Internat. Management Gp, 1988–97; Ballet Opera House, Toronto, 1989–90; Trustee: Wigmore Hall; SPNM; Walton Trust, 1988–2000; Britten Pears Foundn, 1989–99; Dartington Summer Sch., 1989–2000; Purcell Tercentenary Trust, 1991–97; Performing Arts Labs, 1993–97; Sidney Nolan Trust, 1996–. Pres., Salisbury Festival, 1988–; Chm., Salisbury Cathedral Fabric Cttee, 1990–; Chm., Rudolf Nureyev Foundn, 1995–. Gen. Advr, Internat. Istanbul Fest, 1993–. Governor, Repton Sch., 1984–94. Hon. FRAM; Hon. GSM; Hon. RNCM. DUniv UCE, 1996. Commendatore, Italian Republic, 1976. *Publication:* In House, 1999. *Recreations:* walking, theatre. *Address:* 5 Royal Crescent, Bath BA1 2LR. *T:* (01225) 335079, *Fax:* (01225) 335108.

TOOMEY, Ralph; Under-Secretary, Department of Education and Science, 1969–78; *b* 26 Dec. 1918; *s* of late James and Theresa Toomey; *m* 1951, Patricia Tizard; two *d*. *Educ:* Cyfarthfa Grammar Sch., Merthyr Tydfil; University Coll., London; Univ. of Caen. Served British and Indian Army, 1940–46. Teacher, Enfield Grammar Sch., 1947; Lecturer, Univ. of London, at Sch. of Oriental and African Studies, 1948. Min. of Education, 1948–60 and 1963–78 (seconded to Govt of Mauritius, 1960–63, Principal Asst Sec. in Colonial Secretary's Office and Min. of Local Govt and Co-operative Develt). A UK Rep., High Council, European Univ. Inst., Florence, 1974–78. DUniv Open, 1979. *Address:* 8 The Close, Montreal Park, Sevenoaks, Kent TN13 2HE. *T:* (01732) 452553. *Club:* Knole Park Golf (Sevenoaks).

TOOTH, Sir (Hugh) John L.; *see* Lucas-Tooth.

TOOZE, Dr John, FRS 1994; Director of Research (formerly Support) Services, Imperial Cancer Research Fund, since 1994; *b* 16 May 1938; *s* of Reginald John Tooze and Doris Edith Tooze (*née* Bull); *m* 1st, 1962, Sarah Margaret Wynn (marr. diss.); two *s* one *d*; 2nd, 1983, Sharon Ann Queally; one *s* one *d*. *Educ:* Handsworth Grammar Sch., Birmingham; Jesus Coll., Cambridge (BA 1961); King's Coll. London (PhD 1965); Harvard Univ. Served Army, 1956–58. King's College London: Asst Lectr in Biophysics, 1961–65; Lectr, 1965–68; Wellcome Res. Fellow, Harvard Univ., 1965–67; Dep. Editor, Nature, 1968–70; Res. Administrator, ICRF, 1970–73; Exec. Sec., EMBO, Heidelberg, 1973–94; Associate Dir, EMBL, 1993–94. Editor: Trends in Biochemistry, 1979–85; EMBO Jl, 1982–. Trustee, Darwin Trust of Edinburgh, 1991–. EMBO Medal, 1986. *Publications:* Molecular Biology of Tumor Viruses, 1973; DNA Tumor Viruses, 1980; (with J. D. Watson) The DNA Story, 1982; (with C. I. Branden) Introduction to Protein Structure, 1991, 2nd edn 1999. *Recreations:* numismatics, English history, gardening. *Address:* Imperial Cancer Research Fund, PO Box No 123, Lincoln's Inn Fields, WC2A 3PX. *T:* (020) 7242 0200. *Club:* Athenæum.

TOPE, family name of **Baron Tope**.

TOPE, Baron *cr* 1994 (Life Peer), of Sutton in the London Borough of Sutton; **Graham Norman Tope,** CBE 1991; Member (Lib Dem) London Assembly, and Leader, Liberal Democrat Group, Greater London Authority, since 2000; *b* 30 Nov. 1943; *s* of late Leslie Tope, Plymouth and Winifred Tope (*née* Merrick), Bermuda; *m* 1972, Margaret East; two *s*. *Educ:* Whitgift Sch., S Croydon. Company Sec., 1965–72; Insce Manager, 1970–72; Dep. Gen. Sec., Voluntary Action Camden, 1975–90. Pres., Nat. League of Young Liberals, 1973–75 (Vice-Chm., 1971–73); Mem., Liberal Party Nat. Council, 1970–76; Exec. Cttee, London Liberal Party, 1981–84. Sutton Council: Councillor 1974–; Leader, Lib Dem (formerly Soc & Lib Dem) Group, 1988–99 (Liberal Gp, 1974–83, Liberal/SDP Alliance Gp, 1983–88); Leader of Opposition, 1984–86; Leader of Council, 1986–99; spokesperson on libraries, heritage, equalities and community safety, 1999–; Greater London Authority: Member: Metropolitan Police Authy, 2000–; Mayor's Adv. Cabinet, 2000–; Chm., Finance, Planning and Best Value Cttee, 2000–. MP (L) Sutton and Cheam, 1972–Feb. 1974; Liberal Party spokesman on environment, Dec. 1972–1974; contested (L) Sutton and Cheam, Oct. 1974. Lib Dem spokesman on educn, H of L, 1994–2000. Vice-Chm., All Party Parly Gp on Libraries, 1998–. Pres., London Lib Dems, 1991–2000; Vice Pres. and Lib Dem European and Internat. spokesperson, Local Govt Assoc., 1997–. Mem., Policy Cttee, AMA, 1989–97; Chm., Policy and Finance Cttee, London Boroughs Assoc., 1994–95. EU Committee of the Regions: UK Rep., 1994–; Mem. Bureau, 1996–; Vice Chm., UK Delegn, 1996–; Pres., European Lib Dem Reform Gp, 1998–; Mem. Council of Europe, CLRAE, 1996–. Vice Chm., 1997–2000, Mem. Leaders' Cttee, 1995–2000, Assoc. of London Govt. Freeman, City of London, 1998; Liveryman, Needlemakers' Co., 1999–. *Publication:* (jtly) Liberals and the Community, 1974. *Address:* 88 The Gallop, Sutton, Surrey SM2 5SA. *T:* (020) 8770 7269.

TOPHAM, Surgeon Captain Lawrence Garth; RN (Retd); Consultant Physician in Geriatric Medicine, Central Hampshire District Winchester and Andover Hospitals, 1974–83; *b* 14 Nov. 1914; *s* of late J. Topham and late Mrs Topham; *m* 1943, Olive Barbara Marshall (VAD), *yr d* of late J. Marshall and late Mrs Marshall; one *s* one *d*. *Educ:* Bradford Grammar Sch.; Univ. of Leeds. MB, ChB 1937; MD 1946; MRCPE 1957; FRCPE 1967; MRCP 1969. Joined RN 1938. Served War: HMS Newcastle and HMS Milford, 1939–41; USN Flight Surgeon's Wings, 1943; RN Fleet Air Arm Pilot's Wings, 1944. Pres., Central Air Med. Bd, 1949; HMS Sheffield, 1951; Med. Specialist and Consultant in Medicine, at RN Hosps, Trincomalee, Haslar and Plymouth, 1952–66; Prof. of Med., RN, and RCP, 1966–71; QHP 1970; retd at own request, from RN, 1971. House Governor and Medical Superintendent, King Edward VII Convalescent Home for Officers, Osborne, IoW, 1971–74. Member: British Nat. Cttee, Internat. Soc. of Internal Medicine; British Geriatric Soc.; Wessex Physicians Club. OStJ (Officer Brother) 1970. *Publications:* several articles in med. jls, especially on subject of diseases of the chest. *Recreations:* Rugby football refereeing, rowing, photography, Oriental cookery. *Address:* Tilings, 3 Holt Close, Wickham, Hants PO17 5EY. *T:* (01329) 832072.

TOPLEY, Keith; *see* Topley, W. K.

TOPLEY, Kenneth Wallis Joseph, CMG 1976; Secretary for Education and Manpower, Hong Kong, 1981–83, retired; *b* 22 Oct. 1922; *s* of William Frederick Topley, MC and Daisy Elizabeth (*née* Wellings); *m* 1st, 1949, Marjorie Doreen Wills (marr. diss.); two *s* two *d*; 2nd, 1989, Barbara Newman Hough. *Educ:* Dulwich Coll.; Aberdeen Univ.; London Sch. of Econs and Pol. Science (BScEcon 1949). Served War, RAFVR, 1941–46 (Flt Lieut). Westminster Bank, 1939–41; Mass-Observation, 1941; Malayan Civil Service, 1950–55: Econ. Affairs Secretariat, Comr Gen.'s Office, and Labour Dept; Hong Kong Civil Service, 1955–83: various appts, 1955–62; Comr for Co-operative Develt and Fisheries, 1962–64; Sec., UGC, 1965–67; Comr for Census and Statistics, 1970–73; Dir of Social Welfare, 1973–74; Dir of Educn, 1974–80; Chm., Cttee to Review Post-Secondary and Technical Educn, 1980–81. Secretary: Univ. of E Asia, Macau, 1984–88; E Asia Open Inst, 1988–90. Commandeur de l'Ordre des Arts et des Lettres (France), 1987. *Recreations:* walking, study of philosophy. *Address:* Guia, 4 Baltic Wharf, Marlborough Road, Oxford OX1 4JX. *Club:* Hong Kong Jockey (Hong Kong).

TOPLEY, (William) Keith, MA; Senior Master of the Supreme Court (Queen's Bench Division) and Queen's Remembrancer, 1990–96; Admiralty Registrar of the Supreme Court, 1986–92; *b* 19 Jan. 1936; *s* of late Bryan Topley and Grizel Hester (*née* Stirling); *m* 1980, Clare Mary Pennington; one *s* by former marriage. *Educ:* Bryanston School; Trinity Coll., Oxford (MA). Called to Bar, Inner Temple, 1959, Bencher, 1990; Master of Supreme Court, QBD, 1980–90. Mem., Bar Council, 1967–68. Mem. Adv. Bd, Coll. of Law, 1992–96. Freeman, City of London, 1993; Mem., Watermen and Lightermen's Co., 1993–. *Publication:* (ed jtly) Supreme Court Practice, 1988, 1991. *Recreations:* reading, writing, sailing. *Address:* 22 Queens Road, Cowes, Isle of Wight PO31 8BJ. *T:* (01983) 299742. *Clubs:* Garrick; Royal Yacht Squadron, Royal London Yacht (Cdre, 1996–98) (Cowes); Bar Yacht (Cdre, 1992–95); New Zealand Golf.

TOPOLSKI, Daniel; freelance writer, motivational speaker and broadcaster; photo-journalist; Oxford Boat-Race coach, 1973–87, consultant since 1995; *b* 4 June 1945; *s* of late Feliks Topolski and Marion Everall; *m* 1998, Susan Gilmore; one *s* two *d*. *Educ:* Lycée Français, London; Westminster Sch.; New Coll., Oxford (BA, Geography 1967; DipSoc Anthropology 1968, MA 1970). Writer and TV broadcaster on travel and sport; BBC TV Researcher and Producer, 1969–73; TV and Radio presenter and commentator, 1982–; expedition leader: Brazil, 1963; Iran (Marco Polo), 1973–74; travel in Africa, North and South America, India, Himalayas, China, Middle East, SE Asia, Australia. Rowing Competitor: Boat Race, Oxford, 1967, 1968; World Championships, 1969–78 (Gold medal 1977); Henley Regatta (4 victories); Rowing Coach: Oxford Boat Race Crew, 1973–87 (12 victories, record 10 in a row); Nat. Women's Squad, 1979–80; Nat. Men's Pair and Women's Pair, 1982; Nat. Men's Pair, Olympics, 1984. Churchill Fellow, 1980. FRGS 1993. Radio Travel Prog. of the Year award for Topolski's Travels, 1993. *Publications:* Muzungu: one man's Africa, 1976; (with Feliks Topolski) Travels with my Father: journey through South America, 1983; Boat Race, 1985; (with Patrick Robinson) True Blue, 1989 (Sports Book of the Year, 1990), 2nd edn 1996 (filmed, 1998); Henley: the Regatta, 1989. *Recreations:* theatre, cinema, rowing (Steward, Henley Regatta), ski-ing, travel, family. *Address:* 69 Randolph Avenue, W9 1DW. *T:* (020) 7289 8939. *Clubs:* Cobden, Woody's; London Rowing (Putney); Leander (Henley).

TOPP, Air Commodore Roger Leslie; AFC 1950 (Bar 1955, 2nd Bar 1957); independent consultant, aviation and defence, 1988–99; *b* 14 May 1923; *s* of William Horace Topp and Kathleen (*née* Peters); *m* 1945, Audrey Jane Jeffery (*d* 1999); one *s* one *d*. *Educ:* North Mundham Sch.; RAF, Cranwell. Served War: Pilot trg, Canada, 1943–44, commissioned 1944; 'E' Sqdn Glider Pilot Regt, Rhine Crossing, 1945. Nos 107 and 98 Mosquito Sqdns, Germany, 1947–50; Empire Test Pilots' Sch. and RAE Farnborough, 1951–54; Commanded No 111 Fighter Sqdn (Black Arrows) Aerobatic Team, 1955–58; Allied Air Forces Central Europe, Fontainbleau, 1959; Sector Operational Centre, Brockzetel, Germany, 1959–61; jssc, Latimer, 1961–62; commanded Fighter Test Sqdn, Boscombe Down, 1962–64; Station Cmdr, RAF Coltishall, 1964–66; Nat. Def. Coll., Canada, 1966–67; Opl Requirements, MoD (Air), London, 1967–69; Multi-role Combat Aircraft Project, Munich, 1969–70; HQ No 38 Gp, Odiham, 1970; Commandant, Aeroplane and Armament Experimental Estabt, Boscombe Down, 1970–72; Dep. Gen. Man., Multi-role Combat Aircraft Develt and Production Agency, Munich, 1972–78; retd from RAF, 1978. Consultant to Ferranti Defence Systems Ltd, Scotland (Aviation and Defence, FRG), 1978–88. *Recreations:* golf, sailing. *Address:* 95 Taverham Road, Taverham, Norwich, Norfolk NR8 6SE. *Club:* Royal Air Force.

TOPPING, Rev. Frank; actor, author and broadcaster; Superintendent Methodist Minister, Barnet Circuit, 1997–2001; *b* 30 March 1937; *s* of late Frank and Dorothy Topping; *m* 1958, June Berry; two *s* one *d*. *Educ:* St Anne's Convent Sch., Birkenhead; St Anselm's Christian Brother Coll., Birkenhead; North West School of Speech and Drama;

Didsbury Coll., Bristol. Served RAF, Cyprus, 1955–57. Leatherhead Rep. Th., 1957–59; Royal Court, Chelsea, 1959; Wolverhampton Rep. Th., 1959; Granada TV, 1960–64; read Theology at Didsbury Coll., Bristol, 1964–67; asst minister at Dome Methodist Mission, Brighton, and methodist univ. chaplain at Sussex, 1967–70; also freelance broadcaster, BBC Radio Brighton, 1967–70; ordained 1970; staff producer, BBC, 1970–80. Song-writing partnership with Donald Swann, 1973–81; two man show, Swann with Topping, played in Jersey, London fringe theatre, then at Ambassadors; presented three one-man plays, Edinburgh Fest. Fringe, 1986. TV appearances: own series, Sunday Best, 1981, and Topping on Sunday, 1982–84; The 5 Minute Show (weekday series), TVS, 1989–90. Author of radio plays: On the Hill, 1974 (Grace Wyndham Goldie UNDA Dove award, 1975); A Particular Star, 1977. Formed Emmaus Theatre Prodns with wife, 1993. *Publications:* Lord of the Morning, 1977; Lord of the Evening, 1979; Lord of my Days, 1980; Working at Prayer, 1981; Pause for Thought with Frank Topping, 1981; Lord of Life, 1982; The Words of Christ: forty meditations, 1983; God Bless You—Spoonbill, 1984; Lord of Time, 1985; An Impossible God, 1985; Wings of the Morning, 1986; Act Your Age, 1989; Laughing in my Sleep (autobiog.), 1993; All the Days of my Life, 1994; Here I Stand …, 1997; Grappling with God on the M25, 1998. *Recreations:* sailing, travel, photography, late night conversation. *Address:* Lamb Cottage, The Cross, Clearwell, Coleford, Glos GL16 8JU. *T:* and *Fax:* (01594) 834728. *Club:* Hurst Castle Sailing (Keyhaven, Hants).

TORDOFF, family name of **Baron Tordoff.**

TORDOFF, Baron *cr* 1981 (Life Peer), of Knutsford in the County of Cheshire; **Geoffrey Johnson Tordoff;** President of the Liberal Party, 1983–84; Lib Dem Chief Whip, House of Lords, 1988–94 (Liberal Chief Whip, 1984–88; Deputy Chief Whip, 1983–84); *b* 11 Oct. 1928; *s* of Stanley Acomb Tordoff and Annie Tordoff (*née* Johnson); *m* 1953, Mary Patricia (*née* Swarbrick); two *s* three *d. Educ:* North Manchester School; Manchester Grammar School; Univ. of Manchester. Contested (L), Northwich 1964, Knutsford 1966, 1970. Chairman: Liberal Party Assembly Cttee, 1974–76; Liberal Party, 1976–79 (and its Campaigns and Elections Cttee, 1980, 1981); Member, Liberal Party Nat. Executive, 1975–84. Chm. of Cttees, H of L, 2001– (Principal Dep. Chm. of Cttees, 1994–2001); Chm., H of L Select Cttee on the EC, 1994–2001. Chm., ME Cttee, Refugee Council, 1990–95. Mem., Press Complaints Commn, 1995–. *Address:* House of Lords, SW1A 0PW.

TORO-HARDY, Alfredo; Ambassador of Venezuela to the Court of St James's, and concurrently to the Republic of Ireland, since 2001; *b* Caracas, 22 May 1950; *s* of Fernando Toro and Ofelia Toro (*née* Hardy); *m* 1st, 1972, Dinorah Carnevali (marr. diss. 1998); two *s* one *d*; 2nd, 2001, Gabriela Gaxiola. *Educ:* Central Univ. of Venezuela (LLB 1973; LLM Internat. Trade Law 1977); Univ. of Paris II (Comparative Law 1974); Internat. Inst. of Public Admin, Paris (Diplomatic Studies 1974); Univ. of Pennsylvania (LLM Corporative Law 1979). Simón Bolívar University, Caracas: Associate Prof., 1989–93; Co-ordinator, Latin American Studies Inst., and Dir, N American Studies Centre, 1989–91; Dir, Diplomatic Acad., with rank of Ambassador, Foreign Affairs Ministry, 1992–94; Ambassador: to Brazil, 1994–97; to Chile, 1997–99; to USA, 1999–2001. Adviser to: Foreign Affairs Cttee, Chamber of Deputies, Congress of Venezuela, 1986–92; Presidential Commn for Reform of the State, 1989–91, and for Border Affairs, 1991–92; to Minister of Foreign Affairs, 1992–94; Mem., Consultative Bd, Nat. Security and Defence Council, 1988–2000. Vis. Schol. and Sen. Fulbright Schol., Princeton Univ., 1986–87; Hon. Prof., Univ. of Brasilia, 1996–97; prof. and guest speaker in several univs and acad. instns in Venezuela, USA, Chile, Brazil, UK and others. Member: Inter-American Peace and Justice Commn, Santiago, 1997–; Inter-American Dialogue, Washington, 1999–. Weekly columnist and collaborator in numerous media publications, in Venezuela, Mexico, Brazil and Chile, including: El Universal, Caracas, 1994–2000; El Globo, Caracas, 1989–97. Host, weekly TV prog., Radio Caracas TV, 1992–94. Holds several Venezuelan and foreign decorations. *Publications* include: Los Libertadores de Venezuela, 1982; Rafael Caldera, 1982; Para qué una Política Exterior?, 1984; Venezuela, Democracia y Política Exterior, 1986; El Desafío Venezolano: Como Influir las Decisiones Políticas Estadounidenses, 1988; La Maldicion de Sísifo: quince años de política exterior Venezolana, 1991; Bajo el Signo de la Incertidumbre, 1992; Las Falacias del Libre Comercio, 1993; De Yalta a Sarajevo: de la guerra fría a la paz caliente, 1993; Del Descalabro Mexicano a la Crisis Venezolana, 1995; El Desorden Global, 1996. *Address:* Venezuelan Embassy, 1 Cromwell Road, SW7 2HR. *T:* (020) 7584 5375.

ToROBERT, Sir Henry Thomas, KBE 1981; Governor and Chairman of the Board of the Bank of Papua New Guinea since its formation, 1973–93; Partner, Deloitte Touche Tohmatsu, PNG, since 1993; Chairman, Credit Corporation (PNG) Ltd, since 1993; *b* Kokopo, 1942. *Educ:* primary educn in East New Britain; secondary educn in Qld, Australia; Univ. of Sydney, Aust. (BEcon. 1965). Asst Research Officer, Reserve Bank of Australia, Port Moresby, 1965 (one of first local officers to join the bank); Dep. Manager, Port Moresby Branch, 1971; Manager of the Reserve Bank, 1972 (the first Papua New Guinean to hold such a position at a time when all banks were branches of the Aust. commercial banks). Member of the cttee responsible for working out a PNG banking system which came into effect by an act of parliament in 1973; Chairman: Management Bd, PNG Bankers' Coll., 1973–; PNG Currency Working Group advising the Govt on arrangements leading to the introduction of PNG currency, the Kina; ToRobert Cttee to look into problems of administration in PNG Public Service, 1979 (ToRobert Report, 1979); Council, PNG Inst. of Applied Social and Econ. Res., 1975–82; Govt Super Task Force on project implementation, 1994–. Pres., PNG Amateur Sports Fedn and PNG Olympic and Commonwealth Games Cttee, 1980–. *Address:* PO Box 898, Port Moresby, Papua New Guinea.

TORONTO, Archbishop of, (RC), since 1990; **His Eminence Aloysius Cardinal Ambrozic;** *b* 27 Jan. 1930; *s* of Aloysius Ambrozic and Helena (*née* Pecar). *Educ:* St Augustine's Seminary, Scarborough, Ont; Angelicum Rome (STL); Biblicum, Rome, 1957–60 (SSL); Univ. of Würzburg, Germany (ThD). Ordained, 1955; Curate, St Teresa's, Port Colborne, Ont, 1955–57; Professor: St Augustine's Seminary, Scarborough, Ont, 1960–67; Toronto Sch. of Theol., 1970–76; Auxiliary Bishop of Toronto, 1976–86; Coadjutor Archbishop of Toronto, 1986–90. Cardinal, 1998. *Publications:* The Hidden Kingdom, 1972; Remarks on the Canadian Catechism, 1974; Oce, posvečeno bodi tvoje ime, 1980. *Recreations:* hiking, swimming. *Address:* 1155 Yonge Street, Toronto, ON M4T 1W2, Canada. *T:* (416) 9340606.

TORONTO, Bishop of, since 1989; **Rt Rev. Terence Edward Finlay;** *b* 19 May 1937; *s* of Terence John Finlay and Sarah McBryan; *m* 1962, Alice-Jean Cracknell; two *d. Educ:* Univ. of Western Ontario (BA); Huron Coll., London, Ont (BTh); Cambridge Univ., Eng. (MA). Deacon 1961, priest 1962; Dean of Residence, Renison Coll., Waterloo, Canada; Incumbent: All Saints, Waterloo, 1964–66; St Aidan's, London, Canada, 1966–68; Rector: St John the Evangelist, London, 1968–78; Grace Church, Brantford, 1978–82; Archdeacon of Brant, 1978–82; Incumbent, St Clement's, Eglinton, Toronto, 1982–86; a Suffragan Bishop, Diocese of Toronto, 1986; Coadjutor Bishop, 1987. DD: (*jure dignitatis*) Huron Coll., 1987; (*hc*) Wycliffe Coll., 1988; (*hc*) Trinity Coll., 1989. *Recreations:* music, ski-ing, travel. *Address:* Synod Office, 135 Adelaide Street E, Toronto, ON M5C 1L8, Canada. *T:* (416) 3636021.

TORONTO, Bishops Suffragan of; *see* Bedford-Jones, Rt Rev. M.; Blackwell, Rt Rev. D. C.

TORPHICHEN, 15th Lord *cr* 1564; **James Andrew Douglas Sandilands;** *b* 27 Aug. 1946; *s* of 14th Lord Torphichen, and Mary Thurstan, *d* of late Randle Henry Neville Vaudrey; *S* father, 1975; *m* 1976, Margaret Elizabeth, *o d* of late William A. Beale and of Mrs Margaret Patten Beale, Peterborough, New Hampshire, USA; four *d. Heir: cousin* Douglas Robert Alexander Sandilands [*b* 31 Aug. 1926; *m* 1949, Ethel Louise Burkitt; one *s*; *m* Suzette Véva (*née* Pernet); two *s*]. *Address:* Calder House, Mid-Calder, West Lothian EH53 0HN.

TORRANCE, Rev. Prof. Iain Richard, TD 1995; DPhil; Professor in Patristics and Christian Ethics, University of Aberdeen, since 1999; Master of Christ's College, Aberdeen, since 2001; a Chaplain to the Queen in Scotland, since 2001; *b* 13 Jan. 1949; *yr s* of Very Rev. Prof. T. F. Torrance, *qv* and of Margaret Edith Spear; *m* 1975, Morag Ann MacHugh, *er d* of Francis John MacHugh and Wendy Anne Lang; one *s* one *d. Educ:* Edinburgh Acad.; Monkton Combe Sch., Bath; Edinburgh Univ. (MA Mental Philosophy, 1971); St Andrews Univ. (BD New Testament, 1974); Oriel Coll., Oxford (DPhil 1980). Chaplain to the Moderator, Gen. Assembly of Ch of Scotland, 1976–77; ordained, 1982; Minister, Northmavine, Shetland, 1982–85; Lecturer: in NT and Christian Ethics, Queen's Coll., Birmingham, 1985–89; in NT and Patristics, Birmingham Univ., 1989–93; Aberdeen University: Lectr in Divinity, 1993–97; Sen. Lectr, 1997–99; Senate Assessor to Univ. Court, 1999–; Head, Dept of Divinity and Religious Studies, 2000–01; Dean, Faculty of Arts and Divinity, 2001–. TA Chaplain, 1982–97; ACF Chaplain, 1996–2000; Convener, Cttee on Chaplains to HM Forces, Gen. Assembly of C of S, 1998–. Member: Dialogue between World Alliance of Reformed Churches and the Orthodox Church, 1992–; Acad. Internat. des Sciences Religieuses, 1997–; Benchmarking Panel for Degrees in Theology and Religious Studies, QAA, 1999–2000. Sec., Soc. for Study of Christian Ethics, 1995–98; Hon. Sec., 1995–98, Hon. Pres., 1998–99, Aberdeen AUT. Judge, Templeton (UK) Award, 1994–99. Co-ed., Scottish Jl of Theol., 1982–. *Publications:* Christology after Chalcedon, 1989; (jtly) Human Genetics: a Christian perspective, 1995; Ethics and the Military Community, 1998; (ed jtly) To Glorify God: essays on modern reformed liturgy, 1999; (ed) Bioethics for the New Millennium, 2000. *Recreation:* historical Scottish culture (buildings, literature, art). *Address:* (home) Concraig Smiddy, Clinterty, Kingswells, Aberdeenshire AB15 8RN. *T:* (01224) 790902; (office) Faculties Office, University of Aberdeen, Regent Walk, Aberdeen AB24 3FX. *T:* (01224) 272084; *e-mail:* i.r.torrance@abdn.ac.uk. *Club:* New (Edinburgh).

TORRANCE, Rev. Professor James Bruce; Professor of Systematic Theology, King's College, University of Aberdeen, and Christ's College, Aberdeen, 1977–89 (Dean of the Faculty of Divinity, 1978–81), now Professor Emeritus; *b* 3 Feb. 1923; *s* of late Rev. Thomas Torrance and Annie Elizabeth Sharp; *m* 1955, Mary Heather Aitken, medical practitioner; one *s* two *d. Educ:* Royal High School, Edinburgh; Edinburgh Univ. (MA Hons Philosophy, 1st Cl.); New Coll., Edinburgh (BD Systematic Theol., Distinction); Univs of Marburg, Basle and Oxford. Licensed Minister of Church of Scotland, 1950; parish of Invergowrie, Dundee, 1954; Lectr in Divinity and Dogmatics in History of Christian Thought, New Coll., Univ. of Edinburgh, 1961; Sen. Lectr in Christian Dogmatics, New Coll., 1972. Visiting Professor: of New Testament, Union Theol. Seminary, Richmond, Va, 1960; of Theology, Columbia Theol. Seminary, Decatur, Ga., 1965, and Vancouver Sch. of Theology, BC, 1974–75, 1988; Regent Coll., Vancouver, 1984, 1988, 1993, 1994, 1995, 1997; Fuller Theol Seminary, Pasadena, 1982, 1984, 1987, 1989, 1991, 1994, 1995; S Africa, 1980, 1984, 1986, 1990; univs and theol schs in Perth, Brisbane, Melbourne, Adelaide and Sydney, 1990, 1993, 1996; in New Zealand, 1987, 1988, 1989; in Fiji, W Samoa, 1993, 1996. *Publications:* (trans. jtly) Oscar Cullmann's Early Christian Worship, 1953; John Duns Scotus in a Nutshell, 1992; Worship, Community and the Triune God of Greece, 1996; contribs: Essays in Christology for Karl Barth (Karl Barth's Festschrift), 1956; Where Faith and Science Meet, 1954; Calvinus Ecclesiae Doctor, 1978; Incarnation (on Nicene-Constantinopolitan Creed, 381 AD), 1981; The Westminster Confession in the Church Today, 1982; Calvinus Reformator, 1982; Calvinus Sacrae Scripturae Professor, 1994; A Passion for Christ, 1999; articles to Biblical and Biographical Dictionaries, Scottish Jl of Theology, Interpretation, Church Service Society Annual, and other symposia; *festschrift:* Christ in Our Place (ed T. Hart and D. Timell), 1991. *Recreations:* beekeeping, fishing, gardening, swimming. *Address:* 3 Greenbank Crescent, Edinburgh EH10 5TE. *T:* (0131) 447 3230.

See also Very Rev. Prof. T. F. Torrance.

TORRANCE, Madeline Mary; see Drake, M. M.

TORRANCE, Samuel Robert, MBE 1995; professional golfer; *b* Largs, 24 Aug. 1953; *s* of Robert and June Torrance; *m* 1995, Suzanne Danielle; one *s* two *d.* Winner: Under-25 Match Play tournament Radici Open, 1972; Zambian Open, 1975; Martini Internat., Wales, 1976; Scottish PGA Championship, 1978, 1980, 1985, 1991, 1993, 1995; Colombian Open, 1979; Australian PGA Championship, 1980; Irish Open, 1981, 1995; Spanish Open, 1982; Portuguese Open, 1982, 1983; Scandinavian Open, 1983; Tunisian Open, 1984; Benson & Hedges Internat., England, 1984; Sanyo Open, Spain, 1984; Monte Carlo Open, 1985; Italian Open, 1987, 1995; German Masters, 1990; Jersey Open, 1991; Catalan Open, 1993; Kronenburg Open, Italy, 1993; Honda Open, Germany, 1993; British Masters, 1995; French Open, 1998; Member: Dunhill Cup team, 1985–95 (winners, 1995); World Cup team, 1976–95; Ryder Cup team, 1981–95 (winners, 1985 and 1995; Captain, 2001–). *Recreations:* snooker, tennis, all sport.

TORRANCE, Very Rev. Prof. Thomas Forsyth, MBE 1945; DLitt, DTh, DThéol, Dr Teol, DD, DSc; FRSE 1979; FBA 1983; Professor of Christian Dogmatics, University of Edinburgh, and New College, Edinburgh, 1952–79; Moderator of General Assembly of Church of Scotland, May 1976–77; *b* 30 Aug. 1913; *e s* of late Rev. T. Torrance, then of Chengtu, Szechwan, China; *m* 1946, Margaret Edith, *y d* of late Mr and Mrs G. F. Spear, The Brow, Combe Down, Bath; two *s* one *d. Educ:* Chengtu Canadian School; Bellshill Academy; Univs of Edinburgh, Oxford, Basel. MA Edinburgh 1934; studies in Jerusalem and Athens, 1936; BD Edinburgh 1937; post-grad. studies, Basel, 1937–38; DLitt Edinburgh 1971. Prof. of Theology, Auburn, NY, USA, 1938–39; post-grad. studies, Oriel Coll., Oxford, 1939–40; ordained minister of Alyth Barony Parish, 1940; Church of Scotland chaplain (with Huts and Canteens) in MEF and CMF, 1943–45; returned to Alyth; DTh Univ. of Basel, 1946; minister of Beechgrove Church, Aberdeen, 1947; Professor of Church History, Univ. of Edinburgh, and New Coll., Edinburgh, 1950–52. Participant, World Conf. on Faith and Order, Lund, 1952; Evanston Assembly of WCC, 1954; Faith and Order Commn of WCC, 1952–62; Participant in Conversations between: Church of Scotland and Church of England, 1950–58; World Alliance of Reformed Churches and Greek Orthodox Church, 1979–. Lectures: Hewett, 1959 (NY, Newton Center and Cambridge, Mass); Harris, Dundee, 1970; Anderson, Presbyterian

Coll., Montreal, 1971; Taylor, Yale, 1971; Keese, Univ. of Chattanooga, 1971; Cummings, McGill Univ., Montreal, 1978; Richards, Univ. of Virginia at Charlottesville, 1978; Staley, Davidson Coll., NC, 1978; Cosgrove, Glasgow, 1981; Warfield, Princeton, 1981; Payton, Pasadena, 1981; Didsbury, Manchester, 1982; Staley, Regent Coll., Vancouver, 1982; William Lyall Meml, Montreal, 1990; Warburton, Lincoln's Inn, 1995. Mem., Académie Internationale des Sciences Religieuses, 1965 (Pres., 1972–81); For. Mem., Société de l'Histoire du Protestantisme Français, 1968; Mem. Soc. Internat. pour l'Etude de la Philosophie Médiévale, 1969; Hon. President: Soc. for Study of Theology, 1966–68; Church Service Soc. of the Church of Scotland, 1970–71; New Coll. Union, 1972–73. Vice-Pres., Inst. of Religion and Theology of GB and Ireland, 1973–76 (Pres., 1976–78); Mem., Center of Theol Inquiry, Princeton, 1982–. Protopresbyter of Greek Orthodox Church (Patriarchate of Alexandria), 1973. Curator: Deutsches Institut für Bildung und Wissen, 1982–; Europäische Akademie für Umweltfragen, 1986–. Membre d'honneur, Acad. Internat. de Philosophie des Scis, 1976. Hon. DD: Presbyterian Coll., Montreal, 1950; St Andrews, 1960; Edinburgh, 1997; Hon. DThéol: Geneva, 1959; Paris, 1959; Dr Teol (*hc*) Oslo, 1961; Hon. DSc Heriot-Watt, 1983; Dr Th (*hc*) Debrecen, 1988. Templeton Foundn Prize, 1978. Cross of St Mark (first class), 1970. *Publications:* The Modern Theological Debate, 1942; The Doctrine of Grace in the Apostolic Fathers, 1949; Calvin's Doctrine of Man, 1949; Royal Priesthood, 1955, 2nd edn 1993; Kingdom and Church, 1956; When Christ Comes and Comes Again, 1957; The Mystery of the Lord's Supper (Sermons on the Sacrament by Robert Bruce), 1958; ed Calvin's Tracts and Treatises, Vols I-III, 1959; The School of Faith, 1959; Conflict and Agreement in the Church, Vol. I, Order and Disorder, 1959; The Apocalypse Today, 1959; Conflict and Agreement in the Church, Vol. II, The Ministry and the Sacraments of the Gospel, 1960; Karl Barth: an Introduction to his Early Theology, 1910–1930, 1962; ed (with D. W. Torrance) Calvin's NT Commentaries, 1959–73; Theology in Reconstruction, 1965; Theological Science, 1969 (Collins Religious Book Award; trans. French, 1990); Space, Time and Incarnation, 1969; God and Rationality, 1971, 2nd edn 1998; Theology in Reconciliation: Essays towards Evangelical and Catholic Unity in East and West, 1975; The Centrality of Christ, 1976; Space, Time and Resurrection, 1976; The Ground and Grammar of Theology, 1980; Christian Theology and Scientific Culture, 1980; (ed) Belief in Science and in Christian Life, 1980; (ed) The Incarnation: ecumenical studies in the Nicene Constantinopolitan Creed, 1981; Divine and Contingent Order, 1981; Reality and Evangelical Theology, 1982; Juridical Law and Physical Law, 1982; (ed) James Clerk Maxwell: A Dynamical Theory of the Electromagnetic Field, 1982; The Meditation of Christ, 1983, 2nd edn 1992; Transformation and Convergence in the Frame of Knowledge, 1984; The Christian Frame of Mind, 1985, 2nd enlarged edn (subtitled Reason, Order and Openness in Theology and Natural Science), 1989; Reality and Scientific Theology, 1985; (ed) Theological Dialogue between Orthodox and Reformed Churches, vol. 1, 1985, vol. 2, 1993; The Trinitarian Faith: the Evangelical Theology of the Ancient Catholic Church, 1988; The Hermeneutics of John Calvin, 1988; (ed) Thomas Torrance, China's First Missionaries, Ancient Israelites, 1988; Karl Barth, Biblical and Evangelical Theologian, 1990; Senso del divino e scienza moderna, 1992; Divine Meaning: studies in Patristic Hermaneutics, 1993; Trinitarian Perspectives: towards doctrinal agreement, 1993; Preaching Christ Today: the Gospel and scientific thinking, 1994; Divine Meaning: studies in patristic hermeneutics, 1995; The Christian Doctrine of God, One Being, Three Persons, 1996; Scottish Theology, 1996; (ed) H. R. Mackintosh, The Person of Jesus Christ, 2000; Editor, Theology and Science at the Frontiers of Knowledge, series, 1985–91; Jt Editor, Church Dogmatics, Vols 1, 2, 3 and 4, by Karl Barth, 1956–69; Emeritus Editor: Scottish Jl Theology; SJT Monographs. *Address:* 37 Braid Farm Road, Edinburgh EH10 6LE. *T:* and *Fax:* (0131) 447 3224; *e-mail:* ttorr@globalnet.co.uk. *Clubs:* New, University (Edinburgh).

See also Rev. Prof. I. R. Torrance, Rev. Prof. J. B. Torrance.

TORRENS-SPENCE, Captain (Frederick) Michael (Alexander), DSO 1941; DSC 1941; AFC 1944; Royal Navy retired; Lord Lieutenant of County Armagh, 1981–89; *b* 10 March 1914; *s* of Lt-Col Herbert Frederick Torrens-Spence and Mrs Eileen Torrens-Spence; *m* 1944, Rachel Nora Clarke; three *s* one *d*. *Educ:* RNC, Dartmouth. Commnd Sub Lieut, 1934; specialised as pilot, 1936; Battle of Taranto, 1940; commanded 815 Naval Air Sqdn, 1941; Battle of Matapan, 1941; Chief Instructor, Empire Test Pilots Sch., 1947–48; Dep. Dir, Air Warfare Div., Naval Staff, 1952–54; commanded HMS Delight, 1955–56, HMS Albion, 1959–61; ADC to the Queen, 1961. Comdr 1946, Captain 1952. Co. Comdt, Ulster Special Constabulary, 1961–70; commanded 2nd (Co. Armagh) Bn, Ulster Defence Regt, 1970–71. High Sheriff, Co. Armagh, 1979. DFC, Greece, 1941. *Address:* Drumcullen House, Ballydugan, Downpatrick, Co. Down BT30 8HZ. *Club:* MCC.

TORRINGTON, 11th Viscount, *cr* 1721; **Timothy Howard St George Byng;** Bt 1715; Baron Byng of Southill, 1721; *b* 13 July 1943; *o s* of Hon. George Byng, RN (*d* on active service, 1944; *o s* of 10th Viscount) and Anne Yvonne Wood (she *m* 2nd, 1951, Howard Henry Masterton Carpenter; 3rd, 1990, Michael Ingram Bostock); *S* grandfather, 1961; *m* 1973, Susan, *d* of M. G. T. Webster, *qv*; three *d*. *Educ:* Harrow; St Edmund Hall, Oxford. Mem., Select Cttee on EEC, H of L, 1984–87 (Chm., Sub-Cttee B (Energy, Transport and Broadcasting), 1985–87). Chm., Baltic Mills Ltd, 1995–. *Recreation:* travel. *Heir: kinsman*, John Launcelot Byng, MC [*b* 18 March 1919; *m* 1955, Margaret Ellen Hardy; one *s* two *d*]. *Address:* Great Hunts Place, Owslebury, Winchester, Hants SO21 1JL. *Clubs:* White's, Pratt's; Muthaiga (Nairobi).

TORRY, Peter James; HM Diplomatic Service; Ambassador to Spain, since 1998; *b* 2 Aug. 1948; *m* 1979, Angela Wakeling Wood, *d* of J. N. Wood, *qv*; three *d*. *Educ:* Dover Coll.; New Coll., Oxford (Open Schol.; BA 1970; Irvine Award, 1968; Rugby Blue, 1968, 1969). Joined FCO, 1970; Third Sec., Havana, 1971; Second Sec., Jakarta, 1974; First Sec., FCO, 1977; Bonn, 1981; First Sec., subseq. Counsellor, FCO, 1985; Washington, 1989; FCO, 1993–98, Dir (Personnel and Security), 1995–98. *Recreations:* golf, walking, ski-ing, books, antique furniture. *Address:* c/o Foreign and Commonwealth Office, SW1A 2AH. *Clubs:* Oxford and Cambridge; Vincent's (Oxford).

TORTELIER, Yan Pascal; Principal Conductor, BBC Philharmonic, since 1992; *b* 19 April 1947; *s* of late Paul Tortelier and of Maud (*née* Martin); *m* 1970, Sylvie Brunet-Moret; two *s*. *Educ:* Paris Conservatoire; general musical studies with Nadia Boulanger; studied conducting with Franco Ferrara in Sienna. Leader and Associate Conductor, Orchestre du Capitole de Toulouse, 1974–82; Principal Conductor and Artistic Dir, Ulster Orchestra, 1989–92. Has conducted all major British orchestras and toured extensively in USA, Canada, Japan, Australia, Scandinavia, E and W Europe. Numerous recordings incl. complete symphonic works of Debussy and Ravel with Ulster Orch., and Hindemith and Dutilleux series with BBC Philharmonic. Hon. DLitt Ulster, 1992. *Publication:* Première orchestration of Ravel's Piano Trio, 1992. *Recreations:* ski-ing, windsurfing, scuba diving, nature. *Address:* c/o IMG Artists Europe, 616 Chiswick High Road, W4 5RX.

TORVILL, Jayne, (Mrs P. L. Christensen), OBE 2000 (MBE 1981); professional ice skater; *b* 7 Oct. 1957; *d* of George Henry Torvill and Betty (*née* Smart); *m* 1990, Philip Lee Christensen. *Educ:* Clifton Hall Grammar Sch. for Girls, Nottingham. Ice dancer, with Christopher Dean, *qv*; British Champions, 1978, 1979, 1980, 1981, 1982, 1983 and 1994; European Champions, 1981, 1982, 1984 and 1994; World Champions, 1981, 1982, 1983 and 1984; World Professional Champions, 1984, 1985, 1990, 1995 and 1996; Olympic Champions, 1984; Olympic Bronze Medallists, 1994. Hon. MA Nottingham Trent, 1994. *Publication:* (with Christopher Dean) Facing the Music, 1995. *Recreations:* dance, theatre, caring for Freddy and Louis, my dogs. *Address:* PO Box 32, Heathfield, E Sussex TN21 0BW. *T:* (01435) 867825.

TORY, Sir Geofroy (William), KCMG 1958 (CMG 1956); HM Diplomatic Service, retired; *b* 31 July 1912; *s* of William Frank Tory and Edith Wreghitt; *m* 1st, 1938, Emilia Strickland; two *s* one *d*; 2nd, 1950, Hazel Winfield (*d* 1985). *Educ:* King Edward VII Sch., Sheffield; Queens' Coll., Cambridge. Apptd Dominions Office, 1935; Private Sec. to Perm. Under-Sec. of State, 1938–39; served War, 1939–43, in Royal Artillery; Prin. Private Sec. to Sec. of State, 1945–46; Senior Sec., Office of UK High Comr, Ottawa, 1946–49; Prin. Sec., Office of UK Rep. to Republic of Ireland, 1949–50; Counsellor, UK Embassy, Dublin, 1950–51; idc 1952; Dep. High Comr for UK in Pakistan (Peshawar), 1953–54, in Australia, 1954–57; Asst Under-Sec. of State, CRO, 1957; High Comr for UK in Fedn of Malaya, 1957–63; Ambassador to Ireland, 1964–66; High Commissioner to Malta, 1967–70. PMN (Malaysia) 1963. *Recreations:* painting, music. *Address:* Cliff Top, Harbour View, Kilbrittain, Co. Cork, Ireland.

TOSELAND, Ronald James, OBE 1991; Deputy Controller, National Air Traffic Services, 1988–91, retired; *b* 7 March 1933; *s* of W. M. and E. M. Toseland; *m* 1954, Joan Mary, *d* of A. R. and D. M. Pickett; two *s*. *Educ:* Kettering Boys' School. RAF Navigator, 1951–61; Air Traffic Control Officer, 1961–91; i/c Heathrow ATC, 1981–83; Dir, Civil Air Traffic Ops, 1983–87; Joint Field Commander, NATS, 1987–88. *Recreations:* music, walking. *Address:* 1 Marshall Place, Oakley Green, Windsor SL4 4QD. *T:* (01753) 863313.

TOSH, (Neil) Murray, MBE 1987; Member (C) Scotland South, Scottish Parliament, since 1999; *b* 1 Sept. 1950; *s* of Neil Ferguson Tosh and Mary Drummond Tosh (*née* Murray); *m* 1970, Christine Hind; two *s* one *d*. *Educ:* Kilmarnock Acad.; Univ. of Glasgow (MA 2nd Cl. Hons); Jordanhill Coll. of Educn (Secondary Teaching Qualif.). Teacher of history, Ravenspark Acad., Irvine, 1975–77; principal teacher of history: Kilwinning Acad., 1977–84; Belmont Acad., Ayr, 1984–99. Mem. (C) Kyle and Carrick DC, 1987–96 (Convener, Housing Cttee and Vice Convener, Planning and Develt Cttee, 1992–96). Scottish Parliament: Convener, Procedures Cttee; Mem., Transport and Envmt Cttee. *Recreations:* hill-walking, reading (historical, political), historic buildings, touring holidays. *Address:* 47A St Ninian's Road, Prestwick, Ayrshire KA9 1SL. *T:* (01292) 470264.

TOTARO, Prof. Burt James, PhD; Lowndean Professor of Astronomy and Geometry, University of Cambridge, since 2000; *b* 8 Aug. 1967. *Educ:* Princeton Univ. (AB 1984); Univ. of Calif at Berkeley (PhD 1989). Mathematical Scis Res. Inst., Berkeley, 1989–90; Dickson Instructor, 1990–93, Asst Prof., 1993–99, Dept of Maths, Univ. of Chicago; Mem., Inst. for Advanced Study, Princeton, 1994–95; Lectr, Dept of Pure Mathematics and Mathematical Statistics, Univ. of Cambridge, 1999. *Recreation:* cats. *Address:* Department of Pure Mathematics and Mathematical Statistics, University of Cambridge, Wilberforce Road, Cambridge CB3 0WB.

TOTNES, Archdeacon of; *see* Gilpin, Ven. R. T.

TOTTEN, William John; Floating Sheriff, based at Glasgow, since 1999; *b* 11 Sept. 1954; *s* of David and Sarah Totten; *m* 1985, Shirley Ann Morrison; one *s*. *Educ:* John Neilson Inst., Paisley; Univ. of Glasgow (LLB Hons 1977). Apprentice, Tindal, Oatts & Rodger, 1977–79; admitted solicitor, 1979; Procurator Fiscal Service, 1979–83; Asst, then Partner, Beltrami & Co., 1983–88; admitted to Faculty of Advocates, 1989; Advocate-Depute, 1993–96; Temp. Sheriff, 1998–99. *Recreations:* cycling, ski-ing, walking, reading, foreign travel. *Address:* Sheriff's Chambers, Sheriff Court House, 1 Carlton Place, Glasgow G5 9DA. *T:* (0141) 429 8888.

TOTTENHAM, family name of **Marquess of Ely**.

TÖTTERMAN, Richard Evert Björnson, Kt Comdr, Order of the White Rose of Finland; Hon. GCVO 1976 (Hon. KCVO 1969); Hon. OBE 1961; DPhil; Finnish Ambassador, retired; *b* 10 Oct. 1926; *s* of Björn B. Tötterman and Katharine C. (*née* Wimpenny); *m* 1953, Camilla Susanna Veronica Huber; one *s* one *d*. *Educ:* Univ. of Helsinki (Jur. lic.); Brasenose Coll., Oxford (DPhil; Hon. Fellow, 1982). Entered Finnish Foreign Service, 1952: served Stockholm, 1954–56; Moscow, 1956–58; Ministry for Foreign Affairs, Finland, 1958–62; Berne, 1962–63; Paris, 1963–66; Dep. Dir, Min. for For. Affairs, Helsinki, 1966; Sec.-Gen., Office of the President of Finland, 1966–70; Sec. of State, Min. for For. Aff., 1970–75; Ambassador: UK, 1975–83; Switzerland, 1983–90, and (concurrently) to the Holy See, 1988–90. Chm. or Mem. of a number of Finnish Govt Cttees, 1959–75, and participated as Finnish rep. in various internat. negotiations; Chm., Multilateral Consultations preparing Conf. on Security and Co-operation in Europe, 1972–73. Holds numerous foreign orders (Grand Cross, Kt Comdr, etc). *Recreations:* music, outdoor life. *Address:* Parkgatan 9 A 11, 00140 Helsinki, Finland.

TOTTLE, Prof. Charles Ronald; Professor of Medical Engineering, University of Bath, 1975–78, now Emeritus, a Pro Vice-Chancellor, 1973–77; Director, Bath Institute of Medical Engineering, 1975–78; Editor, Materials Science, Research Studies Press, 1977–94; *b* 2 Sept. 1920; *m* 1944, Eileen P. Geoghegan; one *d* (one *s* decd). *Educ:* Nether Edge Grammar School; University of Sheffield (MMet). English Electric Co. Ltd, 1941–45; Lecturer in Metallurgy, University of Durham, King's College, 1945–50; Ministry of Supply, Atomic Energy Division, Springfields Works, 1950–51; Culcheth Laboratories, 1951–56 (UKAEA); Head of Laboratories, Dounreay, 1956–57; Deputy Director, Dounreay, 1958–59; Prof. of Metallurgy, 1959–67, Dean of Science, 1966, Univ. of Manchester; Prof. and Head of School of Materials Science, Univ. of Bath, 1967–75; Man. Dir, South Western Industrial Research Ltd, 1970–75. Resident Research Associate, Argonne Nat. Laboratory, Illinois, USA, 1964–65. Vice-Pres., Instn of Metallurgists, 1968–70; Jt Editor, Institution of Metallurgists Series of Textbooks, 1962–70. Governor, Dauntsey's Sch., 1979–88. CEng 1978; FIM; FInstP 1958, CPhys 1985. Hon. MSc Manchester. *Publications:* The Science of Engineering Materials, 1965; An Encyclopaedia of Metallurgy and Materials, 1984; various contribs to metallurgical and engineering jls. *Recreations:* music, model making, gardening, restoration of old metal artefacts. *Address:* 47 Queens Road, Devizes, Wilts SN10 5HP.

TOUCHE, Sir Anthony (George), 3rd Bt *cr* 1920; Deputy Chairman, Friends' Provident Life Office, 1983–96; *b* 31 Jan. 1927; *s* of Donovan Meredith Touche (*d* 1952) (2nd *s* of 1st Bt) and of Muriel Amy Frances (*d* 1983), *e d* of Rev. Charles R. Thorold Winckley; *S* uncle, 1977; *m* 1961, Hester Christina, *er d* of Dr Werner Pleuger; two *s* one *d* (and one *s* decd). *Educ:* Eton College. FCA. Partner in George A. Touche & Co. (later Touche Ross & Co.), 1951; Director of investment trust companies, 1952–90; retired from Touche

Ross & Co., 1968; Touche, Remnant Holdings Ltd, 1965–89. Dir, 1968–90, Dep. Chm., 1977–87, National Westminster Bank. Chairman, Assoc. of Investment Trust Companies, 1971–73. Prime Warden, Goldsmiths' Co., 1987. *Recreations:* music, reading, walking. *Heir: s* William George Touche [*b* 26 June 1962; *m* 1987, Elizabeth Louise, *y d* of Allen Bridges; three *s* one *d*]. *Address:* Stane House, Ockley, Dorking, Surrey RH5 5TQ. *T:* (01306) 627397.

TOUCHE, Sir Rodney (Gordon), 2nd Bt *cr* 1962; *b* 5 Dec. 1928; *s* of Rt Hon. Sir Gordon Touche, 1st Bt, and of Ruby, Lady Touche (formerly Ruby Ann Macpherson) (*d* 1989); *S* father, 1972; *m* 1955, Ouida Ann, *d* of F. G. MacLellan, Moncton, NB, Canada; one *s* three *d*. *Educ:* Marlborough; University Coll., Oxford. *Heir: s* Eric MacLellan Touche [*b* 22 Feb. 1960; *m* 1990, Leeanne Marie Stringer (marr. diss. 1998); one *s* one *d*]. *Address:* 2403 Westmount Place, 1100 8th Avenue SW, Calgary, AB T2P 3T9, Canada. *T:* (403) 2338800.

TOUHIG, James Donnelly, (Don); MP (Lab and Co-op) Islwyn, since 1995; Parliamentary Under-Secretary of State, Wales Office, since 2001; *b* 5 Dec. 1947; *s* of Michael Touhig and Catherine Touhig (*née* Corten); *m* 1968, Jennifer Hughes; two *s* two *d*. *Educ:* St Francis Sch., Aberyschan; E Monmouth Coll., Pontypool. Journalist, 1968–95; Editor, Free Press of Monmouthshire, 1976–88; General Manager: Free Press Gp, 1988–92; (Business Develt) Bailey Gp, 1992–93; Bailey Print, 1993–95. PPS to Chancellor of the Exchequer, 1997–99; an Asst Govt Whip, 1999–2001. Mem., Welsh Select Cttee, 1996–97; Chm., All-Party Alcohol Abuse Gp, 1996–99; Jt Sec., All-Party Police Gp, 1996–97; Sec., Welsh Gp, PLP, 1995–99. Lab. Party Parly Advr to Police Fedn of Eng. and Wales, 1996–98. KSS 1991. *Recreations:* reading, cooking for family and friends, walking. *Address:* House of Commons, SW1A 0AA. *T:* (020) 7219 6435.

TOULMIN, John Kelvin, CMG 1994; QC 1980; **His Honour Judge Toulmin;** a Judge of the Technology and Construction Court of the High Court, since 1998; *b* 14 Feb. 1941; *s* of late Arthur Heaton Toulmin and B. Toulmin (*née* Fraser); *m* 1967, Carolyn Merton (*née* Gullick), barrister-at-law; one *s* two *d*. *Educ:* Winchester Coll.; Trinity Hall, Cambridge (Patterson Law Scholar, 1959; BA 1963, MA 1966); Univ. of Michigan (Ford Foundn Fellow and Fulbright Scholar, 1964; LLM 1965). Called to the Bar, Middle Temple, 1965 (Harmsworth Exhibnr, 1960; Astbury Scholar, 1965; Bencher, 1986); Western Circuit; a Recorder, 1984–97; a Dep. High Court Judge, 1994–97; an Official Referee and a Sen. Circuit Judge, 1997–98; called to Bar of NI, 1989, to Irish Bar, 1991. Commissary for Notarial Appeals, 2001–. Cambridge Univ. Debating Tour, USA, 1963. Chm., Young Barristers, 1973–75; Member: Bar Council, 1971–77, 1978–81 and 1987–90 (Chm., Internat. Practice Cttee, 1987); Supreme Court Rules Cttee, 1976–80; Council of Legal Educn, 1981–83; DHSS Enquiry into Unnecessary Dental Treatment in NHS (Report, 1986). Mem., Internat. Panel of Dist. Mediators, CPR Inst. for Dispute Resolution, NY, 1993; Panelist, WTO Disputes Settlement Body, 1996–; William W. Bishop Jr Fellow, Univ. of Michigan Law Sch., 1993. Council of Bars and Law Societies of Europe (CCBE): Mem. UK delegn, 1983–90, Leader, 1987–90; Mem. then Chm. of the cttee at European Courts of Justice, 1984–93; Vice-Pres., 1991–92; Pres., 1993. Senator, European Bar President's Conf., Vienna, 1994–; Chm., IFSL Internat. Legal Forum, 2001–. Member: Bd of Governors, Maudsley and Bethlem Royal Hosps, 1979–82; SHA, 1982–87; Cttee of Management, Inst. of Psychiatry, 1982– (Chm., 2000–); Bd of Visitors, Univ. of Michigan Law Sch., 1996–; Council, KCL, 1997–. Trustee: Pro Corda, 1992–97; Temple Music Trust, 1993–; Europäische Rechtsakademie, Trier, 1993– (Vice-Chm., 1994–97; Chm., 1997–). Hon. Mem., Law Soc., 1994. Grand Decoration for Merit (Austria), 1995. *Publications:* (contrib.) The Influence of Litigation in Medical Practice, 1977; European Ed., Encyclopaedia of Banking Law, 1990; Consulting Ed., European Legal Systems, 1992; EFTA Legal Systems, 1993; (contrib.) Practitioners' Handbook of EC Law, 1998. *Recreations:* cricket, music, theatre, Burgundy. *Address:* c/o The High Court of Justice, Technology and Construction Court, St Dunstan's House, 133–137 Fetter Lane, EC4A 1HD. *Clubs:* Pilgrims, MCC.

TOULMIN, Stephen Edelston, MA, PhD; Henry R. Luce Foundation Professor, Center for Multiethnic and Transnational Studies, University of Southern California, 1993–2001; Avalon Foundation Professor in the Humanities, Northwestern University, 1986–92, now Emeritus; *b* 25 March 1922; *s* of late G. E. Toulmin and Mrs E. D. Toulmin; *m*; two *s* two *d*. *Educ:* Oundle School; King's College, Cambridge. BA 1943; MA 1946; PhD 1948; MA (Oxon) 1948. Junior Scientific Officer, Ministry of Aircraft Production, 1942–45; Fellow of King's College, Cambridge, 1947–51; University Lecturer in the Philosophy of Science, Oxford, 1949–55; Acting Head of Department of History and Methods of Science, University of Melbourne, Australia, 1954–55; Professor of Philosophy, University of Leeds, 1955–59; Visiting Prof. of Philosophy, NY Univ. and Stanford Univ. (California) and Columbia Univ. (NY), 1959–60; Director, Nuffield Foundation Unit for History of Ideas, 1960–64; Prof. of Philosophy, Brandeis Univ., 1965–69, Michigan State Univ., 1969–72; Provost, Crown College, Univ. of California, Santa Cruz, 1972–73; Prof. in Cttee on Social Thought, Univ. of Chicago, 1973–86. Counsellor, Smithsonian Institution, 1966–75. Thomas Jefferson Lectr, Nat. Endowment for the Humanities, Washington, 1997; Tanner Lectr, Clare Hall, Cambridge, 1998. Hon. DTech Royal Inst. of Technol., Stockholm, 1991. *Publications:* The Place of Reason in Ethics, 1950; The Philosophy of Science: an Introduction, 1953; Metaphysical Beliefs (3 essays: author of one of them), 1957; The Uses of Argument, 1958; Foresight and Understanding, 1961; The Ancestry of Science, Vol. I (The Fabric of the Heavens) 1961, Vol. II (The Architecture of Matter), 1962, Vol. III (The Discovery of Time), 1965; Night Sky at Rhodes, 1963; Human Understanding, vol. 1, 1972; Wittgenstein's Vienna, 1973; Knowing and Acting, 1976; An Introduction to Reasoning, 1979; The Return to Cosmology, 1982; The Abuse of Casuistry, 1987; Cosmopolis, 1989; Beyond Theory, 1996; Return to Reason, 2001; also films, broadcast talks and contribs to learned jls and weeklies. *Address:* 9309 Beverlycrest Drive, Los Angeles, CA 90210-2503, USA.

See also M. E. P. Jones.

TOULSON, Elizabeth, (Lady Toulson), CBE 1999; Chairman, Children's Society, since 2001; *b* 10 Nov. 1948; *d* of late Henry Bertram Chrimes and of Suzanne Isabel Chrimes (*née* Corbett-Lowe); *m* 1973, Roger Grenfell Toulson (*see* Hon. Sir Roger Toulson); two *s* two *d*. *Educ:* Liverpool Univ.; Clare Hall, Cambridge (LLB). Called to the Bar, Inner Temple, 1974. Womens' Royal Voluntary Service: Trustee, 1981–; Vice-Chm., 1989–93; Nat. Chm., 1993–99. Director: Queen Elizabeth Foundn for Disabled People, 1999–; Surrey Voluntary Service Council, 1999 . Gov., Charterhouse Sch., 1998–. *Recreations:* reading, music, walking, tennis, swimming, ski-ing. *Address:* Billhurst Farm, White Hart Lane, Wood Street Village, Guildford, Surrey GU3 3DZ.

TOULSON, Hon. Sir Roger Grenfell, Kt 1996; **Hon. Mr Justice Toulson;** a Judge of the High Court of Justice, Queen's Bench Division, since 1996; Presiding Judge, Western Circuit, since 1997; *b* 23 Sept. 1946; *s* of late Stanley Kilsha Toulson and Lilian Mary Toulson; *m* 1973, Elizabeth Chrimes (*see* E. Toulson); two *s* two *d*. *Educ:* Mill Hill School; Jesus College, Cambridge (MA, LLB). Called to the Bar, Inner Temple, 1969, Bencher, 1995; QC 1986; a Recorder, 1986–96. *Publication:* (with C. M. Phipps) Confidentiality, 1996. *Recreations:* ski-ing, tennis, gardening. *Address:* Royal Courts of Justice, Strand, WC2A 2LL. *Club:* Old Millhillians.

TOVEY, Sir Brian (John Maynard), KCMG 1980; Chairman: Cresswell Associates Ltd, 1988–2001; Fujitsu Europe Telecoms R & D Centre Ltd, 1990–2001; *b* 15 April 1926; *s* of Rev. Collett John Tovey (Canon, Bermuda Cathedral, 1935–38) and Kathleen Edith Maud Tovey (*née* Maynard); *m* 1989, Mary Helen (*née* Lane); one *s* three *d* by previous marriage. *Educ:* St Edward's Sch., Oxford; St Edmund Hall, Oxford, 1944–45; School of Oriental and African Studies, London, 1948–50. BA Hons London. Service with Royal Navy and subseq. Army (Intelligence Corps and RAEC), 1945–48. Joined Government Communications Headquarters as Jun. Asst, 1950; Principal, 1957; Asst Sec., 1967; Under Sec., 1975; Dep. Sec., 1978; Dir, 1978–83, retired. Defence Systems Consultant, 1983–85, and Defence and Political Adviser, 1985–88, Plessey Electronic Systems Ltd; Dir, Plessey Defence Systems Ltd, 1983–85. Chm., IES Gp PLC, 1993–98. Vice-Pres. (Information and Communications Technology), Fedn of Electronics Industry, 1995–97. *Publications:* contrib. Gazette des Beaux-Arts, Art Newspaper. *Recreations:* music, walking, history of art (espec. 16th Century Italian, and historical methodology of Filippo Baldinucci). *Address:* 80 Ryecroft Road, SW16 3EH. *Club:* Naval and Military (Vice-Pres., 1995–).

TOVUE, Sir Ronald, Kt 1987; OBE 1981; Commissioner, Constitution Review Commission, Papua New Guinea, 1995–97; Premier, Provincial Government of East New Britain Province, Papua New Guinea, 1981–87; Member of Provincial Assembly, 1979–87; *b* 14 Feb. 1933; *s* of Apmeledi ToPalanga and Rachael Warurua; *m* 1971, Suluet Tinvil; two *s* one *d*. *Educ:* Pilapila Community Sch.; Kerevat High Sch. Teacher, 1957–76; Magistrate, 1965–74; Commissioner, 1974–76; businessman, 1977–. *Recreations:* golf, reading, gardening, fishing, church activities. *Address:* Ratavul, PO Box 354, Rabaul, Papua New Guinea. *Club:* Rabaul Golf (Rabaul).

TOWER, Maj.-Gen. Philip Thomas, CB 1968; DSO 1944; MBE 1942; National Trust Administrator, Blickling Hall, 1973–82; *b* 1 March 1917; *s* of late Vice-Admiral Sir Thomas Tower, KBE, CB and late Mrs E. H. Tower; *m* 1943, Elizabeth, *y d* of late Thomas Ralph Sneyd-Kynnersley, OBE, MC and late Alice Sneyd-Kynnersley. *Educ:* Harrow; Royal Military Acad., Woolwich. 2nd Lt Royal Artillery, 1937; served in India, 1937–40; served War of 1939–45 (despatches); Middle East, 1940–42; POW Italy, 1942–43; escaped, 1943; Arnhem, 1944; Norway, 1945; Staff Coll., 1948; Instructor at RMA Sandhurst, 1951–53; comd J (Sidi Rezegh) Bty RHA in Middle East, 1954–55; Joint Services Staff Coll., 1955–56; GSO1 Plans, BJSM Washington, DC, 1956–57; comd 3rd Regt RHA, 1957–60; Imperial Defence Coll., 1961; Comd 51 Inf. Bde Gp, 1961–62; Comd 12 Inf. Bde Gp, BAOR, 1962–64; Director of Public Relations (Army), 1965–67; GOC Middle East Land Forces, 1967 (despatches); Comdt, RMA Sandhurst, 1968–72, retd 1972. Col Comdt, Royal Regt of Artillery, 1970–80. County Comr (Norfolk), SJAB, 1975–78. OStJ 1977. *Recreations:* reading, gardening. *Address:* Pythouse, Tisbury, Salisbury, Wiltshire SP3 6PB. *T:* (01747) 870911. *Club:* Army and Navy.

TOWERS, John, CBE 1995; FREng, FIMechE; Deputy Chairman, Concentric Group Plc; Chairman, Rover Group Ltd, since 2000; *b* 30 March 1948; *s* of Jack Towers and Florence Towers (*née* Abley); *m* 1990, Bethanie Williams; one *s* one *d*. *Educ:* Durham Johnston Sch.; Univ. of Bradford (BSc Hons Mech. Engrg). CEng 1974; FREng (FEng 1992); FIMechE 1992; FIIM 1989. Joined Perkins Engines as student apprentice, 1966: Quality Engr, later Mfg Dir and Gen. Manager, 1983–86; Vice-Pres., Internat. Services, Varity Corp. (Canada), 1986–87; Man. Dir, Massey Ferguson Tractors, 1987–88; Rover Group, 1988–96: Mfg Dir, Land Rover, 1988–89; Product Develt Dir, 1989–90; Dir, 1990–91, Man. Dir, Jan.–Dec. 1991, Product Supply; Gp Man. Dir, 1991–94; Gp Chief Exec., 1994–96; Chief Exec., Concentric Gp, 1996–2000. Director: Midland Bank, 1995–96; B. Elliott, 1996–; HatWel Ltd, 1996–. Vis. Prof., Warwick Univ., 1993. Mem., Council for Sci. and Technol., 1993–97. DUniv Central England in Birmingham, 1994. *Recreations:* golf, music. *Address:* Rover Group, PO Box 41, Longbridge, Birmingham B31 2TB. *T:* (0121) 482 2062, *Fax:* (0121) 482 2763.

TOWLE, Bridget Ellen, CBE 2001; Chief Guide, The Guide Association UK, and Chief Commissioner, Commonwealth Girl Guide Associations, 1996–2001; *b* 19 April 1942; *d* of William Henry Towle and late Marjorie Louisa (*née* Hardstaff). *Educ:* Westonbirt Sch.; Univ. of Exeter (BA Gen. Hons, BA Hons); Leicester Poly. (Post Grad. Courses in Textile Technol. and Business Mgt). Teacher, VSO, Uganda, 1965–66; Towles plc: marketing mgt roles, 1966–94; Dir, 1972–94; Jt Man. Dir, 1980–94. Guide Association: various appts, incl. County Comr, Leics, 1985–92. Mem. Council, Univ. of Leicester, 2000–. FRSA 1999. Hon. LLD Exeter, 2000. Charity Trustee of the Year, Charity Times, 2000. *Recreations:* decorative arts, walking. *Address:* c/o The Guide Association, 17–19 Buckingham Palace Road, SW1W 0PT.

TOWNDROW, Ven. Frank Noel; Archdeacon of Oakham, 1967–77, now Archdeacon Emeritus; Residentiary Canon of Peterborough, 1966–77, now Canon Emeritus; a Chaplain to the Queen, 1975–81; *b* 25 Dec. 1911; *e s* of F. R. and H. A. Towndrow, London; *m* 1947, Olive Helen Weinberger (*d* 1978); one *d* (one *s* decd). *Educ:* St Olave's Grammar Sch.; King's Coll., Cambridge; Coll. of Resurrection, Mirfield. Curate, Chingford, E4, 1937–40; Chaplain, RAFVR, 1940–47; Rector of Grangemouth, Stirlingshire, 1947–51; Vicar of Kirton Lindsey, Lincs, 1951–53; Rector of Greenford, Middx, 1953–62; Vicar of Ravensthorpe, E Haddon and Rector of Holdenby, 1962–66. *Recreation:* modern history. *Address:* 17 Croake Hill, Swinstead, Grantham, Lincs NG33 4PE. *T:* (01476) 550478.

TOWNELEY, Sir Simon (Peter Edmund Cosmo William), KCVO 1994; Lord-Lieutenant and Custos Rotulorum of Lancashire, 1976–96; *b* 14 Dec. 1921; *e s* of late Col A. Koch de Gooreynd, OBE and Baroness Norman, CBE; assumed surname and arms of Towneley by royal licence, 1955, by reason of descent from *e d* and senior co-heiress of Col Charles Towneley of Towneley; *m* 1955, Mary, MBE (*d* 2001), 2nd *d* of Cuthbert Fitzherbert; one *s* six *d*. *Educ:* Stowe; Worcester Coll., Oxford (MA, DPhil; Ruffini Scholar). Served War of 1939–45, KRRC. Lectr in History of Music, Worcester Coll., Oxford, 1949–55. Mem., Agricultural Lands Tribunal, 1960–92. Dir, Granada Television, 1981–92. CC Lancs, 1961–64; JP 1956; DL 1970; High Sheriff of Lancashire, 1971. Mem. Council, Duchy of Lancaster, 1986–96. Patron, Nat. Assoc. for Mental Health (North-West). Pres., NW of England and IoM TA&VRA, 1987–92; Chm., Northern Ballet Theatre, 1969–86; Member: Bd of Governors, Royal Northern Coll. of Music, 1961–98; Council, 1971–97, Court, 1971–98, Univ. of Manchester; Trustee: Historic Churches Preservation Trust, 1984–93; British Museum, 1988–93. Hon. Col, Duke of Lancaster's Own Yeomanry, 1979–88. CRNCM 1990; Hon. Fellow, Lancashire Polytechnic, 1987. Hon. DMus Lancaster, 1994. KStJ; KCSG. *Publications:* Venetian Opera in the Seventeenth Century, 1954 (repr. 1968); contribs to New Oxford History of Music. *Address:* Dyneley, Burnley, Lancs BB11 3RE. *T:* (01282) 423322. *Clubs:* Boodle's, Pratt's, Beefsteak.

See also Sir P. G. Worsthorne.

TOWNEND, James Barrie Stanley; QC 1978; a Recorder of the Crown Court, since 1979; *b* 21 Feb. 1938; *s* of late Frederick Stanley Townend and Marjorie Elizabeth Townend (*née* Arnold); *m* 1970, Airelle Claire (*née* Nies); one step *d. Educ:* Tonbridge Sch.; Lincoln Coll., Oxford (MA). National Service in BAOR and UK, 1955–57: 2nd Lieut, 18th Medium Regt, RA. Called to Bar, Middle Temple, 1962, Bencher, 1987; Head of Chambers, 1982–99. Chairman: Sussex Crown Court Liaison Cttee, 1978–89; Family Law Bar Assoc., 1986–88; Member: Kingston and Esher DHA, 1983–86; Bar Council, 1984–88; Supreme Court Procedure Cttee, 1986–88. Asst Boundary Comr, 2000–. *Recreations:* sailing, fishing, writing verse. *Address:* 1 King's Bench Walk, Temple, EC4Y 7DB. *T:* (020) 7583 6266.

TOWNEND, John Coupe; Director for Europe, Bank of England, since 1999; *b* 24 Aug. 1947; *s* of Harry Norman Townend and Joyce Dentith (*née* Coupe); *m* 1969, Dorothy Allister; three *s. Educ:* Liverpool Inst. High Sch. for Boys; London Sch. of Economics (BSc Econ; MSc). With Bank of England, 1968–: First Head, Wholesale Markets Supervision Div., 1986–90; Head, Gilt-Edged and Money Markets Div., 1990–94; Dep. Dir, 1994–98. *Publications:* articles in econ. jls. *Recreations:* running, trekking, opera, birds. *Address:* Bank of England, Threadneedle Street, EC2R 8AH. *T:* (020) 7601 4541.

TOWNEND, John Ernest; *b* 12 June 1934; *s* of Charles Hope Townend and Dorothy Townend; *m* 1963, Jennifer Ann; two *s* two *d. Educ:* Hymers Coll., Hull. FCA (Plender Prize). Articled Clerk, Chartered Accountants, 1951–56; National Service: Pilot Officer, RAF, 1957–59; J. Townend & Sons Ltd (Hull) Ltd: Co. Sec./Dir, 1959–67; Man. Dir, 1967–77; Chm., 1977–; Vice-Chm., Surrey Building Soc., 1984–93; Dir, AAH Hldgs, 1989–94. Mem., Hull City Council, 1966–74 (Chm., Finance Cttee, 1968–70); Chm., Humber Bridge Bd, 1969–71; Member, Humberside County Council, 1973–79: Cons. Leader of Opposition, 1973–77; Leader, 1977–79; Chm., Policy Cttee, 1977–79. Mem., Policy Cttee, Assoc. of County Councils, 1977–79. MP (C) Bridlington, 1979–97, E Yorks, 1997–2001. PPS to Minister of State for Social Security, 1981–83. Mem., Treasury and Civil Service Select Cttee, 1983–92; Chm., Cons. Small Business Cttee, 1988–92; Vice Chm., Cons. back bench Finance Cttee, 1983–91, 1997–2001 (Chm., 1993–97). Member: Council of Europe, 1992–2001; WEU, 1992–2001. Chm., Merchant Vintners Co., 1964–. *Recreations:* swimming, tennis. *Address:* Sigglesthorne Hall, Sigglesthorne, E Yorks HU11 5QA. *Club:* Carlton.

TOWNEND, His Honour John Philip; a Circuit Judge, 1987–2001; *b* 20 June 1935; *o s* of Luke and Ethel Townend; *m* 1st, 1959; two *s* one *d*; 2nd, 1981, Anne Glover; one step *s* one step *d. Educ:* St Joseph's Coll., Blackpool; Manchester Univ. (LLB). National Service, 1957–58. Called to the Bar, Gray's Inn, 1959; Lectr in Law, Gibson and Weldon College of Law, 1960–65; Asst Legal Advr, Pilkington Bros, 1966–68; Legal Advr, Honeywell Ltd and G. Dew Ltd, 1968–70; joined chambers of Mr Stewart Oakes, Manchester, 1970. *Publications:* articles in various jls on legal topics. *Recreations:* classical music, jazz, food and wine, a decreasing number of active games, mountain walking. *Address:* c/o The Crown Court, Crown Square, Manchester M60 9DJ. *Clubs:* Fairhaven Golf; Lytham Tennis and Hockey.

TOWNEND, Warren Dennis; HM Diplomatic Service; Consul-General, Washington, since 2001; *b* 15 Nov. 1945; *s* of Dennis Jennings Townend and Mary Elizabeth Townend (*née* Knowles); *m* 1978, Ann Mary Riddle; three *s* one *d. Educ:* Netheredge Grammar Sch.; Abbeydale Grammar Sch. Joined Diplomatic Service, 1964; FO 1964–69; Vice Consul, Hanoi, 1969–70; Vice Consul (Commercial), Hamburg, 1970–73; Second Sec. (Commercial), Dacca, 1973–75; FCO, 1976–79; Second, later First, Sec., Bonn, 1979–84; First Sec. (Commercial), Bangkok, 1984–87; FCO, 1987–91; Dep. Consul-Gen. and Dep. Dir-Gen. for Trade and Investment Promotion in Germany, Düsseldorf, 1991–96; Consul-Gen., Shanghai, 1996–2000. *Recreations:* cycling, DIY, travel. *Address:* c/o Foreign and Commonwealth Office, King Charles Street, SW1A 2AH. *Club:* British Chamber of Commerce (Shanghai).

TOWNES, Charles Hard; University Professor of Physics, 1967–86, Professor in the Graduate School, since 1994, University of California, USA; *b* Greenville, South Carolina, 28 July 1915; *s* of Henry Keith Townes and Ellen Sumter (*née* Hard); *m* 1941, Frances H. Brown; four *d. Educ:* Furman Univ. (BA, BS); Duke Univ. (MA); California Institute of Technology (PhD). Assistant in Physics, California Inst. of Technology, 1937–39; Member Techn Staff, Bell Telephone Labs, 1939–47; Associate Prof. of Physics, Columbia Univ., 1948–50; Prof. of Physics, Columbia Univ., 1950–61; Exec. Director, Columbia Radiation Lab., 1950–52; Chairman, Dept of Physics, Columbia Univ., 1952–55; Vice-President and Director of Research, Inst. for Defense Analyses, 1959–61; Provost and Professor of Physics, MIT, 1961–66; Institute Professor, MIT, 1966–67. Guggenheim Fellow, 1955–56; Fulbright Lecturer, University of Paris, 1955–56, University of Tokyo, 1956; Lecturer, 1955, 1960, Dir, 1963, Enrico Fermi Internat. Sch. of Physics; Lectures: Scott, Univ. of Cambridge, 1963; Centennial, Univ. of Toronto, 1967; Rajiv Gandhi, India, 1997; Weinberg, Oak Ridge Nat. Lab., 1997; Henry Norris Russell, AAS, 1998. Dir, Bulletin of Atomic Scientists, 1964–69. Board of Editors: Review of Scientific Instruments, 1950–52; Physical Review, 1951–53; Journal of Molecular Spectroscopy, 1957–60; Columbia University Forum, 1957–59. Fellow: American Phys. Society (Richtmyer Lecturer, 1959; Member Council, 1959–62, 1965–71; President, 1967); Inst. of Electrical and Electronics Engrs; Chairman, Sci. and Technology Adv. Commn for Manned Space Flight, NASA, 1964–69; Member: President's Science Adv. Cttee, 1966–69 (Vice-Chm., 1967–69); Scientific Adv. Bd, US Air Force, 1958–61; Soc. Française de Physique (Member Council, 1956–58); Nat. Acad. Scis (Mem. Council, 1969–72); American Acad. Arts and Sciences; American Philos. Society; American Astron. Society; American Assoc. of Physics Teachers; Société Royale des Sciences de Liège; Pontifical Acad., 1983; Nat. Acad. of Engrg, 1999; Foreign Member: Royal Society, 1976; Russian Acad. of Scis, 1994; Hon. Mem., Optical Soc. of America. Trustee: Salk Inst. for Biological Studies, 1963–68; Rand Corp., 1965–70; Carnegie Instn of Washington, 1965–; Calif Inst. of Technol., 1979–; California Acad. of Scis, 1987–96. Chairman: Space Science Bd, Nat. Acad. of Sciences, 1970–73; Science Adv. Cttee, General Motors Corp., 1971–73; Bd of Dirs, General Motors, 1973–86; Perkin-Elmer Corp., 1966–85. Trustee: Pacific Sch. of Religion, 1983–93; Center for Theol. and Natural Sci., 1989–; Grad. Theol Union, 1993–; California Vocations, 1994–; Enshrinee, Engrg and Sci. Hall of Fame, Ohio, 1983. Holds numerous honorary degrees. Research Corp. Annual Award, 1958; Comstock Prize, Nat. Acad. of Sciences, 1959; Stuart Ballantine Medal, Franklin Inst., 1959, 1962; Rumford Premium, Amer. Acad. of Arts and Sciences, 1961; Thomas Young Medal and Prize, Inst. of Physics and Physical Soc., England, 1963; Nobel Prize for Physics (jointly), 1964; Medal of Honor, Inst. of Electrical and Electronics Engineers, 1967; C. E. K. Mees Medal, Optical Soc. of America, 1968; Churchman of the Year Award, Southern Baptist Theological Seminary, 1967; Distinguished Public Service Medal, NASA, 1969; Michelson-Morley Award, 1970; Wilhelm-Exner Award (Austria), 1970; Medal of Honor, Univ. of Liège, 1971; Earle K. Plyler Prize, 1977; Niels Bohr Internat. Gold Medal, 1979; Nat. Medal of Sci., 1983; Commonwealth Award, 1993; Frederic Ives/James Quinn Medal, Optical Soc. of America, 1996; Frank Annunzio Award, Columbus Fellowship Foundn, 1999. National Inventors Hall of Fame, 1976; S Carolina Hall of Fame, 1977. Hon. Citizen: Kwangju, Korea, 1996; Pusan, Korea, 1997. Officier, Légion d'Honneur (France), 1990. *Publications:* (with A. L. Schawlow) Microwave Spectroscopy, 1955; (ed) Quantum Electronics, 1960; (ed with P. A. Miles) Quantum Electronics and Coherent Light, 1964; Making Waves, 1995; How the Laser Happened: adventures of a scientist, 1999; many scientific articles on microwave spectroscopy, molecular and nuclear structure, quantum electronics, radio and infra-red astrophysics; fundamental patents on masers and (with A. L. Schawlow) lasers. *Address:* Department of Physics, University of California, Berkeley, CA 94720, USA. *T:* (510) 6421128. *Clubs:* Cosmos (Washington, DC); Bohemian (San Francisco).

TOWNSEND, Prof. Alain Robert Michael, PhD; FRS 1992; Professor of Molecular Immunology, since 1992, and Fellow of New College, since 1998, University of Oxford. *Educ:* St Mary's Hosp. Med. Sch., London Univ. (MB BS 1977); PhD London 1984; MA Oxon. MRCP 1979. Oxford University: Lectr in Clin. Immunology, 1985–92; Fellow, Linacre Coll., 1985–98. *Address:* Institute of Molecular Medicine, John Radcliffe Hospital, Headington, Oxford OX3 9DU. *T:* (01865) 222328; 6 Polstead Road, Oxford OX2 6TN.

TOWNSEND, Albert Alan, FRS 1960; PhD; Reader (Experimental Fluid Mechanics), Cavendish Laboratory, University of Cambridge, 1961–85 (Assistant Director of Research, 1950–61); Fellow of Emmanuel College, Cambridge, since 1947; *b* 22 Jan. 1917; *s* of A. R. Townsend and D. Gay; *m* 1950, V. Dees; one *s* two *d. Educ:* Telopea Park IHS; Melbourne and Cambridge Universities. PhD 1947. *Publications:* The Structure of Turbulent Shear Flow, 1956; papers in technical journals. *Address:* Emmanuel College, Cambridge CB2 3AP.

TOWNSEND, Bryan Sydney, CBE 1994; Chairman, Midlands Electricity plc (formerly Midlands Electricity Board), 1986–96 (Chief Executive, 1990–92); *b* 2 April 1930; *s* of Sydney and Gladys Townsend; *m* 1951, Betty Eileen Underwood; one *s* two *d. Educ:* Wolverton Technical Coll. CEng, FIEE; FIMgt. Trainee, Northampton Electric Light & Power Co., 1946–50; successive appts, E Midlands, Eastern and Southern Electricity Bds, 1952–66; Southern Electricity Board: Swindon Dist Manager, 1966–68; Newbury Area Engr, 1968–70; Asst Chief Engr, 1970–73; Dep. Chief Engr, SE Electricity Bd, 1973–76; Chief Engr, S Wales Electricity Bd, 1976–78; Dep. Chm., SW Electricity Bd, 1978–86. Non-executive Director: JBA plc; GPU Inc.; Applecourt Develt. *Recreation:* golf.

TOWNSEND, Dr Christina, CPsychol; FIPD; Chief Executive, Edexcel Foundation (formerly Business & Technology Education Council), 1994–2001; *b* 10 Jan. 1947; *d* of Sidney Townsend and Vera (*née* Wallis). *Educ:* Dursley Grammar Sch., Glos; Leeds Univ. (BSc Psychol.); Birmingham Univ. (MSc); UWIST (PhD). CPsychol 1969; FIPD (FIPM 1991). Lectr, UWIST, 1973–75; Sen. Res. Officer, MSC, 1976–78; Asst Dir, Ashridge Mgt Coll., 1978–80; Hd of Div., Inst. of Manpower Studies, 1981–84; NHS Training Authority, subseq. Directorate: Dir, Res. Educn and Trng, 1984–88; Chief Exec., 1988–91; Nat. Trng Dir and Chief Exec., 1991–93. Dep. Chm., Personnel Standards Lead Body, 1991–94; Director: City Technol. Colls Trust, 1994–95; Mgt Charter Initiative, 1994–95; Further Educn Develt Agency, 1994–97; Member Council: Nat. Forum for Mgt Educn and Develt, 1994–99; Inst. for Employment Studies, 1998–; Mem. Bd, British Trng Internat., 1999–. Gov., Corp. of Cambridge Regl Coll., 1997–. MInstD 1991 (Mem., Nat. Employment Cttee, 1991–97); CIMgt 1994; FRSA 1992. *Recreations:* travelling, hill-walking, theatre, circuit training. *Club:* Royal Society of Medicine.

TOWNSEND, Sir Cyril (David), Kt 1997; Director, Council for the Advancement of Arab–British Understanding, since 1995 (Joint Chairman, 1982–92); *b* 21 Dec. 1937; *s* of late Lt-Col Cyril M. Townsend and Lois (*née* Henderson); *m* 1976, Anita, MA, *d* of late Lt-Col F. G. W. Walshe and Mrs Walshe; two *s. Educ:* Bradfield Coll.; RMA Sandhurst. Commnd into Durham LI; served in Berlin and Hong Kong; active service in Cyprus, 1958 and Borneo, 1966; ADC to Governor and C-in-C Hong Kong, 1964–66; Adjt 1DLI, 1966–68. A Personal Assistant: to Edward Heath, 1968–70; to Sir Desmond Plummer, Ldr of GLC, 1970–73; Mem. Conservative Research Dept, 1970–74. MP (C) Bexleyheath, Feb. 1974–1997. PPS to Minister of State, DHSS, 1979; Member: Select Cttee on Violence in the Family, 1975; Select Cttee on Foreign Affairs, 1982–83; Vice-Chairman: Cons. Parly Defence Cttee, 1985–93 (Jt Sec., 1982–85); Cons. Parly Foreign Affairs Cttee, 1991–96; Chairman: Select Cttee on Armed Forces Bill, 1981; British-Cyprus Parly Gp, 1983–92; All-Party Freedom for Rudolf Hess Campaign, 1977–87; Bow Gp Standing Cttee on Foreign Affairs, 1977–84; (and Co-Founder) South Atlantic Council, 1983–95; Organizing Cttee, Argentine-British Conference, 1988–90; UN Parly Gp, 1992–96; Chm., Cons. ME Council, 1992–95 (Jt Vice-Chm., 1988–92); Vice-Chairman: Friends of Cyprus, 1980–92 (Mem., Exec. Cttee); Hansard Soc., 1988–97; Member: Exec. Cttee, UK Branch, CPA, 1992–93; Exec. Bd, UK Cttee, UNICEF, 1995–2000; Vice-Pres., UNA, 1996–; Pres., SW Reg., UNA, 1999–; Jt Hon. Pres., Islamic Res. Acad.; Gov., Centre for World Dialogue, Nicosia, 1998–. Member: Nat. Cttee, British-Arab Univ. Assoc.; RIIA; South Atlantic Council. Mem., SE London Industrial Consultative Gp, 1975–83. Pres., Bexley Arthritis Care, 1990–96. Trustee, Lord Caradon Lecture Trust. Fellow, Industry and Parliament Trust, 1982. Introduced Protection of Children Act, 1978. Parly Observer, Presidential Election, Lebanon, 1982; Ldr, Parly Delegn to Iran, 1988; EU Election Observer for elections in Palestine, 1996. *Publications:* Helping Others to Help Themselves: voluntary action in the eighties, 1981; Cyprus and NATO's Southern Flank, 1986; contribs to Contemporary Review and political jls; weekly column in Al-Hayat. *Recreations:* books, music, exercise, exploring Cornwall. *Address:* Council for the Advancement of Arab-British Understanding, 21 Collingham Road, SW5 0NU.

TOWNSEND, Brig. Ian Glen; Secretary General, Royal British Legion, since 1996; *b* 7 Feb. 1941; *s* of Kenneth Townsend and Irene (*née* Singleton); *m* 1st, 1964, Loraine Jean (marr. diss. 1988), *d* of late William A. H. Birnie, USA; twin *d*; 2nd, 1989, Susan Natalie, *d* of late Comdr Frank A. L. Heron-Watson, Dalbeattie; two step *s. Educ:* Dulwich Coll.; RMA, Sandhurst (psc †). Commnd RA, 1961; served UK, Norway, Singapore, Brussels and Germany, 1961–71; RMCS, 1971–72; Staff Coll., Camberley, 1972–73; MoD, BAOR and NATO, 1973–85; Comdr Artillery, 1st Armd Div., BAOR, 1986–88; ACOS, Trng, HQ UKLF, 1988–91. Hon. Col, 27 Field Regt, 1988–92. Dir, Sales and Marketing, Land Systems, 1991–93, Mil. Advr, 1993–96, VSEL; Director: Townsend Associates, 1993–96; Legion Enterprise Ltd, 1999; RBL Training Coll., 2000–. Trustee: Officers' Assoc., 1996–; Mil. Mus. of the Pacific, 1997–; Desert Rats 7th Armd Div. Commemoration Fund, 1998–. Freeman, City of London, 1999. FInstM 1988; Mem., ACENVO, 1997. Gov., Salisbury Coll., 2001–. *Publications:* articles in professional jls. *Recreations:* ski-ing, walking, painting, music, theatre. *Address:* Royal British Legion, 48 Pall Mall, SW1Y 5JY. *T:* (020) 7973 7218, *Fax:* (020) 7973 7340. *Clubs:* Army and Navy, Royal Over-Seas League.

TOWNSEND, Jean Ann, (Mrs P. B. Townsend); *see* Corston, J. A.

TOWNSEND, Mrs Joan, MA, MSc; Headmistress, Oxford High School, GPDST, 1981–96; *b* 7 Dec. 1936; *d* of Emlyn Davies and Amelia Mary Davies (*née* Tyrer); *m* 1960,

William Godfrey Townsend, Prof. Emeritus, Cranfield Univ.; two *d*. *Educ:* Somerville Coll., Oxford (Beilby Schol.; BA (Cl.I), MA); University College of Swansea, Univ. of Wales (MSc). School teaching and lecturing of various kinds, including: Tutor, Open University, 1971–75; Lectr, Oxford Polytechnic, 1975–76; Head of Mathematics, School of S Helen and S Katharine, Abingdon, 1976–81. FRSA 1986. *Publication:* paper in Qly Jl Maths and Applied Mech., 1965. *Address:* Silver Howe, 62 Iffley Turn, Oxford OX4 4HN. *T:* (01865) 715807.

TOWNSEND, Lady Juliet Margaret, LVO 1981; Lord-Lieutenant of Northamptonshire, since 1998; *b* 9 Sept. 1941; *d* of 2nd Earl of Birkenhead, TD; *m* 1970, John Richard Townsend; three *d*. *Educ:* Westonbirt Sch.; Somerville Coll., Oxford. Lady in Waiting to Princess Margaret, 1965–71, Extra Lady in Waiting, 1971–. High Sheriff of Northamptonshire, 1991–92. *Publications:* The Shell Guide to Northamptonshire, 1968; Escape from Meerut, 1971. *Address:* Newbottle Manor, Banbury, Oxon OX17 3DD. *T:* (01295) 811295.

TOWNSEND, Mrs Lena Moncrieff, CBE 1974; Member, Race Relations Board, 1967–72; *b* 3 Nov. 1911; twin *d* of late Captain R. G. Westropp, Cairo, Egypt; *m* (twice); two *s* one *d*. *Educ:* Downe House, Newbury; Somerville Coll., Oxford; Heidelberg Univ., Germany. During War of 1939–45 was an Organiser in WVS and in Women's Land Army, and then taught at Downe House. Mem. for Hampstead, LCC, 1955–65; Alderman, London Borough of Camden, 1964–67; Mem. for Camden, GLC, 1967–70; Alderman, GLC, 1970–77, and Dep. Chm., 1976–77; Inner London Education Authority: Dep. Leader, later Leader, 1967–70; Leader of the Opposition, 1970–71; Chm., Management Panel, Burnham Cttee, 1967–70; Mem., Women's European Cttee, 1972–75. Pres., Anglo-Egyptian Assoc., 1961–87 (when wound-up); Executive Member: British Section, European Union of Women, 1970–81; National Council, European Movement (British Council), 1970–86 (Mem., Speaker's Panel); Cons. Gp for Europe, 1967–88 (Founder Mem.); British Section, Internat. Union of Local Authorities and Council of European Municipalities, 1975–97 (rep. on Jt Twinning Cttee, 1975–83); London Europe Soc., 1977– (a Vice-Pres. 1999–); Arkwright Arts Trust, 1971–84 (Chm., 1971–73). Mem., House Cttee, New End Hosp., then Hampstead Cttee, Royal Free Hosp., 1953–65. Mem. Exec. Cttee, Contemporary Dance Trust, 1968–75. Chm., Students' Accommodation Cttee, Univ. of London, 1977–86 (and Mem., Intercollegiate Halls Management Cttee); Member: Council, Westfield Coll., London Univ., 1965–89; Cons Nat. Adv. Cttee on Education, 1976–82; Governor: Barrett Street Coll., later London Coll. of Fashion, 1958–86 (Chm., 1967–86); Old Vic Trust, 1976–88; Hampstead Parochial Primary Sch., 1979–93. Hon. Vice Pres., Local Govt Gp for Europe, 1998. Patron, Lewis Carroll Soc. Hon. Fellow, QMW (Hon. Fellow, Westfield Coll., 1983). *Recreations:* once foreign languages, travel, the arts, gardening; now knitting, sewing, entertaining grandchildren and watching television. *Address:* 16 Holly Mount, NW3 6SG. *T:* (020) 7435 8555.

TOWNSEND, Michael John; Chief Executive, Woodland Trust, since 1997; *b* 12 July 1957; *s* of John and Kathleen Townsend; *m* 1991, Amanda Adkins; two *s*. *Educ:* University Coll. of N Wales (BSc Hons Forestry 1986). MICFor 1990. Project leader, VSO, Kenya, 1980–83; Regl Manager, EFG plc, 1986–92; Michael Townsend Forestry & Landscapes, 1992–95; Woodland Ops Dir, Woodland Trust, 1995–97. *Recreations:* hill-walking, gardening. *Address:* The Woodland Trust, Autumn Park, Dysart Road, Grantham, Lincs NG31 6LL.

TOWNSEND, Prof. Peter Brereton; Professor of Social Policy, University of Bristol, 1982–93, now Emeritus; *b* 6 April 1928; *s* of late Philip Brereton Townsend and Alice Mary Townsend (*née* Southcote); *m* 1st, 1949, Ruth (*née* Pearce); four *s*; 2nd, 1977, Joy (*née* Skegg); one *d*; 3rd, 1985, Jean Ann Corston, *qv*; one step *s* one step *d*. *Educ:* Fleet Road Elementary Sch., London; University Coll. Sch., London; St John's Coll., Cambridge Univ.; Free Univ., Berlin. Research Sec., Political and Economic Planning, 1952–54; Research Officer, Inst. of Community Studies, 1954–57; Research Fellow and then Lectr in Social Administration, London Sch. of Economics, 1957–63; Prof. of Sociology, 1963–81, Pro-Vice-Chancellor (Social Policy), 1975–78, Univ. of Essex; Dir, Sch. of Applied Social Studies, Bristol Univ., 1983–85 and 1988–93. Vis. Prof. of Sociology, Essex Univ., 1982–86; Michael Harrington Distinguished Vis. Prof. of Social Sci., CUNY, 1991–92; Vis. Prof. of Social Policy, 1998–99, Centennial Prof. of Internat. Social Policy, 1999–, LSE; Vis. Prof. of Internat. Social Policy, Univ. of Wales, Swansea, 1998–. Chm., 1965–66, Vice Pres., 1989–, Fabian Society (Chairman: Social Policy Cttee, 1970–82; Res. and Pubns Cttee, 1983–86). President: Psychiatric Rehabilitation Assoc., 1968–83; Child Poverty Action Gp, 1989– (Chm., 1969–89); SW Region, MENCAP, 1989–93; Disability Alliance, 1999– (Chm., 1974–99). Member: Chief Scientist's Cttee, DHSS, 1976–78; Govt Working Gp on Inequalities and Health, 1977–80; MSC Working Gp on Quota Scheme for Disabled, 1983–85; Chm., Steering Gp on Allocation of NHS Resources, Nat. Assembly for Wales, 2000. UNESCO consultant on poverty and development, 1978–80; Consultant: to GLC on poverty and the labour market in London, 1985–86; to Northern RHA on Inequalities of Health, 1985–86; to a consortium of 7 metropolitan boroughs on deprivation and shopping centres in Greater Manchester, 1987–88; to Islington Borough Council on deprivation and living standards, 1987–88; to UN for world summit on social develt, 1994–95; to UNDP on social safety net in Georgia, 1994; to UNDP and IILS on patterns and causes of social exclusion, 1994; to Ministry of Foreign Affairs, Denmark, 1997–2000; to EC on Eur. Social Policy Forum, 1998; Chm., C4 Commn on Poverty, 1996. DU Essex, 1990; DLitt Teeside, 1994; DUniv: Open, 1995; York, 2000; Hon. DSc Edinburgh, 1996; Hon. DArts Lincolnshire and Humberside, 1997. *Publications:* The Family Life of Old People, 1957; National Superannuation (co-author), 1957; Nursing Homes in England and Wales (co-author), 1961; The Last Refuge: a survey of residential institutions and homes for the aged in England and Wales, 1962; The Aged in the Welfare State (co-author), 1965; The Poor and the Poorest (co-author), 1965; Old People in Three Industrial Societies (co-author), 1968; (ed) The Concept of Poverty, 1970; (ed) Labour and Inequality, 1972; The Social Minority, 1973; Sociology and Social Policy, 1975; Poverty in the United Kingdom: a survey of household resources and standards of living, 1979; (ed) Labour and Equality, 1980; Inequalities in Health (co-author), 1980; Manifesto (co-author), 1981; (ed jtly) Disability in Britain, 1981; The Family and Later Life, 1981; (ed jtly) Responses to Poverty: lessons from Europe, 1984; (jtly) Inequalities of Health in the Northern Region, 1986; Poverty and Labour in London, 1987; (jtly) Health and Deprivation: inequalities and the North, 1987; (jtly) Service Provision and Living Standards in Islington, 1988; (jtly) Inequalities in Health: the Black report and the health divide, 1988, 3rd edn 1993; The International Analysis of Poverty, 1993; A Poor Future, 1996; (jtly) The Poverty and Social Exclusion Survey of Britain, 2000; (ed jtly) Breadline Europe: the measurement of poverty, 2001; The Making of International Social Policy, 2001. *Recreations:* athletics, gardening.

TOWNSEND, Dr Ralph Douglas; Headmaster, Oundle School, since 1999; *b* 13 Dec. 1951; *s* of Harry Douglas Townsend and Neila Margaret McPherson; *m* 1973, Cathryn Julie Arnold; one *s* one *d*. *Educ:* Scotch Coll., WA; Univ. of Western Australia (BA 1973); Univ. of Kent at Canterbury (MA 1975); Keble Coll., Oxford (MA 1983; DPhil 1981). Assistant Master: Dover Coll., 1975–77; Abingdon Sch., 1977–78; Sen. Scholar, Keble Coll., Oxford, 1978–81; Jun. Res. Fellow and Dean of Degrees, Lincoln Coll., Oxford, 1983–85; Asst Master, then Head of English, Eton Coll., 1985–89; Head Master, Sydney Grammar Sch., Australia, 1989–99. Gen. Editor, Studies in Early Australian History and Letters (series), 1995–99. *Publications:* (ed) The XYZ Letters, 1996; numerous articles in Dictionnaire de Spiritualité. *Recreations:* music, reading, recumbency. *Address:* Oundle School, Peterborough PE8 4EN. *T:* (01832) 272251. *Club:* Australian (Sydney).

TOWNSEND, Susan, (Sue); writer; *b* 2 April 1946. *Educ:* South Wigston Girls' High Sch. FRSL 1994. Writer and Presenter, Think of England, BBC TV, 1991. *Publications:* The Secret Diary of Adrian Mole Aged 13¾, 1982; The Growing Pains of Adrian Mole, 1984; Bazaar and Rummage, Groping for Words, and Womberang (plays), 1984; The Great Celestial Cow (play), 1985; The Secret Diary of Adrian Mole (play), 1985; Rebuilding Coventry, 1988; Mr Bevans Dream, 1989; Ten Tiny Fingers, Nine Tiny Toes (play), 1989; Adrian Mole From Minor to Major, 1991; The Queen and I, 1992 (adapted for stage, 1994); Adrian Mole—the Wilderness Years, 1993; Ghost Children, 1997; The Cappuccino Years, 1999. *Recreations:* mooching about, reading, looking at pictures, canoeing. *Address:* Bridge Works, Knighton Fields Road West, Leicester LE2 6LH. *T:* (0116) 283 1176. *Club:* Groucho.

TOWNSHEND, family name of **Marquess Townshend**.

TOWNSHEND, 7th Marquess *cr* 1787; **George John Patrick Dominic Townshend;** Bt 1617; Baron Townshend of Lynn Regis, 1661; Viscount Townshend of Raynham, 1682; *b* 13 May 1916; *s* of 6th Marquess Townshend and Gladys Ethel Gwendolen Eugenie (*d* 1959), *e d* of late Thomas Sutherst, barrister; *S* father, 1921; *m* 1st, 1939, Elizabeth (marr. diss. 1960; she *m* 1960, Brig. Sir James Gault, KCMG, MVO, OBE; she *d* 1989), *o d* of Thomas Luby, ICS; one *s* two *d*; 2nd, 1960, Ann Frances (*d* 1988), *d* of Arthur Pellew Darlow; one *s* one *d*. Norfolk Yeomanry TA, 1936–40; Scots Guards, 1940–45. Chairman: Anglia Television Gp plc, 1971–86; Anglia Television Ltd, 1958–86; Survival Anglia, 1971–86; Anchor Enterprises Ltd, 1967–88; AP Bank Ltd, 1975–87; East Coast Grain Ltd, 1982–90; D. E. Longe & Co. Ltd, 1982–90; Norfolk Agricultural Station, 1973–87; Raynham Farm Co. Ltd, 1957–; Vice-Chairman: Norwich Union Life Insurance Society Ltd, 1973–86; Norwich Union Fire Insurance Society Ltd, 1975–86; Director: Scottish Union & National Insurance Co., 1968–86; Maritime Insurance Co. Ltd, 1968–86; London Merchant Securities plc, 1964–95; Norwich Union (Holdings) plc, 1981–86; Napak Ltd, 1982–90; Riggs Nat. Corp., Washington, 1987–89. Chairman, Royal Norfolk Agricultural Association, 1978–85. Hon. DCL East Anglia, 1989. DL Norfolk, 1951–61. *Heir: s* Viscount Raynham, *qv*. *Address:* Raynham Hall, Fakenham, Norfolk NR21 7EP. *T:* (01328) 862133. *Clubs:* White's, MCC; Norfolk (Norwich).

TOWNSHEND, Peter Dennis Blandford; composer, performer, publisher, author; *b* London, 19 May 1945; *s* of Clifford and Betty Townshend; *m* 1968, Karen Astley; one *s* two *d*. *Educ:* Acton County Grammar Sch.; Ealing Art Coll. Mem., The Who, rock group 1963–83; Editor, Faber & Faber, 1983–; *recordings* include: with The Who: Tommy, 1969 (musical, filmed 1975, Grammy Award 1993, staged NY (Tony Award for best score), 1993, Toronto (Dora Mavor Moore Award), 1994, London, 1996 (Olivier Award, 1997)); Quadrophenia, 1973; singles: My Generation; I Can See For Miles; Can't Explain; Substitute; Pinball Wizard; solo: Empty Glass, 1980; Iron Man, 1989; Psychoderelict, 1993. Ivor Novello Award, 1981; British Phonographic Industry Lifetime Achievement Award, 1983. BRIT Award for contribn to British Music, 1988; Living Legend Award, Internat. Rock Awards, 1991; Q Lifetime Achievement Award, 1997; Ivor Novello Lifetime Achievement Award, 2001. *Publication:* Horse's Neck, 1986. *Recreation:* sailing. *Address:* Box 305, Twickenham TW1 1TT.

TOWRY, Peter; *see* Piper, Sir D. T.

TOY, Rev. Canon John, PhD; Chancellor of York Minster, 1983–99 (also Librarian and Guestmaster); Residentiary Canon, York Minster, 1983–99, now Emeritus; Prebendary of Laughton-en-le-Morthen, 1994–99; *b* 25 Nov. 1930; *e s* of late Sidney Toy, FSA and late Violet Mary (*née* Doudney); *m* 1963, Mollie, *d* of Eric and Elsie Tilbury; one *s* one *d*. *Educ:* Epsom County Grammar Sch.; Hatfield Coll., Durham (BA 1st cl. Hons. Theol. 1953, MA 1962). PhD Leeds, 1982. Ordained deacon, 1955, priest, 1956; Curate, St Paul's, Lorrimore Sq., Southwark, 1955–58; Student Christian Movement Sec. for S of England, 1958–60; Chaplain: Ely Theol Coll., 1960–64; St Andrew's Church, Gothenburg, Sweden, 1965–69; St John's College, York: Lectr in Theology, 1969; Sen. Lectr, 1972; Principal Lectr, 1979–83; Prebendary of Tockerington, 1983–94. *Publications:* Jesus, Man for God, 1988; (jtly) A Pilgrim Guide to York, 1997; contrib. to learned jls and cathedral booklets. *Recreations:* Scandinavia, history, architecture. *Address:* 11 Westhorpe, Southwell, Notts NG25 0ND. *T:* (01636) 812609; *e-mail:* john.toy@virgin.net.

TOY, Sam, OBE 1994; Chairman and Managing Director, Ford Motor Co. Ltd, 1980–86; Chairman, Norman Cordiner Ltd, Inverness, 1991–96; *b* 21 Aug. 1923; *s* of Edward and Lillian Toy; *m* 1st, 1944, Jean Balls; one *s*; 2nd, 1950, Joan Franklin Rook; two *s* one *d*; 3rd, 1984, Janetta McMorrow. *Educ:* Falmouth Grammar Sch.; Fitzwilliam Coll., Cambridge (MA; Hon. Fellow, 1984). Pilot (Flt Lieut), RAF, 1942–48. Graduate trainee, Ford Motor Co. Ltd, 1948; thereafter, all business career with Ford Motor Co. Ltd. Mem. Council, SMMT, 1975– (Vice-Pres., 1982–86; Pres., 1986–87; Dep. Pres., 1987–88). Chm., UK 2000 Scotland, 1988–96. *Recreations:* trout and salmon fishing, golf. *Address:* 4 Millbrook Close, Liss, Hants GU33 7SR. *T:* (01730) 892631. *Clubs:* Lord's Taverners', Eccentric.

TOYE, Bryan Edward; JP; Chairman, Toye & Co. and associated companies, since 1969; *b* 17 March 1938; *s* of Herbert Graham Donovan Toye and late Marion Alberta Toye (*née* Montignani); *m* 1982, Fiona Ann, *d* of G. H. J. Hogg, Wellington, NZ; three *s* one *d*. *Educ:* St Andrew's Prep. Sch., Eastbourne; Stowe Sch. Joined Toye & Co., 1956; Dir, Toye Kenning & Spencer, 1962–; Dir, Toye & Co., 1966; Dep. Chm., Futurama Sign Gp Ltd, 1992–96; Mem. Adv. Bd, The House of Windsor Collection Ltd, 1994–95; non-executive Director: Trehaven Trust Ltd, 1990–97; Naval Manning Agency, 1999–. Mem., Lloyd's, 1985–91. Alderman, Ward of Lime Street, City of London, 1983–96; Master, Gold and Silver Wyre Drawers' Co., 1984; Member, Court of Assistants: Broderers' Co. (Master, 1996–97); Guild of Freemen of City of London, 1986–97 (Mem., 1983–); Goldsmiths' Co., 1992– (Liveryman, 1985–92). Pres., Royal Warrant Holders' Assoc., 1991–92 (Mem. Council, 1983–; Hon. Auditor, 1998–). Mem. Council, NSPCC, London, 1966–69; Chm., Greater London Playing Fields Assoc., 1988–90; Mem. Council, London Playing Fields Soc., 1990–92; Policy and Resources Cttee, King George's Fund for Sailors, 1990–92. Trustee: (founder Mem.) Queen Elizabeth Scholarship Trust, 1990–96; Britain-Australia Bicentennial Trust; Black Country Museum (London Gp), 1991–97; British Red Cross, 1993– (Vice Pres. London Br., 1993–). Governor: City of London Sch., 1985–88; King Edward's Sch., Witley, 1988–93; Bridewell Royal Hosp., 1989–96; Christ's Hosp., 1989–96; City of London Freemen's Sch., 1993–96. Mem. Ct, RCA, 1983–86. Hon. Mem., Ct of Assts, HAC, 1983–96; Hon.

Col 55 Ordnance Co. RAOC (V), 1988–93; Hon. Col, 124 Havering Petroleum Sqdn RLC (V), 1994–2000; Hon. Ordnance Officer, Tower of London, 1994–. Member: TA&VRA for Gtr London, 1992–99; City of London TA&VRA, 1992–99. Member: Royal Soc. of St George, London Br., 1981–; Huguenot Soc., 1985–; Cttee, Old Stoic Soc., 1985–92; Stewards' Enc., Henley Royal Regatta. FInstD 1966; FIMgt 1983; FRSA 1989; MCIPS 1991. JP: City of London, 1983–96 (Chm. Bench, 1990–96); Hereford & Worcs, Supplemental list, 1996. OStJ 1980. *Recreations:* cricket, squash, shooting, sailing, swimming, tennis, gardening, classical music, Rugby, entertaining. *Address:* Toye & Co., 19/21 Great Queen Street, WC2B 5BE. *T:* (020) 7242 0471, *Fax:* (020) 7831 8692. *Clubs:* Royal Automobile, Wig and Pen, City Livery (Pres., 1988–89), MCC; Middlesex Co. RFC; Wasps FC (Trustee and Vice-Pres.); Leander (Henley).

TOYE, Prof. John Francis Joseph; Director, Globalisation and Development Strategies Division, UN Committee on Trade and Development, Geneva, since 1998; Fellow, Institute of Development Studies, University of Sussex, since 1987 (Director, 1987–97); *b* 7 Oct. 1942; *s* of late John Redmond Toye and Adele Toye (*née* Francis); *m* 1967, Janet Reason; one *s* one *d*. *Educ:* Christ's Coll., Finchley; Jesus Coll., Cambridge (schol.; MA); Harvard Univ. (Frank Knox Vis. Fellow); Sch. of Oriental and African Studies, Univ. of London (MScEcon; PhD). Asst Principal, HM Treasury, 1965–68; Res. Fellow, SOAS, Univ. of London, 1970–72; Fellow (later Tutor), Wolfson Coll., Cambridge, 1972–80, and Asst Dir of Develt Studies, Cambridge Univ., 1977–80; Dir, Commodities Res. Unit Ltd, 1980–85; Prof. of Develt Policy and Planning and Dir, Centre for Develt Studies, University Coll. of Swansea, 1982–87. Hon. Fellow, Univ. of Birmingham, Inst. of Local Govt Studies, 1986. Member: Council, ODI, 1988–; Adv. Cttee on Econ. and Social Res., ODA, 1989–95. *Publications:* (ed) Taxation and Economic Development, 1978; (ed) Trade and Poor Economies, 1979; Public Expenditure and Indian Development Policy 1960–70, 1981; Dilemmas of Development, 1987; (jtly) Does Aid Work in India?, 1990; (jtly) Aid and Power, 1991; Structural Adjustment and Employment Policy, 1995; numerous articles in acad. jls. *Recreations:* walking, music. *Address:* c/o UNCTAD, Palais des Nations, Geneva 1211, Switzerland.

TOYE, Wendy, CBE 1992; theatrical and film director; choreographer, actress, dancer; *b* 1 May 1917. First professional appearance as Peasblossom in A Midsummer Night's Dream, Old Vic, 1929; principal dancer in Hiawatha, Royal Albert Hall, 1931; Marigold, Phœbe in Toad of Toad Hall and produced dances, Royalty, Christmas, 1931–32; in early 1930s performed and choreographed for the very distinguished Camargo Society of Ballet; guest artist with Sadler's Wells Ballet and Mme Rambert's Ballet Club; went to Denmark as principal dancer with British Ballet, organized by Adeline Genée, 1932; danced in C. B. Cochran's The Miracle, Lyceum, 1932; masked dancer in Ballerina, Gaiety, 1933; member of Ninette de Valois' original Vic Wells Ballet, principal dancer for Ninette de Valois in The Golden Toy, Coliseum, 1934; toured with Anton Dolin's ballet (choreog. for divertissements and short ballets), 1934–35; in Tulip Time, Alhambra, then Markova-Dolin Ballet as principal dancer and choreog., 1935; in Love and How to Cure It, Globe, 1937. Arranged dances and ballets for many shows and films including most of George Black's productions for next 7 years, notably Black Velvet in which also principal dancer, 1939. Shakespearean season, Open Air Theatre, 1939. *Theatre productions:* Big Ben, Bless the Bride, Tough at the Top (for C. B. Cochran), Adelphi; The Shepherd Show, Prince's; Co-Director and Choreographer, Peter Pan, New York; And So To Bed, New Theatre; Co-Director and Choreographer, Feu d'Artifice, Paris; Night of Masquerade, Q; Second Threshold, Vaudeville; Choreography for Three's Company in Joyce Grenfell Requests the Pleasure, Fortune; Wild Thyme, Duke of York's; Lady at the Wheel, Lyric, Hammersmith; Majority of One, Phœnix; Magic Lantern, Saville; As You Like It, Old Vic; Virtue in Danger, Mermaid and Strand; Robert and Elizabeth, Lyric; On the Level, Saville; Midsummer Night's Dream, Shakespeare quatercentenary Latin American tour, 1964; Soldier's Tale, Edinburgh Festival, 1967; Boots with Strawberry Jam, Nottingham Playhouse, 1968; The Great Waltz, Drury Lane, 1970; Showboat, Adelphi, 1971; She Stoops to Conquer, Young Vic, 1972; Cowardy Custard, Mermaid, 1972; Stand and Deliver, Roundhouse, 1972; R loves J, Chichester, 1973; The Confederacy, Chichester, 1974; The Englishman Amused, Young Vic, 1974; Follow The Star, Chichester, 1974, Westminster Theatre, 1976; Made in Heaven, Chichester, 1975; Make Me a World, Chichester, 1976; Once More with Music (with Cicely Courtneidge and Jack Hulbert), 1976; Oh, Mr Porter, Mermaid, 1977; Dance for Gods, Conversations, 1979; Colette, Comedy, 1980; Gingerbread Man, Watermill, 1981; This Thing Called Love, Ambassadors, 1983; (Associate Prod.) Singin' in the Rain, Palladium, 1983; (dir and narr.) Noel and Gertie, Monte Carlo and Canada; (Associate Prod.) Barnham, Manchester, 1984, Victoria Palace, 1985; Birds of a Feather, 1984, and Mad Woman of Chaillot, 1985, Niagara-on-the-Lake; Gala for Joyce Grenfell Tribute, 1985; (Associate Prod.) Torvill and Dean World Tour, 1985; Once Upon a Mattress, Watermill, 1985; Kiss Me Kate, Aarhus and Copenhagen, 1986; Unholy Trinity, Stephenville Fest., 1986; Laburnam Grove, Palace Th. Watford, 1987; Miranda, Chichester Fest., 1987; Get the Message, Molecule, 1987; Songbook, Watermill, 1988; Mrs Dot, Watford, 1988; When That I Was, Manitoba, 1988; Oh! Coward, Hong Kong, 1989; Cinderella, Palace Th., Watford, 1989; Penny Black, Wavendon, 1990; Moll Flanders, Watermill, 1990; Heaven's Up, Playhouse, 1990; Mrs Pat's Profession (workshop with Cleo Laine), Wavendon, 1991; The Drummer, Watermill, 1991; Sound of Music, Sadler's Wells, 1992; See How They Run, Watermill, 1992; Vienna, 1993; Under their Hats, King's Head, 1994, Vienna, 1995; The Anastasia File, 1994, Lloyd George Knew My Father, 1995, Warts and All, Rogues to Riches, 1996, Watermill; Finale Gala, Sadler's Wells, 1996; *Opera Productions:* Bluebeard's Castle (Bartok), Sadler's Wells and Brussels; The Telephone (Menotti), Sadler's Wells; Russalka (Dvořák), Sadler's Wells; Fledermaus, Coliseum and Sadler's Wells; Orpheus in the Underworld, Sadler's Wells and Australia; La Vie Parisienne, Sadler's Wells; Seraglio, Bath Festival, 1967; The Impresario, Don Pasquale (for Phoenix Opera Group), 1968; The Italian Girl in Algiers, Coliseum, 1968; La Cenerentola; Merry Widow, 1979, Orpheus in the Underworld, 1981, ENO North; The Mikado, Nat. Opera Co., Ankara, 1982; Italian Girl in Algiers, ENO, 1982; La Serva Padrona and Der Apotoker, Aix-en-Provence Fest., 1991. *Films directed:* The Stranger Left No Card; The Teckman Mystery; Raising a Riot; The Twelfth Day of Christmas; Three Cases of Murder; All for Mary; True as a Turtle; We Joined the Navy; The King's Breakfast; Cliff in Scotland; A Goodly Manor for a Song; Girls Wanted—Istanbul; Trial by Jury (TV). Retrospectives of films directed: Festival de Films des Femmes International, Créteil, Paris, 1990; Tokyo Film Fest., 1991. Productions for TV, etc, inc. Golden Gala, ATV, 1978; Follow the Star, BBC2, 1979; Stranger in Town, Anglia, 1981. Dir concert, Till We Meet Again, RFH, 1989. Advisor, Arts Council Trng Scheme, for many years; Member: Council, LAMDA; (original) Accreditation Bd instig. by Nat. Council of Drama Training for acting courses, 1981–84; Grand Council, Royal Acad. of Dancing; 1st directors' rep. on Equity Council, 1974– (Dir, Sub-Cttee, 1971–). Committee Member: Wavendon Allmusic Scheme; Vivian Ellis Award Scheme; Richard Stilgoe Award Scheme. Trained with Euphen MacLaren, Karsavina, Dolin, Morosoff, Legat, Rambert. Hon. DLitt City, 1996. Silver Jubilee Medal, 1977. *Address:* c/o Jean Diamond, London Management, Noel House, 2–4 Noel Street, W1V 3RB.

TOYN, His Honour Richard John; a Circuit Judge 1972–92; *b* 24 Jan. 1927; *s* of Richard Thomas Millington Toyn and Ethel Toyn; *m* 1955, Joyce Evelyn Goodwin; two *s* two *d*. *Educ:* Solihull Sch.; Bristol Grammar Sch.; Bristol Univ. (LLB). Royal Army Service Corps, 1948–50. Called to the Bar, Gray's Inn, 1950. Mem., Parole Bd, 1978–80. Contributing Ed., Butterworths County Court Precedents and Pleadings, 1985. *Recreations:* music, drama, photography.

TOYNBEE, Polly; columnist, The Guardian, 1977–88 and since 1998; writer; *b* 27 Dec. 1946; *d* of late Philip Toynbee, and of Anne Powell; *m* 1970, Peter Jenkins (*d* 1992); one *s* two *d* and one step *d*. *Educ:* Badminton Sch.; Holland Park Comprehensive; St Anne's Coll., Oxford. Reporter, The Observer, 1968–71; Editor, The Washington Monthly, USA, 1972–73; Feature Writer, The Observer, 1974–76; Social Affairs Editor, News and Current Affairs, BBC, 1988–95; Associate Editor and columnist, The Independent, 1995–98. Contested (SDP) Lewisham E, 1983. Gov., LSE, 1988–99. Member: Home Office Cttee on Obscenity and Censorship, 1980; DoH Adv. Cttee on the Ethics of Xenotransplantation, 1996; DoH Nat. Screening Cttee, 1996–. Catherine Pakenham Award for Journalism, 1975; British Press Award, 1977, 1982, 1986 (Columnist of the Year); BBC What the Papers Say Award, 1996 (Commentator of the Year); Magazine Writer of the Year, PPA, 1996; George Orwell Prize, 1997. *Publications:* Leftovers, 1966; A Working Life, 1970 (paperback 1972); Hospital, 1977 (paperback 1979); The Way We Live Now, 1981; Lost Children, 1985; (with David Walker) Did Things Get Better? an audit of Labour's successes and failures, 2001. *Address:* The Guardian, 119 Farringdon Road, EC1R 3ER. *T:* (020) 7278 2332.

TOYNE, Prof. Peter; DL; Chairman: Royal Liverpool Philharmonic Society, since 2000; Liverpool Culture Co., since 2000; *b* 3 Dec. 1939; *s* of Harold and Doris Toyne; *m* 1969, Angela Wedderburn; one *s*. *Educ:* Ripon Grammar Sch.; Bristol Univ. (BA); The Sorbonne. Res. Asst, Univ. of Lille, 1964; Univ. of Exeter: Lectr in Geography, 1965–76; Sen. Lectr in Geography and Sub Dean of Social Studies, 1976–78; Dir, DES Credit Transfer Feasibility Study, 1978–80; Hd of Bishop Otter Coll., Chichester, and Dep. Dir (Academic), W Sussex Inst. of Higher Educn, 1980–83; Dep. Rector, NE London Polytechnic, 1983–86; Rector, Liverpool Poly., 1986–92, then Vice-Chancellor and Chief Exec., Liverpool John Moores Univ., 1992–2000 (Hon. Fellow, 2000). Sen. Inspector, Theol Colls, 1980–. Chm., Guidance Accreditation Bd, 1999–; Member: Council, Industrial Soc., 1997–2000; C of E Archbishops' Council, 1999–. Chairman: Trustees, Rodolfus Choir, 1995–; Trustees, Liverpool St George's Hall, 1996–2000; Groundwork St Helens, Knowsley, Sefton & Liverpool, 1997–. Pres., Liverpool YMCA, 1997–. Hon. Life Pres., Liverpool Organists' Assoc., 2000–. Hon. Col, 33 Signal Regt (V), 1999–. FRSA; CIMgt; FICPD; Fellow, Eton Coll., 1996–. Hon. DEd CNAA, 1992. DL 1990, High Sheriff 2001, Merseyside. *Publications:* World Problems, 1970; Techniques in Human Geography, 1971; Organisation, Location and Behaviour, 1974; Recreation and Environment, 1974; Toyne Report: Credit Transfer, 1979; Toyne Report: Environmental Education, 1993; numerous articles in geographical, educnl jls, festschriften and popular press. *Recreations:* railways (model and real), liturgy, music (especially sacred). *Address:* Cloudeslee, Croft Drive, Caldy, Wirral CH48 2JW; *e-mail:* peter.toyne@talk21.com. *Club:* Athenæum (Liverpool).

TOYNE SEWELL, Maj.-Gen. Timothy Patrick; DL; Director, Goodenough College (formerly The London Goodenough Trust for Overseas Graduates), since 1995; *b* 7 July 1941; *s* of late Brig. E. P. Sewell, CBE and of E. C. M. Sewell, MBE (*née* Toyne); *m* 1965, Jennifer Lesley Lunt; one *s* one *d*. *Educ:* Bedford Sch.; RMA, Sandhurst. psc 1973; jsdc 1985; rcds 1988. Commnd KOSB, 1961; ADC to Governor of Aden, 1962–63; helicopter pilot, 2 RGJ and 2 Para, 1966–69; Staff College, 1973; GSO 1, staff of CDS, 1979–81; CO, 1 KOSB, 1981–83; CoS, British Forces Falkland Is, 1983–84; Sen. Directing Staff (Army), JSDC, 1984–85; Comdr, 19 Infantry Bde, 1985–87; RCDS, 1988; Comdr, British Mil. and Adv. Team, Zimbabwe, 1989–91; Comdt, RMA, 1991–94, retired. Team Ldr, Tri Service Study into Services Recruiting Orgns, 1994–95. Col, KOSB, 1995–2001. Dir, Disability Sport England, 1998–99. Gov., Haileybury, 1993–; Mem. Council, QMW, 1996–. DL Greater London, 1999. *Recreations:* racquet sports, golf, fishing, music. *Clubs:* Royal Over-Seas League, Caledonian.

TOZZI, Keith, CEng, FICE; Group Chief Executive, Mid-Kent Holdings plc, since 2000; *b* 23 Feb. 1949; *s* of Edward Thomas Tozzi and Winifred Tozzi (*née* Killick); *m* 1986, Maria Cecilia Buckley; two *s* one *d*. *Educ:* Dartford Grammar Sch.; City Univ. (BSc Hons); Univ. of Kent (MA). Civil Engr, Thames Water, 1973–75; Southern Water plc: Water Manager, 1975–81; Ops Manager, 1981–86; Engrg Manager, 1986–88; Divl Dir, 1988–92; Gp Technical Dir, 1992–96; Chm., Nat. Jt Utilities Gp, 1993–96; Chief Exec., BSI, 1997–2000. Chm., IPID.com Ltd, 2000–; non-exec. Dir, Legal & General UK Select Investment Trust, 2000–. *Publications:* articles in newspapers. *Recreations:* gardening, reading, classic cars. *Address:* Littleworth House, Littleworth, W Sussex RH13 8JF. *T:* (01403) 710488. *Club:* Athenæum.

TOZZI, Nigel Kenneth; QC 2001; *b* 31 Aug. 1957; *s* of Ronald Kenneth Tozzi and Doreen Elsie Florence Tozzi; *m* 1983, Sara Louise Clare Cornish; two *s* one *d*. *Educ:* Hitchin Boys' Grammar Sch.; Exeter Univ. (LLB 1st Cl. Hons); Inns of Court Sch. of Law (1st Cl.). Called to the Bar, Gray's Inn, 1980; in practice as Barrister, specialising in commercial, insce and professional negligence litigation, 1980–. *Recreations:* playing hockey, watching cricket, theatre, cinema. *Address:* 4 Pump Court, Temple, EC4Y 7AN. *T:* (020) 7842 5555. *Club:* Sevenoaks Hockey.

TRACE, Anthony John; QC 1998; *b* 23 Oct. 1958; *s* of Comdr Peter Trace, RD and bar, RNR, and Anne Trace (*née* Allison-Beer); *m* 1986, Caroline Tessa Durrant, *e d* of His Honour A. H. Durrant, *qv*; three *s* one *d*. *Educ:* Vinehall Prep. Sch.; Uppingham Sch.; Magdalene Coll., Cambridge (MA 1st Cl. Hons). Called to the Bar, Lincoln's Inn, 1981. Dep. Managing Ed., Receivers, Administrators and Liquidators' Qly, 1993–. Vice-Chm., Chancery Bar Assoc., 2001– (Hon. Sec., 1997–2001). Founder Mem., Campaign for Real Gin, 1978. Trustee, Uppingham Sch., 1999–. Freeman, City of London, 1981; Liveryman, Co. of Musicians, 1982. Jt Winner, Observer Mace Debating Championship, 1981. Internat. Editl Bd, Briefings in Real Estate Finance, 2000–. *Publications:* (contrib.) Butterworths European Law Service (Company Law), 1992; (contrib.) Butterworths Practical Insolvency, 1999. *Recreations:* stalking, shooting, fishing, the Turf, music, messing about in boats. *Address:* Maitland Chambers, 7 Stone Buildings, Lincoln's Inn, WC2A 3SZ. *T:* (020) 7406 1200. *Clubs:* Athenæum; Pitt (Cambridge).

TRACEY, Prof. Ian; Organist and Master of the Choristers, Liverpool Cathedral, since 1980; Professor, Fellow and Organist, Liverpool John Moores University (formerly Liverpool Polytechnic), since 1988; *b* 27 May 1955; *s* of William Tracey and Helene Mignon Tracey (*née* Harris). *Educ:* Trinity Coll. of Music, London (FTCL); St Katharine's Coll., Liverpool (PGCE). Chorus Master, Royal Liverpool Philharmonic Soc., 1985–; Liverpool City Organist (formerly Consultant Organist, City of Liverpool), 1986–; Dir of music, BBC Daily Service, 1998–. Gov., Liverpool Coll., 1993–. FRSA 1988. NW Arts Award for Classical Music, 1994. *Address:* 6 Cathedral Close, Liverpool Cathedral, Liverpool L1 7BR. *T:* (0151) 708 8471. *Club:* Artists' (Liverpool).

TRACEY, Richard Patrick; JP; strategic marketing and public affairs consultant, since 1997; Director, In Addition Ltd, since 1999; *b* 8 Feb. 1943; *o s* of late P. H. (Dick) Tracey and Hilda Tracey; *m*, Katharine Gardner; one *s* three *d. Educ:* King Edward VI Sch., Stratford-upon-Avon; Birmingham Univ. (LLB Hons). Leader Writer, Daily Express, 1964–66; Presenter/Reporter, BBC Television and Radio, 1966–78: internat. news and current affairs (The World at One, PM, Today, Newsdesk, 24 Hours, The Money Prog.); feature programmes (Wheelbase, Waterline, Motoring and the Motorist, You and Yours, Checkpoint); also documentaries; Public Affairs Consultant/Advisor, 1978–83. Non-executive Director: Tallack Golf Course Construction Ltd, 1987–91; Ranelagh Ltd, 1992–96. Member: Econ. Res. Council, 1981–2000; ISIS Assoc., 1981–92. Various Conservative Party Offices, 1974–81; Dep. Chm., Greater London Cons. Party, 1981–83; Mem., Cons. National Union Exec. Cttee, 1981–83. Contested (C) Northampton N, Oct. 1974. MP (C) Surbiton, 1983–97; contested (C) Kingston and Surbiton, 1997. PPS to Min. of State for Trade and Industry (IT), 1984–85; Parly Under Sec. of State, DoE (with special responsibility for sport), 1985–87. Member: Select Cttee on Televising H of C, 1988–92; Selection Cttee, 1992–94; Public Accounts Cttee, 1994–97. Chm., Cons. Parly Greater London MP's Cttee, 1990–97 (Jt Sec., 1983–84); Sec., Cons. Parly Media Cttee, 1983–84. Fellow, Industry and Parlt Trust, 1984. JP SW London (Wimbledon PSD), 1977. Freeman, City of London, 1984. Mem., Inst. of Advanced Motorists, 1993. *Publications:* (with Richard Hudson-Evans) The World of Motor Sport, 1971; (with Michael Clayton) Hickstead—the first twelve years, 1972; articles, pamphlets. *Recreations:* riding, boating, debating. *Address:* 49 Earlsfield Road, SW18 3DA. *Club:* Wig and Pen.

TRACEY, Stanley William, OBE 1986; professional pianist, composer and arranger, since 1943; *b* 30 Dec. 1926; *s* of Stanley Clark Tracey and Florence Louise Tracey; *m* 1st, 1946, Joan; 2nd, 1954, Jean; 3rd, 1960, Florence Mary, (Jackie); one *s* one *d. Educ:* Tooting, Graveney and Ensham Schools. Leading own small group, 1965–, orchestra, 1969–. Hon. RAM 1984. Fellow, City of Leeds Coll. of Music, 1993. Numerous records of own compositions and arrangements; compositions include: Under Milk Wood suite, 1965; Genesis, 1986; 500 other titles. Hon. DLitt Herts, 1997. Awards include: BASCA Award, 1984; voted best jazz composer, Wire/Guardian, 1989; voted best album of year, Big Band, 1989; pianist of the year, British Jazz Awards, 1992; best album of year, British Jazz Awards, 1993; best arranger/composer, British Jazz Awards, 1995, 1997, BT Jazz Awards, 1999; Jazz Medal, Co. of Musicians, 1997. *Address:* 19 St Augusta Court, Batchwood View, St Albans, Herts AL3 5SS. *T:* (01727) 852595.

TRACEY, Stephen Frederick T.; *see* Thorpe-Tracey.

TRACY; *see* Hanbury-Tracy, family name of Baron Sudeley.

TRACY, Rear-Adm. Hugh Gordon Henry, CB 1965; DSC 1945; *b* 15 Nov. 1912; *e s* of Comdr A. F. G. Tracy, RN; *m* 1938, Muriel, *d* of Maj.-Gen. Sir R. B. Ainsworth, CB, DSO, OBE; two *s* one *d. Educ:* Nautical Coll., Pangbourne. Joined RN, 1929; Lieut, 1934; served in HMS Shropshire, Hawkins and Furious, in Admiralty and attended Advanced Engineering course before promotion to Lt-Comdr, 1942; Sen. Engineer, HMS Illustrious, 1942–44; Asst to Manager, Engineering Dept, HM Dockyard Chatham, 1944–46; Comdr 1946; served in HMS Manxman, Admiralty, RN Engineering Coll. and HM Dockyard Malta; Captain, 1955; Asst Director of Marine Engineering, Admiralty, 1956–58; CO HMS Sultan, 1959–60; Imperial Defence Coll., 1961; CSO (Tech.) to Flag Officer, Sea Training, 1962–63; Rear Admiral, 1963; Director of Marine Engineering, Ministry of Defence (Navy), 1963–66; retired, 1966. Pres., Wilts Gardens Trust, 1992–97 (Chm., 1985–89). *Recreations:* gardening, plant ecology. *Address:* 21a Sion Hill, Bath BA1 2UL.

TRAEGER, Tessa; photographer of still life portraiture and landscape; *b* 30 April 1938; *d* of Thomas Cecil Grimshaw and Joan Hannah (*née* Dearsley); *m* 1965, Ronald S. Traeger (*d* 1968). *Educ:* Guildford High Sch. for Girls; Guildford Sch. of Art. Freelance photographer of private and commissioned work, 1960–, incl. Vogue UK, 1975–91. *Exhibitions:* Photographers' Gall., 1978; Gall. Ratié, Paris, 1979; Neal St Gall., 1980; John Hansard Gall., Southampton, 1983; Sheffield Fine Art, 1988; M Gall., Hamburg, 1993; Ardeche Fest. des Arts, France, annually 1994–98; Michael Hoppen Gall., London, 1997; Witkin Gall., NY, 1997; James Danziger Gall., NY, 1999; Association Gall., London, 2000; *collections:* V&A Mus.; Bibliothèque National, Paris; Metropolitan Mus. of Art, NY; Citibank Private Bank, London, and many private collections. Contrib. to Oral Hist. of British Photography for Nat. Sound Archive, British Liby, 1996. Silver Award, 1979, Gold Award, 1982, DAAD; Lion d'Or, Cannes Advertising Fest., 1994; Silver Award, Assoc. of Fashion, Advertising and Editorial Photographers, 1997 and 1998. *Publications:* (with A. Boxer) Summer Winter Cookbook, 1978; (with A. Boxer) A Visual Feast, 1991 (Andre Simon Award); (with M. Harrison) Ronald Traeger New Angles: a memoir (to accompany exhibn at V&A Mus.), 1999. *Recreations:* gardening, walking in N Devon, restoring 16th century manor house. *Address:* 7 Rossetti Studios, 72 Flood Street, SW3 5TF.

See also N. T. Grimshaw.

TRAFFORD; *see* de Trafford.

TRAFFORD, Ian Colton, OBE 1967; Publisher, The Times Supplements, 1981–88, retired; *b* 8 July 1928; *s* of late Dr Harold Trafford and Laura Dorothy Trafford; *m* 1st, 1949, Nella Georgara (marr. diss. 1964); one *d*; 2nd, 1972, Jacqueline Carole Trenque. *Educ:* Charterhouse; St John's Coll., Oxford. Feature writer and industrial correspondent, The Financial Times, 1951–58; UK Correspondent, Barrons Weekly, New York, 1954–60; Director, Industrial and Trade Fairs Holdings Ltd, 1958–71, Managing Director, 1966–71; Director-General British Trade Fairs in: Peking, 1964; Moscow, 1966; Bucharest, 1968; Sao Paulo, 1969; Buenos Aires, 1970; Man. Dir, Economist Newspaper, 1971–81; Chm., Economist Intelligence Unit, 1971–79; Dep. Chm., Times Books Ltd, 1981–86. Local Dir, W London Board, Commercial Union Assce, 1974–83. OBE awarded for services to exports. *Address:* Grafton House, 128 Westhall Road, Warlingham, Surrey CR6 9HF. *T:* (01883) 622048.

TRAHAIR, John Rosewarne, CBE 1990; DL; Chairman, Plymouth District Health Authority, 1981–90; *b* 29 March 1921; *s* of late Percy Edward Trahair and Edith Irene Trahair; *m* 1948, Patricia Elizabeth (*née* Godrich); one *s* one *d. Educ:* Leys Sch.; Christ's Coll., Cambridge (MA). FCIS. Served with Royal Artillery, 1941–46 (Captain). Finance Dir, Farleys Infant Food Ltd, 1948–73; Dir 1950–74, Dep. Chm. 1956–74, Western Credit Holdings Ltd. Chairman: Moorhaven HMC, 1959–66; Plymouth and District HMC, 1966–74; Member: SW Regional Hosp. Bd, 1965–74 (Vice-Chm. 1971–73, Chm. 1973–74); South Western RHA, 1974–81. Mem., Devon CC, 1977–81. Pres., Devon County Agricl Assoc., 1993–. High Sheriff, Devon, 1987–88; DL Devon, 1989. *Recreations:* sailing, walking. *Address:* West Park, Ivybridge, South Devon PL21 9JP. *T:* (01752) 892466. *Club:* Royal Western Yacht.

TRAILL, Sir Alan Towers, GBE 1984; QSO 1990; Hon. Secretary and Treasurer, ARIAS (Insurance Arbitration Society), since 1997; *b* 7 May 1935; *s* of George Traill and Margaret Eleanor (*née* Matthews); *m* 1964, Sarah Jane (*née* Hutt); one *s. Educ:* St Andrew's Sch., Eastbourne; Charterhouse; Jesus Coll., Cambridge (MA). ACIArb 1991. Underwriting Member of Lloyd's, 1963–89; Man. Dir, Colburn Traill Ltd, 1989–96. British Insurance Brokers Association: Mem. Council, 1978–79; Chairman: Reinsurance Brokers Cttee, 1978–79; UK/NZ 1990 Cttee, 1989–90. Member, Court of Common Council, City of London, 1970; Alderman for Langbourn Ward, 1975–; Sheriff, 1982–83; Lord Mayor of London, 1984–85. Master: Cutlers' Co., 1979–80; Musicians' Co., 1999–Nov. 2000. Dir, City Arts Trust, 1980–. Trustee, Morden Coll., 1995–. Mem. Adv. Cttee, 1995–, Educn Cttee, 1998–, LSO. Gov., Treloar Coll., 1986–; Almoner, Christ's Hosp. Foundn, 1980–. KStJ 1985. *Recreations:* shooting, ski-ing, DIY, travel, opera, assisting education. *Address:* Wheelers Farm, Thursley, Godalming, Surrey GU8 6QE.

TRAIN, Christopher John, CB 1986; Deputy Under Secretary of State, Home Office, and Director-General, Prison Service, 1983–91; *b* 12 March 1932; *s* of late Keith Sydney Sayer Train and Edna Ashby Train; *m* 1957, Sheila Mary Watson; one *s* one *d. Educ:* Nottingham High Sch.; Christ Church Oxford (BA Lit. Hum., MA). Served Royal Navy, 1955–57; Assistant Master, St Paul's Sch., W Kensington, 1957–67; Principal, Home Office, 1968; Asst Sec., Home Office, 1972; Secretary, Royal Commn on Criminal Procedure, 1978–80; Asst Under Sec. of State, Home Office, 1980–83. Vis. Prof., Dept of Management Sci., Strathclyde Univ., 1992–95. Pres., Suffolk Horse Soc., 1989–90. *Publications:* Quietest Under the Sun: a history of Clunbury in the Clun Valley, 1996; The Walls and Gates of Ludlow: their origin and early days, 1999; A Country Education: a history of the schools at Clunbury, 1999; Of Steam and Sheep: the story of Craven Arms, 2000. *Recreations:* collecting and writing cricket books, jogging, local history. *Clubs:* MCC; Vincent's (Oxford).

TRAIN, David, MC 1945; PhD; FCGI, FRPharmS, FRSC; FREng, FIChemE; Partner, 1961–82, Senior Partner, 1980–82, Senior Consultant, 1982–88, Cremer and Warner, Consulting Engineers and Scientists; *b* 27 Feb. 1919; *s* of Charles and Elsie Louisa Train; *m* 1943, Jeanne Catherine, *d* of late William R. and M. M. Edmunds; two *s. Educ:* Lady Hawkins' Grammar Sch., Kington; School of Pharmacy, Univ. of London; Northampton Coll. of Advanced Technology; Imperial Coll., Univ. of London. Fairchild Schol. 1940, MPS 1941, Hewlett Exhibn 1941; BPharm 1942, PhC 1942; BScChemEng 1949, PhD 1956, DIC 1956. ARIC 1949; FRSH 1972; FCGI 1982 (ACGI 1949); FREng (FEng 1983). Apprenticed to F. T. Roper and Daughter, Kington, 1935–38. War service: St John's Hosp. Reserve, 1939; RAMC (non-med.), NW Europe, 1942–45; 212 Fd Amb. 53rd Welsh (Lieut). Lectr in Pharmaceutical Engrg Science, 1949–59, Reader, 1959–61, Fellow, 1991–, Sch. of Pharmacy, London; Vis. Prof., Univ. of Wisconsin, 1959. Examiner: for Pharm. Soc. of Gt Brit., 1949–56; IChemE, 1956–66; Mem. Bd of Studies in Chem. Engrg, Univ. of London, 1958–94. Jt Hon. Secretary: Brit. Pharm. Conf., 1958–64; IChemE, 1972–77; Member: Adv. Cttee on Oil Pollution of the Sea, 1973–84; Parly Gp for Engrg Develt, 1987–; Air Pollution Control Assoc., USA, 1971–84; Fédn Internat. Pharmaceutique, 1970–82. Gov., Bromley Coll. of Further Educn, 1987–95. Liveryman: Worshipful Soc. of Apothecaries, 1975–; Worshipful Co. of Engineers, 1983–. *Publications:* various, on compression of powders, protection of the environment, acidic emissions, hazards in medicaments, preventative toxicology. *Recreations:* gardening, travelling. *Address:* 3 Grayland Close, Bromley, BR1 2PA. *T:* (020) 8464 4701.

TRAINOR, Prof. Richard Hughes, DPhil; FRHistS; Vice-Chancellor, and Professor of Social History, University of Greenwich, since 2000; *b* 31 Dec. 1948; *s* of William Richard Trainor and Sarah Frances (*née* Hughes); *m* 1980, Dr Marguerite Wright Dupree; one *s* one *d. Educ:* Brown Univ. (BA); Princeton Univ. (MA); Merton Coll., Oxford (Rhodes Scholar; MA); Nuffield Coll., Oxford (DPhil 1982). FRHistS 1990. Jun. Res. Fellow, Wolfson Coll., Oxford, 1977–79; Lectr, Balliol Coll., Oxford, 1978–79; University of Glasgow: Lectr in Econ. Hist., 1979–89; Sen. Lectr in Econ. and Social Hist., 1989–95; Prof. of Social Hist., 1995–2000; Dir, Design and Implementation of Software in Hist. Project, 1985–89; Co-Dir, Computers in Teaching Initiative Centre for Hist., Archaeol. and Art Hist., 1989–99; Dean and Hd of Planning Unit, Faculty of Social Sci., 1992–96; Vice-Principal, 1996–2000. Member: Wkg party on Educnl Technol. and Innovative Teaching, Cttee of Scottish Univ. Principals', 1991–92; Awareness, Liaison and Trng Cttee, Jt Inf. Systems Cttee, 1997–2001; Cttee on Academic Quality, E-University, 2001–. Convenor, Steering Gp, Learning and Teaching Support Network, 2000–. Pres., Glasgow and W of Scotland Br., HA, 1991–93; Mem. Council, RHistS, 1997–2001; Hon. Sec., Econ. Hist. Soc., 1998–. FRSA 1995. *Publications:* (ed jtly) Historians, Computers and Data: applications in research and teaching, 1991; (ed jtly) Towards an International Curriculum for History and Computing, 1992; (ed jtly) The Teaching of Historical Computing: an international framework, 1993; Black Country Elites: the exercise of authority in an industrialised area 1830–1900, 1993; (ed with R. Morris) Urban Governance: Britain and beyond since 1750, 2000; (jtly) University, City and State: the University of Glasgow since 1870, 2000; contrib. numerous articles to books and jls. *Recreations:* parenting, observing politics, tennis. *Address:* University of Greenwich, Maritime Greenwich Campus, Old Royal Naval College, Park Row, Greenwich, SE10 9LS. *T:* (020) 8331 8880. *Club:* Athenæum.

TRAINOR, Roy; Chairman: ATM Consulting Group, since 1990; Geneshall Ltd, since 1994; *b* 25 Jan. 1948; *s* of Thomas and Miriam Joyce Trainor; *m* 1972, Elizabeth Ann Evans; two *s. Educ:* Kingston Sch., Stafford; Staffordshire Poly. (DMS 1975); Univ. of Warwick (MA 1982). Mgt Trainee, Lotus Ltd, 1965–67; Personnel, Stoke-on-Trent City Council, 1967–68; Personnel Mgt, then Opnl Mgt, then Dir, NHS, 1968–89. Chairman: Stafford Chamber of Commerce and Industry, 1995–96; Foundn NHS Trust, 1996–2001. MIPD, MMS. *Recreations:* walking, reading, travel. *Address:* ATM Consulting Group, The Hayes, 19 Newport Road, Stafford ST16 1BA. *T:* (01785) 224854, *Fax:* (01785) 229155; *e-mail:* roy_trainor@atmconsultinggroup.com; Vine Cottage, Coton Wood, Radmore Lane, Gnosall, Stafford ST20 0EG. *T:* (01785) 822097. *Clubs:* Naval and Military; County (Stafford).

TRANT, Gen. Sir Richard (Brooking), KCB 1982 (CB 1979); DL; Chairman: Hunting Engineering Ltd, 1988–93; Defence Division, Hunting Plc, 1989–96; Irvin Aerospace Ltd, 1993–96; Deputy Chairman, Wilson's Hogg Robinson Ltd, 1988–96; *b* 30 March 1928; *s* of Richard Brooking Trant and Dora Rodney Trant (*née* Lancaster); *m* 1957, Diana Clare, 2nd *d* of Rev. Stephen Zachary and Ruth Beatrice Edwards; one *s* two *d.* Commissioned DCLI, 1947, later RA; served Korean War, 1952–53; Defence Services Staff Coll., India, 1961–62; S Arabia, 1962–65; Jt Services Staff Coll., 1965; commanded 3rd Regt RHA, 1968–71, 5th Airportable Brigade, 1972–74; Dep. Mil. Sec., MoD (Army), 1975–76; Comdr Land Forces, NI, 1977–79; Dir, Army Staff Duties, 1979–82; GOC South East District, 1982–83, Land Dep. C-in-C Fleet during S Atlantic Campaign, 1982; QMG, 1983–86. Col Comdt: RAEC, 1979–86; RA, 1982–87; RAOC, 1984–88; HAC (TA), 1984–92. Special Comr, Duke of York's Royal Mil. Sch., Dover, 1987–93; Comr, Royal Hosp. Chelsea, 1988–94. Defence Advisor, Short Bros, 1987–88; Dir, Eastern Region Technology Centre, 1989–93. Member: Armed Forces Pay Rev. Body, 1988–94; Council, SBAC, 1988–96; Vice Pres., Defence Manufacturers' Assoc., 1989–96. Pres., Beds Chamber of Commerce and Industry, 1993–96; Dir, S Beds Community

Health Trust, 1991–95. Pres., RA Hunt and RA Saddle Club, 1984–90; Admiral, Army Sailing Assoc., 1984–87. Chm., RA Museums Ltd, 1991–96. Chm., Cornwall Heritage Trust, 1991–. DL Cornwall, 1997. Bard, Cornish Gorsedd, 2000. Mem. Court, Cranfield Univ., 1996–; Hon. DSc Cranfield, 1995. CIMgt (CBIM 1985); MInstD 1987. Freeman, City of London, 1984. Order of South Arabia, 3rd Class, 1965. *Recreations:* golf, field sports, natural history, sailing. *Address:* c/o Lloyds TSB, Newquay, Cornwall TR7 1JB. *Club:* Army and Navy.

TRAPNELL, Barry Maurice Waller, CBE 1982; DL; MA, PhD Cantab; Headmaster of Oundle School, 1968–84; Chairman, Cambridge Occupational Analysts, since 1986; *b* 18 May 1924; *s* of Waller Bertram and late Rachel Trapnell; *m* 1951, Dorothy Joan, *d* of late P. J. Kerr, ICS; two *d. Educ:* University College Sch., Hampstead; St John's Coll., Cambridge (Scholar). Research in physical chemistry in Department of Colloid Science, Cambridge, 1945–46, and Royal Institution, London, 1946–50; Commonwealth Fund Fellow, Northwestern Univ., Ill., 1950–51; Lecturer in chemistry: Worcester Coll., Oxford, 1951–54; Liverpool Univ., 1954–57; Headmaster, Denstone Coll., 1957–68. Visiting Lecturer, American Association for Advancement of Science, 1961. Pres., Independent Schools Assoc. Inc., 1984–97; Member: Adv. Cttee on Supply and Training of Teachers; C of E Commn on Religious Education. E Anglian Regl Dir, Index, 1985–92. Mem. Governing Body, Roedean Sch., 1987–92. Director: Southend Estates Gp plc, 1984–86; Thomas Wall Trust, 1984–92. Hon. FCP, 1995. DL: Staffs, 1967; Northants, 1974–84. Hon. Liveryman, Worshipful Co. of Grocers, 1984. *Publications:* Chemisorption, 1955 (Russian edition, 1958; 2nd English edition, 1964); Learning and Discerning, 1966; papers in British and American scientific journals. *Recreations:* several games (represented Cambridge *v* Oxford at cricket and squash rackets, and Gentlemen *v* Players at cricket; won Amateur Championships at Rugby Fives), English furniture and silver. *Address:* 6 Corfe Close, Cambridge CB2 2QA. *T:* (01223) 249278. *Clubs:* Oxford and Cambridge; Hawks (Cambridge); Vincent's (Oxford).

TRAPP, Prof. Joseph Burney, CBE 1990; FSA; FBA 1980; Professor of the History of the Classical Tradition and Director, Warburg Institute, University of London, 1976–90, Hon. Fellow since 1990; *b* 16 July 1925; *s* of H. M. B. and Frances M. Trapp; *m* 1953, Elayne M. Falla; two *s. Educ:* Dannevirke High Sch. and Victoria University Coll., Wellington, NZ (MA). FSA 1978. Alexander Turnbull Library, Wellington, 1946–50; Jun. Lectr, Victoria University Coll., 1950–51; Asst Lectr, Reading Univ., 1951–53; Warburg Institute: Asst Librarian, 1953–66; Librarian, 1966–76. Visiting Professor: Univ. of Toronto, 1969; Univ. of Melbourne, 1980; Iowa State Univ., Princeton Univ., 1984; Univ. of Warwick, 1992–99. J. H. Gray Lectr, Univ. of Cambridge, 1990; Panizzi Lectr, British Liby, 1990; J. P. R. Lyell Reader in Bibliography, Oxford Univ., 1994. Chm., Panizzi Lectures Selection Cttee, 1996–2000 (Mem., 1986–91). Member: Advisory Council: V&A Museum, 1977–83; British Library, 1980–87; Exec. Cttee, British Sch. at Rome, 1983–87, Council, 1984–95; Foreign Sec., British Academy, 1988–95 (Vice-Pres., 1983–85). Chm. and Trustee, Lambeth Palace Liby, 1987–98. Foreign Mem., Royal Swedish Acad. of Letters, History and Antiquities, 1995. *Publications:* (ed) The Apology of Sir Thomas More, 1979; Essays in the Renaissance and the Classical Tradition, 1990; Erasmus, Colet and More ... (Panizzi Lectures), 1991; (ed with L. Hellinga) Cambridge History of the Book in Britain 1400–1557, 1999; articles in learned jls. *Address:* c/o Warburg Institute, Woburn Square, WC1H 0AB.

TRASENSTER, Michael Augustus Tulk, CVO 1954; photographer, ARPS 1979; *b* 26 Jan. 1923; *er s* of late Major William Augustus Trasenster, MC, and late Brenda de Courcy Trasenster; *m* 1950, Fay Norrie Darley, *d* of late Thomas Bladworth Darley, Cantley Hall, Yorkshire; two *d. Educ:* Winchester. Served with 4th/7th Royal Dragoon Guards, 1942–; NW Europe (Tanks, D-Day to V-E Day), 1944; Middle East, 1946; ADC to Governor of South Australia, 1947–49; School of Tank Technology, 1951; Military Secretary and Comptroller to the Governor General of New Zealand, 1952–55. Chevalier of Order of Leopold II of Belgium, with palm, 1944; Belgian Croix de Guerre, with palm, 1944. *Recreations:* painting, reading. *Address:* c/o Royal Bank of Scotland, High Street, Winchester, Hants SO23 9DA.

TRASLER, Prof. Gordon Blair, PhD; FBPsS; JP; first Professor of Psychology, University of Southampton, 1964–94, now Emeritus; Leverhulme Emeritus Fellow, since 1995; *b* 7 March 1929; *s* of Frank Ferrier Trasler and Marian (*née* Blair); *m* 1953, Kathleen Patricia Fegan. *Educ:* Isleworth Grammar Sch.; Bryanston Sch.; University Coll., Exeter (MA); London Univ. (BSc, PhD). FBPsS 1963; CPsychol. Tutorial Asst, UC, Exeter, 1952–53; Psychologist, HM Prisons, Wandsworth and Winchester, 1955–57; Lectr, Southampton Univ., 1957–64. Visiting Lecturer: LSE, 1962–63; Inst. of Criminology, Cambridge Univ., 1968–; Vis. Prof., Univ. of Alberta at Edmonton, 1977. Mem., Winchester Health Authority, 1981–89. Vice-Pres., Inst. for Study and Treatment of Delinquency, 1987– (Chm., 1981–87); Chm., Div. of Criminolog. and Legal Psychol., BPsS, 1980–83. Chief Scientist's Advr, DHSS, 1977–80 and 1983–; Member: Adv. Council on Penal System, 1968–74; Wootton Cttee on Non-custodial penalties, 1968–70; Younger Cttee on Young Adult Offenders, 1970–74; Lord Chancellor's Adv. Cttee for Southampton, 1988–96. Editor-in-chief, British Jl of Criminology, 1980–85. JP Hants, 1978. Sellin-Glueck Award (for outstanding scholarly contribs to criminology), Amer. Soc. of Criminology, 1990. *Publications:* In Place of Parents, 1960; The Explanation of Criminality, 1962; The Shaping of Social Behaviour, 1967; (jtly) The Formative Years, 1968; (with D. P. Farrington) Behaviour Modification with Offenders, 1980; many papers in jls and chapters on psychology and criminology. *Recreations:* reading, photography, writing. *Address:* Fox Croft, Old Kennels Lane, Oliver's Battery, Winchester SO22 4JT. *T:* (01962) 852345.

TRAVERS, John Richard Lewis, FRICS; Senior Partner, Healey & Baker, since 1999; *b* 20 Aug. 1946; *s* of Edward Arthur Reginald Travers and Dorothy May Travers; *m* 1967, Jennifer Auronwyn Williams; two *s* one *d. Educ:* King Edward VI Sch., Aston; BSc Estate Mgt London Univ. Laing Develt Co. Ltd, Manchester, 1973–75; Healey & Baker: retail negotiator, 1975–79, head of Belgian operation, 1979–, Brussels; Mem., Main Bd, 1992–; Dep. Sen. Partner, 1997–99. *Recreations:* golf, tennis, travel. *Address:* 31 Thames Quay, Chelsea Harbour, SW10 0UY. *T:* (020) 7376 7234.

TRAVERSE-HEALY, Prof. Thomas Hector, (Tim), OBE 1989; FIPR, FPA; Director, Centre for Public Affairs Studies, since 1969; Senior Partner, Traverse-Healy Ltd, 1947–93; *b* 25 March 1923; *s* of John Healy, MBE, and Gladys Traverse; *m* 1946, Joan Thompson; two *s* three *d. Educ:* Stonyhurst Coll.; St Mary's Hosp., London Univ. DipCAM. Served War, Royal Marines Commandos and Special Forces, 1941–46. Chairman: Traverse-Healy & Regester Ltd, 1985–87; Charles Barker Traverse-Healy, 1987–89; non-exec. Dir, Charles Barker Hldgs, 1990–92. Mem., Public and Social Policy Cttee, National Westminster Bank, 1974–92; Professional Advr, Corporate Communications, 1990–92; Specialist Advr, CNAA, 1990–92. Prof. of Public Relns, Univ. of Stirling, 1988–97; Visiting Professor: Baylor Univ., Texas, 1988–97; Univ. of Wales, 1990–97; Advisor: Ball State Univ., USA; Westminster Univ. President: Internat. PR Res. and Educn Foundn, 1983–86; Internat. Foundn for PR Studies, 1987–89; Chm., (UK) PR Educn Trust, 1990–92; Mem., Professional Practices Cttee, PR Consultants Assoc., 1987–91; Sec., PR Res. Network, 1994–97. Institute of Public Relations: Mem. 1948, Fellow 1956; Pres. 1967–68; Tallents Gold Medal, 1985; Hon. Fellow 1988; European PR Federation: Vice-Pres. 1965–69; Internat. PR Assoc.: Sec. 1950–61, Pres. 1968–73, Mem. Emeritus, 1982; Presidential Gold Medal, 1985. FRSA 1953; FIPA 1957. Member, US Public Affairs Council, 1975–; Pres., World PR Congress: Tel Aviv, 1970; Geneva, 1973. Congress Foundn Lecture: Boston, 1976; Bombay, 1982; Melbourne, 1988. PR News Award, 1983; PR Week Award, 1987; Page Soc. Award, 1990. *Publications:* numerous published lectures and articles in professional jls. *Recreations:* French politics, Irish Society. *Address:* 19 Bowes Court, Drews Park, Devizes, Wilts SN10 5FQ. *T:* (01380) 725459. *Clubs:* Athenæum; Philippics.

TREACHER, Adm. Sir John (Devereux), KCB 1975; Chairman, Chromatone Intermedia Ltd, since 2000; Director, Contipark SA, since 1994; *b* Chile, 23 Sept. 1924; *s* of late Frank Charles Treacher, Bentley, Suffolk; *m* 1st, 1953, Patcie Jane (marr. diss. 1968), *d* of late Dr F. L. McGrath, Evanston, Ill; one *s* one *d*; 2nd, 1969, Kirsteen Forbes, *d* of late D. F. Landale; one *s* one *d. Educ:* St Paul's School. War service in HM Ships Nelson, Glasgow, Keppel and Mermaid in Mediterranean, Russian convoys; qual. Fleet Air Arm pilot, 1947; CO: 778 Sqdn 1951, 849 Sqdn 1952–53; CO, HMS Lowestoft, 1964–66; CO, HMS Eagle, 1968–70; Flag Officer Carriers and Amphibious Ships and Comdr Carrier Striking Gp 2, 1970–72; Flag Officer, Naval Air Comd, 1972–73; Vice-Chief of Naval Staff, 1973–75; C-in-C Fleet, and Allied C-in-C Channel and Eastern Atlantic, 1975–77. Chief Exec., 1977–81, and Dir, 1977–85, Nat. Car Parks; Chm., Westland Inc., 1983–89; Dep. Chm., Westland Gp, 1986–89 (Dir. 1978–89); Dir, Meggitt PLC, 1989–95; Chm., Interoute Telecommunications plc, 1996–98. Non-press Mem., Press Council, 1978–81; Dir, SBAC, 1983–89. FRAeS 1973. *Recreations:* shooting, boating. *Address:* 22 Newton Road, W2 5LT. *Clubs:* Boodle's, Institute of Directors.

TREACY, Colman Maurice; QC 1990; a Recorder, since 1991; *b* 28 July 1949; *s* of Dr Maurice Treacy and Mary Treacy; *m* (marr. diss.); one *s* one *d. Educ:* Stonyhurst Coll.; Jesus Coll., Cambridge (Open Scholar in Classics; MA). Called to the Bar, Middle Temple, 1971, Bencher, 1999; an Asst Recorder, 1988–91; Head of Chambers, 1994–2000. Mental Health Rev. Tribunal, 1999–; Asst Boundary Comr, 2000–. *Address:* 3 Fountain Court, Steelhouse Lane, Birmingham B4 6DR. *T:* (0121) 236 5854.

TREADGOLD, Hazel Rhona; JP; Central President of the Mothers' Union, 1983–88; *b* 29 May 1936; *m* 1959, Very Rev. John David Treadgold, *qv*; two *s* one *d*. Mothers' Union: has held office, Dioceses of Southwell, Durham and Chichester, and at HQ; Chm., Central Young Families Cttee, 1971–76; a Central Vice-Pres., 1978–83. Archbishop of Canterbury's Co-ordinator, Bishops' Wives Conf., Lambeth, 1988; Member: Women's Nat. Commn, 1980–83; Exec., Women's Council, 1989–91. Gov., Bishop Luffa C of E Comprehensive Sch., 1990–. JP Chichester, 1991. *Recreations:* travel, reading, flower arranging, swimming, theatre. *Address:* 43 Prior's Acre, Boxgrove, W Sussex PO18 0ER. *T:* (01243) 782385. *Clubs:* Parrot; Chichester Festival.

TREADGOLD, Very Rev. John David, LVO 1990; Dean of Chichester, 1989–2001; Chaplain to the Queen, 1983–89; *b* 30 Dec. 1931; *s* of Oscar and Sybil Treadgold; *m* 1959, Hazel Rhona Bailey (*see* H. R. Treadgold); two *s* one *d. Educ:* Nottingham Univ. (BA); Wells Theological College. Deacon 1959, priest 1960; Vicar Choral, Southwell Minster, 1959–64; Rector of Wollaton, Nottingham, 1964–74; Vicar of Darlington, 1974–81; Canon of Windsor and Chaplain to Windsor Great Park, 1981–89. Chaplain, TA, 1962–67; TAVR, 1974–78; Chaplain to High Sheriff: of Nottinghamshire, 1963–64 and 1975–76; of Durham, 1978–79. Chairman: Chichester DAC for the Care of Churches, 1990–99; Trustees, Hosp. of St Mary, 1989–; Morse-Boycott Trust, 1995–. Trustee, Chichester Festival Theatre, 1989–; Vice Pres., Chichester Festivities, 1989–. Patron, Pallant Hse Gall., 1998. ChStJ 1995 (Mem., Council, Order of St John, Sussex, 1994–). Chm. of Govs, Prebendal Sch., Chichester, 1989–; Governor: Slindon Coll., 1995–96; Wycombe Abbey Sch., 1995–2000. FRSA 1991. *Recreations:* musical appreciation; church architecture. *Address:* 43 Prior's Acre, Boxgrove, Chichester, W Sussex PO18 0ER. *T:* (01243) 782385.

TREADGOLD, Sydney William, CBE 1999; FCA; Secretary: Financial Reporting Council, 1990–98; Financial Reporting Review Panel, 1991–98; Accountancy Foundation, 2000–01; *b* 10 May 1933; *s* of Harold Bryan Treadgold and Violet Watson; *m* 1961, Elizabeth Ann White; two *s. Educ:* Larkmead Sch., Abingdon. Chartered accountant (ACA 1960, FCA 1970). Served RAF, 1951–53 (Navigator). Wenn Townsend & Co., Chartered Accountants, 1954–62; Asst Finance Officer, Univ. of Liverpool, 1963–65; Principal: Min. of Aviation, 1965–67; Min. of Technol., 1967–71; Asst Sec., DTI, 1972–78; Under Secretary: Price Commn, 1978–79; Depts of Industry and Trade, 1979–83; DTI, 1983–89; Mem., Accounting Standards Task Gp, 1989–90; Secretary: Accounting Standards Bd, 1990–93; Ind. Regulation of Accountancy Profession Implementation Gp, 1999–2001. FRSA 1988. *Recreations:* nothing serious.

TREADWELL, Charles James, CMG 1972; CVO 1979; HM Diplomatic Service, retired; *b* 10 Feb. 1920; *s* of late C. A. L. Treadwell, OBE, Barrister and Solicitor, Wellington, NZ. *Educ:* Wellington Coll., NZ; University of New Zealand (LLB). Served with HM Forces, 1939–45. Sudan Political Service and Sudan Judiciary, 1945–55; FO, 1955–57; British High Commn, Lahore, 1957–60; HM Embassy, Ankara, 1960–62; HM Embassy, Jedda, 1963–64; British Dep. High Comr for Eastern Nigeria, 1965–66; Head of Joint Information Services Department, Foreign Office/Commonwealth Office, 1966–68; British Political Agent, Abu Dhabi, 1968–71; Ambassador, United Arab Emirates, 1971–73; High Comr to Bahamas, 1973–75; Ambassador to Oman, 1975–79. *Address:* Cherry Orchard Cottage, Buddington Lane, Midhurst, W Sussex GU29 0QP.

TREASURE, Prof. John Albert Penberthy, PhD; *b* 20 June 1924; *s* of Harold Paul Treasure and Constance Frances Treasure; *m* 1954, Valerie Ellen Bell; three *s. Educ:* Cardiff High Sch.; University Coll., Cardiff (BA 1946); Univ. of Cambridge (PhD 1956). Joined British Market Research Bureau Ltd, 1952, Man. Dir 1957; Marketing Dir, J. Walter Thompson Co. Ltd, 1960, Chm. 1967; Dir, J. Walter Thompson Co. USA, 1967, Vice Chm. 1974; Vice-Chm., Saatchi & Saatchi Advertising Ltd (formerly Saatchi & Saatchi Compton Ltd), 1983–89. Chm., Taylor Nelson AGB plc, 1992–97; Director: Rowntree Mackintosh plc, 1976–88; Assi Packaging (UK) Ltd (formerly AFIH Ltd), 1984–94; Household Mortgage Corp. plc, 1986–94. Dean and Prof. of Marketing, City Univ. Business Sch., 1978–82. President: Inst. of Practitioners in Advertising, 1975–77; Market Res. Soc., 1975–78; Nat. Advertising Benevolent Soc., 1977–78; Chm., History of Advertising Trust, 1985–90. Master, Marketors' Co., 2000. *Publications:* articles on marketing, market research and economics in Financial Times, Times, New Soc., Econ. Jl, Commentary, and Advertising Qly. *Recreations:* golf, tennis. *Address:* 20 Queensberry House, Friars Lane, Richmond, Surrey TW9 1NT. *Clubs:* Caledonian, Queen's, Hurlingham; Royal Mid-Surrey Golf (Richmond).

TREDINNICK, David Arthur Stephen; MP (C) Bosworth, since 1987; *b* 19 Jan. 1950; *m* 1983, Rebecca Jane Shott; one *s* one *d. Educ:* Ludgrove Sch., Wokingham; Eton; Mons

Officer Cadet Sch.; Graduate Business Sch., Capetown Univ. (MBA); St John's Coll., Oxford (MLitt 1987). Trainee, E. B. Savoury Milln & Co, Stockbrokers, 1972; Account Exec., Quadrant International, 1974; Salesman, Kalle Infotec UK, 1976; Sales Manager, Word Processing, 1977–78; Consultant, Baird Communications, NY, 1978–79; Marketing Manager, Q1 Europe Ltd, 1979–81; Res. asst to Kenneth Warren, MP, and Angela Rumbold, CBE, MP, 1981–87; Dir, Malden Mitcham Properties (family business), 1985–. Contested (C) Cardiff S and Penarth, 1983. PPS to Minister of State, Welsh Office, 1991–94. Chairman: Select Cttee on Statutory Instruments, 1997–; Jt Cttee on Statutory Instruments, 1997–; Treasurer: All-Party Parly Gp for Alternative and Complementary Medicine, 1991–; Parly Gp for World Govt, 1991–95; Secretary: Cons. backbench Defence Cttee, 1990–91; Cons. backbench Foreign Affairs Cttee, 1990–91. Chm., British Atlantic Gp of Young Politicians, 1989–91; Co-Chm., Future of Europe Trust, 1991–94; Chairman: Anglo East European Trade Co., 1990–97; Ukraine Business Agency, 1992–97. *Address:* House of Commons, SW1A 0AA. *T:* (020) 7219 4514.

TREFETHEN, Prof. Lloyd Nicholas, PhD; Professor of Numerical Analysis, Oxford University, since 1997; Fellow, Balliol College, Oxford, since 1997; *b* 30 Aug. 1955; *s* of Lloyd McGregor Trefethen and Florence Newman Trefethen; *m* 1988, Anne Elizabeth Daman; one *s* one *d*. *Educ:* Harvard Coll. (AB 1977); Stanford Univ. (MS Computer Sci./Numerical Analysis 1980; PhD 1982). NSF Post-doctoral Fellow and Adjunct Asst Prof., Courant Inst. of Mathematical Scis, New York Univ., 1982–84; Massachusetts Institute of Technology: Asst Prof. of Applied Maths, 1984–87; Associate Prof., 1987–91; Cornell University: Associate Prof., 1991–93; Prof. of Computer Sci., 1994–97. *Publications:* Numerical Conformal Mapping, 1986; Numerical Linear Algebra, 1997; Spectral Methods in MATLAB, 2000; numerous technical articles. *Address:* Oxford University Computing Laboratory, Wolfson Building, Parks Road, Oxford OX1 3QD. *T:* (01865) 273886.

TREFGARNE, family name of **Baron Trefgarne**.

TREFGARNE, 2nd Baron, *cr* 1947, of Cleddau; **David Garro Trefgarne;** PC 1989; *b* 31 March 1941; *s* of 1st Baron Trefgarne and of Elizabeth (who *m* 1962, Comdr A. T. Courtney (from whom she obt. a divorce, 1966); *m* 1971, H. C. H. Ker (*d* 1987), Dundee), *d* of C. E. Churchill; *S* father, 1960; *m* 1968, Rosalie, *d* of Baron Lane of Horsell, *qv*; two *s* one *d*. *Educ:* Haileybury; Princeton University, USA. Opposition Whip, House of Lords, 1977–79; a Lord in Waiting (Govt Whip), 1979–81; Parly Under Sec. of State, DoT, 1981, FCO, 1981–82, DHSS, 1982–83, (Armed Forces) MoD, 1983–85; Minister of State: for Defence Support, 1985–86; for Defence Procurement, 1986–89; DTI, 1989–90; elected Mem., H of L, 1999. Chm., Assoc. of Cons. Peers, 2000–. Dir of various companies. Chm., Engrg and Marine (formerly Engrg) Trng Authority, 1994–. Pres., Popular Flying Assoc., 1992–; Hon. President: METCOM, 1990–; British Assoc. of Aviation Consultants, 1994–; Mem. Council, Air League, 1996–. Vice Chm., ACF Assoc., 1992–. Gov., Guildford Sch. of Acting, 1992 ; Life Gov., Haileybury, 1992. Trustee, Mary Rose Trust, 1994–2001; Chm., Brooklands Mus. Trust, 2001–. Awarded Royal Aero Club Bronze Medal (jointly) for flight from England to Australia and back in light aircraft, 1963. *Recreation:* photography. *Heir:* *s* Hon. George Garro Trefgarne, *b* 4 Jan. 1970. *Address:* House of Lords, SW1A 0PW.

TREFUSIS; *see* Fane Trefusis, family name of Baron Clinton.

TREGARTHEN JENKIN, Ian Evers; *see* Jenkin.

TREGEAR, Mary, FBA 1985; Keeper of Eastern Art, Ashmolean Museum, Oxford, 1987–91; *b* 11 Feb. 1924; *d* of late Thomas R. and Norah Tregear. *Educ:* Sidcot Sch., Somerset; West of England Coll. of Art (ATD 1946); London Univ. (BA); MA Oxon. Taught Art, Wuhan, China, 1947–50; Curator/Lectr, Hong Kong Univ., 1956–61; Sen. Asst Keeper, Chinese, Ashmolean Museum, 1961–87. *Publications:* Arts of China, vol. 1 (co-ordinating ed.), 1968; Catalogue of Chinese Greenwares in the Ashmolean Museum, 1976; Chinese Art, 1980 (trans. French and Spanish), 2nd edn 1997; Song Ceramics, 1982; Tesori d'Arte in Cina, 1994 (trans. English, French and Spanish).

TREGLOWN, Prof. Jeremy Dickinson; Professor of English, University of Warwick, since 1993 (Chairman, Department of English and Comparative Literary Studies, 1995–98); *b* 24 May 1946; *s* of late Rev. Geoffrey and of Beryl Treglown; *m* 1st, 1970, Rona Bower (marr. diss. 1982); one *s* two *d*; 2nd, 1984, Holly Eley (*née* Urquhart). *Educ:* Bristol Grammar Sch.; St Peter's Coll. and Hertford Coll., Oxford (MA, BLitt); PhD London. Lecturer: Lincoln Coll., Oxford, 1974–77; University College London, 1977–80; Times Literary Supplement: Asst Editor, 1980–82; Editor, 1982–90. Vis. Fellow: All Souls Coll., Oxford, 1986; Huntington Library, San Marino, Calif, 1988; Mellon Vis. Associate, Calif Inst. of Technol., 1988; Hon. Res. Fellow, UCL, 1991–; Ferris Vis. Prof., Princeton Univ., 1991–92; Jackson Brothers Fellow, Beinecke Liby, Yale, 1999; Leverhulme Res. Fellow, 2001–; Mellon Fellow, Harry Ransom Humanities Res. Center, Univ. of Texas at Austin, 2002. Mem. Council, RSL, 1989–96; FRSL 1991; FEA 2001. FRSA 1990. Chairman of Judges: Booker Prize, 1991; Whitbread Book of the Year Award, 1998. Contributing Editor, Grand Street, NY, 1991–98. *Publications:* Roald Dahl, 1994; Romancing: the life and work of Henry Green, 2000; edited: The Letters of John Wilmot, Earl of Rochester, 1980; Spirit of Wit, 1982; The Lantern Bearers, Essays by Robert Louis Stevenson, 1988; (with B. Bennett) Grub Street and the Ivory Tower: literary journalism and literary scholarship from Fielding to the Internet, 1998; (with D. McVea) Contributors to The Times Literary Supplement 1902–74: a biographical index, 2000; various articles and book introductions. *Address:* 102 Savernake Road, NW3 2JR; Gardens Cottage, Ditchley Park, Enstone, near Chipping Norton, Oxon OX7 4EP.

TREHANE, Sir (Walter) Richard, Kt 1967; Chairman of the Milk Marketing Board, 1958–77; *b* 14 July 1913; *s* of James Trehane and Muriel Yeoman Cowl; *m* 1948, Elizabeth Mitchell (*d* 1999); two *s*. *Educ:* Monkton Combe School, Somerset; University of Reading (BSc (Agric.)). On staff of School of Agriculture, Cambridge, 1933–36; Manager of Hampreston Manor Farm, Dorset, 1936–79. Member: Dorset War Agric. Exec. Cttee, later Dorset Agricl Cttee, 1942–52 (Dep. Chm., 1947–52); MMB, 1947–77 (Vice-Chm., 1952–58; Chm., 1958–77); Mem. (later Vice-Chm.) Avon and Stour Catchment Bd, subseq. Avon & Dorset Rivers Bd, 1944–53; Mem. Dorset County Council and Chm. Secondary Education Cttee, 1946–49; Chm. Dorset National Farmers' Union, 1947–48; Member, Nat. Milk Publicity Council, 1954–77 (1st Pres. 1954–56); Chm. English Country Cheese Council, 1955–77; Pres. British Farm Produce Council, 1963–78 (Chm. 1960–63). Chm. Govg Body, Grassland Research Institute, Hurley, Berks, 1959–78 (Hon. Fellow, 1981); Chm. and Pres. European Cttee on Milk/Butterfat Recording, 1957–60; Director of British Semen Exports Ltd, 1960–77; Vice-President: World Assoc. Animal Production, 1965–68; President: European Assoc. Animal Prodn, 1961–67 (Hon. Pres., 1967–95); British Soc. Animal Prodn, 1954, 1961; British Friesian Cattle Soc., 1969–70; Royal Assoc. British Dairy Farmers, 1968, 1977; Internat. Dairy Fedn, 1968–72, Hon. Pres., 1972–76. Chm., UK Dairy Assoc., 1963–69. Chm., Alfa-Laval Co. Ltd, 1982–84 (Dir, 1977–84); Director: Southern Television, 1969–81; The Rank Organisation Ltd, 1970–84; Beaumont UK, 1980–83. Trustee, UK Farming Scholarship Trust, 1970. Governor: Monkton Combe School, 1957–83; British Nutrition Foundn, 1975–77. FRAgSs 1970. Hon. DSc Reading, 1976. Justus-von-Liebig Prize, Kiel Univ., 1968; Gold Medal, Soc. of Dairy Technology, 1969; Massey-Fergusson Award, 1971. Comdr du Mérite Agricole, 1964. *Address:* Hampreston Manor Farm, Wimborne, Dorset BH21 7LX. *Club:* Farmers'.

TREISMAN, Dr Richard Henry, FRS 1994; Director of Laboratory Research, since 1999, and Head, Transcription Laboratory, since 1988, Imperial Cancer Research Fund; *b* 7 Oct. 1954; *s* of Woolf Benjamin Treisman and Marjorie Elizabeth (*née* Grounsell); *m* 1993, Kathleen Mary Weston; one *d*. *Educ:* Haberdashers' Aske's Sch.; Christ's Coll., Cambridge (BA 1977); ICRF/UCL (PhD 1981). Postdoctoral Fellow, Harvard Univ., 1981–84; Mem., Scientific Staff, Lab. of Molecular Biol., Cambridge, 1984–88; Principal Scientist, ICRF, 1988. Mem., EMBO, 1987. Mem., Festiniog Railway Soc., Porthmadog, 1967–. EMBO Medal, 1995. *Publications:* papers in scientific jls. *Recreations:* piano playing, fell-walking. *Address:* Transcription Laboratory, Room 528, Imperial Cancer Research Fund, 44 Lincoln's Inn Fields, WC2A 3PX. *T:* (020) 7269 3271.

TREITEL, Sir Guenter (Heinz), Kt 1997; DCL; FBA 1977; QC 1983; Vinerian Professor of English Law, Oxford University, 1979–96, now Emeritus; Fellow of All Souls College, Oxford, 1979–96, now Emeritus; *b* 26 Oct. 1928; *s* of Theodor Treitel and Hanna Lilly Treitel (*née* Levy); *m* 1957, Phyllis Margaret Cook; two *s*. *Educ:* Kilburn Grammar School; Magdalen College, Oxford. BA 1949, BCL 1951, MA 1953, DCL 1976. Called to the Bar, Gray's Inn, 1952, Hon. Bencher, 1982. Asst Lectr, LSE, 1951–53; Lectr, University Coll., Oxford, 1953–54; Fellow, Magdalen Coll., Oxford, 1954–79, Fellow Emeritus, 1979; All Souls Reader in English Law, Univ. of Oxford, 1964–79. Vis. Lectr, Univ. of Chicago, 1963–64; Visiting Professor: Chicago, 1968–69 and 1971–72; W Australia, 1976; Houston, 1977; Southern Methodist, 1978, 1988–89, 1994, 2000 (Dist. Vis. Prof.); Virginia, 1978–79 and 1983–84; Santa Clara, 1981; Vis. Scholar, Ernst von Caemmerer Gedächtnisstiftung, 1990. Trustee, British Museum, 1983–98; Mem. Council, National Trust, 1984–93. *Publications:* The Law of Contract, 1962, 10th edn 1999; An Outline of the Law of Contract, 1975, 5th edn 1995; Remedies for Breach of Contract: a comparative account, 1988; Unmöglichkeit, "Impracticability" und "Frustration" im anglo-amerikanischen Recht, 1991; Frustration and Force Majeure, 1994; (jtly) English Private Law, 2000; (jtly) Carver on Bills of Lading, 2001; edited jointly: Dicey's Conflict of Laws, 7th edn 1958; Dicey and Morris, Conflict of Laws, 8th edn 1967; Chitty on Contracts, 23rd edn 1968 to 28th edn 1999; Benjamin's Sale of Goods, 1974, 5th edn 1997. *Recreations:* music, reading. *Address:* All Souls College, Oxford OX1 4AL. *T:* (01865) 279379.

TRELAWNY, Sir John Barry Salusbury-, 13th Bt *cr* 1628; Director, Goddard Kay Rogers and Associates Ltd, 1984–95; Chairman, GKR Group Ltd, 1993–95; *b* 4 Sept. 1934; *s* of Sir John William Robin Maurice Salusbury-Trelawny, 12th Bt and of his 1st wife, Glenys Mary (*d* 1985), *d* of John Cameron Kynoch; *S* father, 1956; *m* 1958, Carol Knox, *yr d* of late C. F. K. Watson, The Field, Saltwood, Kent; one *s* three *d*. *Educ:* HMS Worcester. Subseq. Sub-Lt RNVR (National Service). Dir, The Martin Walter Group Ltd, 1971–74; various directorships, 1974–83; Dir, 1978–83, Jt Dep. Man. Dir 1981–83, Korn/Ferry Internat. Inc. Pres., London Cornish Assoc., 1997–. Pres., Folkestone & Hythe Dist Scout Council, 1980–. FInstM 1974. JP 1973 78. *Heir:* *s* John William Richard Salusbury-Trelawny [*b* 30 March 1960; *m* 1st, 1980, Anita (marr. diss. 1986), *d* of Kenneth Snelgrove; one *s* one *d*; 2nd, 1987, Sandra (marr. diss. 1993), *d* of Joseph Thompson; one *s*]. *Address:* Beavers Hill, Rectory Lane, Saltwood, Kent CT21 4QA. *T:* (01303) 266476. *Clubs:* Army and Navy; Royal Cinque Ports Yacht.

TRELEAVEN, Prof. Philip Colin, PhD; Professor of Computing, since 1985, and Pro-Provost, since 1994, University College London; *b* 15 March 1950; *s* of Frederick Colin and Evelyn Treleaven; *m* 1981, Isabel Gouveia-Lima. *Educ:* Brunel Univ. (BTech); Manchester Univ. (MSc, PhD). Research Fellow, Univ. of Newcastle upon Tyne, 1979–83; Sen. Res. Fellow, Reading Univ., 1983–85. Contested (C): Ealing Southall, 1992; SW London, Eur. Parly elecns, 1994. *Recreation:* politics. *Address:* University College London, Gower Street, WC1E 6BT. *T:* (020) 7380 7288.

TRELFORD, Prof. Donald Gilchrist; journalist and broadcaster; Editor, The Observer, 1975–93; *b* 9 Nov. 1937; *s* of Thomas and late Doris Trelford (*née* Gilchrist); *m* 1st, 1963, Janice Ingram; two *s* one *d*; 2nd, 1978, Kate Mark; one *d*; 3rd, 2001, Claire Bishop. *Educ:* Bablake Sch., Coventry (School Captain, 1956); Open exhibnr in English, Selwyn Coll., Cambridge; MA; University rugby and cricket. Pilot Officer, RAF, 1956–58. Reporter and Sub-Editor, Coventry Standard and Sheffield Telegraph, 1960–63; Editor, Times of Malawi, 1963–66; Correspondent in Africa for The Observer, The Times, and BBC, 1963–66; The Observer: Dep. News Editor, 1966; Asst Man. Editor, 1968; Dep. Editor, 1969; Chief Exec., The Observer Ltd, 1992–93; Prof. and Hd of Dept of Journalism Studies, 1994–2000, Vis. Prof., 2000–, Sheffield Univ. Acting Editor, The Oldie, 1994; Sports columnist, Daily Telegraph, 1993–. Chm., The Baby Channel, 2000–01; Director: Optomen Television, 1988–97; Observer Films, 1989–93; Central Observer TV, 1990–93; Nat. Acad. of Writing, 2000–; London Press Club, 2001–. Ind. Assessor, BBC TV Regl News, 1997. Member: British Executive Cttee, IPI, 1976–2000; Soc. of Editors, 1984–93; Guild of British Newspaper Editors, 1985–2000 (Mem., Parly and Legal Cttee, 1987–91); Council, Media Soc., 1981– (Pres., 1999–); Defence, Press and Broadcasting Cttee, 1986–93; Competition Commn (newspaper panel), 1999–; Vice-Pres., Newspaper Press Fund, 1992– (Appeals Chm., 1991). Member: judging panel, British Press Awards, 1981–; judging panel, Scottish Press Awards, 1985; Olivier Awards Cttee, SWET, 1984–93; Judge: Whitbread Prize, 1992; Sony Radio Awards, 1994; George Orwell Prize, 1998. Mem. Adv. Bd, London Choral Soc., 1991–98; Chm., Soc. of Gentlemen, Lovers of Musick, 1996–. Vice-Pres., British Sports Trust, 1988–; Hon. Advr, NPFA, 1996–. Mem., Jurade de St Emilion, 1997–. Liveryman, Worshipful Co. of Stationers and Newspaper Makers, 1986; Freeman, City of London, 1986. FRSA 1988. Hon. DLitt Sheffield, 1990. Granada Newspaper of the Year Award, 1983, 1993; commended, Internat. Editor of the Year, World Press Rev., NY, 1984. Frequent broadcasts (writer, interviewer and panellist) on TV and radio; presenter: Running Late (C4); LBC Morning Report; TV interviews include: Rajiv Gandhi, Lord Goodman, Sir Leonard Hutton, Gromyko; speaker at internat. media confs in Spain, Egypt, W Germany, USA, India, Turkey, S Africa, Argentina, Kenya, Trinidad, Lebanon, Canada, Russia, Korea and Peru. *Publications:* Siege, 1980; (ed) Sunday Best, 1981, 1982, 1983; (contrib.) County Champions, 1982; Snookered, 1986; (contrib.) The Queen Observed, 1986; (with Garry Kasparov) Child of Change, 1987; (contrib.) Saturday's Boys, 1990; (contrib.) Fine Glances, 1991; Len Hutton Remembered, 1992; (contrib.) One Over Par, 1992; (ed) The Observer at 200, 1992; (with Daniel King) World Chess Championship, 1993; (contrib.) Animal Passions, 1994; W. G. Grace, 1998. *Recreation:* snooker. *Address:* 15 Fowler Road, N1 2EP. *T:* (020) 7226 9356. *Clubs:* Garrick, Beefsteak, Groucho, MCC (Mem., Cttee, 1988–91).

TREMAIN, Rose, FRSL 1983; novelist and playright; *b* 2 Aug. 1943; *d* of Viola Mabel Thomson and late Keith Nicholas Home Thomson, MBE; *m* 1st, 1971, Jon Tremain (marr. diss.); one *d*; 2nd, 1982, Jonathan Dudley (marr. diss.). *Educ:* Sorbonne, Paris; Univ. of East Anglia (BA Hons Eng. Lit.). Part-time Lectr, UEA, 1988–94. Dylan Thomas Prize, 1984; Giles Cooper Award, Best Radio Play, 1984. *Publications: novels:* Sadler's Birthday, 1976; Letter to Sister Benedicta, 1978; The Cupboard, 1981; The Swimming Pool Season, 1984; Restoration, 1989 (Sunday Express Book of the Year Award; filmed, 1996); Sacred Country, 1992 (James Tait Black Meml Prize, 1993; Prix Femina Etranger (France), 1994); The Way I Found Her, 1997; Music and Silence (Whitbread Novel Award), 1999; *short stories:* The Colonel's Daughter, 1982; The Garden of the Villa Mollini, 1986; Evangelista's Fan, 1994; *for children:* Journey to the Volcano, 1985. *Recreations:* gardening, swimming, yoga. *Address:* 2 High House, South Avenue, Thorpe St Andrew, Norwich NR7 0EZ. *T:* (01603) 439682.

TREMAINE, Prof. Scott Duncan, PhD; FRS 1994; FRSC 1994; Professor and Chairman, Department of Astrophysical Sciences, Princeton University, since 1998; Director, Program in Cosmology and Gravity, Canadian Institute for Advanced Research, 1996–July 2002; *b* 25 May 1950; *s* of Vincent Joseph Tremaine and Beatrice Delphine (*née* Sharp). *Educ:* McMaster Univ. (BSc); Princeton Univ. (MA, PhD). Postdoctoral Fellow, CIT, 1975–77; Res. Associate, Inst. of Astronomy, Cambridge, 1977–78; Long-term Mem., Inst. for Advanced Study, Princeton, 1978–81; Associate Prof., MIT, 1981–85; University of Toronto: Prof. of Physics and Astronomy, 1985–97; Dir, Canadian Inst. for Theoretical Astrophysics, 1985–96. Foreign Hon. Mem., Amer. Acad. of Arts and Scis, 1992. *Publications:* (with J. J. Binney) Galactic Dynamics, 1987; papers in jls of physics and astronomy. *Address:* Princeton University Observatory, Peyton Hall, Princeton NJ 08544–1001, USA. *T:* (609) 258 3810.

TREMBLAY, Dr Marc-Adélard, OC 1980; GOQ 1995; Professor of Anthropology, Université Laval, Québec, 1956–94, now Emeritus; *b* Les Eboulements, Qué., 24 April 1922; *s* of Willie Tremblay and Lauretta (*née* Tremblay); *m* 1949, Jacqueline Cyr; one *s* five *d*. *Educ:* Montréal Univ. (AB, LSA (Agricl Sci.)); Laval (MA Sociol.); Cornell Univ. (PhD Anthropol.). Research Associate, Cornell Univ., 1953–56; Université Laval: Vice-Dean, Faculty Social Scis, 1969–71; Head, Anthropology Dept, 1970; Dean, Graduate Sch., 1971–79. Pres., RSC, 1982–85. Comr, Nunavik Commn, 1999–2000. Pres. Council, Order of Quebec, 1998–2000. Hon. LLD: Ottawa, 1982; Guelph, 1984; Univ. of Northern BC, 1994; Carleton Univ., 1995; Univ. Ste Anne, 1997; McGill, 1998. Innis-Gerin Medal, RSC, 1979; Centennial Medal, RSC, 1982; Molson Prize, Canada Council, 1987; Marcel Vincent Medal, French Canadian Assoc. for Advancement of Science, 1988; Internat. Order of Merit, Internat. Biog. Inst., 1990; Esdras Minville Prize in Soc. Scis, Soc. St Jean-Baptiste, 1991. *Publications:* The Acadians of Portsmouth, 1954; (jtly) People of Cove and Woodlot, 1960; (jtly) Les Comportements économiques de la famille salariée, 1964; Les Fondements Sociaux de la Maturation chez l'enfant, 1965; (jtly) Rural Canada in Transition, 1966; (jtly) A Survey of Contemporary Indians of Canada, 1967; Initiation à la recherche dans les sciences humaines, 1968; (jtly) Etude sur les Indiens contemporains du Canada, 1969; (jtly) Les Changements socio-culturels à Saint-Augustin, 1969; (jtly) Famille et parenté en Acadie, 1971; (jtly) Communautés et Culture, 1973 (Eng. trans. 1973); (jtly) Patterns of Amerindian Identity, 1976; (jtly) The Individual, Language and Society in Canada, 1977; L'Identité Québécoise en péril, 1983; (jtly) Conscience et Enquête, 1983; L'Anthropologie à l'Université Laval: fondements historiques, pratiques académiques, dynamismes d'évolution, 1989; Les fondements historiques et théoriques de la practique professionnelle en anthropologie, 1990; over one hundred and seventy-five scientific articles. *Recreations:* gardening, cross-country skiing. *Address:* 835 Nouvelle-Orléans, Sainte Foy, QC G1X 3J4, Canada. *T:* (418) 6535411.

TREMLETT, Ven. Anthony Frank; Archdeacon of Exeter, since 1994; *b* 25 Aug. 1937; *s* of Frank and Sally Tremlett; *m* 1958, Patricia Lapthorn; two *s* one *d*. *Educ:* Plymouth College. Clerk, Management Trainee (Traffic Apprentice), Area Manager, 1953–68, British Rail; Traffic Manager, District Manager, Operations Director, 1968–80, National Carriers (Nat. Freight Corporation). Asst Curate, Southway, Plymouth, 1981–82; Priest-in-Charge, 1982–84; Vicar, 1984–88; RD of Moorside, Plymouth, 1986–88; Archdeacon of Totnes, 1988–94. *Recreations:* music, home and family. *Address:* St Matthew's House, 45 Spicer Road, Exeter EX1 1TA. *T:* (01392) 425432, *Fax:* (01392) 425783.

TREMLETT, George William, OBE 1981; author, journalist and bookseller; Director, Corran Books Ltd, since 1981; Founder Chairman, George Tremlett Ltd, since 1965; *b* 5 Sept. 1939; *s* of late Wilfred George and of Elizabeth Tremlett; *m* 1971, Jane, *o c* of late Benjamin James Mitchell and Mrs P. A. Mitchell; three *s*. *Educ:* Taunton School; King Edward VI School, Stratford upon Avon. Member of Richmond upon Thames Borough Council, 1963–74; Chairman: Further Education Cttee, 1966–68; Barnes School Governors, 1967–73; Schools Cttee, 1972–73; Shene VIth Form Coll. Governors, 1973–74; Housing Cttee, 1972–74; Thames Water Authority, 1973–74. Greater London Council: Mem. for Hillingdon, 1970–73, for Twickenham, 1973–86; Opposition Housing Spokesman, 1974–77; Leader of Housing Policy Cttee, 1977–81. Consultant: Nat. Assoc. of Voluntary Hostels, 1980–84; Local Govt Inf. Unit, 1985–86; Appeal Dir, SHAC and Help the Homeless National Appeal, 1985–. Member: Housing Minister's Adv. Cttee on Co-operatives, 1977–79; Housing Consultative Council for England, 1977–81; Northampton Develt Corp., 1979–83; Stonham Housing Assoc., 1978–92; Chiswick Family Rescue Appeal Fund, 1979–80; Bd, Empty Property Unit, 1985–86; Adv. Panel, BBC Community Prog. Unit, 1985–. Founder Chm., Dylan Thomas Meml Trust, 1985–90. Governor, Kingston Polytechnic and Twickenham Coll. of Technology, 1967–70; Court of City Univ., 1968–74. *Publications:* 17 biographies of rock musicians, 1974–77—on John Lennon, David Bowie, 10cc, Paul McCartney, The Osmonds, Alvin Stardust, Cat Stevens, Cliff Richard, Slade, The Who, David Essex, Slik, Gary Glitter, Marc Bolan, Rod Stewart, Queen and the Rolling Stones (published in many different countries); Living Cities, 1979; (with Caitlin Thomas) Life with Dylan Thomas, 1986; Clubmen, 1987; Homeless but for St Mungo's, 1989; Little Legs, 1989; Rock Gold, 1990; Dylan Thomas: in the mercy of his means, 1991; Gadaffi: the desert mystic, 1993; David Bowie, 1995; (with James Nashold) The Death of Dylan Thomas, 1997. *Recreations:* ornithology, exploring old churches, local history, rock 'n' roll music. *Address:* Corran House, Laugharne, Carmarthenshire SA33 4SJ. *T:* (01994) 427444. *Clubs:* Carlton, Wig and Pen, United and Cecil; Laugharne RFC.

TRENAMAN, Nancy Kathleen, (Mrs M. S. Trenaman); Principal of St Anne's College, Oxford, 1966–84 (Hon. Fellow, since 1984); *b* 1919; *d* of Frederick Broughton Fisher and Edith Fisher; *m* 1967, M. S. Trenaman. *Educ:* Bradford Girls' Grammar School; Somerville College, Oxford (Hon. Fellow, 1977). Board of Trade, 1941–51; Assistant Secretary, Ministry of Materials, 1951–54; Counsellor, British Embassy, Washington, 1951–53; Board of Trade, 1954–66, Under-Sec. 1962–66. Mem., Commn on the Constitution, 1969–73. Chm., Exec. Cttee, LEPRA, 1992–95. *Address:* Flat 2, Fairlawn Flats, Fairlawn, Oxford OX2 8AP. *Club:* Oxford and Cambridge.

TRENCH, family name of **Baron Ashtown**.

TRENCH; *see* Le Poer Trench, family name of Earl of Clancarty.

TRENCH, John; Master of the Supreme Court, Queen's Bench Division, since 1986; *b* 15 Sept. 1932; *s* of late Prince Constantine Lobanow-Rostovsky and Princess Violette Lobanow-Rostovsky (*née* Le Poer Trench); *m* 1st, 1955, Roxane Bibica-Rosetti (marr. diss.); two *s* one *d*; 2nd 1980, Patricia Margaret Skitmore. *Educ:* Oundle; Christ's College, Cambridge (MA). Nat. Service, 1950–52; commissioned The Duke of Wellington's Regt. Called to the Bar, Lincoln's Inn, 1956, practised at the Bar, in London and on the Oxford Circuit, 1956–86. *Recreations:* painting, collecting antique handwriting equipment. *Address:* Royal Courts of Justice, Strand WC2A 2LL.

TRENCH, Sir Peter (Edward), Kt 1979; CBE 1964 (OBE (mil.) 1945); TD 1949; *b* 16 June 1918; *s* of James Knights Trench and Grace Sim; *m* 1940, Mary St Clair Morford; one *s* one *d*. *Educ:* privately; London Sch. of Economics, London Univ.; St John's Coll., Cambridge Univ. BSc (Econ.) Hons. Served in The Queen's Royal Regt, 1939–46: Staff Coll., 1942; AAG, HQ 21 Army Gp, 1944–45 (OBE). Man. Dir, Bovis Ltd, 1954–59; Director: Nat. Fedn of Bldg Trades Employers, 1959–64; Nat. Bldg Agency, 1964–66; Part-time Mem., Nat. Bd for Prices and Incomes, 1965–68. Chm., Y. J. Lovell (Holdings) plc, 1972–83; Director, 1970–83: LEP plc; Haden plc; Capital & Counties plc; Builder Gp plc; Crendon Ltd; Nationwide Building Soc. Vis. Prof. in Construction Management, Reading Univ., 1981–88. Chm., Construction and Housing Res. Adv. Council, 1973–79; Pres., Construction Health Safety Gp, 1974–80; Vice-President: NHBC, 1984– (Chm., 1978–84); Building Centre, 1976–; Member: Review of Housing Finance Adv. Gp, 1975–76; Council, CBI, 1981–83; Council, RSA, 1981–83. Mem. Court of Governors, LSE; Hon. Mem., Architectural Assoc.; Hon. Treasurer, St Mary's Hosp. Med. Sch. JP Inner London, 1963–71. Hon. FCIOB; Hon. FFB; FCIArb; FRSA; CIMgt; Hon. FRIBA; Hon. Mem. CGLI. Hon. DSc Reading, 1986. *Recreations:* tennis, swimming, travelling. *Address:* 4 Napier Close, Kensington, W14 8LX. *T:* (020) 7602 3936. *Club:* MCC.

TRENCHARD, family name of **Viscount Trenchard**.

TRENCHARD, 3rd Viscount *cr* 1936, of Wolfeton; **Hugh Trenchard;** Bt 1919; Baron 1930; Director, Robert Fleming International Ltd, 1998–2000; *b* 12 March 1951; *s* of 2nd Viscount Trenchard, MC and of Patricia, *d* of Admiral Sir Sidney Bailey, KBE, CB, DSO; *S* father, 1987; *m* 1975, Fiona Elizabeth Morrison, *d* of 2nd Baron Margadale, *qv*; two *s* two *d*. *Educ:* Eton; Trinity Coll., Cambridge (BA 1973). Captain, 4th Royal Green Jackets, TA, 1973–80. Entered Kleinwort Benson Ltd, 1973; Chief Rep. in Japan, 1980–85; Gen. Man., Kleinwort Benson Internat. Inc., Tokyo Br., 1985–88; Dir, Kleinwort Benson Ltd, 1986–96; Pres., 1988–95, Rep. in Japan, 1993–95, Dep. Chm., 1995–96, Kleinwort Benson Internat. Incorporated; Director: KB Berkeley Japan Development Capital Ltd, 1987–97; Dover Japan Inc., 1985–87; ACP Hldgs Ltd, 1990–94; Robert Fleming & Co. Ltd, 1996–98; London Pacific Gp Ltd, 1999–. Chm., Securities Cttee, 1993–95, Vice Chm. Council, 1995, European Business Community (Japan); Director: Japan Securities Dealers' Assoc., 1994–95; Bond Underwriters' Assoc. of Japan, 1994–95; Member: Japan Assoc. of Corporate Executives, 1987–95; Council, Japan Soc., 1992–93 and 1995– (Vice-Chm., 1996–2000; Jt Chm., 2000–). Vice-Chm., British-Japanese Parly Gp, 1997–99; Hon. Treas., H of L All-Party Defence Study Gp, 1992–93. Mem. Council, RAF Benevolent Fund, 1991–. *Heir: s* Hon. Alexander Thomas Trenchard, *b* 26 July 1978. *Address:* Standon Lordship, Ware, Herts SG11 1PR.

TREND, Hon. Michael (St John), CBE 1997; MP (C) Windsor, since 1997 (Windsor and Maidenhead, 1992–97); *b* 19 April 1952; *e s* of Baron Trend, PC, GCB, CVO and Patricia Charlotte, *o d* of Rev. Gilbert Shaw; *m* 1987, Jill Elizabeth Kershaw; one *s* two *d*. *Educ:* Tormore Sch., Upper Deal, Kent; Westminster; Oriel Coll., Oxford; Greek Govt Scholar. Toynbee Hall, 1975–76; Sub-Editor, then Managing Editor, TLS, 1976–81; Editor: History Today, 1981–82; Parliamentary House Magazine, 1984–87; Home Editor, Spectator, 1987–90; Chief Leader Writer, Daily Telegraph, 1990–92. PPS to Minister of State, DoH, 1993–94, to Sec. of State for Transport, 1994–95; Dep. Chm., Conservative Party, 1995–98; Opposition frontbench spokesman on European affairs, 1998–2001. Member: Select Cttee on Health, 1992–93; Speaker's Adv. Cttee on Works of Art, 1993–. Mem. Bd, Victoria County History, 1992–98. *Publication:* The Music Makers, 1985. *Recreations:* music, hill walking. *Address:* House of Commons, SW1A 0AA. *T:* (020) 7219 6929. *Club:* Athenæum.

TRENTHAM, Dr David Rostron, FRS 1982; Head of Physical Biochemistry Division, National Institute for Medical Research, Mill Hill, since 1984; *b* 22 Sept. 1938; *s* of John Austin and Julia Agnes Mary Trentham; *m* 1966, Kamalini; two *s*. *Educ:* Univ. of Cambridge (BA Chemistry, PhD Organic Chemistry). Biochemistry Dept, University of Bristol: Jun. Research Fellow (Medical Research Council), 1966–69; Research Associate, 1969–72; Lectr in Biochemistry, 1972–75; Reader in Biochemistry, 1975–77; Edwin M. Chance Prof., Biochemistry and Biophysics Dept, Univ. of Pennsylvania, 1977–84. Colworth Medal (an annual award), Biochemical Soc., UK, 1974; Wilhelm Feldberg Prize, Feldberg Foundn Bd for Anglo-German Scientific Exchange, 1990. *Publications:* numerous research papers in scientific jls. *Address:* Physical Biochemistry Division, National Institute for Medical Research, The Ridgeway, Mill Hill, NW7 1AA. *T:* (020) 8959 3666.

TREPTE, Paul, FRCO; Organist and Master of the Choristers, Ely Cathedral, since 1990; *b* 24 April 1954; *s* of Harry and Ruth Trepte; *m* 1981, Sally Lampard; one *d*. *Educ:* New College, Oxford (MA). Asst Organist, Worcester Cathedral, 1976; Dir of Music, St Mary's, Warwick, 1981; Organist and Master of the Choristers, St Edmundsbury Cathedral, 1985. *Publications:* choral works. *Address:* The Old Sacristy, The College, Ely CB7 4JU. *T:* (01353) 660336.

TRESCOWTHICK, Sir Donald (Henry), AC 1991; KBE 1979; Chairman, Signet Group Holdings Pty Ltd, since 1978; Executive Director, Australian Olympic Committee, since 1992; *b* 4 Dec. 1930; *s* of Thomas Patrick and Elsie May Trescowthick; *m* 1952, Norma Margaret Callaghan; two *s* two *d*. FCPA. Chairman: Charles Davis Ltd, later Harris Scarfe Holdings Ltd, 1972–98; Harris Scarfe, 1976–93. Founder Chm., Victorian Div., Aust. Olympic Team Fund; Emeritus Chm., Sport Australia Hall of Fame, 1996–99; Chairman: Minus Children's Fund, 1975–; Sir Donald and Lady Trescowthick Foundn; Inaugural Chm., 1972–88, Patron, 1972–, Melbourne to Hobart Yacht Race Cttee; Dir, Aust. Ballet Develt, 1978–93. Pres., Peter MacCallum Cancer Inst. Appeal, 1991–94; Patron: DOXA Youth Welfare Foundn; Special Olympics Australia, 1992–98; Team Equestrian Australia, 1993–. Olympic OM, 1981; CLJ 1982; Knight of Magistral Grace, SMO, Malta, 1984; KCSHS 1995. *Recreations:* golf, travel, reading. *Address:* PO Box 93, Toorak, Vic 3142, Australia. *T:* (3) 98266933. *Clubs:* Athenæum, Victoria Racing, Victorian Amateur Turf, Moonee Valley Racing (Melbourne); Geelong Football.

TRESS, Ronald Charles, CBE 1968; BSc (Econ.) London, DSc Bristol; Director, The Leverhulme Trust, 1977–84; *b* Upchurch, Sittingbourne, Kent, 11 Jan. 1915; *er s* of S. C. Tress; *m* 1942, Josephine Kelly (*d* 1993), *d* of H. J. Medland; one *s* two *d*. *Educ:* Gillingham (Kent) County School; Univ. College, Southampton. Gladstone Student, St Deiniol's Library, Hawarden, 1936–37; Drummond Fraser Research Fellow, Univ. of Manchester,

1937–38; Asst Lecturer in Economics, Univ. Coll. of the S West, Exeter, 1938–41; Economic Asst, War Cabinet Offices, 1941–45; Economic Adviser, Cabinet Secretariat, 1945–47; Reader in Public Finance, Univ. of London, 1947–51; Prof. of Political Economy, Univ. of Bristol, 1951–68; Master of Birkbeck Coll., 1968–77, Fellow, 1977–; Mem., Univ. of London Senate, 1968–77, and Court, 1976–77. Managing Editor, London and Cambridge Economic Service, 1949–51; Member: Reorganisation Commn for Pigs and Bacon, 1955–56; Nigeria Fiscal Commn, 1957–58; Departmental Cttee on Rating of Charities, 1958; Devel Commn, 1959–81; Financial Enquiry, Aden Colony, 1959; East Africa Economic and Fiscal Commn, 1960, Uganda Fiscal Commn, 1962; Kenya Fiscal Commn (Chm.), 1962–63; National Incomes Commn, 1963–65; Chm., SW Economic Planning Council, 1965–68; Mem., Cttee of Inquiry into Teachers' Pay, 1974; Chm., Cttee for Univ. Assistance to Adult Educn in HM Forces, 1974–79; Lay Mem., Solicitors' Disciplinary Tribunal, 1975–79; Chm., Lord Chancellor's Adv. Cttee on Legal Aid, 1979–84. Trustee, City Parochial Foundn, 1974–77, 1979–89; Governor, Christ Church Coll., Canterbury, 1975–91; Mem. Council, Kent Univ., 1977–92. Royal Economic Society: Council, 1960–70, Sec.-Gen., 1975–79, Vice-Pres., 1979–. Hon. LLD: Furman Univ., S Carolina, 1973; Exeter, 1976; DUniv Open Univ., 1974; Hon. DSc (SocSc) Southampton, 1978; Hon. DCL Kent, 1984. *Publications:* articles and reviews in Economic Journal, Economica, LCES Bulletin, etc. *Address:* The Red House, 29 Palace Road, East Molesey, Surrey KT8 9DJ. *T:* (020) 8979 0605.

TRETHEWEY, Ven. Frederick Martyn; Archdeacon of Dudley, since 2001; *b* 24 Jan. 1949; *s* of Kendall and Winifred Trethewey; *m* 1971, Margaret (*née* Davidson); one *s* three *d*. *Educ:* Bedford Coll., London Univ. (BA (Hons) English, 1970); Inst. of Educn, London Univ. (PGCE 1971); Oak Hill Theol Coll. (DipTh 1977). Ordained deacon, 1978, priest 1979; Curate: St Mark with St Anne, Tollington Park, London, 1978–82; St Andrew, Whitehall Park, London, 1982–87; Team Vicar, Hornsey Rise, Whitehall Park Team, 1987–88; Vicar, Brockmoor, W Midlands, 1988–2001; Chaplain, Dudley Gp of Hosps, 1988–2000; RD, Himley, 1996–2001. *Recreations:* sport, walking. *Address:* 15 Worcester Road, Droitwich, Worcs WR9 8AA. *T:* (01905) 773301.

TREUHERZ, Julian Benjamin; Keeper of Art Galleries, National Museums and Galleries on Merseyside (Walker Art Gallery, Lady Lever Art Gallery and Sudley), since 1989; *b* 12 March 1947; *s* of late Werner Treuherz and of Irmgard (*née* Amberg). *Educ:* Manchester Grammar Sch.; Christ Church, Oxford (MA); Univ. of East Anglia (MA). Dip. Museums Assoc. 1974. Manchester City Art Gallery: Trainee, 1971; Asst Keeper, 1972–74, Keeper, 1974–89, of Fine Art. Member: Victorian Soc. (Hon. Sec., Manchester Gp, 1972–79, Chm., 1980–83); Cttee, Whitworth Art Gall., 1993–; Cttee, Lakeland Arts (formerly Lake District Art Gall. and Mus.) Trust, 1997–; Cttee, Liverpool Biennial Trust, 1999–. *Publications:* Pre-Raphaelite Paintings from the Manchester City Art Gallery, 1981; Hard Times: social realism in Victorian art, 1987; (with Peter de Figueiredo) Country Houses of Cheshire, 1988; Victorian Painting, 1993; articles in art-historical jls. *Recreations:* playing the piano, cooking, opera. *Address:* Walker Art Gallery, William Brown Street, Liverpool L3 8EL.

TREVELYAN, (Adye) Mary; *see* Fedden, A. M.

TREVELYAN, Dennis John, CB 1981; MA; FCIPD; Principal, Mansfield College, Oxford, 1989–96, Hon. Fellow, 1997; *b* 21 July 1929; *s* of John Henry Trevelyan; *m* 1959, Carol Coombes; one *s* one *d*. *Educ:* Enfield Grammar Sch.; University Coll., Oxford (Scholar). Entered Home Office, 1950; Treasury, 1953–54; Sec. to Parly Under-Sec. of State, Home Office, 1954–55; Principal Private Sec. to Lord President of Council and Leader of House, 1964–67; Asst Sec., 1966; Asst Under-Sec. of State, NI Office, 1972–76; Home Office: Asst Under-Sec. of State, Broadcasting Dept, 1976–77; Dep. Under-Sec. of State and Dir-Gen., Prison Service, 1978–83; First CS Comr and Dep. Sec., Cabinet Office, 1983–89, retd. Secretary: Peppiatt Cttee on a Levy on Betting on Horse Races, 1960; Lord Radcliffe's Cttee of Privy Counsellors to inquire into D Notice Matters, 1967. Vice-Chm., CS Sports Council, 1980–; Vice-Pres., Industrial Participation Assoc., 1987–; Member: Bd of Management, Eur. Inst. of Public Admin, Maastricht, 1984–89; Council, City Univ. Business Sch., 1986–89; ECCTIS Adv. Group, 1990–98; Governor: Ashridge Management Coll., 1985–89; Contemporary Dance Trust, 1986–89; Oxford Centre for Hebrew and Jewish (formerly for Postgraduate Hebrew) Studies, 1992–; Trustee, Dancers Resettlement Fund, 1987–91. FRSA 1986. *Recreation:* music. *Address:* Lindfield, 1 Begbroke Lane, Begbroke, Oxon OX5 1RN. *Clubs:* Athenæum, MCC; Vincent's (Oxford).

TREVELYAN, Edward Norman; Survey Statistician, Governments Division, US Bureau of the Census, since 1999; *b* 14 Aug. 1955; *er s* of Norman Irving Trevelyan, and of Jennifer Mary Trevelyan, *d* of Arthur E. Riddett; *m* 1993, Debbie Mullin-Trevelyan; one *s* one *d*. *Educ:* Univ. of Calif, San Diego (BA History 1981); Univ. of Calif, Santa Barbara (MA Political Sci. 1986; PhD Political Sci. 1998). *Recreation:* yachting (Gold Medal, Soling Class, Olympic Games, 1984). *Address:* 416 Bay City Road, Stevensville, MD 21666, USA. *T:* (410) 6433164; *e-mail:* edward.norman.trevelyan@census.gov.

TREVELYAN, Sir Geoffrey (Washington), 5th Bt *cr* 1874, of Wallington, Northumberland; *b* 4 July 1920; *s* of Rt Hon. Sir Charles Philips Trevelyan, 3rd Bt, PC and Mary Katharine Trevelyan (*d* 1966); *S* brother, 1996; found in 1999 to be rightful claimant to Trevelyan Baronetcy of Nettlecombe, Somerset, *cr* 1662, in abeyance since 1976, but chose not to prove claim nor be entered on the Official Role of the Baronetage as 11th Bt; *m* 1947, Gillian Isabel Wood (MBE 1999) (*d* 2000); one *s* one *d*. *Educ:* Oundle; Trinity Coll., Cambridge (MA). De Havilland Aircraft Co. Ltd, 1941–61; Dir, Chatto and Windus Ltd, 1962–77; Manager, Seatoller House, Keswick, 1978–81; Chm., The Lake Hunts Ltd, 1979–96; freelance technical writer, 1982–92. *Recreations:* hill-walking, gardening, cabinet-making. *Heir:* *s* Peter John Trevelyan [*b* 11 Sept. 1948; *m* 1996, Diane Terry; one *s*]. *Address:* Silkstead, 3 Abbey Mill End, St Albans, Herts AL3 4HN. *T:* (01727) 864866.

TREVELYAN, George Macaulay; Director of Operations, Foot and Mouth Disease, Department for Environment, Food and Rural Affairs (formerly Ministry of Agriculture, Fisheries and Food), since 2001; *b* 1 April 1944; *s* of (Charles) Humphry Trevelyan and Molly Trevelyan (*née* Bennett); *m* 1st, 1966, Susan Pearson; one *s* two *d*; 2nd, 1980, Valerie Preston; one *s*. *Educ:* Queen's Coll., Oxford (BA Mod. Hist.). Joined MAFF, 1967: Principal, 1971; UK spokesman on numerous agricl mgt cttees under Common Agricl Policy, 1973–81; Mem. of Cabinet, EC Commn for Social Affairs, Brussels, 1981–84; Head, Pesticides Safety, Plant Health, and Cereals/Set Aside Divs, 1984–95; Regl Dir (SE), 1989–91; Chief Exec., Intervention Bd, 1995–2001. Councillor (Lab), London Borough of Camden, 1971–74 (Alderman; Chm., Planning and Communications, 1975–76). *Recreations:* nautical, pedestrian. *Address:* 6 Walton Avenue, Henley on Thames, Oxon RG9 1LA. *T:* (01491) 575245.

TREVELYAN OMAN, Julia; *see* Oman.

TREVES, Vanni Emanuele; Partner, Macfarlanes, Solicitors, since 1970 (Senior Partner, 1987–99); Chairman: Channel 4 Television, since 1998; Equitable Life Assurance Society, since 2001; *b* 3 Nov. 1940; *s* of Giuliano Treves (killed in action, 1944), and of Marianna Treves (*née* Baer); *m* 1971, Angela Veronica Fyffe; two *s* one *d*. *Educ:* St Paul's Sch. (Foundn Scholar); University Coll. Oxford (MA); Univ. of Illinois (LLM; Fulbright Scholar). Articled clerk and Solicitor, Macfarlanes, 1963–68; Vis. Attorney, White & Case, New York, 1968–69. Director: Oceonics Group, 1984–96; Saatchi & Saatchi, 1987–90; Chairman: BBA Gp plc, 1989–2000; McKechnie plc, 1991–2000; Fledgeling Equity and Bond Funds, 1992–2000; Dennis Gp (formerly Trinity Holdings) PLC, 1996–99; Dir, Amplifon SpA, 2000–. Solicitor to Royal Acad., 1992–. Chairman: Devel Cttee, Nat. Portrait Gall., 1991–99; Governors, London Business Sch., 1998– (Gov., 1996–); Mem., Devel Bd, NACF, 1998–. Chm., NSPCC Justice for Children Appeal, 1997–2000. Trustee: J. Paul Getty Jr Charitable Trust, 1985–; 29th May 1961 Charitable Trust, 1970–. Vice-Pres., London Fedn of Clubs for Young People (formerly of Boys' Clubs), 1991– (Hon. Treas., 1976–95). Gov., Sadler's Wells Foundn, 1999–. Governor: Coll. of Law, 1999–; Hall Sch., Hampstead, 1983–94. *Recreation:* epicurean pursuits. *Address:* 10 Norwich Street, EC4A 1BD. *T:* (020) 7831 9222. *Clubs:* Boodle's, City of London.

TREVETHIN, 4th Baron **AND OAKSEY,** 2nd Baron; *see under* Oaksey, 2nd Baron.

TREVETT, Peter George; QC 1992; *b* 25 Nov. 1947; *s* of late George Albert Trevett and Janet Trevett; *m* 1972, Vera Lucia dos Santos Ferreira; two *s* one *d*. *Educ:* Kingston Grammar Sch.; Queens' Coll., Cambridge (MA, LLM). Called to the Bar, Lincoln's Inn, 1971 (Mansfield Schol.), Bencher, 2000; in practice at Revenue Bar, 1973–. *Publications:* contribs to legal pubns. *Recreations:* golf, reading, collecting succulent plants, gardening. *Address:* 11 New Square, Lincoln's Inn, WC2A 3QB. *T:* (020) 7242 4017. *Club:* Woking Golf.

TREVIS, Diane Ellen; theatre director; *b* 8 Nov. 1947; *d* of late Joseph Trevis and of Marjorie Trevis; *m* 1986, Dominic John Muldowney, *qv*; one *d*. *Educ:* Waverley Grammar Sch., Birmingham; Sussex Univ. Actress and dir, Glasgow Citizens' Theatre, 1972–80; Arts Council Associate Dir, Palace Theatre, Westcliff, 1982; Director: Royal Shakespeare Company: Taming of the Shrew, Happy End, 1985–86; The Revenger's Tragedy, 1987; Much Ado About Nothing, 1988; Elgar's Rondo, 1993; Royal National Theatre: Irish-Hebrew Lesson, 1981; The Mother, Yerma, School for Wives, A Matter of Life and Death, 1985–86; The Resistible Rise of Arturo Ui, 1991; Inadmissible Evidence, 1993; Happy Birthday Brecht, 1998; Remembrance of Things Past (adapted with Harold Pinter), 2000; Gawain, Royal Opera House, 1991; The Daughter in Law, 1996, The House of Bernarda Alba, 1997, Theatr Clwyd; Human Cannon, Ballad of California, 1997, Awake and Sing, Happy Birthday Brecht, 1998, Univ. of California; Masterclass, Th. Royal, Bath, 1999; Death of a Salesman, Birmingham Rep., 2000; The Voluptuous Tango, Pirate Jenny, Almeida Fest., 2000. *Recreations:* Morocco, movies, mountain walks. *Address:* c/o Royal National Theatre, South Bank, SE1 9PX.

TREVOR, 5th Baron *cr* 1880, of Brynkinalt, co. Denbigh; **Marke Charles Hill-Trevor;** *b* 8 Jan. 1970; *s* of 4th Baron Trevor and of Susan Janet Elizabeth, *o d* of Dr Ronald Bence; *S* father, 1997. *Educ:* Rannoch Sch., Perthshire. *Heir:* *b* Hon. Iain Robert Hill-Trevor [*b* 12 June 1971; *m* 1998, Kate, *yr d* of David Lord; one *d*]. *Address:* Bryn Kinalt, Chirk, Clwyd LL14 5NS. *T:* (01691) 773510.

TREVOR, Brig. Kenneth Rowland Swetenham, CBE 1964 (OBE 1952); DSO 1945; Brigadier (retired 1966); *b* 15 April 1914; 2nd *s* of late Mr and Mrs E. S. R. Trevor, formerly of The Acres, Upton Heath, Chester; *m* 1st, 1941, Margaret Baynham (*d* 1988), *er d* of late Rev. J. H. Baynham, ACG; two *s*; 2nd, 1989, Jeanne Alexander (*née* Holmes Henderson). *Educ:* Oriel House, St Asaph; Rossall; RMC, Camberley. Joined 22nd (Cheshire) Regt, 1934; served in India and with RWAFF in Nigeria. War of 1939–45 (despatches and DSO): No. 1 Commando, N Africa and Burma, 1941–45, as CO, 1943–45; Staff College, Camberley, 1945–46; Bde Major, 29 Infantry Brigade Group, 1949–51; served Korea, 1950–51 (despatches, OBE); GSO1, RMA Sandhurst, 1954–56; Commanded 1st Bn Cheshire Regt, 1956–58; Malaya, 1957–58 (despatches); Deputy Commander, 50 Infantry Brigade Group/Central Area, Cyprus, 1959; Brigade Col Mercian Brigade, 1960–61; Commander, 2 Infantry Brigade Group and Devon/Cornwall Sub District, 1961–64; Commander, British Guiana Garrison, 1963; Inspector of Boys' Training (Army), 1964–66. With Runcorn Devel Corp., 1966–78. Vice-Pres., The Commando Assoc., 1964– (Pres., 1965–66, 1985–86, 1989–90). Pres., Norton Priory Museum Trust, Runcorn, 1994–2000. *Address:* Barrelwell Hill, Chester CH3 5BR. *Club:* Army and Navy.

TREVOR, William, (William Trevor Cox), CBE (Hon.) 1977; CLit 1994; writer; *b* 24 May 1928; *er s* of J. W. Cox; *m* 1952, Jane, *yr d* of C. N. Ryan; two *s*. *Educ:* St Columba's College, Co. Dublin; Trinity College, Dublin. Mem., Irish Acad. Letters. Television plays include: The Mark-2 Wife; O Fat White Woman; The Grass Widows; The General's Day; Love Affair; Last Wishes; Matilda's England; Secret Orchards; Autumn Sunshine. Radio plays include: The Penthouse Apartment; Beyond the Pale (Giles Cooper award, 1980); Travellers; Autumn Sunshine (Giles Cooper award, 1982); Events at Drimaghleen. Hon. DLitt: Exeter, 1984; TCD, 1986; Cork, 1990; Hon. DLit Belfast, 1989. Allied Irish Banks Award for Literature, 1976; Bennett Award, Hudson Review, USA, 1990; David Cohen British Literature Prize, 1999. *Publications:* A Standard of Behaviour, 1956; The Old Boys, 1964 (Hawthornden Prize; as play, produced Mermaid, 1971); The Boarding-House, 1965; The Love Department, 1966; The Day We Got Drunk on Cake, 1967; Mrs Eckdorf in O'Neill's Hotel, 1969; Miss Gomez and the Brethren, 1971; The Ballroom of Romance, 1972 (adapted for BBC TV, 1982); Going Home (play), 1972; A Night with Mrs da Tanka (play), 1972; Marriages (play), 1973; Elizabeth Alone, 1973; Angels at the Ritz, 1975 (RSL award); The Children of Dynmouth, 1976 (Whitbread Novel Award; televised, 1987); Lovers of Their Time, 1978; Other People's Worlds, 1980; Beyond the Pale, 1981 (televised, 1989); Scenes from an Album (play), 1981; Fools of Fortune, 1983 (Whitbread Novel Award); A Writer's Ireland, 1984; The News from Ireland and other stories, 1986; Nights at the Alexandra, 1987; The Silence in the Garden, 1988; (ed) The Oxford Book of Irish Short Stories, 1989; Family Sins and other stories, 1989; Two Lives, 1991; Juliet's Story (for children), 1992; Excursions in the Real World, 1993; Felicia's Journey, 1994 (Whitbread Book of the Year Award; Sunday Express Book of the Year Award; filmed 1999); After Rain and other stories, 1996; Death in Summer, 1998; The Hill Bachelors, 2000.

TREVOR COX, Major Horace Brimson; *b* 1908; *o s* of late C. Horace Cox, Roche Old Court, Winterslow, Wilts and formerly of Whitby Hall, nr Chester; *m* 1957, Gwenda Mary, *d* of Alfred Ellis, Woodford, Essex; one *d*. *Educ:* Eton (played football for Eton Field and Wall game, 1926 and 1927, boxed for Eton, 1925, 1926, 1927); Germany and USA. Major late Welsh Guards (SR); served in France with BEF, 1939–40, and on General Staff, 1940–44; Major AA Comd. HQ, 1944–46, RARO, 1946–61. Studied commercial and political conditions in Germany, 1927–29, in America and Canada, 1929–30, and in Near East (Egypt and Palestine), 1934; contested (C) NE Derbyshire, 1935, Stalybridge and Hyde, 1937; MP (C) County of Chester, Stalybridge and Hyde, 1937–45; Parliamentary

Private Secretary to: Rt Hon. Sir Ronald Cross when Under-Secretary Board of Trade, 1938–39, and when Minister of Economic Warfare, 1939–40; Minister of Health Rt Hon. H. U. Willink, 1945. Hon. Treasr, Russian Relief Assoc., 1945–47. Contested (C) Stalybridge and Hyde, 1945, Birkenhead, 1950; Parly Candidate (C) for Romford and Brentwood, Essex, 1953–55; contested (Ind) Salisbury by-election, 1965; later joined Labour Party; contested (Lab): RDC, Wilts, 1970; Wilts CC, 1973. Member of Exec. County Committee, British Legion, Wilts, 1946–62; Chairman: Salisbury and S Wilts Branch, English-Speaking Union, 1957–63; Salisbury Road Safety Cttee, 1985 (Mem., 1977–85); Mem. Exec. Cttee, CLA, for Wilts, Hants, IoW and Berks. RBL Wilts Co. Award, for 50 yrs service, 2000. Farmer and landowner. Lord of Manor of East Winterslow. *Address:* Roche Old Court, Winterslow, Wilts SP5 1BG. *Club:* Brooks's.

TREVOR-ROPER, family name of **Baron Dacre of Glanton**.

TREVOR-ROPER, Patrick Dacre, MA, MD, BChir Cantab; FRCS, DOMS England; Hon. FCOphth; FZS; FRGS; Consultant Ophthalmic Surgeon: Westminster Hospital, 1947–82; Moorfields Eye Hospital, 1961–81; King Edward VII Hospital for Officers, 1964–86; Teacher of Ophthalmology, University of London, 1953–82; *b* 1916; *yr s* of Dr B. W. E. Trevor-Roper, Alnwick, Northumberland; unmarried. *Educ:* Charterhouse (senior classical schol.); Clare Coll., Cambridge (exhibitioner); Westminster Hospital Medical Sch. (scholar). Served as Captain, NZ Medical Corps, 1943–46, in Central Mediterranean Forces. Held resident appointments, Westminster Hospital and Moorfields Eye Hospital. Vice-Pres., Ophthalmol Soc. of UK; Chm., Ophth. Qualifications Cttee, 1974–; Founder Mem., Internat. Acad. of Ophthalmology, 1976; FRSocMed (Pres., Ophthalmol Sect., June 1978–80). Formerly: Examnr for Diploma of Ophthalmology, RCS; Mem., Ophth. Group Cttee, BMA; Mem., London Med. Cttee. Hon. Member: Brazilian Society of Ophthalmology, 1958; Ophthalmological Soc. of NZ, 1975; Hon. dipl., Peruvian and Columbian Societies of Otolaryngology and Ophthalmology, 1958; President, etc., of various clubs in connection with sports, music and drama, both hospital and county. Freeman, City of London; Liveryman, Soc. of Spectaclemakers. Doyne medal, 1980; (first) de Lancey medal, RSocMed; Lettsomian Medal, Med. Soc. of London, 1994. Editor, Trans Ophthalmol Soc., UK, 1949–88; Member Editorial Board: Modern Medicine, 1975–; Annals of Ophth., 1972–86; The Broadway, 1946–83. *Publications:* (ed) Music at Court (Four 18th century studies by A. Yorke-Long), 1954; Ophthalmology, a Textbook for Diploma Students, 1955, new edn 1962; Lecture-notes in Ophthalmology, 1960, 7th edn 1986 (trans. French, Spanish, Portuguese, Polish, Malay); (ed) International Ophthalmology Clinics VIII, 1962; The World Through Blunted Sight: an inquiry into the effects of disordered vision on character and art, 1971, 3rd edn 1990; The Eye and Its Disorders, 1973, new edn 1984; (ed) Recent Advances in Ophthalmology, 1975; (ed) The Bowman Lectures, 1980; (ed) Procs 6th Congress of European Ophth. Soc., 1980; Ophthalmology (pocket consultant series), 1981, 2nd edn 1985; miscellaneous articles in medical and other journals. *Recreations:* music, travel. *Address:* Flat 3, Fitzrovia Apartments, 365 Euston Road, NW1 3AR. *T:* (020) 7387 9670; Long Crichel House, near Wimborne, Dorset BH21 5JU. *Clubs:* Athenæum, Beefsteak.

See also Baron Dacre of Glanton.

TREW, Francis Sidney Edward, CMG 1984; HM Diplomatic Service, retired; Ambassador to Bahrain, 1984–88; *b* 22 Feb. 1931; *s* of Harry Francis and Alice Mary Trew; *m* 1958, Marlene Laurette Regnery; three *d*. *Educ:* Taunton's Sch., Southampton. Served Army, 1949–51; 2nd Lieut, Royal Hampshire Regt. FO, 1951; Lebanon, 1952; Amman, 1953; Bahrain, 1953–54; Jedda, 1954–56; Vice-Consul, Philadelphia, 1956–59; Second Sec., Kuwait, 1959–62; FO, 1962; seconded as Sec., European Conf. on Satellite Communications, 1963–65; Consul, Guatemala City, 1965–70; First Sec., Mexico City, 1971–74; FCO, 1974–77; Consul, Algeciras, 1977–79; FCO, 1980–81; High Comr at Belmopan, Belize, 1981–84. Mem. Bd, Devon Community Housing Soc., 1994–. Order of Aztec Eagle (Mexico), 1975. *Recreations:* carpentry, fishing. *Address:* The Orchard, Higher Trickeys, Morebath, Devon EX16 9AL.

TREW, Peter John Edward, FCIS, FCT, FCIArb, MICE; Director, Rush & Tompkins Group plc, 1973–90 (Chairman of Executive Committee, 1986–87); *b* 30 April 1932; *s* of late Antony Trew, DSC; *m* 1st, 1955, Angela (marr. diss. 1985; she *d* 1991), *d* of Kenneth Rush, CBE; two *s* one *d*; 2nd, 1985, Joan, *d* of Allan Haworth. *Educ:* Diocesan Coll., Rondebosch, Cape. Royal Navy, 1950–54; served HMS Devonshire, Unicorn and Charity. Chartered Inst. of Secretaries Sir Ernest Clarke Prize, 1955. Contested (C) Dartford, 1966; MP (C) Dartford, 1970–Feb. 1974; Jt Sec., Cons. Parly Finance Cttee, 1972–74; Mem., Select Cttee on Tax Credits, 1972–73. Chm., Kent West Cons. European Constituency Council, 1978–80. Mem. Council, CBI, 1975–83 (Mem., Econ. and Fin. Policy Cttee, 1980–86). Foundn FCT, 1979; FCIArb 1989. *Publication:* The Boer War Generals, 1999. *Address:* 1 Painshill House, Cobham, Surrey KT11 1DL. *T:* (01932) 863315.

TREWAVAS, Prof. Anthony James, PhD; FRS 1999; FRSE; Professor of Plant Biochemistry, Edinburgh University, since 1990; *b* 17 June 1939; *s* of Clifford John Trewavas and Phyllis (*née* Timms); *m* 1963, Valerie Leng; one *s* two *d*. *Educ:* Roan Grammar Sch.; University Coll. London (BSc 1961; PhD 1964). Sen. Res. Fellow, Univ. of East Anglia, 1964–70; University of Edinburgh: Lectr, 1970–84; Reader, 1984–90. Visiting Professor: Michigan State Univ., 1973; Univ. of Illinois, 1980; Univ. of Alberta, 1983; Univ. of Calif, Davis, 1985; Univ. of Mexico City, 1987; Univ. of Bonn, 1989; Univ. of Milan, 1996. FRSE 1993; FRSA 1995. *Publications:* Molecular and Cellular Aspects of Calcium in Plant Development, 1985; (with David Jennings) Plasticity in Plants, 1986; 180 res. papers. *Recreations:* music, reading, thinking, good wine. *Address:* Old Schoolhouse, Croft Street, Penicuik, Midlothian EH26 9DH. *T:* (01968) 673372.

TRIBE, Geoffrey Reuben, OBE 1968; Controller, Higher Education Division, British Council, 1981–83, retired; *b* 20 Feb. 1924; *s* of late Harry and Olive Tribe; *m* 1st, 1946, Sheila Mackenzie (marr. diss. 1977); 2nd, 1978, Malvina Anne Butt. *Educ:* Southern Grammar Sch., Portsmouth; University Coll. London (BA). Served War, Royal Hampshire Regt (Lieut), 1942–45. Teaching, 1948–58. Appointed to British Council, 1958; Asst Regional Rep., Madras, 1958–63; Regional Dir, Mwanza, 1963–65; Regional Rep., E Nigeria, 1965–67; Asst Controller, Personnel and Staff Recruitment, 1968–73; Controller, Arts Div., 1973–79; Representative, Nigeria, 1979–81. *Recreations:* walking, writing. *Address:* Holly Cottage, St Andrews View, Fontmell Magna, Shaftesbury, Dorset SP7 0QY. *T:* (01747) 812036.

TRIBE, Rear-Admiral Raymond Haydn, CB 1964; MBE 1944; DL; *b* 9 April 1908; *s* of Thomas and Gillian Ada Tribe; *m* 1938, Alice Mary (*née* Golby); no *c*. Served War of 1939–45 (MBE, despatches twice). Commander, 1947; Captain, 1955; Rear-Admiral, 1962. Inspector-General, Fleet Maintenance, and Chief Staff Officer (Technical) to C-in-C Home Fleet, 1962–65; retired from Royal Navy, Sept. 1965. Distinguished Battle Service Medal of Soviet Union, 1943. CC Berks, 1970–77. DL Berks, 1975. *Recreations:* gardening, painting.

TRICHET, Jean-Claude Anne Marie Louis; Governor, Bank of France, since 1993; *b* 20 Dec. 1942; *s* of Jean Trichet and Georgette (*née* Vincent-Carrefour); *m* 1965, Aline Rybalka; two *s*. *Educ:* Ecole Nat. des Mines, Nancy; Inst. d'Etudes Politiques, Paris; Ecole Nat. d'Admin. Inspector of Finances, 1971–76; Sec.-Gen., Business Restructuring Interministerial Cttee, 1976–78; Advisor: Ministry of Finance, 1978; President's Secretariat, 1978–81; Dep. Asst Sec., later Asst Sec., Treasury, 1981–86; Chief of Staff to Minister of Finance, 1986–87; Under-Sec., Treasury, 1987–93. Member, Board of Directors: BIS, 1993–; Eur. Central Bank (formerly Eur. Monetary Inst.), 1994–; Gov., IBRD, 1993–. Chevalier, Légion d'honneur (France); Officier, Ordre National du Mérite (France); many foreign decorations. *Address:* Banque de France, 39 rue Croix des Petits Champs, 75001 Paris, France; 5 rue de Beaujolais, 75001 Paris, France.

TRICKER, Prof. Robert Ian, DLitt; FCA; FCMA; Hon. Professor, University of Hong Kong, since 1996; Director, International Corporate Policy Group (formerly Corporate Policy Group, Oxford), since 1979; *b* 14 Dec. 1933; *m* 1st, 1958, Doreen Murray (marr. diss. 1982); two *d*; 2nd, 1982, Gretchen Elizabeth Bigelow. *Educ:* King Henry VIII Sch., Coventry; Harvard Business Sch., USA. MA, JDipMA; DLitt CNAA, 1983. Articled Clerk, Daffern & Co., 1950–55; Sub-Lt, RNVR, 1956–58; Controller, Unbrako Ltd, 1959–64; Directing Staff, Iron & Steel Fedn Management Coll., 1965; Barclays Bank Prof. of Management Information Systems, Univ. of Warwick, 1968–70; Director, Oxford Centre for Management Studies, 1970–79, Professorial Fellow, 1979–84 (P. D. Leake Res. Fellow, 1966–67); Res. Fellow, Nuffield Coll., Oxford, 1979–84 (Vis. Fellow, 1971–79); Dir, Management Develt Centre of Hong Kong, 1984–86; Prof. of Finance and Accounting, Univ. of Hong Kong, 1986–96. Hon. Prof., Warwick Univ., 1996–2000; Hon. Res. Fellow, Exeter Univ., 1996–2000. Institute of Chartered Accountants in England and Wales: Mem. Council, 1979–84; Mem. Educn and Trng Directorate, 1979–82; Chairman: Examination Cttee, 1980–82; Tech. and Res. Cttee, 1982–84. Member: Council, ICMA, 1969–72; Management and Industrial Relations Cttee, SSRC, 1973–75; Chm., Independent Inquiry into Prescription Pricing Authority for Minister for Health, 1976. Member: Nuffield Hosp. Management Cttee, 1972–74; Adv. Panel on Company Law, Dept of Trade, 1980–83; Company Affairs Cttee, Inst. of Directors, 1980–84; Standing Commn on CS Salaries and Conditions of Service, Hong Kong, 1989–96. Editor, Corporate Governance—an international review, 1992–2000. *Publications:* The Accountant in Management, 1967; Strategy for Accounting Research, 1975; Management Information and Control Systems, 1976, 2nd edn 1982; The Independent Director, 1978; Effective Information Management, 1982; Governing the Institute, 1983; Corporate Governance, 1984; The Effective Director, 1986; The Director's Manual, 1990; International Corporate Governance, 1993; Harnessing Information Power, 1994; The Economist Pocket Director, 1996, 3rd edn 1999; Corporate Governance, 2000. *Address:* The Hill House, 22/23 St Peter's Hill, Brixham, Devon TQ5 9TE; *e-mail:* BobTricker@aol.com.

TRICKETT, Jon Hedley; MP (Lab) Hemsworth, since Feb. 1996; *b* 2 July 1950; *s* of Lawrence and Rose Trickett; *m* 1969 (marr. diss.); one *s* one *d*; *m* 1994, Sarah Balfour. *Educ:* Hull Univ. (BA Politics); Leeds Univ. (MA Pol Sociol). Builder/plumber, to 1985. Joined Labour Party, 1971; Leeds City Council: Councillor, Beeston Ward, 1985–96; Chair: Finance Cttee, 1986–89; Housing Cttee, 1988–89; Leader, 1989–96. Chm., Leeds City Development Co., 1989–96; Member of Board: Leeds Development Corp., 1992–96; Leeds Health Care, 1992–96; Director: Leeds/Bradford Airport, 1988–96; Leeds Playhouse, 1988–96; Leeds Theatre Co., 1988–96. PPS to Minister Without Portfolio, 1997–98; to Sec. of State for Trade and Industry, 1998. Mem., Public Accounts Select Cttee, 2001–. Mem., GMBATU. *Recreations:* cycling, sail-boarding. *Address:* 18 Market Street, Hemsworth, West Yorkshire WF9 4LB. *T:* (01977) 722290; House of Commons, SW1A 0AA. *Clubs:* Cyclists Touring; West Yorkshire Sailing.

TRICKEY, Edward Lorden, FRCS; Dean, Institute of Orthopaedics, London University, 1981–87, retired; Consultant Orthopaedic Surgeon, Royal National Orthopaedic Hospital, London, and Edgware General Hospital, 1960–85, retired; *b* 22 July 1920; *s* of E. G. W. Trickey and M. C. Trickey; *m* 1944, Ivy Doreen Harold; two *s* one *d*. *Educ:* Dulwich College; King's College, London Univ. (MB BS). Consultant Orthopaedic Surgeon, Ashton under Lyne, 1957–60. *Publications:* various articles on orthopaedic trauma and knee joint surgery. *Recreations:* cricket, bridge. *Address:* 43 Beverley Gardens, Stanmore, Mddx HA7 2AP. *T:* (020) 8863 6964. *Clubs:* MCC, Middlesex CC.

TRICKEY, Very Rev. (Frederick) Marc; Dean of Guernsey, since 1995; Rector of St Martin de la Bellouse, Guernsey, 1977–Aug. 2002; Priest-in-charge of Sark, since 1996; *b* 16 Aug. 1935; *s* of Alan Paul Trickey and Isabella Livingston (*née* Gunn); *m* 1963, Elisabeth Marriette Plummer; one *s* one *d*. *Educ:* Bristol Grammar Sch.; St John's Coll., Univ. of Durham (BA (Hons) Psychol. 1962; DipTh 1964). Commercial trainee, Nat. Smelting Co. Ltd, Avonmouth, Bristol, 1954–59. Ordained deacon, 1964, priest, 1965; Asst Curate, St Lawrence, Alton, Hants, 1964–68; Rector of St John with Winnall, Winchester, 1968–77. Mem., General Synod of C of E, 1995–2000. Hon. Canon of Winchester Cathedral, 1995–. Pres., States of Guernsey Ecclesiastical Cttee, 1995–. Chm., Panel of Appeal, States Public Assistance Authy, 1985–96; Mem., Broadcasting Cttee, 1977–, Bd of Industry, 1982–95, States of Guernsey. *Publication:* Your Marriage, 1987. *Recreations:* singing, embroidery, walking, photography. *Address:* (until Aug. 2002) St Martin's Rectory, Guernsey, Channel Islands GY4 6RR. *T:* (01481) 238303, *Fax:* (01481) 237710; (from Aug. 2002) L'Espérance, La Route des Camps, St Martin's, Guernsey GY4 6AD. *T:* (01481) 238441.

TRICKEY, Jane Elizabeth; *see* Hutt, J. E.

TRIER, Peter Eugene, CBE 1980; FREng, FIEE; FInstP, FIMA; Pro-Chancellor, Brunel University, 1980–99; Director of Research and Development, Philips Electronics UK, 1969–81, retired; *b* Darmstadt, 12 Sept. 1919; *s* of Ernst and Nellie Trier; *m* 1st, 1946, Margaret Nora Holloway (*d* 1998); three *s*; 2nd, 2000, Teresa Watson (*née* Keogh). *Educ:* Mill Hill Sch.; Trinity Hall, Cambridge (Wrangler 1941; MA); MSc Open 1997. Royal Naval Scientific Service, 1941–50; Mullard Research Labs, 1950–69, Dir, 1953–69. Dir, Mullard Ltd and other Philips subsidiaries, 1957–85; Main Bd Dir, Philips Electronics, 1969–85. Specialist Advr, House of Lords Select Cttee on Sci and Technol., 1982–84; Member: Electronics Res. Council, MoD, 1963–80 (Chm., 1976–80); Defence Scientific Adv. Council, 1975–85 (Chm., 1981–85); ACARD sub-group on Annual Review of Govt-funded R&D, 1984–86 (Chm., 1985–86). Vice-Pres., IEE, 1974–77 (Faraday Lectr, 1968–69); Pres., IMA, 1982–83; FREng (FEng 1978; Hon. Sec. for Electrical Engrg, 1985–87; Chm., Membership Cttee, 1987–90); Pres., Electronic Engrg Assoc., 1980–81. Member: Management Cttee, Royal Instn, 1978–81; Adv. Bd, RCDS, 1980–90. Brunel University: Mem. Council, 1969–99 (Chm., 1973–78); Chm., Supervisory Bd, Brunel Inst. of Bio-Engineering, 1983–97; Chairman: Engrg Adv. Cttee, UWIST, 1983–86; Technol. Faculty Adv. Bd, Polytechnic South West, subseq. Plymouth Univ., 1989–93; External Examr in Maths: Polytechnic of Central London, 1983–86; Coventry Polytechnic, 1986–92. Mem., Management Cttee, The Wine Soc., 1977–92. Liveryman,

Co. of Scientific Instrument Makers, 1968–. Hon. DTech Brunel, 1975. Glazebrook Medal and Prize, Inst. of Physics, 1984. *Publications:* Strategic Implications of Microelectronics, 1982; Mathematics and Information, 1983; papers in scientific and technical jls. *Recreations:* travel, mathematics, Trier family history, railway history. *Address:* 49 Castlemaine Avenue, Croydon, CR2 7HW. *T:* (020) 8681 5915. *Clubs:* Royal Commonwealth Society, Old Millhillians.

TRIESMAN, David Maxim; General Secretary, Labour Party, since 2001; *b* 30 Oct. 1943; *s* of Michael Triesman and Rita (*née* Lubran). *Educ:* Stationers' Co. Sch., London; Univ. of Essex (BA Hons, MA Philosophy); King's Coll., Cambridge. FSS 1984. Res. Officer in Addiction, Inst. of Psychiatry, 1970–74; ASTMS secondment, 1974–75; Sen. Lectr and co-ord. postgrad. res., Poly. of S Bank, 1975–84; Dep. Sec. Gen. (Nat. Negotiating Sec.), NATFHE, 1984–93; Gen. Sec., AUT, 1993–2001. Vis. Prof. in Social Econ., S Lawrence Univ., 1977; Vis. Fellow in Econs, Wolfson Coll., Cambridge, 2000–. Member: Greater London Manpower Bd, 1981–86; Home Office Consultative Cttee on Prison Educn, 1980–83; Burnham Further and Higher Educn Cttee, 1980–84; Univ. Entrance and Schs Exams Bd for Soc. Sci., 1980–84; Standing Cttee on Business and the Community, HEFCE, 1999–. Mem., Kensington, Chelsea and Westminster AHA, 1976–82. Member: Industrial Relns Public Appointments Panel, DTI, 1996–2001; Indep. Review of Higher Educn Pay and Conditions, 1998–99; Cabinet Office Better Regulation Task Force, 2000–01; Treasury Public Services Productivity Panel, 2000–; British N American Cttee, 1999–. Non-executive Chairman: Mortgage Credit Corp., 1978–2001; Victoria Mgt Ltd, 2000–01. Chm., Usecolor Foundn, 2001. Member: Fabian Soc., 1974–; Charles Rennie Mackintosh Soc., Glasgow, 1986–; Highgate Literary and Scientific Inst., 1990–. Mem. Council, Ruskin Coll., Oxford, 2000–. Hon. Fellow, Nene Coll. of Higher Educn, 1995. FRSA 1990. *Publications:* The Medical and Non-Medical Use of Drugs, 1969; (with G. Viani) Football Mania, 1972; Football in London, 1985; (jtly) College Administration, 1988; Managing Change, 1991; Can Unions Survive (Staniewski Meml Lect.), 1999; Higher Education for the New Century, 2000. *Recreations:* football, art, reading, walking. *Address:* Millbank Tower, Millbank, SW1P 4GT. *Clubs:* Reform; Middlesex CC; Tottenham Hotspurs' Supporters.

TRIGGER, Ian James Campbell; His Honour Judge Trigger; a Circuit Judge, since 1993; *b* 16 Nov. 1943; *s* of late Walter James Trigger and Mary Elizabeth Trigger; *m* 1971, Jennifer Ann Downs; two *s*. *Educ:* Ruthin Sch.; UCW, Aberystwyth (LLB); Downing Coll., Cambridge (MA, LLM). Called to the Bar, Inner Temple, 1970 (major scholarship, 1967); Lectr in Law, UWIST, 1967–70; practice on Northern Circuit, 1970–93. Pt-time Pres., Mental Health Review Tribunal, 1995–; pt-time Chm., Immigration Appeal Tribunal, 1999–. Hon. Chm., Denbighshire Br., CPRW, 1996–. *Recreations:* gardening, walking, spending time with family. *Address:* Queen Elizabeth II Law Courts, Derby Square, Liverpool L2 1XA. *T:* (0151) 473 7373.

TRIMBLE, Rt Hon. David; *see* Trimble, Rt Hon. W. D.

TRIMBLE, Jenifer, (Mrs M. R. Trimble); *see* Wilson-Barnett, J.

TRIMBLE, Rt Hon. (William) David; PC 1998; MP (UU) Upper Bann, since May 1990; Leader, Ulster Unionist Party, since 1995; Member (UU) Upper Bann, and First Minister, Northern Ireland Assembly, since 1998; *b* 15 Oct. 1944; *s* of William and Ivy Trimble; *m* 1978, Daphne Orr; two *s* two *d*. *Educ:* Bangor Grammar Sch.; Queen's University Belfast (LLB). Called to the Bar of Northern Ireland, 1969; Lectr, 1968, Sen. Lectr, 1977, Faculty of Law, QUB. Mem., Constitutional Convention, 1975–76. (Jtly) Nobel Peace Prize, 1998. *Publications:* Northern Ireland Housing Law, 1986; NI Law Reports, 1975–90. *Recreations:* music, reading. *Address:* House of Commons, SW1A 0AA.

TRIMLESTOWN, 21st Baron *cr* 1461 (Ire.), of Trimlestown, co. Meath; **Raymond Charles Barnewall;** *b* 29 Dec. 1930; *yr s* of 19th Baron Trimlestown and Muriel (*d* 1937), *d* of Edward Oskar Schneider; *S* brother, 1997. *Educ:* Ampleforth. *Address:* Autumn Cottage, Chiddingfold, Surrey.

TRIMMER, Sir Jon (Charles), KNZM 1999; MBE 1974; Senior Artiste, Royal New Zealand Ballet, since 1993; *b* 18 Sept. 1939; *s* of Charles Trimmer and Lily Pamela (*née* Arrowsmith); *m* 1963, Jacqui de Joux Oswald. *Educ:* Wellington Tech. Coll. Art Sch., NZ. Joined Royal NZ Ballet, 1958; with Sadler's Wells, London, 1960–61; Australian Ballet, 1965–66; Royal Danish Ballet, 1969–71; has performed in 5 Royal Command Performances in NZ and overseas; rôles in dramatic plays on stage and TV. Patron, several arts and dance socs in NZ. Fulbright Scholar, NY, 1981. Turnofsky Award, NZ, 1986. Commemoration Medal (NZ), 1990. *Recreations:* pottery, gardening, writing short stories, painting. *Address:* 29 Ocean Road, Paekakariki, Kapiti Coast, New Zealand.

TRINDER, Frederick William; Charity Commissioner, 1984–85; *b* 18 Nov. 1930; *s* of Charles Elliott Trinder and Grace Johanna Trinder (*née* Hoadly); *m* 1964, Christiane Friederike Brigitte Dorothea (*née* Hase) (*d* 1994); one *s*. *Educ:* Ruskin Coll., Oxford (Dip. Pols and Econs); LSE, Univ. of London (BSc). Admitted Solicitor, 1966; Legal Asst/Sen. Legal Asst, Charity Commn, 1966–74; Dep. Charity Comr, 1974–84. Mem., BBC and IBA Central Appeals Adv. Cttees, 1986–92. Trustee, Charities Official Investment Fund, 1988–. Mem., Wandsworth BC, 1953–56, 1959–62. *Recreations:* travel, gardening, music. *Address:* 37 The Common, West Wratting, Cambridge CB1 5LR. *T:* (01223) 290469.

TRINICK, Christopher John; Director of Education and Cultural Services (formerly Chief Education Officer), Lancashire County Council, since 1996; *b* 26 Dec. 1948; *s* of George Herbert Trinick and Mary Elizabeth Trinick (*née* Burton); *m* 1976, Pamela May Hall; three *d*. *Educ:* Northumberland Coll. of Educn (Teacher's Cert. 1971); Univ. of Newcastle (BPhil 1980); Brunel Univ. (MA 1984). Teacher, Kelvin Hall, Hull, 1971–75; Head of House, Seaton Burn High Sch., N Tyneside, 1975–79; Professional Asst, Ealing LBC, 1979–82; Special Educnl Needs Prin. Officer, Bradford MBC, 1982–87; Dep. Chief Educn Officer, Salford City Council, 1987–91; Dir of Educn, Solihull MBC, 1991–96. Dir, E Lancs TEC, 1996–99; Treasurer: Soc. of Educn Officers, 1997–; Schs Curriculum Award, 1997–; Sec., Primary Educn Study Gp, 1997–. Mem. Bd, Foundn for IT in Local Govt, 1992–. *Recreations:* gardening, outdoors, fly fishing. *Address:* County Hall, Preston PR1 8RJ; 11 Uplands Chase, Fulwood, Preston PR2 7AW. *T:* (01772) 261646.

TRIPP, Rt Rev. Howard George; an Auxiliary Bishop and Vicar General in Southwark, (RC), since 1980; Titular Bishop of Newport, since 1980; *b* 3 July 1927; *s* of late Basil Howard Tripp and Alice Emily Tripp (*née* Haslett). *Educ:* John Fisher School, Purley; St John's Seminary, Wonersh. Priest, 1953; Assistant Priest: Blackheath SE3, 1953–56; East Sheen, 1956–62; Asst Diocesan Financial Sec., 1962–68; Parish Priest, East Sheen, 1965–71; Dir, Southwark Catholic Children's Soc., 1971–80. Chm., London Churches Gp, 1993–98; Mem., Churches Together in Britain and Ireland, 1998–. *Recreation:* vegetable gardening. *Address:* 8 Arterberry Road, SW20 8AJ. *T:* (020) 8946 4609, *Fax:* (020) 8947 9117; *e-mail:* htripp@ukgateway.net.

TRIPP, (John) Peter, CMG 1971; Consultant, Al-Tajir Bank, since 1986; *b* 27 March 1921; *s* of Charles Howard and Constance Tripp; *m* 1948, Rosemary Rees Jones; one *s* one *d*. *Educ:* Bedford Sch.; Sutton Valence Sch.; L'Institut de Touraine. Served War of 1939–45: Royal Marines, 1941–46. Sudan Political Service, 1946–54. Foreign (subsequently Diplomatic) Service, 1954–81; Political Agent, Trucial States, 1955–58; Head of Chancery, Vienna, 1958–61; Economic Secretary, Residency Bahrain, 1961–63; Counsellor 1963; Political Agent, Bahrain, 1963–65; sabbatical year at Durham Univ., 1965; Amman, 1966–68; Head of Near Eastern Dept, FCO, 1969–70; Ambassador to Libya, 1970–74; High Comr in Singapore, 1974–78; Ambassador to Thailand, 1978–81. Political Adviser, Inchcape Gp, 1981–86; Chm., Private Investment Co. for Asia (UK), 1981–84. County Councillor (Ind.), Powys, 1985–87. Chairman: Anglo-Thai Soc., 1983–88; Montgomeryshire Br., CPRW, 1990–94. *Recreations:* theatre, gardening. *Address:* Tanyffridd, Llanfechain, Powys SY22 6UE.

TRIPPIER, Sir David (Austin), Kt 1992; RD 1983; JP; DL; Chairman, Murray VCT plc, since 1995; *b* 15 May 1946; *s* of late Austin Wilkinson Trippier, MC and Mary Trippier; *m* 1975, Ruth Worthington, Barrister; three *s*. *Educ:* Bury Grammar School. Commnd Officer, Royal Marines Reserve, 1968 (qualif. parachutist, 1970; sc 1982). Member of Stock Exchange, 1968–; Chm., W. H. Ireland PLC, Stockbrokers, 1994–. Mem., Rochdale Council, 1969–78, Leader Cons. Gp, 1974–76. MP (C) Rossendale, 1979–83, Rossendale and Darwen, 1983–92; contested (C) Rossendale and Darwen, 1992. Sec., Cons. Parly Defence Cttee, 1980–82; PPS to Minister for Health, 1982–83; Parliamentary Under-Secretary of State: (Minister for Small Firms and Enterprise) DTI, 1983–85; Dept of Employment, 1985–87; DoE, 1987–89; Minister of State (Minister for the Envmt and Countryside), DoE, 1989–92. Dep. Chm., Cons. Party, 1990–91. Nat. Vice Chm., Assoc. of Cons. Clubs, 1980–84. Chairman: Tepnel Diagnostics PLC, 1992–94; Envirosystems Ltd, 1992–99; Davenham Gp, 1994–96; Marketing Manchester Ltd, 1996–99; Vector Investments Ltd, 1996–2000; Director: Dunlop Heywood & Co., 1992–99; St Modwen Properties, 1992–; Sir David Trippier & Associates, 1992–; Murray Income plc, 1996–; Nord Anglia Educn PLC, 1996–; Camfil Air Filters Ltd, 1998–2000; Consultant: Halliwell Landau, 1992–; Waste Management, 1992–97; Halliday Meecham, 1992–99. President: Manchester Chamber of Commerce and Industry, 1999–2000; Royal Lancs Agricl Soc., 1999–2000. Chm., Tidy Britain Gp, 1996–98. Governor, Manchester Grammar Sch., 1993–. Pres., Northern Reg., RM Assoc., 1988–93; Chm., NW of England Reserve Forces and Cadets Assoc., 2000–; Vice-Chm., RFCA (RM), 1999–. Hon. Col, RM Reserve, Merseyside, 1996–. JP Rochdale, 1975; DL Lancs, 1994, High Sheriff, Lancs, 1997–98. OStJ 2000. *Publications:* Defending the Peace, 1982; New Life for Inner Cities, 1989; Lend Me Your Ears (autobiog.), 1999. *Recreations:* gardening, tennis. *Address:* Dowry Head, Helmshore, Rossendale, Lancs BB4 4AE. *Club:* St James's (Manchester).

TRISTAM, Brother; *see* Holland, Brother T. K.

TRITTON, Alan George, CBE 1999; DL; Director, Barclays Bank Ltd, 1974–91; Chairman: Plantation and General Investments, 1994–96; University Life Assurance Society, 1994–99; Permanent Insurance Co. Ltd, 1995–99; a Vice-President, Equitable Life Assurance Society, 1983–99 (Director, 1976–99); *b* 2 Oct. 1931; *s* of George Henton Tritton, Lyons Hall, Essex, and Iris Mary Baillie, Lochloy; *m* 1st, 1958, Elizabeth Clare d'Abreu (marr. diss.); two *s* one *d*; 2nd, 1972, Diana Marion Spencer. *Educ:* Eton. Member of British Schools Exploring Soc. Expedn, Arctic Norway, 1949. Lt, 1st Batt. Seaforth Highlanders, active service Pahang, Malaya, 1950–52. Leader, S Orkneys Survey Station, 1952–54, and Antarctic Relief Voyage, 1954, Falkland Islands Dependencies Survey; entered Barclays Bank Ltd, 1954; local Dir, 54 Lombard Street, 1964; Dir, Barclays Bank UK Management Ltd, 1972; India Adv, Barclays Bank, 1992–95. A Vice-Pres., Royal Geographical Soc., 1983–86 (Mem. Council, 1975–96, Hon. Treas., 1984–96). Member: Cttee, British Trans-Arctic Expedn, 1966–69; Cttee, British Everest SW Face Expedn, 1974–75; Cttee of Management, Mount Everest Foundn, 1976–80; Friends' Cttee, Scott Polar Research Inst., 1976–80. Chairman: Westminster Abbey Investment Cttee, 1976–94; Calcutta Tercentenary Trust, 1989; Member: Council, Internat. Chamber of Commerce, 1975–90 (Hon. Treas. 1985); Council, Foundn for Aviation and Sustainable Tourism, New Delhi, 1994–; Finance Cttee, 1997–, Council, 1999–, Royal Asiatic Soc.; Court, Essex Univ., 1995–. Trustee: Brentwood Cathedral Trust, 1996–; Falkland Is Conservation Trust, 1998–. High Sheriff, 1992, DL 1993, Essex. *Recreations:* travelling, shooting. *Clubs:* Boodle's, Pratt's, Antarctic, Geographical, Essex; Tollygunge (Calcutta).

TRITTON, Major Sir Anthony (John Ernest), 4th Bt *cr* 1905; *b* 4 March 1927; *s* of Sir Geoffrey Ernest Tritton, 3rd Bt, CBE, and Mary Patience Winifred (*d* 1960), *d* of John Kenneth Foster; *S* father, 1976; *m* 1957, Diana, *d* of Rear-Adm. St J. A. Micklethwait, CB, DSO, and of Clemence Penelope Olga Welby-Everard; one *s* one *d*. *Educ:* Eton. Commissioned 3rd Hussars, Oct. 1945; retired as Major, 1964, The Queen's Own Hussars. *Recreations:* shooting, fishing. *Heir:* *s* Jeremy Ernest Tritton, *b* 6 Oct. 1961. *Address:* River House, Heytesbury, Wilts BA12 0EE. *Club:* Cavalry and Guards.

TRITTON, (Elizabeth) Clare, (Clare McLaren-Throckmorton; Mrs Andrew McLaren); QC 1988; Chief Executive, Throckmorton Estates; *b* 18 Aug. 1935; *d* of Prof. Alfonsus d'Abreu and Elizabeth d'Abreu (*née* Throckmorton); *m* 1st, 1958, Alan Tritton, *qv* (marr. diss. 1971); two *s* one *d*; 2nd, 1973, Andrew McLaren; name changed to McLaren-Throckmorton by deed poll, 1991, following death of uncle, Sir Robert Throckmorton, 11th Bt. *Educ:* Convent of the Holy Child Jesus, Mayfield, St Leonards; Univ. of Birmingham (BA Hons English). Called to the Bar, Inner Temple, 1968. Lived and worked in USA, France, Germany and Italy, intermittently, 1952–86; Centre Organiser, WVS, 1963–64; Charlemagne Chambers, Brussels, 1985–89; founded own Chambers, European Law Chambers, 1987. Chm., Bar European Group, 1982–84; Vice Chm., Internat. Practice Cttee, Gen. Council of the Bar, 1988–91; Chm., Sub Cttee on Eur. Legislation, Hansard Commn on Legislative Reform, 1991–93. Member: Council, Bow Gp, 1963–65; Eur. Cttee, British Invisible Exports Council, 1989–93; Monopolies and Mergers Commn, 1993–97. Dir, Severn Trent plc, 1991–. Indep. Mem., Council, FIMBRA, 1991–98. Trustee Dir, Birmingham Royal Ballet Trust Co Ltd, 1996–. Founder, Bar European News, 1983. *Publications:* articles in law magazines on EEC and private internat. law. *Recreations:* reading, gardening, children, travel. *Address:* Coughton Court, Alcester, Warwicks B49 5JA. *T:* (01789) 400777; Manor House, Molland, South Molton, North Devon EX36 3ND. *T:* (01769) 550325.

TROLLOPE, Andrew David Hedderwick; QC 1991; a Recorder of the Crown Court, since 1989; *b* 6 Nov. 1948; *s* of Arthur George Cecil Trollope and Rosemary (*née* Hodson); *m* 1978, Anne Forbes; two *s*. *Educ:* Charterhouse; Univ. of Nancy. Called to the Bar, Inner Temple, 1971; Asst Recorder, 1985–89. Chm., N London Bar Mess, 1998–2001. Member: South Eastern Circuit Cttee, 1990–93, 1994–97; Cttee, Criminal Bar Assoc., 1991–; Internat. Relns Cttee, Bar Council; Council of Mgt, British Inst. of Internat. and Comparative Law. Fellow, Soc. of Advanced Legal Studies. *Recreations:* opera, jazz, swimming, tennis, sailing, travel. *Address:* 1 Middle Temple Lane, Temple, EC4Y 9AA. *T:* (020) 7583 0659. *Clubs:* Garrick, Hurlingham.

See also J. Trollope.

TROLLOPE, Sir Anthony (Simon), 17th Bt *cr* 1642, of Casewick, Lincolnshire; Marketing Executive with Ricegrowers Co-operative Ltd; *b* 31 Aug. 1945; *s* of Sir Anthony Owen Clavering Trollope, 16th Bt and of Joan Mary Alexis, *d* of Alexis Robert Gibbs; *S* father, 1987; *m* 1969, Denise, *d* of Trevern and Vida Thompson; two *d*. *Educ:* Univ. of Sydney (BA 1969). Breeder, in partnership with his wife, of Anglo-Arabian horses and Rhodesian Ridgeback dogs. Mem., Australian Marketing Inst., 1988–. *Heir: b* Hugh Irwin Trollope [*b* 31 March 1947; *m* 1971, Barbara Anne, *d* of William Ian Jamieson; one *s* two *d*]. *Address:* 28 Midson Road, Oakville, NSW 2765, Australia. *Clubs:* Gordon Rugby, Rhodesian Ridgeback, Arab Horse Society of Australia, Castle Hill RSL (Sydney).

TROLLOPE, Joanna, OBE 1996; writer; *b* 9 Dec. 1943; *er d* of Arthur George Cecil Trollope and Rosemary Trollope (*née* Hodson); *m* 1st, 1966, David Roger William Potter, *qv*; two *d*; 2nd, 1985, Ian Bayley Curteis, *qv* (marr. diss. 2001); two step *s*. *Educ:* Reigate County Sch. for Girls; St Hugh's Coll., Oxford (Gamble Scholar; MA 1972). Inf. and Research Dept, Foreign Office, 1965–67; teaching posts, 1967–79, incl. Farnham Girls' Grammar Sch., adult educn, English for foreigners and at Daneshill Sch. Writer in Residence, Victoria Magazine, USA, 1999. Chm., DNH Adv. Cttee on Nat. Reading Initiative, 1996–97; Mem. Govt Adv. Body, Nat. Year of Reading, 1998. Vice President: Trollope Soc., 1995–; West Country Writers' Assoc., 1998–; Mem. Council, Soc. of Authors, 1997–. Trustee, Joanna Trollope Charitable Trust, 1995–. Patron, Glos Community Foundn, 1994–. *Publications:* Eliza Stanhope, 1978; Parson Harding's Daughter, 1979 (reissued under pseudonym Caroline Harvey, 1995); Leaves from the Valley, 1980; The City of Gems, 1981; The Steps of the Sun, 1983 (reissued under pseudonym Caroline Harvey, 1996); Britannia's Daughters: a study of women in the British Empire, 1983; The Taverners' Place, 1986 (reissued under pseudonym Caroline Harvey, 2000); The Choir, 1988 (televised, 1995); A Village Affair, 1989; A Passionate Man, 1990; The Rector's Wife, 1991 (televised, 1994); The Men and the Girls, 1992; A Spanish Lover, 1993; (ed) The Country Habit: an anthology, 1993; The Best of Friends, 1995; Next of Kin, 1996; Other People's Children, 1998 (televised, 2000); Marrying the Mistress, 2000; The Girl from the South, 2002; *as Caroline Harvey:* Legacy of Love, 1992; A Second Legacy, 1993; A Castle in Italy, 1993; The Brass Dolphin, 1997; contribs to newspapers and magazines. *Recreations:* reading, conversation, very long baths. *Address:* c/o Peters, Fraser & Dunlop, Drury House, 34–43 Russell Street, WC2B 5HA.
See also A. D. H. Trollope.

TRONCHETTI PROVERA, Marco; Chairman, Pirelli & Co., Milan, since 1999; Chairman and Chief Executive Officer, Pirelli SpA, Milan, since 1996; *b* Milan, 1948; three *c*. *Educ:* Bocconi Univ., Milan (grad. 1971). Founder, holding co. in field of maritime transportation, 1973–86; joined Pirelli Gp, 1986; Partner, Pirelli & Co., 1986–; Man. Dir and Gen. Manager, Société Internationale Pirelli SA, Basle, 1988–92; Pirelli SpA: Man. Dir and Gen. Manager, Finance and Admin and Gen. Affairs, 1991–92; Exec. Dep. Chm. and Man. Dir, 1992–96; Dep. Chm., Pirelli & Co., 1995–99. Chairman: CAMFIN SpA, Milan; Il Sole 24 Ore. Dep. Chm., Confindustria (Confedn of Italian Industries), 2000–. Italian Chm., Council for US and Italy. *Address:* Pirelli SpA, Viale Sarca 202, 20126 Milan, Italy.

TROOP, Patricia Ann, (Mrs P. A. Dittner), CBE 2001; FRCP, FFPHM; Deputy Chief Medical Officer, Department of Health, since 1999; *b* 5 April 1948; *d* of John Ronald Troop and Phoebe Margaret Troop; *m* 1979, Michael Dittner; one *s* one *d*. *Educ:* Manchester Univ. Med. Sch. (MB ChB 1971; MSc Community Medicine 1979); MA Cantab 1988. MFCM 1980, FFPHM (FFCM 1986); FRCP 2001. Dir of Public Health, Cambridge HA, 1988–91; Associate Lectr, Faculty of Medicine, Cambridge Univ., 1988–; Chief Executive: Cambridge HA, 1990–93; Cambs Family Health Services, 1992–93; Director of Public Health: East Anglia RHA, 1993–95; Anglia and Oxford, then Eastern, Regl Office, NHS Exec., DoH, 1995–99. Mem. and Vice-Chm., Cambs TEC, 1992–93. Vis. Prof., LSHTM, 2000. Mem., Lucy Cavendish Coll., Cambridge, 1990–99. *Publications:* articles in various med. jls. *Recreations:* family, horse riding, watercolours. *Address:* (office) Richmond House, 79 Whitehall, SW1A 2NS; 47a Lode Way, Haddenham, Ely, Cambs CB6 3UL. *T:* (01353) 741087.

TROSS, Jonathan Edward Simon; Grade 2, Head of Constitution Secretariat, Cabinet Office, since 2000; *b* 21 Jan. 1949; *s* of late Francis Tross and Audrey (*née* Payne); *m* 1972, Ann Humphries; one *s* one *d*. *Educ:* Chislehurst and Sidcup Grammar Sch.; University Coll., Oxford (BA Hons Modern Hist., 1970). Teacher in Kenya, 1971; Department of Health and Social Security: grad. trainee, 1972; Principal, 1977–84; Asst Sec., Supplementary Benefits Review, 1984–87; Asst Dir, Corporate Div., Barclays Bank, on secondment, 1987–90; Pharmaceutical Industry Br., DoH, 1990–91; G3, Head of Planning and Finance Div., 1991–94, G2, Dir of Corporate Mgt, 1994–99, DSS. *Recreations:* football, reading, theatre, walking, allotment. *Address:* Cabinet Office, 70 Whitehall, SW1A 2AS. *T:* (020) 7270 5907. *Club:* Fulham Football.

TROTMAN, Baron *cr* 1999 (Life Peer), of Osmotherley in the county of North Yorkshire; **Alexander James Trotman,** Kt 1996; Chairman, Imperial Chemical Industries, since 2002 (Director, since 1997); *b* 22 July 1933. *Educ:* Boroughmuir Sch., Edinburgh; Michigan State Univ. (MBA). Various positions, Ford of Britain, 1955–67; Dir, Car Product Planning, Ford Europe, 1967–69; positions in Car Product Planning and Sales Planning Depts, Ford US, 1969–75; Chief Car Planning Manager, Ford Motor Co., 1975–79; Vice Pres., European Truck Ops, 1979–83; President: Ford Asia-Pacific, 1983–84; Ford of Europe, 1984–88; Exec. Vice Pres., North American Automotive Ops, 1989–93; Pres., Ford Automotive Gp, 1993; Chm. and CEO, Ford Motor Co., 1993–98. Member, Board of Directors: IBM Corp., 1995–; NY Stock Exchange, 1996–. *Address:* House of Lords, SW1A 0PW. *Club:* Royal Air Force.

TROTMAN, Andrew Frederick; JP; MA; Head Master, St Peter's School, York, since 1995; *b* 9 Dec. 1954; *s* of Campbell Grant Trotman and late Audrey Trotman; *m* 1980, Mary Rosalind Spencer; one *s* one *d*. *Educ:* Alleyne's Grammar Sch., Stevenage; Balliol Coll., Oxford (MA English Language and Lit. 1977); Cert Ed Oxon 1978. Asst Master, Radley Coll., 1978–84; Housemaster, Abingdon Sch., 1984–90; Dep. Rector, Edinburgh Acad., 1991–95. MInstD 1997. JP City of York, 1998. *Recreations:* walking, rowing, music, bagpiping. *Address:* St Catherine's, 11 Clifton, York YO30 6AA. *T:* (01904) 622590. *Club:* East India.

TROTMAN-DICKENSON, Sir Aubrey (Fiennes), Kt 1989; Principal, University of Wales College of Cardiff, 1988–93; Vice-Chancellor, University of Wales, 1975–77, 1983–85 and 1991–93; *b* 12 Feb. 1926; *s* of late Edward Newton Trotman-Dickenson and Violet Murray Nicoll; *m* 1953, Danusia Irena Hewell; two *s* one *d*. *Educ:* Winchester Coll.; Balliol Coll., Oxford (MA, BSc); PhD Manchester; DSc Edinburgh. Fellow, National Research Council, Ottawa, 1948–50; Asst Lecturer, ICI Fellow, Manchester Univ., 1950–53; E. I. du Pont de Nemours, Wilmington, USA, 1953–54; Lecturer, Edinburgh Univ., 1954–60; Professor, University College of Wales, Aberystwyth, 1960–68; Principal; UWIST, Cardiff, 1968–88; UC Cardiff, 1987–88. Chm., Job Creation Programme, Wales, 1975–78. Member: Welsh Council, 1971–79; Planning and Transport Res. Adv. Council, DoE, 1975–79. Tilden Lectr, Chem. Soc., 1963. Hon. LLD Wales, 1995. *Publications:* Gas Kinetics, 1955; Free Radicals, 1959; Tables of Bimolecular Gas Reactions, 1967; (ed) Comprehensive Inorganic Chemistry, 1973; contrib. to learned journals. *Address:* Syston Court, Bristol BS16 9LU. *T:* (0117) 937 2109.

TROTTER, Major Alexander Richard; JP; Lord-Lieutenant of Berwickshire, since 2000; Chairman, Meadowhead Ltd (formerly Mortonhall Park Ltd), since 1974; *b* 20 Feb. 1939; *s* of late Major H. R. Trotter, TD, and of Rona Trotter (*née* Murray); *m* 1970, Julia Henrietta, *d* of Capt. Sir Peter McClintock Greenwell, 3rd Bt, TD; three *s*. *Educ:* Eton Coll.; City of London Tech. Coll. Served Royal Scots Greys, 1956–68; Manager, Charterhall Estate and Farm, 1969–; Vice Chm., Border Grain, Ltd, 1984–. Dir, Timber Growers GB Ltd, 1977–82. Scottish Landowners' Federation: Mem. Council, 1975–; Convener, 1982–85; Vice Pres., 1986–96; Pres., 1996–2001; Mem., NCC and Chm., Scottish Cttee, 1985–90; Mem., UK Cttee, Euro Year of the Envmt, 1986–88. Gen. Comr for Income Tax, Berwickshire, 1973–. Mem. (Ind.), Berwickshire CC, 1969–75 (Chm., Roads Cttee, 1974–75). Mem., Royal Co. of Archers, 1977–. DL 1987, JP 2000, Berwickshire. *Recreations:* golf, bridge, country sports. *Address:* Charterhall, Duns, Berwickshire TD11 3RE. *T:* (home) (01890) 840210; (office) (01890) 840301; *Fax:* (01890) 840651; *e-mail:* alex@charterhall.net. *Clubs:* Pratt's; New (Edinburgh).

TROTTER, David; *see* Trotter, W. D.

TROTTER, Dame Janet (Olive), DBE 2001 (OBE 1991); Director, University of Gloucestershire (formerly Cheltenham and Gloucester College of Higher Education), since 1990; *b* 29 Oct. 1943; *d* of Anthony George Trotter and Joyce Edith Trotter (*née* Patrick). *Educ:* Derby Lonsdale Coll. of Educn (Cert Ed); BD (ext.) London Univ.; Inst. of Educn, London Univ. (MA); Henley Mgt Coll. (MSc Brunel Univ.). Teacher: St Leonards Secondary Sch., 1965–67; Chartham Secondary Sch., 1967–69; Rochester Grammar Sch. for Girls, 1969–73; Lectr, King Alfred's Coll., Winchester, 1973–84; Vice Principal, St Martin's Coll., Lancaster, 1985–86; Principal, St Paul and St Mary's Coll., Cheltenham, 1986–90. Mem. and Chm., Glos HA, 1991–96; Chair, S and W Reg., NHS Exec., DoH, 1996–2001. Member: HEFCE, 1992–97; TTA, 1994–99. Hon. DTech. Pecs, Hungary, 1996. *Publications:* various articles. *Recreations:* cycling, music. *Address:* University of Gloucestershire, PO Box 220, The Park, Cheltenham, Glos GL50 2QF. *T:* (01242) 532701.

TROTTER, Sir Neville (Guthrie), Kt 1997; JP; DL; FCA; FCIT, FRAeS; Consultant, Grant Thornton, Chartered Accountants, since 1983 (Thornton Baker, 1974–83); *b* 27 Jan. 1932; *s* of Captain Alexander Trotter and Elizabeth Winifred Trotter (*née* Guthrie); *m* 1983, Caroline, *d* of late Captain John Farrow, RN retd and Oona Farrow (*née* Hall); one *d*. *Educ:* Shrewsbury; King's Coll., Durham (BCom). Short service commn in RAF, 1955–58. Partner, Thornton Baker & Co., Chartered Accountants, 1962–74. Dir, Romag Plc; former Director: MidAmerican Energy Hldgs Co.; Wm Baird; Darchem. Director: NE Chamber of Commerce, Trade and Industry; Northern Business Forum; Founder Chm., British-American Chamber of Commerce, NE of England, 1999–; Pres., Northern Defence Industries, 2000–. Member: Appeal Council, British Olympic Assoc.; Great North Eastern Railway Business Forum; Council, European Atlantic Gp; Consultant, Go Ahead Gp Plc. Mem., Newcastle City Council, 1963–74 (Alderman, 1970–74; Chm., Finance Cttee, Traffic Highways and Transport Cttee, Theatre Cttee). Mem., CAA Airline Users Cttee, 1973–79. Mem., Tyne and Wear Metropolitan Council, 1973–74; Vice-Chm., Northumberland Police Authority, 1970–74. MP (C) Tynemouth, Feb. 1974–1997. Chm., Cons. Party Shipping and Shipbuilding Cttee, 1979–85, 1994–97 (Vice-Chm., 1976–79); Secretary: Cons. Party Industry Cttee, 1981–83; Cons. Party Transport Cttee, 1983–84; Mil. Sec., Cons. Party Aviation Cttee, 1976–79; Member: Industry Sub-Cttee, Select Cttee on Expenditure, 1976–79; Select Cttee on Transport, 1983–92; Select Cttee on Defence, 1993–97; Parly Defence Study Group, 1980–97; Armed Forces Parly Scheme (RAF), 1990–91; formerly Chm., All-Party Gp for Prevention of Solvent Abuse. Private Member's Bills: Consumer Safety, 1978; Licensing Amendment, 1980; Intoxicating Substances Supply (Glue Sniffing), 1985. Hon. Advr, All-Pty Defence Study Gp, H of L, 1997–. Pres., North Area Cons. Party, 1996–. Vice President: British Marine Equipment Council; British Maritime Charitable Foundn; Soc. for Prevention of Solvent and Volatile Substance Abuse, 1989–. Former Member: Northern Economic Planning Council; Tyne Improvement Commn; Tyneside Passenger Transport Authority; Industrial Relations Tribunal; Council, RUSI. Member: UK Defence Forum, 1997–; Steering Cttee, Parly Maritime Gp, 1997–; Atlantic Council; NE RFCA (formerly TAVRA), 1997–; US Naval Inst.; USAF Assoc.; Council, US Navy League in UK; Railway Studies Assoc. Pres., Tyneside Br., RM Assoc., 2001–. Hon. Col, Royal Marine Reserve, 1998–. FRAeS 1998; FCIT 1998. Freeman, City of London, 1978; Mem., Co. of Chartered Accountants, 1978. JP Newcastle upon Tyne, 1973; DL Tyne and Wear, 1997. *Recreations:* aviation, gardening, fell-walking, study of foreign affairs, defence and industry. *Clubs:* Royal Air Force; Northern Counties (Newcastle upon Tyne).

TROTTER, Sir Ronald (Ramsay), Kt 1985; FCA; New Zealand business executive; Chairman, Fletcher Challenge Ltd, 1981–95 (Chief Executive, 1981–87); *b* Hawera, 9 Oct. 1927; *s* of Clement George Trotter, CBE and Annie Euphemia Trotter (*née* Young); *m* 1955, Margaret Patricia, *d* of James Rainey; three *s* one *d*. *Educ:* Collegiate School, Wanganui; Victoria Univ. of Wellington; Lincoln Coll., Canterbury (BCom, Cert. in Agric.). FCA 1976. Wright Stephenson & Co., 1958–72: Dir, 1962–68; Man. Dir, 1968–70; Chm. and Man. Dir, 1970–72; Chm. and Man. Dir, Challenge Corp., 1972–81. Chairman: Telecom Corp. of New Zealand Ltd, 1987–90; Post Office Bank, 1989; Ciba-Geigy New Zealand Ltd, 1990–96; Wrightson Ltd, 1993–98; Toyota New Zealand Ltd, 1994–2001 (Dir, 1990–94); Director: Reserve Bank of NZ, 1986–88; Australia and New Zealand Banking Gp, 1988–97 (Inaugural Mem., Internat. Bd of Advice, 1986–93); Air New Zealand Ltd, 1989–98; Ciba-Geigy Australia Ltd, 1991–96; Wrightson Farmers Finance Ltd, 1993–98; Mem., Internat. Adv. Bd, Proudfoot plc, 1992–95. Trustee and Chm., NZ Inst. of Economic Research, 1973–86; Chairman: Overseas Investment Commn, 1974–77; NZ Business Roundtable, 1985–90; Pacific Basin Econ. Council, 1985–90 (Internat. Pres., 1986–88); Museum of NZ, 1995– (Mem., Project Develt Bd, 1988–92). Hon. LLD Victoria Univ. of Wellington, 1984; Hon. DCom Lincoln, 1999. Bledisloe Medal, Lincoln Coll., 1988. NZ Business Hall of Fame, 1999. Silver Jubilee Medal, 1977; NZ Commemoration Medal, 1990. *Address:* Te Kowhai Road, RDI Otaki, New Zealand. *T:* (4) 2933947, *Fax:* (4) 2937339. *Club:* Wellington (Wellington, NZ).

TROTTER, Thomas Andrew, FRCO; Organist, St Margaret's Church, Westminster Abbey, since 1982; Organist to the City of Birmingham, since 1983; *b* 4 April 1957; *s* of late His Honour Richard Stanley Trotter and Ruth Elizabeth Trotter. *Educ:* Malvern Coll.; Royal Coll. of Music, 1974–76 (schol.; ARCM) (organ schol., St George's Chapel, Windsor, 1975–76); King's Coll., Cambridge (organ schol., 1976–79; MA). John Stewart of Rannock Schol. in Sacred Music, Cambridge Univ., 1979; Countess of Munster schol. for further organ studies with Marie-Claire Alain in Paris. Début at Royal Fest. Hall, 1980; Prom. début, 1986; regular broadcasts for Radio 2 and Radio 3; has performed at fests throughout UK and in Europe; concert tours to Australia, USA and Far East; organ recordings. Walford Davies Prize, RCM, 1976; First prize and Bach prize, St Albans Internat. Organ Competition, 1979; Prix de Virtuosité, Conservatoire Rueil-Malmaison, 1981. *Address:* c/o The Town Hall, Birmingham B3 3DQ. *T:* (0121) 605 5116.

TROTTER, Prof. (Wilfred) David, PhD; Quain Professor of English Language and Literature, University College London, since 1991; *b* 25 July 1951; *s* of late Wilfred Robert Trotter and Enid Beatrice Trotter (*née* Roulston). *Educ:* Gonville and Caius Coll., Cambridge (BA, PhD). Res. Fellow, Magdalene Coll., Cambridge, 1975–77; University College London: Lectr in English, 1977–87; Reader, 1987–90; Prof. of English, 1990–91. Vis. Prof., CIT, 1988–89. *Publications:* The Poetry of Abraham Cowley, 1979; The Making of the Reader, 1984; Circulation: Defoe, Dickens and the economies of the novel, 1988; The English Novel in History 1895–1920, 1993; (jtly) A Companion to Edwardian Fiction, 1997; Cooking with Mud: the idea of mess in nineteenth century art and fiction, 2000. *Address:* Department of English, University College London, Gower Street, WC1E 6BT. *T:* (020) 7387 7050.

TROUBRIDGE, Sir Thomas (Richard), 7th Bt *cr* 1799, of Plymouth; FCA; Partner, PricewaterhouseCoopers (formerly Price Waterhouse), since 1989; *b* 23 Jan. 1955; *s* of Sir Peter Troubridge, 6th Bt and of Hon. Venetia Daphne (who *m* 2nd, Captain W. F. E. Forbes, *qv*), *d* of 1st Baron Weeks; *S* father, 1988; *m* 1984, Hon. Rosemary Douglas-Pennant, *yr d* of Baron Penrhyn, *qv*; two *s* one *d*. *Educ:* Eton College; Durham Univ. (BSc Eng). ACA 1980, FCA 1991. Joined Price Waterhouse, 1977. *Recreations:* sailing, ski-ing. *Heir: s* Edward Peter Troubridge, *b* 10 Aug. 1989. *Address:* The Manor House, Elsted, Midhurst, W Sussex GU29 0JY. *T:* (01730) 825286. *Clubs:* Hurlingham; Itchenor Sailing.

TROUGHTON, Peter, PhD; Chairman, 4RF Ltd, since 1999; *b* 26 Aug. 1943; *s* of late Frank Sydney Troughton and of Joan Vera Troughton (*née* Root); *m* 1967, Joyce Uncles; two *s*. *Educ:* City Univ. (BSc Eng); University College London (PhD). Technical apprentice, Plessey Co., then Post Office apprentice, 1959; PO scholarship, 1964; research for PhD, 1967; develt of microprocessor techniques for control of telephone switching systems, 1970; Dep. Gen. Manager, South Central Telephone Area, 1977; Head of Ops, Prestel, 1979; Gen. Manager, City Telephone Area, 1980; Regional Dir, British Telecom London, 1983; Man. Dir, British Telecom Enterprises, 1984–86; Dir and Partner, Alan Patricof Associates, 1986–88, non-exec. Dir, 1988–90; Man. Dir and Chief Exec. Officer, Telecom Corp. of NZ, 1988–92; Chairman: Trans Power (NZ National Power Grid) Estabt Bd, 1990–92; Marine Air Systems, then MAS Technology Ltd, 1993–98; Troughton, Swier and Associates, 1996–99. Director: Crown Health Enterprise Develt Unit, NZ, 1992–93; Electricity Supply Industry Reform Unit, Vic, Australia, 1993–95. Advr to NZ govt, 1993–94; Special Advr to Vic. Govt on reform and privatisation of electricity, gas and aluminium industries, 1995–99; Advr to Australian Davos Connection, World Econ. Forum, for conf. on energy in 21st century, 1998–. Mem., State Owned Enterprises Steering Cttee, 1992–93. Mem., NZ Business Round Table, 1988–92; Chm., Twyford and Dist Round Table, 1981–82. NZ Chief Exec. of the Year Award, 1991. NZ Commemoration Medal, 1990. *Publications:* articles and papers on microwave systems, computers, communications, and on restructuring, regulation and privatisation of utility industries. *Recreations:* travel, archaeology, bridge. *Club:* Wellington (NZ).

TROUGHTON, Peter John Charles; Chief Executive, First Arrow Investment Management Ltd, since 2000; Director, Five Arrows Ltd, since 2001; *b* 18 June 1948; *s* of Sir Charles (Hugh Willis) Troughton, CBE, MC, TD and (Constance) Gillean (*née* Mitford), DL; *m* 1977, Sarah Rose, *d* of Sir Timothy Colman, *qv*; one s two *d*. *Educ:* Radley Coll.; Trinity Coll., Cambridge (MA Hons); Harvard Business Sch. (AMP 1987). Joined HM Diplomatic Service 1970; FCO, 1970–72; Jakarta, 1972–75; First Sec., FCO, 1975–79; W. H. Smith Gp plc, 1979–95: Managing Director: News, 1988–91; Retail, 1991–93; UK Retailing, 1993–95; Dir, 1991–95; Chief Exec., Rothschild Asset Mgt Internat. Ltd, 1995–99. Non-executive Director: East Anglian Daily Times, 1984–89; Community Media Ltd, 1989–91; Eastern Counties Newspaper Gp, 1991–; Lowland Investment Trust, 1990–. Trustee: Nat. Gall., 1988–96 (Mem., Publications Cttee, 1982–88); Nat. Gall. Trust, 1996– (Hon. Treas., 2001–); Chm., National Gallery Publications Ltd, 1988–96. Gov., St Mary's Sch., Calne, 1992–. *Recreations:* reading, walking, ski-ing, stalking. *Address:* The Lynch House, Upper Wanborough, near Swindon, Wilts SN4 0BZ. *T:* (01793) 790385. *Clubs:* Brooks's, Pratt's.

TROUNSON, Rev. Ronald Charles, MA; Rector (non-stipendiary), Easton-on-the-Hill, 1994–99 (Rector, Easton-on-the-Hill and Collyweston with Duddington and Tixover, 1989–94); Rural Dean of Barnack, 1991–94; *b* 7 Dec. 1926; *s* of Edwin Trounson and Elsie Mary Trounson (*née* Bolitho); *m* 1952, Leonora Anne Keate; two *s* three *d*. *Educ:* Plymouth Coll.; Emmanuel Coll., Cambridge (Schol.); Ripon Hall, Oxford (MA). Deacon, 1956; Priest, 1957. National Service, RAF, 1948–50. Asst Master, Scaitcliffe Sch., Englefield Green, Surrey, 1950–52; Sixth Form Classics Master, Plymouth Coll., 1953–58; Asst Curate, St Gabriel's, Plymouth, 1956–58; Chaplain, Denstone Coll., 1958–76; Second Master, 1968–76, Bursar, 1976–78; Principal of St Chad's College and Lectr in Classics, Univ. of Durham, 1978–88. Chm. of Governors, Durham High Sch., 1990–94. Fellow, Woodard Corporation, 1983. FRSA 1984. *Address:* 6 Western Avenue, Easton-on-the-Hill, Stamford PE9 3NB.

TROUP, Sir Anthony; *see* Troup, Sir J. A. R.

TROUP, Vice-Adm. Sir (John) Anthony (Rose), KCB 1975; DSC and Bar; *b* 18 July 1921; *s* of late Captain H. R. Troup, RN and N. M. Troup (*née* Milne-Thompson); *m* 1st, 1943, B. M. J. Gordon-Smith (marr. diss. 1952); two *s* one *d*; 2nd, 1953, C. M. Hope; two *s* one *d*. *Educ:* Naut. Trng Coll., HMS Worcester, 1934; RNC Dartmouth, 1936; war service includes: Submarines Turbulent and Strongbow, 1941–45 (dispatches, 1942); HMS Victorious, 1956–59; Comd 3rd Submarine Sqdn, 1961–63; HMS Intrepid, 1966–68; Flag Officer Sea Training, 1969–71; Comdr Far East Fleet, 1971; Flag Officer Submarines and NATO Comdr Submarines, Eastern Atlantic, 1972–74; Flag Officer, Scotland and NI, and NATO Comdr Norlant, 1974–77. *Recreations:* sailing, shooting, gardening. *Address:* Bridge Gardens, Hungerford, Berks RG17 0DL. *Clubs:* Army and Navy; Royal Yacht Squadron.

TROUSDELL, Maj.-Gen. Philip Charles Cornwallis, CB 2000; Commandant, Royal Military Academy Sandhurst, since 2001; *b* 13 Aug. 1948; *s* of late Col Philip James Cornwallis Trousdell, OBE and of Doreen Mary Trousdell (*née* Durdle); *m* 1986, Sally Caroline Slade Parker; one *s* two *d*. *Educ:* Berkhamstead; RMA, Sandhurst. Commnd Royal Irish Rangers, 1968; CO, 1st Bn, 1989–91; commanded 48 Gurkha Bde, 1992–93; Dir, Public Relns (Army), 1994–97; COS, HQ Land Comd, 1997–2000; Dep. Comdr (Ops) Stabilisation Force, Bosnia Herzegovina, 2000. Col, Queen's Own Gurkha Transport Regt, 1993–; Dep. Col, 1996–2001, Col, 2001–, Royal Irish Regt; Col Comdt, Media Ops Gp (Vol.), 2001–. *Recreations:* bonfires, reading, bicycling, wine. *Address:* Royal Military Academy Sandhurst, Camberley, Surrey GU15 4PQ. *Club:* Army and Navy.

TROWBRIDGE, Martin Edward O'Keeffe, CBE 1987; FCGI; public affairs, environmental, regulatory and EC consultant; Chairman, since 1973, and Chief Executive, since 1987, Martin Trowbridge Ltd; *b* 9 May 1925; *s* of late Edward Stanley Trowbridge and Ida Trowbridge (*née* O'Keeffe); *m* 1946, Valerie Ann Glazebrook; one *s*. *Educ:* Royal College of Science, Imperial Coll. of Science and Technology, London Univ. (BSc Eng (Chem. Eng); ACGI 1946); Amer. Management Assoc. Coll., NYC (Dip. Bus. Studies). Technical Officer, ICI (Billingham Div.) Ltd, 1946–48; Division Manager, HWP/Fluor, 1948–53; Technical Dir, Sharples Co., 1953–57; Man. Dir, Sharples Co., 1957–59; Internat. Man. Dir, Sharples Corp., 1959–63; Group Managing Director: Pennwalt International Corp., 1963–72; Pegler-Hattersley Ltd, 1972–73; Dir Gen., Chemical Industries Assoc., 1973–87. Member: Process Plant Working Party, NEDO, 1970–77; Chemicals EDC, NEDO, 1973–87; Process Plant EDC, NEDO, 1977–80; CBI Council; CBI Heads of Sector Group; CBI Europe Cttee; Eur. Chem. Ind. PR Council, Brussels; CEFIC R&D Cttee, Brussels; Anglo-German Gp for Chem. Ind.; Anglo-French Gp for Chem. Ind.; ESRC Govt Industry Relns Cttee, 1973–87; Adv. Cttee, Eur. Business Inst., 1984–90; Bd, NRPB, 1987–91; IMRO Ltd, 1988–95. Chm., NEDO Task-Group on Tech., Research and Develt; Pres., Conseil d'Administration/CEFIC, Brussels, 1984–87 (Mem., 1973–87). Chm., Professional Develt Cttee, IChemE; Mem. Council, IChemE, 1987–89. Trustee, Chemical Ind. Museum, 1985–89. Hinchley Medal, IChemE, 1946; Internat. Medal, SCI, 1987. *Publications:* Purification of Oils for Marine Service, 1960; Scaling Up Centrifugal Separation Equipment, 1962; Collected Poems, 1963; Centrifugation, 1966; Exhibiting for Profit, 1969; Market Research and Forecasting, 1969; The Financial Performance of Process and Plant Companies, 1970; Poems for the Second Half, 1975; The Particular World of Directors General, 1987. *Recreations:* having fun, painting, shooting, mineralogy, print making, kitsch, wooden containers.

TROWBRIDGE, Rear-Adm. Sir Richard (John), KCVO 1975; Governor of Western Australia, 1980–83; *b* 21 Jan. 1920; *s* of A. G. Trowbridge, Andover, Hants; *m* 1955, Anne Mildred Perceval; two *s*. *Educ:* Andover Grammar Sch.; Royal Navy. Joined RN as Boy Seaman, 1935. War of 1939–45: commissioned as Sub Lieut, Dec. 1940 (despatches Aug. 1945). Comdr, 1953; commanded Destroyer Carysfort, 1956–58; Exec. Officer, HMS Bermuda, 1958–59, and HMS Excellent, 1959–60; Captain, 1960; commanded Fishery Protection Sqdn, 1962–64; completed course IDC, 1966; commanded HMS Hampshire, 1967–69; Rear-Adm., 1970; Flag Officer Royal Yachts, 1970–75. An Extra Equerry to the Queen, 1970–. Younger Brother of Trinity Hse, 1972. KStJ 1980. *Recreations:* fishing, sailing, golf; most outdoor pursuits. *Address:* Old Idsworth Garden, Finchdean, Waterlooville PO8 0BA. *T:* (01705) 412714. *Club:* Army and Navy.

TROWELL, Prof. Brian Lewis, PhD; Heather Professor of Music and Fellow of Wadham College, University of Oxford, 1988–96, now Emeritus; *b* 21 Feb. 1931; *s* of Richard Lewis and Edith J. R. Trowell, *m* 1958, Rhianon James; two *d*. *Educ:* Christ's Hospital; Gonville and Caius Coll., Cambridge. MA 1959; PhD 1960. Asst Lectr, later Lectr, in Music, Birmingham Univ., 1957–62; freelance scholar, conductor, opera producer, lecturer and editor, 1962–67; Head of BBC Radio opera, 1967–70; Reader in Music, 1970, Professor of Music, 1973, King Edward Prof. of Music, 1974–88, KCL. Regents' Prof., Univ. of California at Berkeley, 1970; Vis. Gresham Prof. of Music, City Univ., 1971–74. Pres., Royal Musical Assoc., 1983–88. Hon. RAM, 1972; Hon. FGSM, 1972; FRCM 1977; FTCL 1978; Fellow: Curwen Inst., 1987; KCL, 1997. Chm., Editorial Cttee, Musica Britannica, 1983–93. *Publications:* The Early Renaissance, Pelican History of Music vol. ii, 1963; Four Motets by John Plummer, 1968; (ed jtly) John Dunstable: Complete Works, ed M. F. Bukofzer, 2nd edn, 1970; (ed) Invitation to Medieval Music, vol. 3 1976, vol. 4 1978; opera translations; contrib. dictionaries of music and articles in learned journals. *Recreations:* theatre, reading, gardening. *Address:* 5 Tree Lane, Iffley Village, Oxford OX4 4EY.

TROWER, William Spencer Philip; QC 2001; *b* 28 Dec. 1959; *s* of Anthony Gosselin Trower and Catherine Joan Trower (*née* Kellett); *m* 1986, Mary Louise Chastel de Boinville; four *d*. *Educ:* Eton Coll.; Christ Church, Oxford (MA); City Univ. (Dip. Law). Called to the Bar, Lincoln's Inn, 1983. *Publication:* (ed jtly) The Law and Practice of Corporate Administrations, 1994. *Recreations:* family, gardening, countryside, country sports. *Address:* 3–4 South Square, Gray's Inn, WC1R 5HP. *T:* (020) 7696 9900. *Club:* Garrick.

TROWSDALE, Prof. John, PhD; Professor of Immunology, and Head of Division of Immunology, Department of Pathology, University of Cambridge, since 1997; *b* 8 Feb. 1949; *s* of Roy R. Trowsdale and Doris Trowsdale (*née* Graham); *m* 1971, Susan Price; two *s* one *d*. *Educ:* Beverley Grammar Sch.; Univ. of Birmingham (BSc 1970; PhD 1973). European Fellow, Biochemical Soc., Gif-sur-Yvette, France, 1973–75; Res. Fellow, Scripps Clinic and Res. Foundn, Calif, 1975–78; SRC Res. Fellow, Genetics Lab., Univ. of Oxford, 1978–79; Imperial Cancer Research Fund: ICRF Fellow, 1979–82; Res. Scientist, 1982–85; Sen. Scientist, 1986–90; Prin. Scientist, 1990–97. Member: Council, European Fedn of Immunogenetics, 1995–98; Sci. Adv. Bd, Onyvax, 1997–; Chm., Histocompatibility and Immunogenetics Affinity Gp, British Soc. of Histocompatibility and Immunogenetics, 1996–99. FMedSci 2000. *Publications:* (jtly) Advanced Immunology, 1996; res. papers in science jls. *Recreations:* playing rock, jazz and classical music, painting. *Address:* Department of Pathology, Tennis Court Road, Cambridge CB2 1QP. *T:* (01223) 333711.

TROYAT, Henri; Légion d'Honneur; writer; Member of the French Academy, 1959; *b* Moscow, 1 Nov. 1911; *m* 1948, Marguerite Saintagne; one *s*, and one step *d*. *Educ:* Paris. *Publications: novels:* l'Araigne (Prix Goncourt, 1938) (The Web, 1984); Les Semailles et les Moissons (5 vols), 1957; Tant que la Terre durera (3 vols), 1960; La Lumière des Justes (5 vols), 1963; Viou, 1980; Le Pain de l'Etranger, 1982 (The Children, 1983); Le Bruit solitaire du Coeur, 1985; A demain, Sylvie, 1986; Le Troisième Bonheur, 1987; Treachery, 1990; Aliocha, 1991; Youri, 1992; Le Défi d'Olga, 1995; l'Affaire Cremonnière, Juliette Drouet, 1997; Le Fils du Satrape, 1998; Namouna ou la Chaleur Animale, 1999; La Ballerine du Saint-Petersbourg, 2000; *biographies:* Pushkin, Dostoievsky, Tolstoi, Gogol, Catherine la Grande, Pierre le Grand, Alexandre 1er, Ivan le Terrible, Tchekhov, Gorki, Flaubert, Turgenev, Maupassant, Zola, Verlaine, Nicolas II, Baudelaire, Balzac, Rasputin; Terribles Tsarines, 1999. *Address:* Académie Française, Quai de Conti, 75006 Paris, France.

TRUDGILL, Prof. Peter John, FBA 1989; Professor of English Linguistics, University of Fribourg, since 1998; *b* 7 Nov. 1943; *s* of John Trudgill and Hettie Jean Trudgill (*née* Gooch); *m* 1980, Jean Marie Hannah. *Educ:* City of Norwich Sch.; King's Coll., Cambridge (BA; MA 1966); Edinburgh Univ. (Dip Gen Linguistics 1967; PhD 1971). Asst Lectr, Lectr, Reader, Prof., Dept of Linguistic Sci., Univ. of Reading, 1970–86; Reader, 1986–87, Prof. of Sociolinguistics, 1987–92, Essex Univ.; Prof. of English Linguistics, Univ. of Lausanne, 1993–98. Vis. Prof. at Univs of Hong Kong, Bergen, Aarhus, Illinois, Stanford, Osmania, Tokyo International Christian, ANU, Texas Austin, Toronto, Canterbury (NZ). Fellow: Norwegian Acad. of Sci and Letters, 1995; Royal Norwegian

Acad. of Scis, 1996. Hon PhD Uppsala, 1995. *Publications:* The Social Differentiation of English in Norwich, 1974; Sociolinguistics: an introduction, 1974, 4th edn 2000; Accent, Dialect and the School, 1975; Sociolinguistic Patterns in British English, 1978; (with A. Hughes) English Accents and Dialects, 1979; (with J. K. Chambers) Dialectology, 1980; (with J. M. Hannah) International English, 1982, 3rd edn 1994; On Dialect, 1983; Coping with America, 1983, 2nd edn 1985; Language in the British Isles, 1984; Applied Sociolinguistics, 1984; Dialects in Contact, 1986; The Dialects of England, 1990; (with J. K. Chambers) English Dialects: studies in grammatical variation, 1991; (with L. Andersson) Bad Language, 1991; Introducing Language and Society, 1992; Dialects, 1994; (with L. Bauer) Language Myths, 1998. *Recreations:* Norwich City FC, playing the 'cello. *Address:* English Seminar, Université de Fribourg, Miséricorde, 1700 Fribourg, Switzerland. *T:* (26) 3007907.

TRUDINGER, Prof. Neil Sidney, PhD; FRS 1997; FAA; Professor of Mathematics, since 1973, Dean, School of Mathematical Sciences, since 1992, Australian National University; *b* 20 June 1942; *s* of Laurence Robert Trudinger and Dorothy Winifred Trudinger; *m* 1st, 1964, Patricia Robyn Saunders; one *s* one *d*; 2nd, 1991, Tess Rosario Valdez. *Educ:* Univ. of New England, Australia (BSc Hons 1962); Stanford Univ., USA (MS 1965; PhD 1966). FAA 1978. Courant Instructor, New York Univ., 1966–67; Lectr, then Sen. Lectr, Macquarie Univ., Australia, 1967–70; Reader, then Prof., Univ. of Qld, 1970–73; Australian National University: Head, Dept of Pure Maths, 1973–78; Director: Commonwealth Special Res. Centre for Mathematical Analysis, 1982–96; Centre for Maths and its Applications, 1991–93; Prof., Northwestern Univ., 1989–93. *Publications:* Elliptic Partial Differential Equations of the Second Order, 1977, 2nd edn 1983. *Address:* School of Mathematical Sciences, Australian National University, Canberra, ACT 0200, Australia. *T:* (2) 62492957.

TRUE, Nicholas Edward, CBE 1993; Private Secretary to Leader of the Opposition, House of Lords, since 1997; *b* 31 July 1951; *s* of Edward Thomas True and Kathleen Louise True (*née* Mather); *m* 1979, Anne-Marie Elena Kathleen Blanco Hood; two *s* one *d*. *Educ:* Nottingham High Sch.; Peterhouse, Cambridge (BA Hons 1973; MA 1978). Mem., Cons. Res. Dept, 1975–82; Asst to Cons. Party Dep. Leader, 1978–82; Special Advr to Sec. of State for Health and Social Security, 1982–86; Dir, Public Policy Unit, 1986–90; Dep. Head, Prime Minister's Policy Unit, 1991–95; Special Advr, Prime Minister's Office, 1997. Councillor (C), Richmond-upon-Thames, 1986–90, 1998–. Trustee: Olga Havel Foundn, 1990–94; Sir Harold Hood's Charitable Trust, 1996–. *Publications:* articles in newspapers, jls etc; pamphlets and papers on policy matters. *Recreations:* Byzantium, Italy, gardens, cricket. *Address:* 114 Palewell Park, East Sheen, SW14 8JH. *T:* (020) 8876 9628; Contrada Salino 15, San Ginesio, Macerata, Italy. *Clubs:* Beefsteak, Travellers.

TRUEMAN, Frederick Sewards, OBE 1989; writer and broadcaster; *b* Stainton, Yorks, 6 Feb. 1931; *s* of late Alan Thomas Trueman; *m* 1st, 1955, Enid (marr. diss.); one *s* two *d* (incl. twin *s* and *d*); 2nd, Veronica Wilson (*née* Lundy). *Educ:* Maltby Secondary Sch. Apprentice bricklayer, 1946; worked in tally office of Maltby Main pit, 1948–51; Nat. service, RAF, 1951–53. Played club cricket, 1945–48; Yorks Fedn cricket tour, 1948; played for Yorks CCC, 1949–68 (took 2304 wickets in first class games, incl. 100 wickets in a season twelve times; also made 3 centuries); county cap, 1951; captained Yorkshire 31 times, 1962–68; played 6 one day matches for Derby CCC, 1972; first Test series, against India, 1952; MCC tours to WI, 1953–54, 1959–60, and to Australia, 1958–59, 1962–63 (took a total of 307 Test wickets, 1952–65, incl. 10 in a match and 7 in an innings three times, and was first bowler to take 300 Test wickets, 1963). Journalist, Sunday People, 1957–; anchorman, Indoor League series, Yorks TV; cricket commentator for BBC. *Publications:* Fast Fury, 1961; Cricket, 1963; Book of Cricket, 1964; The Freddie Trueman Story, 1966; Ball of Fire (autobiog.), 1976; (with John Arlott) On Cricket, 1977; Thoughts of Trueman Now, 1978; (with Frank Hardy) You Nearly Had Him That Time, 1978; My Most Memorable Matches, 1982; (with Trevor Bailey) From Larwood to Lillee, 1983; (with Don Mosey) Fred Trueman's Yorkshire, 1984; (with Trevor Bailey) The Spinners' Web, 1988; (with Peter Grosvenor) Fred Trueman's Cricket Masterpieces: classic tales from the pavilion, 1990; (with Don Mosey) Champion Times, 1994; (with Don Mosey) Talking Cricket: with friends past and present, 1997; Fred Trueman's Dales Journey, 1998. *Recreations:* ornithology, working for children's charities. *Address:* c/o BBC, Broadcasting House, W1A 1AA. *Clubs:* Yorkshire County Cricket (Hon. Life Mem.), MCC (Hon. Life Mem.), Lord's Taverners, Variety of GB, Forty, Saint Cricket; Ilkley Golf.

TRULUCK, Maj. Gen. Ashley Ernest George, CB 2001; CBE 1997; Chief Executive, Greater London Magistrates' Courts Authority, since 2001; *b* 7 Dec. 1947; *s* of Maj. George William Truluck, RA and Elizabeth Truluck (*née* Kitchener); *m* 1976, Jennifer Bell; one *s* one *d*. *Educ:* Harvey's Sch.; RMA Sandhurst; BA. Regtl duty, Gurkha Signals, Malaya, Hong Kong, Nepal, 1969–74; ADC to Maj. Gen., Bde of Gurkhas, and Comdr FARELF, 1974–75; sc, 1978–79; GSO2, MoD, 1980–81; Sqn Comdr, BAOR, UK, 1982–84; Dir, Staff RMCS, 1984–86; Regt Comdr, BAOR, 1986–88; Col Army Staff Duties, 1989–90; HCSC, 1990; Comdt, Royal Sch. of Signals, 1991–92; RCDS, 1993; Brig. Gen. Staff, Land Comd, 1994–96; Dir, Attack Helicopter, MoD, 1997–98; Exec. ACOS, SHAPE, 1998–2000. Col Comdt, RCS, 2001–. Chm., London Criminal Justice Bd, 2001. FIMgt 1992; MInstD 2001. *Recreations:* offshore sailing, hill walking, sketching. *Address:* GLMCA, 185 Marylebone Road, NW1 5QL; *e-mail:* Truluck@compuserve.com. *Clubs:* Army and Navy, Ocean Cruising.

TRUMPINGTON, Baroness *cr* 1980 (Life Peer), of Sandwich in the County of Kent; **Jean Alys Barker;** PC 1992; an Extra Baroness in Waiting to the Queen, since 1998; *d* of late Arthur Edward Campbell-Harris, MC and late Doris Marie Robson; *m* 1954, William Alan Barker (*d* 1988); one *s*. *Educ:* privately in England and France. Land Girl to Rt Hon. David Lloyd George, MP, 1940–41; Foreign Office, Bletchley Park, 1941–45; European Central Inland Transport Orgn, 1945–49; Sec. to Viscount Hinchingbrooke, MP, 1950–52. Conservative Councillor, Cambridge City Council, Trumpington Ward, 1963–73; Mayor of Cambridge, 1971–72; Deputy Mayor, 1972–73; Conservative County Councillor, Cambridgeshire, Trumpington Ward, 1973–75; Hon. Councillor of the City of Cambridge, 1975–. A Baroness in Waiting (Government Whip), 1983–85 and 1992–97; Parly Under-Sec. of State, DHSS, 1985–87, MAFF, 1987–89; Minister of State, MAFF, 1989–92. UK Delegate to UN Status of Women Commn, 1979–82. Member: Air Transport Users' Cttee, 1972–80 (Dep. Chairman 1978–79, Chm. 1979–80); Bd of Visitors to HM Prison, Pentonville, 1975–81; Mental Health Review Tribunal, 1975–81. Gen. Commissioner of Taxes, 1976–83. Pres., Assoc. of Heads of Independent Schs, 1980–89. Steward, Folkestone Racecourse, 1980–92. Hon. Fellow, Lucy Cavendish Coll., Cambridge, 1980. Hon. FRCPath 1992; Hon. ARCVS 1994; Hon. Mem., BVA, 1995. JP Cambridge, 1972–75, South Westminster, 1976–82. *Recreations:* bridge, racing, collecting antiques, needlepoint. *Address:* House of Lords, SW1A 0PW. *Clubs:* Farmers', Grillions.

TRUNDLE, Shirley Jean, OBE 1999; Director, Opportunities and Diversity Group, Department for Work and Pensions, since 2001; *b* 28 Feb. 1958; *d* of Derek and Jean Hayles; *m* 1979, John Malcolm Trundle; one *s* two *d*. *Educ:* Guildford High Sch.; Newnham Coll., Cambridge (MA); St Catharine's Coll., Cambridge (MPhil). Entered DES, subseq. DFE, then DFEE, 1981; Private Sec. to Sec. of State for Educn and Sci., 1986–87; Principal, 1987–93; Divl Manager, Higher Educn Policy and Funding, 1993–96; Sec. to Nat. Cttee of Inquiry into Higher Educn (Dearing Cttee), 1996–97; Head, Childcare Unit, 1998–99; Dir, Opportunity and Diversity Gp. *Recreations:* family, music, food. *Address:* Department for Work and Pensions, Caxton House, Tothill Street, SW1H 9NF.

TRURO, Bishop of, since 1997; **Rt Rev. William Ind;** *b* 26 March 1942; *s* of William Robert and Florence Emily Ind; *m* 1967, Frances Isobel Bramald; three *s*. *Educ:* Univ. of Leeds (BA); College of the Resurrection, Mirfield. Asst Curate, St Dunstan's, Feltham, 1966–71; Priest in charge, St Joseph the Worker, Northolt, 1971–74; Team Vicar, Basingstoke, 1974–87; Director of Ordinands, dio. of Winchester, 1982–87; Hon. Canon of Winchester, 1985–87; Bishop Suffragan of Grantham, 1987–97; Dean of Stamford, 1988–97. *Recreations:* bird watching, cricket watching, orchid finding. *Address:* Lis Escop, Truro, Cornwall TR3 6QQ. *T:* (01872) 862657.

TRURO, Dean of; *see* Moxon, Very Rev. M. A.

TRUSCOTT, Sir George (James Irving), 3rd Bt *cr* 1909; *b* 24 Oct. 1929; *s* of Sir Eric Homewood Stanham Truscott, 2nd Bt, and Lady (Mary Dorcas) Truscott (*née* Irving) (*d* 1948); *S* father, 1973; *m* 1962, Yvonne Dora (*née* Nicholson); one *s* one *d*. *Educ:* Sherborne School. *Heir: s* Ralph Eric Nicholson Truscott, *b* 21 Feb. 1966. *Address:* BM QUILL, London WC1N 3XX.

TRUSCOTT, Ian Derek; QC (Scot.) 1997; *b* 7 Nov. 1949; *s* of Derek and Jessie Truscott; *m* 1972, Julia Elizabeth Bland; four *s*. *Educ:* Edinburgh Univ. (LLB Hons 1971); Leeds Univ. (LLM 1974). Solicitor, 1973–87; admitted to Faculty of Advocates, 1988; called to the Bar, Gray's Inn, 1995. Vis. Prof. of Law, Strathclyde Univ., 1999–. *Recreations:* walking, snow dome collecting. *Address:* Advocates' Library, Parliament Square, Edinburgh EH1 1RF. *T:* (0131) 226 5071; Old Square Chambers, 1 Verulam Buildings, Gray's Inn, WC1R 5LQ. *T:* (020) 7269 0300. *Club:* Royal Northern and University (Aberdeen).

TRUSCOTT, Dr Peter; political analyst, since 1999; Visiting Research Fellow, Institute for Public Policy Research; *b* 20 March 1959; *s* of late Derek Truscott and of Dorothy Truscott; *m* 1991, Svetlana, *d* of late Col Prof. Nicolai Chernicov and Svetlana Chernicova. *Educ:* Newton Abbot Grammar Sch.; Exeter Coll., Oxford (History Prize; BA 1981, MA 1985, DPhil 1986, Modern History). Labour Party Organiser, 1986–89; NACRO, 1989–94. Mem. Cttee, Herts Assoc., NACRO, 1993–94. Councillor, Colchester Borough Council, 1988–92; contested (Lab) Torbay, 1992. Member: TGWU, 1986–; MSF, 1999–; Co-op Party, 1987–; posts in Trade Union and Labour movements. MEP (Lab) Hertfordshire, 1994–99; contested (Lab) Eastern Reg., 1999. European Parliament: Labour Party spokesman on foreign affairs and defence, 1997–99; Vice-Pres., Cttee on Security and Disarmament, 1994–99; Mem., Foreign Affairs Cttee, 1994–99; Substitute Member: Regl Policy Cttee, 1994–97; Economic, Monetary and Industrial Policy Cttee, 1997–99. Mem., Internat. and Domestic Sub-Cttee, Labour Party NEC, 1996–97. Sch. governor, 1988–92. *Publications:* Russia First, 1997; numerous articles. *Recreations:* walking, music, country dancing, swimming, leafletting. *Address:* 31 Artillery Mansions, 75 Victoria Street, SW1H 0HZ. *Club:* William Morris Labour (South Oxhey).

TRUSTRAM EVE; *see* Eve, family name of Baron Silsoe.

TRUSWELL, Prof. (Arthur) Stewart, Hon. AO 2001; MD, DSc, FRCP, FFPHM, FRACP; Professor of Human Nutrition, University of Sydney, since 1978; *b* 18 Aug. 1928; *s* of George Truswell and Molly Truswell (*née* Stewart-Hess); *m* 1st, 1956, Sheila McGregor (marr. diss. 1983); four *s*; 2nd, 1986, Catherine Hull; two *d*. *Educ:* Ruthin Sch., Clwyd; Liverpool Univ.; Cape Town Univ. (MB, ChB 1952, MD 1959); DSc Sydney 1998. FRCP 1975; FFCM 1979; FRACP 1980. Registrar in Pathology, Cape Town Univ., 1954; Registrar in Med., Groote Schuur Hosp., 1955–57; Research Bursar, Clin. Nutrition Unit, Dept. of Med., Cape Town Univ., 1958 and 1959; Adams Meml Trav. Fellowship to London, 1960; Sen. Fellow, Clin. Nutrition, Tulane Univ., USA, 1961; Res. Officer, Clin. Nutrition Unit, Cape Town Univ., 1962; Sen. Mem., Scientific Staff, MRC Atheroma Research Unit, Western Infirmary, Glasgow, 1963 and 1964; full-time Lectr, then Sen. Lectr in Med. and Consultant Gen. Physician, Cape Town Univ. and Groote Schuur Hosp., 1965–71; Warden of Med. Students' Residence, Cape Town Univ., 1967–69; Prof. of Nutrition and Dietetics, Queen Elizabeth Coll., London Univ., 1971–78. Vice-Pres., Internat. Union of Nutritional Sciences, 1985–93; Member, numerous cttees, working parties, editorial bds and socs related to nutrition. *Publications:* Human Nutrition and Dietetics, 7th edn (with S. Davidson, R. Passmore, J. F. Brock), 1979; ABC of Nutrition, 1986, 3rd edn 1999; (with J. I. Mann) Essentials of Human Nutrition, 1998; numerous research papers in sci. jls on various topics in human nutrition. *Recreations:* gardening, walking (esp. on mountains). *Address:* 23 Woonona Road, Northbridge, NSW 2063, Australia; Human Nutrition Unit, Department of Biochemistry, Sydney University, Sydney, NSW 2006, Australia. *T:* (2) 93513726, *Fax:* (2) 93516022.

TRUSWELL, Paul Anthony; MP (Lab) Pudsey, since 1997; *b* 17 Nov. 1955; *s* of John and Olive Truswell; *m* 1981, Suzanne Clare Evans; two *s*. *Educ:* Firth Park Comprehensive Sch., Sheffield; Leeds Univ. (BA Hons 1977). Journalist, Yorkshire Post newspapers, 1977–88; Local Govt Officer, Wakefield MDC, 1988–97. Member: Leeds HA, 1982–90; Leeds FHSA, 1992–96. Mem. (Lab) Leeds CC, 1982–97. Mem., Envmtl Audit Select Cttee, 1997–99. *Recreations:* playing any sport demanded by my children, photography, cinema. *Address:* House of Commons, SW1A 0AA. *T:* (020) 7219 3504; (constituency office) 10A Greenside, Pudsey, W Yorks LS28 8PU. *T:* (0113) 2293553. *Club:* Civil Service.

TRYON, family name of **Baron Tryon**.

TRYON, 3rd Baron *cr* 1940, of Durnford; **Anthony George Merrik Tryon,** OBE 2001; DL; *b* 26 May 1940; *s* of 2nd Baron Tryon, PC, GCVO, KCB, DSO, and of Etheldreda Josephine, *d* of Sir Merrik Burrell, 7th Bt, CBE; *S* father, 1976; *m* 1973, Dale Elizabeth (*d* 1997), *d* of Barry Harper; two *s* two *d* (of whom one *s* one *d* are twins). *Educ:* Eton. Page of Honour to the Queen, 1954–56. Captain Wessex Yeomanry, 1972. Dir, Lazard Bros & Co. Ltd, 1976–83; Chairman: English & Scottish Investors Ltd, 1977–88; Swaine Adeney Brigg, 1991–93. Chm., Salisbury Cathedral Spire Trust, 1985–. Pres., Anglers Conservation Assoc., 1985–. DL Wilts, 1992. *Recreations:* fishing and shooting. *Heir: s* Hon. Charles George Barrington Tryon, *b* 15 May 1976. *Address:* The Manor House, Great Durnford, near Salisbury, Wilts SP4 6BB. *T:* (01722) 782225. *Clubs:* White's, Pratt's.

TRYTHALL, Maj.-Gen. Anthony John, CB 1983; Director of Army Education, 1980–84; Director: Brassey's (UK) Ltd (formerly Brassey's Defence Publishers Ltd),

1984–97 (Managing Director, 1984–87; Executive Deputy Chairman, 1988–95); Brassey's (US) Inc., 1984–95; *b* 30 March 1927; *s* of Eric Stewart Trythall and Irene (*née* Hollingham); *m* 1952, Celia Haddon; two *s* one *d*. *Educ:* Lawrence Sheriff Sch., Rugby; St Edmund Hall, Oxford (BA Hons Mod. Hist., 1947, DipEd 1951); Institute of Education, London Univ. (Academic DipEd 1962); King's College, London (MA in War Studies, 1969). National Service as RAEC Officer, UK, Egypt and Akaba, 1947–49; teaching, 1951–53; Regular RAEC Officer, 1953; seconded to Malay Regt for service at Fedn Mil. Coll., Port Dickson, 1953–56; WO, 1957–62; BAOR, 1962–66; Inspector, 1967–68; Educn Adviser, Regular Commns Bd, 1969–71; Head of Officer Educn Br., 1971–73; Chief Inspector of Army Educn, and Col Res., 1973–74; MoD, 1974–76; Chief Educn Officer, UKLF, 1976–80. Col Comdt, RAEC, 1986–89. Member: Council, Royal United Services Instn for Def. Studies, 1978–84; London Univ. Bd of War Studies, 1983–95; Chm. Bd, British Military Studies Gp, 1996 (Mem., 1984–99). Chm., Gallipoli Meml Lecture Trust, 1986–89, 1999–2000 (Trustee, 1984–2000). Chm. Bd of Govs, Selwyn Sch., Glos, 1997–. 1st Prize, Trench-Gascoigne Essay Competition, 1969. *Publications:* Boney Fuller: the intellectual general, 1977 (USA, as Boney Fuller: soldier, strategist and writer); (contrib.) The Downfall of Leslie Hore-Belisha in the Second World War, 1982; Fuller and the Tanks in Home Fires and Foreign Fields, 1985; articles in Army Qly, Jl of RUSI, British Army Rev., and Jl of Contemp. Hist. *Address:* c/o Royal Bank of Scotland, Holt's Branch, Lawrie House, Victoria Road, Farnborough, Hants GU14 7NR. *Club:* Naval and Military.

TSANG, Sir Donald Yam-kuen, KBE 1997 (OBE 1993); Chief Secretary for Administration, Hong Kong Special Administrative Region, since 2001; *b* 7 Oct. 1944; *m* 1969, Selina Pou; two *s*. *Educ:* Harvard Univ. (MPA). Joined Govt of Hong Kong, 1967: Dep. Dir of Trade, responsible for trade with N America, 1984; Dep. Sec., Gen. Duties, responsible for Sino-British Jt Declaration, 1985; Dir of Admin, Office of Chief Sec., 1989–91; Dir-Gen. of Trade, 1991–93; Sec. for Treasury, 1993–95; Financial Sec., Hong Kong, 1995–97, HKSAR, 1997. *Recreations:* golf, music. *Address:* Government Secretariat, Central Government Offices, Lower Albert Road, Hong Kong. *T:* 28102323.

TS'ONG, Fou; *see* Fou Ts'ong.

TSUI, Prof. Daniel C., PhD; Arthur LeGrand Doty Professor, Department of Electrical Engineering, Princeton University, since 1982; *b* Henan, China, 1939; US citizen; *m* Linda Varland. *Educ:* Pui Ching Middle Sch., Hong Kong; Augustana Coll., Rock Island, Ill; Univ. of Chicago (PhD 1967). Res. Associate, Univ. of Chicago, 1967–68; Mem. Technical Staff, Bell Labs, Murray Hill, NJ, 1968–82. Fellow, AAAS; Mem., US NAS, 1987. Nobel Prize for Physics (jtly), 1998; Benjamin Franklin Award in Physics, 1998. *Publications:* contribs to jls. *Address:* Department of Electrical Engineering, Princeton University, Princeton, NJ 08544, USA.

TSUI, Prof. Lap-Chee, OC 1991; PhD; FRS 1991; FRSC 1989; Geneticist-in-Chief and Senior Research Scientist, since 1983, Sellers Chair in Cystic Fibrosis Research, since 1989, Director, Centre for Applied Genomics, since 1998, Hospital for Sick Children, Toronto; Professor, Department of Molecular and Medical Genetics, since 1990, University Professor, since 1994, University of Toronto; *b* 21 Dec. 1950; *s* of Jing-Lue Hsue and Hui-Ching Wang; *m* 1977, Lan Fong (Ellen); two *s*. *Educ:* Chinese Univ. of Hong Kong (BSc Biol. 1972; MPhil 1974); Univ. of Pittsburgh (PhD Biol Scis 1979). Asst Prof. 1983–88, Associate Prof. 1988–90, Depts of Med. Genetics and Med. Biophysics, Univ. of Toronto; Dir, Cystic Fibrosis Res. Prog., Hosp. for Sick Children, Toronto, 1995–99. Mem. of team which identified first DNA marker linked to cystic fibrosis on chromosome 7, 1985; led team which isolated the gene responsible for cystic fibrosis and defined the principal mutation, 1989. Chairman: Gordon Res. Conf. on Human Molecular Genetics, 1995; Genome Canada Task Force, 1998–99; Internat. Sci. Prog. Cttee, Human Genome Meeting 2000, 1999–2000. Trustee, Educn Foundn, Fedn of Chinese Canadian Professionals, Ontario. Eminent Scientist, Inst. of Physical and Chemical Res., Japan, 2000; Vis. Prof., Shantou Univ. Med. Sch., China, 2000. Hon. DCL: Univ. of King's Coll., Halifax, 1991; St Francis Xavier, Antigonish, NS, 1994; Hon. DSc: Univ. of New Brunswick, Fredericton, 1991; Chinese Univ. of Hong Kong, 1992. Paul di Sant'Agnese Distinguished Scientific Achievement Award, Cystic Fibrosis Foundn, USA, 1989; Gold Medal of Honor, Pharmaceutical Manufacturers' Assoc., Canada, 1989; Centennial Award, RSCan, 1989; Maclean's Honor Roll, 1989; Award of Excellence, Genetic Soc. Canada, 1990; Courvoisier Leadership Award, 1990; Gairdner Internat. Award, 1990; Cresson Medal, Franklin Inst., 1992; Mead Johnson Award, 1992; Sarsdedt Res. Prize, 1993; Sanremo Internat. Award, 1993; Lecocq Prize, Acad. des Scis, Inst de France, 1994; Henry Friesen Award, 1995; Medal of Honour, Canadian Med. Assoc., 1996; Community Service Award, Toronto Biotechnol. Initiative, 1998; Distinguished Scientist Award, MRC (Canada), 2000. *Publications:* numerous papers in learned jls and invited papers and reviews. *Recreations:* cooking, travel, sightseeing. *Address:* Department of Genetics, Hospital for Sick Children, 555 University Avenue, Toronto, ON M5G 1X8, Canada. *T:* (416) 8136015, *Fax:* (416) 8134931.

TSUJI, Yoshifumi; Chairman, Nissan Motor Co. Ltd, since 1996; *b* Kagawa Prefecture, Japan, 6 Feb. 1928; *m*. *Educ:* Faculty of Engrg, Univ. of Tokyo. Joined Nissan Motor Co. Ltd, 1954: General Manager: Prodn Control and Engrg Dept No 1, Yokohama Plant, 1978–80; Engrg Dept No 1, 1980–83; Engrg Dept No 1 and Cost Mgt Office, 1983–84; Tochigi Plant, 1984–87 (Gen. Manager Mfg Dept No 4, 1985–87); Dir and Mem. Bd, 1985–; Man. Dir i/c Product Planning, Marketing Gp No 1, 1987–89; Exec. Man. Dir, 1989–90; Exec. Vice Pres., 1990–92; Pres., 1992–96. Chm., Japan Automobile Manufactures Assoc. Inc., 1996–. Vice Chm., Fedn of Econ. Orgn, 1997–. Blue Ribbon Medal (Japan), 1995; Order of Queen Isabel la Católica (Spain), 1995. *Recreations:* golf, reading. *Address:* Nissan Motor Co. Ltd, 17–1 Ginza 6-chome, Chuo-ku, Tokyo 104–0061, Japan. *T:* (3) 35435523.

TUAM, Archbishop of, (RC), since 1995; **Most Rev. Michael Neary;** *b* 15 April 1946. Ordained priest, 1971; Titular Bishop of Quaestoriana and Auxiliary Bishop of Tuam, 1992–95. *Address:* Archbishop's House, Tuam, Co. Galway, Ireland. *T:* (93) 24166, *Fax:* (93) 28070.

TUAM, KILLALA AND ACHONRY, Bishop of, since 1998; **Rt Rev. Richard Crosbie Aitken Henderson,** DPhil; *b* 27 March 1957; *s* of Baron Henderson of Brompton, KBE; *m* 1985, Anita Julia Whiting; one *s* two *d*. *Educ:* Westminster Sch.; Magdalen Coll., Oxford (MA, DPhil 1984); St John's Coll., Nottingham (DipTh Univ. of Nottingham 1984; Dip Pastoral Studies 1986). Ordained deacon, 1986, priest, 1987; Curate, Chinnor with Emmington and Sydenham, Dio. Oxford, 1986–89; Diocese of Cork, Cloyne and Ross: Incumbent, Abbeystrewry Union, 1989–95; Ross Union, 1995–98; Canon, Cork and Ross Cathedrals, 1993–95; Prebendary of Cork, 1995–98; Dean of Ross, 1995–98. *Recreation:* woodwork. *Address:* Bishop's House, Knockglass, Crossmolina, Co. Mayo, Ireland. *T:* (96) 31317.
See also Hon. L. D. J. Henderson.

TUCK, Anne Victoria, (Vicky); Principal, Cheltenham Ladies' College, since 1996; *b* 9 Jan. 1953; *m* 1977, Peter John Tuck; two *s*. *Educ:* Univ. of Kent (BA Hons French and Italian); Univ. of London Inst. of Educn (PGCE); Univ. de Lille et de Paris (Dip. Supérieur de Droit et de français des Affaires); Univ. of South Bank (MA). French and Italian teacher, Putney High Sch., 1976–81; Hd of Mod. Langs, Bromley High Sch., 1981–86; Lectr, Inst. of Educn, London Univ., 1991–94; Dep. Hd, City of London Sch. for Girls, 1994–96. *Address:* Cheltenham Ladies' College, Bayshill Road, Cheltenham, Glos GL50 3EP.

TUCK, Anthony; *see* Tuck, J. A.

TUCK, Sir Bruce (Adolph Reginald), 3rd Bt *cr* 1910; *b* 29 June 1926; *o s* of Major Sir (William) Reginald Tuck, 2nd Bt, and Gladys Emily Kettle (*d* 1966), *d* of late N. Alfred Nathan, Wickford, Auckland, New Zealand, and *widow* of Desmond Fosberry Kettle, Auckland Mounted Rifles; *S* father, 1954; *m* 1st, 1949, Luise (marr. diss., in Jamaica, 1964), *d* of John C. Renfro, San Angelo, Texas, USA; two *s*; 2nd, 1968, Pamela Dorothy Nicholson, *d* of Alfred Nicholson, London; one *d*. *Educ:* Canford School, Dorset. Lieutenant, Scots Guards, 1945–47. *Heir:* s Richard Bruce Tuck, *b* 7 Oct. 1952. *Address:* PO Box 274, Montego Bay, Jamaica.

TUCK, Clarence Edward Henry; Civil Service Commissioner, 1977–83; *b* 18 April 1925; *s* of Frederick and May Tuck; *m* 1950, Daphne Robinson; one *s* one *d*. *Educ:* Rendcomb Coll., Cirencester; Merton Coll., Oxford. BA 1949. Served in Royal Signals, 1943–47. Inland Revenue, 1950; Min. of Supply, 1950–55; seconded to Nigerian Federal Govt, Lagos, 1955–57; Ministry of: Supply, 1957–59; Aviation, 1959–60; Defence, 1960–62; Aviation, 1962–66; IDC, 1967; Min. of Technology, 1968–70; Trade and Industry, 1970; CSD, 1971; Trade and Industry, 1973; Dept of Energy, 1974; Civil Service Dept, 1976; Management and Personnel Office, 1981; Dir, Civil Service Selection Board, 1977–81. Asst Principal, 1950; Principal, 1953; Asst Sec., 1962; Under-Sec., 1970.

TUCK, Prof. (John) Anthony, MA, PhD; FRHistS; Professor of Medieval History, University of Bristol, 1990–93, now Emeritus; *b* 14 Nov. 1940; *s* of Prof. John Philip Tuck, *qv*; *m* 1976, Amanda, *d* of Dr L. J. Cawley, Carlton Husthwaite, near Thirsk, Yorks; two *s*. *Educ:* Newcastle upon Tyne Royal Grammar Sch.; Jesus Coll., Cambridge (BA, MA, PhD). FRHistS 1987. Lecturer in History, 1965–75, Sen. Lectr, 1975–78, Univ. of Lancaster; Master of Collingwood Coll., and Hon. Lectr in History, Univ. of Durham, 1978–87; Reader in Medieval History, Univ. of Bristol, 1987–90. Res. Associate, New DNB, 1998–. Hon. Life Fellow, Collingwood Coll., Durham Univ., 1998. Clerk, Stapleford Parish Council, 2000–. *Publications:* Richard II and the English Nobility, 1973; Crown and Nobility 1272–1461, 1985, 2nd edn 1999; contribs to English Historical Rev., Northern History, etc. *Recreations:* walking, gardening. *Address:* 26 Church Street, Stapleford, Cambridge CB2 5DS.
See also R. F. Tuck.

TUCK, Prof. John Philip; Professor of Education, University of Newcastle upon Tyne (formerly King's College, University of Durham) 1948–76, now Emeritus; *b* 16 April 1911; *s* of late William John and Annie Tuck, Uplyme, Lyme Regis; *m* 1936, Jane Adelaide (*d* 2001), *d* of late George William Wall and Maria Ellen Wall, Ulceby, N Lincs; two *s*. *Educ:* Strand School; Jesus College, Cambridge. BA Hons English and History, Class I, 1933; Cambridge certificate in Education, 1934; Adelaide Stoll Bachelor Research Scholar, Christ's College, 1935; MA 1937. English Master: Gateshead Grammar School, 1936; Manchester Central High School, 1938; Wilson's Grammar School, 1939 and 1946. Served War of 1939–45, East Surrey Regt, and Army Education Corps, N Africa, Sicily, Italy, Austria. Lecturer in Education, King's College, Newcastle upon Tyne, 1946–48. Mem. Council, GPDST, 1976–84. FRSA 1970. Hon. Fellow, Coll. of Speech Therapists, 1966. *Address:* 7 Chesterford House, Southacre Drive, Chaucer Road, Cambridge CB2 2TZ. *T:* (01223) 324655.
See also J. A. Tuck, R. F. Tuck.

TUCK, Jonathan Philip; Deputy to the Director, University Library Services and to Bodley's Librarian, University of Oxford, since 1998; Fellow, Wolfson College, Oxford, since 1998; *b* 6 Sept. 1952; *s* of Philip Charles Tuck and Janetta Margaret Tuck; *m* 1982, Ann Lambert; one *s*. *Educ:* Portsmouth Grammar Sch.; Univ. of Manchester (MA); MA Oxon 1998. ALA 1981. John Rylands University Library of Manchester: Asst Librarian, 1978–90; Sub-Librarian, 1990–94; Asst Dir and Head of Admin, 1994–96; Asst Dir and Dep. Univ. Librarian, 1996–97. *Publications:* contrib. articles on aspects of librarianship and library collections. *Recreations:* book collecting, sport, especially cricket, football, Portsmouth Football Club. *Address:* Bodleian Library, Broad Street, Oxford OX1 3BG. *T:* (01865) 287107.

TUCK, Prof. Richard Francis, PhD; FBA 1994; Professor of Government, Harvard University, since 1995; *b* 9 Jan. 1949; *s* of Prof. John Philip Tuck, *qv*; *m* 1st, 1970, Mary Polwarth (marr. diss. 1993); two *s*; 2nd, 1993, Anne Malcolm; one *d*. *Educ:* Royal Grammar Sch., Newcastle upon Tyne; Jesus Coll., Cambridge (BA 1970; PhD 1976; Hon. Fellow 1997). Cambridge University: Research Fellow, 1970, Fellow, 1971–97, Jesus Coll.; Univ. Asst Lectr in History, 1973–77; Lectr in History, 1977–95; Reader in Political Theory, 1995. Vis. Fellow, Princeton Univ., 1989; Carlyle Lectr, Oxford, 1991. Foreign Hon. Mem., Amer. Acad. of Arts and Scis, 1992. *Publications:* Natural Rights Theories, 1979; Hobbes, 1989; Hobbes' Leviathan, 1991; Philosophy and Government 1572–1651, 1993. *Recreations:* repairing houses, looking after children. *Address:* Department of Government, Littauer Center, Harvard University, Cambridge, MA 02138–3001, USA; 9 Park Terrace, Cambridge CB1 1JH.

TUCK, Prof. Ronald Humphrey; Professor of Agricultural Economics, University of Reading, 1965–86 (part-time, 1982–86), now Emeritus; *b* 28 June 1921; *s* of Francis Tuck and Edith Ann Tuck (*née* Bridgewater); *m* Margaret Sylvia Everley (*d* 1990); one *s* two *d*. *Educ:* Harrow County Sch.; Corpus Christi Coll., Oxford. War Service, RAOC and REME, mainly N Africa and Italy, 1941–45 (despatches). Univ. of Reading, Dept of Agric. Economics: Research Economist, 1947–49; Lecturer, 1949–62; Reader, 1962–65; Head of Dept of Agricultural Economics and Management, Univ. of Reading, and Provincial Agricultural Economist (Reading Province), 1965–81; Dean, Faculty of Agriculture and Food, Univ. of Reading, 1971–74. *Publications:* An Essay on the Economic Theory of Rank, 1954; An Introduction to the Principles of Agricultural Economics, 1961 (Italian trans., 1970); reviews etc in Jl of Agric. Economics and Economic Jl. *Recreations:* reading, music, drawing, walking. *Address:* 211 Kidmore Road, Caversham, Reading RG4 7NW. *T:* (0118) 954 6563.

TUCK, Vicky; *see* Tuck, A. V.

TUCKER, Andrew Victor Gunn; HM Diplomatic Service; Ambassador to Azerbaijan, since 2000; *b* 20 Dec. 1955; *s* of Kenneth Gunn Tucker and Megan Tucker; *m* 1986, Judith Anne Gibson. *Educ:* Calday Grange Grammar Sch., Wirral; University Coll., Oxford (BA Hons 1978; MA 1986). MIL 1988. Jt Tech. Lang. Service, 1978–81; joined

HM Diplomatic Service, 1981: Second Sec., Dar es Salaam, 1982–85; First Secretary: on loan to Cabinet Office, 1985–87; and Press Attaché, Moscow, 1987–90; Dep. Hd, CSCE Unit, FCO, 1991–93; on loan to Auswärtiges Amt, 1993–94; Bonn, 1994–97; Dep. High Comr, Nairobi, and concurrently Alternate Perm. Rep. to UNEP and UN Centre for Human Settlements (Habitat), 1997–2000; Counsellor, FCO, 2000. *Recreations:* theatre, long walks, music, crosswords. *Address:* c/o Foreign and Commonwealth Office, King Charles Street, SW1A 2AH. *Clubs:* Royal Commonwealth Society, Royal Over-Seas League.

TUCKER, Brian George, CB 1976; OBE 1963; Deputy Secretary, Department of Energy, 1974–81; Member, UKAEA, 1976–81; *b* 6 May 1922; *s* of late Frank Ernest Tucker and May Tucker; *m* 1948, Marion Pollitt; three *d. Educ:* Christ's Hospital. Entered Home Civil Service, 1939, as Clerical Officer, Admty; successive postings at home, in Africa, the Middle East, Ceylon and Hong Kong till 1953; promoted Executive Officer, 1945; Higher Executive Officer, 1949. Min. of Power, Asst Principal, 1954, Principal, 1957; seconded to HMOCS, 1957–62, Asst Sec., Govt of Northern Rhodesia; returned to MOP, 1962, Principal Private Sec. to Minister, 1965–66, Asst Sec., 1966, Under-Sec., Ministry of Technology, 1969–70, Cabinet Office, 1970–72, DTI, 1972–73; Dep. Sec., 1973. *Recreations:* gardening, music. *Address:* 1 Sondes Place Drive, Dorking, Surrey RH4 3ED. *T:* (01306) 884720.

TUCKER, Clive Fenemore, CB 1996; Director, International Affairs, Department for Education and Skills (formerly Department for Education and Employment), since 1995; *b* 13 July 1944; *s* of William Frederick Tucker and Joan Tucker; *m* 1978, Caroline Elisabeth Macready; two *d. Educ:* Cheltenham Grammar Sch.; Balliol Coll., Oxford (BA). Entered Ministry of Labour, 1965; Private Sec. to Perm. Sec., 1968–70; Department of Employment, later Department for Education and Employment: Principal, 1970; Asst Sec., 1978; Grade 4, 1986; Under Sec., 1987. Chm., EU Employment Cttee, 2001–. Non-exec. Dir, RTZ Chemicals, 1987–90. Mem., Fulbright Commn, 1998–. *Recreations:* opera, looking at pictures, tennis. *Address:* c/o Department for Education and Skills, Caxton House, Tothill Street, SW1H 9NF.

TUCKER, Elizabeth Mary; Head Mistress, Headington School, Oxford, 1982–96; *b* 20 July 1936; *d* of late Harold and Doris Tucker. *Educ:* Cheltenham Ladies' College; Newnham College, Cambridge (BA Classical Tripos 1958); King's College London (PGCE). Assistant Mistress, Queen Anne's School, Caversham, 1959–64; Head of Classics, Notting Hill and Ealing High School, GPDST, 1964–72; Head Mistress, Christ's Hospital, Hertford, 1972–82. Associate, Newnham Coll., Cambridge, 1986–99. Corporate Mem., Cheltenham Ladies' Coll., 1994. Trustee: Bloxham Project, 1982–; Channing Sch., Highgate, 2001– (Mem. Council, 1995–2000). *Recreations:* music (piano), friends and family. *Address:* 78 Manor Drive, N20 0DU. *Club:* University Women's.

TUCKER, His Honour (Henry John) Martin; DL; QC 1975; a Circuit Judge, 1981–99; Resident Judge, Winchester Combined Court Centre, 1994–99; *b* 8 April 1930; *s* of late P. A. Tucker, LDS, RCS and Mrs Dorothy Tucker (*née* Hobbs); *m* 1957, Sheila Helen Wateridge, LRAM; one *s* four *d. Educ:* St Peter's Sch., Southbourne; Downside Sch.; Christ Church, Oxford (MA). Called to Bar, Inner Temple, 1954; Dep. Chm., Somerset QS, 1971; a Recorder of the Crown Court, 1972–81. Pres., Council of HM Circuit Judges, 1993. DL Hampshire, 1996. *Recreations:* walking occasionally; gardening gently; listening to music. *Address:* Chingri Khal, Sleepers Hill, Winchester, Hants SO22 4NB. *T:* (01962) 853927.

TUCKER, Martin; *see* Tucker, H. J. M.

TUCKER, Prof. Maurice Edwin, PhD; CGeol, FGS; Professor of Geological Sciences, University of Durham, since 1993; Master, University College, Durham, since 1998; *b* 6 Nov. 1946; *s* of Edwin Herlin and Winifred Tucker; *m* 1970, Vivienne; one *s* one *d. Educ:* Durham Univ. (BSc 1st cl. Hons Geol. 1968); Reading Univ. (PhD Sedimentol. 1971). CGeol; FGS 1973. Lecturer: Univ. of Sierra Leone, 1971–72; UC Cardiff, Univ. of Wales, 1973–74; Univ. of Newcastle, 1975–82; Lindemann Trust Fellow, Univ. of Calif, Berkeley, 1980–81; Lectr, 1983–86, Sen. Lectr, 1986–88, Reader, 1988–93, Univ. of Durham. Pres., Internat. Assoc. of Sedimentologists. 1998–. Geological Society: Moiety of Lyell Fund, 1983; Coke Medal, 1994. *Publications:* Sedimentary Petrology, 1981, 3rd edn 2001; Field Description of Sedimentary Rocks, 1982; Carbonate Sedimentology, 1990; Sedimentary Rocks in the Field, 1996; *edited:* Modern and Ancient Lake Sediments, 1978; Techniques in Sedimentology, 1988; Carbonate Platforms, 1990; Carbonate Diagenesis, 1990; Calcretes, 1991; Dolomites, 1994; res. papers in carbonate sedimentol. and limestones. *Recreations:* tennis, ski-ing, scuba diving, North American auto licence plates. *Address:* Department of Geological Sciences, University of Durham, Durham DH1 3LE. *T:* (0191) 374 2524; University College, The Castle, Durham DH1 3RW. *T:* (0191) 374 3861.

TUCKER, Paul Michael William; Deputy Director, Financial Stability, Bank of England, since 1999; *b* 24 March 1958; *s* of Brian William Tucker and Helen May Tucker (*née* Lloyd). *Educ:* Trinity Coll., Cambridge (BA Maths, and Philosophy). Joined Bank of England, 1980; Bank Supervisor, 1980–84, and 1987; seconded to merchant bank as corporate financier, 1985–86; seconded to Hong Kong Govt as Advr to Hong Kong Securities Review Cttee, 1987–88; Mkts Area, 1988–89; Private Sec. to Gov., 1989–92; Gilt-Edged and Money Mkts Div., 1993–96 (Hd of Div., 1994–96); Hd of Monetary Assessment and Strategy Div., 1997–98. Mem., Monetary Policy Cttee Secretariat, 1997–. *Address:* Bank of England, Threadneedle Street, EC2R 8AH. *T:* (020) 7601 4444.

TUCKER, Peter Louis; Adviser to the President, Sierra Leone, 1998–99; *b* 11 Dec. 1927; *s* of Peter Louis Tucker and Marion Tucker; *m* 1st, 1955, Clarissa Mary Harleston; three *s* one *d* (and one *d* decd); 2nd, 1972, Teresa Josephine Ganda; one *s. Educ:* Fourah Bay Coll., Sierra Leone (MA Latin, Dunelm); Jesus Coll., Oxford (MA Jurisp.); DipEd. Called to Bar, Gray's Inn, 1970; practised as barrister, Sierra Leone, 1983–84. Teacher, 1952–57; Education Officer, 1957–61; Secretary, Training and Recruitment, Sierra Leone Civil Service, 1961–63; Establishment Sec., 1963–66; Sec. to the Prime Minister and Head of Sierra Leone Civil Service, 1966–67; Asst Director, UK Immigrants Advisory Service, 1970–72; Principal Admin. Officer, Community Relations Commn, 1972–74, Dir of Fieldwork and Admin., 1974–77; Dir of Legal and Gen. Services, and Sec., 1977, Chief Exec., 1977–82, CRE; Comr and Chm., Sierra Leone Population Census, 1984; Special Envoy on Foreign Aid to Sierra Leone and Chm., Nat. Aid Co-ordinating Cttee, 1986–90; Chairman: National Constitutional Review Commn, 1990–91; Nat. Policy Adv. Cttee, 1998–99. DCL (*hc*) Sierra Leone. Papal Medal Pro Ecclesia et Pontifice, 1966. *Publications:* The Tuckers of Sierra Leone 1665–1914, 1997; Origin and Philosophy of the Sierra Leone People's Party, 2001; miscellaneous booklets, articles and reports for Community Relations Commission and Govt of Sierra Leone. *Recreations:* photography, listening to music, the internet. *Address:* Flat 5, Merewood Court, 60 Carew Road, Eastbourne, E Sussex BN21 2JR. *T:* and *Fax:* (01323) 727998.

TUCKER, Sir Richard (Howard), Kt 1985; a Judge of the High Court of Justice, Queen's Bench Division, 1985–2000; *b* 9 July 1930; *s* of Howard Archibald Tucker (His Honour Judge Tucker), and Margaret Minton Tucker; *m* 1st, 1958, Paula Mary Bennett Frost (marr. diss. 1974); one *s* two *d*; 2nd, 1975, Wendy Kate Standbrook (*d* 1988); 3rd, 1989, Jacqueline Suzanne Rossvell Thomson, *widow* of William Thomson, artist. *Educ:* Shrewsbury Sch.; The Queen's Coll., Oxford (MA; Hon. Fellow, 1992). 2nd Lieut, RAOC, 1948–50. Called to Bar, Lincoln's Inn, 1954; Bencher, 1979; Treasurer, 2002. QC 1972; a Recorder, 1972–85; Mem. Senate, Inns of Court and the Bar, 1984–86; Dep. Leader, 1984–85, and Presiding Judge, 1986–90, Midland and Oxford Circuit. Member: Employment Appeal Tribunal, 1986–2000; Parole Bd, 1996– (Vice-Chm., 1998–2000). *Recreations:* sailing, shooting, gardening, model railways. *Address:* Treasury Office, Lincoln's Inn, WC2A 3TL. *Clubs:* Garrick; Leander (Henley-on-Thames); Bar Yacht.

TUCKEY, Andrew Marmaduke Lane; Senior Adviser, Bridgewell, since 2001; *b* 28 Aug. 1943; *s* of late Henry Lane Tuckey and of Aileen Rosemary Newson Tuckey; *m* 1st, 1967, Margaret Louise (*née* Barnes) (marr. diss. 1998); one *s* two *d*; 2nd, 1998, Tracy Elisabeth (*née* Long); one *d. Educ:* Plumtree Sch., Zimbabwe. Chartered Accountant, 1966. Dixon Wilson, Chartered Accountants, 1962–66; British American Tobacco, 1966–68; Baring Brothers & Co., Ltd, 1968–95: Dir, 1973–81; Man. Dir, 1981–89; Chm., 1989–95; Dep. Chm., Barings plc, 1989–95; Advisor: Baring Brothers Ltd, 1995–96; Phoenix Securities Ltd, 1996–97; Senior Adviser, Donaldson, Lufkin & Jenrette, 1997–2000; Credit Suisse First Boston, 2000–01. Dir, Dillon, Read Holding Inc., 1991–95. Member: Federal Reserve Bank of New York Internat. Capital Markets Adv. Cttee, 1992–95; Financial Law Panel, 1993–97; Council, Baring Foundn, 1994–96. Dir, Friends of Covent Garden, 1981–98 (Treas., 1981–96); Dir, Royal Opera House, 1992–95; Trustee: Esmée Fairbairn Charitable Trust, 1986–99; Classic FM Charitable Trust, 1992–99. *Recreations:* music, tennis. *Address:* Bridgewell Ltd, 21 New Street, EC2M 4HR. *Clubs:* White's, City of London, Roehampton.

See also Rt Hon. Sir S. L. Tuckey.

TUCKEY, Rt Hon. Sir Simon (Lane), Kt 1992; PC 1998; **Rt Hon. Lord Justice Tuckey;** a Lord Justice of Appeal, since 1998; *b* 17 Oct. 1941; *s* of late Henry Lane Tuckey and of Aileen Rosemary Newsom Tuckey; *m* 1964, Jennifer Rosemary (*née* Hardie); one *s* two *d. Educ:* Plumtree School, Zimbabwe. Called to Bar, Lincoln's Inn, 1964, Bencher, 1989; QC 1981; a Recorder, 1984–92; a Judge of the High Court of Justice, QBD, 1992–98; a Judge, Employment Appeal Tribunal, 1993–98; Presiding Judge, Western Circuit, 1995–97; Judge in Charge, Commercial List, 1997–98. Chm., Review Panel, Financial Reporting Council, 1990–92. Mem., Judicial Studies Bd, 1993–95 (Chm., Civil and Family Cttee, 1993–95). *Recreations:* sailing, tennis. *Address:* Royal Courts of Justice, Strand, WC2A 2LL.

See also A. M. L. Tuckey.

TUCKMAN, Frederick Augustus, (Fred), OBE 1990; FCIS, FCIPD; *b* 9 June 1922; *s* of Otto and Amy Tina Tuchmann (*née* Adler); *m* 1966, Patricia Caroline Myers; two *s* one *d. Educ:* English and German schools; London School of Economics, 1946–49 (BScEcon). Served RAF, 1942–46. Commercial posts, 1950–65; Management Consultant and Partner, HAY Gp, 1965–85; Managing Director, HAY GmbH, Frankfurt, 1970–80; Partner, HAY Associates, 1975–85; Chm., Suomen HAY, OY, Helsinki, 1973–81; consultant assignments in Europe, Africa and N America. Hon. Sec., Bow Gp, 1958–59; Councillor, London Borough of Camden, 1965–71 (Chm., Library and Arts, 1968–71). Mem. (C) Leicester, European Parliament, 1979–89; contested (C) Leicester, Eur. Parly elecn, 1989. Mem. Council, Inst. of Personnel Management, 1963–70. Chm., Greater London Area, CPC, 1968–70. European Parliament: Budget Cttee, 1979–81; Social and Employment Cttee, 1981–89 (Cons. spokesman, 1984–89); substitute Mem., Economic and Monetary Cttee, 1979–87; substitute Mem., Budgetary Control Cttee, 1984–87; First Vice Pres., Latin American Delegn, 1982–85; Mem., Israel Delegn, 1987–89; Chm., Internat. Gp on Small Business, 1985–86. UK Chm., European Year of Small Business, 1983; Vice Chm., Small Business Bureau, London, 1985–89. Pres., Anglo-Jewish Assoc., 1989–95 (Vice-Pres., 1995–); Vice Pres., Eur. Medium and Small Units, 1985–90. Cross, Order of Merit (FRG), 1989. *Recreations:* reading, arguing, travel, swimming; priority—family. *Address:* 6 Cumberland Road, Barnes, SW13 9LY. *T:* (020) 8748 2392. *Clubs:* Athenæum, Carlton.

TUCKWELL, Anthony David, MA; National Director, National Educational Assessment Centre, since 2000; Headmaster, King Edward VI Grammar School, Chelmsford, 1984–99; *b* 4 July 1943; *s* of Alec William Tuckwell and Muriel Florence Tuckwell (*née* Green); *m* 1967, Kathleen Olivia Hatton. *Educ:* St Peter's Coll., Oxford (MA); Oxford Univ. Dept of Educn (DipEd); MBA Leeds Metropolitan 1995. History Master, Southern Grammar Sch. for Boys, Portsmouth, 1966–69; St John's College, Southsea: Hd of Hist., 1970–73; Sen. Teacher (Curriculum Co-ordinator), 1973–78; Dep. Headmaster, Sale Co. Grammar Sch. for Boys, 1979–83. Mem. Bd of Dirs, Chelmsford Cathedral Fest. Ltd, 1999–. FRSA 1994. *Publications:* (contrib.) School Leadership in the 21st Century, 1996; (contrib.) Living Headship: voices, value, vision, 1999; That Honourable and Gentlemanlike House: a history of King Edward VI Grammar School, Chelmsford 1551–2001, 2000. *Recreations:* music, literature, gardening, travel. *Address:* 28 Oaklands Crescent, Chelmsford, Essex CM2 9PP.

TUCKWELL, Barry Emmanuel, AC 1992; OBE 1965; horn soloist, retired; conductor; Conductor and Music Director, Maryland Symphony Orchestra, 1982–98; *b* 5 March 1931; *s* of late Charles and Elizabeth Tuckwell, Australia; *m* 1st, 1958, Sally Eelin Newton; one *s* one *d*; 2nd, 1971, Hilary Jane Warburton; one *s*; 3rd, 1992, Susan Terry Levitan. *Educ:* various schs, Australia; Sydney Conservatorium. FRCM 1993. Melbourne Symph. Orch., 1947; Sydney Symph. Orch., 1947–50; Hallé Orch., 1951–53; Scottish Nat. Orch., 1953–54; Bournemouth Symphony Orch., 1954–55; London Symph. Orch., 1955–68; founded Tuckwell Wind Quintet, 1968; Conductor, Tasmanian Symphony Orch., 1979–83; Guest Conductor, Northern Sinfonia, 1993–97. Mem. Chamber Music Soc. of Lincoln Center, 1974–81; Horn Prof., Royal Academy of Music, 1963–74; Pres., Internat. Horn Soc., 1969–77, 1992–94. Has played and conducted annually throughout Europe, GB, USA and Canada; has appeared at many internat. festivals, incl. Salzburg and Edinburgh; took part in 1st Anglo-Soviet Music Exchange, Leningrad and Moscow, 1963; toured: Far East, 1964 and 1975; Australia, 1970–95; S America, 1976; USSR, 1977; People's Republic of China, 1984. Many works dedicated to him; has made numerous recordings. Editor, complete horn literature for G. Schirmer Inc. Hon. RAM, 1966; Hon. GSM, 1967. Harriet Cohen Internat. Award for Solo Instruments, 1968; Grammy Award Nominations. *Publications:* Playing the Horn, 1978; The Horn, 1981. *Club:* Athenæum.

TUDGE, Colin Hiram, FLS; author; Research Fellow, Centre for the Philosophy of Social and Natural Sciences, London School of Economics, since 1995; *b* 22 April 1943; *s* of late Cyril Tudge and Maisie Tudge; *m* 1966, Rosemary Shewan (marr. diss. 2001); one *s* two *d. Educ:* Dulwich Coll.; Peterhouse, Cambridge (MA 1966). Writer on various magazines, 1965–80; Features Ed., New Scientist, 1980–85; presenter, BBC Radio 3, 1985–90; freelance author and broadcaster, 1990–. FLS 1995. *Publications:* The Famine

Business, 1977; (with M. Allaby) Home Farm, 1977; Future Cook, 1980; The Food Connection, 1985; Food Crops for the Future, 1988; Global Ecology, 1991; The Engineer in the Garden, 1993; The Day Before Yesterday, 1995; Neanderthals, Bandits and Farmers, 1998; The Second Creation, 2000; The Variety of Life, 2000; In Mendel's Footnotes, 2001. *Recreations:* walking, talking, chess. *Address:* 75 Delawyk Crescent, SE24 9JD. *T:* (020) 7274 2116.

TUDHOPE, James Mackenzie, CB 1987; Chairman of Social Security Appeal Tribunals, 1987–91; *b* 11 Feb. 1927; *m* Margaret Willock Kirkwood, MA Glasgow; two *s. Educ:* Dunoon Grammar School; Univ. of Glasgow (BL 1951). Admitted Solicitor, 1951. Private legal practice, 1951–55; Procurator Fiscal Depute, 1955, Senior PF Depute, 1962, Asst PF, 1968–70, Glasgow; PF, Kilmarnock, 1970–73, Dumbarton, 1973–76; Regional Procurator Fiscal: S Strathclyde, Dumfries and Galloway at Hamilton, 1976–80; for Glasgow and Strathkelvin, 1980–87. Hon. Sheriff, N Strathclyde, 1989–. Mem. Council, Law Soc. of Scotland, 1983–86. *Recreation:* serendipity. *Address:* Point House, Dundonald Road, Kilmarnock, Ayrshire KA1 1TY.

TUDOR, Rev. Dr (Richard) John, Hon. BA; Hon. Development Officer, Harris Manchester College, Oxford, since 1995; *b* 8 Feb. 1930; *s* of Charles Leonard and Ellen Tudor; *m* 1956, Cynthia Campbell Anderson; one *s* one *d. Educ:* Clee Grammar Sch., Grimsby; Queen Elizabeth's, Barnet; Univ. of Manchester, 1951–54 (BA Theology). Served RAF, 1948–51. Junior Methodist Minister, East Ham, London, 1954–57; Ordained, Newark, 1957; Minister, Thornton Cleveleys, Blackpool, 1957–60; Superintendent Minister: Derby Methodist Mission, 1960–71 (Chaplain to Mayor of Derby, Factories and Association with Derby Football Club); Coventry Methodist Mission, 1971–75 (Chaplain to Lord Mayor); Brighton Dome Mission, 1975–81; Westminster Central Hall, London, 1981–95; Free Church Chaplain, Westminster Hosp., 1982–93; Chaplain to Ancient Order of Foresters Charity Stewards, 1989–, to Lord Mayor of Westminster, 1993–94. Hon. DD Texas Wesleyan Univ., Fort Worth, USA, 1981; Hon. Texan, 1965; Freeman of Fort Worth, 1970. *Publication:* Word for all Seasons, 1992. *Recreations:* motoring, cooking, photography, the delights of family life. *Address:* Harris Manchester College, Oxford OX1 3TD. *T:* (01865) 271007.

TUDOR-CRAIG, Pamela; *see* Wedgwood, Pamela Lady.

TUDOR EVANS, Sir Haydn, Kt 1974; a Judge of the High Court of Justice, Queen's Bench Division, 1978–94 (Family Division, 1974–78); *b* 20 June 1920; 4th *s* of John Edgar Evans and Ellen (*née* Stringer); *m* 1947, Sheilagh Isabella Pilkington; one *s. Educ:* Cardiff High Sch.; West Monmouth School; Lincoln College, Oxford. RNVR, 1940–41. Open Scholar, Lincoln Coll., Oxford (Mod. History), 1940; Stewart Exhibitioner, 1942; Final Hons Sch., Mod. History, 1944; Final Hons Sch., Jurisprudence, 1945. Cholmeley Scholar, Lincoln's Inn, 1946; called to the Bar, Lincoln's Inn, 1947, Bencher 1970. QC 1962; Dep. Chm., Kent QS, 1968–72; Recorder of Crown Court, 1972–74; a Judge, Employment Appeal Tribunal, 1982–88. *Recreation:* watching Rugby, racing and cricket. *Address:* 30 Stanford Road, Kensington, W8 5PZ. *Clubs:* Garrick, MCC.

TUDOR JOHN, William; Chairman and Managing Director, European Commitment Committee, Lehman Brothers, since 2000; *b* 26 April 1944; *s* of Tudor and Gwen John; *m* 1967, Jane Clark; three *d. Educ:* Cowbridge Sch., S Wales; Downing Coll., Cambridge (MA). Asst Solicitor, Allen & Overy, 1969–71; Banker, Orion Bank Ltd, 1971–72; Allen & Overy: Partner, 1972–2000; Head of Banking Dept, 1972–92; Man. Partner, 1992–94; Sen. Partner, 1994–2000. Non-executive Chairman: Sutton Seeds (Hldgs) Ltd, 1978–93; Horticultural & Botanical Hldgs Ltd, 1985–93; non-exec. Dir, Woolwich plc, 2000. Associate Fellow, Downing Coll., Cambridge, 1985–92, 1997–. Member: Law Soc., 1969–; City of London Solicitors' Co., 1974–; IBA, 1978–; Financial Law Panel, 1996–. Chm., Law Foundn Adv. Council, Oxford Univ., 1998–; Mem., Adv. Bd, Oxford Univ. Develt Prog., 1999–. Non-exec. Dir, Nat. Film and Television Sch., 2000–. Steward of Appeal, BBB of C, 1978–. Freeman, City of London, 1994; Liveryman, Co. of Gunmakers, 1994–. *Recreations:* Rugby football as an observer, music as a listener, shooting and reading as a participant, daughters' banker. *Address:* (office) 1 Broadgate, EC2M 7HA; (home) Willian Bury, Willian, Herts SG6 2AF. *T:* (01462) 683532; *e-mail:* tj@william.fsnet.co.uk. *Clubs:* City; Cardiff and County (Cardiff).

TUDWAY QUILTER, David C.; *see* Quilter.

TUFFIN, Alan David, CBE 1993; General Secretary, Union of Communication Workers, 1982–93; *b* 2 Aug. 1933; *s* of Oliver Francis and Gertrude Elizabeth Tuffin; *m* 1957, Jean Elizabeth Tuffin; one *s* one *d. Educ:* Eltham Secondary Sch., SE9. Post Office employment, London, 1949–69; London Union Regional Official for UCW, 1957–69; National Official, 1969; Deputy General Secretary, 1979. Member: TUC Gen. Council, 1982–93 (Pres., 1992–93); HSC, 1986–96; Employment Appeal Tribunal, 1995–. Dir, Trade Union Fund Managers Ltd (formerly Trade Union Unit Trust), 1985–; non-exec. Dir, Remploy Ltd, 1999. FRSA 1990. *Recreations:* reading, squash, West Ham United FC. *Address:* c/o TUFM Ltd, Congress House, Great Russell Street, WC1B 3LQ.

TUFNELL, Col Greville Wyndham; DL; Development Officer, National Star Centre for Disabled Youth, 1982–95; Lieutenant, Queen's Body Guard of the Yeomen of the Guard, since 1993; *b* 7 April 1932; *s* of K. E. M. Tufnell, MC and E. H. Tufnell (*née* Dufaur); *m* 1st, 1962, Hon. Anne Rosemary Trench (*d* 1992), *d* of 5th Baron Ashtown, OBE and *widow* of Capt. Timothy Patrick Arnold Gosselin; three *d*, and one step *d*; 2nd, 1994, Susan Arnot Burrows. *Educ:* Eton; RMA, Sandhurst. Commnd Grenadier Guards, 1952; Adjt, 2nd Bn, 1959–61; GSO 3, War Office, 1962–63; Staff Coll., 1964; Maj. 1965; DAQMG, London Dist, 1966–67; GSO 2, HQ 2 Div., 1969–71; Lt Col 1971; comdg 1st Bn, 1971–73 (despatches, 1972); Bde Maj., Household Div., 1974–76; Col 1976; Lt Col comdg Grenadier Guards, 1976–78; retd 1979. Queen's Body Guard of Yeomen of the Guard: Exon, 1979; Ensign, 1985; Clerk of the Cheque and Adjutant, 1987. Freeman, City of London, 1961; Liveryman, Grocers' Co., 1965–. DL Glos, 1994. *Recreations:* shooting, fishing, gardening. *Address:* The Manor House, Ampney St Peter, Cirencester, Glos GL7 5SH. *Clubs:* Cavalry and Guards; MCC.

TUFTON, family name of **Baron Hothfield**.

TUGENDHAT, family name of **Baron Tugendhat**.

TUGENDHAT, Baron *cr* 1993 (Life Peer), of Widdington in the County of Essex; **Christopher Samuel Tugendhat,** Kt 1990; Chairman, Abbey National plc, since 1991; non-executive Director: Eurotunnel plc, since 1991; Rio Tinto plc, since 1997; *b* 23 Feb. 1937; *er s* of late Dr Georg Tugendhat; *m* 1967, Julia Lissant Dobson; two *s. Educ:* Ampleforth Coll.; Gonville and Caius Coll., Cambridge (Pres. of Union; Hon. Fellow 1998). Financial Times leader and feature writer, 1960–70. MP (C) City of London and Westminster South, 1974–76 (Cities of London and Westminster, 1970–74); Mem., 1977–85, a Vice-Pres., 1981–85, EEC Commn. Director: Sunningdale Oils, 1971–76; Phillips Petroleum International (UK) Ltd, 1972–76; National Westminster Bank, 1985–91 (Dep. Chm., 1990–91); The BOC Group, 1985–96; Commercial Union Assce, 1988–91; LWT (Hldgs), 1991–94; Chm., Blue Circle Industries PLC, 1996–2001. Chm., CAA, 1986–91. Chairman: RIIA (Chatham House), 1986–95; Adv. Council, European Policy Forum, 1998–; Governor, Council of Ditchley Foundn, 1986–; Vice-Pres., British Lung Foundn, 1986–. Chancellor, Univ. of Bath, 1998–. Hon. LLD Bath, 1998. *Publications:* Oil: the biggest business, 1968; The Multinationals, 1971 (McKinsey Foundn Book Award, 1971); Making Sense of Europe, 1986; (with William Wallace) Options for British Foreign Policy in the 1990s, 1988; various pamphlets and numerous articles. *Recreations:* being with his family, reading, conversation. *Address:* 35 Westbourne Park Road, W2 5QD. *Clubs:* Athenæum, Royal Anglo-Belgian.
See also M. G. Tugendhat.

TUGENDHAT, Michael George; QC 1986; a Recorder, since 1994; a Deputy High Court Judge, since 1995; a Judge of the Courts of Appeal of Jersey and Guernsey, since 2000; *b* 21 Oct. 1944; *s* of late Georg Tugendhat and Maire Littledale; *m* 1970, Blandine de Loisne; four *s. Educ:* Ampleforth Coll.; Gonville and Caius Coll., Cambridge (Scholar; MA); Yale Univ. Henry Fellowship. Called to the Bar, Inner Temple, 1969, Bencher, 1988. Mem., Bar Council, 1992–94. Chm., Civil Law Working Party on Corruption, 1999. Mem., Mgt Cttee, Prog. in Comparative Media Law & Policy, Oxford Univ. Centre for Socio-Legal Studies, 1998–. Fellow, Inst. Advanced Legal Studies, 1999–. *Publications:* (contrib.) Restitution and Banking Law, 1998; (contrib.) Yearbook of Copyright and Media Law, 2000; (contrib.) Halsbury's Laws of England, 4th edn; occasional contribs to legal jls. *Address:* 5 Raymond Buildings, Gray's Inn, WC1R 5BP. *T:* (020) 7242 2902. *Club:* Brooks's.
See also Baron Tugendhat.

TUITA, Sir Mariano (Kelesimalefo), KBE 1992 (OBE 1975); Cross of Solomon Islands, 1985; Managing Director, L. K. P. Hardware Ltd, since 1985; *b* Solomon Is, 12 Nov. 1932; *s* of late Joachim Alick and Ann Maria Tangoia Hagota; *m* 1957, Luisa Mae; three *s* six *d. Educ:* St Joseph's Sch., Tenaru on Guadacanal. Mem. for Lau, Malaita Local Govt Council, 1958–60; Pres., Malaita Council, 1960–68; Member: first Solomon Is Legislative Council, 1960–65; for N Malaita Constituency, 1965–67; for NE Malaita Constituency, 1967–69; Governing Council for Lau and Baelelea, 1970–73; for Lau and Baelelea, Legislative Assembly, Solomon Is Nat. Parlt, 1976–80. *Address:* L. K. P. Hardware Ltd, PO Box 317, Honiara, Solomon Islands. *T:* 22594 and 23848.

TUITE, Sir Christopher (Hugh), 14th Bt *cr* 1622; Controller, The Nature Conservancy; *b* 3 Nov. 1949; *s* of Sir Dennis George Harmsworth Tuite, 13th Bt, MBE, and of Margaret Essie, *d* of late Col Walter Leslie Dundas, DSO; *S* father, 1981; *m* 1976, Deborah Ann, *d* of A. E. Martz, Punxsutawney, Pa; two *s. Educ:* Univ. of Liverpool (BSc Hons); Univ. of Bristol (PhD). Research Officer, The Wildfowl Trust, 1978–81. *Publications:* contribs to Jl of Animal Ecology, Jl of Applied Ecology, Freshwater Biology, Wildfowl. *Heir: s* Thomas Livingstone Tuite, *b* 24 July 1977. *Address:* c/o HSBC, 33 The Borough, Farnham, Surrey GU9 7NJ.

TUIVAGA, Hon. Sir Timoci (Uluiburotu), Kt 1981; CF 1995; **Hon. Mr Justice Tuivaga;** Chief Justice of Fiji, 1980–87, and since 1988; *b* 21 Oct. 1931; *s* of Isimeli Siga Tuivaga and Jessie Hill; *m* 1958, Vilimaina Leba Parrott Tuivaga; three *s* one *d. Educ:* Univ. of Auckland (BA). Called to Bar, Gray's Inn, 1964, and NSW, 1968. Native Magistrate, 1958–61; Crown Counsel, 1965–68; Principal Legal Officer, 1968–70; Acting Director of Public Prosecutions, 1970; Crown Solicitor, 1971; Puisne Judge, 1972; Acting Chief Justice, 1974; sometime Acting Gov.-Gen., 1983–87. *Recreations:* golf, gardening. *Address:* 228 Ratu Sukuna Road, Suva, Fiji. *T:* 301782. *Club:* Fiji Golf (Suva).

TULLIBARDINE, Marquess of; Bruce George Ronald Murray; *b* 6 April 1960; *s* and *heir* of Duke of Atholl, *qv*; *m* 1984, Lynne Elizabeth, *e d* of Nicholas Andrew; two *s* one *d. Heir: s* Earl of Strathtay and Strathardle, *qv. Address:* PO Box 1522, Louis Trichardt, 0920, South Africa.

TULLO, Carol Anne; Controller of HM Stationery Office, Queen's Printer of Acts of Parliament and Government Printer for Northern Ireland, since 1997; Queen's Printer for Scotland, since 1999; *b* 9 Jan. 1956; *d* of Edward Alan Dodgson and late Patricia Dodgson; *m* 1979, Robin Brownrigg Tullo; one *s* one *d. Educ:* Hull Univ. (LLB Hons 1976). Called to the Bar, Inner Temple, 1977; Publishing Dir, Sweet & Maxwell Ltd, 1990–96; Consultant, Thomson Legal and Professional Gp, 1996–97. Vis. Prof., City Univ., 2000–. *Address:* HM Stationery Office, St Clements House, 2–16 Colegate, Norwich NR3 1BQ. *T:* (01603) 723012.

TULLY, (William) Mark, OBE 1985; freelance journalist and broadcaster, since 1994; *b* 24 Oct. 1935; *s* of late William Scarth Carlisle Tully, CBE and of Patience Treby Tully; *m* 1960, Frances Margaret (*née* Butler); two *s* two *d. Educ:* Twyford School, Winchester; Marlborough College; Trinity Hall, Cambridge (MA; Hon. Fellow, 1994). Regional Dir, Abbeyfield Soc., 1960–64; BBC, 1964–94: Asst, Appointments Dept, 1964–65; Asst, then Actg Rep., New Delhi, 1965–69; Prog. Organiser and Talks Writer, Eastern Service, 1969–71; Chief of Bureau, Delhi, 1972–93; South Asia Correspondent, 1993–94. Padma Shri (India), 1992. Presenter, The Lives of Jesus, BBC TV series, 1996. *Publications:* (with Satish Jacob) Amritsar: Mrs Gandhi's last battle, 1985; (with Z. Masani) From Raj to Rajiv, 1988; No Full Stops in India, 1991; The Heart of India (short stories), 1995; The Lives of Jesus, 1996. *Recreations:* fishing, bird watching, reading. *Address:* 1 Nizamuddin (East), New Delhi 110 013, India. *T:* (11) 4629687/4602878. *Clubs:* Oriental; Press, India International, Gymkhana (Delhi), Bengal (Calcutta).

TULVING, Prof. Endel, PhD; FRS 1992; FRSC; Tanenbaum Chair in Cognitive Neuroscience, Rotman Research Institute, Baycrest Centre, Toronto, since 1992; University Professor Emeritus in Psychology, University of Toronto, since 1992; *b* 26 May 1927; *s* of Juhan Tulving and Linda (*née* Soome); *m* 1950, Ruth Mikkelsaar; two *d. Educ:* Hugo Treffner Gymnasium; Univ. of Heidelberg; Univ. of Toronto (BA, MA); Harvard Univ. (Foundn Fellow, 1954–55; PhD). FRSC 1979. Teaching Fellow, Harvard Univ., 1955–56; University of Toronto: Lectr, 1956–59; Asst Prof. of Psychol., 1959–62; Associate Prof., 1962–65; Prof., 1965–70; Prof. of Psychol., Yale Univ., 1970–75; University of Toronto: Prof. of Psychol., 1972–92; Chm., Dept of Psychol., 1974–80; Univ. Prof., 1985–92. Vis. Scholar, Univ. of Calif., Berkeley, 1964–65; Fellow, Center for Advanced Study in Behavioural Scis, Stanford, Calif., 1972–73; Commonwealth Vis. Prof., Univ. of Oxford, 1977–78; Distinguished Res. Prof. of Neurosci., Univ. of Calif., Davis, 1993–98; Clark Way Harrison Dist. Vis. Prof. of Psychology and Cognitive Neurosci., Washington Univ., 1996–. Izaak Walton Killam Meml Scholarship, 1976; Guggenheim Fellow, 1987–88; William James Fellow, Amer. Psychol Soc., 1990. For. Hon. Mem., Amer. Acad. Arts and Scis, 1986; For. Associate, Nat. Acad. Scis, USA, 1988; Foreign Member: Royal Swedish Acad. Scis, 1991; Academia Europaea, 1996. Hon. MA Yale, 1969; Hon. PhD Umeå, Sweden, 1982; Hon. DLitt: Waterloo, Canada, 1987; Laurentian, Canada, 1988; Hon. DPsych Tartu, Estonia, 1989; Hon. ScD Queen's Univ., Ontario, 1996. Warren Medal, Soc. of Exptl Psychologists, 1982; Dist. Scientific Contrib. Award, Amer. Psychol Assoc., 1983; Award for Dist. Contribs to Psychol. as a Science, Canadian Psychol Assoc., 1983; Izaak Walton Killam Prize in Health Scis, Canada

Council, 1994; Gold Medal Award, Amer. Psychol Foundn, 1994; McGovern Award in the behavioral scis, AAAS, 1996. *Publications:* Elements of Episodic Memory, 1983; (ed jtly) Organization of Memory, 1972; Memory Systems 1994, 1994; Oxford Handbook of Memory, 2000; articles in scientific jls. *Recreations:* tennis, walking, chess, bridge. *Address:* 45 Bâby Point Crescent, Toronto, ON M6S 2B7, Canada. *T:* (416) 7623736.

TUMIM, Sir Stephen, Kt 1996; HM Chief Inspector of Prisons for England and Wales, 1987–95; *b* 15 Aug. 1930; *yr s* of late Joseph Tumim, CBE (late Clerk of Assize, Oxford Circuit) and late Renée Tumim; *m* 1962, Winifred Borthwick (*see* W. L. Tumim); three *d. Educ:* St Edward's Sch., Oxford; Worcester Coll., Oxford (Scholar; Hon. Fellow, 1994). Called to Bar, Middle Temple, 1955, Bencher, 1990. A Recorder of the Crown Court, 1977–78; a Circuit Judge, 1978–96; a Judge of Willesden County Court, 1980–87. Principal, St Edmund Hall, Oxford, 1996–98. Chm., Nat. Deaf Children's Soc., 1974–79. Chairman: Friends of Tate Gall., 1983–90; British Art Market Standing Cttee, 1990–95; Koestler Award Trust, 1993–; Pres., Royal Lit. Fund, 1990–. Pres., Unlock, 1997–. Fellow, Royal Philanthropic Soc., 1994. Hon. FRCPsych 1993; Hon. Fellow: LSE, 1993; UEA, 1994; Oxford Brookes Univ, 1995; Hon. Sen. Fellow, Cayman Is Law Sch., 1994. High Steward, Wallingford, 1995–2001. DUniv: Stirling, 1993; Open, 1997; UCE, 1997; Hon. LLD: Leicester, UWE, 1994; Birmingham, Essex, Southampton, 1995; Keele, Exeter, 1996. *Publications:* Great Legal Disasters, 1983; Great Legal Fiascos, 1985; Crime and Punishment, 1997; occasional reviews. *Recreations:* books and pictures. *Clubs:* Garrick, Beefsteak.

TUMIM, Winifred Letitia, (Lady Tumim), OBE 1992; Chair, National Council for Voluntary Organisations, 1996–2001; *b* 3 June 1936; *d* of Algernon Malcolm Borthwick and Edith Wylde Borthwick (*née* Addison); *m* 1962, Sir Stephen Tumim, *qv*; three *d. Educ:* Lady Margaret Hall, Oxford (PPE Hons 1958; MA); SOAS, London Univ. (Dip. Linguistics 1979). Non-exec. Dir, Parkside Health NHS Trust, 1992–98. Chairman: Sec. of State's Youth Treatment Service Gp, 1991–95; Ind. Adv. Gp on Teenage Pregnancy, 2000–; Mem., Warnock Cttee of Enquiry on Educn of Handicapped Children, 1974–78. Member: Council, Vol. Council for Handicapped Children, 1981–87; GMC, 1996–; Council for Charitable Support, 1996–; Vice-Chm., Family Housing Assoc., 1983–88; Chairman: RNID, 1985–92; NCVO/Charity Commn On Trust Wkg Party, 1992; Council for Advancement of Communication with Deaf People, 1994–97. Gov., Mary Hare Grammar Sch. for The Deaf, 1974–90. Trustee: Nat. Portrait Gall., 1992–99; City Parochial Foundn, 1989–2001; Charities Aid Foundn, 1996–. FRSA 1989. *Recreations:* painting watercolurs, gardening, classical music, modern ceramics, tribal rugs. *T:* (020) 7713 6161.

TUNBRIDGE, William Michael Gregg, MD; FRCP; Director of Postgraduate Medical Education and Training, Oxford University, since 1994; Professorial Fellow of Wadham College, Oxford, since 1994; *b* 13 June 1940; *s* of Sir Ronald Ernest Tunbridge, OBE and of Dorothy (*née* Gregg); *m* 1965, Felicity Katherine Edith Parrish; two *d. Educ:* Kingswood Sch., Bath; Queens' Coll., Cambridge (MA, MD); University Coll. Hosp. House appointments: UCH, 1964–65; Mpilo Hosp., Bulawayo, 1965–66; Manchester Royal Infirmary, 1967–68; Tutor in Medicine, Univ. of Manchester, 1969–70; Registrar, Hammersmith Hosp., 1970–72; Sen. Res. Associate, Univ. of Newcastle, 1972–75; Sen. Registrar in Medicine, Durham, 1975–76; MRC Travelling Fellow, Liège, 1976–77; Consultant Physician, Newcastle Gen. Hosp. and Sen. Lectr in Medicine, Univ. of Newcastle upon Tyne, 1977–94; Hon. Consultant Physician, Oxford Radcliffe Hosps (formerly Radcliffe Infirmary, Oxford), 1994–. President: Thyroid Club, 1994–96; Endocrine Section, Union of European Med. Specialists, 1994–98. *Publications:* (with P. D. Home) Diabetes and Endocrinology in Clinical Practice, 1991; (with R. I. S. Bayliss) Thyroid Disease: the facts, 3rd edn, 1998; (ed) Rationing of Health Care in Medicine, 1993. *Recreation:* walking. *Address:* Coppermill, Church Lane, Weston on the Green, Bicester, Oxon OX25 3QS. *T:* (01869) 350691. *Club:* Athenæum.

TUNG Chee Hwa; Chief Executive, Hong Kong Special Administrative Region, since 1997; *b* 29 May 1937; *s* of C. Y. Tung and Tung Koo Lee-ching; *m* 1961, Betty Tung Chiu Hung Ping; two *s* one *d. Educ:* Liverpool Univ. (BSc Marine Engrg 1960). Chm. and CEO, Orient Overseas (International) Ltd, 1986–96. Advr, Hong Kong Affairs, 1992–; Member: Exec. Council, Hong Kong Govt, 1992–96; Eighth Chinese People's Political Consultative Cttee, 1993–; Vice-Chm., Prep. Cttee, HKSAR, 1995–. Member: Hong Kong/Japan Business Co-operation Cttee, 1991–96; Hong Kong/US Economic Co-operation Cttee, 1993–96. Hon. LLD Liverpool, 1997. *Recreations:* hiking, Tai Chi, swimming, reading. *Address:* Suite 705–708, Asia Pacific Finance Tower, Citibank Plaza, 3 Garden Road, Hong Kong. *T:* (852) 2878 3383, *Fax:* (852) 2509 0575.

TUNNELL, Hugh James Oliver Redvers; HM Diplomatic Service, retired; Ambassador to Bahrain, 1992–95; *b* 31 Dec. 1935; *s* of late Heather and Oliver Tunnell; *m* 1st, 1958, Helen Miller (marr. diss.); three *d*; 2nd, 1979, Margaret, *d* of Sir Richard John Randall; two *d. Educ:* Chatham House Grammar School, Ramsgate. Royal Artillery, 1954–56. FO, 1956–59; Amman, 1959–62; Middle East Centre for Arab Studies, 1962–63; served FO, Aden, CRO, Damascus and FO, 1964–67; UK Delegn to European Communities, 1968–70; FCO, 1970–72; Kuwait, 1972–76; FCO, 1976–79; Head of Chancery, Muscat, 1979–83; Consul Gen., Brisbane, 1983–88; Comr-Gen., British Section, EXPO 88, 1987–88; Consul Gen., Jedda, 1989–92. Mem. Cttee, Bahrain Soc., 1996–. *Recreations:* water sports, tennis. *Club:* Brisbane (Brisbane).

TUNNICLIFFE, Denis, CBE 1993; Chief Executive, London Transport, 1998–2000 (Member of Board, 1993–2000); *b* 17 Jan. 1943; *s* of Arthur Harold and Ellen Tunnicliffe; *m* 1968, Susan Dale; two *s. Educ:* Henry Cavendish Sch., Derby; University Coll. London (State Schol.; BSc (Special)); College of Air Training, Hamble. Pilot, BOAC, 1966–72; British Airways, 1972–86; Chief Exec., International Leisure Group, Aviation Div., 1986–88; Man. Dir, London Underground Ltd, 1988–98. Councillor, Royal Bor. of New Windsor, 1971–75; Councillor, Royal County of Berkshire, 1974–77; Dist Councillor, Bracknell, 1979–83. FCIT 1990; CIMgt (CBIM 1991). *Recreations:* flying, boating, church, travelling. *Clubs:* Royal Air Force, Royal Automobile.

TUNSTALL, Dr David Prestwich, FInstP; FRSE; Reader in Physics, University of St Andrews, since 1978; *b* 15 July 1939; *s* of Henry Brian Tunstall and Emmeline Grace Tunstall (*née* Denman); *m* 1963, Rosemarie Bebbington; two *s* one *d. Educ:* Sir John Talbots Sch., Whitchurch; UCNW, Bangor (BSc *summa cum laude*; PhD). FInstP 1985; FRSE 1990. Post-doctoral Fellow: Zurich, 1963–64; Grenoble, 1964–66; Lectr, 1966–75, Sen. Lectr, 1975–78, Univ. of St Andrews. Visiting Fellow: Cornell Univ., 1973–74; UCLA, 1979. *Publications:* (jtly) Nuclear Magnetic Resonance, 1973; The Metal Non-Metal Transition in Disordered Systems, 1978; (ed jtly) High Temperature Superconductivity, 1991; contrib. to learned jls. *Recreations:* hill walking, ski-ing, tennis. *Address:* 4 West Acres, St Andrews, Fife KY16 9UD. *T:* (01334) 473507; *e-mail:* d.p.tunstall@st-and.ac.uk.

TUOHY, Denis John; broadcaster and journalist; *b* 2 April 1937; *s* of late John Vincent Tuohy and Anne Mary, (Nan), Tuohy (*née* Doody); *m* 1st, 1960, Moya McCann (marr. diss. 1988); two *s* two *d*; 2nd, 1998, Elizabeth Moran. *Educ:* Clongowes Wood Coll., Co. Kildare; Queen's Univ., Belfast (BA Hons Classics). Eisenhower Fellow, USA, 1967. BBC: Newscaster and Reporter, NI, 1960–64; Presenter, Late Night Line Up, 1964–67; Reporter and Presenter: 24 Hours, 1967–71; Panorama, 1974–75; Reporter, Man Alive, 1971–72; Presenter, Tonight, 1975–79; Thames Television: Reporter, This Week, 1972–74; Presenter, People and Politics, 1973–74; Presenter and Reporter: TV Eye, 1979–86; This Week, 1986–92; Newscaster, ITN, 1994–; Presenter, Something Understood, BBC Radio 4, 1995–; reporter on numerous documentaries for BBC and ITV, incl. A Life of O'Reilly, 1974; Mr Truman, why did you drop the second bomb?, 1975; Do You Know Where Jimmy Carter Lives?, 1977; To Us a Child (prod jtly by Thames TV and UNICEF), 1986; The Blitz, 1991; The Real Dad's Army, 1998; The Law and the "Lunatic", 1999. Columnist, The Tablet, 1998–. *Publications:* articles in Listener, New Statesman, Scotsman, Independent, etc. *Recreations:* theatre, cinema, Rugby, cricket. *Address:* 9 Thurnby Court, Wellesley Road, Twickenham, Middx TW2 5RY.

TUOHY, Thomas, CBE 1969; Managing Director, British Nuclear Fuels Ltd, 1971–73; *b* 7 Nov. 1917; *s* of late Michael Tuohy and Isabella Tuohy, Cobh, Eire; *m* 1949, Lilian May Barnes (*d* 1971); one *s* one *d. Educ:* St Cuthberts Grammar Sch., Newcastle; Reading Univ. (BSc). Chemist in various Royal Ordnance Factories, 1939–46. Manager: Health Physics, Springfields Nuclear Fuel Plant, Dept Atomic Energy, 1946; Health Physics, Windscale Plutonium Plant, 1949; Plutonium Piles and Metal Plant, Windscale, 1950; Works Manager: Springfields, 1952; Windscale, UKAEA, 1954; Windscale and Calder Hall: Dep. Gen. Manager, 1957; Gen. Manager, 1958; Man. Dir, Production Gp, UKAEA, 1964–71. Managing Director: Urenco, 1973–74; Vorsitzender der Geschäftsführung Centec GmbH, 1973–74; Dep. Chm., Centec, 1973–74; former Dir, Centec-Algermann Co. Mem. Council, Internat. Inst. for Management of Technology, 1971–73. *Publications:* various technical papers on reactor operation and plutonium manufacture. *Recreations:* gardening, travel. *Address:* Ingleberg, Beckermet, Cumbria CA21 2XX. *T:* (01946) 841226.

TUPMAN, William Ivan, DPhil; Director General of Internal Audit, Ministry of Defence, 1974–81; *b* 22 July 1921; *s* of Leonard and Elsie Tupman; *m* 1945, Barbara (*née* Capel); two *s* one *d. Educ:* Queen Elizabeth's Hosp., Bristol; New Coll., Oxford (Exhibnr; MA, DPhil). Served War, 1942–45, RN (Lieut RNVR). Entered Admiralty as Asst Principal, 1948; Private Sec. to Parly Sec., 1950–52; Principal, 1952; Civil Affairs Adviser to C-in-C, Far East Station, 1958–61; Private Sec. to First Lord of the Admiralty, 1963; Asst Sec., 1964; IDC, 1967.

TUPPER, Sir Charles Hibbert, 5th Bt *cr* 1888, of Armdale, Halifax, Nova Scotia; retired; *b* 4 July 1930; *o s* of Sir James Macdonald Tupper, 4th Bt, formerly Assistant Commissioner, Royal Canadian Mounted Police, and of Mary Agnes Jean Collins; *S* father, 1967; *m* (marr. diss. 1976); one *s. Heir: s* Charles Hibbert Tupper [*b* 10 July 1964; *m* 1987, Elizabeth Ann Heaslip; one *d*]. *Address:* 955 Marine Drive, Apt 1101, West Vancouver, BC V7T 1A9, Canada.

TURBOTT, Sir Ian (Graham), Kt 1968; AO 1997; CMG 1962; CVO 1966; Foundation Chancellor, University of Western Sydney, 1989, Emeritus Chancellor, since 2001; *b* Whangarei, New Zealand, 9 March 1922; *s* of late Thomas Turbott and late E. A. Turbott, both of New Zealand; *m* 1952, Nancy Hall Lantz (*d* 1999), California, USA; three *d. Educ:* Takapuna Grammar School, Auckland, NZ; Auckland University; Jesus College, Cambridge; London University. NZ Forces (Army), 1940–46: Solomon Is area and 2 NZEF, Italy. Colonial Service (Overseas Civil Service): Western Pacific, Gilbert and Ellice Is, 1948–56; Colonial Office, 1956–58; Administrator of Antigua, The West Indies, 1958–64; also Queen's Representative under new constitution, 1960–64; Administrator of Grenada and Queen's Representative, 1964–67; Governor of Associated State of Grenada, 1966–68. Partner, Spencer Stuart and Associates Worldwide, 1973–84; Chairman: Spencer Stuart and Associates Pty Ltd, 1970–84; Chloride Batteries Australia Ltd, 1978–85; I. T. Graham Investments plc, 1982–; TNT Security Pty Ltd; Stuart Brooke Consultants Pty Ltd, Sydney, 1974–82; 2MMM Broadcasting Co. Pty Ltd; Melbourne F/M Radio Pty Ltd, 1986–93; Penrith Lakes Develt Corp., 1980–; Essington Ltd, 1984–89; New World Pictures (Aust.) Ltd, 1986–89; Triple M FM Radio Group, 1986–93; Cape York Space Agency Ltd, 1987–89; Hoyts Media Ltd, 1991–93; Dir, Hoyts Entertainment Ltd, 1990–93; Dep. Chm., Adv. Bd, Amer. Internat. Underwriting (Aust.) Ltd; Director: Standard Chartered Bank Australia Ltd, 1980–91; Capita Financial Gp, 1979–91; Newcastle F/M P/L, 1983–94. Chairman: Internat. Piano Competition Ltd, Sydney, 1977–84; Duke of Edinburgh's Award Scheme, NSW, 1984–. Chm., Japan Entrepreneurs and Presidents Assoc., Australia, 1996–. Governor, NSW Conservatorium of Music, 1974–89. FRSA; FAIM; FAICD. Hon Consul for Cook Is in Australia, 1995. JP 1972. Hon. DLitt Western Sydney, 1993. CStJ 1964. Silver Jubilee Medal, 1977; Guadalcanal Medal (Solomon Is), 1998. Holds 1939–45 Star, Pacific Star, Italy Star, Defence Medal, War Medal, New Zealand Service Medal. *Publications:* Lands of Sun and Spice, 1996; Nancy—my beloved, 2000; various technical and scientific, 1948–51, in Jl of Polynesian Society (on Pacific area). *Recreations:* boating, farming, cricket, fishing. *Address:* 8/8 Lauderdale Avenue, Fairlight, NSW 2094, Australia; 38 MacMasters Parade, MacMasters Beach, NSW 2251, Australia. *Clubs:* Australian (Sydney); Royal Sydney Yacht.

TURCAN, Henry Watson; a Recorder of the Crown Court, since 1985; *b* 22 Aug. 1941; *s* of late Henry Hutchison Turcan and Lilias Cheyne; *m* 1969, Jane Fairrie Blair; one *s* one *d. Educ:* Rugby School; Trinity College, Oxford (BA, MA). Called to the Bar, Inner Temple, 1965; Bencher, 1992. Legal Assessor to General Optical Council, 1983–. Special Adjudicator, Immigration Appeals, 1998–. *Recreations:* hunting, shooting, fishing, golf. *Address:* 4 Paper Buildings, Temple, EC4Y 7EX. *T:* (020) 7353 3420. *Clubs:* Royal and Ancient Golf (St Andrews); Hon. Company of Edinburgh Golfers (Muirfield).

TURCAN, William James; Chief Executive, Elementis (formerly Harrisons & Crosfield plc), 1994–98; *b* 4 Jan. 1943; *m* 1967, Elisabeth Margaret Stewart; three *s* one *d. Educ:* Rugby Sch.; Trinity Coll., Oxford (MA). Binder Hamlyn, 1965–70; Pauls Malt, 1970–86; Finance Dir, Pauls plc, 1986–88; Finance Dir, Harrisons & Crosfield, 1988–94. Bd Mem., Glenrothes New Town Develt Corp., 1983–86.

TURCOTTE, His Eminence Cardinal Jean-Claude; *see* Montreal, Archbishop of, (RC).

TURECK, Rosalyn; concert artist; conductor; writer; teacher; *b* Chicago, 14 Dec. 1914; *d* of Samuel Tureck and Monya (*née* Lipson); *m* 1964, George Wallingford Downs (*d* 1964). *Educ:* Juilliard Sch. of Music, NY. Piano studies with Sophia Brilliant-Liven, Jan Chiapusso and Olga Samaroff; harpsichord with Gavin Williamson. Member Faculty: Philadelphia Conservatory of Music, 1935–42; Mannes School, NYC, 1940–44; Juilliard School of Music, 1943–53; Columbia University, NY, 1953–55; Professor of Music: Univ. of California, San Diego, 1966–72; Univ. of Maryland, 1981–85; Yale Univ., 1991–93. Vis. Prof., Washington Univ., 1963–64; Visiting Fellow: St Hilda's Coll., Oxford, 1974 (Hon. Life Fellow, 1974); Wolfson Coll., Oxford, 1975; Lectures: educnl instns in USA, S America, Canada, Israel, Russia and Europe; Royal Instn of GB, and

Boston Univ., 1993; Smithsonian Instn, 1994; Regents' Lectr, Univ. of Calif, 1995; Oxford Univ. (and master classes), 1995. Has appeared as soloist and conductor of leading orchestras in US, Europe and Israel, and toured US, Canada, South Africa, South America; début solo recital, Chicago, 1924; NY début, Carnegie Hall, 1936; European début, Copenhagen, 1947, since when has toured extensively in Europe, and played at festivals in Edinburgh, Venice, Holland, Wexford, Schaffhausen, Bath, Brussels World Fair, Glyndebourne, Barcelona, Puerto Rico, St Petersburg, etc, and in major Amer. festivals including Mostly Mozart Festival, NY, Caramoor, Detroit, etc; extensive tours: India, Australia and Far East, 1971; S America, 1986–; Spain, 1986–; Rome and Florence, 1996–; Europe and US, 1998–99. Founder: Composers of Today, 1949–53; also Director: Tureck Bach Players, London, 1957 (conductor, 1960–72), NY, 1981–86; Internat. Bach Soc., Inst. for Bach Studies, 1968–93; Tureck Bach Inst. Inc., 1981; Tureck Bach Res. Foundn, Oxford, 1994. Hon. Member, GSMD, London, 1961; Member: Royal Musical Assoc., London; Inc. Soc. of Musicians, London; Amer. Musicological Soc; Amer. Br., New Bach Soc. Editor, Tureck/Bach Urtext series, 1979–. Numerous recordings, 1945–. Hon. Dr of Music, Colby Coll., USA, 1964; Hon. DMus: Roosevelt Univ., 1968; Wilson Coll., 1968; Oxon, 1977; Music and Arts Inst. of San Francisco, 1987. Has won numerous awards, USA, UK, Germany and S America. Officer's Cross, Order of Merit, Fed. Republic of Germany, 1979. *Television films:* Fantasy and Fugue: Rosalyn Tureck plays Bach, 1972; Rosalyn Tureck plays on Harpsichord and Organ, 1977; Joy of Bach, 1978; Bach and Tureck at Ephesus, 1985; Tureck on Television, 1999; also many appearances, US. *Publications:* An Introduction to the Performance of Bach, 1960; Authenticity, 1994; (contrib.) Music and Mathematics, 1995; edited: Bach: Sarabande, C minor, 1950; (transcribed) Paganini: Moto Perpetuo, 1950; (Urtext and performance edns) Bach: Italian Concerto, 1983, 2nd edn 1991; J. S. Bach, Lute Suite in E minor, set for classical guitar, 1984, Lute Suite in C minor, 1985; Authenticity, 1994; Interaction: the journal of the Tureck Bach Research Foundation, Vol. I, 1997, Vol. II, 1998, Vol. III, 1999; many articles. *Address:* Hotel El Paraiso, Ctra Cádiz, Km 167-Apdo 134, 29680 Estepona-Marbella, Spain. *Club:* Century (NY).

TURING, Sir John Dermot, 12th Bt *cr* 1638 (NS), of Foveran, Aberdeenshire; solicitor; *b* 26 Feb. 1961; *s* of John Ferrier Turing (*d* 1983) and of Beryl Mary Ada, *d* of late Herbert Vaughan Hann; *S* kinsman, Sir John Leslie Turing, 11th Bt, 1987; *m* 1986, Nicola J., *er d* of M. D. Simmonds; two *s*. *Educ:* Sherborne School, Dorset; King's College, Cambridge; New College, Oxford. *Heir: s* John Malcolm Ferrier Turing, *b* 5 Sept. 1988. *Address:* 5 Carlton Bank, Station Road, Harpenden, Herts AL5 4SU.

TURMEAU, Prof. William Arthur, CBE 1989; PhD; FRSE; CEng, FIMechE; Chairman, Scottish Environment Protection Agency, 1995–99; Principal and Vice-Chancellor, Napier University, 1992–94 (Principal, Napier College, subseq. Napier Polytechnic of Edinburgh, 1982–92); *b* 19 Sept. 1929; *s* of Frank Richard Turmeau and Catherine Lyon Linklater; *m* 1957, Margaret Moar Burnett, MA, BCom; one *d*. *Educ:* Stromness Acad., Orkney; Univ. of Edinburgh (BSc); Moray House Coll. of Educn; Heriot-Watt Univ. (PhD). FIMechE, CEng, 1971; FRSE 1990. Royal Signals, 1947–49. Research Engr, Northern Electric Co. Ltd, Montreal, 1952–54; Mechanical Engr, USAF, Goose Bay, Labrador, 1954–56; Contracts Manager, Godfrey Engrg Co. Ltd, Montreal, 1956–61; Lectr, Bristo Technical Inst., 1962–64; Napier College: Lectr and Sen. Lectr, 1964–68; Head, Dept of Mechanical Engrg, 1968–75; Asst Principal and Dean, Faculty of Technology, 1975–82. Member: CICHE, British Council, 1982–92; CVCP, 1992–94 (Mem., Cttee of Dirs of Polytechnics, 1982–92); Standing Conf. of Rectors and Vice-Chancellors of European Univs, 1990–94; Cttee of Scottish Univ. Principals, 1992–94; Scottish Div. Cttee, Inst. of Dirs, 1992–94; Acad. Standards Cttee, IMechE, 1994–. Dir, ASH Scotland, 1996–. Trustee, Dynamic Earth Charitable Trust, 1994–. Mem. Court, Edinburgh Acad., 1993–99. Dr *hc* Edinburgh, 1992; DEd *hc* Napier, 1995. *Publications:* various papers relating to higher educn. *Recreations:* modern jazz, Leonardo da Vinci. *Address:* 71 Morningside Park, Edinburgh EH10 5EZ. *T:* (0131) 447 4639. *Club:* Caledonian.

TURNAGE, Mark-Anthony; composer; *b* 1960; *m* Helen Reed; two *s*. *Educ:* Royal College of Music. Mendelssohn Scholar, Tanglewood, USA, 1983. Composer in Association: City of Birmingham Symphony Orchestra, 1989–93; ENO, 1995–2000; Associate Composer, BBC SO, 2000–. *Compositions include: stage:* Greek, 1988 (BMW prizes for best opera and best libretto, Munich Biennale, 1988); The Silver Tassie (opera), 2000 (Outstanding Achievement in Opera (jtly), Laurence Olivier Awards, and South Bank Show Award for opera, 2001); *vocal:* Lament for a Hanging Man, 1983; Greek Suite, 1989; Some Days, 1989; Twice Through The Heart, 1997; *orchestral:* Night Dances, 1981; Three Screaming Popes, 1989; Momentum, 1991; Drowned Out, 1993; Your Rockaby (saxophone concerto), 1994; Dispelling the Fears, 1995; Four-Horned Fandango, 1996; Silent Cities, 1998; Evening Songs, 1999; Another Set To, 2000; *ensemble:* On All Fours, 1985; Kai, 1990; Three Farewells, 1990; Blood on the Floor, 1996; About Time, 1999; Bass inventionS, 2000; A Quick Blast, 2001; *instrumental:* Sleep on, 1992. *Relevant publication:* Mark-Anthony Turnage, by Andrew Clements, 2000. *Address:* c/o Van Walsum Management Ltd, 4 Addison Bridge Place, W14 8XP. *T:* (020) 7371 4343.

TURNBERG, family name of **Baron Turnberg**.

TURNBERG, Baron *cr* 2000 (Life Peer), of Cheadle in the county of Cheshire; **Leslie Arnold Turnberg,** Kt 1994; MD; FRCP, FMedSci; Chairman, Public Health Laboratory Service Board, since 1997; *b* 22 March 1934; *s* of Hyman and Dora Turnberg; *m* 1968, Edna Barme; one *s* one *d*. *Educ:* Stand Grammar Sch., Whitefield; Univ. of Manchester (MB, ChB 1957, MD 1966). MRCP 1961, FRCP 1973; FRCPE 1993; FRCP(I) 1993; FRCPSGlas 1994; FRCS 1996; FCPS(Pak). Junior medical posts: Manchester Jewish Hosp.; Northern Hosp.; Ancoats Hosp.; Manchester Royal Infirmary, 1957–61 and 1964–66; Registrar, UCH, 1961–64; Lectr, Royal Free Hosp., 1967; Res. Fellow, Univ. of Texas South-Western Med. Sch., Dallas, Texas, 1968; University of Manchester: Lectr, then Sen. Lectr, 1968–73; Dean, Fac. of Medicine, 1986–89; Prof. of Medicine, 1973–97. Chm., Specialist Training Authy, 1996–98. Hon. Consultant Physician, Salford HA, 1973–97. Member: Salford HA, 1974–81 and 1990–92; NW RHA, 1986–89. Scientific Advr, Assoc. Med. Res. Charities, 1997–. Royal College of Physicians: Mem. Council, 1989–92; Pres., 1992–97; Chairman: Educn Cttee, 1990–92; Wking Gp on Communication, 1991–92; British Society of Gastroenterology: Mem. Council, 1989–92; Chm., Res. Cttee, 1991–92; Pres., 1999–2000; President: Med. Section, Manchester Med. Soc., 1992–93; Medical Protection Soc., 1997–; Founder FMedSci 1998 (Vice Pres., 1998–). Hon. FFOM 1993; Hon. FRACP 1994; Hon. FRCOphth 1996; Hon. FRCOG 1996; Hon. FFPM 1997; Hon. Fellow: Acad. of Medicine, Singapore, 1994; Coll. of Medicine, S Africa, 1994. Hon. DSc: Salford, 1996; Manchester, 1998; London, 2000. *Publications:* Electrolyte and Water Transport Across Gastro-intestinal Epithelia, 1982; Clinical Gastroenterology, 1989; pubns on mechanisms of intestinal absorption and secretion in health and disease and on clinical gastroenterology. *Recreations:* reading, antiquarian books, walking, talking. *Address:* House of Lords, SW1A 0AA.

TURNBULL, Sir Andrew, KCB 1998 (CB 1990); CVO 1992; Permanent Secretary, HM Treasury, since 1998; *b* 21 Jan. 1945; *s* of Anthony and Mary Turnbull; *m* 1967, Diane Clarke; two *s*. *Educ:* Enfield Grammar Sch.; Christ's Coll., Cambridge (BA). ODI Fellow working as economist, Govt of Republic of Zambia, Lusaka, 1968–70; Asst Principal, HM Treasury, 1970; Principal, 1972; on secondment to staff of IMF, 1976–78; Asst Sec., HM Treasury, 1978; Private Sec. to the Prime Minister, 1983–85; Under Sec., 1985; Hd of Gen. Expenditure Policy Gp, HM Treasury, 1985–88; Principal Private Sec. to Prime Minister, 1988–92; Dep. Sec. (Public Finance), 1992, Second Permanent Sec. (Public Expenditure), 1993–94, HM Treasury; Permanent Sec., DoE, later DETR, 1994–98. Cdre, CS Sailing Assoc., 1996–; Chm., CS Sports Council, 2001–. *Recreations:* walking, opera, golf. *Address:* HM Treasury, Parliament Street, SW1P 3AG. *Club:* Tottenham Hotspur.

TURNBULL, Rt Rev. (Anthony) Michael (Arnold); *see* Durham, Bishop of.

TURNBULL, David Knight Thomas, FCA; Director: Worldbeater Solutions Ltd, since 2000; XXX Building Ltd, since 1999; *b* 13 Dec. 1948; *s* of Stanley Thomas Turnbull and Lalla Turnbull (*née* Knight); *m* 1972, Monica Belton; one *s* one *d*. *Educ:* Stationers' Co. Sch.; Westfield Coll., London Univ. (BSc). FCA 1975. With Coopers & Lybrand, Sheffield and Iran, 1972–79; Amalgamated Metal Corporation plc: Gp Chief Acct, 1980–84; Corporate Controller, 1984–86; Gen. Manager, Business Develt, 1986–89; Finance Director: PO Counters Ltd, 1989–94; British Council, 1994–2000. Sec., Interstate Programmes Ltd, 2000–. *Recreations:* anything old, watching Rugby. *Address:* Halfway Grange, Chantry View Road, Guildford, Surrey GU1 3XR. *T:* (01483) 569285.

TURNBULL, Jeffrey Alan, CBE 1991; FREng; FICE, FIHT; Consultant, Mott MacDonald Group Ltd, 1994–96 (Chairman and Director, 1989–94); *b* 14 Aug. 1934; *s* of Alan Edward Turnbull and Alice May (*née* Slee); *m* 1957, Beryl (*née* Griffith); two *s* one *d*. *Educ:* Newcastle upon Tyne Royal Grammar Sch.; Liverpool Coll. of Technology. DipTE 1964; CEng; FIHT 1966; FICE 1973; FREng (FEng 1992). National Service, RE, 1956–58. Jun. Engr, Cheshire CC, 1951–55; Engr, Herefordshire CC, 1955–59; Resident Engr, Berks CC, 1959–66; Mott Hay & Anderson, 1966–: Chief Designer (Roads), 1968; Associate, 1973; Dir, Mott Hay & Anderson International Ltd, 1975–88; Dir, Mott Hay & Anderson, 1978–88; Dir, 1983–88, Chief Exec., 1987–88, Mott Hay & Anderson Holdings Ltd. *Publication:* (contrib.) Civil Engineer's Reference Book, 4th edn 1988. *Recreations:* walking, France. *Address:* 63 Higher Drive, Banstead, Surrey SM1 1PW. *T:* (020) 8393 1054. *Club:* Royal Automobile.

TURNBULL, John William; JP; Chief Executive, Hereford and Worcester County Council, 1993–97; *b* 12 May 1934; *s* of Henry W. Turnbull and Janet Turnbull; *m* 1956, Sheila Batey; two *d*. *Educ:* Westminster Coll.; LSE (BScEcon); London Inst. of Educn (MA, DipEd). Teacher, 1957–68; Lectr, 1968–70; Educn Officer, 1970–76; Dep. County Educn Officer, Leics, 1977–83; County Educn Officer, Hereford and Worcester, 1984–93. Advr, ACC, 1985 (Advr, Soc. Services Cttee, 1995–97); Mem. Bd, Midlands Examining Gp, 1989–93; Chm., W Midlands Exam. Bd, 1991–93; Mem., Nat. Youth Bureau, 1990–93. Clerk to Lord Lieutenancy, 1993–97. Governor, Further Educn Staff Coll., 1990–93. JP S Worcs, 1998. *Publications:* articles on educn and administration. *Recreations:* reading, playing piano, bowls. *Address:* The Riddings, Bricklehampton, Pershore, Worcs WR10 3HQ.

TURNBULL, Malcolm Bligh; Managing Director, Turnbull & Partners Pty Ltd, Investment Bankers, Sydney, 1987–97 and since 2001; *b* 24 Oct. 1954; *s* of late Bruce Bligh Turnbull and Coral (*née* Lansbury); *m* 1980, Lucinda Mary Forrest Hughes; one *s* one *d*. *Educ:* Sydney Grammar Sch.; Sydney Univ. (BA, LLB); Brasenose Coll., Oxford (Rhodes Schol. (NSW) 1978, BCL 1980). Journalist, Nation Review, 1975; Political Correspondent: TCN–9, Sydney, 1976; The Bulletin, 1977–78; Journalist, Sunday Times, London, 1979; admitted to NSW Bar, 1980; Barrister, Sydney, 1980–82; Gen. Counsel and Secretary, Consolidated Press Holdings Ltd, 1983–85; Partner: Turnbull McWilliam, Solicitors, Sydney, 1986–87; Turnbull & Co., Solicitors, 1987–90; Jt Man. Dir, Whitlam Turnbull & Co. Ltd, Investment Bankers, Sydney, 1987–90; Man. Dir and Chm., Goldman Sachs Australia, 1997–2001. Chm., Australian Republican Movement, 1993–2000 (Dir, 1991–); Deleg., Constitutional Convention, 1998; Dep. Hon. Fedl Treas., Liberal Party of Australia, 2001–. Chairman: Axiom Forest Resources Ltd, 1991–92; FTR Holdings Ltd, 1995–97 (Dir, 1995–); OzEmail Ltd, 1995–99 (Dir, 1995–99); Dir, Reach Ltd, 2001–. *Publications:* The Spycatcher Trial, 1988; The Reluctant Republic, 1993; Fighting for the Republic, 1999. *Recreations:* riding, swimming. *Address:* GPO Box 4298, Sydney, NSW 2001, Australia; *e-mail:* turnbullm@ozemail.com.au. *Clubs:* Australian, Tattersall's (Sydney); Athenæum (Philadelphia).

TURNBULL, Mark; *see* Turnbull, W. M.

TURNBULL, Rt Rev. Michael; *see* Durham, Bishop of.

TURNBULL, (Wilson) Mark, RIBA; FRIAS, FLI; Principal, Mark Turnbull Landscape Architect, since 1999; Chairman: Turnbull Jeffrey Partnership, Landscape Architects, since 1999 (Principal, 1982–99); Envision, since 1999; Member, Royal Fine Art Commission for Scotland, since 1996; *b* 1 April 1943; *s* of Wilson and Margaret Turnbull. *Educ:* Edinburgh Coll. of Fine Art (DipArch (distinction in Design) 1968); Univ. of Pennsylvania (MLA 1970). RIBA 1977; MBCS 1984; FLI 1989; FRIAS 1991. Architect and Landscape Architect, Wallace, McHarg, Roberts and Todd, Landscape Architects and Regl Planners, Philadelphia, 1968–70; Asst Prof., Dept of Architecture, Univ. of S Calif, LA, 1970–74; Envmtl Consultant: US Atomic Energy Commn, 1971, 1974; Kamnitzer, Marks, Lappin and Vreeland, Architects and Regl Planners, LA, 1973–74; Associate, 1974–77, Partner, 1977–82, W. J. Cairns and Partners, Envmtl Consultants, Edinburgh; Partner, Design Innovations Res., 1978–82. Dir, Friday.net, 1999–. Member: Council, Cockburn Assoc., Edinburgh Civic Trust, 1984–95; Countryside Commn for Scotland, 1988–92; Chm., Edinburgh Green Belt Initiative, 1988–92; Vice-Chm., Edinburgh Green Belt Trust, 1991–. *Publications:* numerous articles on landscape architecture, computer visualisation and design methods in jls. *Recreation:* sailing. *Address:* Mark Turnbull Landscape Architect, Craig an Tuirc House, Balquhidder, Perthshire FK19 8NY. *T:* (01877) 384728.

TURNER, family name of **Baron Netherthorpe** and **Baroness Turner of Camden**.

TURNER OF CAMDEN, Baroness *cr* 1985 (Life Peer), of Camden in Greater London; **Muriel Winifred Turner;** *b* 18 Sept. 1927; *m* 1955, Reginald Thomas Frederick Turner (*d* 1995), MC, DFC. Asst Gen. Sec., ASTMS, 1970–87. Member: Occupational Pensions Board, 1978–93; Central Arbitration Cttee, 1980–90; TUC General Council, 1981–87; Equal Opportunities Commission, 1982–88. Junior Spokesperson on Social Security, 1986–96, Principal Opposition Spokesperson on Employment, 1988–96, H of L. Chm., Ombudsman Council, PIA, 1994–97. Hon. LLD Leicester, 1991. *Address:* House of Lords, SW1A 0PW.

TURNER, Adair; *see* Turner, J. A.

TURNER, Alan B.; *see* Brooke Turner.

TURNER, Amédée Edward; QC 1976; *b* 26 March 1929; *s* of Frederick William Turner and Ruth Hempson; *m* 1960, Deborah Dudley Owen; one *s* one *d*. *Educ:* Temple Grove, Heron's Ghyll, Sussex; Dauntsey Sch., Wilts; Christ Church, Oxford (MA). Called to Bar, Inner Temple, 1954; practised patent bar, 1954–57; Associate, Kenyon & Kenyon, patent attorneys, NY, 1957–60; London practice, 1960–; Senior Counsel: APCO Europe, Brussels, 1995–; WorldSpace Ltd, 1999–; of Counsel, Oppenheimer Wolff and Donnelly, Brussels, 1994–. Dir, CJA Consultants Ltd, 1999–. Contested (C) Norwich N, gen. elections, 1964, 1966, 1970. European Parliament: MEP (C) Suffolk, 1979–94; contested (C) Suffolk and SW Norfolk, 1994; Hon. MEP, 1994; EDG spokesman on energy res. and technol., 1984–89; Chief Whip, EDG, 1989–92; joined EPP Gp, 1992; Mem., EPP Gp Bureau, 1992–94; Chm., Civil Liberties and Internal Affairs Cttee, 1992–94; Vice Chm., Legal Cttee, 1979–84; Member: Economic and Monetary Cttee, 1979–84; ACP Jt Cttee, 1980–94; Transport Cttee, 1981–84; Energy Cttee, 1984–94; Legal Affairs Cttee, 1984–89. Mem., Exec. Cttee, European League for Econ. Co-operation, 1996–. *Publications:* The Law of Trade Secrets, 1962, supplement, 1968; The Law of the New European Patent, 1979; many Conservative Party study papers on defence, oil and Middle East. *Recreations:* garden design, art deco collection, fish keeping, oil painting. *Address:* Penthouse 7, Bickenhall Mansions, Bickenhall Street, W1U 6BS. *T:* (020) 7935 2949, *Fax:* (020) 7935 2950; 5 New Square, Lincoln's Inn, WC2A 3RJ. *T:* (020) 7404 0404; The Barn, Westleton, Saxmundham, Suffolk IP17 3AN. *T:* (01728) 648235; La Combe de la Boissière, St Maximin, Uzès 30700, France, *T:* 466220869; *e-mail:* amedee.edward.turner@ukbar.com. *Clubs:* Carlton, Coningsby, United & Cecil.

TURNER, Andrew John; MP (C) Isle of Wight, since 2001; *b* Coventry, 24 Oct. 1953; *s* of late Eustace Albert Turner and Joyce Mary Turner (*née* Lowe). *Educ:* Rugby Sch.; Keble Coll., Oxford (BA 1976, MA 1981); Birmingham Univ. (PGCE 1977); Henley Mgt Centre. Teacher of Econs and Geog., Rushden Boys' Comp. Sch., 1977, Lord Williams's Sch., Thame, 1978–84; Res. Officer, Cons. Central Office, 1984–86; Special Advr to Sec. of State for Social Services, 1986–88; Dir, Grant-maintained Schools Foundn, 1988–97; Dep. Dir, Educn Unit, IEA, 1998–2000; Head of Policy and Resources, Educn Dept, Southwark BC, 2000–01. Educn Consultant, 1997–2001, Dir, 2000–, Empire Packet Co. FRSA. *Recreations:* walking, the countryside, old movies, avoiding gardening. *Address:* House of Commons, SW1A 0AA; (home) 2 Northwood Place, Cowes, Isle of Wight PO31 7TN; (constituency office) 24 The Mall, Carisbrooke Road, Newport, Isle of Wight PO30 1BW. *T:* (01983) 530808. *Club:* Oxford and Cambridge.

TURNER, Ven. Antony Hubert Michael; Archdeacon of the Isle of Wight, 1986–96, now Archdeacon Emeritus; *b* 17 June 1930; *s* of Frederick George and Winifred Frances Turner; *m* 1956, Margaret Kathleen (*née* Phillips); one *s* two *d*. *Educ:* Royal Liberty Grammar School, Romford, Essex; Tyndale Hall, Bristol. FCA 1963 (ACA 1952); DipTh (Univ. of London), 1956. Deacon, 1956; Priest, 1957; Curate, St Ann's, Nottingham, 1956–59; Curate in Charge, St Cuthbert's, Cheadle, Dio. Chester, 1959–62; Vicar, Christ Church, Macclesfield, 1962–68; Home Sec., Bible Churchmen's Missionary Soc., 1968–74; Vicar of St Jude's, Southsea, 1974–86; RD of Portsmouth, 1979–84; Priest i/c, St Mary, Rotterdam, 1999–2000. Church Commissioner, 1983–93. Vice Chm., C of E Pensions Bd, 1988–97. *Recreations:* photography, caravanning. *Address:* 15 Avenue Road, Hayling Island, Hants, PO11 0LX. *T:* (023) 9246 5881.

TURNER, Barry Horace Page, PhD; writer and editor; *b* 4 Oct. 1937; *o s* of Laurence and Esther Turner; *m* 1st, 1965, Sandra Hogben (marr. diss. 1972); 2nd, 1974, Gunilla Nordquist (marr. diss. 1986); one *s* one *d*; 3rd, 1997, Mary Elizabeth Fulton. *Educ:* King Edward VII Grammar Sch., Bury St Edmunds; London School of Economics (BSc Econs 1961; PhD 1966); Inst. of Educn, London Univ. (DipEd 1962). Dep. Editor, New Education, 1966–68; Educn Corresp., Observer, 1969–71; Reporter and Presenter, BBC Current Affairs, Thames TV, Yorkshire TV, Granada TV, 1969–77; Mktg Dir, Macmillan Press, 1977–81. Editor: The Writer's Handbook, annually 1988–; The Statesman's Yearbook, annually 1997–. *Plays:* (jtly) Henry Irving, 1995; Agate, 1997. *Publications:* (jtly) Adventures in Education, 1969; Free Trade and Protection, 1971; Equality for Some, 1974; A Place in the Country, 1974; Sweden, 1976; The Other European Community, 1982; (jtly) The Playgoer's Companion, 1983; A Jobbing Actor, 1984; Richard Burton, 1987; East End, West End, 1990; Marks of Distinction, 1988; . . . And the Policeman Smiled, 1991; The Long Horizon, 1993; Quest for Love, 1994; (jtly) When Daddy Came Home, 1995; The Writer's Companion, 1996; contribs to The Times, Sunday Times. *Recreations:* theatre, old movies, lunch. *Address:* 34 Ufton Road, N1 5BX. *T:* (020) 7241 0116; Le Bernet, 32480 La Romieu, France. *T:* 562288841. *Clubs:* Garrick, Chelsea Arts.

TURNER, Prof. Bryan Stanley, PhD, DLitt; Professor of Sociology, University of Cambridge, since 1998; *b* 14 Jan. 1945; *s* of Stanley W. Turner and Sophie (*née* Brooks); *m* 1996, Eileen Haywood Richardson. *Educ:* Univ. of Leeds (BA 1966; PhD 1970); Flinders Univ. (DLitt 1976). Lecturer: Univ. of Aberdeen, 1969–74; Univ. of Lancaster, 1974–78; Sen. Lectr, 1979–80, Reader, 1980–82, Univ. of Aberdeen; Prof. of Sociology, Univ. of Flinders, 1982–88; Prof. of Gen. Social Sci., Univ. of Utrecht, 1988–90; Professor of Sociology: Univ. of Essex, 1990–92; Deakin Univ., 1992–98. FASSA 1988. Editor: (jtly) Body & Society, 1994–; Citizenship Studies, 1997–; (jtly) Jl of Classical Sociology. *Publications include:* Weber and Islam, 1974; For Weber, 1981; Religion and Social Theory, 1983; The Body and Society, 1984; Citizenship and Capitalism, 1986; Medical Power and Social Knowledge, 1987; Regulating Bodies, 1992; Orientalism, Postmodernism and Globalism, 1994; (ed) The Blackwell Companion to Social Theory, 1996; Classical Sociology, 1999. *Recreations:* gardening, tourism, walking, collecting books. *Address:* Department of Social and Political Sciences, Free School Lane, Cambridge CB2 3RQ. *T:* (01223) 334527.

TURNER, Prof. Cedric Edward, CBE 1987; FREng; Emeritus Professor and Senior Research Fellow, Imperial College, London, since 1991; *b* 5 Aug. 1926; *s* of Charles Turner and Mabel Evelyn (*née* Berry); *m* 1953, Margaret Dorothy (*née* Davies); one *s* two *d*. *Educ:* Brockenhurst Grammar Sch.; University Coll., Southampton (now Univ. of Southampton) (BScEng); DScEng, PhD London. CEng, FIMechE, FREng (FEng 1989). Res. Asst, Imperial Coll., 1948–52; Academic Staff, Imperial Coll., 1952–76 and 1979–: Prof. of Materials in Mech. Engrg, 1975–91; seconded NPL and Brit. Aerospace, 1976–78. Hon. Prof., Shenyang Inst. of Aeronautical Engrg, Shenyang, China, 1987; Leverhulme Emeritus Fellow, 1990–92. Silver Medal, Plastics Inst., 1963; James Clayton Prize, IMechE, 1981. *Publications:* Introduction to Plate and Shell Theory, 1965; (jtly) Post Yield Fracture Mechanics, 1979, 2nd edn 1984; contribs to Proc. Royal Soc., Proc. IMechE, Jl Strain Anal., Amer. Soc. Test & Mat., etc. *Recreations:* fracture mechanics, travel, reading, friend of Kirkaldy Testing Museum, London. *Address:* The Corner House, 17 Meadway, Epsom, Surrey KT19 8JZ. *T:* (01372) 722989.

TURNER, Rev. Christopher Gilbert; Hon. Assistant Curate, Hook Norton with Great Rollright, Swerford and Wigginton, since 1992; Headmaster, Stowe School, 1979–89; *b* 23 Dec. 1929; *s* of late Theodore F. Turner, QC; *m* 1961, Lucia, *d* of late Prof. S. R. K. Glanville (Provost of King's Coll., Cambridge); one *s* one *d* (and one *d* decd). *Educ:* Winchester Coll. (Schol.); New Coll., Oxford (Exhibnr, MA); Oxford Ministry Course. Asst Master, Radley Coll., 1952–61; Senior Classics Master, Charterhouse, 1961–68; Headmaster, Dean Close Sch., 1968–79. Schoolmaster Student at Christ Church, Oxford, 1967. Foundation Member of Council, Cheltenham Colleges of Educn, 1968. Mem., HMC Cttee, 1974–75, 1987–88; Chm., Common Entrance Cttee, 1976–80; Gov., Chipping Norton Sch., 1996–. Ordained deacon, 1992, priest, 1993. *Publications:* chapter on History, in Comparative Study of Greek and Latin Literature, 1969; chapter on Dean Close in the Seventies, in The First Hundred Years, 1986. *Recreations:* music (violin-playing), reading, walking, different forms of manual labour; OUBC 1951. *Address:* Rosemullion, High Street, Great Rollright, near Chipping Norton, Oxon OX7 5RQ. *T:* (01608) 737359.

See also Hon. Sir M. J. Turner.

TURNER, Christopher John, CBE 1990 (OBE 1977); Partner, DCGlobal, since 1998; consultant, EBRD TurnAround Management programme (Balkans); *b* 17 Aug. 1933; *s* of Arthur Basil Turner and Joan Meddows (*née* Taylor); *m* 1961, Irene Philomena de Souza; two *d* (one *s* decd). *Educ:* Truro Cathedral Sch.; Jesus Coll., Cambridge (MA). Served RAF, Pilot Officer (Navigator), 1951–53. Tanganyika/Tanzania: Dist Officer, 1958–61; Dist Comr, 1961–62; Magistrate and Regional Local Courts Officer, 1962–64; Sec., Sch. Admin, 1964–69; Anglo-French Condominium of New Hebrides: Dist Agent, 1970–73; Develt Sec., 1973; Financial Sec., 1975; Chief Sec., 1977–80; Admin. Officer (Staff Planning), Hong Kong, 1980–82; Governor: Turks and Caicos Islands, 1982–87; Montserrat, WI, 1987–90. Manager, Internat. Business Develt, 1990–92, consultant on regl business develt, Santa Domingo, 1990–91, McLane (Wal Mart), Texas; Man. Dir, McLane (UK), 1993; Vice Pres. Develt, McLane Internat., 1994–96; Dir of Mkting, Cambridge Myers (Strasburger Enterprises Inc.), Texas, 1996–98. Vanuatu Independence Medal, 1981. *Recreations:* ornithology, photography, diving, tropical gardening. *Address:* 98 Christchurch Road, Winchester SO23 9TE. *T:* (01962) 870775; (office) 22 Shirlock Road, NW3 2HS. *T:* (020) 7284 4154.

TURNER, Colin Francis; Senior District Judge (formerly Senior Registrar), Family Division of High Court, 1988–91, retired (Registrar, 1971–88); *b* 11 April 1930; *s* of Sidney F. and Charlotte C. Turner; *m* 1951, Josephine Alma Jones; two *s* one *d*. *Educ:* Beckenham Grammar Sch.; King's Coll., London. LLB 1955. Entered Principal Probate Registry, 1949; District Probate Registrar, York, 1965–68. MBOU. Hon. Mem., London Nat. History Soc., 1998. *Publications:* (ed jtly) Rayden on Divorce, 9th, 11th, 12th and 13th edns, consulting editor to 14th edn; an editor of Supreme Court Practice, 1972–90; (jtly) Precedents in Matrimonial Causes and Ancillary Matters, 1985. *Recreations:* birding, fishing. *Address:* Lakers, Church Road, St Johns, Redhill, Surrey RH1 6QA. *T:* (01737) 761807.

TURNER, Colin William; Rector, Glasgow Academy, 1983–94; *b* 10 Dec. 1933; *s* of William and Joyce Turner; *m* 1958, Priscilla Mary Trickett; two *s* two *d*. *Educ:* Torquay Grammar Sch.; King's Coll., London (BSc; AKC). Edinburgh Academy: Asst Master, 1958–82; OC CCF, 1960–74; Head, Maths Dept, 1973–75; Housemaster, 1975–82. *Recreations:* mountaineering, gardening, local history. *Address:* Leat, Lower Down, Bovey Tracey, Devon TQ13 9LF. *T:* (01626) 832266.

TURNER, Sir Colin (William Carstairs), Kt 1993; CBE 1985; DFC 1944; President, The Colin Turner Group, International Media Representatives and Marketing Consultants, 1988–97 (Chairman, 1985–88); *b* 4 Jan. 1922; *s* of late Colin C. W. Turner, Enfield; *m* 1949, Evelyn Mary, *d* of late Claude H. Buckard, Enfield; three *s* one *d*. *Educ:* Highgate Sch. Served War of 1939–45 with RAF, 1940–45, Air observer; S. Africa and E Africa, 223 Squadron; Desert Air Force, N. Africa, 1942–44; commissioned, 1943; invalided out as Flying Officer, 1945, after air crash; Chm., 223 Squadron Assoc., 1975–93; Pres., Enfield Br., 1979–93, Chm., 1994–99, Pres., 2000–March 2002, Sheringham and Dist Br., RAFA. Mem., Enfield Borough Council, 1956–58. Pres., Overseas Press and Media Association, 1965–67, Life Pres., 1982 (Hon. Secretary, 1967; Hon. Treasurer, 1974–82; Editor, Overseas Media Guide, 1968, 1969, 1970, 1971, 1972, 1973, 1974); Chm., PR Cttee, Commonwealth Press Union, 1970–87; Chm., Cons. Commonwealth and Overseas Council, 1976–82 (Dep. Chm. 1975); Vice-Pres., Cons. Foreign and Commonwealth Council, 1985–94; Mem., Nat. Exec., Cons. Party, 1946–53, 1968–73, 1976–82; President: Enfield North Cons. Assoc., 1984–93 (Chm., 1979–84); North Norfolk Cons. Assoc., 1996–99; Chm., Cons. Europ. Constituency Council, London N, 1984–89. Contested (C) Enfield (East), 1950 and 1951; MP (C) Woolwich West, 1959–64. Editor, The Cholmeleian, 1982–95 (Pres., Old Cholmeleian Soc., 1985–86). *Recreations:* gardening, do-it-yourself, fishing. *Address:* The Thatched House, Balfour Road, West Runton, Norfolk NR27 9QJ. *T:* (01263) 837229.

TURNER, David Andrew; QC 1991; a Recorder of the Crown Court, since 1990; *b* 6 March 1947; *s* of late James and of Phyllis Turner; *m* 1978, Mary Christine Moffatt; two *s* one *d*. *Educ:* King George V Sch., Southport; Queens' Coll., Cambridge (MA, LLM). Called to the Bar, Gray's Inn, 1971, Bencher, 2001; Asst Recorder, 1987–90. *Recreations:* squash, music. *Address:* Pearl Assurance House, Derby Square, Liverpool L2 9XX. *T:* (0151) 236 7747. *Club:* Liverpool Racquet.

TURNER, David George Patrick; QC 2000; a Recorder, since 2000; *b* 11 July 1954; *s* of George P. Turner and Elsie B. Turner (*née* McClure); *m* 1978, Jean Patricia Hewett; two *s*. *Educ:* Foyle Coll., Londonderry; King's Coll. London (LLB, AKC 1975). Called to the Bar, Gray's Inn, 1976; in practice at the Bar, 1976–; Asst Recorder, 1997–2000. Chancellor, Diocese of Chester, 1998–. Reader, 1981–, Churchwarden, 1983–, All Souls, Langham Place. *Address:* 14 Gray's Inn Square, Gray's Inn, WC1R 5JP. *T:* (020) 7242 0858.

TURNER, Prof. David Warren, FRS 1973; Fellow of Balliol College, Oxford, 1967–94, now Emeritus Fellow; Professor of Electron Spectroscopy, Oxford, 1985–94, now Emeritus Professor; *b* 16 July 1927; *s* of Robert Cecil Turner and Constance Margaret (*née* Bonner); *m* 1954, Barbara Marion Fisher; one *s* one *d*. *Educ:* Westcliff High Sch.; Univ. of Exeter. MA, BSc, PhD, DIC. Lectr, Imperial Coll., 1958; Reader in Organic Chemistry, Imperial Coll., 1965; Oxford University: Lectr in Physical Chem., 1968; Reader in Physical Chemistry, 1978; Reader in Electron Spectroscopy, 1984. Lectures: Kahlbaum, Univ. of Basle, 1971; Van Geuns, Univ. of Amsterdam, 1974; Harkins, Chicago Univ., 1974; Kistiakowski, Harvard, 1979; Liversidge, RSC, 1981–82. Tilden Medal, Chemical Soc., 1967; Harrison Howe Award, Amer. Chem. Soc., 1973. Hon. DTech, Royal Inst., Stockholm, 1971; Hon. DPhil Basle, 1980; Hon. DSc Exeter, 1999. *Publications:* Molecular Photoelectron Spectroscopy, 1970; contrib. Phil. Trans Royal Soc., Proc. Royal Soc., Jl Chem. Soc., etc. *Recreations:* music, gardening, tinkering with gadgets. *Address:* Balliol College, Oxford OX1 3BJ.

TURNER, Dennis; MP (Lab and Co-op) Wolverhampton South East, since 1987; *b* 26 Aug. 1942; *s* of Mary Elizabeth Peasley and Thomas Herbert Turner; *m* 1976, Patricia Mary Narroway; one *s* one *d*. *Educ:* Stonefield Secondary Modern School, Bilston; Bilston College of Further Education; Bilston Black Country. Office boy, salesman, market trader, steel worker, partner in worker co-operative. Mem. (Lab), Wolverhampton BC, 1966–86 (Chairman of Committees: Social Services, 1972–79; Educn, 1979–86; Econ. Develt, 1982–85; Housing, 1985–86). An Opposition Whip, 1993–97; PPS to Sec. of State for Internat. Develt, 1997–2001. Mem., Educn Select Cttee, 1989–94; Chairman: H of C Catering Cttee, 1997–; All-Party Gp on Further Educn. *Address:* House of Commons, SW1A 0AA. *T:* (020) 7219 4210; Ambleside, King Street, Bradley, Bilston, W Midlands WV14 8PQ. *Club:* Springvale Sports and Social (Bilston).

TURNER, Prof. Denys Alan, DPhil; Norris Hulse Professor of Divinity, University of Cambridge, since 1999; Fellow of Peterhouse, Cambridge, since 1999; *b* 5 Aug. 1942; *s* of Alan Turner and Barbara Turner (*née* Mason); *m* 1969, Marie Lambe; two *s* one *d. Educ:* Nat. Univ. of Ireland (BA 1962; MA 1965); St Edmund Hall, Oxford (DPhil 1975). Asst Lectr, 1967–74, Coll. Lectr, 1974–76, in Philosophy, UC, Dublin; Lectr, 1976–89, Sen. Lectr, 1989–95, in Philosophy of Religion, Dept of Theology and Religious Studies, Univ. of Bristol; H. G. Wood Prof. of Theology, Univ. of Birmingham, 1995–99. *Publications:* Marxism and Christianity, 1983; Eros and Allegory: medieval exegesis of the Song of Songs, 1995; The Darkness of God: negativity in Christian mysticism, 1995. *Recreations:* mediaeval church architecture, classical music from Ockeghem to Mahler, gardens. *Address:* Faculty of Divinity, West Road, Cambridge CB3 9BS. *T:* (01223) 763020.

TURNER, Dr Desmond Stanley; MP (Lab) Brighton Kemptown, since 1997; *b* 17 July 1939; *s* of Stanley and Elsie Turner; *m* 1st, 1966, Lynette Gwyn-Jones (marr. diss. 1987); one *d*; 2nd, 1997, Lynn Rogers. *Educ:* Luton Grammar Sch.; Imperial Coll., London (BSc); University Coll. London (MSc); PhD London; Brighton Univ. (PGCE). ARCS. Junior posts, Royal Free and St Mary's Hosps Schs of Medicine, 1963–67; Research Associate and Hon. Lectr, Guy's Hosp. Med. Sch., 1967–71; Research Fellow and Hon. Lecturer: Univ. of Surrey, 1971–76; Univ. of Sussex, 1974–78; Chm. and Man. Dir, Martlet Brewery, 1979–83; science teacher, 1984–95. R. D. Lawrence Meml Fellowship, British Diabetes Assoc., 1970–72. *Publications:* research papers and reviews. *Recreations:* sailing, fencing. *Address:* 49 Queen's Park Terrace, Brighton BN2 2YZ. *T:* (01273) 687732.

TURNER, Donald William, CEng, FICE; Director: Turner Associates, since 1986; Atlantic Ltd, since 1994; *b* 17 Aug. 1925; *s* of William John Turner and Agnes Elizabeth Jane (*née* Bristow); *m* 1947, Patricia (*née* Stuteley); one *s* one *d. Educ:* Wanstead County High Sch.; Birmingham Univ. Served War, Army, 1943–45. Subseq. completed engrg trng in Britain; then took up post in Australia with Qld Railways, 1949. Left Qld, 1954; joined firm of UK consulting engrs and then worked in W Africa on rly and highway construction until 1960. Returned to UK, but remained with consultants until 1966, when joined BAA; Chief Engr, Heathrow Airport, 1970; Dir of Planning and Bd Mem., 1973; Dir of Privatisation, 1985–86; Chm., British Airports International, 1984–87. Dir, London Underground, 1985–93. *Address:* 27 Kingsway Court, Hove, Sussex BN3 2LP.

TURNER, Dudley Russell Flower, CB 1977; Secretary, Advisory, Conciliation and Arbitration Service, 1974–77; *b* 15 Nov. 1916; *s* of Gerald Flower Turner and Dorothy May Turner (*née* Gillard), Penang; *m* 1941, Sheila Isobel Stewart; one *s* one *d. Educ:* Whitgift Sch.; London Univ. (BA Hons). Served RA (Captain), 1940–46. Entered Ministry of Labour, 1935; HM Treasury, 1953–56; Principal Private Secretary to Minister of Labour, 1956–59; Assistant Secretary: Cabinet Office, 1959–62, Ministry of Labour, 1962–64, 1966; Under-Sec., Ministry of Labour, 1967; Asst Under-Sec. of State, Dept of Employment and Productivity, 1968–70; Under-Sec., Trng Div., 1970–72, Manpower Gen. Div., 1972–73, Dept of Employment; Sec., Commn on Industrial Relations, 1973–74. Imperial Defence Coll., 1965. Pres., East Surrey Decorative and Fine Arts Soc., 1986– (Chm., 1980–86). *Recreations:* music, gardening. *Address:* 9 Witherby Close, Croydon, Surrey CR0 5SU. *Club:* Civil Service.

TURNER, Captain Ernest John Donaldson, CBE 1968; DSO 1942; DSC 1941, RN retd; French Croix de Guerre 1941; Vice Lord-Lieutenant of Dunbartonshire, since 1986; *b* 21 March 1914; *s* of Ernest Turner (*d* 1916, HMS Hampshire) and Margaret Donaldson; *m* 1940, Catherine Chalmers; one *d. Educ:* Hermitage Academy; Glasgow Technical College; Royal Navy; sowc, IDC. Joined Merchant Navy as Cadet, 1930; RN from RNR, 1937; specialised in submarines, 1939; served in submarines, 1941–68; Commodore, Submarines, 1964; Captain i/c Clyde, 1965–68, during building of Faslane Polaris Base; officer recruitment (after retiring), 1968–80; PA to Chm., Whyte & Mackay Distillers Ltd, 1980–82. *Recreations:* hockey and golf, holidays abroad. *Address:* Langcroft, Buchanan Castle, Drymen, by Glasgow G63 0HX. *T:* (01360) 60274. *Clubs:* Victory; Buchanan Castle Golf.

TURNER, Geoffrey Howard; Chief Executive, Securities Institute, since 1997; *b* 23 July 1945; *s* of Charles William Turner and Evelyn Doris (*née* Harris); *m* 1975, Margaret Linda Donaldson; two *d. Educ:* King's Sch., Chester; St Edmund Hall, Oxford (BA, MA; Special Dip. Social Studies). With Simon & Coates, stockbrokers, 1968–70; British India Steam Navigation Co., 1970–73; Stock Exchange, 1973–90: Asst Manager, 1973–75, Manager, 1975–78, Membership Dept; Secretary: Wilson Evidence Cttee, 1978; Planning Cttee, 1977–78; Restrictive Practices Case Cttee, 1978–83; Head of Membership, 1983–86; Dir of Membership, 1986–90; Dir of Authorisation, Securities Assoc., 1986–92; Dir of Public Affairs, SFA, 1993–94; Chief Exec., Assoc. of Private Client Investment Managers and Stockbrokers, 1994–97. *Recreations:* visiting country churches, collecting books and prints. *Address:* 44 Roundwood Lane, Harpenden, Herts AL5 3BU. *T:* (01582) 769882. *Clubs:* City of London; Vincent's (Oxford); Leander (Henley).

TURNER, Rt Rev. Geoffrey Martin; Bishop Suffragan of Stockport, 1994–2000; *b* 16 March 1934; *s* of Ernest Hugh Turner and Winifred Rose Turner (*née* Martin); *m* 1959, Gillian Chope; two *s* one *d. Educ:* Bideford Grammar Sch.; Sandhurst; Oak Hill Theol Coll. Ordained deacon, 1963, priest, 1964; Assistant Curate: St Stephen, Tonbridge, 1963–66; St John, Heatherlands, dio. of Salisbury, 1966–69; Vicar: St Peter, Derby, 1969–73; Christ Church, Chadderton, dio. of Manchester, 1973–79; Rector of Bebington, 1979–93; Rural Dean, Wirral North, 1989–93; Hon. Canon, Chester Cathedral, 1989–93; Archdeacon of Chester, 1993–94. *Recreations:* sport, literature. *Address:* 23 Lang Lane, West Kirby, Wirral CH48 5HG. *T:* (0151) 625 8504, *Fax:* (0151) 626 0422.

TURNER, George, PhD; *b* 9 Aug. 1940; *s* of late George and Jane Turner; *m* Lesley Duggan; two *d*, and one step *s* one step *d. Educ:* Laxton Grammar Sch.; Imperial Coll., London (BSc Hons); Gonville and Caius Coll., Cambridge (PhD Physics 1967). Formerly Lectr in electronic engrg, Univ. of E Anglia. Mem. (Lab) Norfolk CC, 1977–97. Contested (Lab) Norfolk NW, 1992; MP (Lab) Norfolk NW, 1997–2001; contested same seat, 2001. *Address:* 47 Gayton Road, King's Lynn PE30 4EF.

TURNER, Prof. Grenville, FRS 1980; FInstP; Professor of Isotope Geochemistry, Manchester University, since 1988; *b* 1 Nov. 1936; *o s* of Arnold and Florence Turner, Todmorden, Yorks; *m* 1961, Kathleen, *d* of William and Joan Morris, Rochdale, Lancs; one *s* one *d. Educ:* Todmorden Grammar Sch.; St John's Coll., Cambridge (MA); Balliol Coll., Oxford (DPhil). FInstP 1991. Asst Prof., Univ. of Calif at Berkeley, 1962–64; Lectr, Sheffield Univ., 1964–74, Sen. Lectr, 1974–79, Reader, 1979–80, Prof. of Physics, 1980–88. Vis. Associate in Nuclear Geophysics, Calif Inst. of Technol., 1970–71. Mem. Council, Royal Soc., 1990–92. Fellow: Meteoritical Soc., 1980 (Leonard Medal, 1999); American Geophysical Union, 1998; Geochemistry Fellow, Geochemical Soc. and European Assoc. of Geochemistry, 1996. Rumford Medal, Royal Soc. 1996. *Publications:* scientific papers. *Recreations:* photography, walking, theatre. *Address:* 42 Edgehill Road, Sheffield S7 1SP. *T:* (office) (0161) 275 3800; *e-mail:* grenville.turner@man.ac.uk.

TURNER, Harry Edward; Chairman, Amcom Resources plc, since 1995; *b* 28 Feb. 1935; *s* of Harry Turner and Bessie Elizabeth Jay; *m* 1956, Carolyn Bird; one *s* one *d. Educ:* Sloane Grammar Sch., Chelsea. Served Middlesex Regt, Austria, 2nd Lieut, 1953–55. Sales Representative, Crosse & Blackwell Foods, 1955–56; Advertising Executive: Daily Herald, 1956–58; Kemsley Newspapers, 1958–60; Feature Writer and Advtsg Manager, TV International Magazine, 1960–62; Sales Dir, Westward Television, 1962–80; Dir of Marketing, 1980–85, Man. Dir, 1985–92, Television South West; Dir, ITN, 1987–92. Dir, Prince of Wales Trust, 1988–. FRSA 1986. *Publications:* The Man Who Could Hear Fishes Scream (short stories), 1978; The Gentle Art of Salesmanship, 1985; So You Want To Be a Sales Manager, 1987; Innocents in the Boardroom, 1991; The Venetian Chair, 1998. *Recreations:* tennis, riding, ski-ing, literature, travel. *Address:* Four Acres, Lake Road, Deepcut, Surrey GU16 6RB. *T:* (01252) 835527; Villa Providencia, 9 Flores de Calahonda, Marbella, Spain. *Club:* Garrick.

TURNER, Hugh Wason, CMG 1980; Director, National Gas Turbine Establishment, 1980–83, retired; *b* 2 April 1923; *s* of Thomas W. Turner and Elizabeth P. Turner (*née* Pooley); *m* 1950, Rosemary Borley; two *s* two *d. Educ:* Dollar Academy; Glasgow University. BSc Hons (Mech. Eng); CEng; FRAeS. Aeroplane and Armament Experimental Establishment, 1943–52; Chief Tech. Instructor, Empire Test Pilots School, 1953; A&AEE (Prin. Scientific Officer), 1954–64; Asst Director, RAF Aircraft, Min. of Technology, 1965–68; Superintendent, Trials Management, A&AEE, 1968–69; Division Leader, Systems Engineering, NATO MRCA Management Agency (NAMMA), Munich, 1969–74; Chief Superintendent, A&AEE, 1974–75; DGA1 (Dir Gen., Tornado), MoD (PE), 1976–80. *Recreations:* ski-ing, model building, photography, DIY. *Address:* Lavender Cottage, 1 Highcliff Road, Lyme Regis, Dorset DT7 3EW. *T:* (01297) 442310.

TURNER, James; QC 1998; *b* 23 Nov. 1952; *s* of late James Gordon Melville Turner, GC and of Peggy Pamela Hare (*née* Masters); *m* 1979, Sheila Green (separated); three *s* two *d. Educ:* Robertsbridge Co. Secondary Modern Sch.; Bexhill Grammar Sch.; Univ. of Hull (LLB Hons). Called to the Bar, Inner Temple, 1976. *Publication:* (contrib. editor) Archbold: Criminal Pleading, Evidence and Practice, annually, 1992–. *Recreations:* eating, reading, cinema. *Address:* 1 King's Bench Walk, Temple, EC4Y 7DB. *T:* (020) 7936 1500.

TURNER, Prof. James Johnson, FRS 1992; Research Professor in Chemistry, University of Nottingham, 1995–97, now Emeritus (Professor of Inorganic Chemistry, 1979–95); *b* 24 Dec. 1935; *s* of Harry Turner and Evelyn Turner (*née* Johnson); *m* 1961, Joanna Margaret Gargett; two *d. Educ:* Darwen Grammar Sch.; King's Coll., Cambridge (MA, PhD 1960; ScD 1985). CChem; FRSC. Research Fellow, King's Coll., Cambridge, 1960; Harkness Fellow, Univ. of Calif, Berkeley, 1961–63; University of Cambridge: Univ. Demonstrator, 1963–68; Univ. Lectr, 1968–71; College Lectr, 1963–71, Admissions Tutor, 1967–71, King's Coll.; Prof. and Head of Dept of Inorganic Chemistry, Univ. of Newcastle upon Tyne, 1972–78; Nottingham University: Hd of Chem. Dept, 1982–85, 1991–93; Pro-Vice-Chancellor, 1986–90. Visiting Professor: Univ. of Western Ontario, 1975; Texas, 1977; MIT, 1984; Chicago, 1986. Science and Engineering Research Council (formerly SRC): Mem., 1974–77, Chm., 1979–82, Chemistry Cttee; Mem., Science Bd, 1979–86; Mem. Council, 1982–86. Royal Society of Chemistry: Mem., 1974–77, Vice-Pres., 1982–84 and 1991–93, Pres., 1993–95, Dalton Council; Tilden Lectr, 1978; Liversidge Lectr, 1991; Mem. Council, Royal Soc., 1997–99. *Publications:* papers mainly in jls of Chem. Soc. and Amer. Chem. Soc. *Recreation:* walking. *Address:* School of Chemistry, University of Nottingham, University Park, Nottingham NG7 2RD. *T:* (0115) 951 3452.

TURNER, Janet; *see* Kear, J.

TURNER, Janet Mary, (Mrs Paul Griffin); QC 1996; barrister; *b* 16 Nov. 1957; *d* of Cecil Sidney Turner and Gwendoline Joyce Turner (*née* Loseby); *m* 1983, Paul Griffin; one *s* one *d. Educ:* Wycombe Abbey Sch.; Bristol Univ. (LLB 1st cl. Hons). Called to the Bar, Middle Temple, 1979 (Harmsworth Schol.); practising in field of commercial litigation, 1979–2000; legal consultant, 2000–. Member: London Common Law and Commercial Bar Assoc., 1986– (Sec., 1990–97); Commercial Bar Assoc., 1989–. *Recreations:* food and wine, collecting ephemera, restoring French home, gardening. *Address:* 3 Verulam Buildings, Gray's Inn, WC1R 5NT. *T:* (020) 7831 8441.

TURNER, John, CB 1999; Under Secretary, Department for Education and Employment (formerly Department of Employment), 1988–99; Member, Civil Service Appeal Board, since 2000; *b* 22 April 1946; *s* of late William Cecil Turner and Hilda Margaret Turner; *m* 1971, Susan Georgina Kennedy; two *s* one *d. Educ:* Ramsey Abbey Grammar Sch.; Northwood Hills Grammar Sch. Entered Civil Service, 1967; Principal, DoI, 1979; MSC, 1981–84; Asst Sec., Dept of Employment, 1985; Prin. Pvte Sec. to Rt Hon. Lord Young of Graffham and Rt Hon. Norman Fowler, 1986–87; Small Firms and Tourism Div., Dept of Employment, 1989; Dep. Chief Exec., Employment Service, 1989–94; Govt Regl Dir for Eastern Reg., 1994–96; Dir of Jobcentre Services, Employment Service, 1997–99. Trustee, Rathbone CI, 2001–. *Recreations:* music, reading, the outdoors. *Address:* 25 Bole Hill Close, Sheffield S6 5ED. *T:* (0114) 266 1067.

TURNER, Prof. John Derfel; Sarah Fielden Professor of Education, University of Manchester, 1985–94, now Professor Emeritus; *b* 27 Feb. 1928; *s* of Joseph Turner and Dorothy Winifred Turner; *m* 1951, Susan Broady Hovey; two *s. Educ:* Manchester Grammar Sch.; Univ. of Manchester (BA 1948; MA 1951; Teacher's Diploma 1951). Education Officer, RAF, 1948–50; teacher, Prince Henry's Grammar Sch., Evesham, 1951–53; Lectr in English, 1953–56, Sen. Lectr in Educn, 1956–61, Nigerian Coll. of Arts, Science and Technology; Lectr in Educn, Univ. of Exeter Inst. of Education, 1961–64; Prof. of Educn and Dir, Sch. of Educn, 1964–70, and Pro-Vice-Chancellor, 1966–70, Univ. of Botswana, Lesotho and Swaziland, Emeritus Prof., 1970; University of Manchester: Prof. of Educn and Dir of Sch. of Educn, 1970–76; Dean, Faculty of Educn, 1972–74 and 1986–91; Prof. of Adult and Higher Educn, 1976–85; Pro Vice-Chancellor, 1981–94. Rector, University Coll. of Botswana, Univ. of Botswana and Swaziland, 1981–82 and Vice-Chancellor, Univ. of Botswana, 1982–84. Chairman: Univs Council for Educn of Teachers, 1979–81 and 1988–91 (Vice-Chm., 1976–79); Council of Validating Univs, 1990–94; Presidential Commn on Higher Educn in Namibia, 1991–92, on Education, Culture and Training in Namibia, 1999; Member: UK Nat. Commn for UNESCO, 1975–81; IUC Working Parties on East and Central Africa and on Rural

Development, 1975–81; Educn Sub-Cttee, UGC, 1980–81; Educn Cttee and Further Educn Bd, CNAA, 1979–81; Chm., European Develt Fund/IUC Working Party on Academic Develt of Univ. of Juba, 1977–78; Chm. and Mem. Council, Social Studies Adv. Cttee, Selly Oak Colleges, 1975–81. Pres., Coll. of Teachers (formerly Coll. of Preceptors), 1994– (Hon. FCP 1985). Chm., Bd of Governors, Abbotsholme Sch., 1980–98. Chm. Editl Bd, Internat. Jl of Educn and Develt, 1978–81; Ed., Jl of Practice in Educn for Develt, 1994–99. Hon. Fellow, Bolton Inst. of Higher Educn, 1988. Hon. LLD Ohio Univ., 1982; Hon. DLitt Botswana, 1995. *Publications:* Introducing the Language Laboratory, 1963; (ed with A. P. Hunter) Educational Development in Predominantly Rural Countries, 1968; (ed with J. Rushton) The Teacher in a Changing Society, 1974; (ed with J. Rushton) Education and Deprivation, 1975; (ed with J. Rushton) Education and Professions, 1976; (ed) The Reform of Educational Systems to Meet Local and National Needs, 1994; (ed) The State and the School, 1996; school text books and contribs to edited works and to jls. *Recreations:* reading, music, theatre, walking; Methodist local preacher. *Address:* 13 Firswood Mount, Gatley, Cheadle, Cheshire SK8 4JY. *T:* (0161) 283 8429, *Fax:* (0161) 282 1022; *e-mail:* jdturner@cwcom.net. *Club:* Royal Commonwealth Society.

TURNER, Rt Hon. John Napier; PC (Can.) 1965; CC (Can.) 1995; QC (Can.); Leader of the Liberal Party of Canada, and Leader of the Opposition, 1984–90; Partner, Miller Thomson, Toronto, since 1990; *b* 7 June 1929; *s* of Leonard Turner and Phyllis Turner (*née* Gregory); *m* 1963, Geills McCrae Kilgour; three *s* one *d*. *Educ:* Normal Model Public Sch., Ottawa, Ont.; Ashbury Coll., 1939–42; St Patrick's Coll., 1942–45; Univ. of BC; Oxford Univ. BA (PolSci, Hons) BC, 1949; Rhodes Scholar, Oxford Univ., BA (Juris.) 1951; BCL 1952; MA 1957. Joined Stikeman, Elliott, Tamaki, Mercier & Turner, Montreal, Quebec; practised with them after being called to English Bar, 1953, Bar of Quebec, 1954 and Bar of Ont., 1968; QC (Ont and Que) 1968; with McMillan Binch, Toronto, 1976–84. MP for Montreal-St Lawrence-St Georges, 1962–68, Ottawa-Carleton, 1968–76, Vancouver Quadra, 1984–93; Parly Sec. to Minister of Northern Affairs and Nat. Resources, 1963–65; Minister without Portfolio, Dec. 1965–April 1967; Registrar-Gen. of Canada, April 1967–Jan. 1968; Minister of Consumer and Corporate Affairs, Dec. 1967–July 1968; Solicitor-Gen., April-July 1968; Minister of Justice and Attorney-Gen. of Canada, July 1968–Jan. 1972; Minister of Finance, Jan. 1972–Sept. 1975; resigned as MP, Feb. 1976; Prime Minister of Canada, June–Sept. 1984. Barbados Bar, 1969; Yukon and Northwest Territories, 1969; Trinidad Bar, 1969; British Columbia, 1969. Hon. LLD: Univ. of New Brunswick, 1968; York Univ., Toronto, 1969; Univ. of Toronto, 1996; Hon. DCL Mt Allison Univ., NB, 1980. *Publications:* Senate of Canada, 1961; Politics of Purpose, 1968. *Recreations:* tennis, canoeing, ski-ing; Canadian Track Field Champion 1948, Mem. English Track and Field Team. *Address:* (office) 20 Queen Street West, Suite 2500, Toronto, ON M5H 3S1, Canada; (home) 59 Oriole Road, Toronto, ON M4V 2E9, Canada.

TURNER, Prof. John Stewart, FAA 1979; FRS 1982; Foundation Professor of Geophysical Fluid Dynamics, Australian National University, 1975–95, now Emeritus; *b* Sydney, Aust., 11 Jan. 1930; *s* of Ivan Stewart Turner and Enid Florence (*née* Payne); *m* 1959, Sheila Lloyd Jones; two *s* one *d*. *Educ:* North Sydney Boys' High Sch.; Wesley Coll., Univ. of Sydney (BSc, MSc); Trinity Coll., Univ. of Cambridge (PhD). FInstP 1969. Research Officer, CSIRO cloud physics group, 1953–54 and 1960–61; 1851 Exhibition Overseas Schol., 1954–57; postdoctoral research post, Univ. of Manchester, 1958–59; Rossby Fellow, then Associate Scientist, Woods Hole Oceanographic Instn, 1962–66; Asst Director of Research, then Reader, Dept of Applied Mathematics and Theoretical Physics, Univ. of Cambridge, 1966–75; Fellow of Darwin Coll., Cambridge, 1974; Overseas Fellow, Churchill Coll., Cambridge, 1985; Fairchild Scholar, CIT, 1993. Matthew Flinders Lectr, Aust. Acad. of Science, 1990. Member, Australian Marine Sciences and Technologies Adv. Cttee (AMSTAC), 1979–84. Associate Editor, Journal of Fluid Mechanics, 1975–95; Mem. Editorial Adv. Board, Deep-Sea Research, 1974–84. *Publications:* Buoyancy Effects in Fluids, 1973, paperback 1979; papers in various scientific jls. *Recreations:* bushwalking, photography, home handyman. *Address:* (office) Research School of Earth Sciences, Australian National University, Canberra, ACT 0200, Australia. *T:* (2) 61254530; (home) 2/28 Black Street, Yarralumla, ACT 2600, Australia.

TURNER, His Honour John Turnage; a Circuit Judge, 1976–98; Resident Judge at Ipswich, 1984–98; *b* 12 Nov. 1929; *s* of Wilfrid Edward and May Martha Turner; *m* 1956, Gillian Mary Rayner; two *d*. *Educ:* Earls Colne Grammar School. Called to the Bar, Inner Temple, 1952. *Recreations:* music appreciation, travelling, watching cricket, philately. *Club:* MCC.

TURNER, (Jonathan) Adair; Vice Chairman, Merrill Lynch Europe, since 2000; *b* 5 Oct. 1955; *s* of Geoffrey Vincent Turner and Kathleen Margaret (*née* Broadhurst); *m* 1985, Orna Ni Chionna; two *d*. *Educ:* Gonville and Caius Coll., Cambridge (MA Hist. and Econs 1978). Chm., Cambridge Univ. Cons. Assoc., 1976; Pres., Cambridge Union Soc., 1977. BP, 1979; with Chase Manhattan Bank, 1979–82; McKinsey & Co., 1982–95: Principal, 1988; Dir, 1994–95; Dir Gen., CBI, 1995–99. Dir, United News and Media, 2000–; non-exec., Chm., Group.Trade.com, 2000. Mem., National Skills Taskforce, 1998–2000. Vis. Prof., 1999–, and Chair, Policy Cttee, Centre for Economic Performance, 1999–, LSE. Member: BOTB, 1995–99; NACETT, 1996; Bd, BITC, 1996–99. *Publication:* Just Capital: the liberal economy, 2001. *Recreations:* ski-ing, opera, children.

TURNER, Mark George; QC 1998; a Recorder, since 2000; *b* 27 Aug. 1959; *s* of Jeffrey Turner and Joyce Turner; *m* 1988, Caroline Sophia Bullock; three *d*. *Educ:* Sedbergh Sch.; Queen's Coll., Oxford (BA). Called to the Bar, Gray's Inn, 1981; in practice as barrister, Northern Circuit, 1982–; Asst Recorder, 1997–2000. Treas., Gray's Inn Circuit Cttee, 1996–. *Publications:* Occupational Rhinitis, 1998; Occupational Asthma, 1998. *Recreations:* quizzes, computers, classical music, history. *Address:* Deans Court Chambers, 24 St John Street, Manchester M3 4DF. *T:* (0161) 834 4097.

TURNER, Hon. Sir Michael (John); Hon. Mr Justice Turner, Kt 1985; a Judge of the High Court of Justice, Queen's Bench Division, since 1985; *b* 31 May 1931; *s* of late Theodore F. Turner, QC; *m* 1st, 1956, Hon. Susan Money-Coutts (marr. diss. 1965); one *s* one *d*; 2nd, 1965, Frances Deborah (marr. diss.), *d* of Rt Hon. Sir David Croom-Johnson, DSC, VRD, PC; two *s*; 3rd, 1995, Ingrid Maria Fear (*née* Ortner). *Educ:* Winchester; Magdalene Coll., Cambridge (BA). Called to Bar, Inner Temple, 1954 (Bencher 1981); a Recorder, 1972–85; QC 1973–85. Chm., E Mids Agricultural Tribunal, 1979–82. Mem., Judicial Studies Bd, 1988–93 (Co-Chm., Civil and Family Cttee, 1988–93). *Recreations:* horses, walking, listening to music. *Address:* Royal Courts of Justice, Strand, WC2A 2LL. *Club:* Boodle's.

See also C. G. Turner.

TURNER, Michael John, CBE 1999; FRAeS; Chief Operating Officer, BAE SYSTEMS, since 1999; *b* 5 Aug. 1948; *s* of Thomas Turner and Hilda Turner (*née* Pendlebury); *m* 1st, 1972, Rosalind Thomas (marr. diss.); two *s*; 2nd, 1985, Jean (*née* Crotty); two step *d*. *Educ:* Didsbury Tech. High Sch.; Manchester Poly. (BA). ACIS 1973; FRAeS 1991. With British Aerospace, subsequently BAE SYSTEMS, 1966–: undergrad. apprentice, Hawker Siddeley Aviation, Manchester, 1966; Contracts Manager (Mil.), 1978–80; Exec. Dir, Admin, 1981–84, Manchester Div.; Division Director and General Manager: Kingston and Dunsfold, 1984–86; Weybridge, Kingston and Dunsfold, 1986–87; Exec. Vice-Pres., Defence Mktg, 1988–92; Chm. and Man. Dir, Regl Aircraft, 1992–99; Main Bd Dir, 1994; Gp Man. Dir, 1997–98; Exec. Dir, 1998–99; Mem., Supervisory Bd, Airbus, 1998–. Pres., SBAC, 1996–97. *Recreations:* golf, cricket, Rugby, Manchester United. *Address:* BAE SYSTEMS, Stirling Square, 6 Carlton Gardens, SW1Y 5AD.

TURNER, Michael Ralph, FRSA; Group Managing Director, 1976–88, Chief Executive, 1982–88, Associated Book Publishers PLC; Chairman, Associated Book Publishers (UK) Ltd, 1977–90; *b* 26 Jan. 1929; *s* of Ralph Victor Turner and May Turner; *m* 1955, Ruth Baylis (*d* 1997); two *s* two *d*. *Educ:* Newport Sch., Essex; Trinity Coll., Cambridge (BA Hons). Served RAF, Transport Comd, 1947–49. Jun. Editor, J. M. Dent & Sons, 1949–50; Methuen & Co.: Jun. Editor, 1953; subseq. Publicity and Promotion Manager, and Dir; Associated Publishers Ltd: Marketing Dir, 1973; Asst Gp Man. Dir, 1975; Gp Man. Dir, 1976. Chm., Methuen Inc., New York, 1981–88; Pres., Carswell Co. Ltd, Toronto, 1982–84; Dir, ABP Investments (Aust.) Pty Ltd, 1976–88; Sen. Vice-Pres., Publishing Information Gp, Internat. Thomson Orgn Ltd, 1987–89. Chairman: Book Marketing Council, 1981–84; Book Trust, 1990–92; Member: Book Trade Working Party, 1973–74; Council, Publishers Assoc., 1981–90 (Vice-Pres., 1985–87 and 1989–90; Pres., 1987–89; Chm., Home Trade and Services Council, 1989–90); National Council and Exec., NBL, 1980–87; British Library Adv. Council, 1989–94; Centre for the Book Adv. Cttee, 1990–95; Publishing Bd, Design Council, 1991–94. Chm., Soc. of Bookmen, 1992–94. FRSA 1984. *Publications:* The Bluffer's Guide to the Theatre, 1967; Parlour Poetry, 1967; (with Antony Miall) The Parlour Song Book, 1972; (with Antony Miall) Just a Song at Twilight, 1975; (with Antony Miall) The Edwardian Song Book, 1982; (with Michael Geare) Gluttony, Pride and Lust and Other Sins from the World of Books, 1984; Do You Scratch Your Bottom in the Bath, 1998; (with Leslie Lonsdale-Cooper) translations of Hergé's Tintin books, 1958–95. *Recreations:* reading, music, theatre, maritime painting and models. *Address:* Paradise House, Boscastle, Cornwall PL35 0BL. *T:* (01840) 250250. *Club:* Garrick.

TURNER, Neil; MP (Lab) Wigan, since Sept. 1999; *b* 16 Sept. 1945; *m* 1971, Susan Beatrice; one *s*. Quantity surveyor, AMEC Construction, 1963–92. Member (Lab): Wigan CBC, 1972–74; Wigan MBC, 1975–2000 (Chairman: Highways and Works Cttee, 1980–97; Best Value Rev. Panel, 1998–2000). Chairman: Public Services Cttee, AMA, 1995–97; Quality Panel, LGA, 1997–99. *Address:* House of Commons, SW1A 0AA; Gerrard Winstanley House, Crawford Street, Wigan WN1 1NG. *T:* (01942) 242047. *Club:* St Thomas's Labour (Marsh Green, Wigan).

TURNER, Norman Henry, CBE 1977; Official Solicitor to the Supreme Court of Judicature, 1970–80; *b* 11 May 1916; *s* of late Henry James Turner, MA and Hilda Gertrude Turner; *m* 1st, 1939, Dora Ardella (*née* Cooper) (*d* 1990); three *s* two *d*; 2nd, 1991, Mona Florence Mackenzie. *Educ:* Nottingham High School. Articled, Nottingham, 1933; admitted Solicitor (Hons), 1938; joined Official Solicitor's Dept, 1948; Asst Official Solicitor, 1958. *Address:* 62 Walcote Drive, West Bridgford, Nottingham NG2 7GS. *T:* (0115) 923 3565.

TURNER, Peter; *see* Turner, T. P.

TURNER, Air Vice-Marshal Peter, CB 1979; MA; Bursar and Steward, Wolfson College, Cambridge, 1979–89; *b* 29 Dec. 1924; *s* of late George Allen and of Emma Turner; *m* 1949, Doreen Newbon; one *s*. *Educ:* Tapton House Sch., Chesterfield. Served War of 1939–45; 640 Sqdn, 1943–45; Nos 51, 242 and 246 Sqdns, 1945–48; psa 1961; NATO staff, 1963–67; jssc 1967; Chief Equipment and Secretarial Instructor, RAF Coll., Cranwell, 1967–68; Comd Accountant, HQ Air Support Comd, 1968–69; Station Comdr, RAF Uxbridge, 1969–71; RCDS, 1972; Dir of Personnel (Ground) (RAF), MoD, 1973–75; AOA, HQ RAF Support Command, 1975–79, and Head of RAF Admin. Branch, 1976–79. MA Cantab 1979. *Recreation:* retrospective contemplation. *Address:* Hedge End, Potton Road, Hilton, Huntingdon PE28 9NG. *Club:* Royal Air Force.

TURNER, Ven. (Peter) Robin, CB 1999; Chaplain, Dulwich College, since 1998; *b* 8 March 1942; *s* of late Ronald James Turner and Irene Bertha (*née* Stocker); *m* 1967, Elizabeth Mary Kennen; two *s*. *Educ:* Dulwich Coll.; King's Coll. London (AKC); St Luke's Coll., Exeter (PGCE); Open Univ. (BA); Westminster Coll., Oxford (MTh). Ordained deacon, 1966, priest, 1967; Asst Curate, Crediton, 1966–69; Chaplain, RAF: Locking, 1970; Waddington, 1971–72; Nicosia, 1972–74; Little Rissington, 1975–76; Coltishall, 1976–78; Chaplains' Sch., 1978–81; Religious Progs Advr, British Forces Broadcasting Service, Germany, 1981–84; Chaplain, RAF: Odiham, 1984–85; Gutersloh, 1985–88; RAF Coll., Cranwell, 1988–89; Assistant Chaplain-in-Chief: RAF, Germany, 1989–91; RAF Strike Command, 1991–93; QHC, 1991–98; Principal, RAF Chaplains' Sch., 1993–95; Chaplain-in-Chief and Archdeacon, RAF, 1995–98, now Archdeacon Emeritus. Freeman, City of London, 2001. FRSA 2000. *Recreations:* choral singing, classical music, reading history and biography, armchair cricket, wine and its enjoyment. *Address:* (office) Dulwich College, SE21 7LD. *T:* (020) 8299 9218; (home) 161 Westwood Park, Forest Hill, SE23 3QL. *T:* (020) 8699 7036; *e-mail:* turnerpr@dulwich.org.uk. *Club:* Royal Air Force.

TURNER, Peter William; District Secretary, Hereford and Worcester, Transport and General Workers' Union, 1969–91, retired; *m* Maureen Ann Turner (*née* Hill), Councillor, JP. *Educ:* Bordesley Green Infant and Junior Sch.; Saltley Grammar Sch. (until 1940); various Trade Union weekend courses. Appointed District Officer, TGWU, 1969; District Sec., CSEU, 1974–76; seconded as Industrial Advr to DoI, 1976–78. Member of various cttees including: Chemical Industry Area Productivity Cttee, 1969–76 (Vice-Chm., 1970–72, Chm., 1972–74); TUC Regional Educn Adv. Cttee, 1970–76; Birmingham Crime Prevention Panel, 1973–76; W Midlands Conciliation Cttee on Race Relations, 1974–76; DoE Working Party on Race Relations, 1974–76; Teaching Co. Management Cttee, 1977–82. Member: Birmingham Trades Council, 1956–76; Local Appeals Tribunal, 1969–74. *Recreations:* motoring, motor cycling, caravanning, do-it-yourself, reading, electronics, amateur radio (M0CHY). *Address:* 2 Oakleigh Road, Droitwich, Worcs WR9 0RP.

TURNER, Phil; Member, since 1971, and Chair of Leisure and Community Services, since 1998, Camden Borough Council; *b* 7 June 1939; *s* of William Morris Turner and Eileen Lascelles Turner; *m* 1963, Gillian Sharp (*d* 1988); one *s* two *d* (and one *s* decd). *Educ:* Beckenham and Penge Grammar School for Boys; University Coll. London (BScEcon). National Coal Board, later British Coal: Management Trainee, 1961–63; Hd of Information, Purchasing and Stores, 1963–65; O & M Officer, 1965–66; Hd of Admin, R & D Dept, 1966–68; Hd of Manpower Planning, 1968–73; Staff Manager, Opencast Exec., 1973–78; Hd of Conditions of Service, 1978–80; Dep. Dir of Staff Pay and

Conditions, 1980–86; Head of Employment Policy, 1986–89. Joined Labour Party, 1963; Chair, Hampstead Labour Party, 1968–70; Camden Borough Council, 1971–: Chair: Building Works and Services Cttee, 1978–80 and 1986–89; Staff and Management Services Cttee, 1990–93; Leisure Services Cttee, 1993–97, 1998–; Corporate Services Cttee, 1997–98; Leader of Council, 1982–86, Dep. Leader, 1992–93 and 1994–95. Member: Assoc. of London Authorities, 1983–86; Policy Cttee, AMA, 1984–86; Vice Chair, Assoc. of London Govt Arts and Leisure Cttee, 1995–2000; Chair: London Steering Gp, Euro '96, 1995–96; London Sport Bd, 1996–2000. Contested (Lab): Cities of London and Westminster South, Feb. and Oct. 1974; (Lab) Hampstead and Highgate, 1987. *Recreations:* family, travelling, book collecting, Woodcraft Folk camps. *Address:* 33 Minster Road, NW2 3SH. *T:* (020) 7794 8805.

TURNER, Richard Keith, CEng, FIHT, FILT; Chief Executive, Freight Transport Association, since 2001; *b* 2 Oct. 1994; *s* of Richard Louis Turner and Queenie Kate Turner; *m* 1968, Jenny Georgina Whitehead; two *s* one *d*. *Educ:* E Barnet Grammar Sch.; Leeds Univ. (BSc Civil Engrg 1965; MSc Traffic Engrg Planning 1972). CEng 1972. Grad. Engr, Herts CC, 1965–67; Sen. Engr, Leeds CC, 1967–73; Freight Transport Association: Highways and Traffic Advr, 1973–83; Dir of Planning, 1983–95; Dep. Dir Gen., 1995–2001. FIHT 1980; FILT 1993; MInstCE 1972. *Publications:* numerous papers on transport planning and freight. *Recreations:* big DIY, cycling, swimming. *Address:* Freight Transport Association, Hermes House, St John's Road, Tunbridge Wells, Kent TN4 9UZ. *T:* (01892) 552281.

TURNER, Robert Edward, (Ted); American broadcasting company executive; Vice-Chairman, Time Warner Inc., later AOL-Time Warner, 1996–2000; Chairman and President, Turner Broadcasting System Inc., 1970–96; *b* 19 Nov. 1938; *s* of Robert Edward Turner and Florence Turner (*née* Rooney); *m* 1st, Judy Nye (marr. diss.); one *s* one *d*; 2nd, 1965, Jane Shirley Smith (marr. diss. 1988); one *s* two *d*; 3rd, 1991, Jane Fonda (marr. diss. 2001). *Educ:* Brown Univ. Gen. Manager, Turner Advertising, 1960–63; Pres. and Chief Exec. Officer, various Turner cos, 1963–70. Pres., Atlanta Braves, 1976–; Chm. of Bd, Atlanta Hawks, 1977–. Won America's Cup in yacht Courageous, 1977. Pres's Award, 1979, 1989, Ace Special Recognition Award, 1980, Nat. Cable TV Assoc.; Special Award, Edinburgh Internat. TV Fest., 1982; Lifetime Achievement Award, NY Internat. Film and TV Fest., 1984; Tree of Life Award, Jewish Nat. Fund, 1985. *Publication:* (jtly) The Racing Edge, 1979. *Address:* c/o AOL-Time Warner, 75 Rockefeller Plaza, New York 10019–6908, USA.

TURNER, Prof. Robert Kerry, CBE 2000; Professor of Environmental Sciences, University of East Anglia, since 1991; *b* 10 Aug. 1948; *s* of Ben Rees Turner and Eunice Ann Turner; *m* 1971, Merryl Noreen Eborne; one *s*. *Educ:* UC, Swansea (BSc Econs 1970); UC, Cardiff (Cert Ed 1971); Leicester Univ. (MA (Dist) 1972). Lectr in Econs, Coventry Poly., 1974–76; Sen. Res. Fellow, Dept of Econs, Leicester Univ., 1976; Lectr, 1977–88, Sen. Lectr, 1989–91, Sch. of Envmtl Scis, UEA. Chair, Foresight Panel on Natural Resources and the Envmt, OST/DTI, 1995–99; Member: Bd, NRA, 1991–96; Regl Envmtl Protection Agency Cttee (Anglian Reg.), Envmt Agency, 1996–; Envmt Cttee, Broads Authy, 1996– (Vice Chair, 1996–2000; Chair, 2000–). Ed.-in-Chief, Envmtl and Resource Econs Jl, 1999–; Jt Ed., Regl Envmtl Change Jl, 1999–. FRSA 1991. Hon. FCIWEM. *Publications:* Household Waste: separate collection recycling, 1983; *jointly:* Economics of Planning, 1977; Environmental Planning and Management, 1983; Economics of Natural Resources and the Environment, 1990 (trans. Italian, 1992, Spanish, 1995); Elementary Environmental Economics, 1994; Blueprint III, 1993; *edited:* Sustainable Environmental Management: principles and practice, 1988, 2nd edn, 1993; *edited jointly:* Bibliography of Environmental Economics, vols 1 and 2, 1976; Progress in Resource Management and Environmental Planning, vol. 2, 1980, vol. 3, 1981, vol. 4, 1983; Wetlands: market and intervention failure, 1991; Economic Incentives and Environmental Policy, 1994; Ecosystems and Nature, 1999; Perspectives on Integrated Coastal Zone Management, 1999; Economics of Coastal and Water Resources, 2000; Managing a Sea: the ecological economics of the Baltic Sea, 2000; over 150 contribs to books, articles in jls and reports. *Recreations:* outdoor environment, tennis. *Address:* School of Environmental Sciences, University of East Anglia, Norwich NR4 7TJ. *T:* (01603) 593176.

TURNER, Robert Lockley; Senior Master of the Supreme Court, Queen's Bench Division, and Queen's Remembrancer, since 1996; *b* 2 Sept. 1935; *s* of James Lockley Turner and Maud Beatrice Turner; *m* 1963, Jennifer Mary Leather; one *s* one *d*. *Educ:* Clifton Coll.; St Catharine's Coll., Cambridge (BA 1957, MA 1973). Called to the Bar, Gray's Inn, 1958, Bencher, 2000. Commnd Gloucestershire Regt (28th/61st), 1959 (2nd Lieut); transf. to Army Legal Services, 1960 (Captain); Major 1962; retd from Army, 1966 (GSM with clasp South Arabia, 1966). Practised at Common Law Bar in London and on Midland and Oxford Circuit, 1967–84; a Recorder of the Crown Court, 1981–84; Master of Supreme Court, QBD, 1984–96. Prescribed Officer for Election Petitions, 1996–. Advisor to Law Reform Commn, Malta, 1993–99. Assessor, Access to Justice Inquiry, 1994–96. Mem., Notarial Qualifications Bd, 1999–. Vis. Fellow, Inst. of Internat. Maritime Law, Malta, 1998–99. Hon. FICM 1997. Hon. Steward, Westminster Abbey, 1985–; Churchwarden, St Matthew's, Midgham, 1990–92. Freeman, City of London, 1997; Liveryman, Scriveners' Co., 1999–. Chief Advisory Ed., Atkin's Court Forms, 1997–. *Publications:* (ed jtly) Supreme Court Practice, 1988–99; The Office of the Queen's Bench Master, 1990; (ed jtly) Chitty and Jacob, Queen's Bench Forms, 1992; (ed jtly) High Court Litigation Manual, 1992; Annual Practice, 1995; Civil Procedure, 1999. *Recreations:* watercolour painting, gothic churches. *Address:* Royal Courts of Justice, WC2A 2LL. *Clubs:* Army and Navy; Royal Fowey Yacht (Fowey).

TURNER, Ven. Robin; *see* Turner, Ven. P. R.

TURNER, Stephen Gordon; General Secretary, British Association of Journalists, since 1992; *b* 27 July 1935; *s* of John Turner and Lillian Turner (*née* Wiseman); *m* 1st, 1955, Jean Florence Watts (marr. diss. 1978); two *s* one *d*; 2nd, 1979, Deborah Diana Thomas; one *d*. *Educ:* Triptons Secondary Modern Sch., Dagenham; Royal Liberty Grammar Sch., Romford. Royal Signals radio mechanic, 1953–55. Reporter: Romford Times, 1955–56; Ilford Recorder, 1956; Bristol Evening World, 1957; freelance journalist, 1958–68; News sub-editor: Ipswich Evening Star, 1969; Daily Mail, 1969–71; Features sub-editor, 1971–73, Public Opinion Editor, 1973–90, Daily Mirror; Gen. Sec., NUJ, 1990–92. Independent Councillor, Colchester BC, 1967–68. Mem., NUJ, 1955–92; Father of the Chapel, Daily Mirror, 1976–78, 1986–90. *Address:* 2 Beach Street, Deal, Kent CT4 7AH.

TURNER, Ted; *see* Turner, R. E.

TURNER, (Thomas) Peter; Evaluation Consultant, since 1985; *b* 8 May 1928; *s* of Thomas Turner and Laura Crawley; *m* 1952, Jean Rosalie Weston; one *s* one *d*. *Educ:* Ilford County High Sch.; London University. BSc (1st Class Hons), Maths and Physics. GEC, North Wembley, 1947–50; Armament Design Establishment, 1950–54; Air Ministry (Science 3), 1954–58 and 1962–63; Chief Research Officer, RAF Maintenance Command, 1958–62; Police Research and Development Branch, Home Office, 1963–68; Civil Service Dept (OR), 1968–73; Head of Treasury/CSD Joint Operational Research Unit, 1973–76; Head of Operational Res., CSD, 1977–81, HM Treasury, 1981–84. *Address:* 8 Waring Drive, Green St Green, Orpington, Kent BR6 6DW. *T:* (01689) 851189.

TURNER, Wilfred, CMG 1977; CVO 1979; HM Diplomatic Service, retired; Director, Transportation Systems and Market Research Ltd (Transmark), 1987–90; *b* 10 Oct. 1921; *s* of late Allen Turner and Eliza (*née* Leach); *m* 1947, June Gladys Tite; two *s* one *d*. *Educ:* Heywood Grammar Sch., Lancs; London Univ. BSc 1942. Min. of Labour, 1938–42. Served War, REME, 1942–47. Min. of Labour, 1947–55; Brit. High Commn, New Delhi (Asst Lab. Adviser), 1955–59; Senior Wages Inspector, Min. of Labour, 1959–60; Min. of Health (Sec., Cttee on Safety of Drugs, 1963–66), 1960–66. Joined HM Diplomatic Service, 1966; Commonwealth Office, 1966; First Sec.: Kaduna, Nigeria, 1966–69; Kuala Lumpur, 1969–73; Dep. High Comr, and Commercial/Economic Counsellor, Accra, 1973–77; High Comr to Botswana, 1977–81. Dir and Chief Exec., Southern Africa Assoc., 1983–88. Member: Cttee, Zambia Soc., 1983–91; Central Council, Royal Commonwealth Soc., 1987–94; RIIA, 1987–; Royal African Soc., 1987–. *Recreation:* hill walking. *Address:* 44 Tower Road, Twickenham TW1 4PE. *T:* (020) 8892 1593.

TURNER, Dr William; Regional Medical Officer, Yorkshire Regional Health Authority, 1976–86, retired; *b* 23 Feb. 1927; *s* of Clarence and Mabel Turner; *m* 1950, Patricia Bramham Wilkinson; one *s* two *d*. *Educ:* Prince Henry's Grammar Sch., Otley, Yorks; Leeds Univ. MB, ChB; DPH, FFCM; LLB. House Officer, Leeds Gen. Infirmary, 1950–51; RAMC, 1951–53; Gen. Practitioner, 1953–55; Public Health Trng, 1955–60; Medical Officer of Health: Hyde, 1960–63; Huddersfield, 1963–67; Bradford, 1967–74; Area MO, Bradford, 1974–76. Member: Standing Med. Adv. Cttee, 1978–82; NHS Steering Gp on Health Services Inf., 1979–84. *Publications:* contrib. BMJ, Medical Officer. *Address:* Bentcliffe, 1 Premiere Park, Ilkley, West Yorks LS29 9RQ. *T:* (01943) 600114.

TURNER LAING, Sophie Henrietta, (Mrs C. Comninos); Controller, Programme Acquisition, BBC, since 1998; *b* 7 Sept. 1960; *d* of Graham Turner Laing and Gilly Laing (now Drummond), DL; *m* 1987, Carlo Comninos; one *s* one *d*. *Educ:* Oakdene Sch., Bucks. Variety Club of GB, 1979–80; KM Campbell Pty Ltd, Australia, 1980–82; Sales Exec., 1982–85, Sales Dir, 1986–89, Henson Internat. TV; Jt Founder and Dep. Man. Dir, Hit Entertainment, 1989–95; Vice Pres., Broadcasting, Flextech TV, 1995–98; Acting Dir, Marketing and Communications, BBC, 2001. Member: BAFTA, 2000; Variety Club of GB, 2001. *Recreations:* film, theatre, ski-ing. *Address:* 74 Denbigh Street, SW1V 2EX. *T:* (020) 7976 6844.

TURNER-SAMUELS, David Jessel; QC 1972; barrister; *b* 5 April 1918; *s* of late Moss Turner-Samuels, QC, MP, and Gladys Deborah Turner-Samuels (*née* Belcher); *m* 1939, Norma Turner-Samuels (*née* Verstone) (marr. diss. 1975); one *s* one *d*; *m* 1976, Norma Florence Negus, *qv*. *Educ:* Westminster Sch. Called to Bar, Middle Temple, 1939 (Bencher 1980); admitted to Trinidad Bar, 1976, Antigua Bar, 1997, St Lucia Bar, 1998. Served War of 1939–45, in Army, 1939–46. *Publication:* (jointly) Industrial Negotiation and Arbitration, 1951. *Recreation:* getting away from it all. *Address:* 4E Oak Lodge, Lythe Hill Park, Haslemere, Surrey GU27 3TF. *T:* (01428) 651970; New Court, Temple, EC4Y 9BE. *T:* (020) 7353 7613.

TURNER-SAMUELS, Norma Florence, (Mrs D. J. Turner-Samuels); *see* Negus, N. F.

TURNER-WARWICK, Prof. Dame Margaret (Elizabeth Harvey), DBE 1991; MA, DM, PhD; FRCP; Chairman, Royal Devon and Exeter Health Care NHS Trust, 1992–95; President, Royal College of Physicians, 1989–92; Consultant Physician, Brompton Hospital, since 1965 (Professor of Medicine (Thoracic Medicine), 1972–87, Dean, 1984–87, Cardiothoracic Institute, now Emeritus Professor); *b* 19 Nov. 1924; *d* of William Harvey Moore, QC, and Maud Baden-Powell; *m* 1950, Richard Trevor Turner-Warwick, *qv*; two *d*. *Educ:* Maynard Sch., Exeter; St Paul's Girls' Sch.; Lady Margaret Hall, Oxford (Open Schol. 1943; Hon. Fellow, 1990). DM Oxon, 1956; PhD London, 1961; FRCP 1969; FFOM 1983; FRACP 1983; FRCPE 1990; FFPHM 1990; FRCPGlas 1991; FRCGP 1991; FRCPI 1992. University Coll. Hosp., 1947–50: Tuke silver medal, Filliter exhibn in Pathology, Magrath Schol. in Medicine, Atchison Schol.; Postgrad. trng at UCH and Brompton Hosp., 1950–61; Cons. Physician: (Gen. Med.), Elizabeth Garrett Anderson Hosp., 1961–67; Brompton and London Chest Hosps, 1967–72. Sen. Lectr, Inst. of Diseases of the Chest, 1961–72. Lectures: Marc Daniels, 1974, Phillip Ellman, 1980, Tudor Edwards, 1985, Harveian, 1994, RCP; Lettsomian, Med. Soc. of London, 1982. Pres., British Thoracic Soc., 1982–85; Chairman: Central Academic Council, BPMF, 1982–85; Asthma Res. Council (Chm., Med. Res. Cttee, 1982–87); Conf. of Colleges and their Faculties in UK, 1990–92; UKCCCR, 1991–97; Member: MRC Systems Bd (DHSS nomination), 1982–85; Council, British Lung Foundn, 1984–90; Gen. Council, King's Fund, 1991; Council, BHF, 1994–; Mem. Council and Vice-Pres., ASH, 1990–. University of London: Mem. Senate, 1983–87; Mem., Academic Council, 1983–87; Mem., Scholarships Cttee, 1984–87; Mem., Cttee of Extramural Studies, 1984–87. Member: Nuffield Bioethics Council, 1993–; Round Table on Sustainable Develt, 1995–98. Fellow, UCL, 1991; FIC 1996. Founder FMedSci 1998. Hon. Fellow: Girton Coll., Cambridge, 1993; Green Coll., Oxford, 1993; Imperial Coll., London, 1996. Hon. FACP 1988; Hon. FRCP&S (Canada) 1990; Hon. FRCAnaes 1991; Hon. FCMSA 1991; Hon FRCPath 1992; Hon. FRCS 1993; Hon. FRCR 1994. Hon. Bencher, Middle Temple, 1990. Hon. Member: Assoc. of Physicians of GB and Ireland, 1991; S German and Australasian Thoracic Socs; Member; Alpha Omega Alpha, USA, 1987; Acad. of Malaysia, 1991. Hon. DSc: New York, 1985; Exeter, 1990; London, 1990; Hull, 1991; Sussex, 1992; Oxford, 1992; Cambridge, 1993; Leicester, 1998. Osler Meml Medal, Univ. of Oxford, 1995. *Publications:* Immunology of the Lung, 1978; (jtly) Occupational Lung Diseases: research approaches and methods, 1981; chapters in various textbooks on immunology and thoracic medicine, particularly fibrosing lung disorders and asthma; contrib. original articles: Lancet, BMJ, Quarterly Jl Med., Thorax, Tubercle, Jl Clin. Experimental Immunology, etc. *Recreations:* her family and their hobbies, gardening, country life, watercolour painting, violin playing. *Address:* Pynes House, Thorverton, Exeter EX5 5LT.

TURNER-WARWICK, Richard Trevor, CBE 1991; MA, MSc, DM Oxon, MCh; Hon. DSc; FRCP, FRCS, FRCOG, Hon. FACS; Hon. FRACS; specialist in reconstruction and functional restoration of the urinary tract; Emeritus Surgeon and Urologist to the Middlesex Hospital (Senior Surgeon, 1969–90); Hon. Senior Lecturer, London University Institute of Urology, since 1962; Hon. Consultant Urologist, Royal Prince Alfred Hospital, Sydney, since 1980; Robert Luff Foundation Fellow in Reconstructive Surgery, since 1990; *b* 21 Feb. 1925; *s* of W. Turner Warwick, FRCS; *m* 1950, Margaret Elizabeth Harvey Moore (*see* Dame Margaret Turner-Warwick); two *d*. *Educ:* Bedales School; Oriel Coll., Oxford; Middlesex Hosp. Medical School. Pres. OUBC, 1946; Mem. Univ. Boat Race Crew, Isis Head of River crew and Univ. Fours, 1946; Winner OU Silver Sculls, 1946; BSc thesis in neuroanatomy, 1946. Sen. Broderip Schol., Lyell Gold Medallist and Freeman Schol., Middx Hosp., 1949; surgical trng at

Middx Hosp. and St Paul's Hosp., London, and Columbia Presbyterian Med. Centre, NY, 1959. Hunterian Prof. of RCS, 1957, 1976; Comyns Berkeley Travelling Fellowship to USA, 1959. British Assoc. of Urological Surgeons: Mem. Council, 1975–78 and 1982–92; Pres., 1988–90; Fellow, 1961; St Peter's Medal, 1978; Member: Council, Royal Coll. of Surgeons, 1980–92; RCOG, 1990–92; Internat. Soc. of Urology, 1966–; European Soc. of Urology; Soc. of Pelvic Surgeons, 1963; Founder Mem., 1969, Pres., 1985, Internat. Continence Soc.; Corresp. Member: Amer. Assoc. of Genito Urinary Surgeons, 1972 (Harry Spence Medal, 1998); American and Australasian Urological Assocs. Fellow UCL, 1992. Fellow: Assoc. of Surgeons of GB and Ireland, 1960; Australasian Soc. Urology, 1989; Hon. FRACS 1981; Hon. FACS 1997. Hon. DSc New York, 1985. Moynihan Prize of Assoc. of Surgeons, 1957; Victor Bonney Prize, RCOG, 1987; Valentine Medal, NY Acad. of Medicine, 1992. *Publications:* various articles in scientific jls, contributing to surgery, to develt of operative procedures for the reconstruction and restoration of function of the urinary tract, and to design of surgical instruments. *Recreations:* water, family, fishing, gardening. *Address:* Pynes House, 9 Silver Street, Thorverton, Exeter EX5 5LT. *T:* (01392) 861173, *Fax:* (01392) 860940. *Clubs:* Vincent's (Oxford); The Houghton (Stockbridge); Leander (Henley); Ottery St Mary Fly Fishers.

TURNEY, Alan Harry, CB 1991; Assistant Under Secretary of State, Fire and Emergency Planning Department, Home Office, 1986–92; *b* 20 Aug. 1932; *s* of late Harry Landry Turney and Alice Theresa Turney (*née* Bailey); *m* 1957, Ann Mary Dollimore. *Educ:* St Albans Grammar Sch.; London School of Economics (BScEcon). Asst Principal, Home Office, 1961; Asst Private Sec. to Home Sec., 1962–65; Principal, 1965; Asst Sec., Broadcasting Dept, 1976; Rayner Review of Forensic Science Service, 1981; Criminal Dept, 1981–82; Prison Dept, 1982–86. *Recreations:* Rugby Union football, touring provincial France, enjoying the garden. *Address:* Brookfield Cottage, Bury End, Nuthampstead, Royston, Herts SG8 8NG. *T:* (01763) 848935.

TURNOUR, family name of **Earl Winterton**.

TURNQUEST, Sir Orville (Alton), GCMG 1995; QC (Bahamas) 1992; Governor-General of the Bahamas, 1995–2001; *b* 19 July 1929; *y s* of late Robert Turnquest and Gwendolyn Turnquest; *m* 1955, Edith Louise Thompson; one *s* two *d*. *Educ:* Govt High Sch.; Univ. of London (LLB). Articled 1947–53; called to Bahamas Bar, 1953; called to the Bar, Lincoln's Inn, 1960; Counsel and Attorney of Supreme Ct; Notary Public; private practice, 1953–92; stipendiary and circuit magistrate and coroner, 1959; law tutor and Mem., Exam. Bd, Bahamas Bar, 1965–92. Chancellor, Dio. of Nassau and Bahamas. Sec.-Gen., Progressive Liberal Party, 1960–62; MP South Central, Nassau, 1962–67, Montagu, 1982–94; Opposition Leader in Senate, 1972–79; Dep. Leader, Free Nat. Movement, 1987–94; Attorney-Gen., 1992–94; Minister of Justice, 1992–93, of Foreign Affairs, 1992–94; Dep. Prime Minister, 1993–94. Pres., Bahamas Bar Assoc.; Chm., Bahamas Bar Council, 1970–72. Pres., CPA, 1992–93. Member: Anglican Central Educnl Authy; Nat. Cttee of United World Colls; Bd of Govs, St John's Coll. and St Anne's High Sch. Patron, Bahamas Games. *Recreations:* tennis, swimming, music, reading. *Address:* c/o Government House, PO Box N-8301, Nassau, Bahamas.

TUROK, Prof. Neil Geoffrey, PhD; Professor of Mathematical Physics, University of Cambridge, since 1996; *b* 16 Nov. 1958; *s* of Benjamin and Mary Turok; *m* 1992, Corinne Francesca Squire; one *d*. *Educ:* Churchill Coll., Cambridge (BA); Imperial Coll., London (PhD). Postdoctoral Fellow, Univ. of California, Santa Barbara, 1983–85; Advanced Res. Fellow, 1985–87, Reader in Theoretical Physics, 1991–92, Imperial Coll.; Associate Scientist, Fermilab, Ill, 1987–88; Asst Prof., 1988–91, Associate Prof., 1992–95, Prof., 1995, Princeton Univ. David and Lucile Packard Fellow, 1992–97. James Clerk Maxwell Prize, Inst. of Physics, 1992. *Publications:* over 100 articles in Nuclear Physics B, Phys. Review, Phys. Review Letters, New Scientist, Scientific American. *Recreations:* jazz, nature, playing with Ruby. *Address:* Department of Applied Mathematics and Theoretical Physics, Silver Street, Cambridge CB3 9EW. *T:* (01223) 337872, *Fax:* (01223) 337918.

TURPIN, James Alexander, CMG 1966; HM Diplomatic Service, retired; *b* 7 Jan. 1917; *s* of late Samuel Alexander Turpin; *m* 1942, Kathleen Iris Eadie; one *d*. *Educ:* King's Hosp., Dublin; Trinity Coll., Dublin (schol., 1st cl. Hons, Gold Medal, MA). Asst Lectr, Trinity College, Dublin, 1940. Served Army (Royal Irish Fusiliers), 1942–46. Joined Foreign Service, 1947; Mem., UK Delegn to OEEC, Paris, 1948; 1st Sec., 1949; FO, 1950; Warsaw, 1953; Tokyo, 1955; Counsellor, 1960; seconded to BoT, 1960–63; Counsellor (Commercial), The Hague, 1963–67; Minister (Economic and Commercial), New Delhi, 1967–70; Asst Under-Sec. of State, FCO, 1971–72; Ambassador to the Philippines, 1972–76; retired, 1977. Chm., British-Philippine Soc., 1986–88. *Publications:* New Society's Challenge in the Philippines, 1980; The Philippines: problems of the ageing New Society, 1984. *Recreations:* tennis, music, swimming, wine, cookery. *Address:* 12 Grimwood Road, Twickenham, Middlesex TW1 1BX.

TURPIN, Kenneth Charlton; Provost of Oriel College, Oxford, 1957–80, and Hon. Fellow since 1980; Vice-Chancellor, Oxford University, 1966–69 (Pro-Vice Chancellor, 1964–66, 1969–79); Member, Hebdomadal Council, 1959–77; *b* 13 Jan. 1915; *e s* of late Henry John Turpin, Ludlow. *Educ:* Manchester Grammar Sch.; Oriel College, Oxford. Treasury, 1940–43; Asst Private Sec. to C. R. Attlee, Lord President and Dep. Prime Minister, 1943–45; 2nd Asst Registrar, University Registry, Oxford, 1945–47; Sec. of Faculties, Univ. of Oxford, 1947–57; professorial fellow, Oriel Coll., 1948; Hon. Fellow Trinity Coll., Dublin, 1968. A Church Commissioner, 1984–89. *Recreations:* gardening, walking. *Address:* 13 Apsley Road, Oxford OX2 7QX. *Clubs:* Athenæum; Vincent's (Oxford).

TURTON, Eugenie Christine, (Genie), CB 1996; Director General, Urban and Rural Policy Housing and Construction, Department for Transport, Local Government and the Regions (formerly Department of the Environment, Transport and the Regions), since 2000; *b* 19 Feb. 1946; *d* of Arthur Turton and Georgina (*née* Fairhurst); *m* 1st, 1968, Richard Gordon (marr. diss. 1972); 2nd, 1974, Gerry Flanagan (marr. diss. 1978). *Educ:* Nottingham Girls' High Sch. (GPDST); Girton Coll., Cambridge (schol.; MA). Research student (G. C. Winter Warr Studentship), Univ. of Cambridge, 1967–70; joined CS as Asst Principal, MoT (later DoE), 1970; Private Sec. to Parly Under Sec. of State, 1973–74; Principal, 1974–80; Prin. Private Sec. to successive Secretaries of State for Transport, 1978–80; Asst Sec., 1980–86; seconded to Midland Bank International, 1981–82, and to Cabinet Office/MPO (Machinery of Govt Div.), 1982–85; Under Sec., DoE, 1986–91; Director: Heritage and Royal Estate (formerly Ancient Monuments and Historic Bldgs), 1987–90; Inner Cities, 1990–91; Dep. Sec., DoE, 1991–94; Dir, Citizen's Charter Unit, Cabinet Office, 1994–97; Dir, Govt Office for London, 1997–2000. Non-exec. Dir, Woolwich Building Soc., 1987–91. Trustee, Pilgrim Trust, 1991–. Mem. Council, City Univ., 2000–. *Recreations:* books, music, shopping, gardening. *Address:* Department for Transport, Local Government and the Regions, Eland House, Bressenden Place, SW1E 5DU.

TURTON, Victor Ernest; Managing Director: V. E. Turton (Tools) Ltd; V. E. Turton (Wholesalers) Ltd; *b* 29 June 1924; *s* of H. E. Turton; *m* 1951, Jean Edith Murray; two *d*. *Educ:* Paget Secondary Modern Sch.; Aston Techn. Coll.; Birmingham Central Techn. Coll. Birmingham City Councillor (Lab) Duddeston Ward, 1945–63; Saltley Ward, 1970–71; Alderman, Birmingham, 1963–70 and 1971–74, Hon. Alderman, 1974–; Lord Mayor of Birmingham, 1971–72, Dep. Lord Mayor, 1972–73; West Midlands County Council: Mem., 1974–77, 1981–86; Vice-Chm., 1983–84, Chm., 1984–85; Chm., Airport Cttee, 1974–77; Member: Airport and Fire Bde Cttee; Transportation Cttee. Chm., Birmingham Airport, 1959–66; Dir, Birmingham Exec. Airways, 1983–89. Chairman: Smallholdings and Agric. Cttee, 1954–58; West Midlands Regional Adv. Cttee for Civil Aviation, 1966–72; Jt Airports Cttee of Local Authorities, 1975–77. Vice Pres., Heart of England Tourist Bd, 1977– (Chm., 1975–77). Chm., Hall Green Div. Labour Party, 1957–59. Former Governor, Coll. of Technology (now Univ. of Aston in Birmingham). *Recreations:* football, cricket, table tennis, philately. *Address:* 121 Maypole Lane, King's Heath, Birmingham B14 4PF. *Club:* Rotary (Birmingham).

TURVEY, Garry, CBE 1991; Director-General, Freight Transport Association, 1984–93; *b* 11 Oct. 1934; *s* of Henry Oxley Turvey and Annie Maud Braley; *m* 1960, Hilary Margaret Saines; three *s*. *Educ:* Morecambe Grammar School. FCIS; FCILT. Metropolitan Vickers Ltd, Manchester, 1956–58; AEI Manchester Ltd, 1958–60; Asst Sec., 1960–67, Sec., 1967–69, Traders' Road Transport Assoc.; Sec., 1969–84 and Dep. Dir-Gen., 1974–84, Freight Transport Assoc. Freeman, City of London, 1994; Liveryman, Carmen's Co., 1994. *Recreations:* cricket, fly-fishing, gardening. *Address:* 139 Imberhorne Lane, East Grinstead, West Sussex RH19 1RP. *T:* (01342) 325829. *Clubs:* Royal Automobile, MCC.

TURVEY, Ralph, DSc (Econ); economist; Visiting Professor of Economics, London School of Economics, 1973–75 and since 1990; Associate Director of Regulation Initiative, London Business School, since 1990; *b* 1 May 1927; *s* of John and Margaret Turvey; *m* 1957, Sheila Bucher (*d* 1987); one *s* one *d*. *Educ:* Sidcot School; London School of Economics; Uppsala University. Lectr, then Reader, in Economics, at London School of Economics, 1948–64, with interruptions. Vis. Lectr, Johns Hopkins Univ., 1953; Ford Foundation Vis. Res. Prof., Univ. of Chicago, 1958–59; Economic Section, HM Treasury, 1960–62; Center of Economic Research, Athens, 1963. Chief Economist, The Electricity Council, 1964–67. Member, NBPI, 1967–71, Jt Dep. Chm. 1968–71; Economic Advr, Scientific Control Systems Ltd, 1971–75; Economic Advr, then Chief Statistician, ILO, 1975–89; Dir, Dept of Labour Information and Statistics, ILO, until 1989; Res. Fellow, Statistics Canada, 1989–90. Member: Nat. Water Council, 1974–75; Inflation Accounting Cttee, 1974–75; NZ Adv. Cttee on price indices, 1991; RPI Adv. Cttee, 1992–94; Canadian and Swedish adv. cttees on consumer price indices, 1992–. Chm., Centre for the Study of Regulated Industries, 1993–. Governor, Kingston Poly., 1972–75. *Publications:* The Economics of Real Property, 1957; Interest Rates and Asset Prices, 1960; (joint author) Studies in Greek Taxation, 1964; Optimal Pricing and Investment in Electricity Supply, 1968; Economic Analysis and Public Enterprises, 1971; Demand and Supply, 1971; (joint author) Electricity Economics, 1977; Consumer Price Indices, 1989; (ed and joint author) Developments in International Labour Statistics, 1989; Consumer Price Indexes, 1999; papers on economic hist. of Victorian London and on electricity pricing. *Recreation:* walking. *Address:* 30 Sloane Gardens, SW1W 8DJ. *Club:* Reform.

TUSA, John; Managing Director, Barbican Centre, since 1995; *b* 2 March 1936; *s* of late John Tusa, OBE and Lydia Sklenarova; *m* 1960, Ann Hilary Dowson; two *s*. *Educ:* Trinity Coll., Cambridge (BA 1st Cl. Hons History). BBC general trainee, 1960; Producer, BBC External Services, 1962; freelance radio journalist, 1965; Presenter: BBC Radio 4 The World Tonight, 1968; BBC2 Newsnight, 1979–86; Man. Dir, World Service, BBC, 1986–92; Presenter, One O'Clock News, BBC TV, 1993–95. Chm., London News Radio, 1993–94. Pres., Wolfson Coll., Cambridge, 1993. Chairman: Adv. Cttee, Govt Art Collection, 1993–; BBC Marshall Plan of the Mind Trust, 1992–99; Member: Council, RIIA, 1984–90, 1991–95; Board, Public Radio Internat. (formerly American Public Radio), 1990–99; Adv. Cttee, London Internat. String Quartet Competition, 1991– (Vice-Chm. of Board, 1995–); Board, ENO, 1994–; Trustee: Nat. Portrait Gall., 1988–2000; Thomson Foundn, 1992–95; Wigmore Hall Trust, 1993–95 (Chm., 1999–); Design Mus. Trust, 1999–2000; BM, 2000–. Hon. FRIBA 2001; Hon. RAM 1999; Hon. GSMD 1999; Hon. Mem., ISM, 2001. Hon. LLD London, 1993; DUniv Heriot-Watt, 1993; Hon. DLitt City, 1997. TV Journalist of the Year, RTS 1983; Richard Dimbleby Award, BAFTA, 1984; BPG Award for outstanding contribn to radio, 1991; Presenter of the Year, RTS, 1995. Knight First Class, Order of the White Rose (Finland), 1998. *Publications:* Conversations with the World, 1990; A World in Your Ear, 1992; (with Ann Tusa): The Nuremberg Trial, 1983; The Berlin Blockade, 1988; Art Matters: reflecting on culture, 1999. *Recreations:* tennis, chamber music, listening. *Address:* Barbican Centre, Silk Street, EC2Y 8DS. *T:* (020) 7382 7001; 16 Canonbury Place, NI 2NN. *T:* (020) 7704 2451.

TUSHINGHAM, Rita; actress; *b* 14 March 1942; *d* of John Tushingham; *m* 1962, Terence William Bicknell (marr. diss. 1976); two *d*; *m* 1981, Ousama Rawi (marr. diss. 1996). *Educ:* La Sagesse Convent, Liverpool. Student, Liverpool Playhouse, 1958–60. BBC Personality of the Year, Variety Club of GB, 1988. *Stage appearances:* Royal Court Theatre: The Changeling, 1960; The Kitchen, 1961; A Midsummer Night's Dream, 1962; Twelfth Night, 1962; The Knack, 1962; other London theatres: The Giveaway, 1969; Lorna and Ted, 1970; Mistress of Novices, 1973; My Fat Friend, 1981; Children, Children, 1984. *Films:* A Taste of Honey, 1961 (Brit. Film Acad. and Variety Club awards for Most Promising Newcomer, 1961; NY Critics, Cannes Film Festival and Hollywood Foreign Press Assoc. awards); The Leather Boys, 1962; A Place to Go, 1963; Girl with Green Eyes, 1963 (Variety Club award); The Knack, 1964 (Silver Goddess award, Mexican Assoc. of Film Corresps); Dr Zhivago, 1965; The Trap, 1966; Smashing Time, 1967; Diamonds For Breakfast, 1967; The Guru, 1968; The Bed-Sitting Room, 1970; Straight on till Morning, 1972; Situation, 1972; Instant Coffee, 1973; Rachel's Man, 1974; The Human Factor, 1976; Pot Luck, 1977; State of Shock, 1977; Mysteries, 1978; Incredible Mrs Chadwick, 1979; The Spaghetti House Siege, 1982; Flying, 1984; A Judgement in Stone, 1986; Single Room, 1986; Resurrected, 1989; Dante and Beatrice in Liverpool, 1989; Hard Days' Hard Nights, 1990; Paper Marriage, 1991; Rapture of Deceit, 1991; Desert Lunch, 1992; An Awfully Big Adventure, 1994; The Boy from Mercury, 1995; Under The Skin, 1996; Swing, 1998; Out of Depth, 1998; Home Ground, 2000. *TV appearances include:* Red Riding Hood (play), 1973; No Strings (own series), 1974; Don't Let Them Kill Me on Wednesday, 1980; Confessions of Felix Krull, 1980; Seeing Red, 1983; Pippi Longstocking, 1984; The White Whale — The Life of Ernest Hemingway (film), 1987; cameo appearance in Bread, 1988; Sunday Pursuit; Gütt, Ein Journalist, 1991; Hamburg Poison, 1992; Family Secrets (film), 1995; I Was Eddie Mostyn, 1995; Shadow Play, 2001; Patty and Chips with Scraps (BBC radio play), 1997. *Recreations:* interior decorating, cooking, watercolour painting. *Address:* c/o Wim Hance, London Management, 2–4 Noel Street, W1V 3RB.

TUSTIN, Rt Rev. David; Hon. Assistant Bishop of Lincoln, since 2001; Bishop Suffragan of Grimsby, 1979–2000; *b* 12 Jan. 1935; *s* of John Trevelyan Tustin and Janet Reynolds;

m 1964, Mary Elizabeth (*née* Glover); one *s* one *d*. *Educ:* Solihull School; Magdalene Coll., Cambridge (MA Hons); Geneva Univ. (Cert. in Ecumenical Studies); Cuddesdon Coll., Oxford. Philip Usher Memorial Scholar (in Greece), 1957–58; deacon 1960, priest 1961; Curate of Stafford, 1960–63; Asst Gen. Sec., C of E Council on Foreign Relations and Curate of St Dunstan-in-the-West, Fleet St, 1963–67; Vicar of S Paul's, Wednesbury, 1967–71; Vicar of Tettenhall Regis, 1971–79; RD of Trysull, 1977–79. Canon and Prebendary of Lincoln Cathedral, 1979–2000. Co-Chm., Anglican/Lutheran Internat. Commn, 1986–98; Pres., Anglican/Lutheran Soc., 1986–99; Mem., Gen. Synod of C of E, 1990–2000 (Chm., Council for Christian Unity, 1993–98). DD Lambeth 1998. *Recreations:* music, family life, languages, travel. *Address:* The Ashes, Tunnel Road, Wrawby, Brigg, N Lincs DN20 8SF.

TUTI, Rt Rev. Dudley, KBE 1988 (OBE 1974); Paramount Chief of Santa Ysabel, since 1975; Chairman: Solomon Islands Credit Union, since 1982; Ysabel Timber Co. Ltd, since 1991; Chairman, Santa Ysabel Council of Chiefs, since 1984; *b* 1919; *s* of John Tariniu and Daisy Mele Pago; *m* 1957, Naomi Tate; one *s* seven *d* (and one *s* decd). *Educ:* St John's Coll., Auckland, NZ. Deacon, 1946; priest, 1954. Headmaster, Vureas Boys' Sch., 1954–56; District Priest and Rural Dean of Santa Ysabel, 1956–63; consecrated Bishop (by the Archbishop of NZ), 1963; Asst Bishop, dio. of Melanesia, 1963–75; Bishop and Archdeacon, Central Solomons, 1968–75; Vicar-General, dio. of Melanesia, 1971–75; Bishop of Santa Ysabel, 1975–82. Mem., Law Reform Commn, Solomon Is, 1995–98. Chm., Ysabel Community Trust, 1991–96. *Address:* PO Box 35, Jejevo, Buala, Santa Ysabel, Solomon Islands. *T:* 35135.

TUTIN, Mrs Winifred Anne, (Winifred Pennington), PhD; FRS 1979; Principal Scientific Officer, Freshwater Biological Association, 1967–81, retired; *b* 8 Oct. 1915; *d* of Albert R. Pennington and Margaret S. Pennington; *m* 1942, Thomas Gaskell Tutin, FRS (*d* 1987); one *s* three *d*. *Educ:* Barrow-in-Furness Grammar Sch.; Reading Univ. (BSc, PhD). Research posts with Freshwater Biological Assoc., 1940–45; Demonstrator and Special Lectr, Univ. of Leicester, 1947–67; Hon. Reader in Botany, Univ. of Leicester, 1971–79, Hon. Professor, 1980–. Foreign Member, Royal Danish Academy, 1974. *Publications:* (as Winifred Pennington): The History of British Vegetation, 1969, 2nd edn 1974; (with W. H. Pearsall) The Lake District, 1973; papers in New Phytologist, Jl of Ecology, Phil. Trans of Royal Society, and others. *Recreations:* gardening, plain cooking. *Address:* Priory Cottage, North Street, Kingsclere, Newbury, Berks RG20 5QY.

TUTT, Prof. Norman Sydney; Executive Director of Housing and Social Services, London Borough of Ealing, since 2001 (Director of Social Services, 1999–2001); *b* 8 June 1944; *s* of Sydney Robert Tutt and Stella May Tutt; *m* 1966, Diana Patricia Hewitt; two *s*. *Educ:* Chislehurst and Sidcup Grammar Sch.; Univ. of Keele (BA); Univ. of Leeds (MSc); Univ. of Nottingham (PhD). Clin. Psychologist, Nottingham, 1966–69; Resident Psychologist, St Gilbert's Approved Sch., 1969–73; Professional Advr, Northampton Social Services, 1973–74; Sen. Develt Officer, London Boroughs Children Reg. Planning Cttee, 1974–75; Principal Social Work Services Officer, DHSS, 1975–79; Prof. of Applied Social Studies, 1979–92 (on leave of absence, 1989–92), and Hon. Prof., 1992–95, Lancaster Univ.; Dir of Social Services, Leeds CC, 1989–93; Exec. Dir, Social Information Systems, 1993–98. Man., Gulbenkian Commn on Violence to Children, 1995–96. Vis. Prof., Faculty of Community Health Scis, Univ. of Wales Inst. at Cardiff (formerly Cardiff Inst.), 1994–2000. Mem. Council, ASA, 1996–. Mem. Bd, Hanover Housing Assoc., 1996–99. *Publications:* Care or Custody, 1975; (ed) Violence, 1975; (ed) Alternative Strategies for Coping with Crime, 1978; (ed) A Way of Life for the Handicapped, 1983; Children in Custody, 1987; (ed) Children and Homicide, 1996; contributor to other pubns. *Recreations:* work, wine, walks, cracking jokes. *Address:* Coote, Rowdell Road, Northolt, Middx UB5 6AJ; Le Grand Margantinet, 61330 Torchamp, France. *Clubs:* as with Groucho Marx he would not join a club which would have him as a member.

TUTT, Roger Clive, CMG 1994; MBE 1966; HM Diplomatic Service, retired; *b* 22 March 1939; *s* of Clive Pritchard Tutt and Ada (*née* Kyle); *m* 1966, Gwen Leeke; two *s* one *d*. *Educ:* Bristol GS; Ledbury GS; Bristol Univ. (BA Econ). Bristol Univ. expedn to India and S America, 1960-61; Asst Administrator, Turks and Caicos Is, 1963-66; entered HM Diplomatic Service, 1966: Second Secretary: Copenhagen, 1967-69; Lusaka, 1969-71; First Secretary: FCO, 1971-74; Regl Inf. Officer, Barbados, 1974-79; FCO, 1979-87; Counsellor: UKMIS NY, 1987-89; FCO, 1989-94. *Recreations:* conserving a small piece of rural Gloucestershire, travel. *Clubs:* Reform, Royal Commonwealth Society.

TUTTE, Prof. William Thomas, OC 2001; FRS 1987; FRSC 1958; Professor of Mathematics, University of Waterloo, Ontario, 1962–85, Professor Emeritus since 1985; *b* 14 May 1917; *s* of William John Tutte and Annie Tutte (*née* Newell); *m* 1949, Dorothea Geraldine Mitchell. *Educ:* Cambridge and County High Sch.; Cambridge Univ. (BA, MA, PhD). Fellow of Trinity Coll., Cambridge, 1942–49; Lectr to Associate Prof., Univ. of Toronto, 1948–62. *Publications:* Connectivity in Graphs, 1966; Introduction to the Theory of Matroids, 1971; Graph Theory, 1984; Graph Theory as I have known it, 1998; papers in mathematical jls. *Address:* Apt 804, 25 Westmount Road North, Waterloo, ON N2L 5G7, Canada.

TUTU, Most Rev. Desmond Mpilo; Archbishop of Cape Town and Metropolitan of Southern Africa, 1986–96, now Archbishop Emeritus; Chair, Truth and Reconciliation Commission, 1995–99; *b* Klerksdorp, Transvaal, 7 Oct. 1931; *s* of Zachariah and Aletta Tutu; *m* 1955, Leah Nomalizo Shenxane; one *s* three *d*. *Educ:* Johannesburg Bantu High Sch.; Bantu Normal Coll., Pretoria (Higher Teachers' Dip. 1953); Univ. of S Africa (BA 1954); St Peter's Theol Coll., Johannesburg (LTh 1960); King's Coll. London (BD 1965, MTh 1966; FKC 1978). Schoolmaster: Madibane High Sch., Johannesburg, 1954; Munsieville High Sch., Krugersdorp, 1955–57. Theological coll. student, 1958–60; deacon 1960, priest 1961, St Mary's Cathedral, Johannesburg. Curate: St Alban's Church, Benoni, 1960–61; St Philip's Church, Alberton, 1961–62; St Alban's, Golders Green, London, 1962–65; St Mary's, Bletchingley, Surrey, 1965–66; Lecturer: Federal Theol Seminary, Alice, CP, 1967–69; Univ. of Botswana, Lesotho and Swaziland, Roma, Lesotho, 1970–72; Associate Dir, Theol Education Fund (WCC) based in Bromley, Kent, and Hon. Curate, St Augustine's, Grove Park, 1972–75; Dean of Johannesburg, 1975–76; Bishop of Lesotho, 1976–78; Gen. Sec., South African Council of Churches, 1978–85; Rector, St Augustine's Parish, Soweto, 1981–85; Bishop of Johannesburg, 1985–86. Woodruff Vis. Prof., Emory Univ., 1998–2000. Chancellor, Univ. of Western Cape, Cape Town, 1988–. Pres., All Africa Conference of Churches, 1987–97. Trustee, Phelps Stoke Fund, New York. Holds over fifty hon. degrees from academic institutions in UK, Europe and USA. Athena Prize, Onassis Foundation, 1980; Nobel Peace Prize, 1984; Albert Schweitzer Humanitarian Award, Emmanuel Coll., Boston, 1988. Order of Meritorious Service, Gold (S Africa), 1996; Order of Southern Cross (Brazil), 1987; Order of Merit of Brasilia (Brazil), 1987; Grand Cross of Merit (Germany), 1996. *Publications:* Crying in the Wilderness, 1982; Hope and Suffering, 1983; The Words of Desmond Tutu, 1989; The Rainbow People of God, 1994; No Future Without Forgiveness, 1999; articles and reviews. *Recreations:* music, reading, jogging. *Address:* PO Box 3162, Cape Town 8000, S Africa.

TWEEDDALE, 13th Marquis of, *cr* 1694; **Edward Douglas John Hay;** Lord Hay of Yester, 1488; Earl of Tweeddale, 1646; Viscount Walden, Earl of Gifford, 1694; Baron Tweeddale (UK), 1881; Hereditary Chamberlain of Dunfermline; *b* 6 Aug. 1947; *s* of 12th Marquis of Tweeddale, GC, and of Sonia Mary, *d* of 1st Viscount Ingleby; *S* father, 1979. *Educ:* Milton Abbey, Blandford, Dorset; Trinity Coll., Oxford (BA Hons PPE). *Heir: yr* twin *b* Lord Charles David Montagu Hay; *b* 6 Aug. 1947.

TWEEDIE, Prof. Sir David (Philip), Kt 1994; Chairman, International Accounting Standards Board, since 2000; *b* 7 July 1944; *s* of Aidrian Ian Tweedie and Marie Patricia Tweedie (*née* Phillips); *m* 1970, Janice Christine Brown; two *s*. *Educ:* Grangemouth High Sch.; Edinburgh Univ. (BCom, PhD). CA 1972. Accountancy trng, Mann, Judd, Gordon (Glasgow), 1969–72; Edinburgh University: Lectr in Accounting, 1973–78; Associate Dean, Fac. of Social Scis, 1975–78; Technical Dir, Inst. of Chartered Accountants, Scotland, 1978–81; Nat. Res. Partner, KMG Thomson McLintock, 1982–87; Nat. Tech. Partner, KPMG Peat Marwick McLintock, 1987–90; Chm., Accounting Standards Bd, 1990–2000. Visiting Professor of Accounting: Univ. of Lancaster, 1978–88; Univ. of Bristol, 1988–2000; Edinburgh Univ., 1999–. UK and Irish Representative: Internat. Auditing Practices Cttee, 1983–88; Internat. Accounting Standards Cttee, 1995–2000; Auditing Practices Committee, Consultative Committee of Accountancy Bodies: Mem., 1985–90; Vice-Chm., 1986–88; Chm., 1989–90. Institute of Chartered Accountants in England and Wales: Mem. Council, 1989–91; Mem., Financial Reporting Council, 1990–2000; Chm., Urgent Issues Task Force, 1990–2000. Hon. DSc (Econ) Hull, 1993; Hon. LLD: Lancaster, 1993; Exeter, 1997; Dundee, 1998; Hon. DLitt Heriot-Watt, 1996; Hon. DBA Napier, 1999. Centenary Award, Chartered Accountants Founding Socs, 1997; CIMA Award, 1998. *Publications:* (with T. A. Lee) The Private Shareholder and the Corporate Report, 1977; Financial Reporting, Inflation and the Capital Maintenance Concept, 1979; (with T. A. Lee) The Institutional Investor and Financial Information, 1981; (with G. Whittington) The Debate on Inflation Accounting, 1984; contribs to professional and acad. accounting jls and books. *Recreations:* athletics and Rugby (watching, not participating, sadly), walking, gardening. *Address:* c/o Inernational Accounting Standards Board, 30 Cannon Street, EC4M 6XH. *T:* (020) 7246 6410.

TWEEDSMUIR, 3rd Baron *cr* 1935, of Elsfield, Oxford; **William de l'Aigle Buchan;** *b* 10 Jan. 1916; 2nd *s* of 1st Baron Tweedsmuir, PC, GCMG, GCVO, CH and Susan Charlotte (*d* 1977), *d* of Hon. Norman Grosvenor; *S* brother, 1996; *m* 1st, 1939, Nesta Crozier (marr. diss. 1946); one *d*; 2nd, 1946, Barbara (marr. diss. 1960; she *d* 1969), 2nd *d* of E. N. Ensor; three *s* three *d* (incl. twin *d*); 3rd, 1960, Sauré Cynthia Mary, *y d* of Maj. G. E. Tatchell; one *s*. *Educ:* Eton; New Coll., Oxford. Sqdn Leader, RAFVR. *Publications:* John Buchan: a memoir, 1982; The Rags of Time (autobiog.), 1990; *novels:* Kumari, 1955; Helen All Alone, 1961; The Blue Pavilion, 1966. *Heir:* *s* Hon. John William Howard de l'Aigle [*b* 25 May 1950; *m* 1977, Amanda Jocelyn, *d* of Sir Gawain Westray Bell, KCMG, CBE; two *s*]. *Club:* Travellers.

See also Hon. U. M. B. Buchan, Baron Stewartby, C. T. Wide.

TWEEDY, Colin David, OBE 2000; Chief Executive, Arts & Business (formerly Director General, Association for Business Sponsorship of the Arts), since 1983; *b* 26 Oct. 1953; *s* of Clifford Harry Tweedy, of Abbotsbury, Dorset and Kitty Audrey (*née* Matthews). *Educ:* City of Bath Boys' Sch.; St Catherine's Coll., Oxford (MA). Manager, Thorndike Theatre, Leatherhead, 1976–78; Corporate Finance Officer, Guinness Mahon, 1978–80; Asst Dir, Streets Financial PR, 1980–83. Chm., Comité Européen pour le Rapprochement de l'Economie et de la Culture; Mem. Council, Japan Festival, 1991; Director: Covent Garden International Festival; Oxford Stage Co.; Crusaid; Mariinsky Theatre Trust; Member: UK Nat. Cttee, European Cinema and TV Year, 1988–89; Council for Charitable Support. Trustee, Serpentine Gall. Sec., Global Adv. Bd, Mariinsky Theatre. Selector, Discerning Eye 2000 exhibn; a Judge, PR Week Awards, 2000; Mem. Adv. Panel, Whitbread Bk Awards. Freeman, City of London, 1978. FRSA. *Publication:* A Celebration of Ten Years' Business Sponsorship of the Arts, 1987. *Recreations:* the arts in general, opera, theatre and contemporary art in particular, Italy, food, travel. *Address:* Arts & Business, Nutmeg House, 60 Gainsford Street, Butlers Wharf, SE1 2NY. *T:* (020) 7378 8143, *Fax:* (020) 7407 7527; *e-mail:* head.office@AandB.org.uk. *Club:* Home House.

TWELVETREE, Eric Alan; Member, Executive Committee, Field Studies Council, 1978–2001; *b* 26 Dec. 1928; *m* 1953, Patricia Mary Starkings; two *d*. *Educ:* Stamford Sch., Lincs; qualif. IPFA and ACCA. Served with Borough Councils: Gt Yarmouth, Ipswich, Stockport, Southampton; County Councils: Gloucestershire, Kent; County Treasurer, Essex CC, 1974–87. Pres., Soc. of County Treasurers, 1986–87. Dir, Chelmsford Hospice, then Farleigh Hospice, Chelmsford, 1991–99. *Recreations:* silversmithing, bookbinding, watercolours. *Address:* 12 Cherry Orchard Road, Tetbury, Glos GL8 8HX.

TWIGG, (John) Derek; MP (Lab) Halton, since 1997; *b* 9 July 1959; *s* of Kenneth and Irene Twigg; *m* 1988, Mary Cassidy; one *s* one *d*. *Educ:* Bankfield High Sch., Widnes; Halton Coll. of Further Educn. Civil service posts, Department of Employment, and DFE, then DFEE, 1975–96; political consultant, 1996–97. Member (Lab): Cheshire CC, 1981–85; Halton DC, 1983–97. PPS to Minister of State, DTI, 1999–2001, to Sec. of State, DTLR, 2001–. Mem., Public Accounts Cttee, 1998–99. *Recreations:* Liverpool Football Club, various sporting activities, walking, reading history. *Address:* House of Commons, SW1A 0AA. *T:* (020) 7219 3000.

TWIGG, Stephen; MP (Lab) Enfield, Southgate, since 1997; *b* 25 Dec. 1966; *s* of Ian David Twigg and late Jean Barbara Twigg. *Educ:* Southgate Comprehensive Sch.; Balliol Coll., Oxford (BA Hons). Pres., NUS, 1990–92; Parliamentary Officer: British Sect., Amnesty Internat., 1992–93; NCVO, 1993–94; researcher, office of Margaret Hodge, MP, 1994–96. Mem. (Lab), Islington LBC, 1992–97. Gen. Sec., Fabian Soc., 1995–96. Member: Select Cttee on Modernisation of H of C, 1998–2000; Select Cttee on Educn and Employment, 2000–01. Chairman: Labour Campaign for Electoral Reform, 1998–2001; Lab. Friends of Israel, 1998–2001. Mem. Exec., Fabian Soc., 1997–. Dir, Crime Concern, 1997–; Dir, Foreign Policy Centre, 1998–. *Recreations:* swimming, travel, food. *Address:* House of Commons, SW1A 0AA. *T:* (020) 7219 6554, *Fax:* (020) 7219 0948; *e-mail:* twiggs@parliament.uk.

TWIGGY; *see* Lawson, Lesley.

TWIN, Prof. Peter John, OBE 1991; FRS 1993; Professor of Experimental Physics, University of Liverpool, since 1987; *b* 26 July 1939; *s* of Arthur James and Hilda Ethel Twin; *m* 1963, Jean Esther Leatherland; one *s* one *d*. *Educ:* Sir George Monoux Grammar Sch., Walthamstow; Univ. of Liverpool (BSc Hons, PhD). University of Liverpool: Lectr, 1964–73; Sen. Lectr, 1973–79; Reader, 1979–87; Head, Nuclear Structure Facility, Daresbury Lab., SERC, 1983–87. Vis. Prof., Univ. of Alberta, 1968–69. Reader, dio. of Chester, 1991–. Tom Bonner Prize, APS, 1991; John Price Wetherill Medal, Benjamin Franklin Inst., USA, 1991. *Publications:* numerous papers in learned jls. *Address:* Oliver Lodge Laboratory, University of Liverpool, Liverpool L69 3BX. *T:* (0151) 794 3378.

TWINE, Derek Milton, FCIPD; Chief Executive, Scout Association, since 1996; *b* 1 May 1951; *s* of late Edward Montague Twine and Winifred May Twine (*née* Milton); *m* 1974, Rhoda, *d* of Very Rev. R. J. N. Lockhart; one *s* one *d*. *Educ:* Reigate GS; UCNW, Bangor (BA Hons Educn 1st cl.). FCIPD (FITD 1987). Researcher, 1973–75, Lectr in Education, 1975–76, Univ. of Wales; Scout Association: Dir, Venture Scout Trng, 1976–79; Dir of Programme, 1979–85; Exec. Comr (Programme and Trng), 1985–96. Member: Youth Panel, Nat. Trust, 1978–85; Voluntary Sector Panel, RSA, 1990–96; Mgt Cttee, Educn and Standards, Nat. Youth Agency, 1991–95 (Chm., 1993–95); National Society for Voluntary Youth Service: Mem., Exec. Cttee, 1979–82; Chm., Develt Project, 1979–82; Chm., Trng Managers' Gp, 1990–96. Trustee: Whitechapel Foundn, 1996–; Croatia Sunrise City Support, 1996–99. Gov., Davenant Foundn Sch., 1994–. *Publications:* various articles in youthwork and educnl jls. *Recreations:* church activities, theatre, cooking, cross-country running. *Address:* Scout Association, Gilwell Park, Chingford, E4 7QW. *T:* (020) 8433 7100, *Fax:* (020) 8433 7108.

TWINING, Prof. William Lawrence, FBA 1997; Research Professor of Law, University College London, since 1996 (Quain Professor of Jurisprudence, 1983–96); *b* 22 Sept. 1934; *s* of Edward Francis Twining and Helen Mary Twining (*née* Dubuisson); *m* 1957, Penelope Elizabeth Wall Morris; one *s* one *d*. *Educ:* Charterhouse School; Brasenose College, Oxford (BA 1955; MA 1960; DCL 1990); Univ. of Chicago (JD 1958). Lectr in Private Law, Univ. of Khartoum, 1958–61; Sen. Lectr in Law, University Coll., Dar-es-Salaam, 1961–65; Prof. of Jurisprudence, The Queen's Univ., Belfast, 1965–72; Prof. of Law, Univ. of Warwick, 1972–82. Mem., Cttee on Legal Educn in N Ireland, 1972–74; President: Soc. of Public Law Teachers of Law, 1978–79; UK Assoc. for Legal and Social Philosophy, 1980–83; Chairman: Bentham Cttee, 1982–2000; Commonwealth Legal Educn Assoc., 1983–93; vis. appts in several Univs. Hon. LLD: Univ. of Victoria, BC, 1980; Edinburgh, 1994; QUB, 1999; Southampton Inst., 2000. General Editor: Law in Context series, 1966–; Jurists series, 1979–. *Publications:* The Karl Llewellyn Papers, 1968; Karl Llewellyn and the Realist Movement, 1973; (with David Miers) How to Do Things with Rules, 1976, 4th edn 1999; (with J. Uglow) Law Publishing and Legal Information, 1981; (ed) Facts in Law, 1983; Theories of Evidence, 1985; (ed) Legal Theory and Common Law, 1986; (ed with R. Tur) Essays on Kelsen, 1986; (ed jtly) Learning Lawyers' Skills, 1989; (ed jtly) Access to Legal Education and the Legal Profession, 1989; Rethinking Evidence, 1990; (ed) Issues of Self-determination, 1991; (with T. Anderson) Analysis of Evidence, 1991; (with E. Quick) Legal Records in the Commonwealth, 1994; Blackstone's Tower: the English Law School, 1994; Law in Context: enlarging a discipline, 1997; Globalisation and Legal Theory, 2000. *Address:* 10 Mill Lane, Iffley, Oxford OX4 4EJ.

TWINN, Ian David, PhD; Director of Public Affairs, Incorporated Society of British Advertisers, since 1998; *b* 26 April 1950; *s* of David Twinn and Gwynneth Irene Twinn; *m* 1973, Frances Elizabeth Holtby; two *s*. *Educ:* Netherhall Secondary Modern School, Cambridge; Cambridge Grammar School; University College of Wales, Aberystwyth (BA hons); University of Reading (PhD). Senior Lecturer in Planning, Polytechnic of the South Bank, 1975–83. MP (C) Edmonton, 1983–97; contested (C) same seat, 1997. PPS to Minister of State for Industry, 1985–86, to Dep. Chm. of Cons. Party, 1986–88, to Minister of State for Energy, 1987–90, to Minister of State for the Environment, 1990–92, to Paymaster Gen., 1992–94. Contested (C) London Reg., EP elecns, 1999. Vice Chm., British Caribbean Assoc., 1986–. FRSA 1989; FRGS (MIBG 1972). Comdr, Order of Honour (Greece), 2000. *Recreations:* collecting secondhand books, renovating antique furniture. *Address:* 85 Calton Avenue, SE21 7DF. *T:* (020) 8299 4210.

TWINN, John Ernest; Director General Guided Weapons and Electronics, Ministry of Defence, 1978–81, retired; *b* 11 July 1921; *s* of late Col Frank Charles George Twinn, CMG and Lilian May Twinn (*née* Tomlinson); *m* 1950, Mary Constance Smallwood; three *d*. *Educ:* Manchester Grammar Sch.; Christ's Coll., Cambridge (MA). FIEE 1981. Air Min., 1941; Telecommunications Research Estabt (later Royal Radar Estabt), 1943; Head of Guided Weapons Gp, RRE, 1965; Head of Space Dept, RAE, 1968; Head of Weapons Dept, RAE, 1972; Asst Chief Scientific Advr (Projects), MoD, 1973; Dir Underwater Weapons Projects (Naval), 1976. *Recreations:* sailing, music, genealogy. *Address:* Timbers, 9 Woodway, Merrow, Guildford, Surrey GU1 2TF. *T:* (01483) 568993.

TWISK, Russell Godfrey; Editor-in-Chief, British Reader's Digest, since 1988; *b* 24 Aug. 1941; *s* of late K. Y. Twisk and of Joyce Brunning; *m* 1965, Ellen Elizabeth Banbury; two *d*. *Educ:* Salesian Coll., Farnborough. Harmsworth Press, Dep. Editor, Golf Illustrated, 1960; Sub Editor, Sphere; freelance journalist, 1962; joined BBC, editorial staff Radio Times, 1966; Deputy Editor, Radio Times, 1971; Development Manager, BBC, 1975; Editor, The Listener, 1981–87. Director: Reader's Digest, 1988–; Berkeley Magazines Ltd, 1990–. Has edited numerous BBC publications; radio critic for The Observer, 1989–94; Publisher, BBC Adult Literacy Project. Mem., Press Complaints Commn, 1999–. Dir, Greenwich and Docklands Internat. Fest., 1999–. Governor, London College of Printing, 1967–87 (Chm., 1974, 1978). Chm., Reader's Digest Trust, 1988–99. Chm., National Campaign Cttee, Charities Aid Foundn, 1991–94. Chm., BSME, 1990; Pres., Media Soc., 1993–95. Trustee, Christian Responsibility in Public Affairs, 1997–. *Recreations:* running, map reading, watching horses race. *Address:* The Old Barn, East Harting, near Petersfield, Hants GU31 5LZ. *Clubs:* Reform, Groucho.

TWISLETON-WYKEHAM-FIENNES; *see* Fiennes.

TWISS, (Lionel) Peter, OBE 1957; DSC 1942 and Bar 1943; marine consultant; Director and General Manager, Hamble Point Marina Ltd, 1978–88; formerly Chief Test Pilot of Fairey Aviation Ltd; *b* 23 July 1921; *m* 1944, Constance Tomkinson (marr. diss.; she *d* 1996); *m* 1950, Mrs Vera Maguire (marr. diss.); one *d* (and one *d* decd), one step *s* one step *d*; *m* 1960, Cherry (marr. diss.), *d* of late Sir John Huggins, GCMG, MC; one *d*; *m* 1964, Mrs Heather Danby (*d* 1988), Titchfield; one step *s* one step *d*. *Educ:* Sherborne Sch. Joined Fleet Air Arm, 1939; served on catapult ships, aircraft-carriers, 1941–43; night fighter development, 1943–44; served in British Air Commn, America, 1944. Empire Test Pilots School, Boscombe Down, 1945; Test Pilot, Fairey Aviation Co. Ltd, 1946, Chief Test Pilot, 1957–60. Dir, Fairey Marine Ltd, 1968–78. Mem., Lasham Gliding Soc. Holder of World's Absolute Speed Record, 10 March 1956. *Publication:* Faster than the Sun, 1963, 2nd edn 2000. *Address:* Nettleworth, 33 South Street, Titchfield, Hants PO14 4DL. *T:* (01329) 843146. *Clubs:* Royal Southern Yacht; Surrey and Hants Gliding.

TWIST, Kenneth Lyndon, CEng, FIMinE; HM Chief Inspector of Mines, 1992–96; *b* 13 Jan. 1938; *s* of Joseph and Sarah Ellen Twist; *m* 1959, Emily Owens; three *s*. *Educ:* Wigan and Dist Mining & Technical Coll. (Dip. Mining Engrg). Colliery Manager's Cert., 1963. FIMinE 1979. Dep. General Manager, Agecroft, 1969–76; Health and Safety Executive: Inspector of Mines, 1976–87; Principal Dist Inspector of Mines, 1987–91; Dep. Chief Inspector of Mines, 1991–92. Chm., Safety in Mines Res. Adv. Bd, HSC, 1992–96. *Publications:* papers in Mining Engineer, Jl of Instn of Mining Engrs. *Recreations:* gardening, reading, computing, golf. *Address:* Ridgeway, Sunnyridge Avenue, Marford, Wrexham LL12 8TE. *T:* (01978) 855638.

TWITCHETT, Prof. Denis Crispin, FBA 1967; Gordon Wu Professor of Chinese Studies, Princeton University, 1980–94; *b* 23 Sept. 1925; *m* 1956, Umeko (*née* Ichikawa); two *s*. *Educ:* St Catharine's Coll., Cambridge. Lectr in Far-Eastern History, Univ. of London, 1954–56; Univ. Lectr in Classical Chinese, Univ. of Cambridge, 1956–60; Prof. of Chinese, SOAS, London Univ., 1960–68; Prof. of Chinese, Univ. of Cambridge, 1968–80. Vis. Prof., Princeton Univ., 1973–74, 1978–79. Principal Editor, Cambridge History of China, 1977–. *Publications:* (ed with A. F. Wright) Confucian Personalities, 1962; The Financial Administration under the T'ang dynasty, 1963, 2nd edn 1971; (ed with A. F. Wright) Perspectives on the T'ang, 1973; (ed with P. J. M. Geelan) The Times Atlas of China, 1975; (ed) Cambridge History of China, Vol. 10 1978, Vol. 3 1979, Vol. 11 1980, Vol. 12 1983, Vol. 1 1986, Vol. 13 1986, Vol. 7 1987, Vol. 14 1987, Vol. 15 1990, Vol. 6 1994, Vol. 8 1998; Printing and Publishing in Medieval China, 1983; Reader in T'ang History, 1986; The Writing of Official History in T'ang China, 1992; The Historian, his Readers, and the Passage of Time, 1997. *Address:* 24 Arbury Road, Cambridge CB4 2JE; 211 Jones Hall, Princeton, NJ 08544-1008, USA.

TWITE, Robin, OBE 1982; Director, Environmental Program, Israel-Palestine Center for Research and Information, Jerusalem, since 1997; *b* 2 May 1932; *s* of Reginald John Twite and May Elizabeth Walker; *m* 1st, 1958, Sally Randall (marr. diss.); 2nd, 1980, Sonia Yaari; one *s* three step *d*. *Educ:* Lawrence Sheriff School, Rugby; Balliol College, Oxford (BA History 1955). Asst Editor, Schoolmaster, weekly jl of NUT, 1956–58; British Council, 1958–73: served in Israel and London as Sec., Overseas Students Fees Awards Scheme; Sec., Open Univ. of Israel, 1973–76; British Council, 1976–88: adviser on adult and further educn, 1977–79; regional rep., Calcutta, 1980–84; Controller, Books, Libraries and Inf. Div., 1984–88. Hebrew University, Jerusalem: Advr to Chm., Res. Authy, 1988–91; Develt Advr, Truman Res. Inst. for Peace, 1991–93; Dir, Conflict Resolution Project, Leonard Davis Inst. for Internat. Relns, 1994–97. *Publications:* (ed) The Future of Jerusalem, 1993; (ed) Israeli-Arab Negotiations, 1993; (ed) Our Shared Environment: environmental problems of Israel, the West Bank and Gaza, 1994. *Recreations:* travel, music making, local history. *Address:* 36 Ezor Gimel, Ein Kerem, Jerusalem, Israel. *T:* (2) 6410023.

TWYCROSS, Dr Robert Geoffrey, FRCP, FRCR; Director, WHO Collaborating Centre for Palliative Cancer Care, since 1988; Consultant Physician, Sir Michael Sobell House, Churchill Hospital, 1976–2001; Macmillan Clinical Reader in Palliative Medicine, Oxford University, 1988–2001, and Fellow of St Peter's College, Oxford, 1987–2001; *b* 29 Jan. 1941; *s* of Jervis and Irene Twycross; *m* 1964, Deirdre Maeve, *d* of John Richard Campbell; two *s* three *d*. *Educ:* St John's Sch., Leatherhead; St Peter's Coll., Oxford (BA 1962; BM BCh 1965; MA 1965; DM 1977). MRCP 1969, FRCP 1980; FRCR 1996; FRSocMed 1989. Hosp. appts, Oxford, Lancaster, Epsom and Manchester, 1966–71; Res. Fellow, St Christopher's Hospice, London, 1971–76; Vis. MO, St Joseph's Hospice, London, 1971–76. Academic Dir, Oxford Internat. Centre for Palliative Cancer Care, 1992–. Visiting Professor: RSocMed of USA Foundation, 1979; Sir Ernest Finch, Sheffield, 1994; Palliative Medicine, Univ. del Salvador, Buenos Aires, 1999–; Lectures: Abbott, Amer. Soc. of Regl Anaesthesia, 1980; Rendle Short, Christian Med. Fellowship, 1984; Archbishop Dwyer Meml, 1993. Chm., Internat. Sch. for Cancer Care, 1987; Member: WHO Expert Adv. Panel on Cancer, 1985; Bd, Pallium Foundn, Netherlands, 1993; founder mem., numerous internat. care assocs. Dir, palliativedrugs.com, 2000–. Aid and Co-operation Medal, Poland, 1993; Founder's Award, Nat. Hospice Orgn, USA, 1994; Serturner Prize, Serturner Soc., 1995. *Publications:* The Dying Patient, 1975; (ed) Pain Relief in Cancer, vol. 3 No 1, 1984; A Time to Die, 1984; (ed) Edinburgh Symposium on Pain Control and Medical Education, 1989; Pain Relief in Advanced Cancer, 1994; Introducing Palliative Care, 1995, 3rd edn 1999; Symptom Management in Advanced Cancer, 1995, 3rd edn (with A. Wilcock) 2001; (with A. Wilcock and S. Thorp) Palliative Care Formulary, 1998; (ed jtly) Lymphoedema, 2000; with S. A. Lack: Symptom Control in Far-Advanced Cancer: pain relief, 1983; Therapeutics in Terminal Cancer, 1984; Oral Morphine in Advanced Cancer, 1984, (sole author) 3rd edn 1997; Control of Alimentary Symptoms in Far-Advanced Cancer, 1986; Oral Morphine: information for patients, families and friends, 1987, (sole author) 2nd edn, as Morphine and the relief of cancer pain, 1999; contribs to learned jls. *Recreations:* gardening, walking, reading, theatre. *Address:* Tewsfield, Netherwoods Road, Oxford OX3 8HF.

TWYFORD, Donald Henry, CB 1990; Under Secretary, Export Credits Guarantee Department, 1981–89, Director and Chairman of Project Group Board, 1986–89; *b* 4 Feb. 1931; *s* of Henry John Twyford and Lily Hilda (*née* Ridler). *Educ:* Wembley County School. Joined Export Credits Guarantee Dept, 1949; Principal, 1965; seconded to Dept of Trade: Principal (Commercial Relations with East Europe), 1972–75; Asst Secretary (Country Policy), 1976; Establishment Officer, 1979–81; Under Secretary, Head of Services Group (internat. and country policy), ECGD, 1981–85; Hd of Project Underwriting Gp, 1985–89. Chairman, European Policy Coordination Group, 1981. Pres., Jávea Internat. Fest. Cttee, 2001–; Vice-Pres., Jávea Internat. Civic Soc., 1999–; Pres., Penya Británica, 1999–. *Recreations:* gardening (especially growing exotic plants), music, travel. *Address:* Cami de la Sabatera 33, Jávea 03739, Alicante, Spain.

TWYMAN, Paul Hadleigh; management consultant; Chairman, Political Strategy Ltd, since 1988; Director: Nationwide (formerly Nationwide Anglia) Building Society, since 1987 (Anglia Building Society, 1983–87); Connex Transport UK Ltd, since 1999; *s* of late Lawrence Alfred Twyman and Gladys Mary (*née* Williams). *Educ:* Leyton County High Sch.; Chatham House Sch., Ramsgate; Univ. of Sheffield (BAEcon); London Sch. of Econs and Pol Science (MScEcon). Schoolteacher, 1964; Asst Principal, BoT, 1967; Secretariat, Commn on Third London Airport, 1969; Private Sec. to Sec. of State for Trade and Industry, 1971; Dept of Industry, 1975; Anti-Dumping Unit, Dept of Trade, 1976; Asst Sec., and Head of Overseas Projects Group, Dept of Trade, 1978; Dept of Transport, 1983; Cabinet Office, 1984; Under Sec., and Dir, Enterprise and Deregulation Unit, Dept of Employment, 1985. Econ. Adviser to Chm. of Conservative Party, and Head of Econ. Section, Cons. Res. Dept, 1987. Contested (C) Greater Manchester W, European Parly elecn, 1989. Dir, D'Arcy Masius Benton & Bowles, 1990–96; Corporate Strategy Dir, Bates Dorland Ltd, later Bates UK, 1996–99. Mem., Thanet DC, 1991–95. Hon. Comptroller, 1998–99, Vice-Chm., 1999–, Lambeth Community Police Consultative Gp. Associate Mem., Kensington, Chelsea and Westminster HA, 1996–. Trustee, Opportunity Internat. (UK), 1995–. Gov., City of Westminster Coll., 1999–. Mem., British Pteridological Soc. FIMgt; MCIT; FRSA. *Recreations:* family and friends, gardening, hill walking, observing gorillas.

TYACKE, Maj.-Gen. David Noel Hugh, CB 1970; OBE 1957; Controller, Army Benevolent Fund, 1971–80; *b* 18 Nov. 1915; *s* of Capt. Charles Noel Walker Tyacke (killed in action, March 1918) and late Phoebe Mary Cicely (*née* Coulthard), Cornwall; *m* 1940, Diana, *d* of Aubrey Hare Duke; one *s*. *Educ:* Malvern Coll.; RMC Sandhurst. Commissioned DCLI, 1935; India, 1936–39; France and Belgium, 1939–40; India and Burma, 1943–46; Instructor, Staff Coll., Camberley, 1950–52; CO 1st Bn DCLI, 1957–59; Comdr 130 Inf. Bde (TA), 1961–63; Dir of Administrative Planning (Army), 1963–64; Brig. Gen. Staff (Ops), Min. of Defence, 1965–66; GOC Singapore Dist.,

1966–70, retired. Col, The Light Infantry, 1972–77. Mem., Malvern Coll. Council, 1978–88. *Recreations:* walking, motoring, bird-watching. *Address:* c/o Lloyds TSB, Cox's & King's Branch, 7 Pall Mall, SW1Y 5NA.
See also S. J. Tyacke.

TYACKE, Sarah Jacqueline, (Mrs Nicholas Tyacke), CB 1998; FSA; FRHistS; Chief Executive and Keeper of Public Records, Public Record Office, since 1992; *b* 29 Sept. 1945; *d* of late Colin Walton Jeacock and Elsie Marguerite Stanton; *m* 1971, Nicholas, *s* of Maj.-Gen. D. N. H. Tyacke, *qv*; one *d. Educ:* Chelmsford County High Sch.; Bedford Coll., London (BA Hons History). FSA 1985; FRHistS 1994. Asst Keeper, Map Room, BM, 1968; Dep. Map Librarian, British Liby, 1973–85; undertook govt scrutiny of BL preservation (under Efficiency Unit, Cabinet Office), 1985–86; Director of Special Collections, British Library, 1986–91. Chm., European Co-ordinating Bd, 1992–96, a Vice-Pres., 1996–2000, Internat. Council on Archives; Jt Hon. Sec., Hakluyt Soc., 1984–95 (Vice Pres., 1995–97, Pres., 1997–); Vice-Chm., Professional Bd, IFLA, 1987–89; a Vice-Pres., RHistS, 2000–. Dir, Imago Mundi, 1987–; Trustee, Mappa Mundi, 1989–96. Hon. Fellow, RHBNC, 1999. Hon. DPhil Guildhall, 1996. *Publications:* Copernicus and the New Astronomy (with H. Swiderska), 1973; (ed jtly with H. M. Wallis) My Head is a Map: essay and memoirs in honour of R. V. Tooley, 1973; London Map-Sellers 1660–1720, 1978; (with John Huddy) Christopher Saxton and Tudor map-making, 1980; (ed) English map-making 1500–1650: historical essays, 1983; Catalogue of maps, charts and plans in the Pepys Library, Magdalene College, Cambridge, 1989; contribs to archival, library and cartographic jls, incl. The Library, Imago Mundi, Cartographic Jl. *Recreations:* the sea, travel, hill-walking, painting. *Address:* Public Record Office, Kew, Richmond, Surrey TW9 4DU.

TYBULEWICZ, Albin, CPhys, FInstP; Scientific Editor, Quantum Electronics, 1994–2000; *b* Poland, 1 March 1929; *s* of Julian and Elżbieta Tybulewicz (*née* Świgost); *m* 1959, Tuliola Sylwina Bryl; one *s* one *d. Educ:* schools in Poland, Russia, Iran, India; St Mary's High Sch., Bombay. BSc London 1952. CPhys 1985; FInstP 1967. Research Officer, BICC, 1953–56; Asst Editor, 1956–63, Editor, 1963–67, Physics Abstracts and Current Papers in Physics; Editor: Soviet Physics—Semiconductors, 1967–92; Soviet Jl of Quantum Electronics, 1970–92; Soviet Physics—Solid State (jtly with Prof. L. Azaroff), 1982–92. Founder and Chm., Food for Poland Fund, 1980–84. Mem. Prog. Adv. Bd, Polish Satellite TV (Polonia), 1997–. Fellow, Amer. Phys. Soc.; Hon. Fellow, Inst. of Translation and Interpreting (Mem. Council, 1986–94, 1995–2001; Vice-Chm., 1999–2001). Natthorst Non-Literary Prize, Fedn Internat. des Traducteurs, 1990. *Publications:* American Institute of Physics Translation Manual, 1983; trans of numerous Russian physics monographs; contribs to physics and professional jls on language and translation. *Recreations:* theatre, reading, Polish community affairs in England, politics in Poland. *Address:* 2 Oak Dene, West Ealing, W13 8AW. *T:* (020) 8997 8822, *Fax:* (020) 8810 9272; *e-mail:* tybulewicz@aol.com. *Club:* Wig and Pen.

TYDEMAN, John Peter; Head of BBC Radio Drama, 1986–94; *b* 30 March 1936; *s* of George Alfred Tydeman and Gladys (*née* Johnson). *Educ:* Feltonfleet; Hertford GS; Trinity Coll., Cambridge (MA). Nat. Service, 2 Lieut RA, 1954–56. Joined BBC, 1959; producer, 1962–80; Asst Head, Radio Drama, 1980–86. Dir of stage, radio and television plays. Prix Italia, 1970; Prix Futura, 1979 and 1983; Broadcasting Press Guild Award, 1983; Sony Award, 1994. *Recreations:* theatre, travel, reading, the company of friends. *Address:* Flat 7, 88 Great Titchfield Street, W1W 6SE. *T:* (020) 7636 3886. *Club:* Garrick.

TYE, Alan Peter, RDI 1986; Partner, Alan Tye Design (Industrial & Product Designers), since 1962; *b* 18 Sept. 1933; *s* of Chang Qing Tai and Emily Tai (*née* Thompson); *m* 1966, Anita Birgitta Göethe Tye; three *s* two *d. Educ:* Regent Street Polytechnic Sch. of Architecture. RIBA 1959; FCSD (FSIAD 1979). Qualified as architect, 1958; with Prof. Arne Jacobsen, Copenhagen, 1960–62; formed Alan Tye Design, 1962; incorporated HID Ltd, 1977; launched Healthy Individual Design Practice Method (HID), 1992. Mem., Selection Cttee, Council of Industrial Design, 1967; Civic Trust Award Assessor, 1968, 1969; Vis. Tutor, RCA, 1978–83, External Examr, 1987–90; Specialist Adviser on Industrial Design, CNAA, 1980; London Region Assessor, RIBA, 1981 and 1988; RSA Bursary Judge, 1983–; External Examr, Design Res. for Disability, London Guildhall Univ., 1998–. Convenor, Faculty of RDI, RSA, 1991–. Guest Prof., Royal Danish Acad. of Fine Arts, 1996. Internat. Design Prize, Rome, 1962; Council of Industrial Design Award, 1965, 1966, 1981; British Aluminium Design Award, 1966; 1st Prize, GAI Award, 1969; Observer (London) Design Award, 1969; Ringling Mus. of Art (Fla) Award, 1969; Gold Medal, Graphic Design, 1970; 1st Prize, GAI Award, Internat. Bldg Exhibn, 1971; British Aluminium Eros Trophy, 1973; 4 Awards for Design Excellence, Aust., 1973; Commendation for Arch., 1977; Internat. Award, Inst. of Business Designers (NY), 1982; Internat. Bldg Exhibits Top Design Award, 1983, 1985; Resources Council of America Design Award, 1987; RIBA Regl Design Award, 1995; other design awards. *Publication:* (with Dermot O'Flynn) Healthy Industrial Design, 1995. *Recreations:* tai chi, aikido. *Address:* Great West Plantation, Tring, Herts HP23 6DA. *T:* (01442) 825353.

TYLER, Anne; writer; *b* 25 Oct. 1941; *d* of Lloyd Parry Tyler and Phyllis Mahon Tyler (*née* Mahon); *m* 1963, Taghi M. Modarressi, MD (*d* 1997); two *d. Educ:* Duke Univ. (BA). Mem., AAIL. AAIL Award for Literature, 1977; Nat. Book Critics Circle Award for fiction, 1985. *Publications:* If Morning Ever Comes, 1964; The Tin Can Tree, 1965; A Slipping Down Life, 1970; The Clock Winder, 1972; Celestial Navigation, 1974; Searching for Caleb, 1976; Earthly Possessions, 1977; Morgan's Passing, 1980; Dinner at the Homesick Restaurant, 1982; The Accidental Tourist, 1985; Breathing Lessons, 1988 (Pulitzer Prize for fiction, 1989); Saint Maybe, 1991; Tumble Tower (for children), 1993; Ladder of Years, 1995; A Patchwork Planet, 1998; Back When We Were Grownups, 2001. *Address:* 222 Tunbridge Road, Baltimore, MD 21212, USA.

TYLER, Maj.-Gen. Christopher, CB 1989; CEng, FIMechE; Secretary, Royal Humane Society, since 1995; *b* 9 July 1934; *s* of Maj.-Gen. Sir Leslie Tyler, KBE, CB, and late Louie Teresa Tyler (*née* Franklin); *m* 1958, Suzanne, *d* of late Eileen Whitcomb and Patrick Whitcomb; one *s* three *d. Educ:* Beaumont College; RMA Sandhurst; Trinity Coll., Cambridge (MA). Commissioned REME, 1954; served UK and BAOR, 1959–65; Army Staff Course, 1966–67; Weapons Staff, 1968–70 and 1972–74; CO 1st Parachute Logistic Regt, 1974–76; MoD, 1976–80; Chief Aircraft Engineer, Army Air Corps, 1980–82; DEME (Management Services), Logistic Exec., 1982–83; Comd Maint., HQ 1 (BR) Corps, 1983–85; Dep. Comdt, RMCS, 1985–87; DCOS (Support), HQ Allied Forces N Europe, 1987–89. Resident Gov. and Keeper of the Jewel House, HM Tower of London, 1989–94. Col Comdt, REME, 1989–94; Hon. Col, REME (V), 1994–2000. External Mem. of Council, Parachute Regt, 1993–98; Trustee: Tower Hill Improvement Trust, 1990–; Ulysses Trust, 1992–94. Governor: St Mary's Sch., Ascot, 1995–; St John's, Beaumont, 1996–. Liveryman, Turners' Co., 1979– (Master, 2000–01). *Recreations:* Rugby football (RFU Panel Referee, 1957–59 and 1967–73 and Chm., Army and Combined Services, 1985–86), tennis, squash. *Address:* Oak Cottage, Stratfield Saye, Reading, Berks RG7 2EB. *T:* (0118) 933 2562. *Club:* Hawks (Cambridge).

TYLER, Ven. Leonard George; Rector of St Michael and St Mary Magdalene, Easthampstead, 1973–85, retired; *b* 15 April 1920; *s* of Hugh Horstead Tyler and Mabel Adam Stewart Tyler; *m* 1946, Sylvia May Wilson; one *s* two *d. Educ:* Darwen Grammar School; Liverpool University; Christ's College, Cambridge; Westcott House. Chaplain, Trinity College, Kandy, Ceylon, 1946–48; Principal, Diocesan Divinity School, Colombo, Ceylon, 1948–50; Rector, Christ Church, Bradford, Manchester, 1950–55; Vicar of Leigh, Lancs, 1955–66 (Rural Dean, 1955–62); Chaplain, Leigh Infirmary, 1955–66; Archdeacon of Rochdale, 1962–66; Principal, William Temple College, Manchester, 1966–73. Anglican Adviser to ABC Television, 1958–68. *Publications:* contributor to Theology. *Address:* 11 Ashton Place, Kintbury, Hungerford, Berks RG17 9XS. *T:* (01488) 658510.

TYLER, Prof. Lorraine Komisarjevsky, PhD; FBA 1995; MRC Research Professor, University of Cambridge, since 1998 and Director (formerly Co-Director), Centre for Speech and Language, since 1990; *b* 11 Jan. 1945; *d* of James and Anne Komisarjevsky; *m* 1982, William D. Marslen-Wilson, *qv*; one *s* one *d. Educ:* Leicester Univ. (BA); Chicago Univ. (PhD 1977). Sen. Res. Fellow, Max Planck Inst. for Psycholinguistics, 1977–85; Lectr, Dept of Psychology, Cambridge Univ., 1985–90; Prof. of Psychology, Birkbeck Coll., Univ. of London, 1990–98. *Publications:* Spoken Language Comprehension, 1992; contrib. Brain and Lang., Jl of Memory and Lang., Psychological Rev., Cognition, etc. *Address:* Department of Experimental Psychology, University of Cambridge, Downing Street, Cambridge CB2 3EB. *T:* (01223) 766457.

TYLER, Paul Archer, CBE 1985; MP (Lib Dem) North Cornwall, since 1992; public affairs consultant; Director, Western Approaches Public Relations Ltd, Launceston, Cornwall, since 1987 (Managing Director, 1987–92); *b* 29 Oct. 1941; *s* of Oliver Walter Tyler and Ursula Grace Gibbons Tyler (*née* May); *m* 1970, Nicola Mary Ingram; one *s* one *d. Educ:* Mount House Sch., Tavistock; Sherborne Sch.; Exeter Coll., Oxford (MA). Pres., Oxford Univ. Liberal Club, 1962. Royal Inst. of British Architects: Admin. Asst, 1966; Asst Sec., 1967; Dep. Dir Public Affairs, 1971; Dir Public Affairs, 1972. Man. Dir, Cornwall Courier newspaper gp, 1976–81; Exec. Dir, Public Affairs Div., Good Relations plc, 1982–84; Chief Exec., 1984–86, Chm., 1986–87, Good Relations Public Affairs Ltd; Dir, Good Relations plc, 1985–88; Sen. Consultant, Good Relations Ltd, 1987–92. County Councillor, Devon, 1964–70; Mem., Devon and Cornwall Police Authority, 1965–70; Vice-Chm., Dartmoor Nat. Park Cttee, 1965–70; Chm., CPRE Working Party on the Future of the Village, 1974–81; Vice-President: ACRE; ACC; BTCV; Mem. Bd of Shelter (Nat. Campaign for the Homeless), and rep. in Devon and Cornwall, 1975–76. Sec., L/SDP Jt Commn on Employment and Industrial Recovery, 1981–82. Chm., Devon and Cornwall Region Liberal Party, 1981–82; Chm., Liberal Party NEC, 1983–86. Campaign Adviser to Rt Hon. David Steel, and Mem., Alliance Campaign Planning Gp, 1986–87. Contested (L): Totnes, 1966; Bodmin, 1970, 1979; Beaconsfield, 1982; contested (Soc & Lib Dem) Cornwall and Plymouth, European Parly Election, 1989. MP (L) Bodmin, Feb.–Sept. 1974. Parly Liberal spokesman on housing and transport, 1974; Parly adviser to RIBA, 1974; Lib Dem spokesman on agriculture and rural affairs, 1992–97, on transport, 1994–95, on food, 1997–99; Lib Dem Chief Whip, 1997–2001; Shadow Leader of House, 1997–. Member: Select Cttee on Modernisation of H of C, 1997–; Jt Select Cttee on Parly Privilege, 1997–99. *Publications:* A New Deal for Rural Britain (jtly), 1978; Country Lives, Country Landscapes, 1996. *Recreations:* sailing, gardening, walking. *Address:* Church Stile, Launceston, Cornwall PL15 8AT. *Club:* Launceston Liberal Democrat (Cornwall).

TYNAN, Prof. Michael John, MD, FRCP; Professor of Paediatric Cardiology, Guy's Hospital, 1982–99; *b* 18 April 1934; *s* of late Jerry Joseph Tynan and Florence Ann Tynan; *m* 1958, Eirlys Pugh Williams. *Educ:* Bedford Modern School; London Hospital. MD, BS. Senior Asst Resident, Children's Hosp., Boston, Mass, 1962; Registrar, Westminster Hosp., 1964; Registrar, later Lectr, Hosp. for Sick Children, Great Ormond St, 1966; consultant paediatric cardiologist, Newcastle Univ. Hospitals, 1971, Guy's Hosp., 1977. *Publications:* (jtly) Paediatric Cardiology, a textbook, vol. 5, 1983; articles on nomenclature and classification of congenital heart disease and on heart disease in children. *Recreations:* singing, watching cricket, playing snooker. *Address:* 5 Ravensdon Street, SE11 4AQ. *T:* (020) 7735 7119. *Clubs:* Athenæum; Borth and Ynyslas Golf.

TYNAN, William; MP (Lab) Hamilton South, since Sept. 1999; *b* 18 Aug. 1940; *s* of late James and Mary Tynan; *m* 1964, Elizabeth Mathieson; three *d. Educ:* St Joseph's Sch.; St Mungo's Acad.; Stow Coll. Press toolmaker, 1961–88. Joined AEU (subseq. AEEU), 1966: shop steward and convener, 1966; Member: Mid Lanark Dist Cttee, 1969; Divl Cttee, 1976; Nat. Cttee, 1977–88; full-time Union Official, 1988–99: Dist Sec., 1988–96; Regl Officer, 1996–99; Political Officer, 1991; Scottish Political Sec., 1993. Member: Parly Select Cttee on NI, 2001–; European Scrutiny Cttee, 2001–; Convenor, Scottish Labour Gp of MPs, 2001–. Joined Labour Party, 1969: Mem. Exec. and Gen. Mgt Cttee, Hamilton N and Hamilton S Constituency Parties, 1979–; Chm., Hamilton S CLP, 1987; Member: Scottish Labour Policy Forum, 1998; Scottish Exec., 1982–88. *Recreations:* golf, swimming, cycling, gardening, DIY. *Address:* House of Commons, SW1A 0AA. *T:* (020) 7219 6285; 6 East Scott Terrace, Hamilton ML3 6SF. *T:* (office) (01698) 454925.

TYNDALL, Nicholas John; Chief Officer, National Marriage Guidance Council, 1968–86; *b* 15 Aug. 1928; *s* of Rev. Edward Denis Tyndall and Nora Mildred Tyndall; *m* 1953, Elizabeth Mary (*née* Ballard); two *s* two *d. Educ:* Marlborough College; Jesus College, Cambridge. BA. HM Prison and Borstal Service, 1952–68; Training Officer, Cruse-Bereavement Care, 1987–91, retd. Dir, Council of Europe Co-ordinated Research Fellowship on Marriage Guidance and Family Counselling, 1973–75; Mem., Home Office/DHSS Working Party on Marriage Guidance, 1976–78; Chairman: British Assoc. for Counselling, 1976–78; Marriage and Marriage Guidance Commn of Internat. Union of Family Organisations, 1971–86; Training Cttee, Nat. Assoc. of Bereavement Socs, 1993–99. Mem., Gen. Synod of Church of England, 1981–88. Fellow, British Assoc. for Counselling, 1997. *Publication:* Counselling in the Voluntary Sector, 1993. *Recreations:* Morris dancing (Squire, Icknield Way Morris Men, 1998–2000). *Address:* 18 Stanford Road, Faringdon, Oxon SN7 7AQ.
See also Rev. T. Tyndall.

TYNDALL, Rev. Canon Timothy; Chief Secretary, Advisory Council for the Church's Ministry, 1985–90; *b* 24 April 1925; *s* of Rev. Denis Tyndall and Nora Tyndall; *m* 1953, Dr Ruth Mary Turner (*d* 1998); two *s* twin *d. Educ:* Jesus Coll., Cambridge (BA). Parish Incumbent: Newark, 1955; Nottingham, 1960; Sunderland, 1975. *Address:* 29 Kingswood Road, Chiswick, W4 5EU. *T:* (020) 8994 4516.
See also N. J. Tyndall.

TYRE, Colin Jack; QC (Scot.) 1998; *b* 17 April 1956; *s* of James Harrison Tyre and Lilias Carmichael Tyre (*née* Kincaid); *m* 1982, Elaine Patricia Carlin; one *s* two *d. Educ:* Dunoon Grammar Sch.; Univ of Edinburgh (LLB Hons); Université d'Aix-Marseille (DESU). Admitted Solicitor, 1980; admitted to Faculty of Advocates, 1987. Lectr in Law, Univ. of Edinburgh, 1980–83; Tax Editor, CCH Editions Ltd, 1983–86; Standing Junior Counsel: MoD (PE), 1991–95; Scottish Office Envmt Dept (in planning matters), 1995–98. Mem.,

Special Cttee, Tax Law Consultative Bodies, 1993–. Mem., UK Delegn to CCBE, 1999–. *Publications:* CCH Inheritance Tax Reporter, 1986; (jtly) Tax for Litigation Lawyers, 2000; contrib. Stair Memorial Encyclopaedia, learned jls. *Recreations:* mountain walking, golf, orienteering, music (especially popular). *Address:* Advocates' Library, Parliament House, Edinburgh EH1 1RF. *T:* (0131) 226 5071.

TYREE, Sir (Alfred) William, Kt 1975; OBE 1971; electrical engineer, chief executive and chairman; *b* Auckland, NZ, 4 Nov. 1921; *s* of J. V. Tyree and A. Hezeltine (who migrated to Australia, 1938); *m* 1946, Joyce, *d* of F. Lyndon; two *s* one *d. Educ:* Auckland Grammar School; Sydney Technical Coll. (Dip. in Elec. Engrg). FIE (Aust) 1968 (Peter Nicol Russell Mem. Award 1985); FIEE 1983. Founded Tyree Industries Ltd and Westralian Transformers and subsids, 1956; Founder and Chairman: Alpha Air (Sydney) Pty Ltd; Technical Components Pty Ltd; Tycan Australia Pty Ltd; Tyree Holdings Pty Ltd; A. W. Tyree Transformers Pty Ltd; Wirex Pty Ltd; A. W. Tyree Foundation. Mem., Aust. Inst. of Co. Dirs; Councillor: Australian Industry Gp (formerly Metal Trades Industries Assoc.) (Mem., Nat. Exec.); Aust. Chamber of Manufrs. Hon. Fellow, Univ. of Sydney, 1985; Hon. Life Governor, Aust. Postgrad. Fedn in Medicine, 1985. Hon. DSc Univ. of NSW, 1986. James N. Kirby Medal, IProdE, Australia, 1980; IEEE USA Centennial Medal, 1984. *Recreations:* ski-ing, photography, water ski-ing, yachting, tennis, music, golf, sail board riding, computers. *Address:* 60 Martin Place, Sydney, NSW 2000, Australia; (home) 3 Lindsay Avenue Darling Point, NSW. *Clubs:* Royal Aero, American National, Royal Automobile (NSW); Royal Prince Alfred Yacht, Royal Motor Yacht, Cruising Yacht, Kosciusko Alpine, RAC, Australian Golf.

TYRELL-KENYON; *see* Kenyon.

TYRER, Christopher John Meese; His Honour Judge Tyrer; a Circuit Judge, since 1989; *b* 22 May 1944; *s* of late Jack Meese Tyrer and of Margaret Joan Tyrer (*née* Wyatt); *m* 1974, Jane Beckett, JP, LLB, MA, barrister; one *s* one *d. Educ:* Wellington College; Bristol University. LLB hons. Called to the Bar, Inner Temple, 1968. Asst Recorder, 1979–83; a Recorder, 1983–89. Governor: St John's Sch., Lacey Green, 1984–92; Speen Sch., 1984–96 (Chm., 1989–91 and 1995–96); Misbourne Sch., 1993– (Vice Chm., 1995–2000, Chm., 2000–). Mem., Bucks Assoc. of Govs of Primary Schs, 1989–90. *Recreations:* music, boating, following Wycombe Wanderers Football Club. *Address:* Randalls Cottage, Loosley Row, Princes Risborough, Bucks HP27 0NU. *T:* (01844) 344650; Royal Courts of Justice, Strand, WC2A 2LL. *T:* (020) 7947 6430. *Club:* Reform.

TYRER, Prof. Peter Julian, MD; Professor of Community Psychiatry, since 1991, and Head of Department of Public Mental Health, since 1997, Imperial College School of Medicine; *b* 13 Aug. 1940; *s* (identical twin) of Frank Herbert Tyrer and Mary (May) Jane Tyrer; *m* 1967, Ann Anderson; one *s* two *d. Educ:* King Edward Sch., Birmingham; Gonville and Caius Coll., Cambridge (BA 1962; MB, BChir 1966; MD 1975); St Thomas's Hosp. Med. Sch., London. FRCPsych 1979; FRCP 1993. House Officer in Psychological Medicine, St Thomas' Hosp., 1966–67; Sen. House Officer in Medicine, Burton-on-Trent Gen. Hosp., 1967–68; Registrar in Psychiatry: St John's Hosp., Aylesbury, 1968–69; Maudsley Hosp., 1969–70; MRC Clin. Res. Fellow, 1970–73; Sen. Lectr in Psychiatry, Univ. of Southampton, 1973–79; Cons. Psychiatrist, Mapperley Hosp., Nottingham, 1979–88; Sen. Lectr in Community Psychiatry, St Mary's Hosp. Med. Sch., 1988–91. Andrew Woods Prof., Univ. of Iowa, 1986. European Pres., Internat. Soc. for Study of Personality Disorders, 1995–98. FMedSci 1999. Gaskell Bronze Medal and Res. Prize, RCPsych, 1973. *Publications:* The Role of Bodily Feelings in Anxiety, 1976; Insomnia, 1978; Stress, 1980; (ed) Drugs in Psychiatric Practice, 1982, 2nd edn 1997; How to Stop Taking Tranquillisers, 1986; (with D. Steinberg) Models for Mental Disorder, 1987, 3rd edn 1998; Personality Disorders: diagnosis, management and course, 1988, 2nd edn 2000; (ed) Psychopharmacology of Anxiety, 1989; Classification of Neurosis, 1989; (with C. Freeman) Research Methodology in Psychiatry: a beginner's guide, 1989, 3rd edn 2002; (with B. Puri) Sciences Basic to Psychiatry, 1992, 2nd edn 1998; (with P. Casey) Social Function in Psychiatry: the hidden axis of classification exposed, 1993; Anxiety: a multidisciplinary review, 1999. *Recreations:* jousting with social workers, anthropo-phytomorphy, doggerel. *Address:* 52 West Park Avenue, Kew Gardens, Surrey TW9 4AL. *T:* (020) 8876 7996.

TYRIE, Andrew Guy; MP (C) Chichester, since 1997; *b* 15 Jan. 1957; *s* of late Derek and of Patricia Tyrie. *Educ:* Felsted Sch.; Trinity Coll., Oxford (MA); Coll. of Europe, Bruges; Wolfson Coll., Cambridge (MPhil). BP, 1981–83; Cons. Res. Dept, 1983–84; Special Adviser: to Sec. of State for the Envmt, 1985; to Minister for Arts, 1985–86; to Chancellor of the Exchequer, 1986–90; Fellow, 1990–91, Woodrow Wilson Scholar, 1991, Nuffield Coll., Oxford; Sen. Economist, EBRD, 1992–97. Contested (C) Houghton and Washington, 1992. Member: Select Cttee on Public Admin, 1997–2001; Treasury Select Cttee, 2001–; Public Accounts Commn, 1997–. *Publications:* The Prospects for Public Spending, 1996; Sense on EMU, 1998; Reforming the Lords: a Conservative approach, 1998; Leviathan at Large: the new regulator for the financial markets, 2000; Mr Blair's Poodle: an agenda for reviving the House of Commons, 2000; pamphlets. *Recreation:* golf. *Address:* House of Commons, SW1A 0AA. *Clubs:* MCC, Royal Automobile.

TYRIE, Peter Robert; Managing Director, Eton Town House Group, since 1999; *b* 3 April 1946; *m* 1972, Christine Mary Tyrie; three *s* (and one *d* decd). *Educ:* Westminster College Hotel Sch. (BSc Hotel Admin). Manager, Inverurie Hotel, Bermuda, 1969–71; Resident Man., Portman Hotel, London, 1971–73; Project Dir, Pannell Kerr Forster, 1973–77; Operations Dir, Penta Hotels, 1977–80; Managing Director: Gleneagles Hotels plc, 1980–86; Mandarin Oriental Hotel Gp, 1986–89; Balmoral Internat. Hotels, 1989–98. Director: Bell's Whisky, 1983; Dragon Trust, Edinburgh Fund Managers, 1989–. FHCIMA 1977. *Recreations:* squash, shooting, fishing, Rugby, classic cars. *Address:* Ravelston Brae, 36 Ravelston Dykes Road, Edinburgh EH4 3NZ. *T:* (0131) 346 7874, (office) (020) 7432 8400.

TYRONE, Earl of; Henry Nicholas de la Poer Beresford; *b* 23 March 1958; *s* and *heir* of 8th Marquess of Waterford, *qv*; *m* 1986, Amanda, *d* of Norman Thompson; two *s* one *d. Educ:* Harrow School. *Heir: s* Baron Le Poer, *qv. Address:* Kennel House, Curraghmore, Portlaw, Co. Waterford, Ireland.

TYROR, John George, OBE 1999; JP; Director of Safety, United Kingdom Atomic Energy Authority, 1990–92, retired; *b* 5 Nov. 1930; *s* of John Thomas Tyror and Nora Tyror (*née* Tennant); *m* 1956, Sheila Wylie; one *s* one *d. Educ:* Manchester Univ. (BSc 1st cl. Hons Maths, MSc); Trinity Hall, Cambridge. FInstP. Asst Lectr, Univ. of Leeds, 1955–56; AEA Harwell, 1956–59; Atomic Energy Estabt, Winfrith, 1959–63; Reactor Develt Lab., Windscale, 1963–66; Winfrith, 1966–87 (Asst Dir, 1979–87); Dir, Safety and Reliability Directorate, Culcheth, 1987–90. Mem. Adv. Cttee on Safety of Nuclear Installations, 1992–95, Mem. Nuclear Safety Adv. Cttee, 1995–98, HSC. JP Macclesfield, 1976. *Publication:* An Introduction to the Neutron Kinetics of Nuclear Power Reactors, 1970. *Recreations:* tennis, golf, food and wine, antique map collecting, grandfather. *Clubs:* Lancashire CC, Knutsford Golf, Broadstone Golf, East Dorset Lawn Tennis and Croquet.

TYRRELL, Alan Rupert; QC 1976; FCIArb; a Recorder of the Crown Court, 1972–98; a Deputy High Court Judge, 1990–98; Barrister-at-Law; *b* 27 June 1933; *s* of Rev. T. G. R. Tyrrell, and Mrs W. A. Tyrrell, MSc; *m* 1960, Elaine Eleanor Ware, LLB; one *s* one *d. Educ:* Bridport Grammar Sch.; London Univ. (LLB). FCIArb 1993. Called to the Bar, Gray's Inn, 1956, Bencher, 1986. Mem., Criminal Injuries Compensation Bd, 1999– (Mem., Appeal Panel, 2000–). Chm. of the Bar Eur. Gp, 1986–88; Chm. of the Internat. Practice Cttee, Bar Council (co-opted to Bar Council), 1988. Lord Chancellor's Legal Visitor, 1990–; Arbitrator, Internat. Chamber of Commerce, Paris, 1999–. Dir, Papworth Hosp. NHS Trust, 1993–2000. Council Mem., Med. Protection Soc., 1990–98. Chm. London Reg., and Mem. Nat. Exec., Nat. Fedn of Self-Employed, 1978–79. Mem. (C) London E, European Parlt, 1979–84; contested same seat, 1984, 1989. *Publications:* (ed) Moore's Practical Agreements, 10th edn 1965; Students' Guide to Europe, 1984; The Legal Professions in the New Europe, 1992, 2nd edn 1996; Public Procurement in Europe: enforcement and remedies, 1997. *Recreation:* bridge. *Address:* 15 Willifield Way, Hampstead Garden Suburb, NW11 7XU. *T:* (020) 8455 5798; Francis Taylor Building, Temple, EC4Y 7BY. *T:* (020) 7797 7250. *Address:* Vaisse Lardin, 51 avenue Montaigne, 75008 Paris, France. *Club:* Athenæum.

TYRRELL, Dr David Arthur John, CBE 1980; FRCP, FRCPath; FRS 1970; Director, MRC Common Cold Unit, 1982–90, retired; *b* 19 June 1925; *s* of Sidney Charles Tyrrell and Agnes Kate (*née* Blewett); *m* 1950, Betty Moyra Wylie; two *d* (one *s* decd). *Educ:* Sheffield University (MB, ChB Hons; MD Hons). FRCP 1965. Junior hosp. appts, Sheffield, 1948–51; Asst, Rockefeller Inst., New York, 1951–54; Virus Research Lab., Sheffield, 1954–57; MRC Common Cold Unit, Salisbury, 1957–90; Dep. Dir of Clin. Res. Centre, Northwick Park, Harrow, and Head of Div. of Communicable Diseases, 1970–84. Chairman: (first), Adv. Cttee on Dangerous Pathogens, 1981–91; Consultative Cttee on Res. into Spongiform Encephalopathies, 1989–90; Spongiform Encephalopathy Adv. Cttee, 1990–95; Biol Sub-Cttee, Cttee on Safety of Medicines, 1989–92; Task Force on Chronic Fatigue Syndrome/Myalgic Encephalomyelitis/Post Viral Fatigue Syndrome, 1993–99. Managing Trustee, Nuffield Foundn, 1977–92. Sir Arthur Sims Commonwealth Travelling Prof., 1985. Hon. DSc Sheffield, 1979; Hon. DM Southampton, 1990. Stewart Prize, BMA, 1977; Ambuj Nath Bose Prize, 1983, Conway Evans Prize, 1986, RCP. *Publications:* Common Colds and Related Diseases, 1965; Interferon and its Clinical Potential, 1976; (jtly) Microbial Diseases, 1979; The Abolition of Infection: hope or illusion?, 1982; numerous papers on infectious diseases and viruses. *Recreations:* music-making, gardening, walking; various Christian organizations. *Address:* Ash Lodge, Dean Lane, Whiteparish, Salisbury, Wilts SP5 2RN. *T:* and *Fax:* (01794) 884352.

TYRRELL, Prof. (Henry John) Valentine, FRSC; Vice-Principal, King's College London (KQC), 1985–87, retired; *b* 14 Feb. 1920; *s* of John Rice Tyrrell and Josephine (*née* McGuinness); *m* 1st, 1947, Sheila Mabel (*née* Straw) (*d* 1985); three *s* three *d*; 2nd, 1986, Dr Bethan Davies. *Educ:* state schools; Jesus Coll., Oxford. DSc. Chemical Industry, 1942–47; Sheffield Univ., 1947–65; Chelsea College: Professor of Physical and Inorganic Chemistry, 1965–84; Head of Dept, 1972–82; Vice-Principal, 1976–84; Principal, 1984–85. Royal Institution of Great Britain: Sec., 1978–84; Vice-Pres., 1978–84, 1987–89, 1991–94; Chm. Council, 1987–89. *Publications:* Diffusion and Heat Flow in Liquids, 1961; Thermometric Titrimetry, 1968; Diffusion in Liquids, 1984; papers in chemical and physical jls. *Recreations:* foreign travel, gardening. *Address:* 5 Chapel Lane, Wilmslow, Cheshire SK9 5HZ. *Clubs:* Athenæum, Royal Institution.

TYRRELL, Prof. John, DPhil; Professorial Fellow, Music Department, Cardiff University, since 2000; *b* Salisbury, Southern Rhodesia, 17 Aug. 1942; *s* of Henry John Ranger Tyrrell and Florence Ellen Tyrrell (*née* Wright). *Educ:* St John's Coll., Johannesburg; Univ. of Cape Town (BMus); Lincoln Coll., Oxford (DPhil 1969). Associate Ed., Musical Times, 1972–76; Desk Ed., Grove's Dictionary of Music, 1973–76; University of Nottingham: Lectr in Music, 1976–89; Reader in Opera Studies, 1989–96; Prof., 1996–97; Exec. Ed., The New Grove Dictionary of Music and Musicians, 1997–2000 (Dep. Ed., 1996–97). British Acad. Res. Reader in the Humanities, 1992–94. Chm., Music Libraries Trust, 1999–. *Publications:* (with R. Wise) A Guide to International Congress Reports in Music 1900–1975, 1979; Leoš Janáček: Kát'a Kabanová, 1982; Czech Opera, 1988 (Czech trans. 1992); Janáček's Operas: a documentary account, 1992; (ed and trans.) Intimate Letters: Leoš Janáček to Kamila Stösslová, 1994; (ed with Charles Mackerras) Janáček's Jenůfa, 1996; (jtly) Janáček's Works: a catalogue of the music and writings of Leoš Janáček, 1997; (ed and trans.) Zdenka Janáčková: my life with Janáček, 1998. *Recreations:* gardening, walking. *Address:* Music Department, Cardiff University, 31 Corbett Road, Cardiff CF1 3EB. *T:* (029) 2087 4816.

TYRRELL, Robert James; Development Partner, Cognosis Strategy Consultants, since 1999; Chairman: Sociovision UK, since 2001; Global Future Forum Europe, since 2001; *b* 6 June 1951; *s* of Peter John Tyrrell and Mair (*née* Harries); *m* 1983, Jean Linda McKerrow; two *d. Educ:* St Peter's Coll., Oxford (MA, PPE), LSE (MSc Phil with dist.). Academic research, Sussex and Glasgow Univs, 1972–74; joined James Morrell & Associates, 1974; Perkins Engines, 1977; Futures Group, USA, 1980; Man. Dir, 1986–92, Chief Exec., 1992–95, Exec. Chm., 1995–96, Henley Centre for Forecasting. Chm., Internat. Res. Inst. on Social Change, Paris, 1999–2000. Vis. Prof., City Univ. Business Sch., 1994–. Director: New Solutions, 1997–2000; La Table du Pain, Luxembourg, 1999–; Sociovision, Paris, 2000–. Member: Adv. Council of Demos, 1992– (Trustee, 2001–); Steering Cttee, Econ. Beliefs and Behaviour Prog., ESRC, 1994–99; Council, Conservative Party Policy Forum, 1999–. Presenter: Opinions, C4, 1994; Analysis, BBC Radio, 1997–. FRSA. *Publications:* (ed jtly) Britain in the 1980s, 1974; (ed jtly) Britain 2001, 1977; (ed jtly) Planning for Social Change, 1991; Things Can Only Get... Different, 2001. *Recreations:* cycling, ski-ing, theatre, reading, family, holistic thinking. *Address:* Warberry Lodge, Lansdown Road, Bath BA1 5RB.

TYRRELL, Valentine; *see* Tyrrell, H. J. V.

TYRWHITT, Sir Reginald (Thomas Newman), 3rd Bt *cr* 1919; *b* 21 Feb. 1947; *er s* of Admiral Sir St John Tyrwhitt, 2nd Bt, KCB, DSO, DSC and Bar (*d* 1961), and of Nancy (Veronica) Gilbey (who *m* 1965, Sir Godfrey Agnew, KCVO, CB); *S* father, 1961; *m* 1972, Sheila Gail (marr. diss. 1980 and annulled 1984), *d* of William Alistair Crawford Nicoll, Liphook, Hants; *m* 1984, Charlotte, *o d* of late Captain and the Hon. Mrs Angus Hildyard, Goxhill Hall, Goxhill, N Lincs; one *s* one *d. Educ:* Downside. 2nd Lieut, RA, 1966, Lieut 1969; RARO 1969. *Recreations:* shooting, fishing, drawing. *Heir: s* Robert St John Hildyard Tyrwhitt, *b* 15 Feb. 1987.

TYSOE, John Sidney; Chairman, Yorkshire Electricity Group, 1992–94; *b* 14 March 1932; *s* of Florence Alice Tysoe (*née* Gypps) and late Sidney George Tysoe; *m* 1953, Ann Dunham; two *s* one *d. Educ:* Harrow Weald County Grammar Sch.; City of London Coll. FCCA, CPFA, CompIEE. Nat. Service Commn, RN, 1950–52. Exchequer and Audit Dept, 1953–65; Southern Electricity Bd, 1966–67; Head, Special Investigations and Asst Management Accountant, BR, 1967–68; Asst and Dep. Financial Advr, Electricity Council, 1969–77; Chief Accountant and Financial Dir, Southern Electricity Bd, 1978–85; Dep. Chm., Yorkshire Electricity Bd, 1985–89; Gp Man. Dir, Yorkshire

Electricity Gp, 1989–92. Mem. Council, CBI, 1993–94. *Recreations:* walking, woodcarving, theatre.

TYSON, Prof. Laura D'Andrea, PhD; Dean of London Business School, since 2002; *b* 28 June 1947; *m* Erik Tarloff; one *s*. *Educ:* Smith Coll. (BA 1969); MIT (PhD 1974). Asst Prof., Dept of Econs, Princeton Univ., 1974–77; University of California, Berkeley: Prof. of Econs, 1977–2002; Prof., 1990–2002, Dean, 1998–2002, Haas Sch. of Business; Dir, Inst. of Internat. Studies, 1990–92; Dir of Res., Berkeley Roundtable on Internat. Economy, 1988–92; Dist. Teaching Award, 1982. Chairman: US President's Council of Econ. Advrs, 1993–95; Nat. Econ. Council, 1995–96; Principal, Law and Econs Consulting Gp, 1997–; Mem., Council on Foreign Relations, 1987–. Fellow, Nat. Fellows Prog., Hoover Inst., 1978–79. *Publications:* The Yugoslav Economic System and its Performance in the 1970s, 1980; (ed with Egon Neuberger) The Impact of External Economic Disturbances on the Soviet Union and Eastern Europe, 1980; (ed with John Zysman) American Industry in International Competition: political and economic perspectives, 1983; Economic Adjustment in Eastern Europe, 1984; (ed with Ellen Comisso) Power, Purpose and Collective Choice: economic strategy in socialist states, 1986; (ed with William T. Dickens and John Zysman) The Politics of Productivity: the real story of why Japan works, 1989; Who's Bashing Whom? trade conflict in high technology industries, 1992; articles in professional jls. *Address:* London Business School, Regent's Park, NW1 4SA. *T:* (020) 7262 5050.

TYSON, Monica Elizabeth; Editor, A La Carte, 1986–87, retired; *b* 7 June 1927; *d* of F. S. Hill and E. Hill; *m* 1st, 1950, P. M. Lyon (marr. diss. 1958); one *d*; 2nd, 1960, R. E. D. Tyson. *Educ:* George Watson's Ladies Coll.; Edinburgh Coll. of Domestic Science. Asst Home Editor, Modern Woman, 1958–60; Ideal Home: Domestic Planning Editor, 1960–64; Asst Editor, 1964–68; Editor, 1968–77; Editor: Woman's Realm, 1977–82; Special Assignments, IPC Magazines, 1982–84; Mother, 1984–86. *Recreations:* travelling, reading. *Address:* Ramsgate, Kent.

TYSZKIEWICZ, Zygmunt Jan Ansgary, CMG 1998; President, Lanckoronski Foundation, since 1996; *b* 4 Feb. 1934; *s* of Count Jan Michal Tyszkiewicz and Anna Maria Tyszkiewicz (*née* Princess Radziwill); *m* 1958, Kerstin Barbro Ekman; two *s* two *d*. *Educ:* Downside Sch.; Sidney Sussex Coll., Cambridge (BA Hons Mod. and Medieval Langs). Officer, XII Royal Lancers, 1956–57. Joined Shell International Petroleum, 1957: Man. Dir, Shell-BP Tanzania, 1970–73; Gen. Manager, Shell Hellas, 1979–85; Sec. Gen., UNICE, Brussels, 1985–98. Member: Bd, Eur. Foundn for Mgt Develt, Brussels, 1985–98; Adv. Council, Involvement and Participation Assoc., London, 1998–. Gov., Eur. Policy Forum, London, 1998–. Hon. DBA Robert Gordon Univ., 2000. Kt of Malta, 1994; Kt, Order of Dannebrog (Denmark), 1997; Comdr, Order of Leopold (Belgium), 1998. *Publications:* contrib. numerous articles on European and business issues in UK and European jls. *Recreations:* family holidays in Corfu, Greece, politics of European integration. *Address:* 5 Champneys Walk, Cambridge CB3 9AW. *T:* (01223) 302816, *Fax:* (01223) 368596; *e-mail:* ZygTysz@aol.com; (May–Sept.) Kouloura, 49100 Corfu Greece. *T:* (663) 91662, *Fax:* (663) 91663. *Clubs:* Cavalry and Guards; Cercle Royal Gaulois Artistique et Littéraire (Brussels).

TYTE, David Christopher, CB 1997; PhD; Director Rationalisation, Defence Evaluation and Research Agency, Ministry of Defence, 1991–97; *b* 19 Aug. 1937. *Educ:* Dulwich Coll.; Imperial Coll., London (PhD, BSc). CEng, FInstP, MIEE. NRC Post Doctoral Fellow, Univ. of Western Ontario, 1962–65; Asst Prof., York Univ., Toronto, 1965–67; joined MoD, 1967; Dep. Dir (Underwater), Admiralty Res. Estabt, 1987–89; Technical Dir, DRA, 1989–91.

TYZACK, David Ian Heslop; QC 1999; **His Honour Judge Tyzack;** a Circuit Judge, since 2000; *b* 21 March 1946; *s* of late Ernest Rudolf Tyzack and Joan Mary Tyzack (*née* Palmer); *m* 1973, Elizabeth Anne Cubitt; one *s* one *d*. *Educ:* Allhallows Sch., Rousdon; St Catharine's Coll., Cambridge (MA 1969). Called to the Bar, Inner Temple, 1970; in practice at the Bar, Western Circuit, 1971–2000; Asst Recorder, 1996–2000; Recorder, 2000; a Dep. High Ct Judge, 2000–. Chm., Devon and Cornwall Br., Family Law Bar Assoc., 1992–2000. Mem., Devonshire Assoc. Churchwarden, Farringdon Ch, Devon, 1992–. *Publication:* (contrib.) Essential Family Practice, 2001. *Recreations:* gardening, house in France, ski-ing, church. *Address:* Southernhay Chambers, 33 Southernhay East, Exeter EX1 1NX. *T:* (01392) 255777, *Fax:* (01392) 412021.

TYZACK, Margaret Maud, OBE 1970; *b* 9 Sept. 1931; *d* of Thomas Edward Tyzack and Doris Moseley; *m* 1958, Alan Stephenson; one *s*. *Educ:* St Angela's Ursuline Convent; Royal Academy of Dramatic Art. Trained at RADA (Gilbert Prize for Comedy). First engagement, Civic Theatre, Chesterfield. Vassilissa in The Lower Depths, Royal Shakespeare Co., Arts Theatre, 1962; Lady MacBeth, Nottingham, 1962; Miss Frost in The Ginger Man, Royal Court, London, 1964; Madame Ranevsky in The Cherry Orchard, Exeter and Tour, 1969; Jacqui in Find Your Way Home, Open Space Theatre, London, 1970; Queen Elizabeth in Vivat! Vivat Regina!, Piccadilly, 1971; Tamora in Titus Andronicus, Portia in Julius Caesar and Volumnia in Coriolanus, Royal Shakespeare Co., Stratford-on-Avon, 1972; Portia in Julius Caesar, and Volumnia in Coriolanus, RSC, Aldwych, 1973; Maria Lvovna in Summerfolk, RSC, Aldwych, and NY, 1974–75; Richard III, All's Well That Ends Well, Ghosts, Stratford, Ont., 1977; People Are Living There, Manchester Royal Exchange, 1979; Martha, in Who's Afraid of Virginia Woolf?, Nat. Theatre, 1981 (Best Actress, Olivier Award); Countess of Rossilion, in All's Well That Ends Well, RSC Barbican and NY, 1983; An Inspector Calls, Greenwich, 1983; Tom and Viv, Royal Court, 1984, also New York, 1985; Mornings at Seven, Westminster, 1984; Night Must Fall, Greenwich, 1986; Lettice and Lovage, Globe, 1987 (Variety Club of GB Award for Best Stage Actress), and New York, 1990 (Tony award); The Importance of Being Earnest, Aldwych, 1993; An Inspector Calls, Aldwych, 1994; Indian Ink, Aldwych, 1995; Talking Heads, Chichester, 1996, and Comedy, 1996–97; The Family Reunion, RSC, 1999. *Films:* Ring of Spies, 2001: A Space Odyssey, The Whisperers, A Clockwork Orange, The Legacy, The King's Whore. *Television series include:* The Forsyte Saga; The First Churchills; Cousin Bette, 1970–71; I, Claudius, 1976; Quatermass, 1979; The Winter's Tale; Young Indiana Jones, 1992. Actress of the Year Award (BAFTA) for Queen Anne in The First Churchills, 1969. *Address:* c/o Representation Joyce Edwards, 275 Kennington Road, SE11 6BY. *T:* (020) 7735 5736, *Fax:* (020) 7820 1845.

U

UCHIDA, Mitsuko, Hon. CBE; pianist; *b* 20 Dec. 1948; *d* of Fujio and Yasuko Uchida. *Educ:* Hochschule für Musik, Vienna. First recital at age of 14 in Vienna; performs regularly with orchestras worldwide incl. Berlin Philharmonic, Vienna Philharmonic, Cleveland, etc.; performed complete Mozart piano sonatas in London, 1982, Tokyo, 1983, and NY, 1991; Schubert and Schoenberg recitals in Salzburg, London, Vienna, NY, Tokyo, etc, 1994–96; repertoire ranges from J. S. Bach to Messiaen. Recordings include: complete piano sonatas and concertos of Mozart; Beethoven's piano concertos; Debussy's Etudes; Schumann's Carnaval; Schoenberg piano concerto. Has won many prizes for recordings. *Recreations:* sleeping, listening to music. *Address:* c/o Van Walsum Management, 4 Addison Bridge Place, W14 8XP. *T:* (020) 7371 4343.

UDDIN, family name of **Baroness Uddin**.

UDDIN, Baroness *cr* 1998 (Life Peer), of Bethnal Green in the London Borough of Tower Hamlets; **Pola Manzila Uddin;** *b* 17 July 1959; *m* 1976, Komar Uddin; four *s*, one *d*. Youth and Community Worker, YWCA, 1980–82; Liaison Officer, Tower Hamlets Social Services, 1982–84; Manager: Women's Health Project, 1984–88; Asian Family Counselling Service, 1989–90; Social Worker, Manager and subseq. Mgt Consultant, London Borough of Newham Social Services, 1993–98. Mem. (Lab), Tower Hamlets LBC, 1990–98 (Dep. Leader, Lab Gp, 1993–94; Dep. Leader, Council, 1994–96; served on educn, social services and policy and resources cttees). Mem., H of L European Communities Cttee. Member: CPA; IPU; CETSW. *Address:* House of Lords, SW1A 0PW. *T:* (020) 7219 3000.

UDEN, Martin David; HM Diplomatic Service; International Director, Invest-UK, since 2001; *b* 28 Feb. 1955; *s* of Rodney Frederick Uden and Margaret Irene Uden (*née* Brunt); *m* 1982, Fiona Jane Smith; two *s*. *Educ:* Ravensbourne Sch. for Boys; Queen Mary Coll., London Univ. (LLB). Called to the Bar, Inner Temple, 1977; joined FCO, 1977; Second Sec., Seoul, 1978–81; Second, later First Sec., FCO, 1981–86; First Sec., Bonn, 1986–90; FCO, 1990–93; Dep. Head, CSCE Unit, FCO, 1993–94; Pol Counsellor and Consul-Gen., Seoul, 1994–97; Econ., then Trade/Econ., Counsellor, Ottawa, 1997–2001. *Publications:* (with T. Bennett) Korea: caught in time, 1997; Times Past in Korea, 2002. *Address:* c/o Foreign and Commonwealth Office, King Charles Street, SW1A 2AH.

UFF, Prof. John Francis, PhD; FREng, FICE; FCIArb; QC; international arbitrator, advocate and engineer; Nash Professor of Engineering Law, University of London, since 1991; a Recorder, since 1998; *b* 30 Jan. 1942; *s* of Frederick and Eva Uff; *m* 1967, Diana Muriel Graveson; two *s* one *d*. *Educ:* Stratton Sch.; King's College London (BSc (Eng), PhD; FKC 1997). Asst engineer, Rendel Palmer & Tritton, 1966–70; Vis. Lectr in civil engineering, 1963–68; called to the Bar, Gray's Inn, 1970, Bencher, 1993; practice at Bar, Keating Chambers, 1970–, Head of Chambers, 1992–97; Asst Recorder, 1993–98; a Dep. Judge, Technology and Construction Court, 1999–. Dir, Centre of Construction Law and Management, KCL, 1987–99; arbitrator in construction disputes; lectr to professional bodies in engineering law and arbitration. Member: Standing Cttee on Structural Safety, 1984–90; Bldg Users Insurance against Latent Defects Cttee, DoE, 1986–88; Adv. Cttee on arbitration law, DTI, 1993–95. Chairman: Indep. Commn of Inquiry into Yorks Water, 1996; Public Inquiry into Southall Rail Accident, 1997–99; Jt Chm., Public Inquiry into Rail Safety Systems, 1999–2000. Member, Council: ICE, 1982–85; Soc. Construction Law, 1990–98. Vice-Pres., KCL Assoc., 1993–95. FREng (FEng 1995). Prin. Ed., book series of Centre of Construction Law and Mgt, KCL, on construction law, management, environment law and dispute resolution, 1988–. President's Medal, Soc. Construction Law, 2000. *Publications:* Construction Law, 1974, 7th edn 1999; (contrib.) Commentary on Institution of Civil Engineers Conditions of Contract, 4th edn 1978 to 7th edn, as Keating on Building Contracts, 2000; (jtly) ICE Arbitration Practice, 1986; (jtly) Methods of Procurement in Ground Investigation, 1986; (principal draftsman) Construction Industry Model Arbitration Rules, 1998; (contrib.) Chitty on Contracts, 28th edn 1999; technical papers in civil engineering; papers and articles in engineering law and procedure. *Recreations:* playing with violins, painting, farming. *Address:* 10 Essex Street, Outer Temple, WC2R 3AA. *T:* (020) 7240 6981; Ashtead Farm, Selside, Cumbria. *Clubs:* Athenæum, Ronnie Scott's.

UFFEN, Kenneth James, CMG 1977; HM Diplomatic Service, retired; Ambassador and UK Permanent Representative to OECD, Paris, 1982–85; *b* 29 Sept. 1925; *s* of late Percival James Uffen, MBE, former Civil Servant, and late Gladys Ethel James; *m* 1954, Nancy Elizabeth Winbolt; one *s* two *d*. *Educ:* Latymer Upper Sch.; St Catharine's Coll., Cambridge. HM Forces (Flt-Lt, RAFVR), 1943–48; St Catharine's Coll., 1948–50; 3rd Sec., FO, 1950–52; Paris, 1952–55; 2nd Sec., Buenos Aires, 1955–58; 1st Sec., FO, 1958–61; 1st Sec. (Commercial), Moscow, 1961–63; seconded to HM Treasury, 1963–65; FCO, 1965–68; Counsellor, Mexico City, 1968–70; Economic Counsellor, Washington, 1970–72; Commercial Counsellor, Moscow, 1972–76; Res. Associate, IISS, 1976–77; Ambassador to Colombia, 1977–82. *Recreations:* music, gardens. *Address:* 40 Winchester Road, Walton-on-Thames, Surrey KT12 2RH.

UGANDA, Archbishop of, since 1994; **Most Rev. Livingstone Mpalanyi-Nkoyoyo;** *b* 1937. *Educ:*; Buwalasi Coll., Uganda; Legon Trinity Coll., Ghana; East Bond Coll., England. Car mechanic; chauffeur to Bishop Lutaaya, dio. of W Buganda; ordained deacon, 1969, priest, 1970; served in parish: Kasubi, 1969–75; Nsangi, 1975–77; Archdeacon of Namirembe, 1977–79; Suffragan Bishop: dio. of Namirembe, 1980–81; dio. of Mukono, 1981–94. *Address:* PO Box 14123, Kampala, Uganda. *T:* (office) (41) 270218; (residence) (41) 271138.

ULLENDORFF, Prof. Edward, MA Jerusalem, DPhil Oxford; FBA 1965; Professor of Semitic Languages, School of Oriental and African Studies, University of London, 1979–82, now Professor Emeritus (Professor of Ethiopian Studies, 1964–79; Head of Africa Department, 1972–77); *b* 25 Jan. 1920; *s* of late Frederic and Cilli Ullendorff; *m* 1943, Dina Noack. *Educ:* Gymnasium Graues Kloster; Universities of Jerusalem and Oxford. Chief Examiner, British Censorship, Eritrea, 1942–43; Editor, African Publ., British Ministry of Information, Eritrea–Ethiopia, 1943–45; Assistant Political Secretary, British Military Admin, Eritrea, 1945–46; Asst Secretary, Palestine Government, 1947–48; Research Officer and Librarian, Oxford Univ. Inst. of Colonial Studies, 1948–49; Scarbrough Senior Research Studentship in Oriental Languages, 1949–50; Reader (Lectr, 1950–56) in Semitic Languages, St Andrews Univ., 1956–59; Professor of Semitic Languages and Literatures, University of Manchester, 1959–64. Carnegie Travelling Fellow to Ethiopia, 1958; Research Journeys to Ethiopia, 1964, 1966, 1969. Catalogued Ethiopian Manuscripts in Royal Library, Windsor Castle. Chairman: Assoc. of British Orientalists, 1963–64; Anglo-Ethiopian Soc., 1965–68 (Vice-Pres. 1969–77); Pres., Soc. for Old Testament Study, 1971; Vice-Pres., RAS, 1975–79, 1981–85. Joint Organizer, 2nd Internat. Congress of Ethiopian Studies, Manchester, 1963. Chm., Editorial Bd, Bulletin of SOAS, 1968–78; Mem., Adv. Bd, British Library, 1975–83. Vice-Pres., British Acad., 1980–82; Schweich Lectr, British Acad., 1967. FRAS; Hon. Fellow: SOAS, 1985; Oxford Centre for Hebrew Studies, 1998; Foreign Fellow, Accademia Lincei, 1998. Imperial Ethiopian Gold Medallion, 1960; Haile Sellassie Internat. Prize for Ethiopian studies, 1972. MA Manchester, 1962; Hon. DLitt St Andrews, 1972; Hon. Dr Phil Hamburg, 1990. *Publications:* The definite article in the Semitic languages, 1941; Exploration and Study of Abyssinia, 1945; Catalogue of Ethiopian Manuscripts in the Bodleian Library, Oxford, 1951; The Semitic Languages of Ethiopia, 1955; The Ethiopians, 1959, 3rd edn 1973; (with Stephen Wright) Catalogue of Ethiopian MSS in Cambridge University Library, 1961; Comparative Semitics in Linguistica Semitica, 1961; (with S. Moscati and others) Introduction to Comparative Grammar of Semitic Languages, 1964; An Amharic Chrestomathy, 1965, 2nd edn 1978; The Challenge of Amharic, 1965; Ethiopia and the Bible, 1968; (with J. B. Pritchard and others) Solomon and Sheba, 1974; annotated and trans., Emperor Haile Sellassie, My Life and Ethiopia's Progress (autobiog.), 1976; Studies in Semitic Languages and Civilizations, 1977; (with M. A. Knibb) Book of Enoch, 1978; The Bawdy Bible, 1979; (jtly) The Amharic Letters of Emperor Theodore of Ethiopia to Queen Victoria, 1979; (with C. F. Beckingham) The Hebrew Letters of Prester John, 1982; A Tigrinya Chrestomathy, 1985; Studia Aethiopica et Semitica, 1987; The Two Zions, 1988; From the Bible to Enrico Cerulli, 1990; H. J. Polotsky (1905–1991), 1992; From Emperor Haile Sellassie to H. J. Polotsky, 1995; Joint Editor of Studies in honour of G. R. Driver, 1962; Joint Editor of Ethiopian Studies, 1964; articles and reviews in journals of learned societies; contribs to Encyclopaedia Britannica, Encyclopaedia of Islam, etc; Joint Editor, Journal of Semitic Studies, 1961–64. *Recreations:* music, motoring in Scotland. *Address:* 4 Bladon Close, Oxford OX2 8AD.

ULLMANN, (Frederick) Ralph, MA; Headmaster, Wellingborough School, since 1993; *b* 29 July 1945; *s* of late Prof. Walter Ullmann, FBA and Elizabeth Ullmann (*née* Knapp); *m* 1980, Alison Kemp; two *s* one *d*. *Educ:* Trinity Coll., Cambridge (schol.; MA; PGCE). FCollP (ACP). History Teacher, and Head of Gen. Studies, Bishop's Stortford Coll., 1968–72; Head of History and Sen. Housemaster, Bloxham Sch., 1972–85; Headmaster, Ruthin Sch., 1986–93. Member: SHA, 1986– (Mem. Council, 1997–); HMC, 1993– (Member: Community Service Cttee, 1995–2001; Professional Develt Cttee, 1997–; Cttee, 1998–99; Sec., 1998, Chm., 1999, Midland Div.). Founding Dir, Bd, Castle Theatre and Arts Centre, Wellingborough, 1994–98. Mem. Adv. Bd, Rudolf Kempe Soc., 2000–. *Recreations:* photography, music, wine. *Address:* Wellingborough School, Northants NN8 2BX. *T:* (01933) 222427. *Club:* East India.

ULLMANN, Liv (Johanne); actress; *b* Tokyo, 16 Dec. 1938; *d* of late Viggo Ullmann and of Janna (*née* Lund), Norway; *m* 1st, 1960, Dr Gappe Stang (marr. diss. 1965); 2nd, 1985, Donald Saunders. *Educ:* Norway; London (dramatic trng). Stage début, The Diary of Anne Frank (title role), Stavanger, 1956; major roles, National Theatre and Norwegian State Theatre, Oslo; Amer. stage début, A Doll's House, New York Shakespeare Festival, 1974–75; Anna Christie, USA, 1977; The Bear, La Voix humaine, Australia, 1978; I Remember Mama, USA, and Ghosts (Ibsen), Broadway, 1979; British theatre début, Old Times, Guildford, 1985. Wrote and dir. short film, Parting, 1981. Twelve hon. doctorates, including Brown, Smith Coll., Tufts and Haifa. *Films:* Pan, 1965; The Night Visitor, 1971; Pope Joan, 1972; The Emigrants, 1972 (Golden Globe Award); The New Land, 1973 (Best Actress, Nat. Soc. of Film Critics, USA); Lost Horizon, 1973; 40 Carats, 1973 (Golden Globe Award); Zandy's Bride, 1973; The Abdication, 1974; The Wild Duck, 1983; The Bay Boy, 1985; Let's Hope it's a Girl, 1987; Mosca Addio, 1987; Time of Indifference, 1987; La Amiga, 1987; The Ox, 1993; *director:* Sophie, 1993; Kristin Lavrandsdatter (also wrote screenplay), 1995; Private Confessions, 1996; Faithless, 2000; (*dir. by Ingmar Bergman*): Persona, 1966; The Hour of the Wolf, 1968 (Best Actress, Nat. Soc. of Film Critics, USA); Shame, 1968 (Best Actress, Nat. Soc. of Film Critics, USA); The Passion of Anna, 1969; Cries and Whispers, 1972; Scenes from a Marriage, 1974; Face to Face, 1976; The Serpent's Egg, 1977; The Autumn Sonata, 1978 (5 NY Film Critics awards). Goodwill Ambassador, UNICEF, 1980–; Vice Pres., Internat. Rescue Cttee. Peer Gynt Award, Norway (1st female recipient). Commander, Order of St Olav (Norway), 1994. *Publications:* (autobiog.) Changing, 1977; Choices, 1984. *Address:* c/o Robert Lantz, 888 Seventh Avenue, New York, NY 10106, USA; c/o London Management, 2–4 Noel Street, W1V 3RB.

ULLMANN, Ralph; *see* Ullmann, F. R.

ULLRICH, Kay Morrison; Member (SNP) West of Scotland, Scottish Parliament, since 1999; *b* 5 May 1943; *d* of John Dallas Morrison and Charlotte McMillan Morrison (*née* Neil); *m* 1st, 1964, Andrew Jofre (marr. diss.); one *s* one *d*; 2nd, 1976, Grady Ullrich. *Educ:*

Ayr Acad.; Queen's Coll., Glasgow (CQSW). Schools swimming instructor, N Ayrshire, 1973–81; sch. social worker, 1984–86, hosp. social worker, 1986–92, Strathclyde; sen. court social worker, E Ayrshire, 1992–97. Spokesperson on health and community care and Mem., Health and Community Care Cttee, Scottish Parlt, 1999–. Vice-Pres., SNP, 1997–99. Contested (SNP): Cunninghame S, 1983 and 1987; Motherwell S, 1992; Monklands E, June 1994. *Recreations:* swimming, travel, meeting friends. *Address:* Scottish Parliament, Edinburgh EH99 1SP. *T:* (0131) 348 5668; Tulsa, Montgomeryfield, Dreghorn, Irvine KA11 4HB. *T:* (01294) 213331.

ULLSTEIN, Augustus Rupert Patrick Anthony; QC 1992; a Recorder, since 1999; *b* 21 March 1947; *s* of Frederick Charles Leopold Ullstein and Patricia (*née* Guinness); *m* 1970, Pamela Margaret Wells; two *s* two *d*. *Educ:* Bradfield Coll., Berks; LSE (LLB Hons). Called to the Bar, Inner Temple, 1970; in practice as barrister, 1970–; an Asst Recorder, 1993–99. *Publications:* (Supervising Editor) Pelling and Purdie, Matrimonial Injunctions, 1982. *Recreations:* my children, after dinner speaking. *Address:* 29 Bedford Row, Holborn, WC1R 4HE. *T:* (020) 7831 2626.

ULLSWATER, 2nd Viscount *cr* 1921, of Campsea Ashe, Suffolk; **Nicholas James Christopher Lowther;** PC 1994; Private Secretary, Comptroller and Equerry to Princess Margaret, Countess of Snowdon, since 1998; *b* 9 Jan. 1942; *s* of Lieut John Arthur Lowther, MVO, RNVR (*d* 1942), and Priscilla Violet (*d* 1945), *yr d* of Reginald Everitt Lambert; *S* great-grandfather, 1949; *m* 1967, Susan, *d* of James Howard Weatherby; two *s* two *d*. *Educ:* Eton; Trinity Coll., Cambridge. Captain, Royal Wessex Yeomanry, T&AVR, 1973–78. A Lord in Waiting (Govt Whip), H of L, 1989–90; Parly Under-Sec. of State, Dept of Employment, 1990–93; Capt. of Corps of Gentlemen at Arms (Govt Chief Whip), H of L, 1993–94; Minister of State (Minister for Construction and Planning), DoE, 1994–95. *Heir: s* Hon. Benjamin James Lowther, *b* 26 Nov. 1975. *Address:* The Old Rectory, Docking, King's Lynn, Norfolk PE31 8LJ. *T:* (01485) 518822.

ULRICH, Walter Otto; Deputy Secretary, Department of Education and Science, 1977–87; *b* 1 April 1927. Ministry of Works: Asst Principal, 1951; Principal, 1955; Treasury 1958–60; Principal Private Sec. to Minister of Public Building and Works, 1963–65; Asst Sec., 1965; Min. of Housing and Local Govt, 1966; DoE, 1970; Under-Sec., 1972; Cabinet Office, 1974–76. *Address:* 46 Grinstead Lane, Lancing, W Sussex BN15 9DZ. *T:* (01903) 762169.

ULSTER, Earl of; Alexander Patrick Gregers Richard Windsor; *b* 24 Oct. 1974; *s* of HRH The Duke of Gloucester and HRH The Duchess of Gloucester. *Educ:* Eton Coll.; King's Coll., London Univ. (BA War Studies 1996); RMA, Sandhurst. Commnd King's Royal Hussars, 1998.

See under Royal Family.

UNDERHILL, Prof. Allan Edward, PhD, DSc; CChem, FRSC; Professor of Inorganic Chemistry, University College of North Wales, then University of Wales, Bangor, 1983–99, now Emeritus; *b* 13 Dec. 1935; *s* of Albert Edward Underhill and Winifred Underhill (*née* Bailey); *m* 1960, Audrey Jean Foster; one *s* one *d*. *Educ:* Univ. of Hull (BSc 1958; PhD 1962); DSc Wales 1983. Res. Chemist, ICI Ltd, 1961–62; Lectr, Loughborough CAT, 1962–65; University College of North Wales (Bangor): Lectr, 1965–74; Sen. Lectr, 1974–83; Dean, Faculty of Sci., 1985–87, 1994–95; Pro-Vice-Chancellor, 1995–99. *Publications:* over 250 res. papers in RSC jls, Nature, etc. *Recreations:* theatre, walking, photography. *Address:* 4 Pennywell, Darwins Wood, Shrewsbury SY3 8BY. *T:* (01743) 243448.

UNDERHILL, Herbert Stuart; President, Victoria (BC) Press, 1978–79; Publisher, Victoria Times, 1971–78, retired; *b* 20 May 1914; *s* of Canon H. J. Underhill and Helena (*née* Ross); *m* 1937, Emma Gwendolyn MacGregor; one *s* one *d*. *Educ:* University Sch., Victoria, BC. Correspondent and Editor, The Canadian Press, Vancouver, BC, Toronto, New York and London, 1936–50; Reuters North American Editor, 1950; Asst General Manager, Reuters, 1958; Managing Editor, 1965–68; Dep. Gen. Manager, with special responsibility for North and South America and Caribbean, 1963–70. Director: Canadian Daily Newspaper Publishers' Assoc., 1972–76; The Canadian Press, 1972–78. *Publication:* The Iron Church, 1984. *Recreations:* travel, reading. *Address:* 308 Beach Drive, Victoria, BC V8S 2M2, Canada.

UNDERHILL, Prof. Michael James, PhD; FREng; Professor of Electronics, University of Surrey, since 1992; *b* 22 March 1939; *s* of Gp Capt. (retd) Rev. Wilfrid Underhill, DSC and Barbara Nowell Underhill (*née* James); *m* 1977, Gillian Brown; two *s*. *Educ:* St John's Sch., Leatherhead; Oriel Coll., Oxford (Schol.; Bible Schol.; Capt. of Boats, 1959–60; BA Physics 1960; MA); Univ. of Surrey (PhD Electronics 1972). FIEE 1982; FREng (FEng 1982). Philips Res. Labs (formerly Mullard Res. Labs), 1960–84 (Head of Systems Div., 1982–84); Tech. Dir, MEL (Philips), 1984–90; Engrg Dir, Thorn EMI Sensors Div., 1990–91; Head of Dept, Electronic and Electrical Engrg, 1992–96, Dean of Engrg, 1996–97, Univ. of Surrey (Vis. Lectr on Systems Engrg, 1968–82; Vis. Prof., 1984–90). Chm., European Frequency and Time Forum, 1996. Member: NATS Res. Adv. Council, 1996–99; Defence Science Adv. Council, 1982–96 (Chm., various bds and cttees). Institution of Electrical Engineers: Mem. Council, 1992–; Chm., Electronics Div., 1993–94; Chm., Surrey Centre, 1996–97; P. Perring Thoms Award, 1981; J. J. Thomson Award, 1993. Parish Councillor, Rusper, 1977–83. FRSA 1992. *Publications:* 48 patents; 60 papers on frequency control, phase noise, radio and other electronic systems. *Recreations:* licensed radio amateur since 1956, amateur dramatics (Trustee and Pres., Ifield Barn Theatre Club), jazz piano, hack and bash gardening. *Address:* University of Surrey, Guildford, Surrey GU2 7XH. *T:* (01483) 879134.

UNDERHILL, Nicholas Edward; QC 1992; a Recorder, since 1994; Attorney General to the Prince of Wales, since 1998; *b* 12 May 1952; *s* of late Judge Underhill, QC and Rosalie Jean Underhill (who *m* 1989, William Anderson Beaumont, *qv*); *m* 1987, Nina Grunfeld; two *s* two *d*. *Educ:* Winchester Coll.; New Coll., Oxford (MA Hons). Called to the Bar, Gray's Inn, 1976, Bencher, 2000. A Dep. High Court Judge, 1998–; a Judge of the Employment Appeal Tribunal, 2000–. Vice-Chm., Bar Pro Bono Unit, 2000–. *Publication:* The Lord Chancellor, 1978. *Address:* Fountain Court, Temple, EC4Y 9DH. *T:* (020) 7583 3335, *Fax:* (020) 7353 0329; *e-mail:* nunderhill@fountaincourt.co.uk.

UNDERWOOD, Ashley Grenville; QC 2001; *b* 28 Dec. 1953; *s* of Dennis William Underwood and Brenda Margarita Underwood; *m* 1982, Heather Kay Leggett; one *d*. *Educ:* London Sch. of Econs (LLB Hons). Called to the Bar, Gray's Inn, 1976; Hd of Chambers, 1999–. *Recreations:* motorcycling, classic cars, conversation. *Address:* (chambers) 2 Field Court, Gray's Inn, WC1R 5BB. *T:* (020) 7405 6114.

UNDERWOOD, Prof. James Cresseé Elphinstone, MD; FRCPath; Joseph Hunter Professor of Pathology, University of Sheffield, since 1983; Consultant Histopathologist, Sheffield Teaching Hospitals NHS Trust, since 1974; *b* 11 April 1942; *s* of John and Mary Underwood; *m* 1st, 1966 (marr. diss. 1986); one *s* one *d*; 2nd, 1989, Alice Cameron Underwood; one *s*. *Educ:* Downside Sch.; St Bartholomew's Hosp. Med. Coll. (MB BS 1965; MD 1973). MRCS, LRCP 1965; MRCPath 1972, FRCPath 1984. SHO, then Registrar in Pathology, St Bartholomew's Hosp., London, 1966–69; University of Sheffield: Lectr in Pathology, 1969–73; Sen. Lectr, 1974–82; Reader, 1983. MRC Clinical Res. Fellow, Chester Beatty Res. Inst., London, 1973–74; Wellcome-Ramaciotti Res. Fellow, Univ. of Melbourne, 1981. Vice-Pres., RCPath, 1999–2002; Pres., British Div., Internat. Acad. Pathology, 2000–02. Ed., Histopathology, 1995–. Hon. Member: Japanese Soc. Pathology, 1996; Hungarian Soc. Pathologists, 1996. *Publications:* Introduction to Biopsy Interpretation and Surgical Pathology, 1981, 2nd edn 1987; General and Systematic Pathology, 1992, 3rd edn 2000; papers on tumour pathology, chronic liver disease and the autopsy. *Recreations:* music, art, photography, walking. *Address:* Department of Pathology, Medical School, University of Sheffield, Beech Hill Road, Sheffield S10 2RX. *T:* (0114) 271 2501.

UNDERWOOD, John Morris; Director (formerly Partner), Clear Communication, since 1991; *b* 8 Nov. 1953; *s* of John Edward Underwood and Ella Lillian Morris Underwood; *m* 1987, Susan Clare Inglish; two *s*. *Educ:* Univ. of Sheffield (BSc hons); University Coll., Cardiff (Graduate Dip. in Journalism). BBC trainee journalist, 1976–78; regional TV reporter, 1978–80; TV reporter, ITN, 1980–82; home affairs corresp., ITN, 1982–83; freelance TV producer and presenter, 1983–89; Exec. Producer, House of Commons Cttee TV, 1989–90; Dir of Campaigns and Communications, Labour Party, 1990–91. Mem., Mgt Bd, Catalyst think tank, 1998–. Editor, New Century, 1993–95. *Publication:* The Will to Win: John Egan and Jaguar, 1989. *Recreations:* theatre, walking. *Address:* 10 Percival Road, SW14 7QE. *T:* (020) 8876 8884.

UNDERWOOD, Susan Lois, FMA; Chief Executive, North East Museums, Libraries and Archives Council (formerly Director, North of England Museums Service, later North East Museums), since 1990; Commissioner, English Heritage, since 1997; *b* 6 Aug. 1956; *d* of John and Lois Underwood; one *s* one *d*. *Educ:* Univ. of St Andrews (MA Hons); Univ. of Leicester (Mus. Studies Grad. Cert.). FMA 1994. Curator, Nat. Railway Mus., York, 1983–85; Keeper of Local Hist., Scunthorpe Mus. and Art Gall., 1985–88; Dep. Dir, N of England Museums Service, 1989–90. *Recreations:* the arts, travelling, my children. *Address:* North East Museums, Libraries and Archives Council, House of Recovery, Bath Lane, Newcastle upon Tyne NE4 5SQ. *T:* (0191) 222 1661.

UNERMAN, Sandra Diane; Deputy Solicitor, Department for Transport, Local Government and the Regions (formerly Department of the Environment, then Department of the Environment, Transport and the Regions), since 1992; *b* 23 Aug. 1950; *d* of Cecil Unerman and Renee Unerman (*née* Goldberg). *Educ:* Gartlett Sch.; Orange Hill Grammar Sch.; Bristol Univ. (BA Hons History). Called to the Bar, Inner Temple, 1973; Legal Dept, DoE, later DETR, then DTLR, 1974–. UK Civil Service Fellow, Humphrey Inst., Univ. of Minnesota, 1989–90. *Publication:* Trial of Three (novel), 1979. *Recreations:* writing, reading, listening to music, theatre going, folklore, needlework, conversation. *Address:* Department for Transport, Local Government and the Regions, Great Minster House, 76 Marsham Street, SW1P 3DR.

UNGER, Michael Ronald; General Manager, Jazz FM (North West), since 2000; *b* 8 Dec. 1943; *s* of Ronald and Joan Maureen Unger; *m* 1st, 1966, Eunice Dickens (marr. diss. 1992); one *s* (one *d* decd); 2nd, 1993, Noorah Ahmed. *Educ:* Wirral Grammar School. Trainee journalist, Thomson Regional Newspapers, Stockport, 1963; Reading Evening Post, 1965–67; Perth Daily News, W Australia, 1967–71; Daily Post, Liverpool, 1971, Editor, 1979–82; Editor: Liverpool Echo, 1982–83; Manchester Evening News, 1983–97. Dir, Guardian and Manchester Evening News plc, 1983–97. Chm., NW Arts Bd, 1991–93; Mem., Broadcasting Standards Commn, 1999–2000. Trustee: Scott Trust, 1986–97; The Lowry, 1994–; Youth Charter for Sport, 1994–2000; NW Film Archives, 1998–. *Publication:* (ed) The Memoirs of Bridget Hitler, 1979. *Recreations:* theatre, reading, walking.

UNGERER, Jean Thomas, (Tomi); writer and graphic artist; Ambassador for Childhood and Education, Council of Europe; *b* Strasbourg, 28 Nov. 1931; *s* of Theo Ungerer and Alice (*née* Essler); *m* 1970, Yvonne Wright; two *s* one *d*. *Educ:* Strasbourg; Ecole Municipale des Arts Décoratifs, Strasbourg. Moved to USA, 1956; joined Harper's, 1957; worked for Amer. magazines and in advertising; moved to Nova Scotia, 1971, to Ireland, 1976; exhibitions: (first) Berlin, 1962; Strasbourg, 1975; Louvre, Paris, 1981; RFH, London, 1985. Chargé de Mission, Jack Lang, Ministre de la Culture, commission inter-ministérielle Franco-Allemande, 1987–94; Pres. and Founder, Culture Bank, Strasbourg, 1990; Founder, European Centre of Yiddish Cultures, 1999. Burckhardt Prize, Goethe Foundn, 1983; Andersen Prize, Denmark, 1998; French culture prize, 1998, European culture prize, 1999. Commandeur des Arts et des Lettres (France), 1985; Officier, Légion d'Honneur (France), 1990; Cross of Merit (Germany), 1992; numerous other prizes and awards. *Films include:* The Three Robbers, 1972; Beast of Monsieur Racine, 1975. *Publications:* over 130 books in English, French and German, including: Horrible, 1958; Inside Marriage, 1960; The Underground Sketchbook, 1964; The Party, 1966; Fornicon, 1970; Compromises, 1970; The Poster Art of Tomi Ungerer, 1971; Testament, 1985; Once in a Lifetime, 1985; Far Out is not Far Enough, 1985; Joy of Frogs, 1985; Testament, 1985; Cats As Cats Can, 1997; Tomi: a Nazi childhood, 1998; Tortoni Tremolo, 1998; Otto, 1999; Europolitan, 1998; S & M, 2000; Vrai, 2000; The Blue Cloud, 2000; Otto, 2001; *for children:* The Mellops series: The Mellops go Diving for Treasure; Crictor, 1958; Adelaide, 1959; Christmas Eve at the Mellops', 1960; Emile, 1960; Rufus, 1961; The Three Robbers, 1962; Snail, Where Are You?, 1962; One, Two, Where's My Shoe?, 1964; The Brave Vulture Orlando, 1966; Moon Man, 1967; Zeralda's Ogre, 1967; Ask Me a Question, 1968; The Hat, 1970; The Beast of Monsieur Racine, 1971; I am Papa Snap and These are My Favourite No Such Stories, 1971; No Kiss for Mother, 1973; Allumette, 1974; Flix, 1997. *Address:* Diogenes Verlag AG, Sprecherstrasse 8, 8032 Zürich, Switzerland; Centre Tomi Ungerer, Musées de Strasbourg, 4 rue de la Haute Montée, Strasbourg 67000, France.

UNGLEY, John Guilford Gordon; Master of the Supreme Court, Queen's Bench Division, since 1997; a Recorder, since 1989; *b* 30 Jan. 1939; *s* of Harold Gordon Ungley and Ella Gwyneth Reay Ungley (*née* Heslop); *m* 1976, Elizabeth Metcalfe (*née* Mayall); one *d*, and two step *d*. *Educ:* Charterhouse. Queen's Royal Irish Hussars, 1960–61. Called to the Bar, Gray's Inn, 1965; in practice at the Bar, Western Circuit, 1966–97; Asst Recorder, 1986–89. *Recreation:* sailing. *Address:* Royal Courts of Justice, Strand, WC2A 2LL. *T:* (020) 7947 6433. *Clubs:* Bar Yacht, Royal Solent Yacht.

UNRUH, Prof. William George, PhD; FRS 2001; FRSC 1984; Professor of Physics, University of British Columbia, since 1984; Fellow, Canadian Institute for Advanced Research, since 1987; *b* 28 Aug. 1945; *s* of Benjamin Unruh and Anne Unruh (*née* Janzen); *m* 1974, Patricia Truman; one *s*. *Educ:* Univ. of Manitoba (BSc Hons 1967); Princeton Univ. (MA 1969; PhD 1971). FAPS 2000. NSERC (Rutherford) Post Doctoral Fellow, Birkbeck Coll., 1971–72; Miller Fellow, Univ. of Calif, Berkeley, 1973–74; Asst Prof., McMaster Univ., 1974–76; Asst Prof., Univ. of BC, 1976–81; Dir, Cosmology Prog., Canadian Inst. for Advanced Res., 1987–97. Sloan Medal, Sloan Foundn, 1978; Rutherford Medal, RSC, 1982; Herzberg Medal, 1983, Medal of Achievement, 1996,

Canadian Assoc. of Physicists; Steacie Prize, Steacie Foundn, 1984; Sci. and Engrg Gold Medal, Sci. Council of BC, 1990; Killam Prize in Natural Scis, Canadian Council, 1995; Mathematical Physics Prize, Canadian Assoc. of Physicists and Centre Recherche du Mathématique, 1996. *Publications:* (ed with G. Semenoff) The Early Universe, 1987; contrib. numerous papers to scientific jls. *Address:* Department of Physics and Astronomy, University of British Columbia, Vancouver, BC V6T 1Z1, Canada. *T:* (604) 8223273. *Club:* X (Univ. of BC, Vancouver).

UNSWORTH, Barry Forster; author; *b* 10 Aug. 1930; *s* of Michael Unsworth and Elsie (*née* Forster); *m* 1st, 1959, Valerie Irene Moor (marr. diss. 1991); three *d*; 2nd, 1992, Aira Pohjanvaara-Buffa. *Educ:* Stockton Grammar Sch.; Manchester Univ. (BA Hons English). FRSL 1973. *Publications:* The Partnership, 1966; The Greeks Have a Word for It, 1967; The Hide, 1970; Mooncranker's Gift (Heinemann Award), 1973; The Big Day, 1976; Pascali's Island, 1980; The Rage of the Vulture, 1982; Stone Virgin, 1985; Sugar and Rum, 1990; Sacred Hunger (jtly, Booker Prize), 1992; Morality Play, 1995; After Hannibal, 1996; Losing Nelson, 1999. *Recreations:* gardening, viticulture, bird-watching. *Address:* c/o Giles Gordon, Curtis Brown, Haymarket House, 28/29 Haymarket, SW1Y 4SP.

UNSWORTH, Sir Edgar (Ignatius Godfrey), Kt 1963; CMG 1954; QC (N Rhodesia) 1951; *b* 18 April 1906; *yr s* of John William and Minnie Unsworth; *m* 1964, Eileen, *widow* of Raymond Ritzema. *Educ:* Stonyhurst Coll.; Manchester Univ. (LLB Hons). Barrister-at-Law, Gray's Inn, 1930; private practice, 1930–37. Parly Cand. (C) for Farnworth, General Election, 1935. Crown Counsel: Nigeria, 1937; N Rhodesia, 1942; Solicitor-General: N Rhodesia, 1946; Fedn of Malaya, 1949; Chm. of Cttees, N Rhodesia, 1950; Attorney-General, N Rhodesia, 1951–56. Acting Chief Sec. and Dep. to Governor of N Rhodesia for periods during 1953, 1954 and 1955; Attorney-General, Fedn of Nigeria, 1956–60; Federal Justice of Federal Supreme Court of Nigeria, 1960–62; Chief Justice, Nyasaland, 1962–64; Director of a Course for Government Officers from Overseas, 1964–65; Chief Justice of Gibraltar, 1965–76; Justice of Appeal, Gibraltar, 1976–81. Member Rhodesia Railways Arbitration Tribunal, 1946; Chm., Commn of Enquiry into Central African Airways Corp., 1947; Mem., British Observers' Group, Independence Elections, Rhodesia, 1980 (submitted independent report). *Publication:* Laws of Northern Rhodesia (rev. edn), 1949. *Recreations:* gardening, bridge. *Address:* 12 Brock Street, Bath BA1 2LW; Pedro El Grande 9, Sotogrande, Provincia de Cadiz, Spain. *Clubs:* Bath and County (Bath); Royal Gibraltar Yacht.

UNWIN, Sir Brian; *see* Unwin, Sir J. B.

UNWIN, Rev. Canon Christopher Philip, TD 1963; MA; Archdeacon of Northumberland, 1963–82; *b* 27 Sept. 1917; *e s* of Rev. Philip Henry and Decima Unwin. *Educ:* Repton Sch.; Magdalene Coll., Cambridge; Queen's Theological Coll., Birmingham. Deacon, 1940, Priest, 1941. Asst Curate of: Benwell, 1940–43; Sugley, 1944–47; Vicar of: Horton, Northumberland, 1947–55; Benwell, 1955–63. *Recreations:* reading, walking. *Address:* 60 Sandringham Avenue, Benton, Newcastle upon Tyne NE12 8JX. *T:* (0191) 270 0418.

UNWIN, David Charles; QC 1995; *b* 12 May 1947; *s* of Peter Unwin and Rosemary (*née* Locket); *m* 1969, Lorna Bullivant; one *s* one *d*. *Educ:* Clifton Coll.; Trinity Coll., Oxford. Called to the Bar, Middle Temple, 1971; Jun. Counsel to Attorney Gen. in charity matters, 1987–95. *Recreations:* music, mountaineering, windsurfing. *Address:* 7 Stone Buildings, Lincoln's Inn, WC2A 3SZ. *Club:* Climbers'.

UNWIN, David Storr; author; *b* 3 Dec. 1918; *e s* of Sir Stanley Unwin, KCMG, and Alice Mary Storr; *m* 1945, Periwinkle, *yr d* of late Captain Sidney Herbert, RN; twin *s* and *d*. *Educ:* Abbotsholme. League of Nations Secretariat, Geneva, 1938–39; George Allen & Unwin Ltd, Publishers, 1940–44. *Publications:* The Governor's Wife, 1954 (Authors' Club First Novel Award, 1955); A View of the Heath, 1956; Fifty Years with Father: a Relationship (autobiog.), 1982; *for children:* (under pen name David Severn) Rick Afire!, 1942; A Cabin for Crusoe, 1943; Waggon for Five, 1944; Hermit in the Hills, 1945; Forest Holiday, 1946; Ponies and Poachers, 1947; Dream Gold, 1948; The Cruise of the Maiden Castle, 1948; Treasure for Three, 1949; My Foreign Correspondent through Africa, 1950; Crazy Castle, 1951; Burglars and Bandicoots, 1952; Drumbeats!, 1953; The Future Took Us, 1958; The Green-eyed Gryphon, 1958; Foxy-boy, 1959; Three at the Sea, 1959; Clouds over the Alberhorn, 1963; Jeff Dickson, Cowhand, 1963; The Girl in the Grove, 1974; The Wishing Bone, 1977. *Recreations:* travel, gardening. *Address:* Garden Flat, 31 Belsize Park, NW3 4DX. *Club:* PEN.

UNWIN, Eric Geoffrey; Chief Executive Officer, since 2000, and Member of Board, Cap Gemini Ernst and Young (formerly Cap Gemini); Executive Chairman, Hoskyns Group, since 1988; *b* 9 Aug. 1942; *s* of Maurice Doughty Unwin and Olive Milburn (*née* Watson); *m* 1967, Margaret Bronia Element; one *s* one *d*. *Educ:* Heaton Grammar School, Newcastle upon Tyne; King's College, Durham Univ. (BSc Hons Chemistry). Cadbury Bros, 1963–68; joined John Hoskyns & Co., 1968; Managing Dir, Hoskyns Systems Development, 1978; Dir, 1982, Man. Dir, 1984, Hoskyns Group; Chief Operating Officer, 1993–2000, and Vice Chm., Exec. Bd, 1996–2000, Cap Gemini Sogeti, then Cap Gemini. Chm., Cap Programmator AB, 1993–2000; Non-executive Director: Volmac Software Groep NV, 1992–; Gemini Consulting Hldg SA, 1994–2000; United News & Media plc, 1995–. Pres., Computing Services Assoc., 1987–88. Mem., ITAB, 1988–91. CIMgt (CBIM 1984; Mem., Bd., 1990–94). Freeman, City of London, 1987; Founder Mem., and Liveryman, Co. of Information Technologists, 1987. *Recreations:* golf, riding, ski-ing. *Address:* 17 Park Village West, NW1 4AE. *Clubs:* Royal Automobile; Hendon Golf, Hunstanton Golf, Morfontaine Golf, Royal West Norfolk Golf.

UNWIN, Sir (James) Brian, KCB 1990 (CB 1986); President, European Investment Bank, 1993–99, now Hon. President; Director, Dexia SA, since 2000; President, European Centre for Nature Conservation, since 2001; *b* 21 Sept. 1935; *s* of Reginald Unwin and Winifred Annie Walthall; *m* 1964, Diana Susan, *d* of Sir D. A. Scott, *qv*; three *s*. *Educ:* Chesterfield School; New College, Oxford (MA; Hon. Fellow, 1997); Yale University (MA). Asst Principal, CRO, 1960; Private Sec. to British High Commissioner, Salisbury, 1961–64; 1st Secretary, British High Commission, Accra, 1964–65; FCO, 1965–68; transferred to HM Treasury, 1968; Private Sec. to Chief Secretary to Treasury, 1970–72; Asst Secretary, 1972; Under Sec., 1976; seconded to Cabinet Office, 1981–83; Dep. Sec., HM Treasury, 1983–85; Dir, Eur. Investment Bank, 1983–85; Dep. Sec., Cabinet Office, 1985–87; Chm., Bd of HM Customs and Excise, 1987–93. Chm., Supervisory Bd, European Investment Fund, 1994–99; Gov., EBRD, 1993–99. Pres., Customs Co-operation Council, 1991–92. Chm., Civil Service Sports Council, 1989–93. Member: IMPACT Adv. Bd, 1990–93; Bd of Dirs, ENO, 1993–94, 2000– (Sec., 1987–93); Bd, Centre d'Etudes Prospectives, 1996–2000; Bd, Foundation Pierre Werner, 1998–2000. Hon. Pres., Euronem, Athens, 2000–. Gold Medal, Fondation du Mérite Européen, 1995. *Recreations:* opera, bird watching, Wellingtoniana, cricket. *Clubs:* Reform; Kingswood Village (Surrey).

UNWIN, Ven. Kenneth; Archdeacon of Pontefract, 1981–92, now Emeritus; *b* 16 Sept. 1926; *s* of Percy and Elsie Unwin; *m* 1958, Beryl Riley; one *s* four *d*. *Educ:* Chesterfield Grammar School; St Edmund Hall, Oxford (MA Hons); Ely Theological Coll. Assistant Curate: All Saints, Leeds, 1951–55; St Margaret, Durham City (in charge, St John's, Neville's Cross), 1955–59; Vicar: St John Baptist, Dodworth, Barnsley, 1959–69; St John Baptist, Royston, Barnsley, 1969–73; St John's, Wakefield, 1973–82. Hon. Canon, Wakefield Cathedral, 1980–92. RD of Wakefield, 1980–81. Proctor in Convocation, 1972–82. *Address:* 2 Rockwood Close, Skipton, Yorks BD23 1UG. *T:* (01756) 791323.
See also Sir J. D. Acland, Bt.

UNWIN, Dr (Peter) Nigel (Tripp), FRS 1983; Scientist, Medical Research Council Laboratory of Molecular Biology, Cambridge, 1968–80 and since 1987; Senior Research Fellow, Trinity College, Cambridge, since 1988; *b* 1 Nov. 1942; *s* of Peter Unwin and Cara Unwin (*née* Pinckney); *m* 1968, Janet Patricia Ladd; one *s* one *d*. *Educ:* Univ. of Otago, NZ (BE); Univ. of Cambridge (PhD 1968). Prof. of Structural Biol., then Cell Biol., Stanford Univ. Sch. of Medicine, Calif, 1980–87. Founder FMedSci 1998. Hon. FRMS 1989. Ernst Ruska Award, Ernst Ruska Foundn, 1980; Rosenstiel Award, Brandeis Univ., Mass, 1991; Louis Jeantet Prize for Medicine, Jeantet Foundn, Geneva, 1996; Gregori Aminoff Prize, Royal Swedish Acad. of Scis, 1999. *Recreation:* mountaineering. *Address:* 19/20 Portugal Place, Cambridge CB5 8AF.

UNWIN, Peter William, CMG 1981; HM Diplomatic Service, retired; Chairman, David Davies Memorial Institute of International Studies, since 2001 (Director, 1995–2001); *b* 20 May 1932; *s* of Arnold and Norah Unwin; *m* 1955, Monica Steven; two *s* two *d*. *Educ:* Ampleforth; Christ Church, Oxford. Army, 1954–56; FO, 1956–58; British Legation, Budapest, 1958–61; British Embassy, Tokyo, 1961–63; FCO, 1963–67; British Information Services, NY, 1967–70; FCO, 1970–72; Bank of England, 1973; British Embassy, Bonn, 1973–76; Head of Personnel Policy Dept, FCO, 1976–79; Fellow, Center for Internat. Affairs, Harvard, 1979–80; Minister (Economic), Bonn, 1980–83; Ambassador to: Hungary, 1983–86; Denmark, 1986–88; a Dep. Sec. Gen. of the Commonwealth, 1989–93. Chairman: British-Hungarian Soc., 1993–2000 (Pres., 2000–); Abbeyfield Internat., 1996–March 2002; Vice Chm., UK Cttee, UNICEF, 1996–2000. *Publications:* Voice in the Wilderness: Imre Nagy and the Hungarian Revolution, 1991; Baltic Approaches, 1996; Hearts, Minds & Interests: Britain's place in the world, 1998; Where East Met West: a Central European journey, 2000; contrib. The European, Evening Standard, Independent, International Affairs, International Relations, The Observer, The Times and The Tablet. *Address:* 30 Kew Green, Richmond, Surrey TW9 3BH. *T:* (020) 8940 8037. *Club:* Oxford and Cambridge.

UPDIKE, John Hoyer; freelance writer; *b* 18 March 1932; *s* of late Wesley R. and Linda G. Updike; *m* 1st, 1953, Mary E. Pennington (marr. diss.); two *s* two *d*; 2nd, 1977, Martha Bernhard. *Educ:* Harvard Coll. Worked as journalist for The New Yorker magazine, 1955–57. *Publications: poems:* Hoping for a Hoopoe (in America, The Carpentered Hen), 1958; Telephone Poles, 1968; Midpoint and other poems, 1969; Tossing and Turning, 1977; Facing Nature, 1985; Collected Poems, 1993; *novels:* The Poorhouse Fair, 1959; Rabbit, Run, 1960; The Centaur, 1963; Of the Farm, 1966; Couples, 1968; Rabbit Redux, 1972; A Month of Sundays, 1975; Marry Me, 1976; The Coup, 1979; Rabbit is Rich (Pulitzer Prize), 1982; The Witches of Eastwick, 1984 (filmed 1987); Roger's Version, 1986; S., 1988; Rabbit at Rest, 1990 (Pulitzer Prize 1991); Memories of the Ford Administration, 1993; Brazil, 1994; Rabbit Angstrom: a tetralogy, 1995; In the Beauty of the Lilies, 1996; Toward the End of Time, 1998; Gertrude and Claudius, 2000; *short stories:* The Same Door, 1959; Pigeon Feathers, 1962; The Music School, 1966; Bech: A Book, 1970; Museums and Women, 1973; Problems, 1980; Bech is Back, 1982; (ed) The Year's Best American Short Stories, 1985; Trust Me, 1987; The Afterlife and other stories, 1995; Bech at Bay: a quasi-novel, 1998; Licks of Love, 2001; *miscellanies:* Assorted Prose, 1965; Picked-Up Pieces, 1976; Hugging the Shore, 1983; Just Looking: essays on art, 1989; Odd Jobs: essays and criticism, 1991; Golf Dreams, 1997; More Matter, 1999; *autobiography:* Self-Consciousness: Memoirs, 1989; *play:* Buchanan Dying, 1974. *Address:* Beverly Farms, MA 01915, USA.

UPRICHARD, Dame Mary (Elizabeth), DBE 1998 (OBE 1983); President, UK Central Council for Nursing, Midwifery and Health Visiting, 1993–98 (Member of Council, 1980–93); *b* 23 March 1938; *d* of late Norman Uprichard and Rebecca Uprichard (*née* Gracey). *Educ:* Grosvenor Grammar Sch., Belfast. RSCN, RGN, RM, MTD. Sch. of Midwifery, Belfast, 1974–83; Dir of Midwifery Educn, NI Coll. of Midwifery, 1983–97. Chairman: Nat. Bd for Nursing, Midwifery and Health Visiting, 1988–93 (Mem. Bd, 1980–93); Nurses Welfare Service, 1999–; Member: EC Adv. Cttee on Training of Midwives, 1984–98; Council for Professions Supplementary to Medicine, 1997–; Council on Social Responsibility, Methodist Church in Ireland, 1994–. *Address:* 29 Glenview Avenue, Belfast BT5 7LZ. *T:* (028) 9079 1466.

UPSHAW, Dawn; American soprano; *b* 17 July 1960; *m* Michael Nott; two *c*. *Educ:* Illinois Wesleyan Univ. (BA Music 1982); Manhattan Sch. of Music (MA 1984). Joined NY Metropolitan Opera, 1984; début, Rigoletto, 1984; other productions include: Magic Flute, Wolf Trap Fest., 1985, Aix-en-Provence Fest., 1988; Death in the Family, Opera Co. of St Louis, 1986; Béatrice et Bénédict, 1993, Theodora, 1996, Glyndebourne Fest.; The Rake's Progress, Stravinsky Fest., Paris, 1996; El Niño, Châtelet, Paris, 2000; numerous recitals and concerts with major orchestras and chamber gps. Numerous recordings (Grammy Awards). (Jtly) Winner, Naumburg Competition, 1985. *Address:* c/o IMG Artists, Lovell House, 616 Chiswick High Road, W4 5RX.

UPTON, Prof. Graham, PhD; Vice-Chancellor, Oxford Brookes University, since 1997; *b* 30 April 1944; *m* 1st, 1966, Jennifer Ann Clark (marr. diss. 1984); one *s* one *d*; 2nd, 1986, Bebe Speed; one *s* one *d*. *Educ:* Univ. of Sydney (BA, Dip Educn 1966; MA 1969); Univ. of New South Wales (MEd 1973); UC Cardiff, Univ. of Wales (PhD 1978). CPsychol 1988; FBPsS 1996. Teacher, New South Wales, 1966–70; Lectr in Educn, Sydney Teachers' Coll., 1970–71; Lectr in Special Educn, Leeds Poly., 1972–74; University College, Cardiff, 1974–88: Lectr; Sen. Lectr; Reader; Hd of Dept of Educn; Dean, Collegiate Faculty of Educn; Dean, Faculty of Educn and Prof. Studies; University of Birmingham: Prof. of Educnl Psychology and Special Educn and Hd, Sch. of Educn, 1988–93; Pro-Vice-Chancellor, 1993–97. Non-exec. Dir, Oxford Bio-Innovation, 1999–. Member Board: Milton Keynes, Oxon and Bucks Local Learning and Skills Council, 2001–; Oxford Playhouse, 2001–. Mem. Adv. Council, Oxford Trust, 2001–. Governor, Headington Sch., 1999–. AcSS 2000. FRSA 1999. Hon. Fellow, Birmingham Coll. of Food, Tourism and Leisure Studies, 1997. *Publications:* Physical and Creative Activities for the Mentally Handicapped, 1979; Behaviour Problems in the Comprehensive School, 1980; Educating Children with Behaviour Problems, 1983; Staff Training and Special Educational Needs, 1991; Special Educational Needs, 1992; Special Education in Britain After Warnock, 1993; Emotional and Behavioural Difficulties in Schools, 1994; The Voice of the Child, 1996; Pupils with Severe Learning Difficulties who Present Challenging Behaviour, 1996; Stresses in Special Educational Needs Teachers, 1996; Sound Practice, 1997; Effective Schooling for Pupils with Emotional and

Behavioural Difficulties, 1998. *Recreations:* family life, good food, DIY. *Address:* Headington Hill Hall, Headington, Oxford OX3 0BP. *T:* (01865) 484801. *Club:* Royal Over-Seas League.

UPTON, Robert Ian William; Secretary-General, Royal Town Planning Institute, since 1996; *b* 20 Aug. 1951; *s* of late Ronald Alfred Upton and of Iris Eveline Upton; *m* 1987, Mary Faith Higgins; two *d.* *Educ:* Dulwich Coll.; Magdalene Coll., Cambridge (MA); Harvard Business Sch. Hong Kong Government, 1972–91: Clerk of Councils, 1982–84; Sec., Educn Commn, 1985–86; Dep. Sec. for Security, 1986–89; Dir of Planning, 1989–91. Chief Exec., Rushmoor BC, 1992–96. *Recreations:* reading, walking, book-hunting. *Address:* Royal Town Planning Institute, 41 Botolph Lane, EC3R 8DL. *T:* (020) 7929 9494.

UPWARD, Mrs Janet; with Birmingham Family Health Services Authority, 1991–96. *Educ:* Newnham College, Cambridge (BA (Geog. Hons) 1961; MA 1966); Univ. of Birmingham (MSocSci 1993). Sec., National Fedn of Consumer Gps, 1972–82; Mem., 1978–84, Dep. Chm., 1978–83, Domestic Coal Consumers' Council; Chm., National Consumer Congress, 1981–83; Chief Officer, S Birmingham CHC, 1983–90. *Address:* 61 Valentine Road, Birmingham B14 7AJ. *T:* (0121) 689 2597.

URE, James Mathie, OBE 1969; British Council Representative, India, and Minister (Education), British High Commission, New Delhi, 1980–84; *b* 5 May 1925; *s* of late William Alexander Ure, and Helen Jones; *m* 1950, Martha Walker Paterson; one *s* one *d.* *Educ:* Shawlands Acad., Glasgow; Glasgow Univ. (MA); Trinity Coll., Oxford (BLitt). Army Service, 1944–47. Lectr, Edinburgh Univ., 1953–59; British Council: Istanbul, 1956–57; India, 1959–68; Dep. Controller, Arts Div., 1968–71; Rep., Indonesia, 1971–75; Controller, Home Div., 1975–80. *Publications:* Old English Benedictine Office, 1952; (with L. A. Hill) English Sounds and Spellings, 1962; (with L. A. Hill) English Sounds and Spellings—Tests, 1963; (with J. S. Bhandari and C. S. Bhandari) Read and Act, 1965; (with C. S. Bhandari) Short Stories, 1966.

URE, Sir John (Burns), KCMG 1987 (CMG 1980); LVO 1968; HM Diplomatic Service, retired; author; company director; *b* 5 July 1931; *s* of late Tam Ure; *m* 1972, Caroline, *d* of late Charles Allan, Roxburghshire; one *s* one *d.* *Educ:* Uppingham Sch.; Magdalene Coll., Cambridge (MA); Harvard Business Sch. (AMP). Active Service as 2nd Lieut with Cameronians (Scottish Rifles), Malaya, 1950–51; Lieut, London Scottish (Gordon Highlanders) TA, 1952–55. Book publishing with Ernest Benn Ltd, 1951–53; joined Foreign (subseq. Diplomatic) Service, 1956; 3rd Sec. and Private Sec. to Ambassador, Moscow, 1957–59; Resident Clerk, FO, 1960–61; 2nd Sec., Leopoldville, 1962–63; FO, 1964–66; 1st Sec. (Commercial), Santiago, 1967–70; FCO, 1971–72; Counsellor, and intermittently Chargé d'Affaires, Lisbon, 1972–77; Head of South America Dept, FCO, 1977–79; Ambassador to Cuba, 1979–81; Asst Under-Sec. of State, FCO, 1981–84; Ambassador to Brazil, 1984–87, to Sweden, 1987–91. UK Comr Gen., Expo 92, 1990–92. Director: Thomas Cook Group, 1991–99; Sotheby's Scandinavia AB, 1991–99; CSE Aviation, 1992–94; Consultant: Robert Fleming & Co. (merchant bankers), 1995–98; Ecosse Films, 1997–99; European Risk Mgt Consultants, 1997–2000; Sotheby's Scandinavia, 1999–. Chairman: panel of judges, Thomas Cook Travel Book of the Year Award, 1991–2000; Anglo-Swedish Soc., 1992–96; Anglo-Brazilian Chamber of Commerce, 1994–96. Trustee, Leeds Castle Foundn, 1995–. Life Fellow and Mem. Council, RGS, 1982–84; Regular guest lectr on foreign tours. Comdr, Mil. Order of Christ, Portugal, 1973. *Publications:* Cucumber Sandwiches in the Andes, 1973 (Travel Book Club Choice); Prince Henry the Navigator, 1977 (History Guild Choice); The Trail of Tamerlane, 1980 (Ancient History Club Choice); The Quest for Captain Morgan, 1983; Trespassers on the Amazon, 1986; Central and South America sections, in RGS History of World Exploration, 1990; A Bird on the Wing: Bonnie Prince Charlie's flight from Culloden retraced, 1992; Diplomatic Bag, 1994; The Cossacks, 1999; travel articles in Daily and Sunday Telegraph; book reviews in TLS; biographies for DNB. *Recreation:* travelling uncomfortably in remote places and writing about it comfortably afterwards. *Address:* Netters Hall, Hawkhurst, Kent TN18 5AT. *T:* (01580) 752191. *Clubs:* Beefsteak, Pilgrims.

URMSON, James Opie, MC 1943; Emeritus Professor of Philosophy, Stanford University; Emeritus Fellow of Corpus Christi College, Oxford; *b* 4 March 1915; *s* of Rev. J. O. Urmson; *m* 1940, Marion Joyce Drage; one *d.* *Educ:* Kingswood School, Bath; Corpus Christi College, Oxford. Senior Demy, Magdalen College, 1938; Fellow by examination, Magdalen College, 1939–45. Served Army (Duke of Wellington's Regt), 1939–45. Lecturer of Christ Church, 1945–46; Student of Christ Church, 1946–55; Professor of Philosophy, Queen's College, Dundee, University of St Andrews, 1955–59; Fellow and Tutor in Philosophy, CCC, Oxford, 1959–78. Visiting Associate Prof., Princeton Univ., 1950–51. Visiting Lectr, Univ. of Michigan, 1961–62, 1965–66, and 1969; Stuart Prof. of Philosophy, Stanford, 1975–80. *Publications:* Philosophical Analysis, 1956; The Emotive Theory of Ethics, 1968; Berkeley, 1982; Aristotle's Ethics, 1988; The Greek Philosophical Vocabulary, 1990; edited: Encyclopedia of Western Philosophy, 1960; J. L. Austin: How to Do Things with Words, 1962; (with G. J. Warnock) J. L. Austin: Philosophical Papers, 2nd edn, 1970; translations from ancient Greek; articles in philosophical jls. *Recreations:* gardening, music. *Address:* 5 Appleton Road, Cumnor, Oxford OX2 9QH. *T:* (01865) 862769.

URQUHART, Sir Brian (Edward), KCMG 1986; MBE 1945; Scholar-in-Residence, Ford Foundation, 1986–96; an Under-Secretary-General, United Nations, 1974–86; *b* 28 Feb. 1919; *s* of Murray and Bertha Urquhart; *m* 1st, 1944, Alfreda Huntington (marr. diss. 1963); two *s* one *d*; 2nd, 1963, Sidney Damrosch Howard; one *s* one *d.* *Educ:* Westminster; Christ Church, Oxford (Hon. Student, 1985). British Army: Dorset Regt and Airborne Forces, N Africa, Sicily and Europe, 1939–45; Personal Asst to Gladwyn Jebb, Exec. Sec. of Preparatory Commn of UN, London, 1945–46; Personal Asst to Trygve Lie, 1st Sec.-Gen. of UN, 1946–49; Sec., Collective Measures Cttee, 1951–53; Mem., Office of Under-Sec.-Gen. for Special Political Affairs, 1954–71; Asst Sec.-Gen., UN, 1972–74; Exec. Sec., 1st and 2nd UN Conf. on Peaceful Uses of Atomic Energy, 1955 and 1958; active in organization and direction of UN Emergency Force in Middle East, 1956; Dep. Exec. Sec., Preparatory Commn of Internat. Atomic Energy Agency, 1957; Asst to Sec.-Gen.'s Special Rep. in Congo, July–Oct. 1960; UN Rep. in Katanga, Congo, 1961–62; responsible for organization and direction of UN peace-keeping ops and special political assignments. Hon. LLD: Yale, 1981; Tufts, 1985; Grinnell, 1986; State Univ. NY, 1986; Warwick, 1989; DUniv: Essex, 1981; City Univ. NY, 1986; Hon. DCL Oxford, 1986; Hon. DHL Colorado, 1987; Hon. DLitt Keele, 1987. *Publications:* Hammarskjold, 1972; A Life in Peace and War (autobiog.), 1987; Decolonization and World Peace, 1989; (with Erskine Childers) A World in Need of Leadership: tomorrow's United Nations, 1990; Ralph Bunche: an American life, 1993; (with Erskine Childers) Renewing the United Nations System, 1994; A World in Need of Leadership: tomorrow's United Nations, a fresh appraisal, 1996; various articles and reviews on internat. affairs. *Address:* 50 West 29th Street, New York, NY 10001, USA; Howard Farm, Tyringham, MA 01264, USA. *T:* (212) 6796358. *Club:* Century (New York).

URQUHART, Rt Rev. David Andrew; *see* Birkenhead, Bishop Suffragan of.

URQUHART, James Graham, CVO 1983; FCIT, FIMH; Chairman, Fiox Ltd, 1990–92 (Director, 1988–90); *b* 23 April 1925; *s* of James Graham Urquhart and Mary Clark; *m* 1949, Margaret Hutchinson; two *d.* *Educ:* Berwickshire High Sch. Served War, RAF, 1941–44. Management Trainee, Eastern Region, BR, 1949–52; Chief Controller, Fenchurch Street, 1956–59; Dist Traffic Supt, Perth, 1960–62; Divl Operating Supt, Glasgow, 1962–64; Divl Manager, Glasgow and SW Scotland, 1964–67; Asst Gen. Man., Eastern Reg., 1967–69; BR Bd HQ: Chief Ops Man., 1969–72; Exec. Dir, Personnel, 1972–75; Gen. Manager, London Midland Reg., BR, 1975–76; BR Bd: Exec. Mem., Operations and Productivity, 1977–83; Mem., Exports, 1983–85; Chairman: British Transport Police, 1977–86; BRE-Metro, 1978–86; BR Engrg Ltd, 1979–85; Freightliners, 1983–85; Transmark, 1983–86. Director: Waterslides PLC, 1987–89; Park Air Electronics Ltd, 1987–91; Systems Connection Group PLC, 1988–92; CVC Ltd, 1988–91; Sonic Tape PLC, 1988–90. Mem., Industrial Tribunal, 1987–90. MIPM, MInstM, CIMgt. *Recreations:* golf, travel, gardening. *Address:* 12 Durlston Point, 78 Park Road, Swanage, Dorset BH19 2AE. *T:* (01929) 421574.

URQUHART, Lawrence McAllister, CA; Chairman, BAA plc, 1998–April 2002 (Director, since 1993); *b* 24 Sept. 1935; *s* of Robert and Josephine Urquhart; *m* 1961, Elizabeth Catherine Burns; three *s* one *d.* *Educ:* Strathallan; King's Coll., London (LLB). Price Waterhouse & Co., 1957–62; Shell International Petroleum, 1962–64; P. A. Management Consultants, 1964–68; Charterhouse Gp, 1968–74; TKM Gp, 1974–77; Burmah Oil, subseq. Burmah Castrol, 1977–99: Gp Man. Dir, 1985–88; Chief Exec., 1988–93; Chm., 1990–98; non-exec. Dir, 1998–99. Chairman: English China Clays, 1995–99 (Dir, 1991–99); Scottish Widows plc (formerly Scottish Widows' Fund and Life Assurance Soc.), 1995– (non-exec. Dir, 1992–); non-executive Director: Imerys SA, 1999–; Lloyds TSB Bank plc, 2000–; Lloyds TSB Group plc, 2000–. *Recreations:* golf, music. *Address:* BAA plc, 130 Wilton Road, SW1V 1LQ. *Club:* Frilford Heath Golf.

URQUHART, His Honour Peter William Gordon; a Circuit Judge, 1992–2001; *b* 18 March 1934; *s* of Gordon Eldridge Urquhart and Constance Margaret (*née* Taylor); *m* 1965, Carolyn Hemingway Hines; one *s* one *d.* *Educ:* Liverpool Coll.; Peterhouse, Cambridge (MA, LLB). Admitted solicitor, 1960. Member: Lord Chancellor's Legal Aid Adv. Cttee, 1974–80; Equal Opportunities Commn, 1977–82. *Recreations:* book collecting, reading, gardening, early music, jazz. *Address:* Braehead, 19 Poplar Road, Prenton, Merseyside CH43 5TB. *T:* (0151) 652 4043. *Club:* Athenæum (Liverpool).

URSELL, Prof. Fritz Joseph, FRS 1972; Emeritus Professor of Applied Mathematics, Manchester University, since 1990 (Beyer Professor of Applied Mathematics, 1961–90); *b* Düsseldorf, 28 April 1923; *m* 1959, Katharina Renate (*née* Zander); two *d.* *Educ:* Clifton; Marlborough; Trinity College, Cambridge (BA 1943; MA 1947; ScD 1957); MSc Manchester, 1965. Admiralty Service, 1943–47; ICI Fellow in Applied Mathematics, Manchester Univ., 1947–50. Fellow (Title A), Trinity Coll., Cambridge, 1947–51; Univ. Lecturer in Mathematics, Cambridge, 1950–61; Stringer Fellow in Natural Sciences, King's Coll., Cambridge, 1954–60. Georg Weinblum Lectr in Ship Hydrodynamics, Hamburg and Washington, 1986; Stewartson Lectr in Fluid Mechanics, 1991. FIMA 1964 (Gold Medal, 1994). *Publication:* Collected Papers 1946–1992, 1994. *Address:* 28 Old Broadway, Manchester M20 3DF. *T:* (0161) 445 5791; *e-mail:* fritz@ma.man.ac.uk.

URSELL, Rev. Philip Elliott; Principal of Pusey House, Oxford, since 1982; *b* 3 Dec. 1942; *o s* of late Clifford Edwin Ursell and Hilda Jane Ursell (*née* Tucker). *Educ:* Cathays High Sch.; University Coll. Cardiff (Craddock Wells Exhibnr; BA); St Stephen's House, Oxford. MA Oxon. Curate of Newton Nottage, Porthcawl, 1968–71; Asst Chaplain of University Coll. Cardiff, 1971–77; Chaplain of Polytechnic of Wales, 1974–77; Chaplain, Fellow and Dir of Studies in Music, Emmanuel Coll., Cambridge, 1977–82. Select Preacher, Harvard Univ., 1982, 1983, 1996, 1997; Univ. Preacher, Harvard Summer Sch., 1985. Warden, Soc. of Most Holy Trinity, Ascot Priory, 1985–. Examining Chaplain to the Bishop of London, 1987–. Mem. Governing Body, Church in Wales, 1971–77. *Recreations:* fine wines, opera, championing lost causes. *Address:* Pusey House, Oxford OX1 3LZ. *T:* (01865) 278415; Ascot Priory, Berks SL5 8RT. *T:* (01344) 885157.

URWICK, Sir Alan (Bedford), KCVO 1984; CMG 1978; Serjeant at Arms, House of Commons, 1989–95; *b* 2 May 1930; *s* of late Col Lyndall Fownes Urwick, OBE, MC and Joan Wilhelmina Saunders (*née* Bedford); *m* 1960, Marta, *o d* of Adhemar Montagne; three *s.* *Educ:* Dragon Sch.; Rugby (Schol.); New Coll., Oxford (Exhibr). 1st cl. hons Mod. History 1952. Joined HM Foreign (subseq. Diplomatic) Service, 1952; served in: Brussels, 1954–56; Moscow, 1958–59; Baghdad, 1960–61; Amman, 1965–67; Washington, 1967–70; Cairo, 1971–73; seconded to Cabinet Office as Asst Sec., Central Policy Review Staff, 1973–75; Head of Near East and N Africa Dept, FCO, 1975–76; Minister, Madrid, 1977–79; Ambassador to Jordan, 1979–84; Ambassador to Egypt, 1985–87; High Comr to Canada, 1987–89. Chm., Anglo-Jordanian Soc., 1997–2001. KStJ 1982. Grand Cordon, first class, Order of Independence (Jordan), 1984. *Address:* The Moat House, Slaugham Place, near Haywards Heath, Sussex RH17 6AL.

URWIN, Rt Rev. Lindsay Goodall; *see* Horsham, Bishop Suffragan of.

URWIN, (Terence) Peter; public sector consultant; Director of Administration and County Solicitor, Northumberland County Council, 1990–2000; *b* 28 Oct. 1948; *s* of John Robson Urwin; *m* 1971, Mary Theresa Smith; one *d.* *Educ:* Durham Johnston Sch.; Liverpool Univ. (LLB Hons). Solicitor. Durham County Council: Asst Solicitor, 1973–74; Asst Clerk of the Council, 1974–86; Dep. County Solicitor, 1986–90. Clerk to the Lieutenancy, Northumberland, 1990–2000. Secretary, Northumberland Advisory Committee: Justices of the Peace, 1990–2000; Gen. Comrs of Income Tax, 1990–2000. Mem. Council, Law Soc., 1997–2001. *Recreations:* Rugby, walking, crosswords. *Address:* Buckburns, Brancepeth Village, Durham City DH7 8DT. *T:* (0191) 378 3086.

USBORNE, Peter; *see* Usborne, T. P.

USBORNE, Richard Alexander; writer; *b* 16 May 1910; *s* of Charles Frederick Usborne, ICS, and Janet Muriel (*née* Lefroy); *m* 1938, Monica (*d* 1986), *d* of Archibald Stuart MacArthur, Wagon Mound, New Mexico, USA; one *s* one *d.* *Educ:* Summer Fields Preparatory Sch.; Charterhouse; Balliol Coll., Oxford. BA Mods and Greats; MA 1981. Served War, 1941–45: Army, SOE and PWE, Middle East, Major, Gen. List. Advertising agencies, 1933–36; part-owner and Editor of What's On, 1936–37; London Press Exchange, 1937–39; BBC Monitoring Service, 1939–41; Asst Editor, Strand Magazine, 1946–50; Dir, Graham & Gillies Ltd, Advertising, retd, 1970; Custodian, National Trust, 1974–81. *Publications:* Clubland Heroes, 1953 (rev. 1975, 1983); (ed) A Century of Summer Fields, 1964; Wodehouse at Work, 1961, rev. edn, as Wodehouse at Work to the End, 1977; (ed) Sunset at Blandings, 1977; (ed) Vintage Wodehouse, 1977; A Wodehouse Companion, 1981; (ed) Wodehouse 'Nuggets', 1983; (ed) The Penguin Wodehouse Companion, 1988; After Hours with P. G. Wodehouse, 1991; adaptations of Wodehouse novels and stories for BBC radio serials. *Recreations:* reading, writing light verse. *Address:* The Charterhouse, Charterhouse Square, EC1M 6AN. *T:* (020) 7608 0140.

USBORNE, (Thomas) Peter; Founder and Managing Director, Usborne Publishing Ltd, since 1973; *b* 18 Aug. 1937; *s* of Thomas George Usborne and Gerda (*née* Just); *m* 1964, Cornelie Tücking; one *s* one *d*. *Educ:* Summer Fields Sch., Oxford; Eton Coll.; Balliol Coll., Oxford (BA); INSEAD, Fontainebleau, France (MBA 1966). Co Founder and Man. Dir, Private Eye mag., 1962–65; Sen. Scientist, Metra Sigma Martech, 1967–68; Asst to Chm., BPC Publishing Ltd, 1969–70; Publishing Dir, Macdonald Educnl, 1970–73. *Recreations:* flying, gardening, France. *Clubs:* Garrick, Groucho.

USHER, Sir Andrew (John), 8th Bt *cr* 1899, of Norton, Ratho, Midlothian and of Wells, Hobkirk, Roxburghshire; interior decorator and builder; *b* 8 Feb. 1963; *er s* of Sir John Usher, 7th Bt and of Rosemary Margaret, *d* of Col Sir Reginald Houldsworth, 4th Bt, OBE, TD; *S* father, 1998; *m* 1987, Charlotte Louise Alexandra, *o d* of R. B. Eldridge; two *s*. *Educ:* Hilton Coll., S Africa. *Heir:* *s* Rory James Andrew Usher, *b* 11 June 1991. *Recreations:* golf, fishing.

USHER, Sir Leonard (Gray), KBE 1986 (CBE 1971); CF 1997; JP; Secretary, Fiji Press Council, 1985–94; Chairman, Suva Stock Exchange, 1978–92; *b* 29 May 1907; *s* of Robert Usher and Mary Elizabeth (*née* Johnston); *m* 1st, 1940, Mary Gertrude Lockie (marr. diss. 1962; she *d* 1997); one *s* one *d*; 2nd, 1962, Jane Hammond Derné (*d* 1984). *Educ:* Auckland Grammar Sch., NZ; Auckland Training Coll. (Trained Teachers Cert. B); Auckland Univ. (BA). Headmaster, Levuka Public Sch., Provincial Schs, Queen Victoria Sch., 1930–43; Fiji Govt PRO, 1943–56; Exec. Dir, Fiji Times and Herald Ltd, 1957–73; Editor, Fiji Times, 1958–73; Org. Dir, Pacific Is News Assoc., 1974–85 (Councillor and Life Mem., 1985–). Chm., Fiji Develt Bank, 1978–82; Dep. Chm., Nat. Bank of Fiji, 1974–83. Mem., Suva CC, 1962–71, 1975–77; Mayor of Suva, 1966–70, 1975–76. Chm., Fiji Coll. of Honour, 1995–97. *Publications:* Satellite Over The Pacific, 1975; 50 Years in Fiji, 1978; (jtly) Suva—a history and guide, 1978; Levuka School Century, 1979; (jtly) This is Radio Fiji, 1979; The Lodge of Fiji 1882–1982, 1982; (ed) Pacific News Media, 1986; Mainly About Fiji, 1987; 60 Years in Fiji, 1988; Letters From Fiji 1987–1990, 1992; More Letters from Fiji 1990–1994, 1994. *Recreations:* reading, computer programmes, conversation. *Address:* 24 Des Voeux Road, Suva, Fiji. *T:* 302025, *Fax:* 303025; PO Box 13250, Suva, Fiji. *Clubs:* Defence, Fiji, United, Ex-Servicemen's (Fiji); Royal Automobile (Sydney).

USTINOV, Sir Peter (Alexander), Kt 1990; CBE 1975; FRSA, FRSL; actor, dramatist, film director; Chancellor, Durham University, since 1992; Rector of the University of Dundee, 1971–73; Goodwill Ambassador for UNICEF, 1969; *b* London, 16 April 1921; *s* of late Iona Ustinov and Nadia Benois, painter; *m* 1st, 1940, Isolde Denham (marr. diss. 1950); one *d*; 2nd, 1954, Suzanne Cloutier (marr. diss. 1971); one *s* two *d*; 3rd, 1972, Hélène du Lau d'Allemans. *Educ:* Westminster School. Served in Army, Royal Sussex Regt and RAOC, 1942–46. Author of plays: House of Regrets, 1940 (prod Arts Theatre 1942); Blow Your Own Trumpet, 1941 (prod Playhouse [Old Vic] 1943); Beyond, 1942 (prod Arts Theatre, 1943); The Banbury Nose, 1943 (prod Wyndham's, 1944); The Tragedy of Good Intentions, 1944 (prod Old Vic, Liverpool, 1945); The Indifferent Shepherd (prod Criterion, 1948); Frenzy (adapted from Swedish of Ingmar Bergman, prod and acted in St Martin's, 1948); The Man in the Raincoat (Edinburgh Festival, 1949); The Love of Four Colonels (and acted in, Wyndham's, 1951); The Moment of Truth (Adelphi, 1951); High Balcony, 1952 (written 1946); No Sign of the Dove (Savoy, 1953); The Empty Chair (Bristol Old Vic, 1956); Romanoff and Juliet (Piccadilly, 1956, film, 1961; musical, R loves J, Chichester, 1973); Photo Finish (prod and acted in it, Saville, 1962); The Life in My Hands, 1963; The Unknown Soldier and his Wife, 1967 (prod and acted in it, Chichester, 1968, New London, 1973); Halfway up the Tree (Queen's), 1967; compiled, prod and acted in The Marriage, Edinburgh, 1982; wrote and acted in Beethoven's Tenth (Vaudeville, 1983, 1987–88); An Evening with Peter Ustinov, (Haymarket), 1990, 1991, 1994. Co-Author of film: The Way Ahead, 1943–44. Author and Director of films: School for Secrets, 1946; Vice-Versa, 1947. Author, director, producer and main actor in film Private Angelo, 1946; acted in films: One of Our Aircraft is Missing, 1941; The Way Ahead, 1944; Odette, Quo Vadis, Hotel Sahara, 1950; Beau Brummell, The Egyptian, We're No Angels, 1954; Lola Montez, 1955; The Spies, 1955; I Girovaghi, 1956; An Angel Flew Over Brooklyn, 1957; Spartacus, 1960 (Academy Award, Best Supporting Actor, 1961); The Sundowners, 1961; Romanoff and Juliet, 1961; Topkapi (Academy Award, Best Supporting Actor), 1964; John Goldfarb, Please Come Home, 1964; Blackbeard's Ghost, 1967; The Comedians, 1968; Hot Millions, 1968; Viva Max, 1969; Big Truck and Poor Clare, 1971; One of our Dinosaurs is Missing, 1974; Logan's Run, 1975; Treasure of Matecumbe, 1977; Un Taxi Mauve, 1977; The Last Remake of Beau Geste, 1977; Death on the Nile, 1978 (Best Film Actor, Variety Club of GB); Ashanti, The Thief of Baghdad, 1979; Charlie Chan and the Curse of the Dragon Queen, 1981; Evil under the Sun, 1981; Appointment with Death, 1988; The French Revolution, 1989; Lorenzo's Oil, 1992; The Phoenix and the Magic Carpet, 1994; Stiff Upper Lips, 1998; director, producer and actor in film Billy Budd, 1961; director and actor in films: Hammersmith is Out, 1971; Memed My Hawk, 1984. Directed operas at: Covent Garden, 1962; Hamburg Opera, 1968, 1985, 1987; Paris Opera, 1973; Edinburgh Fest., 1973, 1981; Deutsche Oper, Berlin, 1978; Piccola Scala, Milan, 1981, 1982; Dresden Opera, 1993; Bolshoi, 1997. Master's Course (opera direction), Salzburg, 1986. Acted in: revues: Swinging the Gate, 1940, Diversion, 1941; plays: Crime and Punishment, New Theatre, 1946; Love in Albania, St James's, 1949; King Lear, Stratford, Ont, 1979; Beethoven's Tenth, Berlin, 1987; directed Lady L, 1965; *television:* Omnibus: the life of Samuel Johnson (Emmy Award), 1957–58; Barefoot in Athens (Emmy Award), 1966; Storm in Summer (Emmy Award), 1970; The Mighty Continent (series), 1974; Einstein's Universe (series), 1979; 13 at Dinner, 1985; Dead Man's Folly, 1985; World Challenge (series), 1985; Peter Ustinov's Russia (series), 1987; Peter Ustinov in China, 1987 (ACE Award, 1988); Around the World in 80 Days, 1988–89; Secret Identity of Jack the Ripper, 1989; Ustinov aboard the Orient Express, 1992; Ustinov Meets Pavarotti, 1993; Inside the Vatican, 1994; The Old Curiosity Shop, 1995; Haydn Gala, 1995; Sir Peter Ustinov in Thailand, Sir Peter Ustinov in Hong Kong, 1995; Paths of Gods, 1995; Planet Ustinov, 1998; Alice in Wonderland, 2000; Victoria and Albert, 2001. Member: British Film Academy; Acad. of Fine Arts, Paris, 1988. Pres., World Federalist Movt, 1992–; Mem., British USA Bicentennial Liaison Cttee, 1973–. Hon. doctorates include: Hon. DMus Cleveland Inst. of Music, 1967; Hon. DHL Georgetown Univ., 1988; Hon. LLD Ottawa, 1991; Hon. DLitt Durham, 1992; Hon. Dr St Michael's Coll., Toronto, 1995; Dr *hc* Free Flemish Univ., Brussels, 1995. Benjamin Franklin Medal, Royal Society of Arts, 1957; UNICEF award, 1978, 1995; Gold Medal, City of Athens, 1990; Medal of the Greek Red Cross, 1990; Medal of Honour, Charles Univ., Prague, 1991; Grammy Award; Britannia Award, LA Br., BAFTA, 1992; Critics' Circle Award, 1993; German Cultural Award, 1994; German Bambi, 1994; Internat. Child Survival Award, UNICEF, 1995; Rudolph Valentino Award for Lifetime Achievement in Motion Pictures, 1995; Norman Cousins Global Governance Award, World Federalist Movt, 1995. Order of the Smile (for dedication to idea of internat. assistance to children), Warsaw, 1974; Commandeur des Arts et des Lettres (France), 1985; Order of El Istiglal (Jordan); Order of Yugoslav Flag (Yugoslavia); Ordem Nacional do Cruzerio do Sul (Brazil), 1994. *Publications:* House of Regrets, 1943; Beyond, 1944; The Banbury Nose, 1945; Plays About People, 1950; The Love of Four Colonels, 1951; The Moment of Truth, 1953; Romanoff and Juliet (Stage and Film); Add a Dash of Pity (short stories), 1959; Ustinov's Diplomats (a book of photographs), 1960; The Loser (novel), 1961; The Frontiers of the Sea, 1966; Krumnagel, 1971; Dear Me (autobiog.), 1977; Overheard (play), 1981; My Russia, 1983; Ustinov in Russia, 1987; The Disinformer, 1989; The Old Man and Mr Smith, 1990; Ustinov at Large (compilation of articles in The European), 1991; Still at Large (compilation of articles in The European), 1993 and 1995; Quotable Ustinov, 1995; Monsieur René, 1998; contributor short stories to Atlantic Monthly. *Recreations:* lawn tennis, squash, collecting old masters' drawings, music. *Address:* The Ustinov Foundation Office, Höhenberg Strasse 20, 82340 Feldafing, Germany. *Clubs:* Garrick, Savage, Royal Automobile, Arts Theatre, Queen's.

UTEEM, Cassam; President, Republic of Mauritius, since 1992; *b* 22 March 1941; *s* of Omar and Aisha Uteem; *m* 1967, Zohra Uteem; two *s* one *d*. *Educ:* Univ. of Mauritius (Dip. Soc. Work); Univ. of Paris VII (LèsL, MPsychol). Mem., Municipal Council, Port Louis, 1969, 1977–79, 1986–88 (Lord Mayor, 1986); MLA Port Louis East/Maritime, 1982–92; Minister of Employment, Social Security and National Solidarity, 1982–83; Opposition Whip, 1983–87; Chm., Public Accounts Cttee, 1988–90; Dep. Prime Minister and Minister of Industry and Industrial Technol., 1990–92. Hon. DCL Mauritius, 1994; Dr *hc* Aix Marseilles III, 1994. Grand Commander, Order of Star and Key of the Indian Ocean (Republic of Mauritius), 1993. *Recreations:* reading, walking. *Address:* State House, Le Reduit, Mauritius. *T:* 4543021.

UTLEY, (Clifton) Garrick; journalist and broadcaster, since 1964; contributor, CNN, New York, since 1997; *b* 19 Nov. 1939; *s* of late Clifton Maxwell Utley and of Frayn Garrick Utley; *m* 1973, Gertje Rommeswinkel. *Educ:* Carleton Coll., Northfield, Minn, USA (BA 1961); Free Univ., Berlin. Correspondent, NBC News: Saigon, Vietnam, 1964–65; Berlin, Germany, 1966–68; Paris, France, 1969–71; NY, 1971–72; London (Senior European Correspondent), 1973–79; New York (Chief Foreign Correspondent), 1980–93; Chief Foreign Correspondent, ABC News, London, 1993–96. Numerous documentary films on foreign affairs. Hon. LLD: Carleton Coll., 1979; Pomona Coll., 2001. *Recreations:* music, conversation, languages. *Address:* 19 East 88th Street, New York, NY 10128, USA. *Club:* Century (New York).

UTLEY, Prof. James Henry Paul; Professor of Organic Chemistry, Queen Mary and Westfield College (formerly at Queen Mary College), University of London, 1983–2001, now Emeritus; *b* 11 Sept. 1936; *s* of Victor Eric Utley and Lena Beatrice Utley; *m* 1959, Hazel Wendler (*née* Brown); two *s* two *d*. *Educ:* E. P. Collier Sch., Reading; Univ. of Hull (BSc, PhD); Technische Hogeschool, Delft; University College London; DSc London. CChem, FRSC. NATO Research Fellowships, 1961–62; Queen Mary, later Queen Mary and Westfield College, London: Lectr, 1963–76; Reader in Organic Chemistry, 1976–83; Head of Chemistry, 1987–91, 1997–99; Dean, Faculty of Natural Scis, 1991–94; Mem. Council, 1991–94. Guest Professor: Univ. of Aarhus, 1973; Univ. of Münster, 1985; Ecole Normale Supérieure, Paris, 1994; Univ. of Texas at Austin, 1995. M. M. Baizer Award, Electrochem. Soc., USA, 2000. *Publications:* research and review articles in internat. learned jls. *Recreations:* walking, bowls, jazz. *Address:* Department of Chemistry, Queen Mary, University of London, Mile End Road, E1 4NS. *T:* (020) 7882 5023. *Club:* Heathfield (Wandsworth Common).

UTSUMI, Yoshio; Secretary-General, International Telecommunication Union, United Nations, since 1999; *b* 14 Aug. 1942; *m* 1970, Masako Okubo; one *s* one *d*. *Educ:* Univ. of Tokyo (BA Law); Univ. of Chicago (MA Pol Sci.). Joined Min. of Posts and Telecommunications (MPT), Japan, 1966; Prof. of Public Admin, MPT Postal Coll., 1972–73; First Sec., i/c ITU Affairs, Perm. Mission of Japan, Geneva, 1978–81; Dir, Computer Communication Div. and of Policy Div., Communications Policy Bureau, 1982–86; Dir, Fund Mgt Div., Postal Life Insurance Bureau, 1986–88; Dir, Gen Affairs Div., Broadcasting Bureau, 1988–89; Asst Vice-Minister, 1990–91; Dep. Dir-Gen., Communications Policy Bureau, 1991–93; Dir-Gen., Internat. Affairs Dept, 1993–95; Dep. Minister for Internat. Affairs, 1995–96; Dir-Gen. of Posts, 1996–97; Dep. Minister, 1997-99. Chm., ITU Plenipotentiary Conf., 1994. *Address:* International Telecommunication Union, Place des Nations, 1211 Geneva 20, Switzerland.

UTTING, Sir William (Benjamin), Kt 1991; CB 1985; President, National Institute for Social Work, since 1997 (Chairman, 1991–97); *b* 13 May 1931; *s* of John William Utting and Florence Ada Utting; *m* 1954, Mildred Jackson; two *s* one *d*. *Educ:* Great Yarmouth Grammar Sch.; New Coll., Oxford (MA; Hon. Fellow, 1996); Barnett House, Oxford. Probation Officer: Co. Durham, 1956–58; Norfolk, 1958–61; Sen. Probation Officer, Co. Durham, 1961–64; Principal Probation Officer, Newcastle upon Tyne, 1964–68; Lectr in Social Studies, Univ. of Newcastle upon Tyne, 1968–70; Dir of Social Services, Kensington and Chelsea, 1970–76; Chief Social Work Officer, DHSS, 1976–85; Chief Inspector, Social Services Inspectorate, DHSS, subseq. DoH, 1985–91. Member: Chief Scientist's Res. Cttee, DHSS, 1973–76; SSRC, 1979–83; ESRC, 1984; Cttee on Standards in Public Life, 1994–2001. Member Council: Goldsmiths' Coll., 1993– (Dep. Chair, 1995–99; Chair, 2000–); Caldecott Community, 1998–. Chairman: Mary Ward House Trust, 1997–; Forum on Children and Violence, 1997–2000; Vice-Pres., Nat. Family Mediation, 1997–; Pres., Mental Health Foundn, 1999– (Trustee, 1988–97; Vice-Pres., 1997–99); Trustee: Joseph Rowntree Foundn, 1991– (Dep. Chm., 2001–); CSV, 1991–97; Family Fund Trust, 1996–2000. Hon. DLitt: UEA, 1992; East London, 1998; Hon. DCL Northumbria, 1997; Hon. DSc Kingston, 2000. *Publications:* Children in the Public Care, 1991; People Like Us, 1997; contribs to professional jls. *Recreations:* literature, music, art. *Address:* 76 Great Brownings, SE21 7HR. *T:* (020) 8670 1201.

UXBRIDGE, Earl of; Charles Alexander Vaughan Paget; *b* 13 Nov 1950; *s and heir* of 7th Marquess of Anglesey, *qv*; *m* 1986, Georganne Elizabeth Elliott, *d* of Col John Alfred Downes, MBE, MC; one *s* one *d*. *Educ:* Dragon School, Oxford; Eton; Exeter Coll., Oxford; Sussex Univ. (MA, DPhil). *Heir:* *s* Lord Paget de Beaudesert, *qv*. *Address:* Plâs-Newydd, Llanfairpwll, Gwynedd LL61 6DZ.

UZIELL-HAMILTON, Adrianne Pauline; Her Honour Judge Uziell-Hamilton; a Circuit Judge, since 1990; *b* 14 May 1932; *e d* of late Dr Marcus and Ella Grantham; *m* 1952, Mario Reginald Uziell-Hamilton (*d* 1988); one *s* one *d*. *Educ:* Maria Gray's Academy for Girls and privately. Called to the Bar, Middle Temple, 1965; *ad eundem* Mem., Inner Temple, 1976–; Head of Chambers, 1976–90; a Recorder, 1985–90. Vice-Chm., Ethics Cttee, Nat. Hosp., 1993–95 (Mem., 1991–95); Member: Legal Aid Panel, 1969–90; Parole Bd, 1994–96; General Council of the Bar, 1970–74 (Exec. Cttee, 1973–74). Pres., Mental Health Review Tribunals, 1988. Gov., North London Univ. (formerly Polytechnic of N London), 1986–2000. FRSA. *Publications:* articles on marriage contracts. *Recreations:* collecting ballet and theatre costume design, cooking for friends, conversation.

See also F. Hamilton.

V

VACHON, His Eminence Cardinal Louis-Albert, CC (Canada) 1969; OQ 1985; FRSC 1974; Officier de l'Ordre de la fidélité française, 1963; Archbishop (RC) of Quebec and Primate of Canada, 1981–90; *b* 4 Feb. 1912; *s* of Napoléon Vachon and Alexandrine Gilbert. *Educ:* Laval Univ. (PhD Philosophy, 1947); PhD Theology, Angelicum, Rome, 1949. Ordained priest, 1938; Prof. of Philosophy, 1941–47, Prof. of Theology, 1949–55, Laval Univ. Superior, Grand Séminaire de Québec, 1955–59; Superior General, 1960–77; Auxiliary Bishop of Quebec, 1977–81; Cardinal, 1985. Vice-Rector of Laval Univ., 1959–60, Rector, 1960–72. Mem., Royal Canadian Soc. of Arts. Hon. FRCP&S (Canada), 1972. Hon. doctorates: Montreal, McGill and Victoria, 1964; Guelph, 1966; Moncton, 1967; Queen's, Bishop's and Strasbourg, 1968; Notre-Dame (Indiana), 1971; Carleton, 1972; Laval, 1982. Centennial Medal, 1967. KHS 1985; KM 1987. *Publications:* Espérance et Présomption, 1958; Vérité et Liberté, 1962; Unité de l'Université, 1962; Apostolat de l'universitaire catholique, 1963; Mémorial, 1963; Communauté universitaire, 1963; Progrès de l'université et consentement populaire, 1964; Responsabilité collective des universitaires, 1964; Les humanités aujourd'hui, 1966; Excellence et loyauté des universitaires, 1969; Pastoral Letters, 1981. *Recreations:* reading, beaux arts. *Address:* 1 rue des Remparts, Quebec, QC G1R 5L7, Canada.

VAEA, Baron of Houma; Chairman: National Reserve Bank Board, since 1989; Shipping Corporation of Polynesia; *b* 15 May 1921; *s* of Viliami Vilai Tupou and Tupou Seini Vaea; *m* 1952, Tuputupu Ma'afu; three *s* three *d. Educ:* Wesley College, Auckland, NZ. RNZAF, 1942–45; Tonga Civil Service, 1945–53; ADC to HM Queen Salote, 1954–59; Governor of Ha'apai, 1959–68; Commissioner and Consul in UK, 1969; High Comr in UK, 1970–72; Minister for Labour, Commerce and Industries, 1973–91; Actg Dep. Prime Minister, 1986; Prime Minister of Tonga, 1991–2000; Minister of Agric. and Forestry, for Marine and Ports, responsible for Telecommunications, 1991–2000. Chairman: Tonga Telecommunications Commn, 1991–2000; Tonga Broadcasting Commn, 1991–2000; Chm., Tonga Investment Ltd, 1991–. Given the title Baron Vaea of Houma by HM The King of Tonga, 1970. *Recreations:* fishing, tennis. *Heir: e s* Albert Tu'ivanuavou Vaea, *b* 19 Sept. 1957. *Address:* PO Box 262, Nuku'alofa, Tonga.

VAI, Sir Mea, Kt 1996; CBE 1988; ISO 1980; retired public servant, Papua New Guinea; *b* 7 Aug. 1933; *s* of late Rev. Vai Hekure and Konio Toua; *m* 1956, Reia Gau; four *s* two *d. Educ:* Administrative Coll., PNG (matriculation). Started employment with Dept of Dist Services and Native Affairs, Australian Admin, 1949; served in Depts of Home Affairs, Education, Foreign Affairs and Trade, PNG; retired 1990. *Recreations:* reading, camping, hiking, swimming. *Address:* PO Box 240, Konedobu, Port Moresby, Papua New Guinea. *T:* 3212610. *Club:* Aviat Social (Port Moresby).

VAISEY, David George, CBE 1996; FSA; FRHistS; Bodley's Librarian, Oxford, 1986–96, now Emeritus; Keeper of the Archives, Oxford University, 1995–2000; Professorial Fellow then Fellow by Special Election, Exeter College, Oxford, 1975, now Emeritus; *b* 15 March 1935; *s* of William Thomas Vaisey and Minnie Vaisey (*née* Payne); *m* 1965, Maureen Anne (*née* Mansell); two *d. Educ:* Rendcomb Coll., Glos (schol.); Exeter Coll., Oxford (Exhibnr; BA Mod. Hist., MA). 2nd Lieut, Glos Regt and KAR, 1955–56. Archivist, Staffordshire CC, 1960–63; Asst then Sen. Asst Librarian, Bodleian Liby, 1963–75; Dep. Keeper, Oxford Univ. Archives, 1966–75; Keeper of Western Manuscripts, Bodleian Liby, 1975–86. Vis. Prof., Liby Studies, UCLA, 1985. Hon. Res. Fellow, Dept of Library, Archive and Information Studies, UCL, 1987–. Member: Royal Commn on Historical Manuscripts, 1986–98; Adv. Council on Public Records, 1989–94; Expert Panel on Museums, Libraries and Archives, Heritage Lottery Fund, 1999–; Archive, Libraries and Information Adv. Cttee, English Heritage, 1999–; Chm., Nat. Council on Archives, 1988–91. Vice-Pres., British Records Assoc., 1998–; Pres., Soc. of Archivists, 1999–. FRHistS 1973; FSA 1974. Hon. Fellow, Kellogg Coll., Oxford, 1996. Encomienda, Order of Isabel the Catholic (Spain), 1989. *Publications:* Staffordshire and The Great Rebellion (jtly), 1964; Probate Inventories of Lichfield and District 1568–1680, 1969; (jtly) Victorian and Edwardian Oxford from old photographs, 1971; (jtly) Oxford Shops and Shopping, 1972; (jtly) Art for Commerce, 1973; Oxfordshire: a handbook for students of local history, 1973, 2nd edn 1974; The Diary of Thomas Turner 1754–65, 1984; articles in learned jls and collections. *Address:* 12 Hernes Road, Oxford OX2 7PU.

VAIZEY, Lady; Marina Vaizey; writer, lecturer and art critic; Editor, National Art Collections Fund Publications, 1991–94 (Editorial Consultant, 1994–98); *b* 16 Jan. 1938; *o d* of late Lyman and Ruth Stansky; *m* 1961, Lord Vaizey (*d* 1984); two *s* one *d. Educ:* Brearley Sch., New York; Putney Sch., Putney, Vermont; Radcliffe Coll., Harvard Univ. (BA Medieval History and Lit.); Girton Coll., Cambridge (BA, MA). Art Critic: Financial Times, 1970–74; Sunday Times, 1974–91; Dance Critic, Now!, 1979–81. Member: Arts Council, 1976–79 (Mem. Art Panel, 1973–79, Dep. Chm., 1976–79); Advisory Cttee, DoE, 1975–81; Paintings for Hospitals, 1974–90; Cttee, Contemporary Art Soc., 1975–79, 1980–94 (Hon. Sec., 1988–94); Hist. of Art and Complementary Studies Bd, CNAA, 1978–82; Photography Bd, CNAA, 1979–81; Fine Art Bd, CNAA, 1980–83; Passenger Services Sub-Cttee, Heathrow Airport, 1979–83; Visual Arts Adv. Cttee, British Council, 1987–; Crafts Council, 1988–94; Art Wkg Gp, National Curriculum, DES, 1990–91; Cttee, 20th Century Soc., 1995–98; Gov., South Bank Bd, 1993–; Trustee: Nat. Museums and Galleries on Merseyside, 1986–2001 (Pres., Friends of NMGM, 1994–); Geffrye Museum, London, 1990–; Imperial War Museum, 1991–; London Open House, 1996–; Assoc. for Cultural Exchange, 1998–; Internat. Rescue Cttee UK, 1998–; Exec. Dir, Mitchell Prize for the Hist. of Art, 1976–87. Governor: Camberwell Coll. of Arts and Crafts, 1971–82; Bath Acad. of Art, Corsham, 1978–81. Curated: Critic's Choice, Tooth's, 1974; Painter as Photographer, touring exhibn, UK, 1982–85; Shining Through, Crafts Council, 1995. Turner Prize Judge, 1997. *Publications:* 100 Masterpieces of Art, 1979; Andrew Wyeth, 1980; The Artist as Photographer, 1982; Peter Blake, 1985; Christiane Kubrick, 1990; Christo, 1990; Sorensen, 1994; Picasso's Ladies, 1998; Sutton Taylor, 1999; Felim Egan, 1999; (with Charlotte Gere) Great Women Collectors, 1999; (ed) Art, the Critics' Choice, 1999; Magdalene Odundo, 2001. *Address:* 24 Heathfield Terrace, Chiswick, W4 4JE. *T:* (020) 8994 7994, *Fax:* (020) 8995 8057; *e-mail:* marina@vaizey.demon.co.uk.

VAJDA, Christopher Stephen; QC 1997; *b* 6 July 1955; *s* of late Stephen Vajda and of Heidi Vajda (*née* Schmalhorst). *Educ:* Winchester Coll.; Corpus Christi Coll., Cambridge (MA); Inst d'Etudes Européennes, Brussels (Licence speciale en droit européen). Called to the Bar, Gray's Inn, 1979, NI, 1996. Mem., Supplementary Panel, Treasury Counsel, 1993–97. *Publication:* (contrib.) Bellamy & Child, Common Market Law of Competition, 3rd edn 1987, 5th edn 2001. *Recreations:* architecture, opera, theatre, tennis. *Address:* Monckton Chambers, 4 Raymond Buildings, Gray's Inn, WC1R 5DP. *T:* (020) 7405 7211. *Club:* Royal Automobile.

VAJPAYEE, Atal Bihari; Member, Lok Sabha, 1957–62, 1967–84 and since 1991; Prime Minister of India, May 1996 and since 1998; Leader, Bharatiya Janata Party Parliamentary Party, 1980–84, 1986–91, and since 1993; *b* Gwalior, Madhya Pradesh, 25 Dec. 1926; *s* of Shri Krishna Bihari; unmarried. *Educ:* Victoria Coll., Gwalior; D.A.V. Coll., Kanpur (MA). Journalist and social worker. Arrested in freedom movement, 1942; Founder Mem., Jana Sangh, 1951–77; Leader, Jana Sangh Parly Party, 1957–77; Pres., Bharatiaya Jana Sangh, 1968–73; detained 26 June 1975, during Emergency; Founder Member: Janata Party, 1977–80; Bharatiya Janata Party, 1980– (Pres., 1980–86). Mem., Rajya Sabha, 1962–67 and 1986–91; Minister of External Affairs, 1977–79; Leader of the Opposition, Lok Sabha, 1993–98; Chairman: Cttee on Govt Assurances, 1966–67; Public Accounts Cttee, 1969–70, 1991–92; Cttee on Petitions, 1990–91. Member: Parly Goodwill Mission to E Africa, 1965; Parly Delegns to Australia, 1967, Eur. Parlt, 1983; Member: Indian Delegation: to CPA meetings in Canada, 1966, Zambia, 1980, IOM, 1984; to IPU Confs in Japan, 1974, Sri Lanka, 1975, Switzerland, 1984; to UN Gen. Assembly, 1988, 1989, 1990, 1991. Mem., Nat. Integration Council, 1958–62, 1967–73, 1986, 1991–. President: All India Station Masters and Asst Station Masters Assoc., 1965–70; Pandit Deen Dayal Upadhyay Smarak Samiti, 1968–84; Pandit Deen Dayal Upadhyaya Janma Bhumi Smarak Samiti, 1979–. Formerly Editor: Rashtra-dharma; Panchajanya; Veer Arjun. *Publications:* Lok Sabha Mein Atalji (collection of speeches); Qaidi Kavirai ki Kundaliyan; New Dimensions of India's Foreign Policy; Sansad Mein Teen Dashak (collection of speeches). *Address:* (office) South Block, New Delhi 110011, India; Shinde ki Chhawni, Gwalior, MP, India; 7 Race Course Road, New Delhi 110001, India. *T:* (11) 3018939.

VALE, Brian, CBE 1994 (OBE 1977); Regional Director for Middle East and North Africa, British Council, 1995; retired; *b* 26 May 1938; *s* of Leslie Vale and May (*née* Knowles); *m* 1966, Margaret Mary Cookson; two *s. Educ:* Sir Joseph Williamson's Mathematical Sch., Rochester; Keele Univ. (BA, DipEd); King's Coll., London (MPhil). HMOCS, N Rhodesia, 1960–63; Assistant to Comr for N Rhodesia, London, 1963–64; Educn Attaché, Zambia High Commn, London, 1964–65; British Council: Rio de Janeiro, 1965–68; Appts Div., 1968–72; Educn and Sci. Div., 1972–75; Rep., Saudi Arabia, 1975–78; Dep. Controller, Educn and Sci. Div., 1978–80; Dir Tech. Educn and Trng Orgn for Overseas Countries, 1980–81; Controller, Sci., Technol. and Educn Div., 1981–83; Rep. in Egypt, and Cultural Counsellor, British Embassy, Cairo, 1983–87; Asst Dir Gen., 1987–90; Dir, Spain, and Cultural Attaché, British Embassy, Madrid, 1991–95. Chm., Internat. Family Health, 1998–. FRSA. Medalha Merito Tamandaré (Brazil), 1997. *Publications:* Independence or Death: British sailors and Brazilian independence, 1996; A War Betwixt Englishmen: Argentina versus Brazil in the River Plate 1825–30, 1999; A Frigate of King George: life and duty on HMS Doris 1807–1829, 2001; contribs to specialist jls on naval hist. *Recreations:* reading, talking, naval history. *Address:* 40 Gloucester Circus, SE10 8RY. *T:* (020) 8858 6233.

VALENTIA, 15th Viscount *cr* 1622 (Ireland); **Richard John Dighton Annesley;** Bt 1620; Baron Mountnorris 1628; farmer in Zimbabwe, since 1957; *b* 15 Aug. 1929; *s* of 14th Viscount Valentia, MC, MRCS, LRCP, and Joan Elizabeth (*d* 1986), *d* of late John Joseph Curtis; *S* father, 1983; *m* 1957, Anita Phyllis, *o d* of William Arthur Joy, Bristol; two *s* one *d* (and one *s* decd). *Educ:* Marlborough; RMA Sandhurst. BA Univ. of S Africa. Commnd RA, 1950; retd, rank of Captain, 1957. Schoolmaster, Ruzawi Prep. Sch., Marondera, Zimbabwe, 1977–83. *Recreations:* sport, shooting, fishing, leisure riding. *Heir: s* Hon. Francis William Dighton Annesley [*b* 29 Dec. 1959; *m* 1982, Shaneen Hobbs; two *d*].

VALENTINE, Rt Rev. Barry, MA, BD, LTh, DD; Rector, Parish of Salt Spring Island, British Columbia, 1989–95; *b* 26 Sept. 1927; *s* of Harry John Valentine and Ethel Margaret Purkiss; *m* 1st, 1952, Mary Currell Hayes; three *s* one *d*; 2nd, 1984, Shirley Carolyn Shean Evans. *Educ:* Brentwood Sch.; St John's Coll., Cambridge; McGill Univ., Montreal. Curate, Christ Church Cath., Montreal, 1952; Incumbent, Chateauguay-Beauharnois, 1954; Dir, Religious Educn, Dio. Montreal, 1957; Rector of St Lambert, PQ, 1961; Exec. Officer, Dio. Montreal, 1965; Dean of Montreal, 1968; Bishop Coadjutor of Rupert's Land, 1969; Bishop of Rupert's Land, 1970–82; Chaplain, Univ. of British Columbia, 1984–85; Asst Bishop of Maryland, 1986–89. Interim Rector, St Paul's Parish, Washington, 1997. Chancellor, 1970, Res. Fellow, 1983, St John's Coll., Winnipeg. Hon. DD: St John's Coll., Winnipeg, 1969; Montreal Dio. Theol Coll., 1970. *Publication:* The Gift that is in you, 1984. *Recreations:* music, theatre, walking, reading. *Address:* 111 Carlin Avenue, Salt Spring Island, BC V8K 2J5, Canada.

VALENTINE, Caroline, (Mrs Malcolm Valentine); *see* Charles, Caroline.

VALENTINE, (Christopher) Robert; Executive Director, Learning and Skills Council, Nottinghamshire; *b* 28 March 1948; *s* of Robert and Barbara Valentine; *m* 1969, Aline Margaret Wielding; one *s* one *d*. *Educ:* Sheffield Univ. (BA Hons, CertEd, MPhil). Lectr, Granville Coll., Sheffield, 1969; Lectr and Sen. Lectr, Stannington Coll., Sheffield, 1970–81; seconded to Manpower Services Commn, 1981; seconded to Further Education Staff Coll., 1983; joined Notts LEA, 1985; Dep. Dir of Educn, 1991–94, Dir of Educn, 1994–2000, Notts CC. *Recreations:* wildfowling, rough shooting, game shooting, trout fishing, Manchester United FC. *Address:* Learning and Skills Council, Castle Marina R9, Castle Marina Park, Nottingham NG7 1TN.

VALIANT, Prof. Leslie Gabriel, FRS 1991; T. Jefferson Coolidge Professor of Computer Science and Applied Mathematics, Harvard University, since 2001; *b* 28 March 1949; *s* of Leslie Valiant and Eva Julia (*née* Ujlaki); *m* 1977, Gayle Lynne Dyckoff; two *s*. *Educ:* Tynemouth High Sch.; Latymer Upper Sch.; King's Coll., Cambridge (MA); Imperial Coll., London (DIC); Warwick Univ. (PhD). Vis. Asst Prof., Carnegie Mellon Univ., Pittsburgh, 1973–74; Lecturer: Leeds Univ., 1974–76; Edinburgh Univ., 1977–81, Reader 1981–82; Gordon McKay Prof. of Computer Sci. and Applied Maths, Harvard Univ., 1982–2001. Vis. Prof., Harvard Univ., 1982; Vis. Fellow, Oxford Univ. Computing Lab. and Merton Coll., Oxford, 1987–88; Guggenheim Fellow, 1985–86. Fellow, Amer. Assoc. for Artificial Intelligence, 1992; Mem., NAS, 2001. Nevanlinna Prize, IMU, 1986; Knuth Prize, ACM/IEEE, 1997. *Publications:* Circuits of the Mind, 1994; research papers in scientific jls. *Address:* Division of Engineering and Applied Sciences, Harvard University, 33 Oxford Street, Cambridge, MA 02138, USA. *T:* (617) 4955817.

VALIN, Reginald Pierre; business consultant; *b* 8 March 1938; *s* of Pierre Louis Valin and Molly Doreen Valin; *m* 1960, Brigitte Karin Leister; one *d*. *Educ:* Emanuel School. Bank of America, 1959–60; Charles Barker & Sons Ltd, later Charles Barker City, 1960–79: Dir, 1971–73; Man. Dir, 1973–76; Chief Exec., 1976–79; Founder Dir, Valin Pollen, subseq. The VPI Gp: Chm. and Chief Exec., 1979–89, Dep. Chm., 1989–90. Dir, Tallisfield, 1999–. *Address:* 38 Monckton Court, Melbury Road, W14 8NF. *T:* (020) 7371 1872.

VALIOS, Nicholas Paul; QC 1991; a Recorder of the Crown Court, since 1986; *b* 5 May 1943; *s* of Nicholas William and Elizabeth Joan Valios; *m* 1967, Cynthia Valerie Horton; one *s* one *d*. *Educ:* Stonyhurst Coll., Lancs. Called to the Bar, Inner Temple, 1964; Mem., SE Circuit. *Recreations:* windsurfing, golf, reading, computers. *Address:* Francis Taylor Building, Temple, EC4Y 7BY. *T:* (020) 7353 7768.

VALLANCE, Air Vice-Marshal Andrew George Buchanan, OBE 1987; FRAeS; Executive Assistant to Chief of Staff, Command Group, Supreme Headquarters Allied Powers Europe, since 2000; *b* 7 April 1948; *s* of George Charles Buchanan Vallance and Dorothy Mabel Vallance (*née* Wooton); *m* 1972, Katharine Ray Fox; one *s* one *d*. *Educ:* RAF Coll., Cranwell; RAF Staff Coll. (psa 1980); Queens' Coll., Cambridge (MPhil Internat. Relns 1988). Commnd RAF, 1969; sqdn pilot with Nos 9, 617 and 27 Sqdns; Flight Comdr, No 50 Sqdn, 1977–79; Personal SO to Air Mem. for Personnel, 1981; OC No 55 Sqdn, 1982–84; Personal SO to CAS, 1984–87; Dir of Defence Studies, 1988–90; Chief of Mil. Co-op., SHAPE, 1991–93; OC RAF Wyton, 1993–95; Dep. Dir, Nuclear Policy, MoD, 1995; Chief, Special Weapons Br., SHAPE, 1996–98; COS, Reaction Forces Air Staff, NATO, 1998–2000; COS and Dep. C-in-C, RAF Personnel Trng Comd, 2000. FRAeS 1999. Member: RUSI, 1988–; IISS, 1988–. *Publications:* Air Power, 1989; RAF Air Power Doctrine, 1990; The Air Weapon, 1995; contrib. numerous articles to various defence jls. *Recreations:* military history, classical music, structural gardening, strategic studies. *Address:* Lloyds TSB, West Bromwich; EACOS CSI, Command Group, SHAPE, BFPO 26. *Club:* Royal Air Force.

VALLANCE, Dr Elizabeth Mary, (Lady Vallance); JP; Founder and Chairman, me too, since 1999; *b* 8 April 1945; *e d* of William Henderson McGonnigill and Hon. Jean, *d* of 1st Baron Kirkwood; *m* 1967, Sir Iain David Thomas Vallance, *qv*; one *s* one *d*. *Educ:* Univ. of St Andrews (MA); LSE (MSc); Univ. of London (PhD); London Business Sch. (Sloan Fellow). Queen Mary College, later Queen Mary and Westfield College, University of London: Asst Lectr, Lectr, Sen. Lectr, Reader in Govt and Politics, 1968–85; Head, Dept of Politics, 1985–88; Vis. Prof., 1990–96; Hon. Fellow, 1997. Chm., St George's Healthcare NHS Trust, 1993–99; Director: HMV Group, 1990–97; Norwich Union plc, 1995–2000; Charter European Trust plc, 1998–; PPP Healthcare Medical Trust, 1999–; CGNU plc, 2000–. Chm., NHS Adv. Cttee on Distinction Awards, 2000–. Chm. of Govs, James Allen's Girls' Sch., 1991–94; Chm. Council, Inst. of Educn, Univ. of London, 2000–. Member: Adv. Council, Citizenship Foundn, 1988–; Council, Dulwich Picture Gallery Trust, 1995–2000; Council, RSA, 1997–; Adv. Council, NCVO, 1998–. Trustee: Royal Anniversary Trust, 1994–; St George's Hosp. Special Trustees, 1999–2001. Patron, Donaldson Coll., Edinburgh, 1998. FRSA 1991. JP Inner London, 1993. *Publications:* (ed) The State, Society and Self-destruction, 1975; Women in the House, 1979; (with Davies) Women in Europe, 1982; (with Radice and Willis) MP: the job of a backbencher, 1988; (with Mahoney) Business Ethics in a New Europe, 1992; Business Ethics at Work, 1995; contribs to other books, academic acticles, journalism. *Recreations:* writing, reading novels, ski-ing, opera. *Address:* Institute of Education, 20 Bedford Way, WC1H 0AL. *T:* (020) 7612 6004.

VALLANCE, Sir Iain (David Thomas), Kt 1994; Vice-Chairman, Royal Bank of Scotland, since 1994; *b* 20 May 1943; *s* of late Edmund Thomas Vallance and Janet Wright Bell Ross Davidson; *m* 1967, Elizabeth Mary McGonnigill (*see* E. M. Vallance); one *s* one *d*. *Educ:* Edinburgh Acad.; Dulwich Coll.; Glasgow Acad.; Brasenose Coll., Oxford (Hon. Fellow, 1997); London Grad. Sch. of Business Studies (MSc). Joined Post Office, 1966; Director: Central Finance, 1976–78; Telecommunications Finance, 1978–79; Materials Dept, 1979–81; British Telecommunications: a Corp. Dir, 1981–2001; Board Mem. for Orgn and Business Systems, 1981–83; Man. Dir, Local Communications Services Div., 1983–85; Chief of Operations, 1985–86; Chief Exec., 1986–95; Chm., 1987–2001 (part-time 1998–2001). Director: Royal Bank of Scotland, 1993–; Mobil Corp., 1996–99. Pres., CBI, 2000–July 2002 (Mem., Pres.'s Cttee, 1988–); Member, President's Committee: (also Adv. Council), BITC, 1988–; Eur. Foundn for Quality Management, 1988–96. Chm., Eur. Adv. Cttee, New York Stock Exchange, 2000– (Mem., 1995–); Member: Internat. Adv. Bd, British-American Chamber of Commerce, 1991–; Bd, Scottish Enterprise, 1998–2001. Vice Pres., Princess Royal Trust for Carers, 1999– (Chm., 1991–98); Trustee, Monteverdi Trust, 1993–; Dep. Chm., Financial Reporting Council, 2001–. Patron, Loughborough Univ., 1996–. Freeman, City of London, 1985; Liveryman, Wheelwrights' Co., 1986–. Hon. Gov., Glasgow Acad., 1993–. Fellow, London Business School, 1989. Hon. DSc: Ulster, 1992; Napier, 1994; City, 1996; Hon. DTech: Loughborough, 1992; Robert Gordon, 1994; Hon. DBA Kingston, 1993; Hon. DEng Heriot-Watt, 1995. *Recreations:* hill walking, music. *Address:* c/o 81 Newgate Street, EC1A 7AJ.

VALLANCE, Michael Wilson; Headmaster of Bloxham School 1982–91; *b* 9 Sept. 1933; *er s* of late Vivian Victor Wilson Vallance and Kate Vallance, Wandsworth and Helston; *m* 1970, Mary Winifred Ann, *d* of John Steele Garnett; one *s* two *d*. *Educ:* Brighton Coll.; St John's Coll., Cambridge (MA). On staff of United Steel Companies Ltd, 1952–53; awarded United Steel Companies Scholarship (held at Cambridge), 1953; Asst Master, Abingdon School, 1957–61; Asst Master, Harrow School, 1961–72; Headmaster, Durham Sch., 1972–82. Chairman: Cttee of Northern ISIS, 1976–77; NE Div., HMC, 1981–82. World Challenge Expeditions Ltd: Consultant, 1991–; Dir, 1992–96; Chm. Bd, 1995–96. Chm., Council for the Registration of Schools Teaching Dyslexic Pupils, (formerly Nat. Registration Council), 1992–96 (Chm., Trustees, 1996–98). Trustee, Bloxham Project, 1987–91. FRSA 1997. *Recreations:* reading, cricket, gardens (sitting in), the sea. *Address:* 22 Foxholes Hill, Exmouth, Devon EX8 2DQ. *T:* (01395) 271633. *Clubs:* MCC, Jesters.

VALLANCE, Philip Ian Fergus; QC 1989; *b* 20 Dec. 1943; *o s* of Aylmer Vallance and Helen Gosse; *m* 1973, Wendy, *d* of J. D. Alston; one *s* one *d*. *Educ:* Bryanston; New Coll., Oxford (BA Mod. Hist). Called to the Bar, Inner Temple, 1968. *Recreations:* cooking, drystone walling. *Address:* (chambers) 4–5 Gray's Inn Square, Gray's Inn, WC1R 5JP. *T:* (020) 7404 5252. *Club:* Travellers.

VALLANCE-OWEN, Prof. John, MA, MD, FRCP, FRCPI, FRCPath; Visiting Professor, Imperial College of Science, Technology and Medicine, at Hammersmith Hospital, since 1988; Consultant Physician, Wellington Hospital, London, since 1999; *b* 31 Oct. 1920; *s* of late Prof. E. A. Owen; *m* 1950, Renee Thornton; two *s* two *d*. *Educ:* Friar's Sch., Bangor; Epsom Coll.; St John's Coll., Cambridge (de Havilland Schol. from Epsom); London Hosp. (Schol.). BA 1943; MA, MB, BChir Cantab, 1946; MD Cantab 1951; FRCP 1962; FRCPath 1971; FRCPI 1973. Various appts incl. Pathology Asst and Med. 1st Asst, London Hosp., 1946–51; Med. Tutor, Royal Postgrad. Med. Sch., Hammersmith Hosp., 1952–55 and 1956–58; Rockefeller Trav. Fellowship, at George S. Cox Med. Research Inst., Univ. of Pennsylvania, 1955–56; Cons. Phys. and Lectr in Medicine, Univ. of Durham, 1958–64; Cons. Phys., Royal Victoria Infirmary and Reader in Medicine, Univ. of Newcastle upon Tyne, 1964–66; Prof. of Medicine, QUB, 1966–82; Consultant Physician: Royal Victoria Hosp., Belfast, 1966–82 (Chm., Med. Div., 1979–81); Belfast City Hosp., 1966–82; Forster Green Hosp., Belfast, 1975–82 (Chm., Med. Staff Cttee, 1979–82); Dir of Med. Services, Maltese Is, 1981–82; Chinese University of Hong Kong: Foundation Prof. and Chm., Dept of Medicine, 1983–88; Associate Dean, Faculty of Medicine, 1984–88; Consultant Physician, London Ind. Hosp., 1988–99. Hon. Consultant in Medicine: to Hong Kong Govt, 1984–88; to the British Army in Hong Kong, 1985–88. Med. Advr on Clinical Complaints, NE Thames RHA, 1989–96, S Thames RHA, 1995–96. Member: Standing Med. Adv. Cttee, Min. of Health and Social Services, NI, 1970–73; Specialist Adv. Cttee (General Internal Medicine) to the Govt; Northern Health and Social Services Bd, Dept of Health and Soc. Services, NI; Mem., Exec. Cttee, Assoc. of Physicians of GB and Ireland, 1976–79; Regional Adviser for N Ire, to RCP, 1970–75 and Councillor, RCP, 1976–79 (Oliver-Sharpey Prize, RCP, 1976); Councillor, RCPI, 1978–82; Mem. Research Cttee, Brit. Diabetic Assoc.; Brit. Council Lectr, Dept Medicine, Zürich Univ., 1963; 1st Helen Martin Lectr, Diabetic Assoc. of S Calif, Wm H. Mulberg Lectr, Cincinnati Diabetes Assoc., and Lectr, Brookhaven Nat. Labs, NY, 1965; Brit. Council Lectr, Haile Selassie Univ., Makerere UC and S African Univs, 1966; Guest Lecturer: Japan Endocrinological Soc., 1968; Madrid Univ., 1969; Endocrine Soc. of Australia, 1970; Bologna Univ., 1976. Hon. FRCPI 1970; Hon. FHKCP 1996. *Publications:* Essentials of Cardiology, 1961 (2nd edn 1968); Diabetes: its physiological and biochemical basis, 1976; papers in biochem., med., and scientific jls on carbohydrate and fat metabolism and aetiology of diabetes mellitus and related conditions, with special reference to insulin antagonism. *Recreations:* tennis, golf, music. *Address:* 10 Spinney Drive, Great Shelford, Cambridge CB2 5LY. *T:* (01223) 842767; 17 St Matthews Lodge, Oakley Square, NW1 1NB. *T:* (020) 7388 3644; Cuildochart, Killin, Perthshire FK2 8SS. *T:* (01567) 820337. *Clubs:* East India, Royal Society of Medicine (Life Mem.); Gog Magog Golf (Cambridge); United Services Recreation (Hong Kong).

VALLANCE WHITE, James Ashton, CB 1997; Fourth Clerk at the Table and Clerk of the Judicial Office, House of Lords, since 1983; Registrar of Lords' Interests, since 1996; Clerk to Committee for Privileges (Peerage Claims); *b* 25 Feb. 1938; *s* of Frank Ashton White and Dieudonnée Vallance; *m* 1987, Anne O'Donnell. *Educ:* Allhallows School; Albert Schweitzer College, Switzerland; St Peter's College, Oxford (MA). Clerk, House of Lords, 1961; Clerk of Committees, 1971–78; Chief Clerk, Public Bill Office, 1978–83. *Address:* 14 Gerald Road, SW1W 9EQ. *T:* (020) 7730 7658; Biniparrell, San Luis, Menorca. *T:* (971) 151476. *Clubs:* Brooks's, Beefsteak.

VALLAT, Prof. Sir Francis Aimé, GBE 1982; KCMG 1962 (CMG 1955); QC 1961; Barrister-at-Law; Emeritus Professor of International Law, University of London; *b* 25 May 1912; *s* of Col Frederick W. Vallat, OBE; *m* 1st, 1939, Mary Alison Cockell (marr. diss. 1973); one *s* one *d*; 2nd, 1988, Patricia Maria Morton Anderson (*d* 1995); 3rd, 1996, Joan Olive Parham. *Educ:* University College, Toronto (BA Hons); Gonville and Caius Coll., Cambridge (LLB). Called to Bar, Gray's Inn, 1935, Bencher, 1971; Assistant Lecturer, Bristol Univ., 1935–36; practice at Bar, London, 1936–39; RAFVR (Flt Lieut), 1941–45; Asst Legal Adviser, Foreign Office, 1945–50; Legal Adviser, UK Permanent Deleg. to UN, 1950–54; Deputy Legal Adviser, FO, 1954–60, Legal Adviser, 1960–68; Dir of Internat. Law Studies, 1968–76, Reader, 1969–70, Prof., 1970–76, KCL; practice in internat. law, 1968–2001. (On leave of absence) Actg Director, Inst. of Air and Space Law, and Vis. Prof. of Law, McGill Univ., 1965–66. Dir of Studies, Internat. Law Assoc., 1969–73. UK Mem., UN Fact Finding Panel, 1969–. Associate Mem., Institut de Droit International, 1965, elected Mem. 1977, Emeritus Mem., 1999; Member: Internat. Law Commn, 1973–81 (Chm. 1977–78); Permanent Court of Arbitration, 1980–92; Curatorium, Hague Acad., 1982–98 (Vice-Pres., 1993–98). Jt Vice-Pres., David Davies Meml Inst. of Internat. Relations Studies, 1982–2001. Expert Consultant, UN Conf. on Succession of States in respect of Treaties, 1977–78. Dr en dr. *hc*, Lausanne Univ., 1979. *Publications:* International Law and the Practitioner, 1966; Introduction to the Study of Human Rights, 1972; articles in British Year Book of International Law and other journals. *Recreation:* restoration of antiques. *Address:* The Coach House, Church Road, West Lavington, Midhurst, West Sussex GU29 0EH. *Clubs:* Sloane, Hurlingham.

VALLELY, Paul; writer and broadcaster; Associate Editor, The Independent and The Independent on Sunday, since 2000; *b* 11 Nov. 1951; *s* of late Victor Terence Vallely and Mary Frances Vallely (*née* Mannion); *m* 1st, 1972, Heather Cecilia Neil (marr. diss.); one *d*; 2nd, 2000, Christine Lesley Morgan; one *s*. *Educ:* St Mary's Coll. Grammar Sch., Middlesbrough; Univ. of Leeds (BA Philosophy and English). Reporter, Feature Writer, Theatre Critic, Yorkshire Post, 1974–80; Asst Features Editor, Sunday Telegraph Magazine, 1980–82; Radio Critic, The Listener, 1980–82; Feature Writer, Mail on Sunday, 1982–84; Home News Reporter and Corresp. in Africa, Belfast and NY, The Times, 1984–89; Sen. Foreign Writer, Religious Affairs Editor, News Editor and Asst Editor, Sunday Correspondent, 1989–90; Land Reform Study, Philippines, Brazil, Eritrea, Christian Aid, 1990; Editor of Irish edn, Sunday Times, 1991–92; Oped Feature Writer, Daily Telegraph, 1992–94; Dep. Editor, The European, 1994; Editor, News Review, Sunday Times, 1994–95; Feature Writer, Leader Writer and Columnist, The

Independent, 1995–; Exec. Editor, Independent on Sunday, 1999–2000. Columnist: The Tablet, 1996–99; Third Way, 1995–. La Casas Lecture, Blackfriars, Oxford, 2000. Panellist, Moral Maze, 1996, Vice or Virtue, 1997, Radio 4. Chair, Catholic Inst. for Internat. Relations, 1995–2001 (Trustee, 1993–2001). Media Adviser: Christian Aid, 1990–93; CAFOD, 1993–; Trustee, Traidcraft, 1992–95; Chair, Traidcraft Exchange, 1995–99. *Publications:* (with David Blundy) With Geldof in Africa, 1985; (with Bob Geldof) Is That It?, 1986; Bad Samaritans: First World ethics and Third World debt, 1990; Promised Lands: stories of power and poverty in the Third World, 1992; (for children) Daniel and the Mischief Boy, 1993; (ed) The New Politics: Catholic social teaching for the 21st century, 1999. *Address:* The Independent, PO Box 165, Sale, Cheshire M33 2YA. *T:* (0161) 973 3456; *e-mail:* p.vallely@independent.co.uk. *Club:* Royal Commonwealth Society.

VALLINGS, Vice-Adm. Sir George (Montague Francis), KCB 1986; Secretary, Chartered Institute of Management Accountants, 1987–95; *b* 31 May 1932; *s* of Robert Archibald Vallings and Alice Mary Joan Vallings (*née* Bramsden); *m* 1964, Tessa Julia Cousins; three *s*. *Educ:* Belhaven Hill, Dunbar; Royal Naval College, Dartmouth. Midshipman, HMS Theseus, 1950–51; HMS Scarborough, 1961–63; HMS Defender, 1967–68; HMS Bristol, 1970–73; Naval Adviser and RNLO Australia, 1974–76; Captain F2, HMS Apollo, 1977–78; Dir, Naval Ops and Trade, 1978–80; Commodore, Clyde, 1980–82; Flag Officer: Gibraltar, 1983–85; Scotland and NI, 1985–87. Chm., STA Race Cttee, 1988–96. *Recreations:* family and sport. *Address:* c/o HSBC, Surbiton Branch, 1 Victoria Road, Surbiton KT6 4LF. *Clubs:* Royal Ocean Racing; Woking Golf.

VALLIS, Rear-Adm. Michael Anthony, CB 1986; FREng, CEng; *b* 30 June 1929; *s* of R. W. H. Vallis and S. J. Dewsnup; *m* 1959, Pauline Dorothy Abbott, Wymondham, Leics; three *s* one *d*. *Educ:* RN College, Dartmouth; RN Engineering College, Plymouth; RN College, Greenwich. MIMechE, FIMarE. RN Service, 1943–86. *Recreations:* fishing, gardening, walking, food and wine, theatre. *Address:* 4A St Stephen's Close, Bath, BA1 5PP. *Club:* Royal Over-Seas League.

VAN ALLAN, Richard; principal bass; Director, National Opera Studio, 1986–2001; *b* 28 May 1935; *s* of Joseph Arthur and Irene Hannah Van Allan; *m* 1976, Elisabeth Rosemary (marr. diss. 1986); one *s* one *d* (and one *s* decd). *Educ:* Worcester College of Education (DipEd Science); Birmingham School of Music. Glyndebourne, 1964; Welsh National Opera, 1968; English National Opera, 1969 (Mem. Bd of Dirs, 1995–98); Royal Opera House, Covent Garden, 1971; performances also: l'Opéra de Paris, Bordeaux, Nice, Toulouse, Rome, Brussels; USA: Boston, San Diego, Phoenix, Houston, Austin, San Antonio, New Orleans, NY; Argentina: Buenos Aires; Spain: Madrid and Barcelona; Hong Kong; Victoria State Opera, Melbourne. Recordings incl. Don Giovanni, Così fan tutte (Grammy Award), Luisa Miller, L'Oracolo, Britten's Gloriana. Hon. RAM 1987; FBSM 1991. Sir Charles Santley Memorial Award, Musicians' Co., 1996. *Recreations:* shooting, tennis, golf. *Address:* 18 Octavia Street, SW11 3DN.

VAN ALLEN, Prof. James Alfred; Professor of Physics and Head of Department of Physics (of Physics and Astronomy, 1959–85), 1951–85, Carver Professor of Physics, 1972–85, now Regent Distinguished Professor, University of Iowa, USA; *b* Iowa, 7 Sept. 1914; *s* of Alfred Morris and Alma Olney Van Allen; *m* 1945, Abigail Fithian Halsey II; two *s* three *d*. *Educ:* Public High School, and Iowa Wesleyan Coll., Mount Pleasant, Iowa (BSc); University of Iowa, Iowa City (MSc, PhD). Research Fellow, then Physicist, Carnegie Instn of Washington, 1939–42; Physicist, Applied Physics Lab., Johns Hopkins Univ., Md, 1942. Ordnance and Gunnery Officer and Combat Observer, USN, 1942–46, Lt-Comdr 1946. Supervisor of High-Altitude Research Group and of Proximity Fuze Unit, Johns Hopkins Univ., 1946–50. Leader, various scientific expeditions to Central and S Pacific, Arctic and Antarctic, for study of cosmic rays and earth's magnetic field, using Aerobee and balloon-launched rockets, 1949–57. Took part in promotion and planning of International Geophysical Year, 1957–58; developed radiation measuring equipment on first American satellite, Explorer I, and subseq. satellites (discoverer of Van Allen Radiation Belts of the earth, 1958); has continued study of earth's radiation belts, aurorae, cosmic rays, energetic particles in interplanetary space, planetary magnetospheres. Research Fellow, Guggenheim Memorial Foundation, 1951; Research Associate (controlled thermonuclear reactions), Princeton Univ., Project Matterhorn, 1953–54; Regents' Fellow, Smithsonian Inst., 1981. Acting Ed., Jl of Geophysical Research—Space Physics, 1991–92. Mem., Space Science Bd of Nat. Acad. of Sciences, 1958–70, 1980–83; Fellow: American Phys. Society; Amer. Geophysical Union (Pres., 1982–84), etc; Member: Nat. Acad. of Sciences; RAS; Royal Swedish Acad. of Sciences; Founder Member, International Acad. of Astronautics, etc. Holds many awards and hon. doctorates; Gold Medal, RAS, 1978; US Nat. Medal of Sci., 1987; Crafoord Prize, Royal Swedish Acad. of Scis, 1989; Nansen Award and Prize, Norwegian Acad. of Sci. and Letters, 1990. *Publications:* (ed and contrib.) Scientific Uses of Earth Satellites, 1956, 2nd edn 1958; (jtly) Pioneer: first to Jupiter, Saturn and beyond, 1980; Origins of Magnetospheric Physics, 1983; (ed) Cosmic Rays, the Sun, and Geomagnetism: the works of Scott E. Forbush, 1993; 924 Elementary Problems and Answers in Solar System Astronomy, 1993; numerous articles in learned journals and contribs to scientific works. *Address:* Department of Physics and Astronomy, University of Iowa, Iowa City, IA 52242, USA; 5 Woodland Mounds Road, Iowa City, IA 52245, USA.

van ANDEL, Dr Katharine Bridget, (Mrs T. H. van Andel); *see* Pretty, Dr K. B.

VAN CAENEGEM, Baron Raoul Charles Joseph; Ordinary Professor of Medieval History and of Legal History, University of Ghent, Belgium, 1964–92, now Emeritus; *b* 14 July 1927; *s* of Joseph Van Caenegem and Irma Barbaix; created Baron, 1994; *m* 1954, Patricia Mary Carson; two *s* one *d*. *Educ:* Univ. of Ghent (LLD 1951; PhD 1953); Univ. of Paris; London Univ. Ghent University: Assistant to Prof. of Medieval Hist., 1954; Lectr, 1960. Vis. Fellow, UC, Cambridge, 1968; Arthur L. Goodhart Prof. in Legal Science, and Vis. Fellow of Peterhouse, Cambridge Univ., 1984–85; Erasmus Lectr on the History and Civilization of the Netherlands, Harvard Univ., 1991. Corresp. Fellow, Medieval Acad. of Amer., 1971; Corresp. FBA 1982; Sir Henry Savile Fellow, Merton Coll., Oxford, 1989. Mem. Acad. of Scis, Brussels, 1974; For. Mem., Acad. of Scis, Amsterdam, 1977. Hon. Dr: Tübingen, 1977; Catholic Univ., Louvain, 1984; Paris, 1988. Francqui Prize, Brussels, 1974; Solvay Prize, Brussels, 1990. *Publications:* Royal Writs in England from the Conquest to Glanvill: studies in the early history of the common law, 1959; The Birth of the English Common Law, 1973, 2nd edn 1988; Geschiedenis van Engeland (History of England), 1982, 2nd edn 1997; Judges, Legislators and Professors: chapters in European legal history, 1987; An Historical Introduction to Private Law, 1992; An Historical Introduction to Western Constitutional Law, 1995; Introduction aux sources de l'histoire médiévale, 1997; (contrib.) International Encyclopaedia of Comparative Law, 1973. *Recreations:* wine (Bordeaux, Alsace), swimming, classical music, bridge. *Address:* Veurestraat 47, 9051 Afsnee, Belgium. *T:* (9) 2226211. *Club:* Universitaire Stichting (Brussels).

VANCE, Charles Ivan; actor, director and theatrical producer; *b* 6 Dec. 1929; *s* of Eric Goldblatt and Sarah (*née* Freeman); *m* 1959, Hon. Imogen Moynihan; one *d*. *Educ:* Royal Sch., Dungannon; Queen's Univ., Belfast. FInstD 1972; FRSA 1975. Early career as broadcaster; acting debut with Anew MacMaster Co., Gaiety, Dublin, 1949; dir, first prodn, The Glass Menagerie, Arts, Cambridge, 1960; founded Civic Theatre, Chelmsford, 1962; i/c rep. cos, Tunbridge Wells, Torquay, Whitby and Hastings, 1962; as Dir of Charles Vance Prodns, created Eastbourne Theatre Co., 1969; dir. own adaptation of Wuthering Heights, 1972; wrote and staged four pantomimes, 1972–75; devised and dir. The Jolson Revue, 1974 (staged revival, Australia, 1978; world tour, 1981); played Sir Thomas More in A Man for All Seasons, and dir, Oh! What a Lovely War, Greenwood, 1975; purchased Leas Pavilion Theatre, Folkestone, 1976 (HQ of own theatre organisation until 1985); prod and dir. world tour of Paddington Bear, 1978; produced: Cinderella, Stafford, 1981; Aladdin, Bognor, 1981; (London and national tours): Stop the World—I Want to Get Off (revival), 1976; Salad Days (revival), 1977; (also dir.) In Praise of Love, 1977; Witness for the Prosecution, (revival), 1979, 1992; Hallo Paris, 1980; This Happy Breed (revival), 1980; Starlite Spectacular, 1981; The Kingfisher (revival), 1981; The Hollow (revival), 1982 (also dir.); The Little Hut, Australia (also dir.), 1982; Cinderella, 1982, 1983, 1984, 1992 (also dir.); Aladdin, 1982 (also wrote); Lady Chatterley's Lover, 1983; The Mating Game, 1983; The Sleeping Beauty, The Gingerbread Man, The Wizard of Oz, 1983; Dick Whittington, Jack and the Beanstalk, Pinocchio, Jesus Christ Superstar (revival), 1984; Mr Cinders (revival), 1985; Policy for Murder, 1984 (also dir.); Jane Eyre, 1985 (also wrote and dir.), (revival) 1996; Oh Calcutta! (revival), 1985–86; Wuthering Heights (own adaptation), 1987; The Creeper (revival tour), 1994; directed: Verdict (revival), 1984; Alice in Wonderland, 1985 (also wrote); Dick Whittington, Aladdin, Jack and the Beanstalk, Cinderella, 1986–87 (also wrote); Dénouement (also prod), 1988; Spiders Web (Agatha Christie Centenary Prodn) (also prod), 1990; The Mousetrap, USA (also prod), 1990; Daisy Pulls it Off (also prod), 1991; Gaslight (also prod), 1991; Time and Time Again (also prod), 1991; My Cousin Rachel (also prod), 1992; Godspell (also prod), 1993–94; Peter Pan, 1993; Dick Whittington, 1994, 1998, 2001; Brideshead Revisited (also prod), 1995; Cinderella, 1995, 1996, 1997, 2001; Jack and the Beanstalk, 1995, 1998, 2000; Eye Witness (prod), 1996; Babes in the Wood, 1996; Aladdin, 1996, 1997, 1999, 2000; Lettice and Lovage (prod.), 1977; Huckleberry Finn, 1997–98 (tour); Snow White, 1997, 1998, 1999; Kind Hearts and Coronets (tour), The Thirty-Nine Steps, 1998, 2000; The Ladykillers, What the Butler Saw, 1999 (tour); Passport to Pimlico, 2000 (tour); The Lady Vanishes, 2001; Oh What a Lovely War, 2001; Me and My Girl (revival), 2001; Bedside Manners, 2001; The Lavender Hill Mob, 2002; Who Killed Agatha Christie?, 2002. Controlled: Floral Hall Th., Scarborough, 1984–86; Beck Th., Hillingdon, 1986–90; Grand Opera House York, 1988–89; controls Summer Th., Manor Pavilion, Sidmouth, 1987–; rep. seasons: Harlow Playhouse, 1993–94; Grand Th., Wolverhampton, 1994–; Wyvern, Swindon, 1996–97; Lyceum, Crewe, 1996–; Palace, Westcliff, 1997; Alhambra, Bradford, 1997; launched first UK Dinner Theatre, Imperial Hotel, Torquay, 1990. Theatrical Management Association: Mem. Council, 1969; Pres., 1971–73 and 1973–76; Exec. Vice-Pres., 1976– (also of Council of Reg. Theatre). Advisor to Govt of Ghana on bldg Nat. Theatre, 1969. Director: Theatres Investment Fund, 1975–83; Entertainment Investments Ltd, 1980–82; International Holiday Investments, 1980–87; Southern Counties Television, 1980–87; Channel Radio, 1981–86; Gateway Broadcasting Ltd, 1982; Prestige Plays Ltd, 1987–; Operations Dir, Contemporary Theatre Ltd, 1992–94; Trustee Dir, Folkestone Theatre Co., 1979–85. Chairman: Provincial Theatre Council, 1971–87; Standing Adv. Cttee on Local Authority and the Theatre, 1977–90 (Vice-Chm., 1975–77); Gala and Fund-raising Cttee, British Theatre Assoc., 1986–89; Standing Adv. Cttee on Local Authority and the Performing Arts, 1990–93. Vice-Chairman: Theatres Adv. Council, resp. for theatres threatened by devolt, 1974–; (also dir.) Festival of Brit. Theatre, 1975–; Irving Soc., 1972–. Member: Theatres Nat. Cttee, 1971–; Drama Adv. Panel, SE Arts Assoc., 1974–85; Prince of Wales' Jubilee Entertainments Cttee, 1977; Entertainment Exec. Cttee, Artists' Benev. Fund, 1980–; Court, Guild of Thespians, 1998. Gov., Acad. of Live and Recorded Arts, 2000– (Chm.). Mem., Variety Club of GB, 1984–; Life Mem., Equity, 1995; Patron, Voluntary Arts Network, 1992–; Vice-Pres., E Sussex Br., RSPCA, 1975–; Member: Rotary Internat., 1971–; Rotary Club of London, 1986–. Founded Vance Offord (Publications) Ltd, publishers of British Theatre Directory, British Theatre Review, and Municipal Entertainment, 1971; Chm., Platform Publications Ltd, 1987–; Editor in Chief, Team Publishing, 1986–87; Editor, Amateur Stage, and Preview, 1987–. Chambellain, Ordre de Coteaux de Champagne, 1993. *Publications:* British Theatre Directory, 1972, 1973, 1974, 1975; (ed) Amateur Theatre Yearbook, 1989, 1991, 1993, 1995, 1997, 2000; Agatha Christie, The Theatrical Celebration, 1990; Community Arts Directory, 2001; *plays:* Wuthering Heights, 1992; Jane Eyre, 1996. *Recreations:* sailing (crossed Atlantic single-handed, 1956), cooking (Cordon Bleu, 1957), travelling, animals. *Address:* Hampden House, 2 Weymouth Street, W1W 5BT. *Clubs:* Hurlingham, Royal Automobile, Royal Over-Seas League, Directors', Kennel (Mem. Cttee, 1989–), Dorchester, Groucho, Wig and Pen, Home House, Lord's Taverners.

VANCE, Cyrus Roberts, Hon. KBE 1994; Secretary of State, USA, 1977–80; barrister-at-law; *b* Clarksburg, W Va, 27 March 1917; *m* 1947, Grace Elsie Sloane; one *s* four *d*. *Educ:* Kent Sch.; Yale Univ. (BA 1939); Yale Univ. Law Sch. (LLB 1942). Served War, USNR, to Lieut (s.g.), 1942–46. Asst to Pres., The Mead Corp., 1946–47; admitted to New York Bar, 1947; Associate and Partner of Simpson Thacher & Bartlett, New York, 1947–60, Partner, 1956–60, 1967–77 and 1980–98. Special Counsel, Preparedness Investigation Sub-cttee of Senate Armed Services Cttee, 1957–60; Consulting Counsel, Special Cttee on Space and Astronautics, US Senate, 1958; Gen. Counsel, Dept of Defense, 1961–62; Sec. of the Army, 1962–64; Dep. Sec. of Defense, 1964–67; Special Rep. of the President: in Civil Disturbances in Detroit, July–Aug. 1967 and in Washington, DC, April 1968; in Cyprus, Nov.–Dec. 1967; in Korea, Feb. 1968; one of two US Negotiators, Paris Peace Conf. on Vietnam, May 1968–Feb. 1969; Personal Envoy of UN Secretary-General: in Yugoslavia crisis, 1991–93; to Nagorno-Karabakh, 1992; to South Africa, 1992; Mem., Commn to Investigate Alleged Police Corruption in NYC, 1970–72. Mem., Bd of Govs, Federal Reserve Bank of NY (Chm., 1989–91). Pres., Assoc. of Bar of City of New York, 1974–76. Mem. Bd of Trustees: Rockefeller Foundn, 1970–77, 1980–82 (Chm., 1975–77); Yale Univ., 1968–78, 1980–87; Amer. Ditchley Foundn, 1980– (Chm., 1981–); Mayo Foundn, 1980–90. Hon. degrees: Marshall, 1963; Trinity Coll., 1966; Yale, 1968; West Virginia, Bowling Green, 1969; Salem Coll., 1970; Brandeis, 1971; Amherst, W Virginia Wesleyan, 1974; Harvard, Colgate, Gen. Theol Seminary, Williams Coll., 1981. Medal of Freedom (US), 1969. *Publications:* The Choice is Ours, 1983; Hard Choices, 1983. *Address:* Simpson Thacher & Bartlett, 425 Lexington Avenue, New York, NY 10017–3954, USA. *T:* (212) 4557190.

VANCOUVER, Archbishop of, (RC), since 1991; **Most Rev. Adam Exner;** *b* 24 Dec. 1928. *Educ:* St Joseph's Coll., Yorkton, Sask; Gregorian Univ., Rome (LPH 1954; STB 1956 STL 1958); Ottawa Univ. (STD 1960). Entered novitiate, Oblates of Mary Immaculate, St Norbert, Manitoba, 1950; ordained Roviano, Rome, 1957; St Charles Scholasticate, Battleford, Saskatchewan: Prof., 1960–64 and 1971–72; Rector and Superior, 1965–71; Prof. of Moral Theology, Newman Theol Coll., Edmonton, Alberta,

1972–74; Bishop of Kamloops, BC, 1974–82; Archbishop of Winnipeg, 1982–91. Secretary: BC and Yukon Conf. of Bishops, 1974–79 (Chm., 1991–); Conf. of Catholic Bishops, 1974–80. Canadian Conference of Catholic Bishops: Mem., Admin. Bd, 1976–83; Rep. of Western Conf. of Bishops, 1981–83; Mem., Episcopal Commn for Christian Educn, 1983–88; Mem., Social Communications Commn, 1989–91; Rep. of W Reg. of Bishops on Permanent Council, 1989–93; Mem., Cttee on Sexual Abuse, 1990–92; Mem., Theol. Commn, 1991–93, 1995– (Pres., 1993–95); Mem., Working Gp Residential Schs, 1992–95; Mem., Progs and Priorities Cttee, 1993–95; Chm., Catholic Orgn for Life and Family, 1995–. Chm., Conf. of Bishops of Manitoba, 1983–91; Member: Sacred Congregation for Bishops, 1984–90; Nat. Catholic-Lutheran Dialogue, 1987–89. Chaplain, Knight of Columbus, 1974–82; Liaison Bp and Chaplain, Catholic Sch. Trustees Assoc. of BC, 1974–82; Mem., St Paul's Coll. Bd, Univ. of Manitoba, 1982. *Publications:* contrib. to Catholic Press, 1960–82. *Recreations:* playing piano and accordian, golf, working out, cross country ski-ing, jogging. *Address:* 150 Robson Street, Vancouver, BC V6B 2A7, Canada.

VAN CULIN, Rev. Canon Samuel; Secretary General, Anglican Consultative Council, 1983–94; *b* 20 Sept. 1930; *s* of Samuel Van Culin and Susie (*née* Mossman). *Educ:* High School, Honolulu; Princeton University (AB); Virginia Theological Seminary (BD). Ordained 1955; Curate, St Andrew's Cathedral, Honolulu, 1955–56; Canon Precentor and Rector, Hawaiian Congregation, 1956–58; Asst Rector, St John, Washington DC, 1958–60; Gen. Sec., Laymen International, Washington, 1960–61; Asst Sec., Overseas Dept, Episcopal Church, USA, 1962–68; Sec. for Africa and Middle East, Episcopal Church, USA, 1968–76; Executive, World Mission, 1976–83. Hon. Canon: Canterbury Cathedral, 1983; Ibadan, Nigeria, 1983; Jerusalem, 1984; Southern Africa, 1989; Honolulu, 1991. Hon. DD: Virginia Seminary, 1977; Gen. Theol Seminary, 1983. *Recreations:* music, swimming. *Address:* 16A Burgate, Canterbury, Kent CT1 2HG. *Clubs:* Athenæum; Princeton, Huguenot Society (New York).

VandeLINDE, Prof. (Vernon) David, PhD; Vice-Chancellor, University of Warwick, since 2001; *b* Charleston, W Virginia, 9 Aug. 1942; *s* of Vernon Geno VandeLinde and Ava Mae (*née* Scott); *m* 1964, Marjorie Ann Park; two *s*. *Educ:* Carnegie-Mellon Univ. (BS 1964; MS 1965; PhD 1968). Johns Hopkins University: Asst Prof., Elec. Engrg, 1967–74; Associate Prof., 1974–77; Prof., 1977–92; Dean, Sch. of Engrg, 1978–92; Vice-Chancellor, Univ. of Bath, 1992–2001. Chm., Overseas Res. Students Awards Scheme Cttee, UUK (formerly CVCP), 1993–; Mem., Council for Science and Technology, 2000–. *Address:* University of Warwick, Coventry CV4 7AL.

VANDEN-BEMPDE-JOHNSTONE; *see* Johnstone.

van den BERGH, Maarten Albert; Chairman, Lloyds TSB Group plc, since 2001 (Deputy Chairman, 2000–01); *b* 19 April 1942; *s* of Sidney James van den Bergh and Maria van den Bergh (*née* Mijers); *m* 1965, Marjan Désirée Kramer; two *d*. *Educ:* Univ. of Groningen (Drs Econs). Joined Shell Gp, 1968; East and Australasia Area Co-ordinator, 1981–84; Dep. Gp Treas., Shell Internat., 1984–86; Chm., Shell cos in Thailand, 1987–89; Regl Co-ordinator, Western Hemisphere and Africa, Shell Internat., 1989–92; Gp Man. Dir, Royal Dutch/Shell Gp, 1992–2000; Vice-Chm., Cttee of Man. Dirs, and Pres., Royal Dutch Petroleum Co., 1998–2000; Director: Shell Petroleum Co. Ltd, 1992–; Royal Dutch Petroleum Co., 1992–; Shell Petroleum NV, 1992–. Dir, British Telecommunications plc, 2000–. Advr to Chief Exec., HKSAR, 1998–. *Recreations:* European history, collector of Asian antiques. *Address:* Lloyds TSB Group plc, 71 Lombard Street, EC3P 3BS. *T:* (020) 7356 2074. *Clubs:* Soc. De Witte, 't Jagertje (The Hague).

van den BERGH, Prof. Sidney, OC 1994; FRS 1988; astronomer, Dominion Astrophysical Observatory, Victoria, British Columbia, since 1977; *b* 20 May 1929; *s* of S. J. van den Bergh and S. M. van den Berg; *m* 1st, 1957, Roswitha Koropp (marr. diss.); one *s* two *d*; 2nd, 1978, Gretchen Krause (*d* 1987); 3rd, 1990, Paulette Brown. *Educ:* Princeton Univ. (AB); Ohio State Univ. (MSc); Göttingen Univ. (Dr rer. nat.). Asst Prof., Ohio State Univ., 1956–58; progressively, Asst Prof., Associate Prof., Prof., Univ. of Toronto, 1958–77; Dir, Dominion Astrophys. Observatory, 1977–86. Res. Associate, Mt Wilson and Palomar Observatories, 1967–68. ARAS 1984. Hon. DSc: St Mary's Univ., 1995; Univ. of Victoria, 2001. NRCC President's Research Medal, 1988. *Publications:* approx. 625 articles in various scholarly jls. *Recreations:* photography, archaeology. *Address:* Dominion Astrophysical Observatory, 5071 West Saanich Road, Victoria, BC V9E 2E7, Canada.

van den BROEK, Hans, Grand Cross Order of Oranje Nassau; Hon. GCMG; President, Netherlands Institute for International Relations, since 2000; *b* 11 Dec. 1936; *m* 1965, Josephine van Schendel; two *d*. *Educ:* Univ. of Utrecht (Law degree). Lawyer, Rotterdam, 1965–68; Enka Bv., Arnhem: Sec., Man. Bd, 1969–73; Commercial Manager, 1973–76. Member: Lower House of Parliament, Netherlands, 1976–78; Exec., Catholic People's Party, 1978–81; State Sec. for Foreign Affairs, 1981–82; Minister for Foreign Affairs, 1982–93. Mem., CEC, later EC, 1993–99. Grand Cross: Order of Merit (Italy); Order of Isabel la Católica (Spain); Nat. Order of Merit (France); Order of Merit (Germany); Order of the Rising Sun (Japan). *Address:* c/o Netherlands Institute for International Relations, Clinquendael 7, 2597 VH The Hague, The Netherlands.

VAN DEN HOVEN, Helmert Frans; *see* Hoven.

VAN der BIJL, Nigel Charles; His Honour Judge Van der Bijl; a Circuit Judge, since 2001; *b* 28 April 1948; *s* of late Nicholas Alexander Christian Van der Bijl and of Mollie Van der Bijl; *m* 1974, Loba Nassiri; one *s* one *d*. *Educ:* Trinity Coll., Dublin (BA Hons Classics, LLB). Called to the Bar, Inner Temple, 1973; Co. Sec., Internat. Div., Beecham Pharmaceutical, 1973–74; Legal Manager, Shahpur Chemical Co. Ltd and Nat. Iranian Oil Co., Tehran, 1974–77; in private practice as barrister, specialising in crime and in European and human rights law, 1977–2001; a Recorder, 1996–2001. Friend, British Sch. of Athens, 1996–. *Address:* c/o The Law Courts, Chaucer Road, Canterbury, Kent CT1 1ZA.

VANDERFELT, Sir Robin (Victor), KBE 1973 (OBE 1954); Secretary-General, Commonwealth Parliamentary Association, 1961–86; *b* 24 July 1921; *y s* of late Sydney Gorton Vanderfelt, OBE, and Ethel Maude Vanderfelt (*née* Tremayne); *m* 1962, Jean Margaret Becker (*d* 1996), *d* of John and Eve Steward; two *s* (and one step *s* one step *d*). *Educ:* Haileybury; Peterhouse, Cambridge. Served War in India and Burma, 1941–45. Asst Secretary, UK Branch, CPA, 1949–59; Secretary, 1960–61. Secretary, UK Delegn, Commonwealth Parly Conf., India, 1957; as Sec.-Gen., CPA, served as Secretary to Parliamentary Conferences throughout Commonwealth, 1961–85, also attended many area and regional confs and Confs of Commonwealth Speakers and Clerks. Mem. Internat. Services Bd, RIPA, 1986–89; Governor: Queen Elizabeth House, Oxford, 1980–87; E-SU, 1984–89. *Recreation:* gardening. *Address:* No 6 Saddler's Mead, Wilton, Salisbury, Wilts SP2 0DE. *T:* (01722) 742637. *Clubs:* Royal Commonwealth Society, Royal Over-Seas League, English-Speaking Union.

van der LOON, Prof. Piet; Professor of Chinese, University of Oxford, and Fellow of University College, Oxford, 1972–87, now Emeritus Professor and Emeritus Fellow; *b* 7 April 1920; *m* 1947, Minnie C. Snellen; two *d*. *Educ:* Univ. of Leiden. Litt. Drs Leiden, MA Cantab. Univ. Asst Lectr, Cambridge, 1948; Univ. Lectr, Cambridge, 1949. *Publications:* Taoist Books in the Libraries of the Sung Period, 1984; The Classical Theatre and Art Song of South Fukien, 1992; articles in Asia Major, T'oung Pao, Jl Asiatique. *Recreations:* travel, gardening. *Address:* Midhurst, Old Boars Hill, Oxford OX1 5JQ. *T:* (01865) 739318.

VANDERMEER, (Arnold) Roy; QC 1978; a Recorder of the Crown Court, 1972–97; a Deputy High Court Judge, since 1989; *b* London, 26 June 1931; *o s* of late William Arnold Vandermeer and Katherine Nora Vandermeer; *m* 1964, Caroline Veronica (*née* Christopher); one *s* two *d*. *Educ:* Dame Alice Owen's Sch., Islington; King's Coll., London (LLB). Called to Bar, Gray's Inn, 1955, Bencher, 1988. Flt-Lt, RAF, 1955–58. Chairman: Greater Manchester Structure Plan Examination in Public, 1978; County of Avon Structure Plan Examination in Public, 1983. Inspector, Heathrow Terminal 5 and associated enquiries, 1995–. *Recreations:* reading, watching cricket, golf. *Address:* The Field House, Barnet Lane, Elstree, Herts WD6 3QU. *T:* (020) 8953 2244. *Club:* MCC.

van der MEER, Dr Simon; Ridder Nederlandse Leeuw, 1985; Senior Engineer, CERN, Geneva (European Organisation for Nuclear Research), 1956–90; *b* 24 Nov. 1925; *s* of Pieter van der Meer and Jetske Groeneveld; *m* 1966, Catharina M. Koopman; one *s* one *d*. *Educ:* Technical University, Delft, Netherlands; physical engineer. Philips Research Laboratories, Eindhoven, 1952–56. Hon. degrees: Univ. of Geneva, 1983; Amsterdam, 1984; Genoa, 1985. Nobel Prize for Physics (jtly), 1984. *Recreation:* literature. *Address:* 4 chemin des Corbillettes, 1218 Grand-Saconnex, Switzerland. *T:* (22) 7984305.

VANDERMERWE, Prof. Sandra, DBA; Professor of International Marketing and Services, Management School, Imperial College of Science, Technology and Medicine, University of London, since 1996; Chairman, Great Minds Consulting Ltd, since 1995; *b* 8 Aug. 1946; *d* of late David Fortes and of Myra Fortes; *m* 1973, Andre Vandermerwe; two *d*. *Educ:* Univ. of Cape Town (BA 1966); Grad. Sch. of Business, Univ. of Cape Town (MBA 1972); Grad. Sch. of Business, Univ. of Stellenbosch (DBA 1974). Senior Lecturer: Dept of Business Sci., Univ. of Cape Town, 1973–76; Grad. Sch. of Business, Univ. of Stellenbosch, 1976–79; Prof., and Head of Mktg Dept, Univ. of Witwatersrand, 1979–82; Vis. Prof. of Mktg, Internat. Mgt Inst., Geneva, 1983–85; Prof. of Internat. Mktg and Services, IMD-Internat. Inst. for Mgt Develt, Lausanne, 1985–96 (also Dir, several exec. progs). Mem. Bd, Internat. Health Insurance. Consultant on implementing customer-focused transformation, major internat. cos; speaker on Executive progs for business schs incl. INSEAD, London Business Sch., Templeton Coll., Oxford, and Vrije Univ., Netherlands. Mem., editl bds, and reviewer for internat. academic and mgt jls. FRSA 1996. Several awards. *Publications:* From Tin Soldiers to Russian Dolls: creating added value through services, 1993; (jtly) Cases in European Marketing Management, 1994; (jtly) Competing Through Services, 1994; The 11th Commandment: transforming to 'own' customers, 1995; Customer Capitalism: getting increasing returns in new market spaces, 1999; numerous articles in prof. jls. *Recreations:* jogging, animals, meditation. *Address:* Management School, Imperial College of Science, Technology and Medicine, 53 Prince's Gate, SW7 2PG. *T:* (020) 7594 9155.

van der VEEN, Air Vice-Marshal Marten; Senior Bursar, and Fellow, since 1999, Balliol College, Oxford; *b* 22 Jan. 1946; *s* of Lourens Jan van der Veen and Esmé Lily van der Veen (*née* Edwards); *m* 1968, Susan Mary Wallers; two *s*. *Educ:* King's Coll. Sch., Wimbledon; Magdalen Coll., Oxford (MA Engrg Sci. and Econs); RAF Coll., Cranwell (Aerosystems course). Exchange Officer with French Air Force, Paris, 1978–79; RAF Staff Coll., 1980; Dir of Defence Studies, RAF, 1985–88; Station Comdr, RAF Cosford, 1989–90; Dir, Support Policy, RAF, 1991–93; Station Comdr, RAF St Athan and Air Officer, Wales, 1994–95; last Commandant, RAF Staff Coll., Bracknell, 1996; DG Support Mgt, RAF, 1997. FRAeS 1998. *Recreations:* travel, classical music, opera, social tennis, inevitable DIY. *Address:* Balliol College, Oxford OX1 3BJ. *Club:* Royal Air Force.

van der WATEREN, Jan Floris, FLA; Keeper and Chief Librarian, National Art Library, 1988–2000; *b* 14 May 1940; *s* of late Jacob van der Wateren and of Wilhelmina (*née* Labuschagne). *Educ:* Potchefstroom Univ., S Africa (MA); University Coll. London (Postgrad. Dip. Librarianship). ALA 1971, FLA 1995. Lectr in Philosophy, Potchefstroom Univ., 1962–64; Asst Librarian, Univ. of London Inst. of Educn, 1967–71; Dep. Librarian, Sir Banister Fletcher Liby, RIBA, 1971–78; British Architectural Library: Managing Librarian, 1978–83; Dir and Sir Banister Fletcher Librarian, 1983–88. Sec., British Architectural Liby Trust, 1983–88. Hon. FRIBA 1995. FRSA 1994. *Publications:* articles, reviews for librarianship jls. *Address:* 52 Blenheim Crescent, W11 1NY. *T:* (020) 7221 6221; *e-mail:* jan.vanderwateren@ukgateway.net.

van der WERFF, Jonathan Ervine; His Honour Judge van der Werff; a Circuit Judge, since 1986; Resident Judge, Inner London Crown Court, since 1993; *b* 23 June 1935; *s* of H. H. J. van der Werff; *m* 1968, Katharine Bridget, *d* of Major J. B. Colvin, Withypool, Som; two *d*. *Educ:* St Piran's Sch., Maidenhead; Harrow; RMA, Sandhurst. Commnd in Coldstream Guards, 1955; Adjt 1st Bn, 1962–63; Major 1967, retired 1968. Called to Bar, Inner Temple, 1969; a Recorder, 1986; Resident Judge, Croydon Law Courts, 1989–93; Sen. Circuit Judge, 1993. *Address:* The Crown Court, Inner London Sessions House, Newington Causeway, SE1 6AZ. *Clubs:* Boodle's, Pratt's, Something; Bembridge Sailing.

VANDER ZALM, Hon. William N.; Premier of the Province of British Columbia, 1986–91; MLA (Social Credit Party) for Richmond, British Columbia; *b* Noordwykerhout, Holland, 29 May 1934; *s* of Wilhelmus Nicholaas van der Zalm and Agatha C. Warmerdam; *m* 1956, Lillian Mahalick; two *s* two *d*. *Educ:* Phillip Sheffield Sen. Secondary Sch., Abbotsford, BC. Purchased Art Knapp Nurseries Ltd, and became Co. Pres., 1956. Alderman 1965, Mayor 1969, Surrey Municipal Council. Minister of Human Resources, BC, 1975; Minister of Municipal Affairs and Minister responsible for Urban Transit Authority, 1978; Minister of Educn and Minister responsible for BC Transit, 1982; Leader, BC Social Credit Party, 1986–. Established Fantasy Garden World, major tourist attraction in Richmond, BC, 1983–. *Publication:* The Northwest Gardener's Almanac, 1982. *Recreations:* gardening, fishing, soccer. *Address:* Normandy Manor, 3553 Arthur Drive, Ladner, BC V4K 3N2, Canada. *Clubs:* Union (Victoria, BC); Hon. Member: Victoria Golf, Royal Vancouver Yacht, Royal Victoria Yacht.

VAN de WALLE, Leslie; Chief Executive Officer, Shell South America and Africa, since 2001; *b* 27 March 1956; *s* of Philippe Van de Walle and Luce Van de Walle; *m* 1982, Domitille Noel; two *d*. *Educ:* Hautes Etudes Commerciales, Paris. Managing Director: Schweppes Benelux, 1990–92; Schweppes France and Benelux, 1992–93; Schweppes Spain and Portugal, 1993–94; Snacks Div., Continental Europe UB, 1994–95; Chief Executive Officer: UB Continental Europe, 1996–97; McVities Gp, 1998; Chief Exec.,

United Biscuits Gp, 1999–2000. *Recreations:* golf (handicap 6), travel. *Address:* Flat 6, 25 Stanhope Gardens, SW7 5QX. *Clubs:* Foxhills Golf (Surrey); Chantilly Golf (France).

VANDORE, Peter Kerr; QC (Scot.) 1982; *b* 7 June 1943; *s* of James Vandore and Janet Kerr Fife; *m* 1970, Hilary Ann Davies; two *d. Educ:* Berwickshire High Sch., Duns; Edinburgh Univ. (MA Hons Hist.; LLB). Called to the Scottish Bar, 1968; Standing Counsel to Sec. of State for Scotland, for private legislation procedure, 1975–86. Mem., Legal Aid Central Cttee, 1972–85. *Publications:* contribs to Juridical Rev.

VANDYK, Neville David, PhD; Editor, Solicitors' Journal, 1968–88; *b* 6 Sept. 1923; *yr s* of late Arthur Vandyk, solicitor, and Constance Vandyk (*née* Berton); *m* 1956, Paula (*née* Borchert); one *d. Educ:* St Paul's Sch.; London School of Economics, Univ. of London (BCom 1947, PhD 1950). Admitted Solicitor, 1957. HM Forces, incl. service in India, Burma and Japan, 1942–46; research asst, LSE, 1951–52; with Herbert Oppenheimer, Nathan & Vandyk, Solicitors, 1953–58; Asst Editor, 1958, Managing Editor, 1963, Solicitors' Journal; Member for its duration, Law Society's Constitution Cttee prior to the adoption in 1969 of their revised Bye-Laws, 1966–68. Founder Mem., W London Law Soc. (Pres., 1970–71); Mem. Council, Medico-Legal Soc., 1963–66, Vice-Pres. 1966–67, and 1985–90, Hon. Treas. 1967–85; Founder Mem., Assoc. of Disabled Professionals, Vice-Chm. 1972–80; Mem. for its duration, Royal Bor. of Kensington and Chelsea's Working Gp on the Disabled and their Families, 1980–81. Governor (nominated by Univ. of London) William Blake County Secondary Sch., 1957–70. Freeman 1962, Liveryman 1963, Worshipful Co. of Solicitors of City of London. Founder's Meml Lecture, Brit. Council for Rehabilitation of the Disabled, 1971; Hon. Prof. of Legal Ethics, Univ. of Birmingham, 1981–83. Life Member: Burma Star Assoc., RAFA; Hon. Life Mem., British Legal Assoc., 1989. *Publications:* Tribunals and Inquiries, 1965; Accidents and the Law, 1975, 2nd edn 1979; (title) National Health Service, in Halsbury's Laws of England, 3rd edn 1959, 4th edn 1982. *Address:* c/o Law Society Records Office, Ipsley Court, Berrington Close, Redditch, Worcs B98 0TD.

VANDYKE PRICE, Pamela Joan; freelance writer and lecturer on wine, since 1956; *b* 21 March 1923; *o c* of Harry Norman Walford, MBE, and Florence Amélie Halliday; *m* 1950, Alan Vandyke Price, MB BS, MRCP (*d* 1955). *Educ:* privately; Somerville Coll., Oxford (MA Hons); Central Sch. of Speech and Drama. Various odd jobs, 1943–53; occasional adult educn lects, S Wales, 1951–52; Household Ed., House & Garden, 1953–55; Ed., Wine & Food, 1967–69; formerly: consumer contributor to Spectator; wine correspondent: The Times; Sunday Times; Observer; contribs to The Guardian, provincial newspapers and trade jls. Has made frequent radio broadcasts. Circle of Wine Writers: Mem.; formerly Cttee Mem., Programme Sec., Chm., and Pres.; Hon. Trustee in Perpetuity; Hon. Mem., Internat. Food & Wine Soc. Glenfiddich Gold Medal and Trophy, 1971, Silver Medal, 1973. Chevalier du Mérite Agricole (France), 1981. *Publications:* Cooking with Wine, Spirits, Beer and Cider, 1959; France: a food and wine guide, 1960; Casserole Cooking, 1961; The Art of the Table, 1962; Cooking with Spices, 1964; Century Companion to the Wines of Bordeaux, 1971, rev. edn 1982 (trans. French, German and Dutch); Eating and Drinking in France Today, 1972; Wine Lovers' Handbook, 1972; Wines and Spirits, 1972; A Dictionary of Wines and Spirits, 1974; The Taste of Wine, 1975 (trans. French, German, Dutch and Japanese); Entertaining with Wine, 1976; Century Companion to the Wines of Champagne, 1979 (trans. French, German and Dutch); The Penguin Book of Spirits and Liqueurs, 1979, Dictionary of Wines and Spirits, 1980, rev. edn 1987; Understanding Wines and Spirits, 1981; Enjoying Wine: a taster's companion, 1982; The Penguin Wine Book, 1984; (with C. Fielden) Alsace Wines and Spirits, 1984; Wine: lore, legends and traditions, 1985 (Book of Year: Wine Mag., 1986; Wine Guild, 1986); Wine's Company, 1986; French Vintage, 1986; France for the Gourmet Traveller, 1988; Wines of the Graves, 1988; (ed) Christie's Wine Companion, 1989; Woman of Taste (autobiog.), 1990. *Recreation:* making wine vinegar. *Address:* 8 Queen's Gate, SW7 5EL.

VANE; *see* Fletcher-Vane, family name of Baron Inglewood.

VANE, family name of **Baron Barnard**.

VANE, Sir John (Robert), Kt 1984; FRS 1974; Hon. President, William Harvey Research Institute, since 1997 (Director, 1986–90; Director-General, 1990–97); Professor of Pharmacology and of Medicine, New York Medical College, since 1986; *b* 29 March 1927; *s* of Maurice Vane and Frances Florence Vane (*née* Fisher); *m* 1948, Elizabeth Daphne Page; two *d. Educ:* Birmingham Univ. (BSc Chemistry, 1946); St Catherine's Coll., Oxford (BSc Pharmacology, 1949; DPhil 1953; DSc 1970; Hon. Fellow, 1983). Stothert Research Fellow of Royal Soc., 1951–53; Asst Prof. of Pharmacology, Yale Univ., 1953–55; Sen. Lectr in Pharmacology, Inst. of Basic Medical Sciences, RCS, 1955–61; Reader in Pharmacology, RCS, Univ. of London, 1961–65; Prof. of Experimental Pharmacology, RCS, Univ. of London, 1966–73; Gp Res. and Develt Dir, Wellcome Foundn, 1973–85. Visiting Professor: King's Coll., London, 1976; Charing Cross Hosp. Med. Sch., 1979; Harvard Univ., 1979; St Marianna Univ., Japan, 1993. British Pharmacological Soc.: Meetings Sec., 1967–70; Gen. Sec., 1970–73; For. Sec., 1979–85; Hon. Mem., 1985; a Vice Pres., Royal Soc., 1985–87. Founder FMedSci 1998. Mem., Royal Acad. of Medicine, Belgium, 1978 (Hon. Foreign Mem., 1983). Foreign Member: Royal Netherlands Acad. of Arts and Scis, 1979; Polish Acad. of Scis, 1980; For. Associate, US Nat. Acad. of Scis, 1983; For. Hon. Mem., Amer. Acad. of Arts and Scis, 1982; Hon. Member: Polish Pharmacological Soc., 1973; Japanese Pharm. Soc., 1990; Alpha Omega Alpha Honor Med. Soc., USA, 1990; Polish Acad. of Medicine, 1995; Hon. FACP 1978; Hon. FRCP 1983; Hon. FRCPath 1990; Hon. FRCS 1995; Hon. FFPM 1996; Hon. Fellow: Swedish Soc. of Medical Scis, 1982; Royal Acad. of Medicine, Spain, 1996; QMW, 1996. Hon. DM: Krakow, 1977; Vienna, 1993; Hon. Dr René Descartes Univ., Paris, 1978; Hon. DSc: Mount Sinai Med. Sch., NY, 1980; Aberdeen, 1983; NY Med. Coll., 1984; Birmingham, 1984; Camerino, 1984; Catholic Univ., Louvain, 1986; London, 1995; DUniv Surrey, 1984; Dr *hc* Buenos Aires, 1986; Hon. DPharm Milan, 1993; Hon. Dr Med. Surg. Florence, 1991. (Jtly) Albert Lasker Basic Med. Res. Award, 1977; Baly Medal, RCP, 1977; (jtly) Peter Debye Prize, Univ. of Maastricht, 1980; Feldberg Foundn Prize, 1980; Ciba Geigy Drew Award, Drew Univ., 1980; Dale Medal, Soc. for Endocrinol., 1981; Nobel Prize for Physiology or Medicine (jtly), 1982; Galen Medal, Apothecaries' Soc., 1983; Biol Council Medal, 1983; Louis Pasteur Foundn Prize, Calif, 1984; Royal Medal, Royal Soc., 1989; Special Award, Tsukuba City, Japan, 1990; Meml Prize, Fernandez-Cruz Foundn, 1991; Golden Medal Medicus Magnus, Polish Acad. of Medicine, 1995. Freeman: Scranton, USA, 1988; Taipei, Taiwan, 1989; New Orleans, USA, 1995. *Publications:* (ed jtly) Adrenergic Mechanisms, 1960; (ed jtly) Prostaglandin Synthetase Inhibitors, 1974; (ed jtly) Metabolic Functions of the Lung, Vol. 4, 1977; (ed jtly) Handbook of Experimental Pharmacology, 1978; (ed jtly) Prostacyclin, 1979; (ed jtly) Interactions Between Platelets and Vessel Walls, 1981; (ed jtly) Endothelin, Vol. I, 1989, Vol. II, 1991, Vol. III, 1993, Vol. IV, 1995; (ed jtly) Aspirin and Other Salicylates, 1992; (ed jtly) Prostacyclin: new perspectives in basic research and novel therapeutic indications, 1992; (ed jtly) Therapeutic Applications of Prostaglandins, 1993; (ed jtly) The Endothelial Cell in Health and Disease, 1995; (ed jtly) Improved Non-steroid Anti-inflammatory Drugs, 1995; (ed jtly) New Targets in Inflammation: inhibitors of Cox-2 or adhesion molecules, 1996; (ed jtly) Eicosanoids, Aspirin and Asthma, 1998; (ed jtly) Selective Cox-2 Inhibitors: pharmacology, clinical effects and therapeutic potential, 1998; numerous papers in learned jls. *Recreations:* photography, travel, underwater swimming. *Address:* William Harvey Research Institute, St Bartholomew's and The Royal London School of Medicine and Dentistry, Charterhouse Square, EC1M 6BQ. *Clubs:* Athenæum, Garrick.

VANE-TEMPEST-STEWART, family name of **Marquess of Londonderry**.

VANE-WRIGHT, Richard Irwin; Keeper of Entomology, Natural History Museum, since 1998; *b* 26 July 1942; *s* of Gerald Vane Wright, (James Wright) and late Jessie Margaret (*née* Baldwin); *m* 1987, Hazel June Whitehead; two *d. Educ:* University Coll. London (BSc 1st Cl. Hons Zool. 1967). British Museum (Natural History), subseq. Natural History Museum: Asst (Scientific), 1961–63; SO, Dept Entomology, 1967–84; Dep. Keeper of Entomology, 1984–90; Individual Merit Researcher (Band 2), 1990–98. Fellow, Wissenschaftskolleg, Berlin, 1993–94. Karl Jordan Medal, Lepidopterists' Soc., USA, 1989. *Publications:* (with P. R. Ackery) The Biology of Butterflies, 1984, 2nd edn 1989; (with P. R. Ackery) Milkweed Butterflies, 1984; (jtly) Carcasson's African Butterflies, 1995; numerous contribs to books and science jls. *Recreations:* jazz, walking, woodwork, books, clocks, craneflies, butterflies, conservation. *Address:* Department of Entomology, Natural History Museum, Cromwell Road, SW7 5BD. *Club:* Tetrapods.

VANEZIS, Prof. Peter, OBE 2001; MD, PhD; FRCPath, FRCPGlas; Regius Professor of Forensic Medicine and Science, since 1993 and Director, Human Identification Centre, since 1994, University of Glasgow; *b* 11 Dec. 1947; *s* of Savvas Vanezis and Efrosini Vanezis; *m* 1981, Maria Galatariotis; one *s* one *d. Educ:* Wanstead High Sch.; Bristol Univ. (MB ChB, MD); PhD London; DMJ Path; MRCPGlas. Jun. appt, St Olave's Hosp. (Guy's), 1973–74; Jun. Lectr, Lectr and Sen. Lectr in Forensic Medicine, London Hosp. Med. Coll., 1974–90; Reader and Head of Dept of Forensic Medicine and Toxicology, Charing Cross and Westminster Med. Sch. and Hon. Consultant, Riverside AHA, 1990–93. External Examiner in Forensic Pathology: Postgrad. Med. Inst., Sri Lanka, 1995–; Coll. of Pathologists, Hong Kong, 1999–; Ext. Examiner in Forensic Medicine, Univ. of Malaysia, 2001–. Vis. Prof., Inst. of Forensic Medicine, Singapore, 2000–. Hon. Consultant: Tower Hamlets AHA, 1982–90; the Armed Forces, 1992–; Gtr Glasgow Health Bd, 1993–; Medico-legal Inst., Santiago, 1994–; Govt of Republic of Cyprus, 1984–. Pres., British Acad. of Forensic Scis, 1996–97; mem., numerous forensic science socs, UK and USA. Mem., Editl Bds (Path), Science and Justice, Jl of Clinical Path, Amer. Jl Forensic Medicine & Path. *Publications:* Pathology of Neck Injury, 1989; Suspicious Death-Scene Investigation, 1996; articles on forensic medicine and science in learned jls. *Recreations:* painting, golf. *Address:* Department of Forensic Medicine and Science, The University, Glasgow G12 8QQ. *T:* (0141) 330 4573.

VAN GELDER, Prof. Gerard Jan Henk, PhD; Laudian Professor of Arabic, University of Oxford, since 1998; Fellow, St John's College, Oxford, since 1998; *b* 10 June 1947; *s* of Gerard Jan Van Gelder and Hendrika Venmans; *m* 1973, Sheila Maureen Ottway; two *d. Educ:* Univ. of Amsterdam (doctoral); Univ. of Leiden (PhD 1982). Librarian, Inst. for Modern Near East, Univ. of Amsterdam, 1973–75; Lectr in Arabic, Univ. of Groningen, 1975–98. Mem., Royal Netherlands Acad. of Arts and Scis, 1997. *Publications:* Beyond the Line: classical Arabic literary critics on the coherence and unity of the poem, 1982; Two Arabic Treatises on Stylistics, 1987; The Bad and the Ugly: attitudes towards invective poetry (Hijā') in classical Arabic literature, 1989; Of Dishes and Discourse, 2000; books in Dutch; contrib. articles in learned jls and encyclopaedias. *Recreation:* music and musicology, especially early music. *Address:* The Oriental Institute, Pusey Lane, Oxford OX1 2LE. *T:* (01865) 278200; 48 Merrivale Square, Oxford OX2 6QX.

van HASSELT, Marc; Headmaster, Cranleigh School, 1970–84; *b* 24 April 1924; *s* of Marc and Helen van Hasselt; *m* 1st, 1949, Geraldine Frances Sinclair (marr. diss. 1976); three *s* one *d*; 2nd, 1989, Tessa Carolyn, *d* of Mrs B. Gofton-Salmond. *Educ:* Sherborne; Selwyn Coll., Cambridge (MA); Corpus Christi Coll., Oxford (DipEd). Served War of 1939–45 (despatches): commissioned in Essex Yeomanry, RHA, 1944; served North-West Europe (D-day). Lecturer in Commonwealth Studies, RMA, Sandhurst, 1950–58; Asst Master, Oundle School, 1959–70 (Housemaster, Sanderson House, 1963–70). Member: Admiralty Interview Bd, 1972–86; Army Scholarship Bd, 1972–86. Chairman: Castle Court Sch., 1988–95; Walhampton Sch., 1990–97; Gov., Canford Sch., 1985–95. *Publications:* occasional articles and reviews. *Recreations:* cruising under sail, governing schools. *Address:* Carrick Corner, New Road, Keyhaven, Lymington, Hants SO41 0TN. *T:* (01590) 644690; rue Lyvet, 22690 Vicomte-sur-Rance, France. *Clubs:* Royal Cruising; Royal Lymington Yacht.

VAN KLAVEREN, Adrian; Head of Newsgathering, BBC News, since 2000; *b* 31 Dec. 1961; *s* of late Arthur Van Klaveren and Thelma Van Klaveren; *m* 1990, Julie Stringer; two *s. Educ:* Bristol Grammar Sch.; St John's Coll., Oxford (BA Modern Hist.). Joined BBC, 1983; news trainee, 1983–85; producer, TV News, 1985–90; Sen. Producer, Panorama, 1990–91; Deputy Editor: Nine O'Clock News, 1992–94; Newsnight, 1994; Hd, Local Progs, BBC W Midlands, 1995–96; News Ed., Newsgathering, 1996–2000. *Recreations:* football (especially Spurs), cricket, political biography. *Address:* BBC Television Centre, Wood Lane, W12 7RJ. *T:* (020) 8576 7994.

van KUFFELER, John Philip de B.; *see* de Blocq van Kuffeler.

van MAURIK, Ernest Henry, OBE 1944; HM Diplomatic Service, retired; *b* 24 Aug. 1916; *s* of late Justus van Maurik and Sybil van Maurik (*née* Ebert), BEM; *m* 1945, Winifred Emery Ritchie Hay (*d* 1984); one *s* one *d. Educ:* Lancing Coll.; Ecole Sup. de Commerce, Neuchatel, Switzerland. Worked in Tea Export, Mincing Lane, 1936–39. Commnd as 2nd Lt, in Wiltshire Regt, 1939; seconded to Special Ops Exec., 1941–46; demob. with hon. rank of Lt-Col (subst. Major), 1946. Joined Foreign Office, 1946; Moscow, 1948–50; West Germany and West Berlin, 1952–56; Buenos Aires, 1958–62; Copenhagen, 1965–67; Rio de Janeiro, 1968–71; FCO, 1971–75. Officier de la Couronne (Belgium), 1944. *Recreations:* golf, gardening, languages. *Address:* Mountfield Cottage, Wickhurst Road, Weald, Sevenoaks, Kent TN14 6LY. *T:* (01732) 452173. *Club:* Special Forces.

VAN MIERT, Karel; President, Nyenrode University, Netherlands Business School, since 2000; *b* 17 Jan. 1942; *m* 1971, Annegret Sinner; one *s. Educ:* Univ. of Ghent; European Univ. Centre, Nancy. With Sicco Mansholt, 1968–70; Asst in Internat. Law, New Univ. of Brussels, 1971–73; Office of Vice-Pres. of EC, 1973–75; Head of Private Office of Minister of Economic Affairs, Belgium, 1977; part-time Lectr on European Instns, Free Univ. of Brussels, 1978; Mem., European Parlt, 1979–85; Mem., Belgian Chamber of Reps, 1985–88; Mem., CEC, then EC, 1989–99. Vice-Chm., Socialist Internat., 1986–89. *Publications:* papers on European integration. *Address:* Nyenrode University, Netherlands Business School, Straatweg 25, 3621 BG Breukelen, Netherlands.

VANN, (William) Stanley, DMus(Lambeth); *b* 15 Feb. 1910; *s* of Frederick and Bertha Vann; *m* 1934, Frances Wilson; one *s* one *d*. *Educ:* privately. BMus London; FRCO; ARCM. Asst Organist, Leicester Cath., 1931–33; Chorus Master, Leicester Phil. Soc., 1931–36; Organist and Choirmaster, Gainsborough Parish Ch., Dir of Music, Queen Elizabeth Grammar Sch. and High Sch., Gainsborough, Conductor, Gainsborough Mus. and Orch. Socs, also Breckin Choir, Doncaster, 1933–39; Organist and Choirmaster, Holy Trinity PC, Leamington Spa, Founder-Conductor, Leamington Bach Choir and Warwicks Symph. Orch., and Dir of Music, Emscote Lawn Sch., Warwick, 1939–49. Served War of 1939–45, RA, final rank Captain. Master of Music, Chelmsford Cath., Conductor, Chelmsford Singers, Founder Conductor, Essex Symph Orch., Prof., Trinity Coll. of Music, London, 1949–53; Master of Music, Peterborough Cath., Conductor, Peterborough Phil. Choir and Orch., 1953–77, retired. Conductor, St Mary's Singers, 1984–. Examiner, TCL, 1953–77; Mem. Council and Examr RCO, 1972–98; Mem., ISM; Adjudicator, Brit. Fed. of Festivals, Canadian Fed. Fest. and Hong Kong Fest., 1950–84; Chairman: Peterborough Music Fest., 1953–; Eastern Area Council, British Fedn of Music Festivals, 1982–90; President: Essex Symph. Orch., 1990–; Peterborough Children's Choir, 1994–; Gildenburgh Choir, 1997–. Patron, Precincts Soc., 1985–. DMus Lambeth 1971 (for eminent services to church music); Hon. FTCL 1953. *Publications:* seven settings of Missa Brevis and Missa Sancti Pauli; Billingshurst Mass; three settings of Rite A Communion Service; two settings of Rite B Communion Service; Evening Services in E minor and C major and for Rochester, Gloucester, Hereford, Lincoln, Lichfield, Peterborough, Chester, Salisbury, York, Chichester, Ripon and Worcester Cathedrals; over 100 anthems, motets, carols, organ works and choral arrangements of folk-songs and of Handel; five sets of Preces and Responses and a Collection of Anglican Chants. *Recreations:* railway modelling, painting, gardening. *Address:* Holly Tree Cottage, Wansford, Peterborough PE8 6PL. *T:* (01780) 782192.

VANNECK, family name of **Baron Huntingfield**.

VANNET, Alfred Douglas; Sheriff of South Strathclyde, Dumfries and Galloway at Airdrie and Lanark, since 2001; *b* 31 July 1949; *s* of William Peters Vannet and Jean Farquhar Low or Vannet; *m* 1979, Pauline Margaret Renfrew; one *s* one *d*. *Educ:* High Sch. of Dundee; Univ. of Dundee (LLB 1973). Solicitor in private practice, Oban, 1973–76; Procurator Fiscal Depute, Dundee, 1976–77; Procurator Fiscal Depute, then Sen. Procurator Fiscal Depute, Glasgow, 1977–84; Crown Office, Edinburgh: Head of Appeals Section, 1984–87; Asst Solicitor, Law Officers' Secretariat, 1987–88; Dep. Crown Agent, 1990–94; Solicitor to Public Inquiry into Piper Alpha Disaster, 1988–90; Regional Procurator Fiscal: Grampian Highland and Islands, 1994–97; Glasgow and Strathkelvin, 1997–2000; floating Sheriff, all Scotland, 2000. Mem., Criminal Courts Rules Council, 1997–2000. Member: Forensic Sci. Soc., 1985–; Internat. Assoc. of Prosecutors, 1997–2000; Council, Scottish Medico-Legal Soc., 1997–2000. Hon. Mem., Royal Faculty of Procurators in Glasgow, 1997. FRSA 1995. *Recreations:* music, dog walking. *Address:* Sheriff Court House, Graham Street, Airdrie ML6 6EE. *T:* (01236) 751121; *e-mail:* sheriff.advannet@scotcourts.gov.uk.

VANNI d'ARCHIRAFI, Raniero; Italian Ambassador to Spain, 1983–87 and 1995–98; *b* 7 June 1931; *m* 1956, Simonetta Fiocca; two *s*. *Educ:* Univ. of Rome (Degree in Law). Joined Italian Diplomatic Service; served on Permanent Representation of Italy to EC, Brussels, 1961–66; Counsellor, Directorate General for Econ. Affairs, 1969–73; 1st Counsellor, Madrid, 1973; Minister Plenipotentiary, EC Summit, Feb. 1980; Head, Cabinet of Minister of Foreign Affairs, 1980–83; Ambassador to FRG, 1987–89; Director General for: Econ. Affairs, 1989–91; Political Affairs, 1991–93; Mem., CEC, later EC, 1993–95. Gran Cruz, Isabela la Católica (Spain), 1986; Cavaliere di Gran Croce della Rep. Italiana, 1990. *Address:* Calle Lagasca 107, 28006 Madrid, Spain.

VAN ORDEN, Brig. Geoffrey Charles, MBE 1973; Member (C) Eastern Region, England, European Parliament, since 1999; *b* 10 April 1945; *s* of Thomas and Mary Van Orden; *m* 1974, Frances Elizabeth Weir; three *d*. *Educ:* Sandown Sch.; Mons OCS; Univ. of Sussex (BA Hons Pol Sci.); Indian Defence Services Staff Coll. (psc). Commnd Intelligence Corps, 1964; operational service in Borneo, NI and BAOR; Directing Staff, Führungs Akademie der Bundeswehr, 1985–88; COS and ACOS, G2 Berlin (British Sector), 1988–90; Assessment Staff, Cabinet Office, 1990; Res. Associate, IISS and Service Fellow, Dept of War Studies, KCL, 1990–91; Head, Internat. Mil. Staff Secretariat, NATO HQ, 1991–94; retd and trans. to Regular Reserve, 1994; Sen. Official, EC (Directorate-Gen. Ext. Relations), 1995–99. Mem., IISS, 1991–. Founder Mem., Anglo-German Officers' Assoc., 1991. Member: Friends of the Union, 1997–; Countryside Alliance, 1999–; Bow Gp, 1999–. Freeman, City of London; Freeman, Co. of Painter-Stainers, 1991. *Publications:* various articles on foreign and security policy issues. *Address:* 88 Rectory Lane, Chelmsford, Essex CM1 1RF. *T:* (01245) 345141; European Parliament, Rue Wiertz, 1047 Brussels, Belgium. *T:* (2) 2845332. *Club:* Army and Navy.

van RIEMSDIJK, John Theodore, CIMechE; Keeper of Mechanical and Civil Engineering, Science Museum, 1976–84; author and broadcaster; *b* 13 Nov. 1924; *s* of late Adrianus Kors van Riemsdijk and Nora Phyllis van Riemsdijk (*née* James); *m* 1957, Jocelyn Kilma Arfon-Price. *Educ:* University College Sch.; Birkbeck Coll. (BA). Served SOE, 1943–46. Manufacturer of gearing, 1946–54; Science Museum: Asst, 1954; Lectr, 1961; Educn Officer, 1969. Engaged in setting up Nat. Railway Mus., York, 1973–75. *Publications:* Pregrouping Railways, 1972; Pictorial History of Steam Power, 1980; Compound Locomotives, 1982, 2nd edn 1994; Science Museum Books; contribs to: BBC Publications; Newcomen Soc. Trans, Procs of IMechE. *Recreations:* oil painting, making models. *Address:* Le Moulin du Gavot, St Maximin, 30700 Uzès, Gard, France. *T:* 466227378.

van ROIJEN, Jan Herman Robert Dudley; Knight, Order of the Netherlands Lion; Officer, Order of Orange Nassau; Netherlands Ambassador to the Court of St James's, 1995–99, and concurrently to Iceland; *b* 17 Dec. 1936; *s* of late Dr Jan Herman van Roijen and Anne (*née* Jonkvrouw Snouck Hurgronje); *m* 1963, Jonkvrouw Caroline H. W. Reuchlin; one *s* two *d*. *Educ:* Groton Sch., Mass, USA; Univ. of Utrecht (LLM 1961). Mil. service, Platoon Comdr in New Guinea, 1962. Foreign Service, 1963–; served Jakarta, Paris (NATO), Brussels (NATO), Saigon (chargé d'Affaires); Counsellor and Dep. Chief of Mission: Athens, 1975; Ottawa, 1978; Minister and Dep. Chief of Mission, Jakarta, 1981; Dep. Dir-Gen., Internat. Co-operation, Min. of Foreign Affairs, 1983; Ambassador, Tel Aviv, 1986; Principal Dir of Personnel, Diplomatic Budget and Buildings, Min. of Foreign Affairs, 1990; Ambassador, Jakarta, 1992. *Recreations:* tennis, ski-ing. *Address:* Jagerslaan 9 Zuid, 2243 EH Wassenaar, Netherlands. *T:* (70) 5144470. *Clubs:* Brooks's; The Haagsche (The Hague).

van SCHOONHETEN, Baron Willem Oswald B.; *see* Bentinck van Schoonheten.

VÄNSKÄ, Osmo; Music Director, Lahti Symphony Orchestra, since 1988; Chief Conductor, BBC Scottish Symphony Orchestra, since 1996; *b* Finland, 1953. *Educ:* trained as clarinettist; Sibelius Acad., Helsinki (conducting, under Jorma Panula). Formerly clarinettist, Helsinki Philharmonic Orch.; Artistic Dir, Icelandic SO, 1993–96; Guest Conductor of orchestras in Europe, USA, Australia and Japan. First Prize, Internat. Young Conductors' Competition, Besançon, 1982. *Address:* c/o Harrison Parrott Ltd, 12 Penzance Place, W11 4PA.

van WACHEM, Lodewijk Christiaan; Knight, Order of the Netherlands Lion, 1981; Commander, Order of Orange-Nassau, 1990; Hon. KBE 1988 (Hon. CBE 1977). mechanical engineer, Netherlands; Chairman, Supervisory Board, Royal Dutch Petroleum Co., The Hague, since 1992 (Managing Director, 1976–82; President, 1982–92); *b* Pangkalan Brandan, Indonesia, 31 July 1931; *m* 1958, Elisabeth G. Cristofoli; two *s* one *d*. *Educ:* Technological Univ., Delft (mech. engr). Joined BPM, The Hague, 1953; Mech. Engr, Compania Shell de Venezuela, 1954–63; Shell-BP Petr. Develt Co. of Nigeria: Chief Engr, 1963–66; Engrg Manager, 1966–67; Brunei Shell Petr. Co. Ltd: Head of Techn. Admin., 1967–69; Techn. Dir, 1969–71; Head of Prod. Div., SIPM, The Hague, 1971–72; Chm. and Managing Dir, Shell-BP Petr. Develt Co. of Nigeria, 1972–76; Co-ordinator, Exploration and Prod., SIPM, The Hague, 1976–79; Mem. Presidium, Bd of Dirs, Shell Petroleum NV, 1976–92; Man. Dir, Shell Petroleum Co. Ltd, 1976–92; Chm., Cttee of Man. Dirs, Royal Dutch/Shell Gp of Cos, 1985–92. Chm., Shell Oil Co., USA, 1982–92; Dir, Shell Canada Ltd, 1982–92. Public Service Star (Singapore), 1998. *Address:* Carel van Bylandtlaan 30, 2596 HR The Hague, Holland. *T:* (70) 3772118.

VARADHAN, Prof. Srinivasa, PhD; FRS 1998; Professor of Mathematics, Courant Institute, New York University, since 1972; *b* 2 Jan. 1940; *s* of S. V. Rangaiyengar and S. R. Janaki; *m* 1964, Vasundara Narayanan; two *s*. *Educ:* Madras Univ. (BSc Hons, MA); Indian Statistical Inst. (PhD 1963). Courant Institute, New York University: Vis. Member, 1963–66; Asst Prof., 1966–68; Associate Prof., 1968–72; Dir, 1980–84 and 1992–94. Fellow, Amer. Acad. Arts and Sci., 1988; Associate Fellow, Third World Acad. Scis, 1988; Mem., NAS, 1995. *Publications:* Multi-dimensional Diffusion Processes, 1979; On Diffusion Problems and Partial Differential Equations, 1980; Large Deviations and Applications, 1984. *Recreations:* travel, tennis, squash, bridge. *Address:* Courant Institute, New York University, 251 Mencer Street, New York, NY 10012, USA. *T:* (212) 9983334.

VARAH, Rev. Dr (Edward) Chad, CH 2000; CBE 1995 (OBE 1969); Rector, Lord Mayor's Parish Church of St Stephen Walbrook, in the City of London, since 1953; Senior Prebendary of St Paul's Cathedral, since 1997 (a Prebendary, 1975–97); Founder, The Samaritans (to befriend the suicidal and despairing), 1953, President of London Branch, 1974–86 (Director, 1953–74); President, Befrienders International (Samaritans Worldwide), 1983–86 (Chairman 1974–83); *b* 12 Nov. 1911; *e s* of Canon William Edward Varah, Vicar of Barton-on-Humber, and Mary (*née* Atkinson); *m* 1940, Doris Susan Whanslaw, OBE (*d* 1993); four *s* (three of them triplets) one *d*. *Educ:* Worksop Coll., Notts; Keble Coll., Oxford (Hon. Fellow 1981); Lincoln Theol. Coll.; Exhibnr in Nat. Sci. (Keble); BA Oxon (Hons in PPE), 1933, MA 1943. Secretary: OU Russian Club, 1931; OU Slavonic Club, 1932; Founder Pres., OU Scandinavian Club, 1931–33. Deacon, 1935, Priest, 1936. Curate of: St Giles, Lincoln, 1935–38; Putney, 1938–40; Barrow-in-Furness, 1940–42; Vicar of: Holy Trinity, Blackburn, 1942–49; St Paul, Clapham Junction, 1949–53. Staff Scriptwriter-Visualiser for Eagle and Girl, 1950–61; Sec., Orthodox Churches Aid Fund, 1952–69; Pres., Cttee for Publishing Russian Orthodox Church Music, 1960–76; Chm., The Samaritans (Inc.), 1963–66; Pres., Internat. Fedn for Services of Emergency Telephonic Help, 1964–67. Consultant: Forum Magazine, 1967–2001; Assoc. for Crisis Intervention, China, 1994–. Patron, Outsiders' Club, 1984–; Terrence Higgins Trust, 1987–99; Founder, 1992, Sec., 1999–, Men Against Genital Mutilation of Girls. Hon. Liveryman, Worshipful Co. of Carmen, 1977, Worshipful Co. of Grocers, 1994. Freedom, City of Lincoln, 1999. Hon. LLD: Leicester, 1979; St Andrews, 1993; Leeds, 1995; Hon. DSc City, 1993; Hon. DLitt De Montfort, 1998; Hon. DA Lincs and Humberside, 2000. Roumanian Patriarchal Cross, 1968. Albert Schweitzer Gold Medal, 1972; Louis Dublin Award, Amer. Assoc. Suicidology, 1974; with Befrienders International, Prix de l'Institut de la Vie, 1978; Honra ao Mérito Medal, São Paulo TV, Brazil, 1982; Pride of Britain Award for Lifetime Achievement, 2000. *Publications:* Notny Sbornik Russkogo Pravoslavnogo Tserkovnogo Peniya, vol. 1 Bozhestveniya Liturgia, 1962, vol. 2 Pt 1 Vsenoshchnaya, 1975; (ed) The Samaritans, 1965; Samariter: Hilfe durchs Telefon, 1966; Vänskap som hjälp, 1971; (TV play) Nobody Understands Miranda, 1972; (ed) The Samaritans in the 70s, 1973, rev. edn 1977; Telephone Masturbators, 1976; (ed) The Samaritans in the 80s, 1980, rev. edn as The Samaritans: befriending the suicidal, 1984, 2nd edn 1988; Before I Die Again (autobiog.), 1992; Limp, 1993. *Recreations:* reading, listening to music, watching videos of nature programmes on television. *Address:* St Stephen's Church, 39 Walbrook, EC4N 8BN. *T:* (020) 7283 4444, (020) 7626 8242. *Clubs:* Athenæum, Walbrook; Oxford Union.

VARCOE, (Christopher) Stephen; baritone; *b* 19 May 1949; *s* of Philip William and Mary Northwood Varcoe; *m* 1972, Melinda Davies; two *s* two *d* (and one *s* decd). *Educ:* King's School, Canterbury; King's College, Cambridge (MA). Freelance concert and opera singer, 1970–; Calouste Gulbenkian Foundation Fellowship, 1977. *Publications:* Sing English Song: a practical guide to the language and repertoire, 2000; (contrib.) Cambridge Companion to Singing, 2000. *Recreations:* painting, gardening, building.

VARCOE, Jeremy Richard Lovering Grosvenor, CMG 1989; HM Diplomatic Service, retired; part-time Immigration Adjudicator, since 1995; *b* 20 Sept. 1937; *s* of late Ronald A. G. Varcoe and Zoe E. Varcoe (*née* Lovering); *m* 1st, 1961, Wendy Anne Moss (*d* 1991); two *d*; 2nd, 1995, Ruth Murdoch (*née* Wallis). *Educ:* Charterhouse; Lincoln Coll., Oxford (MA). National Service, Royal Tank Regt, 2nd Lieut, 1956–58. HMOCS: District Officer, Swaziland, 1962–65. Called to the Bar, Gray's Inn, 1966; Lectr in Law, Univ. of Birmingham, 1967–70; joined HM Diplomatic Service, 1970; FCO, 1970–72; Dep. Secretary General, Pearce Commn on Rhodesian Opinion, 1972; First Sec., Ankara, 1972–74, Lusaka, 1974–78; FCO, 1978–79; Commercial Counsellor, Kuala Lumpur, 1979–82; Head of Southern African Dept, FCO, 1982–84; Counsellor, Ankara, 1984–85; on special leave with Standard Chartered Bank, Istanbul, 1985–87; Ambassador to Somalia, 1987–89; Minister/Dep. High Comr, Lagos, 1989–90; Asst Under-Sec. of State, FCO, 1990–92. Co-ordinator, London Economic Summit, 1991. Dir Gen., United World Colls, 1992–94; Dep. Dir, Develt Office, Oxford Univ., 1995–96. *Publication:* Legal Aid in Criminal Proceedings—a Regional Survey, 1970. *Recreations:* sailing, golf. *Address:* Dozmary House, Romsey Road, King's Somborne, Stockbridge, Hants SO20 6PR.

VARCOE, Stephen; *see* Varcoe, C. S.

VARDY, Sir Peter, Kt 2001; Chairman, Reg Vardy plc, since 1982; *b* 4 March 1947; *s* of late Reginald Vardy and of Sarah Vardy; *m* 1971, Margaret; two *s* one *d* (and one *s* decd.). *Educ:* Chorister Sch.; Durham Sch. Began work in family business, Reg Vardy Ltd (motor dealership), at age of 16; built co. to become one of largest UK motor retail gps; floated on Stock Exchange, 1989. Sponsor and Chm., Emmanuel Coll., Gateshead (City Tech.

Coll.), 1990. Hon. DBA. *Address:* (office) Houghton House, Wessington Way, Sunderland, Tyne and Wear SR5 3RJ.

VARFIS, Grigoris; Member (Socialist), European Parliament, 1984–89; *b* 1927. *Educ:* Univ. of Athens; Univ. of Paris. Journalist, Paris, 1953–58; OECD, 1958–62; Econ. Adviser to permt Greek delegn to EEC, 1963–74; Dir-Gen., Econ. Min. of Co-ordination, 1974–77; Man. Dir in chemical industry, 1977–81; Vice-Minister of Foreign Affairs, 1981–84; Greek Comr to EC, 1985–88 (responsible for structural funds and consumer protection, 1986–88). *Address:* Kypseli, Aegina 18010, Greece.

VARGAS LLOSA, Mario; writer; *b* Arequipa, Peru, 28 March 1936; *m* 1st, 1955, Julia Urquidi (marr. diss. 1964); 2nd, 1965, Patricia Llosa Urquidi; two *s* one *d. Educ:* Univ. Nacional Mayor de San Marcos, Lima (BA); Univ. of Madrid (PhD 1959). Journalist and broadcaster, Lima and Paris; Lectr, QMC, 1967; Writer in Residence, Wilson Center, Smithsonian Instn, 1980; Vis. Fellow, Wissenschaftskolleg, Berlin, 1991–92; Visiting Professor: Washington State Univ., 1968; KCL, 1969; Univ. de Puerto Rico, 1969; Columbia Univ., 1975; Cambridge Univ., 1977; Syracuse Univ., 1988; Florida Internat. Univ., 1991; Harvard Univ., 1992–93; Princeton Univ., 1993; Georgetown Univ., 1994, 1999; Oxford Univ., 2000. Founder of political party, Movimiento Libertad, 1988; Presidential candidate, Peru, 1990. Pres., PEN Club Internat., 1976–79. Member: Acad. Peruana de la Lengua, 1975; Royal Spanish Acad., 1994. Biblioteca Breve prize (Spain), 1963; Rómulo Gallegos Internat. Literature prize (Venezuela), 1967; Ritz Paris Hemingway prize (France), 1985; Asturias prize (Spain), 1986; Planeta prize (Spain), 1993; Cervantes prize (Spain), 1994; Jerusalem prize (Israel), 1995. Congressional Medal of Honour (Peru), 1981; Légion d'honneur (France), 1985; Chevalier, Ordre des Arts et des Lettres (France), 1993. *Publications:* Los jefes (short stories), 1958; *novels:* La ciudad y los perros, 1962; La casa verde, 1965; Los cachorros, 1967; Conversación en la Catedral, 1969; Historia secreta de una novela, 1971; Pantaleón y las visitadoras, 1973; La tía Julia y el escribidor, 1977 (filmed as Tune in Tomorrow, 1990); La guerra del fin del mundo, 1981; La historia de Mayta, 1984; ¿Quién mató a Palomino Molero?, 1986; El hablador, 1987; Elogio de la madrastra, 1988; Lituma en los Andes, 1993; Los cuadernos de Don Rigoberto, 1997; La fiesta del Chivo, 2000; *plays:* La señorita de Tacna, 1981; Kathie y el hipopótamo, 1981; La Chunga, 1986; El loco de los balcones, 1993; *non-fiction:* Contra viento y marea (essays), vols I and II, 1986, vol. III, 1990; El pez en el agua (autobiog.), 1993; Desafíos a la libertad (essays), 1994; Making Waves (essays), 1996. *Address:* Las Magnolias 295-6° Piso, Barranco, Lima 04, Peru. *Fax:* (1) 4773518; c/o Faber & Faber Ltd, 3 Queen Square, WC1N 3AU. *Fax:* (020) 7465 0034.

VARLEY, family name of **Baron Varley**.

VARLEY, Baron *cr* 1990 (Life Peer), of Chesterfield in the County of Derbyshire; **Eric Graham Varley;** PC 1974; DL; Director: Ashgate Hospice Ltd, 1987–96; Cathelco Ltd, since 1989; Laxgate Ltd, 1991–92; *b* 11 Aug. 1932; *s* of Frank Varley, retired miner, and Eva Varley; *m* 1955, Marjorie Turner; one *s. Educ:* Secondary Modern and Technical Schools; Ruskin Coll., Oxford. Apprentice Engineer's Turner, 1947–52; Engineer's Turner, 1952–55; Mining Industry (Coal) Craftsman, 1955–64. National Union of Mineworkers: Branch Sec., 1955–64; Mem. Area Exec. Cttee, Derbyshire, 1956–64. Chm., and Chief Exec., Coalite Gp, 1984–89; N and E Midlands Regl Dir, 1987–89, Midlands and N Wales Regl Dir, 1989–91, Lloyds Bank PLC. MP (Lab) Chesterfield, 1964–84; Asst Govt Whip, 1967–68; PPS to the Prime Minister, 1968–69; Minister of State, Min. of Technology, 1969–70; Chm., Trade Union Gp of Labour MPs, 1971–74; Secretary of State: for Energy, 1974–75; for Industry, 1975–79; Principal Opposition Spokesman on employment, 1979–83; Treasurer, Labour Party, 1981–83. Mem., H of L European Communities Select Cttee, 1991–96. Vis. Fellow, Nuffield Coll., 1977–81. DL Derbys, 1989. *Recreations:* reading, gardening, music, sport. *Address:* c/o House of Lords, SW1A 0PW.

VARLEY, Dame Joan (Fleetwood), DBE 1985 (CBE 1974); Director, Local Government Organisation, Conservative Central Office, 1976–84; *b* 22 Feb. 1920; *d* of late F. Ireton and Elizabeth Varley. *Educ:* Cheltenham Ladies' College; London School of Economics (BSc Econ). Section Officer, WAAF, 1944–46. Conservative Agent, Shrewsbury, 1952–56; Dep. Central Office Agent, NW Area, 1957–65; Dep. Dir Orgn, 1966–74, Dir, Central Admin, 1975–76, Cons. Central Office. Chm., Friends of St James Norlands Assoc., 1986–95; Pro Chancellor, Univ. of Greenwich Court of Governors, 1992–94 (Vice-Chm., 1986–91, Chm., 1991–92, Thames Polytechnic Court of Governors); pt-time Mem., Panel of VAT Tribunals, 1986–94. DUniv Greenwich, 1995. *Recreations:* gardening, walking. *Address:* 9 Queensdale Walk, W11 4QQ. *T:* (020) 7727 1292. *Club:* St Stephen's Constitutional.

VARLEY, John Silvester; Director, since 1998 and Group Finance Director, since 2000, Barclays Bank plc; *b* 1 April 1956; *m* 1981, Carolyn Thorn Pease; one *s* one *d. Educ:* Downside Sch.; Oriel Coll., Oxford (MA 1st cl. Hons History). Admitted Solicitor, 1979; Commercial Law Dept, Frere Cholmeley, Solicitors, 1979–82; Asst Dir, Corporate Finance Dept, Barclays Merchant Bank, 1982–86; Barclays de Zoete Wedd: Corporate Finance Div., 1986–89; Man. Dir, BZW Asia, 1989–91; Dep. Chief Exec., Global Equities Div., 1991–94; Dir, Odey Asset Management, 1994–95; Chairman: BZW Asset Management, 1995–96; BZW Property Investment Management, 1995–96; Dir, BZW Barclays Global Investors, 1995–96; Chm., Barclays Asset Management Gp, 1996–98; Chief Exec., Retail Finance Services, Barclays Bank plc, 1998–2000. *Address:* c/o Barclays Bank plc, 54 Lombard Street, EC3P 3AH. *T:* (020) 7699 3260; *e-mail:* john.varley@barclays.co.uk. *Clubs:* Brooks's, Army and Navy.

VARLEY, Rosemary Margaret, (Rosie); Regional Chairman, Eastern (formerly Anglia and Oxford) Region, NHS Executive, Department of Health, since 1997; *b* 22 Dec. 1951; *d* of late Ratcliffe Bowen Wright, MD, FRCOG and of Dr Margaret Bowen Wright (*née* Williams); *m* 1976, Andrew Iain Varley; one *s* one *d. Educ:* New Hall, Chelmsford; Durham Univ. (BA Hons); Manchester Univ. (MA Econ). Various acad. posts, Manchester Univ., 1978–83; Mem., W Suffolk HA, 1984–92; Chm., Mid Anglia Community NHS Trust, 1992–97. Indep. Mem., E of England Regl Assembly, 1999–. Member: Mental Health Rev. Tribunal, 1995–; Disability Appeal Tribunal, 1992–. Chm., Gen. Optical Council, 1999–. FRSocMed 1999. *Publications:* contrib. various articles in health jls and mgt textbooks. *Recreations:* walking, travel, sailing, extended family, home and dog. *Address:* 72 Southgate Street, Bury St Edmunds, Suffolk IP33 2BJ. *T:* (01284) 753135; *e-mail:* rvarley@doh.gov.uk.

VARMUS, Prof. Harold Eliot, MD; President and Chief Executive Officer, Memorial Sloan-Kettering Cancer Center, New York City; *b* 18 Dec. 1939; *s* of Frank Varmus and Beatrice Barasch Varmus; *m* 1969, Constance Louise Casey; two *s. Educ:* Freeport High Sch., NY; Amherst Coll., Mass (BA 1961); Harvard Univ. (MA 1962); Columbia Univ., NY (MD 1966). Surgeon, US Public Health Service, 1968–70; Dept of Microbiology, Univ. of California Medical Center, San Francisco: Lectr, 1970–72; Asst Prof., 1972–74; Associate Prof., 1974–79; Prof. of Microbiology and Immunology, 1979–93 (Dept of Biochem. and Biophys, 1982–93); Amer. Cancer Soc. Prof. of Molecular Virology, 1984–93; Dir, NIH, Bethesda, Md, 1993–99. Scientific Consultant, Chiron Corp., 1982–87; Member, Scientific Adv. Bd: Merck Corp., 1985–88; Gilead Corp., 1988–. Associate Editor: Cell, 1974–78, 1979–; Virology, 1974–84; Genes and Develt, 1986–; Editor, Molecular and Cellular Biol., 1984–88; Mem., Editl Bd, Trends in Genetics, 1989–. Member: Special Grants Cttee, Calif. Div., Amer. Cancer Soc., 1973–76; Breast Cancer Virus Wkg Gp, Virus Cancer Program, 1973–74. Bd of Scientific Counselors, Div. of Cancer Biol. and Diagnosis, 1983–87, Nat. Cancer Inst.; Virology Study Section, NIH, 1976–80. Member: AAAS; Amer. Soc. Microbiology; Amer. Soc. Biochem. and Molecular Biol; Amer. Soc. Virology; Nat. Acad. Scis, 1984; Amer. Acad. Arts and Scis, 1988. Hon. DSc: Amherst Coll., 1984; Columbia Univ., 1990. Numerous awards and prizes incl. (jtly) Nobel Prize for Physiology or Medicine, 1989. *Address:* Memorial Sloan-Kettering Cancer Center, 1275 York Avenue, NYC 10021, USA.

VARNAM, Ivor; Deputy Director, Royal Armament Research and Development Establishment, 1974–82, retired; *b* 12 Aug. 1922; *s* of Walter Varnam and Gertrude Susan Varnam (*née* Vincent); *m* 1942, Doris May Thomas; two *s. Educ:* Alleyn's Coll., Dulwich; University Coll., Cardiff; Birkbeck Coll., London. BSc Wales 1944; BSc (Hons) London 1952. Served War, RAF, 1940–46 (commnd 1944). Joined Tannoy Products, 1946; Atomic Energy Research Estabt, 1947; Siemens Bros., 1948; Royal Armament Research and Development Estabt, 1953–60 and 1962–82 (Defence Research Staff, Washington, USA, 1960–62), as: Supt Mil. ADP Br., 1964; Supt GW Br., 1967; Prin. Supt Systems Div., 1969; Head, Applied Physics Dept, 1972. *Publications:* official reports. *Recreations:* gardening, photography, bridge, music.

VARNEY, David Robert; Chairman, mmO$_2$ (formerly BT Wireless), since 2001; *b* 11 May 1946; *s* of Robert Kitchener Frederick Varney and Winifred Gwendoline Williams; *m* 1971, Patricia Ann Billingham; one *s* one *d. Educ:* Brockley County Grammar Sch.; Surrey Univ. (BSc); Manchester Univ. (MBA). Joined Shell Refining Co., 1968; various appts in UK, Australia, Holland and Sweden, 1968–90; Head of Mkting, Branding and Product Develt, SIPCO, 1990–91; Man. Dir, Downstream Oil, Shell UK, 1991–95; Dir (responsible for Shell's oil products business in Europe), Shell Internat. Petroleum Co., 1996; Chief Exec., BG Group plc, 1997–2000. Non-exec. Dir, Cable and Wireless, 1999–2000. Member: Bd, Oil, Gas and Petrochemicals Supplies Office, 1997–99; Public Service Productivity Panel, 2000–; Policy Commn on Future of Farming and Food, 2001–. Vice-Chm., Council, Univ. of Surrey, 2001– (Mem., 1994–). *Recreations:* opera, Formula 1 motor racing, Rugby. *Address:* River Thatch, The Abbotsbrook, Bourne End, Bucks SL8 5QU. *Clubs:* Royal Automobile, Royal Society of Medicine.

VARNISH, Peter, OBE 1982; FREng, FIEE; Director of Technology (Partnership), Defence Evaluation and Research Agency, Farnborough, since 2000; *b* 30 May 1947; *s* of John Varnish and Ilma Varnish (*née* Godfrey); *m* 1968, Shirley-Anne Bendelow; two *s. Educ:* Warwick Sch.; UCNW, Bangor (BSc Hons 1968). CEng 1987; FIEE 1989; FREng (FEng 1995). Res., Services Electronics Res. Lab., Baldock, 1968–75; Scientific Advr to MoD, British Embassy, Washington, 1975–79; Res. Area Co-ordinator for Electrical Warfare in UK, ASWE Portsdown, 1979–81; Officer i/c, ASWE Funtington, 1981–84; Head: Radar Div., ASWE Portsdown, 1984–86; Signature Control, ARE Funtington, 1986–88; Electronic Warfare and Weapons Dept, ARE Portsdown, 1988–90; Dir, Above Water Weapons, DRA, 1990–92; RCDS 1992; Dir, SDI Participation Office, 1993; Dir of Sci. for Ballistic Missile Defence, MoD, 1993–95; Defence Evaluation and Research Agency: Dir, Internat. Business Develt, 1995–98; Dir, Business Develt, 1998–2000. Non-executive Director: Schvink Environmental Hldgs, 1999–; EMC Gp Hldgs, 2000–. Mem., Defence Scientific Adv. Council, 1991–99. Chairman: Common Defence Forum, 1988; Military Microwaves, 1990; Stealth Conf., 1990; Milcon, Abu Dhabi, 1995, 1997, 1999; Singapore Internat. Defence Conf., 1997, 1999. SMIEE; MIMgt; MInstD 1995. FRSA 1996. Several patents on stealth technology, radar. *Publications:* numerous papers on electron bombarded semiconductor devices, radar, electronic warfare, Stealth, SDI, ballistic missile defence and res. policy, defence globalisation, technol. of modern warfare. *Recreations:* Rugby football, classical music, photography, furtherance of science in UK, travelling, being a grandparent. *Address:* 1 Greatfield Way, Rowlands Castle, Hants PO9 6AG. *T:* (023) 9241 2440; *e-mail:* pvarnish@dera.gov.uk. *Club:* Naval and Military.

VASARY, Tamàs; pianist and conductor; Music Director and Principal Conductor, Budapest Symphony Orchestra, since 1993; Principal Conductor, Bournemouth Sinfonietta, 1989–97, Conductor Laureate, 1997–98; *b* 11 Aug. 1933; *s* of Jozsef Vàsàry and Elizabeth (*née* Baltazàr); *m* 1967, Ildiko (*née* Kovàcs). *Educ:* Franz Liszt Music Academy Budapest. First concert at age of 8 in Debrecen, Hungary; First Prize, Franz Liszt Competition, Budapest, 1947; prizes at internat. competitions in Warsaw, Paris, Brussels, Rio de Janeiro; Bach and Paderewski medals, London, 1961; début in London, 1961, in Carnegie Hall, NY, 1961; plays with major orchestras and at festivals in Europe, USA, Australasia and Far East; 3 world tours. Conducting debut, 1970; Musical Dir, Northern Sinfonia Orch., 1979–82; conducts worldwide. Records Chopin, Debussy, Liszt, Rachmaninov (in Germany), Brahms, Mozart, Honnegger, Respighi, Martinu, Beethoven. *Recreations:* yoga, writing, sports. *Address:* c/o IMG Artists, 616 Chiswick High Road, W4 5RX.

VASCONCELLOS, Josefina Alys Hermes de, MBE 1985; Hon. DLitt; sculptor; Founder, The Harriet Trust, Beached Trawler adapted for Nature-observation Base for Young Disabled; *b* 26 Oct. 1904; *d* of late H. H. de Vasconcellos, Brazilian Consul-General in England, and Freda Coleman; *m* 1930, Delmar Banner (*d* 1983), painter. *Educ:* sculpture: London, Paris, Florence; Royal Academy Schools. Former FRBS. Exhibits RA, Leicester Galls; High Altar and Statue, Varengeville, Normandy, 1925; Bronze St Hubert, Nat. Gall. of Brazil, 1926; Music in Trees, in stone, Southampton Gall., 1933; Ducks, in marble, Glasgow Art Gall., 1946; exhibn with husband, of 46 sculptures in 20 materials at RWS Gall., 1947; Episcopal Crook, in perspex, for Bristol Cathedral, 1948; Refugees, in stone, Sheffield Art Gall., 1949; Last Chimera, Canongate Kirk, Edinburgh; 8ft Christ (in Portland Stone), Nat. War Meml to Battle of Britain, Aldershot, 1950; two works, Festival of Britain, Lambeth Palace, 1951; sculpture exhibn, with husband, RWS Galls, 1955; War Memorial, St Bees School, 1955; two figures, St Bees Priory, 1955; life-size Mary and Child and design group of 11 sculptures by 11 collaborators, for Nativity, St Paul's Cathedral, Christmas 1955; Mary and Child bought for St Paul's, 1956; life-size Resurrection for St Mary, Westfield, Workington, 1956–57; Madonna and Child, St James's, Piccadilly, (now in Burrswood, Dorothy Kerin Trust), 1957; Rising Christ in St Bartholomew the Great, Smithfield; Winter, carving in Perspex, Oldham Gallery, 1958; Nativity (for ruins of Coventry Cathedral), 1958; Flight into Egypt, for St Martin-in-the-Fields, 1958 (now in Cartmel Priory); War Memorial, Reredos of carved oak, Rossall School Chapel, 1959; Nativity Set, life-size figures, St Martin-in-the-Fields, annually in Trafalgar Sq.; Winged Victory Crucifix, Clewer Church, 1964, and Canongate Kirk, Edinburgh; life-size Holy Family, Liverpool Cathedral and Gloucester Cathedral, 1965; life-size Virgin and Child, Blackburn Cathedral, 1974; Reunion, Bradford Univ., 1977, rededicated as Reconciliation when cast taken for two bronzes, 1995 (for Coventry Cathedral and Hiroshima Peace Park Hall, bronze casts also for grounds of Stormont, NI, and for site on remains of Berlin Wall, 1999); Return of the Carpenter, group of 10 life-size children, Samlesbury Hall, 1978; life-size Holy Family, for St Martin-in-the-Fields, 1983, 1992; life-size Holy Family, in cold cast stone, Norwich Cathedral, 1985; Revelation XXI, 'and God shall wipe the tears from their eyes', life-size two figure group, in plaster, for Lake Artists Exhibn, Grasmere, 1986; life-size Virgin and Child, Ambleside Parish Church, 1988; Reredos, Wordsworth Chapel, 1988; life-size Mary and Babe, Carlisle Cathedral, 1989; Sea Legend, in bronze, Hutton in the Forest, 1990; Childline to God, life-size figures of Christ, angels and 4 children, the Fratery, Carlisle Cathedral, 1990; life-size Holy Family, Manchester Cathedral, 1992 (exhibited Lake Artists Exhibn); Father Forgive, Rydal Hall, 1993; St Michael, life-size bronze, Cartmel Priory, 1995; The Weight of our Sins, St Martin-in-the-Fields, 1999–2000; Escape to Light, Brougham Hall, 2001; one man exhibn, A Christmas Exhibition of Sculpture, Painting and Poems, Manchester Cath., 1991–92; Heroic Fragment (life-size body), in memory of glider pilots, Mus. of Army Flying, Middle Wallop, 2000; sculptures at Dallas, Tulsa, Chicago, USA; Portraits: bronze of Lord Denning, 1969; Bishop Fleming; Rev. Austen Williams; Mario Borelli; and Rev. Dr M. S. Israel. Documentary film Out of Nature (on her work), 1949; BBC programme, Viewpoint TV, 1968; film, Moments of Truth, Border TV, 1993. President: Guild of Lakeland Craftsmen, 1971–73; Cumbria Sculptors, 1999–; Brother, Art Workers Guild. Mem., Inst. of Patentees and Inventors; Hon. Member, Glider Pilots Regimental Assoc. Founder, Childrise, 2000. Hon. DLitt Bradford, 1977. Jean Masson Davidson Medal, Soc. of Portrait Sculptors. *Publications:* Woodcut illustrations for The Cup (Poems by F. Johnson), 1938; (contrib.) They Became Christians (ed Dewi Morgan), 1966; *relevant publication:* Sculptor: Josefina de Vasconcellos, by Linda Clifford, 2000. *Recreation:* tiny garden. *Address:* Catlands Foot Farm, Catlands Hill, Mealsgate, Wigton, Cumbria CA7 1DJ. *Club:* Reynolds.

VASEY, Rt Rev. Mgr Kevin, OBE 1990; QHC 1999; Principal Roman Catholic Chaplain and Vicar General (Army), Ministry of Defence, since 1997; *b* 8 April 1949; *s* of late Frederick Vasey and of Edna Mary Vasey (*née* Stoddart). *Educ:* St Mary's Primary Sch., Hartlepool; St Mary's Coll., Middlesbrough; Ushaw College. Ordained priest, 1973; Curate, St Mary's Cathedral, Newcastle upon Tyne and Dio. Tribunal Asst, 1973–76; Royal Army Chaplains' Department: TA commn, 1976–79; Regular Army commn, 1979; Dortmund Garrison, 1979–81; 3 Inf. Bde, 1981; 8 Inf. Bde, 1981–82; 12 Armd Bde, 1982–84; Dhekelia Garrison, 1984–85; RMA, Sandhurst, 1985–88; Sen. RC Chaplain, HQ NI, 1988–90; 1 (Br) Corps, 1990–93; HQ ARRC, 1993–94; HQ BAOR, 1994–95; HQ UK Support Comd (Germany), 1995; 4th Div., 1995–97. *Recreations:* performing arts, travel. *Address:* Ministry of Defence Chaplains (A), Trenchard Lines, Upavon, Pewsey, Wilts SN9 6BE. *T:* (01980) 615803. *Club:* Army and Navy.

VASQUEZ, Hon. Sir Alfred (Joseph), Kt 1988; CBE 1974; QC (Gibraltar) 1986; *b* 2 March 1923; *s* of Alfred Joseph Vasquez and Maria Josefa (*née* Rugeroni); *m* 1950, Carmen, *o d* of Lt-Col Robert Sheppard-Capurro, OBE, JP; three *s* one *d*. *Educ:* Mount St Mary's Sch., Millfield; Fitzwilliam Coll., Cambridge (MA). Gibraltar Defence Force, 1943–45; The Gibraltar Regt, 1957–64, Captain. Called to the Bar, Inner Temple, 1950; called to Gibraltar Bar, 1950; Sen. Partner, Vasquez Benady & Co., 1950–91; Consultant, Triay & Triay, barristers and solicitors, 1995–. Speaker, Gibraltar Hse of Assembly, 1970–89; Mayor of Gibraltar, 1970–76. Vice-Chm., Gibraltar Bar Council, 1996–98. Pres., Gibraltar Oxford & Cambridge Soc. Hon. Fellow, World Innovation Foundn, 2000. KHS 1989. *Recreations:* golf, shooting, gardening, bridge. *Address:* St Vincent House, Rosia Parade, Gibraltar. *T:* 73710. *Clubs:* Royal Gibraltar Yacht; Sotogrande Golf (Spain).

VASSAR-SMITH, Sir John (Rathborne), 4th Bt *cr* 1917, of Charlton Park, Charlton Kings, Co. Gloucester; Headmaster, St Ronan's Preparatory School, 1972–97; *b* 23 July 1936; *o s* of Major Sir Richard Rathborne Vassar-Smith, 3rd Bt and Mary Dawn, *d* of Sir Raymond Woods, CBE; *S* father, 1995; *m* 1971, Roberta Elaine, *y d* of Wing Comdr N. Williamson; two *s*. *Educ:* Eton. *Heir: s* Richard Rathborne Vassar-Smith, *b* 29 Dec. 1975. *Address:* 24 Haywards Close, Wantage, Oxon OX12 7AT.

VASSILIOU, Dr George Vassos; Leader, United Democrats (formerly Free Democrats Movement), Cyprus, since 1993; President of Cyprus, 1988–93; *b* 20 May 1931; *s* of Vassos Vassiliou and Fofo Vassiliou; *m* Androulla Georgiades; one *s* two *d*. *Educ:* Univs of Geneva, Vienna and Budapest (DEcon). Market researcher, Reed Paper Group, UK; Founder: Middle East Marketing Research Bureau, 1962 (Chm. and Man. Dir); Middle East Centres for Management and Computing Studies, 1984; Cyprus Branch, Inst. of Directors (Hon. Sec.). Vis. Prof., Cranfield School of Management, 1985–. MP (United Democrats), Cyprus, 1993. Head, Cyprus negotiating team for accession to EU, 1998–. Member: Bd and Exec. Cttee, Bank of Cyprus, 1987–88; Econ. Adv. Council, Church of Cyprus, 1982–88; Educn Adv. Council, 1983–88; Inter Action Council, 1994–. Chm. Bd, World Inst. for Develt Econs Res. of UN Univ., Helsinki, 1999– (Mem., 1995–). Member, Board of Governors: Shimon Peres Inst. for Peace, 1997–; Centre for Eur. Policy Studies, Brussels, 1997–. Dr *hc:* Univ. of Athens; Univ. of Econs, Budapest. Grand Cross: Legion of Honour (France); Order of the Saviour (Greece); Order of Republic of Italy; Standard (Flag) Order (Hungarian People's Republic); Grand Collar, Order of Austria. *Publications:* Marketing in the Middle East, 1976, etc. *Address:* 21 Academia Avenue, Aglandjia, PO Box 22098, Nicosia 1583, Cyprus.

VASSYLENKO, Volodymyr; Ambassador of the Ukraine to the Court of St James's, and non-resident Ambassador to Ireland, since 1998; *b* Kyiv, Ukraine, 16 Jan. 1937; *m;* one *s* one *d*. *Educ:* Kyiv State Univ. (degree, 1964; DSc 1977). Teaching Public Internat. Law, Human Rights Law, Internat. Humanitarian Law and Law of Internat. Orgn, Ukrainian Inst. Internat. Relns, Kyiv State Univ., 1964–93; Legal Advr to Min. of Foreign Affairs, Ukraine, 1972–93; Sen. Legal Advr to Parliament of Ukraine and Mem., Constitutional Commn, 1991–93; Ambassador to Belgium, The Netherlands and Luxembourg, and Permanent Rep. to EU and N Atlantic Co-operation Council, 1993–95; Ambassador-at-Large, Min. of Foreign Affairs, 1995–98; Permanent Rep. to IMO, 1998–. Rep. of Ukraine to internat. confs; Rep. to UN Commn on Human Rights, 1989–91 and 1996–98; Mem., Ukrainian Delegn to CIS sunmmits, 1991, 1992. Member: Consultative Council to Min. of Justice, Ukraine; Supervisory Bd, Ukrainian Legal Foundn. Sec., Adv. and Governing Councils, 1972–78, Mem., 1978–92, Inst. Internat. Relns, Kyiv State Univ. Mem., Grand Council, Popular Democratic People's Movement of Ukraine, 1969–91. Vice-Pres., Ukrainian Assoc. for UN, 1989–98. *Publications:* International Law, 1971; *monographs:* State Responsibility for International Offences, 1976; Sanctions in International Law, 1982; Legal Aspects of Participation of the Ukrainian SSR in International Relations, 1985; Protection Mechanisms for International Law and Order, 1986; Fundamentals of International Law, 1988; contrib. numerous articles in public internat. law and constitutional protection of human rights. *Address:* Embassy of the Ukraine, 60 Holland Park, W11 3SJ. *T:* (020) 7727 6312.

VAUGHAN, family name of **Earl of Lisburne.**

VAUGHAN, Viscount; David John Francis Malet Vaughan; artist; *b* 15 June 1945; *e s* of 8th Earl of Lisburne, *qv*; *m* 1973, Jennifer Jane Sheila Fraser Campbell, artist, *d* of James and Dorothy Campbell, Invergarry; one *s* one *d*. *Educ:* Ampleforth Coll.

VAUGHAN, Rt Rev. Benjamin Noel Young; Hon. Assistant Bishop, Swansea and Brecon, since 1988; *b* 25 Dec. 1917; *s* of late Alderman and Mrs J. O. Vaughan, Newport, Pembs; *m* 1st, 1945, Nesta Lewis (*d* 1980); 2nd, 1987, Magdalene Reynolds. *Educ:* St David's Coll., Lampeter (BA; Hon. Fellow, 1990); St Edmund Hall, Oxford (MA); Westcott House, Cambridge. Deacon, 1943; priest, 1944; Curate of: Llannon, 1943–45; St David's, Carmarthen, 1945–48; Tutor, Codrington Coll., Barbados, 1948–52; Lecturer in Theology, St David's Coll., Lampeter, and Public Preacher, Diocese of St David's, 1952–55; Rector, Holy Trinity Cathedral, Port of Spain, and Dean of Trinidad, 1955–61; Bishop Suffragan of Mandeville, 1961–67; Bishop of British Honduras, 1967–71; Assistant Bishop and Dean of Bangor, 1971–76; Bishop of Swansea and Brecon, 1976–87. Examining Chaplain to Bishop of Barbados, 1951–52, to Bishop of Trinidad, 1955–61; Commissary for Barbados, 1952–55. Formerly Chairman: Nat. Council for Educn in British Honduras; Govt Junior Secondary Sch.; Provincial Commn on Theological Educn in WI; Provincial Cttee on Reunion of Churches, Christian Social Council of British Honduras; Ecumenical Commn of British Honduras; Agric. Commn of Churches of British Honduras; Pres., Belize Church Assoc., 1974–98. Chairman: Provincial Cttee on Missions, Church in Wales; Church and Society Dept, Council of Churches for Wales; Adv. Cttee on Church and Society, Church in Wales, 1977; Judge of Provincial Court, Church in Wales. Pres., Council of Churches for Wales, 1980–82. Member: Council, St David's Univ. Coll., Lampeter, 1976–89 (Sub-Visitor, 1987–); Council and Ct, Swansea Univ. Coll., 1976–89; Ct, Univ. of Wales, 1986–89. Chm. of Govs, Christ Coll., Brecon, 1976–87. Sub-Prelate, OStJ, 1977; Order of Druids, Gorsedd y Beirdd. *Publications:* Structures for Renewal, 1967; Wealth, Peace and Godliness, 1968; The Expectation of the Poor, 1972. *Address:* 4 Caswell Drive, Caswell, Swansea, West Glamorgan SA3 4RJ. *T:* (01792) 360646.

VAUGHAN, David Arthur John; QC 1981; QC (NI) 1981; a Recorder, since 1994; a Deputy High Court Judge, since 1997; a Judge of the Courts of Appeal of Jersey and Guernsey, since 2000; *b* 24 Aug. 1938; *s* of late Captain F. H. M. Vaughan, OBE, RN and J. M. Vaughan; *m* 1st, 1967, (marr. diss.); 2nd, 1985, Leslie Anne Fenwick Irwin; one *s* one *d*. *Educ:* Eton Coll.; Trinity Coll., Cambridge (MA). 2nd Lieut, 14th/20th King's Hussars, 1958–59. Called to the Bar, Inner Temple, 1962, Bencher, 1988. Vis. Prof., European Law, Durham Univ., 1989–2000. Leader, European Circuit, Bar of England and Wales, 2001–. Member: Bar Council, 1968–72, 1984–86; Bar Cttee, 1987–88; International Relations Committee of Bar Council, 1968–86 (Chm., 1984–86); Bar/Law Soc. Working Party on EEC Competition Law, 1977– (Chm., 1978–88); UK Delegation to Consultative Committee of the Bars and Law Societies of the European Communities, 1978–81 (Chm., Special Cttee on EEC Competition Law, 1978–88); Law Adv. Cttee, British Council, 1982–85; Bar European Gp, 1978– (Founder and Chm., 1978–80, Hon. Vice-Pres., 1990–); EEC Section, Union Internationale des Avocats, 1987–91 (Chm., 1987–91); Adv. Bd, Centre for Europ. Legal Studies, Cambridge Univ., 1991–; Council of Management, British Inst. of Internat. and Comparative Law, 1992–; Chm., Mgt Cttee, Lord Slynn of Hadley Eur. Law Foundn, 1999–. Trustee, Wye Foundn, 1997–2000 (Chm., Steering Gp, Wye Habitat Improvement Project, 1999–2000). Chm. Editl Bd, European Law Reports, 1997–; Member, Editorial Board: Eur. Business Law Review, 1998–. Cambridge Yearbook of European Legal Studies, 1999–; Consulting editor for numerous pubns on EC Law. FRSA 1997. Bronze Medal, Bar of Bordeaux, 1985. *Publications:* co-ordinating editor, vols on European Community Law, Halsbury's Laws of England, 1986; (ed) Vaughan on Law of the European Communities, 2 vols, 1986, 2nd edn 1993–98. *Recreation:* fishing. *Address:* 50 Oxford Gardens, W10 5UN. *T:* (020) 8960 5865; (020) 8969 0707; Brick Court Chambers, 7–8 Essex Street, WC2R 3LD. *T:* (020) 7379 3550; avenue d'Auderghem 36, 1040 Brussels, Belgium. *T:* (2) 2303161. *Clubs:* Brooks's, Pratt's.

VAUGHAN, Elizabeth, (Mrs Ray Brown), FRAM; international operatic mezzo-soprano (formerly soprano); *b* Llanfyllin, Montgomeryshire; *m* 1968, Ray Brown (Gen. Manager, D'Oyly Carte Opera); one *s* one *d*. *Educ:* Llanfyllin Grammar Sch.; RAM (ARAM, LRAM); Kathleen Ferrier Prize. Joined Royal Opera House; rôles in: Benvenuto Cellini; La Bohème; Midsummer Night's Dream; Madama Butterfly; Rigoletto; Simon Boccanegra; La Traviata; Il Trovatore; Turandot; Don Giovanni; Un Ballo in Maschera; Ernani; Nabucco; Aida; Cassandra; La Forza del Destino; Tosca; Idomeneo; Macbeth; Gloriana; Salome; Katya Kabanova; Hansel and Gretel; The Carmelites; Suor Angelica. Frequent appearances with: ENO; WNO; Opera North; Scottish Opera; Vienna State Opera; Deutsche Oper, Berlin; Hamburg State Opera; Metropolitan Opera, NY; Paris Opera. Professor of Singing: Welsh Coll. of Music and Drama, 1987–94; Guildhall School of Music, 1989–; RNCM, 1994–96. Has toured in: Europe; USA; Australia; Canada; Japan; S America. Hon. DMus Wales, 1989. *Recreations:* tapestry, antiques, cookery. *Address:* c/o IMG, Lovell House, 616 Chiswick High Road, W4 5RX.

VAUGHAN, Sir Gerard (Folliott), Kt 1984; FRCP; *b* Xinavane, Portuguese E Africa, 11 June 1923; *s* of late Leonard Vaughan, DSO, DFC, and Joan Vaughan (*née* Folliott); *m* 1955, Joyce Thurle (*née* Laver); one *s* one *d*. *Educ:* privately in E Africa; London Univ.; Guy's Hosp. MB, BS 1947; MRCP 1949; Academic DPM London 1952; FRCP 1966; FRCPsych 1972. Consultant Staff, Guy's Hosp., 1958–79, now Consultant Emeritus. Alderman: LCC, 1955–61; LCC Streatham, 1961–64; GLC Lambeth, 1966–70; Alderman, GLC, 1970–72; Chm., Strategic Planning Cttee GLC, 1968–71; Mem., SE Economic Planning Council, 1968–71. Contested (C) Poplar, 1955. MP (C) Reading, 1970–74, Reading South, 1974–83, Reading East, 1983–97. Minister for Health, DHSS, 1979–82; Minister of State (Consumer Affairs), Dept of Trade, 1982–83. Member: Select Cttee on Educn, 1983–93; Select Cttee on Sci. and Technol., 1993–97. Chm., Party and Scientific Cttee, 1991–94. Parly Mem., MRC, 1973–76. Governor, UCL, 1959–68. Liveryman, Worshipful Co. of Barbers (Master, 1992–93). Hon. FASI (FFAS 1978); Hon. FRCS 1993. *Publications:* various professional and general literary publications. *Recreations:* painting, fishing. *Clubs:* Carlton, White's.

VAUGHAN, Prof. John Patrick, CBE 1998; MD; FRCPE, FFPHM; Professor of Epidemiology and Public Health (formerly Health Care Epidemiology), London School of Hygiene and Tropical Medicine, University of London, 1987–2000, now Emeritus; *b* 27 Dec. 1937; *s* of Thomas Frances Gerald Vaughan and Ellalline (*neé* Norwood); *m* 1st, 1960, Patricia Elspeth Pooley; two *s*; 2nd, 1975, Pauline Winifred Macaulay; two step *s* one step *d*. *Educ:* Bishop Wordsworth GS, Salisbury (Holgate and Folliott Prizes); Guy's Hosp. Med. Sch. (MB BS 1961; MD 1978). FRCPE 1982; FFPHM 1988. Specialist physician, Papua New Guinea, 1966–68; Head, Dept of Epidemiology and Biostats, Univ. of Dar es Salaam, 1969–73; Sen. Lectr in Epidem. and Public Health, Med. Sch., Nottingham, 1973–75; London School of Hygiene and Tropical Medicine: Sen. Lectr, 1975–83; Dir, Trop. Epidem. Unit, 1975–79; Reader, 1983–87; Head of Dept of Public Health and Policy, 1989–93; on secondment as Dir, Public Health Scis Div., Internat.

Centre for Diarrhoeal Disease Res., Dhaka, 1995–98. Visiting Professor: Pelotas Fed. Univ., Brazil, 1986–90; Andalucian Sch. of Public Health, Spain, 1994. Specialist Advr in Public Health to World Bank, 1989; hon. consultancies include: NHS, 1975–; MRC; WHO, in foreign countries; Sen. Health and Population Advr, DFID, 1998–99; Advr in Public Health to Perf. and Innovation Unit, Cabinet Office, 2000–01. Member: Amnesty Internat.; WWF; Dorset Trust for Nature Conservation. Founder and Editor, Health Policy and Planning Jl, 1985–93. Okeke and William Simpson Prizes for best student, LSHTM, 1969. *Publications:* (jtly) Community Health, 1981; (ed jtly and contrib.) Refugee Community Health Care, 1983; (jtly) Community Health Workers: the Tanzanian experience, 1987; (jtly) In the Shadow of the City: community health and the urban poor, 1988; (with R. Morrow) Manual of Epidemiology for District Health Management, 1989 (trans. French, Portuguese, Spanish, Turkish); (jtly) Health System Decentralization: concepts, issues and country experience, 1990 (trans. French, Spanish, Indonesian); (ed with C. Normand) Europe without Frontiers: the implications for health, 1993; (contrib.) Disease Control Priorities in Developing Countries, 1993; monographs on health and medicine; contrib. learned jls on health and epidemiology. *Recreations:* travel, yachting, reading, art history, wild life, natural history. *Address:* Department of Public Health and Policy, London School of Hygiene and Tropical Medicine, Keppel Street, WC1E 7HT. *T:* (020) 7636 8636.

VAUGHAN, Prof. Leslie Clifford, FRCVS; Professor of Veterinary Surgery, 1974–91, now Emeritus, and Vice-Principal, 1982–91, Royal Veterinary College; *b* 9 Jan. 1927; *s* of Edwin Clifford and Elizabeth Louise Vaughan; *m* 1951, Margaret Joyce Lawson; one *s* one *d*. *Educ:* Bishop Gore Grammar School, Swansea; Royal Veterinary College, Univ. of London (DVR 1967; DSc 1970; FRVC 1995). FRCVS 1957. Lectr in Veterinary Surgery, RVC, 1951; Reader, London Univ., 1968; Prof. of Vet. Orthopaedics, 1972. Junior Vice-Pres., 1986, Pres., 1987–88, Senior Vice-Pres., 1988–89, 1989–90, RCVS. Francis Hogg Prize for contribs to small animal medicine and surgery, RCVS, 1962; Simon Award for small animal surgery, 1966, Bourgelat Prize, 1975, British Small Animal Vet. Assoc.; Victory Medal, Central Vet. Soc., 1982; Dalrymple-Champneys Cup and Medal, BVA, 1995. *Publications:* papers in sci jls. *Recreations:* gardening, watching rugby football. *Address:* 26 Burywick, Harpenden, Herts AL5 2AH.

VAUGHAN, Prof. Peter Rolfe, FREng; FICE; Professor of Ground Engineering, Imperial College, London, 1987–94, now Emeritus, and Senior Research Fellow; *b* 10 March 1935; *s* of Ernest Alfred Vaughan and Clarrice Marjorie Vaughan. *Educ:* Luton Grammar Sch.; Imperial Coll., London (BSc Eng, PhD, DSc). FREng (FEng 1991). Industry; postgraduate studies; work on Kainji Dam, Nigeria, 1964–67; academic staff, Imperial Coll., 1969–. Dir, Geotechnical Consulting Group, 1982–. *Publications:* numerous technical papers. *Recreations:* fishing, eating and drinking. *Address:* Department of Civil Engineering, Imperial College, SW7 2AZ. *T:* (020) 7594 6081.

VAUGHAN, Rt Rev. Peter St George; Area Bishop of Ramsbury, 1989–98; Hon. Assistant Bishop, diocese of Bradford, 1998–2001; *b* 27 Nov. 1930; *s* of late Dr Victor St George Vaughan and Dorothy Marguerite Vaughan; *m* 1961, Elisabeth Fielding Parker; one *s* two *d*. *Educ:* Charterhouse; Selwyn Coll., Cambridge (MA Theology 1959); Ridley Hall, Cambridge; MA Oxon (by incorporation) 1963. Nat. Service, 1949–51, Lt RAPC. Ordained deacon 1957, priest 1958; Asst Curate, Birmingham Parish Church, 1957–62; Chaplain to Oxford Pastorate, 1963–67; Asst Chaplain, Brasenose Coll., Oxford, 1963–67; Vicar of Christ Church, Galle Face, Colombo, 1967–72; Precentor of Holy Trinity Cathedral, Auckland, NZ, 1972–75; Principal of Crowther Hall, CMS Training Coll., Selly Oak Colleges, Birmingham, 1975–83; Archdeacon of Westmorland and Furness, 1983–89. Hon. Canon: Carlisle Cathedral, 1983–89; Salisbury Cathedral, 1989–98, now Emeritus; Bradford Cathedral, 1998–2001. Commissary for Bishop of Colombo, 1984–. *Recreations:* gardening, reading, people. *Address:* Willowbrook, Downington, Lechlade-on-Thames, Glos GL7 3DL.

VAUGHAN, Prof. Robert Charles, FRS 1990; Professor of Mathematics, Pennsylvania State University, since 1999; *b* 1945. Imperial College, London, 1972–97: Prof. of Pure Maths, 1980–97; EPSRC (formerly SERC) Senior Fellow, 1992–96; Vis. Prof. of Maths, Univ. of Michigan, Ann Arbor, 1997–98. *Publication:* The Hardy-Littlewood Method, 1981, 2nd edn 1997. *Address:* Department of Mathematics, McAllister Building, Pennsylvania State University, University Park, PA 16802, USA.

VAUGHAN, Roger, PhD; FREng; FRINA; Chairman, Safinah Ltd, since 1999; *b* 14 June 1944; *s* of late Benjamin Frederick Vaughan and Marjorie (*née* Wallace); *m* 1st, 1968 (marr. diss.); three *s* two *d*; 2nd, 1987, Valerie (*née* Truelove); one step *s* (and one step *s* decd). *Educ:* Newcastle Univ. (BSc Hons Naval Architecture and Shipbuilding 1966, PhD 1971). FREng (FEng 1990). Student apprentice, Vickers Gp, 1962; Shipbuilding Develt Engr, Swan Hunter Shipbuilders Ltd, 1970–71; Dir, 1971–81, Man. Dir, 1978–81, A&P Appledore Ltd; Dir, Performance Improvement and Productivity, British Shipbuilders, 1981–86; took part in privatisation of Swan Hunter, 1986; Joint Chief Exec., Swan Hunter, 1988–93; Chief Exec., Sch. of Mgt, Newcastle Univ., 1995–99. Non-exec. Dir, Newcastle City Health NHS Trust, 1996–2001; Dir, Northern Sinfonia Concert Soc. Ltd, 1996–. Vis. Prof., Sch. of Mgt, Univ. of Newcastle, 2000–. Member: Nat. Curriculum Council, 1992–94; Council, Newcastle Univ., 1992–95 (Chm., Engrg Design Centre, 1990–94). Pres., Shipbuilders and Shiprepairers Assoc., 1991–93. FRSA 1993. Shipbuilding Gold Medal, NECInst, 1969. *Recreations:* music, theatre, ballet, opera, sailing, walking, reading. *Address:* Correslaw, Netherwitton, Morpeth, Northumberland NE61 4NW.

VAUGHAN, Roger Davison, OBE 1986; FREng; General Manager, Fast Reactor Projects, National Nuclear Corporation Ltd, 1977–88, retired; Director, Fast Reactor Technology Ltd, 1984–88; *b* 2 Oct. 1923; *s* of late David William and Olive Marion Vaughan; *m* 1951, Doreen Stewart; four *s*. *Educ:* University High Sch., Melbourne; Univ. of Melbourne, Aust. (BMechE). Engineer Officer, RAAF, 1945–46. Chemical Engr, Commonwealth Serum Laboratories, 1946–47; Works apprenticeship, C. A. Parsons & Co., 1948–49; Chief Engr, C. A. Parsons Calcutta, 1950–53; AERE, Harwell, 1954; Chief Engineer: Nuclear Power Plant Co., 1955–59 (Director, 1958); The Nuclear Power Group, 1960–75 (Dir, 1960–75); Manager, Technology Div., Nuclear Power Co., 1976–77. Chairman: Gas-cooled Breeder Reactor Assoc., Brussels, 1970–88; Energy Jt Venture Study Gp, Engrg Council, 1996–98; Member: Bd, BSI, 1989–92 (Chm., BSI Engineering Council, 1983–88); BSI Standards Bd, 1992–96. FIMechE (Mem. Council, 1977–81, 1985–89; Chm., Power Industries Div., 1985–89); FREng (FEng 1981). *Publications:* papers in jls of IMechE, Brit. Nuc. Energy Soc., World Energy Conf. *Recreations:* skiing, mountain walking; questionable performer on piano and clarinet. *Address:* Otterburn House, Manor Park South, Knutsford, Cheshire WA16 8AG. *T:* (01565) 632514. *Club:* Himalayan (Bombay).

VAUGHAN, Tom; *see* Phillips, T. R. V.

VAUGHAN-JACKSON, Oliver James, VRD 1951; FRCS; Consulting Orthopaedic Surgeon to London Hospital, since 1971; *b* 6 July 1907; *e s* of Surgeon Captain P. Vaughan-Jackson, RN, Carramore, Ballina, County Mayo; *m* 1939, Joan Madeline (*d* 1996), *er d* of E. A. Bowring, CBE, St Johns, Newfoundland; two *s*. *Educ:* Berkhamsted School; Balliol Coll., Oxford; The London Hospital. Kitchener Scholar; BA, BM, BCh Oxon, 1932; MRCS, LRCP, 1932; FRCS 1936. Surgical Registrar, The London Hosp. Surgeon Lieut-Comdr RNVR, Retd, Surgical specialist, Roy. Naval Hosp., Sydney, Australia. Sen. Registrar (Orthopædic), The London Hosp.; Orthopaedic Surgeon to: The London Hosp., 1946–71; St Bartholomew's Hosp., Rochester, 1947–70; Medway Hosp., 1970–71; Claybury Mental Hosp., 1946–64; Halliwick Cripples Sch., 1946–71; Cons. In Orthopaedics to Royal Navy, 1956–71; Vis. Prof. of Orthopaedics, Memorial Univ. of Newfoundland, 1971–73; Senior Consultant in Orthopaedics at St John's Gen. Hosp., St Clare Mercy Hosp. and Janeway Child Health Centre, St John's, Newfoundland, 1971–73. Sen. Fellow, British Orthopædic Assoc.; Fellow: RSM (Pres., Section of Orthopædics, 1968–69); Med. Soc. London; Mem., Soc. Internat. de Chirurgie Orthopédique et de Traumatologie; Hon. Mem., British Soc. for Surgery of the Hand. Trustee, Meml Univ. of Newfoundland's Harlow Campus Trust, 1988–91. Former Mem., Editorial Board of Jl of Bone and Joint Surgery. Hon. DSc Memorial Univ. of Newfoundland, 1973. *Publications:* Sections on: Arthrodesis (Maingot's Techniques in British Surgery), 1950; Arthrodesis of the Hip, and Osteotomy of the Upper End of Femur (Operative Surgery, ed Rob and Smith), 1958; Surgery of the Hand; Orthopædic Surgery in Spastic conditions; Peripheral Nerve Injuries (Textbook of British Surgery, ed Sir Henry Souttar and Prof. J. C. Goligher), 1959; The Rheumatoid Hand; Carpal Tunnel Compression of the Median Nerve (Clinical Surgery, ed Rob and Smith), 1966; Surgery in Arthritis of the Hand, in Textbook of Rheumatic Diseases, 1968; The Rheumatoid Hand, in Operative Surgery, 2nd edn, 1971; contribs to Jl of Bone and Joint Surgery, etc. *Recreations:* gardening, photography. *Address:* 25 Barton Farm, Cerne Abbas, Dorchester, Dorset DT2 7LF.

VAUX OF HARROWDEN, 10th Baron *cr* 1523; **John Hugh Philip Gilbey;** *b* 4 Aug. 1915; 2nd *s* of William Gordon Gilbey (*d* 1965) and Grace Mary Eleanor, 8th Baroness Vaux of Harrowden (*d* 1958); *S* brother, 1977; *m* 1939, Maureen Pamela (*d* 1999), *e d* of Hugh Gilbey; three *s* one *d*. *Educ:* Ampleforth College; Christ Church, Oxford (BA 1937). Formerly Major, Duke of Wellington's Regt; served War of 1939–45. *Heir:* *s* Hon. Anthony William Gilbey [*b* 25 May 1940; *m* 1964, Beverley Anne, *o d* of Charles Alexander Walton; two *s* two *d*].

VAUX, John Esmond George; Speaker's Counsel, House of Commons, since 2000; *b* 3 Sept. 1948; *s* of Arthur Ernest Vaux and Marjory May Vaux; *m* 1980 Jenny Lennox; one *s* one *d*. *Educ:* Gosport Co. Grammar Sch.; Selwyn Coll., Cambridge (MA). Legal Dept, MAFF, 1979–90 (on secondment to EC, 1983–85); Cabinet Office Legal Advr, and Hd, European Div., Treasury Solicitor's Dept, 1990–97; Speaker's Counsel (European Legislation), H of C, 1997–2000. *Address:* House of Commons, SW1A 0AA. *T:* (020) 7219 3776.

VAUX, Maj.-Gen. Nicholas Francis, CB 1989; DSO 1982; Consultant and Managing Director, International Security Company (formerly UK-Russia Security Group), since 1993; Major General Royal Marines Commando Forces, 1987–90, retired; *b* 15 April 1936; *s* of late Harry and of Penelope Vaux; *m* 1966, Zoya Hellings; one *s* two *d*. *Educ:* Stonyhurst College. Commissioned RM, 1954; served Suez, 1956; Far East, 1958–61; West Indies Frigate, 1962–64; Staff Coll., Camberley, 1969; MoD (Army), 1975–77; Special Advisor, USMC, 1979–81; CO 42 Commando RM, 1981–83; Falklands, 1982; RCDS, 1985. *Publication:* March to the South Atlantic, 1986. *Recreations:* field sports. *Address:* National Westminster Bank, Old Town Street, Plymouth PL1 1DG. *Clubs:* Farmers', Special Forces.

VAVALIDIS, Barbara Joan; *see* Donoghue, B. J.

VAVASOUR, Sir Eric (Michel Joseph Marmaduke), 6th Bt *cr* 1828, of Haslewood, Yorkshire; Chief Engineer, BAL Broadcast, since 1999 (Senior Engineer, 1997–99); *b* 3 Jan. 1953; *s* of Hugh Bernard Moore Vavasour (*d* 1989) and Monique Pauline Marie Madeleine (*née* Beck) (*d* 1982); *S* kinsman, 1997; *m* 1976, Isabelle Baudouin Françoise Alain Cécile Cornelie Ghislaine (*née* van Hille); two *s* one *d*. *Educ:* St Joseph's Coll., Stoke-on-Trent; Manchester Univ. (BSc). AMIEE. BCRA, 1977; Matthey Printed Products Ltd, 1979; BAL (UK) Ltd, 1985. Mem., Soc. of Motion Picture and Television Engineers (USA), 1994–. *Heir:* *s* Joseph Ian Hugh André Vavasour, *b* 22 Jan. 1978. *Address:* 15 Mill Lane, Earl Shilton, Leicester LE9 7AW.

VAVER, Prof. David, JD; Reuters Professor of Intellectual Property and Information Technology Law, University of Oxford, since 1998; Fellow, St Peter's College, Oxford, and Director, Oxford Intellectual Property Research Centre at St Peter's College, since 1998; *b* 28 March 1946; *s* of Ladislav and Pola Vaver; *m* 1978, Judith Maxine McClenaghan; one *s* one *d*. *Educ:* Auckland Grammar Sch.; Univ. of Auckland (BA French 1969; LLB Hons 1970); Univ. of Chicago (JD 1971); MA Oxon 1998. Called to the Bar, NZ, 1970; Asst Prof. of Law, Univ. of BC, 1971; Lectr, 1972–74, Sen. Lectr in Law, 1974–78, Univ. of Auckland; Res. Dir, later Dir, Legal Res. Foundn, Auckland, 1972–78; Associate Prof. of Law, Univ. of BC, 1978–85; Prof. of Law, Osgoode Hall Law Sch., York Univ., Toronto, 1985–98. Editor-in-Chief, Intellectual Property Jl, 1984–98. Consultant on copyright law reform to Dept of Canadian Heritage, 1989–98. *Publications:* Intellectual Property Law: copyright, patents, trade-marks, 1997; Copyright Law, 2000; numerous contribs to edited books and legal jls on intellectual property and contract law. *Recreations:* music, art, wine. *Address:* St Peter's College, Oxford OX1 2DL. *T:* (01865) 278900.

VAZ, (Nigel) Keith (Anthony Standish); MP (Lab) Leicester East, since 1987; *b* Aden, 26 Nov. 1956; *m* 1993, Maria Fernandes; one *s* one *d*. *Educ:* St Joseph's Convent, Aden; Latymer Upper Sch., Hammersmith; Gonville and Caius Coll., Cambridge (BA 1979); Coll. of Law, Lancaster Gate. Solicitor, Richmond-upon-Thames BC, 1982; Senior Solicitor, Islington BC, 1982–85; Solicitor, Highfields and Belgrave Law Centre, Leicester, 1985–87. Contested (Lab): Richmond and Barnes (gen. election), 1983; Surrey W (European Parlt election), 1984. Opposition front bench spokesman on inner cities and urban areas, 1992–97; PPS to Attorney Gen. and Solicitor Gen., 1997–99; Parly Sec., Lord Chancellor's Dept, 1999; Minister of State (Minister for Europe), FCO, 1999–2001. Mem., Home Affairs Select Cttee, 1987–92; Chairman: Unison Gp of MPs, 1996–99; Indo-British Parly Gp, 1997–99; Yemen Parly Gp, 1997–99; Vice Chm., PLP Internat. Develt Gp, 1997–99. Chm., City 2020, Urban Policy Commn, 1993–99; Member: Nat. Adv. Cttee, Crime Concern, 1989–93; Bd, British Council, 1999. Mem., Clothing and Footwear Inst., 1988–94. Vice Pres., Assoc. of Dist Councils, 1993–97. Patron, Gingerbread, 1990–92; Jt Patron, UN Year of Tolerance, 1995; Pres., Leicester and S Leics RSPCA, 1988–99. Chm. Bd, Patrons into Leadership. Columnist: Tribune; Catholic Herald; New Life (Gujarat Samachar). President: Hillcroft FC; Thurnby Lodge

Boys' Club FC. *Address:* 144 Uppingham Road, Leicester LE5 0QF. *T:* (0116) 212 2020. *Clubs:* Safari (Leicester); Scraptoft Valley Working Men's.

VEAL, Group Captain John Bartholomew, CBE 1956; AFC 1940; Civil Aviation Safety Adviser, Department of Trade and Industry, 1972–74, retired; *b* 28 September 1909; *er s* of John Henry and Sarah Grace Veal; *m* 1933, Enid Marjorie Hill (*d* 1987); two *s*. *Educ:* Christ's Hosp. Special trainee, Metropolitan-Vickers, 1926–27; commissioned in RAF as pilot officer, 1927; served in Nos 4 and 501 Squadrons and as flying Instructor at Central Flying School, transferring to RAFO, 1932; Flying-Instructor, Chief Flying Instructor, and Test Pilot, Air Service Training Ltd, 1932–39; recalled to regular RAF service, 1939; commanded navigation and flying training schools, 1939–43; Air Staff No. 46 Transport Group, 1944 and Transport Command, 1945–46 (despatches); released from RAF, 1946, to become Deputy Director of Training, Ministry of Civil Aviation; Director of Air Safety and Training, 1947; Director of Operations, Safety and Licensing, 1952; Deputy Director-General of Navigational Services, Ministry of Transport and Civil Aviation, 1958; Director-General of Navigational Services, Ministry of Aviation, 1959–62; Chief Inspector of Accidents, Civil Aviation Department, Board of Trade (formerly Min. of Aviation), 1963–68; Dir Gen. of Safety and Operations, DTI (formerly BOT), 1968–72. FRAeS 1967 (AFRAeS 1958). *Address:* Woodacre, Horsham Road, Cranleigh, Surrey GU6 8DZ. *T:* (01483) 274490. *Club:* Royal Air Force.

VEAL, Kevin Anthony; Sheriff of Tayside Central and Fife, since 1993; *b* 16 Sept. 1946; *s* of George Algernon Veal and Pauline Grace Short; *m* 1969, Monica Flynn; two *s* two *d*. *Educ:* St Joseph's Primary Sch., Dundee; Lawside Acad., Dundee; Univ. of St Andrews (LLB 1966). Partner, Burns Veal & Gillan, Dundee, 1971–93; Temp. Sheriff, 1984–93. Dean, Faculty of Procurators and Solicitors in Dundee, 1991–93; part-time Tutor, Dept of Law, Univ. of Dundee, 1978–85. Mem., Court, Abertay Dundee Univ., 1998–. Musical Dir, Cecilian Choir, Dundee, 1975–. KCHS 1998 (KHS 1989); KSG 1993. *Recreations:* choral music, organ playing, classical music, hill-walking. *Address:* Sheriff Court House, Market Street, Forfar, Angus DD8 3LA; Viewfield, 70 Blackness Avenue, Dundee DD2 1JL. *T:* (01382) 668633.

VEALE, Sir Alan (John Ralph), Kt 1984; FREng; Chairman: Rossmore Warwick Ltd, 1986–88; RFS Industries Ltd, 1987–92; Exeter Enterprise Ltd, since 1990; *b* 2 Feb. 1920; *s* of Leslie H. Veale and Eleanor Veale; *m* 1946, Muriel Veale; two *s* (and one *s* decd). *Educ:* Exeter School; Manchester College of Technology (AMCT). FIMechE, FIEE; FREng (FEng 1980). Manufacturing Dir, AEI Turbine Generators Ltd, 1963; Director and General Manager: Heavy Plant Div., AEI, 1966; Motor Control Group, AEI, 1967; Managing Director: GEC Diesels Ltd, 1969; GEC Power Engineering Ltd, 1970–85; Dir, GEC plc, 1973–85; Chm., Fairey Gp, 1987; Dir, Throgmorton Trust PLC, 1986–90. Pres., IProdE, 1985–86. CIMgt. Hon. DSc Salford, 1984. *Recreations:* sailing, walking. *Address:* 41 Northumberland Road, Leamington Spa CV32 6HF. *T:* (01926) 424349.

VEASEY, Josephine, CBE 1970; opera singer (mezzo soprano), retired; teaching privately, since 1982; vocal consultant to English National Opera, 1985–94; *b* London, 10 July 1930; *m* (marr. diss.); one *s* one *d*. Joined chorus of Royal Opera House, Covent Garden, 1949; a Principal there, 1955– (interval on tour, in opera, for Arts Council). Teacher of voice production, RAM, 1983–84. Has sung at Royal Opera House, Glyndebourne, Metropolitan (NY), La Scala, and in France, Germany, Spain, Switzerland, South America; operatic Roles include: Octavian in Der Rosenkavalier; Cherubino in Figaro; name role in Iphigenie; Dorabella in Cosi fan Tutte; Amneris in Aida, Fricka in Die Walküre; Fricka in Das Rheingold; name role in Carmen; Dido and Cassandra in the Trojans; Marguerite in The Damnation of Faust; Charlotte in The Sorrows of Werther; Eboli, Don Carlos; name role, Orfeo; Adalgesa in Norma; Rosina in The Barber of Seville; Kundry in Parsifal; Gertrude in Hamlet, 1980. Concerts, 1960–70 (Conductors included Giulini, Bernstein, Solti, Mehta, Sargent). Verdi's Requiem; Monteverdi's Combattimento di Tancredi e Clorinda, Aix Festival, 1967; various works of Mahler; two tours of Israel (Solti); subseq. sang in Los Angeles (Mehta); then Berlioz: Death of Cleopatra, Royal Festival Hall, and L'enfance du Christ, London and Paris; Rossini's Petite Messe Solennelle, London and Huddersfield (with late Sir Malcolm Sargent); Handel's Messiah, England, Munich, Oporto, Lisbon; Berlioz' Romeo and Juliette, London, and Bergen Festival; Rossini's Stabat Mater, Festival d'Angers and London, 1971; Berlioz' Beatrice and Benedict, NY, and London; Emperor in 1st perf. Henze's We Come to the River, Covent Garden, 1976. Has sung Elgar's Dream of Gerontius all over England. Frequently makes recordings. Hon. RAM, 1972. *Recreations:* grandchildren, gardening. *Address:* 5 Meadow View, Whitchurch, Hants RG28 7BL.

VEDRINE, Hubert Yves Pierre; Minister of Foreign Affairs, France, since 1997; *b* 31 July 1947; *s* of Jean and Suzanne Vedrine; *m* 1974, Michèle Froment; two *s*. *Educ:* Lycée Albert-Camus; Univ. of Nanterre; Institute d'Etudes Politiques; Ecole Nationale d'Administration. Chargé de mission, Min. of Culture, 1974–78; Head, Dept of Architecture, Min. of the Envmt, 1978–79; Co-ordinator, Cultural Relations, Near and Middle East, Min. of Foreign Affairs, 1979–81; Head, Dept for Technical Co-operation on Health, Housing, Public Admin and Human Science, 1979–81; Technical Advr, External Affairs, Office of Sec.-Gen. of the Pres., 1981–86; Maître des requêtes, Conseil d'Etat, 1986; Advr and Spokesman, 1988–91, Sec.-Gen., 1991–95, Office of the Pres.; Partner, Jeantet & Associés, barristers, 1996–97. *Publications:* Mieux aménager sa ville, 1979; articles in jls. *Address:* Ministère des Affaires Etrangères, 37 Quai d'Orsay, 75700 Paris, France.

VEEDER, Van Vechten; QC 1986; a Recorder, since 2000; *b* 14 Dec. 1948; *s* of John Van Vechten Veeder and Helen Letham Townley; *m* 1st, 1970; one *s* one *d*; 2nd, 1991, Marie Lombardi; one *d*. *Educ:* Ecole Rue de la Ferme, Neuilly, Paris; Clifton College, Bristol; Jesus College, Cambridge. Called to the Bar, Inner Temple, 1971, Bencher, 2000. *Recreations:* sailing, travelling, reading. *Address:* Essex Court Chambers, 24 Lincoln's Inn Fields, WC2A 3ED. *T:* (020) 7813 8000, *Fax:* (020) 7813 8080.

VEIL, Simone Annie, Hon. DBE 1998; Chevalier de l'Ordre national du Mérite; Member, Constitutional Council, since 1998; Magistrate; *b* Nice, 13 July 1927; *d* of André Jacob and Yvonne (*née* Steinmetz); *m* 1946, Antoine Veil, Inspecteur des Finances, President, A. V. Consultants; three *s*. *Educ:* Lycée de Nice; Lic. en droit, dipl. de l'Institut d'Etudes Politiques, Paris; qualified as Magistrate, 1956. Deported to Auschwitz and Bergen-Belsen, March 1944–May 1945. Ministry of Justice, 1957–69; Technical Advr to Office of Minister of Justice, 1969; Gen.-Sec., Conseil Supérieur de la magistrature, 1970–74. Minister of Health, France, 1974–76; Minister of Health and Social Security, 1976–79; Minister of Social Affairs, Health and Urban Develt, 1993–95. European Parliament: Member, 1979–93; Pres., 1979–82; Chm., Liberal and Democratic Reformist Gp, 1984–89. Pres., Haut Conseil à l'Intégration, 1997–99. Monismanie Prize, 1978; Onassis Foundn Prize, Athens, 1980; Charlemagne Prize, Prix Louise Weiss, 1981; Louise Michel Prize, 1983; Jabotinsky Prize, 1983; Prize for Everyday Courage, 1984; Special Freedom Prize, Eleanor and Franklin Roosevelt Foundn, 1984; Fiera di Messina Prize, 1984; Living Legacy Award, San Diego, Univ. d'Acadie, 1987; Johanna Lowenherz Prize, Neuwied, 1987; Thomas Dehler Prize, Munich, 1988. Dr *hc* Princeton, 1975; Institut Weizmann, 1976; Yale, Cambridge, Edinburgh, Jerusalem, 1980; Georgetown, Urbino, 1981; Yeschiva, Sussex, 1982; Free Univ., Brussels, 1984; Brandeis, 1989; Glasgow, 1995; Pennsylvania, 1997. *Publication:* (with Prof. Launay and Dr Soulé) les Données psycho-sociologiques de l'Adoption, 1969. *Address:* 11 place Vauban, 75007 Paris, France; (office) 10 rue de Rome, 75008 Paris, France.

VELTMAN, Prof. Dr Martinus Justinus Godefridus; McArthur Professor of Physics, University of Michigan, 1981–97, Emeritus Professor, since 1997; *b* Netherlands, 27 June 1931; *s* of Gerard P. H. Veltman and Goverdina Veltman (*née* Vissers); *m* 1960, Anna M. M. Swart; two *s* one *d*. *Educ:* Univ. of Utrecht (PhD 1963). Fellow and Staff Mem., CERN, Geneva, 1961–66; Prof. of Theoretical Physics, Univ. of Utrecht, 1966–81. High Energy Physics Prize, Eur. Physics Soc., 1993; Nobel Prize for Physics, 1999. Comdr, Order of Dutch Lion (Netherlands), 1999; Officier, Légion d'Honneur (France), 2000. *Publications:* Diagrammatica, 1994; Facts and Mysteries in Particle Physics, 2001. *Recreation:* billiards. *Address:* Physics Department, University of Michigan, Ann Arbor, MI 48109, USA. *Club:* Probus '83 (Bilthoven, Netherlands).

VENABLES, Rt Rev. Gregory James; Rector of St Saviour's, Belgrano and Coadjutor Bishop of Argentina, since 2000; *b* 6 Dec. 1949; *s* of Rev. Dudley James Venables and May Norah Venables (*née* Saddington); *m* 1970, Sylvia Margaret Norton; one *s* two *d*. *Educ:* Chatham House; Kingston Univ.; Christchurch Coll., Canterbury. Computer Systems Officer, Sterling Winthrop, 1971–72; English master, Holy Cross Sch., Broadstairs, 1974–77; Headmaster, St Andrews Coll., Asuncion, Paraguay, 1978–89; ordained deacon, March 1984, priest, Nov. 1984; Asst Curate, St Helen's and St Giles, Rainham with St Mary's, Wennington, dio. of Chelmsford, 1990–93; Asst Bishop, dio. of Peru and Bolivia, 1993–95; Bishop of Bolivia, and Vice-Primate, Province of the Southern Cone of America, 1995–2000. *Publication:* Look to the Scars, 1973. *Recreations:* reading, music, walking. *Address:* Casilla de Correo 4293, Correo Central, 1000 Buenos Aires, Argentina; 25 de Mayo 282, 1002 Buenos Aires, Argentina. *T:* (11) 43424618, *Fax:* (11) 43310234; *e-mail:* diocesisanglibue@arnet.com.ar.

VENABLES, (Harold) David (Spenser), CB 1993; Official Solicitor to the Supreme Court, 1980–93; *b* 14 Oct. 1932; *s* of late Cedric Venables and Gladys Venables (*née* Hall); *m* 1964, Teresa Grace, *d* of late J. C. Watts; one *d* one *s*. *Educ:* Denstone College. Admitted Solicitor, 1956. Pilot Officer, Royal Air Force, 1957–58. Legal Assistant, Official Solicitor's Office, 1960; Secretary, Lord Chancellor's Cttee on the Age of Majority, 1965–67; Asst Official Solicitor, 1977–80. *Publications:* A Guide to the Law Affecting Mental Patients, 1975; The Racing Fifteen-Hundreds: a history of voiturette racing 1931–40, 1984; Napier: the first to wear the Green, 1998; First Among Champions: the Alfa Romeo Grand Prix cars, 2000; contributor, Halsbury's Laws of England, 4th edn. *Recreations:* vintage cars, motoring and military history. *Address:* 11 Onslow Road, Hove, Sussex BN3 6TA. *T:* (01273) 502374.

VENABLES, Richard William Ogilvie; Member of Council and Board, Direct Mail Services Standards Board, 1983–95; *b* 23 Feb. 1928; *s* of late Canon and Mrs E. M. Venables; *m* 1952, Ann Richards; three *s* two *d*. *Educ:* Marlborough Coll.; Christ Church, Oxford (BA, MA). Joined former Mather and Crowther Ltd, as trainee, 1952; Account Group Director, 1965; Board Member, 1966; Mem. Executive Cttee, 1972; Managing Director, 1974; joined Board of Ogilvy and Mather International, 1975; Chm., Ogilvy Benson and Mather Ltd, 1978–81; retired early, 1981, to pursue new career in the making of violins, violas, lutes, harpsichords. Chm., Apple and Pear Develt Council, 1980–83. *Recreations:* fly fishing, hill walking, cabinet making, golf. *Address:* First Field, Combe Hay, Bath BA2 8RD. *T:* (01225) 833694.

VENABLES, Robert; QC 1990; *b* 1 Oct. 1947; *s* of Walter Edwin Venables, MM, and Mildred Daisy Robson Venables. *Educ:* Merton Coll., Oxford (MA); London School of Economics (LLM). FTII. Called to Bar, Middle Temple, 1973, Bencher, 1999; private practice as barrister, 1976–. Lecturer: Merton Coll., Oxford, 1972–75; UCL, 1973–75; Official Fellow and Tutor in Jurisprudence, St Edmund Hall, Oxford, and CUF Lectr, Oxford Univ., 1975–80; Fellow, St Edmund Hall, Oxford, 1992–. Chartered Institute of Taxation: Council Mem., 1999–; Chartered Tax Adviser, 1999. Pres., Key Haven Pubns plc, 1990–. Treasurer, CRUSAID, 1991–96 (Pres. Council, 1996–); Dir, Yves Guihannec Foundn, 1992–. Consulting Editor: Personal Tax Planning Review; Corporate Tax Review; Offshore and Internat. Taxation Review; EC Tax Jl; Taxation Ed., Charities Law and Practice Review. *Publications:* Inheritance Tax Planning, 1986, 4th edn 2000; Preserving the Family Farm, 1987, 2nd edn 1989; Non-Resident Trusts, 1988, 8th edn 2000; Tax Planning and Fundraising for Charities, 1989, 3rd edn 2000; Hold-Over Relief, 1990; The Company Car, 1990; Tax Planning Through Trusts—Inheritance Tax, 1990; National Insurance Contributions Planning, 1990; Capital Gains Tax Planning for Non-UK Residents, 1991, 3rd edn 1999. *Recreation:* music making. *Address:* 24 Old Buildings, Lincoln's Inn, WC2A 3UP. *T:* (020) 7242 2744, *Fax:* (020) 7831 8095; *e-mail:* taxchambers@compuserve.com. *Club:* Travellers.

VENABLES, Robert Michael Cochrane; Consultant, Bircham & Co., Solicitors, since 1997; *b* 8 Feb. 1939; *s* of late Cdre Gilbert Henry Venables, DSO, OBE, RN and Muriel Joan Haes; *m* 1972, Hazel Lesley Gowing, BSc; two *s* two *d*. *Educ:* Portsmouth Grammar Sch. Admitted solicitor, 1962; in private practice, London, Petersfield and Portsmouth, 1962–70; Treasury Solicitor's Department: Legal Asst, 1970; Sen. Legal Asst, 1973; Asst Treasury Solicitor, 1980; Charity Comr, 1989–97. Adminr and Dir, Cobbe Collection Trust, 1997–99. Mem. Council, Law Soc., 1993–; Pres., City of Westminster Law Soc., 1997–98. Trustee: Incorp. Council of Law Reporting for Eng. and Wales, 1999–; SolCare, 1997– (Chm., 1998–); Law Soc. Charity; Old Portsmouthian Charity, 1999–. Chm., Legal Sect., FDA, 1981–83 (Mem. Exec. Cttee, 1981–83, 1987–92). FRSA 1995. *Recreations:* opera, theatre, collecting domestic anachronisms. *Address:* c/o Bircham & Co., 1 Dean Farrar Street, SW1H 0DY. *T:* (020) 7222 8044, *Fax:* (020) 7222 2340.

VENABLES, Terence Frederick; *b* 6 Jan. 1943; *m* Yvette; two *d*. *Educ:* Dagenham. Played at football clubs: Chelsea, 1958–66 (Captain, 1962); Tottenham Hotspur, 1966–68 (winners FA Cup 1967); Queen's Park Rangers, 1968–73; represented England at all levels; Club Manager: Crystal Palace, 1976–80 (took club from 3rd Div. to top of 1st Div.); QPR, 1980–84 (won 2nd Div. title, 1980); Barcelona, 1984–87 (won Spanish championship, 1984); Tottenham Hotspur, 1987–93 (won FA Cup, 1991; Chief Exec., 1991–93); Coach: England football team, 1994–96; Australian football team, 1996–98; Chm., Portsmouth FC, 1996–98; Head Coach, Crystal Palace FC, 1998–99. *Publications:* They Used to Play on Grass, 1971; (with Gordon Williams) TV detective series Hazell: Hazell plays Solomon, 1974; Hazell and the Three Card Trick, 1975; Hazell and the Menacing Jester, 1976; (with Neil Hanson) Terry Venables: the Autobiography, 1994; (with Jane Nottage) Venables' England, 1996; The Best Game in the World, 1996.

VENABLES-LLEWELYN, Sir John (Michael) Dillwyn-, 4th Bt *cr* 1890; farmer, since 1975; *b* 12 Aug. 1938; *s* of Sir Charles Michael Dillwyn-Venables-Llewelyn, 3rd Bt,

MVO, and of Lady Delia Mary Dillwyn-Venables-Llewelyn, *g d* of 1st Earl St Aldwyn; *S* father, 1976; *m* 1st, 1963, Nina (marr. diss. 1972), *d* of late Lt J. S. Hallam; two *d*; 2nd, 1975, Nina Gay Richardson Oliver (*d* 1995); one *d* decd. *Recreation:* racing vintage cars. *Address:* Llysdinam, Newbridge-on-Wye, Llandrindod Wells, Powys LD1 6NB.

VENDLER, Helen Hennessy, PhD; author and poetry critic; Porter University Professor, Harvard University, since 1990; *b* Boston, Mass, 30 April 1933; *d* of George and Helen Hennessy (*née* Conway); one *s*. *Educ:* Emmanuel Coll., Boston, Mass (AB 1954); Harvard Univ. (PhD 1960). Instructor, Cornell Univ., 1960–63; Lectr, Swarthmore Coll. and Haverford Coll., Pa, 1963–64; Asst Prof., Smith Coll., Northampton, Mass, 1964–66; Associate Prof., 1966–68, Prof., 1968–85, Boston Univ.; Harvard University: Kenan Prof., 1985–1990; Associate Acad. Dean, 1987–92; Sen. Fellow, Harvard Soc. Fellows, 1981–93. Fulbright Lectr, Univ. of Bordeaux, 1968–69; Vis. Prof., Harvard Univ., 1981–85. Poetry Critic, New Yorker, 1978–. Member: Educnl Adv. Bd, Guggenheim Foundn, 1991–; Pulitzer Prize Bd, 1991–. Overseas Fellow, Churchill Coll., Cambridge, 1980; Stewart Parnell Fellow, Magdalene Coll., Cambridge, 1996, Hon. Fellow, 1996. Holds numerous hon. degrees, including: DLitt: Columbia, 1987; Washington, 1991; DHL: Toronto, 1992; TCD, 1993; Cambridge, 1997; NUI, 1998. Awards include: Nat. Book Critics Award, 1980; Keats-Shelley Assoc. Award, 1994; Truman Capote Award, 1996. *Publications:* Yeats's Vision and the Later Plays, 1963; On Extended Wings: Wallace Stevens' longer poems, 1969; The Poetry of George Herbert, 1975; Part of Nature, Part of Us, 1980; The Odes of John Keats, 1983; Wallace Stevens: words chosen out of desire, 1984; (ed) Harvard Book of Contemporary American Poetry, 1985; Voices and Visions: the poet in America, 1987; The Music of What Happens, 1988; Soul Says, 1995; The Given and the Made, 1995; The Breaking of Style, 1995; Poems, Poets, Poetry, 1995; The Art of Shakespeare's Sonnets, 1997; Seamus Heaney, 1998. *Address:* Department of English, Harvard University, Barker Center, Cambridge, MA 02138-3929, USA.

VENGEROV, Maxim; violinist and conductor; *b* 20 Aug. 1974; *s* of Alexander Vengerov, oboist, and Larissa Vengerov; studied with Galina Turtschaninova, then Zakhar Bron. Has performed in recitals worldwide; has appeared with major orchestras throughout the world, including: NY Philharmonic, 1991; Berlin Philharmonic; LPO; LSO; Chicago SO; LA Philharmonic; Vienna Philharmonic; San Francisco SO; Concertgebouw (tour of Italy and S America), 1994. Envoy for Music, UNICEF, 1997–. Numerous recordings. First Prize: Jun. Wieniawski Competition, Lublin, 1985; Carl Flesch Internat. Violin Competition, London, 1990. *Address:* c/o Askonas Holt, Lonsdale Chambers, 27 Chancery Lane, WC2A 1PF.

VENKATARAMAN, Ramaswamy; President of India, 1987–92 (Vice-President, 1984–87); *b* 4 Dec. 1910; *s* of Ramaswami Iyer; *m* 1938, Janaki; three *d*. *Educ:* Madras Univ. (MA, LLB). Formerly in practice as a lawyer, Madras High Court and Supreme Court; prominent trade union leader, also political and social worker. Mem., Provisional Parlt, 1950, Mem., Lok Sabha, 1952–57 and (for Madras S), 1977–84; Leader of the House, Madras Legislative Council, and Minister of Industries, 1957–67; Mem., Planning Commn, Madras, 1967–71. Minister of: Finance and Industry, 1980–82; Defence, 1982–84. Sec., Madras Provincial Bar Fedn, 1947–50. Chm., Nat. Research and Develt Corp. Leader, Indian delegation to ILO, 1958, and delegate, UN Gen. Assembly, 1953–61. Chm., Kalakshetra Foundn; Mem. Internat. Jury, Gandhi Peace Prize Award; Trustee: Jawaharlal Nehru Meml Fund; Indira Gandhi Nat. Centre for the Arts. *Address:* 5 Safdarjang Road, New Delhi 110011, India. *T:* (11) 3794366, *Fax:* (11) 3014925.

VENKITARAMAN, Prof. Ashok Ramakrishnan, PhD; Ursula Zoellner Professor of Cancer Research, University of Cambridge, since 1998; Fellow, New Hall, Cambridge, since 1998; Deputy Director, Medical Research Council Cancer Cell Unit, Cambridge, since 2001; *b* 14 Oct. 1960; *s* of Prof. Avittathur R. Venkitaraman and Vasanti Venkitaraman (*née* Ramaratnam); *m* 1984, Dr Rajini Ramana; one *s* one *d*. *Educ:* Christian Med. Coll., Vellore, India (MB BS 1984); University Coll. London (PhD 1988); MA Cantab 1993. House Physician, Christian Med. Coll. Hosp., Vellore, India, 1983–84; Fellow, Lady Tata Meml Trust, UCL and Charing Cross and Westminster Med. Sch., 1985–88; MRC Laboratory of Molecular Biology, Cambridge: Fellow, Beit Meml Trust, 1988–91; Mem., Scientific Staff, 1991–98. FMedSci 2001. *Publications:* numerous contribs to scientific and med. jls. *Address:* Department of Oncology, Cambridge Institute for Medical Research, Addenbrooke's Hospital, Hills Road, Cambridge CB2 2XY. *T:* (01223) 336901.

VENNER, Rt Rev. Stephen Squires; *see* Dover, Bishop Suffragan of.

VENNING, Philip Duncombe Riley, FSA; Secretary, Society for the Protection of Ancient Buildings, since 1984; *b* 24 March 1947; *s* of late Roger Venning and of Rosemary (*née* Mann); *m* 1987, Elizabeth Frances Ann, *d* of M. A. R. Powers; two *d*. *Educ:* Sherborne Sch.; Trinity Hall, Cambridge (MA). Times Educational Supplement, 1970–81 (Asst Editor, 1978–81); freelance journalist and writer, 1981–84. Mem., Westminster Abbey Fabric Commn, 1998–. Mem. Council, Nat. Trust, 1992–2001; Trustee, 1995, Exec., 1997–, Historic Churches Preservation Trust. FSA 1989; FRSA 1990. *Publications:* contribs to books and other pubns on educn and on historic buildings. *Recreations:* exploring Britain, book collecting. *Address:* 17 Highgate High Street, N6 5JT.

VENNING, Robert William Dawe; Principal Establishment and Finance Officer, Cabinet Office, 1993–96; *b* 25 July 1946; *s* of Tom William Dawe and Elsie Lillian Venning; *m* 1969, Jennifer Mei-Ling Jackson; one *s* one *d*. *Educ:* Midhurst Sch.; Univ. of Birmingham (BA Special Hons Philosophy 1968). Tutor in Philosophy, Univ. of Birmingham, 1968; Lectr in Logic and Scientific Method, Lanchester Polytechnic, 1969; Department of Health and Social Security: Admin. Trainee, 1971; Private Sec. to Minister for Disabled, 1974; Principal, 1975; Private Sec. to Minister for Health, 1981; Asst Sec., 1983; Under Sec., HA Personnel Div., DoH, 1990–93. Non-Exec. Dir, Compel plc, 1990–93. *Recreations:* playing classical and flamenco guitar; electronics and computing. *Address:* 53 Gloucester Road, Kingston, Surrey KT1 3QZ.

VENTRY, 8th Baron *cr* 1800 (Ire.); **Andrew Wesley Daubeny de Moleyns;** Bt 1797; Director, Burgie Lodge Farms Ltd, since 1970; Marketing Manager, Unico (UK) Ltd, since 1994; *b* 28 May 1943; *s* of Hon. Francis Alexander Innys Eveleigh Ross de Moleyns (*d* 1964) (2nd *s* of 6th Baron) and of Joan (now Joan Springett), *e d* of Harold Wesley; assumed by deed poll, 1966, surname of Daubeny de Moleyns; *S* uncle, 1987; *m* 1st, 1963, Nelly Renée (marr. diss. 1979), *d* of Abel Chaumillon; one *s* two *d*; 2nd, 1983, Jill Rosemary, *d* of C. W. Oramon; one *d*. *Educ:* Edge Grove; Aldenham. Farmer, 1961–; in electronics, 1986–. *Recreations:* shooting, stalking, photography, sailing, ski-ing. *Heir:* *s* Hon. Francis Wesley Daubeny de Moleyns, *b* 1 May 1965.

VENTURI, Robert; architect; Principal, Venturi, Scott Brown and Associates, Inc., since 1989 (Venturi, Rauch and Scott Brown, 1980–89); *b* 25 June 1925; *s* of Robert Charles Venturi and Vanna Venturi (*née* Lanzetta); *m* 1967, Denise Scott Brown; one *s*. *Educ:* Princeton Univ. (AB 1947, MFA 1950). Designer, Oskar Stonorov, 1950, Eero Saarinen & Assoc., 1950–53; Rome Prize Fellow, Amer. Acad. in Rome, 1954–56; designer, Louis I Kahn, 1957; Principal: Venturi, Cope and Lippincott, 1958–61; Venturi and Short, 1961–64; Venturi and Rauch, 1964–80. Associate Prof., Univ. of Pennsylvania, 1957–65; Charlotte Shepherd Davenport Prof. of Architecture, Yale, 1966–70. Works include: Vanna Venturi House, 1961, Guild House, 1961, Franklin Court, 1972, Inst. for Sci. Inf. Corp. HQ, 1978 (all Philadelphia); Allen Meml Art Museum Addition (Oberlin, Ohio), 1973; Gordon Wu Hall (Princeton), 1980; Seattle Art Mus., 1984; Sainsbury Wing, Nat. Gall., London, 1986; Fisher and Bendheim Halls, 1986, Princeton Campus Center, 1996, Princeton Univ.; Gordon and Virginia MacDonald Med. Res. Labs (with Payette Associates), 1986, Gonda (Goldschmeid) Neuroscience and Genetics Res. Center (with Lee, Burkhart, Liu Inc.), 1993, UCLA; Charles P. Stevenson Jr Library, Bard Coll., 1989; Roy and Diana Vagelos Labs (with Payette Associates), Univ. of Penn, 1990; Regl Govt Bldg, Toulouse, France, 1992; Kirifuri resort facilities, Nikko, Japan, 1992; Congress Ave Bldg, Yale Univ. Sch. of Medicine (with Payette Associates), 1998. Fellow: Amer. Inst. of Architects; Amer. Acad. in Rome; Accad. Nazionale di San Luca; Amer. Acad. of Arts and Letters; Amer. Acad. of Arts and Scis; Hon. FFRIAS; Hon. RIBA. Hon. DFA: Oberlin Coll., 1977; Yale, 1979; Univ. of Pennsylvania, 1980; Princeton Univ., 1983; Philadelphia Coll. of Art, 1985; Hon. LHD NJ Inst. of Technology, 1984. James Madison Medal, Princeton Univ., 1985; Thomas Jefferson Meml Foundn Medal, Univ. of Virginia, 1983; Pritzker Architecture Prize, Hyatt Foundn, 1991; US Nat. Medal of Arts, 1992; Benjamin Franklin Medal, RSA, 1993. *Publications:* A View from the Campidoglio: selected essays, 1953–84 (with Denise Scott Brown), 1984; Complexity and Contradiction in Architecture, 1966, 2nd edn 1977; Learning from Las Vegas (with Denise Scott Brown and Steven Izenour), 1972, 2nd edn 1977; Iconography and Electronics upon a Generic Architecture, 1996; articles in periodicals. *Recreation:* travel. *Address:* Venturi, Scott Brown and Associates, Inc., 4236 Main Street, Philadelphia, PA 19127, USA. *T:* (215) 4870400.

VENUGOPAL, Dr Sriramashetty, OBE 1992; FRCGP; Principal in General Practice, Aston, Birmingham, since 1967; *b* 14 May 1933; *s* of Satyanarayan and Manikyamma Sriramashetty; *m* 1960, Subhadra Venugopal; one *s* one *d*. *Educ:* Osmania Univ., Hyderabad, India (BSc, MB BS); Madras Univ. (DMRD). MRCGP 1990, FRCGP 1997; MFPHM 1998. Medical posts, Osmania Hosp., State Med. Services, Hyderabad, Singareni Collieries, 1959–65; Registrar, Radiology, Selly Oak Hosp., Birmingham, 1965–66; Registrar, Chest Medicine, Springfield Hosp., Grimsby, 1966–67; Hosp. Practitioner, Psychiatry, All Saints Hosp., Birmingham, 1972–94. Member: Working Group, DHSS, 1984–; Local Med. Cttee, 1975–; Dist. Med. Cttee, 1978–; GMC, 1984–99; West Birmingham HA, 1982– (Chm., sub-cttee on needs of ethnic minorities, 1982–85); Birmingham FPC, 1984–; Birmingham Community Liaison Adv. Cttee, 1985. Vice-Chm., Birmingham Div., BMA, 1986–87 (Chm., 1985–86). Mem., Local Review Cttee for Winson Green Prison, 1981–83. Founder Mem., Overseas Doctors' Assoc., 1975–81 (Dep. Treasurer, 1975–81; Nat. Vice-Chm., 1981–87; Inf. and Adv. Service, 1981–99; Nat. Chm., 1987–93; Pres., 1993–99); Founder Mem. and Chm., Link House Council, 1975–89. Founder Mem., Osmania Grad. Med. Assoc. in UK, 1984–. Vice-Chm., Hyderabad Charitable Trust, 1985–. FRSocMed 1986; FRIPHH 1988; FRSH 1997. *Publications:* contribs to learned jls on medico-political topics. *Recreations:* medical politics, music, gardening. *Address:* Aston Health Centre, 175 Trinity Road, Aston, Birmingham B6 6JA. *T:* (0121) 328 3597; 24 Melville Road, Edgbaston, Birmingham B16 9JT. *T:* (0121) 454 1725. *Club:* Aston Rotary (Pres., 1984–85).

VERCOE, Rt Rev. Whakahuihui; *see* Aotearoa, Bishop of.

VERDI, Prof. Richard Frank, PhD; Professor of Fine Art, since 1989, and Director, Barber Institute of Fine Arts, since 1990, University of Birmingham; *b* 7 Nov. 1941; *s* of Frank and Anne Verdi. *Educ:* Univ. of Michigan (BA 1963); Univ. of Chicago (MA 1966); Courtauld Inst. of Art, Univ. of London (PhD 1976). Lectr in Hist. of Art, Univ. of Manchester, 1969–71; Lectr, 1971–81, Sen. Lectr, 1981–89, in Hist. of Art, Univ. of York. FRSA 1999. *Publications:* Klee and Nature, 1984; Cézanne and Poussin: the classical vision of landscape, 1990; Cézanne, 1992; Nicolas Poussin 1594–1665, 1995. *Recreations:* music, literature, natural history. *Address:* Barber Institute of Fine Arts, University of Birmingham, Edgbaston, Birmingham B15 2TS. *T:* (0121) 414 3485.

VERE OF HANWORTH, Lord; James Malcolm Aubrey Edward de Vere Beauclerk; *b* 2 Aug. 1995; *s* and *heir* of Earl of Burford, *qv*.

VERE-HODGE, Michael John Davy; QC 1993; a Recorder, since 1989; *b* 2 July 1946; *s* of Nicholas and Anne Vere-Hodge; *m* 1978, Jane Gilmour Semple (marr. diss. 2001); one *s* one *d*. *Educ:* Winchester Coll.; Grenoble Univ. Called to the Bar, Gray's Inn, 1970. *Recreations:* clay shooting, fishing. *Address:* 2 King's Bench Walk, Temple, EC4Y 7DE. *T:* (020) 7353 1746.

VEREKER, family name of **Viscount Gort**.

VEREKER, Sir John (Michael Medlicott), KCB 1999 (CB 1992); Permanent Secretary, Department for International Development (formerly Overseas Development Administration), 1994–Feb. 2002; Governor and Commander-in-Chief of Bermuda, from Feb. 2002; *b* 9 Aug. 1944; *s* of late Comdr C. W. M. Vereker and M. H. Vereker (*née* Whatley); *m* 1971, Judith Diane, *d* of Hobart and Alice Rowen, Washington, DC; one *s* one *d*. *Educ:* Marlborough Coll.; Keele Univ. (BA Hons 1967). Asst Principal, ODM, 1967–69; World Bank, Washington, 1970–72; Principal, ODM, 1972; Private Sec. to successive Ministers of Overseas Develt, 1977–78; Asst Sec., 1978; Prime Minister's Office, 1980–83; Under Sec., 1983–88, and Principal Finance Officer, 1986–88, ODA, FCO; Dep. Sec., DES, then DFE, 1988–93. Chm., Students Loans Co. Ltd, 1989–91. Mem. Council, Inst. of Manpower Studies, 1989–92; Member Board: British Council, 1994–; IDS, 1994–; VSO, 1994–. CIMgt 1995. FRSA 1999. Hon. DLitt Keele, 1997. *Address:* c/o Foreign and Commonwealth Office, King Charles Street, SW1A 2AH.

VEREY, David John; Deputy Chairman, Cazenove & Co., since 2001; *b* 8 Dec. 1950; *s* of late Michael John Verey, TD and Sylvia Mary Verey; *m* 1st, 1974, Luise Jaschke (marr. diss. 1990); two *s* one *d*; 2nd, 1990, Emma Katharine Broadhead (*née* Laidlaw). *Educ:* Eton College; Trinity College, Cambridge (MA). Lazard Brothers: joined 1972; Dir, 1983; Dep. Chief Exec., 1985; Chief Exec., 1990–2001; Chm., 1992–2001. Dir, Pearson plc, 1996–2000. Trustee, Tate Gall., 1992– (Chm., Bd of Trustees, 1998–). Fellow, Eton Coll., 1997–. *Recreations:* stalking, bridge, gardening, travel. *Address:* Cazenove & Co., 12 Tokenhouse Yard, EC2R 7AN.

VERHEUGEN, Günter, Hon. GCVO 1998; Member, European Commission, since 1999; *b* Bad Kreuznach, 28 April 1944; *s* of Leo Verheugen and Leni (*née* Holzhäuser); *m* 1st, Helga (*d* 1983); 2nd, 1987, Gabriele (*née* Reimann). *Educ:* studied history, sociol. and politics in Cologne and Bonn. Trainee, Neue Rhein-Neue Ruhr Zeitung, 1963–65; Head: Public Relns Div., Min. of Interior, W Germany, 1969–74; Analysis and Inf. task force, Foreign Office, 1974–76; Federal Party Manager, 1977–78, Gen. Sec., 1978–82, FDP. Mem. (SPD) Bundestag, 1983–99 (Mem., Foreign Affairs Cttee, 1983–99; Chm.,

EU special cttee, 1992). Chm., Socialist Internat. Peace, Security and Disarmament Council, 1997–99. Chm., Radio Broadcasting Council, Deutsche Welle, 1990–99. Joined SPD, 1982: spokesman of Nat. Exec., 1986–87; Editor-in-Chief, Vorwärts (SPD newspaper), 1987–88; Dep. foreign policy spokesman and Chm., UN wkg gp of parly gp, 1991–93; Chm., Bavarian SPD gp in Bundestag, 1993–95; Sec., parly gp, 1993; Fed. Party Manager, 1993–95; Dep. Chm., parly gp for foreign, security and develt policy, 1994–97; Chm., Kulmbach-Lichtenfels dist, 1996–99; Mem., Upper Franconia regl exec., 1996–99; Co-ordinator for internat. relns of SPD and SPD parly gp, 1997–99; Mem., Nat. Exec., 1997–. Mem., Cttee for Envmt and Develt, Protestant Ch, Germany, 1998–. Officer's Cross, Order of Merit (Germany), 1994; Order of Merit (Bavaria), 1997; Kt Comdr's Cross, Order of Merit (Italy), 1982. *Publications:* Der Ausverkauf: Macht und Verfall der FDP, 1984; (jtly) Halbzeit in Bonn: die BRD zwei Jahre nach der Wende, 1985; Apartheid, Südafrika und die deutschen interessen am Kap, 1986; and numerous others. *Address:* European Commission, Rue de la Loi 200, 1049 Brussels, Belgium. *T:* (2) 2991111.

VERHOFSTADT, Guy; Prime Minister of Belgium, since 1999; *b* 11 April 1953; *s* of Marcel Verhofstadt and Gaby (*née* Stockmans); *m* 1981, Dominique Verkinderen; one *s* one *d*. *Educ:* Koninklijk Atheneum, Ghent; Univ. of Ghent (LLM 1975). Attorney, Ghent Bar, 1975–94. Pol Sec. to Nat. Pres., Party for Freedom and Progress, 1977–81; Mem. (Party for Freedom and Progress) Ghent-Ekklo, House of Reps, Belgium, 1978–84, 1985–95; Dep. Prime Minister and Minister for the Budget, Scientific Res. and the Plan, 1985–88; Pres., shadow cabinet, 1988–91; Minister of State, 1995–; Senator (Flemish Liberals and Democrats), and Vice Pres., Senate, 1995–99. Mem., City of Ghent Council, 1976–82. Nat. Pres., Party for Freedom and Progress, 1982–85, 1989–92; Nat. Pres., Flemish Liberals and Democrats, 1992–95, 1997–99. Vice-Pres. and Rapporteur, Rwanda Investigation Commn, Senate, 1996–97. *Publications:* Angst, afgunst en het algemeen belang, 1994; De Gelgische ziekte, 1997; pamphlets, articles, contribs to books. *Address:* Prime Minister's Office, Wetstraat 16, 1000 Brussels, Belgium. *T:* (2) 5010211, *Fax:* (2) 5116953.

VERITY, Anthony Courtenay Froude, MA; Master, Dulwich College, 1986–95; *b* 25 Feb. 1939; *s* of Arthur and Alice Kathleen Verity; *m* 1962, Patricia Ann Siddall; one *s* one *d*. *Educ:* Queen Elizabeth's Hosp., Bristol; Pembroke Coll., Cambridge (MA). Assistant Master: Dulwich Coll., 1962–65; Manchester Grammar Sch., 1965–69; Head of Classics, Bristol Grammar Sch., 1969–76; Headmaster, Leeds Grammar Sch., 1976–86. Educnl Advr to Emir of Qatar, 1996. Chm., Schools' Arabic Project, 1988–96. Trustee, Dulwich Picture Gallery, 1994–96. Editor, Greece and Rome, 1971–76. *Publications:* Latin as Literature, 1971; contribs to Jl of Arabic Lit. *Recreations:* music, fell-walking. *Address:* The Reddings, Cliburn, Penrith, Cumbria CA10 3AL. *Club:* Athenæum.

VERMES, Prof. Geza, FBA 1985; Professor of Jewish Studies, 1989–91, now Professor Emeritus, and Fellow of Wolfson College, 1965–91, now Fellow Emeritus, Oxford University; Director, Oxford Forum for Qumran Research, Oxford Centre for Hebrew and Jewish Studies (formerly for Postgraduate Hebrew Studies), since 1991; *b* 22 June 1924; *s* of late Ernö Vermes and Terézia Riesz; *m* 1st, 1958, Pamela Hobson (*d* 1993); 2nd, 1996, Margaret Unarska. *Educ:* Univ. of Budapest; Coll. St Albert de Louvain, Louvain Univ. Licencié en Histoire et Philologie Orientales (avec la plus grande distinction), 1952; DTheol 1953; MA Oxon 1965, DLitt 1988. Asst Editor, Cahiers Sioniens, Paris, 1953–55; research worker, CNRS, Paris, 1955–57; Lectr, later Sen. Lectr in Divinity, Newcastle Univ., 1957–65; Reader in Jewish Studies, Oxford Univ., 1965–89; Chm. of Curators of Oriental Inst., Oxford, 1971–74; Chm. Bd of Faculty of Oriental Studies, Oxford, 1978–80; Emeritus Governor, Oxford Centre for Postgrad. Hebrew Studies (Governor, 1972–92). Vis. Prof. in Religious Studies, Brown Univ., 1971; Rosenstiel Res. Fellow, Univ. of Notre Dame, 1972; Dist. Vis. Prof. in Judeo-Christian Studies, Tulane Univ., 1982; Vis. Prof. of History, Univ. of Calif, San Diego, 1995; Vis. Prof. in Hebrew Studies, Peter Pázmány Univ., Budapest, 1996. Lectures: Margaret Harris in Religion, Dundee Univ., 1977; Riddell Meml, Newcastle Univ., 1981; Igor Kaplan Visiting, Toronto Sch. of Theology, 1985, 1987; Inaugural, Geza Vermes Lectures in Hist. of Religions, Univ. of Leicester, 1997; Gunning, Univ. of Edinburgh, 1998. Pres., British Assoc. for Jewish Studies, 1975, 1988; Pres., European Assoc. for Jewish Studies, 1981–84. Editor, Jl of Jewish Studies, 1971–. Hon. DD: Edinburgh, 1989; Durham, 1990; Hon. DLitt Sheffield, 1994. W. Bacher Medallist, Hungarian Acad. of Scis, 1996. *Publications:* Les manuscrits du désert de Juda, 1953; Discovery in the Judean Desert, 1956; Scripture and Tradition in Judaism, 1961; The Dead Sea Scrolls in English, 1962, 4th edn 1995 (trans. Portuguese); Jesus the Jew, 1973 (trans. Spanish, French, Japanese, Italian, Portuguese, German, Hungarian); Post-Biblical Jewish Studies, 1975; (with Pamela Vermes) The Dead Sea Scrolls: Qumran in perspective, 1977 (trans. Spanish), 3rd edn 1994; The Gospel of Jesus the Jew, 1981; (ed jtly) Essays in Honour of Y. Yadin, 1982; Jesus and the World of Judaism, 1983 (trans. Portuguese, Hungarian); (ed and rev., with F. G. B. Millar and M. D. Goodman) E. Schürer, The History of the Jewish People in the Age of Jesus Christ I–III, 1973–87 (trans. Spanish, Italian); (with M. D. Goodman) The Essenes according to the Classical Sources, 1989; The Religion of Jesus the Jew, 1993 (trans. Spanish, Portuguese); (ed) Pamela Vermes, The Riddle of the Sparks, 1993; The Complete Dead Sea Scrolls in English, 1997; Providential Accidents (autobiog.), 1998 (trans. Hungarian); (ed with P. S. Alexander) Discoveries in the Judaean Desert, vol. 26, 1998; An Introduction to the Complete Dead Sea Scrolls, 1999; The Dead Sea Scrolls, 2000; The Changing Faces of Jesus, 2000 (trans. Italian, Hungarian). *Recreations:* watching wild life, correcting proofs. *Address:* Oriental Institute, Pusey Lane, Oxford OX1 2LE; West Wood Cottage, Foxcombe Lane, Boars Hill, Oxford OX1 5DH. *T:* (01865) 735384, *Fax:* (01865) 735034; *e-mail:* geza.vermes@orinst.ox.ac.uk.

VERNEY, family name of **Baron Willoughby de Broke**.

VERNEY, Sir Edmund Ralph, 6th Bt *cr* 1818, of Claydon House, Buckinghamshire; *b* 28 June 1950; *o s* of Sir Ralph Bruce Verney, 5th Bt, KBE and of Mary (*née* Vestey); *S* father, 2001; *m* 1982, Daphne Fausset-Farquhar; one *s* one *d*. *Educ:* Harrow; York Univ. FRICS. Mem., Nat. Council, CLA, 1990–2001 (Chm., Bucks Br., 1996–99). Prime Warden, Dyers' Co., 2001–02. High Sheriff, Bucks, 1998–99. *Heir:* *s* Andrew Nicholas Verney, *b* 9 July 1983. *Address:* Claydon House, Middle Claydon, Bucks MK18 2EX.

VERNEY, (Sir) (John) Sebastian, (3rd Bt *cr* 1946, of Eaton Square, City of Westminster; *S* father, 1993, but does not use the title). *Heir:* *cousin* Christopher Ralph Evelyn Verney [*b* 4 Oct. 1948; *m* 1976, Madeliene Lindberg].

VERNEY, His Honour Sir Lawrence (John), Kt 1993; TD 1955; DL; Recorder of London, 1990–98; *b* 19 July 1924; *y s* of Sir Harry Verney, 4th Bt, DSO; *m* 1972, Zoë Auriel, *d* of Lt-Col P. G. Goodeve-Docker. *Educ:* Harrow; Oriel Coll., Oxford. Called to Bar, Inner Temple, 1952, Bencher, 1990. Dep. Chm., Bucks QS, 1962–71; Dep. Chm., Middlesex Sessions, then a Circuit Judge, 1971–90. Editor, Harrow School Register, 1948–; Governor, Harrow Sch., 1972–87. Master, Co. of Pattenmakers, 1988. Hon. Col 1 (RBY) Signal Sqdn, 1997–99. DL Bucks 1967. Hon. LLD London Guildhall, 1998. OStJ 1992. *Address:* Windmill House, Church Lane, Oving, Aylesbury, Bucks HP22 4HL.
See also Rt Rev. S. E. Verney.

VERNEY, Sir Sebastian; *see* Verney, Sir J. S.

VERNEY, Rt Rev. Stephen Edmund, MBE 1945; Assistant Bishop, diocese of Oxford, since 1991; *b* 17 April 1919; 2nd *s* of late Sir Harry Verney, 4th Bt, DSO and Lady Rachel Verney (*née* Bruce); *m* 1st, 1947, Priscilla Avice Sophie Schwerdt (*d* 1974); one *s* three *d*; 2nd, 1981, Sandra Ann Bailey; (one *s* decd). *Educ:* Harrow School; Balliol College, Oxford (MA). Curate of Gedling, Nottingham, 1950; Priest-in-charge and then first Vicar, St Francis, Clifton, Nottingham, 1952; Vicar of Leamington Hastings and Diocesan Missioner, Dio. Coventry, 1958; Canon Residentiary, Coventry Cathedral, 1964; Canon of Windsor, 1970; Bishop Suffragan of Repton, 1977–85. *Publications:* Fire in Coventry, 1964; People and Cities, 1969; Into the New Age, 1976; Water into Wine, 1985; The Dance of Love, 1989. *Recreations:* conversation and aloneness; music, gardening, travel. *Address:* Charity School House, Church Road, Blewbury, Oxon OX11 9PY. *Club:* English-Speaking Union.
See also Sir L. J. Verney.

VERNON, family name of **Baron Lyveden**.

VERNON, 11th Baron *cr* 1762; **Anthony William Vernon-Harcourt;** founder and Chairman, Monks Partnership Ltd, since 1980; *b* 29 Oct. 1939; *s* of William Ronald Denis Vernon-Harcourt, OBE and Nancy Everil (*née* Leatham); *S* kinsman, 2000; *m* 1966, Cherry Stanhope, *er d* of T. J. Corbin; three *s* one *d*. *Educ:* Eton; Magdalene Coll., Cambridge. MInstD. *Heir:* *s* Hon. Simon Anthony Vernon-Harcourt, *b* 24 Aug. 1969. *Recreations:* Church of England, cycling, motorcycling, countryside issues. *Address:* Monks Farm, Debden Green, Saffron Walden, Essex CB11 3LX.

VERNON, David Bowater; Under Secretary, Inland Revenue, 1975–84; *b* 14 Nov. 1926; *s* of Lt-Col Herbert Bowater Vernon, MC, and Ivy Margaret Vernon; *m* 1954, Anne de Montmorency Fleming, *d* of late John and Margaret Fleming; three *s* three *d*. *Educ:* Marlborough Coll.; Oriel Coll., Oxford (MA). RA, 1945–48 (Lieut). Inland Revenue, 1951–84. *Recreation:* gardening. *Address:* 6 Hurstwood Park, Tunbridge Wells, Kent TN4 8YE.

VERNON, Diana Charlotte; Headmistress, Woldingham School, since 2000; *b* 30 April 1961; *d* of Roderick W. P. Vernon and Jennifer F. F. Vernon (*née* Tyrrell). *Educ:* St Michael's, Burton Park; Durham Univ.; King's Coll., London (PGCE). Editl Asst, John Wiley & Sons Ltd, 1982–84; Account Executive: Business Image PR, 1984–85; Grayling, 1985–87; Corporate Communications Executive: Thorn EMI, 1987–89; London Internat. Gp, 1989–93; Housemistress and Dir of PR, Downe House, Newbury, 1994–2000. Governor: Lilian Baylis, London, 1985–; Flexlands Sch., Chobham, 1994–; Prince's Mead Sch., Winchester, 2000–. *Recreations:* theatre, cookery, travel, swimming. *Address:* Woldingham School, Marden Park, Woldingham, Surrey CR3 7YA. *T:* (01883) 349431. *Club:* Seaview Yacht (Isle of Wight).

VERNON, Kenneth Robert, CBE 1978; Deputy Chairman and Chief Executive, North of Scotland Hydro-Electric Board, 1973–88; *b* 15 March 1923; *s* of late Cecil W. Vernon and Jessie McGaw, Dumfries; *m* 1946, Pamela Hands, Harrow; one *s* three *d* (and one *d* decd). *Educ:* Dumfries Academy; Glasgow University. BSc, FEng, FIEE, FIMechE. BTH Co., Edinburgh Corp., British Electricity Authority, 1948–55; South of Scotland Electricity Bd, 1955–56; North of Scotland Hydro-Electric Bd, 1956: Chief Electrical and Mech. Engr, 1964; Gen. Man., 1966; Bd Mem., 1970. Dir, British Electricity International Ltd, 1976–88; Mem. Bd, Northern Ireland Electricity Service, 1979–85. *Publications:* various papers to technical instns. *Recreations:* fishing, gardening. *Address:* 10 Keith Crescent, Edinburgh EH4 3NH. *T:* (0131) 332 4610.

VERNON, Sir Michael; *see* Vernon, Sir William M.

VERNON, Sir Nigel (John Douglas), 4th Bt *cr* 1914; Director, Bain Hogg Ltd UK Division, subseq. Aon Risk Services UK, 1987–99; *b* 2 May 1924; *s* of Sir (William) Norman Vernon, 3rd Bt, and Janet Lady Vernon (*d* 1973); *S* father, 1967; *m* 1947, Margaret Ellen (*née* Dobell) (*d* 1999); one *s* one *d* (and one *s* decd). *Educ:* Charterhouse. Royal Naval Volunteer Reserve (Lieutenant), 1942–45. Spillers Ltd, 1945–65; Director: Castle Brick Co Ltd, 1965–71; Deeside Merchants Ltd, 1971–74; Travel Finance Ltd, 1971–87. *Recreations:* golf, shooting, gardening. *Heir:* *s* James William Vernon, FCA [*b* 2 April 1949; *m* 1981, Davinia, *er d* of Christopher David Howard, Ryton, Shrewsbury; two *s* one *d*]. *Address:* Top-y-Fron Hall, Kelsterton, near Flint, N Wales CH6 5TF. *T:* (01244) 830010. *Clubs:* Naval, Army and Navy.

VERNON, Sir (William) Michael, Kt 1995; Chairman, Royal National Lifeboat Institution, 1989–96 (Deputy Chairman, 1980–89; Vice-President, 1975–2001, now Life Vice-President; *b* 17 April 1926; *o surv. s* of late Sir Wilfred Vernon; *m* 1st, 1952, Rosheen O'Meara; one *s*; 2nd, 1977, Mrs Jane Colston (*née* Kilham-Roberts) (*d* 1998); 3rd, 2001, Mrs Penelope Cuddeford (*née* Skelton). *Educ:* Marlborough Coll.; Trinity Coll., Cambridge. MA 1948. Lieut, Royal Marines, 1944–46. Joined Spillers Ltd, 1948: Dir, 1960; Jt Man. Dir, 1962; Chm. and Chief Exec., 1968–80; Chm., Granville Meat Co. Ltd, 1981–94. Director: EMI Ltd, 1973–80; Strong & Fisher (Hldgs) plc, 1980–90; Chm., Famous Names Ltd, 1981–85. Pres., Nat. Assoc. of British and Irish Millers, 1965; Vice-Chm., Millers' Mutual Assoc., 1968–80; Pres., British Food Export Council, 1977–80. CIMgt. Bronze Medal, RHS, 1956. *Recreations:* shooting, boating. *Address:* Fyfield Manor, Andover, Hants SP11 8EN. *Clubs:* Royal Ocean Racing (Cdre 1964–68); Royal Yacht Squadron.

VERNON-HARCOURT, family name of **Baron Vernon**.

VERPLAETSE, Viscount Alfons Remi Emiel; Governor, National Bank of Belgium, 1989–99, now Hon. Governor; *b* Zulte, Belgium, 19 Feb. 1930; created Viscount, 1999; *s* of Leon Verplaetse and Alida Baert; *m* 1954, Odette Vanhee; three *s* two *d*. *Educ:* Catholic Univ. of Louvain (Licentiate of Commercial and Consular Scis). Joined National Bank of Belgium, 1953: Attaché, 1960–62; Asst Advr, 1962–66; Advr, 1966–74; Inspector Gen., 1974–80; Sen. Economist, 1980–82; on secondment to Social and Econ. Cabinet of Prime Minister as Dep. Chief of Cabinet, 1982–83, Chief of Cabinet, 1983–88; Dir, 1985–88; Vice-Governor, 1988–89. Gov., IMF, 1989–; Deputy Governor: IBRD, 1989–; IFC, 1989–; IDA, 1989–. Dir, European Fund for Monetary Co-operation, 1989–; Mem. Council, European Monetary Inst., 1994–. Grand Officier, Ordre de la Couronne (Belgium), 1991; Grande Ufficiale, Ordine al Merito (Italy), 1986; Officier de la Légion d'Honneur (France), 1994. *Address:* National Bank of Belgium, Boulevard de Berlaimont 14, 1000 Bruxelles, Belgium. *T:* (2) 2214777.

VERTOVEC, Dr Steven Allen; Research Reader in Anthropology, University of Oxford, since 1997; Senior Research Fellow, Linacre College, Oxford, since 1997;

Director, ESRC Transnational Communities Research Programme, since 1997; *b* 2 July 1957; *s* of Frank J. Vertovec and Dorothea M. Vertovec; *m* 1994, Astrid Gräfe; one *s* one *d*. *Educ:* Immaculate Conception High Sch., Elmhurst, Ill; Univ. of Colorado, Boulder (BA); Univ. of Calif, Santa Barbara (MA); Nuffield Coll., Oxford (DPhil 1988). Res. Fellow, Sch. of Geography, Oxford Univ., 1991–93; Principal Res. Fellow, Centre for Res. in Ethnic Relns, Univ. of Warwick, 1994–97. Regents' Fellow, Univ. of Calif, 1980–82; Overseas Res. Student Award, CVCP, 1983–86; Res. Fellow, Alexander von Humboldt-Stiftung, 1993–94; Vis. Fellow, Inst. Ethnology, Free Univ., Berlin, and Inst. Eur. Ethnology, Humboldt Univ., Berlin, 1993–94. *Publications:* (jtly) South Asians Overseas: migration and ethnicity, 1990; Aspects of the South Asian Diaspora, 1991; Hindu Trinidad: religion, ethnicity and socio-economic change, 1992; (with A. Rogers) The Urban Context: ethnicity, social networks and situational analysis, 1995; (with C. Peach) Islam in Europe: the politics of religion and community, 1997; (with A. Rogers) Muslim European Youth: reproducing religion, ethnicity and culture, 1998; Migration and Social Cohesion, 1999; (with R. Cohen) Migration, Diasporas and Transnationalism, 1999; The Hindu Diaspora: comparative patterns, 2000; contrib. articles to Religion, Ethnic and Racial Studies, Social and Economic, Ethnology, New Community, Etnolog, Contribs to Indian Sociology, Social Compass, Internat. Social Sci. Jl. *Address:* Institute of Social and Cultural Anthropology, University of Oxford, 51 Banbury Road, Oxford OX2 6PE.

VERULAM, 7th Earl of, *cr* 1815; **John Duncan Grimston;** Bt 1629; Baron Forrester (Scot.), 1633; Baron Dunboyne and Viscount Grimston (Ire.), 1719; Baron Verulam (Gt. Brit.), 1790; Viscount Grimston (UK), 1815; Director, Kleinwort Benson Private Bank, since 2001; *b* 21 April 1951; *s* of 6th Earl of Verulam and Marjorie Ray (*d* 1994), *d* of late Walter Atholl Duncan; *S* father, 1973; *m* 1976, Dione Angela, *e d* of Jeremy Smith, *qv*; three *s* one *d*. *Educ:* Eton; Christ Church, Oxford (MA 1976). Dir, Baring Brothers Ltd, 1987–96.; ABN-AMRO Bank NV, 1996–2000. Chm., Grimston Trust Ltd, 1982–. *Heir: s* Viscount Grimston, *qv*. *Address:* Gorhambury, St Albans, Herts AL3 6AH. *T:* (01727) 855000. *Clubs:* White's, Beefsteak.

VESEY, family name of **Viscount de Vesci**.

VESSEY, Prof. Martin Paterson, CBE 1994; FRS 1991; Professor of Public Health (formerly Social and Community Medicine), University of Oxford, 1974–2000, now Emeritus; Fellow of St Cross College, Oxford, since 1973; *b* 22 July 1936; *s* of Sidney J. Vessey and Catherine P. Vessey (*née* Thomson); *m* 1959, Anne Platt; two *s* one *d*. *Educ:* University College Sch., Hampstead; University Coll. London (Fellow, 1992); University Coll. Hosp. Med. Sch., London. MB, BS London 1959; MD London 1971; FFCM RCP 1972; MA Oxon 1974; MRCPE 1978; FRCPE 1979; FRCGP 1983; FRCP 1987; FRCOG 1989; FFFP 1995. Scientific Officer, Dept of Statistics, Rothamsted Exper. Stn, 1960–65; House Surg. and House Phys., Barnet Gen. Hosp., 1965–66; Mem. Sci. Staff, MRC Statistical Research Unit, 1966–69; Lectr in Epidemiology, Univ. of Oxford, 1969–74. Chairman: Adv. Cttee on Breast Cancer Screening, DHSS, subseq. DoH, 1987–99; Adv. Cttee on Cervical Cancer Screening, DoH, 1996–; Member: Cttee on Safety of Medicines, 1980–92, 1996–98; Royal Commn on Environmental Pollution, 1984–89. Founder FMedSci 1998. *Publications:* many sci. articles in learned jls, notably on med. aspects of fertility control, safety of drugs, and epidemiology of cancer. *Recreations:* motoring, fine arts, conservation. *Address:* 8 Warnborough Road, Oxford OX2 6HZ. *T:* (01865) 552698.

VEST, Prof. Charles Marstiller, PhD; President, Massachusetts Institute of Technology, since 1990; *b* 9 Sept. 1941; *m* 1963, Rebecca McCue; one *s* one *d*. *Educ:* West Virginia Univ.; Univ. of Michigan (MSc 1964; PhD 1967). Asst Prof., then Associate Prof., 1968–77, Prof. of Mechl Engrg, 1977–90, Univ. of Michigan. *Publication:* Holographic Interferometry, 1979. *Address:* Office of the President, Massachusetts Institute of Technology, Cambridge, MA 02139, USA.

VESTEY, family name of **Baron Vestey**.

VESTEY, 3rd Baron *cr* 1922, of Kingswood; **Samuel George Armstrong Vestey;** Bt 1913; DL; Master of the Horse, since 1999; *b* 19 March 1941; *s* of late Captain the Hon. William Howarth Vestey (killed in action in Italy, 1944; *o s* of 2nd Baron Vestey and Frances Sarah Howarth) and of Pamela Helen Fullerton, *d* of George Nesbitt Armstrong; *S* grandfather, 1954; *m* 1st, 1970, Kathryn Mary (marr. diss. 1981), *er d* of John Eccles, Moor Park, Herts; two *d*; 2nd, 1981, Celia Elizabeth, *d* of late Major Guy Knight, MC, Lockinge Manor, Wantage, Oxon; two *s* one *d*. *Educ:* Eton. Lieut, Scots Guards. Chairman: Steeplechase Co. (Cheltenham), 1990–; Vestey Group Ltd, 1995–. Chm., Meat Training Council, 1991–95. President: London Meat Trade and Drovers Benevolent Assoc., 1973; Inst. of Meat, 1978–83; Three Counties Agricl Soc., 1978; Royal Bath and W of England Soc., 1994; BHS, 1994–97; Glos Assoc. of Boys' Clubs, 1979–. Patron, Glos CCC, 1997–. Liveryman, Butchers' Co. DL Glos, 1982. GCStJ 1987 (Chancellor of the Order, 1988–91, Lord Prior, 1991–). *Recreations:* racing, shooting, cricket. *Heir: s* Hon. William Guy Vestey [*b* 27 Aug. 1983. Page of Honour to the Queen, 1995–97]. *Address:* Stowell Park, Northleach, Glos GL54 3LE. *Clubs:* White's, Turf; Jockey (Newmarket); Melbourne (Melbourne).

VESTEY, Edmund Hoyle; DL; Director, Vestey Group Ltd, 1993–2000; *b* 19 June 1932; *o s* of late Ronald Arthur Vestey and Florence Ellen McLean, *e d* of Col T. G. Luis, VD; *m* 1960, Anne Moubray, *yr d* of Gen. Sir Geoffry Scoones, KCB, KBE, CSI, DSO, MC; four *s*. *Educ:* Eton. 2nd Lieut Queen's Bays, 1951; Lieut, City of London Yeomanry. Chairman: Blue Star Line, 1971–96; Associated Container Transportation (Australia), 1979–82, 1985–88. Pres., Gen. Council of British Shipping, later Chamber of Shipping, 1981–82, 1992–94. FRSA; FCIT 1982. Joint Master, Thurlow Foxhounds; Chm., Masters of Foxhounds Assoc., 1992–96. President: Essex County Scout Council, 1979–87; E of England Agricl Soc., 1995. High Sheriff, Essex, 1977; DL Essex, 1978; DL Suffolk, 1991. *Address:* Little Thurlow Hall, Haverhill, Suffolk CB9 7LQ; Iolaire Lodge, Lochinver, Sutherland IV27 4LU; Sunnyside Farmhouse, Hawick, Roxburghshire TD9 9SS. *Clubs:* Cavalry and Guards, Carlton.

VESTEY, Sir (John) Derek, 2nd Bt *cr* 1921; *b* 4 June 1914; *s* of John Joseph Vestey (*d* 1932) and Dorothy Mary (*d* 1918), *d* of John Henry Beaver, Gawthorpe Hall, Bingley, Yorkshire; *g s* of Sir Edmund Vestey, 1st Bt; *S* grandfather, 1953; *m* 1938, Phyllis Irene, *o d* of H. Brewer, Banstead, Surrey; one *s* one *d*. *Educ:* Leys Sch., Cambridge. Served War of 1939–45: Flt-Lieut, RAFVR, 1940–45. *Heir: s* Paul Edmund Vestey [*b* 15 Feb. 1944; *m* 1971, Victoria Anne Scudamore, *d* of John Salter, Tiverton, Devon; three *d*. *Educ:* Radley]. *Address:* Park Penthouse, 355 Kings Road, Chelsea, SW3 5ES. *T:* (020) 7352 5940. *Clubs:* Royal Over-Seas League, MCC.

VIALA, Prof. Alain Bernard Jean; Professor of French Studies and Fellow of Wadham College, University of Oxford, since 1997; Professor of French Literature, University of Paris III, Sorbonne Nouvelle, since 1985; *b* 20 Nov. 1947; *s* of Ernest and Marie Viala. *Educ:* Ecole Normale Supérieure, Cachan; (Agregé des lettres; DèsL). Lecturer: Ecole Nationale de Chimie, 1972–78; Ecole d'Artillerie, 1973–74; Asst Prof., Univ. Sorbonne Nouvelle, 1978–84. Guest Professor: Univ. of Liège, 1988; Univ. of Tel Aviv, 1996. Pres., Commn des Programmes de Lettres, Min. of Educn, France, 1993–. *Publicaitons:* Savoir-lire, 1982; Naissance de l'écrivain, 1985; Racine: la stratégie du caméléon, 1990; Approches de la réception, 1993; Le théâtre en France, 1996. *Address:* Wadham College, Oxford OX1 3PN. *T:* (01865) 277574.

VICARY, Rev. Douglas Reginald; Canon Residentiary and Precentor of Wells Cathedral, 1975–88; *b* 24 Sept. 1916; *e s* of R. W. Vicary, Walthamstow; *m* 1947, Ruth, *y d* of late F. J. L. Hickinbotham, JP, and of Mrs Hickinbotham, Edgbaston; two *s* two *d*. *Educ:* Sir George Monoux Grammar Sch., Walthamstow; Trinity Coll., Oxford (Open Scholar), Wycliffe Hall, Oxford. 1st Class Nat. Sci. 1939; BSc 1939, MA 1942; Diploma in Theology with distinction, 1940; deacon, 1940; priest, 1941. Curate of St Peter and St Paul, Courteenhall, and Asst Chaplain and House Master, St Lawrence Coll., Ramsgate, while evacuated at Courteenhall, Northampton, 1940–44; Chaplain, Hertford Coll., Oxford, 1945–48; Tutor at Wycliffe Hall, 1945–47, Chaplain 1947–48; Dir of Religious Education, Rochester Diocese, 1948–57; Sec., CACTM Exams Cttee and GOE, 1952–57; Dir, Post-Ordination Training, 1952–57, Headmaster of King's School, Rochester, 1957–75; Chaplain to HM the Queen, 1977–86. Minor Canon, Rochester Cathedral, 1949–52; Canon Residentiary and Precentor, 1952–57; Hon. Canon, 1957–75. Exam. Chaplain to Bishop of Rochester, 1950–88, to Bishop of Bath and Wells, 1975–87. Mem., Archbishops' Liturgical Commn, 1955–62. Mem. Court, Kent Univ., 1965–75. FRSA 1970. *Publications:* (contrib.) Canterbury Chapters, 1976; contrib. DNB. *Recreations:* music, architecture, hill-walking, reading. *Address:* 8 Tor Street, Wells, Somerset BA5 2US. *T:* (01749) 679137.

VICK, His Honour Arnold Oughtred Russell; QC 1980; a Circuit Judge, 1982–2001; a Designated Family Judge, 1991–2001; *b* 14 Sept. 1933; *yr s* of late His Honour Judge Sir Godfrey Russell Vick, QC and late Lady Russell Vick, JP, *d* of J. A. Compston, KC; *m* 1959, Zinnia Mary, *e d* of Thomas Brown Yates, Godalming; two *s* one *d*. *Educ:* The Leys Sch., Cambridge; Jesus Coll., Cambridge (MA). Pilot, RAF, 1952–54. Called to Bar, Inner Temple, 1958; Mem. Gen. Council of the Bar, 1964–68; Prosecuting Counsel to the Post Office, 1964–69; Dep. Recorder, Rochester City QS, 1971; a Recorder of the Crown Court, 1972–82; Principal Judge for Civil Matters in Kent, 1990–98. Mem., Lord Chancellor's County Court Rules Cttee, 1972–80; Recorder, SE Circuit Bar Mess, 1978–80. Gov., New Beacon Sch., Sevenoaks, 1982–2000. Master, Curriers' Co., 1976–77. *Publication:* A Hundred Years of Golf at Wildernesse, 1990. *Recreations:* golf, cricket, bridge. *Address:* Little Hermitage, Wildernesse Avenue, Seal, Sevenoaks, Kent TN15 0ED. *T:* (01732) 761686. *Clubs:* MCC; Hawks (Cambridge); Wildernesse (Captain 1978) (Sevenoaks); Royal Worlington and Newmarket Golf; Senior Golfers.

VICK, Graham; Director of Productions, Glyndebourne Festival Opera, since 1994; Founder and Artistic Director, Birmingham Opera Company (formerly City of Birmingham Touring Opera); *b* 30 Dec. 1953. Trained as a singer and conductor. Associate Dir, English Music Theatre; Dir of Productions, Scottish Opera, 1984–87. *Productions* include: Scottish Opera: La vie parisienne, 1985; Hedda Gabler, 1985; Carmen, 1986; Don Giovanni, Billy Budd, 1987; Opera Theatre of St Louis: Die Entführung aus dem Serail, 1986; Vanessa, 1988; City of Birmingham Touring Opera, later Birmingham Opera Co.: The Magic Flute, 1988; Ghanashyam—a Broken Branch, 1989; The Ring, 1990; Les Boréades, 1992; Silas Marner, 1994; The Adventures of Vixen Sharp-Ears, 1998; The Two Widows, 1999; Wozzeck, 2001; Royal Opera House, Covent Garden: Un rè in ascolto, 1989; Die Meistersinger, 1993; King Arthur, 1995; The Midsummer Marriage, 1995; The Merry Widow, 1997; Falstaff, 1999; English National Opera: Ariadne auf Naxos, 1983; Madam Butterfly, 1986; Eugene Onegin, 1989; Timon of Athens, 1991; Figaro's Wedding, 1991; Fidelio, 1996; Tales of Hoffmann, 1998; Musica nel Chiostro, Batignano, Italy: Tolomeo; Zaïde, 1981; King Priam, 1990; Candide, 1993; Glyndebourne Festival Opera: Queen of Spades, 1992; Eugene Onegin, 1994; Ermione, 1995; Manon Lescaut, 1997; Così fan tutte, 1998; Pelléas et Mélisande, 1999; Le Nozze di Figaro, Don Giovanni, 2000; Opera North: Mahagonny, 1995; Così fan tutte; The Magic Flute; Opéra Bastille, Paris: Un rè in ascolto, 1991; Mahagonny; Peter Grimes, 2001; Ariadne, Netherlands Opera; Don Giovanni, New Israeli Opera, 1994; Metropolitan Opera, NY: Lady Macbeth of Mtsensk; Moses und Aron, 1999; War and Peace, Kirov Theatre, Leningrad; La Scala, Milan: Outis (Berio), 1996; Macbeth, 1997. *Address:* c/o Ingpen & Williams, 26 Wadham Road, SW15 2LR.

VICKERMAN, Prof. Keith, FRS 1984; FRSE 1971; Regius Professor of Zoology, University of Glasgow, 1984–98; *b* 21 March 1933; *s* of Jack Vickerman and Mabel Vickerman (*née* Dyson); *m* 1961, Moira Dutton, LLB; one *d*. *Educ:* King James' Grammar School, Almondbury; University College London (Fellow, 1985). BSc 1955; PhD 1960; DSc 1970. Wellcome Trust Lectr, Zoology Dept, UCL, 1958–63; Royal Soc. Tropical Res. Fellow, UCL, 1963–68; Glasgow University: Reader in Zoology, 1968–74; Prof., 1974–98; Head of Dept of Zoology, 1979–85. Leeuwenhoek Lectr, Royal Soc., 1994. Mem., WHO Panel of Consultant Experts on Parasitic Diseases, 1973–98. Mem. Council, Royal Soc., 1996–97. Founder FMedSci 1998. Gold Medal for Zoology, Linnean Soc., 1996. *Publications:* The Protozoa (with F. E. G. Cox), 1967; numerous papers on protozoa (esp. trypanosomes) in scientific and med. jls. *Recreations:* sketching, gardening. *Address:* Division of Environmental and Evolutionary Biology, Graham Kerr Building, University of Glasgow, Glasgow G12 8QQ. *T:* (0141) 330 4433, *Fax:* (0141) 330 5973; *e-mail:* k.vickerman@bio.gla.ac.uk; 16 Mirrlees Drive, Glasgow G12 0SH. *T:* (0141) 586 7794.

VICKERS, Andrew Julian; Assistant Attending Research Methodologist, Memorial Sloan-Kettering Cancer Center, New York, since 1999; *b* 11 Feb. 1967; *s* of Jeffrey Vickers and Angela Vickers; *m* 1996, Caroline Batzdorf; one *s* one *d*. *Educ:* Girton Coll., Cambridge; Green Coll., Oxford. Joined Res. Council for Complementary Medicine, 1993; Dir of Res., 1997–99; estabd registry of randomised trials in complementary medicine for Cochrane Collaboration, 1995. Ed., Complementary Therapies in Medicine, 1996–99. Principal investigator, NHS funded trial of acupunture for headache, 1998–. Mem., R&D Cttee, Prince of Wales initiative for Integrated Medicine, 1996–98. *Publications:* Complementary Medicine and Disability, 1993; Health Options: complementary therapies for cerebral palsy and related conditions, 1994; Massage and Aromatherapy: a guide for health professionals, 1996; (ed) Examining Complementary Medicine: the sceptical holist, 1998; (jtly) ABC of Complementary Medicine, 2000; contrib. numerous papers to peer-reviewed health-related jls. *Recreations:* cooking, Ultimate Frisbee, running, guitar. *e-mail:* andrewline@earthlink.net.

VICKERS, Prof. Brian William, PhD, LittD; FBA 1998; Professor of English Literature, and Director, Centre for Renaissance Studies, ETH Zürich, since 1975; *b* 13 Dec. 1937; *s* of William Morgan Davies and Josephine Davies (*née* Grant); *m* 1st, 1962, Ilse-Renate Freiling (marr. diss. 1989); two *d*; 2nd, 1989, Sabine Köllmann; one *s* one *d*. *Educ:* St Marylebone Grammar Sch.; Trinity Coll., Cambridge (BA 1st Cl. Hons English 1962; Charles Oldham Shakespeare Schol., 1961; Sen. Schol., 1962); PhD 1967, LittD 1996

Cantab. Cambridge University: Res. Fellow, Churchill Coll., 1964–65; Asst Lectr in English, 1964–68; Fellow and Dir of Studies in English, Downing Coll., 1966–71; Univ. Lectr in English, 1968–72; Prof. of English Lit., Univ. of Zürich, 1972–75. Vis. Fellow, All Souls Coll., Oxford, 1980–81; Fellow, Wissenschaftskolleg zu Berlin, 1986–87. Shakespeare Lecture, British Acad., 1992. Pres., Internat. Soc. for History of Rhetoric, 1977–79. Member of Editorial Board: Renaissance Studies, 1994–; Annals of Science, 1995–; Isis, 1999–. *Publications:* (ed) Henry Mackenzie: the man of feeling, 1967; Francis Bacon and Renaissance Prose, 1968; The Artistry of Shakespeare's Prose, 1968, rev. edn 1979; (ed) Essential Articles for the Study of Francis Bacon, 1968; (ed) The World of Jonathan Swift, 1968; (ed) Seventeenth Century Prose, 1969; Classical Rhetoric in English Poetry, 1970, rev. edn 1989; Towards Greek Tragedy, 1973; (ed) Shakespeare: the critical heritage, 6 vols, 1623–1692, 1974, 1693–1733, 1974, 1733–1752, 1975, 1753–1765, 1976, 1765–1774, 1979, 1774–1801, 1981; (ed jtly) Hooker: the laws of ecclesiastical polity, 1976; Shakespeare's Coriolanus, 1976; (ed) Rhetoric Revalued, 1982; (ed) Occult and Scientific Mentalities in the Renaissance, 1984 (trans. Spanish 1980); (ed) Arbeit, Musse, Meditation: Betrachtungen zur Vita activa und Vita contemplativa, 1985, rev. edn 1991; (ed) Public and Private Life in the Seventeenth Century: the Mackenzie-Evelyn debate, 1986; (ed) English Science: Bacon to Newton, 1987; In Defence of Rhetoric, 1988 (trans. Italian 1994), rev. edn 1997; Returning to Shakespeare, 1989; Appropriating Shakespeare: contemporary critical quarrels, 1993; (ed) Francis Bacon, 1996; (ed) Francis Bacon: history of the reign of King Henry VII, 1998; (ed) Francis Bacon: the essays and counsels, civil and moral, 1999; (ed) English Renaissance Literary Criticism, 1999; Counterfeiting Shakespeare: the politics of attribution, 2001; (Gen. Ed.) series, Shakespeare: the critical tradition: King John, 1996; Richard II, 1998; A Midsummer Night's Dream, 1999; Measure for Measure, 2001; articles and reviews in learned jls. *Recreations:* music, sport, film. *Address:* Centre for Renaissance Studies, ETH Zentrum, 8092 Zürich, Switzerland. *T:* (1) 6324004, *Fax:* (1) 6321063; *e-mail:* vickers@english.gess.ethz.ch; (home) Langacherstrasse 4c, 8127 Forch, Switzerland. *T:* (1) 9804212.

VICKERS, Eric, CB 1979; Director of Defence Services, Department of the Environment, 1972–81; *b* 25 April 1921; *s* of late Charles Vickers and late Ida Vickers; *m* 1945, Barbara Mary Jones; one *s* one *d*. *Educ:* King's School, Grantham. Joined India Office, 1938; RAF (Fl/Lt Coastal Command), 1941–46; Ministry of Works, 1948; Principal, 1950; Assistant Secretary, 1962; Imperial Defence College, 1969; Dir of Home Estate Management, DoE, 1970–72. *Recreation:* photography, music, wine appreciation. *Address:* 46 Stamford Road, Oakham, Rutland LE15 6JA. *T:* (01572) 724166.

VICKERS, James Oswald Noel, OBE 1977; General Secretary, Civil Service Union, 1963–77 (Deputy General Secretary, 1960–62); *b* 6 April 1916; *s* of Noel Muschamp and Linda Vickers; *m* 1940, Winifred Mary Lambert; one *s* one *d*. *Educ:* Stowe Sch.; Queens' Coll., Cambridge. Exhibnr, BA Hons Hist., MA. Served War, HM Forces, 1939–45. Warden, Wedgwood Memorial Coll., 1946–49; Educn Officer, ETU, and Head of Esher Coll., 1949–56. Member: Civil Service Nat. Whitley Council, 1962–77 (Chm. Staff Side, 1975–77); TUC Inter-Union Disputes Panel, 1970–77; TUC Non-Manual Workers Adv. Cttee, 1973–75; Fabian Soc. Trade Union and Industrial Relations Cttee, 1964–81 (Chm. 1973–78; Vice-Chm., 1978–79); UCL Coll. Cttee, 1974–79; Council, Tavistock Inst., 1976–80; Employment Appeal Tribunal, 1978–86; CS Appeal Bd, 1978–86. *Publications:* contrib. to Fabian pamphlets. *Recreations:* bird-watching, gardening, travel. *Address:* 5 The Butts, Brentford, Mddx TW8 8BJ. *T:* (020) 8560 3482.

VICKERS, John Stuart, DPhil; FBA 1998; Director General of Fair Trading, since 2000; *b* 7 July 1958; *s* of Aubrey and Kay Vickers; *m* 1991, Maureen Freed; one *s* two *d*. *Educ:* Eastbourne Grammar Sch.; Oriel Coll., Oxford (BA PPE 1979); MPhil Econs Oxon 1983; DPhil Econs Oxon 1985. Financial Analyst, Shell UK, 1979–81; Fellow, All Souls Coll., Oxford, 1979–84; Roy Harrod Fellow in Economics of Business and Public Policy, Nuffield Coll., Oxford, 1984–90; Drummond Prof. of Political Economy, Oxford Univ., 1991– (on leave); Fellow, All Souls Coll., Oxford, 1991–; Exec. Dir, Chief Economist, and Mem. Monetary Policy Cttee, Bank of England, 1998–2000. Vis. Fellow, Princeton, 1988; Vis. Lectr, Harvard, 1989, 1990; Vis. Prof., London Business Sch., 1996. Fellow, Econometric Soc., 1998. *Publications:* (jtly) Privatization: an economic analysis, 1988; (jtly) Regulatory Reform, 1994; articles in econ. jls on industrial organisation, regulation, competition, monetary policy. *Address:* Office of Fair Trading, Fleetbank House, 2–6 Salisbury Square, EC4Y 8JX. *T:* (020) 7211 8920.

VICKERS, Jon, CC (Canada) 1968; dramatic tenor; *b* Prince Albert, Saskatchewan, 29 Oct. 1926; *m* 1953, Henrietta Outerbridge; three *s* two *d*. Studied under George Lambert, Royal Conservatory of Music, Toronto. Made debut with Toronto Opera Company, 1952; Stratford (Ontario) Festival, 1956. Joined Royal Opera House, Covent Garden, 1957. First sang at: Bayreuth Festival, 1958; Vienna State Opera, San Francisco Opera, and Chicago Lyric, 1959; Metropolitan, New York, and La Scala, Milan, 1960; Buenos Aires, 1962; Salzburg Festival, 1966; appeared in other opera houses of Argentina, Austria, Brazil, France, Germany, Greece, Mexico and USA. *Films:* Carmen; Pagliacci; Otello; Norma; Peter Grimes; Fidelio; Samson et Delilah. Has made many recordings. Presbyterian. Hon. Dr: University of Saskatchewan, 1963; Bishop's Univ., 1965; Univ. West Ontario, 1970; Brandon Univ., 1976; Laval Univ., 1977; Univ. of Guelph, 1978; Illinois, 1983; Queens, Canada, 1984; Toronto, 1987. RAM 1977. Canada Centennial Medal, 1967; Critics' Award, London, 1978; Grammy Award, 1979.

VICKERS, Prof. Michael Douglas Allen, OBE 2000; Professor of Anaesthetics, University of Wales College of Medicine (formerly Welsh National School of Medicine), 1976–95, now Emeritus; Vice Provost, University of Wales College of Medicine, 1990–93; *b* 11 May 1929; *s* of George and Freda Vickers; *m* 1959, Ann Hazel Courtney; two *s* one *d*. *Educ:* Abingdon Sch.; Guy's Hosp. Med. Sch. (MB, BS). FFARCS. Lectr, RPMS, 1965–68; Consultant Anaesthetist, Birmingham AHA, 1968–76. Chm., N Glamorgan NHS Trust, 1996–2000. Mem. Bd, Faculty of Anaesthetists, 1971–85; President: Assoc. of Anaesthetists of GB and Ireland, 1982–84 (Hon. Sec., 1974–76; John Snow Lectr, 1982); European Acad. of Anaesthesiology, 1988–91 (Sec., 1982–84); World Fedn of Socs of Anaesthesiologists, 1996–2000 (Chm., Exec. Cttee, 1988–92; Sec. Gen., 1992–96). FRSocMed (Pres., Sect. of Anaesthetics, 1998–99). Hon. FANZCA. Editor: European Journal of Anaesthesiology, 1983–94; Today's Anaesthetist, 1994–2001. *Publications:* (jtly) Principles of Measurement for Anaesthetists, 1970 (2nd edn, as Principles of Measurement, 1981, 3rd edn 1991); (jtly) Drugs in Anaesthetic Practice, 3rd edn 1968, to 8th edn 1999; Medicine for Anaesthetists, 1977, 4th edn 1999; (jtly) Ethical Issues in Anaesthesia, 1994; (jtly) Objective Structured Clinical Examinations for Anaesthetists, 1995. *Recreations:* music, theatre. *Address:* North Pines, 113 Cyncoed Road, Cardiff CF23 6AD. *T:* (029) 2075 3698.

VICKERS, Rt Rev. Michael Edwin; Area Bishop of Colchester, 1988–94; Assistant Bishop, Diocese of Blackburn, since 1994; *b* 13 Jan. 1929; *s* of William Edwin and Florence Alice Vickers; *m* 1960, Janet Cynthia Croasdale; three *d*. *Educ:* St Lawrence Coll., Ramsgate; Worcester Coll., Oxford (BA Mod. History 1952; MA 1956); Cranmer Hall, Durham (DipTheol with distinction, 1959). Company Secretary, Hoares (Ceylon) Ltd, 1952–56; Refugee Administrator for British Council for Aid to Refugees, 1956–57; Lay Worker, Diocese of Oklahoma, 1959; Curate of Christ Church, Bexleyheath, 1959–62; Sen. Chaplain, Lee Abbey Community, 1962–67; Vicar of St John's, Newland, Hull, 1967–81; Area Dean, Central and North Hull, 1972–81; Archdeacon of E Riding, 1981–88. Chm., York Diocesan House of Clergy, 1975–85; Canon and Prebendary of York, 1981–88. Mem., Gen. Synod, 1975–88 (Proctor in Convocation, 1975–85). *Recreations:* gardening, fell-walking, travel, drama. *Address:* 2 Collingham Park, Lancaster LA1 4PD. *T:* (01524) 848492.

VICKERS, Lt-Gen. Sir Richard (Maurice Hilton), KCB 1983; CVO 1998 (LVO 1959); OBE 1970 (MBE 1964); an Extra Gentleman Usher to the Queen, since 1998 (a Gentleman Usher, 1986–98); *b* 21 Aug. 1928; *s* of Lt-Gen. W. G. H. Vickers, CB, OBE; *m* 1957, Gaie, *d* of Maj.-Gen. G. P. B. Roberts, CB, DSO, MC; three *d*. *Educ:* Haileybury and Imperial Service Coll.; RMA. Commissioned Royal Tank Regt, 1948; 1st RTR, BAOR, Korea, Middle East, 1948–54; Equerry to HM The Queen, 1956–59; Brigade Major, 7 Armd Bde, 1962–64; 4th RTR, Borneo and Malaysia, 1964–66; CO The Royal Dragoons, 1967–68, The Blues and Royals, 1968–69; Comdr, 11th Armd Brigade, 1972–74; Dep. Dir of Army Training, 1975–77; GOC 4th Armoured Div., 1977–79; Comdt, RMA, 1979–82; Dir-Gen. of Army Training, 1982–83. Dir Gen., Winston Churchill Meml Trust, 1983–93. *Recreations:* squash, flyfishing. *Club:* Cavalry and Guards.

VICKERS, Roger Henry, FRCS; Orthopaedic Surgeon to HM the Queen, since 1992; Consultant Orthopaedic Surgeon: St George's Hospital, since 1980; King Edward VII Hospital for Officers, since 1992; Civilian Consultant Orthopaedic Surgeon to the Army, since 1992; *b* 26 July 1945; *s* of late Dr H. Renwick Vickers, FRCP and of Penelope Evelyn (*née* Peck); *m* 1972, Joanna, *d* of late John Francis Mordaunt; two *s* two *d*. *Educ:* Winchester Coll.; Magdalen Coll., Oxford (MA); St Thomas's Hosp. (BM, BCh 1970). FRCS 1975. Sen. Orthopaedic Registrar, Charing Cross, St Mary's and Royal Nat. Orthopaedic Hosps, 1977–80; Consultant Orthopaedic Surgeon, St James' Hosp., London, 1980–88. Mem. Council, Med. Defence Union, 1983–. Non-exec. Dir, Med. Sickness Soc., 1998–. *Recreations:* sailing, Real tennis. *Address:* 11 Edenhurst Avenue, SW6 3PD; 149 Harley Street, W1G 6DE. *Clubs:* Hurlingham; Seacourt; Hayling Island Sailing.

VICKERS, Dr Tony; Project Manager, UK Human Genome Mapping Project, 1990–92; *b* 6 July 1932; *s* of Harry and Frances Vickers; *m* 1964, Anne Dorothy Wallis (marr. diss. 1986); two *d*. *Educ:* Manchester Grammar Sch.; Sidney Sussex Coll., Cambridge (MA, PhD). University of Cambridge: Demonstrator, 1956; Lectr in Physiology, 1961–72; Fellow, Sidney Sussex Coll., 1956–70; Headquarters Office, MRC, 1972–84 (Head of Medical Div., 1980–84); UK Administrator, Ludwig Inst. for Cancer Res., 1985–89. Member of Council: BAAS, 1969–72, 1982–85 (Pres., Biomed. Scis Sect., 1977); Cancer Res. Campaign, 1980–85 (Mem., Scientific Cttee, 1979–85); Paterson Labs, Manchester, 1984–85. Chm., Tenovus Sci. Adv. Cttee, 1987–91; Mem. Res. Cttee, Clatterbridge Centre for Oncology and Cancer Res. Trust, 1994–99. Governor, Beatson Inst., Glasgow, 1983–85. *Address:* 42 Bengeo Street, Hertford, Herts SG14 3ET.

VICKERY, Prof. Brian Campbell, FLA, FIInfSc; Professor of Library Studies and Director, School of Library Archive and Information Studies, University College London, 1973–83, now Professor Emeritus; *b* 11 Sept. 1918; *s* of Adam Cairns McCay and Violet Mary Watson; *m* 1st, 1945, Manuletta McMenamin; one *s* one *d*; 2nd, 1970, Alina Gralewska. *Educ:* King's Sch., Canterbury; Brasenose Coll., Oxford. MA. Chemist, Royal Ordnance Factory, Somerset, 1941–45; Librarian, ICI Ltd, Welwyn, 1946–60; Principal Scientific Officer, Nat. Lending Library for Sci. and Technology, 1960–64; Librarian, UMIST, 1964–66; Head of R&D, Aslib, 1966–73. *Publications:* Classification and Indexing in Science, 1958, 3rd edn 1975; On Retrieval System Theory, 1961, 2nd edn 1965; Techniques of Information Retrieval, 1970; Information Systems, 1973; Information Science, 1987, 2nd edn 1992; Online Search Interface Design, 1993; (ed) Fifty Years of Information Progress, 1994; Scientific Communication in History, 2000; articles in professional jls. *Recreations:* reading history, poetry, philosophy; music and theatre; personal computing. *Address:* 9 Clover Close, Cumnor Hill, Oxford OX2 9JH. *T:* (01865) 863306.

VICTOR, Ed; Chairman and Managing Director, Ed Victor Ltd, since 1977; *b* 9 Sept. 1939; *s* of Jack Victor and Lydia Victor; *m* 1st, 1963, Michelene Dinah Samuels (marr. diss.); two *s*; 2nd, 1980, Carol Lois Ryan; one *s*. *Educ:* Dartmouth Coll. USA (BA *summa cum laude* 1961); Pembroke Coll., Cambridge (MLitt 1963). Began as art books editor, later editorial Dir, Weidenfeld & Nicolson, 1964–67; editorial Dir, Jonathan Cape Ltd, 1967–71; Senior Editor, Alfred A. Knopf Inc., NY, 1972–73; literary agent and Dir, John Farquharson Ltd (lit. agents), 1974–76; founded Ed Victor Ltd (lit. agency), 1977. Council Mem., Aids Crisis Trust, 1986–98. Vice-Chm., Almeida Theatre, 1994– (Dir, 1993–). Trustee, The Arts Foundn, 1991–. *Recreations:* golf, tennis, travel, opera. *Address:* 10 Cambridge Gate, Regent's Park, NW1 4JX. *T:* (020) 7224 3030. *Clubs:* Garrick, Beefsteak.

VICTORY, Louis Eamonn Julian; Chief Executive, Cumbria County Council, since 2000; *b* 14 Feb. 1948; *s* of Gerald Louis Victory and Doris Mabel Victory; *m* 1969, Sian Anne Bees Davies (marr. diss. 1996); three *d*. *Educ:* Cambridge Grammar Sch.; Christ's Coll., Cambridge (MA). DipArch; RIBA 1974. Architect in public and private practice, Birmingham, Oxon and Dyfed, 1972–90; Nottinghamshire County Council: Dep. Co. Architect, 1990; Dep. Dir, 1991, Dir, 1992–95, Construction and Design; Dir, Envmt, 1995–2000. *Recreations:* travelling, observing, recording (and sometimes making) townscape and landscape. *Address:* Cumbria County Council, The Courts, Carlisle, Cumbria CA3 8NA. *T:* (01228) 606301.

VICUÑA, Francisco O.; *see* Orrego-Vicuña.

VIDAL, Gore; author; *b* 3 Oct. 1925; *s* of Eugene and Nina Gore Vidal. *Educ:* Phillips Exeter Academy, New Hampshire, USA (grad. 1943). Army of the US, 1943–46: Private to Warrant Officer (jg) and First Mate, Army FS-35, Pacific Theatre Ops. Democratic-Liberal candidate for US Congress, 1960; candidate for Democratic nomination for election to US Senate from California, 1982. Apptd to President Kennedy's Adv. Council of the Arts, 1961–63. Hon. DLitt Brown Univ., 1988, etc. Chevalier de l'Ordre des Arts et des Lettres (France), 1995. *Publications: novels:* Williwaw, 1946; In a Yellow Wood, 1947; The City and the Pillar, 1948; The Season of Comfort, 1949; A Search for the King, 1950; Dark Green, Bright Red, 1950; The Judgment of Paris, 1952; Messiah, 1954; Julian, 1964; Washington, DC, 1967; Myra Breckinridge, 1968 (filmed 1969); Two Sisters, 1970; Burr, 1973; Myron, 1975; 1876, 1976; Kalki, 1978; Creation, 1981; Duluth, 1983; Lincoln, 1984; Empire, 1987; Hollywood, 1989; Live from Golgotha, 1992; The Smithsonian Institution, 1998; The Golden Age, 2000; *essays:* Rocking the Boat, 1962; Reflections upon a Sinking Ship, 1969; Homage to Daniel Shays (collected essays 1952–72), 1972; Matters of Fact and of Fiction, 1977; The Second American Revolution (UK title, Pink Triangle and Yellow Star and other essays (1976–1982)), 1982;

Armageddon?, 1987; At Home, 1988; A View from the Diner's Club, 1991; Screening History, 1992; United States: essays 1952–1992, 1993 (Nat. Book Award, 1994); Virgin Islands: essays 1992–1997, 1997; The Last Empire: essays 1992–2000; *short stories:* A Thirsty Evil, 1956; *travel:* Vidal in Venice, 1987; *memoir:* Palimpsest, 1995; *plays:* Visit to a Small Planet (NY prod.), 1957; The Best Man (NY prod.), 1960, 2000; Romulus (adapted from F. Dürrenmatt) (NY prod.), 1962; Weekend (NY prod.), 1968; On the March to the Sea (German prod.), 1962; An Evening with Richard Nixon (NY prod.), 1972; *screenplays;* from 1955: Wedding Breakfast, 1957; Suddenly Last Summer, 1958; The Best Man (Critic's Prize, Cannes), 1964, etc; *television plays:* 1954–56: The Death of Billy the Kid (translated to screen as The Lefthanded Gun, 1959, and as Gore Vidal's Billy the Kid, 1989), etc; *literary and political criticism for:* NY Review of Books, New Yorker, Nation, TLS, etc. *Recreations:* as noted above. *Address:* La Rondinaia, 84010 Ravello, (Salerno), Italy. *Club:* Athenæum.

VIERTEL, Deborah Kerr; *see* Kerr, D. J.

VIGARS, Della, (Mrs Paul Vigars); *see* Jones, D.

VIGARS, Robert Lewis; *b* 26 May 1923; *s* of late Francis Henry Vigars and Susan Laurina May Vigars (*née* Lewis); *m* 1962, Margaret Ann Christine, *y d* of late Sir John Walton, KCIE, CB, MC, and Lady Walton; two *d. Educ:* Truro Cathedral Sch.; London Univ. (LLB (Hons)). Served War of 1939–45: RA and Royal Corps of Signals, 1942–47; attached Indian Army (Captain), 1944–47; Captain, Princess Louise's Kensington Regt, TA, 1951–54. Qualified as solicitor (Hons), 1948. Partner, Simmons & Simmons, London, EC2, 1951–75. Member: Kensington Borough Council, 1953–59; London and Home Counties Traffic Adv. Cttee, 1956–58; London Roads (Nugent) Cttee, 1958–59; LCC and GLC Kensington (formerly South Kensington), 1955–86; Environmental Planning Cttee, GLC, 1967–71 (Chm.); Strategic Planning Cttee, GLC, 1971–73 (Chm.); Leader of Opposition, ILEA, 1974–79; Chm. of the GLC, 1979–80; Mem., Standing Conf. on London and SE Regional Planning and SE Economic Planning Council, 1968–75. Gen. Comr of Income Tax (Highbury), 1988–98; Mem., Central London Valuation Tribunal, 1989–95. Dir, Heritage of London Trust, 1985–; Mem., Historic Buildings and Monuments Commn for England, 1986–88 (Mem., London Adv. Cttee, 1986–92 (Chm. 1986–88)); Trustee, Historic Chapels Trust, 1993–. Mem. Court, London Univ., 1977–82. Chm., Kensington Soc., 1994–99. *Recreation:* mountain walking. *Club:* Hurlingham.

VIGGERS, Peter John; MP (C) Gosport, since Feb. 1974; *b* 13 March 1938; *s* of late J. S. Viggers and E. F. Viggers (later Mrs V. E. J. Neal), Gosport; *m* 1968, Jennifer Mary McMillan, MB, BS, LRCP, MRCS, DA, *d* of late Dr R. B. McMillan, MD, FRCP, Guildford, and late Mrs J. T. C. McMillan, MA, MIB; two *s* one *d. Educ:* Portsmouth Grammar Sch.; Trinity Hall, Cambridge (MA 1961). Chm., Cambridge Univ. Cons. Assoc., 1960. Solicitor 1967. Royal Canadian Air Force (pilot), 1956–58; commnd 457 (Wessex) Regt, RA (TA), 1963. PPS to Solicitor-General, 1979–83, to Chief Sec. of HM Treasury, 1983–85; Parly Under-Sec. of State (Industry Minister), NI Office, 1986–89. Chm., Select Cttee on Armed Forces Bill, 1986, 1996; Member: Select Cttee on Members' Interests, 1991–93; Select Cttee on Defence, 1992–97, 2000– (Vice-Chm., 2000–); Exec., British-American Parly Gp, 2000– (Jt Treas., 2000–); Vice-Chm., British-Japanese Parly Gp, 1999– (Chm., 1992–99); UK Delegate: Jt IPU and UN Conf. on Conventional Disarmament, Mexico City, 1985; N Atlantic Assembly, 1981–86, 1992– (Vice-Chm., Political Cttee, 1995–97; Chm., 2000–). Chm. and dir of public and private cos, 1972–; Chm., Tracer Petroleum Corp., 1996–98; Dir, Emerald Energy PLC, 1998–. Underwriting Member of Lloyd's (Council Mem., 1992–96); Chm. Trustees, Lloyd's Pension Fund, 1996–. Mem., Management Cttee, RNLI, 1979–89, Vice-Pres., 1989–. Dir and Trustee, HMS Warrior 1860, 1995–. *Recreations:* beagling, opera, travel. *Address:* House of Commons, SW1A 0AA. *Club:* House of Commons Yacht (Cdre, 1984–85; Adm., 1997–).

VIGNOLES, Roger Hutton, ARCM; pianoforte accompanist and conductor; *b* 12 July 1945; *s* of late Keith Hutton Vignoles and of Phyllis Mary (*née* Pearson); *m* 1st, 1972, Teresa Ann Elizabeth Henderson (marr. diss. 1982); 2nd, 1982, Jessica Virginia, *d* of late Prof. Boris Ford; one *s* one *d. Educ:* Canterbury Cathedral Choir Sch.; Sedbergh Sch.; Magdalene Coll., Cambridge (BA, BMus); Royal College of Music, London (ARCM). Accompanist of national and internat. reputation, regularly appearing with the most distinguished internat. singers and instrumentalists, both in London and provinces and at major music festivals (*eg* Aldeburgh, Cheltenham, Edinburgh, Brighton, Bath, Salzburg, Prague, etc) and broadcasting for BBC Radio 3 and television. International tours incl. USA, Canada, Australia-New Zealand, Hong Kong, Scandinavia, and recitals at Opera Houses of Cologne, Brussels, Frankfurt, Lincoln Center, NY, San Francisco, Tokyo, Carnegie Hall, NY, Venice, Paris, Munich, Berlin, etc. Repetiteur: Royal Opera House, Covent Garden, 1969–71; English Opera Group, 1968–74; Australian Opera Company, 1976. Professor of Accompaniment, 1974–81, Prince Consort Prof. of Piano Accompaniment, 1996–, RCM; Consultant Prof. of Accompaniment, RAM, 1989–; Artistic Dir, Young Brahms Fest., QEH, 1992. Has conducted: Buxton Fest., 1992; Bath and Wessex Opera, 1993; Hallé Orch., 1993, etc. Gramophone recordings of extensive vocal and chamber music repertoire. Hon. RAM 1984. *Recreations:* drawing, painting, looking at pictures, swimming, sailing. *Address:* 1 Ascham Street, Kentish Town, NW5 2PB. *T:* (020) 7267 3187.

VILE, Prof. Maurice John Crawley; Professor Emeritus of Political Science, University of Kent at Canterbury; *b* 23 July 1927; *s* of Edward M. and Elsie M. Vile; two *s. Educ:* London Sch. of Economics. BSc (Econ) 1951; PhD London, 1954; MA Oxford, 1962. FRHistS 1989. Lectr in Politics, Univ. of Exeter, 1954–62; Fellow of Nuffield Coll., Oxford, 1962–65; Lectr in Politics, Magdalen Coll., Oxford, 1963–64; University of Kent: Reader in Politics and Govt, 1965–68; Prof. of Political Sci., 1968–84; Dir of Internat. Progs, 1984–87; Dean of Faculty of Social Scis, 1969–75; Pro-Vice-Chancellor, 1975–81; Dep. Vice-Chancellor, 1981–84; Dir of British Progs, Boston Univ., 1989–94; Dir of Res., Canterbury Christ Church Coll., 1994–99. Visiting Professor: Univ. of Massachusetts, 1960; Smith College, Mass., 1961. Royer Lectr, Univ. of Calif., Berkeley, 1974. Hon. DCL Kent, 1993. *Publications:* The Structure of American Federalism, 1961; Constitutionalism and the Separation of Powers, 1967, 2nd edn 1998; Politics in the USA, 1970, 5th edn 1999; Federalism in the United States, Canada and Australia (Res. Paper No 2, Commn on the Constitution), 1973; The Presidency (Amer. Hist. Documents Vol. IV), 1974. *Address:* Little Cob, Garlinge Green, Petham, Canterbury, Kent CT4 5RT. *T:* (01277) 700432.

VILIKOVSKÝ, Ján, PhD; Head: Slovak Centre for Literary Translation, since 1997; Centre for Information on Literature, since 2001; *b* 13 July 1937; *s* of late Prof. Ján Vilikovský and Dr Júlia Vilikovská (*née* Bárdošová); *m* 1st, 1962, Božica Štúrová (*d* 1985); two *d*; 2nd, 1992, Mária Horváthová. *Educ:* Comenius Univ., Bratislava (BA 1959; MA 1975; PhD 1982). Editor, Slovak Writers' Publishing House, 1959–70; Asst Prof., Inst. of Translators, 1970–74; Asst Prof., Dept of English and American Studies, Comenius Univ., 1974–90; Sec.-Gen., Slovak Translators' Assoc., 1986–90; Dir, Tatran Publishers, 1990–92; Ministry of Foreign Affairs, 1992; Ambassador of Czechoslovakia, 1992; Ambassador of Slovak Republic to UK, 1993–96. Asst Gen. Sec., RECIT (European Network of International Centres of Literary Translators), 2000–. Ján Holý Prize for Translation, 1969, 1980. *Publications:* Slovak-English Dictionary, 1959, 5th edn 1992; Preklad ako tvorba (Translation as a creative process), 1984; contribs to learned jls; translations from English and American literature. *Recreations:* classical music, reading, talking. *Address:* Zálužická 7, 821 01 Bratislava, Slovakia.

VILJOEN, Marais, DMS 1976; State President of the Republic of South Africa, 1979–84; *b* 2 Dec. 1915; *s* of Gabriel François Viljoen and Magdalena Debora (*née* de Villiers); *m* 1940, Dorothea Maria Brink; one *d. Educ:* Jan van Riebeeck High Sch., Cape Town; Univ. of Cape Town. After leaving school, employed in Dept of Posts and Telegraphs, 1932–37; on editorial staff, Die Transvaler newspaper, 1937–40; manager, Transvaler book trade business, Potchefstroom, 1940; co-founder and provincial leader of Nat. Youth League, 1940–45; organiser of Transvaal National Party, 1945–49; Member, Provincial Council, Transvaal, 1949–53; Information Officer, Transvaal National Party, several years from 1951; Chairman, Inf. Service of Federal Council, National Party of S Africa, 1969–74; Dep. Chm., Nat. Party, Transvaal, 1966–75. MP Alberton, 1953–76; Dep. Minister of Labour and of Mines, 1958–61; various other ministerial offices, incl. Interior and Immigration, until 1966; Cabinet appointments, 1966–: Minister of Labour and of Coloured Affairs, 1966–69, also of Rehoboth Affairs, 1969–70; Minister of Labour and of Posts and Telecommunications, 1970–76. President of the Senate, 1976–79. Special Cl., Grand Collar, Order of Good Hope, Republic of S Africa, 1981. *Recreations:* golf, bowls, reading. *Address:* PO Box 5555, Pretoria, 0001, Republic of South Africa.

VILJOEN, Theo Leon; His Honour Judge Viljoen; a Circuit Judge, since 1992; *b* 25 Aug. 1937; *s* of Robert Bartlett Viljoen and Cecilia Jacoba Viljoen (*née* van der Walt); *m* 1967, Dorothy Nina Raybould, *d* of late Prof. S. G. Raybould; two *d. Educ:* Afrikaanse Hoër Seunskool; Univ. of Pretoria. Called to the Bar, Middle Temple, 1972; a Recorder, 1991–92. Legal Assessor, UKCC, 1987–92. Mem., Parole Bd, 1997–. Mem., N Lambeth and Kennington Gardens Guild. *Recreations:* walking, gardening, wine. *Address:* 2 Harcourt Buildings, Temple, EC4Y 9DB. *T:* (020) 7583 9020.

VILLIERS; *see* Child Villiers, family name of Earl of Jersey.

VILLIERS; *see* de Villiers.

VILLIERS, family name of **Earl of Clarendon.**

VILLIERS, Charles Nigel, FCA; Deputy Chairman, Abbey National plc, 1999–2001; *b* 25 Jan. 1941; *s* of Robert Alexander and Elizabeth Mary Villiers; *m* 1970, Sally Priscilla Magnay; one *s* one *d. Educ:* Winchester Coll.; New Coll., Oxford (MA German and Russian). Arthur Andersen & Co., 1963–67; ICFC, 1967–72; County Bank Ltd, 1972–86; Dir, 1974; Dep. Chief Exec., 1977; Chm. and Chief Exec., 1984–85; Exec. Chm., 1985–86; Exec. Dir, National Westminster Bank, 1985–88; Chief Exec., NatWest Investment Bank Ltd (estab. June 1986 incorporating the business of County Bank Ltd), 1986–88; Chm., County NatWest Ltd, 1986–88; Man. Dir of Corporate Develt, then Abbey Nat. Building Soc.), Abbey National plc, 1988–99. Non-exec. Dir, DTZ Hldgs, 1997–. *Recreations:* opera, ski-ing, tennis. *Club:* Reform.

VILLIERS, Theresa Anne; Member (C) London Region, European Parliament, since 1999; *b* 5 March 1968; *d* of George and Virginia Villiers; *m* 1999, Sean Wilken. *Educ:* Univ. of Bristol (LLB Hons 1990); Jesus Coll., Oxford (BCL Hons 1991). Called to the Bar, Inner Temple, 1992; Barrister specialising in chancery, insolvency and entertainment law, 1994–95; Lectr in Law, King's Coll., London, 1995–99. Treas. and economic spokesman for Cons. delegn to EP, 1999–; EP Rapporteur for banking capital adequacy rules, 2000–. *Publications:* (with Sean Wilken) Waiver, Variation and Estoppel, 1998; Tax Harmonisation: the impending threat, 2001; various articles in legal jls, incl. Lloyd's Maritime and Commercial Law Qly. *Recreations:* in-line skating, ski-ing, water ski-ing. *Address:* Conservative Central Office, 32 Smith Square, SW1P 3HH. *T:* (020) 7984 8227. *Club:* Middlesex CC.

VINCENT, family name of **Baron Vincent of Coleshill.**

VINCENT OF COLESHILL, Baron *cr* 1996 (Life Peer), of Shrivenham, in the County of Oxfordshire; **Field Marshal Richard Frederick Vincent,** GBE 1990; KCB 1984; DSO 1972; FIMechE; FRAeS; Chairman: Hunting Defence Ltd, since 1996; Hunting Engineering Ltd, since 1998 (Director, since 1996); Hunting Brae, since 1997; *b* 23 Aug. 1931; *s* of late Frederick Vincent and Frances Elizabeth (*née* Coleshill); *m* 1955, Jean Paterson, *d* of Kenneth Stewart and Jane (*née* Banks); one *s* one *d* (and one *s* decd). *Educ:* Aldenham Sch.; RMCS. Commnd RA, National Service, 1951; Germany, 1951–55; Gunnery Staff, 1959; Radar Res. Estabt, Malvern, 1960–61; BAOR, 1962; Technical Staff Training, 1963–64; Staff Coll., 1965; Commonwealth Bde, Malaysia, 1966–68; MoD, 1968–70; Comd 12th Light Air Def. Regt, Germany, UK and NI, 1970–72; Instr, Staff Coll., 1972–73; Greenlands Staff Coll., Henley, 1974; Mil. Dir of Studies, RMCS, 1974–75; Comd 19 Airportable Bde, 1975–77; RCDS, 1978; Dep. Mil. Sec., 1979–80; Comdt, Royal Military College of Science, 1980–83; Master-Gen. of the Ordnance, MoD, 1983–87; VCDS, 1987–91; CDS, 1991–92; Chm. of Mil. Cttee, NATO, 1993–96. Master Gunner, St James's Park, 1996–2000. Non-exec. Dir, Vickers Defence Systems Ltd, 1996–. Mem., Commn on Britain and Europe, RIIA, 1996. Col Commandant: REME, 1981–87; RA, 1983–2000; Hon. Colonel: 100 (Yeomanry) Field Regt RA, TA, 1982–91; 12th Air Defence Regt, 1987–91. Vice Pres., Officers' Pension Soc., 1997–. President: Combined Services Winter Sports Assoc., 1983–90; Army Ski-ing Assoc., 1983–87. Kermit Roosevelt Lectr, 1988; Vis. Fellow, Australian Coll. of Defence and Strategic Studies, 1995–99. Vice-Pres., 1996–2000, Pres., 2000–, Defence Manufacturers Assoc. Chancellor, Cranfield Univ., 1998–; Member: Court, Cranfield Inst. of Technol., 1981–83; Court, Greenwich Univ., 1997–; Adv. Council, RMCS, 1983–91; Governor: Aldenham Sch., 1987–; ICSTM, 1995– (Chm., 1996–; Fellow, 1996). Freeman: City of London, 1992; Wheelwrights' Co., 1997; Mem., Guild of Freemen, 1992. FRAeS 1990; FIMechE 1990. Hon. DSc Cranfield, 1985. Order of Merit (1st cl.) (Jordan), 1991; Commander, Legion of Merit (USA), 1993. *Publications:* contrib. mil. jls and pubns. *Recreation:* seven grandchildren. *Address:* c/o HSBC, Shaftesbury, Dorset SP7 8JX.

VINCENT, Anthony Lionel; Legal Adviser, Department of Foreign Affairs and Trade, Canberra, 1993–97; *b* 18 Oct. 1933; *s* of Harold Francis Vincent and Lesley Allison Vincent; *m* 1958, Helen Frances Beasley; one *s* one *d. Educ:* Univ. of Western Australia, Perth (LLB); Univ. of Oxford (BCL). Joined Dept of Foreign Affairs, Aust., 1958; served: Karachi, 1959–61; Hong Kong, 1963–66; Singapore, 1966–69; Belgrade, 1972–74; Paris, 1977–80; Australian Ambassador to: Iraq, 1981–83; GDR, 1984; Dep. High Comr in London, 1984–87; Asst Sec., Treaties and Sea Law Br., 1987–89, Intelligence and Defence Br., 1989–90, Dept of Foreign Affairs and Trade, Canberra; Ambassador to Czech and Slovak Federal Republic, subseq. to Czech and Slovak Republics, 1990–93. *Recreations:*

drawing, painting, reading. *Address:* 56 Blackwall Reach Parade, Bicton, WA 6157, Australia.

VINCENT, Prof. Colin Angus; Professor of Electrochemistry, since 1989, Master, since 1996 and Deputy Principal, since 2001, of the United College, University of St Andrews; *b* 4 March 1938; *s* of Harold Frederick Vincent and Helen McEachern Vincent; *m* 1964, Doris Susan Cole; one *s* one *d*. *Educ:* Oban High Sch.; Univ. of Glasgow (BSc; PhD; DSc). AMIEE; CChem, FRSC 1976; FRSE 1992. Assistant, Univ. of Glasgow, 1963–65; Lectr, Univ. of Illinois, 1965–67; University of St Andrews: Lectr, 1967–76; Sen. Lectr; 1976–84; Reader, 1984–89; Head, School of Chemistry, 1990–97; Vice-Principal, United Coll., 1996–2001; Vice-Chancellor and Acting Principal, 2000. Galvani Medal, Italian Chem. Soc., 1998. *Publications:* (jtly) Alkali Metal, Alkaline: earth metal and ammonium halides in amide solvents, 1980; Modern Batteries, 1984, 2nd edn 1997; Polymer Electrolyte Reviews, vol. 1, 1987, vol. 2, 1989; more than 120 papers in learned jls. *Recreations:* squash, hill walking, opera. *Address:* College Gate, University of St Andrews, St Andrews, Fife KY16 9AJ. *T:* (01334) 462548.

VINCENT, Prof. Ewart Albert; Professor of Geology, and Fellow of University College, Oxford, 1967–86, now Emeritus; *b* 23 Aug. 1919; *o s* of Albert and Winifred Vincent, Aylesbury; *m* 1944, Myrtle Ablett; two *d*. *Educ:* Reading Sch.; Univ. of Reading. BSc (Reading) 1940; PhD 1951; MA (Oxon) 1952; MSc (Manch.) 1966. FGS. Chemist, Min. of Supply, 1940–45; Geologist, Anglo-Iranian Oil Co., 1945–46; Lectr in Mineralogy and Crystallography, Univ. of Durham, 1946–51; Lectr in Geology, Oxford Univ., 1951–56; Reader in Mineralogy, Oxford Univ., 1956–62; Prof. of Geology, Manchester Univ., 1962–66. Visiting Professor: Univ. of Kuwait, 1970; Washington and Lee Univ., Va, 1980. Mem. NERC, 1975–78. Vice-Pres., Internat. Assoc. of Volcanology, 1968–71; Pres., Mineralogical Soc. of GB, 1974–76; Mem. Council, Geol Soc., 1973–76. Fellow, Mineralogical Soc. of Amer. Hon. Corresp. Mem., Soc. Géol. de Belgique. Awarded Wollaston Fund, Geol Soc. London, 1961. *Publications:* scientific papers in learned jls. *Recreations:* music, photography. *Address:* 2 Linch Farm, Wytham, Oxford OX2 8QP. *T:* (01865) 723170; Department of Earth Sciences, Parks Road, Oxford OX1 3PR. *T:* (01865) 272000.

VINCENT, Rev. Irvin James; Supernumerary Minister, Taunton Methodist Church, since 1999; *b* 22 July 1932; *s* of Amy Mary Catharine Vincent (*née* Nye) and Vince Thomas Vincent; *m* 1959, Stella Margaret (*née* Chaplin); one *s* two *d*. *Educ:* Mitcham Grammar School; Didsbury College (Methodist), Bristol. BA Open Univ. Accountancy, 1948; National Service, RAF, 1950–52; Local Govt, 1952–55; theological training, 1955–59; Methodist Circuit, Stonehouse and Dursley, 1959–61; entered RN as Chaplain, 1961; Malta, 1968–72; exchange with USN, 1976–78; Principal Chaplain, Church of Scotland and Free Churches (Navy), 1984–86; QHC, 1984–86; Minister, Temple Methodist Church, Taunton, 1986–97; Hon. Associate Minister, Westminster Central Hall, 1997–99. *Recreations:* all sport, reading, family. *Address:* 20 Wesley Close, The Grange, Taunton, Som TA1 4YA.

VINCENT, Rev. Dr John James; Methodist Minister, Sheffield Inner City Ecumenical Mission (Superintendent, 1970–97); Director, Urban Theology Unit, 1969–97, Director Emeritus, since 1997; President of the Methodist Conference, 1989–90; *b* 29 Dec. 1929; *s* of late David Vincent and Ethel Beatrice Vincent (*née* Gadd); *m* 1958, Grace Johnston, *d* of late Rev. Wilfred Stafford, Bangor, Co. Down; two *s* one *d*. *Educ:* Manchester Grammar Sch.; Richmond Coll.; London Univ. (BD 1954); Drew Univ., USA (STM 1955); Basel Univ., Switzerland (DTheol 1960). Sgt, RAMC, 1948–49. Minister, Manchester and Salford Mission, 1956–62; Supt, Rochdale Mission, 1962–69; Founder and Leader, The Ashram Community, 1967–. Visiting Professor of Theology: Boston Univ., and New York Theol Seminary, 1969–70; Drew Univ., 1977; Adjunct Prof. of Theol., New York Theol Seminary, 1979–88. Hon. Lectr in Biblical Studies, 1990–; supervisor, doctoral prog. in Contextual, Urban and Liberation Theologies, 1993–, Sheffield Univ. Chairman: NW Campaign for Nuclear Disarmament, 1957–63; Alliance of Radical Methodists, 1970–76; Urban Mission Trng Assoc., 1982–90; Trustee Savings Bank Depositors Assoc. (also litigant in High Court and H of L, TSB *v* Vincent), 1986; Jt Co-ordinator, British Liberation Theol. Inst., 1990–; Co-Chair, Urban Theologians Internat., 1993–; Member: Studiorum Novi Testamenti Societas, 1961–; Council, Christian Orgns for Social, Political and Econ. Change, 1981–91; Exec., Assoc. of Centres of Adult Theol. Educn, 1984–90. Jt Ed., British Liberation Theology series, 1995, 1997, 1999. *Publications:* Christ in a Nuclear World, 1962; Christian Nuclear Perspective, 1964; Christ and Methodism, 1965; Here I Stand, 1967; Secular Christ, 1968; The Race Race, 1970; The Jesus Thing, 1973; Stirrings: essays Christian and Radical, 1975; Alternative Church, 1976; Disciple and Lord: discipleship in the Synoptic Gospels, 1976; Starting All Over Again, 1981; Into the City, 1982; OK, Let's Be Methodists, 1984; Radical Jesus, 1986; Mark at Work, 1986; Britain in the Nineties, 1989; Discipleship in the Nineties, 1991; A Petition of Distress from the Cities (to the Queen and Govt), 1993; (ed jtly) The Cities: Methodist report, 1997; Hope from the City, 2000; *relevant publication:* Urban Christ: responses to John Vincent, ed I. K. Duffield, 1997. *Recreations:* jogging, writing. *Address:* 178 Abbeyfield Road, Sheffield S4 7AY. *T:* (0114) 243 6688, *T:* and *Fax:* (Urban Theology Unit) (0114) 243 5342; *e-mail:* john@utu.sheffield.fsnet.co.uk.

VINCENT, Prof. John Russell; Professor of History, University of Bristol, since 1984; *b* 20 Dec. 1937; *s* of late Prof. J. J. Vincent and M. Monica Vincent, MSc, PhD (*née* Watson); *m* 1972, Nicolette Elizabeth Kenworthy; one *s* (and one *s* decd). *Educ:* Bedales Sch.; Christ's Coll., Cambridge. Lectr in Modern British History, Cambridge Univ., 1967–70; Prof. of Modern History, Univ. of Bristol, 1970–84. Chm., Bristol Br., NCCL, 1972–74. *Publications:* The Formation of the Liberal Party, 1966 (2nd edn as The Formation of the British Liberal Party 1857–68, 1980); Poll Books: How Victorians voted, 1967; (ed with A. B. Cooke) Lord Carlingford's Journal, 1971; (ed with M. Stenton) McCalmont's Parliamentary Poll Book 1832–1918, 1971; (with A. B. Cooke) The Governing Passion: Cabinet Government and party politics in Britain 1885–86, 1974; (ed) Disraeli, Derby and the Conservative Party: the political journals of Lord Stanley 1849–69, 1978; Gladstone and Ireland (Raleigh Lecture), 1979; (ed) The Crawford Papers: the journals of David Lindsay, Twenty-Seventh Earl of Crawford and Tenth Earl of Balcarres during the years 1892 to 1940, 1984; Disraeli, 1990; (ed) The Derby Diaries 1869–1878, 1995; (contrib.) Twentieth-Century Britain: an encyclopaedia, 1995; An Intelligent Person's Guide to History, 1995; (contrib.) Why Tory Governments Fall, 1996. *Recreation:* journalism. *Address:* The Graduate Centre, 7 Woodland Road, Bristol BS8 1TB. *T:* (0117) 928 8892.

VINCENT, Leonard Grange, CBE 1960; FRIBA, FRTPI, Distinction Town Planning (RIBA); formerly architect and town planner, and Principal Partner, Vincent and Gorbing, Architects and Planning Consultants; *b* 13 April 1916; *s* of late Godfrey Grange Vincent; *m* 1942, Evelyn (*née* Gretton); twin *s* one *d*. *Educ:* Forest House School. Trained as architect in London, 1933, and subsequently as a town planner; experience in private practice and local government. Served War of 1939–45: Royal Engineers (Major); mostly overseas, in Western Desert, and Italian campaigns with 8th Army, 1940–45. Formerly Chief Architect and Planner, Stevenage Development Corporation. *Publications:* various technical and planning articles in technical press. *Recreations:* archaeology, painting. *Address:* Medbury, Rectory Lane, Stevenage, Hertfordshire SG1 4BX. *T:* (01438) 351175.

VINCENT, Prof. Nigel Bruce; Mont Follick Professor of Comparative Philology, University of Manchester, since 1987; *b* 24 Sept. 1947; *s* of Denis George Vincent and Peggy Eliza Vincent; *m* 1st, 1971, Janet Elizabeth Hutchinson (marr. diss. 1999); two *d*; 2nd, 1999, Merethe Damsgård Sørensen; one *d*. *Educ:* Sexey's Sch., Bruton; Trinity Hall, Cambridge (BA 1st cl. hons Mod. and Medieval Langs 1970); Darwin Coll., Cambridge (Dip. Linguistics 1971). Lecturer: Birkbeck Coll., London, 1973–74; Univ. of Lancaster, 1974–76; Univ. of Hull, 1976–81; Univ. of Cambridge, 1981–87 (Fellow, Trinity Hall, 1983–87); Res. and Graduate Dean of Arts, Univ. of Manchester, 1992–96. British Acad. Res. Reader, 1996–98. Visiting Professor: Univ. of Pavia, 1983; Univ. of Rome, 1986; Ecole Pratique des Hautes Etudes, Paris, 1993; Australian Linguistic Inst., La Trobe Univ., 1994; Univ. of Copenhagen, 1997; Melbourne Univ., 2000; Erskine Fellow, Univ. of Canterbury, NZ, 2000. Member: Res. Grants Bd, ESRC, 1988–91; Council, Philological Soc., 1982–86, 1989–94, 1995–99 (Pres., 2000–); Res. Gp Leader, EUROTYP Project, ESF, 1990–94; Humanities Res. Bd, 1994–96; Chm., Res. Assessment Panels, HEFCE, 1992, 1996. Vice Pres., Società di Linguistica Italiana, 1990–92; Pres., Internat. Soc. of Historical Linguistics, 1993–95. Mem. Bd, British Inst. in Paris, 1999–. Editor, Jl of Linguistics, 1984–93. *Publications:* (jtly) Studies in the Romance Verb, 1982; (jtly) The Romance Languages, 1988; (jtly) Parameters of Morphosyntactic Change, 1997; articles in jls. *Recreations:* wine, all things Italian. *Address:* Department of Linguistics, University of Manchester, Manchester M13 9PL. *T:* (0161) 275 3194; 48 Lower Lane, Chinley, High Peak SK23 6BD. *T:* (01663) 750943; *e-mail:* nigel.vincent@man.ac.uk.

VINCENT, Robin Anthony, CBE 2001; International Court Management Consultant, United Nations and British Council, since 2001; *b* 27 Feb. 1944; *s* of late John Kenneth Vincent and of Ivy Elizabeth Ann Vincent (*née* Grayer); *m* 1971, Hazel Ruth Perkins; two *s*. *Educ:* King's Sch., Worcester. Clerk, Worcs QS, 1962–70; Sen. Asst and Dep. Clerk, Worcs County Justices, 1970–72; Higher Executive Officer: Worcester Crown Court, 1972–76; Worcs County Court, 1976–77; Court Business Officer, 1977–79; Sen. Exec. Officer (Personnel), Circuit Administrator's Office, Birmingham, 1979–80; Chief Clerk, Worcester Crown Court, 1980–82; Principal Chief Clerk, Manchester Crown Court, 1982–86; Head of Division, Lord Chancellor's Department: Court Service Develt, London, 1986–91; Personnel Mgt, 1991–93; Judicial Appts, 1993; Circuit Administrator, Northern Circuit, LCD, then Court Service Agency, 1993–2001. *Recreations:* cricket (playing), music, drinking red wine with Steve Baines. *Address:* The Moorings, 33 Grange Road, Bramhall, Stockport, Cheshire SK7 3BD. *T:* (0161) 440 9526. *Clubs:* Old Vigornians (Worcester); Eggington Cricket (Leighton Buzzard); Stockport Georgians (Stockport).

VINCENT, Sir William (Percy Maxwell), 3rd Bt *cr* 1936; Managing Director, Cambridge Associates (UK) Ltd, since 1995; *b* 1 Feb. 1945; *o s* of Sir Lacey Vincent, 2nd Bt, and Helen Millicent, *d* of Field Marshal Sir William Robert Robertson, 1st Bt, GCB, GCMG, GCVO, DSO; *S* father, 1963; *m* 1976, Christine Margaret, *d* of Rev. E. G. Walton; three *s*. *Educ:* Eton College. 2nd Lieutenant, Irish Guards, 1964–67. Jt Man. Dir, 1987–92, and Investment Dir, 1986–92, Touche Remnant & Co. and Touche Remnant Holdings; Dir, Touche Remnant & Co., 1985–92; Dir, M & G (N America) Ltd, 1992–95. Dir, Save and Prosper Investment Management, 1980–85. *Recreations:* water skiing, sailing. *Heir:* *s* Edward Mark William Vincent, *b* 6 March 1978. *Address:* Whistlers, Buriton, Petersfield, Hampshire GU31 5RU. *T:* (01730) 263532.

VINCENT BROWN, Kenneth; *see* Brown.

VINE, David Martin; broadcaster and promotions consultant, since 1960; *b* 3 Jan. 1935; *s* of Dorothy and Harold Vine; *m* Mandy; two *s* two *d*. *Educ:* Barnstaple Grammar Sch. Journalist: North Devon Journal-Herald, 1953; Western Morning News, 1956; Westward Television, 1960; presenter, 1965–2001, consultant, 2001–, BBC TV; programmes include: The Superstars, Question of Sport, Wimbledon, Horse of Year Show, World Snooker Championships (25 years), Ski Sunday (21 years), fourteen Summer and Winter Olympic Games, Miss World. *Publication:* The Superstars, 1984. *Recreation:* relaxing.

VINE, Prof. Frederick John, FRS 1974; Professorial Fellow, School of Environmental Sciences, University of East Anglia, since 1998 (Professor, 1974–98); *b* 17 June 1939; *s* of Frederick Royston Vine and Ivy Grace Vine (*née* Bryant); *m* 1964, Susan Alice McCall; one *s* one *d*. *Educ:* Latymer Upper Sch., Hammersmith; St John's Coll., Cambridge (BA, PhD). Instructor, 1965–67, and Asst Professor, 1967–70, Dept of Geological and Geophysical Sciences, Princeton Univ., NJ, USA; Reader, 1970–74, Dean, 1977–80 and 1993–98, School of Environmental Sciences, UEA. *Publications:* (jtly) Global Tectonics, 1990, 2nd edn 1996; articles in Nature, Science, Phil. Trans Roy. Soc. London, etc. *Recreations:* walking, camping. *Address:* 144 Christchurch Road, Norwich NR2 3PG.

VINE, Jeremy; Presenter, Newsnight, BBC, since 1999; *b* 17 May 1965; *s* of Dr Guy and Diana Vine. *Educ:* Epsom Coll.; Durham Univ. (BA Hons English Lit. 1986). Coventry Evening Telegraph, 1986–87; joined BBC, 1987: News Trainee, 1987–89; Programme Reporter, Today, 1989–93; Political Corresp., 1993–97; Africa Corresp., 1997–99. *Address:* c/o Room G680, BBC Television Centre, Wood Lane, W12 7RJ. *T:* (020) 8624 9800. *Club:* Soho House.

VINE, Col (Roland) Stephen, FRCPath, FZS; Chief Inspector, Cruelty to Animals Act (1876), Home Office, 1962–75; *b* 26 Dec. 1910; *s* of late Joseph Soutter Vine and of Josephine Vine (*née* Moylan); *m* 1935, Flora Betty, *d* of Charles Strutton Brookes, MBE, Dovercourt; three *d*. *Educ:* Southend-on-Sea High Sch.; Guy's Hosp. BSc; MRCS, LRCP, FRCPath, FZS(Scientific). Royal Army Medical Corps, 1934–60 (incl. War of 1939–45). Home Office, 1960–75. Former Mem., Council, Res. Defence Soc., 1977–85. *Publications:* chapter in: Biomedical Technology in Hospital Diagnosis, 1972; Animals in Scientific Research, 1983; articles in RAMC Jl. *Recreations:* gardening, bowling. *Address:* Shola, Fielden Road, Crowborough, Sussex TN6 1TR. *T:* (01892) 661381. *Club:* Civil Service.

VINE, Roy; Vice-Chairman, Barclays Bank plc, 1982–84; *b* 1923; *m* 1945, Dorothy A. Yates; one *s* one *d*. *Educ:* Taunton's Sch., Southampton. Served RAF (Flt Lieut), 1942–46 and 1951–53. Vice-Chm., Barclays Bank UK Ltd, 1982–84; Dir, Barclays Bank plc, 1979–84 (Gen. Man., 1972; Senior Gen. Man., 1979–81). Director: First Nat. Finance Corp. plc, 1984–93; First Nat. Bank Plc (formerly First Nat. Securities Ltd), 1985–90; First Nat. Commercial Bank Ltd, 1990–93. FCIB 1951. *Recreations:* golf, football, music. *Address:* Summerfold, Itchen Abbas, Winchester SO21 1AX.

VINEALL, Anthony John Patrick; Chairman, School Teachers' Review Body, since 1996; *b* 17 March 1932; *s* of George John Charles Vineall and Helen Fairley Vineall (*née* Bradshaw); *m* 1962, Dorothy Earnshaw; two *s*. *Educ:* Leeds Grammar Sch.; New Coll., Oxford (MA PPE). FIPD 1982. Nat. Service, commnd RA, 1951. Unilever: personnel posts in Animal Foods, Frozen Food, and in Ghana, 1955–67; Co. Personnel Manager, Walls Meat, 1967–70; Personnel Dir, SSC&B Lintas, 1970–75; Dir, Unilever UK Hldgs and Nat. Personnel Manager, 1975–81; Head of Corporate Mgt Develt, 1981–92. Chm., Tavistock and Portman NHS Trust, 1993–99. Member: Council, Foundn for Mgt Educn, 1976–92; CBI Employment Policy Cttee, 1977–81; Doctors' and Dentists' Pay Review Body, 1990–93; Review of Armed Forces Career and Rank Structure, 1994–95; Chairman: Exec. Cttee, Industrial Soc., 1982–85; Careers Res. Adv. Centre, 1991–96 (Mem. Council, 1981–); Vice Pres., Centre for Internat. Briefing, Farnham Castle, 1996– (Chm. Govs, 1987–96). Gov., Guildford Royal Grammar Sch., 1994–. *Recreations:* gardening, travel, bridge. *Address:* Ways End, 34 Abbotswood, Guildford GU1 1UZ.

VINELOTT, Sir John (Evelyn), Kt 1978; Judge of the High Court of Justice, Chancery Division, 1978–95; *b* 15 Oct. 1923; *s* of George Frederick Vine-Lott and Vera Lilian Vine-Lott (*née* Mockford); *m* 1956, Sally Elizabeth, *d* of His Honour Sir Walker Kelly Carter, QC; two *s* one *d*. *Educ:* Queen Elizabeth's Gram. Sch., Faversham, Kent; Queens' Coll., Cambridge (MA). War Service, Sub-Lieut RNVR, 1942–46. Called to Bar, Gray's Inn, 1953 (Atkin Scholar; Bencher, 1974; Treas., 1993); QC 1968; practised at the Chancery Bar. Chairman: Insolvency Rules Adv. Cttee, 1984–92; Trust Law Cttee, 1995–. Président, L'association de Bousquetara, 1989–. *Publications:* essays and articles on Revenue and Administration Law, in specialist periodicals. *Address:* 22 Portland Road, W11 4LG. *T:* (020) 7727 4778. *Club:* Garrick.

VINEN, William Frank, (Joe), FRS 1973; Professor of Physics, 1962–74, Poynting Professor of Physics, 1974–97, University of Birmingham, now Emeritus Professor of Physics; *b* 15 Feb. 1930; *o s* of Gilbert Vinen and Olive Maud Vinen (*née* Roach); *m* 1960, Susan-Mary Audrey Master; one *s* one *d*. *Educ:* Watford Grammar Sch.; Clare College, Cambridge. Research Fellow, Clare College, 1955–58. Royal Air Force, 1948–49. Demonstrator in Physics, Univ. of Cambridge and Fellow of Pembroke Coll., 1958–62. Hon. Life Fellow, Coventry Univ. (formerly Poly.), 1989. Simon Meml Prize, Inst. of Physics, 1963; Holweck Medal and Prize, Inst. of Physics and French Physical Soc., 1978; Rumford Medal, Royal Soc., 1980. *Recreation:* good food. *Address:* 52 Middle Park Road, Birmingham B29 4BJ. *T:* (0121) 475 1328.

VINER, Her Honour Monique Sylvaine, (Mrs M. S. Gray), CBE 1994; QC 1979; a Circuit Judge, 1990–99; *b* 3 Oct. 1926; *d* of late Hugh Viner and Eliane Viner; *m* 1958, Dr Pieter Francis Gray; one *s* three *d*. *Educ:* Convent of the Sacred Heart, Roehampton; St Hugh's Coll., Oxford (MA; Hon. Fellow, 1990). In teaching, publishing, factory and shop work, 1947–50. Called to the Bar, Gray's Inn, 1950, Bencher, 1988. A Recorder, 1986–90. Chm. of five Wages Councils, 1952–94; Mem., Industrial Court, 1976. *Recreations:* talking, reading, tennis, music, piano, walking, gardening, cooking, bird watching, history. *Address:* Old Glebe, Waldron, Heathfield, East Sussex TN21 0RB. *T:* (01435) 863865, *Fax:* (01435) 862599; *e-mail:* Monique@oldglebe.fsbusiness.co.uk.

VINES, Prof. David Anthony, PhD; Fellow and Tutor in Economics, Balliol College, Oxford, since 1992; Professor of Economics, University of Oxford, since 2000; Adjunct Professor of Economics, Research School of Pacific and Asian Studies, Australian National University, since 1991; *b* 8 May 1949; *s* of Robert Godfrey and Vera Frances Vines; *m* 1st, 1979, Susannah Lucy Robinson (marr. diss. 1992); three *s*; 2nd, 1995, Jane Elizabeth Bingham; two step *s*. *Educ:* Scotch Coll., Melbourne; Melbourne Univ (BA 1971); Cambridge Univ. (BA 1974; MA 1977; PhD 1984). Cambridge University: Fellow, Pembroke Coll., 1976–85; Res. Officer and Sen. Res. Officer, Dept of Applied Econs, 1979–85; Adam Smith Prof. of Political Economy, Univ. of Glasgow, 1985–92; Reader in Econs, Oxford Univ., 1997–2000; Res. Fellow, Centre for Econ. Policy Res., London, 1985–. Board Member: Channel 4 Television, 1987–92; Glasgow Develt Agency, 1990–92. Economic Consultant to Sec. of State for Scotland, 1987–92; Consultant, IMF, 1988, 1989. Economic and Social Research Council: Member: Econ. Affairs Cttee, 1985–87; Res. Progs Bd, 1992–93; Dir, Res. Prog. on Global Econ. Instns, 1994–2000. Mem. Academic Panel, HM Treasury, 1986–. Mem. Council, Royal Economic Soc., 1988–92. Bd Mem., Analysys, 1989–. Comr, BFI Enquiry into the Future of the BBC, 1992. Bd Mem., Scottish Early Music Consort, 1990–. *Publications:* (with J. E. Meade and J. M. Maciejowski) Stagflation, Vol. II: Demand Management, 1983; (with D. A. Currie) Macroeconomic Interactions Between North and South, 1988; (jtly) Macroeconomic Policy: inflation, wealth and the exchange rate, 1989; (with G. Hughes) Deregulation and the Future of Commercial Television, 1989; (with A. Stevenson) Information, Strategy, and Public Policy, 1991; (with D. A. Currie) North South Interactions and International Macroeconomic Policy, 1995; (with Peter Drysdale) Europe, East Asia and APEC, 1998; (jtly) The Asian Financial Crises, 1999; (with Chris Gilbert) The World Bank: structure and policies, 2000; papers on international macroeconomics, balance of payments and economic policy, in professional jls. *Recreations:* hillwalking, music. *Address:* Balliol College, Oxford OX1 3BJ. *T:* (01865) 277719, *Fax:* (01865) 277803.

VINES, Eric Victor, CMG 1984; OBE 1971; HM Diplomatic Service, retired; *b* 28 May 1929; *s* of late Henry E. Vines; *m* 1953, Ellen-Grethe Ella Küppers; one *s*. *Educ:* St Dunstan's Coll., London; St Catharine's Coll., Cambridge (MA). Army service, 1947–49. Joined Commonwealth Relations Office, 1952; Colombo, 1954–55; 1st Sec., Singapore, 1958–61; Canberra, 1961–65; Diplomatic Service Administration Office, 1965–68; 1st Sec., Information, Mexico City, 1968–70; Counsellor, Exec. Sec.-Gen., SEATO Conf., London, 1971; Head, Cultural Exchange Dept, FCO, 1971–74; Counsellor (Commercial), Tel Aviv, 1974–77, Stockholm, 1977–80; Consul-Gen., Barcelona, 1980–83; Ambassador to Mozambique, 1984–85; Ambassador to Uruguay, 1986–89; Staff Assessor, FCO, 1991–94. Chm., British-Uruguayan Soc., 1995–; Vice-Chm., Britain–Mozambique Soc., 1999–2000. Trustee: Centre for S African Studies, York Univ., 1989–94; Gemini Ethiopian Trust, 1990–99. *Recreations:* opera, archaeology. *Address:* 80 Farquhar Road, SE19 1LT. *Club:* Royal Commonwealth Society.

VINES, Sir William (Joshua), AC 1987; Kt 1977; CMG 1969; FASA, ACIS; psc; Chairman, ANZ Banking Group, 1982–89 (Director, since 1976); Director, Dalgety Australia Ltd, 1980–91 (Chairman, 1970–80); grazier at Tara, Queensland, 1965–82 and Cliffdale, Currabubula, NSW, 1982–97; *b* 27 May 1916; *s* of P. V. Vines, Canterbury, Victoria, Australia; *m* 1st, 1939, Thelma J. (*d* 1988), *d* of late F. J. Ogden; one *s* two *d*; 2nd, 1990, Judith Anne Ploeg, *d* of late T. E. Raynsford. *Educ:* Haileybury College, Brighton Beach, Victoria. Managing Director: Internat. Wool Secretariat, 1961–69 (Board Mem., 1969–79); Berger, Jenson & Nicholson Ltd, 1960 (Dir, 1961–69); Dalgety Australia Ltd, 1971–76 (Chm., 1970–80); Group Managing Director, Lewis Berger & Sons Ltd, 1955–61; Director: Lewis Berger & Sons (Aust.) Pty Ltd & Sherwin Williams Co. (Aust.) Pty Ltd, 1952–55; Goodlass Wall & Co. Pty Ltd, 1947–49; Dalgety Ltd; Dalgety New Zealand Ltd, 1969–80; Port Phillip Mills Pty Ltd, 1969–88; Wiggins Teape Ltd (UK), 1970–79; Tubemakers of Australia Ltd, 1970–86 (Dep. Chm., 1973–86); Associated Pulp & Paper Mills Ltd, 1971–83 (Dep. Chm. 1977, Chm. 1979–83); Conzinc Rio Tinto of Australia, 1977–84; Grindlays Hldgs, subseq. ANZ UK Hldgs, 1985–89; Grindlays Bank, 1987–89; Chm., Thorn Holdings Pty Ltd, 1969–74. Vice-President Melbourne Legacy, 1949–51; Pres. Building Industry Congress, Vic., 1954–55. Chm., Aust. Wool Commn, 1970–72; Mem. Exec., CSIRO, 1973–78; Chm. Council, Hawkesbury Agric. Coll., 1975–85. Mem., Australia New Zealand Foundn, 1979–84. Chm., The Sir Robert Menzies Meml Trust, 1978–92. Served War of 1939–45 (despatches, C-in-C's commendation for gallantry, El Alamein), 2nd AIF, 2/23 Aust. Inf. Bn, Middle East, New Guinea and Borneo, Capt. Hon. DSc Econ Sydney, 1993. *Address:* 1/10 West Street, Balgowlah, NSW 2093, Australia. *T:* (2) 99481147. *Clubs:* Union (Sydney); RACV (Melbourne).

VINEY, Hon. Anne Margaret, (Hon. Mrs Viney); JP; barrister; Part-time Chairman, Social Security Appeal Tribunals, 1987–96; *b* 14 June 1926; *d* of late Baron Morton of Henryton, PC, MC, and Lady Morton of Henryton; *m* 1947, Peter Andrew Hopwood Viney; one *s* two *d*. *Educ:* Priorsfield, Godalming, Surrey. Called to the Bar, Lincoln's Inn, 1979. Councillor, Kensington and Chelsea BC, 1960–62. Helped to found London Adventure Playground Assoc., 1962 (Sec. 1962–69); Chm., Consumer Protection Adv. Cttee, 1973–82. JP, 1961; Mem., Inner London Juvenile Court panel, 1961–87 (Chm. 1970). *Recreations:* conversation, playing poetry game. *Address:* Worth House, Worth Matravers, near Swanage, Dorset BH19 3LQ.

VINEY, Elliott (Merriam), DSO 1945; MBE 1946; TD; DL; FSA; Director: British Printing Corporation Ltd, 1964–75; Hazell, Watson & Viney Ltd, 1947–78; *b* 21 Aug. 1913; *s* of late Col. Oscar Viney, TD, DL, and Edith Merriam; *m* 1950, Rosamund Ann Pelly; two *d*. *Educ:* Oundle; Univ. Coll., Oxford. Bucks Bn, Oxford and Bucks Light Infantry (TA), 1932–46. Governor and Trustee, Museum of London, 1972–88. Pres., British Fedn of Master Printers, 1972–73. Master, Grocers' Company, 1970–71. County Dir, Bucks St John Amb. Assoc., 1953–55; Trustee, Bucks Historic Churches Trust, 1957; Pres., Bucks Archaeol. Soc., 1979–98 (Hon. Sec., 1954–79); Pres., CPRE (Bucks), 1990–93 (Chm., 1976–90); Chm., Bucks Record Soc., 1986–99. JP 1950, DL 1952, High Sheriff, 1964, Buckinghamshire. Editor: Oxford Mountaineering, 1935; Climbers' Club Jl, 1936–39; (jt) Records of Bucks, 1947–74. *Publications:* The Sheriffs of Buckinghamshire, 1965; (jtly) Old Aylesbury, 1976. *Recreations:* conservation, music. *Address:* Cross Farmhouse, Quainton, Aylesbury, Bucks HP22 4AR. *Clubs:* Alpine; County Hall (Aylesbury).

VINING, Rowena Adelaide, OBE 1979 (MBE 1964); HM Diplomatic Service, retired; *b* 25 Sept. 1921; *er d* of late Col Percival Llewellyn Vining and Phyllis Servante Vining. *Educ:* privately, and at Chiddingstone Castle, Edenbridge, Kent. Foreign Office, 1941–52 (war service in Italy, Indonesia, 1943–45). Commonwealth Relations Office, 1952–55; Second Secretary: Karachi, 1955–58; Sydney, 1958–62; First Sec.: CRO, 1962–65; Canberra, 1965–67; Commonwealth Office (later Foreign and Commonwealth Office), 1967–71; Vienna, 1972–74; Consul, Florence and Consul-General, San Marino, 1974–78; Dep. UK Permanent Rep. to the Council of Europe, 1978–81; Consul-General, Strasbourg, 1979–80. Staff Assessor, FCO, 1983–86. *Recreations:* gardening, music. *Address:* Dorchester Cottage, Greywell, Hook, Hants RG29 1BT.

VINSON, family name of **Baron Vinson**.

VINSON, Baron, *cr* 1985 (Life Peer), of Roddam Dene in the County of Northumberland; **Nigel Vinson,** LVO 1979; DL; entrepreneur; Founder, 1952, Chairman, 1952–72, Plastic Coatings Ltd; Founder Director, Centre for Policy Studies, 1974–80; Vice-President, Institute of Economic Affairs, since 1998 (Trustee, since 1972; Chairman of the Trustees, 1989–96); *b* Nettlestead Place, Kent, 27 Jan. 1931; *s* of late Ronald Vinson and Bettina Vinson (*née* Southwell-Sander); *m* 1972, Yvonne Ann Collin; three *d*. *Educ:* Pangbourne Naval Coll. Lieut, Queen's Royal Regt, 1949–51. Plastic Coatings Ltd: started in a Nissen hut, 1952, flotation, 1969; Queen's Award to Industry, 1971. Director: Fleming High Income Growth Trust (formerly Fleming Tech. Trust), 1972–; BAA, 1973–80; Electra Investment Trust, 1975–98 (Dep. Chm., 1990–98); Barclays Bank UK, 1982–88. Member: Crafts Adv. Cttee, 1971–77; Design Council, 1973–80; Dep. Chm., CBI Smaller Firms Council, 1979–84; Chairman: CoSIRA, 1980–82; Rural Develt Commn, 1980–90 (Mem., 1978–90); Industry Year Steering Cttee, RSA, 1985–87; Pres., Industrial Participation Assoc., 1979–89 (Chm., 1971–78). Hon. Dir, Queen's Silver Jubilee Appeal, 1976–78; Member: Northumbrian Nat. Parks Countryside Cttee, 1977–89; Regional Cttee, Nat. Trust, 1977–84. Chm., NE Region, PYBT, 1995–98; Pres., NE Civic Trust, 1999–2001. Council Mem., St George's House, Windsor Castle, 1990–96. FRSA, CIMgt. DL Northumberland, 1990. *Publications:* Personal and Portable Pensions for All, 1984; Owners All, 1985; Take upon Retiring, 1998. *Recreations:* fine art and craftmanship, horses, farming. *Address:* 34 Kynance Mews, SW7 4QR. *T:* (01668) 217230. *Clubs:* Boodle's, Pratt's.

VINTER, (Frederick Robert) Peter, CB 1965; *b* 27 March 1914; *e s* of P. J. Vinter (Headmaster, Archbishop Holgate's Grammar Sch., York, 1915–37) and Harriet Mary (*née* Cammack); *m* 1938, Margaret (*d* 1998), *d* of S. I. Rake, Pembroke; two *s*. *Educ:* Haileybury Coll.; King's Coll., Cambridge (MA). Min. of Economic Warfare, 1939; Cabinet Office, 1943; HM Treasury, 1945–69, Third Sec., 1965–69; Dep. Sec., Min. of Technology and DTI, 1969–73. Overseas Adviser to CEGB, 1973–79; Dir (non-Exec.), Vickers Ltd, 1974–80. Nuffield Travelling Fellowship (in India), 1950–51.

VINTON, Alfred Merton; Chairman, Electra Partners Ltd (formerly Electra Kingsway Managers, then Electra Fleming Ltd), since 1995; *b* 11 May 1938; *s* of Alfred Merton Vinton and Jean Rosalie Vinton (*née* Guiterman); *m* 1st, 1963, Mary Bedell Weber; two *s* one *d*; 2nd, 1983, Anna-Maria Hawser (*née* Dugan-Chapman); one *s* one *d*. *Educ:* Harvard College (AB Econs 1960). US Navy Lieut (JG), 1960–62. J. P. Morgan, 1962–88; Chief Operating Officer, N. M. Rothschild & Sons, 1988–92; Chief Exec. Officer, Entreprises Quilmes SA, 1992–94; Director: Sand Aire Investments plc, 1995–; Sagitta Investment Advrs Ltd, 1996–2001; Unipart Ltd, 1998–; Amerindo Internet Fund plc, 2000–; Lambert Howarth Gp plc, 2000–. *Recreations:* tennis, riding, music. *Address:* Stoke Albany House, Market Harborough, Leics LE16 8PT. *T:* (01858) 535227. *Clubs:* White's, Mark's; Queen's; Harvard (NY).

VIOT, Jacques Edmond; Commandeur de la Légion d'Honneur; Commandeur de l'Ordre National du Mérite; President: France-Great Britain Association, since 1987; French section, Franco-British Council, since 1992; Alliance Française de Paris, since 1994; *b* 25 Aug. 1921; *m* 1950, Jeanne de Martimprey de Romécourt. *Educ:* Bordeaux and Paris Lycées; Ecole Normale Supérieure; Ecole Nationale d'Administration. Foreign Office (European Dept), 1951–53; Second Sec., London, 1953–57; First Sec., Rabat, 1957–61; Tech. Advisor to Foreign Minister, 1961–62; Head of Technical Co-operation, FO, 1962–68; Dir for Personnel and Gen. Admin, 1968–72; Ambassador to Canada, 1972–77; Gen. Inspector for Foreign Affairs, 1977–78; Directeur de Cabinet to Foreign Minister, 1978–81; Gen. Inspector for Foreign Affairs, 1981–84; Ambassador to the Court of St James's, 1984–86; Ambassadeur de France, 1986; Chm., Review Cttee on Foreign Affairs, Paris, 1986–87. Chm. Entrance Examination Bd, Ecole Nat. d'Admin, 1987. Fellow, St Antony's College, Oxford. *Address:* 19 rue de Civry, 75016 Paris, France.

VIRANI, Nazmudin Gulamhusein; Chairman and Chief Executive, Control Securities PLC, property and leisure company, 1985–92; *b* 2 March 1948; *s* of Gulamhusein Virani and Fatma Virani; *m* 1970, Yasmin Abdul Rasul Ismail; two *s* one *d*. *Educ:* Aga Khan Sch., Kampala, Uganda. Left Uganda for UK, 1972; founded Virani gp of companies, 1972 (Chm. and Chief Exec.); Chm. and Chief Exec., Belhaven PLC, 1983–86. *Recreations:* cricket, travel, philanthropy.

VIS, Dr Rudolf Jan; MP (Lab) Finchley and Golders Green, since 1997; *b* 4 April 1941; *s* of late Laurens and Helena Vis; *m* Dr Joan Hanin (marr. diss.); one *s*; *m* Jacqueline Suffling; twin *s*. *Educ:* Univ. of Maryland (BSc Econ 1970); LSE (MSc Econ 1972); Brunel Univ. (PhD Econ 1976). Dutch military service, 1960–64; USAF Base, Spain, 1964–65; Hotel Fleissig, Amsterdam, 1966; Fox Language Inst., USA, 1967; Lectr in Econs, Poly. of East London, later Univ. of East London, 1971–97. *Recreations:* walking through London, bridge. *Address:* House of Commons, SW1A 0AA. *T:* (020) 7219 4562.

VISHNEVSKAYA, Galina; soprano; *b* 25 Oct. 1926; *m* 1955, Mstislav Rostropovich, *qv*; two *d*. *Educ:* studied with Vera Garina. Toured with Leningrad Light Opera Co., 1944–48, with Leningrad Philharmonic Soc., 1948–52; joined Bolshoi Theatre, 1952. Concert appearances in Europe and USA, 1950–; first appeared at Metropolitan Opera, NY, 1961. Rôles include: Leonora in Fidelio, Tatiana in Eugene Onegin, Iolanta. Has sung in Britain at Festival Hall, Aldeburgh Festival, Edinburgh Festival, Covent Garden, Rostropovich Festival, Snape; Dir, Iolanta, Aldeburgh Fest., 1988. Makes concert tours with her husband. Has made many recordings. *Publication:* Galina (autobiog.), 1984. *Address:* c/o Victor Hochhauser, 4 Oak Hill Way, NW3 7LR.

VISSER, John Bancroft; Director of Administration, Science and Engineering Research Council (formerly Science Research Council), 1974–88; *b* 29 Jan. 1928; *o s* of late Gilbert and Ethel Visser; *m* 1955, Astrid Margareta Olson; two *s* one *d*. *Educ:* Mill Hill Sch.; New Coll., Oxford (Exhibnr). Entered Civil Service, Asst Principal, Min. of Supply, 1951; Principal, 1956; Min. of Aviation, 1959; Admin. Staff Coll., 1965; Asst Sec., 1965; Min. of Technology, 1967; Royal Coll. of Defence Studies, 1970; Civil Service Dept, 1971; Procurement Exec., MoD, 1971; Under-Sec., 1974; Sec. of Nat. Defence Industries Council, 1971–74. *Recreations:* sport, music, gardening, walking. *Address:* Rosslyn, 3 Berkeley Road, Cirencester, Glos GL7 1TY. *T:* (01285) 652626. *Club:* Old Millhillians.

VITORIA, Dr Mary Christine; QC 1997; *m* Prof. Clive Ashwin. *Educ:* Bedford Coll., London (BSc, PhD Chemistry); LLB (ext.) London Univ. Called to the Bar, Lincoln's Inn, 1975; Lectr in Law, QMC, 1977; in practice at the Bar, 1978–. Editor: Reports of Patent Cases, 1995–; Fleet Street Reports, 1995–. *Publications:* (jtly) Modern Law of Copyright and Designs, 1980, 3rd edn 2000; (contrib.) Halsbury's Laws of England, 4th edn. *Recreations:* opera, bird watching. *Address:* 8 New Square, Lincoln's Inn, WC2A 3QP. *T:* (020) 7405 4321.

VITORINO, António; Member, European Commission, since 1999; *b* 12 Jan. 1957; *m*; two *c*. *Educ:* Lisbon Law Sch. (law degree 1981; Master in Law and Pol Sci. 1986). Lawyer, 1982; Asst Prof., Lisbon Law Sch., 1982; Prof., Lisbon Autonomous Univ., 1986; Judge, Constitutional Court of Portugal, 1989–94; Vice-Pres., Portugal Telecom Internacional, 1998–99; Prof., Internat. Univ., 1998–99. Deputy (Socialist Party) Portuguese Parlt, 1980–83, 1985–89; Sec. of State for Parly Affairs, 1984–85, for Admin and Justice, Macao govt, 1986–87; Dep. Prime Minister and Minister of Defence, 1995–97; Mem., European Parlt, 1994–96. Member: Jt EP and Portuguese Parlt Cttee on European Integration, 1980–84; Sino-Portuguese Jt Liaison Gp on Macao, 1987–89. *Publications:* books on European affairs, constitutional law and pol sci. *Address:* European Commission, rue de la Loi 200, 1049 Brussels, Belgium.

VIVIAN, family name of **Barons Swansea** and **Vivian**.

VIVIAN, 6th Baron *cr* 1841; **Nicholas Crespigny Laurence Vivian;** Bt 1828; *b* 11 Dec. 1935; *s* of 5th Baron Vivian and Victoria (*d* 1985), *er d* of late Captain H. G. L. Oliphant, DSO, MVO; *S* father, 1991; *m* 1st, 1960, Catherine Joyce (marr. diss. 1972), *y d* of late James Kenneth Hope, CBE; one *s* one *d*; 2nd, 1972, Carol, *e d* of F. Alan Martineau, MBE; two *d*. *Educ:* Eton; Madrid Univ. CO 16th/5th The Queen's Royal Lancers, 1976–79; Col, MoD, 1980–84; Dep. Comdr Land Forces and Chief of Staff, Cyprus, 1984–87; Brig., 1987; Comdr, British Communication Zone (Antwerp), 1987–90. Conservative; Hon. Sec., All-Party Defence Study Gp, H of L; Mem., Statutory Instruments Cttee, 1997–; elected Mem., H of L, 1999. Member: IPU; CPA; Dep. Chm., Assoc. of Cons. Peers, 1998–. Comr, Royal Hosp. Chelsea, 1994–2000; Special Trustee, Chelsea and Westminster Hosp., 1996–. Hon. Col, 306 Field Hosp. RAMC(V), 1995–2001. *Recreation:* travel. *Heir:* *s* Hon. Charles Crespigny Hussey Vivian, *b* 20 Dec. 1966. *Address:* House of Lords, SW1A 0PW. *Clubs:* White's, Cavalry and Guards.

VIVIAN, Michael Hugh; Full-time Board Member, 1974–80, and Deputy Chairman, 1978–80, Civil Aviation Authority; *b* 15 Dec. 1919; *s* of Hugh Vivian and Mary (*née* Gilbertson); *m* 1st, 1951, June Stiven (*d* 1980); one *s* one *d*; 2nd, Joy D. Maude. *Educ:* Uppingham; Oxford. Served War: RAF (139 Sqdn), Flying Instructor, Test Pilot, 1940–44. Min. of Civil Aviation, 1945; Private Sec. to Parly Sec. for Civil Aviation, 1945–46; various operational appts, 1947–61; Dep. Dir of Flight Safety, 1961–66; Dir of Flight Safety, 1966–67; Dir of Advanced Aircraft Ops, 1967–71; Civil Aviation Authority, 1972: Dir-Gen. Safety Ops, 1972–74; Gp Dir, Safety Services, 1974–78; Dir, CSE Aviation Ltd, 1980–82. *Recreations:* golf, vintage cars. *Address:* Willow Cottage, The Dickredge, Steeple Aston, Bicester, Oxfordshire OX25 4RS. *T:* (01869) 347171. *Club:* Royal Air Force.

VLESSING, Suzanna; *see* Taverne, S.

VOBE, Helen Mary; *see* Jones, H. M.

VOCKLER, Rt Rev. John Charles, (Rt Rev. Brother John-Charles); engaged in writing and research and active preaching and teaching ministry; Founder, and Superior, Franciscan Order of the Divine Compassion, since 1990; *b* 22 July 1924; *e s* of John Thomas Vockler and Mary Catherine Vockler (*née* Widerberg), Sydney, New South Wales. *Educ:* Sydney Boys' High Sch.; after studying accountancy, matriculated by private study and correspondence (Metropolitan Business Coll. and Internat. Correspondence Schs, Sydney) to the Univ. of Sydney; Moore Theol Coll.; St John's Theol College, Morpeth, NSW; Australian Coll. of Theology (LTh 1948; Hey Sharp Prize for NT Greek); Univ. of Queensland (BA (1st cl. Hons History) 1953; Univ. Gold Medal for outstanding achievement, 1953; Walter and Eliza Hall Foundn Travelling Scholarship, 1953); Fulbright Schol., 1953; BA Univ. of Adelaide, *aegr.*, 1961; Gen. Theol Seminary, NY (MDiv 1954; STM 1956). Junior Clerk, W. R. Carpenter & Co. Ltd, Sydney, NSW, 1939–43. Deacon, 1948; priest, 1948; Asst Deacon, Christ Church Cathedral, Newcastle, 1948; Asst Priest, 1948–50; Vice-Warden of St John's Coll., Univ. of Queensland, 1950–53; Acting Chaplain, C of E Grammar Sch. for Boys, Brisbane, 1953; Acting Vice-Warden, St John's Coll., Morpeth and Lectr in Old Testament, 1953; Asst Priest, Cathedral of S John the Divine, NY and Chaplain, St Luke's Home for Aged Women and the Home for Old Men and Aged Couples, 1953–54; Australian Delegate to Anglican Congress, 1954; Fellow and Tutor, GTS, 1954–56; Asst Priest, St Stephen's Church, West 69th Street, NY, 1955; Priest-in-charge, St Stephen's, New York, 1956; Asst Priest, parish of Singleton, NSW, 1956–59; Lecturer in Theology, St John's Theol Coll., Morpeth, NSW, 1956–59; Secretary, Newcastle Diocesan Board of Education, 1958–59; Titular Bishop of Mount Gambier and Assistant Bishop of Adelaide (Coadjutor, 1959; title changed to Assistant, 1961), until 1962; also Archdeacon of Eyre Peninsula, 1959–62; Vicar-General, Examining Chaplain to Bishop of Adelaide, 1960–62; Bishop of Polynesia, 1962–68. Society of St Francis: entered Soc., 1969; professed, 1972; Chaplain, Third Order, European Province, 1972–74; made life profession, 1975; Guardian, Friary of St Francis, Brisbane, 1975–77, Islington, NSW, 1978–79; Minister Provincial, Pacific Province, 1976–81; Archivist, Amer. Province, 1985–89; left SSF, 1990; Vicar, Trinity Church, Monmouth, Ill, 1990–93; Adjunct Prof. of Ascetical Theology, Nashotah House Seminary, 1991–93; received into Anglican Catholic Church, USA, 1994: Commissary in USA for Bishop of Australia, 1994–98; Hon. Asst Bishop, dio. of Australia, 1994; Asst Bp to the Metropolitan, 1995–97; Chm., Dept of Ministry, 1996–, Dept of Evangelism, 1997; VG, dio. of Australia, 1998–; Dean, Holyrood Seminary, Liberty, NY, 1995–97 (Sub-Dean for Acad. Affairs, 1994–95); Prof. of Ascetical and Pastoral Theol., 1997. Warden: Community of St Clare, Newcastle, NSW, 1975–80; Soc. of Sacred Advent, Qld, 1976–80 (Priest Associate, 1975–); Poor Clares of Reparation, Mt Sinai, NY, 1982–83 (Bishop Protector, 1987–93); Spiritual Dir, Community of the Holy Spirit, NY, 1988–89; Bishop Visitor, Order of the Incarnation, NY, 1990–93 (Spiritual Advr, 1988–89); Spiritual Dir to Bishops and Priests of the Catholic and Apostolic Church of N America, 1988–97; Confessor Extraordinary, Soc. of St John the Evangelist, Cambridge, Mass, 1987–89; Chaplain to Monmouth Community Hosp., 1990–93. Collegial Mem., House of Bishops, Episcopal Church, USA, 1983–93; Member: House of Bishops' Cttee on Religious Life, 1986–89; Episcopal Synod of America, 1989–93. President, Harry Charman's All Races Sports and Social Club, Suva, Fiji, 1962–68, Hon. Life Vice-Pres., 1968; Chairman: S Pacific Anglican Council, 1963–68; Council of Pacific Theol Coll., 1963–68; President: Fiji Council of Social Services, 1964–68; Fiji Branch, Royal Commonwealth Soc., 1966–68. Writing Grant, Literature Bd of Australia Council, 1979, 1981. Member: Soc. of Authors; Australian Soc. of Authors; PEN (International), Sydney Br. and New York Br.; Guild of Writers Inc., NY; Christian Writers' Fellowship (USA); Aust. Professional Writers' Services; Penman Club (UK); National Writers' Club (USA); Federated Clerks Union of Aust., 1978–81; Internat. Center for Integrative Studies, NY 1983–93; Internat. Ecumenical Fellowship; Guild of All Souls; Confraternity of the Blessed Sacrament; Soc. of Mary; Catholic and Evangelical Mission; Anglican Pacifist Fellowship; Fellowship of Reconciliation; Fellowship of S Alban and S Sergius; Anglican Fellowship of Prayer, USA; Fellowship of Three Kings, Haddington, Scotland; Amnesty Internat., USA (Mem., Urgent Action Gp); Soc. of the Holy Cross, 1992–94; The Living Rosary of Our Lady and St Dominic, 1992–. Priest Associate, Shrine of Our Lady, Walsingham and Priory of Our Lady of Pew, Westminster Abbey, 1978–96; Associate, Guild of St Vincent, 1985–93; Priest Mem., OGS, 1952–75. Sec., Adv. Council for Religious Communities in Aust. and Pacific, 1976–80. Permission to officiate in various dioceses, UK, NZ, USA, Australia, 1969–93. Vice-Pres. and Mem. Council, USPG, 1973–74; Vice-Pres., Missions to Seamen, 1963–69; Hon. Asst Bp of Worcester, 1972–73; Assistant Bishop: Chelmsford, 1973–74; Southwark, 1974–75; Assisting Bishop, dio. of Quincy, USA, 1990–93; Hon. Canon of Southwark, 1975, Canon Emeritus 1975; Hon. Mission Chaplain, dio. Brisbane, 1975–79. Examnr for Aust. Coll. of Theology, 1975–76 and 1979. Patron: Monarchist League, 1993–; King Kigali V's Fund for Rwandan Children, 1993–; Mem., Australian Monarchist League, 1998–. ThD (*jure dig.*) ACT, 1961; STD (*hc*) Gen. Theological Seminary, NY, 1961; BD (*ad eund.*) Melbourne College of Divinity, 1960. Bronze Medal, Royal Aust. Life Saving Soc., 1939; Bishop's Cross, dio. of Long Is, 1989. *Publications:* Can Anglicans Believe Anything—The Nature and Spirit of Anglicanism, 1961 (NSW); Forward Day by Day, 1962; (ed) Believing in God (by M. L. Yates), 1962 (Australian edn), revd edn 1983 (US); One Man's Journey, 1972; St Francis: Franciscanism and the Society of St Francis, 1980; A School of Prayer, 1998; Seven Deadly Sins, Seven Grace-full Virtues, and Seven Mystical or Spiritual Gifts, 1999; contributions to: Preparatory Volume for Anglican Congress, Toronto, 1963; Anglican Mosaic, 1963; Mutual Responsibility: Questions and Answers, 1964; All One Body (ed T. Wilson), 1968; Australian Dictionary of Biography (4 articles); St Mark's Review, Australian Church Quarterly, The Anglican, The Young Anglican, Pacific Journal of Theology, New Zealand Theological Review, weekly feature, Newcastle Morning Herald, NSW; book reviews in Amer. theol jls; Aust. corresp. to New Fire, 1980–81; book review Editor, New York Episcopalians, 1986–91; Contributing Ed., The Trinitarian, 1995–. *Recreations:* classical music, detective stories, theatre, films, prints and engravings. *Address:* PO Box 1053, Natchitoches, LA 71458, USA; 825 Second Street, Natchitoches, LA 71458, USA. *Clubs:* Tonga (Nukualofa); St John's Coll. (Brisbane) (Hon Mem., 1976–); Returned Services League (Toronto, NSW); Gallipoli Legion (Newcastle); Royal Commonwealth Society (NSW).

VOELCKER, Christopher David, TD 1967; a District Judge (Magistrates' Courts) (formerly Metropolitan Stipendiary Magistrate), 1982–2001; *b* 10 May 1933; *s* of Eric Voelcker and Carmen Muriel Lyon Voelcker (*née* Henstock); *m* 1st, 1964, Sybil Russell Stoneham (marr. diss. 1985); two *d*; 2nd, 1991, Petrina Alexandra Keany (*née* Holdsworth). *Educ:* Wellington Coll., Berks. Called to Bar, Middle Temple, 1955. National Service, 8th King's Royal Irish Hussars, 1952–53. 3/4 County of London Yeomanry (Sharpshooters) TA, 1953–60; Kent and County of London Yeomanry (Sharpshooters) TA, 1960–67. An Asst Recorder, 1985–89; a Recorder, 1989–94. Member: Inner London Probation Cttee, 1986–92; Recruitment and Trng Cttee, Central Council of Probation for England and Wales, 1988–91. *Recreations:* military history, gardening, preserved railways. *Address:* 6 Pump Court, Temple, EC4Y 7AR. *T:* (020) 7353 7242. *Club:* Cavalry and Guards.

VOGEL, Dr Dieter H.; Chairman, Deutsche Bank AG; *b* 14 Nov. 1941; *m* 1970, Ursula Gross; two *c*. *Educ:* primary sch., Berchtesgaden; secondary sch., Frankfurt; Tech. Univ. of Darmstadt (Dip. Mech. Engrg); Tech. Univ. of Munich (Dr.Ing). Asst Prof., Thermic Turbo Engines, Tech. Univ. of Munich, 1967–69; Vice-Pres., Printing Div., Bertelsmann AG, 1970–74; Pegulan Ag, 1975–85 (Chm., 1978); Vice-Chm., Mgt Bd, Batig (BAT Industries), 1978–85; Thyssen Group, 1986–98: Chm., Thyssen Handelsunion AG, 1986–96; Mem., Exec. Bd, 1986–91, Dep. Chm., 1991–96, Chm., 1996–98, Thyssen AG. *Recreation:* ski-ing. *Address:* Koenigsallee 60A, 40212 Düsseldorf, Germany.

VOGEL, Hans-Jochen, Hon. CBE; Dr jur; Chairman: Social Democratic Party (SPD), Federal Republic of Germany, 1987–91; Gegen Vergessen-Für Demokratie eV; *b* 3 Feb. 1926; *s* of Dr Hermann Vogel and Caroline (*née* Brinz); *m* 1st, 1951, Ilse Leisnering (marr. diss. 1970); one *s* two *d*; 2nd, 1972, Liselotte Sonnenholzer. *Educ:* Göttingen and Giessen; Univs of Marburg and Munich (Dr jur 1950). Army service, 1943–45 (PoW). Admitted Bavarian Bar, 1951; Legal Asst, Bavarian Min. of Justice, 1952–54; District Court Counsel, Traunstein, 1954–58; staff of Bavarian State Chancellery, 1955–58; Munich City Council,

1958, Oberbürgermeister (Chief Executive), Munich, 1960–72 (re-elected, 1966); Vice-Pres., Org. Cttee, Olympic Games, 1972. Mayor of West Berlin, Jan.–June 1981, leader of opposition, 1981–83. Chm., Bavarian SPD, 1972–77; Mem. (SPD) Bundestag, 1972–94; Minister of regional planning, housing and urban develt, 1972–74; Minister of Justice, 1974–81; Leader of the Opposition, 1983–91. Bundesverdienstkreuz; Bavarian Verdienstorden. *Publications:* Städte im Wandel, 1971; Die Amtskette: Meine 12 Münchner Jahre, 1972; Reale Reformen, 1973; Nachsichten, 1996. *Recreations:* mountaineering, swimming, reading history. *Address:* Gegen Vergessen-Für Demokratie eV, Max Planck Strasse 3, 53177 Bonn, Germany. *T:* (228) 933890, *Fax:* (228) 9338920.

VOGELPOEL, Pauline, (Mrs R. D. Mann), MBE 1962; Vice-President, Contemporary Art Society, since 1984; *d* of late Pieter Vogelpoel and Yvonne Vogelpoel, Mozambique; *m* 1975, Richard David Mann, *s* of F. A. Mann, CBE, FBA. *Educ:* Herschel School, Cape Town; University of Cape Town (BA). Joined Contemporary Art Society, 1954, as Organising Secretary; Director 1976–82. Zurich Editor, Harpers & Queen Magazine, 1982–86. Member: Adv. Council, Victoria and Albert Museum, 1977–82; Internat. Council, Tate Gall., 1997–. *Publications:* occasional journalism. *Recreations:* cooking, music, junkshops, pugs. *Address:* Hebelstrasse 15, 4056 Basle, Switzerland.

VOGT, Dr Marthe Louise, FRS 1952; Dr med Berlin, Dr phil Berlin; PhD Cantab; *b* 1903; *d* of Oskar Vogt and Cécile Vogt (*née* Mugnier). *Educ:* Auguste Viktoria-Schule, Berlin; University of Berlin. Research Assistant, Department of Pharmacology, Berlin Univ., 1930; Research Assistant and head of chemical division, Kaiser Wilhelm Institut für Hirnforschung, Berlin, 1931–35; Rockefeller Travelling Fellow, 1935–36; Research Worker, Dept of Pharmacology, Cambridge Univ., 1935–40; Alfred Yarrow Research Fellow of Girton Coll., 1937–40; Member Staff of College of Pharmaceutical Society, London, 1941–46; Lecturer, later Reader, in Pharmacology, University of Edinburgh, 1947–60; Head of Pharmacology Unit, Agricultural Research Council Institute of Animal Physiology, 1960–68. Vis. Associate Prof. in Pharmacology, Columbia Univ., New York, 1949; Vis. Prof., Sydney 1965, Montreal 1968. Life Fellow, Girton Coll., Cambridge, 1970. For. Hon. Mem., Amer. Acad. of Arts and Scis, 1977. Hon. Fellow RSM 1980. Corresp. Mem., Deutsche Physiologische Gesellschaft, 1976; Hon. Member: Physiological Soc., 1974; British Pharmacological Soc., 1971; Hungarian Acad. of Scis, 1981; British Assoc. for Psychopharmacol., 1983. Hon. DSc: Edinburgh, 1974; Cambridge, 1983. Royal Medal, Royal Soc., 1981. *Publications:* papers in neurological, physiological and pharmacological journals. *Address:* Chateau La Jolla Terrace, 7544 La Jolla Boulevard, La Jolla, CA 92037, USA.

VOLCKER, Paul A.; Frederick H. Schultz Professor of International Economic Policy, Princeton University, 1988–96, now Emeritus; Chairman, James D. Wolfensohn Incorporated, 1988–96; *b* Cape May, New Jersey, 5 Sept. 1927; *s* of Paul A. Volcker and Alma Louise Klippel; *m* 1954, Barbara Marie Bahnson (*d* 1998); one *s* one *d*. *Educ:* Princeton Univ. (AB *summa cum laude*); Harvard Univ. (MA); LSE. Special Asst, Securities Dept, Fed. Reserve Bank, NY, 1953–57; Financial Economist, Chase Manhattan Bank, NYC, 1957–62; Vice-Pres. and Dir of Forward Planning, 1965–69; Dir, Office of Financial Analysis, US Treasury Dept, 1962–63; Dep. Under-Sec. for Monetary Affairs, 1963–65; Under-Sec. for Monetary Affairs, 1969–74; Senior Fellow, Woodrow Wilson Sch. of Public and Internat. Affairs, Princeton Univ., 1974–75; Pres. NY Federal Reserve Bank, 1975–79; Chairman: American Federal Reserve Board, 1979–87; J. Rothschild, Wolfensohn & Co., 1992–95. Chairman: Trilateral Commn, 1992–2001; Group of Thirty, 2000– (Mem., 1989–); Internat. Accounting Standards Cttee, IASC Foundn, 2001–. *Address:* 151 E 79th Street, New York, NY 10021, USA; (office) 610 Fifth Avenue, Suite 420, New York, NY 10020, USA. *T:* (212) 2187878.

VOLGER, Dr Hendrik Cornelis; Manager, Sittingbourne Research Centre, and Director, Shell Research Ltd, 1989–93; *b* 6 March 1932; *s* of Ferdinand Pieter and Marijtje Spaans Volger; *m* 1959, Aaltje Roorda; two *d*. *Educ:* Univ. of Groningen (PhD). Lieut, Special Branch, Royal Dutch Air Force, 1958–59; Ramsay Fellow, UCL, 1959–60; Shell Research BV, Amsterdam, 1960 and 1969–75; Shell Development Co., USA, 1968–69; Director: Shell Milstead Lab., 1975–77; Shell Biotech. Res., 1977–83; Product Res. Lab., Amsterdam, 1983–89. Mem., Royal Dutch Akademie of Science, 1987. AKZO Prize, 1972. *Publications:* Organic Chemistry, 1956; Organometal Complexes, 1961; Homogenous Catalysis, 1965. *Recreations:* tennis, gardening.

VOLHARD, Christiane N.; *see* Nüsslein-Volhard.

VOLLRATH, Prof. Lutz Ernst Wolf; Professor of Histology and Embryology, University of Mainz, Germany, since 1974; *b* 2 Sept. 1936; *s* of Pastor Richard Hermann Vollrath and Rita (*née* Brügmann); *m* 1963, Gisela (*née* Dialer); three *d*. *Educ:* Ulrich von Hutten-Schule, Berlin; Univs of Berlin, Kiel and Tübingen. Dr med Kiel, 1961. Wissenschaftlicher Assistent, Dept of Anatomy, Würzburg, Germany, 1963; Res. Fellow, Dept of Anatomy, Birmingham, 1964; Wissenschaftlicher Assistent, Dept of Anatomy, Würzburg, 1965–71 (Privatdozent, 1968; Oberassistent, 1969; Universitätsdozent, 1970); King's College London: Reader in Anatomy, 1971; Prof. of Anatomy, 1973–74. Hon. Mem., Romanian Soc. of Anatomists, 1996; Corresp. Mem., Saxonian Acad. of Scis in Leipzig, 1998; Hon. Mem., Anatomy Assoc., Costa Rica, 1999. Editor: Cell & Tissue Research, 1978–96; Annals of Anatomy, 1992–. *Publications:* (co-editor) Neurosecretion: the final neuroendocrine pathway, 1974; The Pineal Organ, 1981; (ed) Handbook of Microscopic Anatomy (formerly Handbuch der mikr. Anat. des Menschen) (series), 1978–; research publications on histochemistry and ultrastructure of organogenesis and various aspects of neuroendocrinology, in Annals of Anatomy, Z Zellforsch., Histochemie, Phil. Trans Royal Society B, Erg. Anat. Entw.gesch. *Recreations:* gardening, tennis. *Address:* c/o Anatomisches Institut, 55099 Mainz, Saarstr. 19/21, Germany.

von DOHNÁNYI, Christoph; Principal Conductor, Philharmonia Orchestra, London, since 1997; *b* 8 Sept. 1929; *m* 1st, 1957, Renate Zillessen (marr. diss.); one *s* one *d*; 2nd, 1979, Anja Silja, *qv*; one *s* two *d*. *Educ:* 2 years' law study; Musikhochschule, Munich; Florida State Univ.; with grandfather Ernst von Dohnányi in USA. Coach and asst conductor, Frankfurt Opera, 1953; Gen. Music Dir, Lübeck and Kassel, 1957–68; Chief Conductor, Radiosymphonie Orch., Cologne, 1964–70; London début with LPO, 1965; Gen. Music Dir, Frankfurt Opera, 1968–77; Dir, Städtische Bühnen, Frankfurt, 1972–77; Intendant and Chief Conductor, Hamburg Opera, 1977; Music Dir, Cleveland Orch., 1984–99; Guest Conductor of major orchestras and opera houses in Europe, Israel and USA; Artistic Advr, l'Orch. de Paris, 1998–. Numerous recordings; honours, music prizes and hon. doctorates. *Address:* c/o Harrison Parrott, 12 Penzance Place, W11 4PA.

von ETZDORF, Georgina Louise, RDI 1997; Artistic Director, Georgina von Etzdorf, since 1981; *b* 1 Jan. 1955; *d* of late Roderick Rudiger von Etzdorf and of Audrey von Etzdorf (*née* Catterns). *Educ:* Downe House; St Martin's Sch. of Art; Camberwell Sch. of Art (BA Hons 1977). Freelance textile designer, 1978–79; freelance designer, developing designs from paper work and silk screens on to fabric, 1979–80; Founder, Georgina von Etzdorf Partnership, 1981; artistic dir of team producing biannual collections of clothing and accessories, 1992–. Lectures and teaching posts: Cooper Hewitt Mus., NYC; Nova Scotia Sch. of Art and Design; Glasgow Coll. of Art; St Martin's Sch. of Art; Royal Coll. of Art; Crafts Council. *Exhibitions:* Smithsonian Instn's Nat. Mus. of Design, Washington; Cooper Hewitt Mus., NY; V & A. Hon. DDes Winchester Sch. of Art, Univ. of Southampton, 1996. Enterprise Award for Small Businesses, Radio 4, 1984; British Apparel Export Award, 1986; Manchester Prize for Art and Industry, British Gas Award, 1988. *Recreations:* singing, dancing, playing the ukelele. *Address:* Odstock Road, Odstock, Salisbury, Wilts SP5 4NZ. *T:* (01722) 343000, *Fax:* (01722) 338541. *Club:* Chelsea Arts.

von HASE, Karl-Günther, Hon. GCVO 1972; Hon. KCMG 1965; Hon. President, Deutsch-Englische Gesellschaft, Düsseldorf, since 1993 (Chairman, 1982–93); *b* 15 Dec. 1917; *m* 1945, Renate Stumpff; five *d*. *Educ:* German schools. Professional Soldier, 1936–45; War Academy, 1943–44; Training College for Diplomats, 1950–51; Georgetown Univ., Washington DC, 1952. German Foreign Service: German Embassy, Ottawa, 1953–56; Spokesman, Foreign Office Bonn, 1958–61; Head, West European Dept, 1961–62; Spokesman of German Federal Government, 1962–67; State Secretary, Min. of Defence, German Federal Govt, 1968–69; German Ambassador to the Court of St James's, 1970–77; Dir-Gen., Zweites Deutsches Fernsehen, 1977–82. Hon. LLD Manchester, 1987. Holds German and other foreign decorations. *Recreations:* shooting, music. *Address:* Am Stadtwald 60, 53177 Bonn, Germany.

von KLITZING, Prof. Klaus, PhD; Director, Max-Planck-Institut für Festkörperforschung, Stuttgart, since 1985; *b* 28 June 1943; *s* of Bogislav and Anny von Klitzing; *m* 1971, Renate Falkenberg; two *s* one *d*. *Educ:* Technische Univ., Braunschweig (Dipl Phys); Univ. of Würzburg (PhD; Habilitation (univ. teaching qual.). Prof., Technische Univ., München, 1980–84; Hon. Prof., Univ. of Stuttgart, 1985. Nobel Prize for Physics, 1985. *Address:* Max-Planck-Institut für Festkörperforschung, Heisenbergstrasse 1, 70569 Stuttgart, Federal Republic of Germany. *T:* (711) 6891570.

von KUENHEIM, Eberhard; Chairman: Executive Board, 1970–93, Supervisory Board, since 1993, BMW AG, Munich; *b* 2 Oct. 1928, E Prussia. *Educ:* Stuttgart Technical Univ. (Diplom-Ingenieur; MSc). Technical Dir, Machine tool factory, Hanover, 1954–65; joined QUANDT Gp, 1965; Dep. Chm., Exec. Bd., Industriewerke Karlsruhe Augsburg AG, 1968–70. Mem. Supervisory Board: Bayerische Vereinsbank, Munich; Royal Dutch Petroleum Co.; Münchner Rückversicherungsges; Delton AG. Mem. Senate, Max Planck Soc. for Advancement of Scis. Hon. Senator, Munich Technical Univ. Hon. doctorates: Clausthal-Zellerfeld Technical Univ.; Munich Technical Univ. *Address:* 80788 Munich, Petuelring 130, Germany.

von MALLINCKRODT, Georg Wilhelm, Hon. KBE 1997; President, Schroders plc, since 1995 (Chairman, 1984–95; Director, since 1977); Chairman, Schroders Incorporated, New York, since 1985; Chairman, J. Henry Schroder Bank AG, Zurich, since 1984; *b* 19 Aug. 1930; *s* of Arnold Wilhelm von Mallinckrodt and Valentine von Mallinckrodt (*née* von Joest); *m* 1958, Charmaine Brenda Schroder; two *s* two *d*. *Educ:* Salem, West Germany. Agfa AG Munich, 1948–51; Münchmeyer & Co., Hamburg, 1951–53; Kleinwort Sons & Co., London, 1953–54; J. Henry Schroder Banking Corp., New York, 1954–55; Union Bank of Switzerland, Geneva 1956; J. Henry Schroder Banking Corp., NY, 1957–60; J. Henry Schroder & Co., subseq. J. Henry Schroder Wagg & Co., London, 1960–85, Director, 1967–; Chm. and Chief Exec. Officer, J. Henry Schroder Bank & Trust Co., NY, 1984–86. Director: Schroder Asseily & Co., 1981–; Schroders Australia Hldgs Ltd, Sydney, 1984–; NM UK, 1986–90; Euris SA, Paris, 1987–; Schroder Internat. Merchant Bankers, 1988–2000; Siemens plc, 1989–; Foreign & Colonial German Investment Trust PLC, 1992–98. Vice-Pres., German Chamber of Industry and Commerce in UK, 1971–; Member: Europ. Adv. Cttee, McGraw Hill Inc., USA, 1986–89; Supervisory Bd, Trader.com, 2000; Dir, Europ. Arts Foundn, 1987–; Pres., German-British Chamber of Industry and Commerce, 1992–95. Member: British N American Cttee, 1988–; City Adv. Gp, CBI, 1990–. Pres., German YMCA, London, 1961–; Member: Ct of Benefactors, Oxford Univ., 1990–; Nat. Art Collection Develt Fund, 1995–; BM Develt Trust, 1995–; Trustee, Prague Heritage Fund, 1992. FRSA 1986; CIMgt (CBIM 1986). Hon. DCL Bishop's Univ., Canada, 1994. Verdienstkreuz am Bande des Verdienstordens (FRG), 1986; Verdienstkreuz 1 Klasse des Verdienstordens (FRG), 1990. *Recreations:* music, gardening, shooting, ski-ing. *Address:* Schroders plc, 120 Cheapside, EC2V 6DS. *T:* (020) 7658 6000.

von MOLTKE, Gebhardt; Permanent Representative of the Federal Republic of Germany to NATO, since 1999; *b* 28 June 1938; *s* of late Hans-Adolf von Moltke and Davida, Gräfin Yorck von Wartenburg; *m* 1965, Dorothea Bräuer; one *s* one *d*. *Educ:* Univs of Grenoble, Berlin, Freiburg (Law); qualified as lawyer, 1967. German Trade Unions, 1967–68; Fed. Republic of Germany Diplomatic Service, 1968–: served Liverpool, Cabinet of Foreign Minister, Moscow, Jaoundé/Cameroon, and Foreign Office Personnel Dept; Washington Embassy, 1982–86; Head, US Desk, Foreign Office, 1986–91; Asst Sec.-Gen. for Political Affairs, NATO HQ, Brussels, 1991–97; Ambassador to UK, 1997–99. *Recreations:* music, art (Italian drawings), reading, tennis. *Address:* NATO, Boulevard Léopold III, 1110 Brussels, Belgium.

VONNEGUT, Kurt, Jr; writer; *b* Indianapolis, 11 Nov. 1922; *m* 1st, 1945, Jane Marie Cox (marr. diss. 1979; decd); one *s* two *d*; 2nd, 1979, Jill Krementz. *Educ:* Cornell Univ.; Carnegie Inst. of Technol.; Univ. of Chicago. Served War, US Army, 1942–45 (POW). Reporter, Chicago City News Bureau, 1945–47; PRO, GEC, Schenectady, 1947–50; freelance writer, 1950–65; Lectr, Writers' Workshop, Univ. of Iowa, 1965–67; Guggenheim Fellow, 1967–68; Lectr in English, Harvard, 1970; Dist. Prof., City Coll., New York, 1973–74. Mem., National Inst. of Arts and Letters. *Publications:* Player Piano, 1951; The Sirens of Titan, 1959; Mother Night, 1961; Cat's Cradle, 1963; God Bless You, Mr Rosewater, 1964; Welcome to the Monkey House (short stories), 1968; Slaughterhouse-Five, 1969; Happy Birthday, Wanda June (play), 1970; Between Time and Timbuktu or Prometheus-5 (TV script), 1972; Breakfast of Champions, 1973; Wampeters, Foma and Granfalloons (essays), 1974; Slapstick, or Lonesome No More, 1976; Jailbird, 1979; (with Ivan Chermayeff) Sun Moon Star, 1980; Palm Sunday (autobiog.), 1981; Deadeye Dick, 1982; Galapagos, 1985; Bluebeard, 1988; Hocus Pocus, 1990; Fates Worse Than Death (essays and speeches), 1991; Timequake, 1997; Bagombo Snuff Box, 1999. *Address:* c/o Donald C. Farber Esq., 6th Floor, 750 Lexington Avenue, New York, NY 10022, USA.

von OTTER, Anne Sofie; singer (mezzo-soprano); *b* Stockholm, 9 May 1955. *Educ:* Stockholm Acad. of Music; GSMD; vocal studies with Vera Rozsa, 1981–. With Basle Opera, 1983–85; freelance, 1985–; appearances at most major opera houses incl. Covent Garden, 1985–; Metropolitan Opera, 1985–; La Scala, Milan, 1987–; Geneva, Aix-en-Provence, Paris, Vienna, Chicago, Berlin and Munich; has also given recitals in many European countries. Rôles include: Mozart: Cherubino, Sextus, Idamante, Dorabella, Ramiro; Strauss: Octavian, Clairon, Componist; Bellini: Romeo; Rossini: Tancredi, Cenerentola; Gluck: Orfeo; Monteverdi: Nerone; Handel: Ariodante. Major recordings include: Così fan tutte; Orfeo ed Euridice; Hansel and Gretel; Der Rosenkavalier; Le

Nozze di Figaro; Idomeneo; Ariodante; Werther; Les Contes d'Hoffmann; La Damnation de Faust; Nuits d'Eté, Mahler cycles, and lieder by Mahler, Brahms, Grieg, Wolf, etc. *Address:* c/o IMG, Lovell House, 616 Chiswick High Road, W4 5RX. *T:* (020) 8747 9977.

von PLOETZ, Dr Hans-Friedrich; Ambassador of the Federal Republic of Germany to the Court of St James's, since 1999; *b* 12 July 1940; *m* 1971, Päivi Leinonen; two *s*. Diplomatic posts in: Morocco, 1967–68; Helsinki, 1968–73; Min. for Foreign Affairs, 1973–78; Washington, 1978–80; Min. for Foreign Affairs, 1980–88; Dep. Perm. Rep. of Germany, 1988–89, Ambassador and Perm. Rep. of Germany, 1989–93, on NATO Council; Dir-Gen. for Eur. Integration, Bonn, 1993–94; State Sec., Min. for Foreign Affairs, Bonn, 1994–99. *Recreations:* music, golf, gardening. *Address:* German Embassy, 23 Belgrave Square, SW1X 8PZ. *T:* (020) 7824 1302, *Fax:* (020) 7824 1315.

von REITZENSTEIN, Hans-Joachim Freiherr; *see* Leech, John.

von RICHTHOFEN, Baron Hermann, Hon. GCVO 1992; Permanent Representative of the Federal Republic of Germany to NATO, 1993–98; *b* 20 Nov. 1933; *s* of Baron Herbert von Richthofen and Baroness Gisela von Richthofen (*née* Schoeller); *m* 1966, Christa, Countess von Schwerin; one *s* two *d*. *Educ:* Univs of Heidelberg, Munich and Bonn; Dr in law Cologne Univ. 1963. Joined Diplomatic Service of FRG, 1963; served Boston, Mass, 1963–64; FO, 1964–66; Saigon, 1966–68; Jakarta, 1968–70; FO, 1970–74; Dep. Hd, Sect. for Internat. Law, FO, 1974; Hd, Sect. for For. Policy, Perm. Mission to GDR, 1975–78; Hd of Dept for German and Berlin Affairs, FO, 1978–80; seconded to Fed. Chancellery as Hd of Intra-German Policy Unit, 1980–86; Dir Gen. of Legal Div., 1986, of Political Div., and Political Dir, 1986–88, FO; Ambassador to UK, 1988–93. Chm., British-German Assoc., Berlin, 1998–. Gov., Ditchley Foundn, 1988–93, 1996–. Trustee, 21st Century Trust, 1998–. Hon. LLD Birmingham. ER 1961, RR 1985; Officer's Cross, Order of the Knights of Malta, 1967; Commander's Cross: Order of Merit (Italy), 1979; Legion of Honour (France), 1987; Grand Officer's Cross, Order of Infante D. Henrique (Portugal), 1988; Knight Commander's Cross, 2nd class (Austria), 1989; Grand Cross, Order of Merit (FRG), 1999; Grand Cross, Order of Merit (Luxembourg), 2000. *Recreations:* ski-ing, swimming, gardening, reading history, arts. *Address:* Beckerstrasse 6a, 12157 Berlin, Germany.

von SCHRAMEK, Sir Eric (Emil), Kt 1982; architect; Chairman, von Schramek and Dawes Pty Ltd, 1963–91; Consultant to Hames Sharley International, Architects and Planners, 1989–97; *b* 4 April 1921; *s* of Emil and Annie von Schramek; *m* Edith, *d* of Dipl. Ing. W. Popper; one *s* two *d*. *Educ:* Stefans Gymnasium, Prague; Technical Univ., Prague. DiplIngArch; Life Fellow: RAIA; Inst. of Arbitrators and Mediators of Aust. Town Planner, Bavaria, 1946–48; Sen. Supervising Architect, Dept of Works and Housing, Darwin, NT, 1948–51; Evans, Bruer & Partners (later von Schramek and Dawes), 1951–91: work includes multi-storey office buildings in Adelaide (Nat. Mutual Centre; State Govt Insce Bldg; Wales House; Qantas Bldg, etc); Wesley House, Melbourne; Westpac House, Hobart; AMP Bldg and Qantas Bldg, Darwin; numerous churches throughout Australia and New Guinea. National Pres., Building Science Forum of Aust., 1970–72; President: RAIA (SA Chapter), 1974–76; Inst. of Arbitrators, Aust. (SA Chapter), 1977–80. Vis. Lectr, Univ. of Adelaide; former Vis. Lectr, S Australian Inst. of Technol. Past National Dep. Chm., Austcare; past Councillor, Council of Professions; past Chm., Commn on Worship and other Depts, Lutheran Church of Australia. Hon. Associate (Arch.), SA Inst. of Technology, 1989. KSJ 1995. *Publications:* contribs and articles in architectural pubns. *Recreations:* music, reading, golf. *Address:* The Olives, PO Box 457, Yankalilla, SA 5203, Australia. *T:* (8) 85583341.

von WECHMAR, Baron Rüdiger, Hon. GCVO 1986; Member (FDP) for Germany, European Parliament, 1989–94; *b* 15 Nov. 1923; *s* of Irnfried von Wechmar and Ilse (*née* von Binzer); *m* 1961, Dina-Susanne (Susie) (*née* Woldenga); one *d* (one *s* one *d* of previous marr.). *Educ:* Oberrealschule, Berlin; Univ. of Minnesota, USA (as prisoner of war). MA Journalism. Army, 3rd Reconnaissance Battalion, Western Desert and PoW Camp, 1941–46. Journalist, 1946–58; joined German Foreign Service as Consul, New York, 1958; Dir, German Inf. Centre, NY; Dep. Head, Govt Press and Inf. Office, Bonn, 1969; State Sec. and Chief Govt Spokesman, 1972; Perm. Rep. to UN, 1974–81; Pres., UN Security Council, 1977–78; Pres., 35th Gen. Assembly, UN, 1980–81; Ambassador to Italy, 1981–83; Ambassador to UK, 1983–88. Commander's Cross, Order of Merit (FRG), 1980; decorations from UK, Sweden, Norway, Japan, Netherlands, Egypt, Mexico, Italy, Romania. Paul Klinger Award, DAG, 1973; UN Peace Gold Medal, 1980. *Address:* Hiltenspergerstrasse 15, 80798 München, Germany.

von WEIZSÄCKER, Freiherr Carl-Friedrich, Dr Phil; University Professor Emeritus; *b* Kiel, 28 June 1912; *m* 1937, Gundalena (*née* Wille); three *s* one *d*. *Educ:* Universities of Berlin, Leipzig, Göttingen, Copenhagen, 1929–33. Dr.phil 1933, Dr.phil.habil, 1936, Univ. Leipzig; Asst., Inst. of Theor. Physik, Univ. of Leipzig, 1934–36; Wissenschaftl. Mitarb., Kaiser Wilhelm Inst., Berlin, 1936–42; Dozent, Univ. of Berlin, 1937–42; pl. ao. Prof. Theor. Physik, Univ. of Strassburg, 1942–44; Kaiser-Wilhelm-Inst., Berlin and Hechingen, 1944–45; Hon. Prof., Univ. Göttingen and Abt. Leiter, Max Planck Inst. für Physik, Göttingen, 1946–57; Ord. Prof. of Philosophy, Univ. of Hamburg, 1957–69. Hon. Prof., Univ. of Munich, and Dir, Max-Planck-Institut on the preconditions of human life in the modern world, 1970–80. Gifford Lecturer, Glasgow Univ., 1959–61. Member: Deutsche Akademie der Naturforscher Leopoldina, Halle; Akademie der Wissenschaften, Göttingen; Joachim-Jungius-Gesellschaft der Wissenschaften, Hamburg; Bayerische Akademie der Wissenschaften, München; Österreichische Akademie der Wissenschaften, Wien; Sächsische Akademie der Wissenschaften zu Leipzig. Verdienstorden der Bundesrepublik Deutschland, 1959–73; Orden Pour le Mérite für Wissenschaften und Künste, 1961; Max Planck Medal, 1957; Goethe Prize (Frankfurt) 1958; Friedenspreis des deutschen Buchhandels, 1963; Erasmus Prize (with Gabriel Marcel), 1969; Templeton Prize for Progress in Religion (jtly), 1989. Hon. Dr theol: Univ. Tübingen, 1977; Univ. Basel, 1989; Hon. Dr iur Free Univ., Amsterdam, 1977; Hon. LLD: Alberta, Canada, 1981; Aberdeen, 1989; Hon. Dr rer. nat. Karl-Marx-Univ., Leipzig, 1987. Dr.phil *hc*: Technische Univ., Berlin, 1987; Aachen, 1988. *Publications:* Die Atomkerne, 1937; Zum Weltbild der Physik, 11th edn, 1970 (English, London, 1952); Die Geschichte der Natur, 7th edn, 1970 (English, Chicago, 1949); Physik der Gegenwart (with J. Juilfs), 2nd edn, 1958 (Engl., 1957); Die Verantwortung der Wissenschaft im Atomzeitalter, 5th edn, 1969; Atomenergie und Atomzeitalter, 3rd edn, 1958; Bedingungen des Friedens, 1963, 5th edn, 1970; Die Tragweite der Wissenschaft, 1964; Der ungesicherte Friede, 1969; Die Einheit der Natur, 1971, 3rd edn, 1972; (ed) Kriegsfolgen und Kriegsverhütung, 1970, 3rd edn, 1971; Voraussetzungen der naturwissenschaftlichen Denkens, 1972, 2nd edn, 1972; Fragen zur Weltpolitik, 1975; Wege in der Gefahr, 1976; Der Garten des Menschlichen, Beiträge zur geschichtlichen Anthropologie, 1977; Deutlichkeit, Beiträge zu politischen und religiösen Gegenwartsfragen, 1978; Der bedrohte Friede, 1981; Wahrnehmung der Neuzeit, 1983; Aufbau der Physik, 1985; Die Zeit drängt — Eine Weltversammlung der Christen für Gerechtigkeit, Frieden und die Bewahrung der Schöpfung, 1986; Bewusstseinswandel, 1988; Bedingungen der Freiheit, 1990; Der Mensch in seiner Geschichte, 1991; Zeit und Wissen, 1992; Der bedrohte Friede-heute, 1994; Wohin gehen wir?, 1994; Grosse Physiker, 1999; *relevant publication:* bibliography in Einheit und Vielheit, Festschrift ... ed Scheibe and Süssmann, 1973. *Recreations:* hiking, chess. *Address:* 82319 Starnberg, Maximilianstrasse 14c, Germany.

See also R. von Weizsäcker.

von WEIZSÄCKER, Richard, Dr jur; President of the Federal Republic of Germany, 1984–94; *b* 15 April 1920; *s* of late Baron Ernst von Weizsäcker; *m* 1953, Marianne von Kretschmann; three *s* one *d*. *Educ:* Berlin and Bern; Univs of Oxford, Grenoble and Göttingen (Dr jur). Army service, 1938–45 (Captain, wounded). Formerly with Allianz Lebensversicherung, Stuttgart and Robeco-Gruppe, Amsterdam. Member: Robert Bosch Foundn, Stuttgart; Synod and Council, German Evangelical Church, 1969– (Pres., Congress). Joined Christian Democratic Union, 1954: Mem., Fed. Board; Chm., Gen. Policy Commn, 1971–74; Chm., Basic Prog. Commn, 1974–77; Dep. Chm., CDU/CSU Parlt Gp, 1972–79; Presidential candidate, 1974; First Chm., Berlin CDU, 1981–83. Mem., Bundestag, 1969–81, Vice-Pres., 1979–81; Governing Mayor of West Berlin, 1981–84. Royal Victorian Chain, 1992. *Address:* (office) Am Kupfergraben 7, 10117 Berlin, Germany.

See also Carl-Friedrich von Weizsäcker.

von WINTERFELDT, (Hans) Dominik; Managing Partner, Boyden International GmbH, since 1996; Partner, Boyden World Corporation, New York, since 1996; *b* 3 July 1937; *s* of late Curt von Winterfeldt and Anna Franziska Margaretha Luise (*née* Petersen); *m* 1966, Cornelia Waldthausen; one *s* one *d*. *Educ:* German schools; Stanford-INSEAD, Fontainebleau (Industriekaufmann). DipICC. Joined Hoechst AG, Frankfurt/Main, 1957; Asst Manager, Hoechst Colombiana Ltda, 1960; Commercial Manager, Pharmaceuticals, Hoechst Peruana SA, 1963; General Manager, Hoechst Dyechemie W. L. L., Iraq, 1965; Man. Dir, Hoechst Pakistan Ltd and Hoechst Pharmaceuticals Ltd, 1967; Hoechst UK Ltd: Dep. Man. Dir, 1972; Man. Dir and Chief Exec., 1975; Exec. Chm., 1984; Dir (Corporate PR and Communications), 1987–94; Dir, Cassella AG, 1994–95. Member: British Deer Soc., 1979–; British Assoc. for Shooting and Conservation, 1979–. *Recreations:* music, deer stalking, golf. *Address:* Boyden International GmbH, Ferdinandstrasse 6, 61348 Bad Homburg, Germany. *T:* (6172) 180200.

VORDERMAN, Carol Jean, MBE 2000; broadcaster and author; *b* 24 Dec. 1960; *d* of Anton Joseph Maria Vorderman and Edwina Jean Vorderman; *m* 1st, 1985, Christopher Mather (marr. diss. 1987); 2nd, 1990, Patrick John King; one *s* one *d*. *Educ:* Blessed Edward Jones High Sch., Rhyl; Sidney Sussex Coll., Cambridge (MA). Mem., Action into Engrg Task Force, DTI, 1995. Founder Mem. and Trustee, NESTA, 1998–. Television programmes include: Countdown, 1982–; World Chess Championship (Kasparov *v* Short), 1993; Tomorrow's World, 1994–95; Computers Don't Bite, 1997; Mysteries with Carol Vorderman, 1997–98; Dream House, 1998–99; Carol Vorderman's Better Homes, 1999–; Carol Vorderman's Better Gardens, 1999–2000; Find a Fortune, 1999–; Star Lives (formerly Stars and Their Lives), 1999–; Tested to Destruction, 1999; Pride of Britain Awards Ceremony, 2000, 2001. Columnist: Daily Telegraph, 1996–98; Mirror, 1998–. FRSA 1997. Hon. Fellow, Univ. of Wales, Bangor, 1999. Hon. MA Bath, 2000. *Publications:* Dirty, Loud and Brilliant, 1988; Dirty, Loud and Brilliant Too, 1989; How Mathematics Works, 1996; (with R. Young) Carol Vorderman's Guide to the Internet, 1998, 2nd edn 2001; Maths Made Easy, 1999; Science Made Easy, 2000; English Made Easy, 2000; Educating and Entertaining Your Children Online with Carol Vorderman, 2001. *Address:* c/o John Miles Organisation, Cadbury Camp Lane, Clapton-in-Gordano, Bristol BS20 7SB. *T:* (01275) 854675.

VOS, Geoffrey Charles; QC 1993; *b* 22 April 1955; *s* of Bernard Vos and Pamela Celeste Rose (*née* Heilbuth); *m* 1984, Vivien Mary Fieldhouse (*née* Dowdeswell); one *d* and one step *s* two step *d*. *Educ:* University College Sch., London; Gonville and Caius Coll., Cambridge (BA, MA). Called to the Bar, Inner Temple, 1977; Bencher, Lincoln's Inn, 2000. Chm., Chancery Bar Assoc., 1999–2001 (Hon. Sec., 1994–97; Vice-Chm., 1997–99). Bar Council: Chm., Fees Collection Cttee, 1995–; Vice Chm., Professional Standards Cttee, 2001. *Recreations:* farming, wine, photography. *Address:* 3 Stone Buildings, Lincoln's Inn, WC2A 3XL. *Clubs:* Oxford and Cambridge; Worcestershire Golf.

VOS, His Honour Geoffrey Michael; a Circuit Judge, 1978–94; *b* 18 Feb. 1927; *s* of Louis and Rachel Eva Vos; *m* 1955, Marcia Joan Goldstone (marr. diss. 1977); two *s* two *d*; *m* 1981, Mrs Anne Wilson. *Educ:* St Joseph's College, Blackpool; Gonville and Caius College, Cambridge. MA, LLB. Called to the Bar, Gray's Inn, 1950. A Recorder of the Crown Court, 1976–78. *Recreations:* swimming, walking. *Address:* c/o The Crown Court, The Law Courts, Quayside, Newcastle upon Tyne NE1 3LA. *T:* (0191) 201 2000.

VOSPER, Christopher John; QC 2000; a Recorder, since 1998; *b* 4 Oct. 1952; *s* of John Darvel Vosper and Hettie Vosper; *m* 1982, Ann Prosser Bowen; one *s* one *d*. *Educ:* Cowbridge Grammar Sch.; Pembroke Coll., Oxford (MA). Called to the Bar, Middle Temple, 1977; in practice as barrister, 1977–. *Address:* 3 Mayals Road, Blackpill, Swansea SA3 5BT; (chambers) Farrar's Building, Temple, EC4Y 7BD.

VOWLES, Paul Foster; Academic Registrar, University of London, 1973–82; *b* 12 June 1919; *s* of late E. F. Vowles and G. M. Vowles, Bristol; *m* 1948, Valerie Eleanor Hickman; one *s* two *d*. *Educ:* Bristol Grammar Sch.; Corpus Christi Coll., Oxford (schol.; MA). Served Gloucestershire Regt and King's African Rifles, 1939–46 (despatches, Major). Asst Secretary: Appts Bd, Univ. of Birmingham, 1947–48; Inter-University Council for Higher Educn Overseas, 1948–51; Registrar, Makerere University Coll., E Africa, 1951–63; Sen. Asst to Principal, Univ. of London, 1964–68; Warden, Lillian Penson Hall, 1965–69; External Registrar, 1968–73. Mem., 1983–89, Vice-Chm., 1986–89, Westfield Coll. Council. Hon. Fellow, QMW (Fellow, 1991). *Address:* 13 Dale Close, Oxford OX1 1TU. *T:* (01865) 244042. *Club:* Athenæum.

VRAALSEN, Tom; Commander, Royal Order of Saint Olav 1987; Norwegian Ambassador to Finland, since 2001; *b* 26 Jan. 1936; *m* 1977, Viebecke Strøm; two *d*. *Educ:* Arhus Sch. of Econs and Business Admin, Denmark (MEcon). Entered Norwegian Foreign Service, 1960; served Peking, Cairo, Manila, 1960–71; Head of Div., Min. of Foreign Affairs, 1971–75; Minister-Counsellor, Perm. Mission of Norway to UN, NY, 1975–81; Dir-Gen., Min. of Foreign Affairs, 1981–82; Ambassador, Perm. Mission of Norway to UN, NY, 1982–89; Minister of Develt Assistance, 1989–90; Dir of Information, Saga Petroleum, 1991–92; Asst Sec. Gen., Min. of Foreign Affairs, 1992–94; Ambassador to: UK, 1994–96; USA, 1996–2001; Special Envoy of UN Sec.-Gen. for humanitarian affairs, Sudan, 1998–. *Address:* Rehbinderintie 17, 00150 Helsinki, Finland.

VREDELING, Hendrikus, (Henk); Member, and Vice-President (responsible for Employment and Social Affairs), Commission of European Communities, 1977–80; *b* 20 Nov. 1924. *Educ:* Agricultural Univ., Wageningen. Member: Second Chamber of States-

General, Netherlands, 1956–73; European Parliament, 1958–73; Socio-Economic Adviser to Agricultural Workers' Union, Netherlands, 1950–73; Minister of Defence, Netherlands, 1973–76. Member: Dutch Emancipation Council, 1981–85; Dutch Council on Peace and Security, 1987–94. *Address:* Rembrandtlaan 13A, 3712 AJ Huis ter Heide, Netherlands.

VULLIAMY, Shirley, (Mrs J. S. P. Vulliamy); *see* Hughes, S.

VUONG THUA PHONG; Ambassador of Vietnam to the Court of St James's, since 1998; *b* 25 Oct. 1956; *m* Ngo Thi Phi Nga; two *s*. *Educ:* Soviet Union. Dep. Dir, Policy Planning Dept, Min. of Foreign Affairs, Vietnam; Private Sec. to Foreign Minister, 1994–98. Member: RIIA; London Diplomatic Assoc. *Recreation:* golf. *Address:* Embassy of Vietnam, 12 Victoria Road, W8 5RD. *Club:* London Golf.

VYVYAN, Maj.-Gen. Charles Gerard Courtenay, CB 1998; CBE 1990 (MBE 1974); Defence Attaché and Head of British Defence Staff, Washington, 1997–2000; *b* 29 Sept. 1944; *er s* of John Michal Kenneth Vyvyan and Elizabeth Mary Lowder Vyvyan; *m* 1989, Elizabeth Frances (LVO 1998), 3rd *d* of Sir John Paget, 3rd Bt, Haygrass, Taunton. *Educ:* Winchester Coll.; Balliol Coll., Oxford (BA Mod. Hist. 1966; MA 1991); Nat. Defence Coll., Pakistan (MSc, Defence and Strategic Studies). Commnd, Royal Green Jackets (Rifle Bde), 1967; Sultan of Oman's Armed Forces, 1975–76; Staff Coll., 1978; CO 1st Bn RGJ, 1984–86; Col GS Mil. Ops, 1986–87; Comdr 3 Inf. Bde, 1988–90; student, Nat. Defence Coll., Pakistan, 1990–91; DCS, HQ UKLF, 1991–94; COS, UKLF, later HQ Land Command, 1994–97. Col Comdt, 1 RGJ, 1994–2000. Gov., Cranleigh Sch., 2000–. *Recreations:* mountains, gardens, travel, fishing, Alexander the Great. *Address:* c/o Barclays Bank, PO Box 333, High Street, Oxford OX1 3HS. *Clubs:* Boodle's, Beefsteak.

VYVYAN, Sir (Ralph) Ferrers (Alexander), 13th Bt *cr* 1645, of Trelowarren, Cornwall; *b* 21 Aug. 1960; *s* of Sir John Stanley Vyvyan, 12th Bt and of his 3rd wife, Jonet Noël, *e d* of Lt-Col Alexander Hubert Barclay, DSO, MC; *S* father, 1995; *m* 1986, Victoria Arabella, *y d* of M. B. Ogle; four *s*. *Educ:* Charterhouse; Sandhurst; Architectural Assoc. *Heir: s* Joshua Drummond Vyvyan, *b* 10 Oct. 1986. *Address:* Trelowarren, Mawgan, Helston, Cornwall TR12 6AF.

W

WADDELL, Gordon Herbert; Chairman, Shanks Group plc (formerly Shanks & McEwan), since 1992; *b* Glasgow, 12 April 1937; *s* of late Herbert Waddell; *m* 1st, 1965, Mary (marr. diss. 1971), *d* of H. F. Oppenheimer, *qv*; 2nd, 1973, Kathy May, *d* of W. S. Gallagher. *Educ:* St Mary's Sch., Melrose; Fettes Coll., Edinburgh; Cambridge Univ. (BA); Stanford Univ. (MBA). Rugby Blue, Cambridge Univ., 1958, 1959, 1961; Member, British Isles Rugby Touring Team: to Australia and NZ, 1959; to South Africa, 1962; eighteen rugby caps for Scotland. MP (Progressive Party) for Johannesburg North, April 1974–Nov. 1977. Dir, E. Oppenheimer & Son Ltd, 1965–87; Exec. Dir, Anglo American Corp. of South Africa Ltd, 1971–87; Chairman: Johannesburg Consolidated Investment Co. Ltd, 1981–87; Rustenburg Platinum Mines Ltd, 1981–87; South African Breweries Ltd, 1984–87; Fairway Group plc (formerly Fairway (London)), 1989–98; Ryan Gp (formerly Digger), 1991–95; Gartmore Scotland Investment Trust, 1991–; Tor Investment Trust, 1992–96; Mersey Docks and Harbour Co., 1992–; Director: Cadbury Schweppes, 1988–97; Scottish Nat. Trust, 1988–96; London and Strathclyde Trust, 1989–96. *Recreation:* golf. *Address:* Flat A, 43 Elm Park Gardens, SW10 9PA; Corbet Tower, Morebattle, Kelso TD5 8AQ. *Clubs:* Hawks (Cambridge); Honourable Company of Edinburgh Golfers; Royal and Ancient (St Andrews).

WADDELL, Sir James (Henderson), Kt 1974; CB 1960; Deputy Chairman, Police Complaints Board, 1977–81; *b* 5 Oct. 1914; *s* of D. M. Waddell and J. C. Fleming; *m* 1940, Dorothy Abbie Wright; one *s* one *d*. *Educ:* George Heriot's Sch.; Edinburgh Univ. Assistance Board, 1936; Ministry of Information, 1940; Reconnaissance Corps, 1942; Ministry of Housing and Local Government, 1946; Under-Secretary, 1955; Under-Secretary, Cabinet Office, 1961–63; Dep.-Secretary, Min. of Housing and Local Government, 1963–66; Dep. Under-Sec., Home Office, 1966–75. *Address:* Long Meadow, East Lavant, Chichester, W Sussex PO18 0AH. *T:* (01243) 527129.

WADDELL, Rear-Adm. William Angus, CB 1981; OBE 1966; *b* 5 Nov. 1924; *s* of late James Whitefield Waddell and Christina Waddell (*née* Maclean); *m* 1950, Thelma Evelyn Tomlins; one *s* one *d*. *Educ:* Glasgow Univ. (BSc (Hons) Maths and Nat. Phil.; Cleland Gold Medal). CEng; FIEE. Midshipman, Sub Lieut RNVR (Special Branch), HMS Ranee, HMS Collingwood, 1945–47; Instr Lieut, HMS Collingwood, HMS Glasgow, HMS Siskin, HMS Gambia, 1947–59 (RMCS 1956–57); Instr Comdr, HMS Albion, 1959–61; Staff of Dir, Naval Educn Service, 1961–63; Sen. British Naval Officer, Dam Neck, Virginia, 1963–66; Officer i/c RN Polaris Sch., 1966–68; Instr Captain, Staff of SACLANT (Dir, Inf. Systems Gp), 1969–72; Dean, RN Coll., Greenwich, 1973–75; Dir Naval Officer Appointments (Instr), 1975–78; Rear-Adm. 1979; Chief Naval Instructor Officer, 1978–81 and Flag Officer, Admiralty Interview Bd, 1979–81. ADC to HM the Queen, 1976–79. Assoc. Teacher, City Univ., 1973–75; Sec. and Chief Exec., RIPH&H, 1982–90. Hon. FRIPHH 1990. *Publication:* An Introduction to Servomechanisms (with F. L. Westwater), 1961, repr. 1968. *Address:* c/o National Westminster Bank, 80 Lewisham High Street, SE13 5JJ.

WADDINGTON, family name of **Baron Waddington**.

WADDINGTON, Baron *cr* 1990 (Life Peer), of Read in the County of Lancashire; **David Charles Waddington,** GCVO 1994; PC 1987; DL; QC 1971; Governor and Commander-in-Chief of Bermuda, 1992–97; a Recorder of the Crown Court, 1972–99; *b* 2 Aug. 1929; *o s* of late Charles Waddington and of Mrs Minnie Hughan Waddington; *m* 1958, Gillian Rosemary, *d* of late Alan Green, CBE; three *s* two *d*. *Educ:* Sedbergh; Hertford Coll., Oxford (Hon. Fellow, 1998). President, Oxford Univ. Conservative Assoc., 1950. 2nd Lieut, XII Royal Lancers, 1951–53. Called to Bar, Gray's Inn, 1951, Bencher, 1985. Contested (C): Farnworth Div., 1955; Nelson and Colne Div., 1964; Heywood and Royton Div., 1966; MP (C): Nelson and Colne, 1968–Sept. 1974; Clitheroe, March 1979–1983; Ribble Valley, 1983–90; a Lord Comr, HM Treasury, 1979–81; Parly Under-Sec. of State, Dept of Employment, 1981–83; Minister of State, Home Office, 1983–87; Parly Sec., HM Treasury and Govt Chief Whip, 1987–89; Sec. of State, Home Office, 1989–90; Lord Privy Seal and Leader of H of L, 1990–92. DL Lancs 1991. *Address:* Stable House, Sabden, near Clitheroe, Lancs BB7 9HP; Flat 4, 39 Chester Way, SE11 4UR.

WADDINGTON, Prof. David James; Professor of Chemical Education, University of York, 1978–2000, now Emeritus; *b* 27 May 1932; *s* of late Eric James and Marjorie Edith Waddington; *m* 1957, Isobel Hesketh; two *s* one *d*. *Educ:* Marlborough College; Imperial College, Univ. of London (BSc, ARCS, DIC, PhD). Head of Chemistry Dept, 1959, Head of Science Dept, 1961, Wellington College; York University: Sen. Lectr, 1965; Head Chemistry Dept, 1983–92; Pro-Vice-Chancellor, 1985–91. Hon. Prof., Mendeleev Univ. of Chem. Technol., Moscow, 1998–; Vis. Prof., IPN, Univ of Kiel, 2000–. President: Educn Div., Royal Soc. of Chem., 1981–83; Inst. of Sci. Technol., 1995–2000; Sec., 1977, Chm., 1981–86, Cttee on Teaching of Chemistry, IUPAC; Sec., 1986–89, Chm., 1990–94, Cttee on Teaching of Science, ICSU. Liveryman, Salters' Co., 2001–. Nyholm Medal, RSC, 1985; Brasted Award, ACS, 1988. Nat. Order of Scientific Merit (Brazil), 1997. *Publications:* Organic Chemistry, 1962; (with H. S. Finlay) Organic Chemistry Through Experiment, 1965; (with R. O. C. Norman) Modern Organic Chemistry, 1972; (with A. Kornhauser and C. N. R. Rao) Chemical Education in the 70s, 1980; (ed) Teaching School Chemistry, 1985; (ed) Education, Industry and Technology, 1987; (jtly) Introducing Chemistry: the Salters' approach, 1989; Chemistry: the Salters' approach, 1990; (jtly) Salters' Advanced Chemistry, 1994; (ed) Science for Understanding Tomorrow's World: global change, 1994; Global Environmental Change Science: education and training, 1995; (with J. N. Lazonby) Partners in Chemical Education, 1996; (jtly) Salters' Higher Chemistry, 1999; (jtly) The Essential Chemical Industry, 1999. *Recreations:* golf, gardening. *Address:* Department of Chemistry, University of York, York YO10 5DD.

WADDINGTON, Leslie; Chairman, Waddington Galleries, since 1966; *b* Dublin, 9 Feb. 1934; *s* of late Victor and Zelda Waddington; *m* 1st, 1967, Ferriel Lyle (marr. diss. 1983); two *d*; 2nd, 1985, Clodagh Frances Fanshawe. *Educ:* Portora Royal School; Sorbonne; Ecole du Louvre (Diplômé). Formed Waddington Galleries with father, 1957. Chm., Modern Painting Sect., 1994–, Pictura Sect., 1996–2000, Maastricht Art Fair. Sen. Fellow, RCA, 1993. *Recreations:* chess, backgammon, reading. *Address:* 11 Cork Street, W1S 3LT. *T:* (020) 7851 2200.

WADDINGTON, Very Rev. Robert Murray; Dean of Manchester, 1984–93, now Emeritus; *b* 24 Oct. 1927; *s* of Percy Nevill and Dorothy Waddington. *Educ:* Dulwich Coll.; Selwyn Coll., Cambridge; Ely Theological Coll. MA (2nd cl. Theol.). Asst Curate St John's, Bethnal Green, 1953–55; Chaplain, Slade Sch., Warwick, Qld, Aust., 1955–59; Curate, St Luke's, Cambridge, 1959–61; Headmaster, St Barnabas Sch., Ravenshoe, N Qld, Aust., 1961–70; Oxford Univ. Dept of Education, 1971–72; Residentiary Canon, Carlisle Cathedral, and Bishop's Adviser for Education, 1972–77; Gen. Sec., C of E Bd of Education and Nat. Soc. for Promoting Religious Education, 1977–84. Superior, Oratory of the Good Shepherd, 1987–90. *Recreations:* cooking, films, sociology. *Address:* 6 Waverley Street, York YO31 7QZ. *T:* (01904) 670200.

WADDINGTON, Susan Andrée; Consultant on Europe and Lifelong Learning, since 2000; *b* 23 Aug. 1944; *m* 1966, Ivan Waddington; one *s* one *d*. *Educ:* Blyth GS, Norwich; Leicester Univ. (BA; MEd). Assistant Director of Education: Derbys CC, 1988–90; Birmingham CC, 1990–94. Mem. (Lab) Leics CC, 1973–91. MEP (Lab) Leicester, 1994–99. Contested (Lab): Leics NW, 1987; E Midlands Reg., EP, 1999. *Address:* 5 Roundhill Road, Leicester LE5 5RJ; *e-mail:* office@sue-waddington.co.uk.

WADDS, Mrs Jean Casselman, OC 1982; Member, Royal Commission on Economic Union and Development Prospects for Canada, 1983–85; *b* 16 Sept. 1920; *d* of Hon. Earl Rowe and Treva Lennox Rowe; *m* 1st, 1946, Clair Casselman; one *s* one *d*; 2nd, 1964, Robert Wadds (marr. diss. 1977). *Educ:* Univ. of Toronto (BA); Weller Business Coll. First elected to Canadian House of Commons (Riding Grenville-Dundas), 1958; re-elected: 1962, 1963, 1965; defeated (Riding Grenville-Carlton), 1968. Member, Canada's Delegn to United Nations, 1961; Parliamentary Sec. to Minister of Health and Welfare, 1962. National Sec., Progressive Conservative Party, 1971–75; Member, Ontario Municipal Bd, 1975–79. Canadian High Comr to UK, 1980–83. Former Director: Bell Canada; Royal Trustco Ltd; Air Canada; Celanese Canada Inc.; Canadian Pacific Ltd. Adv. Bd, Norman Paterson Sch. of Internat. Affairs, Carleton Univ., Ont. Freeman, City of London, 1981. Hon. DCL Acadia Univ., NS, 1981; Hon. LLD St Thomas Univ., NB, 1983; hon. degrees: Univ. of Toronto, 1985; Dalhousie Univ., NS, 1985. Hon. Fellowship Award, Bretton Hall Coll., W Yorks, 1982; Hon. Patron, Grenville Christian Coll., Brockville, 1981. *Recreations:* walking, swimming. *Address:* PO Box 579, Prescott, ON K0E 1T0, Canada.

WADDY, Rev. Lawrence Heber; retired; Lecturer in Classics, University of California, San Diego, 1969–80; *b* 5 Oct. 1914; *s* of late Archdeacon Stacy Waddy, Secretary of SPG, and Etheldred (*née* Spittal). *Educ:* Marlborough Coll.; Balliol Coll., Oxford (Domus Exhibitioner in Classics, Balliol, 1933; 1st Class Hon. Mods., Oxford, 1935; de Paravicini Scholar, 1935; Craven Scholar, 1935; 2nd Class Lit. Hum., 1937; BA 1937; MA 1945). Deacon, 1940; Priest, 1941; Chaplain, RNVR, 1942–46; Assistant Master: Marlborough Coll., 1937–38; Winchester Coll., 1938–42 and 1946–49 (Chaplain, 1946); Headmaster, Tonbridge Sch., 1949–62; Education Officer, School Broadcasting Council, 1962–63; Chaplain to The Bishop's School, La Jolla, California, 1963–67; Headmaster, Santa Maria Internat. Acad., Chula Vista, Calif, 1967–69; Vicar, Church of the Good Samaritan, University City, 1970–74; Hon. Asst, St James', La Jolla, 1974–94. Examining Chaplain to the Bishop of Rochester, 1959–63; Hon. Canon of Rochester, 1961–63; Hon. Canon of San Diego, 1997. Select Preacher: Cambridge Univ., 1951; Oxford Univ., 1954–56. *Publications:* Pax Romana and World Peace, 1950; The Prodigal Son (musical play), 1963; The Bible as Drama, 1974; Faith of Our Fathers, 1975; Symphony, 1977; Drama in Worship, 1978; Mayor's Race, 1980; A Parish by the Sea, 1988; First Bible Stories, 1994; Shakespeare Remembers, 1994; Florence Nightingale, 1995; Jonah, 1995. *Address:* 5910 Camino de la Costa, La Jolla, CA 92037, USA.

WADE, family name of **Baron Wade of Chorlton**.

WADE OF CHORLTON, Baron *cr* 1990 (Life Peer), of Chester in the County of Cheshire; **(William) Oulton Wade,** Kt 1982; JP; farmer and cheese master; company director; consultant; Chairman, NIMTECH; *b* 24 Dec. 1932; *s* of Samuel Norman Wade and Joan Ferris Wade (*née* Wild); *m* 1959 Gillian Margaret Leete, Buxton, Derbys; one *s* one *d*. *Educ:* Birkenhead Sch.; Queen's Univ., Belfast. Jt Treas., Cons. Party, 1982–90; Chm., Parly Rural Economy Gp. Pres., Campus Ventures Ltd; Director: Murray Vernon (Holdings) Ltd; Cartmel PR Ltd; President: Combined Heat and Power Assoc.; Fedn of Econ. Develt Authorities; UK Rep., Internat. Business Adv. Council, UNIDO. JP Cheshire 1967. Freeman, City of London, 1980; Liveryman, Farmers' Co., 1980–. *Publications:* contribs to Dairy Industries Internat., Jl of Soc. of Dairy Technol. *Recreations:* politics, reading, shooting, food, travel. *Address:* House of Lords, Westminster, SW1A 0PW. *Clubs:* Chester City (Chester); St James's (Manchester).

WADE, Charles; *see* Wade, R. C. B.

WADE, Prof. Sir (Henry) William (Rawson), Kt 1985; QC 1968; FBA 1969; MA; LLD (Cantab); DCL (Oxon); Master of Gonville and Caius College, Cambridge, 1976–88; Barrister-at-Law; *b* 16 Jan. 1918; *s* of late Colonel H. O. Wade and of E. L. Rawson-Ackroyd; *m* 1st, 1943, Marie (*d* 1980), *d* of late G. E. Osland-Hill; two *s*; 2nd,

1982, Marjorie, *d* of late Surgeon-Capt. H. Hope-Gill, RN, and *widow* of B. C. Browne. *Educ:* Shrewsbury Sch. (Governor, 1977–85); Gonville and Caius Coll., Cambridge. Henry Fellow, Harvard Univ., 1939; temp. officer, Treasury, 1940–46. Called to the Bar, Lincoln's Inn, 1946; Hon. Bencher, 1964. Fellow of Trinity Coll., Cambridge, 1946–61, Hon. Fellow, 1991; University Lecturer, 1947; Reader, 1959; Prof. of English Law, Oxford Univ., 1961–76; Fellow, St John's College, Oxford, 1961–76, Hon. Fellow, 1976; Rouse Ball Prof. of English Law, Cambridge Univ., 1978–82. Lectr, Council of Legal Education, 1957; British Council Lectr in Scandinavia, 1958, and Turkey, 1959; Cooley Lectr, Michigan Univ., 1961; Vithalbai Patel Lectr, New Delhi, 1971; Chettyar Lectr, Madras, 1974; Chitaley Lectr, New Delhi, 1982; Cassel Lectr, Stockholm, 1987; Nambyar Lectr, India, 1992. Vice-Pres., British Acad., 1981–83. Member: Council on Tribunals, 1958–71; Relationships Commn, Uganda, 1961; Royal Commn on Tribunals of Inquiry, 1966. Hon. LittD Cantab, 1998. *Publications:* The Law of Real Property, 1957 (with Rt Hon. Sir Robert Megarry), 6th edn 2000; Administrative Law, 1961, 8th edn (with Dr C. F. Forsyth) 2000; Towards Administrative Justice, 1963; (with Prof. B. Schwartz) Legal Control of Government, 1972; Constitutional Fundamentals (Hamlyn Lectures), 1980, rev. edn 1989; articles in legal journals; broadcast talks. *Recreations:* climbing, gardening. *Address:* 1A Ludlow Lane, Fulbourn, Cambridge CB1 5BL. *T:* (01223) 881745; Gonville and Caius College, Cambridge CB2 1TA. *T:* (01223) 332400, *Fax:* (01223) 332456. *Club:* Alpine.

WADE, Joseph Frederick; General Secretary, National Graphical Association, 1976–84; Visiting Professor, University of Strathclyde, 1985–88; *b* 18 Dec. 1919; *s* of James and Ellen Wade; *m* Joan Ann; two *s*. *Educ:* elementary sch., Blackburn, Lancs. Trained as compositor, The Blackburn Times, 1934–40; served UK and overseas, East Lancs Regt and RAOC, 1940–46; newspaper compositor, 1946–56. Full-time Trade Union official, Typographical Assoc., 1956; Nat. Officer, NGA, 1964; Asst Gen. Sec., NGA, 1968; Gen. Sec., NGA, 1976, NGA '82 (after amalgamation) 1982. Member: Exec. Cttee, Printing and Kindred Trades Fedn, 1971–74; Exec. Cttee, Internat. Graphical Fedn, 1976–85 (Vice-Pres.); TUC Printing Industries Cttee, 1976–84; TUC Gen. Council, 1983–84; Printing and Publishing Industry Training Bd, 1977–82; Printing Industries EDC, 1979–84. Mem., Blackburn County Borough Council, 1952–56. *Recreations:* walking, Scrabble, gardening. *Address:* 10 Spring Vale, Swarthmoor, Ulverston, Cumbria LA12 0XA.

WADE, Prof. Kenneth, FRS 1989; CChem, FRSC; Professor of Chemistry, Durham University, 1983–98, now Emeritus; *b* Sleaford, Lincs, 13 Oct. 1932; 2nd *s* of Harry Kennington Wade and Anna Elizabeth (*née* Cartwright); *m* 1962, Gertrud Rosmarie Hetzel; one *s* two *d*. *Educ:* Carre's Grammar Sch., Sleaford; Nottingham Univ. (BSc, PhD; DSc 1970). Postdoctoral research assistant: Cambridge Univ., 1957–59; Cornell Univ., 1959–60; Lectr in Inorganic Chemistry, Derby Coll. of Technology, 1960–61; Durham University: Lectr 1961–71, Sen. Lectr 1971–77, Reader 1977–83, in Chemistry; Chm., Dept of Chemistry, 1986–89. Vis. Res. Fellow, Loker Hydrocarbon Res. Inst., USC, LA, 1979–. Visiting Professor: Technical Univ., Warsaw, 1974; Free Univ., Amsterdam, 1977–78; Univ. of S California, 1979 and 1984–85; Notre Dame Univ., 1983; McMaster Univ., 1984; Western Ontario Univ., 1991. Tilden Lectr, 1987–88, Mond Lectr, 1998–99, RSC; Emanuel Merck Lectr, Darmstadt, 1994. Pres., Dalton Div., RSC, 1995–97. Main Gp Element Award, RSC, 1982. *Publications:* (jtly) Organometallic Compounds: the main group elements, 1967; (jtly) Principles of Organometallic Chemistry, 1968; Electron Deficient Compounds, 1971; (jtly) The Chemistry of Aluminium, Gallium, Indium and Thallium, 1973; (jtly) Organometallic Chemistry, 1976; Hypercarbon Chemistry, 1987; Electron Deficient Boron and Carbon Clusters, 1990; many papers (res. and rev. articles) in learned jls. *Recreations:* (a) musing, (b) musing, (c) walking. *Address:* Chemistry Department, Durham University Science Laboratories, South Road, Durham DH1 3LE. *T:* (0191) 3743122.

WADE, Prof. Owen Lyndon, CBE 1983; MD; FRCP; FRCPI; FFPM; Professor of Therapeutics and Clinical Pharmacology, 1971–86, now Emeritus, and Pro-Vice-Chancellor and Vice-Principal, 1985–86, University of Birmingham; *b* 17 May 1921; *s* of J. O. D. Wade, MS, FRCS, and Kate Wade, Cardiff; *m* 1948, Margaret Burton, LDS; three *d*. *Educ:* Repton; Cambridge; University College Hospital, London. Senior Scholar, Emmanuel Coll., Cambridge, 1941; Achison and Atkinson Morley Schol., UCH, 1945; Resident Medical Officer, UCH, 1946; Clinical Assistant, Pneumoconiosis Research Unit of the Medical Research Council, 1948–51; Lecturer and Sen. Lecturer in Medicine, Dept of Medicine, University of Birmingham, 1951–57; Whitla Prof. of Therapeutics and Pharmacology, Queen's Univ., Belfast, 1957–71; Dean, Faculty of Medicine and Dentistry, Univ. of Birmingham, 1978–84. Rockefeller Travelling Fellowship in Medicine, 1954–55; Research Fellow, Columbia Univ. at Department of Medicine, Presbyterian Hospital, New York, 1954–55; Consultant, WHO. Chm., Cttee on the Review of Medicines, 1978–84; Chm., Jt Formulary Cttee for British Nat. Formulary, 1978–86. Mem. GMC, 1981–84. Hon. MD QUB, 1989. *Publications:* (with J. M. Bishop) The Cardiac Output and Regional Blood Flow, 1962; Adverse Reactions to Drugs, 1970, 2nd edn with L. Beeley, 1976; The Romance of Remedies, 1996; When I Dropped the Knife, 1996. *Recreations:* books, travel and sailing. *Address:* c/o The Medical School, Birmingham University, Birmingham B15 2TT. *Club:* Athenæum.

WADE, Rebekah; Editor, News of the World, since 2000; *b* 27 May 1968; *d* of late Robert Wade and of Deborah Wade. *Educ:* Appleton Hall, Cheshire; Sorbonne, Paris. Features Editor, then Associate Editor, subseq. Dep. Editor, News of the World, 1989–98; Dep. Ed., The Sun, 1998–2000. Founder Mem. and Pres., Women in Journalism. *Address:* News of the World, 1 Virginia Street, E1 9BD. *T:* (020) 7782 4406.

WADE, (Richard) Charles (Bathurst); His Honour Judge Wade; a Circuit Judge, since 2000; *b* 16 Dec. 1946; *s* of David Ison Wade and Margaret Elizabeth Lucy Wade (*née* Wainwright); *m* 1972, Juliet Ann Jehring; one *s* three *d*. *Educ:* Malvern Coll. Admitted Solicitor, 1972; in private practice, 1972–89; County Court Registrar, 1989–91; Dist Judge, 1991–2000. Trustee: Gloucester Acad. of Music and Performing Arts, 1992–99; Harnhill Centre of Christain Healing. Mem. Council, Cheltenham and Gloucester Coll. of Higher Educn, 1999–2000. *Recreations:* gardening, music, walking.

WADE, Richard Lawrence; writer, producer, and campaigner for the modernisation of English orthography; *b* 5 July 1938; *s* of Wilfred George Wade and Frances Mary (*née* Smith); *m* 1st, 1962, Angela Lee Mikhelson (marr. diss. 1995); two *d*; 2nd, 1996, Angela Claire Mills (*née* Thomson). *Educ:* Bedford Sch.; New Coll., Oxford (MA Oriental Studies; Pres., OU Gymnastics Club (Half Blue)). Management Trainee, Unilever Ltd, 1961–63; BBC TV, 1963–75: dir and producer, 1963–70; Editor, Tomorrow's World, 1970–75; Chief Asst, Radio 4 and Hd of Radio 4, 1975–83; Chief Asst to Man. Dir, BBC Radio, 1983–86; Marketing Dir, BITC, 1986–88; Man. Dir, Business in the Cities, 1988–89; Dir Gen., Advertising Assoc., 1990–93; Fellow and Dir of Develt, St Edmund Hall, Oxford, 1993–96. Chm., Freespeling Ltd. Chm., Direct Marketing Assoc. (UK) Ltd, 1991–92. Mem., Calderdale Partnership, Halifax, 1987–89. Mem., BAFTA, 1968–. Freeman, City of London, 1988. *Recreations:* ski-ing, conversation, photography. *Address:* 49 Park Town, Oxford OX2 6SL. *T:* (01865) 511984. *Club:* Oxford and Cambridge.

WADE, R(obert) Hunter; New Zealand diplomat, retired; *b* 14 June 1916; *s* of R. H. Wade, Balclutha, NZ; *m* 1941, Avelda Grace Petersen (*d* 1990); one *s* two *d* (and one *s* decd). *Educ:* Waitaki; Otago Univ. NZ Treasury and Marketing Depts, 1939; NZ Govt diplomatic appts, Delhi, Simla, Sydney, Canberra, 1941–49; Head of Eastern Political Div., Dept of External Affairs, Wellington, NZ, 1949; NZ Embassy, Washington, 1951; NZ High Commn, Ottawa, 1956; Director of Colombo Plan Bureau, Colombo, 1957; Dir, External Aid, Wellington, 1959; Comr for NZ in Singapore and British Borneo, 1962; High Comr in Malaya/Malaysia, 1963–67; Dep. High Comr in London, 1967–69; NZ Ambassador to Japan and Korea, 1969–71; Dep. Sec.-Gen. of the Commonwealth, 1972–75; NZ Ambassador to Federal Republic of Germany and to Switzerland, 1975–78. Represented New Zealand at Independence of: Uganda, 1962; Botswana, 1966; Lesotho, 1966. Pres., Asiatic Soc. of Japan, 1971. *Address:* 12 Pleasant Place, Howick, Auckland, New Zealand. *Club:* Northern (Auckland).

WADE, Air Chief Marshal Sir Ruthven (Lowry), KCB 1974 (CB 1970); DFC 1944; Chief of Personnel and Logistics, Ministry of Defence, 1976–78, retired 1978; Director, Acatos and Hutcheson, since 1979; *b* 1920. *Educ:* Cheltenham Coll.; RAF Coll., Cranwell. RAF, 1939; served War of 1939–45, UK and Mediterranean (DFC); psa, 1953; HQ 2nd Tactical Air Force, Germany; RAF Flying Coll.; Gp Captain 1960; Staff Officer, Air HQ, Malta; Comdr, Bomber Comd station, RAF Gaydon, 1962–65; Air Cdre, 1964; idc 1965; Air Exec. to Deputy for Nuclear Affairs, SHAPE, 1967–68; AOC No 1 (Bomber) Gp, Strike Comd, 1968–71; Air Vice-Marshal, 1968; Dep. Comdr, RAF Germany, 1971–72; ACAS (Ops), 1973; Vice Chief of Air Staff, 1973–76; Air Marshal, 1974; Air Chief Marshal, 1976. *Address:* White Gables, Westlington, Dinton, Aylesbury, Bucks HP17 8UR. *T:* (01296) 748884.

WADE, (Sarah) Virginia, OBE 1986 (MBE 1969); tennis player; commentator, BBC Television, since 1980; *b* 10 July 1945; *d* of late Eustace Holland Wade and of Joan Barbara Wade. *Educ:* Sussex Univ. (BSc). Won tennis championships: US Open, 1968; Italian, 1971; Australian, 1972; Wimbledon, 1977; played for GB in Wightman Cup and Federation Cup 20 times (record); Captain, GB team. Mem. Cttee, All England Lawn Tennis Club, 1983–91. Hon. LLD Sussex, 1985. Elected into Internat. Tennis Hall of Fame, 1989. *Publications:* Courting Triumph, 1978; Ladies of the Court, 1984. *Address:* c/o IMG, Pier House, Strand on the Green, W4 3NN. *T:* (020) 8233 5000.

WADE, Sir William; see Wade, Sir H. W. R.

WADE-GERY, Sir Robert (Lucian), KCMG 1983 (CMG 1979); KCVO 1983; Senior Consultant to: Barclays Private Bank, since 1999; Fellow, All Souls College, Oxford, since 1997; *b* 22 April 1929; *o s* of late Prof. H. T. Wade-Gery; *m* 1962, Sarah, *er d* of A. D. Marris, CMG; one *s* one *d*. *Educ:* Winchester; New Coll., Oxford (1st cl. Hon. Mods 1949 and Lit. Hum. 1951; Hon. Fellow, 1985). Fellow, All Souls Coll., Oxford, 1951–73, 1987–89. Joined HM Foreign (now Diplomatic) Service, 1951; FO (Economic Relations Dept), 1951–54; Bonn, 1954–57; FO (Private Sec. to Perm. Under-Sec., later Southern Dept), 1957–60; Tel Aviv, 1961–64; FO (Planning Staff), 1964–67; Saigon, 1967–68; Cabinet Office (Sec. to Duncan Cttee), 1968–69; Counsellor 1969; on loan to Bank of England, 1969; Head of Financial Policy and Aid Dept, FCO, 1969–70, Under-Sec., Central Policy Review Staff, Cabinet Office, 1971–73; Minister, Madrid, 1973–77; Minister, Moscow, 1977–79; Dep. Sec. of the Cabinet, 1979–82; High Comr to India, 1982–87. Dir, Barclays Capital (formerly BZW), 1987–99 (Vice-Chm., 1994–99). Hon. Treas., IISS, 1991–. Chm., Anglo-Spanish Soc., 1995–98. Chm. of Govs, SOAS, 1990–99. *Recreations:* walking, sailing, travel, history. *Address:* The Old Vicarage, Cold Aston, Cheltenham GL54 3BW. *T:* (01451) 821115, *Fax:* (01451) 822496; 14 Hill View, 2 Primrose Hill Road, NW3 3AX. *T:* (020) 7722 4754, *Fax:* (020) 7586 5966. *Clubs:* Boodle's, Beefsteak.

WADHAM, John; Director, Liberty (National Council for Civil Liberties), since 1995; *b* 24 Jan. 1952; *s* of late Ernest George Wadham and of Unity Winifred Wadham (*née* Errington); partner, Alison Macnair. *Educ:* London School of Economics (BSc 1974); Surrey Univ. (CQSW 1978; MSc 1979). Legal Advr, Wandsworth Law Centres, 1978–86; articled clerk, Birnberg & Co., Solicitors, 1987–90; admitted Solicitor, 1989; Legal Officer, 1990–92, Dir of Law, 1992–95, NCCL, later Liberty. Mem., Human Rights Act Task Force, 1999–2001. Editor, Cases and Comment: the European Human Rights Law Review, 1995–; Series Editor, Blackstone's Human Rights Act series, 2000–. Hon. Fellow of Law, Univ. of Kent at Canterbury, 1992. *Publications:* (jtly) Fuel Rights Handbook, 2nd edn 1981 to 6th edn 1988; (contrib.) The Penguin Guide to the Law, 3rd edn, 1992, 4th edn, 2001; (ed) Your Rights: the Liberty guide, 5th edn 1994 to 7th edn 2000; Blackstone's Guide to the Human Rights Act 1998, 1999, 2nd edn 2000; Blackstone's Guide to the Freedom of Information Act 2000, 2001; articles in newspapers and legal jls. *Recreation:* flying (private pilot). *Address:* Liberty, 21 Tabard Street, SE1 4LA. *T:* (020) 7403 3888.

WADHAMS, Dr Peter, FRGS; Reader in Polar Studies, Cambridge University, since 1992; *b* 14 May 1948; *s* of late Frank Cecil Wadhams and of Winifred Grace Wadhams (*née* Smith); *m* 1980, Maria Pia Casarini. *Educ:* Palmer's Sch., Grays, Essex; Churchill Coll., Cambridge (BA Phys. 1969; MA 1972; ScD 1994); graduate res., Scott Polar Res. Inst. (PhD 1974). Res. Scientist, Bedford Inst. of Oceanography, Dartmouth, Canada, 1969–70 (asst to Sen. Scientist on Hudson '70 expedn, first circumnavigation of Americas); Fellow, NRC Canada, 1974–75 (Inst. Ocean Scis, Victoria, BC); Scott Polar Research Institute, 1976–: leader, Sea Ice Gp, 1976; Asst Dir of Res., 1981; Dep. Dir, 1983–87; Dir, 1987–92; Sen. Res. Fellow, Churchill Coll., Cambridge, 1983–93. Leader, 29 field ops in Arctic, 5 in Antarctic; UK Deleg., Arctic Ocean Scis Bd, 1984–; Member: IAPSO Commn on Sea Ice, 1987– (Pres., 1999–); SCAR Gp of specialists in Antarctic Sea Ice, 1989–; IASC Wkg Gp on Global Change, 1992–; Co-ordinator, Internat. Prog. for Antarctic Buoys, World Climate Res. Prog., 1999–. Vis. Prof., Naval Postgrad. Sch., Monterey, 1980–81; Green Schol Scripps Instn, 1987–88; Walker-Ames Vis. Prof., Univ. of Washington, WA, 1988; Vis. Prof., Nat. Inst. of Polar Res., Tokyo, 1995, 1996–97. W. S. Bruce Prize, RSE 1977; Polar Medal, 1987; Italgas Prize for Envmtl Scis, 1990. *Publications:* (contrib.) The Nordic Seas, 1986; (contrib.) The Geophysics of Sea Ice, 1986; (ed) Ice Technology for Polar Operations, 1990; (contrib.) Microwave Remote Sensing of Sea Ice, 1992; (ed) Advances in Ice Technology, 1992; Marine, Offshore and Ice Technology, 1994; (ed) The Arctic and Environmental Change, 1996; Ice in the Ocean, 2000; numerous sci. papers on glaciology and polar oceanography. *Recreations:* painting, music, sailing. *Address:* 40 Grafton Street, Cambridge CB1 1DS. *T:* (01223) 359433.

WADHWANI, Sushil Baldev, PhD; Member, Monetary Policy Committee, Bank of England, since 1999; *b* 7 Dec. 1959; *s* of Baldev and Meena Wadhwani; *m* 1st, 1991, Anjali Mirgh (marr. diss. 1994); 2nd, 1996, Renu Sakhrani; one *d*. *Educ:* London Sch. of Economics (BSc Econs; MSc Econs 1982; PhD 1986). Lectr, 1984–91, Reader, 1991–92, in Economics, London Sch. of Economics; Dir of Equity Strategy, Goldman Sachs

Internat. Ltd, 1991–95; Dir of Res. and Partner, Tudor Gp, 1995–99. Visiting Professor: City Univ. Business Sch.; LSE. Mem. Council, NIESR, 2000–. Asst Ed., Economic Policy, 1987–89; Mem. Editl Bd, New Economy, 1996–. *Publications:* articles in academic jls. *Address:* Bank of England, Threadneedle Street, EC2R 8AH. *T:* (020) 7601 3235.

WADIA, Jim, FCA; Chief Operating Officer, Linklaters, since 2001; *b* 12 April 1948; *m* 1972, Joelle Garnier; one *s* one *d*. *Educ:* Le Rosey, Rolle, Switzerland; Inns of Court Sch. of Law. Called to the Bar, Inner Temple, 1969. Arthur Andersen: Partner, 1982–2000; Hd, London Tax, 1989–93; Man. Partner, UK, 1993–97; Worldwide Man. Partner, 1997–2000. FRSA 1993. *Recreations:* tennis, theatre. *Address:* 28 Eldon Road, W8 5PT. *T:* (020) 7937 7045, (office) (020) 7456 4982; *e-mail:* jim.wadia@linklaters.com.

WADKINS, Lanny; golfer; *b* 5 Dec. 1949; *s* of Jerry Lanston Wadkins and Frances Ann Wadkins (*née* Burnett); *m* 1971, Rachel Irene Strong; one *d*. *Educ:* Wake Forest Univ., USA. US Amateur Champion, 1970; tournament wins include: US World Series and US PGA, 1977; Tournament Players' Champion, 1979, 1982, 1983; Hawaiian Open, 1988, 1991; mem., US Ryder Cup Team, 1977, Captain, 1995. *Address:* c/o Professional Golfers' Association Tour, 100 Avenue of the Champions, Palm Beach Gardens, FL 33410-9601, USA.

WADSWORTH, Brian; Director, Logistics and Maritime Transport, Department for Transport, Local Government and the Regions (formerly Department of the Environment, Transport and the Regions), since 1999; *b* 18 Jan. 1952; *s* of George David Brian Wadsworth and Betty (*née* Metcalfe); *m* 1987, Anne Jacqueline Beuselinck. *Educ:* Univ. of British Columbia (BA Hons Eng. Lit. 1973). FILog 1998. Entered Department of Transport, 1974; Sec., Review of Main Line Rly Electrification, 1978–79; Sec. to Chief Exec., LB of Hounslow, 1981; Principal: Transport Policy Rev. Unit, 1981–83; London Transport Finance, 1984; Pvte Sec. to Minister of State, 1985; Finance Transport Industries (BA, BAA, NBC privatisations), 1986–89; Sec. to BA plc, 1989–91; Asst Sec., Rlys Policy (BR privatisation), 1991–95; Sec. to British Oxygen plc, 1995; Under Sec., Dir of Finance, 1995–97; Dir, Freight Distbn and Logistics, DETR, 1997–99. Freeman, City of London, 1997; Liveryman, Co. of Carmen, 1997– (Mem., Ct of Assistants, 2000–). *Publication:* Best Methods of Railway Restructuring and Privatisation, 1995. *Recreations:* travel, sailing, music. *Address:* Department for Transport, Local Government and the Regions, Great Minster House, 76 Marsham Street, SW1P 4DR. *T:* (020) 7944 2750.

WADSWORTH, David Grant; Chief Executive, Service Children's Education, Ministry of Defence, since 1997; *b* 30 Dec. 1944; *s* of Fred Wadsworth and Lona Wadsworth (*née* Booth); *m* Marcia Armour (*née* Lyles); one step *s* one step *d*. *Educ:* Hipperholme Grammar Sch., Yorks; Oriel Coll., Oxford (MA 1970); Univ. of Newcastle upon Tyne (MPhil 1992). Teacher, 1966–73; Educn Admin, Leeds CC, 1973–85; Dep. Dir of Educn, Northumberland CC, 1985–89; Chief Educn Officer, Bedfordshire CC, 1989–96. Hon. DEd De Montfort, 1996. Chevalier, l'Ordre des Palmes Académiques (France), 1992; Cavaliere della Ordine al Merito (Italy), 1994. *Recreations:* Rugby and cricket (passively), travel, music, European food and wine. *Address:* HQ SCE, BFPO 40. *T:* (Germany) (2161) 9082372. *Club:* Oxford and Cambridge.

WADSWORTH, James Patrick; QC 1981; **His Honour Judge Wadsworth;** a Circuit Judge, since 2000; *b* 7 Sept. 1940; *s* of Francis Thomas Bernard Wadsworth, Newcastle, and Geraldine Rosa (*née* Brannan); *m* 1963, Judith Stuart Morrison, *e d* of Morrison Scott, Newport-on-Tay; one *s* one *d*. *Educ:* Stonyhurst; University Coll., Oxford (MA). Called to the Bar, Inner Temple, 1963, Bencher, 1988; a Recorder, 1980–2000. Member: Bar Council, 1992–95; Bar Professional Standards Cttee, 1993–95. *Address:* Southwark Crown Court, 1 English Grounds, Southwark, SE1 2HU.

WADSWORTH, Prof. Michael Edwin John, PhD; Director, Medical Research Council National Survey of Health and Development, since 1985, and Visiting Professor, Department of Epidemiology and Public Health Medicine, since 1992, Royal Free and University College Medical School, University College London (formerly University College London Medical School); *b* 20 Jan. 1942; *s* of Cecil and Amelia Wadsworth; *m* 1966, Jane Arnott (marr. diss. 1991); one *s* one *d*; partner, Kit Leighton-Kelly; one *d*. *Educ:* Leeds Univ. (BA, MPhil); London Sch. of Econs (PhD 1976). Research Asst, Dept of Medicine, Guy's Hosp. Med. Sch., 1963–65; Res. Fellow, Dept of Gen. Practice, Univ. of Edinburgh Med. Sch., 1965–68; Res. Scientist, MRC Nat. Survey Health and Devel, 1968–. Hon. MFPHM 1993. *Publications:* (jtly) Health and Sickness, 1971; Roots of Delinquency, 1976; (ed with D. Robinson) Studies in Everyday Medical Life, 1976; (ed with U. Gerhardt) Stress and Stigma, 1985; The Imprint of Time, 1991; (ed with M. G. Marmot) Fetal and Early Childhood Development, 1997; numerous articles in learned jls in medicine and social scis. *Recreations:* music, living. *Address:* 12C Kingsdown Parade, Bristol BS6 5UD. *T:* (0117) 924 4906.

WAGERMAN, Josephine Miriam, OBE 1992; President, Board of Deputies of British Jews, since 2000 (Senior Vice-President, 1997–2000); *b* 17 Sept. 1933; *d* of Emanuel and Jane Barbanel; *m* 1956, Peter Henry Wagerman; one *s* one *d*. *Educ:* John Howard Sch., London; Birkbeck Coll., London Univ. (BA Hons 1955); Inst. of Educn, London Univ. (PGCE 1956; Acad. Dipl. 1959; MA (Ed) 1970). Teacher, Battersea, Highgate, Hackney and Singapore, 1956–73; Jews' Free School: Head of Lower Sch., 1973–76; Dep. Head, 1976–85; Headteacher, 1985–93; Chief Exec., Lennox Lewis Coll., 1994–96. Former Pres., London Br., AMMA; former Member: Teachers' Pay and Conditions of Service Adv. Cttee, ILEA; London Standing Cttee Adv. Cttee on Religious Educn, ILEA; Council, Selly Oak Coll. Centre for Jewish-Christian Relns; Member: Inner Cities Religious Council, DoE, 1994–; Bd of Dirs, and Partnership 2000 Policy Cttee, United Jewish Israel Appeal, 1995–. Trustee and Gov., Central Foundn Schs, London, 1995–. *Recreations:* gardening, cooking, entertaining friends, travel, Art Nouveau silver, Victorian painting. *Address:* Board of Deputies of British Jews, Commonwealth House, 1–19 New Oxford Street, WC1A 1NF. *T:* (020) 8543 5400.

WAGNER, Erica Augusta; writer; Literary Editor, The Times, since 1996; *b* NYC, 24 Sept. 1967; *d* of Arthur Malcolm Wagner and Ellen Franklin Wagner; *m* 1993, Francis Jonathan Gilbert; one *s*. *Educ:* Brearley Sch., NYC; St Paul's Girls' Sch., London; Corpus Christi Coll., Cambridge (BA Hons 1989); UEA (MA Creative Writing 1991). Freelance editor/researcher/journalist, 1992–95; The Times: Asst to Literary Editor, 1995; Dep. Literary Editor, 1996. *Publications:* Gravity: stories, 1997; Ariel's Gift: Ted Hughes, Sylvia Plath and the story of Birthday Letters, 2000. *Recreations:* bridges, cooking, Antarctic dreams. *Address:* c/o Antony Harwood Ltd, Riverbank House, Putney Bridge Approach, SW6 3JD. *T:* (020) 7351 7561.

WAGNER, Gerrit Abram, KBE (Hon.) 1977 (CBE (Hon.) 1964); Kt, Order of Netherlands Lion, 1969; Grand Officer, Order of Oranje Nassau, 1983 (Commander 1977); Chairman, Supervisory Board, Royal Dutch Petroleum Co., 1977–87 (President, 1971–77); *b* 21 Oct. 1916; *m* 1946, M. van der Heul; one *s* three *d*. *Educ:* Leyden Univ. LLM 1939. After a period in a bank in Rotterdam and in Civil Service in Rotterdam and The Hague, joined Royal Dutch Shell Group, 1946; assignments in The Hague, Curaçao, Venezuela, London and Indonesia; apptd Man. Dir, Royal Dutch Petroleum Co. and Shell Petroleum Co. Ltd; Mem. Presidium of Bd of Directors of Shell Petroleum NV, 1964; Dir, Shell Canada Ltd, 1971–77; Chm., Cttee of Man. Dirs, Royal Dutch/Shell Group, 1972–77; Chm., Shell Oil USA, 1972–77. Former Chairman, Supervisory Board: De Nederlandsche Bank NV; Gist-Brocades NV; KLM; Smit Internat.; Vice-Chm., Supervisory Bd, Hoogovens Gp BV, Beverwijk; Member, International Advisory Committee: Chase Manhattan Bank, NY; Robert Bosch, Stuttgart. Hon. Dr Eindhoven, 1986; Hon. LLD Rochester, USA, 1987. Order of Francisco de Miranda, Grand Officer (Venezuela), 1965; Officier Légion d'Honneur (France), 1974. *Address:* 13 Teylingerhorstlaan 13, 2244 EJ Wassenaar, The Netherlands.

WAGNER, Dame Gillian (Mary Millicent), (Lady Wagner), DBE 1994 (OBE 1977); Chairman, Carnegie UK Trust, 1995–2000 (Trustee, since 1980); *b* 25 Oct. 1927; *e d* of late Major Henry Archibald Roger Graham, and of Hon. Margaret Beatrix, *d* of 1st Baron Roborough; *m* 1953, Sir Anthony Wagner, KCB, KCVO; two *s* one *d*. *Educ:* Cheltenham Ladies' Coll.; Geneva Univ. (Licence ès Sciences Morales); London Sch. of Economics (Dip. Social Admin). PhD London 1977. Mem. Council, Barnardo's, 1969–97 (Chm., Exec./Finance Cttee, 1973–78; Chm. Council, 1978–84); Chairman: Nat. Centre for Volunteering (formerly Volunteer Centre), 1984–89 (Pres., 1990–); Review of Residential Care, 1986–88; Ct of Govs, Thomas Coram Foundn for Children, 1990–95; The Leche Trust, 1992–97; Chair, Community Care Inquiry for people with learning difficulties, Mental Health Foundn, 1995–96; President: Skill: Nat. Bureau for Students with Disabilities, 1978–91; IAPS, 1985–90; Abbeyfield, 1995–; Trustee, Princess Royal Trust for Carers, 1992–. Mem. Exec. Cttee, Georgian Gp, 1970–78. Chm. of Governors, Felixstowe Coll., 1980–87; Gov., Nat. Inst. for Social Work, 1988–96. Governor, LSE, 1991–96. FRSA 1995. Hon. DSc Bristol, 1989; Hon. LLD Liverpool, 1990. *Publications:* Barnardo, 1979; Children of the Empire, 1982; The Chocolate Conscience, 1987; various articles on residential care. *Recreations:* gardening, travelling. *Address:* Flat 31, 55 Ebury Street, SW3W 0PA. *T:* (020) 7730 0040; Wyndham Cottage, Crespigny Road, Aldeburgh, Suffolk IP15 5DL. *T:* (01728) 452596. *Club:* Aldeburgh Yacht.

WAGNER, Prof. Leslie, CBE 2000; MA; Vice-Chancellor (formerly Principal and Chief Executive), and Professor, Leeds Metropolitan University, since 1994; *b* 21 Feb. 1943; *s* of Herman and Toby Wagner; *m* 1967, Jennifer Jean Fineberg; one *s* one *d*. *Educ:* Salford Grammar Sch.; Manchester Univ. (MAEcon). Economic Asst and Economic Advr, DEA, 1966–69; Economic Advr, Min. of Technology, 1969–70; Lectr in Econs, Open Univ., 1970–76; Hd of Social Sciences, 1976–82, Prof., 1980, Polytechnic of Central London; Asst Sec. (Academic), Nat. Adv. Body for Local Authy Higher Educn, 1982–85; Dep. Sec., Nat. Adv. Body for Public Sector Higher Educn, 1985–87; Dir, Poly. of N London, 1987–92, then Vice-Chancellor and Chief Exec., Univ. of N London, 1992–93. Member: Bd, Open Learning Foundn, 1990–96 (Chm., 1990–93); Bd, HEQC, 1992–97; Council for Industry and Higher Educn, 1992–; Leeds TEC, 1997–2001; DFEE Skills Task Gp, 1998–2000. Chairman: SRHE, 1994–96; Higher Educn for Capability, 1994–98; Yorks and Humberside Univs Assoc., 1996–99; UUK Wider Participation and Lifelong Learning Gp; Leeds Common Purpose Adv. Gp, 2000–. Councillor (Lab) London Bor. of Harrow, 1971–78, Chm., Educn Cttee, 1972–74. Contested (Lab) Harrow W, Feb. 1974. Dir, Leeds Business Services, 2001–; Mem., Leeds Cares Leadership Gp. Vice-Pres., Utd Synagogue, 1992–93; Chm., Jewish Community Allocations Bd, 1994–96; Mem. Bd, Jewish Chronicle Trust, 1999–. *Publications:* (ed) Readings in Applied Microeconomics, 1973, 2nd edn 1981; (ed) Agenda for Institutional Change in Higher Education, 1982; The Economics of Educational Media, 1982; (jtly) Choosing to Learn: a study of mature students, 1987. *Address:* Leeds Metropolitan University, Calverley Street, Leeds LS1 3HE. *T:* (0113) 283 3100.

WAGSTAFF, Ven. Christopher John Harold; Archdeacon of Gloucester, 1982–2000, now Emeritus; *b* 25 June 1936; *s* of Harold Maurice Wagstaff and Kathleen Mary Wagstaff (*née* Bean); *m* 1964, Margaret Louise (*née* Macdonald); two *s* one *d*. *Educ:* Bishop's Stortford College, Herts; Essex Inst. of Agriculture, Chelmsford (Dipl. in Horticulture 1959); St David's Coll., Lampeter (BA 1962, Dipl. in Theol. 1963). Deacon 1963, priest 1964; Curate, All Saints, Queensbury, 1963–68; Vicar, St Michael's, Tokyngton, Wembley, 1968–73; Vicar of Coleford with Staunton, 1973–83; RD, South Forest, 1975–82. Diocese of Gloucester: Chairman: House of Clergy, 1983–95; Bd of Social Responsibility, 1983–96; Diocesan Trust, 1983–2000; Diocesan Assoc. for the Deaf, 1989–94; DAC, 1988–2000; Adv. Council for Ministry, 1996–2000. Mem., General Synod, 1988–98. Hon. Canon, St Andrew's Cathedral, Njombe, Tanzania, 1993–. Freeman, City of London; Liveryman, Co. of Armourers and Brasiers (Master, 2000–01). *Recreations:* gardening, entertaining, travel. *Address:* Karibuni, 1 Collafield, Littledean, Glos GL14 3LG. *T:* (01594) 825282.

WAGSTAFF, David St John Rivers; a Recorder of the Crown Court, 1974–94; barrister, retired; *b* 22 June 1930; *s* of late Prof. John Edward Pretty Wagstaff and Dorothy Margaret (*née* McRobie); *m* 1970, Dorothy Elizabeth Starkie; two *d*. *Educ:* Winchester Coll. (Schol.); Trinity Coll., Cambridge (Schol., MA, LLB). Called to Bar, Lincoln's Inn, 1954. *Publication:* Man's Relationship with God, or Spiritual Adventure, 1996. *Recreations:* mountaineering, fencing. *Address:* 8 Breary Lane East, Bramhope, Leeds LS16 9BJ. *Clubs:* Alpine; Fell and Rock Climbing (Lake District), Leeds (Leeds).

WAGSTAFF, (Edward) Malise (Wynter); HM Diplomatic Service, retired; psychotherapist; *b* 27 June 1930; *s* of late Col Henry Wynter Wagstaff, CSI, MC, and Jean Mathieson, MB, BS; *m* 1st, 1957, Eva Margot (marr. diss. 1995), *d* of Erik Hedelius; one *s* two *d*; 2nd, 1995, Vivien Rosemary Manton, *d* of Winston and Marjorie Farrar. *Educ:* Wellington Coll.; RMA Sandhurst; Pembroke Coll., Cambridge (MA; Mech Scis Tripos); Staff Coll., Camberley; psc. Commissioned RE, 1949; served in UK, Germany and Gibraltar, 1950–62; seconded to Federal Regular Army, Fedn of S Arabia, 1963–65; Asst Mil. Attaché, Amman, 1967–69 (Major, 1962; GSM; South Arabia Radfan bar). Joined FCO, 1969; served Saigon, 1973, FCO, 1975, Oslo, 1976, Copenhagen, 1978, FCO, 1981; Counsellor, FCO, 1982–92; Advr, later Consultant FCO, 1992–95. Qualified as Psychosynthesis psychotherapist, 1993. Kt, First Degree, Order of Dannebrog, 1979. *Recreations:* God, concern for the bewildered, plumbing. *Address:* c/o Lloyds TSB, 32 Commercial Way, Woking, Surrey GU21 1ER.

WAIAPU, Bishop of, since 1991; **Rt Rev. Murray John Mills;** *b* 29 May 1936; *s* of Robert Claude Mills and Mabel Winifred Mills; *m* 1961, Judith Anne Cotton; two *s* three *d*. *Educ:* Auckland Univ. (BA, MA); St John's Theol Coll. (LTh (First Cl. Hons)). Ordained: Deacon, 1960; Priest, 1961 (dio. of Auckland); Assistant Curate: Papakura, 1960–63; Whangarei, 1963–65; Vicar: Bay of Islands, 1965–70; Matamata, 1970–75; Archdeacon of Waikato, 1976–81; Vicar-Gen., dio. of Waikato, 1978–84; Vicar: Tokoroa, 1981–84; St John's Cathedral, Napier (dio. of Waiapu) and Dean of Waiapu, 1984–91. Examining Chaplain to Bishop of Waikato, 1974–84; Advr in Christian Educn, 1976–81. *Publication:* History of Christ Church, Papakura, 1961. *Recreations:* tramping, gardening, drama, politics, music, reading. *Address:* (home) 8 Cameron Terrace, Napier,

New Zealand. *T:* (6) 8357846; (office) Diocesan Office, PO Box 227, Napier, New Zealand. *T:* (6) 8358230.

WAIARU, Rt Rev. Amos Stanley, OBE 2001; Archbishop of Melanesia, and Bishop of Central Melanesia, 1988–93; *b* 19 April 1944; *s* of late Stanley Qagora and Emma Kaifo; *m* 1976, Mary Marjorie Waiaru (*née* Mwele); one *s* three *d*. *Educ:* Bishop Patteson Theol Coll., Kohimarama, Solomon Is; Pacific Theol Coll., Suva, Fiji Is (DipTh). Tutor, Torgil Training Centre, Vanuatu, 1976; Chaplain, Vureas High School, Vanuatu, 1977–78, Head Master 1979–80; Bishop of Temotu, Solomon Is, 1981–87. Chm., S Pacific Anglican Council, 1991–93. *Recreations:* gardening, fishing. *Address:* Ngafinuatoga Village, Santa Anna, Makira-Ulawa Province, Solomon Islands.

WAIDE, (Edward) Bevan, OBE 1988; Partner, Coopers & Lybrand, 1988–93; Chairman, Oxford Policy Management Ltd, since 1996; *b* 14 Sept. 1936; *s* of William Leathley Waide and Louisa Winifred Waide (*née* Evershed); *m* 1st, 1961, Pu-Chin (marr. diss. 1993); one *s* one *d*; 2nd, 1995, Urmila Kumari, Kathiwada. *Educ:* Farnham Grammar Sch.; Emmanuel Coll., Cambridge (BA); Univ. of California, Berkeley (MA). Teaching Asst, Univ. of California, 1959–61; Sen. Economist, Asia, World Bank, 1962–69; Chief Advr, Min. of Economic Affairs and Develt Planning, Govt of Tanzania, 1969–73; Dir, N Region Strategy Team, DoE, 1973–76; World Bank: Chief Economist, S Asia, 1976–79; Dir, Develt Policy, 1979–82; Dir, Country Policy Dept, 1982–84; Dir, New Delhi Office, 1984–88. Chief Advr, Privatisation, Tanzanian Govt, 1993–97; Advisor, Privatisation: Indonesian Govt, 1979–99; Bangladeshi Govt, 1999–. Mem., Commonwealth Develt Corp., 1990–93. *Publications:* (jtly) India: an industrialising economy in transition, 1989; World Develt Reports, World Bank; Government of Indonesia: privatisation masterplan, 1998; articles on develt and regional planning issues; country reports. *Recreations:* tennis, car restoration. *Address:* Laburnum Cottage, The Butts, Napton-on-the-Hill, Southam, Warwicks CV47 8NW. *T:* (01926) 817024; *e-mail:* bevan@waide.net. *Clubs:* Reform; Vintage Sports Car.

WAIGEL, Dr Theodor; Member for Neu Ulm, Bundestag, since 1972; Chairman, CSU, 1988–99; *b* 22 April 1939; *s* of August Waigel and Genoveva Konrad; *m* 1st, 1966, Karin Hönig; one *s* one *d*; 2nd, 1994, Dr Irene Epple; one *s*. *Educ:* Univ. of Munich; Univ. of Würzburg (Dr jur. 1967). Lawyer, 1967–69. Junge Union: Dist Chm., Krumbach, 1961–70; Regl Chm., Schwaben, 1967–71; Chm., Bavaria, 1971–75; Chairman: CSU Basic Commn, 1973–88; Economy wkg gp, CDU/CSU parly gp, 1980–82; Bavaria gp, CSU, 1982–89; First Dep. Chm., CDU/CSU parly gp, 1982–89. Posts in Min. of Finance, and Min. of Economy and Transport, Bavaria, 1969–72; Minister of Finance, Germany, 1989–98. Governor: German Helsinki Human Rights Cttee; German Soc. of For. Policy. *Address:* Bundeshaus, Platz der Republik, 11011 Berlin, Germany.

WAIKATO, Bishop of, since 1993; **Rt Rev. David John Moxon;** *b* 6 Sept. 1951; *s* of John Rosher Moxon and Joan Moxon; *m*; two *s* two *d*. *Educ:* Freyberg High Sch., Palmerston North; Massey Univ. (MA Hons). MA Oxford Univ. Volunteer service abroad (school leaver scheme), 1970; Univ. Tutor, Educn Dept, Massey Univ., 1974–75; Curate, St Luke's, Havelock North, 1978–81; Vicar, St George's, Gate Pa, Tauronga, 1981–87; Dir, Theol Educn by Extension Unit, Anglican Church of Aotearoa, NZ and Polynesia, 1987–93. Hon. LTh Aotearoa. Gold Duke of Edinburgh Award, 1969. *Recreations:* playing flute, reading, tramping, swimming. *Address:* Bishop's House, 3 Lake Domain Drive, Hamilton, NZ. *T:* (7) 8395308, (office) Anglican Church House, 33 Victoria Street, Hamilton, NZ. *T:* (7) 8382309.

WAINE, Dr Colin, OBE 1990; FRCGP, FRCPath; Director of Health Programmes and Primary Care Development, Sunderland Health Authority, since 1996; Chairman, Council, Royal College of General Practitioners, 1990–93; *b* 12 March 1936; *m* 1959, Gwendoline Jameson; two *d*. *Educ:* King James I Grammar Sch., Bishop Auckland; Medical Sch., King's Coll., Univ. of Durham (MB BS Hons). MRCGP (dist.) 1975, FRCGP 1976, FRCPath 1993. Principal in general practice, Bishop Auckland, 1962–93; Hosp. Practitioner in Paediatrics, Bishop Auckland General Hosp., 1963–88; Gen. Manager, SW Durham HA, 1985–92; Dir of Primary Care, Sunderland Health Commn, 1993–96. Course Organiser (Continuing Educn), Regional Post Grad. Inst., Newcastle upon Tyne, 1978–86. Consultant and UK Delegate, European Health Cttee, Primary Care and Prevention Gp, Council of Europe, Strasbourg, 1983–85. *Publications:* (contrib.) Handbook of Preventative Care for Pre-School Children, 1984; Organisation of Prevention in Primary Care, 1986; Why not care for your diabetic patients?, 1986; (contrib.) Chronic Disease in Medical Audit in General Practice, 1990; contrib. to reports of working parties and papers and articles on diabetes, health care for children, asthma, etc in BMJ, The Practitioner, Cardiology in Practice, Members Reference Books, RCGP. *Recreations:* reading, gardening, music, cricket. *Address:* 42 Etherley Lane, Bishop Auckland, Co. Durham DL14 7QZ. *T:* (01388) 604429.

WAINE, Rt Rev. John, KCVO 1996; Bishop of Chelmsford, 1986–96; Clerk of the Closet to the Queen, 1989–96; *b* June 1930; *s* of late William and Ellen Waine; *m* 1957, Patricia Zena Haikney; three *s*. *Educ:* Prescot Grammar Sch.; Manchester Univ. (BA); Ridley Hall, Cambridge. Deacon 1955, Priest 1956; Curate of St Mary, West Derby, 1955–58; Curate in Charge of All Saints, Sutton, 1958–60; Vicar of Ditton, 1960–64; Vicar of Holy Trinity, Southport, 1964–69; Rector of Kirkby, 1969–75; Bishop Suffragan of Stafford, 1975–78; Bishop of St Edmundsbury and Ipswich, 1978–86. Chm., Churches Main Cttee, 1991–96. Mem., Press Complaints Commn, 1997–. Chm. Council, Univ. of Essex, 1995–2001. Master, Glass Sellers' Co., 1999–2000. ChStJ 1983 (Prelate, 1999). *Recreations:* music, gardening. *Address:* Broadmere, Ipswich Road, Grundisburgh, Woodbridge, Suffolk IP13 6TJ. *T:* (01473) 738296. *Club:* Royal Air Force.

WAINE, Stephen Phillip; His Honour Judge Waine; a Circuit Judge, since 2001; *b* 9 June 1947; *s* of Dr T. E. Waine and late M. F. Waine; *m* 1st, 1976 (marr. diss.); 2nd, 1981, Clare (*née* Pryor); one *s* one *d*. *Educ:* Rugby Sch.; Southampton Univ. (LLB). Called to the Bar, Lincoln's Inn, 1969; a Recorder, Midland and Oxford Circuit, 1992–2001. FCIArb 1999. *Recreations:* ski-ing, golf, gardening, watching sports, reading. *Address:* Nottingham Court Centre, 60 Canal Street, Nottingham NG1 7EL. *Club:* MCC.

WAINWRIGHT, Elizabeth-Anne; *see* Gumbel, E.-A.

WAINWRIGHT, Geoffrey John, MBE 1991; PhD; FSA; Founder, Bluestone Partnership, 1999; *b* 19 Sept. 1937; *s* of Frederick and Dorothy Wainwright; *m* 1977, Judith; one *s* two *d*. *Educ:* Pembroke Docks Sch.; Univ. of Wales (BA); Univ. of London (PhD). FSA 1967; MIFA 1984, Hon. MIFA 1999. Prof. of Archaeology, Univ. of Baroda, India, 1961–63; Inspectorate of Ancient Monuments, English Heritage (formerly part of DoE), 1963–99; Principal Inspector, 1963–90; Chief Archaeologist, 1989–99. Mem., Royal Commn on Ancient and Historical Monuments in Wales, 1987–2000, Vice Chm., 2000–; President: Cornwall Archaeological Soc., 1980–84; Prehistoric Soc., 1982–86; Vice Pres., 1997–2001, Treasurer, 2001–, Soc. of Antiquaries (Dir, 1984–90). Visiting Professor: Univ. of Southampton, 1991–; UCL, 1995–. Fellow, University Coll., Cardiff, 1985. FRSA 1991. Hon. Fellow, Univ. of Wales, Lampeter, 1996. Hon. Mem., Europae Archaeologiae Consilium, 1999. *Publications:* Stone Age in North India, 1964; Coygan Camp, Carms, 1967; Durrington Walls, Wilts, 1971; Mount Pleasant, Dorset, 1979; Gussage All Saints, Dorset, 1979; The Henge Monuments, 1990; numerous articles in learned jls. *Recreations:* Rugby football, walking, food and drink. *Address:* 13 Park Cottages, Crown Road, Twickenham, TW1 3EQ. *T:* (020) 8891 2429; March Pres, Pontfaen, Pembs SA65 9TT.

WAINWRIGHT, Richard Barry; Principal Legal Adviser, European Commission; *b* 10 June 1940; *s* of Denys and Shelagh Wainwright; *m* 1966, Linda Sully; three *s* one *d*. *Educ:* Trinity Coll., Oxford (BA Hons); Inns of Court Sch. of Law. In practice as barrister, 1966–68; Solicitor's Office, Inland Revenue, 1968–69; Legal Advr, British Petroleum Co., 1969–73; with Legal Service, EC, 1973–. *Publications:* contribs to Common Market Law Rev., European Law Rev., Oxford Yearbook of European Law, Revue du Marché Commun. *Recreations:* music, reading, sailing, ski-ing, tennis, golf, walking. *Address:* 5 rue de l'Abreuvoir, 1170 Brussels, Belgium. *T:* (2) 6726803. *Club:* Château Ste Anne (Brussels).

WAINWRIGHT, Richard Scurrah; *b* 11 April 1918; *o s* of late Henry Scurrah and Emily Wainwright; *m* 1948, Joyce Mary Hollis; one *s* two *d* (and one *s* decd). *Educ:* Shrewsbury Sch.; Clare Coll., Cambridge (Open Scholar). BA Hons (History), 1939. Friends Ambulance Unit, NW Europe, 1939–46. Retired Partner, Peat Marwick Mitchell & Co., Chartered Accountants. Pres., Leeds/Bradford Society of Chartered Accountants, 1965–66. MP (L) Colne Valley, 1966–70 and Feb. 1974–87, retired. Chm., Liberal Party Research Dept, 1968–70; Chm., Liberal Party, 1970–72; Mem., Select Cttee on Treasury, 1979–87; Liberal spokesman on the economy, 1979–85, on employment, 1985–87. Dep. Chm., Wider Share Ownership Council, 1968–92. Pres., Yorks Fedn of Lib Dems, 1989–97. *Recreations:* gardening, swimming. *Address:* 8 Dunstarn Lane, Leeds LS16 8EL. *T:* (0113) 267 3938.

WAINWRIGHT, Sam, CBE 1982; Member: Monopolies and Mergers Commission, 1985–91; Post Office Audit Committee, 1989–92; Director, BICC, 1985–90; *b* 2 Oct. 1924; *m* Ruth Strom; three *s* one *d*. *Educ:* Regent Street Polytechnic; LSE (MSc Econ). Financial journalist, Glasgow Herald, 1950; Deputy City Editor, 1952–55; Director: Rea Brothers Ltd (Merchant Bankers), 1960–77 (Managing Dir, 1965–77); Furness Withy & Co. Ltd, 1971–77; Stothert & Pitt Ltd, 1970–77 (Chm., 1975–77); Aeronautical & General Instruments Ltd, 1968–77; Lancashire & London Investment Trust Ltd, 1963–77; Scottish Cities Investment Trust Ltd, 1961–77; Scottish & Mercantile Investment Co. Ltd, 1964–77; AMDAHL (UK), 1987–93; Post Office Corporation: Mem. Bd, 1977–85; Dep. Chm., 1981–85; Man. Dir, Nat. Girobank, 1977–85; Dir Postel Investment Ltd, 1982–85; Dir, 1972–87, Dep. Chm., 1985–86, Chm., 1986–87, Manders (Hldgs). Mem. Council, Soc. of Investment Analysts, 1961–75, Fellow, 1980. Chm., Jigsaw Day Nurseries, 1991–95. Hon. Editor, The Investment Analyst, 1961–74. *Publications:* articles in various Bank Reviews. *Recreations:* reading, bridge, walking. *Address:* Flat 5, 29 Warrington Crescent, W9 1EJ. *T:* (020) 7286 8050. *Club:* Reform.

WAIT, John James; His Honour Judge Wait; a Circuit Judge, since 1997; *b* 19 Sept. 1949; *s* of Eric James Wait and Rachel Wait; *m* 1986, Patricia, (Tricia), Ann Hitchcock; two *s*. *Educ:* Queen Mary's Grammar Sch., Walsall; Nottingham Univ. (LLB 1971). Called to the Bar, Inner Temple, 1972; Lectr in Law, UCW, Aberystwyth, 1972–74; in practice at the Bar, 1974–97; Asst Recorder, 1989–93; a Recorder, 1993–97; Midland and Oxford Circuit. *Recreations:* golf, tennis, sailing. *Address:* Derby Combined Court, Morledge, Derby DE1 2XE. *Clubs:* Moor Hall Golf (Sutton Coldfield), St Enodoc Golf (N Cornwall).

WAITE, Rt Hon. Sir John (Douglas), Kt 1982; PC 1993; a Lord Justice of Appeal, 1993–97; Chairman, UNICEF (UK), since 1997; *b* 3 July 1932; *s* of late Archibald Waite and Betty, *d* of late Ernest Bates; *m* 1966, Julia Mary, *er d* of late Joseph Tangye; three *s* two step *s*. *Educ:* Sherborne Sch.; Corpus Christi Coll., Cambridge (MA). President of Cambridge Union, 1955. Nat. Service, 2nd Lieut, RA, 1951–52. Called to Bar, Gray's Inn, 1956, Bencher, 1981; QC 1975; a Judge of the High Court of Justice, Family Div., 1982–93; Presiding Judge, North Eastern Circuit, 1990–93; Judge, Gibraltar Court of Appeal, 1997–2000. Pres., Employment Appeal Tribunal, 1983–85. Chairman: Special Trustees, Middx and UC Hosps, 1997–; UCL Hosps Charitable Foundn, 1999–. *Recreations:* reading (haphazardly), sailing (uncertainly), gardening (optimistically). *Address:* 33 Cleaver Square, SE11 4EA; 54 Church Street, Orford, Woodbridge, Suffolk IP12 2NT.

WAITE, Terence Hardy, CBE 1992 (MBE 1982); writer and lecturer; Adviser to Archbishop of Canterbury on Anglican Communion Affairs, 1980–92; Fellow Commoner, Trinity Hall, Cambridge, 1992–93; *b* 31 May 1939; *s* of Thomas William Waite and Lena (*née* Hardy); *m* 1964, Helen Frances Watters; one *s* three *d*. *Educ:* Wilmslow and Stockton Heath, Cheshire; Church Army Coll., London; privately in USA and Europe. Lay training adviser to Bishop and Diocese of Bristol, 1964–68; Adviser to Archbishop of Uganda, Rwanda and Burundi, 1968–71; Internat. Consultant working with Roman Catholic Church, 1972–79. Member, National Assembly, Church of England, 1966–68 (resigned on moving to Africa); Co-ordinator, Southern Sudan Relief Project, 1969–71. Founder-Chm., Y Care International, 1985–2000 (Pres., 2000–). Mem., Royal Inst. of International Affairs, 1980–. Paul Harris Fellow, Internat. Rotarian Organisation, 1983–. Vice-Pres., E Cheshire Hospice, Macclesfield, 1992–. Dir, Educational Interactive, 2000–. Member: World Wildlife Council, 1985–; Council, Internat. Year of Shelter for the Homeless, 1987; Central Cttee, Victim Support. Trustee, Butler Trust. Patron: Strode Park Foundn for the Disabled, Herne, Kent, 1985; Bury St Edmunds Volunteer Centre; Rainbow Appeal, 1995; Warrington Male Voice Choir, 1996; Romany Soc.; Lewisham Envmt Trust; Langley House Trust; Suffolk Far East Prisoners of War Soc.; Save our Parsonages; Uganda Soc. for Disabled Children; Pres., Emmaus UK; Ambassador for WWF, 2000. Hon. Pres., 3 cs Appeal, Univ. Hosp. Lewisham. Templeton UK Project Award, 1985. Hon. DCL: City, 1986; Kent at Canterbury, 1986; Durham, 1992; Hon. LLD: Liverpool, 1986; Sussex, 1992; Yale, 1992; Hon. DHL Virginia Commonwealth Univ., 1996. Franklin D. Roosevelt Four Freedom Award, 1992. *Publications:* Taken on Trust, 1993; Footfalls in Memory, 1995; Travels with a Primate, 2000. *Recreations:* music, walking, travel (esp. in remote parts of the world), Jungian studies, international affairs and politics, Left-Handed Society, preservation of old Blackheath. *Address:* Trinity Hall, Cambridge CB2 1TJ. *Clubs:* Travellers; Empire (Toronto).

WAJDA, Andrzej; Polish film and theatre director; Managing Director, Teatr Powszechny, Warsaw, 1989–90; Senator, Polish People's Republic, 1989–91 (one term); *b* 6 March 1926; *s* of Jakub Wajda and Aniela Wajda; *m* 1st, 1967, Beata Tyszkiewicz (marr. diss.); one *d*; 2nd, 1975, Krystyna Zachwatowicz. *Educ:* Acad. Fine Arts, Cracow; Film Acad., Łódź. Asst Stage Manager, 1953; film dir, 1954–; Stage Manager, Teatr Stary, Cracow, 1973. Pres., Polish Film Assoc., 1978–83. Hon. Mem., Union of Polish Artists and Designers, 1977. Dr *hc*: American, Washington, 1981; Bologna, 1988; Jagiellonian, Cracow, 1989. British Acad. Award for Services to Film, 1982; BAFTA Fellowship, 1982;

Hon. Academy Award for lifetime achievement, 2000. Order of Banner of Labour, 1975; Officer's Cross of Polonia Restituta; Officier, Légion d'Honneur (France), 1982; Order of Kirill and Methodius (Bulgaria). *Films:* Generation, 1954; I'm Going to the Sun, 1955; Kanal, 1956 (Silver Palm, Cannes, 1957); Ashes and Diamonds, 1957; Lotna, 1959; Innocent Sorcerers, 1959; Samson, 1960; Serbian Lady Macbeth, 1961; Love at Twenty, 1961; Ashes, 1965; Gates of Paradise, 1967; Everything For Sale, 1968; Jigsaw Puzzle (for TV), 1969; Hunting Flies, 1969; Macbeth (TV), 1969; Landscape After Battle, 1970; The Birch Wood, 1970; Pilatus (TV), 1971; Master and Margaret (TV), 1972; The Wedding, 1972 (Silver Prize, San Sebastian, 1973); The Promised Land, 1974 (Grand Prix, Moscow Film Festival, 1975); The Shadow Line, 1976; A Dead Class (TV), 1976; Man of Marble, 1977; Rough Treatment, 1978; The Orchestral Conductor, 1979; The Maids of Wilko, 1979 (Oscar nomination, 1980); Man of Iron, 1981 (Palme D'Or, Cannes, 1981); Danton, 1982; Love in Germany, 1985; Chronicle of Love Affairs, 1986; The Possessed, 1987; Korczak, 1990; The Ring with the Crowned Eagle, 1992; Nastasya, 1994; The Great Week, 1995; Miss Nobody, 1996; Pan Tacleusz, 2000; *plays:* Hatful of Rain, 1959; Hamlet, 1960, 1980, 1989; Two on the Seesaw, 1960, 1990; The Wedding, 1962; The Possessed, 1963, 1971, 1975; Play Strindberg, 1969; Idiot, 1971, 1975; Sticks and Bones, Moscow, 1972; Der Mittmacher, 1973; November Night, 1974; The Danton Case, 1975, 1978; When Reason is Asleep, 1976; Emigrés, 1976; Nastasia Philipovna (improvisation based on Dostoyevsky's The Idiot), 1977; Conversation with the Executioner, 1977; Gone with the Years, Gone with the Days …, 1978; Antygone, 1984; Crime and Punishment, 1984, 1986, 1987; Miss Julia, 1988; Dybuk, 1988; Lesson of Polish Language, 1988; Nastasya (adapted from The Idiot), 1989, Osaka, 1993; Hamlet IV, 1989; Romeo and Juliet, 1990; The Wedding, 1991; Sonate of Spectres, 1994; Mishima, 1994; Wrocław's Improvisation, 1996. *Publication:* My Life in Film (autobiog.), 1989. *Address:* Film Polski, ul. Mazowiecka 6/8, Warsaw, Poland.

WAKE, Sir Hereward, 14th Bt *cr* 1621; MC 1942; Vice Lord-Lieutenant of Northamptonshire, 1984–91; Major (retired) King's Royal Rifle Corps; *b* 7 Oct. 1916; *e s* of Maj. Gen. Sir Hereward Wake, 13th Bt, CB, CMG, DSO, and Margaret W. (*d* 1976), *er d* of R. H. Benson; *S* father, 1963; *m* 1952, Julia Rosemary, JP, DL, *yr d* of late Capt. G. W. M. Lees, Falcutt House, near Brackley, Northants; one *s* three *d*. *Educ:* Eton; RMC, Sandhurst. Served War of 1939–45 (wounded, MC). Retired from 60th Rifles, 1947, and studied Estate Management and Agriculture. Fellow, Nene Coll., Northampton, 1997. High Sheriff, 1955, DL 1969, Northants. *Heir: s* Hereward Charles Wake [*b* 22 Nov. 1952; *m* 1st, 1977, Lady Doune Ogilvy (marr. diss. 1995), *e d* of Earl of Airlie, *qv*; two *s* one *d* (and one *s* decd); 2nd, 1998, Mrs Joan Barrow]. *Address:* Old School House, Courteenhall, Northampton NN7 2QD. *Club:* Brooks's.

WAKEFIELD, Bishop of, since 1992; **Rt Rev. Nigel Simeon McCulloch;** Lord High Almoner to the Queen, since 1997; *b* 17 Jan. 1942; *s* of late Pilot Officer Kenneth McCulloch, RAFVR, and of Audrey Muriel McCulloch; *m* 1974, Celia Hume Townshend, *d* of Canon H. L. H. Townshend; two *d*. *Educ:* Liverpool College; Selwyn Coll., Cambridge (Kitchener Schol., BA 1964, MA 1969); Cuddesdon Coll., Oxford. Ordained, 1966; Curate of Ellesmere Port, 1966–70; Chaplain of Christ's Coll., Cambridge, 1970–73; Director of Theological Studies, Christ's Coll., Cambridge, 1970–75; permission to officiate, dio. of Liverpool, 1970–73; Diocesan Missioner for Norwich Diocese, 1973–78; Rector of St Thomas' and St Edmund's, Salisbury, 1978–86; Archdeacon of Sarum, 1979–86; Bishop Suffragan of Taunton, 1986–92. Prebendary of Ogbourne, Salisbury Cathedral, 1979–86, of Wanstrow, Wells Cathedral, 1986–92; Canon Emeritus of Salisbury Cathedral, 1989. Took his seat in H of L, 1997. Mem., House of Bishops, Gen. Synod of C of E, 1990–. Chairman: Finance Cttee, ACCM, 1988–92; Decade of Evangelism Steering Gp, 1989–96; C of E Communications Unit, 1993–; C of E Mission, Evangelism and Renewal Cttee, 1996–99. Chaplain to Council of St John: Somerset, 1987–92; SW Yorks, 1992–; Hon. Nat. Chaplain, RBL, 2001–. Chm., Sandford St Martin Trust, 1999–. Pres., Somerset Rural Music Sch., 1986–92; Mem. Council, RSCM, 1984–. Chm., Somerset County Scout Assoc., 1988–92; Pres., Central Yorks Scouts, 1992–. *Publications:* A Gospel to Proclaim, 1992; Barriers to Belief, 1994. *Recreations:* music, brass bands, walking in the Lake District. *Address:* Bishop's Lodge, Woodthorpe Lane, Wakefield, W Yorks WF2 6JL. *Club:* Athenæum.

WAKEFIELD, Dean of; *see* Nairn-Briggs, Very Rev. G. P.

WAKEFIELD, Anne Prudence; Her Honour Judge Anne Wakefield; a Circuit Judge, since 1999; *b* 25 May 1943; *d* of John Arkell Wakefield and Stella Adelaide Wakefield; *m* 1974, James Robert Reid; two *s* one *d*. *Educ:* London Sch. of Economics and Political Science (LLB); Newnham Coll., Cambridge (LLM 1969). Called to the Bar, Gray's Inn, 1968; in practice, 1970–75 and 1987–99; Asst Recorder, 1991–95; a Recorder, 1995–99. Lecturer in Law: LSE, 1969–70; pt-time, QMC, 1983–87. Pt-time Chm., Industrial Tribunals, 1992–99; a Judge of the Employment Appeal Tribunal, 2000–. *Address:* Crown Court, 6–8 Penrhyn Road, Kingston-upon-Thames, Surrey KT1 2BB.

WAKEFIELD, Derek John, CB 1982; Under Secretary, Government Communications Headquarters, 1978–82; *b* 21 Jan. 1922; *s* of Archibald John Thomas and Evelyn Bessie Wakefield; *m* 1951, Audrey Ellen Smith; one *d*. *Educ:* The Commonweal School. Air Ministry, 1939–42 and 1947–52. Served War, Lieut, Royal Pioneer Corps, 1942–47. Government Communications Headquarters, 1952–82. Mem., Airship Assoc. Governor, Barnwood House Trust, Gloucester, 1973–90. *Recreation:* airships. *Club:* Naval and Military.

WAKEFIELD, Sir (Edward) Humphry (Tyrrell), 2nd Bt *cr* 1962; *b* 11 July 1936; *s* of Sir Edward Birkbeck Wakefield, 1st Bt, CIE, and Constance Lalage, *e d* of late Sir John Perronet Thompson, KCSI, KCIE; *S* father, 1969; *m* 1st, 1960, Priscilla (marr. diss. 1964), *e d* of O. R. Bagot; 2nd, 1966, Hon. Elizabeth Sophia (from whom he obt. a divorce, 1971), *e d* of 1st Viscount De L'Isle, VC, KG, PC, GCMG, GCVO, and former wife of G. S. O. A. Colthurst; one *s*; 3rd, 1974, Hon. Katharine Mary Alice Baring, *d* of 1st Baron Howick of Glendale, KG, GCMG, KCVO, and of Lady Mary Howick; one *s* one *d* (and one *s* decd). *Educ:* Gordonstoun; Trinity Coll., Cambridge (MA Hons). Formerly Captain, 10th Royal Hussars. Exec. Vice-Pres., Mallett, America Ltd, 1970–75; Chm., Tyrrell & Moore Ltd, 1978–92; Director: Mallett & Son (Antiques) Ltd, 1971–78; Tree of Life Foundn 1976–. Dir, Spoleto Fest. of Two Worlds, USA and Italy, 1973–80. Chm., Wilderness Trust, 1999–; President: Northumberland Nat. Park Search and Rescue Team; Avison Trust; Patron: Action North East; Medicine and Chernobyl; Centre for Search Res. UK; Shadow Dance UK; formerly Appeals Consultant, London Br., British Red Cross Soc. Mem., Standing Council of Baronetage. Fellow, Pierpont Morgan Library. Mem., Norman Vaughan Antarctic Expedn, 1993. Life Mem., Scott-Polar Inst. FRGS. *Recreations:* riding, writing, music, shooting. *Heir: s* Capt. Maximilian Edward Vereker Wakefield [*b* 22 Feb. 1967; *m* 1994, Lucinda Katharine Elizabeth, *d* of Lt-Col and Mrs David Pipe; two *s*. *Educ:* Milton Abbey; RMA Sandhurst]. *Address:* Chillingham Castle, Chillingham, Northumberland NE66 5NJ; Sedgwick House, Kendal, Cumbria LA8 0JX. *Clubs:* Cavalry and Guards, Turf; Harlequins Rugby Football (Twickenham).
See also G. H. C. Wakefield.

WAKEFIELD, Gerald Hugo Cropper, (Hady); Chairman, J & H Marsh & McLennan (Holdings) Ltd (formerly Bowring Group), 1996–99; *b* 15 Sept. 1938; *s* of Sir Edward Wakefield, 1st Bt, CIE, and (Constance) Lalage, *e d* of Sir John Perronet Thompson, KCSI, KCIE; *m* 1971, Victoria Rose Feilden; one *s*. *Educ:* Eton; Trinity Coll., Cambridge (MA). Started at Lloyd's, 1961; joined C. T. Bowring & Co., 1968, Dir 1983; Guy Carpenter & Co., NY: Dep. Chm., 1990; Pres., 1993; Chm., 1996. *Recreations:* fishing, shooting, ski-ing, opera. *Address:* Bramdean House, Alresford, Hants SO24 0JU. *T:* (01962) 771214. *Clubs:* White's; The Brook (NY).

WAKEFIELD, Hady; *see* Wakefield, G. H. C.

WAKEFIELD, Sir Humphry; *see* Wakefield, Sir E. H. T.

WAKEFIELD, Sir Norman (Edward), Kt 1988; Chairman, Y. J. Lovell (Holdings) plc, 1987–90; *b* 30 Dec. 1929; *s* of Edward and Muriel Wakefield; *m* 1953, Denise Mary Bayliss (*d* 1998); two *s* four *d*. *Educ:* Wallington County Sch.; Croydon and Brixton Technical Colls. Articled student, Wates Ltd, 1947; Man. Dir, Wates Construction Ltd, 1967; Pres., jt venture co., USA, between Wates and Rouse Co., 1970–73; Man. Dir, Holland, Hannen & Cubitts, 1973; Chief Exec., 1977–83, Chm. and Chief Exec., 1983–87, Y. J. Lovell (Holdings). Dep. Chm., Housing Corp., 1990–94. Director: Lloyds Abbey Life, 1986–93; English Estates, 1990–94. Pres., CIOB, 1985–86. Chm., Nelson House Recovery Trust, 1995–. *Recreations:* opera, walking, gardening. *Address:* Blackhurst Hall, Blackhurst Park, Tunbridge Wells, Kent TN2 4RG. *Club:* Arts.

WAKEFIELD, Sir Peter (George Arthur), KBE 1977; CMG 1973; HM Diplomatic Service, retired; art management consultant; Chairman, Asia House, London, since 1993; *b* 13 May 1922; *s* of John Bunting Wakefield and Dorothy Ina Stace; *m* 1951, Felicity Maurice-Jones; four *s* one *d*. *Educ:* Cranleigh Sch.; Corpus Christi Coll., Oxford. Army Service, 1942–47; Military Govt, Eritrea, 1946–47; Hulton Press, 1947–49; entered Diplomatic Service, 1949; Middle East Centre for Arab Studies, 1950; 2nd Sec., Amman, 1950–52; Foreign Office, 1953–55; 1st Sec., British Middle East Office, Nicosia, 1955–56; 1st Sec. (Commercial), Cairo, 1956; Administrative Staff Coll., Henley, 1957; 1st Sec. (Commercial), Vienna, 1957–60; 1st Sec. (Commercial), Tokyo, 1960–63; SE Asia Dept, FO, 1964–66; Consul-General and Counsellor, Benghazi, 1966–69; Econ. and Commercial Counsellor, Tokyo, 1970–72; Econ. and Commercial Minister, Tokyo, 1973; seconded as Special Adviser on the Japanese Market, BOTB, 1973–75; Ambassador to the Lebanon, 1975–78, to Belgium, 1979–82. Director: NACF, 1982–92; UK, Trust for Mus. Exhibns, 1992–99. Chairman: Richmond Theatre Trust, 1989–2001; Heritage Co-ordination Gp, 1992–98. *Recreations:* looking at paintings, collecting pots, restoring ruins. *Address:* Lincoln House, 28 Montpelier Row, Twickenham, Middx TW1 2NQ. *T:* (020) 8892 6390; La Molineta, Frigiliana, near Malaga, Spain. *T:* (52) 533175. *Clubs:* Travellers, Arts.

WAKEFIELD, Robert; His Honour Judge Wakefield; a Circuit Judge, since 1996; *b* 14 Feb. 1946; *s* of Dudley James Wakefield and Violet Harriette Hart; *m* 1977, Anne Jennifer Gregory. *Educ:* Birmingham Univ. (LLB); Brasenose Coll., Oxford (BCL). Called to the Bar, Middle Temple, 1969; Recorder, 1993–96. *Address:* Central London County Court, 13–14 Park Crescent, W1N 4HT. *T:* (020) 7917 5000.

WAKEFIELD, William Barry, CB 1990; Deputy Director (Research), National Commission on Education, 1991–95; *b* 6 June 1930; *s* of Stanley Arthur and Evelyn Grace Wakefield; *m* 1953, Elizabeth Violet (*née* Alexander); three *s* one *d*. *Educ:* Harrow County Grammar Sch.; University Coll., London. BSc; FSS. Statistician, NCB, 1953–62; DES, 1962–67; Chief Statistician, MoD, 1967–72, CSO, 1972–75; Asst Dir, CSO, Cabinet Office, 1975–79; Dir of Statistics, DES, 1979–90. Member, United Reformed Church. *Recreations:* horse racing, gardening, family history. *Address:* Egg Hall Cottage, 14 Birch Street, Nayland, Colchester CO6 4JA.

WAKEFORD, David Ewing, MBE 1992; Chief Executive, Simplified Trade Procedures Board, since 2000; *b* 30 Oct. 1944; *s* of Arthur Ewing Wakeford and late Gertrude Ada Wakeford (*née* Hall); *m* 1968, Pauline Marian Stacey; three *s*. *Educ:* Hadham Hall Sch.; St Mary's Sch., Welwyn; Univ. of Manchester (MSc Polymer and Fibre Sci.). ICI, 1963–99: Res. Chemist, Plastics Div., 1963–78; Purchasing Manager, Petrochemicals and Plastics, 1978–85; Internat. Trade Manager, Head Office, 1985–99; Man. Dir, Global Trade Knowledge, 1999–2000. *Recreations:* sailing, bird-watching, country pursuits. *Address:* (office) 151 Buckingham Palace Road, SW1W 9SS. *T:* (020) 7215 0843.

WAKEFORD, (Geoffrey) Michael (Montgomery), OBE 1995; Clerk to the Worshipful Company of Mercers, 1974–98; Barrister-at-Law; *b* 10 Dec. 1937; *o s* of late Geoffrey and Helen Wakeford; *m* 1966, Diana Margaret Loy Cooper, *y d* of late Comdr W. G. L. Cooper and of Patricia Cooper (*née* Fforde), Aislaby, N Yorks; two *s* two *d*. *Educ:* Downside; Clare Coll., Cambridge (Classical Schol., MA, LLB). Called to Bar, Gray's Inn and South Eastern Circuit, 1961; practised at Common Law Bar until 1971. Apptd Dep. Clerk to the Mercers Co., 1971. Dir, Portman Settled Estates Ltd, 1998–. Mem. Council, Technology Colls Trust (formerly City Technology Colls Trust), 1988–. Hon. Sec., GBA, 1991–99. Governor: London Internat. Film Sch., 1981–85, 1990– (Vice Chm., 1997–); Molecule Theatre, 1986–; The Hall Sch., 1990–97; Thomas Telford Sch., 1990– (Chm., 1997–2001); Bute House Prep. Sch. for Girls, 1991–2000; Emanuel Sch., 1998–; Coll. of Richard Collyer at Horsham, 1999–; Bl. John Roche RC Boys' Sch., 1999– (Vice Chm.); Abingdon Sch., 2000–; Guardian Angels RC Primary Sch., 2000 (Chm.). *Address:* 15 Compton Terrace, N1 2UN. *Club:* Travellers.

WAKEFORD, Richard George; Chief Executive, Countryside Agency, since 1999; *b* 6 Oct. 1953; *s* of (Henry) Eric Wakeford and Mary Elisabeth Wakeford (*née* Parsons); *m* 1976, Susan Mary Beacham; three *s*. *Educ:* Chichester High Sch. for Boys; King's Coll., London (BSc Maths and Physics). Exec. Officer, 1975–80, Asst Private Sec. to Minister of State, 1979–80, DoE; HEO posts, DoE and Dept of Transport, 1980–83; Department of the Environment: Private Sec. to Permt Sec., 1983–85; Planning Inspectorate, 1985–87; Bill Manager, Water Privatisation, 1988–89; Principal, Envmt White Paper Team, 1990; (last) Chief Exec., Crown Suppliers, 1991; Head of Develt Plans and Policies, 1991–94; Asst Sec., Economic and Domestic Secretariat, Cabinet Office, 1994–96; Chief Exec., Countryside Commn, 1996–99. Mid Career Fellow, Princeton Univ., 1987–88. *Publications:* Speeding Planning Appeals, 1986; American Development Control: parallels and paradoxes from a British perspective, 1990. *Recreations:* gardening, photography, built and natural landscape. *Address:* Charingworth Court, Broadway Road, Winchcombe, Glos GL54 5JN. *T:* (01242) 603033.

WAKEFORD, Air Marshal Sir Richard (Gordon), KCB 1976; LVO 1961; OBE 1958; AFC 1952; Director, RAF Benevolent Fund, Scotland, 1978–89; *b* 20 April 1922; *s* of Charles Edward Augustus Wakeford; *m* 1948, Anne Butler; two *s* one *d* (and one *d* decd). *Educ:* Montpelier Sch., Paignton; Kelly Coll., Tavistock. Joined RAF, 1941; flying Catalina flying boats, Coastal Comd, operating out of India, Scotland, N Ireland, 1942–45; flying Liberator and York transport aircraft on overseas routes, 1945–47; CFS 1947; Flying

Instructor, RAF Coll. Cranwell; CFS Examining Wing; ground appts, incl. 2' years on staff of Dir of Emergency Ops in Malaya, 1952–58; comdg Queen's Flight, 1958–61; Directing Staff, RAF Staff Coll., 1961–64; subseq.: comdg RAF Scampton; SASO, HQ 3 Group Bomber Comd; Asst Comdt (Cadets), RAF Coll. Cranwell; idc 1969; Comdr N Maritime Air Region, and Air Officer Scotland and N Ireland, 1970–72; Dir of Service Intelligence, MoD, 1972–73; ANZUK Force Comdr, Singapore, 1974–75; Dep. Chief of Defence Staff (Intell.), 1975–78; HM Comr, Queen Victoria Sch., Dunblane; Vice-Chm. (Air), Lowland T&AVR. Trustee, McRobert Trusts (Chm., 1982–94); Director: Thistle Foundn; Cromar Nominees. President's Medal, Fellowship of Engrg, 1987. CStJ 1986. *Recreations:* golf, fishing. *Address:* Sweethome Cottage, Inchberry Road, Fochabers, Moray IV32 7QA. *T:* (01343) 820436. *Clubs:* Flyfishers', Royal Air Force.

WAKEHAM, family name of **Baron Wakeham**.

WAKEHAM, Baron *cr* 1992 (Life Peer), of Maldon in the County of Essex; **John Wakeham;** PC 1983; JP; DL; FCA; Chairman, Press Complaints Commission, since 1995; *b* 22 June 1932; *s* of late Major W. J. Wakeham and late Mrs E. R. Wakeham; *m* 1st, 1965, Anne Roberta Bailey (*d* 1984); two *s*; 2nd, 1985, Alison Bridget Ward, MBE, *d* of Ven. E. J. G. Ward, *qv*; one *s*. *Educ:* Charterhouse. Chartered Accountant. MP (C) Maldon, Feb. 1974–1983, Colchester South and Maldon, 1983–92; Asst Govt Whip, 1979–81; a Lord Comr of HM Treasury (Govt Whip), 1981; Parly Under-Sec. of State, DoI, 1981–82; Minister of State, HM Treasury, 1982–83; Parly Sec. to HM Treasury and Govt Chief Whip, 1983–87; Lord Privy Seal, 1987–88; Leader of the H of C, 1987–89; Lord Pres. of the Council, 1988–89; Sec. of State for Energy, 1989–92; Minister responsible for co-ordinating develt of presentation of govt policies, 1990–92; Lord Privy Seal and Leader of the H of L, 1992–94. Chm., Royal Commn on Reform of H of L, 1999. Chm., British Horseracing Bd, 1996–98 (Mem., 1995–98). Chancellor, Brunel Univ., 1998–. Mem., Cttee of Mgt, RNLI, 1995–. JP Inner London, 1972; DL Hants, 1997. Hon. PhD Anglia Poly. Univ., 1992; DUniv Brunel, 1998. *Recreations:* farming, sailing, racing, reading. *Address:* House of Lords, SW1A 0PW. *Clubs:* Carlton (Chm. 1992–98), St Stephen's Constitutional, Buck's, Garrick; Royal Yacht Squadron.

WAKEHAM, Prof. William Arnot, FREng; Vice-Chancellor, University of Southampton, since 2001; *b* 25 Sept. 1944; *s* of Stanley William Wakeham; *m* 1st, 1969, Christina Marjorie Stone (marr. diss. 1974); one *s*; 2nd, 1978, Sylvia Frances Tolley; two *s*. *Educ:* Univ. of Exeter (BSc 1966; PhD 1969; DSc 1985). FREng (FEng 1997). Research Associate, Brown Univ., USA, 1969–71; Imperial College, London University: Lectr in Transport Processes, Dept of Chem. Engrg, 1971–78; Reader in Chemical Physics, 1978–85; Prof. in Chemical Physics, 1985–2001; Hd of Dept of Chem. Engrg and Chem. Technology, 1988–96; Pro Rector (Research), 1996–2001; Dep. Rector, 1997–2001. Chm., Commn of IUPAC, 1993–. *Publications:* Intermolecular Forces: their origin and determination, 1981; Forces between Molecules, 1988; The Transport Properties of Fluids, 1987; International Thermodynamic Tables, vol. XI, 1989; Experimental Thermodynamics, vol. III, 1992; numerous articles in learned jls. *Recreations:* water ski-ing, cycling. *Address:* Beacon Down, Rewe, Exeter, Devon. *T:* (office) (023) 8059 2801.

WAKEHURST, 3rd Baron *cr* 1934, of Ardingly; **(John) Christopher Loder;** Chairman: Anglo & Overseas Trust PLC (formerly Anglo-American Securities Corporation), 1980–96 (Director, 1968–96); The Overseas Investment Trust PLC (formerly North Atlantic Securities Corporation), 1980–95; Morgan Grenfell Equity Income Trust PLC, 1991–95; *b* 23 Sept. 1925; *s* of 2nd Baron Wakehurst, KG, KCMG, and Dowager Lady Wakehurst, (Dame Margaret Wakehurst), DBE (*d* 1994); *S* father, 1970; *m* 1956, Ingeborg Krumbholz-Hess (*d* 1977); one *s* one *d*; *m* 1983, Brigid, *yr d* of William Noble, Cirencester. *Educ:* Eton; King's School, nr Sydney, NSW; Trinity College, Cambridge (BA 1948, LLB 1949, MA 1953). Served War as Sub Lieut RANVR and RNVR; South West Pacific, 1943–45. Barrister, Inner Temple, 1950. Chm., Morgan Grenfell Trust Managers Ltd, 1991–94; Director: Mayfair & City Properties plc, 1984–87; The Nineteen Twenty-Eight Investment Trust plc, 1984–86; Morgan Grenfell Latin American Cos Trust, 1994–96; Chm. and Dir, Hampton Gold Mining Areas, 1981–86; Chairman: Continental Illinois Ltd, 1973–84; Philadelphia National Ltd, 1985–90; Dep. Chm., London and Manchester Gp, 1970–95 (Dir, 1966–95). Trustee: The Photographers' Gallery Ltd, 1979–90; Photographers' Trust Fund, 1986–91. CStJ. *Heir: s* Hon. Timothy Walter Loder, *b* 28 March 1958. *Address:* Trillinghurst Oast, Ranters Lane, Goudhurst, Kent TN17 1HL. *Clubs:* City of London, Chelsea Arts.

WAKELEY, Amanda Jane; fashion designer; Creative Director, Amanda Wakeley, since 1999; *b* 15 Sept. 1962; *d* of Sir John Cecil Nicholson Wakeley, 2nd Bt, *qv*. *Educ:* Cheltenham Ladies' Coll. Worked, in fashion industry, NY, 1983–85, for private commns, 1987–90; Founder, Amanda Wakeley label, 1990; collections, incl. a mainline designer range, elements range and bridal collection, sold in UK, Europe, USA, Far East and Middle East; Chelsea shop opened 1993. Co-Chm., Fashion Targets Breast Cancer Appeal Cttee, 1996, 1998 and 2000 (raised over £3 million). British Fashion Award for Glamour, 1992, 1993 and 1996. *Recreations:* water ski-ing, driving, snow ski-ing, roller-blading, travel, music. *Address:* 79–91 New Kings Road, SW6 4SQ. *T:* (020) 7471 8804.

WAKELEY, Sir John (Cecil Nicholson), 2nd Bt *cr* 1952; FRCS; Consultant Surgeon, West Cheshire Group of Hospitals, 1961–88, retired; *b* 27 Aug. 1926; *s* of Sir Cecil Pembrey Grey Wakeley, 1st Bt, KBE, CB, MCh, FRCS, and Elizabeth Muriel (*d* 1985), *d* of James Nicholson-Smith; *S* father, 1979; *m* 1954, June Leney; two *s* one *d*. *Educ:* Canford School. MB, BS London 1950; LRCP 1950, FRCS 1955 (MRCS 1950), FACS 1973. Lectr in Anatomy, Univ. of London, 1951–52. Sqdn Ldr, RAF, 1953–54. Councillor, RCS, 1971–83; Member: Mersey Regional Health Authority, 1974–78; Editorial Bd, Health Trends, DHSS, 1968–71; Examiner for Gen. Nursing Council for England and Wales, 1954–59; Consultant Adviser in Surgery to RAF, 1981–89, Hon. Consultant Advr, 1990–. Liveryman: Worshipful Soc. of Apothecaries; Worshipful Co. of Barbers; Freeman of City of London. FACS 1973. CStJ 1959. *Publications:* papers on leading med. jls, incl. British Empire Cancer Campaign Scientific Report, Vol. II: Zinc 65 and the prostate, 1958; report on distribution and radiation dosimetry of Zinc 65 in the rat, 1959. *Recreations:* music, photography, bird-watching. *Heir: s* Nicholas Jeremy Wakeley [*b* 17 Oct. 1957; *m* 1991, Sarah Ann, *d* of Air Vice-Marshal B. L. Robinson, *qv*]. *Address:* Mickle Lodge, Mickle Trafford, Chester CH2 4EB. *T:* (01244) 300316. *Club:* Council Club of Royal College of Surgeons.
See also A. J. Wakeley.

WAKELING, Rt Rev. John Denis, MC 1945; Bishop of Southwell, 1970–85; *b* 12 Dec. 1918; *s* of Rev. John Lucas Wakeling and Mary Louise (*née* Glover); *m* 1941, Josephine Margaret, *d* of Dr Benjamin Charles Broomhall and Marion (*née* Aldwinckle); two *s* (and one *s* decd). *Educ:* Dean Close Sch., Cheltenham; St Catharine's Coll., Cambridge. MA Cantab 1944. Commnd Officer in Royal Marines, 1939–45 (Actg Maj.). Ridley Hall, Cambridge, 1946–47. Deacon, 1947; Priest, 1948. Asst Curate, Barwell, Leics, 1947; Chaplain of Clare Coll., Cambridge, and Chaplain to the Cambridge Pastorate, 1950–52; Vicar of Emmanuel, Plymouth, 1952–59; Prebendary of Exeter Cathedral, 1957, Prebendary Emeritus, 1959; Vicar of Barking, Essex, 1959–65; Archdeacon of West Ham, 1965–70. Entered House of Lords, June 1974. Chairman: Archbishops' Council on Evangelism, 1976–79; Lee Abbey Council, 1976–84. Hon. DD Nottingham, 1985. *Recreations:* formerly cricket and hockey (Cambridge Univ. Hockey Club, 1938, 1939, 1945, 1946, English Trials Caps, 1939, 1946–49), gardening, water colours, fly fishing. *Address:* 50 St Ann Place, Salisbury, Wilts SP1 2SU. *T:* (01722) 322016. *Club:* Hawks (Cambridge).

WAKELING, Richard Keith Arthur; Chairman, Polar Capital (formerly Henderson) Technology Trust PLC, since 1996; *b* 19 Nov. 1946; *s* of late Eric George Wakeling and Dorothy Ethel Wakeling; *m* 1971, Carmen; three *s*. *Educ:* Churchill Coll., Cambridge (MA). Called to the Bar, Inner Temple, 1971. Group Treasurer, BOC Group, 1973–83; Finance Dir, John Brown, 1983–86; Finance Dir, 1986–88, Acting Chief Exec., 1988–89, Charter Consolidated; Dep. Chief Exec., 1990, Chief Exec., 1991–94, Johnson Matthey. Dep. Chm., Celtic Group Holdings Ltd, 1994–97; Director: Costain, 1992–96; Laura Ashley Holdings, 1994–95; Logica, 1995–; Staveley Industries, 1995–99; Henderson Geared Income & Growth Trust (formerly HTR Income and Growth Split Trust), 1995–; Oxford Instruments plc, 1995–; MG plc, 1999–2000; Brunner Investment Trust plc, 2000–. *Recreations:* mediaeval history and architecture, golf, music, gardening. *Address:* 46 The Bourne, Southgate, N14 6QS.

WAKEMAN, Sir Edward Offley Bertram, 6th Bt *cr* 1828, of Perdiswell Hall, Worcestershire; *b* 31 July 1934; *s* of Captain Sir Offley Wakeman, 4th Bt, CBE and his 2nd wife, Josceline Ethelreda (*d* 1996), *e d* of Maj.-Gen. Bertram Revely Mitford, CB, CMG, DSO; *S* half-brother, 1991. *Heir:* none.

WAKERLEY, Richard MacLennon; QC 1983; **His Honour Judge Wakerley;** a Senior Circuit Judge, since 2001; *b* 7 June 1942; *s* of late Charles William Wakerley and Gladys MacLennon Wakerley; *m* Marian Heather Dawson; two *s* two *d*. *Educ:* De Aston Sch., Market Rasen; Emmanuel Coll., Cambridge (MA). Called to the Bar, Gray's Inn, 1965, Bencher, 1991. Practised on Midland and Oxford Circuit, 1965–2001 (Dep. Leader, 1989–92, Leader, 1992–96); a Recorder, 1982–2001; Hon. Recorder of Birmingham, 2001–. *Recreations:* theatre, bridge, gardening. *Address:* Crown Court, Queen Elizabeth II Law Courts, 1 Newton Street, Birmingham B4 7NA. *T:* (0121) 681 3345.

WAKLEY, His Honour Bertram Joseph, MBE 1945; a Circuit Judge, 1973–92; *b* 7 July 1917; *s* of Major Bertram Joseph Wakley and Hon. Mrs Dorothy Wakley (*née* Hamilton); *m* 1953, Alice Margaret Lorimer. *Educ:* Wellington Coll.; Christ Church, Oxford. BA 1939, MA 1943. Commnd S Lancs Regt, 1940; Captain 1941; Major 1943; served N Africa, Italy, Greece (despatches). Called to Bar, Gray's Inn, 1948. A Recorder of the Crown Court, 1972–73. Reader, Diocese of Southwark, 1977–96. *Publications:* History of the Wimbledon Cricket Club, 1954; Bradman the Great, 1959; Classic Centuries, 1964. *Recreations:* cricket, golf. *Address:* 4 The Watergardens, Warren Road, Kingston Hill, Surrey KT2 7LF. *T:* (020) 8546 7587. *Clubs:* Carlton, MCC, Roehampton.

WALBANK, Frank William, CBE 1993; FBA 1953; MA; Rathbone Professor of Ancient History and Classical Archæology in the University of Liverpool, 1951–77, now Professor Emeritus; Dean, Faculty of Arts, 1974–77; *b* 10 Dec. 1909; *s* of A. J. D. and C. Walbank, Bingley, Yorks; *m* 1935, Mary Woodward (*d* 1987), *e d* of O. C. A. and D. Fox, Shipley, Yorks; one *s* two *d*. *Educ:* Bradford Grammar School; Peterhouse, Cambridge (Hon. Fellow, 1984). Scholar of Peterhouse, 1928–31; First Class, Parts I and II Classical Tripos, 1930–31; Hugo de Balsham Research Student, Peterhouse, 1931–32; Senior Classics Master at North Manchester High School, 1932–33; Thirlwall Prize, 1933; Asst Lecturer, 1934–36, Lecturer, 1936–46, in Latin, Professor of Latin, 1946–51, University of Liverpool; Public Orator, 1956–60; Hare Prize, 1939. J. H. Gray Lectr, Univ. of Cambridge, 1957; Andrew Mellon Vis. Prof., Univ. Pittsburgh, 1964; Myres Memorial Lectr, Univ. of Oxford, 1964–65; Sather Prof., Univ. of Calif (Berkeley), 1971. Pres., Cambridge Phil Soc., 1982–84; Member Council: Classical Assoc., 1944–48, 1958–61 (Pres. 1969–70); Roman Soc., 1948–51 (Vice-Pres., 1953–; Pres., 1961–64); Hellenic Soc., 1951–54, 1955–56; Classical Journals Bd, 1948–66; British Acad., 1960–63; British Sch. at Rome, 1979–87. Mem., Inst. for Advanced Study, Princeton, 1970–71; Foreign Mem., Royal Netherlands Acad. of Arts and Sciences, 1981–; Corresp. Mem., German Archaeol Inst., 1987–. Hon. Mem., Israel Soc. for Promotion of Classical Studies, 1992–. Hon. DLitt Exeter, 1988; Hon. DHL Louisville, 1996. Kenyon Medal, British Acad., 1989; Steven Runciman Prize, Anglo-Hellenic Soc., 1989. Kentucky Col, 1995. *Publications:* Aratos of Sicyon, 1933; Philip V of Macedon, 1940; Latin Prose Versions contributed to Key to Bradley's Arnold, Latin Prose Composition, ed J. F. Mountford, 1940; The Decline of the Roman Empire in the West, 1946; A Historical Commentary on Polybius, Vol. i, 1957, Vol. ii, 1967, Vol. iii, 1979; The Awful Revolution, 1969; Polybius, 1972; The Hellenistic World, 1981; Selected Papers: Studies in Greek and Roman history and historiography, 1985; (with N. G. L. Hammond) A History of Macedonia, Vol. III: 336–167 BC, 1988; chapters in: The Cambridge Economic History of Europe, Vol. II, 1952, 2nd edn 1987; A Scientific Survey of Merseyside, 1953; (ed jtly and contrib.) Cambridge Ancient History, Vol. VII pt 1, 1984, pt 2, 1989, Vol VIII 1989; contribs to: the Oxford Classical Dictionary, 1949; Chambers' Encyclopædia, 1950; Encyclopædia Britannica, 1960 and 1974; English and foreign classical books and periodicals. *Address:* 64 Grantchester Meadows, Cambridge CB3 9JL. *T:* (01223) 364350.
See also D. J. Thompson.

WALBY, Christine Mary; independent consultant in social services and children's services matters, since 1996; *b* 9 Feb. 1940; *d* of Kathleen Walby (*née* Bradburn) and late James Walby. *Educ:* University College of Wales, Aberystwyth (BA, DipEd); Manchester Univ. (Dip. Social Admin and Social Work); University College Cardiff (MSc Econ). Youth Leader Trainer, 1961–64; Social Worker, Children's Dept, Cheshire, 1964–70; Training Officer, Salford; Tutor, Manchester Univ.; Area Officer, Salford Social Services, 1970–74; Principal Officer, S Glam Social Services, 1974–81; Divl Dir, Berks Social Services, 1981–87; Dir, Social Services, Solihull MDC, 1987–91; Dir of Social Services, Staffs CC, 1991–96. Sen. Vis. Res. Fellow, Keele Univ, 1994–; Hon. Res. Fellow, Univ. of Wales Swansea, 1998–. Mem., Human Fertilization and Embryology Authy, 1991–93. Chm., Early Childhood Unit Adv. Gp, Nat. Children's Bureau, 1995–99; Trustee: Office for Children's Rights Comr; Children in Wales, 1998–; Member: Nat. Commn of Inquiry into Prevention of Child Abuse, 1994–96; Hon. Mem. Council, NSPCC. Chm., Homestart, 1999–. *Publications:* Who Am I?: identity, adoption and human fertilization (with Barbara Symons), 1990; contrib. professional jls. *Recreations:* mountain walking, bird watching, theatre, music.

WALCOTT, Sir Clyde (Leopold), KA 1993; GCM 1991; OBE 1966; Chairman, 1993–97, Chairman of Cricket Committee, 1997–2000, International Cricket Council; *b* 17 Jan. 1926; *s* of late Frank Eyre Walcott and Ruth Walcott (*née* Morris); *m* 1951, Muriel Edith Ashby; two *s*. *Educ:* Harrison Coll., Barbados. Début for Barbados Cricket IX, 1942; played for Barbados, 1942–55, for British Guiana, 1955–64 (record highest score of 314 not out for Barbados *v* Trinidad, 1946); 44 caps for WI, 1947–60 (scored record 5 centuries in single Test series, *v* Australia, 1955). Chief Personnel Officer and Dir, Barbados Shipping and Trading Co. Ltd, 1980–91, retd. Mem., Barbados Public Service

Commn, 1982–87. Barbados Employers' Confederation: Pres., 1978–81; Trustee, 1987–91; President: Guyana Cricket Bd of Control, 1968–70; WI Cricket Bd of Control, 1988–93 (Chm., Selection Cttee, 1973–88); Hon. Life Vice-Pres., Barbados Cricket Assoc. *Publication:* Island Cricketers, 1958. *Recreations:* cricket, football. *Address:* Wildey Heights, St Michael, Barbados, WI. *T:* 4294638. *Club:* MCC (Hon. Life Mem.).

WALCOTT, Derek Alton; poet and playwright; *b* Castries, St Lucia, 23 Jan. 1930; twin *s* of late Warwick and Alix Walcott; *m* 1954, Fay Moston (marr. diss. 1959); one *s*; *m* 1962, Margaret Ruth Maillard (marr. diss.); two *d*; *m* Norline Metivier (marr. diss.). *Educ:* St Mary's Coll., St Lucia; Univ. of WI (BA 1953). Formerly teacher at schs in St Lucia and Grenada, and at Kingston Coll., Jamaica. Founded Trinidad Theatre Workshop, 1958. Lecturer: Rutgers Univ.; Yale Univ. Visiting Professor: Columbia Univ., 1981; Harvard Univ., 1982; Boston Univ., 1985–. Hon. DLitt Univ. of WI, 1972. Heinemann Award, RSL, 1966, 1983; Cholmodeley Award, 1969; Queen's Gold Medal for Poetry, 1989; Nobel Prize for Literature, 1992. Order of the Hummingbird (Trinidad and Tobago), 1969. *Publications include:* In a Green Night, 1962; Selected Poems, 1964; Castaway, 1965; Gulf and other poems, 1969; Another Life, 1973; Sea Grapes, 1976; Joker of Seville, 1979; Remembrance, and Pantomime, 1980; The Star-Apple Kingdom, 1980; The Fortunate Traveller, 1982; Midsummer, 1984; Collected Poems 1948–84, 1986; The Arkansas Testament, 1988; Three Plays: The Last Carnival, Beef No Chicken, A Branch of the Blue Nile, 1988; Collected Poems, 1990; Poems 1965–80, 1992; Omeros, 1990 (W. H. Smith Literary Award, 1991); Selected Poetry, 1993; Odyssey, 1993; The Bounty, 1997; (jtly) Homage to Robert Frost, 1998; What the Twilight Says (essays), 1998; Tiepolo's Hound, 2000. *Address:* c/o Faber & Faber, 3 Queen Square, WC1N 3AU; PO Box GM926, Castries, St Lucia, West Indies.

WALCOTT, Prof. Richard Irving, PhD; FRS 1991; FRSNZ; Professor of Geology, Victoria University, Wellington, New Zealand, 1985–99, now Emeritus; *b* 14 May 1933; *s* of James Farrar Walcott and Lilian Stewart (*née* Irving); *m* 1960, Genevieve Rae Lovatt; one *s* two *d*. *Educ:* Victoria Univ., Wellington (BSc Hons 1962; PhD 1965; DSc 1980). Meteorological Asst, Falkland Is Dependencies Survey, 1955–58; Post-doctoral Fellow, Geophysics Dept, Univ. of BC, 1966–67; Research Scientist: Earth Physics Br., Dept of Energy, Mines and Resources, Ottawa, 1967–74; Geophysics Div., Dept Sci. and Industrial Res., Wellington, NZ, 1975–84. FRSNZ 1982; Fellow, American Geophysical Union, 1993. Hector Medal, Royal Soc. NZ, 1994; Charles Whitten Medal, Amer. Geophysical Union, 1999. *Recreations:* tramping, gardening. *Address:* 24 Mahoe Street, Eastbourne, Wellington, New Zealand. *T:* (4) 5628040.

WALD, Prof. Nicholas John, FRCP, FFPHM, FRCOG, FMedSci; CBiol, FIBiol; Professor and Head of Department of Environmental and Preventive Medicine, since 1983, and Chairman, Wolfson Institute of Preventive Medicine, 1991–95 and since 1997, Bart's and The London School of Medicine and Dentistry, Queen Mary and Westfield College (formerly St Bartholomew's Hospital Medical College), University of London; Hon. Consultant, St Bartholomew's Hospital, since 1983; *b* 31 May 1944; *s* of Adolf Max Wald and Frieda (*née* Shatsow); *m* 1966, Nancy Evelyn Miller; three *s* one *d*. *Educ:* Owen's Sch., EC1; University Coll. London; University Coll. Hosp. Med. Sch. (MB BS); DSc (Med) London 1987. FRCP 1986 (MRCP 1971); FFPHM (FFCM 1982; MFCM 1980); FRCOG 1992; CBiol, FIBiol 2000. VSO, India, 1966. Ho. appts, UCH and Barnet Gen. Hosp., 1968–69; Med. Registrar, UCH, 1970; Member: MRC Sci. Staff, MRC Epidemiology and Med. Care Unit, 1971; Sci. Staff, ICRF (formerly DHSS) Cancer Epidem. and Clin. Trials Unit, 1972–82, Dep. Dir, 1982–83. Wellcome Vis. Prof. in Basic Med. Scis, at Foundn for Blood Res., USA, 1980, then Hon. Sen. Res. Scientist. Hon. Dir, Cancer Screening Gp, CRC, 1989–2000. Chairman: MRC Smoking Res. Rev. Cttee, 1986–89; MRC Study Monitoring Cttee of Randomised Trial of Colo-rectal Cancer Screening, 1986–; MRC Volatile Substance Abuse Wkg Party, 1985–87; NE Thames Reg. Breast Cancer Res. Cttee, 1988–96; Nat. Inst. of Child Health and Human Develt Wkg Gp on Quality Control of Alpha-fetoprotein Measurement, 1978; Steering Cttee for MRC Multicentre Aneurysm Screening Study, 1997–; Member: MRC Neurosciences Bd, 1962–86; MRC Steering Cttee of Randomised Trial of Multivitamins and Neural Tube Defects, 1983–92; DHSS Cttee on Med. Aspects of Contamination of Air, Soil and Water, 1985–89; DHSS Cttee on Carcinogenicity of Chemicals in Food, Consumer Products and the Environment, 1984–89; DHSS Indep. Sci. Cttee on Smoking and Health, 1983–91; DoH (formerly DHSS) Adv. Cttee on Breast Cancer Screening, 1986–; Central R&D Cttee, 1991–95; CMO's Health of the Nation Wkg Gp, 1991–97; DoH Population Screening Panel, 1992–98; CMO's Scientific Cttee on Tobacco and Health, 1993–; Folic Acid Sub-gp, DoH Cttee on Med. Aspects of Food and Nutrition Policy, 1996–; Antenatal Sub-gp, DoH Nat. Screening Cttee, 1997–; Nat. Screening Cttee, HPV/LBC Pilots Steering Gp, 2000–; Adv. Gp for Evaluation of UK Colorectal Cancer Screening Pilot, 2000; ACOST Med. Res. and Health Cttee, 1991–92; RCP Cttee on Ethical Issues in Medicine, 1988–; RCP Computer Cttee, 1988–92, and special Adv. Gp to the RCP Med. IT Cttee, 1992–; Physiol. and Pharmacol. Panel, Wellcome Trust, 1995–2000; MRC Scientific Adv. Cttee on Gulf War Syndrome, 1996–97; Adv. Gp on Nuclear Test Veterans, 2000; Council of Trustees, Foundn for Study of Infant Deaths, 2000; Cttee on Environmental Tobacco Smoke, Nat. Acad. of Sci., USA, 1985–86. Inaugural Ed., Jl of Medical Screening, 1994. William Julius Mickle Fellow, Univ. of London, 1990. Founder FMedSci 1998; Mem., Assoc. of Physicians of GB and Ire. Joseph P. Kennedy Jr Foundn Award for Scientific Res., 2000. *Publications:* (ed) Antenatal and Neonatal Screening, 1984; (ed with Sir Richard Doll) Interpretation of Negative Epidemiological Evidence for Carcinogenicity, 1985, 2nd edn (ed with Ian Leck) 2000; (ed jtly) UK Smoking Statistics, 1988; (ed with Sir Peter Froggatt) Nicotine, Smoking and the Low Tar Programme, 1989; (ed with J. Baron) Smoking and Hormone Related Disorders, 1990; (jtly) International Smoking Statistics, 1993; articles in sci. jls on screening for neural tube defects, Down's Syndrome and other disorders, on health effects of tobacco, on the aetiology and prevention of cancer, cardiovascular disease and congenital malformations. *Recreations:* ski-ing, boating, economics. *Address:* Department of Environmental and Preventive Medicine, Wolfson Institute of Preventive Medicine, Bart's and The London School of Medicine and Dentistry, Charterhouse Square, EC1M 6BQ. *T:* (020) 7882 6269; 9 Park Crescent Mews East, W1N 5HB. *T:* (020) 7636 2721. *Club:* Athenæum.

WALDECK, Adrienne May; *see* Page, A. M.

WALDEGRAVE, family name of **Earl Waldegrave** and **Baron Waldegrave of North Hill**.

WALDEGRAVE, 13th Earl, *cr* 1729; **James Sherbrooke Waldegrave;** Bt 1643; Baron Waldegrave 1685; Viscount Chewton 1729; *b* 8 Dec. 1940; *e s* of 12th Earl Waldegrave, KG, GCVO and Mary Hermione (*d* 1995), *d* of Lt-Col A. M. Grenfell, DSO; *S* father, 1995; *m* 1986, Mary Alison Anthea (marr. diss. 1996), *d* of late Sir Robert Furness, KBE, CMG, and Lady Furness; two *s*. *Educ:* Eton Coll.; Trinity Coll., Cambridge. *Heir: s* Viscount Chewton, *qv*. *Address:* Chewton House, Chewton Mendip, Radstock BA3 4LL. *Clubs:* Beefsteak; Leander.

WALDEGRAVE OF NORTH HILL, Baron *cr* 1999 (Life Peer), of Chewton Mendip in the county of Somerset; **William Arthur Waldegrave;** PC 1990; a Managing Director, Dresdner Kleinwort Wasserstein, since 1998; *b* 15 Aug. 1946; *yr s* of 12th Earl Waldegrave, KG, GCVO and Mary Hermione (*née* Grenfell); *m* 1977, Caroline Burrows (*see* Caroline Waldegrave); one *s* three *d*. *Educ:* Eton; Corpus Christi Coll., Oxford (Hon. Fellow, 1991); Harvard Univ. (Kennedy Fellow). Fellow, All Souls Coll., Oxford, 1971–86 and 1999–. Central Policy Review Staff, Cabinet Office, 1971–73; Political Staff, 10 Downing Street, 1973–74; Head of Leader of Opposition's Office, 1974–75; GEC Ltd, 1975–81. MP (C) Bristol West, 1979–97; contested (C) same seat, 1997. Parly Under-Sec. of State, DES, 1981–83, DoE, 1983–85. Minister of State for the Environment and Countryside, 1985–87, for Planning, 1986–88, and for Housing, 1987–88, DoE; Minister of State, FCO, 1988–90; Sec. of State for Health, 1990–92; Chancellor of the Duchy of Lancaster, 1992–94; Minister of Agric., Fisheries and Food, 1994–95; Chief Sec. to HM Treasury, 1995–97. Director: Waldegrave Farms Ltd, 1975–; Bristol and West plc (formerly Bristol and West Bldg Soc.), 1997–; Henry Sotheran Ltd, 1998–; Finsbury Life Scis Investment Trust, 1998–. Mem., IBA Adv. Council, 1980–81. Trustee, Rhodes Trust, 1992–. Founder Trustee and Chm., Bristol Cathedral Trust, 1989–. JP Inner London Juvenile Court, 1975–79. *Publication:* The Binding of Leviathan, 1977. *Address:* 66 Palace Gardens Terrace, W8 4RR. *Clubs:* White's, Beefsteak, Pratt's; Clifton (Bristol).

WALDEGRAVE, Caroline Linda Margaret, (Lady Waldegrave of North Hill), OBE 2000; Founding Principal, since 1975, and Managing Director, since 1977, Leith's School of Food and Wine Ltd; *b* 14 Aug. 1952; *y d* of Major Philip Richard Miles Burrows and Molly Burrows (*née* Hollins); *m* 1975, Hon. William Waldegrave (*see* Baron Waldegrave of North Hill); one *s* three *d*. *Educ:* Convent of the Sacred Heart, Woldingham, Surrey. Mem., HEA, 1985–88. Chm., Guild of Food Writers, 1991–93. Pres., Portobello Trust, 1987–2000. *Publications:* The Healthy Gourmet, 1986; Low Fat Gourmet, 1987; *jointly:* Leith's Cookery Course, 1980; Leith's Cookery School, 1985; Leith's Cookery Bible, 1991, 2nd edn 1996; Leith's Complete Christmas, 1992; Children's Cookery, 1993; Leith's Fish Bible, 1995; Leith's Easy Dinner Parties, 1995; Leith's Healthy Eating, 1996; Children's Fun to Cook Book, 1996; Sainsbury Book of Children's Cookery, 1997. *Recreations:* bridge, tennis. *Address:* c/o Leith's School of Food and Wine Ltd, 21 St Albans Grove W8 5BP. *T:* (020) 7229 0177.

WALDEN, (Alastair) Brian; television presenter and journalist; Chairman, Paragon, since 1996; *b* 8 July 1932; *s* of W. F. Walden; *m* Hazel Downes, *d* of William A. Downes; one *s* (and three *s* of former marriages). *Educ:* West Bromwich Grammar School; Queen's College and Nuffield College, Oxford; Pres., Oxford Union, 1957. University Lecturer. MP (Lab): Birmingham, All Saints, 1964–74; Birmingham, Ladywood, 1974–77. Mem., W Midland Bd, Central TV, 1981–84. Columnist: London Standard, 1983–86; Thomson Regional Newspapers, 1983–86; Sunday Times, 1986–90. Presenter: Weekend World, LWT, 1977–86; The Walden Interview, ITV, 1988 and 1989; Walden, LWT, 1990–94; Walden on Labour Leaders, BBC, 1997; Walden on Heroes, BBC, 1998; Walden on Villains, BBC, 1999. Shell International Award, 1982; BAFTA Richard Dimbleby Award, 1985; Aims of Industry Special Free Enterprise Award, 1990; TV Times Favourite TV Current Affairs Personality, 1990; Television and Radio Industries Club ITV Personality of the Year, 1991. *Publication:* The Walden Interviews, 1990. *Recreations:* chess, reading. *Address:* Landfall, Fort Road, St Peter Port, Guernsey GY1 1ZU.

WALDEN, David Peter; Head of Social Care Policy, Department of Health, since 1999; *b* 23 Sept. 1954; *s* of Gerald Walden and Shirley Walden (*née* Rothfeld); *m* 1981, Janet Day; one *s* one *d*. *Educ:* Newcastle upon Tyne Royal Grammar Sch.; St John's Coll., Oxford (BA Modern Hist. 1977). DHSS, subseq. DoH, 1977–: Principal, 1982; Management Side Secretary: Nurses' and Midwives' Whitley Council, 1982–85; NHS Consultants' Negotiating Body, 1985–86; Private Sec. to Dep. Chm., NHS Mgt Bd, 1986–87; Asst Sec., Doctors' Pay and Conditions, 1989–90; on secondment as Personnel Dir, Poole Hosp. NHS Trust, 1991–93; Hd, Community Care Br., DoH, 1993–96; Hd, Health Promotion Div., DoH, 1996–99. *Address:* Department of Health, Wellington House, 133–155 Waterloo Road, SE1 8UG. *T:* (020) 7972 4045.

WALDEN, George Gordon Harvey, CMG 1981; writer; *b* 15 Sept. 1939; *s* of G. G. Walden; *m* 1970, Sarah Nicolette Hunt; two *s* one *d*. *Educ:* Latymer Upper Sch.; Jesus Coll., Cambridge; Moscow Univ. (post-graduate). Research Dept, Foreign Office, 1962–65; Chinese Language Student, Hong Kong Univ., 1965–67; Second Secretary, Office of HM Chargé d'Affaires, Peking, 1967–70; First Sec., FCO (Soviet Desk), 1970–73; Ecole Nationale d'Administration, Paris, 1973–74; First Sec., HM Embassy, Paris, 1974–78; Principal Private Sec. to Foreign and Commonwealth Sec., 1978–81; sabbatical year, Harvard, 1981; Head of Planning Staff, FCO, 1982–83; retired from HM Diplomatic Service, 1983. MP (C) Buckingham, 1983–97. PPS to Sec. of State for Educn and Science, 1984–85; Parly Under-Sec. of State, DES, 1985–87. Chm. of Judges, Booker Prize, 1995. Columnist, Evening Standard, 1991–. *Publications:* Ethics and Foreign Policy, 1990; We Should Know Better: solving the education crisis, 1996; Lucky George (memoir), 1999; The New Elites: making a career in the masses, 2000. *Address:* 14 Ashchurch Terrace, W12 9SL.

WALDEN, Rt Rev. Graham Howard; *see* Murray, Bishop of The.

WALDEN, Herbert Richard Charles, CBE 1986; part-time Member, Building Societies Commission, 1986–94; *b* 6 Oct. 1926; *s* of Reginald George Walden and Matilda Ethel Walden; *m* 1950, Margaret Walker (*d* 1995); two *d*. *Educ:* Westgate Sch., Warwick. FCIS; FCIB. War service, 1944–47, Royal Warwickshire Regt and Royal Leicestershire Regt (UK and Gold Coast) (Captain). Asst Sec., Warwick Building Soc., 1955, Gen. Manager 1962; Gen. Manager, Rugby and Warwick Building Soc. (on merger), 1967; Gen. Manager, Heart of England Building Soc. (on merger), 1974, Dir and Gen. Manager, 1974–86. Mem. Bd, Housing Corp., 1985–88. Chm., Midland Assoc. of Building Socs, 1972–73, Vice-Pres., 1986; Vice President: Building Societies Assoc., 1994– (Mem. Council, 1974–86, Dep. Chm. 1981–83, Chm., 1983–85); CBSI, 1988–93. Mem., Warwick BC, 1955–63; Chm., S Warwickshire HMC, 1964–72; Mem., Warwick Schs Foundn, 1962–90 (Chm., 1986–90); Trustee, various Warwick Charities; Founder Pres., Rotary Club of Warwick, 1965; Vice Pres., Warwickshire Scout Assoc., 1969– (Hon. Treas., 1958–68). Mem., Finance Cttee, Northgate Methodist Church, Warwick. Chm., Warwicks Adv. Cttee, Tax Comrs, 1983–96 (Mem., 1969–96). *Recreation:* watching cricket. *Address:* Fieldgate House, 24 Hill Wootton Road, Leek Wootton, Warwick CV35 7QL. *T:* (01926) 854291. *Club:* Naval and Military.

WALDEN, Ian Mennie, MBE 1972; Chief Executive, British Lung Foundation, since 1997; *b* 23 Oct. 1940; *s* of Col Frank Walden, MBE, DL, and Mollie Walden (*née* Mennie); *m* 1st, 1965, Anne Frances Lacey (marr. diss.); three *s*; 2nd, 1995, Christine Anne Osbourn; one *d*, and two step *d*. *Educ:* Haileybury. Served Royal Marines, 1958–89, including: active service in ME, FE and NI; Temp. Equerry to Duke of Edinburgh, 1976; briefer to CDS, during Falklands War, 1980–82; CO, Commando Logistic Regt, 1983–85; Dep. COS, Trng and Reserve Forces, 1985–87; Dir, Jt Ops Centre, MoD, 1987–89; Campaign Manager, St John Ambulance, 1992–93; Dir, Internat. Spinal Res. Trust,

1993–97. Mem., Harpenden Lions, 2001–. *Recreations:* woodwork, badminton, family life (most of the time!). *Address:* 50 Lyndhurst Drive, Harpenden, Herts AL5 5RJ. *T:* (01582) 462067.

WALDER, Edwin James, CMG 1971; NSW Civil Service, retired; *b* 5 Aug. 1921; *s* of Edwin James Walder and Dulcie Muriel Walder (*née* Griffiths); *m* 1944, Norma Cheslin; two *d*. *Educ:* North Newtown High Sch.; Univ. of Sydney (BEc). FRAIPA 1983. Apptd NSW Civil Service, 1938; NSW State Treasury: 1945; Asst Under-Sec. (Finance), 1959–61; Dep. Under-Sec., 1961–63; Under-Sec. and Comptroller of Accounts, 1963–65; Pres., Metrop. Water, Sewerage and Drainage Bd, Sydney, 1965–81. Member: State Pollution Control Commn, 1971–81; Metropolitan Waste Disposal Authority (Sydney), 1971–81; management consultant and co. dir, 1981–92. *Recreations:* genealogy, internet browsing. *Address:* 44 Del Monte Place, Copacabana, NSW 2251, Australia. *Clubs:* Central Coast League's (Gosford); Avoca Beach Bowling; Probus (Avoca Beach, and Broadwater Central Coast).

WALDER, Ruth Christabel, (Mrs Wesierska), OBE 1956; *b* 15 Jan. 1906; *d* of Rev. Ernest Walder; *m* 1955, Maj.-Gen. George Wesierski (*d* 1967), formerly Judge Advocate General of the Polish Forces. *Educ:* Cheltenham Ladies' College. General Organiser, National Federation of Women's Institutes, 1934–40; Admiralty, 1940–41; Relief Department, Foreign Office, 1942–44; UNRRA, Sec. Food Cttee of Council for Europe, 1944–47; Secretary United Nations Appeal for Children (in the UK), 1948; National General Secretary, YWCA of Great Britain, 1949–67. Lectr for the European Community, 1970–. Defence Medal, 1946. Polish Gold Cross of Merit, 1969. *Publication:* (as Ruth Walder Wesierska) They built a Jolly Good Mess (memoirs, in Europe 1939–45), 1987. *Address:* Westhope, Langton Herring, Weymouth, Dorset DT3 4HZ. *T:* (01305) 871233. *Clubs:* Naval and Military; Royal Dorset Yacht.

WALDHEIM, Dr Kurt; President of the Republic of Austria, 1986–92; *b* 21 Dec. 1918; *m* 1944, Elisabeth Ritschel Waldheim; one *s* two *d*. *Educ:* Consular Academy, Vienna; Univ. of Vienna (Dr Jr 1944). Entered Austrian foreign service, 1945; served in Min. for Foreign Affairs; Mem., Austrian Delegn to Paris, London and Moscow for negotiations on Austrian State Treaty, 1945–47; 1st Sec., Embassy, Paris, 1948–51; apptd Counsellor and Head of Personnel Div., Min. of Foreign Affairs, 1951–55; Permanent Austrian Observer to UN, 1955–56; Minister Plenipotentiary to Canada, 1956–58; Ambassador to Canada, 1958–60; Dir-Gen. for Political Affairs, Min. of Foreign Affairs, 1960–64; Permanent Rep. of Austria to UN, 1964–68 (Chm., Outer Space Cttee of UN 1965–68 and 1970–71); Federal Minister for Foreign Affairs, 1968–70; Candidate for the Presidency of Republic of Austria, 1971; Permanent Rep. of Austria to UN, 1970–Dec. 1971; Sec.-Gen. of UN, 1972–81. Guest Prof. of Diplomacy, Georgetown Univ., Washington DC, 1982–84. Chm., InterAction Council for Internat. Co-operation, 1983–85. Hon. LLD: Chile, Carleton, Rutgers, Fordham, 1972; Jawaharlal Nehru, Bucharest, 1973; Wagner Coll., NY, Catholic Univ. of America, Wilfrid Laurier, 1974; Catholic Univ. of Leuven, Charles Univ., Hamilton Coll., Clinton, NY, 1975; Denver, Philippines, Nice, 1976; American Univ., Kent State, Warsaw, Moscow State Univ., Mongolian State Univ., 1977; Atlanta Univ., Humboldt Univ., Univ. of S Carolina, 1979; Notre Dame, USA, 1980. George Marshall Peace Award, USA, 1977; Dr Karl Renner Prize, City of Vienna, 1978. *Publications:* The Austrian Example, 1971, English edn 1973; The Challenge of Peace, 1977, English edn 1980; Building the Future Order, 1980; In the Eye of the Storm, 1985; Die Antwort, 1996. *Recreations:* sailing, swimming, skiing, horseback riding. *Address:* 1 Lobkowitz-Platz, 1010 Vienna, Austria.

WALDMANN, Prof. Herman, FRS 1990; Professor and Head of Department of Pathology, Oxford University, since 1994; Fellow of Lincoln College, Oxford, since 1994; *b* 27 Feb. 1945; *s* of Leon and Rene Ryfka Waldmann; *m* 1971, Judith Ruth Young. *Educ:* Sir George Monoux Grammar Sch., Walthamstow; Sidney Sussex Coll., Cambridge (BA); London Hosp. Med Coll. (MB BChir); PhD Cantab. MRCPath, MRCP. Cambridge University: Dept of Pathology, 1971–94; Fellow, King's Coll., 1985–94; Kay Kendall Prof. of Therapeutic Immunology, 1989–93. Founder FMedSci 1998. Hon. Fellow, QMW, 1996. Graham Bull Prize for Clinical Res., RCP, 1991. *Publications:* Limiting Dilution Analysis (with Dr I. Lefkovits), 1977, 2nd edn 1998; The Immune System (with Dr I. McConnell and A. Munro), 1981; (ed) Monoclonal Antibodies, 1988; many scientific papers. *Recreations:* family, (less) food, friends, travel, music. *Address:* Sir William Dunn School of Pathology, South Parks Road, Oxford OX1 3RE.

WALDNER, Benita Maria F.; *see* Ferrero-Waldner.

WALDRON-RAMSEY, Waldo Emerson; Barrister and Attorney-at-Law; international consultant; *b* 1 Jan. 1930; *s* of Wyatt and Delcina Waldron-Ramsey; *m* 1954, Shiela Pamella Beresford, Georgetown, Guyana; one *s* two *d*. *Educ:* Barbados; Hague Academy; London Sch. of Economics; Yugoslavia. LLB Hons; BSc (Econ) Hons; PhD. Called to Bar, Middle Temple; practised London Bar and SW Circuit, 1957–60; Marketing Economist, Shell International, 1960–61; Tanzanian Foreign Service, 1961–70; High Comr for Barbados in UK, and Ambassador to France, Netherlands and Germany, 1970–71; Ambassador and Perm. Rep. for Barbados to UN, 1971–76. UN Legal Expert: in field of human rights, 1967–71; on Israel, 1968–71. Chairman: Sunny Investment & Finance Gp of Cos, 1994–; Edutech (Pty) Ltd, Windhoek, Cape Town, a nd Gabarone, 1994–. Mem., National Exec., Barbados Labour Party, 1980–. Senator, Parlt of Barbados, 1983–85. Editor, Beacon Newspaper, 1982–86. Member: Amer. Acad. of Political and Social Sciences; Amer. Soc. of Internat. Law; Amer. Inst. of Petroleum (Marketing Div.). Hon. Fellow, Hebrew Univ. of Jerusalem, 1972. DSc (Pol. Econ.) Univ. of Phnom-Penh, 1973; Hon. LLD Chung-Ang Univ., Republic of Korea, 1975. Grand Officer (1st Class), Nat. Order of Honneur et Mérite, Republic of Haiti, 1968; Grand Officier, Ordre Nat. de l'Amitié et Mérite, Khymèr, 1973; Order of Distinguished Diplomatic Service Merit, Gwangwha (1st Class), Republic of Korea, 1974. *Recreations:* cricket, tennis, bridge, travel. *Address:* (chambers) 50 Swan Street, Bridgetown, Barbados. *T:* 4278280, 4242021; (chambers) 26 Court Street, Brooklyn, New York 11225, USA; The Monticello, 30 Park Avenue, Mount Vernon, New York 10550, USA. *T:* (London) (020) 7229 4870; (N Carolina) (919) 7650080. *Clubs:* Royal Automobile; Lincoln Lodge (Connecticut).

WALES, Archbishop of, since 2000; **Most Rev. Rowan Douglas Williams,** FBA 1990; Bishop of Monmouth, since 1992; *b* 14 June 1950; *s* of Aneurin Williams and Nancy Delphine Williams; *m* 1981, Hilary Jane Paul; one *s* one *d*. *Educ:* Dynevor School, Swansea; Christ's College, Cambridge (BA 1971, MA 1975); Christ Church and Wadham College, Oxford (DPhil 1975; DD 1989). Lectr, College of the Resurrection, Mirfield, 1975–77; ordained deacon, 1977, priest, 1978; Chaplain, Tutor and Director of Studies, Westcott House, Cambridge, 1977–80; Cambridge University: Univ. Lectr in Divinity, 1980–86; Fellow and Dean of Clare Coll., 1984–86; Lady Margaret Prof. of Divinity, and Canon of Christ Church, Oxford, 1986–92. Hon. Asst Priest, St George's, Cambridge, 1980–83; Canon Theologian, Leicester Cathedral, 1981–92. Examining Chaplain to Bishop of Manchester, 1987–92. Hon. Fellow: UC, Swansea, 1993; Clare Coll., Cambridge, 1994; Univ. of Wales Coll., Newport, 2000. Hon. DTheol Erlangen, 1999; Hon. DD Nashotah Hse, USA. *Publications:* The Wound of Knowledge, 1979; Resurrection, 1982; The Truce of God, 1983; (with Mark Collier) Beginning Now; peacemaking theology, 1984; Arius: heresy and tradition, 1987; (ed) The Making of Orthodoxy, 1989; Teresa of Avila, 1991; Open to Judgement, 1994; After Silent Centuries, 1994; Sergii Bulgakov: towards a Rusian political theology, 1999; On Christian Theology, 1999; Lost Icons, 2000; Christ on Trial, 2000; (ed jtly) Love's Redeeming Work: the Anglican quest for holiness, 2001; contribs to Theologische Realencylklopädie, Jl of Theological Studies, Downside Review, Eastern Churches Review, Sobornost, New Blackfriars. *Recreations:* music, fiction, languages. *Address:* Bishopstow, Newport, Gwent NP9 4EA. *T:* (01633) 263510.

WALES, Daphne Beatrice; Chairman, Board for Mission and Unity, General Synod of the Church of England, 1983–88; *b* 6 Dec. 1917; *d* of Frederick James Wales and Lilian Frederica (*née* Whitnall). Dep. Principal, Bank of England, retd. Mem., General Synod, 1975–90 (Mem., Panel of Chairmen, 1983); Chm., St Albans Diocese House of Laity, 1979–85. Chm., Highway Trust, 1992–99 (Vice-Chm., 1983–92); Gov., Partnership for World Mission, 1978–90; Trustee, S American Missionary Soc., 1983–97 (Vice-Chm., 1989–97). Mem. Council, Oak Hill Theol Coll., 1981–91. *Address:* 41 Park Road, Watford, Herts WD17 4QW. *T:* (01923) 225643.

WALES, Prof. Kathleen Margaret; Professor of Modern English Language, since 1996, Dean of Learning and Teaching, Faculty of Arts, since 2000, University of Leeds; *b* 8 Feb. 1946; *d* of Richard Derwent and Yvonne Derwent (*née* Atkins); *m* 1st, 1971, Brian Wales (marr. diss. 1988); one *s*; 2nd, 1993, David Bovey. *Educ:* Darlington High Sch. for Girls; Royal Holloway Coll., Univ. of London (BA 1st Cl. Hons English). Royal Holloway College, later Royal Holloway and Bedford New College, University of London: Lectr in English Lang., 1968–88; Sen. Lectr, 1988–94; Reader, 1994–95; Prof., 1995–96; Hd, English Dept, 1995–96. Sen. Res. Fellow, British Acad./Leverhulme Trust, 1992–93; Vis. Res. Fellow, Lucy Cavendish Coll., Univ. of Cambridge, 1999–2000. FRSA 1996; FEA 2001. Ed., Jl Lang. and Lit., 1996–. *Publications:* Dictionary of Stylistics, 1989, 2nd rev. edn 2001; The Language of James Joyce, 1992; (ed) Feminist Linguistics in Literary Criticism, 1994; Personal Pronouns in Present-Day English, 1996; (ed jtly) Shakespeare's Dramatic Language: a reader's guide, 2000; numerous book chapters; contrib. articles to learned jls. *Recreations:* buying and selling twentieth-century collectables and children's books and toys at antique fairs and flea markets, keeping fit, collecting elephants, writing children's joke-books, water-colour painting. *Address:* 31 Newton Road, Little Shelford, Cambridge CB2 5HL. *T:* (01223) 846494.

WAŁĘSA, Lech, Hon. GCB 1991; President of Poland, 1990–95; *b* Popowo, 29 Sept. 1943; *s* of late Bolesław Wałęsa and Feliksa Wałęsa; *m* 1969, Danuta; four *s* four *d*. *Educ:* Lipno primary and tech. schools; trained as electrician. Lenin Shipyard, Gdańsk, 1966–76, 1980–90 (Chm., Strike Cttees, 1970, 1980); founder Chm., Nat. Co-ordinating Commn of Indep. Autonomous Trade Union Solidarity (NSZZ Solidarność), 1981–82; in custody, 1981–82; returned to Gdańsk Shipyard, 1983; Leader, (outlawed) Solidarity, 1983–88, (re-instated) Solidarity, 1988–90. Dr *hc*, including: Alliance Coll., Cambridge, Mass, 1981; Harvard, 1983; Gdańsk, 1990; Connecticut State, 1996. Nobel Peace Prize, 1983. Presidential Medal of Freedom (USA); Grand Cross, Legion of Honour (France); Order of Merit (Italian Republic); Order of Pius, 1st Cl. (Holy See); Grand Ribbon, Order of Leopold (Belgium). *Publication:* A Path of Hope: An Autobiography, 1987. *Address:* ul. Waly Jagiellonskie 1, 80–853 Gdańsk, Poland.

WALEY, Daniel Philip, FBA 1991; PhD; Keeper of Manuscripts, British Library, 1973–86 (Keeper of Manuscripts, British Museum, 1972–73); *b* 20 March 1921; *er s* of late Hubert David Waley and Margaret Hendelah Waley; *m* 1945, Pamela Joan Griffiths; one *s* one *d* (and one *d* decd). *Educ:* Dauntsey's Sch.; King's Coll., Cambridge (MA, PhD). Historical Tripos, Cambridge, 1939–40 and 1945–46 (cl. 1). Served War, 1940–45. Fellow of King's Coll., Cambridge, 1950–54. Asst Lectr in Medieval History, London School of Economics and Political Science, Univ. of London, 1949–51, Lectr, 1951–61, Reader in History, 1961–70, Prof. of History, 1970–72. Hon. Res. Fellow, Westfield Coll., London, 1986; Emer. Fellow, Leverhulme Trust, 1986–87. British Acad. Italian Lectr, 1975. Corresp. Fellow, Deputazione di Storia Patria per l'Umbria, 1991. Serena Medal, British Acad., 1990. *Publications:* Mediaeval Orvieto, 1952; The Papal State in the 13th Century, 1961; Later Medieval Europe, 1964, 3rd edn (with P. Denley) 2001; The Italian City Republics, 1969, 3rd edn 1988; British Public Opinion and the Abyssinian War, 1935–36, 1975; (ed) George Eliot's Blotter: A Commonplace-Book, 1980; (contrib.) Storia d'Italia, ed by G. Galasso, vol. 7, 1987; Siena and the Sienese in the Thirteenth Century, 1991; (ed) J. K. Hyde, Literacy and Its Uses: studies on late medieval Italy, 1993; (contrib.) Il Libro Bianco di San Gimignano, vol. 1, 1996; A Liberal Life: Sydney, Earl Buxton, 1853–1934, 1999; contributor to: Dizionario Biografico degli Italiani, English Hist. Review, Trans Royal Hist. Soc., Papers of British Sch. at Rome, Jl of Ecclesiastical Hist., Jl of the History of Ideas, Rivista Storica Italiana, Rivista di Storia della Chiesa in Italia, Procs Brit. Acad., British Library Jl, Bull. of John Rylands Liby, Sussex Archaeol Collections, etc. *Recreation:* walking. *Address:* 33 Greyfriars Court, Court Road, Lewes, E Sussex BN7 2RF.

WALEY-COHEN, Hon. Joyce Constance Ina; (Joyce, Hon. Lady Waley-Cohen), MA; President, Independent Schools Information Service Council, 1981–85 (Member, 1972–80); *b* 20 Jan. 1920; *o d* of 1st Baron Nathan, PC, TD, and Eleanor Joan Clara, *d* of C. Stettauer; *m* 1943, Sir Bernard Nathaniel Waley-Cohen, 1st Bt, (*d* 1991); two *s* two *d*. *Educ:* St Felix Sch., Southwold; Girton Coll., Cambridge (MA). Member: Governing Body, St Felix Sch., 1945–83 (Chm., 1970–83); Westminster Hosp. Bd of Governors, 1952–68; Chairman: Westminster Children's Hosp., 1952–68; Gordon Hosp., 1961–68; Governing Bodies of Girls' Schools' Assoc., 1974–79 (Mem., 1963); Ind. Schs Jt Council, 1977–80. Governor: Taunton Sch., 1978–90; Wellington Coll., 1979–90. JP Mddx 1949–59, Somerset 1959–86. *Recreations:* hunting, spinning, family life. *Address:* Honeymead, Simonsbath, Minehead, Somerset TA24 7JX. *T:* (01643) 831242.

WALEY-COHEN, Sir Stephen (Harry), 2nd Bt *cr* 1961, of Honeymead, Co. Somerset; Managing Director: Victoria Palace Theatre, since 1989; Mousetrap Productions, since 1993; Savoy Theatre Management, since 1997; *b* 22 June 1946; *s* of Sir Bernard Nathaniel Waley-Cohen, 1st Bt and Hon. Joyce Constance Ina Waley-Cohen, *qv*; *S* father, 1991; *m* 1st, 1972, Pamela Elizabeth (marr. diss.), *yr d* of J. E. Doniger; two *s* one *d*; 2nd, 1986, Josephine Burnett, *yr d* of late Duncan M. Spencer; two *d*. *Educ:* Wellesley House Sch.; Eton (Oppidan Scholar); Magdalene Coll., Cambridge (MA Hons). Financial journalist, Daily Mail, 1968–73; Publisher, Euromoney, 1969–83; Chief Exec., Maybox Theatres, 1984–89; Chairman: Thorndike Holdings, management training, 1989–98; Bridge Underwriting Agents (formerly Willis Faber & Dumas (Agencies)), 1992–99 (Dir, 1988–99); Policy Portfolio, 1993–97; Portsmouth & Sunderland Newspapers, 1998–99 (Dir, 1994–99); First Call Gp, 1996–98; Director: Badgworthy Land Co., 1982–; St Martin's Theatre, 1989–; Theatresoft, 1992–97; Theatre Investment Fund, 1992–; Exeter Selected Assets (formerly Preferred Capital) Investment Trust, 1992–; Man. Dir, Vaudeville Th., 1996–2001. Chm., Mousetrap Foundn for the Arts, 1996–; Mem., SOLT (formerly SWET), 1984– (Mem., Finance Cttee, 1989–; Chm., 1996–); Chm., Olivier

Awards Cttee, 1995–. Mem. Council, JCA Charitable Foundn (formerly Jewish Colonisation Assoc.), 1985– (Pres., 1992–); Chairman: Exec. Cttee, British American Project for Successor Generation, 1986–92; Mowbray Trust for Reproductive Immunology, 1996–. Trustee, Theatres Trust, 1998–. Member: Public Affairs Cttee, British Field Sports Soc., 1972–92; Cttee, Devon & Somerset Staghounds, 1974–. Mem., UCL Finance Cttee, 1984–89; Governor, Wellesley House Sch., 1974–97. Contested (C) Manchester, Gorton, Feb. and Oct. 1974. *Recreations:* family, theatre, hunting. *Heir: s* Lionel Robert Waley-Cohen, *b* 7 Aug. 1974. *Address:* 1 Wallingford Avenue, W10 6QA. *T:* (020) 8968 6268; Honeymead, Simonsbath, Somerset TA24 7JX. *T:* (01643) 831584. *Club:* Garrick.

WALFORD, Sir Christopher (Rupert), Kt 1995; TEM 1972; Lord Mayor of London, 1994–95; *b* 15 Oct. 1935; *s* of John Rupert Charles Walford, MBE and Gladys Irene Walford (*née* Sperrin); *m* 1967, Anne Elizabeth Viggars; two *s* (and one *s* decd). *Educ:* Charterhouse; Oriel College, Oxford (MA; Hon. Fellow, 1995). Solicitor (Hons). National Service, commissioned RA, 1954–56; HAC 1957–72 (to Warrant Officer). Allen & Overy, 1959–96 (Partner, 1970–96). Councillor, Kensington, 1962–65, Kensington & Chelsea, 1964–82, Dep. Mayor, 1974–75, Mayor, 1979–80; Alderman, Ward of Farringdon Within, 1982–2002; Sheriff, City of London, 1990–91. Member: Council, CGLI, 1984–98; Council, and Policy and Exec. Cttees, Inst. of Directors, 1986–94; Court of Assistants and Finance Cttee, Corp. of Sons of the Clergy, 1989–98; Trustee: St Paul's Cathedral Choir Sch. Foundn, 1985–97; Guildhall Sch., Music and Drama Foundn, 1989–97; Morden Coll., 1991–. Vice-Pres., Bridewell Royal Hosp., 1996–2002 (Gov., 1984–2002). Governor, Hon. Irish Soc., 1997–2000; Mem. Bd of Govs, London Guildhall Univ., 1997–. Freeman, City of London, 1964; Liveryman: Makers of Playing Cards Co., 1978 (Master, 1987); City of London Solicitors Co., 1983 (Master, 1993). FRSA. Hon. DCL City, 1994; Hon. LLD Ulster, 2000. *Recreations:* listening to music (especially opera), kitchen bridge, watching Rugby football and cricket, horse racing, hill walking. *Address:* 17 Market Place, Masham, Ripon, N Yorks HG4 4EG. *T:* (01765) 688420, *Fax:* (01765) 689471; *e-mail:* crwalford@aol.com. *Clubs:* Athenæum, East India, MCC.

WALFORD, Dr Diana Marion; Director, Public Health Laboratory Service, 1993–Sept. 2002; Principal, Mansfield College, Oxford, from Oct. 2002; *b* 26 Feb. 1944; *d* of Lt-Col Joseph Norton, LLM, and Thelma Norton (*née* Nurick); *m* 1970, Arthur David Walford, LLB; one *s* one *d*. *Educ:* Calder High Sch. for Girls, Liverpool; Liverpool Univ. (George Holt Medal, Physiol.; J. H. Abram Prize, Pharmacol.; BSc (1st C1. Hons Physiol.) 1965; MB ChB 1968; MD 1976); London Univ. (MSc (Epidemiology) 1987). FRCP 1990 (MRCP 1972); FRCPath 1986 (MRCPath 1974); MFPHM 1989, FFPHM 1994. Ho. Officer posts, Liverpool Royal Inf., 1968–69; Sen. Ho. Officer posts and Sen. Registrar, St Mary's Hosp., Paddington, and Northwick Park Hosp., Harrow, 1969–75; MRC Research (Training) Fellow, Clin. Res. Centre, 1975–76; Sen. MO 1976–79, PMO 1979–83, SPMO (Under Sec.), 1983–89, Dep. CMO, 1989–92, DHSS, subseq. Dept of Health. Hon. Consultant Haematologist, Central Middlesex Hosp., 1977–87. Mem., British Soc. for Haematology, 1978–; Founder Mem., British Blood Transfusion Soc., 1983–; Hon. Life Mem., British Assoc. of Med. Managers. Gov., Ditchley Foundn, 2000–. FRSocMed. *Publications:* chapters on haematological side effects of drugs in: Meyler's Side Effects of Drugs, 9th edn 1980; Side Effects of Drugs Annual, 1980; Drug-Induced Emergencies, 1980; articles on alpha-thalassaemia. *Recreations:* theatre, painting, travel. *Address:* (until Sept. 2002) Public Health Laboratory Service, 61 Colindale Avenue, NW9 5DF; *T:* (020) 8200 1295; (from Oct. 2002) Mansfield College, Mansfield Road, Oxford OX1 3TF.

WALFORD, Prof. Geoffrey, PhD; Professor of Education Policy, University of Oxford, since 2000; Fellow, Green College, Oxford, since 1995; *b* 30 April 1949. *Educ:* Univ. of Kent (BSc Physics 1971; PhD 1975); Open Univ. (BA Sociol. and Educn 1975; MSc 1985; MBA 1996); St John's Coll., Oxford (MPhil Sociol. 1978; MA 1995); Inst. of Educn, Univ. of London (MA Educnl Admin 1986). Aston University: Lectr in Sociol. of Educn, Dept of Educnl Enquiry, 1979–83; Lectr in Educn Policy and Mgt, 1983–90, Sen. Lectr in Sociol. and Educn Policy, 1990–94, Aston Business Sch.; University of Oxford: Lectr in Educnl Studies (Sociol.), 1995–97; Reader in Educn Policy, 1997–2000. Jt Ed., Brit. Jl Educnl Studies, 1998–. *Publications:* books include: Life in Public Schools, 1986; Restructuring Universities: politics and power in the management of change, 1987; Privatization and Privilege in Education, 1990; (with H. Miller) City Technology College, 1991; (ed) Doing Educational Research, 1991; Choice and Equity in Education, 1994; (ed) Researching the Powerful in Education, 1994; Educational Politics: pressure groups and faith-based schools, 1995; (ed with R. Pring) Affirming the Comprehensive Ideal, 1997; (ed) Doing Research about Education, 1998; (ed) Studies in Educational Ethnography, annually, 1998–; Policy, Politics and Education: sponsored grant-maintained schools and religious diversity, 2000; Doing Qualitative Educational Research, 2001. *Recreations:* travel, walking. *Address:* Department of Educational Studies, University of Oxford, 15 Norham Gardens, Oxford OX2 6PY. *T:* (01865) 274141.

WALFORD, John de Guise; His Honour Judge Walford; a Circuit Judge, since 1993; *b* 23 Feb. 1948; *s* of late Edward Wynn Walford and of Dorothy Ann Walford; *m* 1977, Pamela Elizabeth Russell; one *s* one *d*. *Educ:* Sedbergh Sch.; Queens' Coll., Cambridge (MA). Called to the Bar, Middle Temple, 1971; practice on NE Circuit, 1974; Asst Recorder, 1985–89; Recorder, 1989–93. Standing Counsel (Criminal) to DHSS, NE Circuit, 1991–93. Chancellor, dio. of Bradford, 1999–. *Recreations:* cricket, tennis, opera, watching Middlesbrough FC. *Address:* Law Courts, Russell Street, Middlesbrough TS1 2AE. *Clubs:* Hawks (Cambridge); Free Foresters.

WALFORD, John Howard; President, Solicitors' Disciplinary Tribunal, 1979–88; Senior Legal Officer, Office of the Banking Ombudsman, 1991–96; *b* 16 May 1927; *s* of Henry Howard Walford and Marjorie Josephine Solomon; *m* 1953, Peggy Ann Jessel; two *s* two *d*. *Educ:* Cheltenham College; Gonville and Caius College, Cambridge; MA (Hons). Solicitor, 1950; Bischoff & Co.: Senior Partner, 1979–88; Consultant, 1988–91. Mem. Council, Law Society, 1961–69; Governor, College of Law, 1967–88; Senior Warden, City of London Solicitors' Co., 1980–81, Master, 1981–82. Governor, St John's Hosp. for Diseases of the Skin, 1967–82; Chm., Appeal Cttee, Skin Disease Research Fund, 1974–93; Mem., Bd of Management, Petworth Cottage Nursing Home (Chm., 1988–93). Mem., Arbitration Panel, The Securities and Futures Authority Consumer Arbitration Scheme, 1988–94. Hon. Mem., British Assoc. of Dermatologists, 1993. Commander, Order of Bernardo O'Higgins, Chile, 1972. *Address:* Pheasant Court, Northchapel, near Petworth, W Sussex GU28 9LJ. *Clubs:* Garrick, City Law; Leconfield Flyfishing.

WALFORD, John Thomas, OBE 1985; a Vice President, Multiple Sclerosis Society of Great Britain and Northern Ireland, since 1995 (Deputy General Secretary, 1965–77; General Secretary, 1977–95); *b* 6 Feb. 1933; *s* of Frederick Thomas Walford and Rose Elizabeth Walford; *m* 1st, 1955, June Muriel Harding (marr. diss. 1970); two *s* one *d*; 2nd, 1996, Nansi Yvonne Long. *Educ:* Richmond and East Sheen County Grammar Sch. Served RAF, 1951–53. C. C. Wakefield & Co. Ltd, 1949–51 and 1953–55; Stanley Eades & Co., 1955–60; Moo Cow Milk Bars Ltd, 1960–64. DL Greater London, 1988–95. Editor, MS News (qly jl of Multiple Sclerosis Soc.), 1977–95. *Recreation:* collecting Victorian fairings. *Address:* Rhoslyn, Talley, Llandeilo, Carmarthenshire SA19 7AX. *T:* (01558) 685744. *Club:* Royal Society of Medicine.

WALFORD, Lionel Kingsley, PhD; FInstP; EU Sales Director, Jagged Peak Inc.; *b* 19 May 1939; *s* of late Edward Walford and of Muriel (*née* Davies); *m* 1963, Linda Jones; one *d* (and one *d* decd). *Educ:* Whitchurch Grammar Sch., Cardiff; Univ. of Wales (BSc 1st Cl. Hons Physics, 1960); St Catharine's Coll., Cambridge (PhD 1963). FInstP 1972. Southern Illinois University, USA: Asst Prof., 1963–67; Associate Prof., 1967–72; Prof. of Physics, 1972–78; Research Consultant, McDonnell Douglas Corp., 1964–72; joined Welsh Office, 1978: Principal, 1978–84; Sen. Principal seconded to WDA, 1984–85; Dir, Manpower Services in Wales, 1985–88; Asst Sec., 1988–94, Under Sec. (Hd, then Dir), 1994–99, Welsh Office Agriculture Dept. *Publications:* numerous articles in jls on applied physics; one US patent. *e-mail:* lionelw@jaggedpeak.com.

WALKER, family name of **Barons Walker of Doncaster** and **Walker of Worcester**.

WALKER OF DONCASTER, Baron *cr* 1997 (Life Peer), of Audenshaw in the co. of Greater Manchester; **Harold Walker,** Kt 1992; PC 1979; DL; *b* 12 July 1927; *s* of Harold and Phyllis Walker; *m* 1984, Mary Griffin; one *d* by former marriage. *Educ:* Manchester College of Technology. Served RN, 1946–48. MP (Lab) Doncaster, 1964–83, Doncaster Central, 1983–97. An Assistant Government Whip, 1967–68; Jt Parly Under-Sec. of State, Dept of Employment and Productivity, 1968–70; Opposition Front-Bench spokesman on Industrial Relations, 1970–74, on Employment, 1979–83; Parly Under-Sec. of State, Dept of Employment, 1974–76; Minister of State, Dept of Employment, 1976–79; Chm. of Ways and Means and Dep. Speaker, H of C, 1983–92. Chm., All Party Gardening and Horticulture Gp, 1997–. DL S Yorks, 1997. Freeman, Borough of Doncaster, 1999. Lifetime Achievement Award, Inst. of Occupational Safety and Health, 1999. *Recreations:* reading, gardening. *Address:* House of Lords, SW1A 0PW. *Clubs:* Westminster, Clay Lane, Doncaster Trades, RN, Catholic (all Doncaster); Wimbledon Village.

WALKER OF WORCESTER, Baron *cr* 1992 (Life Peer), of Abbots Morton in the County of Hereford and Worcester; **Peter Edward Walker;** PC 1970; MBE 1960; *b* 25 March 1932; *s* of Sydney and Rose Walker; *m* 1969, Tessa, *d* of G. I. Pout; three *s* two *d*. *Educ:* Latymer Upper Sch. Member, National Executive of Conservative Party, 1956–70; Nat. Chairman, Young Conservatives, 1958–60; contested (C) Dartford, 1955 and 1959. MP (C) Worcester, March 1961–1992. PPS to Leader of House of Commons, 1963–64; Opposition Front Bench Spokesman: on Finance and Economics, 1964–66; on Transport, 1966–68; on Local Government, Housing, and Land, 1968–70; Minister of Housing and Local Govt, June–Oct. 1970; Secretary of State for: the Environment, 1970–72; Trade and Industry, 1972–74; Opposition Spokesman on Trade, Industry and Consumer Affairs, Feb.-June 1974, on Defence, June 1974–Feb. 1975; Minister of Agric., Fisheries and Food, 1979–83; Sec. of State for Energy, 1983–87, for Wales, 1987–90. Chairman: Thornton & Co., 1991–97; Cornhill Insurance, 1992–; English Partnerships, 1992–98; Kleinwort Benson, 1997–99; Vice Chm., Dresdner Kleinwort Wasserstein (formerly Dresdner Kleinwort Benson), 1999–; non-executive Director: British Gas, 1990–96; Dalgety, 1990–96; Tate & Lyle, 1990–; LIFFE, 1995–. Pres., British German Chamber of Commerce, 1999–. *Publications:* The Ascent of Britain, 1977; Trust The People, 1987; Staying Power (autobiog.), 1991. *Address:* Abbots Morton Manor, Gooms Hill, Abbots Morton, Worcester WR7 4LT. *Clubs:* Carlton (Chm., 1998–); Worcestershire County Cricket, Union and County (Worcester).

WALKER, Rev. Sir Alan, Kt 1981; OBE 1955; Principal, Pacific College for Evangelism, 1989–95, Principal Emeritus, Alan Walker College of Evangelism, since 1995; *b* 4 June 1911; *s* of Rev. Alfred Edgar Walker, former Pres., NSW Methodist Conf., and Violet Louise Walker; *m* 1938, Winifred Garrard Walker (*née* Channon); three *s* one *d*. *Educ:* Leigh Theological Coll., Sydney; Univ. of Sydney (BA, MA); Bethany Biblical Seminary, Chicago. Minister, Cessnock, NSW, 1939–44; Supt, Waverley Methodist Mission, 1944–54; Dir, Australian Mission to the Nation, 1953–56; Vis. Professor: of Evangelism, Boston Sch. of Theology, 1957; of Evangelism and Preaching, Claremont Sch. of Theol., USA, 1973; Supt, Central Methodist Mission, Sydney, 1958–78; Dir, World Evangelism, World Methodist Council, 1978–87. Deleg. to First Assembly of WCC, Amsterdam, 1948; Adviser to: Aust. Delegn at UN, 1949; Third Ass. of WCC, New Delhi, 1962; Fourth Ass., WCC, Uppsala, 1968; Missions to: Fiji, S Africa, S America, Singapore and Malaysia, Sri Lanka, 1962–75; Founder, Sydney Life Line Tel. Counselling Centre, 1963 (Pres., Life Line Internat., 1966–87); Sec., NSW Methodist Conf., 1970, Pres., 1971; lectures, various times, USA. Hon. DD Bethany Biblical Sem., 1954. Inst. de la Vie award, Paris, for services to humanity, 1978; (with Lady Walker) World Methodist Peace Award, 1986. Order of Jerusalem, 1999. *Publications include:* There is Always God, 1938; Everybody's Calvary, 1943; Coal Town, 1944; Heritage Without End, 1953; The Whole Gospel for the Whole World, 1957; The Many Sided Cross of Jesus, 1962; How Jesus Helped People, 1964; A Ringing Call to Mission, 1966; The Life Line Story, 1967 (USA, As Close as the Telephone); Breakthrough, 1969; God, the Disturber, 1973 (USA); Jesus, the Liberator, 1973 (USA); The New Evangelism, 1974 (USA); Love in Action, 1977; Life Grows with Christ, 1981; Life Ends in Christ, 1983; Standing Up To Preach, 1983; Your Life Can Be Changed, 1985; Life in the Holy Spirit, 1986; Try God, 1990; Herald of Hope, 1994; The Contrast Society of Jesus, 1997; *relevant publication:* Conscience of the Nation, by Don Wright, 1997. *Recreations:* swimming, tennis. *Address:* 14 Owen Stanley Avenue, Beacon Hill, NSW 2100, Australia. *T:* (2) 4513923.

WALKER, Prof. Alan Cyril, PhD; FRS 1999; Distinguished Professor of Anthropology and Biology, Pennsylvania State University, since 1996 (Professor of Anthropology and Biology, 1995–96); *b* 23 Aug. 1938; *s* of Cyril Walker and Edith (*née* Tidd); *m* 1st, 1963, Patricia Dale Larwood (marr. diss.); one *s*; 2nd, 1976, Patty Lee Shipman. *Educ:* St John's Coll., Cambridge (BA 1962); Royal Free Hosp., London (PhD 1967). BM Scientific Associate, 1963–64; Asst Lectr in Anatomy, Royal Free Hosp. Sch. of Medicine, 1965; Lectr in Anatomy, Makerere UC, Kampala, 1965–69; Hon. Keeper of Paleontology, Uganda Mus., 1967–69; Sen. Lectr in Anatomy, Univ. of Nairobi, 1969–73; Harvard University: Vis. Lectr, Dept of Anatomy, 1973–74, Associate Prof. of Anatomy, 1974–78, Med. Sch.; Associate Prof. of Anthropol., 1974–78; Res. Associate, Peabody Mus., 1974–78; Mem., Cttee of Profs in Evolutionary and Organismic Biol., 1974–78; Prof. of Cell Biol. and Anatomy, Johns Hopkins Univ. Sch. of Medicine, 1978–95 (part-time, 1995–97). Associate Editor: Amer. Jl Physical Anthropol., 1974–79; Jl Human Evolution, 1994–98. John Simon Guggenheim Meml Foundn Fellow, 1986; John D. and Catherine T. MacArthur Foundn Fellow, 1988–93; Phi Beta Kappa Schol., 1995. Mem., American Acad. of Arts and Scis, 1996. DSc Chicago, 2000. Internat. Fondation Fyssen Prize, 1998; Faculty Scholar's Medal, Pennsylvania State Univ., 1999. *Publications:* (ed jtly) Prosimian Biology, 1974; (jtly) Structure and Function of the Human Skeleton, 1985; (ed with R. Leakey) The Nariokotome Homo Erectus Skeleton, 1993; (with P. Shipman) The Wisdom of the Bones, 1996 (Rhône-Poulenc Prize, 1997); contrib. numerous papers to jls and edited books. *Address:* Department of Anthropology, 409 Carpenter Building, Pennsylvania State University, University Park, PA 16802, USA. *T:* (814) 8653122.

WALKER, Alexander; Film Critic, London Evening Standard, since 1960; *b* Portadown, N Ireland, 22 March 1930; *s* of Alfred and Ethel Walker. *Educ:* Portadown Grammar Sch.; The Queen's Univ., Belfast (BA); Collège d'Europe, Bruges; Univ. of Michigan, Ann Arbor. Lecturer in political philosophy and comparative govt, Univ. of Michigan, 1952–54. Features editor, Birmingham Gazette, 1954–56; leader writer and film critic, The Birmingham Post, 1956–59; columnist, Vogue magazine, 1974–86. Frequent broadcaster on the arts on radio and television; author: TV series Moviemen; BBC Radio series Film Star; author and co-producer of TV programmes on History of Hollywood, Garbo and Chaplin. Member: British Screen Adv. Council (formerly Wilson Interim Action Cttee on the Film Industry), 1977–92; Bd of Govs, BFI, 1989–95. Chevalier de l'Ordre des Arts et des Lettres, 1981. Critic of the Year, in annual British Press awards, 1970, 1974, 1998, commended, 1985; Award of Golden Eagle, Philippines, for services to internat. cinema, 1982. *Publications:* The Celluloid Sacrifice: aspects of sex in the movies, 1966; Stardom: the Hollywood phenomenon, 1970; Stanley Kubrick Directs, 1971; Hollywood, England: the British film industry in the sixties, 1974; Rudolph Valentino, 1976; Double Takes: notes and afterthoughts on the movies 1956–76, 1977; Superstars, 1978; The Shattered Silents: how the talkies came to stay, 1978; Garbo, 1980; Peter Sellers: the authorized biography, 1981; Joan Crawford, 1983; Dietrich, 1984; (ed) No Bells on Sunday: journals of Rachel Roberts, 1984; National Heroes: British cinema industry in the seventies and eighties, 1985; Bette Davis, 1986; trans., Benayoun, Woody Allen: beyond words, 1986; Vivien: the life of Vivien Leigh, 1987; It's Only a Movie, Ingrid: encounters on and off screen, 1988; Elizabeth: the life of Elizabeth Taylor, 1990; (jtly) Zinnemann: an autobiography, 1992; Fatal Charm: the life of Rex Harrison, 1992; Audrey: her real story, 1994; (contrib.) Screen Violence, 1996; Projections 8, 1998; Stanley Kubrick, Director, 1999; contributor to many British and foreign publications. *Recreations:* ski-ing, persecuting smokers. *Address:* 1 Marlborough, 38–40 Maida Vale, W9 1RW. *T:* (020) 7289 0985.

WALKER, Alexandra Margaret Jane; Director, Human Resources, Inland Revenue, since 2000; *b* 31 Oct. 1945; *d* of late Frederic Douglas Walker and Hertha Julie (*née* Freiin Gemmingen von Massenbach); one *d*. *Educ:* Nikolaus Cusanus Gymnasium, Bonn; Lady Margaret Hall, Oxford (Schol.; BA Lit. Hum.). Joined MoD as admin. trainee, 1973; Principal, 1976; on secondment to: Plessey Co., 1979–81; LSE as Nancy Seear Fellow in Industrial Relns, 1981–82; Asst Sec. and Hd of Civilian Mgt (Industrial Relns), 1983–86; rcds 1987; Counsellor, British Embassy, Bonn, 1988–92; Asst Under-Sec. of State (Service Personnel), 1993–97; Dir Gen. Future Hd Office, 1997–2000. *Recreations:* walking the coastline, amateur cello playing, counselling. *Address:* c/o Inland Revenue, Somerset House, Strand WC2B 1LB.

WALKER, (Alfred) Cecil; JP; *b* 17 Dec. 1924; *s* of Alfred George Walker and Margaret Lucinda Walker; *m* 1953, Ann May Joan Verrant; two *s*. *Educ:* Methodist College. Senior Certificate. In timber business with James P. Corry & Co. Ltd, Belfast, 1941–83, Departmental Manager, 1952. MP (UU) Belfast N, 1983–2001 (resigned seat Dec. 1985 in protest against Anglo-Irish Agreement; re-elected Jan. 1986); contested same seat, 2001. JP Belfast, 1966. *Recreations:* sailing, sea angling. *Address:* 1 Wynnland Road, Newtownabbey, Northern Ireland BT36 6RZ. *T:* (028) 9083 3463. *Club:* Down Cruising.

WALKER, Andrew Douglas; Senior Partner, Lovells, since 2000; *b* 6 May 1945; *s* of Malcolm Douglas Walker and Jean Catherine Walker (*née* Ross-Scott); *m* 1973, Hilary Georgina Smith. *Educ:* Giggleswick Sch.; Exeter Coll., Oxford (MA 1966). Admitted Solicitor, England and Wales, 1970, Hong Kong, 1982; articled, 1968–70, Solicitor, 1971–75, Wilkinson Kimbers & Staddon; Lovell, White & King: Solicitor, 1970–71; Partner, 1975; Hong Kong office, 1982–87; Managing Partner, 1987–88; Lovell White Durrant (formed from merger with Durrant Presse): Managing Partner, 1988–93; Sen. Partner, 1996–2000; Lovells formed 2000, from merger with Boesbeck Droste. *Recreations:* opera, classical music, ornithology. *Address:* Lovells, 65 Holborn Viaduct, EC1A 2DY; 11 St Ann's Terrace, NW8 6PH. *T:* (020) 7586 9697. *Club:* Hong Kong.

WALKER, Andrew John; Chief Executive, McKechnie plc, since 1997; Director, Ultra Electronics Holdings plc, since 1996; *b* 27 Sept. 1951; *s* of John Kenneth Walker, MD and Mary Magdaline (*née* Browne); *m* 1981, Pippa Robinson; two *s* one *d*. *Educ:* Ampleforth; Gonville and Caius Coll., Cambridge (MA). MIMechE. Chief Exec., SWALEC, 1993–96. *Address:* McKechnie plc, Leighswood Road, Aldridge, Walsall, West Midlands WS9 8DS.

WALKER, Andrew John; Director of Finance and Administration, House of Commons, since 1997; *b* 4 Jan. 1955; *s* of Edward Geoffrey Walker and Raymonde Dorothy Walker; *m* 1987, Alison Aitkenhead; two *s* one *d*. *Educ:* Newcastle-under-Lyme High Sch.; Univ. of Birmingham (BA Ancient Near Eastern Studies). Inland Revenue, 1976–89; Principal, Fiscal Policy Gp, HM Treasury, 1989–91; Asst Dir, Human Resources Strategy and Planning, Inland Revenue, 1992–96. *Address:* House of Commons, SW1A 0AA. *T:* (020) 7219 5460.

WALKER, Angus Henry; Partner, Mitchell Madison Group, 1996–98; *b* 30 Aug. 1935; *s* of late Frederick William Walker and of Esther Victoria (*née* Wrangle); *m* 1st, 1968, Beverly Phillpotts (*see* B. J. Anderson) (marr. diss. 1976); 2nd, 1979, Ann (*née* Griffiths), *widow* of Richard Snow; two *d* and two step *d*. *Educ:* Erith Grammar Sch., Kent; Balliol Coll., Oxford (Domus Scholar; 1st Cl. Hons BA Mod. Hist. 1959; Stanhope Prize, 1958; MA 1968). Nat. Service, 1954–56 (commnd RA). Senior Scholar, St Antony's Coll., Oxford, 1959–63; HM Diplomatic Service, 1963–68: FO, 1963–65; First Sec., Washington, 1965–68. Lectr, SSEES, London Univ., 1968–70; Univ. Lectr in Russian Social and Political Thought, Oxford, and Lectr, Balliol Coll., 1971–76; Fellow, Wolfson Coll., Oxford, 1971–76; Dir, SSEES, London Univ., 1976–79; British Petroleum Co. Plc, 1979–84; Dir, Corporate Strategy, British Telecom PLC, 1985–88; Managing Director: Strategic Planning Associates, 1988–91; A. T. Kearney, 1991–94. Co-opted Mem., Arts Sub-Cttee, UGC, for enquiry into Russian in British Univs, 1978–79; Governor, Centre for Economic Policy Res., 1986–89. CompIEE 1988. *Publications:* trans. from Polish: Political Economy, by Oskar Lange, vol. 1, 1963; Marx: His Theory in its Context, 1978, 2nd edn 1989. *Address:* Barclays Bank plc, 126 Station Road, Edgware, HA8 7RY. *Club:* Reform.

WALKER, Hon. Anna Elizabeth Blackstock, (Hon. Mrs Walker); Director General, Energy, Department of Trade and Industry, since 1998; *b* 5 May 1951; *d* of Baron Butterworth, *qv*; *m* 1983, Timothy Edward Hanson Walker, *qv*; three *d*. *Educ:* Benenden Sch., Kent; Bryn Mawr Coll., USA; Lady Margaret Hall, Oxford (MA History). British Council, 1972–73; CBI, 1973–74; joined Department of Trade, 1975: Commercial Relations and Exports Div. (ME), 1975; Post and Telecommunications Div., 1976; Private Sec. to Sec. of State for Industry, 1977–78; Shipping Policy Div. (Grade 7), 1979–82; Finance Div., 1983–84; Interdeptl Rev. of Budgetary Controls, 1985; Cabinet Office (on secondment), 1986; Personnel Div. (Grade 6), 1987–88; Competition Policy Div. (Grade 5), 1988–91; Dir, Competition, 1991–94, Dep. Dir Gen., 1994–98, Oftel; Dep. Dir Gen., Energy, DTI, 1998. *Recreations:* travel, theatre, cycling. *Address:* c/o Department of Trade and Industry, 1 Victoria Street, SW1H 0ET. *T:* (020) 7215 5400.

WALKER, Annabel; *see* Carr, E. A.

WALKER, Gen. Sir Antony (Kenneth Frederick), KCB 1987; Director-General, British Institute of Facilities Management, since 1998; *b* 16 May 1934; *o s* of late Kenneth Walker and Iris Walker; *m* 1961, Diana Merran Steward (marr. diss. 1983); one *s* one *d*; *m* 1991, Sqn Ldr Hannah Watts, WRAF. *Educ:* Merchant Taylors' School; RMA Sandhurst. Commissioned into Royal Tank Regt, 1954; served BAOR, Libya, Ghana, Northern Ireland, Hong Kong, Cyprus; Instructor, Staff Coll., 1971–73; CO 1st Royal Tank Regt, 1974–76 (despatches); Col GS HQ UK Land Forces, 1976–78; Comdr Task Force Golf (11 Armd Bde), 1978–80; Dep. Mil. Sec. (A), 1980–82; Comdr, 3rd Armoured Div., 1982–84; Chief of Staff, HQ UKLF, 1985–87; Dep. CDS (Commitments), MoD, 1987–89; Comdt, RCDS, 1990–92. Sec.-Gen., Opsis (Nat. Assoc. for Educn, Trng and Support of Blind and Partially Sighted People), 1992–96. Mil. Advr, Porton Internat. plc, 1992–94; Sen. Mil. Advr, Electronic Data Systems Ltd, 1994; Business Develt Dir, John Mowlem. Col Comdt, Royal Tank Regt, 1983–94 (Rep., 1985–91). Mem. Council, RUSI, 1982–85 and 1990–94. Governor, Centre for Internat. Briefing, Farnham Castle, 1987–91. Chairman: Army Bobsleigh Assoc., 1983–92; British Bobsleigh Assoc., 1992– (Mem. Council, 1989–); President: Services' Dry Fly Fishing Assoc., 1988–92; Combined Services' Winter Sports Assoc., 1990–92. Mem., Council of Management, Salisbury Festival, 1988–96 (Vice-Chm., 1990–93; Chm., 1994–96). Trustee, Tank Mus., 1994–. *Recreations:* bird watching, fly-fishing, music, practical study of wine. *Address:* British Institute of Facilities Management, 67 High Street, Saffron Walden, Essex CB10 1AA; c/o National Westminster Bank plc, PO Box 237, 72–74 High Street, Watford, Herts WD1 2BQ. *Club:* Royal Air Force (Associate).

WALKER, Sir (Baldwin) Patrick, 4th Bt *cr* 1856; *b* 10 Sept. 1924; *s* of late Comdr Baldwin Charles Walker, *o s* of Sir Francis Walker, 3rd Bt and Mary, *d* of F. P. Barnett of Whalton, Northumberland; *S* grandfather, 1928; *m* 1948, Joy Yvonne (marr. diss. 1954); *m* 1954, Sandra Stewart; *m* 1966, Rosemary Ann, *d* of late Henry Hollingdrake; one *s* one *d*; *m* 1980, Vanessa Hilton. *Educ:* Gordonstoun. Served Royal Navy, Fleet Air Arm, 1943–58. Lieut, RN, retired. *Heir:* *s* Christopher Robert Baldwin Walker, *b* 25 Oct. 1969. *Address:* 5 Voortrekker Road, Blanco 6531, South Africa.

WALKER, Bill; *see* Walker, W. C.

WALKER, (Brian) Stuart, RDI 1989; freelance film production designer, since 1990; *b* 5 March 1932; *s* of William and Annie Walker; *m* 1961, Adrienne Elizabeth Atkinson (marr. diss.); two *d*; *m* 2000, Francesca Boyd; one *s*. *Educ:* Blackpool Sch. of Art (Intermediate Exam. in Arts and Crafts; Nat. Diploma in Painting (1st cl. Hons)); RA Schs (RA Dip.). BBC Television, 1958–90: Design Assistant, 1958; Designer, 1961; Sen. Designer, 1970. BAFTA Award for TV Design, 1983, 1990; RTS Award for Production Design, 1988. *Address:* c/o Casarotto Marsh Ltd, National House, 60–66 Wardour Street, W1V 4ND. *T:* (020) 7287 4450.

WALKER, Brian Wilson; consultant in ecology and development, since 1996; Executive Director, Earthwatch Europe, 1989–95; *b* 31 Oct. 1930; *s* of Arthur Walker and Eleanor (*née* Wilson); *m* 1954, Nancy Margaret Gawith; one *s* five *d*. *Educ:* Heversham Sch., Westmorland; Leicester Coll. of Technology; Faculty Technology, Manchester Univ. Management Trainee, Sommerville Bros, Kendal, 1952–55; Personnel Man., Pye Radio, Larne, 1956–61; Bridgeport Brass Ltd, Lisburn: Personnel Man., 1961–66; Gen. Man. (Develt), 1966–69; Gen. Man. (Manufrg), 1969–74; Dir Gen., Oxfam, 1974–83; Dir, Independent Commn on Internat. Humanitarian Issues, 1983–85; Pres., Internat. Inst. for Envmt and Develt, 1985–89. Chairman: Band Aid—Live Aid Projects Cttee, 1985–90; SOS Sahel, 1988–95. Founder Chm., New Ulster Movt, 1969–74; Founder Pres., New Ulster Movt Ltd, 1974. Member: Standing Adv. Commn on Human Rights for NI, 1975–77; World Commn on Food and Peace, 1989–95. Mem., Editl Cttee, World Resources Report, 1985–95. Trustee: Cambodia Trust, 1989–95; Internat. Inst. for Environment and Develt, 1989–95; Artizan Trust, 1992–99; Nginn Karet Foundn, 1996–. Chm. Govs, Dallam Sch., Cumbria, 1996–. Eponymous annual lecture inaugurated Oxford Univ., 1996. Hon. MA Oxon, 1983. Kt, Sov. Order of St Thomas of Acre; Kentucky Colonel, 1966. *Publications:* Authentic Development—Africa, 1986; various political/religious papers on Northern Ireland problem and Third World subjects. *Recreations:* gardening, Irish politics, classical music, active Quaker. *Address:* Biskets, Church Hill, Arnside, Cumbria LA5 0DW. *Club:* Athenæum.

WALKER, Carl, GC 1972; Police Inspector, 1976–82; *b* 31 March 1934; English; *m* 1955, Kathleen Barker; one *s*. *Educ:* Kendal Grammar Sch., Westmorland. RAF Police, 1952–54 (Corporal). Lancashire Police, Oct. 1954–March 1956, resigned; Blackpool Police, 1959–82 (amalgamated with Lancashire Constabulary, April 1968); Sergeant, 1971. Retired 1982, as a result of the injuries sustained from gunshot wounds on 23 Aug. 1971 during an armed raid by thieves on a jeweller's shop in Blackpool (GC). *Recreations:* Rugby; Cumberland and Westmorland wrestling, photography, walking. *Address:* 9 Lawnswood Avenue, Poulton-Le-Fylde, Blackpool FY6 7ED.

WALKER, Catherine Marguerite Marie-Therese; French couturier; Founder, The Chelsea Design Company Ltd, 1978; *b* Pas de Calais; *d* of Remy Baheux and Agnes (*née* Lefebvre); *m* John Walker (decd); two *d*. *Educ:* Univ. of Lille; Univ. of Aix-en-Provence. Dir, Film Dept, French Inst., London, 1970; Lecture Dept, French Embassy, London, 1971. Hon. Bd Mem., 1999–, and Donor Patron, Gilda's Club; Founder Sponsor, Haven Trust, Catherine Walker Tree of Life (fund-raising mural/sculpture). FRSA 2000. Designer of the Year Award: for British Couture, 1990–91; for Glamour, 1991–92. *Publication:* Catherine Walker, An Autobiography by the Private Couturier to Diana, Princess of Wales, 1998. *Address:* The Chelsea Design Co., 65 Sydney Street, Chelsea, SW3 6PX. *T:* (020) 7352 4626.

WALKER, Cecil; *see* Walker, A. C.

WALKER, Sir (Charles) Michael, GCMG 1976 (KCMG 1963; CMG 1960); HM Diplomatic Service, retired; Chairman, Commonwealth Scholarship Commission in the UK, 1977–87; *b* 22 Nov. 1916; *s* of late Col C. W. G. Walker, CMG, DSO; *m* 1945, Enid Dorothy, *d* of late W. A. McAdam, CMG; one *s* one *d*. *Educ:* Charterhouse; New Coll., Oxford. Clerk of House of Lords, June 1939. Enlisted in Army, Oct. 1939, and served in RA until 1946 when released with rank of Lt-Col. Dominions Office, 1947; First Sec., British Embasssy, Washington, 1949–51; Office of United Kingdom High Comr in Calcutta and New Delhi, 1952–55; Establishment Officer, Commonwealth Relations Office, 1955–58. Imperial Defence Coll., 1958; Asst Under-Sec. of State and Dir of Establishment and Organisation, CRO, 1959–62; British High Commissioner in: Ceylon, 1962–65 (concurrently Ambassador to Maldive Islands, July-Nov. 1965), Malaysia,

1966–71; Sec., ODA, FCO, 1971–73; High Comr, India, 1974–76. Chm., Festival of India Trust, 1980–83. Hon. DCL City, 1980. *Recreations:* fishing, gardening, golf. *Address:* Herongate House, West Chiltington Common, Pulborough, Sussex RH20 2NL. *T:* (01798) 813473. *Club:* Sloane.

See also Sir R. N. O. Couper, Bt.

WALKER, Charls E., PhD; Consultant, Washington, DC, since 1973; *b* Graham, Texas, 24 Dec. 1923; *s* of Pinkney Clay and Sammye McCombs Walker; *m* 1949, Harmolyn Hart, Laurens, S Carolina; one *s* one *d.* *Educ:* Univ. of Texas (MBA); Wharton Sch. of Finance, Univ. of Pennsylvania (PhD). Instructor in Finance, 1947–48, and later Asst and Associate Prof., 1950–54, at Univ. of Texas, in the interim teaching at Wharton Sch. of Finance, Univ. of Pennsylvania; Associate Economist, Fed. Reserve Bank: of Philadelphia, 1953, of Dallas, 1954 (Vice-Pres. and Economic Advr, 1958–61); Economist and Special Asst to Pres. of Republic Nat. Bank of Dallas, 1955–56 (took leave to serve as Asst to Treasury Sec., Robert B. Anderson, April 1959–Jan. 1961); Exec. Vice-Pres., Amer. Bankers Assoc., 1961–69. Under-Sec. of the Treasury, 1969–72, Dep. Sec., 1972–73. Chm., American Council for Capital Formation; Mem. Council on Foreign Relations; Founder Chm., Bretton Woods Cttee. Adjunct Prof. of Finance and Public Affairs, Univ. of Texas at Austin, 1985–; Dist. Vis. Prof., Emory Univ., 2000–. Chm., Nafta Inst., 1998–. Dist. Alumnus, Univ. of Texas, 1994. Hon. LLD Ashland Coll., 1970. Alexander Hamilton Award, US Treasury, 1973; Award for Outstanding Contribs to Minority Enterprise and Educn, Urban League, 1973; Beker Award, Nat. Council on Econ. Educn. Co-editor, The Banker's Handbook, 1988–. *Publications:* (ed) New Directions in Federal Tax Policy, 1983; (ed) The Consumption Tax, 1987; (ed) The US Savings Challenge, 1990; contribs to learned jls, periodicals. *Recreations:* golf, fishing, music. *Address:* 10120 Chapel Road, Potomac, MD 20854, USA. *T:* (301) 2995414. *Clubs:* Congressional Country, Burning Tree Golf (Bethesda, Md); Cripple Creek Country (Bethany Beech, Delaware).

WALKER, (Christopher) Roy, CB 1992; Chief Officer, Joint Nature Conservation Committee, 1993–96; *b* 5 Dec. 1934; *s* of late Christopher Harry Walker and Dorothy Jessica Walker; *m* 1961, Hilary Mary Biddiscombe; two *s.* *Educ:* Sir George Monoux Grammar Sch., E17; Sidney Sussex Coll., Cambridge (BA); Université Libre de Bruxelles. National Service, Essex Regt, 1952–54. BoT, 1958; CSD, 1968; Private Sec. to Lord Privy Seal, 1968–71; Treasury, 1973; DTI, 1973; Dept of Energy, 1974; Cabinet Office, 1974; Dept of Energy, 1975; Under Secretary: DES, 1977; Dept. of Employment, 1986; seconded as Dir, Business in the Cities, 1989; Dep. Head of Sci. and Technol. Secretariat, Cabinet Office, 1989–92. *Recreations:* hill walking, sailing. *Clubs:* Chipstead Sailing (Sevenoaks); Medway Yacht.

WALKER, Prof. David Alan, PhD, DSc; FRS 1979; Professor of Photosynthesis, University of Sheffield, 1988–93, now Emeritus; *b* 18 Aug. 1928; *s* of Cyril Walker and Dorothy Walker (*née* Dobson); *m* 1956, Shirley Wynne Walker (*née* Mason); one *s* one *d.* *Educ:* King's Coll., Univ. of Durham (BSc, PhD, DSc). Royal Naval Air Service, 1946–48. Lecturer, 1958–63, Reader, 1963–65, Queen Mary Coll., Univ. of London; Reader, Imperial Coll., Univ. of London, 1965–70; University of Sheffield: Prof. of Biology, 1970–84; Prof. and Dir, Res. Inst. for Photosynthesis, 1984–88. Leverhulme Emeritus Fellow, 1991–93. Corresp. Mem., Amer. Soc. Plant Physiol., 1979; MAE 1994. Alexander von Humboldt Prize, Alexander von Humboldt Foundn, Bonn, 1991. *Publications:* Energy Plants and Man, 1979, 2nd edn 1992; (with G. E. Edwards) C3, C4—Mechanisms, Cellular and Environmental Regulation of Photosynthesis, 1983; The Use of the Oxygen Electrode and Fluorescence Probes in Simple Measurements of Photosynthesis, 1987, 2nd edn 1990; A Leaf in Time, 1999; Like Clockwork, 2000; papers, mostly in field of photosynthesis. *Recreations:* changing the Biddlestone landscape, singing the Sheffield Carols, philosophising in The Cross Keys. *Address:* 6 Biddlestone Village, Morpeth, Northumberland NE65 7DT. *T:* (01669) 630235; *e-mail:* david@alegba.demon.co.uk.

WALKER, Sir David (Alan), Kt 1991; Senior Adviser, Morgan Stanley International Ltd, since 2001; *b* 31 Dec. 1939; *m* 1963, Isobel Cooper; one *s* two *d.* *Educ:* Chesterfield Sch.; Queens' Coll., Cambridge (MA; Hon. Fellow, 1989). Joined HM Treasury, 1961; Private Sec. to Joint Permanent Secretary, 1964–66; seconded to Staff of International Monetary Fund, Washington, 1970–73; Asst Secretary, HM Treasury, 1973–77; joined Bank of England as Chief Adviser, then Chief of Economic Intelligence Dept, 1977; a Dir, 1982–93 (non-exec., 1988–93); Chairman: Johnson Matthey Bankers, later Minories Finance, 1985–88; SIB, 1988–92; Agricl Mortgage Corp., 1993–94; Dep. Chm., Lloyds Bank plc, 1992–94; Dir, Morgan Stanley Inc., 1994–97; Exec. Chm., Morgan Stanley Gp (Europe) plc, subseq. Morgan Stanley Dean Witter (Europe) Ltd, 1994–2000; Chm., Morgan Stanley Internat. Inc., 1995–2000; Mem., Mgt Bd, Morgan Stanley Dean Witter, 1997–2000. Chm., Steering Gp, Financial Markets Gp, LSE, 1986–93. Pt-time Mem. of Bd, CEGB, 1987–89; non-exec. Director: National Power, 1990, 1993–94; British Invisibles, 1993–; Reuters Holdings, 1994–2000. Mem., 1993–, and Treas., 1998–, The Group of Thirty. Nominated Mem., Council of Lloyd's, 1988–92 (Chm., Inquiry into LMX Spiral, 1992). Governor, Henley Management Coll., 1993–99. FRSA 1987; CIMgt (CBIM 1986). *Recreations:* music, long-distance walking. *Address:* Morgan Stanley International Ltd, 25 Cabot Square, Canary Wharf, E14 4QA. *Clubs:* Reform, Garrick.

WALKER, David Bruce; Member (part-time), British Coal Corporation, 1988–95; *b* 30 Aug. 1934; *s* of Noel B. Walker and June R. Walker (*née* Sutherland); *m* 1961, Leonora C. Freeman; two *s.* *Educ:* Knox Grammar Sch., Wahroonga, NSW; Univ. of Sydney (BSc (Hons), MSc, Geology). Demonstrator in Geology: Univ. of Sydney, 1956–58; Bristol Univ., 1958–59; British Petroleum Co., 1959–85: worked as geologist in UK, Gambia, Algeria, Libya, Colombia, Kuwait, Iran and US; Vice-Pres., Production Planning, USA, 1974–77; Regional Coordinator, Western Hemisphere, 1977–79; Controller, BP Exploration, 1979–80; Chief Executive, BP Petroleum Development (UK), 1980–82; Dir, Resources Development, BP Australia, 1982–85; Chief Exec., Britoil plc, 1985–88. Chairman: Sun Internat. Exploration and Production Co., 1988–91; Sun Oil Britain, 1988–91. Distinguished Lectr, Soc. of Petroleum Engineers, 1976. President, UK Offshore Operators Assoc., 1982. *Recreations:* music, gardening. *Address:* Spring Cottage, Chetnole, Sherborne, Dorset DT9 6PF. *T:* (01935) 872604.

WALKER, David Critchlow, CMG 1993; CVO 1988 (MVO 1976); HM Diplomatic Service, retired; High Commissioner to Bangladesh, 1996–99; *b* 9 Jan. 1940; *s* of John Walker and Mary Walker (*née* Cross); *m* 1965, Tineke van der Leek; three *s.* *Educ:* Manchester Grammar Sch.; St Catharine's Coll., Cambridge (BA,MA,DipEd). Assistant Lecturer, Dept of Geography, Manchester Univ., 1962; Commonwealth Relations Office, 1963; Third Secretary, British Embassy, Mexico City, 1965; Second Secretary, Brussels, 1968; First Secretary: FCO, 1970; Washington, 1973; First Sec., later Counsellor, FCO, 1978–83; Consul General, São Paulo, 1983–86; Minister, Madrid, 1986–89; Counsellor, FCO, 1989–92; High Comr, Ghana, and non-resident Ambassador, Togo, 1992–96. *Address:* 7 The Crescent, Thirsk YO7 1DE.

WALKER, Prof. David Maxwell, CBE 1986; QC (Scot.) 1958; FBA 1976; FRSE 1980; Regius Professor of Law, Glasgow University, 1958–90, now Professor Emeritus and Senior Research Fellow; Dean of the Faculty of Law, 1956–59; Senate Assessor on University Court, 1962–66; *b* 9 April 1920; *o s* of James Mitchell Walker, Branch Manager, Union Bank of Scotland, and Mary Paton Colquhoun Irvine; *m* 1954, Margaret Knox, OBE, MA, *yr d* of Robert Knox, yarn merchant, Brookfield, Renfrewshire. *Educ:* High School of Glasgow (Mackindlay Prizeman in Classics); Glasgow, Edinburgh and London Universities. MA (Glasgow) 1946; LLB (Distinction), Robertson Schol., 1948; Faulds Fellow in Law, 1949–52; PhD (Edinburgh), 1952; Blackwell Prize, Aberdeen Univ., 1955; LLB (London), 1957; LLD (Edinburgh), 1960; LLD (London), 1968; LLD (Glasgow), 1985. Served War of 1939–45, NCO Cameronians; commissioned HLI, 1940; seconded to RIASC, 1941; served with Indian Forces in India, 1942, Middle East, 1942–43, and Italy, 1943–46, in MT companies and as Brigade Supply and Transport Officer (Captain). HQ 21 Ind. Inf. Bde, 8 Ind. Div. Advocate of Scottish Bar, 1948; Barrister, Middle Temple, 1957; QC (Scotland) 1958; practised at Scottish Bar, 1948–53; studied at Inst. of Advanced Legal Studies, Univ. of London, 1953–54; Prof. of Jurisprudence, Glasgow Univ., 1954–58. Dir, Scottish Univs' Law Inst., 1974–80. Trustee, Hamlyn Trust, 1954–93. Vice-Pres., RSE, 1985–88. Governor: Scottish College of Commerce, 1957–64; High School of Glasgow (and Chm., Educational Trust), 1974–. Hon. Sheriff of Lanarkshire at Glasgow, 1966–82. FSAScot 1966; FRSA 1991. Hon. LLD Edinburgh, 1974. *Publications:* (ed) Faculty Digest of Decisions, 1940–50, Supplements, 1951 and 1952; Law of Damages in Scotland, 1955; The Scottish Legal System, 1959, 8th edn 2001; Law of Delict in Scotland, 1966, 2nd edn 1981; Scottish Courts and Tribunals, 1969, 5th edn 1985; Principles of Scottish Private Law (2 vols), 1970, 4th edn (4 vols), 1988–89; Law of Prescription and Limitation in Scotland, 1973, 5th edn 1996; Law of Civil Remedies in Scotland, 1974; Law of Contracts in Scotland, 1979, 3rd edn 1995; Oxford Companion to Law, 1980; (ed) Stair's Institutions (6th edn), 1981; (ed) Stair Tercentenary Studies, 1981; The Scottish Jurists, 1985; Legal History of Scotland, vol. I, 1988, vol. II, 1990, vol. III, 1995, vol. IV, 1996, vol. V, 1998, vol. VI, 2001; Scottish Part of Topham and Ivamy's Company Law, 12th edn 1955, to 16th edn 1978; contribs to collaborative works; articles in legal periodicals; *festschrift:* Obligations in Context, ed A. J. Gamble, 1990. *Recreations:* motoring, book collecting, Scottish history. *Address:* 1 Beaumont Gate, Glasgow G12 9EE. *T:* (0141) 339 2802.

WALKER, Rt Rev. David Stuart; *see* Dudley, Area Bishop of.

WALKER, Maj.-Gen. Derek William Rothwell; Manager, CBI Overseas Scholarships, 1980–89, retired; *b* 12 Dec. 1924; *s* of Frederick and Eileen Walker; *m* 1950, Florence Margaret Panting; two *s* (and one *s* decd). *Educ:* Mitcham County Grammar Sch.; Battersea Polytechnic. FIMechE 1970–89; FIEE 1971–89. Commissioned REME, 1946; served: Middle East, 1947–50 (despatches 1949); BAOR, 1951–53; Far East, 1954–56 (despatches 1957); Near East, 1960–62; Far East, 1964–67; psc 1957. Lt-Col 1964, Col 1970, Brig. 1973. Appts include: Comdr, REME Support Group, 1976–77; Dir, Equipment Engineering, 1977–79. Mem. Council, IEE, 1975–79; Pres., SEE, 1979–81. *Recreations:* fishing, sailing, wine-making. *Address:* 26 Cranford Drive, Holybourne, Alton, Hants GU34 4HJ.

WALKER, Desmond; *see* Le Cheminant, Air Chief Marshal Sir P. de L.

WALKER, Rt Rev. Dominic Edward William Murray; *see* Reading, Area Bishop of.

WALKER, Prof. Donald, FRS 1985; Professor of Biogeography, Institute of Advanced Studies, Australian National University, Canberra, 1969–88; *b* 14 May 1928; *s* of Arthur Walker and Eva (*née* Risdon); *m* 1959, Patricia Mary Smith; two *d.* *Educ:* Morecambe Grammar School; Sheffield Univ. (BSc); MA, PhD Cantab. Commission, RAF (Nat. Service), 1953–55. Research Scholar and Asst in Res., later Sen. Asst, Sub-Dept of Quaternary Res., Cambridge Univ., 1949–60; Fellow of Clare College, 1952–60 (Asst Tutor, 1955–60); Reader in Biogeography, ANU, 1960–68; Head of Dept of Biogeography and Geomorphology, ANU, 1969–88. Hon. Prof., Chinese Acad. of Science, 1986–. *Publications:* articles on plant ecology, palaeoecology and related topics in sci. jls. *Recreations:* pottery, architecture, prehistory. *Address:* 8 Galali Place, Aranda, ACT 2614, Australia. *T:* (2) 62513136.

WALKER, Edward William F.; *see* Faure Walker.

WALKER, Prof. Frederick, MD; FRCPath; Regius Professor of Pathology, University of Aberdeen, 1984–2000, now Emeritus; Consultant Pathologist, Grampian Health Board, 1984–2000; *b* 21 Dec. 1934; *s* of Frederick James Walker and Helen Stitt Halliday; *m* 1st, 1963, Cathleen Anne Gordon, BSc (marr. diss.); two *d*; 2nd, 1998, Jean Winifred Keeling. *Educ:* Kirkcudbright Academy; Univ. of Glasgow. MB ChB 1958; PhD 1964; MD 1971; MRCPath 1966, FRCPath 1978. Lectr in Pathology, Univ. of Glasgow, 1962–67; Vis. Asst Prof., Univ. of Minnesota, 1964–65; Sen. Lectr in Pathology, Univ. of Aberdeen, 1968–73; Foundation Prof. of Pathology, Univ. of Leicester, 1973–84. Chm., Nat. Quality Assurance Adv. Panel (Histopathology and Cytology), 1991–96; Mem. Council, RCPath, 1990–93; Chm. and Gen. Sec., Pathol Soc. of GB and Ireland, 1992–2000 (Mem. Cttee, 1990–92). Editor, Jl of Pathology, 1983–93. *Publications:* papers in scientific and med. jls. *Recreations:* writing, walking. *Address:* 9 Forres Street, Edinburgh EH3 6BJ. *T:* (0131) 225 9673.

WALKER, George Alfred; Chief Executive: Walkers International, 1992; Premier Telesports Plc, since 1994; *b* 14 April 1929; *s* of William James Walker and Ellen (*née* Page); *m* 1957, Jean Maureen Walker (*née* Hatton); one *s* two *d.* *Educ:* Jubilee Sch., Bedford, Essex. Formerly boxer and boxing manager; Amateur Boxing Champion, GB, 1951. *Recreations:* ski-ing, ocean racing, climbing. *Address:* Pell House, High Road, Fobbing, Essex SS17 9JJ.

WALKER, Dr George Patrick Leonard, FRS 1975; G. A. Macdonald Professor of Volcanology, University of Hawaii, 1981–96, Professor Emeritus since 1999; *b* 2 March 1926; *s* of Leonard Richard Thomas Walker and Evelyn Frances Walker; *m* 1958, Hazel Rosemary (*née* Smith); one *s* one *d.* *Educ:* Wallace High Sch., Lisburn, N Ire.; Queen's Univ., Belfast (BSc, MSc); Univ. of Leeds (PhD 1956); Univ. of London (DSc 1982). Research, Univ. of Leeds, 1948–51; Asst Lectr and Lectr, Imperial Coll., 1951–64; Reader in Geology, Imperial Coll., 1964–79; Captain J. Cook Res. Fellow, Royal Soc. of NZ, 1978–80. Visiting Professor: Bristol Univ.; Cheltenham & Gloucester Coll. of Higher Educn. Fellow: Geol Soc. of America, 1987; Amer. Geophysical Union, 1988. Awarded moiety of Lyell Fund of Geological Soc. of London, 1963, Lyell Medal, 1982; Wollaston Medal, 1995. Hon. Member: Visindafjelag Íslendinga, (Iceland), 1968; Royal Soc. of NZ, 1987. Hon. DSc Iceland, 1988. McKay Hammer Award, Geol Soc. of NZ, 1982. Icelandic Order of the Falcon, Knight's Class, 1980. *Publications:* scientific papers on mineralogy, the geology of Iceland, and volcanology. *Recreation:* visiting volcanoes. *Address:* Geology Department, Bristol University, Bristol BS8 1RJ; Geology Department, Cheltenham & Gloucester College of Higher Education, Glos GL50 4AZ.

WALKER, George Robert, OBE 1992; Director-General, International Baccalaureate Organisation, since 1999; *b* 25 Jan. 1942; *s* of William Walker and Celia Walker (*née* Dean); *m* 1968, Jennifer Anne Hill; one *s* one *d*. *Educ:* Watford Boys' Grammar Sch.; Exeter Coll., Oxford (MA, MSc); Univ. of Cape Town (LRSM). Science teacher, Watford Grammar Sch., 1966–68; Lectr in Educn, Univ. of York, 1969–73; Dep. Headmaster, Carisbrooke High Sch., 1973–76; Headmaster: Heathcote Sch., Stevenage, 1977–81; Cavendish Sch., Hemel Hempstead, 1981–91; Dir-Gen., Internat. Sch. of Geneva, 1991–99. Chm., Centre for Study of Comprehensive Schs, 1980–85. Member: HMC, 1982–99; Nat. Curriculum Sci. Working Gp, 1987–88. Educn Advr to ICI plc, 1990–91. Hon. Sen. Vis. Fellow, Univ. of York, 1988–91; Vis. Prof., Univ. of Bath, 1997–. *Publications:* (jtly) Modern Physical Chemistry, 1981, 3rd edn 1986; Comprehensive Themes, 1983; contrib. to TES, Educn, etc. *Recreations:* piano-playing, mountain walking. *Address:* International Baccalaureate Organisation, 15 route des Morillons, 1218 Grand-Saconnex, Geneva, Switzerland. *T:* (22) 7917740.

WALKER, Gordon; *see* Walker, T. G.

WALKER, Guy; *see* Walker, W. G.

WALKER, Sir Harold (Berners), KCMG 1991 (CMG 1979); HM Diplomatic Service, retired; President, CARE International, 1997–2001; *b* 19 Oct. 1932; *s* of late Admiral Sir Harold Walker, KCB, RN, and Lady Walker (*née* Berners); *m* 1960, Jane, *d* of late Capt. C. J. L. Bittleston, CBE, DSC, RN; one *s* two *d*. *Educ:* Winchester; Worcester Coll., Oxford. BA 1955. 2nd Lieut RE, 1951–52. Foreign Office, 1955; MECAS, 1957; Asst Political Agent, Dubai, 1958; Foreign Office, 1960; Principal Instructor, MECAS, 1963; First Sec., Cairo, 1964; Head of Chancery and Consul, Damascus, 1966; Foreign Office (later FCO), 1967; First Sec. (Commercial), Washington, 1970; Counsellor, Jedda, 1973; Dep. Head, Personnel Operations Dept, FCO, 1975–76, Head of Dept, 1976–78; Corpus Christi Coll., Cambridge, 1978; Ambassador to Bahrein, 1979–81, to United Arab Emirates, 1981–86, to Ethiopia, 1986–90, to Iraq, 1990–91; retd 1992. Member: Commonwealth War Graves Commn, 1992–97; Bd, CARE International UK, 1992–2001 (Chm., 1994–97); Pres., Friends of Imperial War Mus., 1992–97. Chm., Bahrain Soc., 1993–99. Mem. of Corp., Woking Sixth Form Coll., 1996–99. Associate Fellow, RUSI, 1992–97. *Address:* 39 Charlwood Street, SW1V 2DU. *Club:* Oxford and Cambridge.

WALKER, His Honour Judge Harry; *see* Walker, P. H. C.

WALKER, Major Sir Hugh (Ronald), 4th Bt *cr* 1906; *b* 13 Dec. 1925; *s* of Major Sir Cecil Edward Walker, 3rd Bt, DSO, MC, and Violet (*née* McMaster); *S* father, 1964; *m* 1971, Norna, *er d* of Lt-Cdr R. D. Baird, RNR; two *s*. *Educ:* Wellington Coll., Berks. Joined Royal Artillery, 1943; commissioned Sept. 1945; 2 iC, RA Range, Benbecula, Outer Hebrides, 1964–66; Commanding No 1 Army Information Team, in Aden and Hong Kong, 1966–68; Larkhill, 1969–73, retired. Mem., Assoc. of Supervisory and Executive Engineers. *Recreation:* horses. *Heir:* *s* Robert Cecil Walker, *b* 26 Sept. 1974. *Address:* Ballinamona, Hospital, Kilmallock, Co. Limerick, Ireland.

WALKER, Rev. Dr James Bernard; Chaplain, since 1993, and Assistant Director, Student Support Services (formerly Assistant Hebdomadar), since 1998, St Andrews University; *b* 7 May 1946; *s* of Rev. Dr Robert B. W. Walker and Grace B. Walker; *m* 1972, Sheila Mary Easton; three *s*. *Educ:* Hamilton Academy, Lanarkshire; Edinburgh Univ. (MA 1st cl. Hons Mental Philosophy 1968; BD 1st cl. Hons Systematic Theol. 1971); Merton Coll., Oxford (DPhil 1981). Church of Scotland minister, ordained 1975, Dundee; Associate Minister, Mid Craigie Parish Church linked with Wallacetown Parish Church, Dundee, 1975–78; Minister, Old and St Paul's Parish Church, Galashiels, 1978–87; Principal, Queen's Coll., Birmingham, 1987–93. *Publications:* Israel — Covenant and Land, 1986; (contrib.) Politique et Théologie chez Athanase d' Alexandrie (ed C. Kannengiesser), 1974; (contrib.) God, Family and Sexuality (ed D. W. Torrance), 1997. *Recreations:* golf, tennis, swimming, hill walking. *Address:* The Chaplaincy Centre, University of St Andrews, 3a St Mary's Place, St Andrews, Fife KY16 9UY. *T:* (01334) 462865.

WALKER, James Findlay, QPM 1964; Commandant, National Police College, 1973–76; *b* 20 May 1916; *m* 1941, Gertrude Eleanor Bell (*d* 1993); one *s*. *Educ:* Arbroath High Sch., Angus, Scotland. Joined Metropolitan Police, 1936. Served War, 1943–46: commissioned Black Watch; demobilised rank Captain. Served in Metropolitan Police through ranks to Chief Supt, 1963; Staff of Police Coll., 1963–65; Asst Chief Constable: W Riding Constabulary, 1965–68; W Yorks Constabulary, 1968–70; Dep. Chief Constable, W Yorks Constabulary, 1970–73. *Recreations:* gardening, golf. *Address:* 33 Cortachy Crescent, Kirriemuir, Angus DD8 4TP.

WALKER, Sir James (Graham), Kt 1972; MBE 1963; Part Owner of Cumberland Santa Gertrudis Stud and Camden Park, Greenwoods and Wakefield sheep properties; *b* Bellingen, NSW, 7 May 1913; *s* of late Albert Edward Walker and Adelaide Walker, Sydney, NSW; *m* 1939, Mary Vivienne Maude Poole; two *s* three *d*. *Educ:* New England Grammar Sch., Glen Innes, NSW. Councillor, Longreach Shire Council, 1953– (Chm., 1957–91); Vice-Pres., Local Authorities of Qld, 1966, Sen. Vice-Chm., 1972–89. Dep. Chm., Longreach Pastoral Coll., since inception, 1966–78, Chm. 1978–89. Exec. Mem., Central Western Queensland Local Authorities' Assoc. and Queensland Local Authorities' Assoc., 1964–79. Chm., Central Western Electricity Bd, 1966–76; Dep. Chm., Capricornia Electricity Bd, 1968–76, Chm., 1976–85; Dep. Chm., Longreach Printing Co. Chm., Santa Gertrudis Assoc., Australia, 1976–77. Past Asst Grand Master, United Grand Lodge of Qld, 1970. Session Clerk, St Andrews Church, Longreach, 1948–78. Nat. Chm., Stockman's Hall of Fame and Out Back Heritage Centre, 1983–90. Fellow, Internat. Inst. of Community Service, 1975; Paul Harris Rotary Fellow, Longreach Rotary Club, 1985. Freeman, City of London, 1990. Hon. LLD Queensland Univ., 1985. *Recreations:* bowls, golf, surfing, painting. *Address:* Camden Park, Longreach, Queensland 4730, Australia. *T:* (7) 46581331. *Clubs:* Queensland, Tattersall's (Brisbane); Longreach, Longreach Rotary, Diggers (Longreach).

WALKER, Sir James Heron, 5th Bt *cr* 1868; *b* 7 April 1914; *s* of Major Sir Robert Walker, 4th Bt and Synolda, *y d* of late James Thursby-Pelham; *S* father, 1930; *m* 1st, 1939, Angela Margaret, *o d* of Victor Alexandre Beaufort; one *s* (one *d* decd); 2nd, 1972, Sharrone, *er d* of David Read; one *s*. *Educ:* Eton Coll.; Magdalene Coll., Cambridge. *Recreations:* long haired Dachshunds, music. *Heir:* *s* Victor Stewart Heron Walker [*b* 8 Oct. 1942; *m* 1st, 1969, Caroline Louise (marr. diss. 1982), *d* of late Lt-Col F; E. B. Wignall; two *s* one *d*; 2nd, 1982, Svea, *o d* of late Captain Ernst Hugo Gothard Knutson Borg and of Mary Hilary Borg]. *Address:* Oakhill, Port Soderick, Isle of Man.
See also Baron Cornwallis.

WALKER, Jane Helen; *see* Darbyshire, J. H.

WALKER, Janey Patricia Winifred, (Mrs Hamish Mykura); Managing Editor Commissioning, Channel 4 Television, since 1999; *b* 10 April 1958; *d* of Brig. Harry Walker and Patricia Walker; *m* 1997, Hamish Mykura; twin *d*. *Educ:* Brechin High Sch.; Benenden Sch.; York Univ. (BA Hist./Politics); Univ. of Chicago (Benton Fellow). BBC News and Current Affairs, 1983–89; The Late Show, BBC, 1990–94; Editor, Edge prog., WNET, and dir, BBC NY, 1994–95; Wall to Wall TV, London, 1995–96; Commng Ed. Arts, Channel 4, 1996–99. *Recreations:* walking, art. *Address:* c/o Channel 4 Television, 124 Horseferry Road, SW1P 2TX. *T:* (020) 7396 4444.

WALKER, Jeremy; Chief Executive, North Yorkshire County Council, since 1999; *b* 12 July 1949; *m* 1968, Patricia June Lockhart; two *s* one *d*. *Educ:* Brentwood Sch., Essex; Univ. of Birmingham (BA 1971). Dept of Employment, 1971–73; Pvte Sec. to Chm., MSC, 1974–75; HSE, 1975–76; Econ. Secretariat, Cabinet Office, 1976–78; MSC, 1978–82; Exchange Officer, Australian Dept of Employment and Industrial Relations, 1982–84; Manpower Services Commission: Regl Employment Manager, 1984–86; Hd, Community Prog. and New Job Trng Scheme, 1986–88; Regl Dir, Yorks and Humberside, Trng Agency and Dept of Employment, 1988–94; Regl Dir, Govt Office for Yorks and the Humber, 1994–99. Member: Bd, Yorks and Humberside Arts, 1994–99; Council, Leeds Univ., 1992–2000; N Yorks TEC, 1999–2001; Court, Univ. of York, 2001–. Trustee: W Yorks Police Community Trust, 1996–99; York and N Yorks Community Trust, 2000–. *Recreations:* running a smallholding, gardening. *Address:* (office) County Hall, Northallerton, N Yorks DL7 8AD.

WALKER, John; *see* Walker, N. J.

WALKER, John; Under Secretary, Scottish Development Department, 1985, retired; *b* 16 Dec. 1929; *s* of John Walker and Elizabeth White Fish; *m* 1952, Rena Robertson McEwan; two *d*. *Educ:* Falkirk High School. Entered Civil Service, Min. of Labour, as clerical officer, 1946. National Service, RAF, 1948–50. Asst Principal, Dept of Health for Scotland, 1958; Scottish Home and Health Dept: Principal, 1960; Secretary, Cttee on General Medical Services in the Highlands and Islands, 1964–67; Asst Sec., 1969; Scottish Development Dept, 1975–78; Under Sec., Scottish Home and Health Dept, 1978–85. Asst Comr, Scottish Local Govt Boundary Commn, 1987–94. *Recreations:* grandparenthood, anti-social bridge, blethering to Rena. *Address:* 8/1 Back Dean, Ravelston Terrace, Edinburgh EH4 3UA. *T:* (0131) 343 3811.

WALKER, His Honour John David; DL; a Circuit Judge, 1972–89; *b* 13 March 1924; *y s* of late L. C. Walker, MA, MB (Cantab), BCh, and late Mrs J. Walker, Malton; *m* 1953, Elizabeth Mary Emma (*née* Owbridge); one *s* two *d*. *Educ:* Oundle (1937–42); Christ's Coll., Cambridge (1947–50); BA 1950, MA 1953. War of 1939–45: commissioned Frontier Force Rifles, Indian Army, 1943; demob., Captain, 1947. Called to the Bar, Middle Temple, 1951; a Recorder, 1972. A Pres., Mental Health Review Tribunals, 1986–96. Mem., Parole Bd, 1992–95. DL Humberside, subseq. ER of Yorks, 1985. *Recreations:* shooting, fishing. *Address:* 19 St Mary's Manor, North Bar Within, Beverley, E Yorks HU17 8DE. *Club:* Lansdowne.

WALKER, John Eric Austin; *see* Austin, J. E.

WALKER, Sir John (Ernest), Kt 1999; DPhil; FRS 1995; Director, MRC Dunn Human Nutrition Unit, Cambridge, since 1998; Fellow, Sidney Sussex College, Cambridge, since 1997; *b* 7 Jan. 1941; *s* of Thomas Ernest Walker and Elsie (*née* Lawton); *m* 1963, Christina Jane Westcott; two *d*. *Educ:* Rastrick Grammar Sch., W Yorks; St Catherine's Coll., Oxford (BA; DPhil 1969; Hon. Fellow, 1998). Vis. Research Fellow, Univ. of Wisconsin, 1969–71; NATO Res. Fellow, CNRS, Gif-sur-Yvette, France, 1971–72; EMBO Res. Fellow, Pasteur Inst., Paris, 1972–74; Staff Scientist, MRC Lab. of Molecular Biol., Cambridge, 1974–98. Mem., EMBO, 1983. Founder FMedSci 1998. Hon. DSc Oxon, 1999. Johnson Foundn Prize, Univ. of Pennsylvania, 1994; Ciba Medal and Prize, Biochem. Soc., 1995; Peter Mitchell Medal, European Bioenergetics Conf., 1996; Nobel Prize for Chemistry, 1997; Messel Medal, SCI, 2000. *Publications:* research papers and reviews in scientific jls. *Recreations:* cricket, opera music, walking. *Address:* MRC Dunn Human Nutrition Unit, Hills Road, Cambridge CB2 2XY.

WALKER, Air Marshal Sir John (Robert), KCB 1992; CBE 1978; AFC; Ministry of Defence, 1989–95; *b* 26 May 1936. rcds; psc. SASO, Strike Comd, 1985–87; Dep. CoS (Ops), HQ AAFCE, 1987–89. Wing Comdr 1970; Gp Capt. 1975; Air Cdre 1980; Air Vice-Marshal 1986; Air Marshal 1991.

WALKER, Julian Fortay, CMG 1981; MBE 1960; HM Diplomatic Service, retired; Special Adviser on Syria, 1987–93, and on Iraq, 1990–93, Research and Analysis Department, Foreign and Commonwealth Office; *b* 7 May 1929; *s* of Kenneth Macfarlane Walker, FRCS, and Eileen Marjorie Walker (*née* Wilson); *m* 1983, Virginia Anne Austin (*née* Stevens) (marr. diss. 1995); three step *d*. *Educ:* Harvey Sch., Hawthorne, New York; Stowe; Bryanston; Cambridge Univ. (MA). National Service, RN, 1947–49; Cambridge, 1949–52; London Univ. Sch. of African and Oriental Studies, 1952. Foreign Service: MECAS, 1953; Asst Political Agent, Trucial States, 1953–55; 3rd and 2nd Sec., Bahrain Residency, 1955–57; FCO and Frontier Settlement, Oman, 1957–60; 2nd and 1st Sec., Oslo, 1960–63; FCO News Dept Spokesman, 1963–67; 1st Sec., Baghdad, 1967; 1st Sec., Morocco (Rabat), 1967–69; FCO, 1969–71; Political Agent, Dubai, Trucial States, 1971, Consul-Gen. and Counsellor, British Embassy, Dubai, United Arab Emirates, 1971–72; Cambridge Univ. on sabbatical leave, 1972–73; Political Advr and Head of Chancery, British Mil. Govt, Berlin, 1973–76; NI Office, Stormont Castle, 1976–77; Dir, MECAS, 1977–78; Ambassador to Yemen Arab Republic and Republic of Jibuti, 1979–84; Ambassador to Qatar, 1984–87. *Publications:* (ed) The UAE Internal Boundaries and Boundaries with Oman, 8 vols, 1994; Tyro on the Trucial Coast, 1999. *Recreations:* skiing, sailing, tennis, music, cooking.

WALKER, Julian Guy Hudsmith, CB 1991; independent engineering consultant, since 1994; Director General, Policy and Special Projects, Ministry of Defence, 1992–94, retired; *b* 2 Oct. 1936; *s* of Nathaniel and Frieda Walker; *m* 1960, Margaret Burns (*née* Jamieson). *Educ:* Winchester College; Southampton Univ. (BSc Mech Eng). CEng, FIMechE. Hawker Aircraft Co., 1958–61; Logistic Vehicles, FVRDE, WO, subseq. MoD, 1961–69; Ministry of Defence: Special Projects, MVEE, 1970–80; Head, Vehicle Engrg Dept, 1980–84; Scientific Adviser (Land), 1984–87; Dir, Estabts and Research (B), 1987–89; Head, RARDE, Chertsey, 1989–92. *Recreations:* vintage cars, photography, wood-turning, Wombling, solving practical problems.

WALKER, Kathrine S.; *see* Sorley Walker.

WALKER, Linda, (Mrs P. B. Walker); *see* Sutcliffe, L.

WALKER, Lorna Margaret S.; *see* Secker-Walker.

WALKER, Malcolm Conrad, CBE 1995; Chairman, Iceland Group plc (formerly Iceland Frozen Foods plc), 1973–2001 (Chief Executive, 1973–2000); *b* 11 Feb. 1946; *s* of Willie Walker and Ethel Mary Walker; *m* 1969, Nest Rhianydd; one *s* two *d*. *Educ:* Mirfield Grammar Sch. Trainee Manager, F. W. Woolworth & Co., 1964–71; Jt Founder,

Iceland Frozen Foods, 1970. Non-exec. Dir, DFS Furniture Co. plc, 1993–. *Recreations:* ski-ing, sailing, shooting, stalking, business, home and family. *Address:* PO Box 3182, Chester CH3 9ZD.

WALKER, Sir Michael; *see* Walker, Sir C. M.

WALKER, Michael; His Honour Judge Michael Walker; a Circuit Judge, since 1978; *b* 13 April 1931; *m* 1959, Elizabeth Mary Currie; two *s.* *Educ:* Chadderton Grammar Sch.; Sheffield Univ. (LLM). Called to the Bar, Gray's Inn, 1956; joined North Eastern Circuit, 1958; a Recorder of the Crown Court, 1972–78; Hon. Recorder of Sheffield, 1996; authorised to sit in Ct of Appeal (Criminal Div.), 1997.

WALKER, Dr Michael John; Headmaster, King Edward VI Grammar School, Chelmsford, since 1999; *b* 24 Nov. 1955; *s* of Stephen Thomas Walker and Sheila Walker (*née* Ereaut); *m* 1977, Rita Bridget Carpenter; one *s* two *d.* *Educ:* Corpus Christi Coll., Cambridge (BA Hons Hist. 1977; CertEd 1979; MA 1980; PhD 1985). Asst Prof. of History, Birmingham-Southern Coll., Birmingham, Alabama, 1977–78; Asst Master, Dulwich Coll., 1982–86; Hd of History, Gresham's Sch., Norfolk, 1986–89; King Edward VI Grammar School, Chelmsford: Sen. Teacher, 1989–90; Dep. Head (Middle Sch.), 1990–92; Dep. Head (Sixth Form), 1992–99. *Recreations:* painting, drawing, tennis, squash, walking, travel. *Address:* King Edward VI Grammar School, Broomfield Road, Chelmsford, Essex CM1 3SX. *T:* (01245) 353510, *Fax:* (01245) 344741.

WALKER, Gen. Sir Michael (John Dawson), GCB 2000 (KCB 1995); CMG 1997; CBE 1990 (OBE 1982); Chief of the General Staff, since 2000; Aide de Camp General to the Queen, since 1997; *b* 7 July 1944; *s* of William Hampden Dawson Walker and Dorothy Helena Walker (*née* Shiach); *m* 1973, Victoria Margaret Holme; two *s* one *d.* *Educ:* Milton Sch., Bulawayo; Woodhouse Grove Sch., Yorks; RMA Sandhurst. Commissioned Royal Anglian Regt, 1966; Regtl and Staff duties, 1966–82; Staff Coll., 1976–77; MA to CGS, 1982–85; CO 1 Royal Anglian Regt, 1985–87; Comdr, 20th Armoured Brigade, 1987–89; COS, 1 (Br) Corps, 1989–91; GOC NE District and Comdr, 2nd Inf. Div., 1991–92; GOC Eastern District, 1992; ACGS, MoD, 1992–94; Comdr, ACE Rapid Reaction Corps, 1994–97; Comdr, Land Component Peace Implementation Force, Bosnia, 1995–96; C-in-C, Land Comd, 1997–2000. Colonel Commandant: Queen's Div., 1991–2000; AAC, 1994–; Col, Royal Anglian Regt, 1997– (Dep. Col, 1991–97). *Recreations:* ski-ing, sailing, shooting, golf, family. *Address:* Ministry of Defence, Old War Office Building, Whitehall, SW1A 2EU.

WALKER, Sir Michael Leolin F.; *see* Forestier-Walker.

WALKER, Hon. Sir Miles Rawstron, Kt 1997; CBE 1991; Chief Minister, Isle of Man, 1986–96; *b* 13 Nov. 1940; *s* of George Denis Walker and Alice (*née* Whittaker); *m* 1966, Mary Lilian Cowell; one *s* one *d.* *Educ:* Arbory Primary Sch.; Castle Rushen High Sch.; Shropshire Coll. of Agric. Company Dir, farming and retail dairy trade, 1960–. Mem. and Chm., Arbory Parish Comrs, 1970–76; Mem., House of Keys for Rushen, 1976–. Hon. LLD Liverpool, 1994. *Address:* Magher Feailley, Main Road, Colby, Isle of Man. *T:* (01624) 833728.

WALKER, Prof. Nigel David, CBE 1979; MA Oxon, PhD Edinburgh, DLitt Oxon; Wolfson Professor of Criminology and Fellow of King's College, Cambridge, 1973–84 (Director, Institute of Criminology, 1973–81); *b* 6 Aug. 1917; *s* of David B. Walker and Violet Walker (*née* Johnson); *m* 1939, Sheila Margaret Johnston; one *d.* *Educ:* Tientsin Grammar Sch.; Edinburgh Academy; Christ Church, Oxford (Hon. Scholar). Served War, Infantry officer (Camerons and Lovat Scouts), 1940–46. Scottish Office, 1946–61; Gwilym Gibbon Fellow, Nuffield Coll., 1958–59; University Reader in Criminology and Fellow of Nuffield Coll., Oxford, 1961–73. Visiting Professor: Berkeley, 1965; Yale, 1973; Stockholm, 1978; Cape Town, 1984. Chairman: Home Secretary's Adv. Council on Probation and After-care, 1972–76; Study Gp on Legal Training of Social Workers, 1972–73; President: Nat. Assoc. of Probation Officers, 1980–84; British Soc. of Criminology, 1984–87; Member: Home Sec.'s TV Research Cttee, 1963–69; Adv. Council on Penal System, 1969–73; Cttee on Mentally Abnormal Offenders, 1972–75; Working Party on Judicial Training and Information, 1975–78; Floud Cttee on Dangerous Offenders; Hodgson Cttee on Profits of Crime; Parole Bd, 1986–89. Hon. LLD: Leicester, 1976, Edinburgh 1985. Hon. FRCPsych 1987. *Publications:* Delphi, 1936 (Chancellor's Prize Latin Poem); A Short History of Psychotherapy, 1957 (various trans); Morale in the Civil Service, 1961; Crime and Punishment in Britain, 1965; Crime and Insanity in England, 2 vols, 1968 and 1972; Sentencing in a Rational Society, 1969 (various trans.); Crimes, Courts and Figures, 1971; Explaining Misbehaviour (inaug. lecture), 1974; Treatment and Justice (Sandoz lecture), 1976; Behaviour and Misbehaviour, 1977; Punishment, Danger and Stigma, 1980; Sentencing Theory Law and Practice, 1985, 2nd edn (jtly) 1997; Crime and Criminology, 1987; (jtly) Public Attitudes to Sentencing, 1988; Why Punish?, 1991 (Italian and Chinese trans.); (jtly) Dangerous People, 1996; Aggravation, Mitigation and Mercy, 1999; reports, articles, etc. *Recreation:* chess. *Address:* King's College, Cambridge CB2 1ST. *Club:* Royal Society of Medicine.

WALKER, (Noel) John; Chief Executive, British Urban Regeneration Association, since 2000; *b* 18 Dec. 1948; *s* of Robert and Nora Walker; *m* 1979, Pamela Gordon; two *s.* *Educ:* Liverpool Univ. (BSc 1970); Trent Polytechnic (DipTP 1972). Planning Officer, Hartlepool BC, 1972–74; Sen. Planner, Cleveland CC, 1974; travelled abroad, 1974–75; Milton Keynes Development Corporation: Employment Planner, 1975–76; Head of Policy Evaluation, 1976–78; Dep. Planning Manager, 1978–79; Planning Manager, 1979–80; Dir of Planning, 1980–87; Dep. Gen. Manager, 1987–92; Chief Exec., Commn for the New Towns, 1992–99; Dir, Competition for future use of Millennium Dome, 1999–2000. Chairman: Bucks Manpower Cttee, 1982–83; Milton Keynes IT Exchange, 1983–86. Founder Mem., Nat. Energy Foundn, 1988– (Trustee, 1999–). Dep. Chm., Milton Keynes Housing Assoc., 1986–89; Board Member: Milton Keynes Marketing, 1992–93; Telford Develt Agency, 1992; Peterborough Develt Agency, 1992–94. Trustee: Bletchley Park Trust, 2000–; Milton Keynes Parks Trust, 2000–. FRSA 1997. Hon. DArts De Montfort, 1998. *Recreations:* squash, gardening, travelling. *Address:* Fullers Barn, The Green, Loughton, Milton Keynes MK5 8AW.

WALKER, Patricia Kathleen Randall; *see* Mann, P. K. R.

WALKER, Sir Patrick; *see* Walker, Sir B. P.

WALKER, Sir Patrick (Jeremy), KCB 1990; *b* 25 Feb. 1932; *s* of late Reginald Plumer Walker, sometime Chief Accountant, East African Railways, and Gladys Walker; *m* 1955, Susan Mary Hastings; two *s* one *d.* *Educ:* King's Sch., Canterbury; Trinity Coll., Oxford (MA). Uganda Admin, 1956–62; Security Service, 1963–92, Dir Gen., 1988–92. Trustee, Leonard Cheshire Foundn, 1994– (Chm., Govs, 2000–). Gov., UC Northampton (formerly Nene Coll. of Higher Educn), 1997–. *Recreations:* music, African history, art. *Clubs:* Oxford and Cambridge, MCC.

WALKER, Paul Ashton; Chief Executive: Sage Group plc, since 1984; Sage Software Ltd; *b* 17 May 1957. *Educ:* Univ. of York (BA). ACA. With Arthur Youngs, 1979–84. Non-executive Director: Airtours plc; The Gadget Shop Ltd. *Address:* Sage Group plc, Sage House, Benton Park Road, Newcastle upon Tyne NE7 7LZ.

WALKER, Dr Paul Crawford; Senior Partner, Independent Public Health, since 1994; *b* 9 Dec. 1940; *s* of Joseph Viccars Walker and Mary Tilley (*née* Crawford); *m* 1963, Barbara Georgina Bliss; three *d.* *Educ:* Queen Elizabeth Grammar Sch., Darlington; Downing Coll., Cambridge (MA); University College Hospital Med. Sch. (MB, BChir); Edinburgh Univ. (DipSocMed); Harvard Bus. Sch. (Program for Health Systems Management, 1980). FFPHM (FFCM 1980). Dep. Medical Officer of Health and Dep. Principal Sch. MO, Wolverhampton County Borough Council, 1972–74; District Community Physician, Staffordshire AHA, 1974–76; Area MO, Wakefield AHA, 1976–77; Regional MO, NE Thames RHA, 1978–85; Dist Gen. Manager, Frenchay HA, 1985–88; Hon. Consultant in Community Medicine, Bristol and Weston HA, 1988–89; Dir of Public Health, Norwich HA, 1989–93; Sen. Lectr in Applied Epidemiology, Univ. of Wales Coll. of Medicine, 1993–94. Hon. Sen. Lectr, Dept of Community Medicine, LSHTM, 1983–85; Co-Dir, Centre for Health Policy Res., UEA, 1990–93; Vis. Prof., QMC, London Univ., 1985; Vis. Fellow, UWE, 1999–. Governor, Moorfields Eye Hosp., 1981–82; Vice-Chm., Professional Adv. Gp, NHS Trng Authy, 1986–88; Member: Bd of Management, LSHTM, 1983–85; Adv. Cttee on Drug Misuse, 1983–87; Exec. Cttee, Greater London Alcohol Adv. Service, 1978–85; NHS Computer Policy Cttee, 1984–85; Editl Bd, Jl of Management in Medicine, 1985–; Norwich HA, 1989–93; Frenchay Mental Handicap Trust, 1986–88; Frenchay Mental Health Trust, 1986–88; Norwich and Norfolk Care Trust, 1991–; Frenchay Community Care Trust, 1994–; Peckham Pioneer Health Centre Ltd, 1994–96. Chm., Welsh Food Alliance, 1998–; Director: S Bristol Advice Services, 1998–; Bristol Health Co-op., 1999–. Vice-Pres., Socialist Health Assoc., 1999–; Sec., Public Health Assoc. Cymru, 1998–. Mem. (Lab), Bristol CC, 1995–99; Member: Avon and Som Police Authy, 1998–99; Avon Probation Cttee, 1997–99. JP Epping and Ongar, 1980–85. Captain, RAMC (V). *Publications:* Healthy Norfolk People, 1990; (ed) Helping People with Disabilities in East Anglia, 1991; contribs to medical and health service jls. *Recreations:* music, natural history, railway history. *Address:* Chagford, 8 Church Avenue, Sneyd Park, Bristol BS9 1LD; *e-mail:* paul@crawfordwalker.freeserve.co.uk. *Club:* Athenæum.

WALKER, Paul James; QC 1999; FCIArb; *b* Wellington, NZ, 1954; *s* of James Edgar Walker and Dawne Walker (*née* McGowan); *m* 1988, Josephine Andrews; one *d.* *Educ:* St Peter's Coll., Adelaide; Magdalen Coll., Oxford (BA Law, BCL). FCIArb 1992. Called to the Bar, Gray's Inn, 1979; barrister in private practice, 1980–; Sen. Lectr in Law, Victoria Univ. of Wellington, 1994–96; Dir, NZ Inst. Public Law, 1996. Counsel to BSE Inquiry, 1998–2000. Fellow, Arbitrators and Mediators Inst., NZ, 1994. *Publications:* (ed with S. Rogers) Studies in Insurance Law, 1996; (ed jtly) Commercial Regulation and Judicial Review, 1998. *Address:* Brick Court Chambers, 7 Essex Street, WC2R 3LD. *T:* (020) 7379 3550.

WALKER, Pauline Ann, (Mrs D. D. Walker); *see* Oliver, P. A.

WALKER, Rt Rev. Peter Knight, MA, DD; Bishop of Ely, 1977–89; an Hon. Assistant Bishop, diocese of Oxford, 1989–95; *b* 6 Dec. 1919; *s* of late George Walker and Eva Muriel (*née* Knight); *m* 1973, Mary Jean, JP 1976, *yr d* of late Lt-Col J. A. Ferguson, OBE. *Educ:* Leeds Grammar Sch. (Schol.); The Queen's Coll., Oxford (Hastings schol.; Cl. 2 Classical Hon. Mods. 1940, Cl. 1 Lit. Hum. 1947; MA Oxon 1947; Hon. Fellow, 1981); Westcott House, Cambridge. MA Cantab by incorporation, 1958; Hon. DD Cantab, 1978. Served in RN (Lieut, RNVR, Atlantic, Indian Ocean, Mediterranean), 1940–45. Asst Master: King's Sch., Peterborough, 1947–50; Merchant Taylors' Sch., 1950–56. Ordained, 1954; Curate of Hemel Hempstead, 1956–58; Fellow, Dean of Chapel and Lectr in Theology, Corpus Christi Coll., Cambridge, 1958–62 (Asst Tutor, 1959–62), Hon. Fellow, 1978; Principal of Westcott House, Cambridge, 1962–72; Commissary to Bishop of Delhi, 1962–66; Hon. Canon of Ely Cathedral, 1966–72; Bishop Suffragan of Dorchester, and Canon of Christ Church, Oxford, 1972–77. Entered H of L, 1984. Select Preacher: Univ. of Cambridge, 1962, 1967 (Hulsean), 1986; Univ. of Oxford, 1975, 1980, 1990, 1996; Examining Chaplain to Bishop of Portsmouth, 1962–72. Chm., Hosp. Chaplaincies Council, 1982–86. Pres., British Sect., Internat. Bonhoeffer Soc., 1987–96. A Governor, St Edward's Sch., Oxford, 1975–96. Hon. Fellow: St John's Coll., Cambridge, 1989; St Edmund's Coll., Cambridge, 1989. *Publications:* The Anglican Church Today: rediscovering the middle way, 1988; contrib. to: Classical Quarterly; Theology, etc. *Address:* 19 St Mark's Court, Barton Road, Cambridge CB3 9LE. *T:* (01223) 363041. *Club:* Cambridge County.

WALKER, Prof. Peter Martin Brabazon, CBE 1976; FRSE; Honorary Professor and Director, MRC Mammalian Genome Unit, 1973–80; *b* 1 May 1922; *e s* of Major Ernest Walker and Mildred Walker (*née* Heaton-Ellis), Kenya; *m* 1st, 1943, Violet Norah Wright (*d* 1985); one *s* three *d*; 2nd, 1986, Joan Patricia Taylor; one *d.* *Educ:* Haileybury Coll.; Trinity Coll., Cambridge, 1945. BA, PhD. Tool and instrument maker, 1939 (during War); Scientific Staff, MRC Biophysics Research Unit, King's Coll., London, 1948; Royal Society Research Fellow, Edinburgh, 1958; Univ. of Edinburgh: Lectr in Zoology, 1962; Reader in Zoology, 1963; Professor of Natural History, 1966–73. Member: Biological Research Bd, MRC, 1967 (Chm., 1970–72); MRC, 1970–72; Ext. Scientific Staff, MRC, 1980–84; Chief Scientist Cttee, Scottish Home and Health Dept, 1973–85; Chm., Equipment Res. Cttee, Scottish Home and Health Dept, 1973–79; Mem. Council, Imp. Cancer Res. Fund, 1971–94; Chm., Imp. Cancer Res. Fund Scientific Adv. Cttee, 1975–85; Mem., Scientific Adv. Cttee of European Molecular Biology Lab., 1976–81. General Editor: Chambers Science & Technology Dictionary, 1985–94; Chambers Biology Dictionary, 1989; Chambers Air and Space Dictionary, 1990; Chambers Earth Sciences Dictionary, 1991; Larousse Dictionary of Science and Technology, 1994–95; Chambers Dictionary of Science and Technology, 1998–99. *Publications:* contribs to the molecular biology of the genetic material of mammals in: Nature; Jl of Molecular Biology, etc. *Recreations:* gardening, design of scientific instruments, railway history. *Address:* Drumlaggan, The Ross, Comrie, Perthshire PH6 2JT. *T:* (01764) 670303.

WALKER, Philip Andrew Geoffrey; Editor, Daily Star, 1994–98; *b* 28 July 1944; *m* 1st, 1965, Stella Kaspar; one *s* three *d*; 2nd, 1987, Sharon Ring. *Educ:* Howardian High Sch., Cardiff. South Wales Echo, 1962–64; Daily Sketch, 1964–65; Evening Post, Reading, 1966–68; Daily Mail, 1968–69; Asst Editor, Daily Mirror, 1969–80; Associate Editor, Daily Express, 1980–83; Dep. Editor, Daily Mirror, 1983–88; freelance journalist, 1988–90; Dep. Editor, Daily Star, 1990–94. *Recreation:* natural history.

WALKER, His Honour Philip Henry Conyers, (Harry); a Circuit Judge, 1979–99; *b* 22 Dec. 1926; *o c* of Philip Howard and Kathleen Walker; *m* 1953, Mary Elizabeth Ross; two *s* two *d.* *Educ:* Marlborough; Oriel Coll., Oxford. MA, BCL (Oxon); DipTh (London). Army (6 AB Sigs), 1944–48 (despatches, 1948). Solicitor in private practice, 1954–79; a Recorder of the Crown Court, 1972–79. Mem., Church Assembly, Nat. Synod of C of E, 1960–80. Chm., Agricultural Land Tribunal (Yorks & Lancs), 1977–79;

Dep. Chm., Agricultural Land Tribunal (Western), 1989–99; Mem., Criminal Law Revision Cttee, 1981–. *Recreations:* fishing, shooting, sailing, walking. *Address:* Pond House, Askwith, Otley, West Yorks LS21 2JN. *T:* (01943) 463196.

WALKER, Dr Ranginui Joseph Isaac, DCNZM 2001; PhD. Professor of Maori Studies and Head of Department, Auckland University, 1993–97, now Professor Emeritus; Amorange (Executive), Manukau Institute of Technology, since 2000; *b* 1 March 1932; *s* of Isaac Walker and Wairata Walker; *m* 1953, Deirdre Patricia Dodson; two *s* one *d. Educ:* Univ. of Auckland (PhD Anthropol. 1970). Asst teacher (primary), 1953–62; Lectr, Auckland Teachers' Coll., 1962–66; Auckland University: Asst Lectr, 1967–69; Lectr (Contg Educn), 1970–85; Associate Prof., 1986–93; Pro Vice-Chancellor (Maori), 1996–97. Elsdon Best Meml Medal, Jl of Polynesian Soc., 1997. *Publications:* Years of Anger, 1987; Struggle Without End, 1990; The Walker Papers, 1996; He Tipua: a biography of Sir Apirana Ngata, 2001. *Recreations:* reading, boating, fishing, diving. *Address:* 124B Gowing Drive, Meadowbank, Auckland, New Zealand. *T:* (9) 5288381.

WALKER, Raymond Augustus; QC 1988; a Recorder, since 1993; *b* 26 Aug. 1943; *s* of Air Chief Marshal Sir Augustus Walker, GCB, CBE, DSO, DFC, AFC and Lady Walker; *m* 1976, June Rose Tunesi; one *s. Educ:* Radley; Trinity Hall, Cambridge (BA). Called to the Bar, Middle Temple, 1966. *Recreations:* golf, tennis, ski-ing, sailing, opera. *Address:* 4 King's Bench Walk, Temple, EC4Y 7DL. *T:* (020) 7353 0375. *Clubs:* Garrick; Royal West Norfolk Golf, Sunningdale Golf.

WALKER, Raymond James, OBE 1991; Special Adviser on International Electronic Data Interchange to Department of Trade and Industry, since 1996; *b* 13 April 1943; *s* of Cyril James Walker and Louie Walker; *m* 1969, Mary Eastwood Whittaker (marr. diss. 1995); one *d*; *m* 1996, Anne Troye. *Educ:* St Audreys', Hatfield; University of Lancaster. BA (Hons). Personnel Director, Saracen Ltd, 1971–73; Jt Man. Dir, Carrington Viyella Exports Ltd, 1973–78; Export Dir, Carrington Viyella Home Furnishings (DORMA), 1978–83; Chief Exec., SITPRO, 1983–96. Co-Chm., Jt Electronic Data Interchange Cttee, UN Econ. Commn for Europe, 1985–87; Rapporteur for Western Europe, UN-Electronic Data Interchange for Admin, Commerce and Transport, 1987–. Amer. Nat. Standards Inst. Award, 1986; Electronic Data Interchange Award, Internat. Data Exchange Assoc., 1988. *Recreations:* collecting wine labels, a fascination for maps, growing clematis. *T:* (office) (020) 8318 7616. *Clubs:* Royal Automobile; Belle Toute (Lancaster).

WALKER, Richard; His Honour Judge Richard Walker; a Circuit Judge, since 1989; *b* 9 March 1942; *s* of Edwin Roland Walker and Barbara Joan (*née* Swann); *m* 1969, Angela Joan Hodgkinson; two *d. Educ:* Epsom Coll.; Worcester Coll., Oxford (MA). Called to the Bar, Inner Temple, 1966; in practise at the Bar, 1966–89; Asst Boundary Comr, 1979–88; a Recorder, 1989. Judicial Mem., Mental Health Review Tribunal, 1991–. Commissary Gen., City and Dio. of Canterbury, 1995–. *Publication:* (ed jtly) Carter-Ruck on Libel and Slander, 3rd edn 1985, 4th edn 1992. *Address:* c/o 1 Brick Court, Temple, EC4Y 9BY. *T:* (020) 7353 8845.

WALKER, Richard Alwyne F.; *see* Fyjis-Walker.

WALKER, Richard John Boileau, CVO 2000; MA; FSA; picture cataloguer; *b* 4 June 1916; *s* of Comdr Kenneth Walker and Caroline Livingstone-Learmonth; *m* 1946, Margaret, *d* of Brig. Roy Firebrace, CBE; one *s* two *d. Educ:* Harrow; Magdalene Coll., Cambridge (MA); Courtauld Institute of Art. Active service, RNVR, 1939–45. British Council, 1946; Tate Gallery, 1947–48; Min. of Works Picture Adviser, 1949–76; Curator of the Palace of Westminster, 1950–76; Nat. Portrait Gallery Cataloguer, 1976–85; Royal Collection Cataloguer, 1985–91; Nat. Trust Cataloguer, 1990–2001. Trustee: Nat. Maritime Museum, 1977–84; Army Museums Ogilby Trust, 1979–90. *Publications:* Catalogue of Pictures at Audley End, 1950 and 1973; Old Westminster Bridge, 1979; Regency Portraits, 1985; Palace of Westminster: a catalogue, 4 vols, 1988; Royal Collection: the 18th century miniatures, 1992; Miniatures in the Ashmolean Museum, 1997; The Nelson Portraits, 1998 (Anderson Prize, Soc. for Nautical Res.); (with Hugh Tait) The Athenæum Collection, 2000. *Recreations:* looking at pictures and finding quotations. *Address:* 31 Cadogan Place, SW1X 9RX. *T:* (020) 7235 1801. *Clubs:* Athenæum, Oxford and Cambridge.

WALKER, Robert; HM Diplomatic Service, retired; *b* 1 May 1924; *s* of Young and Gladys Walker, Luddendenfoot, Yorks; *m* 1949, Rita Thomas; one *s* one *d. Educ:* Sowerby Bridge Grammar Sch.; Peterhouse, Cambridge. Commissioned RNVR 1944; served in minesweepers in home waters. Cambridge, 1942–43 and 1946–48; BA Hons History, 1948; MA 1963. Joined CRO, 1948; served Peshawar and Karachi, 1949–51; New Delhi, 1955–59; Sen. First Sec., Accra, 1962–64; Dep. British High Comr, in Ghana, 1964–65; FCO, 1965–68. IDC, 1969; Commercial Counsellor, Ankara, 1970–71; Dep. High Comr, Nairobi, 1971–72. Dep. Registrar, Hull Univ., 1972–79. Mem., Craven DC, 1984–98 (Chm., 1991–92 and 1996–97). Contested (L): Haltemprice, Feb. and Oct. 1974, 1979; Humberside, European election, 1979; South Ribble, 1983. Mem., Liberal Party Council, 1976–87; Chm., Yorkshire Liberal Fedn, 1977–81. Mem. Council, Lancaster Univ., 1986–94. Founder Mem. and first Chm., Ribblesdale Trust, 1987–94. Mem. Cttee, Yorkshire Dales Nat. Park, 1992–98. *Recreations:* golf, travel. *Address:* 13 Acacia Grove, West Dulwich, SE21 8ER. *T:* (020) 8670 7029.

WALKER, Rt Hon. Sir Robert, Kt 1994; PC 1997; **Rt Hon. Lord Justice Walker;** a Lord Justice of Appeal, since 1997; *b* 17 March 1938; *s* of late Ronald Robert Antony Walker and Mary Helen Walker (*née* Welsh); *m* 1962, Suzanne Diana Leggi; one *s* three *d. Educ:* Downside Sch.; Trinity Coll., Cambridge (BA). Called to Bar, Lincoln's Inn, 1960, Bencher 1990; QC 1982; in practice at Chancery Bar, 1961–94; a Judge of the High Court of Justice, Chancery Div., 1994–97. *Address:* c/o Royal Courts of Justice, Strand, WC2A 2LL.

WALKER, Robert M.; Group Chief Executive, Severn Trent plc, since 2000; *b* 3 Feb. 1945; *s* of Arthur Norman Walker and Nancy (*née* Waugh); *m* 1970, Patricia Douglass; one *s* one *d. Educ:* Hampton Sch.; Magdalen Coll., Oxford (BA Hons Modern History 1966). Procter & Gamble Ltd, 1966–70; McKinsey & Co. Inc., 1970–76; PepsiCo Inc., 1976–99 (Div. Pres.). *Club:* Oxford and Cambridge.

WALKER, Sir Rodney (Myerscough), Kt 1996; Chairman: UK Sports Council, since 1998; Rugby Football League, since 1993; *b* 10 April 1943; *s* of Norman and Lucy Walker; *m* 1974, Anne Margaret Aspinall; two *s. Educ:* Thornes House Grammar Sch. CEng. Founder Chm., Myerscough Holdings, 1976; activities incl. grass concrete, civil engrg, motor retail, and develt. Chairman: W Yorks Broadcasting, 1986–; Leicester City plc, 1997–; Donington Park Estates, 1999–. Chairman: Sports Council of GB, 1994–96; English Sports Council, 1996–98; Vice-Chm., Rugby League Internat. Fedn, 1998–99. Mem., Wakefield HA, 1982–90; Chairman: Bradford Hosps NHS Trust, 1990–96; NHS Trust Fedn, 1993–95 (Pres., 1995–97). Chm., Wakefield Theatre Trust, 1981–99, now Hon. Life Pres.; Vice Chm., Yorks Sculpture Park, 1984–. Trustee: Nat. Mining Mus. for England, 1993–; English Nat. Stadium Trust, 1998–; Chm., Wembley Nat. Stadium Ltd, 2000–. Gov., SportsAid Foundn, 1994–. FInstD; FRSA. KLJ 1997. *Recreations:* golf, theatre, travel. *Address:* Walker House, Bond Street, Wakefield WF1 2QP. *T:* (01924) 379443; Pine Lodge, Home Farm, Woolley, Wakefield WF4 2JS. *T:* (01226) 384089.

WALKER, Comdr Roger Antony Martineau-, LVO 1994; RN; Clerk to Trustees, United Westminster Almshouses Foundation, since 1997; *b* 15 Oct. 1940; *s* of Antony Philip Martineau-Walker and Sheila Hazeal Mayoh Wilson; *m* Inger Lene Brag-Nielsen; two *s. Educ:* Haileybury and Imperial Service College, Hertford; BRNC Dartmouth. Commissioned RN, 1962; served Malta, Singapore and Sarawak, 1962–65; Torpedo and Antisubmarine Course, HMS Vernon, 1968; HMS Galatea, 1973–76; NDC Latimer, 1977–78; Naval and Defence Staff, MoD, 1978–83; Naval Manpower Planning, with special responsibility for introd. of longer career for ratings (2nd Open Engagement), 1983–85; operational staff (UK commitments), 1985–87; Head, Naval Sec's Policy Staff, 1987–90; Pvte Sec. to Duke and Duchess of Kent, 1990–93. Bursar, Royal Sch. for Daughters of the Army, 1995–96. *Recreations:* fishing, photography, music. *Address:* 13 The Peak, Rowlands Castle, Hants PO9 6AH. *Club:* Army and Navy.

WALKER, Ronald Jack; QC 1983; a Recorder, since 1986; *b* 24 June 1940; *s* of Jack Harris Walker and Ann Frances Walker; *m* 1st, 1964, Caroline Fox (marr. diss. 1997); two *s*; 2nd, 1999, Clare Oonagh Jane Devitt; one *d. Educ:* Owen's School, London; University College London. LLB (Hons). Called to the Bar, Gray's Inn, 1962, Bencher, 1993. Mem. Gen. Council of the Bar, 1993–96 (Chm. Professional Conduct Cttee, 1993–94). *Publications:* English Legal System (with M. G. Walker), 1967, 7th edn 1994; contributing ed., Bullen & Leake & Jacob's Precedents of Pleadings, 13th edn 1990; (ed) Butterworths Professional Negligence Service, 1999. *Address:* 12 King's Bench Walk, Temple, EC4Y 7EL. *T:* (020) 7583 0811. *Club:* Travellers.

WALKER, Roy; *see* Walker, C. R.

WALKER, Sarah Elizabeth Royle, (Mrs R. G. Allum), CBE 1991; mezzo-soprano; *d* of Elizabeth Brownrigg and Alan Royle Walker; *m* 1972, Graham Allum. *Educ:* Pate's Grammar School for Girls, Cheltenham; Royal College of Music. FRCM 1987; LRAM. Prince Consort Prof. of Singing, RCM, 1993–; vocal performance consultant, GSMD, 1999–. Pres., Cheltenham Bach Choir, 1986–. Major appearances at concerts and in recital in Britain, America, Australia, New Zealand, Europe; operatic débuts include: Coronation of Poppea, Kent Opera, 1969, San Francisco Opera, 1981; La Calisto, Glyndebourne, 1970; Les Troyens, Scottish Opera, 1972, Wien Staatsoper, 1980; Principal Mezzo Soprano, ENO, 1972–77; Die Meistersinger, Chicago Lyric Opera, 1977; Werther, Covent Garden, 1979; Giulio Caesare, Le Grand Théâtre, Genève, 1983; Capriccio, Brussels, 1983; Teseo, Sienna, 1985; Samson, NY Metropolitan Opera, 1986; numerous recordings and video recordings, incl. title rôle in Britten's Gloriana. FGSM 2000. *Recreations:* interior design, encouraging her husband with the gardening. *Address:* 152 Inchmery Road, SE6 1DF. *Fax:* (020) 8461 5659; *e-mail:* megamezzo@sarahwalker.com. *Club:* University Women's.

WALKER, Sheila Mosley, (Mrs Owen Walker), CBE 1981; JP; Chief Commissioner, Girl Guides Association, 1975–80; *b* 11 Dec. 1917; *yr d* of late Charles Eric Mosley Mayne, Indian Cavalry, and Evelyn Mary, *d* of Sir Thomas Skewes-Cox, MP; *m* 1st, 1940, Major Bruce Dawson, MC, Royal Berkshire Regt (killed, Arnhem, 1944); one *s* one *d*; 2nd, 1955, Henry William Owen, *s* of late Sir Henry Walker, CBE; one step *s* one step *d. Educ:* St Mary's Hall, Brighton; St James' Secretarial Coll., London. Midlands Regional Chief Comr, 1970–75, Vice-Pres., 1988–, Girl Guides Assoc. Vice-Chm., CPRE, 1988–95. JP Nottingham City, 1970. *Recreations:* children, animals, all country and nature conservation. *Address:* Dingley Hall, near Market Harborough, Leics LE16 8PJ. *T:* (01858) 535388. *Club:* New Cavendish (Chm. Bd, 1983–93).

WALKER, Simon Edward John; Communications Secretary to the Queen, since 2000; *b* 28 May 1953; *s* of Louis Charles Vivian Walker and Joan Wallace Walker (*née* Keith); *m* 1980, Mary Virginia Strang; one *s* one *d. Educ:* South African Coll. Sch.; Balliol Coll., Oxford (BA PPE; MA 1978). Personal Asst to Lord Sainsbury, 1974–75; reporter, TV NZ, Wellington, 1975–79; Knight Journalism Fellow, Stanford Univ., 1979–80; Communications Dir, NZ Labour Party, 1980–84; Director: Communicor Govt and PR, 1984–87; NZ Centre for Independent Studies, Auckland, 1987–89; Eur. Public Affairs, Hill & Knowlton PR, London, 1989–90; Man. Dir, Hill & Knowlton, Belgium, 1990–94; Partner, Brunswick PR, 1994–98 (on secondment to Policy Unit, 10 Downing St, 1996–97); Dir of Communications, British Airways, 1998–2000. Non-exec. Dir, Comair Ltd (SA), 2000–. *Publication:* Rogernomics: reshaping New Zealand's economy, 1989. *Recreations:* family, reading, music, travel. *Address:* Buckingham Palace, SW1A 1AA. *T:* (020) 7930 4832. *Club:* Travellers.

WALKER, Stuart; *see* Walker, B. S.

WALKER, Terence William, (Terry Walker); *b* 26 Oct. 1935; *s* of William Edwin and Lilian Grace Walker; *m* 1959, Priscilla Dart (marr. diss. 1983); two *s* one *d*; *m* 1983, Rosalie Fripp. *Educ:* Grammar Sch. and Coll. of Further Educn, Bristol. Employed by Courage (Western) Ltd at Bristol for 23 yrs, Mem. Chief Accountant's Dept. MP (Lab) Kingswood, Feb. 1974–1979; Second Church Estates Comr, 1974–79. Contested (Lab): Kingswood, 1983; Bristol NW, 1987. Member: Avon CC, 1981–96 (Vice-Chm., 1992–93; Chm., 1993–94), S Glos Unitary Council, 1996– (Dep. Leader Labour Gp); Chairman: Avon Public Protection Cttee, 1981–86; Avon Combined Fire Authy, 1996–. *Recreations:* cricket, football. *Address:* 28 Cherington Road, Westbury-on-Trym, Bristol BS10 5BJ. *T:* (0117) 962 3027.

WALKER, Dr (Thomas) Gordon, OBE 2000; FInstP; Chief Executive, Council for the Central Laboratory of Research Councils, 2000–01; retired; *b* 4 Nov. 1936; *s* of James Smart Walker and Mary Margaret McIntosh Walker; *m* 1960, Una May Graham Stevenson; one *s* one *d. Educ:* Uddingston Grammar Sch.; Univ. of Glasgow (BSc, PhD). Rutherford High Energy Laboratory, National Institute for Research in Nuclear Science, later Rutherford Appleton Laboratory, Science and Engineering Research Council: Res. Physicist, 1960–71; Gp Leader, 1971–80; Head: Instrumentation Div., 1980–83; Technology Div., 1983–87; Dep. Dir, 1987–94; Head, 1994–96; Dir, R&D, CCLRC, 1996–2000. Mem., Renewable Energy Adv. Cttee, DTI, 1980–. Chief Sci. Advr (Civil Defence), Oxfordshire CC, 1983–93. Chm., Mgt Cttee, Didcot CAB, 1991–97; Pres., Didcot Rotary Club, 1977–78. Chm., Harwell Parish Council, 1988–91. *Publications:* papers in sci. jls on experimental particle physics. *Recreations:* golf, gardening. *Address:* Tudor Cottage, Burr Street, Harwell, Didcot OX11 0DU. *T:* (01235) 835418. *Club:* Frilford Heath Golf.

WALKER, Ven. Thomas Overington; Archdeacon of Nottingham, 1991–96, now Emeritus; *b* 7 Dec. 1933; *m* 1957, Molly Anne Gilmour; one *s* two *d. Educ:* Keble Coll., Oxford (BA 1958; MA 1961); Oak Hill Theol Coll. Ordained 1960. Curate: St Paul, Woking, dio. of Guildford, 1960–62; St Leon, St Leonards, dio. of Chichester, 1962–64; Travelling Sec., Inter-Varsity Fellowship, 1964–67; Succentor, Birmingham Cathedral,

1967–70; Vicar, Harborne Heath, 1970–91; Priest-in-charge, St Germain, Edgbaston, 1983–91; Rural Dean, Edgbaston, 1989–91; Hon. Canon, Birmingham Cathedral, 1980–91. Proctor in Convocation, 1985–92. *Publications:* Renew Us By Your Spirit, 1982; The Occult Web, 1987, 3rd edn 1989; From Here to Heaven, 1987; Small Streams Big Rivers, 1991. *Recreations:* sport, music, reading, dry stone walling. *Address:* 6 Cornbrook, Clee Hill, Ludlow, Shropshire SY8 3QQ. *T:* (01584) 890176.

WALKER, Prof. Thomas William, ONZM 2000; ARCS; DSc; DIC; Professor of Soil Science, Lincoln College, New Zealand, 1961–79, now Emeritus; *b* 22 July 1916; *m* 1940, Edith Edna Bott; four *d. Educ:* Loughborough Grammar School; Royal College of Science. Royal Scholar and Kitchener Scholar, 1935–39; Salter's Fellow, 1939–41; Lecturer and Adviser in Agricultural Chemistry, Univ. of Manchester, 1941–46. Provincial Advisory Soil Chemist, NAAS, 1946–51; Prof. of Soil Science, Canterbury Agric. Coll., New Zealand, 1952–58; Prof. of Agric., King's Coll., Newcastle upon Tyne, 1958–61. Bledisloe Medal, Lincoln Univ., 1997; Gold Medal, Royal Soc. of NZ, 1998. *Publications:* Vegetable Growers Handbook for New Zealanders, 1992; numerous research. *Recreations:* fishing, gardening. *Address:* 843 Cashmere Road, Christchurch 3, New Zealand.

WALKER, Hon. Sir Timothy (Edward), Kt 1996; **Hon. Mr Justice Timothy Walker;** a Judge of the High Court of Justice, Queen's Bench Division, and a Judge of the Commercial Court, since 1996; *b* 13 May 1946; *s* of George Edward Walker, solicitor, and Muriel Edith Walker; *m* 1968, Mary (*née* Tyndall); two *d. Educ:* Harrow Sch. (Totland Entrance Schol.; Clayton Leaving Schol.); University Coll., Oxford (Plumptre Schol., 1965; 1st Cl. Hons Jurisprudence, 1967; MA). Asst Lectr in Law, King's Coll., London, 1967–68; Profumo Schol., Inner Temple, 1968; Eldon Law schol., 1969; called to the Bar, Inner Temple, 1968, Bencher, 1996; QC 1985; a Recorder of the Crown Court, 1986–96. *Address:* Royal Courts of Justice, Strand, WC2A 2LL.

WALKER, Timothy Edward Hanson, CB 1998; Director-General, Health and Safety Executive, since 2000; *b* 27 July 1945; *s* of late Harris and of Elizabeth Walker; *m* 1st, 1969, Judith Mann (*d* 1976); one *d*; 2nd, 1983, Hon. Anna Butterworth (*see* Hon. A. E. B. Walker); two *d. Educ:* Tonbridge Sch.; Brasenose Coll., Oxford (BA Chemistry, 1967; MA, DPhil 1969). Weir Jun. Res. Fellow, University Coll., Oxford, and Exhibnr of Royal Commn of 1851, Oxford and Paris, 1969; Harkness Fellow, Commonwealth Fund of New York, 1971, Univ. of Virginia, 1971 and Northwestern Univ., 1972; Strategic Planner, GLC, 1974; Principal, Dept of Trade, 1977; Sloan Fellow, London Business Sch., 1983; Department of Trade and Industry: Asst Sec., 1983; Dir (Admin), Alvey Programme, 1983; Head, Policy Planning Unit, 1985; Principal Private Sec. to successive Secs of State for Trade and Industry, 1986; Under Sec., 1987; Dir, Inf. Engrg Directorate, 1987; Head, Atomic Energy Div., Dept of Energy, then DTI, 1989–95; Dep. Sec., 1995, and Dir Gen., Immigration and Nationality Directorate, 1995–98, Home Office; Comr and Dep. Chm., HM Customs and Excise, 1998–2000. Non-exec. Dir, ICI Chemicals and Polymers Ltd, 1988–89. UK Gov., IAEA, 1989–94; non exec. Dir, Govt Div., UKAEA, 1994–95. Chm., Assembly of Donors, Nuclear Safety Account, EBRD, 1993–95. Governor, St Anne's Sch., Wandsworth, 1977–82. FRSA 2000. *Publications:* contribs to scientific jls. *Recreations:* cookery, gardening, collecting modern prints. *Address:* Health and Safety Executive, Rose Court, 2 Southwark Bridge, SE1 9HS.

WALKER, Victoria Patricia Ann, (Mrs F. A. Woods Walker); *see* Woods, V. P. A.

WALKER, William Connoll, (Bill), OBE 1998; FIPM; Chairman, Walker Associates, since 1975; *b* 20 Feb. 1929; *s* of Charles and Williamina Walker; *m* 1956, Mavis Evelyn Lambert; three *d. Educ:* Logie Sch., Dundee; Trades Coll., Dundee; College for Distributive Trades. FIPM 1968; FIMgt. Message boy, 1943–44; office boy, 1944–46; commissioned RAF, 1946–49; Sqdn Leader, RAFVR, 1949–; salesman, public service vehicle driver, general manager, 1949–59; RAF, 1959–65; training and education officer, furnishing industry, 1965–67; company director, 1967–79; pt-time presenter, TV progs, 1969–75. MP (C) Perth and E Perthshire, 1979–83, Tayside N, 1983–97; contested (C) Tayside N, 1997. Director: Stagecoach Malaŵi, 1989–94; Stagecoach Internat. Services, 1989–94; Chm., Aerotech Marketing, 1995–. Chm., Scotland and NI Air Cadet Council, 1997–; Hon. Pres., Air Cadet Gliding, 1994–. FRSA 1970. *Recreations:* RAFVR, gliding, caravanning, walking, youth work. *Address:* Longacres, Burrelton, Perthshire PH13 9NY. *T:* (01828) 670407. *Club:* Royal Air Force.

WALKER, (William) Guy, CBE 1993; Chairman, Van den Bergh Foods Ltd, 1985–98; UK National Manager, Unilever plc, 1995–98; *b* 1 March 1936; *s* of Arthur and Margaret Walker; *m* 1st, 1960, Elizabeth Barbette Lawrence (*d* 1980); one *s* two *d*; 2nd, 1983, Marian Farrow Norrie, *qv*; two step *d. Educ:* Cheltenham Coll.; St John's Coll., Cambridge (MA 1958). Salesman, W. M. Sowry, S Africa, 1960; Trainee, Unilever, 1961–64; Manager: Batchelor Foods, 1964–78; Unilever, Rotterdam, 1978–82; Chm., Batchelor Foods, 1982–85. Mem., BBSRC, 1997–2000. Pres., Food and Drink Fedn, 1995–97. Mem. (C), Sheffield CC, 1967–71. Dir and Treas., Britain in Europe Campaign, 2000–. Chm., Brighton Festival Trust, 2000–. Gov., Varndean Coll., Brighton. *Recreations:* golf, ski-ing. *Address:* c/o Van den Bergh Foods Ltd, Manor Royal, Crawley, West Sussex RH10 2RQ. *Club:* Sussex CC (Mem. Cttee).

WALKER, William MacLelland; QC (Scot.) 1971; Social Security Commissioner, since 1988; a Child Support Commissioner, since 1993; *b* 19 May 1933; *s* of late Hon. Lord Walker; *m* 1957, Joan Margaret, *d* of late Charles Hutchison Wood, headmaster, Dundee; one *d. Educ:* Edinburgh Academy; Edinburgh Univ. (MA, LLB). Advocate, 1957; Flying Officer, RAF, 1957–59; Standing Junior Counsel: Min. of Aviation, 1963–68; BoT (Aviation), 1968–71; Min. of Technology, 1968–70; Dept of Trade and Industry (Power), 1971; Min. of Aviation Supply, 1971. Hon. Sheriff, various Sheriffdoms, 1963–71. Chairman: Industrial Tribunals in Scotland, 1972–88; VAT Tribunals, 1985–88. *Recreations:* shooting, travel, photography. *Address:* 58B Manor Place, Edinburgh EH3 7EH; Edenside, Gordon, Berwickshire TD3 6LB. *Clubs:* Royal Air Force; New (Edinburgh); Naval de Portimão (Portimão, Portugal).

WALKER-ARNOTT, Edward Ian; Consultant, Herbert Smith, since 2000 (Senior Partner, 1992–2000); *b* 18 Sept. 1939; *s* of late Charles Douglas Walker-Arnott and Kathleen Margaret (*née* Brittain); *m* 1971, (Phyllis) Jane Ricketts; one *s* two *d. Educ:* Haileybury Coll.; London Univ. (LLB ext.); University Coll. London (LLM; Fellow, 1999; Vis. Prof., 2000–). Admitted solicitor, 1963; Partner, Herbert Smith, 1968–2000. Dir, Sturge Hldgs, 1989–95. Member: Cork Cttee on Review of Insolvency Law, 1977–82; Insolvency Practitioners Tribunal, 1987–. Mem. Council of Lloyds, 1983–88. Mem. Bd, RNT, 2000–. Governor: S Bank Bd, 1999–; The Wellcome Trust, 2000–. Member, Governing Body: Haileybury Coll., 1969–98; Benenden Sch., 1987–93. Author, report for Arts Council of England on relationship with Royal Opera House, Covent Garden (Walker-Arnott Report), 1997. *Recreations:* reading, gardening, cycling, watching sport. *Address:* Manuden Hall, Manuden, near Bishop's Stortford, Herts CM23 1DY. *Club:* City of London.

WALKER-HAWORTH, John Leigh; *b* 25 Oct. 1944; *s* of William and Julia Walker-Haworth; *m* 1976, Caroline Mary Blair Purves; two *s. Educ:* Charterhouse; Pembroke College, Oxford. Called to the Bar, Inner Temple, 1967. Dir, 1981–93, Vice Chm., 1993–95, S. G. Warburg & Co.; Man. Dir, 1995–97, Advr, 1997–2000, UBS Warburg. Dep. Chm., Takeover Panel, 1997– (Dir-Gen., City Panel on Takeovers and Mergers, 1985–87). Governor: Sutton's Hosp., Charterhouse, 1997–; Charterhouse Sch., 2000–. *Address:* 6 Chancellor House, Hyde Park Gate, SW7 5DQ.

WALKER-OKEOVER, Sir Peter (Ralph Leopold), 4th Bt *cr* 1886; DL; *b* 22 July 1947; *s* of Colonel Sir Ian Peter Andrew Monro Walker-Okeover, 3rd Bt, DSO, TD, and of Dorothy Elizabeth, *yr d* of Captain Josceline Heber-Percy; *S* father, 1982; *m* 1st, 1972, Catherine Mary Maule (marr. diss. 1991), *d* of Colonel George Maule Ramsay; two *s* one *d*; 2nd, 1993, Patricia Margaret Sevier, *er d* of Laurance Sanderson. *Educ:* Eton; RMA Sandhurst. Captain, Blues and Royals, retired. DL Staffs, 1992. *Heir: s* Andrew Peter Monro Walker-Okeover, *b* 22 May 1978. *Address:* Okeover Hall, Ashbourne, Derbyshire DE6 2DE; House of Glenmuick, Ballater, Aberdeenshire.

WALKER-SMITH, Sir (John) Jonah, 2nd Bt *cr* 1960, of Broxbourne, Co. Herts; a Recorder of the Crown Court, since 1980; *b* 6 Sept. 1939; *s* of Baron Broxbourne (Life Peer), QC, TD and Dorothy (*d* 1999), *d* of late L. J. W. Etherton; *S* to baronetcy of father, 1992; *m* 1974, Aileen Marie Smith; one *s* one *d. Educ:* Westminster School; Christ Church, Oxford. Called to Bar, Middle Temple, 1963. *Heir: s* Daniel Derek Walker-Smith, *b* 26 March 1980. *Address:* 11 Doughty Street, WC1N 2PG. *Club:* Garrick.

WALKINE, Herbert Cleveland, CMG 1990; CVO 1994; OBE 1985; Secretary to the Cabinet, Bahamas, 1987–94; *b* 28 Nov. 1929; *s* of late Herbert Granville Walkine and Rebecca Walkine; *m* 1966, Julliette Pam Maria Sherman; three *d. Educ:* Government High Sch., Nassau; Bahamas Teachers' Coll.; Univ. of Manchester. Started career as teacher; served as District Commissioner, 1958–68; Asst Sec., 1968, First Asst Sec., 1969, Dep. Perm. Sec., 1970, Under Sec., 1972, Perm. Sec., 1974–87, Bahamas. *Recreations:* fishing, reading, watching boxing matches. *Address:* PO Box CB 13333, Nassau, Bahamas. *T:* 3255979.

WALL, Alfreda, (Mrs D. R. Wall); *see* Thorogood, A.

WALL, (Alice) Anne, (Mrs Michael Wall), DCVO 1982 (CVO 1972; MVO 1964); Extra Woman of the Bedchamber to HM the Queen, since 1981; *b* 1928; *d* of late Admiral Sir Geoffrey Hawkins, KBE, CB, MVO, DSC and late Lady Margaret Montagu-Douglas-Scott, *d* of 7th Duke of Buccleuch; *m* 1975, Commander Michael E. St Q. Wall, Royal Navy. *Educ:* Miss Faunce's PNEU School. Asst Press Sec. to the Queen, 1958–81. *Address:* Ivy House, Lambourn, Hungerford, Berks RG17 8PB. *T:* (01488) 72348; (020) 7582 0692.

WALL, Brian Owen, CEng, FRINA; RCNC; Chief Naval Architect, Ministry of Defence, 1985–90; *b* 17 June 1933; *s* of Maurice Stanley Wall and Ruby Wall; *m* 1960, Patricia Thora Hughes; one *s. Educ:* Newport High School, Mon; Imperial Coll. of Science and Technology; RN Coll., Greenwich. BSc Eng. ACGI. MoD Bath: Ship Vulnerability, 1958–61; Submarine Design, 1961–66; Head of Propeller Design, Admiralty Experiment Works, Haslar, 1966–71; Staff of C-in-C Fleet, Portsmouth, 1971–73; Submarine Support and Modernisation Group, MoD Bath, 1973–77; RCDS 1977; MoD Bath: Ship Production Div., 1978–79; Project Director, Vanguard Class, 1979–84; Dir, Cost Estimating and Analysis, 1985. Gov., Imperial Coll., London, 1991–99. *Recreations:* photography, chess, music, walking. *Address:* Wychwood, 39 High Bannerdown, Batheaston, Bath BA1 7JZ.

WALL, Prof. Charles Terence Clegg, FRS 1969; Professor of Pure Mathematics, 1965–99, and Senior Fellow, since 1999, Liverpool University; *b* 14 Dec. 1936; *s* of late Charles Wall, schoolteacher; *m* 1959, Alexandra Joy, *d* of late Prof. Leslie Spencer Hearnshaw; two *s* two *d. Educ:* Marlborough Coll.; Trinity Coll., Cambridge. PhD Cantab 1960. Fellow, Trinity Coll., 1959–64; Harkness Fellow, Princeton, 1960–61; Univ. Lectr, Cambridge, 1961–64; Reader in Mathematics, and Fellow of St Catherine's Coll., Oxford, 1964–65. SERC Sen. Fellowship, 1983–88. Royal Soc. Leverhulme Vis. Prof., CIEA, Mexico, 1967. Pres., London Mathematical Soc., 1978–80 (Mem. Council, 1973–80 and 1992–96); Hon. Mem., Irish Math. Soc., 2001. Fellow, Royal Danish Academy, 1990. Sylvester Medal, Royal Soc., 1988. *Publications:* Surgery on Compact Manifolds, 1970; A Geometric Introduction to Topology, 1972; (with A. A. du Plessis) The Geometry of Topological Stability, 1995; papers on various problems in geometric topology, singularity theory, and related algebra. *Recreations:* reading, walking, gardening, home winemaking. *Address:* 5 Kirby Park, West Kirby, Wirral, Merseyside CH48 2HA. *T:* (0151) 625 5063.

WALL, David (Richard), CBE 1985; Dance Consultant, Remedial Dance Clinic, since 1991; Ballet Master, English National Ballet Co., since 1994; *b* 15 March 1946; *s* of Charles and Dorothy Wall; *m* 1967, Alfreda Thorogood, *qv*; one *s* one *d. Educ:* Royal Ballet Sch. Joined Royal Ballet Co., Aug. 1964. Promotion to: Soloist, Aug. 1966; Junior Principal Dancer, Aug. 1967; Senior Principal Dancer, Aug. 1968; during period of employment danced all major roles and had many ballets created for him; retired from dancing, 1984. Assoc. Dir, 1984–87, Dir, 1987–91, Royal Acad. of Dancing. Guest repetiteur, London City Ballet, 1993–. Evening Standard Award for Ballet, 1977. *Recreations:* music, theatre. *Address:* 34 Croham Manor Road, South Croydon, Surrey CR2 7BE.

WALL, Rt Rev. Eric St Quintin; Bishop Suffragan of Huntingdon, 1972–80; *b* 19 April 1915; *s* of Rev. Sydney Herbert Wall, MA, and Ethel Marion Wall (*née* Wilkins); *m* 1942, Doreen Clare (*née* Loveley); one *s* one *d. Educ:* Clifton; Brasenose Coll., Oxford (MA); Wells Theol. College. Deacon, 1938; priest, 1939; Curate of Boston, 1938–41; Chaplain, RAFVR, 1941–45; Vicar of Sherston Magna, 1944–53; Rural Dean of Malmesbury, 1951–53; Vicar of Cricklade with Latton, 1953–60; Hon. Chaplain to Bp of Bristol, 1960–66; Hon. Canon, Bristol, 1960–72; Diocesan Adviser on Christian Stewardship, Dio. Bristol, 1960–66; Proc. Conv., 1964–69; Vicar, St Alban's, Westbury Park, Bristol, 1966–72; Rural Dean of Clifton, 1967–72; Canon Residentiary of Ely, 1972–80. *Recreation:* golf. *Address:* Forest House, Cinder Hill, Coleford, Glos GL16 8HQ. *T:* (01594) 832424.

WALL, James Francis, (Frank), CMG 1999; Head of Shipping Policy 3 Division, Department of the Environment, Transport and the Regions (formerly Department of Transport), since 1993; *b* 6 Jan. 1944; *s* of late James Wall, MA and Elizabeth Wall (*née* O'Sullivan); *m* 1970, Eileen Forrester McKerracher; two *d. Educ:* Belvedere Coll., SJ; University Coll., Dublin (BA 1966); Univ. of Liverpool (MCD 1968). MRTPI 1970. Asst to Prof. H. Myles Wright, Dublin Regl Planning Consultant, 1965–66; Planner then Sen. Planner, Antrim and Ballymena Develt Commn, 1968–71; Planning Officer, NI Min. of Develt, 1971–72; Asst, S Hants Plan Technical Unit, 1972–74; Sen. Planning Officer, Hants CC, 1974; Planning Officer, then Principal Planning Officer, DoE, 1974–82;

Principal, 1982, Asst Sec., 1993, Dept of Transport. Chm., UK Search and Rescue Strategy Cttee, 2000. *Publications:* contrib. conf. proc. and articles in maritime law jls. *Recreations:* Flower Class Corvettes, the Boeing 707-348C. *Address:* Collingwood, Elvetham Road, Fleet, Hants GU13 8HH.

WALL, Prof. Jasper V., PhD; Visiting Professor, Department of Astrophysics, University of Oxford, since 1998; *b* 15 Jan. 1942; *s* of late Philip Errington Wall and Lilian Margaret (*née* Blackburn); *m* 1969, Jennifer Anne Lash; one *s* one *d*. *Educ:* Vankleek Hill Collegiate Inst.; Queen's Univ., Kingston (BSc 1963); Univ. of Toronto (MASc 1966); Australian Nat. Univ. (PhD 1970). Res. Scientist, Australian Nat. Radio Astronomy Observatory, Parkes, NSW, 1970–74; Leverhulme Fellow, RAS, 1974–75, Jaffé Donation Fellow, Royal Soc., 1975–79, Cavendish Lab.; Hd, Astrophysics and Astrometry Div., Royal Greenwich Observatory, 1979–87; Officer-in-Charge, Isaac Newton Gp of Telescopes, La Palma, Canary Is, 1987–90; Royal Greenwich Observatory: Hd, Technol. Div., 1990–91; Hd, Astronomy Div., 1991–95; Dep. Dir, 1991–93; Head, 1993–95; Dir, 1995–98. Vis. Reader, Univ. of Sussex, 1980–90. FRAS 1975 (Mem. Council, 1992–96; Vice-Pres., 1996); FRSA 1998. Chm., Editl Bd, Astronomy & Geophysics, 1999–. *Publications:* (ed jtly) Modern Technology and its Influence on Astronomy, 1986; Optics in Astronomy, 1993; (jtly) The Universe at High Redshifts, 1997; numerous papers in professional jls on observational cosmology and statistics for astronomers. *Recreations:* hiking, running, ski-ing, music. *Address:* Nuclear and Astrophysics Laboratory, Keble Road, Oxford OX1 3RH. *T:* (01865) 273296; *e-mail:* jvw@astro.ox.ac.uk.

WALL, Sir John (Anthony), Kt 2000; CBE 1994; Chairman, Royal National Institute for the Blind, 1990–2000; Partner, Lawrence Graham, solicitors, 1977–93 (Consultant, 1993–95); *b* 4 June 1930; *s* of George and Edith Wall; *m* 1st, 1956, Joan Reeve (*d* 1991); four *s*; 2nd, 1996, Friedel Lawrence (*d* 1999). *Educ:* Worcester Coll. for the Blind; Balliol Coll., Oxford (MA). Legal Officer, NALGO, 1956–74; Partner, Middleton Lewis, 1974–77; Dep. Master of High Court, Chancery Div., 1990–. Mem., Supreme Ct Rule Cttee, 1993–99. Pres., European Blind Union, 1996– (Mem. Bd, 1990–; Sec.-Gen., 1992–96); Jt Hon. Sec., Soc. of Visually Impaired Lawyers (formerly Blind Lawyers), 1993–. Vice-Pres., British Chess Fedn, 1991–. Gold Medal, IBCA Correspondence Chess Olympiad, 1987. *Publications:* articles in learned periodicals. *Recreation:* chess (Oxford *v* Cambridge 1949 and 1951). *Address:* 36 Broadmead Avenue, Worcester Park, Surrey KT4 7SW. *T:* (020) 8330 2309. *Club:* Reform.

WALL, Sir (John) Stephen, KCMG 1996 (CMG 1990); LVO 1983; HM Diplomatic Service; Head of European Secretariat, Cabinet Office, since 2000 (on secondment); *b* 10 Jan. 1947; *s* of John Derwent Wall and Maria Laetitia Wall (*née* Whitmarsh); *m* 1975, Catharine Jane Reddaway, *d* of late G. F. N. Reddaway, CBE and of Jean Reddaway, OBE; one *s*. *Educ:* Douai Sch.; Selwyn Coll., Cambridge (BA; Hon. Fellow, 2000). FCO 1968; Addis Ababa, 1969–72; Private Sec. to HM Ambassador, Paris, 1972–74; First Sec., FCO, 1974–76; Press Officer, No 10 Downing Street, 1976–77; Asst Private Sec. to Sec. of State for Foreign and Commonwealth Affairs, 1977–79; First Sec., Washington, 1979–83; Asst Head, later Head, European Community Dept, FCO, 1983–88; Private Secretary: to Foreign and Commonwealth Sec., 1988–90; to the Prime Minister, 1991–93; Ambassador to Portugal, 1993–95; Ambassador and UK Perm. Rep. to EU, Brussels, 1995–2000. *Recreations:* walking, photography, reading. *Address:* c/o Cabinet Office, 70 Whitehall, SW1A 2AS. *Club:* Wimbledon Football.

WALL, Malcolm Robert; Chief Operating Officer, United Business Media plc, since 2000; *b* 24 July 1956; *s* of Maj. Gen. Robert Percival Walter Wall, *qv* and Patricia Kathleen Wall; *m* 1985, Elizabeth Craxford; three *d*. *Educ:* Allhallows Sch., Lyme Regis; Univ. of Kent (BA Hons). Sales Dir, Anglia TV, 1987; Sales and Mktg Dir, Granada TV, 1988–92; Dep. CEO, Meridian Broadcasting, 1992–94; Man. Dir, Anglia TV, 1994–96; Dep. CEO, 1996–99, CEO, 1999–2000, United Broadcasting and Entertainment. Chm., Harlequin FC, 1997–2000. *Recreations:* sport, reading, television. *Address:* c/o United Business Media plc, Ludgate House, 245 Blackfriars Road, SE1 9UY. *Clubs:* Royal Automobile, MCC.

WALL, Mrs Michael; *see* Wall, A. A.

WALL, Hon. Sir Nicholas (Peter Rathbone), Kt 1993; **Hon. Mr Justice Wall;** a Judge of the High Court of Justice, Family Division, since 1993; *b* 14 March 1945; *s* of late Frederick Stanley Wall and of Margaret Helen Wall; *m* 1973, Margaret Sydee, JP; four *c*. *Educ:* Dulwich College; Trinity Coll., Cambridge (Scholar; MA). Pres., Cambridge Union Soc., 1967; Mem., combined univs debating tour, USA, 1968. Called to the Bar, Gray's Inn, 1969, Bencher, 1993; QC 1988; Asst Recorder, 1988–90; a Recorder, 1990–93; Family Div. Liaison Judge, Northern Circuit, 1996–. Mem., Lord Chancellor's Adv. Bd on Family Law, 1997– (Chm., Children Act Sub-Cttee, 1998–). *Publications:* (ed jtly) Supplements to Rayden and Jackson on Divorce, 15th edn, 1988–91; (ed jtly) Rayden and Jackson on Divorce, 16th edn, 1991–97, 17th edn 1997; (ed and contrib.) Rooted Sorrows: psychoanalytic contributions to assessments and decisions in the family justice system, 1996; (contrib.) Divided Duties: care planning within the family justice system, 1998; A Handbook for Expert Witnesses in Children Act Cases, 2000; papers in med. and legal jls. *Recreations:* collecting, binding and restoring books, theatre, opera, walking, composing clerihews. *Address:* Royal Courts of Justice, Strand, WC2A 2LL.

WALL, Maj.-Gen. Robert Percival Walter, CB 1978; Member, North East Thames Regional Health Authority, 1990–94; Chairman, Essex Family Health Services Authority, 1990–96; *b* 23 Aug. 1927; *s* of Frank Ernest and Ethel Elizabeth Wall; *m* 1st, 1953 (marr. diss. 1985); two *s* one *d*; 2nd, 1986, Jennifer Hilary Anning. Joined Royal Marines, 1945; regimental soldiering in Commandos, followed by service at sea and on staff of HQ 3 Commando Bde RM, 1945–58; psc(M) 1959; jssc 1961; Asst Sec., Chiefs of Staff Secretariat, 1962–65; 43 Commando RM, 1965–66; Naval Staff, 1966–68; Directing Staff, JSS Coll., 1969–71; Col GS Commando Forces and Dept of Commandant General RM, 1971–74; course at RCDS, 1975; Chief of Staff to Commandant General, RM, 1976–79. Dir, Land Decade Educnl Council, 1982–90. Chm., Essex FPC, 1985–90. Vice-Pres., River Thames Soc., 1983– (Chm., 1978–83); Mem. Council, Thames Heritage Trust, 1980–83; Pres., Blackheath Football Club (RFU), 1983–85; Council, Officers' Pension Soc., 1980–91. Freeman of City of London, 1977; Freeman, Co. of Watermen and Lightermen of River Thames, 1979. FIMgt; FRSA 1985. JP: City of London, 1982–92; Essex, 1992. *Recreations:* cricket, rugby, walking, reading. *Address:* c/o Barclays Bank, Metropolitan Essex Group, Barking, Essex IQ11 8GY. *Clubs:* Army and Navy, MCC.

See also M. R. Wall.

WALL, Sir Robert (William), Kt 1987; OBE 1980; Pro-Chancellor, University of Bristol, 1990–98; *b* 27 Sept. 1929; *s* of William George and Gladys Perina Wall; *m* 1968, Jean Ashworth; one *d* (and one *s* decd). *Educ:* Monmouth School; Bristol Coll. of Technology. HND MechEng; AMRAeS, TechEng. Student apprentice, Bristol Aeroplane Co., 1947–52; commissioned RAF Eng. Branch, and Mountain Rescue Service, 1955–57; management posts with British Aircraft Corp., 1957–67, Chief Ratefixer, 1969–75, Manager, Cost Control, 1975–88. Bristol City Council: Councillor 1959; Alderman 1971; re-elected Councillor 1974; Leader, Cons. Gp, 1974–97; Chm., Public Works Cttee, 1968–72; Dep. Leader, 1971–72, Council Leader, 1983–84. Mem., Bristol Develt Corp., 1993–96. Chairman: Bristol Cons. Assoc., 1979–88; Western Area Provincial Council, Nat. Union of Cons. and Unionist Assocs, 1988–91. Mem. Council, Univ. of Bristol, 1974–98 (Chairman: GP Cttee, 1979–87; Buildings Cttee, 1987–91; Audit Cttee, 1991–98); Governor, Bristol Old Vic Theatre Trust, 1974–87, and 1988–93; Mem. Council, SS Great Britain Project, 1975–; Chm., Rail Users' Cons. Cttee for W England, 1982–98. Mem., Audit Commn, 1986–94. Pres., Bristol Soc. of Model and Experimental Engrs, 1972–2000. FCIT. Freeman, Co. of Watermen and Lightermen. Hon. MA Bristol, 1982; Hon. DEng Bristol, 1999. *Publications:* Bristol Channel Pleasure Steamers, 1973; Ocean Liners, 1978 (trans. German, French, Dutch), 2nd edn 1984; Air Liners, 1980; Bristol: maritime city, 1981; The Story of HMS Bristol, 1986; Quayside Bristol, 1992; Ocean Liner Postcards, 1998; Brabazon, 1999; Bristol Aircraft, 2000. *Recreations:* writing maritime history, collecting postcards, hill walking. *Address:* 1 Ormerod Road, Stoke Bishop, Bristol BS9 1BA. *T:* (0117) 968 2910; The Glebe, Winsford, Somerset TA24 7BJ. *Clubs:* Bristol Savages, Clifton (Bristol).

WALL, Sir Stephen; *see* Wall, Sir J. S.

WALL, Prof. William Douglas, PhD, DLit; CPsychol, FBPsS; Professor of Educational Psychology, Institute of Education, University of London, 1973–78, now Professor Emeritus; *b* 22 Aug. 1913; *s* of late John Henry Wall and Ann McCulloch Wall, Wallington, Surrey; *m* 1st, 1936, Doris Margaret (*née* Satchel) (marr. diss. 1960); two *s* one *d*; 2nd, 1960, Ursula Maria (*née* Gallusser); one *s*. *Educ:* Univ. Coll. London, 1931–34 (BA Hons); Univ. Coll. London/Univ. of Birmingham, 1944–48 (PhD (Psychol.)); DLit (London) 1979. Mem., Social Psych. Sect., Child and Educnl Psych. Sect., BPsS. Univ. of Birmingham Educn Dept, 1945–53; Reader, 1948–53; Head, Educn and Child Develt Unit, UNESCO, Paris, 1951–56; Dir, Nat. Foundn for Educnl Res. in England and Wales, 1956–68; Dean, Inst. of Educn, Univ. of London, 1968–73; Scientific Advr, Bernard van Leer Foundn, 1978–82. Visiting Professor: Univ. of Michigan, 1957; Univ. of Jerusalem, 1962; Univ. of Tel Aviv, 1967. Chm., Internat. Project Evaluation of Educnl Attainment, 1958–62; Mem., Police Trng Council, 1970–78; Co-Dir, 1958–75, and Chm., Nat. Child Develt Study, 1958–78; Mem. Council, Internat. Children's Centre, Paris, 1970–78. *Publications:* (many trans. various langs): Adolescent Child, 1948 (2nd edn, 1952); Education and Mental Health, 1955; Psychological Services for Schools, 1956; Child of our Times, 1959; Failure in School, 1962; Adolescents in School and Society, 1968; Longitudinal Studies and the Social Sciences, 1970; Constructive Education for Children, 1975; Constructive Education for Adolescents, 1977; Constructive Education for Handicapped, 1979; contrib: British Jl Educnl Psych.; British Jl Psych., Educnl Res. (Editor, 1958–68), Educnl Rev., Enfance, Human Develt, Internat. Rev. Educn. *Recreations:* painting (one-man exhibitions: Windsor, 1986, 1988; London, 1987; Open Studio, Visual Images Gp, 1993), church architecture, gardening. *Address:* La Geneste, Rose Hill, Burnham, Bucks SL1 8LW.

WALLACE, family name of **Barons Wallace of Coslany** and **Wallace of Saltaire**.

WALLACE OF COSLANY, Baron *cr* 1974 (Life Peer), of Coslany in the City of Norwich; **George Douglas Wallace;** *b* 18 April 1906; *e s* of late George Wallace, Cheltenham Spa, Gloucestershire; *m* 1932, Vera Randall, Guildford, Surrey; one *s* one *d*. *Educ:* Central School, Cheltenham Spa. Mem. of Management Cttee, in early years, of YMCA at East Bristol and Guildford; Mem. Chislehurst-Sidcup UDC, 1937–46; has been Divisional Sec. and also Chm., Chislehurst Labour Party; also Chm. of Parks and Cemeteries Cttee of UDC, Schools Manager and Member of Chislehurst, Sidcup and Orpington Divisional Education Executive; Mem., Cray Valley and Sevenoaks Hosp. Management Cttee; Chm., House Cttee, Queen Mary's Hosp.; Vice-Chm., Greenwich and Bexley AHA, 1974–77. Joined Royal Air Force, reaching rank of Sergeant. Served in No 11 Group Fighter Command, 1941–45. MP (Lab) Chislehurst Div. of Kent, 1945–50; Junior Govt Whip, 1947–50; MP (Lab) Norwich North, Oct. 1964–Feb. 1974; PPS: to Lord President of the Council, Nov. 1964–65; to Sec. of State for Commonwealth Affairs, 1965; to Minister of State, Min. of Housing and Local Govt, 1967–68; Mem. Speaker's Panel of Chairmen, 1970–74; a Lord in Waiting (Govt Whip), 1977–79; opposition spokesman and Whip, H of L, 1979–84. Delegate to Council of Europe and WEU, 1975–77. Member: Commonwealth Parly Assoc.; Commonwealth War Graves Commn, 1970–86; Kent CC, 1952–57. *Recreations:* interested in Youth Movements and social welfare schemes. *Address:* 44 Shuttle Close, Sidcup, Kent DA15 8EP. *T:* (020) 8300 3634.

WALLACE OF SALTAIRE, Baron *cr* 1995 (Life Peer), of Shipley in the County of West Yorkshire; **William John Lawrence Wallace;** Professor of International Relations, London School of Economics, since 1999; *b* 12 March 1941; *s* of William E. Wallace and Mary A. Tricks; *m* 1968, Helen Sarah Rushworth (*see* H. S. Wallace); one *s* one *d*. *Educ:* Westminster Abbey Choir School (Sen. Chorister, 1954); St Edward's Sch., Oxford; King's Coll., Cambridge (Exhibnr, 1959; BA Hist 1962); Nuffield Coll., Oxford; Cornell Univ. (PhD Govt 1968). Lectr in Govt, Univ. of Manchester, 1967–77; Dep. Dir, RIIA, 1978–90; Sen. Res. Fellow in European Studies, St Antony's Coll., Oxford, 1990–95; Prof. of Internat. Studies, Central European Univ., Budapest, 1994–97; Reader in Internat. Relns, LSE, 1995–99. Contested (L): Huddersfield West, 1970; Manchester Moss Side, Feb. and Oct. 1974; Shipley, 1983 and 1987. Vice-Chm., Liberal Party Policy Cttee, 1977–87. Editor, Jl of Common Market Studies, 1974–78. Hon. Dr, Free Univ. of Brussels, 1992. Ordre pour la Mérite (France), 1995. *Publications:* Foreign Policy and the Political Process, 1972; The Foreign Policy Process in Britain, 1977; (with Helen Wallace) Policy-making in the European Union, 1977, 4th edn 2000; (with Christopher Tugendhat) Options for British Foreign Policy in the 1990s, 1988; The Transformation of Western Europe, 1990; Regional Integration: the West European experience, 1994; Why vote Liberal Democrat?, 1997. *Address:* Department of International Relations, London School of Economics, Houghton Street, WC2A 2AD.

WALLACE OF SALTAIRE, Lady; *see* Wallace, H. S.

WALLACE, Albert Frederick, CBE 1963 (OBE 1955); DFC 1943; Controller of Manpower, Greater London Council, 1978–82; *b* 22 Aug. 1921; *s* of Major Frederick Wallace and Ada Wallace; *m* 1940, Evelyn M. White; one *s* one *d*. *Educ:* Roan School, Blackheath, SE3. MIPM, MIMgt, MILGA. Regular Officer, Royal Air Force, 1939–69: served war of 1939–45, with 40 Sqn, 93 Sqn, 214 Sqn, 620 Sqn; overseas service in Egypt (Canal Zone), S Rhodesia, India, Cyprus; sc 1944–45; NDC 1959–60; sowc 1963; retired in rank of Group Captain. Regional Advisory Officer, Local Authorities Management Services and Computer Cttee, 1969–71; Asst Clerk of the Council, Warwickshire CC, 1971–73; County Personnel Officer, W Midlands CC, and Dir, W Midlands PTA, 1973–78. *Recreations:* golf, bridge. *Address:* Flat 14, Kepplestone, Staveley Road, Eastbourne BN20 7JY. *T:* (01323) 730668. *Club:* Royal Air Force.

WALLACE, Angus; *see* Wallace, W. A.

WALLACE, Ben; *see* Wallace, R. B. L.

WALLACE, Charles William, CMG 1983; CVO 1975; HM Diplomatic Service, retired; *b* 19 Jan. 1926; *s* of Percival Francis and Julia Wallace; *m* 1957, Gloria Regina de Ros Ribas (*née* Sanz-Agero). *Educ:* privately and abroad. HM Foreign (later Diplomatic) Service, 1949; served: Asuncion; Barcelona; Bari; Bahrain; Tegucigalpa; Guatemala; Panama; Foreign Office; Baghdad; Buenos Aires; Montevideo; FO, later FCO, Asst Head of American Dept; Counsellor 1969; Rome and Milan; Mexico City; Ambassador: Paraguay, 1976–79; Peru, 1979–83; Uruguay, 1983–86. Freeman, City of London, 1981. *Publication:* The Valedictory, 1992. *Recreations:* sailing, fishing. *Address:* c/o Lloyds Private Banking, 50 Grosvenor Street, W1X 9FH.

WALLACE, Lt-Gen. Sir Christopher (Brooke Quentin), KBE 1997 (OBE 1983; MBE 1978); Commandant, Royal College of Defence Studies, since 2001; *b* 3 Jan. 1943; *s* of Major Robert Quentin Wallace, RA and Diana Pamela Wallace (*née* Galtrey); *m* 1969, Delicia Margaret Agnes Curtis; one *s* one *d*. *Educ:* Shrewsbury Sch.; RMA Sandhurst. Commissioned 1962; CO 3rd Bn Royal Green Jackets, 1983–85; Comdr, 7th Armd Brigade, 1986–88; Dir, Public Relations (Army), 1989–90; Comdr, 3rd Armd Div., 1990–93; Comdt, Staff Coll., Camberley, 1993–94; Perm. Jt HQ Implementation Team Leader, 1994–96; Chief of Jt Ops, Perm. Jt HQ (UK), Northwood, 1996–99. Rep. Col Comdt, Royal Green Jackets, 1995–98; Col Comdt, Light Div., 1998–99; Dep. Col Comdt, AGC, 1992–99. Pres., Army Golf Assoc., 1995–2000; Mem., RUSI Council, 1996–2000. Chm. Trustees, RGJ Mus., 1999–; Trustee, Imperial War Mus., 1999–. *Recreations:* golf, bird-watching, military history. *Address:* c/o RHQ The Royal Green Jackets, Peninsula Barracks, Winchester, Hants SO23 8TS. *Club:* Sunningdale Golf.

WALLACE, Prof. David James, CBE 1996; DL; PhD; FRS 1986; CEng, FREng, FInstP; FRSE; Vice-Chancellor, Loughborough University, since 1994; *b* 7 Oct. 1945; *s* of Robert Elder Wallace and Jane McConnell Wallace (*née* Elliot); *m* 1970, Elizabeth Anne Yeats; one *d*. *Educ:* Hawick High Sch.; Univ. of Edinburgh (BSc, PhD). FRSE 1982; FInstP 1991; FREng (FEng 1998). Harkness Fellow, Princeton Univ., 1970–72; Lecturer in Physics, 1972–78, Reader in Physics, 1978–79, Southampton Univ.; Tait Prof. of Mathematical Physics, 1979–93, Hd of Physics, 1984–87, Edinburgh Univ. Assoc. Dir, Res. Inst. on Pattern Recognition, RSRE, Malvern, 1986–90. Director: Edinburgh Concurrent Supercomputer, 1987–89; Edinburgh Parallel Computing Centre, 1990–93. Science and Engineering Research Council, subseq. Engineering and Physical Sciences Research Council: Chm., Physics Cttee, 1987–90; Chm., Science Bd, 1990–94; Mem. Council, 1990–98; Chm., Technical Opportunities Panel, 1994–98. European Commission: Mem., High Performance Computing and Networking Adv. Cttee, 1991–92; Physics Panel, Human Capital and Mobility Prog., 1991–94; Large Scale Facilities Evaluation Panel, 1995–97; European Sci. and Technol. Assembly, 1997–98. Chairman: CVCP/SCOP Task Force on sport in higher educn, 1995–97; Value for Money Steering Gp, HEFCE, 1997–; Member: Royal Soc. sci. and industl award Cttees, 1990–95; SHEFC, 1993–97; LINK Bd, OST, 1995–98; LINK/Teaching Co. Scheme Bd, 1999–. Non-executive Director: Scottish Life Insurance Co., 1999–2001; Taylor & Francis Gp plc, 2000–. Pres., Physics Sect., BAAS, 1994. FRSA. DL Leics, 2001. Maxwell Medal of Inst. of Physics, 1980. *Publications:* in research and review jls, in a number of areas of theoretical physics. *Recreations:* running, eating at La Potinière, mycophagy. *Address:* Loughborough University, Loughborough LE11 3TU. *T:* (01509) 222001.

WALLACE, (Dorothy) Jacqueline H.; *see* Hope-Wallace.

WALLACE, Fleming; *see* Wallace, J. F.

WALLACE, Graham Martyn, FCMA; Chief Executive, Cable and Wireless plc, since 1999; *b* 26 May 1948; *s* of Ronald and May Wallace; *m* 1974, Denise Margaret Wallace (*née* Dyer); one *s* one *d*. *Educ:* Imperial College, London (BSc Eng; ACGI). Graduate trainee, Turner & Newall, 1969–72; Co. Accountant, Brandhurst Co. Ltd, 1972–74; various finance and mgt posts, Rank Xerox, 1974–83; Planning Manager, Imperial Gp, 1983–85; Finance Dir, Imperial Leisure and Retailing, 1985–86; Head of Finance and Planning, 1986–89, Finance Dir, 1989–92, Granada Gp plc; Chief Executive: Granada UK Rental, 1992–95; Granada Restaurants and Services, 1995–97; Cable & Wireless Communications plc, 1997–99. Non-executive Director: Barclays PLC, 2001–; Barclays Bank PLC, 2001–. *Address:* Cable and Wireless plc, 124 Theobalds Road, WC1X 8RX. *T:* (020) 7315 4000.

WALLACE, Helen Richenda, (Mrs D. Papp); Editor, BBC Music Magazine, since 1999; *b* 19 Nov. 1966; *d* of Dr Ian Wallace and Richenda Ponsonby; *m* 2000, David Papp. *Educ:* St Peter's Coll., Oxford (MA English); Guildhall Sch. of Music and Drama (LGSM); London Coll. of Printing (Dip. Periodical Journalism). Features Ed., The Music Mag., 1991–92; Ed., The Strad, 1992–94; Dep. Ed., BBC Music Mag., 1994–99; Editor-in-Chief, South Bank mag., 2000–. *Address:* BBC Music Magazine, Woodlands, 80 Wood Lane, W12 0TT. *T:* (020) 8433 3283.

WALLACE, Prof. Helen Sarah, (Lady Wallace of Saltaire), CMG 2000; PhD; FBA 2000; Director, Robert Schuman Centre, European University Institute, since 2001; *b* 25 June 1946; *d* of Edward Rushworth and Joyce Rushworth; *m* 1968, William John Lawrence Wallace (*see* Baron Wallace of Saltaire); one *s* one *d*. *Educ:* St Anne's Coll., Oxford (MA Classics); Coll. of Europe, Bruges (Dip. Eur. Studies 1968); Univ. of Manchester (PhD 1975). Lectr, UMIST, 1974–78; Lectr, then Sen. Lectr, CS Coll., 1978–85 (on secondment to FCO, 1979–80); Dir, Eur. Programme, RIIA, 1985–92; Dir, 1992–98, Co-Dir, 1998–2001, Sussex European Inst. Dir, One Europe or Several? Programme, ESRC, 1998–2001. Serves on various editl and adv. bds, incl. Mem., Res. Council, Eur. Univ. Inst., Florence, 1999–. Chevalier, Ordre Nationale du Mérite (France), 1996. *Publications:* (ed jtly) Policy Making in the European Union, 1977, 4th edn 2000; (jtly) The Council of Ministers of the European Union, 1997; contrib. numerous articles on European integration. *Recreations:* gardening, travelling. *Address:* Robert Schuman Centre, European University Institute, Via dei Roccettini 9, 50016 San Domenico di Fiesole, Italy. *T:* (055) 4685 792.

WALLACE, Ian Alexander; JP; Headmaster, Canford School, 1961–76; *b* 5 Oct. 1917; *s* of late Very Rev. A. R. Wallace and Winifred, *d* of late Rev. H. C. Sturges; *m* 1947, Janet Glossop; two *s* two *d*. *Educ:* Clifton; Corpus Christi College, Cambridge (open scholar). Classical Tripos, Part I, 1st Cl.; Theological Tripos Part I, 2nd Cl. Div. One. Served War of 1939–45, Mountain Artillery, NW Frontier, India, 1941; School of Artillery, India, 1942–43; Arakan, 1944; Mandalay, 1945 (despatches). Rossall School: Assistant Master, 1946; Housemaster, 1951–61. SW Regional Sec., Independent Schools Careers Organisation, 1976–84; Project Manager for India, GAP Activity Projects, 1984–89; Wilts Regional Dir, HOST, 1992–95. Governor: Portsmouth Grammar Sch., 1977–89; King's Sch., Bruton, 1977–92. JP Poole Borough, 1966. *Address:* Steeple Close, Hindon, Salisbury, Wilts SP3 6DJ.

WALLACE, Ian Bryce, OBE 1983; Hon. RAM; Hon. RCM; singer, actor and broadcaster; *b* London, 10 July 1919; *o s* of late Sir John Wallace, Kirkcaldy, Fife (one-time MP for Dunfermline), and Mary Bryce Wallace (*née* Temple), Glasgow; *m* 1948, Patricia Gordon Black, Edenwood, Cupar, Fife; one *s* one *d*. *Educ:* Charterhouse; Trinity Hall, Cambridge (MA). Served War of 1939–45, (invalided from) RA, 1944. London stage debut in The Forrigan Reel, Sadler's Wells, 1945. Opera debut, as Schaunard, in La Bohème, with New London Opera Co., Cambridge Theatre, London, 1946. Sang principal roles for NLOC, 1946–49, incl. Dr Bartolo in Il Barbiere di Siviglia. Glyndebourne debut, Masetto, Don Giovanni, Edin. Fest., 1948. Regular appearances as principal *buffo* for Glyndebourne, both in Sussex and at Edin. Fest., 1948–61, incl. perfs as Don Magnifico in La Cenerentola, at Berlin Festwoche, 1954. Italian debut: Masetto, Don Giovanni, at Parma, 1950; also Don Magnifico, La Cenerentola, Rome, 1955, Dr Bartolo, Il Barbiere di Siviglia, Venice, 1956, and Bregenz Fest., 1964–65. Regular appearances for Scottish Opera, 1965–, incl. Leporello in Don Giovanni, Pistola in Falstaff, Duke of Plaza Toro in The Gondoliers. Don Pasquale, Welsh Nat. Opera, 1967, Dr Dulcamara, L'Elisir d'Amore, Glyndebourne Touring Opera, 1968. Devised, wrote and presented three series of adult education programmes on opera, entitled Singing For Your Supper, for Scottish Television (ITV), 1967–70. Recordings include: Gilbert and Sullivan Operas with Sir Malcolm Sargent, and humorous songs by Flanders and Swann. Theatrical career includes: a Royal Command Variety Perf., London Palladium, 1952; Cesar in Fanny, Theatre Royal, Drury Lane, 1956; 4 to the Bar, Criterion, 1960; Toad in Toad of Toad Hall, Queen's, 1964. Regular broadcaster, 1944–: radio and TV, as singer, actor and compere; a regular panellist on radio musical quiz game, My Music; acted in series, Porterhouse Blue, Channel 4 TV, 1987. President: ISM, 1979–80; Council for Music in Hosps, 1987–99. Hon. DMus St Andrews, 1991. Sir Charles Santley Meml Award, Musicians' Co., 1984. *Publications:* Promise Me You'll Sing Mud (autobiog.), 1975; Nothing Quite Like It (autobiog.), 1982; Reflections on Scotland, 1988. *Recreations:* walking, reading, sport watching, going to the theatre, singing a song about a hippopotamus to children of all ages. *Address:* c/o Peters, Fraser & Dunlop, Drury House, 34–43 Russell Street, WC2B 5HA. *T:* (020) 7344 1010. *Clubs:* Garrick, MCC; Stage Golfing Society.

WALLACE, Sir Ian (James), Kt 1982; CBE 1971 (OBE (mil.) 1942); Director, Coventry Motor and Sundries Co. Ltd, 1986–92; Chairman, SNR Bearings (UK) Ltd, 1975–85; *b* 25 Feb. 1916; *s* of John Madder Wallace, CBE; *m* 1942, Catherine Frost Mitchell, *e d* of Cleveland S. Mitchell; one *s* (one *d* decd). *Educ:* Uppingham Sch.; Jesus Coll., Cambridge (BA). Underwriting at Lloyd's, 1935–39. War Service, Fleet Air Arm: Cmdr (A) RNVR, 1939–46. Harry Ferguson Ltd from 1947: Dir 1950; later Massey Ferguson Ltd, Dir Holdings Board until 1970. Coventry Conservative Association: Treas., 1956–68; Chm., 1968–88; Pres., 1988–92; Pres., S Worcs Cons. Assoc., 1992–96; Life Pres., Mid Worcs Cons. Assoc., 1996–; Chm., W Midlands Cons. Council, 1967–70 (Treas., 1962–67); Pres., W Midlands Area Cons. Council. Member: Severn-Trent Water Authority, 1974–82; W Midlands Econ. Planning Council, 1965–75; Vice-Chm., Midland Regional Council, CBI, 1964, Chm., 1967–69; President: Coventry Chamber of Commerce, 1972–74; Birmingham and Midland Inst., 1992–93. Pres., Hereford and Worcester (formerly Worcs County) Rifle Assoc., 1983–. *Recreations:* rifle shooting, horology. *Address:* Little House, 156 High Street, Broadway, Worcs WR12 7AJ. *T:* (01386) 852414. *Clubs:* Carlton, North London Rifle.

WALLACE, Ian Norman Duncan; QC 1973; *b* 21 April 1922; *s* of late Duncan Gardner Wallace, HBM Crown Advocate in Egypt, Paymaster-Comdr RNR and Eileen Agnes Wallace. *Educ:* Loretto; Oriel Coll., Oxford (MA). Served War of 1939–45: Ordinary Seaman RN, 1940; Lieut RNVR, 1941–46. Called to Bar, Middle Temple, 1948; Western Circuit, 1949. Vis. Scholar, Berkeley Univ., Calif, 1977–; Vis. Prof., Centre of Construction Law and Management, KCL, 1987–. Mem. Editl Bd, Construction Law Jl, 1984–. *Publications:* (ed) Hudson on Building and Civil Engineering Contracts, 8th edn 1959, to 11th edn 1995; Building and Civil Engineering Standard Forms, 1969; Further Building and Engineering Standard Forms, 1973; The International Civil Engineering Contract, 1974, supplement 1980; The ICE Conditions (5th edn), 1978; Construction Contracts: principles and policies in Tort and Contract, vol. I 1986, vol. II 1996; draftsman, Singapore Institute of Architects Forms of Contract, 1980, and subseq. revisions; contrib. Law Qly Review, Jl of Internat. Law and Commerce, Construction Law Jl, Internat. Construction Law Rev., Arbitration Internat. *Recreations:* shooting, keeping fit, foreign travel. *Address:* 53 Holland Park, W11 3RS. *T:* (020) 7727 7640. *Clubs:* Lansdowne, Hurlingham.

WALLACE, Ivan Harold Nutt, CB 1991; Senior Chief Inspector, Department of Education, Northern Ireland, 1979–95; *b* 20 Feb. 1935; *s* of late Harold Wallace and Annie McClure Wallace; *m* 1962, Winifred Ervine Armstrong; two *d*. *Educ:* Grosvenor High Sch., Belfast; QUB (BSc 1957). MRSC 1963. School Teacher: Leeds Central High Sch., 1957–60; Foyle Coll., Londonderry, 1960–69; Inspector of Schools, NI, 1969–75; Sen. Inspector, 1975–77; Staff Inspector, 1977–78; Chief Inspector, 1978–79. Hon. Prof., Sch. of Educn, QUB, 1996–2001. *Recreations:* music, walking, bell-ringing. *Address:* 25 Tudor Oaks, Holywood, Co. Down, N Ireland BT18 0PA.

WALLACE, (James) Fleming; QC (Scot) 1985; Counsel to Scottish Law Commission, 1979–93; *b* 19 March 1931; *s* of James F. B. Wallace, SSC and Margaret B. Gray, MA; *m* 1st, 1964, Valerie Mary (*d* 1986), *d* of Leslie Lawrence, solicitor, and Madge Lawrence, Ramsbury, Wilts; two *d*; 2nd, 1990, Linda Ann, solicitor, *d* of Robert Grant, civil engineer, and Alice Grant. *Educ:* Edinburgh Academy; Edinburgh University (MA 1951; LLB 1954). Served RA, 1954–56 (2nd Lieut); TA 1956–60. Admitted Faculty of Advocates, 1957; practised at Scottish Bar until 1960; Parly Draftsman and Legal Secretary, Lord Advocate's Dept, London, 1960–79. Part-time Chm., Industrial Tribunals, Scotland, 1993–2001. Volunteer, CAB, 2001–. *Publication:* The Businessman's Lawyer (Scottish Section), 1965, 2nd edn 1973. *Recreations:* hill walking, choral singing, golf. *Address:* 24 Corrennie Gardens, Edinburgh EH10 6DB.

WALLACE, Rt Hon. James (Robert); PC 2000; QC (Scot.) 1997; Member (Lib Dem) Orkney, Scottish Parliament, since 1999; Deputy First Minister of the Scottish Executive and Minister of Justice, since 1999; *b* 25 Aug. 1954; *s* of John F. T. Wallace and Grace Hannah Wallace (*née* Maxwell); *m* 1983, Rosemary Janet Fraser; two *d*. *Educ:* Annan Academy; Downing College, Cambridge (BA 1975, MA 1979); Edinburgh University (LLB 1977). Chm., Edinburgh Univ. Liberal Club, 1976–77. Called to the Scots Bar, 1979; practised as Advocate, 1979–83. Contested Dumfriesshire (L), 1979; contested South of Scotland (L), European Parlt election, 1979. Mem., Scottish Liberal Exec., 1976–85; Vice-Chm. (Policy), Scottish Liberal Party, 1982–85; Hon. Pres., Scottish Young Liberals, 1984–85; Leader, Scottish Liberal Democrats, 1992–. MP Orkney and Shetland, 1983–2001 (L 1983–88, Lib Dem 1988–2001). Liberal spokesman on defence, 1985–87; Deputy Whip, 1985–87, Chief Whip, 1987–88; first Lib Dem Chief Whip, 1988–92; Alliance spokesman on Transport, 1987; Lib Dem spokesman on employment and training, 1988–92, on fisheries, 1988–97, on Scottish affairs, 1992–, on maritime affairs, 1994–97. *Recreations:* golf, music, travel. *Address:* Northwood House, Tankerness, Orkney KW17 2QS. *T:* (01856) 861383; *e-mail:* jim.wallace.msp@scotland.parliament.uk. *Clubs:* Caledonian; Scottish Liberal (Edinburgh).

WALLACE, Prof. James Stuart, PhD; Deputy Director, and Director of Hydrology, NERC Centre for Ecology & Hydrology, since 2000; *b* 20 June 1952; *s* of Joseph Wallace and Anne Wallace (*née* Keenan); *m* 1974, Josephine Marie Richardson; one *s* three *d*. *Educ:* Lisburn Tech. Coll.; Queen's Univ., Belfast (BSc 1973); Univ. of Nottingham (PhD 1978). NERC Institute of Hydrology: Envmtl Physicist, 1978–; Head: Vegetation Water Use Section, 1989–93; Hydrological Processes Div., 1993–96; Dir, 1996–2000. Vis. Prof. in Hydrology, Univ. of Reading, 1997–. Consultant to UNDP Global Envmt Facility, 1995; Hydrological Advr to UK Perm. Rep. to WMO, 1999. Chairman: Jt UNESCO/WMO Task Force for Hydrology for Envmt, Life and Policy initiative, 1999–; UK Inter-Deptl Cttee on Hydrology, 2000–. Vice-Pres., Internat. Cttee on Atmosphere-Soil-Vegetation Relns, 1996. *Publications:* (ed jtly) Soil Water Balance in the Sudano-Sahelian Zone, 1991; papers on hydrological processes in Qly Jl RMetS, Proc. Royal Soc., Agric. and Forest Meteorology, etc. *Recreations:* gardening, golf, motorcycling with Gromit. *Address:* Centre for Ecology & Hydrology, Maclean Building, Crowmarsh Gifford, Wallingford, Oxon OX10 8BB. *T:* (01491) 838800; *e-mail:* jsw@ceh.ac.uk.

WALLACE, Hon. Sir John (Hamilton), KNZM 1997; Judge of the High Court of New Zealand, 1982–96; *b* 9 Sept. 1934; *s* of G. H. and C. I. Wallace; *m* 1961, Elizabeth Ann Goodwin; one *s* one *d*. *Educ:* King's Coll., Auckland; Auckland Univ.; Merton Coll., Oxford (MA 1958). Called to the Bar, Gray's Inn, 1958; admitted as Barrister and Solicitor, NZ, 1959; QC 1974. Chairman: Equal Opportunities Tribunal, 1978–82; Human Rights Commn, 1984–89; Royal Commn on the Electoral System, 1985–86; Pres., Electoral Commn, 1994–96; Dep. Pres., Law Commn, 1991–96; Member: Contracts and Commercial Law Reform Cttee, 1974–85; Royal Commn on the Courts, 1976–78. Pres., Auckland Law Soc., 1980–81; Vice Pres., NZ Law Soc., 1981–82. Fellow, Internat. Acad. of Trial Lawyers, 1981. *Recreations:* golf, walking. *Club:* Auckland.

WALLACE, John Malcolm Agnew; JP; Vice Lord-Lieutenant, Dumfries and Galloway (District of Wigtown), since 1990; *b* 30 Jan. 1928; *s* of John Alexander Agnew Wallace and Marjory Murray Wallace; *m* 1955, Louise Haworth-Booth; one *s* two *d*. *Educ:* Brooks Sch., USA; Harrow; West of Scotland Agricultural College. Farmer. JP Stranraer, 1970; DL Dumfries and Galloway, 1971. *Address:* Lochryan, Stranraer DG9 8QY. *T:* (01581) 200284.

WALLACE, John Williamson, OBE 1995; Pirincipal, Royal Scottish Academy of Music and Drama, since 2002; freelance soloist, composer, conductor; *b* 14 April 1949; *s* of Christopher Kidd Wallace and Ann Drummond Allan; *m* 1971, Elizabeth Jane Hartwell; one *s* one *d*. *Educ:* Buckhaven High Sch.; King's Coll., Cambridge (MA); York Univ.; Royal Acad. of Music (ARAM 1983; FRAM 1990). ARCM 1968; FRSAMD 1993; Hon. RCM 1985. Asst Principal Trumpet, LSO, 1974–76; Prin. Trumpet, Philharmonia Orch., 1976–94; founded The Wallace Collection (brass-interest music gp), 1986; Principal Trumpet, London Sinfonietta, 1987–2001; Artistic Dir of Brass, RAM, 1993–2001. Trumpet solo recordings. Mercedes-Benz Prize, 1991. *Publications:* Five Easy Pieces, 1984; First Book of Trumpet Solos, 1985; Second Book of Trumpet Solos, 1985, 2nd edn 1987; Grieg's Seven Lyric Pieces, 1985; Kornukopia, 1986; Prime Number, 1990; Odd Number and Even Number, 1991; (jtly) Music Through Time, 1995; (ed jtly) Cambridge Companion to Brass Instruments, 1997. *Address:* Royal Scottish Academy of Music and Drama, 100 Renfrew Street, Glasgow G2 3DB.

WALLACE, Lawrence James, OC 1972, CVO 1983; OBC 1990; Deputy Minister to the Premier of British Columbia, 1980–81; *b* Victoria, BC, Canada, 24 April 1913; *s* of John Wallace and Mary Wallace (*née* Parker); *m* 1942, Lois Leeming; three *d*. *Educ:* Univ. of British Columbia (BA); Univ. of Washington, USA (MEd). Served War, Lt-Comdr, Royal Canadian Navy Voluntary Reserve, 1941–45. Joined British Columbia Govt, as Dir of Community Programmes and Adult Educn, 1953; Dep. Provincial Sec., 1959–77, Dep. to Premier, 1969–72; Agent-General for British Columbia in UK and Europe, 1977–80. General Chairman: four centennial celebrations, marking founding of Crown Colony of British Columbia in 1858, union of Crown Colonies of Vancouver Is. and British Columbia, 1866, Canadian Confedn, 1867, and joining into confedn by British Columbia in 1871. Former Dir, Provincial Capital Commn; Vice Chm., BC Press Council; Past Chm., Inter-Provincial Lottery Corp., Queen Elizabeth II Schol. Cttee, and Nancy Green Schol. Cttee; Hon. Trustee, British Columbia Sports Hall of Fame. Director: Sen. Citizens Lottery; BC Forest Museum; Adv. Bd, Salvation Army; Canadian Council of Christians and Jews; President: Duke of Edinburgh Awards Cttee, BC; McPherson Playhouse Foundn; Hon. Pres., Univ of Victoria Alumni; Hon. Co-Chm., Operation Eye Sight, BC; Chm., Historic Royal Theatre Renovations and Restoration; Hon. Member: BC High Sch. Basketball Assoc.; BC Recreation Assoc.; Hon. Life Mem., BC Legislative Press Gallery, 1984. Freeman of City of London, 1978. Hon. LLD: British Columbia, 1978; Royal Roads Military Coll., 1994. Named British Columbia Man of the Year, 1958, and Greater Vancouver Man of the Year, 1967; Canadian Centennial Medal, 1967; Comdr Brother, OStJ, 1969; City of Victoria Citizenship Award, 1971; Silver Jubilee Medal, 1977; 125 Confederation Medal; Good Servant Award, Canadian Council of Christians and Jews, 1980; Peakes Meml Citizenship Award, 1991. Hon. Chief: Alberni, Gilford and Southern Vancouver Is Indian Bands. *Recreations:* gardening, community activities. *Address:* 1345 Fairfield Road, Victoria, BC V8S 1E4, Canada.

WALLACE, Major Malcolm Charles Robarts; Director of Regulation, Jockey Club, since 1994; *b* 12 June 1947; *s* of Lionel John Wallace and Maureen Winefride (*née* Robarts); *m* 1st, 1974, Caroline Anne Doyne-Ditmas (marr. diss. 1990); one *s* one *d*; 2nd, 1991, Mrs Jane Thelwall; two *s*. *Educ:* Blackrock College, Co. Dublin. Student pupil with Lt-Col J. Hume-Dudgeon at Burton Hall, Co. Dublin, 1965–67; Mons Officer Cadet Sch.; commissioned RA, 1967; gun line officer, 18 Light Regt, Hong Kong; 3rd Regt RHA, 1969; King's Troop RHA, 1970 (long equitation course, RAVC Melton Mowbray); Troop Comdr, 19 Field Regt, 1974; Adjutant 101 Northumbrian Field Artillery, 1976; Staff Officer, HQ UKLF, 1978–82; Comd King's Troop RHA, 1982–85, retired. Dir Gen., BEF, 1985–94. Chef d'Equipe to British Internat. and Olympic Three Day Event Teams, 1979–84; Chef de Mission, Equestrian Team, Olympic Games, Seoul, 1988 and Barcelona, 1992. Freeman, Saddlers' Co., 1985. *Publication:* The King's Troop Royal Horse Artillery, 1984. *Recreations:* field and equestrian sports, golf, gardening. *Address:* Fishponds Farm, Stoke Albany, Market Harborough LE16 8PZ. *T:* (01858) 535250, *Fax:* (01858) 535499. *Club:* Cavalry and Guards.

WALLACE, Marjorie Shiona, MBE 1994; Founder, and Chief Executive, SANE, mental health charity, since 1989; broadcaster, author, journalist; *d* of William Wallace and Doris Tulloch; *m* Count Andrzej Skarbek; three *s* one *d*. *Educ:* Rodeane; Johannesburg; Parsons' Mead, Ashtead; University College London (BA Hons Psych and Phil). Television: The Frost Programme, 1966–68; ITV religious programmes, 1966–68; LWT current affairs, 1968–69; Dir/reporter, current affairs, BBC TV, 1969–72; Insight team (thalidomide campaign), feature writer, Sunday Times, 1972–89, incl. Forgotten Illness (Schizophrenia) campaign, The Times, 1985–89; Guardian Res. Fellow, Nuffield Coll., Oxford, 1989–91. Estabd SANELINE, and Prince of Wales Internat. Res. Centre, Oxford. Institute of Psychiatry: Member: Cttee of Management, 1989–; Ethics Cttee (Res.), 1991–; Schiz. Adv. Panel, 1991–. Chm., Friends of Open Air Theatre, 1991–. Numerous internat. presentations and speeches, also broadcasts on TV and radio; TV documentaries: Whose Mind Is It?, 1988; Circles of Madness, 1994. Campaigning Journalist of the Year, British Press Awards, 1982, 1986; John Pringle Meml Award, 1986; Oddfellows Book Trust Prize, 1987; Snowdon Special Award, 1988; Medical Journalist of the Year, 1988; Evian Health Award, 1991, and Best Use of Media award, 1995. *Publications:* (jtly) On Giant's Shoulders, 1976 (also original TV screenplay (Internat. Emmy award), 1979); (jtly) Suffer the Children: the story of Thalidomide, 1978; (jtly) The Superpoison, The Dioxin Disaster, 1980; The Silent Twins, 1986 (also TV screenplay); Campaign and Be Damned, 1991. *Recreations:* poetry, music, piano, Victorian ballads, opera, dining out. *Address:* SANE, Cityside House, 40 Adler Street, E1 1EE. *T:* (020) 7375 1002; 26 Bisham Gardens, N6 6DD. *T:* (020) 8341 0435. *Club:* Groucho.

WALLACE, Ven. Martin William; Archdeacon of Colchester, since 1997; *b* 16 Nov. 1948; *s* of Derek Philip William and Audrey Sybil Wallace; *m* 1971, Diana Christine Wallace; one *s* one *d*. *Educ:* Varndean Grammar Sch., Brighton; Tauntons Sch., Southampton; King's Coll., London (BD (Hons); AKC; Winchester Schol.); St Augustine's Theol Coll., Canterbury. Ordained deacon, 1971, priest, 1972; Assistant Curate: Attercliffe, Sheffield, 1971–74; New Malden, Surrey, 1974–77; Vicar, St Mark's, Forest Gate, 1977–93 and Priest-in-charge, Emmanuel, 1985–89, All Saints, 1991–93, Forest Gate; Chaplain, Forest Gate Hosp., 1977–80; Rural Dean, Newham, 1982–91; Chelmsford Diocesan Urban Officer, 1991–93; Priest-in-charge, Bradwell and St Lawrence, 1993–97; Industrial Chaplain, Maldon and Dengie, 1993–97. Hon. Canon, Chelmsford Cathedral, 1989–97. *Publications:* Healing Encounters in the City, 1987; City Prayers, 1994; Pocket Celtic Prayers, 1996; Celtic Resource Book, 1998. *Recreations:* local history, gardening, Celtic culture. *Address:* 63 Powers Hall End, Witham, Essex CM8 1NH. *T:* (01376) 513130.

WALLACE, Moira Paul, OBE 1997; Director, Social Exclusion Unit, Cabinet Office (on secondment), since 1997; *b* 15 Aug. 1961; *d* of Prof. and Mrs W. V. Wallace. *Educ:* Coleraine High Sch.; Emmanuel Coll., Cambridge (MA Mod. Langs 1983); Harvard Univ. (Kennedy Schol.; AM Comparative Lit. 1985). HM Treasury, 1985–: Private Sec. to Chancellor of Exchequer, 1987–90; Grade 5, 1995; Econ. Affairs Private Sec. to Prime Minister, 1995–97; Grade 3, 1998. Vis. Fellow, Nuffield Coll., Oxford, 1999–. *Address:* Social Exclusion Unit, Cabinet Office, 35 Great Smith Street, SW1P 3BQ. *T:* (020) 7276 2081.

WALLACE, Reginald James, CMG 1979; OBE 1961; Chairman, Abbey National Gibraltar Ltd, 1987–2000; *b* 16 Aug. 1919; *s* of James Wallace and Doris (*née* Welch); *m* 1st, 1943, Doris Barbara Brown, MD, FRCS, MRCOG (decd); one *d*; 2nd, 1973, Maureen Coady (*d* 1983); 3rd, 1983, Marilyn Ryan (*née* Gareze); one *d*. *Educ:* John Gulson Sch., Coventry; Tatterford Sch., Norfolk; Leeds Univ. (BA); Queen's Coll., Oxford. Served War, 1939–46, 7th Rajput Regt, Indian Army (Major). Gold Coast/Ghana Admin. Service, 1947–58; Sen. District Comr, 1955; Asst Chief Regional Officer, Northern Region, 1957; Regional Sec., 1958; Financial Sec., British Somaliland, 1958–60; War Office, 1961–66; HM Treasury, 1966–78; seconded to Solomon Is, as Financial Sec. (later Financial Adviser), 1973–76; seconded, as British Mem., Anglo/French Mission on Admin. Reform in the Condominium of the New Hebrides, 1977; Governor of Gilbert Is, 1978 to Independence, July 1979; Financial and Develt Sec., Gibraltar, 1979–83. Chm., Norwich Union Fire Insurance Soc. (Gibraltar) Ltd, 1984–99. *Recreations:* walking, music. *Club:* Royal Commonwealth Society.

WALLACE, Richard Alexander; Principal Finance Officer, Welsh Office, 1990–97; *b* 24 Nov. 1946; *s* of Lawrence Mervyn and late Norah Wallace; *m* 1970, Teresa Caroline Harington Smith; three *c* (and one *c* decd). *Educ:* Bembridge and Sandown C of E Primary Schools; Clifton Coll. Prep. Sch.; Clifton Coll.; King's Coll., Cambridge (MA). Asst Master, Woking County GS for Boys, 1967; Min. of Social Security, 1968; Principal, DHSS, 1972, Asst Sec., 1981; transf. to Welsh Office, 1986; Under Sec., 1988.

WALLACE, (Robert) Ben (Lobban); Member (C) North East Scotland, Scottish Parliament, since 1999; *b* 15 May 1970. *Educ:* Millfield Sch., Somerset; RMA Sandhurst. Ski Instructor, Austrian Nat. Ski Sch., 1987–89; commissioned, Scots Guards, 1991; Platoon Comdr, 1991–93 (despatches, 1992); Ops Officer, 1993, Intelligence, 1994–97; Co. Comdr, 1997; served N Ireland, Central America, BAOR, Egypt, Cyprus; retired 1999. *Recreations:* ski-ing, sailing, Rugby, horse racing. *Address:* Scottish Parliament, Edinburgh EH99 1SP. *T:* (0131) 348 5651. *Clubs:* Cavalry and Guards; Royal Perth Golfing.

WALLACE, Theodore; *see* Wallace, W. T. O.

WALLACE, Walter Wilkinson, CVO 1977; CBE 1973 (OBE 1964); DSC 1944; Foreign and Commonwealth Office, 1980–99; *b* 23 Sept. 1923; *s* of late Walter Wallace and Helen Wallace (*née* Douglas); *m* 1955, Susan Blanche, *d* of Brig. F. W. B. Parry, CBE; one *s* one *d*. *Educ:* George Heriot's, Edinburgh. Served War, Royal Marines, 1942–46 (Captain). Joined Colonial Service, 1946; Asst Dist Comr, Sierra Leone, 1948; Dist Comr, 1954; seconded to Colonial Office, 1955–57; Sen. Dist Comr, 1961; Provincial Comr, 1961; Develt Sec., 1962–64; Estabt Sec., Bahamas, 1964–67; Sec. to Cabinet, Bermuda, 1968–73; HM Commissioner, Anguilla, 1973; Governor, British Virgin Islands, 1974–78. Constitutional Comr, St Helena, 1987, Cayman Islands, 1991, Turks and Caicos Is, 1992, British Virgin Islands, 1993, Falkland Islands, 1995. *Recreation:* golf. *Address:* Becketts, Itchenor, Sussex PO20 7DE. *T:* (01243) 512438. *Club:* Army and Navy.

WALLACE, (Wellesley) Theodore (Octavius); Chairman, VAT and Duties (formerly VAT) Tribunal, since 1989 (part-time, 1989–92); Special Commissioner of Income Tax, since 1992; *b* 10 April 1938; *s* of late Dr Caleb Paul Wallace and Dr Lucy Elizabeth Rainsford (*née* Pigott); *m* 1988, Maria Amelia Abercromby, *d* of Sir Ian Abercromby, Bt, *qv*; one *s* one *d*. *Educ:* Charterhouse; Christ Church, Oxford. 2nd Lt, RA, 1958; Lt, Surrey Yeomanry, TA, 1959–62. Called to the Bar, Inner Temple, 1963. Mem., Lincoln's Inn (*ad eundem*), 1973. Hon. Sec., Taxation of Sub-cttee, Soc. of Cons. Lawyers, 1974–92. Trustee, Trinity Fields Trust, Wandsworth. Contested (C): Pontypool, Feb. 1974; S Battersea, Oct. 1974, 1979. *Publication:* (jtly with John Wakeham) The Case Against Wealth Tax, 1968. *Recreations:* lawn tennis, ski-ing, golf. *Address:* 46 Belleville Road, SW11 6QT. *T:* (020) 7228 7740; Whitecroft, W Clandon, Surrey GU4 7TD. *T:* (01483) 222574.

WALLACE, Prof. (William) Angus, FRCS, FRCSE; Professor of Orthopaedic and Accident Surgery, School of Medical and Surgical Sciences, University of Nottingham, since 1985; *b* 31 Oct. 1948; *s* of late Dr William Bethune Wallace and Dr Frances Barret Wallace (*née* Early), Dundee; *m* 1971, Jacqueline Vera Studley; two *s* one *d*. *Educ:* Dundee High Sch.; Univ. of St Andrews (MB ChB 1972); FRCSE 1977; Cert. of Orthopaedic Higher Specialist Trng 1984; FRCSE (Orth) 1985; FRCS 1997. Jun. House Officer, Dundee Royal Infirmary and Maryfield Hosp., 1972–73; Sen. House Officer, Derby, 1974–75; Registrar (Basic Surg. Trng), Newcastle and Gateshead Hosps, 1975–77;

Orthopaedic Registrar, Nottingham Hosps, 1978–81; MRC Res. Fellow, 1979; Lectr (Hon. Sen. Registrar) in Orthopaedic Surgery, Univ. of Nottingham, 1981–84; Vis. Res. Fellow, Toronto Western Hosp., Canada, 1983; Med. Dir, North Western Orthotic Unit, and Med. Advr, Dept of Orthopaedic Mechanics, Univ. of Salford, 1984–85. Mem., ABC Club, 1988–. Member: RSocMed 1988; Council, RCSE, 1990–2000 (Vice-Pres., 1997–2000); Dean, Faculty of Medical Informatics, RSCE, 2000–. Chm., Nat. Sports Medicine Inst. of UK, 1999–. Sir Walter Mercer Gold Medal, RCSE, 1985; Weigelt-Wallace Award for exceptional med. care, Univ. of Texas, 1995; Great Scot Sci. and Medicine Award, Sunday Mail, Scotland, 1995; People of the Year Award, RADAR, 1995. *Publications:* Shoulder Arthroscopy, 1992; Management of Disasters and their Aftermath, 1994; Joint Replacement of the Shoulder and Elbow, 1998; A Handbook of Sports Medicine, 1999; numerous articles in learned jls on osteoporosis, shoulder surgery and sports medicine. *Recreations:* narrow boating, information technology, DIY. *Address:* High Trees, Foxwood Lane, Woodborough, Nottingham NG14 6ED. *T:* (0115) 965 2372, *Fax:* (0115) 965 4638; *e-mail:* Angus.Wallace@rcsed.ac.uk.

WALLACE-HADRILL, Prof. Andrew Frederic, DPhil; Director, British School at Rome, since 1995; Professor of Classics, University of Reading, since 1987 (on leave of absence); *b* 29 July 1951; *s* of John Michael Wallace-Hadrill and Anne (*née* Wakefield); *m* 1976, Josephine Claire Braddock; one *s* one *d.* *Educ:* Rugby Sch.; Corpus Christi Coll., Oxford (MA); St John's Coll., Oxford (DPhil). Fellow and Dir of Studies in Classics, Magdalene Coll., Cambridge, 1976–83; Lectr in Ancient History, Univ. of Leicester, 1983–87; Head, Dept of Classics, Reading Univ., 1988–94. Editor, Jl of Roman Studies, 1991–95. *Publications:* Suetonius: the scholar and his Caesars, 1983, 2nd edn 1995; (ed) Patronage in Ancient Society, 1989; (ed with J. W. Rich) City and Country in the Ancient World, 1991; Augustan Rome, 1993; Houses and Society in Pompeii and Herculaneum, 1994; (ed with R. Laurence) Domestic Space in the Roman World: Pompeii and beyond, 1997. *Address:* The British School at Rome, via Gramsci 61, Rome, Italy.

WALLEN, Ella Kathleen, MA (Oxon); Headmistress, St Mary's School, Wantage, 1977–80; *b* 15 Feb. 1914. *Educ:* Camden School for Girls; St Hugh's College, Oxford. History Mistress, Queen Victoria High School, Stockton-on-Tees, 1937–41; Senior History Mistress, High School for Girls, Gloucester, 1942–59; Headmistress: Queen Victoria High School, Stockton-on Tees, 1959–65; Bedford High Sch., 1965–76. *Address:* 10 Dove House Close, Upper Wolvercote, Oxford OX2 8BG.

WALLENBERG, Jacob; Chairman of the Board, Skandinaviska Enskilda Banken, since 1998; *b* 13 Jan. 1956; *s* of Peter Wallenberg, *qv* and Suzanne Fleming; *m* Marie Wehtje; one *s* two *d.* *Educ:* Univ. of Pennsylvania (BSc Econ 1980; MBA 1981). Joined J. P. Morgan, NY, 1981; Hambros Bank, London, 1983; Enskilda Securities, London, 1984, then with Skandinaviska Enskilda Banken, Sweden; Dep. Man. Dir, Investor, 1990–92; rejoined Skandinaviska Enskilda Bank Gp, 1993; Dep. Chief Operating Officer, 1994, Chief Operating Officer, 1995–97, Enskilda Div.; Pres. and CEO, Skandinaviska Enskilda Banken, 1997. *Recreations:* golf, sailing, downhill ski-ing, shooting. *Address:* Skandinaviska Enskilda Banken, PO Box 16067, 10322 Stockholm, Sweden. *T:* (8) 221900.

WALLENBERG, Marcus; President and Chief Executive Officer, Investor AB, since 1999; *b* 2 Sept. 1956; *s* of Marc and Olga Wallenberg; *m* Fanny Sachs; four *c.* *Educ:* Georgetown Univ., Washington (BSc Foreign Service). Lieut, Royal Swedish Naval Acad., 1977. Citibank NA, New York, 1980–82; Deutsche Bank AG, Frankfurt and Hamburg, 1983; S. G. Warburg Co. Ltd, London, 1983; Citicorp, Hong Kong, 1984; Skandinaviska Enskilda Banken, Stockholm and London, 1985–90; Dir, Stora Feldmuhle AG, Dusseldorf, 1990–93; Exec. Vice Pres., Investor AB, 1993–99. Vice Chairman: L. M. Ericsson; Saab AB. Holds numerous directorships. *Recreations:* sports, tennis, sailing, ski-ing, hunting. *Address:* Investor AB, Arsenalsgatan 8C, 10332 Stockholm, Sweden. *T:* (8) 6142000.

WALLENBERG, Peter, Order of Wasa, 1974; King's Medal 12th Class, 1983; Hon. KBE 1989; First Vice Chairman, Skandinaviska Enskilda Banken, 1984–96 (Vice Chairman, 1980–84); Chairman: Investor AB, 1982–97; Wallenberg Foundation, since 1982; *b* Stockholm, 26 May 1926; *s* of Marcus Wallenberg and Dorothy (*née* Mackay); *m* (marr. diss.); two *s* one *d.* *Educ:* Stockholm Univ. (LLB 1953). Various positions within Atlas Copco Gp, 1953–68; Man. Dir, Atlas Copco MCT AB, 1968–70; Dep. Man. Dir, Atlas Copco AB, 1970–74; Industrial Advr to Skandinaviska Enskilda Banken, 1974–80. Mem. Bd, Stockholm Sch. of Econs, 1976–. Pres., ICC, 1989–90. Hon. Dr: Stockholm Sch. of Econ., 1984; Augustana Coll., Ill, 1985; Upsala Coll., NJ, 1989; Georgetown, Wash, 1990. Seraphime Medal, 2000. Orden de Isabel la Católica (Spain), 1979; Comdr, Légion d'Honneur (France), 1987; Comdr 1st Cl. Order of Lion of Finland, 1988; Comdr l'Ordre de Léopold (Belgium), 1989; Grand Cross, Ordem do Merito e Industrial (Portugal), 1990; Grand Cross, Order of Gregorius the Great (Vatican), 1991; Comdr 1st Cl., Royal Norwegian Order of Merit, 1992. *Recreations:* hunting, sailing, tennis. *Address:* Investor AB, 103 32 Stockholm, Sweden.

See also J. Wallenberg.

WALLER, Gary Peter Anthony; *b* 24 June 1945; *s* of late John Waller and of Elizabeth Waller. *Educ:* Rugby Sch.; Univ. of Lancaster (BA Hons). Chairman: Lancaster Univ. Conservative Assoc., 1965; Spen Valley Civic Soc., 1978–80; Vice-Chm., Nat. Assoc. of Cons. Graduates, 1970–73 and 1976–77. Member: Exec. Cttee, Cons. Nat. Union, 1976–77; Management Cttee, Bradford and Dist Housing Assoc., 1976–90. Exec. Sec., Wider Share Ownership Council, 1973–76. Contested (C): Kensington, Bor. Council elecns, 1971, 1974; Leyton, GLC elecn, 1973; Rother Valley, parly elecn, Feb. and Oct. 1974. MP (C) Brighouse and Spenborough, 1979–83, Keighley, 1983–97; contested (C) Keighley, 1997. PPS to Sec. of State for Transport, 1982–83. Chm., Select Cttee on Information, 1992–97 (Mem., 1991–97); Member: H of C Select Cttee on Transport, 1979–82; Jt Cttee on Consolidation Bills, 1982–92; Select Cttee on Finance and Services, 1992–97; Chm., All Party Wool Textile Gp, 1984–89 (Sec., 1979–83); Vice-Chairman: Parly Food and Health Forum, 1985–97; Parly IT Cttee, 1987–97 (Treas., 1981–87); Cons. Parly Transport Cttee, 1992–94, 1996–97 (Sec., 1985–87, 1988–92); Secretary: Cons. Parly Sport and Recreation Cttee, 1979–81; Yorkshire Cons. Members, 1979–83; All-Party Rugby League Gp, 1989–97; Hon. Secretary: Parly and Scientific Cttee, 1988–91; Parly Univs Gp, 1995–97. Mem. Council, Consumers' Assoc., 1995–; Pres., Brighouse Citizens Advice Bureau, 1979–83; Vice-Pres., Newham S Cons. Assoc., 1979–95 (Chm., 1971–74). Vice-President: Inst. of Trading Standards Admin, 1988–; Keighley Sea Cadets, 1984–; Friends of the Settle–Carlisle Railway, 1987–; AMA, 1992–97. Governor: George Green's Sch., Tower Hamlets, 1968–70; Isaac Newton Sch., N Kensington, 1971–73; Manager, Moorend C of E Primary Sch., Cleckheaton, 1977–80. *Recreations:* music, photography, sport. *Address:* 12 Plane Tree House, Duchess of Bedford's Walk, W8 7QT. *T:* (020) 7937 9034; *e-mail:* gary.waller@which.net. *Club:* Carlton.

WALLER, Rt Hon. Sir (George) Mark, Kt 1989; PC 1996; **Rt Hon. Lord Justice Waller;** Lord Justice of Appeal, since 1996; *b* 13 Oct. 1940; *s* of Rt Hon. Sir George Waller, OBE; *m* 1967, Rachel Elizabeth, *d* of His Honour Judge Beaumont, *qv*; two *s* (and one *s* decd). *Educ:* Oundle Sch.; Durham Univ. (LLB). Called to the Bar, Gray's Inn, 1964, Bencher, 1988; QC 1979; a Recorder, 1986–89; a Judge of the High Court of Justice, QBD, 1989–96; Presiding Judge, NE Circuit, 1992–95; Judge i/c Commercial List, 1995–96. Chm., Judicial Studies Bd, 1999–. *Recreations:* tennis, golf. *Address:* Royal Courts of Justice, Strand, WC2A 2LL. *Clubs:* Garrick, MCC; Huntercombe Golf.

WALLER, Guy de Warrenne, MA, MSc; Headmaster, Cranleigh School, since 1997; *b* 10 Feb. 1950; *s* of late Col Desmond de Warrenne Waller and of Angela Mary Waller (*née* Wright); *m* 1980, Hilary Ann Farmbrough; four *d.* *Educ:* Hurstpierpoint Coll.; Worcester Coll., Oxford (MA; Hon. Sec., OUCC; cricket blue, 1974; hockey blue, 1974, 1979); Wolfson Coll., Oxford (MSc). Head of Chemistry and Housemaster, Radley Coll., 1974–93; Headmaster, Lord Wandsworth Coll., 1993–97. *Publications:* Thinking Chemistry, 1980; Advancing Chemistry, 1982; Condensed Chemistry, 1985. *Recreations:* sports, keeping up with family and friends, chess, music. *Address:* Crane House, Cranleigh School, Cranleigh, Surrey GU6 8QQ. *T:* (01483) 542001. *Clubs:* MCC; Ladykillers Hockey.

WALLER, Rt Rev. John Stevens; an Assistant Bishop, diocese of Bath and Wells, since 1987; *b* 18 April 1924; *m* 1951, Pamela Peregrine; two *s* three *d.* *Educ:* St Edward's School, Oxford; Peterhouse, Cambridge (MA); Wells Theol Coll. War service with RNVR, 1942–46. Deacon 1950, priest 1951, London; Leader, Strood Gp of Parishes, 1967–72, Team Rector of Strood 1972–73; Rector of St Nicholas, Harpenden, Herts, 1973–79; Bishop Suffragan of Stafford, 1979–87; Team Vicar, Long Sutton and Long Load, Som, 1987–89. *Address:* 102 Harnham Road, Salisbury, Wilts SP2 8JW. *T:* (01722) 329739.

WALLER, Hon. Sir Mark; *see* Waller, Hon. Sir G. M.

WALLER, Philip Anthony; District Judge, Principal Registry of the Family Division, since 1994; *b* 12 Oct. 1952; *s* of Robert Waller and Olive (*née* Deakin); *m* 1978, Linda Andrews; two *d.* *Educ:* Whitgift Sch.; Univ. of Exeter (LLB Hons 1974); Inns of Court Sch. of Law. Called to the Bar, Inner Temple, 1975; with Reed, Smith, Shaw & McClay, Attorneys, Pittsburgh, USA, 1976; practised London, 1977–93. Mem., Ecclesiastical Law Soc., 1988–. *Publication:* (co-ed) Rayden and Jackson's Law and Practice in Divorce and Family Matters, 17th edn 1997. *Recreations:* choral singing, early music, historic houses and gardens, wine, France. *Address:* Principal Registry, Family Division, First Avenue House, 42–49 High Holborn, WC1V 6NP.

WALLER, Rev. Dr Ralph; Principal, and Tutor in Theology, Harris Manchester (formerly Manchester) College, University of Oxford, since 1988; Director, Farmington Institute for Christian Studies, since 2001; *b* 11 Dec. 1945; *s* of Christopher Waller and Ivy (*née* Miller); *m* 1968, Carol Roberts; one *d.* *Educ:* John Leggott Grammar Sch., Scunthorpe; Richmond Coll. Divinity Sch., Univ. of London (BD); Univ. of Nottingham (MTh); King's Coll. London (PhD 1986); MA Oxon. VSO in India, teaching maths and PE, and House Master, Shri Shivajh Mil. Sch., Poona, 1967–68; Maths Master, Riddings Comprehensive Sch., Scunthorpe, 1968–69; Methodist Minister, Melton Mowbray, 1972–75; ordained, 1975; Minister, Elvet Methodist Ch, Durham City, and Methodist Chaplain, Univ. of Durham, 1975–81; Chaplain, St Mary's Coll. and St Aidan's Coll., Univ. of Durham, 1979–81; Chaplain, Tutor in Theol. and Resident Tutor, Westminster Coll., Oxford, 1981–88; University of Oxford: Chm., Faculty of Theol., 1995–97; Chm., Envmtl Cttee, 1997–2000; Mem., Hebdomadal Council, 1997–2000. Hon. DLitt Menlo Coll., Calif, 1994; Hon. DHum Ball State Univ., Indiana, 1998. UK Templeton Prize, 1993. *Publications:* (contrib.) Truth, Liberty and Religion, 1986; (ed with Benedicta Ward) Christian Spirituality, 1999. *Recreations:* swimming, walking, browsing round second-hand bookshops. *Address:* Harris Manchester College, Mansfield Road, Oxford OX1 3TD. *T:* (01865) 271006. *Club:* Oxford and Cambridge.

WALLER, Sir Robert William, 9th Bt *cr* 1780, of Newport, Co. Tipperary; employed by the General Electric Co. of America as an Industrial Engineer, 1957–91; *b* 16 June 1934; *s* of Sir Roland Edgar Waller, 8th Bt, and Helen Madeline, *d* of Joseph Radl, Matawan, New Jersey, USA; *S* father, 1958; is a citizen of the United States; *m* 1960, Carol Anne, *d* of J. E. Hines (marr. diss. 1975; remarried 1997); two *s* two *d* (and one *s* decd). *Educ:* St Peter's Prep. Sch.; Newark Coll. of Engrg; Fairleigh Dickinson University. *Heir:* *s* John Michael Waller [*b* 14 May 1962; *m* 1986, Maria Renee Gonzalez; four *s* two *d*]. *Address:* 5 Lookout Terrace, Lynnfield, MA 01940, USA.

WALLER, Stephen Philip; His Honour Judge Stephen Waller; a Circuit Judge, since 1996; *b* 2 Jan 1950; *s* of Ronald Waller and Susannah Waller; *m* 1st, 1974, Anne Brooksbank (marr. diss.); one *s* one *d*; 2nd, 1986, Jennifer Welch; one *d.* *Educ:* Mill Hill Sch.; University College London (LLB Hons). Called to the Bar, Inner Temple, 1972.

WALLEY, Dr Francis, CB 1978; FREng; consulting engineer; Consultant to the Ove Arup Partnership; *b* 30 Dec. 1918; *s* of late Reginald M. Walley and Maria M. Walley; *m* 1946, Margaret, *yr d* of late Rev. Thomas and Margaret J. Probert; two *d.* *Educ:* Cheltenham Grammar Sch.; Bristol Univ. MSc, PhD; FICE (Mem. Council, 1978–81); FIStructE (Vice-Pres., 1982–83; Hon. Treasurer, 1981; Hon. Sec., 1979–81); FREng (FEng 1985); Lewis Kent Award, IStructE, 1985. Entered Min. of Home Security as Engr, 1941: reported to CIGS on allied bombing of Pantellaria, 1943; Member: British Bombing Survey Unit, France, 1944–45; Jt UK/USA Survey Unit of Nagasaki and Hiroshima, 1945. Min. of Works, 1945; Suptg Civil Engr, 1963; Dep. Dir of Building Develt, 1965; Dir of Estate Management Overseas, 1969; Dir of Post Office Services, 1971; Under-Sec., Dir of Civil Engineering Services, DoE, 1973–78. I/c of Civil Defence Structures, British Atomic Trials, Aust., 1954; Mem., British Govt team looking at building construction in USSR, 1966. Mem., Standing Cttee on Structural Safety, 1977–88; Chairman: BSI Code Cttee for Structural Use of Concrete, 1987–; ISO Cttee of Design of Concrete Structures, 1989–. Diamond Jubilee Lecture, British Cement Assoc., 1995; James Sutherland Lecture, IStructE, 2000. *Publications:* Prestressed Concrete Design and Construction, 1954; (with Dr S. C. C. Bate) A Guide to the Code of Practice CP 115, 1960; (contrib.) Historic Concrete, 2000; several papers to ICE and techn. jls. *Recreations:* gardening, furniture-making. *Address:* 13 Julien Road, Coulsdon, Surrey CR5 2DN. *T:* (020) 8660 3290.

See also Sir John Walley.

WALLEY, Joan Lorraine; MP (Lab) Stoke-on-Trent North, since 1987; *b* 23 Jan. 1949; *d* of late Arthur Walley and Mary Walley; *m* 1980, Jan Ostrowski; two *s.* *Educ:* Biddulph Grammar School; Hull Univ. (BA); University Coll. Swansea (Dip. Community Work). Alcoholics Recovery Project, 1970–73; Swansea City Council, 1974–78; Wandsworth Borough Council, 1978–79; NACRO, 1979–82. Mem., Lambeth Borough Council, 1982–86 (Chair: Health and Consumer Services Cttee; Assoc. of London Authorities Public Protection Cttee). Opposition front-bench spokesman on envmtl protection, 1988–90, on transport, 1990–95. Mem., Envmtl Audit Select Cttee, 1997–; Vice-Chm., All Party Football Gp; Chm., Associate Envmt Gp. Pres., West Midlands Home and Water Safety Council, 1990–. Vice-President: Inst. of Environmental Health Officers, 1987–; Socialist Envmt and Resources Assoc. Member: UNISON; Globe Internat. Hon. Pres.,

235 (1st Stoke-on-Trent) Sqn, ATC. *Address:* House of Commons, SW1A 0AA. *Clubs:* Newchapel Sports and Social Inst.; Fegg Hayes Sports and Social.

WALLEY, Sir John, KBE 1965; CB 1950; retired as Deputy Secretary, Ministry of Social Security, 1966 (Ministry of Pensions and National Insurance, 1958–66); *b* Barnstaple, Devon, 3 April 1906; *e s* of late R. M. Walley; *m* 1934, Elisabeth Mary, *e d* of late R. H. Pinhorn, OBE; two *s* two *d*. *Educ:* Hereford High Sch.; Hereford Cathedral Sch.; Merton Coll., Oxford; Postmaster, 1924–28; Hons Maths and Dip., Pol. and Econ. Sci. Ministry of Labour: Asst Principal, 1929; Sec., Cabinet Cttee on Unemployment, 1932; Principal, 1934; Asst Sec., Min. of National Service, 1941; promoted Under-Sec. to take charge of legislation and other preparations for Beveridge Nat. Insce Scheme, in new Min. of National Insurance, 1945; Chm., Dental Benefit Council, 1945–48. Chm., Hampstead Centre, National Trust, 1969–79, Pres., 1980–90. *Publications:* Social Security-Another British Failure?, 1972; contribs: to The Future of the Social Services, ed Robson and Crick, 1970; on Children's Allowances, in Family Poverty, ed David Bull, 1971; vol. in British Oral Archive of Political and Administrative History, 1980; articles in journals and the press on Social Security matters. *Address:* Brookland House, 24 High Street, Cottenham, Cambs CB4 8SA. *T:* (01954) 250931.

See also F. Walley.

WALLEY, Keith Henry, FREng, FIChemE; Managing Director, Shell Chemicals UK Ltd, 1978–84; *b* 26 June 1928; *s* of Eric Henry James Walley and Rose Walley; *m* 1950, Betty Warner; one *s* one *d*. *Educ:* Hinckley Grammar School; Loughborough College (Dip. Chem. 1949, Dip. Chem. Eng. 1952). FIChemE 1972; FREng (FEng 1981). Commissioned RAOC 1949–51. Joined Royal Dutch/Shell Group, 1952; served in Holland, 1952–69; Works Manager, Shell Chemicals, Carrington, 1970–71; Head, Manufacturing Economic and Ops, The Hague, 1972–73; Gen. Man., Base Chemicals Shell International Chemicals, 1974–77; Jt Man. Dir, Shell UK Ltd, 1978–84; Chm., International Military Services, 1985–91 (Dir, 1984–91); Dep. Chm., Johnson Matthey, 1986–91 (Dir, 1985–91). Non-executive Director: John Brown plc, 1984–86; Reckitt & Colman plc, 1986–90. Vis. Prof., UCL, 1986–. Pres., Soc. of Chemical Industry, 1984–86 (Vice-Pres., 1981–84); Member Council: Chem. Ind. Assoc., 1978–84 (Chm., Educn and Sci. Policy Cttee, 1980–84); IChemE, 1983– (Vice-Pres., 1985; Pres., 1987); Royal Acad. (formerly Fellowship) of Engineering, 1984–. CIMgt (CBIM 1982). Hon. DSc Loughborough, 1989. *Publications:* papers in chem. jls and planning jls. *Recreations:* the Pyrenees, opera, tennis, ski-ing. *Club:* Athenæum.

WALLFISCH, Raphael; 'cellist; *b* 15 June 1953; *s* of Peter Wallfisch, pianist; *m*; one *s*. *Educ:* Univ. of Southern California; studies with Amaryllis Fleming, Amadeo Baldovino, Derek Simpson and Gregor Piatigorsky. London début, QEH, 1974. 1st recordings of compositions by Bax, Strauss and others; numerous other recordings. Won Gaspar Cassado Internat. Cello competition, 1977. *Address:* c/o Clarion/Seven Muses, 47 Whitehall Park, N19 3TW; 24 Versailles Road, SE20 8AX.

WALLINGTON, Susan Margaret; *see* Bullock, S. M.

WALLIS, (Diana) Lynn; Artistic Director, Royal Academy of Dance (formerly of Dancing), since 1994; *b* 11 Dec. 1946; *d* of Dennis Blackwell Wallis and Joan Wallis. *Educ:* Tonbridge Grammar Sch. for Girls; Royal Ballet Upper Sch. FISTD. Royal Ballet Touring Co., 1965–68; Royal Ballet School: Ballet Mistress, 1969–81; Dep. Principal, 1981–84; National Ballet of Canada: Artistic Co-ordinator, 1984–86; Associate Artistic Dir, 1986–87; Co-Artistic Dir, 1987–89; Dep. Artistic Dir, English National Ballet, 1990–94. *Recreations:* music, theatre, cinema.

WALLIS, Diana Paulette; Member (Lib Dem) Yorkshire and the Humber, European Parliament, since 1999; *b* 28 June 1954; *d* of John Frederick Wallis and Jean Elizabeth Wallis (*née* Jones); *m* 1989, Stewart David Arnold. *Educ:* N London Poly. (BA Hist.); Univ. of Kent at Canterbury (MA Local Govt); Coll. of Law, Chester. Admitted Solicitor, 1983. Mem. (Lib Dem) Humberside CC, subseq. E Riding of Yorks UA, 1994–99 (Dep. Leader, 1995–99). European Parliament: Mem., Legal Affairs Cttee, 1999–; Vice-Pres., delegn to Iceland, Norway and Switzerland, 1999–. *Address:* (constituency office) Land of Green Ginger, Hull HU1 2EA. *T:* (01482) 609943. *Club:* National Liberal.

WALLIS, Edmund Arthur, FREng; Chairman, Powergen (formerly PowerGen), since 1996 (Chief Executive, 1988–2001); *b* 3 July 1939; *s* of late Reuben Wallis and of Iris Mary Cliff; *m* 1964, Gillian Joan Mitchell; two *s*. CEng 1978; MIEE 1971; MIMechE 1972; FREng (FEng 1995). Central Electricity Generating Board: Stn Manager, Oldbury Nuclear Power Stn, 1977–79; Dir of System Op., 1981–86; Divl Dir of Ops, 1986–88. Non-executive Director: BSI, 1992–97; LucasVarity plc, 1995–99 (Chm., 1998–99); London Transport, 1999–; Indep. non-exec. Dir, Mercury European Privatisation Trust plc, 1994–; Mem. Adv. Bd, RWE, Germany, 1994–98. Lay Mem. Council, Aston Univ., 1992–98. Chm., Birmingham Royal Ballet Trust, 1996–. CIMgt (CBIM 1991; AMBIM 1973). *Address:* Powergen, Westwood Way, Westwood Business Park, Coventry CV4 8LG.

WALLIS, Frederick Alfred John E.; *see* Emery-Wallis.

WALLIS, Jeffrey Joseph; retail consultant; *b* 25 Nov. 1923; *s* of Nathaniel and Rebecca Wallis; *m* 1948, Barbara Brickman; one *s* one *d*. *Educ:* Owen's; Coll. Aeronautical Engrg. Man. Dir, Wallis Fashion Group, 1948–80. Mem., Monopolies and Mergers Commn, 1981–85. Formerly Member: CNAA; Clothing Export Council; NEDC (Textiles). Involved in art educn throughout career; various governorships. *Recreations:* motor racing, motor boating, industrial design. *Address:* 37 Avenue Close, NW8 6DA. *T:* (020) 7722 8665.

WALLIS, Prof. Kenneth Frank, FBA 1994; Professor of Econometrics, University of Warwick, 1977–2001, now Emeritus; *b* 26 March 1938; *s* of late Leslie Wallis and Vera Daisy Wallis (*née* Stone); *m* 1963, Margaret Sheila Campbell. *Educ:* Wath-on-Dearne GS; Manchester Univ. (BSc, MScTech); Stanford Univ. (PhD). Mem. Exec., NUS, 1961–63. Lectr, then Reader, in Stats, LSE, 1966–77; Dir, ESRC Macroeconomic Modelling Bureau, 1983–99. Mem., HM Treasury Academic Panel, 1980–2001 (Chm., 1987–91). Member Council: Royal Stat. Soc., 1972–76; Royal Econ. Soc., 1989–94; Econometric Soc., 1995–97 (Fellow, 1975). Hon. Dr Groningen, 1999. *Publications:* Introductory Econometrics, 1972; Topics in Applied Econometrics, 1973; (ed with D. F. Hendry) Econometrics and Quantitative Economics, 1984; Models of the UK Economy 1–4, 1984–87; (ed) Macroeconometric Modelling, 1994; Time Series Analysis and Macroeconometric Modelling, 1995; (ed with D. M. Kreps) Advances in Economics and Econometrics: theory and applications, 1997; articles in learned jls. *Recreations:* travel, music, gardening, swimming. *Address:* Department of Economics, University of Warwick, Coventry CV4 7AL. *T:* (024) 7652 3055; 4 Walkers Orchard, Stoneleigh, Warwicks CV8 3JG. *T:* (024) 7641 4271.

WALLIS, Lynn; *see* Wallis, D. L.

WALLIS, Sir Peter (Gordon), KCVO 1992; CMG 1990; HM Diplomatic Service, retired; High Commissioner to Malta, 1991–94; *b* 2 Aug. 1935; *s* of late Arthur Gordon Wallis, DFC, BScEcon, and Winifred Florence Maud Wallis; *m* 1965, Delysia Elizabeth (*née* Leonard); three *s* one *d*. *Educ:* Taunton and Whitgift Schools; Pembroke Coll., Oxford (MA). Ministry of Labour and National Service, 1958; HM Customs and Excise, 1959 (Private Sec., 1961–64); HM Diplomatic Service, 1968; Tel Aviv, 1970; Nairobi, 1974; Counsellor (Econ. and Comm.), Ankara, 1977; RCDS, 1981; Cabinet Office, 1982; Hd, Perm. Under-Sec.'s Dept, FCO, 1983; Minister, Pretoria, 1987; Minister, British Liaison Office, 1989, and subseq. Acting High Comr, 1990, Windhoek, Namibia; Political Advr to Jt Comdr, British Forces in the Gulf, Jan.–April 1991, to Comdr, British Forces, SE Turkey and N Iraq, May–July 1991. Advr to Learmont Enquiry into Prison Security, 1995. Head, UK delegn to EC monitor mission, Balkans, 1996, 1997, 1998, 1999. *Recreations:* reading, writing, music, sport. *Address:* Parsonage Farm, Curry Rivel, Somerset TA10 0HG.

WALLIS, Peter Ralph; Deputy Controller, Aircraft Weapons and Electronics, Ministry of Defence, 1980–84; *b* 17 Aug. 1924; *s* of Leonard Francis Wallis and Molly McCulloch Wallis (*née* Jones); *m* 1949, Frances Jean Patricia Cowie; three *s* one *d*. *Educ:* University College Sch., Hampstead; Imperial Coll. of Science and Technology, London (BSc(Eng)). CEng 1967; FIEE 1967; FIMA 1968. Henrici and Siemens Medals of the College, 1944. Joined Royal Naval Scientific Service 1944; work at Admty Signal and Radar Estab. till 1959, Admty Underwater Weapons Estab. till 1968; Asst Chief Scientific Advr (Research), MoD, 1968–71, Dir Gen. Research Weapons, 1971–75, Dir Gen. Guided Weapons and Electronics, 1975–78, Dir Gen. Research A (Electronics) and Dep. Chief Scientist (Navy), 1978–80. Vice Pres., 1992–, Hon. Treas., 1988–, Hampstead Scientific Soc. (Hon. Sec., 1974–90). FCGI. Marconi Award, IERE, 1964. *Publications:* articles in Jl of IEE, IERE and Op. Res. Quarterly. *Recreations:* skiing, mountain walking, archæology, sailing, egyptology, travel. *Address:* 22 Flask Walk, Hampstead, NW3 1HE. *Clubs:* Alpine Ski, Eagle Ski.

WALLIS, Peter Spencer; a District Judge (Magistrates' Courts) (formerly Metropolitan Stipendiary Magistrate), since 1993; a Recorder, since 2000; *b* 31 March 1945; *s* of Philip Wallis and Winifred Wallis; *m* 1970, Ann Margaret Bentham; one *s* one *d*. *Educ:* Maidstone Grammar Sch.; Lincoln Coll., Oxford (MA). Pilot, RAF, 1967–72. Admitted solicitor, 1976. Clerk to: Tonbridge and Malling Justices, 1977–88; Dover and Ashford Justices, 1988–93; Folkestone and Hythe Justices, 1990–93. An Asst Recorder, 1997–2000. Mem. Council, Justices' Clerks' Soc., 1983–93 (Pres., 1993). *Publications:* The Transport Acts 1981 and 1982, 1982, 2nd edn 1985; Road Traffic: guide to Part I of the 1991 Act, 1991; General Editor, Wilkinson's Road Traffic Offences, 13th edn 1987 to 20th edn 2001. *Recreations:* flying, cricket, choral singing. *Address:* c/o Greenwich Magistrates' Court, 9 Blackheath Road, SE10 8PG. *T:* (020) 8694 0033. *Club:* Royal Air Force.

WALLIS, Stuart Michael; Chairman: Euramax International, since 1997; Communisis plc (formerly John Mansfield Group), since 1997; Hay Hall Group Ltd, since 1997; Trident Components Group, since 1999; SSL International plc, since 1996; Protherics plc, since 1999; Worldmark International, since 2000; ElectroTextiles Ltd, since 2000; *b* 8 Oct. 1945; *s* of Stanley Oswald Wallis and Margaret Ethel Wallis; *m* 1971; Eileen; one *s*. *Educ:* Hawesdown Sch., West Wickham, Kent. FCA, ATII. Roland Goodman & Co., 1962–68; Chrysler, 1968–71; Shipton Automation, 1971–73; Star Computer Services, 1973–74; Hestair Gp, 1974–85 (Main Board, 1977); Exec. Dir, Octopus, 1985–87; Main Board Dir, Bowater plc, 1988–94; Chief Exec., Fisons plc, 1994–96; Chairman: Sheffield Forgemasters Ltd, 1996–98; LLP Gp, 1996–98; Tetley Group Ltd, 1999–2000; Yorkshire Gp, 1996–2000. Non-exec. Dir, Boddington Gp, 1993–95. *Recreations:* golf, swimming, ski-ing. *Address:* Devonshire House, 146 Bishopsgate, EC2M 4JX. *Club:* Ashridge Golf.

WALLIS, Sir Timothy (William), Kt 1994; Managing Director, Alpine Deer Group; *b* 9 Sept. 1938; *s* of Arthur Wallis and Janice Blunden; *m* 1974, Prudence Ann Hazledine; four *s*. *Educ:* Christ's Coll., Christchurch. Founding Dir, Tourism Holdings Ltd. Mem. Council, NZ Deer Farmers' Assoc., 1977–84 (Hon. Life Mem.); founding Chm. and Hon. Life Mem., NZ Wapiti Soc. DCom (*hc*) Lincoln Univ., 2000. E. A. Gibson Award, 1980, for contribs to NZ aviation; Sir Arthur Ward Award, 1985, for contribs to agric.; Commem. Medal for services to deer industry, 1990; Sir Jack Newman Award, 1999, for outstanding contrib. to NZ tourism industry. *Recreations:* scuba diving, hunting, fly fishing; represented West Coast-Buller 1958, S Canterbury 1959, at Rugby. *Address:* Benfiddich, Mount Barker, Wanaka, New Zealand.

WALLIS-JONES, His Honour Ewan Perrins; a Circuit Judge (formerly County Court Judge), 1964–84; *b* 22 June 1913; *s* of late William James Wallis-Jones, MBE, and late Ethel Perrins Wallis-Jones; *m* 1940, Veronica Mary (*née* Fowler); one *s* two *d*. *Educ:* Mill Hill Sch.; University Coll. of Wales, Aberystwyth; Balliol Coll., Oxford. LLB Hons Wales, 1934; BA Oxon 1936; MA Oxon 1941. Qualified Solicitor, 1935; called to Bar, Gray's Inn, 1938. Chm., Carmarthenshire QS, 1966–71 (Dep. Chm., 1965–66); Jt Pres., Council of Circuit Judges, 1982. ARPS. *Recreations:* music, reading and photography. *Address:* 25 Cotham Grove, Bristol BS6 6AN. *T:* (0117) 924 8908. *Club:* Royal Photographic Society.

WALLIS-KING, Maj.-Gen. Colin Sainthill, CBE 1975 (OBE 1971); retired; *b* 13 Sept. 1926; *s* of late Lt-Col Frank King, DSO, OBE, 4th Hussars, and Colline Ammabel, *d* of late Lt-Col C. G. H. St Hill; *m* 1962, Lisabeth, *d* of late Swan Swanstrøm, Oslo, Norway; two *d*. *Educ:* Stowe. Commissioned Coldstream Guards, 1945; Liaison Officer with Fleet Air Arm, 1954; Staff Coll., 1960; Regtl Adjutant, Coldstream Guards, 1961; seconded to Para. Regt, 1963; ACOS HQ Land Norway, 1965; Comdr 2nd Bn Coldstream Guards, 1969; Dep. Comdr 8 Inf. Brigade, 1972; Comdr 3 Inf. Brigade, 1973; BGS Intell., MoD, 1975; Dir of Service Intelligence, 1977–80. Dir, Kongsberg Ltd, 1982–87; UK Agent for Norsk Forsvarsteknologi A/S, 1987–93. *Recreations:* equitation, sailing, music, cross-country skiing, fishing. *Address:* c/o Royal Bank of Scotland, Lawrie House, Victoria Road, Farnborough, Hants GU14 7NR. *Club:* Cavalry and Guards.

WALLOP, family name of **Earl of Portsmouth.**

WALLROCK, John; Chairman, Conocean International Consultants Group, Hong Kong, 1984–92; *b* 14 Nov. 1922; *s* of Samuel and Marie Kate Wallrock; *m* 1967, Audrey Louise Ariow; one *s* two *d*. *Educ:* Bradfield Coll., Berks. Cadet, Merchant Navy, 1939; Lieut RNR, 1943; Master Mariner, 1949; J. H. Minet & Co. Ltd, 1950, Dir, 1955–79, Chm., 1972–79; Chairman: Minet Holdings, 1972–82; St Katherine Insurance Co. Ltd, London, 1972–82; Dir, Tugu Insce Co. Ltd, Hong Kong, 1976–84. Underwriting Mem. of Lloyd's, 1951–86. Mem., Council of Management, White Ensign Assoc. Ltd, 1974–83. Liveryman, Master Mariners' Co., 1954–; Freeman, City of London, 1965. FCIB, MNI. *Recreations:* yachting, shooting. *Address:* 14 Lowndes Square, SW1X 9HB; Kits Croft, Up Green, Eversley, Hants RG27 0PE. *Clubs:* East India, Naval; Royal London Yacht, Royal Southern Yacht.

WALLS, Prof. Eldred Wright; Emeritus Professor of Anatomy in the University of London at Middlesex Hospital Medical School (Dean, Medical School, 1967–74); Hon. Consultant Anatomist, St Mark's Hospital; *b* 17 Aug. 1912; 2nd *s* of late J. T. Walls, Glasgow; *m* 1939, Jessie Vivien Mary Robb, MB, ChB, DPH (*d* 1999), *o d* of late R. F. Robb and late M. T. Robb; one *s* one *d*. *Educ:* Hillhead High Sch.; Glasgow Univ. BSc, 1931; MB, ChB (Hons), 1934; MD (Hons), 1947, FRSE, FRCS, FRCSE; Struthers Medal and Prize, 1942. Demonstrator and Lectr in Anatomy, Glasgow Univ., 1935–41; Senior Lectr in Anatomy, University Coll. of S Wales and Monmouthshire, 1941–47; Reader in Anatomy, Middlesex Hospital Medical Sch. 1947–49, S. A. Courtauld Prof. of Anatomy, 1949–74; Lectr in Anatomy, Edinburgh Univ., 1975–82. Past President: Anatomical Soc. of GB and Ireland; Chartered Soc. of Physiotherapy. Lectures: West., UC Cardiff, 1965; Osler, Soc. of Apothecaries, 1967; Astor, Mddx Hosp., 1975; Gordon Taylor, RCS, 1976; Struthers, RCSE, 1983. Farquharson Award, RCSE, 1988. *Publications:* (co-editor) Rest and Pain (by John Hilton) (6th edn), 1950; (co-author) Sir Charles Bell, His Life and Times, 1958; contrib. Blood-vascular and Lymphatic Systems, to Cunningham's Textbook Anat., 1981; contrib. to Journal of Anatomy, Lancet, etc. *Recreation:* annual visit to Lord's. *Address:* 19 Dean Park Crescent, Edinburgh EH4 1PH. *T:* (0131) 332 7164. *Clubs:* MCC; New (Edinburgh).

WALLS, Geoffrey Nowell; Regional Director, Clipsal Industries (Holdings) Ltd, South Asia, since 2000 (Regional Manager, Sharjah, 1998–2000); *b* 17 Feb. 1945; *s* of late Andrew Nowell Walls and of Hilda Margaret Thompson; *m* 1975, Vanessa Bodger; one *s* three *d*. *Educ:* Trinity Grammar Sch., Melbourne; Univ. of Melbourne (BComm 1965). Australian Regular Army, 2nd Lieut RAAOC, 1966–69; Australian Trade Comr Service, 1970–79; served Jakarta, Singapore, Cairo, Beirut, Bahrain, Manila, Baghdad; Regional Dir, Adelaide, Commonwealth Dept of Trade, 1980–83; Gen. Manager, ATCO Industries (Aust) Pty Ltd, 1983–86; Agent Gen. for S Australia in London, 1986–98. Mem., S Australian Cricket Assoc. *Recreations:* golf, tennis, gardening. *Address:* 5 Fourth Chin Bee Road, Singapore 619699.

WALLS, Rev. Brother Roland Charles; Member, Community of the Transfiguration, since 1965; *b* 7 June 1917; *s* of late Roland William Walls and late Tina Josephine Hayward. *Educ:* Sandown Grammar Sch.; Corpus Christi Coll., Cambridge; Kelham Theological Coll. Curate of St James', Crossgates, Leeds, 1940–42; Curate of St Cecilia's, Parson Cross, Sheffield, 1942–45; Licensed preacher, Diocese of Ely, 1945–48; Fellow of Corpus Christi Coll., Cambridge, 1948–62; Lecturer in Theology, Kelham Theological Coll., 1948–51; Chaplain and Dean of Chapel, Corpus Christi Coll., Cambridge, 1952–58; Canon Residentiary, Sheffield Cathedral, 1958–62; Chaplain of Rosslyn Chapel, Midlothian, 1962–68. Examining Chaplain to Bishop of Edinburgh. Lecturer at Coates Hall Theological Coll.; Lecturer in Dogmatics Dept, New Coll., Edinburgh, 1963–74. Received into RC Church, ordained priest, 1983. *Publications:* (contrib.) Theological Word Book (ed A. Richardson), 1950; Law and Gospel, 1980; (contrib.) Dictionary of Christian Spirituality, 1983; (contrib.) Dictionary of Pastoral Counsel, 1984; The Royal Mysteries, 1990. *Recreations:* botany, music, etc. *Address:* The Hermitage, 23 Manse Road, Roslin, Midlothian EH25 9LF.

WALLS, Stephen Roderick; Partner, Compass Partners International, since 1999; *b* 8 Aug. 1947; *s* of late R. W. Walls and of D. M. Walls; *m*; one *s*; *m* 1996, Mrs Ruth Barry, *o d* of J. Nadler. Chartered Accountant. Senior Auditor, Deloitte & Co., 1969; Group Chief Accountant, Lindustries, 1971; Financial Planning Exec., Vernons, 1974; Chesebrough Ponds: Finance Dir, UK and Geneva, 1975; Internat. Finance Dir, Geneva, 1981; Vice-Pres., Finance, 1981–87; Dir of Finance, 1987, Man. Dir, 1988–89, Plessey Co.; Chm., 1990–91, Chief Exec., 1990–92, Wiggins Teape Appleton, later Arjo Wiggins Appleton; Chm., The Albert Fisher Gp, 1992–98. Non-executive Director: Lonrho, 1993–98; Lonrho Africa, 1998–99; Servisair, 1994–99. Mem., Financial Reporting Council, 1990–95. *Recreations:* running, flying, music, theatre. *Address:* c/o Compass Partners International, 4 Grosvenor Place, SW1X 7HJ. *Club:* Royal Automobile.

WALLSTRÖM, Margot; Member, European Commission, since 1999; *b* 28 Sept. 1954; *m* 1984, Håkan Wallström; two *s*. *Educ:* Stockholm Univ. Adminr, Swedish Social Democratic Youth League, 1974–77; Accountant, 1977–79, Sen. Accountant, 1986–87, Alfa Savings Bank, Karlstad; MP (SDP), Sweden, 1979–85; Minister for: Civil Affairs, 1988–91; Culture, 1994–96; Health and Social Affairs, 1996–98; CEO, TV Värmland, 1993–94; Exec. Vice-Pres., Worldview Global Media, Sri Lanka, 1998–99. Mem. Exec. Cttee, Swedish SDP, 1993–. *Address:* European Commission, rue de la Loi 200, 1049 Brussels, Belgium.

WALLWORK, John, FRCSE; Consultant Cardiothoracic Surgeon, since 1981, and Director of Transplantation, since 1989, Papworth Hospital; *b* 8 July 1946; *s* of Thomas and Vera Wallwork; *m* 1973, Elizabeth Ann Medley; one *s* two *d*. *Educ:* Accrington Grammar Sch.; Edinburgh Univ. (BSc Hons Pharm. 1966; MB ChB 1970); MA Cantab 1986. FRCSE 1974; FRCS *ad eundem* 1992. Surgical Registrar, Royal Infirmary, Edinburgh, 1975–76; Senior Registrar: Adelaide Hosp., SA, 1977–78; Royal Infirmary, Glasgow, 1978–79; St Bartholomew's Hosp., 1979–81; Chief Resident in Cardiovascular and Cardiac Transplant Surgery, Stanford Univ. Med. Sch., 1980–81. Lister Prof., RCSE, 1985–86. *Publications:* (with R. Stepney) Heart Disease: what it is and how it is treated, 1987; (ed) Heart and Heart-Lung Transplantation, 1989; numerous papers on cardiothoracic and cardiopulmonary topics. *Recreations:* tennis, conversation, making phone calls from the bath. *Address:* 3 Latham Road, Cambridge CB2 2EG. *T:* (01223) 352827. *Club:* Caledonian.

WALLWORK, John Sackfield, CBE 1982; Director, Daily Mail and General Trust PLC, 1982–91; Managing Director, Northcliffe Newspapers Group Ltd, 1972–82 (General Manager, 1967–71); *b* 2 Nov. 1918; *s* of Peter Wallwork and Clara Cawthorne Wallwork; *m* 1945, Bessie Bray; one *s* one *d*. *Educ:* Leigh Grammar Sch., Leigh, Lancs. FCIS. General Manager, Scottish Daily Mail, Edinburgh, 1959–62; Asst Gen. Man., Associated Newspapers Gp Ltd, London, 1962–66, Dir, 1973–82. Chm., Press Association Ltd, 1973–74 (Dir, 1969–76); Director: Reuters Ltd, 1973–76; Reuters Founders Share Co. Ltd, 1984–87; Reuters Trustee, 1978–84; Member Press Council, 1974–75; Newspaper Society: Mem. Council, 1967–85; Jun. Vice-Pres. 1975; Sen. Vice-Pres., 1976, Pres., 1977–78. Commander, Order of Merit, Republic of Italy, 1973. *Recreation:* reading and more reading. *Address:* Greenfield, Manor Road, Sidmouth, Devon EX10 8RR. *T:* (01395) 513489.

WALLWORTH, Cyril; Assistant Under-Secretary of State, Ministry of Defence, 1964–76; Gwilym Gibbon Fellow, Nuffield College, Oxford, 1975–76; *b* 6 June 1916; *s* of Albert A. Wallworth and Eva (*née* Taylor); unmarried. *Educ:* Oldham High Sch.; Manchester Univ. BA (Hons) History, 1937. Asst Principal, Admiralty, 1939; Asst Private Secretary to First Lord, 1941–45, Principal, 1943; Asst Secretary, 1951; IDC 1960; Under-Secretary, 1964. Liveryman: Basketmakers' Co., 1990; Upholders' Co., 1991. *Recreations:* music, wine, cooking, photography. *Address:* 5 Leinster Mews, W2 3EY. *Clubs:* Hurlingham, Lansdowne, United Wards, City Livery.

WALMSLEY, Baroness *cr* 2000 (Life Peer), of West Derby in the co. of Merseyside; **Joan Margaret Walmsley;** Director, Walmsley Jones Communications, since 1999; *b* 12 April 1943; *d* of Leo Watson and Monica Watson (*née* Nolan); *m* 1st, 1966, John Newan Caro Richardson (marr. diss. 1979); one *s* one *d*; 2nd, 1986, Christopher Roberts Walmsley (*d* 1995); one step *s* two step *d*. *Educ:* Notre Dame High Sch., Liverpool; Univ. of Liverpool (BSc Hons Biology); Manchester Poly. (PGCE). Cytologist, Christie Hosp., Manchester, 1966–67; teacher, Buxton Coll., 1979–87; Mkting Officer, Ocean Youth Club, 1987–88; PR Consultant: Intercommunication, Manchester, 1988–89; Hill & Knowlton UK Ltd, 1989–97; Joan Walmsley Public Relations, 1997–99. *Recreations:* music, theatre, keeping fit, good company. *Address:* House of Lords, SW1A 0PW. *T:* (020) 7219 6047. *Club:* National Liberal.

WALMSLEY, Brian; Under Secretary, Social Security Policy Group, Department of Social Security, 1990–94; *b* 22 April 1936; *s* of late Albert Edward Walmsley and Ivy Doreen Walmsley (*née* Black); *m* 1st, 1956, Sheila Maybury (marr. diss. 1993); two *d*; 2nd, 1994, Margaret Wilson. *Educ:* Prescot Grammar School. National Service, RAF, 1955–57. Joined Min. of Pensions and Nat. Insurance, 1957, later Min. of Social Security and DHSS; Sec. to Industrial Injuries Adv. Council, 1978–79; Asst Sec., 1979; Under Sec., 1985; Civil Service Comr, OMCS, Cabinet Office (on secondment), 1988–90. *Recreations:* following cricket, playing golf, reading, gardening. *Club:* MCC.

WALMSLEY, Rt Rev. Francis Joseph, CBE 1979; Roman Catholic Bishop of the Forces, since 1979; *b* 9 Nov. 1926; *s* of Edwin Walmsley and Mary Walmsley (*née* Hall). *Educ:* St Joseph's Coll., Mark Cross, Tunbridge Wells; St John's Seminary, Wonersh, Guildford. Ordained, 1953; Asst Priest, Woolwich, 1953; Shoreham-by-Sea, Sussex, 1958; Chaplain, Royal Navy, 1960; Principal RC Chaplain, RN, 1975; retired from RN, 1979. Prelate of Honour to HH Pope Paul VI, 1975; ordained Bishop, 1979. *Recreations:* photography, gardening.

WALMSLEY, Prof. Ian Alexander, PhD; Professor of Experimental Physics, University of Oxford, and Fellow of St Hugh's College, Oxford, since 2001; *b* 13 Jan. 1960; *s* of Richard M. and Hazel F. Walmsley; *m* 1986, Katherine Frances Pardee; two *s* one *d*. *Educ:* Imperial Coll., Univ. of London (BSc 1980); Univ of Rochester, NY (PhD 1986). Res. Associate, Cornell Univ., NY, 1986–88; Institute of Optics, University of Rochester, New York: Asst Prof., 1988–94, Associate Prof., 1994–98, Prof., 1998–2000, of Optics; Dir, 2000. Vis. Prof. of Physics, Ulm Univ., 1995. Fellow: Optical Soc. of America, 1997; APS, 2000. *Publications:* contrib. to books and professional jls. *Recreation:* Tae Kwon Do (4th dan, World Assoc.). *Address:* Department of Physics, University of Oxford, Clarendon Laboratory, Parks Road, Oxford OX1 3PU. *T:* (01865) 272205.

WALMSLEY, Nigel Norman; Chairman, Carlton Television, since 1994 (Chief Executive, 1991–94); Executive Director, since 1992 and Deputy Chief Executive, since 2000, Carlton Communications plc; *b* 26 Jan. 1942; *s* of Norman and Ida Walmsley; *m* 1969, Jane Walmsley, broadcaster, author and producer; one *d*. *Educ:* William Hulme's Sch.; Brasenose Coll., Oxford (BA English). Joined the Post Office, 1964; Asst Private Secretary to Postmaster General, 1967; Asst Director of Marketing, Post Office, 1973–75; Asst Sec., Industrial Planning Division of Dept of Industry, 1975–76; Director of Marketing, Post Office, 1977–81, Board Mem. for Marketing 1981–82; Man. Dir, Capital Radio, 1982–91; Chm., GMTV, 1994–96. Board Member: Ind. Radio News, 1983–91; South Bank Centre, 1985–92 and 1997–; Director: The Builder Gp, 1986–92; General Cable plc, 1994–97; non-executive Chm., Central Television, 1996–; non-executive Director: Energis plc, 1997–; ONdigital plc, 1997–; de Vere plc, 2001–. Chm., GLAA, 1985–86; Vice Chm., Advertising Assoc., 1992–. *Recreation:* intensive inactivity. *Address:* 26 Belsize Road, NW6 4RD. *T:* (020) 7586 1950.

WALMSLEY, Peter James, MBE 1975; Director-General (formerly Director) of Petroleum Engineering Division, Department of Energy, 1981–89; *b* 29 April 1929; *s* of George Stanley and Elizabeth Martin Walmsley; *m* 1970, Edna Fisher; three *s* one *d*. *Educ:* Caterham Sch., Surrey; Imperial Coll., London (BSc; ARSM). Geologist: Iraq Petroleum Co., 1951–59; BP Trinidad, 1959–65; BP London, 1965–72; Exploration Manager, BP Aberdeen, 1972–78; Dep. Chief Geologist, BP London, 1978–79; Regional Exploration Manager, BP London, 1979–81. Chairman, Petroleum Exploration Soc. of Gt Britain, 1971–72; Pres., RSM Assoc., 1995–96. *Publications:* contribs to various learned jls on North Sea geology. *Recreations:* home and garden. *Address:* Elm Tree Cottage, 10 Great Austins, Farnham, Surrey GU9 8JG.

WALMSLEY, Sir Robert, KCB 1995; FREng, FIEE; Chief of Defence Procurement, Ministry of Defence, since 1996; Chief Executive, Defence Procurement Agency, since 1999; *b* Aberdeen, 1 Feb. 1941; *s* of late Prof. Robert Walmsley, TD, FRCPE, FRCSE and of Dr Isabel Mary Walmsley; *m* 1967, Christina Veronica Melvill; one *s* two *d*. *Educ:* Fettes Coll.; RN Coll., Dartmouth; Queens' Coll., Cambridge (MA MechScis); RN Coll., Greenwich (MSc Nuclear Sci.). FIEE 1994; FREng (FEng 1998). HMS Ark Royal, 1962–63; HMS Otus, 1964–66; HMS Churchill, 1968–72; Ship Dept, MoD, 1973–74; HM Dockyard, Chatham, 1975–78; MoD, PE, 1979–80; Chm., Naval Nuclear Technical Safety Panel, 1981–83; Naval Staff, 1984; MoD, PE, 1985–86; Dir Operational Requirements (Sea), 1987–89; ACDS (Communications, Command, Control and Information Systems), 1990–93; Dir Gen. Submarines, Chief Naval Engr Officer and Sen. Naval Rep. in Bath, 1993–94; Controller of the Navy, in rank of Vice-Adm., 1994–96. FRSA 1997. *Recreations:* fly fishing, West Ham United FC, Scotland. *Address:* Ministry of Defence, Old War Office Building, Whitehall, SW1A 2EU. *Club:* Army and Navy.

WALPOLE, family name of **Baron Walpole**.

WALPOLE, 10th Baron *cr* 1723, of Walpole; **Robert Horatio Walpole;** Baron Walpole of Wolterton, 1756; *b* 8 Dec. 1938; *s* of 9th Baron Walpole, TD and of Nancy Louisa, OBE, *y d* of late Frank Harding Jones; *S* father, 1989; *m* 1st, 1962, S. Judith Schofield (later S. J. Chaplin, OBE, MP; marr. diss. 1979; she *d* 1993); two *s* two *d*; 2nd, 1980, Laurel Celia, *o d* of S. T. Ball; two *s* one *d*. *Educ:* Eton; King's College, Cambridge (MA, Dip Agric). Member, Norfolk CC, 1970–81 (Chm. of various cttees). Elected Mem., H of L, 1999. Chairman: Area Museums Service for South East England, 1976–79; Norwich School of Art, 1977–87; Textile Conservation Centre, 1981–88 (Pres. 1988); East Anglian Tourist Board, 1982–88. Hon. Fellow, St Mary's UC, Strawberry Hill, 1997. JP Norfolk, 1972. *Heir: s* Hon. Jonathan Robert Hugh Walpole, *b* 16 Nov. 1967. *Address:* Mannington Hall, Norwich NR11 7BB. *T:* (01263) 587763. *Clubs:* none on principle.

WALPORT, Prof. Mark Jeremy, PhD; FRCP, FRCPath, FMedSci; Professor of Medicine, and Head of Division of Medicine, since 1997, Imperial College School of Medicine; *b* 25 Jan. 1953; *s* of Samuel Walport and Doreen Walport (*née* Music); *m* 1986, Julia Elizabeth Neild; one *s* three *d*. *Educ:* St Paul's Sch., London; Clare Coll., Cambridge; Middlesex Hosp. Med. Sch., London (MA, MB BChir; PhD 1986). FRCP 1990; FRCPath 1997. House Officer, Middlesex Hosp. and Queen Elizabeth II Hosp., Welwyn, 1977–78; SHO, 1978–80; Hon. Registrar, Brompton Hosp., 1980; Registrar, Hammersmith Hosp., 1980–82; MRC Trng Fellow, MRC Mechanisms in Tumour

Immunity Unit, Cambridge, 1982–85; Harrison-Watson Student, Clare Coll., Cambridge, 1982–85; Royal Postgraduate Medical School, now Imperial College School of Medicine: Sen. Lectr in Rheumatology, 1985–90; Reader in Rheumatological Medicine, 1990–91; Prof. of Medicine, 1991; Vice Dean for Res., 1994–97; Hon. Cons. Physician, Hammersmith Hosp., 1985–; Dir, R&D, Hammersmith Hosps Trust, 1994–98. Member: Scientific Adv. Bd, Cantab Pharmaceuticals, Cambridge, 1989–; R&D Adv. Bd, SmithKline Beecham, 1998–. Member: Council, British Soc. for Rheumatology, 1989–95 (Chm., Heberden Cttee, 1993–95); Wkg Cttee on Ethics of Xenotransplantation, Nuffield Bioethics Council, 1995–96; Council, British Soc. for Immunology, 1998–; Chairman: Ethics Cttee, Hammersmith and Queen Charlotte's SHA, 1990–94; Molecular and Cell Panel, Wellcome Trust, 1998–2000. Philip Ellman Lecture, RCP, 1995 (Graham Bull Prize in Clin. Sci., 1996). Founder FMedSci 1998 (Registrar, 1998–). Gov., Wellcome Trust, 2000–. Asst Ed., British Jl of Rheumatology, 1990–97; Series Ed., British Med. Bulletin, 1998–; Ed., Clin. and Exptl Immunology, 1998–2000. Roche Prize for Rheumatology, 1991. *Publications:* (jtly) Immunobiology, 3rd edn 1997, 4th edn 1999; (ed jtly) Clinical Aspects of Immunology, 5th edn 1993; papers in sci. jls on immunology and genetics of rheumatic diseases. *Recreations:* natural history, food. *Address:* Division of Medicine, Imperial College School of Medicine, Hammersmith Hospital, Du Cane Road, W12 0NN. *T:* (020) 8383 3299.

WALSALL, Archdeacon of; *see* Sadler, Ven. A. G.

WALSBY, Prof. Anthony Edward, PhD; FRS 1993; Melville Wills Professor of Botany, University of Bristol, since 1980. *Educ:* Birmingham Univ. (BSc); PhD London. Asst Lectr, then Lectr in Botany, Westfield Coll., London Univ., 1965–71; Miller Fellow, Univ. of Calif. at Berkeley, 1971–73; Lectr, then Reader, Department of Marine Science–Marine Biology, UCNW, Bangor, 1973–80. *Address:* School of Biological Sciences, University of Bristol, Woodland Road, Bristol BS8 1UG. *T:* (0117) 928 7490; *e-mail:* a.e.walsby@bristol.ac.uk.

WALSH, Arthur Stephen, CBE 1979; FREng, FIEE; Chairman, Simoco International Ltd, since 1997; *b* 16 Aug. 1926; *s* of Wilfred and Doris Walsh; *m* 2nd, 1985, Judith Martha Westenborg. *Educ:* Selwyn Coll., Cambridge (MA). FIEE 1974; FREng (FEng 1980). GEC Group, 1952–79: various sen. appts within the Group; Managing Director: Marconi Space and Defence Systems, 1969–86; Marconi Co., 1982–85; Dir, GEC, 1983; Chief Exec., 1985–91, Chm., 1989–91, STC. Chairman: Telemetrix plc, 1991–97; Nat. Transcommunications Ltd, 1991–96; Dir, FKI plc, 1991–99. Hon. DSc: Ulster, 1988; Southampton, 1993. *Recreations:* ski-ing, golf. *Address:* Aiglemont, Trout Rise, Loudwater, Rickmansworth, Herts WD3 4JS. *T:* (01923) 770883.

WALSH, Colin Stephen, FRCO; Organist and Master of the Choristers, Lincoln Cathedral, since 1988; *b* 26 Jan. 1955. *Educ:* Portsmouth Grammar Sch.; St George's Chapel, Windsor Castle (Organ Scholar); Christ Church, Oxford (Organ Scholar; MA 1980). DipEd 1978. ARCM 1973; FRCO 1976. Asst Organist, Salisbury Cathedral, 1978–85; Master of the Music, St Alban's Cathedral, 1985–88. Recitals in UK (incl. Royal Festival Hall), France, Scandinavia, Czechoslovakia and USA. Recordings incl. French organ music, esp. by Vierne. *Recreations:* walking, dining out, theatre, travel. *Address:* 12 Minster Yard, Lincoln LN2 1PJ. *T:* (01522) 532877.

WALSH, Rt Rev. (Geoffrey David) Jeremy; Bishop Suffragan of Tewkesbury, 1986–95; *b* 7 Dec. 1929; *s* of late Howard Wilton Walsh, OBE and Helen Maud Walsh (*née* Lovell); *m* 1961, Cynthia Helen, *d* of late F. P. Knight, FLS, VMH, and H. I. C. Knight, OBE; two *s* one *d. Educ:* Felsted Sch., Essex; Pembroke Coll., Cambridge (MA Econ.); Lincoln Theological Coll. Curate, Christ Church, Southgate, London, 1955–58; Staff Sec., SCM, and Curate, St Mary the Great, Cambridge, 1958–61; Vicar, St Matthew, Moorfields, Bristol, 1961–66; Rector of Marlborough, Wilts, 1966–76; Rector of Elmsett with Aldham, 1976–80; Archdeacon of Ipswich, 1976–86. Hon. Canon, Salisbury Cathedral, 1973–76. *Recreations:* gardening, golf, bird-watching. *Address:* 6 Warren Lane, Martlesham Heath, Ipswich IP5 3SH. *T:* (01473) 620797.

WALSH, Graham Robert, FCA; Deputy Chairman, Moss Bros Group plc, 1999–2001 (Director, 1988–2001); *b* 30 July 1939; *s* of Robert Arthur Walsh and Ella Marian (*née* Jacks); *m* 1967, Margaret Ann Alexander; one *s* one *d. Educ:* Hurstpierpoint Coll., Sussex. Qualified as chartered accountant, 1962; joined Philip Hill Higginson Erlangers (now Hill Samuel & Co. Ltd), 1964; Director, Hill Samuel, 1970, resigned 1973; Dir, 1973–87, Head of Corporate Finance Div., and Mem. Management Cttee, 1981–87, Morgan Grenfell & Co. Ltd; Man. Dir, Bankers Trust Co., 1988–91; Director: Morgan Grenfell Group plc (formerly Morgan Grenfell Holdings), 1985–87; Armitage Shanks Group Ltd, 1973–80; Phoenix Opera Ltd, 1970–87; Ward White Group plc, 1981–89; Rush & Tompkins Gp plc, 1988–90; Haslemere Estates, 1989–92; Rodamco UK BV, 1992–98. Dir Gen., Panel on Takeovers and Mergers, 1979–81; Chm., Issuing Houses Assoc., 1985–87 (Dep. Chm., 1979 and 1983–85). Gov., Dulwich Coll. Prep. Sch., 1995–97. *Recreations:* opera, theatre, music, gardening. *Address:* 19 Alleyn Park, Dulwich, SE21 8AU. *T:* (020) 8670 0676.

WALSH, Henry George; Deputy Chairman, Building Societies Commission, 1991–95; *b* 28 Sept. 1939; *s* of James Isidore Walsh and Sybil Bertha Bazeley; *m* 1999, Elizabeth Long; one *d*; two *d* by previous *m. Educ:* West Hill High Sch., Montreal; McGill Univ.; Churchill Coll., Cambridge. HM Treasury, 1966–74; Private Secretary to Chancellor of the Duchy of Lancaster, 1974–76; HM Treasury, 1976–78; Cabinet Office Secretariat, 1978–80; Counsellor (Economic), Washington, 1980–85; HM Treasury: Hd of Monetary Policy Div., 1985–86; Hd of IMF and Debt Div., 1986–89; Hd of Financial Instns and Markets Gp, 1989–91. *Recreations:* golf, model railways, being taken for walks by Labrador retrievers. *Address:* 60 Roxburgh Road, SE27 0LD. *Club:* Dulwich and Sydenham Hill Golf.

WALSH, Rt Rev. Jeremy; *see* Walsh, Rt Rev. G. D. J.

WALSH, Jill P.; *see* Paton Walsh.

WALSH, John; Director, J. Paul Getty Museum, 1983–2000, now Director Emeritus; Vice-President, J. Paul Getty Trust, 1998–2000; *b* 9 Dec. 1937; *s* of John J. Walsh and Eleanor Walsh (*née* Wilson); *m* 1961, Virginia Alys Galston; two *s* one *d. Educ:* Yale Univ. (BA 1961); Univ. of Leyden, Netherlands, Columbia Univ. (MA 1965; PhD 1971). Lectr, Research Asst, Frick Collection, NY, 1966–68; Metropolitan Museum of Art, NY: Associate for Higher Educn, 1968–71; Associate Curator and Curator, 1970–75, Vice-Chm., 1974–75, Dept of European Paintings; Columbia University: Adjunct Associate Prof., 1972–75; Prof. of Art History, Barnard Coll., 1975–77; Mrs Russell W. Baker Curator of Paintings, Museum of Fine Arts, Boston, 1977–83. Vis Prof. of Fine Arts, Harvard, 1979. Member: Governing Bd, Yale Univ. Art Gallery, 1975–; Bd of Fellows, Claremont Grad. Sch. and Univ. Center, 1988–2000; Assoc. of Art Museum Dirs, 1983–2001 (Trustee, 1986–90; Pres., 1989); Amer. Antiquarian Soc., 1984–. Mem., Amer. Acad. of Arts and Scis, 1997. Hon. LHD: Wharton Coll., 2000; Wheaton Coll., 2000. *Publications:* Things in Place: landscapes and still lifes by Sheridan Lord, 1995; Jan Steen, The Drawing Lesson, 1996; (with D. Gribbon) The J. Paul Getty Museum and its Collections: a museum for the new century, 1997; numerous contribs to learned jls. *Address:* c/o J. Paul Getty Museum, 1200 Getty Center Drive, Ste 1000, Los Angeles, CA 90049-1679, USA. *Club:* Century Association (NY).

WALSH, John Henry Martin; feature writer, Independent, since 1996 (Literary Editor, 1995–96); *b* 24 Oct. 1953; *s* of Martin Walsh and Anne Walsh (*née* Durkin); partner, Carolyn Clare Hart; one *s* two *d. Educ:* Wimbledon Coll.; Exeter Coll., Oxford (BA Hons); University Coll., Dublin (MA). Advertisement Dept, Tablet Magazine, 1977; Publicity Dept, Victor Gollancz, 1978–79; Associate Editor, The Director, 1979–83; freelance writer, 1983–87; Literary Editor, 1987, Features and Literary Editor, 1988, Evening Standard; Literary Editor, Sunday Times, 1988–92; Editor, Independent Magazine, 1993–95. Presenter, Books and Company, BBC Radio 4, 1995–97. Artistic Dir, Cheltenham Festival of Literature, 1997–98. Chm. Judges, Forward Poetry Prize, 2000. *Publications:* Growing Up Catholic, 1989; The Falling Angels, 1999. *Recreations:* drinking, talking, music. *Address:* 88 Croxted Road, Dulwich, SE21 8NP. *T:* (020) 8670 5859. *Club:* Groucho.

WALSH, John P.; *see* Pakenham-Walsh.

WALSH, Sir John (Patrick), KBE 1960; Professor of Dentistry and Dean and Director, University of Otago Dental School, 1946–72; *b* 5 July 1911; *s* of John Patrick Walsh and Lillian Jane (*née* Burbidge), Vic, Australia; *m* 1934, Enid Morris; one *s* three *d. Educ:* Ormond Coll.; Melbourne Univ. BDSc 1st Cl. Hons Melbourne; LDS Victoria, 1936; MB, BS Melbourne, 1943; DDSc Melbourne, 1950; FDSRCS 1950; FDSRCS Edinburgh, 1951; MDS NUI, 1952; FRSNZ 1961; FACD 1962; Hon. FACDS, 1967; Hon. DSc Otago, 1975. Hosp. and teaching appointments in Melbourne till 1946. MO, RAAF, 1945–46. Consultant, WHO Dental Health Seminars: Wellington, 1954; Adelaide, 1959. Speaker: 11th and 12th Internat. Dental Congresses, London and Rome; Centennial Congress of Amer. Dental Assoc., New York, 1959; 12th, 14th and 15th Australian Dental Congresses. Chairman: Dental Council of NZ, 1956–72; Mental Health Assoc. of Otago, 1960. Dominion Pres., UNA, 1960–64. Member: MRC of NZ, 1950–72 (Chm. Dental Cttee, 1947–60); Scientific Commn; Fedn Dentaire Internat., 1954–61; Council, Univ. of Otago, 1958–63; Nat. Commn for UNESCO, 1961–69; Educn Commn, 1961–; Expert Panel on Dental Health, WHO, 1962; Nat. Council, Duke of Edinburgh's Award, 1963–68. CC, Dunedin, 1968–73. Pres., Dunedin Rotary Club, 1960, Governor Dist 298, 1966–67. Paul Harris Fellow, 1981. Hon. Mem., American Dental Assoc., 1969–; List of Honour, FDI, 1969–. Holds hon. degrees. *Publications:* A Manual of Stomatology, 1957; Living with Uncertainty, 1968; Psychiatry and Dentistry, 1976; numerous articles in scientific literature. *Recreation:* retirement. *Address:* Elizabeth Knox Home, 10 Ranfurly Road, Epsom, Auckland 3, New Zealand. *T:* (9) 5207102.

See also Dame E. A. Hanan.

WALSH, Dr Julia M.; non-executive Director: British Energy, since 1996; Southalls Hygiene Services, since 1996; David A. Hall Ltd, since 1996; Chairman, AVL Holdings, since 1997, Chief Exec., ADAS, 1991–95. *Address:* c/o British Energy, 10 Lockside Place, Edinburgh EH12 9DF.

WALSH, (Mary) Noëlle; Editor, The Good Deal Directory, since 1992; Director, The Value for Money Company Ltd, since 1992; *b* 26 Dec. 1954; *d* of late Thomas Walsh and of Mary Kate Ferguson; *m* 1988, David Heslam; one *s* one *d. Educ:* Univ. of East Anglia (BA Hons European Studies (History and German)). Editorial Asst, PR Dept, St Dunstan's Orgn for the War-Blinded, 1977–79; News Editor, Cosmopolitan, 1979–85; Editor, London Week newspaper, 1985–86; freelance writer, 1986; Dep. Editor, 1986–87, Editor, 1987–91, Good Housekeeping; Dep. Editor, You and Your Family, Daily Telegraph, 1992; Editor, The Good Deal Directory monthly newsletter, 1992–97; Founder, gooddealdirectory website. Member: Network; 300 Group; Forum UK. FRSA. *Publications:* Hot Lips, the Ultimate Kiss and Tell Guide, 1985; (co-ed) Ragtime to Wartime: the best of Good Housekeeping 1922–39, 1986; (co-ed) The Home Front: the best of Good Housekeeping 1939–1945, 1987; (co-ed) The Christmas Book: the best of Good Housekeeping at Christmas 1922–1962, 1988; (ed jtly) Food Glorious Food: eating and drinking with Good Housekeeping 1922–1942, 1990; Things my Mother Should Have Told Me, 1991; Childhood Memories, 1991; (ed) The Good Deal Directory, annually, 1994–; (ed) The Good Deal Directory Food Guide, 1993; (ed) The Home Shopping Handbook, 1994; Baby on a Budget, 1995; Wonderful Weddings that won't cost a fortune, 1995; The Factory Shopping and Sightseeing Guide to the UK, 1996; The Good Mail Order Guide, 1996; contrib. to Sunday Times annual Good Deal Guide. *Recreation:* medieval Irish history. *Address:* Cottage by the Church, Filkins, Lechlade, Glos GL7 3JS.

WALSH, Michael Jeffrey; Chief Executive Officer, Europe, Africa and Middle East, Ogilvy and Mather, since 1994; *b* 1 Oct. 1949; *s* of Kenneth Francis Walsh and Edith Walsh; *m* 1983, Sally Elizabeth Hudson; one *s* one *d. Educ:* Hulme Grammar Sch., Oldham; Durham Univ. (BA Hons Geog.). Joined Young and Rubicam as grad. trainee, 1972; Dir, 1980–83; New Business Dir, 1981–83; Mem., Exec. Cttee, 1982–83; Ogilvy and Mather, 1983–: Man. Dir, UK, 1986–89; Chairman: UK, 1989–90; UK Gp, 1990–99. Vice-Chm. and Trustee, BRCS, 1994–. Worldwide Trustee, WWF, 1996–99. *Recreations:* collecting children's books, antiques, golf, tennis, sailing. *Address:* Ogilvy and Mather, 10 Cabot Square, Canary Wharf, E14 4QB. *T:* (020) 7345 3366. *Clubs:* Royal Automobile, Mark's, Annabel's; Highgate Golf, Royal West Norfolk Golf, Hunstanton Golf.

WALSH, Maj.-Gen. Michael John Hatley, CB 1980; CBE 1996; DSO 1968; Director of Overseas Relations, St John's Ambulance, 1989–95; *b* 10 June 1927; *s* of Captain Victor Michael Walsh, late Royal Sussex, and Audrey Walsh; *m* 1952, Angela, *d* of Col Leonard Beswick; two *d. Educ:* Sedbergh Sch. Commnd, KRRC, 1946; served in Italy, Malaya, Germany, Cyprus, Suez, Aden, Australia and Singapore; Bde Maj. 44 Parachute Bde, 1960–61; GSO1 Defence Planning Staff, 1966; CO 1 Para Bn, 1967–69; Col AQ 1 Div., 1969–71; Comdr, 28 Commonwealth Bde, 1971–73; BGS HQ BAOR, 1973–76; GOC 3rd Armoured Div., 1976–79; Dir of Army Training, MoD, 1979–81. Hon. Col, 1st Bn Wessex Regt, TA, 1981–89. Chief Scout of the UK and Dependent Territories, 1982–88; Vice Pres., Scout Assoc., 1988–. Council Mem., Operation Raleigh, 1984; Royal National Life-boat Institution: Member: Cttee of Management, 1988–; Search and Rescue Sub-cttee, 1989–99; Fund Raising Sub-cttee, 1991–; Vice Pres., 1998–. Kt Pres., Hon. Soc. of Knights of the Round Table, 1988–95 (Kt 1986–); Mem., St John Council, Wilts, 1989–99, London, 1995–2000. DL Greater London, 1986–99. Freeman, City of London, 1987. KStJ 1993 (Mem., Chapter Gen., 1989–99). *Recreations:* athletics, boxing (Life Pres., Army Boxing Assoc., 1986), parachuting (Pres., Army Parachute Assoc., 1979–81), sailing, Australian Rules football, photography. *Address:* c/o Barclays Bank, James Street, Harrogate. *Club:* Royal Yacht Squadron (Cowes).

WALSH, Michael Thomas; Head, International Department, Trades Union Congress, since 1980; *b* 22 Oct. 1943; *s* of Michael Walsh and late Bridget (*née* O'Sullivan); *m* 1972, Margaret Patricia Blaxhall; two *s* two *d*. *Educ:* Gunnersbury Grammar Sch.; Exeter Coll., Oxford (Hons degree PPE). International Dept, TUC, 1966; Deputy Overseas Labour Adviser, FCO, 1977–79. Member: Economic and Social Committee of the European Community, 1976–77 and 1979–80; World of Work Cttee, Catholic Bishops' Conf. of England and Wales, 1992–. Member: Wilton Park Academic Council, 1994–; Governing Body, Plater Coll., Oxford, 1995–. *Recreations:* cricket, historical research, music. *Address:* 77 Uvedale Road, Enfield EN2 6HD.

WALSH, Lt-Col Noel Perrings; Under Secretary, and Director of Home Regional Services, Department of the Environment, 1976–79; *b* 25 Dec. 1919; *s* of late John and Nancy Walsh; *m* 1st, 1945, Olive Mary (*d* 1987), *y d* of late Thomas Walsh, Waterford; three *s* one *d*; 2nd, 1988, Mary Ruth, *d* of late Rev. R. D. M. Hughes. *Educ:* Purbrook Park Grammar Sch.; Open Univ.; Birmingham Univ. (MSocSc). Served Army, 1939–66; India, 1941–44; Arakan Campaign, 1944–45; DAQMG, 52 (L) Div., 1951–53; GSO2 RA, HQ BAOR, 1955–57; GSO1 PR, MoD Army, 1964–66; retired Lt-Col, RA, 1966. Entered Home Civil Service as Principal, MPBW, 1966; Regional Director: Far East, 1969–70; Midland Region, 1970–75. Vice-Chm., Midland Study Centre for Building Team, 1982–90; Regional Chm., W Midlands Council, CIOB, 1988–90. Vice-Pres., W Midlands Central SSAFA, 1995– (Chm., 1991–95); Chm., RBL Birmingham Poppy Appeal, 1996–2001; Vice Chm., Birmingham Ex-Service Appeals Cttee, 2001–. FCIOB 1972; FIMgt (FBIM 1978); FRSA 1987. *Recreations:* gardening, economic history, gauge O railway modelling. *Address:* 25 Oakfield Road, Selly Park, Birmingham B29 7HH. *T:* (0121) 472 2031. *Club:* Naval and Military.

WALSH, Most Rev. Patrick Joseph; *see* Down and Connor, Bishop of.

WALSH, Robin; Controller, BBC Northern Ireland, 1991–94; *b* 6 Feb. 1940; *s* of Charles and Ellen Walsh; *m* 1964, Dorothy Beattie; two *d*. *Educ:* Foyle College, Londonderry; Royal Belfast Academical Inst. Reporter, Belfast Telegraph, 1958–65; Reporter/News Editor, Ulster TV, 1965–74; BBC: News Editor, NI, 1974–81; Dep. Editor, TV News, 1982–85; Managing Editor, News and Current Affairs—TV, 1985–88; Asst Controller, News and Current Affairs, Regions, 1988–90. *Recreations:* cricket, walking. *Address:* Holly Lodge, 3A Ballymullan Road, Crawfordsburn, Co. Down NI BT19 1JG. *T:* (028) 9185 2709.

WALSH, Terence Michael; His Honour Judge Walsh; a Circuit Judge, North East Circuit, since 2001; *b* 10 March 1945; *s* of late Gerrard Walsh and of Freda Alice Walsh (now Kay); *m* 1969, Pauline Totham; two *s* one *d*. *Educ:* Belle View Boys' Grammar Sch., Bradford. Admitted as solicitor, 1974; Sen. Partner, Chivers Walsh Smith, Solicitors, Bradford, 1991–2001. Dep. Registrar, later Dep. Dist Judge, 1984–94; Asst Recorder, 1989–94; Recorder, 1994–2001. Pres., Bradford Law Soc., 1990–91; Mem., Children's Panel, Law Soc., 1994–. Consulting Ed., Practitioner's Guides, 1991–. *Publications:* Child Care and the Courts, 1988; Child Protection Handbook, 1995. *Recreations:* history, music, walking. *Address:* Leeds Combined Court Centre, Oxford Row, Leeds LS1 3BG. *T:* (0113) 283 0040.

WALSH, Most Rev. William; *see* Killaloe, Bishop of, (RC).

WALSHAM, Sir Timothy (John), 5th Bt *cr* 1831, of Knill Court, Herefordshire; horticulturalist; *b* 26 April 1939; *o s* of Rear Adm. Sir John Walsham, 4th Bt, CB, OBE and of Sheila Christina, *o d* of Comdr B. Bannerman, DSO; *S* father, 1992. *Educ:* Sherborne. Peninsular & Oriental Shipping Company, 1960–67; Royal Fleet Auxiliary Service, 1968–72. *Recreation:* horticulture. *Heir: cousin* Percy Robert Stewart Walsham [*b* 6 April 1904; *m* 1937, Tamara Ellis (*d* 1981); one *s* one *d*]. *Address:* Beckford Close, Tisbury, Wiltshire SP3 6QT.

WALSINGHAM, 9th Baron *cr* 1780; **John de Grey,** MC 1952; Lieut-Colonel, Royal Artillery, retired, 1968; *b* 21 Feb. 1925; *s* of 8th Baron Walsingham, DSO, OBE, and Hyacinth (*d* 1968), *o d* of late Lt-Col Lambart Henry Bouwens, RA; *S* father, 1965; *m* 1963, Wendy, *er d* of E. Hoare, Southwick, Sussex; one *s* two *d*. *Educ:* Wellington Coll.; Aberdeen Univ.; Magdalen Coll., Oxford; RMCS. BA Oxon, 1950; MA 1959. Army in India, 1945–47; Palestine, 1947; Oxford Univ., 1947–50; Foreign Office, 1950; Army in Korea, 1951–52; Hong Kong, 1952–54; Malaya, 1954–56; Cyprus, Suez, 1956; Aden, 1957–58; Royal Military Coll. of Science, 1958–60; Aden, 1961–63; Malaysia, 1963–65. Co. Dir, 1968–96. *Heir:* *s* Hon. Robert de Grey [*b* 21 June 1969; *m* 1995, Josephine Elizabeth, *d* of Richard Haryott; one *s* one *d*]. *Address:* The Hassocks, Merton, Thetford, Norfolk IP25 6QP. *T:* (01953) 885385, *Fax:* (01953) 885385; *e-mail:* hassocks@lineone.net. *Clubs:* Army and Navy, Special Forces; Norfolk County (Norwich).

WALTER, Harriet Mary, CBE 2000; actress; *b* 24 Sept. 1950; *d* of late Roderick Walter and of Xandra Carandini (*née* Lee). *Educ:* Cranborne Chase Sch.; LAMDA. Associate Artist, RSC, 1987–. *Theatre:* Ragged Trousered Philanthropists, Joint Stock Co., 1978; Hamlet, Cloud Nine, Royal Court, 1980; Nicholas Nickleby, RSC, 1980; Seagull, Royal Court, 1981; RSC seasons, 1981–83: Midsummer Night's Dream; All's Well That Ends Well (also on Broadway, 1983); The Castle, RSC, 1985; Merchant of Venice, Royal Exchange, Manchester, 1987; RSC seasons, 1987–89: Cymbeline; Twelfth Night; Three Sisters; Question of Geography (Best Actress, Olivier Awards, 1988); Duchess of Malfi, RSC, 1989–90; Three Birds Alighting on a Field, Royal Court, 1991–92, NY, 1994; Arcadia, 1993, The Children's Hour, 1994, National; Old Times, Wyndham's, 1995; Sweet Panic, Hampstead, Hedda Gabler, Chichester, 1996; Ivanov, Almeida, 1997; The Late Middle Classes, Watford and UK tour, 1999; Macbeth, RSC, 1999; Life x 3, RNT, 2000, transf. Old Vic, 2001; The Royal Family, Th. Royal, Haymarket, 2001; *television:* The Imitation Game, 1980; Cherry Orchard, 1981; The Price, 1985; Lord Peter Wimsey, 1987; Benefactors, 1989; They Never Slept, 1990; The Men's Room, 1991; Ashenden, 1991; Inspector Morse, 1992; Hard Times, 1994; A Dance to the Music of Time, 1997; Unfinished Business, 1998; Macbeth, 1999; many radio performances (Sony Award, Best Actress, 1988 and 1992); *films:* Reflections, 1983; Turtle Diary, 1985; The Good Father, 1986; Milou en Mai, 1990; The Hour of the Pig, 1993; Sense and Sensibility, 1996; The Governess, 1998; Bedrooms and Hallways, 1998; Onegin, 1999; Villa des Roses, 2000. *Publications:* Other People's Shoes, 1999; contribs to: Clamorous Voices, 1988; Players of Shakespeare, Vol. III, 1993; Mothers by Daughters, 1995; Renaissance Drama in Action, 1999. *Address:* c/o Conway van Gelder, 18–21 Jermyn Street, SW1Y 6HP. *T:* (020) 7287 0077.

WALTER, Kenneth Burwood, CVO 1978; Full-time Member, British Airports Authority, 1975–77; *b* 16 Oct. 1918; *s* of late Leonard James Walter and Jesse Florence Walter; *m* 1940, Elsie Marjorie Collett (*d* 1997); two *s*. *Educ:* St Dunstan's Coll., SE6. Dept of Civil Aviation, Air Ministry, 1936. Served War, Royal Artillery (Anti Aircraft and Field), home and Far East, 1940–46. Ministries of: Civil Aviation; Transport and Civil Aviation; Aviation, 1946–66; British Airports Authority: Dep. Dir Planning, 1966; Dir Planning, 1972; Airport Dir, Heathrow, 1973–77. MCIT, ARAeS. *Publications:* various papers on airports. *Recreations:* music, swimming, fishing, gardening. *Address:* 7 Willersley Avenue, Orpington, Kent BR6 9RT.

WALTER, Neil Douglas; New Zealand Secretary of Foreign Affairs and Trade, since 1999; *b* 11 Dec. 1942; *s* of Ernest Edward Walter and Anita Walter (*née* Frethey); *m* 1966, Berys Anne (*née* Robertson); one *s* two *d*. *Educ:* New Plymouth Boys' High School; Auckland University (MA). Second Sec., Bangkok, 1966–70; First Sec., NZ Mission to UN, NY, 1972–76; Official Sec., Tokelau Public Service, Apia, 1976–78; Minister, Paris and NZ Permt Deleg. to Unesco, 1981–85; Dep. High Comr for NZ in London, 1985–87; Asst Sec., Ministry of External Relations, NZ, 1987–90; NZ Ambassador to Indonesia, 1990–94; Dep. Sec., Ministry of Foreign Affairs and Trade, NZ, 1994–98; NZ Ambassador to Japan, 1998–99. *Recreations:* sport, reading. *Address:* Ministry of Foreign Affairs and Trade, Private Bag 18901, Wellington, New Zealand.

WALTER, Robert John; MP (C) Dorset North, since 1997; *b* 30 May 1948; *s* of Richard and Irene Walter; *m* 1970, Sally Middleton (*d* 1995); two *s* one *d*; *m* 2000, Barbara Gorna; one step *s* one step *d*. *Educ:* Lord Weymouth Sch., Warminster; Aston Univ. (BSc 1971). Farmer, S Devon; Mem., Stock Exchange, 1983–; internat. banker. Dir and Vice Pres., Aubrey G. Lanston & Co., Inc., 1986–97. Vice Pres., Cons. Gp for Europe, 1995–97 (Vice Chm., 1984–86; Dep. Chm., 1989–92; Chm., 1992–95). Contested (C) Bedwellty, 1979. Opposition spokesman on constitutional affairs and Wales, 1999–2001. Mem., Health Select Cttee, 1997–99; Eur. Legislation Select Cttee, 1998–99; Vice-Chm., Cons. Agric. Cttee, 1997–99; Sec., Cons. Eur. Affairs Cttee, 1997–99; Treasurer: All Party British–Japanese Parly Gp, 1997–; All Party Gp on Charities and Vol. Sector, 1997–; British–Caribbean Parly Gp, 1997–; Vice Chairman: All Party Gp on Lupus, 2000–; All Party British-Turkish Parly Gp; All Party Human Rights Gp; Associate, British-Irish Parly Body, 1997–. Hon. Sec., 1999–, Rear Cdre, 2001–, H of C Yacht Club. Chm. Bd of Governors, Tachbrook Sch., 1980–2000. Freeman, City of London, 1983; Liveryman, Needlemakers' Co., 1983. *Address:* House of Commons, SW1A 0AA. *Clubs:* Constitutional (Blandford); Conservative (Wimborne).

WALTERS, Sir Alan (Arthur), Kt 1983; Vice-Chairman and Director, AIG Trading Group, Inc., 1991–2001; Professor of Economics, Johns Hopkins University, Maryland, 1976–91; *b* 17 June 1926; *s* of James Arthur Walters and Claribel Walters (*née* Heywood); *m* 1975, Margaret Patricia (Paddie) Wilson; one *d* of former marr. *Educ:* Alderman Newton's Sch., Leicester; University Coll., Leicester (BSc (Econ) London); Nuffield Coll., Oxford (MA). Lectr in Econometrics, Univ. of Birmingham, 1951; Visiting Prof. of Economics, Northwestern Univ., Evanston, Ill, USA, 1958–59; Prof. of Econometrics and Social Statistics, Univ. of Birmingham, 1961; Cassel Prof. of Economics, LSE, 1968–76. Vis. Prof. of Econs, MIT, 1966–67; Vis. Fellow, Nuffield Coll., Oxford, 1982–84; Sen. Fellow, Amer. Enterprise Inst., 1983– (Boyer Lectr, 1983). Economic Adviser to World Bank, 1976–80, 1984–88; Chief Econ. Advr to the Prime Minister (on secondment), 1981–84, 1989. Mem. Commission on Third London Airport (the Roskill Commission), 1968–70. Contested (Referendum) Cities of London and Westminster, 1997. Fellow, Econometric Soc., 1971. Hon. Fellow, Cardiff Univ., 2001. Hon. DLitt Leicester, 1981; Hon. DSocSc: Birmingham, 1984; Francisco Marroquin Univ., Guatemala, 1994. *Publications:* Growth Without Development (with R. Clower and G. Dalton), 1966 (USA); Economics of Road User Charges, 1968; An Introduction to Econometrics, 1969 (2nd edn 1971); Economics of Ocean Freight Rates (with E. Bennathan), 1969 (USA); Money in Boom and Slump, 1970 (3rd edn 1971); Noise and Prices, 1974; (with R. G. Layard) Microeconomic Theory, 1977; (with Esra Bennathan) Port Pricing and Investment Policy for Developing Countries, 1979; Britain's Economic Renaissance, 1986; Sterling in Danger, 1990; The Economics and Politics of Money, 1998. *Recreations:* music, Thai porcelain. *Address:* 3 Chesterfield Hill, W1X 7RP. *Club:* Political Economy.

WALTERS, Sir Dennis, Kt 1988; MBE 1960; *b* 28 Nov. 1928; *s* of late Douglas L. Walters and Clara Walters (*née* Pomello); *m* 1st, 1955, Vanora McIndoe (marr. diss. 1969); one *s* one *d*; 2nd, 1970, Hon. Celia (*née* Sandys) (marr. diss. 1979); one *s*; 3rd, 1981, Bridgett, *d* of late J. Francis Shearer; one *s* one *d*. *Educ:* Downside; St Catharine's College (Exhibitioner), Cambridge (MA). War of 1939–45: interned in Italy; served with Italian Resistance Movement behind German lines after Armistice, 1943–44; repatriated and continued normal educn, 1944. Chm., Fedn of Univ. Conservative and Unionist Assocs, 1950; Personal Asst to Lord Hailsham throughout his Chairmanship of Conservative Party; Chm., Coningsby Club, 1959. Contested (C) Blyth, 1959 and Nov. 1960; MP (C) Westbury Div. of Wilts, 1964–92. Jt Hon. Sec., Conservative Parly Foreign Affairs Cttee, 1965–71, Jt Vice-Chm., 1974–78; Jt Chm., Euro-Arab Parly Assoc., 1978–81; Mem., UK Parly Delegn to UN, 1966; UK Deleg. to Council of Europe and Assembly of WEU, 1970–73. Introduced Children and Young Persons (Amendment) Bill, 1985 (Royal Assent, 1986). Pres., Cons. ME Council, 1992– (Chm., 1980–92). Director: The Spectator, 1983–84; Middle East Internat., 1971–90 (Chm., 1990–). Chm., Asthma Research Council, 1968–88; Vice Pres., Nat. Asthma Campaign, 1989–. Chm., UK/Saudi Jt Cultural Cttee, 1988–; Joint Chairman: Council for Advancement of Arab British Understanding, 1970–82 (Jt Vice-Chm., 1967–70); Kuwait British Friendship Soc., 1996–; Mem., Kuwait Investment Adv. Cttee, 1969–. Governor, British Inst. of Florence, 1965–95. Comdr, Order of Cedar of Lebanon, 1969. *Publication:* Not Always with the Pack (autobiographical memoirs), 1989 (trans. Italian, rev. edn, as Benedetti Inglesi Benedetti Italiani, 1991). *Address:* 43 Royal Avenue, SW3 4QE. *T:* (020) 7730 9431; Orchardleigh, Corton, Warminster, Wilts BA12 0SZ. *T:* (01985) 850369. *Club:* Boodle's.

WALTERS, Sir Donald, Kt 1983; Chairman, Llandongh Hospital NHS Trust, 1992–98; *b* 5 Oct. 1925; *s* of Percival Donald and Irene Walters; *m* 1950, Adelaide Jean McQuistin; one *s*. *Educ:* Howardian High Sch., Cardiff; London School of Economics and Political Science (LLB). Called to Bar, Inner Temple, 1946; practised at Bar, Wales and Chester circuit, 1948–59. Dir, 1959–85, Dep. Man. Dir, 1975–85, Chartered Trust plc. Member: Welsh Develt Agency, 1980–93 (Dep. Chm., 1984–92); Develt Bd for Rural Wales, 1984–99; Dir, WNO, 1985–2000 (Vice-Chm., 1990); Chm., Wales Council for Voluntary Action, 1987–93; Mem. Council, Cardiff Univ. (formerly UWCC), 1988– (Chm., 1988–98). High Sheriff, S Glamorgan, 1987–88. Treas., Friends of Llandaff Cathedral, 1998–. Hon. LLD Wales, 1990; Hon. Dr Glamorgan, 1997. *Recreations:* gardening, walking. *Address:* 120 Cyncoed Road, Cardiff CF23 6BL. *T:* (029) 2075 3166.

WALTERS, Geraint Gwynn, CBE 1958; Director for Wales, Ministry of Public Building and Works and Department of the Environment, 1966–72, retired; *b* in the Welsh Colony in Patagonia, 6 June 1910; *s* of Rev. D. D. Walters; *m* 1st, 1942, Doreena Owen (*d* 1959); 2nd, 1968, Sarah Ann Ruth Price; no *c*. *Educ:* various schools in Argentina and Wales; University Coll., Bangor (BA). Gladstone Prizeman, Foyle Prizeman. Schoolmaster, 1933–35; political organizer on staff of Rt Hon. David Lloyd George, 1935–40; Min. of Information, 1940–45; Dep. Regional Dir of Inf., Bristol and Plymouth, 1942–45; Principal, Min. of Works HQ, 1945–48; Dir for Wales, Min. of Works, 1948–63; Dir, Far East Region, Min. of Public Building and Works, 1963–66. Chm., Royal Inst. of Public Admin (S Wales Br.), 1960–61; Hon. Mem. of Gorsedd, 1961; Pres., St David's Soc. of

Singapore, 1965; Leader of Welsh Overseas, at Nat. Eisteddfod of Wales, 1965; Chm., Argentine Welsh Soc., 1976–78, Pres., 1979–82. Chm., Civil Service Sports Council for Wales, 1970–72. Govt Housing Comr for Merthyr Tydfil, 1972–73; Member: Welsh Bd for Industry, 1948–62; Housing Production Bd for Wales; Cttee of Inquiry on Welsh Television, 1963. Mem. Council, Univ. of Wales Inst. of Science and Technology, 1970–87 (Vice-Chm., 1980–83); Mem. Court, Univ. of Wales, 1982–88; Life Mem. Court, Univ. of Wales Coll. of Cardiff, 1989–. *Recreations:* reading Talking Books, radio, travel. *Address:* 1 The Mount, Cardiff Road, Llandaff, Cardiff CF5 2AR. *T:* (029) 2056 8739. *Clubs:* Civil Service; Cardiff and County (Cardiff).

WALTERS, Ian, FIMechE; Chief Executive, Training and Employment Agency, Northern Ireland, since 1995; *b* 20 March 1943; *s* of John and Olive Walters; *m* 1968, Carol Ann Flanders; two *s* one *d*. *Educ:* Moseley Hall Grammar Sch., Cheadle; Univ. of Manchester (BSc; DipTechSc 1966). AMIEE 1970; MIGasE 1972; FIMechE 1997. With Parkinson Cowan Measurement, rising to Factory Manager, Manchester, then Belfast, 1966–72; Dep. Principal, then Principal, Dept of Commerce, NI, 1972–80; Industrial Development Board for Northern Ireland: Dir, then Sen. Dir, IDB N America, NY, 1980–84; Executive Director: Food Div., 1985–89; Internat. Mktg Div., 1989–91; Internat. Repn Div., 1991–92; Corporate Services Group: Actg Dep. Chief Exec., 1992–93; Sen. Exec. Dir, Jan.–Oct. 1993; Dir, Business Support Div., Trng and Employment Agency, 1993–95. MIMgt 1993; FRSA 2000. Chm., Bd of Govs, Groomsport Primary Sch., 1990–. Hon. Dr Rocky Mountain Coll., Montana, 1999. *Recreations:* photography, swimming, gardening. *Address:* (office) Adelaide House, 39–49 Adelaide Street, Belfast BT2 8FD. *T:* (028) 9025 7803.

WALTERS, John Latimer; QC 1997; *b* 15 Sept. 1948; *o s* of late John Paton Walters and Charlotte Alison Walters (*née* Cunningham); *m* 1st, 1970, Victoria Anne Chambers (marr. diss. 1987; she *d* 1996); 2nd, 1990, Caroline Elizabeth, *d* of late John Vipond Byles and of Doreen Violet Byles, Norwich; two *d*, and one step *s*. *Educ:* Rugby Sch.; Balliol Coll., Oxford (MA; Wylie Prize, 1970). FCA. Called to the Bar, Middle Temple, 1977 (Astbury Scholar); practice at Revenue Bar, 1978–. Local Preacher in the Methodist Church (Diss Circuit). *Recreations:* gardening, painting, design and work embroidery, genealogy, singing, esp. hymns, formerly Lieder. *Address:* Gray's Inn Tax Chambers, Gray's Inn, WC1R 5JA. *T:* (020) 7242 2642.

WALTERS, Rear-Adm. John William Townshend, CB 1984; Chairman, Industrial Tribunals, 1984–98; Deputy Chairman, Data Protection Tribunal, 1985–98; *b* 23 April 1926; *s* of William Bernard Walters and Lilian Martha Walters (*née* Hartridge); *m* 1949, Margaret Sarah Patricia Jeffkins; two *s* one *d*. *Educ:* John Fisher Sch., Purley, Surrey. Called to Bar, Middle Temple, 1956. Special Entry to RN, 1944; Secretary: to Flag Officer Middle East, 1962–64; to Naval Secretary, 1964–66; jssc 1967; Supply Officer, HMS Albion, 1967–69; Secretary to Chief of Fleet Support, 1969–72; Chief Naval Judge Advocate, 1972–75; Captain Naval Drafting, 1975–78; Director Naval Administrative Planning, 1978–80; Defence Deleg., UN Law of the Sea Conf., 1980–81; ACDS (Personnel and Logistics), 1981–84, retired. *Address:* 60 Chiltley Way, Liphook, Hants GU30 7HE. *T:* (01428) 723222. *Clubs:* Army and Navy, Royal Naval Sailing Association.

WALTERS, Joyce Dora; Headmistress, Clifton High School, Bristol, 1985–95; *m* 1979, Lt-Col Howard C. Walters (*d* 1983); one *s*. *Educ:* St Anne's College, Oxford. Headmistress, St Mary's, Calne, 1972–85. *Recreations:* travelling, reading, cooking. *Address:* 4 Longwood House, Failand, Bristol BS8 3TL. *T:* (01275) 392092.

WALTERS, Julie, OBE 1999; actress; *b* 22 Feb. 1950; *d* of late Thomas and Mary Walters; *m* 1997, Grant Roffey; one *d*. *Educ:* Holly Lodge Grammar Sch., Smethwick; Manchester Polytechnic (Teaching Certificate). *Theatre:* Educating Rita, 1980 (Drama Critics' Most Promising Newcomer Award; Variety Club Best Newcomer); Having a Ball, Lyric, Hammersmith, 1981; Fool for Love, NT, 1984; Macbeth, Leicester Haymarket, 1985; When I was a Girl I used to Scream and Shout, Whitehall, 1986; Frankie and Johnny in the Clair de Lune, Comedy, 1989; The Rose Tattoo, Playhouse, 1991; All My Sons, RNT, 2000 (Best Actress, Laurence Olivier Awards, 2001). *Films:* Educating Rita, 1983 (Variety Club of GB's Award for best film actress; BAFTA Award for best actress; Hollywood Golden Globe Award); She'll be Wearing Pink Pyjamas, 1985; Car Trouble, 1986; Personal Services, 1987 (British Video Award, Best Actress); Prick Up Your Ears, 1987; Buster, 1988; Killing Dad, 1989; Stepping Out (Variety Club Best Film Actress), 1991; Just Like a Woman, 1992; Clothes in the Wardrobe, 1992; Wide Eyed and Legless, 1993; Bambino Mio, 1994; Pat and Margaret, 1994; Sister My Sister, 1995; Intimate Relations, 1996; Girls' Night, 1998; Titanic Town, 1999; Billy Elliot (Evening Standard Award, Best Actress; BAFTA Award, Best Supporting Actress), 2000; Harry Potter and the Philosopher's Stone, 2001; *Television:* series include: Wood and Walters, 1981–82; Victoria Wood as Seen on TV, 1984, 2nd series, 1986; The Secret Diary of Adrian Mole, 1985; Victoria Wood Series, 1989; GBH, 1991; Jake's Progress, 1995; Melissa, 1997; Dinnerladies, 1998–99; film: Little Red Riding Hood, 1995; serial: Oliver Twist, 1999; also television plays, incl. monologues in series, Talking Heads, 1988, 1998. Show Business Personality of the Year, Variety Club of GB, 2001. *Publication:* Baby Talk, 1990. *Recreations:* reading, television, travel. *Address:* ICM, 76 Oxford Street, W1N 0AX.

WALTERS, Prof. Kenneth, PhD, DSc; FRS 1991; Professor of Applied Mathematics, University of Wales, Aberystwyth, since 1973; *b* 14 Sept. 1934; *s* of late Trevor Walters and of Lilian (*née* Price); *m* 1963, Mary Ross Eccles; two *s* one *d*. *Educ:* University Coll. of Swansea (BSc 1956; MSc 1957; PhD 1959; DSc 1984; Hon. Fellow, 1992). Dept of Mathematics, University Coll. of Wales, Aberystwyth: Lectr, 1960–65; Sen. Lectr, 1965–70; Reader, 1970–73. Vis. Fellow, Peterhouse, Cambridge, 1996. Pres., European Soc. of Rheology, 1996–2000; Chm., Internat. Cttee on Rheology, 2000–. Church Warden, St Michael's, Aberystwyth, 1993–99, 2001–. For. Associate, NAE, USA, 1995. Dr *hc* Joseph Fourier, Grenoble, 1998. Gold Medal, British Soc. of Rheology, 1984. *Publications:* Rheometry, 1975; (ed) Rheometry: industrial applications, 1980; (with M. J. Crochet and A. R. Davies) Numerical Simulation of non-Newtonian Flow, 1984; (with H. A. Barnes amd J. F. Hutton) An Introduction to Rheology, 1989; (with D. V. Boger) Rheological Phenomena in Focus, 1993; (with R. I. Tanner) Rheology: an historical perspective, 1998. *Recreation:* golf. *Address:* Department of Mathematics, University of Wales, Penglais, Aberystwyth, Ceredigion SY23 3BZ. *T:* (01970) 622750; 8 Pen y Graig, Aberystwyth, Dyfed SY23 2JA. *T:* (01970) 615276.

WALTERS, Max; *see* Walters, S. M.

WALTERS, Michael Quentin; Senior Partner, Theodore Goddard, Solicitors, 1983–89; *b* 14 Oct. 1927; *s* of late Leslie Walters and Helen Marie Walters; *m* 1954, Lysbeth Ann Falconer (*d* 1999). *Educ:* Merchant Taylors' School; Worcester College, Oxford. MA. Served Army, 1946–48, 2nd Lieut. Joined Theodore Goddard, 1951; admitted Solicitor, 1954. Chm., EIS Group plc, 1977–94; Deputy Chairman: Martonair International plc, 1980–86; Tilbury Douglas plc, 1991–96; Dir, Delta plc, 1980–95. Mem., Management Cttee, Inst. of Neurology, 1986–91. *Recreations:* fishing, gardening, reading. *Address:* Derryfield Cottage, Ashton Keynes, Swindon, Wilts SN6 6PA. *T:* (01285) 861362.

WALTERS, Minette Caroline Mary; crime writer, since 1992; *b* 26 Sept. 1949; *d* of Capt. Samuel Henry Desmond Jebb and Minette Colleen Helen Jebb (*née* Paul); *m* 1978, Alex Hamilton Walters; two *s*. *Educ:* Godolphin Sch.; Durham Univ. (BA). Magazine journalist, 1972–77; freelance journalist and writer, 1977–82. John Creasey Award, 1992, Gold Dagger Award, 1994, CWA; Edgar Allen Poe Award, 1994. *Publications:* The Ice House, 1992; The Sculptress, 1993; The Scold's Bridle, 1994; The Dark Room, 1995; The Echo, 1997; The Breaker, 1998; The Shape of Snakes, 2000. *Recreations:* crosswords, jigsaw puzzles, DIY, cinema, TV, Radio 4, sailing, reading, wine. *Address:* c/o Gregory & Radice, Authors' Agents, 3 Barb Mews, W6 7PA. *T:* (020) 7610 4676.

WALTERS, Sir Peter (Ingram), Kt 1984; Joint Deputy Chairman, Glaxo SmithKline, since 2000 (Director, 1989–2000, Chairman, 1994–2000, SmithKline Beecham); Deputy Chairman, HSBC Holdings, 1992–2001; *b* 11 March 1931; *s* of late Stephen Walters and of Edna Walters (*née* Redgate); *m* 1st, 1960, Patricia Anne (*née* Tulloch) (marr. diss. 1991); two *s* one *d*; 2nd, 1992, Meryl Marshall. *Educ:* King Edward's Sch., Birmingham; Birmingham Univ. (BCom). NS Commn; RASC, 1952–54; British Petroleum Co., 1954–90: Man. Dir, 1973–90; Chm., 1981–90; Vice-Pres., BP North America, 1965–67; Chairman: BP Chemicals, 1976–81; BP Chemicals Internat., 1981; Blue Circle Industries PLC, 1990–96; Dep. Chm., Thorn EMI, later EMI, 1990–99 (Dir, 1989–99). Dir, 1981–89, Dep. Chm., 1988–89, Nat. Westminster Bank; Chm., Midland Bank, 1991–94. Member: Indust. Soc. Council, 1975–90; Post Office Bd, 1978–79; Coal Industry Adv. Bd, 1981–85; Inst. of Manpower Studies, 1986–88 (Vice-Pres., 1977–80; Pres., 1980–86); Gen. Cttee, Lloyds Register of Shipping, 1976–90; President's Cttee, CBI, 1982–90; President: Soc. of Chem. Industry, 1978–80; Gen. Council of British Shipping, 1977–78; Inst. of Directors, 1986–92. Chm. Governors, London Business Sch., 1987–91 (Governor, 1981–91); Governor Nat. Inst. of Economic and Social Affairs, 1981–90; Mem. Foundn Bd, 1982–83, Chm., 1984–86, Internat. Management Inst.; Trustee: Nat. Maritime Museum, 1983–90; E Malling Res. Station, 1983–; Inst. of Economic Affairs, 1986–. Pres., Police Foundn (Chm., Trustees, 1985–2001). Hon. DSocSc Birmingham, 1986; DUniv Stirling, 1987. Comdr, Order of Leopold (Belgium), 1984. *Recreations:* golf, gardening, sailing. *Address:* 22 Hill Street, W1X 7FU. *Club:* Athenæum.

WALTERS, Sir Roger (Talbot), KBE 1971 (CBE 1965); RIBA, FIStructE; architect in private practice, 1984–87; *b* 31 March 1917; 3rd *s* of Alfred Bernard Walters, Sudbury, Suffolk; *m* 1st, 1946, Gladys Evans (marr. diss.); 2nd, 1976, Claire Myfanwy Chappell. *Educ:* Oundle; Architectural Association School of Architecture; Liverpool University; Birkbeck Coll., London Univ. (BA 1980, BSc 2000). Diploma in Architecture, 1939. Served in Royal Engineers, 1943–46. Office of Sir E. Owen Williams, KBE, 1936; Directorate of Constructional Design, Min. of Works, 1941–43; Architect to Timber Development Assoc., 1946–49; Principal Asst Architect, Eastern Region, British Railways, 1949–59; Chief Architect (Development), Directorate of Works, War Office, 1959–62; Dep. Dir-Gen., R&D, MPBW, 1962–67; Dir-Gen., Production, 1967–69; Controller General, 1969–71; Architect and Controller of Construction Services, GLC, 1971–78; Principal, The Self-Employed Agency, 1981–83. Hon. FAIA. *Address:* 46 Princess Road, NW1 8JL. *T:* (020) 7722 3740. *Club:* Reform.

WALTERS, Sam Robert, MBE 1999; Artistic Director, Orange Tree Theatre, since 1971 (Founder, 1971); *b* 11 Oct. 1939; *s* of Denbigh Robert Walters and Elizabeth Walters (*née* Curry); *m* 1964, Auriol Smith; two *d*. *Educ:* Felsted Sch., Essex; Merton Coll., Oxford (MA PPE); LAMDA. Actor, 1963–67; Resident Dir, Worcester Repertory Co., Swan Theatre, 1967–69; Dir, Jamaica Theatre Co. and Jamaica Theatre Sch., 1970–71; freelance dir, West End, regl theatres, and in Israel and Holland, 1970–; at Orange Tree Theatre has dir. premières of plays by Alan Ayckbourn, Rodney Ackland, Harley Granville Barker, Vaclav Havel and James Saunders, amongst many others. *Recreations:* no time, alas! *Address:* Orange Tree Theatre, 1 Clarence Street, Richmond TW9 2SA. *T:* (020) 8940 0141.

WALTERS, S(tuart) Max, ScD; VMH; Director, University Botanic Garden, Cambridge, 1973–83, retired; *b* 23 May 1920; *s* of Bernard Walters and Ivy Dane; *m* 1948, Lorna Mary Strutt; two *s* one *d*. *Educ:* Penistone Grammar Sch.; St John's Coll., Cambridge. 1st cl. hons Pt I Nat. Scis Tripos 1940 and Pt II Botany 1946; PhD 1949. Research Fellow, St John's Coll., 1947–50; Curator of Herbarium, Botany Sch., Cambridge, 1948–73; Lectr in Botany 1962–73; Fellow of King's Coll., Cambridge, 1964–84. VMH 1984; Linnean Medal for Botany, 1995. *Publications:* (with J. S. L. Gilmour) Wild Flowers, 1954; (with J. Raven) Mountain Flowers, 1956; (ed, with F. H. Perring) Atlas of the British Flora, 1962; (with F. H. Perring, P. D. Sell and H. L. K. Whitehouse) A Flora of Cambridgeshire, 1964; (with D. Briggs) Plant Variation and Evolution, 1969, 3rd edn 1997; The Shaping of Cambridge Botany, 1981; Wild and Garden Plants, 1993; (with E. A. Stow) Darwin's Mentor: John Stevens Henslow 1796–1861, 2001. *Address:* 1 Symonds Lane, Grantchester, Cambridge CB3 9NU. *T:* (01223) 841295.

WALTHER, Robert Philippe, FIA; Group Chief Executive, Clerical Medical Investment Group, since 1995; *b* 31 July 1943; *s* of Prof. D. P. Walther and Barbara (*née* Brook); *m* 1969, Anne Wigglesworth. *Educ:* Charterhouse; Christ Church, Oxford (MA). FIA 1970. Clerical Medical Investment Group: Investment Manager, 1974–85; Investment Dir, 1985–94; Dep. Man. Dir, 1994–95. *Recreations:* hockey, golf, sailing, bridge. *Address:* Ashwells Barn, Chesham Lane, Chalfont St Giles, Bucks HP8 4AS. *T:* (01494) 875575. *Club:* Oxford and Cambridge.

WALTON, family name of **Baron Walton of Detchant.**

WALTON OF DETCHANT, Baron *cr* 1989 (Life Peer), of Detchant in the County of Northumberland; **John Nicholas Walton,** Kt 1979; TD 1962; FRCP; Warden, Green College, University of Oxford, 1983–89; *b* 16 Sept. 1922; *s* of Herbert Walton and Eleanor Watson Walton; *m* 1946, Mary Elizabeth Harrison; one *s* two *d*. *Educ:* Alderman Wraith Grammar Sch., Spennymoor, Co. Durham; Med. Sch., King's Coll., Univ. of Durham. MB, BS (1st Cl. Hons) 1945; MD (Durham) 1952; DSc (Newcastle) 1972; MA(Oxon) 1983; FRCP 1963 (MRCP 1950). Ho. Phys., Royal Victoria Inf., Newcastle, 1946–47; service in RAMC, 1947–49; Med. Registrar, Royal Vic. Inf., 1949–51; Research Asst, Univ. of Durham, 1951–56; Nuffield Foundn Fellow, Mass. Gen. Hosp. and Harvard Univ., 1953–54; King's Coll. Fellow, Neurological Res. Unit, Nat. Hosp., Queen Square, 1954–55; First Asst in Neurology, Newcastle upon Tyne, 1956–58; Cons. Neurologist, Newcastle Univ. Hosps, 1958–83; Prof. of Neurology, 1968–83, and Dean of Medicine, 1971–81, Univ. of Newcastle upon Tyne. Numerous named lectureships and overseas visiting professorships. Member: MRC, 1974–78; GMC, 1971–89 (Chm. Educn Cttee, 1975–82; Pres., 1982–89); President: BMA, 1980–82; Royal Soc. of Medicine, 1984–86 (Hon. Fellow, 1988); ASME 1982–94; Assoc. of British Neurologists, 1987–88; World Fedn Neurol., 1989–97 (First Vice-Pres., 1981–89; Chm., Res. Cttee); Chm., Hamlyn Nat. Commn on Educn, 1991–95; UK Rep., EEC Adv. Cttee, Med. Educn, 1975–83; Editor-in-Chief, Jl of Neurological Sciences, 1966–77; Chm., Muscular Dystrophy Gp of GB, 1970–95, etc. Chm., H of L Select Cttee on Med. Ethics, 1993–94; Mem., H of L Select Cttee on Sci. and Technol., 1992–97, 1999–2001 (Chm., Sub-Cttee 1, 1994–96 and 1999–2001). Col (late RAMC) and OC 1 (N) Gen. Hosp. (TA), 1963–66;

Hon. Col 201(N) Gen. Hosp. (T&AVR), 1971–77. Freeman, City of London, 1978. Founder FMedSci 1998. Foreign Member: Norwegian Acad. of Sci. and Letters, 1987; Venezuelan Acad. of Medicine, 1992; Russian Acad. of Med. Scis, 1993; Hon. Mem., Osler Soc. of London; Hon. Foreign Member: Amer. Neurological Assoc., Amer. Acad. of Neurology, Assoc. Amer. Phys., Amer. Osler Soc., Japan Osler Soc., and of Canadian, French, German, Australian, Austrian, Belgian, Spanish, Polish, Venezuelan, Thai, Japanese, Russian and Brazilian Neurological Assocs. Hon. FACP 1980; Hon. FRCPE 1981; Hon. FRCP (Can) 1984; Hon. FRCPath 1993; Hon. FRCPsych 1993; Hon. Fellow, Inst. of Educn, Univ. of London, 1994. Dr de l'Univ. (Hon.) Aix-Marseille, 1975; Hon. DSc: Leeds, 1979; Leicester, 1980; Hull, 1988; Oxford Brookes, 1994; Durham, 2002; Hon. MD: Sheffield, 1987; Mahidol, Thailand, 1998; Hon. DCL Newcastle, 1988; Laurea *hc* Genoa, 1992. Hon. Freeman, Newcastle upon Tyne, 1980. *Publications:* Subarachnoid Haemorrhage, 1956; (with R. D. Adams) Polymyositis, 1958; Essentials of Neurology, 1961, 6th edn 1989; Disorders of Voluntary Muscle, 1964, 6th edn (ed jtly) 1994; Brain's Diseases of the Nervous System, 7th edn 1969, 10th edn 1993; (with F. L. Mastaglia) Skeletal Muscle Pathology, 1982, 2nd edn 1991, etc; (ed jtly) The Oxford Companion to Medicine, 1986; The Spice of Life (autobiog.), 1993; (ed jtly) The Oxford Medical Companion, 1994; numerous chapters in books and papers in sci. jls. *Recreations:* cricket, golf and other sports, reading, music. *Address:* 13 Norham Gardens, Oxford OX2 6PS. *T:* (01865) 512492. *Clubs:* Athenæum, Oxford and Cambridge.

WALTON, Arthur Halsall, FCA; Partner in Lysons, Haworth & Sankey, 1949–85; *b* 13 July 1916; *s* of Arthur Walton and Elizabeth Leeming (*née* Halsall); *m* 1958, Kathleen Elsie Abram; three *s*. *Educ:* The Leys School. Articled in Lysons & Talbot, 1934; ACA 1940. Military Service, 1939–48: commnd Lancs Fusiliers, 1940. Inst. of Chartered Accountants: Mem. Council 1959; Vice-Pres., 1969; Dep. Pres. 1970; Pres. 1971. *Recreation:* reading. *Address:* 19 Cavendish Mews, Wilmslow SK9 1PW. *Club:* St James's (Manchester).

WALTON, Christopher Thomas; His Honour Judge Walton; a Circuit Judge, since 1997; *b* 20 March 1949; *s* of George Edward Taylor Walton and Margaret Walton; *m* 1992, Brenda Margaret Laws. *Educ:* St Cuthbert's GS, Newcastle upon Tyne; Downing Coll., Cambridge (MA). Called to the Bar, Middle Temple, 1973; a Recorder, 1992–97; North Eastern Circuit. *Publication:* (gen. ed.) Charlesworth & Percy on Negligence, 9th edn 1996. *Recreations:* tennis, golf, suffering with Newcastle United FC, history, music, Scottish art. *Address:* Newcastle Group Manager's Office, North Eastern Circuit, 3rd Floor, Merchant House, 30 The Cloth Market, Newcastle upon Tyne NE1 1EE.

WALTON, Ven. Geoffrey Elmer; Archdeacon of Dorset, 1982–2000, now Archdeacon Emeritus; *b* 19 Feb. 1934; *s* of Harold and Edith Margaret Walton; *m* 1961, Edith Mollie O'Connor; one *s*. *Educ:* St John's Coll., Univ. of Durham (BA); Queen's Coll., Birmingham (DipTh). Asst Curate, Warsop with Sookholme, 1961–65; Vicar of Norwell, Notts, 1965–69; Recruitment and Selection Sec., ACCM, 1969–75; Vicar of Holy Trinity, Weymouth, 1975–82; RD of Weymouth, 1980–82; Non-Residentiary Canon of Salisbury, 1981–2000. Chairman: E Dorset Housing Assoc., 1991–; Dorset County Scout Council, 1995–. *Recreations:* conjuring, religious drama. *Address:* Priory Cottage, 6 Hibberds Field, Cranborne, Dorset BH21 5QL. *T:* (01725) 517167.

WALTON, John William Scott; Director of Statistics, Board of Inland Revenue, 1977–85; *b* 25 Sept. 1925; *s* of late Sir John Charles Walton, KCIE, CB, MC, and late Nelly Margaret, Lady Walton, *d* of late Prof. W. R. Scott. *Educ:* Marlborough; Brasenose Coll., Oxford. Army (RA), 1943–47. Mutual Security Agency, Paris, 1952; Inland Revenue, 1954; Central Statistical Office, 1958, Chief Statistician, 1967, Asst Dir, 1972. *Publications:* (contrib. jtly) M. Perlman, The Organization and Retrieval of Economic Knowledge, 1977; articles in The Review of Income and Wealth, Economic Trends, Business Economist, Statistical News. *Club:* Oxford and Cambridge.

WALTON, Sarah Louise; *see* Rowland-Jones, S. L.

WALTON, William Stephen; Chief Education Officer, Sheffield, 1985–90; *b* 28 March 1933; *s* of Thomas Leslie Walton and Ena Walton (*née* Naylor); *m* 1964, Lois Elicia Petts; three *d* (incl. twins). *Educ:* King's School, Pontefract; Univ. of Birmingham (BA). RAF, gen. duties (flying), 1951–55. Production Management, Dunlop Rubber Co., 1958–61; Derbyshire Local Educn Authy School Teacher, 1961–67; Educational Administration: Hull, 1967–70; Newcastle upon Tyne, 1970–79; Sheffield 1979–90. Visiting Professor: Univ. of Simon Fraser, BC, 1990–91; Univ. of Portland, Oregon, 1990–91. Pres., Soc. of Educn Officers, 1989–90; Chm., Sch. Curriculum Industry Partnership/Mini Enterprise Schs Project, 1990–95. Dir, Outward Bound, 1989–95. Registered Inspector of Schools, 1993–. Hon. Fellow, Sheffield City Polytechnic, 1990. *Recreation:* travel. *Address:* 3 Bentham Road, Chesterfield, Derbyshire S40 4EZ. *T:* (01246) 203769. *Club:* Royal Air Force.

WALWYN, Peter Tyndall; racehorse trainer, 1960–99; *b* 1 July 1933; *s* of late Lt-Col Charles Lawrence Tyndall Walwyn, DSO, OBE, MC, Moreton in Marsh, Glos; *m* 1960, Virginia Gaselee, *d* of A. S. Gaselee, MFH; one *s* one *d*. *Educ:* Amesbury Sch., Hindhead, Surrey; Charterhouse. Leading trainer on the flat, 1974, 1975; leading trainer, Ireland, 1974, 1975; a new record in earnings (£373,563), 1975. Major races won include: One Thousand Guineas, 1970, Humble Duty; Oaks Stakes, 1974, Polygamy; Irish Derby, 1974, English Prince, and 1975, Grundy; King George VI and Queen Elizabeth Stakes, Ascot, 1975, Grundy; Epsom Derby, 1975, Grundy. Chm., Lambourn Trainers' Assoc., 1989–; Member: Jockey Club, 1999–; Council of Mgt, Animal Health Trust, 1998–. Trustee, Lambourn Valley Housing Trust, 1996–. *Publication:* Handy All the Way: a trainer's life, 2000. *Recreations:* foxhunting, shooting. *Address:* Windsor House, Lambourn, Berks RG17 8NR. *T:* (01488) 71347. *Club:* Turf.

WAMIRI, Sir Akapite, KBE 1999; *b* 1938; *s* of Wamiri and Okero Simelupo; *m* 1963, Aime Robuna; two *s* three *d* (and one *d* decd). *Educ:* primary sch.; Teaching Cert. Primary sch. teacher, SDA Church, 1962–70; carpenter, 1970–72; public motor vehicle operator, 1972–75; Man. Dir and Proprietor, 1975–2000. PNG Businessman of the Year, 1993. *Recreation:* watching Rugby League games. *Address:* PO Box 477, Goroka, Papua New Guinea. *T:* 7321818, 7321652.

WANAMAKER, Zoë, Hon. CBE 2001; actor; *b* 13 May; *d* of late Sam Wanamaker, Hon. CBE, and Charlotte (*née* Holland); *m* 1994, Gawn Grainger. *Stage includes:* A Midsummer Night's Dream, 69 Theatre Co., 1970; repertory at Royal Lyceum, 1971–72, Oxford Playhouse, 1974–75 and Nottingham, 1975–76; Royal Shakespeare Company: The Devil's Disciple, Ivanov, Wild Oats, 1976; Captain Swing, The Taming of the Shrew, Piaf, 1978 (NY, 1980); Once in a Lifetime, 1979 (Olivier Award); Comedy of Errors, Twelfth Night, The Time of your Life, 1983; Mother Courage (Drama magazine award), 1984; Othello, 1989; National Theatre: The Importance of Being Earnest, 1982; The Bay at Nice, Wrecked Eggs, 1986; Mrs Klein, 1988, transf. Apollo, 1989; The Crucible, 1990; Battle Royal, 1999; West End: The Last Yankee, Young Vic, 1993; Dead Funny, Hampstead, transf. Vaudeville, 1994; The Glass Menagerie, Donmar, transf. Comedy, 1995; Sylvia, Apollo, 1996; The Old Neighbourhood, Duke of York's, 1998; Boston Marriage, Donmar, 2001; Chichester: Electra, 1997 (Olivier Award, Variety Club Award, 1998), transf. Princeton and NY, 1998–99; Loot, NY, 1986; *films include:* Inside the Third Reich, The Hunger, 1982; The Raggedy Rawney, 1987; Amy Foster, 1996; Wilde, 1997; Harry Potter and the Philosopher's Stone, 2001; *television includes:* Strike, 1981; Richard III, 1982; Enemies of the State, 1982; The Edge of Darkness, 1985; Paradise Postponed, 1985; Once in a Lifetime, 1987; The Dog it was that Died, 1988; Prime Suspect, 1991; Love Hurts, 1992, 1993, 1994; The Blackheath Poisonings, 1992; Momento Mori, 1992; The Countess Alice, 1992; The Widowing of Mrs Holroyd, 1995; A Dance to the Music of Time, 1997; Leprechauns, 1999; David Copperfield, 1999; Gormenghast, 2000; My Family, 2000; Adrian Mole: the Cappuccino Years, 2001; has also appeared in radio plays. Hon. DLitt: S Bank, 1995; Amer. Internat. Univ., London, 1999. Callaway Award, US, 1998. *Address:* c/o Peggy Thompson, 1st & 2nd Floor Offices, 296 Sandycombe Road, Kew, Richmond, Surrey TW9 3NG.

WANDSWORTH, Archdeacon of; *see* Gerrard, Ven. D. K. R.

WANG Gungwu, Prof., CBE 1991; FAHA; Director, East Asian Institute, Singapore, since 1997; Distinguished Professorial Fellow, Institute of Southeast Asian Studies, since 1999; Vice-Chancellor, University of Hong Kong, 1986–95; *b* 9 Oct. 1930; *s* of Wang Fo Wen and Ting Yien; *m* 1955, Margaret Lim Ping-Ting; one *s* two *d*. *Educ:* Anderson Sch., Ipoh, Malaya; Nat. Central Univ., Nanking, China; Univ. of Malaya, Singapore (BA Hons, MA); Univ. of London (PhD 1957). University of Malaya, Singapore: Asst Lectr, 1957–59; Lectr, 1959; University of Malaya, Kuala Lumpur: Lectr, 1959–61; Sen. Lectr, 1961–63; Dean of Arts, 1962–63; Prof. of History, 1963–68; Australian National University: Prof. of Far Eastern History, 1968–86, Emeritus Prof., 1988; Dir, Res. Sch. of Pacific Studies, 1975–80; Univ. Fellow, 1996–. Rockefeller Fellow, 1961–62, Sen. Vis. Fellow, 1972, Univ. of London; Vis. Fellow, All Souls Coll., Oxford, 1974–75; John A. Burns Distinguished Vis. Prof. of History, Univ. of Hawaii, 1979; Rose Morgan Vis. Prof. of History, Univ. of Kansas, 1983. Dir, East Asian History of Science Foundation Ltd, 1987–95. MEC, Hong Kong, 1990–92. Co-Patron, Asia-Link, Melbourne, 1994–. Chairman: Australia-China Council, 1984–86; Envmt Pollution Cttee, HK, 1988–93; Adv. Council on the Envmt, 1993–95; Council for the Performing Arts, HK, 1989–94; Asia-Pacific Council, Griffith Univ., 1997–; Member: Commn of Inquiry on Singapore Riots, 1964–65; Internat. Adv. Panel, E-W Center, Honolulu, 1979–91; Cttee on Aust.-Japan Relations, 1980–81; Regional Council, Inst. of SE Asian Studies, Singapore, 1982–; Admin. Bd, Assoc. of SE Asian Instns of Higher Learning, 1986–92; Council, Chinese Univ. of Hong Kong, 1986–95; Exec. Council, WWF, HK, 1987–95; Council, Asia-Aust. Inst., Sydney, 1991–95, 1999–; Council, Asia Soc., HK, 1991–95; Council, IISS, 1992–2001; Nat. Arts Council, Singapore, 1996–2000; Nat. Heritage Bd, Singapore, 1997–; Nat. Library Bd, 1997–; Bd, Social Sci. Council, NY, 2000–; Council, Nat. Univ. of Singapore, 2000–; Vice-Chm., Chinese Heritage Centre, Singapore, 2000–. President: Internat. Assoc. of Historians of Asia, 1964–68, 1988–91; Asian Studies Assoc. of Aust., 1979–80; Australian Acad. of the Humanities, 1980–83 (Fellow 1970); Hon. Corresp. Mem. for Hong Kong, RSA, 1987 (Fellow 1987; Chm., Hong Kong Chapter, 1992–95); Co-patron, Asia Link, Univ. of Melbourne, 1994–. Mem., Academia Sinica, 1992. For. Hon. Mem., Amer. Acad. of Arts and Scis., 1995; Hon. Mem., Chinese Acad. of Social Scis, 1996. Editor: (also Councillor), Jl of Nanyang Hsueh-hui, Singapore, 1958–68; (also Vice-Pres.), Jl of RAS, Malaysian Br., 1962–68; Gen. Editor, East Asian Historical Monographs series for OUP, 1968–95. Hon. Fellow, SOAS, London Univ., 1996. Hon. DLitt: Sydney, 1992; Hull, 1998; Hon. LLD: Monash, 1992; ANU, 1996; Melbourne, 1997; DUniv: Soka, 1993; Griffith, 1995. *Publications:* The Nanhai Trade: a study of the early history of Chinese trade in the South China Sea, 1958, 2nd edn 1998; A Short History of the Nanyang Chinese, 1959; Latar Belakang Kebudayaan Pendudok di-Tanah Melayu: Bahagian Kebudayaan China (The Cultural Background of the Peoples of Malaysia: Chinese culture), 1962; The Structure of Power in North China during the Five Dynasties, 1963; (ed) Malaysia: a survey, 1964; (ed jtly) Essays on the Sources for Chinese History, 1974; (ed) Self and Biography: essays on the individual and society in Asia, 1975; China and the World since 1949: the impact of independence, modernity and revolution, 1977; (ed jtly) Hong Kong: dilemmas of growth, 1980; Community and Nation: essays on Southeast Asia and the Chinese, 1981; (ed jtly) Society and the Writer: essays on literature in modern Asia, 1981; Dongnanya yu Huaren (Southeast Asia and the Chinese), 1987; Nanhai Maoyi yu Nanyang Huaren (Chinese Trade and Southeast Asia), 1988; (ed with J. Cushman) Changing Indentities of Southeast Asian Chinese since World War II, 1988; Lishi di Gongneng (The Functions of History), 1990; China and the Chinese Overseas, 1991 (Zhongguo yu Haiwai Huaren, 1994); The Chineseness of China: selected essays, 1991; Community and Nation: China, Australia and Southeast Asia, 1992; The Chinese Way: China's position in international relations, 1995; (ed with S. L. Wong) Hong Kong's Transition, 1995; (ed) Global History and Migrations, 1997; (ed) Xianggang shi Xinbian (Hong Kong History: new perspectives), 2 vols, 1997; (ed with S. L. Wong) Hong Kong in the Asia-Pacific Region, 1997; (ed with S. L. Wong) Dynamic Hong: business and culture, 1997; (ed with L. C. Wang) The Chinese Diaspora, 2 vols, 1998; China and Southeast Asia, 1999; (ed with J. Wong) Hong Kong in China, 1999; (ed with J. Wong) China: two decades of reform and change, 1999; The Chinese Overseas: from earthbound China to the quest for autonomy, 2000; Joining the Modern World: inside and outside China, 2000; (ed with Y. Zheng) Reform, Legitimacy and Dilemmas: China's politics and society, 2000; Don't Leave Home: migration and the Chinese, 2001; Sino-Malay Encounters, 2001; contribs to collected vols on Asian history; articles on Chinese and Southeast Asian history in internat. jls. *Recreations:* music, reading, walking. *Address:* East Asian Institute, National University of Singapore, Arts Link, Singapore 119260. *T:* 7752033, *Fax:* 7756607.

WANGARATTA, Bishop of, since 1998; **Rt Rev. (Ralph) David Farrer;** *b* 7 May 1944; *s* of Alexander John Farrer and Jacquelyn Mary Westacott Farrer (*née* Pattison); *m* 1969, Helen Belfield Walker; two *s*. *Educ:* Mentone Grammar Sch.; Ringwood High Sch.; St Barnabas Theol Coll. (ThL Hons; ThSchol Hons). Asst Curate, Good Shepherd, Plympton, SA, 1968–71; ordained priest, 1969; Priest i/c, St John the Baptist, Hillcrest, SA, 1971–73; Asst Priest, St Peter, Eastern Hill, Melbourne, 1973–75; Vicar: Christ Church, Brunswick, Vic, 1975–90; St Mary, Nottingham, 1988–89 (exchange); St Peter, Eastern Hill, 1990–98. Canon, St Paul's Cathedral, Melbourne, 1985–98; Archdeacon: La Trobe, Vic, 1994–96; Melbourne, 1996–98. Dir, Inst. for Spiritual Studies, Melbourne, 1990–98. Chaplain to Parlt, Vic, 1992–98. CHLJ 1991; CMLJ 1996. *Publications:* Orthodoxy Down Under: tracts for our times, 1983; Wilderness Transformed, 1992. *Recreations:* reading, travel, golf. *Address:* Bishop's Lodge, Wangaratta, Vic 3677, Australia. *Club:* Melbourne (Melbourne).

WANLESS, Derek, FCIB; Group Chief Executive, National Westminster Bank plc, 1992–99; *b* 29 Sept. 1947; *s* of Norman Wanless and Edna (*née* Charlton); *m* 1971, Vera West; one *s* four *d*. *Educ:* Royal Grammar Sch., Newcastle upon Tyne; King's Coll., Cambridge (BA 1st cl. Hons Maths, MA). MIS 1973. Joined National Westminster Bank, 1970; appts include: Area Dir, NE Area, 1982–85, W Yorks, 1985–86; Dir of Personal Banking, 1986–88; Gen. Manager, UK Branch Business, 1989–90; Chief Exec., UK Financial Services, 1990–92; Dir, 1991–99; Dep. Gp Chief Exec., Feb.–March 1992.

Chairman: Adv. Cttee on Business and Envmt set up by Secs of State for Envmt and Trade and Ind., 1993–95 (Mem., 1991–93); Nat. Forum for Mgt Educn and Develt, 1996– (Mem. Council, 1993–); Member: Envmtl Management Wkg Gp, 1991–93; Financial Sector Wkg Gp, 1993– (Chm., 1991–93); Business in the Envmt, 1992–; EC Consultative Forum, on the Envmt, 1994–96; World Business Council for Sustainable Develt (formerly World Industry Council for the Envmt), 1993–; Statistics Commn, 2000–. FRSA 1991; CIMgt (CBIM 1992). Freeman, City of London, 1992. Hon. DSc City, 1995. *Recreations:* all sports, chess, music, walking, gardening. *Club:* Reform.

WANLESS, Peter Thomas; Director of Strategy and Communications, Department for Education and Skills (formerly Department for Education and Employment), since 1998; *b* 25 Sept. 1964; *s* of Thomas and Pam Wanless; *m* 1999, Beccy King. *Educ:* Sheldon Sch., Chippenham; Univ. of Leeds (BA Hons Internat. History and Politics). HM Treasury, 1986–94; Private Sec. to Treasury Chief Sec., 1992–94; Head of Information, Dept of Employment, 1994–95; Head of Private Finance Policy, HM Treasury, 1996–98. *Recreations:* cricket, football, eating and drinking. *Address:* (office) Sanctuary Buildings, Great Smith Street, SW1P 3BT. *T:* (020) 7925 5092.

WANSTALL, Hon. Sir Charles Gray, Kt 1974; Chief Justice of Queensland, Australia, 1977–82; *b* 17 Feb. 1912; *m* 1938, Olwyn Mabel, *d* of C. O. John; one *d*. *Educ:* Roma and Gympie State Schs; Gympie High Sch., Queensland, Australia. Called to Queensland Bar, 1933. High Court, 1942. MLA (Liberal) for Toowong, 1944–50; Pres., Liberal Party of Australia (Qld Div.), 1950–53. QC 1956; Judge, Supreme Court, Qld, 1958; Sen. Puisne Judge, 1971. *Recreations:* reading, photography. *Address:* 26/36 Jerdanefield Road, St Lucia, Brisbane, Queensland 4067, Australia. *Clubs:* Queensland (Brisbane); St Lucia Bowling.

WAPSHOTT, Nicholas Henry; North America Correspondent, The Times, since 2001; *b* 13 Jan. 1952; *s* of Raymond Gibson Wapshott and Olivia Beryl Darch; *m* 1980, Louise Nicholson; two *s*. *Educ:* Dursley County Primary Sch.; Rendcomb Coll., Cirencester; Univ. of York (BA Hons). The Scotsman, 1973–76; The Times, 1976–84; The Observer, 1984–92, Political Editor, 1988–92; Editor: The Times Magazine, 1992–97; The Saturday Times, 1997–2001. *Publications:* Peter O'Toole, 1982; (with George Brock) Thatcher, 1983; The Man Between: a biography of Carol Reed, 1990; Rex Harrison, 1991; (with Tim Wapshott) Older: a biography of George Michael, 1998. *Recreations:* cinema, music, elephants. *Address:* The Times, 1 Pennington Street, E98 1TT. *T:* (020) 7782 5000. *Clubs:* Garrick, Morton's.

WARBURTON, Col Alfred Arthur, CBE 1961; DSO 1945; DL; JP; Chairman, SHEF Engineering Ltd, 1970–75; Company Director since 1953; *b* 12 April 1913; *s* of late A. V. Warburton. *Educ:* Sedbergh. Served War of 1939–45, with Essex Yeomanry; Lt-Col comdg South Notts Hussars Yeomanry, 1953–58; Hon. Col 1966–76; Col DCRA 49th Inf. Div. TA, 1958–60; ADC to the Queen, 1961–66; Chm., Notts Cttee TA&VR Assoc. for E Midlands, 1970–78. Director, John Shaw Ltd, Worksop, 1953–66. President: East Midlands Area, Royal British Legion, 1976–77, 1981–82, 1986–87, 1991–92; Notts County Royal British Legion, 1979–95. DL 1966, High Sheriff 1968, JP 1968, Notts. *Recreations:* shooting, fishing, gardening. *Address:* Wigthorpe House, Wigthorpe, Worksop, Notts S81 8BT. *T:* (01909) 730357. *Club:* Cavalry and Guards.

WARBURTON, Dame Anne (Marion), DCVO 1979 (CVO 1965), CMG 1977; HM Diplomatic Service, 1957–85; President, Lucy Cavendish College, Cambridge, 1985–94; *b* 8 June 1927; *d* of Captain Eliot Warburton, MC and Mary Louise (*née* Thompson), US. *Educ:* Barnard Coll., Columbia Univ. (BA); Somerville Coll., Oxford (BA, MA; Hon. Fellow, 1977); MA Cantab 1985. Economic Cooperation Administration, London, 1949–52; NATO Secretariat, Paris, 1952–54; Lazard Bros, London, 1955–57; entered Diplomatic Service, Nov. 1957; 2nd Sec., FO, 1957–59; 2nd, then 1st Sec., UK Mission to UN, NY, 1959–62; 1st Sec., Bonn, 1962–65; 1st Sec., DSAO, London, 1965–67; 1st Sec., FO, then FCO, 1967–70; Counsellor, UK Mission to UN, Geneva, 1970–75; Head of Guidance and Information Policy Dept, FCO, 1975–76; Ambassador to Denmark, 1976–83; Ambassador and UK Permanent Rep. to UN and other internat. organisations, Geneva, 1983–85. Dep. Leader, UK Delegn to UN Women's Conf., Nairobi, 1985; Leader, EC Investigative Mission: Abuse of Bosnian Muslim Women, 1992–93; Mem., Cttee on Standards in Public Life, 1994–97. Member: Equal Opportunities Commn, 1986–88; British Library Bd, 1989–95; Council, UEA, 1991–97. Governor, ESU, 1992–96. Hon. LLD Arkansas, 1994. Verdienstkreuz, 1st Class (West Germany), 1965; Grand Cross, Order of Dannebrog, 1979; Lazo de Dama, Order of Isabel la Católica (Spain), 1988. *Recreations:* travel, dog-walking, enjoying the arts. *Address:* Ansted, Thornham Magna, Eye, Suffolk IP23 8HB. *Clubs:* Oxford and Cambridge, English-Speaking Union.

WARBURTON, David; Senior National Officer: GMB (formerly General, Municipal, Boilermakers and Allied Trades Union), 1973–95; APEX (white collar section of GMB), since 1990; *b* 10 Jan. 1942; *s* of Harold and Ada Warburton; *m* 1966, Carole Anne Susan Tomney; two *d*. *Educ:* Cottingley Manor Sch., Bingley, Yorks; Coleg Harlech, Merioneth, N Wales. Campaign Officer, Labour Party, 1964; Educn Officer, G&MWU, 1965–66, Reg. Officer, 1966–73. Secretary: Chemical Unions Council; Rubber Industry Jt Unions, 1980–86; Health Care Textile Unions, 1988–; Chm., Paper and Packaging Industry Unions, 1988–92. Mem., Europ. Co-ord. Cttee, Chem., Rubber and Glass Unions, 1975–81. Chm., Chem. and Allied Industries Jt Indust. Council, 1973–86; Mem., Govt Industrial Workers Jt Consultative Cttee, 1988–92; Sec., Home Office Jt Indust. Council, 1989–; Treas., Electricity Supply Nat. Jt Council, 1990–; Member: Industrial Tribunal, 1995–99; Employment Tribunal, 1999–. Vice-Pres., Internat. Fedn of Chemical, Energy and Gen. Workers, 1986–94. Member: NEDC, 1973–86; Commonwealth Develt Corp., 1979–87; TUC Energy Cttee, 1978–92; Nat. Jt Council for Civil Air Transport, 1992–95; Chm., TUC Gen. Purposes Cttee, 1984–95; Dir, Union Liaison Services, 1995–. Nat. Sec., UK Friends of Palestine, 1983–. Campaign Dir, Friends of The Speaker, 1996–2000. *Publications:* Pharmaceuticals for the People, 1973; Drug Industry: which way to control, 1975; UK Chemicals: The Way Forward, 1977; Economic Detente, 1980; The Case for Voters Tax Credits, 1983; Forward Labour, 1985; Facts, Figures and Damned Statistics, 1987. *Recreations:* music, American politics, flicking through reference books, films of the thirties and forties. *Address:* 47 Hill Rise, Chorleywood, Rickmansworth, Herts WD3 2NY. *T:* (01923) 778726.

WARBURTON, Prof. Geoffrey Barratt, FREng; Hives Professor of Mechanical Engineering, University of Nottingham, 1982–89; *b* 9 June 1924; *s* of Ernest McPherson and Beatrice Warburton; *m* 1952, Margaret Coan; three *d*. *Educ:* William Hulme's Grammar School, Manchester; Peterhouse, Cambridge (Open Exhibition in Mathematics, 1942; 1st cl. Hons in Mechanical Sciences Tripos, 1944; BA 1945; MA 1949); PhD Edinburgh, 1949. FREng (FEng 1985). Junior Demonstrator, Cambridge Univ., 1944–46; Asst Lecturer in Engineering, Univ. Coll. of Swansea, 1946–47; Dept of Engineering, Univ. of Edinburgh: Assistant, 1947–48, Lecturer, 1948–50 and 1953–56; ICI Research Fellow, 1950–53; Head of Post-graduate School of Applied Dynamics, 1956–61; Nottingham University: Prof. of Applied Mechanics, 1961–82; a Pro-Vice-Chancellor, 1984–88. Vis. Prof., Dept of Civil Engrg, Imperial Coll., 1990–97. FRSE 1960; FIMechE 1968. Rayleigh Medal, Inst. of Acoustics, 1982. Editor, Earthquake Engineering and Structural Dynamics, 1988–96 (Associate Editor, 1972–88); Member, Editorial Boards: Internat. Jl of Mechanical Sciences, 1967–92; Internat. Jl for Numerical Methods in Engineering, 1969–96; Jl of Sound and Vibration, 1971–96. *Publications:* The Dynamical Behaviour of Structures, 1964, 2nd edn 1976; research on mechanical vibrations, in several scientific journals. *Address:* 18 Grangewood Road, Wollaton, Nottingham NG8 2SH.

WARBURTON, Ivor William; Director, Business Development and Industry Affairs, Virgin Rail Group, 1997–99; *b* 13 Aug. 1946; *s* of late Dennis and of Edna Margaret Warburton; *m* 1969, Carole-Ann Ashton (marr. diss. 1982); three *d*. *Educ:* Dulwich Coll.; Queens' Coll., Cambridge (MA); Univ. of Warwick (MSc). FCIT 1989; FCIM 1994. British Railways, 1968–97: graduate trainee, 1968–70; local ops posts, London Midland Region, 1970–73; Divl Passenger Manager, Bristol, 1974–78; Overseas Tourist Manager, 1978–82; Regional Passenger Manager, York, 1982–83; Dir, Passenger Marketing Services, 1984–85; Asst Gen. Manager, London Midland Region, 1985–87; Employee Relations Manager, 1987–88; Dir of Operations, 1988–90; Gen. Manager, London Midland Region, 1990–92; Dir, 1992–95, Man. Dir, 1995–97, InterCity West Coast. Chm., Assoc. of Train Operating Cos, 1997–99. Pres., Railway Study Assoc., 1993–94. *Recreations:* Chinese language and culture, music, opera, handicapped scouting, Marketors' Livery Company. *Address:* 34 St Clair's Road, Croydon CR0 5NE. *T:* (020) 8681 6421.

WARBURTON, John Kenneth, CBE 1983; Director General, Birmingham Chamber of Commerce and Industry, 1994 (Chief Executive, 1978–94); *b* 7 May 1932; *s* of Frederick and Eva Warburton; *m* 1960, Patricia Gordon; one *d*. *Educ:* Newcastle-under-Lyme High Sch.; Keble Coll., Oxford (MA Jurisprudence). Called to Bar, Gray's Inn, 1977. London Chamber of Commerce, 1956–59; Birmingham Chamber of Commerce and Industry, 1959–94. President, British Chambers of Commerce Executives, 1979–81; Member: Steering Cttee, Internat. Bureau of Chambers of Commerce, 1976–94; Nat. Council, Assoc. of British Chambers of Commerce, 1978–94; European Trade Cttee and Business Link Gp, BOTB, 1979–87; E European Trade Council, BOTB, 1984–93; Review Body on Doctors' and Dentists' Remuneration, 1982–92; MSC Task Gp on Employment Trng, 1987; Disciplinary Panels, FIMBRA, 1989–93; Lord Chancellor's Birmingham Adv. Cttee, 1993–99; Chm., Adv. Council, W Midlands Industrial Develt Assoc., 1983–86. Mediator, Centre for Dispute Resolution, 1994–. Director: National Garden Festival 1986 Ltd, 1983–87; National Exhibition Centre Ltd, 1989–95. Chm., Birmingham Macmillan Nurses Appeal, 1994–97; Dep. Chm., Birmingham Children's Hosp. Appeal, 1996–98. Vol. advr, BESO, Slovakia, 1994, and Mongolia, 1995. Companion, BITC, 1992–. Trustee, Holy Child Sch., Edgbaston, 1992–96; Gov., Newman Coll., 1993– (Exec. Chm., 1999–); Life Mem., Court, Brimingham Univ. (Gov., 1982–99). FRSA. DUniv UCE, 1999. *Address:* 35 Hampshire Drive, Edgbaston, Birmingham B15 3NY. *T:* (0121) 454 6764.

WARBURTON, Richard Maurice, OBE 1987; Director General, Royal Society for the Prevention of Accidents, 1979–90; *b* 14 June 1928; *s* of Richard and Phylis Agnes Warburton; *m* 1952, Lois May Green; two *s*. *Educ:* Wigan Grammar Sch.; Birmingham Univ. (BA 1st Cl. Hons). Flying Officer, RAF, 1950–52. HM Inspector of Factories, 1952–79; Head of Accident Prevention Advisory Unit, Health and Safety Executive, 1972–79. *Recreations:* golf, gardening, fell walking. *Address:* Cornaa, Wyfordby Avenue, Blackburn, Lancs BB2 7AR. *T:* (01254) 56824.

WARCHUS, Matthew; freelance theatre director; *b* 24 Oct. 1966; *s* of Michael Warchus and Rosemary Warchus. *Educ:* Bristol Univ. (BA 1st Cl. Hons Music and Drama). Associate Dir, W Yorkshire Playhouse, 1992–94. Plays directed include: Sejanus: his fall, Edinburgh, 1988; The Suicide, 1989, Coriolanus, 1990–91, NYT; Master Harold and the Boys, Bristol Old Vic, 1990; West Yorkshire Playhouse, 1992–94: Life is a Dream, 1992; Who's Afraid of Virginia Woolf, 1992; Fiddler on the Roof, 1992; The Plough and the Stars, 1993; Death of a Salesman, 1994; Betrayal, 1994; True West, 1994; Much Ado About Nothing, Queen's, 1993; The Life of Stuff, Donmar Warehouse, 1993; Henry V, 1994, The Devil is an Ass, 1995, RSC; Troilus and Cressida, Opera North, 1995; Volpone, RNT, 1995; Peter Pan, W Yorks Playhouse, 1995; The Rake's Progress, WNO, 1996; Art, Wyndham's, 1996, NY, 1998; Falstaff, Opera North and ENO, 1997; Hamlet, 1997, The Unexpected Man, Duchess, 1998, NY 2000, RSC; Life x 3, RNT, transf. Old Vic, 2000. Film: Simpatico (also screenplay), 1999. *Address:* c/o Royal Shakespeare Company, Royal Shakespeare Theatre, Stratford-upon-Avon CV37 6BB.

WARD, family name of **Earl of Dudley** and of **Viscount Bangor**.

WARD, Prof. Alan Gordon, CBE 1972 (OBE 1959); Procter Professor of Food and Leather Science, Leeds University, 1961–77, now Emeritus; *b* 18 April 1914; *s* of Lionel Howell Ward and Lily Maud Ward (*née* Morgan); *m* 1938, Cicely Jean Chapman; one *s* two *d*. *Educ:* Queen Elizabeth's Grammar Sch., Wimborne; Trinity Coll., Cambridge (schol.). BA (Cantab) 1935; MA (Cantab) 1940; FInstP 1946; FIFST 1966; CPhys; FSLTC 1986. Lectr in Physics and Mathematics, N Staffs Technical Coll., 1937–40; Experimental Officer, Min. of Supply, 1940–46; Sen. Scientific Officer, Building Research Station, 1946–48; Principal Scientific Officer, 1948–49; Dir of Research, The British Gelatine and Glue Research Assoc., 1949–59; Prof. of Leather Industries, Leeds Univ., 1959–61. Chm., Food Standards Cttee set up by Minister of Agriculture, 1965–79. Hon. FIFST 1979; Hon. FAIFST 1979. *Publications:* Nature of Crystals, 1938; Colloids, Their Properties and Applications, 1945; The Science and Technology of Gelatin, 1977; papers in Trans. Far. Soc., Jl Sci. Instr, Biochem. Jl, etc. *Recreations:* music, gardening. *Address:* 35 Templar Gardens, Wetherby, West Yorkshire LS22 7TG. *T:* (01937) 584177.

WARD, Rt Hon. Sir Alan Hylton, Kt 1988; PC 1995; **Rt Hon. Lord Justice Ward;** a Lord Justice of Appeal, since 1995; *b* 15 Feb. 1938; *s* of late Stanley Victor Ward and of Mary Ward; *m* 1st, 1963 (marr. diss. 1982); one *s* two *d*; 2nd, 1983, Helen (*née* Gilbert); one *d* (and one twin *d* decd). *Educ:* Christian Brothers Coll., Pretoria; Univ. of Pretoria (BA, LLB); Pembroke Coll., Cambridge (MA, LLB; Hon. Fellow, 1998). Called to the Bar, Gray's Inn, 1964, Bencher, 1988; QC 1984; a Recorder, 1985–88; a Judge of the High Court, Family Div., 1988–95; Family Div. Liaison Judge, Midland and Oxford Circuit, 1990–95. Formerly an Attorney of Supreme Court of South Africa. Mem., Matrimonial Causes Procedure Cttee, 1982–85. Consulting Editor, Children Law and Practice, 1991–. *Recreation:* in between reading and writing boring judgments, trying to remember what recreation is. *Address:* Royal Courts of Justice, Strand, WC2A 2LL. *Club:* MCC.

WARD, (Albert Joseph) Reginald; Chief Executive, Reg Ward Associates, since 1993; *b* 5 Oct. 1927; *s* of Albert E. and Gwendolene M. E. Ward, Lydbook, Glos; *m* 1954, Betty Anne Tooze; one *s* one *d*. *Educ:* East Dean Grammar Sch., Cinderford, Glos; Univ. of Manchester (BA Hons History). HM Inspector of Taxes, 1952–65; Chief Administrator, County Architects Dept, Lancashire CC, 1965–68; Business Manager, Shankland Cox & Associates, 1968–69; Corporation Secretary, Irvine New Town Development Corporation, 1969–72; Chief Executive: Coatbridge Borough Council, 1972–74; London

Borough of Hammersmith, 1974–76; Hereford and Worcester CC, 1976–80; LDDC, 1981–88; Kent European Enterprise, 1988–89; ISLEF, Danish develt co., 1989–92. Mem., Duke of Edinburgh's Commn into Housing, 1986–87. Hon. Fellow, QMC, 1987; Fellow, Univ. of London. FRSA. *Recreations:* walking, tennis, music, architecture and urban design. *Address:* Abbot's Court, Deerhurst, Gloucester GL19 4BX. *T:* (01684) 274881.

WARD, Mrs Ann Sarita; non-executive Director, Lambeth, Southwark, Lewisham Family Health Services Authority, 1991–96; *b* 4 Aug. 1923; *d* of Denis Godfrey and Marion Phyllis Godfrey; *m* Frank Ward (*d* 1991); one *s*. *Educ:* St Paul's Girls' Sch., Hammersmith. Professional photographer; photo journalist, Daily Mail, 1962–67, Daily Mirror, 1967–70; award winner, British Press Photographs of Year, 1967. Councillor, London Bor. of Southwark, 1971–86 (Dep. Leader, 1978–83); Chm., ILEA, 1981–82. Pol Advr to Barbara Follett, MP, 1996–2001. Contested (Lab) Streatham, 1970. Associate Mem., Camberwell HA, 1990–93 (Mem., 1982–90). Special Trustee, KCH, 1983–88. Bd Mem., Internat. Shakespeare Globe Centre, 1988–92; Hon. Vice Pres., Friends of Shakespeare's Globe, 1992– (Chm., 1987–92). Co-ordinator, Emily's List UK, 1992–96. *Recreations:* theatre, gardening. *Address:* 49 Pound Avenue, Stevenage, Herts SG1 3JB. *T:* (01438) 220221.

WARD, Cecil, CBE 1989; JP; Town Clerk, Belfast City Council, 1979–89; *b* 26 Oct. 1929; *s* of William and Mary Caroline Ward. *Educ:* Technical High Sch., Belfast; College of Technology, Belfast. Employed by Belfast City Council (formerly Belfast County Borough Council), 1947–89; Asst Town Clerk (Administration), 1977–79. Mem., Local Govt Staff Commn, 1983–89. Member: Arts Council NI, 1980–85, 1987–89; Bd, Ulster Mus., 1989–95; Dir, Ulster Orchestra Soc., 1980–94 (Chm., 1990–94). Mem., Senate, QUB, 1990–2001. Mem., Bd, Mater Hosp., 1994–2002. JP Belfast, 1988. Hon. MA QUB, 1988. *Recreations:* music, reading, hill walking. *Address:* 24 Thornhill, Malone, Belfast, Northern Ireland BT9 6SS. *T:* (028) 9066 8950; Hatter's Field, Drumawier, Greencastle, Co. Donegal, Ireland.

WARD, (Charles John) Nicholas, FCA; Chairman: Ryan Group Ltd, since 1995; ADAS Holdings, since 1998; *b* 1 Aug. 1941; *s* of John Newman Ward and Vivienne Grainger Ward; *m* 1967, Deirdre Veronica Shaw; two *d*. *Educ:* Charterhouse; INSEAD (MBA 1968). FCA 1964. Engaged in retailing, distribution, healthcare, leisure and property sectors with several cos. Chm., NHS Supplies Authy, 1995–98; Dep. Chm., Albert E. Sharp Hldgs, 1996–98. Chairman: Nat. Assoc. for Lay Visiting, 1992–96 (Pres., 1996–); Make a Difference Team, 1994–96; The Volunteering Partnership, 1995–96; British Liver Trust, 1999–; Co-Chm., The Volunteering Partnership Forum for England, 1996–. Liveryman, Tylers and Bricklayers' Co., 1963– (Master, 1991–92). *Address:* Bacon House, Greatworth, near Banbury, Oxon OX17 2DX. *T:* (01295) 712732; Flat 12, 77 Warwick Square, SW1V 2AR. *T:* (020) 7834 9175. *Clubs:* Carlton, Royal Society of Medicine.

WARD, Christopher John; Editorial Director and Joint Founder, Redwood Publishing, since 1983; *b* 25 Aug. 1942; *s* of John Stanley Ward and Jacqueline Law-Hume Costin; *m* 1st, 1971 (marr. diss.); one *s* two *d*; 2nd, 1990, Nonie Niesewand (*née* Fogarty). *Educ:* King's Coll. Sch., Wimbledon. Successively on staff of Driffield Times, 1959, and Newcastle Evening Chronicle, 1960–63; reporter, sub-editor, then feature writer and columnist, 1963–76, Daily Mirror; Assistant Editor: Sunday Mirror, 1976–79; Daily Mirror, 1979–81; Editor, Daily Express, 1981–83. Dir, Acorn Computer plc, 1983–99. Trustee, 1994–2000, Mem. Council, Scotland, 2000–, WWF. Mark Boxer award, British Soc. of Magazine Eds, 1995. *Publications:* How to Complain, 1974; Our Cheque is in the Post, 1980. *Recreations:* walking in the Scottish Borders, shooting. *Address:* Glenburn Hall, Jedburgh TD8 6QB. *T:* (01835) 862291. *Club:* Savile.

WARD, Christopher John Ferguson; solicitor; *b* 26 Dec. 1942; *m* Janet Ward, JP, LLB; one *s* one *d* and two *s* one *d* by former marr. *Educ:* Magdalen College Sch.; Law Society Sch. of Law. MP (C) Swindon, Oct. 1969–June 1970; contested (C) Eton and Slough, 1979. Mem., Berks CC, 1965–81 (Leader of the Council and Chm., Policy Cttee, 1979–81). Gov., Chiltern Nursery Trng Coll., 1975–97 (Chm., 1988–91). Treas., United & Cecil Club, 1993 (Hon. Sec., 1982–87). *Address:* Ramblings, Maidenhead Thicket, Berks SL6 3QE. *T:* (office) (01635) 517111; *e-mail:* cfward@aol.com.

WARD, (Christopher) John (William); Development Director, English National Opera, since 1997; *b* 21 June 1942; *s* of late Thomas Maxfield and of Peggy Ward; *m* 1970, Diane Lelliott (marr. diss. 1988); partner, 1982, Susan Corby. *Educ:* Oundle Sch.; Corpus Christi Coll., Oxford (BA LitHum); Univ. of East Anglia (Graduate DipEcon). Overseas and Economic Intelligence Depts, Bank of England, 1965; General Secretary, Bank of England Staff Organisation, 1973; Gen. Sec., Assoc. of First Div. Civil Servants, 1980; Head of Development, Opera North, 1988–94. Dir of Corporate Affairs, W Yorks Playhouse, 1994–97. *Recreations:* opera, theatre, football. *Address:* ENO, London Coliseum, St Martin's Lane, WC2N 4ES. *Club:* Swindon Town Supporters.

WARD, Claire Margaret; MP (Lab) Watford, since 1997; *b* 9 May 1972; *d* of Frank and Catherine Ward. *Educ:* Loreto Coll., St Albans; Univ. of Hertfordshire (LLB Hons); Brunel Univ. (MA). Trainee Solicitor, Pattinson & Brewer, 1995–97; qualif. Solicitor, 1998–. Mem. (Lab) Elstree and Borehamwood Town Council, 1994–98 (Mayor, 1996–97). PPS to Minister of State for Health, 2001–. Mem., NEC, Lab. Party, 1991–95. Mem., Select Cttee on Culture, Media and Sports, 1997–2001. Jt Sec., All Party Film Industry Gp, 1997–. Patron, Young European Movement, 1999. *Recreations:* films, Association Football (Watford FC season ticket holder), eating out. *Address:* House of Commons, SW1A 0AA. *Club:* Reform.

WARD, Colin; Chief Executive, Student Loans Co., since 1996; *b* 23 June 1947; *s* of Simon Myles Ward and Ella May McConnell; *m* 1969, Marjory Hall Milne. *Educ:* Daniel Stewart's Coll., Edinburgh; Heriot-Watt Univ. (BA 1970). CA 1974. Ernst & Young, Edinburgh, 1970–74; Price Waterhouse, Glasgow, 1974–75; BSC, 1975–77; SDA, latterly Chief Accountant, 1977–90; Student Loans Co., 1990–: Loans Dir, 1990–92; Asst Man. Dir, 1992–96; Main Board, 1994–. Loans Scheme consultant to Hungarian Govt, 1999–2000. *Recreations:* sailing, gardening, classical music. *Address:* Student Loans Co., 100 Bothwell Street, Glasgow G2 7JD. *T:* (0141) 306 2010.

WARD, David; Partner, Atkinson Ritson (formerly Atkinson & North), Solicitors, Carlisle, 1964–98, now Consultant; President, The Law Society, 1989–90; *b* 23 Feb. 1937; *s* of Rev. Frank Ward, Darfield, Yorks, and Elizabeth Ward (*née* Pattinson), Appleby, Westmorland; *m* 1978, Antoinette, *d* of Maj.-Gen. D. A. B. Clarke, CB, CBE; two *s* one *d*. *Educ:* Dame Allan's Sch., Newcastle upon Tyne; Queen Elizabeth Grammar Sch., Penrith; St Edmund Hall, Oxford (BA). Admitted solicitor, 1962. Articled Clerk, 1959, Assistant, 1962, Atkinson & North. Mem., Lord Chancellor's Adv. Cttee on Legal Educn and Conduct, 1991–97. Mem. Council, 1972–91, Vice-Pres., 1988–89, Law Soc.; Pres., Carlisle and District Law Soc., 1985–86. Pres., Carlisle Mountaineering Club, 1985–88. Methodist local preacher, 1955–. *Recreations:* mountaineering, choral and church music. *Address:* The Green, Caldbeck, Wigton, Cumbria CA7 8ER. *T:* (01697) 478220.

WARD, Rev. David Conisbee; Non-stipendiary Minister, St George's, Tolworth, since 1995; *b* 7 Jan. 1933; *s* of late Sydney L. Ward and Ivy A. Ward; *m* 1958, Patricia Jeanette (*née* Nobes); one *s* one *d*. *Educ:* Kingston Grammar Sch.; St John's Coll., Cambridge (Scholar, MA). Asst Principal, Nat. Assistance Bd, 1956, Principal, 1961; Asst Sec., DHSS, 1970, Under Sec., 1976–83. Southwark Ordination Course, 1977–80; Deacon, 1980; Priest, 1981; Non-Stipendiary Curate, St Matthew, Surbiton, 1980–83; Curate, Immanuel Church, Streatham Common, 1983–84, parish priest, 1984–87; Vicar, St Paul's, Hook, Surrey, 1987–93; NSM, All Saints, Kingston, 1993–95. Councillor (Lib Dem) Kingston-upon-Thames, 1994–98 (Dep. Mayor, 1996–97). Governor, Kingston GS, 1988–. FRSA 2000. *Publication:* (with G. W. Evans) Chantry Chapel to Royal Grammar School: the history of Kingston Grammar School 1299–1999, 2000. *Recreations:* member Kingstonian FC; Pitcairn Islands Study Group (philately). *Address:* 50 Elgar Avenue, Tolworth, Surbiton, Surrey KT5 9JN. *T:* (020) 8399 9679. *Club:* Civil Service.

WARD, David Gordon; HM Diplomatic Service; Ambassador to the Dominican Republic, since 1998, and (non-resident) to Haiti, since 1999; *b* 25 July 1942; *s* of late Major Gordon Alec Ward, MBE and of Irene Ward; *m* 1st, 1966, Rosemary Anne Silvester (marr. diss. 1979); two *s* one *d*; 2nd, 1980, Margaret (*née* Martin); one *s* one *d*, and one step *s*. *Educ:* Rutlish Sch., Merton. With CRO, 1961–65; entered FCO, 1965; Montevideo, 1967–70; Dakar (also accredited to Nouakchott, Bamako and Conakry), 1970–74; FCO, 1974–76; Victoria, 1977–80; Libreville, 1980; Luxembourg, 1981–83; Consul, Oporto, 1983–87; FCO, 1988–90; Harare, 1990–95; FCO, 1995–98. Hon. Cavaleiro da Confrariá do Vinho do Porto, 1986. *Recreations:* theatre, visual arts, tennis. *Address:* c/o Foreign and Commonwealth Office, SW1A 2AH.

WARD, Donald Albert; *b* 30 March 1920; *s* of Albert and Rosie Ward; *m* 1948, Maureen Molloy; five *s*. *Educ:* Brewery Road Elementary Sch.; Southend-on-Sea High Sch.; The Queen's Coll., Oxford. BA(Hons)(Maths); MA. Served War, Indian Army (RIASC), 10th Indian Div., Middle East and Italy, 1940–45 (despatches). Min. of Food, 1946–53; Export Credits Guarantee Dept, 1953–74 (Under-Sec., 1971–74); Sec. Gen., Internat. Union of Credit and Investment Insurers (Berne Union), 1974–86. *Address:* 54 Highlands Road, Leatherhead, Surrey KT22 8NJ.

See also M. Ward.

WARD, Ven. Edwin James Greenfield, LVO 1963; Archdeacon of Sherborne, 1968–84; Archdeacon Emeritus and Canon Emeritus of Salisbury Cathedral, since 1985; Extra Chaplain to the Queen, since 1989 (Chaplain, 1955–89); *b* 26 Oct. 1919; *er s* of Canon F. G. Ward, MC, lately of Canberra, Australia; *m* 1946, Grizell Evelyn Buxton (*d* 1985); one *s* two *d*. *Educ:* St John's, Leatherhead; Christ's Coll., Cambridge (MA). Served King's Dragoon Guards, 1940; Reserve, 1946. Ordained 1948; Vicar of North Elmham, Norfolk, 1950–55; Chaplain, Royal Chapel, Windsor Great Park, 1955–67; Rector of West Stafford, 1967–84. Mem. of Council, Marlborough Coll., 1969–88; Visitor, Milton Abbey School, 1991–94 (Mem., Bd of Govs, 1983–91). *Recreation:* fishing. *Address:* 14 Arle Close, Alresford, Hants SO14 9BG. *T:* (01962) 735501.

See also Baron Wakeham.

WARD, Frank Dixon; *see* Dixon Ward.

WARD, Graham Norman Charles, FCA; FInstE; Senior Partner, World Energy and Utilities Group, PricewaterhouseCoopers, since 2000; President, Institute of Chartered Accountants in England and Wales, 2000–01; *b* 9 May 1952; *s* of late Ronald Charles Edward Ward and of Hazel Winifred Ward (*née* Elis); *m* 1975, Ingrid Imogen Sylvia Baden-Powell (marr. diss. 1981); two *s*; *m* 1993, Ann Mistri; one *s*. *Educ:* Jesus Coll., Oxford (Boxing Blue; MA). ACA 1977, FCA 1983; CIGasE 1997; FInstE 1999. Price Waterhouse, subseq. PricewaterhouseCoopers: articled clerk, 1974–77; Personal Technical Asst to Chm., Accounting Standards Cttee, 1978–79; on secondment to HM Treasury, 1985; Partner, 1986; Dir, Electricity Services Europe, 1990–94; Direct Business Devel, 1993–94; Chm., World Utilities Gp, 1994–96; Dep. Chm., World Energy Gp, 1996–98; World Utilities Leader, 1998–2000. Member: Panel on Takeovers and Mergers, 2000–01; Financial Reporting Council, 2001– (Dep. Chm., 2001–01). Chairman: Consultative Cttee of Accountancy Bodies, 2000–01; Power Sector Wkg Gp, Trade Partners UK, 2001–; Mem. Council, Soc. of Pension Consultants, 1988–90; Mem., Auditing Practices Bd, 2001–; Member: Cttee, British Energy Assoc., 1997– (Vice-Chm., 1998–2001; Chm., 2001–); Exec. Council, Parly Gp for Energy Studies, 1998–. Chairman: Young Chartered Accountants' Gp, 1980–81; London Soc. of Chartered Accountants, 1989–90 (Mem. Cttee, 1983–91); Chartered Accountants in the Community, 1996–; Mem. Council, ICAEW, 1991– (Vice-Pres., 1998–99; Dep. Pres., 1999–2000). Vice Pres., Epilepsy Res. Foundn, 1997–. Vice President: Univ. of Oxford Amateur Boxing Club, 1990–; Soc. of Conservative Accountants, 1992–; President: Jesus Coll. Assoc., 1990–91; Chartered Accountant Students' Soc. of London, 1992–96 (Vice-Pres., 1987–92). FRSA 1996. Freeman: City of London, 1994; Co. of Chartered Accountants in England and Wales, 1994 (Mem., Ct of Assts, 1997–). *Publications:* The Work of a Pension Scheme Actuary, 1987; Pensions: your way through the maze, 1988. *Recreations:* boxing, Rugby, opera, ballet. *Address:* PricewaterhouseCoopers, No 1 London Bridge, SE1 9QL. *T:* (020) 7804 3101. *Clubs:* Carlton; Vincent's (Oxford).

WARD, Hubert, OBE 1996; MA; Headmaster (formerly Principal), English College, Prague, 1992–96; *b* 26 Sept. 1931; *s* of Allan Miles Ward and Joan Mary Ward; *m* 1958, Elizabeth Cynthia Fearn Bechervaise; one *s* two *d*. *Educ:* Westminster Sch.; Trinity Coll., Cambridge. Asst Master (Maths), Geelong C of E Grammar Sch., Victoria, 1955–66; Asst Master (Maths), Westminster Sch., London, 1966–69; Headmaster, King's Sch., Ely, 1970–92. Mem. (L) Cambs CC, 1985–89. JP Cambs, 1976–92. *Publication:* (with K. Lewis) Starting Statistics, 1969. *Recreations:* rowing, sailing, bird-watching. *Address:* 1 The Green, Mistley, Manningtree, Essex CO11 1EU.

WARD, Prof. Ian Macmillan, FRS 1983; FInstP, FIM; Research Professor and Technical Director, Centre for Industrial Polymers, University of Leeds, since 1994 (Professor of Physics, 1970–94, and Cavendish Professor, 1987–94); *b* 9 April 1928; *s* of Harry Ward and Joan Moodie (*née* Burt); *m* 1960, Margaret (*née* Linley); two *s* one *d*. *Educ:* Royal Grammar Sch., Newcastle upon Tyne; Magdalen Coll., Oxford (MA, DPhil). FInstP 1965; FIM (FPRI 1974). Technical Officer, ICI Fibres, 1954–61; seconded to Division of Applied Mathematics, Brown Univ., USA, 1961–62; Head of Basic Physics Section, ICI Fibres, 1962–65, ICI Research Associate, 1964; Sen. Lectr in Physics of Materials, Univ. of Bristol, 1965–69; Chm., Dept of Physics, Univ. of Leeds, 1975–78, 1987–89; Dir, Interdisciplinary Res. Centre in Polymer Sci. and Technol., Univs of Leeds, Bradford and Durham, 1989–94. Secretary, Polymer Physics Gp, Inst. of Physics, 1964–71, Chm. 1971–75; Chairman, Macromolecular Physics Gp, European Physical Soc., 1976–81; Pres., British Soc. of Rheology, 1984–86. Hon. DSc Bradford, 1993. A. A. Griffith Medal, 1982; S. G. Smith Meml Medal, Textile Inst., 1984; Swinburne Medal, Plastics and Rubber Inst., 1988; Charles Vernon Boys Medal, Inst. of Physics, 1993. *Publications:* Mechanical Properties of Solid Polymers, 1971, 2nd edn 1983; (ed) Structure and Properties of Oriented Polymers, 1975, 2nd edn 1997; (ed jtly) Ultra High Modulus Polymers, 1979; (with D. Hadley) An Introduction to the Mechanical Properties of Solid

Polymers, 1993; (ed jtly) Solid Phase Processing of Polymers, 2000; contribs to Polymer, Jl of Polymer Science, Jl of Materials Science, Proc. Royal Soc., etc. *Recreations:* music, walking. *Address:* Kirskill, 2 Creskeld Drive, Bramhope, Leeds LS16 9EL. *T:* (0113) 267 3637.

WARD, John; *see* Ward, C. J. W.

WARD, Most Rev. John Aloysius, OFM Cap; Archbishop of Cardiff, (RC), 1983–2001; *b* 24 Jan. 1929; *s* of Eugene Ward and Hannah Ward (*née* Cheetham). *Educ:* Prior Park College, Bath. Entered Franciscan Friary, 1945; first vows 1946; solemn profession, 1950; ordained Priest, 1953; Diocesan Travelling Mission, Menevia, 1954–60; Guardian and Parish Priest, Peckham, London, 1960–66; Provincial Definitor (Councillor), 1963–69; Provincial Dir of Vocations, 1963–69; Provincial Deleg. to Secular Order of Franciscans, 1966–69; Minister Provincial, 1969–70; General Definitor (Councillor) , Rome, 1970–80; Bishop Coadjutor of Menevia, 1980–81; Bishop of Menevia, 1981–83.

WARD, Sir John (Devereux), Kt 1997; CBE 1973; BSc; CEng, FICE, FIStructE; *b* 8 March 1925; *s* of late Thomas Edward and Evelyn Victoria Ward; *m* 1955, Jean Miller Aitken; one *s* one *d. Educ:* Romford County Technical Sch.; Univ. of St Andrews (BSc). Navigator, RAF, 1943–47; student, 1949–53. Employed, Consulting Engineers, 1953–58, Taylor Woodrow Ltd, 1958–79; Man. Dir, Taylor Woodrow Arcon, Arcon Building Exports, 1976–78. MP (C) Poole, 1979–97. PPS to: Financial Sec. to Treasury, 1984–86; Sec. of State for Social Security, 1987–89; Prime Minister, 1994–97. UK Rep. to Council of Europe and WEU, 1983–87, 1989–94. Chm., British Gp, IPU, 1993–94 (Mem., Exec. Cttee, 1982–94). Chm., Wessex Area Conservatives, 1966–69; Conservative Party: Mem., Nat. Union Exec., 1965–78 (Mem., Gen. Purposes Cttee, 1966–72, 1975–78); Mem., Central Bd of Finance, 1969–78; Vice-Chm., Cons. Trade and Industry Cttee, 1983–84.

WARD, John MacQueen, CBE 1995; Chairman: Scottish Homes, since 1996; Scottish Post Office Board, since 1997; Chairman, Macfarlane Group plc (formerly MacFarlane Group (Clansman)), since 1998; *b* 1 Aug. 1940; *m* Barbara MacIntosh; one *s* three *d. Educ:* Edinburgh Acad.; Fettes Coll. CA. IBM UK Ltd: Plant Controller, 1966–75; Dir, Inf. Systems for Europe, 1975–79; Manufacturing Controller, 1979–81; Dir, Havant Plant, 1982–90 (numerous quality awards); Dir, UK Public Service Business, 1991–95; Res. Dir, Scotland and N England, 1991–96. Chm., European Assets Trust, 1995–; non-exec. Dir, Dunfermline Building Soc., 1995–. Chairman: Scottish CBI, 1993–95; Scottish Qualifications Authy, 2000–. Chm. or former Chm., advisory bodies and councils in Scotland. *Recreations:* walking, DIY, reading. *Address:* Scottish Homes, 91 Haymarket Terrace, Edinburgh EH12 5HE. *T:* (0131) 479 5220. *Club:* New (Edinburgh).

WARD, John Stanton, CBE 1985; NEAC; RP 1952; artist and portrait painter; *b* 10 Oct. 1917; *s* of Russell Stanton and Jessie Elizabeth Ward; *m* 1950, Alison Christine Mary Williams; four *s* twin *d. Educ:* St Owen's School, Hereford; Royal College of Art. Royal Engineers, 1939–46. Vogue Magazine, 1948–52. ARA 1956, RA 1966, resigned 1997; former Vice-Pres., Royal Soc. of Portrait Painters. Mem. Exec., Nat. Art-Collections Fund, 1976–87. Trustee, Royal Acad. Has held exhibitions at Agnews Gallery, Maas Gallery, and at Hazlitt Gooden & Fox, 1994, 1996, 1998. Freeman: City of Hereford, 1991; City of Canterbury. Hon. DLitt Kent, 1982. *Recreation:* book illustration. *Address:* Bilting Court, Bilting, Ashford, Kent TN25 4HF. *T:* (01233) 812478. *Clubs:* Athenæum, Harry's Bar.

WARD, Rev. Prof. (John Stephen) Keith, FBA 2001; Regius Professor of Divinity, University of Oxford, since 1991; Canon of Christ Church, Oxford, since 1991; *b* 22 Aug. 1938; *s* of John George Ward and Evelyn (*née* Simpson); *m* 1963, Marian Trotman; one *s* one *d. Educ:* UCW, Cardiff (BA 1962); Linacre Coll., Oxford (BLitt 1968); Trinity Hall, Cambridge (MA 1972); Westcott House, Cambridge. DD Oxon, 1998; DD Cantab, 1999. Ordained priest of Church of England, 1972. Lecturer in Logic, Univ. of Glasgow, 1964–69; Lectr in Philosophy, Univ. of St Andrews, 1969–71; Lectr in Philosophy of Religion, Univ. of London, 1971–75; Dean of Trinity Hall, Cambridge, 1975–82. F. D. Maurice Prof. of Moral and Social Theology, Univ. of London, 1982–85; Prof. of History and Phil. of Religion, King's Coll. London, 1985–91. Jt Editor, Religious Studies, 1990–98. Jt Pres., World Congress of Faiths, 1992–2001. *Publications:* Ethics and Christianity, 1970; Kant's View of Ethics, 1972; The Divine Image, 1976; The Concept of God, 1977; The Promise, 1981; Rational Theology and the Creativity of God, 1982; Holding Fast to God, 1982; The Living God, 1984; Battle for the Soul, 1985; Images of Eternity, 1987; The Rule of Love, 1989; Divine Action, 1990; A Vision to Pursue, 1991; Religion and Revelation, 1994; Religion and Creation, 1996; God, Chance and Necessity, 1996; God, Faith and the New Millennium, 1998; Religion and Human Nature, 1998; Religion and Community, 2000. *Recreations:* music, walking. *Address:* Christ Church, Oxford OX1 1DP. *T:* (01865) 276246.

WARD, Joseph Haggitt; *b* 7 July 1926; *s* of Joseph G. and Gladys Ward; *m* 1961, Anthea Clemo; one *s* one *d. Educ:* St Olave's Grammar School; Sidney Sussex College, Cambridge. Asst Principal, Min. of National Insurance, 1951; Private Sec. to Minister of Social Security, 1966–68; Asst Sec., 1968; Min. of Housing, later DoE, 1969–72; DHSS, 1972; Under-Sec. (pensions and nat. insce contributions), DHSS, 1976–86. *Recreations:* music, history of music. *Address:* 34 Uffington Road, SE27 0ND. *T:* (020) 8670 1732.

WARD, Sir Joseph James Laffey, 4th Bt *cr* 1911; *b* 11 Nov. 1946; *s* of Sir Joseph George Davidson Ward, 3rd Bt, and Joan Mary Haden (*d* 1993), *d* of Major Thomas J. Laffey, NZSC; *S* father, 1970; *m* 1968, Robyn Allison, *d* of William Maitland Martin, Rotorua, NZ; one *s* one *d. Heir: s* Joseph James Martin Ward; *b* 20 Feb. 1971.

WARD, Keith; *see* Ward, J. S. K.

WARD, His Honour Malcolm Beverley; a Circuit Judge, Midland and Oxford Circuit, 1979–97; *b* 3 May 1931; *s* of Edgar and Dora Mary Ward; *m* 1958, Muriel Winifred, *d* of Dr E. D. M. Wallace, Perth; two *s* two *d. Educ:* Wolverhampton Grammar Sch.; St John's Coll., Cambridge (Open Mathematical Schol.; MA, LLM). Called to the Bar, Inner Temple, 1956; practised Oxford (later Midland and Oxford) Circuit; a Recorder of the Crown Court, 1974–79. Governor, Wolverhampton Grammar Sch., 1972– (Chm., 1981–). *Recreations:* golf, music, (in theory) horticulture. *Address:* 1 Fountain Court, Birmingham B4 6DR.

WARD, Malcolm Stanley; Managing Editor, The Peninsula, Qatar, since 1995; *b* 24 Sept. 1951; *s* of Hugh Ward and Rebecca Ward (*née* Rogerson). *Educ:* Gilberd School, Colchester. Dep. Editor, Gulf News, Dubai, 1978–79; Editor, Woodham and Wickford Chronicle, Essex, 1979–81; Dep. Editor, Gulf Times, Qatar, 1981–84; Dep. Editor, 1984–86, Dir and Editor, 1986–91, Daily News, Birmingham; Editor, Metro News, Birmingham, 1991–92; Ed., Evening News, Worcester, 1992–95. *Recreations:* writing, travel, soccer, driving, tennis. *Address:* 3 Rectory Park Avenue, Sutton Coldfield, West Midlands B75 7BL. *T:* (0121) 329 2589.

WARD, Mary Angela, MBE 1996; Co-Founder, and Artistic Director, since 1974, Chicken Shed Theatre Co.; *b* 2 Dec. 1944; *d* of Patrick O'Dwyer and Dot O'Dwyer (*née* Johnson); *m* 1971, Manus Ward; two *s. Educ:* Ilford Ursuline High Sch.; Digby Stuart Coll. Teacher, 1966–85; with Jo Collins, founded Chicken Shed Th. Co., 1974, with aim of producing pieces of theatrical and musical excellence to open the performing arts to all, incl. those denied access elsewhere. DUniv Middx, 1998. *Recreation:* Chicken Shed! *Address:* Chicken Shed Theatre Co., Chase Side, Southgate, N14 4PE. *T:* (020) 8351 6161, ext. 204.

WARD, Michael; Chief Executive, London Development Agency, since 2000; *b* 15 Oct. 1949; *s* of Donald Albert Ward, *qv*; partner, Hilary Knight; one *s* one *d. Educ:* Wimbledon Coll., London; University Coll., Oxford (BA PPE 1972); Birkbeck Coll., London (MA Social and Econ. Hist. 1980). Mem. (Lab), GLC, 1981–86 (Chm., Industry and Employment Cttee, 1981–86; Dep. Leader, 1985–86). Dir, Centre for Local Econ. Strategies, Manchester, 1987–2000. Chm., Manchester City Labour Party, 1995–2000. *Address:* London Development Agency, Romney House, 43 Marsham Street, SW1P 3PY. *T:* (020) 7983 4802.

WARD, Michael Jackson, CBE 1980; British Council Director, Germany, 1990–91, retired; *b* 16 Sept. 1931; *s* of late Harry Ward, CBE, and Dorothy Julia Ward (*née* Clutterbuck); *m* 1955, Eileen Patricia Foster; one *s* one *d. Educ:* Drayton Manor Grammar Sch.; University Coll. London (BA); Univ. of Freiburg; Corpus Christi Coll., Oxford. HM Forces, 1953–55; 2nd Lieut Royal Signals. Admin. Officer, HMOCS, serving as Dist Comr and Asst Sec. to Govt, Gilbert and Ellice Is; British Council, 1961–91: Schs Recruitment Dept, 1961–64; Regional Rep., Sarawak, 1964–68; Dep. Rep., Pakistan, 1968–70; Dir, Appointments Services Dept, 1970–72; Dir, Personnel Dept, 1972–75; Controller, Personnel and Appts Div., 1975–77; Representative, Italy, 1977–81; Controller, Home Div., 1981–85; Asst Dir-Gen., 1985–90. Hon. Mem., British Council, 1991. *Recreations:* music, golf. *Address:* 1 Knapp Rise, Haslingfield, Cambridge CB3 7LQ; *e-mail:* mjward@spanner.org. *Club:* Gog Magog Golf.

WARD, Michael John; Chairman, Charlton Triangle Homes Ltd, since 1999; *b* 7 April 1931; *s* of late Stanley and Margaret Ward; *m* 1953, Lilian Lomas; two *d. Educ:* Mawney Road Jun. Mixed Sch., Romford; Royal Liberty Sch., Romford; Bungay Grammar Sch.; Univ. of Manchester. BA (Admin). FIPR. Education Officer, RAF, 1953–57; Registrar, Chartered Inst. of Secretaries, 1958–60; S. J. Noel-Brown & Co. Ltd: O&M consultant to local authorities, 1960–61; Local Govt Officer to Labour Party, 1961–65; Public Relns consultant to local authorities, 1965–70; Press Officer, ILEA, 1970–74 and 1979–80; Public Relns Officer, London Borough of Lewisham, 1980–84; Dir of Information, ILEA, 1984–86; Public Affairs Officer, Gas Consumers Council, 1986–88; Exec. Officer to Rt Hon. Paddy Ashdown, MP, 1988–89; Asst Gen. Sec., Public Relations, Assoc. of Chief Officers of Probation, 1989–95. Administrator, Blackheath Cator Estate Residents Ltd, 1995–2001. Contested: (Lab) Peterborough, 1966, 1970, Feb. 1974; (SDP/Alliance) Tonbridge and Malling, 1987. MP (Lab) Peterborough, Oct. 1974–1979; PPS to Sec. of State for Educn and Science, 1975–76, to Minister for Overseas Develt, 1976, to Minister of State, FCO, 1976–79. Sponsored Unfair Contract Terms Act, 1977. Councillor, Borough of Romford, 1958–65; London Borough of Havering: Councillor, 1964–78; Alderman, 1971–78; Leader of Council, 1971–74. Labour Chief Whip, London Boroughs Assoc., 1968–71; Member, Essex River Authority, 1964–71; Greenwich DHA, 1982–85; Greenwich and Bexley FPC, 1982–85; SE London Valuation Tribunal, 1997–. FRSA 1992. *Recreations:* gardens, music. *Address:* 55 Bridge House, Valetta Way, Rochester, Kent ME1 1LQ.

WARD, Michael Phelps, CBE 1983; FRCS; FRGS; Emeritus Consultant Surgeon: City and East London Area Health Authority (Teaching) (Consultant Surgeon, 1964–93); St Andrew's Hospital, Bow (Consultant Surgeon, 1964–93); Newham Hospital (Consultant Surgeon, 1983–93); Lecturer in Clinical Surgery, London Hospital Medical College, 1975–93; *b* 26 March 1925; *s* of late Wilfrid Arthur Ward, CMG, MC and Norah Anne Phelps; *m* 1957, Felicity Jane Ewbank; one *s. Educ:* Marlborough Coll., Wilts; Peterhouse, Cambridge (Ironmongers' Co. Exhibn); London Hosp. Med. Coll. BA Hons Cantab 1945, MA 1961; MB BChir 1949, MD 1968. FRCS 1955. Ho. Surg., Surgical Registrar, Sen. Surgical Registrar, London Hosp.; Asst Resident, Royal Victoria Hosp., Montreal, Canada; Consultant Surg., Poplar Hosp., E14, 1964–75; Hunterian Prof., RCS, 1954. Served RAMC, Captain, 1950–52. Fellow, Assoc. of Surgs of Gt Britain. Master, Soc. of Apothecaries, 1993–94 (Mem., Court of Assts, 1986). Mount Everest Reconnaissance Expedn, 1951; Mount Everest Expedn, 1953 (1st Ascent); Scientific Expedn to Everest Region, 1960–61 (Leader, 1st Winter Ascents of Amadablam and other peaks); Scientific Expedns to Bhutan Himal, 1964 and 1965; scientific and mountaineering expedn to Pamirs West Kun Lun, China, 1980–81; Royal Soc./Chinese Acad. of Sciences Tibet Geotraverse, 1985–86. FRSocMed; FRGS 1964. Dickson Asia Lectr, RGS, 1966, 1985; Monkton Copeman Lectr, Soc. of Apothecaries, 1994. Cuthbert Peek Award, RGS, 1973; Founder's (Royal) Medal, RGS, 1982; Cullum Medal, Amer. Geog. Soc., 1954. Chm., Mount Everest Foundn, 1978–80. *Publications:* Mountaineers' Companion, 1966; In this Short Span, 1972; Mountain Medicine, 1975; (jtly) High Altitude Medicine and Physiology, 1989, 3rd edn 2000; many scientific and medical papers on the effects of great altitude, exposure to cold, and on exercise; also on exploratory journeys to Nepal, Bhutan, Chinese Central Asia and Tibet. *Recreations:* mountaineering, ski-ing. *Clubs:* Alpine (Vice-Pres., 1968–69; Hon. Mem., 1993); Cambridge Alpine (Pres., 1986–95).

WARD, Nicholas; *see* Ward, C. J. N.

WARD, Peter Simms; a District Judge (Magistrates' Courts), Manchester, since 2001; *b* 20 June 1943; *s* of Norman and Marie Ward; *m* 1974, Monica Stalker; three *s. Educ:* Bolton Sch.; Bristol Univ. (LLB). Articled to J. J. Rothwell, Solicitor, Salford; admitted Solicitor, 1969; Partner, Rothwell & Evans, Solicitors, Salford, Gtr Manchester, 1969–94; Provincial Stipendiary Magistrate, subseq. Dist Judge (Magistrates' Courts), Merseyside, 1994–2001. *Recreations:* reading, walking, swimming. *Address:* City Magistrates' Court, Crown Square, Manchester M60 1PR. *T:* (0161) 832 7272.

WARD, Maj.-Gen. Sir Philip (John Newling), KCVO 1976; CBE 1972 (OBE 1969); Lord-Lieutenant of West Sussex, 1994–99 (Vice Lord-Lieutenant, 1990–94); *b* 10 July 1924; *s* of George William Newling Ward and Mary Florence Ward; *m* 1948, Pamela Ann Glennie; two *s* two *d.* Commnd Welsh Guards, 1943; Adjt, RMA Sandhurst, 1960–62; Bde Major, Household Bde, 1962–65; Comdg 1st Bn Welsh Guards, 1965–67; Comdr Land Forces, Gulf, 1969–71; GOC London Dist and Maj.-Gen. comdg Household Div., 1973–76; Comdt, RMA, 1976–79. Communar of Chichester Cathedral, 1980–83. Dir, Public Affairs, Internat. Distillers and Vintners (UK), 1980–89; Chm., Peter Hamilton Security Consultants, 1986–90; Director: W & A Gilbey (formerly Gilbey Vintners), 1983–89; Morgan Furze, 1983–89; Justerini & Brooks, 1987–89; Southern Reg., Lloyds Bank, 1983–90. Pres., S of England Agricl Soc., 1994–95 (Vice Patron and Life Gov., 1996); Chairman: Queen Alexandra Hosp. Home, 1979–98; Royal Soldiers Daughters School, 1980–83; Governor and Comdt, Church Lads and Church Girls Bde., 1980–86. Patron, Chichester Cathedral Trust, 1995. Freeman, City of London, 1976. DL West

Sussex, 1981, High Sheriff, 1985–86. KStJ 1994. *Recreation:* gardening. *Address:* 15 Tarrant Wharf, Arundel, W Sussex BN18 9NY. *Clubs:* Cavalry and Guards (Chm., 1987–90), Buck's.

WARD, Phillip David; Director of Finance, Department for Transport, Local Government and the Regions (formerly Department of the Environment, Transport and the Regions), since 2001; *b* 1 Sept. 1950; *s* of Frederick William Ward and Phyllis Mavis Ward; *m* 1974, Barbara Patricia, (Pip), Taylor; two *d. Educ:* Sir John Talbot's GS, Whitchurch; Sheffield Univ. (BJur 1973). Department of the Environment, later Department of the Environment, Transport and the Regions: Admin Trainee, 1973–78; Hackney/Islington Inner City Partnership, 1978–80; Principal, Local Govt Finance Directorate, 1980–85; Asst Sec., Local Govt Finance Review, 1985–90; Principal Private Sec. to Sec. of State for the Envmt, 1990–92; Dir (Under Sec.), Construction Sponsorship, 1992–97; Dir, Energy, Envmt and Waste, 1997–2001. *Recreations:* sailing, Rugby, cinema. *Address:* (office) Floor 11/E14, Ashdown House, 123 Victoria Street, SW1E 6DE. *T:* (020) 7890 6970. *Club:* Fishers Green Sailing.

WARD, Rear-Adm. Rees Graham John, FIEE; Capability Manager (Strategic Deployment), Ministry of Defence, 1999–June 2002; *b* 1 Oct. 1949; *s* of John Walter Ward and Helen Burt Ward (*née* Foggo); *m* 1st, 1973, Christina Glen Robertson (marr. diss.); two *s*; 2nd, 1980, Phyllis Gentry Pennington; two *d. Educ:* Queens' Coll., Cambridge (MA); Cranfield Univ. (MSc). FIEE 1998. Joined RN, 1967; served: HMS Russel, 1972–73; HMS Brighton, 1977–79; MoD PE, 1981–83; jsdc 1984; HMS Ark Royal, 1984–87; MA to Controller of Navy, 1988–89; Asst DOR (Sea), 1990–92; MA to Chief of Defence Procurement, 1992–94; DOR (Sea), 1995–97; rcds 1998; hcsc 1999; ACDS, Operational Requirements (Sea Systems), 1999. Rep. GB and Scotland at athletics cross country running, 1972–77. *Recreations:* reading, running marathons. *Address:* Ministry of Defence, Whitehall, SW1A 2HB. *Club:* Hawks (Cambridge).

WARD, Reginald; *see* Ward, A. J. R.

WARD, Reginald George; Director, Analysis and Research (formerly Statistics and Economic Office), Inland Revenue, since 1994; *b* 6 July 1942; *s* of Thomas George and Ada May Ward; *m* 1964, Chandan Mistry; two *s* one *d. Educ:* Leicester, Aberdeen and Oxford Universities; London Business Sch. Lectr in Economics, St Andrews Univ., 1965; Analyst, National Cash Register, 1969; Economist, ICL, 1970; DTI, 1971; Chief Statistician: HM Treasury, 1978; Cabinet Office, 1982; Dir, Business Statistics Office, DTI, 1986; Asst Dir, CSO, 1989–94. *Recreation:* sailing. *Address:* Room F11, Somerset House, WC2R 1LB.

WARD, Prof. Richard Hugh, PhD; Professor of Biological Anthropology and Fellow of Linacre College, Oxford University, since 1996. *Educ:* Univ. of Auckland, NZ (BA, BSc, MA); PhD Michigan. Lectr, Auckland Univ., until 1974; Asst Prof. of Anthropology and Res. Affiliate in Child Develt, 1974–78, Associate Prof. in Epidemiology and Biostats, 1978–80, Univ. of Washington; Associate Prof. of Med. Genetics, Univ. of British Columbia, 1980–96. Mem., N Amer. Human Genome Diversity Cttee, 1993–96. *Publications:* contrib. to learned jls. *Address:* Linacre College, Oxford OX1 3JA.

WARD, Maj.-Gen. Robert William, CB 1989; MBE 1972; DL; plantsman, landscape and garden design consultant, since 1992; *b* 17 Oct. 1935; *s* of late Lt-Col William Denby Ward and Monica Thérèse Ward (*née* Collett-White); *m* 1966, Lavinia Dorothy Cramsie; two *s* one *d. Educ:* Rugby School; RMA Sandhurst. Commissioned Queen's Bays (later 1st Queen's Dragoon Guards), 1955; served Jordan, Libya, BAOR, Borneo and Persian Gulf; MA to C-in-C BAOR, 1973–75; CO 1st Queen's Dragoon Guards, 1975–77; Col GS Staff Coll., 1977–79; Comdr 22 Armd Brigade, 1979–82; RCDS Canada, 1982–83; Asst Chief of Staff, Northern Army Group, 1983–86; GOC Western Dist, 1986–89, retd. Col, 1st Queen's Dragoon Guards, 1991–97; Hon. Col, Royal Mercian and Lancastrian Yeomanry, 1995–2001. Sec., Game Conservancy, Shropshire, 1993–2000; Chairman: Nat. Meml Arboretum, 1996–98; Shropshire Parks and Gardens Trust, 1996–2001. Pres., SSAFA, Shropshire, 1994–. DL Shropshire, 2000. *Recreations:* gardening, outdoor sports, country pursuits, travel, food, wine. *Clubs:* Cavalry and Guards, MCC, I Zingari.

WARD, Robin William; Director-General, West Yorkshire Passenger Transport Executive, 1976–82; *b* 14 Jan. 1931; *s* of William Frederick and Elsie Gertrude Ward; *m* 1974, Jean Catherine Laird; three *s. Educ:* Colston's Sch., Bristol; University Coll. London. BScEcon, 1st Cl. Hons. Pilot Officer/Flying Officer, RAF Educn Br., 1954–55. Various posts, London Transport Exec., 1955–67; seconded to Brit. Transport Staff Coll. as mem. staff and latterly Asst Principal (incl. course at Harvard Business Sch.), 1967–70; Industrial Relations Officer, London Transport Exec., 1970–74; Dir of Personnel, W Yorks Passenger Transport Exec., 1974–76. *Recreations:* Scottish country dancing; trying to learn the piano. *Address:* 29 Stanley Street, Palmwoods, Qld 4555, Australia.

WARD, His Honour Roy Livingstone; QC 1972; a Circuit Judge, 1979–94; *b* 31 Aug. 1925; *m* 1972, Barbara Anne (*née* Brockbank) (marr. diss); one *s* one *d. Educ:* Taunton Sch.; Pembroke Coll., Cambridge. BA(Hons). Served RAF, 1943–47 (commnd 1945). Called to Bar, Middle Temple, 1950. A Recorder of the Crown Court, 1972–79. *Address:* Tethers End, Shelsley Drive, Colwall, Worcs WR13 6PS. *Club:* Oxford and Cambridge.

WARD, Rt Rev. Simon B.; *see* Barrington-Ward.

WARD, Tony, OBE 1998; Group Services Director, BAA plc, since 1999 (Group Human Resources Director, 1997–99); *b* 20 Feb. 1950; *s* of Kenneth H. Ward and Elsie M. Ward; *m* 1972, Margaret Harrison; one *d. Educ:* Univ. of Leeds (BSc 1st Class Hons 1972). Personnel Manager, Stone Platt Industries, 1972–81; Personnel Director (Divisional), GrandMet, 1981–91; Dir of Human Resources, Kingfisher plc, 1992–97. Mem., 1990–95, Dep. Chm., 1993–95, CRE. Chm., Equal Opportunities Panel, CBI. FCIPD; FRSA. *Recreations:* golf, art. *Address:* BAA plc, 130 Wilton Road, SW1V 1LQ. *Club:* Lambourne.

WARD, William Alan H.; *see* Heaton-Ward.

WARD, William Alec; HM Diplomatic Service, retired; *b* 27 Nov. 1928; *s* of William Leslie Ward and Gladys Ward; *m* 1955, Sheila Joan Hawking; two *s* two *d. Educ:* King's Coll. Sch., Wimbledon; Christ Church, Oxford. HM Forces, 1947–49. Colonial Office, 1952; Private Sec. to Permanent Under-Sec., 1955–57; Singapore, 1960–64; seconded to CRO, 1963; Karachi, 1964–66; Islamabad, 1966–68; joined HM Diplomatic Service, 1968; FCO, 1968–71; Salisbury, 1971–72; Dep. High Comr, Colombo, 1973–76; High Comr, Mauritius, 1977–81. *Recreations:* music, walking. *Address:* The Grange, Ellesmere, Shropshire SY12 9DE.

WARD-BOOTH, Maj.-Gen. John Antony, OBE 1971; DL; Consultant, Francis Graves and Partners, 1989–95; *b* 18 July 1927; *s* of Rev. J. Ward-Booth and Mrs E. M. Ward-Booth; *m* 1952, Margaret Joan, *d* of Rev. A. W. Hooper, MC, MA and G. Hooper; one *s* two *d* (and one *s* decd). *Educ:* Worksop College, Notts. Joined Army, 1945; commnd into Worcestershire Regt in India, 1946; served India and Middle East, 1946–48; regular commn Bedfordshire and Hertfordshire Regt, 1948; served BAOR, Far East, Nigeria and Congo, 1950–63, trans. to Parachute Regt, 1963; commanded 3rd Bn, Parachute Regt, 1967–69; Hong Kong, 1969–70; Comdr, 16 Parachute Bde, 1970–73; Nat. Defence Coll., Canada, 1973–74; DAG, HQ BAOR, 1974–75; Dir, Army Air Corps, 1976–79; GOC Western District, 1979–82. Dep. Col, Royal Anglian Regt, 1982–87. Sec., Eastern Wessex TAVRA, 1982–89. Hon. Vice-Pres., Army Rugby Union, 1982. Governor: Enham Village Centre, 1982–97; Clayesmore Sch., Dorset, 1985–2000 (Chm., 1989–94). DL Hants, 1988. *Recreations:* sailing, golf, cricket. *Address:* 19 St Peter's Close, Goodworth Clatford, Andover, Hants SP11 7SF. *Club:* MCC.

WARD-JACKSON, Mrs (Audrey) Muriel; *b* 30 Oct. 1914; *d* of late William James Jenkins and Alice Jenkins (*née* Glyde); *m* 1946, George Ralph Norman Ward-Jackson (*d* 1982); no *c. Educ:* Queenswood, Hatfield, Herts; Lady Margaret Hall, Oxford (MA). Home Civil Service (Ministries of Works, Town and Country Planning, Housing and Local Government, and Central Econ. Planning Staff, HM Treasury): Asst Principal, 1937; Principal, 1942; Asst Sec., 1946–55. A Director (concerned mainly with Finance), John Lewis Partnership, 1955–74; John Lewis Partnership Ltd: Dir, 1957–74; Dir, John Lewis Properties Ltd, 1969–74; Chm., John Lewis Partnership Pensions Trust, 1964–74. On Civil Service Arbitration Tribunal, 1959–64; Chm., Consumers Cttees (Agric. Marketing), 1971–75; Member: Nat. Savings Review Cttee, 1971–73; Royal Commn on Standards of Conduct in Public Life, 1974–76. A Governor, British Film Inst., 1962–65; Mem. Council, Bedford Coll., London Univ., 1967–72. *Recreation:* swimming. *Address:* 91 The Cloisters, Pegasus Grange, White House Road, Oxford OX1 4QQ. *T:* (01865) 725486.

WARD-JONES, Norman Arthur, CBE 1990; VRD 1959; Chairman, Gaming Board for Great Britain, 1986–92 (Member, 1984–92); *b* 19 Sept. 1922; *s* of Alfred Thomas Ward-Jones and Claire Mayall Lees; *m* 1962, Pamela Catherine Ainslie (*née* Glessing). *Educ:* Oundle Sch.; Brasenose Coll., Oxford. Solicitor 1950. War service, Royal Marines (Captain), 1941–46; RM Reserve, 1948–64, Lt-Col and CO RMR (City of London), 1961–64; Hon. Col 1968–74. Solicitor, Lawrance Messer & Co., Sen. Partner, 1981–85, retired 1989. Hon. Solicitor, Magistrates' Assoc., 1960–85. Chm; East Anglian Real Property Co. Ltd, 1970–80, non-exec. Dir, 1980–89. Pres., Brasenose Soc., 1991–92. JP N Westminster PSD, 1966–92. *Recreation:* wine drinking. *Address:* The Cottage, Barnhorne Manor, 75 Barnhorn Road, Little Common, Bexhill-on-Sea, East Sussex TN39 4QU. *Club:* East India.

WARD-THOMAS, Evelyn, (Mrs Michael Ward-Thomas); *see* Anthony, Evelyn.

WARD THOMAS, Gwyn Edward; *see* Thomas.

WARDALE, Sir Geoffrey (Charles), KCB 1979 (CB 1974); Second Permanent Secretary, Department of the Environment, 1978–80; *b* 29 Nov. 1919; *m* 1944, Rosemary Octavia Dyer; one *s* one *d. Educ:* Altrincham Grammar Sch.; Queens' Coll., Cambridge (Schol.). Army Service, 1940–41. Joined Ministry of War Transport as Temp. Asst Princ., 1942; Private Sec. to Perm. Sec., 1946; Princ., 1948; Asst Sec., 1957; Under-Sec., Min. of Transport, later DoE, 1966; Dep. Sec., 1972. Led inquiry: into the Open Structure in the Civil Service (The Wardale Report), 1981; into cases of fraud and corruption in PSA, 1982–83. Mem. Council, Univ. of Sussex, 1986–92; Chm., Brighton Coll. Council, 1985–90. President: Friends of Lewes Soc., 1992–97; Lewes Area CABx, 1989–99. *Recreations:* transport history, painting, listening to music. *Address:* 89 Paddock Lane, Lewes, East Sussex BN7 1TW. *T:* (01273) 473468.

WARDELL, Gareth Lodwig; *b* 29 Nov. 1944; *s* of John Thomas Wardell and Jenny Ceridwen Wardell; *m* 1967, Jennifer Dawn Evans; one *s. Educ:* London Sch. of Econs and Pol. Science (BScEcon, MSc). Geography Master, Chislehurst and Sidcup Technical High Sch., 1967–68; Head of Econs Dept, St Clement Danes Grammar Sch., 1968–70; Sixth Form Econs Master, Haberdashers' Aske's Sch., Elstree, 1970–72; Educn Lectr, Bedford Coll. of Physical Educn, 1972–73; Sen. Lectr in Geography, Trinity Coll., Carmarthen, 1973–82. MP (Lab) Gower, Sept. 1982–1997. A Forestry Comr, 1999–. Mem. Bd, Envmt Agency, 1997–. Lay Mem., GMC, 1995–. *Publications:* articles on regional issues in British Econ. Survey. *Recreations:* cycling, cross-country running.

WARDINGTON, 2nd Baron *cr* 1936, of Alnmouth in the County of Northumberland; **Christopher Henry Beaumont Pease;** *b* 22 Jan. 1924; *s* of 1st Baron Wardington and Hon. Dorothy Charlotte (*d* 1983), *er d* of 1st Baron Forster; *S* father, 1950; *m* 1964, Margaret Audrey Dunfee, *d* of John and Eva White; one *s* two *d* (adopted). *Educ:* Eton. Served War of 1939–45, in Scots Guards, 1942–47, Captain. Partner in Stockbroking firm of Hoare Govett Ltd, 1947–86. Alderman of Broad Street Ward, City of London, 1960–63. Mem., Council of Foreign Bondholders, 1967–81. Comr, Public Works Loan Bd, 1969–73. Trustee, Royal Jubilee Trusts, 1967–90; Chm., Athlone Trust, 1983–. Pres., Friends of the British Library, 1999– (Chm., 1988–94). *Recreations:* cricket, golf, book collecting. *Heir: b* Hon. William Simon Pease [*b* 15 Oct. 1925; *m* 1962, Hon. Elizabeth Jane Ormsby-Gore, *d* of 4th Baron Harlech, KG, PC, GCMG]. *Address:* Wardington Manor, Banbury, Oxon OX17 1SW. *T:* (01295) 750202; 29 Moore Street, SW3. *T:* (020) 7584 5245. *Clubs:* Royal Automobile, Garrick, Roxburghe; All England Lawn Tennis.

WARDLAW, Sir Henry (John), 21st Bt *cr* 1631, of Pitreavie; *b* 30 Nov. 1930; *s* of Sir Henry Wardlaw, 20th Bt, and Ellen (*d* 1977), *d* of John Francis Brady; *S* father, 1983; *m* 1962, Julie-Ann, *d* of late Edward Patrick Kirwan; five *s* two *d. Educ:* Melbourne Univ. (MB, BS). *Heir: s* (Henry) Justin Wardlaw [*b* 10 Aug. 1963; *m* 1988, Rachel Jane, *y d* of James Kennedy Pitney]. *Address:* Mandalay, 75–77 Two Bays Road, Mount Eliza, Vic 3930, Australia.

WARDLE, Charles Frederick; Public Affairs Director, Harrods Ltd, 2001; *b* 23 Aug. 1939; *s* of late Frederick Maclean Wardle; *m* 1964, Lesley Ann, *d* of Sidney Wells; one *d. Educ:* Tonbridge Sch.; Lincoln Coll., Oxford; Harvard Business Sch. MA Oxon 1968; MBA Harvard. Asst to Pres., American Express Co., NY, 1966–69; Merchant Banking, London, 1969–72; Chairman: Benjamin Priest Gp plc, 1977–84 (Dir, 1972–74, Man. Dir, 1974–77); Warne, Wright and Rowland, 1978–84; Dir, Asset Special Situations Trust plc, 1982–84. CBI: Mem. Council, 1980–84; Mem., W Midlands Regional Council, 1980–84. MP (C) Bexhill and Battle, 1983–2001. PPS: to Minister of State (Health), 1984; to Sec. of State for Social Services, 1984–87; to Sec. of State for Scotland, 1990–92; Parly Under-Sec. of State, Home Office, 1992–94, DTI, 1994–95. Member Select Committee: on Trade and Industry, 1983–84; on Treasury and Civil Service, 1990–91. Chm., Cons. One Nation Forum, 1989–90. Member: Commercial and Econ. Cttee, EEF, 1981–83; Midlands Cttee, InstD, 1981–83. FRGS 1977. *Recreations:* books, sport, travel.

WARDLE, (John) Irving; Drama Critic, The Independent on Sunday, 1990–95; *b* 20 July 1929; *s* of John Wardle and Nellie Partington; *m* 1958, Joan Notkin (marr. diss.); *m* 1963, Fay Crowder (marr. diss.); two *s*; *m* 1975, Elizabeth Grist; one *s* one *d. Educ:* Bolton Sch.; Wadham Coll., Oxford (BA); Royal Coll. of Music (ARCM). Joined Times Educational Supplement as sub-editor, 1956; Dep. Theatre Critic, The Observer, 1960; Drama Critic,

The Times, 1963–89. Editor, Gambit, 1973–75. Play: The Houseboy, prod Open Space Theatre, 1974, ITV, 1982. *Publications:* The Theatres of George Devine (biog.), 1978; Theatre Criticism, 1992. *Recreation:* piano playing. *Address:* 51 Richmond Road, New Barnet, Herts EN5 1SF. *T:* (020) 8440 3671.

WARE, Anna, (Mrs T. D. O. Ware); *see* Pavord, A.

WARE, Cyril George, CB 1981; Under-Secretary, Inland Revenue, 1974–82; *b* 25 May 1922; *s* of Frederick George Ware and Elizabeth Mary Ware; *m* 1946, Gwennie (*née* Wooding); two *s* one *d. Educ:* Leyton County High Sch. Entered Inland Revenue as Tax Officer, 1939; Inspector of Taxes, 1949; Sen. Principal Inspector, 1969. *Recreations:* music, woodwork, gardening, swimming. *Address:* 86 Tycehurst Hill, Loughton, Essex IG10 1DA. *T:* (020) 8508 3588.

WARE, Michael John, CB 1985; QC 1988; barrister-at-law; Solicitor and Legal Adviser, Department of the Environment, 1982–92; *b* 7 May 1932; *s* of Kenneth George Ware and Phyllis Matilda (*née* Joynes); *m* 1966, Susan Ann Maitland; three *d. Educ:* Cheltenham Grammar Sch.; Trinity Hall, Cambridge (BA(Law), LLB). Called to Bar, Middle Temple. Nat. Service, 2/Lieut RASC, 1954–56. Board of Trade (later Dept of Trade and Industry): Legal Asst, 1957–64; Sen. Legal Asst, 1964–72; Asst Solicitor, 1972–73; Dir, Legal Dept, Office of Fair Trading, 1973–77; Under Secretary: Dept of Trade, 1977–81; DoE, 1982. Chm., Meat Hygiene Appeals Tribunals for England and Wales, 1993–. *Address:* 12 Hill Road, Haslemere, Surrey GU27 2JN.

WAREING, Robert Nelson; MP (Lab) Liverpool, West Derby, since 1983; *b* 20 Aug. 1930; *s* of late Robert Wareing and late Florence Wareing (*née* Mallon); *m* 1962, Betty Coward (*d* 1989). *Educ:* Ranworth Square Sch., Liverpool; Alsop High Sch., Liverpool; Bolton Coll. of Educn. BSc (Econ) London Univ., 1956. RAF, 1948–50. Administrative Asst, Liverpool City Bldg Surveyor's Dept, 1946–56; Lecturer: Brooklyn Technical Coll., Birmingham, 1957–59; Wigan and Dist Mining and Technical Coll., 1959–63; Liverpool Coll. of Commerce, 1963–64; Liverpool City Inst. of Further Educn, 1964–72; Central Liverpool Coll. of Further Educn, 1972–83. Merseyside County Council: Mem., 1981–86; Chief Whip, Labour Gp, 1981–83; Chm., Economic Develt Cttee, 1981–83; Chm., Merseyside Economic Develt Co. Ltd, 1981–86. A Vice-Pres., AMA, 1984–97. Joined Labour Party, 1947: Pres., Liverpool Dist Labour Party, 1974–81; Mem., MSF. Introduced Chronically Sick and Disabled Persons Bill, 1983; Asst Labour Whip, 1987–92, with responsibility for health and social security, employment, sport, environment and foreign affairs. Mem., Select Cttee on Foreign Affairs, 1992–97. Chm., British–Yugoslav Parly Gp, 1994– (Vice-Chm., 1985–94); Sec., British–Russian Parly Gp, 1997– (Vice Pres., 1992–97); Treasurer: British-Azerbaijan Parly Gp, 1997–; British-Ukranian Parly Gp, 1999–. *Recreations:* watching soccer (especially Everton FC), concert-going and ballet, motoring and travel. *Address:* House of Commons, SW1A 0AA.

WARHURST, Alan, CBE 1990; Director, Manchester Museum, 1977–93; *b* 6 Feb. 1927; *s* of W. Warhurst; *m* 1953, Sheila Lilian Bradbury; one *s* two *d. Educ:* Canon Slade Sch., Bolton; Manchester Univ. (BA Hons History 1950). FSA 1958; FMA 1958. Commnd Lancashire Fusiliers, 1947. Asst, Grosvenor Museum, Chester, 1950–51; Asst Curator, Maidstone Museum and Art Gallery, 1951–55; Curator, Northampton Museum and Art Gallery, 1955–60; Director: City Museum, Bristol, 1960–70; Ulster Museum, 1970–77. Vice-Pres., NW Museum and Art Gallery Service, subseq. NW Museums Service, 1997– (Dep. Chm., 1987–92; Chm., 1992–97). Mem., Museums and Galls Commn, 1994–99. Chm., Irish Nat. Cttee, ICOM, 1973–75; President: S Western Fedn Museums and Galls, 1966–68; Museums Assoc., 1975–76; N Western Fedn of Museums and Art Galls, 1979–80; Hon. Sec., Univ. Museums Gp, 1987–93. Trustee, Boat Mus., Ellesmere Port, 1990–92. Chm., Hulme Hall Cttee, Univ. of Manchester, 1986–93; Gov., Hulme Hall Trust Foundn, 1994–2000. Hon. MA Belfast, 1982. *Publications:* various archaeological and museum contribs to learned jls. *Address:* Calabar Cottage, Woodville Road, Altrincham, Cheshire WA14 2AL.

WARING, Sir (Alfred) Holburt, 3rd Bt *cr* 1935; *b* 2 Aug. 1933; *s* of Sir Alfred Harold Waring, 2nd Bt, and Winifred (*d* 1992), *d* of late Albert Boston, Stockton-on-Tees; *S* father, 1981; *m* 1958, Anita, *d* of late Valentin Medinilla, Madrid; one *s* two *d. Educ:* Rossall School; Leeds College of Commerce. Director: SRM Plastics Ltd; Waring Investments Ltd; Property Realisation Co. Ltd. *Recreations:* golf, squash, swimming. *Heir: s* Michael Holburt Waring, *b* 3 Jan. 1964. *Address:* Earls Croft, 30 Russell Road, Moor Park, Northwood, Middlesex HA6 2LR. *T:* (01923) 824570. *Club:* Moor Park Golf (Rickmansworth).

WARK, Kirsty Anne; journalist and television presenter, since 1976; *b* 3 Feb. 1955; *d* of James Allan Wark and Roberta Eason Forrest; *m* 1990, Alan Clements; one *s* one *d. Educ:* Wellington Sch., Ayr; Edinburgh Univ. (BA 1976). Joined BBC, 1976: radio then TV producer, politics and current affairs progs, 1977–90; formed independent prodn co. with husband, 1990; Presenter: The Late Show, and Edinburgh Nights, 1990–93; Newsnight, 1993–; One Foot In The Past, 1993–2000; Words With Wark, 1995–99; Building a Nation, 1998; Gen. Elections, Scottish Gen. Elections and Referendum, and Rough Justice, 1998–; The Kirsty Wark Show, 1999–2001. Patron: Playbus Assoc., 1998–; TAG Theatre Co., 1998–; Scottish Blind Golf Soc., 2000–; Nat. AIDS Trust, 2000–; Maggies Centre, 2001–; Mem. Council, The Prince's Trust, 2000–. Hon. FRIAS 2000; Hon. FRIBA 2001. Hon. DLitt Abertay, 1995; Dr *hc* Edinburgh, 2000; Hon. LLD Aberdeen, 2001. Scotland Journalist of Year, 1993, Scotland Presenter of Year, 1997, BAFTA; Scot of the Year, 1998. *Publication:* Restless Nation, 1997. *Recreations:* reading, tennis, beachcombing, architecture, cooking, film, music. *Address:* Wark, Clements & Co. Ltd, The Tollgate, 19 Marine Crescent, Glasgow G51 1HD. *T:* (0141) 429 1750.

WARKE, Rt Rev. Robert Alexander; Bishop of Cork, Cloyne and Ross, 1988–98; *b* 10 July 1930; *s* of Alexander and Annie Warke; *m* 1964, Eileen Charlotte Janet Minna Skillen; two *d. Educ:* Mountmellick National School; The King's Hospital; Trinity Coll., Dublin (BA 1952, BD 1960); Union Theol Seminary, New York (Dip. in Ecumenical Studies). Ordained, 1953; Curate: St Mark's, Newtownards, 1953–55; St Catherine's, Dublin, 1956–59; Rathfarnham, Dublin, 1959–64; Rector: Dunlavin, Hollywood and Ballymore-Eustace, 1964–67; Drumcondra, North Strand and St Barnabas, 1967–71; Zion, Dublin, 1971–88; Archdeacon of Dublin, 1980–88. *Publications:* St Nicholas Church and Parish, 1967; Light at Evening Time, 1986; The Passion according to St Matthew, 1990; Ripples in the Pool, 1993; In Search of the Living God, 2000. *Recreations:* following sport, theatre, reading. *Address:* 6 Kerdiff Park, Naas, Co. Kildare, Ireland.

WARKENTIN, Juliet; Partner, The Fourth Room, since 2000; *b* 10 May 1961; *d* of John and Germaine Warkentin; *m* 1991, Andrew Lamb. *Educ:* Univ. of Toronto (BA History). Editor: Toronto Life Fashion Magazine, 1989–91; Drapers Record Magazine, 1993–96; Marie Claire, 1996–98; Man. Dir, Mktg and Internet Develt, Arcadia Gp plc, 1998–2000. National Magazine Award, Canada, 1990; PPA Business Editor of the Year, 1995. *Address:* The Fourth Room, 34 Bedford Row, WC1R 4JH. *T:* (020) 7430 5900.

WARLOW, Prof. Charles Picton, MD; FRCP, FRCPE, FRCPGlas, FMedSci; Professor of Medical Neurology and Hon. Consultant Neurologist, University of Edinburgh, since 1987; *b* 29 Sept. 1943; *s* of Charles Edward Picton Warlow and Nancy Mary McLennan (*née* Hine); *m* 1976, Ilona McDowall; two *s* one *d. Educ:* Haileybury and Imperial Service Coll.; Sidney Sussex Coll., Cambridge (BA 1st Cl. Hons 1965; MB BChir with Dist. in Medicine 1968; MD 1975); St George's Hosp. Med. Sch. FRCP 1983; FRCPE 1987; FRCPGlas 1993. Clinical Reader in Neurology and Hon. Consultant Neurologist, Univ. of Oxford, 1977–86; Fellow, Green Coll., Oxford, 1979–86; Head, Dept of Clinical Neuroscis, Univ. of Edinburgh, 1990–93 and 1995–98. Pres., Assoc. of British Neurologists, 2001–. Founder FMedSci 1998. *Publications:* Handbook of Clinical Neurology, 1991; (with G. J. Hankey) Transient Ischaemic Attacks of the Brain and Eye, 1994; (jtly) Stroke: a practical guide to management, 1996, 2nd edn 2001. *Recreations:* sailing, photography, mountains, theatre. *Address:* Department of Clinical Neurosciences, Western General Hospital, Crewe Road, Edinburgh EH4 2XU. *T:* (0131) 537 2081.

WARMAN, Oliver Byrne, RBA 1984; ROI 1989; Chief Executive, Federation of British Artists, 1984–92; *b* 10 June 1932. *Educ:* Stowe; Exeter Univ.; Balliol Coll., Oxford. Commissioned Welsh Guards, 1952; GSO3 Cabinet Office; Instructor, Intelligence Centre; Staff College; RMCS; retired 1970. Dir, Public Relations, Ship and Boat Builders Fedn, 1970; Director: Ashlyns, 1978; Tulsemead, 1983. First exhibited RA, 1980; exhib. at RBA, RWA, NEAC, RSMA, ROI; work in public collections, incl. US Embassy, Sultanate of Oman and Crown Commn. Officer, ROI, 1998–. Gold Medal, 1997, Gourlay Prize, 1998, ROI. *Publications:* Arnhem 1944, 1970; articles on wine and military history, 1968–. *Recreations:* France, food, wine, sailing, painting, mongrel dogs. *Address:* La Grange de l'Herbey, Merri, 61160 Trun, Orne, France; *e-mail:* oliverwarman@aol.com. *Clubs:* Cavalry and Guards, Chelsea Arts; Royal Cornwall Yacht.

WARMINGTON, Sir David (Marshall), 5th Bt *cr* 1908, of Pembridge Square, Royal Borough of Kensington; Corporate Adviser, Western Provident Association, since 2000; *b* 14 Feb. 1944; *s* of Sir Marshall Warmington, 3rd Bt and his 2nd wife, Eileen Mary Warmington (*d* 1969); *S* half-brother, 1996; *m* 1st, 1966, Susan Mary Chapman (marr. diss. 1980); two *s*; 2nd, 1981, Eileen Victoria Johnston. *Educ:* Charterhouse; Madrid Univ., Spain. Director: Malaŵi Finance Co., 1975–77; Balfour Wiliamson Inc., NY, 1980–83; British Chamber of Commerce, Mexico, 1981–83; American British Cowdray Hosp., Mexico, 1982–83; Elders Finance Group Ltd, London, 1985–87; Man. Dir, Marbella Times, 1988–90; Man. Dir, Internat. Product Design Inc., 1991–99. *Recreations:* golf, tennis, horse racing. *Heir: s* Rupert Marshall Warmington, *b* 17 June 1969. *Address:* 139 Highlands Heath, Putney, SW15 3TZ. *T:* (home) (020) 8780 5740; Finca Montanchez, Alhaurin El Grande, 29120 Málaga, Spain. *Clubs:* MCC; Wimbledon Park Golf; El Prat (Barcelona).

WARNE, Maj.-Gen. Antony M.; *see* Makepeace-Warne.

WARNE, (Ernest) John (David), CB 1982; Secretary, Institute of Chartered Accountants in England and Wales, 1982–90; *b* 4 Dec. 1926; *m* 1st, 1953, Rena Wolfe (*d* 1995); three *s*; 2nd, 1997, Irene Zajac. *Educ:* Univ. of London (BA(Hons)). Civil Service Commission, 1953; Asst Comr and Principal, Civil Service Commn, 1958; BoT, later DTI and Dept of Industry: Principal, 1962; Asst Sec., 1967; Under-Sec., 1972; Dir for Scotland, 1972–75; Under-Secretary: Personnel Div., 1975–77; Industrial and Commercial Policy Div., 1977–79; Dep. Sec., Dep. Dir-Gen., OFT, 1979–82. *Recreations:* reading, collecting prints, languages. *Address:* 16 Carlton Mews, Wells, Somerset BA5 1SG. *T:* (01749) 671286.

WARNE, (Frederick) John (Alford), CB 2000; Director, Organised and International Crime, Home Office, since 1996; *b* 7 March 1944; *m* (marr. diss); two *s. Educ:* Liskeard Grammar Sch., Cornwall. Home Office: Pvte Sec. to Minister of State, 1966–69; Principal, 1974–83; Asst Sec., 1984–93; Under-Sec., Police Dept, 1993–95. *Recreations:* Chelsea FC, exploring Cornwall. *Address:* Home Office, 50 Queen Anne's Gate, SW1H 9AT.

WARNER, family name of **Baron Warner**.

WARNER, Baron *cr* 1998 (Life Peer), of Brockley in the London Borough of Lewisham; **Norman Reginald Warner;** Adviser to the Government on family policy and related matters, since 1998; Chairman, Youth Justice Board for England and Wales, since 1998; *b* 8 Sept. 1940; *s* of Albert Henry Edwin Warner and Laura Warner; *m* 1961, Anne Lesley Lawrence (marr. diss. 1981); one *s* one *d*; *m* 1990, Suzanne Elizabeth Reeve (*see* S. E. Warner); one *s. Educ:* Dulwich College; University of California, Berkeley (MPH). Min. of Health, 1959; Asst Private Sec. to Minister of Health, 1967–68, to Sec. of State for Social Services, 1968–69; Executive Councils Div., DHSS, 1969–71; Harkness Fellowship, USA, 1971–73; NHS Reorganisation, DHSS, 1973–74; Principal Private Sec. to Sec. of State for Social Services, 1974–76; Supplementary Benefits Div., 1976–78; Management Services, DHSS, 1979–81; Regional Controller, Wales and S Western Region, DHSS, 1981–83; Gwilym Gibbon Fellow, Nuffield Coll., Oxford, 1983–84; Under Sec., Supplementary Benefits Div., DHSS, 1984–85; Dir of Social Services, Kent CC, 1985–91; Man. Dir, Warner Consultancy and Trng Services Ltd, 1991–97. Sen. Fellow in European Social Welfare and Chm., European Inst. of Social Services, Univ. of Kent, 1991–97. Chm., City and E London FHSA, 1991–94. Mem., Local Govt Commn, 1995–96. Chm., Expert Panel for UK Harkness Fellowships, 1994–97. Chairman: Nat. Inquiry into Selection, Develt and Management of Staff in Children's Homes, 1991–92 (report, Choosing with Care, 1992); Govt Task Force on Youth Justice, 1997–. Mem. Nat. Mgt Cttee, Carers Nat. Assoc., 1991–94. Trustee: Leonard Cheshire Foundn, 1994–96; MacIntyre Care, 1994–97; Royal Philanthropic Soc., 1992–99 (Chm., 1993–98); Chairman: Residential Forum, 1994–97; Include, 2000–01; NCVO, 2001–. *Publications:* (ed) Commissioning Community Alternatives in European Social and Health Care, 1993; articles in Jl of Public Admin., Community Care, The Guardian, Local Govt Chronicle, etc. *Recreations:* reading, cinema, theatre, exercise. *Address:* House of Lords, SW1A 0PW.

WARNER, Lady; *see* Warner, S. E.

WARNER, Prof. Anne Elizabeth, FRS 1985; Professor of Developmental Biology, University College London, since 1986; *b* 25 Aug. 1940; *d* of late James Frederick Crompton Brooks and of Elizabeth Marshall; *m* 1963, Michael Henry Warner. *Educ:* Pate's Grammar School for Girls, Cheltenham; University College London (BSc); Nat. Inst. for Med. Res. (PhD). Res. Associate, Middlesex Hosp. Med. Sch., 1968–71, Lectr in Physiology 1971–75, Sen. Lectr 1975–76, Royal Free Hosp Sch. of Medicine; Sen. Lectr in Anatomy, 1976–80, Reader in Anatomy, 1980–86, Fellow, 1993, UCL. *Publications:* papers in scientific jls. *Address:* University College London, Gower Street, WC1E 6BT.

WARNER, Deborah; free-lance theatre director, since 1980; *b* 12 May 1959; *d* of Ruth and Roger Warner. *Educ:* Sidcot Sch., Avon; St Clare's Coll., Oxford; Central Sch. of

Speech and Drama. Founder, 1980, and Artistic Dir, 1980–86, Kick Theatre Co.; Resident Dir, RSC, 1987–89; Associate Dir, Royal Nat. Theatre, 1989–98. *Productions:* Kick Theatre Co.: The Good Person of Szechwan, 1980; Woyzeck, 1981, 1982; The Tempest, 1983; Measure for Measure, 1984; King Lear, 1985; Coriolanus, 1986; Royal Shakespeare Co.: Titus Andronicus, 1987 (Laurence Olivier and Evening Standard Awards for Best Dir); King John, Electra, 1988; Electra (also in Paris), 1991; Royal National Theatre: The Good Person of Sichuan, 1989; King Lear, 1990; Richard II, 1995 (filmed, 1997); The Diary of One Who Vanished (also ENO), 1999; other productions: Wozzeck, Opera North, 1993 and 1996; Coriolan, Salzburg Fest., 1993 and 1994; Hedda Gabler, Abbey Theatre, Dublin, and Playhouse, 1991 (Laurence Olivier Award for Best Dir and Best Prodn); Don Giovanni, Glyndebourne Festival Opera, 1994 and 1995 (also Channel 4); Footfalls, Garrick, 1994; The Waste Land, Brussels, Dublin, Paris, Toronto, Montreal, NY, Cork, London, Adelaide, Brighton, Bergen, Perth, 1995–99 (televised, 1995); Une Maison de Poupée, Paris, 1996; The Turn of the Screw, Royal Opera, 1997; Bobigny (S Bank Arts Award; Evening Standard Award), 1998; Tower Project (London Internat. Fest. of Theatre), 1999; St John Passion, Coliseum, 2000; Medea, Abbey Th., Dublin, 2000, Queen's, 2001; The Angel Project, Perth Internat. Arts Festival, 2000; Fidelio, Glyndebourne, 2001. *Film:* The Last September, 2000. Officier de l'Ordre des Arts et des Lettres (France). *Recreation:* travelling. *Address:* c/o Conway van Gelder, 18–21 Jermyn Street, SW1Y 6HP. *T:* (020) 7287 0077; c/o Askonas Holt, Lonsdale Chambers, 27 Chancery Lane, WC2A 1PF. *T:* (020) 7400 1700.

WARNER, Sir (Edward Courtenay) Henry, 3rd Bt, *cr* 1910; *m*; three *s*. *Heir: s* Philip Courtenay Thomas Warner, *b* 3 April 1951.

WARNER, Sir Edward (Redston), KCMG 1965 (CMG 1955); OBE 1948; HM Diplomatic Service, retired; *b* 23 March 1911; *s* of late Sir George Redston Warner, KCVO, CMG, and Margery Catherine (*née* Nicol); *m* 1943, Grizel Margaret Clerk Rattray; three *s* one *d*. *Educ:* Oundle; King's College, Cambridge. Entered Foreign Office and Diplomatic Service, 1935; UK Delegation to OEEC, Paris, 1956–59; Minister at HM Embassy, Tokyo, 1959–62; Ambassador to Cameroon, 1963–66; UK Rep., Econ. and Social Council of UN, 1966–67; Ambassador to Tunisia, 1968–70. *Address:* The Old Royal Oak, High Street, Blockley, Glos GL56 9EX. *Club:* Oxford and Cambridge.

WARNER, Francis (Robert Le Plastrier); poet and dramatist; Dean of Degrees, since 1984, and Emeritus Fellow, since 1999, St Peter's College, Oxford; *b* Bishopthorpe, Yorks, 21 Oct. 1937; *s* of Rev. Hugh Compton Warner and Nancy Le Plastrier (*née* Owen); *m* 1st, 1958, Mary Hall (marr. diss. 1972); two *d*; 2nd, 1983, Penelope Anne Davis; one *s* one *d*. *Educ:* Christ's Hosp.; London Coll. of Music; St Catharine's Coll., Cambridge (Choral Exhibitioner; BA, MA; Hon. Fellow, 1999). Supervisor in English, St Catharine's Coll., Cambridge, 1959–65; Staff Tutor in English, Cambridge Univ. Bd of Extra-Mural Studies, 1963–65; Oxford University: Fellow and Tutor, 1965–99, Fellow Librarian, 1966–76, and Vice-Master, 1987–89, St Peter's Coll.; University Lectr (CUF), 1965–99; Pro-Proctor, 1989–90, 1996–97, 1999–2000; Chm., Examiners, English Hon. Mods, 1993. Foreign Academician, Acad. de Letras e Artes, Portugal, 1993. Messing Internat. Award for distinguished contribs to Literature, 1972. Benemerenti Silver Medal, Kts of St George, Constantinian Order (Italy), 1990. *Publications: poetry:* Perennia, 1962; Early Poems, 1964; Experimental Sonnets, 1965; Madrigals, 1967; The Poetry of Francis Warner, USA 1970; Lucca Quartet, 1975; Morning Vespers, 1980; Spring Harvest, 1981; Epithalamium, 1983; Collected Poems 1960–84, 1985; Nightingales: poems 1985–96, 1997; Cambridge: a poem, 2001; *plays:* Maquettes, a trilogy of one-act plays, 1972; Requiem: Pt 1, Lying Figures, 1972, Pt 2, Killing Time, 1976, Pt 3, Meeting Ends, 1974; A Conception of Love, 1978; Light Shadows, 1980; Moving Reflections, 1983; Living Creation, 1985; Healing Nature: the Athens of Pericles, 1988; Byzantium, 1990; Virgil and Caesar, 1993; Agora: an epic, 1994; King Francis 1st, 1995; Goethe's Weimar, 1997; Rembrandt's Mirror, 2000; *edited:* Eleven Poems by Edmund Blunden, 1965; Garland, 1968; Studies in the Arts, 1968; *relevant publications:* by G. Pursglove: Francis Warner and Tradition, 1981; Francis Warner's Poetry: a critical assessment, 1988. *Recreations:* grandchildren, cathedral music, travel. *Address:* St Peter's College, Oxford OX1 2DL. *T:* (01865) 278900; St Catharine's College, Cambridge CB2 1RL. *T:* (01223) 338300. *Club:* Athenæum.

WARNER, Prof. Sir Frederick (Edward), Kt 1968; FRS 1976; FREng; Visiting Professor, Essex University, since 1983; *b* 31 March 1910; *s* of Frederick Warner; *m* 1st, Margaret Anderson McCrea; two *s* two *d*; 2nd, Barbara Ivy Reynolds. *Educ:* Bancrofts Sch.; University Coll., London. Pres., Univ. of London Union, 1933. Chemical Engr with various cos, 1934–56; self-employed, 1956–. Joined Cremer and Warner, 1956, Senior Partner 1963–80. Inst. of Chemical Engrs: Hon. Sec., 1953; Pres., 1966; Mem. Council, Engrg Instns, 1962; President: Fedn Européenne d'Assocs nationales d'Ingénieurs, 1968–71 (European Engr, 1987); Brit. Assoc. for Commercial and Industrial Educn, 1977–89; Inst. of Quality Assurance, 1987–90; Vice- Pres., BSI, 1976–80 and 1983–89 (Chm., Exec. Bd, 1973–76; Pres., 1980–83). Missions and Consultations in India, Russia, Iran, Egypt, Greece, France. Assessor, Windscale Inquiry, 1977. Chairman: Cttee on Detergents, 1970–74; Process Plant Working Party, 1971–77; Sch. of Pharmacy, Univ. of London, 1971–79; CSTI, 1987–90; Member: Royal Commn on Environmental Pollution, 1973–76; Adv. Council for Energy Conservation, 1974–79; Treasurer, SCOPE (Scientific Cttee on Problems of Environment), 1982–88 (Chm., Environmental Consequences of Nuclear Warfare, 1983–88). Vis. Professor: Imperial Coll., 1970–78 and 1993–2001; UCL, 1970–86; Pro-Chancellor, Open Univ., 1974–79; Member Court: Cranfield Inst. of Technology; Essex Univ.; Fellow UCL, 1967. FREng (FEng 1976). Hon. FRSC 1991; Hon. Fellow: UMIST, 1986; Sch. of Pharmacy, 1979. Ordinario, Accademia Tiberina, 1969. Hon. DTech, Bradford, 1969; Hon. DSc: Aston, 1970; Cranfield, 1978; Heriot-Watt, 1978; Newcastle, 1979; DUniv: Open, 1980; Essex, 1992. Gold Medal, Czecho-Slovak Soc. for Internat. Relations, 1969; Medal, Insinöö-riliitto, Finland, 1969; Leverhulme Medal, Royal Soc., 1978; Buchanan Medal, 1982; Environment Medal, Technical Inspectorate of the Rheinland, 1984; Gerard Piel Award, 1991; World Fedn of Engrg Organs Medal for World Engrg Excellence, 1993. Hon. Mem., Koninklijk Instituut van Ingenieurs, 1972; Academico Correspondiente, AI Mexico, 1972. *Publications:* Problem in Chemical Engineering Design (with J. M. Coulson), 1949; Technology Today (ed de Bono), 1971; Standards in the Engineering Industries, NEDO, 1977; Risk Assessment, Royal Soc., 1982; (ed jtly) Treatment and Handling of Wastes, 1992; (ed jtly) Radioecology since Chernobyl, 1992; (ed) Risk Analysis, Perception and Assessment, 1992; (ed) Quality 2000, 1992; (ed jtly) Nuclear Test Explosions, 1998; papers on Kuwait oil fires, nuclear winter, underground gasification of coal, air and water pollution, contracts, planning, safety, professional and continuous education. *Recreations:* monumental brasses, ceramics, gardens. *Address:* Essex University, Colchester CO4 3SQ. *T:* (01206) 873370. *Club:* Athenæum.

WARNER, Sir Gerald (Chierici), KCMG 1995 (CMG 1984); HM Diplomatic Service, retired; Intelligence Co-ordinator, Cabinet Office, 1991–96; *b* 27 Sept. 1931; *s* of Howard Warner and Elizabeth (*née* Chierici); *m* 1st, 1956, Mary Wynne Davies (*d* 1998), DMath, Prof., City Univ.; one *s* two *d*; 2nd, 2000, Catherine Mary Humphrey. *Educ:* Univ. of Oxford (BA). 2 Lieut, Green Howards, 1949–50; Flight Lt, RAFVR, 1950–56. Joined HM Diplomatic Service, 1954; 3rd Sec., Peking, 1956–58; 2nd Sec., Rangoon, 1960–61; 1st Sec., Warsaw, 1964–66, Geneva, 1966–68; Counsellor, Kuala Lumpur, 1974–76; FCO, 1976–90, retd. Mem., Police Complaints Authy, 1990–91. Member: Adv. Bd, Tavistock Inst., 1998–; Glos Council for Drugs and Alcohol, 1997–. *Address:* c/o Coutts & Co., 1 Cadogan Place, SW1X 9PX.

WARNER, Graeme Christopher; Sheriff of Grampian, Highland and Islands, 1992–98; Part-time Sheriff, since 2000 (Temporary Sheriff, 1998–2000); *b* 20 Oct. 1948; *s* of Richard James Lewis Warner and Jean McDonald McIntyre or Warner; *m* 1st, 1976, Rachel Kidd Gear (marr. diss. 1994); one *s* one *d*; 2nd, 1996, Jean Raeburn. *Educ:* Belmont House, Glasgow; Strathallan, by Perth; Edinburgh Univ. (LLB). NP, WS. Law Apprentice, 1969–71; Law Assistant, 1971–72; Partner: Boyd, Janson & Young, WS, Leith, 1972–76; Ross Harper & Murphy, WS, Edinburgh, 1976–88; Macbeth, Currie & Co., WS, Edinburgh, 1989–91, Consultant, 1999–2000. *Recreation:* staying alive! *Address:* 6 Mortonhall Road, Edinburgh EH9 2HW. *T:* (0131) 668 2437. *Club:* Royal Northern and University (Aberdeen).

WARNER, Sir Henry; *see* Warner, Sir E. C. H.

WARNER, Sir Jean-Pierre (Frank Eugene), Kt 1981; Judge of the High Court of Justice, Chancery Division, 1981–94; a Judge of the Restrictive Practices Court, 1982–94; *b* 24 Sept. 1924; *s* of late Frank Cloudesley ffolliot Warner and of Louise Marie Blanche Warner (*née* Gouet); *m* 1950, Sylvia Frances, *d* of Sir Ernest Goodale, CBE, MC; two *d*. *Educ:* Sainte Croix de Neuilly; Ecole des Roches; Harrow; Trinity Coll., Cambridge (MA). Served in Rifle Bde, 1943–47, Actg Major, GSO2 (Ops) GHQ Far East. Called to Bar, Lincoln's Inn, 1950 (Cassel Schol.), Bencher 1966, Treasurer 1985; Mem. Gen. Council of Bar, 1969–72. Junior Counsel: to Registrar of Restrictive Trading Agreements, 1961–64; to Treasury (Chancery), 1964–72; QC 1972; Advocate-Gen., Ct of Justice of European Communities, 1973–81. Councillor: Royal Borough of Kensington, 1959–65 (Chm., Gen. Purposes Cttee, 1963–65); Royal Borough of Kensington and Chelsea, 1964–68. Dir, Warner & Sons Ltd and subsids, 1952–70. Pres., UK Assoc. for European Law, 1983–89 (Vice-Pres., 1975–83). Hon. Mem., Soc. of Public Teachers of Law, 1982. Hon. LLD: Exeter, 1983; Leicester, 1984; Edinburgh, 1987. Liveryman, Worshipful Co. of Weavers, 1957. Chevalier du Tastevin, 1952, Commandeur 1960; Mem., Confrérie St Etienne d'Alsace, 1981. Grand Cross, Order of Merit, Luxembourg, 1998. *Recreation:* sitting in the sun with a cool drink. *Address:* 32 Abingdon Villas, W8 6BX. *T:* (020) 7937 7023.

WARNER, John Charles; His Honour Judge Warner; a Circuit Judge, since 1996; *b* 30 Aug. 1945; *s* of late Frank Charles Warner and Kathleen Moyra Warner; *m* 1975, Kathleen Marion Robinson; one *s* one *d*. *Educ:* King Edward's Sch., Birmingham. Solicitor, 1969; Partner, Adie Evans & Warner, 1971–96; Asst Recorder, 1988–92; Recorder, 1992–96. Mem., Birmingham Duty Solicitor Cttee, 1985–96. *Address:* c/o The Court Service, Combined Court Centre, Victoria Square, Stafford ST16 2QQ. *T:* (01785) 255219.

WARNER, Prof. John Oliver, MD; FRCPCH; Professor of Child Health, University of Southampton, since 1990; *b* 19 July 1945; *s* of Henry Paul Warner and Ursula Mina Warner; *m* 1st, 1968, Wendy Margaret Cole (marr. diss. 1989); one *s* two *d*; 2nd, 1990, Jill Amanda Price; two *d*. *Educ:* Sheffield Univ. Med. Sch. (MB ChB 1968; DCH 1970; MD 1979). FRCP 1986 (MRCP 1972); FRCPCH 1997. Gen. prof. trng, Children's Hosp. and Royal Hosp., Sheffield, 1968–72; Great Ormond Street Children's Hospital: Registrar, 1972–74; research, 1974–77; Sen. Registrar, 1977–79; Consultant, 1979–90, Sen. Lectr, 1979–88, Reader, 1988–90, London Cardiothoracic Inst., Brompton Hosp. FRSocMed; FMedSci 1999. *Publications:* A Colour Atlas of Paediatric Allergy, 1994; The Bronchoscope—Flexible and Rigid—in Children, 1995; (ed jtly) Textbook of Pediatric Asthma: an international perspective, 2001; over 200 papers in med jls. *Recreations:* cricket, horse riding. *Address:* Compass Copse, 48 Wilderness Heights, West End, Southampton SO18 3PS. *Club:* MCC.

WARNER, Marina Sarah, FRSL; writer and critic; *b* 9 Nov. 1946; *d* of Esmond Pelham Warner and Emilia (*née* Terzulli); *m* 1st, 1971, Hon. William Shawcross, *qv*; one *s*; 2nd, 1981, John Dewe Mathews. *Educ:* Lady Margaret Hall, Oxford (MA Mod. Langs, French and Italian). FRSL 1985. Getty Schol., Getty Centre for Hist. of Art and Humanities, Calif, 1987–88; Vis. Fellow, BFI, 1992; Whitney J. Oakes Fellow, Princeton Univ., 1996; Tinbergen Prof., Erasmus Univ., Rotterdam, 1991; Mellon Prof., Univ. of Pittsburgh, 1997; Visiting Professor: Univ. of Ulster, 1995; QMW, 1995–; York Univ., 1996–; Dist. Vis. Prof., Stanford Univ., 2000; Visiting Fellow: Trinity Coll., Cambridge, 1998; Humanities Res. Centre, Warwick Univ., 1999; All Souls Coll., Oxford, 2001; Hon. Res. Fellow, Birkbeck Coll., Univ. of London, 1999–. Lectures: Reith, 1994; Tanner, Yale Univ., 1999; Clarendon, Oxford Univ., 2001. Mem. Adv. Bd, Royal Mint, 1986–93. Member: Council, Charter 88, 1990–98; Cttee of Management, Nat. Council for One-Parent Families, 1990–99; Adv. Council, British Liby, 1992–98; Cttee, London Liby, 1997–2000; Literature Panel, Arts Council, 1992–98; Council, Inst. of Historical Res., Univ. of London, 1999–2000; Cttee, PEN, 2001–. Hon. DLitt: Exeter, 1995; York, 1997; St Andrews, 1998; Hon. Dr: Sheffield Hallam, 1995; North London, 1997; East London, 1999. Libretti: The Legs of the Queen of Sheba, 1991; In the House of Crossed Desires, 1996. *Publications:* The Dragon Empress, 1972; Alone of All Her Sex: the myth and the cult of the Virgin Mary, 1976; Queen Victoria's Sketchbook, 1980; Joan of Arc: the image of female heroism, 1981; Monuments and Maidens: the allegory of the female form, 1985; L'Atalante, 1993; Managing Monsters: six myths of our time (Reith Lectures), 1994; From the Beast to the Blonde: on fairy tales and their tellers, 1994; The Inner Eye: art beyond the visible, 1996; No Go the Bogeyman: scaring, lulling and making mock, 1998; *fiction:* In a Dark Wood, 1977; The Skating Party, 1983; The Lost Father, 1988; Indigo, 1992; The Mermaids in the Basement, 1993; (ed) Wonder Tales, 1994; The Leto Bundle, 2001; *children's books:* The Impossible Day, 1981; The Impossible Night, 1981; The Impossible Bath, 1982; The Impossible Rocket, 1982; The Wobbly Tooth, 1984; *juvenile:* The Crack in the Teacup, 1979; pamphlet in Counterblasts series; short stories, arts criticism, radio and television broadcasting. *Recreations:* friends, travels, reading. *Address:* c/o Rogers, Coleridge & White, 20 Powis Mews, W11 1NJ.

WARNER, Suzanne Elizabeth, (Lady Warner); Deputy Chairman, Broadcasting Standards Commission, since 1998; *b* 12 Aug. 1942; *d* of Charles Clifford Reeder and Elizabeth Joan Armstrong Reeder; *m* 1st, 1967, Jonathan Reeve (marr. diss. 1980); one *s*; 2nd, 1990, Norman Reginald Warner (*see* Baron Warner); one *s*. *Educ:* Badminton Sch., Bristol; Univ. of Sussex (BA Hons History); Univ. of Cambridge (Dip. Criminology). Home Office Res. Unit, 1966–67; Personal Assistant to Sec. of State for Social Services, DHSS, 1968–70; Principal, DHSS, 1970–73; Central Policy Review Staff, 1973–74; Asst Sec., DHSS, 1979–85; Sec., 1985–88, Actg Chm., 1987–88, ESRC; Exec. Dir, Food from Britain, 1988–90; Chief Exec., Foundn for Educn Business Partnerships, 1990–91; Personal Advr to Dep. Chm., BT plc, 1991–93; Hd of Gp Govt Relations, 1993–96, Gp Dir of Govt Relations, 1996–97, Cable and Wireless plc. Member: Management Bd, Sci.

Policy Support Unit, Royal Soc., 1991–93; Technology Foresight Steering Gp, OST, 1994–97; Council, Industry and Parlt Trust, 1994–97; Acad. Council, Wilton Park, 1995– (Chm., 1999–). University of Sussex: Mem. Adv. Bd, Sci. Policy Res. Unit, 1998–; Mem., Court, 2000–; Vice-Chm. of Council, 2001–. Non-executive Director: SE Thames RHA, 1993–; S Thames RHA, 1994–; Broadmoor Hosp. Authy, 1996–98. Chm. Trustees, Botanic Gardens Conservation Internat., 1999–. *Recreations:* family life, cooking, gardening, reading, films. *Address:* Broadcasting Standards Commission, 7 The Sanctuary, SW1P 3JS.

WARNOCK, family name of **Baroness Warnock**.

WARNOCK, Baroness *cr* 1985 (Life Peer), of Weeke in the City of Winchester; **Helen Mary Warnock,** DBE 1984; Mistress of Girton College, Cambridge, 1985–91; *b* 14 April 1924; *d* of late Archibald Edward Wilson, Winchester; *m* 1949, Sir Geoffrey Warnock (*d* 1995); two *s* three *d*. *Educ:* St Swithun's, Winchester; Lady Margaret Hall, Oxford (Hon. Fellow 1984). Fellow and Tutor in Philosophy, St Hugh's Coll., Oxford, 1949–66; Headmistress, Oxford High Sch., GPDST, 1966–72; Talbot Res. Fellow, Lady Margaret Hall, Oxford, 1972–76; Sen. Res. Fellow, St Hugh's Coll., Oxford, 1976–84 (Hon. Fellow, 1985). Member: IBA, 1973–81; Cttee of Inquiry into Special Educn, 1974–78 (Chm.); Royal Commn on Environmental Pollution, 1979–84; Adv. Cttee on Animal Experiments, 1979–85 (Chm.); SSRC, 1981–85; UK Nat. Commn for Unesco, 1981–84; Cttee of Inquiry into Human Fertilization, 1982–84 (Chm.); Cttee of Inquiry into Validation of Public Sector Higher Educn, 1984; Cttee on Teaching Quality, PCFC, 1990 (Chm.); European Adv. Gp on Bioethics, 1992–94; Archbishop of Canterbury's Adv. Gp on Medical Ethics, 1992–; Chm., Educn Cttee, GDST (formerly GPDST), 1994–2001. Visitor, RHBNC, 1997–2001. Gifford Lectr, Univ. of Glasgow, 1991–92; Reed Tuckwell Lectr, Univ. of Bristol, 1992. Leverhulme Emeritus Fellow, 1992–94. FRCP 1979; FRSocMed 1989; Hon. FIC 1986; Hon. FBA 2000. Hon. Fellow, Hertford Coll., Oxford, 1997. Hon. degrees: Open, Essex, Melbourne, Manchester, Bath, Exeter, Glasgow, York, Nottingham, Warwick, Liverpool, London and St Andrews Univs.; Leeds Polytechnic; Leicester Polytechnic; King Alfred's Coll., Winchester. Albert Medal, RSA, 1999. *Publications:* Ethics since 1900, 1960, 3rd edn 1978; J.-P. Sartre, 1963; Existentialist Ethics, 1966; Existentialism, 1970; Imagination, 1976; Schools of Thought, 1977; (with T. Devlin) What Must We Teach?, 1977; Education: a way forward, 1979; A Question of Life, 1985; Teacher Teach Thyself (Dimbleby Lect.), 1985; Memory, 1987; A Common Policy for Education, 1988; Universities: knowing our minds, 1989; The Uses of Philosophy, 1992; Imagination and Time, 1994; (ed) Women Philosophers, 1996; An Intelligent Person's Guide to Ethics, 1998; A Memoir, 2000; Is There a Right to Have Children?, 2001. *Recreations:* music, gardening. *Address:* 3 Church Street, Great Bedwyn, Wilts SN8 3PE. *T:* (01672) 870214.

WARR, John James; Deputy Chairman, Clive Discount Co. Ltd, 1973–87, retired; President of the MCC, 1987–88; *b* 16 July 1927; *s* of late George and Florence May Warr; *m* 1957, Valerie Powell (*née* Peter) (*d* 2000); two *d*. *Educ:* Ealing County Grammar Sch.; Emmanuel Coll., Cambridge (BA Hons 1952). Served RN, 1945–48. Man. Dir, Union Discount Co., 1952–73. Chm., Racecourse Assoc., 1989–93. Mem., Jockey Club, 1977–. Pres., Berks CCC, 1990–. *Recreations:* racing, cricket, golf, good music. *Address:* Orchard Farm, Touchen End, Maidenhead, Berks SL6 3TA. *T:* (01628) 622994. *Clubs:* Saints and Sinners (Chm., 1991–92), MCC, XL, I Zingari; Temple Golf, Berkshire Golf.

WARRELL, Prof. David Alan, DM; DSc; FRCP, FRCPE, FMedSci; Professor of Tropical Medicine and Infectious Diseases, University of Oxford, since 1987; Fellow, St Cross College, Oxford, since 1977; *b* 6 Oct. 1939; *s* of Alan and late Mildred Warrell; *m* 1975, Dr Mary Jean Prentice; two *d*. *Educ:* Portsmouth Grammar Sch.; Christ Church, Oxford (MA, BCh 1964; DM 1970; DSc 1990). MRCS 1965; FRCP 1977; FRCPE 1999. Oxford Univ. Radcliffe Travelling Fellow, Univ. of Calif at San Diego, 1969–70; Sen. Lectr, Ahmadu Bello Univ., Zaria, Nigeria, 1970–74; Lectr, RPMS, London, 1974–75; Consultant Physician, Radcliffe Infirmary, Oxford, 1975–79; Founding Dir, Wellcome-Mahidol Univ. Oxford Tropical Medicine Research Programme in Bangkok, 1979–86; Founding Dir, Centre for Tropical Medicine, Univ. of Oxford, 1991–2001, now Emeritus. Vis. Prof., Mahidol Univ., 1997–. WHO Consultant on malaria, rabies and snake bite, 1979–. Chm., MRC's AIDS Therapeutic Trials Cttee, 1987–93; Mem., MRC's Tropical Medicine Res. Bd, 1986–89; Advr to MRC on tropical medicine, 2001–. Hon. Consultant Malariologist to the Army, 1989–; Hon. Med. Advr, RGS, 1993–. Pres., Internat. Fedn of Tropical Medicine, 1996–2000; Pres., RSTM&H, 1997–99. Delegate, OUP, 1999–. RCP Lectures: Marc Daniels, 1977; Bradshaw, 1989; Croonian, 1996; College, 1999; Harveian, 2001. Scientific FZS 1976; FRGS 1989. Founder FMedSci 1998. Hon. Fellow, Ceylon Coll. of Physicians, 1985. Chalmers Medal, RSTM&H, 1981; Ambuj Nath Bose Prize, RCP, 1994. *Publications:* Rabies—the Facts, 1977, 2nd edn 1986; (ed) Oxford Textbook of Medicine, 1983, 3rd edn 1995; (ed) Essential Malariology, 3rd edn 1993, 4th edn 2001; Expedition Medicine, 1998; chapters in textbooks of medicine; papers in learned jls (Lancet, New England Jl of Medicine, etc) on respiratory physiology, malaria, rabies, infectious diseases and snake bite. *Recreations:* book collecting, music, bird watching, hill walking. *Address:* University of Oxford, Nuffield Department of Clinical Medicine, John Radcliffe Hospital, Headington, Oxford OX3 9DU. *T:* (01865) 220968 and 221332, *Fax:* (01865) 220984. *Club:* Royal Society of Medicine.

WARRELL, David Watson, MD; FRCOG; urological gynaecologist, 1969–94; Chairman, Mid-Cheshire Hospitals NHS Trust, 1994–97; *b* 20 June 1929; *s* of late Charles Warrell and Sarah (*née* Gill); *m* 1955, Valerie Jean Fairclough; one *s* one *d*. *Educ:* Sheffield Univ. MB ChB 1953; MD 1964; FRCOG 1970. Sen. Lectr and Hon. Consultant Obstetrician and Gynaecologist, Jessop Hosp. for Women, 1965–69; St Mary's Hosp., Manchester, 1969–94: established Dept of Urological Gynaecology; Med. Dir, 1991–92, Chief Exec., 1992–94, Central Manchester Health Care Trust. Blair Bell Travelling Fellowship, 1967. *Publications:* chapters and papers on urinary control in women. *Recreations:* farming, hill-walking. *Address:* Beudy y Chain, Llanfaglan, Caernarfon, Gwynedd LL54 5RA.

WARRELL, Ernest Herbert, MBE 1991; Organist, King's College, London, 1980–91 (Lecturer in Music, KCL, 1953–80); *b* 23 June 1915; *er s* of Herbert Henry Warrell and Edith Peacock; *m* 1952, Jean Denton Denton; two *s* one *d*. *Educ:* Loughborough School. Articled pupil (Dr E. T. Cook), Southwark Cath., 1938; Asst Organist, Southwark Cath., 1946–54; Organist, St Mary's, Primrose Hill, 1954–57; Lectr in Plainsong, RSCM, 1954–59; Organist, St John the Divine, Kennington, SW9, 1961–68; Organist and Dir of Music, Southwark Cathedral, 1968–76; Musical Dir, Gregorian Assoc., 1969–82. Chief Examiner in Music, Internat. Baccalaureate, 1984–89; Examinations Sec., Guild of Church Musicians, 1991–97. Hon. FCTL 1977; FKC 1979; Hon. FGCM 1988. *Publications:* Accompaniments to the Psalm Tones, 1942; Plainsong and the Anglican Organist, 1943; (ed jtly) An English Kyriale, 1988. *Recreation:* sailing. *Address:* 41 Beechhill Road, Eltham, SE9 1HJ. *T:* (020) 8850 7800. *Clubs:* Special Forces, Little Ship; Royal Scots (Edinburgh).

WARREN, Very Rev. Alan Christopher; Provost of Leicester, 1978–92, now Provost Emeritus; *b* 27 June 1932; *s* of Arthur Henry and Gwendoline Catherine Warren; *m* 1957, Sylvia Mary (*née* Matthews); three *d*. *Educ:* Dulwich College; Corpus Christi Coll., Cambridge (Exhibnr, MA); Ridley Hall, Cambridge. Curate, St Paul's, Margate, 1957–59; Curate, St Andrew, Plymouth, 1959–62; Chaplain of Kelly College, Tavistock, 1962–64; Vicar of Holy Apostles, Leicester, 1964–72; Coventry Diocesan Missioner, 1972–78; Hon. Canon, Coventry Cathedral, 1972–78; Proctor in Convocation, 1977–78, 1980–85. Mem., Cathedral Statutes Commn, 1981–85. Trustee, St Martin's, Birmingham, 1979–. Chm., Leicester Council of Christians and Jews, 1985–92; President: Leicester Council of Churches, 1985–92; Leicester Civic Soc., 1983–92. Tutor, Adult Educn, Norfolk, 1993–99; Dir of Music, W Norfolk Choral Soc., 1993–2000. Chm., Hunstanton Arts Fest. Cttee, 1994–99. Mem., MCC, 1960–76. Pres., Alleyn Club, 1991–92 (Vice-Pres., 1990–91). *Publications:* Putting it Across, 1975; The Miserable Warren, 1991; articles on church music, evangelism and sport in Church Times and other journals; *compositions:* Incarnatus for Organ, 1960; Piano Sonata, 1996. *Recreations:* music, golf, steam trains. *Address:* 9 Queens Drive, Hunstanton, Norfolk PE36 6EY. *T:* (01485) 534533. *Clubs:* Free Foresters; Hunstanton Golf.

See also Ven. N. L. Warren, R. H. C. Warren.

WARREN, Alastair Kennedy, TD 1953; Editor, Dumfries and Galloway Standard, 1976–86; *b* 17 July 1922; *s* of John Russell Warren, MC, and Jean Cousin Warren; *m* 1952, Ann Lindsay Maclean; two *s*. *Educ:* Glasgow Acad.; Loretto; Glasgow Univ. (MA Hons). Served War of 1939–45; HLI, 1940–46; Major, 1946. Served 5/6th Bn HLI (TA) 1947–63. Sales Clerk, Stewarts & Lloyds Ltd, 1950–53; joined editorial staff of The Glasgow Herald as Sub-Editor, 1954; Leader Writer, 1955–58; Features Editor, 1958–59; Commercial Editor, 1960–64; City Editor, 1964–65; Editor, 1965–74; Regional Editor, Scottish and Universal Newspapers Ltd, 1974–76. Provost of New Galloway and Kells Community Council, 1978–81; Chairman: Loch Arthur Village Community (Camphill Movt), 1985–92; Nithsdale Council of Voluntary Service, 1988–91 (Pres., 1992–). Hon. Pres., Galloway Community Coll. *Publications:* Pebbles on the Beach (poems), 1999; Then and Now and Next (poems), 2000; contribs to various periodicals. *Recreations:* swimming, hill walking, marathon running. *Address:* Rathan, New Galloway, Castle Douglas DG7 3RN. *T:* (01644) 420257.

WARREN, Sir (Brian) Charles (Pennefather), 9th Bt *cr* 1784; *b* 4 June 1923; *o s* of Sir Thomas Richard Pennefather Warren, 8th Bt, CBE; *S* father, 1961; *m* 1st, 1976, Cola (marr. diss. 1983), *d* of Captain E. L. Cazenove, Great Dalby, Leics; 2nd, 1996, Rosemary, *d* of B. W. Day, OBE, Hovingham, Yorks. *Educ:* Wellington College. Served War of 1939–45; Lt, 1943–45, 2nd Bn Irish Guards. *Recreation:* hunting. *Address:* Saffron Hill, Doneraile, Co. Cork, Ireland. *Club:* Cavalry and Guards.

WARREN, Rt Rev. Cecil Allan; Rector, Old Brampton and Loundsley Green, 1983–88; Assistant Bishop, Diocese of Derby, 1983–88; *b* 25 Feb. 1924; *s* of Charles Henry and Eliza Warren; *m* 1947, Doreen Muriel Burrows. *Educ:* Sydney Univ. (BA 1950); Queen's Coll., Oxford (MA 1959). Deacon 1950, priest 1951, Dio. of Canberra and Goulburn; appointments in Diocese of Oxford, 1953–57; Canberra, 1957–63; Organising Sec. Church Society, and Director of Forward in Faith Movement, Dio. of Canberra and Goulburn, 1963–65; Asst Bishop of Canberra and Goulburn, 1965–72; Bishop of Canberra and Goulburn, 1972–83. *Publication:* A Little Foolishness: an autobiographical history, 1993. *Address:* 2/19 Sidney Street, Toowoomba, Qld 4350, Australia.

WARREN, Sir Charles; *see* Warren, Sir B. C. P.

WARREN, David Alexander; HM Diplomatic Service; Director, Business Group, Trade Partners UK, British Trade International, since 2000; *b* 11 Aug. 1952; *s* of late Alister Charles Warren and of Celia Warren (*née* Golding); *m* 1992, Pamela, *d* of late Benjamin Ivan Pritchard and of Violet Pritchard (*née* Sherman). *Educ:* Epsom Coll.; Exeter Coll., Oxford (MA English; Pres., Oxford Union Soc., 1973). Entered HM Diplomatic Service, 1975; FCO, 1975–77; Third, later Second, then First Sec., Tokyo, 1977–81; FCO, 1981–87; First Sec. and Hd of Chancery, Nairobi, 1987–90; FCO, 1990–91; on secondment as Hd, Internat. Div., Sci. and Technol. Secretariat, later OST, then OPSS, Cabinet Office, 1991–93; Counsellor (Commercial), Tokyo, 1993–98; Hd, Hong Kong Dept, later China Hong Kong Dept, FCO, 1998–2000. *Recreations:* books, history of theatre and music hall. *Address:* c/o Foreign and Commonwealth Office, King Charles Street, SW1A 2AH; c/o British Trade International, Kingsgate House, 66–74 Victoria Street, SW1E 6SW. *Club:* Oxford and Cambridge.

WARREN, Sir (Frederick) Miles, ONZ 1995; KBE 1985 (CBE 1974); FNZIA; ARIBA; Senior Partner, Warren & Mahoney, Architects Ltd, since 1958; *b* Christchurch, 10 May 1929. *Educ:* Christ's Coll., Christchurch; Auckland Univ. DipArch; ARIBA 1952; FNZIA 1965. Founded Warren & Mahoney, 1958. Award-winning designs include: Christchurch Town Hall and Civic Centre; NZ Chancery, Washington; Canterbury Public Library; Michael Fowler Centre, Wellington; St Patrick's Church, Napier; Ohinetahi, Governors Bay; Rotorua Dist Council Civic Offices; Mulholland Hse, Wanganui; Parkroyal Hotel, Christchurch. Pres., Canterbury Soc. of Arts, 1972–76. Gold Medal, NZIA, 1960, 1964, 1969, 1973; Nat. Awards, NZIA, 1980, 1981, 1983–86, 1988, 1989, 1990, 1991. *Publication:* Warren & Mahoney Architects, 1990. *Recreation:* making a garden. *Address:* 65 Cambridge Terrace, Christchurch 1, New Zealand.

WARREN, Prof. Graham Barry, PhD; FRS 1999; Professor of Cell Biology, Yale University Medical School, since 1999; *b* 25 Feb. 1948; *s* of Joyce Thelma and Charles Graham Thomas Warren; *m* 1966, Philippa Mary Adeline (*née* Temple-Cole); four *d*. *Educ:* Willesden County Grammar Sch.; Pembroke Coll., Cambridge (MA, PhD). MRC Fellow, Nat. Inst. for Med. Research, 1972–75; Royal Soc. Stothert Research Fellow, Dept of Biochemistry, Cambridge, 1975–77; Research Fellow, Gonville & Caius Coll., Cambridge, 1975–77; Group Leader then Senior Scientist, European Molecular Biology Lab., Heidelberg, 1977–85; Prof. and Hd of Dept of Biochemistry, Dundee Univ., 1985–88; Prin. Scientist, ICRF, 1989–99. Mem., EMBO, 1986. *Publications:* papers in learned jls on cell biology. *Recreation:* woodworking. *Address:* 12 Elmwood Road, New Haven, CT 06515-2242, USA; Department of Cell Biology, Yale University School of Medicine, 333 Cedar Street, New Haven, CT 06520-8002, USA. *T:* (203) 7855058, *Fax:* (203) 7854301; *e-mail:* graham.warren@yale.edu.

WARREN, Ian Scott; Senior Master of the Supreme Court (Queen's Bench Division) and Queen's Remembrancer, 1988–90 (Master, 1970–90); *b* 30 March 1917; *er s* of Arthur Owen Warren and Margaret Cromarty Warren (*née* Macnaughton); *m* 1st, 1943, Barbara (marr. diss.), *er d* of Walter Myrick, Tillsonburg, Ont.; four *s* one *d*; 2nd, Jeanne Hicklin (marr. diss.), *d* of late Frederick and Lydia Shaw, Crosland Moor; 3rd, 1987, Olive Sybil, *d* of late James Charles Montgomerie Wilson. *Educ:* Charterhouse (Exhbnr); Magdalene Coll., Cambridge (Exhbnr); BA 1938, MA 1950. Colonial Administrative Service, 1938–41, serving Gold Coast (Asst DC, 1940); RAF, 1942–46; Flying Badge and commissioned, 1943; Flt Lieut, 1944. Called to Bar, Lincoln's Inn, 1947, Bencher 1967;

practised at Common Law Bar, London, 1947–70. *Publications:* Verses from Lincoln's Inn (jtly), 1975; Aesop's Fables: a selection, 1982. *Recreations:* ski-ing, walking, poetry. *Clubs:* Garrick, MCC.

WARREN, Jack Hamilton, OC 1982; principal trade policy advisor, Government of Quebec, 1986–94; *b* 10 April 1921; *s* of Tom Hamilton Warren and Olive Sykes (*née* Horsfall); *m* 1953, Hilary Joan Titterington; two *s* two *d*. *Educ:* Queen's Univ., Kingston, (BA). Served War, with Royal Canadian Navy. Public Service, 1945–79: Dept of External Affairs; Dept of Finance; diplomatic postings in Ottawa, London, Washington, Paris and Geneva; Asst Dep. Minister of Trade and Commerce, 1958; Chm., Council of Representatives, 1960, and Chm., Contracting Parties, 1962 and 1964, GATT; Dep. Minister: Dept of Trade and Commerce, 1964; Dept of Industry, Trade and Commerce, 1969; High Comr for Canada in London, 1971–74; Ambassador to USA, 1975–77; Ambassador, and Canadian Co-ordinator for the Multilateral Trade Negotiations, 1977–79; Vice-Chm., Bank of Montreal, 1979–86; Director: Royal Insurance Co. of Canada, 1980–91; Pratt and Whitney, Canada, 1983–91; PACCAR of Canada Ltd, 1984–91. Dep. Chm. (N America), Trilateral Commn, 1985–91. Hon. LLD Queen's, Ont, 1974. Outstanding Achievement Award, Public Service of Canada, 1975. *Recreations:* fishing, gardening, ski-ing. *Address:* 37 Larrimac Road, Chelsea, QC J9B 2C4, Canada. *Clubs:* Rideau (Ottawa); White Pine Fishing, Larrimac Golf (Canada).

WARREN, John; QC 1994; a Recorder, Midland and Oxford Circuit, since 1993; *b* 25 Aug. 1945; *s* of Frank Warren and Dora Warren (*née* Thomas); *m* 1968, Anne Marlor; one *s* one *d* (twins). *Educ:* Chadderton Grammar Sch., near Oldham; Univ. of Nottingham (LLB). Called to the Bar, Gray's Inn, 1968. *Recreations:* opera and classical music, supporting Nottingham Forest FC, doing The Times crossword in bed with my wife. *Address:* 1 High Pavement, Nottingham NG1 1HF. *T:* (0115) 941 8218. *Clubs:* Nottingham, Keyworth and Ruddington Rotary (Nottingham).

WARREN, Sir Kenneth (Robin), Kt 1994; Eur Ing, CEng, FRAeS; FCIT, FILT; consultant in engineering; director of a number of companies; *b* 15 Aug. 1926; *s* of Edward Charles Warren and Ella Mary Warren (*née* Adams); *m* 1962, Elizabeth Anne Chamberlain, MA Cantab and MA Lond; one *s* two *d*. *Educ:* Midsomer Norton; Aldenham; London Univ.; De Havilland Aeronautical Technical Sch. Fulbright Scholar, USA, 1949; Research Engineer, BOAC, 1951–57; Personal Asst to Gen. Manager, Smiths Aircraft Instruments Ltd, 1957–60; Elliott Automation Ltd, 1960–69; Military Flight Systems: Manager, 1960–63; Divisional Manager, 1963–66; Marketing Manager, 1966–69. MP (C) Hastings, 1970–83, Hastings and Rye, 1983–92. Mem., Select Cttee on Science and Technology, 1970–79 (Chm., Offshore Engrg Sub-Cttee, 1975–76); Mem., Council of Europe, 1973–80; Chm., WEU, Science, Technology and Aerospace Cttee, 1976–79; Chm., Cons. Parly Aviation Cttee, 1975–77; PPS to Sec. of State for Industry, 1979–81, to Sec. of State for Educn and Sci., 1981–83; Chairman: Select Cttee on Trade and Industry, 1983–92; British Soviet Parly Gp, 1986–92. Former branch officer, G&MWU. Chairman: Computer Security Adv. Bd, LSE, 1991–2001; Anglo-Japanese Adv. Bd on Financial Regulation, 1999–. President: British Resorts Assoc., 1987–92; Inst. of Travel Mgt, 1999–. Hon. Vice Pres., WEU, 1996–. Liveryman: Coachmakers' Co.; GAPAN; Freeman, City of London. FRSA. Hon. Fellow, Exeter Univ., 1994. *Publications:* various papers on aeronautical engineering and management, in USA, UK, Hungary, Netherlands and Japan. *Recreations:* mountaineering, flying, gardening. *Address:* Woodfield House, Goudhurst, Kent TN17 2NN. *T:* (01580) 211590, *Fax:* (01580) 212152. *Clubs:* Athenæum, Garrick, Special Forces.

WARREN, Maurice Eric; Chairman, Aggregate Industries plc, 1997–2000; *b* 21 June 1933; *s* of Frederick Leonard and Winifred Warren; *m* 1954, Molly Warren; one *s* one *d*. *Educ:* St Brendan's Coll., Bristol. Certified Accountant, FCCA. Crosfield & Calthrop, 1958–74 (Dir, 1970–74); Managing Director: Dalgety Crosfields, 1974–76; Dalgety Agriculture Ltd, 1976–81; Dalgety UK Ltd, 1981–87; Dir, 1982, Chief Exec., 1989–93, Chm., 1993–96, Dalgety PLC. Chairman: S Western Electricity, 1993–95; CAMAS, 1994–97; Great Western Holdings, 1996–98. *Recreation:* golf.

WARREN, Prof. Michael Donald, MD, FRCP, FFPHM; Emeritus Professor of Social Medicine, University of Kent, since 1983; *b* 19 Dec. 1923; *s* of late Charles Warren and Dorothy Gladys Thornton Reeks; *m* 1946, Joan Lavina Peacock; one *s* two *d*. *Educ:* Bedford Sch.; Guy's Hosp.; London Sch. of Hygiene and Tropical Medicine. MB 1946, MD 1952; DPH 1952, DIH 1952; MRCP 1969, FRCP 1975; FFCM 1972; Hon. FFPHM 1991. Sqdn Ldr RAF, Med. Branch, 1947–51; Dep. MOH, Metropolitan Borough of Hampstead, 1952–54; Asst Principal MO, LCC, 1954–58; Sen. Lectr and Hon. Consultant in Social Medicine, Royal Free Hosp. Sch., Royal Free Hosp. and London Sch. of Hygiene and Tropical Medicine, 1958–64; Sen. Lectr in Social Medicine, LSHTM, 1964–67; Reader in Public Health, Univ. of London, 1967–71; Prof. of Community Health, Univ. of London, 1978–80; Dir, Health Services Res. Unit, and Prof. of Social Medicine, Univ. of Kent, 1971–83, jtly with Specialist in Community Medicine (Epidemiology and Health Services Res.), SE Thames RHA, 1980–83. Chm., Soc. of Social Medicine, 1982–83. Academic Registrar, Faculty of Community Medicine, Royal Colls of Physicians, 1972–77. Jt Editor, British Jl of Preventive and Social Medicine, 1969–72. *Publications:* (jtly) Public Health and Social Services, 4th edn 1957, 6th edn 1965; (ed jtly) Management and the Health Services, 1971; (jtly) Physiotherapy in the Community, 1977; (jtly) Physically Disabled People Living at Home, 1978; (ed jtly) Recalling the Medical Officer of Health, 1987; (jtly) Health Services for Adults with Physical Disabilities, 1990; The Genesis of the Faculty of Community Medicine, 1997; A Chronology of State Medicine, Public Health, Welfare and Related Services in Britain 1066–1999, 2000; contribs to BMJ, Lancet, Internat. Jl of Epidemiology. *Recreations:* enjoying gardens, genealogy, reading, listening to music. *Address:* 2 Bridge Down, Bridge, Canterbury, Kent CT4 5AZ. *T:* (01227) 830233. *Clubs:* Royal Society of Medicine; Kent County Cricket.

WARREN, Sir Miles; *see* Warren, Sir F. M.

WARREN, Nicholas Roger; QC 1993; a Recorder, since 1999; *b* 20 May 1949; *s* of Roger Warren and Muriel (*née* Reeves); *m* 1st, 1978 (marr. diss. 1989); two *s* one *d*; 2nd, 1994, Catherine Graham-Harrison. *Educ:* Bryanston Sch.; University Coll., Oxford. Called to the Bar, Middle Temple, 1972, Bencher, 2001. *Recreations:* music, sailing. *Address:* Wilberforce Chambers, 8 New Square, Lincoln's Inn, WC2A 3QP.

WARREN, Ven. Norman Leonard; Archdeacon of Rochester, 1989–2000; *b* 19 July 1934; *s* of Arthur Henry Warren and Gwendoline Catharine Warren; *m* 1961, Yvonne Sheather; three *s* two *d*. *Educ:* Dulwich College; Corpus Christi Coll., Cambridge (MA). Asst Curate, Bedworth, 1960–63; Vicar, St Paul's, Leamington Priors, 1963–77; Rector of Morden, 1977–89; RD of Merton, 1984–88. Musical Editor: Hymns for Today's Church, 1982; Jesus Praise, 1982; Sing Glory, 1999. *Publications:* Journey into Life, 1964; The Way Ahead, 1965; Directions, 1969; What's the Point?, 1986; The Path of Peace, 1988; A Certain Faith, 1988; Is God there?, 1990; Why Believe?, 1993; (ed) Responsorial Psalms of the Alternative Services Book, 1994. *Recreations:* cricket, soccer and Rugby, walking, music. *Address:* 1 Sandling Way, St Mary's Island, Chatham, Kent ME4 3AZ. *T:* (01634) 891363.

See also Very Rev. A. C. Warren, R. H. C. Warren.

WARREN, Peter Francis; Chairman, Hammond Communications, since 1994; non-executive Chairman, Radio Advertising Bureau, 1995–2001; *b* 2 Dec. 1940; *s* of Francis Joseph Warren and Freda Ruth Hunter; *m* 1962, Susan Poole; two *s* one *d*. *Educ:* Finchley Grammar School. Deputy Managing Director, Ogilvy Benson & Mather Ltd, 1977; Director, Ogilvy & Mather International Inc., 1978; Man. Dir, Ogilvy Benson & Mather Ltd, 1978; Chairman: Ogilvy & Mather (Hldgs), subseq. The Ogilvy Gp (Hldgs) Ltd, 1981–90; Ogilvy & Mather Europe, 1988–90; Consultant, Ogilvy & Mather Worldwide, 1991 (Dir, 1985–90). Dir, Abbott Mead Vickers, 1992–99. *Address:* 31 Welbeck Street, W1G 8ET. *T:* (020) 7935 5430.

WARREN, Prof. Peter Michael, PhD; FSA; FBA 1997; Professor of Ancient History and Classical Archaeology, 1977–2000, now Emeritus, and Senior Research Fellow, since 2001, University of Bristol; *b* 23 June 1938; *s* of Arthur George Warren and Alison Joan Warren (*née* White); *m* 1966, Elizabeth Margaret Halliday; one *s* one *d*. *Educ:* Sandbach Sch.; Llandovery Coll.; University College of N Wales, Bangor (Ellen Thomas Stanford Schol.; BA 1st Cl. Hons Greek and Latin); Corpus Christi Coll., Cambridge (Exhibnr; BA Classical Tripos Pt II 1962; MA 1966; PhD 1966; Fellow, 1965–68); student, British Sch. at Athens, 1963–65. FSA 1973. Research Fellow in Arts, Univ. of Durham, 1968–70; Asst Director, British Sch. at Athens, 1970–72; University of Birmingham: Lectr in Aegean Archaeol., 1972–74; Sen. Lectr, 1974–76; Reader, 1976; Bristol University: Dean, Faculty of Arts, 1988–90; Pro-Vice-Chancellor, 1991–95; Fellow, 1995–96. Vis. Prof., Univ. of Minnesota, 1981; Geddes-Harrower Prof. of Greek Art and Archaeol., Univ. of Aberdeen, 1986–87; Neubergh Lectr, Univ. of Göteborg, 1986. Dir of excavations, Myrtos, Crete, 1967–68; Debla, Crete, 1971; Knossos, 1971–73, 1978–82, 1997. Member: Managing Cttee, British Sch. at Athens, 1973–77, 1978–79, 1986–90, 1994–98, 1999– (Chm., 1979–83); Council, Soc. for Promotion of Hellenic Studies, 1978–81; Pres., Bristol Anglo-Hellenic Cultural Soc., 1987–97. Bristol and Gloucestershire Archaeological Society: Vice-Chm. Council, 1980–81; Chm., 1981–84; Vice-Pres., 1989–93; Pres., 2000–01. Hon. Fellow, Archaeol Soc. of Athens, 1987; Corresp. Fellow, Soc. for Cretan Historical Studies, 1992; Corresp. Mem., Österreichische Akad. der Wissenschaften, 1997. Hon. Dr Univ. of Athens, 2000. *Publications:* Minoan Stone Vases, 1969; Myrtos, an Early Bronze Age Settlement in Crete, 1972; The Aegean Civilizations, 1975, 2nd edn 1989; Minoan Religion as Ritual Action, 1988; (with V. Hankey) Aegean Bronze Age Chronology, 1989; articles on Aegean Bronze Age, particularly Minoan archaeology, in archaeol, science and classical jls. *Recreations:* contemporary British politics, Manchester United, history of Greek botany. *Address:* Claremont House, Merlin Haven, Wotton-under-Edge, Glos GL12 7BA. *T:* (01453) 842290.

WARREN, Peter Tolman, CBE 1998; PhD; Consultant, World Humanity Action Trust, 1999–2001 (Director, 1997–99), now Trustee; *b* 20 Dec. 1937; *s* of late Hugh Alan Warren and Florence Christine Warren (*née* Tolman); *m* 1961, Angela Mary (*née* Curtis); two *s* one *d*. *Educ:* Whitgift Sch., Croydon; Queens' Coll., Cambridge (MA, PhD); CGeol. Geological Survey of GB, 1962; Chief Scientific Adviser's Staff, Cabinet Office, 1972; Private Sec. to Lord Zuckerman, 1973–76; Science and Technology Secretariat, Cabinet Office, 1974–76; Safety Adviser, NERC, 1976–77; Dep. Exec. Sec., 1977–85, Exec. Sec., 1985–97, Royal Soc. Mem. Council, Parly and Scientific Cttee, 1992– (Vice-Pres., 1995–97, 2001–). Member: Council, GDST (formerly GPDST), 1989–; Ct of Governors and Council, Nat. Mus and Galls of Wales, 2000–. Vice-President: Geol Soc., 1992–96; BAAS, 1997–; Chm., Cambridge Soc. (Surrey Br.), 2000–. Editor, Monographs of Palaeontographical Soc., 1968–77. *Publications:* (ed) Geological Aspects of Development and Planning in Northern England, 1970; (co-author) Geology of the Country around Rhyl and Denbigh, 1984; papers on geology in learned jls. *Recreations:* geology, gardening. *Address:* 34 Plough Lane, Purley, Surrey CR8 3QA. *T:* (020) 8660 4087. *Club:* Athenæum.

WARREN, Prof. Raymond Henry Charles, MusD; Stanley Hugh Badock Professor of Music, University of Bristol, 1972–94; *b* 7 Nov. 1928; *s* of Arthur Henry Warren and Gwendoline Catherine Warren; *m* 1953, Roberta Lydia Alice Smith; three *s* one *d*. *Educ:* Bancroft's Sch.; Corpus Christi Coll., Cambridge (MA, MusD). Music Master, Wolverstone Hall Sch., 1952–55; Queen's University Belfast: Lectr in Music, 1955–66; Prof. of Composition, 1966–72; Resident Composer, Ulster Orchestra, 1967–72. Compositions incl. 3 symphonies, 3 string quartets and 6 operas. *Publications: compositions:* The Passion, 1963; String Quartet No 1, 1967; Violin Concerto, 1967; Songs of Old Age, 1971; Continuing Cities (oratorio), 1989; Opera Workshop, 1995. *Recreation:* walking. *Address:* 9 Cabot Rise, Portishead, Bristol BS20 6NX. *T:* (01275) 844289.

See also Very Rev. A. C. Warren, Ven. N. L. Warren.

WARREN, Stanley Anthony Treleaven, CB 1984; CEng, FRINA, FIMechE; RCNC; Director General Submarines, Ministry of Defence (Procurement Executive), 1979–85, retired; *b* 26 Sept. 1925; *s* of Stanley Howard Warren and Mabel Harriett (*née* Ham); *m* 1950, Sheila Glo May (*née* Rowe); two *s* one *d*. *Educ:* King's Coll., Univ. of London (BSc 1st Cl. Hons Engrg); RNC, Greenwich (1st Cl. Naval Architecture). FRINA 1967; FIMechE 1970. Sub-Lieut, RN, 1945–47; Constructor Lieut, RCNC, 1947–51; Royal Yacht Britannia design, 1951–54; frigate modernisations, 1954–57; Constructor, HM Dockyard, Malta, 1957–60; Admiralty Constructor Overseer, John Brown and Yarrow, 1960–64; Polaris Submarine design, 1964–67; Chief Constructor and Principal Naval Overseer, Birkenhead, 1967–72; Asst Dir and Invincible Class Proj. Manager, 1972–76; Dep. Dir of Submarines (Polaris), MoD (PE), 1976–79. *Publications:* contribs to learned societies. *Recreations:* golf, travel, gardening.

WARREN EVANS, (John) Roger, FCIOB; consultant and lecturer, trading as Lexikon, since 1995; Director, Estates & Agency Holdings plc, since 1995; *b* 11 Dec. 1935; *s* of Thomas and Mary Warren Evans; *m* 1966, Elizabeth M. James; one *s* one *d*. *Educ:* Leighton Park Sch., Reading; Trinity Coll., Cambridge (BA History, 1st Cl.); London Sch. of Economics. Called to Bar, Gray's Inn, 1962. Television Interviewer, Anglia Television, 1960–61; Research Officer, Centre for Urban Studies, London, 1961; practice at Bar, 1962–69; Legal Correspondent, New Society, 1964–68; general management functions with Bovis Gp, in construction and develt, 1969–74, incl. Man. Dir, Bovis Homes Southern Ltd, 1971–74; Under-Secretary, DoE, 1975; Industrial Advr on Construction, DoE, 1975–76; Man. Dir, Barratt Develts (London), Ltd, 1977–79; Dir, Swansea Centre for Trade and Industry, 1979–85; Man. Dir, Demos Ltd, 1985–87; SavaCentre Property Develt Manager, 1987–88; Regl Property Dir, J. Sainsbury plc, 1988–94. Member: Welsh Consumer Council, 1992–95; Cttee, Community Selfbuild Agency, 1995–99. Mem. Bd, Assoc. of Self Employed, 1995–96. Gov., Gillespie Primary Sch., Islington, 1993–96. Trustee: Inst. of Community Studies, 1975–2001; Mutual Aid Centre, 1975–; Aquaterra Leisure, 1999–; Croeso Trust, 2000–. Member: Hackney BC, 1971–73; Mumbles Community Council, Swansea, 1999–. FCIOB 1976. Hon. Fellow, Coll. of Estate Mgt,

1982. *Recreation:* tennis. *Address:* 23 St Peter's Road, Newton, Swansea SA3 4SB. *T:* (01792) 368003.

WARREN-GASH, Haydon Boyd; HM Diplomatic Service; Foreign and Commonwealth Office, since 2001; *b* 8 Aug. 1949; *s* of Alexis Patrick and Cynthia Warren-Gash; *m* 1973, Caroline Emma Bowring Leather; one *s* one *d.* *Educ:* Sidney Sussex Coll., Cambridge (MA Econs). Joined Foreign and Commonwealth Office, 1971; language training, SOAS, London Univ., 1972 (on secondment); Third Sec., Ankara, 1973–76; Second, subseq. First, Sec., Madrid, 1977–80; First Sec., FCO, 1980–82; Private Sec. to Minister of State, 1982–85; First Sec. (Commercial), Paris, 1985–89; Asst Head, Southern European Dept, FCO, 1989–91; Dep. High Comr, Nairobi, 1991–94; Hd, Southern European Dept, FCO, 1994–97; Ambassador to Côte d'Ivoire, to Niger, Burkino Faso and Liberia, 1997–2001. *Recreation:* entomology. *Address:* c/o Foreign and Commonwealth Office, King Charles Street, SW1A 2AH. *Club:* Muthaiga (Nairobi).

WARRENDER, family name of **Baron Bruntisfield**.

WARRENDER, Hon. Robin Hugh; Senior Consultant, Aon Insurance Services Ltd (formerly Bain Hogg Ltd), since 1999 (non-executive Director, 1994–99); *b* 24 Dec. 1927; 3rd *s* of 1st Baron Bruntisfield, MC; *m* 1951, Gillian, *d* of Leonard Rossiter; one *s* two *d.* *Educ:* Eton; Trinity Coll., Oxford. Underwriting Member of Lloyd's, 1953; Tudor & Co. (Insurance) Ltd, 1958–62; Managing Director, Fenchurch Insurance Holdings Ltd, 1963–69; Dep. Chm., A. W. Bain & Sons Ltd, 1970; Chairman: Bain Dawes PLC and other group companies, 1973–85; London Wall Hldgs Ltd, 1986–94. Director: Comindus S. A. (France), 1980–82; Worms & Co., 1981–83; Varity Corporation, 1982–96; Varity Holdings Ltd, 1982–91; Heritable Group Holdings Ltd, 1983–94; Société Centrale Préservatrice Foncière Assurances, 1986–89; Gp Athena, 1989–93. Mem. Council and Cttee of Lloyd's, 1983–86. Mem. Council, Bath Univ., 1979–82; Hon. Treas., Governing Cttee, Royal Choral Soc., 1979–. *Recreations:* shooting, gardening, bridge. *Address:* Capps Lodge House, Fulbrook, Burford, Oxon OX18 4DB. *T:* (01993) 822262. *Club:* White's.
See also Baron Colgrain.

WARRINGTON, Bishop Suffragan of, since 2000; **Rt Rev. David Willfred Michael Jennings;** *b* 13 July 1944; *s* of late Rev. Willfred Jennings and Nona Jennings (*née* de Winton); *m* 1969, Sarah Catherine Fynn, *d* of Dr Robert Fynn of Harare, Zimbabwe; three *s.* *Educ:* Radley Coll.; King's Coll., London (AKC 1966). Ordained deacon, 1967, priest, 1968; Assistant Curate: St Mary, Walton on the Hill, Liverpool, 1967–69; Christchurch Priory, Christchurch, Hants, 1969–73; Vicar: Hythe, Southampton, 1973–80; St Edward, Romford, 1980–92; Rural Dean of Havering, 1985–92; Archdeacon of Southend, 1992–2000. Non-residentiary Canon, Chelmsford Cathedral, 1987–92. *Recreation:* exploring the buildings of the British Isles. *Address:* 34 Central Avenue, Eccleston Park, Prescot, Merseyside L34 2QP. *T:* (0151) 426 1897.

WARRINGTON, Archdeacon of; *see* Bradley, Ven. P. D. D.

WARRINGTON, Prof. Elizabeth Kerr, FRS 1986; Professor of Clinical Neuropsychology, 1982–96, now Emeritus, and Hon. Consultant, since 1996, National Hospital for Neurology and Neurosurgery; *d* of late Prof. John Alfred Valentine Butler, FRS and Margaret Lois Butler; one *d.* *Educ:* University College London (BSc 1954; PhD 1960; DSc 1975; Fellow 1994). Research Fellow, Inst. of Neurology, 1956; National Hospital: Senior Clinical Psychologist, 1960; Principal Psychologist, 1962; Top Grade Clinical Psychologist, 1972–82. Dr (*hc*) Psiccologia, Bologna, 1998; DUniv York, 1999. *Publications:* (with R. A. McCarthy) Cognitive Neuropsychology, 1990; numerous papers in neurological and psychological jls. *Recreations:* gardening, entertaining granddaughters. *Address:* Dementia Research Group, Institute of Neurology, Queen Square, WC1N 3BG. *T:* (020) 7837 3611.

WARRY, Peter Thomas, CEng, FIEE, FIMechE; FCMA; Chairman, Victrex plc, since 1999; *b* 31 Aug. 1949; *s* of William Vivian Warry and Pamela Warry; *m* 1981, Rosemary Furbank; one *d.* *Educ:* Clifton Coll., Bristol; Merton Coll., Oxford (MA); LLB London Univ. CEng 1979; FIEE 1995; FIMechE 1995; FCMA 1983. Man. Dir, Self-Changing Gears Ltd, 1979–82; Gp Man. Dir, Aerospace Engineering plc, 1982–84; Director: Plessey Telecoms, 1986–87; Norcros plc, 1988–94; Nuclear Electric plc, 1995–96; British Energy plc, 1996–98; Chief Exec., Nuclear Electric Ltd, 1996–98. Non-executive Director: Heatherwood & Wexham Park Hosps NHS Trust, 1992–95; PTS Gp plc, 1995–98; Kier Group plc, 1998–; Office of the Rail Regulator, 1999–; BSS Gp plc, 1999–. Special Advr, Prime Minister's Policy Unit, 1984–86; Mem., Deregulation Task Force, DTI, 1993–94. Indust. Prof., Warwick Univ., 1993–. *Recreations:* squash, tennis, walking, archeology, history. *Address:* Coxhorne, London Road, Cheltenham GL52 6UY. *T:* (01242) 518552.

WARSI, Perween, MBE 1997; Managing Director, S&A Foods Ltd, since 1987; *b* 10 Aug. 1956; *m* 1972, Dr Talib Warsi; two *s.* Started S&A Foods from own kitchen, 1986; founded business, 1987; entered partnership with Hughes Foods Gp, 1988; with husband, completed mgt buy-out, 1991; S&A Foods began exporting, 1995; company created 1300 jobs in inner-city Derby, achieved annual growth rate of 40–50%, and has recd 28 awards, 1995–. Mem., Govt Adv. Cttee on Competitiveness, 1997–. Non-exec. Dir, Century 106 FM Radio, 1997–. Hon. MBA Derby, 1997; Hon. DBA Internat. Mgt Centres, 1999. Midlands Business Woman of Year Award, 1994; RADAR People of Year Award, 1995; Woman Entrepreneur of World Award, 1996. *Address:* S&A Foods Ltd, Sir Francis Ley Industrial Park, 37 Shaftesbury Street South, Derby DE23 8YH. *T:* (01332) 270670, *Fax:* (01332) 270523.

WARTNABY, Dr John; Keeper, Department of Earth and Space Sciences, Science Museum, South Kensington, 1969–82; *b* 6 Jan. 1926; *o s* of Ernest John and Beatrice Hilda Wartnaby; *m* 1962, Kathleen Mary Barber, MD, MRCP, DPM; one *s* one *d.* *Educ:* Chiswick Grammar Sch.; Chelsea Coll. (BSc 1946); Imperial Coll. of Science and Technology (DIC 1950); University Coll., London (MSc 1967; PhD 1972). FInstP 1971. Asst Keeper, Dept of Astronomy and Geophysics, Science Museum, 1951; Deputy Keeper, 1960. *Publications:* Seismology, 1957; The International Geophysical Year, 1957; Surveying, 1968; papers in learned jls. *Recreations:* country walking, Zen. *Address:* 11 Greenhurst Lane, Oxted, Surrey RH8 0LD. *T:* (01883) 714461.

WARWICK; *see* Turner-Warwick.

WARWICK, 9th Earl of, *cr* 1759; **Guy David Greville;** Baron Brooke 1621; Earl Brooke 1746; *b* 30 Jan. 1957; *s* of 8th Earl of Warwick and of Sarah Anne Chester Greville (*née* Beatty; now Mrs Harry Thomson Jones); *S* father, 1996; *m* 1st, 1981, Susan McKinlay Cobbold (marr. diss. 1992); one *s;* 2nd, 1996, Louisa Heenan. *Educ:* Summerfields; Eton; Ecole des Roches. *Recreations:* girls, surfing. *Heir:* *s* Lord Brooke, *qv.* *Address:* 19 Walter Street, Claremont, WA 6010, Australia. *Club:* White's.

WARWICK OF UNDERCLIFFE, Baroness *cr* 1999 (Life Peer), of Undercliffe in the county of West Yorkshire; **Diana Warwick;** Chief Executive, Universities UK (formerly Committee of Vice Chancellors and Principals), since 1995; *b* 16 July 1945; *d* of Jack and Olive Warwick; *m* 1969. *Educ:* St Joseph's Coll., Bradford; Bedford Coll., Univ. of London (BA Hons). Technical Asst to the Gen. Sec., NUT, 1969–72; Asst Sec., CPSA, 1972–83; Gen. Sec., AUT, 1983–92; Chief Exec., Westminster Foundn for Democracy, 1992–95. Mem., Cttee on Standards in Public Life, 1994–2000. Member: Bd, British Council, 1985–95; Employment Appeal Tribunal, 1987–; Exec. and Council, Industrial Soc., 1987–; TUC Gen. Council, 1989–92; Council, Duke of Edinburgh's Seventh Commonwealth Study Conf., 1991; Chm., VSO, 1994–. Gov., Commonwealth Inst., 1988–95. Trustee, Royal Anniversary Trust, 1991–93. FRSA 1984. Hon. DLitt Bradford, 1993; DUniv Open, 1998. *Recreations:* theatre, looking at pictures. *Address:* Universities UK, Woburn House, 20 Tavistock Square, WC1H 9HQ. *T:* (020) 7419 4111.

WARWICK, Bishop Suffragan of, since 1996; **Rt Rev. Anthony Martin Priddis;** *b* 15 March 1948; *s* of Ted and Joan Priddis; *m* 1973, Kathy Armstrong; two *s* one *d.* *Educ:* Corpus Christi Coll., Cambridge (BA 1969; MA 1973); New Coll., Oxford (DipTh 1971; MA 1975); Cuddesdon Coll., Oxford. Ordained deacon, 1972, priest, 1973; Asst Curate, New Addington, 1972–75; Chaplain, Christ Church, Oxford, 1975–80; Team Vicar, High Wycombe, 1980–86; Priest-in-charge, 1986–90, Rector, 1990–96, Amersham. Rural Dean of Amersham, 1992–96. *Publications:* (contrib.) Study of Spirituality, 1986. *Recreations:* walking the dogs, music, golf, gardening, watching sport. *Address:* Warwick House, 139 Kenilworth Road, Coventry CV4 7AP. *T:* (024) 7641 6200, *Fax:* (024) 7641 5254; *e-mail:* bishwarwick@clara.net.

WARWICK, Archdeacon of; *see* Paget-Wilkes, Ven. M. J. J.

WARWICK, Hannah Cambell Grant; *see* Gordon, H. C. G.

WARWICK, Prof. Kevin, PhD; FIEE; Professor of Cybernetics, University of Reading, since 1988; *b* 9 Feb. 1954; *s* of Stanley and Jessie Allcock; *née* Kevin Warwick Allcock; adopted Warwick as surname by Deed Poll, 1974; *m* 1st, 1974, Sylvia Margaret Walsh (marr. diss. 1991); one *s* one *d;* 2nd, 1991, Irena Vorackova. *Educ:* Lawrence Sheriff Sch., Rugby; Aston Univ. (BSc); Imperial Coll., London (PhD 1982; DIC 1982); DSc (Eng) London 1993. FIEE 1987. British Telecom Apprentice, 1970–76; Res. Asst, Imperial Coll., London, 1982; Lectr, Newcastle upon Tyne Univ., 1982–85; Res. Lectr, Oxford Univ., 1985–87; Sen Lectr, Warwick Univ., 1987–88. FCGI 1992. Mem., Aventis Books Cttee, Royal Soc., 2000–01. Presenter, Royal Instn Christmas Lectures, 2000. Hon. Mem., Acad. of Scis, St Petersburg, 1999. DrSc Czech Acad. of Scis, 1994. Future of Health Technol. Award, MIT, 2000. *Publications:* (ed jtly) Neural Nets for Control and Systems, 1992; March of the Machines, 1997; In the Mind of the Machine, 1998; QI: The Quest for Intelligence, 2000; contribs to books and jls on control, robotics, machine intelligence and cyborgs. *Recreations:* soccer (Reading FC supporter), travel, theatre. *Address:* Department of Cybernetics, University of Reading, Whiteknights, Reading RG6 6AY. *T:* (0118) 931 8210, *Fax:* (0118) 931 8220.

WARWICK THOMPSON, Paul; Director, Smithsonian Cooper-Hewitt National Design Museum, New York, since 2001; *b* 9 Aug. 1959; *s* of Sir Michael Thompson, *qv;* *m* 1984, Adline Finlay; one *s* one d. *Educ:* Bryanston Sch.; Univ. of Bristol (BA Jt Hons); Univ. of East Anglia (MA, PhD). Design Council, 1987–88; Design Museum, 1988–2001, Dir, 1992–2001. *Recreations:* theatre, cinema, gardening.

WASHINGTON, Neville James Cameron, OBE 1992; Chief Executive, Coal Authority, 1994–97; *b* 8 May 1948; *s* of Peter Washington and Sybil Joan Washington (*née* Cameron); *m* 1980, Jennifer Anne Frideswide Kekewich; two *s* one *d.* *Educ:* Marlborough Coll.; Trinity Hall, Cambridge (MA). Research on chimpanzee behaviour, Gombe, Tanzania, 1969–70. Joined Queen's Own Highlanders (Seaforth & Camerons), 1971; Army Staff Coll., Camberley, 1982; jsdc 1987; comd 3rd Bn, UDR, 1987–89 (despatches); left Army in rank of Lieut-Col, 1992. Dir of Human Resources, Victoria Infirmary, Glasgow, 1992–94. *Recreations:* sheep, hunting. *Address:* Rottenrow, Crosshands, by Mauchline, Ayrshire KA5 2TN.

WASS, Sir Douglas (William Gretton), GCB 1980 (KCB 1975; CB 1971); Senior Adviser, Nomura International plc, since 1998 (Chairman, 1986–98); Permanent Secretary to HM Treasury, 1974–83, and Joint Head of the Home Civil Service, 1981–83; *b* 15 April 1923; *s* of late Arthur W. and late Elsie W. Wass; *m* 1954, Dr Milica Pavičić; one *s* one *d.* *Educ:* Nottingham High Sch.; St John's Coll., Cambridge (MA; Hon. Fellow, 1982). Served War, 1943–46: Scientific Research with Admiralty, at home and in Far East. Entered HM Treasury as Asst Principal, 1946; Principal, 1951; Commonwealth Fund Fellow in USA, 1958–59; Vis. Fellow, Brookings Instn, Washington, DC, 1959; Private Sec.: to Chancellor of the Exchequer, 1959–61; to Chief Sec. to Treasury, 1961–62; Asst Sec., 1962; Alternate Exec. Dir, Internat. Monetary Fund, and Financial Counsellor, British Embassy, Washington, DC, 1965–67; HM Treasury: Under-Sec., 1968; Dep. Sec., 1970–73; Second Permanent Sec., 1973–74. Chairman: Equity & Law, subseq. Axa Equity & Law, Life Assurance Soc., 1986–95 (Dir, 1984–95); NCM (Credit Insce), 1991–95; Director: Barclays Bank, 1984–87; De La Rue Company plc, 1984–93; Equitable Cos Inc., 1992–95; Equitable Life Assurance Soc., USA, 1992–93; NCM (NV), Amsterdam, 1992–95; Soho Theatre Co., 1996–2000. Administrateur, Axa SA (formerly Cie du Midi), 1987–95; Consultant to Coopers & Lybrand, 1984–86. Chairman: British Selection Cttee of Harkness Fellowships, 1981–84; UN Adv. Gp on Financial Flows for Africa, 1987–88; SIB Adv. Cttee on Pension Transfers, 1993–94; Syndicate on the Government of Univ. of Cambridge, 1988–89. Pres., Market Res. Soc., 1987–91. Dep. Chm., Council of Policy Studies Inst, 1981–85; Vice-Pres., 1984–91, and Mem. Adv. Bd, Constitutional Reform Centre; Vice Chm., Africa Capacity Building Foundn, 1991–98; Governor, Ditchley Foundn, 1981–2000; Member, Council: Centre for Econ. Policy Res., 1983–90; Employment Inst., 1985–92; Univ. of Bath, 1985–91; British Heart Foundn, 1990–96; ODI, 1991–98. Lectures: Reith, BBC, 1983; Shell, St Andrews Univ., 1985; Harry Street Meml, Univ. of Manchester, 1987. Hon. DLitt Bath, 1985. *Publications:* Government and the Governed, 1984; articles in newspapers and jls. *Address:* 6 Dora Road, SW19 7HH. *T:* (020) 8946 5556. *Club:* Reform.
See also S. Wass.

WASS, Sasha, (Mrs N. R. A. Hall); QC 2000; a Recorder, since 2000; *b* 19 Feb. 1958; *d* of Sir Douglas William Gretton Wass, *qv;* *m* 1986, Nigel R. A. Hall; one *s* one *d.* *Educ:* Wimbledon High Sch.; Liverpool Univ. (LLB Hons). Called to the Bar, Gray's Inn, 1981; Asst Recorder, 1997–2000. Criminal Bar Association: Mem. Cttee, 1992–; Treas., 1997–99. *Address:* 6 King's Bench Walk, Temple, EC4Y 7DR. *T:* (020) 7583 0410.

WASSALL, Philip Hugh; a District Judge (Magistrates' Courts) (formerly Provincial Stipendiary Magistrate, Devonshire), since 1994; a Recorder, since 2000; *b* 11 March 1950; *s* of Derek William Wassall and Avril Mary Holden Wassall; *m* 1991, Julia Lesley; two *d.* *Educ:* Aldridge Grammar Sch.; Chelmsford Coll. (LLB Hons ext. London). Criminal Law Clerk, 1969–75; Articled Clerk, 1976–78; Solicitor, 1979–94. *Recreations:* golf, information technology, cooking, music, walking. *Address:* Plymouth Magistrates' Court, St Andrew Street, Plymouth PL1 2DP. *T:* (01752) 206200.

WASSERMAN, Gordon Joshua; Special Adviser and Chief of Staff to Police Commissioner, City of Philadelphia, since 1998; *b* Montreal, 26 July 1938; *s* of late John J. Wasserman, QC, and Prof. Rachel Chait Wasserman, Montreal; *m* 1964, Cressida Frances, *yr d* of late Rt Hon. Hugh Gaitskell, PC, CBE, MP, and Baroness Gaitskell; two *d*. *Educ:* Westmount High Sch., Montreal; McGill Univ. (BA); New Coll., Oxford (MA). Rhodes Scholar (Quebec and New Coll.), 1959; Sen. Research Scholar, St Antony's Coll., Oxford, 1961–64; Lectr in Economics, Merton Coll., Oxford, 1963–64; Research Fellow, New Coll., Oxford, 1964–67; joined Home Office as Economic Adviser, 1967, Sen. Econ. Adviser, 1972, Asst Sec., 1977–81; Head, Urban Deprivation Unit, 1973–77; Civil Service Travelling Fellowship in USA, 1977–78; Under Sec., Central Policy Review Staff, Cabinet Office, 1981–83; Asst Under Sec. of State, Home Office (Head, Police Science and Technology Gp), 1983–95; Special Advr (Sci. and Technol.) to Police Comr, NYC, 1996–98. Member: Exec., ELITE Gp, 1993–96; Bd, SEARCH Gp Inc., USA, 1994–. Trustee, McGill Univ. (Canada) Trust, 1995–96. Fellow, Koret Inst., USA, 1996–98. Vice-Pres., English Basket Ball Assoc., 1983–86. *Recreations:* gardening, walking, opera, music. *Address:* 200 West 86th Street, New York, NY 10024, USA. *Clubs:* Reform, Beefsteak.

WASTELL, Cyril Gordon, CBE 1975; Secretary General of Lloyd's, 1967–76, retired; *b* 10 Jan. 1916; *s* of Arthur Edward Wastell and Lilian Wastell; *m* 1947, Margaret Lilian (*née* Moore); one *d*. *Educ:* Brentwood Sch., Essex. Joined Staff of Corporation of Lloyd's, 1932; apart from war service (Lieut Royal Corps of Signals), 1939–46, progressed through various depts and positions at Lloyd's, until retirement. *Recreations:* reading, gardening under duress, walking, crosswords, various trivial pursuits. *Address:* Candys, Burgmann's Hill, Lympstone, Devon EX8 5HP.

WATERFIELD, Giles Adrian, FSA; Joint Director, Attingham Summer School, since 1995; Director, Royal Collection Studies, since 1995; *b* 24 July 1949; *s* of late Anthony and Honor Waterfield. *Educ:* Eton College; Magdalen College, Oxford (BA); Courtauld Institute (MA). FSA 1991. Education Officer, Royal Pavilion, Art Gallery and Museums, Brighton, 1976–79; Dir, Dulwich Picture Gall., 1979–96. Consultant Curator, Compton Verney, 1996–98. Mem., Museums Expert Panel, 1996–2000, Trustee, 2000–, Heritage Lottery Fund. Mem. Exec. Cttee, London Library, 1999–. Vice-Pres., NADFAS, 1998–. Judge, Mus. of the Year Awards, Nat. Heritage, 1999. Trustee: Holburne Mus., Bath, 1999–; Edward James Foundn, 1999–. *Publications:* Faces, 1983; (ed) Collection for a King (catalogue), 1985; Soane and After, 1987; Rich Summer of Art, 1988; (ed) Palaces of Art, 1991; (ed) Art for the People, 1994; (ed) Soane and Death, 1996; (contrib.) Art Treasures of England (catalogue), 1998; (contrib.) In Celebration: the art of the country house (catalogue), 1998; The Long Afternoon (novel), 2000; articles in Apollo, Art Newspaper, Burlington Magazine, Connoisseur, Country Life, London Review, TLS. *Recreations:* historic buildings, theatre. *Address:* 48 Claylands Road, SW8 1NZ.

WATERFIELD, John Percival; *b* Dublin, 5 Oct. 1921; *er s* of late Sir Percival Waterfield, KBE, CB; *m* 1st, 1950, Margaret Lee Thomas (*d* 1990); two *s* one *d*; 2nd, 1991, Tilla Hevesi Vahanian (*d* 1999). *Educ:* Dragon Sch.; Charterhouse (schol.); Christ Church, Oxford (schol.). Served War of 1939–45: 1st Bn, The King's Royal Rifle Corps (60th Rifles), Western Desert, Tunisia, Italy and Austria (despatches). Entered HM Foreign (subseq. Diplomatic) Service, 1946; Third Secretary, Moscow, 1947; Second Secretary, Tokyo, 1950; Foreign Office, 1952; First Secretary, Santiago, Chile, 1954; HM Consul (Commercial), New York, 1957; FO, 1960; Ambassador to Mali Republic, 1964–65, concurrently to Guinea, 1965; duties connected with NATO, 1966; Counsellor and Head of Chancery, New Delhi, 1966–68; Head of Western Organizations Dept, FCO, 1969; Man. Dir, BEAMA, 1971; Principal Estabs and Finance Officer, NI Office, 1973–79; on secondment to Internat. Military Services Ltd, 1979–80; retired from public service, 1980; company dir and consultant, 1980–84. *Address:* 5 North Street, Somerton, Somerset TA11 7NY. *T:* (01458) 272389.

WATERFIELD, Prof. Michael Derek, PhD; FRCPath, FMedSci; FRS 1991; Director of Research, Ludwig Institute for Cancer Research, since 1986 and Courtauld Professor of Biochemistry, since 1991, University College London; *b* 14 May 1941; *s* of Leslie N. Waterfield and Kathleen A. (*née* Marshall); *m* 1982, Sally E. James, MB BS, PhD; two *d*. *Educ:* Brunel Univ. (BSc 1963); Univ. of London (PhD 1967). FRCPath 1994. Res. Fellow, Harvard Univ. Med. Sch., 1967–70; Sen. Res. Fellow, CIT, 1970–72; Hd, Protein Chem. Lab., ICRF Labs, 1972–86; Head, Dept of Biochem. and Molecular Biology, UCL, 1991–2001. Scientific Adv. Bd, Baxter Healthcare (US), 1987–. Trustee: ICRF, 2000–; Inst. of Cancer Res., 2000–; Breakthrough Breast Cancer, 2000–; EMF Trust, 2001–. Founder FMedSci 1998. Hon. MD Ferrara, Italy, 1991. *Publications:* numerous articles in scientific jls on biochem. and molecular biol. as applied to cancer research. *Recreation:* pottering about the garden and kitchen. *Address:* Chantemerle, Speen Lane, Newbury, Berks RG13 1RN.

WATERFORD, 8th Marquess of, *cr* 1789; **John Hubert de la Poer Beresford;** Baron Le Poer, 1375; Baronet, 1668; Viscount Tyrone, Baron Beresford, 1720; Earl of Tyrone, 1746; Baron Tyrone (Great Britain), 1786; *b* 14 July 1933; *er s* of 7th Marquess and Juliet Mary (who *m* 2nd, 1946, Lieut-Colonel John Silcock), 2nd *d* of late David Lindsay; *S* father, 1934; *m* 1957, Lady Caroline Wyndham-Quin, *yr d* of 6th Earl of Dunraven and Mount-Earl, CB, CBE, MC; three *s* one *d*. *Educ:* Eton. Lieut, RHG Reserve. *Heir: s* Earl of Tyrone, *qv*. *Address:* Curraghmore, Portlaw, Co. Waterford. *T:* (51) 387102, *Fax:* (51) 387481. *Club:* White's.

WATERFORD AND LISMORE, Bishop of, (RC), since 1993; **Most Rev. William Lee,** DCL; *b* 2 Dec. 1941; *s* of John Lee and Bridget Ryan. *Educ:* Newport Boys' Nat. Sch.; Rockwell Coll.; Maynooth Coll. (BA, BD, LPh, DCL); Gregorian Univ., Rome. Ordained priest, 1966; Catholic Curate, Finglas, West Dublin, 1969–71; Bursar, 1971–87, President, 1987–93, St Patrick's Coll., Thurles. *Recreations:* reading, walking, golf. *Address:* Bishop's House, John's Hill, Waterford, Ireland. *T:* (51) 874463, *Fax:* (51) 852703.

WATERHOUSE, David Martin; Regional Director for South Asia and Pacific, British Council, 1994–97; *b* 23 July 1937; *s* of Rev. John W. Waterhouse and Dr Esther Waterhouse; *m* 1966, Verena Johnson; one *s* two *d*. *Educ:* Kingswood Sch., Bath; Merton Coll., Oxford (MA). Joined British Council, 1961; Enugu, Nigeria, 1962–65; Glasgow, 1965–68; Ndola, Zambia, 1968–71; Inst. of Educn, London Univ., 1971–72; Representative: Nepal, 1972–77; Thailand, 1977–80; Dir, Personnel Management Dept, 1980–85; Rep., Nigeria, 1985–89; Controller, Home Div., subseq. Dir, Exchanges and Training Div., British Council, 1989–91; Dir, Germany, 1991–93. Chm., Hoffman de Visme Foundn, 1998–. *Recreations:* walking, music. *Address:* 54 Grand Avenue, N10 3BP.

WATERHOUSE, Frederick Harry; systems consultant and advisor, since 1995; *b* 3 June 1932; *m* 1954, Olive Carter; two *d*. *Educ:* King Edward's, Aston, Birmingham; London Univ. (BScEcon). Associate Mem., CIMA. Chief Accountant, Copper Div., Imperial Metal Industries, 1967–70; Asst Chief Accountant, Agricl Div., ICI, 1970–72; Chief Accountant, Plant Protection Div., ICI, 1972–78; Dir, Société pour la Protection d'Agriculture (SOPRA), France, 1976–78; Dir, Solplant SA, Italy, 1976–78; Bd Member, Finance and Corporate Planning, The Post Office, 1978–79; Treasurer's Dept, ICI Ltd, Millbank, 1979–82. Partner, Bognor Antiques, 1984–87; Chief Accountant, Jelkeep Ltd, Deerhyde Ltd and Thawscroft Ltd, Selsey, 1988–94. *Recreations:* golf, gardening, sailing. *Address:* Pendennis, Fishers, St Lawrence, Ventnor, Isle of Wight PO38 1UU.

WATERHOUSE, Keith Spencer, CBE 1991; FRSL; writer; *b* 6 Feb. 1929; 4th *s* of Ernest and Elsie Edith Waterhouse; *m* 1984, Stella Bingham (marr. diss. 1989); one *s* one *d* (and one *d* decd) from previous marriage. *Educ:* Leeds. Journalist in Leeds and London, 1950–; Columnist with: Daily Mirror, 1970–86; Daily Mail, 1986–; Contributor to various periodicals; Mem. Punch Table, 1979. Mem., Kingman Cttee on Teaching of English Language, 1987–88. Hon. Fellow, Leeds Metropolitan Univ. (formerly Poly.), 1991. Granada Columnist of the Year Award, 1970; IPC Descriptive Writer of the Year Award, 1970; IPC Columnist of the Year Award, 1973; British Press Awards Columnist of the Year, 1978, 1991; Granada Special Quarter Century Award, 1982; Edgar Wallace Trophy, London Press Club, 1996; Gerald Barry Lifetime Achievement Award, What the Papers Say awards, 2000. Films (with Willis Hall) include: Billy Liar; Whistle Down the Wind; A Kind of Loving; Lock Up Your Daughters. Plays: Mr and Mrs Nobody, 1986; Jeffrey Bernard is Unwell, 1989 (Evening Standard Best Comedy Award, 1990), revived 1999; Bookends, 1990; Our Song, 1992; Good Grief, 1998; Bing-Bong!, 1999; plays with Willis Hall include: Billy Liar, 1960 (from which musical Billy was adapted, 1974); Celebration, 1961; All Things Bright and Beautiful, 1963; Say Who You Are, 1965; Whoops-a-Daisy, 1968; Children's Day, 1969; Who's Who, 1972; The Card (musical), 1973; Saturday, Sunday, Monday (adaptation from de Filippo), 1973; Filumena (adaptation from de Filippo), 1977; Worzel Gummidge, 1981; Budgie (musical), 1988. TV series: Budgie, Queenie's Castle, The Upper Crusts, Billy Liar, The Upchat Line, The Upchat Connection, Worzel Gummidge, West End Tales, The Happy Apple, Charters and Caldicott, Andy Capp; TV films: Charlie Muffin, 1983; This Office Life, 1985; The Great Paper Chase, 1988. *Publications: novels:* There is a Happy Land, 1957; Billy Liar, 1959; Jubb, 1963; The Bucket Shop, 1968; Billy Liar on the Moon, 1975; Office Life, 1978; Maggie Muggins, 1981; In the Mood, 1983; Thinks, 1984; Our Song, 1988; Bimbo, 1990; Unsweet Charity, 1992; Good Grief, 1997; Soho, 2001; *plays:* Jeffrey Bernard Is Unwell and other plays, 1991; (with Willis Hall) include: Billy Liar, 1960; Celebration, 1961; All Things Bright and Beautiful, 1963; Say Who You Are, 1965; Who's Who, 1974; Saturday, Sunday, Monday (adaptation from de Filippo), 1974; Filumena (adaptation from de Filippo), 1977; *general:* (with Guy Deghy) Café Royal, 1956; (ed) Writers' Theatre, 1967; The Passing of The Third-floor Buck, 1974; Mondays, Thursdays, 1976; Rhubarb, Rhubarb, 1979; Daily Mirror Style, 1980, rev. and expanded edn, Newspaper Style, 1989; Fanny Peculiar, 1983; Mrs Pooter's Diary, 1983; Waterhouse At Large, 1985; Collected Letters of a Nobody, 1986; The Theory and Practice of Lunch, 1986; The Theory and Practice of Travel, 1989; English Our English, 1991; Sharon & Tracy & The Rest, 1992; City Lights, 1994; Streets Ahead, 1995. *Recreation:* lunch. *Address:* 84 Coleherne Court, Old Brompton Road, SW5 0EE. *Club:* Garrick.

WATERHOUSE, Dame Rachel (Elizabeth), DBE 1990 (CBE 1980); PhD; Chairman, Consumers' Association, 1982–90 (Member Council, 1966–96, Deputy Chairman, 1979–82); *b* 2 Jan. 1923; *d* of Percival John Franklin and Ruby Susanna Franklin; *m* 1947, John A. H. Waterhouse; two *s* two *d*. *Educ:* King Edward's High Sch., Birmingham; St Hugh's Coll., Oxford (BA 1944, MA 1948); Univ. of Birmingham (PhD 1950). WEA and Extra-mural tutor, 1944–47. Birmingham Consumer Group: Sec., 1964–65, Chm. 1966–68, Mem. Cttee, 1968–; Member: Nat. Consumer Council, 1975–86; Consumers' Consultative Cttee of EEC Commn, 1977–84; Price Commn, 1977–79; Council, Advertising Standards Authority, 1980–85; NEDC, 1981–91; BBC Consultative Gp on Industrial and Business Affairs, 1984–89; Richmond Cttee on Microbiol Safety of Food, 1989–90; HSC, 1990–95; Adv. Cttee on Microbiological Safety of Food, 1991–95. Ministerial nominee to Potato Marketing Bd, 1969–81; Chm., Council for Licensed Conveyancers, 1986–89; Member: Home Office Working Party on Internal Shop Security, 1971–73; Adv. Cttee on Asbestos, 1976–79; Council for the Securities Industry, 1983–85; Securities and Investments Board, 1985–92; Organising Cttee, Marketing of Investments Bd, 1985–86; Council, Office of the Banking Ombudsman, 1985–95; Duke of Edinburgh's Inquiry into British Housing, 1984–85; Adv. Bd, Inst. of Food Res., 1988–93. Pres., Inst. of Consumer Ergonomics, Univ. of Loughborough, 1980–90 (Chm., 1970–80); Vice-President: Nat. Fedn of Consumer Gps, 1980–96; Birmingham Centre for Business Ethics, 1999–; Member: Council, Birmingham and Midland Inst., 1993 (Pres., 1992); Court of Govs, Univ. of Birmingham, 1992–; Provost, Selly Oak Colls, 1997–2000. Chm., Birmingham Gp, Victorian Soc., 1966–67, 1972–74; Vice-Chm., Lunar Soc., 1996–98 (Chm., 1990–96). Trustee: Joseph Rowntree Foundn, 1990–98; Affirming Catholicism, 1991–2001; Gov., Foundn of Lady Katherine Leveson, 2001–. Hon. FGIA (Hon. CGIA 1988). Hon. DLitt Univ. of Technology, Loughborough, 1978; Hon. DSocSc Birmingham, 1990; Hon. DSc Aston, 1998. *Publications:* The Birmingham and Midland Institute 1854–1954, 1954; A Hundred Years of Engineering Craftsmanship, 1957; Children in Hospital: a hundred years of child care in Birmingham, 1962; (with John Whybrow) How Birmingham became a Great City, 1976; King Edward VI High School for Girls 1883–1983, 1983. *Address:* 252 Bristol Road, Birmingham B5 7SL. *T:* (0121) 472 0427.

WATERHOUSE, Roger William; Vice-Chancellor, University of Derby, since 1992; *b* 29 April 1940; *s* of Ronald Waterhouse and Dorthy May Waterhouse (*née* Holmes); *m* 1st, 1962, Mania Jevinsky (marr. diss.); one *s* two *d*; 2nd, 1979, Jacqueline Mary Dymond; one *s* one *d*. *Educ:* Corpus Christi Coll., Oxford (BA, MA Phil. & Psychol.). Lectr, Shoreditch Coll., 1961–62; Teacher, Kibbutz Ma'abarot, Israel, 1962–64; Hd of Econs, Myers Grove Comprehensive Sch., Sheffield, 1966–68; Asst Lectr, Lectr, Sen. Lectr and Principal Lectr, Hendon Coll. of Technol., 1968–73; Hd, Dept of Humanities and Dean of Humanities, Middx Poly., 1973–86; Dep. Dir (Acad. Planning), Wolverhampton Poly., 1986–89; Dir, Derbys Coll. of Higher Educn, 1989–92. Chm., Derbyshire Careers Service Ltd, 1995–. FRSA 1993. *Publications:* A Heidegger Critique, 1981; jl articles on modern European philosophy, higher educn, credit accumulation and transfer. *Recreation:* wood-turning. *Address:* University of Derby, Kedleston Road, Derby DE22 1GB. *T:* (01332) 591000.

WATERHOUSE, Sir Ronald (Gough), Kt 1978; Judge of the High Court of Justice, Family Division, 1978–88, Queen's Bench Division, 1988–96; *b* Holywell, Flintshire, 8 May 1926; *s* of late Thomas Waterhouse, CBE, and Doris Helena Waterhouse (*née* Gough); *m* 1960, Sarah Selina, *d* of late Captain E. A. Ingram and Diana Mary Ingram (*née* Leigh-Bennett); one *s* two *d*. *Educ:* Holywell Grammar Sch.; St John's Coll., Cambridge. RAFVR, 1944–48. McMahon Schol., St John's Coll., 1949; Pres., Cambridge Union Soc., 1950; MA, LLM; called to Bar, Middle Temple, 1952 (Harmsworth Schol.), Bencher, 1977, Treas., 1995; Wales and Chester Circuit, Leader, 1978; QC 1969; a Recorder of the Crown Court, 1972–77; Presiding Judge, Wales and Chester Circuit, 1980–84; a Judge, Employment Appeal Tribunal, 1979–87. Mem. Bar Council, 1961–65. Deputy Chairman: Cheshire QS, 1964–71; Flintshire QS, 1966–71. Contested (Lab) West Flintshire, 1959. Chairman: Inter-departmental Cttee of Inquiry on Rabies, 1970; Cttees of Investigation for GB and England and Wales, under Agricultural Mkting Act, 1971–78; Local Govt Boundary Commn for Wales, 1974–78; Tribunal of Inquiry into Child Abuse in N Wales Children's Homes, 1996–2000; Ind. Supervisory Authy for Hunting, 2000–. Pres., CAB, Royal Courts of Justice, 1992–98 (Chm., 1981–92). A Vice-Pres., Zoological Soc. of London, 1981–84 and 1992–93 (Mem. Council, 1972–89, 1991–93). President: Llangollen Internat. Musical Eisteddfod, 1994–97; St John's Wood Soc., 1994–96. Hon. LLD Wales, 1986. *Recreations:* music, golf. *Address:* Greystone House, Walford, Ross-on-Wye, Herefordshire HR9 5RJ. *Clubs:* Garrick, Pilgrims, MCC; Cardiff and County (Cardiff).

See also J. B. Thompson.

WATERLOW, Anthony John; Chairman and Managing Director, Kodak, 1992–97; *b* 14 July 1938; *s* of George Joseph Waterlow and Sylvia Netta Waterlow; *m* 1st, 1962, Sheila; three *s*; 2nd, 1992, Ann. *Educ:* Harrow County Grammar Sch.; Ealing College; Chartered Inst. of Management Accountants. Joined Kodak as accountant trainee, 1954. *Recreation:* bridge. *Address:* c/o Kodak Ltd, Kodak House, Hemel Hempstead, Herts HP1 1JU. *T:* (01442) 261122.

WATERLOW, Sir Christopher Rupert, 5th Bt *cr* 1873; Lighting Cameraman, QVC, The Shopping Channel; *b* 12 Aug. 1959; *s* of (Peter) Rupert Waterlow (*d* 1969) and Jill Elizabeth (*d* 1961), *e d* of E. T. Gourlay; *S* grandfather, 1973. *Educ:* Stonyhurst Coll., Lancs; Ravensbourne Coll. (HND Professional Broadcasting Technical Ops, 1999). Fellow and Assessment Officer, Inst. of Videography; Mem., Guild of Television Cameramen. *Recreations:* playing and listening to music, supporting Wasps RFC. *Heir: cousin* Nicholas Anthony Waterlow [*b* 30 Aug. 1941; *m* 1965, Rosemary (*d* 1998), *o d* of W. J. O'Brien; two *s* one *d*]. *Address:* 78 Portland Road, Bromley, Kent BR1 5AZ. *Club:* Stonyhurst Association.

WATERLOW, Sir (James) Gerard, 4th Bt *cr* 1930; management consultant; *b* 3 Sept. 1939; *s* of Sir Thomas Gordon Waterlow, 3rd Bt, CBE and Helen Elizabeth (*d* 1970), *yr d* of Gerard A. H. Robinson; *S* father, 1982; *m* 1965, Diana Suzanne, *yr d* of Sir Thomas Skyrme, *qv*; one *s* one *d*. *Educ:* Marlborough; Trinity College, Cambridge. *Recreations:* tennis, bridge. *Heir: s* (Thomas) James Waterlow [*b* 20 March 1970; *m* 1999, Theresa, *y d* of Captain Francis Walsh]. *Address:* Rushall Lodge, Pewsey, Wilts SN9 6EN. *Club:* Lansdowne.

WATERLOW, Prof. John Conrad, CMG 1970; MD, ScD; FRCP; FRS 1982; FRGS; Professor of Human Nutrition, London School of Hygiene and Tropical Medicine, 1970–82, now Emeritus; *b* 13 June 1916; *o s* of Sir Sydney Waterlow, KCMG, CBE, HM Diplomatic Service; *m* 1939, Angela Pauline Cecil Gray; two *s* one *d*. *Educ:* Eton Coll.; Trinity Coll., Cambridge (MD, ScD); London Hosp. Med. College. Mem., Scientific Staff, MRC, 1942; Dir, MRC Tropical Metabolism Research Unit, Univ. of the West Indies, 1954–70. For. Associate Mem., Nat. Acad. of Scis, USA, 1992. *Publications:* numerous papers on protein malnutrition and protein metabolism. *Recreation:* mountain walking. *Address:* 15 Hillgate Street, W8 7SP; Parsonage House, Oare, Marlborough, Wilts SN8 4JA. *Club:* Savile.

WATERMAN, Fanny, CBE 2000 (OBE 1971); FRCM; Chairman, Leeds International Pianoforte Competition, since 1963, also Chairman of Jury, since 1981; *b* 22 March 1920; *d* of Myer Waterman and Mary Waterman (*née* Behrmann); *m* 1944, Dr Geoffrey Michael de Keyser (*d* 2001); two *s*. *Educ:* Allerton High Sch., Leeds; Tobias Matthay, Cyril Smith, Royal College of Music, London (FRCM 1972). Concert pianist, teacher of international reputation. Vice-President: European Piano-Teachers Assoc., 1975–; World Fedn of Internat. Music Competitions, 1992–; Trustee, Edward Boyle Meml Trust, 1981–96. Governor, Harrogate Fest., 1983–99; Vice-Pres., Harrogate Internat. Fest., 1999–. Founded (with Marion Harewood) Leeds International Pianoforte Competition, 1961. Member of International Juries: Beethoven, Vienna, 1977, 1993; Casagrande, Terni, 1978, 1994; Munich, 1979, 1986; Bach, Leipzig, 1980, 1984, 1988; Calgary, 1982; Gina Bachauer, Salt Lake City, 1982, 1984; Viña del Mar (Chm.), 1982, 1987, 1992; Maryland, 1983; Cologne, 1983, 1986, 1989, 1996; Pretoria, 1984, 1992; Santander, 1984; Rubinstein, Israel (Vice-Pres.), 1986, 1989; Tchaikowsky, Moscow, 1986; Vladigerov, Bulgaria, 1986; Lisbon, 1987, 1991; Canadian Broadcasting Corp., Toronto, 1989; first Internat. Pianoforte Competitions, China, 1994, and Korea, 1995. Piano Progress series on ITV Channel 4. Hon. MA 1966, Hon. DMus 1992, Leeds; DUniv York, 1995. Dist. Musician Award, ISM, 2000. *Publications:* (with Marion Harewood): series of Piano Tutors, 1967–: 1st Year Piano lessons: 1st Year Repertoire; 2nd Year Piano lessons: 2nd Year Repertoire; 3rd Year Piano lessons: 3rd Year Repertoire; Duets and Piano Playtime, 1978; Recital Book for pianists, Book 1, 1981; Sonatina and Sonata Book, 1982; Four Study Books for Piano (Playtime Studies and Progress Studies), 1986; (with Paul de Keyser) Young Violinists Repertoire books, 1–4; Fanny Waterman on Piano Playing and Performing, 1983; Music Lovers Diary, 1984–86; Merry Christmas Carols, 1986; Christmas Carol Time, 1986; Nursery Rhyme Time, 1987; Piano for Pleasure, Bks 1 and 2, 1988; Me and my Piano series, Book 1, 1988, Book 2, 1989, repertoire and duets, Books 1 and 2, 1992, superscales for the young pianist, 1995; Animal Magic, 1989; Monkey Puzzles, Books 1 and 2, 1990; (with Wendy Thompson) Piano Competition: the story of the Leeds, 1990; Young Pianist's Dictionary, 1992. *Recreations:* travel, reading, voluntary work, cooking. *Address:* Woodgarth, Oakwood Grove, Leeds LS8 2PA. *T:* (0113) 265 5771.

WATERMAN, Peter Alan; record producer; Chairman, PWL Empire, since 1983; *b* 15 Jan. 1947; *s* of John Waterman and Stella Waterman; *m* 1st, 1970, Elizabeth Reynolds (marr. diss. 1974); one *s*; 2nd, 1980, Julie Reeves (marr. diss. 1984); one *s*; 3rd, 1991, Denise Gyngell; two *d*. *Educ:* Frederick Bird Secondary Sch. Disc jockey at local pubs and Mecca dance hall, 1961–83; arts and repertoire man for various record cos, 1973–; formed Loose Ends Prodns with Peter Collins, 1977–83; Founder Partner with M. Stock and M. Aitken, Stock Aitken Waterman, 1984–93. Has produced numerous charity records. Waterman Railway Trust formed 1994. Awards for songwriting and for records produced include: BPI Best British Producer Award, 1988; Music Week Top Producers Award, 1987, 1988 and 1989; Ivor Novello Award, 1987, 1988 and 1989. *Recreations:* railways, models and the real thing, car collection. *Address:* (office) 4/7 The Vineyard, Sanctuary Street, SE1 1QL. *T:* (020) 7403 0007.

WATERPARK, 7th Baron *cr* 1792; **Frederick Caryll Philip Cavendish,** Bt 1755; Director, D. T. Dobie (East Africa) Ltd, 1995–2000; *b* 6 Oct. 1926; *s* of Brig.-General Frederick William Laurence Sheppard Hart Cavendish, CMG, DSO (*d* 1931) and Enid, Countess of Kenmare (she *m* 3rd, 1933, as his 3rd wife, 1st Viscount Furness, who *d* 1940; 4th, as his 2nd wife, 6th Earl of Kenmare), *d* of Charles Lindeman, Sydney, New South Wales, and *widow* of Roderick Cameron, New York; *S* uncle, 1948; *m* 1951, Daniele, *e d* of Roger Guirche, Paris; one *s* two *d*. *Educ:* Eton. Lieut, 4th and 1st Bn Grenadier Guards, 1944–46. Served as Assistant District Commandant Kenya Police Reserve, 1952–55, during Mau Mau Rebellion. Man. Dir, Spartan Air Services, 1955–60; Dep. Chm. and Man. Dir, CSE International Ltd, 1984–90; Dep. Chm., 1984–90, Chief Exec., 1990, CSE Aviation Ltd; Director: Handley Page Ltd, 1968–70; Airborn Group plc, 1990–93. Trustee, RAF Mus., 1994–2000. Founder Mem., Air Sqdn. *Heir: s* Hon. Roderick Alexander Cavendish [*b* 10 Oct. 1959; *m* 1989, Anne, *d* of Hon. Luke Asquith; two *s*]. *Address:* (home) 74 Elm Park Road, SW3 6AU. *Club:* Cavalry and Guards.

WATERS, Alan Victor; HM Diplomatic Service; High Commissioner, Solomon Islands, since 1998; *b* 10 April 1942; *s* of late George and Ruth Waters; *m* 1977, Elizabeth Ann Newman; one *s* one *d*. *Educ:* Judd Sch., Tonbridge. Joined CO, 1958, CRO, 1961; Freetown, 1963–66; UKDEL to ECSC, Luxembourg, 1967–68; Prague, 1968–70; Anguilla, 1970–71; Peking, 1971–73; FCO, 1973–76; Second Secretary: Kinshasa, 1976–80; Dep. High Commn, Bombay, 1980–83; FCO, 1984–86; First Secretary: FCO, 1986–87; Copenhagen, 1987–91; FCO, 1991–95; acting Adminr, Tristan da Cunha, 1995–96; First Sec., Islamabad, 1996–98. *Recretations:* walking, cricket, golf, tennis, philately. *Address:* c/o Foreign and Commonwealth Office, SW1A 2AH. *Club:* Kent CC.

WATERS, Gen. Sir (Charles) John, GCB 1995 (KCB 1988); CBE 1981 (OBE 1977); JP; DL; Deputy Supreme Allied Commander, Europe, 1993–94; Aide-de-Camp General to The Queen, 1992–95; *b* 2 Sept. 1935; *s* of Patrick George Waters and Margaret Ronaldson Waters (*née* Clark); *m* 1962, Hilary Doyle Nettleton; three *s*. *Educ:* Oundle; Royal Military Academy, Sandhurst. Commissioned, The Gloucestershire Regt, 1955; GSO2, MO1 (MoD), 1970–72; Instructor, GSO1 (DS), Staff Coll., Camberley, 1973–74; Commanding Officer, 1st Bn, Gloucestershire Regt, 1975–77; Colonel General Staff, 1st Armoured Div., 1977–79; Comdr 3 Infantry Bde, 1979–81; RCDS 1982; Dep. Comdr, Land Forces, Falkland Islands, May-July 1982; Comdr 4th Armoured Div., 1983–85; Comdt, Staff Coll., Camberley, 1986–88; GOC and Dir of Ops, NI, 1988–90; C-in-C, UKLF, 1990–93. Col, The Gloucestershire Regt, 1985–91; Col Comdt, POW Div., 1988–91; Hon. Colonel: Royal Wessex Yeomanry, 1991–97; Royal Devonshire Yeomanry, 1991–97. President: (Army) Officers' Assoc., 1997–; Devon RBL, 1998–. Mem. Adv. Council, Victory Meml Mus., Arlon, Belgium 1989–97; Mem. Council, Cheltenham Coll., 1991–97; Dep. Chm. Council, Nat. Army Mus., 1997–; Gov., Colyton Primary Sch., 1997–. Admiral: Army Sailing Assoc., 1990–93; Infantry Sailing Assoc., 1990–93. Kermit Roosevelt Lectr, USA, 1992. FRSA 1993. JP Axminster and Honiton, 1998; DL Devon, 2001. *Recreations:* sailing, ski-ing, painting, gardening. *Address:* c/o Lloyds TSB, Colyton, Devon EX13 6JS. *Clubs:* Army and Navy, Beefsteak; British Keil Yacht.

WATERS, David Ebsworth Benjamin; QC 1999; a Recorder, since 1990; *b* 24 April 1945; *s* of William Thomas Ebsworth Waters and Esther Jane Waters; *m* 1st, 1971, Susan Jennifer Bulmer (marr. diss. 1986); two *d*; 2nd, 1996, Sonia Jayne Bound. *Educ:* Greenhill Grammar Sch., Tenby. Admitted Solicitor, 1969; called to the Bar, Middle Temple, 1973; Junior Treasury Counsel, 1989–94, Sen. Treasury Counsel, 1994–99, CCC. *Recreations:* golf, fishing. *Address:* 1 Hare Court, Temple, EC4Y 7BE. *T:* (020) 7353 3982. *Clubs:* MCC; Royal Wimbledon Golf, Woking Golf.

WATERS, David Watkin; Lt Comdr RN; *b* 2 Aug. 1911; *s* of Eng. Lt William Waters, RN, and Jessie Rhena (*née* Whitemore); *m* 1946, Hope Waters (*née* Pritchard); one step *s* one step *d*. *Educ:* RN Coll., Dartmouth. Joined RN, 1925; Cadet and Midshipman, HMS Barham, 1929; specialised in Aviation (Pilot), 1935. Served War of 1939–45: Fleet Air Arm, Malta (PoW, Italy, Germany, 1940–45). Admlty, 1946–50; retd, 1950. Admlty Historian (Defence of Shipping), 1946–60; Head of Dept of Navigation and Astronomy, Nat. Maritime Museum, 1960–76, and Sec. of Museum, 1968–71; Dep. Dir, 1971–78. Pres., British Soc. for Hist. of Sci., 1976–78 (Vice-Pres., 1972–74, 1978–81). Vis. Prof. of History, Simon Fraser Univ., Burnaby, BC, 1978; Regents' Prof., UCLA, 1979; Caird Res. Fellow, Nat. Maritime Museum, 1979–83; Alexander O. Victor Res. Fellow, John Carter Brown Library, Brown Univ., Providence, RI, 1990. Chm., Japan Animal Welfare Soc., 1972–80. Gold Medal, Admiralty Naval History, 1936, and Special Award, 1946; FRHistS 1951; Fellow, Inst. Internac. da Cultura Portuguesa, 1966; FSA 1970. Hon. Member: Royal Inst. of Navigation, 1989 (Fellow 1959); Scientific Instrument Soc., 1989; Acad. de Marinha Portuguesa, 1989; Soc. for Nautical Res., 1996. *Publications:* The True and Perfect Newes of Syr Francis Drake, 1955; (with F. Barley) Naval Staff History, Second World War, Defeat of the Enemy attack on Shipping, 1939–1945, 1957, 2nd edn 1997; The Art of Navigation in England in Elizabethan and Early Stuart Times, 1958, 2nd edn 1978; The Sea—or Mariner's Astrolabe, 1966; The Rutter of the Sea, 1967; (with Hope Waters) The Saluki in History, Art, and Sport, 1969, 2nd edn 1984; (with G. P. B. Naish) The Elizabethan Navy and the Armada of Spain, 1975; Science and the Techniques of Navigation in the Renaissance, 1976; (with Thomas R. Adams) English Maritime Books relating to ships and their construction and operation at sea printed before 1801, 1995; Navigation and Hydrography in the Great Age of Discovery, 2002; contrib.: Jl RIN; RUSI; Mariners' Mirror; American Neptune; Jl RN Scientific Service; Jl British Soc. of History of Science; Navy International; Revista da Universidade de Coímbra. *Recreations:* maritime history, history of technology (medieval, Renaissance and Scientific Revolution, and Chinese sailing craft). *Address:* Saffron Cottage, 6 Brewery Row, Little Compton, Moreton-in-Marsh, Glos GL56 0RY. *Club:* English-Speaking Union.

WATERS, Donald Henry, OBE 1994; CA; Chief Executive, 1987–97, and Deputy Chairman, 1993–97, Grampian Television PLC; *b* 17 Dec. 1937; *s* of late Henry Lethbridge Waters, WS, and Jean Manson Baxter; *m* 1962, June Leslie, *d* of late Andrew Hutchison; one *s* two *d*. *Educ:* George Watson's, Edinburgh; Inverness Royal Acad. Mem. ICA(Scot.) 1961; CA 1961. Dir, John M. Henderson and Co. Ltd, 1972–75; Grampian Television: Company Sec., 1975; Dir of Finance, 1979. Chairman: Glenburnie Properties, 1993–97 (Dir, 1976–93); Central Scotland Radio, 1994–96; Director: Scottish TV and Grampian Sales Ltd, 1980–98; Blenheim Travel, 1981–91; Moray Firth Radio, 1982–97; Independent Television Publications Ltd, 1987–90; Cablevision (Scotland) PLC, 1987–91; GRT Bus Group, 1994–96; British Linen Bank, 1995–99; British Linen Bank Gp, 1995–99; Aberdeen Royal Hosp. NHS Trust, 1996–99; Scottish Post Office Bd, 1996–; Digital 3 and 4 Ltd, 1997–98; Scottish Media Group plc, 1997–; James Johnston of Elgin Ltd, 1999–; North Bd, Bank of Scotland, 1999–. Vis. Prof. of Film and Media Studies, Stirling Univ., 1992–. Mem., BAFTA, 1980– (Scottish Vice Chm., 1992–); Chm., Celtic Film and Television Assoc., 1994–96 (Trustee for Scotland, 1990–94); Dir, ITVA, 1994–97. Mem. Council, CBI Scotland, 1994–2001. Chairman: Police Dependent Trust, Aberdeen, 1991–96; Project Steering Gp, New Royal Aberdeen Children's Hosp., 1999–; Jt Chm., Grampian Cancer MacMillan Appeal, 1999–; Member: Council, Cinema and Television Benevolent Fund, 1986–99; Grampian & Islands Family Trust, 1986–. Governor: Univ. of Aberdeen, 1998–99; Robert Gordon's Coll., 1998–99. Burgess of Guild, Aberdeen, 1979– (Assessor, 1998 2001). FRTS 1998 (Mem., 1988); FRSA. *Recreations:* gardening, travel, hillwalking. *Address:* Balquhidder, Milltimber, Aberdeen AB13 0JS. *T:* (01224) 867131. *Clubs:* Royal Northern (Chm., 1987–88), University (Aberdeen).

WATERS, Gen. Sir John; *see* Waters, Gen. Sir C. J.

WATERS, Keith Stuart, FCA; Clerk, Fishmongers' Company, since 1994 (Assistant Clerk, 1987–93); *b* 18 March 1951; *s* of late Thomas Charles Waters and of Elsie Lillian (*née* Addison); *m* 1976, Elizabeth Jane Weeks; one *s* two *d*. *Educ:* Leigh GS; Wigan Tech. Coll.; Univ. of Newcastle upon Tyne (BA 1973). FCA 1976. Deloitte Haskins & Sells,

Manchester, 1973–77; audit senior, Peat Marwick Mitchell, Kingston, Jamaica, 1978; with Price Waterhouse: audit senior, Miami, Fla, 1979–80; Manager, Melbourne, Aust., 1980–82; Sen. Manager, London, 1982–85; Gp Financial Accountant, Guinness plc, 1985–87. *Recreations:* theatre, concerts, ballet, tennis, watersports, running, food and wine. *Address:* The Cow Shed, Bard Hill, Salthouse, Norfolk NR25 7XB. *T:* (01263) 740227.

WATERS, Malcolm Ian; QC 1997; *b* 11 Oct. 1953; *s* of Ian Power Waters and Yvonne Waters (*née* Mosley). *Educ:* Whitgift Sch.; St Catherine's Coll., Oxford (MA, BCL). Called to the Bar, Lincoln's Inn, 1977; in practice, 1978–. *Publications:* (co-editor) Wurtzburg & Mills, Building Society Law, 15th edn, 1989 (with annual updates); (jtly) The Building Societies Act 1986, 1987. *Recreations:* music, opera, theatre, gardening. *Address:* 11 Old Square, Lincoln's Inn, WC2A 3TS. *T:* (020) 7430 0341.

WATERS, Sir (Thomas) Neil (Morris), Kt 1995; PhD; DSc; Vice-Chancellor, Massey University, 1983–95, Emeritus Professor, 1995; *b* New Plymouth, 10 April 1931; *s* of Edwin Benjamin Waters and Kathleen Emily (*née* Morris); *m* 1959, Joyce Mary, *d* of Ven. T. H. C. Partridge. *Educ:* Auckland Univ. (BSc 1953; MSc 1954; PhD 1958; DSc 1969); FNZIC 1977. Sen. Res. Fellow, UKAEA, 1958–60; Auckland University: Lectr in Chemistry, 1961–62; Sen. Lectr, 1963–65; Associate Prof., 1966–69; Prof., 1970–83, Emeritus Prof., 1984–; Asst Vice-Chancellor, 1979–81; Acting Vice-Chancellor, 1980. Visiting Scientist: Univ. of Oxford, 1964, 1971; Northwestern Univ., Illinois, 1976. Chm., NZ Vice-Chancellors' Cttee, 1985–86, 1994 (Mem., 1983–95). DLitt Massey, 1995. *Address:* Box 25–463, St Heliers, Auckland, New Zealand.

WATERSON, Nigel Christopher; MP (C) Eastbourne, since 1992; *b* 12 Oct. 1950; *s* of James Waterson and Katherine (*née* Mahon); *m* 1999, Dr Barbara Judge. *Educ:* Leeds Grammar Sch.; Queen's Coll., Oxford (MA Jurisprudence); College of Law. Called to the Bar, Gray's Inn, 1973; admitted solicitor, 1979. Pres., Oxford Univ. Cons. Assoc., 1970. Res. Asst to Sally Oppenheim, MP, 1972–73. Cllr, London Borough of Hammersmith, 1974–78. Chairman: Bow Gp, 1986–87 (Hon. Patron, 1993–95); Hammersmith Cons. Assoc., 1987–90; Hammersmith and Fulham Jt Management Cttee, 1988–90; Member: Cons. Gtr London Area Exec. Cttee, 1990–91; Soc. of Cons. Lawyers Exec. Cttee, 1993–97; Conservative Political Centre: Mem., Adv. Cttee, 1986–90; Mem., Gtr London Gen. Purposes Cttee, 1990–91. Pres., SE Area Cons. Educn Adv. Cttee, 1993–. PPS to Minister of State, DoH, 1995, to Dep. Prime Minister, 1996–97; an Opposition Whip, 1997–99; Opposition spokesman on local govt and housing, 1999–2001. Mem., Select Cttee on Nat. Heritage, 1995–96; Vice Chairman: Cons. Backbench Tourism Cttee, 1992–97; Cons. Backbench Transport Cttee, 1992–97; Sec., Cons. Backbench Shipping and Shipbuilding Cttee, 1992–97; Vice Chairman: All-Party Daylight Extra Gp, 1993–97; All-Party British Greek Gp, 1993–; Sec., British Cyprus Gp, CPA, 1992–. Member: London West European Constituency Council, 1987–91; Management Cttee, Stonham Housing Assoc. Hostel for Ex-Offenders, 1988–90. *Publications:* papers on an Alternative Manifesto, 1973, the future of Hong Kong, and on shipping. *Recreations:* sailing, polo, reading, music. *Address:* House of Commons, SW1A 0AA. *Clubs:* Coningsby; Eastbourne Constitutional; Guards' Polo; Sussex CC.

WATERSTON, Dr Charles Dewar, FRSE; formerly Keeper of Geology, Royal Scottish Museum; *b* 15 Feb. 1925; *s* of Allan Waterston and Martha Dewar (*née* Robertson); *m* 1965, Marjory Home Douglas. *Educ:* Highgate Sch., London; Univ. of Edinburgh (BSc 1st Cl. Hons 1947; Vans Dunlop Scholar, PhD 1949; DSc 1980). FRSE 1958. Asst Keeper, Royal Scottish Museum, 1950–63, Keeper, 1963–85. Member: Scottish Cttee, Nature Conservancy, 1969–73; Adv. Cttee for Scotland, Nature Conservancy Council, 1974–82; Chairman's Cttee, 1978–80, Exec. Cttee, 1980–82, Council for Museums and Galleries in Scotland; Adv. Cttee on Sites of Special Scientific Interest, 1992–95; Gen. Sec., RSE, 1986–91 (Mem. Council, 1967–70; Vice-Pres., 1980–83; Sec., 1985–86); Hon. Sec., Edinburgh Geol Soc., 1953–58 (Pres., 1969–71). Chm., Judges Panel, Scottish Mus. of Year Award, 1999–2000. Keith Prize, 1969–71, Bicentenary Medal, 1992, RSE; Clough Medal, Edinburgh Geol Soc., 1984–85; (first) A. G. Brighton Medal, Geol Curators' Gp, 1992. *Publications:* (with G. Y. Craig and D. B. McIntyre) James Hutton's Theory of the Earth: the lost drawings, 1978; (with H. E. Stace and C. W. A. Pettitt) Natural Science Collections in Scotland, 1987; Collections in Context, 1997; (with D. Guthrie) The Royal Society Club of Edinburgh 1820–2000, 1999; technical papers in scientific jls, chiefly relating to extinct arthropods and the history of geology. *Address:* 9/7 Trinity Way, East Trinity Road, Edinburgh EH5 3PY.

WATERSTONE, David George Stuart, CBE 1991; UK Chairman, Ansaldo Ltd, 1995–98; Chairman, ADAS Holdings Ltd, 1997–98; *b* 9 Aug. 1935; *s* of Malcolm Waterstone and Sylvia Sawday; *m* 1st, 1960, Dominique Viriot (marr. diss.); one *s* two *d*; 2nd, 1988, Sandra Packer (*née* Willey). *Educ:* Tonbridge; St Catharine's Coll., Cambridge (MA). HM Diplomatic Service, 1959–70; Sen. Exec., IRC, 1970–71; BSC, 1971–81: Board Mem., 1976–81; Man. Dir, Commercial, 1972–77; subseq. Executive Chairman, BSC Chemicals, 1977–81, and Redpath Dorman Long, 1977–81; Chief Exec., Welsh Develt Agency, 1983–90; Chief Exec., Energy and Technical Services Gp plc, 1990–95. Director: Portsmouth and Sunderland Newspapers, 1983–99; Hunting, 1995–2000; Precoat Internat., 1995–. Chm., Combined Heat and Power Assoc., 1993–95. *Recreations:* sailing, walking, painting, furniture making. *Address:* 1 Prior Park Buildings, Prior Park Road, Bath BA2 4NP. *T:* (01225) 427346. *Club:* Reform.

See also T. J. S. Waterstone.

WATERSTONE, Timothy John Stuart; Founder, Waterstone's Booksellers, 1982; Founder, Chairman, Daisy & Tom children's stores, since 1996; *b* 30 May 1939; *s* of Malcolm Waterstone and Sylvia Sawday; *m* 1st, Patricia Harcourt-Poole (marr. diss.); two *s* one *d*; 2nd, Clare Perkins (marr. diss.); one *s* two *d*; 3rd, Mary Rose, (Rosie), *d* of Rt Hon. Michael Alison, *qv*; two *d*. *Educ:* Tonbridge; St Catharine's College, Cambridge (MA). Carritt Moran, Calcutta, 1962–64; Allied Breweries, 1964–73; W. H. Smith, 1973–81; Founder Chm., Chm. and Chief Exec., Waterstone's Booksellers Ltd, 1982–93; Chairman: Priory Investments Ltd, 1990–95; Golden Rose Radio (London Jazz FM), 1992–93; INB plc, 1999–; HMV Media Gp plc (merged businesses of Waterstone's and HMV), 1998–2001; Dep. Chm., Sinclair-Stevenson Ltd, 1989–92; Member of Board: Yale Univ. Press, 1992–; Future Start, 1992–; Virago Press., 1995–96; Hill Samuel UK Emerging Cos Investment Trust PLC, 1996–; National Gallery Co. Ltd, 1996–; Downing Classic VCT, 1998–. Chm., DTI Working Gp on Smaller Quoted Cos and Private Investors, 1999–. Chm., Shelter 25th Anniversary Appeal Cttee, 1991–92. Member: Bd of Trustees, English International (Internat. House), 1987–92; Bd, London Philharmonic Orch., 1990–97 (Trustee, 1995–98); Portman House Trust, 1994–96; Chairman: Acad. of Ancient Music, 1990–95; London Internat. Festival of Theatre, 1991–92; Elgar Foundn, 1992–98; King's Coll. Library Bd, 2000–. Co-Founder BOOKAID, 1992–93. Adv. Mem., Booker Prize Management Cttee, 1986–93; Chm. of Judges, Prince's Youth Business Trust Awards, 1990. *Publications:* novels: Lilley & Chase, 1994; An Imperfect Marriage, 1995; A Passage of Lives, 1996. *Recreation:* being with Rosie Alison. *Address:* c/o Ed Victor Ltd, 6 Bayley Street, WC1B 3HB. *Club:* Garrick.

See also D. G. S. Waterstone.

WATERTON, Sqdn Leader William Arthur, GM 1952; AFC 1942, Bar 1946; *b* Edmonton, Canada, 18 March 1916. *Educ:* Royal Military College of Canada; University of Alberta. Cadet Royal Military College of Canada, 1934–37; Subaltern and Lieut, 19th Alberta Dragoons, Canadian Cavalry, 1937–39; served RAF, 1939–46: Fighter Squadrons; Training Command; Transatlantic Ferrying Command; Fighter Command; Meteorological Flight; Fighter Experimental Unit; CFE High Speed Flight World Speed Record. Joined Gloster Aircraft Co. Ltd, 1946. 100 km closed circuit record, 1947; Paris/London record (618.5 mph), 1947; "Hare and Tortoise" Helicopter and jet aircraft Centre of London to Centre of Paris (47 mins), 1948. Chief Test Pilot Gloster Aircraft Co. Ltd, 1946–54. Prototype trials on first Canadian jet fighter, Canuck and British first operational delta wing fighter, the Javelin. *Publications:* The Comet Riddle, 1956; The Quick and The Dead, 1956; aeronautical and meteorological articles. *Recreations:* sailing, riding, photography, motoring, shooting. *Address:* RR #4, Owen Sound, ON N4K 5N6, Canada. *Club:* Royal Military College of Canada (Kingston, Ont.).

WATERWORTH, Alan William; JP; Lord-Lieutenant of Merseyside, since 1993 (Vice Lord-Lieutenant, 1989–93); *b* 22 Sept. 1931; *s* of late James and Alice Waterworth, Liverpool; *m* 1955, Myriam, *d* of late Edouard Baete and Magdelaine Baete, formerly of Brussels; three *s* one *d*. *Educ:* Uppingham Sch.; Trinity Coll., Cambridge (MA). National Service, commnd King's Regt, 1950. Waterworth Bros Ltd: progressively, Dir, Man. Dir, Chm., 1954–69. Gen Comr, Inland Revenue, 1965–72. Dir, NHS Hosp. Trust, Liverpool, 1992–93. Member: Skelmersdale Develt Corp., 1971–85 (Dep. Chm., 1979–85); Merseyside Police Authority, 1984–92; Cttee, Merseyside Br., Inst. of Dirs, 1965–77 (Chm., 1974–77). Chm., IBA Adv. Cttee for Radio on Merseyside, 1975–78. Chairman: Liverpool Boys' Assoc., 1967–75; Merseyside Youth Assoc., 1971–75; Everton FC, 1973–76 (Dir, 1970–93). Mem. Council, Liverpool Univ., 1993–. Trustee, Nat. Museums and Galls on Merseyside, 1994–. JP Liverpool 1961 (Chm., Juvenile Panel, 1974–83; Chm. of Bench, 1985–89); DL Co. Merseyside 1986, High Sheriff, Co. Merseyside, 1992. Hon. Col, Merseyside Cadet Force, 1994–. Hon. Fellow, Liverpool John Moores, 1995. KStJ 1994. *Recreations:* local history, bibliomania. *Address:* Crewood Hall, Kingsley, Cheshire WA6 8HR. *T:* (01928) 788316. *Clubs:* Army and Navy; Athenæum, Artists' (Liverpool).

WATES, Andrew Trace Allan; Chairman, Wates Group (formerly Wates Ltd), since 2000; *b* 16 Nov. 1940; 4th *s* of Sir Ronald Wallace Wates and of Phyllis Mary Wates (*née* Trace); *m* 1965, Sarah Mary de Burgh Macartney; four *s* (and one *s* decd). *Educ:* Oundle Sch.; Emmanuel Coll., Cambridge (BA Estate Mgt 1960). Joined Wates, 1964; Dir, Wates Construction, 1972–2000; Chairman: Wates Leisure Gp, later Pinnacle Leisure Gp, 1972–99; Wates Estate Agency Services, 1976–2000; Director: Wates Ltd, 1973–2000; Wates Hldgs, 1973–. Chairman: United Racecourses Ltd, 1996–; Leisure and Media plc, 2001–; Director: Racecourse Hldgs Trust, 1996; Barnard and Hill Ltd, 1999; Fontwell Park plc, 1991–2001. Mem. Bd of Mgt, Royal Albert and Alexandra Sch., 1996–. Mem., Jockey Club, 1977–. *Recreations:* horse-racing, shooting, fishing, golf. *Address:* Henfold House, Beare Green, Dorking, Surrey RH5 4RW. *T:* (01306) 631324. *Clubs:* White's, Turf.

See also M. E. Wates, P. C. R. Wates.

WATES, Sir Christopher (Stephen), Kt 1989; BA; FCA; Chairman, Wates Holdings, since 2000; Chief Executive, Wates Group (formerly Wates Building Group), 1984–2000; *b* 25 Dec. 1939; *s* of Norman Edward Wates and Margot Irene Sidwell; *m* 1965, Sandra Mouroutsos (marr. diss. 1975); three *d*; *m* 1992, Georgina Ferris McCallum. *Educ:* Stowe School; Brasenose College, Oxford (BA 1962; Rugby blue, 1961; Hon. Fellow, 1993). FCA 1975 (ACA 1965). Financial Director, Wates Ltd, 1970–76. Chm., Criterion Hldgs, 1981–96. Director: Electra Investment Trust, 1980–93; Equitable Life Assurance Society, 1983–94; Scottish Ontario Investment Co. Ltd, 1978–83; 3i Smaller Quoted Cos Trust (formerly North British Canadian Investment Co., then NB Smaller Cos Trust), 1983–98 (Chm., 1996–98); Wates City of London Properties plc, 1984–2000; Mem., 1980–89, Chm., 1983–89, English Industrial Estates Corp.; Chm., Keymer Brick & Tile Co. Ltd, 1985–89. A Church Comr, 1992–96. Governor of Council, 1984–, Chm., 1997–, Goodenough Coll. (formerly London House for Overseas Graduates, then London Goodenough Trust) (Dep. Chm., 1989–96); Trustee: Chatham Historic Dockyard Trust, 1984–87; Science Museum, 1987–; Lambeth Palace Library, 1990–. Chm., Industrial Soc., 1998. FRSA 1988. Hon. Mem., RICS, 1990. *Address:* Tufton Place, Northiam, near Rye, East Sussex TN31 6HL. *T:* (01797) 252125.

WATES, Michael Edward, CBE 1998; Chairman, Wates Group (formerly Wates Ltd), 1974–2000; *b* 19 June 1935; 2nd *s* of Sir Ronald Wallace Wates and of Phyllis Mary Wates (*née* Trace); *m* 1959, Caroline Josephine Connolly; four *s* one *d*. *Educ:* Oundle School; Emmanuel College, Cambridge (MA); Harvard Business Sch. (PMD 1963). Served RM, 1953–55. Joined Wates 1959; Director: Wates Construction, 1963; Wates Built Homes, 1966. Mem., Nat. Housebuilding Council, 1974–80. Chm., British Bloodstock Agency plc, 1986–92; Member: Council, Thoroughbred Breeders Assoc., 1978–82 (Chm., 1980–82); Horserace Betting Levy Bd, 1987–90. King's College Hospital: Deleg., Sch. of Medicine and Dentistry, 1983–; Chm., Equipment Cttee, 1983–91; Special Trustee, 1985 (Chm., Trustees, 1985). Hon. FRIBA. *Address:* Manor House, Langton Long, Blandford Forum, Dorset DT11 9HS. *T:* (01258) 455241.

See also A. T. A. Wates, P. C. R. Wates.

WATES, Paul Christopher Ronald, FRICS; Managing Director, 1984–94, Chairman, 1994–2001, Wates City of London Properties plc; *b* 6 March 1938; 3rd *s* of Sir Ronald Wallace Wates and of Phyllis Mary Wates (*née* Trace); *m* 1965, Annette Beatrice Therese Randag; three *s* three *d*. *Educ:* Coll. of Estate Mgt; London Business Sch. Chesterton & Sons, 1958–59; Nat. Service, 14th/20th King's Hussars, 1959–61; joined Wates Ltd, 1962; Director: Wates Built Homes Ltd, 1965–; Wates Ltd, 1969–; Wates Gp, 1969–; Non-exec. Dir, 3i Smaller Quoted Cos Trust plc, 1998. Chm., C&G. FRSA. Mem. Court, Clothworkers' Co. Gov., Emanuel Sch., Wandsworth. *Address:* Bellasis House, Mickleham, Dorking, Surrey RH5 6DH. *T:* (01737) 843003. *Clubs:* Turf, Cavalry & Guards, MCC.

See also A. T. A. Wates, M. E. Wates.

WATHEN, Julian Philip Gerard; Chairman: Hall School Charitable Trust, 1972–97; City of London Endowment Trust for St Paul's Cathedral, since 1983; *b* 21 May 1923; *s* of late Gerard Anstruther Wathen, CIE, and Melicent Louis (*née* Buxton); *m* 1948 Priscilla Florence Wilson; one *s* two *d*. *Educ:* Harrow. Served War, 60th Rifles, 1942–46. Third Secretary, HBM Embassy, Athens, 1946–47. Barclays Bank DCO, 1948; Ghana Director, 1961–65; General Manager, 1966; Sen. Gen. Manager, Barclays Bank International, 1974; Vice Chm., 1976; Vice Chairman: Barclays Bank, 1979–84; Banque du Caire, Barclays International, 1976–83; Dep. Chm., Allied Arab Bank, 1977–84; Director: Barclays Australia International, 1973–84; Barclays Bank of Kenya, 1975–84; Mercantile & General Reinsurance Co., 1977–91. Pres., Royal African Soc., 1984–89 (Chm., 1978–84). Member Council: Goodenough Coll. (formerly London House for Overseas Graduates, then London Goodenough Trust), 1971– (Vice-Chm., 1984–89); Book Aid Internat.,

1988–; Governor: St Paul's Sch., 1981–99 (Chm., 1995–99); St Paul's Girls' Sch., 1981–; SOAS, 1983–92; Overseas Develt Inst., 1984–96; Dauntsey's Sch., 1985–; Abingdon Sch., 1985–95; Dep. Chm., Thomas Telford Sch., 1990–97. Mem. Cttee, GBA, 1986–94. Master, Mercers' Co., 1984–85. *Address:* Woodcock House, Owlpen, Dursley, Glos GL11 5BY. *T:* (01453) 860214; 1 Montagu Place, Marylebone, W1H 2EW. *T:* (020) 7935 8569. *Club:* Travellers.

WATHERSTON, John Anthony Charles; Registrar of the Privy Council, since 1998; *b* 29 April 1944; *yr s* of Sir David Watherston, KBE, CMG and of Lady Watherston; *m* 1976, Jane (*née* Chaytor), *widow* of John Atkinson; one *s*, and one step *s* one step *d*. *Educ:* Winchester Coll.; Christ Church, Oxford (BA Jurisp. 1966; MA 1970). Called to the Bar, Inner Temple, 1967; Lord Chancellor's Department: Legal Asst, 1970–74; Sec., Phillimore Cttee on Law of Contempt of Court, 1971–74; Sen. Legal Asst, 1974–80; Private Sec. to Lord Chancellor, 1975–77; Asst Solicitor (Grade 5), 1980–85, 1988–98; Sen. Crown Counsel, Attorney Gen.'s Chambers, Hong Kong, 1985–88. Lay Reader, Chelsea Old Church, Dio. of London, 1995–; Mem., London Diocesan Synod, 2000–. *Address:* Judicial Committee of the Privy Council, Downing Street, SW1A 2AJ.

WATKIN, Prof. David John, LittD; FSA; Fellow of Peterhouse, Cambridge, since 1970; Professor of History of Architecture, University of Cambridge, since 2001; *b* 7 April 1941; *o s* of Thomas Charles and late Vera Mary Watkin. *Educ:* Farnham Grammar Sch.; Trinity Hall, Cambridge (Exhibnr; BA (1st Cl. Hons Fine Arts Tripos); PhD; LittD 1994). University of Cambridge: Librarian, Fine Arts Faculty, 1967–72; University Lectr in History of Art, 1972–93; Head, Dept of History of Art, 1989–92; Reader in Hist. of Architecture, 1993–2001. Mem., Historic Bldgs Council for England, then Historic Bldgs Adv. Cttee, Historic Bldgs and Monuments Commn for England, 1980–95. Hon. FRIBA 2001. Hon. DArts De Montfort Univ., 1996. *Publications:* Thomas Hope (1769–1831) and the Neo-Classical Idea, 1968; (ed) Sale Catalogues of Libraries of Eminent Persons, vol. 4, Architects, 1970; The Life and Work of C. R. Cockerell, RA, 1974 (Alice Davis Hitchcock medallion, 1975); The Triumph of the Classical, Cambridge Architecture 1804–34, 1977; Morality and Architecture, 1977 (trans. French, Italian, Japanese and Spanish); English Architecture, a Concise History, 1979, 2nd edn 2000; The Rise of Architectural History, 1980; (with Hugh Montgomery-Massingberd) The London Ritz, a Social and Architectural History, 1980; (with Robin Middleton) Neo-Classical and Nineteenth-century Architecture, 1980 (trans. French, German and Italian); (jtly) Burke's and Savills Guide to Country Houses, vol. 3, East Anglia, 1981; The Buildings of Britain, Regency: a Guide and Gazetteer, 1982; Athenian Stuart, Pioneer of the Greek Revival, 1982; The English Vision: The Picturesque in Architecture, Landscape and Garden Design, 1982; (contrib.) John Soane, 1983; The Royal Interiors of Regency England, 1984; Peterhouse: an architectural record 1284–1984, 1984; A History of Western Architecture, 1986 (trans. Dutch, German and Italian), 3rd edn 2000; (with Tilman Mellinghoff) German Architecture and the Classical Ideal: 1740–1840, 1987 (trans. Italian); (contrib.) The Legacy of Rome: a new appraisal, 1992; (contrib.) Public and Private Doctrine: essays in English history presented to Maurice Cowling, 1993; (contrib.) The Golden City: essays on the architecture and imagination of Beresford Pite, 1993; Creations and Recreations: Alec Cobbe, thirty years of design and painting, 1996; Sir John Soane: enlightenment thought and the Royal Academy lectures, 1996 (Sir Banister Fletcher Award, 1997); Sir John Soane: the Royal Academy lectures, 2000; Morality and Architecture Revisited, 2001; (ed) Alfred Gilbey: a memoir by some friends, 2001; (contrib.) New Offerings, Ancient Treasures: studies in medieval art for George Henderson, 2001; (contrib.) William Beckford, 1760–1844: an eye for the magnificent, 2001. *Address:* Peterhouse, Cambridge CB2 1RD; Albany, Piccadilly, W1J 0AU. *Clubs:* Beefsteak, Home House, Brooks's; University Pitt (Cambridge).

WATKINS, Dr Alan Keith; Chairman, Senior plc (formerly Senior Engineering Group), 1996–2001 (Director, 1994–2001; Deputy Chairman, 1995–96); *b* 9 Oct. 1938; *s* of late Wilfred Victor Watkins and Dorothy Hilda Watkins; *m* 1963, Diana Edith Wynne (*née* Hughes); two *s*. *Educ:* Moseley Grammar School, Birmingham; Univ. of Birmingham (BSc Hons, PhD). FIM (Mem. Council, 1990–95); CEng; FIMfgE (Vice-Pres., 1991); FIEE (Mem. Council, 1991–92). Lucas Research Centre, 1962; Lucas Batteries, 1969, subseq. Manufacturing Dir; Lucas Aerospace, 1975; Man. Dir, Aerospace Lucas Industries, 1987–89; Man. Dir and Chief Exec., Hawker Siddeley Gp, 1989–91; London Transport: Chief Exec., 1992–94; Vice-Chm., 1992–93; Dep. Chm., 1993–94. Director: Dobson Park Industries plc, 1992–95; Hepworth plc, 1995–98; Chm., High Duty Alloys Ltd, 1997–2000. Member: DTI Aviation Cttee, 1985–89; Review Bd for Govt Contracts, 1993–. Member Council: SBAC, 1982–89 (Vice-Pres., 1988–89); CBI, 1992–94. Vice-Pres., EEF, 1989–91, 1997–2001. *Recreations:* tennis, veteran and vintage cars, hot-air ballooning, photography. *Club:* Olton Golf.

WATKINS, Alan (Rhun); journalist; Political Columnist, Independent on Sunday, since 1993; *b* 3 April 1933; *o c* of late D. J. Watkins, teacher, Tycroes, Carmarthenshire, and Violet Harris; *m* 1955, Ruth Howard (*d* 1982); one *s* one *d* (and one *d* decd). *Educ:* Amman Valley Grammar Sch., Ammanford; Queens' Coll., Cambridge (MA, LLM). Chm., Cambridge Univ. Labour Club, 1954. National Service, FO, Educn Br., RAF, 1955–57. Called to Bar, Lincoln's Inn, 1957. Research Asst to W. A. Robson, LSE, 1958–59; Editorial Staff, Sunday Express, 1959–64 (New York Corresp., 1961; Actg Political Corresp., 1963; Crossbencher Columnist, 1963–64); Political Columnist: Spectator, 1964–67; New Statesman, 1967–76; Sunday Mirror, 1968–69; Observer, 1976–93; Columnist, Evening Standard, 1974–75; Rugby Columnist: Field, 1984–86; Independent, 1986–; Drink Columnist, Observer Magazine, 1992–93. Mem. (Lab) Fulham Bor. Council, 1959–62. Dir, The Statesman and Nation Publishing Co. Ltd, 1973–76. Chm., Political Adv. Gp, British Youth Council, 1978–81. Awards: Granada, Political Columnist, 1973; British Press, Columnist, 1982, commended 1984. Hon. Fellow, Univ. of Wales, Lampeter, 1999. *Publications:* The Liberal Dilemma, 1966; (contrib.) The Left, 1966; (with A. Alexander) The Making of the Prime Minister 1970, 1970; Brief Lives, 1982; (contrib.) The Queen Observed, 1986; Sportswriter's Eye, 1989; A Slight Case of Libel, 1990; A Conservative Coup, 1991, 2nd edn 1992; (contrib.) The State of the Nation, 1997; The Road to Number 10, 1998; (contrib.) Secrets of the Press, 1999; A Short Walk Down Fleet Street, 2000. *Recreation:* watching cricket. *Address:* 54 Barnsbury Street, N1 1ER. *T:* (020) 7607 0812. *Clubs:* Beefsteak, Garrick.

WATKINS, Brian, CMG 1993; HM Diplomatic Service, retired; Immigration Adjudicator (part time), since 1993; *b* 26 July 1933; *s* of late James Edward Watkins and late Gladys Anne Watkins (*née* Fletcher); *m* 1st, 1957 (marr. diss. 1978); one *s*; 2nd, 1982, Elisabeth, *d* of A. and M. Arfon-Jones; one *d*. *Educ:* London School of Economics (BSc Econ); Worcester College, Oxford. Solicitor. Flying Officer, RAF, 1955–58. HMOCS, Sierra Leone, 1959–63; Local Govt, 1963–66; Administrator, Tristan da Cunha, 1966–69; Lectr, Univ. of Manchester, 1969–71; HM Diplomatic Service, 1971; FCO, 1971–73; New York, 1973–75; seconded to N Ireland Office, 1976–78; FCO, 1978–81; Counsellor, 1981; Dep. Governor, Bermuda, 1981–83; Consul General and Counsellor (Economic, Commercial, Aid), Islamabad, 1983–86; Consul Gen., Vancouver, 1986–90; High Comr to Swaziland, 1990–93. First Pres., Council of Immigration Judges, 1997–2000, now Emeritus. Swazi Rep. on Council, British Commonwealth Ex-Services League, 1993– (Mem. Exec. Cttee, 1996–; Hon. Legal Advr, 2001–); Patron, Friends of Swaziland Hospice (UK), 1997–; Chm., Swaziland Soc., 1998–. OStJ 1994 (Chm., Monmouthshire Council, 1996–; Mem., Welsh Chapter, 1996–). *Recreations:* reading history and spy stories, watching theatre, dancing. *Address:* c/o Royal Bank of Scotland, Drummonds Branch, Charing Cross, SW1A 2DX. *Clubs:* Athenæum, Royal Commonwealth Society; Cardiff and County (Cardiff).

WATKINS, David James; Senior Director, and Director of Policing and Security, Northern Ireland Office, since 1998; *b* 3 Aug. 1948; *s* of John Walter Watkins and Elizabeth Watkins (*née* Buckley); *m* 1974, Valerie Elizabeth Graham; one *s* one *d*. *Educ:* Royal Belfast Academical Instn; Trinity Coll., Dublin (BA Hons Modern Langs). Public Expenditure Control Div., NI Dept of Finance and Personnel, 1972–77; State Aids Directorate, DGIV, Eur. Commn, 1978–79; NI Dept of Econ. Develt, 1979–86; Private Sec. to Sec. of State for NI, 1986–88; Dep. Chief Exec., IDB, 1989–92; Dir, Central Secretariat, 1992–98. *Recreations:* reading, gardening, holidays in France. *Address:* Northern Ireland Office, Stormont, Belfast BT4 3SG. *T:* (028) 9052 8138.

WATKINS, David John; Director, Council for the Advancement of Arab-British Understanding, 1983–90 (Joint Chairman, 1979–83); company director and consultant; *b* 27 Aug. 1925; *s* of Thomas George Watkins and Alice Elizabeth (*née* Allen); unmarried. *Educ:* Bristol. Member: Bristol City Council, 1954–57; Bristol Educn Cttee, 1958–66; Labour Party, 1950–; Amalgamated Engineering and Electrical Union (formerly Amalgamated Engineering Union), 1942–; Sec., AEU Gp of MPs, 1968–77. Contested Bristol NW, 1964. MP (Lab) Consett, 1966–83; Mem., House of Commons Chairmen's Panel, 1978–83. Sponsored Employers Liability (Compulsory Insurance) Act, 1969, and Industrial Common Ownership Act, 1976 as Private Member's Bills; introd Drained Weight Bill, 1973, and Consett Steel Works Common Ownership Bill, 1980. Chm., Labour Middle East Council, 1974–83; Treas., Internat. Co-ord Cttee, UN Meeting of Non-Governmental Organisations on Question of Palestine, 1985–90. Dir, 1987–, Chm., 1990–, Courtlands Estate (Richmond) Ltd (Vice Chm., 1988–90). Hon. Treas., Med. Aid for Palestinians, 1995– (Trustee, 1984–). *Publications:* Labour and Palestine, 1975; Industrial Common Ownership, 1978; The World and Palestine, 1980; The Exceptional Conflict, 1984; Palestine: an inescapable duty, 1992; Seventeen Years in Obscurity, 1996. *Recreations:* reading, listening to music, swimming. *Address:* 1 Carisbrooke House, Courtlands, Sheen Road, Richmond, Surrey TW10 5AZ. *Club:* Royal Commonwealth Society.

WATKINS, Prof. Eric Sidney, MD; FRCSE; Consultant Neurosurgeon, London Hospital, 1958–2001; Professor of Neurosurgery, University of London, 1972–93, now Emeritus; *b* 6 Sept. 1928; *s* of Wallace and Jessica Watkins; four *s* two *d*. *Educ:* Prescot Grammar Sch.; Univ. of Liverpool Med. Sch. (BSc Hons Neurophysiol. 1949; MB ChB 1952; MD 1956); MD New York 1962. FRCSE 1969. House physician and house surgeon, Walton and Stanley Hosps, Liverpool, 1952–53; Capt., RAMC, 1953–56; Specialist in Physiol., W African Council for Med. Res., Lagos, 1954–56; Registrar in Gen. Surgery and Orthopaedic Surgery, Weston-super-Mare Gen. Hosp. and Winford Orthopaedic Hosp., Bristol, 1956–58; Registrar in Neurosurgery, Radcliffe Infirmary, Oxford, 1958–61; MRC Res. Fellow, Middx and Maida Vale Hosp., 1961–62; Prof. of Neurosurgery, SUNY, Upstate Med. Center, 1962–69. Consultant Surgeon, Formula One Constructors' Assoc., 1978–2001. Pres., Med. Safety and Res. Commns, Fedn Internat. de l'Automobile (World Governing Body of Motor Sport), 1981–2001. Prince Michael of Kent RAC Centennial Award for Contributions to Motor Sport, 1998. *Publications:* Stereotaxic Anatomy of Thalmus and Basal Ganglia, 1969; Stereotaxic Anatomy of Cerebellum and Brain Stem, 1976; Life at the Limit: triumph and tragedy in Formula One, 1996; Beyond the Limit, 2001. *Recreation:* fly fishing. *Address:* The Princess Grace Hospital, 42–52 Nottingham Place, W1M 3FD. *Clubs:* Athenæum, Royal Automobile.

WATKINS, Dr George Edward, CBE 2000; Chairman and Managing Director, Conoco (UK) Ltd, since 1993; *b* 19 Aug. 1943; *s* of George Robert Leonard Watkins and Laura Watkins; *m* 1966, Elizabeth Mary Bestwick; two *s*. *Educ:* Leeds Univ. (BSc Mining, MSc Geophysics; PhD Geophysics 1968); Stanford Univ., Calif (MS Mgt). Geophysicist, Shell Internat. Petroleum Co., 1968–73; Conoco (UK) Ltd: Geophysicist, 1973–80; Dir, Exploration, 1980–84; Dir, Prodn, 1985–90; Vice Pres., Exploration Prodn, Conoco Inc., Houston, 1990–93. Sloan Fellow, Stanford Univ., 1984–85. Vice Chm., Scottish Enterprise Grampian, 1999–. Chm., UK Oil & Gas Industry Safety Leadership Forum, 1997–2000. Pres., UKOOA, 1996. Van Weelden Award, Eur. Assoc. Exploration Geophysicists, 1967. *Recreations:* cinema, gardening, walking, fishing. *Address:* 12 Rubislaw Den South, Aberdeen AB15 4BB. *T:* (01224) 208706.

WATKINS, Gerwyn Rhidian; a District Judge (Magistrates' Courts) (formerly Stipendiary Magistrate), South Glamorgan, since 1993; *b* 22 Jan. 1943; *s* of late William Watkins and Margaret Watkins (*née* Evans); *m* 1966, Eleanor Margaret Hemingway; two *s*. *Educ:* Ardwyn Grammar Sch., Aberystwyth; University Coll. of Wales, Aberystwyth (LLB). Articled to Thomas Andrews, Bracknell, 1966–68; Court Clerk, Cardiff Magistrates' Court, 1968–71; Justices' Clerk: Bromsgrove and Redditch, 1971–74; Vale of Glamorgan, 1974–93. Pres., Barry Rotary Club, 1990–91. *Address:* Magistrates' Court, Fitzalan Place, Cardiff CF2 1RZ. *T:* (029) 2046 3040.

WATKINS, Rev. Gordon Derek; Secretary, London Diocesan Advisory Committee, 1984–94; *b* 16 July 1929; *s* of Clifford and Margaret Watkins; *m* 1957, Beryl Evelyn Whitaker. *Educ:* St Brendan's College, Clifton. Nat. Service, RAOC, 1947–49. Staff of W. D. & H. O. Wills, 1944–51; deacon 1953, priest 1954; Curate, Grafton Cathedral, NSW, 1953–56; Vicar of Texas, Qld, 1957–61; Curate, St Wilfrid's, Harrogate, 1961–63; Vicar of Upton Park, 1963–67; Rector: Great and Little Bentley, 1967–73; Great Canfield, 1973–78; Pastoral Sec., Dio. London, 1978–84; Vicar, St Martin-within-Ludgate, City and Dio. of London, 1984–89; Priest Vicar, Westminster Abbey, 1984–90; Priest in Ordinary to the Queen, 1984–96. Freeman, City of London, 1984. *Recreations:* reading, music, country life. *Address:* 21 Cramond Place, Dalgety Bay, Dunfermline, Fife KY11 9LS.

WATKINS, Maj.-Gen. Guy Hansard, CB 1986; OBE 1974; Chief Executive, Royal Hong Kong Jockey Club, 1986–96; *b* 30 Nov. 1933; *s* of Col A. N. M. Watkins and Mrs S. C. Watkins; *m* 1958, Sylvia Margaret Grant; two *s* two *d*. *Educ:* The King's Sch., Canterbury; Royal Military Academy, Sandhurst. Commissioned into Royal Artillery, 1953; CO 39 Medium Regt RA, 1973; Comd Task Force 'B'/Dep. Comd 1 Armd Div., 1977; Director, Public Relations (Army), 1980; Maj. Gen. RA and GOC Artillery Div., 1982; Dir Gen., Army Manning and Recruiting, 1985; retd 1986. Chm., Sportal Racing, 1999; Director: British Bloodstock Agency, 1996–2001; Racecourse Holdings Trust, 1996–. *Recreations:* racing, golf, fishing, ski-ing. *Address:* The Mill House, Fittleworth, near Pulborough, West Sussex RH20 1EP. *T:* (01798) 865717, *Fax:* (01798) 865684. *Clubs:* Oriental; Hong Kong Jockey, Shek O (Hong Kong); W Sussex Golf.

WATKINS, Prof. Hugh Christian, MD, PhD; FRCP, FMedSci; Field Marshal Alexander Professor of Cardiovascular Medicine, University of Oxford, since 1996; Fellow, Exeter College, Oxford, since 1996; *b* 7 June 1959; *s* of David Watkins, MB, BCh, and late Gillian Mary Watkins; *m* 1987, Elizabeth Bridget Hewett; one *s* one *d*. *Educ:* Gresham's Sch., Norfolk; St Bartholomew's Hosp. Med. Sch., London (BSc 1st Cl. Hons; MB, BS; Brackenbury & Bourne Prize in Gen. Medicine, 1984); PhD 1995, MD 1995, London. MRCP 1987, FRCP 1997. House Physician, Professorial Med. Unit, St Bartholomew's Hosp., 1984–85; Senior House Officer: in Medicine, John Radcliffe Hosp., Oxford, 1985–87; in Neurology, St Bartholomew's, 1987; Registrar, Medicine and Cardiology, St Thomas' Hosp., London, 1987–89; Lectr in Cardiological Scis, St George's, London, 1990–94, Hon. Sen. Lectr, 1995; Res. Fellow in Medicine, Harvard Med. Sch. and Brigham & Women's Hosp., Boston, 1990–94; Asst Prof. of Medicine, Harvard Med. Sch. and Associate Physician, Brigham & Women's Hosp., 1995. BHF Clinical Scientist Fellow, 1990. Goulstonian Lectr, RCP, 1998. FMedSci 1999. Golden Stethoscope Award for Clinical Teaching, Oxford Univ. Med. Sch., 1986; Young Res. Worker Prize, British Cardiac Soc., 1992. *Publications:* papers in scientific jls incl. New England Jl Medicine, Jl Clinical Investigation, Cell, Nature Genetics. *Recreations:* photography, Oriental porcelain. *Address:* Department of Cardiovascular Medicine, John Radcliffe Hospital, Oxford OX3 9DU. *T:* (01865) 220257, *Fax:* (01865) 768844.

WATKINS, Prof. Jeffrey Clifton, PhD; FMedSci; FRS 1988; FIBiol; Hon. Professor of Pharmacology, 1989–99, and Leader of Excitatory Amino Acid Group, Department of Pharmacology, 1973–99, School of Medical Sciences (formerly The Medical School), Bristol (Hon. Senior Research Fellow, 1983–89); *b* 20 Dec. 1929; *s* of Colin Hereward and Amelia Miriam Watkins; *m* 1973, Beatrice Joan Thacher; one *s* one *d*. *Educ:* Univ. of Western Australia (MSc 1954); Univ. of Cambridge (PhD 1954). Research Fellow, Chemistry Department: Univ. of Cambridge, 1954–55; Univ. of Yale, 1955–57; Res. Fellow, 1958–61, Fellow, 1961–65, Physiology Dept, ANU; Scientific Officer, ARC Inst. of Animal Physiology, Babraham, Cambridge, 1965–67; Res. Scientist, MRC Neuropsychiatry Unit, Carshalton, Surrey, 1967–73; Senior Research Fellow, Depts of Pharmacology and Physiology, The Med. Sch., Bristol, 1973–83. MAE 1989; FIBiol 1998; FMedSci 1999. *Publications:* The NMDA Receptor, 1989, 2nd edn 1994; approx. 250 pubns in learned jls, eg Jl of Physiol., Brit. Jl of Pharmacol., Nature, Brain Res., Exptl Brain Res., Eur. Jl of Pharmacol., Neuroscience, Neuroscience Letters, Jl of Neuroscience. *Address:* 8 Lower Court Road, Lower Almondsbury, Bristol BS32 4DX. *T:* (01454) 613829.

WATKINS, Penelope Jill, (Mrs M. J. Bowman); a District Judge (Magistrates' Courts) (formerly Stipendiary Magistrate), Mid-Glamorgan, since 1995, and South Wales, since 1996; a Recorder, since 2000; *b* 19 April 1953; *d* of Laurence Gordon Watkins and Dorothy Ernestine Watkins; *m* 1977, Michael James Bowman. *Educ:* Howell's Sch., Llandaff; Henbury Sch., Bristol; Somerville Coll., Oxford (BA Jurisp. 1974; MA). Called to the Bar, Lincoln's Inn, 1975; Inner London Magistrates' Courts Service: Dep. Chief Clerk, serving at London Courts, 1976–90; Dep. Training Officer, 1983–86; Justices' Clerk: Wells Street, 1990–91; Camberwell Green, 1991–95. An Asst Recorder, 1998–2000. *Recreations:* reading, music, travel. *Address:* Pontypridd Magistrates' Court, Union Street, Pontypridd CF37 1SD. *T:* (01443) 480750.

WATKINS, Peter Rodney; education consultant, since 1991; Office for Standards in Education Inspector, 1993–98; *b* 8 Oct. 1931; *s* of late Frank Arthur Watkins and Mary Gwyneth Watkins (*née* Price); *m* 1971, Jillian Ann Burge (marr. diss. 1998); two *d*. *Educ:* Solihull Sch.; Emmanuel Coll., Cambridge (Exhibnr; Hist. Tripos Pts I and II 1952, 1953; Cert. in Educn 1954; MA 1957). Flying Officer, RAF, 1954–56; History Master, East Ham Grammar Sch., 1956–59; Sixth Form Hist. Master, Brentwood Sch., 1959–64; Sen. Hist. Master, Bristol Grammar Sch., 1964–69; Headmaster, King Edward's Five Ways Sch., Birmingham, 1969–74; Headmaster, Chichester High Sch. for Boys, 1974–79; Principal, Price's Sixth Form Coll., Fareham, 1980–84; Dep. Chief Exec., Sch. Curriculum Develt Cttee, 1984–88, Nat. Curriculum Council, 1988–91. Exec., SHA, 1980–84. Chm., Christian Educn Movement, 1980–87. Reader, St Peter's, Bishop's Waltham, dio. of Portsmouth, 1989–. *Publications:* The Sixth Form College in Practice, 1982; Modular Approaches to the Secondary Curriculum, 1986; St Barnabas' Church, Swanmore 1845–1995, 1995; Swanmore since 1840, 2001. *Recreations:* travel, fell walking, local history, theology, cooking. *Address:* 7 Crofton Way, Swanmore, Southampton SO32 2RF. *T:* (01489) 894789.

WATKINS, Rt Hon. Sir Tasker, VC 1944; GBE 1990; Kt 1971; PC 1980; DL; a Lord Justice of Appeal, 1980–93; Deputy Chief Justice of England, 1988–93; *b* 18 Nov. 1918; *s* of late Bertram and Jane Watkins, Nelson, Glam; *m* 1941, Eirwen Evans; one *d* (one *s* decd). *Educ:* Pontypridd Grammar Sch. Served War, 1939–45 (Major, the Welch Regiment). Called to Bar, Middle Temple, 1948, Bencher 1970; QC 1965; Deputy Chairman: Radnor QS, 1962–71; Carmarthenshire QS, 1966–71; Recorder: Merthyr Tydfil, 1968–70, Swansea, 1970–71; Leader, Wales and Chester Circuit, 1970–71; Judge of the High Court of Justice, Family Div., 1971–74, QBD, 1974–80; Presiding Judge, Wales and Chester Circuit, 1975–80; Sen. Presiding Judge for England and Wales, 1983–91. Counsel (as Deputy to Attorney-General) to Inquiry into Aberfan Disaster, 1966. Chairman: Mental Health Review Tribunal, Wales Region, 1960–71; Judicial Studies Bd, 1979–80. Pres., Univ. of Wales Coll. of Medicine, 1987–98. Pres., British Legion, Wales, 1947–68; Mem., TA Assoc., Glamorgan and Wales, 1947–. Chm., Welsh RU Charitable Trust, 1975–; Pres., Welsh RU, 1993–. DL Glamorgan, 1956. Hon. FRCS 1992. Hon. Fellow, Amer. Coll. of Trial Lawyers, 1985. Hon. LLD: Wales, 1979; Glamorgan, 1996. KStJ 2000. *Address:* Fairwater Lodge, Fairwater Road, Llandaff, Glamorgan CF5 2LE. *T:* (029) 2056 3558; 5 Pump Court, Middle Temple, EC4Y 7AP. *T:* (020) 7353 1993. *Clubs:* Army and Navy; Cardiff and County (Cardiff); Glamorgan Wanderers Rugby Football (Pres., 1968–).

See also J. Griffith Williams.

WATKINS, Thomas Frederick; Director, Chemical Defence Establishment, Porton, 1972–74; *b* 19 Feb. 1914; *s* of late Edward and late Louisa Watkins; *m* 1939, Jeannie Blodwen Roberts (*d* 2000); two *d*. *Educ:* Cowbridge Grammar Sch.; Univ. of Wales, Cardiff. BSc Hons Wales 1935; MSc Wales 1936; FRIC 1947. Joined Scientific Staff of War Dept, 1936; seconded to Govt of India, 1939–44; seconded to Dept of Nat. Defence, Canada, 1947–49; Head of Research Section, CDRE, Sutton Oak and Min. of Supply CDE, Nancekuke, 1949–56; Supt Chemistry Research Div., CDE, Porton, 1956; Asst Dir Chemical Research, CDE, Porton, 1963; Dep. Dir, CDE, Porton, 1966. *Publications:* various papers on organic chemistry. *Recreation:* gardening. *Address:* 34 Harnwood Road, Salisbury, Wilts SP2 8DB. *T:* (01722) 335135.

WATKINS, Dr Winifred May, FMedSci; FRS 1969; Visiting Professor and Senior Research Fellow, Imperial College School of Medicine (formerly Royal Postgraduate Medical School), University of London, since 1990; Head of Division of Immunochemical Genetics, Clinical Research Centre, Medical Research Council, 1976–89; *b* 6 Aug. 1924; *d* of Albert E. and Annie B. Watkins. *Educ:* Godolphin and Latymer Sch., London; Univ. of London. PhD 1950; DSc 1963. FRCPath 1983. Research Asst in Biochemistry, St Bartholomew's Hosp. Med. Sch., 1948–50; Beit Memorial Research Fellow, 1952–55; Mem. of Staff of Lister Inst. of Preventive Medicine, 1955–75; Wellcome Travelling Research Fellow, Univ. of California, 1960–61; Reader in Biochemistry, 1965; Prof. of Biochemistry, Univ. of London, 1968–75; William Julius Mickle Fellow, London Univ., 1971. Mem. Council, Royal Soc., 1984–86. Hon. Member: Internat. Soc. of Blood Transfusion, 1982; British Blood Transfusion Soc., 1996; Japanese Biochemical Soc., 1990; British Biochem. Soc., 2000; Foreign Member: Polish Acad. of Sciences, 1988; Royal Swedish Acad. of Scis, 1998. Governor: Dulwich Coll., 1987–95; Alleyn's Sch., Dulwich, 1995–97. Founder FMedSci 1998. Hon. FRCP 1990. Hon. DSc Utrecht, 1990. Landsteiner Memorial Award (jtly), 1967; Paul Ehrlich-Ludwig Darmstädter Prize (jtly), 1969; Kenneth Goldsmith Award, British Blood Transfusion Soc., 1986; Royal Medal, Royal Soc., 1988; Franz Oehlecker Medal, German Soc. of Transfusion Medicine and Immunohaematology, 1989; (jtly) Philip Levine Award, Amer. Soc. of Clin. Pathologists, 1990. *Publications:* various papers in biochemical and immunological jls. *Address:* Department of Haematology, Imperial College School of Medicine, Hammersmith Hospital, Du Cane Road, W12 0NN. *T:* (020) 8383 2171, *Fax:* (020) 8742 9335; *e-mail:* w.watkins@ic.ac.uk.

WATKINSON, Angela Eileen; MP (C) Upminster, since 2001; *b* 18 Nov. 1941; *m* 1961, Roy Michael Watkinson; one *s* two *d*. *Educ:* Wanstead County High Sch.; Anglia Poly. (HNC 1989). Bank of NSW, 1958–64; Special Sch. Sec., Essex CC, 1976–88; Cttee Clerk, Barking and Dagenham BC, 1988–89; Cttee Manager, Basildon DC, 1989–94. Member (C): Havering BC, 1994–98; Essex CC, 1997–. *Address:* (office) 23 Butts Green Road, Hornchurch, Essex RM11 2JS; c/o House of Commons, SW1A 0AA.

WATKINSON, John Taylor; solicitor; Director, Interconnect Communications Ltd, since 1986; *b* 25 Jan. 1941; *s* of William Forshaw Watkinson; *m* 1969, Jane Elizabeth Miller; two *s* two *d*. *Educ:* Bristol Grammar Sch.; Worcester Coll., Oxford. Schoolmaster, Rugby Sch., Warwicks, 1964–71. Called to the Bar, Middle Temple, 1971; practised, Midland Circuit, 1972–74, South East Circuit, 1978–79; Solicitor of the Supreme Ct, 1986–; Principal, Watkinson & Co., 1989–95. MP (Lab) Gloucestershire West, Oct. 1974–1979; PPS to Sec. of State, Home Office, 1975–79; Member: Public Accounts Cttee, 1976–79; Expenditure Cttee, 1978–79; Speakers' Conf. on Northern Ireland, 1979; Hon. Sec., Anglo-Swiss Parly Gp, 1977–79; Mem. and Rapporteur, Council of Europe and WEU, 1976–79; Rapporteur, first Europ. Declaration on the Police. Contested: (Lab) Warwick and Leamington, 1970; (SDP) Glos West, 1983, 1987. Financial Reporter, BBC TV, 1979–82. Dir, Wyedean Review Ltd, 1987–. Advr to Polish, Macedonian, Bulgarian, Latvian, Austrian, Moroccan, Mauritian, Norwegian, Bosnian, Belarusian, Czech Republic, Slovakian, Ukrainian, Cypriot and Romanian Govts on telecommunications, postal and broadcasting laws and regulatory regimes, 1992–93. Visitor, Onley Borstal, Warwicks, 1970–71. Mem., NUJ. Amateur Rugby Fives Champion (Singles 3 times, Doubles 4 times), 1964–70. *Publications:* (jtly) UK Telecommunications Approval Manual, 1987; Telecommunications Approval Report, 1987; European Telecommunications Manual, 1990. *Recreations:* rackets, Real tennis, cricket, golf. *Address:* Clanna Lodge, Alvington, Lydney, Glos GL15 6AJ.

WATLING, His Honour Rev. (David) Brian; QC 1979; a Circuit Judge, 1981–2001; Resident Judge, Chelmsford Crown Court, 1997–2001; Hon Curate, Nayland with Wissington, since 1990; *b* 18 June 1935; *o s* of late Russell and Stella Watling; *m* 1964, Noelle Louise Bugden. *Educ:* Charterhouse; King's Coll., London (LLB). Sub-Lieut RNR. Called to Bar, Middle Temple, 1957, Lincoln's Inn, 1998; Advocate, Gibraltar, 1980. Various Crown appts, 1969–72; Treasury Counsel, Central Criminal Court, 1972–79; a Recorder of the Crown Court, 1979–81. Vis. Lectr, 1978–80, Vis. Prof. in Criminal Law, 1980–84, University Coll. at Buckingham (now Univ. of Buckingham). Diocese of St Edmundsbury and Ipswich: Reader 1985; deacon 1987; priest 1988. Chm., Mistley Bk Club, 1989–94; Pres., Dedham Vale Soc., 1994–. *Publication:* (contrib.) Serving Two Masters, 1988. *Recreations:* sailing, hill walking, theatre and ballet, fireside reading, the company of old friends. *Address:* The Manse, Nayland, Colchester, Essex CO6 4HX. *Clubs:* Garrick; Royal Harwich Yacht; Aldeburgh Yacht.

WATSON, family name of **Barons Manton** and **Watson of Richmond**.

WATSON OF INVERGOWRIE, Baron *cr* 1997 (Life Peer), of Invergowrie in Perth and Kinross; **Michael Goodall Watson;** Member (Lab) Glasgow Cathcart, Scottish Parliament, since 1999; *b* 1 May 1949; *s* of late Clarke Watson and Senga (*née* Goodall). *Educ:* Invergowrie Primary Sch., Dundee; Dundee High Sch.; Heriot-Watt Univ., Edinburgh (BA 2nd Cl. Hons Econs and Industrial Relns). Development Officer, WEA, E Midlands Dist, 1974–77; full-time official, ASTMS, then MSF, 1977–89. Dir, PS Public Affairs Consultants, then PS Communications Consultants Ltd, Edinburgh, 1997–99. MP (Lab) Glasgow Central, 1989–97. Mem., Public Accounts Cttee, 1995–97. Mem., Scottish Exec. Cttee, Labour Party, 1987–90; Chm., PLP Overseas Develt Aid Cttee, 1991–97. *Publications:* Rags to Riches: the official history of Dundee United Football Club, 1985; Year Zero: an inside view of the Scottish Parliament, 2001. *Recreations:* supporting Dundee United FC, reading, especially political biographies, running. *Address:* Scottish Parliament, Edinburgh EH99 1SP; *e-mail:* mike.watson.msp@scottish.parliament.uk.

WATSON OF RICHMOND, Baron *cr* 1999 (Life Peer), of Richmond in the London Borough of Richmond-upon-Thames; **Alan John Watson,** CBE 1985; Chairman: Corporate Television Networks (CTN), since 1992; Burson-Marsteller UK, since 1994; Burson-Marsteller Europe, since 1996; Director, Burson-Marsteller Worldwide, since 1992; *b* 3 Feb. 1941; *s* of Rev. John William Watson and Edna Mary (*née* Peters); *m* 1965, Karen Lederer; two *s*. *Educ:* Diocesan Coll., Cape Town, SA; Kingswood Sch., Bath, Somerset; Jesus Coll., Cambridge (Open Schol. in History 1959, State Schol. 1959; MA Hons). Vice-Pres., Cambridge Union; Pres., Cambridge Univ. Liberal Club. Research Asst to Cambridge Prof. of Modern History on post-war history of Unilever, 1962–64. General trainee, BBC, 1965–66; Reporter, BBC TV, The Money Programme, 1966–68; Chief Public Affairs Commentator, London Weekend Television, 1969–70; Reporter, Panorama, BBC TV, 1971–74; Presenter, The Money Programme, 1974–75; Head of TV, Radio, Audio-Visual Div., EEC, 1975–79; Dir, Charles Barker City Ltd, 1980–85 (Chief Exec., 1980–83); Dep. Chm., Sterling PR, 1985–86; Chairman: City and Corporate Counsel Ltd, 1987–94; Threadneedle Publishing Gp, 1987–94; Corporate Vision Ltd, 1989–98. Mem. Bd, Y & R Partnership, 1999–. Mem., Exec. Bd, Unicef, 1985–92; Mem. Bd, POW Business Leaders Forum, 1996–; non-exec. Dir, Community and Charities Cttee, BT Bd, 1996–. Pres., Liberal Party, 1984–85. Vice Chm., European Movt, 1995–. Presenter: You and 1992, BBC 1 series, 1990; The Germans, Channel 4, 1992; Key Witness, Radio 4, 1996. Vis. Prof. in English Culture and European Studies, Louvain Univ., 1990–; Hon. Prof., German Studies, Birmingham Univ., 1997–. Chairman: RTS, 1992–94 (Mem. Council, 1989–95; FRTS 1992); CBI Media Industries Gp, 1995–98. Pres., British-German Assoc., 2000– (Chm., 1992–2000). Pres., Heathrow Assoc. for Control of Aircraft Noise, 1992–95. Chm., Chemistry Adv. Bd, Cambridge Univ., 1999–; Mem. Adv. Council, John Smith Meml Trust, 1998–. Chm. of Govs,

Westminster Coll., Oxford, 1988–94; Governor: Kingswood Sch., 1984–90; ESU, 1993– (Internat. Dep. Chm., 1995–99; Chm., 2000–); Trustee, British Studies Centre, Humboldt Univ., Berlin, 1998–. Hon. FIPR 1998. Hon. DHL St Lawrence Univ., 1992. Grand Prix Eurodiaporama of EC for European TV Coverage, 1974. Order of Merit (Germany), 1995, Grand Cross, 2001. *Publications:* Europe at Risk, 1972; The Germans: who are they now?, 1992 (German, US, Japanese, Polish and Chinese edns); Thatcher and Kohl: old rivalries renewed, 1996. *Recreation:* historical biography. *Address:* Cholmondeley House, 3 Cholmondeley Walk, Richmond upon Thames, Surrey TW9 1NS; Somerset Lodge, Nunney, Somerset BA11 4NP. *Clubs:* Brooks's, Royal Automobile, Kennel.

WATSON, Adam; *see* Watson, John Hugh A.

WATSON, Alan; *see* Watson, W. A. J.

WATSON, Alan; Deputy Parliamentary Commissioner for Administration, since 2000; Deputy Scottish Parliamentary Commissioner for Administration, since 2000; Deputy Welsh Administration Ombudsman, since 2000; *b* 23 Nov. 1942; *s* of late Dennis Watson and of Dorothy Watson; *m* 1st, 1966, Marjorie Eleanor Main (marr. diss.); one *s* one *d*; 2nd, 1991, Susan Elizabeth Beare (*née* Dwyer); one step *s*. *Educ:* King Edward VI Grammar Sch., Morpeth. Min. of Pensions and Nat. Insce, later Min. of Social Security, then DHSS, 1962–76; Staff Inspection, CSD, 1976–80; Mgt Trng, DSS, 1980–84; Investigations Manager with Parly Comr for Admin, 1984–89; Personnel, DSS, 1989–92; Dir, Field Ops, with Contributions Agency, 1992–94; Dir of Investigations, with Parly Comr for Admin, 1994–2000. *Recreations:* cricket, football, football referee, walking, books. *Address:* Office of the Parliamentary Commissioner, Millbank Tower, Millbank, SW1P 4QP.

WATSON, Prof. Alan Albert; JP; FRCPath; Regius Professor of Forensic Medicine, University of Glasgow, 1985–92, now Emeritus; *b* 20 Feb. 1929; *s* of Wilfrid Roy Watson and Gladys Cusden or Watson; *m* 1955, Jeannette Anne Pitts or Watson; three *s*. *Educ:* Reading Sch.; St Mary's Hosp. Med. Sch., Univ. of London (MB BS); MA Cantab; FRCPGlas; DMJ; DTM&H (Antwerp); BD Glasgow. Director, Ntondo Hosp., Zaire, 1958; Lectr in Pathology, Glasgow Univ., 1964; Asst Pathologist, Cambridge Univ., 1969, Fellow, Queens' Coll., Cambridge, 1970; Sen. Lectr, Forensic Medicine, Glasgow, 1971. District Court Judge, 1982; JP Glasgow, 1982–93, Kilmarnock and Loudoun Dist, 1993–. Fellow, Royal Belgian Acad. of Medicine, 1983. *Publications:* Legal Aspects of Dental Practice, 1975; Forensic Medicine, 1989; Lecture Notes on Forensic Medicine, 1989; contribs to Jls of Forensic Medicine, and Pathology. *Address:* 76 Arrol Drive, Ayr KA7 4AW. *T:* (01292) 266365.

WATSON, Prof. Alan Andrew, FRS 2000; FRAS, FInstP; Professor of Physics, University of Leeds, since 1984; *b* 26 Sept. 1938; *s* of William John Watson and Elsie Robinson; *m* 1973, Susan Lorraine Cartman; one *s* one *d*. *Educ:* Daniel Stewart's College, Edinburgh; Edinburgh Univ. (BSc 1st cl. hons Physics 1960; PhD 1964). FInstP 1998. Asst Lectr, Univ. of Edinburgh, 1962–64; University of Leeds: Lectr, 1964–76; Reader in Particle Cosmic Physics, 1976–84; Chm., Physics Dept, 1989–93; Pro Vice-Chancellor, 1994–97; Hd, Dept of Physics and Astronomy, 1997–2000. Science and Engineering Research Council: Member: Astronomy and Planetary Science Bd, 1986–90; Nuclear Physics Bd, 1987–90; Chm., Ground Based Facilities Cttee, PPARC, 1996–99. Mem., Cosmic Ray Commn, IUPAP, 1991–95. Member, Editorial Board: Astroparticle Physics, 1992–; Nuclear Instruments and Methods, 1993–. *Publications:* contribs to Physical Review Letters, Astrophysical Jl, Jl of Physics, Nuclear Instruments and Methods, Astroparticle Physics, Nature. *Recreations:* malt whisky tasting, golf, watching Scotland win Calcutta Cup games, theatre. *Address:* Department of Physics and Astronomy, University of Leeds, Leeds LS2 9JT. *T:* (0113) 233 3888; *e-mail:* a.a.watson@leeds.ac.uk. *Club:* Crail Golfing Society.

WATSON, Rear-Adm. Alan George, CB 1975; Served Royal Navy, 1941–77; Asst Chief of Naval Staff, 1974–77, retired. Pres., Church of England Soldiers', Sailors' and Airmen's Clubs, 1997–.

WATSON, Sir Andrew; *see* Watson, Sir J. A.

WATSON, Maj.-Gen. Andrew Linton, CB 1981; Lieutenant Governor and Secretary, Royal Hospital, Chelsea, 1984–92; *b* 9 April 1927; *s* of Col W. L. Watson, OBE, and Mrs D. E. Watson (*née* Lea); *m* 1952, Mary Elizabeth, *d* of Mr and Mrs A. S. Rigby, Warrenpoint, Co. Down; two *s* one *d*. *Educ:* Wellington Coll., Berks. psc, jssc, rcds. Commnd The Black Watch, 1946; served, 1946–66: with 1st and 2nd Bns, Black Watch, in UK, Germany, Cyprus and British Guiana; with UN Force, Cyprus; as GSO 2 and 3 on Staff, UK and Germany; GSO 1 HQ 17 Div./Malaya Dist, 1966–68; CO 1st Bn The Black Watch, UK, Gibraltar and NI, 1969–71; Comdr 19 Airportable Bde, Colchester, 1972–73; RCDS, 1974; Comdr British Army Staff, and Military Attaché, Washington, DC, 1975–77; GOC Eastern District, 1977–80; COS, Allied Forces, Northern Europe, 1980–82. Col, The Black Watch, 1981–92. Chm., Inner London Br., Army Benevolent Fund, 1980–2000; Trustee, Royal Cambridge Home for Soldiers' Widows, 1992–2001. *Recreations:* golf, walking, classical music. *Address:* c/o Royal Bank of Scotland, 12 Dunkeld Road, Perth PH1 5RB. *T:* (01738) 21777. *Club:* Pitt.

WATSON, Sir Andrew Michael M.; *see* Milne-Watson.

WATSON, (Angus) Gavin; Chairman, Fortunegate Community Housing, since 1998; *b* 14 April 1944; *s* of late H. E. and M. Watson; *m* 1967, Susan Naomi Beal (marr. diss. 1991); two *s* (and one *d* decd). *Educ:* Carlisle Grammar School; Merton College, Oxford; Peterhouse, Cambridge. Joined Dept of the Environment, 1971; Private Office, Secretary of State, 1975–77; Asst Sec., 1980–86; Under Secretary, 1986–97: Hd, Directorate of Public Housing Mgt and Resources, 1986–91; Hd, Water Directorate, Jun.–July 1991; Hd, Directorate of Envmtl Policy and Analysis, 1991–94; Hd, Cities, Countryside and Private Finance Directorate, 1994–95; Hd, Govt Offices Central Unit, 1995–97. *Recreations:* looking at buildings, industrial archaeology, fell walking. *Address:* 19 Castle Street, Bishop's Castle, Shropshire SY9 5BU. *T:* (01588) 630444.

WATSON, Anthony Gerard; Editor, Yorkshire Post, since 1989; *b* 28 May 1955; *s* of George Maurice Watson and Ann (*née* McDonnell); *m* 1st, 1982, Susan Ann Gutteridge (marr. diss. 1994); two *s* one *d*; 2nd, 1994, Sylvie Helen Pask; one *s* one *d*. *Educ:* St John Fisher Sch., Peterborough. N Staffs Polytechnic (BA Pol. and Internat. Relns). Journalist with E Midlands Allied Press, Peterborough, 1977–79; joined Westminster Press—Evening Despatch, Darlington, 1979, News Editor, 1983–84; Yorkshire Post, 1984–86; Researcher, World in Action, Granada TV, 1986–88; Dep. Editor, Yorkshire Post, 1988–89. Provincial Journalist of the Year, British Press Awards, 1987. *Address:* Yorkshire Post, Wellington Street, Leeds LS1 1RF. *T:* (0113) 243 2701.

WATSON, Anthony Heriot, CBE 1965; *b* 13 April 1912; *s* of William Watson and Dora Isabel Watson (*née* Fisher); *m* 1946, Hilary Margaret Fyfe. *Educ:* St Paul's Sch.; Christ Church, Oxford; University Coll., London. Statistical Officer, British Cotton Industry Research Assoc., 1936. Min. of Supply, 1940: Statistician; Asst Dir of Statistics; Min. of Aircraft Production, 1942; Statistician, Dept of Civil Aviation, Air Ministry, 1945; Chief Statistician: Min. of Civil Aviation, 1951; Min. of Transport and Civil Aviation, 1954; Min. of Aviation, 1959; Min. of Transport, 1964, Dir of Statistics, 1966; DoE, 1970; retired 1973. *Publication:* (ed with D. L. Munby and contrib.) Inland Transport Statistics: Great Britain 1900–1970, vol. 1, 1978. *Recreations:* music, garden. *Address:* 9 Kirk Park, Edinburgh EH16 6HZ. *T:* (0131) 664 7428.

WATSON, Antony Edward Douglas; QC 1986; *b* 6 March 1945; *s* of William Edward Watson and Margaret Watson (*née* Douglas); *m* 1972, Gillian Mary Bevan-Arthur; two *d*. *Educ:* Sedbergh School; Sidney Sussex College, Cambridge (MA). Called to the Bar, Inner Temple, 1968. Dep. Chm., Copyright Tribunal, 1994–97. *Publication:* (jtly) Terrell on Patents (1884), 13th edn 1982, 14th edn 1994. *Recreations:* wine, opera, country pursuits. *Address:* The Old Rectory, Milden, Suffolk IP7 7AF. *T:* (01449) 740227.

WATSON, Barbara Joan; Her Honour Judge Watson; a Circuit Judge, since 2000; *b* 13 Oct. 1950; *d* of Gordon Smith Watson and Joan Watson; *m* 1975, James David Heyworth (marr. diss. 1982); one *s*. *Educ:* Nelson Grammar Sch., Lancs; Southampton Univ. (LLB Hons 1972). Called to the Bar, Gray's Inn, 1973; in practice as barrister, Northern Circuit, 1973–75 and 1981–2000; Lectr in Law, Manchester Poly., 1973–80; Asst Recorder, 1992–97; Recorder, 1997–2000. *Recreations:* opera, travel, watching Rugby Union. *Address:* The Law Courts, Openshaw Place, Ringway, Preston PR1 2LL. *T:* (01772) 823300.

WATSON, Sir Bruce (Dunstan), Kt 1985; Chairman, M.I.M. Holdings Limited, 1983–91 (Chief Executive Officer, 1981–90); *b* 1 Aug. 1928; *s* of James Harvey and Edith Mary (Crawford); *m* 1952, June Kilgour; one *s* two *d*. *Educ:* University of Queensland (BE (Elec) 1949, BCom 1957). Engineer, Tasmanian Hydro Electricity Commn, 1950–54, Townsville Regional Electricity Board, 1954–56; MIM Group of Companies: Engineer, Copper Refineries Pty Ltd, Townsville, 1956–69; Mount Isa Mines Ltd, 1970–73; Group Industrial Relations Manager, MIM Group, Brisbane, 1973–75; First Gen. Man., Agnew Mining Co., WA, 1975–77; M.I.M. Holdings Ltd, Brisbane: Director, 1977; Man. Dir. 1980; Man. Dir and Chief Exec. Officer, 1981. Director: Asarco Inc., 1985–90; National Australia Bank, 1984–91, 1992–98; Boral, 1990–99; Mem., Supervisory Bd, Metallgesellschaft AG, 1988–93. Member: Business Council of Australia, 1983–90; Exec. Cttee, Australian Mining Industry Council, 1980–90 (Pres., 1985–87); President: Australian Inst. of Mining and Metallurgy, 1992; Australian Inst. of Co. Dirs, 1992–95. Mem., Qld Corrective Services Commn, 1997–99 (Chm., 1998–99); Chm. Council, Qld Inst. of Med. Res., 1998–. Bd Mem., Australian Management Coll., Mt Eliza, 1980–91. Hon. DEng Queensland, 1989; DUniv Griffith 1992. *Recreation:* golf. *Address:* 272 Jesmond Road, Figtre Pocket, Brisbane, Qld 4069, Australia. *T:* (7) 33781536.

WATSON, (Daniel) Stewart, CB 1967; OBE 1958; *b* 30 Dec. 1911; *s* of Reverend Dr William Watson, DD, DLitt, and Mary Mackintosh Watson; *m* 1939, Isabel (*née* Gibson) (*d* 1991); one *s*. *Educ:* Robert Gordon's Coll.; Aberdeen University. Student Apprentice, British Thomson Houston, Rugby, 1933, Research Engr, 1936. Scientific Officer, Admiralty, 1938–; Dir, Admiralty Surface Weapons Establishment, 1961–68; Dep. Chief Scientist (Naval), MoD, 1968–72; Dir Gen. Establishments, Resources Programme A, MoD, 1972–73. *Publications:* contribs to IEEJ. *Recreations:* thoroughbred cars; caravanning. *Address:* 28 Longhope Drive, Wrecclesham, Farnham, Surrey GU10 4SN. *T:* (01252) 733126.

WATSON, Sir David (John), Kt 1998; Director, and Professor of the History of Ideas, University of Brighton (formerly Brighton Polytechnic), since 1990; *b* 22 March 1949; *s* of late Lewis James Watson and Berenice Nichols; *m* 1975, Betty Pinto Skolnick; one *d* one *s*. *Educ:* Cheshunt Grammar School; Eton College; Clare College, Cambridge (MA); Univ. of Pennsylvania (PhD). Sen. Lectr, Principal Lectr in Humanities, Crewe and Alsager Coll. of Higher Educn, 1975–81; Dean, Modular Course, Asst Dir, Dep. Dir, Oxford Polytechnic, 1981–90. Member: Council, CNAA, 1989–93 (Mem., 1977–93); PCFC, 1988–93; HEFCE, 1992–96; Paul Hamlyn Foundn Nat. Commn on Educn, 1991–93; Open Univ. Validation Bd, 1992–2001; Nat. Cttee of Inquiry into Higher Educn (Dearing Cttee), 1996–97; Chairman: Univs Assoc. for Contg Educn, 1994–98; Steering Cttee for ESRC Teaching and Learning Prog., 1998–; SE England Cultural Consortium, 1999–; UUK Longer Term Strategy Gp, 1999–. *Publications:* Margaret Fuller, 1988; Managing the Modular Course, 1989; (jtly) Developing Professional Education, 1992; Arendt, 1992; (jtly) Managing the University Curriculum, 1994; (jtly) Continuing Education in the Mainstream, 1996; (jtly) Lifelong Learning and the University, 1998; Managing Strategy, 2000; (jtly) New Directions in Professional Higher Education, 2000; papers on history of American and British ideas, higher education policy. *Recreations:* tennis, music (piano and saxophone), cricket. *Address:* University of Brighton, Mithras House, Lewes Road, Brighton BN2 4AT. *T:* (01273) 642001.

WATSON, Very Rev. Derek Richard; Dean of Salisbury, since 1996; *b* 18 Feb. 1938; *s* of Richard Goodman and Honor Joan Watson; *m* 1985, Rev. Sheila Anne Atkinson. *Educ:* Uppingham Sch.; Selwyn Coll., Cambridge (MA 1965); Cuddesdon Coll., Oxford. Ordained deacon, 1964, priest, 1965; Asst Curate, All Saints, New Eltham, 1964–66; Chaplain, Christ's Coll., Cambridge, 1966–70; Domestic Chaplain to Bishop of Southwark, 1970–73; Vicar, St Andrews and St Mark's, Surbiton, 1973–78; Canon Treasurer, Southwark Cathedral and Diocesan Dir of Ordinands and Post Ordination Training, 1978–82; Rector, St Luke and Christchurch, Chelsea, 1982–96. Chm., Chelsea Festival, 1993–96. *Recreations:* swimming, cycling. *Address:* The Deanery, 7 The Close, Salisbury, Wilts SP1 2EF.

WATSON, Sir Duncan (Amos), Kt 1993; CBE 1986; Principal Assistant Treasury Solicitor, Common Law, 1978–86; Chairman, Executive Council, Royal National Institute for the Blind, 1975–90; *b* 10 May 1926; *m* 1954, Mercia Casey, Auckland, NZ. *Educ:* Worcester College for the Blind; St Edmund Hall, Oxford (BA). Solicitor. Chm., Access Cttee for England, 1989–93; Pres., World Blind Union, 1988–92. *Address:* 19 Great Russell Mansions, WC1B 3BE.

WATSON, Gavin; *see* Watson, A. G.

WATSON, Gerald Walter; Chairman, Centaur Trust, since 1999; *b* 13 Dec. 1934; *s* of Reginald Harold Watson and Gertrude Hilda Watson (*née* Ruffell); *m* 1961, Janet Rosemary (*née* Hovey); one *s* two *d*. *Educ:* King Edward VI, Norwich School; Corpus Christi Coll., Cambridge (MA). National Service, RAF Regt, 1953–55. War Office, 1958–64; MoD, 1964–69; Civil Service Dept, 1969–73; Northern Ireland Office, 1973–75; CSD, 1975–81; HM Treasury, 1981–86; Dir, Central Computer and Telecommunications Agency, 1978–82; Partner, Banking Gp, Ernst & Young (formerly Arthur Young), 1989–98. Dep. Chm., Building Socs Commn, 1986–88. *Recreations:* opera and theatre going, equestrian sports. *Address:* Topcroft Lodge, Bungay, Suffolk NR35 2BB.

WATSON, Graham Robert; Member (Lib Dem) South West Region, England, European Parliament, since 1999 (Somerset and North Devon, 1994–99); *b* 23 March 1956; *s* of late Gordon Graham Watson and of Stephanie Revill-Johnson; *m* 1987, Rita Giannini; one *s* one *d*. *Educ:* City of Bath Boys' Sch.; Heriot-Watt Univ. (BA Hons Mod. Langs). Freelance interpreter and translator, 1979–80; Administrator, Paisley Coll. of Tech., 1980–83; Head, Private Office of Rt Hon. David Steel, MP, 1983–87; Sen. Press Officer, TSB Group, 1987–88; HSBC Holdings: Public Affairs Manager, 1988–91; Govt Affairs Manager, 1992–94. *Publications:* (ed) The Liberals in the North-South Dialogue, 1980; (ed) To the Power of Ten, 2000; articles on politics in magazines and nat. newspapers. *Recreations:* sailing, walking. *Address:* European Parliament, 1040 Brussels, Belgium. *T:* (2) 2845626; Liberal Democrat Office, Bagehot's Foundry, Beards Yard, Langport, Som TA10 9PS. *T:* (01458) 252265. *Club:* Royal Commonwealth Society.

WATSON, Henry, CBE 1969; QPM 1963; Chief Constable of Cheshire, 1963–74; *b* 16 Oct. 1910; *s* of John and Ann Watson, Preston, Lancs; *m* 1933, Nellie Greenhalgh; two *d*. *Educ:* Preston Victoria Junior Technical Coll. Admitted to Inst. of Chartered Accountants, 1934; joined Ashton-under-Lyne Borough Police, 1934; King's Lynn Borough Police, 1942; Norfolk County Constabulary, 1947; Asst Chief Constable, Cumberland and Westmorland, 1955, Chief Constable, 1959. CStJ 1973. *Recreation:* golf. *Address:* Gorgate Road, Hoe, Dereham, Norfolk NR20 4BG.

WATSON, Maj.-Gen. (Henry) Stuart (Ramsay), CBE 1973 (MBE 1954); *b* 9 July 1922; *yr s* of Major H. A. Watson, CBE, MVO and Mrs Dorothy Bannerman Watson, OBE; *m* 1965, Susan, *o d* of Col W. H. Jackson, CBE, DL; two *s* one *d*. *Educ:* Winchester College. Commnd 2nd Lieut 13th/18th Royal Hussars, 1942; Lieut 1943; Captain 1945; Adjt 13/18 H, 1945–46 and 1948–50; psc 1951; GSO2, HQ 1st Corps, 1952–53; Instr RMA Sandhurst, 1955–57; Instr Staff Coll. Camberley, 1960–62; CO 13/18 H, 1962–64; GSO1, MoD, 1964–65; Col GS, SHAPE, 1965–68; Col, Defence Policy Staff. MoD, 1968; idc 1969; BGS HQ BAOR, 1970–73; Dir Defence Policy, MoD, 1973–74; Sen. Army Directing Staff, RCDS, 1974–76. Col, 13th/18th Royal Hussars, 1979–90. Exec. Dir, 1977–85, Dep. Dir Gen., 1985–88, Inst. of Dirs; Dir, Treasurers' Dept, Cons. Central Office, 1992–94. *Recreations:* golf, gardening. *Address:* The White Cross, Askett, Princes Risborough, Bucks HP27 9LR. *T:* and *Fax:* (01844) 347601. *Clubs:* Cavalry and Guards; Huntercombe Golf.

WATSON, Dr Iain Arthur; Integrated Project Team Leader, BOWMAN and Land Digitization, Ministry of Defence, since 1999; *b* 21 Nov. 1947; *s* of Alastair Cameron Watson and Lilian Ellen Watson (*née* Smith); *m* 1st, 1968, Janet Marshall (marr. diss. 1995); one *s* one *d*; 2nd, 1998, Pamela Chambers (*née* Low). *Educ:* Stratford Grammar Sch.; Dundee Univ. (BSc Pure Maths 1970; MSc Maths 1972; PhD 1976). Ministry of Defence: Underwater Research, Portland, 1974–89; Director: IT Systems, 1989–91; IT Strategy, 1991–92; Fleet Support (Communications and Inf. Systems), 1992–97; Dir Gen., Command Inf. Systems, 1997–99. *Recreations:* dinghy sailing, basketball, car restoration, ski-ing, history. *Address:* Defence Procurement Agency, Ministry of Defence, Abbey Wood #147, Bristol BS34 8JH. *T:* (0117) 913 3240.

WATSON, Sir (James) Andrew, 5th Bt *cr* 1866; a Recorder, since 1989; *b* 30 Dec. 1937; *s* of Sir Thomas Aubrey Watson, 4th Bt and Ella Marguerite, *y d* of late Sir George Farrar, 1st Bt, DSO; *S* father, 1941; *m* 1965, Christabel Mary, *e d* of K. R. M. Carlisle and Hon. Mrs Carlisle; two *s* one *d*. *Educ:* Eton. Called to the Bar, Inner Temple, 1966. *Heir: s* Roland Victor Watson, *b* 4 March 1966. *Address:* Talton House, Newbold-on-Stour, Stratford-upon-Avon, Warwickshire CV37 8UB. *T:* (01789) 450212.

WATSON, Prof. James Dewey; President, Cold Spring Harbor Laboratory, since 1994 (Director, 1968–94); *b* 6 April 1928; *s* of James D. and Jean Mitchell Watson; *m* 1968, Elizabeth Lewis; two *s*. *Educ:* Univ. of Chicago (BS); Indiana Univ. (PhD); Clare Coll., Cambridge (Hon. Fellow, 1967). Senior Res. Fellow in Biology, California Inst. of Technology, 1953–55; Harvard University: Asst Prof. of Biology, 1956–58; Associate Prof., 1958–61; Prof. of Molecular Biology, 1961–76. Dir, Nat. Center for Human Genome Res., NIH, 1989–92. Newton-Abraham Vis. Prof., Oxford, 1994. Member: US National Acad. Sciences, 1962–; Amer Acad. of Arts and Sciences, 1958; Royal Danish Acad. 1962; Amer. Philosophical Soc., 1977; Foreign Member: Royal Soc., 1981; Acad. of Scis, Russia (formerly USSR), 1989; NAS, Ukraine, 1995. Hon. FIBiol 1995; Hon. Fellow, Tata Inst. of Fundamental Res., Bombay, 1996. Hon. degrees include: Hon. DSc: Chicago, 1961; Indiana, 1963; Long Island, 1970; Adelphi, 1972; Brandeis, 1973; Albert Einstein Coll. of Medicine, 1974; Hofstra, 1976; Harvard, 1978; Rockefeller, 1980; Clarkson Coll., 1981; SUNY, 1983; Rutgers, 1988; Bard Coll., 1991; Univ. of Stellenbosch, S Africa, 1993; Fairfield Univ., Conn, 1993; Cambridge, 1993; Oxford, 1995; Melbourne, 1996; Univ. of Judaism, LA, 1999; London, Illinois Wesleyan, 2000; Widener, Dartmouth, 2001; Hon. MD: Buenos Aires, 1986; Charles Univ., Prague, 1998; Hon. LLD Notre Dame, 1965. Awards include: Nobel Prize for Physiology or Medicine (jointly), 1962; Carty Medal, US NAS, 1971; Kaul Foundn Award for Excellence, 1992; Copley Medal, Royal Soc., 1993; Nat. Biotechnol. Venture Award, 1993; Nat. Medal of Science, USA, 1997; Mendel Medal, Czechoslovakia, 1998; Univ. of Chicago Medal, 1998; Heald Award, Illinois Inst. of Technol., 1999; NY Acad. of Medicine Award, 1999; Univ. Medal, SUNY, 2000; UCL Prize, 2000; (jtly) Benjamin Franklin Medal, APS, 2001. Liberty Medal, City of Philadelphia, 2000. US Presidential Medal of Freedom, 1977. *Publications:* (jtly) Molecular Biology of the Gene, 1965, 4th edn 1986; The Double Helix, 1968; (with John Tooze) The DNA Story, 1981; (with others) The Molecular Biology of the Cell, 1983, 3rd edn 1994; (with John Tooze and David T. Kurtz) Recombinant DNA: a short course, 1984, 2nd edn (with others) 1992; A Passion for DNA, 2000; scientific papers on the mechanism of heredity. *Recreation:* tennis. *Address:* Bungtown Road, Cold Spring Harbor, NY 11724, USA. *Clubs:* Century, Piping Rock, Brook (New York).

WATSON, James Kay Graham, PhD; FRS 1987; FRSC 1990; Principal Research Officer, National Research Council of Canada, since 1987 (Senior Research Officer, 1982–87); *b* Denny, Stirlingshire, 20 April 1936; *s* of Thomas Watson and Mary Catherine (*née* Miller); *m* 1981, Carolyn Margaret Landon Kerr, *e d* of late Robert Reid Kerr. *Educ:* Denny High Sch.; High School of Stirling; Univ. of Glasgow (BScChem, PhD). Postdoctoral Fellow: UCL, 1961–63; Nat. Res. Council, Ottawa, 1963–65; Univ. of Reading, 1965–66; Lectr in Chem. Physics, Univ. of Reading, 1966–71; Vis. Associate Prof. of Physics, Ohio State Univ., Columbus, 1971–75; SRC Sen. Res. Fellow in Chemistry, Univ. of Southampton, 1975–82. Fellow, American Physical Soc., 1990. Award for Theoretical Chemistry and Spectroscopy, Chemical Soc., 1974; Plyler Prize, Amer. Phys. Soc., 1986; H. M. Tory Medal, Royal Soc. of Can., 1999. *Publications:* 140 articles on molecular physics and spectroscopy in learned jls. *Recreations:* music, golf, tree-watching. *Address:* 183 Stanley Avenue, Ottawa, ON K1M 1P2, Canada. *T:* (613) 7457928; (business) Steacie Institute for Molecular Sciences, National Research Council of Canada, Ottawa, ON K1A OR6, Canada. *T:* (613) 9900739; *e-mail:* james.watson@nrc.ca.

WATSON, James Kenneth, FCA; Chairman: Alldays (formerly Watson & Philip) plc, 1994–99; NFC plc (formerly National Freight Consortium), 1991–94 (Finance Director, 1982–84; Deputy Chairman, 1985–90); *b* 16 Jan. 1935; *s* of James and Helen Watson; *m* 1959, Eileen Fay Waller (marr. diss. 1998); two *s* one *d*; *m* 2001, Sylvia Grace Bailey. *Educ:* Watford Grammar Sch.; Stanford Univ., California, USA. Baker Sutton & Co., Chartered Accountants, 1964; Financial Controller, Times Group, 1968; Finance Director: British Road Services Ltd, 1970–76; Nat. Freight Corp., later Nat. Freight Co., 1977–82. Non-executive Director: Gartmore, 1993–96; Henlys Group, 1994–2000; National Express, 1994–. Chm., Inst. of Management, 1993–96. *Publications:* contribs to transport, management and financial press. *Recreations:* cricket, theatre, history. *Address:* Benton Potts, Hawridge Common, near Chesham, Bucks HP5 2UH. *Clubs:* Royal Automobile, MCC.

WATSON, Prof. James Patrick; Professor of Psychiatry, Guy's, King's and St Thomas' School of Medicine of King's College London (formerly UMDS), 1974–2000, now Emeritus; *b* 14 May 1936; *e s* of Hubert Timothy Watson and Grace Emily (*née* Mizen); *m* 1962, Dr Christine Mary Colley; four *s*. *Educ:* Roan Sch. for Boys, Greenwich; Trinity Coll., Cambridge; King's Coll. Hosp. Med. Sch., London. MA, MD; FRCP, FRCPsych, DPM, DCH. Qualified, 1960. Hosp. appts in Medicine, Paediatrics, Pathology, Neurosurgery, at King's Coll. Hosp. and elsewhere, 1960–64; Registrar and Sen. Registrar, Bethlem Royal and Maudsley Hosps, 1964–71; Sen. Lectr in Psychiatry, St George's Hosp. Med. Sch., and Hon. Consultant Psychiatrist, St George's Hosp., 1971–74. Member: British Assoc. for Behavioural Psychotherapy; British Psychological Soc.; Soc. for Psychotherapy Res.; Assoc. of Sexual and Marital Therapists. Mem., various bodies concerned with interfaces between counselling and psychotherapy, religion and medicine. *Publications:* (ed jtly) Personal Meanings, 1982; papers on gp, family, marital and behavioural psychotherapy, treatment of phobias, hospital ward environmental effects on patients, postnatal depression, community psychiatry, in BMJ, Lancet, British Jl of Psychiatry, British Jl of Med. Psychology, British Jl of Clin. Psychology, Behaviour Research and Therapy. *Recreations:* mountains; music, especially opera, especially Mozart. *Address:* 36 Alleyn Road, SE21 8AL. *T:* (020) 8670 0444.

WATSON, Ven. Jeffrey John Seagrief; Archdeacon of Ely, since 1993; *b* 29 April 1939; *s* of late John Cole Watson and of Marguerite Freda Rose Watson; *m* 1969, Rosemary Grace Lea; one *s* one *d*. *Educ:* University College Sch., Hampstead; Emmanuel Coll., Cambridge (MA Hons Classics); Clifton Theol Coll., Bristol. Curate: Christ Church, Beckenham, 1965–69; St Jude, Southsea, 1969–71; Vicar: Christ Church, Winchester, 1971–81; Holy Saviour, Bitterne, 1981–93; Examining Chaplain to Bishop of Winchester, 1976–93; RD of Southampton, 1983–93; Hon. Canon: Winchester Cathedral, 1991–93; Ely Cathedral, 1993–. Mem., Gen. Synod, 1985–95; Chm., C of E Vocations Adv. Sub-Cttee, 1991–99; Chm., Ministry Div. Candidates' Panel, 1999–. *Recreations:* photography, barbershop singing, walking, travel (when I have time and money!). *Address:* St Botolph's Rectory, 1a Summerfield, Cambridge CB3 9HE. *T:* (01223) 515725, *Fax:* (01223) 571322; *e-mail:* archdeacon.ely@ely.anglican.org.

WATSON, Jenny; communications and human rights consultant; Deputy Chair, Equal Opportunities Commission, since 2000; Director, Banking Code Standards Board, since 2001; *b* 25 Jan. 1964; *d* of Ronald Watson and Phyllis Watson (*née* Avery). *Educ:* Coopers' Co. and Coborn Sch., Upminster; Sheffield Hallam Univ. (BA Communications Studies); Univ. of Westminster (MA 20th Century British Hist.). Promotions Manager, Liberty (NCCL), 1993–95; Campaign and Communications Manager, and Co-ordinator, Human Rights Develt Network, Charter 88, 1996–98; Media and PR Manager, Victim Support, 1999; Comr, EOC, 1999–2000; Develt Dir, Human Rights Act Res. Unit, KCL, 2000–01. Chair, Indep. Transparency Rev. Panel, Nirex UK, 2001–. Chm., Fawcett Soc., 1997–2001. Mem., Mgt Cttee, Liby of Women, London Guildhall Univ., 2001–. *Recreations:* gardening, singing (Mem., London Philharmonic Choir), reading, walking, campaigning. *Address:* Equal Opportunities Commission, 36 Broadway, SW1H 0XH. *T:* (020) 7222 1110.

WATSON, John, FRCS, FRCSE; Consultant Plastic Surgeon to: Queen Victoria Hospital, East Grinstead, 1950–77, now Hon. Consultant; King Edward VII Hospital for Officers, 1963–87; London Hospital, 1963–82; *b* 10 Sept. 1914; *s* of late John Watson; *m* 1941, June Christine Stiles; one *s* three *d*. *Educ:* Leighton Park, Reading; Jesus Coll., Cambridge; Guy's Hospital. MRCS, LRCP 1938; MA, MB, BChir (Cantab) 1939; FRCS(Ed.) 1946; FRCS 1963. Served as Sqdn Ldr (temp.) RAF, 1940–46 (despatches twice). Marks Fellow in Plastic Surgery, Queen Victoria Hosp., E Grinstead, 1947–50; Consultant Plastic Surgeon, Queen Victoria Hospital, East Grinstead, and Tunbridge Wells Gp of Hospitals, 1950–77. Gen. Sec., Internat. Confedn for Plastic and Reconstructive Surgery, 1971–75; Hon. Mem. Brit. Assoc. of Plastic Surgeons, 1979– (Hon. Sec., 1960–62, Pres., 1969); Hon. MRSocMed. *Publications:* numerous articles on plastic surgery in techn. jls and scientific periodicals. Chapters in: Textbook of Surgery, Plastic Surgery for Nurses, Modern Trends in Plastic Surgery, Clinical Surgery. *Recreations:* fishing, astronomy. *Address:* Iddons, Henley's Down, Catsfield, Battle, East Sussex TN33 9BN. *T:* (01424) 830226.

WATSON, Sir John Forbes I.; *see* Inglefield-Watson.

WATSON, John Grenville Bernard, OBE 1998; Chairman, Bradford Community NHS Trust, since 1996; Vice Chairman, Yorkshire Building Society, since 2000; *b* 21 Feb. 1943; *s* of Norman V. Watson and Ruby E. Watson; *m* 1965, Deanna Wood; one *s* two *d*. *Educ:* Moorlands Sch., Leeds; Bootham Sch., York; College of Law, Guildford. Articled, 1962, qualified as solicitor, 1967; joined John Waddington Ltd as managerial trainee, 1968; Export Director, Plastona John Waddington Ltd, 1972; Marketing Dir, 1975, Man. Dir, 1977, Waddington Games Ltd, responsible for Security Printing Div., 1984–89, for Johnsen & Jorgensen, 1988–89; Director: John Waddington PLC, 1979–89; Goddard Kay Rogers (Northern) Ltd, 1989–92; Chief Exec., Bradford City Challenge Ltd, 1992–97. Dir, Yorkshire Building Soc., 1995–. Mem., Leeds Develt Corp., 1988–92. Joined Young Conservatives, 1965; Chairman, Yorkshire YC, 1969; Personal Asst to Rt Hon. Edward Heath, 1970; Chm., Nat. YC, 1971; contested (C) York, general elections, Feb. and Oct. 1974. MP (C): Skipton, 1979–83; Skipton and Ripon, 1983–87. Chm., Conservative Candidates Assoc., 1975–79. Mem., Parly Select Cttee on Energy, 1980–82; PPS, NI Office, 1982–83; PPS, Dept of Energy, 1983–85. Chm., British Atlantic Gp of Young Political Leaders, 1982–84; Nat. Vice Pres., Young Conservative Orgn, 1984–86. Pres., British Youth Council, 1980–83. *Recreations:* bungee jumping, impersonating Elvis Presley. *Address:* Evergreen Cottage, Main Street, Kirk Deighton, Leeds LS22 4DZ. *T:* (01937) 588273.

See also V. H. Watson.

WATSON, (John Hugh) Adam, CMG 1958; Professor, Center for Advanced Studies, University of Virginia, 1980–95; *b* 10 Aug. 1914; *er s* of Joseph Charlton Watson and Alice (*née* Tate); *m* 1950, Katharine Anne Campbell; two *s* one *d*. *Educ:* Rugby; King's Coll., Camb. Entered the Diplomatic Service, 1937; Brit. Legation, Bucharest, 1939; Brit. Embassy, Cairo, 1940; Brit. Embassy, Moscow, 1944; FO, 1947; Brit. Embassy,

Washington, 1950; Head of African Dept, Foreign Office, 1956–59; appointed British Consul-General at Dakar, 1959; British Ambassador: to the Federation of Mali, 1960–61; to Senegal, Mauritania and Togo, 1960–62; to Cuba, 1963–66; Under-Secretary, Foreign Office, 1966–68; Diplomatic Adviser, British Leyland Motor Corp., 1968–73. Gwilym Gibbon Fellow, Nuffield Coll., Oxford, Oct. 1962–Oct. 1963. Vis. Fellow, ANU, 1973; Vis. Prof., Univ. of Virginia, 1978. Dir Gen., Internat. Assoc. for Cultural Freedom, 1974. *Publications:* The War of the Goldsmith's Daughter, 1964; Nature and Problems of Third World, 1968; (ed) The Origins of History, 1981; Diplomacy: the dialogue between States, 1982; (with Hedley Bull) The Expansion of International Society, 1984; The Evolution of International Society, 1992; The Limits of Independence, 1997; various plays broadcast by BBC. *Address:* Sharnden Old Manor, Mayfield, East Sussex TN20 6QA. *T:* (01435) 872441; 1871 Field Road, Charlottesville, VA 22903, USA. *T:* (804) 2958295. *Club:* Brooks's.

WATSON, (Leslie) Michael (Macdonald) S.; *see* Saunders Watson.

WATSON, Prof. Newton Frank, RIBA; Haden/Pilkington Professor of Environmental Design and Engineering, and Head, Bartlett School of Architecture and Planning, University College London, 1985–88, now Emeritus Professor; Dean of the Faculty of Environmental Studies, 1986–88; *b* 29 July 1923; *s* of Frank Watson and Amy Watson (*née* Cole); *m* 1944, Bridget Williams; two *d. Educ:* Holywell Grammar Sch.; King's Coll., Univ. of Durham. BArch. Wartime service, RWF (Lieut). Asst architect in practice, 1951–55; Res. Fellow, Nuffield Foundn Div. for Architectural Studies, 1955–57; Lectr in Arch., Poly. of N London, 1957–60; Lectr/Sen. Lectr in Arch., UCL, 1960–69; Bartlett Prof. of Architecture, UCL, 1969–85. Vis. Prof., Dept. of Arch., Univ. of California at Berkeley, 1965–66; Vis. Scholar, Sch. of Design, N Carolina State Univ., 1989. Awards (jtly) by Illuminating Soc. of Amer. for lighting design of London Stock Exchange, 1974, and Tate Gall., 1980. *Publications:* (jtly) in Design for Research, 1986; contribs to professional jls on lighting design (CIBSE medal (jtly) 1982, for contrib. Preferred Lighting Levels for Viewing Works of Art. *Recreations:* etching, France. *Address:* 1b Oval Road, NW1 7EA. *T:* (020) 7485 4796. *Club:* Athenæum.

WATSON, Dr Peter, OBE 1988; FREng; Chief Executive, AEA Technology, since 1994; *b* 9 Jan. 1944; *m* 1966, Elizabeth Buttery; two *s. Educ:* Univ. of Leeds (BSc 1966); Univ. of Waterloo, Canada (MSc 1968; PhD 1971). FIMechE; FREng (FEng 1998); FCIPS. PSO, British Railways Res., 1971–76; GKN Technology Ltd, 1976–89 (Chm., 1982–89); Chm., GKN Axles Ltd, 1986–91; Technical Dir, British Railways, 1991–94. Non-executive Director: Spectris (formerly Fairey) Plc, 1997–; Martin Currie Enhanced Income Trust, 2000–. Pres., Engrg Integrity Soc., 1988–. Chm., Engrg Policy Cttee, Sheffield Hallam Univ., 1990–; Mem. Bd, Univ. of Wolverhampton, 1993–. Hon. FAPM. FRSA 1988. *Publications:* numerous articles on metal fatigue and management. *Address:* 49 Suckling Green Lane, Codsall, Wolverhampton, W Midlands WV8 2BT. *T:* (01902) 845252.

WATSON, Most Rev. Peter Robert; *see* Melbourne, Archbishop of.

WATSON, Vice-Adm. Sir Philip (Alexander), KBE 1976; LVO 1960; *b* 7 Oct. 1919; *yr s* of A. H. St C. Watson; *m* 1948, Jennifer Beatrice Tanner; one *s* two *d. Educ:* St Albans School. FIEE 1963; CIMgt (CBIM 1973). Sub-Lt RNVR, 1940; qual. Torpedo Specialist, 1943; transf. to RN, 1946; Comdr 1955; HM Yacht Britannia, 1957–59; Captain 1963; MoD (Ship Dept), 1963; Senior Officers' War Course, 1966; comd HMS Collingwood, 1967; Dep. Dir of Engrg (Ship Dept), MoD, 1969; Dir Gen. Weapons (Naval), MoD, 1970–77; Chief Naval Engineer Officer, 1974–77. Rear-Adm. 1970; Vice-Adm. 1974. Director: Marconi International Marine Co. Ltd, 1977–86; Marconi Radar Systems Ltd, 1981–86 (Chm., 1981–85); Consultant, GEC–Marconi Ltd, 1986–87. Mem. Council, IEE, 1975–78, 1982–91, Chm. South East Centre, 1982–83. Adm. Pres., Midland Naval Officers Assoc., 1979–85, Vice Pres., 1985–. *Address:* The Hermitage, Bodicote, Banbury, Oxon OX15 4BZ. *T:* (01295) 263300.

WATSON, Richard (Eagleson Gordon) Burges, CMG 1985; HM Diplomatic Service, retired; Ambassador to Nepal, 1987–90; *b* 23 Sept. 1930; *er s* of late Harold Burges Watson and Marjorie Eleanor (*née* Gordon); *m* 1966, Ann Rosamund Clarke; two *s* three *d. Educ:* King Edward VI Sch., Bury St Edmunds; St John's Coll., Cambridge. RA, 1948–50. Joined HM Foreign (subseq. Diplomatic) Service, 1954; Tokyo, 1954–60; FO, 1960–63; Bamako (Mali), 1963–66; British Delegn to OECD, 1966–69; FCO, 1969–71; Vis. Student, Woodrow Wilson Sch., Princeton, 1971–72; Tokyo, 1972–76; Brussels, 1976–78; FCO, 1978–81; Foundn for Internat. Research and Studies, Florence, 1981–82; FCO, 1982–83; Minister (Commercial) and Consul-Gen., Milan, 1983–86. *Recreations:* travel, bridge, walking. *Address:* Highfield House, Gloucester Road, Painswick GL6 6QN. *T:* (01452) 814763. *Clubs:* Travellers, Hurlingham.

WATSON, Sir Ronald (Matthew), Kt 1997; CBE 1989; Member (C), Sefton Metropolitan Borough Council, 1974–91 and since 1992; Deputy Leader, Conservative Group, Local Government Association, 1996–2000; *b* 24 May 1945; *s* of Ralph and Rheta Mary Watson; *m* 1966, Lesley Ann McLean; one *s* one *d. Educ:* South Shields GS; Waterloo GS. General Manager: Laycock Travel Services, 1970–92; Morrisons Travel Agents, 1970–92. Mem. (C), Southport CBC, 1969–74; Leader, Sefton MBC, 1983–87. Leader, Cons. Gp, AMA, 1992–97. Non-exec. Dir, Southport & Formby, subseq. Sefton, HA, 1991–. Mem., EU Cttee of the Regions, 1998–. Consultant, Eur. Advice Unit, Barnetts, Solicitors, Southport, 1994–. Mem., Audit Commn, 1995–. Founder Mem. and Fellow, Tourism Soc., 1978; Fellow, Inst. of Travel and Tourism, 1989. *Recreation:* writer on jazz and blues. *Address:* 7 Carnoustie Close, Oxford Road, Birkdale, Southport PR8 2FB.

WATSON, Roy William, CBE 1983; Director General, National Farmers' Union, 1979–85, retired; *b* 7 Feb. 1926; *s* of William and Eleanor Maud Watson; *m* 1st, 1947, Margaret Peasey; two *s*; 2nd, 1977, Phyllis Frances Brotherwood (*née* Farrer). *Educ:* Alleyn's Sch., Dulwich. Intelligence Corps, 1945–48. National Farmers' Union, 1948–85: Asst Dir General, 1973–78; Dep. Dir General, 1978. Mem., UK Employer Delegn to ILO, 1961–76; formerly Mem., ILO Permanent Agric. Cttee and Cttee on Rural Develt; Employer Deleg. to World Employment Conf., 1976. *Recreations:* music, military history, golf, gardening. *Address:* Galilee, 44 Greenway, Frinton-on-Sea, Essex CO13 9AL. *T:* (01255) 679651.

WATSON, Prof. Stephen Roger; Principal, Henley Management College, since 2001; Fellow of Emmanuel College, Cambridge, since 1968; *b* 29 Aug. 1943; *s* of John C. Watson and Marguerite F. R. Watson; *m* 1969, Rosemary Victoria Tucker; one *s* one *d. Educ:* University College Sch., Hampstead; Emmanuel Coll., Cambridge (BA 1964, MA 1968, PhD 1969). Research Fellow, Emmanuel Coll., Cambridge, 1968–70; Shell International, 1970–71; Cambridge University: Univ. Lectr in Operational Research, Engineering Dept, 1971–86; Tutor, Emmanuel Coll., 1973–85; Peat, Marwick Prof. of Management Studies, 1986–94; Dir, Judge Inst. of Management Studies, 1990–94; Dean, Lancaster Univ. Mgt Sch., 1994–2001. Director: Cambridge Decision Analysts Ltd, 1984–95; Environmental Resources Management, 1989–95. *Publications:* Decision Synthesis (with D. M. Buede), 1987; papers in learned jls. *Recreations:* singing, development issues. *Address:* Henley Management College, Greenlands, Henley-on-Thames, Oxon RG9 3AU. *T:* (01491) 418831.

WATSON, Stewart; *see* Watson, D. S.

WATSON, Maj.-Gen. Stuart; *see* Watson, Maj.-Gen. H. S. R.

WATSON, Thomas; MP (Lab) West Bromwich East, since 2001; *b* 8 Jan. 1967; *s* of Tony and Linda Watson; *m* 2000, Siobhan Corbu. *Educ:* Hull Univ. Fundraiser, Save the Children, 1988–89; Account Manager, P. Barker & Associates, 1989–90; Chair, Nat. Orgn of Labour Students, 1992–93; Dep. Gen. Election Co-ordinator, Labour Party, 1993–97; Nat. Political Organiser, AEEU, 1997–2001. *Recreation:* Playstation 2. *Address:* House of Commons, SW1A 0AA. *Club:* West Bromwich Labour.

WATSON, Thomas Sturges; professional golfer, since 1971; *b* 4 Sept. 1949; *s* of Raymond Etheridge Watson and Sarah Elizabeth Watson (*née* Ridge); *m* 1973, Linda Tova Rubin (marr. diss. 1998); one *s* one *d. Educ:* Stanford Univ. (BS 1971). Championships include: Open, 1975, 1977, 1980, 1982, 1983; US Open, 1982; Masters, 1977, 1981; Mem., Ryder Cup team, 1977, 1981, 1983, 1989, Captain, 1993. *Address:* 1901 W 47th Place, Suite 200, Shawnee Mission, KS 66205, USA.

WATSON, Victor Hugo, CBE 1987; DL; *b* 26 Sept. 1928; *s* of Norman Victor and Ruby Ernestine Watson; *m* 1952, Sheila May Bryan; two *d. Educ:* Clare Coll., Cambridge (MA). Served Royal Engineers (2nd Lieut), 1946–48. Joined John Waddington Ltd, 1951; Chm., 1977–93, retired. Director: Leeds & Holbeck Building Soc., 1985–99 (Pres., 1989–91); Stylo PLC, 1993–99; Topps Tiles PLC, 1997–; Black i Ltd, 1998–. Pres., Inst. of Packaging, 1984–. DL West Yorks, 1991. Hon. LLD Leeds, 1994. *Recreations:* music, golf, sailing. *Address:* Moat Field, Moor Lane, East Keswick, Leeds LS17 9ET.

WATSON, Prof. William, CBE 1982; MA; FBA 1972; FSA; Professor of Chinese Art and Archaeology in University of London, at the School of Oriental and African Studies, 1966–83, now Emeritus, and Head of the Percival David Foundation of Chinese Art, 1966–83; *b* 9 Dec. 1917; *s* of Robert Scoular Watson and Lily Waterfield; *m* 1940, Katherine Sylvia Mary, *d* of Mr and Mrs J. H. Armfield, Ringwood, Hants; four *s. Educ:* Glasgow High Sch.; Herbert Strutt Sch.; Gonville and Caius Coll., Cantab (Scholar; tripos in Modern and Medieval Langs). Served Intelligence Corps, 1940–46, Egypt, N Africa, Italy, India, ending as Major. Asst Keeper, British Museum, first in Dept of British and Medieval Antiquities, then in Dept of Oriental Antiquities, 1947–66. Slade Prof. of Fine Art, Cambridge University, 1975–76. Trustee, BM, 1980–90. Pres., Oriental Ceramic Soc., 1981–84. Hon. DLitt Chinese Univ. of Hong Kong, 1984. Sir Percy Sykes Meml Medal, 1973. *Publications:* The Sculpture of Japan, 1959; Archaeology in China, 1960; China before the Han Dynasty, 1961; Ancient Chinese Bronzes, 1961; Jade Books in the Chester Beatty Library, 1963; Cultural Frontiers in Ancient East Asia, 1971; The Genius of China (catalogue of Burlington House exhibn), 1973; Style in the Arts of China, 1974; L'Art de l'Ancienne Chine, 1980; (ed) Catalogue of the Great Japan Exhibition (at Burlington House 1981–82); Tang and Liao Ceramics, 1984; Pre-Tang Ceramics of China, 1991; The Arts of China to AD 900, 1995; Collected Papers, 2 vols, 1997, 1998; The Arts of China 900–1620, 2000. *Recreation:* exploring N Wales, Romanesque France and Spain. *Address:* Cefn y Maes, Parc, Bala, Gwynedd LL23 7YS. *T:* (01678) 540302.

WATSON, William Albert, CB 1989; PhD; FRCVS; Director, Veterinary Laboratories, Ministry of Agriculture, Fisheries and Food, 1986–90; international veterinary consultant, 1990–97; *b* 8 March 1930; *s* of Henry Watson and Mary Emily Watson; *m* 1956, Wilma, *d* of Rev. Theodorus Johannas Henricus Steenbeck; one *s* one *d. Educ:* Preston Grammar School; University of Bristol (PhD, BVSc). Private practice, Garstang, Lancs, 1954–55; Asst Vet. Investigation Officer, Weybridge, 1954–56, Leeds, 1956–66; Animal Health Expert, FAO, Turkey, 1966–67; Vet. Investigation Officer, Penrith, 1967–71; Dep. Regional Vet. Officer, Nottingham, 1971–75; Regional Vet. Officer, Edinburgh, 1975–77; Asst Chief Vet. Officer, Tolworth, 1977–84; Dep. Dir, Vet. Labs, Weybridge, 1984–86. External Examr, London, Liverpool, Dublin and Edinburgh Univs. *Publications:* contribs to vet. jls and textbooks. *Recreations:* fishing, gardening, restoration of listed property, farming.

WATSON, Prof. William Alexander Jardine; Ernest P. Rogers Professor of Law, University of Georgia, since 1989; *b* 27 Oct. 1933; *s* of James W. and Janet J. Watson; *m* 1st, 1958, Cynthia Betty Balls, MA, MLitt (marr. diss.); one *s* one *d*; 2nd, 1986, Harriett Camilla Emanuel, BA, MS, JD, LLM; one *d. Educ:* Univ. of Glasgow (MA 1954, LLB 1957); Univ. of Oxford (BA (by decree) 1957, MA 1958, DPhil 1960, DCL 1973). Lectr, Wadham Coll., Oxford, 1957–59; Lectr, 1959–60, Fellow, 1960–65, Oriel Coll., Oxford; Pro-Proctor, Oxford Univ., 1962–63; Douglas Prof. of Civil Law, Univ. of Glasgow, 1965–68; Prof. of Civil Law, Univ. of Edinburgh, 1968–79; University of Pennsylvania: Prof. of Law and Classical Studies, 1979–84; Dir, Center for Advanced Studies in Legal Hist., 1980–89; Nicholas F. Gallichio Prof. of Law, 1984–86; Univ. Prof. of Law, 1986–89. Visiting Professor of Law: Tulane Univ., 1967; Univ. of Virginia, 1970 and 1974; Univ. of Cape Town, 1974 and 1975; Univ. of Michigan, 1977. Mem. Council, Stair Soc., 1970–; Hon. Mem., Speculative Soc., 1975. Hon. LLD Glasgow, 1993. *Publications:* (as Alan Watson): Contract of Mandate in Roman Law, 1961; Law of Obligations in Later Roman Republic, 1965; Law of Persons in Later Roman Republic, 1967; Law of Property in Later Roman Republic, 1968; Law of the Ancient Romans, 1970; Roman Private Law Around 200 BC, 1971; Law of Succession in Later Roman Republic, 1971; Law Making in Later Roman Republic, 1974; Legal Transplants, An Approach to Comparative Law, 1974, 2nd edn 1993; (ed) Daube Noster, 1974; Rome of the Twelve Tables, 1975; Society and Legal Change, 1977; The Nature of Law, 1977; The Making of the Civil Law, 1981; Sources of Law, Legal Change, and Ambiguity, 1984; The Evolution of Law, 1985, enlarged edn as The Evolution of Western Private Law, 2000; (ed) The Digest of Justinian (4 vols), 1986; Failures of the Legal Imagination, 1988; Slave Law of the Americas, 1989; Roman Law and Comparative Law, 1991; The State, Law and Religion: pagan Rome, 1991; Studies in Roman Private Law, 1991; Legal Origins and Legal Change, 1991; The State, Law and Religion: archaic Rome, 1992; Joseph Story and the Comity of Errors, 1993; International Law in Archaic Rome, 1993; The Spirit of Roman Law, 1995; Jesus and the Jews, 1995; The Trial of Jesus, 1995; Jesus and the Law, 1996; The Trial of Stephen, 1996; Jesus: a profile, 1998; Ancient Law and Modern Understanding, 1989; Law Out of Context, 2000; various articles. *Recreations:* Roman numismatics, shooting. *Address:* Law School, University of Georgia, Herty Drive, Athens, GA 30602, USA.

WATT; *see* Gibson-Watt.

WATT, Very Rev. Alfred Ian; Dean of the United Diocese of St Andrews, Dunkeld and Dunblane, 1989–98; *b* 1934. *Educ:* Edinburgh Theol Coll. Deacon, 1960, priest 1961, Diocese of Brechin; Curate, St Paul's Cathedral, Dundee, 1960–63; Precentor, 1963–66;

Rector of Arbroath, 1966–69; Provost of St Ninian's Cathedral, Perth, 1969–82; Canon, 1982–89; Rector, St Paul's, Kinross, 1982–95. Convenor, Mission Bd of General Synod, 1982–87. *Address:* 33 Stirling Road, Milnathort, Kinross KY13 7XS.

WATT, Charlotte Joanne, (Mrs G. L. Watt); *see* Erickson, Prof. C. J.

WATT, Prof. David Anthony, PhD; Professor of Computing Science, University of Glasgow, since 1995; *b* 5 Nov. 1946; *s* of Francis Watt and Mary Watt (*née* Stuart); *m* 1974, Helen Dorothy Day; one *s* one *d*. *Educ:* Univ. of Glasgow (BSc (Eng) 1st Cl. Hons; Dip. Comp. Sci. (Dist.); PhD 1974). University of Glasgow: programmer, Computing Service, 1969–72 and 1974; Department of Computing Science: Lectr, 1974–85; Sen. Lectr, 1985–90; Reader, 1990–95; Head of Dept, 1993–96; Vice-Dean, Faculty of Sci., 1996–. Vis. Associate Prof., Univ. of Calif, Santa Cruz, 1981–82; Vis. Res. Associate, Univ. of Calif, Berkeley, 1985. *Publications:* (with W. Findlay) Pascal: an introduction to methodical programming, 1978, 3rd edn 1985; (jtly) Ada: language and methodology, 1987; Programming Language Concepts and Paradigms, 1990; Programming Language Syntax and Semantics, 1991; Programming Language Processors: compilers and interpreters, 1993. *Recreations:* chess, running, science, history, politics. *Address:* Department of Computing Science, University of Glasgow, Glasgow G12 8QQ. *T:* (0141) 330 4470.

WATT, Prof. Donald C.; *see* Cameron Watt.

WATT, Hamish; writer, politician, farmer; Rector of Aberdeen University, 1985–88; *b* 27 Dec. 1925; *s* of Wm Watt and Caroline C. Allan; *m* 1948, Mary Helen Grant (marr. diss. 1989); one *s* two *d*. *Educ:* Keith Grammar Sch.; St Andrews Univ. Engaged in farming (dairy and sheep). Subseq. company director, quarries. Contested (C), Caithness, 1966; contested (SNP): Banff, 1970; Moray, 1983. MP (SNP) Banff, Feb. 1974–1979. Regional and Dist Councillor (SNP), Moray, 1985–90 (Chm., Educn Cttee, 1986–90). Columnist, after-dinner speaker, story writer. JP Moray, 1984. Hon. LLD Aberdeen, 1988. *Address:* Mill of Buckie, Buckie, Banffshire AB5 2AA. *T:* (01542) 832591. *Clubs:* Farmers', Whitehall Court.

WATT, Surgeon Vice-Adm. Sir James, KBE 1975; MS, FRCS; Medical Director-General (Navy), 1972–77; *b* 19 Aug. 1914; *s* of Thomas Watt and Sarah Alice Clarkson. *Educ:* King Edward VI Sch., Morpeth; Univ. of Durham. MB, BS 1938; MS 1949; FRCS 1955; MD 1972; FRCP 1975. Served War, RN, FE and N Atlantic, 1941–46 (despatches, 1945). Surgical Registrar, Royal Vic. Infirm., Newcastle upon Tyne, 1947; Surgical Specialist: N Ire., 1949; RN Hosp., Hong Kong, 1954; Consultant in Surgery, RN Hospitals: Plymouth, 1956; Haslar, 1959; Malta, 1961; Haslar, 1963; Jt Prof. of Naval Surgery, RCS and RN Hosp., Haslar, 1965–69; Dean of Naval Medicine and MO i/c, Inst. of Naval Medicine, 1969–72. Chm., RN Clin. Research Working Party, 1969–77; Chm. Bd of Trustees, Naval Christian Fellowship, 1968–75; President: Royal Naval Lay Readers Soc., 1973–83; Inst. of Religion and Medicine, 1989–91. QHS 1969–77. Surg. Comdr 1956; Surg. Captain 1965; Surg. Rear-Adm. 1969; Surg. Vice-Adm. 1972. Mem., Environmental Medicine Res. Policy Cttee, MRC, 1974–77. Thomas Vicary Lectr, RCS, 1974; University House Vis. Fellow, ANU, 1986. FICS 1964; Fellow: Assoc. of Surgeons of GB and Ire.; Med. Soc. of London (Mem. Council, 1976; Lettsomian Lectr, 1979; Pres., 1980–81; Vice-Pres., 1981–83); RSocMed (Pres., 1982–84; Hon. FRSocMed 1998); FSA 1991; Hon. FRCSE; Hon. Fellow, Royal Acad. of Medicine in Ireland, 1983; Member: Brit. Soc. for Surgery of the Hand; Internat. Soc. for Burns Injuries; Corr. Mem., Surgical Research Soc., 1966–77; Mem. Editorial Bd, Brit. Jl of Surgery, 1966–77. FRGS 1982; Mem. Council, RGS, 1985–88. Pres., ECHO, 1989–; Vice-Pres., Churches' Council for Health and Healing, 1987–99. Trustee: Marylebone Centre Trust, 1989–93; Medical Soc. of London, 1986–. Gov., Epsom Coll., 1990–. Pres., Smeatonian Soc. of Civil Engineers, 1996 (Hon. Mem., 1978–). Hon. Freeman, Co. of Barbers, 1978. Hon. DCh Newcastle, 1978. Errol-Eldridge Prize, 1968; Gilbert Blane Medal, 1971. CStJ 1972. *Publications:* edited: Starving Sailors, 1981; Talking Health, 1988; What is Wrong with Christian Healing?, 1993; The Church, Medicine and the New Age, 1995; papers on: burns, cancer chemotherapy, peptic ulceration, hyberbaric oxygen therapy, naval medical history. *Recreations:* mountain walking, music. *Address:* 7 Cambisgate, Church Road, Wimbledon, SW19 5AL. *Club:* Royal Over-Seas League.

WATT, Sir James H.; *see* Harvie-Watt.

WATT, James Wilfrid, CVO 1997; HM Diplomatic Service; Head, Consular Division, Foreign and Commonwealth Office, since 2000; *b* 5 Nov. 1951; *s* of late Anthony James MacDonald Watt and Sona Elvey (*née* White); *m* 1980, Elizabeth Ghislaine Villeneuve (*d* 1998), *d* of Marcel Villeneuve and Lorna Oliver Tudsbery; one *s* one *d*. *Educ:* Ampleforth Coll., York; Queen's Coll., Oxford (MA Mod. Langs 1974). Kleinwort Benson, 1974–75; freelance broadcaster and interpreter, Madrid, 1975–77; entered HM Diplomatic Service, 1977; MECAS, 1978; FCO, 1979–80; Abu Dhabi, 1980–83; FCO, 1983–85; UK Permanent Mission to UN, NY, 1985–89; Dep. Hd, UN Dept and Hd, Human Rights Unit, FCO, 1989–92; Dep. Hd of Mission and Consul Gen., Amman, 1992–96; Dep. High Comr, Islamabad, 1996–98; Res. Studentship, SOAS, 1999–2000. *Recreations:* good company, landscapes, tea. *Address:* c/o Foreign and Commonwealth Office, King Charles Street, SW1A 2AH. *Club:* Athenæum.

WATT, John Gillies McArthur; QC (Scot.) 1992; *b* 14 Oct. 1949; *s* of Peter Julius Watt and Nancy (*née* McArthur); *m* 1st, 1972, Catherine (marr. diss. 1988), *d* of Robert Russell, Toronto, Canada; two *d*; 2nd, 1988, Susan, *d* of Dr Tom C. Sparks, Ardmore, Oklahoma, and Breckenridge, Colorado, USA. *Educ:* Clydebank High Sch.; Glasgow Univ.; Edinburgh Univ. (LLB 1971). Solicitor, 1974–78; Advocate at Scottish Bar, 1979; Advocate Depute *ad hoc*, 1990; Temporary Sheriff, 1991; called to the Bar, Middle Temple, 1992. *Recreations:* shooting, ski-ing, sailing, opera. *Address:* 51 Northside Circle, PO Box 2794, Silverthorne, CO 80498, USA. *T:* (970) 3334900, *Fax:* (970) 5137392. *Clubs:* Lansdowne; Royal Western Yacht (Glasgow).

WATT, His Honour Robert; QC (NI) 1964; County Court Judge, 1971–89; *b* 10 March 1923; *s* of John Watt, schoolmaster, Ballymena, Co. Antrim; *m* 1951, Edna Rea; one *d*. *Educ:* Ballymena Academy; Queen's Univ., Belfast (LLB). Called to Bar, Gray's Inn, 1946; called to Bar of Northern Ireland, 1946; Sen. Crown Prosecutor Counties Fermanagh and Tyrone. *Recreation:* sailing. *Address:* 12 Deramore Drive, Belfast BT9 5JQ. *Club:* Royal North of Ireland Yacht.

WATT, Prof. W(illiam) Montgomery; Professor of Arabic and Islamic Studies, University of Edinburgh, 1964–79; *b* Ceres, Fife, 14 March 1909; *o c* of late Rev. Andrew Watt; *m* 1943, Jean Macdonald, *er d* of late Prof. Robert Donaldson; one *s* four *d*. *Educ:* George Watson's Coll., Edinburgh; University of Edinburgh; Balliol Coll., Oxford; University of Jena; Cuddesdon Coll. Warner Exhibition (Balliol), 1930; Ferguson Schol. in Classics, 1931; MA, PhD (Edinburgh); MA, BLitt (Oxon). Asst Lecturer, Moral Philosophy, University of Edinburgh, 1934–38; Curate, St Mary Boltons, London, 1939–41; Curate, Old St Paul's, Edinburgh, 1941–43; Arabic specialist to Bishop in Jerusalem, 1943–46; Lecturer, Ancient Philosophy, University of Edinburgh, 1946–47; Lectr, Sen. Lectr and Reader in Arabic, Univ. of Edinburgh, 1947–64. Visiting Professor: of Islamic Studies, University of Toronto, 1963; Collège de France, Paris, 1970; of Religious Studies, Univ. of Toronto, 1978; of Arab Studies, Georgetown Univ., 1978–79. Chairman, Assoc. of British Orientalists, 1964–65. Editor, series, Islamic Surveys, 1961–79. Hon. DD Aberdeen, 1966; Hon. DLitt Hamdard Univ., Karachi, 1998. Levi Della Vida Medal, Los Angeles, 1981. *Publications:* Free Will and Predestination in Early Islam, 1949; The Faith and Practice of al-Ghazali, 1953; Muhammad at Mecca, 1953; Muhammad at Medina, 1956; The Reality of God, 1958; The Cure for Human Troubles, 1959; Islam and the Integration of Society, 1961; Muhammad Prophet and Statesman, 1961; Islamic Philosophy and Theology, 1962, new enlarged edn, 1986; Muslim Intellectual, 1963; Truth in the Religions, 1963; Islamic Spain, 1965; Islam (in Propyläen Weltgeschichte, XI), 1965; A Companion to the Qur'an, 1967; What is Islam?, 1968; Islamic Political Thought, 1968; Islamic Revelation and the Modern World, 1970; Bell's Introduction to the Qur'an, 1970; The Influence of Islam on Medieval Europe, 1972; The Formative Period of Islamic Thought, 1973; The Majesty that was Islam, 1974; Der Islam, i, 1980, ii, 1985; Islam and Christianity Today, 1984; Muhammad's Mecca, 1988; Islamic Fundamentalism and Modernity, 1988; Early Islam, 1991; Muslim-Christian Encounters, 1991; Islamic Creeds: a selection, 1994; Religious Truth for Our Time, 1995; A Short History of Islam, 1995; contribs learned journals. *Address:* 2 Bridgend, Dalkeith, Midlothian EH22 1JT. *T:* (0131) 663 3197.

WATT, Emeritus Prof. William Smith, MA (Glasgow and Oxon); FBA 1989; Regius Professor of Humanity in the University of Aberdeen, 1952–79, Vice-Principal, 1969–72; *b* 20 June 1913; *s* of John Watt and Agnes Smith; *m* 1944, Dorothea, *e d* of R. J. Codrington Smith; one *s*. *Educ:* University of Glasgow; Balliol Coll., Oxford (Snell Exhibitioner and Hon. Scholar). First Class Hons in Classics, Glasgow Univ., 1933; Ferguson Schol., 1934; Craven Schol., 1934; First Class, Classical Moderations, 1935; Hertford Schol., 1935; Ireland Schol., 1935; First Class, Lit. Hum., 1937. Lecturer in Greek and Greek History, University of Glasgow, 1937–38; Fellow and Tutor in Classics, Balliol Coll., Oxford, 1938–52. Civilian Officer, Admiralty (Naval Intelligence Div.), 1941–45. Convener, Scottish Univs Council on Entrance, 1973–77. Governor, Aberdeen Coll. of Educn, 1958–75 (Chm. of Governors 1971–75). Pres., Classical Assoc. of Scotland, 1983–88. *Publications:* (ed) Ciceronis Epistulae ad Quintum fratrem, etc, 1958, 1965; (ed) Ciceronis Epistularum ad Atticum Libri I-VIII, 1965; (ed) Ciceronis Epistulae ad familiares, 1982; (ed with P. J. Ford) George Buchanan's Miscellaneorum Liber, 1982; (ed) Vellei Paterculi Historiae, 1988; many articles in classical periodicals. *Address:* 38 Woodburn Gardens, Aberdeen AB15 8JA. *T:* (01224) 314369. *Club:* Business and Professional (Aberdeen).

WATTERS, David George; Chief Executive (formerly General Secretary), Primary Immunodeficiency Association, since 1994; *b* 14 Jan. 1945. *Educ:* Stromness Acad., Orkney Is. Church of Scotland lay worker, 1964–68; Social Worker, St Martin-in-the-Fields, 1968–73; Director: Threshold Centre, 1973–78; Alone In London Service, 1978–81; Gen. Sec., Haemophilia Soc., 1981–93. Churchwarden, All Saints, Tooting, 1978–84 and 1994–98. JP Inner London, 1980–2000. *Recreations:* music, photography, birdwatching, travel, Cornwall, Orkney, theology, reading. *Address:* 81c Trinity Road, SW17 7SQ. *T:* (020) 8672 3888.

WATTLEY, Graham Richard; Director, Driver and Vehicle Licensing Directorate, Department of Transport, 1985–90, retired; *b* 12 March 1930; *s* of R. C. H. Wattley and Sylvia Joyce Wattley (*née* Orman); *m* 1st, 1953, Yvonne Heale (*d* 1990); one *s* two *d*; 2nd, 1997, M. Rose Daniel (*née* Dawson). *Educ:* Devonport High School. Pilot Officer, RAF, 1949–50. Min. of Works, 1950–71; Dept of the Environment, 1971–73; Department of Transport, 1973–90: Asst Sec., DVLC Computer Div., 1978–85; Under Sec., 1986. Treas., Dewi Sant Housing Assoc., 1991–95. Mem., Governing Body, Church in Wales, 1992–94. Warden, St Paul's Church, Sketty, 1991–96. Walk Leader, HF Holidays, 1994–. *Recreations:* walking, cooking, bird-watching. *Address:* 36 The Ridge, Derwen Fawr, Swansea SA2 8AG. *T:* (01792) 290408. *Club:* Civil Service.

WATTS, Prof. Anthony, PhD; DSc; Professor of Biochemistry, University of Oxford, since 1996; C. W. Maplethorpe Fellow in Biological Sciences, St Hugh's College, Oxford, since 1983; *b* 7 Jan. 1950; *s* of late Wilfred Thomas Watts and of Ingrid Hiltraud Watts; *m* 1972, Valerie Maud Lewis; one *s* two *d*. *Educ:* Ludlow Grammar Sch.; Leeds Univ. (BSc; PhD 1976); St Hugh's Coll., Oxford (MA; DSc 1995). Max Planck Res. Fellow, Göttingen, 1976–80; University of Oxford: Deptl Demonstrator, 1980–83; New Blood Lectr, 1983–88; BBSRC Sen. Res. Fellow, 1997–; Rutherford Appleton Laboratory, Didcot: Sen. Scientist, ISIS Facility, 1996–; Dir, Nat. Biol Solid State NMR Facility, 1997–. Fulbright Fellow and Vis. Prof., Harvard Univ., 1987; Fellow, IACR, 1998; Willsmore Fellow, Melbourne Univ., 2000. Lectr, Aust. and NZ Magnetic Resonance Soc., 1998. Moses Gomberg Lectr, USA. Chm., ESF Network on Molecular Dynamics of Biomembranes, 1990–92; UK rep., Membrane Commn, IUPAB, 1994–; Mem. Cttee, then Chm., BBSRC Biol Neutron Adv. Panel and Mem., ISIS Scheduling Panels, 1995–99. Member: Cttee, Biochem. Soc. of GB, 1989–98; Cttee, Biophysical Soc., 1998–. Principal Ed., Biophysical Chem., 1994–; Managing Ed., European Biophysics Jl, 1997–. 350th Commemorative Medal, Helsinki Univ., 1990; SERC-CNRS Maxime Hanss Prize for Biophysics, 1992; Morton Medal, British Biochem. Soc., 1999. *Publications:* (with J. J. H. H. M. de Pont) Progress in Protein-Lipid Interactions, Vol. 1 1985, Vol. 2 1986; Protein-Lipid Interactions, 1993; numerous contribs to learned jls. *Address:* Biomembrane Structure Unit, Department of Biochemistry, South Parks Road, Oxford OX1 3QU. *T:* (01865) 275268; *e-mail:* awatts@bioch.ox.ac.uk.

WATTS, Prof. Anthony Brian, PhD; Professor of Marine Geology and Geophysics, University of Oxford, since 1990; *b* 23 July 1945; *s* of Dennis Granville Watts and of late Vera (*née* Fisher); *m* 1970, Mary Tarbit; two *d*. *Educ:* University Coll. London (BSc); Univ. of Durham (PhD). Post-Doctoral Fellow, Nat. Res. Council of Canada, 1970–71; Res. Scientist, Lamont-Doherty Geol Observatory, Palisades, NY, 1971–81; Arthur D. Storke Meml Prof. of Geol Scis, Columbia Univ., NY, 1981–90. Fellow, Amer. Geophysical Union, 1986; MAE 1999. A. I. Levorsen Meml Award, Amer. Assoc. Petroleum Geologists, 1981; Rosenstiel Award, Univ. of Miami, 1982; Murchison Medal, Geol Soc., 1993. *Publications:* numerous articles in scientific jls. *Recreations:* cricket, carpentry. *Address:* Department of Earth Sciences, University of Oxford, Parks Road, Oxford OX1 3PR. *T:* Oxford (01865) 272032. *Club:* Geological Society.

WATTS, Sir Arthur (Desmond), KCMG 1989 (CMG 1977); QC 1988; barrister; *b* 14 Nov. 1931; *o s* of Col A. E. Watts, MA (Cantab); *m* 1957, Iris Ann Collier, MA (Cantab); one *s* one *d*. *Educ:* Haileybury and Imperial Service College; Royal Military Academy, Sandhurst; Downing Coll., Cambridge (Schol.; BA 1954; LLM (First Cl.) 1955; MA; Whewell Schol. in Internat. Law, 1955; Hon. Fellow, 1999). Called to Bar, Gray's Inn, 1957, Bencher, 1996. Legal Asst, Foreign Office, 1956–59; Legal Adviser, British Property Commn (later British Embassy), Cairo, 1959–62; Asst Legal Adviser, FO, 1962–67; Legal Adviser, British Embassy, Bonn, 1967–69; Asst Solicitor, Law Officers Dept, 1969–70; Legal Counsellor, FCO, 1970–73; Counsellor (Legal Advr), Office of UK Permanent

Rep. to EEC, 1973–77; Legal Counsellor, 1977–82, Dep. Legal Advr, 1982–87, Legal Advr, 1987–91, FCO. High Rep's Special Negotiator on Succession Issues, former Yugoslavia, 1996–2001; Mem., Panel of Arbitrators, UN Law of the Sea Convention, 1998–. Member: Bd of Management, British Inst. of Internat. and Comparative Law, 1987–; Bd, Inst. of Advanced Legal Studies, 1988–91; Adv. Bd, Inst für Internationales Recht, Kiel Univ., 1989–; Inst de Droit Internat., 1997– (Assoc. Mem., 1991–97). Pres., British Br., Internat. Law Assoc., 1992–98 (Hon. Pres., 1998–). Mem. Editl Cttee, British Year Book of International Law, 1991–. *Publications:* Legal Effects of War, 4th edn (with Lord McNair), 1966; (with C. and A. Parry and J. Grant) Encyclopaedic Dictionary of International Law, 1986; (with Sir Robert Jennings) Oppenheim's International Law, vol. 1, 9th edn 1992; International Law and the Antarctic Treaty System, 1992; (with W. F. Danspeckgruber) Self-Determination and Self-Administration, 1997; The International Law Commission 1949–1998 (3 vols), 1999–2000; contribs to: British Year Book of Internat. Law; Internat. and Comparative Law Quarterly, and other internat. law publications. *Recreation:* cricket (County Cap, Shropshire, 1955; in Antarctica, 1985). *Address:* 20 Essex Street, WC2R 3AL.

WATTS, David Leonard; MP (Lab) St Helens North, since 1997; *b* 26 Aug. 1951; *s* of Leonard and Sarah Watts; *m* 1972, Avril Davies; two *s*. *Educ:* Huyton Hey Secondary Sch. Labour Party Orgnr, until 1992; Researcher for John Evans, MP, 1992–97. PPS to Minister of State, MoD, 2000–01, to Minister of State (Minister of Transport), DTLR, 2001–. *Recreations:* reading, football, travel. *Address:* Anne Ward House, 1 Mill Street, St Helens, Merseyside WA10 1PX.

WATTS, Diana; *see* Ellis, D.

WATTS, Donald Walter, AM 1998; PhD; FTSE; FRACI; FACE; FAIM; Dean, Research and Postgraduate Studies, University of Notre Dame Australia, since 1995; *b* 1 April 1934; *s* of late Horace Frederick Watts and Esme Anne Watts; *m* 1960, Michelle Rose Yeomans; two *s*. *Educ:* Hale Sch., Perth; University of Western Australia (BSc Hons, PhD); University College London. FRACI 1967. Post-Doctoral Fellow, UCL, 1959–61; University of Western Australia: Sen. Lectr, 1962; Reader, 1969; Associate Prof., 1971; Personal Chair in Physical and Inorganic Chemistry, 1977–79; Dir, W Australian Inst. of Tech., 1980–86, renamed Vice-Chancellor, Curtin Univ. of Tech., Jan.–June 1987; Pres. and Vice-Chancellor, Bond Univ., Australia, 1987–90, now Emeritus. Vis. Scientist, Univ. of S California, 1967; Visiting Professor: Australian National Univ., 1973; Univ. of Toronto, 1974; Japan Foundn Vis. Fellow, 1984. Chairman: Aust. Cttee of Dirs and Principals in Advanced Education Ltd, 1986–87; NT Employment and Trng Authy, 1991–93; NT Trade Develt Zone Authy, 1993–95. Member: Aust. Science and Technol. Council, 1984–90; Technology Develt Authority of WA, 1984–87; Chm., Australian Space Council, Canberra, 1993–95. Chairman: Advanced Energy Systems Ltd, 1997– (Dir, 1995–); Technical Trng Inst. Pty Ltd, 2001–. Hon. Fellow, Marketing Inst. of Singapore, 1987. Hon. DTech Curtin, 1987; Hon. DEd WA. *Publications:* Chemical Properties and Reactions (jtly) (Univ. of W Aust.), 1978 (trans. Japanese, 1987); (jtly) Chemistry for Australian Secondary School Students (Aust. Acad. of Sci.), 1979; (jtly) The School Chemistry Project—a secondary school chemistry syllabus for comment, 1984; Earth, Air, Fire and Water, and associated manuals (Aust. Acad. of Sci. Sch. Chem. Project), 1984; numerous papers on phys. and inorganic chemistry in internat. jls; several papers presented at nat. and internat. confs. *Recreations:* tennis (Mem. Interstate Tennis Team, 1952–53), squash (Mem. Interstate Squash Team, 1957–66), golf. *Address:* University of Notre Dame Australia, 19 Mouat Street, Fremantle, WA 6160, Australia. *Clubs:* Royal Kings Park Tennis (Perth); Nedlands Tennis (Nedlands); Lake Karrinyup Golf (Karrinyup); Vines Resort (Swan Valley).

WATTS, Edward, (Ted), FRICS; property advisor; Chairman, Watts & Partners, 1967–99; *b* 19 March 1940; *s* of Edward Samuel Window Watts and Louise Coffey; *m* 1960, Iris Josephine Frost; two *s* (one *d* decd). *Educ:* SW Essex Technical Coll. FRICS 1971 (ARICS 1962). Established own practice, 1967 (surveyors, architects and engineers). Founder Chm., Hyde Housing Assoc., 1967–70 (Mem., 1967–85). Director: Surveyors Hldgs, 1983–88; People Need Homes, 1991–97; WASP, 1994–98; Buildingcare, 1994–97; Avilla Develts Ltd, 1998–; non-executive Director: WSP Gp, 1993–; Thamesmead Town, 1994–2000; Mem. Adv. Bd, Property Hldgs, 1992–96. Chairman: Technical Cttee, Bldg Conservation Trust, 1984–86; Empty Homes Agency, 1997–; Tilfen Ltd, 1999–; Blackheath Preservation Trust Ltd, 2001–. Member: ARCUK, 1991–97; Urban Villages Gp, 1992–96; Bd, Coll. of Estate Management, 1994–96; Ministerial Adv. Bd, Property Advrs to the Civil Estate. Royal Institution of Chartered Surveyors: Pres., 1991–92; Mem., Gen. Council, 1982–95; Dir, RICS Journals Ltd, 1982–88 (Chm., 1986–88). FIMgt (FBIM 1982). Freeman, City of London, 1985; Liveryman, Chartered Surveyors' Co., 1985–. Hon. DSc South Bank, 1992. *Recreations:* sailing, cruising, racing offshore. *Address:* 37 Langton Way, SE3 7TJ. *T:* (020) 8858 2334. *Clubs:* Royal Ocean Racing; Royal Lymington Yacht (Hants); Island Sailing (Cowes, IoW).

WATTS, Helen Josephine, (Mrs Michael Mitchell), CBE 1978; FRAM; concert, lieder and opera singer (contralto), retired 1985; *b* 7 Dec. 1927; *d* of Thomas Watts and Winifred (*née* Morgan); *m* 1980, Michael Mitchell. *Educ:* Sch. of St Mary and St Anne, Abbots Bromley; Royal Academy of Music (LRAM). FRAM 1961 (Hon. ARAM 1955). *Recreation:* gardening.

WATTS, Jane Angharad, (Mrs C. D. G. Ross), FRCO; concert organist, since 1980; *b* 7 Oct. 1959; *d* of J. Maldwyn Watts and J. Leonora Watts; *m* 1985, Callum David George Ross; one *s*. *Educ:* Royal Coll. of Music (ARCM 1978, LRAM 1979); postgrad. studies with Mme Marie-Claire Alain, Paris. FRCO 1980; GRSM 1981. Débuts: BBC Radio, 1980; BBC TV, 1981; RFH, with LPO, 1983; recital, 1986; BBC Prom. Concerts, 1988; Organist and accompanist, Bach Choir, 1991–. Numerous engagements throughout UK, 1980–, with orchestras incl. BBC Nat. Orch. of Wales, LPO, Ulster Orch., London Mozart Players, etc; recital series incl. complete cycle of Widor Organ Symphonies, Brangwyn Hall, Swansea, 1999 and 2000 and St John's Smith Square, 2001; has performed in USA, Europe, Hong Kong, Barbados, Australia and NZ, 1991–. Numerous recordings incl. recitals in Westminster Abbey, Salisbury Cathedral, Chartres Cathedral, Orleans Cathedral, Belfast, Glasgow, Sydney, Brisbane and Wellington. Performer of Year, RCO, 1986. *Recreations:* cookery, maintaining links with with Wales and Welsh-speaking community. *Address:* c/o Callum Ross, Yr Ysgubor, 10 Bury Farm Close, Horton Road, Slapton, Bucks LU7 9DS. *T:* (01525) 222729; c/o Phillip Truckenbrod Concert Artists, PO Box 331060, West Hartford, CT 06133-1060, USA. *T:* (860) 5607800. *Club:* London Welsh.

WATTS, John Arthur, FCA; *b* 19 April 1947; *s* of late Arthur and Ivy Watts; *m* 1974, Susan Jennifer Swan; one *s* three *d*. *Educ:* Bishopshalt Grammar Sch., Hillingdon; Gonville and Caius Coll., Cambridge (MA). Qual. as chartered accountant, 1972; FCA 1979. Chairman: Cambridge Univ. Cons. Assoc., 1968; Uxbridge Cons. Assoc., 1973–76; Mem., Hillingdon Bor. Council, 1973–86 (Leader, 1978–84). MP (C) Slough, 1983–97; contested (C) Reading E, 1997. PPS: to Minister for Housing and Construction, 1984–85; to Minister of State, Treasury, 1985; Minister of State, Dept of Transport, 1994–97. Chm., Treasury and CS Select Cttee, 1992–94 (Mem., 1986–94). *Recreation:* reading. *Address:* The Hustings, 34 West Lane Close, Keeston, Haverfordwest, Pembs SA61 6EW.

WATTS, Sir John (Augustus Fitzroy), KCMG 2000; CBE 1988; President of the Senate, Grenada, 1967, 1985–90 and since 1995; *b* 31 May 1923; *s* of Cecil and Pearl Watts; *m* 1963, Dorothy Paterson. *Educ:* Michigan State Univ. (BSc); New York Univ. (DDS 1952). Founder and Leader, Grenada Nat. Party, 1955; Mem. and Dep. Speaker, Grenada Legislative Council, 1962–67; Leader of Opposition, Senate, 1968–72. Director: Caribbean Hotel Assoc., 1965–67; Grenada Airports Authy, 1985–90; Chairman: Grenada Tourist Bd, 1959–67, 1980–90; Carnival Develt Cttee, 1960–65; Pres., Caribbean Tourist Assoc., 1965–67. *Recreations:* music, golf, politics. *Address:* Church Street, St George's, Grenada, West Indies. *T:* 4402606. *Clubs:* Rotary of Grenada (Dist Gov., 1974–75; Pres., 1996); Grenada Golf and Country (St George's).

WATTS, Col John Cadman, OBE 1959; MC 1946; FRCS 1949; first Professor of Military Surgery, Royal College of Surgeons, 1960–64; *b* 13 April 1913; *s* of John Nixon Watts, solicitor, and Amy Bettina (*née* Cadman); *m* 1938, Joan Lilian (*née* Inwood); three *s* one *d*. *Educ:* Merchant Taylors' Sch.; St Thomas's Hospital. MRCS, LRCP, 1936; MB, BS, 1938. Casualty Officer, Resident Anæsthetist, House Surgeon, St Thomas's Hospital, 1937; Surgical Specialist, RAMC, 1938–60, serving in Palestine, Egypt, Libya, Syria, Tunisia, Italy, France, Holland, Germany, Malaya, Java, Japan, and Cyprus. Hunterian Professor, RCS, 1960; Conslt Surgeon, Bedford Gen. Hosp., 1966–76. Co. Comr, St John Ambulance Brigade, 1970. British Medical Association: Chm., N Beds Div., 1971; Mem. Council, 1972–74; Chm., Armed Forces Cttee, 1978–82; Pres., Ipswich Div., 1982–83. OStJ 1970. *Publications:* Surgeon at War, 1955; Clinical Surgery, 1964; Exploration Medicine, 1964. *Recreations:* sailing, gardening. *Address:* 1 Athenrye Court, Cumberland Street, Woodbridge, Suffolk IP12 4AP. *T:* (01394) 382618. *Clubs:* Deben Yacht (Woodbridge); United Hospitals Sailing (Burnham-on-Crouch).

WATTS, John Francis, BA; educational writer; Principal, Countesthorpe College, Leicestershire, 1972–81; *b* 18 Oct. 1926; *s* of John Weldon Watts and Norah K. Watts; *m* 1st, 1950, Elizabeth Hamilton (marr. diss.); four *s* one *d*; 2nd, 1985, Madeleine Marshall. *Educ:* West Buckland Sch.; Univ. of Bristol (BA). First Headmaster, Les Quennevais Sch., Jersey, CI, 1964–69; Lectr, Univ. of London, 1969–72. Chm., Nat. Assoc. for Teaching of English (NATE), 1974–76. *Publications:* Encounters, 1965, 2nd edn 1983; Contact, 1970 (Australia); Interplay, 1972; Teaching, 1974; The Countesthorpe Experience, 1977; Towards an Open School, 1980; Hearings, 1994; contrib. to various publications. *Address:* Kingfisher Barn, Kings Lane, Weston, Beccles, Suffolk NR34 8TX.

WATTS, Lt-Gen. Sir John Peter Barry Condliffe, KBE 1988 (CBE 1979; OBE 1972); CB 1985; MC 1960; Chief of Defence Staff, Sultan of Oman's Armed Forces, 1984–87; *b* 27 Aug. 1930; *m*; seven *c*. *Educ:* Westminster Sch.; Phillips Acad., Andover, USA; RMA Sandhurst. Commissioned, RUR, 1951 (Royal Irish Rangers, 1968); served Hong Kong, Malaya (despatches), Cyprus, Oman (MC), BAOR, Borneo and South Arabia; 48 Gurkha Inf. Bde, 1967–69; CO 22 SAS Regt, 1970–72; Directing Staff, Staff Coll., 1972–74; MoD, 1974; Comdr, SAS Gp, 1975–78; Comdr, Sultan of Oman's Land Forces, 1979–84.

WATTS, Mark Francis; Member (Lab) South East Region, England, European Parliament, since 1999 (Kent East, 1994–99); *b* 11 June 1964; *s* of Albert Charles Watts and Carole Emmah Watts (*née* Fleischman); *m* 1988, Kim McEachan; two *s*. *Educ:* Maidstone Grammar Sch.; LSE (BSc Econ; MSc Econ). Planning Officer, Royal Borough of Kingston-upon-Thames, 1988–94. Spokesman on transport, EP, 1995–. Co-Chm., Eur. Transport Safety Council, 1996–. Maidstone Borough Council: Councillor, 1986–96; Leader, Lab. Gp, 1990–94. Pres., Old Maidstonians Soc., 1996–97. *Recreations:* walking, enjoying the countryside, spending time with my family, swimming. *Address:* European Office, 29 Park Road, Sittingbourne, Kent ME10 1DR. *T:* (01795) 477880, *Fax:* (01795) 437224; *e-mail:* mfwatts1@aol.com. *Club:* Whitstable Labour.

WATTS, Philip Beverley, FInstP, FRGS, FGS; Group Managing Director, since 1997, and Chairman, Committee of Managing Directors, since 2001, Royal Dutch/Shell Group; Managing Director, since 1997, and Chairman, since 2001, Shell Transport and Trading plc; *b* 25 June 1945; *s* of Samuel Watts and Phillippa (*née* Wale); *m* 1966, Janet Lockwood; one *s* one *d*. *Educ:* Wyggeston Grammar Sch., Leicester; Univ. of Leeds (BSc Hons Physics, MSc Geophysics). FInstP 1980; FInstPet 1990; FRGS 1998; FGS 1998. Sci. teacher, Methodist Boys High Sch., Freetown, Sierra Leone, 1966–68; joined Shell International, 1969: seismologist, Indonesia, 1970–74; geophysicist, UK/Europe, 1974–77; Exploration Manager, Norway, 1978–81; Div. Head, Malaysia, Brunei, Singapore, London, 1981–83; Exploration Dir, UK, 1983–85; Head, Exploration & Production Liaison—Europe, The Hague, 1986–88; Head, Exploration & Production Econs and Planning, The Hague, 1989–91; Man. Dir, Nigeria, 1991–94; Regl Co-ordinator—Europe, The Hague, 1994–95; Dir, Planning, Envmt and Ext. Affairs, London, 1996–97. Member: Exec. Cttee, World Business Council for Sustainable Develt, 1998–; Governing Body, ICC UK, 1997– (Chm., 1998–); ICC Exec. Bd (Worldwide), 1997–2000. *Club:* Travellers. *Recreations:* travel, gardening, reading. *Address:* Shell Centre, SE1 7NA. *T:* (020) 7934 5554.

WATTS, Rolande Jane Rita; *see* Anderson, R. J. R.

WATTS, Thomas Rowland, (Tom), CBE 1978; Chartered Accountant; *b* 1 Jan. 1917; *s* of late Thomas William Watts and late Daisy Maud Watts (*née* Bultitude); *m* 1955, Hester Zoë Armitstead; one *s* two *d*. *Educ:* Gresham's Sch., Holt. Served War, TA, 1939–41, Royal Marines (Captain), 1941–46. Articled to Price Waterhouse & Co., 1934–39, Partner, 1963–82. Dir, Jarrold & Sons Ltd, Norwich, 1982–87. Chm., Accounting Standards Cttee (UK and Ireland), 1978–82; Mem. Council, Inst. of Chartered Accountants in England and Wales, 1974–82; Mem. City EEC Cttee, 1974–82; Adviser to Dept of Trade on EEC company law, 1974–83; Vice-Pres. d'honneur, Groupe d'Etudes des experts comptables de la CEE, 1979–88 (Vice-Pres., 1975–79); Chm., EEC Liaison Cttee of UK Accountancy Bodies, 1986–88; Chm., Dental Rates Study Gp, 1982–85. A Gen. Comr of Income Tax, 1986–92. Hon. Vis. Prof., City of London Polytech., 1983–86. Liveryman, Chartered Accountants' Co., 1977–. Chartered Accountants Founding Socs' Centenary Award, 1982. *Publications:* editor, various professional books; papers in professional jls. *Address:* 13 Fitzwalter Road, Colchester, Essex CO3 3SY. *T:* (01206) 573520.

WATTS, His Honour Victor Brian; a Circuit Judge, 1980–99; *b* 7 Jan. 1927; *o s* of Percy William King Watts and Doris Millicent Watts; *m* 1965, Patricia Eileen (*née* Steer); one *s* one *d*. *Educ:* Colfe's Grammar Sch.; University Coll., Oxford. MA(Oxon): BCL. Called to the Bar, Middle Temple, 1950; subseq. Western Circuit; a Recorder of the Crown Court, 1972–80. Flying Officer, Royal Air Force, 1950–52. Churchwarden, St Peter's Church, Hammersmith, 1984–90. *Publications:* Landlord and Tenant Act, 1954; Leading Cases on the Law of Contract, 1955; occasional articles of a legal nature. *Recreations:* the arts, travel, tennis, riding. *Address:* 28 Abinger Road, W4 1EL. *T:* (020) 8994 4435. *Club:* Hurlingham.

WATTS, Vincent Challacombe, OBE 1998; Vice-Chancellor, University of East Anglia, since 1997; Chairman, East of England Development Agency, since 1998; *b* 11 Aug. 1940; *s* of Geoffrey Watts and Lilian Watts (*née* Pye); *m* 1967, Rachel Rosser (*d* 1998), Prof. of Psychiatry, UCL Med. Sch.; one *s* one *d*. *Educ:* Sidcot Sch.; Peterhouse, Cambridge (MA 1966); Birmingham Univ. (MSc 1967). FCA 1976; FIMC 1986. Joined Andersen Consulting, 1963, Partner, 1976–97; seconded to: Dept of Health as Founder Mem., Operational Res. Unit, 1970–71; HM Treasury, 1974; Financial Management Unit, Cabinet Office/HM Treasury, 1982–85. *Publications:* papers on performance evaluation in health services. *Recreations:* sailing, squash, satisfying curiosity. *Address:* University of East Anglia, Norwich NR4 7TJ. *Clubs:* Oxford and Cambridge; Jesters.

WATTS, William Arthur, MA, ScD; Provost, Trinity College, Dublin, 1981–91; *b* 26 May 1930; *s* of William Low Watts and Bessie (*née* Dickinson); *m* 1954, Geraldine Mary Magrath; two *s* one *d*. *Educ:* Trinity Coll., Dublin (MA, ScD). Lecturer in Botany, Univ. of Hull, 1953–55; Trinity College, Dublin: Lectr in Botany, 1955–65; Fellow, 1970; Professor of Botany, 1965–80; Prof. of Quaternary Ecology, 1980–81. Adjunct Prof. of Geology, Univ. of Minnesota, 1975–. Pres., RIA, 1982–85; Governor: National Gallery of Ireland, 1982–85; Marsh's Library, 1981–; Member: Dublin Inst. for Advanced Studies, 1981–; Scholarship Exchange Bd, Ireland, 1982–. Chairman: Federated Dublin Voluntary Hosps, 1983–; Mercer's Hosp., 1975–83; Mercer's Hosp. Foundn, 1983–; Health Res. Bd, Ireland, 1987–89. Hon. LLD QUB, 1990; Hon. DSc NUI, 1991. *Publications:* numerous articles on aspects of quaternary ecology. *Recreations:* walking, conservation studies, music. *Address:* Room 24.02, Trinity College, Dublin 2. *T:* (1) 772941. *Club:* Kildare Street and University (Dublin).

WAUCHOPE, Sir Roger (Hamilton) Don-, 11th Bt *cr* 1667 (NS), of Newton Don; chartered accountant, South Africa; Partner, Deloitte & Touche, since 1972; *b* 16 Oct. 1938; *s* of Sir Patrick George Don-Wauchope, 10th Bt and Ismay Lilian Ursula (who later *m* George William Shipman), *d* of Sidney Richard Hodges; *S* father, 1989; *m* 1963, Sallee, *yr d* of Lt-Col Harold Mill-Colman, OBE, AMICE, Durban; two *s* one *d*. *Educ:* Hilton Coll., Natal; Univ. of Natal, Durban; Univ. of Natal, Pietermaritzburg (Higher Diploma in Taxation). *Heir:* *s* Dr Andrew Craig Don-Wauchope, *b* 18 May 1966. *Address:* Newton, 53 Montrose Drive, Pietermaritzburg 3201, Natal, South Africa. *T:* (331) 471107; PO Box 365, Pietermaritzburg 3200, Natal, South Africa. *Clubs:* Victoria Country (Chm., 1993–95) (Pietermaritzburg); Durban Country (Durban); Old Hiltonian (Chm., 1992–97).

WAUGH, Andrew Peter; QC 1998; *b* 6 Nov. 1959; *m* 1980, Catrin Prys Davies; four *s*. *Educ:* City Univ. (BSc 1st Cl. Hons 1980; DipLaw 1981). Called to the Bar, Gray's Inn, 1982; in practice as barrister, 1982–; specialist in Intellectual Property Law. *Recreations:* Association football, food, wine. *Address:* 3 New Square, Lincoln's Inn, WC2A 3RS. *T:* (020) 7405 1111.

WAUGH, Rev. Eric Alexander; Vice-Chancellor, His People Christian Education Institute, Cape Town, South Africa, since 1998 (Dean, His People Institute, 1996–98); *b* 9 May 1933; *s* of Hugh Waugh and Marion Waugh (*née* McLay); *m* 1955, Agnes-Jean (Sheena) Saunders; two *s*. *Educ:* Glasgow Univ.; Edinburgh Univ. (LTh). Local government officer, 1948–64. Assistant Minister, High Church, Bathgate, 1969–70; Missionary, Kenya Highlands, 1970–73; Minister, Mowbray Presbyterian Church, Cape Town, 1973–78; Missioner, Presbyterian Church of Southern Africa, 1978–85; Minister, City Temple, URC, 1986–91; Missioner, Kingdom Communications Trust, S Africa, 1992–95. *Recreations:* hill walking, gardening. *Address:* 86 Main Street, Redding, Falkirk FK2 9UH. *T:* (01324) 715948; *e-mail:* eawaugh@aol.com; His People Christian Education Institute, PO Box 275, Rondebosch 7700, Cape Town, South Africa.

WAVERLEY, 3rd Viscount *cr* 1952, of Westdean; **John Desmond Forbes Anderson;** *b* 31 Oct. 1949; *s* of 2nd Viscount Waverley and of Myrtle Ledgerwood; *S* father, 1990; *m* 1994, Dr Ursula Barrow, *qv*; one *s*. *Educ:* Malvern. Elected Mem., H of L, 1999. *Heir:* *s* Hon. Forbes Alastair Rupert Anderson, *b* 15 Feb. 1996. *Address:* c/o House of Lords, SW1A 0PW.

WAVERLEY, Viscountess; *see* Barrow, U. H.

WAWRZYNSKI, Dana R.; *see* Ross-Wawrzynski.

WAX, Ruby; actor and comedian; *b* 19 April 1953; *d* of Edward Wax and Berta Wax (*née* Goldmann); *m* 1988, Edward Richard Morison Bye; one *s* two *d*. *Educ:* Evanston High Sch.; Berkeley Univ.; RSAMD. *Theatre:* Crucible, 1976; Royal Shakespeare Co., 1978–82; Stressed (one-woman show), 2000; *television:* Not the Nine O'Clock News, 1982–83; Girls on Top, 1983–85; Don't Miss Wax, 1985–87; Hit and Run, 1988; Full Wax, 1987–92; Ruby Wax Meets . . ., 1996, 1997, 1998; Ruby, 1997, 1998, 1999, 2000; Ruby's American Pie, 1999, 2000; Hot Wax, 2001; *films:* Miami Memoirs, 1987; East Meets Wax, 1988; Class of '69; Ruby Takes a Trip, 1992. *Address:* c/o Peters Fraser & Dunlop, Drury House, 34–43 Russell Street, WC2B 5HA.

WAXMAN, Prof. Jonathan Hugh, MD; FRCP; Professor of Oncology, Imperial College, University of London, since 1999; *b* 31 Oct. 1951; *s* of David Waxman and Shirley Waxman (*née* Friedman); *m* 1993, Clare Taylor; one *s* one *d*. *Educ:* Haberdashers' Aske's Sch., Elstree; University Coll. London (BSc); University Coll. Hosp. (MB BS 1975; MD 1986). MRCP 1978, FRCP 1988. House Officer, UCH and Addenbrooke's Hosp., Cambridge, 1975–76; SHO, UCH, London Chest Hosp. and St Mary's Hosp., London, 1976–78; Registrar, St Mary's Hosp., 1979–81; ICRF Res. Fellow, St Bartholomew's Hosp., 1981–86; Consultant Physician, Hammersmith Hosp., 1986–99. Founder Mem., All Party Gp on Cancer, 1998–. Founder Chm., Prostate Cancer Charity, 1996–. *Publications:* The New Endocrinology of Cancer, 1987; The Molecular Biology of Cancer, 1989; Urological Oncology, 1992; Interleukin 2, 1992; Molecular Endocrinology of Cancer, 1996; The Fifth Gospel, 1997; Cancer Chemotherapy Treatment Protocols, 1998; Cancer and the Law, 1999; Treatment Options in Urological Oncology, 2001; The Prostate Cancer Book, 2001; contrib. various scientific papers on cancer res. *Recreations:* family and friends. *Address:* Department of Oncology, Hammersmith Hospital, Du Cane Road, W12 0NN. *T:* (020) 8383 4651.

WAY, Col Anthony Gerald, MC 1944; Member, HM Body Guard of the Honourable Corps of Gentlemen at Arms, 1972–90 (Standard Bearer, 1988–90); *b* 5 Nov. 1920; *s* of Roger Hill Way and Brenda Lathbury; *m* 1st, 1946, Elizabeth Leslie Richmond (*d* 1986); one *s* one *d*; 2nd, 1989, Mrs Anthea Methven, St Martin's Abbey, by Perth. *Educ:* Stowe Sch.; RMC Sandhurst. Joined Grenadier Guards, 1939, 2nd Lieut; served in N Africa and Italy; CO, 3rd Bn, 1960–61; Lt-Col comdg Grenadier Guards, 1961–64. *Recreations:* shooting, gardening. *Address:* Kincairney, Dunkeld, Perthshire PH8 0RE. *T:* (01738) 710304.

WAYWELL, Prof. Geoffrey Bryan, FSA 1979; Professor of Classical Archaeology, King's College, University of London, since 1987; Director, Institute of Classical Studies, University of London, since 1996; *b* 16 Jan. 1944; *s* of Francis Marsh Waywell and Jenny Waywell; *m* 1970, Elisabeth Ramsden; two *s*. *Educ:* Eltham Coll.; St John's Coll., Cambridge (BA, MA, PhD). Walston Student, Cambridge Univ., 1965–67; School Student, British Sch. at Athens, 1966–67; King's College, London: Asst Lectr in Classics, 1968; Lectr in Classics, 1970; Reader in Classical Archaeology, 1982; Hon. Curator, Ashmole Archive, 1985. Dir of excavations at ancient Sparta, 1989–. *Publications:* The Free-Standing Sculptures of the Mausoleum at Halicarnassus in the British Museum, 1978; The Lever and Hope Sculptures, 1986; Sculptors and Sculpture of Caria and the Dodecanese, 1997; numerous articles and reviews in archaeol and classical jls. *Recreations:* music, excavating. *Address:* Institute of Classical Studies, Senate House, Malet Street, WC1E 7HU. *T:* (020) 7862 8701.

WEAIRE, Prof. Denis Lawrence, PhD; FRS 1999; Erasmus Smith's Professor of Natural and Experimental Philosophy, since 1984, Fellow, since 1987, Trinity College, Dublin; *b* 17 Oct. 1942; *s* of Allen Maunder Weaire and Janet Eileen (*née* Rea); *m* 1969, Colette Rosa O'Regan; one *s*. *Educ:* Belfast Royal Acad.; Clare Coll., Cambridge (MA Maths; PhD 1968). Harkness Fellow, Calif and Chicago, 1964–66; researcher, Cavendish Lab., Univ. of Cambridge, 1966–69; Fellow, Clare Coll., Cambridge, 1967–69; Res. Fellow, Harvard Univ., 1969–70; Yale University: Instructor, 1970–72; Asst Prof., 1972–73; Heriot-Watt University: Associate Prof., 1973–74; Sen. Lectr, 1974–77; Reader, 1977–79; Prof. of Exptl Physics, UC Dublin, 1980–84 (Hd of Dept, 1983–84); Trinity College, Dublin: Hd of Dept, 1984–89; Dean of Science, 1989–92. Ed., Jl Physics: Condensed Matter, 1994–97. Pres., Eur. Physical Soc., 1997–99 (Vice Pres., 1996–97 and 1999–2000). MRIA 1987; MAE 1998. Dr *hc* Tech. Univ., Lisbon, 2001. *Publications:* (ed jtly) Tetrahedrally Bonded Amorphous Semiconductors, 1974; (ed with D. Pettifor) The Recursion Method, 1985; (with P. G. Harper) Introduction to Physical Mathematics, 1985; (ed with C. Windsor) Solid State Science, 1987; (ed jtly) Tradition and Reform, 1988; (ed jtly) Epioptics, 1995; (ed) The Kelvin Problem, 1997; (ed with J. Banhart) Foams and Films, 1999; (ed) Richard Helsham's Course of Lectures on Natural Philosophy, 1999; (with S. Hutzler) The Physics of Foams, 1999; (with T. Aste) The Pursuit of Perfect Packing, 2000; contrib. numerous scientific papers. *Recreations:* theatre, humorous writing. *Address:* 26 Greenmount Road, Terenure, Dublin, Republic of Ireland. *T:* (1) 4902063. *Club:* University and Kildare Street (Dublin).

WEALE, Prof. Albert Peter, PhD; FBA 1998; Professor of Government, University of Essex, since 1992; *b* 30 May 1950; *s* of Albert Cecil and Margaret Elizabeth Weale; *m* 1st, 1976, Jane Leresche (marr. diss. 1987); 2nd, 1994, Janet Felicity Harris. *Educ:* St Luke's Primary Sch., Brighton; Varndean Grammar Sch., Brighton; Clare Coll., Cambridge (BA Theol.; PhD Social and Political Scis 1977). Sir James Knott Fellow, Dept of Politics, Univ. of Newcastle upon Tyne, 1974–76; University of York: Lectr, Dept of Politics, 1976–85; Asst Dir, Inst. for Res. in Social Scis, 1982–85; Prof. of Politics, UEA, 1985–92. Mem., Nuffield Council on Bioethics, 1998. King's Fund: Chm. Grants Cttee, 1997; Mem. Mgt Cttee, 1997. FRSA 1993. *Publications:* Equality and Social Policy, 1978; Political Theory and Social Policy, 1983; The New Politics of Pollution, 1992; Democracy, 1999; *jointly:* Lone Mothers, Paid Work and Social Security, 1984; Controlling Pollution in the Round, 1991; The Theory of Choice, 1992; Environmental Governance in Europe, 2000; *edited:* Cost and Choice in Health Care, 1988; (with L. Roberts) Innovation and Environmental Risk, 1991; (jtly) Environmental Standards in the European Community in an Interdisciplinary Framework, 1994; (with P. Lehning) Citizenship, Democracy and Justice in the New Europe, 1997; articles in learned jls. *Recreations:* walking, music, the company of friends. *Address:* Department of Government, University of Essex, Wivenhoe Park, Colchester, Essex CO4 3SQ. *T:* (01206) 872127.

WEALE, Anthony Philip; Secretary of Faculties, since 1984 and Academic Registrar, since 1999, University of Oxford; Fellow of Worcester College, Oxford, since 1982; *b* 4 Dec. 1945; *s* of Geoffrey Arthur Weale and Jocelyn Mary Weale (*née* Weeks); *m* 1975, Katharine O'Connell; two *d*. *Educ:* Kimbolton Sch.; University Coll., Oxford (Scholar; MA 1st Cl., Honour Sch. of Jurisprudence; Martin Wronker Prize for Law, 1967). GKN Ltd, 1967–71; Admin. Service, Oxford Univ., 1971–; Sec., Medical Sch., 1977–84. Treas., Historic Towns Trust, 1975–. Governor: Pusey House, Oxford, 1977–85; Kimbolton Sch., 2001–. *Recreations:* family, dabbling in military and political history. *Address:* University Offices, Wellington Square, Oxford OX1 2JD. *T:* (01865) 270013; 90 Staunton Road, Headington, Oxford OX3 7TR. *T:* (01865) 761530.

WEALE, Martin Robert, CBE 1999; Director, National Institute of Economic and Social Research, since 1995; *b* 4 Dec. 1955; *s* of Prof. R. A. Weale and M. E. Weale. *Educ:* Clare Coll., Cambridge (BA 1977). ODI Fellow, Nat. Statistical Office, Malawi, 1977–79; University of Cambridge: Research Officer, Dept of Applied Econs, 1979–87; Lectr, Faculty of Econs and Politics, 1987–95; Fellow, Clare Coll., 1981–95. Houblon-Norman Fellow, Bank of England, 1986–87. Mem., Stats Commn, 2000–. Hon. FIA 2001. *Publications:* (with J. Grady) British Banking, 1986; (jtly) Macroeconomic Policy: inflation, wealth and the exchange rate, 1989; (with J. Sefton) Reconciliation of National Income and Expenditure, 1995. *Recreations:* bridge, music, travel. *Address:* 63 Noel Road, N1 8HE. *T:* (020) 7359 8210. *Club:* Athenæum.

WEARE, Trevor John, OBE 1990; PhD; Chairman, HR Wallingford Group, Ltd, since 1999; *b* 31 Dec. 1943; *s* of Trevor Leslie Weare and Edna Margaret (*née* Roberts); *m* 1964, Margaret Ann Wright; two *s*. *Educ:* Aston Technical Coll.; Imperial College of Science and Technology (BSc Physics, PhD). Post-doctoral Research Fellow: Dept of Mathematical Physics, McGill Univ., Montreal, 1968–70; Dept of Theoretical Physics, Univ. of Oxford, 1970–72; Sen. Scientific Officer, Hydraulics Res. Station, 1972; Principal Scientific Officer, 1975; Sen. Principal Scientific Officer, Head of Estuaries Div., 1978; Chief Scientific Officer, DoE, 1981; Chief Exec., Hydraulics Res. Ltd, then HR Wallingford Gp Ltd, 1984–99. *Publications:* numerous contribs to scientific jls on theoretical High Energy Nuclear Physics, and on computational modelling in Civil Engineering Hydraulics; archaeological paper in Oxoniensia. *Recreations:* music, walking, archaeology. *Address:* 14 Trenithick Meadow, Mount Hawke, Truro, Cornwall TR4 8GN. *T:* (01209) 890082.

WEARING, Gillian; artist; *b* 1963; Goldsmiths' Coll., Univ. of London (BA Hons Fine Art 1990). *Solo exhibitions:* Maureen Paley/Interim Art, London, 1994, 1996–97, 1999; Hayward Gall., 1995; Le Consortium, Dijon, 1996; Jay Gorney Modern Art, NY, Chisenhale Gall., London, Kunsthaus Zürich, 1997; Centre d'Art Contemporain, Geneva, 1998; De Vleeshal, Middleburg, The Netherlands, 1999; Serpentine Gall., Regen Projects, LA, Contemp. Art Center, Cincinnati, 2000; Bluecoat Gall., Liverpool, la Caixa, Madrid, Musée d'Art Moderne, Paris, Museo do Chiado, Lisbon, Kunstverein München, Angel Row Gall., Nottingham, 2001; *group exhibitions* include: BT Young Contemporaries, UK tour, 1993; Brilliant! New Art from London, Walker Art Center, Minneapolis, 1995; Life/Live, Musée d'Art Moderne, Paris, 1996; Pandaemonium, London Fest. of Moving Images, ICA, 1996; Sensation, RA, and Mus. für Gegenwart,

Berlin, 1998; Real/Life: new British art, Japanese Mus. tour, 1998; Let's Entertain, Walker Art Centre, Minneapolis, 2000; New British Art, Tate Britain, London, 2000; Century City, Tate Modern, London, 2001; exhibns in Europe. Turner Prize, 1997. *Address:* c/o Maureen Paley/Interim Art, 21 Herald Street, E2 6JT. *T:* (020) 7729 4112.

WEATHERALL, Sir David (John), Kt 1987; DL; MD, FRCP; FRCPE 1983; FRS 1977; Regius Professor of Medicine, University of Oxford, 1992–2000; Student of Christ Church, Oxford, 1992–2000; Hon. Director: Molecular Haematology Unit, Medical Research Council, 1980–2000; Institute for Molecular Medicine, University of Oxford, 1988–2000; *b* 9 March 1933; *s* of late Harry and Gwendoline Weatherall; *m* 1962, Stella Mayorga Nestler; one *s*. *Educ:* Calday Grange Grammar Sch.; Univ. of Liverpool (MB, ChB 1956; MD 1962); MA Oxon 1974. FRCP 1967; FRCPath 1969. Ho. Officer in Med. and Surg., United Liverpool Hosps, 1956–58; Captain, RAMC, Jun. Med. Specialist, BMH, Singapore, and BMH, Kamunting, Malaya, 1958–60; Research Fellow in Genetics, Johns Hopkins Hosp., Baltimore, USA, 1960–62; Sen. Med. Registrar, Liverpool Royal Infirmary, 1962–63; Research Fellow in Haematology, Johns Hopkins Hosp., 1963–65; Consultant, WHO, 1966–70; Univ. of Liverpool: Lectr in Med., 1965–66; Sen. Lectr in Med., 1966–69; Reader in Med., 1969–71; Prof. of Haematology, 1971–74; Consultant Physician, United Liverpool Hosps, 1966–74; Nuffield Prof. of Clinical Medicine, Univ. of Oxford, 1974–92; Fellow, Magdalen Coll., Oxford, 1974–92, Emeritus 1992–. Mem. Soc. of Scholars, and Centennial Schol., Johns Hopkins Univ., 1976; Physician-in-Chief *pro tem.*, Peter Bent Brigham Hosp., Harvard Med. Sch., 1980. RSocMed Foundn Vis. Prof., 1981; Sims Commonwealth Vis. Prof., 1982; Phillip K. Bondy Prof., Yale, 1982. K. Diamond Prof., Univ. of Calif in San Francisco, 1986; HM Queen Elizabeth the Queen Mother Fellow, Nuffield Prov. Hosps Trust, 1982. Lectures: Watson Smith, RCP, 1974; Foundn, RCPath, 1979; Darwin, Eugenics Soc., 1979; Croonian, RCP, 1984; Fink Meml, Yale, 1984; Sir Francis Frazer, Univ. of London, 1985; Roy Cameron, RCPath, 1986; Hamm Meml, Amer. Soc. of Haematology, 1986; Still Meml, BPA, 1987; Harveian, RCP, 1992. President: British Soc. for Haematology, 1980–; Internat. Soc. of Haematology, 1992; BAAS, 1992–93; Chm., Med. and Scientific Adv. Panel, Leukaemia Res. Fund, 1985–89; Mem. Council, Royal Soc., 1989– (Vice Pres., 1990–91); Mem., MRC, 1994–96; Trustee, Wellcome Trust, 1990–. Founder FMedSci 1998. DL Oxfordshire, 2000. Foreign Member: Nat. Acad. of Scis, USA, 1990; Inst. of Medicine, Nat. Acad. of Scis, USA, 1991; Hon. Member: Assoc. of Physicians of GB and Ireland, 1968 (Pres., 1989); Assoc. of Amer. Physicians, 1976; Amer. Soc. of Haematology, 1982; Eur. Molecular Biology Orgn, 1983; Amer. Acad. of Arts and Scis, 1988; Alpha Omega Alpha Honor Med. Soc., USA, 1988; Hon. Fellow, Royal Coll. Physicians, Thailand, 1988; Hon. FRACP 1986; Hon. FRCOG 1988; Hon. FIC 1989; Hon. FACP 1991; Hon. FRSocMed 1998. Hon. Fellow, Green Coll., Oxford, 1993. Hon. DSc: Manchester, 1988; Edinburgh, 1989; Leicester, 1991; Aberdeen, 1991; London, 1993; Keele, 1993; Oxford Brookes, 1995; South Bank, 1995; Exeter, 1998; Hon. MD: Leeds, 1988; Sheffield, 1989; Nottingham, 1993; Hon. DHL Johns Hopkins, 1990; Hon. LLD: Liverpool, 1992; Bristol, 1994. Ambuj Nath Bose Prize, RCP, 1980; Ballantyne Prize, RCPE, 1982; Stratton Prize, Internat. Soc. Haematology, 1982; Feldberg Prize, 1984; Royal Medal, Royal Soc., 1989; Gold Medal, RSM, 1992; Conway Evans Prize, RCP and Royal Soc., 1992; Buchanan Medal, Royal Soc., 1994; (jtly) Helmut Horten Res. Award, 1995; Manson Medal, 1998. Commandeur de l'Ordre de la Couronne (Belgium), 1994. *Publications:* (with J. B. Clegg) The Thalassaemia Syndromes, 1965, 4th edn 2001; (with R. M. Hardisty) Blood and its Disorders, 1973, 2nd edn 1981; The New Genetics and Clinical Practice, 1982, 3rd edn 1991; (ed, with J. G. G. Ledingham and D. A. Warrell) Oxford Textbook of Medicine, 1983, 3rd edn 1995; Science and the Quiet Art, 1995; many papers on Abnormal Haemoglobin Synthesis and related disorders. *Recreations:* music, oriental food. *Address:* 8 Cumnor Rise Road, Cumnor Hill, Oxford OX2 9HD. *T:* (01865) 222360.

WEATHERALL, Vice-Adm. Sir James (Lamb), KCVO 2001; KBE 1989; HM Marshal of the Diplomatic Corps, 1992–2001; *b* 28 Feb. 1936; *s* of Alwyn Thomas Hirst Weatherall and Olive Catherine Joan Weatherall (*née* Cuthbert); *m* 1962, Hon. Jean Stewart Macpherson, *d* of 1st Baron Drumalbyn, KBE, PC; two *s* three *d*. *Educ:* Glasgow Academy; Gordonstoun School. Joined RN 1954; commanded HM Ships: Soberton, 1966–67; Ulster, 1970–72; Tartar, 1975–76; Andromeda, 1982–84 (incl. Falklands conflict); Ark Royal, 1985–87; with SACEUR, 1987–89; Dep. Supreme Allied Comdr Atlantic, 1989–91. Chairman: Sea Cadet Council, 1992–98; Sea Cadet Assoc., 1992–98 (Sea Cadet Medal, 1998). Pres., Internat. Social Service (UK), 1996–. Trustee, Marwell Preservation Trust, 1992– (Chm., 1999–). Chm., Lord Mayor of London's Appeal, 1997–98. Chairman, Board of Governors: Box Hill Sch., 1993– (Trustee, 1992–); Gordonstoun Schs, 1996– (Gov., 1994–). Mem., Ct of Assts, Shipwrights' Co., 1989– (Prime Warden, 2001–April 2002); Younger Brother, Corp. of Trinity House, 1986–. Chm., Royal Soc. of St George, 2001–. *Recreations:* stamp collecting, fishing. *Address:* Craig House, Ashton Lane, Bishop's Waltham, Hampshire SO32 1FS. *Club:* Royal Navy of 1765 and 1785.

WEATHERALL, Miles, MA, DM, DSc; FIBiol; medical scientist; *b* 14 Oct. 1920; *s* of Rev. J. H. and Mary Weatherall; *m* 1944, Josephine A. C. Ogston; three *d*. *Educ:* Dragon School and St Edward's School, Oxford; Oriel College, Oxford (Open Schol. in Nat. Sci., 1938; BA, BSc 1941; BM 1943; MA 1945; DM 1951; DSc 1966). FIBiol 1972. Lecturer in Pharmacology, Edinburgh University, 1945; Head of Dept of Pharmacology, London Hosp. Med. Coll., 1949–66; Prof. of Pharmacology, Univ. of London, 1958–66; Wellcome Research Laboratories: Head, Therapeutic Res. Div., 1967–75; Dep. Dir, 1969–74; Dir of Estblt, 1974–79. Member: Adv. Cttee on Pesticides and other Toxic Chemicals, 1964–66; Council, Pharmaceutical Soc., 1966–70; Council, Roy. Soc. Med., 1972–82 (Hon. Sec. 1974–82); Comr, Medicines Commn, 1979–81. Chm., Sci. Co-ord. Cttee, Arthritis and Rheumatism Council, 1983–88. Chm., Council, Chelsea Coll., Univ. of London, 1970–83. Hon. Lecturer: UCL, 1968–89; KCL, 1979–82; Hon. Fellow: Chelsea Coll., London, 1984; KCL, 1985. Mem. Cttee, Wine Soc., 1964–72. *Publications:* Statistics for Medical Students (jointly with L. Bernstein), 1952; Scientific Method, 1968; (ed jtly) Safety Testing of New Drugs, 1984; In Search of a Cure, 1990; The Search and the Girl (novel), 2001; papers in scientific and medical journals. *Recreations:* writing, gardening, cooking. *Address:* Willows, Charlbury, Oxford OX7 3PX. *Club:* Royal Society of Medicine.

WEATHERBY, Jonathan Roger; Chairman, Weatherbys Group Ltd, since 1993; *b* 30 Nov. 1959; *s* of Christopher Nicholas Weatherby and Alison Beatrix (*née* Pease); *m* 1993, Sophie Frances Cliffe-Jones; two *s* two *d*. *Educ:* Eton Coll. Joined Weatherbys, 1979; Dir, 1988–. Chairman: Gazelle Investments Ltd, 1992–; Wild Boar Inns Ltd, 1994–. Mem., Jockey Club, 1997–. *Recreations:* horse-racing, soccer, hunting. *Address:* Weatherbys Group Ltd, Sanders Road, Wellingborough, Northants NN8 4BX. *T:* (01933) 440077. *Clubs:* White's, Turf.

WEATHERHEAD, Alexander Stewart, OBE 1985; TD 1964 (clasp 1973); Partner, 1960–97 and Senior Partner, 1992–97, Tindal Oatts & Rodger, then Tindal Oatts Buchanan and McIlwraith, subsequently Tindal Oatts, and Brechin Tindal Oatts, Solicitors, Glasgow (Consultant, 1997–98); *b* Edinburgh, 3 Aug. 1931; *er s* of Kenneth Kilpatrick Weatherhead and Katharine Weatherhead (*née* Stewart); *m* 1972, Harriett Foye, *d* of Rev. Dr Arthur Organ, Toronto, Canada; two *d*. *Educ:* Glasgow Acad.; Glasgow Univ. MA 1955, LLB 1958. Served in RA, 1950–52, 2nd Lieut, 1950. Solicitor, 1958; Temp. Sheriff, 1985–92. Hon. Vice-Pres., Law Society of Scotland, 1983–84 (Mem. Council, 1971–84); Member: Royal Faculty of Procurators in Glasgow, 1960– (Mem. Council, 1992–2001; Dean, 1992–95; Hon. Mem., 1997); Council, Soc. for Computers and Law, 1973–86 (Vice-Chm., 1973–82; Chm., 1982–84; Hon. Mem., 1986); Mem., Royal Commn on Legal Services in Scotland, 1976–80. Trustee, Nat. Technol. and Law Trust (formerly Nat. Law Library Trust), 1979–86; Examr in Conveyancing, Univ. of Aberdeen, 1984–86. Dir, Glasgow Chamber of Commerce, 1992–95. Mem., Local Res. Ethics Cttee, Royal Infirmary, Glasgow, 1999–. Joined TA, 1952; Lt-Col Comdg 277 (A&SH) Field Regt, RA (TA), 1965–67; The Lowland Regt (RA(T)), 1967 and Glasgow & Strathclyde Univs OTC, 1971–73; Col 1974; TAVR Col Lowlands (West), 1974–76; ADC (TAVR) to the Queen, 1977–81; Member: TAVR Assoc. Lowlands, 1967–2000 (Vice-Chm., 1987–90; Chm., 1990–93); RA Council for Scotland, 1972–2001 (Vice Chm., 1997–2001). Hon. Col, Glasgow and Strathclyde Univs OTC, 1982–98. Commodore, Royal Western Yacht Club, 1995–98 (Vice Cdre, 1991–95; Hon. Sec., 1981–84). *Recreations:* sailing, reading, music, tennis. *Address:* 52 Partickhill Road, Glasgow G11 5AB. *T:* (0141) 334 6277. *Clubs:* New (Edinburgh); Royal Highland Yacht (Oban); Royal Western Yacht, Clyde Cruising (Glasgow).

WEATHERHEAD, Very Rev. James Leslie, CBE 1997; Principal Clerk of the General Assembly of the Church of Scotland, 1985–93 and 1994–96 (Moderator, 1993–94); Chaplain to the Queen in Scotland, 1991–2001, Extra Chaplain, since 2001; *b* 29 March 1931; *s* of Leslie Binnie Weatherhead, MBE, MM and Janet Hood Arnot Smith or Weatherhead; *m* 1962, Dr Anne Elizabeth Shepherd; two *s*. *Educ:* High Sch., Dundee; Univ. of Edinburgh (MA, LLB; Senior Pres., Students' Repr. Council, 1953–54); New Coll., Univ. of Edinburgh (Pres., Univ. Union, 1959–60). Temp. Acting Sub-Lieut RNVR (Nat. Service), 1955–56. Licensed by Presb. of Dundee, 1960; ordained by Presb. of Ayr, 1960; Asst Minister, Auld Kirk of Ayr, 1960–62; Minister, Trinity Church, Rothesay, 1962–69; Minister, Old Church, Montrose, 1969–85. Convener, Business Cttee of Gen. Assembly, 1981–84. Mem., Broadcasting Council for Scotland, BBC, 1978–82. Hon. DD Edinburgh, 1993. *Publication:* (ed) The Constitution and Laws of the Church of Scotland, 1997. *Recreations:* sailing, music. *Clubs:* Victory Services; RNVR Yacht.

WEATHERILL, family name of **Baron Weatherill**.

WEATHERILL, Baron *cr* 1992 (Life Peer), of North East Croydon in the London Borough of Croydon; **Bruce Bernard Weatherill;** PC 1980; DL; *b* 25 Nov. 1920; *s* of late Bernard Weatherill, Spring Hill, Guildford, and Annie Gertrude (*née* Creak); *m* 1949, Lyn, *d* of late H. T. Eatwell; two *s* one *d*. *Educ:* Malvern College. Served War of 1939–45; commissioned 4/7th Royal Dragoon Guards, 1940; transferred to Indian Army, 1941 and served with 19th King George V's Own Lancers, 1941–45 (Captain). Man. Dir, Bernard Weatherill Ltd, 1957–70, President, 1992, First Chm., Guildford Young Conservatives, 1946–49; Chm., Guildford Cons. Assoc., 1959–63; Vice-Chm., SE Area Prov. Council, 1962–64; Member National Union of Cons. Party 1963–64. MP (C) Croydon NE, 1964–83 (When elected Speaker); MP Croydon NE and Speaker of The House of Commons, 1983–92; an Opposition Whip, 1967; a Lord Comr of HM Treasury, 1970–71; Vice-Chamberlain, HM Household, 1971–72; Comptroller of HM Household, 1972–73; Treasurer of HM Household and Dep. Chief Govt Whip, 1973–74; Opposition Dep. Chief Whip, 1974–79; Chm. of Ways and Means and Dep. Speaker, 1979–83. Convenor, Cross Bench Peers, 1995–99. Chairman: Commonwealth Speakers and Presiding Officers, 1986–88; Industry and Parlt Trust, 1994–. Pres., CPA, 1986. High Bailiff of Westminster Abbey, 1989–99. Freeman of City of London, 1949; Freeman of Borough of Croydon, 1983. Hon. Bencher, Lincoln's Inn, 1988. DL Kent, 1992. Hon. LLD Coll. of William and Mary, Va, 1989; Hon. DCL: Kent, 1990; Denver, 1992; DUniv Open, 1993. KStJ 1992; Vice-Chancellor, Order of St John of Jerusalem, 1992–99. Hilal-e-Pakistan 1993. *Recreation:* playing with grandchildren. *Address:* Emmetts House, Ide Hill, Kent TN14 6BA.

See also Hon. B. R. Weatherill.

WEATHERILL, Hon. Bernard Richard; QC 1996; a Recorder, since 2000; *b* 20 May 1951; *er s* of Baron Weatherill, *qv*; *m* 1977, Sally Maxwell Fisher (marr. diss. 2001); one *s* one *d*. *Educ:* Malvern Coll.; Principia Coll., Illinois, USA; Kent Univ. (BA Hons). Called to the Bar, Middle Temple, 1974; an Asst Recorder, 1998–2000. Non-exec. Dir, A. Cohen & Co. plc, 1989–2000. Mem., General Council of the Bar, 1990–95 (Mem., Professional Conduct Cttee, 1998–99); Chm., Bar Services Co. Ltd, 2000–. FCIArb 1999. *Recreations:* lawn tennis, Real tennis, golf, wine, avoiding gardening. *Address:* Enterprise Chambers, 9 Old Square, Lincoln's Inn, WC2A 3SR. *Clubs:* Hurlingham: All England Lawn Tennis, Royal Tennis Court, Bar Lawn Tennis Society, Jesters; Royal Wimbledon Golf.

WEATHERILL, Prof. Stephen Robson; Jacques Delors Professor of European Community Law, University of Oxford, since 1998; Fellow, Somerville College, Oxford, since 1998; *b* 21 March 1961. *Educ:* Queens' Coll., Cambridge (MA); Univ. of Edinburgh (MSc). Brunel Univ., 1985; Reading Univ., 1986–87; Manchester Univ., 1987–90; Nottingham Univ., 1990–97, Jean Monnet Prof. of European Law, 1995–97. *Publications:* Cases and Materials on EC Law, 1992, 5th edn 2000; (with P. Beaumont) EC Law, 1993, 3rd edn 1999; Law and Integration in the European Union, 1995; (with G. Howells) Consumer Protection Law, 1995; EC Consumer Law and Policy, 1997; (with H. Micklitz) European Economic Law, 1997. *Address:* Somerville College, Oxford OX2 6HD. *T:* (01865) 270600.

WEATHERLEY, Christopher Roy, MD; FRCS, FRCSE, FRCSE (Orth); Consultant Spinal Surgeon, since 1987, Director, Spinal Unit, since 1993, Royal Devon & Exeter Hospital; Consultant Spinal Surgeon, Princess Elizabeth Orthopaedic Hospital, Exeter, since 1987; *b* 26 Sept. 1943; *s* of Dudley Graham Weatherley and Hilda Ada Weatherley (*née* Wilson). *Educ:* Queen Elizabeth's Sch., Crediton; Liverpool Univ. Med. Sch. (MB ChB; MD 1968). FRCSE 1973; FRCS 1974; FRCSE (Orth) 1984. Sen. Res. Associate, MRC Decompression Sickness Unit, Newcastle upon Tyne, 1973–76; Sen. Registrar in Orthopaedics, Robert Jones and Agnes Hunt Orthopaedic Hosp., 1979–87. Eur. Res. Fellow, Inst. Calôt, Berck-Plage, France, 1981–82; Consultant Spinal Surgeon, St Vincent's Hosp., Melbourne, 1985–86. Hon. Civilian Consultant, RN, 1991. Fellow, Brit. Orthopaedic Assoc., 1983; FRSocMed 1991. Member: Exec. Cttee, Brit. Scoliosis Soc., 1993– (Sec. and Treas., 1996–99); Council, Brit. Scoliosis Res. Foundn, 1998–; Eur. Cervical Spine Soc., 1984. Gold Medal Lectr, Old Oswestrians Annual Meeting, 2000. *Publications:* contrib. chapters in books, editorials and papers on: decompression sickness and dysbaric osteonecrosis; spinal tumours; scoliosis; back pain; surgical approaches to the spine; spinal fusion; ankylosing spondylitis; stress fractures in fast bowlers. *Recreations:* the fine line, the creation of myths. *Address:* 1 The Quadrant, Wonford Road, Exeter, Devon EX2 4LE. *T:* (01392) 272951. *Club:* Royal Society of Medicine.

WEATHERSTON, (William) Alastair (Paterson), CB 1993; Under Secretary, Scottish Office Education Department, 1989–95; *b* 20 Nov. 1935; *s* of William Robert Weatherston and Isabella (*née* Paterson); *m* 1961, Margaret Jardine; two *s* one *d. Educ:* Peebles High Sch.; Edinburgh Univ. (MA Hons History). Asst Principal, Dept of Health for Scotland and Scottish Educn Dept, 1959–63; Private Sec. to Permanent Under Sec. of State, Scottish Office, 1963–64; Principal, Scottish Educn Dept, 1964–72, Cabinet Office, 1972–74; Assistant Secretary: SHHD, 1974–77; Scottish Educn Dept, 1977–79; Central Services, Scottish Office, 1979–82; Dir, Scottish Courts Admin, 1982–86; Fisheries Sec., Dept of Agric. and Fisheries for Scotland, 1986–89. Sec., Gen. Council, Univ. of Edinburgh, 1997–2001. *Recreations:* reading, music. *Address:* 1 Coltbridge Terrace, Edinburgh EH12 6AB. *T:* (0131) 337 3339.

WEATHERSTONE, Sir Dennis, KBE 1990; Director, J. P. Morgan & Co., New York; *b* 29 Nov. 1930; *s* of Henry and Gladys Weatherstone; *m* 1959, Marion Blunsum; one *s* three *d. Educ:* Northwestern Polytechnic, London. Morgan Guaranty Trust Co., subseq. J. P. Morgan & Co.: Sen. Vice-Pres., 1972–77; Exec. Vice-Pres., 1977–79; Treas., 1977–79; Vice-Chm., 1979–80; Chm., Exec. Cttee, 1980–86; Pres., 1987–89; Chm. and Chief Exec., 1990–94. *Address:* J. P. Morgan & Co., 60 Wall Street, New York, NY 10260, USA.

WEATHERSTONE, Robert Bruce, TD 1962; CA; Chairman, Lothian Health Board, 1986–90; *b* 14 May 1926; *s* of Sir Duncan Mackay Weatherstone, MC, TD, and late Janet Pringle; *m* 1954, Agnes Elaine Jean Fisher; one *s* one *d. Educ:* Edinburgh and Dollar Academies. CA 1951. Served Royal Marines, 44 Commando, 1944–47. Dir/Sec., J. T. Salvesen Ltd, 1954–62; Dir and Mem., Management Cttee, Christian Salvesen Ltd, 1962–83; Dir, Lothian Region Transport plc, 1986–92. Chm., Leith Enterprise Trust, 1983–88; Vice-Pres., Leonard Cheshire Foundn, 1996– (Trustee, 1973–96). *Recreations:* hill-walking, ornithology. *Address:* 27 Ravelston Garden, Edinburgh EH4 3LE. *T:* (0131) 337 4035. *Club:* New (Edinburgh).

WEAVER, (Christopher) Giles (Herron), FCA; Chairman, Murray Emerging Growth & Income Trust plc; *b* 4 April 1946; *s* of Lt Col John Weaver and Ursula (*née* Horlick); *m* 1975, Rosamund Betty Mayhew; two *s* two *d. Educ:* Eton Coll.; London Business Sch. (MSc 1973). FCA 1978. Dir, UK and Pensions Investment, Ivory & Sime, 1976–86; Man. Dir, Pension Mgt, Prudential Corp., 1986–90; Murray Johnstone Ltd, 1990: Chief Investment Officer, 1990–93; Man. Dir, 1993–99; Chm., 1999–2000. Non-executive Director: Helical Bar, 1993–; James Finlay, 1996–; Charter Eur. Trust, 1997–; Atrium Underwriting, 1998–; Aberdeen Asset Management plc. Trustee and Dep. Chm., Nat. Galls of Scotland, 1998–; Chm., HHA in Scotland, 1999–. *Recreations:* ski-ing, golf, tennis, bridge. *Address:* Grey Walls, Gullane, E Lothian EH31 2EG. *T:* (01620) 843205. *Clubs:* Hurlingham, Queen's; New (Edinburgh); Hon. Company of Edinburgh Golfers (Muirfield).

WEAVER, Leonard John, CBE 1990; Chairman: The Engineering Link, since 1996; Shorterm Group, since 1999; *b* 10 June 1936; *s* of late A. W. Weaver, HMOCS, and of B. I. M. Weaver (*née* Geleyns); *m* 1963, Penelope Ann Sturge-Young; five *s* one *d. Educ:* St Mary's Sch.; Battersea Coll. of Advanced Technology (Surrey Univ.); MA London. CEng, FIEE, FIM, FIMechE, FIMC. Served Kenya Regt, 1955–57. AEI, 1962–64; PYE-TMC, 1964–66; Consultant, Dir and Man. Dir, P-E Internat., 1966–82; Chairman: Polymark Internat., 1982–92; Manifold Industries, 1982–95; Pearson Engineering, 1985–88; Jones & Shipman, 1988–98; Eutech Engrg Servs, 1995–2001. Member: NEDO Prod. Control Adv. Gp (Chm., 1980–82); NEDO Advanced Manfg Systems Gp, 1983–86; SERC Teaching Co. Mangt Cttee, 1983–86; Jt DTI/SERC Advanced Manfg Tech. Cttee, 1983–91 (Chm., 1987–91); SERC Engrg Bd, 1987–91; Indust. Develt Adv. Bd, 1989–95; Innovation Adv. Bd, 1991–93; Steering Bd, NPL, 1993–95. Member Council: Inst. of Mgt (formerly BIM), 1978–83, 1991–98 (Vice Chm., 1993–97); Inst. of Mgt Consultants, 1978–86 (Pres., 1983–84); IProdE, 1980–91 (Pres., 1990–91); IEE, 1991–96. Mem. Bd of Dirs, Soc. of Manfg Engrs, USA, 1998– (Hon. Mem., 1990). Freeman, City of London, 1984; Sen. Warden, 1999–2000, Master, 2000–01, Engrs' Co. CIMgt (CBIM 1980); FRSA, FSME. DUniv Surrey, 1991. Sandforth Smith Award, Inst. of Management Consultants, 1984; Internat. Engineer of the Year, San Fernando Valley Engrs Council, 1985; Calif. State Legis. Commend., 1985. *Publications:* contribs to professional jls. *Recreations:* book collecting, cricket. *Address:* Crab Apple Court, Oxshott Road, Leatherhead, Surrey KT22 0DQ. *T:* (01372) 843647. *Clubs:* Reform, City Livery, MCC.

WEAVER, Oliver; QC 1985; *b* 27 March 1942; *s* of Denis Weaver and late Kathleen (*née* Lynch); *m* 1964, Julia Mary (*née* MacClymont); one *s* two *d. Educ:* Friends' Sch., Saffron Walden; Trinity Coll., Cambridge (MA, LLM). President, Cambridge Union Society, 1963. Called to the Bar, Middle Temple, 1965; Lincoln's Inn, 1969. Mem. Bar Council, 1981–84; Vice-Chm., Bar Law Reform Cttee, 1987–89; Member: Incorporated Council of Law Reporting, 1987–93; Panel of Chairmen of Authorisation and Disciplinary Tribunals, Securities and Futures Authy (formerly Securities Assoc., then Securities and Futures Assoc.), 1988–93. Retired due to ill-health, 1993. *Recreations:* fishing, racing, gun dogs. *Address:* Kennel Farm, Albury End, Ware, Herts SG11 2HS. *T:* (01279) 771331.

WEBB, Sir Adrian (Leonard), Kt 2000; DLitt; Vice-Chancellor, University of Glamorgan, since 1993; *b* 19 July 1943; *s* of Leonard and Rosina Webb; *m* 1st, 1966, Caroline Williams (marr. diss. 1995); two *s*; 2nd, 1996, Monjulee Dass. *Educ:* Birmingham Univ. (1st cl. Hons BSocSci 1965); LSE (MSc (Econ) 1966); DLitt Loughborough 1993. Lectr, LSE, 1966–74; Res. Dir, Personal Social Services Council, 1974–76; Loughborough University: Prof. of Social Policy, 1976–93; Dir, Centre for Res. in Social Policy, 1983–90; Dean, then Pro Vice-Chancellor, subseq. Sen. Pro Vice-Chancellor, 1986–93. Member: Nat. Cttee of Inquiry into Higher Educn (Dearing Cttee), 1996–97; BBC Broadcasting Council for Wales, 1998–. Non-exec. Dir, E Glamorgan NHS Trust, 1997–. FRSA. *Publications:* Change, Choice and Conflict in Social Policy, 1975; Planning Need and Scarcity: essays on the personal social services, 1986; The Economic Approach to Social Policy, 1986; Social Work, Social Care and Social Planning, 1987; Joint Approaches to Social Policy: rationality and practice, 1988; contribs on social policy to scholarly and professional periodicals. *Recreations:* walking, painting (water colour), ornithology. *Address:* University of Glamorgan, Pontypridd, Mid Glam CF37 1DL. *T:* (01443) 480480.

WEBB, Rear-Adm. Arthur Brooke, CB 1975; retired; *b* 13 June 1918; *m* 1949, Rachel Marian Gerrish; three *d.* Joined Royal Navy, 1936. Comdr 1954, Captain 1963, Rear-Adm. 1973. *Recreations:* gardening, walking, survival. *Address:* Shearwater, Downderry, Torpoint, Cornwall PL11 3LL.

WEBB, Prof. Colin Edward, MBE 2000; DPhil; FRS 1991; FInstP; Professor, Department of Physics, University of Oxford, since 1992; Senior Research Fellow, Jesus College, Oxford, since 1988; Founder and Chairman, Oxford Lasers Ltd, since 1977; *b* 9 Dec. 1937; *s* of Alfred Edward Webb and Doris (*née* Collins); *m* 1st, 1964, Pamela Mabel Cooper White (*d* 1992); two *d*; 2nd, 1995, Margaret Helen (*née* Dewar); two step *d. Educ:* Univ. of Nottingham (BSc 1960); Oriel Coll., Oxford (DPhil 1964). FInstP 1985. Mem., Technical Staff, Bell Labs, Murray Hill, NJ, 1964–68; University of Oxford: AEI Res. Fellow in Physics, Clarendon Lab., 1968–71; Univ. Lectr, 1971–90; Tutorial Fellow, Jesus Coll., 1973–88; Reader, Dept of Physics, 1990–92; Hd of Atomic and Laser Physics, 1995–99. Visiting Professor: Dept of Pure and Applied Physics, Univ. of Salford, 1987–; Dept of Mechanical Engrg, Cranfield Univ., 1999–. Fellow, Optical Soc. of America, 1988. Hon. DSc Salford, 1996. Duddell Medal and Prize, 1985, Glazebrook Medal and Prize, 2001, Inst. of Physics; Clifford Paterson Lect. and Medal, Royal Soc., 1999. *Publications:* contribs on lasers, laser mechanisms and applications to learned jls. *Recreations:* travel, photography, music, reading. *Address:* Clarendon Laboratory, Parks Road, Oxford OX1 3PU. *T:* (01865) 272210.

WEBB, Colin Thomas; Editor-in-Chief, Press Association, 1986–94 (Director, 1989–96; General Manager, 1994–96); *b* 26 March 1939; *e s* of late William Thomas and Ada Alexandra Webb; *m* 1970, Margaret Frances, *y d* of late Maurice George and Joan Rowden Cheshire; two *s* one *d. Educ:* Portsmouth Grammar School. Reporter, Portsmouth Evening News, Surrey Mirror, Press Assoc., Daily Telegraph, The Times; Royal Army Pay Corps Short Service Commission (to Captain), 1960–64; Home News Editor, The Times, 1969–74; Editor, Cambridge Evening News, 1974–82; Dep. Editor, The Times, 1982–86; Journalist Dir, Times Newspaper Holdings, 1983–86. Member: Core Cttee, British Executive Internat. Press Inst., 1984–96; Council, Commonwealth Press Union, 1985–96; Lord Chancellor's Adv. Bd on Family Law, 1997–2001; Consultative Council, BBFC, 2000–. Nat. Trustee, Lloyds TSB Foundn for England and Wales, 2000–. Gov., Univ. of Portsmouth, 2001– (Hon. Fellow, 1991). *Publication:* (co-author with The Times News Team) Black Man in Search of Power, 1968. *Recreations:* family, walking, history books. *Address:* Fairfield House, Pine Grove, West Broyle, Chichester, West Sussex PO19 3PN. *T:* (01243) 771870. *Club:* Garrick.

WEBB, Prof. David Charles, PhD; Professor of Finance, and Director, Financial Markets Group Research Centre, London School of Economics, since 1991; *b* 13 July 1953; *s* of Charles Ronald Webb and Margaret Jane Webb (*née* Oldham). *Educ:* Grangefield Grammar Sch., Stockton upon Tees; Univ. of Manchester (BA Econs 1974; MA Econs 1975); London School of Economics (PhD 1979). Lectr, Univ. of Bristol, 1978–84; Lectr, 1984–90, Reader in Economics, 1991, LSE. Vis. Associate Prof., Queen's Univ., Canada, 1982–84; Vis. Prof. of Economics, Univ. of Iowa, 1991. Consultant, Asian Develt Bank, 1998–; Mem., Adv. Bd, Centro de Estudios Monetarios y Financieros, Madrid, 1998–. Editor, Economica, 1989–97; Associate Editor, Jl of Banking and Finance, 1997–. *Publications:* articles in Econs and Finance, Qly Jl of Econs, Internat. Econ. Review, Econ. Jl and Jl of Public Econs. *Recreations:* ski-ing, football. *Address:* Financial Markets Group, London School of Economics, Houghton Street, WC2A 2AE. *T:* (020) 7955 6301.

WEBB, Prof. Edwin Clifford; Emeritus Professor, University of Queensland and Macquarie University; Vice-Chancellor, Macquarie University, 1976–86; *b* 21 May 1921; *s* of William Webb and Nellie Webb; *m* 1st, 1942, Violet Sheila Joan (*née* Tucker) (marr. diss. 1987); one *s* four *d* (and one *s* decd); 2nd, 1988, Miriam Margaret Therese (*née* Armstrong). *Educ:* Poole Grammar Sch.; Cambridge Univ. (BA, MA, PhD). FRACI 1968. Cambridge University: Beit Meml Res. Fellow, 1944–46; Univ. Demonstrator in Biochem., 1946–50; Univ. Lectr in Biochem., 1950–62; University of Queensland: Foundn Prof. of Biochem. and Head of Dept, 1962–70; Dep. Vice-Chancellor (Academic), 1970–76. Pres., Australasian Council on Chiropractic and Osteopathic Educn, 1991–96. Hon. DSc: Queensland, 1978; Macquarie, 1988. *Publications:* Enzymes, 1959, 3rd edn 1979; 56 scientific papers. *Recreations:* music, theatre. *Address:* 34 Sorbonne Close, Sippy Downs, Qld 4556, Australia.

WEBB, George Hannam, CMG 1984; OBE 1974; HM Diplomatic Service, retired; *b* 24 Dec. 1929; *s* of George Ernest Webb, HM Colonial Service, Kenya, and Mary Hannam (*née* Stephens); *m* 1956, Josephine (later MA Cantab; JP Surrey), *d* of late Richard Chatterton, Horncastle; two *s* two *d. Educ:* Malvern Coll.; King's Coll., Cambridge (MA). Served 14/20th King's Hussars, 1948–49; Parachute Regt (TA), 1950–53. Joined Colonial Administration, Kenya, 1953: District Officer, Central Nyanza, 1954–56; N Nyanza, 1956–57; District Commissioner, Moyale, 1958–60; Secretariat, Nairobi, 1960–62; retired 1963 and joined HM Diplomatic Service; First Sec., Bangkok, 1964–67; Accra, 1969–73; Counsellor, Tehran, 1977–79, Washington, 1980–82; retd 1985. Dir, Management Develt, 1985–89, Sen. Fellow, 1989–93, City Univ. Member Council: Royal Soc. for Asian Affairs, 1984–91; Friends of Nat. Army Museum, 1988–95; Gresham Coll., 1988–2000; Horatian Soc., 1991–2001; Trustee: Hakluyt Soc., 1986–; Encounter, 1989–91. Liveryman, Scriveners' Co., 1989–. Editor, *Kipling Journal*, 1980–2001. *Publications:* The Bigger Bang: growth of a financial revolution, 1987; (ed with Sir Hugh Cortazzi) Kipling's Japan, 1988; contribs to learned jls. *Recreation:* books. *Address:* Weavers, Danes Hill, Woking GU22 7HQ. *T:* (01483) 761989. *Clubs:* Travellers (Chm., 1987–91), Beefsteak, Royal Commonwealth Society.

WEBB, Prof. John Stuart, FREng; Professor of Applied Geochemistry in the University of London, 1961–79, now Emeritus, and Senior Research Fellow, 1979–89, Imperial College of Science and Technology; *b* 28 Aug. 1920; *s* of Stuart George Webb and Caroline Rabjohns Webb (*née* Pengelly); *m* 1946, Jean Millicent Dyer; one *s. Educ:* Westminster City School; Royal School of Mines, Imperial College of Science and Technology (BSc, ARSM, 1941). Served War of 1939–45, Royal Engineers, 1941–43. Geological Survey of Nigeria, 1943–44; Royal School of Mines, Imperial Coll., 1945–; Beit Scientific Research Fellow, 1945–47; PhD, DIC, in Mining Geology, 1947; Lecturer in Mining Geology, 1947–55; Reader in Applied Geochemistry, 1955–61. DSc, 1967. Mem., Home Office Forensic Science Cttee, 1969–75. Mem. Council, Instn of Mining and Metallurgy, 1964–71, and 1974–83, Vice Pres., 1971–73, Pres., 1973–74; Mem. Bd, Council Engineering Instns, 1973–74; Reg. Vice-Pres. (Europe), Soc. of Econ. Geologists, USA, 1979–81. Mem., Royal Soc. Wkg Pty on Environmental Geochem. and Health, 1979–83. FREng (FEng 1979). Hon. Mem., Assoc. Exploration Geochemists, USA, 1977; Hon. FIMM 1980. Consolidated Goldfields of SA Gold Medal, IMM, 1953; William Smith Medal, Geol Soc. of London, 1981. *Publications:* (with H. E. Hawkes) Geochemistry in Mineral Exploration, 1962, 2nd edn (with A. W. Rose) 1979; (jtly) Geochemical Atlas of Northern Ireland, 1973; (jtly) Wolfson Geochemical Atlas of England and Wales, 1978; contrib. to scientific and technical jls. *Recreations:* amateur radio, meteorology. *Address:* Stone Cottage, Lyons Road, Slinfold, Horsham, Sussex RH13 7QT. *T:* (01403) 790243.

WEBB, Prof. Joseph Ernest, PhD (London) 1944, DSc (London) 1949; CBiol, FIBiol; FLS; FZS; Professor of Zoology, 1960–80, and Vice-Principal, 1976–80, Westfield College, University of London, now Emeritus Professor; *b* 22 March 1915; *s* of Joseph Webb and Constance Inman Webb (*née* Hickox); *m* 1940, Gwenlilian Clara Coldwell (*d* 1994); three *s. Educ:* Rutlish School; Birkbeck College, London (BSc 1940). FZS 1943;

CBiol, FIBiol 1963; FLS 1972. Research Entomologist and Parasitologist at The Cooper Technical Bureau, Berkhamsted, Herts, 1940–46; Lecturer, Univ. of Aberdeen, 1946–48; Senior Lecturer, 1948–50, Professor of Zoology, 1950–60, University Coll., Ibadan, Nigeria. Hon. Fellow, QMW (formerly Westfield Coll.), 1986. *Publications:* (jointly): Guide to Invertebrate Animals, 1975, 2nd edn 1978; Guide to Living Mammals, 1977, 2nd edn 1979; Guide to Living Reptiles, 1978; Guide to Living Birds, 1979; Guide to Living Fishes, 1981; Guide to Living Amphibians, 1981; various on insect physiology, insecticides, systematics, populations, tropical ecology, marine biology and sedimentology. *Recreations:* art, music, photography, gardening. *Address:* 43 Hill Top, NW11 6EA. *T:* (020) 8458 2571. *Club:* Athenæum.

WEBB, Prof. Leslie Roy; Vice-Chancellor, Griffith University, since 1985; *b* 18 July 1935; *s* of Leslie Hugh Charles Webb and Alice Myra Webb; *m* 1966, Heather, *d* of late H. Brown; one *s* one *d.* *Educ:* Wesley College, Univ. of Melbourne (BCom 1957); Univ. of London (PhD 1962). FASSA 1986; FAIM 1989; FACE 1997. Sen. Lectr in Economics, Univ. of Melbourne, 1964–68; Reader in Economics, La Trobe Univ., 1968–72; University of Melbourne: Truby Williams Prof. of Economics, 1973–84, Prof. Emeritus, 1984; Pro-Vice-Chancellor, 1982–84; Chm., Academic Bd, 1983–84. Vis. Prof., Cornell, 1967–68. Chairman: Bd, Qld Tertiary Admissions Centre, 1986, 1991, 1992 (Mem., 1985–); Australian-Amer. Educnl Foundn (Fulbright Program), 1986–90 (Mem., 1985–89); Member: Conf. of Qld Vice-Chancellors, 1985– (Chm., 1988); Bd of Dirs, Australian Vice-Chancellors' Cttee, 1991–94; Cttee, Sir Robert Menzies Australian Studies Centre, Univ. of London, 1990–92; Bd of Govs, Foundn for Develt Co-operation, 1990–. Consultant, UN Conf. on Trade and Develt, 1974–75; Chm., Cttee of Inquiry into S Australian Dairy Industry, 1977; Mem., Council of Advice, Bureau of Industry Economics, 1982–84; Pres., Victoria Branch, Econ. Soc. of Aust. and NZ, 1976. Award for outstanding achievement, US Inf. Agency, 1987. Joint Editor, The Economic Record, 1973–77. Cavaliere dell'Ordine al Merito (Italy), 1995. *Publication:* (ed jtly) Industrial Economics: Australian studies, 1982. *Recreations:* music, art. *Address:* Griffith University, Kessels Road, Nathan, Qld 4111, Australia. *T:* (7) 38757340.

WEBB, Margaret Elizabeth Barbieri; *see* Barbieri, M. E.

WEBB, Maysie (Florence), CBE 1979; BSc; Deputy Director, British Museum, 1971–83 (Assistant Director 1968–71); *b* 1 May 1923; *d* of Charles and Florence Webb. *Educ:* Kingsbury County School; Northern Polytechnic. Southwark Public Libraries, 1940–45; A. C. Cossor Ltd, 1945–50; British Non-Ferrous Metals Research Assoc., 1950–52; Mullard Equipment Ltd, 1952–55; Morgan Crucible Co. Ltd, 1955–60; Patent Office Library, 1960–66; Keeper, National Reference Library of Science and Invention, 1966–68. General Comr in England and Wales, 1976–2002. Trustee of the Royal Armouries, 1984–90. *Recreations:* family and friends, thinking.

WEBB, Michael Alfred Healey; Consultant in Occupational Medicine; Deputy Chief Commander, St John Ambulance, since 1999; *b* 10 Oct. 1934; *s* of Alfred Webb and Lily Margaret Webb (*née* Beeson); *m* 1962, Shirley Ann Parsons; one *s* one *d.* *Educ:* Sir Walter St John's Grammar Sch.; King's Coll., London; King's Coll. Hosp. Med. Sch. MRCS, LRCP 1961; DIH 1978; FFOM 1996. Various posts as occupational health physician to: EMAS, 1973–78; Commonwealth Smelting Ltd, 1978–81; Post Office, 1981–94. Med. Dir, St John Ambulance Assoc., 1991–96; Dir-Gen., St John Ambulance, 1996–99. KStJ 1996. *Publication:* (jtly) First Aid Manual, 7th edn 1997. *Recreations:* gardening, home maintenance. *Address:* 48 Offington Avenue, Worthing, W Sussex BN14 9PJ.

WEBB, Pauline Mary, FKC; retired; author and broadcaster; *b* 28 June 1927; *d* of Rev. Leonard F. Webb. *Educ:* King's Coll., London Univ. (BA, AKC, FKC 1985); Union Theological Seminary, New York (STM). BA English Hons (King's), 1948; Teacher's Diploma, London Inst. of Educn, 1949. Asst Mistress, Thames Valley Grammar Sch., 1949–52; Editor, Methodist Missionary Soc., 1955–66; Vice-Pres., Methodist Conf., 1965–66; Dir, Lay Training, Methodist Church, 1967–73; Area Sec., Methodist Missionary Soc., 1973–79; Chm., Community and Race Relns Unit, BCC, 1976–79; Organiser, Religious Broadcasting, BBC World Service, 1979–87. Vice-Chm., Central Cttee, WCC, 1968–75; Jt Chm., World Conf. on Religion and Peace, 1989–93. Pres., Feed the Minds, 1998–. Hon Life Mem., World Assoc. of Christian Communication, 1998. Hon. Dr in Protestant Theology, Univ. of Brussels, 1984; Hon. DSL Victoria Univ., Toronto, 1985; Hon. DHL Mt St Vincent Univ., Nova Scotia, 1987; Hon. DD Birmingham, 1997. *Publications:* Women of Our Company, 1958; Women of Our Time, 1960; Operation-Healing, 1964; All God's Children, 1964; Are We Yet Alive?, 1966; Agenda for the Churches, 1968; Salvation Today, 1974; Eventful Worship, 1975; Where are the Women?, 1979; Faith and Faithfulness, 1985; Celebrating Friendship, 1986; Evidence for the Power of Prayer, 1987; Candles for Advent, 1989; (ed jtly) Dictionary of the Ecumenical Movement, 1991; She Flies Beyond, 1993; (ed) The Long Struggle: the World Council of Churches' involvement with South Africa, 1994; (ed) All Loves Excelling, 1997; Worship in Every Event, 1998; Living by Grace (anthol.), 2001. *Address:* 14 Paddocks Green, Salmon Street, NW9 8NH. *Club:* BBC.

WEBB, Richard Murton Lumley; Chairman, Morgan Grenfell & Co. Ltd, 1989–96; *b* 7 March 1939; *s* of Richard Henry Lumley Webb and Elizabeth Martin (*née* Munro Kerr); *m* 1966, Juliet Wendy English Devenish; one *s* one *d.* *Educ:* Winchester Coll.; New Coll., Oxford (BA Modern Hist.). Mem., Inst. Chartered Accountants of Scotland, 1965. Brown Fleming & Murray, 1961–68; Morgan Grenfell & Co. Ltd, 1968–96; Morgan Grenfell Gp PLC, 1988–96. Chairman: Medway Housing Society Ltd, 1996–; Wax Lyrical Ltd, 1997–99; Dir, Scottish Provident Instn, 1997–2001. *Address:* 12 Gwendolen Avenue, Putney, SW15 6EH. *Club:* Hurlingham.

WEBB, Robert Stopford; QC 1988; General Counsel and Head of Government and Industry Affairs, Safety, Security and Environment, British Airways, since 1998; *b* 4 Oct. 1948; *s* of late Robert Victor Bertram Webb, MC and of Isabella Raine Webb (*née* Hinks); *m* 1975, Angela Mary Freshwater; two *s.* *Educ:* Wycliffe Coll.; Exeter Univ. (LLB 1970). Called to the Bar, Inner Temple, 1971 (Bencher, 1997), and Lincoln's Inn, 1996; a Recorder, 1993–98; Western Circuit. Director: Air Mauritius, 1998–; London Stock Exchange, 2001–. Chm., Air Law Gp, RAeS, 1988–93 (FRAeS 1992); English Bar Rep., Internat. Bar Assoc., 1994–99; Chm., Internat. Relations Cttee, Bar Council, 1997–98; Member: Commn d'Arbitrage Aerien et Spatial, Paris, 1994–; Bd, Internat. Acad. of Trial Lawyers, 1994– (Fellow, 1990). *Recreations:* fly-fishing, golf, conservation. *Address:* British Airways PLC, Waterside (HBB3), PO Box 365, Harmondsworth UB7 0GB. *T:* (020) 8738 6870, *Fax:* (020) 8738 9964. *Clubs:* Royal Automobile, Reform; Royal Wimbledon Golf, Royal Lytham St Anne's Golf, Prestbury Golf.

WEBB, Simon, CBE 1991; Policy Director, Ministry of Defence, since 2001; *b* 21 Oct. 1951; *s* of Rev. Canon Bertie Webb and Jane Webb (*née* Braley); *m* 1975, Alexandra Jane Culme-Seymour; one *s* one *d.* *Educ:* King's Sch., Worcester (Schol.); Hertford Coll., Oxford (Meeke Schol.; MA). Entered MoD, 1972: Asst Private Sec. to Minister of State, 1975; Principal, 1977; Public Enterprises, HM Treasury, 1982–85; Dir of Resources and Progs (Warships), MoD, 1985–88; Rand Corp., Santa Monica, Calif, 1988–89; Head, Agency Team, MoD, 1989; Private Sec. to Sec. of State for Defence, 1989–92; Minister (Defence Material), Washington, 1992–96; Dir Gen. Resources, PE, MoD, 1996–98; Team Leader, Smart Procurement, 1998–99; Asst Under Sec. of State (Home & Overseas), subseq. Dir Gen., Operational Policy, MoD, 1999–2001. Edgell Sheppee Prize for Engrg and Econs. *Publication:* Defense Acquisition and Free Markets, 1990. *Recreations:* cycling, gardens, golf. *Address:* Ministry of Defence, Metropole Building, Northumberland Avenue, WC2N 5BP. *T:* (020) 7218 9000. *Club:* Reform.

WEBB, Steven John; MP (Lib Dem) Northavon, since 1997; *b* 18 July 1965; *s* of Brian and Patricia Webb; *m* 1993, Rev. Helen Edwards; one *s* one *d.* *Educ:* Hertford Coll., Oxford (1st Cl. BA Hons PPE). Economist, Inst. for Fiscal Studies, 1986–95; Prof. of Social Policy, Bath Univ., 1995–97. *Publication:* (with Alissa Goodman and Paul Johnson) Inequality in the UK, 1997. *Recreations:* church organ, oboe. *Address:* (constituency office) Poole Court, Poole Court Drive, Yate BS37 5PP.

WEBB, Sir Thomas (Langley), Kt 1975; *b* 25 April 1908; *s* of Robert Langley Webb and Alice Mary Webb; *m* 1942, Jeannette Alison Lang; one *s* one *d.* *Educ:* Melbourne Church of England Grammar Sch. Joined Huddart Parker Ltd, 1926 (Man. Dir, 1955–61). Served War, AIF, 1940–45. Dir, Commercial Bank of Aust., 1960–78 (Chm., 1970–78); Dir and Vice-Chm., McIlwraith McEacharn Ltd, 1961–92. Vice-Pres. and Hon. Treas., Royal Victorian Eye and Ear Hosp., 1963–82. *Recreations:* golf, tennis. *Address:* 18 Chastleton Avenue, Toorak, Victoria 3142, Australia. *T:* (3) 98275259. *Clubs:* Australian, Melbourne, Royal Melbourne Golf, Royal South Yarra Tennis (all Melbourne).

WEBB, William Grierson; freelance conductor and teacher; Musical Director, South Coast Opera, since 1998; *b* 16 Oct. 1947; *s* of Horace James Harry Webb and Marjorie Cairns (*née* Grierson); *m* 1984, Elizabeth Jean Shannon; two *s.* *Educ:* Rugby School; Merton Coll., Oxford (MA); Salzburg Mozarteum (Dip.). Hon. FLCM. Conductor, Trier Opera House, Germany, 1973–76; Asst General Administrator, Scottish Nat. Orchestra, 1976–78; Founder Administrator, Nat. Youth Orchestra of Scotland, 1978–87; Dep. Dir, 1987–90, Artistic Dir, 1991–96, London Coll. of Music; Associate Artistic Dir, The Rehearsal Orch., 1994–98. Musical Dir, Aberdeen Internat. Youth Festival, 1989–91. Dir, Chase Lodge Music, 1997–. Chm., Mendelssohn and Boise Scholarship Foundns, 1992–94. *Publications:* (trans.) Tyrol through the Ages, 1973; The Music of John McLeod, 1979. *Address:* Chase Lodge, Herbert Road, Bournemouth BH4 8HD.

WEBB-CARTER, Maj. Gen. Sir Evelyn (John), KCVO 2000; OBE 1989; General Officer Commanding London District and Major General Commanding Household Division, 1997–2000; *b* 30 Jan. 1946; *s* of Brig. Brian Webb-Carter, DSO, OBE and Rosemary Webb-Carter (*née* Hood); *m* 1973, Hon. Anne Celia Wigram, *yr d* of Baron Wigram, *qv*; one *s* two *d.* *Educ:* Wellington Coll.; RMA Sandhurst. Commissioned Grenadier Guards, 1966; Commanded: 1st Bn Grenadier Guards, 1985–88; 19 Mechanised Bde, 1991–93; Multi National Div. (SW) in Bosnia, 1996–97. Regtl Lt-Col, Grenadier Guards, 1995–2000; Col, Duke of Wellington's Regt, 1999–; Hon. Regtl Col, King's Troop, RHA, 2001–. Chm., Mounted Infantry Club, 1993–; Pres., Army Boxing Assoc., 1998–2000. *Recreations:* hunting, military history, riding in foreign parts. *Clubs:* Boodle's; Banja Luka Hunt (Bosnia).

WEBBER; *see* Lloyd Webber.

WEBBER, Prof. Bryan Ronald, PhD; FRS 2001; CPhys, FInstP; Professor of Theoretical Physics, University of Cambridge, since 1999; Fellow, Emmanuel College, Cambridge, since 1973; *b* 25 July 1943; *s* of Frederick Ronald Webber and Iris Evelyn Webber (*née* Hutchings); *m* 1968, Akemi Horie. *Educ:* Colston's Sch., Bristol; Queen's Coll., Oxford (MA); Univ. of Calif, Berkeley (PhD 1969). CPhys, FInstP 1987. Physicist, Lawrence Berkeley Nat. Lab., Calif, 1969–71; Department of Physics, University of Cambridge: Res. Asst, 1971–73; Demonstrator, 1973–78; Lectr, 1978–94; Reader, 1994–99. *Publications:* (jtly) QCD and Collider Physics, 1996; contrib. articles on high energy physics. *Address:* Cavendish Laboratory, Madingley Road, Cambridge CB3 0HE. *T:* (01223) 337200.

WEBBER, Howard Simon; Chief Executive, Criminal Injuries Compensation Authority, since 1999; *b* 25 Jan. 1955; *s* of Manny and Josie Webber; *m* 1978, Sandra Wagman; one *s.* *Educ:* Univ. of Birmingham (LLB 1976); Harvard Univ. (MPA 1987). Joined Home Office, 1976; seconded to Royal Commn on Criminal Procedure, 1979–80 and Cabinet Office, 1986; Harkness Fellow, USA, 1986–87; Prison Bldg Budget Manager, Home Office, 1987–88; Dir, Incentive Funding, 1988–91, Hd, Policy and Planning, 1991–94, Arts Council; Manager, Public Sector MBA, Cabinet Office, 1994; Hd, Voluntary Services Unit/Active Community Unit, Home Office, 1995–99. *Publication:* (jtly) A Creative Future: a national strategy for the arts and media, 1993. *Recreations:* travel, the arts. *Address:* Criminal Injuries Compensation Authority, Morley House, 26–30 Holborn Viaduct, EC1A 2JQ. *T:* (020) 7842 6802.

WEBBER, Rev. Canon Lionel Frank; Rector of Basildon, 1976–2001; Chaplain to the Queen, since 1994; *b* 12 July 1935; *s* of Nellie and Sydney Webber; *m* 1961, Jean Thomas; one *d.* *Educ:* Danetree Road Co. Secondary Sch., Ewell; Kelham Theol Coll.; St Michael's Theol Coll., Llandaff. Ordained deacon, 1960, priest, 1961; Curate: The Saviour, Bolton, 1960–63; Holy Trinity, Aberavon, 1963–65; Rector, Stowell Meml Parish Ch., Salford, 1965–69; Vicar, Holy Trinity, Aberavon, 1969–74; Team Vicar, Stantonbury, Milton Keynes, 1974–76. Hon. Canon, Chelmsford Cathedral, 1984–2001. Chaplain: British Racing Drivers' Club; RNSA. *Recreations:* motor racing, sailing.

WEBBER, Roy Seymour, IPFA, FCCA; Town Clerk and Chief Executive, Royal Borough of Kensington and Chelsea, 1979–90; *b* 8 April 1933; *s* of A. E. and A. M. Webber; *m* 1960, Barbara Ann (*née* Harries); one *s* three *d.* *Educ:* Ipswich School. Ipswich CBC, 1949–55; Coventry CBC, 1955–58; St Pancras BC, 1958–61; IBM (UK) Ltd, 1961–62; Woolwich BC, 1962–65; Greenwich LBC, 1965–68; Royal Borough of Kensington and Chelsea: Dep. Borough Treasurer, 1968–73; Director of Finance, 1973–79. *Recreation:* walking. *Address:* 11 River Park, Marlborough, Wilts SN8 1NH. *T:* (01672) 511426.

WEBER, Catherine Elisabeth Dorcas; *see* Bell, C. E. D.

WEBER, Prof. Jonathan Norden, FRCP, FRCPath; Jefferiss Professor of Genito-Urinary Medicine and Communicable Diseases, Imperial College and St Mary's Hospital, since 1991; Chairman, Wright-Fleming Institute, Imperial College School of Medicine, since 2000; *b* 29 Dec. 1954; *s* of Dr Geoffrey Norden Weber and Rosalie Weber; *m* 1996, Dr Sophie Elisabeth Day; three *s.* *Educ:* Gonville and Caius Coll., Cambridge (BA 1976); St Bartholomew's Med. Sch. (MB BChir 1979). FRCP 1993; FRCPath 1997. Wellcome Trust Res. Fellow, St Mary's Hosp. Med. Sch., 1982–85; Wellcome Trust Lectr in Cell and Molecular Biol., Inst. Cancer Res., 1985–88; Sen. Lectr, Dept of Medicine, RPMS, 1988–91. FMedSci 2000. *Publications:* The Management of AIDS Patients, 1986; contribs to The Lancet, etc. *Recreations:* motor-bikes, boats. *Address:* 50 St Paul's Road, Islington, N1 2QW. *T:* (020) 7226 4579; *e-mail:* j.weber@ic.ac.uk.

WEBER, Jürgen; Chairman, Executive Board, Lufthansa German Airlines, since 1991; *b* 17 Oct. 1941; *m* 1965, Sabine Rossberg; one *s* one *d*. *Educ:* Stuttgart Tech. Univ. (Dipl. Ing. Aeronautical Engrg 1965); MIT (Sen. Mgt Trng 1980). Joined Lufthansa, 1967: Engrg Div., 1967–74; Director: Line Maintenance Dept, 1974–78; Aircraft Engrg Subdiv., 1978–87; Chief Operating Officer (Tech.), 1987–89; Dep. Mem., Exec. Bd, 1989–90; Chief Exec., Tech., 1990–91. *Recreations:* jogging, ski-ing. *Address:* Deutsche Lufthansa AG, Lufthansa Basis, 60546 Frankfurt, Germany. *T:* (69) 6962200.

WEBER, Prof. Richard Robert, Jr, PhD; Churchill Professor of the Mathematics for Operational Research, Cambridge University, since 1994; Fellow, since 1978 and Vice President, since 1996, Queens' College, Cambridge; *b* 25 Feb. 1953; *s* of Richard Robert Weber and Elizabeth Bray. *Educ:* Walnut Hills High Sch., USA; Solihull Sch.; Downing Coll., Cambridge (BA 1974; MA 1978; PhD 1980). Cambridge University: Asst Lectr and Lectr in Engrg, 1978–92; Reader in Management Sci., Engrg, 1992–94; Queens' College: Res. Fellow, 1977–78; Tutor, 1979–92; Dir of Studies (Maths), 1985–94. *Publications:* numerous articles on stochastic systems, scheduling and queueing theory. *Recreations:* hiking, travel. *Address:* Queens' College, Cambridge CB3 9ET; Statistical Laboratory, Centre for Mathematic Science, Wilberforce Road, Cambridge CB3 0WD. *T:* (01223) 335570, 337944.

WEBLIN, Harold; Chairman, Liberty's, 1984–95 (Chief Executive, 1984–93); *b* 10 April 1930; *s* of E. W. Weblin and B. Weblin; *m* 1954, June Weblin (decd); two *s*. *Educ:* Walpole Grammar School, London. General Manager, Way-In, Harrods, 1948–71; General Manager, Liberty's, 1971–84. *Recreation:* gardening.

WEBSTER, Very Rev. Alan Brunskill, KCVO 1988; Dean of St Paul's, 1978–87, now Dean Emeritus; *b* 1918; *s* of Rev. J. Webster; *m* 1951, M. C. F. Falconer; two *s* two *d*. *Educ:* Shrewsbury School; Queen's College, Oxford (MA, BD). Ordained, 1942; Curate of Attercliffe Parishes, Sheffield, 1942; Curate of St Paul's, Arbourthorne, Sheffield, 1944; Chaplain and Vice Principal, Westcott House, 1946; Vicar of Barnard Castle, 1953; Warden, Lincoln Theol Coll., 1959–70; Dean of Norwich, 1970–78. Pres., Cathedral Camps, 1981–2000. Hon. DD City Univ., 1983. *Publications:* Joshua Watson, 1954; Broken Bones May Joy, 1968; Julian of Norwich, 1974 (rev. edn 1980); contributed: The Historic Episcopate, 1954; Living the Faith, 1980; Strategist for the Spirit, 1985; Preaching from the Cathedrals, 1998. *Recreations:* gardening, writing. *Address:* 20 Beechbank, Norwich, Norfolk NR2 2AL. *T:* (01603) 455833.

WEBSTER, Alec, FCCA; CIGasE; Regional Chairman, British Gas Wales, 1989–92; *b* 22 March 1934; *s* of Clifford Webster and Rose Webster (*née* Proctor); *m* 1958, Jean Thompson; one *s* two *d*. *Educ:* Hull Univ. (BScEcon Hons). Chief Accountant, British Gas Southern, 1974; Controller of Audit and Investigations, British Gas, 1979; Treas., British Gas, 1981; Reg. Dep. Chm., British Gas Southern, 1984. Pres., Chartered Assoc. of Certified Accountants, 1989–90. Chairman: Hendref Building Preservation Trust, 1992–; Darwin Centre for Biology and Medicine, 1993–. FRSA 1990. *Recreations:* sailing, mountaineering, wood carving. *Address:* Tŷ Carreg, 2 Maillards Haven, Penarth, S Glam CF64 5RF.

WEBSTER, Alistair Stevenson; QC 1995; a Recorder, since 1996 (Assistant Recorder, 1992–96); *b* 28 April 1953; *s* of His Honour I. S. Webster, *qv*; *m* 1977, Barbara Anne Longbottom; two *d*. *Educ:* Hulme Grammar Sch., Oldham; Brasenose Coll., Oxford (BA Hons Jurisp.). Called to the Bar, Middle Temple, 1976; practice on Northern Circuit, 1976–. Hon. Sec., Northern Circuit, 1988–93; Mem., Bar Council, 1995–96. *Recreations:* cricket, tennis, ski-ing, football. *Address:* Lincoln House Chambers, 1 Brazennose Street, Manchester M2 5EL. *T:* (0161) 832 5701. *Clubs:* Manchester Racquets; Rochdale Racquets; I Volenti CC.

WEBSTER, Maj.-Gen. Bryan Courtney, CB 1986; CBE 1981; Director of Army Quartering, 1982–86; *b* 2 Feb. 1931; *s* of Captain H. J. Webster, Royal Fusiliers (killed in action, 1940) and late M. J. Webster; *m* 1957, Elizabeth Rowland Waldron Smithers, *d* of Prof. Sir David Smithers; two *s* one *d*. *Educ:* Haileybury College; RMA Sandhurst. Commissioned Royal Fusiliers, 1951; ADC to GOC, 16 Airborne Div., 1953–55; served BAOR, Korea, Egypt, Malta, Gibraltar, Hong Kong; Directing Staff, Staff Coll., 1969–70; Comd 1st Bn Royal Regt of Fusiliers, 1971–73; Comd 8th Inf. Brigade, 1975–77 (Despatches); Dep. Col, Royal Regt of Fusiliers (City of London), 1976–89; Nat. Defence Coll., India, 1979; Staff appts, Far East, MoD, incl. Dir of Admin Planning (Army), 1980–82. Chm., Army Benevolent Fund, Surrey, 1986–2000. Mem. Council, Wine Guild of UK, 1995–2001. Pres., CPRE Hants, 2001–. FIMgt. Freeman, City of London, 1984. *Recreations:* ornithology, shooting, wine. *Address:* c/o HSBC, 69 High Street, Sevenoaks, Kent TN13 1LB.

WEBSTER, Charles, DSc; Senior Research Fellow, All Souls College, Oxford, since 1988; Reader in the History of Medicine, University of Oxford, 1972–88; Director, Wellcome Unit for the History of Medicine, 1972–88; Fellow of Corpus Christi College, Oxford, 1972–88. FBA 1982–99. *Publications:* (ed) Samuel Hartlib and the Advancement of Learning, 1970; The Great Instauration, 1975; From Paracelsus to Newton, 1982; Problems of Health Care: the National Health Service before 1957, 1988; (ed) Aneurin Bevan on the National Health Service, 1991; (ed) Caring for Health, History and Diversity, 1993; Government and Health Care: the British National Health Service 1958–1979, 1996; The National Health Service: a political history, 1998. *Address:* All Souls College, Oxford OX1 4AL. *T:* (01865) 279379.

WEBSTER, Dr Cyril Charles, CMG 1966; Chief Scientific Officer, Agricultural Research Council, 1971–75 (Scientific Adviser, 1965–71); *b* 28 Dec. 1909; *s* of Ernest Webster; *m* 1947, Mary, *d* of H. R. Wimhurst; one *s* one *d*. *Educ:* Beckenham County Sch.; Wye Coll.; Selwyn Coll., Cambridge; Imperial Coll. of Tropical Agriculture, Trinidad. Colonial Agricultural Service, 1936–57: Nigeria, 1936–38; Nyasaland, 1938–50; Kenya (Chief Research Officer), 1950–55; Malaya (Dep. Dir of Agriculture), 1956–57; Prof. of Agriculture, Imperial Coll. of Tropical Agriculture, Univ. of W Indies, 1957–60; Dir, Rubber Research Inst. of Malaya, subseq. of Malaysia, 1961–65; Dir-Gen., Palm Oil Research Inst. of Malaysia, 1978–80. JMN, 1965. *Publications:* (with P. N. Wilson) Agriculture in the Tropics, 1966, 3rd edn 1998; (with W. J. Baulkwill) Rubber, 1989; scientific papers in agricultural jls. *Address:* 5 Shenden Way, Sevenoaks, Kent TN13 1SE. *T:* (01732) 453984.

WEBSTER, David; Chairman, Trans-Atlantic Dialogue on Broadcasting and the Information Society, since 1988; consultant to international companies and institutions; *b* 11 Jan. 1931; *s* of Alec Webster and Clare Webster; *m* 1st, 1955, Lucy Law (marr. diss.), Princeton, NJ; two *s*; 2nd, 1981, Elizabeth Drew, author, Washington, DC. *Educ:* Taunton Sch.; Ruskin Coll., Oxford. British Broadcasting Corporation: Sub-Editor, External Services News Dept, 1953–59; Producer, Panorama, 1959–64; Exec. Producer, Enquiry, and Encounter, BBC-2, 1964–66; Dep. Editor, Panorama, 1966, Editor, 1967–69; Exec. Editor, Current Affairs Group, 1969, Asst Head, 1970; BBC Rep. in USA, 1971–76; Controller, Information Services, 1976–77; Dir, Public Affairs, 1977–80; Dir, US, BBC, 1981–85. Mem., Bd of Management, BBC, 1977–85. Resident Associate, Carnegie Endowment, 1985–87; Sen. Fellow, Annenberg Washington Program on Communications Policy Studies, 1987–92. Pres., RadioSar Internat., 1991–97. Special Adviser, Communications Studies and Planning Internat., 1987–88; Chm., Internat. Disaster Communications Project, 1987–91. Mem., Twentieth Century Fund Task Force on the Flow of the News, 1978. Mem. Adv. Council, Ditchley Foundn of US, 1981–; Mem., Nat. Adv. Cttee for the William Benton Fellowship Prog., Univ. of Chicago, 1983–89. Fellow, Internat. Council, National Acad. of Television Arts and Sciences, USA, 1980– (Chm., Internat. Council, 1974 and 1975). *Address:* 3000 Woodland Drive, Washington, DC 20008, USA. *T:* (202) 2986373, *Fax:* (202) 2986374; *e-mail:* Dwebsweb@aol.com. *Club:* Century Association (NY).

See also S. H. E. Kitzinger.

WEBSTER, David Gordon Comyn; Chairman, Safeway plc, since 1997; *b* 11 Feb. 1945; *s* of Alfred Edward Comyn Webster and Meryl Mary Clutterbuck; *m* 1972, Pamela Gail Runnicles; three *s*. *Educ:* Glasgow Acad.; Glasgow Univ. (LLB). Lieut, RNR, retd 1970. Admitted Solicitor, 1968; Corporate Finance Manager, Samuel Montagu & Co., 1969–72; Finance Dir, Oriel Foods Ltd, 1973–76; Co-Founder and Finance Dir, 1977–89, Dep. Chm., 1989–97, Argyll Gp, now Safeway plc. Non-executive Director: Reed International plc, 1992–; Reed Elsevier, 1993–; Elsevier NV, 1999–. Mem., Nat. Employers Liaison Cttee, 1992–. Pres., Inst. of Grocery Distribn, 2001–. *Recreations:* military history, ski-ing, sailing, gardening, walking. *Address:* 6 Millington Road, Hayes, Middx UB3 4AY. *T:* (020) 8848 8744.

WEBSTER, David MacLaren; QC 1980; **His Honour Judge MacLaren Webster;** a Circuit Judge, since 1987 (Resident Judge, Salisbury); *b* 21 Dec. 1937; *s* of late John MacLaren Webster and Winning McGregor Webster (*née* Rough); *m* 1964, Frances Sally McLaren, RE, *o d* of late Lt-Col J. A. McLaren and of Mrs H. S. Scammell; three *s*. *Educ:* Hutchesons', Glasgow; Christ Church, Oxford (MA (Eng. Lang. and Lit.)); Conservatoire d'Art Dramatique and Sorbonne (French Govt Schol. 1960–61). Radio and television work in drama and current affairs, Scotland, incl. Dixon of Dock Green, A Nest of Singing Birds, and Muir of Huntershill, 1949–64; called to the Bar, Gray's Inn, 1964; Western Circuit; a Dep. Circuit Judge, 1976–79; a Recorder, 1979–87; Hon. Recorder of Salisbury. Chairman: Salisbury & Dist Family Mediation Service, 1987–2001; Area Criminal Justice Liaison Cttee for Hants, Dorset and IoW, 1994–99; Area Criminal Justice Strategy Cttee, Hants and IoW, 2000–. Member: Bar Council, 1972–74; Senate of Inns of Court and Bar, 1974–79, 1982–85 (Senate Representative, Commonwealth Law Conf., Edinburgh, 1977); Matrimonial Causes Rules Cttee, 1976–79; Crown Court Rules Cttee, 1983–87; Western Circuit Univs Liaison Cttee, 1978–84. Chm., Salisbury Safety Partnership, 1998–. Gold Medal, LAMDA, 1954; LRAM 1955. President, Oxford Univ. Experimental Theatre Club, 1958–59; Secretary, Mermaid's, 1958; Chm., Bar Theatrical Soc., 1976–86. Governor, Port Regis Sch., 1983–94. *Recreations:* finding time for theatre, sailing, cricket, reading, training Souka and Jupiter. *Address:* c/o The Law Courts, Winchester, Hants SO23 9EL. *Clubs:* Garrick, MCC; Bar Yacht.

WEBSTER, Derek Adrian, CBE 1979; Chairman and Editorial Director, Scottish Daily Record and Sunday Mail Ltd, 1974–86; *b* 24 March 1927; *s* of James Tulloch Webster and Isobel Webster; *m* 1966, Dorothy Frances Johnson; two *s* one *d*. *Educ:* St Peter's, Bournemouth. Served RN, 1944–48. Reporter, Western Morning News, 1943; Staff Journalist, Daily Mail, 1949–51; joined Mirror Group, 1952; Northern Editor, Daily Mirror, 1964–67; Editor, Daily Record, 1967–72; Director: Mirror Gp Newspapers, 1974–86; Clyde Cable Vision, 1983–87. Mem., Press Council, 1981–84 (Jt Vice-Chm., 1982–83). Vice-Chm., Age Concern (Scotland), 1977–83; Hon. Vice-Pres., Newspaper Press Fund, 1983–; Mem. Council, CPU, 1984–86. *Recreations:* travel, photography. *Address:* 6 Park Circus Place, Glasgow G3 6AN. *T:* (0141) 353 6330.

WEBSTER, Henry George, CBE 1974; FSAE; Chairman, SKF Steel UK, 1982–87; retired; *b* Coventry, 27 May 1917; *s* of William George Webster; *m* 1943, Margaret, *d* of H. C. Sharp; one *d* decd. *Educ:* Welshpool County Sch.; Coventry Technical Coll. Standard Motor Co. Ltd: apprenticed, 1932; Asst Technl Engr, 1938–40; Dep. Chief Inspector, 1940–46; Asst Technl Engr, 1946–48; Chief Chassis Engr, 1948–55; Chief Engr, 1955–57; Dir and Chief Engr, Standard-Triumph Internat., 1957–68; Technical Dir, Austin Morris Div., British Leyland UK Ltd, 1968–74; Group Engineering Dir, Automotive Products, 1974–83. Joined original Instn of Automobile Engrs, as a grad., 1937 (Sec. of Grad. Section, Coventry Br. of Instn, 1941–45); transf. to Associate Mem., 1946, Mem., 1964. MSAE, 1958; FSAE, 1976; FRSA. Freeman, City of Coventry. *Recreation:* golf. *Address:* The Old School House, Barrowfield Lane, Kenilworth, Warwickshire CV8 1EP. *T:* (01926) 853363.

WEBSTER, His Honour Ian Stevenson; a Circuit Judge, 1981–95; *b* 20 March 1925; *s* of late Harvey Webster and Annabella Stevenson Webster (*née* McBain); *m* 1951, Margaret (*née* Sharples); two *s*. *Educ:* Rochdale Grammar Sch.; Manchester Univ. Sub. Lieut (A), RNVR, 1944. Called to the Bar, Middle Temple, 1948; Assistant Recorder: of Oldham, 1970; of Salford, 1971; a Recorder of the Crown Court, 1972–76, 1981; Chm., Industrial Tribunals for Manchester, 1976–81; Liaison Judge: for Burnley, Reedley and Accrington Benches, 1981–86; for Rochdale, Middleton and Heywood Benches, 1987–95; Resident Judge, Burnley, 1985–95. Hon. Recorder, Burnley, 1991–95. *Club:* Rochdale Golf.

See also A. S. Webster.

WEBSTER, Janice Helen, WS; Secretary, Scottish Law Agents Society, since 1998; part-time Chairman: Social Security Appeals Tribunal, since 1996; Disability Appeal Tribunal, since 1999; legal expert to Council of Europe, since 1993; *b* 2 April 1944; *d* of James Bell Reid and Janet (*née* Johnston); *m* 1968, R. M. Webster; two *d*. *Educ:* Edinburgh Univ. (LLB 1964). Solicitor and Notary Public. Legal Asst, then Sen. Solicitor, Falkirk Town Council, 1967–71; in private practice, Alston Nairn & Hogg, Edinburgh, 1971–74; Dep. Sec., Law Soc. of Scotland, 1974–80; Crown Counsel, then Magistrate, Govt of Seychelles, 1980–82; Law Society of Scotland, 1982–90 (Dep. Sec., Dir, European Affairs and Sec., Scottish Lawyers' European Gp); Dir Gen., CCBE, 1991–93; Consultant, Bell & Scott, WS, Edinburgh, 1994–96. Mem., Scottish Records Adv. Council, 1995–2000. Director: Scottish Archive Network, 1998–; Franco-British Lawyers' Soc. Ltd, 1998–. Member: Council, WS Soc., 1998–2000; Governing Council, Erskine Stewart's Melville, 1998–. Ed., Human Rights and UK Practice, 1999–. *Publication:* (with R. M. Webster) Professional Ethics and Practice for Scottish Solicitors, 3rd edn 1996. *Recreations:* singing, walking, gardening. *Club:* New (Edinburgh).

WEBSTER, Rev. Prof. John Bainbridge, PhD; Lady Margaret Professor of Divinity, University of Oxford, and Canon of Christ Church, Oxford, since 1996; *b* 20 June 1955; *s* of Gordon and Ruth Webster; *m* 1978, Jane Goodden; two *s*. *Educ:* Clare Coll., Cambridge (MA, PhD 1982). Stephenson Fellow, Dept of Biblical Studies, Univ. of Sheffield, 1981–82; ordained deacon, 1983, priest, 1984; Dep. Sen. Tutor, Tutor in Systematic Theology, and Chaplain, St John's Coll., Univ. of Durham, 1982–86; Wycliffe College, University of Toronto: Associate Prof. of Systematic Theology, 1986–93;

Professor, 1993–95; Ramsay Armitage Prof., 1995–96. *Publications:* Eberhard Jüngel: an introduction to his theology, 1986; (ed) The Possibilities of Theology, 1994; Barth's Ethics of Reconciliation, 1995; Barth's Moral Theology, 1998; (ed) Theology after Liberalism, 2000; (ed) The Cambridge Companion to Karl Barth, 2000; Karl Barth, 2000; Word and Church, 2001. *Address:* Christ Church, Oxford OX1 1DP.

WEBSTER, John Lawrence Harvey, CMG 1963; *b* 10 March 1913; *s* of late Sydney Webster, Hindhead, and Elsie Gwendoline Webster (*née* Harvey); *m* 1st, 1940, Elizabeth Marshall Gilbertson (marr. diss., 1959); two *d*; 2nd, 1960, Jessie Lillian Royston-Smith. *Educ:* Rugby Sch.; Balliol College, Oxford (MA). District Officer, Colonial Administrative Service, Kenya, 1935–49; Secretary for Development, 1949–54; Administrative Sec., 1954–56; Sec. to Cabinet, 1956–58; Permanent Sec., Kenya, 1958–63; on retirement from HMOCS, with the British Council, 1964–80, in Thailand, Sri Lanka, Hong Kong, Istanbul and London. *Recreations:* travel, reading, swimming. *Address:* Timbercroft, 11 Pevensey Road, West Worthing, Sussex BN11 5NP. *T:* (01903) 248617. *Clubs:* Royal Commonwealth Society; Leander; Nairobi (Kenya).

WEBSTER, Vice-Adm. Sir John (Morrison), KCB 1986; retired 1990; painter; President, Royal Naval Benevolent Trust, 1991–98; *b* 3 Nov. 1932; *s* of late Frank Martin Webster and Kathleen Mary (*née* Morrison); *m* 1962, Valerie Anne Villiers; two *d* (one *s* decd). *Educ:* Pangbourne College. Joined RN, 1951; specialised navigation, 1959; RAN, 1959–61; HMS Lowestoft, 1961–63; BRNC Dartmouth, 1963–65; HMS Dido, 1965–67; RN Tactical Sch., 1967–69; in command HMS Argonaut, 1969–71; MoD Navy, 1971–73; RNLO Ottawa, 1974–76; in command HMS Cleopatra and 4th Frigate Sqdn, 1976–78; MoD, Director Naval Warfare, 1980–82; Flag Officer Sea Trng, 1982–84; C of S to C-in-C Fleet, 1984–86; Flag Officer Plymouth, Naval Base Comdr Devonport, Comdr Central Sub Area Eastern Atlantic and Comdr Plymouth Sub Area Channel, 1987–90. Lt-Comdr 1963, Comdr 1967, Captain 1973, Rear-Adm. 1982, Vice-Adm. 1985. Younger Brother of Trinity House, 1970–. Mem., Armed Forces Art Soc., 1967– (Chm., 1990–96). One-man exhibitions of paintings: Canada, 1976; Winchester, 1980; London, 1982, 1984, 1986, 1988, 1991, 1993, 1996, 1999. Governor: Canford Sch., 1984–; Pangbourne College, 1990–2000 (Chm., 1992–2000). Associate, RSMA, 1998. *Recreations:* painting, sailing. *Address:* Old School House, Soberton, Hants SO32 3PF. *Clubs:* Royal Cruising, Royal Naval Sailing Association.

WEBSTER, Prof. John Paul Garrett, PhD; Professor of Agricultural Business Management, Imperial College of Science, Technology and Medicine (formerly at Wye College), University of London, since 1991; *b* 16 July 1942; *s* of Leonard Garrett Webster and Dorothy Agnes Webster (*née* White); *m* 1972, Dr Amanda Jane Hetigin; one *s* one *d*. *Educ:* Reading Univ. (BSc); Wye Coll., London Univ. (PhD). FIAgrM 1995. Wye College: Asst Lectr, 1965–67; Lectr in Agricl Econs, 1967–76; Sen. Lectr, 1976–81; Reader, 1981–91. Visiting appointments: Makerere Univ., Uganda, 1970–71; Drapers Lectr, Univ. of New England, Australia, 1974–75; Economist, Internat. Rice Res. Inst., Philippines, 1980–81; Prof., Lincoln Univ., NZ, 1999–2000. Indep. Mem., Adv. Cttee on Pesticides, MAFF, 1992–99. Pres., Agricl Econs Soc., 1999–2000. FIMgt (FBIM 1985); FRSA 1987. Hon. Freeman, Farmers' Co., 2000. *Publications:* articles in Jl Agricl Econs, Amer. Jl Agricl Econs, Farm Mgt, etc. *Recreation:* water polo. *Address:* Imperial College of Science, Technology and Medicine, South Kensington, SW7 2AZ. *T:* (020) 7594 2857. *Club:* Farmers'.

WEBSTER, Prof. Keith Edward, PhD; Professor of Anatomy and Human Biology (formerly Professor of Anatomy), King's College, University of London, 1975–2000; *b* 18 June 1935; *e s* of Thomas Brotherwick Webster and Edna Pyzer; 1st marr. diss. 1983; two *s*; 2nd marr. diss. 1990. *Educ:* UCL (BSc 1957, PhD 1960); UCH Med. Sch. (MB, BS 1962). University Coll. London: Lectr in Anatomy, 1962–66; Sen. Lectr in Anat., 1966–74; Reader in Anat., 1974–75. Symington Prize, British Anatomical Soc., 1966. *Publications:* A Manual of Human Anatomy, Vol. 5: The Central Nervous System (with J. T. Aitken and J. Z. Young), 1967; papers on the nervous system in Brain Res., Jl of Comp. Neurol., Neuroscience and Neurocytology. *Recreation:* Mozart, Wagner and language: the deification of the unspeakable.

WEBSTER, Maj. Michael; *see* Webster, R. M. O.

WEBSTER, Michael George Thomas; Chairman, DRG plc (formerly Dickinson Robinson Group), 1985–87 (Director, 1976–87; Deputy Chairman, 1983–85); *b* 27 May 1920; *s* of late J. A. Webster, CB, DSO, and late Constance A. Webster, 2nd *d* of late Richard and Lady Constance Combe; *m* 1947, Mrs Isabel Margaret Bucknill, *d* of late Major J. L. Dent, DSO, MC; three *d*. *Educ:* Stowe; Magdalen Coll., Oxford (MA). Commnd Grenadier Guards, 1940–46: NW Europe Campaign, 1944–45 (despatches). Joined Watney Combe Reid & Co. Ltd, 1946; Chm., Watney Combe Reid, 1963–68; Watney Mann Ltd: Vice-Chm., 1965–70; Chm., 1970–72; Chm., Watney Mann & Truman Holdings, 1974; Director: Grand Metropolitan Ltd, 1972–74; National Provident Instn, 1973–85; Chm., Fitch Lovell PLC, 1977–83. Master of Brewers' Co., 1964–65; a Vice-Pres., The Brewers' Soc., 1975–. Gov., Gabbitas Truman & Thring, 1986–90 (Chm., Truman and Knightley Educnl Trust, 1985–87). Chm., Aldenham Sch. Governing Body, 1977–84. High Sheriff, Berks, 1971; DL Berks, 1975–90. *Recreations:* fishing, golf. *Address:* Little Manor Farm, Dummer, Basingstoke, Hants RG25 2AD. *Clubs:* Cavalry and Guards, MCC.
See also Viscount Torrington.

WEBSTER, Patrick; a Chairman, Industrial, then Employment, Tribunals, Cardiff Region, 1965–2000 (full-time Chairman, 1976–93); a Recorder, 1972–93; *b* 6 Jan. 1928; *s* of late Francis Glyn Webster and Ann Webster; *m* 1955, Elizabeth Knight; two *s* four *d*. *Educ:* Swansea Grammar Sch.; Rockwell Coll., Eire; St Edmund's Coll., Ware; Downing Coll., Cambridge (BA). Called to Bar, Gray's Inn, 1950. Practised at Bar, in Swansea, 1950–75; Chm., Medical Appeals Tribunal (part-time), 1971–75. *Recreations:* listening to music, watching rowing and sailing. *Address:* Langland, 24 Maillard's Haven, Penarth, South Glam CF64 5RF. *T:* (029) 2070 4758. *Clubs:* Penarth Yacht; Beechwood (Swansea).

WEBSTER, Paul; film producer; Chief Executive, FilmFour Ltd (formerly Head of Film Division, Channel 4), since 1998; *b* 19 Sept. 1952. Co-Dir, Osiris Film, London, 1979–81; Founder, Palace Pictures, 1982–88; launched Working Title Films, LA, 1990–92; Head of Prodn, Miramax Films, 1995–97 (films incl. The English Patient, Welcome to Sarajevo, Wings of the Dove). Producer: The Tall Guy, 1988; Drop Dead Fred, 1990; Bob Roberts, 1992; Romeo is Bleeding, 1993; Little Odessa, 1994; The Pallbearer, 1995; Gridlock'd, 1996; The Yards, 1998. Mem. Council and Film Council, BAFTA. *Address:* FilmFour Ltd, 76–78 Charlotte Street, W1P 1LX.

WEBSTER, Hon. Sir Peter (Edlin), Kt 1980; a Judge of the High Court of Justice, Queen's Bench Division, 1980–92; *b* 16 Feb. 1924; *s* of Herbert Edlin Webster and Florence Helen Webster; *m* 1955, Susan Elizabeth Richards (marr. diss.); one *s* two *d*; *m* 1968, Avril Carolyn Simpson, *d* of Dr John Ernest McCrae Harrison. *Educ:* Haileybury; Merton Coll., Oxford (MA). RNVR, 1943–46 and 1950, Lieut (A). Imperial Tobacco Co., 1949; Lectr in Law, Lincoln Coll., Oxford, 1950–52; called to Bar, Middle Temple, 1952; Bencher, 1972; Standing Jun. Counsel to Min. of Labour, 1964–67; QC 1967; a Recorder of the Crown Court, 1972–80. Mem., Council of Justice, 1955–60, 1965–70; Mem., General Council of the Bar, 1967–74, and of Senate of the Inns of Court and the Bar, 1974–81 (Vice-Chm. 1975–76; Chm., 1976–77); Chairman: London Common Law Bar Assoc., 1975–79; Judicial Studies Bd, 1981–83 (Mem., 1979–83); Review Bd for Govt Contracts, 1993–; Mem., City Disputes Panel, 1994–. Dir, Booker McConnell, 1978–79. FCIArb 1993. *Address:* Ivy Cottage, Bratton, Wilts BA13 4RQ.

WEBSTER, Philip George; Political Editor, The Times, since 1993; *b* 2 June 1949; *s* of Bertie and Eva Webster; *m* 1974, Gill Bloomfield. *Educ:* Rockland St Mary Primary Sch.; County GS; Wymondham Coll.; Harlow Coll. (NCTJ Cert.). Eastern Counties Newspapers, 1967–73; The Times: Parly Reporter, 1973–81; Pol Reporter, 1981–86; Chief Pol Correspondent, 1986–93. *Recreations:* golf, ski-ing, cricket, squash, football. *Address:* 3 Wyke Close, Syon Lane, Osterley TW7 5PE. *T:* (020) 8847 1210. *Clubs:* Richmond Golf, Rookery Park Golf.

WEBSTER, Maj. (Richard) Michael (Otley); Clerk of the Course and Manager, Bangor-on-Dee, since 1996; Clerk of the Course, Chester, since 2001; one of HM Body Guard, Honourable Corps of Gentlemen-at-Arms, since 1993; *b* 11 Aug. 1942; *s* of Brig. Frederick Richard Webster and Beryl Helena Sellars (*née* Otley); *m* 1971, Joanna Gay Enid Simpson, *d* of Lt-Col R. H. O. Simpson, DSO; two *s*. *Educ:* Charterhouse; RMA, Sandhurst. Commnd RA, 1962; Army Staff Coll., 1975; CO, King's Troop, RHA, 1976–78. United Racecourses, 1979–96; Clerk of the Course: Kempton Park, 1980–96; Lingfield Park, 1986–87; Epsom, 1988–95. Member: Horseracing Adv. Council, 1987–90; Nat. Jt Pitch Council, 2000–. *Recreations:* cricket, racing, shooting, walking. *Address:* Coopers Farm, Hartley Wespall, Hook, Hants RG27 0BQ. *Club:* Army and Navy.

WEBSTER, Prof. Robert Gordon, FRS 1989; Professor of Virology and Molecular Biology, St Jude Children's Research Hospital, Memphis, USA; *b* 5 July 1932; *s* of Robert Duncan Webster and Mollie Sherriffs; *m* 1957, Marjorie Freegard; two *s* one *d*. *Educ:* Otago Univ., NZ (BSc, MSc); Australian Nat. Univ., Canberra (PhD). Virologist, NZ Dept of Agric., 1958–59; Postdoctoral Fellow, Sch. of Public Health, Univ. of Michigan, Ann Arbor (Fullbright Schol.), 1962–63; Res. Fellow, then Fellow, Dept of Microbiology, John Curtin Med. Sch., ANU, 1964–67; Associate Mem., then Mem., Dept of Virology and Molecular Biol., 1968–88, apptd Head of Dept and Rose Marie Thomas Prof., 1988, St Jude Children's Res. Hosp. Fogarty Internat. Sen. Fellow, Nat. Inst. for Med. Res., MRC, London, 1978–79. Mem., Nat. Acad. of Sci., USA, 1998. *Publications:* contribs on influenza viruses etc. to learned jls, incl. Virology, Nature, and Cell. *Recreations:* gardening, sea-fishing, walking. *Address:* Department of Virology and Molecular Biology, St Jude Children's Research Hospital, 332 N Lauderdale Street, Memphis, TN 38105-2794, USA. *T:* (901) 5220403. *Club:* Royal Society of Medicine.

WEBSTER, Prof. Robin Gordon MacLennan, OBE 1999; ARSA 1995; RIBA; FRIAS; Head, Scott Sutherland School of Architecture, Robert Gordon University, Aberdeen, since 1984; Principal, Robin Webster & Associates, Architects, since 1984; *b* 24 Dec. 1939; *s* of Gordon Webster and Sheila Webster; *m* 1967, Katherine Crichton; one *s* two *d*. *Educ:* Glasgow Acad.; Rugby Sch.; St John's Coll., Cambridge (MA); University Coll., London (MA Arch). ARIBA 1967; FRIAS 1996. Partner, Spence & Webster, 1972–84. Comr, Royal Fine Art Commn for Scotland, 1990–98. Winner, internat. competition for new Parly bldg at Westminster, 1972; Joint Winner: internat. competition for Manhattan West Side, NY, 1991; Sci. and Engrg Lib. and Inf. Centre, Univ. of Edinburgh, 1997. *Publication:* Stonecleaning, and the nature, soiling and decay mechanisms of stone, 1992. *Recreations:* looking at buildings, drawing. *Address:* 6 Park Road, Cults, Aberdeen AB15 9HR. *T:* and *Fax:* (01224) 867140; *e-mail:* rwebster@garthdee-rgu.fsnet.co.uk.

WECHSLER, David Keith; Chief Executive, London Borough of Croydon, since 1993; *b* 17 June 1946; *s* of Bernard James Victor Wechsler and late Kathleen Nora Wechsler (*née* Ramm); *m* 1968, Muriel-Anne (Polly) Stuart; one *s* one *d*. *Educ:* Sloane Sch., Chelsea; Leicester Univ. (BA Social Sci.). London Borough of Croydon: grad. trainee, 1970–72; Corporate Planner, 1972–79; Hd, Exec. Office, 1979–87; Dep. Chief Exec., 1987–91; Dir, Econ. and Strategic Develt, 1991–93. Director: S London TEC, 1993–99; Croydon Business Venture, 1993–. *Publications:* articles on corporate planning and local govt mgt in specialist jls. *Recreations:* sailing, music, swimming, making ice cream. *Address:* London Borough of Croydon, Taberner House, Park Lane, Croydon, Surrey CR9 3JS. *T:* (020) 8686 4433.

WEDD, George Morton, CB 1989; consultant; South-West Regional Director, Departments of the Environment and Transport, Bristol, 1983–90; *b* 30 March 1930; *s* of Albert Wedd and Dora Wedd; *m* 1953, Kate Pullin; two *s* one *d*. *Educ:* various schs in Derbyshire; St John's Coll., Cambridge (BA 1951). Joined Min. of Housing and Local Govt (later DoE), 1951; Principal, 1957; Asst Sec., 1966; Under Sec., 1976. *Address:* The Lodge, High Littleton, Somerset BS39 6HG.

WEDDERBURN, family name of **Baron Wedderburn of Charlton.**

WEDDERBURN OF CHARLTON, Baron *cr* 1977 (Life Peer), of Highgate; **(Kenneth) William Wedderburn;** QC 1990; FBA 1981; Cassel Professor of Commercial Law, London School of Economics, University of London, 1964–92, now Professor Emeritus and Hon. Fellow; *b* 13 April 1927; *o s* of Herbert J. and Mabel Wedderburn, Deptford; *m* 1st, 1951, Nina Salaman; one *s* two *d*; 2nd 1962, Dorothy E. Cole; 3rd, 1969, Frances Ann Knight; one *s*. *Educ:* Aske's Hatcham School; Whitgift School; Queens' College, Cambridge (MA 1951; LLB 1949; Chancellor's Medal for English Law). Royal Air Force, 1949–51. Called to the Bar, Middle Temple, 1953. Fellow, 1952–64, Tutor, 1957–60, Hon. Fellow, 1997, Clare College, Cambridge; Asst Lectr, 1953–55, Lectr 1955–64, Faculty of Law, Cambridge University. Visiting Professor: UCLA Law Sch., 1967; Harvard Law Sch., 1969–70. Staff Panel Mem., Civil Service Arbitration Tribunal; Chm., Independent Review Cttee, 1976–; Mem., Cttee on Industrial Democracy, 1976–77. Independent Chm., London and Provincial Theatre Councils, 1973–93. Hon. Pres., Industrial Law Soc., 1997–. Gen. Editor, Modern Law Review, 1971–88; Mem. Editl Bd, Internat. Labour Law Reports, 1975–. Hon. Doctor of Jurisprudence, Pavia, 1987; Hon. Doctor of Econs, Siena, 1991; Hon. LLD Stockholm, 1995. *Publications:* The Worker and the Law, 1965, 3rd edn 1986; Cases and Materials on Labour Law, 1967; (with P. Davies) Employment Grievances and Disputes Procedures in Britain, 1969; (ed) Contracts, Sutton and Shannon, 1956, 2nd edn 1963; (Asst Editor) Torts, Clerk and Lindsell, 1969, 1975, 1982, 1989, 1995, 2000; (ed with B. Aaron) Industrial Conflict, 1972; (with S. Sciarra *et al*) Democrazia Politica e Democrazia Industriale, 1978; (ed with Folke Schmidt) Discrimination in Employment, 1978; (with R. Lewis and J. Clark) Labour Law and Industrial Relations, 1983; (ed with W. T. Murphy) Labour, Law and the Community, 1983; (with S. Ghimpu and B. Veneziani) Diritto del Lavoro in Europa, 1987; Social

Charter, European Company and Employment Rights, 1990; Employment Rights in Britain and Europe, 1991; (with M. Rood *et al*) Labour Law in the post-Industrial Era, 1994; Labour Law and Freedom, 1995; I Diritti del Lavoro, 1998; articles in legal and other jls. *Recreation:* Charlton Athletic Football Club. *Address:* 29 Woodside Avenue, N6 4SP. *T:* (020) 8444 8472.

WEDDERBURN, Sir Andrew John Alexander O.; *see* Ogilvy-Wedderburn.

WEDDERBURN, Prof. Dorothy Enid Cole; Senior Research Fellow, Imperial College, London, since 1981; Principal, Royal Holloway and Bedford New College, 1985–90, and a Pro-Vice-Chancellor, 1986–88, University of London; *b* 18 Sept. 1925; *d* of Frederick C. Barnard and Ethel C. Barnard. *Educ:* Walthamstow High Sch. for Girls; Girton Coll., Cambridge (MA). Research Officer, subseq. Sen. Res. Officer, Dept of Applied Economics, Cambridge, 1950–65; Imperial College of Science and Technology: Lectr in Industrial Sociology, 1965–70, Reader, 1970–77, Prof., 1977–81; Dir, Industrial Sociol. Unit, 1973–81; Head, Dept of Social and Economic Studies, 1978–81; Principal, Bedford Coll., 1981–85. Mem. Court, Univ. of London, 1981–90. Vis. Prof., Sloan Sch. of Management, MIT, 1969–70. Mem. SSRC, 1976–82; Chm., SERC/SSRC Jt Cttee, 1980–82. Chm., Cttee of Inquiry into Women Imprisonment, Prison Reform Trust, 1998–2000. Member: Govt Cttee on the Pay and Condition of Nurses, 1974–75; (part-time), Royal Commn on the Distribution of Income and Wealth, 1974–78; Council, Advisory Conciliation and Arbitration Service, 1976–82; Cttee of Vice-Chancellors and Principals, 1988–90; Bd, Anglo-German Foundn, 1987–; Bd of Governors, London Guildhall Univ. (formerly City of London Polytechnic), 1989–99; Council, Loughborough Univ., 1990–93; Court, City Univ., 1992–; Council, Goldsmiths' Coll., London Univ., 1993–2000. Mem., Kensington, Chelsea and Westminster DHA, 1993–. Hon. Pres., Fawcett Soc., 1986–. Hon. Fellow: Ealing Coll. of Higher Educn, 1985; RHBNC, 1991; Hon. FIC 1986. Hon. DLitt: Warwick, 1984; Loughborough, 1989; DUniv Brunel, 1990; Hon. LLD Cambridge, 1991; Hon. DSc City, 1991; Hon. DSocSc Southampton, 1999; Hon. PhD London Guildhall, 2000. *Publications:* White Collar Redundancy, 1964; Redundancy and the Railwayman, 1964; Enterprise Planning for Change, 1968; (with J. E. G. Utting) The Economic Circumstances of Old People, 1962; (with Peter Townsend) The Aged in the Welfare State, 1965; (jtly) Old Age in Three Industrial Societies, 1968; (with Rosemary Crompton) Workers' Attitudes and Technology, 1972; (ed) Poverty, Inequality and Class Structure, 1974; Justice for Women: the case for reform, 2000; contrib. Jl of Royal Statistical Soc.; Sociological Review; New Society, etc. *Recreations:* politics, walking, cooking. *Address:* Management School, Imperial College of Science, Technology and Medicine, 52/53 Princes Gate, Exhibition Road, SW7 2AZ; Flat 5, 65 Ladbroke Grove, W11 2PD.

See also Professor G. A. Barnard.

WEDDERSPOON, Very Rev. Alexander Gillan; Dean of Guildford, 1987–2001, now Emeritus; *b* 3 April 1931; *s* of Rev. Robert John Wedderspoon and Amy Beatrice Woolley; *m* 1968, Judith Joyce Wynne Plumptre; one *s* one *d*. *Educ:* Westminster School; Jesus Coll., Oxford (MA, BD); Cuddesdon Theological Coll. Nat. Service, 1949–51; commnd, RA. Ordained 1961; Curate, Kingston Parish Church, 1961–63; Lectr in Religious Education, Univ. of London, 1963–66; Education Adviser, C of E Schools Council, 1966–69; Sec. of Commn on Religious Education, 1966–69; Priest in charge, St Margaret's, Westminster, 1969–70; Canon Residentiary, Winchester Cathedral, 1970–87. *Recreations:* walking, travel. *Address:* c/o Cathedral Office, Stag Hill, Guildford GU2 5UP.

WEDELL, Prof. (Eberhard Arthur Otto) George; Professor of Communications Policy, University of Manchester, 1983–92, Professor Emeritus since 1992; Vice President, European Institute for the Media, 1993–97 (Director, 1983–90; Director-General, 1991–93); *b* 4 April 1927; *er s* of late Rev. Dr H. Wedell and Gertrude (*née* Bonhoeffer); *m* 1948, Rosemarie (*née* Winckler); three *s* one *d*. *Educ:* Cranbrook; London School of Economics (BSc Econ., 1947). Ministry of Education, 1950–58; Sec., Bd for Social Responsibility, Nat. Assembly of Church of England, 1958–60; Dep. Sec., ITA, 1960–61, Secretary, 1961–64; Prof. of Adult Educn and Dir of Extra-Mural Studies, Manchester Univ., 1964–75; Vis. Prof. of Employment Policy, Manchester Business Sch., 1975–83; Senior Official, European Commn, 1973–82. Emeritus Fellow, Leverhulme Trust, 1994–96. Contested (L) Greater Manchester West, 1979, (L-SDP Alliance) Greater Manchester Central, 1984, European Parly elections; Chm., British Liberals in EEC, 1980–82; Vice-President: Greater Manchester Liberal Party, 1984–88; EC-ACP Cultural Foundn, 1992–94. Chairman: Wyndham Place Trust, 1983–; Beatrice Hankey Foundn, 1984–; Christians and the Future of Europe, 1997–99. Director, Royal Exchange Theatre Company, 1968–89, Hon. Mem., 1989. Patron, Mosscare Housing Assoc., 1998–. FRSA; FRTS. Hon. MEd Manchester, 1968; Dr *hc* Internat. Journalistics Inst., Kazakstan, 1994. Lord of the Manor of Clotton Hoofield in the County Palatine of Chester. Letters Patent of Armorial Ensigns, 1997. Chevalier de l'Ordre des Arts et des Lettres (France), 1989; Verdienstkreuz (1 Klasse) des Verdienstordens (Germany), 1991; Comdr, Order of Merit (Portugal), 1993. *Publications:* The Use of Television in Education, 1963; Broadcasting and Public Policy, 1968; (with H. D. Perraton) Teaching at a Distance, 1968; (ed) Structures of Broadcasting, 1970; (with R. Glatter) Study by Correspondence, 1971; Correspondence Education in Europe, 1971; Teachers and Educational Development in Cyprus, 1971; (ed) Education and the Development of Malawi, 1973; (with E. Katz) Broadcasting in the Third World, 1977 (Nat. Assoc. of Educational Broadcasters of USA Book of the Year Award, 1978); (with G. M. Luyken and R. Leonard) Mass Communications in Western Europe, 1985; (ed) Making Broadcasting Useful, 1986; (with G. M. Luyken) Media in Competition, 1986; (ed and contrib.) Europe 2000: what kind of television?, 1988; (with P. Crookes) Radio 2000, 1991; (with R. Rocholl) Vom Segen des Glaubens, 1995; (ed and contrib.) No Discouragement, 1997; (with A. J. Tudesq) Television and Democracy in Africa, 1998; (with B. Luckham) Television at the Crossroads, 2001; (contrib.) New DNB; general editor, Media Monographs, 1985–93. *Recreations:* gardening, theatre, reading. *Address:* 18 Cranmer Road, Manchester M20 6AW. *T:* (0161) 445 5106; Vigneau, Lachapelle, 47350 Seyches, France. *T:* 553838871. *Clubs:* Athenæum; St James's (Manchester).

See also Ven. H. Lockley.

WEDGWOOD, family name of **Baron Wedgwood.**

WEDGWOOD, 4th Baron *cr* 1942, of Barlaston; **Piers Anthony Weymouth Wedgwood;** Director, Waterford Wedgwood, since 2000; *b* 20 Sept. 1954; *s* of 3rd Baron Wedgwood and of Lady Wedgwood (Jane Weymouth, *d* of W. J. Poulton, Kenjockety, Molo, Kenya); *S* father, 1970; *m* 1985, Mary Regina Margaret Kavanagh Quinn, *d* of late Judge Edward Thomas Quinn and of Helen Marie Buchanan Quinn of Philadelphia; one *d*. *Educ:* Marlborough College; RMA Sandhurst. Royal Scots, 1973–80. GSM for N Ireland, 1976. *Heir: cousin* John Wedgwood, CBE, MD, FRCP [*b* 28 Sept. 1919; *m* 1st, 1943, Margaret (marr. diss. 1971), *d* of A. S. Mason; three *s* two *d*; 2nd, 1972, Joan, *d* of J. Ripsher]. *Address:* Waterford Wedgwood plc, Barlaston, Stoke-on-Trent, Staffordshire ST12 9ES.

WEDGWOOD, Sir (Hugo) Martin, 3rd Bt *cr* 1942, of Etruria, Co. Stafford; *b* 27 Dec. 1933; *s* of Sir John Hamilton Wedgwood, 2nd Bt, TD and Diana Mildred (*d* 1976), *d* of late Col Oliver Hawkshaw, TD; *S* father, 1989; *m* 1963, Alexandra Mary Gordon Clark, *er d* of late Judge Alfred Gordon Clark; one *s* two *d*. *Educ:* Eton; Trinity Coll., Oxford. Mem., Stock Exchange, 1973–91; Partner, Laurence, Prust and Co., 1973–84; Dir, Smith New Court Far East Ltd, 1986–91. *Heir: s* Ralph Nicholas Wedgwood, *b* 10 Dec. 1964. *Recreation:* ceramics. *Club:* Oriental.

WEDGWOOD, John Alleyne, CBE 1984; MA, FCIS; Chairman, Southern Electricity Board, 1977–84; *b* 26 Jan. 1920; *s* of Rev. Charles Henry Wedgwood and Myrtle Winifred Perry; *m* 1st, 1942, Freda Mary Lambert (*d* 1963); one *s*; 2nd, 1974, Lilian Nora Forey (*d* 1992); 3rd, 1992, Jeanette May England. *Educ:* Monkton Combe Sch.; Queens' Coll., Cambridge (MA Hons Hist. Tripos). FCIS, CompIEE. Served War, Lincs Regt and Durham LI, 1940–46 (Actg Major). Asst Principal, Min. of Fuel and Power, 1946–48; Admin. Officer, British Electricity Authority, 1948–55; Dep. Sec., London Electricity Bd, 1955–58; Dep. Sec., Electricity Council, 1958–65, Sec., 1965–74; Dep. Chm., S Eastern Elec. Bd, 1974–77. President: Inst. of Chartered Secs and Administrators, 1976; Electric Vehicle Assoc., 1983–86; Chm. Bd of Management, Electrical and Electronics Industries Benevolent Assoc., 1977–83. Member: Worshipful Co. of Scriveners, 1973–; SE Econ. Planning Council, 1975–79. Founder Master, Worshipful Co. of Chartered Secs and Administrators, 1978. Freeman, City of London, 1973. *Recreations:* gardening, music, railways, ornithology. *Address:* Bexington, 9 Roberts Grove, Wokingham, Berks RG41 4WR. *T:* (0118) 978 5901. *Club:* Phyllis Court (Henley).

WEDGWOOD, Pamela, Lady, (Pamela Tudor-Craig), PhD; FSA; Medieval art historian; *b* 26 June 1928; *d* of Herbert Wynn Reeves and Madeline Marion Wynn Reeves (*née* Brows); *m* 1st, 1956, Algernon James Riccarton Tudor-Craig (*d* 1969); one *d*; 2nd, 1982, Sir John Hamilton Wedgwood, 2nd Bt (*d* 1989). *Educ:* Courtauld Inst. Fine Art, Univ. of London (BA 1st Cl. Hons Hist. of Art 1949; PhD 1952). FSA 1958. Lectr at American Colls in UK, 1969–96. Mem., Cathedrals Adv. Commn, 1973–88; Chm., Wall Paintings Cttee, and Vice-Chm., Panel Paintings Cttee, 1975–92, Vice Chm., Paintings Cttee, 1992–96, Council for Care of Churches; Member, Architectural Advisory Panel: Westminster Abbey, 1979–98; Exeter Cathedral, 1985–90; Member, Fabric Committee: Lincoln Cathedral, 1986–92; Peterborough Cathedral, 1987–96; Southwell Minster, 1984–2001. Founder, Cambs Historic Churches Trust, 1982; Mem., Sussex Historic Churches Trust, 1996–. Founder, Annual Harlaxton Symposium of English Medieval Studies, 1984. Hon. Member: SPAB; Richard III Soc. TV broadcasts, incl. series, The Secret Life of Paintings, 1986–87; contribs to numerous radio programmes. Hon. DHum William Jewell Coll., USA, 1983. *Publications:* Richard III (exhibn catalogue), 1973; (with R. Foster) The Secret Life of Paintings, 1986; contrib. numerous chapters and articles in books and exhibn catalogues; contrib. to History Today, Church Times and other scholarly jls. *Recreations:* walking dogs on Downs, swimming. *Address:* 9 St Anne's Crescent, Lewes, E Sussex BN7 1SB. *T:* (01273) 479564.

WEE CHONG JIN, Hon.; Chief Justice of the Supreme Court, Singapore, 1963–90; *b* 28 Sept. 1917; *s* of late Wee Gim Puay and Lim Paik Yew; *m* 1955, Cecilia Mary Henderson; three *s* one *d*. *Educ:* Penang Free Sch.; St John's Coll., Cambridge. Called to Bar, Middle Temple, 1938; admitted Advocate and Solicitor of Straits Settlement, 1940; practised in Penang and Singapore, 1940–57; Puisne Judge, Singapore, 1957. Hon. DCL Oxon, 1987. *Recreation:* golf. *Address:* 80 Raffles Place #29–20, UOB Plaza 2, Singapore 048624.

WEE KIM WEE, Hon. GCB 1989; President of Singapore, 1985–93; *b* 4 Nov. 1915; *m* 1936, Koh Sok Hiong; one *s* six *d*. *Educ:* Pearl's Hill School; Raffles Instn. Joined Straits Times, 1930; United Press Assoc., 1941 and 1945–59; Straits Times, 1959–73 (Dep. Editor, Singapore); High Comr to Malaysia, 1973–80; Ambassador to Japan, 1980–84 and to Republic of Korea, 1981–84; Chm., Singapore Broadcasting Corp., 1984–85. Formerly Member: Rent Control Bd, Film Appeal Cttee; Land Acquisition Bd; Bd of Visiting Justices; Nat. Theatre Trust; former Chm., Singapore Anti-Tuberculosis Assoc.; former Pres., Singapore Badminton Assoc. and Vice-Pres., Badminton Assoc. of Malaya. JP 1966. Hon. DLitt Nat. Univ. of Singapore, 1994. Public Service Star, 1963; Meritorious Service Medal, 1979. Order of Temasek, 1st cl. (Singapore), 1993; Most Esteemed Family Order Laila Utama (Brunei), 1990.

WEEDEN, Air Vice Marshal John; Director of Legal Services (RAF) and Royal Air Force Prosecuting Authority, Ministry of Defence, since 1997; *b* 21 June 1949; *s* of Denis Claude Weeden and Winifred Marion Weeden; *m* 1971, Marjanne Dita De Boer; three *s* two *d*. *Educ:* Brighton Coll.; Univ. of Bristol (LLB Hons). SSC 1973. Articled to Griffith Smith, Brighton, 1971–73, Asst Solicitor, 1973–74; joined RAF Legal Br. as Flight Lieut, 1974; worked in UK and Europe, undertaking court martial prosecutions and gen. legal work involving administrative, internat. and operational law; Deputy Director: Cyprus, 1984–87; Germany, 1991–92; Legal Services (RAF), MoD, 1992–97. *Recreations:* golf, photography, cars. *Address:* HQ Personnel and Training Command, RAF Innsworth, Gloucester GL3 1EZ. *T:* (01452) 712612. *Club:* Royal Air Force.

WEEDON, Prof. Basil Charles Leicester, CBE 1974; DSc; PhD; FRS 1971; FRSC; Vice-Chancellor, Nottingham University, 1976–88; *b* 18 July 1923; *s* of late Charles William Weedon; *m* 1959, Barbara Mary Dawe; one *s* one *d*. *Educ:* Wandsworth Sch.; Imperial Coll. of Science and Technology (ARCS; DIC). Research Chemist, ICI Ltd (Dyestuffs Div.), 1943–47; Lecturer in Organic Chemistry, Imperial Coll., 1947–55, Reader, 1955–60; Prof. of Organic Chemistry, QMC, 1960–76, Fellow, 1984; Hon. Prof., Nottingham Univ., 1988–. Chm., Food Additives and Contaminants Cttee, 1968–83; Mem., EEC Scientific Cttee for Food, 1974–81; Scientific Editor, Pure and Applied Chemistry, 1960–75. Member: UGC, 1974–76; Council, National Stone Centre, 1985–93 (Chm. Council, 1985–91). Chm., E Midlands Reg., Electricity Consumers' Cttee, 1990–94. Tilden Lecturer, Chemical Society, 1966. Hon. DTech Brunel Univ., 1975; Hon. LLD Nottingham, 1988. Meldola Medal, Roy. Inst. of Chemistry, 1952. *Publications:* A Guide to Qualitative Organic Chemical Analysis (with Sir Patrick Linstead), 1956; scientific papers, mainly in Jl Chem. Soc. *Address:* Sheepwash Grange, Heighington Road, Canwick, Lincoln LN4 2RJ. *T:* (01522) 522488.

WEEDON, Dudley William, BSc(Eng), CEng, FIEE; retired; *b* 25 June 1920; *s* of Reginald Percy and Ada Kate Weedon; *m* 1951, Monica Rose Smith; two *s* one *d*. *Educ:* Colchester Royal Grammar Sch.; Northampton Polytechnic. Marconi's Wireless Telegraph Co., 1937–48; Cable & Wireless Ltd, 1949–82 (Dir, 1979–82); Chm., Energy Communications Ltd, 1980–82. *Recreation:* sailing. *Address:* 103 Lexden Road, Colchester, Essex CO3 3RB.

WEEKES, Rt Rev. Ambrose Walter Marcus, CB 1970; FKC; Assistant Bishop, Diocese in Europe, since 1988; *b* 25 April 1919; *s* of Lt-Comdr William Charles Tinnoth Weekes, DSO, RNVR, and Ethel Sarah Weekes, JP. *Educ:* Cathedral Choir Sch., Rochester; Sir Joseph Williamson's Sch., Rochester; King's Coll., London; AKC 1941, FKC 1972; Scholae Cancellarii, Lincoln. Asst Curate, St Luke's, Gillingham, Kent,

1942–44; Chaplain, RNVR, 1944–46, RN 1946–72; HMS: Ganges, 1946–48; Ulster, 1948–49; Triumph, 1949–51; Royal Marines, Deal, 1951–53; 3 Commando Bde, RM, 1953–55; HMS: Ganges, 1955–56; St Vincent, 1956–58; Tyne, 1958–60; Ganges, 1960–62; 40 Commando, RM, 1962–63; MoD, 1963–65; HMS: Eagle, 1965–66; Vernon, 1966–67; Terror, and Staff of Comdr Far East Fleet, 1967–68; HMS Mercury, 1968–69; Chaplain of the Fleet and Archdeacon for the Royal Navy, 1969–72; QHC, 1969–72; Chaplain of St Andrew, Tangier, 1972–73; Dean of Gibraltar, 1973–77; Assistant Bishop, Diocese of Gibraltar, 1977, until creation of new diocese, 1980; Suffragan Bishop of Gibraltar in Europe, 1980–86; Dean, Pro-Cathedral of the Holy Trinity, Brussels, 1980–86; Hon. Asst Bishop of Rochester, 1986–88; Hon. Canon of Rochester Cathedral, 1986–88; Chaplain at Montreux, Switzerland, 1988–92. *Recreations:* yachting, music. *Address:* Charterhouse, Charterhouse Square, EC1M 6AN. *Clubs:* Army and Navy, MCC.

WEEKES, Anesta Glendora; QC 1999; a Recorder, since 2000; *b* 10 June 1955; *d* of late Joseph Weekes and of Sarah Weekes. *Educ:* Keele Univ. (BA Hons). Called to the Bar, Gray's Inn, 1981; in practice at the Bar, specialising in employment and criminal law; Counsel to Stephen Lawrence Inquiry, 1999; Asst Recorder, 1999–2000. *Recreations:* music, dance, travel books. *Address:* 36 Bedford Row, WC1R 4JH. *T:* (020) 7421 8000. *Club:* Royal Commonwealth Society.

WEEKES, Sir Everton (de Courcy), KCMG 1995; GCM; OBE; international bridge player; former international cricketer; *b* Bridgetown, Barbados, 26 Feb. 1925. *Educ:* St Leonard's Sch., Bridgetown. First class début, 1944, for Barbados; played for Barbados, 1944–64 (Captain), for West Indies, 1947–58 (48 Test matches; 15 centuries, incl. 5 double centuries in England, 1950); on retirement from Test cricket, held world record for five consecutive centuries (*v* England and India), 1948–49, and for seven consecutive half-centuries. *Address:* c/o West Indies Cricket Board of Control, Letchworth Complex, The Garrison, St Michael, Barbados, West Indies.

WEEKES, Mark K.; *see* Kinkead-Weekes.

WEEKES, Philip Gordon, CBE 1993 (OBE 1977); CEng, FIMinE; Chairman: S. V. Waste Services Ltd, since 1992; Goitre Tower Anthracite Ltd, 1994–99; *b* 12 June 1920; *s* of Albert Edwin and Gwladys Magdaline Weekes; *m* 1944, Branwen Mair Jones; two *s* two *d*. *Educ:* Tredegar County Sch.; University Coll., Cardiff (BSc Hons; Fellow, 1982). Jun. official, Tredegar Iron & Coal Co., 1939. Served War, RAF, 1942–44. Manager: Wyllie Colliery, Tredegar (Southern) Colliery Co., 1946; Oakdale Colliery, 1948; seconded to Colonial Office, 1950; Colliery Agent, S Wales, 1951; HQ Work Study Engr, 1952; Gp Manager, Area Prod. Manager, in various areas in S Wales, 1954; Dir of Studies, NCB Staff Coll., 1964; Dep. Dir (Mining), S Midlands Area, 1967; Chief Mining Engr, Nat. HQ, 1970; Dir-Gen. of Mining, Nat. HQ, 1971; Area Dir, S Wales Coalfield, 1973–85; part-time Mem., NCB, 1977–84. Chm., 1992 Garden Fest. Wales Ltd, 1987–94. Member: Prince of Wales' Cttee, 1978–89; IBA Wales Adv. Cttee, 1983–90. Gov., United World Coll. of the Atlantic, 1981–95. *Address:* Hillbrow, Llantwit Major, South Glamorgan CF61 1RE. *Club:* Cardiff and County.

WEEKS, John Henry; QC 1983; **His Honour Judge Weeks;** a Circuit Judge, since 1991; *b* 11 May 1938; *s* of Henry James and Ada Weeks; *m* 1970, Caroline Mary, *d* of Lt Col J. F. Ross; one *s* two *d*. *Educ:* Cheltenham Coll.; Worcester Coll., Oxford (MA). Called to Bar, Inner Temple, 1963, Bencher, 1996; in practice in Chancery, 1963–91. *Publication:* Limitation of Actions, 1989. *Recreation:* walking the dog. *Address:* Brympton d'Evercy, Yeovil, Somerset BA22 8TD. *T:* (01935) 862528.

WEEPLE, Edward John; Head of Lifelong Learning Group, Scottish Executive Enterprise and Lifelong Learning Department, since 1999; *b* 15 May 1945; *s* of Edward Weeple and Mary Catherine (*née* McGrath); *m* 1970, Joan (*née* Shaw); three *s* one *d*. *Educ:* St Aloysius' Coll., Glasgow; Glasgow Univ. (MA). Asst Principal, Min. of Health, 1968–71; Private Sec. to Minister of Health, 1971–73; Principal: DHSS, 1973–78; Scottish Econ. Planning Dept, 1978–80; Assistant Secretary: SHHD, 1980–85; Dept of Agriculture and Fisheries for Scotland, 1985–90; Under Sec., Scottish Office Industry Dept, 1990–95; Hd of Further and Higher Educn, Trng and Sci., then Lifelong Learning, Gp, Scottish Office Educn and Industry Dept, 1995–99. *Address:* (office) Victoria Quay, Edinburgh EH6 6QQ. *T:* (0131) 244 0623; 19 Lauder Road, Edinburgh EH9 2JG. *T:* (0131) 668 1150.

WEETCH, Kenneth Thomas; *b* 17 Sept. 1933; *s* of Kenneth George and Charlotte Irene Weetch; *m* 1961, Audrey Wilson; two *d*. *Educ:* Newbridge Grammar Sch., Mon; London School of Economics. MSc(Econ), DipEd (London Inst. of Educn). National Service: Sgt, RAEC, Hong Kong, 1955–57; Walthamstow and Ilford Educn Authorities and Research at LSE, 1957–64; Head of History Dept, Hockerill Coll. of Educn, Bishop's Stortford, 1964–74. Contested (Lab): Saffron Walden, 1970; Ipswich, 1987. MP (Lab) Ipswich, Oct. 1974–1987. PPS to Sec. of State for Transport, 1976–79. Member: Lab Select Cttee on Home Affairs, 1981–83; Select Cttee on Parly Comr for Administration, 1983–87. *Recreations:* walking, reading, watching Association football, playing the piano in pubs, eating junk food. *Address:* 4 Appleby Close, Ipswich, Suffolk IP2 9XS. *Club:* Silent Street Labour (Ipswich).

WEIDENBAUM, Murray Lew, PhD; Hon. Chairman, Weidenbaum Center on the Economy, Government and Public Policy, since 2001; Mallinckrodt Distinguished University Professor, Washington University, 1971–81 and since 1982; *b* 10 Feb. 1927; *m* 1954, Phyllis Green; one *s* two *d*. *Educ:* City Coll., NY; Columbia Univ. (MA); Princeton Univ. (PhD 1958). Fiscal Economist, Budget Bureau, Washington, 1949–57; Corp. Economist, Boeing Co., Seattle, 1958–63; Sen. Economist, Stanford Res. Inst., 1963–64; Washington University, St Louis, 1964–81, 1982–: Prof. and Chm. of Dept of Econs, 1966–69; Dir, 1975–81 and 1983–95, and Chm., 1995–2001, Center for the Study of Amer. Business; Asst Sec., Treasury Dept, Washington, 1969–71 (on secondment). Chairman: Council of Economic Advisers, USA, 1981–82; Congressional Commn on Trade Deficit, 1999–2000. Hon. LLD: Baruch Coll., 1981; Evansville, 1983. Mem., Free Market Hall of Fame, 1983. Nat. Order of Merit, Republic of France, 1985. *Publications:* Federal Budgeting, 1964; Economic Impact of the Vietnam War, 1967; Modern Public Sector, 1969; Economics of Peacetime Defense, 1974; Government-Mandated Price Increases, 1975; Business, Government, and the Public, 1977, 6th edn (as Business and Government in the Global Marketplace), 1999; The Future of Business Regulation, 1980; Rendezvous with Reality: the American economy after Reagan, 1988; Small Wars, Big Defense, 1992; The Bamboo Network, 1996. *Address:* Weidenbaum Center, Washington University, Campus Box 1027, St Louis, MO 63130–4899, USA.

WEIDENFELD, family name of **Baron Weidenfeld.**

WEIDENFELD, Baron *cr* 1976 (Life Peer), of Chelsea; **Arthur George Weidenfeld,** Kt 1969; Chairman, Weidenfeld & Nicolson Ltd since 1948, and associated companies; *b* 13 Sept. 1919; *o s* of late Max and Rosa Weidenfeld; *m* 1st, 1952, Jane Sieff; one *d*; 2nd, 1956, Barbara Connolly (*née* Skelton) (marr. diss. 1961; she *d* 1996); 3rd, 1966, Sandra Payson Meyer (marr. diss. 1976); 4th, 1992, Annabelle Whitestone. *Educ:* Piaristen Gymnasium, Vienna; University of Vienna (Law); Konsular Akademie (Diplomatic College). BBC Monitoring Service, 1939–42; BBC News Commentator on European Affairs on BBC Empire & North American service, 1942–46. Wrote weekly foreign affairs column, News Chronicle, 1943–44; Founder: Contact Magazine and Books, 1945; Weidenfeld & Nicolson Ltd, 1948. One year's leave as Political Adviser and Chief of Cabinet of President Weizmann of Israel. Consultant, Bertelsmann Foundn, 1992–; Mem. Bd, Herbert-Quandt-Foundn, Bad Homburg, 1999–; Chm., Cheyne Capital, 2000–. Columnist, Die Welt am Sonntag, 1999–. Jt Vice-Pres., Campaign for Oxford, 1992–95; Vice-Chm., Oxford Develt Prog., 1995–. Chm., Bd of Governors, Ben Gurion Univ. of the Negev, Beer-Sheva, 1996– (Vice-Chm., 1976–96); Governor: Univ. of Tel Aviv, 1980–; Weizmann Inst. of Science, 1964–; Bezalel Acad. of Arts, Jerusalem, 1985–; Hon. Senator, Univ. of Bonn, 1997. Member: South Bank Bd, 1986–99; ENO Bd, 1988–98; Trustee, Nat. Portrait Gall., 1988–95. Hon. Fellow: St Peter's Coll., Oxford, 1992; St Anne's Coll., Oxford, 1994. Hon. PhD Ben Gurion Univ. of the Negev, 1984; Hon. MA Oxon, 1992; Hon. DLitt Exeter, 2001. Charlemagne Medal for European Media, Aachen, Germany, 2000. Golden Kt's Cross with Star, Order of Merit (Austria), 1989; Chevalier, Légion d'Honneur (France), 1990; Kt Comdr, Cross, Badge and Star, Order of Merit (Germany), 1991. *Publications:* The Goebbels Experiment, 1943 (also publ. USA); Remembering My Good Friends (autobiog.), 1994. *Recreations:* travel, opera. *Address:* 9 Chelsea Embankment, SW3 4LE. *Clubs:* Athenæum, Garrick.

See also C. A. Barnett.

WEIGHELL, Sidney; General Secretary, National Union of Railwaymen, 1975–83; Member, Trades Union General Council, 1975–83; *b* 31 March 1922; *s* of John Thomas and Rose Lena Weighell; *m* 1st, 1949, Margaret Alison Hunter (killed, 1956); one *s* (one *d*; killed, 1956); 2nd, 1959, Joan Sheila Willetts. *Educ:* Church of England Sch., Northallerton, Yorks. Joined LNER, Motive Power Dept, 1938. Elected to: NUR Exec., 1953; full-time NUR Official, 1954; Asst Gen. Sec., 1965. Labour Party Agent, 1947–52; Mem., Labour Party Exec., 1972–75. Non-exec. Dir, BAA plc (formerly BAA), 1987–88 (pt-time Bd Mem., 1983–87); Mem., Programme Consultative Panel, Tyne Tees TV Ltd, 1984–87. Pres., Great Yorks Rly Preservation Soc., 1986–; Mem., Ditchley Foundn, 1983–89 (Gov., 1983–92). *Publications:* On the Rails, 1983; A Hundred Years of Railway Weighells (autobiog.), 1984. *Recreations:* trout fishing, swimming, gardening; professional footballer, Sunderland FC, 1945–47. *Address:* Blenheim, 2 Moor Park Close, Beckwithshaw, near Harrogate, North Yorkshire HG3 1TR.

WEILER, Terence Gerard, OBE 1993; *b* 12 Oct. 1919; *s* of Charles and Clare Weiler; *m* 1952, Truda, *d* of Wilfrid and Mary Woollen; two *s* two *d*. *Educ:* Wimbledon College; University College, London. Army (RA and Queen's Royal Regiment), 1940–45; UCL, 1937–39 and 1946–47; Home Office: Asst Principal, 1947; Principal, 1948; Asst Sec., 1958; Asst Under-Sec. of State, 1967–80; Mem., Prisons Board, 1962–66, 1971–80; Chm., Working Party: on Habitual Drunken Offenders, 1967–70; on Adjudication Procedures in Prisons, 1975. *Recreations:* cinema, crime fiction. *Address:* 4 Vincent Road, Isleworth, Mddx TW7 4LT. *T:* (020) 8560 7822.

WEILL, Michel Alexandre D.; *see* David-Weill.

WEINBERG, Prof. Felix Jiri, FRS 1983; CPhys, FInstP; Emeritus Professor of Combustion Physics, University of London, since 1993; Senior Research Fellow, Imperial College, University of London, since 1993 (Professor of Combustion Physics, 1967–93); consultant to numerous industrial and government research organisations in UK and USA; *b* 2 April 1928; *s* of Victor Weinberg and Nelly Marie (*née* Altschul); *m* 1954, Jill Nesta (*née* Piggott); three *s*. *Educ:* Univ. of London (BSc ext.); Imperial Coll., London (PhD, DIC, DSc). Lecturer 1956–60, Sen. Lectr 1960–64, Reader in Combustion, 1964–67, Dept of Chemical Engrg and Chem. Technology, Imperial Coll. Director, Combustion Inst., 1978–88 (Chm. British Sect., 1975–80); Founder and first Chm., Combustion Physics Gp, Inst. of Physics, 1974–77, and Rep. on Watt Cttee on Energy, 1979–85; Mem. Council, Inst. of Energy, 1976–79; Mem., Royal Institution. Leverhulme Emeritus Fellow, 1994. FCGI 1998. Foreign Associate, Amer. NAE, 2001. DSc *hc* Israel Inst. of Technol., Haifa, 1990. Combustion Inst. Silver Combustion Medal 1972, Bernard Lewis Gold Medal 1980; Rumford Medal, Royal Soc., 1988; ItalGas Prize for Res. and Innovation in Energy Scis, Turin Acad., 1991. *Publications:* Optics of Flames, 1963; Electrical Aspects of Combustion, 1969; (ed) Combustion Institute European Symposium, 1973; Advanced Combustion Methods, 1986; over 200 papers in Proc., jls and symposia of learned socs. *Recreations:* Eastern philosophies, travel, archery. *Address:* Department of Chemical Engineering, Imperial College, SW7 2BY. *T:* (020) 7594 5580; 59 Vicarage Road, SW14 8RY. *T:* (020) 8876 1540.

WEINBERG, Sir Mark (Aubrey), Kt 1987; Chairman: J Rothschild Assurance, since 1991; Life Assurance Holding Corporation, since 1994; Joint Chairman, 1991–96 and Chairman, since 1996, St James's Place Capital; *b* 9 Aug. 1931; *s* of Philip and Eva Weinberg; *m* 1st, 1961, Sandra Le Roith (*d* 1978); three *d*; 2nd, 1980, Anouska Hempel; one *s*. *Educ:* King Edward VII Sch., Johannesburg; Univ. of the Witwatersrand (BCom, LLB); London Sch. of Econs (LLM). Called to the Bar, South Africa, 1955. Barrister, S Africa, 1955–61; Man. Dir, Abbey Life Assurance Co., 1961–70; Hambro Life Assurance, subseq. Allied Dunbar Assurance: Man. Dir, 1971–83; Chm., 1984–90. Chm., Organizing Cttee, Marketing of Investments Bd, 1985–86; Dep. Chm., Securities and Investment Bd, 1986–90 (Mem., 1985–90); Trustee, Tate Gall., 1985–92. Hon. Treas., NSPCC, 1983–91. *Publication:* Take-overs and Mergers, 1962, 5th edn 1989. *Recreations:* bridge, ski-ing. *Address:* Spencer House, 27 St James's Place, SW1A 1NR. *T:* (020) 7514 1909. *Club:* Portland.

WEINBERG, Prof. Steven, PhD; Josey Regental Professor of Science, University of Texas, since 1982; *b* 3 May 1933; *s* of Fred and Eva Weinberg; *m* 1954, Louise Goldwasser; one *d*. *Educ:* Cornell Univ. (AB); Copenhagen Institute for Theoretical Physics; Princeton Univ. (PhD). Instructor, Columbia Univ., 1957–59; Research Associate, Lawrence Berkeley Laboratory, 1959–60; Faculty, Univ. of California at Berkeley, 1960–69; full prof., 1964; on leave: Imperial Coll., London, 1961–62; Loeb Lectr, Harvard, 1966–67; Vis. Prof., MIT, 1967–69; Prof., MIT, 1969–73; Higgins Prof. of Physics, Harvard Univ., and concurrently Senior Scientist, Smithsonian Astrophysical Observatory, 1973–83 (Sen. Consultant, 1983–). Morris Loeb Vis. Prof., Harvard Univ., 1983–; Dir, Jerusalem Winter Sch. of Theoretical Physics, 1983–94. Lectures: Richtmeyer, Amer. Assoc. of Physics Teachers, 1974; Scott, Cavendish Lab., 1975; Silliman, Yale Univ., 1977; Lauritsen, Calif Inst. of Technol., 1979; Bethe, Cornell, 1979; Schild, Texas, 1979; de Shalit, Weizmann Inst., 1979; Henry, Princeton, 1981; Harris, Northwestern, 1981; Cherwell-Simon, Oxford, 1983; Bampton, Columbia, 1983; Einstein, Israel Acad. of Arts and Sciences, 1984; Hilldale, Wisconsin, 1985; Dirac, Cambridge, 1986; Klein, Stockholm, 1989; Brittin, Colorado, 1992; Gibbs, Amer. Math. Soc., 1996; Bochner, Rice, 1997; Witherspoon, Washington, 2001. Mem., Science Policy Cttee, Superconducting Supercollider Lab., 1989–93. Fellow, Amer. Acad. of Arts and Scis; Member: US Nat.

Acad. of Scis; Amer. Philosophical Soc.; Phil Soc. of Texas (Pres., 1994); IAU; Amer. Historical Assoc.; Texas Inst. of Letters; For. Mem., Royal Soc.; Hon. ScD: Knox Coll. 1978; Chicago, 1978; Rochester, 1979; Yale, 1979; City Univ. of New York, 1980; Clark, 1982; Dartmouth Coll., 1984; Columbia, 1990; Salamanca, 1992; Padua, 1992; Barcelona, 1996; Hon. PhD Weizmann Inst., 1985; Hon. DLitt, Washington Coll., 1985. J. R. Oppenheimer Prize, 1973; Heinemann Prize in Mathematical Physics, 1977; Amer. Inst. of Physics—US Steel Foundn Science Writing Award, 1977; Elliott Cresson Medal of Franklin Inst., 1979; (jtly) Nobel Prize in Physics, 1979; Madison Medal, Princeton, 1991; US Nat. Medal of Sci., 1991; Gemant Prize, Amer. Inst. of Physics, 1997; Pizzi Prize, govts of Sicily and Palermo, 1998; Lewis Thomas Prize, Rockefeller Univ., 1999. Co-editor, CUP Monographs on Mathematical Physics; Mem., Bd of Dirs, Daedalus, 1990–. *Publications:* Gravitation and Cosmology: principles and applications of the general theory of relativity, 1972; The First Three Minutes: a modern view of the origin of the universe, 1977; The Discovery of the Subatomic Particles, 1982; (jtly) Elementary Particles and the Laws of Physics, 1988; Dreams of a Final Theory, 1993; The Quantum Theory of Fields, vol. I, 1995, vol. II, 1996, vol. III, 2000; Facing Up, 2001; numerous articles in learned jls. *Recreation:* reading history. *Address:* Physics Department, University of Texas, Austin, TX 78712, USA. *T:* (512) 4714394. *Clubs:* Saturday (Boston, Mass); Cambridge Scientific (Cambridge, Mass); Headliners, Tuesday (Austin, Texas).

WEINBERGER, Caspar Willard, Hon. GBE 1988; Secretary of Defense, United States of America, 1981–87; Chairman, Forbes Magazine, since 1993 (Publisher, 1989–93); *b* San Francisco, Calif, 18 Aug. 1917; *s* of Herman and Cerise Carpenter (Hampson) Weinberger; *m* 1942, Jane Dalton; one *s* one *d. Educ:* Harvard Coll. (AB *magna cum laude*); Harvard Law Sch. (LLB). Member: Phi Beta Kappa; Amer. Bar Assoc.; State Bar of Calif; Dist of Columbia Bar. Served in Infantry, Private to Captain, AUS, 1941–45 (Bronze Star). Law Clerk to US Ct of Appeals Judge William E. Orr, 1945–47; with law firm Heller, Ehrman, White & McAuliffe, 1947–69, partner, 1959–69. Member, Calif Legislature from 21st Dist, 1952–58; Vice-Chm., Calif Republican Central Cttee, 1960–62, Chm. 1962–64; Chm., Commn on Calif State Govt Organization and Economy, 1967–68; Dir of Finance, Calif, 1968–69; Chm., Fed. Trade Commn, 1970; Dep. Dir, 1970–72, Dir 1972–73, Office of Management and Budget; Counsellor to the President, 1973; Sec., HEW, 1973–75. Gen. Counsel, Vice-Pres., Dir, Bechtel gp of companies, 1975–81; Counsel, Rogers & Wells Internat. Law Firm, 1988–94; former Dir, Pepsi Co. Inc., Quaker Oats Co. Distinguished Vis. Prof., Edinburgh Univ., 1988. Formerly staff book reviewer, San Francisco Chronicle; moderator weekly TV prog., Profile, Bay area, station KQED, San Francisco, 1959–68; host, World Business Review, public TV, 1996–99. Frank Nelson Doubleday (Smithsonian) Lectr, 1974; Chm., Pres.'s Commn on Mental Retardation, 1973–75; Chm., USA–Republic of China Economic Council, 1991–94; Member: Nat. Econ. Commn, 1988–89; Pres's For. Intelligence Adv. Bd, 1988–90; Chatham House Foundn Inc., 1999–; former Member: Trilateral Commn; Adv. Council, Amer. Ditchley Foundn; Bd of Trustees, St Luke's Hosp., San Francisco; Trustee, Winston Churchill Meml Trust, 1994–; former Nat. Trustee, Nat. Symphony, Washington, DC; former Treas., Episcopal Dio. of California. Hon. LLD Leeds, 1989; Hon. DLitt Buckingham, 1995. Medal of Freedom, with Distinction (USA), 1987; Grand Cordon, Order of Rising Sun (Japan), 1988; Order of Brilliant Star, with Grand Cordon (China), 1988; Hilal-i-Pakistan (Pakistan), 1989. *Publications:* Fighting for Peace: seven critical years in the Pentagon, 1990; (with P. Schweizer) The Next War, 1996; contributed a semi-weekly column for a number of Calif newspapers. *Address:* Forbes Magazine, 1101 17th Street NW, Suite 406, Washington, DC 20036, USA; Forbes Magazine, 60–5th Avenue, New York, NY 10011, USA. *Clubs:* Century (NY); Bohemian (San Francisco); Harvard (San Francisco/Washington DC).

WEINER, Edmund Simon Christopher; Deputy Chief Editor, Oxford English Dictionary, 1993–98 and since 2001 (Co-Editor, 1984–93; Principal Philologist, 1998–2001); Supernumerary Fellow, Kellogg College (formerly Rewley House), Oxford, since 1991; *b* 27 Aug. 1950; *s* of Prof. Joseph Sidney Weiner and Marjorie Winifred (*née* Daw); *m* 1973, Clare (Christine) Mary Wheeler; two *s* one *d. Educ:* Westminster; Christ Church, Oxford (BA Eng. Lang. and Lit.; MA). Lectr, Christ Church, Oxford, 1974–77; Mem. Staff, A Supplement to The Oxford English Dictionary, 1977–84. *Publications:* Oxford Guide to English Usage, 1983, 2nd edn (with A. Delahunty) 1993; (ed jtly) The Oxford English Dictionary, 2nd edn, 1989; (with Sylvia Chalker) The Oxford Dictionary of English Grammar, 1994; (with Sidney Greenbaum) The Oxford Reference Grammar, 2000. *Recreations:* language, music, family life, the Church, history. *Address:* Oxford University Press, Great Clarendon Street, Oxford OX2 6DP. *T:* (01865) 556767.

WEINSTEIN, Harvey; film producer; Co-Chairman, Miramax Films Corporation; *b* 1952. Films produced include: Playing for Keeps, 1986; Scandal, 1989; Strike it Rich, Hardware, 1990; A Rage in Harlem, 1991; The Crying Game, 1992; The Night We Never Met, Benefit of the Doubt, True Romance, 1993; Mother's Boys, Like Water for Chocolate, Pulp Fiction, Pret-a-Porter, 1994; Smoke, A Month by the Lake, The Crossing Guard, The Journey of August King, Things To Do In Denver When You're Dead, The Englishman Who Went Up A Hill But Came Down A Mountain, Blue in the Face, Restoration, 1995; Scream, The Pallbearer, The Last of the High Kings, Jane Eyre, Flirting with Disaster, The English Patient, Emma, The Crow: City of Angels, Beautiful Girls, 1996; Addicted to Love, Air Bud, Cop Land, Good Will Hunting, Scream 2, Jackie Brown, 1997; Velvet Goldmine, Shakespeare in Love, Rounders, The Prophecy II, A Price Above Rubies, Playing by Heart, The Mighty, Little Voice, Heaven, Halloween H20: Twenty Years Later, The Faculty, B. Monkey, Phantoms, Senseless, Ride, Wide Awake, Night Watch, 54, Talk of Angels, 1998; Guinevere, Allied Forces, Wasteland, She's All That, My Life So Far, The Yards, 1999; Scary Movie, Boys and Girls, The Crow: Salvation, Reindeer Games, Love's Labour's Lost, Scream 3, About Adam, 2000; Bounce, 2001. *Publication:* (with Robert Weinstein) The Art of Miramax: the inside story. *Address:* Miramax Films Corporation, 375 Greenwich Street, New York, NY 10013, USA.

WEINSTOCK, family name of **Baron Weinstock.**

WEINSTOCK, Baron *cr* 1980 (Life Peer), of Bowden in the County of Wiltshire; **Arnold Weinstock,** Kt 1970; BSc (Econ), FSS; Managing Director, General Electric Co. plc, 1963–96, now Chairman Emeritus; *b* 29 July 1924; *s* of Simon and Golda Weinstock; *m* 1949, Netta, *d* of Sir Michael Sobell; one *d* (one *s* decd). *Educ:* LSE, Univ. of London (BSc Stats). Junior administrative officer, Admiralty, 1944–47; engaged in finance and property development, group of private companies, 1947–54; Radio & Allied Industries Ltd (later Radio & Allied Holdings Ltd), 1954–63 (Managing Director); General Electric Co. Ltd, Director 1961. Dir, Rolls-Royce (1971) Ltd, 1971–73. Vice Pres., Friends of the Ravenna Fest., 1993–94; Trustee: British Museum, 1985–96; Royal Philharmonic Soc., Foundn Fund, 1984–92. Mem., Jockey Club. Hon. FRCR 1975. Hon. Fellow: Peterhouse, Cambridge, 1982; LSE, 1985. Hon. Bencher, Gray's Inn, 1982. Hon. DSc: Salford, 1975; Aston, 1976; Bath, 1978; Reading, 1978; Ulster, 1987; Hon. LLD: Leeds, 1978; Wales, 1985; Keele, 1997; Hon. DTech Loughborough, 1981; DUniv Anglia Poly. Univ., 1994; Hon. DEconSc London, 1997. Commendatore nell' Ordine al Merito (Italy), 1991; Officier, Légion d'Honneur (France), 1992. *Recreations:* racing, music. *Address:* 7 Grosvenor Square, W1X 9LA.

WEINSTOCK, Anne Josephine, CBE 1993; Chief Executive, Connexions Service, since 2000; *b* 28 Dec. 1950; *d* of late Dr Kevin Maher and Brenda Maher; *m* 1976, Dr Harold Weinstock; one *s* two *d. Educ:* Manchester Victoria Univ. (BA Hons Econs). Manager: Stopover hostel for homeless girls, 1972–73; Lance Project for Single Homeless, 1973–75; Regl Manager, then Principal Organiser, NACRO, 1975–79; Mem., Home Office Parole Bd, 1979–84; Chief Executive: Rathbone Soc., 1985–94; Community Industry, 1994–95; Rathbone CI, 1995–99; Dir, Millennium Volunteers, 1999–2000 (on secondment). Director: Manchester TEC, 1989–98; Manchester Careers Partnership, 1995–98; Member: NW FEFC, 1995–98; Govt Skills Task Force, 1998–2000; Chm., Equality NW, 1997–. Fellow, Univ. of Central Lancs, 2001–. *Publications:* contrib. articles on raising standards in educn and trng, impact of league tables, alternative educn for disaffected youth, and encouraging young people to become volunteers. *Recreations:* running, walking, swimming, friends and family, reading. *Address:* Beechwood, 4 Pinfold Lane, Whitefield, Manchester M45 7JS. *T:* (0161) 796 2683, *Fax:* (0161) 796 1384; *T:* (Connexions) (0114) 259 3595.

WEIR, family name of **Baron Inverforth** and **Viscount Weir.**

WEIR, 3rd Viscount *cr* 1938; **William Kenneth James Weir;** Chairman: The Weir Group PLC, 1983–99; Balfour Beatty (formerly BICC) plc, since 1996; Director: St James's Place Capital (formerly J. Rothschild Holdings) plc, since 1985 (Vice-Chairman, 1985–95); Canadian Pacific Ltd, since 1989; *b* 9 Nov 1933; *e s* of 2nd Viscount Weir, CBE, and Lucy (*d* 1972), *d* of late James F. Crowdy, MVO; *S* father, 1975; *m* 1st, 1964, Diana (marr. diss.), *o d* of Peter L. MacDougall; one *s* one *d*; 2nd, 1976, Mrs Jacqueline Mary Marr (marr. diss.), *er d* of late Baron Louis de Chollet; 3rd, 1989, Marina, *d* of late Marc Sevastopoulo; one *s. Educ:* Eton; Trinity Coll., Cambridge (BA). Dir, BSC, 1972–76; Dir, 1977–91, Dep. Chm., 1991–96, BICC Ltd. Dir, 1970, Chm., 1975–82, Great Northern Investment Trust Ltd; Co-Chm., RIT and Northern plc, 1982–83; Chairman: Major British Exporters, 1992–; British Water, 1998–2000. Member: London Adv. Cttee, Hongkong & Shanghai Banking Corp., 1980–92; Court, Bank of England, 1972–84; Export Guarantees Adv. Council, 1992–98. Chm., Engrg Design Res. Centre, 1989–91; Pres., BEAMA, 1988–89, 1994–95; Vice Pres., China-Britain Trade Gp, 1994–. Chm., Patrons of Nat. Galls of Scotland, 1985–95. Mem., Queen's Body Guard for Scotland (Royal Co. of Archers). FRSA. Hon. FREng (Hon. FEng 1993). Hon. DEng Glasgow, 1993. *Recreations:* shooting, golf, fishing. *Heir: s* Hon. James William Hartland Weir, *b* 6 June 1965. *Address:* Rodinghead, Mauchline, Ayrshire KA5 5TR. *T:* (01563) 884233. *Club:* White's.

WEIR, Hon. Lord; David Bruce Weir; a Senator of the College of Justice in Scotland, 1985–97; *b* 19 Dec. 1931; *yr s* of late James Douglas Weir and Kathleen Maxwell Weir (*née* Auld); *m* 1964, Katharine Lindsay, *yr d* of Hon. Lord Cameron, KT, DSC; three *s. Educ:* Kelvinside Academy; Glasgow Academy; The Leys Sch., Cambridge; Glasgow Univ. (MA, LLB). Royal Naval Reserve, 1955–64, Lieut RNR. Admitted to Faculty of Advocates, 1959; Advocate Depute for Sheriff Court, 1964; Standing Junior Counsel: to MPBW, 1969; to DoE, 1970; QC (Scot.) 1971; Advocate Depute, 1979–82; Justice of Ct of Appeal, Botswana, 1999–. Chairman: Medical Appeal Tribunal, 1972–77; Pensions Appeal Tribunal for Scotland, 1978–84 (Pres., 1984–85); NHS Tribunal, Scotland, 1983–85; Member: Criminal Injuries Compensation Bd, 1974–79 and 1984–85; Transport Tribunal, 1979–85; Parole Bd, Scotland, 1989–92. Mem., Law Adv. Cttee, 1988–95, Chm., Scottish Law Cttee, 1994–95, British Council. Governor, Fettes Coll., 1986–95 (Chm., 1989–95). Mem. Bd, Scottish Internat. Piano Competition, 1997–. Vice-Chm., S Knapdale Community Council, 1998–. *Publication:* (contrib.) The Laws of Scotland: Stair Memorial Encyclopaedia, 1990. *Recreations:* sailing, music. *Address:* Lochead House, Achahoish, Lochgilphead, Argyll PA31 8PA. *T:* (01880) 770208. *Clubs:* New (Edinburgh); Royal Cruising; Royal Highland Yacht.

WEIR, Rear-Adm. Alexander Fortune Rose, CB 1981; DL; Senior Associate, McMullen Associates (formerly Captain Colin McMullen and Associates), Marine Consultants, since 1982; *b* 17 June 1928; *s* of late Comdr Patrick Wylie Rose Weir and Minna Ranken Forrester Weir (*née* Fortune); *m* 1953, Ann Ross Hamilton Crawford, Ardmore, Co. Londonderry; four *d. Educ:* Royal Naval Coll., Dartmouth. Cadet, 1945–46; Midshipman, 1946–47; Actg Sub-Lieut under trng, HMS Zephyr, Portland, 1947; Sub-Lieut professional courses, 1947–48; Sub-Lieut and Lieut, HMS Loch Arkaig, Londonderry Sqdn, 1949–51; ADC to Governor of Victoria, Aust., 1951–53; HMS Mariner, Fishery Protection Sqdn, Home waters and Arctic, 1953–54; qual. as Navigating Officer, 1954; HMS St Austell Bay, WI, Navigating Officer, 1955–56; HMS Wave, Fishery Protection Sqdn, Home, Arctic and Iceland, 1956–58; Lt-Comdr, advanced navigation course, 1958; Staff ND Officer, Flag Officer Sea Trng at Portland, Dorset, 1958–61; HMS Plymouth, Staff Officer Ops, 4th Frigate Sqdn, Far East Station, 1961–62; Comdr 1962; Trng Comdr, BRNC Dartmouth, 1962–64; Comd, HMS Rothesay, WI Station, 1965–66; Staff of C-in-C Portsmouth, Staff Officer Ops, 1966–68; 2nd in Comd and Exec. Officer, HMS Eagle, 1968–69; Captain 1969; jssc 1969–70; Pres., Far East Comd Midshipman's Bd, 1970; Asst Dir Naval Operational Requirements, MoD(N), 1970–72; Captain (F) 6th Frigate Sqdn (8 ships) and HMS Andromeda, 1972–74; NATO Def. Coll., Rome, 1974–75; ACOS Strategic Policy Requirements and Long Range Objectives, SACLANT, 1975–77; Captain HMS Bristol, 1977–78; Rear-Adm. 1978; Dep. Asst Chief of Staff (Ops) to SACEUR, 1978–81. FIMgt (FBIM 1979); AVCM 1982. Member: Nautical Inst.; Royal Inst. of Navigation. Licenced Royal Naval Lay Reader, 1981; Licensed Lay Reader: Westbourne Parish, dio. Chichester, 1982; St Kew Parish, dio. Truro, 1984–; Warden of Readers, dio. Truro, 1995–2000; Lay Canon, Truro Cathedral, 1996, now Emeritus. JP: Chichester, 1982–84; Bodmin, 1985–97; DL Cornwall, 1993. *Recreations:* sailing, shooting, golf. *Address:* Tipton, St Kew, Bodmin, Cornwall PL30 3ET. *T:* (01208) 841289, *Fax:* (01208) 841675; *e-mail:* weiralec@cs.com; (office) Maunsell House, Beckenham BR3 4DE. *T:* (020) 8663 6565. *Clubs:* Naval, Royal Navy 1765 and 1785, Institute of Directors; Royal Yacht Squadron, Royal Yachting Association, Royal Naval Sailing Association.

WEIR, David Bruce; *see* Weir, Hon. Lord.

WEIR, Prof. David Thomas Henderson; Professor of Management, CERAM, France, since 2001; Chairman, Forever Broadcasting, Yorkshire, since 2000; *b* 10 April 1939; *s* of late Johnstone Mather Weir and Irene Florence Brooks; *m* 1st, 1959, Janeen Elizabeth Whitson Fletcher; one *s* one *d*; 2nd, 1967, Mary Willows; one *s. Educ:* Ilkley Grammar Sch.; Bradford Grammar Sch.; Queen's Coll., Oxford (Hastings Scholar, Sir William Akroyd's Scholar, MA, Dip PSA). Research and lecturing, Univs of Aberdeen, Leeds, Hull, Manchester, 1961–72; Sen. Lectr, Manchester Business Sch., 1972–74; University of Glasgow: Prof. of Organizational Behaviour, 1974–89; Head, Dept of Management Studies, 1981–89; Dean, Scottish Business Sch., 1977–79; Chm., Glasgow Business Sch., 1985–89; Dir and Prof. of Mgt, Univ. of Bradford Mgt Centre, 1989–97; Dean and Dir, Newcastle Business Sch., and Prof. of Mgt, Univ. of Northumbria at Newcastle,

1998–2000, now Prof. Emeritus. Visiting Professor: Bolton Inst., 1993; Southampton Inst., 1994; (in Mgt Develt) Lancaster Sch. of Mgt, 2000–; Barrie Turner Meml Lectr, Middlesex Univ., 1998. Dir, Gulliver Foods, 1980–81; Arbitrator, Dairy Industry, Scotland, 1985–89. Consultant, World Bank, Unesco, SDA and many companies. Member: Sociology and Social Admin Cttee, SSRC, 1976–78; Cttee of Inquiry, Engrg Profession (Finniston Cttee), 1977–79; Teaching Co. Cttee, SERC, 1983–87 (Chm., 1986–87); CNAA, 1986–89; Incorp. of Gardeners of Glasgow, 1985; Conseil Scient. de l'Univ. des eaux de vies, Segonzac, 1989; Strategic Audit Panel for Review of Dutch Business Educn, Eur. Foundn for Mgt Educn, 1994–95. Chm., Assoc. of Business Schs, 1994–96; Mem. Council, Nat. Forum for Management Educn and Develt, 1994–96. Member Council: Prague Internat. Business Sch., 1992; Cyprus Internat. Business Sch., 1990. CIMgt (FBIM 1984); FRSA. Burgess, City of Glasgow, 1985; Ambassador for Bradford, 1996–. *Publications:* with Eric Butterworth: Sociology of Modern Britain, 1970, 3rd edn 1980; Social Problems of Modern Britain, 1972; New Sociology of Modern Britain, 1984; Men and Work in Modern Britain, 1973; (with Camilla Lambert) Cities in Modern Britain, 1974; (jtly) Computer Programs for Social Scientists, 1972; (with Gerald Mars) Risk Management: theories and models, 2000; (with Gerald Mars) Risk Management: practice and prevention, 2000; The Fourth Paradigm: management in the Arab world, 2002. *Recreations:* playing cricket, supporting Leeds United FC, listening to music, fell walking, wine appreciation. *Address:* CERAM, Rue Dostoievski, BP 085, Sophia Antipolis, 06902, France; *e-mail:* David.Weir@Cote-azur.cci.fr. *Clubs:* Athenæum, Groucho, Ebury Court.

WEIR, Dame Gillian (Constance), DBE 1996 (CBE 1989); concert organist; Prince Consort Professor, Royal College of Music, since 1999; *b* 17 Jan. 1941; *d* of Cecil Alexander Weir and Clarice M. Foy Weir; *m* 1st, 1967, Clive Rowland Webster (marr. diss. 1971); 2nd, 1972, Lawrence Irving Phelps (*d* 1999). *Educ:* Royal College of Music, London. LRSM, LRAM, LTCL; Hon. FRCO. Winner of St Albans Internat. Organ Competition, 1964; Début, 1965: Royal Festival Hall, solo recital; Royal Albert Hall, concerto soloist, opening night of Promenade Concerts; since then, worldwide career solely as touring concert organist; concerto appearances with all major British orchestras, also with Boston Symphony, Seattle Symphony, Württemberg Chamber Orch., and others; solo appearances at leading internat. Festivals, incl. Bath, Aldeburgh, Edinburgh, English Bach, Europalia, Europe and USA (AGO Nat. Conventions, RCCO Diamond Jubilee Nat. Convention, etc). Frequent radio and television appearances: BBC Third Prog., USA, Australasia, Europe; TV film, Toccata: two weeks in the life of Gillian Weir, 1981 (shown NZ TV 1982); presenter and performer, The King of Instruments, TV series BBC2 and Europe, Australia etc, 1989; many first performances, incl. major works by Fricker, Connolly, Camilleri, Messiaen. Master-classes, adjudicator internat. competitions, UK, Europe, N America, Japan. President: Incorp. Assoc. of Organists, 1981–83; ISM, 1992–93; RCO, 1994–96 (Hon. Fellow and Mem. Council, 1977–); Hon. RAM, 1989; Hon. FRCM 2000. Hon. Fellow, Royal Canadian Coll. of Organists, 1983. Hon. DMus: Victoria Univ. of Wellington, NZ, 1983; Hull, 1999; Exeter, 2001; Hon. DLitt Huddersfield, 1997; DUniv UCE, 2001. Internat. Performer of the Year Award, NY Amer. Guild of Organists, 1981; Internat. Music Guide's Musician of the Year Award, 1982; Turnovsky Prize for outstanding achievement in the arts, Turnovsky Foundn for the Arts, NZ, 1985; Silver Medal, Albert Schweitzer Assoc., Sweden, 1998; Evening Standard Award for outstanding performance, 1999. Recordings include complete organ works of Messiaen, 1994, and of Franck, 1997. *Publications:* contributor to: Grove's Internat. Dictionary of Music and Musicians, 1980; musical jls and periodicals. *Recreation:* theatre. *Address:* 78 Robin Way, Tilehurst, Berks RG31 4SW.
See also Sir R. B. Weir.

WEIR, Col James Mathieson Knight, OBE (mil.) 1988; TD 1971 (clasp 1977); FRICS; Vice Lord-Lieutenant of Rutland, since 1997; Chairman, Rutland County Council, 1997–99; *b* 3 March 1931; *s* of James Weir and Elspet Mathieson Weir (*née* Knight); *m* 1961, Mary, *d* of Thomas Maden; two *s*. *Educ:* George Heriot's Sch., Edinburgh; Heriot-Watt Coll.; Royal Sch. of Military Engrg. FRICS 1954. Nat. Service, 1954–57; commnd RE; served UK, Germany, Belgium and Holland. Territorial Army: RE in Scotland, 1958–74; attached 4 Armd Div., 1974–81; Territorial, Auxiliary & Volunteer Reserve Association: Mem., Council, 1996–2000; Mem. for E Midlands, 1983–2000; Chm., Leics and Rutland Cttee, 1996–2000; Chm., ACF Cttee, E Midlands, 1998–2000; Co. Comdt, Leics and Northants ACF, 1982–92 (Hon. Col, Leics, Northants and Rutland ACF, 1995–); Mem., ACFA Council, 1998–. Director: Mitchell Construction Kinnear Moodie Gp, 1966–73; Jeakins Weir Ltd, 1973–. Mem. Bd, Anglian Water Authy, 1981–87. Mem. (C), Leics CC, 1981–93 (Chm., Public Protection Cttee, 1989–93); Mem., Leics Police Authy, 1986–93; Chm., Rutland & Melton Police/Community Consultative Cttee, 1990–93; Mem. (C), Rutland DC, 1991–97 (Vice Chm., 1996–97). DL: Leics, 1984–97; Rutland, 1997. Chm., Leics and Rutland Campaign Army Benevolent Fund, 1989–99. Constituency Conservative Association: Chm., Rutland & Stamford, 1982–83; Rutland & Melton, 1983–85 and 1991–94. Trustee: Peterborough Cathedral Preservation Trust, 1988–; Oakham Sch., 1989–; Governor: C of E Co. Primary Sch., Oakham, 1984–92; Rutland Sixth Form Coll., 1985–93; Vale of Catmose Coll., 1986–95. *Recreations:* golf, visual arts, Rugby Union. *Address:* Swooning House, Oakham, Rutland LE15 6JD. *T:* (01572) 724273. *Club:* Army and Navy.

WEIR, Judith, CBE 1995; composer; *b* 11 May 1954; *d* of Jack and Ishbel Weir. *Educ:* King's Coll., Cambridge (MA). Cramb Fellow, Glasgow Univ., 1979–82; Fellow-Commoner, Trinity Coll., Cambridge, 1983–85; Composer-in-Residence, RSAMD, Glasgow, 1988–91; Fairbairn Composer in assoc. with CBSO, 1995–98; Artistic Dir, Spitalfields Fest., 1998–2000 (Jt Artistic Dir, 1994–97). Critics' Circle Award for outstanding contrib. to British musical life, 1994; Lincoln Center Stoeger Award, 1996. *Publications include: compositions:* King Harald's Saga, 1979; The Consolations of Scholarship, 1985; Missa Del Cid, 1988; Heaven Ablaze In His Breast, 1989; Music Untangled, 1991–92; Heroic Strokes of the Bow, 1992; Moon and Star, 1995; Forest, 1995; Piano Concerto, 1997; Storm, 1997; *operas:* A Night at the Chinese Opera, 1987; The Vanishing Bridegroom, 1990; Blond Eckbert, 1994. *Address:* c/o Chester Music, 8/9 Frith Street, W1D 3JB. *T:* (020) 7434 0066.

WEIR, Michael; MP (SNP) Angus, since 2001; *b* 24 March 1957; *s* of James and Elizabeth Weir; *m* 1985, Anne Jack; two *d*. *Educ:* Arbroath High Sch.; Aberdeen Univ. (LLB). Solicitor: Charles Wood and Son, Kirkcaldy, 1981–83; Myers and Wills, Montrose, 1983–84; J. & D. G. Shiell, Brechin, 1984–2001. Mem. (SNP), Angus DC, 1984–88. Contested (SNP) Aberdeen S, 1987. Pres., Aberdeen Univ. Student Nationalist Assoc., 1979; Mem., Nat. Exec., Young Scottish Nationalists, 1982. *Address:* House of Commons, SW1A 0AA; SNP Office, Marketgate, Arbroath, Angus DD11 1AT. *T:* (01241) 874522.

WEIR, Sir Michael (Scott), KCMG 1980 (CMG 1974); HM Diplomatic Service, retired; Director, 21st Century Trust, 1990–2000; *b* 28 Jan. 1925; *s* of Archibald and Agnes Weir; *m* 1953, Alison Walker; two *s* two *d*; *m* 1976, Hilary Reid (OBE 1998); two *s*. *Educ:* Dunfermline High School; Balliol College, Oxford. Served RAF (Flt Lt), 1944–47; subseq. HM Diplomatic Service; Foreign Office, 1950; Political Agent, Trucial States, 1952–54; FO, 1954–56; Consul, San Francisco, 1956–58; 1st Secretary: Washington, 1958–61; Cairo, 1961–63; FO, 1963–68; Counsellor, Head of Arabian Dept, 1966; Dep. Political Resident, Persian Gulf, Bahrain, 1968–71; Head of Chancery, UK Mission to UN, NY, 1971–73; Asst Under-Sec. of State, FCO, 1974–79; Ambassador, Cairo, 1979–85. Pres., Egypt Exploration Soc., 1988–; Chm., British Egyptian Soc., 1990–. *Recreations:* golf, music. *Address:* 37 Lansdowne Gardens, SW8 2EL. *Clubs:* Rye Golf, Royal Wimbledon Golf.

WEIR, Peter James; barrister; Member (UU) North Down, Northern Ireland Assembly, since 1998; *b* 21 Nov. 1968; *s* of James Weir and Margaret Lovell Weir. *Educ:* Ballyholme Primary Sch.; Bangor Grammar Sch.; Queen's Univ., Belfast (LLB Law and Accountancy; MSSc; Cert. Professional Legal Studies). Called to the Bar, NI, 1992; Lectr in Constitutional and Admin. Law, Univ. of Ulster, 1993. Mem., NI Forum, 1996–98. Chm., Ulster Young Unionist Council, 1993–95. Mem., Senate, QUB, 1997–. *Publications:* (jtly) The Anglo-Irish Agreement: three years after, 1988; (jtly) Unionism, National Parties and Ulster, 1991. *Recreations:* sport, history, reading. *Address:* 6 Vernon Park, Bangor, Co. Down BT20 4PH. *Fax:* (028) 9145 8895; (office) 77A High Street, Bangor, Co. Down BT20 5BD. *T:* (028) 9052 0320.

WEIR, Peter Lindsay, AM 1982; film director, since 1969; *b* 21 Aug. 1944; *s* of Lindsay Weir and Peggy Barnsley Weir; *m* 1966, Wendy Stites; one *s* one *d*. *Educ:* Scots Coll., Sydney; Vaucluse High Sch.; Sydney Univ. Short Film: Homesdale, 1971; Feature Films: The Cars That Ate Paris, 1973; Picnic at Hanging Rock, 1975; Last Wave, 1977; The Plumber (for TV), 1979; Gallipolli, 1980; The Year of Living Dangerously, 1982; Witness, 1985; The Mosquito Coast, 1986; Dead Poets Society, 1989; Green Card, 1991; Fearless, 1994; The Truman Show, 1998. *Address:* c/o Australian Film Commission, 8 West Street, North Sydney, NSW 2060, Australia.

WEIR, Richard Stanton; Director-General, Institutional Fund Managers' Association, 1989–95; *b* 5 Jan. 1933; *o s* of Brig. R. A. Weir, OBE and Dr M. L. Cowan; *m* 1961, Helen Eugenie Guthrie; one *d*. *Educ:* Repton Sch., Derbys; Christ Church, Oxford (MA). Called to the Bar, Inner Temple, 1957. Commnd 3rd Carabiniers (Prince of Wales' Dragoon Guards), 1952. Head of Legal Dept, Soc. of Motor Mfrs and Traders Ltd, 1958–61; Exec., British Motor Corp. Ltd, 1961–64; Dep. Co. Sec., Rank Organisation Ltd, 1964–67; Head of Admin, Rank Leisure Services, 1967–69; Sec., CWS Ltd, 1969–74; Dir, 1975–81, Dir-Gen., 1987–89, Retail Consortium; Sec. Gen. (Chief Exec.), BSA, 1981–86; Dir, British Retailers' Assoc., 1987–89. Mem., Consumer Protection Adv. Cttee set up under Fair Trading Act, 1973, 1973–76. Pres., Old Reptonians Soc., 1998. *Recreations:* reading, walking, shooting. *Address:* PO Box 427, Umhlali, Kwazulu, Natal 4390, Republic of South Africa. *Club:* Oxford and Cambridge.

WEIR, Sir Roderick (Bignell), Kt 1984; JP; Chairman, Rod Weir Co. Ltd; Director, New Zealand Enterprise Trust; *b* 14 July 1927; *s* of Cecil Alexander Weir and Clarice Mildred Foy; *m* 1952, Loys Agnes Wilson (*d* 1984); one *d*; *m* 1986, Anna Jane Mcfarlane. *Educ:* Wanganui Boys' Coll., NZ. Various positions to regional manager, Dalgety NZ Ltd, Wanganui, 1943–63; formed stock and station co., Rod Weir & Co. Ltd, 1963; formed Crown Consolidated Ltd, 1976; Dir, 1980–98, Chm., 1988–98, McKechnie Pacific Ltd; Chm., Danaflex Packaging Corp. Ltd, 1990–98; former Chm., Rangatira Ltd; former Dir, NZ SO. Patron, Massey Coll. Business & Property Trust. Past President: NZ Stock and Station Agents' Assoc.; Asean Business Council. Mem., NZ Inst. of Econ. Res. Inc.; Board Member and Patron: Massey Univ. Foundn; Medic Alert; Wellington Sch. of Medicine; Wellington Med. Res. Foundn; Mem., Adv. Bd, Salvation Army; Dir, Winston Churchill Meml Trust; Trustee: Wanganui Old Boys' Assoc.; Waitangi Foundn (UK). JP NZ 1972. Hon. DSc Massey, 1993. *Recreations:* fishing, shooting, boxing. *Address:* The Grove, 189 Main Road, Waikanae, New Zealand. *T:* and *Fax:* (4) 2936373. *Clubs:* Wellington (Wellington); Heretaunga (Lower Hutt); Levin (Levin).
See also Dame Gillian Weir.

WEIR, Stuart Peter; Director and Joint Editor, Democratic Audit of the United Kingdom, and Senior Research Fellow, Human Rights Centre, Essex University, since 1991; Visiting Professor, Essex Univerity, since 1999; *b* 13 Oct. 1938; *e s* of Robert Hendry Weir, CB and Edna Frances (*née* Lewis); *m* 1st, 1963, Doffy Burnham; two *s*; 2nd, 1987, Elizabeth Ellen Bisset; one *s* two *d*. *Educ:* Peter Symonds Sch., Winchester; Brasenose Coll., Oxford (BA Hons Modern History). Feature writer, Oxford Mail, 1964–67; diarist, The Times, 1967–71; Dir, Citizens Rights Office, CPAG, 1971–75; Founding Editor, Roof magazine, 1975–77; Dep. Editor, New Society, 1977–84; Editor: New Socialist, 1984–87; New Statesman, 1987–88, New Statesman and Society, 1988–90. WEA and Adult Educn lectr, 1969–73. Founder Chair, Family Rights Gp, 1975; Founder and Exec. Mem., Charter 88, 1988–95; Chm., Charter 88 Trust, 1991–92. Associate Consultant, British Council, 1997–; Consultant, State of Democracy Project, Inst. for Democracy and Electoral Assistance, Stockholm, 1998–2001. Member: Exec., CPAG and Finer Jt Action Cttee, 1970–84; (Founding), Labour Co-ordinating Cttee, 1979. Active in anti-racist and community groups, Oxford and Hackney, 1964–72; Mem. (Lab), London Bor. of Hackney Council, 1972–76. Mem., Human Rights Commn, Helsinki Citizens Assembly, 1990–92; Sen. Internat. Facilitator, EU Democracy and Governance Project, Namibia, 1994–95; Facilitator, Parly Reform Project, Zimbabwe, 1996–98; Trustee: Civil Liberties Trust, 1990–97; The Scarman Trust, 1997–99. Columnist: Community Care, 1973–75; London Daily News, 1987; script consultant: Spongers, BBC TV, 1977; United Kingdom, BBC TV, 1980–81; editorial consultant: The People's Parliament, 1994–96; C4 Dispatches, Behind Closed Doors, 1995. *Publications:* (contrib.) Towards Better Social Services, 1973; Social Insecurity, 1974; Supplementary Benefits: a social worker's guide, 1975; (ed and contrib.) Manifesto, 1981; (contrib.) The Other Britain, 1982; (contrib.) Consuming Secrets, 1982; (with W. Hall) EGO-TRIP, 1994; (with W. Hall) Behind Closed Doors, 1995; Consolidating Parliamentary Democracy in Namibia, 1995; (with F. Klug and K. Starmer) Pillars of Liberty: political rights and freedoms in the UK, 1996; (jtly) Making Votes Count, 1997; (with D. Beetham) Political Power and Democratic Control in Britain, 1998; (jtly) Voices of the People, 2001; (jtly) The IDEA Handbook on Democracy Assessments, 2001. *Recreations:* cooking, football, being with my children. *Address:* Butts Orchard, Butts Batch, Wrington, Bristol BS40 5LN.

WEISKRANTZ, Lawrence, FRS 1980; Professor of Psychology, Oxford University, 1967–93, now Emeritus; Fellow, Magdalen College, Oxford, 1967–93, now Emeritus; *b* 28 March 1926; *s* of Dr Benjamin Weiskrantz and Rose (*née* Rifkin); *m* 1954, Barbara Collins; one *s* one *d*. *Educ:* Girard College; Swarthmore; Univs of Oxford and Harvard. Part-time Lectr, Tufts University, 1952; Research Assoc., Inst. of Living, 1952–55; Sen. Postdoctoral Fellow, US Nat. Res. Council, 1955–56; Research Assoc., Cambridge Univ., 1956–61; Asst Dir of Research, Cambridge Univ., 1961–66; Reader in Physiological Psychology, Cambridge Univ., 1966–67. Member: US Nat. Acad. of Scis, 1987; Council, Royal Soc., 1988–89. Ferrier Lectr, Royal Soc., 1989; Hughlings Jackson Lectr/Medallist, RSM, 1990; Camp Lectr, Stanford Univ., 1997. Kenneth Craik Research Award, St John's Coll., Cambridge, 1975–76; Williams James Award, Amer. Psychol Soc.,

1992. Dep. Editor, Brain, 1981–; Co-Editor, Oxford Psychology Series, 1979–. *Publications:* (jtly) Analysis of Behavioural Change, 1967; The Neuropsychology of Cognitive Function, 1982; Animal Intelligence, 1985; Blindsight, 1986; Thought Without Language, 1988; Consciousness Lost and Found, 1997; articles in Science, Nature, Quarterly Jl of Experimental Psychology, Jl of Comparative and Physiological Psychology, Animal Behaviour. *Recreations:* music, walking. *Address:* Department of Experimental Psychology, South Parks Road, Oxford OX1 3UD.

WEISMAN, Malcolm, OBE 1997; Barrister-at-law; a Recorder of the Crown Court, since 1980; *s* of David and Jeanie Pearl Weisman; *m* 1958, Rosalie, *d* of Dr and Mrs A. Spiro; two *s*. *Educ:* Harrogate Grammar Sch.; Parmiter's Sch.; London School of Economics; St Catherine's Coll., Oxford (MA). Blackstone Pupillage Prize. Chaplain (Sqdn Ldr), Royal Air Force, 1956; called to Bar, Middle Temple, 1961; Head of Chambers, 1982–90. Asst Comr of Parly Boundaries, 1976–85; Special Adjudicator, Immigration Appeals, 1998–. Mem., Bar Disciplinary Cttee, Inner Temple, 1990–. Senior Jewish Chaplain, HM Forces, 1972; Religious advisor to small congregations, and Hon. Chaplain, Oxford, Cambridge and new universities, 1963–; Chm. and Sec.-Gen., 1981–92, Pres., 1993–94, Allied Air Forces in Europe Chief of Chaplains Cttee; Sec., Former Chiefs of Chaplains Assoc., 1994; Mem. Exec., USA Jewish Chaplains Assoc., 1992–; Member: MoD Adv. Cttee on Chaplaincy, 1972–; Exec., CCJ, 1998–; Bd, Three Faiths Forum, 1998–. Mem., Cabinet of the Chief Rabbi, 1967–; Hon. Chaplain to: Lord Mayor of Westminster, 1992–93; Mayor of Barnet, 1994–95; Assoc. of Jewish Ex-Servicemen and Women, 1999–. Hon. Vice-Pres., Monash Br., RBL, 1992–. Mem., Senior Common Room, Essex, Kent and Lancaster Univs, 1964–; Fellow, Centre for Theol. and Soc. (formerly Inst. of Theology), Univ. of Essex, 1992– (Mem. Council, 2000–). Member of Court: Univ. of Lancaster, 1970–; Univ. of Kent, 1970–; Warwick Univ., 1983–; Univ. of East Anglia, 1985–; Essex Univ., 1990–; Sussex Univ., 1992–; Mem. Council, Selly Oak Coll., Birmingham, 1992–; Gov., 1980–, Trustee, 1994–, Parmiter's Sch.; Gov., Carmel Coll., 1995–98. Trustee: B'nai B'rith Music Fest., 1995–; Internat. Multi-faith Chaplaincy, Univ. of Derby, 2000. Patron, Jewish Nat. Fund (formerly Holy Land Trust), 1993–. B'nai B'rith Award for Outstanding Communal Service, 1980; Chief Rabbi's Award for Excellence, 1993; US Jewish Military Special Chaplains' Chaplain Award, 1998; Inter-faith Gold Medallion, Internat. CCJ, 2001. Editor, Menorah Jl, 1972–. *Recreations:* travelling, reading, doing nothing. *Address:* 1 Gray's Inn Square, WC1R 5AA. *T:* (020) 7405 8946, *Fax:* (020) 7405 1617.

WEISS, Mrs Althea McNish; *see* McNish, A. M.

WEISS, John Roger; Group Director, Underwriting, Export Credits Guarantee Department, since 1995; *b* 27 Dec. 1944; *s* of Ernst and Betsy Weiss; *m* 1967, Hazel Kay Lang. *Educ:* St Helen's Coll., Thames Ditton. Tax Officer, Inland Revenue, 1961–64; ECGD, 1964–: Dir, Asset Management Gp, 1990–95. *Recreations:* music, walking. *Address:* Export Credits Guarantee Department, 2 Exchange Tower, Harbour Exchange Square, E14 9GS. *T:* (020) 7512 7376.

WEISS, Prof. Nigel Oscar, FRS 1992; Professor of Mathematical Astrophysics, Cambridge University, since 1987; Fellow of Clare College, Cambridge, since 1965; *b* 16 Dec. 1936; *s* of Oscar and Molly Weiss; *m* 1968, Judith Elizabeth Martin; one *s* two *d*. *Educ:* Hilton College, Natal; Rugby School; Clare College, Cambridge (BA 1957; PhD 1962; ScD 1993). Research Associate, UKAEA Culham Lab., 1962–65; Cambridge University: Lectr, Dept of Applied Maths and Theoretical Physics, 1965–79; Reader in Astrophysics, 1979–87; Sen. Fellow, SERC, 1987–92; Chm., Sch. of Physical Scis, 1993–98. Visiting Professor: Sch. of Math. Scis, QMC, then QMW, London, 1986–96; Dept of Applied Maths, Univ. of Leeds, 2001–; temporary appointments: MIT; Max Planck Inst. für Astrophysik, Munich; Nat. Solar Observatory, New Mexico; Harvard-Smithsonian Center for Astrophysics; Sci. Univ. of Tokyo. Pres., Royal Astronomical Soc., 2000–May 2002. *Publications:* papers on solar and stellar magnetic fields, astrophysical and geophysical fluid dynamics and nonlinear systems. *Recreation:* travel. *Address:* Department of Applied Mathematics and Theoretical Physics, Silver Street, Cambridge CB3 9EW. *T:* (01223) 337910; 10 Lansdowne Road, Cambridge CB3 0EU. *T:* (01223) 355032.

WEISS, Prof. Robert Anthony, (Robin), PhD; FRCPath; FRS 1997; Professor of Viral Oncology, University College London, since 1999; *b* 20 Feb. 1940; *s* of Hans Weiss and Stefanie Löwensohn; *m* 1964, Margaret Rose D'Costa; two *d*. *Educ:* University College London (BSc, PhD). Lecturer in Embryology, University Coll. London, 1963–70; Eleanor Roosevelt Internat. Cancer Research Fellow, Univ. of Washington, Seattle, 1970–71; Visiting Associate Prof., Microbiology, Univ. of Southern California, 1971–72; Staff Scientist, Imperial Cancer Research Fund Laboratories, 1972–80, Gustav Stern Award in Virology, 1973; Institute of Cancer Research: Dir, 1980–89; Prof. of Viral Oncology, 1984–98; Dir of Res., 1990–96. Researching into viruses causing cancer and AIDS. Founder FMedSci 1998. Hon. FRCP 1998. *Publications:* RNA Tumour Viruses, 1982, 2nd edn (2 vols) 1985; various articles on cell biology, virology and genetics. *Recreations:* music, natural history. *Address:* Windeyer Institute of Medical Sciences, 46 Cleveland Street, W1P 6DB. *T:* (020) 7679 9554, *Fax:* (020) 7679 9555; *e-mail:* r.weiss@ucl.ac.uk.

WEISSBERG, Prof. Peter Leslie, MD; FRCP, FRCPE; British Heart Foundation Professor of Cardiovascular Medicine, since 1994, and Fellow of Wolfson College, since 1993, Cambridge University; *b* 4 Oct. 1951; *s* of Edmund and Dorcas Alfreda Weissberg; *m* 1976, Alison (*née* Prowse), MB ChB; two *s*. *Educ:* Warwick Sch.; Univ. of Birmingham (MB ChB Hons 1976; MD 1985). MRCP 1978, FRCP 1992; FRCPE 1996. Lectr in Cardiovascular Medicine, Univ. of Birmingham, 1983–88; MRC Res. Fellow, Baker Inst., Melbourne, Australia, 1985–87; University of Cambridge: BHF Sen. Res. Fellow, 1988–92; Lectr in Medicine, 1993–94. FESC 1994; FMedSci 1999. *Publications:* numerous contribs to sci. jls. *Address:* Division of Cardiovascular Medicine, ACCI, Level 6, Box 110,Addenbrooke's Hospital, Hills Road, Cambridge CB2 2QQ. *T:* (01223) 331504, *Fax:* (01223) 331505.

WEISSKOPF, Prof. Victor Frederick; Professor of Physics, Massachusetts Institute of Technology, 1946–73, now Emeritus (Chairman, Department of Physics, 1967–73); *b* 19 Sept. 1908; *m* 1st, 1934, Ellen Margrete Tvede (*d* 1989); one *s* one *d*; 2nd, 1991, Duscha Schmid. *Educ:* Göttingen, Germany. PhD 1931. Research Associate: Berlin Univ., 1932; Eidgenossiche Technische Hochschule (Swiss Federal Institute of Technology), Zürich, 1933–35; Inst. for Theoretical Physics, Copenhagen, 1936; Asst Professor of Physics, Univ. of Rochester, NY, USA, 1937–43; Dep. Division Leader, Manhattan Project, Los Alamos, USA, 1943–45; Director-Gen., CERN, Geneva, 1961–65 (on leave of absence from MIT). Chm., High Energy Physics Adv. Panel, AEC, 1967–75. Mem., Nat. Acad. of Sciences, Washington, 1954; Pres., Amer. Acad. of Arts and Sciences, 1976–79; Corresp. Member: French Acad. of Sciences, 1957; Scottish Acad. of Scis, 1959; Royal Danish Scientific Soc., 1961; Bavarian Acad. of Scis, 1962; Austrian Acad. of Scis, 1963; Spanish Acad. of Scis, 1964; Soviet Acad. of Scis, 1976; Pontifical Acad. of Scis, 1976. Hon. Fellow: Weizmann Inst., Rehovot, Israel, 1962; Inst. of Physics, France, 1980. Hon. PhD: Manchester, 1961; Uppsala, 1964; Yale, 1964; Chicago, 1967; Hon. DSc: Montreal, 1959; Sussex, 1961; Lyon, 1962; Basle, 1962; Bonn, 1963; Genève, 1964; Oxford, 1965; Vienna, 1965; Paris, 1966; Copenhagen, 1966; Torino, 1968; Yale, 1968; Upsala, 1969; Harvard, 1984; Graz, 1985. Cherwell-Simon Memorial Lecturer, Oxford, 1963–64. Planck Medal, 1956; Gamov Award, 1969; Prix Mondial Del Duca, 1972; Killian Award, 1973; Smoluchovski Medal, Polish Physical Soc., 1979; Nat. Medal of Science, 1979; Wolf Prize (Israel), 1981; Enrico Fermi Award, 1989; Nat. Acad. Public Welfare Medal, 1991; Compton Award, 1992. Légion d'Honneur (France), 1959; Pour le Mérite Order, Germany, 1978; Grosse Goldene Ehrenzeichen (Austria), 2000. *Publications:* Theoretical Nuclear Physics, 1952; Knowledge and Wonder, 1962; Physics in the XX Century, 1972; Concepts of Particle Physics, 1984; The Privilege of Being a Physicist, 1989; The Joy of Insight, 1991; papers on theoretical physics in various journals. *Address:* 20 Bartlett Terrace, Newton, MA 02459, USA.

WEISSMÜLLER, Alberto Augusto, FCIB; President and Chief Executive Officer, A. A. Weissmüller Ltd, since 1992; General Partner, The Stillwaters Group, Washington, since 1992; *b* 2 March 1927; *s* of late Carlos Weissmüller and Michela Cottura; *m* 1976, Joan Ann Freifrau von Süsskind-Schwendi (*née* Smithson); one *s* one *d* by previous *m*. *Educ:* Univ. of Buenos Aires, Argentina; Illinois Inst. of Technol., Chicago, USA. Civil Engr, 1952; FCIB (FIB 1977). The Lummus Co., New York, 1958–59; Office of Graham Parker, NY, 1960–62; Bankers Trust Co., NY, 1962–71: Edge Act subsid., 1962–64; Asst Treasurer, and Mem., Bd of Corporation Financiera Nacional, Colombia, 1964–65; Asst Vice-Pres., 1965–67; Vice-Pres., 1967–71; Rome Rep., 1968–71; Man. Dir, Bankers Trust Finanziaria, SpA, Rome, 1970–71; Crocker National Bank, San Francisco, seconded to United Internat. Bank (now Unibank Ltd), London, as Chief Exec., 1971–79; Chief Adviser, Bank of England, 1979–81; Chief Exec. (UK), Banca Commerciale Italiana, 1981–82; Chm., BCI Ltd, London, 1981–83; Dir, N American Bancorp Inc. (a subsid. of Banca Commerciale Italiana), 1982–87; Rep. of Banca Commerciale Italiana in Washington, 1983–92 and in Mexico City, 1987–92. *Publication:* Castles from the Heart of Spain, 1977. *Recreations:* medieval fortified and Palladian architecture, photography (architectural). *Address:* A. A. Weissmüller Ltd, 13801 Deakins Lane, Germantown, MD 20874, USA.

WEITZ, Dr Bernard George Felix, OBE 1965; DSc; MRCVS; FIBiol; Chief Scientist, Ministry of Agriculture, Fisheries and Food, 1977–81; *b* London, 14 Aug. 1919; *m* 1945, Elizabeth Shine; one *s* one *d*. *Educ:* St Andrew, Bruges, Belgium; Royal Veterinary College, London. MRCVS 1942; DSc London 1961. Temp. Research Worker, ARC Field Station, Compton, Berks, 1942; Research Officer, Veterinary Laboratory, Min. of Agric. and Fisheries, 1942–47; Asst Bacteriologist, Lister Inst. of Preventive Medicine, Elstree, Herts, 1947; Head of Serum Dept, 1952; Dir, Nat. Inst. for Res. in Dairying, Univ. of Reading, Shinfield, Berks, 1967–77. Vis. Prof., Dept of Agriculture and Horticulture, Univ. of Reading, 1980–88. Member: ARC, 1978–81; NERC, 1978–81. Hon. FRASE, 1977. *Publications:* many contribs to scientific journals on Immunology and Tropical Medicine. *Recreations:* music, croquet. *Address:* 21 Hartley Close, Charlton Kings, Cheltenham, Glos GL53 9DN.

WEITZMAN, Peter; QC 1973; a Recorder of the Crown Court, 1974–98; *b* 20 June 1926; *s* of late David Weitzman, QC, and Fanny Weitzman; *m* 1954, Anne Mary Larkam; two *s* two *d*. *Educ:* Cheltenham Coll.; Christ Church, Oxford (MA). Royal Artillery, 1945–48. Called to Bar, Gray's Inn, 1952; Bencher, 1981; Leader, Midland and Oxford Circuit, 1988–92 (Dep. Leader, 1985–88). Mem., Senate of Inns of Court, 1980–81, 1984–92. Member: Mental Health Review Tribunal, 1986–98; Criminal Injuries Compensation Bd, 1986–2000; Criminal Injuries Compensation Appeals Panel, 2000–. *Recreations:* hedging and ditching. *Address:* 21 St James's Gardens, W11 4RE; Little Leigh, Kingsbridge, Devon TQ7 4AG.

WEIZMAN, Maj.-Gen. Ezer; President of Israel, 1993–2000; *b* Tel Aviv, 15 June 1924; *s* of Yechiel Weizman and Yehudit Weizman; *m* 1950, Reuma Schwartz; one *d* (one *s* decd). Joined RAF, 1942; fighter pilot, 1944; served ME and FE; co-founder, Israeli Air Force, 1947; fighter pilot, War of Independence, 1948–49; Comdr, first Israeli fighter sqdn, 1949; RAF Staff Coll., 1952; Air Base Comdr, 1953–57; Maj.-Gen. and Comdr, Israeli Air Force, 1958–66; Dep. COS, Israel Defence Forces, 1966–69; retd, 1969. Israeli Government: Mem., Knesset, 1977–92; Minister: of Tspt, 1969–70; of Defence, 1977–80; for Arab Affairs, 1984–88; of Sci. and Technol., 1988–90. *Publications:* On Eagles' Wings, 1974; The Battle for Peace, 1981. *Address:* Beit Amot Mishpat, 8 Shaul Hamelech Boulevard, Tel Aviv, Israel.

WELANDER, Rev. Canon David Charles St Vincent; Canon Residentiary and Librarian, Gloucester Cathedral, 1975–91, now Emeritus; *b* 22 Jan. 1925; *s* of late Ernest Sven Alexis Welander, Orebro and Uppsala, Sweden, and Louisa Georgina Downes Welander (*née* Panter); *m* 1952, Nancy O'Rorke Stanley; two *s* three *d*. *Educ:* Unthank Coll., Norwich: London Univ. (BD 1947, Rubie Hebrew Prize 1947); ALCD (1st Cl.) 1947; Toronto Univ., 1947–48 (Hon. Mem. Alumni, Wycliffe Coll., 1948). FSA 1981. Deacon 1948, Priest 1949; Asst Curate, Holy Trinity, Norwich, 1948–51; Chaplain and Tutor, London Coll. of Divinity, 1952–56; Vicar: of Iver, Bucks, 1956–62; of Christ Church, Cheltenham, 1963–75; Rural Dean of Cheltenham, 1973–75. Member: Council, St Paul's and St Mary's Colls of Educn, Cheltenham, 1963–78; Council, Malvern Girls' Coll., 1982–91; Bishops' Cttee on Inspections of Theol Colls, 1967–81; Sen. Inspector of Theol Colls, 1970–84; Mem., Gen. Synod of C of E, 1970–85. Mem., Cathedrals Cttee, English Heritage, 1990–94. Trustee: Church Patronage Trust, 1969–78; Stained Glass Mus., 1986–. *Publications:* History of Iver, 1954; Gloucester Cathedral, 1979; The Stained Glass of Gloucester Cathedral, 1984; Gloucester Cathedral: its history, art and architecture, 1990; Gloucester Cathedral, A Visitor's Handbook, 2001; contrib. Expository Times, etc. *Recreations:* walking, church architecture, music. *Address:* 1 Sandpits Lane, Sherston Magna, near Malmesbury, Wilts SN16 0NN. *T:* (01666) 840180.

WELBOURN, Prof. Richard Burkewood, MA, MD, FRCS; Professor of Surgical Endocrinology, Royal Postgraduate Medical School, University of London, 1979–82, now Emeritus Professor; *b* 1919; *y s* of late Burkewood Welbourn, MEng, MIEE, and Edith Welbourn, Rainhill, Lancs; *m* 1944, Rachel Mary Haighton, BDS, Nantwich, Cheshire; one *s* four *d*. *Educ:* Rugby School; Emmanuel College, Cambridge; Liverpool University. MB, BChir 1942; FRCS 1948; MA, MD Cambridge, 1953. War of 1939–45: RAMC. Senior Registrar, Liverpool Royal Infirmary, 1948; Research Asst, Dept of Surgery, Liverpool Univ., 1949. Fellow in Surgical Research, Mayo Foundation, Rochester, Minn, 1951. Professor of Surgical Science, Queen's University of Belfast, 1958–63; Surgeon, Royal Victoria Hospital, Belfast, 1951–63 and Belfast City Hosp., 1962–63; Prof. of Surgery, Univ. of London and Dir, Dept of Surgery, RPMS and Hammersmith Hosp., 1963–79; Hon. Consultant Surgeon, Hammersmith Hosp., 1979–82. Consultant Adviser in Surgery to Dept of Health and Social Security, 1971–79; Consultant (Vis. Schol., res. in hist. of Endocrine Surgery), Dept of Surgery, UCLA, 1983–89. Member: Council, MRC, 1971–75; Council, Royal Postgraduate Med. Sch., 1963–82. Hunterian Professor, RCS, 1958 (James Berry Prize, 1970); Harvey Lectr, Yale

Univ., 1995. Member: Society of Sigma XI; British Medical Association; Internat. Assoc. of Endocrine Surgeons, 1979– (Peter Heimann Lectr, 1989; Distinguished Service Award, 1991); Internat. Soc. of Surgery, 1979–; British Soc. of Gastro-enterology and Assoc. of Surgeons; 58th Member King James IV Surgical Association Inc.; Fellow, West African Coll. of Surgeons; FRSocMed (former Mem. Council, Section of Endocrinology, former Vice-Pres., Section of Surgery); Hon. Fellow Amer. Surgical Assoc.; Hon. Mem., Soc. for Surgery of the Alimentary Tract; formerly: Pres., Surgical Res. Soc. (Hon. Mem.); British Assoc. of Endocrine Surgeons (Hon. Mem.); Chm., Assoc. of Profs of Surgery; Mem., Jt Cttee for Higher Surgical Training; formerly Examr in Surgery, Univs of Manchester, Glasgow, Oxford, Sheffield, Edinburgh, QUB, and Liverpool; formerly Examr in Applied Physiology, RCS. Chm., Editorial Cttee, Journal of Medical Ethics, 1974–81; former Member: Editorial Cttee, Gut; Exec. Cttee, British Jl of Surgery. Formerly: Pres., Internat. Surgical Gp; Chm. Governing Body, Inst. of Medical Ethics; Pres., Prout Club. Hon. Mem., Royal Coll. of Surgeons of Univs of Denmark, 1978; Hon. FACS 1984. Hon. MD Karolinska Inst., Stockholm, 1974; Hon. DSc QUB, 1985. Biennial Medal and Prize, Internat. Soc. of Surgery, 1995. *Publications:* (with D. A. D. Montgomery) Clinical Endocrinology for Surgeons, 1963, rev. edn, Medical and Surgical Endocrinology, 1975; (with A. S. Duncan and G. R. Dunstan) Dictionary of Medical Ethics, 1977, 2nd edn 1980, American edn 1981; The History of Endocrine Surgery, 1990; chapters in books and papers, mainly on gastro-intestinal and endocrine surgery and physiology, and history of endocrinology, in med. and surg. jls. *Recreations:* reading, writing without deadlines, gardening, music. *Address:* 2 The Beeches, Tilehurst, Reading RG31 6RQ. *T:* (0118) 942 9258.

WELBY, Sir (Richard) Bruno (Gregory), 7th Bt *cr* 1801; *b* 11 March 1928; *s* of Sir Oliver Charles Earle Welby, 6th Bt, TD, and Barbara Angela Mary Lind (*d* 1983), *d* of late John Duncan Gregory, CB, CMG; *S* father, 1977; *m* 1952, Jane Biddulph, *y d* of late Ralph Wilfred Hodder-Williams, MC; three *s* one *d. Educ:* Eton; Christ Church, Oxford (BA 1950). *Heir: s* Charles William Hodder Welby [*b* 6 May 1953; *m* 1978, Suzanna, *o d* of Major Ian Stuart-Routledge, Harston Hall, Grantham; three *d*]. *Address:* Denton Manor, Grantham, Lincs NG32 1JX.

WELCH, Andrew Richard; Theatre Director (formerly Festival Director), Chichester Festival Theatre, since 1998; *b* 5 Feb. 1949; *s* of Richard Joseph Welch and Ruth Jordan Welch; *m* 1980, Louisa Mary Emerson; two *s. Educ:* Bedford Sch., Bedford; UC of Swansea, Univ. of Wales (BA). Dir, Arts Centre, Univ. of Warwick, 1977–81; General Manager: Hong Kong Arts Centre, 1981–84; Theatre Royal, Plymouth, 1984–90; Producer, Carnival Films and Theatre Ltd, 1990–95; Chief Exec., Theatre of Comedy Ltd, 1996–98. Man. Dir, Armada Prodns, 1987–. *Recreations:* music, walking. *Address:* 12 Westwood Road, SW13 0LA. *T:* (020) 8876 9292.

WELCH, Rear Adm. John Edwin Nugent, CB 1996; Chief of Naval Staff, New Zealand, 1994–97; *b* 14 Jan. 1941; *s* of Robert Nugent Welch and Mary Helen Anne Welch; *m* 1966, Adrienne Sandford Cox; three *s. Educ:* King's High Sch., Dunedin, NZ; Britannia Royal Naval Coll., Dartmouth. Service at sea, Pacific and Far East, 1961–66; Long Gunnery Course, HMS Excellent, 1967–68; i/c HMNZS Mako, 1968–69; service at sea, Far East, 1969–70; ashore, 1971–72; service at sea, 1972–75; i/c HMNZS Inverell, 1976–77; jssc, Australia, 1978; i/c HMNZS Otago, Far East and USA, 1978–80; staff appts, 1981–82; i/c HMNZS Canterbury, 1983–84; Capt. 1985; staff appts, Wellington, 1985–87; NZ Defence Advr, Ottawa, 1988–90; staff appts, 1991–97; Cdre 1992; Rear Adm 1994. Naval Gen. Service Medal, 1964; NZ Armed Forces Award, 1985. Silver Jubilee Medal, 1977. *Recreations:* trout fishing, golf, reading, sailing. *Address:* 9 Rangitira Avenue, Takapuna, Auckland, New Zealand. *T:* (9) 4891237; *e-mail:* welchfam@clear.net.nz. *Clubs:* Auckland Central Rotary; Waitemata Golf.

WELCH, Sir John K.; *see* Kemp-Welch.

WELCH, Sir John (Reader), 2nd Bt *cr* 1957; Partner, Wedlake Bell, 1972–96; Chairman, John Fairfax (UK) Ltd, 1977–90; *b* 26 July 1933; *s* of Sir (George James) Cullum Welch, 1st Bt, OBE, MC, and Gertrude Evelyn Sladin Welch (*d* 1966); *S* father, 1980; *m* 1962, Margaret Kerry, *o d* of late K. Douglass, Killara, NSW; one *s* twin *d. Educ:* Marlborough College; Hertford Coll., Oxford (MA). National service in Royal Signals, 1952–54 (2nd Lt); TA, 1954–62 (Capt., Middlesex Yeomanry). Admitted a solicitor, 1960. Partner, Bell Brodrick & Gray, 1961–71. Ward Clerk of Walbrook Ward, City of London, 1961–74, Common Councilman, 1975–86 (Chm., Planning and Communications Cttee, 1981, 1982); Registrar of Archdeaconry of London, 1964–99. Governor: City of London Sch. for Girls, 1977–82; Haberdashers' Aske's Schs, Elstree, 1981–85 and 1990–91. FRSA. Liveryman, Haberdashers' Co., 1955 (Court of Assistants, 1973; Master, 1990–91); Freeman, Parish Clerks' Co. (Master, 1967). Chm., Cttee of Management, London Homes for the Elderly, 1980–90; Pres., Grand Charity of Freemasons, 1985–95; Sen. Grand Warden, United Grand Lodge of England, 1998–2000. CStJ 1981. *Recreations:* piano, walking. *Heir: s* James Douglass Cullum Welch, *b* 10 Nov. 1973. *Address:* 28 Rivermead Court, Ranelagh Gardens, SW6 3RU. *Clubs:* City Livery (Hon. Solicitor, 1983–90, Pres., 1986–87), Walbrook Ward (Chm., 1978–79), Hurlingham.

WELCH, Prof. Robert Anthony, PhD; FEA; Director, Centre for Irish Literature and Bibliography, since 1994, and Dean, Faculty of Arts, since 2000, University of Ulster; *b* 25 Nov. 1947; *s* of Patrick Welch and Kathleen Kearney; *m* 1970, Angela O'Riordan; three *s* one *d. Educ:* University Coll., Cork (BA Hons 1968; MA 1971); Univ. of Leeds (PhD 1974). Lecturer: Sch. of English, Univ. of Leeds, 1971–73; in English, Univ. of Ife, Nigeria, 1973–74; Sch. of English, Univ. of Leeds, 1974–84; Prof. and Head of Dept, Univ. of Ulster, Coleraine, 1984–94. Mem. 1990–96, Vice Chm. 1992–93, Arts Council of NI. Chm., Internat. Assoc. for Study of Ireland's Literatures, 1988–91. Founding FEA, 2000. *Publications:* Irish Poetry from Moore to Yeats, 1980; A History of Verse Translation from the Irish, 1988; Changing States: transformations in modern Irish literature, 1993; Muskerry (poems), 1993; The Kilcolman Notebook (novel), 1994; (ed) Oxford Companion to Irish Literature, 1996; Secret Societies (poems), 1997; Groundwork (novel), 1997; The Blue Formica Table (poems), 1998; The Abbey Theatre: 1899–1999, 1999. *Recreations:* gardening, fishing. *Address:* Faculty of Arts, University of Ulster, Coleraine, Northern Ireland BT52 1SA. *Clubs:* Carlton; Kildare Street and University (Dublin).

WELCHMAN, Charles Stuart; His Honour Judge Welchman; a Circuit Judge, since 1998; *b* 7 April 1943; *s* of late Edward James Welchman and Marjorie (*née* Williams, later Parsons); *m* 1972, Rosemary Ann Fison, *d* of late Dr Thomas Notley Fison and of Nancy Jean Laird Fison; one *s* one *d. Educ:* W Buckland Sch.; Exeter Tech. Coll.; University Coll. London (LLB Hons 1965). Called to the Bar, Gray's Inn, 1966 (Mould Scholar 1966); a Recorder, 1994–98. Mem., Exec. Cttee, Professional Negligence Bar Assoc., 1996–98. *Recreations:* inland waterways, fishing, theatre, jazz. *Address:* Snaresbrook Crown Court, The Court House, Hollybush Hill, E11 1DW. *Clubs:* 100; Surrey County Cricket.

WELD FORESTER, family name of **Baron Forester.**

WELDON, Sir Anthony (William), 9th Bt *cr* 1723; *b* 11 May 1947; *s* of Sir Thomas Brian Weldon, 8th Bt, and of Marie Isobel (who *m* 1984, 6th Earl Cathcart, CB, DSO, MC), *d* of Hon. William Joseph French; *S* father, 1979; *m* 1980, Mrs Amanda Wigan, *d* of Major Geoffrey and Hon. Mrs North; two *d. Educ:* Sherborne. Formerly Lieutenant, Irish Guards. Dir, Bene Factum Publishing Ltd, 1983–. *Publication:* (ed) Breakthrough: handling career opportunities and changes, 1994. *Recreations:* stalking, fishing, antiquarian books, champagne. *Heir: cousin* Kevin Nicholas Weldon [*b* 19 April 1951; *m* 1973, Catherine Main; one *s*]. *Clubs:* White's, Stranded Whales.

WELDON, Duncan Clark; theatrical producer; Chairman and Managing Director, Duncan C. Weldon Productions Ltd, since 1964; *b* 19 March 1941; *s* of Clarence Weldon and Margaret Mary Andrew; *m* 1974, Janet Mahoney; one *d. Educ:* King George V School, Southport. Formerly a photographer; first stage production, A Funny Kind of Evening, with David Kossoff, Theatre Royal, Bath, 1965; co-founder, Triumph Theatre Productions, 1970; Director: Triumph Proscenium Productions Ltd, 1994–; Malvern Festival Theatre Trust Ltd, 1997–; Artistic Dir, Chichester Festival Theatre, 1995–97. First London production, Tons of Money, Mayfair Theatre, 1968; productions in the West End include: When We are Married, 1970 (also 1996); The Chalk Garden, Big Bad Mouse, The Wizard of Oz, 1971; Lord Arthur Savile's Crime, Bunny, The Wizard of Oz, 1972; Mother Adam, Grease, The King and I, 1973; Dead Easy, 1974; The Case in Question, Hedda Gabler, Dad's Army, Betzi, On Approval, 1975; 13 Rue de l'Amour, A Bedful of Foreigners, Three Sisters, The Seagull, Fringe Benefits, The Circle, 1976; Separate Tables, Stevie, Hedda Gabler, On Approval, The Good Woman of Setzuan, Rosmersholm, Laburnum Grove, The Apple Cart, 1977; Waters of the Moon, Kings and Clowns, The Travelling Music Show, A Family, Look After Lulu, The Millionairess, 1978; The Crucifer of Blood, 1979; Reflections, Rattle of a Simple Man, The Last of Mrs Cheyney, Early Days, 1980; Virginia, Overheard, Dave Allen, Worzel Gummidge, 1981; Murder In Mind, Hobson's Choice (also 1995), A Coat of Varnish, Captain Brassbound's Conversion, Design for Living, Uncle Vanya (also 1996), Key for Two, The Rules of the Game, Man and Superman, 1982; The School for Scandal, DASH, Heartbreak House, Call Me Madam, Romantic Comedy, Liza Minnelli, Beethoven's Tenth, Edmund Kean, Fiddler on the Roof, A Patriot for Me, Cowardice, Great and Small, The Cherry Orchard, Dial 'M' for Murder, Dear Anyone, The Sleeping Prince, Hi-De-Hi!, 1983; Hello, Dolly!, The Aspern Papers, Strange Interlude, Serjeant Musgrave's Dance, Aren't We All?, American Buffalo, The Way of the World, Extremities, 1984; The Wind in the Willows, The Lonely Road, The Caine Mutiny Court-Martial, Other Places, Old Times (also 1995), The Corn is Green, Waste, Strippers, Guys and Dolls, Sweet Bird of Youth, Interpreters, Fatal Attraction, The Scarlet Pimpernel, 1985; The Apple Cart, Across From the Garden of Allah, Antony and Cleopatra, The Taming of the Shrew, Circe & Bravo, Annie Get Your Gun, Long Day's Journey Into Night, Rookery Nook, Breaking the Code, Mr and Mrs Nobody, 1986; A Piece of My Mind, Court in the Act!, Canaries Sometimes Sing, Kiss Me Kate, Melon, Portraits, Groucho: a Life In Review, A Man for All Seasons, You Never Can Tell, Babes in the Wood, 1987; A Touch of the Poet, The Deep Blue Sea, The Admirable Crichton, The Secret of Sherlock Holmes, A Walk in the Woods, Richard II, Orpheus Descending, 1988; Richard III (also 1999), The Royal Baccarat Scandal, Ivanov, Much Ado About Nothing, The Merchant of Venice, Veterans Day, Another Time, The Baker's Wife, London Assurance, 1989; Salome, Bent, An Evening with Peter Ustinov (also 1994), The Wild Duck, Henry IV, Kean, Love Letters (also 1999), Time and the Conways, 1990; The Homecoming, The Philanthropist, The Caretaker, Becket, Tovarich, The Cabinet Minister, 1991; Talking Heads (also 1996), A Woman of No Importance, Lost in Yonkers, Trelawny of the "Wells", Cyrano de Bergerac, 1992; Relative Values, Two Gentlemen of Verona, Macbeth, 1993; Travesties, A Month in the Country, Rope, Arcadia, Home, Saint Joan, Lady Windermere's Fan, The Rivals, 1994; Dangerous Corner, Cell Mates, The Duchess of Malfi, Taking Sides, Communicating Doors, The Hothouse, 1995; The Cherry Orchard (RSC), 1996; Live and Kidding, The Herbal Bed (RSC), Life Support, A Letter of Resignation, The Magistrate, Electra, 1997; New Edna—The Spectacle, Rent, 1998; The Prisoner of Second Avenue (RSC), Hay Fever, The Importance of Being Earnest, Collected Stories, 1999; Enigmatic Variations, Napoleon, God Only Knows, 2000; presented on Broadway: Brief Lives, 1974; Edmund Kean, Heartbreak House, 1983; Beethoven's Tenth, 1984; Strange Interlude, Aren't We All?, 1985; Wild Honey, 1986; Blithe Spirit, Pygmalion, Breaking the Code, 1987; Orpheus Descending, The Merchant of Venice, 1989; Taking Sides, 1996; Electra, 1999; has also presented in Europe, Australia, Canada and Hong Kong. *Television:* Co-producer, Into the Blue, 1997. *Address:* Suite 4, Waldorf Chambers, 11 Aldwych, WC2B 4DA. *T:* (020) 7343 8800.

WELDON, Fay, CBE 2001; writer; *b* 22 Sept. 1931; *d* of Frank Birkinshaw and Margaret Jepson; *m* 1962, Ron Weldon (*d* 1994); four *s*; *m* 1995, Nicolas Fox. *Educ:* Hampstead Girls' High Sch.; St Andrews Univ. (MA 1952). Has written or adapted numerous television and radio plays, dramatizations, and series, and ten stage plays. Chm. of Judges, Booker McConnell Prize, 1983. Hon. DLitt St Andrews, 1990. *Libretto:* A Small Green Space, 1989. *Publications:* The Fat Woman's Joke, 1967; Down Among the Women, 1972; Female Friends, 1975; Remember Me, 1976; Little Sisters, 1977 (as Words of Advice, NY, 1977); Praxis, 1978 (Booker Prize Nomination); Puffball, 1980; Watching Me, Watching You (short stories), 1981; The President's Child, 1982; The Life and Loves of a She-Devil, 1984 (televised, 1986; filmed as She-Devil, 1990); Letters to Alice—on First Reading Jane Austen, 1984; Polaris and other Stories, 1985; Rebecca West, 1985; The Shrapnel Academy, 1986; Heart of the Country, 1987 (televised, 1987); The Hearts and Lives of Men, 1987; The Rules of Life, 1987; Leader of the Band, 1988; (for children) Wolf the Mechanical Dog, 1989; The Cloning of Joanna May, 1989 (televised, 1992); (for children) Party Puddle, 1989; Darcy's Utopia, 1990; (contrib.) Storia 4: Green, 1990; Moon over Minneapolis or Why She Couldn't Stay (short stories), 1991; Life Force, 1992; Growing Rich, 1992; Affliction, 1994; Splitting, 1995; (with David Bailey) The Lady is a Tramp: portraits of Catherine Bailey, 1995; Wicked Women, 1995; Worst Fears, 1996; (for children) Nobody Likes Me!, 1997; Big Women, 1998 (televised, 1998); A Hard Time to Be a Father (short stories), 1998; Godless in Eden: a book of essays, 1999; Rhode Island Blues, 2000; The Bulgari Connection, 2001. *Address:* c/o Casarotto Co. Ltd, National House, 62/66 Wardour Street, W1V 3HP.

WELEMINSKY, Judith Ruth; Senior Consultant, Compass Partnership, since 1997 (Consultant, 1994–97); *b* 25 Oct. 1950; *d* of Dr Anton Weleminsky and Gerda Weleminsky (*née* Loewenstamm); partner, Robert James Armstrong Smith; two *d. Educ:* Birmingham Univ. (BSc Hons Psych); Lancaster Univ. (MA Organisational Psych). Personnel and Training Officer, Lowfield (Storage and Distbn), 1973–75; Community Relations Officer, Lambeth, 1975–78; Equal Opportunities Officer, Wandsworth, 1978–80; Employment Development Officer, NACRO, 1980–82; Dir, Nat. Fedn of Community Orgns, 1982–85; Dir, Nat. Schizophrenia Fellowship, 1985–90; Dir, NCVO, 1991–94; Associate, Centre for Voluntary Sector and Not for Profit Mgt, City Univ. Bus. Sch., 1994–97. Partner, Mentoring Dirs, 1995–97. Bd Mem., Children and Family Court Adv. Support Service, 2001–. Trustee: Cosmopolitan Develt Trust, 1997–; Makaton Vocabulary Develt Project, 1998–. FRSA. *Recreations:* family, friends, food.

Address: Compass Partnership, 203–209 North Gower Street, NW1 2NJ. *T:* (020) 7391 9911.

WELFARE, Jonathan William; Chief Executive, Elizabeth Finn Trust (formerly Distressed Gentlefolk's Aid Association), since 1998; *b* 21 Oct. 1944; *s* of late Kenneth William Welfare and of Dorothy Patience Athol Welfare (*née* Ross); *m* 1969, Deborah Louise Nesbitt; one *s* three *d. Educ:* Bradfield Coll., Berks; Emmanuel Coll., Cambridge (MA Econs and Land Economy 1969; boxing blue). Economist, Drivers Jonas & Co., 1966–68; Consultant, Sir Colin Buchanan and Partners, 1968–70; Economist and Corporate Planning Manager, Milton Keynes Develt Corp., 1970–74; Economist, then Dep. Chief Exec., S Yorks CC, 1974–84; Director: Landmark Trust, 1984–86; Oxford Ventures Gp, 1986–90; Man. Dir, Venture Link Investors, 1990–95; Chief Exec., Bristol 2000, 1995–96; mgt consultant, 1995–98. Director: Oxford Innovation, 1987–96; Granite TV, 1988–; Interconnect Ltd, 1990–94; Calidair Ltd, 1990–95; Meridian Software, 1990–95. Trustee: Oxford Trust, 1985– (Chm., 1985–95); Northmoor Trust, 1986–99 (Chm., 1986–95). FRSA 1992. Freeman: City of London, 1991; Co. of Information Technologists, 1991. *Recreations:* family, cricket, fishing, resisting potentially misplaced development. *Address:* Wilton House, High Street, Hungerford, Berks RG17 0NF. *T:* (01488) 684228; (office) 1 Derry Street, W8 5HY. *T:* (020) 7396 6700. *Club:* Hawks (Cambridge).

WELLAND, Colin, (Colin Williams); actor, playwright; *b* 4 July 1934; *s* of John Arthur Williams and Norah Williams; *m* 1962, Patricia Sweeney; one *s* three *d. Educ:* Newton-le-Willows Grammar Sch.; Bretton Hall Coll.; Goldsmiths' Coll., London (Teacher's Dip. in Art and Drama; Hon. Fellow, 2000). Art teacher, 1958–62; entered theatre, 1962; Library Theatre, Manchester, 1962–64; television, films, theatre, 1962–. Freelance sports writer: The Observer; The Independent. Films (actor): Kes; Villain; Straw Dogs; Sweeney; Dancing through the Dark; (original screenplay): Yanks, 1978; Chariots of Fire, 1980 (won Oscar, Evening Standard and Broadcasting Press Guild Awards, 1982); Twice in a Lifetime, 1986; A Dry White Season, 1989; War of the Buttons, 1994; television (actor): The Fix; Bramwell, 1998. Plays (author): Say Goodnight to Grandma, St Martin's, 1973; Roll on Four O'clock, Palace, 1981. Award winning TV plays include: Roll on Four O'clock, Kisses at 50, Leeds United, Jack Point, Your Man from Six Counties, Bambino Mio. Best TV Playwright, Writers Guild, 1970, 1973 and 1974; Best TV Writer, and Best Supporting Film Actor, BAFTA Awards, 1970; Broadcasting Press Guild Award (for writing), 1973. *Publications:* Northern Humour, 1982; plays: Roomful of Holes, 1972; Say Goodnight to Grandma, 1973. *Recreations:* sport, theatre, cinema, politics, dining out. *Address:* c/o Peters, Fraser & Dunlop, Drury House, 34–43 Russell Street, WC2B 5HA.

WELLBELOVED, James; commercial consultant; Director General, National Kidney Research Fund, 1984–93; *b* 29 July 1926; *s* of Wilfred Henry Wellbeloved, Sydenham and Brockley (London), and Paddock Wood, Kent; *m* 1948, Mavis Beryl Ratcliff; two *s* one *d. Educ:* South East London Technical College. Boy seaman, 1942–46. MP (Lab 1965–81, SDP 1981–83) Erith and Crayford, Nov. 1965–1983; Parly Private Secretary: Minister of Defence (Admin), 1967–69; Sec. of State for Foreign and Commonwealth Affairs, 1969–70; an Opposition Whip, 1972–74; Parly Under-Sec. of State for Defence (RAF), MoD, 1976–79. UK Rep., North Atlantic Assembly, 1972–76, 1979–82. Dep. Chm., London MPs Parly Gp, 1970–81; Chairman: River Thames Gp; All Party Parly Camping and Caravanning Gp, 1967–74; Nat. Whitley Council, MoD, 1976–79; Member: Ecclesiastical Cttee, 1971–76; RACS Political Purposes Cttee, 1973–83; PLP Liaison Cttee, 1974–78; Defence Council, 1976–79; Unrelated Live Transplant Regulatory Authority, 1990–97; Vice Chm., Labour Party Defence Gp, 1970–81. Contested (SDP) 1983, (SDP/Alliance) 1987, Erith and Crayford. Dir, Assoc. of Former MPs, 1983–. Dir, Greenwich and Bexley Cottage Hospice, 1998–. Pres., British Transplant Organ Donor Soc., 1992–97. Nat. Vice-Pres., Camping and Caravanning Club, 1974–. Former Governor, Greenwich Hosp. Sch. *Publication:* Local Government, 1971. *Recreations:* camping, travel. *Address:* 9 Woodstock Close, Bexley, Kent DA5 3JT.

WELLBY, Rear-Adm. Roger Stanley, CB 1958; DSO 1940; DL; retired; Head of UK Services Liaison Staff in Australia and Senior Naval Adviser to UK High Commissioner, 1956–59; *b* 28 April 1906; *o s* of Dr Stanley Wellby and Marian Schwann; *m* 1936, Elaine, *d* of late Sir Clifford Heathcote-Smith; three *s. Educ:* RNC, Dartmouth. Qualified as Torpedo Officer, 1931; Commander, 1939; Special Service in France, 1940 (DSO, Croix de Guerre); Captain, 1947; Imperial Defence College; Rear-Adm. 1956. Dep. Comr-in-Chief, St John Ambulance Brigade, 1963–71; Comr, St John Ambulance Brigade, Bucks, 1971–75. DL Bucks 1972. KStJ 1966. *Recreation:* hockey, for Navy. *Address:* 17 Honey Banks, Wendover, Bucks HP22 6NA. *T:* (01296) 624507.

WELLER, Sir Arthur (Burton), Kt 1997; CBE 1988; Chairman, Citadel Reinsurance Company Ltd, since 1984; *b* 9 Nov. 1929; *s* of Thomas Burton Weller and Mary Johnston Weller (*née* Norman); *m* 1962, Margaret Marea Piper (*née* Callinan); one *s* one *d. Educ:* Trinity Acad., Edinburgh. Master Mariner, 1957. Chm., Sirius Insurance Co., 1969–91. Chairman: Britain-Australia Bicentennial Schooner Trust, 1986–; Maritime Trust, 1989–96 (Mem. Council, 1977; Hon. Warden, 1996–); HM Bark Endeavour Foundn, 1991–2000; Trustee, Nat. Maritime Mus., 1990–97. *Recreations:* reading, breeding Angus cattle. *Address:* Flat 16, Arlington House, Arlington Street, SW1A 1RL; Mittabah, Exeter, NSW 2579, Australia; *e-mail:* arthurw@attglobal.net. *Clubs:* Hong Kong Yacht (Hong Kong); Royal Sydney Yacht Squadron (Sydney); St Botolph (Boston).

WELLER, Prof. Ian Vincent Derrick, MD; FRCP; Professor, since 1991, and Head of Department of Sexually Transmitted Diseases, since 1994, Royal Free and University College Medical School of University College London (formerly University College London Medical School); *b* 27 March 1950; *s* of Derrick Charles William Weller and Eileen Weller; *m* 1972, Darryl McKenna; two *d. Educ:* Westlain Grammar Sch., Brighton; St Bartholomew's Hosp. Med. Sch. (BSc 1st Cl. Hons 1971; MB BS 1974; MD 1983). MRCP 1977, FRCP 1990. House physician, Med. Unit, St Bartholomew's Hosp. and house surgeon, Hackney Hosp., 1975; SHO rotation, Northwick Park Hosp., 1976–77; Med. Registrar rotation, St Mary's Hosp., London, 1977–79; Ingram Res. Fellow, then Hon. Lectr and MRC Trng Fellow, Acad. Dept of Medicine, Royal Free Hosp., 1979–82; Lectr and Hon. Sen. Registrar, Acad. Dept of Genito-Urinary Medicine, 1982–84, Wellcome Trust Sen. Lectr in Infectious Diseases, 1984–88, Middx Hosp. Med. Sch.; Reader in Genito-Urinary Medicine, UCL Med. Sch., 1988–91. Member: Genito-Urinary Specialist Cttee, RCP, 1994–; MRC Committees: AIDS Res. Co-ordinating Cttee, 1994–; AIDS Therapeutics Cttee, 1987– (Dep. Chm., 1995–; Chm., Anti-viral Sub-gp), 1990–; Mem., Adv. Gp to HEA, 1994–; Vice Co-Chair, Cttee on Safety of Medicines, 1999–. Mem., Eur./Australian Internat. Co-ordinating Cttee for trials in HIV infection and AIDS, 1989– (Mem., Virology Sub-gp, 1990–); also mem. internat. cttees on res. and drug therapy relating to HIV and AIDS; Mem. various *ad hoc* wkg parties for EEC and Eur. Medicines Evaluation Agency. *Publications:* contrib. chapters in proc. and books; numerous papers in peer reviewed jls and articles. *Recreations:* golf, walking, farming. *Address:* Department of Sexually Transmitted Diseases, Royal Free and University College Medical School, Mortimer Market Centre, Mortimer Market, off Capper Street, WC1E 6AU.

WELLER, Dr Thomas Huckle; Richard Pearson Strong Professor of Tropical Public Health, Harvard University, 1954–85, Emeritus 1985 (Head, Department of Tropical Public Health, 1954–81); Director, Center for Prevention of Infectious Diseases, Harvard School of Public Health, 1966–81; *b* 15 June 1915; *s* of Carl V. and Elsie H. Weller; *m* 1945, Kathleen R. Fahey; two *s* two *d. Educ:* University of Michigan (AB, MS); Harvard (MD). Fellow, Departments of Comparative Pathology and Tropical Medicine and Bacteriology, Harvard Medical School, 1940–41; Intern, Children's Hosp., Boston, 1941–42. Served War, 1942–45: 1st Lieut to Major, Medical Corps, US Army. Asst Resident in Medicine, Children's Hosp., 1946; Fellow, Pediatrics, Harvard Medical School, 1947; Instructor, Dept Tropical Public Health, Harvard School of Public Health, 1948; Assistant Professor, 1949; Associate Professor, 1950. Asst Director, Research Div. of Infectious Diseases, Children's Medical Center, Boston, 1949–55; Dir, Commission on Parasitic Diseases, Armed Forces Epidemiological Bd, 1953–59, Mem. 1959–72; Mem. Trop. Med. and parasitology study sect., US Public Health Service, 1953–56. Diplomate, American Board of Pediatrics, 1948; Amer. Acad. of Arts and Sciences, 1955; National Academy of Sciences, USA. Consultant on tropical medicine and infectious diseases to foundations and industries, 1985–. Hon. FRSTM&H, 1987. Hon. LLD Michigan, 1956; Hon. DSc: Gustavus Adolphus Coll., 1975; Univ. of Mass Med. Sch., 1986; Hon. LHD Lowell, 1977. Mead Johnson Award of Amer. Acad. of Pediatrics (jointly), 1954; Kimble Methodology Award (jointly), 1954; Nobel Prize Physiology or Medicine (jointly), 1954; Ledlie Prize, 1963; United Cerebral Palsy Weinstein-Goldenson Award, 1974; Bristol Award, Infectious Diseases Soc. of America, 1980; First Scientific Achievement Award, VZV Res. Foundn, 1993; Walter Reed Medal, Amer. Soc. of Tropical Medicine and Hygiene, 1996. *Publications:* numerous scientific papers on *in vitro* cultivation of viruses and on helminth infections of man. *Recreations:* gardening, photography. *Address:* 56 Winding River Road, Needham, MA 02492–1025, USA. *Club:* Harvard (Boston).

WELLER, Walter; Principal Guest Conductor, National Orchestra of Spain, since 1987; *b* 30 Nov. 1939; *s* of Walter and Anna Weller; *m* 1966, Elisabeth Samohyl; one *s. Educ:* Realgymnasium, Vienna; Akademie für Musik, Vienna (degree for violin and piano). Founder of Weller Quartet, 1958–69; Member, Vienna Philharmonic, 1958–69. First Leader, 1960–69; Conductor, Vienna State Opera, 1969–75; Guest Conductor with all main European and American Orchestras, also in Japan and Israel, 1973–; Principal Conductor and Artistic Adviser, Royal Liverpool Philharmonic Orch., 1977–80; Principal Conductor, RPO, 1980–85; Principal Conductor and Music Dir, Royal Scottish Nat. Orch., 1992–97, now Conductor Emeritus. Artistic Dir, Allgemeine Musikges. Basel, 1994–95. Many recordings (Grand Prix du disque Charles Cros). Medal of Arts and Sciences, Austria, 1968; Great Silver Cross of Honour, Austria, 1998. *Recreations:* magic, model railway, sailing, swimming, stamp-collecting, ski-ing. *Address:* c/o Harrison-Parrott Ltd, 12 Penzance Place, W11 4PA.

WELLESLEY, family name of **Earl Cowley** and of **Duke of Wellington.**

WELLINGS, David Gordon; Group Chief Executive, Cadbury Schweppes plc, 1993–96; *b* 13 Dec. 1940; *s* of Gordon Henry and Muriel Wellings; *m* 1962, Jennifer Christine Simpson; one *s* one *d. Educ:* Manchester Grammar Sch.; Oriel Coll., Oxford (MA Mod. Langs). Joined Cadbury Bros Ltd, 1962; Marketing Dir, Associated Fisheries & Food, 1970–73; Man. Dir, Northray Foods Ltd, 1973–78; Dir, Fish Ops, Ross Foods Ltd, 1978–82; Chm. and Chief Exec., Golden Wonder/HP Foods, 1982–86; Managing Director: Cadbury Ltd, 1986–89; Gp Confectionery, Cadbury Schweppes plc, 1989–93. *Recreations:* ornithology, golf. *Club:* Oxford and Cambridge.

WELLINGS, Sir Jack (Alfred), Kt 1975; CBE 1970; Chairman, 1968–87, Managing Director, 1963–84, The 600 Group Ltd; *b* 16 Aug. 1917; *s* of Edward Josiah and Selina Wellings; *m* 1946, Greta, *d* of late George Tidey; one *s* two *d. Educ:* Selhurst Grammar Sch.; London Polytechnic. Vice-Pres., Hawker Siddeley (Canada) Ltd, 1954–62; Dep. Man. Dir, 600 Group Ltd, 1962. Member: NCB, 1971–77; NEB, 1977–79; part-time Mem., British Aerospace, 1980–87; non-exec. Dir, Clausing Corp., USA, 1982–84. *Address:* Boundary Meadow, Collum Green Road, Stoke Poges, Bucks SL2 4BB. *T:* (01753) 662978.

WELLINGTON, 8th Duke of, *cr* 1814; **Arthur Valerian Wellesley,** KG 1990; LVO 1952; OBE 1957; MC 1941; DL; Baron Mornington, 1746; Earl of Mornington, Viscount Wellesley, 1760; Viscount Wellington of Talavera and Wellington, Somersetshire, Baron Douro, 1809; Earl of Wellington, Feb. 1812; Marquess of Wellington, Oct. 1812; Marquess Douro, 1814; Prince of Waterloo, 1815, Netherlands; Count of Vimeiro, Marquess of Torres Vedras and Duke of Victoria in Portugal; Duke of Ciudad Rodrigo and a Grandee of Spain, 1st class; *b* 2 July 1915; *s* of 7th Duke of Wellington, KG, and Dorothy Violet (*d* 1956), *d* of Robert Ashton, Croughton, Cheshire; *S* father, 1972; *m* 1944, Diana Ruth, *o d* of Maj.-Gen. D. F. McConnel; four *s* one *d. Educ:* Eton; New Coll., Oxford. Served War of 1939–45 in Middle East (MC), CMF and BLA. Lt-Col Comdg Royal Horse Guards, 1954–58; Silver Stick-in-Waiting and Lt-Col Comdg the Household Cavalry, 1959–60; Comdr 22nd Armoured Bde, 1960–61; Comdr RAC 1st (Br.) Corps, 1962–64; Defence Attaché, Madrid, 1964–67, retired; Col-in-Chief, The Duke of Wellington's Regt, 1974–; Hon. Col 2nd Bn, The Wessex Regt, 1974–80; Dep. Col, The Blues and Royals, 1999–. Director: Massey Ferguson Holdings Ltd, 1967–89; Massey Ferguson Ltd, 1973–84. President: Game Conservancy, 1976–81 (Dep. Pres., 1981–87); SE Branch, Royal British Legion, 1978; BSJA, 1980–82; Rare Breeds Survival Trust, 1984–87; Council for Environmental Conservation, 1983–87; Atlantic Salmon Trust, 1983–; Nat. Canine Defence League, 1996–; Labrador Retriever Club, 1997–; Vice-President: Zool Soc. of London, 1983–89; Kennel Club, 1985–; Mem. Council, RASE, 1976– (Dep. Pres., 1993). HM's Rep. Trustee, Bd of Royal Armouries, 1983–95; Trustee, WWF (UK), 1985–90. Hampshire CC 1967–74; DL Hants, 1975. Pres., Hampshire Assoc. of Parish and Town Councils, 1994–99. Governor of Wellington Coll., 1964–. Pres., Pitt Club. OStJ. Officier, Légion d'Honneur (France); Kt Grand Cross: Order of St Michael of the Wing (Portugal), 1984; Order of Isabel the Catholic (Spain), 1986. *Heir: s* Marquess of Douro, *qv. Address:* Stratfield Saye House, Basingstoke, Hants RG27 0AS; Apsley House, 149 Piccadilly, W1V 9FA. *Club:* Cavalry and Guards.

WELLINGTON (NZ), Archbishop of, (RC), since 1979; **His Eminence Cardinal Thomas Stafford Williams,** ONZ 2000; DD; Metropolitan of New Zealand; *b* 20 March 1930; *s* of Thomas Stafford Williams and Lillian Maude Kelly. *Educ:* Holy Cross Primary School, Miramar; SS Peter and Paul Primary School, Lower Hutt; St Patrick's Coll., Wellington; Victoria University Coll., Wellington; St Kevin's Coll., Oamaru; Holy Cross Coll., Mosgiel; Collegio Urbano de Propaganda Fide, Rome (STL); University Coll., Dublin (BSocSc); Hon. DD. Assistant Priest, St Patrick's Parish, Palmerston North, 1963–64; Director of Studies, Catholic Enquiry Centre, Wellington, 1965–70; Parish Priest: St Anne's Parish, Leulumoega, W Samoa, 1971–75; Holy Family Parish, Porirua, NZ, 1976–79. Cardinal, 1983. *Address:* Viard, 21 Eccleston Hill, Wellington 1, New Zealand. *T:* (4) 4961795.

WELLINGTON (NZ), Bishop of, since 1998; **Rt Rev. Dr Thomas John Brown;** *b* 16 Aug. 1943; *s* of Ernest Robert Brown and Abby Brown; *m* 1965, Dwyllis Lyon; one *s* two *d*. *Educ:* Otago Univ.; St John's Theol Coll., Auckland (LTh, STh); Graduate Theol Union, Berkeley, Univ. of California (DMin). Curate: St Matthew, Christchurch, NZ, 1972–74; St James the Greater, Leicester, UK, 1974–76; Vicar: Upper Clutha, 1976–79, St John, Roslyn, 1979–85, Dio. Dunedin, NZ; St James, Lower Hutt, Dio. Wellington, 1985–91; Archdeacon of Belmont, 1987–91; Asst Bishop and Vicar General, Diocese of Wellington, 1991–98. *Publications:* Ministry At The Door, 1981; Learning From Liturgy, 1984; (contrib.) Growing in Newness of Life, 1993; (contrib.) Designer Genes, 2000; (contrib.) Gene Technology in New Zealand: scientific issues and implications, 2000. *Recreations:* golf, fly-fishing, reading, swimming. *Address:* Bishopscourt, 20 Eccleston Hill, Thorndon, Wellington, New Zealand.

WELLINGTON, Peter Scott, CBE 1981; DSC; PhD; ARCS; FLS; FIBiol; FRAgS; Director, National Institute of Agricultural Botany, 1970–81; *b* 20 March 1919; *er s* of late Robert Wellington, MBE, MC; *m* 1947, Kathleen Joyce, *widow* of E. H. Coombe; one *s* one *d*. *Educ:* Kelly Coll.; Imperial Coll. of Science. BSc 1946. Observer, Fleet Air Arm, 1940–45 (Lt-Comdr (A) RNVR). Research Asst 1948–52, Chief Officer 1953–61, Official Seed Testing Stn for England and Wales; Asst Dir 1961–68, Dep. Dir 1968–69, Nat. Inst. of Agricultural Botany. Vice-Pres., Internat. Seed Testing Assoc., 1953–56 (Chm. Germination Cttee, 1956–70); Chief Officer, UK Variety Classification Unit, 1965–70; Chm., Technical Working Group, Internat. Convention for Protection of Plant Varieties, 1966–68; Mem., Governing Body, Nat. Seed Develt Orgn Ltd, 1982–87. *Publications:* (with V. Silvey) Crop and Seed Improvement: a history of the National Institute of Agricultural Botany 1919–1996, 1997; papers on germination of cereals and weeds, seed-testing and seed legislation. *Recreations:* gardening, walking, reading. *Address:* Colescus, Gorran Haven, St Austell, Cornwall PL26 6JJ. *T:* (01726) 842065.

WELLINK, Arnout Henricus Elisabeth Maria; Executive Director, since 1982, President, since 1997, De Nederlandsche Bank; *b* 27 Aug. 1943; *m* 1989, Monica Victoria Volmer; three *s* two *d*. *Educ:* Gymnasium B; Leyden Univ. (law degree 1968); Univ. of Rotterdam (PhD Econs 1975). Teaching asst in econs, and staff mem., Leyden Univ., 1965–70; Ministry of Finance: staff mem., 1970–75; Hd, Directorate Gen. for Financial and Econ. Policy, 1975–77; Treas. Gen., 1977–81. Dir, BIS, Basle, 1997–; Member: Council, Eur. Monetary Inst., 1997–98; Governing Council, European Central Bank, 1998–. Vice-Chm., Bd, Westeinde Hosp. and Ursula Clinic, 1987–; Mem., Bd of Trustees, Mus. Meermanno Westreenianum, 1994–. Chm., King William I Foundn, 1997–; Member: Bd, Foundn for Orthopaedic Patients' Interests, 1995–; Foundn for Postgrad. Med. Trng in Indonesia, 1997–; N. G. Pierson Fund Foundn, 1997–. Kt, Order of Lion (Netherlands), 1981. *Address:* De Nederlandsche Bank NV, PO Box 98, 1000 AB Amsterdam, The Netherlands. *T:* (20) 5242150, *Fax:* (20) 5242525.

WELLS, Dean of; *see* Lewis, Very Rev. R.

WELLS, Archdeacon of; *see* Acworth, Ven. R. F.

WELLS, Dr Alan Arthur, OBE 1982; FRS 1977; FREng; Director-General, The Welding Institute, 1977–88; *s* of Arthur John Wells and Lydia Wells; *m* 1950, Rosemary Edith Alice Mitchell; four *s* one *d*. *Educ:* City of London Sch.; Univ. of Nottingham (BScEng); Clare Coll., Cambridge (PhD). FREng (FEng 1978); MIMechE (Hon. FIMechE 1999); Hon. FWeldI. British Welding Res. Association: Asst Dir, 1956; Dep. Dir (Scientific), 1963; Queen's University of Belfast: Prof. of Struct. Science, 1964; Head of Civil Engrg Dept, 1970–77; Dean, Faculty of Applied Science and Technol., 1973–76; Professorial Fellow, 1990. Hon. Dr, Faculty of Engrg, Univ. of Gent, 1972; Hon. DSc Glasgow, 1982; Hon. DScEng QUB, 1986. *Publications:* Brittle Fracture of Welded Plate (jtly), 1967; res. papers on welding technol. and fracture mechanics. *Recreation:* handyman about the house and garden. *Address:* Grove House, Mepal, Ely, Cambs CB6 2AR. *T:* (01353) 778620. *Club:* Athenæum.

WELLS, Andrew Mark; Director, Regional Co-ordination Unit, Cabinet Office, since 2000; *b* 22 Feb. 1955; *s* of Richard Frederick Wells and Eunice Mary Wells (*née* Williams). *Educ:* Bristol Grammar Sch.; St John's Coll., Cambridge (MA Maths 1976). Grad. trainee, 1976–83, Principal, Local Govt Finance, 1983–87, DoE; on loan as Principal, Econ. Secretariat, Cabinet Office, 1987–90; Department of the Environment: Divl Manager, Local Govt Rev. Team, 1990–92; Hd, London Policy Unit, 1992–93; Divisional Manager: Local Authy Housing, 1993–96; Water Supply and Regulation, 1996–99; on loan as Dir, Modernising Govt, Cabinet Office, 1999–2000. *Recreations:* walking, squash. *Address:* Regional Co-ordination Unit, Riverwalk House, 157–161 Millbank, SW1P 4RR. *T:* (020) 7217 3552.

WELLS, Bowen; *b* 4 Aug. 1935; *s* of late Reginald Laird Wells and of Agnes Mary Wells (*née* Hunter); *m* 1975, Rennie Heyde; two *s*. *Educ:* St Paul's School; Univ. of Exeter (BA Hons); Regent St Polytechnic School of Management (Dip. Business Management). National Service, RN (promoted to Sub Lt), 1954–56. Schoolmaster, Colet Court, 1956–57; sales trainee, British Aluminium, 1957–58; Univ. of Exeter, 1958–61; Commonwealth Development Corporation, 1961–73; Owner Manager, Substation Group Services Ltd, 1973–79. MP (C) Hertford and Stevenage, 1979–83, Hertford and Stortford, 1983–2001. Parliamentary Private Secretary: to Minister of State for Employment, 1982–83; to Minister of State at Dept of Transport, 1992–94; an Asst Govt Whip, 1994–95; a Lord Comr of HM Treasury (Govt Whip), 1994–97. Member: For. Affairs Select Cttee, 1981–92; European Legislation Select Cttee, 1983–92; Chairman: Select Cttee on Internat. Develt, 1997–2001; UN Parly Gp, 1983–92; British-Caribbean Gp, 1983–95; Jt Hon. Sec., Parly Cons. Trade and Industry Gp, 1984–91 (Vice-Chm., 1983–84); Sec., All Party Overseas Develt Gp., 1984–94; Sec., Cons. Envmt Cttee, 1991–92; Mem., 1922 Exec.; Mem., British-American Gp, 1985. Mem., UK Br. Exec., CPA, 1984–2001 (Treas., 1997–); Treas., Internat. CPA. Trustee, Industry and Parlt Trust, 1985–2001. Gov., Inst. of Development Studies, 1980–94. *Recreations:* music, walking, gardening cooking, sailing.

WELLS, Brigid; *see* Wells, J. B. E.

WELLS, Sir Christopher (Charles), 3rd Bt *cr* 1944, of Felmersham, co. Bedford; *b* 12 Aug. 1936; *s* of Sir Charles Maltby Wells, 2nd Bt and of Katharine Boulton Wells; *S* father, 1996; *m* 1st, 1960, Elizabeth Florence Vaughan (marr. diss. 1983), *d* of I. F. Griffiths; two *s* two *d*; 2nd, 1985, Lynda Ann Cormack; one *s*. *Educ:* McGill Univ., Montreal (BSc); Univ. of Toronto (MD). MD in family practice, retired 1995. Assoc. Prof., Faculty of Medicine, Univ. of Toronto, 1975–95. *Heir: s* Michael Christopher Gruffydd Wells, *b* 24 Oct. 1966. *Address:* 1268 Seaforth Crescent, RR#3, Lakefield, ON K0L 2H0, Canada.

WELLS, Hon. Clyde (Kirby); Chief Justice of Newfoundland, since 1999; *b* 9 Nov. 1937; *s* of Ralph Pennell Wells and Maude Wells (*née* Kirby); *m* 1962, Eleanor, *d* of Arthur and Daisy Bishop; two *s* one *d*. *Educ:* All Saints Sch., Stephenville Crossing; Memorial Univ., Newfoundland (BA 1959); Dalhousie Univ. Law Sch. (LLB 1962). Served with Canadian Army, JAG's Office, 1962–64; called to the Bar, Nova Scotia, 1963, Newfoundland, 1964; Partner, Barry and Wells, and successor law firms, 1964–81; Senior Partner, Wells & Co., 1981–87; QC (Can.) 1977; Counsel, O'Reilly, Noseworthy, 1996–98; Justice, Court of Appeal, Newfoundland, 1998–99. Dir, 1978–87, and Chm., 1985–87, Newfoundland Light & Power Co. Ltd. MHA (L): Humber East, 1966–71; Windsor-Buchans, Dec. 1987–1989; Bay of Islands, 1989–96; Minister of Labour, 1966–68; Leader of Liberal Party, 1987; Premier of Newfoundland and Labrador, 1989–96. Hon. LLD Memorial, Newfoundland, 1996. *Address:* Court of Appeal, 287 Duckworth Street, PO Box 937, St John's, NF A1C 5M3, Canada; 3 Glenridge Crescent, St John's, NF A1A 1T4, Canada.

WELLS, Prof. David Arthur; Professor of German, Birbeck College, University of London, since 1987; *b* 26 April 1941; *s* of Arthur William Wells and Rosina Elizabeth (*née* Jones). *Educ:* Christ's Hosp., Horsham; Gonville and Caius Coll., Cambridge; Univs of Strasbourg, Vienna and Münster. Mod. and Med. Langs Tripos, BA 1963, Tiarks Studentship 1963–64, MA, PhD Cantab 1967. Asst Lectr 1966–67, Lectr 1967–69, in German, Univ. of Southampton; Lectr in German, Bedford Coll., Univ. of London, 1969–74; Sec., London Univ. Bd of Staff Examiners in German, 1973–74; Tutor, Nat. Extension Coll., Cambridge, 1966–74; Prof. of German, QUB, 1974–87. Lecture tour of NZ univs, 1975. Mem., Managing Body, Oakington Manor Jun. Mixed and Infant Sch., London Bor. of Brent, 1972–74. Hon. Treasurer: Assoc. for Literary and Linguistic Computing, 1973–78; MHRA, 2001– (Hon. Sec., 1969–2001); Sec.-Gen., Internat. Fedn for Modern Langs and Lits, 1981–. Editor, MHRA Ann. Bull. of Modern Humanities Research Assoc., 1969–; Jt Editor, The Year's Work in Modern Language Studies, 1976– (Editor, 1982). FRSA 1983. *Publications:* The Vorau Moses and Balaam: a study of their relationship to exegetical tradition, 1970; The Wild Man from the Epic of Gilgamesh to Hartmann von Aue's Iwein, 1975; A Complete Concordance to the Vorauer Bücher Moses (Concordances to the Early Middle High German Biblical Epic), 1976; contribs to MHRA Style Book: Notes for Authors and Editors, 1971, 4th edn 1991; articles, monographs and reviews in learned jls. *Recreations:* travel, theatre, music. *Address:* School of Languages, Linguistics and Culture, Birkbeck College, 43 Gordon Square, WC1H 0PD. *T:* (020) 7631 6103.

WELLS, David George; Managing Director, Service (formerly Servicing and Installation), British Gas plc, 1993–96; *b* 6 Aug. 1941; *s* of George Henry Wells and Marian (*née* Trolley); *m* 1967, Patricia Ann Fenwick; two *s*. *Educ:* Market Harborough Grammar Sch.; Reading Univ. (BA). FCA 1966. Hancock, Gilbert & Morris, 1962–67; Esso Chemical Ltd, 1967–69; joined Gas Council, 1969; Investment Accountant (Investment Appraisal), 1970–73; British Gas Corporation: Chief Accountant, Admin, 1973–76; Chief Investment Accountant, 1976; Dir of Finance, SE Reg., 1976–83; Dep. Chm., W Midlands Reg., 1983–88; Regl Chm., S Eastern, 1988–93; Man. Dir, Regl Services, 1993. Director: Metrogas Bldg Soc., 1978–86 (Dep. Chm., 1979–83); Port Greenwich Ltd, 1989–. Chm., S London Trng and Enterprise Council, 1989–93. CIGasE 1988; CIMgt (CBIM 1990); FRSA 1991. *Recreations:* world travel, walking, reading, photography, gardening. *Address:* 11 Parklands, Ice House Wood, Oxted, Surrey RH8 9DP.

WELLS, Dominic Richard Alexander; Editor in Chief, AOL UK (formerly Editorial Director, AOL Bertelsmann Online), since 1999; *b* 7 March 1963; *s* of Prof. Colin M Wells and Catherine Wells; partner, Elizabeth Hitchcock; two *s*. *Educ:* Winchester Coll.; New Coll., Oxford (BA Hons Modern History). Gofer, Muller, Blond & White Publishing Ltd, 1985–86; Sub-Editor, London's Alternative Magazine, 1986–87; Time Out magazine: Sub-Editor, then Chief Sub-Editor, subseq. Dep. Editor, 1987–92; Editor, 1992–98. Editor of the Year, BSME, 1992, 1994, 1995, 1998. *Recreation:* anything with my children. *Address:* 45A Grove Lane, Camberwell, SE5 8SP. *T:* (020) 7703 6546; *e-mail:* dominicwells@aol.com. *Club:* London Press.

WELLS, Doreen Patricia, (Doreen, Marchioness of Londonderry); dancer and actress; Ballerina of the Royal Ballet, 1955–74; *m* 9th Marquess of Londonderry, *qv* (marr. diss. 1989); two *s*. *Educ:* Walthamstow; Bush Davies School; Royal Ballet School. Engaged in Pantomime, 1952 and 1953. Joined Royal Ballet, 1955; became Principal Dancer, 1960; has danced leading roles in Noctambules, Harlequin in April, Dance Concertante, Sleeping Beauty, Coppelia, Swan Lake, Sylvia, La Fille mal Gardée, Two Pigeons, Giselle, Invitation, Rendezvous, Blood Wedding, Raymonda, Concerto, Nutcracker, Romeo and Juliet, Concerto No 2 (Ballet Imperial); has created leading roles in Toccata, La Création du Monde, Sinfonietta, Prometheus, Grand Tour; also played leading roles in musical shows. Choreographer and Co-Dir, Canterbury Pilgrims for the Canterbury Fest., 2000; Reader, 600th anniv. of Geoffrey Chaucer, Southwark Cathedral and Westminster Abbey. Patron: British Ballet Orgn; ISTD Ballet; Chelmsford Ballet Co.; Liverpool Proscenium Youth Ballet Co.; Liverpool Th. Sch. and Coll. Ltd; Tiffany School; Sch. of Dancing, Reiki Master, 1997. Adeline Genée Gold Medal, 1954. *Recreations:* classical music, reading, theatre-going.

WELLS, Prof. George Albert, MA, BSc, PhD; Professor of German, Birkbeck College, University of London, 1968–88, now Emeritus; *b* 22 May 1926; *s* of George John and Lilian Maud Wells; *m* 1969, Elisabeth Delhey. *Educ:* University College London (BA, MA German; PhD Philosophy; BSc Geology). Lecturer in German, 1949–64, Reader in German, 1964–68, University Coll. London. Hon. Associate, Rationalist Press Assoc., 1989 (Dir, 1974–89). Mem., Acad. of Humanism, 1983– (Humanist Laureate, 1983). *Publications:* Herder and After, 1959; The Plays of Grillparzer, 1969; The Jesus of the Early Christians, 1971; Did Jesus Exist?, 1975, 2nd edn 1986; Goethe and the Development of Science 1750–1900, 1978; The Historical Evidence for Jesus, 1982; The Origin of Language: aspects of the discussion from Condillac to Wundt, 1987; (ed and contrib.) J. M. Robertson (1856–1933), Liberal, Rationalist and Scholar, 1987; Religious Postures, 1988; Who Was Jesus? a critique of the New Testament record, 1989; Belief and Make Believe: critical reflections on the sources of credulity, 1991; What's in a Name?: reflections on language, magic and religion, 1993; The Jesus Legend, 1996; The Jesus Myth, 1998; The Origin of Language, 1999; articles in Jl of History of Ideas, Jl of English and Germanic Philology, German Life and Letters, Question, Trivium, Wirkendes Wort. *Recreation:* walking. *Address:* 35 St Stephen's Avenue, St Albans, Herts AL3 4AA. *T:* (01727) 851347.

WELLS, Howard James Cowen; Chairman, Central Council of Physical Recreation, since 2001; *b* 9 Jan. 1947; *s* of late Harold Arthur James Wells and Joan Wells (*née* Cowen, now Moore); *m* 1971, Linda Baines; one *s* one *d*. *Educ:* Leeds Univ. (BEd, Cert Ed); Carnegie Coll. (Dip. in Phys. Educn). Head of Boys' Phys. Educn, Brooklands Sch., Leighton Buzzard, 1970–72; Lectr-in-Charge of Phys. Recreation, Hitchin Coll., 1972–74; Dep. Dir, Bisham Abbey Nat. Sports Centre, 1975–81; Operations Manager, 1981–84, Chief Exec., 1984–89, Jubilee Sports Centre, Hong Kong; Chief Executive: Hong Kong Sports Develt Bd, 1989–96; UK Sports Council, 1996–98; Watford Assoc. FC, 1998–99; Ipswich Town FC, 1999–2000. Chm., Spa Club Ltd; Dep. Chm., Only for Sport Mgt Ltd; Dir, Premier Sport & Media Ltd. Mem., Saudi Arabian-UK Memorandum of Understanding Gp in Sport, 1996–. Governor, Ashlyns Sch., Berkhamsted, 1996–.

Publication: Start Living Now, 1979. *Recreations:* Football Association (full qualifying coaching licence, 1973), theatre, travel. *Address:* CCPR, Francis House, Francis Street, SW1P 1DE. *Clubs:* Oriental, Scribes.

WELLS, Jack Dennis; Executive Director, Aircraft Owners and Pilots Association, since 1991 (Vice-Chairman, 1996–98); Assistant Director, Central Statistical Office, 1979–88; *b* 8 April 1928; *s* of late C. W. Wells and H. M. Wells (*née* Clark); *m* 1st, 1953, Jean Allison; one *s* one *d*; 2nd, 1987, Cynthia Palmer. *Educ:* Hampton Grammar Sch.; Polytechnic of Central London. AIS 1955. Ministry of Fuel and Power, 1947; Royal Air Force, 1947–49; Min. of (Fuel and) Power, 1949–69; Private Secretary to Paymaster General, 1957–59; Chief Statistician, Dept of Economic Affairs, 1969; Min. of Technology, 1969; HM Treasury, 1970; Dept of (Trade and) Industry, 1971–79. Pres., CS Aviation Assoc., 1988–. Sec. and Dir, Gen. Aviation Awareness Council, 1997–. Past Chairman, Old Hamptonians Assoc. *Publications:* contribs to Long Range Planning, Economic Trends, Statistical News, Review of Income and Wealth, Jl of Banking and Finance, BIEC Yearbook. *Recreations:* cricket, jazz, travel. *Clubs:* Civil Service, United Services, MCC.

WELLS, James Henry; Member (DemU) South Down, Northern Ireland Assembly, since 1998; *b* 27 April 1957; *s* of Samuel Henry Wells and Doreen Wells; *m* 1983, Violet Grace Wallace; one *s* two *d*. *Educ:* Lurgan Coll.; Queen's Univ., Belfast (BA Hons Geog. 1979; DipTP 1981). Mem. (DemU) South Down, NI Assembly, 1982–86; research asst, RSPB, 1987–88; Asst Regl Public Affairs Manager, NI Reg., NT, 1989–98. *Recreations:* birdwatching, hill-walking. *Address:* 2 Belfast Road, Ballynahinch, Co. Down BT24 8DZ.

WELLS, (Jennifer) Brigid (Ellen), (Mrs Ian Wells); Chairman Assessor, Civil Service Selection Board, 1989–95; *b* 18 Feb. 1928; *d* of Dr Leonard John Haydon, TD, MA Cantab, MB BCh and Susan Eleanor Haydon (*née* Richmond), actress; *m* 1962, Ian Vane Wells; three *d*. *Educ:* schools in UK, USA, Canada; Edinburgh Univ.; Lady Margaret Hall, Oxford (scholar; BA Mod. Hist.; MA); PG Dip. Couns., Univ. of Brighton, 1995. Commonwealth Relations Office, 1949; UK High Commn, NZ, 1952–54; Private Sec. to Parly Under-Sec. of State, CRO, 1954–56; MAFF, 1956–62; teaching: LCC, 1962–63; Haringey, 1967; Camden Sch. for Girls, 1969–75 (to Head of Dept); Head of Dept, St David's and St Katharine's, Hornsey, 1975–77; Headmistress, Brighton and Hove High Sch., GPDST, 1978–88. Qualified team inspector: OFSTED, 1994–; ISI (formerly ARCS), 1995–. Chm. designate, W Sussex Ambulance NHS Trust, 1992–93. Member: Local Radio Council, 1980–82; Broadcasting Complaints Commn, 1986–93 (Chm., Jan.–June 1992); Chairman: Educn Cttee, GSA, 1987–88; SE Region, GSA, 1984–86. Project Manager (USA), GAP, 1989–91; Mem., British Atlantic Council, 1988–93; Governor, Woldingham Sch., 1989–97; Comr, Duke of York's Royal Mil. Sch., Dover, 1993–. Chm., Friends of GPDST (now GDST), 1991–. JP Inner London, 1972–77, Brighton and Hove, 1980–98. *Publications:* articles in learned jls. *Recreations:* gardening, travel. *Address:* Cherry Trees, Bradford Road, Lewes, E Sussex BN7 1RD. *T:* (01273) 477491.

WELLS, Prof. John Christopher, PhD; FBA 1996; FIL; Professor of Phonetics, University College London, since 1988; *b* 11 March 1939; *s* of Rev. Philip Cuthbert Wells and Winifred May (*née* Peaker). *Educ:* St John's Sch., Leatherhead; Trinity Coll., Cambridge (BA 1960; MA 1964); University Coll., London (MA 1962; PhD 1971). FIL 1982. University College London: Asst Lectr in Phonetics, 1962–65; Lectr, 1965–82; Reader, 1982–88; Head, Dept of Phonetics and Linguistics, 1990–2000. Sec., Internat. Phonetic Assoc., 1973–86; Pres., World Esperanto Assoc., 1989–95; Mem., Esperanto Acad., 1971–. Editor, Jl Internat. Phonetic Assoc., 1971–87. Contribs to radio and TV programmes. *Publications:* Concise Esperanto and English Dictionary, 1969; (with G. Colson) Practical Phonetics, 1971; Jamaican Pronunciation in London, 1973; (jtly) Jen Nia Mondo 1, 1974 (trans. Italian, Icelandic, Swedish, Finnish; (jtly) Jen Nia Mondo 2, 1977; Lingvistikaj aspektoj de Esperanto, 1978, 2nd edn 1989 (trans. Danish; Accents of English (three vols and cassette), 1982; Geiriadur Esperanto/Kimra vortaro, 1985; (pronunciation editor) Universal Dictionary, 1987; (pronunciation editor) Hutchinson Encyclopedia, 8th edn 1988, and subsequent editions; Longman Pronunciation Dictionary, 1990, 2nd edn 2000; articles in learned jls and collective works. *Recreations:* reading, walking, running. *Address:* Department of Phonetics and Linguistics, University College London, Gower Street, WC1E 6BT. *T:* (020) 7380 7175; 5 Poplar Road, SW19 3JR. *T:* (020) 8542 0302; *e-mail:* j.wells@ucl.ac.uk.

WELLS, Sir John (Julius), Kt 1984; DL; *b* 30 March 1925; *s* of A. Reginald K. Wells, Marlands, Sampford Arundel, Som; *m* 1948, Lucinda Meath-Baker; two *s* two *d*. *Educ:* Eton; Corpus Christi College, Oxford (MA). War of 1939–45: joined RN as ordinary seaman, 1942; commissioned, 1943, served in submarines until 1946. Contested (C) Smethwick Division, General Election, 1955. MP (C) Maidstone, 1959–87. Chairman: Cons. Party Horticulture Cttee, 1965–71, 1973–87; Horticultural sub-Cttee, Select Cttee on Agriculture, 1968; Parly Waterways Group, 1974–80; Vice-Chm., Cons. Party Agriculture Cttee, 1970; Mem., Mr Speaker's Panel of Chairmen, 1974. Hon. Freeman, Borough of Maidstone, 1979. DL Kent, 1992. Kt Comdr, Order of Civil Merit (Spain), 1972; Comdr, Order of Lion of Finland, 1984. *Recreations:* country pursuits. *Address:* Mere House Barn, Mereworth, Kent ME18 5NB.

WELLS, Malcolm Henry Weston, FCA; Director, Carclo Engineering Group PLC, 1982–97 (Deputy Chairman, 1987–93); *b* 26 July 1927; *s* of late Lt-Comdr Geoffrey Weston Wells; *m* 1952, Elizabeth A. Harland, *d* of late Rt Rev. M. H. Harland, DD; one *s* one *d*. *Educ:* Eton Coll. ACA 1951, FCA 1961. Served RNVR, 1945–48. Peat, Marwick Mitchell, 1948–58; Siebe Gorman and Co. Ltd, 1958–63; Charterhouse Japhet, 1963–80 (Chm., 1973–80); Dir, Charterhouse Gp, 1971–80; Chairman: Charterhouse Petroleum PLC, 1977–82; Granville Business Expansion Funds, 1983–93; BWD Securities, 1987–95; London rep., Bank in Liechtenstein, 1981–85; Director: Bank in Liechtenstein (UK) Ltd, 1985–90; Nat. Home Loans Corp., 1989–93. Mem., CAA, 1974–77. Mem. Solicitors' Disciplinary Tribunal, 1975–81. *Recreation:* sailing. *Address:* 100 Palace Gardens Terrace, W8 4RS. *Clubs:* Hurlingham; West Wittering Sailing.

WELLS, Petrie Bowen; *see* Wells, B.

WELLS, Richard Burton, QPM 1987; Chief Constable, South Yorkshire Police, 1990–98; Director, E-Quality Leadership, since 1998; *b* 10 Aug. 1940; *s* of Walter Percival Wells and Daphne Joan Wells (*née* Harris); *m* 1970, Patricia Ann Smith; one *s* one *d*. *Educ:* Sir Roger Manwood's Grammar Sch., Sandwich; Priory Sch. for Boys, Shrewsbury; St Peter's Coll., Oxford (Open Exhibnr 1959; BA 1962; MA 1965); principal educn, 36 yrs with the police service. Constable, Bow Street, 1962–66; Sergeant, Notting Hill, 1966–68; Special Course, Police Staff Coll., 1966–67; Inspector, Leman St, and Hendon Police Trng Sch., 1968–73; Chief Inspector, Notting Hill, 1973–76; Supt, Hampstead, 1976–79; Chief Supt, Hammersmith and New Scotland Yard, 1979–82; Sen. Command Course, Police Staff Coll., 1981; Comdt, Hendon Training Sch., 1982–83; Dep. Asst Comr, Dir of Public Affairs, New Scotland Yard, 1983–86; Dep. Asst Commissioner, OC NW London, 1986–90. Chairman: Media Adv. Gp, ACPO, 1992–98; Nat. Conf. of Police Press and PROs, 1994–98; Personnel and Trng Cttee, ACPO, 1996–98 (Sec., 1993–96). Sec., Provincial Police Award Selection Cttee, 1990–98. Member: Rathbone Corporate Partnership Gp, 1993–98; Selection Cttee, Fulbright Fellowship in Police Studies, 1991–98; Forensic Psychotherapy Course Adv. Gp, 1990–98; Barnsley City Challenge Bd, 1992–98; Sheffield Common Purpose Adv. Gp and Council, 1993–98. President: Young Enterprise Bd for S Yorks and S Humberside, 1993–98; Deepcar Brass Band, 1992–98; Patron: S Yorks Br., RLSS, 1990–98; Weston Park Hosp. Cancer Care Appeal, 1993–98. President: St Peter's Soc., Oxford Univ., 1989–96; Police Athletics Assoc. Men's Hockey, 1996–98 (Vice Pres., 1989–96). Mem., St John Council for S and W Yorks, 1990–98. Freeman, City of London, 1992. CIMgt (CBIM 1991). Chm. Editl Bd, Policing Today, 1994–98. *Publications:* (contrib.) Leaders on Leadership, 1996; (contrib.) Learning Organisations in the Public Sector, 1997. *Recreations:* walking, painting (watercolour, gloss and emulsion), T'ai Chi, genealogy, local history. *Address:* Bidwell Farm, Upottery, Devon EX14 9PP. *T:* (01404) 861122.

WELLS, Ven. Roderick John; Archdeacon of Stow, 1989–2001, and of Lindsey, 1994–2001, now Archdeacon Emeritus; *b* 17 Nov. 1936; *s* of Leonard Arthur and Dorothy Alice Wells; *m* 1969, Alice Louise Scholl; one *s* two *d*. *Educ:* Durham Univ. (BA Hons Theol.); Hull Univ. (MA). Insurance clerk, 1953–55 and 1957–58. RAF, 1955–57 (Radar Mechanic). Asst Master, Chester Choir School, 1958–59; Asst Curate, St Mary at Lambeth, 1965–68, Priest-in-Charge 1968–71; Rector of Skegness, 1971–78; Team Rector, West Grimsby Team Ministry (Parish of Great and Little Coates with Bradley), 1978–89; Area Dean of Grimsby and Cleethorpes, 1983–89. *Recreations:* music (pianist and organist), walking, geology. *Address:* 2 Althorpe Road, Oakham, Rutland LE15 6FD.

WELLS, Ronald Alfred, OBE 1965; BSc, FRSC, FIMM; retired; *b* 11 February 1920; *s* of Alfred John Wells and Winifred Jessie (*née* Lambert); *m* 1953, Anne Brebner Lanshe; two *s*. *Educ:* Birkbeck College, London; Newport Technical College. Service with Government Chemist, 1939–40; Royal Naval Scientific Service, 1940–47; Joined Nat. Chemical Laboratory, 1947; Mem. UK Scientific Mission, Washington, 1951–52; Head of Radio-chemical Group, 1956; Head of Div. of Inorganic and Mineral Chemistry, 1963; Deputy Director, Nov. 1963; Director of National Chemical Laboratory, 1964; Dir of Research, TBA Industrial Products Ltd, 1965–70, Jt Man. Dir, 1970–77; Man. Dir, AMFU Ltd (Turner & Newall), 1977–81; Gp Scientist, Turner & Newall, 1981–83; industrial consultant, 1983–87. Director: Salford Univ. Industrial Centre Ltd, 1981–82; Rochdale Private Surgical Unit, 1975–81; non-exec. Dir, Eversave (UK) Ltd, 1984–85. Mem. Council, Royal Inst. Chemistry, 1965–68. *Publications:* numerous contribs to Inorganic Chromatography and Extractive Metallurgy. *Recreations:* gardening, golf, mineralogy. *Address:* Westbury, 19 First Avenue, Charmandean, Worthing, Sussex BN14 9NJ. *T:* (01903) 233844.

WELLS, Rosemary; writer and illustrator of children's books, since 1968; *b* 29 Jan. 1943; *m* Thomas M. Wells; two *d*. Mem., Soc. of Illustrators, NY. Best Illustrated Book of the Year, New York Times (twice); Horn Best Book of the Year; Notable Book, American Library Assoc. (40 times); numerous other awards. *Publications* include: Noisy Nora, 1973; Benjamin and Tulip, 1973; Timothy Goes to School, 1981; Voyage to the Bunny Planet, 1992; Edward Unready for School, 1995; My Very First Mother Goose, 1996; Bunny Cakes, 1997; Bunny Money, 1997; The Bear Went Over the Mountain, 1998; The Itsy-Bitsy Spider, 1998; Max's Toys, 1998; Max's Bath, 1998. *Address:* 66 Linden Circle, Briarcliff Manor, NY 10510, USA. *T:* (914) 9239234.

WELLS, Prof. Stanley William; Professor of Shakespeare Studies, and Director of the Shakespeare Institute, University of Birmingham, 1988–97, now Emeritus Professor and Hon. Fellow; General Editor of the Oxford Shakespeare since 1978; *b* 21 May 1930; *s* of Stanley Cecil Wells and Doris Wells; *m* 1975, Susan Elizabeth Hill, *qv*; two *d* (and one *d* decd). *Educ:* Kingston High Sch., Hull; University Coll., London (BA; Fellow, 1995); Shakespeare Inst., Univ. of Birmingham (PhD). Fellow, Shakespeare Inst., 1962–77: Lectr, 1962; Sen. Lectr, 1971; Reader, 1973–77; Hon. Fellow, 1979–88; Head of Shakespeare Dept, OUP, 1978–88. Sen. Res. Fellow, Balliol Coll., Oxford, 1980–88. Consultant in English, Wroxton Coll., 1964–80. Chm., Membership Cttee, 1991–99, Collections Cttee, 1992–99, RSC; Mem., Exec. Council, 1976–, Exec. (formerly F and GP) Cttee, 1991–, Royal Shakespeare Theatre (Gov., 1974–, Vice Chm. of Govs, 1991–); Dir, Royal Shakespeare Theatre Summer Sch., 1971–98. Pres., Shakespeare Club of Stratford-upon-Avon, 1972–73; Chm., Internat. Shakespeare Assoc., 1996–2001, Exec., 2001– (Vice-Chm., 1991–96); Member: Council, Malone Soc., 1967–90; Exec. Cttee, Shakespeare's Birthplace, 1976–78, 1988– (Trustee, 1975–81, 1984–; Chm. Trustees, 1991–); Trustee, Rose Theatre, 1991–; Dir, Globe Theatre, 1992– (Trustee, 1998–); Pres., Wolverhampton Shakespeare Soc., 1992–93. Governor, King Edward VI Grammar Sch. for Boys, Stratford-upon-Avon, 1973–77. Guest lectr, British and overseas univs; Lectures: British Acad. Annual Shakespeare, 1987; Hilda Hulme Meml, 1987; first annual Globe, 1990; Melchiori, Rome, 1991; Walter Clyde Curry Annual Shakespeare, Vanderbilt Univ., 1998. Hon. DLitt Furman Univ., SC, 1978; Hon. DPhil Munich, 1999. Walcott Award, LA, 1995. Associate Editor: New Penguin Shakespeare, 1967–; New DNB, 1998–; Editor, Shakespeare Survey, 1980–99. *Publications:* (ed) Thomas Nashe, Selected Writings, 1964; (ed, New Penguin Shakespeare): A Midsummer Night's Dream, 1967, Richard II, 1969, The Comedy of Errors, 1972; Shakespeare, A Reading Guide, 1969 (2nd edn 1970); Literature and Drama, 1970; (ed, Select Bibliographical Guides): Shakespeare, 1973 (new edn 1990), English Drama excluding Shakespeare, 1975; Royal Shakespeare, 1977, 2nd edn 1978; (compiled) Nineteenth-Century Shakespeare Burlesques (5 vols), 1977; Shakespeare: an illustrated dictionary, 1978, 2nd edn 1985, revised as Oxford Dictionary of Shakespeare, 1998; Shakespeare: the writer and his work, 1978; (ed with R. L. Smallwood) Thomas Dekker, The Shoemaker's Holiday, 1979; (with Gary Taylor) Modernizing Shakespeare's Spelling, with three studies in the text of Henry V, 1979; Re-Editing Shakespeare for the Modern Reader, 1984; (ed) Shakespeare's Sonnets, 1985; (ed with Gary Taylor *et al*) The Complete Oxford Shakespeare, 1986; (ed) The Cambridge Companion to Shakespeare Studies, 1986; (with Gary Taylor *et al*) William Shakespeare: a textual companion, 1987; An Oxford Anthology of Shakespeare, 1987; Shakespeare: a dramatic life, 1994, rev. edn as Shakespeare: the poet and his plays, 1997; (ed with E. A. Davies) Shakespeare and the Moving Image, 1994; (ed with R. Warren) Twelfth Night, 1994; (ed) Shakespeare in the Theatre: an anthology of criticism, 1997; (ed) Summerfolk, 1997; William Shakespeare: the quiz book, 1998; (ed) King Lear, 2000; (ed with C. M. S. Alexander) Shakespeare and Race, 2001; (ed with M. de Grazia) The Cambridge Companion to Shakespeare, 2001; (ed with Michael Dobson) The Oxford Companion to Shakespeare, 2001; contrib. Shak. Survey, Shak. Qly, Shak. Jahrbuch, Theatre Notebook, Stratford-upon-Avon Studies, TLS, etc. *Recreations:* music, theatre, the countryside. *Address:* Longmoor Farmhouse, Ebrington, Glos GL55 6NW. *T:* (01386) 593352.

WELLS, Susan Elizabeth, (Mrs Stanley Wells); *see* Hill, S. E.

WELLS, Thomas Umfrey, MA; Headmaster, Wanganui Collegiate School, New Zealand, 1960–80; *b* 6 Feb. 1927; *s* of Athol Umfrey and Gladys Colebrook Wells; *m* 1953, Valerie Esther Brewis; two *s* one *d*. *Educ:* King's College, Auckland, New Zealand;

Auckland University (BA); (Orford Studentship to) King's College, Cambridge. BA 1951; MA 1954. Assistant Master, Clifton College, 1952–60 (Senior English Master, 1957–60). Pres., NZ Assoc. of Heads of Independent Secondary Schs, 1972–75. Member: Univs Entrance Bd, 1972–80; HMC; Tongariro Forest Park Promotion Cttee, 1984–87; Taumarunui and Dist Promotion and Develt Council, 1985–; Executive Member: CKC Visual Arts Trust, 1986– (Chm., 1986–91); Wanganui River Floats Coalition, 1987–; Taumarunui Community Arts Council, 1987–; Trustee: Avonlea, 1984–; Outdoor Pursuits Centre, Tawhiti-kuri, 1985–90; Taumarunui Museum Trust, 1987–. Synodsman, 1985–, Mem. Standing Cttee, 1989–, Waikato Dio.; Mem. of Vestry, Taumarunui Anglican Church, 1981–. Pres., Taumarunui Cricket Club Assoc., 1984–86, Patron, 1986–; Mem., Rotary Club of Wanganui, 1961–80 (Pres., 1979–80), of Taumarunui, 1980–95, of Te Awamuta, 1995–; Chm., Dist 993 Rotaract Cttee, 1983–85. *Recreations:* reading, theatre, cricket (NZU Blue, 1948–49 (Capt., 1949); Cambridge Blue, 1950), tennis, fishing; formerly Rugby football (Cambridge Blue, 1951; England Final Trial, 1951; Trial, 1954; Bristol, 1952–56; Glos, 1953–56). *Address:* c/o Windsor Court Rest Home, Sandes Street, Ohaupo, New Zealand. *Clubs:* MCC; Hawks (Cambridge).

WELLS, Sir William (Henry Weston), Kt 1997; FRICS; President, Chesterton International plc, London, since 1998 (Partner, since 1965); Chairman, NHS Appointments Commission, since 2001; *b* 3 May 1940; *s* of Sir Henry Wells, CBE, and Lady Wells; *m* 1966, Penelope Jean Broadbent; two *s* (and one *s* decd). *Educ:* Radley Coll.; Magdalene Coll., Cambridge (BA). Joined Chesterton, 1959; Chairman: Land and House Property Gp, 1977 (Dir, 1972–76); Frincon Holdings Ltd, 1977–87; Chesterton plc, 1984–98. Director: London Life Assoc., 1984–89; AMP (UK) plc, 1994–; Pearl Gp Ltd (formerly Pearl Assurance), 1994–; Norwich and Peterborough Bldg Soc., 1994–; NFC plc, 1996–2000; AMP (UK) Holdings, 1997–; NPI Ltd, 1999–; Nat. Provident Life Ltd, 1999–; Exel plc, 2000–. Mem. Council, NHS Trust Fedn, 1991–93 (Vice Chm., 1992–93). Chairman: Hampstead HA, 1982–90; Royal Free Hampstead NHS Trust, 1990–94; S Thames RHA, 1994–96; S Thames Region, NHS Exec., DoH, 1996–99; Regl Chm., SE, NHS Exec., 1999–2001. Member: Board of Governors, Royal Free Hosp., 1968–74; Camden and Islington AHA, 1974–82; Chm., Special Trustees of Royal Free Hosp., 1979–2001; Member, Council: Royal Free Hosp. Sch. of Medicine, 1977–91; UMDS, Guy's and St Thomas' Hosps, 1994–98; St George's Hosp. Med. Sch., 1994–98; Univ. of Surrey, 1998– (Vice Chm., 1999–2000, Chm., 2001–); KCL, 1998–2001; City Univ., 1999–2001; Member: Delegacy, King's Coll. Sch. of Medicine and Dentistry, 1994–98; Council and Mgt Cttee, King's Fund, 1995–. Pres., Royal Free Hosp. Retirement Fellowship, 1994–. Hon. Treasurer: RCN, 1988–; Nat. Assoc. of Leagues of Hosp. Friends, 1992–. Mem. Council, Priory of England and the Is, 2000–. *Recreations:* family, philately, gardening. *Club:* Boodle's.

WELSBY, John Kay, CBE 1990; President, Institute of Logistics and Transport, since 1999; *b* 26 May 1938; *s* of late Samuel and Sarah Ellen Welsby; *m* 1964, Jill Carole Richards; one *s* one *d*. *Educ:* Heywood Grammar Sch.; Univ. of Exeter (BA); Univ. of London (MSc). FCIT 1990. Govt Economic Service, 1966–81; British Railways Board: Dir, Provincial Services, 1982–84; Managing Dir, Procurement, 1985–87; Mem. Bd, 1987–99; Chief Exec., 1990–98; Chm., 1995–99; Director: London & Continental Rlys Ltd, 1999–; LCR Finance plc, 1999–. Chm., CIT, 1998–99. Member: Business Adv. Council, Northwestern Univ., Evanston, Ill., 1995–. CIMgt 1991. Freeman, City of London, 1992; Liveryman, Carmen's Co., 1992. *Publications:* articles on economic matters. *Recreations:* walking, music, swimming. *Address:* Yew Tree Cottage, Ibworth, Tadley, Hants RG26 5TJ.

WELSBY, Rev. Canon Paul Antony; Canon Residentiary and Vice-Dean of Rochester Cathedral, 1966–88, Canon Emeritus since 1988; Permission to Officiate, Diocese of Rochester, since 1988; Chaplain to the Queen, 1980–90; *b* 18 Aug. 1920; *m* 1948, Cynthia Mary Hosmer; one *d*. *Educ:* Alcester Grammar Sch.; University Coll., Durham (MA); Lincoln Theological Coll.; Univ. of Sheffield (PhD). Curate at Boxley, Kent, 1944–47; Curate, St Mary-le-Tower, Ipswich, 1947–52; Rector of Copdock with Washbrook, 1952–66; Rural Dean of Samford, 1964–66. Director of Post-Ordination Training for Dio. of Rochester, 1966–88; Examining Chaplain to Bp of Rochester, 1966–88, Personal Chaplain 1988–90. Member, Church Assembly, 1964–70, General Synod, 1970–80; Chm., House of Clergy at Gen. Synod and Prolocutor of Convocation of Canterbury, 1974–80. *Publications:* A Modern Catechism, 1956; Lancelot Andrewes, 1958; How the Church of England Works, 1960, new edn, 1985; The Unwanted Archbishop, 1962; The Bond of Church and State, 1962; Sermons and Society, 1970; (contrib.) Oxford Dictionary of the Christian Church, 2nd edn, 1974, 3rd edn 1997; A History of the Church of England 1945–80, 1984; (contrib.) Faith and Fabric: a history of Rochester Cathedral 604–1994, 1996; contrib. Theology. *Recreations:* reading detective fiction and biographies, visiting National Trust properties. *Address:* 20 Knights Ridge, Pembury, Kent TN2 4HP. *T:* (01892) 823053.

WELSER-MÖST, Franz; Music Director, Zürich Opera, since 1995; Music Director designate, Cleveland Orchestra, from Sept. 2002; *b* 16 Aug. 1960. Music Director, LPO, 1990–96; conducts Bayerischer Rundfunk, Vienna Philharmonic, Salzburg Fest., Berlin Philharmonic and all major US orchestras; numerous recordings. Awards from USA and UK. *Address:* c/o Van Walsum Management Ltd, 4 Addison Bridge Place, W14 8XP. *T:* (020) 7371 4343.

WELSH, Andrew Paton; Member (SNP) Angus, Scottish Parliament, since 1999; *b* 19 April 1944; *s* of William and Agnes Welsh; *m* 1971, Sheena Margaret Cannon; one *d*. *Educ:* Univ. of Glasgow. MA (Hons) History and Politics; DipEd, 1980. Teacher of History, 1972–74; Lectr in Public Admin and Economics, Dundee Coll. of Commerce, 1979–83; Sen. Lectr in Business and Admin. Studies, Angus Technical Coll., 1983–87. MP (SNP) South Angus, Oct. 1974–1979; contested (SNP) Angus E, 1983; MP (SNP) Angus E, 1987–97, Angus, 1997–2001. SNP Parly Chief Whip, 1978–79, 1987–97; SNP spokesman on: housing, 1974–78; self employed affairs and small businesses, 1975–79, 1987–2001; agriculture, 1976–79, 1987–2001; local govt, 1987–97; local govt, housing and educn, 1997–2001. Member: Scottish Affairs Select Cttee, 1992–2001; Speaker's Panel of Chairmen, 1997–2001. Scottish Parliament: Mem., Corporate Body, 1999–; Convenor, Audit Cttee, 1999–; Mem., Commn of Accounts, 2000–. SNP Exec. Vice Chm. for Admin, 1979–87; SNP Vice-Pres., 1987–. Mem., Angus District Council, 1984–87; Provost of Angus, 1984–87. *Recreations:* music, horse riding, languages. *Address:* 31 Market Place, Arbroath, Angus DD11 1HR. *T:* (01241) 439369, *Fax:* (01241) 871561. *Club:* Glasgow University Union.

WELSH, Prof. Dominic; *see* Welsh, J. A. D.

WELSH, Frank Reeson; writer; Director, Grindlays Bank, 1971–85; *b* 16 Aug. 1931; *s* of F. C. Welsh and D. M. Welsh; *m* 1954, Agnes Cowley; two *s* two *d*. *Educ:* Gateshead and Blaydon Grammar Schools; Magdalene Coll., Cambridge (schol.; MA). With John Lewis Partnership, 1954–1958; CAS Group, 1958–64; Man. Dir, William Brandt's Sons & Co. Ltd, 1965–72; Chairman: Hadfields Ltd, 1967–79; Jensen Motors Ltd, 1968–72; Cox & Kings, 1972–76; Dir, Henry Ansbacher & Co., 1976–82. Member: British Waterways Board, 1975–81; Gen. Adv. Council, IBA, 1976–80; Royal Commn on Nat. Health Service, 1976–79; Health Educn Council, 1978–80. Dir, Trireme Trust, 1983–. Vis. Lectr and Alcoa Schol., Graduate Sch. of Business Studies, Univ. of Tennessee, Knoxville, 1979–85. CIMgt. *Publications:* The Profit of the State, 1982; (contrib.) Judging People, 1982; The Afflicted State, 1983; First Blood, 1985; (with George Ridley) Bend'Or, Duke of Westminster, 1985; Uneasy City, 1986; Building the Trireme, 1988; Companion Guide to the Lake District, 1989, 2nd edn 1997; Hong Kong: a history (US edn as A Borrowed Place), 1993, 2nd edn 1997; A History of South Africa, 1998; Dangerous Deceits, 1999. *Recreation:* sailing. *Club:* Oxford and Cambridge.

WELSH, Ian; Chief Executive, Kilmarnock Football Club, 1997–99 and since 2000; *b* 23 Nov. 1953; *m* 1977, Elizabeth McAndrew; two *s*. *Educ:* Prestwick Acad.; Ayr Acad.; Glasgow Univ. (MA Hons Eng. Lit. and Hist.); Jordanhill Coll. (Dip. in Educnl Mgt); Open Univ. (MA). Former professional football player, Kilmarnock FC; English teacher: James Hamilton Acad., Kilmarnock, 1977–80; Auchinleck Acad., 1980–97 (Dep. Head Teacher, 1992–97); Dir of Human Resources and Public Affairs, Prestwick Internat. Airport, 1997. Member (Lab): Kyle and Carrick Council, 1984–95 (Leader, 1990–92); S Ayrshire Council, 1995–99 (Leader); MSP (Lab) Ayr, 1999. Director: Borderline Theatre Co., 1990–; Prestwick Internat. Airport, 1992–97. FRSA. *Address:* 35 Ayr Road, Prestwick, Ayrshire KA9 1SY.

WELSH, Prof. (James Anthony) Dominic, DPhil; Professor of Mathematics, since 1992, and Chairman of Mathematics, 1996–2001, Oxford University; Fellow of Merton College, Oxford, since 1966; *b* 29 Aug. 1938; *s* of late James Welsh and Teresa Welsh (*née* O'Callaghan); *m* 1966, Bridget Elizabeth Pratt; two *s* (and one *s* decd). *Educ:* Bishop Gore Grammar Sch., Swansea; Merton Coll., Oxford (MA DPhil); Carnegie Mellon Univ. (Fulbright Scholar). Bell Telephone Labs, Murray Hill, 1961; Oxford University: Jun. Lectr, Mathematical Inst., 1963–66; Tutor in Maths, Merton Coll., 1966–90; Reader in Maths, 1990–92. Vis. appts, Univs of Michigan, Waterloo, Calgary, Stockholm, North Carolina; John von Neumann Prof., Univ. of Bonn, 1990–91. Chm., British Combinatorial Cttee, 1983–87. *Publications:* (ed) Combinatorial Mathematics and its Applications, 1971; (ed jtly) Combinatorics, 1973; Matroid Theory, 1976; (with G. R. Grimmett) Probability: an introduction, 1986; Codes and Cryptography, 1988, German edn, 1991; (ed jtly) Disorder in Physical Systems, 1990; Complexity: knots, colourings and counting, 1993; articles in math. jls. *Recreations:* real tennis, rugby, walking. *Address:* Merton College, Oxford OX1 4JD; South Lodge, Rose Lane, Oxford OX1 4DT. *T:* (01865) 247449.

WELSH, Michael Collins; *b* 23 Nov. 1926; *s* of Danny and Winnie Welsh; *m* 1950, Brenda Nicholson; two *s*. *Educ:* Sheffield Univ. (Dept of Extramural Studies, Day Release Course, three years); Ruskin Coll., Oxford. Miner from age of 14 years. Member, Doncaster Local Authority, 1962–69. MP (Lab) Don Valley, 1979–83, Doncaster North, 1983–92. *Club:* Carcroft Village Workingmen's (Carcroft, near Doncaster).

WELSH, Michael John; Chief Executive, Action Centre for Europe Ltd, since 1995; *b* 22 May 1942; *s* of Comdr David Welsh, RN, and Una Mary (*née* Willmore); *m* 1963, Jennifer Caroline Pollitt; one *s* one *d*. *Educ:* Dover Coll.; Lincoln Coll., Oxford (BA (Hons) Jurisprudence). Proprietors of Hays Wharf Ltd, 1963–69; Levi Strauss & Co. Europe Ltd, 1969–79 (Dir of Market Development, 1976). Chm., Chorley and S Ribble NHS Trust, 1994–98. MEP (C) Lancashire Central, 1979–94; contested (C) Lancashire Central, Eur. Parly elecns, 1994; Chm., Cttee for Social Affairs and Employment, Eur. Parlt, 1984–87. Mem. (C) Lancs CC, 1997– (Opposition finance spokesman). Chm., Positive Europe Gp, 1988–94. *Recreations:* amateur drama, sailing, rough walking. *Address:* Watercrook, 181 Town Lane, Whittle le Woods, Chorley, Lancs PR6 8AG. *T:* (01257) 276992. *Club:* Carlton.

WELSH, Maj.-Gen. Peter Miles, OBE 1983; MC 1967; President, Regular Commissions Board, 1983–85; *b* 23 Dec. 1930; *s* of William Miles Moss O'Donnel Welsh and Mary Edith Margaret Gertrude Louise Welsh (*née* Hearn); *m* 1974, June Patricia McCausland (*née* Macadam); two step *s* one step *d*. *Educ:* Winchester College; RMA Sandhurst. Commissioned, KRRC, 1951; Kenya Regt, 1958–60; student, Staff Coll., 1961; Malaya and Borneo, 1965–66; Royal Green Jackets, 1966; JSSC, 1967; Instructor, Staff Coll., 1968–71; CO 2 RGJ, 1971–73; Comd 5 Inf. Bde, 1974–76; RCDS, 1977; HQ BAOR, 1978–80; Brig., Light Div., 1980–83. *Recreations:* shooting, fishing, vegetable gardening, cooking, golf. *Clubs:* MCC, Free Foresters, I Zingari, Jesters; Berks Golf.

WELTEKE, Ernst; President, Deutsche Bundesbank, since 1999; *b* Korbach, 21 Aug. 1942. *Educ:* Univ. of Marburg; Univ. of Frankfurt am Main (Dip. Volkswirt). Apprentice agricl machine mechanic, 1959–62; Office of Prime Minister of Hesse, 1972–74; MP (SDP) Hesse, 1974–95; Minister of Econs, Transport and Technol., 1991–94; Minister of Finance, 1994–95; Pres., Land Central Bank, Hesse, and Mem., Central Bank Council, Deutsche Bundesbank, 1995–99. Chm., Parly Gp, SDP, 1984–Apr. 1987 and Feb. 1988–1991. *Address:* Deutsche Bundesbank, Postfach 10 06 02, 60006 Frankfurt am Main, Germany.

WEMYSS, 12th Earl of *cr* 1633, **AND MARCH,** 8th Earl of *cr* 1697; **Francis David Charteris,** KT 1966; Lord Wemyss of Elcho, 1628; Lord Elcho and Methil, 1633; Viscount Peebles, Baron Douglas of Neidpath, Lyne and Munard, 1697; Baron Wemyss of Wemyss (UK), 1821; President, The National Trust for Scotland, 1967–91, now President Emeritus (Chairman of Council, 1946–69); Lord Clerk Register of Scotland and Keeper of the Signet, since 1974; *b* 19 Jan. 1912; *s* of late Lord Elcho (killed in action, 1916) and Lady Violet Manners (she *m* 2nd, 1921, Guy Holford Benson (decd), and *d* 1971), 2nd *d* of 8th Duke of Rutland; *S* grandfather, 1937; *m* 1st, 1940, Mavis Lynette Gordon, BA (*d* 1988), *er d* of late E. E. Murray, Hermanus, Cape Province; one *s* one *d* (and one *s* and one *d* decd); 2nd, 1995, Shelagh Kathleen Kennedy, *d* of George Ernest Thrift, Vancouver. *Educ:* Eton; Balliol College, Oxford. Assistant District Commissioner, Basutoland, 1937–44. Served with Basuto Troops in Middle East, 1941–44. Lieut, Queen's Body Guard for Scotland, Royal Company of Archers; Lord High Comr to Gen. Assembly of Church of Scotland, 1959, 1960, 1977; Chairman: Scottish Cttee, Marie Curie Meml Foundn, 1952–86; Royal Commn on Ancient and Historical Monuments, Scotland, 1949–84; Scottish Churches Council, 1964–71; Hon. Pres., The Thistle Foundn; Mem., Central Cttee, WCC, 1961–75; Mem., Royal Commn on Historical Manuscripts, 1975–85. Consultant, Wemyss and March Estates Management Co. Ltd; formerly Director: Standard Life Assurance Co. Ltd; Scottish Television Ltd. Lord-Lieut, E Lothian, 1967–87. Hon. LLD St Andrews, 1953; DUniv Edinburgh, 1983. *Heir:* *s* Lord Neidpath, *qv*. *Address:* Gosford House, Longniddry, East Lothian EH32 0PX. *Club:* New (Edinburgh).

See also D. H. Benson.

WEMYSS, Rear-Adm. Martin La Touche, CB 1981; *b* 5 Dec. 1927; *s* of late Comdr David Edward Gillespie Wemyss, DSO, DSC, RN, and Edith Mary Digges La Touche; *m* 1st, 1951, Ann Hall (marr. diss. 1973); one *s* one *d*; 2nd, 1973, Elizabeth Loveday Alexander; one *s* one *d*. *Educ:* Shrewsbury School. CO HMS Sentinel, 1956–57; Naval

Intell. Div., 1957–59; CO HMS Alliance, 1959–60; CO Commanding Officers' Qualifying Course, 1961–63; Naval Staff, 1963–65; CO HMS Cleopatra, 1965–67; Naval Asst to First Sea Lord, 1967–70; CO 3rd Submarine Sqdn, 1970–73; CO HMS Norfolk, 1973–74; Dir of Naval Warfare, 1974–76; Rear-Adm., 1977; Flag Officer, Second Flotilla, 1977–78; Asst Chief of Naval Staff (Ops), 1979–81. Clerk to Brewers' Co., 1981–91. *Recreations:* sailing, shooting. *Address:* The Old Post House, Emberton, near Olney, Bucks MK46 5BX. *T:* (01234) 713838. *Clubs:* White's, Army and Navy.

WEN, Eric Lewis; freelance writer and music producer; Director, Biddulph Recordings, since 1989; *b* 18 May 1953; *s* of Adam and Mimi Wen; *m* 1989, Louise Anne, *d* of Sir Brian Barder, *qv*; two *d*. *Educ:* Columbia Univ. (BA); Yale Univ. (MPhil); Cambridge Univ. Lecturer: Guildhall Sch. of Music, 1978–84; Goldsmiths' Coll., Univ. of London, 1980–84; Mannes Coll. of Music, NY, 1984–86; Editor: The Strad, 1986–89; The Musical Times, 1988–90. *Publications:* (contrib.) Schenker Studies, 1989; (contrib.) Trends in Schenkerian Research, 1990; (ed) The Fritz Kreisler Collection, 1990; (contrib.) Cambridge Companion to the Violin, 1992; (ed) The Heifetz Collection, 1995; contrib. various music jls. *Recreations:* music, chess, cooking. *Address:* 1825 Second Avenue #4N, New York NY 10128, USA.

WENBAN-SMITH, (William) Nigel, CMG 1991; HM Diplomatic Service, retired; Secretary General, Commonwealth Magistrates' and Judges' Association, 1993–94; *b* 1 Sept. 1936; *s* of William Wenban-Smith, CMG, CBE; *m* 1st, 1961, Charlotte Chapman-Andrews (marr. diss 1975; she *m* 2nd, Sir Peter Leslie, *qv*); two *s* two *d*; 2nd, 1976, Charlotte Susanna Rycroft (*d* 1990); two *s*; 3rd, 1993, Frances Catharine Barlow; two step *d*. *Educ:* King's Sch., Canterbury; King's Coll., Cambridge (BA); MA Buckingham 2000. National Service, RN. Plebiscite Supervisory Officer, Southern Cameroons, 1960–61; Asst Principal, CRO, 1961–65 (Private Sec. to Parly Under Sec., 1963–64); Second Sec., Leopoldville, 1965–67; First Sec. and (1968) Head of Chancery, Kampala, 1967–70; FCO, 1970–74; Dublin, 1975; Commercial Sec., Brussels, 1976–78; Commercial Counsellor, Brussels, 1978–80; on loan to Cabinet Office, 1980–82; Hd of E Africa Dept and Comr, British Indian Ocean Territory, FCO, 1982–85; National Defence Coll. of Canada, 1985–86; Deputy High Comr, Ottawa, 1986–89; High Comr, Malaŵi, 1990–93. Chm., Friends of the Chagos Assoc., 1996–. *Recreations:* walking, gardening. *Address:* 2 Shirlock Road, NW3 2HS.

WENDT, Henry, Hon. CBE 1995; Chairman: SmithKline Beecham, 1989–94; Global Health Care Partners, DLJ Merchant Banking, since 1997; *b* 19 July 1933; *s* of Henry Wendt and Rachel L. (*née* Wood); *m* 1956, Holly Peterson; one *s* one *d*. *Educ:* Princeton Univ. (AB 1955). Joined SmithKline & French Labs, 1955: various positions in Internat. Div.; Pres., 1976–82; Chief Exec. Officer, 1982–87; Chm., 1987–89 (merger of SmithKline Beckman and Beecham, 1989). Director: Arjo Wiggins Appleton plc, 1990–92; West Marine Inc., 1997–; Wilson Greatbatch Ltd, 1997–; Computerised Med. Systems, 1997–; Charles River Labs, 2000–. Trustee: Amer. Enterprises Inst.; Philadelphia Museum of Art; HFT Develt Trust. Order of the Rising Sun with Gold and Silver Star (Japan), 1994. *Publication:* Global Embrace, 1993. *Recreations:* sailing, flyfishing, tennis, viticulture. *Address:* Quivira Vineyard, 4900 West Dry Creek Road, Healdsburg, CA 95448, USA. *Clubs:* Flyfishers'; Links, New York Yacht (NYC).

WENDT, Robin Glover, CBE 1996; DL; Vice-Chairman, NCH, since 2000; *b* 7 Jan. 1941; *er s* of late William Romilly Wendt and Doris May (*née* Glover), Preston, Lancs; *m* 1965, Prudence Ann Dalby; two *d*. *Educ:* Hutton GS, Preston; Wadham Coll., Oxford Univ. (BA 1962; MA 1992). Asst Principal 1962, Principal 1966, Min. of Pensions and Nat. Insurance; Principal Private Sec. to Sec. of State for Social Services, 1970; Asst Sec., DHSS, 1972; Dep. Sec., 1975, Chief Exec., 1979–89, Cheshire CC; Clerk of Cheshire Lieutenancy, 1979–90; Sec., ACC, 1989–97; Chief Exec., Nat. Assoc. of Local Councils, 1997–99. Member: Social Security Adv. Cttee, 1982–; PCFC, 1989–93; Council, RIPA, 1989–92; Council for Charitable Support, 1991–97; DoH Wider Health Working Gp, 1991–97; Adv. Bd, Fire Service Coll., 1992–96; Citizenship Foundn Adv. Council, 1993–97; Joseph Rowntree Foundn Income and Wealth Inquiry, 1993–95; Royal Commn on Long-Term Care of the Elderly, 1997–99; Bd, FAS, 1997–99; Council, NCH (formerly NCH Action for Children), 1997–; Bd, YMCA Chester, 1997–. Mem., S Cheshire HA, 2001–. Chairman: Cheshire Rural Forum, 2000–; Chester in Partnership, 2001–. Mem. Exec., Chester Music Soc., 1999–; Chm., Chester Summer Music Fest., 2001–. Pres., Cheshire Assoc. of Town and Parish Councils, 1997–. Trustee, Indep. Living Funds, 1993–2000. DL Cheshire, 1990. *Publications:* various articles and reviews on public service issues. *Recreations:* music, swimming, following sport, travel, journalism. *Address:* 28 Church Lane, Upton, Chester CH2 1DJ. *T:* (01244) 382786.

WENGER, Arsène; Manager, Arsenal Football Club, since 1996; *b* 22 Oct. 1949. *Educ:* Strasbourg Univ. (BEc 1974). Amateur football player, Mutzig, then Mulhouse, 1969–78; professional football player, Strasbourg, 1978–83 (Coach, Youth team, 1981–83); Player/Coach, Cannes, 1983; Manager: AS Nancy, 1984–87; AS Monaco, 1987–94; Nagoya Grampus Eight, Japan, 1995–96. Arsenal won Premier League and FA Cup, 1998. *Address:* Arsenal Football Club, Arsenal Stadium, Highbury, N5 1BU.

WENGER, (John) Patrick; Chief Executive, Royal Doulton PLC, 1997–99; *b* 23 Nov. 1943; *s* of Richard John Wenger and Hilda Wenger (*née* Hardy); *m* 1969, Sheila Ann Baddeley; one *s* one *d*. *Educ:* Repton; N Staffs Tech. Coll. (Pottery Managers Dip.; Ceramic Technicians Dip.); Harvard (AMP). Allied English Potteries: Mgt trainee, 1960–65; works manager, 1966; PA to Man. Dir, 1967–68; Gen. Works Manager, 1969–70; Asst Chief Exec., Paragon Div., 1971; Exec. i/c Paragon, following merger with Royal Doulton, 1972–84; Chief Executive: Hotel and Airlines Div., 1985–86; Ext. Sales Div., 1986–89; Internat. Sales Dir, 1989–93; Chief Operating Officer (following demerger from Pearson PLC), 1993–97. Retired due to serious car accident whilst in Australia in business. *Recreations:* sailing, golf, tennis, hockey, cricket, travel. *Address:* Foxley, Mill Lane, Standon, near Eccleshall, Staffs ST21 6RP. *Club:* British Pottery Manufacturers (Stoke-on-Trent).

WENNER, Michael Alfred; HM Diplomatic Service, retired; President, Wenner Communications Co. (formerly Wenner Trading Co.), since 1982; *b* 17 March 1921; *s* of Alfred E. Wenner and of Simone Roussel; *m* 1st, 1950, Gunilla Cecilia Ståhle (*d* 1986), *d* of Envoyé Nils K. Ståhle, CBE, and Birgit Olsson; four *s*; 2nd, 1990, Holly (Raven) Adrianne Johnson, *d* of Adrian W. Johnson and Ophelia A. Matley. *Educ:* Stonyhurst; Oriel College, Oxford (Scholar). Served E Yorks Regt, 1940; Lancs Fusiliers and 151 Parachute Bn, India, 1941–42; 156 Bn, N Africa, 1943; No 9 Commando, Italy and Greece, 1944–45. Entered HM Foreign Service, 1947; 3rd Sec., Stockholm, 1948–51; 2nd Sec., Washington, 1951–53; Foreign Office, 1953–55; 1st Sec., Tel Aviv, 1956–59; Head of Chancery, La Paz, 1959–61, and at Vienna, 1961–63; Inspector of Diplomatic Establishments, 1964–67; Ambassador to El Salvador, 1967–70. Commercial Advr, Consulate-Gen. of Switzerland in Houston, 1974–91. Hon. Mem., Consular Corps of Houston, 1992–. *Publications:* Advances in Controlled Droplet Application, Agrichemical Age, 1979; So It Was (memoirs), 1993; Telephone Tales, 1996. *Recreations:* fly-fishing, old maps, choral singing, elocution. *Address:* 7917 Westwood Drive, Houston, TX 77055, USA. *T:* and *Fax:* (713) 4659169; Laythams Farm, Slaidburn, Clitheroe, Lancs BB7 3AJ. *T:* (01200) 446677.

WENT, David; Group Chief Executive, Irish Life & Permanent PLC, since 1999 (Managing Director, Irish Life, 1998); *b* 25 March 1947; *s* of Arthur Edward James Went and Phyllis (*née* Howell); *m* 1972, Mary Christine Milligan; one *s* one *d*. *Educ:* High Sch., Dublin; Trinity Coll., Dublin (BA Mod; LLB). Called to the Bar, King's Inns, Dublin, 1970. Graduate Trainee, Citibank, Dublin, 1970; Gen. Manager, Citibank, Jeddah, 1975–76; Dir 1976, Chief Exec. 1982, Ulster Investment Bank; Ulster Bank: Dep. Chief Exec., 1987; Chief Exec., 1988–94; Chief Exec., Coutts Gp, 1994–97. Chm., NI Bankers' Assoc., 1988–89; President: Irish Bankers' Fedn, 1991–92; Inst. of Bankers in Ireland, 1993–94. *Recreations:* tennis, reading, theatre. *Address:* Irish Life & Permanent, Lower Abbey Street, Dublin 1, Ireland. *T:* (1) 7042717. *Clubs:* Kildare Street and University (Dublin); Fitzwilliam Lawn Tennis; Royal Belfast Golf; Royal North of Ireland Yacht.

WENT, Rt Rev. John Stewart; *see* Tewkesbury, Bishop Suffragan of.

WENTWORTH, Maurice Frank Gerard, CMG 1957; OBE 1946; *b* 5 Nov. 1908; *s* of F. B. Wentworth, Finchley, N3; *m* 1962, Belinda Margaret, *d* of late B. S. Tatham and Mrs Tatham, Mickleham, Surrey; one *s* one *d*. *Educ:* Haileybury; University Coll., London (BA). Military Service, 1939–46, Lieutenant-Colonel. Gold Coast: Inspector of Schools, 1930; Sen. Education Officer, 1945; Principal, Teacher Training Coll., Tamale, 1946; Administrative Officer Class I, 1951; Permanent Secretary, 1953; Establishment Secretary, 1954–57 (Ghana Civil Service); Chairman: Public Service Commission: Sierra Leone, 1958–61; E African High Commn, 1961–64; Appointments Officer, ODM, 1964–73. *Address:* Castania, Burton Street, Marnhull, Sturminster Newton, Dorset DT10 1JJ.

WENTWORTH, Stephen; Fisheries Director, Department for Environment, Food and Rural Affairs (formerly Fisheries Secretary, Ministry of Agriculture, Fisheries and Food), since 1993; *b* 23 Aug. 1943; *s* of Ronald Wentworth, OBE and Elizabeth Mary Wentworth (*née* Collins); *m* 1970, Katharine Laura Hopkinson; three *d*. *Educ:* King's College Sch., Wimbledon; Merton Coll., Oxford (MA, MSc). Joined Ministry of Agriculture, Fisheries and Food, 1967; seconded to CSSB, 1974, and to FCO, as First Sec., UK Perm. Repn to EEC, Brussels, 1976; Head of Beef Div., 1978; seconded to Cabinet Office, 1980; Head of: Milk Div., 1982; European Communities Div., 1985; Under-Sec. and Head of Meat Gp, 1986; Head of Livestock Products Gp, 1989; Head of EC and External Trade Policy Gp, 1991. *Address:* Department for Environment, Food and Rural Affairs, Nobel House, Smith Square, SW1P 3JR; *e-mail:* stephen.wentworth@defra.gsi.gov.uk.

WERNER, Alfred Emil Anthony; Chairman, Pacific Regional Conservation Center, 1975–82, retired; *b* 18 June 1911; *o s* of late Professor Emil Alphonse Werner, Dublin; *m* 1939, Marion Jane Davies; two *d*. *Educ:* St Gerard's School, Bray; Trinity College, Dublin. MSc (Dublin Univ.) and ARIC 1936; MA (Dublin) and DPhil (Univ. of Freiburg im Breisgau) 1937; Hon. ScD (Dublin) 1971. Lecturer in Chemistry, TCD, 1937; Reader in Organic Chemistry, TCD, 1946; Research Chemist, National Gallery, 1948; Principal Scientific Officer, British Museum Research Laboratory, 1954, Keeper, 1959–75. Prof. of Chemistry, Royal Acad., 1962–75. FSA 1958; FMA 1959 (President, 1967); MRIA 1963. Pres., International Institute for the Conservation of Artistic and Historic Works, 1971 (Hon. Treasurer, 1962). *Publications:* The Scientific Examination of Paintings, 1952; (with H. Roosen-Runge) Codex Lindisfarnensis, Part V, 1961; (with H. J. Plenderleith) The Conservation of Antiquities and Works of Art, 1972; articles in scientific and museum journals. *Recreations:* chess, travelling. *Address:* Smalls Farm, Groton, Sudbury, Suffolk CO10 5EG. *T:* (01787) 210231; 11/73 South Street, Bellerive, Tas 7018, Australia. *T:* (3) 62446959. *Clubs:* Athenæum; Tasmanian (Hobart).

WERNER, Ronald Louis, AM 1980; MSc, PhD; company director; President, New South Wales Institute of Technology, 1974–86; Emeritus Professor, University of Technology, Sydney, since 1988; *b* 12 Sept. 1924; *s* of Frank Werner and Olive Maude Werner; *m* 1948, Valerie Irene (*née* Bean); two *s* one *d*. *Educ:* Univ. of New South Wales (BSc (1st Cl. Hons; Univ. Medal); MSc, PhD). FRACI. Sen. Lectr, 1954–60, Associate Prof., 1961–67, Head of Dept of Phys. Chemistry, 1964–67, Univ. of New South Wales; Dep. Dir, 1967–68, Director, 1968–73, NSW Inst. of Technology. Chm., NSW Advanced Educn Bd, 1969–71; Trustee, Mus. of Applied Arts and Scis, 1973–86 (Pres., Bd of Trustees, 1976–84); Chairman: Conf. of Dirs of Central Insts of Technology, 1975; ACDP, 1982–83; Member: Science and Industry Forum, Aust. Acad. of Science, 1971–76; Council for Tech. and Further Educn, 1970–85; Hong Kong UPGC, 1972–90; NSW Bicentennial Exhibition Cttee, 1985–88; Adv. Council, Univ. of Western Sydney, 1986–88; Governor, College of Law, 1972–76. Director: NRMA Ltd, 1977–95; NRMA Life Ltd, 1985–95; NRMA Travel Ltd, 1986–95; Open Road Publishing Co., 1986–95; NRMA Sales & Service, 1986–95; NRMA Finance Ltd, 1992–95. Councillor, Nat. Roads and Motorists Assoc., 1977–95. DUniv Univ. of Tech., Sydney, 1988. *Publications:* numerous papers in scientific jls. *Recreations:* yachting, golf. *Address:* 13 Capri Close, Clareville, NSW 2107, Australia.

WESIERSKA, Ruth Christabel, (Mrs George Wesierska); *see* Walder, R. C.

WESIL, Dennis; Senior Director, Posts, 1971–75, and Member, 1975, Post Office Management Board; *b* 18 Feb. 1915; *e s* of Jack and Polly Wesil, London; *m* 1941, Kathleen, *d* of H. S. McAlpine; two *d*. *Educ:* Central Foundation Sch.; University Coll., London. Entered London telephone service as Asst Supt of Traffic, 1937; PO Investigation Branch, 1941; Asst Postal Controller, 1947; Principal, GPO Headqrtrs, 1953; Dep. Chief Inspector of Postal Services, 1961; Asst Sec. in charge of Postal Mechanisation Branch, 1963; Dep. Dir, NE Region (GPO), 1966; Director: NE Postal Region, 1967; London Postal Region, 1970–71. *Recreations:* reading, golf. *Address:* 2 Stoneleigh, Martello Road South, Poole, Dorset BH13 7HQ. *T:* (01202) 707304; *e-mail:* dwesil@talk21.com.

WESKER, Arnold, FRSL 1985; playwright; director; Founder Director of Centre Fortytwo, 1961 (dissolved 1970); Chairman, British Centre of International Theatre Institute, 1978–82; President, International Playwrights' Committee, 1979–83; *b* 24 May 1932; *s* of Joseph Wesker and Leah Perlmutter; *m* 1958, Dusty Bicker; two *s* two *d*. *Educ:* Upton House School, Hackney. Furniture Maker's Apprentice, Carpenter's Mate, 1948; Bookseller's Asst, 1949 and 1952; Royal Air Force, 1950–52; Plumber's Mate, 1952; Farm Labourer, Seed Sorter, 1953; Kitchen Porter, 1953–54; Pastry Cook, 1954–58. Former Mem., Youth Service Council. Hon. Fellow, QMW, 1995. Hon. LittD UEA, 1989; Hon. DHL Denison, Ohio, 1997. Author of plays: The Kitchen, produced at Royal Court Theatre, 1959, 1961, 1994 (filmed, 1961); Trilogy of plays (Chicken Soup with Barley, Roots, I'm Talking about Jerusalem) produced Belgrade Theatre (Coventry), 1958–60, Royal Court Theatre, 1960; Chips with Everything, Royal Court, 1962, Vaudeville, 1962 and Plymouth Theatre, Broadway, 1963; The Four Seasons, Belgrade Theatre (Coventry) and Saville, 1965; Their Very Own and Golden City, Brussels and Royal Court, 1966 (Marzotto Drama Prize, 1964); The Friends, Stockholm and London, 1970 (also dir); The Old Ones, Royal Court, 1972; The Wedding Feast, Stockholm, 1974, Leeds 1977; The

Journalists, Coventry (amateur), 1977, Yugoslav TV, 1978, Germany, 1981; The Merchant, subseq. entitled Shylock, Stockholm and Aarhus, 1976, Broadway, 1977, Birmingham, 1978; Love Letters on Blue Paper, Nat. Theatre, 1978 (also dir); Fatlips (for young people), 1978; Caritas (Scandinavian Project commission), 1980, Nat. Theatre, 1981, adapted as opera libretto (music by Robert Saxton), 1991; Sullied Hand, 1981, Edinburgh Festival and Finnish TV, 1984; Four Portraits (Japanese commn), Tokyo, 1982, Edinburgh Festival, 1984; Annie Wobbler, Suddeutscher Rundfunk, Germany, Birmingham and New End Theatre, 1983, Fortune Theatre, 1984, New York, 1986; One More Ride on the Merry-Go-Round, Leicester, 1985; Yardsale, Edinburgh Fest. and Stratford-on-Avon (RSC Actors' Fest.), 1985 (also dir); When God Wanted A Son, 1986; Whatever Happened to Betty Lemon (double-bill with Yardsale), Lyric Studio, 1987 (also dir); Little Old Lady (for young people), Sigtuna, Sweden, 1988; The Mistress, 1988, Rome (also dir); Beorhtel's Hill, Towngate, Basildon, 1989; Three Women Talking, 1990, Chicago, 1992; Letter to a Daughter, 1990; Blood Libel, 1991; Wild Spring, 1992, Tokyo, 1994; Denial, Bristol Old Vic, 2000. *Film scripts:* Lady Othello, 1980; Homage to Catalonia, 1990; Maudie, 1995 (adapted from Diary of Jane Somers, by Doris Lessing). *Television:* (first play) Menace, 1963; Breakfast, 1981; (adapted) Thieves in the Night, by A. Koestler, 1984; (adapted) Diary of Jane Somers, by Doris Lessing, 1989; Barabbas, 2000. *Radio:* Yardsale, 1984; Bluey (Eur. Radio Commn), Cologne Radio 1984, BBC Radio 3, 1985 (adapted as stage play, 1993). *Publications:* Chicken Soup with Barley, 1959; Roots, 1959; I'm Talking about Jerusalem, 1960; The Wesker Trilogy, 1960; The Kitchen, 1961; Chips with Everything, 1962; The Four Seasons, 1966; Their Very Own and Golden City, 1966; The Friends, 1970; Fears of Fragmentation (essays), 1971; Six Sundays in January, 1971; The Old Ones, 1972; The Journalists, 1974 (in Dialog; repr. 1975); Love Letters on Blue Paper (stories), 1974, 2nd edn 1990; (with John Allin) Say Goodbye! You May Never See Them Again, 1974; Words—as definitions of experience, 1976; The Wedding Feast, 1977; Journey Into Journalism, 1977; Said the Old Man to the Young Man (stories), 1978; The Merchant, 1978; Fatlips (for young people), 1978; The Journalists, a triptych (with Journey into Journalism and A Diary of the Writing of The Journalists), 1979; Caritas, 1981; The Merchant, 1983; Distinctions, 1985; Yardsale, 1987; Whatever Happened to Betty Lemon, 1987; Little Old Lady, 1988; Shoeshine, 1989; Collected Plays: vols 1 and 5, 1989, vols 2, 3, 4 and 6, 1990, vol. 7, 1994; As Much As I Dare (autobiog.), 1994; Circles of Perception, 1996; Break, My Heart, 1997; Denial, 1997; The Birth of Shylock and the Death of Zero Mostel (journals), 1997; The King's Daughters (stories), 1998; Barabbas (TV play), 2000; Groupie (radio play), 2001; Longitude (play), 2001. *Address:* Hay-on-Wye, Hereford HR3 5RJ.

WESLEY, Mary; *see* Siepmann, M. A.

WEST; *see* Sackville-West, family name of Baron Sackville.

WEST, Adm. Sir Alan (William John), KCB 2000; DSC 1982; Commander-in-Chief Fleet, since 2001; Commander-in-Chief East Atlantic and Commander Allied Naval Forces North, since 2001; *b* 21 April 1948; *m* 1973, Rosemary Anne Linington Childs; two *s* one *d*. *Educ:* Windsor Grammar Sch.; Clydebank High Sch. Joined RN 1965; seagoing appts, 1966–73; CO HMS Yarnton, 1973; qualified Principal Warfare Officer, 1975; HMS Juno, 1976; HMS Ambuscade, 1977; RN Staff Course, 1978; qualified Advanced Warfare Officer, 1978; HMS Norfolk, 1979; CO HMS Ardent, 1980; Naval Staff, 1982; CO HMS Bristol, 1987; Defence Intell. Staff, 1989; RCDS 1992; Higher Comd and Staff Course, Camberley, 1993; Dir, Naval Staff Duties, 1993; Naval Sec., 1994–96; Comdr UK Task Gp, and Comdr Anti Submarine Warfare Striking Force, 1996–97; Chief of Defence Intelligence, 1997–2001. Yr Brother, Trinity House. President: Royal Naval Fencing; St Barbara Assoc.; Bollington Sea Cadet Corps; Ardent Assoc.; Ship Recognition Corps; Assoc. of Service Yacht Clubs. Cdre, RNSA. *Recreations:* sailing, military and local history. *Address:* JSU Warrior, Eastbury Park, Northwood, Middx HA6 3HP. *Clubs:* Army and Navy, Royal Navy of 1765 and 1785, Anchorites; Royal Yacht Squadron.

WEST, Brian John; media consultant; Director and Chief Executive, Association of Independent Radio Companies, 1983–95; *b* 4 Aug. 1935; *s* of Herbert Frank West and Nellie (*née* Painter); *m* 1st, 1960, Patricia Ivy White (marr. diss. 1986); 2nd, 1987, Gillian Bond. *Educ:* Tiffin Sch., Kingston upon Thames. Sub-Lt (O), Fleet Air Arm, RN, 1956–58. Journalist, Richmond Herald, Surrey Comet and Western Morning News, 1952–60; Surrey Comet: Asst Editor, 1960–64; Editor, 1964–70; Editor, Leicester Mercury, 1970–74; Head of Advertising and PR, Littlewoods Orgn Plc, 1974–83. Founder Pres., Assoc. of European Radios, 1992–93; Council Mem., Advertising Assoc., 1987–95; Dir, Radio Jt Audience Res. Ltd, 1992–94. Churchill Fellow, 1995; Beaverbrook Foundn Fellow, 1995; Fellow, Radio Acad., 1995. *Publication:* Radio Training in the United States, 1996. *Recreations:* music, riding, walking, gardening, photography, cherishing my wife. *Address:* Greenbank, Glyndwr Road, Gwernymynydd, Mold CH7 5LP. *T:* (01352) 752669, *Fax:* (01352) 752168; *e-mail:* BriGilW@cs.com.

WEST, Christopher John; Solicitor to HM Land Registry, since 1991; *b* 4 May 1941; *s* of George William West and Kathleen Mary West; *m* 1978, Susan Elizabeth Kirkby; one *d*. *Educ:* Raynes Park County Grammar Sch.; Inns of Court Sch. of Law. Called to the Bar, Lincoln's Inn, 1966. Exec. Officer, Charity Commn, 1961; HM Land Registry, 1969–; Sen. Land Registrar, 1983; Dist Land Registrar, Tunbridge Wells Dist land Registry, 1987. *Publications:* (contrib.) Land Registration (jtly) and Land Charges, to Halsbury's Laws of England, 4th edn, 1977; (contrib.) Atkin's Court Forms, 1978, 1987; (with T. B. F. Ruoff) Concise Land Registration Practice and Land Registration Forms, 1982; (ed jtly) Ruoff and Roper's Registered Conveyancing, 5th edn 1986, looseleaf edn updated bi-annually 1991–. *Recreations:* theatre, jazz, watching cricket. *Address:* (office) 32 Lincoln's Inn Fields, WC2A 3PH. *T:* (020) 7917 5994.

WEST, David Arthur James; Assistant Under Secretary of State (Naval Personnel), Ministry of Defence, 1981–84, retired; *b* 10 Dec. 1927; *s* of Wilfred West and Edith West (*née* Jones). *Educ:* Cotham Grammar Sch., Bristol. Executive Officer, Air Ministry, 1946; Higher Executive Officer, 1955; Principal, 1961; Assistant Secretary, 1972; Asst Under Sec. of State, 1979. *Address:* 66 Denton Road, East Twickenham TW1 2HQ. *T:* (020) 8892 6890.

WEST, David Thomson, CBE 1982; *b* 10 March 1923; *m* 1958, Marie Sellar; one *s* one *d*. *Educ:* Malvern Coll.; St John's Coll., Oxford. Served in RNVR, 1942–45; HM Diplomatic Service, 1946–76; served in Foreign Office, Office of Comr General for UK in SE Asia, HM Embassies, Paris, Lima, and Tunis; Counsellor, 1964; Commercial Inspector, 1965–68; Counsellor (Commercial) Berne, 1968–71; Head of Export Promotion Dept, FCO, 1971–72; seconded to Civil Service Dept as Head of Manpower Div., 1972–76; transf. to Home Civil Service, 1976, retired 1983. *Address:* The Manor House, Great Sampford, Essex CB10 2RL. *T:* (01799) 586305. *Club:* Garrick.

WEST, Prof. Donald James; Professor of Clinical Criminology 1979–84, now Emeritus, and Director 1981–84, University of Cambridge Institute of Criminology; Fellow of Darwin College, Cambridge, 1967–91, now Emeritus; Hon. Consultant Psychiatrist, National Health Service, 1961–86, retired; *b* 9 June 1924; *s* of John Charles and Jessie Mercedes West. *Educ:* Merchant Taylors' Sch., Crosby; Liverpool Univ. (MD). LittD Cambridge. FRCPsych. Research Officer, Soc. for Psychical Research, London, and pt-time graduate student in psychiatry, 1947–50; in hospital practice in psychiatry, 1951–59; Sen. Registrar, Forensic Psychiatry Unit, Maudsley Hosp., 1957–59; Inst. of Criminology, Cambridge, 1960–. Leverhulme Emeritus Fellow, 1988–89. Mental Health Act Comr, 1989–97. Vice Pres., 1981–, and former Pres., British Soc. of Criminology; Pres., Soc. for Psychical Research, 1963–65, 1984–87, 1998–; Chm., Forensic Section, World Psychiatric Assoc., 1983–89; Chm., Streetwise Youth, 1986–92. *Publications:* Psychical Research Today, 1954 (revd edn 1962); Eleven Lourdes Miracles (med. inquiry under Parapsych. Foundn Grant), 1957; The Habitual Prisoner (for Inst. of Criminology), 1963; Murder followed by Suicide (for Inst. of Criminology), 1965; The Young Offender, 1967; Homosexuality, 1968; Present Conduct and Future Delinquency, 1969; (ed) The Future of Parole, 1972; (jtly) Who Becomes Delinquent?, 1973; (jtly) The Delinquent Way of Life, 1977; Homosexuality Re-examined, 1977; (ed, jtly) Daniel McNaughton: his trial and the aftermath, 1977; (jtly) Understanding Sexual Attacks, 1978; Delinquency: its roots, careers and prospects, 1982; Sexual Victimisation, 1985; Sexual Crimes and Confrontations, 1987; (jtly) Children's Sexual Encounters with Adults, 1990; Male Prostitution, 1992; (ed) Sex Crimes, 1994; (ed with R. Green) Sociolegal Controls on Homosexuality: a multi-nation comparison, 1997; various contribs to British Jl of Criminology, Criminal Behaviour and Mental Health and Jl Soc. for Psychical Res. *Recreations:* travel, parapsychology. *Address:* 32 Fen Road, Milton, Cambridge CB4 6AD. *T:* (01223) 860308.

WEST, Edward Mark, CMG 1987; Deputy Director-General, Food and Agriculture Organization of the United Nations, 1982–86; *b* 11 March 1923; *m* 1948, Lydia Hollander; three *s*. *Educ:* Hendon County Sch.; University Coll., Oxford (MA). Served RA (W/Lieut), 1943; ICU BAOR (A/Captain), 1945. Asst Principal, Colonial Office, 1947; Private Sec., PUS, Colonial Office, 1950–51, Principal, 1951–58; Head of Chancery, UK Commn, Singapore, 1958–61; Private Secretary to Secretary of State, Colonial Affairs, 1961–62; Private Secretary to Secretary of State for Commonwealth and Colonial Affairs, 1963; Asst Sec., ODM, 1964–70; Food and Agriculture Organization: Director, Programme and Budget Formulation, 1970; Asst Dir-Gen., Administration and Finance Dept, 1974; Asst Dir-Gen., Programme and Budget Formulation, 1976; Special Rep., Internat. Conf. on Nutrition, 1992. Mem. Corp., Trinity Coll. of Music, 1992–. *Address:* 10 Warwick Mansions, Cromwell Crescent, SW5 9QR.

WEST, Emma Louise; *see* Johnson, E. L.

WEST, Lt-Col George Arthur Alston-Roberts-, CVO 1988; DL; Comptroller, Lord Chamberlain's Office, 1987–90 (Assistant Comptroller, 1981–87); an Extra Equerry to the Queen, since 1982; *b* 1937; *s* of Major W. R. J. Alston-Roberts-West, Grenadier Guards (killed in action 1940) and late Mrs W. R. J. Alston-Roberts-West; *m* 1970, Hazel, *d* of late Sir Thomas and Lady Cook. *Educ:* Eton Coll.; RMA, Sandhurst. Commissioned into Grenadier Guards, Dec. 1957; served in England, Northern Ireland, Germany and Cyprus; retired, 1980. Dir, Care Ltd, 1991–95. DL Warwicks, 1988. *Address:* Atherstone Hill Farm, Stratford-on-Avon, Warwicks CV37 8NF. *Clubs:* Boodle's, Pratt's.

WEST, Rt Hon. Henry William; PC (N Ire) 1960; Leader, Ulster Unionist Party, 1974–79; *b* 27 March 1917; *s* of late W. H. West, JP; *m* 1956, Maureen Elizabeth Hall; four *s* three *d*. *Educ:* Enniskillen Model School; Portora Royal School. Farmer. MP for Enniskillen, NI Parlt, 1954–72; Mem. (U), Fermanagh and S Tyrone, NI Assembly, 1973–75; Parly Sec. to Minister of Agriculture, 1958; Minister of Agriculture, 1960–67, and 1971–72; MP (UUUC) Fermanagh and South Tyrone, Feb.-Sept. 1974; Mem. (UUUC), for Fermanagh and South Tyrone, NI Constitutional Convention, 1975–76. N Ireland representative on British Wool Marketing Board, 1950–58; President, Ulster Farmers' Union, 1955–56. High Sheriff, Co. Fermanagh, 1954. *Address:* Rossmere, Rossahilly, Enniskillen, Northern Ireland BT94 2FP. *T:* (028) 6632 3060.

WEST, Jeffrey James; Deputy Director of Conservation, and Director, Conservation Management, English Heritage, since 1998; *b* 15 Oct. 1950; *s* of Walter Edward West and late (Frances) Margaret West (*née* Tatam); *m* 1987, Juliet Elizabeth Allan. *Educ:* Bedford Modern Sch.; Worcester Coll., Oxford (BA PPE 1972; BPhil Politics 1974; MA 1976). Joined Ancient Monuments Inspectorate, Department of Environment, 1974: Asst Inspector, 1974–79; Inspector, 1979–81; seconded as Principal, Local Govt Finance, DoE, 1981–83; Principal Inspector of Historic Buildings, DoE, later English Heritage, 1983–86; English Heritage: Regl Dir of Historic Properties (Midlands and E Anglia), 1986–97; Actg Dir of Historic Properties, 1997–98. Member: Council, Royal Archaeol Inst., 1980–83; Res. and Recording Cttee, ICOMOS (UK), 1997–. *Publications:* contrib. articles, notes and reviews on individual historic bldgs and theory and practice of conservation in learned jls. *Recreations:* philosophy, garden history, gardening. *Address:* The Cottage, Bayliss Yard, Charlbury, Oxford OX7 3RS. *T:* (01608) 811136.

WEST, Prof. John Clifford, CBE 1977; PhD, DSc; FREng, FIEE; FRGS; Vice-Chancellor and Principal, University of Bradford, 1979–89; *b* 4 June 1922; *s* of J. H. West and Mrs West (*née* Ascroft); *m* 1946, Winefride Mary Turner; three *d*. *Educ:* Hindley and Abram Grammar School; Victoria Univ., Manchester (PhD 1953; DSc 1957). Matthew Kirtley Entrance Schol., Manchester Univ., 1940. Electrical Lieutenant, RNVR, 1943–46. Lecturer, University of Manchester, 1946–57; Professor of Electrical Engineering, The Queen's University of Belfast, 1958–65; University of Sussex: Prof. of Electrical and Control Engineering, 1965–78; Founder Dean, Sch. of Applied Scis, 1965–73, Pro-Vice-Chancellor, 1967–71; Dir, Phillips' Philatelic Unit, 1970–78. Director, A. C. E. Machinery Ltd, 1966–79. Member: UGC, 1973–78 (Chm., Technology Sub-Cttee, 1973–78); Science Res. Council Cttee on Systems and Electrical Engineering, 1963–67; Science Res. Council Engrg Bd, 1976–79; Vis. Cttee, Dept of Educn and Science, Cranfield; Civil Service Commn Special Merit Promotions Panel, 1966–72; Naval Educn Adv. Cttee, 1965–72; Crawford Cttee on Broadcasting Coverage, 1973–74; Inter-Univ. Inst. of Engrg Control, 1967–83 (Dir, 1967–70); Chairman: Council for Educnl Technology, 1980–85; Educn Task Gp, IStructE, 1988–89. Pres., IEE, 1984–85 (Dep. Pres. 1982–84); Chm., Automation and Control Div., IEE, 1970–71. Vice-Chm., Yorkshire Cancer Res. Campaign, 1989– (Treas., 1989–97). Chm., Internat. Commn on Higher Educn, Botswana, 1990; UK deleg., Conf. on Higher Educn, Madagascar, 1992. Member: Royal Philatelic Soc., 1960–; Sociedad Filatélica de Chile, 1970–; Chm., British Philatelic Council, 1980–81; Trustee, Nat. Philatelic Trust, 1989–; Keeper of the Roll of Distinguished Philatelists, 1992–, Signatory, 2000. FRPSL 1970; Fellow, Inst. of Paper Conservation, 1980; FREng (FEng 1983). Hon. FInstMC 1984; Hon. FIEE 1992. Hon. DSc Sussex, 1988; DUniv Bradford, 1990. Hartley Medal, Inst. Measurement and Control, 1979; International Philatelic Gold Medal: Seoul, 1994; Seville, 1996. *Publications:* Textbook of Servomechanisms, 1953; Analytical Techniques for Non-Linear Control Systems, 1960; papers in Proc. IEE, Trans Amer. IEE, Brit. Jl of Applied Physics, Jl of Scientific Instruments, Proc. Inst. Measurement and Control. *Recreations:* philately, postal history. *Address:* North End House, 19 The Street, Stedham,

West Sussex GU29 0NQ. *T:* (01730) 810833, *Fax:* (01730) 810834; *e-mail:* johnwest.sted@quista.net. *Club:* Athenæum.

WEST, John James; Member (Lab), since 1981, Leader, since 1997, Lancashire County Council (Deputy Leader, 1989–97); *b* 19 April 1939; *s* of John West and Teresa West (*née* Campbell); two *s*. *Educ:* St Mary's RC Sch., Dublin; Dublin Univ. (BA Econs and Hist. 1961); Harris Coll., Preston and Poole Tech. Coll. (Dip Business Studies 1974); Open Univ. MInstTA 1976; MCIT 1978. Dep. Manager/Dep. Chm. of Bd, Preston Borough Transport Ltd, 1961–92. Freelance pt-time Lectr in Econs and History. Chair, Superannuation Panel, 1984–, Finance Cttee, 1985–, Lancs CC; Exec. Mem., LGA, 1994–. Chairman: Lancashire Waste Services Ltd, 1991–; Lancashire Co-op Develt Agency, 1991–; non-executive Director: Preston and S Ribble Develt Agency, 1997–; Preston Acute Hosp. NHS Trust, 1997–. *Recreations:* reading (especially ancient history), watching most sports. *Address:* (home) 17 Carlton Drive, Frenchwood, Preston PR1 4PP; (office) County Hall, Pitt Street, Preston PR1 8XJ. *T:* (01772) 263355.

WEST, Kenneth, CChem, FRSC; Deputy Chairman, ICI Fibres Division, 1980–84 (Technical Director, 1977–80); *b* 1 Sept. 1930; *s* of Albert West and Ethel Kirby (*née* Kendall); *m* 1980, Elizabeth Ann Borland (*née* Campbell); one step *s*, and three *d* by a previous marriage. *Educ:* Archbishop Holgate's Grammar Sch., York; University Coll., Oxford (BA). Customer Service Manager, ICI Fibres, 1960; Res. and Engrg Manager, FII, 1967; Director: South African Nylon Spinners, Cape Town, 1970; Fibre Industries Inc., N Carolina, 1974; Man. Dir, TWA, 1984–85; Dir, Water Res. Council, 1984–85. Dir, Seahorse Internat. Ltd, 1987–89. Mem., British Assoc. of the Var. FRSA. *Recreations:* sailing, flying, music, wine, amateur dramatics. *Address:* La Salamandre, Route de Repenti, 83340 Le Luc, France. *Clubs:* Don Mills Variety; Oxford and Cambridge (Var Br.); Yacht International (Bormes les Mimosas).

WEST, Martin Litchfield, DPhil, DLitt; FBA 1973; Senior Research Fellow, All Souls College, University of Oxford, since 1991; *b* 23 Sept. 1937; *s* of Maurice Charles West and Catherine Baker West (*née* Stainthorpe); *m* 1960, Stephanie Roberta Pickard (*see* S. R. West); one *s* one *d*. *Educ:* St Paul's Sch.; Balliol Coll., Oxford (MA 1962; DPhil 1963; DLitt 1994). Chancellor's Prizes for Latin Prose and Verse, 1957; Hertford and de Paravicini Schols, 1957; Ireland Schol., 1957; Conington Prize, 1965. Woodhouse Jun. Research Fellow, St John's Coll., Oxford, 1960–63; Fellow and Praelector in Classics, University Coll., Oxford, 1963–74 (Hon. Fellow 2001); Prof. of Greek, Bedford Coll., then at RHBNC, London Univ., 1974–91. Corresp. Mem., Akademie der Wissenschaften zu Göttingen, 1991; MAE 1998. Editor of Liddell and Scott's Greek-English Lexicon, 1965–81. Internat. Balzan Prize for Classical Antiquity, 2000. *Publications:* (ed) Hesiod, Theogony, 1966; (ed with R. Merkelbach) Fragmenta Hesiodea, 1967; Early Greek Philosophy and the Orient, 1971; Sing Me, Goddess, 1971; (ed) Iambi et Elegi Graeci, 1971–72; Textual Criticism and Editorial Technique, 1973; Studies in Greek Elegy and Iambus, 1974; (ed) Hesiod, Works and Days, 1978; (ed) Theognidis et Phocylidis fragmenta, 1978; (ed) Delectus ex Iambis et Elegis Graecis, 1980; Greek Metre, 1982; The Orphic Poems, 1983; (ed) Carmina Anacreontea, 1984; The Hesiodic Catalogue of Women, 1985; (ed) Euripides, Orestes, 1987; Introduction to Greek Metre, 1987; Hesiod (trans.), 1988; (ed) Aeschyli Tragoediae, 1990; Studies in Aeschylus, 1990; Ancient Greek Music, 1992; Greek Lyric Poetry (trans.), 1993; The East Face of Helicon, 1997; (ed) Homeri Ilias, 2 vols, 1998 and 2000; Studies in the Text and Transmission of the Iliad, 2001; (with E. Pöhlmann) Documents of Ancient Greek Music, 2001; articles in classical periodicals. *Recreation:* strong music. *Address:* All Souls College, Oxford OX1 4AL.

WEST, Michael Charles B.; *see* Beresford-West.

WEST, Nigel; *see* Allason, R. W. S.

WEST, Norman; Member (Lab) Yorkshire South, European Parliament, 1984–98; *b* 26 Nov. 1935; *m*; two *s*. *Educ:* Barnsley; Sheffield Univ. Miner. Mem., South Yorks CC (Chm., Highways Cttee; Mem., anti-nuclear working party). Member: NUM; CND. Mem., Energy, Research and Technology Cttee, European Parlt, 1984–98. *Address:* 43 Coronation Drive, Birdwell, Barnsley, South Yorks S10 5RJ.

WEST, Peter; BBC television commentator/anchorman, 1950–86; commentaries for radio, 1947–85; Chairman, West Nally Group (sports marketing), 1971–83; *b* 12 Aug. 1920; *s* of Harold William and Dorcas Anne West; *m* 1946, Pauline Mary Pike; two *s* one *d*. *Educ:* Cranbrook Sch.; RMC, Sandhurst. Served War of 1939–45: Duke of Wellington's Regt. TV/Radio commentaries every year: on Test matches, 1952–86; on Wimbledon, 1955–82; on Rugby Union, 1950–85; Olympics, 1948–60–64–68–72–76. Rugby Football Correspondent of The Times, 1971–82. TV shows: Chairman of: Why?, 1953; Guess my Story, 1953–54–55. Introduced: At Home, 1955; First Hand and It's Up to You, 1956–57; Box Office, 1957; Come Dancing, 1957–72 (incl.); Be Your Own Boss and Wish You Were Here, 1958; Get Ahead, 1958–62; Good Companions, 1958–62; First Years at Work (Schs TV), 1958–69 (incl.); Miss World, 1961–66 (incl.); Facing West (HTV, Bristol), 1986–88. Children's TV: introd.: Question Marks, 1957; Ask Your Dad, 1958; What's New?, 1962–63–64. Radio: introd.: What Shall We Call It?, 1955; Sound Idea, 1958; Morning Call, 1960–61; Treble Chance, 1962; Sporting Chance, 1964; Games People Play, 1985. Pres., Cheltenham Cricket Soc., 1984–. Editor, Playfair Cricket Annual, 1948–53. *Publications:* The Fight for the Ashes, 1953; The Fight for the Ashes, 1956; Flannelled Fool and Muddied Oaf (autobiog.), 1986; Clean Sweep, 1987; Denis Compton—Cricketing Genius, 1989. *Recreations:* gardening, rubber bridge. *Address:* The Paddock, Duntisbourne Abbotts, Cirencester, Glos GL7 7JW. *T:* (01285) 821380.

WEST, Prunella Margaret Rumney, (Mrs T. L. West); *see* Scales, Prunella.

WEST, Prof. Richard Gilbert, FRS 1968; FSA; FGS; Fellow of Clare College, Cambridge, since 1954; Professor of Botany, University of Cambridge, 1977–91; *b* 31 May 1926; *m* 1st, 1958; one *s*; 2nd, 1973, Hazel Gristwood (*d* 1997); two *d*. *Educ:* King's School, Canterbury; Univ. of Cambridge. Cambridge University: Demonstrator in Botany, 1957–60; Lecturer in Botany, 1960–67; Dir, Subdept of Quaternary Research, 1966–87; Reader in Quaternary Research, 1967–75; Prof. of Palaeoecology, 1975–77. Member: Council for Scientific Policy, 1971–73; NERC, 1973–76; Ancient Monuments Bd for England, 1980–84. Darwin Lecturer to the British Association, 1959; Lyell Fund, 1961, Bigsby Medal, 1969, Lyell Medal, 1988, Geological Society of London. Hon. MRIA. *Publications:* Pleistocene Geology and Biology, 1968, 2nd edn 1977; (jtly) The Ice Age in Britain, 1972, 2nd edn 1981; The Pre-glacial Pleistocene of the Norfolk and Suffolk coasts, 1980; Pleistocene Palaeoecology of Central Norfolk, 1991; Plant Life in the Quaternary Cold Stages, 2000. *Address:* 3A Woollards Lane, Great Shelford, Cambs CB2 5LZ. *T:* (01223) 842578; Clare College, Cambridge CB2 1TL.

WEST, Prof. Richard John, FRCP, FRCPCH; Medical Postgraduate Dean to South and West Region, and Hon. Professor, University of Bristol, 1991–99; *b* 8 May 1939; *s* of late Cecil J. West and of Alice B. West (*née* Court); *m* 1962, Jenny Winn Hawkins; one *s* two *d*. *Educ:* Tiffin Boys' Sch.; Middlesex Hospital Medical School (MB, BS, MD). FRCP 1979; FRCPCH 1997. Research Fellow, Inst. of Child Health, London, 1971–73; Sen. Registrar, Hosp. for Sick Children, London, 1973–74; Lectr, Inst. of Child Health, 1974–75; Sen. Lectr, 1975–91, Dean, 1982–87, St George's Hosp. Med. Sch.; Consultant Paediatrician, St George's Hosp., 1975–91; Hon. Consultant Paediatrician, Royal Hosp. for Sick Children, Bristol, 1991–99. Member: Wandsworth HA, 1981–82, 1989–90; SW Thames RHA, 1982–88. Member: DoH Clinical Outcomes Gp, 1991–96; Steering Gp on Undergraduate Med. and Dental Educn and Res., 1992–. Member, Governing Body: Inst. of Med. Ethics, 1985–2001(Gen. Sec., 1989–99); Tiffin Boys' Sch., 1983–86; Wimbledon High Sch., 1988–91. *Publications:* Family Guide to Children's Ailments, 1983; Royal Society of Medicine Child Health Guide, 1992; research papers on metabolic diseases, incl. lipid disorders. *Recreations:* windmills, medical history, travel, archaeology. *Address:* 4 Old Vicarage Place, Apsley Road, Bristol BS8 2TD. *T:* (0117) 973 8311.

WEST, Samuel Alexander Joseph; actor; *b* 19 June 1966; *s* of Timothy Lancaster West, *qv* and Prunella Margaret Rumney West (*see* Prunella Scales). *Educ:* Alleyn's Sch., Dulwich; Lady Margaret Hall, Oxford (BA Hons Eng. Lit.). First professional stage appearance, The Browning Version, Birmingham Rep., 1985; London début, Les Parents Terribles, Orange Tree, Richmond, 1988; West End début, A Life in the Theatre, Haymarket, 1989; *theatre* includes: Hidden Laughter, Vaudeville, 1990; Royal National Theatre: The Sea, 1991; Arcadia, 1993; Antony and Cleopatra, 1998; Cain (Byron), Chichester, 1992; The Importance of Being Earnest, Manchester, 1993; Henry IV parts I & II, English Touring Th., 1996; Richard II, 2000, Hamlet, 2001, RSC; *television* includes: serials: Stanley and the Women, 1990; Over Here, 1995; Out of the Past, 1998; Hornblower, 1998; films: Frankie and Johnny, 1985; Voices in the Garden, 1991; A Breed of Heroes, 1995; Persuasion, 1995; Longitude, 2000; *films* include: Reunion, 1989; Howards End, 1991; Archipel (in French), 1992; Carrington, 1994; A Feast at Midnight, 1995; Jane Eyre, 1995; Stiff Upper Lips, 1996; The Ripper, 1997; Rupert's Land, 1997; Notting Hill, 1998; Pandaemonium, 1999; Iris, 2001; *radio* includes: more than thirty plays; regular reader for Poetry Please. Reciter and reader for concerts with orchs incl. Royal Opera, BBC SO and CBSO. Mem. Council, Equity, 1996–2000. *Recreations:* photography, travelling, poker, supporting Wimbledon FC. *Address:* c/o Peters Fraser & Dunlop, 503/4 The Chambers, Chelsea Harbour, SW10 0XF. *T:* (020) 7344 1010. *Clubs:* Groucho, Cobden.

WEST, Dr Stephanie Roberta, FBA 1990; Senior Research Fellow in Classics and Fellow Librarian, Hertford College, Oxford, since 1990; *b* 1 Dec. 1937; *d* of Robert Enoch Pickard and Ruth (*née* Batters); *m* 1960, Martin Litchfield West, *qv*; one *s* one *d*. *Educ:* Nottingham High Sch. for Girls; Somerville Coll., Oxford (1st cl. Classics Mods 1958, 1st cl. Lit. Hum. 1960; Gaisford Prize for Greek Verse Composition 1959; Ireland Scholar 1959, Derby Scholar 1960); MA 1963, DPhil 1964, Oxon. Oxford University: Mary Ewart Res. Fellow, Somerville Coll., 1965–67; Lecturer: in Classics, Hertford Coll., 1966–90; in Greek, Keble Coll., 1981–. Mem. Council, GPDST, 1974–87. *Publications:* The Ptolemaic Papyri of Homer, 1967; Omero, Odissea 1 (libri I–IV), 1981; (with A. Heubeck and J. B. Hainsworth) A commentary on Homer's Odyssey 1, 1988; articles and reviews in learned jls. *Recreations:* opera, curious information. *Address:* 42 Portland Road, Oxford OX2 7EY. *T:* (01865) 556060.

WEST, Dr Stephen Craig, FMedSci; FRS 1995; Principal Scientist, Imperial Cancer Research Fund, since 1989; *b* 11 April 1952; *s* of Joseph and Louise West; *m* 1985, Phyllis Fraenza. *Educ:* Univ. of Newcastle upon Tyne (BSc 1974; PhD 1977). Post-doctoral Research Associate: Univ. of Newcastle upon Tyne, 1977–78; Dept of Molecular Biophysics and Biochemistry, and Therapeutic Radiology, Yale Univ., 1978–83 (Res. Scientist, Dept of Therapeutic Radiology, 1983–85); Sen. Scientist, ICRF, 1985–89. Mem., EMBO, 1994–; FMedSci 2000. Hon. Prof., UCL, 1997–. *Publications:* numerous res. papers in biochem. and molecular biol. *Recreations:* squash, ski-ing, music. *Address:* Imperial Cancer Research Fund, Clare Hall Laboratories, South Mimms, Potters Bar, Herts EN6 3LD.

WEST, Prof. Thomas Summers, CBE 1988; FRS 1989; FRSE, FRSC; Director, Macaulay Institute for Soil Research, Aberdeen, 1975–87; Honorary Research Professor, University of Aberdeen, 1983–87, now Emeritus; *b* 18 Nov. 1927; *s* of late Thomas West and Mary Ann Summers; *m* 1952, Margaret Officer Lawson, MA; one *s* two *d*. *Educ:* Tarbat Old Public Sch., Portmahomack; Royal Acad., Tain; Aberdeen Univ. (BSc 1st Cl. Hons Chemistry, 1949); Univ. of Birmingham (PhD 1952, DSc 1962). FRSC (FRIC 1962); FRSE 1979. Univ. of Birmingham: Sen. DSIR Fellow, 1952–55; Lectr in Chem., 1955–63; Imperial Coll., London: Reader in Analytical Chem., 1963–65; Prof. of Analytical Chem., 1965–75. Royal Society: Mem., British National Cttee for Chem., and Chm., Analytical Sub-cttee, 1965–82; Mem., Internat. Cttee, 1990–92; Mem., Internat. Exchanges Cttee, 1992– (Chm. Panel III). Sec. Gen., IUPAC, 1983–91 (Pres., Analytical Div., 1977–79); Pres., Soc. for Analytical Chem., 1969–71; Chm., Finance Cttee, ICSU, 1990–92; Mem., British Nat. Cttee for IUPAC, RSC, 1990–98; Hon. Sec., Chemical Soc., 1972–75 (Redwood Lectr, 1974); Hon. Member: Bunseki Kagakukai (Japan), 1981; Fondation de la Maison de la Chimie (Paris), 1985. Meldola Medal, RIC, 1956; Instrumentation Medal, 1976, and Gold Medal, 1977, Chemical Soc.; Johannes Marcus Medal for Spectroscopy, Spectroscopic Soc. of Bohemia, 1977. *Publications:* Analytical Applications of Diamino ethane tetra acetic acid, 1958, 2nd edn 1961; New Methods of Analytical Chemistry, 1964; Complexometry with EDTA and Related Reagents, 1969. *Recreations:* gardening, motoring, reading, music, family history research. *Address:* 31 Baillieswells Drive, Bieldside, Aberdeen AB15 9AT. *T:* (01224) 868294; *e-mail:* ⟨tswest@dialstart.net⟩.

WEST, Timothy Lancaster, CBE 1984; actor and director; *b* 20 Oct. 1934; *s* of late Harry Lockwood West and Olive Carleton-Crowe; *m* 1st, 1956, Jacqueline Boyer (marr. diss.); one *d*; 2nd, 1963, Prunella Scales, *qv*; two *s*. *Educ:* John Lyon Sch., Harrow; Regent Street Polytechnic. Entered profession as asst stage manager, Wimbledon, 1956; first London appearance, Caught Napping, Piccadilly, 1959; Mem., RSC, 1964–66; Prospect Theatre Co., 1966–72: Dr Samuel Johnson, Prospero, Bolingbroke, young Mortimer in Edward II, King Lear, Emerson in A Room with a View, Alderman Smuggler in The Constant Couple, and Holofernes in Love's Labour's Lost; Otto in The Italian Girl, 1968; Gilles in Abelard and Heloise, 1970; Robert Hand in Exiles, 1970; Gilbert in The Critic as Artist, 1971; Sir William Gower in Trelawny (musical), Bristol, 1972; Falstaff in Henry IV Pts I and II, Bristol, 1973; Shpigelsky in A Month in the Country, Chichester, 1974 (London, 1975); Brack in Hedda Gabler, RSC, 1975; Iago in Othello, Nottingham, 1976; with Prospect Co.: Harry in Staircase, 1976, Claudius in Hamlet, storyteller in War Music, and Enobarbus in Antony and Cleopatra, 1977; Ivan and Gottlieb in Laughter, and Max in The Homecoming, 1978; with Old Vic Co.: Narrator in Lancelot and Guinevere, Shylock in The Merchant of Venice, 1980; Beecham, Apollo, 1980, NZ, 1983, Dublin, 1986; Uncle Vanya, Australia, 1982; Stalin in Master Class, Leicester, 1983, Old Vic, 1984; Charlie Mucklebrass in Big in Brazil, 1984; The War at Home, Hampstead, 1984; When We Are Married, Whitehall, 1986; The Sneeze, Aldwych, 1988; Bristol Old Vic: The Master Builder, 1989; The Clandestine Marriage, Uncle Vanya, 1990; James Tyrone, in

Long Day's Journey into Night, 1991, also at NT; Andrew in It's Ralph, Comedy, 1991; King Lear, Dublin, 1992; Willie Loman in Death of a Salesman, Theatr Clwyd, 1993; Christopher Cameron in Himself, Southampton, 1993; Sir Anthony Absolute in The Rivals, Chichester, 1994; Macbeth, Theatr Clwyd, 1994; Mail Order Bride, 1994, Getting On, 1995, W Yorks Playhouse; Twelve Angry Men, Comedy, 1996; Falstaff, in Henry IV Pts 1 and 2, Old Vic, 1997; Gloucester, in King Lear, RNT, 1997; The Birthday Party, Piccadilly, 1999; The Master Builder, tour, 1999; The External, tour, 2001; Luther, RNT, 2001. *Directed:* plays for Prospect Co., Open Space, Gardner Centre, Brighton, and rep. at Salisbury, Bristol, Northampton and Cheltenham; own season, The Forum, Billingham, 1973; Artistic Dir, Old Vic Co., 1980–81. *Television includes:* Edward VII, 1973; Hard Times, 1977; Crime and Punishment, 1979; Brass, 1982–84, 1990; The Last Bastion, 1984; The Nightingale Saga, Tender is the Night, 1985; The Monocled Mutineer, 1986; The Train, 1987; A Shadow on the Sun, 1988; The Gospels, Framed, 1992; Bramwell, 1998; Bedtime, 2001; *plays:* Richard II, 1969; Edward II, The Boswell and Johnson Show, 1970; Horatio Bottomley, 1972; Churchill and the Generals, 1979 (RTS Award); The Good Doctor Bodkin Adams, 1986; What the Butler Saw, Harry's Kingdom, When We Are Married, Breakthrough at Reykjavik, 1987; Strife, The Contractor, 1988; Blore, MP, Beecham, 1989; Survival of the Fittest, 1990; Bye Bye Columbus, 1991; Reith to the Nation, Smokescreen, 1993; Hiroshima, Eleven Men Against Eleven, Cuts, 1995; The Place of the Dead, 1996; King Lear, 1997; Midsomer Murders, 1999; Murder in Mind, 2000. *Films:* The Looking-Glass War, 1968; Nicholas and Alexandra, 1970; The Day of the Jackal, 1972; Hedda, 1975; Joseph Andrews, and The Devil's Advocate, 1976; William Morris, 1977; Agatha, and The 39 Steps, 1978; The Antagonists, 1980; Murder is Easy, and Oliver Twist, 1981; Cry Freedom, 1986; Consuming Passions, 1987; Ever After, 1997; Joan of Arc, 1998; Iris, 2001. Compiles and dir. recital progs; sound broadcaster. Chairman: All Change Arts Ltd, 1986–; LAMDA, 1992–. Pres., Soc. for Theatre Res., 1999–. FRSA 1992. DUniv Bradford, 1993; Hon. DLitt: West of England, 1994; East Anglia, 1996; Westminster, 1999. *Publications:* I'm Here, I Think, Where are You? (collected letters), 1994; A Moment Towards the End of the Play, 2001. *Recreations:* theatre history, travel, music, old railways. *Address:* c/o Gavin Barker Associates Ltd, 2D Wimpole Street, W1G 0EB. *Clubs:* Garrick, Groucho.

See also S. A. J. West.

WEST AFRICA, Archbishop of, since 1993; **Most Rev. Robert Garshong Allotey Okine;** Bishop of Koforidua-Ho, Ghana, since 1981; *b* 12 July 1937; *s* of late Robert Cudjoe Okine and Miriam Naadjah Decker; *m* 1967, Juliana Sakai (*née* Nerquaye-Tetteh); two *s* two *d*. *Educ:* Anglican Church schs, Gold Coast and Gambia; Methodist Boys' High Sch., Bathurst, The Gambia; Adisadel Coll., Cape Coast, Ghana; Theol Coll., SSM, Kelham (GOE 1964); Inst. of Pastoral Educn, London, Ont. (CertCPE 1972); Huron Coll., Univ. of W Ontario, Canada (BMin 1973); Vanderbilt Univ., Nashville, USA (MA 1975; EdS 1975). Ordained deacon 1964, priest 1965; Asst Curate, St Andrew's, Sekondi, 1964–66; Chaplain and teacher, Adisadel Coll., Cape Coast, 1966–68; Rector: St James, Agona-Swedru, 1968–69; Bishop Aglionby Meml Parish, Tamale, 1969–71; Assistant Priest: St Anne's, Byron, and St George's, London, Ont., Canada, 1971–73; Holy Trinity Episcopal Church, Nashville, USA, 1973–75; Christ Church Parish, Cape Coast, 1975–81; Headmaster, Acad. of Christ the King, 1976–81; Principal, St Nicholas Theol Coll., 1976–81; Archdeacon of Koforidua and Rector, St Peter's, Koforidua, Feb.–Oct. 1981. Hon. Canon, Cathedral Church of Most Holy Trinity, Accra, 1979–81. Chairman: Bd of Educn, Anglican Educn Unit; Human Resources Develt Desk, Jt Anglican Diocesan Council; Provincial Liturgical Commn. Gov., Adisadel Coll., 1987–. Patron, YMCA (Eastern), 1984–. Hon. DD W Ontario, 1982. *Recreations:* entertaining, watching good movies, listening to all brands of music. *Address:* Bishopslodge, PO Box 980, Koforidua, Ghana, West Africa. *T:* (81) 2329.

WEST CUMBERLAND, Archdeacon of; *see* Davis, Ven. A. N.

WEST HAM, Archdeacon of; *see* Fox, Ven. M. J.

WEST INDIES, Archbishop of, since 1998; **Most Rev. Drexel Wellington Gomez,** CMG 1994; Bishop of Nassau and the Bahamas, since 1995; *b* 1937; *m* Carrol Gomez; four *c*. *Educ:* Codrington Coll., Barbados (DipTh 1957); Durham Univ. (BA 1959). Ordained 1959; parochial work, Bahamas, 1962–64; Tutor, Codrington Coll., 1964–68; Sec. and Treas., dio. of Bahamas, 1970–72; Bishop of Barbados, 1972–93; Provincial Sec., Church in the Province of the West Indies, until 1999. *Address:* PO Box N-656, Nassau, Bahamas.

WEST-KNIGHTS, Laurence James; QC 2000; a Recorder, since 1999; *b* 30 July 1954; *o s* of late Major Jan James West-Knights and Amy Winifred West-Knights (*née* Gott); *m* 1st, 1979 (marr. diss. 1983); 2nd, 1992, Joanne Anita Florence Ecob; one *s* two *d*. *Educ:* Perse Sch., Cambridge; Hampton Sch.; Emmanuel Coll., Cambridge (MA 1976). FCIArb 1993. RNR, 1979–94 (Lt Comdr 1993, retd). Called to the Bar, Gray's Inn, 1977; W Circuit; in practice at the Bar, 1977–; Asst Recorder, 1994–99. Chm., Steering Cttee, IT Industry Enquiry into Govt IT Contracts, 2000; Member: IT Cttees, Bar Council, 1996–; Incorporated Council of Law Reporting, 1997–; IT and the Courts, 1998– (Mem., Civil Litigation Wkg Party, 1997–); Founder Mem., and Exec. Dir, British and Irish Legal Information Inst., 1999–. Jt Chm., Soc. for Computers and Law, 2001– (Mem. Council, 1995–). Lay Chm., PCC, Christ Church, Turnham Green, 1998–2001 (Mem., 1997–2001). Mem. Editl Bd, Jl of Judicial Studies Bd, 1997–2001. Writer, LawOnLine.cc legal web site, 1997–. *Publications:* (contrib.) Researching the Legal Web, 1997; (contrib.) Jordan's Civil Court Service, 1999–; numerous papers and articles on free access to the law via the Internet. *Recreations:* sailing, scuba diving, cricket, languages, family. *Address:* 4 Paper Buildings, Temple, EC4Y 7EX. *T:* (020) 7353 3366, *Fax:* (020) 7353 5778; *e-mail:* law@west-knights.com. *Clubs:* Whitefriars, Royal Naval Volunteer Reserve Yacht, Bar Yacht; Royal Solent Yacht, Surrey CC.

WEST-RUSSELL, His Honour Sir David (Sturrock), Kt 1986; President of Industrial Tribunals for England and Wales, 1984–91; *b* 17 July 1921; *o s* of late Sir Alexander West-Russell and late Agnes West-Russell (*née* Sturrock); *m* Christine (*née* Tyler); one *s* two *d*. *Educ:* Rugby; Pembroke Coll., Cambridge. Served war: Buffs, 1940; commissioned Queen's Own Cameron Highlanders, 1941; Parachute Regt, 1942–46; N Africa, Italy, France, Greece, Norway and Palestine (despatches, Major). Management Trainee, Guest Keen and Nettlefold, 1948–50; Harmsworth Law Scholar, 1952; called to Bar, Middle Temple, 1953, Bencher, 1986; SE Circuit; Dep. Chm., Inner London Quarter Sessions, 1966–72; Circuit Judge, 1972; Sen. Circuit Judge, Inner London Crown Court, 1979–82, Southwark Crown Court, 1983–84. Mem., Departmental Cttee on Legal Aid in Criminal Proceedings, 1964–65. Comr (NI Emergency Provisions Act), 1974–80; Chairman: Lord Chancellor's Adv. Cttee on Appts of Magistrates for Inner London, 1976–87; Home Sec's Adv. Bd on Restricted Patients, 1985–91; Inner London Probation Cttee, 1988–89 (Mem., 1979–89); Member: Lord Chancellor's Adv. Cttee on the Trng of Magistrates, 1980–85; Judicial Studies Bd, 1980–84, 1987–90; Parole Bd, 1980–82; Parole Review Cttee, 1987–88; Criminal Injuries Compensation Bd, 1991–95. Pres., Inner London Magistrates' Assoc., 1979–85; Jt Pres., Council of HM Circuit Judges, 1985. *Address:* Old Sarum Cottage, Teffont Magna, Salisbury, Wilts SP3 5QX. *Club:* Garrick.

WESTABY, Stephen, FRCS; Senior Cardiac Surgeon, John Radcliffe Hospital, since 1986; *b* 27 July 1948; *s* of Kenneth and Doreen Westaby; *m* 1st, 1974, Jane Elizabeth Axon (marr. diss. 1983); one *d*; 2nd, 1985, Sarah Catherine MacDougal; one *s*. *Educ:* Charing Cross Hosp. Med. Sch., Univ. of London (BSc Biochemistry 1969; MB BS 1972; MS 1986). FRCS 1986. Surgical training: Addenbrooke's Hosp., Hammersmith Hosp., RPMS, Hosp. for Sick Children, Great Ormond Street, Harefield Hosp., Middlesex Hosp., Univ. of Alabama; adult and paediatric surgeon; specialist surgeon in congenital heart disease, thoracic aortic surgery, valvular and coronary heart disease; pioneer in artificial heart technology; developed first artificial heart res. prog., UK; established Oxford Heart Centre, John Radcliffe Hosp., internat. teaching centre for valve and aortic surgery. Member: Soc. for Thoracic Surgery, USA, 1995; Amer. Assoc. for Thoracic Surgery, 1998; European Assoc. for Cardiothoracic Surgery, 1998. Editor, Jl of Circulatory Support. *Publications:* editor/joint author: Wound Care, 1985; Stentless Bioprosthesis, 1995, 2nd edn 1999; Landmarks in Cardiac Surgery, 1997; Surgery of Acquired Aortic Valve Disease, 1997; Principles and Practice of Critical Care, 1997; Trauma Pathogenesis and Treatment, 1998; Ischemic Heart Disease: surgical management, 1998; Cardiothoracic Trauma, 1999; 40 chapters in books, and over 200 scientific papers. *Recreations:* writing, shooting, breeding llamas. *Address:* Oxford Heart Centre, John Radcliffe Hospital, Headley Way, Headington, Oxford OX3 9DU. *T:* (01865) 220269, 220268; *e-mail:* swestaby@ahf.org.uk.

WESTBROOK, Eric Ernest, CB 1981; painter and writer; *b* 29 Sept. 1915; *s* of Ernest James and Helen Westbrook; *m* 1st, 1942, Ingrid Nyström; one *d*; 2nd, 1964, Dawn Sime (*d* 2001). *Educ:* Alleyn's Sch., Dulwich; various schools of art. Lecturer for Arts Council of Gt Britain, 1943; Director, Wakefield City Art Gallery, Yorks, 1946; Chief Exhibitions Officer, British Council, 1949; Director: Auckland City Art Gallery, NZ, 1952–55; National Gallery of Victoria, Melbourne, Aust., 1956–73; Director (Permanent Head), Ministry for the Arts, Victoria, 1973–80, retired. Hon. LLD Monash, 1974. Chevalier de l'Ordre des Arts et Lettres (France), 1972; Palmes Académiques, 1989. *Publications:* Birth of a Gallery, 1968; various articles and reviews in arts and museum pubns. *Recreations:* music, gardening. *Address:* Houghton Park, Odgers Road, Castlemaine, Vic 3450, Australia. *T:* (3) 54724171.

WESTBROOK, Michael John David, OBE 1988; composer, pianist and band-leader; *b* 21 March 1936; *s* of Philip Beckford Westbrook and Vera Agnes (*née* Butler); *m* 1976, Katherine Jane (*née* Duckham), singer, songwriter and painter; one *s* one *d* of previous marriage. *Educ:* Kelly Coll., Tavistock; Plymouth Coll. of Art (NDD); Hornsey Coll. of Art (ATD). Formed first band at Plymouth Art Sch., 1958; moved to London, 1962, and has since led a succession of groups incl. The Mike Westbrook Brass Band, formed with Phil Minton in 1973, The Mike Westbrook Orch., 1974–, Westbrook Trio (with Kate Westbrook and Chris Biscoe), formed in 1982, Kate Westbrook Mike Westbrook Duo, 1995–, and Westbrook & Company, 1998–. Has toured extensively in Britain and Europe, and performed in Australia, Canada, NY, Singapore and Hong Kong. Has written commissioned works for fests in Britain, France and other European countries, composed music for theatre, radio, TV and films, and made numerous LPs. Principal compositions/recordings include: Marching Song, 1967; Metropolis, 1969; Tyger: a celebration of William Blake (with Adrian Mitchell), 1971, also The Westbrook Blake, 1980 and Glad Day, 1999; Citadel/Room 315, 1974; On Duke's Birthday (dedicated to the memory of Duke Ellington), 1984; Off Abbey Road, 1988; Bean Rows and Blues Shots (saxophone concerto), 1991; Coming Through Slaughter (opera), 1994; Bar Utopia (lyrics by Helen Simpson), 1995; Blues for Terenzi, 1995; Cable Street Blues, 1997; The Orchestra of Smith's Academy, 1998; Classical Blues, 2001; TV scores incl. Caught on a Train, 1983; film scores: Moulin Rouge, 1990; Camera Makes Whoopee, 1996; with Kate Westbrook: concert works incorporating European poetry and folk song, notably The Cortège, for voices and jazz orch., 1979, and London Bridge is Broken Down, for voice, jazz orch. and chamber orch., 1987; also a succession of music-theatre pieces, including: Mama Chicago, 1978; Westbrook-Rossini, 1984; The Ass (based on poem by D. H. Lawrence), 1985; Pier Rides, 1986; Quichotte (opera), 1989; Goodbye Peter Lorre, 1991; Measure for Measure, 1992; Good Friday 1663 (TV opera), 1994; Stage Set, 1996; Love Or Infatuation, 1997; Platterback, 1998; Jago (opera), 2000. *Recreation:* walking by the Erme Estuary. *Address:* Brent House, Holbeton, near Plymouth, Devon PL8 1LX.

WESTBROOK, Sir Neil (Gowanloch), Kt 1988; CBE 1981; Chairman and Managing Director, Central Manchester Holdings Ltd, since 1960; Chairman, Trafford Park Estates PLC, 1963–98; *b* 21 Jan. 1917; *s* of Frank and Dorothy Westbrook; *m* 1945, Hon. Mary Joan Fraser, *o d* of 1st Baron Strathalmond, CBE; one *s* one *d*. *Educ:* Oundle Sch.; Clare Coll., Cambridge (MA). FRICS. Served War of 1939–45: Sapper, 1939; Actg Lt-Col 1945 (despatches). Chm., NW Industrial Council, 1982–87; Member: Council, CBI North West Region, 1982–88 (Chairman: NW Inner Cities Studies Gp, 1985; NW Working Party on Derelict Land Clearance, 1986); Inst. of Directors Greater Manchester Branch Cttee, 1972–86. Treas., Manchester Conservative Assoc., 1964–73, Dep. Chm., 1973–74, Chm., 1974–83; Chairman: Greater Manchester Co-ordinating Cttee, NW Area Cons. Assoc., 1977–86; Exchange Div. Cons. Assoc., 1973; Manchester Euro South Cons. Assoc., 1978–84; Member: NW Area F and GP Cttee, Cons. Party, 1974–87; Nat. Union Exec. Cttee, 1975–81; Cons. Bd of Finance, 1984–87. Mem., Manchester City Council, 1949–71; Dep. Leader 1967–69; Lord Mayor 1969–70. Chm., North Western Art Galleries and Museums Service, 1965–68; Mem., Exec. Cttee, Museums Assoc., 1965–69. Pres., Central Manchester Br., Arthritis and Rheumatism Council, 1970. Member: Duke of Edinburgh's Award Scheme Cttee, Manchester Area, 1972–75; Bd, Manchester YMCA, 1960–73. Mem., Chartered Auctioneers & Estate Agents Agricl Cttee, 1949–70; Mem., ABCC Rating Cttee, 1971–74. *Recreations:* football, fishing, horse racing. *Address:* c/o Central Manchester Holdings, Castle Hill, Prestbury, Cheshire SK10 4AR. *Clubs:* Carlton; Manchester Tennis and Racquets.

WESTBROOK, Roger, CMG 1990; HM Diplomatic Service, retired; Chairman, Spencer House, since 2000; *b* 26 May 1941; *e s* of Edward George Westbrook and Beatrice Minnie Westbrook (*née* Marshall). *Educ:* Dulwich Coll.; Hertford Coll., Oxford (MA Modern History). Foreign Office, 1964; Asst Private Sec. to Chancellor of Duchy of Lancaster and Minister of State, FO, 1965; Yaoundé, 1967; Rio de Janeiro, 1971; Brasilia, 1972; Private Sec. to Minister of State, FCO, 1975; Head of Chancery, Lisbon, 1977; Dep. Head, News Dept, FCO, 1980; Dep. Head, Falkland Is Dept, FCO, 1982; Overseas Inspectorate, FCO, 1984; High Comr, Negara Brunei Darussalam, 1986–91; Ambassador to Zaire, 1991–92; High Comr, Tanzania, 1992–95; Ambassador to Portugal, 1995–99. UK Comr, EXPO 98, Lisbon. Chm., Anglo-Portuguese Soc., 2000–. *Recreations:* doodling, sightseeing, theatre, reading, dining. *Address:* 33 Marsham Court, Marsham Street, SW1P 4JY.

WESTBURY, 5th Baron *cr* 1861; **David Alan Bethell,** CBE 1994; MC 1942; DL; *b* 16 July 1922; *s* of Captain The Hon. Richard Bethell (*d* 1929; *o c* of 3rd Baron); *S* brother, 1961; *m* 1947, Ursula Mary Rose James, CBE; two *s* one *d*. *Educ:* Harrow. 2nd Lieut 1940, Capt. 1944, Scots Guards. Equerry to the Duke of Gloucester, 1946–49. DL N Yorks, formerly NR Yorks, 1973. GCStJ 1988 (KStJ 1977). *Heir:* *s* Hon. Richard Nicholas

Bethell, MBE 1979 [*b* 29 May 1950; *m* 1st, 1975; one *s* two *d*; 2nd, 1993, Charlotte Sarah-Jane, *d* of Jack Gore. *Educ:* Harrow; RMA Sandhurst. Major Scots Guards, retired]. *Address:* Grange Cottage, Thirlby, Thirsk, N Yorks YO7 2DT. *T:* (01845) 597161.

WESTBURY, Prof. Gerald, OBE 1990; FRCP, FRCS; Professor of Surgery, 1982–89, now Professor Emeritus, and Dean, 1986–92, Institute of Cancer Research; Hon. Consultant Surgeon, Royal Marsden Hospital, 1982–89; *b* 29 July 1927; *s* of Lew and Celia Westbury; *m* 1965, Hazel Frame; three *d. Educ:* St Marylebone Grammar Sch.; Westminster Med. Sch., Univ. of London (MB, BS (Hons) 1949); FRCS 1952; FRCP 1976. House Surg., Westminster and Royal Northern Hosps, 1949–50; RAF Med. Service, 1950–52; RSO, Brompton Hosp., 1952–53; Registrar and Sen. Registrar, Westminster Hosp., 1953–60; Fellow in Surgery, Harvard Med. Sch., 1957; Cons. Surg., Westminster Hosp., 1960–82 (Hon. Cons. Surgeon, 1982–89); Hon. Cons. in Surgery to the Army, 1980–89. Pres., British Assoc. of Surgical Oncology, 1989–92. Examiner, Univs of London, Edinburgh, Cambridge, Hong Kong; Hunterian Prof., RCS, 1963; Honyman Gillespie Lectr, Univ. of Edinburgh, 1965; Semon Lectr and Haddow Lectr, RSM, 1982; Gordon-Taylor Lectr, RCS, 1989. Fellow, Inst. of Cancer Res., 2000; Hon. FRCSE, 1993. Walker Prize, RCS, 1990. *Publications:* medical articles and contribs to text books. *Recreations:* music, bird watching. *Club:* Athenæum.

WESTCOTT, Prof. John Hugh, DSc(Eng), PhD, DIC; FRS 1983; FREng; FCGI, FInstD; Emeritus Professor of Control Systems, and Senior Research Fellow, Imperial College of Science and Technology; Chairman, Feedback plc, 1958–99; *b* 3 Nov. 1920; *s* of John Stanley Westcott and Margaret Elisabeth Westcott (*née* Bass); *m* 1950, Helen Fay Morgan; two *s* one *d. Educ:* Wandsworth Sch.; City and Guilds Coll., London; Massachusetts Inst. of Technology. Royal Commission for the Exhibition of 1851 Senior Studentship; Apprenticeship BTH Co., Rugby. Radar Research and Develt Estabt, 1941–45; Lectr, Imperial Coll., 1950; Reader, 1956; Prof., 1961; Head of Computing and Control Dept, 1970–79. Control Commn for Germany, 1945–46. Consultant to: Bataafsche Petroleum Maatschappij (Shell), The Hague, Holland, 1953–58; AEI, 1955–69; ICI, 1965–69; George Wimpey & Son, 1975–80; Westland plc, 1983–85. Chm., Control and Automation Div., Instn of Electrical Engrs, 1968–69. Mem., Exec. Council of Internat. Fedn of Automatic Control, 1969–75; Chm., United Kingdom Automation Council, 1973–79; Pres., Inst. of Measurement and Control, 1979–80. Mem., Adv. Council, RMCS, 1986–; Governor, Kingston Polytechnic, 1974–80. FREng (FEng 1980). Hon. FIEE; Hon. FInstMC. *Publications:* An Exposition of Adaptive Control, 1962; monographs and papers, mainly on Control Systems and related topics. *Recreations:* gardening, reading. *Address:* (home) 8 Fernhill, Oxshott, Surrey KT22 0JH; Department of Electrical Engineering, Imperial College, SW7 2BT. *T:* (020) 7594 6240.

See also N. J. Westcott.

WESTCOTT, Dr Nicholas James, CMG 1999; HM Diplomatic Service; Minister-Counsellor (Trade and Transport), Washington, since 1999; *b* 20 July 1956; *s* of Prof. John Hugh Westcott and Helen Fay Westcott (*née* Morgan); *m* 1989, Miriam Pearson; one *s* one *d. Educ:* Epsom Coll.; Sidney Sussex Coll., Cambridge (MA; PhD History 1982). Entered Foreign and Commonwealth Office, 1982; on secondment to EC, 1984–85; UK Perm. Rep. to EC, Brussels, 1985–89; FCO, 1989–93; Head of Common Foreign and Security Policy Unit, 1992–93; Dep. High Comr, Dar es Salaam, 1993–96; Head of Economic Relations Dept, FCO, 1996–98. *Publications:* (contrib.) Africa and the Second World War, 1986; (with P. Kingston and R. G. Tiedemann) Managed Economies in World War II, 1991; articles in jls. *Recreations:* walking, reading, music. *Address:* Foreign and Commonwealth Office, King Charles Street, SW1A 2AH.

WESTENRA, family name of **Baron Rossmore**.

WESTHEIMER, Prof. Gerald, FRS 1985; Professor of Neurobiology, University of California, Berkeley, since 1989 (Professor of Physiology, 1967–89; Head of Division of Neurobiology, 1989–92); *b* Berlin, 13 May 1924; *s* of late Isaac Westheimer and Ilse Westheimer (*née* Cohn). *Educ:* Sydney Tech. Coll. (Optometry dip. 1943, Fellowship dip. 1949); Univ. of Sydney (BSc 1947); Ohio State Univ. (PhD 1953); postdoctoral training at Marine Biol. Lab., Woods Hole, 1957 and at Physiolog. Lab., Cambridge, 1958–59. Australian citizen, 1945; practising optometrist, Sydney, 1945–51; faculties of Optometry Schools: Univ. of Houston, 1953–54; Ohio State Univ., 1954–60; Univ. of California, Berkeley, 1960–67. Associate: Bosch Vision Res. Center, Salk Inst., 1984–92; Neurosciences Res. Program, NY, 1985–95; Chairman: Visual Scis Study Sect., NIH, 1977–79; Bd of Scientific Counsellors, Nat. Eye Inst., 1981–83; Bd of Editors, Vision Research, 1986–91; service on numerous professional cttees. Adjunct Prof., Rockefeller Univ., NY, 1992–. Fellow or Member, scientific socs, UK and overseas; Fellow, Amer. Acad. of Arts and Scis. Lectures: Sackler, in Med. Sci., Tel Aviv Univ., 1989; Perception, Eur. Conf. on Visual Perception, 1989; D. O. Hebb, McGill Univ., Canada, 1991; Ferrier, Royal Soc., 1992; Wertheimer, Frankfurt Univ., 1998. Hon. DSc: New South Wales, 1988; SUNY, 1990. Tillyer Medal, Optical Soc. of America, 1978; Proctor Medal, Assoc. for Res. in Vision and Ophthalmology, 1979; von Sallmann Prize, Coll. of Physicians and Surgeons, Columbia Univ., 1986; Prentice Medal, Amer. Acad. of Optometry, 1986; Bicentennial Medal, Aust. Optometric Assoc., 1988. *Publications:* research articles in sci. and professional optometric and ophth. jls; edtl work for sci. jls. *Recreations:* chamber music (violin), foundation and history of sensory physiology. *Address:* 582 Santa Barbara Road, Berkeley, CA 94707, USA; *e-mail:* gwest@socrates.berkeley.edu. *Club:* Cosmos (Washington).

WESTLAKE, Peter Alan Grant, CMG 1972; MC 1943; *b* 2 Feb. 1919; *s* of A. R. C. Westlake, CSI, CIE, and late Dorothy Louise (*née* Turner); *m* 1943, Katherine Spackman (*d* 1990); two *s. Educ:* Sherborne; Corpus Christi Coll., Oxford; Military College of Science. Served with 1st Regt RHA (Adjt 1942), and on the staff (despatches). HM Foreign Service (now Diplomatic Service), 1946–76: served in Japan and at Foreign Office; Joint Services Staff College, 1954; Israel, 1955; Japan, 1957; Administrative Staff Coll., 1961; Counsellor: Foreign Office, 1961; Washington, 1965; British High Commn, Canberra, 1967–71; Minister, Tokyo, 1971–76. Pres., Asiatic Soc. of Japan, 1972–74. UK Comr-General, Internat. Ocean Expo, Okinawa, 1975. BD Wales 1981, MSc Wales, 1981; Deacon, Church in Wales, 1981, priest 1982. FRAS. Order of the Rising Sun, Japan. *Publications:* The Proud Walkers, 1992; Holy Island, 1992; Equations of motion for the Earth's crust, 1993; The Troy Game, 1995; Atlas for the ascent of Pan, 1998; Winter-Fire-Shed, 2000. *Address:* 53 Church Street, Beaumaris, Anglesey LL58 8AB.

WESTLEY, Stuart Alker, MA; Master of Haileybury, since 1996; *b* 21 March 1947; *s* of Arthur Bancroft Westley and Gladys Westley; *m* 1979, Mary Louise Weston; one *d. Educ:* Lancaster Royal GS; Corpus Christi Coll., Oxford (BA 1969; MA 1972). Professional cricketer, 1969–71; Mathematics Teacher, King Edward VII Sch., Lytham, 1969–72; Housemaster and Dir of Studies, Framlingham Coll., 1973–84; Dep. Headmaster, Bristol Cathedral Sch., 1984–89; Principal, King William's Coll., IOM, 1989–96. *Recreations:* golf, fly fishing, gardening, architecture, choral and classical music, computers. *Address:* The Master's Lodge, Haileybury, Hertford SG13 7NG. *T:* (01992) 706222. *Club:* East India, Devonshire, Sports and Public Schools.

WESTMACOTT, Peter John, CMG 2000; LVO 1993; HM Diplomatic Service; Ambassador to Turkey, since 2002; *b* 23 Dec. 1950; *s* of Prebendary Ian Field Westmacott and Rosemary Patricia Spencer Westmacott; *m* 1972, Angela Margaret Lugg (marr. diss. 1999); two *s* one *d. Educ:* Taunton Sch.; New Coll., Oxford (MA). Entered FCO 1972; served Tehran 1974, Brussels, 1978; First Sec., Paris, 1980; Private Sec. to Minister of State, FCO, 1984; Head of Chancery, Ankara, 1987; Dep. Private Sec. to Prince of Wales, 1990; Counsellor, Washington, 1993; Dir, Americas, FCO, 1997; Dep. Under-Sec. of State, FCO, 2000–01. *Recreations:* tennis, ski-ing. *Address:* c/o Foreign and Commonwealth Office, SW1A 2AH.

WESTMACOTT, Richard Kelso; Chairman, Country Gardens plc, since 1998; *b* 20 Feb. 1934; *s* of Comdr John Rowe Westmacott, RN and Ruth Pharazyn; *m* 1965, Karen Husbands; one *s* one *d. Educ:* Eton College. Royal Navy, 1952–54. Hoare & Co., 1955; Mem., Stock Exchange, 1960; Chairman: Hoare Govett Ltd, 1975–90; Security Pacific Hoare Govett (Holdings) Ltd, 1985–90; Dep. Chm., Maritime Trust, 1992–99. Dir, Prudential-Bache Internat. Bank Ltd, 1996–. Master, Mercers' Co., 1998–99; Younger Brother, Trinity House, 2000–. *Recreations:* sailing, shooting. *Address:* 9 Alexander Square, SW3 2AY. *Clubs:* White's; Royal Yacht Squadron.

WESTMEATH, 13th Earl of, *cr* 1621; **William Anthony Nugent;** Baron Delvin, by tenure temp. Henry II; by summons, 1486; Senior Master, St Andrew's School, Pangbourne, 1980–88; *b* 21 Nov. 1928; *s* of 12th Earl of Westmeath and Doris (*d* 1968), 2nd *d* of C. Imlach, Liverpool; *S* father, 1971; *m* 1963, Susanna Margaret, *o d* of J. C. B. W. Leonard, *qv*; two *s. Educ:* Marlborough Coll. Captain, RA, retired. Staff of St Andrew's Sch., Pangbourne, 1961–88. *Heir: s* Hon. Sean Charles Weston Nugent, *b* 16 Feb. 1965. *Address:* Farthings, Rotten Row Hill, Bradfield, Berks RG7 6LL. *T:* (0118) 974 4426.

WESTMINSTER, 6th Duke of, *cr* 1874; **Gerald Cavendish Grosvenor,** OBE 1995; TD 1994; DL; Bt 1622; Baron Grosvenor, 1761; Earl Grosvenor and Viscount Belgrave, 1784; Marquess of Westminster, 1831; *b* 22 Dec. 1951; *s* of 5th Duke of Westminster, TD, and Viola Maud (*d* 1987), *d* of 9th Viscount Cobham, KCB, TD; *S* father, 1979; *m* 1978, Natalia, *d* of Lt-Col H. P. J. Phillips; one *s* three *d. Educ:* Harrow. Commnd Queen's Own Yeomanry, RAC, TA, 1973; Captain, 1979; Major, 1985; Lt-Col, 1992; Comd, 1993–95; Col, 1995–97; Dep. Comdr, 143 W Midlands Bde, 1997–99; Brig., TA HQ AG, 2000–. Director: Internat. Students Trust, 1976–93; Claridges Hotel Ltd, 1981–93; Marcher Sound Ltd, 1982–97; Grosvenor Estate Hldgs, 1989–; Westminster Christmas Appeal Trust Ltd, 1989–94; NW Business Leadership Team Ltd, 1990–97; BITC, 1991–95; Manchester Olympic Games Co-ordinating Cttee Ltd, 1991–94. Governor: Royal Agricl Soc. of England; Chester Teacher Training Coll., 1979; Pro-Chancellor, Univ. of Keele, 1986–93; Chancellor, Manchester Metropolitan Univ., 1993–. President: NW Industrialists' Council, 1979–93; Chester City Conservative Assoc., 1977–93; RNIB, 1986–; Arthritis Care, 1987–; Spastics Soc., 1985–; Game Conservancy; London Fedn of Boys' Clubs; Abbeyfield Soc., 1989–; Nat. Kidney Res. Fund; Drug and Alcohol Foundn; BLESMA, 1992–; Manchester Commonwealth Games; Vice-Pres., RBL, 1993–. Member, Committee: Rural Target Team, Business in the Community; N Amer. Adv. Gp, BOTB; Nat. Army Mus.; Prince's Youth Business Trust; US Inf. Agency; Winston Churchill Meml Trust; Chm., RICS Foundn, 2000–. Patron: Worcs CCC (Pres., 1984–86); British Holstein Soc.; British Kidney Patients Assoc.; Dyslexia Inst., 1989–98. Trustee: TSB Foundn for England and Wales; Grosvenor Estate; Westminster Abbey Trust; Westminster Foundn; Westminster Housing Trust. Freeman: Chester, 1973; England, 1979; City of London, 1980. Liveryman: GAPAN; Gunmakers' Co.; Weavers' Co.; Armourers and Braziers' Co.; Marketors' Co.; Goldsmiths' Co.; Fishmongers' Co. DL Cheshire, 1982. FRSA; FRAS; FCIM; FCIOB; Fellow, Liverpool John Moores Univ., 1990. Hon. MRICS; Hon. Fellow, Univ. of Central Lancs, 2001. Hon. LLD Liverpool, 2000; Hon. DLitt Salford, 2000. Hon. Colonel: 7 Regt AAC, 1993–; Northumbrian Univs OTC; Royal Mercian and Lancastrian Yeomanry, 2001–; Col in Chief, Royal Westminster Regt. KStJ 1991. *Recreations:* shooting, fishing, scuba diving. *Heir: s* Earl Grosvenor, *qv. Address:* Eaton Hall, Chester, Cheshire CH4 9EJ. *Clubs:* Brooks's, Cavalry, MCC; Royal Yacht Squadron.

See also Lady J. M. Dawnay.

WESTMINSTER, Archbishop of, (RC), since 2000; **His Eminence Cardinal Cormac Murphy-O'Connor;** *b* 24 Aug. 1932; *s* of late Dr P. G. Murphy-O'Connor and Ellen (*née* Cuddigan). *Educ:* Prior Park Coll., Bath; English Coll., Rome; Gregorian Univ. PhL, STL. Ordained Priest, 1956. Asst Priest, Portsmouth and Fareham, 1956–66; Sec. to Bp of Portsmouth, 1966–70; Parish Priest, Parish of the Immaculate Conception, Southampton, 1970–71; Rector, English College, Rome, 1971–77; Bishop of Arundel and Brighton, 1977–2000. Cardinal, 2001. Chairman: Bishops' Cttee for Europe, 1978–83; Cttee for Christian Unity, 1983–2000; Dept for Mission and Unity, Bishops' Conf. of England and Wales, 1993–; Jt Chm., ARCIC-II, 1983–2000; Pres., Catholic Bps' Conf. of England and Wales, 2000–. Member: Congregation for the Sacraments and Divine Worship, 2001–; Admin of Patrimony of Holy See, 2001; Council for Study of Orgnl and Econ. Problems of the Holy See, 2001–. DD Lambeth, 1999. *Recreations:* music, sport. *Address:* Archbishop's House, Westminster, SW1P 1QJ.

WESTMINSTER, Auxiliary Bishops of, (RC); *see* O'Brien, Rt Rev. J. J., Roche, Rt Rev. A., and Stack, Rt Rev. G.

WESTMINSTER, Dean of; *see* Carr, Very Rev. A. W.

WESTMORLAND, 16th Earl of, *cr* 1624; **Anthony David Francis Henry Fane;** Baron Burghersh, 1624; Director, Phillips Auctioneers, since 1997; *b* 1 Aug. 1951; *s* of 15th Earl of Westmorland, GCVO and of Jane, *d* of Lt-Col Sir Roland Lewis Findlay, 3rd Bt; *S* father, 1993; *m* 1985, Caroline Eldred, *d* of Keon Hughes; one *d. Educ:* Eton. Mem., Orbitex North Pole Expedn, 1990. Life Pres., St Moritz Sporting Club. *Heir: b* Hon. Harry St Clair Fane [*b* 19 March 1953; *m* 1984, Tessa, *d* of Captain Michael Philip Forsyth-Forrest; one *s* one *d*]. *Address:* London SW10. *Club:* Turf.

WESTMORLAND AND FURNESS, Archdeacon of; *see* Howe, Ven. G. A.

WESTON, Bryan Henry; Chairman: Manweb plc (formerly Merseyside and North Wales Electricity Board), 1985–94; The National Grid Holding, 1991–93; *b* 9 April 1930; *s* of Henry James Weston and Rose Grace Weston; *m* 1956, Heather West; two *s* two *d. Educ:* St George Grammar School, Bristol; Bristol, Rutherford and Oxford Technical Colleges. CEng, FIEE; CIMgt. South Western Electricity Board: Commercial Manager, 1973–75; Bd Mem., 1975; Exec. Mem., 1975–77; Dep. Chm., Yorkshire Electricity Bd, 1977–85. *Recreations:* caravanning, walking, gardening. *Address:* Fountainhead Cottage, Brassey Green, near Tarporley, Cheshire CW6 9UG. *T:* (01829) 733523.

WESTON, Christopher John; Life President, Phillips Son & Neale (Chairman and Chief Executive, 1972–98); Chairman and Chief Executive Officer, Plaxbury Group, since 1998; *b* 3 March 1937; *s* of Eric Tudor Weston and Evelyn Nellie Weston; *m* 1969, Josephine Annabel Moir; one *d. Educ:* Lancing Coll. FIA (Scot.). Director: Phillips,

1964–98; Foreign and Colonial Pacific Investment Trust, 1984–99; Hodder Headline Plc (formerly Headline Book Publishing PLC), 1986–99 (Chm., 1997–99); Foreign & Colonial Enterprise Trust plc, 1987–99; Chm., Bradford Peters (Holdings) Ltd, 1977–. Chm., Council, Quit-Soc. of Non Smokers, 1993–. Liveryman, Painters-Stainers' Co. FRSA (Mem. Council, 1985). *Recreations:* theatre, music. *Address:* 5 Hillside Close, Carlton Hill, NW8 0EF. *T:* (020) 7372 5042. *Club:* Oriental.

WESTON, Rev. Canon David Wilfrid Valentine, PhD; Residentiary Canon of Carlisle Cathedral, since 1994; Canon Librarian, since 1995; *b* 8 Dec. 1937; *s* of Rev. William Valentine Weston and Mrs Gertrude Hamilton Weston; *m* 1984, Helen Strachan Macdonald, *d* of James and Barbara Macdonald; two *s*. *Educ:* St Edmund's Sch., Canterbury; Lancaster Univ. (PhD 1993). Entered Nashdom Abbey, 1960; deacon, 1967, priest, 1968; Novice Master, 1969–74; Prior, 1971–74; Abbot, 1974–84; Curate, St Peter's, Chorley, 1984–85; Vicar, St John the Baptist, Pilling, 1985–89; Domestic Chaplain to Bishop of Carlisle, 1989–94. Chm., Carlisle Tourism Forum, 1996–98. Freeman, City of London; Liveryman of Salters' Co. *Publication:* Carlisle Cathedral History, 2000. *Address:* 3 The Abbey, Carlisle, Cumbria CA3 8TZ.

See also Bishop Suffragan of Knaresborough.

WESTON, Rt Rev. Frank Valentine; *see* Knaresborough, Bishop Suffragan of.

WESTON, Galen; *see* Weston, W. G.

WESTON, Garfield Howard, (Garry); Chairman: Associated British Foods plc, 1967–2000 (Chief Executive, 1969–99); Fortnum and Mason, 1979–2000; Wittington Investments Ltd UK, 1979–2000; British Sugar PLC, 1991–2000; *b* 28 April 1927; *s* of late Willard Garfield Weston and Reta Lila Howard; *m* 1959, Mary Ruth, *d* of late Major-Gen. Sir Howard Kippenberger; three *s* three *d*. *Educ:* Sir William Borlase School, Marlow; New College, Oxford; Harvard University (Economics). Managing Director: Ryvita Co. Ltd, UK, 1951–54; Weston Biscuit Co., Aust., 1954–67; Vice-Chm., Associated British Foods Ltd, 1960; Chm., George Weston Holdings Ltd, 1978. *Recreations:* gardening, tennis, walking. *Address:* Weston Centre, Bowater House, 68 Knightsbridge, SW1X 7LQ. *T:* (020) 7589 6363.

WESTON, Hon. Hilary Mary; Lieutenant Governor of Ontario, since 1997; *b* 12 Jan. 1942; *d* of Michael Frayne and Noel Elizabeth Guerrini; *m* 1966, Willard Galen Weston, *qv*; one *s* one *d*. *Educ:* Loretto Abbey, Dalkey. Dep. Chm., Holt, Renfrew & Co., 1986–96; Design Dir, Windsor, Florida, 1988–96. Founder, Ireland Fund of Canada, 1979. Hon. DLittS Univ. of St Michael's Coll., Toronto, 1997; Hon. LLD: Western Ontario, 1997; UC of Cape Breton, 1999; Toronto, 2000. DStJ 1997. *Publications:* (jtly) In a Canadian Garden, 1989; (jtly) At Home in Canada, 1995. *Recreations:* tennis, riding. *Address:* Queen's Park, Toronto, ON M7A 1A1, Canada. *T:* (416) 3257780; Fort Belvedere, Ascot, Berks SL5 7SD. *Clubs:* Toronto, York, National, Granite, Royal Canadian Yacht (Toronto).

WESTON, Sir John; *see* Weston, Sir P. J.

WESTON, John Pix, BSc(Eng), BSc(Econ); CEng, FIEE; investment consultant, since 1984; *b* 3 Jan. 1920; *s* of John Pix Weston and Margaret Elizabeth (*née* Cox); *m* 1948, Ivy (*née* Glover); three *s*. *Educ:* King Edward's Sch., Birmingham, 1931–36; Univ. of Aston, 1946–50 (BSc(Eng), Hons); Univ. of London (LSE), 1954–57 (BSc(Econ), Hons). CEng 1953, FIEE 1966; FSS 1958; FREconS 1958; FIMgt (FBIM 1977). Mil. Service, 1939–46, S Africa and Albania. City of Birmingham: Police Dept, 1936–39; Electricity Supply Dept, 1939–48; Midlands Electricity Bd, 1948–50; English Electricity Co., 1950–51; NW Elec. Bd, 1951–58; Eastern Elec. Bd, 1958–60; Dep. Operating Man., Jamaica Public Services Co., 1960–61; Principal Asst Engr, Midlands Elec. Bd, 1961–64; Asst Ch. Commercial Officer, S of Scotland Elec. Bd, 1964–66; Sen. Econ. Adviser to Mrs Barbara Castle, MoT, 1966–69; Sen. Econ. and Chartered Engr, IBRD, 1968–70; Michelin Tyre Co., France, 1970–72; Dir of Post Experience Courses, Open Univ., 1972–75; Dir Gen., RoSPA, 1975–77; Gen. Sec., Birmingham Anglers' Assoc., 1977; Industrial Develt Officer, Argyll and Bute, 1977–79; Health, Safety and Welfare Officer, Newcastle Polytechnic, and Central Safety Advr, Northants CC, 1979; Chief Admin. Officer and Clerk to Governors, W Bromwich Coll. of Comm. and Tech., 1979–85. Hon. Sec. and Treasurer, Assoc. of Coll. Registrars and Administrators (W Midlands), 1982–85. Council Mem., Midlands Counties Photographic Fedn, 1984–86; Hon. Prog., Competition and Outings Sec. and Council Mem., Birmingham Photographic Soc., 1981–86; MIES 1963; Mem., Assoc. of Public Lighting Engrs, 1962. Chm., Upper Marlbrook Residents' Assoc., 1982–87; Treasurer, Laugharne Cons. Assoc., 1991–94 (Asst Treasurer, 1990–91). Member: Narbeth and Dist Probus Club, 1988–96; St Clears Probus Club, 1989–96 (Pres., 1990–91); Tenby Probus Club, 1990–96. Page Prize, IEE, 1950; Rosebery Prize, Univ. of London, 1957. SBStJ 1962. *Publications:* papers, reports and other contribs on electricity, highways, educn (espec. function and progress of the Open University), safety, etc, to public bodies, congresses and conferences, UK and abroad. *Recreations:* cine photography, gardening, swimming, fell walking. *Address:* Brook Mill & Woodside, Brook, Pendine, Carmarthenshire SA33 4NX. *T:* (01994) 427477. *Clubs:* Farmers', St John House; Birmingham Press.

See also J. P. Weston.

WESTON, John Pix, CBE 1994; FRAeS; FREng; Director, since 1994, Chief Executive, since 1998, BAE SYSTEMS (formerly British Aerospace) plc (Group Managing Director, 1996–98); *b* 16 Aug. 1951; *s* of John Pix Weston, *qv* and Ivy (*née* Glover); *m* 1974, Susan West; one *s* one *d*. *Educ:* King's Sch., Worcester; Trinity Hall., Cambridge (MA Eng.). CEng 1992; FRAeS 1992. British Aerospace: undergrad. apprenticeship, 1970–74; sales appts on Jaguar and Tornado projects, 1974–82; on secondment to MoD Sales Orgn, 1982–85; Military Aircraft Division, Warton: ME Sales Manager, Project Manager, Al Yamamah Project and Exec. Dir, Saudi Ops, 1985–89; Dir, 1989–92; Man. Dir, 1990–92; Chm. and Man. Dir, British Aerospace Defence Ltd, 1992–96. Mem., Prime Minister's Council for Science and Technol., 2000–. Mem., President's Cttee, 2000–, Chm., Europe Cttee, 2001–, CBI; Vice-Pres., RUSI, 2000–. FREng 2000; FRSA. *Recreations:* ski-ing, photography, hill-walking. *Address:* BAE SYSTEMS plc, Stirling Square, 6 Carlton Gardens, SW1Y 5AD. *T:* (01252) 384820.

WESTON, John William, CB 1979; Principal Assistant Solicitor, Board of Inland Revenue, 1967–80; *b* 3 Feb. 1915; *s* of Herbert Edward Weston, MA, and Emma Gertrude Weston; *m* 1943, Frances Winifred (*née* Johnson); two *s* one *d*. *Educ:* Berkhamsted Sch., Herts. Solicitor, 1937. Joined Inland Revenue, 1940; Sen. Legal Asst, 1948; Asst Solicitor, 1954. *Recreation:* golf. *Address:* 5 Dickerage Road, Kingston Hill, Surrey KT1 3SP. *T:* (020) 8942 8130.

WESTON, Dame Margaret (Kate), DBE 1979; BScEng (London); CEng, MIEE, FINucE; FMA; Director of the Science Museum, 1973–86; *b* 7 March 1926; *o c* of late Charles Edward and Margaret Weston. *Educ:* Stroud High School; College of Technology, Birmingham (now Univ. of Aston). Engineering apprenticeship with General Electric Co. Ltd, followed in 1949 by development work, very largely on high voltage insulation problems. Joined Science Museum as an Assistant Keeper, Dept of Electrical Engineering and Communications, 1955; Deputy Keeper, 1962; Keeper, Dept of Museum Services, 1967–72. Member: Ancient Monuments Bd for England, 1977–84; 1851 Commission, 1987–96; Museums and Galleries Commission, 1988–96; Steering Gp, Museum in Docklands, 1986–90. Member: SE Elec. Bd, 1981–90; BBC Sci. Consultative Gp, 1986–89. Trustee: Hunterian Mus., 1981–; Brooklands, 1987–; Fleet Air Arm Mus., 1992–2000; British Empire and Commonwealth Mus., Bristol, 1999– (Chm., 1999–); RCS. Horniman Public Museum and Public Park: Chm. Trust, 1990–96; Mem. Develt Cttee, 1996–; Pres., Friends, 1996–; Pres., Horniman Mus., Trust, 1997–. Governor, Imperial Coll., 1974–90 (FIC 1975); Governor and Mem. Management Council, Ditchley Foundn, 1984–. Pres., Heritage Railways Assoc. (formerly Assoc. of Railway Preservation Socs, then Assoc. of Independent Railways and Preservation Socs), 1985–. FMA 1976; Sen. Fellow, RCA, 1986; FRSA (Mem. Council, 1985–90); CIMgt. Hon. Fellow, Newnham Coll., Cambridge, 1986. Hon. DEng Bradford, 1984; Hon. DSc: Aston, 1974; Salford, 1984; Leeds, 1987; Loughborough, 1988; DUniv Open, 1987. *Address:* 7 Shawley Way, Epsom, Surrey KT18 5NZ. *T:* (01737) 355885.

WESTON, Sir Michael (Charles Swift), KCMG 1991; CVO 1979; HM Diplomatic Service, retired; UK Permanent Representative to Conference on Disarmament, Geneva (with personal rank of Ambassador), 1992–97; *b* 4 Aug. 1937; *s* of late Edward Charles Swift Weston and Kathleen Mary Weston (*née* Mockett); *m* 1st, 1959, Veronica Anne Tickner (marr. diss. 1990); two *s* one *d*; 2nd, 1990, Christine Julia Ferguson; one *s* one *d*. *Educ:* Dover Coll.; St Catharine's Coll., Cambridge (Exhibitioner). BA, MA. Joined HM Diplomatic Service, 1961; 3rd Sec., Kuwait, 1962; 2nd Sec., FCO, 1965; 1st Secretary: Tehran, 1968; UK Mission, New York, 1970; FCO, 1974; Counsellor, Jedda, 1977; RCDS, 1980; Counsellor (Information), Paris, 1981; Counsellor, Cairo, 1984; Head of Southern European Dept, FCO, 1987; Ambassador to Kuwait, 1990–92. Member: UN Sec.-Gen.'s Gp of Experts on Small Arms, 1998–99; Special Immigration Appeals Commn, 1999–. *Recreations:* tennis, squash, walking. *Address:* Beech Farm House, Beech Lane, Matfield, Kent TN12 7HG. *T:* and *Fax:* (01892) 824921. *Club:* Oxford and Cambridge.

WESTON, Sir (Philip) John, KCMG 1992 (CMG 1985); HM Diplomatic Service, retired; British Permanent Representative to the United Nations, 1995–98; *b* 13 April 1938; *s* of late Philip George Weston and Edith Alice Bray (*née* Ansell); *m* 1967, Margaret Sally Ehlers; two *s* one *d*. *Educ:* Sherborne; Worcester Coll., Oxford. 1st Cl. Hons, Honour Mods Classics and Lit. Hum. Served with Royal Marines, 1956–58. Entered Diplomatic Service, 1962; FO, 1962–63; Treasury Centre for Admin. Studies, 1964; Chinese Language student, Hong Kong, 1964–66; Peking, 1967–68; FO, 1969–71; Office of UK Permanent Representative to EEC, 1972–74; Asst Private Sec. to Sec. of State for Foreign and Commonwealth Affairs (Rt Hon. James Callaghan, Rt Hon. Anthony Crosland), 1974–76; Counsellor, Head of EEC Presidency Secretariat, FCO, 1976–77; Vis. Fellow, All Souls Coll., Oxford, 1977–78; Counsellor, Washington, 1978–81; Hd Defence Dept, FCO, 1981–84; Asst Under-Sec. of State, FCO, 1984–85; Minister, Paris, 1985–88; Dep. Sec. to Cabinet, Cabinet Office, 1988–89 (on secondment); Dep. Under-Sec. of State (Defence), FCO, 1989–90; Political Dir, FCO, 1990–91; Ambassador and UK Perm. Rep. to N Atlantic Council (NATO), 1992–95, to Perm. Council of WEU, 1992–95. Non-executive Director: British Telecommunications, 1998–; Rolls Royce, 1998–; Hakluyt and Co. Ltd, 2001–. Trustee, 1999–, and Chm. Bd of Patrons, 2000–, Nat. Portrait Gall. Council Mem., IISS; Gov., Ditchley Foundn; Gov., Sherborne Sch., 1995– (Chm., 2000–). Trustee, Amer. Associates of the Royal Acad. Trust, 1998–. Hon. Pres., Community Foundn Network, 1999–. *Recreations:* fly-fishing, birds, running, poetry. *Address:* 13 Denbigh Gardens, Richmond, Surrey TW10 6EN. *Club:* Garrick.

WESTON, W(illard) Galen, OC 1990; Chairman, George Weston Ltd, Toronto, since 1978 (President, 1974–96); *b* England, 29 Oct. 1940; *s* of W. Garfield Weston and Reta Lila (*née* Howard); *m* 1966, Hon. Hilary Mary Frayne (*see* Hon. H. M. Weston); one *s* one *d*. Chairman: Loblaw Companies Ltd; Holt Renfrew & Co. Ltd; Weston Foods Ltd; Wittington Investments Ltd; Vice-Chm., Fortnum & Mason plc (UK); Director: Canadian Imperial Bank of Commerce; Associated British Foods plc (UK); Brown Thomas Group Ltd (Eire). Pres. and Trustee, W. Garfield Weston Foundation, Canada; Chm. and Trustee, United World Colls of Canada Inc. Hon. LLD Univ. of Western Ont. *Recreations:* golf, tennis. *Address:* Suite 2001, George Weston Ltd, 22 St Clair Avenue East, Toronto, ON M4T 2S3, Canada. *T:* (416) 9222500, *Fax:* (416) 9224394. *Clubs:* Guards' Polo; Toronto, York (Toronto); Lyford Cay (Bahamas); Windsor (Florida).

WESTON, William John; Chief Executive, Royal Parks Agency, since 2000; *b* 4 July 1949; *s* of Eric Gordon and Pauline Violet Weston; *m* 1978, Patricia April (*decd*); two *d*; *m* 1995, Jane Henriques; one step *s* one step *d*. *Educ:* Wymondham Coll., Norfolk; Royal Manchester Coll. of Music; Poly. of Central London. Concerts Manager, Bournemouth SO, 1971–73; City Arts Administrator, Southampton CC, 1973–77; Administrator, Irish Th. Co., Dublin, 1977–80; Exec. Dir and Creator, W Yorks Playhouse, Leeds, 1980–93; freelance TV producer, 1993–95; Gen. Manager, RSC, 1995–2000. *Recreations:* the arts, walking, gardening, open spaces, jazz, sailing. *Address:* The Royal Parks, The Old Police House, Hyde Park, W2 2UH.

WESTWELL, Alan Reynolds, OBE 1996; PhD, MSc; CEng, MIMechE, MIEE; FCIT; Managing Director and Chief Executive, Dublin Buses Ltd, since 1997; *b* 11 April 1940; *s* of Stanley Westwell and Margaret (*née* Reynolds); *m* 1967, Elizabeth Aileen Birrell; two *s* one *d*. *Educ:* Old Swan Coll.; Liverpool Polytechnic (ACT Hons); Salford Univ. (MSc 1983); Keele Univ. (PhD 1991). Liverpool City Transport Dept: progressively, student apprentice, Technical Asst, Asst Works Manager, 1956–67; Chief Engineer: Southport Corporation Transport Dept, 1967–69; Coventry Corp. Transport Dept, 1969–72; Glasgow Corp. Transport Dept, 1972–74; Director of Public Transport (responsible for bus/rail, airport, harbours), Tayside Regional Council, 1974–79; Dir Gen., Strathclyde PTE, 1979–86; Chm., Man. Dir and Chief Exec., Strathclyde Buses Ltd, 1987–90; Man. Dir and Chief Exec., Greater Manchester Buses Ltd, 1990–93, Greater Manchester Buses North Ltd, 1993–97. Professional Advr, COSLA, 1976–86. President: Scottish Council of Confedn of British Road Passenger Transport, 1982–83 (Vice-Pres., 1981–82); Bus and Coach Council, UK, 1989–90 (Vice Pres., 1985–88; Sen. Vice-Pres., 1988–89). Mem., Parly Road Transport Cttee, 1986–97. Chm., IMechE, Automobile Div., Scottish Centre, 1982–84; Mem. Council, CIT, UK, 1986–89 (Chm. Scottish Centre, 1983–84). International Union of Public Transport: Vice Pres., 1997; Member: Management Cttee, 1991–; Internat. Metropolitan Railway Cttee, 1979–86; Internat. Gen. Commn on Transport and Urban Life (formerly Internat. Commn, Traffic and Urban Planning), 1986–; UITP-EU (formerly European Action) Cttee, 1988–; Chm., UK Members, 1993–97. *Publications:* various papers. *Recreations:* swimming, music, reading. *Address:* 6 Amberley Drive, Hale Barns, Cheshire WA15 0DT. *T:* (0161) 980 3551.

WESTWOOD, family name of **Baron Westwood**.

WESTWOOD, 3rd Baron *cr* 1944, of Gosforth; **William Gavin Westwood;** *b* 30 Jan. 1944; *s* of 2nd Baron Westwood and of Marjorie, *o c* of Arthur Bonwick; *S* father, 1991; *m* 1969, Penelope, *e d* of Dr C. E. Shafto; two *s*. *Educ:* Fettes. *Recreations:* golf, music, reading. *Heir: s* Hon. (William) Fergus Westwood, *b* 24 Nov. 1972. *Address:* Ferndale, Clayton Road, Newcastle upon Tyne NE2 1TL. *T:* (0191) 212 0567; *e-mail:* lordwestwood@hotmail.com.

WESTWOOD, Dr Albert Ronald Clifton, FREng, FIM; FInstP; Chairman and Chief Executive, Council for the Central Laboratory of Research Councils in the United Kingdom, 1998–2000; *b* 9 June 1932; *s* of Albert Sydney Westwood and Ena Emily (*née* Clifton); *m* 1956, Jean Mavis Bullock; two *d*. *Educ:* Univ. of Birmingham (BSc Hons 1953; PhD 1956; DSc 1968). FInstP 1967; FIM 1998. Joined Research Institute for Advanced Studies, subseq. Martin Marietta Labs, Baltimore, 1958, Dir, 1974–84; Martin Marietta Corporation: Corporate Dir, R&D, 1984–87; Vice Pres., R&D, 1987–90, Res. and Technol., 1990–93; Vice Pres., Res. and Exploratory Technol., Sandia Nat. Labs, 1993–96. Chairman: Commn on Engrg and Technical Systems, Nat. Res. Council, 1992–97; Cttee on Global Aspects of Intellectual Properties Rights in Sci. and Technol., Nat. Res. Council, 1992–93; and various govt, academic, civic, music and humanities councils and adv. bds. President: Industrial Res. Inst., US, 1989–90; Minerals, Metals and Materials Soc., 1990 (Fellow, 1990). Fellow, Amer. Soc. for Materials Internat., 1974; FAAAS 1986; FREng (FEng 1996). Member: US NAE, 1980; Royal Swedish Acad. Engrg Scis, 1989; Russian Acad. Engrg, 1995. Pianist and arranger accompanying wife in concerts and recitals in US and around world. Has received awards, prizes and lectureships in recognition of scientific and managerial contribs. *Publications:* (ed) Environment Sensitive Mechanical Behavior, 1966; (ed) Mechanisms of Environment Sensitive Cracking of Materials, 1977; scientific papers. *Recreations:* music, theatre, arts, travel. *Address:* 13539 Canada Del Oso, High Desert, Albuquerque, NM 87111, USA.

WESTWOOD, Dr David, QPM 2001; Chief Constable, Humberside Police, since 1999; *b* 1 April 1948; *s* of late Sqdn Ldr William Westwood and Judith Westwood (*née* Green); *m* 1969, Wendy Stevenson; three *s* one *d*. *Educ:* Collyers Sch., Horsham; Lady Margaret Hall, Oxford (MA Juris.); Bristol Poly. (PhD 1991). Constable, Sussex Police, 1963–73; Constable to Supt, Avon and Somerset Police, 1973–92; Chief Supt, Humberside Police, 1992–95; Asst Chief Constable, Merseyside Police, 1995–97; Dep. Chief Constable, Humberside Police, 1997–99. Hd, Business Area for Race and Community Relns, ACPO, 2000–. *Recreations:* theatre, organic gardening. *Address:* Humberside Police Headquarters, Queens Gardens, Kingston upon Hull HU1 3DJ. *T:* (01482) 220105.

WESTWOOD, Vivienne, OBE 1992; fashion designer; *b* 8 April 1941; *née* Vivienne Isabel Swire; two *s*. In partnership with Malcolm McLaren 1970–83, designed a series of influential avant-garde collections shown at 430 King's Rd, World's End, Chelsea; solo career, 1984–; opened Vivienne Westwood shop, 6 Davies St, W1, 1990, also flagship shop, 44 Conduit St, W1; shops opened in Manchester and Leeds; collections: Pirate, Savage, London, 1981; Buffalo, London, 1982; Punkature, Witches, Hypnos (also Tokyo), Paris, 1983; Clint Eastwood, Mini Crini (also NY), Paris, 1984; Harris Tweed, Pagan I, London, 1987; Time Machine, Civilizade, London, 1988; Voyage to Cythera, Pagan V, London, 1989; Portrait, Cut & Slash, Cut Slash & Pull, 1990; Dressing Up, Salon, Paris, 1991; Always on Camera, Grand Hotel, Paris, 1992; Anglomania, Café Society, Paris, 1993; On Liberty, Erotic Zones, Paris, 1994; Vive la Cocotte, Les Femmes, Paris, 1995; Vivienne Westwood Man, Milan, 1996; Storm in a Teacup, Vive la Bagatelle, Paris, 1996; Man, Milan, 1996–; Red Label, London, 1997–, Paris, 1998–, New York, 1999–; Five Centuries Ago, Tied to the Mast, Paris, 1997; Dressed to Scale, La Belle Hélène, Paris, 1998; Gold Label, Paris, 1999–; Exploration, Paris, 2000; Wild Beauty, Paris, 2001. Launched fragrance, Boudoir, 1998, Libertine, 2000. Professor of Fashion: Acad. of Applied Arts, Vienna, 1989–91; Hochschule der Künste, Berlin, 1993–. Hon. Sen. FRCA 1992. British Designer of the Year, British Fashion Council, 1990, 1991; Queen's Award for Export, 1998. *Address:* Westwood Studios, 9–15 Elcho Street, SW11 4AU.

WETHERED, Julian Frank Baldwin; Director, International Division, United States Banknote Corporation, 1992–94; *b* 9 Nov. 1929; *s* of late Comdr Owen Francis McTier Wethered, RN retd and Betty (*née* Baldwin); *m* 1st, 1952, Britt Eva Hindmarsh (marr. diss. 1971); one *s* one *d*; 2nd, 1973, Antonia Mary Ettrick Roberts; two *s*. *Educ:* Eton Col.; Jesus Coll., Cambridge (BA Hons Hist. 1952; MA). National Service, RM, HMS Diadem, 1948–49. Trainee, Expandite Ltd, 1952–54; Sales Rep., Remington Rand, 1955–56; Thomas De La Rue and Co.: trainee, 1956; Mem., PA Study Team, 1957; Printing Preliminaries Manager, Currency Div., 1958–62; Special Rep., Africa, 1963–67; Manager, Banknote Printing Co., 1968–69; Regl Manager, FE, 1970–75; Associate Dir of Sales, Africa and FE, 1976–83; Regl Dir, FE, De La Rue Co. plc, 1984–88; Associate Dir of Sales, Thomas De La Rue & Co., 1989. Dir Gen., RoSPA, 1990–91. Chm., Riding for the Disabled Assoc. of Singapore, 1987–88. Pres., British Business Assoc. of Singapore, 1988. FInstD; FRSA. *Recreations:* sailing, riding, the arts. *Address:* Brunton Barn, Collingbourne Kingston, Marlborough, Wilts SN8 3SE. *Club:* Travellers.

WETHERELL, Gordon Geoffrey; HM Diplomatic Service; Ambassador to Luxembourg, since 2000; *b* 11 Nov. 1948; *s* of Geoffrey and late Georgette Maria Wetherell; *m* 1981, Rosemary Anne Myles; four *d*. *Educ:* Bradfield Coll., Berks; New Coll., Oxford (BA 1969; MA 1975); Univ. of Chicago (MA 1971). Joined HM Diplomatic Service, 1973; FCO (concurrently British Embassy, Chad), 1973–74; E Berlin, 1974–77; First Sec., FCO, 1977; UK Delegn to Comprehensive Test Ban Negotiations, Geneva, 1977–80; New Delhi, 1980–83; FCO, 1983–85; on secondment to HM Treasury, 1986–87; Asst Head, European Communities Dept (External), FCO, 1987–88; Counsellor and Dep. Head of Mission, Warsaw, 1988–92; Counsellor (Politico-Military), Bonn, 1992–94; Hd, Personnel Services Dept, FCO, 1994–97; Ambassador to Ethiopia and (non-res.) to Eritrea and Djibouti, 1997–2000. *Recreations:* tennis, reading, travel, Manchester United Football Club. *Address:* c/o Foreign and Commonwealth Office, King Charles Street, SW1A 2AH. *Club:* Oxford and Cambridge.

WETTON, Hilary John D.; *see* Davan Wetton.

WETTON, Philip Henry Davan, CMG 1993; HM Diplomatic Service, retired; Consul-General, Milan, 1990–96; *b* 21 Sept. 1937; *s* of late Eric Davan Wetton, CBE and Kathleen Valerie Davan Wetton; *m* 1983, Roswitha Kortner. *Educ:* Westminster; Christ Church, Oxford (MA). Unilever Ltd, 1958–65; FCO, 1965–68; served Tokyo, Osaka and FCO, 1968–73; Head of Division, later Director, Secretariat of Council of Ministers of European Communities, 1973–83; Counsellor, Seoul, 1983–87; FCO, 1987–90. Founded Philip Wetton Chair of Astrophysics, Oxford, 2000. *Recreations:* rowing, music, astronomy. *Address:* Aller's End, East Kennett, Marlborough, Wilts SN8 4EY.

See also H. J. Davan Wetton.

WETZEL, Dave; Partner, Yun Kim's Oriental Cuisine Restaurant, Brentford, since 1997; Vice-Chair, Transport for London, since 2000; Chair, London Buses, since 2000; *b* 9 Oct. 1942; *s* of Fred Wetzel and Ivy Donaldson; *m* 1973, Heather Allman; two *d*. *Educ:* Spring Grove Grammar Sch.; Southall Technical Coll., Ealing Coll., and the Henry George Sch. of Social Sciences (part-time courses). Student apprentice, 1959–62; Bus Conductor/Driver, 1962–65, Bus Official, 1965–69, London Transport; Br. Manager, Initial Services, 1969–70; Pilot Roster Officer, British Airways, 1970–74 (ASTMS Shop Steward); Political Organiser, London Co-op., 1974–81; Member (Lab) for Hammersmith N, GLC, 1981–86 (Transport Cttee Chair, 1981–86); Mem. (Lab) Hounslow Borough Council, 1964–68, 1986–94 (Dep. Leader and Chair, Environmental Planning, 1986–87; Leader, 1987–91). Proprietor, Granny's Attic Antique Shop, Mevagissey, 1994–99. Contested (Lab): Richmond upon Thames, Twickenham, 1979; Mevagissey, Restormel DC, 1995; St Austell West, Cornwall CC, 1997. Vice-Chm., Public Transport Cttee, AMA, 1993–94; Mem. Management Cttee, Hounslow Community Transport and Central London Dial-a-Ride, 1991–94. Dir, DaRT (Dial-a-Ride and Taxicard Users), 1989–94. Pres., W London Peace Council, 1982–94; Chair, Labour Land Campaign, 1982–. Mem. Bd, Riverside Studios, Hammersmith, 1983–86. Founder and co-ordinator, Trade Union and Co-op Esperanto Gp, 1976–80. Pres., Thames Valley Esperanto Soc., 1982–94; Vice-Pres., Transport Studies Soc., London Univ., 1992–99 (Pres., 1991–92). Vice Chm., Mevagissey Chamber of Commerce, 1996–98. Mem. Editl Bd, Voice of the Unions, 1975–79; Editor, Civil Aviation News, 1978–81. FRSA 2001. *Recreations:* politics, Esperanto, land campaigning. *Address:* Yun Kim's, 9 York Parade, Great West Road, Brentford, Middlesex TW8 9AA. *T:* (020) 8569 7223.

WEYLAND, Joseph; Ambassador of Luxembourg to the Court of St James's, since 1993; *b* 24 April 1943; *s* of Adolphe Weyland and Marie Kox; *m* 1st, 1969, France Munhowen; two *s*; 2nd, 1993, Bénédicte Boucqueau. *Educ:* LLD, and Dip. of Inst. d'Etudes Politiques, Univ. of Paris. Foreign Ministry, Luxembourg, 1968; served Bonn and EEC, Brussels; Ambassador to UN, NY, 1982; Perm. Rep. to EEC, Brussels, 1985 (Mem., Intergovt. Conf. leading to Single European Act, 1985, later Chm., Intergovt Conf. on Political Union leading to Treaty of Maastricht, 1991; Sec.-Gen., Foreign Ministry, Luxembourg, 1992. Mem., Reflection Gp, IGC, 1995. *Publication:* (jtly) Le Traité de Maastricht, 1993. *Recreations:* art, sports, music. *Address:* 27 Wilton Crescent, SW1X 8SD. *T:* (020) 7235 6961, *Fax:* (020) 7235 9734. *Club:* Rotary.

WEYMAN, Anne Judith, OBE 2000; FCA; Chief Executive, fpa (formerly Family Planning Association), since 1996; *b* 1 Feb. 1943; *d* of Stanley Weyman and Rose Weyman; *m* 1977, Christopher Leonard Bulford; one *d*. *Educ:* Tollington GS; Bristol Univ. (BSc Physics); London Sch. of Econs (BScSoc). FCA 1973. Articled Clerk and Audit Manager, Finnie, Ross, Welch & Co., Chartered Accts, 1964–68; Audit Manager, Foster Weyman & Co., Chartererd Accts, 1968–69; Research Officer: LSE, 1972–74; Queen Mary's Hosp., Roehampton, 1974–77; Hd of Finance and Admin, Internat. Secretariat, Amnesty Internat., 1977–86; Dir of Inf. and Public Affairs and Co. Sec., Nat. Children's Bureau, 1986–96. Chm., Pinter Publishers Ltd, 1989–95. Mem. (Lab), Westminster CC, 1978–82. Mem., NW Thames RHA, 1978–80. Vice-Chm., Sexual Health Strategy Reference Gp, 1999–2000; Member: Ind. Adv. Gp on Teenage Pregnancy, 2000–; Women's Nat. Commn, 1999–. Hon. Pres., Sex Educn Forum (Founder, 1987). *Publications:* (with J. Westergaard and P. Wiles) Modern British Society: a bibliography, 1977; (with J. Unell) Finding and Running Premises, 1985; (with S. Capper and J. Unell) Starting and Running a Voluntary Group, 1989; (with Y. Carter and C. Moss) RCGP Handbook of Sexual Health in Primary Care, 1998; (with M. Duggan) Individual Choices, Collective Responsibility: sexual health, a public health issue, 1999; (jtly) Sexual and Reproductive Health and Rights in the UK: 5 years on from Cairo, 1999; articles on health, mental health and sex educn. *Recreations:* reading, gardening. *Address:* fpa, 2–12 Pentonville Road, N1 9FP. *T:* (020) 7837 5432.

WEYMES, John Barnard, OBE 1975; HM Diplomatic Service, retired; Managing Director, Cayman Islands News Bureau, Grand Cayman, 1981–83; *b* 18 Oct. 1927; *s* of William Stanley Weymes and Irene Innes Weymes; *m* 1978, Beverley Pauline Gliddon; three *c* (by a previous marr.). *Educ:* Dame Allan's Sch., Newcastle upon Tyne; King's Coll., Durham Univ., Newcastle upon Tyne. Served HM Forces, 1945–48. Foreign Office, 1949–52; 3rd Sec., Panama City, 1952–56; 2nd Sec., Bogotá, 1957–60; Vice-Consul, Berlin, 1960–63; Dep-Consul, Tamsui, Taiwan, 1963–65; 1st Sec., FCO, 1965–68; Prime Minister's Office, 1968–70; Consul, Guatemala City, 1970–74; 1st Sec., FCO, 1974–77; Consul-Gen., Vancouver, 1977–78; Ambassador to Honduras, 1978–81. *Recreations:* outdoor sport, partic. cricket; chess, reading. *Address:* Holmesdale, Lower Lane, Dalwood, Axminster, Devon EX13 7EG. *T:* (01404) 881114. *Clubs:* MCC, Middlesex County Cricket; Sedlescombe Cricket.

WEYMOUTH, Viscount; Ceawlin Henry Laszlo Thynn; *b* 6 June 1974; *s* and *heir* of Marquess of Bath, *qv*.

WHADDON, Baron *cr* 1978 (Life Peer), of Whaddon in the County of Cambridgeshire; **(John) Derek Page;** Chairman, Daltrade, since 1983; *b* 14 Aug. 1927; *s* of John Page and Clare Page (*née* Maher); *m* 1st, 1948, Catherine Audrey Halls (*d* 1979); one *s* one *d*; 2nd, 1981, Angela Rixson. *Educ:* St Bede's College, Manchester; London University. External BSc (Soc.). MP (Lab) King's Lynn, 1964–70; contested (Lab) Norfolk NW, Feb. 1974. Chairman: Skorimpex-Rind, 1985–; Cambridge Chemical Co. Ltd, 1991–2000 (Dir, 1962–2000); Crag Group Ltd, 1996–. Mem., Council of Management, CoSIRA, 1975–82; Mem., E Anglia Economic Planning Council, 1975–80. Golden Insignia of Order of Merit (Poland), 1989. *Club:* Reform.

WHALE, John Hilary; journalist; Editor, Church Times, 1989–95; *b* 19 Dec. 1931; *s* of late Rev. Dr John Seldon Whale and Mary Whale (*née* Carter); *m* 1957, Judith Laurie Hackett; one *s*. *Educ:* Winchester; Corpus Christi College, Oxford. BA Lit Hum 1955, MA 1958. Lieut, Intelligence Corps, 1950–51 (Nat. Service). Writing, acting and teaching, 1954–58; Section Anglaise, French radio, Paris, 1958–59; ITN, 1960–69: Political Corresp., 1963–67; US Corresp., Washington, 1967–69; Sunday Times, 1969–84: political staff, 1969–79; Religious Affairs Corresp., 1979–84; Asst Editor, 1981–84; leader-writer throughout; Head of Religious Programmes, BBC TV, 1984–89. Dir, London programme, Univ. of Missouri Sch. of Journalism, 1980–83. Churchwarden, St. Mary's, Barnes, 1976–81. *Publications:* The Half-Shut Eye, 1969; Journalism and Government, 1972; The Politics of the Media, 1977; One Church, One Lord, 1979 (Winifred Mary Stanford Prize, 1980); (ed) The Pope from Poland, 1980; Put it in Writing, 1984; (contrib.) Why I am Still an Anglican, 1986; The Future of Anglicanism, 1988; contribs to books, quarterlies, weeklies. *Address:* 45 Shakespeare Road, W3 6SE. *T:* (020) 8993 7952.

WHALEN, Sir Geoffrey (Henry), Kt 1995; CBE 1989; FIMI, FIPD; Deputy Chairman, Peugeot Motor Co. plc, since 1990 (Managing Director, 1984–95); *b* 8 Jan. 1936; *s* of Henry and Mabel Whalen; *m* 1961, Elizabeth Charlotte; two *s* three *d*. *Educ:* Magdalen College, Oxford. MA Hons Modern History. National Coal Board, Scotland (industrial relations), 1959–66; Divl Personnel Manager, A. C. Delco Div., General Motors, Dunstable, 1966–70; British Leyland, 1970–78; Personnel Dir, Leyland Cars, 1975–78; Personnel Dir, Rank Hovis McDougall Bakeries Div., 1978–80; Personnel and Indust. Rel. Dir, Talbot Motor Co., 1980–81, Asst Man. Dir, 1981–84. Director: Coventry

Building Soc., 1992– (Chm., 1999–); Novar (formerly Caradon) plc, 1996–; Federal Mogul Corp., 1998–; Chairman: Hills Precision Components Ltd, 1990–2001; Camden Motors Ltd, 1996–. Pres., SMMT, 1988–90 and 1993; Vice Pres., Inst. of Motor Industry, 1986–; Chm., Coventry and Warwicks TEC, 1990–94. FIMI 1986; FCGI 1989; CIMgt (CBIM 1987). Hon. DBA Coventry Univ., 1995. Midlander of the Year Award, Bass Mitchells & Butlers Ltd, 1988; Midlands Businessman of the Year, 1992. Chevalier de la Légion d'Honneur (France), 1990. *Address:* Victoria Lodge, 8 Park Crescent, Abingdon, Oxon OX14 1DF. *Club:* Oxford and Cambridge.

WHALLEY, Jeffrey; Chairman: British Aluminium plc, since 1996; FKI, 1991–99; *b* 20 Nov. 1942; *s* of William Henry and Elsie Whalley; *m* 1st, 1965, Maureen Ann Ivers (marr. diss. 1995); three *s*; 2nd, 1996, Karn Jane Jamieson. *Educ:* Grammar School and Polytechnic. Managing Director: Dynamo Electrical Services, 1970–75; Whipp & Bourne Switchgear, 1975–80; FKI Electricals, 1980–87; Man. Dir and Dep. Chm., FKI Babcock, 1987–89; Jt Dep. Chm., Babcock International, 1989–95; Man. Dir, Gartland & Whalley Securities, later Gartland Whalley & Barker Ltd, 1989–95 (Dir, 1995–). Non-exec. Dir, Towcester Racecourse Ltd, 1998–. FRSA; CIMgt; FInstD. *Recreations:* tennis, fishing, football. *Clubs:* Carlton, Royal Automobile.

WHALLEY, John Mayson, FRTPI; FRIBA; PPLI; Principal, JMW International, since 1994; Design Co-ordinator, Kishiwada Port Development Corporation, Osaka, Japan, since 1997; *b* 14 Sept. 1932; *s* of George Mayson Whalley and Ada Florence Cairns; *m* 1966, Elizabeth Gillian Hide; one *s* two *d*. *Educ:* Grammar Sch., Preston; Univ. of Liverpool (BArch, 1st Cl. Hons; MCivic Des.); Univ. of Pennsylvania (MLandscape Arch). Sir Charles Reilly Medal and Prize for thesis design, 1956; Leverhulme and Italian Govt Fellowships for study in Scandinavia and Univ. of Rome, 1957; Fulbright Schol., 1958; Manchester Soc. of Architects Winstanley Fellowship, 1965. Asst architect to Sir Frederick Gibberd, Harlow, 1956; architect/landscape architect: Oskar Stonorov, Philadelphia, 1958–60; Grenfell Baines and Hargreaves Building Design Partnership, Preston, 1960–62; Associate, 1963–68, Sen. Partner, 1968–93, Derek Lovejoy & Partners. Chm., NW Region, RIBA, 1984–85; President: Manchester Soc. of Architects, 1980–81; Landscape Inst., 1985–87; Mem. Council, National Trust, 1989–94; Trustee and Dir, Rural Heritage Trust; Chm., Rivington Heritage Trust, 1997–. Civic Trust awards: W Burton Power Stn, 1968; Cheshire Constabulary HQ, 1969; Rochdale Canal, 1973; Royal Life Offices, Peterborough, 1992; design competitions 1st prizes: Cergy-Pontoise, 1970; La Courneuve, Paris, 1972; Liverpool Anglican Cathedral precinct, 1982; Urban Park, Vitoria-Gasteiz, 1991; Regional Park, Mito City, Japan, 1992; Garden Festivals: Liverpool, 1982; Stoke-on-Trent, 1983; Glasgow, 1985. Civic Trust awards assessor, 1970–94; UN Tech. Expert, Riyadh, 1975. Mem., Ordre des Architectes de France; FRSA. Contribs to radio and TV. *Publications:* Selected Architects Details, 1958; articles in professional jls. *Recreation:* using imagination–to play jazz piano, opening for Lancashire and England, playing twenty pounds salmon and owning French vineyard! *Address:* Dilworth House, Longridge, Preston, Lancs PR3 3ST. *T:* and *Fax:* (01772) 783262; *e-mail:* maysonwhalley@netscapeonline.co.uk. *Clubs:* Ronnie Scott's; St James's (Manchester).

WHALLEY, Richard Carlton; Chairman, Ewden Associates Ltd, since 1981; *b* Quetta, India, 4 July 1922; *s* of Frederick Seymour Whalley, MC, FCGI, MIMechE, and Gwendolen, *d* of Sir William Collingwood; *m* 1945, Mary Christian Bradley; two *s* twin *d*. *Educ:* Shrewsbury Sch.; 151 OCTU, Aldershot. Served War: Private, Royal Berkshire Regt, 1940; commissioned 2nd Lieut, Royal Corps of Signals, 1942; Captain and Adjt, 2nd Div. Signals, India, Assam, Burma, 1942–45 (despatches). War Office, AG II (O), 1945–48; GHQ Singapore, 1948–51. Vulcan Foundry Ltd: Asst Sec., 1952–58; Commercial Manager, 1958–60; Dep. Gen. Manager, 1960–65; Manager, English Electric Diesel Engine Div., 1965–67; Dir and Gen. Manager, Glacier Metal Co., 1968–70. 1970–78: Dep. Chm. and Managing Dir, Millspaugh Ltd; Chm. and Managing Dir, C. A. Harnden Ltd, Westbury Engrg Ltd, Hargreaves & Jennings Ltd, and T. Rowbottom Ltd; Director: Bertram-Scott Ltd; Sulzer Bros (UK) Ltd; Mem., Bd of British Shipbuilders (with special responsibility for personnel, indust. relations, and trng), 1978–80. Chairman: F. & M. Ducker Ltd, 1981–84; A. Spafford & Co. Ltd, 1981–82; Pennine Plastics Ltd, 1981–82; Eaton and Booth Ltd, 1984–87; (also Chief Exec.) Eaton and Booth Rolling Mills Ltd, 1984–87; John King and Co. Ltd, 1985–87; Director: Estridge & Ropner Ltd, 1981–84; Sheffield Photoco, 1983–84; Dep. Chm., Malacarp Group, 1982–84. Freeman, Co. of Cutlers in Hallamshire, 1986. *Recreations:* rowing, walking. *Address:* Sunnybank Farm, Bolsterstone, Sheffield S36 3ST. *T:* (0114) 288 3116. *Clubs:* National Liberal; London Rowing.

WHALLEY, Prof. William Basil; Professor of Chemistry and Head of Department of Pharmaceutical Chemistry, School of Pharmacy, 1961–82, now Emeritus Professor of Chemistry, University of London; *b* 17 Dec. 1916; *s* of William and Catherine Lucy Whalley; *m* 1945, Marie Agnes Alston; four *s* one *d*. *Educ:* St Edward's College, Liverpool; Liverpool University. BSc Hons 1938; PhD 1940; DSc 1952; FRIC 1950. MOS and ICI 1940–45. Lecturer, 1946–55, Sen. Lectr, 1955–57, Reader, 1957–61, in Organic Chemistry, at Liverpool University. *Publications:* contrib. on organic chemistry to several books: *eg* Heterocyclic Compounds, Vol. 7, Edited R. C. Elderfield, Wiley (New York); many pubns in Jl of Chem. Soc., Jl Amer. Chem. Soc., etc. *Recreations:* music and mountaineering. *Address:* 9 Peaks Hill, Purley, Surrey CR8 3JG. *T:* (020) 8668 2244.

WHALLEY, Maj.-Gen. William Leonard, CB 1985; *b* 19 March 1930; *m* 1955, Honor Mary (*née* Golden); one *d*. *Educ:* Sir William Turner's Sch., Coatham. Joined Army (Nat. Service), 1948; sc 1962; Commander, RAOC, 1st Div., 1968–71; Dir of Ordnance Services, BAOR, 1980–83; Dir Gen. of Ordnance Services, MoD, 1983–85. Colonel Commandant: RAOC, 1986–93; RLC, 1993. Life Vice-Pres., Army Boxing Assoc. (Chm., 1983–85). Pres., Little Aston Br., Conservative Assoc., 1996– (Chm., 1987–96, 1998–). Chm. of Govs, Brooke Weston (formerly Corby) City Technol. Coll., 1991–96 (Project Dir, 1989–91). Pres., RAOC Charitable Trust, 1996–2000. *Recreations:* bridge, computers, cabinet making. *Address:* HSBC, 8 High Street, Sutton Coldfield, West Midlands B72 1XB.

WHARNCLIFFE, 5th Earl of, *cr* 1876; **Richard Alan Montagu Stuart Wortley;** Baron Wharncliffe 1826; Viscount Carlton 1876; *b* 26 May 1953; *s* of Alan Ralph Montagu-Stuart-Wortley (*d* 1986) and Virginia Anne (*d* 1993), *d* of W. Martin Claybaugh; *S* cousin, 1987; *m* 1979, Mary Elizabeth Reed; three *s*. *Heir: s* Viscount Carlton, *qv*. *Address:* 74 Sweetser Road, N Yarmouth, ME 04097, USA.

WHARTON, 12th Baron *cr* 1544–45; **Myles Christopher David Robertson;** *b* 1 Oct. 1964; *e s* of Baroness Wharton (11th in line) and Henry McLeod Robertson; *S* mother, 2000; *m* 1998, Caroline Laura, *d* of John David Jeffrey. *Educ:* King's Coll., Wimbledon. *Heir: b* Hon. Christopher James Robertson, *b* 24 Dec. 1969.

WHARTON, Rt Rev. John Martin; *see* Newcastle, Bishop of.

WHARTON, Michael Bernard; author and journalist; 'Peter Simple' Columnist, Daily and Sunday Telegraph, since 1957; *b* 19 April 1913; *s* of Paul Nathan and Bertha Wharton; *m* 1st, 1936, Joan Atkey (marr. diss. 1947); one *s*; 2nd 1952, Catherine Mary Derrington (marr. diss. 1972; she *d* 1992); one *d*; 3rd, 1974, Susan Moller. *Educ:* Bradford Grammar Sch.; Lincoln Coll., Oxford. Army service, Royal Artillery and General Staff, 1940–46. Scriptwriter and Producer, BBC, 1946–56; (with Colin Welch) writer of Peter Simple column, Daily Telegraph, 1957–60. *Publications: as Michael Wharton:* (ed) A Nation's Security, 1955; Sheldrake (novel), 1958; The Missing Will (autobiog.), 1984; A Dubious Codicil (autobiog.), 1991; editor and mainly writer of anthologies of Peter Simple column, 1963, 1965, 1969, 1971, 1973, 1975, 1978, 1980, 1984, 1987; Far Away is Close at Hand: 40 years of Peter Simple, 1995; Peter Simple's Century, 1999; *under pseudonym Simon Crabtree:* Forgotten Memories, 1941; Hector Tumbler Investigates, 1943.

WHATLEY, Prof. Frederick Robert, FRS 1975; Sherardian Professor of Botany, Oxford University, 1971–91; Fellow of Magdalen College, Oxford, since 1971; *b* 26 Jan. 1924; *s* of Frederick Norman Whatley and Maud Louise (*née* Hare); *m* 1951, Jean Margaret Smith Bowie; two *d*. *Educ:* Bishop Wordsworth's Sch., Salisbury; (Scholar) Selwyn Coll., Cambridge University (BA, PhD). Benn W. Levy Student, Cambridge, 1947. Sen. Lectr. in Biochemistry, Univ. of Sydney, 1950–53; Asst Biochemist, Univ. of California at Berkeley, 1954–58; Associate Biochemist, 1959–64; Guggenheim Fellowship (Oxford and Stockholm), 1960; Prof. of Botany, King's Coll., London, 1964–71. Vis. Fellow, ANU, 1979. *Publications:* articles and reviews in scientific jls. *Address:* 50 Church Road, Sandford-on-Thames, Oxford OX4 4XZ.

WHATMOUGH, Rev. Michael Anthony; Vicar, St Mary Redcliffe, Bristol, since 1993; *b* 14 Oct. 1950; *s* of Derrick and Molly Whatmough; *m* 1975, Jean Macdonald Watt; two *s* two *d*. *Educ:* Exeter Univ. (BA 1972); Edinburgh Univ. (BD 1981). ARCO 1972. Teacher of music, Forrester High Sch., Edinburgh, 1973–74; Sub-Organist, Old St Paul's Church, Edinburgh, 1973–78; Music Master, George Watson's Coll., Edinburgh, 1974–78; ordained deacon, 1981, priest, 1982; Curate, St Hilda and St Fillan, Edinburgh, 1981–84; Vis. Lectr in Music, Faculty of Divinity, Edinburgh Univ., 1981–84; Curate and Rector, Salisbury St Thomas, 1984–93; Rural Dean, Salisbury, 1990–93. *Recreations:* harpsichord playing, drinking the wine from our own vineyard. *Address:* The Vicarage, 10 Redcliffe Parade West, Bristol BS1 6SP. *T:* (0117) 929 1487; *e-mail:* tony.whatmough@bigfoot.com.

WHEADON, Richard Anthony; Principal, Elizabeth College, Guernsey, 1972–88, retired; *b* 31 Aug. 1933; *s* of Ivor Cecil Newman Wheadon and Margarita Augusta (*née* Cash); *m* 1961, Ann Mary (*née* Richardson); three *s*. *Educ:* Cranleigh Sch. Balliol Coll., Oxford. MA (Physics). Commissioned RAF, 1955 (Sword of Honour); Air Radar Officer, 1955–57; Asst Master, Eton Coll., 1957–66; Dep. Head Master and Head of Science Dept, Dauntsey's Sch., 1966–71. Mem., Wilts Educn Cttee's Science Adv. Panel, 1967–71. Rowed bow for Oxford, 1954, for GB in European Championships and Olympic Games, 1956; Captain RAF VIII, 1956 and 1957; Olympic Selector and Nat. Coach, 1964–66. Contingent Comdr, Dauntsey's Sch. CCF, 1969–70. Reader, C of E, dio. of Winchester, 1995–; Member: Guernsey Standing Adv. Council for Religious Educn, 1997–; Diocesan Readers' Selection Bd, 1998–. *Publication:* The Principles of Light and Optics, 1968. *Recreations:* French horn, photography, electronics, singing, sailing, words. *Address:* L'Enclos Gallienne, Rue du Court Laurent, Torteval, Guernsey, Channel Islands GY8 0LH. *T:* (01481) 264988.

WHEARE, Thomas David, MA; Headmaster of Bryanston School, since 1983; *b* 11 Oct. 1944; *s* of late Sir Kenneth Wheare, CMG, FBA, and of Lady (Joan) Wheare; *m* 1977, Rosalind Clare Spice; two *d*. *Educ:* Dragon Sch.; Magdalen College Sch., Oxford; King's Coll., Cambridge (BA, MA); Christ Church, Oxford (DipEd). Assistant Master, Eton College, 1967–76; Housemaster of School House, Shrewsbury School, 1976–83. Chm., HMC, 2000 (Hon. Treas., 1993–98). FRSA 1989. *Recreations:* music, supporting Arsenal FC. *Address:* Bryanston School, Blandford, Dorset DT11 0PX. *T:* (01258) 484632.

WHEAT, Rev. Fr (Charles Donald) Edmund, SSM; Vicar, St Thomas', Middlesbrough, since 2001; *b* 17 May 1937; *s* of Charles and Alice Wheat. *Educ:* Kelham Theol Coll.; Nottingham Univ. (BA); Sheffield Univ. (MA). Curate, St Paul's, Arbourthorne, Sheffield, 1962–67; licensed, Dio. Southwell, 1967–70; Mem., SSM, 1969–; Chaplain, St Martin's Coll., Lancaster, 1970–73; Prior, SSM Priory, Sheffield, 1973–75; Curate, St John, Ranmoor and Asst Chaplain, Sheffield Univ., 1975–77, Chaplain 1977–80; Provincial, English Province, 1981–91, Dir, 1982–89, Provincial Bursar, 1992–98, Provincial of European Province, 1999–2001, SSM; Vicar, All Saints', Middlesbrough, 1988–95; Prior, St Antony's Priory, Durham, 1998–2001. Chaplain: Whitelands Coll., 1996–97; Order of the Holy Paraclete, Whitby, 1997–98. Mem., Gen. Synod, 1975–80. *Recreations:* reading, watching soap operas. *Address:* St Thomas' House, 154 Carisbrooke Avenue, Thorntree, Middlesbrough TS11 4RJ.

WHEATCROFT, Patience Jane, (Mrs A. Salter); Business and City Editor, The Times, since 1997; *b* 28 Sept. 1951; *d* of Anthony Wheatcroft and Ruth Wheatcroft (*née* Frith); *m* 1976, Anthony Salter; two *s* one *d*. *Educ:* Univ. of Birmingham (LLB). Dep. City Ed., The Times, 1984–86; Asst City Ed., Daily Mail, 1986–88; Ed., Retail Week, 1988–93; Dep. City Ed., Mail on Sunday, 1994–97. *Recreations:* ski-ing, opera, day-dreaming, talking. *Address:* The Times, 1 Pennington Street, E98 1TB. *T:* (020) 7782 5000.

WHEATCROFT, Stephen Frederick, OBE 1974; Director, Aviation and Tourism International Ltd, since 1983; *b* 11 Sept. 1921; *s* of late Percy and Fanny Wheatcroft; *m* 1st, 1943, Joy (*d* 1974), *d* of late Cecil Reed; two *s* one *d*; 2nd, 1974, Alison, *d* of late Arnold Dessau; two *s*. *Educ:* Latymer Sch., N9; London Sch. of Economics (BSc(Econ) 1942; Hon. Fellow, 1998). Served War, Pilot in Fleet Air Arm, 1942–45. Commercial Planning Manager, BEA, 1946–53; Simon Research Fellow, Manchester Univ., 1953–55; private practice as Aviation Consultant, 1956–72; retained as Economic Adviser to BEA. Commns for Govts of: Canada, India, W Indies, E African Community, Afghanistan; Consultant to World Bank; Assessor to Edwards Cttee on British Air Transport in the Seventies; Mem. Bd, British Airways (Dir of Economic Develt), 1972–82. Governor, London Sch. of Economics. FRAeS, FCIT (Pres., 1978–79); FAIAA. *Publications:* Economics of European Air Transport, 1956; Airline Competition in Canada, 1958; Air Transport Policy, 1966; Air Transport in a Competitive European Market, 1986; European Liberalisation and World Air Transport, 1990; Europe's Senior Travel Market, 1993; Aviation and Tourism Policies, 1994; Europe's Youth Travel Market, 1995; articles in professional jls. *Recreation:* travel. *Address:* (office) 6 Cheyne House, 18 Chelsea Embankment, SW3 4LA. *T:* (020) 7352 4150. *Club:* Reform.

WHEATLEY, Hon. Lord; Hon. John Francis Wheatley; a Senator of the College of Justice in Scotland, since 2000; *b* 9 May 1941; *s* of John Thomas Wheatley (Baron Wheatley, PC) and late Agnes Nichol; *m* 1970, Bronwen Catherine Fraser; two *s*. *Educ:* Mount St Mary's Coll., Derbyshire; Edinburgh Univ. (BL). Called to the Scottish Bar, 1966; Standing Counsel to Scottish Develt Dept, 1971; Advocate Depute, 1975; Sheriff of Tayside Central and Fife, at Dunfermline, 1979–80, at Perth, 1980–2000; Temp. High Ct Judge, 1992; QC (Scot.) 1993. *Recreations:* gardening, music. *Address:* Braefoot Farmhouse, Crook of Devon, Fossoway, Kinross-shire KY13 7UL. *T:* (01577) 840212.

WHEATLEY, Alan Edward, FCA; Chairman: Special Utilities (formerly Foreign and Colonial Special Utilities) Investment Trust plc, since 1993; IntaMission, since 2001; *b* 23 May 1938; *s* of late Edward and of Margaret Wheatley (*née* Turner); *m* 1962, Marion Frances (*née* Wilson); two *s* one *d*. *Educ:* Ilford Grammar School. Chartered Accountant. Norton Slade, 1954–60, qualified 1960; joined Price Waterhouse, 1960; admitted to partnership, 1970; Mem., Policy Cttee, 1981–92; Sen. Partner (London Office), 1985–92; Chm., 3i Gp, 1992–93; Dep. Chm., Ashtead Gp, 1994–. Non-executive Director: EBS Investments (Bank of England sub.), 1977–90; British Steel plc (formerly BSC), 1984–94; Babcock International Gp, 1993–; Legal & General Gp, 1993–; Forte, 1993–96; N M Rothschild & Sons, 1993–99; Chm., New Court Financial Services Ltd, 1996–99; Govt Dir, Cable & Wireless, 1981–84, non-exec. Dep. Chm., 1984–85. Mem., Ind. Develt Adv. Bd, 1985–92. Trustee, V&A Mus., 1996–99. Governor, Solefield School, 1985–95. *Recreations:* golf, bridge. *Address:* Highcroft, Kippington Road, Sevenoaks, Kent TN13 2LN. *Club:* Wildernesse (Seal, Kent).

WHEATLEY, Rear-Adm. Anthony, CB 1988; General Manager, National Hospital for Neurology and Neurosurgery, Queen Square, 1988–96; *b* 3 Oct. 1933; *yr s* of late Edgar C. Wheatley and Audrey G. Barton Hall; *m* 1962, Iona Sheila Haig; one *d*. *Educ:* Berkhamsted School. Entered RN Coll., Dartmouth, 1950; RNEC, Manadon, 1953–57; HMS Ceylon, 1958–60; HMS Ganges, 1960–61; HMS Cambrian, 1962–64; Staff of RNEC, Manadon, 1964–67; Staff of Comdr British Navy Staff, Washington, 1967–69; HMS Diomede, 1970–72; Staff of C-in-C Fleet, 1972–74; Exec. Officer, RNEC Manadon, 1975–76; MoD Procurement Exec., 1977–79; British Naval Attaché, Brasilia, 1979–81; RCDS course 1982; HMS Collingwood (in Command), 1982–85; Flag Officer, Portsmouth, Naval Base Comdr and Head of Establishment of Fleet Maintenance and Repair Orgn, Portsmouth, 1985–87. Trustee: Nat. Soc. for Epilepsy, 1996–; Friends of the Elderly, 1997–. *Recreations:* cricket, golf, music. *Address:* 7 The Hollies, New Barn, Kent DA3 7HU. *Clubs:* Army and Navy; Free Foresters, Incogniti, Royal Navy Cricket.

WHEATLEY, Rev. Canon Arthur; Priest in Charge of St Columba's, Grantown-on-Spey and St John's, Rothiemurchus, 1983–95; Hon. Assistant Priest, Grantown-on-Spey, since 1996; *b* 4 March 1931; *s* of George and Elizabeth Wheatley; *m* 1959, Sheena Morag Wilde; two *s* two *d*. *Educ:* Alloa Academy; Coates Hall Theol Coll., Edinburgh. Deacon 1970, priest 1970, Dio. Brechin; 1st Curate's title, St Salvador's with St Martin's, Dundee, 1970–71; Curate in Charge, St Ninian's Mission, Dundee, 1971–76; Rector of Holy Trinity, Elgin with St Margaret's Church, Lossiemouth, Dio. Moray, Ross and Caithness, 1976–80; Canon of St Andrew's Cathedral, 1978–80; Provost, 1980–83; Canon of Inverness Cathedral, 1985–. Episcopalian Chaplain to HM Prison, Porterfield, 1980–; Anglican Chaplain to RAF Unit, Grantown-on-Spey, 1984–95. *Recreations:* fishing, bee keeping. *Address:* The Cot, 15 Broomhill Court, Nethy Bridge, Inverness-shire PH25 3EH. *T:* (01479) 821576.

WHEATLEY, Prof. David John, MD; British Heart Foundation Professor of Cardiac Surgery, University of Glasgow, since 1979; Hon. Consultant Cardiac Surgeon, Glasgow Royal Infirmary, since 1979; *b* 2 Aug. 1941; *s* of John Henry Wheatley and Dorothy Wheatley (*née* Price); *m* 1964, Ann Marie Lamberth; two *d*. *Educ:* South African Coll., Cape Town; Univ. of Cape Town Med. Sch. (MB ChB 1964; ChM 1976; MD 1979). FRCSE 1969; FRCSGlas 1979; FRCPE 1997; FRCS 1998. Senior Registrar: Nat. Heart Hosp., London, 1972–73; Mearnskirk Hosp., Glasgow, 1974–76; Sen. Lectr, Royal Infirmary, Edinburgh, 1976–79. Mem. Council, RCSE, 1986–90, 1992–97, 1997–Sept. 2002; President: Soc. of Cardiothoracic Surgeons of GB and Ireland, 1996–98; European Assoc. for Cardiothoracic Surgery, 1998–99. Founder FMedSci 1998. *Publications:* Surgery of Coronary Artery Disease, 1986; author or jt author of 175 articles on cardiac surgery. *Recreations:* piano, classical music, opera. *Address:* 13 Lochend Drive, Bearsden, Glasgow G61 1ED. *T:* (home) (0141) 942 1381; (office) (0141) 211 4987.

WHEATLEY, Derek Peter Francis; QC 1981; Barrister-at-Law; Member, Joint Law Society/Bar Council Working Party on Banking Law, 1976–94; 3rd *s* of late Edward Pearse Wheatley, company director, and Gladys Wheatley; *m* 1955, Elizabeth Pamela, *d* of John and Gertrude Reynolds; two *s* one *d*. *Educ:* The Leys Sch., Cambridge; University Coll., Oxford (MA). Served War of 1939–45, Army, 1944–47: (short univ. course, Oxford, 1944); commissioned into 8th King's Royal Irish Hussars, 1945, Lieut. University Coll., Oxford, 1947–49; called to the Bar, Middle Temple, 1951; Deputy Coroner: to the Royal Household, 1959–64; for London, 1959–64; Recorder of the Crown Court, 1972–74. Chief Legal Advr to Lloyds Bank, 1976–89. Member: Commercial Court Cttee, 1976–90; Senate of Inns of Court and the Bar, 1975–78, 1982–85; Exec. Cttee, Bar Council, 1982–85; Bar Council, 1986–90, 1995–96, 1999–2000 (Member: Professional Standards Cttee, 1986–88; F and GP Cttee, 1988–); Chm., Bar Assoc. for Commerce, Finance and Industry, 1982–83 and 1999–2000 (Vice-Pres., 1986–); Sen. Vice-Chm., Employed Bar Assoc. (Chm., 1999–2000). Chm., Legal Cttee, Cttee of London and Scottish Bankers, 1985–87. FRSA 1994. *Publications:* articles in legal jls and The Times, etc. *Recreation:* sailing. *Address:* Three The Wardrobe, Old Palace Yard, Richmond, Surrey TW9 1PA. *T:* (020) 8940 6242, *Fax:* (020) 8332 0948; *e-mail:* derek.wheatley@virgin.net. *Clubs:* Roehampton, Sloane; Bar Yacht.

WHEATLEY, John Derek, CBE 1993; Member, National Rivers Authority, 1989–96 (Chief Executive, 1991–92); *b* 24 July 1927; *s* of Leslie Sydney and Lydia Florence Wheatley; *m* 1956, Marie Gowers; one *s* one *d*. *Educ:* Sir Thomas Rich's Sch., Gloucester; Loughborough Coll., 1944–46 (Teacher's Cert.); Carnegie College of Physical Educn, 1952–53 (DipPE). Served RAF, 1946–52; Surrey Education Authority, 1953–54; Central Council of Physical Recreation: London and SE, 1954–58; Secretary, Northern Ireland, 1959–69; Principal Regional Officer, SW, 1970–72; Sports Council: Regional Director, SW, 1972–80; Director of Administrative Services, Headquarters, 1980–83; Dir Gen., 1983–88. Chm., Nat. Small-Bore Rifle Assoc., 1989–95. *Recreations:* gardening, music.

WHEATLEY, Hon. John Francis; *see* Wheatley, Hon. Lord.

WHEATLEY, Oswald Stephen, (Ossie), CBE 1997; Chairman, Sports Council for Wales, 1990–99; company director; *b* 28 May 1935; *s* of late Harold Wheatley and Laura Wheatley (*née* Owens); *m* 1964, Christine Mary Godwin (*d* 2000); one *s* (two *d* decd). *Educ:* King Edward's Sch., Birmingham; Caius Coll., Cambridge (MA Econs and Law). 2nd Lieut, RA, 1954. Cambridge Cricket Blue, 1957–58; played for Warwicks CCC, 1957–1960; Glamorgan CCC, 1961–69 (Captain, 1961–66); Chm., Glamorgan CCC, 1977–84. Test and County Cricket Board: Test Selector, 1972–74; Chairman: Discipline Cttee, 1978–83; Cricket Cttee, 1987–95; Mem., England Cttee, 1989–93; Chm., Cricket Foundn, 1996–. Member: Sports Council of GB, 1984–88 and 1990–96; UK Sports Council, 1997–99; Broadcasting Council for Wales, 1990–95; Sch. Exam and Assessment Council, 1992–93. Chm., Nat. Sports Medicine Inst., St Bartholomew's Hosp., 1991–96. Hon. Fellow, Univ. of Wales Inst., 1995. Freeman, City of Newcastle-upon-Tyne, 1976. *Recreations:* sport, art. *Address:* Low Fell, City, Cowbridge, Vale of Glamorgan CF71 7RW. *Clubs:* MCC, Free Foresters, Cardiff and County; Glamorgan CC.

WHEATLEY, Ven. Paul Charles; Archdeacon of Sherborne and Priest in Charge of West Stafford with Frome Billet, since 1991; *b* 27 May 1938; *s* of Charles Lewis and Doris Amy Wheatley; *m* 1963, Iris Mary Lacey; two *s* one *d*. *Educ:* Wycliffe Coll.; St John's Coll., Durham (BA 1961); Lincoln Theol Coll. Ordained deacon 1963, priest 1964; Curate, Bishopston, Bristol, 1963–68; Youth Chaplain, dio. of Bristol, 1968–73; Team Rector, Dorcan, Swindon, 1973–79; Rector, Ross, Hereford, 1979–81; Team Rector, Ross with Brampton Abbots, Bridstow, Peterstow, 1979–91; Prebendary, Hereford Cathedral, 1987–91; Ecumenical Officer, Hereford, 1987–91; Hon. Canon, Salisbury Cathedral, 1991–. *Recreations:* travel, gardening, opera, model railways. *Address:* The Rectory, West Stafford, Dorchester, Dorset DT2 8AB. *T:* (01305) 264637, *Fax:* (01305) 260640.

WHEATLEY, Rt Rev. Peter Williams; *see* Edmonton, Area Bishop of.

WHEATLEY, Philip Martin; Deputy Director General, HM Prison Service, since 1999; *b* 4 July 1948; *s* of Alan Osborne Wheatley and Ida Mary Wheatley; *m* 1st, 1969, Merryll Angela Francis (marr. diss. 1989); one *s* one *d*; 2nd, 1990, Anne Eleanor Roy. *Educ:* Leeds Grammar Sch.; Sheffield Univ. (LLB Hons). HM Prison Service: Prison Officer, 1969–70; Asst Gov., 1970; Hull Prison, 1971–74; Prison Service Coll., 1974–78; Leeds Prison, 1978–82; Dep. Gov., Gartree Prison, 1982–86; Governor, Hull Prison, 1986–90; Prison Service Area Manager for E Midlands, 1990–92; Asst Dir, Custody Gp, Prison Service HQ, 1992–95; Dir of Dispersals, i/c 6 highest security prisons, 1995–99. Mem., Prisons Bd, 1995–. *Recreations:* good wine, good food and holidays to enjoy them. *Address:* HM Prison Service Headquarters, Room 506, Cleland House, Page Street, SW1P 4LN.

WHEATON, Rev. Canon David Harry; Vicar of Christ Church, Ware, 1986–96; Chaplain to The Queen, 1990–2000; *b* 2 June 1930; *s* of Harry Wheaton, MBE, and Kathleen Mary (*née* Frost); m 1956, Helen Joy Forrer; one *s* two *d*. *Educ:* Abingdon Sch.; St John's Coll., Oxford (Exhibnr; MA); London Univ. (BD (London Bible Coll.)); Oak Hill Theol Coll. NCO, Wiltshire Regt, 1948–49. Deacon, 1959; priest, 1960; Tutor, Oak Hill Coll., 1954–62; Rector of Ludgershall, Bucks, 1962–66; Vicar of St Paul, Onslow Square, S Kensington, 1966–71; Chaplain, Brompton Chest Hosp., 1969–71; Principal Oak Hill Theol Coll., 1971–86; RD of Hertford, 1988–91. Hon. Canon, Cathedral and Abbey Church of St Alban, 1976–96, now Canon Emeritus. *Publications: contributed to:* Baker's Dictionary of Theology, 1960; New Bible Dictionary, 1962; New Bible Commentary (rev.), 1970, 21st century edn 1994; Lion Handbook to the Bible, 1973, 3rd edn 1999; Evangelical Dictionary of Theology, 1984; Here We Stand, 1986; Restoring the Vision, 1990. *Recreations:* walking, carpentry and do-it-yourself. *Address:* 43 Rose Drive, Chesham, Bucks HP5 1RR. *T:* (01494) 783862.

WHEELER, Rev. Andrew Charles; Archbishop's Secretary for the Anglican Communion, 2000–01; *b* 14 April 1948; *s* of Charles Hildred Wheeler and Ruth Goss Wheeler (*née* Rhymes); *m* 1979, Susan Jane Snook; one *s* one *d*. *Educ:* Corpus Christi Coll., Cambridge (MA); Makerere Univ., Kampala (MA); Leeds Univ. (PGCE); Trinity Coll., Bristol (BA Theol.). Asst Master in Hist., Harrogate Granby High Sch., 1972–75; theol teacher, for CMS, Bishop Gwynne Coll., Mundri, Sudan, 1977–86; ordained deacon, 1988, priest, 1988; Asst Curate, Aldbourne, Salisbury dio., 1988–89; Hon. Curate, All Saints Cathedral, Cairo, with resp. for care of Sudanese refugees, 1989–92; Theol Trng Co-ordinator, New Sudan Council of Churches, 1992–96; Sudan Church Res. Project Dir, 1996–2000. *Publications:* (Gen. Ed.) Faith in Sudan series, 10 vols, 1997–2000 (ed and contrib. to vols 1, 5 and 6); (jtly) Day of Devastation, Day of Contentment: the history of the Sudanese Church across 2000 years, 2000. *Recreations:* music, walking, squash.

WHEELER, Sir Anthony; *see* Wheeler, Sir H. A.

WHEELER, Captain Arthur Walter; RN retd; CEng; Keeper, HMS Belfast, 1983–88; *b* 18 Oct. 1927; *s* of Walter Sidney Wheeler and Annie Ethel Marsh; *m* 1st, 1957, Elizabeth Jane Glendinning Bowman (marr. diss. 1968); two *s*; 2nd, 1968, Mary Elvis Findon; one *s*. *Educ:* Woodhouse Sch., Finchley; HMS Fisgard, Torpoint; RN Engineering Coll., Manadon. FIMechE, MIMarE. Joined Royal Navy as artificer apprentice, 1943; served in cruiser Birmingham, 1947–50. Progressively, Sub Lieut 1950 to Captain 1974. Served in frigate Palliser and aircraft carriers Bulwark, Hermes and Ark Royal 1954–74; Sea Trng Staff at Portland, 1961–63; MoD, Ship Dept, 1966–70 and 1975–78; CSO(Engrg) to Flag Officer Third Flotilla, 1979–80; HMS Daedalus in comd, 1980–82, retired. Received into RC Church, 1987. *Recreations:* painting and drawing, music and opera, English history.

WHEELER, Arthur William Edge, CBE 1979 (OBE 1967); Chairman, Foreign Compensation Commission, 1983–2001; a Social Security Commissioner, 1992–98; a Child Support Commissioner, 1993–98; *b* 1 Aug. 1930; *e s* of Arthur William Wheeler and Rowena (*née* Edge); *m* 1956, Gay; two *s* one *d*. *Educ:* Mountjoy Sch.; Trinity Coll., Dublin (Reid Prof.'s Prize, MA, LLB). Called to the Irish Bar, King's Inns, 1953; called to the Bar, Gray's Inn, 1960; practised at Irish Bar, 1953–55; Crown Counsel, Nigeria, 1955; Legal Sec. (Actg), Southern Cameroons, and Mem. Exec. Council and House of Assembly, 1958; Principal Crown Counsel, Fedn of Nigeria, 1961; Northern Nigeria: Dep. Solicitor Gen., 1964; Dir of Public Prosecutions, 1966; High Court Judge, 1967; Chief Judge (formerly Chief Justice), Kaduna State of Nigeria, 1975; Comr for Law Revision, northern states of Nigeria, 1980. Mem., Body of Benchers, Nigeria, 1975; Associate Mem., Commonwealth Parly Assoc. *Recreations:* sport (university colours for hockey and assoc. football; Nigerian hockey internat.), music. *Clubs:* Royal Commonwealth Society, MCC.

WHEELER, Charles (Cornelius-), CMG 2001; journalist and broadcaster, since 1940; *b* 26 March 1923; *s* of late Wing-Comdr Charles Cornelius-Wheeler, RFC and RAFVR, and Winifred (*née* Rees); *m* 1962, Dip Singh; two *d*. *Educ:* Cranbrook School. Began journalism as tape-boy, Daily Sketch, 1940. Served War, Royal Marines, 1942–46; Captain 1944 (despatches NW Europe). Sub-editor, BBC Latin American Service, 1947–49; German Service Correspondent in Berlin, 1950–53; Talks writer, European Service, 1954–56; Producer, Panorama, 1956–58; S Asia Correspondent, 1958–62; Berlin Corresp., 1962–65; Washington Corresp., 1965–68; Chief Correspondent: USA, 1969–73; Europe, 1973–76; BBC Television News, 1977; Panorama, 1977–79; Newsnight, 1980–95. Documentaries include: The Kennedy Legacy, 1970; Battle for Berlin, 1985; The Road to War (series), 1989; Bloody Sunday in Tbilisi, 1989; Beyond Reasonable Doubt, 1990; The Legacy of Martin Luther King, 1993; D-Day: the Battle of Normandy, 1994; Burma: the forgotten war, 1995; Wheeler on America (series), 1996; The LBJ Tapes, 1997; Why Stephen?, 1999; The White House Tapes (series), 1999; The Evacuation (series), 1999; The Peacetime Conscripts (series), 2000; The Nationbuilders, 2001; Death Row on Trial, 2001. DUniv Open, 1992; Hon. DLitt Sussex, 1995. TV Journalist of the Year, RTS, 1988; Internat. Documentary Award, RTS, 1989; James Cameron Meml Award, City Univ., 1990; RTS Special Commendation, 1992; Cyril

Bennett Award, RTS, 1993; Harvey Lee Award, BPG, 1995; TV Journalist of the Year, BPG, 1996; RTS Judges' Award, 1996; BAFTA Special Award, 1997; Home Documentary Award, RTS, 1999; Sony Radio Speech Award, 2000. *Publication:* The East German Rising (with Stefan Brant), 1955. *Recreations:* gardening, travel. *Address:* 10A Portland Road, W11 4LA.

WHEELER, Prof. David John, FRS 1981; Professor of Computer Science, Cambridge University, 1978–94, now Emeritus; Fellow of Darwin College, Cambridge, 1967–94, now Emeritus; *b* 9 Feb. 1927; *s* of Arthur William Wheeler and Agnes Marjorie (*née* Gudgeon); *m* 1957, Joyce Margaret Blackler; one *s* two *d. Educ:* Camp Hill Grammar Sch., Birmingham; Hanley High Sch., Stoke on Trent; Trinity Coll., Cambridge. Research Fellow, Trinity Coll., Cambridge, 1951–57; Visiting Asst Prof., Univ. of Illinois, USA, 1951–53; Asst Director of Research, Cambridge Univ., 1956–66; Reader in Computer Science, Cambridge Univ., 1966–78. Fellow, Assoc. of Computing Machinery, 1994. *Publication:* The Preparation of Programs for an Electronic Digital Computer, 1951. *Address:* 131 Richmond Road, Cambridge CB4 3PS. *T:* (01223) 351319.

WHEELER, Frank Basil, CMG 1990; HM Diplomatic Service, retired; Chairman, British-Chilean Chamber of Commerce, since 1997; *b* 24 April 1937; *s* of late Harold Gifford Wheeler and Winifred Lucy Wheeler (*née* Childs); *m* 1st, 1959, Catherine Saunders Campbell (*d* 1979); one *s*; 2nd, 1984, Alyson Ruth Lund (*née* Powell) (marr. diss. 1989); 3rd, 1991, Susana Plaza Larrea. *Educ:* Mill Hill Sch. HM Forces, 1956–58. HM Foreign Service, 1958–: Foreign Office, 1958–61; Third Sec. (Commercial), Moscow, 1961–63; Asst Private Sec. to Minister of State, FO, 1963–65; Second Sec. (Commercial), Berne, 1965–67; First Sec., FO (later FCO), 1967–72; Wellington, 1972–75; FCO, 1975–77; Counsellor and Head of Chancery, Prague, 1977–79; Inspector, 1979–82; Head of Personnel Policy Dept, FCO, 1982–84; Counsellor and Head of Chancery, UK Delegn to NATO, Brussels, 1984–86; Counsellor, on loan to DTI, 1986–89; Ambassador: to Ecuador, 1989–93; to Chile, 1993–97. Internat. Advr, FA, 1997–2000; Advr, InterClubNet plc, 2001. *Recreations:* music, tennis. *Address:* 53 Shelton Street, WC2H 9HE.

WHEELER, Sir (Harry) Anthony, Kt 1988; OBE 1973; RSA, FRIBA, FRIAS; President, Royal Scottish Academy, 1983–90; Senior Partner, 1954–86, Consultant, 1986–89, Wheeler & Sproson, Architects and Planning Consultants, Edinburgh and Kirkcaldy; *b* 7 Nov. 1919; *s* of Herbert George Wheeler and Laura Emma Groom; *m* 1944, Dorothy Jean Campbell; one *d. Educ:* Stranraer High Sch.; Royal Technical Coll., Glasgow; Glasgow School of Art; Univ. of Strathclyde (BArch). DipTP. Glasgow Sch. of Architecture, 1937–48 (war service, Royal Artillery, 1939–46); John Keppie Scholar and Sir Rowand Anderson Studentship, 1948; RIBA Grissell Gold Medallist, 1948, and Neale Bursar, 1949. Assistant: to City Architect, Oxford, 1948; to Sir Herbert Baker & Scott, London, 1949; Sen. Architect, Glenrothes New Town, 1949–51; Sen. Lectr, Dundee Sch. of Arch., 1952–58; commenced private practice in Fife, 1952. Principal works include: Woodside Shopping Centre and St Columba's Parish Church, Glenrothes; Reconstruction of Giles Pittenweem; Redevelopment of Dysart and of Old Buckhaven; Town Centre Renewal, Grangemouth; Students' Union, Univ. of St Andrews; Hunter Building, Edinburgh Coll. of Art; St Peter's Episcopal Ch, Kirkcaldy; Leonard Horner Hall, and Students' Union, Heriot-Watt Univ.; Bank of Scotland, and Royal Bank of Scotland, Dunfermline; Community and Outdoor Centre, Linlithgow. Member: Royal Fine Art Commn for Scotland, 1967–86; Scottish Housing Adv. Cttee, 1971–75; Trustee, Scottish Civic Trust, 1970–83; Pres., Royal Incorpn of Architects in Scotland, 1973–75; Vice-Pres., RIBA, 1973–75. FRSA; RSA 1975 (ARSA 1963; Treasurer, 1978–80; Sec., 1980–83); Hon. RA 1983; Hon. RHA 1983; Hon. RGI 1987. Hon. DDes Robert Gordon's Inst. of Technology, 1991. Hon. Pres., Saltire Soc., 1995. 22 Saltire Awards and Commendations for Housing and Reconstruction; 12 Civic Trust Awards and Commendations. *Publications:* articles on civic design and housing in technical jls. *Recreations:* making gardens, sketching and water colours, fishing, music and drama. *Address:* South Inverleith Manor, 31/6 Kinnear Road, Edinburgh EH3 5PG. *T:* (0131) 552 3854. *Clubs:* New, Scottish Arts (Edinburgh).

WHEELER, Air Chief Marshal Sir (Henry) Neil (George), GCB 1975 (KCB 1969; CB 1967); CBE 1957 (OBE 1949); DSO 1943; DFC 1941 (Bar 1943); AFC 1954; *b* 8 July 1917; *s* of late T. H. Wheeler, South African Police; *m* 1942, Elizabeth, *d* of late W. H. Weightman, CMG; two *s* one *d. Educ:* St Helen's College, Southsea, Hants. Entered Royal Air Force College, Cranwell, 1935; Bomber Comd, 1937–40; Fighter and Coastal Comds, 1940–45; RAF and US Army Staff Colls, 1943–44; Cabinet Office, 1944–45; Directing Staff, RAF Staff Coll., 1945–46; FEAF, 1947–49; Directing Staff, JSSC, 1949–51; Bomber Comd, 1951–53; Air Min., 1953–57. Asst Comdt, RAF Coll., 1957–59; OC, RAF Laarbruch, 1959–60; IDC, 1961; Min. of Defence, 1961–63; Senior Air Staff Officer, HQ, RAF Germany (2nd TAF), Sept. 1963–66; Asst Chief of Defence Staff (Operational Requirements), MoD, 1966–67, Deputy Chief of Defence Staff, 1967–68; Commander, FEAF, 1969–70; Air Mem. for Supply and Organisation, MoD, 1970–73; Controller, Aircraft, MoD Procurement Exec., 1973–75. ADC to the Queen, 1957–61. Director: Rolls-Royce Ltd, 1977–82; Flight Refuelling (Holdings) Ltd, 1977–85. Chm., Anglo-Ecuadorian Soc., 1986–88. Vice-Pres., Air League; Liveryman, GAPAN, 1980, Master, 1986–87. FRAeS; CIMgt. *Address:* Boundary Hall, Cooksbridge, Lewes, East Sussex BN8 4PT. *Clubs:* Royal Air Force, Flyfishers'.

WHEELER, Rt Hon. Sir John (Daniel), Kt 1990; PC 1993; JP; DL; Chairman, Service Authorities for National Criminal Intelligence Service and National Crime Squad, since 1997; *b* 1 May 1940; *s* of late Frederick Harry Wheeler and of Constance Elsie (*née* Foreman); *m* 1967, Laura Margaret Langley; one *s* one *d. Educ:* county sch., Suffolk; Staff Coll., Wakefield. Home Office: Asst Prison Governor, 1967–74; Res. Officer (looking into causes of crime and delinquency and treatment of offenders), 1974–76; Dir-Gen., BSIA, 1976–88 (Hon. Mem., 1990). Dir, National Supervisory Council for Intruder Alarms, 1977–88. Chairman: Nat. Inspectorate of Security Guard Patrol and Transport Services, 1982–92; Security Systems Inspectorate, 1987–90; Inspectorate of the Security Industry, 1992–93. Chm. and non-exec. dir, various cos, 1976–93, 1997–. Chm., Capital Link, 1997–. MP (C) City of Westminster, Paddington Div., 1979–83, Westminster N, 1983–97. Minister of State, NI Office, 1993–97. Member: Home Office Crime Prevention Cttee, 1976–92; Cons. Party National Adv. CPC Cttee, 1978–80; Home Affairs Select Cttee, 1979–92 (Chm., 1987–92); Chairman: Home Affairs Sub-Cttee, Race Relations and Immigration, 1980–87; All Party Penal Affairs Gp, 1986–93 (Vice-Chm., 1979–86); Vice-Chairman: Cons. Home Affairs Cttee, 1987–92 (Jt Sec., 1980–87); British Pakistan Parly Gp, 1987–93; Chm., Cons. Greater London Area Members' Cttee, 1983–90 (Jt Sec., 1980–83). Mem., Lloyd's, 1986–97. Pres., Paddington Div., St John Ambulance, 1998–99 (Vice Pres., 1990–98). Freeman, City of London, 1987. JP Inner London, 1978; DL Greater London, 1989; Rep. DL, LB of Merton, 1997. James Smart Lecture, SHHD, 1991 (Silver Medal). KStJ 1997 (Mem. Council, Order of St John for London, 1990–; Mem., Chapter Gen., 1993–99; Registrar, 1997–99, Sub-Chancellor, 1999–, Order of St John; Trustee and Mem. Priory Chapter for England and the Islands, 1999–). Hilal-i-Quaid-i-Azam (Pakistan), 1991. *Publications:* Who Prevents Crime?, 1980; (jtly) The Standard Catalogue of the Coins of the British Commonwealth, 1642 to present day, 1986. *Recreation:* enjoying life. *Address:* PO Box 890, SW1P 1XW.

WHEELER, Sir John (Hieron), 3rd Bt *cr* 1920; formerly Chairman, Raithby, Lawrence & Co. Ltd, retired 1973; *b* 22 July 1905; 2nd *s* of Sir Arthur Wheeler, 1st Bt; *S* brother, Sir Arthur (Frederick Pullman) Wheeler, 1964; *m* 1929, Gwendolen Alice (*née* Oram); two *s. Educ:* Charterhouse. Engaged in Print. Served War of 1939–45, Trooper, RTR, 1941–45. After the war, returned to printing. *Recreations:* whittling, dry stone walling. *Heir: s* John Frederick Wheeler [*b* 3 May 1933; *m* 1963, Barbara Mary, *d* of Raymond Flint, Leicester; two *s* one *d*]. *Address:* 39 Morland Avenue, Leicester LE2 2PF. *Club:* Wig and Pen.

WHEELER, (John) Stuart; Chief Executive, since 1974, and Chairman, since 1985, IG Group (formerly IG Index); *b* 30 Jan. 1935; adopted by late Capt. Alexander Hamilton Wheeler and Betty Lydia Wheeler; *m* 1979, Teresa Anne Codrington; three *d. Educ:* Eton Coll.; Christ Church, Oxford (LLB Hons). Nat Service, 2nd Lieut, Welsh Guards, 1953–55. Called to the Bar, Inner Temple, 1959, in practice as barrister, 1959–62; Asst Manager, Investment Dept, Hill Samuel, 1962–68; Manager, Investment Dept, J. H. Vavasseur, 1968–73; First Nat. Finance Corp., 1973. Coronation Medal, 1953. *Recreations:* tennis, bridge. *Address:* IG Group plc, Friars House, 157–168 Blackfriars Road, SE1 8EZ. *T:* (020) 7896 0011. *Clubs:* White's, Queen's, Portland.

WHEELER, Air Vice-Marshal Leslie William Frederick; Independent Inspector for Public Inquiries and Chairman of Appointments Boards for Civil Service Commissioners and Ministry of Defence, 1984–94; *b* 4 July 1930; *s* of late George Douglas Wheeler and Susan Wheeler; *m* 1960, Joan, *d* of late Harry Carpenter and of Evelyn Carpenter; two *d. Educ:* Creighton School, Carlisle. Commnd, 1952; Egypt and Cyprus, 1954–56; Specialist in Signals, 1958; Aden, 1958–60; V-force (Valiants), 1961–65; India (Staff Coll.), 1965–66; Headquarters Signals Command, 1966–69; OC 360 Sqdn, 1970–72; Dir, RAF Staff Coll., 1972–74; Electronic Warfare and Recce Operations, MoD, 1975–77; Stn Comdr, RAF Finningley, 1977–79; Air Cdre Policy & Plans, Headquarters RAF Support Comd, 1979–83; Dir-Gen., Personal Services (RAF), MoD, 1983–84, retired. *Recreations:* walking, golf, philately. *Address:* c/o HSBC, Brampton, Cumbria CA8 1NQ. *Club:* Royal Air Force.

WHEELER, Sir Neil; *see* Wheeler, Sir H. N. G.

WHEELER, Raymond Leslie, RDI 1995; FRAeS; FRINA; *b* 25 Oct. 1927; *s* of Edmund Francis Wheeler and Ivy Geraldine Wheeler; *m* 1950, Jean McInnes; one *s* two *d. Educ:* Southampton Univ. (BSc (Eng) 1949); Imperial Coll., London (MSc (Eng) 1953; DIC). FRAeS 1974; FRINA 1975. Apprentice, 1945–48, Aircraft stressman, 1953–62, Chief Stressman, 1962–65, Saunders Roe Ltd, then Saunders Roe Div. of Westland Aircraft Ltd; Chief Structural Designer and Project Engr, SRN4 (world's largest hovercraft), 1965; British Hovercraft Corp. Ltd, subseq. Westland Aerospace Ltd: Chief Designer, 1966–85; Technical Dir, 1972–85; Dir, 1985–91. *Publications:* (with A. E. Tagg) From Sea to Air: the heritage of Sam Saunders, 1989; From River to Sea: the marine heritage of Sam Saunders, 1993; Saunders Roe, 1998. *Recreations:* gardening, photography, pottery, painting, archaeology, sport. *Address:* Brovacum, 106 Old Road, East Cowes, Isle of Wight PO32 6AX.

WHEELER, Gen. Sir Roger (Neil), GCB 1997 (KCB 1993); CBE 1983; Constable, HM Tower of London, since 2001; Chief of the General Staff, 1997–2000; Aide-de-camp General to the Queen, 1996–2000; *b* 16 Dec. 1941; *s* of Maj.-Gen. T. N. S. Wheeler, CB, CBE; *m* 1980, Felicity Hares; three *s* one *d* by former marriage. *Educ:* All Hallows Sch., Devon. Early Army service in Borneo and ME, 1964–70; Bde Major, Cyprus Emergency, 1974; Mem., Lord Carver's Staff, Rhodesia talks, 1977; Bn Comd, Belize, Gibraltar, Berlin and Canada, 1979–82; COS, Falkland Is, June–Dec. 1982; Bde Comd, BAOR, 1985–86; Dir, Army Plans, 1987–89; Comdr, 1st Armoured Div., BAOR, 1989–90; ACGS, MoD, 1990–92; GOC and Dir of Military Ops, NI, 1993–96; C-in-C, Land Comd, 1996–97. Col, Royal Irish Regt, 1996–2001; Col Comdt, Intell. Corps, 1996–2000. Hon. Colonel: QUB OTC, 2000–; Oxford Univ. OTC, 2000–. President: Army RFU, 1995–99; Army Rifle Assoc., 1995–2000; Mem. Council, NRA, 2000–. Non-executive Director: Thales plc, 2001–; Affinitas, 2001–. Pres., Ex Services Mental Welfare Soc., Combat Stress, 2001–. Patron, Police Foundn, 2001–. FRGS 2000. Hon. Liveryman, Painter-Stainers' Co. Hon. Fellow, Hertford Coll., Oxford. *Recreations:* fly-fishing, cricket, shooting, ornithology. *Clubs:* Army and Navy, Royal Commonwealth Society; Stragglers of Asia CC, Devon Dumplings CC.

WHEELER, (Selwyn) Charles (Cornelius-); *see* Wheeler, C. C.

WHEELER, Stuart; *see* Wheeler, J. S.

WHEELER-BENNETT, Richard Clement; Chairman of the Council, Marie Curie Cancer Care (formerly Marie Curie Memorial Foundation), 1990–2000; *b* 14 June 1927; *s* of Dr Clement Wheeler-Bennett and Enid Lucy (*née* Boosey); *m* 1954, Joan Ellen Havelock (marr. diss.); two *d* (one *s* decd); *m* 2001, Hon. Lady Smith-Ryland. *Educ:* Radley; Christ Church, Oxford (MA); Harvard Business Sch. Served Royal Marines, 1944–48. First Nat. City Bank of NY, 1951–66, Manager 1960–66; Australia and New Zealand Banking Group, 1966–80; Exec. Dir, 1967–78; Gen. Manager Europe, 1978–80; Chm., Thomas Borthwick & Sons Ltd, 1980–85; Director: Fleming Technology Trust, 1983–90; Fleming Internat. High Income Investment Trust, 1990–92; ANZ Grindlays Bank, 1993–96. Pres. Dir Gen., Boucheries Bernard SA, Paris, 1980–85. Chm., British Overseas and Commonwealth Banks Assoc., 1980. Founder Chm., Prospect Housing Assoc., 1965–77. Chm. of Govs, Springfields Sch., Calne, 1991–. Chm., Roehampton Club Ltd, 1988–92. Freeman, City of London; Liveryman, Butchers' Co. *Recreations:* flyfishing, golf, shooting, viticulture. *Address:* The Old Hall, Medbourne, Market Harborough, Leics LE16 8DZ. *T:* (01858) 565543. *Clubs:* Brooks's, Pratt's, MCC.

WHEELER-BOOTH, Sir Michael (Addison John), KCB 1994; Special Lecturer in Politics, Magdalen College, Oxford, since 1998; Clerk of the Parliaments, 1991–97; *b* 25 Feb. 1934; *s* of Addison James Wheeler and Mary Angela Wheeler-Booth (*née* Blakeney-Booth); *m* 1982, Emily Frances Smith; one *s* two *d. Educ:* Leighton Park Sch.; Magdalen Coll., Oxford (Exhibnr; MA). Nat. Service, Midshipman (Sp.) RNVR, 1952–54. A Clerk, House of Lords, 1960–97; seconded as Private Secretary to Leader of House and Government Chief Whip, 1965; seconded as Jt Sec., Inter-Party Conference on House of Lords Reform, 1967; Clerk of the Journals, 1970–74, 1983–90; Chief Clerk, Overseas and European Office, 1972, Principal Clerk, 1978; Reading Clerk, 1983; Clerk Asst, 1988. Treas. and Co-Ed. Jl, Soc. of Clerks at the Table in Commonwealth Parlts, 1962–65. Comr, Welsh Nat. Assembly Standing Orders, 1998–99. Chm., Study of Parliament Gp, 1984–87; Mem., Royal Commn on H of L reform, 1999. Waynflete Lectr, 1998, Vis. Fellow, 1997–98, Magdalen Coll., Oxford. Trustee: History of Parliament Trust, 1991–97; Industry and Parliament Trust, 1994–97. Gov., Magdalen Coll. Sch., 2001–. *Publications:* (contrib.) Griffith and Ryle, Parliament, 1989; (ed jtly) Halsbury's Laws of

England on Parliament, 4th edn 1997; contribs to parly jls. *Recreations:* reading, ruins, swimming, opera, the countryside. *Address:* Northfields, Sandford St Martin, Chipping Norton, Oxon OX7 7AG. *T:* (01608) 683632; 4 Polstead Road, Oxford OX2 6TN. *T:* (01865) 514040, 276108, *Fax:* (01865) 516048. *Clubs:* Brooks's, Garrick.

WHEELHOUSE, Keith Oliver B.; *see* Butler-Wheelhouse.

WHEEN, Natalie Kathleen; broadcaster and writer; *b* Shanghai, China, 29 July 1947; *d* of late Edward Leslie Lee Wheen and Galina (*née* Yourieff). *Educ:* Downe House, Newbury; London Univ. (BMus 1967); Royal Coll. of Music (ARCM). BBC, 1968–80: radio studio manager; attachments as Asst Producer, BBC TV Music and Arts, 1970; Radio 3 Music Producer, Manchester and London, 1971–72; Asst Producer, Music Now, Radio 3, 1972–73; Producer, Music Now, Talking About Music and various documentaries, 1973–80 (Best Music Documentary, Imperial Tobacco Soc. Authors Awards for Radio, 1978); London Arts Corresp., Canadian Broadcasting; freelance broadcaster, 1980–; Presenter: Kaleidoscope, Radio 4, 1980–95; Mainly for Pleasure, subseq. In Tune, Radio 3, 1980–97; Music Review, World Service; Cardiff Singer of the World, BBC2, 1993, 1995 and 1997; presenter, Classic FM: Week-end Afternoons, 1999–; Access All Areas, 2000–01; Tonight at 11, 2001–; contributor: The Food Programme, R4; The Influence of Effluent, R4, 1998; Compère, Gramophone Awards, 1995 and 1996; interviews, Third Ear, etc; interviewer and co-producer: Tippett's Time, C4, 1995; Visions of Paradise Intervals, R3, 1995; documentaries on arts subjects. Partner, Worsley Wheen prodns, 1983–88; indep. media prodn with Natalie Wheen & Associates. Contributing Editor, 3 mag., 1983–86. Jury Member: Sony Awards for Radio, 1994; Prudential Awards for the Arts, 1996. Director/Trustee: Hackney Music Develt Trust, 1995–; Creative Dance Artists Trust, 1995–96; Matthew Hawkins and the Fresh Dances Gp, 1995–97. Lectr and Workshop Leader in presentation and communication skills; Consultant, GSMD, 1991–92; Presenter, British Airways In-flight Light Classics Channel, 1991–95. Mem. Council, ENO Works, 1996–. Governor, Downe House Sch., 1986–98. *Publications:* (jtly) A Life on the Fiddle: Max Jaffa's Autobiography, 1991; publications on trng and employment for Careers and Occupational Information Centre, and Dept of Employment. *Recreations:* olives, fishing, whisky, laughter, anarchy. *Address:* c/o Simpson Fox Associates, 52 Shaftesbury Avenue, W1D 6LP.

WHELAN, Michael George; Practice Director, T. V. Edwards (Solicitors), since 2000; *b* 13 Oct. 1947; *s* of George Henry Whelan and Vera Frances Whelan (*née* Davies); *m* 1st, 1968, Veronica Gemma Merron (marr. diss. 1986); one *s* one *d*; 2nd, 1987, Anne Vivien Williams, JP; one *s*. *Educ:* Univ. of London (BSc(Econ) Hons, MSc(Econ)). Operational Manager, Walton Hosp., Liverpool, then Good Hope Hosp., Sutton Coldfield, and Hope Hosp., Salford, 1964–72; Tutor in Management, and Principal Trng Officer, N Western RHA, 1972–74; Deputy Chief Officer: Tameside and Glossop HA, 1974–78; Surrey AHA, 1978–80; Chief Officer, SW Surrey HA, 1980–85; Gp Manager, Healthcare, KPMG Management Consultants,1985–90; Partner, Pannell Kerr Forster, 1990–92; Chief Exec., Parkinson's Disease Soc., 1992–94; healthcare business consultant, 1994–97; Principal, Watson Wyatt Actuaries and Consultants, 1997–98; Chief Exec., Thomson, Snell & Passmore, Solicitors, 1998–2000. AIPM 1975; FHSM 1980. *Recreations:* music, entertaining, family, gardening, literature. *Address:* Chambord, 46 Pewley Way, Guildford, Surrey GU1 3QA.

WHELAN, Prof. Michael John, MA, PhD, DPhil; FRS 1976; FInstP; Professor of Microscopy of Materials, Department of Materials, University of Oxford, 1992–97, now Emeritus Professor; Fellow of Linacre College, Oxford, since 1967; *b* 2 Nov. 1931; *s* of William Whelan and Ellen Pound. *Educ:* Farnborough Grammar Sch.; Gonville and Caius Coll., Cambridge. FInstP 1976. Fellow of Gonville and Caius Coll., 1958–66; Demonstrator in Physics, Univ. of Cambridge, 1961–65; Asst Dir of Research in Physics, Univ. of Cambridge, 1965–66; Reader, Dept of Materials, Univ. of Oxford, 1966–92. Hon. Prof., Univ. of Sci. and Technol. Beijing, China, 1995. C. V. Boys Prize, Inst. of Physics, 1965; Hughes Medal, Royal Soc., 1988; Distinguished Scientist Award, Microscopy Soc. of Amer., 1998. *Publications:* (co-author) Electron Microscopy of Thin Crystals, 1965; Worked Examples in Dislocations, 1990; numerous papers in learned jls. *Recreation:* gardening. *Address:* 18 Salford Road, Old Marston, Oxford OX3 0RX. *T:* (01865) 244556.

WHELAN, Terence Leonard; editorial consultant; Editor, Ideal Home Magazine, 1977–95; *b* 5 Dec. 1936; *s* of Thomas James and Gertrude Beatrice Whelan; *m* 1972, Margaret Elizabeth Bowen; one *d*, and two *s* from previous marriage. *Educ:* Oakfield Secondary School. NDD 1955; MSTD 1972. Studied Graphic Design at Beckenham College of Art, 1953–56. Art Editor, Publishers, Condé Nast, working on Vogue Pattern Book, Vogue South Africa and British Vogue, 1959–68; gained a number of Design and Art Direction awards during this period; Art Editor, 1968–74, Asst Editor/Art Director, 1974–77, Ideal Home magazine. FRSA 1993. Editor of the Year, Special Interest Section, British Soc. of Magazine Editors, 1988. *Publications:* writer and broadcaster on home improvements. *Address:* 12 Bromefield, Stanmore, Middlesex HA7 1AB. *T:* and *Fax:* (020) 8952 5114.

WHELAN, Prof. William Joseph, PhD, DSc; FRS 1992; Professor of Biochemistry and Molecular Biology, University of Miami School of Medicine, since 1967 (Chairman of Department, 1967–91); *b* 14 Nov. 1924; *s* of William Joseph Whelan and Jane Antoinette Whelan (*née* Bertram); *m* 1951, Margaret Miller Birnie (*d* 1993). *Educ:* Univ. of Birmingham, England (BSc Hons 1944; PhD 1948; DSc 1955). Asst Lectr, Univ. of Birmingham, 1947–48; Asst Lectr, Lectr and Sen. Lectr, UCNW, Bangor, 1948–55; Sen. Mem., Lister Inst. of Preventive Medicine, Univ. of London, 1956–64; Prof. and Head, Dept of Biochemistry, Royal Free Hosp. Sch. of Medicine, Univ. of London, 1964–67. Co-Dir, Miami Nature Biotech. Winter Symposia, 1968–99. Dir, Enterprise Florida Technol. Develt Bd (formerly Enterprise Florida Innovation Partnership), 1993–98. President: Portland Press Inc., 1995–98; Frontiers of Knowledge Inc., 1999–. Pres., Internat. Union of Biochemistry and Molecular Biol., 1997–2000. FAAAS 1989. Hon. MRCP 1985; Hon. Mem., Biochemical Soc., 1993. Hon. DSc La Trobe, 1997. Alsberg Medal, 1967; Ciba Medal, 1968; Saare Medal, 1979; FEBS Millennium Medal, 2000. Editor-in-Chief: Trends in Biochemical Sciences, 1975–78; BioEssays, 1984–89; Fedn Procs, 1986–87; FASEB Jl, 1987–96; IUBMB Life, 2000–. *Recreations:* publishing, travel. *Address:* Department of Biochemistry and Molecular Biology, University of Miami School of Medicine (M823), PO Box 016129, Miami, FL 33101–6129, USA. *T:* (305) 2436267, *Fax:* (305) 3245665; *e-mail:* wwhelan@miami.edu. *Club:* Athenæum.

WHELDON, Juliet Louise, CB 1994; HM Procurator General and Treasury Solicitor, since 2000; *b* 26 March 1950; *d* of late John Wheldon and of Ursula Mabel Caillard. *Educ:* Sherborne School for Girls; Lady Margaret Hall, Oxford (1st Cl. Hons Mod. Hist.). Called to the Bar, Gray's Inn, 1975, Bencher 1999. Treasury Solicitor's Dept, 1976–83; Law Officers Dept, 1983–84; Treasury Solicitor's Dept, 1984–86; Asst Legal Sec. to the Law Officers, 1986–87; Hd of Central Adv. Div., Treasury Solicitor's Dept (Under-Sec.), 1987–89; Legal Sec. to the Law Officers, 1989–97; Legal Advr to Home Office, 1997–2000. Hon. QC 1997. *Address:* Queen Anne's Chambers, 28 Broadway, SW1H 9JS; *e-mail:* thetreasurysolicitor@treasury-solicitor.gsi.gov.uk.

WHELER, Sir Edward (Woodford), 14th Bt *cr* 1660, of City of Westminster; Company Secretary, Robert Lewis (St James's) Ltd, 1981–90; *b* 13 June 1920; *s* of Sir Trevor Wood Wheler, 13th Bt, and Margaret Idris (*d* 1987), *y d* of late Sir Ernest Birch, KCMG; *S* father, 1986; *m* 1945, Molly Ashworth (*d* 2000), *e d* of Thomas Lever, Devon; one *s* one *d*. *Educ:* Radley College. Joined Army (RA), 1940; commnd Royal Sussex Regt, 1941; attached 15 Punjab Regt, IA, 1941–45; BAOR, 1945–47. Oversea Audit Service, Uganda and Ghana, 1948–58; Automobile Association of East Africa, Kenya, 1958–70; Benson & Hedges Ltd, 1971–81, Director 1979–81. Liveryman, Co. of Pipe Makers and Tobacco Blenders, 1980; Freeman, City of London, 1980. *Heir:* *s* Trevor Woodford Wheler [*b* 11 April 1946; *m* 1974, Rosalie Margaret, *d* of late Ronald Thomas Stunt; two *s*].

WHELON, Charles Patrick Clavell; a Recorder of the Crown Court, 1978–97; *b* 18 Jan. 1930; *s* of Charles Eric Whelon and Margaret Whelon; *m* 1968, Prudence Mary (*née* Potter); one *s* one *d*. *Educ:* Wellington Coll.; Pembroke Coll., Cambridge (MA Hons). Called to Bar, Middle Temple, 1954. Liveryman of Vintners' Co., 1952–. *Recreations:* gardening, cartooning. *Address:* Russets, Pyott's Hill, Old Basing, Hants RG24 8AP. *T:* (01256) 469964.

WHELTON, David William; pianist, organist, music administrator; Managing Director, Philharmonia Orchestra, since 1988; *b* 16 June 1954; *s* of William and Nora Whelton; *m* 1977, Caroline Rachel Gardner; one s. Dir of Music, Royal GS, Guildford, 1979–83; Music Officer, Yorks Arts Assoc., 1983–85; Principal Arts Officer, Leeds CC, 1985–86; Music Officer, Arts Council of GB, 1986–88. Director: Assoc. of British Orchestras, 1997–; Internat. Musicians Seminar, Prussia Cove, 1998–. Trustee: Mayfield Valley Arts Trust, 1986–; Philharmonia Trust, 1988–. *Recreations:* gardening, architecture, history. *Address:* Philharmonia Orchestra, First Floor, 125 High Holborn, WC1V 6QA. *T:* (020) 7242 5001.

WHENT, Sir Gerald Arthur, Kt 1995; CBE 1989; Deputy Chairman, Vodafone Group PLC, 1997–98 (Chief Executive, 1988–96); *b* 1 March 1927; *m* 1st, Coris Dorothy (*née* Bellman-Thomas); one *s* one *d*; 2nd, Sarah Louise (*née* Donaldson); two step *s* one step *d*. *Educ:* St Mary's College, Southampton. Dent Allcroft & Co.: Management Trainee, 1952; Asst Div. Manager, 1957; Div. Manager, 1959–62; Plessey Co.: Dept Manager, 1962; Div. Gen. Manager, 1966–69; Dir, Racal Recorders, 1970–72; Man. Dir, Racal Comsec, 1973–76; Man. Dir, Racal-Tacticom, 1977–80; Chm. and Man. Dir, Racal Radio Group, 1980–85; Dir, Racal Electronics plc, 1982–; Chm. and Chief Exec., Racal Telecommunications Group, 1983–88. *Recreations:* golf, ski-ing, horse riding, chess, bridge. *Address:* Raffin Stud, West Soley, Chilton Foliat, Hungerford RG17 0TN.

WHETNALL, Andrew Donard, CB 1996; Director for Local Government, Department for Transport, Local Government and the Regions (formerly Department of the Environment, Transport and the Regions), since 1996; *b* 18 May 1948; *s* of late Donard and of Joan Whetnall (*née* Mummery); *m* 1972, Jane Lepel Glass; two *s* two *d*. *Educ:* King's Norton Grammar Sch.; Univ. of Sussex (MA). Joined DoE, 1975; Principal, Dept of Transport, 1980–83; Department of the Environment: Principal, 1983–87, Asst Sec., 1987–88, Inner Cities; Water Legislation, 1988–89; Head, Machinery of Govt Div., Cabinet Office, 1989–96 (Under Sec., 1993). *Recreations:* reading, music. *Address:* Department for Transport, Local Government and the Regions, Eland House, Bressenden Place, SW1E 5DU. *T:* (020) 7944 4198.

WHETSTONE, Rear-Adm. Anthony John, CB 1982; Member, Advisory Committee on Historic Wreck Sites, since 1996; *b* 12 June 1927; *s* of Albert Whetstone; *m* 1951, Elizabeth Stewart Georgeson; one *s* two *d*. *Educ:* King Henry VIII School, Coventry. Joined RN, 1945; specialised in submarines, 1949; Commanded: HMS Sea Scout, 1956–57; HMS Artful, 1959–61; HMS Repulse, 1968–70; HMS Juno, 1972–73; HMS Norfolk, 1977–78; Flag Officer Sea Training, 1978–80; Asst Chief of Naval Staff (Operations), 1981–83. Director-General: Cable TV Assoc., 1983–86; Nat. Television Rental Assoc., 1983–87. Dep. Sec., Defence Press and Broadcasting Cttee, 1987–92. Dir, DESC Ltd, 1991–96. Nat. Pres., Submariners Assoc., 1988–May 2002. Chm. Trustees, Royal Navy Submarine Mus., 1990–98. FIMgt (FBIM 1979). *Recreations:* hill walking, fishing, amateur dramatics (Chm., Civil Service Drama Fedn, 1985–92). *Address:* 17 Anglesey Road, Alverstoke, Hants PO12 2EG. *Club:* Army and Navy.
See also N. K. Whetstone.

WHETSTONE, (Norman) Keith, OBE 1983; VRD; journalist and editorial consultant; *b* 17 June 1930; *yr s* of Albert and Anne Whetstone; *m* 1952, Monica Joan Clayton, Leamington Spa; three *s*. *Educ:* King Henry VIII Sch., Coventry. Served Royal Navy, 1949–50, 1951–52; Lt Comdr (S) RNVR, retired, 1965. Coventry Evening Telegraph, 1950–51; Western Morning News, 1952–55; Birmingham Post, 1955–58; Coventry Evening Telegraph, 1958–63; Editor, Cambridge Evening News, 1964–70; Editor, Coventry Evening Telegraph, 1970–80; Editor-in-Chief: Birmingham Evening Mail series, 1980–84; Birmingham Post and Birmingham Evening Mail series, 1984–86; Dir, Birmingham Post & Mail Ltd, 1980–86. Nat. Pres., Guild of British Newspaper Editors, 1976–77. Mem. Press Council, 1980–86. *Recreations:* theatre, Rugby football (Pres., Old Coventrians RFC, 2000), golf. *Address:* 4 The Green, Meriden, Coventry CV7 7PE. *T:* (01676) 522654; Niaudon, 46220 Prayssac, Lot, France. *T:* 565224661.
See also A. J. Whetstone.

WHEWAY, Albert James; Director, Hogg Robinson Travel Ltd, since 1976; *b* 6 April 1922; *s* of Albert and Alice Wheway; *m* 1st, 1946, Joan Simpson; 2nd, 1984, Susannah Mary Gray (*née* Luesby). *Educ:* Kimberworth School, Rotherham. Cooper Bros (later Cooper Lybrand), 1946–53; S. G. Warburg, 1953–57; industry, 1957–63; Ionian Bank, 1963–70; internat. industry and commerce, 1970–; Chm., Hogg Robinson Group plc, 1983–87. *Recreations:* art collecting, music. *Address:* Beaumont, Duddington, near Stamford, Lincs PE9 3QE. *T:* (01780) 444237; Bilancia, Cappella Alta, Lucca, Italy. *T:* (583) 394473.

WHICHER, Peter George, CEng; FRAeS; MIEE; Principal, INECO, since 1994; *b* 10 March 1929; *o s* of late Reginald George Whicher and Suzanne (*née* Dexter); *m* 1st, 1962, Susan Rosemary Strong (*d* 1989); one *s* one *d*; 2nd, 1992, Margaret Rosemary (*née* Rickman). *Educ:* Chichester High School. BSc(Eng) London 1948; CEng, MIEE 1957. STC, 1948–51; Flying Officer, RAF, 1951–53; Min. of Aviation, 1953; Principal Expert in Telecommunications, Eurocontrol Agency, Paris, 1962–64; Cabinet Office, 1964–66; Asst Dir, Telecommunications R & D, and Manager, Skynet Satellite Communications Project, Min. of Technology, 1967–71; Superintendent, Communications Div., RAE, 1971–73; Dir, Air Radio, MoD(PE), 1973–76; RCDS, 1977; Dir, Defence Sci. (Electronics), MoD, 1978–81; Dep. Dir, RAE, 1981–84. Consultant, Logica, 1985–94. FRAeS 1985. *Publications:* reports and papers for professional instns. *Recreations:* sailing, innovation, arts. *Address:* Widgers Wood, Sheets Health, Brookwood, Woking, Surrey GU24 0EJ. *Clubs:* Royal Ocean Racing; Offshore Cruising.

WHICKER, Alan Donald; television broadcaster (Whicker's World); writer; *b* 2 Aug. 1925; *o s* of late Charles Henry Whicker and late Anne Jane Cross. *Educ:* Haberdashers' Aske's Sch. Capt., Devonshire Regt; Dir, Army Film and Photo Section, with 8th Army and US 5th Army. War Corresp. in Korea, Foreign Corresp., novelist, writer, television and radio broadcaster. Joined BBC TV, 1957: Tonight programme (appeared nightly in filmed reports from around the world, studio interviews, outside broadcasts, Eurovision, and Telstar, incl. first Telstar two-way transmission at opening of UN Assembly, NY, 1962); TV Series: Whicker's World, 1959–60; Whicker Down Under, 1961; Whicker on Top of the World!, 1962; Whicker in Sweden, Whicker in the Heart of Texas, Whicker Down Mexico Way, 1963; Alan Whicker Report series: The Solitary Billionaire (J. Paul Getty), etc; wrote and appeared in own series of monthly documentaries on BBC 2, subseq. repeated on BBC 1, under series title, Whicker's World, 1965–67 (31 programmes later shown around the world); BBC radio programmes and articles for The Listener, etc; left BBC, 1968. Various cinema films, incl. The Angry Silence. Mem., successful consortium for Yorkshire Television, 1967. Completed 16 Documentaries for Yorkshire TV during its first year of operation, incl. Whicker's New World series, and Specials on Gen. Stroessner of Paraguay, Count von Rosen, and Pres. Duvalier of Haiti; Whicker in Europe; Whicker's Walkabout; Broken Hill—Walled City; Gairy's Grenada; documentary series, World of Whicker; Whicker's Orient; Whicker within a Woman's World, 1972; Whicker's South Seas, Whicker way out West, 1973; Whicker's World, series on cities, 1974–77; Whicker's World—Down Under, 1976; Whicker's World: US, 1977 (4 progs); India, 1978 (7 progs); Indonesia, 1979; California, 1980 (6 progs); Peter Sellers Meml programme, 1980; Whicker's World Aboard the Orient Express, 1982; Around Whicker's World in 25 Years (3 YTV retrospect. progs), 1982; BBC TV, 1982–92; Whicker's World—the First Million Miles (6 retrospect. progs), 1982; Whicker's World—a Fast Boat to China (4 QE2 progs), 1984; Whicker! (10 talk shows), 1984; Whicker's World—Living with Uncle Sam (10 progs), 1985; Whicker's World—Living with Waltzing Matilda (10 progs), 1987–88; Whicker's World—Hong Kong (8 progs), 1990; Whicker's World—a Taste of Spain (8 progs), 1992; returned to ITV for: Around Whicker's World—the Ultimate Package! (4 progs), 1992; Whicker's World—The Absolute Monarch (the Sultan of Brunei), 1992; South Africa: Whicker's Miss World, and Whicker's World—The Sun King, 1993; South-East Asia: Whicker's World Aboard the real Orient Express; Whicker—the Mahathir Interview (Dr Mahathir Mohammed, PM of Malaysia); Pavarotti in Paradise, 1994; updated 27 progs for Travel Channel, 1996 and 4 for Yorkshire-Tyne Tees, 1997; Auntie's Greatest Hits, BBC TV, 1998. BBC Radio: Chm., Start the Week; Whicker's Wireless World (3 series), 1983; Around Whicker's World (6 progs), 1998; Whicker's Week, 1999; Whicker's New World (7 progs), 1999; Whicker's World Down Under (6 Progs); The Fabulous Fifties (4 progs), 2000; The History of Television - It'll Never Last! (6 progs), 2001. FRSA 1970. Various awards, 1963–, incl. Screenwriters' Guild, best Documentary Script, 1963; Guild of Television Producers and Directors Personality of the Year, 1964; Silver Medal, Royal Television Soc., 1968; Dumont Award, Univ. of California, 1970; Best Interview Prog. Award, Hollywood Festival of TV, 1973; Dimbleby Award, BAFTA, 1978; TV Times Special Award, 1978; first to be named in RTS Hall of Fame for outstanding creative contribution to British TV, 1993; Travelex travel writers' Special Award for outstanding achievement in travel journalism, 1998. *Publications:* Some Rise by Sin, 1949; Away—with Alan Whicker, 1963; Best of Everything, 1980; Within Whicker's World: an autobiography, 1982; Whicker's Business Traveller's Guide (with BAA), 1983; Whicker's New World, 1985; Whicker's World Down Under, 1988; Whicker's World—Take 2, 2000; Sunday newspaper columns; contrib. various internat. pubns. *Recreations:* people, photography, writing, travel, and reading (usually airline timetables). *Address:* Le Gallais Chambers, St Helier, Jersey JE4 8YD.

WHIFFEN, David Hardy, MA, DPhil (Oxon), DSc (Birmingham); FRS 1966; FRSC; Professor of Physical Chemistry, 1968–85, Head of School of Chemistry, 1978–85, Pro-Vice-Chancellor, 1980–83, University of Newcastle upon Tyne (Dean of Science, 1974–77); *s* of late Noël H. and Mary Whiffen; *m* Jean P. Bell (*d* 1998); four *s*. *Educ:* Oundle School; St John's College, Oxford (Scholar). Sometime Commonwealth Fund Fellow, Sen. Student of Commn for 1851 Exhibition. Formerly: Lectr in Chemistry, Univ. of Birmingham; Supt, Molecular Science Div., NPL. Vice-Chm., Newcastle HA, 1983–85 (Mem., Newcastle AHA, 1978–82, Newcastle HA, 1982–85). Pres., Faraday Div., RSC, 1981–83. *Publications:* Spectroscopy, 1966; The Royal Society of Chemistry: the first 150 years, 1991; papers in scientific jls.

WHINERAY, Sir Wilson (James), KNZM 1998; OBE 1961; Chairman: Carter Holt Harvey Ltd, since 1993 (Director, since 1987; Deputy Managing Director, 1987–93); National Bank of New Zealand Ltd, since 1998 (Director, since 1993); *b* 10 July 1935; *s* of Bruce Ludlow Whineray and Ida Cecilia Whineray (*née* Billany); *m* 1959, Elisabeth Eve Seymour; one *s* two *d*. *Educ:* Auckland GS; Auckland Univ. (BCom 1964); Grad. Sch. of Business Admin, Harvard Univ. (MBA 1969). Played Rugby for All Blacks, 1957–65, Capt., 1958–65; 32 Tests, 30 as Captain. State Advances Corp. of NZ, 1958–64; Dominion Breweries Ltd, 1964–67; joined Alex Harvey Industries Ltd, 1969; became Carter Holt Harvey Ltd, 1985. Chm., Hillary Commn, 1993–98. Gov., NZ Sports Fedn, 1981–. Col Comdt, NZ SAS, 1997–. NZ Sportsman of the Year, 1965. *Address:* 15 Arney Crescent, Remuera, Auckland, New Zealand.

WHINNEY, Rt Rev. Michael Humphrey Dickens; Hon. Assistant Bishop, Diocese of Birmingham, since 1996 (Assistant Bishop, 1988–95); Canon Residentiary, Birmingham Cathedral, 1992–95; *b* 8 July 1930; *s* of late Humphrey Charles Dickens Whinney and Evelyn Lawrence Revell Whinney (*née* Low); great-great-grandson of Charles Dickens; *m* 1958, Veronica (*née* Webster); two *s* one *d*. *Educ:* Charterhouse; Pembroke Coll., Cambridge (BA 1955, MA 1958); Ridley Hall, Cambridge; General Theological Seminary, NY (STM 1990). National Service commission, RA, 1949 (served in 5th Regt, RHA and Surrey Yeo. Queen Mary's Regt). Articled clerk to Chartered Accountants, Whinney Smith & Whinney (now Ernst Young), 1950–52. Curate, Rainham Parish Church, Essex, 1957–60; Head, Cambridge University Mission Settlement, Bermondsey, 1960–67, Chaplain, 1967–72; Vicar, St James' with Christ Church, Bermondsey, 1967–73; Archdeacon and Borough Dean of Southwark, 1973–82; Bishop Suffragan of Aston, 1982–85; Bishop of Southwell, 1985–88. *Address:* Moorcroft, 3 Moor Green Lane, Moseley, Birmingham B13 8NE.

WHIPPLE, Prof. Fred Lawrence; Senior Scientist, Smithsonian Astrophysical Observatory, since 1973; Director, Smithsonian Institution Astrophysical Observatory, 1955–73; Phillips Professor of Astronomy, Harvard University, 1968–77; *b* 5 Nov. 1906; *s* of Harry Lawrence Whipple and Celestia Whipple (*née* MacFarland); *m* 1st, 1928, Dorothy Woods (divorced 1935); one *s*; 2nd, 1946, Babette Frances Samelson; two *d*. *Educ:* Long Beach High School, Calif; UCLA; Univ. of California, Berkeley. Lick Observatory Fellow, 1930–31; Staff Member, Harvard Univ., 1931–; Instructor, 1932–38; Lecturer, 1938–45; Assoc. Prof., 1945–50; Professor, 1950–77; Chm. Dept of Astronomy, 1949–56. US Nat. Cttee of Internat. Geophysical Year: Chm. Techn. Panel on Rocketry, 1955–59; Member: Techn. Panel on Earth Satellite Program, 1955–59; Working Group on Satellite Tracking and Computation, 1955–58; Scientific Advisory Bd to USAF, 1953–62; Cttee on Meteorology, Nat. Acad. of Sciences, Nat. Research Coun., 1958–61; Special Cttees on Space Techn., Nat. Advisory Cttee for Aeronautics, 1958–63 (now NASA), US; Space Sciences Working Group on Orbiting Astronomical Observatories, Nat. Acad. of Sciences (Mem. Nat. Acad. of Sciences, 1959–); Advisory Panel to Cttee on Sci. and Astronautics of US House of Representatives, 1960–73; Amer. Philosophical Soc., Philadelphia; Amer. Acad. of Arts and Sciences, Boston; New York Acad. of Science, NY; several technical societies. Associate, Royal Astronomical Soc., 1970–. Benjamin Franklin Fellow, RSA, 1968–. Editor: Smithsonian Contributions to Astrophysics, 1956–73; Planetary and Space Science, 1958–. Hon. degrees: MA, Harvard Univ., 1945; DSc, Amer. Internat. Coll., 1958; DLitt, North-eastern Univ., 1961; DS: Temple Univ., 1961; Arizona, 1979; LLD, CW Post Coll. of Long Island Univ., 1962. J. Lawrence Smith Medal of Nat. Acad. of Sciences, 1949; Donohue Medals, 1932, 1933, 1937, 1940, 1942 (received two medals that year); Presidential Certificate of Merit, 1948; Exceptional Service Award, US Air Force Scientific Adv. Bd, 1960; Space Flight Award, Amer. Astron. Soc., 1961; President's Award for Distinguished Federal Civilian Service, 1963; Space Pioneers Medallion, 1968; NASA Public Services Award, 1969; Kepler Medal, AAAS, 1971; Nat. Civil Service League's Civil Service Award, 1972; Henry Medal, Smithsonian Instn, 1973; Alumnus of the Year Award, UCLA, 1976; Gold Medal, Royal Astronomical Soc., 1983; Bruce Gold Medal, Astronomical Soc. of Pacific, 1986; UCLA Medal, 1997; other foreign awards. Depicted on postal stamp, Mauritania, 1986 (in recognition of contribn to understanding of comets, and to commemorate Halley's Comet) and on stamp of St Vincent, 1994. *Publications:* Earth, Moon and Planets, 1942, 3rd edn 1968; Orbiting the Sun, 1981; The Mystery of Comets, 1985; many technical papers in various astronomical and geophysical journals and books; popular articles in magazines and in Encyclopædia Britannica. *Recreation:* cultivation of roses. *Address:* Smithsonian Astrophysical Observatory, 60 Garden Street, Cambridge, MA 02138, USA. *T:* (617) 8647383.

WHISH, Prof. Richard Peter; Professor of Law, King's College London, since 1991; *b* 23 March 1953; *s* of Thomas Stanton Whish and Avis Mary Whish (*née* Sullivan). *Educ:* Clifton Coll., Bristol; Worcester Coll., Oxford (BA 1st Cl. Hons 1974; BCL 1st Cl. Hons 1978). Qualified as solicitor, 1977; University of Bristol: Lectr in Law, 1978–88; Reader in Commercial Law, 1988–90; Partner, Watson, Farley and Williams (Solicitors), London, 1989–98. Mem., Exec. Council, Centre for European Law, KCL, 1991–. Chm., Adv. Body to Dir Gen. of Gas and Electricity Mgt, 2000–01. Member: Adv. Cttee, Centre for Study of Regulated Industries, 1991–; Adv. Panel, Dir Gen. of Fair Trading, 2001–; Editl Bd, European Business Law Review, 1994–. FRSA 1995. *Publications:* (jtly) Conveyancing Solutions, 1987; (Gen. Ed.) Butterworth's Competition Law, 1991; Competition Law, 3rd edn 1993; (jtly) Merger Cases in the Real World: a study of merger control procedures, 1994; (ed) Halsbury's Laws of England, Vol. 47, 4th edn 1994; The Competition Act, 1998; numerous articles, case-notes and book reviews in legal periodicals and books. *Recreations:* opera and music, travelling (in particular in the sub-continent), gardening, conservation, Bristol Rovers FC. *Address:* 14 Glebe House, 15 Fitzroy Mews, W1T 6DP; *e-mail:* richard.whish@kcl.ac.uk.

WHISHAW, Anthony Popham Law, RA 1989 (ARA 1980); RWA 1992; *b* 22 May 1930; *s* of Robert Whishaw and Joyce (*née* Wheeler); *m* 1957, Jean Gibson; two *d*. *Educ:* Tonbridge Sch.; Chelsea Sch. of Art (Higher Cert); Royal College of Art (ARCA 1955). Travelling Schol., RCA; Abbey Minor Schol.; Spanish Govt Schol.; Abbey Premier Schol., 1982; Lorne Schol., 1982–83. John Moores Minor Painting Prize, 1982; (jtly) 1st Prize, Hunting Group Art Awards, 1986. *One-man exhibitions:* Libreria Abril, Madrid, 1957; Rowland Browse and Delbranco, London, 1960, 1961, 1963, 1965, 1968; ICA, 1971; New Art Centre, 1972; Folkestone Arts Centre, 1973; Hoya Gall., London, 1974; Oxford Gall., Oxford, 1974; ACME, London, 1978; Newcastle upon Tyne Polytech. Gall., 1979; (with Martin Froy) New Ashgate Gall., Farnham, 1979; Nicola Jacobs Gall., London 1981; From Landscape, Kettle's Yard, Cambridge, Ferens Gall., Hull, Bede Gall., Jarrow, 1982–84; Works on Paper, Nicola Jacobs Gall., 1983; Paintings, Nicola Jacobs Gall., 1984; Mappin Art Gall., Sheffield, 1985; Large Paintings, RA 1986; Reflections after Las Meninas (touring): Royal Acad., and Hatton Gall., Newcastle upon Tyne, 1987; Mead Gall., Warwick Univ., John Hansard Gall., Southampton Univ., and Spacex Gall., Exeter, 1988; Infaust Gall., Shanghai and Hamburg, 1989; Blason Gall., London, 1991; artspace, London, 1992, 1994 and 1995; RWA Bristol, 1993; Barbican, 1994 and tour, Mappin Gall., Sheffield, Royal Albert Meml Mus., Exeter, 1994, Newport Mus. and Art Gall., Bolton Metropolitan Mus. and Art Gall., 1995; Maclaurin Gall., Ayr, Huddersfield Gall., Royal Hibernian Acad. of Arts, Gallagher Gall., Dublin, Hatton Gall., Newcastle, 1994; Art First, London, 1997; Friends' Room, Royal Acad., 2000; Stephen Lacey Gall., London, 2000. *Group exhibitions:* Gimpel Fils, AIA Gall., Café Royal Centen., Towards Art (RCA), Camden Arts Centre, London, Ashmoleum Mus., Oxford, 1957–72; Brit. Drawing Biennale, Teesside, 1973; British Landscape, Graves Art Gall., Sheffield, Chichester Nat. Art, 1975; Summer Exhibn, RA, 1974–81; British Painting, 1952–77, RA, 1977; London Group, Whitechapel Open, 1978, A Free Hand, Arts Council (touring show), 1978; The British Art Show, Arts Council (touring), Recent Arts Council Purchases and Awards, Serpentine Gall., First Exhibition, Nicola Jacobs Gall., Tolly Cobbold (touring), 55 Wapping Artists, London, 1979; Four Artists, Nicola Jacobs Gall., Sculpture and Works on Paper, Nicola Jacobs, Wapping Open Studios, Hayward Annual, Hayward Gall., Whitechapel Open, Whitechapel Gall., John Moore's Liverpool Exhibn 12, 1980, Exhibn 13, 1982, Walker Art Gall., Liverpool; London Gp, S London Art Gall., Wapping Artists, 1981; Images for Today, Graves Art Gall., Sheffield, 1982; Nine Artists (touring), Helsinki, 1983; Tolly Cobbold/Eastern Arts Fourth (touring), 1983; Three Decades 1953–83, RA, 1983; Romantic Tradition in Contemporary British Painting (touring), Murcia and Madrid, Spain, and Ikon Gall., Birmingham, 1988. *Works in collections:* Arts Council of GB, Tate Gall., Coventry Art Gall., Leicester Art Gall., Nat. Gall. of Wales, Sheffield City Art Galls, Financial Times, Shell-BP, Museo de Bahia, Brazil, Nat. Gall. of Victoria, Melb., Seattle Mus. of Art, Bank of Boston, Chantrey Bequest, W Australia Art Gall., Bayer Pharmaceuticals, DoE, Nat. Westminster Bank, Power Art Gall., Aust. European Parlt, Ferens Art Gall, Museum, Murcia, Spain, Alliance & Leicester, Rosehaven PLC, Royal Academy, Linklater and Paines, Mus. of Contemp. Art, Helsinki, Christchurch, Kensington, Long Term Credit Bank of Japan, Andersen Consulting, Ashikaga Bank of Tokyo, Tetrapak, Zeneca, RWA, Deutsche Morgan-Grenfell, Mercury Asset Mgt, Ladbrokes, Crown Commodities, Stanhope, Baring Asset Mgt, St Anne's Coll., Oxford. *Recreations:* chess, badminton. *Address:* 7a Albert Place, Victoria Road, W8 5PD. *T:* (020) 7937 5197.

WHISHAW, Sir Charles (Percival Law), Kt 1969; solicitor (retired); *b* 29 October 1909; 2nd *s* of late Montague Law Whishaw and Erna Louise (*née* Spies); *m* 1936, Margaret Joan (*d* 1989), *e d* of late Col T. H. Hawkins, CMG, RMLI; one *s* two *d*. *Educ:* Charterhouse; Worcester College, Oxford. Called to Bar, Inner Temple, 1932; Solicitor, 1938; Partner in Freshfields, 1943–74. Trustee, Calouste Gulbenkian Foundn, 1956–81. Member: Iron and Steel Holding and Realisation Agency, 1953–67; Council, Law Soc., 1967–76. Comdr, Order of Prince Henry (Portugal), 1981. *Address:* Clare Park, near Farnham, Surrey GU10 5DT. *T:* (01252) 855065, 850681.

WHISTON, John Joseph; Director of Programmes, Yorkshire Tyne Tees Productions, since 1998; *b* 10 Oct. 1958; *s* of Peter Rice Whiston and Kathleen Whiston (*née* Parker); partner, Kate Symington; one *s* two *d*. *Educ:* Edinburgh Acad.; Balliol Coll., Oxford (BA Eng.). Joined BBC, 1982: follow spot operator, for Rowan Atkinson, 1982; gen. trainee, 1983–85; Producer, Music and Arts, 1985–94; Head: Youth and Entertainment Features, 1994–96; Entertainment and Features, 1996–98. Motoring corresp., Vogue, 1991–93. *Recreations:* collecting power tools, watching bad television. *Address:* 68 Stamford Road, Bowdon, Cheshire WA14 2JF. *T:* (0161) 928 6979.

WHITAKER, family name of **Baroness Whitaker**.

WHITAKER, Baroness *cr* 1999 (Life Peer), of Beeston in the county of Nottinghamshire; **Janet Alison Whitaker;** Chair, Working Men's College for Men and Women Corporation, since 1998; *b* 20 Feb. 1936; *d* of late Alan Harrison Stewart and Ella Stewart (*née* Saunders); *m* 1964, Benjamin Charles George Whitaker, *qv*; two *s* one *d*. *Educ:* Nottingham High Sch. for Girls; Girton Coll., Cambridge (Major Scholar); Bryn Mawr Coll., USA (Farley Graduate Fellow); Harvard Univ. (Radcliffe Fellow). Teacher, Lycée Français de Londres, 1958–59; Editor, André Deutsch Ltd, 1961–66; Health and Safety Executive, 1974–88: Hd of Gas Safety, 1983–86; Hd of Nuclear Safety Admin, 1986–88; Department of Employment: Hd of Health and Safety Br., 1988–92; Hd of Sex Equality Div., 1992–96; Leader, UK delegn to Fourth UN Conf. on Women, 1995. Member: Sub Cttee on Social Affairs, Educn and Home Affairs, EU Select Cttee, H of L, 1999–; Jt Cttee on Human Rights, 2000–. Member: OECD Wkg Pty on Rôle of Women in the Economy, 1992–96; Employment Tribunals, 1996–2000; ACORD Gender Cttee, 1996–; SOS Sahel Mgt Cttee, 1997–; Population Concern, 1998–; Immigration Audit Complaints Cttee, 1998–99. Chair, Camden Racial Equality Council, 1999. Assessor, Citizen's Charter Chartermark Unit, 1996. Dir, Tavistock & Portman NHS Trust, 1997–2001. Member: Friends Provident Cttee of Reference, 2000–; Adv. Council, Transparency Internat. (UK), 2001. Trustee: Runnymede Trust, 1997–; One World Trust, 2000–. Mem., Fabian Soc., 1970. FRSA 1993. *Recreation:* travelling hopefully. *Address:* House of Lords, SW1A 0PW. *Club:* Reform.

WHITAKER, Benjamin Charles George, CBE 2000; author; Executive Director, Gulbenkian Foundation (UK), 1988–99; *b* 15 Sept. 1934; 3rd *s* of late Maj.-Gen. Sir John Whitaker, 2nd Bt, CB, CBE, and late Lady Whitaker (*née* Snowden), Babworth, Retford, Notts; *m* 1964, Janet Alison Stewart (*see* Baroness Whitaker); two *s* one *d*. *Educ:* Eton; New Coll., Oxford. BA (Modern History). Called to Bar, Inner Temple, 1959 (Yarborough-Anderson Scholar). Practised as Barrister, 1959–67. Extra-mural Lectr in Law, London Univ., 1963–64. MP (Lab) Hampstead, 1966–70; PPS to Minister of: Overseas Development, 1966; Housing and Local Govt, 1966–67; Parly Sec., ODM, 1969–70. Exec. Dir, Minority Rights Group, 1971–88. Member: UN Human Rights Sub-Commn, 1975–88 (Vice-Chm., 1979); Goodman Cttee on Charity Law Reform, 1974–76; UK Nat. Commn for UNESCO, 1978–85; Speaker's Commn on Citizenship, 1989–90; Nat. Lottery Charities (Community Fund) Bd, 2000–; Chairman: UN Working Gp on Slavery, 1976–78; Defence of Literature and Arts Soc., 1976–82; City Poverty Cttee, 1971–83; Friends of Regent's Park, 1991–93; Foundns Forum, 1996–98. Judge: NCR Book Award, 1990; RIBA Architecture Awards, 1992. Lieut, Order of Merit (Portugal), 1993. *Publications:* The Police, 1964; (ed) A Radical Future, 1967; Crime and Society, 1967; Participation and Poverty, 1968; Parks for People, 1971; (ed) The Fourth World, 1972; The Foundations, 1974; The Police in Society, 1979; (contrib.) Human Rights and American Foreign Policy, 1979; UN Report on Slavery, 1982; (ed) Teaching about Prejudice, 1983; A Bridge of People, 1983; (ed) Minorities: a question of human rights?, 1984; UN Report on Genocide, 1985; The Global Connection, 1987; (contrib.) The United Kingdom—The United Nations, 1990; Gen. Editor, Sources for Contemporary Issues series (7 vols), 1973–75. *Address:* 16 Adamson Road, NW3 3HR.

WHITAKER, David Haddon, OBE 1991; Chairman, J. Whitaker & Sons, Ltd, 1982–97 (Director, 1966–97; Editorial Director, 1980–91); *b* 6 March 1931; *s* of late Edgar Haddon Whitaker, OBE and of Mollie Marian, *y d* of George and Louisa Seely; *m* 1st, 1959, Veronica Wallace (decd); two *s* two *d*; 2nd, 1976, Audrey Miller (marr. diss. 1979); 3rd, 1994, Marguerite van Reenen. *Educ:* Boscastle Infants' Sch.; Marlborough Coll.; St John's Coll., Cambridge. Joined family firm of publishers, J. Whitaker & Sons, Ltd, 1955; Dir, 1966; Editor, The Bookseller, 1977–79. Member: Adv. Panel, Internat. Standard Book Numbering Agency (Berlin), 1979–97 (Chm., 1990–97); Adv. Panel, Registrar for Public Lending Right, 1983–93 (Chm., 1989–93); Standing Cttee on Technology, Booksellers' Assoc., 1984–89; Library and Information Services Council, 1985–89; Chairman: Information and Library Services Lead Body for Nat. Vocational Qualifications, 1992–95; British Nat. Bibliography Res. Fund, 1992–2001. Chairman: Soc. of Bookmen, 1984–86; Book Trade Electronic Data Interchange Standards Cttee, 1987–90. Hon. Vice-Pres., LA, 1990. Hon. Fellow, Amer. Nat. Inst. of Standards Orgns, 1997. *Recreations:* reading, walking. *Address:* 4 Ufton Grove, N1 4HG. *T:* (020) 7241 3501, *Fax:* (020) 7241 5177. *Clubs:* Garrick, Thames Rowing; Leander (Henley-on-Thames).

WHITAKER, (Edwin) John, MBE 1991; show-jumper; *b* 5 Aug. 1955; *er s* of Donald Whitaker and Enid (*née* Lockwood); *m* 1979, Claire Barr; one *s* two *d*. British champion, 1992, 1993; other European championship wins: team and individual silver medals, 1983 (Ryan's Son); team gold and individual bronze, 1985 (Hopscotch); team gold and individual silver, 1987 (Milton); individual and team gold, 1989 (Milton). World Cup gold medals, 1990, 1991 (Milton); Olympic individual and team silver medals, 1980, and team silver medal, 1984 (Ryan's Son); jumping Derby, 1983 (Ryan's Son), 1998 (Gammon), 2000 (Virtual Village Welham); King George V Gold Cup, 1986 (Ryan's Son), 1990 (Milton), 1997 (Virtual Village Welham); Aachen Grand Prix, 1997 (Virtual Village Welham). Leading Jumper of the Year, Horse of the Year Show, 1993, 1998; numerous other wins and awards. *Address:* c/o British Show Jumping Association, Stoneleigh, Warwicks CV8 2LR.

See also M. Whitaker.

WHITAKER, John; *see* Whitaker, E. J.

WHITAKER, Sir John James Ingham, (Sir Jack), 4th Bt *cr* 1936, of Babworth, Nottinghamshire; farmer; *b* 23 Oct. 1952; *o s* of Sir James Herbert Ingham Whitaker, 3rd Bt, OBE and Mary Elisabeth Lander Whitaker (*née* Johnston); *S* father, 1999; *m* 1981, Elizabeth Jane Ravenscroft Starke; one *s* three *d*. *Educ:* Eton; Bristol Univ. (BSc). FCA; AMIEE. High Sheriff, Notts, 2001. *Heir:* *s* Harry James Ingham Whitaker, *b* 16 March 1984. *Address:* Babworth Hall, Retford, Notts DN22 8EP. *T:* (01777) 860964.

WHITAKER, Michael; show-jumper; *b* 17 March 1960; *yr s* of Donald Whitaker and Enid (*née* Lockwood); *m* 1980, Veronique Dalems, *d* of Dino Vastapane. British champion, 1984, 1989; other European championship wins: Junior, 1978; team gold medal, 1985 (Warren Point); team gold, 1987 (Amanda); team gold and individual silver, 1989 (Monsanta); team silver and individual silver, 1995; team bronze, 1997; Olympic silver medal, 1984 (Amanda); Jumping Derby: 1980 (Owen Gregory); 1991 and 1992 (Monsanta); 1993 (My Messieur); King George V Gold Cup: 1982 (Disney Way); 1989 (Didi); 1992, 1994 (Midnight Madness); bareback high jump record, Dublin, 1980. *Address:* c/o British Show Jumping Association, Stoneleigh, Warwicks CV8 2LR.

See also E. J. Whitaker.

WHITAKER, Sheila; Director, London Film Festival, 1987–96; *b* 1 April 1936; *d* of Hilda and Charles Whitaker. *Educ:* Cathays High Sch. for Girls, Cardiff; Kings Norton Grammar Sch. for Girls, Birmingham; Univ. of Warwick (BA Hons). Secretarial and admin. posts in commerce and industry, 1956–68; Chief Stills Officer, National Film Archive, 1968–74; Univ. of Warwick, 1975–78; Dir, Tyneside Cinema, Tyneside Film Festival, Newcastle upon Tyne, 1979–84; Head, Programming: NFT, 1984–90; Article 27, 2000–. Dir, Film London Ltd, 1997–. Dir, Free Form Arts Trust, 2000–. Mem. Jury, Venice Internat. Film Festival, 1992. Founder and Co-Editor, Writing Women, 1981–84; Gen. Editor, Tyneside Publications, 1984. Hon. DLitt Newcastle, 1997. Chevalier des Arts et des Lettres (France), 1996. *Publications:* (ed jtly) Life and Art: the new Iranian cinema, 1999; An Argentine Passion: Maria Luisa Bemberg and her films, 2000; contribs to Framework, Screen, Sight and Sound, Guardian, Observer. *Recreations:* reading, pottering in the garden, trying to play the piano. *Address:* 9 Buckingham Road, N1 4DG. *Club:* Groucho.

WHITAKER, Thomas Kenneth; Chancellor, National University of Ireland, 1976–96; Member, Council of State, Ireland, 1991–97; Chairman, Constitution Review Group, 1995–96; President, Royal Irish Academy, 1985–87; *b* 8 Dec. 1916; *s* of Edward Whitaker and Jane O'Connor; *m* 1941, Nora Fogarty; five *s* one *d*. *Educ:* Christian Brothers' Sch., Drogheda; London Univ. (External Student; BScEcon, MScEcon). Irish CS, 1934–69 (Sec., Dept of Finance, 1956–69); Governor, Central Bank of Ireland, 1969–76; Dir, Bank of Ireland, 1976–85. Dir, Arthur Guinness Son & Co. Ltd, 1976–84. Chairman: Bord na Gaeilge, 1975–78; Agency for Personal Service Overseas, 1973–78; Mem., Seanad Éireann, 1977–82. Jt Chm., Anglo-Irish Encounter, 1983–89. Former Pres., Econ. and Social Res. Inst.; Chm. Council, Dublin Inst. for Advanced Studies. Freeman of Drogheda, 1999. Hon. DEconSc National Univ. of Ireland, 1962; Hon. LLD: Univ. of Dublin, 1976; Queen's Univ. of Belfast, 1980; Hon. DSc NUU, 1984; Hon. PhD Dublin City Univ., 1995. Commandeur de la Légion d'Honneur, France, 1976. *Publications:* Financing by Credit Creation, 1947; Economic Development, 1958; Interests, 1983. *Recreations:* fishing, golf, music. *Address:* 148 Stillorgan Road, Donnybrook, Dublin 4, Ireland. *T:* (1) 2693474.

WHITBREAD, Samuel Charles; JP; Director: Whitbread plc, 1972–2001 (Chairman, 1984–92); S. C. Whitbread Farms, since 1985; Lord-Lieutenant of Bedfordshire, since 1991; *b* 22 Feb. 1937; *s* of late Major Simon Whitbread and of Helen Beatrice Margaret (*née* Trefusis); *m* 1961, Jane Mary Hayter; three *s* one *d*. *Educ:* Eton College. Beds and Herts Regt, 1955–57. Joined Board, Whitbread & Co., 1972, Dep. Chm., Jan. 1984. Director: Whitbread Investment Co., 1977–93; Sun Alliance Gp, 1989–92; Chm., Hertfordshire Timber Supplies, 2000–. Chm., Mid-Beds Conservative Assoc., 1969–72 (Pres., 1986–91). President: Shire Horse Soc., 1990–92; E of England Agricl Soc., 1991–92; St John Council for Beds, 1991–; Beds RFCA (formerly Beds TA&VRA), 1991–; E Anglia RFCA, 2000– (Vice-Pres., E Anglia TA&VRA, 1991–2000). Bedfordshire: JP, 1969–83, 1991; High Sheriff, 1973–74; DL, 1974; County Councillor, 1974–82. FLS; FRSA. Bledisloe Gold Medal, RASE, 1989. KStJ 1992. *Recreations:* shooting, painting, music. *Address:* Southill Park, Biggleswade, Beds SG18 9LL. *T:* (01462) 813272. *Club:* Brooks's.

WHITBURN, Vanessa Victoria; Editor, The Archers, BBC Radio, since 1991; additional responsibility for Radio Drama in the Midlands, BBC, since 1995; *b* 12 Dec. 1951; *d* of Victor D. Whitburn and Eileen Whitburn. *Educ:* Mount St Mary's Convent, Exeter; Univ. of Hull (BA Hons). Studio Manager, BBC, 1974–76; Asst Floor Manager, BBC TV, 1976–77; Producer and Sen. Producer, Radio Drama, Pebble Mill, 1977–88; Producer, Brookside, Channel 4, 1988–90; Producer and Director, BBC TV, Pebble Mill, 1990–91. *Publication:* The Archers: the official inside story, 1996. *Recreations:* opera, theatre, spending time with friends, travel. *Address:* Radio Drama Department, BBC in the Midlands, Pebble Mill Road, Birmingham, W Midlands B5 7QQ.

WHITBY, Bishop Suffragan of, since 1999; **Rt Rev. Robert Sidney Ladds,** SSC; *b* 15 Nov. 1941; *s* of late Sidney Ladds and of Joan Dorothy Ladds (*née* Cant); *m* 1964, Roberta Harriet Sparkes; three *s*. *Educ:* Christ Church Coll., Canterbury (CertEd 1970, BEd Hons 1971, London Univ.); Canterbury Sch. of Ministry. LRSC 1972; FRSC (FCS 1972). Industrial res. chemist, 1959–68; schoolmaster, 1971–80; ordained deacon, 1980, priest, 1981; Asst Curate, St Leonard, Hythe, 1980–83; Rector of Bretherton, 1983–91; Chaplain, Bishop Rawstorne Sch., 1983–86; Bishop of Blackburn's Chaplain for Ministry, 1986–90; Bishop's Audit Officer, 1990–91; Rector of Preston, 1991–97; Hon. Canon, Blackburn, 1993–97; Archdeacon of Lancaster, 1997–99. Commissary for Northern Province to Bp of Taejon, S Korea, 1997–99; Vice-Pres., Korea Mission Partnership, 1999–. Superior-Gen., Soc. of Mary, 2000–. *Recreations:* gardening, beekeeping, fell-walking, bonsai, church architecture. *Address:* Nant Escob, 60 West Green, Stokesley, Middlesbrough TS9 5BD.

WHITBY, Charles Harley; QC 1970; a Recorder of the Crown Court, Western Circuit, 1972–98; *b* 2 April 1926; *s* of late Arthur William Whitby and Florence Whitby; *m* 1981, Eileen Scott. *Educ:* St John's, Leatherhead; Peterhouse, Cambridge. Open Schol., Peterhouse, 1943; served RAFVR, 1944–48; BA (History) 1st cl. 1949, MA 1951. Called to Bar, Middle Temple, 1952 (Bencher, 1977; Lent Reader, 1996); Mem. Bar Council, 1969–71, 1972–78. Member: Criminal Injuries Compensation Bd, 1975–2000; Criminal Injuries Compensation Appeals Panel, 2000–. Chm. Council, St John's Sch., Leatherhead, 1985–97 (Mem., 1977–97). *Publications:* contrib. to Master and Servant in Halsbury's Laws of England, 3rd edn, Vol. 25, 1959 and Master and Servant in Atkin's Encyclopaedia of Court Forms, 2nd edn, Vol. 25, 1962. *Recreations:* golf, watching soccer, boating, fishing, swimming, theatre, cinema. *Address:* 12 King's Bench Walk, Temple, EC4Y 7EL. *T:* (020) 7583 0811. *Clubs:* Oxford and Cambridge, Royal Automobile (Steward, 1985–), Garrick; Woking Golf.

WHITBY, Mrs Joy; Director, Grasshopper Productions Ltd; *b* 27 July 1930; *d* of James and Esther Field; *m* 1954, Anthony Charles Whitby (*d* 1975); three *s*. *Educ:* St Anne's Coll., Oxford. Schools Producer, BBC Radio, 1956–62; Children's Producer, BBC Television, 1962–67; Executive Producer, Children's Programmes, London Weekend Television, 1967–70; freelance producer and writer, 1970–76; Head of Children's Programmes, Yorkshire TV, 1976–85. Dir, Bd of Channel 4, 1980–84; Member: Adv. Panel for Youth, Nat. Trust, 1985–89; Bd, Unicorn Theatre, 1987–92. Trustee, Internat. Childcare Trust, 1995–97. Devised for television: Play School, 1964; Jackanory, 1965; The Book Tower, 1979; Under the Same Sky (EBU Drama Exchange), 1984. Independent film productions: Grasshopper Island, 1971; A Pattern of Roses, 1983; Emma and Grandpa, 1984; East of the Moon, 1988; The Angel and the Soldier Boy, 1989 (ACE Award, 1991); On Christmas Eve, 1992; The Mousehole Cat, 1993; The Story of Arion and the Dolphin, 1996; Mouse and Mole, 1997–. BAFTA Award and Prix Jeunesse: for Play School, 1965; for The Book Tower, 1980 (also BAFTA Award, 1983); Eleanor

Farjeon Award for Services to Children's Books, 1979. *Publications:* Grasshopper Island, 1971; Emma and Grandpa (4 vols), 1984.

WHITE, family name of **Baron Annaly** and **Baroness James of Holland Park**.

WHITE, Adrian Edwin, CBE 1993; Founder Chairman, Biwater plc, since 1968; Governor of the BBC, 1995–2000; *b* 25 July 1942; *s* of Raymond Gerard White and Lucy Mildred White (*née* Best); *m* 1971, Gillian Denise Evans; four *s* one *d. Educ:* Cray Valley Technical High; City of London Coll. Chartered Water Engineer; FCIWEM. Biwater plc (holding co. for Biwater Industries, Biwater International and other cos), 1968–. Chm., British Water Industries Gp, 1992–93; Founder Chm., British Water, 1993–98. Vice-Pres., Small Business Bureau, 1980–90; Governor, Engineering, World Economic Forum, 1989–; Mem., Overseas Projects Bd, DTI, 1993–95. Chm., Epsom Healthcare NHS Trust, 1990–94, 1997–99. Pres., Epsom Medical Equipment Fund, 1999–. Founder, Denbies Charitable Trust. Owner, Denbies Wine Estate, 1986–. Governor: Stanway Sch., 1984–94; Queen Elizabeth's Foundn for Disabled People, 1989–; Parkside Sch., 1994–96; Chm. Bd of Governors, Millfield Schs, 1997–. Winner, Free Enterprise Award, 1985. *Recreations:* family, golf, theatre. *Address:* Biwater plc, Biwater House, Station Approach, Dorking, Surrey RH4 1TZ. *T:* (01306) 740740; Denbies, Ranmore Common, Dorking, Surrey RH5 6SP. *T:* (01306) 886640. *Club:* Wisley Golf.
See also Rev. B. R. White.

WHITE, Aidan Patrick; General Secretary, International Federation of Journalists, since 1987; *b* 2 March 1951; *s* of Thomas White and Kathleen Ann McLaughlin. *Educ:* King's Sch., Peterborough. Dep. Gp Editor, Stratford Express, 1977–79; journalist, The Guardian, 1980–87. Mem., Press Council, 1978–80. National Union of Journalists: Mem. Exec. Council, 1974, 1976, 1977; Treasurer, 1984–86; Chm., National Newspapers Council, 1981. Chm., EC Inf. Soc. Forum Wkg Gp, 1996–98. Member: Exec. Council, ICFTU, 1989–; Steering Cttee, ETUC, 1997–. *Publications:* on ethics of journalism for UNESCO, UNICEF and Council of Europe. *Address:* 10 Avenue Ferne Francard, 1310 La Hulpe, Belgium. *T:* (2) 6541016; *e-mail:* aidan.white@ifj.org.

WHITE, Alan, CMG 1985; OBE 1973; HM Diplomatic Service, retired; Ambassador to Chile, 1987–90; *b* 13 Aug. 1930; *s* of William White and Ida (*née* Hall); *m* 1st, 1954, Cynthia Maidwell; two *s* one *d*; 2nd, 1980, Clare Corley Smith. SSC Army 1954 (Capt.); Hong Kong, 1959–63; MoD (Central), 1965; First Sec., FO (later FCO), 1966; Mexico City, 1969; First Sec., UK Disarmament Delegn, Geneva, 1974; Counsellor (Commercial), Madrid, 1976; Counsellor and Head of Chancery, Kuala Lumpur, 1980–83; Hd, Trade Relns and Exports Dept, FCO, 1983–85; Ambassador to Bolivia, 1985–87. *Recreations:* reading, travel. *Address:* c/o Foreign and Commonwealth Office, SW1A 2AH.

WHITE, Andrew; QC 1997; *b* 25 Jan. 1958; *s* of Peter White and late Sandra Jeanette White (*née* Lovelace); *m* 1987, Elizabeth Denise Rooney; two *s. Educ:* University Coll. Cardiff (LLB Hons). Called to the Bar, Lincoln's Inn (Hardwick Schol., Megarry Schol.) 1980; in practice at the Bar, 1981–. *Publication:* (contrib.) Encyclopaedia of Forms and Precedents, vol. 5: building and engineering contracts, 5th edn (1986). *Recreations:* farming, sailing, music. *Address:* 1 Atkin Building, Gray's Inn, WC1R 5AT. *T:* (020) 7404 0102.

WHITE, Antony Dennis Lowndes; QC 2001; *b* 22 Jan. 1959; *s* of Albert Dennis White and Marion Seymour White; partner, Kate Ursula Macfarlane; one *s* two *d. Educ:* Huish's Grammar Sch., Taunton; Clare Coll., Cambridge (MA). Called to the Bar, Middle Temple, 1983; called to the Gibraltar Bar, 1998. *Publications:* (with S. Greer) Abolishing the Diplock Courts, 1986; (contrib.) Justice Under Fire, 1988; (contrib.) The Jury Under Attack, 1988. *Recreations:* classic cars, walking, swimming, cooking, wine, modern literature, contemporary art. *Address:* Matrix Chambers, Griffin Building, Gray's Inn, WC1R 5LN. *T:* (020) 7404 3447.

WHITE, Rev. Barrington Raymond; Principal, Regent's Park College, Oxford, 1972–89, now Principal Emeritus (Senior Research Fellow and Tutor in Ecclesiastical History, 1989–99); *b* 28 Jan. 1934; *s* of Raymond Gerard and Lucy Mildred White; *m* 1957, Margaret Muriel Hooper; two *d. Educ:* Chislehurst and Sidcup Grammar Sch.; Queens' Coll., Cambridge (BA Theol, MA); Regent's Park Coll., Oxford (DPhil). Ordained, 1959; Minister, Andover Baptist Church, 1959–63; Tutor in Ecclesiastical History, Regent's Park Coll., Oxford, 1963–72. First Breman Prof. of Social Relations, Univ. of N Carolina at Asheville, 1976. FRHistS 1973. *Publications:* The English Separatist Tradition, 1971; Association Records of the Particular Baptists to 1660, Part I, 1971, Part II, 1973, Part III, 1974; Authority: a Baptist view, 1976; Hanserd Knollys and Radical Dissent, 1977; contrib. Reformation, Conformity and Dissent, ed R. Buick Knox, 1977; The English Puritan Tradition, 1980; contrib. Biographical Dictionary of British Radicals in the Seventeenth Century, ed Greaves and Zaller, 1982–84; The English Baptists of the Seventeenth Century, 1983; (contrib.) A Transcription of the Glasshouse Yard Church Book 1832 to 1857, 2000; contribs to Baptist Qly, Jl of Theological Studies, Jl of Ecclesiastical History, Welsh Baptist Studies. *Recreation:* recorded music. *Address:* Regent's Park College, Oxford OX1 2LB.
See also A. E. White.

WHITE, Brian Arthur Robert; MP (Lab) Milton Keynes North East, since 1997; *b* 5 May 1957; *s* of Edward and Jean White; *m* 1984, Leena Lindholm; two step *s. Educ:* Methodist Coll., Belfast. Systems analyst: HM Customs, 1977–83 (consultant, 1983–84); Canada Life Assurance, 1984–86; Abbey National, 1986–97. *Address:* House of Commons, SW1A 0AA; 43 Bradwell Road, Bradville, Milton Keynes MK13 7AX.

WHITE, Bryan Oliver; HM Diplomatic Service, retired; consultant on Latin American affairs; *b* 3 Oct. 1929; *s* of Thomas Frederick White and Olive May Turvey; *m* 1958, Helen McLeod Jenkins; one *s* two *d. Educ:* The Perse Sch.; Wadham Coll., Oxford (Lit.Hum.). HM Forces, 1948–49; FO, 1953; Kabul, Vienna, Conakry, Rio de Janeiro, the Cabinet Office, and Havana, 1953–79; Counsellor, Paris, 1980–82; Head of Mexico and Central America Dept, FCO, 1982–84; Ambassador to Honduras and (non-resident) to El Salvador, 1984–87; Consul-Gen., Lyon, 1987–89. *Recreation:* the Romance languages. *Address:* 14 Stonebridge Lane, Fulbourn, Cambridge CB1 5BW.

WHITE, Hon. Byron R(aymond); Associate Justice of the Supreme Court of the United States, 1962–93; *b* Fort Collins, Colorado, 8 June 1917; *s* of Alpha White, Wellington, Colorado; *m* 1946, Marion Lloyd Stearns, *d* of Dr Robert L. Stearns; one *s* one *d. Educ:* Wellington High Sch.; Univ. of Colorado; Oxford Univ. (Rhodes Scholar); Yale Univ. Law Sch (before and after War). Served War of 1939–45: USNR, Naval Intell., Pacific (two Bronze Stars). Law Clerk to Chief Justice of the United States, 1946–47; law practice in Denver, Colorado, 1947–60, with firm of Lewis, Grant, Newton, Davis and Henry (later Lewis, Grant and Davis). Dep. Attorney-Gen., 1961–62. Phi Beta Kappa, Phi Gamma Delta. As a Democrat, he was a prominent supporter of John F. Kennedy in the Presidential campaign of 1960. *Recreations:* fishing, walking. *Address:* c/o US Supreme Court, 1 First Street NE, Washington, DC 20543, USA.

WHITE, (Charles) John (Branford); HM Diplomatic Service; High Commissioner, Barbados and the Eastern Caribbean States, since 2001; *b* 24 Sept. 1946; *s* of Frederick Bernard White and Violet Phyllis White (*née* Palmer); *m* 1975, Judith Margaret Lewis. *Educ:* Taunton Sch.; Brentwood Sch.; Pembroke Coll., Cambridge (Trevelyan Schol., MA); University Coll. London (MSc 1983). ODI Fellow, Govt of Botswana, 1968–71; ODA, 1971–77; Economic Advr, E Africa Develt Div., ODM, 1977–82; ODA, 1983–86; Asst Head, Economic Relations Dept, FCO, 1986–90; First Sec., Lagos, 1990–93; Dep. Hd of Mission, Consul Gen. and Counsellor, Tel Aviv, 1993–97; Hd, S Atlantic and Antarctic, subseq. UK Overseas Territories, Dept, FCO, and Comr (non-resident), British Antarctic Territory and British Indian Ocean Territory, 1997–2001. *Recreations:* golf, skiing. *Address:* c/o Foreign and Commonwealth Office, King Charles Street, SW1A 2AH. *Clubs:* Ski Club of Great Britain; Royal Mid-Surrey Golf; Nairobi (Kenya).

WHITE, Prof. Sir Christopher (John), Kt 2001; CVO 1995; PhD; FBA 1989; Director, Ashmolean Museum, Oxford, 1985–97; Fellow of Worcester College, 1985–97, and Professor of the Art of the Netherlands, 1992–97, now Professor Emeritus, Oxford University; *b* 19 Sept. 1930; *s* of late Gabriel Ernest Edward Francis White, CBE and Elizabeth Grace Ardizzone; *m* 1957, Rosemary Katharine Desages; one *s* two *d. Educ:* Downside Sch.; Courtauld Institute of Art, London Univ. BA (Hons) 1954, PhD 1970. Served Army, 1949–50; commnd, RA, 1949. Asst Keeper, Dept of Prints and Drawings, British Museum, 1954–65; Director, P. and D. Colnaghi, 1965–71; Curator of Graphic Arts, Nat. Gall. of Art, Washington, 1971–73; Dir of Studies, Paul Mellon Centre for Studies in British Art, 1973–85; Adjunct Prof. of History of Art, Yale Univ., 1976–85; Associate Dir, Yale Center for British Art, 1976–85. Dutch Govt Schol., 1956; Hermione Lectr, Alexandra Coll., Dublin, 1959; Adjunct Prof., Inst. of Fine Arts, New York Univ., 1973 and 1976; Conference Dir, European-Amer. Assembly on Art Museums, Ditchley Park, 1975; Visiting Prof., Dept of History of Art, Yale Univ., 1976. Trustee: V & A Mus., 1997–; Mauritshuis, The Hague, 1999–. Gov., British Inst. of Florence, 1994–. Dir, Burlington Magazine, 1981– (Chm., 1996–2002). Reviews Editor, Master Drawings, 1967–80. *Publications:* Rembrandt and his World, 1964; The Flower Drawings of Jan van Huysum, 1965; Rubens and his World, 1968; Rembrandt as an Etcher, 1969, 2nd edn 1999; (jtly) Rembrandt's Etchings: a catalogue raisonné, 1970; Dürer: the artist and his drawings, 1972; English Landscape 1630–1850, 1977; The Dutch Paintings in the Collection of HM The Queen, 1982; (ed) Rembrandt in Eighteenth Century England, 1983; Rembrandt, 1984; Peter Paul Rubens: man and artist, 1987 (Eugène Baie Prize, 1983–87); (jtly) Drawing in England from Hilliard to Hogarth, 1987; (jtly) Rubens in Oxford, 1988; (jtly) One Hundred Old Master Drawings from the Ashmolean Museum, 1991; (jtly) The Dutch and Flemish Drawings at Windsor Castle, 1994; Anthony van Dyck: Thomas Howard, the Earl of Arundel, 1995; Dutch, Flemish and German Paintings in the Ashmolean Museum, 1999; (ed jtly) Rembrandt by Himself, 1999; film (script and commentary), Rembrandt's Three Crosses, 1969; various exhibn catalogues; contribs to Burlington Mag., Master Drawings, etc. *Recreation:* husbandry. *Address:* 34 Kelly Street, NW1 8PH. *T:* (020) 7485 9148; Shingle House, St Cross, Harleston, Norfolk IP20 0NT. *T:* (01986) 782264; *e-mail:* cjwhite@ukonline.co.uk.

WHITE, Sir Christopher (Robert Meadows), 3rd Bt *cr* 1937, of Boulge Hall, Suffolk; *b* 26 Aug. 1940; *s* of Sir (Eric) Richard Meadows White, 2nd Bt, and Lady Elizabeth Mary Gladys (*d* 1950), *o d* of 6th Marquess Townshend; *S* father, 1972; *m* 1st, 1962, Anne Marie Ghislaine (marr. diss. 1968), *yr d* of Major Tom Brown, OBE; 2nd, 1968, Dinah Mary Sutton (marr. diss. 1972), Orange House, Heacham, Norfolk; 3rd, 1976, Ingrid Carolyn Jowett, *e d* of Eric Jowett, Great Baddow; two step *s. Educ:* Bradfield Coll., Berks. Imperial Russian Ballet School, Cannes, France, 1961; schoolmaster, 1961–72; Professore, Istituto Shenker, Rome, and Scuola Specialisti Aeronauta, Macerata, 1962–63; Housemaster, St Michael's Sch., Ingoldisthorpe, Norfolk, 1963–69. Hon. Pres., Warnborough House, Oxford, 1973–. Lieutenant, TA, Norfolk, 1969. *Recreations:* dogs, vintage cars, antiques. *Address:* c/o Mrs Edwin Steinschaden-Silver, Pinkney Court, Malmesbury, Wilts SN16 0PD.

WHITE, Christopher Stuart S.; *see* Stuart-White.

WHITE, Prof. David Clifford Stephen, DPhil; Director of Science and Technology, Biotechnology and Biological Sciences Research Council, since 1997; *b* 8 March 1941; *s* of late Clifford George White and of Joyce Beatrice White (*née* Lawley); *m* 1st, 1965, Ailsa Pippin (marr. diss.); one *s* one *d*; 2nd, 1987, Patricia Spallone. *Educ:* Berkhamsted Sch.; New Coll., Oxford (BA 1962; MA 1967; DPhil 1967). Deptl Demonstrator, Dept of Zool., Univ. of Oxford, 1967–71; Department of Biology, University of York: Lectr, 1971–86; Sen. Lectr, 1986–90; Reader, 1990–95; Prof., 1995–97; Head of Dept, 1990–97. *Publications:* Biological Physics, 1973; The Kinetics of Muscle Contraction, 1973. *Recreations:* walking, gardening. *Address:* (office) Polaris House, North Star Avenue, Swindon SN2 1UH. *T:* (01793) 413267.

WHITE, Sir David Harry, Kt 1992; DL; Chairman, Mansfield Brewing, since 1993; Director, 1970–88, a Deputy Chairman, 1988–90, Chairman of Trustees, 1986–2000, National Freight Consortium; *b* 12 Oct. 1929; *s* of late Harry White, OBE, FCA, and Kathleen White; *m* 1971, Valerie Jeanne White; one *s* four *d. Educ:* Nottingham High Sch.; HMS Conway. Master Mariner's F. G. Certificate. Sea career, apprentice to Master Mariner, 1944–56; Terminal Manager, Texaco (UK) Ltd, 1956–64; Operations Manager, Gulf Oil (GB) Ltd, 1964–68; Asst Man. Dir, Samuel Williams Dagenham, 1968–70; Trainee to Gp Managing Director, British Road Services Ltd, 1970–76; Group Managing Director: British Road Services, 1976–82; Pickfords, 1982–84; NFC Property Gp, 1984–87; Chm., Nottingham HA, 1986–98; Director (non-executive): BR Property Bd, 1985–87; Y. J. Lovell Ltd, 1987–94; Hilda Hanson Ltd, 1996–; James Bell (Nottingham) Ltd, 1997–; Nottingham Forest FC, 1999–; Alkane plc, 2000–; non-exec. Chm., EPS Ltd, 1997–2000. Mem., British Coal Corp., 1993–94; Chm., Coal Authy, 1994–99. Chairman: Nottingham Develt Enterprise, 1987–93; Bd of Governors, Nottingham Trent Univ. (formerly Nottingham Poly.), 1989–99. Trustee, Djanogly City Technology Coll., 1989–99. Hon-Pres., Notts County Branch, RSPCA, 1987–. Governor, Nottingham High Sch., 1987–99. DL Notts, 1989. Hon. DBA Nottingham Trent, 1999. *Recreations:* football supporter (Nottingham Forest), walking. *Address:* Whitehaven, 6 Croft Road, Edwalton, Nottingham NG12 4BW. *Club:* Royal Automobile.

WHITE, David Thomas, (Tom), CBE 1990; Principal and Chief Executive, NCH Action for Children (formerly National Children's Home), 1990–96; *b* 10 Oct. 1931; *s* of Walter Henry White and Annie White; *m* 1956, Eileen May Moore; two *d* (and one *s* decd). *Educ:* Council Primary and Maesydderwen Grammar Sch., Ystradgynlais, Swansea Valley; University Coll., Swansea (Social Sci.); London School of Economics (Social Work). Clerical Officer, CS, 1947–54; National Service, RAF, 1951–53. Social work and management posts, Devon CC, 1957–61; Dep. Children's Officer, Monmouthshire, 1961–65; Dep. County Children's Officer, Lancs, 1965–70; Dir of Social Services, Coventry, 1970–85; Dir of Social Work, Nat. Children's Home, 1985–90. Past President:

Assoc. of Child Care Officers; Assoc. of Directors of Social Services; Gov., Nat. Inst. of Social Work, 1973–96 (Hon. Fellow, 1996); Chm., Nat. Foster Care Assoc., 1996–99. Mem. (Lab), Coventry CC, 1996–. *Publication:* (contrib.) Social Work, the Media and Public Relations, 1991. *Recreations:* gardening, golf, walking. *Address:* 102 Kenilworth Road, Coventry CV4 7AH. *T:* (024) 7641 9949. *Club:* Coventry Golf (Finham, Coventry).

WHITE, Derek Leslie; HM Diplomatic Service, retired; *b* 18 April 1933; *s* of John William and Hilda White; *m* 1989, Elisabeth Denise Marcelle Lemoine; one *d* from previous marr. *Educ:* Catshill Secondary Sch., Bromsgrove; RAF Apprentice Sch. Served RAF, 1950–63. For. Office (later HM Diplomatic Service), 1963; served Helsinki, Sofia, Algiers; Vice Consul, Tripoli, 1970; FCO, 1972; Commercial Officer, Baghdad, 1975, Second Sec., 1977; Port Louis, 1979; Antananarivo, 1983; FCO, 1984, First Sec., 1985; Consul, Marseilles and Principality of Monaco, 1986; FCO, 1989; High Comr to Kiribati, 1990–93, and concurrently Ambassador to Federated States of Micronesia and to Marshall Is, 1992–93. *Recreations:* sailing, cooking, music. *Address:* Cansargue, 83470 Pourcieux, France. *T:* 494597879.

WHITE, Edward George, OBE 1976; HM Diplomatic Service, retired; *b* 30 June 1923; *s* of late George Johnson White, OBE, ISO, and Edith (*née* Birch); *m* 1st, 1945, Sylvia Shears; two *d*; 2nd, 1966, Veronica Pauline Crosling. *Educ:* Bec Secondary Sch., London SW. Served RAF, 1941–47. Various consular and diplomatic appts in Guatemala, USA, Madagascar, Burma, Thailand and India; Dep. Head of Finance Dept, FCO, 1976–78; Counsellor (Admin), Bonn, 1978–79. Specialist Adviser, Foreign Affairs Cttee, H of C, 1980–87. *Publication:* Nightfighter Navigator, 1994. *Address:* 7 Crosslands, Thurlestone, Kingsbridge, Devon TQ7 3TF. *T:* (01548) 560236.

WHITE, (Edward) Martin (Everatt); *b* 22 Feb. 1938; *s* of Frank and Norah White; *m* 1969, Jean Catherine Armour; one *s* one *d*. *Educ:* Priory Boys' Grammar Sch., Shrewsbury; King's Coll., Cambridge (MA). Solicitor. Asst Solicitor, Lancs County Council, 1962–65; Sen. Asst Solicitor, then Asst Clerk, then Principal Asst Clerk, Kent County Council, 1965–72; Dep. Chief Exec., Somerset County Council, 1972–74; Chief Executive: Winchester City Council, 1974–80; Bucks County Council, 1980–88; Nat. Assoc. of Citizens Advice Bureaux, 1988–90. *Recreations:* gardening, walking, other outdoor pursuits. *Address:* 1 School Lane, Itchen Abbas, Winchester SO21 1BE. *T:* (01962) 779617.

WHITE, Ven. Francis, (Frank); Archdeacon of Sunderland, since 1997; *b* 26 May 1949; *s* of John Edward White and Mary Ellen White; *m* 1982, Alison Mary, *d* of Dr K. R. Dumbell, *qv*. *Educ:* St Cuthbert's GS, Newcastle upon Tyne; Consett Tech. Coll.; UWIST, Cardiff (BScEcon); UC Cardiff (DipSocSci); St John's Coll., Nottingham (Dip. Pastoral Studies); Nottingham Univ. (DipTh); Dir, Youth Action York, 1971–73; Detached Youth Worker, Manchester, 1973–77; Asst Curate, St Nicholas, Durham, 1980–84; Sen. Curate, St Mary and St Cuthbert, Chester-le-Street, 1984–87; Chaplain, Durham HA Hosps, 1987–89; Vicar, St John the Evangelist, Birtley, 1989–97; RD of Chester-le-Street, 1993–97. Proctor in Convocation, Gen. Synod of C of E, 1987–2000. Hon. Canon, Durham Cathedral, 1997. *Recreations:* birdwatching, walking, motor cars, theatre, soccer. *Address:* Greenriggs, Dipe Lane, East Boldon, S Tyneside NE36 0PH. *T:* (0191) 536 2300.

WHITE, His Honour Sir Frank (John), Kt 1997; a Senior Circuit Judge, 1994–97 (a Circuit Judge, 1974–94); *b* 12 March 1927; *s* of late Frank Byron White and Marie-Thérèse Renée White; *m* 1953, Anne Rowlandson, MBE, *d* of late Sir Harold Gibson Howitt, GBE, DSO, MC; two *s* two *d*. *Educ:* Reading Sch.; King's Coll., London (LLB, LLM; FKC 1999). Sub-Lt, RNVR, 1945–47; called to the Bar, Gray's Inn, 1951, Bencher, 1997; Dep. Chm., Berkshire QS, 1970–72; a Recorder of the Crown Court, 1972–74. Pres., Council of HM Circuit Judges, 1990–91. Member: Lord Chancellor's Adv. Cttee on Legal Aid, 1977–83; Judicial Studies Bd, 1985–89; County Court Rule Cttee, 1991–97 (Chm., 1993–97). Mem., General Council of the Bar, 1969–73. Pres., KCL Assoc., 2000–. *Publication:* Bench Notes and Exercises for Assistant Recorders, 1988. *Recreations:* walking, photography. *Address:* 8 Queen's Ride, SW13 0JB. *T:* (020) 8788 8903; Blauvac, Vaucluse, France. *Clubs:* Athenæum, Roehampton.

WHITE, Frank Richard; JP; former executive director and industrial relations adviser; Director, National Training College, GMB (formerly General, Municipal, Boilermakers and Allied Trades Union), 1988–2000; *b* Nov. 1939; *m*; three *c*. *Educ:* Bolton Tech. Coll. Member: Bolton CC, 1963–74; Greater Manchester CC, 1973–75; Bolton DC, 1986–. Member: GMB; IPM; Inst. of Management Services. Contested (Lab): Bury and Radcliffe, Feb. 1974; Bury North, 1983; Bolton NE, 1987. MP (Lab) Bury and Radcliffe, Oct. 1974–1983; PPS to Minister of State, Dept of Industry, 1975–76; Asst Govt Whip, 1976–78; Opposition Whip, 1980–82; opposition spokesman on church affairs, 1980–83. Chairman: All Party Paper Industry Gp, 1979–83; NW Lab Gp, 1979–83; Mem., NW Regional Exec., Labour Party, 1986–88. Director: Lancs Co-op. Develt Agency, 1984–; Bolton/Bury TEC, 1995–; Mem., Greater Manchester Police Authy, 1997–; Mem. Area Bd, United Norwest Co-op, 1994–; Dir, Europ. Foundn Continued Learning, 1995–. President: Bolton United Services Veterans' Assoc., 1988–; Bolton Male Voice Choir, 1992–; Vice-Pres., E Lancs Railway Preservation Soc., 1983–. JP Bolton, 1968 (Chm. Bench, 1993–95). Hon. Fellow, Bolton Inst., 1993. *Address:* 4 Ashdown Drive, Firwood Fold, Bolton, Lancs BL2 3AX.

WHITE, Air Vice-Marshal George Alan, CB 1984; AFC 1973; FRAeS; Commandant, Royal Air Force Staff College, 1984–87; *b* 11 March 1932; *s* of James Magee White and Evangeline (*née* Henderson); *m* 1955, Mary Esmé (*née* Magowan); two *d*. *Educ:* Queen's Univ., Belfast; University of London (LLB). Pilot, 1956; served in RAF Squadrons and OCUs, 1956–64; RAF Staff College, 1964; HQ Middle East Command, 1966–67; 11 Sqn, 1968–70; 5 Sqn, 1970–72; Nat. Defence Coll., 1972–73; in command, RAF Leuchars, 1973–75; Royal Coll. of Defence Studies, 1976; Dir of Ops (Air Defence and Overseas), 1977–78; SASO No 11 Group, 1979–80; Air Cdre Plans, HQ Strike Comd, 1981–82; Dep. Comdr, RAF Germany, 1982–84. FRAeS 1985. *Recreations:* sailing, hill walking, bridge. *Address:* Leithen Lodge, Innerleithen, Peeblesshire EH44 6NW. *Clubs:* Royal Air Force; Royal Scots (Edinburgh).

WHITE, Sir George (Stanley James), 4th Bt *cr* 1904, of Cotham House, Bristol; FSA; clockmaker and horological consultant; Keeper of the Collection of the Worshipful Company of Clockmakers, since 1988; *b* 4 Nov. 1948; *s* of Sir George Stanley Midelton White, 3rd Bt, and of Diane Eleanor, *d* of late Bernard Abdy Collins, CIE; *S* father, 1983; *m* 1st, 1974; one *d*; 2nd, 1979, Elizabeth Jane, *d* of Sir Reginald Verdon-Smith and of Jane Margaret, *d* of V. W. J. Hobbs; one *s* one *d*. *Educ:* Harrow School. Pres., Gloucestershire Soc., 1993; Chm., Adv. Gp on Bldg Conservation, Bristol Univ., 1996–; Member: Gloucester DAC for Care of Churches, 1985– (Clocks Advr, 1986–); Council, Bristol and Glos Archaeological Soc., 1987–2000 (Chm., 1992–95); Council, Nat. Trust, 1998–. Pres., British Horological Inst., 2001 (Pres., Bristol Br., 1993–). Liveryman, Co. of Clockmakers, 1986– (Asst, 1994–; Master, 2001). High Sheriff, Avon, 1989; JP Bristol, 1991–95. FSA 1988. *Publications:* (with E. J. White) St Mary's Church, Hawkesbury, 1980; English Lantern Clocks, 1989; Tramlines to the Stars, 1995; The Clockmakers of London, 1998; contrib. Antiquaries' Jl, Antiquarian Horology, etc. *Heir: s* George Philip James White, *b* 19 Dec. 1987.

WHITE, Maj.-Gen. Gilbert Anthony, MBE 1944; *b* 10 June 1916; *s* of Cecil James Lawrence White and Muriel (*née* Collins); *m* 1939, Margaret Isabel Duncan Wallet; two *d*. *Educ:* Christ's Hosp., Horsham. Member of Lloyd's, 1938. Joined TA Artists Rifles, 1937; TA Commn, E Surrey Regt, 1939; served BEF, 1940, N Africa, 1943–44, Italy, 1944–45; Staff Coll., 1944; Instructor, Staff Coll., Haifa, 1946; with UK Delegn to UN, 1946–48; served on Lord Mountbatten's personal staff in MoD, 1960–61; idc 1965; BAOR, 1966–69; Chief, Jt Services Liaison Orgn, Bonn, 1969–71; retd 1971. Mem. Council, Guide Dogs for the Blind, 1971–92. *Recreations:* golf, racing.

WHITE, Harold Clare, MBE 1967; HM Diplomatic Service, retired; Consul-General, Seattle, 1976–79; *b* 26 Oct. 1919; *s* of Alfred John White and Nora White; *m* 1951, Marie Elizabeth Richardson; two *d*. *Educ:* Grammar Sch., Warrington. Served War, Royal Signals, 1939–45. GPO, 1937–39 and 1946; FO, 1947; Third Sec., Djakarta, 1951; FO, 1955; Vice-Consul, Piraeus, Kirkuk, San Francisco, and Durban, 1957–64; 1st Secretary: Kinshasa, 1964; Kuala Lumpur, 1968; FCO, 1972; Dep. Consul-Gen., Chicago, 1974. *Recreation:* cricket. *Address:* 31 Stuart Avenue, Eastbourne, East Sussex BN21 1UR. *T:* (01323) 731148. *Club:* Civil Service.

WHITE, Harvey, DM; FRCS; Consulting Surgeon: Royal Marsden Hospital, since 1976; King Edward VII Hospital for Officers, since 1983; *b* 10 March 1936; *s* of Arthur White and Doris (*née* Dunstan); *m* 1965, Diana Mary Bannister; one *s* one *d*. *Educ:* Winchester Coll.; Magdalen Coll., Oxford (DM, MCh); St Bartholomew's Hosp. FRCS 1970. St Bartholomew's Hospital: Lectr in Physiol., 1966–71; Sen. Surgical Registrar, 1971–76; Chm., Div. of Surgery, Royal Marsden Hosp., 1987–89. Editor: Oxford Med. Gazette, 1956–57; St Bartholomew's Hosp. Jl, 1960–61; Clinical Oncology, 1983–84; European Jl of Surgical Oncology, 1985–87; Chm., Royal Society of Medicine Press Ltd, 1997–. Hunterian Prof., RCS, 1988; Hunterian Oration, 1993. Vice-Pres., Brit. Assoc. of Surgical Oncology, 1984; Pres., Med. Soc. of London, 1995–96. Mem. Council, Cancer Relief Macmillan Fund, 1991–95. Chm., Brendoncare Foundn of Elderly, 1986–; Trustee, Duchess of Somerset's Almshouses, 1992–. Ernest Miles Medal, Brit. Assoc. of Surgical Oncology, 1989. *Publications:* (jtly) The Greater Omentum, 1983, Russian edn 1989; (jtly) The Omentum and Malignant Diseases, 1984; An Atlas of Omental Transposition, 1987; contrib. to: History of Surgery, 1974; Royal Hospital St Bartholomew, 1974; Surgical Oncology for Nurses, 1978; The Laser in General Surgery, 1979; Oxford Companion to Medicine, 1986; European Handbook of Oncology, 1989; Aird's Companion to Surgery, 1992; contrib. various learned surgical and cancer jls. *Recreations:* dog-walking, rackets and Real tennis, sailing, fishing. *Address:* (office) 149 Harley Street, W1G 6DE. *T:* (020) 7935 4444; 7 Arlington Square, N1 7DS. *T:* (020) 7226 4628; Carley Cottage, Bapton, Wylye, Wilts BA12 0SD. *T:* (01985) 850759. *Clubs:* Garrick, Royal Society of Medicine.

WHITE, Sir Henry Arthur Dalrymple D.; *see* Dalrymple-White.

WHITE, Adm. Sir Hugo (Moresby), GCB 1995 (KCB 1991); CBE 1985; DL; Governor and Commander-in-Chief, Gibraltar, 1995–97; *b* 22 Oct. 1939; *s* of late Hugh Fortescue Moresby White, CMG and Betty Sophia Pennington White; *m* 1966, Josephine Mary Lorimer Pedler; two *s*. *Educ:* Dragon School; Nautical Coll., Pangbourne; Britannia RN Coll., Dartmouth. HMS Blackpool, 1960; submarine training, 1961; HM Submarines Tabard, Tiptoe, Odin, 1961–65; Long Navigation Course, HMS Dryad, 1966; Navigator, HMS Warspite, 1967; First Lieut, HMS Osiris, 1968–69; in Comd, HMS Oracle, 1969–70; Staff, BRNC Dartmouth, 1971–72; Submarine Sea Training, 1973–74; in Comd, HMS Salisbury (cod war), 1975–76; Naval Sec.'s Dept, 1976–78; Naval Plans, 1978–80; in Comd, HMS Avenger (Falklands) and 4th Frigate Sqn, 1980–82; Principal Staff Officer to Chief of Defence Staff, 1982–85; in Comd, HMS Bristol and Flag Captain, 1985–87; Flag Officer Third Flotilla, and Comdr Anti-Submarine Warfare Striking Force, 1987–88; ACNS, 1988–91; Flag Officer Scotland and NI, 1991–92; C-in-C Fleet, Allied C-in-C, Eastern Atlantic, 1992–95, also Allied C-in-C, Channel, 1991–94; Naval Comdr, NW Comd, 1994–95. DL Devon, 1999. *Recreations:* sailing, travelling, gardening, reading. *Address:* c/o Naval Secretary, Victory Building, HM Naval Base, Portsmouth PO1 3LS. *Club:* Army and Navy.

WHITE, Ian; Member (Lab) Bristol, European Parliament, 1989–99; former Partner, McCarthy and White, solicitors. Contested (Lab) SW Reg., EP elecn, 1999.

WHITE, James; Managing Director, Glasgow Car Collection Ltd, 1959–87; *m*; one *s* two *d*. *Educ:* Knightswood Secondary School. Served Eighth Army, War of 1939–45 (African and Italian Stars; Defence Medal). MP (Lab) Glasgow (Pollok), 1970–87. Mem. Commonwealth Parly Assoc. Delegns, Bangladesh, 1973, Nepal, 1981. *Address:* 23 Alder Road, Glasgow G43 2UU.

WHITE, James; author and art historian; Professor of History of Painting, Royal Hibernian Academy, since 1968; *b* 16 Sept. 1913; *s* of Thomas John White and Florence Coffey; *m* 1941, Agnes Bowe; three *s* two *d*. *Educ:* Belvedere Coll., Dublin; privately in European museums and collections. Art Critic: Standard, 1940–50; Irish Press, 1950–59; Irish Times, 1959–62. Curator, Municipal Gallery of Modern Art, Dublin, 1960–64; Director, Nat. Gallery of Ireland, 1964–80. Chm., Irish Arts Council, 1978–84; Hon. Sec., Royal Dublin Soc., 1986–. Ext. Lectr in History of Art, University Coll., Dublin, 1955–77; Visiting Lectr in Univs and Socs in GB, Italy, USA, Canada. Trustee, Chester Beatty Library of Oriental Art, Dublin. Radio and Television contribs: BBC, RTE, and in the USA. Irish Comr to Biennale at Venice and at Paris on various occasions; Organiser of Exhibns in Dublin, London, Paris, etc., incl. Paintings from Irish Collections, 1957. Corresp. Mem., Real Academia de Bellas Artes de San Fernando, 1975. Hon. LLD NUI, 1970. Arnold K. Henry Medal of RCS of Ireland. Chevalier, Légion d'Honneur, 1974; Order of Merit, Govt of Italy, 1977; Commander of the Order of Merit, Federal Republic of Germany, 1983. *Publications:* Irish Stained Glass (with Michael Wynne), 1963; The National Gallery of Ireland, 1968; Jack B. Yeats, 1971; John Butler Yeats and the Irish Renaissance, 1972; Masterpieces of the National Gallery of Ireland, 1978; Pauline Bewick: painting a life, 1985; Gerard Dillon, a Biography, 1993; monographs on Louis Le Brocquy, George Campbell, Brian Bourke; contributor to: Apollo, Art News, Studio, Connoisseur, Blackfriars, Manchester Guardian, The Furrow, Doctrine and Life, Art Notes, Merian, Werk, Das Munster, Hollandsche Art, La Biennale, La Revue Française, Il Milione, Encyclopaedia of Art, etc. *Recreations:* golf, swimming, gardening, bridge. *Address:* 66 Cedars, Herbert Park Lane, Dublin 4. *T:* (1) 6683723. *Club:* Kildare Street and University (Dublin).

WHITE, James Ashton V.; *see* Vallance White.

WHITE, Jeremy Nigel; Chairman, Nettec plc, since 1995; *b* 20 Jan. 1955; *s* of Colin Lawrence White and Drusilla Marie Goodman; *m* 1989, Kim-Marie Klinger; one *s* three *d*. *Educ:* Leeds Grammar Sch.; Leeds Polytechnic (Dip. Management, Accounting and Finance, Marketing); City Univ. (MBA); Pepperdine Univ. (MA Educn and Psychology; Dist Alumni 1995). Man. Dir, RSS Gp, 1975–79; Chm., White Gp Electronics, 1979–85; Britannia Group: Jt Man. Dir, 1985–86; Pres., 1986–88; Chm., Data Safe Inc., 1988–94; Chief Exec. and Dep. Chm., Prince's Youth Business Trust, 1994–95; Dep. Chm., Youthnet UK, 1995–2000; Dir, oneclickHR plc (formerly Vizual Business Tools Ltd), 1997–. Mem., Bd, British-Amer. Chamber of Commerce, S Calif, 1993–94, and other LA orgns, 1992–94. Member: Council, Industry and Parlt Trust, 1984–88 and 1995–; Young Enterprise Nat. Council, 1986–98; Adv. Council Educn and Trng, Inst. of Econ. Affairs, 1996–2000; DoI Business Links Accreditation Adv. Bd, 1996–98; Small and Medium Size Enterprises Task Gp and Basic Skills Gp, Univ. for Industry, 1999–2000. Trustee: Prince of Wales Award for Innovation, 1995–; Technology Coll. Trust, 1998–2000. Gov., Pepperdine Univ., 1993–; Mem. Council, City Univ. Business Sch., 1995–99; Mem. Ct Govs, Univ. of Westminster, 1999–. Mem., BSES exp. to W Himalayas, 1989; flying records: Lisbon to LA, 1990; LA to Albuquerque, 1990; Buenos Aires to LA, 1991; La Paz to LA, 1991. FRGS. *Publications:* The Retail Financial Services Sector, 1985; 21st Century Schools—Educating for the Information Age, 1997. *Recreations:* private flying, collecting. *T:* (020) 7514 9500; *e-mail:* jwhite@nettec.net. *Clubs:* Brooks's, Pilgrims', Royal Geographical.

WHITE, Jeremy Richard, (Jerry); Commissioner for Local Administration in England (Local Government Ombudsman), since 1995; *b* 23 March 1949; *s* of John Robert White and Molly Loiseau; *m* 1st, 1981, Sandra Margaret Smith (marr. diss. 1995); two *s* one *d*; 2nd, 1995, Rosie Cooper; one *d*. *Educ:* Swanage Grammar Sch.; Cosham and Hackney Technical Colls. Sen. Public Health Inspector, Islington, 1970–81; Asst Borough Housing Officer, Haringey, 1981–84; London Borough of Hackney: Head, Environmental Health, 1984–87; Dir, Environmental Health and Consumer Protection, 1987–89; Chief Exec. and Town Clerk, 1989–95. Vis. Prof., Sch. of History and Politics, Middlesex Univ., 1996–; Associate Fellow, Centre for Social History, Univ. of Warwick, 1997–. *Publications:* Rothschild Buildings: life in an East End tenement block 1887–1920, 1980; The Worst Street in North London: Campbell Road, Islington, between the wars, 1986; Fear of Voting: local democracy and its enemies 1894–1994, 1994; (with Michael Young) Governing London, 1996; London in the Twentieth Century: a city and its people, 2001. *Recreations:* reading, music, London. *Address:* Commission for Local Administration, 2 The Oaks, Westwood Way, Coventry CV4 8JB. *T:* (024) 7669 5999. *Club:* Reform.

WHITE, John; *see* White, C. J. B.

WHITE, Rev. Canon John Austin; Canon of Windsor, since 1982; Warden, St George's House, since 2000; *b* 27 June 1942; *s* of Charles White and Alice Emily (*née* Precious). *Educ:* The Grammar Sch., Batley, W Yorkshire; Univ. of Hull (BA Hons); College of the Resurrection, Mirfield. Assistant Curate, St Aidan's Church, Leeds, 1966–69; Asst Chaplain, Univ. of Leeds, 1969–73; Asst Director, post ordination training, Dio. of Ripon, 1970–73; Chaplain, Northern Ordination Course, 1973–82. Dir of Clergy Courses, St George's House, Windsor Castle, 1998–. *Publications:* (with Julia Neuberger) A Necessary End: attitudes to death, 1991; (with L. R. Muir) Nicholas Ferrar: materials for a life, 1997; Phoenix in Flight, 1999; various articles. *Recreations:* medieval iconography, drama, Italy, cooking, poetry. *Address:* 8 The Cloisters, Windsor Castle SL4 1NJ. *T:* (01753) 860409.

WHITE, Hon. Sir John (Charles), Kt 1982; MBE (mil.) 1942; Judge of High Court of New Zealand, retired 1981, sat as retired Judge, 1982–84; *b* 1 Nov. 1911; *s* of Charles Gilbert White and Nora Addison Scott White; *m* 1st, 1943, Dora Eyre Wild (*d* 1982); one *s* three *d*; 2nd, 1987, Margaret Elspeth Maxwell Fletcher. *Educ:* Wellesley Coll., Wellington; John McGlashan Coll., Dunedin; Victoria University Coll., Wellington; Univ. of New Zealand (LLM Hons). Barrister and Solicitor of Supreme Court of New Zealand. Judge's Associate, 1937–38; served War, Middle East, Greece, Crete, N Africa, Italy, 1940–45, ADC to Gen. Freyberg, 2nd NZEF, ME, 1940–45 (final rank Major); formerly Dominion Vice-Pres., New Zealand Returned Services Assoc.; Private practice as barrister and solicitor, Wellington, 1945–66; Pres., Wellington Law Soc., Vice-Pres., NZ Law Soc., 1966; QC and Solicitor General of New Zealand, 1966; Judge of the Supreme Court (now High Court), 1970, retd 1981; Judge Advocate General of Defence Forces, 1966–87. Actg Chief Justice, Solomon Islands, 1984. Pres., Solomon Is Court of Appeal, 1985–87. Royal Comr, Inquiry into 1982 Fiji Gen. Election, 1983. Asst Editor, Sim's Practice & Procedure, 9th edn, 1955, and 10th edn 1966. *Publications:* letters and commentaries in mil. pubns and the press on hist. of NZ Forces in ME during World War II, and world peace through rule of law. *Recreations:* formerly Rugby, cricket, tennis, golf, bowls. *Address:* 23 Selwyn Terrace, Wellington 6001, New Zealand. *T:* (4) 4725502. *Clubs:* Wellington; Dunedin; Melbourne.

WHITE, Prof. John Edward Clement Twarowski, CBE 1983; FSA; Durning-Lawrence Professor of the History of Art, University College London, 1971–90 (Vice-Provost, 1984–88; Pro Provost, 1990–95); *b* 4 Oct. 1924; *s* of Brigadier A. E. White and Suzanne Twarowska; *m* 1950, Xenia Joannides (*d* 1991). *Educ:* Ampleforth College; Trinity College, Oxford; Courtauld Institute of Art, University of London. Served in RAF, 1943–47. BA London 1950; Junior Research Fellow, Warburg Inst., 1950–52; PhD Lond. 1952; MA Manchester 1963. Lectr in History of Art, Courtauld Inst., 1952–58; Alexander White Vis. Prof., Univ. of Chicago, 1958; Reader in History of Art, Courtauld Inst., 1958–59; Pilkington Prof. of the History of Art and Dir of The Whitworth Art Gallery, Univ. of Manchester, 1959–66; Vis. Ferens Prof. of Fine Art, Univ. of Hull, 1961–62; Prof. of the History of Art and Chm., Dept of History of Art, Johns Hopkins Univ., USA, 1966–71. Member: Adv. Council of V&A, 1973–76; Exec. Cttee, Assoc. of Art Historians, 1974–81 (Chm., 1976–80); Art Panel, Arts Council, 1974–78; Vis. Cttee of RCA, 1977–86; Armed Forces Pay Review Body, 1986–92; Chm., Reviewing Cttee on Export of Works of Art, 1976–82 (Mem., 1975–82). Trustee, Whitechapel Art Gall., 1976–93 (Vice-Chm., 1985–93). Membre Titulaire, 1983–95, Membre du Bureau, 1986–92, Comité International d'Histoire de l'Art. *Publications:* Perspective in Ancient Drawing and Painting, 1956; The Birth and Rebirth of Pictorial Space, 1957, 3rd edn 1987 (Italian trans. 1971; French trans. 1992; Spanish trans. 1994); Art and Architecture in Italy, 1250–1400, 1966, 3rd edn 1993 (Spanish trans. 1989); Duccio: Tuscan Art and the Medieval Workshop, 1979; Studies in Renaissance Art, 1983; Studies in Late Medieval Italian Art, 1984; Poems Poèmes Poesie, 1992; Quartet Quartett Quartetto Quatuor, 1993; Trinity Trinita Trinité, 1994; You that I love, 1998; articles in Art History, Art Bulletin, Burlington Magazine, Jl of Warburg and Courtauld Institutes. *Address:* 25 Cadogan Place, SW1X 9SA. *Club:* Athenæum.

WHITE, John Sampson, AO 1982; CMG 1970; Secretary to the Governor, South Australia, 1976–82; *b* 9 June 1916; *s* of late W. J. White; *m* 1941, Dorothy G., *d* of late E. J. Griffin; one *s* one *d*. *Educ:* Black Forest Primary and Adelaide High Schs. AASA. Attorney-General's Dept, 1933–61. Served War, 2nd AIF, 1941–45, Captain. Asst Sec., Industries Develt Cttee, 1950, Sec., 1951–61; Sec., Land Agents' Bd, 1951–61; Sec. to Premier, SA, 1961–65; Mem., SA Superannuation Fund Bd, 1961–74; Sec., Premier's Dept, SA, 1965–74; Agent-Gen. for SA, 1974–76; Comr of Charitable Funds, 1964–74. Member: State Exec. Cttee, Meals on Wheels Inc., 1982–89 (Vice Pres., 1989–91; Pres., 1991–); Exec. Cttee, SA Br., Victoria League for Commonwealth Friendship, 1982–; Bd of Dirs, Service to Youth Council, 1982–84; Casino Supervisory Authy, 1983–86. Mem., Council of Governors, Presb. Girls' Coll., 1958–73. Freeman, City of London. *Recreations:* swimming, tennis. *Address:* 4 Evans Avenue, Mitcham, SA 5062, Australia. *Clubs:* Adelaide, Naval, Military and Air Force (Adelaide).

WHITE, John William, CMG 1981; DPhil; FRS 1993; FRSC; FAA; Professor of Physical and Theoretical Chemistry, Australian National University, Canberra, since 1985 (Pro Vice-Chancellor and Chairman, Board of Institute of Advanced Studies, 1992–94; Dean, Research School of Chemistry, 1995–98); *b* Newcastle, Australia, 25 April 1937; *s* of late George John White and of Jean Florence White; *m* 1966, Ailsa Barbara, *d* of A. A. and S. Vise, Southport, Qld; one *s* three *d*. *Educ:* Newcastle High Sch.; Sydney Univ. (MSc); Lincoln Coll., Oxford (1851 Schol., 1959; MA, DPhil). ICI Fellow, Oxford Univ.; Research Fellow, Lincoln Coll., 1962; University Lectr, Oxford, 1963–85, Assessor, 1981–82; Fellow, St John's Coll., Oxford, 1963–85 (Vice-Pres. 1973). Neutron Beam Coordinator, AERE, Harwell, 1974; Asst Director, 1975, Director 1977–80, Institut Laue-Langevin, Grenoble. Argonne Fellow, Argonne Nat. Lab. and Univ. of Chicago, 1985; Christensen Fellow, St Catherine's Coll., Oxford, 1991. Pres., Soc. of Crystallographers, Aust., 1989–92; Chairman: Nat. Cttee for Crystallography, Aust., 1992–; Neutron Scattering Commn, Internat. Union of Crystallography, 1994–. Sec. for Sci. Policy, and Mem. Council, Aust. Acad. of Sci., 1997–. Chm., Dirs' Adv. Council, Intense Pulsed Neutron Source, Argonne Nat. Lab., and Univ of Chicago, 1989–92. Pres., ISCAST Australia, 1991–. Lectures: Tilden, Chemical Soc., 1975; Liversidge, Sydney Univ., 1985; Hinshelwood, Oxford Univ., 1991; Foundn, Assoc. of Asian Chemical Socs, 1991; H. G. Smith, RACI, 1997–98; T. G. H. Jones Meml, Univ. of Qld, 1998; Hudnall-Cars Distinguished, Univ. of Chicago, 1998; 50th Anniversary, Internat. Union of Crystallography, 1998. Member of Council: Epsom Coll., 1981–85; Wycliffe Hall, Oxford, 1983–85; St Mark's Nat. Theol Centre, Canberra, 1997–. FRSC 1982; FRACI 1985; FAIP 1986; FAA 1991. Marlow Medal, Faraday Soc., 1969; H. G. Smith Medal and Prize, RACI, 1997. *Publications:* various contribs to scientific jls. *Recreations:* family, squash, ski-ing. *Address:* 2 Spencer Street, Turner, ACT 2601, Australia. *T:* (6) 62486836.

WHITE, Sir John (Woolmer), 4th Bt *cr* 1922; *b* 4 Feb. 1947; *s* of Sir Headley Dymoke White, 3rd Bt and Elizabeth Victoria Mary (*d* 1996), *er d* of late Wilfrid Ingram Wrightson; *S* father, 1971; *m* 1987, Joan Borland; one *s*. *Educ:* Hurst Court, Hastings; Cheltenham College; RAC, Cirencester. *Heir:* *s* Kyle Dymoke Wilfrid White, *b* 16 March 1988. *Address:* Salle Park, Norwich, Norfolk NR10 4SG. *Club:* Athenæum.

WHITE, Kenneth James; District Judge, Principal Registry of Family Division, since 1991; *b* 24 March 1948; *s* of Kenneth William John White and Pamela Blanche Emily White (*née* Seth); *m* 1971, Anne Christine Butcher; one *s* one *d*. *Educ:* Gosport County Grammar Sch., Hants; QMC, Univ. of London (LLB Hons 1969). Qualified as Solicitor, 1972; Partner, R. V. Stokes & Co., Solicitors, Portsmouth, 1974, Sen. Partner, 1991. Mem., Family Cttee, Judicial Studies Bd, 1999–. Mem., Portsmouth & Southsea Voluntary Lifeguards, 1968– (Pres. 1985–); Royal Life Saving Society UK: Vice-Pres., 1994–98; Pres., 1998–; Chm., Nat. Lifeguard Cttee, 1992–98; Pres., Wessex Br., 1981; Dir, Internat. Life Saving Fedn, 2000–. *Publications:* (consulting editor) Family Court Reporter, 1992; (contrib.) Atkin's Court Forms, 1994–. *Recreations:* swimming, reading, travel, lifesaving, bowls. *Address:* First Avenue House, High Holborn, WC1V 6HA. *T:* (020) 7936 6000.

WHITE, Lawrence John, CMG 1972; Assistant Secretary, Board of Customs and Excise, 1961–75, retired; *b* 23 Feb. 1915; *s* of Arthur Yirrell White and Helen Christina White; *m* 1936, Ivy Margaret Coates; one *s*. *Educ:* Banbury Grammar Sch. Joined Customs and Excise, 1933; Commonwealth Relations Office, 1948–50; Customs and Excise, 1951–75. *Recreations:* reading, walking. *Address:* Peach Tree Cottage, Fifield, Oxon OX7 6HL. *T:* (01993) 830806.

WHITE, Sir Lynton (Stuart), Kt 1985; MBE (mil.) 1943; TD 1950; DL; Chairman, Hampshire County Council, 1977–85; *b* 11 Aug. 1916; 2nd *s* of Sir Dymoke White, 2nd Bt, JP, DL; *m* 1945, Phyllis Marie Rochfort Worley, *er d* of Sir Newnham Arthur Worley, KBE; four *s* one *d*. *Educ:* Harrow; Trinity College, Cambridge (MA 1938). Associate RIBA, 1947–82. TA 1939, as 2nd Lieut RA; served War of 1939–45: UK, 1939–40; Far East, 1940–45 (despatches, 1943); Hon. Lieut-Col RA, TA, 1946; TARO, 1948–71. Member Hampshire CC, 1970; Vice-Chm., 1976. DL Hants 1977.

WHITE, Marco Pierre; chef; *b* 11 Dec. 1961; *s* of late Frank and Maria Rosa White; *m* 1st, 1988, Alexandra McCarthy (marr. diss.); one *d*; 2nd, 1992, Lisa Butcher (marr. diss.); 3rd, 2000, Matilda Conejero-Caldera; two *s*. *Educ:* Firtree Primary Sch.; Allarton High Sch., Leeds. Commis: Hotel St George, Harrogate, 1978; Box Tree, Ilkley, 1979; Chef de Partie: Le Gavroche, 1981; Tante Claire, 1983; Sous Chef, Manoir aux Quat' Saisons, 1984–85; Proprietor and Chef: Harveys, 1986–93; The Canteen Restaurant, Chelsea Harbour, 1992–96; Restaurant Marco Pierre White, 1993–; Marco Pierre White's Criterion, 1995–; Quo Vadis, 1996–; Oak Room, Le Meridien, 1997–99; MPW Canary Wharf, 1997–; Café Royal Grill Room, 1997–; Mirabelle Restaurant, Curzon St, 1998–. Michelin Stars 1988, 1990, 1995 (youngest and first GB winner of 3 Michelin stars). *Publications:* White Heat, 1990; Wild Food from Land and Sea, 1994; Canteen Cuisine, 1995; Glorious Puddings, 1998; The Mirabelle Cookbook, 1999. *Recreations:* shooting, fishing, bird watching. *Address:* Mirabelle Restaurant, 56 Curzon Street, W1Y 7PF.

WHITE, Martin; *see* White, E. M. E.

WHITE, Martin Andrew C.; *see* Campbell-White.

WHITE, Maj.-Gen. Martin Spencer, CB 1998; CBE 1991; FCIT; FILog; Senior Military Adviser, Ernst & Young, subseq. Cap Gemini Ernst & Young, since 1999; Vice Lord-Lieutenant for the Isle of Wight, since 1999; *b* 25 March 1944; *s* of Harold Spencer White and Mary Elizabeth White; *m* 1966, Fiona Margaret MacFarlane; three *s* one *d*. *Educ:* Sandown GS, IoW; Welbeck Coll.; RMA Sandhurst. FCIT 1992; FILog 1993. Commnd, RASC/RCT, 1966; Staff Coll., Camberley, 1977–78; Comd 4 Div., Transport Regt, 1983–85; Directing Staff, Army Staff Coll., 1985–87; Command: Logistic Support Gp, 1987–89; Force Maintenance Area (Gulf), 1990–91; Transport 1(BR) Corps, 1991–92; RCDS, 1993; Dir of Support, HQ Allied Land Forces Central Europe, 1993–95; Dir-Gen., Logistic Support (Army), 1995–98. Hon. Colonel: Southampton Univ. OTC, 1999–; 165 Regt RLC, 2001–. Governor, Ryde Sch., 1997–. DL Isle of Wight, 1998. *Publication:* Gulf Logistics: Black Adder's war, 1995. *Recreations:* cricket, offshore sailing. *Address:* Grove House, Old Seaview Lane, Seaview, Isle of Wight PO34 5BJ. *Clubs:* Army and Navy; Sea View Yacht.

WHITE, Michael Charles; Associate Editor, since 1989, Political Editor, since 1990, The Guardian; *b* 21 Oct. 1945; *y s* of Henry Wallis White, master mariner of St Just in Penwith, Cornwall and of Kay (*née* Wood); *m* 1973, Patricia Vivienne Gaudin; three *s*. *Educ:* Bodmin Grammar Sch.; University Coll. London (BA Hist. 1966). Reporter: Reading Evening Post, 1966–70; London Evening Standard, 1970–71; The Guardian, 1971–: Parly Sketchwriter, 1977–84; Washington Corresp., 1984–88; Columnist, The Listener, 1989–90; Co-presenter, Week in Westminster, Radio 4, 1989–. Chm., Parly Press Gall., 1994, and Lobby, 1997. Vis. Fellow, Woodrow Wilson Foundn, Princeton, NJ, 1990–. What the Papers Say Sketchwriter of the Year Award, 1982. *Recreation:* dashing about. *Address:* Press Gallery, House of Commons, SW1A 0AA. *T:* (020) 7219 4700; 7 The Avenue, Chiswick, W4 1HA. *T:* (020) 8995 5055. *Club:* Garrick.

WHITE, Michael John; broadcaster and author; *b* 4 April 1955; *s* of Albert E. White and Doris M. White (*née* Harvey). *Educ:* Langdon Sch., London; Mansfield Coll., Oxford (MA Jurisp.). Called to the Bar, Middle Temple, 1978 (non-practising) (Harmsworth Scholar and Middle Temple Advocacy Prize). Contribs to Observer and Guardian; joined Independent, 1986; Music Critic, The Independent on Sunday, 1990–2000. Broadcasts for BBC Radio and TV, Channel 4, Classic FM (voted Britain's least boring music critic); presenter: Best of 3, R3, 1998–2000; Opera in Action, R3; Sound Barrier series, R4, 1999; opera libretti writer; awards judge. Mem., Board of Dirs, Spitalfields Fest., 1992–. *Publications:* Wagner for Beginners, 1995; Opera and Operetta, 1997. *Recreations:* travel, Church of England (occasionally). *Address:* c/o BBC Radio 3, Broadcasting House, W1A 1AA.

WHITE, Michael Simon; theatre and film producer; *b* 16 Jan. 1936; *s* of Victor R. and Doris G. White; *m* 1965, Sarah Hillsdon (marr. diss. 1973); two *s* one *d*; 2nd, 1985, Louise M. Moores, *d* of late Nigel Moores; one *s*. *Educ:* Lyceum Alpinum, Zuoz, Switzerland; Pisa University; Sorbonne, Paris. Asst to Sir Peter Daubeny, 1956–61; *stage:* London productions include: The Connection, 1961; Blood Knot, 1966; American Hurrah, 1967; Oh, Calcutta!, 1970; Joseph and the Technicolor Dreamcoat, 1972; Rocky Horror Show, 1973; Loot, 1975; A Chorus Line, 1976; Sleuth, 1978; Deathtrap, 1978; Annie, 1978; Pirates of Penzance, 1982; On Your Toes, 1984; Metropolis, 1989; Bus Stop, 1990; Crazy for You, 1993; Me and Mamie O'Rourke, 1994; She Loves Me, 1994; Fame, 1995; Voyeurz, 1996; Boys in the Band, 1997; Disney's Beauty and the Beast, 1997; Black Goes with Everything, 2000; Notre-Dame de Paris, 2000; *films:* include: Monty Python and the Holy Grail, 1974; Rocky Horror Picture Show, 1975; The Comic Strip Presents …, 1983; My Dinner with André, 1984; Ploughman's Lunch, 1984; Moonlighting, 1984; Strangers's Kiss, 1985; The Supergrass, 1985; High Season, 1986; Eat the Rich, 1987; White Mischief, 1987; The Deceivers, 1988; Nuns on the Run, 1989; The Pope Must Die, 1991; Robert's Movie, 1993; Widow's Peak, 1994; Enigma, 2000. *Publication:* Empty Seats, 1984. *Recreations:* art, ski-ing, racing. *Address:* 48 Dean Street, W1D 5BF. *T:* (020) 7734 7707, *Fax:* (020) 7734 7727.

WHITE, Neville Helme; Stipendiary Magistrate for Humberside, 1985–99; *b* 12 April 1931; *s* of Noel Walter White and Irene Helme White; *m* 1958, Margaret Jennifer Catlin; two *s* one *d*. *Educ:* Newcastle-under-Lyme High School. RAF, 1949–51. Partner, Grindey & Co., Solicitors, Stoke-on-Trent, 1960–85. Pres., N Staffs Law Soc., 1980–81. Pres., Hull Boys' Club, 1985. *Recreations:* music, walking, gardening, reading, all sports, paintings. *Address:* 8 Solent Place, Evesham, Worcs WR11 6FB.

WHITE, Sir Nicholas (Peter Archibald), 6th Bt *cr* 1802, of Wallingwells, Nottinghamshire; *b* 2 March 1939; *s* of Captain Richard Taylor White, DSO (2 bars), RN (*d* 1995) and of Gabrielle Ursula White (*née* Style); *S* uncle, 1996; *m* 1970, Susan Irene, *d* of G. W. B. Pollock; two *s* one *d*. *Educ:* Harrow. Nat. Service, 2nd Lt 2/10th PWO Gurkha Rifles, 1957–59. Courage Ltd, 1959–84; wine trade, 1984–94; Gulf Eternit Industries, Dubai, UAE, 1994–2000. *Recreations:* tennis, travelling, music. *Heir:* *s* Christopher David Nicholas White, *b* 20 July 1972. *Address:* The Stables, Canon Lane, Wateringbury, near Maidstone, Kent ME18 5PQ.

WHITE, Norman Arthur, PhD; CEng, FIMechE; Eur Ing; corporate executive, international consultant and management academic; *b* Hetton-le-Hole, Durham, 11 April 1922; *s* of late Charles Brewster White and Lillian Sarah (*née* Finch); *m* 1st 1944, Joyce Marjorie Rogers (*d* 1982); one *s* one *d*; 2nd, 1983, Marjorie Iris Rushton. *Educ:* Luton Tech. Coll. (HNC); Manchester Inst. of Sci. and Technol. (AMCT Hons); London Univ. (BSc Eng (Hons)); Univ. of Philippines (MSc); London Polytechnic (DMS); Harvard Business Sch. (grad. AMP 1968); LSE (PhD 1973). CEng; MRAeS; FInstPet; FInstE; FIMechE; FIMM. Industrial apprentice, George Kent, and D. Napier & Son; Flight Test Engr, Mil. Aircraft develt, 1943–45. Royal Dutch/Shell Gp, 1945–72: Petroleum Res. Engr, Thornton Res. Centre, 1945–51; Tech. Manager, Shell Co. of Philippines, 1951–55; Shell International Petroleum: Div. Hd, later Dep. Manager, Product Develt Dept, 1955–61; special assignments in various countries, 1961–63; Gen. Manager, Lubricants, Bitumen and LPG Divs, 1963–66; Dir of Marketing Develt, 1966–68; Chief Exec., New Enterprises Div., London and The Hague, 1968–72; Chm. and Dir, Shell oil and mining cos, UK and overseas, 1963–72. Established Norman White Associates (specialists in technology based enterprises and international resources), 1972, Director and Principal Executive, 1972–94; Energy Adviser: Hambros Bank, 1972–76; Tanks Consolidated Investments, Nassau, 1974–85; Chm./Dir, various petroleum exploration and prodn cos in UK, Netherlands, Canada and USA, 1974–92; Chairman: KBC Advanced Technologies, 1979–90; Tesel plc, 1983–85 (Dir, 1980–85); Ocean Thermal Energy Conversion Systems, 1982–; Process Automation and Computer Systems, 1985–94; Andaman Resources plc, 1986–90; Technology Transfer Centre Surrey Ltd, 1990–97; Delta Media Solutions Ltd, 1990–93; Transnational Satellite Educn Centre, 1991–94; SpaceLink Learning Foundn (formerly Millennium Satellite Centre Ltd), 1995–; Director: Environmental Resources, 1973–87; Henley Centre for Forecasting, 1974–92 (Dep. Chm., 1974–87); Proscyon Partners, 1992–2000; Corporate Adviser: Placer Dome, Vancouver, 1973–78; Kennedy & Donkin Gp, 1986–94; Alcatel-Alsthom, Paris, 1993–96. Mem., Parly and Scientific Cttee, House of Commons, 1977–83, 1987–92. World Energy Council, Member: British Nat. Cttee, 1977–88; Conservation Commn, 1979–87; Internat. Exec. Assembly, 1987–94; World Petroleum Congress: Chm., British Nat. Cttee, 1987–94 (Dep. Chm., 1977–87); Permanent Council, 1979–97; Treasurer, 1983–91, 1994–97; Chm., Develt Cttee, 1989–97; Vice-Pres., 1991–94; Presidential Award, 1997; Member: Bd and World Council, Internat. Road Fedn, Geneva and Washington, 1964–72; UK CAA Cttee of Enquiry on Flight Time Limitations (Bader Cttee), 1972–73; Internat. Energy/Petroleum Delegn to Russia, Rumania, E Germany, Hungary, Venezuela, Japan, Korea, People's Republic of China, Indonesia, India, Mexico, Argentina, Brazil, Iran and Southern Africa, 1979–; Royal Soc./Inst. of Petroleum Delegn to People's Republic of China, 1985; Chm., China Technical Exchange Cttee, 1985–89. Visiting Professor: Arthur D. Little Management Educn Inst., Boston, USA, 1977–79; Henley Management Coll., 1979–89 (Vis. Fellow 1976–79); Manchester Business Sch., 1981–90 (Vis. Industrial Dir 1971–81); City Univ., 1990–96 (ext. examnr, 1983–89); Vis. Lectr, RCDS, 1981–85. London University: Member: Senate, 1974–87; External Council, 1974–84; Governing Bd, Commerce Degree Bureau, 1975–84; Academic Adv. Bd in Engrg, 1976–85; Collegiate Council, 1984–87; Cttee of Mangt, Inst. of US Studies, 1984–92; Mem., Council of Mining and Metallurgical Instns, 1981–87; Member Council: Inst. of Petroleum, 1975–81 (Vice-Pres., 1978–81; Council Award for Meritorious Service, 1996); IMechE, 1980–85, 1987–91 (Chm., Engrg Management Div., 1980–85, Southern Br., 1987–89; Presidential Award for Meritorious Service, 1994); Founder Chm., Jt Bd for Engrg Management, 1990–93 (Chm. Academic Bd, 1994–97; Hon. DipEM 1997). FRSA 1944; FIMgt; MRI; Mem., RIIA; Founder Mem., British Inst. of Energy Econs. Associate, St George's House, Windsor Castle, 1972. Governor: King Edward VI Royal Grammar Sch., Guildford, 1976–; Reigate Grammar Sch., 1976–93. Freeman, City of London, 1983; Liveryman: Worshipful Co. of Engineers, 1984; Co. of Spectacle Makers, 1986; Member: Guild of Freemen, 1986; Co. of World Traders, 1989. *Publications:* Financing the International Petroleum Industry, 1978; The International Outlook for Oil Substitution to 2020, 1983; (contrib.) Handbook of Engineering Management, 1988; contribs to professional jls in UK, Philippines and Canada, on fluid mechanics, petroleum utilization, energy resources, R&D management, project financing and engrg management. *Recreations:* family and various others in moderation, country and coastal walking, wild life, browsing, international affairs, comparative religions, domestic odd-jobbing. *Address:* 9 Park House, 123–125 Harley Street, W1G 6AY. *T:* (020) 7935 7387, *Fax:* (020) 7704 6060; Green Ridges, Downside Road, Guildford, Surrey GU4 8PH. *T:* Guildford (01483) 567523, *Fax:* (01483) 504314. *Clubs:* Athenæum, City Livery, Inst. of Directors, LSE; County (Guildford); Harvard Business (USA).

WHITE, Adm. Sir Peter, GBE 1977 (KBE 1976; CBE 1960; MBE 1944); *b* 25 Jan. 1919; *s* of William White, Amersham, Bucks; *m* 1947, Audrey Eileen (*d* 1991), *d* of Ernest Wallin, Northampton; two *s*. *Educ:* Dover College. Secretary: to Chief of Staff, Home Fleet, 1942–43; to Flag Officer Comdg 4th Cruiser Sqdn, 1944–45; to Asst Chief of Naval Personnel, 1946–47; to Flag Officer, Destroyers, Mediterranean, 1948–49; to Controller of the Navy, 1949–53; to C-in-C Home Fleet and C-in-C Eastern Atlantic, 1954–55; Naval Asst to Chm. BJSM, Washington, and UK Rep. of Standing Group, NATO, 1956–59; Supply Officer, HMS Adamant, 1960–61; Dep. Dir of Service Conditions and Fleet Supply Duties, Admty, 1961–63; idc 1964; CO HMS Raleigh, 1965–66; Principal Staff Officer to Chief of Defence Staff, 1967–69; Dir-Gen. Fleet Services, 1969–71; Port Admiral, Rosyth, 1972–74; Chief of Fleet Support, 1974–77. Consultant, Wilkinson Match Ltd, 1978–79; Associate Director: The Industrial Soc., 1980–88; BITC, 1988–96. Underwriting Member of Lloyd's, 1979–97. Chm., Officers Pension Society, 1982–90. Mem. Foundn Cttee, Gordon Boys' Sch., 1979–89.

WHITE, Peter Richard; Group Chief Executive, Alliance & Leicester plc (formerly Alliance & Leicester Building Society), 1991–99; Chairman, Girobank plc, 1996–99 (Director, 1990–99); *b* 11 Feb. 1942; *m* 1968, Mary Angela Bowyer; one *s* one *d*. *Educ:* St Paul's School. FCA; FCIB, FCT. Price Waterhouse, 1965–69; Management Accountant, Chief Internal Auditor, Financial Controller, Treasurer, Abbey National Building Soc., 1970–82; Gen. Manager (Finance and Management Services), Alliance Building Soc., 1982–85; Alliance & Leicester Building Society: Gen. Manager (Admin. and Treasury), 1985–87; Dir and Gen. Manager (Develt and Treasury), 1987–89; Dep. Group Chief Exec. and Man. Dir, 1989–91. Director: Alliance & Leicester Pensions Investments Ltd, 1989–99; Reckitt Benkiser (formerly Reckitt & Colman), 1997–. Chairman: Metropolitan Assoc. of Buildings Socs, 1994–95; Council of Mortgage Lenders, 1995–98; Audit Cttee, 1997–; Dep. Chm., BSA, 1995–96; Mem. Council, BBA, 1996–99. Trustee: Crimestoppers Trust, 1997–98; Develt Trust (for the Mentally Handicapped), 1997–99. Freeman, City of London, 1996. MInstD; CIMgt. *Recreations:* golf, opera, arts. *Address:* 21 Clareville Grove, South Kensington, SW7 5AU.

WHITE, Peter Robert, FSA; Secretary, Royal Commission on the Ancient and Historical Monuments of Wales, since 1991; *b* 28 Nov. 1944; *y s* of late John Edward White and Lily Agnes Lois White (*née* Powell); *m* 1973, Christine Margaret Joyce Robertson; two *d*. *Educ:* Eastbourne Grammar Sch.; Univ. of Leeds (BA History); Univ. of Southampton. FSA 1988; IHBC 1998. Asst Insp. of Ancient Monuments, MPBW, 1966–71; Insp., 1971–82, Prin. Insp., 1982–89, DoE; Head, Historic Buildings Listing, English Heritage, 1989–91. Member: Res. Cttee on Industrial Archaeol., Council of British Archaeol., 1969–91; Wkg Party on Industrial Archaeol., Council of Europe, 1984–89; Industrial Archaeol. Panel, English Heritage, 1991–; Exec. Cttee, Soc. of Antiquaries of London, 1994– (Mem. Council, 1992–94); Editl Bd, Cardiganshire County History, 1997–; Nat. Adv. Panel, Eur. Assoc. of Archaeologists, 1998–99. Vice-Pres., Royal Archaeol Inst., 1994–99 (Mem. Council, 1975–78, 1991–94). FRSA 1999. Hon. Fellow, UC, Northampton, 1999. *Publications:* contribs to learned jls, particularly on industrial archaeol. *Recreations:* walking, orchestral music. *Address:* (office) Plas Crug, Aberystwyth SY23 1NJ. *T:* (01970) 621201.

WHITE, Richard Michael, MBE 1983; HM Diplomatic Service; Assistant Director, Personnel Services, Foreign and Commonwealth Office, since 2000; *b* 12 July 1950; *s* of Geoffrey Richard White and Frances Kathleen (*née* Kendrick); *m* 1979, Deborah Anne Lewis; one *s* one *d*. *Educ:* King's Sch., Pontefract; Richmond Sch., Yorkshire. VSO, Senegal, 1968–69; entered HM Diplomatic Service, 1969: Attaché, UK Delegn to EEC, Brussels, 1971–74; Persian lang. studies, SOAS, and Yazd, Iran, 1974–75; Third Sec. (Commercial), Tehran, 1975–77; Second Sec. and Asst Private Sec. to Minister of State, Lord Privy Seal, FCO, 1978–79; FCO, 1979–80; Second Sec. (Commercial/Admin) and Consul, Dakar, 1980–84; First Secretary: (Technol.), Paris, 1984–88; FCO, 1988–92; Dep. High Comr, Valletta, 1992–95; FCO, 1996–2000, Hd, Migration and Visa Div., 1997–2000. *Recreations:* surfing the net, short wave radio, genealogy, French cuisine. *Address:* c/o Foreign and Commonwealth Office, King Charles Street, SW1A 2AH.

WHITE, Prof. Robert George, PhD, DSc; FREng; Professor of Vibration Studies, University of Southampton, 1983–98, now Emeritus; *b* 11 Dec. 1939; *s* of N. A. J. White and G. M. White; *m* 1988, Patricia Margaret (*née* Sidley); one step *s* one step *d*. *Educ:* Farnborough Coll. of Technology; Southampton Univ. (PhD 1970; DSc 1992). FInstP 1981; FIOA 1985; FRAeS 1986; FREng (FEng 1995). RAE, Farnborough, 1957–67; Dir, Inst. of Sound and Vibration Res., 1982–89, Inst. of Transducer Technol., 1989–93, Hd of Dept of Aeronautics amd Astronautics, 1995–98, Southampton Univ. *Publications:* (ed jtly) Noise and Vibration, 1982; 190 conf. papers and contribs to jls. *Recreations:* flying, walking. *Address:* 41 Lower Bere Wood, Waterlooville, Hants P07 7NQ.

WHITE, Prof. Robert Stephen, FRS 1994; FGS; Professor of Geophysics, Cambridge University, since 1989; Fellow of St Edmund's College, Cambridge, since 1988; *b* 12 Dec. 1952; 2nd *s* of James Henry White and Ethel Gladys (*née* Cornick); *m* 1976, Helen Elizabeth (*née* Pearce); one *s* one *d*. *Educ:* Market Harborough and West Bridgford Comprehensive Schs; Emmanuel Coll., Cambridge (Sen. Schol., 1972–74; Bachelor Schol., 1974–77; BA, MA, PhD). FRAS 1979; FGS 1989. Research Assistant: Berkeley Nuclear Labs, CEGB, 1970–71; Dept of Geodesy and Geophysics, Cambridge, 1978; postdoctoral schol., Woods Hole Oceanographic Instn, USA, 1978–79; Res. Fellow, Emmanuel Coll., Cambridge, 1979–82; Sen. Asst in Res., 1981–85, Asst Dir of Res., 1985–89, Dept of Earth Scis, Cambridge Univ. Cecil and Ida H. Green Schol., Scripps Instn of Oceanography, UCSD, USA, 1987; Guest Investigator, Woods Hole

Oceanographic Instn, 1988. Bigsby Medal, Geol Soc., 1991; George P. Woollard Award, Geol Soc. Amer., 1997. *Publications:* papers in many internat. jls. *Recreations:* building radio-controlled models, walking. *Address:* Bullard Laboratories, Madingley Road, Cambridge CB3 0EZ. *T:* (01223) 337187, *Fax:* (01223) 360779.

WHITE, Robin Bernard G.; *see* Grove-White.

WHITE, Roger, FSA 1986; Executive Secretary, Garden History Society, 1992–96; *b* 1 Sept. 1950; *s* of Geoffrey and Zoë White. *Educ:* Ifield Grammar School; Christ's College, Cambridge (1st class Hons, Hist. of Art Tripos); Wadham College, Oxford. GLC Historic Buildings Div., 1979–83; Sec., Georgian Gp, 1984–91; Mem., Chiswick House Adv. Panel, 1991–. Trustee, Pell Wall Preservation Trust, 1994–98. Curator, Nicholas Hawksmoor and the Replanning of Oxford, RIBA, 1997, Ashmolean Mus., 1998. Chichele Lectr, All Souls Coll., Oxford, 1999. Contributing Ed., House and Garden, 1994–. *Publications:* John Vardy, 1985; Georgian Arcadia: architecture for the park and garden, 1987; The Architectural Evolution of Magdalen College, Oxford, 1993; Chiswick House and Gardens, 2001; The Architectural Drawings of Magdalen College, Oxford, 2001;contribs to Architectural Hist., Jl of Garden Hist., Country Life. *Recreation:* visiting and writing about historic buildings. *Address:* 142 Weir Road, SW12 0ND.

WHITE, Sandra; Member (SNP) Glasgow, Scottish Parliament, since 1999; *b* 17 Aug. 1951; *d* of Henry Harley and Elizabeth Rodgers; *m* 1971, David White; two *s* one *d.* *Educ:* Garthamlock Sen. Sec. Sch.; Cardonald Coll. of Further Educn; Glasgow Coll. (Social Science degree). Clerkess, Gray Dunn, 1966–68; Timothy Whites, then Boots Chemist, 1968–73; Littlewoods Pools, 1973–88. Member (SNP): Renfrew DC, 1989–; Renfrewshire CC, 1995–. *Recreations:* walking, reading, gardening. *Address:* Scottish Parliament, Edinburgh EH99 1SP. *T:* (0131) 348 5000.

WHITE, Prof. Simon David Manton, PhD; FRS 1997; Director, Max Planck Institute for Astrophysics, since 1994; *b* 30 Sept. 1951; *s* of David and Gwyneth White; *m* 1st, 1984, Judith Dianne Jennings (marr. diss. 1990); 2nd, 1994, Guinevere Alice Mei-Ing Kauffmann; one *s.* *Educ:* Christ's Hosp.; Jesus Coll., Cambridge (BA 1973; MA 1976; PhD 1977); Univ. of Toronto (MSc 1974). Lindemann Fellow, 1977–78, Sen. Res. Fellow, 1980–83, Univ. of Calif at Berkeley; Res. Fellow, Churchill Coll., Cambridge, 1978–80; Associate Prof., 1983–87, Prof., 1987–90, Univ. of Arizona; Sheepshanks Reader, Univ. of Cambridge, 1990–94. Scientific Mem., Max Planck Soc., 1994–. *Publication:* Morphology and Dynamics of Galaxies, 1983. *Recreations:* ski-ing, singing, violin, Morris Dancing. *Address:* Max-Planck-Institut für Astrophysik, Karl-Schwarzschild Strasse, 87548 Garching bei München, Germany. *T:* (89) 300002211.

WHITE, Stephen Fraser; consulting engineer; *b* 13 May 1922; *s* of Robert and Iola White; *m* 1953, Judith Hamilton Cox; two *s* one *d.* *Educ:* Friars, Bangor; Nottingham Univ. BSc; FICE, MIWEM. War Service in Indian Electrical and Mechanical Engineers, discharged 1947. G. H. Hill and Sons, Consulting Civil Engineers, 1947–59; Cardiff Corporation, 1959–62; Engineering Inspector, Min. of Housing and Local Govt, 1962–70; Dir of Water Engineering, Dept of the Environment, 1970–77; Sen. Technical Advr to Nat. Water Council, 1977–83. *Recreations:* golf, bridge. *Address:* Rosehill, 4 Goodens Lane, Great Doddington, Northants NN29 7TY.

WHITE, Air Vice-Marshal Terence Philip, CB 1987; DL; CEng, FIEE; at leisure; *b* 1 May 1932; *s* of Horace Arthur White and Evelyn Annie White (*née* Simpson); *m* 1956, Sheila Mary (*née* Taylor); three *d.* *Educ:* Wellingborough Technical Inst,; Rugby Coll. of Technology and Arts; RAF Engineering College. Electrical engineering apprentice, BTH Co., 1948–53; Junior Design Engineer, BTH Co., 1953; commissioned RAF Signals Officer, 1954–56; RAF Permt commn, Elect. Engr, 1957; attached RAAF, 1958–60; RAF weapons, communications and radar appts, 1963–67; OC Wing, RAF, Fylingdales, 1967–70; RAF Staff Coll., 1971; commanded RAF N Luffenham, 1972–74; Mem., RCDS, 1975; Senior Elect. Engr, HQ RAF Strike Command, 1976–77; Dir, Engineering Policy MoD (Air), 1978–80; Air Officer, Engrg and Supply, HQ RAF Germany, 1981–82; AOC Maintenance Units and AO Maintenance, RAF Support Comd, 1983–87. Vice Chm. (Air), E Midlands TAVRA, 1988–98. Hon. Air Cdre, County of Lincoln RAuxAF Sqn, 1992–; Hon. County Rep., Lincs, RAF Benevolent Fund, 1995–. DL Lincoln, 1994. *Publications:* contribs to RAF and professional jls. *Recreations:* rough shooting, antique and house restoration. *Address:* c/o HSBC, Grantham, Lincs NG31 6LF. *Club:* Royal Air Force.

WHITE, Thomas Anthony B.; *see* Blanco White.

WHITE, Tom; *see* White, D. T.

WHITE, Willard Wentworth, CBE 1995; singer, actor; *b* 10 Oct. 1946; *s* of Egbert and Gertrude White; *m* 1972, Gillian Jackson; three *s* one *d.* *Educ:* Excelsior High Sch., Kingston, Jamaica; Juilliard Sch. of Music. BM. Guest singer, recitalist and recording artist, UK and overseas; singing rôles include Sarastro, Osmin, Sprecher, Leporello, Banquo, King Philip, Grand Inquisitor, Ferrando, Wotan, Klingsor, Hunding, Fafner, King Henry, Orestes, Porgy, Golaud, Pizarro, Prince Khovansky, Mephistopheles (Gounod's Faust and Berlioz's Damnation of Faust); *stage:* title rôle, Othello, RSC, 1989. Prime Minister of Jamaica's Medal of Appreciation, 1987. *Address:* c/o IMG Artists Europe, 616 Chiswick High Road, W4 5RX.

WHITE, William Kelvin Kennedy, CMG 1983; HM Diplomatic Service, retired; *b* 10 July 1930; *y s* of late Kennedy White, JP, Caldy, Cheshire, and Violet White; *m* 1957, Susan Margaret, *y d* of late R. T. Colthurst, JP, Malvern, Worcs; three *s.* *Educ:* Birkenhead Sch.; Merton Coll., Oxford. 2nd Lieut Manchester Regt, 1949–50; Lieut 13th (Lancs) Bn, Parachute Regt, TA, 1950–54. Entered HM Foreign (later Diplomatic) Service, 1954; Foreign Office, 1954–56, attending UN Gen. Assemblies, 1954 and 1955; 3rd Sec., Helsinki, 1956–57; 2nd Sec., Commissioner-General's Office, Singapore, 1957–61; 2nd Sec., then 1st Sec., FO, 1961–66; 1st Sec. (Commercial), Stockholm, 1966–69; 1st Sec., then Counsellor and Head of Republic of Ireland Dept, FCO, 1969–74; Counsellor, New Delhi, 1974–77; Head of South Asian Dept, FCO, 1978–80; Minister, Canberra, 1980–81; Dep. Chief Clerk and Chief Inspector, FCO, 1982–84; High Comr to Zambia, 1984–87; Ambassador to Indonesia, 1988–90. Mem. Council, Univ. of Surrey, 1991–97. *Address:* Church Farm House, North Moreton, near Didcot, Oxon OX11 9BA. *Club:* Moreton CC.

WHITE-COOPER, William Robert, FCII; Chief Executive, Sedgwick Group plc, since 1997; *b* 17 March 1943; *s* of William Ronald White-Cooper and Alison Mary White-Cooper; *m* 1965, Jennifer Margaret Hayward; one *s* three *d.* *Educ:* Diocesan Coll., Cape Town. FCII 1970. Various exec. posts, Price Forbes Gp, S Africa, 1962–83; Chairman: Sedgwick UK Ltd, 1986–89; Sedgwick Europe Ltd, 1989–93; Sedgwick Noble Lowndes Gp, 1993–96. Past Pres., Insce Inst. of London; Mem. Council, Prince of Wales Business Leaders Forum. MInstD. *Recreations:* playing tennis, spectating cricket and Rugby, reading biographies, collecting antiques. *Address:* (office) Sackville House, 143–149 Fenchurch Street, EC3M 6BN. *T:* (020) 7481 5030. *Clubs:* Wentworth Golf; Kelvin Grove, Western Province Cricket (Cape Town).

WHITEFIELD, Gavin; Chief Executive, North Lanarkshire Council, since 2000; *b* 7 Feb. 1956; *s* of late Gavin Whitefield and of Annie Whitefield; *m* 1981, Grace; two *d.* *Educ:* DPA 1990; CPFA 1996. Audit Asst, Exchequer and Audit Dept, 1974–76; Clydesdale District Council: Asst Auditor, 1976–84; Computer Develt Officer, 1984–86; Principal Housing Officer (Finance and Admin), 1986–89; Asst Dir of Housing (Finance and Admin), Motherwell DC, 1989–95; Dir, Housing and Property Services, N Lanarks Council, 1995–2000. *Recreations:* hill walking, football. *Address:* North Lanarkshire Council, PO Box 14, Civic Centre, Motherwell ML1 1TW. *T:* (01698) 302252, *Fax:* (01698) 230265.

WHITEFIELD, Karen; Member (Lab) Airdrie and Shotts, Scottish Parliament, since 1999; *b* 8 Jan. 1970; *d* of William and Helen Whitefield. *Educ:* Calderhead High Sch.; Glasgow Poly. (BA Hons Public Admin and Mgt). Civil Servant, Benefits Agency, 1992; Personal Asst to Rachel Squire, MP, 1992–99. Mem., Girls' Bde, Scotland. *Recreations:* reading, travel, cake decoration, swimming. *Address:* Scottish Parliament, George IV Bridge, Edinburgh EH99 1SP. *T:* (0131) 348 5000.

WHITEHEAD, Dr Alan Patrick Vincent; MP (Lab) Southampton Test, since 1997; Parliamentary Under-Secretary of State, Department for Transport, Local Government and the Regions, since 2001; *b* 15 Sept. 1950; *m*; one *s* one *d.* *Educ:* Southampton Univ. (BA 1973, PhD 1976). Dep. Dir, 1976–79, Dir, 1979–83, Outset; Dir, British Inst. of Industrial Therapy, 1983–92; Prof. of Public Policy, Southampton Inst., 1992–97. Mem. (Lab), Southampton CC, 1980–92 (Leader, 1984–92). Mem., Select Cttee on Envmt, Transport and Regions, 1997–99; Chm., All Party Ports Gp, 1998–2001. Vice Pres., LGA, 1997–. *Address:* House of Commons, SW1A 0AA. *T:* (020) 7219 3000.

WHITEHEAD, Edward Anthony, (Ted); playwright; *b* 3 April 1933; *s* of Edward Whitehead and Catherine Curran; *m* 1st, 1958, Kathleen Horton (marr. diss. 1976); two *d*; 2nd, 1976, Gwenda Bagshaw. *Educ:* Christ's Coll., Cambridge (MA). Military Service, King's Regt (Infantry), 1955–57. *TV plays:* Under the Age; The Peddler; The Proofing Session; The Blonde Bombshell; *TV adaptations:* The Detective; Jumping the Queue; The Life and Loves of a She-Devil; Firstborn; The Free Frenchman; The Cloning of Joanna May; A Question of Guilt; Tess of the D'Urbervilles; The Mayor of Casterbridge; *stage adaptation:* The Dance of Death. Evening Standard Award, and George Devine Award, 1971; BAFTA Award, 1986. *Publications:* The Foursome, 1972; Alpha Beta, 1972; The Sea Anchor, 1975; Old Flames, 1976; The Punishment, 1976; Mecca, 1977; World's End, 1981; The Man Who Fell in Love with his Wife, 1984; Collected Plays, 2001. *Recreations:* soccer, pubs, music. *Address:* c/o Jenne Casarotto, 2nd Floor, National House, 60–66 Wardour Street, W1V 3HP. *T:* (020) 7287 4450.

WHITEHEAD, Frank Ernest; Deputy Director (Statistics), Office of Population Censuses and Surveys, 1987–89; *b* 21 Jan. 1930; *s* of Ernest Edward Whitehead and Isabel Leslie; *m* 1961, Anne Gillian Marston; three *s.* *Educ:* Leyton County High School; London School of Economics. BSc (Econ). National Service, RAF, 1948–49. Rio Tinto Co. Ltd, 1952–54; Professional Officer, Central Statistical Office, Fedn of Rhodesia and Nyasaland, 1955–64; Statistician, General Register Office, 1964–68; Chief Statistician, Min. of Social Security, later DHSS, 1968–77; Head of Social Survey Div., Office of Population Censuses and Surveys, 1977–82; Under Secretary, 1982; Dep. Dir, OPCS, 1982–87. Vice-Pres., Royal Statistical Soc., 1988–89 (Council, 1987–92). *Publications:* Social Security Statistics: reviews of United Kingdom statistical sources, vol. II (ed W. F. Maunder), 1974; contribs to Statistical News, Population Trends. *Recreations:* family history, gardening. *Address:* Bryaton, Morwenstow, N Cornwall EX23 9SU.

WHITEHEAD, His Honour (Garnet) George (Archie), DFC 1944; a Circuit Judge, 1977–89; *b* 22 July 1916; *s* of late Archibald Payne Whitehead and Margaret Elizabeth Whitehead; *m* 1946, Monica (*née* Watson); two *d.* *Educ:* Wisbech. Admitted Solicitor, 1949. Served War, 1939–45, RAF, Pilot, Bomber Comd and Transport Comd; demob. as Flt Lt, 1 Jan. 1947. Articled to Edmund W. Roythorne, MBE, Solicitor, Spalding. Formerly Senior Partner, Roythorne & Co., Solicitor, Boston, Lincs (Partner, 1950–77); a Recorder of the Crown Court, 1972–77. Formerly Alderman, Boston Borough Council; Mayor of Boston, 1969–70. Reader, Diocese of Lincoln. *Recreations:* photography, walking. *Address:* 15 Burton Close, Boston, Lincs PE21 9QW. *T:* (01205) 364977.

WHITEHEAD, Godfrey Oliver, CBE 1987; FICE; Chief Executive, Alfred McAlpine PLC, since 1993; *b* 9 Aug. 1941; *s* of late Clarence Whitehead and Mary Whitehead (*née* Gartside); *m* 1965, Stephanie McAllister; three *s* one *d.* *Educ:* Hulme Grammar Sch., Oldham; Univ. of Bradford (BSc Civil Engrg). FICE 1992. John Laing Plc, 1963–86: Man. Dir, John Laing Construction Ltd, 1982–86; Exec. Dir, John Laing Plc 1983–86; Chm., Jt Venture (Laing-Mowlem-ARC) which built Mt Pleasant Airport, Falkland Is, 1983–86; Chm., John Laing Internat., 1986; Exec. Dir, AMEC Plc, 1986–89; Gp Chief Exec., Babcock Internat. Gp PLC, 1989–93. Non-Exec. Dir, PSA, 1989–91. Manchester Ringway Developments PLC: Chm., 1987–89; Pres., 1989–. Col, Engr and Logistics Staff Corps, TA, 1996 (Major, 1984; Chm., Liaison Cttee, 1991–). Liveryman, Paviors' Co., 1986–. *Recreations:* gardening, shooting, opera. *Address:* Alfred McAlpine PLC, 8 Suffolk Street, SW1Y 4HG; 55 Copperkins Lane, Amersham, Bucks HP6 5RA.

WHITEHEAD, Graham Wright, CBE 1977; President, Jaguar Cars Inc., 1983–90; Chairman, Jaguar Canada Inc., Ontario, 1983–90; Director: Jaguar Cars Ltd, 1982–90; Jaguar plc, 1984–90; *m* Gabrielle Whitehead, OBE; one *s* one *d.* Joined Wolseley Motors, 1945; moved to US, 1959; Pres., BL Motors Inc., later Jaguar Rover Triumph Inc., NJ, 1968–83; Chm., Jaguar Rover Triumph Canada Inc., Ont, 1977–83. President: British-American Chamber of Commerce, NY, 1976–78; British Automobile Manufacturers Assoc., NY; St George's Soc. of NY; Governor, Nat. Assoc. of Securities Dealers, 1987–90. *Address:* 20 Meadow Place, Old Greenwich, CT 06870, USA. *Club:* Riverside Yacht (Conn).

WHITEHEAD, Ian Richard; HM Diplomatic Service; Counsellor (Management), Paris, since 1999; *b* 21 July 1943; *s* of Alexander Guthrie Whitehead and Mary Helen (*née* Crosby-Milligan); *m* 2nd, 1996, Pamela Mitchison; one *d*, and one *d* from previous marriage. *Educ:* Parmiter's Grammar Sch., London. Entered Foreign Office, 1960: 3rd Secretary: Addis Ababa, 1965–69; UK Delegn, NATO, Brussels, 1969–71; Consular Officer, Dubai, 1971–72; Vice Consul, Casablanca, 1972–75; FCO, 1975–78; 2nd Sec., Bridgetown, 1978–83; First Secretary: Paris, 1983–88; FCO, 1988–91; Dep. High Comr, Dar-es-Salaam, 1991–93; Head of Mission, Skopje, 1993–94; Counsellor, FCO, 1994–98; High Comr to Guyana and Ambassador to Suriname, 1998. *Recreations:* football, tennis, reading. *Address:* c/o Foreign and Commonwealth Office, King Charles Street, SW1A 2AH.

WHITEHEAD, Dr John Ernest Michael, FRCPath; Director of Public Health Laboratory Service, 1981–85; *b* 7 Aug. 1920; *s* of Dr Charles Ernest Whitehead and Bertha Whitehead; *m* 1946, Elizabeth Bacchus (*née* Cochran) (*d* 1996); one *s* one *d*. *Educ:* Merchant Taylors' Sch.; Gonville and Caius Coll., Cambridge (MA); St Thomas's Hosp. Med. Sch. (MB BChir, DipBact). Jun. Ho. appts, St Thomas' Hosp., 1944–47; Lectr in Bacteriology, St Thomas's Hosp. Med. Sch., 1948–51; Travelling Fellowship, State Serum Inst., Copenhagen, 1949–50; Asst Bacteriologist, Central Public Health Laboratory, 1952–53; Dep. Dir, Public Health Lab., Sheffield, 1953–58; Dir, Public Health Lab., Coventry, 1958–75; Cons. Microbiologist, Coventry Hosps, 1958–75; Dep. Dir, Public Health Laboratory Service, 1975–81. Hon. Lecturer: Univ. of Sheffield, 1954–58; Univ. of Birmingham, 1962–75. Vice-Pres., RCPath, 1983–86; Member: Adv. Cttee on Dangerous Pathogens, 1981–85; Adv. Cttee on Irradiated and Novel Foods, 1982–86; Expert Adv. Gp on AIDS, 1985; Consultant Advr in Microbiol., DHSS, 1982–85; Specialist Advr to H of C Agric. Cttee, 1988–91, to H of C Social Services Cttee, 1989–90; Temporary Adviser and Chm., Working Gp on Safety Measures in Microbiology, WHO, 1976–82; Chm., Working Gp on Organisation and Administration of Public Health Laboratory Services, Council of Europe, 1977–79. *Publications:* chapters in The Pathological Basis of Medicine, ed R. C. Curran and D. G. Harnden, 1974; papers and reviews in med. microbiology in various med. and scientific jls. *Recreations:* house and garden visiting, modern languages. *Address:* Ashleigh Cottage, The Street, Frampton on Severn, Gloucester GL2 7ED. *T:* (01452) 741698.

WHITEHEAD, Sir John (Stainton), GCMG 1992 (KCMG 1986; CMG 1976); CVO 1978; HM Diplomatic Service, retired; Chairman, Deutsche Morgan Grenfell Trust Bank Ltd (Japan), 1996–99; Senior Adviser, Deutsche Asset Management Group Ltd, 1996–2000; *b* 20 Sept. 1932; *s* of late John William and Kathleen Whitehead; *m* 1964, Carolyn (*née* Hilton); two *s* two *d*. *Educ:* Christ's Hospital; Hertford Coll., Oxford (MA; Hon. Fellow 1991). HM Forces, 1950–52; Oxford, 1952–55; FO, 1955–56; Tokyo, 1956–61; FO, 1961–64; 1st Sec., Washington, 1964–67; 1st Sec. (Economic), Tokyo, 1968–71; FCO, 1971–76, Head of Personnel Services Dept, 1973–76; Counsellor, Bonn, 1976–80; Minister, Tokyo, 1980–84; Dep. Under-Sec. of State (Chief Clerk), FCO, 1984–86; Ambassador to Japan, 1986–92. Non-executive Director: Cadbury Schweppes, 1993–2001; Serco Group, 1994–96; BPB, 1995–; Sen. Advr, Morgan Grenfell, later Deutsche Morgan Grenfell, Gp, 1992–99; Adviser: Cable and Wireless plc, 1992–; Sanwa Bank Ltd, 1993–2000; Tokyo Electric Power Co. Inc., 1993–; Adviser to Board: Inchcape plc, 1992–96; Guinness plc, 1992–97; Mem. Adv. Bd, PowerGen International, 1996–2001. Exec. Consultant, WDA, 1992–94; Advr to Pres. of BoT, 1992–95; Mem. Adv. Panel, ANA, 2000–. Member: UK–Japan 2000 Gp, 1992–2000, UK Japan 21st Century Gp, 2001– (Dir, 1995–); Council, Japan Soc., 1992– (Mem. Exec. Cttee, 1996–2000, Jt Chm., 2000–); Management Council, GB Sasakawa Foundn, 1993–96. Trustee, Monteverdi Choir and Orchestra, 1991–2000; Member: Royal Opera House Trust, 1992–93; Council, Buckingham Univ., 1992–95. Pres., Hertford Soc., 1991–97. *Recreations:* new challenges, music, travel, golf, woodland management. *Address:* Bracken Edge, High Pitfold, Hindhead, Surrey GU26 6BN. *Clubs:* Beefsteak, Oxford and Cambridge, London Capital, MCC; Liphook Golf (Hants).

WHITEHEAD, Phillip; writer and television producer; Member (Lab) East Midlands Region, European Parliament, since 1999 (Staffordshire East and Derby, 1994–99); *b* 30 May 1937; adopted *s* of late Harold and Frances Whitehead; *m* 1967, Christine, *d* of T. G. Usborne; two *s* one *d*. *Educ:* Lady Manners' Grammar Sch., Bakewell; Exeter Coll., Oxford. President, Oxford Union, 1961. BBC Producer, 1961–67, and WEA Lecturer, 1961–65; Editor of This Week, Thames TV, 1967–70. Guild of TV Producers Award for Factual Programmes, 1969; BPG Best Documentary Award and Emmy Award for Best Script, for the Kennedys, 1993. Vice-Chm., Young Fabian Group, 1965; Chm., Fabian Soc., 1978–79 (Centenary Dir, 1983–84). Chairman: New Society Ltd, 1986; Statesman and Nation Publications Ltd, 1985–90; Director: Goldcrest Film and Television Hldgs Ltd, 1984–87; Brook Productions, 1986–97; Brook Lapping Prodns, 1997–. Member: Annan Cttee on Future of Broadcasting, 1974–77; Council, Consumers' Assoc., 1982– (Chm., 1990–94). Vis. Fellow, Goldsmiths' Coll., Univ. of London, 1985–91; MacTaggart Lectr, Edinburgh Internat. Television Festival, 1987. MP (Lab) Derby N, 1970–83; Front bench spokesman on higher educn, 1980–83 and on the arts, 1982–83; Member: Procedure Cttee, 1977–79; Select Cttee on Home Affairs, 1979–81; PLP Liaison Cttee, 1975–79; Council of Europe Assembly, 1975–80. European Parliament: Chm., Intergroup on Consumer Affairs, 1994–99; Mem., Temp. Cttee of Enquiry into BSE, 1996–97; Vice Pres., Delegn to Czech Republic, 1997–. Chm., Eur. PLP, 1999–. Contested (Lab): W Derbys, 1966, Derby N, 1983, 1987. Member: NUJ; RMT. Times columnist, 1983–85; Presenter, Credo series, LWT, 1983–84. FRSA 1983. *Publications:* (jtly) Electoral Reform: time for change, 1982; (contrib.) Fabian Essays in Socialist Thought, 1984; The Writing on the Wall, 1985; (jtly) Stalin, a time for judgment, 1990; (jtly) The Windsors, a Dynasty Revealed, 1994; (jtly) Dynasty: the Nehru/Gandhi story, 1997. *Recreations:* walking, cinema, old model railways. *Address:* Mill House, Rowsley, Matlock, Derbys DE4 2EB. *T:* (01629) 732659.

WHITEHEAD, Dr Roger George, CBE 1992; nutrition consultant; Director, Dunn Nutrition Centre, Medical Research Council, Cambridge and Keneba, The Gambia, 1973–98; Fellow of Darwin College, Cambridge, 1973–2001, now Emeritus Fellow; *b* 7 Oct. 1933; *s* of late Arthur Charles Sanders Whitehead and Eleanor Jane Whitehead (*née* Farrer); *m* 1958, Jennifer Mary Lees; two *s* one *d*. *Educ:* Ulverston Grammar Sch.; Univ. of Leeds (BSc 1956; PhD 1959); MA Cantab 1973. FIBiol 1973; Hon. MRCP 1986, Hon. FRCP 1993; Hon. FRCPCH 1997. Scientific Staff, MRC, 1959–98; Dir, Child Nutrition Unit, Kampala, 1968–73; Vice Master, Darwin Coll., Cambridge, 1989–97. Vis. Prof., KCL, 1992–; Hon. Professor: Shenyang Univ., China, 1995–; Chinese Acad. of Preventive Medicine, 1995–; Fellow, Internat. Union of Nutritional Scis, 1997. Committee on Medical Aspects of Food Policy: Mem., 1975–91; Chm., Dietary Reference Panel, 1987–91; Mem., MAFF Food Adv. Cttee, 1988–95. Hon. Sen. Scientist, Human Nutrition Res., MRC, Cambridge, 1999–. Pres., Nutrition Soc., 1989–92 (Hon. Mem., 2000); Chm., British Nutrition Foundn, 1994–96 (Vice-Chm., 1993–94). Hon. DSc Ulster, 2000. Drummond Prize, Nutrition Soc., 1968; Unesco Science Prize, 1983; British Nutrition Foundn Prize, 1990; Nutricia Internat. Award for Nutritional Sci., 1994. *Publications:* (jtly) Protein-Energy Malnutrition, 1977; (ed) Maternal Nutrition during Pregnancy and Lactation, 1980; (ed) New Techniques in Nutritional Research, 1991; contribs to learned jls. *Recreations:* photography, licensed amateur radio operator, G3ZUK, 5X5NA, C53U. *Address:* Church End, Weston Colville, Cambridge CB1 5PE. *T:* (01223) 290524; *e-mail:* rogergwhitehead@cs.com.

WHITEHEAD, Sir Rowland (John Rathbone), 5th Bt *cr* 1889; *b* 24 June 1930; *s* of Major Sir Philip Henry Rathbone Whitehead, 4th Bt, and 1st wife Gertrude, *d* of J. C. Palmer, West Virginia, USA; *S* father, 1953; *m* 1954, Marie-Louise, *d* of Arnold Christian Gausel, Stavanger, Norway; one *s* one *d*. *Educ:* Radley; Trinity Hall, Cambridge (BA). Late 2nd Lieutenant RA. Chairman: Trustees, Rowland Hill Benevolent Fund, 1982–; Brogdale Trust Appeal, 1995–97; Trustee: Baronets' Trust, 1984– (founder Chm., 1984–89); Standing Council of the Baronetage, 1972– (Chm. Exec. Cttee, 1984–87); Brogdale Horticultural Trust, 1994–; Kelmscott House Trust, 1970–; Royal Aero Club Trust, 1998–. Vice Chm., Tyndale Soc.; Pres., Rising Stars Foundn, Romania. Hon. Mem., British Weights and Measures Assoc., 1998–. Pres., Inst. of Translation and Interpreting, 1996–. Governor, Appleby Grammar Sch., 1964–. Churchwarden, St Mary Abchurch, City of London, 1996–. Freeman, City of London; Master, Co. of Fruiterers', 1995–96; Court, Guild of PR Practitioners, 2000– (Upper Warden, 2001–Sept. 2002). *Recreations:* poetry and rural indolence. *Heir:* s Philip Henry Rathbone Whitehead [*b* 13 Oct. 1957; *m* 1987, Emma, *d* of Captain A. M. D. Milne Home; two *s*. Late Welsh Guards]. *Address:* Sutton House, Chiswick Mall, W4 2PR. *T:* (020) 8994 2710; Walnut Tree Cottage, Fyfield, Lechlade, Glos GL7 3NT. *T:* (01367) 850267. *Club:* Arts.

WHITEHEAD, Ted; *see* Whitehead, E. A.

WHITEHEAD, Prof. Thomas Patterson, CBE 1985; MCB, FRCPath, FRSC; Professor of Clinical Chemistry, University of Birmingham, 1968–87, now Emeritus Professor; Consultant Biochemist, Queen Elizabeth Medical Centre, 1960–87; *b* 7 May 1923; *m* 1947, Doreen Grace Whitton, JP; two *s* one *d*. *Educ:* Salford Royal Technical Coll.; Univ. of Birmingham (PhD). Biochemist to S Warwickshire Hospital Gp, 1950–60. Dean, Faculty of Medicine and Dentistry, Birmingham Univ., 1984–87. Dir, Wolfson Research Laboratories, 1972–84. Council Mem., Med. Research Council, 1972–76; Mem., Health Service Research Bd, 1973–75; Chairman: Div. of Path. Studies, Birmingham, 1974–80; Board of Undergraduate Med. Educn, Birmingham, 1982–84; W Midlands RHA Res. Cttee, 1982–86; DHSS Adv. Cttee on Assessment of Laboratory Standards, 1969–84; W Midlands RHA Scientific Services Cttee, 1984–86; Member: Adv. Bd, CS Occupational Health Service, 1988–96; Med. Adv. Panel on Driving and Alcohol and Substance Abuse, Dept of Transport, 1989–97. Chief Scientific Advr, BUPA Med. Res., London, 1987–91; Consultant to: BUPA Medical Centre, London, 1969–91; BUPA Hosps, London, 1983–91; BUPA Med. R&D, 1991–95; Centro Diagnostico Italiano, Milan, 1972–92; WHO, Geneva, 1974–86; Unilabs Clinical Pathology Services (formerly JS Pathology Services), London, 1983–99. Pres., Assoc. of Clinical Biochemists, 1981–83; Mem. Council, RCPath, 1982–84. Hon. MRCP 1985. Kone Award Lectr, 1983. Wellcome Prize, 1972; Dade Award, Geneva, 1975; Disting. Internat. Services Award, Internat. Fedn of Clinical Chemistry, 1987; Rank Prize for Opto-Electronics, 1991. *Publications:* Quality Control in Clinical Chemistry, 1976; papers in med. and scientific jls. *Recreation:* growing and exhibiting sweet peas. *Address:* 70 Northumberland Road, Leamington Spa CV32 6HB. *T:* (01926) 421974. *Club:* Athenæum.

WHITEHORN, John Roland Malcolm, CMG 1974; a Deputy Director-General, Confederation of British Industry, 1966–78; *b* 19 May 1924; *s* of late Alan and Edith Whitehorn; *m* 1st, 1951, Josephine (*née* Plummer) (marr. diss. 1973; she *d* 1990); no *c*; 2nd, 1973, Marion FitzGibbon (*née* Gutmann). *Educ:* Rugby Sch. (Exhbnr); Trinity Coll., Cambridge (Exhbnr). Served War, 1943–46, RAFVR (Flying Officer). Joined FBI, 1947; Dep. Overseas Dir, 1960; Overseas Dir, 1963; Overseas Dir, CBI, 1965–68; Dir, Mitchell Cotts plc, 1978–86; Consultant Dir, Lilly Industries, 1978–89. Member: BOTB, 1975–78; Bd, British Council, 1968–82; Gen. Adv. Council, BBC, 1976–82. Chm., Cocking Parish Council, 1991–99. *Address:* Casters Brook, Cocking, near Midhurst, W Sussex GU29 0HJ. *T:* (01730) 813537. *Club:* Reform.

See also Katharine Whitehorn.

WHITEHORN, Katharine Elizabeth, (Mrs Gavin Lyall); Columnist, The Observer, 1960–96 (Associate Editor, 1980–88); Agony Aunt, Saga Magazine, since 1997; *b* London; *d* of late A. D. and E. M. Whitehorn; *m* 1958, Gavin Lyall, *qv*; two *s*. *Educ:* Blunt House; Roedean; Glasgow High School for Girls, and others; Newnham Coll., Cambridge. Publisher's Reader, 1950–53; Teacher-Secretary in Finland, 1953–54; Grad. Asst, Cornell Univ., USA, 1954–55; Picture Post, 1956–57; Woman's Own, 1958; Spectator, 1959–61. Member: Latey Cttee on Age of Majority, 1965–67; BBC Adv. Gp on Social Effects of Television, 1971–72; Board, British Airports Authority, 1972–77; Council, RSocMed, 1982–85. Director: Nationwide Building Soc., 1983–91; Nationwide Anglia Estate Agents, 1987–90. Vice-Pres., Patients Assoc., 1983–96. Rector, St Andrews Univ., 1982–85. Advr, Inst. for Global Ethics, 1993–. Patron, Central Middx Relate, 1997–. Mem., ESU. FRSA. Hon. LLD St Andrews, 1985; Hon. DLitt London Guildhall, 2000. Woman That Makes A Difference Award, Internat. Women's Forum, 1992. *Publications:* Cooking in a Bedsitter, 1960; Roundabout, 1961; Only on Sundays, 1966; Whitehorn's Social Survival, 1968; Observations, 1970; How to Survive in Hospital, 1972; How to Survive Children, 1975; Sunday Best, 1976; How to Survive in the Kitchen, 1979; View from a Column, 1981; How to Survive your Money Problems, 1983. *Recreation:* river boat. *Address:* 14 Provost Road, NW3 4ST. *Clubs:* University Women's (Hon. Mem.), Royal Society of Medicine.

See also J. R. M. Whitehorn.

WHITEHOUSE, Dr David Bryn; Executive Director and Trustee, The Corning Museum of Glass, Corning, USA, since 1992 (Chief Curator, 1984–88; Deputy Director, 1988–92); Trustee, The Rockwell Museum, since 1992; *b* 15 Oct. 1941; *s* of Brindley Charles Whitehouse and Alice Margaret Whitehouse; *m* 1st, 1963, Ruth Delamain Ainger; one *s* two *d*; 2nd, 1975, Elizabeth-Anne Ollemans; one *s* two *d*. *Educ:* King Edward's Sch., Birmingham; St John's Coll., Cambridge. MA, PhD; FSA; FRGS. Scholar, British Sch. at Rome, 1963–65; Wainwright Fellow in Near Eastern Archaeology, Univ. of Oxford, 1966–73; Dir, Sīrāf Expedn, 1966–73; Dir, British Inst. of Afghan Studies, 1973–74; Dir, British Sch. at Rome, 1974–84. President: Internat. Union of Institutes, 1980–81; Internat. Assoc. for Hist. of Glass, 1991–95 (Mem. Management Cttee, 1988–95 and 1998–); Mem. Council, Internat. Assoc. for Classical Archaeology, 1974–84. Corresp. Mem., German Archaeological Inst.; Academician, Accademia Fiorentina dell'Arte del Disegno; Fellow: Pontificia Accademia Romana di Archeologia; Accademia di Archeologia, Lettere e Belle Arti, Naples. Ed., Jl of Glass Studies, 1988–. *Publications:* (jtly) Background to Archaeology, 1973; (jtly) The Origins of Europe, 1974; (with Ruth Whitehouse) Archaeological Atlas of the World, 1975; (ed jtly) Papers in Italian Archaeology I, 1978; Siraf III: The Congregational Mosque, 1980; (with David Andrews and John Osborne) Papers in Italian Archaeology III, 1981; (with Richard Hodges) Mohammed, Charlemagne and the Origins of Europe, 1983; (jtly) Glass of the Caesars, 1987; Glass of the Roman Empire, 1988; (jtly) Treasures from The Corning Museum of Glass, 1992; Glass: a pocket dictionary, 1993; English Cameo Glass, 1994; Roman Glass in The Corning Museum of Glass, Vol. I, 1997, Vol. II, 2001; Ancient Glass from Ed-Dur, 1998; The Corning Museum of Glass: a decade of glass collecting 1990–1999, 2000; (with Stefano Carboni) Glass of the Sultans, 2001; many papers in Iran, Antiquity, Med. Archaeol., Papers of Brit. Sch. at Rome, Jl of Glass Studies, etc. *Address:* The Corning Museum of Glass, One Museum Way, Corning, NY 14830–2253, USA. *T:* (607) 9748424; *e-mail:* whitehoudb@cmog.org. *Club:* Athenæum.

WHITEHOUSE, David Rae Beckwith; QC 1990; a Recorder, since 1987; *b* 5 Sept. 1945; *s* of late (David) Barry (Beckwith) Whitehouse, MA, MD, FRCS, FRCOG and Mary Beckwith Whitehouse, JP; *m* 1971, Linda Jane, *d* of Eric Vickers, CB and Barbara Mary Vickers; one *s*. *Educ:* Ellesmere College; Choate Sch., Wallingford, Conn., USA;

Trinity College, Cambridge (MA). English-Speaking Union Scholarship, 1964. Called to the Bar, Gray's Inn, 1969; in practice on SE Circuit, specialising in criminal law, licensing and tribunals. Criminal cases include: Last Tango in Paris (obscene pubns); George Davis (five robbery trials and two appeals); Handless Corpse Murder; Cyprus Spy trial; murder trial of Lennie The Guv'nor McLean; Colombian Cartel and Mafia drug trials; fraud cases include: Barlow Clowes (investment and co. takeover fraud); Norton plc (rights issue fraud); Abbey National plc (corruption); local authy frauds involving W Wilts and Brent Councils; read The Sun for defamation and contempt, 1969–76. Member: Criminal Bar Assoc., 1969–; Central Criminal Court Bar Mess, 1970– (Cttee, 1981–84); Internat. Bar Assoc. (Business Crime section), 1990–. *Recreations:* the arts, esp. architecture, music and cinema; walking, wild gardening. *Address:* 3 Raymond Buildings, Gray's Inn, WC1R 5BH. *T:* (020) 7400 6400, *Fax:* (020) 7242 4221.

WHITEHOUSE, Prof. (Julian) Michael (Arthur), MD; FRCP, FRCR, FRCPE, FMedSci; Professor Emeritus, Imperial College School of Medicine, London; Vice Principal for Undergraduate Medicine, Imperial College School of Medicine and Professor of Medical Oncology, University of London, 1997–2000; *b* 2 June 1940; *s* of Arthur Arnold Keer Whitehouse and Kathleen Ida Elizabeth (*née* Elliston); *m* 1965, Diane France de Saussure; one *s* two *d*. *Educ:* Queens' Coll., Cambridge (BA 1963; MB, BChir 1966; MA 1967; MD 1975); St Bartholomew's Hosp. Med. Coll., London. FRCP 1979; FRCR 1992; FRCPE 1994. Sen. Lectr and Actg Dir, ICRF Dept of Med. Oncology, and Hon. Consultant Physician, St Bartholomew's Hosp., London, 1975–76; Prof. of Med. Oncology and Dir, CRC Wessex Regl Med. Oncology Unit, Univ. of Southampton, and Hon. Consultant Physician, Southampton Gen. Hosp., 1976–97; Dean, Charing Cross and Westminster Med. Sch., 1997. Chm., Educn Trng Bd, Eur. Orgn for Res. and Treatment of Cancer, 1997–. Chm. Council, Paterson Inst., Christie Hosp., Manchester, 1997–; Member: Council, CRC, 1997–; GMC Professional Conduct Cttee, 2000–. Dep. Chm. Govs, Canford Sch., Dorset, 1998–; Gov. and Mem. Council, St Swithin's Sch., Winchester, 1996–; Gov., City of London Sch., 2000–. FMedSci 2000. *Publications:* CNS Complications of Malignant Disease, 1979; Recent Advances in Clinical Oncology, 1982, 2nd edn 1986; A Pocket Consultant in Clinical Oncology, 1983; Cancer Investigation and Management, 1984; Cancer: the facts, 1996; contrib. numerous papers in various jls on res. and treatment of cancer. *Recreations:* devising projects, ski-ing, sailing, travelling. *Address:* 25 Chilbolton Avenue, Winchester, Hants SO22 5HE; *e-mail:* m.whitehouse@ic.ac.uk. *Club:* Athenæum.

WHITEHOUSE, Mary, CBE 1980; Founder and President Emeritus, National Viewers' and Listeners' Association (Hon. General Secretary, 1965–80; President, 1980–93); freelance journalist, broadcaster; *b* 13 June 1910; *d* of James and Beatrice Hutcheson; *m* 1940, Ernest R. Whitehouse; three *s*. *Educ:* Chester City Grammar Sch.; Cheshire County Training Coll. Art Specialist: Wednesfield Sch., Wolverhampton, 1932–40; Brewood Grammar Sch., Staffs, 1943; Sen. Mistress, and Sen. Art Mistress, Madeley Sch., Shropshire, 1960–64. Co-founder, "Clean up TV campaign", 1964. *Publications:* Cleaning Up TV, 1966; "Who Does She Think She Is?", 1971; Whatever Happened to Sex?, 1977; A Most Dangerous Woman?, 1982; Mightier than the Sword, 1985; Quite Contrary (autobiog.), 1993. *Recreations:* reading, gardening, walking. *Address:* c/o Abberton Manor, Layer Road, Abberton, Colchester, Essex CO5 7NL.

WHITEHOUSE, Michael; *see* Whitehouse, J. M. A.

WHITEHOUSE, Prof. Norman Harold; Professor of Dental Public Health, and Dean, Dental School, University of Wales College of Medicine, 1993–99 (Pro Vice Chancellor, 1997–99); Chief Executive, University Dental Hospital NHS Trust, 1995–99 (Chief Executive, Cardiff Dental Hospital, 1993–94); *b* 22 April 1938; *y s* of late Norman Lester Whitehouse, builder and Maud Whitehouse, Bloxwich, Walsall, Staffs; *m* 1963, Barbara Palmer; one *s* one *d*. *Educ:* Univ. of Leeds (LDS 1961; BChD 1962); Univ. of Birmingham (DDH 1970); DDPH RCS 1970; FDSRCSE (*ad hominem*) 1995; FDSRCS (by election) 1995. Chief Admin. Dental Officer and Specialist in Community Dental Health, S Glam and E Dyfed HAs, 1974–86; British Dental Association: Sec., 1986–91; Chief Exec. and Sec., 1991–93; Chief Admin. Dental Officer and Dir, Dental Public Health, Mid Glam HA, 1993–99; Hon. Consultant in Dental Public Health, S and Mid Glam HAs, 1993–99. Mem., BroTaf HA, 2000–. *Publications:* contrib. articles in jls. *Recreations:* hill-walking, cross-country ski-ing. *Address:* White Cottage, Craig Penllyn, Cowbridge, Vale of Glamorgan CF71 7RT. *T:* (01446) 774184; *e-mail:* whitehousenh@tesco.net.

WHITEHOUSE, Paul Chapple, QPM 1993; Chief Constable, Sussex Police, 1993–2001; *b* 26 Sept. 1944; *s* of Beatrice and Jack Whitehouse, Cambs; *m* 1970, Elizabeth Dinsmore; one *s* one *d*. *Educ:* Ipswich Sch.; Emmanuel Coll., Cambridge (BA 1967; MA 1969). VSO, Starehe Boys' Centre, Nairobi, 1963–64; Durham Constabulary, 1967–74; Northumbria Police, 1974–83; Asst Chief Constable, Greater Manchester Police, 1983–87; Dep. Chief Constable, W Yorkshire Police, 1987–93. Association of Chief Police Officers: Chairman: Communications Gp, 1995–2001; Personnel Mgt (formerly Personnel and Trng) Cttee, 1998–2001; Vice Chm., Media Adv. Group, 1994–2001; Member: Finance and Resources Cttee, 1994–2001; Inf. Mgt Cttee, 1995–2001. Chm., Brighton and Hove Common Purpose Adv. Gp, 1994–2001; Member Council: IAM, 1993–; NACRO, 1994–; Centre for Crime and Justice Studies, 1997–. Chm., Starehe Endowment Fund (UK), 1994–. *Recreations:* collecting people, IT, steam, disputation, keeping the peace. *Address:* Broadgate Close, Lower Broad Street, Ludlow, Shropshire SY8 1PH. *T:* (01584) 872165, *Fax:* (01584) 872177. *Club:* Oxford and Cambridge.

WHITEHOUSE, Walter Alexander; Professor of Theology, University of Kent, 1965–77; Master of Eliot College, University of Kent, 1965–69, and 1973–75; *b* 27 Feb. 1915; *e s* of Walter and Clara Whitehouse, Shelley, near Huddersfield; *m* 1st, 1946, Beatrice Mary Kent Smith (*d* 1971); 2nd, 1974, Audrey Ethel Lemmon. *Educ:* Penistone Gram. Sch.; St John's Coll., Cambridge; Mansfield Coll., Oxford. Minister of Elland Congregational Church, 1940–44; Chaplain at Mansfield College, Oxford, 1944–47; Reader in Divinity, Univ. of Durham, 1947–65. Principal of St Cuthbert's Soc., Univ. of Durham, 1955–60; Pro-Vice-Chancellor of Univ., and Sub-Warden, 1961–64. Minister at High Chapel, Ravenstonedale, 1977–82. Mem. (Lab), Glos CC, 1989–93. Hon. DD Edinburgh, 1960. *Publications:* Christian Faith and the Scientific Attitude, 1952; Order, Goodness, Glory (Riddell Memorial Lectures), 1959; The Authority of Grace, 1981. *Address:* 5 Penlee Manor Drive, Penzance, Cornwall TR18 4HW.

WHITELAW, Billie, CBE 1991; actress; *b* 6 June 1932; *d* of Perceval and Frances Whitelaw; *m* Robert Muller (*d* 1998), writer; one *s*. *Educ:* Thornton Grammar Sch., Bradford. Appeared in: *plays:* Hotel Paradiso, Winter Garden, 1954 and Oxford Playhouse, 1956; Progress to the Park, Theatre Workshop and Saville, 1961; England our England, Prince's, 1962; Touch of the Poet, Venice and Dublin, 1962; National Theatre, 1963–65: Othello, London and Moscow; Hobson's Choice; Beckett's Play; Trelawny of the Wells; The Dutch Courtesan; After Haggerty, Criterion, 1971; Not I, Royal Court, 1973 and 1975; Alphabetical Order, Mayfair, 1975; Footfalls, Royal Court, 1976; Molly, Comedy, 1978; Happy Days, Royal Court, 1979; The Greeks, Aldwych, 1980; Passion Play, Aldwych, 1981; Rockaby and Enough, NY, 1981, with Footfalls, 1984, NT 1982, Riverside, 1986, Adelaide Fest., 1986, Purchase Fest., NY, 1986; Tales from Hollywood, NT, 1983; Who's Afraid of Virginia Woolf?, Young Vic, 1987; *films:* No Love for Johnny; Charlie Bubbles; Twisted Nerve; The Adding Machine; Start the Revolution Without Me; Leo the Last; Eagle in a Cage; Gumshoe; Frenzy; Night Watch; The Omen; Leopard in the Snow; The Water Babies; An Unsuitable Job for a Woman; Slayground; Shadey; The Chain; The Dressmaker; Maurice; Joyriders; The Krays; Deadly Advice; Jane Eyre; Canterbury Tales (animated film); Quills; *television:* No Trams to Lime Street; Lena Oh My Lena; Resurrection; The Skin Game; Beyond the Horizon; Anna Christie; Lady of the Camellias; The Pity of it all; Love on the Dole; A World of Time; You and Me; Poet Game; Sextet (8 plays); Napoleon and Love (9 plays: Josephine); The Fifty Pound Note (Ten from the Twenties); The Withered Arm (Wessex Tales); The Werewolf Reunion (2 plays); Ghost Trio, and But the Clouds, by Samuel Beckett; Not I; Eustace and Hilda (2 plays); The Serpent Son; Happy Days (dir. by Beckett); Private Schulz; Last Summer's Child; A Tale of Two Cities; Jamaica Inn; Camille; Old Girlfriends; The Secret Garden; Imaginary Friends (mini-series); The Picnic; Three Beckett plays; The 15 Streets; Lorna Doone; The Entertainer; A Murder of Quality; The Cloning of Joanna May; Firm Friends I and II (mini-series); Born to Run; Shooting the Past; A Dinner of Herbs; *radio plays:* The Master Builder; Hindle Wakes; Jane Eyre; The Female Messiah; Alpha Beta; The Cherry Orchard; Vassa Zhelyezhova; Filumena; The Wireless Lady. Lecturer on Beckett: in USA at univs of Santa Barbara, Stanford and Denver, 1985, Smith and Dartmouth Colls, 1992, Franklyn and Marshall Colls, 1993, Albany Univ., NY, 1997; at Balliol Coll., Oxford, 1986; An Informal Evening with Samuel Beckett and lecture tours, USA, 1992–95 and 1996; one-woman Beckett Evening, NY, 1997 and QEH, 1999. Annenberg/Beckett Fellow, Reading Univ., 1993. Silver Heart Variety Club Award, 1961; TV Actress of Year, 1961, 1972; British Academy Award, 1968; US Film Critics Award, 1968; Variety Club of GB Best Film Actress Award, 1977; Evening News Film Award as Best Actress, 1977; Sony Best Radio Actress Award, 1987; Evening Standard Film Award for Best Actress, 1988. Hon. DLitt: Bradford, 1981; St Andrews, 1997; Birmingham, 1997. *Publication:* Billie Whitelaw: who he? (autobiog.), 1995, USA 1996. *Recreation:* pottering about the house. *Address:* c/o Michael Foster, ICM, Oxford House, 76 Oxford Street, W1R 1RB.

WHITELAW, Prof. James Hunter, FRS 1996; FREng; FIMechE; Professor of Convective Heat Transfer, Imperial College, London, since 1974; *b* 28 Jan. 1936; *s* of James Whitelaw and Jean Ross Whitelaw (*née* Scott); *m* 1959, Elizabeth Shields; three *s*. *Educ:* Univ. of Glasgow (BSc 1957; PhD 1961); DSc London 1981. Res. Associate, Brown Univ., 1961–63; Lectr, Imperial Coll., 1963–69; Reader, Imperial Coll., 1969–74. Chair Prof. of Pollution and Combustion, Hong Kong Poly. Univ., 2000–. Editor, Experiments in Fluids, 1983–. FREng (FEng 1991); FCGI 1999. Foreign Associate, US Acad of Engrg, 2000. DSc *hc:* Lisbon, 1980; Valencia, 1996; TCD, 1999; Nat. Technical Univ. of Athens, 2001. *Publications:* (jtly) Data and Formulae Handbook, 1967, 2nd edn 1976; (jtly) Principles and Practice of Laser-Doppler Anemometry, 1976, 2nd edn 1981; (jtly) Engineering Calculation Methods for Turbulent Flow, 1981; ed. 25 vols proc., and published over 350 papers in learned jls, incl. Jl of Fluid Mechanics, Experiments in Fluids, proc. of learned socs. *Recreations:* gardening, music. *Address:* 149a Coombe Lane West, Kingston-upon-Thames, KT2 7DH. *T:* (020) 8942 1836.

WHITELEY, family name of **Baron Marchamley**.

WHITELEY, Sir Hugo Baldwin H., *see* Huntington-Whiteley.

WHITELEY, Dame Jane (Elizabeth), DBE 1990; *b* 14 July 1944; *d* of Major Charles Packe (killed in action, July 1944) and Hon. Margaret Lane Fox; *m* 1st, 1966, Ian Gow, TD, MP (*d* 1990); two *s*; 2nd, 1994, Lt-Col Michael Whiteley. *Educ:* St Mary's School, Wantage. Governor: three special schs in S London, 1968–72; Hankham CP Sch., 1976–85; St Bede's Sch., Eastbourne, 1980–87; Park Coll., Eastbourne, 1985–88; Grenville Coll., Bideford, 1997–; Mem. Council, Cheltenham Coll., 1996–98. Trustee, Ian Gow Meml Fund, 1990–. Freeman, Bor. of Eastbourne, 1992. *Recreations:* playing organ and piano, reading. *Address:* Lower Lewer, Hatherleigh, Okehampton, Devon EX20 3LF.

WHITELEY, Gen. Sir Peter (John Frederick), GCB 1979 (KCB 1976); OBE 1960; DL; Lieutenant-Governor and Commander-in-Chief, Jersey, 1979–84; *b* 13 Dec. 1920; *s* of late John George Whiteley; *m* 1948, Nancy Vivian, *d* of late W. Carter Clayden; two *s* two *d*. *Educ:* Bishop's Stortford Coll.; Bembridge Sch.; Ecole des Roches. Joined Royal Marines, 1940; 101 Bde, 1941; HMS: Resolution, 1941; Renown, 1942; HMNZS Gambia, 1942; seconded to Fleet Air Arm, 1946–50; Adjt 40 Commando, 1951; Staff Coll., Camberley, 1954; Bde Major 3rd Commando Bde, 1957; Instructor, Staff Coll., Camberley, 1960–63; CO 42 Commando, 1965–66 (despatches, Malaysia, 1966); Col GS Dept of CGRM, 1966–68; Nato Defence Coll., 1968; Comdr 3rd Commando Bde, 1968–70; Maj.-Gen. Commando Forces, 1970–72; C of S, HQ Allied Forces Northern Europe, 1972–75; Commandant General, Royal Marines, 1975–77; C-in-C Allied Forces Northern Europe, 1977–79. Col Comdt, RM, 1985–87; Hon. Col, 211 (Wessex) Field Hosp. RAMC (Volunteers), TA, 1985–90. Mem., Council, Union Jack Club, 1985–91; Vice Chm., Theatre Royal, Plymouth, 1991–97; Pres., W Devon Area, 1985–87, Pres., Devon, 1987–96, St John's Ambulance Bde; Vice-Pres., Devon Care Trust, 1995–. Life Trustee, Durrell Wildlife Conservation Trust. Governor: Bembridge Sch., 1981–95; Kelly Coll., 1985–94; St Michael's Sch., Tavistock, 1985–89. Member: Royal Commonwealth Soc., 1981–; Anglo Norse Soc., 1980–; Anglo Danish Soc., 1980–; Jersey Soc. in London, 1984–. Liveryman, Fletchers' Co., 1982 (Hon. Life Liveryman, 1999); Guild of Freemen of City of London: Mem. Ct of Assistants, 1980–; Master, 1987–88. DL Devon, 1987. CIMgt. KStJ 1980; Chevalier, Ordre de la Pléaiade, Assoc. of French Speaking Parliaments, 1984. *Publications:* contribs to Jane's Annual, NATO's Fifteen Nations, RUSI Jl, Nauticus. *Recreations:* music, photography, painting, wood carving, sailing, dogs. *Clubs:* Royal Commonwealth Society; Royal Naval Sailing Assoc.

WHITELEY, Samuel Lloyd; Deputy Chief Land Registrar, 1967–73; Legal Assistant to the Clerk to the Haberdashers' Company 1973–78, Freeman, 1978; *b* 30 April 1913; *s* of Rev. Charles Whiteley and Ann Letitia Whiteley; *m* 1939, Kathleen Jones (*d* 1988); two *d*. *Educ:* George Dixon Sch.; Birmingham Univ. LLB (Hons) 1933. Admitted Solicitor, 1935; HM Land Registry, 1936; seconded Official Solicitor's Dept, 1939; RAF, 1940–46; HM Land Registry, 1946–73. *Recreation:* sport, as a reminiscent spectator. *Address:* 8 Stonehaven Court, Knole Road, Bexhill, Sussex TN40 1LW. *T:* (01424) 213191.

WHITEMAN, Prof. John Robert, PhD; CMath, FIMA; Professor of Numerical Analysis, since 1981, and Public Orator, since 1999, Brunel University; Director, Brunel Institute of Computational Mathematics, since 1976; *b* 7 Dec. 1938; *s* of Robert Whiteman and Rita (*née* Neale); *m* 1964, Caroline Mary Leigh; two *s* (one *d* decd). *Educ:* Bromsgrove Sch.; Univ. of St Andrews (BSc); Worcester Coll., Oxford (DipEd); Univ. of London (PhD). FIMA 1970. Sen. Lectr, RMCS, Shrivenham, 1963–67; Assistant Professor: Univ. of Wisconsin, 1967–68; Univ. of Texas, Austin, 1968–70; Reader in Numerical Analysis, Brunel Univ., 1970–76; Richard Merton Gästprofessor, Univ. of Münster, 1975–76; Brunel University: Hd of Dept of Maths and Statistics, 1982–90; Vice

Principal, 1991–96. Visiting Professor: Univ. of Pisa, 1975; Univ. of Kuwait, 1986; Texas A & M Univ., 1986, 1988, 1989, 1990, 1992; Univ. of Stuttgart, 1989, 1992; Vis. Prof., 1996, Dist. Res. Fellow, 1997–2001, Univ. of Texas at Austin. Lectures: Geary, City Univ., 1986; Robert Todd Gregory, Univ. of Texas, Austin, 1990; Collatz Gedenkkolloquium, Hamburg Univ, 1991; Univ. of Stuttgart, 1995. Member: SERC Maths Cttee, 1981–86 and Science Bd, 1989–91; Bd of Dirs, Eur. Scientific Assoc. for Forming Processes, 1997–. FRSA. Hon. DSc West Bohemia Univ., 1995. Editor, Numerical Methods for Partial Differential Equations, 1985–; Member, Editorial Board: Computer Methods in Applied Mechanics and Engrg; Communications in Applied Numerical Methods; Internat. Jl for Numerical Methods in Fluids; Jl of Mathematical Engrg in Industry; Jl of Engrg Analysis; Computational Mechanics Advances. *Publications:* (ed) The Mathematics of Finite Elements and Applications, vols 1–10, 1973, 1976, 1979, 1982, 1985, 1988, 1991, 1994, 1997, 2000; numerous works on numerical solution of partial differential equations, particularly finite element methods for singularities in elliptic problems and for problems of linear and non linear solid mechanics, incl. viscoelasticity. *Recreations:* walking, swimming, golf, orchestral and choral music. *Address:* Institute of Computational Mathematics, Brunel University, Uxbridge, Middx UB8 3PH. *T:* (01895) 203270; *e-mail:* john.whiteman@brunel.ac.uk.

WHITEMAN, Peter George; QC 1977; barrister-at-law; a Recorder, since 1989; a Deputy High Court Judge, since 1994; Attorney and Counselor at Law, State of New York; *b* 8 Aug. 1942; *s* of David Whiteman and Betsy Bessie Coster; *m* 1971, Katherine Ruth (*née* Ellenbogen); two *d. Educ:* Warwick Secondary Modern Sch.; Leyton County High Sch.; LSE (LLB, LLM with Distinction). Called to the Bar, Lincoln's Inn, 1967, Bencher, 1985; *ad eundem* Middle Temple, 1977. Lectr, London Univ., 1966–70; Prof. of Law, Univ. of Virginia, 1980. Mem., Faculty of Laws, Florida Univ., 1977; Visiting Professor: Virginia Univ., 1978; Univ. of California at Berkeley, 1980. Mem. Cttee, Unitary Tax Campaign (UK), 1982–. Pres., Dulwich Village Preservation Soc., 1987–; Chairman: Dulwich against the Rail Link, 1988–; Dulwich Jt Residents' Cttee, 1991–. Member: Cttee Dulwich Picture Gall., 1989–; Adv. Cttee, Dulwich Estate Govs' Scheme of Management, 1988–. FRSA. Mem. Bd, Univ. of Virginia Jl of Internat. Law, 1981–. *Publications:* Whiteman on Capital Gains Tax, 1967, 4th edn 1988; Whiteman on Income Tax, 1971, 3rd edn 1988; contrib. British Tax Encyc. *Recreations:* tennis, squash, mountain-walking, jogging, croquet. *Address:* Hollis Whiteman Chambers, Queen Elizabeth Building, Temple, EC4Y 9BS. *T:* (020) 7936 3131.

WHITEMAN, Robert Arthur; JP; Executive Director of Resources, London Borough of Lewisham, since 1999; *b* 4 Dec. 1961; *s* of late William Whiteman and of Joan Whiteman (*née* Elliott); *m* 1988, Hilary Barbara Cannon; two *s* one *d. Educ:* Univ. of Essex (BA Hons). IRRV 1988; CPFA 1995. W. H. Smith plc, 1983–86; London Borough of Newham, 1986–88; Corp. of London, 1988; Head of Revenues, London Borough of Camden, 1988–96; Asst Dir of Finance, London Borough of Lewisham, 1996–99. Core Finance Advr to LGA, 1999. JP Newham, 1996. *Publications:* regular contribs to local authy jls. *Recreations:* DIY, music, swimming. *Address:* Lewisham Town Hall, Catford Road, SE6 4RU. *T:* (020) 8314 6000.

WHITEMAN, Ven. Rodney David Carter; Archdeacon of Cornwall, since 2000; *b* Par, Cornwall, 6 Oct. 1940; *s* of Leonard Archibald Whiteman and Sybil Mary (*née* Morshead); *m* 1969, Christine Anne Chelton; one *s* one *d. Educ:* St Austell Grammar School; Pershore Coll. of Horticulture; Ely Theological Coll. Deacon 1964, priest 1965; Curate of Kings Heath, Birmingham, 1964–70; Vicar: St Stephen, Rednal, Birmingham, 1970–79; St Barnabas, Erdington, 1979–89; RD of Aston, 1981–89; Hon. Canon of Birmingham Cathedral, 1985–89; Priest-in-charge of Cardinham with Helland, 1989–94; Hon. Canon of Truro Cathedral, 1989–; Archdeacon of Bodmin, 1989–99. *Recreations:* gardening, music, historic buildings and monuments, walking. *Address:* Archdeacon's House, 3 Knight's Hill, Truro TR1 3UY.

WHITEMORE, Hugh John; dramatist; *b* 16 June 1936; *s* of late Samuel George Whitemore and Kathleen Alma Whitemore (*née* Fletcher); *m* 1st, Jill Brooke (marr. diss.); 2nd, 1976, Sheila Lemon (marr. diss.); one *s*; 3rd, 1998, Rohan McCullough. *Educ:* King Edward VI School, Southampton; RADA. FRSL 1999. *Stage:* Stevie, Vaudeville, 1977; Pack of Lies, Lyric, 1983; Breaking the Code, Haymarket, 1986, transf. Comedy, 1987 (Amer. Math. Soc. Communications Award, 1990); The Best of Friends, Apollo, 1988; It's Ralph, Comedy, 1991; A Letter of Resignation, Comedy, 1997, transf. Savoy, 1998; Disposing of the Body, Hampstead, 1999; God Only Knows, Vaudeville, 2000; *television:* plays and dramatisations include: Elizabeth R (Emmy award, 1970); Cider with Rosie (Writer's Guild award, 1971); Country Matters (Writer's Guild award, 1972); Dummy (RAI Prize, Prix Italia, 1979); Concealed Enemies (Emmy award, Neil Simon Jury award, 1984); The Final Days, 1989; A Dance to the Music of Time, 1997 (Script Prize, Monte Carlo Fest., 1998); *films:* Stevie, 1980; The Return of the Soldier, 1982; 84 Charing Cross Road, 1986 (Scriptor Award, Los Angeles, 1988); Utz, 1992; Jane Eyre, 1996. *Publications:* (contrib) Elizabeth R, 1972; Stevie, 1977, new edn 1984; (contrib.) My Drama School, 1978; (contrib.) Ah, Mischief!, 1982; Pack of Lies, 1983; Breaking the Code, 1986; The Best of Friends, 1988; It's Ralph, 1991; A Letter of Resignation, 1997; Disposing of the Body, 1999; God Only Knows, 2001. *Recreations:* music, movies, reading. *Address:* 67 Peel Street, W8 7PB. *Club:* Garrick.

WHITEN, Prof. (David) Andrew, PhD; FBA 2000; FRSE; FBPsS; Professor of Evolutionary and Developmental Psychology, since 1997, and Wardlaw Professor, since 2000, University of St Andrews; *b* 20 April 1948; *s* of Bernard Wray Whiten and Maisie (*née* Gathercole); *m* 1973, Dr Susie Challoner; two *d. Educ:* Sheffield Univ. (BSc 1st Cl. Hons Zool. 1969); Bristol Univ. (PhD 1973). FBPsS 1991. SSRC Conversion Fellow, Queen's Coll., Oxford, 1972–75; St Andrew's University: Lectr in Psychol., 1975–90; Reader, 1991–97; Leverhulme Res. Fellow, 1997. Vis. Prof., Zurich Univ., 1992; F. M. Bird Prof., Emory Univ., 1995–96; British Acad. Res. Reader, 1999–2001. FRSE 2001. *Publications:* (ed) Natural Theories of Mind: evolution, development and simulation of everyday mindreading, 1991; (ed with E. Widdowson) Natural Diet and Foraging Strategy of Monkeys, Apes and Humans, 1992; (ed with R. Byrne) Machiavellian Intelligence: social expertise and the evolution of intellect, 1988; Machiavellian Intelligence II: extensions and evaluations, 1997 (trans. Japanese 2000); contrib. many articles on evolution and develt of social intelligence and cultural transmission to learned jls. *Recreations:* friends, family, art, painting, film, music, garden. *Address:* School of Psychology, University of St Andrews, St Andrews, Fife KY16 9JU.

WHITEOAK, John Edward Harrison, MA, CPFA; Managing Director (formerly Managing Partner), Whiteoak Associates Ltd (Public Sector Consultancy), since 1998; *b* 5 July 1947; *s* of Frank Whiteoak, farmer, and Marion Whiteoak; *m* 1st, 1969, Margaret Elizabeth Blakey (decd); one *s* two *d*; 2nd, 1983, Karen Lynne Wallace Stevenson, MB ChB, BSc; two *d. Educ:* Sheffield Univ. (MA). CIPFA 1971. Cheshire County Council: Dep. County Treas., 1979–81; County Treas., 1981–94; Gp Dir, Resources, 1994–98; Treas., Cheshire Police Authy, 1995–98. Non-exec. Director: VALPAK Ltd, 1998–; Industrial Properties Ltd, 1997–. Financial Advr, ACC, 1984–97. Lead negotiator on local govt finance for local authorities in England, 1994–97; lead finance advr to English County Councils, 1994–98. Member: Soc. of County Treasurers, 1981–98 (Pres., 1997–98); Accounting Standards Cttee, 1984–87. Chartered Institute of Public Finance and Accountancy: Mem., Technical Cttee, 1986–87 and 1991–; Mem., Accounting Panel, 1984–87 (Chm., 1987); Chm., Financial Reporting Panel, 1991–94; Chm., Corporate Governance Panel, 1994–; Pres., NW Region, 1994–95. *Publications:* (jtly) Public Sector Accounting and Financial Control, 1992; contrib. various professional and management journals. *Recreations:* social golf, tennis, snooker. *Address:* Huntington Hall, Chester CH3 6EA. *T:* (business) (01244) 400860. *Clubs:* Royal Automobile; City (Chester); Eaton Golf, Portal Golf.

WHITEREAD, Rachel; sculptor; *b* 20 April 1963. *Educ:* Brighton Poly. (BA 1st Cl. Hons); Slade Sch. of Art (DipHE). *Exhibitions:* Ghost, Chisenhale Gall., London, 1990; Stedelijk Van-Abbemuseum, Eindhoven, 1993; Mus. of Contemporary Art, Chicago, 1993; Kunsthalle, Basel, ICA, Philadelphia, ICA, Boston, 1994–95; retrospective, Tate Gall., Liverpool, 1996–97; Reina Sofia, Madrid, 1997; Venice Biennale, 1997; Anthony d'Offay Gall., 1998; solo, Serpentine Gall., Scottish Nat. Gall. of Modern Art, 2001. *Public sculptures:* Water Tower Project, NY, 1998; Holocaust Meml, Judenplatz, Vienna, 2000; Monument, Fourth Plinth, Trafalgar Sq., 2001. Prize, Deutscher Akademischer Austauschdienst, Berlin, 1992; Turner Prize, 1993; Prix Eliette von Karajan, 1996. *Address:* c/o Anthony d'Offay Gallery, 9 Dering Street, W1R 9AA. *T:* (020) 7499 4100, *Fax:* (020) 7493 4443.

WHITESIDE, Prof. Derek Thomas, PhD; FBA 1975; University Professor of History of Mathematics and Exact Sciences, Cambridge, 1987–99, now Emeritus; *b* 23 July 1932; *s* of Ernest Whiteside and Edith (*née* Watts); *m* 1962, Ruth Isabel Robinson (*d* 1997); one *s* one *d. Educ:* Blackpool Grammar Sch.; Bristol Univ. (BA); Cambridge Univ. (PhD). Leverhulme Research Fellow, 1959–61; DSIR Research Fellow, 1961–63; Research Asst, 1963–72, Asst Dir of Research, 1972–76, University Reader in History of Mathematics, 1976–87, Univ. of Cambridge. Editor, The Mathematical Papers of Isaac Newton, 1967–. Hon. DLitt Lancaster, 1987. Médaille Koyré, Académie Internat. d'Histoire des Sciences, 1968; Sarton Medal, Amer. History of Sci. Soc., 1977. *Publications:* Patterns of Mathematical Thought in the later Seventeenth Century, 1961; (ed) The Preliminary Manuscripts for Isaac Newton's 1687 Principia: 1684–1685 (in facsimile), 1989; articles in Brit. Jl Hist. Science, Jl for Hist. of Astronomy, Physis, etc; *Festschrift:* The Investigation of Difficult Things, 1992. *Recreation:* looking into space creatively. *Address:* c/o Centre for Mathematical Sciences, Wilberforce Road, Cambridge CB3 0WB.

WHITEWAY, Paul Robin; HM Diplomatic Service; Counsellor and Deputy Head of Mission, Chile, since 2000; *b* 1 Dec. 1954; *s* of Frank Whiteway and Patricia (*née* Callaway); *m* 1st, 1980, Melanie Jane Blew (marr. diss.); one *d*; 2nd, 1996, Maha Georges Yannieh; one *s. Educ:* Henley Grammar Sch.; Merton Coll., Oxford (BA Hons Mod. History; MA). Joined FCO, 1977; Far Eastern Dept, 1977–79; Third, later Second Sec., Dublin, 1980–83; First Secretary: Nuclear Energy Dept, 1984–86; Port Stanley, 1986–87; Mexico and Central America Dept, 1987–88; seconded to MoD (Navy), 1988–90; Dep. High Comr, Uganda, 1990–93; Asst Head, Southern Africa Dept, 1993–96; Counsellor and Dep. Hd of Mission, Syria, 1996–99. *Recreations:* riding, tennis, history, travel. *Address:* c/o Foreign and Commonwealth Office, King Charles Street, SW1A 2AH.

WHITFIELD, family name of **Baron Kenswood**.

WHITFIELD, Adrian; QC 1983; a Recorder of the Crown Court, 1981–2000; *b* 10 July 1937; *s* of Peter Henry Whitfield and Margaret Mary Burns; *m* 1st, 1962, Lucy Caroline Beckett (marr. diss.); two *d*; 2nd, 1971, Niamh O'Kelly; one *s* one *d. Educ:* Ampleforth Coll.; Magdalen Coll., Oxford (Demy; MA). 2nd Lieut, KOYLI (Nat. Service), 1956–58. Called to the Bar, Middle Temple, 1964, Bencher 1990; Member of Western Circuit. Chm., NHS Tribunal, 1993–. *Publications:* contribs on legal matters in medical and dental pubns. *Recreations:* reading, visual arts, travel. *Address:* 47 Faroe Road, W14 0EL. *T:* (020) 7603 8982; 3 Serjeants' Inn, EC4Y 1BQ. *T:* (020) 7427 5000.

WHITFIELD, Alan; transport consultant, since 1998; *b* 19 April 1939; *s* of John J. Whitfield and Annie Fothergill-Rawe; *m* 1964, Sheila Carr; two *s. Educ:* Consett Grammar Sch., Durham; Sunderland and Newcastle Colls of Advanced Technology. MICE 1968; MIMunE 1969; FIHT 1984. Surveyor/Engr, NCB, 1956–62; Engrg Asst, Northumberland CC, 1962–70; Department of Transport: Main Grade Engr, 1970–73; Prin. Professional, 1973–76; Suptg Engr, 1976–80; Dep. Dir, Midlands Road Construction Unit, 1980–83; Dir (Transport), W Midlands Reg. Office, 1983–89; Regl Dir, Eastern Region, DoE and Dept of Transport, 1989; Road Prog. Div., Dept of Transport, 1989–94, Highways Agency, 1994–95. Director: Ove Arup & Partners, 1995–98; Ove Arup & Partners Internat., 1995–98. Associate Consultant, Waterfront Partnership, 1998–. *Publications:* papers on cost benefit analysis, centrifugal testing soils, road design and construction, etc. to IHT, ICE, Inst. Geo. Sci., etc. *Recreations:* bridge, golf, music.

WHITFIELD, Prof. Charles Richard, MD; FRCOG; FRCPGlas; Regius Professor of Midwifery in the University of Glasgow, 1976–92, now Emeritus; *b* 21 Oct. 1927; *s* of Charles Alexander and Aileen Muriel Whitfield; *m* 1953, Marion Douglas McKinney; one *s* two *d. Educ:* Campbell Coll., Belfast; Queen's Univ., Belfast (MD). House Surg. and Ho. Phys. appts in Belfast teaching hospitals, 1951–53; Specialist in Obstetrics and Gynaecology, RAMC (Lt-Col retd), 1953–64; Sen. Lectr/Hon. Reader in Dept of Midwifery and Gynaecology, Queen's Univ., Belfast, 1964–74; Consultant to Belfast teaching hosps, 1964–74; Prof. of Obstetrics and Gynaecology, Univ. of Manchester, 1974–76. Mem. Council, RCOG, 1985–91 (Chairman: Subspecialty Bd, 1984–89; Scottish Exec. Cttee, 1985–91; Higher Trng Cttee, 1989–92). *Publications:* (ed) Dewhurst's Obstetrics and Gynaecology for Postgraduates, 4th edn 1985, 5th edn 1995; papers on perinatal medicine, pregnancy anaemia and other obstetric and gynaec. topics in med. and scientific jls. *Recreations:* food, travel, sun-worship. *Address:* 7 Grange Road, Bearsden, Glasgow G61 3PL.

WHITFIELD, John; solicitor; Senior Partner, family firm of Whitfield Hallam Goodall, of Batley, Dewsbury and Mirfield; *b* 31 Oct. 1941; *s* of Sydney Richard Whitfield and Mary Rishworth Whitfield; *m*; three *s*; *m* 1999, Janet Gissing (*née* Oldroyd). *Educ:* Sedbergh Sch.; Leeds Univ. (LLB). Solicitor, Whitfield Son and Hallam, then Whitfield Hallam Goodall, 1965–. MP (C) Dewsbury, 1983–87. Contested (C): Hemsworth, 1979; Dewsbury, 1987 and 1992. Director: Thomas Carr Ltd, 1989–; Leeds Rugby Football Club Ltd, 1998–. *Recreations:* fishing, shooting, badminton, walking with dogs. *Address:* Haugh Top Farm, Krumlin, Barkisland, Halifax HX4 0EL. *T:* (01422) 822994. *Clubs:* Flyfishers'; Mirfield Constitutional; Tanfield Angling; Leeds Rugby Football.

WHITFIELD, John Flett; JP; DL; Chairman, Surrey Police Authority, 1985–89; Chairman of Police Committee, Association of County Councils, 1985–88; *b* 1 June 1922; *s* of John and Bertha Whitfield; *m* 1946, Rosemary Elisabeth Joan Hartman; two *d. Educ:* Epsom Coll., Surrey. Served War, King's Royal Rifle Corps, 1939–46. HM Foreign

Service, 1946–57; Director, Materials Handling Equipment (GB) Ltd, 1957–61; London Director, Hunslet Holdings Ltd, 1961–64. Director, Sunningdale Golf Club, 1973–77. Councillor: Berkshire CC, 1961–70; Surrey CC, 1970–89 (Chm., 1981–84). Contested (C) Pontefract, General Election, 1964. JP Berkshire 1971–, Chm. Windsor County Bench, 1978–80; DL Surrey 1982, High Sheriff, 1985–86. Chm., Surrey Univ. Council, 1986–88 (Vice-Chm., 1983–86). *Recreations:* golf, foreign languages, bookbinding. *Address:* Moor Cottage, Chobham Road, Sunningdale, Berks SL5 0HU. *T:* (01344) 620997. *Clubs:* Royal and Ancient Golf of St Andrews; Royal Cinque Ports Golf; Sunningdale Golf; Rye Golf; Woking Golf.

WHITFIELD, June Rosemary, (Mrs T. J. Aitchison), CBE 1998 (OBE 1985); actress; *b* 11 Nov. 1925; *d* of John Herbert Whitfield and Bertha Georgina Whitfield; *m* 1955, Timothy John Aitchison (*d* 2001); one *d. Educ:* Streatham Hill High School; RADA (Diploma 1944). Revue, musicals, pantomime, TV and radio; worked with Arthur Askey, Benny Hill, Frankie Howerd, Dick Emery, Bob Monkhouse, Leslie Crowther, Ronnie Barker; first worked with Terry Scott in 1969; *radio:* JW at the BBC, 1997; June Whitfield at the Beeb, 1999; series include: Take It From Here (with Dick Bentley and Jimmy Edwards, 1953–60; The News Huddlines (with Roy Hudd and Chris Emmett), 1984–; JW Radio Special, 1992; Like They've Never Been Gone (with Roy Hudd), 1998–; serials (as Miss Marple): Murder at the Vicarage, 1993; A Pocketful of Rye, 1994; At Bertram's Hotel, 1995; The 4.50 from Paddington, 1996; The Caribbean Mystery, 1997; Nemesis, The Mirror Cracked, 1998; The Body in the Library, 1999; A Murder is Announced, 1999; The Moving Finger, 2001; They Do It With Mirrors, 2001; musical, Gigi, 1997; *films:* Carry on Nurse, 1959; Carry on Abroad, 1972; Bless This House, 1972; Carry on Girls, 1973; Carry On Columbus, 1992; Jude the Obscure, 1996; The Last of the Blonde Bombshells, 2000; *television:* This Is Your Life, 1976 and 1995; guest appearance, Amer. TV series, Friends, 1998; series include: Fast and Loose (with Bob Monkhouse), 1954; Faces of Jim (with Jimmy Edwards), 1962, 1963; Beggar My Neighbour, 1966, 1967; Scott On . . . (with Terry Scott), 1969–73; Happy Ever After, 1974–78; Terry and June, 1979–87; Cluedo, 1990; Absolutely Fabulous, 1993–96, 2001; What's My Line?, 1994, 1995; Common As Muck, 1996; Family Money, 1997; The Secret, 2000; *stage:* An Ideal Husband, Chichester, 1987; Ring Round the Moon, Chichester, 1988; Over My Dead Body, Savoy, 1989; Babes in the Wood, Croydon, 1990, Plymouth, 1991, Cardiff, 1992; Cinderella, Wimbledon, 1994. Freeman, City of London, 1982. Lifetime Achievement Award, British Comedy Awards, 1994; RTS Hall of Fame, 1999. *Publication:* And June Whitfield (autobiog.), 2000. *Address:* c/o April Young, 11 Woodlands Road, Barnes, SW13 0JZ. *T:* (020) 8876 7030.

WHITFIELD, Dr Michael, CChem, FRSC; CBiol, FIBiol; FGS; Vice President, Marine Biological Association, since 2000 (Director and Secretary, 1987–99); Director, Plymouth Marine Laboratory, 1994–96 (Deputy Director, 1988–94); *b* 15 June 1940; *s* of Arthur and Ethel Whitfield; *m* 1961, Jean Ann Rowe (*d* 1984); one *s* three *d. Educ:* Univ. of Leeds (BSc 1st cl. Hons Chem.; PhD Chem.). FRSC 1980; FIBiol 1994. Research Scientist, CSIRO Div. of Fisheries and Oceanography, Cronulla, NSW, 1964–69; Vis. Res. Fellow, KTH Stockholm, 1969, Univ. of Liverpool, 1970; Res. Scientist, Marine Biolog. Assoc., 1970–87. Vice Pres., Sir Alister Hardy Foundn for Ocean Science, 1991–99; Pres., Challenger Soc. for Marine Science, 1996–98. FRSA 1992. Dr (*hc*): Göteborg, 1991; Plymouth, 2000. *Publications:* Ion-selective electrodes for the analysis of natural waters, 1970; Marine Electrochemistry, 1981; Tracers in the Ocean, 1988; Light and Life in the Sea, 1990; Aquatic Life Cycle Strategies, 1999; numerous papers in professional jls. *Recreations:* hill walking, bird watching, photography. *Address:* The Laboratory, Citadel Hill, Plymouth PL1 2PB. *T:* (01752) 633331.

WHITFIELD, Prof. Roderick; Percival David Professor of Chinese and East Asian Art, University of London, since 1993 (Professor of Chinese and East Asian Art, and Head of Percival David Foundation of Chinese Art, 1984–93); *b* 20 July 1937; *s* of late Prof. John Humphreys Whitfield and Joan Herrin, ARCA; *m* 1st, 1963, Frances Elizabeth Oldfield, PhD (marr. diss 1983), *e d* of late Prof. R. C. Oldfield and Lady Kathleen Oldfield; one *s* two *d*; 2nd, 1983, Youngsook Pak, PhD, art historian, *e d* of late Pak Sang-Jon, Seoul. *Educ:* Woodbourne Acad.; King Edward's Sch., Birmingham; Sch. of Oriental and African Studies (Civil Service Interpreter, 2nd cl.); St John's Coll., Cambridge (BA Hons 1960, Oriental Studies Tripos); Princeton Univ. (MA 1963, PhD 1965). Research Associate and Lectr, Princeton, 1965–66; Research Fellow, St John's Coll., Cambridge, 1966–68; Asst Keeper I, Dept of Oriental Antiquities, British Museum, 1968–84. Visiting Professor: Univ. of Heidelberg, 1996; Univ. of Helsinki, 1997; Univ. of Barcelona, 1998. Teetzel Lectr, Univ. of Toronto, 1995. Pres., Circle of Inner Asian Art, 1996–. Trustee, Inst. of Buddhist Studies, 1987–. Corresp. Fellow, Dunhuang Res. Acad., 1999–. Mem. Editl Bd, Artibus Asiae, 1992–. *Publications:* In Pursuit of Antiquity: Chinese paintings of Ming and Ch'ing dynasties in collection of Mr and Mrs Earl Morse, 1969; The Art of Central Asia: the Stein collection at the British Museum, 3 vols, 1983–85; (ed) Treasures from Korea, 1984; (ed) Korean Art Treasures, 1986; (ed) Early Chinese Glass, 1988; Caves of the Thousand Buddhas, 1990; (ed) Problems in Meaning in Early Chinese Ritual Bronzes, 1993; Fascination of Nature: plants and insects in Chinese paintings and ceramics of the Yuan dynasty, 1993; Dunhuang, Caves of the Singing Sands: Buddhist Art from the Silk Road, 2 vols, 1995; (trans. jtly) The Arts of Central Asia: the Pelliot Collection in the Musée Guimet, 1996; (ed jtly) Exploring China's Past: new researches and discoveries in Chinese archaeology, 2000; (jtly) The Mogao Caves, 2000; articles in Asiatische Studien, Buddhica Britannica, Orientations, Burlington Magazine, British Liby Jl and other jls. *Address:* 7 St Paul's Crescent, NW1 9XN. *T:* (020) 7267 2888.

WHITFIELD, Sir William, Kt 1993; CBE 1976; RIBA; Senior Partner, Whitfield Partners, architects. DipArch; DipTP. Prof. of Architecture, Victoria Univ. of Manchester, 1981. Surveyor to the Fabric, St Paul's Cathedral, 1985–90. Mem., Royal Fine Art Commn. Trustee, British Museum. *Address:* Whitfield Partners, 30 Warner Street, EC1R 5EX. *T:* (020) 7837 4040.

WHITFIELD LEWIS, Herbert John; *see* Lewis.

WHITFORD, Hon. Sir John (Norman Keates), Kt 1970; Judge of the High Court, Chancery Division, 1970–88; *b* 24 June 1913; *s* of Harry Whitford and Ella Mary Keates; *m* 1946, Rosemary, *d* of John Barcham Green and Emily Paillard; four *d. Educ:* University College School; Munich University; Peterhouse, Cambridge. President, ADC. Called to the Bar: Inner Temple, 1935; Middle Temple, 1946 (Bencher 1970). Served with RAFVR, 1939–44: Wing Comdr, 1942; Chief Radar Officer and Dep. Chief Signals Officer, Air Headquarters Eastern Mediterranean; Advisor on patents and information exchanged for war purposes, HM Embassy, Washington, 1944–45. QC 1965. Member of Bar Council, 1968–70. Chm., Departmental Cttee on Law Relating to Copyright and Designs, 1974–76. *Address:* 140 High Street, West Malling, Kent ME19 6NE.

WHITHAM, Prof. Gerald Beresford, FRS 1965; Charles Lee Powell Professor of Applied Mathematics, at the California Institute of Technology, Pasadena, Calif, 1983–98, now Emeritus; *b* 13 Dec. 1927; *s* of Harry and Elizabeth Ellen Whitham; *m* 1951, Nancy (*née* Lord); one *s* two *d. Educ:* Elland Gram. Sch., Elland, Yorks; Manchester University. PhD Maths, Manchester, 1953. Lectr in Applied Mathematics, Manchester Univ., 1953–56; Assoc. Prof., Applied Mathematics, New York Univ., 1956–59; Prof., Mathematics, MIT, 1959–62; Prof. of Aeronautics and Maths, 1962–67, Prof. of Applied Maths, 1967–83, CIT. FAAAS 1959. Wiener Prize in Applied Mathematics, 1980. *Publications:* Linear and Nonlinear Waves, 1974; Lectures on Wave Propagation, 1979; research papers in Proc. Roy. Soc., Jl Fluid Mechanics, Communications on Pure and Applied Maths. *Address:* Applied Mathematics 217–50, California Institute of Technology, Pasadena, CA 91125, USA.

WHITING, Alan; Executive Director, Regulation and Compliance, London Metal Exchange, since 1997; *b* 14 Jan. 1946; *s* of Albert Edward and Marjorie Irene Whiting; *m* 1968, Annette Frances Pocknee; two *s* two *d. Educ:* Acklam Hall Grammar Sch., Middlesbrough; Univ. of East Anglia (BA Hons); University College London (MSc Econ). Research Associate and Asst Lectr, Univ. of East Anglia, 1967; Cadet Economist, HM Treasury, 1968; Economic Asst, DEA, and Min. of Technology, 1969; Economist, EFTA, Geneva, 1970; Economist, CBI, 1972; Economic Adviser, DTI, 1974; Sen. Econ. Adviser, 1979; Industrial Policy Div., Dept of Industry, 1983–85; Under Sec., Economics Div., DTI, 1985; Finance and Resource Management Div., DTI, 1989–92; Under Sec., Securities and Investment Services, later Financial Regulation, HM Treasury, 1992–97. Dep. Chm., Council of Mortgage Code Register of Intermediaries, 1999–. *Publications:* (jtly) The Trade Effects of EFTA and the EEC 1959–1967, 1972; (ed) The Economics of Industrial Subsidies, 1975; articles in economic jls. *Recreations:* building, gardening, music, sailing, tennis. *Address:* London Metal Exchange, 56 Leadenhall Street, EC3A 2DX. *Clubs:* Littleton Sailing; Bracknell Lawn Tennis.

WHITING, Prof. Brian, MD; FRCPGlas, FRCPE; Professor of Clinical Pharmacology, 1986–2001, Dean, Faculty of Medicine, and Head of Clinical Medicine Planning Unit, 1992–2000, University of Glasgow; *b* 6 Jan. 1939; *s* of late Leslie George Whiting and of Evelyn Irene Edith Whiting (*née* Goss); *m* 1st, 1967, Jennifer Mary Tait (marr. diss. 1983); two *d*; 2nd, 1990, Marlene Shields (*née* Watson); two step *s. Educ:* Univ. of Glasgow (MB ChB 1964; MD 1970). FRCPGlas 1979; FRCPE 1996. House Officer, Western Infirmary and Stobhill Gen. Hosp., Glasgow, 1964; University of Glasgow: Department of Materia Medica: Hutchison Res. Schol., 1965; Registrar in Medicine, 1966–68; Lectr and Sen. Registrar in Clinical Pharmacol., 1969–77; Sen. Lectr and Consultant Physician, 1977–82; Reader in Clinical Pharmacol., 1982–86; Hd, Div. of Clinical Pharmacol., Dept of Medicine and Therapeutics, 1989–91. Dir, Clinical Pharmacokinetics Lab., Stobhill Gen. Hosp., Glasgow, 1980–90. Vis. Scientist, Div. of Clinical Pharmacol., Univ. of Calif, San Francisco, 1978–79; Internat. Union of Pharmacol. Vis. Consultant, India and Nepal, 1985; Visiting Professor of Clinical Pharmacology: Univ. of Auckland, 1987; (British Council) Japan, 1988; British Council and Internat. Union of Pharmacol., India and Nepal, 1990. Non-exec. Mem., Gtr Glasgow Health Bd, 1994–2000. Member: Assoc. of Physicians of GB and Ireland, 1985–; GMC, 1991–96. Founder FFPM (by Dist.) 1990; Founder FMedSci 1998. *Publications:* (ed jtly) Lecture Notes on Clinical Pharmacology, 1982, 6th edn 2001; contrib. numerous articles or book chapters, principally in field of clinical pharmacology. *Recreations:* painting, music (listening and composition), mountaineering. *Address:* 2 Milner Road, Glasgow G13 1QL. *T:* (0141) 959 2324.

WHITING, Clifford Hamilton, ONZ 1999; artist; Kaihautu (Leader), Te Papa Tongarewa Museum of New Zealand, 1993–2000; *b* 6 May 1936; *s* of Frank Whiting and Huriana Herewini (Whanau A-Apanui Tribal Gp); *m* 1957, Heather Leckie; three *s. Educ:* Wellington Teachers' Coll.; Dunedin Teachers' Coll. (Trained Teachers' Cert.). Art Advr, Dept of Educn, 1958–71; Lectr in Art, Palmerston North Teachers' Coll., 1972–81; freelance artist, multi media murals, illustrations, photography, print-making, carving, engraving and painting, 1981–. Mem. and Chm., Maori and S Pacific Arts Council and TeWakaToi, 1980–94; Vice-Chm., QEII Arts Council, 1990–93. Hon. DLitt Massey, 1996. *Publication:* Mataora, 1996. *Recreations:* fishing, yachting, diving. *Address:* 24 Gould Street, Russell, Bay of Islands, New Zealand. *T:* (9) 4037726.

WHITING, Rev. Peter Graham, CBE 1984; Minister, Beechen Grove Baptist Church, 1985–95; *b* 7 Nov. 1930; *s* of late Rev. Arthur Whiting and Olive Whiting; *m* 1960, Lorena Inns; two *s* three *d. Educ:* Yeovil Grammar Sch.; Irish Baptist Theol Coll., Dublin. Ordained into Baptist Ministry, 1956. Minister, King's Heath, Northampton, 1956–62; commnd RAChD, 1962; Regtl Chaplain, 1962–69 (Chaplain to 1st Bn The Parachute Regt, 1964–66); Sen. Chaplain, 20 Armd Bde and Lippe Garrison, BAOR, 1969–72; Staff Chaplain, HQ BAOR, 1973–74; Sen. Chaplain, 24 Airportable Bde, 1974–75; Dep. Asst Chaplain Gen., W Midland Dist, Shrewsbury, 1975–78 (Sen. Chaplain, Young Entry Units, 1976–78); Asst Chaplain Gen., 1st British Corps, BAOR, 1978–81; Dep. Chaplain Gen. to the Forces (Army), 1981–84. QHC 1981–85. *Address:* 5 Pook Lane, Warblington, Havant, Hants PO9 2TH.

WHITLAM, Hon. (Edward) Gough, AC 1978; QC 1962; Member: Executive Board of Unesco, 1985–89 (Australian Ambassador to Unesco, 1983–86); Constitutional Commission, 1986–88; Prime Minister of Australia, 1972–75; *b* 11 July 1916; *s* of late H. F. E. Whitlam, Australian Crown Solicitor and Aust. rep. on UN Human Rights Commission; *m* 1942, Margaret Elaine, AO, *d* of late Mr Justice Dovey, NSW Supreme Court; three *s* one *d. Educ:* University of Sydney. BA 1938; LLB 1946. RAAF Flight Lieut, 1941–45. Barrister, 1947; MP for Werriwa, NSW, 1952–78; Mem., Jt Parly Cttee on Constitutional Rev., 1956–59; Leader, 1973 and 1975, Dep. Leader, 1977, Constnl Conventions; Deputy Leader, Aust. Labor Party, 1960, Leader, 1967–77; Leader of the Opposition, 1967–72 and 1976–77; Minister for Foreign Affairs, 1972–73. Vis. Fellow, 1978–79, First Nat. Fellow, 1980–81, ANU; Fellow, Univ. of Sydney Senate, 1981–83, 1986–89; Visiting Professor: Harvard Univ., 1979; Univ. of Adelaide, 1983. Chairman: Australia–China Council, 1986–91; Australian Nat. Gall., 1987–90. Pres., Australian Sect., Internat. Commn of Jurists, 1982–83. Founder, Hanoi Architectural Heritage Foundn, 1993. FAHA 1993. Corresp. Mem., Acad. of Athens, 1992. Hon. DLitt: Sydney, 1981; Wollongong, 1989; La Trobe, Wodonga, 1992; Univ. of Technol., Sydney, 1995; Hon. LLD Philippines, 1974. Silver Plate of Honour, Socialist Internat., 1976; Mem. of Honour, IUCN, 1988; Redmond Barry Award, Australian Library and Info. Assoc., 1994. Grand Cross, Order of Makarios III (Cyprus), 1983; Grand Comdr, Order of Honour (Greece), 1996; Order of the Phoenix (Greece), 1998; Grand Officer, Order of Merit (Italy), 1999 (Comdr, 1997). *Publications:* The Constitution *versus* Labor, 1957; Australian Foreign Policy, 1963; Socialism within the Constitution, 1965; Australia, Base or Bridge?, 1966; Beyond Vietnam: Australia's Regional Responsibility, 1968; An Urban Nation, 1969; A New Federalism, 1971; Urbanised Australia, 1972; Australian Public Administration and the Labor Government, 1973; Australia's Foreign Policy: New Directions, New Definitions, 1973; Road to Reform: Labor in Government, 1975; The New Federalism: Labor's Programs and Policies, 1975; Government of the People, for the People—by the People's House, 1975; On Australia's Constitution, 1977; Reform During Recession, 1978; The Truth of the Matter, 1979, 2nd edn 1983; The Italian Inspiration in English Literature, 1980; A Pacific Community, 1981; The Cost of Federalism, 1983; The Whitlam Government 1972–75, 1985; International Law-Making, 1989; Australia's Administrative Amnesia, 1990; Living with the United States: British Dominions and

New Pacific States, 1990; National and International Maturity, 1991; Human Rights in One Nation, 1992; Abiding Interests, 1997; An Italian Notebook, 2001. *Address:* 100 William Street, Sydney, NSW 2011, Australia.

See also N. R. Whitlam.

WHITLAM, Michael Richard, CBE 2000; charity consultant; Mike Whitlam - Solutions for Charity, since 2001; *b* 25 March 1947; *s* of late Richard William Whitlam and Mary Elizabeth Whitlam (*née* Land); *m* 1968, Anne Jane McCurley; two *d. Educ:* Morley Grammar Sch.; Tadcaster Grammar Sch.; Coventry Coll. of Educn, Univ. of Warwick (Cert. of Educn); Home Office Prison Dept Staff Coll. (Qual. Asst Governor Prison Dept); Cranfield Coll. of Technology (MPhil 1988). Biology teacher, Ripon, 1968–69; Asst Governor, HM Borstal, Hollesley Bay and HM Prison, Brixton, 1969–74; Dir, Hammersmith Teenage Project, NACRO, 1974–78; Dep. Dir/Dir, UK ops, Save the Children Fund, 1978–86; Chief Exec., RNID, 1986–90; Dir-Gen., BRCS, 1991–99; Chief Exec., Mentor Foundn (Internat.), 1999–2001. Board Member: Britcross Ltd, 1991–99; British Red Cross Events Ltd, 1991–99; British Red Cross Trading, 1991–99; REACH, 1997–; Chm., Sound Advantage plc, 1988–90. Member: Exec. Council, Howard League, 1974–84; Community Alternative Young Offenders Cttee, NACRO, 1979–82; Exec. Council, Nat. Children's Bureau, 1980–86; Bd, City Literary Inst., 1989–90; Bd, Charity Appointments Ltd, 1990–; Chairman: London Intermediate Treatment Assoc., 1980–83; Assoc. of Chief Execs of Nat. Voluntary Orgns, 1988– (Mem. Policy and Res. Gp, 1994–); Prisoners Abroad, 1999–. FRSA 1995; CIMgt 1997. Mem., URC. *Publications:* numerous papers on juvenile delinquency and charity management. *Recreations:* painting, walking, family activities, voluntary organisations, politics, visiting France, cooking. *Address:* (office) 40 Pepys Close, Ickenham, Middx UB10 8NY. *T:* (01895) 678169; *e-mail:* m.whitlam@btinternet.com. *Club:* New Cavendish.

WHITLAM, Nicholas Richard; Chairman, Whitlam & Co., since 1990; President, NRMA Ltd, since 1996 (Deputy President, 1995–96); Chairman, NRMA Insurance Ltd, NRMA Building Society Ltd, and other NRMA companies, since 1996 (Deputy Chairman, NRMA Insurance Ltd, 1995–96); *b* 6 Dec. 1945; *s* of Hon. (Edward) Gough Whitlam, *qv*; *m* 1973, Sandra Judith Frye; two *s* one *d. Educ:* Sydney High Sch.; Harvard Coll. (AB Hons); London Business Sch. (MBA). Morgan Guaranty Trust Co., 1969–75; American Express Co., 1975–78; Banque Paribas, 1978–80; Comr, Rural Bank of New South Wales, 1980–81, then Man. Dir, State Bank of New South Wales, 1981–87; Man. Dir, Whitlam Turnbull & Co. Ltd, 1987–90; Dep. Chm., Export Finance and Insurance Corp., 1991–94; Advr, Asian Capital Partners, 1993–96. Board Member: Aust. Trade Commn, 1985–91; Integral Energy Aust., 1996–99. Board Member: Aust. Graduate Sch. of Management, 1982–97 (Chm., 1988–97; Chm., Adv. Council, 1997–99; Mem., Adv. Council, 1999–); Aust. Sports Foundn, 1986–95; Chm., Sydney Symphony Orch., 1991–96; Mem. Symphony Council, 1996–; Trustee, Sydney Cricket and Sports Ground, 1984–88. DUniv NSW, 1996. *Recreations:* swimming, cycling. *Address:* 388 George Street, Sydney, NSW 2000, Australia. *T:* (2) 92215560, *Fax:* (2) 92215646. *Clubs:* Hong Kong; Tattersall's (Chm., 1993–96), Whale Beach Surf (Sydney).

WHITLEY, Elizabeth Young, (Mrs H. C. Whitley); social worker and journalist; *b* 28 Dec. 1915; *d* of Robert Thom and Mary Muir Wilson; *m* 1939, Henry Charles Whitley (Very Rev. Dr H. C. Whitley, CVO; *d* 1976); two *s* two *d* (and one *s* decd). *Educ:* Laurelbank School, Glasgow; Glasgow University. MA 1936; courses: in Italian at Perugia Univ., 1935, in Social Science at London School of Economics and Glasgow School of Social Science, 1938–39. Ran Girls' Clubs in Govan and Plantation, Glasgow, and Young Mothers' Clubs in Partick and Port Glasgow; Vice-Chm. Scottish Association of Girls' Clubs and Mixed Clubs, 1957–61, and Chm. of Advisory Cttee, 1958–59. Broadcast regular programme with BBC (Scottish Home Service), 1953. Member: Faversham Committee on AID, 1958–60; Pilkington Committee on Broadcasting, 1960–62. Columnist, Scottish Daily Express. Adopted as Parly candidate for SNP by West Perth and Kinross, 1968. *Publications:* Plain Mr Knox, 1960; The Two Kingdoms: the story of the Scottish covenanters, 1977; descriptive and centenary articles for Scottish papers, particularly Glasgow Herald and Scotland's Magazine. *Recreations:* reading, gardening. *Address:* The Glebe, Southwick, by Dumfries DG2 8AR. *T:* (01387) 780276.

WHITLEY, His Honour John Reginald; a Circuit Judge, 1986–96; Resident Judge, Portsmouth Combined Court Centre, 1988–96; *b* 22 March 1926; *o s* of late Reginald Whitley and of Marjorie Whitley (*née* Orton); *m* 1966, Susan Helen Kennaway; one *d. Educ:* Sherborne Sch.; Corpus Christi Coll., Cambridge. Served War, Army, Egypt, Palestine, 1944–48; commissioned, KRRC, 1945. Called to the Bar, Gray's Inn, 1953; Western Circuit, 1953; a Recorder, 1978–86. *Recreation:* golf. *Address:* Kingsrod, Friday's Hill, Kingsley Green, near Haslemere, Surrey GU27 3LL.

WHITLEY, Oliver John; Managing Director, External Broadcasting, British Broadcasting Corporation, 1969–72, retired; *b* 12 Feb. 1912; *s* of Rt Hon. J. H. Whitley, and Marguerite (*née* Marchetti); *m* 1939, Elspeth Catherine (*née* Forrester-Paton); four *s* one *d. Educ:* Clifton Coll.; New Coll., Oxford. Barrister-at-Law, 1935; BBC, 1935–41. Served in RNVR, 1942–46; Coastal Forces and Combined Ops. BBC 1946–: seconded to Colonial Office, 1946–49; Head of General Overseas Service, 1950–54; Assistant Controller, Overseas Services, 1955–57; Appointments Officer, 1957–60; Controller, Staff Training and Appointments, 1960–64; Chief Assistant to Dir-Gen., 1964–68. Valiant for Truth Award, Order of Christian Unity, 1974. *Recreations:* reading and gardening. *Address:* Greenacre, Ganavan Road, Oban, Argyll PA34 5TU. *T:* (01631) 562555.

WHITLOCK, William Charles; *b* 20 June 1918; *s* of late George Whitlock and Sarah Whitlock, Sholing, Southampton; *m* 1943, Jessie Hilda, *d* of George Reardon of Armagh; five *s. Educ:* Itchen Gram. Sch.; Southampton Univ. Army Service, 1939–46. Apptd full-time Trade Union Officer, Area Organiser of Union of Shop, Distributive and Allied Workers, 1946. President, Leicester and District Trades Council, 1955–56; President, Leicester City Labour Party, 1956–57; President, North-East Leicester Labour Party, 1955–56, and 1958–59. Member East Midlands Regional Council of Labour Party, 1955–67, Vice-Chairman 1961–62, Chairman 1962–63. MP (Lab) Nottingham N, Oct. 1959–1983; Opposition Whip, House of Commons, 1962–64; Vice-Chamberlain of the Household, 1964–66; Lord Comr of Treasury, March 1966–July 1966; Comptroller of HM Household, July 1966–March 1967; Dep. Chief Whip and Lord Comr of the Treasury, March-July 1967; Under Sec. of State for Commonwealth Affairs, 1967–68; Parly Under-Sec. of State, FCO, 1968–69. Contested (Lab) Nottingham N, 1983. DPhil *hc* Ukranian Free Univ., 1986.

WHITMORE, Sir Clive (Anthony), GCB 1988 (KCB 1983); CVO 1983; Director: Morgan Crucible Co. PLC, since 1994; N. M. Rothschild & Sons Ltd, since 1994; *b* 18 Jan. 1935; *s* of Charles Arthur Whitmore and Louisa Lilian Whitmore; *m* 1961, Jennifer Mary Thorpe; one *s* two *d. Educ:* Sutton Grammar Sch., Surrey; Christ's Coll., Cambridge (BA). Asst Principal, WO, 1959; Private Sec. to Permanent Under-Sec. of State, WO, 1961; Asst Private Sec. to Sec. of State for War, 1962; Principal, 1964; Private Sec. to Permanent Under-Sec. of State, MoD, 1969; Asst Sec., 1971; Asst Under-Sec. of State (Defence Staff), MoD, 1975; Under Sec., Cabinet Office, 1977; Principal Private Sec. to the Prime Minister, 1979–82; Dep. Sec., 1981; Permanent Under-Secretary of State: MoD, 1983–88; Home Office, 1988–94. Director: Racal Electronics, 1994–2000; Boots Co., 1994–2001. Mem., Security Commn, 1998–. Chancellor, De Montfort Univ., 1995–97; Chm. Council, Inst. of Educn, Univ. of London, 1995–2000. *Recreations:* gardening, listening to music. *Address:* c/o N. M. Rothschild & Sons Ltd, 19 St Swithin's Lane, EC4P 4DU.

WHITMORE, David John Ludlow, FCA; Managing Partner, Global Assurance and Business Advisory Markets, Andersen, since 2001; *b* 20 July 1959; *s* of Dr John L. Whitmore and Joan C. Whitmore (*née* Hale); *m* 1984, Monica Mary Boyd; two *s* one *d. Educ:* Carisbrooke High Sch., IoW; Univ. of Warwick (BSc Hons Accounting and Financial Analysis). ACA 1984, FCA 1989; CPA(US) 1988. Joined Arthur Andersen, 1980; worked in: London, 1980–84; LA, 1984–86; World HQ, Chicago, 1986–87; LA, 1987–89; London, 1989–; Partner, 1991; Head, Commercial Assce and Business Adv. Practice, 1995–97; Managing Partner, UK Assurance and Business Adv. Practice, 1997–2001. *Recreations:* golf, tennis, reading. *Address:* (office) 1 Surrey Street, WC2R 2PS. *T:* (020) 7438 3655. *Clubs:* Royal Automobile; Liphook Golf; Freshwater Bay Golf (IoW).

WHITMORE, Sir John (Henry Douglas), 2nd Bt *cr* 1954; Senior Partner, Performance Consultants, since 1998; *b* 16 Oct. 1937; *s* of Col Sir Francis Henry Douglas Charlton Whitmore, 1st Bt, KCB, CMG, DSO, TD, and Lady Whitmore (*née* Ellis Johnsen); *S* father, 1961; *m* 1st, 1962, Gunilla (marr. diss. 1969), *e d* of Sven A. Hansson, OV, KLH, Danderyd, and *o d* of Mrs Ella Hansson, Stockholm, Sweden; one *d*; 2nd, 1977, Diana Elaine, *e d* of Fred A. Becchetti, California, USA; one *s. Educ:* Stone House, Kent; Eton; Sandhurst; Cirencester. Active in personal development and social change; retired professional racing driver; business trainer and sports psychologist. *Publications:* The Winning Mind, 1987; Superdriver, 1988; Coaching for Performance, 1992; Need, Greed or Freedom, 1997; Mind Games, 1998. *Recreations:* ski-ing, squash. *Heir: s* Jason Whitmore, *b* 26 Jan. 1983. *Address:* Southfield, Leigh, near Tonbridge TN11 8PJ. *Club:* British Racing Drivers.

WHITNEY, Prof. David John; Director, Clinical Management Unit, Keele University, since 2001; *b* 1 Sept. 1950; *s* of Leonard and Joyce Susannah Whitney; *m* 1979, Pauline Jane; one *s* two *d. Educ:* Exeter Univ. (BA Hons); London Univ. (MA). Dep. House Governor, Moorfields Eye Hosp, 1982–85; Regl Dir of Planning, Trent RHA, 1985–90; Chief Exec., Central Sheffield Univ. Hosps NHS Trust, 1991–2001. Prof. Associate, Sheffield Centre for Health and Related Res., Univ. of Sheffield, 1995–. *Recreations:* soccer, tennis, squash, art, music. *Address:* Bryce, Hill Lane, Hathersage, Hope Valley S32 1AY.

WHITNEY, John Norton Braithwaite; Chairman, Caspian Publishing Ltd, since 1996; *b* 20 Dec. 1930; *s* of Dr Willis Bevan Whitney and Dorothy Anne Whitney; *m* 1956, Roma Elizabeth Hodgson; one *s* one *d. Educ:* Leighton Park Friends' Sch. Radio producer, 1951–64; formed Ross Radio Productions, 1951, and Autocue, 1955; founded Radio Antilles, 1963; Founder Dir, Sagitta Prodns, 1968–82; Man. Dir, Capital Radio, 1973–82; Dir Gen., IBA, 1982–89; Dir, The Really Useful Group Ltd, 1990–97 (Man. Dir, 1989–90; Chm., 1990–95); Chm., Trans World Communications plc, 1992–94. Dir, Duke of York's Theatre, 1979–82. Chm., Friends' Provident Ethical Investment Trust plc, 1992–; Dir, Friends' Provident Life Office, 1982– (Chm., Friends' Provident Stewardship Cttee of Reference, 1985–2000); Chairman: Radio Joint Audience Research Ltd, 1992–; Sony Music Pace Partnership (National Bowl), 1992–95; Enterprise Radio Hldgs Ltd, 1994–96; Radio Partnership, 1996–99; Director: VCI plc, 1995–98; Galaxy Media Corp. plc, 1997–2000; Far Pavilions Ltd, 1997–; Bird & Co. International, 1999– (Chm.). Chm., Assoc. of Indep. Local Radio Contractors, 1973, 1974, 1975 and 1980. Wrote, edited and devised numerous television series, 1956–82. Chm., Sony Radio Awards Cttee, 1991–97; Vice Pres., Japan Festival 1991, 1991–92 (Chm., Festival Media Cttee, 1991); Trustee, Japan Educn Trust, 1993–; Member: Bd, NT, later RNT, 1982–94 (Trustee, Pension and Life Assce, RNT, 1994–); Films, TV and Video Adv. Cttee, British Council, 1983–89; RCM Centenary Develt Fund (formerly Appeals Cttee), 1982– (Chm., Media and Events Cttee, 1982–94); Bd, City of London Sinfonia, 1994–2001; Exec. Cttee, Musicians Benevolent Fund, 1995–2001; Council: Royal London Aid Society, 1966–90; TRIC, 1979–89 (Pres., 1985–86; Companion, 1989–); Fairbridge (formerly Drake Fellowship, then Fairbridge Drake Soc.), 1981–96 (Vice Pres., 1996–); RSA, 1994–99; Council for Charitable Support, 1989–92; Bd, Open Coll., 1987–89; Chm., British Amer. Arts Assoc., 1992–95. Pres., London Marriage Guidance Council, 1983–90; Vice President: Commonwealth Youth Exchange Council, 1982–83; RNID, 1988–; Chm., Trustees, Soundaround (National Sound Magazine for the Blind), 1981–2000 (Life Pres., 2000); Chm., Artsline, 1983–2000 (Life Pres., 2001); Trustee: Venture Trust, 1982–86; Hosp. Broadcasting Assoc. Patron, MusicSpace Trust, 1990–; Governor: English Nat. Ballet (formerly London Festival Ballet), 1989–91; Bd, Performing Arts and Technol. Sch., 1992–2001; Chm., Theatre Investment Fund, 1990–2001. Fellow and Vice Pres., RTS, 1986–89; Fellow, Radio Acad., 1996; Mem., BAFTA. FRSA; Hon. RCM. *Recreations:* chess, photography, sculpture. *Address:* Heathcoat House, 20 Savile Row, W1S 3PR. *Clubs:* Garrick, Pilgrims, Buck's.

WHITNEY, Sir Raymond (William), Kt 1997; OBE 1968; *b* 28 Nov. 1930; *o s* of late George Whitney, Northampton; *m* 1956, Sheila Margot Beswick Prince; two *s. Educ:* Wellingborough Sch.; RMA, Sandhurst; London Univ. (BA (Hons) Oriental Studies). Commnd Northamptonshire Regt, 1951; served in Trieste, Korea, Hong Kong, Germany; seconded to Australian Army HQ, 1960–63; resigned and entered HM Diplomatic Service, 1964; First Sec., Peking, 1966–68; Head of Chancery, Buenos Aires, 1969–72; FCO, 1972–73; Dep. High Comr, Dacca, 1973–76; FCO, 1976–78, Hd of Information Res. Dept and Hd of Overseas Inf. Dept, 1976–78. MP (C) Wycombe, April 1978–2001. PPS to Treasury Ministers, 1979–80; Parly Under-Sec. of State, FCO, 1983–84, DHSS, 1984–86. Vice-Chm., Cons. Employment Cttee, 1980–83; Chm., Cons. For. Affairs Cttee, 1981–83; Mem., Public Accounts Cttee, 1981–83; Vice-Chairman: Parly Latin-America Gp, 1997–2001 (Chm., 1987–97); All-Party China Gp, 1997–2001; All-Party Hospice Gp, 1997–2001; Sec., All-Party Parly Argentine Gp, 1997–2001; Chm., Positive European Gp, 1993–2001. Chm., Mountbatten Community Trust (formerly Mountbatten Training), 1987–. Chm., The Cable Corp., 1989–96. *Publications:* National Health Crisis—a modern solution, 1988; articles on Chinese and Asian affairs in professional jls. *Recreations:* theatricals, golf, bridge, walking. *Address:* The Dial House, Sunninghill, Berks SL5 0AG. *T:* (01344) 623164.

WHITROW, Benjamin John; actor; *b* 17 Feb. 1937; *s* of Philip and Mary Whitrow; *m* 1972, Catherine Cook; one *s* one *d. Educ:* RADA (Leverhulme Schol.). *Stage:* Nat. Theatre, 1967–74; West End productions: Otherwise Engaged, Queen's, 1975; Dirty Linen, Arts, 1976; Ten Times Table, Globe, 1978; Passion Play, Aldwych, 1980; Uncle Vanya, Vaudeville, 1986; Noises Off, Savoy, 1983; Man for All Seasons, Savoy, 1987; Falstaff, Merry Wives of Windsor, RSC, 1992; Wild Oats, RNT, 1996; The Invention of

Love, RNT, 1998; The Rivals, RSC, 2000; Henry IV Part II, 2001; *films:* Quadrophenia, 1979; Clockwise; Personal Services, 1987; *television* includes: Pride and Prejudice, 1995; Tom Jones, 1997. *Recreations:* golf, reading, bridge. *Address:* c/o Lou Coulson, 37 Berwick Street, W1F 8RS. *T:* (020) 7734 9633.

WHITSEY, Fred; Gardening Correspondent, Daily Telegraph, since 1971; *b* 18 July 1919; *m* 1947, Patricia Searle. *Educ:* outside school hours, and continuously since then. Assistant Editor, Popular Gardening, 1948–64, Associate Editor, 1964–67, Editor, 1967–82. Gardening correspondent, Sunday Telegraph, 1961–71. Vice-Pres., RHS, 1996–. Gold Veitch Meml Medal, RHS, 1979; VMH 1986; Lifetime Achievement Award, Garden Writers' Guild, 1994. *Publications:* Sunday Telegraph Gardening Book, 1966; Fred Whitsey's Garden Calendar, 1985; Garden for All Seasons, 1986; contribs to Country Life and The Garden. *Recreations:* gardening, music. *Address:* Avens Mead, 20 Oast Road, Oxted, Surrey RH8 9DU.

WHITSON, Keith Roderick; Group Chief Executive, HSBC Holdings plc, since 1998 (Director, since 1994); *b* 25 March 1943; *s* of William Cleghorn Whitson and Ellen (*née* Wade); *m* 1968, Sabine Marita, *d* of Ulrich Wiechert; one *s* two *d*. *Educ:* Alleyn's Sch., Dulwich. FCIB. Joined Hong Kong and Shanghai Banking Corporation Ltd, 1961; Manager, Frankfurt, 1978–80; Manager, Indonesia, 1981–84; Asst Gen. Manager, Finance, Hong Kong, 1985–87; Chief Exec. Officer, UK, 1987, Exec. Dir, Marine Midland Bank, NY, 1990–92; Dep. Chief Exec., 1992–94, Chief Exec., 1994–98, Dep. Chm., 1998, Midland Bank. Chm., Merrill Lynch HSBC, 2000–; Director: HSBC Bank Argentina, 1997–; HSBC Bank USA, 1998–; HSBC Bank Canada, 1998–; Dep. Chm. Supervisory Bd, HSBC Trinkaus und Burkhardt Dusseldorf, 1993–. Non-exec. Dir, FSA, 1998–. *Address:* HSBC Holdings plc, 10 Lower Thames Street, EC3R 6AE. *T:* (020) 7260 8000, *Fax:* (020) 7260 9881.

WHITSON, Thomas Jackson, OBE 1985; Commandant, Scottish Police College, 1987–91; *b* 5 Sept. 1930; *s* of Thomas and Susan Whitson; *m* 1953, Patricia Marion Bugden; two *s*. *Educ:* Knox Acad., Haddington. RN, 1949–56. Lothian and Peebles Police, 1956–75: Police Constable, 1956; Detective Constable, 1959; Detective Sergeant, 1966; Inspector, 1969; Chief Inspector, 1972; Superintendent, 1974; Lothian and Borders Police, 1975–80: Chief Superintendent, 1976; Dep. Chief Constable, Central Scotland Police, 1980–87. *Recreations:* golf, curling, angling. *Address:* Glenelg, Orchard Grove, Polmont, Stirlingshire FK2 0XE.

WHITTAKER, Air Vice-Marshal David, CB 1988; MBE 1967; Air Officer Administration and Air Officer Commanding Directly Administered Units, RAF Support Command, 1986–89, retired; *b* 25 June 1933; *s* of Lawson and Irene Whittaker; *m* 1956, Joyce Ann Noble; two *s*. *Educ:* Hutton Grammar School. Joined RAF, 1951; commissioned 1952; served No 222, No 3, No 26 and No 1 Squadrons, 1953–62; HQ 38 Group, 1962–63; HQ 24 Bde, 1963–65; Comd Metropolitan Comms Sqdn, 1966–68; RAF Staff Coll., 1968; Asst Air Adviser, New Delhi, 1969–70; RAF Leeming, 1971–73; Coll. of Air Warfare, 1973; Directing Staff, RNSC Greenwich, 1973–75; Staff of CDS, 1975–76; DACOS (Ops), AFCENT, 1977–80; RCDS 1980; Defence and Air Adviser, Ottawa, 1983–86. *Recreations:* fishing, gardening, travel. *Address:* Seronera, Copgrove, Harrogate, North Yorks HG3 3SZ. *T:* (01423) 340459. *Club:* Royal Air Force.

WHITTAKER, Geoffrey Owen, OBE 1974 (MBE 1962); Governor of Anguilla, 1987–89; retired 1990; *b* 10 Jan. 1932; *s* of late Alfred James Whittaker and Gertrude (*née* Holvey); *m* 1959, Annette Faith Harris; one *s* and one *d*. *Educ:* Nottingham High Sch.; Bristol Univ. (BA). Auditor: Tanganyika, 1956–58; Dominica, 1958–60; Principal Auditor, Windward Is, 1960–64; Dir of Audit, Grenada, 1964–67; Audit Adviser, British Honduras, 1967–69; Colonial Treas., St Helena, 1970–75; Financial Sec. and Actg Governor, Montserrat, 1975–78; Financial Sec., British Virgin Is, 1978–80; Admin Officer, Hong Kong, 1980–87; Finance Br., 1980–83; Principal Asst Sec., Lands and Works Br., 1983–85; Gen. Man., Hong Kong Industrial Estates Corp., 1985–87. *Recreations:* music, Basset hounds, heraldry. *Address:* Ashley, near Market Harborough, Leics.

WHITTAKER, Prof. John Brian, PhD, DSc; FRES; Professor of Ecology, University of Lancaster, since 1987; *b* 26 July 1939; *s* of Roland Whittaker and Freda (*née* Lord); *m* 1964, Helen May Thorley (*d* 1998); two *s*. *Educ:* Bacup and Rawtenstall Grammar Sch.; Univ. of Durham (BSc, PhD, DSc). FRES 1979. Res. Officer, Univ. of Oxford, 1963–66; University of Lancaster: Lectr, then Sen. Lectr, 1966–87; Hd, Dept of Biol Scis, 1983–86 and 1991–94. Mem., Adv. Cttee on Sci., NCC, 1978–81; Chm., Terrestrial Life Scis Cttee, NERC, 1991–95. Pres., British Ecol Soc., 2000–01 (Vice-Pres., 1987–89; Mem. Council, 1970–75, 1984–86); Mem. Council, Freshwater Biol Assoc., 1988–91. *Publications:* Practical Demonstration of Ecological Concepts, 1988; (ed jtly) Toward a More Exact Ecology, 1989; (with D. T. Salt) Insects on dock plants, 1998; contribs to books and jls in insect ecology. *Recreations:* 18th century English furniture, fell-walking, family. *Address:* Division of Biological Sciences, Institute of Environmental and Natural Sciences, Lancaster University, Lancaster LA1 4YQ. *T:* (01524) 65201.

WHITTAKER, Nigel; corporate consultant; UK Chairman, Edelman Public Relations Worldwide, since 1999; *b* 7 Nov. 1948; *s* of late Phillip Whittaker and Joan Whittaker; *m* 1972, Joyce Cadman; three *s*. *Educ:* Caterham Sch.; Clare Coll., Cambridge (MA); Yale Law Sch. (JD). Called to the Bar, Middle Temple, 1974. Roche Products, 1974–77; British Sugar, 1977–82; Woolworth Holdings, subseq. Kingfisher plc, 1982–95 (Exec. Dir, 1983–95). Chairman: Retail Decisions (formerly Card Clear) plc, 1996–; Burson-Marsteller UK, 1997–99; MTI Partners Ltd, 1997–; Madisons Coffee (formerly City Gourmets Hldgs) plc, 1998–; Texstyle World Ltd, 1999–; Eagle Eye Telematics plc, 2000–; Mettoni Gp plc, 2000–; Advance Capital Invest, 2000–; Director: Wickes plc, 1996–2000; Bigsave.com Ltd, 1999–2001. Chm., CBI Distributive Trades Survey, 1986–94; Chm., British Retail Consortium (formerly Retail Consortium), 1995; Mem., UK Ecolabelling Bd (formerly Nat. Adv. Gp on Environmental Labelling), 1993–98. *Recreations:* cricket, car-parking. *Address:* 176 Bickenhall Mansions, Bickenhall Street, W1H 3DF.

WHITTAKER, Stanley Henry, FCA; Director of Finance and Planning, British Railways Board, 1988–91; *b* 14 Sept. 1935; *s* of Frederick Whittaker and Gladys Margaret (*née* Thatcher); *m* 1959, Freda Smith; two *s*. *Educ:* Bec School. ACA 1958, FCA 1969; ACMA 1971. Articled clerk, G. H. Attenborough & Co., Chartered Accountants, 1953–57; Sen. Assistant, Slater, Chapman & Cooke, 1960–62; Partner, Tiplady, Brailsford & Co., 1962–65; Finance Manager, NCB, 1965–68; British Railways: Finance Manager, 1968–74; Corporate Budgets Manager, 1974–78; Sen. Finance Manager, 1978–80; Chief Finance Officer, Western Reg., 1980–82; Director: Budgetary Control, 1982–86; Finance Devel, 1986–87; Group Finance, 1987–88. *Recreations:* flying, ski-ing, industrial archaeology, travel. *Address:* 12 Kennylands Road, Sonning Common, Reading, Berks RG4 9JT. *T:* (0118) 972 2951.

WHITTALL, (Harold) Astley, CBE 1978; CEng; Chairman: B.S.G. International Ltd, 1981–94; Ransomes plc (formerly Ransome, Sims & Jefferies Ltd), 1983–93 (Director 1979–93; Deputy Chairman, 1981–83); *b* 8 Sept. 1925; *s* of Harold and Margaret Whittall; *m* 1952, Diana Margharita Berner. *Educ:* Handsworth Grammar Sch., Birmingham; Handsworth and Birmingham Technical Colls. Gen. Manager, Belliss & Morcom, 1962; Managing Dir, Amalgamated Power Engineering, 1968, Chm., 1977–81; Director: LRC Internat., 1982–85; APV (formerly APV Baker and APV plc), 1982–95; R. Platnauer Ltd, 1984–; Sykes Pickervant, 1987–94; Inchcape Insurance Hldgs, 1988–90; Qualifications for Industry Ltd, 1997–99, 2000–; RTITB Ltd, 1999–. Pres., Engineering Employers' Fedn, 1976–78; Chairman: Engrg ITB, 1985–91; ETA, 1990–94; British Iron and Steel Consumers Council, 1987–91. *Address:* Brook Farmhouse, Whelford, near Fairford, Glos GL7 4DY. *T:* (01285) 712393. *Clubs:* Royal Automobile, St James'.

WHITTALL, Michael Charlton, CMG 1980; OBE 1963; HM Diplomatic Service; Counsellor, Foreign and Commonwealth Office, 1973–91; *b* 9 January 1926; *s* of Kenneth Edwin Whittall and Edna Ruth (*née* Lawson); *m* 1953, Susan Olivia La Fontaine one *d*. *Educ:* Rottingdean; Rugby; Trinity Hall, Cambridge. Served RAF, 1944–48. Foreign Office, 1949; Salonika, 1949; British Middle East Office, 1952; Vice-Consul, Basra, 1953; FO, 1955; Second Secretary, Beirut, 1956; FO, 1958; First Secretary, Amman, 1959. *Recreations:* railways (GWR), birdwatching, photography.

WHITTAM, Prof. Ronald, FRS 1973; Emeritus Professor, Leicester University, since 1983 (Professor of Physiology, 1966–83); *b* 21 March 1925; *e s* of Edward Whittam and May Whittam (*née* Butterworth), Oldham, Lancs; *m* 1957, Christine Patricia Margaret, 2nd *d* of Canon J. W. Lamb; one *s* one *d*. *Educ:* Council and Technical Schools, Oldham; Univs of Manchester and Sheffield and King's College, Cambridge. BSc 1st Class Hons (Manchester); PhD (Sheffield and Cambridge); MA (Oxon). Served RAF, 1943–47. John Stokes Fellow, Dept of Biochem., Univ. of Sheffield, 1953–55; Beit Memorial Fellow, Physiological Lab., Cambridge, 1955–58; Mem. Scientific Staff, MRC Cell Metabolism Research Unit, Oxford, 1958–60; Univ. Lectr in Biochemistry, Oxford, 1960–66; Bruno Mendel Fellow of Royal Society, 1965–66; Dean of Fac. of Science, Leicester Univ., 1979–82. Mem. Editorial Bd of Biochem. Jl, 1963–67; Hon. Sec., 1969–74, Hon. Mem., 1986, Physiological Soc.; Mem. Biological Research Bd of MRC, 1971–74, Co-Chm., 1973–74; Member: Biological Sciences Cttee, UGC, 1974–82; Educn Cttee, Royal Soc., 1979–83; Chm., Biological Educn Cttee, Royal Soc. and Inst Biol., 1974–77. *Publications:* Transport and Diffusion in Red Blood Cells, 1964; scientific papers dealing with cell membranes. *Recreation:* walking. *Address:* 9 Guilford Road, Leicester LE2 2RD.

WHITTAM SMITH, Andreas; President, British Board of Film Classification, since 1998; Chairman, Financial Ombudsman Service Ltd, since 1999; *b* 13 June 1937; *s* of Canon J. E. Smith and Mrs Smith (*née* Barlow); *m* 1964, Valerie Catherine, *d* of late Wing Comdr J. A. Sherry and of Mrs N. W. H. Wyllys; two *s*. *Educ:* Birkenhead Sch., Cheshire; Keble Coll., Oxford (BA) (Hon. Fellow, 1990). *T:* and *Fax:* With N. M. Rothschild, 1960–62; Stock Exchange Gazette, 1962–63; Financial Times, 1963–64; The Times, 1964–66; Dep. City Editor, Daily Telegraph, 1966–69; City Editor, The Guardian, 1969–70; Editor, Investors Chronicle and Stock Exchange Gazette, and Dir, Throgmorton Publications, 1970–77; City Editor, Daily Telegraph, 1977–85; Editor, The Independent, 1986–94; Editor-in-Chief, Independent on Sunday, 1991–94. Dir, 1986–98, Chief Exec., 1987–93, Chm., 1994–95, Newspaper Publishing plc; Dir, Ind. News & Media (UK), 1998–. Vice Pres., Nat. Council for One Parent Families, 1991– (Hon. Treas., 1982–86). Chm., Sir Winston Churchill Archive Trust, 1995–2000. Trustee, Architecture Foundn, 1994–2000. Hon. Fellow: UMIST, 1989; Liverpool John Moores, 2001. Hon. DLitt: St Andrews; Salford; City; Liverpool, 1992; Hon. LLD Bath. Wincott award, 1975; Marketing Man of the Year, Inst. of Marketing, 1987; Journalist of the Year, British Press Awards, 1987; Hemingway Europa Prize, 1988; Editor of the Year, Granada TV What the Papers Say award, 1989. *Recreations:* music, history, walking. *Address:* 31 Brunswick Gardens, W8 4AW. *Club:* Garrick.

WHITTELL, James Michael Scott, CMG 1998; OBE 1984; Chief Executive, Interstate Programmes Ltd, since 1999; *b* 17 Feb. 1939; *s* of late Edward Arthur Whittell and Helen Elizabeth Whittell (*née* Scott); *m* 1962, Eleanor Jane Carling; three *s*. *Educ:* Gresham's School, Holt; Magdalen College, Oxford (MA, BSc); Manchester Univ. Teaching, Sherborne School, 1962–68, Nairobi School, 1968–72; British Council: Ibadan, Nigeria, 1973–76; Enugu, Nigeria, 1976–78; Director General's Dept, 1978–81; Rep., Algiers, 1981–85; Sec. to the British Council and Head of Dir Gen's Dept, 1985–88; seconded to PM's Efficiency Unit, 1988; Rep., subseq. Dir, Nigeria, 1989–92; Dir, Africa and ME Div., 1992; Regl Dir, EC, later EU, 1993–96; Dir, British Council in Europe, 1996–99. *Recreations:* walking, mountaineering, books, music. *Address:* 15 Stratford Grove, SW15 1NU. *Club:* Alpine.

WHITTEMORE, Prof. Colin Trengove; Professor of Agriculture and Rural Economy, and Convenor, School of Agriculture, University of Edinburgh, since 1990; *b* 16 July 1942; *s* of Hugh Ashcroft Whittemore and Dorothea Whittemore (*née* Nance); *m* 1966, Mary Christine Fenwick; one *s* three *d*. *Educ:* Rydal Sch.; Harper Adams Agricl Coll. (NDA); Univ. of Newcastle upon Tyne (BSc, PhD, DSc). FIBiol 1989; FRSE 1994. Lectr, Univ. of Edinburgh, 1970–79; Head, Animal Production Adv. and Develt, E of Scotland Coll. of Agric., 1979–84; University of Edinburgh: Prof. of Animal Prodn, 1984–90; Head, Dept of Agric., 1989–90; Head, Inst. of Ecology and Resource Mgt, 1990–2000. Pres., British Soc. of Animal Sci., 1998–99. Sir John Hammond Award, British Soc. of Animal Prodn, 1983; Res. Gold Medal, RASE, 1984; Oscar della Suinicoltura, Assoc. Mignini, 1987; David Black Award, Meat and Livestock Commn, 1990. *Publications:* Practical Pig Nutrition (with F. W. H. Elsley), 1976; Lactation, 1980; Pig Production, 1980; Elements of Pig Science, 1987; The Science and Practice of Pig Production, 1993, 2nd edn 1998. *Recreations:* ski-ing, horses, the pursuit of science. *Address:* Institute of Ecology and Resource Management, University of Edinburgh, School of Agriculture Building, West Mains Road, Edinburgh EH9 3JG. *T:* (0131) 667 1041; Rowancroft, 17 Fergusson View, West Linton, Peeblesshire EH46 7DJ. *Club:* Farmers'.

WHITTICK, Richard James; Assistant Under-Secretary of State, Home Office, 1967–72; *b* 21 August 1912; *s* of Ernest G. Whittick and Grace M. Shaw; *m* 1938, Elizabeth Mason; two *s*. *Educ:* George Heriot's School; Edinburgh University. British Museum (Natural History), 1936; Home Office, 1940; Principal Private Secretary to Home Secretary, 1952–53; Assistant Secretary, 1953. *Recreations:* gardening, photography (FRPS 1988). *Address:* Coombe Cottage, Coombe, Sherborne, Dorset DT9 4BX. *T:* (01935) 814488.

WHITTINGDALE, John Flasby Lawrance, OBE 1990; MP (C) Maldon and Chelmsford East, since 1997 (Colchester South and Maldon, 1992–97); *b* 16 Oct. 1959; *s* of late John Whittingdale and of Margaret Esmé Scott Napier; *m* 1990, Ancilla Campbell Murfitt; one *s* one *d*. *Educ:* Sandroyd Sch.; Winchester Coll.; University Coll. London (BScEcon). Head of Political Section, Conservative Research Dept, 1982–84; Special Adviser to Sec. of State for Trade and Industry, 1984–87; Manager, N. M. Rothschild & Sons, 1987; Political Sec. to the Prime Minister, 1988–90; Private Sec. to Rt Hon.

Margaret Thatcher, 1990–92. PPS to Minister of State for Educn, 1994–95, for Educn and Employment, 1995–96; an Opposition Whip, 1997–98; Opposition Treasury spokesman, 1998–99; PPS to Leader of the Opposition, 1999–2001; Shadow Sec. of State for Trade and Industry, 2001–. Member, Select Committee: on Health, 1993–97; on Trade and Industry, 2001–; Sec., Conservative Parly Home Affairs Cttee, 1992–94. *Recreations:* cinema, music. *Address:* c/o House of Commons, SW1A 0AA. *Club:* Essex.

WHITTINGHAM, Charles Percival, BA, PhD Cantab; Head of Department of Botany, Rothamsted Experimental Station, 1971–82; *b* 1922; *m* 1946, Alison Phillips; two *d. Educ:* St John's College, Cambridge. Professor of Botany, London University, at Queen Mary College, 1958–64; Head of Dept of Botany, 1967–71, and Prof. of Plant Physiology, 1964–71, Imperial Coll., Univ of London; Dean, Royal Coll. of Science, 1969–71; Hon. Dir, ARC Unit for Plant Physiology, 1964–71. Vis. Prof., Univ. of Nottingham, 1978. *Publications:* Chemistry of Plant Processes, 1964; (with R. Hill) Photosynthesis, 1955; The Mechanism of Photosynthesis, 1974; contrib. to scientific journals. *Recreations:* music, travel. *Address:* Red Cottage, The Green, Brisley, Dereham, Norfolk NR20 5LN.

WHITTINGTON, Prof. Dorothy Allan, CPsychol; Professor of Health Psychology, University of Ulster, since 1999; *b* 14 Dec. 1941; *d* of Eric George Whittington and Margaret Cowan Allan. *Educ:* Hutchesons' Girls' Grammar Sch., Glasgow; Univ. of Glasgow (MA, MEd, Teaching Cert.). AFBPsS 1970; CPsychol 1988. Infant teacher, Glasgow primary schs, 1962–67; Lectr in Psychol., Callendar Park Coll. of Educn, Falkirk, 1967–72; Sen. Lectr in Educn, 1972–73, Principal Lectr in Psychol., 1973–84, Ulster Poly.; University of Ulster: Sen. Lectr in Psychol., 1984–94; Dir, Centre for Health and Social Res., 1990–95; Hd, Sch. of Health Scis, 1994–96; Dir, Health Care Distance Learning, 1997–. Co-founder, NI Parents' Advice Centre, 1978; Mem., Nat. Council, Assoc. for Quality in Health Care, 1989–92. *Publications:* (jtly) Quality Assurance: a workbook for health professionals, 1992 (trans. Italian and Portuguese); with R. Ellis: A Guide to Social Skill Training, 1981; New Directions in Social Skill Training, 1983; Quality Assurance in Health Care, 1993; Quality Assurance in Social Care: an introductory workbook, 1998; contrib. papers and book chapters on social skill, communication in professional contexts, quality and governance in health and social care, needs assessment and prog. evaluation in primary and community care, patient and public involvement in health and social care planning. *Recreations:* sailing, music. *Address:* 8 Coastguard Cottages, Beach Road, Whitehead, Co. Antrim, Northern Ireland BT38 9QS.

WHITTINGTON, Prof. Geoffrey, CBE 2001; Member, International Accounting Standards Board, since 2001; Price Waterhouse Professor of Financial Accounting, Cambridge University, 1988–2001, now Emeritus; Fellow of Fitzwilliam College, Cambridge, 1966–72 and since 1988; *b* 21 Sept. 1938; *s* of late Bruce Whittington and Dorothy Gwendoline Whittington (*née* Gent); *m* 1963, Joyce Enid Smith; two *s. Educ:* Dudley Grammar Sch.; LSE (Leverhulme Schol.; BSc Econ); MA, PhD Cantab. FCA. Chartered Accountancy training, 1959–62; research posts, Dept of Applied Econ., Cambridge, 1962–72; Dir of Studies in Econs, Fitzwilliam Coll., Cambridge, 1967–72; Prof. of Accountancy and Finance, Edinburgh Univ., 1972–75; University of Bristol: Prof. of Accounting and Finance, 1975–88; Head of Dept of Econs, 1981–84; Dean, Faculty of Social Scis, 1985–87. Professorial Res. Fellow, Inst. of Chartered Accountants of Scotland, 1996–2001. Part-time Econ. Adviser, OFT, 1977–83; part-time Mem., Monopolies and Mergers Commn, 1987–96; Academic Advr, 1990–94, Mem., 1994–2001, Accounting Standards Bd; Mem., Adv. Body on Fair Trading in Telecommunications, 1997–98. Hon. DSc (SocSci) Edinburgh, 1998. *Publications:* Growth, Profitability and Valuation (with A. Singh), 1968; The Prediction of Profitability, 1971; Inflation Accounting, 1983; (with D. P. Tweedie) The Debate on Inflation Accounting, 1984; (ed jtly) Readings in the Concept and Measurement of Income, 1986; The Elements of Accounting, 1992; contribs to jls and books in accounting, economics and finance. *Recreations:* music, squash, badminton, walking, usual academic pursuits of reading my own books and laughing at my own jokes. *Address:* International Accounting Standards Board, 30 Cannon Street, EC4M 6XH. *T:* (020) 7246 6411.

WHITTINGTON, Prof. Harry Blackmore, FRS 1971; Woodwardian Professor of Geology, Cambridge University, 1966–83; *b* 24 March 1916; *s* of Harry Whittington and Edith M. (*née* Blackmore); *m* 1940, Dorothy E. Arnold; no *c. Educ:* Handsworth Gram. Sch.; Birmingham University. Commonwealth Fund Fellow, Yale Univ., 1938–40; Lectr in Geology, Judson Coll., Rangoon, 1940–42; Prof. of Geography, Ginling Coll., Chengtu, W China, 1943–45; Lectr in Geology, Birmingham Univ., 1945–49; Harvard Univ.: Vis. Lectr, 1949–50; Assoc. Prof. of Geology, 1950–58; Prof. of Geology, 1958–66. Trustee: British Museum (Nat. History), 1980–89; Uppingham Sch., 1983–91. Hon. Fellow, Geol Soc. of America, 1983. Hon. AM, Harvard Univ., 1950. Medal, Paleontol Soc., USA, 1983; Lyell Medal, 1986, Wollaston Medal, 2001, Geological Soc.; Mary Clark Thompson Medal, US Nat. Acad of Scis, 1990; Lapworth Medal, Palaeontol Assoc., 2000; Medal, Geol Assoc. of Canada, 2000. *Publications:* The Burgess Shale, 1985; Trilobites, 1992; articles in Jl of Paleontology, Bulletin Geol. Soc. of Amer., Quarterly Jl Geol. Soc. London, Phil. Trans. Royal Soc., etc. *Address:* 20 Rutherford Road; Cambridge CB2 2HH. *Club:* Geological.

WHITTINGTON, Thomas Alan, CB 1977; TD 1986; Circuit Administrator, North Eastern Circuit, 1974–81; *b* 15 May 1916; *o s* of late George Whittington, JP and Mary Elizabeth Whittington; *m* 1939, Audrey Elizabeth, *y d* of late Craven Gilpin, Leeds; four *s. Educ:* Uppingham Sch.; Leeds Univ. (LLB). Commnd W Yorks Regt (Leeds Rifles) TA, 1937, serving War of 1939–45 in UK and 14th Army in India (Major). Solicitor of Supreme Court, 1945; Clerk of the Peace, Leeds, 1952–70; Senior Partner, Marklands, Solicitors, Leeds, 1967–70, Consultant, 1981–; Under-Sec., Lord Chancellor's Office, 1970; Circuit Administrator, Northern Circuit, 1970–74. *Recreations:* fishing, gardening. *Address:* The Cottage, School Lane, Collingham, Wetherby LS22 5BQ. *T:* (0113) 257 3881.

WHITTINGTON-SMITH, Marianne Christine, (Mrs C. A. Whittington-Smith); *see* Lutz, M. C.

WHITTLE, Prof. Alasdair William Richardson, DPhil; FBA 1998; Professor of Archaeology, School of History and Archaeology, Cardiff University (formerly University of Wales College of Cardiff), since 1997; *b* 7 May 1949; *s* of late Charles and of Grizel Whittle; *m* 1971, Elisabeth Sampson; three *d. Educ:* Christ Church, Oxford (MA; DPhil 1976). Lectr, UC Cardiff, then Univ. of Wales Coll. of Cardiff, 1978–97. Jt Ed., Proc. Prehistoric Soc., 1988–94. Leader, Avebury Area Excavation Project, 1987–93. Member: Panel for Archaeol., RAEs, 1996, 2001; Ancient Monuments Bd for Wales, 2000–. *Publications:* Neolithic Europe, 1985; Scord of Brouster, 1986; Problems in Neolithic Archaeology, 1988; Europe in the Neolithic, 1996; Sacred Mound, Holy Rings, 1997; The Harmony of Symbols, 1999. *Recreations:* golf, fishing, travel. *Address:* School of History and Archaeology, Cardiff University, PO Box 909, Cardiff CF10 3XU.

WHITTLE, Kenneth Francis, CBE 1987; Chairman, South Western Electricity Board, 1977–87; *b* 28 April 1922; *s* of Thomas Whittle and May Whittle; *m* 1945, Dorothy Inskip; one *s* one *d. Educ:* Kingswood Sch., Bath; Faculty of Technol., Manchester Univ. (BScTech). Served War, Electrical Lieut, RNVR, 1943–46. Metropolitan Vickers Elec. Co. Ltd, 1946–48; NW Div., CEGB, 1948–55; North West Electricity Board: various posts, 1955–64; Area Commercial Officer, Blackburn, 1964–69; Manager, Peak Area, 1969–71; Manager, Manchester Area, 1971–74; Chief Commercial Officer, 1974–75; Dep. Chm., Yorks Elec. Bd, 1975–77. Chairman: British Electrotechnical Approvals Bd, 1985–96; British Approvals Bd for Telecommunications, 1985–96. *Recreation:* golf. *Address:* 8 Cambridge Road, Clevedon, N Somerset BS21 7HX. *T:* (01275) 874017.

WHITTLE, Prof. Peter, FRS 1978; Churchill Professor of Mathematics for Operational Research, University of Cambridge, 1967–94, now Professor Emeritus; Fellow of Churchill College, Cambridge, since 1967; *b* 27 Feb. 1927; *s* of Percy Whittle and Elsie Tregurtha; *m* 1951, Käthe Hildegard Blomquist; three *s* three *d. Educ:* Wellington Coll., New Zealand. Docent, Uppsala Univ., 1951–53; employed New Zealand DSIR, 1953–59, rising to Senior Principal Scientific Officer; Lectr, Univ. of Cambridge, 1959–61; Prof. of Mathematical Statistics, Univ. of Manchester, 1961–67. Sen. Fellow, SERC, 1988–91. Mem., Royal Soc. of NZ, 1981–. Hon. DSc Victoria Univ. of Wellington, NZ, 1987. *Publications:* Hypothesis Testing in Time Series Analysis, 1951; Prediction and Regulation, 1963; Probability, 1970; Optimisation under Constraints, 1971; Optimisation over Time, 1982; Systems in Stochastic Equilibrium, 1986; Risk-sensitive Optimal Control, 1990; Probability via Expectation, 1992; Optimal Control: basics and beyond, 1996; Neural Nets and Chaotic Carriers, 1998; contribs to Jl Roy. Statistical Soc., Proc. Roy. Soc., Jl Stat. Phys, Systems and Control Letters. *Recreations:* variable. *Address:* 268 Queen Edith's Way, Cambridge CB1 8NL; Statistical Laboratory, University of Cambridge CB3 0WB.

WHITTLE, Stephen Charles; Controller of Editorial Policy, BBC, since 2001; *b* 26 July 1945; *s* of Charles William Whittle and Vera Lillian Whittle (*née* Moss); *m* 1988, Claire Walmsley (marr. diss. 1999). *Educ:* St Ignatius College, Stamford Hill; University College London (LLB Hons). Asst Editor, New Christian, 1968–70; Communications Officer, World Council of Churches, Geneva, 1970–73; Editor, One World, WCC, 1973–77; Asst Head, Communications Dept, WCC, 1975–77; BBC: Sen. Producer, Religious Programmes, Manchester, 1977–82; Producer, Newsnight, 1982; Editor, Songs of Praise and Worship, 1983–89; Hd of Religious Progs, 1989–93; Chief Advr, Editl Policy, Policy and Planning Directorate, 1993–96; Director: Broadcasting Standards Council, 1996–97; Broadcasting Standards Commn, 1997–2001. Gov., Eur. Inst. for the Media, 1997–. FRSA. Freeman, City of London, 1990. Sandford St Martin Award for contrib. to religious broadcasting, 1993. *Publications:* Tickling Mrs Smith, 1970; contribs to One World and The Tablet. *Recreations:* cinema, theatre, music, reading, exercise. *Address:* BBC Broadcasting House, Portland Place, W1A 1AA.

WHITTON, Prof. Peter William; Deputy Vice-Chancellor, University of Melbourne, 1979–84, retired; *b* 2 Sept. 1925; *s* of William Whitton and Rosa Bungay; *m* 1950, Mary Katharine White; two *s* three *d. Educ:* Latymer Upper Sch., London; Southampton Univ. (BScEng); Imperial College of Science and Technology, London (DIC, PhD); ME Melbourne 1965. FIE(Aust). Engineering Cadet, English Electric Co., Preston, 1942–46; Wireless Officer, Royal Signals, Catterick and Singapore, 1946–48; Sen. Lectr in Mech. Engrg, Univ. of Melbourne, 1953–56; Head, Engrg Sect., ICI Metals Div. Research Dept, Birmingham, 1956–60; Foundation Prof. and Dean, Faculty of Engrg, Univ. of the West Indies, 1960–64; University of Melbourne: Prof. of Mech. Engrg, 1965–77, Emeritus Prof., 1977–; Dean, Faculty of Engrg, 1966; Principal, Royal Melbourne Inst. of Technology, 1977–78. *Publications:* various papers on metal forming, in Proc. IMechE, London, and Jl of Inst. of Metals, London. *Recreation:* reading. *Address:* 7 Surf Avenue, Beaumaris, Vic 3193, Australia.

WHITTY, family name of **Baron Whitty**.

WHITTY, Baron *cr* 1996 (Life Peer), of Camberwell in the London Borough of Southwark; **John Lawrence Whitty, (Larry);** Parliamentary Under-Secretary of State, Department for Environment, Food and Rural Affairs (formerly Department of the Environment, Transport and the Regions), since 1998; *b* 15 June 1943; *s* of Frederick James and Kathleen May Whitty; *m* 1969, Tanya Margaret (marr. diss. 1986); two *s*; *m* 1993, Angela Forrester. *Educ:* Latymer Upper School; St John's College, Cambridge (BA Hons Economics). Hawker Siddeley Aviation, 1960–62; Min. of Aviation Technology, 1965–70; Trades Union Congress, 1970–73; General, Municipal, Boilermakers and Allied Trade Union (formerly GMWU), 1973–85; Gen. Sec., 1985–94, European Co-ordinator, 1994–97, Labour Party. A Lord in Waiting (Govt Whip), 1997–98. *Recreations:* theatre, cinema, swimming. *Address:* 61 Bimport, Shaftesbury, Dorset SP7 8AZ. *T:* (01747) 854619, (0171) 834 8890.

WHITTY, Prof. Geoffrey James; Director, Institute of Education, University of London, since 2000; *b* 31 Dec. 1946; *s* of Frederick James Whitty and Kathleen May Whitty; *m* 1st, 1969, Gillian Patterson (marr. diss. 1989); one *s* one *d*; 2nd, 1989, Marilyn Toft; one *d. Educ:* Latymer Upper Sch.; St John's Coll., Cambridge (BA, MA); Inst. of Educn, London Univ. (PGCE, MA). Teacher: Lampton Sch., Hounslow, 1969–70; Thomas Bennett Sch., Crawley, 1970–73; Lecturer: Univ. of Bath, 1973–80; KCL, 1981–84; Prof. of Educn, Bristol Poly., 1985–89; Goldsmiths' Prof. of Policy and Mgt, Goldsmiths Coll., Univ. of London, 1990–92; Karl Mannheim Prof. of Sociol. of Educn, Inst. of Educn, 1992–2000. Vis. Prof., Univ. of Wisconsin-Madison, 1979–80. Hon. FCT 2001. Hon. EdD UWE, 2001. *Publications:* (jtly) Society, State and Schooling, 1977; Sociology and School Knowledge, 1985; (jtly) The State and Private Education, 1989; (jtly) Specialisation and Choice in Urban Education, 1993; (jtly) Devolution and Choice in Education, 1998; (jtly) Teacher Education in Transition, 2000. *Recreations:* travel, reading, politics. *Address:* Institute of Education, 20 Bedford Way, WC1H 0AL. *T:* (020) 7612 6004.

See also Baron Whitty.

WHITTY, Niall Richard; Member, Scottish Law Commission, 1995–2000; *b* 28 Oct. 1937; *s* of Richard Hazleton Whitty and Muriel Helen Margaret Scott or Whitty; *m* 1977, Elke Mechthild Maria Gillis; three *s* one *d. Educ:* John Watson's Sch., Edinburgh; Morrison's Acad., Crieff; St Andrews Univ. (MA Hons 1960); Edinburgh Univ. (LLB 1963). Admitted solicitor, 1965. Legal Officer, 1967–70, Sen. Legal Officer, 1970–71, Asst Solicitor, 1977–94, Scottish Office; seconded to legal staff, Scottish Law Commn, 1971–94. Vis. Prof., Sch. of Law, Univ. of Edinburgh, 2000–. Gen. Editor, The Laws of Scotland, Stair Memorial Encyclopaedia, 2000–. *Publications:* contrib. Stair Memorial Encyclopaedia, and legal jls. *Address:* St Martins, Victoria Road, Haddington, East Lothian EH41 4DJ. *T:* (01620) 822234.

WHITWAM, Derek Firth, CEng, FRINA; RCNC; Director of Quality Assurance, Ministry of Defence, 1985–88; *b* 7 Dec. 1932; *s* of Hilton and Marion Whitwam; *m* 1954, Pamela May (*née* Lander); one *s* one *d. Educ:* Royds Hall Sch., Huddersfield; Royal Naval

Coll., Dartmouth; Royal Naval Engineering Coll., Manadon; Royal Naval Coll., Greenwich. Work on ship design, MoD (N) Bath, 1957–65; Rosyth Dockyard, 1965–68; Singapore Dockyard, 1968–70; DG Ships Bath, 1970–77; RCDS 1978; Production Manager, Rosyth Dockyard, 1979–80; Gen. Manager, Portsmouth Dockyard, 1981–84; Principal Dir of Planning and Policy, Chief Exec. Royal Dockyards, 1984–85. *Publications:* papers for Trans Royal Inst. of Naval Architects. *Recreations:* golf, music, walking. *Club:* Bath Golf.

WHITWELL, Stephen John, CMG 1969; MC; HM Diplomatic Service, retired; *b* 30 July 1920; *s* of Arthur Percy Whitwell and Marion Whitwell (*née* Greenwood). *Educ:* Stowe; Christ Church, Oxford. Coldstream Guards, 1941–47; joined HM Foreign Service (now Diplomatic Service), 1947; served: Tehran, 1947; FO, 1949; Belgrade, 1952; New Delhi, 1954; FO, 1958; Seoul, 1961. Polit. Adv. to C-in-C Middle East, Aden, 1964; Counsellor, Belgrade, 1965; Ambassador to Somalia, 1968–70; Head of East-West Contacts Dept, FCO, 1970–71. *Recreations:* reading, painting, looking at buildings. *Club:* Travellers.

WHITWORTH, Diana Storey; Chief Executive, Carers UK (formerly Carers National Association), since 1999; *b* 5 April 1949; *d* of Barrington Allen Whitworth and Rosemary Whitworth (*née* Braithwaite); one *d*; partner, Guy Dehn. *Educ:* Badminton Sch.; King's High Sch., Warwick; South Bank Poly. (MA Applied Eur. Studies). Consumer Advr, London Borough of Hillingdon, 1973–77; Sen. R&D Officer, NACAB, 1980–88; Sen. Policy and Develt Officer, then Hd, Public Affairs, NCC, 1988–99. Chair, Consumer Congress, 1983–85; Member: Adv. Cttee on Work Life Balance, DFEE, 2000–; Commng Bd, Nat. Co-ordinating Centre for NHS Service Delivery and Orgn R&D, 2000–. Mem., Indep. Complaints Panel, Portman Gp, 1998–. Trustee, City Roads, 2000–. Gov., Stoke Newington Sch., 1996–. *Recreations:* reading, gardening, cycling. *Address:* Carers UK, Ruth Pitter House, 20–25 Glasshouse Yard, EC1A 4JT. *T:* (020) 7490 8818.

WHITWORTH, Francis John, OBE 1994; Member, Economic and Social Committee of the European Communities, 1986–98; *b* 1 May 1925; *s* of late Captain Herbert Francis Whitworth, OBE, RNVR, and Helen Marguerite Whitworth (*née* Tait); *m* 1956, Auriol Myfanwy Medwyn Hughes; one *s* one *d*. *Educ:* Charterhouse (Jun. Schol.); Pembroke Coll., Oxford (Holford Schol.; MA Jurisprudence 1949). FIMgt (FBIM 1980; MBIM 1967). Served War, Royal Marines, 1943–46. Called to Bar, Middle Temple, 1950. Joined Cunard Steam-Ship Co., 1950; Personnel Director, 1965, Managing Dir Cunard Line, 1968, Group Admin Dir, 1969; joined British Shipping Fedn as Dep. Dir, Industrial Relations, 1972; Dep. Dir-Gen., Gen. Council of British Shipping, 1980–87; Dir, Internat. Shipping Fedn, 1980–88; Mem., Nat. Maritime Bd, 1962–87. Chairman: Internat. Cttee of Passenger Lines, 1968–71; Atlantic Passenger Steamship Conf., 1970–71; Employers' Gp, Jt Maritime Commn of ILO, 1980–88; Employers' Gp, Internat. Maritime (Labour) Conf. of ILO, 1986–87; Social Affairs Cttee, Comité des Assocs d'Armateurs des Communautés Européennes, 1983–88; Nat. Sea Training Schs, 1980–87; Merchant Navy Officers' Pension Fund Trustees, 1987–93; Member: Industrial Tribunals for England and Wales, 1978–94; Council, Marine Soc., 1988–; Council, Mission to Seafarers (formerly Missions to Seamen), 1988–. Freeman, City of London, 1999; Liveryman, Shipwrights' Co., 1999–. *Recreations:* racing, opera, music, cricket. *Address:* The Old School House, Farley Chamberlayne, Romsey, Hants SO51 0QR. *Club:* Oxford and Cambridge.

WHITWORTH, Maj.-Gen. Reginald Henry, CB 1969; CBE 1963; MA; *b* 27 Aug. 1916; 2nd *s* of late Aymer William Whitworth and late Alice (*née* Hervey), Eton College; *m* 1st, 1946, June Rachel (*d* 1994), *o d* of late Sir Bartle Edwards, CVO, MC, and of Daphne, MBE, *d* of late Sir Cyril Kendall Butler, KBE; two *s* one *d*; 2nd, 1999, Victoria Mary Rose (née Buxton), *widow* of Major David Faulkner, Irish Guards. *Educ:* Eton; Balliol College, Oxford, 1st cl. Hons, Modern History, 1938; Laming Travelling Fellow, Queen's Coll., Oxford, 1938–39. 2nd Lt Grenadier Guards, 1940; War Service in N Africa and Italy, 1943–45; GSO2, 78 Division, 1944; Bde Major, 24 Guards Brigade, 1945–46; comdg 1st Bn Grenadier Guards, 1956–57; Comdr Berlin Infantry Bde, 1961–63; DMS 1, Ministry of Defence, 1964–66; GOC: Yorkshire District, 1966–67; Northumbrian District, 1967–68; Chief of Staff, Southern Command, 1968–70. Bursar and Official Fellow, Exeter College, Oxford, 1970–81. Bronze Star, USA, 1945. *Publications:* Field Marshal Earl Ligonier, 1958; Famous Regiments: the Grenadier Guards, 1974; Gunner at Large, 1988; William Augustus, Duke of Cumberland, 1992. *Recreations:* golf, church crawling, fishing, military history. *Address:* Abbey Farm, Goosey, Faringdon, Oxon SN7 8PA. *T:* (01367) 710252. *Club:* Army and Navy.

WHITWORTH-JONES, Anthony; General Director, The Dallas Opera, since 2000; *b* 1 Sept. 1945; *s* of Henry Whitworth-Jones and Patience Martin; *m* 1974, Camilla (*née* Barlow); one *d*. *Educ:* Wellington College. Mem., Inst. of Chartered Accountants of Scotland. Thomson McLintock & Co., 1970–72; Administrative Dir, London Sinfonietta, 1972–81; Administrator, Glyndebourne Touring Opera and Opera Manager, Glyndebourne Fest. Opera, 1981–89; Gen. Adminr, then Gen. Dir, Glyndebourne Fest. Opera, 1989–98. Dir, SE Arts Bd, 1993–96. Chm., Michael Tippett Musical Foundn, 1998–. Member: Adv. Bd, Voices of Change, Dallas, 2001–; Exec. Bd, Meadows Sch. of the Arts, Southern Methodist Univ., Dallas, 2001–. *Recreations:* enjoying the spirit and countryside of Wales, listening to music other than opera, contemporary art, golf. *Address:* 81 St Augustine's Road, NW1 9RR. *T:* (020) 7284 0908, *Fax:* (020) 7482 7017; 3925D Gilbert Avenue, Dallas, TX 75219, USA. *T:* (214) 4439227, *Fax:* (214) 5267792; *e-mail:* wjdallas@cs.com.

WHYBREW, Edward Graham, (Ted); Partner, Museum Replicas, since 1997; Certification Officer for Trade Unions and Employers' Associations, 1992–2001; *b* 25 Sept. 1938; *s* of Ernest Whybrew and Winifred (*née* Castle); *m* 1967, Julia Helen Baird; one *s* two *d*. *Educ:* Hertford Grammar Sch.; Balliol Coll., Oxford (BA 1961); Nuffield Coll., Oxford. Economist: NEDO, 1963; DEA, 1964–69; Dept of Employment, subseq. EDG, 1969–92; Asst Sec., Employment, Trng and Industrial Relations, 1977–85; Under Sec., Industrial Relations Div., 1985–89; Dir, Personnel and Staff Develt, 1989–92. ACAS Arbitrator. Associate Partner, Jamieson Scott (Exec. Search), 1993–98. *Publication:* Overtime Working in Great Britain, 1968. *Recreations:* watching cricket, ceramic restoration, gardening. *Address:* Grange Lea, Grange Park, Steeple Aston, Bicester, Oxon OX25 4SR.

WHYBROW, Christopher John; QC 1992; *b* 7 Aug. 1942; *s* of Herbert William Whybrow, OBE and Ruby Kathleen Whybrow (*née* Watson); *m* 1st, 1969, Marion Janet Macaulay (marr. diss. 1976); 2nd, 1979, Susan Younge (marr. diss. 1990). *Educ:* Colchester Royal Grammar Sch.; King's Coll., London (LLB). Called to the Bar, Inner Temple, 1965. A Dep. Social Security Comr, 1996–. *Publications:* (contrib.) Atkins Court Forms; contribs to Jl of Planning and Environment Law. *Recreations:* cricket, tennis, gardening, country life. *Address:* Eldon Chambers, Falcon Court, 30–32 Fleet Street, EC4Y 1AA. *Clubs:* Lansdowne, MCC; Leavenheath Cricket.

WHYBROW, John William; Executive Vice-President, Royal Philips Electronics, since 2001; *b* 11 March 1947; *s* of Charles Ernest James Whybrow and Doris Beatrice Whybrow (*née* Abbott); *m* 1968, Paula Miriam Hobart; one *s* one *d*. *Educ:* Hatfield Tech. GS; Imperial Coll., London (BSc Hons Mech. Engrg); Manchester Business Sch. (MBA); ACGI. English Electric, Rugby, 1968–70; Philips Electronics: Northern Operational Res. Gp, 1970–78; Ind. Engrg Head, Mullard Simonstone, 1979–82; Div. Manager, 1982–83, Plant Dir, 1983–87, Mullard Blackburn; Plant Dir, Hazel Grove, 1987–88; Man. Dir, TDS Circuits plc, 1988–90; Tech. Dir, Philips Components, 1990–91; Industrial Dir, 1991–93, Chm. and Man. Dir, 1993–95, Philips Electronics UK; Pres. and CEO, Philips Lighting Holding BV, 1995–2001. Mem. Bd, Royal Philips Electronics, 1998–. Chm., Lumileds Lighting BV, 1997–2000. Director: Teletext Hldgs, 1993–95; (non-exec.), Wolseley PLC, 1997–. MInstD 1993. *Recreations:* sailing, squash. *Address:* Royal Philips Electronics, Rembrandt Tower HRT 24, PO Box 77900, 1070 MX Amsterdam, Netherlands. *Club:* East India.

WHYTE, Duncan; consultant; Chief Executive, Weir Group plc, 1999–2000; *b* 27 July 1946; *s* of Andrew Montgomery Whyte and Margaret Steedman Whyte; *m* 1971, Marion McDonald McCready; one *s*. *Educ:* Kilsyth Acad. CA 1968; ATII 1968. Trainee Chartered Accountant, Paterson and Benzil, 1963–69; Arthur Andersen & Co., 1969–83 (Man. Partner, Edinburgh office, 1980–83); Financial Dir, Kwikfit Hldgs plc, 1983–88; Scottish Power: Exec. Dir, 1988–99; Finance Dir, 1988–93; Chief Operating Officer, 1993–95; Exec. Dir, Multi Utility, 1995–99. Non-exec. Dir, Motherwell Bridge Hldgs Ltd. *Recreations:* golf, badminton, reading history. *Address:* 4 Victoria Crescent, Kilsyth, Glasgow G65 9BJ.

WHYTE, Prof. Iain Boyd, PhD; FRSE; Professor of Architectural History, University of Edinburgh, since 1996; *b* 6 March 1947; *s* of Thomas Boyd Whyte and Mary Whyte (*née* Macpherson); *m* 1973, Deborah Smart; one *s* one *d*. *Educ:* Nottingham Univ. (BA 1969; MPhil 1971); Cornell Univ.; Jesus Coll., Cambridge (PhD 1979); Leeds Univ. (MA 1987). FRSE 1998. British Acad./Wolfson Fellow, 1976–77; Alexander von Humboldt-Stiftung Fellow, 1979–82; Leverhulme Trust Res. Fellow, 1985–87; University of Edinburgh: Lectr in Architecl Hist., 1988–93; Reader, 1993–95. Getty Schol., 1989–90; Getty Sen. Schol., 1998–2000. Trustee, Nat. Galls of Scotland, 1998–. FRSA. *Publications:* Bruno Taut and the Architecture of Activism, 1982 (German edn, 1981); (ed) The Crystal Chain Letters, 1985 (trans. German, 1986); (jtly) Emil Hoppe, Marcel Kammerer, Otto Schönthal, 1989; (introd and co-trans.) Hendrik Petrus Berlage on Style 1886–1909, 1996; (jtly) John Fowler, Benjamin Baker: The Forth Bridge, 1997. *Recreations:* violin playing, sculling. *Address:* 22 Lutton Place, Edinburgh EH8 9PE. *T:* (0131) 668 2899. *Clubs:* Leander (Henley-on-Thames); Akademischer Ruderclub zu Berlin (Berlin).

WHYTE, Very Rev. James Aitken; Moderator of the General Assembly of the Church of Scotland, 1988–89; Professor of Practical Theology and Christian Ethics, University of St Andrews, 1958–87; *b* 28 Jan. 1920; 2nd *s* of late Andrew Whyte, Leith, and late Barbara Janet Pittillo Aitken; *m* 1st, 1942, Elisabeth (*d* 1988), *er d* of Rev. G. S. Mill, MA, BSc, Kalimpong, India; two *s* one *d*; 2nd, 1993, Ishbel Christina Rathie (*née* Macaulay); *widow* of William Rathie, MA. *Educ:* Daniel Stewart's Coll., Edinburgh; University of Edinburgh (Arts and Divinity), MA 1st Cl. Hons Phil., 1942. Ordained, 1945; Chaplain to the Forces, 1945–48; Minister of: Dunollie Road, Oban, 1948–54; Mayfield, Edinburgh, 1954–58; Associate, Hope Park, St Andrews, 1987–96. St Andrews University: Dean, Faculty of Divinity, 1968–72; Principal, St Mary's Coll., 1978–82. Guest Lectr, Inst. for the Study of Worship and Religious Architecture, Birmingham, 1965–66; Lectures: Kerr, Univ. of Glasgow, 1969–72; Croall, Univ. of Edinburgh, 1972–73; Margaret Harris, Univ. of Dundee, 1990. Pres., Soc. for Study of Theol., 1983–84. Hon. LLD Dundee, 1981; Hon. DD St Andrews, 1989; DUniv Stirling, 1994. *Publications:* (ed jtly) Worship Now: Vol. 1, 1972, Vol. 2, 1989; Laughter and Tears, 1993; The Dream of the Perfect Round, 2001; contributor to various dictionaries, composite volumes, journals, etc. *Address:* 13 Hope Street, St Andrews, Fife KY16 9HJ. *Club:* New (Edinburgh).

WHYTE, John Stuart, CBE 1976; MSc(Eng); FREng, FIEE; Chairman, GPT (International) Ltd, 1988–90; *b* High Wycombe, 20 July 1923; *s* of late William W. Whyte and Ethel K. Whyte; *m* 1951, (Edna) Joan (Mary) (*née* Budd) (*d* 1995); one *s* one *d*. *Educ:* The John Lyon Sch., Harrow; Northampton Polytechnic, London Univ. BSc(Eng) (Hons), MSc(Eng). Post Office Radio Laboratory, Castleton, Cardiff, 1949–57; PO Research Station, Dollis Hill: Sen. Exec. Engr, 1957–61; Asst Staff Engr, 1961–65. Asst Sec., HM Treasury, 1965–68; Dep. Dir of Engrg, PO, 1968–71; Dir, Operational Programming, PO, 1971–75; Dir of Purchasing and Supply, 1975–76, Sen. Dir of Develt, 1977–79, Dep. Man. Dir, 1979–81, PO Telecommunications; Engr-in-Chief, Man. Dir (major systems), and Mem. Main Bd, British Telecom, 1981–83; Dir, British Telecommunications Systems Ltd, 1979–83; Chm., Astronet Corp., 1984–85; Pres., 1984–85, Chm., 1985–86, Stromberg Carlson Corp; Chm., Plessey Telecommunications (Internat.) Ltd, 1983–85; Dep. Chm., Plessey Telecommunications and Office Systems Ltd, 1985–88. Manager, Royal Instn, 1971–74 (Vice-Pres., 1972, 1973, 1974), Mem. Cttee of Visitors, 1975–78 (Chm., 1977–78), Chm., Membership Cttee, 1975–77. Mem., Nat. Electronics Council, 1977–2000 (Mem. Exec. Cttee, 1977–2000; Dep. Chm., 1980–2000); Mem. Council, ERA, 1977–83. President: Instn of PO Electrical Engrs, 1977–82; Instn of British Telecommunications Engrs, 1982–83 (Hon. Mem., 1984); Mem. Council, IEE, 1980–84 (Vice-Pres., 1981–84; Chm. Professional Bd, 1981–84). FREng (FEng 1980). Governor, Internat. Council for Computer Communication, 1985–91. Liveryman, Scientific Instrument Makers' Co. Freeman, City of London, 1979. Leader, British Hinku Expedn, 1979; Pres., Assoc. of British Members of Swiss Alpine Club, 1988–90. *Publications:* various articles and papers in professional telecommunications jls. *Recreations:* mountaineering, opera, foreign travel, genealogy. *Address:* Wild Hatch, Coleshill Lane, Winchmore Hill, Amersham, Bucks HP7 0NT. *T:* (01494) 722663. *Clubs:* Alpine; Cambridge University Alpine (Hon.).

WHYTE, (John) Stuart Scott, CB 1986; Under Secretary, Department of Health and Social Security, 1978–86; *b* 1 April 1926; *er s* of late Thomas and Mysie Scott Whyte, Sandycove, Co. Dublin; *m* 1950, Jocelyn Margaret, *o d* of late George Hawley, CBE, Edinburgh; two *s* one *d*. *Educ:* St Andrew's Coll., Dublin; Trinity Coll., Univ. of Dublin. BA 1947; LLB 1948. Asst Principal, Dept of Health for Scotland, 1948; Principal, 1955; Principal Private Sec. to Sec. of State for Scotland, 1959; Asst Sec., Scottish Develt Dept, 1962; Asst Sec., Cabinet Office, 1969; Asst Under-Sec. of State, Scottish Office, 1969–74; Under Sec., Cabinet Office, 1974–78. *Address:* La Bâtisse, Bonin, 47120 Duras, France. *T:* 553837031.

WHYTE, Stuart Scott; *see* Whyte, J. S. S.

WIBLIN, Derek John, CB 1992; Under Secretary, Principal Establishment and Finance Officer, Crown Prosecution Service, 1988–93; *b* 18 March 1933; *s* of late Cyril G. H. Wiblin and of Winifred F. Wiblin (*née* Sandford); *m* 1960, Pamela Jeanne Hamshere; one *s* one *d*. *Educ:* Bishopshalt School, Hillingdon; Birmingham University (BSc Hons Chem 1954). RAF, 1954–57. Courtaulds Ltd, 1957–58; joined DSIR Building Research Station, 1958; Civil Service Commission, 1967–71; Asst Sec., Local Govt Div., DoE, 1971–79;

Ports Div., Dept of Transport, 1979–81; Estabs Div., DoE, 1981–83; Under Sec., Principal Estabt and Finance Officer, Lord Chancellor's Dept, 1984–88. Chm., First Division Pensioners' Gp, 1993–98. *Recreations:* making violins, collecting books. *Address:* 19 Woodwaye, Oxhey, Watford, Herts WD19 4NN. *T:* (01923) 228615. *Clubs:* Athenæum, Royal Air Force.

WICKENS, Prof. Alan Herbert, OBE 1980; FREng, FIMechE; Industrial Professor, Department of Mechanical Engineering, Loughborough University (formerly Loughborough University of Technology), since 1993; *b* 29 March 1929; *s* of late Herbert Leslie Wickens and of Sylvia Wickens; *m* 1st, 1953, Eleanor Joyce Waggott (*d* 1984); one *d*; 2nd, 1987, Patricia Anne McNeil. *Educ:* Ashville Coll., Harrogate; Loughborough Univ. of Technol. (DLC Eng, BScEng London, 1951; DSc Loughborough, 1978). CEng, FIMechE 1971; MRAeS. Res. Engr, Sir W. G. Armstrong Whitworth Aircraft Ltd, Coventry, 1951–55; Gp Leader, Dynamics Analysis, Canadair Ltd, Montreal, 1955–59; Head of Aeroelastics Section, Weapons Res. Div., A. V. Roe & Co., Ltd, Woodford, 1959–62; British Rail: Supt, Res. Dept, 1962–67; Advanced Projs Engr, 1967–68; Dir of Advanced Projs, 1968–71; Dir of Labs, 1971–78; Dir of Research, 1978–84; Dir of Engrg Develt and Research, 1984–89. Loughborough University of Technology: Industrial Prof. of Transport Technol., 1972–76; Prof. of Dynamics, Dept of Mechanical Engrg, 1989–92. Vis. Prof., Dept of Mech. Engrg, Design and Manufacture, Manchester Metropolitan Univ., 1998–. Pres., Internat. Assoc. of Vehicle System Dynamics, 1981–86; Chm., Office of Res. and Experiments, Union Internationale de Chemins de fer, 1988–90. Mem., Amer. Inst. Aeronautics and Astronautics, 1958. FBIS; FRSA. Hon. Fellow, Derbyshire Coll. of Higher Educn, 1984. Hon. DTech CNAA, 1978; Hon. Dr Open Univ, 1980. George Stephenson Res. Prize, IMechE, 1966; (jtly) MacRobert Award, 1975. *Publications:* papers on dynamics of railway vehicles, high speed trains and future railway technology, publ. by IMechE, Amer. Soc. of Mech. Engrs, Internat. Jl of Solids and Structures, and Jl of Vehicle System Dynamics. *Recreations:* gardening, travel, music. *Address:* Ecclesbourne Farmhouse, Ecclesbourne Lane, Idridgehay, Derbys DE56 2SB. *T:* (01773) 550368. *Club:* Royal Air Force.

WICKERSON, Sir John (Michael), Kt 1987; Partner, 1962–98, Consultant, since 1998, Ormerods (previously Ormerod, Morris & Dumont, later Ormerod Wilkinson Marshall, then Ormerod Heap & Marshall); President, Law Society, 1986–87; *b* 22 Sept. 1937; *s* of Walter and Ruth Wickerson; *m* 1963, Shirley Maud Best; one *s*. *Educ:* Christ's Hospital; London University (LLB). Admitted solicitor, 1960; Mem. Council, Law Society, 1969 (Chm., Contentious Business Cttee; Vice-Pres., 1985–86). Member: Matrimonial Causes Rules Cttee, 1982–86; Royal Commn on Criminal Justice, 1991–93. Pres., London Criminal Courts Solicitors Assoc., 1980–81. Chairman: Mansell plc (formerly R. Mansell Ltd), 1994–; Investors' Compensation Scheme Ltd, 1996–2001. Chm., Croydon Community NHS Trust, 1991–98. Hon. Member: Amer. Bar Assoc., 1986; Canadian Bar Assoc., 1986; NZ Law Soc., 1987. *Publication:* Motorist and the Law, 1975, 2nd edn 1982. *Recreation:* golf. *Address:* c/o Ormerods, Green Dragon House, 64–70 High Street, Croydon, Surrey CR0 9XN. *T:* (020) 8686 5000.

WICKES, Charles G.; *see* Goodson-Wickes.

WICKHAM, Prof. Christopher John, DPhil; FBA 1998; Professor of Early Medieval History, University of Birmingham, since 1993; *b* 18 May 1950; *s* of Cyril George Wickham and Katharine Brenda Warington Wickham (*née* Moss); *m* 1990, Dr Leslie Brubaker. *Educ:* Millfield Sch.; Keble Coll., Oxford (BA 1971; DPhil 1975). Lectr, 1977–87, Sen. Lectr, 1987–89, Reader, 1989–93, Univ. of Birmingham. Jt Ed., Past & Present, 1994–. *Publications:* Early Medieval Italy, 1981; The mountains and the city, 1988; (with J. Fentress) Social memory, 1992; Land and power, 1994; Community and Clientele, 1998 (Italian edn, 1995); Legge, pratica e conflitti, 2000. *Recreations:* politics, travel. *Address:* Department of Medieval History, University of Birmingham, Birmingham B15 2TT.

WICKHAM, Daphne Elizabeth, (Mrs J. K. A. Alderson); a District Judge (Magistrates' Courts) (formerly Metropolitan Stipendiary Magistrate), since 1989; *b* 31 Aug. 1946; *d* of late Major Harry Temple Wickham and of Phyllis Wickham (*née* Roycroft); *m* 1983, John Keith Ameers Alderson. *Educ:* Sydenham High Sch.; Chislehurst and Sidcup Girls' Grammar School. Called to the Bar, Inner Temple, 1967. *Recreation:* laughter. *Address:* 3 Temple Gardens, Temple, EC4Y 9AU. *T:* (020) 7353 3102. *Club:* Reform.

WICKHAM, David Ian; Chief Executive, Energis plc, since 2001; *b* 23 Oct. 1957; *s* of Edwin and Betty Wickham; *m* 1982, Joanne Frances Carter; two *s*. *Educ:* St Olave's Grammar Sch., Orpington; S London Coll. (HND Business Studies). Various develt roles in UK, Europe and S Pacific to 1985; Mktg Dir, C&W Systems Ltd, Hong Kong, 1985–87; Mercury Communications Ltd: Gen. Manager, Residential and Operator Services, 1987–91; Mktg Dir, Business and Consumer Services, 1991–94; Man. Dir, Partner Services, 1994–96; Ops Dir, 1996–97; Man. Dir, Internat. and Partner Services, Cable & Wireless Communications Ltd, 1997–98; Chief Exec., Global Network, Cable and Wireless plc, 1998–99; Chief Operating Officer, Energis plc, 1999–2001. *Recreations:* golf, theatre, family, travel. *Address:* Energis plc, Carmelite, 50 Victoria Embankment, EC4Y 0DE. *Club:* London Golf.

WICKHAM, Glynne William Gladstone; Professor of Drama, University of Bristol, 1960–82, now Emeritus, and Senior Research Fellow, since 1995 (Hon. Fellow, 1996); *b* 15 May 1922; *s* of W. G. and Catherine Wickham; *m* 1954, Marjorie Heseltine (*née* Mudford); two *s* one *d*. *Educ:* Winchester College; New College, Oxford. Entered RAF, 1942; commissioned as Navigator, 1943; discharged as Flt Lt, 1946. BA, 1947; DPhil, 1951 (Oxon); President of OUDS, 1946–47. Bristol University: Asst Lectr, Drama Dept, 1948; Sen. Lectr and Head of Dept, 1955; Dean, Faculty of Arts, 1970–72. Worked sporadically as actor, script-writer and critic for BBC, from 1946; attended General Course in Broadcasting, BBC Staff Trg Sch., 1953. Travelled in America on Rockefeller Award, 1953. Visiting Prof., Drama Dept, State Univ. of Iowa, 1960; Ferens Vis. Prof. of Drama, Hull Univ., 1969; Vis. Prof. of Theatre History, Yale Univ., 1970; Killam Res. Prof., Dalhousie Univ., 1976–77; S. W. Brooks Vis. Prof., Univ. of Qld, 1983; Vis. Prof. in British Studies (Drama), Univ. of the South, Sewanee, 1984; Adjunct Prof. (Arts and Letters), Univ. of Notre Dame (London Campus), 1987–96; Hon. Prof., Univ. of Warwick, 1990–95. Lectures: G. F. Reynolds Meml, Univ. of Colorado, 1960; Judith E. Wilson, in Poetry and Drama, Cambridge, 1960–61; Festvortrag, Deutsche Shakespeare Gesellschaft, 1973; Shakespeare, British Acad., 1984; British Council, in Europe, annually 1969–79. Directed: Amer. première, The Birthday Party, for Actors' Workshop, San Francisco, 1960; world première, Wole Soyinka's Brother Jero's Metamorphosis, 1974. Consultant to Finnish National Theatre and Theatre School on establishment of Drama Department in Univ. of Helsinki, 1963. Governor of Bristol Old Vic Trust, 1963–83; Vandyck Theatre, Bristol Univ., renamed Glynne Wickham Studio Theatre, 1983. Consultant to Univ. of E Africa on establishment of a Sch. of Drama in University Coll., Dar-es-Salaam, Tanzania, 1965; Dir, Theatre Seminar, for Summer Univ., Vaasa, Finland, 1965; External Examr to Sch. of Drama in Univ. of Ibadan, Nigeria, 1965–68. Chm., Nat. Drama Conf., Nat. Council of Social Service, 1970–76; Chm., and Chief Exec., Radio West plc (ILR Bristol), 1979–83; Pres., Soc. for Theatre Research, 1976–99; Member: Adv. Cttee, British Theatre Museum, 1974–77; Culture Adv. Panel, UK Nat. Commn to UNESCO, 1984–86. Mem., Edit. Cttee, Shakespeare Survey, 1974–94; Chairman: Adv. Bd, Theatre Research International, 1975–; Gen. Edit. Bd, Theatre in Europe: documents and sources, 1979–. Trustee, St Deiniol's Residential Library, Hawarden, 1985–2000; Dir, Bd of Internat. Shakespeare Globe Centre, 1986–91. Mem., Polish Acad. of Arts and Letters, 1991. Hon. DLitt: Loughborough, 1984; Univ. of the South, Sewanee, 1984. Sam Wanamaker Award for services to the theatre, 1999. *Publications:* Early English Stages 1300–1660, Vol. I (1300–1576), 1959, 2nd edn 1980; Vol. II (1576–1660, Pt 1), 1962; Vol. II (Pt 2), 1972; Vol. III, 1981; Vol. IV, 2001; Editor: The Relationship between Universities and Radio, Film and Television, 1954; Drama in a World of Science, 1962; Gen. Introd. to the London Shakespeare, 6 vols (ed J. Munro), 1958; Shakespeare's Dramatic Heritage, 1969; The Medieval Theatre, 1974, 3rd edn 1987; English Moral Interludes, 1975, 2nd edn 1985; A History of the Theatre, 1985, 2nd edn 1992; English Professional Theatre 1530–1660: a documentary history, 2001. *Recreations:* gardening and travel. *Address:* 6 College Road, Clifton, Bristol BS8 3JB. *T:* (0117) 973 4918. *Clubs:* Garrick, National Liberal.

WICKHAM, John Ewart Alfred, FRCS; specialist in minimally invasive surgery and urology; Surgeon and Senior Research Fellow, Guy's Hospital, 1993–98; Director, Academic Unit, Institute of Urology, University of London, 1979–98; Surgeon: St Peter's Hospital, 1967–95; King Edward VII Hospital, 1972–98; Middlesex Hospital, 1973–95; *b* 10 Dec. 1927; *s* of Alfred James Wickham and Hilda May Wickham (*née* Cummins); *m* 1961, (Gwendoline) Ann Loney; three *d*. *Educ:* Chichester Grammar Sch.; London Univ.; St Bartholomew's Hosp. Med. Coll. (BSc Hons 1953; MB BS 1955; MS 1966). FRCS 1959. Nat. Service, RAF, 1947–49. St Bartholomew's Hosp. and RPMS, 1955–66; Sen. Consultant Urological Surgeon, St Bart's, 1966–85; Sen. Lectr, 1967–92, and Sub Dean, 1967–79, Inst. of Urology; Civilian Consultant Urologist, RAF, 1973–98. Director: Lithotripter Units of London Clinic, 1984–98, and of NE Thames Region, 1987–95; Minimally Invasive Therapy, London Clinic, 1989–99. First Pres., Internat. Soc. of Urological Endoscopy, 1982; President: Urological Sect., RSM, 1984–85; Internat. Soc. of Minimally Invasive Therapy, 1989–2000; Founder Mem., Europ. Soc. of Urology, 1969; Member: Internat. Soc. of Urology, 1970; Italian-Belgian Soc. of Urology, 1980; Irish Soc. of Urology, 1984; American Soc. of Urology, 1990; Japanese Soc. of Urology, 1993. Hon. FRCP 1993; Hon. FRCR 1993. Freeman, City of London; Liveryman, Barber Surgeon's Co., 1971. Hon. MD Gothenburg, 1994. Hunterian Prof. and Medal, RCS, 1967; Cutlers Prize and Medal, Assoc. of Surgeons, 1984; James Berry Medal, RCS, 1985; St Peter's Medal, British Assoc. of Urological Surgeons, 1985; J. K. Latimer Medal, Amer. Urological Assoc., 1990; Cecil Joll Prize, RCS, 1993; Rovsing Medal, Danish Soc. of Surgery, 1993; Cook Medal, RCR, 1998; Galen Medal, Soc. of Apothecaries, 1998. Editor, Jl of Minimally Invasive Therapy, 1990–2000. *Publications:* Urinary Calculus Disease, 1979; Percutaneous Renal Surgery, 1983; Intrarenal Surgery, 1984; Lithotripsy II, 1987; Urinary Stone Metabolic Basis and Clinical Practice, 1989; over 150 papers on urology and minimally invasive surgery. *Recreations:* mechanical engineering, tennis. *Address:* Stowe Maries, Balchins Lane, Westcott, Surrey RH4 3LR. *T:* (01306) 885557. *Clubs:* Athenæum, Royal Automobile.

WICKHAM, His Honour William Rayley; a Circuit Judge, 1975–97; Hon. Recorder of Liverpool and Senior Circuit Judge, Liverpool, 1992–97; *b* 22 Sept. 1926; *s* of late Rayley Esmond Wickham and late Mary Joyce Wickham; *m* 1957, Elizabeth Mary (*née* Thompson); one *s* two *d*. *Educ:* Sedbergh Sch.; Brasenose Coll., Oxford (MA, BCL). Served War of 1939–45, Army, 1944–48. Called to Bar, Inner Temple, 1951. Magistrate, Aden, 1953; Chief Magistrate, Aden, 1958; Crown Counsel, Tanganyika, 1959; Asst to Law Officers, Tanganyika, 1961–63; practised on Northern Circuit, 1963–75; a Recorder of the Crown Court, 1972–75. *Recreations:* fell walking, music, amateur dramatics. *Address:* 115 Vyner Road South, Prenton CH43 7PP.

WICKINS, David Allen; Founder and Chairman, Southern Counties Car Auctions, later The British Car Auction Group, 1946–1989; *b* 15 Feb. 1920; *s* of Samuel Wickins and Edith Hannah Robinson; *m* 1969, Karen Esther Young; one *s* five *d*. *Educ:* St George's College, Weybridge. Trained as chartered accountant with Deloitte & Co., attached to Johannesburg Consolidated Investment Co. and moved to S Africa, 1938, to work on audits for Rhodesian copper mines and sawmills. War of 1939–45: S African Naval Forces (18 months with Eastern Fleet); seconded to RN; served with UK Coastal Forces. Former Chairman: Attwoods plc; Group Lotus plc; Expedier Leisure plc. *Recreations:* tennis, golf, sailing. *Clubs:* St James's, Royal Thames Yacht; Sunningdale Golf.

WICKRAMASINGHE, Prof. (Nalin) Chandra, PhD, ScD; Professor of Applied Mathematics and Astronomy in the School of Mathematics, University of Wales College of Cardiff, since 1988 (Professor and Head of Department of Applied Mathematics and Astronomy, University College, Cardiff, 1973–88); *b* 20 Jan. 1939; *s* of Percival Herbert Wickramasinghe and Theresa Elizabeth Wickramasinghe; *m* 1966, Nelum Priyadarshini Pereira; one *s* two *d*. *Educ:* Royal Coll., Colombo, Sri Lanka; Univ. of Ceylon (BSc); Univ. of Cambridge (MA, PhD, ScD). Commonwealth Scholar, Trinity Coll., Cambridge, 1960; Powell Prize for English Verse, 1961; Jesus College, Cambridge: Research Fellow, 1963–66; Fellow, 1967–73; Tutor, 1970–73; Staff Mem., Inst. of Theoretical Astronomy, Univ. of Cambridge, 1968–73. Visiting Professor: Vidyodaya Univ. of Ceylon, Univ. of Maryland, USA, Univ. of Arizona, USA, Univ. of Kyoto, Japan, 1966–70; Univ. of W Ontario, 1974, 1976; Inst. of Space and Astronautical Studies, Japan, 1993; Univ. of WI, Kingston, Jamaica, 1994; UNDP Cons. and Scientific Advisor to President of Sri Lanka, 1970–81; Dir, Inst. of Fundamental Studies, Sri Lanka, 1982–83 (Vis. Prof., 1997–). Collaborator with Prof. Sir Fred Hoyle, and propounder with Hoyle of the theory of the space origin of life and of microorganisms. Hon. DSc Soka Univ., Japan, 1996. Dag Hammarskjöld Gold Medal in science, Académie Diplomatique de la Paix, 1986; Scholarly Achievement Award, Inst. of Oriental Philosophy, Japan, 1989; Internat. Peace and Culture Award, Soka Gakkai, 1993; Sahabdeen Internat. Award for Science, A. M. M. Sahabdeen Trust Foundn, 1996. Vidya Jyothi (Sri Lanka), 1992. *Publications:* Interstellar Grains, 1967; (with F. D. Kahn and P. G. Mezger) Interstellar Matter, 1972; Light Scattering Functions for Small Particles with Applications in Astronomy, 1973; The Cosmic Laboratory, 1975; (with D. J. Morgan) Solid State Astrophysics, 1976; Fundamental Studies and the Future of Science, 1984; (with F. Hoyle and J. Watkins) Viruses from Space, 1986; (with Daisaku Ikeda) Emergent Perspectives for 2000 AD, 1992; (with D. Ikeda) The Wonders of Life and the Universe, 1993; Glimpses of Life, Time and Space: an anthology of poetry, 1994; Cosmic Dragons: life and death of our planet, 2001; (with F. Hoyle): Lifecloud: the origin of life in the universe, 1978; Diseases From Space, 1979; The Origin of Life, 1980; Evolution From Space, 1981; Space Travellers, the Bringers of Life, 1981; From Grains to Bacteria, 1984; Living Comets, 1985; Archaeopteryx, the Primordial Bird: a case of fossil forgery, 1986; Cosmic Life Force, 1987; Theory of Cosmic Grains, 1991; Our Place in the Cosmos: the unfinished revolution, 1993; Life on Mars?: the case for a cosmic heritage, 1997; Astronomical Origins of Life: steps towards panspermia, 2000; over 300 articles and papers in astronomical and scientific jls; contributor to anthologies of Commonwealth Poetry, incl. Young Commonwealth Poets '65, ed P. L. Brent, 1965. *Recreations:* photography, poetry—both writing and reading, history and philosophy of science. *Address:* School of Mathematics, University of Wales College of Cardiff, Senghenydd Road, Cardiff CF2 4AG. *T:* (029) 2075 2146, *Fax:* (029) 2075 3173; *e-mail:* wickramasinghe@cardiff.ac.uk.; (home) 24 Llwynypia Road, Lisvane, Cardiff CF14 0SY.

See also S. N. Wickramasinghe.

WICKRAMASINGHE, Prof. Sunitha Nimal, PhD, ScD; FRCP, FRCPath; FIBiol; Professor, and Head of Department of Haematology, Imperial College, University of London, 1979–2000, Professor Emeritus, since 2000; *b* 2 July 1941; *s* of Percival Herbert Wickramasinghe and Theresa Elizabeth Wickramasinghe; *m* 1968, Priyanthi Soummia Fernando; one *s* two *d. Educ:* Royal Coll., Colombo; Univ. of Ceylon (MB BS); PhD 1968, ScD 1984, Cantab. FRCPath 1986; FRCP 1991; FIBiol 1982. Gulbenkian Res. Student, Churchill Coll., Cambridge, 1966–68; John Lucas Walker Sen. Student, Univ. of Cambridge, 1968; Clin. Res. Fellow, Univ. of Leeds, 1969; Lectr, 1970–73, Sen. Lectr, 1973–78, Reader in Haematol., 1978–79 , St Mary's Hosp. Med. Sch., Univ. of London; Dep. Dean, ICSM at St Mary's, 1995–97; Hon. Consultant Haematologist: St Mary's Hosp., London, 1979–; Oxford Radcliffe Hosps, 2000–. Vis. Prof. in Haematol., Univ. of Oxford, 2000–. Hon. Fellow, Sri Lanka Coll. of Haematologists, 1999; E. H. Cooray Meml Orator and Gold Medallist, Coll. of Pathologists, Sri Lanka, 1995. Guest Editor: Megaloblastic Anaemia, 1995; Haematological Aspects of Infection, 2000. *Publications:* Human Bone Marrow, 1975; (ed) Blood and Bone Marrow: systemic pathology, 3rd edn 1986; (with N. C. Hughes-Jones) Lecture Notes on Haematology, 5th edn 1991, 6th edn 1996; contrib. papers on abnormal erythropoiesis. *Recreations:* photography, travel, biology. *Address:* 32 Braywick Road, Maidenhead, Berks SL6 1DA. *T:* (01628) 621665.

See also N. C. Wickramasinghe.

WICKREMESINGHE, Sarath Kusum; Chairman: Sri Lankan Airlines Ltd, since 1999; National Development Bank Ltd, Colombo, since 1999; *b* 26 Jan. 1928; *m* 1953, Damayantha Hulugalle. *Educ:* St Thomas' Coll., Mt Lavinia; Univ. of Ceylon (BSc Hons Physics). Exec. in ICI (Export) Ltd, Colombo, 1951–66; Chief Exec., 1966–80, Chm., 1966–94, ICI associate co. in Sri Lanka; Chm., subsid. and associate cos, Coates Internat., 1982–84, BAT, 1985–91, and Standard Chartered Bank, 1989–94; High Comr for Sri Lanka in London, 1995–99. *Address:* 8 Claessen Place, Colombo 5, Sri Lanka. *Clubs:* Hill (Sri Lanka); Ceylon Rugby Football.

WICKS, Allan, CBE 1988; Organist, Canterbury Cathedral, 1961–88; *b* 6 June 1923; *s* of late Edward Kemble Wicks, priest, and Nancie (*née* Murgatroyd); *m* 1955, Elizabeth Kay Butcher; two *d. Educ:* Leatherhead; Christ Church, Oxford. Sub-organist, York Minster, 1947; Organist, Manchester Cathedral, 1954. MusDoc Lambeth, 1974; Hon. DMus Kent, 1985. *Address:* The Old Farm House, Lower Hardres, Canterbury, Kent CT4 5NR. *T:* (01227) 700253.

WICKS, Geoffrey Leonard; a District Judge (Magistrates' Courts) (formerly Metropolitan Stipendiary Magistrate), since 1987; *b* 23 July 1934; *s* of late Leonard James Wicks and Winifred Ellen Wicks; *m* 1st, 1959, Catherine Margaret Shanks (marr. diss. 1977); one *s* one *d*; 2nd, 1978, Maureen Evelyn Neville. *Educ:* Tollington Sch., N10; Law Society's Sch. of Law, London. Admitted Solicitor, 1957. National Service, RASC, 1957–59. Asst Solicitor, LCC, 1959–60; Asst Solicitor, 1960–61, Partner, 1961–79 (Abu Dhabi office, 1978), Oswald Hickson, Collier & Co., Solicitors, London, Chesham, Amersham, Slough; Principal, Geoffrey Wicks & Co., Solicitors, Chesham, Hemel Hempstead, 1979–82; Partner, Iliffes, Solicitors, London, Chesham, 1982–87. Chairman: Family Courts, 1991–97; Youth Courts, 1991–; Mem., Inner London Magistrates' Courts Cttee, 1995–99, 2000–01. Mem., Home Sec.'s Task Force for Youth Justice, 1997–98. Mem., Commonwealth Magistrates' and Judges' Assoc. Member: Chesham Round Table, 1962–75 (Chm. 1968–69, Area Chm. Area 42, 1972–73); Chesham Rotary Club, 1974–77. *Recreations:* walking, opera, ballet. *Address:* c/o Horseferry Road Magistrates' Court SW1P 2AX. *T:* (020) 7805 1103.

WICKS, Malcolm Hunt; MP (Lab) Croydon North, since 1997 (Croydon North West, 1992–97); Parliamentary Under-Secretary of State, Department for Work and Pensions, since 2001; *b* 1 July 1947; *s* of Arthur Wicks and late Daisy (*née* Hunt); *m* 1968, Margaret Baron; one *s* two *d. Educ:* Norfolk House; Elizabeth Coll., Guernsey; NW London Poly.; LSE (BSc Hons Sociology). Fellow, Dept of Social Admin, York Univ., 1968–70; res. worker, Centre for Envmtl Studies, 1970–72; Lectr in Social Admin, Dept of Govt Studies, Brunel Univ., 1970–74; Social Policy Analyst, Urban Deprivation Unit, Home Office, 1974–77; Lectr in Social Policy, Civil Service Coll., 1977–78; Res. Dir and Sec., Study Commn on the Family, 1978–83; Dir, Family Policy Studies Centre, 1983–92; Co-Dir, European Family and Social Policy Unit, 1992. Parly Under-Sec. of State, DFEE, 1999–2001. Sec., PLP Social Security Cttee, 1994–96. Mem., Family Policy Observatory, Eur. Commn, 1987–92. Chm., Winter Action on Cold Homes, 1986–92. Trustee, Nat. Energy Foundn, 1987–. *Publications:* Old and Cold: hypothermia and social policy, 1978; (jtly) Government and Urban Policy, 1983; A Future for All: do we need a welfare state?, 1987; (jtly) Family Change and Future Policy, 1990; contribs to books and periodicals. *Recreations:* walking, music, writing. *Address:* House of Commons, SW1A 0AA. *T:* (020) 7219 3000. *Club:* Ruskin House Labour (Croydon).

WICKS, Sir Nigel (Leonard), GCB 1999 (KCB 1992); CVO 1989; CBE 1979; Chariman, Committee on Standards in Public Life, since 2001; Chairman, CRESTCo, since 2001; *b* 16 June 1940; *s* of late Leonard Charles and Beatrice Irene Wicks; *m* 1969, Jennifer Mary (*née* Coveney) three *s. Educ:* Beckenham and Penge Grammar Sch.; Portsmouth Coll. of Technology; Univ. of Cambridge (MA); Univ. of London (MA). The British Petroleum Co. Ltd, 1958–68; HM Treasury, 1968–75; Private Sec. to the Prime Minister, 1975–78; HM Treasury, 1978–83; Economic Minister, British Embassy, Washington, and UK Exec. Dir, IMF and IBRD, 1983–85; Principal Private Sec. to the Prime Minister, 1985–88; Second Perm. Sec. (Finance), HM Treasury, 1989–2000. Mem. Bd, BNOC, 1980–82. Gov., King's Coll. Sch., Wimbledon, 1993–. *Address:* c/o HM Treasury, Parliament Street, SW1P 3AG.

WICKSTEAD, Cyril; Chairman, Eastern Electricity Board, 1978–82; Member, Electricity Council, 1978–82; *b* 27 Sept. 1922; *s* of John William and Mary Caroline Wickstead; *m* 1948, Freda May Hill; two *s. Educ:* Rowley Regis Central Sch.; City of Birmingham Commercial Coll. FCIS. Served War, Royal Navy (Lieut RNVR), 1942–46. Midland Electric Corporation for Power Distribution Ltd: various positions, 1937–42; Asst Sec., 1946–48; Midlands Electricity Board: Sec., S Staffs and N Worcs Sub-Area, 1948–59; Dep. Sec. of Bd, 1959–63; Sec., 1964–72; Dep. Chm., 1972–77. Freeman, City of London, 1979. *Recreations:* music, gardening, sport (spectator, alas). *Address:* Ryton, Brook Street, Dedham, Colchester, Essex CO7 6AD.

WICKSTEAD, Myles Antony; HM Diplomatic Service; Ambassador to Ethiopia, and Ambassador (non-resident) to Djibouti, since 2000; *b* 7 Feb. 1951; *s* of John Horace Wickstead and Eva Mary Wickstead (*née* Fouracre); *m* 1990, Shelagh Paterson; one *s* one *d. Educ:* Blundell's Sch.; St Andrews Univ. (MA 1st Cl. Hons Eng. Lang. and Lit. 1974); New Coll., Oxford (MLitt). Joined ODM, 1976; Asst Private Sec. to Lord Privy Seal, FCO, 1979–80; Asst to UK Exec. Dir, IMF/IBRD, 1980–84; Principal, ODA, 1984–88; Private Sec. to Minister for Overseas Develt, 1988–90; Head: EC and Food Aid Dept, ODA, 1990–93; British Develt Div. in Eastern Africa, 1993–97; UK Alternate Exec. Dir, World Bank, and Counsellor (Develt), Washington, 1997–2000. *Recreations:* sports, music, travel, flying, two young children. *Address:* c/o Foreign and Commonwealth Office, King Charles Street, SW1A 2AH; The Manor House, Great Street, Norton sub Hamdon, Som TA14 6SJ. *T:* (01935) 881385. *Club:* Muthaiga (Nairobi).

WIDDAS, Prof. Wilfred Faraday, MB, BS; BSc; PhD; DSc; Professor of Physiology in the University of London, and Head of the Department of Physiology, Bedford College, 1960–81, now Professor Emeritus; *b* 2 May 1916; *s* of late Percy Widdas, BSc, mining engineer, and Annie Maude (*née* Snowdon); *m* 1940, Gladys Green (*d* 1983); one *s* two *d. Educ:* Durham School; University of Durham College of Medicine and Royal Victoria Infirmary, Newcastle upon Tyne. MB, BS 1938; BSc 1947; PhD 1953; DSc 1958. Assistant in General Practice, 1938–39. Served in RAMC, 1939–47; Deputy Assistant Director-General Army Medical Services, War Office (Major), 1942–47. Research Fellow, St Mary's Hospital Medical School, 1947–49; Lecturer and Sen. Lecturer in Physiology, St Mary's Hospital Medical School, 1949–55; Senior Lecturer in Physiology, King's College, 1955–56; University Reader in Physiology at King's College, 1956–60. FRSocMed. Mem., Royal Institution of Gt Britain; Hon. Mem., Physiological Society. *Publications:* papers on membrane transporters for glucose, the red cell anion exchanger and bicarbonate permeability; other research papers chiefly in Cytobios. *Recreation:* tennis. *Address:* 16 Linden Grove, Great Linford, Milton Keynes, MK14 5HF. *T:* (01908) 605900.

WIDDECOMBE, Rt Hon. Ann (Noreen); PC 1997; MP (C) Maidstone and The Weald, since 1997 (Maidstone, 1987–97); *b* 4 Oct. 1947; *d* of late James Murray Widdecombe, CB, OBE and of Rita Noreen (*née* Plummer). *Educ:* La Sainte Union Convent, Bath; Univ. of Birmingham; Lady Margaret Hall, Oxford (BA Hons, MA). Marketing, Unilever, 1973–75; Senior Administrator, Univ. of London, 1975–87. Contested (C): Burnley, 1979; Plymouth, Devonport, 1983. PPS to Tristan Garel-Jones, MP, Nov. 1990; Parly Under-Sec. of State, DSS, 1990–93, Dept of Employment, 1993–94; Minister of State: Dept of Employment, 1994–95; Home Office, 1995–97. *Publications:* Layman's Guide to Defence, 1984; The Clematis Tree (novel), 2000. *Recreations:* reading, researching Charles II's escape. *Address:* 39 Searles Road, SE1 4YX. *T:* (020) 7701 6684; Kloof Cottage, Sutton Valence, Maidstone, Kent. *T:* (01622) 843868.

WIDDICOMBE, David Graham; QC 1965; a Recorder, 1985–96; a Deputy High Court Judge, 1983–96; *b* 7 Jan. 1924; *s* of Aubrey Guy Widdicombe and Margaret (*née* Puddy); *m* 1961, Anastasia Cecilia (*née* Leech) (marr. diss. 1983); two *s* one *d. Educ:* St Albans Sch.; Queen's Coll., Cambridge (BA 1st cl. Hons; LLB 1st cl. Hons; MA). Called to the Bar, Inner Temple, 1950, Bencher, 1973; Attorney at Law, State Bar of California, 1986. Mem., Cttee on Local Govt Rules of Conduct, 1973–74; Chairman: Oxfordshire Structure Plan Examination in Public, 1977; Cttee of Inquiry into Conduct of Local Authority Business, 1985–86. *Publication:* (ed) Ryde on Rating, 1968–83. *Address:* 2 Mitre Court Buildings, Temple, EC4Y 7BX. *T:* (020) 7583 1380; 5 Albert Terrace, NW1 7SU. *T:* (020) 7586 5209. *Clubs:* Athenæum, Garrick.

WIDDOWS, Air Commodore Charles; *see* Widdows, Air Commodore S. C.

WIDDOWS, Roland Hewlett, CB 1989; a Deputy Special Commissioner of Income Tax and Chairman (part-time) of Value Added Tax Tribunals, 1990–94; *b* 14 Aug. 1921; *s* of late A. E. Widdows, CB; *m* 1945, Diana Gweneth, *d* of late E. A. Dickson, Malayan Civil Service; two *s* one *d. Educ:* Stowe Sch.; Hertford Coll., Oxford (MA). Served in Royal Navy, Coastal Forces, 1941–45. Called to Bar, Middle Temple, 1948; entered Inland Revenue Solicitor's Office, 1951; Asst Solicitor, 1963; on staff of Law Commission, 1965–70; Lord Chancellor's Office, 1970–77; Under Secretary, 1972; Special Comr of Income Tax, 1977–90, Presiding Comr, 1984–90. *Recreations:* sailing, playing the clarinet. *Address:* 1 Chaucer Drive, Milford-on-Sea, Hants SO41 0SS. *T:* (01590) 644661. *Clubs:* Oxford and Cambridge; Royal Lymington Yacht.

WIDDOWS, Air Commodore (Stanley) Charles, CB 1959; DFC 1941 (despatches); RAF retired; People's Deputy, States of Guernsey, 1973–79; *b* 4 Oct. 1909; *s* of P. L. Widdows, Southend, Bradfield, Berkshire; *m* 1939, Irene Ethel, *d* of S. H. Rawlings, Ugley, Essex; two *s. Educ:* St Bartholomew's School, Newbury; No 1 School of Technical Training, RAF, Halton; Royal Air Force College, Cranwell. Commissioned, 1931; Fighting Area, RAF, 1931–32; RAF Middle East, Sudan and Palestine, 1933–37; Aeroplane and Armament Experimental Estab., 1937–40; OC 29 (Fighter) Sqdn, 1940–41; OC RAF West Malling, 1941–42; Gp Capt., Night Ops, HQ 11 and 12 Gp, 1942; SASO, No 85 (Base Defence) Gp, 1943–44, for Operation Overlord; Gp Capt. Organisation, HQ, Allied Expeditionary Air Force, 1944; OC, RAF Wahn, Germany, 1944–46; RAF Directing Staff, Sen. Officers War Course, RNC, Greenwich, 1946–48; Fighter Command, 1948–54: SASO HQ No 12 Gp; Chief Instructor, Air Defence Wing, School of Land/Air Warfare; Sector Commander, Eastern Sector. Imperial Defence College, 1955; Director of Operations (Air Defence), Air Ministry, 1956–58. Bailiwick Rep., RAF Benevolent Fund, 1973–93. Vice-Pres., Guernsey Scout Assoc., 1990– (Chm., 1974–90). *Address:* Les Granges de Beauvoir, Rohais, St Peter Port, Guernsey GY1 1QT. *T:* (01481) 720219.

WIDDOWSON, Prof. Henry George; Professor of English Linguistics, University of Vienna, since 1998; *b* 28 May 1935; *s* of George Percival Widdowson and Edna Widdowson; *m* 1st, 1966, Dominique Dixmier (marr. diss.); two *s*; 2nd, 1997, Barbara Seidlhofer. *Educ:* Alderman Newton's Sch., Leicester; King's Coll., Cambridge (MA); Univ. of Edinburgh (PhD). Lectr, Univ. of Indonesia, 1958–61; British Council Educn Officer, Sri Lanka, 1962–63; British Council English Language Officer, Bangladesh, 1963–64, 1965–68; Lectr, Dept of Linguistics, Univ. of Edinburgh, 1968–77; Prof. of Educn, Univ. of London, at Inst. of Educn, 1977–; Prof. of Applied Linguistics, Univ. of Essex, 1993–98. Chm., English Teaching Adv. Cttee, British Council, 1982–91; Mem., Kingman Cttee of Inquiry into Teaching of English Language, 1986–88. Editor, Jl of Applied Linguistics, 1980–85. Dr *hc* Oulu, 1994. *Publications:* Stylistics and the Teaching of Literature, 1975, Japanese edn 1989; Teaching Language as Communication, 1978, French edn 1981, Ital. edn 1982, Japanese edn 1991; Explorations in Applied Linguistics I, 1979; Learning Purpose and Language Use, 1983, Italian edn 1986; Explorations in Applied Linguistics II, 1984; (with Randolph Quirk) English in the World, 1985; Aspects of Language Teaching, 1990; Practical Stylistics, 1992; Linguistics, 1996; editor of series: English in Focus; Communicative Grammar; Language Teaching: a scheme for teacher education; Oxford Introductions to Language Study; papers in various jls. *Recreations:* poetry, bird-watching, walking. *Address:* Institut für Anglistik, Universität Wien, Universitätcampus AAKH/Hof 8, Spitalgasse 2–4, 1090 Vienna, Austria. *T:* (1) 427742441.

WIDDUP, Malcolm, CB 1979; retired 1981; Under-Secretary, HM Treasury, 1971–80; *b* 9 May 1920; *s* of John and Frances Ellen Widdup; *m* 1947, Margaret Ruth Anderson; one *s* one *d*. *Educ:* Giggleswick Sch.; Trinity Coll., Oxford (MA). Served War, Army, RA and Staff, 1940–45. Ministry of Food, 1946–53; HM Treasury, 1953–55; Cabinet Office, 1955–57; HM Treasury, 1957–60; Min. of Health, 1960–62; HM Treasury, 1962–66; UK Delegn to OECD, 1966–68; HM Treasury, 1968–80; Sen. Clerk, House of Lords, 1980–81. *Recreations:* gardening, bridge, bowling.

WIDE, Charles Thomas; QC 1995; **His Honour Judge Wide;** a Circuit Judge, since 2001; *b* 16 April 1951; *s* of Nicholas Scott Wide, MC, and Ruth Mildred Norton Wide; *m* 1979, Hon. Ursula Margaret Bridget Buchan, *qv*; one *s* one *d*. *Educ:* The Leys Sch., Cambridge; Exeter Univ. (LLB). Called to the Bar, Inner Temple, 1974; Midland and Oxford Circuit Junior, 1983; Standing Counsel to: HM Customs and Excise (Crime), 1989–95; Inland Revenue (Crime), 1991–95; Asst Recorder, 1991–95; Recorder, 1995–2001. *Recreation:* fell walking. *Address:* Law Courts, 60 Canal Street, Nottingham NG1 7EL. *Club:* Travellers.

WIDE, Hon. Ursula Margaret Bridget; *see* Buchan, Hon. U. M. B.

WIESCHAUS, Prof. Eric Francis, PhD; Professor of Molecular Biology, since 1987, and Squibb Professor, since 1993, Princeton University; *b* 8 June 1947; *s* of Leroy Wieschaus and Marcella Wieschaus (*née* Carner); *m* 1983, Trudi Schüpbach; three *d*. *Educ:* Univ. of Notre Dame, Indiana (BS 1969); Yale Univ. (PhD 1974); Univ. of Zürich. Postdoctoral Fellow, Zool. Inst., Univ. of Zürich, 1975–78; EMBO Fellowship, France, 1976; Vis. Researcher, Center of Pathology, Univ. of California, Irvine, 1977; Group Leader, EMBL, Heidelberg, 1978–81; Asst Prof., 1981–83, and Associate Prof., 1983–87, Princeton Univ. Fellow, Amer. Acad. of Arts and Scis; Mem., Nat. Acad. of Scis. Awards include: John Spangler Niclaus Prize, Yale, 1974; NIHHD Merit Award, 1989; Nobel Prize in Physiology or Medicine (jtly), 1995. *Publications:* From Molecular Patterns to Morphogenesis: the lessons from Drosophila, in the Nobel Prize 1995 (ed T. Fransmyr), 1996; numerous contribs to Jl of Cell Biology and other sci. jls. *Address:* Department of Molecular Biology, Princeton University, Washington Road, Princeton, NJ 08544, USA.

WIESEL, Prof. Elie; Andrew W. Mellon Professor in the Humanities and Professor of Religious Studies, Boston University, since 1976, Professor of Philosophy, since 1988; *b* 30 Sept. 1928; naturalised US citizen, 1963; *m* 1969, Marion Erster; one *s*, one step *d*. *Educ:* The Sorbonne, Univ. of Paris. Distinguished Prof. of Judaic Studies, City Coll., City Univ. of New York, 1972–76; Dist. Vis. Prof. of Literature and Philosophy, Florida Internat. Univ., 1982; Henry Luce Vis. Scholar in the Humanities and Social Thought, Whitney Humanities Center, Yale Univ., 1982–83. Founder and Pres., Elie Wiesel Foundn for Humanity, 1987. Chairman: US Holocaust Meml Council, 1980–86; US President's Commn on the Holocaust, 1979–80; Adv. Bd, World Union of Jewish Students, 1985–; Member, Board of Directors: Nat. Cttee on Amer. Foreign Policy, 1983– (Special Award, 1987); Internat. Rescue Cttee, 1985– (Internat. Vice Pres.); HUMANITAS; Member, Board of Trustees: Elaine Kaufman Cultural Center (formerly Hebrew Arts Sch.), 1980–; Amer. Jewish World Service, 1985–; Yeshiva Univ., 1977–; Member, Board of Governors: Tel-Aviv Univ., 1976 (Hon. Mem., 1988); Haifa Univ., 1977–. Fellow: Jewish Acad. of Arts and Sciences; Amer. Acad. of Arts and Sciences, 1986; Member: Amnesty Internat.; Writers Guild of America (East); Authors' Guild; Writers and Artists for Peace in ME; Royal Norwegian Soc. of Sciences and Letters, 1987; Hon. Life Mem., Foreign Press Assoc., 1960. Holds hon. degrees from univs and colls. Elie Wiesel Chair in Judaic Studies endowed at Connecticut Coll., 1990. Nobel Peace Prize, 1986; other awards include: Anatoly Shcharansky Humanitarian Award, 1983; US Congressional Gold Medal 1985; US Medal of Liberty Award, 1986; Achievement Award, Israel, 1987. Grand Cross: Légion d'Honneur (France), 2001 (Commandeur, 1984; Grand Officier, 1990); Order of the Southern Cross, Brazil, 1987. *Publications:* Night (memoir), 1960; The Jews of Silence (personal testimony), 1966; Legends of Our Time (essays and stories), 1968; One Generation After (essays and stories), 1970; Souls on Fire: portraits and legends of the Hasidic masters, 1972; Messengers of God: portraits and legends of Biblical heroes, 1976; A Jew Today (essays, stories and dialogues), 1978; Four Hasidic Masters, 1978; Images from the Bible, 1980; Le Testament d'un Poète Juif Assassiné, 1980 (Prix Livre-Inter, and Bourse Goncourt, France, 1980; Prix des Bibliothèquaires, France, 1981); Five Biblical Portraits, 1981; Paroles d'étranger (essays, stories and dialogues), 1982; Somewhere a Master, 1982; The Golem, 1983; Signes d'Exode (essays, stories and dialogues), 1985; Against Silence: the voice and vision of Elie Wiesel (collected shorter writings, ed Irving Abrahamson), 3 vols, 1985; Job ou Dieu dans la Tempête (dialogue and commentary with Josy Eisenberg), 1986; The Nobel Address, 1987; (with Albert Friedlander) The Six Days of Destruction, 1988; Silences et Mémoire d'hommes (essays), 1989; From the Kingdom of Memory (reminiscences), 1990; Evil and Exile (dialogues with Philippe-Michaël de Saint-Cheron), 1990; (with John Cardinal O'Connor) A Journey of Faith, 1990; Sages and Dreamers, 1991; Célébration talmudique, 1991; A Passover Haggadah (commentaries), 1993; Tout les Fleuves vont à la Mer (memoirs), vol. I, 1994, English trans., as All Rivers Run to the Sea, 1995; (with Jorge Semprun) Se taire est impossible, 1995; Et la mer n'est pas remplie (memoirs) vol. II, 1996, English trans., as And the Sea is Never Full, 1999; Memoir in Two Voices (with François Mitterrand), 1996; Célébration Prophétique, Portraits et légendes, 1998; King Soloman and His Magic Ring (for children), 1999; Le Mal et L'Exil, Dix ans après (dialogues with Michaël de Saint-Cheron), 1999; D'où viens-tu? (essays), 2001; *novels:* Dawn, 1961; The Accident, 1962; The Town beyond the Wall, 1964; The Gates of the Forest, 1966; A Beggar in Jerusalem, 1970; The Oath, 1973; The Testament, 1980; The Fifth Son, 1985 (Grand Prix de la Littérature, Paris); Twilight, 1988; L'Oublié, 1989 (The Forgotten, 1992); Les juges, 1999; *cantatas:* Ani Maamin, 1973; A Song for Hope, 1987; *plays:* Zalmen, or the Madness of God, 1974; The Trial of God, 1979. *Address:* Boston University, 745 Commonwealth Avenue, Boston, MA 02215, USA. *Clubs:* PEN, Lotos.

WIESEL, Prof. Torsten Nils, MD; Head of Laboratory of Neurobiology, since 1983, and President, since 1992, Rockefeller University; *b* 3 June 1924; *s* of Fritz S. Wiesel and Anna-Lisa Wiesel (*née* Bentzer); *m* 1st, 1956, Teeri Stenhammar (marr. diss. 1970); 2nd, 1973, Ann Yee (marr. diss. 1981); one *d*. *Educ:* Karolinska Inst., Stockholm (MD 1954). Instructor, Dept of Physiol., Karolinska Inst., 1954–55; Asst, Dept of Child Psychiatry, Karolinska Hosp., Stockholm, 1954–55; Fellow in Ophthalmol., 1955–58, Asst Prof. of Ophthalmic Physiol., 1958–59, Johns Hopkins Univ. Med. Sch., Baltimore; Harvard Medical School: Associate in Neurophysiol. and Neuropharmacol., 1959–60; Asst Prof., 1960–67; Prof. of Physiol., 1967–68; Prof. of Neurobiol., 1968–74; Chm., Dept of Neurobiol., 1973–82; Robert Winthrop Prof. of Neurobiol., 1974–83. Scientific Advr, Bristol Myers-Squibb Corp. Lectures: Ferrier, Royal Soc., 1972; Grass, Soc. for Neurosci., 1976. Member: Amer. Physiol Soc.; AAAS; Amer. Acad. of Arts and Scis; Amer. Philosophical Soc.; Soc. for Neurosci. (Pres. 1978–79); Nat. Acad. of Scis; Swedish Physiol Soc.; Harvard Bd of Overseers; Foreign Mem., Royal Soc., 1982; Hon. Mem., Physiolog. Soc., 1982. Has received hon. degrees from univs in Sweden, Norway, Italy and USA. Awards and Prizes: Dr Jules C. Stein, Trustees for Research to Prevent Blindness, 1971; Lewis S. Rosenstiel, Brandeis Univ., 1972; Friedenwald, Assoc. for Res. in Vision and Ophthalmology, 1975; Karl Spencer Lashley, Amer. Phil. Soc., 1977; Louisa Gross Horwitz, Columbia Univ., 1978; Dickson, Pittsburgh Univ., 1979; Ledlie, Harvard Univ., 1980; Soc. for Scholars, Johns Hopkins Univ., 1980; Nobel Prize in Physiology or Medicine, 1981. *Publications:* (contrib.) Physiological and Biochemical Aspects of Nervous Integration, 1968; (contrib.) The Organization of the Cerebral Cortex, 1981; contribs to professional jls, symposia and trans of learned socs. *Address:* Rockefeller University, 1230 York Avenue, New York, NY 10021–6399, USA. *T:* (212) 5707661. *Club:* Harvard (Boston).

WIGAN, Sir Michael (Iain), 6th Bt *cr* 1898, of Clare Lawn, Mortlake, Surrey and Purland Chase, Ross, Herefordshire; journalist and author; *b* 3 Oct. 1951; *s* of Sir Alan Lewis Wigan, 5th Bt, and of Robina, 2nd *d* of Sir Iain Colquhoun of Luss, 7th Bt, KT, DSO; *S* father, 1996; one *s* by Lady Alexandra Hay; *m* 1989, Julia Teresa, *d* of John de Courcy Ling, *qv*; three *s* one *d*. *Educ:* Eton; Exeter Coll., Oxford. *Publications:* The Scottish Highland Estate: preserving an environment, 1991; Stag at Bay, 1993; The Last of the Hunter Gatherers, 1998; Grimersta: the story of a great fishery, 2001. *Recreations:* deer stalking, fishing, literature. *Heir:* *s* Fergus Adam Wigan, *b* 30 April 1990. *Address:* Borrobol, Kinbrace, Sutherland KW11 6UB. *T:* (01431) 831264.

WIGDOR, Lucien Simon, CEng, FRAeS; President, L. S. Wigdor Inc., New Hampshire, since 1984; Managing Director, L. S. Wigdor Ltd, since 1976; *b* Oct. 1919; *s* of William and Adèle Wigdor; *m* 1951, Marion Louise, *d* of Henry Risner; one *s* one *d*. *Educ:* Highgate Sch.; College of Aeronautical Engineering (Dip. 1939). CEng 1989; FRAeS 2001. Served War, RAF, early helicopter pilot, 1940–46 (Sqn Ldr; FAI Helicopter Aviators Cert. No 10); Operational Research, BEA: Research Engr, 1947–51; Manager, Industrial and Corporate Develt, Boeing Vertol Corp., USA, 1951–55; Managing Dir, Tunnel Refineries Ltd, 1955–69, Vice-Chm., 1969–72; Corporate Consultant, The Boeing Company, 1960–72; Dep. Dir-Gen., CBI, 1972–76; Chief Exec., Leslie & Godwin (Holdings) Ltd, 1977–78, Dir 1977–81; Chm., Weir Pumps Ltd, 1978–81; Director: The Weir Group, 1978–81; Rothschild Investment Trust, 1977–82; Zambian Engineering Services Ltd, 1979–84; Rothschild Internat. Investments SA, 1981–82. Special Adviser on Internat. Affairs, Bayerische Hypotheken-SPTund Wechsel-SPTBank AG, 1981–83; Consultant: Lazard Bros, 1982–84; Manufacturing and Financial Services Industries (L. S. Wigdor Inc.), 1984–. *Publications:* papers to Royal Aeronautical Soc., American Helicopter Soc. *Recreations:* ski-ing, experimental engineering. *Address:* Indian Point, Little Sunapee Road, PO Box 1035, New London, NH 03257, USA. *T:* (603) 5264456, *Fax:* (603) 5264963. *Club:* Royal Air Force.

WIGGHAM, Hon. (Edward) Barrie, CBE 1991; JP; Hong Kong Commissioner, USA, 1993–97; *b* 1 March 1937; *s* of Edward and Agnes Wiggham; *m* 1961, Mavis Mitson; two *d* (one *s* decd). *Educ:* Woking Grammar Sch.; Queen's Coll., Oxford (MA Mod. Langs). Hong Kong Government: Admin. Officer, 1961–63; Dist Officer, New Territories, 1963–71; postings in finance, econ., security and information branches, 1971–79; Comr for Recreation and Culture, 1979–83; Regl Sec., 1983–86; seconded to British Embassy, Peking, 1986; Sec., General Duties, 1986–90; Mem. Gov's Exec. Council, 1989–92; Sec. for CS, 1990–93. JP Hong Kong, 1973. *Recreations:* music, people. *Address:* Bauhinia, Litlington, Polegate, E Sussex BN26 5RA. *Clubs:* Royal Commonwealth Society; Hong Kong, Foreign Correspondents, United Services (Hong Kong); George Town, National Press (Washington).

WIGGIN, Sir Alfred William, (Sir Jerry Wiggin), Kt 1993; TD 1970; *b* 24 Feb. 1937; *e s* of late Col Sir William H. Wiggin, KCB, DSO, TD, DL, JP, and late Lady Wiggin, Worcestershire; *m* 1st, 1964, Rosemary Janet (marr. diss. 1982), *d* of David L. D. Orr; two *s* one *d*; 2nd, 1991, Morella Bulmer (*née* Kearton). *Educ:* Eton; Trinity Coll., Cambridge. 2nd Lieut, Queen's Own Warwickshire and Worcestershire Yeomanry (TA), 1959; Major, Royal Yeomanry, 1975–78. Contested (C) Montgomeryshire, 1964 and 1966. MP (C) Weston-super-Mare, 1969–97. PPS to Lord Balniel, at MoD, later FCO, 1970–74, and to Ian Gilmour, MoD, 1971–72; Parly Sec., MAFF, 1979–81; Parly Under-Sec. of State for Armed Forces, MoD, 1981–83. Chm., Select Cttee on Agriculture, 1987–97. Jt Hon. Sec., Conservative Defence Cttee, 1974–75; Vice-Chm., Conservative Agricultural Cttee, 1975–79; Chm., West Country Cons. Gp, 1978–79; Pres., Wells Cons. Assoc., 2000–. Promoted Hallmarking Act, 1973. Chm., Economic Cttee, North Atlantic Assembly, 1990–94. Hon. Col, Warwickshire and Worcs Yeomanry (A) Sqn, Royal Mercian and Lancastrian Yeomanry, 1992–99. Mem. Ct of Assts, Goldsmiths' Co., 1995–. *Address:* The Court, Axbridge, Somerset BS26 2BN. *T:* (01934) 732527. *Clubs:* Beefsteak, Pratt's; Royal Yacht Squadron.

See also W. D. Wiggin.

WIGGIN, Maj. Sir Charles Rupert John, 5th Bt *cr* 1892, of Metchley Grange, Harborne, Staffs; *b* 2 July 1949; *s* of Sir John Wiggin, 4th Bt, MC and his 1st wife, Lady Cecilia Evelyn Anson (*d* 1963), *yr d* of 4th Earl of Lichfield; *S* father, 1992; *m* 1979, Mrs Mary Burnett-Hitchcock; one *s* one *d*. *Educ:* Eton. Major, Grenadier Guards. *Heir:* *s* Richard Edward John Wiggin, *b* 1 July 1980. *Address:* c/o Child & Co., 1 Fleet Street, EC4Y 1BD.

WIGGIN, Sir Jerry; *see* Wiggin, Sir A. W.

WIGGIN, William David; MP (C) Leominster, since 2001; *b* 4 June 1966; *s* of Sir A. W., (Jerry), Wiggin, *qv* and of Rosemary Janet (*née* Orr, now Dale Harris); *m* 1999, Camilla Chilvers. *Educ:* Eton; UCNW, Bangor (BA Hons Pure Econs). Trader: Rayner Coffee Internat., 1988–90; Mitsubishi Corp., 1990–91; Union Bank of Switzerland, 1991–94; Associate Dir, Dresdner Kleinwort Benson, 1994–98; Manager, Commerz Bank, 1998–2001. *Recreations:* motor bikes, diving. *Address:* House of Commons, SW1A 0AA. *Clubs:* Hurlingham, Annabel's.

WIGGINS, (Anthony) John; Member, Court of Auditors of the European Communities, 1993–2001; *b* 8 July 1938; *s* of late Rev. Arthur Wiggins and of Mavis Wiggins (*née* Brown); *m* 1962, Jennifer Anne Walkden; one *s* one *d*. *Educ:* Highgate Sch.; The Hotchkiss Sch., Lakeville, Conn, USA; Oriel Coll., Oxford (MA). Assistant Principal, HM Treasury, 1961; Private Sec. to Permanent Under Sec., Dept of Economic Affairs, 1964–66; Principal: Dept of Economic Affairs, 1966–67; HM Treasury, 1967–69; Harkness Fellow, Harvard Univ., 1969–71 (MPA 1970); Asst Sec., HM Treasury 1972–79; Principal Private Sec. to Chancellor of the Exchequer, 1980–81; Under Sec., Dept of Energy, 1981–84 (Mem. of BNOC, 1982–84); Under Sec., Cabinet Office, 1985–87; Under Sec., 1987–88, Dep. Sec., 1988–92, DES, subseq. DFE, on secondment to HM Treasury, 1992. Sec. to Royal Opera House Develt Bd, 1987–93 (Sec. to cttees, 1982–87). *Recreations:* mountaineering, skiing, opera.

WIGGINS, Bernard; novelist, as Bernard Cornwell, since 1980; *b* 23 Feb. 1944; *s* of Joseph and Margery Wiggins; *m* 1st, 1967, Lindsay Leworthy (marr. diss. 1976); one *d*; 2nd, 1980, Judy Cashdollar. *Educ:* Monkton Combe Sch.; London Univ. (BA ext.). Producer, BBC TV, 1970–76; Hd, Current Affairs TV, BBC NI, 1976–78; Ed., Thames TV News, 1978–80. *Publications:* Sharpe's Eagle, 1981; Sharpe's Gold, 1981; Sharpe's

Company, 1982; Sharpe's Sword, 1983; Sharpe's Enemy, 1984; Sharpe's Honour, 1985; Sharpe's Regiment, 1986; Sharpe's Siege, 1987; Redcoat, 1987; Sharpe's Rifles, 1988; Wildtrack, 1988; Sharpe's Revenge, 1989; Sea Lord, 1989; Sharpe's Waterloo, 1990; Crackdown, 1990; Stormchild, 1991; Sharpe's Devil, 1992; Scoundrel, 1992; Rebel, 1993; Copperhead, 1994; Sharpe's Battle, 1995; Battle Flag, 1995; The Winter King, 1995; The Bloody Ground, 1996; Enemy of God, 1996; Sharpe's Tiger, 1997; Excalibur, 1997; Sharpe's Triumph, 1998; Sharpe's Fortress, 1999; Stonehenge, 2000 BC, 1999; Sharpe's Trafalgar, 2000; Sharpe's Prey, 2001; The Gallows Thief, 2001. *Recreation:* sailing. *Address:* c/o Toby Eady Associates, 9 Orme Court, W2 4RL. *T:* (020) 7792 0092. *Club:* Stage Harbor Yacht (Chatham, Mass).

WIGGINS, Prof. David, FBA 1978; Wykeham Professor of Logic, and Fellow of New College, Oxford University, 1994–2000, now Emeritus Fellow; *b* 8 March 1933; *s* of late Norman Wiggins and Diana Wiggins (*née* Priestley); *m* 1979, Jennifer Hornsby. *Educ:* St Paul's Sch.; Brasenose Coll., Oxford. BA 1955; MA 1958. Asst Principal, Colonial Office, London 1957–58. Jane Eliza Procter Vis. Fellow, Princeton Univ., 1958–59; Lectr, 1959, then Fellow and Lecturer, 1960–67, New College, Oxford; Prof. of Philosophy, Bedford Coll., Univ. of London, 1967–80; Fellow and Praelector in Philosophy, University Coll., Oxford, 1981–89; Prof. of Philosophy, Birkbeck Coll., Univ. of London, 1989–94. Visiting appointments: Stanford, 1964 and 1965; Harvard, 1968 and 1972; All Souls College, 1973; Princeton, 1980; New York Univ., 1988; Fellow, Center for Advanced Study in the Behavioral Sciences, Stanford, 1985–86. Mem., Indep. Commn on Transport, 1973–74; Chm., Transport Users' Consultative Cttee for the South East, 1977–79. Pres., Aristotelian Soc., 1999–2000. Mem., Institut International de Philosophie. For. Hon. Mem., Amer. Acad. of Arts and Scis, 1992. *Publications:* Identity and Spatio–Temporal Continuity, 1967; Truth, Invention and the Meaning of Life, 1978; Sameness and Substance, 1980, 2nd 2001; Needs, Values, Truth: essays in the philosophy of value, 1986, 3rd edn 1998; philosophical articles in Philosophical Review, Analysis, Philosophy, Synthèse, Phil Qly, Ratio; articles on environmental and transport subjects in Spectator, Times, Tribune, and ed collections.

WIGGINS, John; *see* Wiggins, A. J.

WIGGINS, Rt Rev. Maxwell Lester; Bishop of Victoria Nyanza, 1963–76; retired; *b* 5 Feb. 1915; *s* of Herbert Lester and Isobel Jane Wiggins; *m* 1941, Margaret Agnes Evans (decd); one *s* two *d. Educ:* Christchurch Boys' High Sch., NZ; Canterbury University College, NZ (BA). Asst Curate, St Mary's, Merivale, NZ, 1938; Vicar of Oxford, NZ, 1941; CMS Missionary, Diocese Central Tanganyika, 1945; Head Master, Alliance Secondary Sch., Dodoma, 1948; Provost, Cathedral of Holy Spirit, Dodoma, 1949; Principal, St Philip's Theological Coll., and Canon of Cathedral of Holy Spirit, Dodoma, 1954; Archdeacon of Lake Province, 1956; Asst Bishop of Central Tanganyika, 1959; Asst Bishop of Wellington, 1976–81; Pres., NZ CMS, 1986–96 (Gen. Sec., 1982–83). Sen. ChLJ, 1982 96. *Address:* 42 Otara Street, Christchurch 5, New Zealand.

WIGGLESWORTH, Gordon Hardy, RIBA; Consultant, Alan Turner Associates, architects, planning and development consultants, 1988–92 (Director, 1984–88); *b* 27 June 1920; *m* 1952, Cherry Diana Heath; three *d. Educ:* Highgate; University Coll., London; Architectural Association. AADipl; RIBA 1948. Served War of 1939–45: Royal Engineers, 1941–46. Architectural Assoc., 1946–48; private practice and Univ. of Hong Kong, 1948–52; private practice: London, 1952–54; Hong Kong, 1954–56; London, 1956–57. Asst Chief Architect, Dept of Education and Science, 1957–67; Dir of Building Develt, MPBW, later DoE, 1967–72; Principal Architect, Educn, GLC (ILEA), 1972–74; Housing Architect, GLC, 1974–80. Vice-Pres., RIBA, 1980–81. FRSA 1983. *Address:* 53 Canonbury Park South, N1 2JL. *T:* (020) 7226 7734.

WIGGLESWORTH, Jack; Chairman, London International Financial Futures Exchange, 1995–98; *b* 9 Oct. 1941; *s* of Jack Wigglesworth and Gladys Maud Wigglesworth; *m* 1970, Carlota Josefina Paéz; one *s* one *d. Educ:* Jesus Coll., Oxford (MA). Gilt Desk Economist and Bond Salesman, Phillips & Drew, 1963–71; Gilt Desk Bond Salesman, 1971–86, Partner, 1973–86, W. Greenwell & Co.; London International Financial Futures and Options Exchange: Member: Founder Wkg Party, 1980–81; Steering Cttee, 1981–82; Dir, 1982–98; Designed Gilt Contract, 1982; Chm., Membership and Rules Cttee, 1988–92; Dep. Chm., 1992–95. Dir of Marketing, Citifutures Ltd, 1993–97; Chairman: ABN Amro Futures Ltd, 1997–99; CableNet Internat., 2001–. Director: Stace Barr Angerstein plc, 1997–2001; Clivia Ltd, 1998–; Capital Value Brokers Ltd, 1998–. Mem., London Stock Exchange, 1968–91; Director: Securities Inst., 1992–; Futures and Options Assoc., 1995–2000. Mem., Financial Services Adv. Gp, QCA, 1999–2001. Chm., Hackney Educn Action Zone, 1999–; Member: Business Sch. Council, London Guildhall Univ., 1998–; Council, Gresham Coll., 1999–. Hon. DSc City, 1998. *Recreations:* music, films, computers, gardening, boating. *Address:* 3 Deacons Heights, Elstree, Herts WD6 3QY. *T:* (020) 8953 8524. *Clubs:* Athenæum, Oxford and Cambridge, City of London.

WIGGLESWORTH, Mark Harmon; orchestral conductor; Music Director, BBC National Orchestra of Wales, 1996–2000; *b* 19 July 1964; *s* of Martin Wigglesworth and Angela (*née* Field). *Educ:* Bryanston Sch.; Manchester Univ. (BMus); Royal Acad. of Music. Winner, Kondrashin Comp., 1989. Founder and Music Dir, Première Ensemble, 1989–; Associate Conductor, BBC SO, 1991–93; Music Dir, Opera Factory, 1991–94; Prin. Guest Conductor, Swedish Radio SO, 1998–. *Address:* c/o Askonas Holt, Lonsdale Chambers, 27 Chancery Lane, WC2A 1PF. *T:* (020) 7400 1700.

WIGGLESWORTH, Raymond; QC 1999; a Recorder, since 1990; *b* 24 Dec. 1947; *s* of Kenneth Holt Wigglesworth and Marguerite (*née* Lonsdale); *m* 1982, Amanda Jane Littler; two *s* one *d. Educ:* Manchester Univ. (LLB). Called to the Bar, Gray's Inn, 1974; in practice on Northern Circuit, 1974–; Asst Recorder, 1987–90; Standing Counsel to HM Customs and Excise, 1995–99. *Recreations:* mountaineering, ski-ing, golf, sailing. *Address:* 18 St John Street, Manchester M3 4EA. *T:* (0161) 278 1800. *Club:* Wilmslow Golf.

WIGGLESWORTH, William Robert Brian; Director, Reedheath Ltd, since 1994; Joint Director, International Institute for Regulations in Telecommunications, Westminster University, since 1998 (City University, 1994–98); *b* 8 Aug. 1937; *s* of Sir Vincent Wigglesworth, CBE, FRS; *m* 1969, Susan Mary, *d* of late Arthur Baker, JP, Lavenham; one *s* one *d. Educ:* Marlborough; Magdalen College, Oxford (BA). Nat. Service, 2nd Lieut, Royal Signals, 1956–58. Ranks, Hovis McDougall Ltd, 1961–70: trainee; Gen. Manager, Mother's Pride Bakery, Cheltenham; PA to Group Chief Exec.; Gen. Manager, Baughans of Colchester; Board of Trade, 1970; Fair Trading Div., Dept of Prices and Consumer Protection, 1975; Posts and Telecommunications Div., 1978, Inf. Tech. Div., 1982, Dept of Industry; Dep. Dir Gen. of Telecommunications, 1984–94, Actg Dir, 1992–93. Prin. Advr, Telecoms Forum, Internat. Inst. of Communications, 1994–97; Mem. Bd, UKERNA, 1994–98. *Recreations:* fishing, gardening, history. *Address:* Millfield House, Heath Road, Polstead, Colchester CO6 5AN. *T:* (01787) 210590, *Fax:* (01787) 210592; *e-mail:* ww@reedheath.keme.co.uk.

WIGGS, (John) Samuel; His Honour Judge Wiggs; a Circuit Judge, Western Circuit, since 1995; Resident Judge, Bournemouth, since 1999; *b* 23 Nov. 1946; *s* of late Kenneth Ingram Wiggs and of Marjorie Ruth Wiggs (*née* Newton); *m* Elizabeth Jones (decd); *m* Kerry Martley; four *d. Educ:* Chigwell Sch.; Southampton Univ. (LLB). Called to the Bar, Middle Temple, 1970; Recorder, 1991. Chancellor, Dio. of Salisbury, 1997–. *Recreations:* playing the bassoon and organ, gardening, hill walking. *Address:* Courts of Justice, Deansleigh Road, Bournemouth, Dorset BH7 7DS. *T:* (01202) 502800, *Fax:* (01202) 502801.

WIGGS, Roger Sydney William Hale; Group Chief Executive, Securicor plc, 1996–2001, non-executive Director, since 2001; *b* 10 June 1939; *s* of Sydney Thomas Wiggs and Elizabeth Alice Wiggs (*née* Coomber); *m* 1963, Rosalind Anne Francis; four *s. Educ:* Tiffins Sch., Kingston upon Thames. Admitted Solicitor, 1962; Partner, Hextall, Erskine & Co., 1963–74; Overseas Dir, Securicor Ltd, 1974–80; Man. Dir, Securicor Internat. Ltd, 1980–89; Dir, 1977, Dep. Gp Chief Exec., 1985–88, Gp Chief Exec., 1988–96, Securicor Gp plc, and Security Services plc. *Recreations:* sport, particularly soccer, Rugby, motor racing. *Address:* c/o Securicor plc, Sutton Park House, 15 Carshalton Road, Sutton, Surrey SM1 4LD. *T:* (020) 8770 7000.

WIGGS, Samuel; *see* Wiggs, J. S.

WIGHT, Robin, CVO 2000; Chairman, WCRS, since 1987; *b* 6 July 1944; *s* of late Brig. I. L. Wight and of C. P. Wight; *m* 1st (marr. diss.); two *s* one *d*; 2nd (marr. diss.); one *s* one *d. Educ:* Wellington Coll.; St Catharine's Coll., Cambridge. Copywriter: Robert Sharp and Partners, 1966; CDP and Partners, 1967; Creative Director: Richard Cope and Partners, 1968; Euro Advertising, 1968; Creative Partner, Wight, Collins, Rutherford, Scott, 1979. Marketing Adviser to Rt Hon. Peter Walker, 1982–84. Chm., Duke of Edinburgh Award Charter for Business, 1992–. Mem. Council, Arts & Business (formerly ABSA), 1994– (Chm., 1997–). Contested (C) Bishop Auckland, 1987. *Publication:* The Day the Pigs Refused to be Driven to Market, 1972. *Recreations:* horseriding, oenology. *Address:* 6 Lewisham Street, SW1H 9AH.

WIGHTMAN, John Watt, CVO 1998; CBE 1986; RD; WS; Chairman, Craig & Rose plc, 1994–2000; Solicitor to the Queen in Scotland, 1983–99; *b* 20 Nov. 1933; *s* of Robert Johnson Wightman and Edith Wilkinson (*née* Laing); *m* 1962, Isla Fraser MacLeod; one *s* two *d. Educ:* Daniel Stewart's Coll.; Univ. of St. Andrews (MA); Univ. of Edinburgh (LLB). Partner, Morton Fraser, WS, 1961–99. Cdre, RNR, 1982–85; Chairman: Lowland TAVRA, 1992–95; Regl Adv. Cttee for S Scotland, Forestry Commn, 1998–. Dir, Earl Haig Fund Scotland, 2000–. *Recreations:* sailing, fishing, ornithology. *Address:* 10 Ann Street, Edinburgh EH4 1PJ. *T:* (0131) 332 6463. *Clubs:* Naval; Royal Scots (Edinburgh).

WIGHTMAN, Very Rev. William David; Provost of St Andrew's Cathedral, Aberdeen, since 1991; Priest in charge of St Ninian, Aberdeen, since 1991; *b* 29 Jan. 1939; *s* of William Osborne Wightman and Madge Wightman; *m* 1963, Karen Elizabeth Harker; two *s* two *d. Educ:* Alderman Newton's GS, Leicester; George Dixon GS, Birmingham; Univ. of Birmingham (BA Hons Theol.); Wells Theol Coll. Ordained deacon, 1963; priest, 1964; Curate: St Mary and All Saints, Rotherham, 1963–67; St Mary, Castlechurch, Stafford, 1967–70; Vicar: St Aidan, Buttershaw, Bradford, 1970–76; St John the Evangelist, Cullingworth, Bradford, 1976–83; Rector: St Peter, Peterhead, 1983–91; St John Longside, St Drostan, Old Deer and All Saints, Strichen, 1990–91; Chaplain, HM Prison, Peterhead, 1989–91; Dir, Training for Ministry, Dio. of Aberdeen and Orkney, 1989–94. Hon. Canon, Christ Church Cathedral, Hartford, Conn, USA, 1991. *Recreations:* fishing, choral music, swimming, gardening. *Address:* 15 Morningfield Road, Aberdeen AB15 4AP. *T:* (01224) 314765.

WIGHTWICK, Charles Christopher Brooke, MA; educational consultant, since 1991; *b* 16 Aug. 1931; *s* of Charles Frederick Wightwick and Marion Frances Wightwick (*née* Smith); *m* 1st, 1955, Pamela Layzell (marr. diss. 1986); one *s* two *d*; 2nd, 1986, Gillian Rosemary Anderson (*née* Dalziel). *Educ:* St Michael's, Otford Court; Lancing Coll.; St Edmund Hall, Oxford. BA 1954, MA 1958. Asst Master, Hurstpierpoint Coll., 1954–59; Head of German, Denstone Coll., 1959–65; Head of Languages, then Director of Studies, Westminster Sch., 1965–75; Head Master, King's College Sch., Wimbledon, 1975–80; HM Inspector of Schs, 1980–91; Staff Inspector for Mod. Langs, 1988–91. Series Editor, Berlitz Language Reference Handbooks, 1992–. *Publications:* (co-author) Longman Audio-Lingual German, 3 vols., 1974–78; German Grammar Handbook, 1993. *Recreations:* photography, computer programming, running, judo, language learning. *Address:* 19 Nottingham Road, SW17 7EA. *T:* (020) 8767 6161.

WIGLEY, Rt Hon. Dafydd; PC 1997; Member (Plaid Cymru) Caernarfon, National Assembly for Wales, since 1999; industrial economist; *b* 1 April 1943; *s* of Elfyn Edward Wigley, former County Treasurer, Caernarfonshire CC; *m* 1967, Elinor Bennett (*née* Owen), *d* of late Emrys Bennett Owen, Dolgellau; one *s* one *d* (and two *s* decd). *Educ:* Caernarfon Grammar Sch.; Rydal Sch., Colwyn Bay; Manchester Univ. Ford Motor Co., 1964–67; Chief Cost Accountant and Financial Planning Manager, Mars Ltd, 1967–71; Financial Controller, Hoover Ltd, Merthyr Tydfil, 1971–74. Mem., Merthyr Tydfil Borough Council, 1972–74. MP (Plaid Cymru) Caernarfon, Feb. 1974–2001. Mem., Select Cttee on Welsh Affairs, 1983–87. Vice-Chairman: Parly Social Services Gp, 1985–88; All-Party Disablement Gp, 1992–2001; British-Slovene Parly Gp, 1993–2001; Mem., Standing Cttee on Eur. Legislation, 1991–96. Sponsor, Disabled Persons Act, 1981. Pres., Plaid Cymru, 1981–84 and 1991–2000; Leader, Plaid Cymru, Nat. Assembly for Wales, 1999–2000. Contested (Plaid Cymru), N Wales, Eur. Parly elecns, 1994. Vice-Pres., Nat. Fedn of Industrial Develt Authorities, 1981–. Mem., Nat. Cttee for Electoral Reform. Pres., Spastic Soc. of Wales, 1985–90. Pres. (unpaid), S Caernarfonshire Creamery. Fellow, UCNW, Bangor, 1994. *Publications:* An Economic Plan for Wales, 1970; O Ddifri, 1992; Dal Ati, 1993; A Democratic Wales in a United Europe, 1995; A Real Choice for Wales, 1996. *Address:* National Assembly for Wales, Cardiff Bay, Cardiff CF99 1NA.

WIGMORE, His Honour James Arthur Joseph; a Circuit Judge, 1990–2001; *b* 7 Aug. 1928; *s* of Sqdn-Ldr Arthur J. O. Wigmore, MB, and Kathleen (*née* Jowett); *m* 1966, Diana, *d* of Comdr H. J. Holemans, RN; three *d. Educ:* Downside Sch.; Royal Military Acad., Sandhurst; English Coll., Rome. BSc London; PhL, STL, Gregorian Univ., Rome. Served Royal Signals, 1946–52, commnd 1948. Lectured in Philosophy: Downside Abbey, 1960 63; Oscott Coll., 1963–66. Called to the Bar, Inner Temple, 1971; Dep. Coroner, Bristol, 1976–88; a Recorder, 1989. *Club:* Naval and Military.

WIGODER, family name of **Baron Wigoder**.

WIGODER, Baron *cr* 1974 (Life Peer), of Cheetham in the City of Manchester; **Basil Thomas Wigoder;** QC 1966; Vice-President, British United Provident Association, since 1992 (Chairman, 1981–92); *b* 12 Feb. 1921; *s* of late Dr P. I. Wigoder and Mrs R. R. Wigoder, JP, Manchester; *m* 1948, Yoland Levinson; three *s* one *d* (of whom one *s* one *d* are twins). *Educ:* Manchester Gram. Sch.; Oriel Coll., Oxford (Open Scholar, Mod.

Hist.; MA 1946). Served RA, 1942–45. Pres. Oxford Union, 1946. Called to Bar, Gray's Inn, 1946, Master of the Bench, 1972, Vice-Treas., 1988, Treas., 1989. A Recorder of the Crown Court, 1972–84. BoT Inspector, Pinnock Finance (GB) Ltd, 1967. Member: Council of Justice, 1960–; Gen. Council of the Bar, 1970–74; Crown Court Rules Cttee, 1971–77; Council on Tribunals, 1980–86; Home Office Adv. Cttee on Service Candidates, 1984–; Chm., Health Services Bd, 1977–80; a Tribunal Chm., Securities Assoc., 1988–92. Chm., Liberal Party Exec., 1963–65; Chm., Liberal Party Organising Cttee, 1965–66; Liberal Chief Whip, House of Lords, 1977–84 (Dep. Whip, 1976–77). Contested (L): Bournemouth, 1945 and by-election, Oct. 1945; Westbury, 1959 and 1964. Vice-President: Nuffield Hosps, 1981–92; Statute Law Soc., 1984–90; Mem. Court, Nene Coll., 1982–90; Trustee, Oxford Union Soc., 1982–92. *Recreations:* cricket, music. *Address:* House of Lords, SW1A 0PW. *Clubs:* National Liberal, MCC.

WIGRAM, family name of **Baron Wigram**.

WIGRAM, 2nd Baron *cr* 1935, of Clewer; **George Neville Clive Wigram,** MC 1945; JP; DL; *b* 2 Aug. 1915; *s* of Clive, 1st Baron Wigram, PC, GCB, GCVO, CSI, and Nora Mary (*d* 1956), *d* of Sir Neville Chamberlain, KCB, KCVO; *S* father, 1960; *m* 1941, Margaret Helen (*d* 1986), *yr d* of late General Sir Andrew Thorne, KCB, CMG, DSO; one *s* two *d*. *Educ:* Winchester and Magdalen College, Oxford. Page of Honour to HM King George V, 1925–32; served in Grenadier Guards, 1937–57: Military Secretary and Comptroller to Governor-General of New Zealand, 1946–49; commanded 1st Bn Grenadier Guards, 1955–56. Governor of Westminster Hospital, 1967–74. JP Gloucestershire, 1959, DL 1969. *Heir: s* Major Hon. Andrew (Francis Clive) Wigram, MVO, late Grenadier Guards [*b* 18 March 1949; *m* 1974, Gabrielle Diana, *y d* of late R. D. Moore; three *s* one *d*]. *Address:* Poulton Fields, Cirencester, Gloucestershire GL7 5SS. *T:* (01285) 851250. *Club:* Cavalry and Guards.

See also Sir E. J. Webb-Carter.

WIGRAM, Major Sir (Edward) Robert (Woolmore), 8th Bt *cr* 1805, of Walthamstow, Essex; *b* 19 July 1913; *yr s* of Robert Ainger Wigram and Evelyn Dorothy (*née* Henslowe); *S* brother, 2000; *m* 1944, Viva Ann (*d* 1997), *d* of Douglas Bailey; one *d*. *Educ:* Winchester; Trinity Coll., Cambridge (BA 1934). Attached 2nd Bn S Staffordshire Regt, Bangalore, 1935; Major, 19th KGO Lancers, Lahore, 1938. Former master, Westminster Sch. *Heir: cousin* John Woolmore Wigram [*b* 25 May 1957; *m* 1996, Sally Winnington; two *s*]. *Address:* 1 Skipster Hagg, Sinnington, York YO62 7SP.

WIIN-NIELSEN, Aksel Christopher, Fil.Dr; Professor, Geophysical Institute, University of Copenhagen, 1988–94, now Emeritus; *b* 17 Dec. 1924; *s* of Aage Nielsen and Marie Petre (*née* Kristoffersen); *m* 1953, Bente Havsteen (*née* Zimsen); three *d*. *Educ:* Univ of Copenhagen (MSc 1950); Univ. of Stockholm (Fil.Lic. 1957; Fil.Dr 1960). Danish Meteorol Inst., 1952–55; Staff Member: Internat. Meteorol Inst., Stockholm, 1955–58; Jt Numerical Weather Prediction Unit, Suitland, Md, USA, 1959–61; Asst Dir, Nat. Center for Atmospherical Research, Boulder, Colorado, 1961–63; Prof., Dept of Atmospheric and Oceanic Sci., Univ. of Michigan, 1963–73; Dir, European Centre for Medium-Range Weather Forecasts, Reading, 1974–79; Sec.-Gen., WMO, 1980–83; Dir, Danish Meteorol Office, 1984–87. Pres., European Geophysical Soc., 1988–90; Vice-Pres., Danish Acad. of Technical Scis, 1989–92 (Mem., 1984–); Member: Finnish Acad. of Arts and Scis; Royal Swedish Acad. of Sci.; Danish Royal Soc., 1986–; Hon. Member: RMetS; Amer. Meteorol Soc., 1994; European Geophysical Soc., 1998. Hon. DSc: Reading, 1982; Copenhagen, 1986. Buys Ballot Medal, Royal Netherlands Acad., 1982; Wihuri Internat. Prize, Finland, 1983; Rossby Prize, Sweden, 1987; Friedman Rescue Award, Friedman Foundn, Calif., 1993. *Publications:* Dynamic Meteorology, 1970; Predictability, 1987; Fundamentals of Atmospheric Energetics, 1993; over 100 scientific publications. *Address:* C. F. Richs Vej 101A, 2000 Frederiksberg, Denmark.

WILBERFORCE, family name of **Baron Wilberforce**.

WILBERFORCE, Baron *cr* 1964 (Life Peer); **Richard Orme Wilberforce;** PC 1964; Kt 1961; CMG 1956; OBE 1944; a Lord of Appeal in Ordinary, 1964–82; Fellow, All Souls College, Oxford, since 1932; *b* 11 Mar. 1907; *s* of late S. Wilberforce; *m* 1947, Yvette, *d* of Roger Lenoan, Judge of Court of Cassation, France; one *s* one *d*. *Educ:* Winchester; New College, Oxford. Called to the Bar, 1932; served War, 1939–46 (Hon. Brig.); Under Sec., Control Office Germany and Austria, 1946–47; returned to Bar, 1947; QC 1954; Judge of the High Court of Justice (Chancery Division), 1961–64; Bencher, Middle Temple, 1961. Chm. Exec. Council, Internat. Law Assoc., 1966–88; Mem., Permanent Court of Arbitration; President: Fédération Internationale du Droit Européen, 1978; Appeal Tribunal, Lloyd's of London, 1983–87. Jt Pres., Anti-Slavery Soc.; Vice-President: (jt) RCM; David Davies Meml Inst. Chancellor, Univ. of Hull, 1978–94; University of Oxford: High Steward, 1967–90; Visitor: Wolfson Coll., 1974–90; Linacre Coll., 1983–90; Hon. Fellow: New Coll., 1965; Wolfson Coll., 1991. Hon. FRCM. Hon. Comp. Royal Aeronautical Society. Hon. Mem., Scottish Faculty of Advocates, 1978. Hon. DCL Oxon, 1968; Hon. LLD: London, 1972; Hull, 1973; Bristol, 1983. Diplôme d'Honneur, Corp. des Vignerons de Champagne. US Bronze Star, 1944; Grand Cross, St Jean de Penafort (Spain), 1970. *Publications:* The Law of Restrictive Trade Practices, 1956; articles and pamphlets on Air Law and International Law. *Recreations:* the turf, travel, opera. *Address:* House of Lords, SW1A 0PW. *Club:* Athenæum.

WILBRAHAM; *see* Bootle-Wilbraham, family name of Baron Skelmersdale.

WILBRAHAM, Sir Richard B.; *see* Baker Wilbraham.

WILBY, David Christopher; QC 1998; a Recorder, since 2000; *b* 14 June 1952; *s* of Alan and June Wilby; *m* 1976, Susan Arding; one *s* three *d*. *Educ:* Roundhay Sch., Leeds; Downing Coll., Cambridge (MA). Called to the Bar, Inner Temple, 1974; Mem., North Eastern Circuit. Member: Exec. Cttee, Professional Negligence Bar Assoc., 1995–; Bar Council, 1996–99; Chm., Bar Conf., 2000. Mem., Commonwealth Lawyers Assoc., 1995; Associate Mem., American Bar Assoc., 1996. Editor: Professional Negligence and Liability Law Reports, 1995–; Professional Negligence Key Cases, 1999–. *Recreations:* golf, Rugby, Association Football. *Address:* 1 Verulam Buildings, Gray's Inn, WC1R 5LQ. *T:* (020) 7269 0300; Park Lane Chambers, 19 Westgate, Leeds LS1 2RD. *T:* (0113) 228 5000. *Clubs:* Headingley Taverners; Pannal Golf; Harrogate Rugby Union Football.

WILBY, Peter John; Editor, New Statesman, since 1998; *b* 7 Nov. 1944; *s* of Lawrence Edward Wilby and Emily Lavinia Wilby; *m* 1967, Sandra James; two *s*. *Educ:* Kibworth Beauchamp Grammar Sch., Leics; Univ. of Sussex (BA Hons). Reporter, Observer, 1968–72; Education Correspondent: Observer, 1972–75; New Statesman, 1975–77; Sunday Times, 1977–86; Educn Editor, Independent, 1986–89; Independent on Sunday: Home Editor, 1990–91; Dep. Editor, 1991–95; Editor, 1995–96; Books Editor, New Statesman, 1997–98. *Publications:* Parent's Rights, 1983; Sunday Times Good University Guide, 1984; Sunday Times Good Careers Guide, 1985; (ed with Henry Pluckrose): The Condition of English Schooling, 1981; Education 2000, 1982. *Recreations:* reading, cooking, lunching. *Address:* 51 Queens Road, Loughton, Essex IG10 1RR.

WILCOCK, Christopher Camplin, CB 1997; Director, Financial Advisory Services, PricewaterhouseCoopers (formerly Price Waterhouse), 1997–99; *b* 13 Sept. 1939; *s* of late Arthur Camplin Wilcock and Dorothy (*née* Haigh); *m* 1965, Evelyn Clare Gollin; two *d*. *Educ:* Berkhamsted and Ipswich Schs; Trinity Hall, Cambridge (BA 1st Cl. Hons; MA). FO, 1962–63; MECAS, 1963–64; 3rd Sec., Khartoum, 1964–66; FO, 1966–68; 2nd Sec., UK Delegn to NATO, 1968–70; FO, 1970–72; Hosp. Bldg Div., DHSS, 1972–74; Petroleum Prodn, subseq. Continental Shelf Policy Div., Dept of Energy, 1974–78, Asst Sec. 1976; Electricity Div., 1978–81; on secondment to Shell UK Ltd, 1982–83; Department of Energy, subseq. of Trade and Industry: Hd of Finance Br., 1984–86; Dir of Resource Management (Grade 4), 1986–88; Grade 3, 1988; Hd of Electricity Div. A, 1988–91; Hd of Electricity Div., 1991–94; Hd of Electricity and Nuclear Fuels Div., 1994–95; Hd of Nuclear Power Privatization Team, 1995–96. Order of the Two Niles, Fifth Cl. (Sudan), 1965. *Recreations:* reading, history, cinema. *Address:* 22 Luttrell Avenue, SW15 6PF.

WILCOCK, Prof. William Leslie; consultant in industrial instrumentation; Professor of Physics, University College of North Wales, Bangor, 1965–82, now Emeritus; *b* 7 July 1922. *Educ:* Manchester Univ. (BSc, PhD). Instrument Dept, RAE, 1943–45. Asst Lectr in Physics, 1945–48, Lectr, 1950–56, Manchester Univ.; DSIR Res. Fellow, St Andrews Univ., 1948–50; Reader in Instrument Technol., 1956–61, in Applied Physics, 1961–65, Imperial Coll. of Science and Technology, London. Arnold O. Beckman Award, Instrument Soc. of Amer., 1977. Mem., SERC, 1981–85. *Publications:* (contrib.) Principles of Optics, 1959; Advances in Electronics and Electron Physics, vols 12–16 (ed jtly), 1960–61; numerous papers in scientific jls. *Address:* 3 Garth Court, Llandudno LL30 2HF.

WILCOX, Baroness *cr* 1995 (Life Peer), of Plymouth in the County of Devon; **Judith Ann Wilcox;** Director, Cadbury Schweppes plc, since 1997; *d* of John and Elsie Freeman; *m* 1st, 1961, Keith Davenport; one *s*; 2nd, 1986, Sir Malcolm George Wilcox, CBE (*d* 1986). *Educ:* St Dunstan's Abbey, Devon; St Mary's Convent, Wantage; Plymouth Polytechnic. Management of family business, Devon, 1969–79; Financial Dir, Capstan Foods, Devon, 1979–84; Chm., Channel Foods, Cornwall, 1984–89; Pres. Dir Gen., Pecheries de la Morinie, France, 1989–91; Chm., Morinie et Cie, France, 1991–94. Chm., Nat. Consumer Council, 1990–96; Comr, Local Govt Commn, 1992–95; Mem., Prime Minister's Adv. Panel to Citizen's Charter Unit, 1992–97; Chm., Citizen's Charter Complaints Task Force, 1993–95. Board Member: AA, 1991–; Inland Revenue, 1992–95; PLA, 1993– (Vice-Chm., 2000–); non-exec. Dir, Carpetright plc, 1997–. Chairman: All Party Parly Gp for Consumer Affairs and Trading Standards; H of L Sci. Select Cttee Enquiry into Aircraft Cabin Envmt, 2000–01; Member: H of L European Select Cttee, Envmt, Public Health and Consumer Affairs, 1996–; Lord Chancellor's Review of Court of Appeal, 1996–; Tax Law Review Cttee. President: NFCG; Inst. of Trading Standards Admin; Mem., Governing Body, Inst. of Food Res. Vice-Pres., Guide Assoc. Gov., Plymouth Univ. FRSA. *Recreations:* sailing, flyfishing, calligraphy. *Address:* House of Lords, SW1A 0PW. *Club:* St Mawes Sailing.

WILCOX, Albert Frederick, CBE 1967; QPM 1957; Chief Constable of Hertfordshire, 1947–69, retired; *b* 18 April 1909; *s* of late Albert Clement Wilcox, Ashley Hill, Bristol; *m* 1939, Ethel, *d* of late E. H. W. Wilmott, Manor House, Whitchurch, Bristol; one *s* two *d*. *Educ:* Fairfield Grammar School, Bristol. Joined Bristol City Police, 1929; Hendon Police Coll., 1934; Metropolitan Police, 1934–43. Served Allied Mil. Govt, Italy and Austria (Lt-Col), 1943–46. Asst Chief Constable of Buckinghamshire, 1946. Cropwood Fellowship, Inst. of Criminology, Cambridge, 1969. Pres. Assoc. of Chief Police Officers, Eng. and Wales, 1966–67; Chm. of Management Cttee, Police Dependents' Trust, 1967–69. Regional Police Commander (designate), 1962–69. Member, Parole Board, 1970–73. Criminological Res. Fellowship, Council of Europe, 1974–76. Barrister-at-Law, Gray's Inn, 1941. *Publication:* The Decision to Prosecute, 1972. *Address:* 34 Roundwood Park, Harpenden, Herts AL5 3AF.

WILCOX, David John Reed; His Honour Judge David Wilcox; a Judge of the Technology and Construction Court of the High Court, since 1998; *b* 8 March 1939; *s* of Leslie Leonard Kennedy Wilcox and Margaret Ada Reed Wilcox (*née* Rapson); *m* 1962, Wendy Feay Christine Whiteley; one *s* one *d*. *Educ:* Wednesbury Boys' High Sch.; King's Coll., London (LLB Hons). Called to the Bar, Gray's Inn, 1962. Directorate, Army Legal Services (Captain): Legal Staff, 1962–63; Legal Aid, Far East Land Forces, Singapore, 1963–65. Crown Counsel, Hong Kong, 1965–68; Member, Hong Kong Bar, 1968; in practice, Midland and Midland and Oxford Circuits, 1968–85; a Recorder of the Crown Court, 1979–85; a Circuit Judge, 1985–98; an Official Referee, 1996–98. Resident Judge, Great Grimsby Combined Court Centre, 1989–94; County Court Judge: Lincs and S Humberside, 1989–94; Birmingham, 1994–96; Care Judge, Birmingham, 1994–96. Lord Chancellor's Rep., Humberside Probation Cttee, 1989–94. Chm., Nottingham Friendship Housing Assoc., 1970–75. *Recreations:* reading, gardening, travel. *Address:* St Dunstan's House, 133–137 Fetter Lane, EC4A 1HD.

WILCOX, Rt Rev. David Peter; an Assistant Bishop, diocese of Chichester, since 1995; *b* 29 June 1930; *s* of John Wilcox and Stella Wilcox (*née* Bower); *m* 1956, Pamela Ann Hedges; two *s* two *d*. *Educ:* Northampton Grammar School; St John's Coll., Oxford (MA); Lincoln Theological Coll. Deacon 1954, priest 1955; Asst Curate, St Peter's, St Helier, Morden, Surrey, 1954–56; Asst Curate, University Church, Oxford and SCM Staff Secretary in Oxford, 1956–59; on staff of Lincoln Theological Coll., 1959–64; USPG Missionary on staff of United Theological Coll., Bangalore, and Presbyter in Church of S India, 1964–70; Vicar of Great Gransden with Little Gransden, dio. Ely, 1970–72; Canon Residentiary, Derby Cathedral and Warden, E Midlands Joint Ordination Training Scheme, 1972–77; Principal of Ripon College, Cuddesdon and Vicar of All Saints', Cuddesdon, 1977–85; Bishop Suffragan of Dorking, 1986–95. Chm. of Govs, St Mary's Sch., Bexhill-on-Sea. *Recreations:* walking, music, art. *Address:* 4 The Court, Hoo Gardens, Willingdon, Eastbourne BN20 9AX. *T:* (01323) 506108.

WILCOX, Esther Louise, (Mrs Desmond Wilcox); *see* Rantzen, E. L.

WILD, Dr David; Director of Public Health, South West Thames Regional Health Authority, 1989–90, retired; *b* 27 Jan. 1930; *s* of Frederick and Lena Wild; *m* 1954, Dr Sheila Wightman; one *s* one *d*. *Educ:* Manchester Grammar Sch.; Univ. of Manchester (MB, ChB); Univ. of Liverpool (DPH; FFCM, DMA). Deputy County Medical Officer, 1962, Area Medical Officer, 1974, West Sussex; Regional MO, 1982–86, Dir of Prof. Services, 1986–89, SW Thames RHA. Non-exec. Dir, Worthing DHA, 1990–95. Dir, Inf. Unit for Conf. of Med. Royal Colls and their Faculties in UK, 1991–93. Editor (with Dr Brian Williams), Community Medicine, 1978–84. *Publications:* contribs Jl Central Council of Health Educn, Medical Officer, Archives of Disease in Childhood. *Recreation:* conversation. *Address:* 16 Brandy Hole Lane, Chichester, Sussex PO19 4RY. *T:* (01243) 527125.

WILD, His Honour David Humphrey; a Circuit Judge, 1972–92; *b* 24 May 1927; *s* of John S. Wild and Edith Lemarchand; *m* 1963, Estelle Grace Prowett, *d* of James Marshall, Aberdeen and Malaya; one *s*. *Educ:* Whitgift Middle Sch., Croydon. Served War of

1939–45, Royal Navy, 1944–48. Called to Bar, Middle Temple, 1951. Practised, London and SE Circuit, 1951–58, Midland Circuit, 1958–72; resident judge, Cambridge Crown Court, 1973–84. Councillor, Oundle and Thrapston RDC, 1968–72. Mem., St Catharine's Coll., Cambridge, 1973. *Publication:* The Law of Hire Purchase, 1960 (2nd edn, 1964). *Clubs:* Naval and Military, Savile, Sette of Odd Volumes.

WILD, Dr (John) Paul, AC 1986; CBE 1978; FRS 1970; FAA 1962; FTS 1978; Chairman and Chief Executive, Commonwealth Scientific and Industrial Research Organization, 1978–85 (Associate Member of Executive, 1977; Chief, Division of Radiophysics, 1971); *b* 1923; *s* of late Alwyn Howard Wild and late Bessie Delafield (*née* Arnold); *m* 1st, 1948, Elaine Poole Hull (*d* 1991); two *s* one *d*, 2nd, 1991, Margaret Lyndon. *Educ:* Whitgift Sch.; Peterhouse, Cambridge (Hon. Fellow 1982). ScD 1962. Radar Officer in Royal Navy, 1943–47; joined Research Staff of Div. of Radiophysics, 1947, working on problems in radio astronomy, esp. of the sun, later also radio navigation (Interscan aircraft landing system). Dep. Chm., 1973–75, 1980–82, Chm., 1975–80, Anglo-Australian Telescope Bd; Mem. Bd, Interscan (Australia) Pty Ltd, 1978–84. For. Hon. Mem., Amer. Acad. of Arts and Scis, 1961; For. Mem., Amer. Philos. Soc., 1962; Corresp. Mem., Royal Soc. of Scis, Liège, 1969; For. Sec., Australian Acad. of Science, 1973–77. Hon. FIE(Aust), 1991; Hon. FRSA 1991. Hon. DSc: ANU, 1979; Newcastle (NSW), 1982. Edgeworth David Medal, 1958; Hendryk Arctowski Gold Medal, US Nat. Acad. of Scis, 1969; Balthasar van der Pol Gold Medal, Internat. Union of Radio Science, 1969; 1st Herschel Medal, RAS, 1974; Thomas Ranken Lyle Medal, Aust. Acad. of Science, 1975; Royal Medal, Royal Soc., 1980; Hale Medal, Amer. Astronomical Soc., 1980; ANZAAS Medal, 1984; Hartnett Medal, RSA, 1988. *Publications:* numerous research papers and reviews on radio astronomy in scientific jls. *Address:* (Dec.–March) 4/1 Grant Crescent, Griffith, ACT 2603, Australia; (April–Nov.) 800 Avon Road, Ann Arbor, MI 48104, USA.

WILD, (John) Robin; JP; Chief Dental Officer, Department of Health, 1997–2000; *b* 12 Sept. 1941; *s* of John Edward Brooke Wild and Teresa (*née* Ballance); *m* 1965, Eleanor Daphne Kerr; one *s* two *d*. *Educ:* Sedbergh Sch., Cumbria; Edinburgh Univ. (BDS); Dundee Univ. (DPD). DGDP RCS; FDS RCSE. Dental practice, 1965–71; Dental Officer, E Lothian CC, 1971–74; Chief Admin. Dental Officer, Borders Health Bd, 1974–87; Regl Dental Postgrad. Advr, SE Scotland, 1982–87; Dep. Chief Dental Officer, Scottish Office, 1987–93; Chief Dental Officer and Dir of Dental Services, NHS, Scottish Office, 1993–97. Pres., Council of European Chief Dental Officers, 1999–2000; Vice Pres., Commonwealth Dental Assoc., 1997–. JP Scottish Borders, 1982; Chm. Scottish Borders Justices Cttee, 2000–. *Publications:* contribs to Scottish Office Health Bulletin. *Address:* Braehead House, St Boswells, Roxburghshire TD6 0AZ. *T:* (01835) 823203. *Clubs:* Royal Commonwealth Society; Royal Scottish Automobile (Glasgow).

WILD, John Vernon, CMG 1960; OBE 1955; Colonial Administrative Service, retired; *b* 26 April 1915; *m* 1st, 1942, Margaret Patricia Rendell (*d* 1975); one *d* (one *s* decd); 2nd, 1976, Marjorie Mary Lovatt Robertson. *Educ:* Taunton School; King's College, Cambridge. Senior Optime, Cambridge Univ., 1937; Cricket Blue, 1938. Colonial Administrative Service, Uganda: Assistant District Officer, 1938; Assistant Chief Secretary, 1950; Establishment Secretary, 1951; Administrative Secretary, 1955–60; Chairman, Constitutional Committee, 1959. Teacher and Lectr in Mathematics, 1960–76. *Publications:* The Story of the Uganda Agreement; The Uganda Mutiny; Early Travellers in Acholi. *Recreations:* golf, gardening. *Address:* Maplestone Farm, Brede, near Rye, East Sussex TN31 6EP. *T:* (01424) 882261. *Clubs:* Hawks (Cambridge); Rye Golf.

WILD, Paul; *see* Wild, J. P.

WILD, Prof. Raymond, DSc, PhD; CEng, FIMechE, FIEE; Principal, Henley Management College, 1990–2001; *b* 24 Dec. 1940; *s* of Alice Wild and Frank Wild; *m* 1965, Carol Ann Mellor; one *s* one *d*. *Educ:* Stockport College; Bradford University (PhD (Management), MSc (Eng), MSc (Management)). DSc Brunel, 1988; WhF. Engineering apprentice, Crossley Bros, 1957–62, design engineer, 1962–63, research engineer, 1963–65; postgrad. student, Bradford Univ., 1965–66; production engineer, English Electric, 1966–67; Res. Fellow then Senior Res. Fellow, Bradford Univ., 1967–73; Dir of Grad. Studies, Admin. Staff Coll., Henley, 1973–77, Mem., Senior Staff, Henley Management Coll., 1973–2001; Brunel University: Dir, Special Engineering Programme, 1977–84; Hd, Dept of Engrg and Management Systems, 1977–86; Hd, Dept of Prodn Technology, 1984–86; Hd, Dept of Manufacturing and Engrg Systems, 1986–89; Pro-Vice-Chancellor, 1988–89. CIMgt; FRSA. Editor-in-Chief, Internat. Jl of Computer Integrated Manufacturing Systems, 1988–91. *Publications:* The Techniques of Production Management, 1971; Management and Production, 1972, trans. Greek 1984; (with A. B. Hill and C. C. Ridgeway) Women in the Factory, 1972; Mass Production Management, 1972; (with B. Lowes) Principles of Modern Management, 1972; Work Organization, 1975; Concepts for Operations Management, 1977; Production and Operations Management, 1979, 5th edn 1994; Operations Management: a policy framework, 1980; Essentials of Production and Operations Management, 1980, 4th edn 1995; (ed) Management and Production Readings, 1981; Read and Explain (4 children's books on technology), 1982 and 1983, trans. French, Swedish, German, Danish; How to Manage, 1983, 2nd edn 1995; (ed) International Handbook of Production and Operations Management, 1989; (ed) Technology and Management, 1990; papers in learned jls. *Recreations:* writing, restoring houses, travel, painting. *Address:* Broomfield, New Road, Shiplake, Henley on Thames, Oxon RG9 3LA. *T:* (0118) 940 4102.

WILD, Robert; Director, Project Underwriting Group, Export Credits Guarantee Department, 1989–92; *b* 19 April 1932; *s* of Thomas Egan Wild and Janet Wild; *m* 1955, Irene Whitton Martin; two *d*. *Educ:* King Edward VII Sch., Lytham. Board of Trade, 1950; Export Credits Guarantee Dept, 1959. *Recreations:* bird watching, archaeology, reading.

WILD, Robin; *see* Wild, J. R.

WILDASH, Richard James, LVO 1997; HM Diplomatic Service; Deputy High Commissioner, Malaysia, since 1998; *b* 24 Dec. 1955; *s* of Arthur Ernest Wildash and Sheila Howard Wildash; *m* 1981, Elizabeth Jane Walmsley; two *d*. *Educ:* Corpus Christi Coll., Cambridge (MA). Joined HM Diplomatic Service, 1977; FCO, 1977–79: E Berlin, 1979–81; Vice-Consul, Abidjan, 1981–84; FCO, 1984–88; First Secretary: Harare, 1988–92; FCO, 1992–94; New Delhi, 1994–98. AIL 1977, MIL 1990. FRGS 1991. *Recreations:* the arts, travel. *Address:* c/o Foreign and Commonwealth Office, King Charles Street, SW1A 2AH. *Club:* Royal Lake (Kuala Lumpur).

WILDBLOOD, Stephen Roger; QC 1999; a Recorder, since 2000; *b* 18 Aug. 1958; *s* of F. R. J. Wildblood and late P. A. M. Wildblood; *m* 1984, Helena Margaret Jongman; one *s* one *d*. *Educ:* Sheffield Univ. (LLB). Called to the Bar, Inner Temple, 1980; Asst Recorder, 1997–2000. *Publication:* (ed jtly) Encyclopedia of Financial Provision in Family Matters, 1998. *Recreations:* sport, reading, languages. *Address:* Albion Chambers, Broad Street, Bristol BS1 1DR. *T:* (0117) 927 2144.

WILDE, Dr Christian; Joint Senior Partner, Freshfields Bruckhaus Deringer, since 2000; *b* 21 Sept. 1939; *s* of Wolf Wilde and Inge Wilde (*née* Uibeleisen); *m* 1980, Gabriele Rocholl; two *s* one *d*. *Educ:* Univ. of Lausanne; Univ of Hamburg; Univ. of Göttingen (Dr Juris); Univ. of Calif, Berkeley (LLM). Associate, 1970, Partner, 1971–90, Stegemann Sieveking & Lutheroth; Partner, Bruckhaus Westrick Stegemann, 1991–2000. Non-exec. board mem. of several cos. *Recreations:* golf, reading. *Address:* (office) Alsterarkaden 27, 20354 Hamburg, Germany. *T:* (40) 369060; (office) 65 Fleet Street, EC4Y 1HS. *T:* (020) 7936 4000. *Club:* Der Uebersee (Hamburg).

WILDE, Imogen; Director, Curriculum and Communications, Department for Education and Skills (formerly Department for Education and Employment), since 1999; *b* 22 Jan. 1949; *d* of late John William Luxton and of Eva Luxton; *m* 1978, Patrick John Wilde (*d* 1999); two *d*. *Educ:* Colston's Girls' Sch., Bristol; Durham Univ. (BA Hons Hist. 1969). Postgrad. res., Inst. of Historical Research, 1969–71; joined Department of Education and Science, 1971: Sec. to Warnock Cttee on Educn of Children with Special Educnl Needs, 1975–78; Principal Private Sec. to Sec. of State for Educn and Sci., 1982–83; DES, subseq. DFE, 1983–91; Asst Sec., UGC (on secondment), 1986–88; British Petroleum plc (on secondment), 1988–91; various posts DFE, subseq. DfEE, 1991–99, incl. Divl Manager, HE Funding and Orgn, 1997–99. FRSA 2000. *Address:* Department for Education and Skills, Caxton House, 6–12 Tothill Street, SW1H 9NA. *T:* (020) 7273 5012.

WILDE, John; HM Diplomatic Service, retired; High Commissioner to Botswana, 1998–2001; *b* 6 Oct. 1941; *s* of John William and Clara Wilde; *m* 1965, Jeanette Grace Reed; one *s* one *d*. *Educ:* Malet Lambert Sch., Hull. Foreign Office, 1959; served Conakry, Pretoria, Kuwait, Tripoli, FCO and Zagreb, to 1976; Singapore, 1976–79; FCO, 1979–82; Asst to Dep. Governor, Gibraltar, 1982–85; jsdc, 1985; First Sec., FCO, 1985–87; Dep. High Comr, Lilongwe, 1987–91; FCO, 1991–95 (Mem., EC Monitor to former Yugoslavia, 1991; ECMM Service Medal, 1994); High Comr, The Gambia, 1995–98. *Recreations:* golf, music, reading. *Address:* Cedarhurst, 26 Boyne Park, Tunbridge Wells, Kent TN4 8ET.

WILDE, Peter Appleton; HM Diplomatic Service, retired; *b* 5 April 1925; *m* 1950, Frances Elisabeth Candida Bayliss; two *s*. *Educ:* Chesterfield Grammar Sch.; St Edmund Hall, Oxford. Army (National Service), 1943–47; Temp. Asst Lectr, Southampton, 1950; FO, 1950; 3rd Sec., Bangkok, 1951–53; Vice-Consul, Zürich, 1953–54; FO, 1954–57; 2nd Sec., Baghdad, 1957–58; 1st Sec., UK Delegn to OEEC (later OECD), Paris, 1958–61; 1st Sec., Katmandu, 1961–64; FO (later FCO), 1964–69; Consul-Gen., Lourenço Marques, 1969–71; Dep. High Comr, Colombo, 1971–73. Mem., Llanfihangel Rhosycorn Community Council, 1974–83. Member: Management Cttee, Carmarthenshire Pest Control Soc. Ltd, 1974–82; Council, Royal Forestry Soc., 1977–86; Regional Adv. Cttee, Wales Conservancy, Forestry Commn, 1985–87 (Mem., Regional Adv. Cttee, S Wales Conservancy, 1983–85). *Recreation:* forestry. *Address:* Nantyperchyll, Gwernogle, Carmarthen SA32 7RR. *T:* (01267) 223181.

WILDENSTEIN, Daniel Leopold; art historian; President: Foundation Wildenstein, Paris, 1970–90; Wildenstein INstitute, Paris, since 1990; Chairman, Wildenstein & Co Inc., New York, 1967–94 (Vice-President, 1943–59, President, 1959–68); Vice-President, Florence Gould Foundation, since 1983; *b* Verrières-le-Buisson, France, 11 Sept. 1917; *s* of Georges Wildenstein; *m* 1939, Martine Kapferer (marr. diss. 1968); two *s*; *m* 1978, Sylvia Roth. *Educ:* Cours Hattemer; Sorbonne (LèsL 1938). Gp Sec., French Pavilion, World's Fair, 1937; went to US, 1940; with Wildenstein & Co. Inc., New York, 1940–; Director: Wildenstein & Co. Inc., London, 1963–; Wildenstein Arte, Buenos Aires, 1963–. Dir, Gazette des Beaux Arts, 1963–; Dir of Activities, Musée Jacquemart-André, Paris, 1956–62; Musée Chaalis, Institut de France, Paris, 1956–62; organiser of art competitions (Hallmark art award). Mem., French Chamber of Commerce in US (Conseiller), 1942–; Founder (1947) and Mem, Amer. Inst. of France (Sec.). Mem., Institut de France (Académie des Beaux-Arts), 1971; Membre du Haut Comité du Musée de Monaco. *Publications:* Claude Monet, vol. 1, 1975, vols 2 and 3, 1979, vol. 4, 1985, vol. 5, 1992; Edouard Manet, vol. 1, 1976, vol. 2, 1977; Gustave Courbet, vol. 1, 1977, vol. 2, 1978. *Recreation:* horse racing (leading owner, 1977). *Address:* Bauernhofstrasse 14, 8853 Lachen, Switzerland; (office) 57 rue La Boétie, 75008 Paris, France. *T:* (1) 45616161. *Clubs:* Brooks's; Turf and Field, Madison Square Garden (New York); Cercle de Deauville, Tir au Pigeon (Paris); Jockey (Buenos Aires).

WILDING, Christine Mary; Director, British Institute of Florence, since 1998; *b* 7 Oct. 1941; *d* of Lionel Walter Haines and Marjorie Gibson Haines (*née* Hall); *m* 1964, Malcolm David Wilding (marr. diss. 1999); two *s* one *d*. *Educ:* Univ. of Leeds (BA Italian 1962). Various teaching posts, mainly part-time, 1963–78; Res. Asst, Univ. of Aston, 1979–82; Sec., Jt Council of Lang. Assocs, 1982–89; Dir, Assoc. for Lang. Learning, 1989–97. Vis. Lectr, Univs of Warwick and Aston in Birmingham, 1977–79. Co-ordinator, Fest. of Langs and Young Linguists Awards, 1982–92. Chevalier, Ordre des Palmes Académiques (France), 1988. *Publications:* research papers and articles to promote use of foreign langs in business, and to motivate language learning. *Recreations:* cooking, walking, the sea, meeting people. *Address:* British Institute of Florence, Palazzo Lanfredini, Lungarno Guicciardini 9, 50125 Florence, Italy. *T:* (055) 217323.

WILDING, Richard William Longworth, CB 1979; Head of Office of Arts and Libraries, Cabinet Office, 1984–88; *b* 22 April 1929; *er s* of late L. A. Wilding; *m* 1954, Mary Rosamund de Villiers; one *s* two *d*. *Educ:* Dragon Sch., Oxford; Winchester Coll.; New Coll., Oxford (MA). HM Foreign Service, 1953–59; transf. to Home Civil Service, 1959; Principal, HM Treasury, 1959–67; Sec., Fulton Cttee on Civil Service, 1966–68; Asst Sec., Civil Service Dept, 1968–70; Asst Sec., Supplementary Benefits Commn, DHSS, 1970–72; Under-Sec., Management Services, 1972–76, Pay, 1976, CSD; Deputy Secretary: CSD, 1976–81; HM Treasury, 1981–83. Review of Structure of Arts Funding in England, 1989; Review of Redundant Churches Fund, 1990. Trustee, Nat. Museums and Galleries on Merseyside, 1989–97. *Publications:* (with L. A. Wilding) A Classical Anthology, 1954; Key to Latin Course for Schools, 1966; The Care of Redundant Churches, 1990; articles in Jl Public Administration, Social Work Today, Studies. *Recreations:* music, gardening. *Address:* 16 Ashcombe Court, Ilminster, Somerset TA19 0ED. *T:* (01460) 55379. *Club:* Athenæum.

WILDISH, Vice-Adm. Denis Bryan Harvey, CB 1968; *b* 24 Dec. 1914; *s* of late Engr Rear-Adm. Sir Henry William Wildish, KBE, CB; *m* 1941, Leslie Henrietta Jacob; two *d*. *Educ:* RNC Dartmouth; RNEC. Entered Royal Navy, 1932; sea service HM Ships Ramillies, Revenge, Nelson, 1932–39; War service, Atlantic, Mediterranean, FE, HM Ships Prince of Wales, Kedah and Isis (despatches); subseq. various Admiralty appts; HMS Implacable, 1946–48; Planning Staff, Exercise Trident, 1948–49; Asst Naval Attaché, Rome, Berne, 1951–53; HMS Eagle, 1953–56; Asst Dir, then Dir, Fleet Maintenance, 1960–64; Commodore Naval Drafting and i/c HMS Centurion, 1964–66; Adm. Supt, HM Dockyard, Devonport, 1966–70; Dir Gen. of Personal Services and Trng (Navy) and Dep. Second Sea Lord, 1970–72; retired. Rep. RN at cricket, also RN, Combined Services, Devon, and W of England (Divisional Trials), at hockey. *Recreations:* walking, cricket, painting (Mem., Armed Forces Art Soc.). *Address:* 57 The Gatehouse, 354

Seafront, Hayling Island, Hants PO11 0AT. *Clubs:* Army and Navy, MCC; I Zingari, XL, Incogniti, Devon Dumplings, Royal Navy Cricket.

WILDMAN, Maj. Gen. Murray Leslie, CBE 2001; Eur. Ing; CEng, FIEE; Director, Defence Business Solutions Limited, since 2001; *b* 10 Feb. 1947; *s* of Peter Wildman and late Margery Wildman (*née* Littlechild) and step *s* of Elizabeth Susan Wildman (*née* Wood); *m* 1974, Lindsay Anne Johnson. *Educ:* Reading Sch.; Royal Military Coll. of Sci. (BSc (Eng) 1969). CEng 1987; Eur Ing 1991; FIEE 1991. Army service, 1968–2001, mainly in engrg and equipt support field; rcds 1993; Dir, Equipt Support, MoD, 1993–96; Defence Advr, Pretoria, S Africa, 1996–99; Dir Gen., Whole Fleet Mgt, MoD, 1999–2001. FIMgt 1989. MInstD. *Recreations:* ski-ing, classic cars. *Club:* Army and Navy.

WILDOR, Sarah; ballet dancer; *b* 1972; *m* Adam Cooper, *qv*. *Educ:* Royal Ballet Sch. Royal Ballet, 1991–2001: soloist, 1994; Principal, 1999; main rôles include: Juliet, in Romeo and Juliet; Giselle; Ondine; Manon; Anastasia; Cinderella; Titania, in The Dream; Lise, in La Fille Mal Gardée; with Adventures in Motion Pictures, Cinderella, 1998. *Address:* c/o Royal Opera House, Covent Garden, WC2E 9DD.

WILDS, Ven. Anthony Ronald; Archdeacon of Plymouth, since 2001; *b* 4 Oct. 1943; *s* of Ernest and Eva Wilds; *m* 1967, Elizabeth Mary Prince; three *d*. *Educ:* Univ. of Durham (BA 1964); Bishops' Coll., Cheshunt. Ordained deacon, 1966, priest, 1967, Asst Curate, Newport Pagnell, 1966–72; Priest in charge, Chipili, Zambia, 1972–75; Vicar: Chandlers Ford, Hants, 1975–85; Andover, Hants, 1985–97; Rector, Solihull, W Midlands, 1997–2001. *Recreations:* theatre, Rugby union, walking, gardening. *Address:* 33 Leat Walk, Roborough, Plymouth PL6 7AT. *T:* (01752) 793397.

WILDSMITH, Brian Lawrence; artist and maker of picture books for young children; *b* 22 Jan. 1930; *s* of Paul Wildsmith and Annie Elizabeth Oxley; *m* 1955, Aurelie Janet Craigie Ithurbide; one *s* three *d*. *Educ:* de la Salle Coll.; Barnsley Sch. of Art; Slade Sch. of Fine Arts. Art Master, Selhurst Grammar School for Boys, 1954–57; freelance artist, 1975–. Exhibitions include: World of Seven English Picture Book Artists, tour of Japan, 1998–99; one-man shows: Hong Kong, Kobe, Yokohama, Mihara, Imabari, 1992; Nakano, Sumida (both Tokyo), Fukuoka, Sendai, Kuwana, Yamaguchi, 1993; World of Brian Wildsmith, Tokyo and tour of Japan, 1995; New World of Brian Wildsmith, Tokyo and tour of Japan, 1997; World of Nursery Tales, Fukui, 1997; Brian Wildsmith Mus. of Art, Kohoku Tokyu, 1998; Kyoto Mus., 2000; Okazaki Mus. for Children, 2001. Production design, illustrations, titles and graphics for first USA-USSR Leningrad film co-production of the Blue Bird. Brian Wildsmith Museum opened Izukogen, Japan, 1994. Mem. Bd of Visitors, Mazza Galleria, Univ. of Findlay, USA, 1999–. Kate Greenaway Medal, 1962; Soka Gakkai Japan Educn Medal, 1988; USHIO Publication Culture Award, 1991. *Publications:* ABC, 1962; The Lion and the Rat, 1963; The North Wind and the Sun, 1964; Mother Goose, 1964; 1; 2; 3;, 1965; The Rich Man and the Shoemaker, 1965; A Child's Garden of Verses (Lewis Carroll Shelf Award, 1966); The Hare and the Tortoise, 1966; Birds, 1967; Animals, 1967; Fish, 1968; The Miller, the Boy and the Donkey, 1969; The Circus, 1970; Puzzles, 1970; The Owl and the Woodpecker, 1971; The Twelve Days of Christmas, 1972; The Little Wood Duck, 1972; The Lazy Bear, 1973; Squirrels, 1974; Pythons Party, 1974; The Blue Bird, 1976; The True Cross, 1977; What the Moon Saw, 1978; Hunter and his Dog, 1979; Animal Shapes, 1980; Animal Homes, 1980; Animal Games, 1980; Animal Tricks, 1980; The Seasons, 1980; Professor Noah's Spaceship, 1980; Bears Adventure, 1981; The Trunk, 1982; Cat on the Mat, 1982; Pelican, 1982; The Apple Bird, 1983; The Island, 1983; All Fall Down, 1983; The Nest, 1983; Daisy, 1984; Who's Shoes, 1984; Toot Toot, 1984; Give a Dog a Bone, 1985; Goats Trail, 1986; My Dream, 1986; What a Tail, 1986; If I Were You, 1987; Giddy Up …, 1987; Carousel, 1988; The Christmas Story, 1989; The Snow Country Prince, 1990; The Cherry Tree, 1991; The Princess and the Moon, 1991; Over the Deep Blue Sea, 1992; The Easter Story, 1993; Noah's Ark Pop Up, 1994; Saint Francis, 1995; The Creation (pop up), 1995; Brian Wildsmith's Amazing World of Words, 1996; (with HIH Princess Hisako Takamodo) Katie and the Dream Eater, 1996; Joseph, 1997; Exodus, 1998; The Bremen Town Band, 1999; The Seven Ravens, 2000; My Flower, 2000; If Only, 2000; Knock Knock, 2000; Not Here, 2000; Can You Do This?, 2000; How Many, 2000; Jesus, 2000; Mary, 2002; with Rebecca Wildsmith: Wake Up Wake Up, 1993; Whose Hat Was That?, 1993; Look Closer, 1993; What Did I Find?, 1993; Jack and the Meanstalk, 1995. *Recreations:* squash, tennis, music (piano). *Address:* 11 Castellaras, 06370 Mouans-Sartoux, France. *T:* 493752411. *Club:* Reform.

WILDSMITH, Prof. John Anthony Winston, MD; FRCA, FRCPE; Foundation Professor and Head of Department of Anaesthesia, University of Dundee, since 1995; Hon. Consultant Anaesthetist, Tayside University (formerly Dundee Teaching) Hospitals NHS Trust, since 1995; *b* 22 Feb. 1946; *s* of Winston Wildsmith and Phyllis Wildsmith (*née* Jones); *m* 1969, Angela Fay Smith; three *d*. *Educ:* King's Sch., Gloucester; Edinburgh Univ. Med. Sch. (MD). FRCA (FFARCS 1973); FRCPE 1996. Grad. Res. Fellow, Dept of Physiology and Anaesthetics, Univ. of Edinburgh, 1971–72; Rotating Registrar in Anaesthesia, Edinburgh Trng Scheme, 1972–75; Lectr in Anaesthesia, 1975–77; Royal Infirmary of Edinburgh: Consultant Anaesthetist, 1977–95; part-time Sen. Lectr, 1977–95; Clin. Dir of Anaesthesia, Theatres and Intensive Care, 1992–95. Vis. Lectr in Anaesthesia, Harvard Med. Sch., 1983–84. *Publications:* edited jointly: Principles and Practice of Regional Anaesthesia, 1987 (trans. German 1991), 2nd edn 1993; Induced Hypotension, 1991; Conduction Blockade for Postoperative Analgesia, 1991; Anaesthesia for Vascular Surgery, 2000; books, chapters and papers on aspects of regional anaesthesia, acute pain relief, induced hypotension and history of anaesthesia. *Recreations:* golf, travel, wine. *Address:* 6 Castleroy Road, Broughty Ferry, Dundee DD5 2LQ. *T:* (01382) 732451. *Clubs:* Royal Scottish Automobile (Glasgow); Royal Burgess Golfing Soc.

WILEMAN, Margaret Annie, MA; Honorary Fellow, Hughes Hall, Cambridge, since 1973 (President (formerly Principal), 1953–73); *b* 19 July 1908; *e d* of Clement Wileman and Alice (*née* Brinson). *Educ:* Lady Margaret Hall, Oxford, and the University of Paris. Scholar of Lady Margaret Hall, Oxford, 1927; First in Hons School of Mod. Langs, 1930; Zaharoff Travelling Scholar, 1931; Assistant, Abbey School, Reading, 1934; Senior Tutor, Queen's College, Harley Street, 1937; Lecturer, St Katherine's Coll., Liverpool, 1940; Resident Tutor, Bedford College, Univ. of London, 1944–53; Univ. Lectr, and Dir of Women Students, Dept of Educn, Cambridge Univ., 1953–73. Officier, Ordre des Palmes Académiques (France), 2000. *Address:* 5 Drosier Road, Cambridge CB1 2EY. *T:* (01223) 351846. *Club:* University Women's.

WILES, Sir Andrew (John), KBE 2000; PhD; FRS 1989; Professor of Mathematics, Princeton University, 1982–88 and since 1990; *b* 11 April 1953; *s* of Rev. Prof. M. F. Wiles, *qv*; *m*; two *d*. *Educ:* Merton Coll., Oxford (BA 1974; MA 1988; Hon. Fellow); Clare Coll., Cambridge (MA 1977; PhD 1980). Sometime Fellow, Clare Coll., Cambridge; Royal Society Research Professor in Maths and Professorial Fellow of Merton Coll., Oxford University, 1988–90. Solved and proved Fermat's Last Theorem, 1993. Hon. DSc Oxon, 1999. (Jtly) Jun. Whitehead Prize, London Math. Soc., 1988 (Hon. Mem., 2001). *Address:* Department of Mathematics, Princeton University, Fine Hall, Washington Hall, Princeton, NJ 08544, USA.

WILES, Clive Spencer; a District Judge (Magistrates' Courts) (formerly Stipendiary Magistrate), Middlesex, since 1996; *b* 1 Dec. 1942; *s* of late Ernest George Wiles and of Emily Louise Wiles (*née* Cummings); *m* 1996, Lisa Bernadette McCarthy; one step *s* one step *d*, and two *s* from former marriage. *Educ:* Leggatts Sch., Watford. Articled clerk to Clerk to Justices, Watford, 1962–67; admitted Solicitor, 1968; Solicitor, subseq. Partner, Ellis Hancock, Watford, later Hancock Quins, 1968–96. *Recreations:* walking, gardening, reading, photography. *Address:* The Court House, The Hyde, Hendon, NW9 7BY. *T:* (020) 8441 9042.

WILES, Harry; HM Diplomatic Service; Ambassador to Nicaragua, since 2000; *b* 17 June 1944; *s* of John Horace Wiles and Margaret, (Peggy), Wiles; *m* 1966, Margaret Bloom; two *d*. *Educ:* Hull Grammar Sch. Joined Foreign Office, 1964: Ankara, 1966–68; Paris, 1969–72; Algiers, 1972–75; FCO, 1975–78; Vice Consul, Bilbao, 1978–81; Third Sec. (Admin), Jedda, 1981–83; Second Secretary: (Admin), Riyadh, 1983–84; (Commercial), Abu Dhabi, 1984–88; Second, later First, Sec., on loan to ECGD, 1988–90; Consul (Commercial) and Dep. Consul Gen., Barcelona, 1990–94; First Sec. (Commercial), Buenos Aires, 1994–98; Dep. Hd of Security Comd, FCO, 1998–2000. *Recreations:* jogging, Rugby League (spectating), classical music, reading. *Address:* c/o Foreign and Commonwealth Office, King Charles Street, SW1A 2AH.

WILES, Rev. Prof. Maurice Frank, FBA 1981; Canon of Christ Church, Oxford, and Regius Professor of Divinity, 1970–91; *b* 17 Oct. 1923; *s* of late Sir Harold Wiles, KBE, CB, and Lady Wiles; *m* 1950, Patricia Margaret (*née* Mowll); two *s* one *d*. *Educ:* Tonbridge School; Christ's College, Cambridge. Curate, St George's, Stockport, 1950–52; Chaplain, Ridley Hall, Cambridge, 1952–55; Lectr in New Testament Studies, Ibadan, Nigeria, 1955–59; Lectr in Divinity, Univ. of Cambridge, and Dean of Clare College, 1959–67; Prof. of Christian Doctrine, King's Coll., Univ. of London, 1967–70; Bampton Lectr, Univ. of Oxford, 1986. FKC 1972. *Publications:* The Spiritual Gospel, 1960; The Christian Fathers, 1966; The Divine Apostle, 1967; The Making of Christian Doctrine, 1967; The Remaking of Christian Doctrine, 1974; (with M. Santer) Documents in Early Christian Thought, 1975; Working Papers in Doctrine, 1976; What is Theology?, 1976; Explorations in Theology 4, 1979; Faith and the Mystery of God, 1982 (Collins Biennial Religious Book Award, 1983); God's Action in the World, 1986; Christian Theology and Interreligious Dialogue, 1992; A Shared Search, 1994; The Archetypal Heresy, 1996; Reason to Believe, 1999. *Address:* Christ Church, Oxford OX1 1DP.

See also Sir A. J. Wiles.

WILES, Paul Noel Porritt; Director of Research, Development and Statistics, Home Office, since 1999; *b* 24 Dec. 1944; *m* 1989, Merlyn Alice Greenhalgh (*née* Morton); one *s* one *d*, and three step *s*. *Educ:* London Sch. of Economics (BSc Econ. 1967); Trinity Hall, Cambridge (Dip Criminol. 1968). Lectr in Sociology, LSE, 1969–70; Res. Fellow, Inst. of Criminology, Univ. of Cambridge, 1970–72; University of Sheffield: Lectr in Criminology, 1972–76, Sen. Lectr, 1976–88; Dir, Centre for Criminological and Socio-legal Studies, 1985–89; Prof. of Criminology, 1988–99; Dean, Faculty of Law, 1990–96. Mem., Mechanics Inst., Eyam, 1979–. *Publications:* monographs, contribs to books, and papers in learned jls on criminology and socio-legal studies. *Recreation:* fell walking. *Address:* Research, Development and Statistics Directorate, Home Office, 50 Queen Anne's Gate, SW1H 9AT. *T:* (020) 7273 2616.

WILFORD, Sir (Kenneth) Michael, GCMG 1980 (KCMG 1976 CMG 1967); HM Diplomatic Service, retired; *b* Wellington, New Zealand, 31 Jan. 1922; *yr s* of late George McLean Wilford and late Dorothy Veronica (*née* Wilson); *m* 1944, Joan Mary, *d* of Captain E. F. B. Law, RN; three *d*. *Educ:* Wrekin College; Pembroke College, Cambridge. Served in Royal Engineers, 1940–46 (despatches). Entered HM Foreign (subseq. Diplomatic) Service, 1947; Third Sec., Berlin, 1947; Asst Private Secretary to Secretary of State, Foreign Office, 1949; Paris, 1952; Singapore, 1955; Asst Private Sec. to Sec. of State, Foreign Office, 1959; Private Sec. to the Lord Privy Seal, 1960; served Rabat, 1962; Counsellor (Office of British Chargé d'Affaires) also Consul-General, Peking, 1964–66; Visiting Fellow of All Souls, Oxford, 1966–67; Actg Pol Advr to Gov. of Hong Kong, 1967; Counsellor, Washington, 1967–69; Asst Under Sec. of State, FCO, 1969–73; Dep. Under Sec. of State, FCO, 1973–75; Ambassador to Japan, 1975–80. Director: Lloyds Bank Internat., 1982–85; Lloyds Merchant Bank Ltd, 1986–87; Adviser, Baring Internat. Investment Management, 1982–90. Chm., Royal Soc. for Asian Affairs, 1984–94 (Hon. Vice Pres., 1994–); Hon. Pres., Japan Assoc., 1981–. Pres., Old Wrekinian Assoc., 1995–. *Recreations:* golf, gardening. *Address:* Brook Cottage, Abbotts Ann, Andover, Hants SP11 7DS. *T:* (01264) 710509.

WILFORD, Michael James, CBE 2001; architect; Senior Partner, Michael Wilford Architects; *b* 9 Sept. 1938; *s* of James Wilford and Kathleen Wilford; *m* 1960, Angela Spearman; two *s* three *d*. *Educ:* Kingston Tech. Sch.; Northern Poly. Sch. of Architecture; Regent St Poly Planning Sch. (Hons DipArch with Dist.). Sen. Asst to James Stirling and James Gowan, 1960–63; Associate Partner, with James Stirling, 1964–71; Partner, James Stirling, Michael Wilford and Associates, 1971–92; Sen. Partner, Michael Wilford and Partners, 1993–2000. Hon. DLitt Sheffield, 1987; Hon. DSc Newcastle, Australia, 1993. *Publications:* Recent Work of James Stirling, Michael Wilford and Associates, 1990; James Stirling, Michael Wilford and Associates Design Philosophy and Recent Projects, 1990; The Museums of James Stirling and Michael Wilford, 1990; James Stirling and Michael Wilford Architectural Monograph, 1993; James Stirling, Michael Wilford and Associates Buildings and Projects 1975–1992, 1994; Wilford-Stirling-Wilford, 1996; Michael Wilford and Partners, 1999. *Recreation:* earth moving and landscaping. *Address:* Lone Oak Hall, Chuck Hatch, Hartfield, E Sussex TN7 4EX. *T:* (01892) 770980. *Club:* Groucho.

WILK, Christopher David; Chief Curator, Furniture and Woodwork Department, Victoria & Albert Museum, since 1996; *b* 28 Dec. 1954; *s* of Maurice Wilk and Norma Wilk (*née* Bloomberg); *m* 1st, 1980, Susan Harris (marr. diss. 1983); 2nd, 1984, Ann Curtis (marr. diss. 1997); two *d*. *Educ:* Vassar Coll. (AB 1976); Columbia Univ. (MA 1979). Researcher, 1976–78, Curatorial Asst, 1978–79, NY Mus. of Modern Art; freelance curator and writer, 1979–82; Asst Curator, 1982–87, Associate Curator, 1987–88, Brooklyn Mus.; Asst Keeper, 1988–90, Curator and Head of Dept, 1990–96, V&A. Mem., Adv. Council, NACF, 1992–; Member Council: Attingham Trust, 1989–; 20th Century Soc., 1990–97; Furniture History Soc., 1992– (Chm., Ingram Fund, 1995–). *Publications:* Thonet: 150 years of furniture, 1980; Marcel Breuer: furniture and interiors, 1981; Frank Lloyd Wright: the Kaufmann Office, 1993; (ed) Western Furniture, 1996; contribs to learned jls. *Recreations:* cycling, soccer, music. *Address:* Furniture and Woodwork Department, Victoria and Albert Museum, SW7 2RL. *T:* (020) 7942 2286.

WILKES, Prof. Eric, OBE (civil) 1974 (MBE (mil.) 1943); DL; FRCP, FRCGP, FRCPsych; Professor of Community Care and General Practice, Sheffield University, 1973–83, now Emeritus; *b* 12 Jan. 1920; *s* of George and Doris Wilkes; *m* 1953, Jessica Mary Grant; two *s* one *d*. *Educ:* Royal Grammar Sch., Newcastle upon Tyne; King's Coll., Cambridge (MA); St Thomas' Hosp., SE1 (MB, BChir). Lt-Col, Royal Signals, 1944. General Medical Practitioner, Derbyshire, 1954–73. High Sheriff of S Yorkshire, 1977–78. Med. Director, St Luke's Nursing Home, later St Luke's Hospice, Sheffield,

1971–86; Emeritus Consultant, Centre for Palliative and Continuing Care, Trent RHA, 1993. Chairman: Sheffield and Rotherham Assoc. for the Care and Resettlement of Offenders, 1976–83; Sheffield Council on Alcoholism, 1976–83; Prevention Cttee, Nat. Council on Alcoholism, 1980–83; Trinity Day Care Trust, 1979–83; Sheffield Victim Support Scheme, 1983–84; Mem., Nat. Cancer sub cttee, 1979–88; President: Inst. of Religion and Medicine, 1982–83; High Peak Hospice, Chapel and Thornhill House, Great Longstone, Derbyshire, 1992–; Co-Pres., St Luke's Hospice, Sheffield, 1986–; Vice-Pres., Ashgate Hospice, Chesterfield, 1990–; Hon. Vice-Pres., Nat. Hospice Council, 1992–; Trustee, Help the Hospices, 1984–95 (Vice-Chm., 1993–95; Co-Chm., 1984–93). DL Derbys, 1984. Hon. Fellow, Sheffield City Polytechnic, 1985. Hon. MD Sheffield, 1986. *Publications:* The Dying Patient, 1982; Long-Term Prescribing, 1982; various chapters and papers, mainly on chronic and incurable illness. *Recreations:* gardening, walking, natural history. *Address:* Curbar View Farm, Calver, Sheffield S32 3XR. *T:* (01433) 631291.

WILKES, Prof. John Joseph, FSA; FBA 1986; Yates Professor of Greek and Roman Archaeology, University College London, 1992–2001; *b* 12 July 1936; *s* of Arthur Cyril Wilkes and Enid Cecilia Eustance; *m* 1980, Dr Susan Walker; one *s*. *Educ:* King Henry VIII Grammar Sch., Coventry; Harrow County Grammar Sch.; University Coll. London (BA); Univ. of Durham (St Cuthbert's Society) (PhD). FSA 1969. Research Fellow, Univ. of Birmingham, 1961–63; Asst Lectr in History and Archaeology, Univ. of Manchester, 1963–64; Lectr in Roman History, 1964–71, Sen. Lectr 1971–74, Univ. of Birmingham; Prof. of Archaeology of the Roman Provinces, Univ. of London, 1974–92. Chm., Faculty of Archaeology, Hist. and Letters, British Sch. at Rome, 1979–83. Vis. Fellow, Inst. of Humanistic Studies, Pennsylvania State Univ., 1971. Mem., Ancient Monuments Bd for Scotland, 1981–91. Vice-Pres., Soc. for Promotion of Roman Studies, 1978; Pres., London and Middx Archaeological Soc., 1982–85. Corresp. Mem., German Archaeol Inst., 1976. Governor, Mus. of London, 1981–95. Member: Council, British Sch. at Rome, 1988–96; Man. Cttee, British Sch. at Athens, 1990–97. Editor, Britannia, 1980–84. *Publications:* Dalmatia (Provinces of Roman Empire series), 1969; (jtly) Diocletian's Palace: joint excavations in the southeast quarter, Pt 1, Split, 1972; (ed jtly) Victoria County History of Cambridgeshire, vol. VII, Roman Cambridgeshire, 1978; Rhind Lectures (Edinburgh), 1984; Diocletian's Palace, Split (2nd Ian Saunders Meml Lecture, expanded), 1986; (jtly) Strageath: excavations within the Roman Fort 1973–1986, 1989; The Illyrians, 1992; (jtly) Excavations at Sparta 1988–95, reports 1994–98; papers, excavation reports and reviews in learned jls of Britain, Amer., and Europe. *Recreations:* listening to music, watching Association football. *Address:* Institute of Archaeology, University College London, 31–34 Gordon Square, WC1H 0PY. *T:* (020) 7679 7489.

WILKES, Sir Maurice (Vincent), Kt 2000; MA, PhD; FRS 1956; FREng, FIEE, FBCS; Staff Consultant, AT&T Laboratories, Cambridge, since 1999; Head of the Computer Laboratory, Cambridge (formerly Mathematical Laboratory), 1970–80; Professor of Computer Technology, 1965–80, now Emeritus Professor; Fellow of St John's College, since 1950; *b* 26 June 1913; *s* of late Vincent J. Wilkes, OBE; *m* 1947, Nina Twyman; one *s* two *d*. *Educ:* King Edward's School, Stourbridge; St John's College, Cambridge. Mathematical Tripos (Wrangler). Research in physics at Cavendish Lab.; Univ. Demonstrator, 1937. Served War of 1939–45, Radar and Operational Research. Univ. Lecturer and Acting Dir of Mathematical Laboratory, Cambridge, 1945; Dir of Mathematical Laboratory, 1946–70. Computer Engr, Digital Equipment Corp., USA, 1980–86; Mem. for Res. Strategy, Olivetti Res. Bd, 1986–96; Advr on Res. Strategy, Olivetti and Oracle Res. Lab., 1996–99. Adjunct Prof. of Computer Sci. and Elect. Engrg, MIT, 1981–85. Member: Measurement and Control Section Committee, IEE, 1956–59; Council, IEE, 1973–76; First President British Computer Soc., 1957–60, Distinguished Fellow 1973. Mem. Council, IFIP, 1960–63; Chm. IEE E Anglia Sub-Centre, 1969–70; Turing Lectr Assoc. for Computing Machinery, 1967. Foreign Hon. Mem., Amer. Acad. of Arts and Sciences, 1974; Foreign Corresponding Member: Royal Spanish Acad. of Sciences, 1979; Royal Spanish Acad. of Engrg, 1999; Foreign Associate: US Nat. Acad. of Engrg, 1977; US Nat. Acad. of Scis, 1980. FREng (FEng 1976). Hon. DSc: Newcastle upon Tyne, 1972; Hull, 1974; Kent, 1975; City, 1975; Amsterdam, 1978; Munich, 1978; Bath, 1987; Cambridge, 1993; Pennsylvania, 1996; Hon. DTech Linköping, 1975. Harry Goode Award, Amer. Fedn of Inf. Processing Socs, 1968; Eckert-Mauchly Award, Assoc. for Computing Machinery and IEEE Computer Soc., 1980; McDowell Award, IEEE Computer Soc., 1981; Faraday Medal, IEE, 1981; Pender Award, Univ. of Pennsylvania, 1982; C & C Prize, Foundn for C & C Promotions, Tokyo, 1988; Italgas Prize for Computer Science, 1991; Kyoto Prize, Inamori Foundn, 1992; John von Neumann Medal, IEEE, 1997; Mountbatten Medal, Nat. Electronics Council, 1997. *Publications:* Oscillations of the Earth's Atmosphere, 1949; (joint) Preparations of Programs for an Electronic Digital Computer, Addison-Wesley (Cambridge, Mass), 1951, 2nd edn 1958; Automatic Digital Computers, 1956; A Short Introduction to Numerical Analysis, 1966; Time-sharing Computer System, 1968, 3rd edn 1975; (jtly) The Cambridge CAP Computer and its Operating System, 1979; Memoirs of a Computer Pioneer, 1985; Computing Perspectives, 1995; papers in scientific jls. *Address:* AT&T Laboratories, 24a Trumpington Street, Cambridge CB2 1QA. *T:* (01223) 343213. *Club:* Athenæum.

WILKES, Ven. Michael Jocelyn James P.; *see* Paget-Wilkes.

WILKES, Gen. Sir Michael (John), KCB 1991; CBE 1988 (OBE 1980); Lieutenant-Governor and Commander-in-Chief, Jersey, 1995–2000; *b* 11 June 1940; *s* of late Lt-Col Jack Wilkes, OBE, MC and of Phyllis Wilkes; *m* 1966, Anne Jacqueline Huelin; two *s*. *Educ:* King's Sch., Rochester; RMA Sandhurst. Commnd RA, 1960; joined 7 Para Regt, RHA, 1961; served ME Troop, Comdr Special Forces, 1964–67, Radfan, S Arabia, Borneo; Staff Coll., 1971–72; Bde Major RA, HQ3 Armd Div., 1973–74; Battery Comdr Chestnut Troop, 1 RHA (BAOR), 1975–76, CO, 1977–79; Mil. Asst to CGS, 1980–81; COS, 3 Armd Div., 1982–83; Comdr, 22 Armd Bde, 1984–85; Arms Dir, MoD, 1986–88; GOC 3 Armd Div., 1988–90; Comdr UK Field Army and Inspector Gen., TA, 1990–93; ME Advr to MoD, 1992–95; Adjutant Gen., 1993–95. Col Comdt and Pres., HAC, 1992–98. Pres., ACFA, 1999–. Kermit Roosevelt Lectr, 1995. Freeman, City of London, 1993. KStJ 1995. Order of Mil. Merit, 1st class (Jordan), 1994. *Recreations:* sailing, ski-ing, military history. *Clubs:* Naval and Military, Special Forces; Victoria (Jersey); Royal Channel Islands Yacht, St Helier Yacht.

WILKES, Richard Geoffrey, CBE 1990 (OBE (mil.) 1969); TD 1959; DL; FCA; company director; Director, Cassidy, Davis Insurance Group, 1989–99 (Chairman, 1998–99); Partner, Price Waterhouse, Chartered Accountants, 1969–90; *b* 12 June 1928; *s* of Geoffrey W. Wilkes and Kathleen (*née* Quinn); *m* 1953, Wendy Elaine, *d* of Rev. C. Ward; one *s* three *d*. *Educ:* Repton (Exhibnr). ACA 1952; FCA 1957. Partner, Bolton Bullivant, Chartered Accountants, Leicester, 1953–69. Pres., Leics and Northants Soc. of Chartered Accountants, 1967–68; Mem. Council, Inst. of Chartered Accountants in England and Wales, 1969–90 (Dep. Pres., 1979–80; Pres., 1980–81); Chairman: UK Auditing Practices Cttee, 1976–78; CA Compensation Scheme, 1990–98; International Federation of Accountants: UK Rep; Mem. Council, 1983–87; Dep. Pres., 1985–87; Pres., 1987–90; Mem., Internat. Auditing Practices Cttee, 1978–79; Adviser on self-regulation, Lloyd's of London, 1983–85. Governor, CARE for the Mentally Handicapped, 1972–98 (Chm., 1995–98). Commnd RHA, 1947; served TA, RA and Royal Leics Regt, 1948–69; CO 4/5th Bn Royal Leics Regt (TA), 1966–69; Col TAVR E Midlands Dist, 1969–73; ADC (TAVR) to the Queen, 1972–77. Dep. Hon. Col, Royal Anglian Regt (Leics), 1981–88; Vice Chm., E Midlands TA&VRA, 1980–89 (Chm., Leics Co. Cttee, 1980–89); Chm., E Midlands TAVRA Employers Liaison Cttee, 1990–98. Comdt, Leics Special Constab., 1972–79. Chm., Leics SSAFA, 1991–98 (Treas., 1969–91). Mem., Court, Worshipful Co. of Chartered Accountants in England and Wales, 1977–98 (Master, 1991–92). DL Leics, 1967. Internat. Award, ICA, 1990. *Recreations:* shooting, sailing. *Address:* The Hermitage, Foxton, Market Harborough, Leics LE16 7RH. *T:* (01858) 545213. *Club:* Army and Navy.

WILKIE, Alan Fraser; QC 1992; **His Honour Judge Wilkie;** a Circuit Judge, since 1997; a Law Commissioner, since 2000; *b* 26 Dec. 1947; *s* of James and Helen Wilkie; *m* 1972, Susan Elizabeth Musgrave; one *s* one *d*. *Educ:* Hutcheson's Grammar Sch., Glasgow; Manchester Grammar Sch.; Balliol Coll., Oxford (BA, BCL). Lecturer in Law: Exeter Coll., Oxford, 1971–72; Southampton Univ., 1972–74; called to the Bar, Inner Temple, 1974, Bencher, 2001; an Asst Recorder, 1992–95; a Recorder, 1995–97. *Recreations:* music, films, watching football, playing tennis, cycling. *Address:* Law Commission, Conquest House, 37–38 John Street, WC1N 2BQ.

WILKIE, Prof. Alex James, FRS 2001; PhD; Reader in Mathematical Logic, since 1986, and titular Professor, since 1996, University of Oxford; Fellow, Wolfson College, Oxford, since 1986; *b* 1 Aug. 1948; *s* of late Alan George Wilkie and Hilda Grace Wilkie (*née* Mitchell); *m* 1987, Catrin Roberts; one *s* one *d*. *Educ:* University Coll. London (BSc); Bedford Coll., London (MSc, PhD 1972). Lectr in Maths, Univ. of Leicester, 1972–73; Res. Fellow in Maths, Open Univ., 1973–78; Jun. Lectr in Maths, Oxford Univ., 1978–80 and 1981–82; Res. Fellow in Maths, Univ. Paris VII, 1982–83; SERC Advanced Res. Fellow, 1983–84, Lectr in Maths, 1984–86, Univ. of Manchester. Vis. Asst Prof. in Maths, Yale Univ., 1980–81. Carol Karp Prize, Assoc. for Symbolic Logic, 1993. *Publications:* contrib. numerous papers in maths and mathematical logic jls. *Address:* Mathematical Institute, 24-29 St Giles, Oxford OX1 3LB. *T:* (01865) 273540.

WILKIE, Kim Edward Kelvin; Principal, Kim Wilkie Associates, since 1989; *b* 30 Oct. 1955; *s* of Edward Henry Wilkie and Christien Audrey Parsons. *Educ:* Winchester Coll.; New Coll., Oxford (MA); Univ. of California, Berkeley (MLA). MLI (ALI 1987). Marketing Manager, Unilever, 1978–81; Associate, Land Use Consultants, 1984–89. Awards: Amer. Soc. of Landscape Architects, 1984; Francis Tibbalds, RTPI, 1994; Landscape Inst., 1995; RTPI, 1996; Centenary, Country Life, 1997; for Place Design, Envmtl Design Res. Assoc., US, 1999. *Publications:* Thames Landscape Strategy: Hampton to Kew, 1994; Indignation!, 2000. *Recreations:* earth sculpting, rollerblading, bonfires, sea kayaking. *Address:* 34 Friars' Stile Road, Richmond TW10 6NE. *T:* (020) 8332 0304.

WILKIN, Rev. Rose Josephine H.; *see* Hudson-Wilkin.

WILKINS, Baroness *cr* 1999 (Life Peer), of Chesham Bois in the county of Buckinghamshire; **Rosalie Catherine Wilkins;** *b* 6 May 1946; *d* of late Eric Frederick Wilkins and Marjorie Phyllis Elizabeth Wilkins. *Educ:* Univ. of Manchester (BA). PA to Dir, Central Council for the Disabled, 1971–74; Information Officer, MIND (Nat. Assoc. for Mental Health), 1974–78, presenter/researcher, Link magazine programme and documentaries, ATV Network and Central Television, 1975–88; freelance video and documentary producer/presenter on disability issues, 1988–96; Information Officer, Nat. Centre for Independent Living, 1997–99. Snowdon Award (for outstanding work for the benefit of disabled people), Action Research, 1983. *Recreations:* friends, travel, gardening, theatre, cinema. *Address:* 74 Inglethorpe Street, Fulham, SW6 6NX.

WILKINS, Sir Graham John, (Bob), Kt 1980; Chairman, THORN EMI, 1985–89, retired (Chief Executive, 1985–87); President, Beecham Group Ltd, 1984–89 (Chairman and Chief Executive, 1975–84); *b* 22 Jan. 1924; *s* of George William and Anne May Wilkins; *m* 1st, 1945, Daphne Mildred Haynes; 2nd, 1990, Helen Catherine McGregor. *Educ:* Yeovil Sch.; University Coll., South West of England, Exeter (BSc). Dir and Vice-Pres., Beecham (Canada) Ltd, 1954–59; C. L. Bencard Ltd, and Beecham Research Labs Ltd: Asst Man. Dir, 1959; Man. Dir, 1960; Dir, Beecham Pharmaceutical Div., 1962–64; Beecham Group Ltd: Dir and Chm., Pharmaceutical Div., 1964–72; Man. Dir (Pharmaceuticals), 1972; Exec. Vice-Chm., 1974; Chm., ICC UK, 1985–89 (Vice Chm., 1984–85); Director: Beecham Inc., 1967–86; Hill Samuel Gp Ltd, 1977–87; THORN EMI (formerly Thorn Electrical Industries) Ltd, 1978–89; Rowntree, 1985–88 (Dep. Chm., 1988); Courage Pensions, 1989–; Eastern Electricity, 1989–95. Mem., Doctors' and Dentists' Remuneration Rev. Bd, 1980–90 (Chm., 1986–90). Vice-Chm., Proprietary Assoc. of GB, 1966–68; President: Assoc. of Brit. Pharmaceutical Industry, 1969–71 (Vice-Pres., 1968–69); European Fedn of Pharmaceutical Industries Assoc., 1978–82; Chm., Medico-Pharmaceutical Forum, 1971–73 (Vice-Chm., 1969–70). Mem., BOTB, 1977–80. Pres., Advertising Assoc., 1983–89. Mem. Council, Sch. of Pharmacy, London Univ., 1984–2000 (Chm., 1987–2000). Hon. FRCP 1984. *Publications:* various papers on pharmaceutical industry. *Recreations:* golf, theatre-going. *Address:* Alceda, Walton Lane, Shepperton-on-Thames, Middx TW17 8LQ.

WILKINS, John Anthony Francis, MBE 1998; Editor of The Tablet, since 1982; *b* 20 Dec. 1936; *s* of Edward Manwaring Wilkins and Ena Gwendolen Francis. *Educ:* Clifton Coll., Bristol (Scholar); Clare Coll., Cambridge (State Scholar, 1954; Major Scholar and Foundn Scholar; Classical Tripos 1959, Theol Tripos 1961; BA 1961). Served 1st Bn Glos Regt, 1955–57 (2nd Lieut). Planning Div., Marine Dept, Head Office of Esso Petroleum, London, 1962–63; Asst Editor: Frontier, 1964–67; The Tablet, 1967–72; features writer, BBC External Services, 1972–81; Producer, Radio 4, 1978. Vis. Fellow, Clare Coll., Cambridge, 1996. Ondas Radio Prize, 1973; John Harriott Meml Prize, ITC, 1996. *Publications:* (ed) How I Pray, 1993; (ed) Understanding Veritatis Splendor, 1994. *Recreation:* ornithology. *Address:* The Tablet, 1 King Street Cloisters, Clifton Walk, W6 0QZ. *T:* (020) 8748 8484.

WILKINS, Prof. Malcolm Barrett, FRSE 1972; Regius Professor of Botany, University of Glasgow, 1970–2000; *b* 27 Feb. 1933; *s* of Barrett Charles Wilkins and Eleanor Mary Wilkins (*née* Jenkins); *m* 1959, Mary Patricia Maltby; one *s* (one *d* decd). *Educ:* Monkton House Sch., Cardiff; King's Coll., London. BSc 1955; PhD London 1958; AKC 1958; DSc 1972. Lectr in Botany, King's Coll., London, 1958–64; Rockefeller Foundn Fellow, Yale Univ., 1961–62; Research Fellow, Harvard Univ., 1962–63; Lectr in Biology, Univ. of East Anglia, 1964–65; Prof. of Biology, Univ. of East Anglia, 1965–67; Prof. of Plant Physiology, Univ. of Nottingham, 1967–70; Glasgow University: Dean, Faculty of Science, 1984–87; Chm., Sch. of Biol Scis, 1988–92. Darwin Lectr, British Assoc. for Advancement of Science, 1967. Member: Biol. Sci. Cttee of SRC, 1971–74; Governing Body: Hill Farming Res. Orgn, 1971–80; Scottish Crops Research Inst, 1974–89; Glasshouse Crops Res. Inst., 1979–88; W of Scotland Agricl Coll., 1983–92; Exec. Cttee, Scottish Field Studies Assoc.; British Nat. Cttee for Biology, 1977–82; Life Science

Working Gp, ESA, 1983–89 (Chm., 1987–89); Microgravity Adv. Cttee, ESA, 1985–89; NASA Lifesat Science Cttee, 1986–91; Court, Glasgow Univ., 1993–97. Vice-Pres., RSE, 1994–97 (Mem. Council, 1989–92). Trustee, Royal Botanic Gdn, Edinburgh, 1990–99 (Chm., 1994–99; Hon. Fellow, 1999); Adv. Council, Scottish Agricl Coll. Corresp. Mem., Amer. Soc. of Plant Physiologists, 1985. Dir, West of Scotland Sch. Co.; Chm., Laurel Bank Sch. Co. Ltd. Cons. Editor in Plant Biology, McGraw-Hill Publishing Co., 1968–80; Managing Editor, Planta, 1977–2001. *Publications:* (ed) The Physiology of Plant Growth and Development, 1969; (ed) Advanced Plant Physiology, 1984; Plantwatching, 1988; papers in Jl of Experimental Botany, Plant Physiology, Planta, Nature, Proc. Royal Soc. *Recreations:* sailing, fishing, model engineering. *Address:* 5 Hughenden Drive, Glasgow G12 9XS. *T:* (0141) 334 8079; *e-mail:* m.wilkins@vigonline.com; Institute of Biomedical and Life Science, Bower Building, The University, Glasgow G12 8QQ. *T:* (0141) 330 4450. *Clubs:* Caledonian; New (Edinburgh).

WILKINS, Maurice Hugh Frederick, CBE 1963; MA, PhD; FRS 1959; Professor of Bio-physics, 1970–81, Emeritus Professor of Biophysics since 1981, and Fellow, since 1973, King's College, University of London; Director, Medical Research Council Cell Biophysics Unit, 1974–80 (Deputy Director, 1955–70, Director, 1970–72, Biophysics Unit; Director Neurobiology Unit, 1972–74); *b* 15 Dec. 1916; *s* of late Edgar Henry Wilkins and of Eveline Constance Jane (*née* Whittaker), both of Dublin; *m* 1959, Patricia Ann Chidgey; two *s* two *d.* *Educ:* King Edward's Sch., Birmingham: St John's College, Cambridge (Hon. Fellow, 1972). Research on luminescence of solids at Physics Department, Birmingham University, with Ministry of Home Security and Aircraft Production, 1938; PhD 1940; Manhattan Project (Ministry of Supply), Univ. of California (research on separation of uranium isotopes by mass spectrograph), 1944; Lectr in Physics, St Andrews Univ., 1945; MRC Biophysics Unit in Physics Department, King's College, London, 1946; Hon. Lecturer in the sub-department of Biophysics, 1958; Prof. of Molecular Biology, King's Coll., 1963–70. President: British Soc. for Social Responsibility in Science, 1969–91; Food and Disarmament Internat., 1984–. Hon. Mem., Amer. Soc. of Biological Chemists, 1964; For. Hon. Mem., Amer. Acad. of Arts and Scis, 1970. Albert Lasker Award, Amer. Public Health Assoc., 1960. Hon. LLD Glasgow, 1972; Hon. ScD: TCD, 1992; Birmingham, 1992; Hon. DSc London, 1998. (Jt) Nobel Prize for Medicine, 1962. *Publications:* papers in scientific journals on luminescence and topics in bio-physics, *eg* molecular structure of nucleic acids and structure of nerve membranes. *Address:* 30 St John's Park, SE3 7JH. *T:* (020) 8858 1817.

WILKINS, Nancy; barrister-at-law; *b* 16 June 1932; three *s* one *d.* *Educ:* School of St Helen and St Katharine, Abingdon, Berkshire. Called to the Bar, Gray's Inn, Nov. 1962; in practice, Midland Circuit, 1962–85; Dep. Circuit Judge, 1974–78; a Recorder, 1978–85; practised in solicitors' office, 1986–90; retired. *Publication:* An Outline of the Law of Evidence (with late Prof. Sir Rupert Cross), 1964, 5th edn 1980. *Recreation:* trying to grow old gracefully.

WILKINSON; *see* Browne-Wilkinson.

WILKINSON, Rev. Canon Alan Bassindale, PhD, DD; lecturer and writer; honorary priest, Portsmouth Cathedral, since 1988 (Cathedral Chaplain, 1994–2001; diocesan theologian, 1993–2001); *b* 26 Jan. 1931; *s* of late Rev. J. T. Wilkinson, DD; *m* 1975, Fenella Holland; two *s* one *d* of first marriage. *Educ:* William Hulme's Grammar Sch., Manchester; St Catharine's Coll., Cambridge; College of the Resurrection, Mirfield. MA 1958, PhD 1959, DD 1997 Cambridge. Deacon, 1959; priest, 1960; Asst Curate, St Augustine's, Kilburn, 1959–61; Chaplain, St Catharine's Coll., Cambridge, 1961–67; Vicar of Barrow Gurney and Lecturer in Theology, College of St Matthias, Bristol, 1967–70; Principal, Chichester Theol. Coll., 1970–74; Canon and Prebendary of Thorney, 1970–74, Canon Emeritus, 1975; Warden of Verulam House, Dir of Training for Auxiliary Ministry, dio. of St Albans, 1974–75; Lectr in Theology and Ethics, Crewe and Alsager Coll. of Higher Educn, 1975–78; Dir of Training, Diocese of Ripon, 1978–84; Hon. Canon, Ripon Cathedral, 1984; Priest-in-Charge, Darley with Thruscross and Thornthwaite, 1984–88; Tutor, Open Univ., 1988–96. Vis. Fellow, Chichester Inst. of Higher Educn, 1995–97; Fellow, George Bell Inst., Birmingham, 1996–; Vis. Lectr, Portsmouth Univ., 1998–. Hulsean Preacher, 1967–68; Select Preacher, Oxford Univ., 1982. Mem., Bd of Educn, Gen. Synod, 1981–85; Vice-Chm., Leeds Marriage and Personal Counselling Service, 1981–83. Governor: SPCK, 1982–91; Coll. of Ripon and York St John, 1985–88. Scott Holland Trustee, 1993–95, 1998– (Scott Holland Lectr, 1998). *Publications:* The Church of England and the First World War, 1978, 2nd edn 1996; Would You Believe It?, 1983; More Ready to Hear, 1983; Christian Choices, 1983; Dissent or Conform?, 1986; The Community of the Resurrection: a centenary history, 1992; (jtly) An Anglican Companion: words from the heart of faith, 1996, 2nd edn 2001; Christian Socialism: Scott Holland to Tony Blair, 1998; contributor to: Cambridge Sermons on Christian Unity, 1966; Catholic Anglicans Today, 1968; A Work Book in Popular Religion, 1986; Chesterton and the Modernist Crisis, 1990; Britain and the Threat to Stability in Europe, 1993; Forever Building, 1995; The Changing Face of Death, 1997; The Impact of New Labour, 1999; also to: Faith and Unity, Sobornost, Preacher's Quarterly, London Quarterly Holborn Review, Theology, Clergy Review, New Fire, Church Times, Chesterton Review, Internat. Christian Digest, Modern Hist. Rev., New DNB. *Recreations:* gardening, walking, cinema, Victorian architecture. *Address:* 29 Kings Road, Emsworth, Hants PO10 7HN. *T:* (01243) 370457.

WILKINSON, Alexander Birrell; QC (Scot.) 1993; Sheriff of Lothian and Borders at Edinburgh, 1996–2001; *b* 2 Feb. 1932; *o s* of late Captain Alexander Wilkinson, MBE, The Black Watch and Isabella Bell Birrell; *m* 1965, Wendy Imogen, *d* of late Ernest Albert Barrett and R. V. H. Barrett; one *s* one *d.* *Educ:* Perth Academy; Univs of St Andrews and Edinburgh. Walker Trust Scholar 1950, Grieve Prizeman in Moral Philosophy 1952, MA(Hons Classics) 1954, Univ. of St Andrews. National Service, RAEC, 1954–56. Balfour Keith Prizeman in Constitutional Law 1957, LLB (with distinction) 1959, Univ. of Edinburgh. Admitted to Faculty of Advocates, 1959; in practice at Scottish bar, 1959–69; Lecturer in Scots Law, Univ. of Edinburgh, 1965–69; Sheriff of Stirling, Dunbarton and Clackmannan at Stirling and Alloa, 1969–72; Prof. of Private Law, 1972–86, and Dean of Faculty of Law, 1974–76 and 1986, Univ. of Dundee; Sheriff of: Tayside, Central and Fife at Falkirk, 1986–91; Glasgow and Strathkelvin, 1991–96; Temp. Judge of Court of Session and High Court of Justiciary, 1993–. Chancellor: Dio. of Brechin, 1982–98; Dio. of Argyll and the Isles, 1985–98. Chairman: Central Scotland Marriage Guidance Council, 1970–72; Scottish Marriage Guidance Council, 1974–77; Legal Services Gp, Scottish Assoc. of CAB, 1979–83. Pres., Sheriffs' Assoc., 1997–2000 (Vice-Pres., 1995–97). *Publications:* (ed jtly) Gloag and Henderson's Introduction to the Law of Scotland, 8th edn 1980, 9th edn 1987; The Scottish Law of Evidence, 1986; (jtly) The Law of Parent and Child in Scotland, 1993; (contrib.) Macphail's Sheriff Court Practice, 2nd edn 1998; articles in legal periodicals. *Recreations:* collecting books and pictures, reading, travel. *Address:* 25 Glencairn Crescent, Edinburgh EH12 5BT. *T:* (0131) 346 1797. *Club:* New (Edinburgh).

WILKINSON, Prof. Andrew Robert, FRCP, FRCPCH; Professor of Paediatrics, since 1997, and Head of Department of Paediatrics, since 2000, University of Oxford; Fellow, All Souls College, Oxford, since 1992; Director of Neonatal Medicine, John Radcliffe Hospital, Oxford, since 1981; *b* 30 Oct. 1945; *s* of late Rev. Thomas Richard Wilkinson and of (Winifred) Frances Wilkinson (*née* Steel). *Educ:* Heath Grammar Sch., Halifax; Univ. of Birmingham Med. Sch. (MB ChB 1968); Univ. of Calif, San Francisco; MA Oxon 1992. FRCP 1986; FRCPCH 1997. House officer: in medicine and surgery, Dudley Rd Hosp., Birmingham, 1968–69; in paediatrics, Warwick Hosp., 1969; Registrar: in medicine, Stratford-on-Avon, 1971–72; in paediatrics, Gt Ormond St Hosp., Oxford and Southampton, 1973–74; Fellow, Cardiovascular Res. Inst., Univ. of Calif, San Francisco, 1977; Consultant Paediatrician, Oxfordshire HA, 1981–92; Clin. Reader in Paediatrics, Oxford Univ., 1992–97. Pres., British Assoc. of Perinatal Medicine, 1999–. Chm., Acad. Bd, RCPCH, 1997–98. *Publications:* contrib. papers and articles on develts in care of children and specifically neonatal medicine. *Recreations:* sailing, lawn maintenance. *Address:* All Souls College, Oxford OX1 4AL.

See also C. R. Wilkinson.

WILKINSON, Brian; *see* Wilkinson, W. B.

WILKINSON, Prof. Christopher David Wicks, PhD; FRSE; James Watt Professor of Electrical Engineering, Glasgow University, since 1992; *b* 1 Sept. 1940; *s* of Charles Norman Wilkinson and Doris Margaret (*née* Wicks); *m* 1963, Dr Judith Anne Hughes; one *s* two *d.* *Educ:* Balliol Coll., Oxford (BA Physics; MA); Stanford Univ. (PhD Applied Physics). FRSE 1987. Engr, English Electric Valve Co., Chelmsford, 1968; Department of Electronics and Electrical Engineering, Glasgow University: Lectr, 1969–75; Sen. Lectr, 1975–79; Reader, 1979–82; Titular Prof., 1982–92. Vis. Scientist, IBM Res. Centre, Yorktown Heights, USA, 1975–76; Vis. Prof., NTT Labs, Tokyo, 1982. *Publications:* 220 papers on nanoelectronics, optoelectronics and bioelectronics, in learned jls. *Recreations:* hill walker, allotment holder, cooking, theatre. *Address:* 31 Hyndland Road, Glasgow G12 9UY. *T:* (0141) 357 0204.

WILKINSON, Christopher John, OBE 2000; Chairman, Wilkinson Eyre (formerly Chris Wilkinson) Architects Ltd, since 1989; *b* 1 July 1945; *s* of Edward Anthony Wilkinson and Norma Doreen Wilkinson; *m* 1976, Diana Mary Edmunds; one *s* one *d.* *Educ:* St Albans Sch.; Regent Street Poly. (DipArch). RIBA. Architect: Foster Associates, 1973–74; Michael Hopkins Architects, 1975–79; Richard Rogers Partnership, 1979–83; founded Chris Wilkinson Architects, 1983; partnership with James Eyre, 1986–. *Projects include:* Stratford Market Depot, 1997 (FT Architecture Award, British Construction Industry Building Award, RIBA Commercial Architecture Award, Structural Steel Design Awards, Industrial Buildings Award, 1997; Civic Trust Design Award, 1998) and Stratford Station, for Jubilee Line Extension, 1998 (RIBA Category Award, 1999; Civic Trust Award, 2000); South Quay Footbridge, 1997 (AIA Excellence in Design Award, 1997; Civic Trust Design Award, 1998); Hulme Arch, 1997; Challenge of Materials Gall., Science Mus., 1997; *current projects:* Gateshead Millennium Bridge (RA/Bovis Grand Award, 1997); Explore at Bristol (RIBA Award, 2001); HQ for Dyson Appliances Ltd; Magna Millennium Project, Rotherham (RIBA Award, 2001). Member: Council, Steel Construction Inst., 1998–; Urban Panel, English Heritage, 2000–. RIBA Lectr, 1996, 2001. Work exhibited: Science Mus.; RIBA; Architecture Foundn; Design Council Millennium Products touring exhibn. Designer of the Year, CSD, 1996. *Publications:* Supersheds, 1991, 2nd edn 1995 (trans. Japanese 1995); (with James Eyre) Bridging Art and Science, 2001; contribs World Architecture, Architects Jl. *Recreations:* golf, painting, travel. *Address:* 52 Park Hall Road, SE21 8BW. *T:* (020) 8761 7021. *Club:* Dulwich and Sydenham Golf.

WILKINSON, Christopher Richard; Adviser, Directorate General, Information Society (formerly Telecommunications Information Market and Exploitation of Research) (DG XIII), Commission of the European Communities, since 1993; *b* 3 July 1941; *s* of late Rev. Thomas Richard Wilkinson and of Winifred Frances Wilkinson (*née* Steel). *Educ:* Hymers Coll., Kingston upon Hull; Heath Grammar Sch., Halifax; Selwyn Coll., Cambridge (MA). Commonwealth Economic Cttee, 1963–65; OECD, Paris and Madrid, 1965–66; World Bank, Washington DC and Lagos, 1966–73; EEC: Head of Division: Directorate Gen. for Regional Policy, 1973–78; Directorate Gen. for Internal Market and Industrial Affairs, 1978–82; Directorate Gen. for Telecommunications, Information Industries and Innovation, 1983–93. EU Rep., Govtl Adv. Cttee, Internet Corp. for Assigned Names and Numbers, 1999. Mem., Internet Policy Oversight Cttee, 1997–2000. Vis. Fellow, Center for Internat. Affairs, Harvard Univ., 1982–83. Vice-Pres., European School Parents Assoc., Brussels, 1974, 1976–77. *Recreations:* mountain walking, gardening, cooking. *Address:* rue Charles Quint 55, 1000 Brussels, Belgium.

See also A. R. Wilkinson.

WILKINSON, Clive Victor; Chairman, Birmingham Heartlands and Solihull NHS Trust, since 2001; *b* 26 May 1938; *s* of Mrs Winifred Jobson; *m* 1961, Elizabeth Ann Pugh; two *d.* *Educ:* Four Dwellings Secondary Sch., Quinton; Birmingham Modern Sch. Birmingham City Council: Member, 1970–84; Leader, 1973–76 and 1980–82; Leader of Opposition, 1976–80, 1982–84. Dir, Nat. Exhibn Centre, 1973–84; Financial and Commercial Dir, Birmingham Rep. Theatre, 1983–87. Chm., CoSIRA, 1977–80; Dep. Chairman: AMA, 1974–76; Redditch Develt Corp., 1977–81. Chairman: Sandwell DHA, 1986–94; Wolverhampton Health Care NHS Trust, 1995–97; W Midlands Region, NHS Exec., DoH, 1997–2001. Member: Develt Commn, 1977–86; Electricity Consumers Council, 1977–80; Audit Commn, 1987–96; Black Country Develt Corp., 1989–92; Local Govt Commn, 1992–95; Midlands Industrial Assoc., 1978– (Chm., 1980–88). Non-exec. Dir, FSA, 2001–. Chairman: Birmingham Civil Housing Assoc., 1979–; Customer Services Cttee, Severn Trent Region, Office of Water Services, 1990–2001. Mem. Council, Univ. of Birmingham, 1974–84. Trustee, Bournville Village Trust, 1982–. Hon. Alderman, City of Birmingham, 1984. *Recreations:* watching Birmingham City Football Club, playing squash. *Address:* 53 Middle Park Road, Birmingham B29 4BH. *T:* (0121) 475 1829.

WILKINSON, David Anthony, CB 1994; Deputy Head, Economic and Domestic Affairs Secretariat, Cabinet Office, 2001; *b* 27 Nov. 1947; *s* of Ambrose Wilkinson and Doreen (*née* Durden); *m* 1973, Meryl, *d* of Edison and Margaret Pugh; three *d.* *Educ:* Boteler Grammar Sch., Warrington; Wigan and District Mining and Technical Coll.; Bedford Coll., Univ. of London (BA History); London School of Economics; Moscow State Univ. Department of Education and Science, 1974–92: Hd of Inf. Br., 1987–88; Dep. Dir of Establishments, 1988–89; Under Sec., and Hd of Sci. Br., 1989–92; Under Sec., OST, then OPSS, Cabinet Office, 1992–94; RCDS, 1995; Dir, Machinery of Govt and Standards Gp, OPS, 1996–98, Hd of Central Secretariat, 1998–2000, Cabinet Office; Dir of Regl Policy, DETR, 2000–01. *Address:* c/o Cabinet Office, 70 Whitehall, SW1A 2AS. *Club:* Wimbledon Squash and Badminton.

WILKINSON, Dr David George; Head, Division of Developmental Neurobiology, and Genes and Cellular Controls Group, National Institute for Medical Research, since 2000; *b* 8 March 1958; *s* of George Arthur Wilkinson and Barbara May Wilkinson (*née* Hayton);

m 1991, Qiling Xu. *Educ:* Aylesbury Grammar Sch.; Hymers Coll., Hull; Univ. of Leeds (BSc Hons 1979, PhD 1983). Postdoctoral Fellow, Fox Chase Cancer Center, Philadelphia, 1983–86; National Institute for Medical Research: Postdoctoral Fellow, 1986–88; scientific staff, 1988–. Mem., EMBO, 2000. FMedSci 2000. *Publications:* (ed) In Situ Hybridisation, 1992, 2nd edn 1998; (ed jtly) Extracellular Regulators of Differentiation and Development, 1996; contrib. numerous scientific articles to various jls. *Recreations:* natural history, music, poetry. *Address:* Division of Developmental Neurobiology, National Institute for Medical Research, The Ridgeway, Mill Hill, NW7 1AA. *T:* (020) 8959 3666.

WILKINSON, Sir David Graham Brook; *see* Wilkinson, Sir Graham.

WILKINSON, Prof. David Gregor, (Greg), FRCPE; FRCPsych; Professor of Liaison Psychiatry, Liverpool University, since 1994; *b* 17 May 1951; *s* of David Pryde Wilkinson and Joan (*née* McCabe); *m* 1984, Christine Mary Lewis; three *s* one *d*. *Educ:* Lawside Acad., Dundee; Edinburgh Univ. (BSc, MB ChB); MPhil London. FRCPE 1989; FRCPsych 1991. House Physician and Surgeon, Royal Infirmary, Edinburgh, 1975–76; Sen. House Physician, Leith Hosp., 1976–78; Registrar, Maudsley Hosp., 1978–81; Sen. Registrar, Maudsley Hosp. and KCH, 1981–83; Res. Worker and Lectr, then Sen. Lectr, Inst. of Psychiatry, Univ. of London, 1983–89; Sen. Lectr and Reader, Academic Sub-dept of Psychol Medicine in N Wales, 1989–91; Prof. of Psychiatry, London Hosp. Med. Coll., London Univ., 1992–94. Editor, Brit. Jl of Psychiatry, 1993–. *Publications:* Mental Health Practices in Primary Care Settings, 1985; (jtly) Mental Illness in Primary Care Settings, 1986; (jtly) The Provision of Mental Health Services in Britain, 1986; Coping with Stress, 1987, 2nd edn as Understanding Stress, 1993; Depression, 1989; Recognising and Treating Depression in General Practice, 1989; (jtly) The Scope of Epidemiological Psychiatry, 1989; Recognising and Treating Anxiety in General Practice, 1992; Talking About Psychiatry, 1993; (jtly) Psychiatry and General Practice Today, 1994; (jtly) A Carers Guide to Schizophrenia, 1996, 2nd edn 2000; (ed jtly) Textbook of General Psychiatry, 1998; (jtly) Critical Reviews in Psychiatry, 1998, 2nd edn 2000; (jtly) Seminars in Psychosexual Disorders, 1998; (jtly) Treating People with Depression, 1999; Treating People with Anxiety and Stress, 1999; articles in general and specialist med. jls. *Recreations:* family, rural pursuits, being a pimp of discourse. *Address:* Craig y Castell, Bryniau, Dyserth, Denbighshire LL18 6DE. *T:* (01745) 570136.

WILKINSON, David Lloyd; Chief Executive and General Secretary, Cooperative Union, 1975–99; *b* 28 May 1937; *m* 1960; one *s* one *d*. *Educ:* Royds Hall Grammar Sch. ACIS; CSD. *Address:* 2 Old House, Marsden, Huddersfield HD7 6AS. *T:* (01484) 844580.

WILKINSON, Sir Denys (Haigh), Kt 1974; FRS 1956; Vice-Chancellor, University of Sussex, 1976–87 (Emeritus Professor of Physics, 1987); *b* Leeds, Yorks, 5 September 1922; *o s* of late Charles Wilkinson and Hilda Wilkinson (*née* Haigh); *m* 1st, 1947, Christiane Andrée Clavier (marriage dissolved, 1967); three *d*; 2nd, 1967, Helen Sellschop; two step *d*. *Educ:* Loughborough Gram. Sch.; Jesus Coll. Cambridge (Fellow, 1944–59, Hon. Fellow 1961). BA 1943, MA, PhD 1947, ScD 1961. British and Canadian Atomic Energy Projects, 1943–46; Univ. Demonstrator, Cambridge, 1947–51; Univ. Lecturer, 1951–56; Reader in Nuclear Physics, Univ. of Cambridge, 1956–57; Professor of Nuclear Physics, Univ. of Oxford, 1957–59; Prof. of Experimental Physics, Univ. of Oxford, 1959–76, Head of Dept of Nuclear Physics, 1962–76; Student, Christ Church, Oxford, 1957–76, Emeritus Student, 1976, Hon. Student, 1979. Dir, Internat. Sch. of Nuclear Physics, Erice, Sicily, 1975–83. Mem. Governing Board of National Institute for Research in Nuclear Science, 1957–63 and 1964–65; Member: SRC, 1967–70; Wilton Park Acad. Council, 1979–83; Council, ACU, 1980–87; Royal Commn for the Exhibn of 1851, 1983–90 (Chm., Science Scholarships Cttee, 1983–90); British Council, 1987– (Chm., Sci. Adv. Panel and Cttee, 1977–86); Chairman: Nuclear Physics Board of SRC, 1968–70; Physics III Cttee, CERN, Geneva, 1971–75; Radioactive Waste Management Adv. Cttee, 1978–83; Pres., Inst. of Physics, 1980–82; Vice-Pres., IUPAP, 1985–93. Lectures: Welch, Houston, 1957; Scott, Cambridge Univ., 1961; Rutherford Meml, Brit. Physical Soc., 1962; Graham Young, Glasgow Univ., 1964; Queen's, Berlin, 1966; Silliman, Yale Univ., 1966; Cherwell-Simon, Oxford Univ., 1970; Distinguished, Utah State Univ., 1971, 1983, 1988; Goodspeed-Richard, Pennsylvania Univ., 1973 and 1986; Welsh, Toronto Univ., 1975; Tizard Meml, Westminster Sch., 1975; Lauritsen Meml, Cal. Tech., 1976; Herbert Spencer, Oxford Univ., 1976; Schiff Meml, Stanford Univ., 1977; Racah Meml, Hebrew Univ. Jerusalem, 1977; Cecil Green, Univ. of BC, 1978; Distinguished, Univ. of Alberta, 1979; Wolfson, Oxford Univ., 1980; Waterloo-Guelph Distinguished, Guelph Univ., 1981; Herzberg, Ottawa, 1984; Solly Cohen Meml, Hebrew Univ., Jerusalem, 1985; Peter Axel Meml, Univ. of Illinois, 1985; Breit Meml, Yale Univ., 1987; Moon, Birmingham Univ., 1987; Rochester, Durham Univ., 1988; Pegram, Brookhaven Nat. Lab., 1989; W. B. Lewis Meml, Chalk River, Ont, 1989; Humphry Davy, Académie des Sciences, Paris, 1990; Rutherford Meml, Royal Soc., 1991; W. V. Houston Meml, Rice Univ., 1994; Hudspeth, Univ. of Texas at Austin, 1994; Anna McPherson, McGill Univ., 1995; Pickavance Meml, Rutherford Lab., 1997; B. W. Sargent, Queen's Univ., Canada, 1998; Director's Distinguished, Livermore Nat. Lab., 1999. Walker Ames Prof., Univ. of Washington, 1968; Battelle Distinguished Prof., Univ. of Washington, 1970–71; Vis. Prof., Tokyo Univ., 1995; Visiting Scientist: Brookhaven Nat. Lab., 1954–80; TRIUMF, Vancouver, 1987–; Los Alamos Nat. Lab., 1990–93. For. Mem., Royal Swedish Acad. of Scis, 1980; Mem. Acad. Europaea, 1990. Holweck Medal, British and French Physical Socs, 1957; Rutherford Prize, British Physical Soc., 1962; Hughes Medal, Royal Society, 1965; Bruce-Preller Prize, RSE, 1969; Bonner Prize, American Physical Soc., 1974; Royal Medal, Royal Soc., 1980; Guthrie Medal and Prize, Inst. of Physics, 1986; Gold Medal, Centro Cultura Scientifica Ettore Majorana, Sicily, 1988. Hon. Mem., Mark Twain Soc, 1978. Hon. DSc: Saskatchewan, 1964; Utah State, 1975; Guelph, 1981; Queen's, Kingston, 1987; William and Mary, Va, 1989; Hon. FilDr Uppsala, 1980; Hon. LLD Sussex, 1987. Comm. Bontemps Médoc et Graves, 1973. *Publications:* Ionization Chambers and Counters, 1951; (ed) Isospin in Nuclear Physics, 1969; (ed) Progress in Particle and Nuclear Physics, 1978–84; (ed jtly) Mesons in Nuclei, 1979; Our Universes, 1991; papers on nuclear physics and bird navigation. *Recreations:* mediæval church architecture and watching birds. *Address:* Gayles Orchard, Friston, Eastbourne, East Sussex BN20 0BA. *T:* and *Fax:* (01323) 423333.

WILKINSON, Endymion Porter, PhD; Senior fellow, Asia Center, Harvard University; *b* 15 May 1941; *s* of George Curwen Wilkinson and Pamela Algernon Wilkinson (*née* Black). *Educ:* King's Coll., Cambridge (BA 1964; MA 1967); Princeton Univ. (PhD 1970). Teacher, Peking Inst. of Languages, 1964–66; Lectr in History of Far East, SOAS, London Univ., 1970–74; joined European Commn, 1974: Head of Economic and Commercial Section, Tokyo, 1974–79; China Desk, Brussels, 1979–82; Dep. Head, SE Asia Repn, Bangkok, 1982–88; Head, Asia Div., Brussels, 1988–94; Ambassador and Hd of Delegn to China, EC, 1994–2001. *Publications:* The History of Imperial China: a research guide, 1973; Studies in Chinese Price History, 1980; Japan versus Europe: a history of misunderstanding, 1982 (trans. Japanese, Chinese, French, German and Italian); Japan versus the West, 1991; Chinese History: a manual, 1998, 2nd edn 2000; *translations:* The People's Comic Book, 1973; Landlord and Labour in Late Imperial China, by Jing Su and Luo Lun, 1978. *Recreations:* Chinese oracle-bone inscriptions, tropical gardening, swimming. endymion121@yahoo.com.

WILKINSON, Geoffrey Crichton, CBE 1986; AFC; Chief Inspector of Accidents (Aircraft), 1981–86; *b* 7 Nov. 1926; *s* of Col W. E. D. Wilkinson and Mrs E. K. Wilkinson; *m* 1958, Virginia Mary Broom; two *d*. *Educ:* Bedford Sch. Graduate, Empire Test Pilots Sch.; FRAES. Royal Indian Mil. Coll., 1943–44; served RN, 1944–47; aeronautical engrg course, 1948; served RAF, 1949–59 (Air Force Cross, 1956); Turner and Newall, 1959–61; Mercury Airlines, 1961–65; Accidents Investigation Br., 1965–86. Air Medal, USA, 1953. *Recreations:* sailing, skiing, music. *Address:* Buckingham House, 50 Hyde Street, Winchester, Hants SO23 7DY. *T:* (01962) 865823. *Club:* Royal Air Force.

WILKINSON, Sir Graham, 3rd Bt *cr* 1941; Managing Director, S.E.I.C. Services (UK) Ltd, 1985–89; *b* 18 May 1947; *s* of Sir David Wilkinson, 2nd Bt, DSC, and of Sylvia Anne, *d* of late Professor Bosley Alan Rex Gater; *S* father, 1972; *m* 1977, Sandra Caroline Rossdale (marr. diss. 1996); two *d*; *m* 1998, Hilary Jane Griggs, *d* of late W. H. C. Bailey, CBE. *Educ:* Millfield; Christ Church, Oxford. Orion Royal Bank Ltd, 1971–85 (Dir 1979–85); non-executive Director: Galveston-Houston Co., USA, 1986–89; Sovereign Management Corp., USA, 1987–94; Lamport Gilbert Ltd, 1992–97. CStJ 1995. *Clubs:* White's, Royal Ocean Racing; Royal Yacht Squadron.

WILKINSON, Greg; *see* Wilkinson, David Gregor.

WILKINSON, Ven. Guy Alexander; Archdeacon of Bradford, since 1999; *b* 13 Jan. 1948; *m* 1971, Tessa Osbourn; two *s*. *Educ:* Magdalene Coll., Cambridge (BA 1969); Ripon Coll., Cuddesdon. Commn of Eur. Communities; Dir, 1980–85, non-exec. Dir, 1985–87, Express Foods Gp.; ordained deacon 1987, priest 1988; Curate, Caludon, Coventry, 1987–90; Priest i/c, 1990–91, Rector, 1991–94, Ockham with Hatchford; Domestic Chaplain to Bishop of Guildford, 1990–94; Vicar, Small Heath, Birmingham, 1994–99. *Address:* 14 Park Cliffe Road, Bradford BD2 4NS; *e-mail:* guy@gwilkinson.org.uk.

WILKINSON, Hon. Dame Heather; *see* Hallett, Hon. Dame H. C.

WILKINSON, James Hugh; freelance journalist and broadcaster; *b* 19 Sept. 1941; *s* of Hugh Davy Wilkinson and Marjorie Wilkinson (*née* Prout); *m* 1978, Rev. Elisabeth Ann Morse; two *s*. *Educ:* Westminster Abbey Choir Sch.; Sutton Grammar Sch.; King's Coll., London (BSc Hons); Churchill Coll., Cambridge (CertEd). Health and Sci. Corresp., Daily Express, 1964–74; Sci. and Air Corresp., BBC Radio News, 1974–83; Sci. Corresp., BBC News and Current Affairs, 1983–99. Vis. Fellow, Inst. of Food Res., 1992–96. Mem., Educn Cttee, CRC, 1977–82; Mem., Adv. Bd, CIBA Foundn Media Resource Service, 1994–99 (Mem., Steering Cttee, 1985–94). Hon. Steward, Westminster Abbey, 1999– (Sec., Brotherhood of St Edward, 1984–99). Mem., Editl Cttee, Sci. and Public Affairs Jl, 1989–. Founder Mem., Med. Journalists' Assoc. (Chm., 1972–74). Glaxo Wellcome Sci. Writers' Award, 1996. *Publications:* The Conquest of Cancer, 1973; Tobacco: the truth behind the smokescreen, 1986; Green or Bust, 1990. *Recreations:* music, singing, bookbinding, editing The Westminster Abbey Chorister.

WILKINSON, Jeffrey Vernon; Consultant, Apax Partners & Co. (formerly Alan Patricof Associates), since 2000 (Director, 1986–2000; Partner, 1988–2000); Chairman of several private companies, since 1985; *b* 21 Aug. 1930; *s* of late Arthur Wilkinson and Winifred May Allison; *m* 1955, Jean Vera Nurse; two *d*. *Educ:* Mathew Humberstone Foundation Sch.; King's Coll., Cambridge (MA; Fellow Commoner, 2001–); Sorbonne. FBCS, CIMgt. Joined Joseph Lucas as graduate apprentice, 1954; Director, CAV, 1963; Director and General Manager, Diesel Equipment, CAV, 1967; Director: Simon Engineering, 1968; Joseph Lucas, 1974; Dir and Gen. Manager, Lucas Electrical, 1974; Divisional Man. Dir, Joseph Lucas Ltd, 1978; Jt Gp Man. Dir, Lucas Industries plc, 1979–84; Chm. and CEO, Spear & Jackson plc, 1992–2000. Chairman: Automotive Components Manufacturers, 1979–84; Plastics Processing EDC, 1985–87; Mem. Council and Exec., SMMT, 1979–84. Liveryman, Wheelwrights Company, 1971–. *Recreations:* water-skiing, swimming, tennis, reading, theatre, art. *Address:* Hillcroft, 15 Mearse Lane, Barnt Green, Birmingham B45 8HG. *T:* (0121) 447 7750.

WILKINSON, John Arbuthnot Du Cane; MP (C) Ruislip Northwood, since 1979; *b* 23 Sept. 1940; 2nd *s* of late Denys Wilkinson and Gillian Wilkinson, Eton College; *m* 1st, 1969 (marr. diss. 1987); one *d*; 2nd, 1987, Cecilia Cienfuegos, *d* of late Raul Cienfuegos Lyon, Santiago, Chile; one *s*. *Educ:* Eton (King's Scholar); RAF Coll., Cranwell; Churchill Coll., Cambridge (2nd cl. Hons Mod. Hist.; MA). Flight Cadet, RAF Coll., Cranwell, 1959–61 (Philip Sassoon Meml Prize, qualified French Interpreter); commnd 1961; Flying Instructor, No 8 FTS, Swinderby, 1962. Churchill Coll., Cambridge, Oct. 1962–65. Trooper, 21st Special Air Service Regt (Artists'), TA, 1963–65; rejoined RAF 1965; Flying Instructor, RAF Coll., Cranwell, 1966–67; Tutor, Stanford Univ.'s British Campus, 1967; ADC to Comdr 2nd Allied Tactical Air Force, Germany, 1967; resigned RAF, 1967. Head of Universities' Dept, Conservative Central Office, 1967–68; Aviation Specialist, Cons. Research Dept, 1969; Senior Administration Officer (Anglo-French Jaguar Project), Preston Div., British Aircraft Corp., 1969–70; Tutor, Open Univ., 1970–71; Vis. Lectr, OCTU RAF Henlow, 1971–75; Chief Flying Instructor, Skywork Ltd, Stansted, 1974–75; Gen. Manager, General Aviation Div., Brooklands Aviation Ltd, 1975–76; PA to Chm., BAC, 1975–77; Senior Sales Executive, Eagle Aircraft Services Ltd, 1977–78; Sales Manager, Klingair Ltd, 1978–79. MP (C) Bradford W, 1970–Feb. 1974; contested same seat, Feb. and Oct. 1974. PPS to Minister of State for Industry, 1979–80, to Sec. of State for Defence, 1981–82. Chairman: Cons. Parly Aviation Cttee, 1983–85, and 1992–93 (Jt Sec., 1972–74; Vice-Chm., 1979); Cons. Parly Defence Cttee, 1993–94, 1996–97 (Vice-Chm., 1983–85, 1990–91, 1992–93; Sec., 1972–74 and 1980–81); Special Select Cttee on Armed Forces Bill, 1991; Member Select Committee on: Race Relations and Immigration, 1972–74; Sci. and Technol., 1972–74; Defence, 1987–90. Chairman: Anglo-Asian Cons. Soc., 1979–82; European Freedom Council, 1982–90; Cons. Space Sub Cttee, 1986–90 (Vice-Chm., 1983–85). Chm., Horn of Africa Council, 1984–88. Delegate to Council of Europe (Chm., Space Sub-Cttee, 1984–88) and WEU (Chm., Cttee on Scientific, Technological and Aerospace Questions, 1986–89), 1979–90, 2000–; Leader, EDG/EPP Gp, Assembly of WEU, 2000–; Chief Whip, EDG Gp, Council of Europe, 2001–. Parly Industrial Fellow, GKN plc, 1989–90; Postgrad. Fellow, TI plc, 1993; Parly Armed Forces Scheme attachment, RM, 1993–94. Mem., Commonwealth War Graves Commn, 1997–. Pres., London Green Belt Council, 1997–. CRAeS 1997. HQA (Pakistan), 1989; Order of Terra Mariana, 3rd cl. (Estonia), 1999. *Publications:* (jtly) The Uncertain Ally, 1982; British Defence: a blueprint for reform, 1987; pamphlets and articles on defence and politics. *Recreation:* cross country ski-ing. *Address:* c/o House of Commons, SW1A 0AA.

See also R. D. Wilkinson.

WILKINSON, John Francis; Director of Public Affairs, BBC, 1980–85; *b* 2 Oct. 1926; *s* of late Col W. T. Wilkinson, DSO, and Evelyn S. Wilkinson (*née* Ward); *m* 1951, Alison, *d* of late Hugh and Marian Malcolm; two *s* one *d*. *Educ:* Wellington Coll.; Edinburgh

Univ. Naval Short Course, 1944–45; Cambridge and London Univs Colonial Course, 1947–48. Served Royal Navy (Fleet Air Arm trainee pilot, 1945), 1945–47; HM Colonial Service, N Nigeria, 1949; Asst District Officer, Bida, 1949; Asst Sec., Lands and Mines, Kaduna, 1950; Private Sec. to Chief Comr, N Nigeria, 1951; transf. to Nigerian Broadcasting Corp., 1952; Controller: Northern Region, 1952–56; National Programme, Lagos, 1956–58; joined BBC African Service as African Programme Organiser, 1958; East and Central African Programme Organiser, 1961; BBC TV Production Trng Course and attachment to Panorama, 1963; Asst Head, 1964, Head, 1969, BBC African Service; attachment to Horizon, 1972; Head of Production and Planning, BBC World Service, 1976; Secretary of the BBC, 1977–80. Dir, 1986–90, Trustee, 1990–99, The One World Broadcasting Trust. Chm. of Governors, Centre for Internat. Briefing, Farnham Castle, 1977–87, Vice-Pres., 1987–. Vice-Pres., Royal African Soc., 1978–82. MUniv Open, 1989. *Publications:* Broadcasting in Africa, in African Affairs (Jl of Royal African Soc.), 1972; contrib. to Broadcasting in Africa, a continental survey of radio and television, 1974. *Recreations:* sailing, occasional golf. *Address:* Compass Cottage, Box, Minchinhampton, near Stroud, Glos GL6 9HD. *T:* (01453) 833072. *Club:* New Cavendish.

WILKINSON, Rev. Canon Keith Howard; Headmaster, King's School, Canterbury, since 1996; *b* 25 June 1948; *s* of Kenneth John Wilkinson and Grace Winifred (*née* Bowler); *m* 1972, Carolyn Gilbert; two *d. Educ:* Beaumont Leys Coll.; Gateway Sch., Leicester; Univ. of Hull (BA Hons); Emmanuel Coll., Cambridge (Lady Romney Exhibnr, MA status); Westcott House, Cambridge. Hd of Religious Studies, Bricknell High Sch., 1970–72; Hd of Faculty (Humanities), Kelvin Hall Comprehensive Sch., Kingston upon Hull, 1972–74; Deacon 1976; Priest 1977; Asst Priest, St Jude, Westwood, Peterborough, 1977; Asst Master and Chaplain, Eton Coll., Windsor, 1979–84; Sen. Chaplain and Hd of Religious Studies, Malvern Coll., 1984–89; Sen. Tutor, Malvern Coll., 1988–89; Headmaster, Berkhamsted Sch., 1989–96. Hon. Canon, Canterbury Cathedral, 1996–. *Publications:* various articles and reviews. *Recreations:* films, theatre, music, walking, buildings and building, ecology. *Address:* The King's School, Canterbury, Kent CT1 2ES. *T:* (01227) 595501. *Club:* East India.

WILKINSON, Kenneth Henry Pinder; His Honour Judge Wilkinson; a Circuit Judge, since 1996; *b* 5 Aug. 1939; *s* of late Henry Wilkinson and Alice Wilkinson; *m* 1966, Margaret Adams; two *s* one *d. Educ:* Wigan GS; Univ. of Manchester (LLB Hons). Admitted solicitor, 1965; in private practice, 1965–80; Dep. Dist Registrar, 1977–80; Dist Judge, 1980–96; Asst Recorder, 1990–93; Recorder, 1993–96. Chm (part-time), Industrial Tribunal, 1977–80; Member: Matrimonial Causes Rule Cttee, 1978–80; County Court Rule Cttee, 1988–92. Mem., Family Law Cttee, Law Soc., 1976–80. *Publications:* (jtly) A Better Way Out, 1979; (contrib.) Personal Injury Litigation Service, 1984; (with I. S. Goldrein) Commercial Litigation: pre-emptive remedies, 1987, 3rd edn 1996; (with M. De Haas) Property Distribution on Divorce, 1989; (Consult. Ed.) County Court Litigation, 1993. *Recreations:* gardening, music, walking, watching sport. *Address:* Manchester Combined Court Centre, Crown Square, Manchester M60 9DJ.

WILKINSON, Leon Guy, FCIB; a General Commissioner of Income Tax, City of London, since 1989; part-time Member, VAT Tribunal, since 1989; *b* 6 Nov. 1928; *s* of Thomas Guy and Olive May Wilkinson; *m* 1953, Joan Margaret; one *s* one *d. Educ:* Bude Grammar Sch. CMS Oxon. Lloyds Bank: Regional Gen. Man., N and E Midlands, 1976–79; Asst Gen. Man., 1979–83; Gen. Man. (Finance), 1984–86; Chief Financial Officer, 1986–88. *Recreation:* sports. *Address:* Astons, Bishops Down Park Road, Tunbridge Wells, Kent TN4 8XR. *T:* (01892) 541184. *Clubs:* MCC, Royal Over-Seas League; Nevill Golf (Tunbridge Wells).

WILKINSON, Rear-Adm. Nicholas John, CB 1994; Secretary to the Defence, Press and Broadcasting Advisory Committee (DA Notice Secretary), since 1999; *b* 14 April 1941; *s* of late Lt-Col Michael Douglas Wilkinson, RE and Joan Mary Wilkinson (*née* Cosens); *m* 1st, 1969, Penelope Ann Stephenson (marr. diss. 1996); three *s* one *d*; 2nd, 1998, Juliet Rayner (*née* Hockin). *Educ:* English School, Cairo; Cheltenham College; BRNC Dartmouth. Served HM Ships Venus, Vidal and Hermes, 1960–64; RN Air Station, Arbroath, 1964–65; HMS Fife, 1965–67; Asst Sec. to Vice-Chief of Naval Staff, 1968–70; HMS Endurance, 1970–72; Army Staff Course, 1973 (Mitchell Prizewinner); Clyde Submarine Base, 1974–75; Sec. to ACNS (Policy), 1975–77; HMS London, 1977–78; Asst Dir, Naval Officer Appts (SW), 1978–80; Trng Comdr, HMS Pembroke, 1980–82; NATO Defence Coll., Rome, 1982–83; MA to Dir, NATO Internat. Mil. Staff, 1983–85; RCDS, 1986; Dir, Defence Logistics, 1986; Sec. to First Sea Lord, 1989–90; Sen. Mil. Mem., Defence Organisation Study and Project Team, 1991–92; Dir Gen. of Naval Manpower and Trng, 1992–94; Chief Naval Supply and Secretariat Officer, 1993–97; Comdt, JSDC, 1994–97; mgt consultant, 1998–99. Chairman: Assoc. RN Officers, 1998–; Victory Services Assoc., 2001–. *Publications:* articles in The Naval Review. *Recreations:* swimming, cricket, opera, jazz, cuisine périgourdine. *Address:* 37 Burns Road, SW11 5GX. *Clubs:* Savile, MCC.

WILKINSON, Nigel Vivian Marshall; QC 1990; a Recorder, since 1992; *b* 18 Nov. 1949; *s* of late John Marshall Wilkinson and of Vivien Wilkinson; *m* 1974, Heather Carol Hallett (*see* Hon. Dame Heather Hallett); two *s. Educ:* Charterhouse; Christ Church, Oxford (Holford exhibnr; MA). Called to the Bar, Middle Temple, 1972, Bencher, 1997; Astbury Scholar, 1972; Midland and Oxford Circuit, 1972–; an Asst Recorder, 1988–92. Dep. Chm., Appeals Cttee, Cricket Council, 1991–97. Gov., Brambletye Sch., 1992–98. *Recreations:* cricket, golf, theatre. *Address:* 2 Crown Office Row, Temple, EC4Y 7HJ. *T:* (020) 7797 8100. *Clubs:* MCC; Vincent's (Oxford); I Zingari, Butterflies CC, Invalids CC, Armadillos CC, Rye Golf, Royal Wimbledon Golf.

WILKINSON, Prof. Paul; Professor of International Relations, since 1990, and Director, Centre for the Study of Terrorism and Political Violence, since 1999, University of St Andrews; *b* 9 May 1937; *s* of late Walter Ross Wilkinson and of Joan Rosemary (*née* Paul); *m* 1960, Susan Flook; two *s* one *d. Educ:* Lower School of John Lyon; University Coll., Swansea, Univ. of Wales (BA (jt Hons Mod. Hist. and Politics), MA; Hon. Fellow, 1986). Royal Air Force regular officer, 1959–65. Asst Lecturer in Politics, 1966–68, Lectr in Politics, 1968–75, Sen. Lectr in Politics, 1975–77, University Coll., Cardiff; Reader, Univ. of Wales, 1978–79; Prof., Internat. Relations, 1979–89, Hd, Dept of Politics and Internat. Relations, 1985–89, Univ. of Aberdeen; Dir, Res. Inst. for Study of Conflict and Terrorism, 1989–94; Hd, Sch. of History and Internat. Relations, Univ. of St Andrews, 1994–96. Vis. Fellow, Trinity Hall, Cambridge, 1997–98. Mem., IBA Scottish Adv. Cttee, 1982–85. Special Consultant, CBS Broadcasting Co., USA, 1986–91; Security Advr, Internat. Foundn of Airline Passengers Assocs, 1988–. FRSA 1995. Gen. Editor, Key Concepts in International Relations, 1980–; Jt Editor, Terrorism and Political Violence Jl, 1988–; Emeritus Editor, Handbook of Security, 1991–. *Publications:* Social Movement, 1971; Political Terrorism, 1974; Terrorism versus Liberal Democracy, 1976; Terrorism and the Liberal State, 1977, rev. edn 1986; (jtly) Terrorism: theory and practice, 1978; (ed) British Perspectives on Terrorism, 1981; The New Fascists, 1981, rev. edn 1983; Defence of the West, 1983; (jtly) Contemporary Research on Terrorism, 1987; Lessons of Lockerbie, 1989; Terrorist Targets and Tactics: new risks to world order, 1990; Northern Ireland: reappraising Republican violence, 1991; (ed) Technology and Terrorism, 1993; (ed) Terrorism: British perspectives, 1993; Lloyd Inquiry into Legislation against Terrorism, vol. 2 (research report), 1996; (jtly) Aviation Terrorism and Security, 1998; Terrorism Versus Democracy: the liberal state response, 2000; contribs to wide range of jls in Britain, USA and Canada. *Recreations:* modern art, poetry, walking. *Address:* Department of International Relations, North Street, St Andrews, Fife KY16 9AL. *T:* (01334) 462900. *Club:* Savile.

WILKINSON, Sir Philip (William), Kt 1988; FCIB; Director: National Westminster Bank PLC, 1979–90 (Deputy Chairman, 1987–90); HandelsBank NatWest, 1983–90 (Deputy Chairman, 1987–90); *b* 8 May 1927; *m* 1951, Eileen Patricia (*née* Malkin) (*d* 1991); one *s* two d. *Educ:* Leyton County High School. With Westminster Bank, later National Westminster Bank, 1943–90; Chief Executive, Lombard North Central Ltd, 1975; General Manager, Related Banking Services Division, 1978; Dir, 1979–90; Dep. Group Chief Executive, 1980; Group Chief Executive, 1983–87; Chm., NatWest Investment Bank, 1987–89; Director: Internat. Westminster Bank, 1982–90; Nat. Westminster Bank, USA, 1987–90. Director: BAe, 1987–91; Nat. Power, 1990–93. Former Mem., Bd of Banking Supervision, Bank of England; a Vice-Pres., Chartered Inst. of Bankers, 1989–. Dir, ENO, 1987–93. Mem. Council, Imperial Cancer Res. Fund, 1990–2000, a Vice Pres., 2000–; Chm., Wishbone Trust, 1994–. Trustee, Baptist Building Fund, 1987–. Freeman, City of London, 1969. Hon. Fellow, British Orthopaedic Assoc., 2001. *Recreations:* theatre, golf, watching sport. *Address:* Pine Court, Whichert Close, Knotty Green, Beaconsfield, Bucks HP9 2TP. *Club:* Royal Automobile.

WILKINSON, Richard Denys, CVO 1992; HM Diplomatic Service; Director, Americas and Overseas Territories, Foreign and Commonwealth Office, since 2000; *b* 11 May 1946; *y s* of late Denys and Gillian Wilkinson; *m* 1982, Maria Angela Morris; two *s* one *d. Educ:* Eton Coll. (King's Schol.); Trinity Coll., Cambridge (MA, MLitt, Wace Medallist); Ecole Nat. des Langues Orientales Vivantes, Univ. de Paris; Ecole des Langues Orientales Anciennes, Inst. Catholique de Paris. Hayter Postdoctoral Fellow in Soviet Studies, SSEES, London, 1971; joined Diplomatic Service, 1972: Madrid, 1973; FCO, 1977; Vis. Prof., Univ. of Michigan, Ann Arbor, 1980; FCO, 1980; Ankara, 1983; Mexico City, 1985; Counsellor (Information), Paris, 1988; Head of Policy Planning Staff, FCO, 1993–94; Head of Eastern Dept, FCO, 1994–96; Ambassador to Venezuela, 1997–2000. *Publications:* articles and reviews in learned jls. *Recreations:* sightseeing, oriental studies. *Address:* c/o Foreign and Commonwealth Office, SW1A 2AH. *Club:* Oxford and Cambridge.

See also J. A. D. Wilkinson.

WILKINSON, Robert Purdy, OBE 1990; Director of Surveillance, The Stock Exchange, 1984–90; Director of Enforcement and Deputy Chief Executive, The Securities Association, 1987–90; *b* 23 Aug. 1933; *s* of Robert Purdy and Lily Ingham Wilkinson; *m* 1957, June (*née* Palmer); two *d. Educ:* Univ. of Durham (BA). Kleinwort Sons & Co., 1958–62; Estabrook & Co., 1962–64; Partner, W. I. Carr Sons & Co., 1966–81. Stock Exchange: Mem. Council, 1978–81; Cttee Chm., 1980–81; Stock Exchange Inspector, 1981–84. Dir, Tradepoint, 1994–2001. Consultant: Morgan Grenfell Internat., 1991; S Africa Financial Markets Bd, 1991; Johannesburg Stock Exchange, 1991; DTI Inspector, 1987, 1989, 1991; Invesco Gp, 1997– (Dir, 1994–97). Mem., Financial Services Tribunal, 1991–94; Special Advisor: Assoc. of Swiss Stock Exchanges, 1991; Czech Ministry of Finance, 1995; Bulgarian Ministry of Finance, 1997–99; Romanian Securities Commn, 1997–99; Tallinn Stock Exchange, 1999; Jordan Securities Commn, 1999–2001. Testified US Congress Cttee, 1988. Chm. of Govs, Sevenoaks Sch., 1992–2002. *Publications:* various articles on securities regulation and insider dealing. *Recreations:* walking, schools' sport. *Address:* Bessels House, Bessels Green, Sevenoaks, Kent TN13 2PS. *T:* (01732) 457782.

WILKINSON, Prof. (William) Brian, PhD; FGS; FICE; FCIWEM; Senior Consultant, Solutions to Environmental Problems, since 1999; *b* 20 Jan. 1938; *s* of James Edmund Wilkinson and Gladys (*née* Forster); *m* 1962, Gillian Warren; two *s* one *d. Educ:* Univ. of Durham (BSc Hons Civil Engrg, BSc Hons Geol.); Univ. of Manchester (PhD 1968). FGS 1974; FCIWEM (FIWEM 1984); FICE 1989. Asst engr, Babtie Shaw and Morton, Consulting Engrs, 1961–63; Lectr, Dept of Civil Engrg, Univ. of Manchester, 1963–69; Sen. Engr, Water Resources Bd, 1969–74; Sen. Principal Hydrologist, Severn Trent Water Authy, 1974–75; Hd, Water Resources Div., Water Res. Centre, 1975–83; Prof. of Civil Engrg, RMCS, Cranfield Univ., 1983–88; Dir, Inst. of Hydrology, 1988–94, Dir, Centre for Ecology and Hydrology, 1995–99, NERC. Visiting Professor: in Hydrol., Univ. of Reading, 1989–; in Dept of Civil Engrg, Univ. of Newcastle upon Tyne, 2000–. Dir, Oxford Vacs, 1997–99. Mem., Acad. of Experts, 2001. Fellow, Russian Acad. of Nat. Sci., 1997. *Publications:* (ed) Groundwater Quality, Measurement, Prediction and Protection, 1976; (ed jtly) Applied Groundwater Hydrology, 1991; (ed) Groundwater Problems in Urban Areas, 1994; numerous articles covering geotechnics and envmtl sci. *Recreations:* classical music, French wines, water colour painting, karate. *Address:* Vine Cottage, Union Street, Ramsbury, Marlborough, Wilts SN8 2PR. *T:* (01672) 520644; *e-mail:* gb.wilk@dial.pipex.com.

WILKINSON, Dr William Lionel, CBE 1987; FRS 1990; FREng; a Director, British Nuclear Fuels plc, 1984–94; *b* 16 Feb. 1931; *s* of Lionel and Dorothy Wilkinson; *m* 1955, Josephine Anne Pilgrim; five *s. Educ:* Christ's Coll., Cambridge (MA, PhD, ScD). Salters' Res. Schol., Christ's Coll., Cambridge, 1953–56; Lectr in Chem. Engrg, UC Swansea, 1956–59; UKAEA Production Gp, 1959–67; Prof. of Chem. Engrg, Univ. of Bradford, 1967–79; British Nuclear Fuels Ltd: Dep. Dir, 1979–84; Technical Dir, 1984–86; Dep. Chief Exec., 1986–92; Non.-exec. Dir, 1992–94; Dep. Chm., Allied Colloids plc, 1992–98. Vis. Prof. of Chemical Engrg, Imperial Coll., London, 1980–. Chm., British Nuclear Industry Forum, 1992–97; President: Eur. Atomic Forum, 1994–96; British Nuclear Industry Forum, 1997–. Member: SERC, 1981–85; ACOST, 1990–95. FIChemE (Pres., 1980); FREng (FEng 1980). Liveryman, Salters' Co., 1985. Hon. DEng Bradford, 1989. *Publications:* Non-Newtonian Flow, 1960; contribs to sci. and engrg jls on heat transfer, fluid mechanics, polymer processing and process dynamics. *Recreation:* fell-walking. *Address:* Tree Tops, Legh Road, Knutsford, Cheshire WA16 8LP. *T:* (01565) 653344. *Club:* Athenæum.

WILKS, Ann; *see* Wilks, M. A.

WILKS, (David) Michael (Worsley); Chairman, Medical Ethics Committee, British Medical Association, since 1997 (Member, since 1995); *b* 26 May 1949; *s* of Dennis Worsley Wilks and Bridget Wilks (*née* Chetwynd-Stapylton, later Sewter); *m* 1972, Patricia Hackforth (marr. diss. 1992); one *s* two *d. Educ:* St John's Sch., Leatherhead; St Mary's Hosp. Med. Sch., London (MB BS 1972). DObstRCOG 1975. House officer posts at St Mary's Hosp., Paddington and Wembley Hosp., 1972–74; GP trng, London, 1974; Principal in gen. practice, Kensington and Richmond, 1975–92; Metropolitan Police: Sen. Police Surgeon, 1992–97; Principal Forensic Med. Examr, 1997–. Vis. Lectr, Kingston Univ., 1997–. Medical Adviser: Abbeyfield Housing Assoc., 1990–; American Airlines, 1994–; Asst Med. Advr, Richmond Council Housing Dept, 1991–; Educn

Officer, Med. Council on Alcoholism, 1996–; Med. Referee, Sick Doctors' Trust, 1997–. British Medical Association: Member: Trainees Sub-Cttee, 1974–75; Gen. Med. Services Cttee, 1977–89; Med. Ethics Cttee, 1979–86; New Charter Wkg Gp, 1982; Council, 1997–; Hon. Sec., Richmond, Twickenham and Roehampton Div., 1996–. Observer, Standards Cttee, GMC, 1997–; Member: Ethics in Medicine Cttee, RCP, 1998–; Euthanasia wkg party (jtly with RCGP), 1999–. *Publications:* contribs to med. jls on ethical issues, addiction medicine, forensic medicine. *Recreations:* photography, theatre, art, literature, cinema, walking, Mozart. *Address:* c/o BMA, BMA House, Tavistock Square, WC1H 9JP. *Club:* Royal Society of Medicine.

WILKS, Jean Ruth Fraser, CBE 1977; Chairman of Council and Pro-Chancellor, Birmingham University, 1985–89; *b* 14 April 1917; *d* of Mark Wilks. *Educ:* North London Collegiate Sch.; Somerville Coll., Oxford (MA; Hon. Fellow, 1985). Assistant Mistress: Truro High Sch., 1940–43; James Allen's Girls' Sch., Dulwich, 1943–51; Head Mistress, Hertfordshire and Essex High Sch., Bishop's Stortford, Hertfordshire, 1951–64; Head Mistress, King Edward VI High Sch. for Girls, Birmingham, 1965–77. Pres., Assoc. of Head Mistresses, 1972–74; Member: Public Schools Commn, 1968–70; Governing Council of Schools Council, 1972–75; Adv. Council on Supply and Trng of Teachers, 1973–78; Educn Cttee, Royal Coll. of Nursing, 1973–79; University Authorities Panel, 1982–89. University of Birmingham: Mem. Council, 1971–89; Life Mem. Court, 1977; Chm., Academic Staffing Cttee, 1978–85; Dep. Pro-Chancellor, 1979–85. Pres., ASM, Somerville Coll., Oxford, 1982–85. Chm. Governors, Ellerslie, Malvern, 1982–89; Mem. Council, Malvern Coll., 1992–93. FCP 1978. Hon. LLD Birmingham, 1986. *Address:* 4 Hayward Road, Oxford OX2 8LW.

WILKS, (Margaret) Ann; Secretary, Financial Reporting Council, and Financial Reporting Review Panel, since 1998; *b* 11 May 1943; *d* of Herbert Robson and Margaret Robson (*née* Culbert); *m* 1977, Victor Wilks; two *d. Educ:* Putney High Sch., GPDST; Lady Margaret Hall, Oxford (BA Modern Hist., BPhil American Hist.); Univ. of Pennsylvania (Thouron Schol.). Asst Principal, Min. of Power and DTI, 1968–71; Department of Trade and Industry: Private Sec. to Perm. Sec. (Trade) and Parly Sec., 1971–72; Principal, 1972–73; journalist, Economist, 1973–74; Principal: DTI, 1974–76; Cabinet Office, 1976–78; (pt-time) DTI, 1982–84; (pt-time) Asst Sec., DTI, 1984–96 (Hd, Industrial Develt Unit, and Sec., Industrial Develt Adv. Bd, 1991–96); Dir, Metals, Minerals and Shipbuilding, DTI, 1996–98. Mem. Cttee, Thouron Scholarship, 1974–80. *Recreations:* tennis, cookery, theatre, walking, sightseeing. *Address:* Financial Reporting Council, Holborn Hall, 100 Gray's Inn Road, WC1X 8AL. *T:* (020) 7611 9710. *Club:* Coolhurst Lawn Tennis and Squash Rackets.

WILKS, Michael; *see* Wilks, D. M. W.

WILL, Prof. Robert George, CBE 2000; MD; FRCP; Consultant Neurologist, since 1987, and Director, National Creutzfeldt-Jakob Disease Surveillance Unit, since 1990, Western General Hospital, Edinburgh; Professor of Clinical Neurology, University of Edinburgh, since 1998; *b* 30 July 1950; *s* of George and Margaret Will; *m* 1976, Jayne; one *s* one *d. Educ:* Glenalmond Coll.; St John's Coll., Cambridge (MB BChir 1974; MA, MD 1985); London Hosp. Med Coll. FRCP 1994. London Hosp., Nat. Hosp., Queen Sq. and N Middx Hosp., 1974–79; res. at Univ. of Oxford, 1979–82; Registrar, St Thomas' Hosp., 1982–84; Sen. Registrar, Nat. Hosp., Queen Sq. and Guy's Hosp., 1994–97. FMedSci 2001. FRSA 1998. *Publications:* contrib. articles on Creutzfeldt-Jakob Disease. *Address:* 4 St Catherine's Place, Edinburgh EH9 1NU. *T:* (0131) 667 3667.

WILL, Ronald Kerr; Deputy Keeper of Her Majesty's Signet, 1975–83; formerly Senior Partner, Dundas & Wilson, CS, Edinburgh; *b* 22 March 1918; 3rd *s* of late James Alexander Will, WS and late Bessie Kennedy Salmon, Dumfries; *m* 1953, Margaret Joyce, *d* of late D. Alan Stevenson, BSc, FRSE; two *s. Educ:* Merchiston Castle Sch.; Edinburgh Univ. Commnd King's Own Scottish Borderers, 1940; served with 1st Bn and in Staff appts (despatches); psc; GSO2. Writer to the Signet, 1950. Director: Scottish Equitable Life Assce Soc., 1965–88 (Chm., 1980–84); Scottish Investment Trust PLC, 1963–88; Standard Property Investment PLC, 1972–87. Mem. Council on Tribunals, 1971–76 and Chm. of Scottish Cttee, 1972–76. Governor, Merchiston Castle Sch., 1953–76. *Recreations:* fishing, gardening. *Address:* Heriot, 11 Muirfield Park, Gullane, East Lothian EH31 2DS. *T:* (01620) 843283. *Club:* New (Edinburgh).

WILLACY, Michael James Ormerod, CBE 1989; Managing Director (formerly Managing Partner), Michael Willacy Associates Ltd, since 1990; *b* 7 June 1933; *s* of James and Marjorie Willacy (*née* Sanders); *m* 1st, 1961, Merle Louise de Lange; two *s* one *d*; 2nd, 1985, Victoria Stuart John; three *s* one *d. Educ:* Taunton Sch., Somerset. FCIPS. Purchasing Agent, Shell Venezuela, 1964–73; Procurement Advr, Shell Internat., The Hague, 1974–77; Supt., Shell Stanlow, 1978–80; Manager, Shell Wilmslow, 1981–83; Gen. Man., Shell Materials Services, 1983–85; Dir, Central Unit on Purchasing, 1985–90, Procurement Advr, 1991–92, HM Treasury. Chairman: Macclesfield Chamber of Commerce, 1981–83; Macclesfield Business Ventures, 1982–83. Old Tauntonian Association: Gen. Sec., 1978–91; Pres., 1988–89; Vice-Pres., 1990–; Mem. Council, Taunton Sch., 1993–; Chm., St Dunstan's Abbey Sch., Plymouth, 1997–. *Recreations:* golf, travel, gardening. *Address:* Michael Willacy Associates, PO Box 20, Ivybridge PL21 9XS. *Clubs:* Royal Commonwealth Society; Old Tauntonian Association (Taunton).

WILLAN, Edward Gervase, CMG 1964; HM Diplomatic Service, retired; Ambassador to Czechoslovakia, 1974–77; *b* 17 May 1917; *er s* of late Captain F. G. L. Willan, RNR; *m* 1944, Mary Bickley Joy (*d* 1992), *d* of late Lieut-Colonel H. A. Joy, IAOC. *Educ:* Radley; Pembroke Coll., Cambridge (Exhibitioner, MA). Indian Civil Service, 1939–47; 2nd Secretary (from 1948, 1st Secretary) on staff of UK High Commissioner, New Delhi, 1947–49; appointed to HM Diplomatic Service, 1948; Foreign Office, 1949–52; 1st Secretary, HM Embassy, The Hague, 1953–55; 1st Secretary, HM Legation, Bucharest, 1956–58 (Chargé d'Affaires, 1956, 1957 and 1958); Head of Communications Dept, FO, 1958–62; Political Adviser to Hong Kong Government, 1962–65; Head of Scientific Relations Dept, FO, 1966–68; Minister, Lagos, 1968–70; Ambassador at Rangoon, 1970–74. *Recreations:* walking, gardening. *Address:* Cherry Tree Cottage, Shappen Hill, Burley, Hants BH24 4AH.

WILLASEY-WILSEY, Timothy Andrew; HM Diplomatic Service; Counsellor, UK Mission to United Nations, Geneva, since 1999; *b* 12 Sept. 1953; *s* of Maj.-Gen. Anthony Patrick Willasey-Wilsey, CB, MBE, MC, and of Dorothy Willasey-Wilsey (*née* Yates); *m* 1983, Alison Middleton Mackie; three *s. Educ:* Shrewsbury Sch.; Univ. of St Andrews (MA 1st Cl. Hons Mod. Hist. 1976). Metal Box Ltd, 1976–81: Export Sales Manager, 1977–79; Factory Mgt, 1979–81; joined HM Diplomatic Service, 1981; FCO, 1981–83; First Sec., Luanda, 1983–86; Hd of Chancery, later Dep. Hd of Mission, San Jose, Costa Rica, 1986–89; also Consul, San Jose and Managua, 1986–89; FCO, 1989–93; Counsellor (Political), Islamabad, 1993–96; FCO, 1996–99. *Recreations:* political and military history, travel, reading, cricket, ski-ing, tennis, music. *Address:* c/o Foreign and Commonwealth Office, King Charles Street, SW1A 2AH. *Clubs:* Royal Over-Seas League, MCC.

WILLCOCK, His Honour Kenneth Milner; QC 1972; a Circuit Judge, 1972–94. MA; BCL. Called to Bar, Inner Temple, 1950. Dep. Chm., Somerset QS, 1969–71; a Recorder of the Crown Court, 1972.

WILLCOCK, Prof. Malcolm Maurice; Professor of Latin, 1980–91, now Emeritus, and Vice-Provost, 1988–91, University College London; *b* 1 Oct. 1925; *s* of late Dr Maurice Excel Willcock and Evelyn Clarice Willcock (*née* Brooks); *m* 1957, Sheena Gourlay; four *d. Educ:* Fettes Coll.; Pembroke Coll., Cambridge (MA). Served Royal Air Force, 1944–47. Research Fellow, Pembroke Coll., Cambridge, 1951–52; Sidney Sussex College: Fellow, 1952–65; Sen. Tutor, 1962–65; University of Lancaster: first Professor of Classics, 1965–79; Principal, Bowland Coll., 1966–79; Pro-Vice-Chancellor, 1975–79. *Publications:* ed, Plautus, Casina, 1976; Companion to the Iliad, 1976; ed, Iliad of Homer, vol. 1 (Books I–XII) 1978, vol. 2 (Books XIII–XXIV) 1984; ed, Plautus, Pseudolus, 1987. *Recreation:* bridge. *Address:* 1 Lancaster Avenue, SE27. *T:* (020) 8761 5615.

WILLCOCKS, Alison Ann; Head, Bedales School, 1995–2001; *b* 22 July 1952; *d* of Patrick MacNamara and Sibyl MacNamara; *m*; one *s* one *d. Educ:* St Francis Coll., Letchworth; New Hall, Cambridge Univ. (MA Hist.); Birmingham Univ. (BMus). Asst Mistress, Portsmouth High Sch., 1976–79; Bedales Sch., 1980–2001: History teacher, 1980–83; Housemistress, 1983–88; Dep. Head, 1988–94. *Recreations:* writing, music, reading.

WILLCOCKS, Sir David (Valentine), Kt 1977; CBE 1971; MC 1944; conductor; Musical Director of the Bach Choir, 1960–98, Conductor Laureate, since 1998; General Editor, OUP Church Music, since 1961; *b* 30 Dec. 1919; *s* of late T. H. Willcocks; *m* 1947, Rachel Gordon, *d* of late Rev. A. C. Blyth, Fellow of Selwyn Coll., Cambridge; one *s* two *d* (and one *s* decd). *Educ:* Clifton Coll.; King's Coll., Cambridge (MA; MusB). Chorister, Westminster Abbey, 1929–33; Scholar, Clifton Coll., 1934–38; FRCO, 1938; Scholar at College of St Nicolas (RSCM), 1938–39; Organ Scholar, King's Coll., Cambridge, 1939–40; Open Foundation Scholarship, King's Coll., Cambridge, 1940; Stewart of Rannoch Scholarship, 1940. Served War of 1939–45, 5th Bn DCLI, 1940–45. Organ Scholar, King's Coll., Cambridge, 1945–47; Fellow of King's Coll., Cambridge, 1947–51, Hon. Fellow, 1979–; Organist of Salisbury Cathedral, 1947–50; Master of the Choristers and Organist, Worcester Cathedral, 1950–57; Fellow and Organist, King's Coll., Cambridge, 1957–73; Univ. Lectr in Music, Cambridge Univ., 1957–74; Univ. Organist, Cambridge Univ., 1958–74; Dir, RCM, 1974–84. Conductor: Cambridge Philharmonic Soc., 1947; City of Birmingham Choir, 1950–57; Bradford Festival Choral Soc., 1957–74; Cambridge Univ. Musical Soc., 1958–73. President: RCO, 1966–68; ISM, 1978–79; Old Cliftonian Soc., 1979–81; Nat. Fedn of Music Socs, 1980–89; Assoc. of British Choral Dirs, 1993–. Mem. Council, Winston Churchill Trust, 1980–90. Freeman, City of London, 1981. FRSCM 1965; FRCM 1971; FRNCM 1977; FRSAMD 1982; Hon. RAM 1965; Hon. FTCL 1976; Hon. GSM 1980; Hon. FRCCO 1967. Hon. MA Bradford, 1973; Hon. DMus: Exeter, 1976; Leicester, 1977; Westminster Choir Coll., Princeton, 1980; Bristol, 1981; St Olaf Coll., Minnesota, 1991; RCM, 1998; Victoria, BC, 1999; Hon. DLitt Sussex, 1982; Hon. Dr of Sacred Letters, Trinity Coll., Toronto, 1985; Hon. Dr of Fine Arts, Luther Coll., Iowa, 1998; Hon. LLD Toronto, 2001. *Publications:* miscellaneous choral and instrumental works. *Address:* 13 Grange Road, Cambridge CB3 9AS. *T:* (01223) 359559. *Club:* Athenæum.

WILLCOCKS, Lt Gen. Sir Michael (Alan), KCB 2000 (CB 1997), Gentleman Usher of the Black Rod and Serjeant-at-Arms, House of Lords, and Secretary to the Lord Great Chamberlain, since 2001; *b* 27 July 1944; *s* of Henry Willcocks and late Georgina Willcocks (*née* Lawton); *m* 1966, Jean Paton Weir; one *s* two *d. Educ:* St John's Coll.; RMA Sandhurst; London Univ. (BSc Hons). Commnd RA, 1964; served Malaya, Borneo, UK, Germany, 1965–72; Instructor, RMA Sandhurst, 1972–74; MoD, 1977–79; Comd M Battery, RHA, 1979–80; Directing Staff, Staff Coll., 1981–83; CO, 1st Regt, RHA, 1983–85; Dep. ACOS, HQ UKLF, 1985–87; ACOS, Intelligence/Ops, HQ UKLF, 1988; CRA, 4th Armd Div., 1989–90; rcds 1991; ACOS, Land Ops, Joint War HQ, Gulf War, 1991; Dir Army Plans and Programme, 1991–93; Dir Gen. Land Warfare, 1993–94; COS Allied Command Europe Rapid Reaction Corps, 1994–96; COS Land Component Implementation Force, Bosnia-Herzegovina, 1995–96; ACGS, MoD, 1996–99; Dep. Comdr (Ops), Stabilisation Force, Bosnia-Herzegovina, 1999–2000; UK Mil. Rep. to NATO and the EU, 2000–01. Comr, Royal Hosp., Chelsea, 1996–99. Col Comdt, RA, 2000–. Hon. Col, 1 RHA, 1999–. Mem., European-Atlantic Gp, 1994–. MSM (USA), 1996, 2000. *Publications:* Airmobility and the Armoured Experience, 1989. *Recreations:* books, music, tennis, fishing, sailing. *Address:* House of Lords, SW1A 0PW. *Club:* National Liberal.

WILLCOX, James Henry, CB 1988; Clerk of Public Bills, House of Commons, 1982–88, retired; *b* 31 March 1923; *s* of George Henry and Annie Elizabeth Willcox; *m* 1st, 1950, Winsome Rosemarie Adèle Dallas Ross (*d* 1984); one *s* one *d*; 2nd, 1985, Pamela, *widow* of Col John Lefroy Knyvett. *Educ:* St George's Coll., Weybridge; St John's Coll., Oxford (Schol.; MA). Served RNVR, 1942–45. Assistant Clerk, House of Commons, 1947; Sen. Clerk, 1951; Clerk of Standing Committees, 1975–76; Clerk of Overseas Office, 1976–77; Clerk of Private Bills, Examiner of Petitions for Private Bills and Taxing Officer, 1977–82. *Recreations:* walking, gardening. *Address:* Ibthorpe Farm House, Ibthorpe, near Andover, Hants SP11 0BN. *T:* (01264) 736575. *Club:* Garrick.

WILLEBRANDS, His Eminence Cardinal Johannes Gerardus Maria; President, Vatican Secretariat for Promoting Christian Unity, 1969–89, now President Emeritus; Archbishop of Utrecht and Primate of Holland, 1975–83; *b* Netherlands, 4 Sept. 1909. *Educ:* Warmond Seminary, Holland; Angelicum, Rome (Dr Phil.). Priest, 1934; Chaplain, Begijnhof Church, Amsterdam, 1937–40; Prof. of Philosophy, Warmond, 1940; Director, 1945; Pres., St Willibrord Assoc., 1946; organised Catholic Conf. on Ecumenical Questions, 1951; Sec., Vatican Secretariat for Promoting Christian Unity, 1960; Titular Bishop of Mauriana, 1964; Cardinal, 1969; Cardinal with the Title of St Sebastian, Martyr, 1975. Hon. Dr of Letters: St Louis Univ., 1968; St Olaf Coll., USA, 1976; St Thomas' Coll., St Paul's, Minn, 1979; Assumption Coll., Worcester, Mass, 1980; Hon. Dr of Theology: Catholic Univ. of Louvain, 1971; Leningrad Theological Acad, 1973; Catholic Univ., Lublin, Poland, 1985; Catholic Univ., München, 1987; St Michael's UC, Toronto, 1990; Hon. DD Oxon, 1987; Hon. DH Hellenic Coll./Holy Cross Orthodox Sch. of Theol., Brookline, Mass, 1989; Hon. LLD: Notre Dame Univ., 1970; Catholic Univ., Washington, 1974; Seton Hall Univ., NJ, 1987. *Publications:* Oecuménisme et Problèmes Actuels, 1969; Mandatum Unitatis: Beiträge zur Oekumene, 1989; Church and Jewish People, 1992; reports on the ecumenical situation and articles on inter-church relationships. *Address:* Pont. Collegio Olandese, Via Ercole Rosa 1, 00153 Rome, Italy.

WILLEMS, Lodewijk; Ambassador of Belgium to the Court of St James's, since 1997; *b* 6 April 1948; *s* of Frans and Leona Willems-Hendrickx; *m* 1976, Lindsay Edwards; three *s* one *d. Educ:* Univ. of Brussels (Licentiate Pol. Science and Internat. Relns 1971); Yale Univ. (MA Pol. Science 1975). Entered Belgian Diplomatic Service, 1976; Dep. Perm. Rep., IAEA, Vienna, 1977; Advr to Dep. Prime Minister and Minister for Econ. Affairs, 1977–81; Dep. Sec. Gen., Benelux Econ. Union, 1981–85; Political Counsellor, Kinshasa,

1985–88; Chef de Cabinet to Minister for Econ. Affairs, 1988–91; Dep. Perm. Rep. to EU, 1991–92; Chef de Cabinet to Minister of Foreign Affairs, 1992–94; Perm. Rep. (Ambassador rank), UN, Geneva, 1994–97. Mem., Anglo-Belgian Soc., 1997–. Commn for Relief of Belgium Fellow, Belgian-American Educnl Foundn, 1973. Commander, Order of the Crown (Belgium), 1995. *Recreations:* theatre, classical music. *Address:* Belgian Embassy, 103 Eaton Square, SW1W 9AB. *T:* (020) 7470 3700. *Clubs:* Anglo-Belgian, Travellers.

WILLESDEN, Area Bishop of, since 2001; **Rt Rev. Peter Alan Broadbent;** *b* 31 July 1952; *s* of Philip and Patricia Broadbent; *m* 1974, Sarah Enderby; one *s*. *Educ:* Merchant Taylors' Sch., Northwood, Middx; Jesus Coll., Cambridge (MA 1978); St John's Coll., Nottingham (DipTh 1975). Ordained deacon, 1977, priest 1978; Assistant Curate: St Nicholas, Durham City, 1977–80; Emmanuel, Holloway, 1980–83; Chaplain, Poly. of N London, 1983–89; Vicar, Trinity St Michael, Harrow, 1989–94; Archdeacon of Northolt, 1995–2001. Proctor in Convocation, London, 1985–2001. Member: Archbishops' Council, C of E, 1999–2000; Central Governing Body, City Parochial Foundn, 1999–. Mem. (Lab) Islington BC, 1982–89. *Publications:* contrib. to theol books and jls. *Recreations:* football, theatre and film, railways. *Address:* 173 Willesden Lane, NW6 7YN. *T:* (020) 8451 0189, *Fax:* (020) 8451 4606; *e-mail:* bishop.willesden@btinternet.com.

WILLESEE, Hon. Donald Robert; Member of Senate for Western Australia, 1949–75; *b* 14 April 1916; *m*; four *s* two *d*. *Educ:* Carnarvon, Western Australia. Special Minister of State, Minister assisting Prime Minister, Minister assisting Minister for Foreign Affairs and Vice-Pres. of Exec. Council, 1972–73; Minister for Foreign Affairs, 1973–75; Leader of Opposition in the Senate, 1966–67; Deputy Leader of Opposition in Senate, 1969–72; Deputy Leader of Govt in Senate, 1972. *Recreation:* swimming. *Address:* 5 Walton Place, Quinns Rock, WA 6030, Australia.

WILLETT, Allan Robert, CMG 1997; DL; Chairman: Willett International Ltd, since 1983 (Chief Executive, 1983–91); South East England Development Agency, since 1998; *b* 24 Aug. 1936; *s* of Robert Willett and Irene Willett; *m* 1st, 1960, Mary Hillman (marr. diss. 1993); 2nd, 1993, Anne Boardman (*née* Stead). *Educ:* Eastbourne Coll. Commnd Royal E Kent Regt, 1955–57; seconded, KAR, 1955–56. Man. Dir, G. D. Peters Ltd, 1969–71; Chm., Northampton Machinery Co., 1970–74; Dep. Chm., Rowen & Boden, 1973–74; formed Willett Cos, 1974. DL Kent, 2001. *Recreations:* military history, golf, tennis, walking. *Address:* Chairman's Office, Willett International Ltd, Cumberland Cottage, Chilham, Kent CT4 8BX. *T:* (01227) 738800, *Fax:* (01227) 738855; *e-mail:* allan.willett@willett.com. *Club:* Royal Over-Seas League.

WILLETT, Prof. Frank, CBE 1985; FRSE 1979; Emeritus Professor and Hon. Senior Research Fellow, Hunterian Museum, University of Glasgow, since 1990; *b* 18 Aug. 1925; *s* of Thomas Willett and Frances (*née* Latham); *m* 1950, Mary Constance Hewitt; one *s* three *d*. *Educ:* Bolton Municipal Secondary Sch.; University Coll., Oxford. MA (Oxon); Dip. Anthropology (Oxon). War damage clerk, Inland Revenue, 1940; RAF Linguist, Japanese, 1943–44. Keeper, Dept of Ethnology and Gen. Archaeology, Manchester Museum, 1950–58; Hon. Surveyor of Antiquities, Nigerian Federal Govt, 1956–57, 1957–58; Archaeologist and Curator, Mus. of Ife Antiquities, Nigerian Fed. Govt, 1958–63; Supply Teacher, Bolton Educn Cttee, 1963–64; Leverhulme Research Fellow, 1964; Research Fellow, Nuffield Coll., Oxford, 1964–66; Prof. of Art History, African and Interdisciplinary Studies, Northwestern Univ., Evanston, Ill, USA, 1966–76; Dir and Titular Prof., Hunterian Mus. and Art Gall., Glasgow, 1976–90. Research Collaborator, Smithsonian Instn, 1992–. Vis. Fellow, Clare Hall, Cambridge, 1970–71. Curator, RSE, 1992–97. Hon. Corresp. Member, Manchester Literary and Philosophical Soc., 1958–. Leadership Award, Arts Council of the African Studies Assoc., 1995; Bicentenary Medal, RSE, 1997. *Publications:* Ife in the History of West African Sculpture, 1967, rev. edn, Ife: une Civilisation Africaine, 1971; African Art: An Introduction, 1971, rev. edn 1993; (with Ekpo Eyo) Treasures of Ancient Nigeria, 1980; articles in Encyc. Britannica, Man, Jl of Afr. Hist., Afr. Arts, Africa, Jl of Nigerian Historical Soc., Odu, SA Archaeol Bull., Archæometry; many conf. reports and chapters in several books. *Recreations:* relaxing, baiting architects. *Address:* Hunterian Museum, University of Glasgow, Glasgow G12 8QQ. *T:* (0141) 330 4221. *Club:* Royal Commonwealth Society.

WILLETT, Michael John, FRAeS; Board Member, Civil Aviation Authority and Group Director, Safety Regulation, 1992–97; *b* 2 Oct. 1944; *s* of Reginald John Willett and Nora Else Willett; *m* 1st, 1967, Gillian Margaret Pope (marr. diss. 1998); two *s* one *d*; 2nd, 1998, Paulene Ann Parkinson. *Educ:* Grammar Sch., Tottenham; Open Univ. (BA Hons); Open Business Sch. (MBA). RAF, 1963–71; Airline Captain, Laker Airways, 1973–82; Flight Ops Inspectorate, CAA, 1982–92. Mem. (C), W Sussex CC, 1999–2001. Liveryman, GAPAN, 1991– (Warden, 1998–). *Recreation:* horse riding.

WILLETTS, David Lindsay; MP (C) Havant, since 1992; *b* 9 March 1956; *s* of John Roland Willetts and Hilary Sheila Willetts; *m* 1986, Hon. Sarah Harriet Ann, *d* of Lord Butterfield, *qv*; one *s* one *d*. *Educ:* King Edward's Sch., Birmingham; Christ Church, Oxford (BA 1st cl. Hons PPE). Res. Asst to Nigel Lawson, MP, 1978; HM Treasury, 1978–84: Pvte Sec. to Financial Sec., 1981–82; Principal Monetary Policy Div., 1982–84; Prime Minister's Downing Street Policy Unit, 1984–86; Dir of Studies, Centre for Policy Studies, 1987–92. PPS to Chm. of Cons. Party, 1993–94; an Asst Govt Whip, 1994–95; a Lord Comr of HM Treasury (Govt Whip), 1995; Parly Sec., Office of Public Service, Cabinet Office, 1995–96; HM Paymaster General, 1996; Opposition front bench spokesman on employment, 1997–98, on educn and employment, 1998–99, on social security, 1999–2001, on work and pensions, 2001–. Consultant Dir, 1987–92, Chm., 1997, Cons. Res. Dept. Director: Retirement Security Ltd, 1988–94; Electra Corporate Ventures Ltd, 1988–94; Economic Advr, Dresdner Kleinwort Benson, 1997–. Vis. Fellow, Nuffield Coll., Oxford, 1999–. Mem., Social Security Adv. Cttee, 1989–92. Member: Parkside HA, 1988–90; Lambeth, Lewisham and Southwark FPC, 1987–90. *Publications:* Modern Conservatism, 1992; Civic Conservatism, 1994; Blair's Gurus, 1996; Why Vote Conservative?, 1997; (jtly) Is Conservatism Dead?, 1997; Welfare to Work, 1998; After the Landslide, 1999; paper, The Role of the Prime Minister's Policy Unit, 1987 (Haldane Medal, RIPA); various pamphlets. *Recreations:* swimming, reading. *Address:* c/o House of Commons, SW1A 0AA. *T:* (020) 7219 4570. *Club:* Hurlingham.

WILLIAMS; *see* Rees-Williams, family name of Baron Ogmore.

WILLIAMS; *see* Sims-Williams.

WILLIAMS, family name of **Barons Williams of Elvel** and **Williams of Mostyn** and **Baroness Williams of Crosby**.

WILLIAMS OF CROSBY, Baroness *cr* 1993 (Life Peer), of Stevenage in the County of Hertfordshire; **Shirley Vivien Teresa Brittain Williams;** PC 1974; Co-founder, Social Democratic Party, 1981, President, 1982–88; Professor of Elective Politics, John F. Kennedy School of Government, Harvard University, 1988–2000, now Emeritus; *b* 27 July 1930; *d* of late Prof. Sir George Catlin, and late Mrs Catlin, (Vera Brittain); *m* 1st, 1955, Prof. Bernard Arthur Owen Williams (*see* Sir B. A. O. Williams) (marr. diss. 1974); one *d*; 2nd, 1987, Prof. Richard Elliott Neustadt. *Educ:* eight schools in UK and USA; Somerville Coll., Oxford (scholar; MA, Hon. Fellow, 1970); Columbia Univ., New York (Smith-Mundt Scholar). General Secretary, Fabian Soc., 1960–64 (Chm., 1980–81). Contested: (Lab) Harwich, Essex, 1954 and 1955, and Southampton Test, 1959; (SDP) Crosby, 1983; (SDP/Alliance) Cambridge, 1987. MP: (Lab) Hitchin, 1964–74; (Lab) Hertford and Stevenage, 1974–79; (first-elected SDP MP) Crosby, Nov. 1981–1983; PPS, Minister of Health, 1964–66; Parly Sec., Min. of Labour, 1966–67; Minister of State: Education and Science, 1967–69; Home Office, 1969–70; Opposition spokesman on: Social Services, 1970–71, on Home Affairs, 1971–73; Prices and Consumer Protection, 1973–74; Sec. of State for Prices and Consumer Protection, 1974–76; Sec. of State for Educn and Science, 1976–79; Paymaster General, 1976–79. Bd Mem., Rand Corp., Europe, 1993–. Chm., OECD study on youth employment, 1979; Member: Council of Advrs to Praesidium, Ukraine, 1991–97; Adv. Council to UN Sec.-Gen. for Fourth World Women's Conf., Beijing, 1995; EC Comité des Sages, 1995–96; Council, Internat. Crisis Gp, 1998–; Internat. Adv. Cttee, Council on Foreign Relns, NY. Mem., Labour Party Nat. Exec. Cttee, 1970–81. Leader, Liberal Democrat Party, House of Lords, 2001– (Dep. Leader, 1999–2001). Visiting Fellow, Nuffield College, Oxford, 1967–75; Res. Fellow, PSI, 1979–85; Visiting Faculty, Internat. Management Inst., Geneva, 1979–88; Fellow, Inst. of Politics, Harvard, 1979–80 (Mem., Sen. Adv. Council, 1986–99; Acting Dir, 1989–90); Director: Turing Inst., Glasgow, 1985–90; Learning by Experience Trust, 1986–94; Educn Develt Centre, Newton, Mass, 1991–98; Internat. Mgt Inst., Kiev, 1990–2000; Project Liberty, 1990–98; Trustee, The Century Foundn (formerly Twentieth Century Fund), NY, 1978–. Lectures: Godkin, Harvard, 1980; Rede, Cambridge, 1980; Janeway, Princeton, 1981; Regents', Univ. of Calif., Berkeley, 1991; Erasmus, Notre Dame, 2001–02. Hon. Fellow, Newnham Coll., Cambridge, 1977. Hon. DEd CNAA, 1969; Hon. Dr Pol. Econ.: Univ. of Leuven, 1976; Radcliffe Coll., Harvard, 1978; Leeds, 1980; Bath, 1980; Hon. LLD: Sheffield, 1980; Southampton, 1981; Hon. DLitt Heriot-Watt, 1980; Hon. DSc Aston, 1981. *Publications:* Politics is for People, 1981; Jobs for the 1980s; Youth Without Work, 1981; (jtly) Unemployment and Growth in the Western Economies, 1984; A Job to Live, 1985; Snakes and Ladders: a diary of a political life, 1996; (contrib.) Realizing Human Rights, ed. Power and Alison, 2000. *Recreations:* music, poetry, hill walking.

WILLIAMS OF ELVEL, Baron *cr* 1985 (Life Peer), of Llansantffraed in Elvel in the County of Powys; **Charles Cuthbert Powell Williams,** CBE 1980; *b* 9 Feb. 1933; *s* of late Dr Norman Powell Williams, DD, and Mrs Muriel de Lérisson Williams (*née* Cazenove); *m* 1975, Jane Gillian (*née* Portal), DL; one step *s*. *Educ:* Westminster Sch.; Christ Church, Oxford (MA); LSE. British Petroleum Co. Ltd, 1958–64; Bank of London and Montreal, 1964–66; Eurofinance SA, Paris, 1966–70; Baring Brothers and Co. Ltd, 1970–77 (Man. Dir, 1971–77); Chm., Price Commn, 1977–79; Man. Dir 1980–82, Chm. 1982–85, Henry Ansbacher & Co. Ltd; Chief Exec., Henry Ansbacher Holdings PLC, 1982–85. Parly Candidate (Lab), Colchester, 1964. House of Lords: Dep. Leader of Opposition, 1989–92; Opposition spokesman on trade and industry, 1986–92, on energy, 1988–90, on defence, 1990–97, on the envmt, 1992–97. Founder Mem, Labour Econ. Finance and Taxation Assoc. (Vice-Chm., 1975–77, 1979–83). Director: Pergamon Holdings Ltd, 1985–91; Mirror Group Newspapers Ltd, 1985–91, Mirror Group Newspapers PLC, 1991–92. Pres., Campaign for Protection of Rural Wales, 1989–95 (Vice-Pres., 1995–). *Publications:* The Last Great Frenchman: a life of General de Gaulle, 1993; Bradman: an Australian hero, 1996; Adenauer, the Father of the new Germany, 2000. *Recreations:* cricket (Oxford Univ. CC, 1953–55, Captain 1955; Essex CCC, 1953–59); music, real tennis. *Address:* 48 Thurloe Square, SW7 2SX. *T:* (020) 7581 1783; Pant-y-Rhiw, Llansantffraed in Elvel, Powys LD1 5RH. *Clubs:* Reform, MCC.

WILLIAMS OF MOSTYN, Baron *cr* 1992 (Life Peer), of Great Tew in the County of Oxfordshire; **Gareth Wyn Williams;** PC 1999; QC 1978; Lord Privy Seal, Leader of the House of Lords, since 2001; *b* 5 Feb. 1941; *s* of Albert Thomas Williams and Selina Williams; *m* 1st, 1962, Pauline Clarke (marr. diss.); one *s* two *d*; 2nd, 1994, Veena Maya Russell; one *d*. *Educ:* Rhyl Grammar Sch.; Queens' Coll., Cambridge (Open Schol. (History) 1958; Univ. Prize, Jurisprudence 1962; Foundn Schol. 1964; LLB (1st Cl.) 1964; MA 1965). Called to the Bar, Gray's Inn, 1965, Bencher, 1991; a Recorder, 1978–; Leader, Wales and Chester Circuit, 1987–89. Mem., Bar Council, 1986–92 (Chm., 1992). Parly Under-Sec. of State, Home Office, 1997–98; Minister of State, Home Office, 1998–99; Attorney Gen., 1999–2001. Pro-Chancellor, Univ. of Wales, 1994–. Fellow, UCW, Aberystwyth, 1993. *Address:* House of Lords, SW1A 0PW.

WILLIAMS, Adèle; *see* Williams, J. A.

WILLIAMS, Prof. Alan Harold; Professor in the Department of Economics, University of York, since 1968; *b* 9 June 1927; *s* of Harold George Williams and Gladys May Williams (*née* Clark); *m* 1953, June Frances Porter; two *s* one *d*. *Educ:* King Edward's, Birmingham; Univ. of Birmingham (BCom). Lecturer, Exeter Univ., 1954–63; Sen. Lectr and Reader, Univ. of York, 1964–68. Visiting Lecturer: MIT, 1957–58; Princeton, 1963–64; Director of Economic Studies, HM Treasury Centre for Administrative Studies, 1966–68. Member: Yorkshire Water Authority, 1973–76; DHSS Chief Scientists Research Cttee, 1973–78; Royal Commission on the NHS, 1976–78; various SSRC Cttees and Panels, 1973–; Nat. Water Council, 1980–83. Hon. DPhil Lund, 1977. *Publications:* Public Finance and Budgetary Policy, 1963; (with Robert Anderson) Efficiency in the Social Services, 1975; (with Robert Sugden) Principles of Practical Cost-Benefit Analysis, 1978; Being Reasonable about the Economics of Health, 1997; articles in Economica, Jl of Political Econ., Jl of Public Econs, Nat. Tax Jl, Jl of Health Econ., BMJ and elsewhere; numerous conf. papers on various aspects of public expenditure appraisal, esp. health and health care. *Recreations:* music, walking, teasing.

WILLIAMS, Rt Hon. Alan John; PC 1977; MP (Lab) Swansea West since 1964; *b* 14 Oct. 1930; *m* 1957, Mary Patricia Rees, Blackwood, Mon; two *s* one *d*. *Educ:* Cardiff High Sch.; Cardiff College of Technology; University College, Oxford. BSc (London); BA (Oxon). Lecturer in economics, Welsh College of Advanced Technology; Free-lance Journalist. Joined Labour Party, 1950. Member: NATFHE (formerly of ATTI), 1958–; Fabian Society; Co-operative Party; National Union of Students delegation to Russia, 1954. Advr, Assoc. of First Div. Civil Servants, 1982–93. Contested (Lab) Poole, 1959. PPS to Postmaster General, 1966–67; Parly Under-Sec., DEA, 1967–69; Parly Sec., Min. of Technology, 1969–70; Opposition Spokesman on Consumer Protection, Small Businesses, Minerals, 1970–74; Minister of State: Dept of Prices and Consumer Protection, 1974–76; DoI, 1976–79; Opposition spokesman on Wales, 1979–80; Shadow Minister for CS, 1980–83; opposition spokesman on: trade and industry, 1983–87; Wales, 1987–89; Dep. Shadow Leader of the House, 1983–89 and 1988–89; Shadow Sec. of State for Wales, 1987–88. Member: Public Accts Cttee, 1966–67, 1990–; Privileges Cttee, 1994–95, 1997–; Lord Chancellor's Adv. Council on Public Records, 1995–2001; Jt Cttee on Parly Privilege, 1997–; Jt Chm., All-Party Minerals Cttee, 1979–86; Chairman, Welsh PLP, 1966–67; Delegate, Council of Europe and WEU, 1966–67. Sponsored by TSSA

(Mem., 1984–95). Chm., Welsh Br., British–Russia Soc., 1996–. *Address:* House of Commons, SW1A 0AA. *Club:* Clyne Golf.

WILLIAMS, Alan Lee, OBE 1973; Director, Atlantic Council, since 1993 (Director, 1972–74 and 1992–93, Chairman, 1980–83, British Atlantic Committee); *b* 29 Nov. 1930; *m* 1974, Jennifer Ford. *Educ:* Roan Sch., Greenwich; Ruskin Coll., Oxford. National Service, RAF, 1951–53; Oxford, 1954–56; National Youth Officer, Labour Party, 1956–62. Dir-Gen., E-SU, 1979–86; Warden and Chief Exec., Toynbee Hall, 1987–92. MP (Lab) Hornchurch, 1966–70, Havering, Hornchurch, Feb. 1974–1979; PPS to Sec. of State for Defence, 1969–70, 1976; PPS to Sec. of State for NI, 1976–78; Chm., Parly Lab. Party Defence Cttee, 1976–79. Member: FO Adv. Cttee on Disarmament and Arms Control, 1975–79; Council, RUSI, 1975–78; Adv. Council on Public Records, 1977–84; Chm., Delegn to 4th Cttee of UN, NY, 1969; Chm., Transport on Water Assoc.; Deputy Director, European Movement, 1970–71; Vice Pres., European-Atlantic Gp, 1983–; Pres., Atlantic Treaty Assoc., 2000–; Chm., European Working Gp of Internat. Centre for Strategic and Internat. Studies, Washington, 1987–99 (Mem., 1974–); Mem. Council, RUSI, 1968–79; Member: Trilateral Commn, 1976–; Missile Proliferation Study Gp, 2000. Chairman: Cedar Centre, Isle of Dogs, 1991–; Toynbee Housing Assoc., 1993–99. Chm. of Govs, City Coll., 1990–. Freeman: City of London, 1969; Co. of Watermen and Lightermen, 1952–. Fellow, QMW, 1993. DLitt (*hc*) Schiller Internat. Univ., 1987. FRSA. *Publications:* Radical Essays, 1966; Europe or the Open Sea?, 1971; Crisis in European Defence, 1973; The European Defence Initiative: Europe's bid for equality, 1985; The Decline of Labour and the Fall of the SDP, 1989; Islamic Resurgence, 1991; Prospects for a Common European Foreign and Security Policy, 1995; NATO's Future in the Balance: time for a rethink, 1995; NATO and European Defence: a new era of partnership, 1997; NATO's Strategy for Securing the Future, 1999. *Recreations:* reading, history, walking. *Address:* 6 North Several, Blackheath, SE3 0QR. *Clubs:* Reform, Pilgrims.

WILLIAMS, Dr Alan Wynne; *b* 21 Dec. 1945; *s* of late Tom and Mary Hannah Williams; *m* 1973, Marian Williams. *Educ:* Carmarthen Grammar School; Jesus College, Oxford (BA Chem. 1st cl. hons; DPhil). Senior Lecturer in Environmental Science, Trinity College, Carmarthen, 1971–87. MP (Lab) Carmarthen, 1987–97, Carmarthen E and Dinefwr, 1997–2001; contested Carmarthen E and Dinefwr, 2001. *Recreations:* reading, watching sport.

WILLIAMS, Sir Alastair Edgcumbe James D.; *see* Dudley-Williams.

WILLIAMS, Albert; General Secretary, Union of Construction, Allied Trades and Technicians, 1985–92; President, European Federation of Building and Woodworkers, 1988–92; *b* 12 Feb 1927; *s* of William Arthur Williams and Phyllis Williams (*née* Barnes); *m* 1954, Edna Bradley; two *s*. *Educ:* Houldsworth School, Reddish; Manchester School of Building (1st and 2nd year Union of Lancs and Cheshire Insts Certs of Training). Apprentice bricklayer, Manchester City Corp., 1941; Armed Forces, 1944–48; bricklaying for various contractors; Member: Exec., Amalgamated Union of Building Trade Workers, 1958; Exec., Council of UCATT, 1971–92; Construction Ind. Trng Bd, 1979–92; Gen. Council, TUC, 1986–92; Dir, Bldg and Civil Engrg Holidays Scheme Management Ltd, 1979–92; Operatives' Side Sec., Nat. Jt Council for Building Industry, 1984–. Dir, Labour Train Contract Services, 1994–. Chm. of Trustees, Working Class Liby, Salford, 1971–. *Recreations:* poetry and work. *Address:* 3 Cornflower Lane, Shirley, Croydon, Surrey CR0 8XJ.

WILLIAMS, (Albert) Trevor; management scientist; *b* 7 April 1938; *s* of Ben and Minnie Williams; *m* 1st, 1970, Mary Lynn Lyster; three *s*; 2nd, 1978, Deborah Sarah Fraser Duncan (*née* Milne); one *s*, and one step *s* two step *d*. *Educ:* King George V Sch., Southport; Queens' Coll., Cambridge (Open Exhibr; MA); Univ. of Ghana (Rotary Foundn Fellow); Cranfield Institute of Technology (MSc). Commnd RA, 1957. Director: Business Operations Research Ltd, 1965–68; Novy Eddison and Partners, 1971–74; Dep.-Dir for Futures Research, Univ. of Stellenbosch, 1974–78; Dep. Chief Scientific Officer, Price Commission, 1978–79; Advisor on Technology Projects, Scottish Development Agency, 1979; Dir, Henley Centre for Forecasting, 1980–81. Consultant and Sen. Industrial Advr, Monopolies and Mergers Commn, 1982–90; advr to cos in Europe, S Africa and USA, 1989–2001. Various academic appointments, 1968–95, incl. visiting and hon. professorships: Graduate Sch. of Business, Cape Town Univ.; Sussex Univ.; INSEAD; Wisconsin Univ.; Hong Kong Univ.; LSE. Mem., Editl Adv. Bd, Futures, 1984–98. FInstD; MRI. *Publications:* A Guide to Futures Studies, 1976; (contrib.) Futures, 1985–98. *Recreation:* celebrating the new millennium. *Address:* Wyebeere, Ruckhall Common, Hereford HR2 9QU. *T:* (01981) 251439. *Club:* Athenæum.

WILLIAMS, Alexander, CB 1991; FInstP; Government Chemist, 1987–91; *b* 30 March 1931; *s* of Henry and Dorothy Williams; *m* 1957, Beryl Wynne Williams (*née* Williams); one *s*. *Educ:* Grove Park Grammar Sch., Wrexham; University College of North Wales, Bangor (BSc). National Service, REME, 1953–55; Monsanto Chemicals, 1955–56; Southern Instruments, Camberley, 1956–59; National Physical Laboratory: Div. of Radiation Science, 1959–78; Head, Div. of Mechanical and Optical Metrology, 1978–81; Under Sec., Res. and Technology Policy Div., DTI 1981–87. Dir, Assoc. of Official Analytical Chemists, 1989–93. Pres., British Measurement and Testing Assoc., 1995–. Freeman, City of London, 1997; Liveryman, Co. of Scientific Instrument Makers, 1997–. *Publications:* A Code of Practice for the Detailed Statement of Accuracy (with P. J. Campion and J. E. Burns), 1973; numerous papers on measurements of radio-activity etc, to Internat. Jl of Applied Radiation and Isotopes, Nucl. Instruments and Methods, etc. *Recreations:* bell-ringing, music, opera, walking.

WILLIAMS, Sir Alwyn, Kt 1983; PhD; FRS 1967; FRSE, MRIA, FGS; Principal and Vice-Chancellor of University of Glasgow, 1976–88, Hon. Senior Research Fellow in Geology, since 1988; *b* 8 June 1921; *s* of D. Daniel Williams and E. May (*née* Rogers); *m* 1949, E. Joan Bevan; one *s* one *d*. *Educ:* Aberdare Boys' Grammar Sch.; University College of Wales, Aberystwyth (Hon. Fellow, 1990). PhD Wales. Fellow, Univ. of Wales, 1946–48. Harkness Fund Fellow at US National Museum, Washington, DC, 1948–50; Lecturer in Geology in University of Glasgow, 1950–54; Prof. of Geology, 1954–74, Pro-Vice-Chancellor, 1967–74, Queen's Univ. of Belfast; Lapworth Prof. of Geology, and Head of Dept, Univ. of Birmingham, 1974–76. Pres., Palaeontological Assoc., 1968–70. Trustee, British Museum (Nat. History), 1971–79, Chm. of Trustees, 1974–79. Member: Equip. and Phys. Sci. sub-cttees, UGC, 1974–76; NERC, 1974–76; Adv. Council, British Library, 1975–77; Scottish Tertiary Educn Adv. Council, 1983–87; Adv. Bd for the Res. Councils, 1985–88; Chairman: Cttee on Nat. Museums and Galls in Scotland, 1979–81; Cttee on Scottish Agricl Colls, 1989; Scottish Hospitals Endowment Res. Trust, 1989–96; Vice-Chm., Cttee of Vice-Chancellors and Principals, 1979–81. Dir, Scottish Daily Record & Sunday Mail Ltd, 1984–90. Pres., Royal Soc. of Edinburgh, 1985–88. Hon. FRSAMD 1988; Hon. Fellow, Geol Soc. of America, 1970–; For. Mem., Polish Academy of Sciences, 1979–; Hon. Associate, BM (Nat. Hist.), 1981–; Hon. FRCPS; Hon. FDS RCPS; Hon. DSc: Wales, 1974; Belfast, 1975; Edinburgh, 1979; Hon. LLD: Strathclyde, 1982; Glasgow, 1988; Hon. DCL Oxford, 1987; DUniv Paisley, 1993. Bigsby Medal, 1961, Murchison Medal, 1973, Geol Soc.; Clough Medal, Edin. Geol. Soc., 1976; T. Neville George Medal, Glasgow Geol. Soc., 1984. *Publications:* contrib. to Trans Royal Socs of London and Edinburgh, Jl Geological Society; Geological Magazine; Washington Acad. of Sciences; Geological Societies of London and America; Palaeontology; Journal of Paleontology, etc. *Address:* Palaeobiology Unit, The University, Glasgow G12 8QQ; 25 Sutherland Avenue, Pollokshields, Glasgow G41 4HG. *T:* (0141) 427 0589.

WILLIAMS, Anna Maureen, (Mrs G. H. G. Williams); *see* Worrall, A. M.

WILLIAMS, Anthony Neville; Managing Partner Worldwide, Andersen Legal, since 2000; *b* 8 July 1956; *s* of late David Leslie Williams and Rose Williams (*née* Mingay); *m* 1979, Johannah McDonnell; one *s* one *d*. *Educ:* Southampton Univ. (LLB 1978). Admitted Solicitor, England, 1981, Hong Kong, 1985; Solicitor and Barrister, Victoria, Australia, 1986. Solicitor: Turner Garrett & Co., 1981; Coward Chance, 1981–87, Clifford Chance (following merger), 1987–2000; Hong Kong office, 1984–90; Partner, 1988–2000; Man. Partner, Moscow office, 1995–97; Man. Partner, 1998–99. *Publications:* (jtly) Intellectual Property in the People's Republic of China, 1986; (jtly) The Hong Kong Banking Ordinance, 1987. *Recreations:* horse riding, wine. *Address:* Andersen Legal, 2 Arundel Street, WC2R 3DA.

WILLIAMS, Dr Anthony Peter; HM Inspector of Constabulary (non-police), 1993–96; *b* 18 June 1936; *s* of late Dr Emlyn Williams, Principal, Hendon Coll. of Technology, and Gwyneth Mair Williams (*née* Williams); *m* 1964, Vera Georgiadou; one *s* one *d*. *Educ:* St Paul's Sch., London; Keble Coll., Oxford (BA 1961; MA 1965); Birkbeck Coll., London (PhD 1971). Research and teaching, 1961–67; Principal Psychologist, CSSB, 1967–71; Consultant, Hay-MSL Ltd, 1971–76; Head of Personnel, BOC Gases, 1976–78; Consultant and Manager, Hay Associates, NY, 1979–84; Dir of Personnel, World Bank, 1984–88; Worldwide Partner and Dir, Hay Management Consultants, 1989–93. Vis. Sen. Fellow, City Univ. Business Sch., 1997–. Mem., Corporate Governance Wkg Party, Assoc. of Investment Trust Cos, 1999–2000. *Publications:* Just Reward?: the truth about top executive pay, 1994; Who Will Guard the Guardians?: corporate governance in the Millennium, 1999; numerous articles in professional and management jls. *Recreations:* international affairs, use of language, travel, cultural diversity, opera, good food and wine, intelligent conversation, asking difficult questions. *Address:* 49 Talbot Road, W2 5JJ; 51 Bostock Road, Shokan, NY 12481, USA. *Clubs:* Athenæum, Oxford and Cambridge.

WILLIAMS, Sir Arthur (Dennis Pitt), Kt 1991; Chairman, Williams Holdings Ltd, since 1965; *b* 15 Oct. 1928; *s* of Arthur Henry Williams and Dora Ruth Williams; *m* 1st, 1951, Ngaire Garbett; three *s* two *d*; 2nd, 1989, Jeanne Brinkworth; one *s*. *Educ:* Salmerston; Margate College. Served RN, 1944–46. Apprentice carpenter, 1942–44 and 1946–47; carpenter, NZ, 1951–53; builder, 1953–, and property owner. Govt Appointee, Govt Property Services Ltd, 1991. Fellow: NZ Inst. of Builders; Aust. Inst. of Builders; NZ Inst. of Management. NZ Commemorative Medal, 1990. *Recreations:* horse breeding and racing. *Address:* Cranbrook, Cranbrook Grove, Waikanae, New Zealand. *T:* (business) (6) 3647739, *Fax:* (6) 3647605. *Club:* Wellesley (Wellington, NZ).

WILLIAMS, (Arthur) Ronald, OBE 1991; Chief Executive, Publishers Association, since 1998; *b* 29 Oct. 1942; *s* of Alfred Arthur Williams, OBE and Marjory Williams (*née* Heenan); *m* 1st, 1968, Lynne Diana Merrin; two *d*; 2nd, 1993, Antoinette Catherine Naldrett. *Educ:* Rossall Sch., Lancs; Selwyn Coll., Cambridge (MA). HM Diplomatic Service, 1964–79, served Jakarta, Singapore, Budapest and Nairobi (First Sec.); Chief Exec., Timber Growers UK, 1981–87; Exec. Dir, Forestry Industry Council of GB, 1987–97. *Publications:* Montrose: cavalier in mourning, 1975; The Lords of the Isles, 1985; The Heather and the Gale, 1997; Sons of the Wolf, 1998. *Recreations:* fly-fishing, Real tennis, walking, writing, reading. *Address:* Starlings, Wildhern, Andover, Hants SP11 0JE. *T:* (01264) 735389. *Club:* Royal Commonwealth Society.

WILLIAMS, Hon. Atanda F.; *see* Fatayi-Williams.

WILLIAMS, Rev. Austen; *see* Williams, Rev. S. A.

WILLIAMS, Sir Bernard (Arthur Owen), Kt 1999; FBA 1971; Fellow of All Souls College, Oxford, 1951–54 and since 1997; Monroe Deutsch Professor of Philosophy, University of California, Berkeley, since 1988; *b* 21 Sept. 1929; *s* of late O. P. D. Williams, OBE and H. A. Williams; *m* 1955, Shirley Vivienne Teresa Brittain Catlin (*see* Baroness Williams of Crosby) (marr. diss. 1974); one *d*; *m* 1974, Patricia Law Skinner; two *s*. *Educ:* Chigwell Sch., Essex; Balliol Coll., Oxford (BA 1951; MA 1954; Hon. Fellow 1984). RAF (Gen. Duties Br.), 1951–53; Fellow of New Coll., Oxford, 1954–59; Vis. Lectr, Univ. Coll. of Ghana, 1958–59; Lectr in Philosophy, UCL, 1959–64; Prof. of Philosophy, Bedford Coll., London, 1964–67 (Hon. Fellow 1985); Knightbridge Prof. of Philosophy, Cambridge Univ., 1967–79; Fellow, 1967–79 and 1988–, Provost, 1979–87, King's Coll., Cambridge; White's Prof. of Moral Philosophy, Oxford Univ., and Fellow of CCC, Oxford, 1990–96 (Hon. Fellow, 1996). Visiting Professor: Princeton Univ., USA, 1963; Harvard Univ., 1973; Univ. of California, Berkeley, 1986; Sather Prof. of Classics, Univ. of Calif, Berkeley, 1989; Vis. Fellow, Inst. of Advanced Studies, ANU, 1969; Sen. Vis. Fellow, Princeton, 1978, 1991; Gauss Seminar in Criticism, Princeton, 1992. Member: Public Schools Commn, 1965–70; Royal Commn on Gambling, 1976–78; Commn on Social Justice, 1993–94; Ind. Inquiry into the Misuse of Drugs Act (1971), 1997–2000; Chairman: Cttee on Obscenity and Film Censorship, 1977–79; Fitzwilliam Mus. Syndicate, 1984–87. Dir, English Nat. Opera (formerly Sadler's Wells Opera), 1968–86. Foreign Hon. Mem., Amer. Acad. of Arts and Sciences, 1983. FRSA 1993. Hon. LittD Dublin, 1981; Hon. DLitt: Aberdeen, 1987; Keele, 1995; Yale, 2001; Hon. DHL Chicago, 1999. Author and presenter, What is Truth? series, Channel 4, 1988. *Publications:* (ed with A. C. Montefiore) British Analytical Philosophy, 1966; Morality, 1972; Problems of the Self, 1973; A Critique of Utilitarianism, 1973; Descartes: The Project of Pure Enquiry, 1978; Moral Luck, 1981; (ed with A. K. Sen) Utilitarianism and Beyond, 1982; Ethics and the Limits of Philosophy, 1985; Shame and Necessity, 1993; Making Sense of Humanity, 1995; Plato, 1998; articles in philosophical jls, etc. *Recreation:* music, particularly opera. *Address:* All Souls College, Oxford OX1 4AL.

WILLIAMS, Betty; *see* Williams, Elizabeth.

WILLIAMS, Betty Helena; MP (Lab) Conwy, since 1997; *b* 31 July 1944. *Educ:* Ysgol Dyffryn Nantlle; BA (Hons) Wales. Member (Lab): Arfon BC, 1970–91 (Mayor, 1990–91); Gwynedd CC, 1976–93. Contested (Lab) Caernarfon, 1983, Conwy, 1987 and 1992. Mem., Welsh Affairs Select Cttee, 1997–. Hon. Fellow, Univ. of Wales, Bangor. *Address:* House of Commons, SW1A 0AA.

WILLIAMS, Prof. Sir Bruce (Rodda), KBE 1980; Professor of the University of Sydney, since 1967, and Fellow of the Senate, 1994–98 (Vice-Chancellor and Principal, 1967–81); *b* 10 Jan. 1919; *s* of late Rev. W. J. Williams and Helen Baud; *m* 1942, Roma Olive Hotten (*d* 1991); five *d*. *Educ:* Wesley College; Queen's College, University of Melbourne (BA 1939). MA Adelaide 1942; MA(Econ) Manchester, 1963. FASSA 1968. Lecturer in Economics, University of Adelaide, 1939–46 and at Queen's University of

Belfast, 1946–50; Professor of Economics, University College of North Staffordshire, 1950–59; Robert Otley Prof., 1959–63, and Stanley Jevons Prof., 1963–67, Univ. of Manchester; Dir, Technical Change Centre and Vis. Prof., Imperial Coll., London, 1981–86. Vis. Fellow, ANU, 1987, 1988, 1990, 1992–94. Secretary and Joint Director of Research, Science and Industry Committee, 1952–59. Member, National Board for Prices and Incomes, 1966–67; Econ. Adviser to Minister of Technology, 1966–67; Member: Central Advisory Council on Science and Technology, 1967; Reserve Bank Board, 1969–81; Chairman: NSW State Cancer Council, 1967–81; Australian Vice Chancellors Cttee, 1972–74; Aust. Govt Cttee of Inquiry into Educn and Trng, 1976–79; (Australian) Review of Discipline of Engrg, 1987–88; Dep. Chm., Parramatta Hosps Bd, 1979–81. President: Sydney Conservatorium of Music Foundn, 1994–98; Sydney Spring Fest. of New Music, 1999–; Chm., Internat. Piano Comp. of Australia, 1986–. Editor, The Sociological Review, 1953–59, and The Manchester Sch., 1959–67. President Economics Section of British Assoc., 1964. Hon. FIE(Aust) 1989. Hon. DLitt: Keele, 1973; Sydney, 1982; Hon. DEcon Qld, 1980; Hon. LLD: Melbourne, 1981; Manchester, 1982; Hon. DSc Aston, 1982. Kirby Meml Award, IProdE, 1988. *Publications:* The Socialist Order and Freedom, 1942; (with C. F. Carter): Industry and Technical Progress, 1957, Investment in Innovation, 1958, and Science in Industry, 1959; Investment Behaviour, 1962; Investment Proposals and Decisions, 1965; Investment, Technology and Growth, 1967; (ed) Science and Technology in Economic Growth, 1973; Systems of Higher Education: Australia, 1978; Education, Training and Employment, 1979; Living with Technology, 1982; (ed) Knowns and Unknowns in Technical Change, 1985; Attitudes to New Technologies and Economic Growth, 1986; Review of the Discipline of Engineering, 1988; University Responses to Research Selectivity, 1991; Higher Education and Employment, 1994. *Address:* 24 Mansfield Street, Glebe, NSW 2037, Australia; 106 Grange Road, W5 3PJ. *Club:* Athenæum.

WILLIAMS, Rear-Adm. Charles Bernard, CB 1980; OBE 1967; Flag Officer Medway and Port Admiral Chatham, 1978–80, retired; *b* 19 Feb. 1925; *s* of Charles Williams and Elizabeth (*née* Malherbe); *m* 1946, Patricia Mary, *d* of Henry Brownlow Thorp and Ellen Thorp; one *s* one *d*. *Educ:* Graeme Coll., Grahamstown, SA; Royal Naval Engineering Coll., Plymouth. Served in HM Ships Nigeria, Hornet, Triumph, 1946–53; in charge: Flight deck trials unit, 1953; Naval Wing, Nat. Gas Turbine Estabt, 1956; Sen. Engr, HMS Cumberland, 1958; in charge Admiralty Fuel Experimental Station, 1960; Comdr 1960; Engineer Officer, HMS London, 1962; Staff Engr, Flag Officer ME, 1964; Duty Comdr, Naval Ops MoD (N), 1967; Captain 1969; Dep. Manager, Portsmouth Dockyard, 1969; Supt, Clyde Submarine Base, 1972; Captain, HMS Sultan, 1975; Rear-Adm. 1978. Chairman: RYA Yachting Qualifications Cttee, 1976–86; Whitbread Round the World Race, 1981–90. *Recreations:* sailing, walking, music, bridge. *Address:* Green Shutters, Montserrat Road, Lee-on-Solent PO13 9LT. *T:* (023) 9255 0816. *Clubs:* Royal Yacht Squadron; Royal Ocean Racing; Royal Naval Sailing Association (Life Vice Cdre); Lee-on-Solent Sailing; Royal London Yacht (Hon. Mem.); Royal Southern Yacht (Hon. Mem.); Hornet Sailing; Cruising Association of South Africa (Life Mem.).

WILLIAMS, Sir Charles (Othniel), Kt 2000; Executive Chairman, C. O. Williams Construction and group of companies, since 1969; *b* 24 Nov. 1932; *s* of Elliot Williams and Lillian Williams; *m* 1st, 1956, Diane Walcott (marr. diss. 1999); two *s* one *d*; 2nd, 2000, Mary-Ann Gemmell (*née* Stewart-Richardson). *Educ:* Lodge Secondary Sch., Barbados. Overseer, Brighton Plantation, St George, 1951–54; Under Manager: Hothersall Plantation, St John, 1954–56; Guinea Sugar Factory, St John, 1956; Manager, Foster Hall Plantation, St Joseph, 1956–60; leased Foster Hall, 1960–75; founded: C.O. Williams, 1960; C.O. Williams Construction Co. Ltd, 1969. Master Entrepreneur of the Year, Ernst & Young Awards, 1997. *Recreations:* polo, deep-sea fishing, horse-racing. *Address:* Bromefield Plantation House, St Lucy, Barbados. *Clubs:* Barbados Polo, Barbados Turf, Barbados Yacht, Carlton Cricket, Wanderers Cricket (all Barbados).

WILLIAMS, Rt Rev. Christopher; *see* Williams, Rt Rev. J. C. R., Bishop of The Arctic.

WILLIAMS, Christopher Beverley, FRCP; Consultant Physician in Gastrointestinal Endoscopy: Wolfson Unit for Endoscopy, St Mark's Hospital for Colorectal and Intestinal Disorders, since 1975; Endoscopy Unit, London Clinic, since 1975; *b* 8 June 1938; *s* of late Denis John Williams, CBE, MD, FRCP and Dr Joyce Beverley Williams (*née* Jewson); *m* 1970, Christina Janet Seymour, MB, FRCP, *d* of Reginald S. Lawrie, MD, FRCS, FRCP, and Jean E. Lawrie, CBE, MB; one *s* one *d*. *Educ:* Dragon Sch.; Winchester Coll.; Trinity Coll., Oxford (BA Hons Physiol., BM BCh, MA); UCH. MRCS 1965, FRCS 1998; LRCP 1965, MRCP 1968, FRCP 1983. House appointments: UCH, 1965; Whittington and Brompton Hosps, 1966; SHO, Nat. Hosp. for Nervous Diseases, and Hammersmith Hosp., 1966–67; Registrar, UCH, 1968–70; Registrar, 1970–72, Res. Fellow and Hon. Sen. Registrar, 1972–74, St Mark's Hosp.; Consultant Physician, St Bartholomew's Hosp., 1975. Hon. Consultant Physician (Endoscopy): Royal Free Hosp.; Great Ormond Street Hosp. for Sick Children; King Edward VII Hosp. for Officers; St Luke's Hosp. for the Clergy. Vis. Prof., Sydney Univ., 1973; demonstrations, teaching courses and invited lectures world-wide on colonoscopy and colorectal cancer prevention; Foundn Lectr, British Soc. of Gastroenterology, 1976, 1995 (Vice-Pres., Endoscopy, 1987). Member: Soc. of Apothecaries, 1956–; Medical Soc. of London, 1983–; FRSocMed 1970. Hon. FRCS 1999. Mem., several internat. editl bds. *Publications:* (ed jtly) Colorectal Disease, 1981; (jtly) Practical Gastrointestinal Endoscopy, 1983, 4th edn 1996 (trans. Italian 1980, German 1985, French 1986, Spanish 1992, Portuguese, 1998); (jtly) Annual of Gastrointestinal Endoscopy, annually 1988–97; numerous articles and chapters on colonoscopy, colorectal disease and teaching methodology. *Recreations:* travel, fine wine and food, ski-ing, scuba. *Address:* 11 Frognal Way, Hampstead, NW3 6XE. *T:* (020) 7435 4030, *Fax:* (020) 7435 5636; *e-mail:* christopherwilliams@compuserve.com; Wolfson Unit, Northwick Park, HA1 3UJ. *T:* (020) 8235 4225, *Fax:* (020) 8423 3588; *e-mail:* wolfsonendoscopy@ic.ac.uk; London Clinic, 20 Devonshire Place, W1N 2DH. *T:* (020) 8616 7781, *Fax:* (020) 8616 7684.

WILLIAMS, Dr Christopher John Hacon, FRCP; Co-ordinator, Cochrane Cancer Network, Institute of Health Sciences, Oxford, since 1996; *b* 3 Aug. 1946; *s* of Owen Henry Williams and Joyce May Hacon Deavin; *m* 1970, Susan Tennant (marr. diss. 1995); two *d*. *Educ:* Reed's Sch., Surrey; London Univ., St Mary's Hosp. (MBBS); DM Southampton 1980. Jun. posts, London Hosps, 1971–74; Jun. Registrar, Med. Oncology, St Bartholomew's, 1974–75; Postdoctoral Res. Fellow, Stanford Univ., 1975–77; Res. Fellow, 1977–80, Sen. Lectr and Hon. Consultant Physician in Medical Oncology, 1980–96, Southampton Univ. Chairman: MRC Gynaecol Cancer Working Party, 1989–93; MRC Cancer Therapy Cttee, 1994–97; steering cttees and ind. data monitoring cttees for large-scale trials in breast and ovarian cancer; Member: Protocol Rev. Cttee, EORTC, 1993–; Oncology Trials Adv. Cttee, MRC, 1997–; Steering Gp, Cochrane Collaboration, 1998–; Co-ordinator, ICON trials for ovarian carcinoma, 1991–. Mem., Council, Inst. of Health Scis, Oxford, 1997. Mem. Bd of Editors, Annals of Oncology, 1996; Co-ordinating Ed., Cochrane Gynaecol Cancer Collaborative Rev. Gp, 1997–. *Publications:* Recent Advances in Clinical Oncology, 1982; All About Cancer, 1983; Lung Cancer: the facts, 1984; Cancer Investigations and Management, 1985; Cancer: a guide for patients and family, 1986; (with R. B. Buchanan) Medical Management of Breast Cancer, 1987; Textbook of Uncommon Cancer, 1988; Cancer Biology and Management, 1989; (with J. S. Tobias) Cancer: a colour atlas, 1991; Introducing New Treatments for Cancer, 1992 (Medical Textbook of the Year, 1993); Supportive Care of the Cancer Patient, 1997; (jtly) Cancer: a comprehensive guide, 1998; papers on new therapies for cancer, esp. clinical trials and systematic reviews. *Recreations:* active participation in painting and sculpture, writing, gentle walking, wildlife and landscape photography; passive participation in theatre, music, films, books; gathering art objects. *Address:* The Triangle, Sibford Road, Hook Norton, Banbury OX15 5JU. *T:* (01865) 226628; *e-mail:* cwilliams@canet.org.

WILLIAMS, Clifford; Associate Director, Royal Shakespeare Company, 1963–91, Hon. Associate Artist, since 1991; *b* 30 Dec. 1926; *s* of George Frederick Williams and Florence Maud Williams (*née* Gapper); *m* 1st, 1952, Joanna Douglas (marr. diss. 1959); no *c*; 2nd, 1962, Josiane Eugenie Peset; two *d*. *Educ:* Highbury County Grammar Sch. Acted in London (These Mortals, Larissa, Wolves and Sheep, Great Catherine), and repertory theatres, 1945–48; founded and directed Mime Theatre Company, 1950–53; Dir of Productions: at Marlowe Theatre, Canterbury, 1955–56; at Queen's Theatre, Hornchurch, 1957. Directed at Arts Theatre, London: Yerma, 1957; Radio Rescue, 1958; Dark Halo, Quartet for Five, The Marriage of Mr Mississippi (all in 1959); Moon for the Misbegotten, The Shepherd's Chameleon, Victims of Duty (all in 1960); The Race of Adam, Llandaff Festival, 1961. Joined Royal Shakespeare Company, 1961; Directed: Afore Night Come, 1962; The Comedy of Errors, 1963. Productions for RSC in Stratford and London: The Tempest, The Representative, The Comedy of Errors (revival), 1963; Richard II, Henry IV Pts I and II (co-dir), Afore Night Come (revival), The Jew of Malta, 1964; The Merchant of Venice, The Jew of Malta (revival), The Comedy of Errors (revival), 1965; The Meteor, Twelfth Night, Henry IV Pts I and II (co-dir, revivals), 1966; Doctor Faustus, 1968; Major Barbara, 1970; The Duchess of Malfi, 1971; The Comedy of Errors (revival), 1972; The Taming of the Shrew, A Lesson in Blood and Roses, 1973; Cymbeline (co-dir), 1974; The Mouth Organ, Too True to be Good, 1975; Wild Oats, 1976, 1979; Man and Superman, 1977; The Tempest, 1978; The Love-Girl and the Innocent, 1981; The Happiest Days of Your Life, 1984; Il Candelaio, 1986; The Beaux' Stratagem, 1988. Other productions include: Our Man Crichton, 1964, and the Flying Dutchman, 1966, in London; The Gardener's Dog, 1965, and The Merry Wives of Windsor, 1967, for the Finnish National Theatre; Volpone at Yale Univ., 1967; Othello, for Bulgarian Nat. Theatre, Soldiers, New York and London, 1968; Dido and Aeneas, Windsor Festival, Famine, English Stage Soc., 1969; As You Like It, 1967, and Back to Methuselah, 1969, both for the Nat. Theatre of GB; The Winter's Tale, 1969, for Yugoslav Nat. Theatre; Sleuth, London, NY and Paris, 1970; Oh! Calcutta!, London and Paris, 1970; Emperor Henry IV, New York, 1973; As You Like It (revival), New York, What Every Woman Knows, London, Emperor Henry IV, London, 1974; Murderer, London, 1975; Mardi-Gras, London, Carte Blanche, London, 1976; Stevie, The Old Country, Rosmerholm, London, 1977; The Passion of Dracula, London, 1978; Richard III, Mexican Nat. Theatre, 1979; Threepenny Opera, 1979, and The Love-Girl and the Innocent, 1980, Aalborg; Born in the Gardens, London, 1980; Overheard, London, To Grandmother's House We Go, NY, The Carmelites, Aalborg, 1981; Othello, Bad Hersfeld, Chapter 17, London, 1982; Richard III, Madrid, Merry Wives of Windsor, USA, Scheherazade, Festival Ballet, 1983; Pack of Lies, London, 1983, NY, 1985; A Child's Christmas in Wales (revival), USA, 1983; Rise and Fall of the City of Mahagonny, Aalborg, 1984; Aren't We All?, London, 1984, NY, 1985; The Cherry Orchard, Tokyo, 1984; Measure for Measure, Norrköping, St Joan, British tour, 1985; Legends, USA, 1986; Breaking the Code, London, 1986, NY, 1987; Aren't We All?, Australia, 1986; The Importance of Being Earnest, Copenhagen, 1987; A Chorus of Disapproval, British tour, Richard II, London, 1988; Richard III, London, Song at Nightfall, Dorset Music Fest., Wheel of Fire, Mérida Fest., Spain, 1989; Bellman's Opera, Stockholm, 1990; A Slight Hangover, British tour, Painting Churches, Southampton, It's Ralph, London, 1991; Pygmalion, Denmark, Breaking the Code, British tour, Bellman's Opera, London, 1992; A Murder of No Importance, Matters Matrimonial, British tours, 1993; Arsenic and Old Lace, British tour, 1994; Harvey, London, 1995; The Father, NY, 1996, LA, 1998; Separation, Frankfurt, 1997. Also directed plays for the Arena Theatre, Triumph Theatre Co., Theatre Workshop, Guildford, Oxford, Coventry, Windsor, Toronto, Los Angeles, Washington, Houston, Johannesburg, Edinburgh Festival; Malvern Festival; Dir, Man and Superman (film), 1986. Mem. Welsh Arts Council, 1963–72; Chairman: Welsh Nat. Theatre Co., 1968–72; British Theatre Assoc., 1977–90; Chm., British Children's Theatre Assoc., 1968–71; Governor, Welsh Coll. of Music and Drama, 1981–90. Associate Artist of Yugoslav Nat. Theatre, 1969; FTCL 1960; FWCMD 1994. *Publications:* (ed) John O'Keeffe, Wild Oats, 1977; (ed) Frederick Lonsdale, Plays 1, 2000; *plays:* The Disguises of Arlecchino, 1951; The Sleeping Princess, 1953; The Goose Girl, 1954; The Secret Garden, 1955; (with Donald Jonson) Stephen Dedalus, 1956; Matters Matrimonial, 1993; (with Daphne du Maurier) Rebecca, 1994; The Keys of the Kingdom, 1996; Saints and Sinners, 1997; (with Albert Camus) The Fall, 1997; (with Georges Bernanos) The Carmelites, 1998; (with Rex Warner) The Wild Goose Chase, 1998; (after Benjamin Disraeli) Sybil, or The Two Nations, 2000; (after Susan Ferrier) Marriage, 2001; *translations:* Ionesco, The Duel, Double Act, 1979; Pirandello, As You Desire Me, 1981; Chekhov, The Cherry Orchard, 1981. *Recreations:* motor boating, water-ski-ing. *Address:* 62 Maltings Place, Bagleys Lane, SW6 2BY; 12 Chemin Cambarnier Nord, 06650 Opio, France.

WILLIAMS, Colin; *see* Welland, C.

WILLIAMS, Colin Hartley; Partner, Williams & Williams, PR consultants, since 1992; *b* 7 Dec. 1938; *s* of late Gwilym Robert Williams and Margaret (*née* Hartley); *m* 1st, 1964, Carolyn (*née* Bulman) (*d* 1993); one *s* two *d*; 2nd, 1997, Shirley Ann (*née* Lavers). *Educ:* Grangefield Grammar Sch., Stockton-on-Tees; University College of Wales, Aberystwyth (BA). Journalist: Evening Gazette, Middlesbrough, 1960–63; Today Magazine, Odhams Press, 1964; Daily Sketch, 1964–66; Senior Lecturer, International Press Inst., Nairobi, 1967–68; Corporate and Public Relations Executive, 1969–74; Press Officer, Corporation of City of London, 1975–76; Asst Dir, City Communications Centre, 1977, Exec. Dir, 1979–83; Exec. Dir, Cttee on Invisible Exports, 1982–83; Chief Press Relations Manager, 1983–90, Hd of Corporate Communications, 1990–91, Hd of PR Gp, 1991–92, Nat. Westminster Bank. *Recreations:* writing, wine, golf. *Address:* Goodacre House, Goodacres Lane, Lacey Green, Princes Risborough, Bucks HP27 0QD. *T:* (01844) 347271.

WILLIAMS, Ven. Colin Henry; Archdeacon of Lancaster, since 1999; *b* 12 Aug. 1952; *s* of William Henry Williams and Blanche Williams. *Educ:* King George V Grammar Sch. for Boys, Southport; Pembroke Coll., Oxford (BA 1973; MA 1977); Coll. of Law, Chester; St Stephen's House, Oxford (BA Oxon 1981). Asst Solicitor, Gibson, Russell & Adler, solicitors, Wigan, 1974–78; ordained deacon 1981, priest 1982; Asst Curate, St Paul Stoneycroft, Liverpool, 1981–84; Team Vicar, St Aidan, Walton, 1984–89; Domestic Chaplain to Bishop of Blackburn, and Chaplain, Whalley Abbey Retreat and Conf. Centre, 1989–94; Vicar, St Chad, Poulton-le-Fylde, 1994–99. Mem., Gen. Synod of C of E, 1995–. Mem., Meissen Commn, 1996–. *Recreations:* walking, singing, developing knowledge of all things German. *Address:* St Michael's House, Hall Lane, St Michael's-on-Wyre, Preston, Lancs PR3 0TQ. *T:* (01995) 679242, *Fax:* (01995) 679747; *e-mail:* archdeacon.lancaster@ukonline.co.uk.

WILLIAMS, Dafydd Wyn J.; *see* Jones-Williams.

WILLIAMS, Sir Daniel (Charles), GCMG 1996; QC 1996; Governor General of Grenada, since 1996; *b* 4 Nov. 1935; *s* of Adolphus D. Williams and Clare Stanislaus; *m* 1960, Cecilia Patricia Gloria Modeste; one *s* three *d. Educ:* Primary and comprehensive schs, Grenada; LLB London Univ.; Council of Legal Educn, London. Called to the Bar, Lincoln's Inn, 1968; Barrister, 1969–70, 1974–84, 1990–96; Magistrate, St Lucia, 1970–74; MP (New Nat. Party) St David's, Grenada, 1984–89; Minister of Health, Housing and Envmt, 1984–89; Minister of Legal Affairs, and Attorney Gen., 1988–89; Acting Prime Minister, July 1988. Held several lay positions in RC Ch, incl. Chm., Dio. Pastoral Council. Was active Scout, incl. Dist Comr and Dep. Chief Comr; now Chief Scout. *Publications:* Index of Laws of Grenada 1959–79; (contrib.) Modern Legal Systems Cyclopedia: Central America and the Caribbean, vol. 7, 1985; The Office and Duties of the Governor-General of Grenada, 1998; A Synoptic View of the Public Service of Grenada; Prescriptions for a Model Grenada, 2000. *Recreations:* lawn tennis, gardening. *Address:* Government House, St George's, Grenada. *T:* 4402401. *Clubs:* St George's Lions (Pres.) (St George's); Vieux Fort Lions (Pres.) (St Lucia).

WILLIAMS, Prof. David, FRS 1984; (part-time) Research Professor of Mathematics, University of Wales Swansea, since 1999; Professor of Mathematical Sciences, Bath University, 1992–99, now Emeritus; *b* 9 April 1938; *s* of Gwyn Williams and Margaret Elizabeth Williams; *m* 1966, Sheila Margaret Harrison; two *d. Educ:* Jesus College, Oxford (DPhil); Grey College, Durham. Instructor, Stanford Univ., 1962; Lectr, Durham Univ., 1963; Shell Research Lectr, Statistical Lab., and Res. Fellow, Clare Coll., Cambridge, 1966; Lectr, 1969, Prof. of Maths, 1972, University Coll., Swansea; Prof. of Mathematical Stats and Professorial Fellow, Clare Coll., Cambridge Univ., 1985–92. Vis. Fellow, Bath Univ., 1991–92. Hon. Fellow, UC, Swansea, 1991–. *Publications:* Diffusions, Markov processes, and martingales, vol. 1, Foundations, 1979, vol. 2 (with L. C. G. Rogers), Itô calculus, 1987; Probability with martingales, 1991; Weighing the odds, 2001; papers in Séminaire de probabilités and other jls. *Recreations:* music, cycling, walking.

WILLIAMS, Adm. Sir David, GCB 1977 (KCB 1975); DL; Governor and Commander-in-Chief, Gibraltar, 1982–85; a Gentleman Usher to The Queen, 1979–82, an Extra Gentleman Usher, since 1982; *b* 22 Oct. 1921; 3rd *s* of A. E. Williams, Ashford, Kent; *m* 1947, Philippa Beatrice Stevens; two *s. Educ:* Yardley Court Sch., Tonbridge; RN College, Dartmouth. Cadet, Dartmouth, 1935. Graduate, US Naval War Coll., Newport, RI. Served War of 1939–45 at sea in RN. Qual. in Gunnery, 1946; Comdr, 1952; Captain, 1960; Naval Asst to First Sea Lord, 1961–64; HMS Devonshire, 1964–66; Dir of Naval Plans, 1966–68; Captain, BRNC, Dartmouth, 1968–70; Rear-Adm. 1970; Flag Officer, Second in Command Far East Fleet, 1970 72; Vice Adm. 1973; Dir-Gen. Naval Manpower and Training, 1972–74; Adm. 1974; Chief of Naval Personnel and Second Sea Lord, 1974–77; C-in-C Naval Home Comd, and ADC to the Queen, 1977–79, retired. Pres., Ex Services Mental Welfare Soc., 1979–91; Chm. of Council, Missions to Seamen, 1989–93. Member: Commonwealth War Graves Commn, 1980–89 (Vice Chm., 1985–89); Museums and Galleries Commn, 1987–93. Hon. Liveryman, Fruiterers' Co.; KStJ 1982. DL Devon, 1981. *Recreations:* sailing, gardening. *Address:* Barnhill, Stoke Gabriel, Totnes, Devon TQ9 6SJ. *Clubs:* Army and Navy; Royal Dart Yacht; RN Sailing Association; Royal Yacht Squadron.

WILLIAMS, Prof. David Arnold, OBE 2000; PhD, DSc; CPhys, FInstP; FRAS; Perren Professor of Astronomy, University College London, since 1994; *b* 9 Sept. 1937; *s* of James Arnold Williams and Frances Barbara Williams (*née* Begg); *m* 1964, Doreen Jane Bell; two *s. Educ:* Larne Grammar Sch.; Queen's Univ., Belfast (BSc, PhD); Manchester (DSc). CPhys 1968; FInstP 1994; FRAS 1967. Maths Dept, Manchester Coll. of Sci. and Technol., 1963–65; NASA Goddard Space Flight Centre, Md, USA, 1965–67; Lectr, Sen. Lectr, Reader, Maths Dept, 1967–84, Prof. of Theoretical Astrophysics, 1984–94, UMIST. Pres., RAS, 1998–2000. *Publications:* (with J. E. Dyson) The Physics of the Interstellar Medium, 1980, 2nd edn 1997; (with W. W. Duley) Interstellar Chemistry, 1984; (with T. W. Hartquist) The Chemically Controlled Cosmos, 1995; (with T. W. Hartquist) The Molecular Astrophysics of Stars and Galaxies, 1998; contrib. numerous articles in learned jls. *Recreations:* hill-walking, choral singing, beer and wine. *Address:* Department of Physics and Astronomy, University College London, Gower Street, WC1E 6BT.

WILLIAMS, David Claverly, CVO 1970; CBE 1977; *b* 31 July 1917; *s* of late Rev. Canon Henry Williams, OBE, and late Ethel Florence Williams; *m* 1944, Elizabeth Anne Fraser; three *d. Educ:* Christ's Coll., Christchurch, NZ; Victoria Univ. of Wellington. Professional Exam. in Public Administration. Inland Revenue Dept, 1936–39. Served War, 2NZEF, Pacific and Middle East, 1939–46. NZ Forest Service, 1946–60; Official Sec. to the Governor-General of NZ, 1960–77; Sec./Manager, The Wellington Club (Inc.), 1978–82. *Address:* 443 Muritai Road, Eastbourne, New Zealand. *Clubs:* Wellington (Wellington).

WILLIAMS, Sir David (Glyndwr Tudor), Kt 1991; DL; Fellow of Emmanuel College, Cambridge, since 1996; Vice-Chancellor, Cambridge University, 1989–96; *b* 22 Oct. 1930; *s* of late Tudor Williams, OBE (Headmaster of Queen Elizabeth Grammar Sch., Carmarthen, 1929–55), and late Anne Williams; *m* 1959, Sally Gillian Mary Cole; one *s* two *d. Educ:* Queen Elizabeth Grammar Sch., Carmarthen; Emmanuel Coll., Cambridge (MA, LLB, Hon. Fellow 1984). LLM Calif. Nat. Service, RAF, 1949–50. Called to the Bar, Lincoln's Inn, 1956, Hon. Bencher, 1985. Commonwealth Fund Fellow of Harkness Foundn, Berkeley and Harvard, 1956–58; Lecturer: Univ. of Nottingham, 1958–63; Univ. of Oxford, 1963–67 (Fellow of Keble Coll.); University of Cambridge: Fellow, 1967–80, Sen. Tutor and Tutor for Admissions, 1970–76, Emmanuel Coll.; Reader in Public Law, 1976–83; Rouse Ball Prof. of English Law, 1983–92; Pres., Wolfson Coll., 1980–92 (Hon. Fellow, 1993); Prof. of Law, 1996–98. Vis. Fellow, 1974, Dist. Anniv. Fellow, 1996, ANU, Canberra; Allen, Allen and Hemsley Vis. Fellow, Law Dept, Univ. of Sydney, 1985; George P. Smith Dist. Vis. Prof., Indiana Univ., 2000. Lectures: Stevens, Cornell, 1984; Martland, Alberta and Calgary, 1988; Read, Dalhousie, 1989; Fuchs, Indiana, 1993; Laskin, Osgoode Hall, 1993; Samuel Gee, RCP, 1993; Morris of Borth-y-Gest, Bangor, 1993; Wynne Baxter Godfree, Sussex, 1994; Spencer Mason, Auckland, 1994; Harry Street, Manchester, 1999. Pres., Nat. Soc. for Clean Air, 1983–85; Chairman: Animal Procedures Cttee, 1987–90; RAC Adv. Gp on Cars and the Envmt, 1991–92. Member: Clean Air Council, 1971–79; Royal Commn on Environmental Pollution, 1976–83; Commn on Energy and the Environment, 1978–81; Council on Tribunals, 1972–82; Justice/All Souls Cttee on Adminstrative Law, 1978–88; Berrill Cttee of Investigation, SSRC, 1982–83; Marre Cttee on Future of Legal Profession, 1986–88; Sen. Salaries Review Body, 1998–; Univ. Comr, 1988–93. Mem., Amer. Law Inst., 1986; For. Hon. Mem., Amer. Acad. of Arts and Scis, 1994. Mem., Internat. Jury, Indira Gandhi Prize, 1992–. DL Cambs, 1995. Hon. Fellow: Keble Coll., Oxford, 1992; Pembroke Coll., Cambridge, 1993; Trinity Coll., Carmarthen, 1994; Hon. QC 1994. Hon. DLitt: William Jewell Coll., 1984; Loughborough Univ. of Technology, 1988; Davidson Coll., 1992; Hon. LLD: Hull, 1989; Sydney 1990; Nottingham, 1991; Liverpool, 1994; McGill, De Montfort, 1995; Duke, 1996; Cambridge, 1997. *Publications:* Not in the Public Interest, 1965; Keeping the Peace, 1967; articles in legal jls. *Address:* Emmanuel College, Cambridge CB2 3AP. *T:* (01223) 334200.

WILLIAMS, Sir David Innes, Kt 1985; MD, MChir Cambridge, FRCS; Consulting Urologist: Hospital for Sick Children, Great Ormond Street (Urologist, 1952–78); St Peter's Hospital, London (Surgeon, 1950–78); *b* 12 June 1919; *s* of late Gwynne E. O. Williams, MS, FRCS; *m* 1944, Margaret Eileen Harding; two *s. Educ:* Sherborne Sch.; Trinity Hall, Cambridge; Univ. College Hospital (Hon. Fellow, 1986). RAMC, 1945–48 (Major, Surg. Specialist). Urologist, Royal Masonic Hosp., 1963–72; Civilian Consultant Urologist to RN, 1974–84; Dir, BPMF, 1978–86, Pro-Vice-Chancellor, 1985–87, Univ. of London. Mem., 1975–91, Chm., 1982–91, Council, ICRF; Chm., Council for Postgrad. Med. Educn in England and Wales, 1985–88. Mem., Home Sec's Adv. Cttee on Cruelty to Animals, 1975–79. Mem., GMC, 1979–89 (Chm., Overseas Cttee, 1981–88); Vice-Pres., RCS, 1983–85 (Mem. Council, 1974–86; Mem. Jt Consultants Cttee, 1983–85; Hon. Medal, 1987); President: BMA, 1988–89; RSocMed, 1990–92 (Past Pres., Urology Sect.). Pres., Friends of the Wellcome Inst. for History of Medicine, 1998–. Hon. Member: British Assoc. Paediatric Surgeons (Denis Browne Medal, 1977); British Assoc. Urological Surgeons (Past Pres.; St Peter's Medal, 1967); Assoc. Française d'Urologie; Amer. Surgical Assoc.; British Paediatric Assoc.; Amer. Acad. Pediatrics (Urology Medal, 1986). Hon. FACS 1983; Hon. FRCSI 1984; Hon. FDSRCS; Hon. FRSocMed 1993; Hon. FRCPCH 1996. *Publications:* Urology of Childhood, 1958; Paediatric Urology, 1968, 2nd edn 1982; Scientific Foundations of Urology, 1976, 2nd edn 1982; The London Lock, 1995; various contributions to medical journals. *Address:* 66 Murray Road, SW19 4PE. *T:* (020) 8879 1042; The Old Rectory, East Knoyle, Salisbury, Wilts SP3 6AQ. *T:* (01747) 830255.

See also Sir R. E. O. Williams.

WILLIAMS, David John; *b* 10 July 1914; *s* of late James Herbert Williams and late Ethel (*née* Redman); unmarried. *Educ:* Lancing College; Christ Church, Oxford (MA). Called to Bar, Inner Temple, 1939. Postgrad. Dip. in Social Anthropology, LSE, 1965. Served War of 1939–45, Royal Artillery. Practised as Barrister, Norwich, 1946–51; Resident Magistrate, Tanganyika, 1951–56; Senior Resident Magistrate, 1956–60; Judge of High Court of Tanganyika, 1960–62; Lord Chancellor's Office, 1966–79. *Recreations:* the arts and travelling. *Address:* 10e Thorney Crescent, Morgan's Walk, SW11 3TR. *Clubs:* Travellers, Hurlingham.

WILLIAMS, David John, QPM 1992; Chief Constable, British Transport Police, 1997–2001; Associate Director, Reliance Security Services Ltd, since 2001; *b* 7 April 1941; *s* of late John Isaac Williams and Edith (*née* Stoneham); *m* 1962, Johanna Murphy; two *s. Educ:* Ystalyfera Grammar Sch.; University Coll. London (LLB Hons). Called to the Bar, Middle Temple, 1977. Metropolitan Police, 1960–84; FBI Nat. Acad., 1982; on secondment to Home Office Inspectorate, 1983; Herts Constabulary, 1984–89; Dep. Chief Constable, 1989–91, Chief Constable, 1991–97, Surrey Police; Nat. Exec. Inst., USA, 1994. Chm., Traffic Cttee, ACPO, 1995–97. OStJ 1995. Queen's Commendation for Bravery, 1976; Police Long Service and Good Conduct Medal, 1982. *Recreations:* music, Rugby football, walking, golf. *Club:* Royal Over-Seas League.

WILLIAMS, David John, FRCP, FRCPE, FRCS, FRCSE, FRCA, FFAEM; Clinical Director, Accident & Emergency Services, Guy's and St Thomas' Hospitals NHS Trust, since 1993; *b* 23 April 1938; *s* of Frank Williams, CBE and Kathleen Williams; *m* 1977, Ann Andrews (*née* Walker-Watson); one *s* one *d. Educ:* Highgate Sch.; Hotchkiss Sch., USA; Trinity Coll., Cambridge (MA, MB, BChir); St Thomas' Hosp. Med. Sch. MRCGP 1970; FRCP 1982; FFAEM 1993; FRCS 1997; FRCPE 1998; FRCSE 1999; FRCA 2000. Jun. med. posts, St Thomas' Hosp., Kingston Hosp., Guy's–Maudsley Neurosurgical Unit, 1964–65; RMO, Nat. Heart Hosp., 1966, Middlesex Hosp., 1967–70; Registrar, Maudsley Hosp., 1970–71; GP, 1971–72; Consultant, Accident and Emergency Medicine: Middlesex Hosp., 1973–84; St Thomas' Hosp., 1984–93. Sec., Casualty Surgeons Assoc., 1978–84; President: British Assoc. for A&E Medicine, 1987–90; Intercollegiate Faculty of A&E Medicine, 1993–97; Vice-Pres., Eur. Soc. for Emergency Medicine, 2000–; Invited Member Council: RCP, 1994–; RCS, 1994–; Royal Coll. of Anaesthetists, 1994–. Hon. Mem., Amer. Coll. Emergency Physicians, 1990; Hon. Life Mem., British Assoc. for A&E Medicine, 1998. *Recreations:* reading, collecting books, theatre, travel. *Address:* 13 Spencer Hill, Wimbledon, SW19 4PA. *T:* (020) 8946 3785.

WILLIAMS, (David John) Delwyn; company director; *b* 1 Nov. 1938; *s* of David Lewis Williams and Irena Violet Gwendoline Williams; *m* 1963, Olive Elizabeth Jerman; one *s* one *d. Educ:* Welshpool High School; University College of Wales, Aberystwyth. LLB. Sometime Solicitor and company director. MP (C) Montgomery, 1979–83; former Member: Select Cttee on Wales; Statutory Instruments Cttee; Jt Sec., All-Party Leisure and Recreation Industry Cttee. Contested (C) Montgomery, 1983. Former Mem., British Field Sports Soc. *Recreations:* race horse owner; cricket, golf, small bore shooting.

WILLIAMS, David Lincoln; Chairman and Managing Director, Costa Rica Coffee Co. Ltd, since 1988; *b* 10 Feb. 1937; *s* of Lewis Bernard Williams and Eileen Elizabeth Cadogan; *m* 1959, Gillian Elisabeth, *d* of Dr William Phillips; one *s* one *d. Educ:* Cheltenham College. Served RA Gibraltar, 1955–57. Chairman: Allied Windows (S Wales) Ltd, 1971–85; Cardiff Broadcasting PLC, 1979–84; Allied Profiles Ltd, 1981–96; Chm. and Man. Dir, John Williams of Cardiff PLC, 1983–88 (Dir, 1968–88). Chm., Cox (Penarth), 1987–94. President, Aluminium Window Assoc., 1971–72. Member: CBI Welsh Council, 1986–89; Welsh Arts Council, 1987–94 (Chm., Music Cttee, 1988–94). Pres., Vale of Glamorgan Festival, 1995– (Chm., 1978–95); Director: Cardiff Bay Opera House Trust, 1994–97; WNO, 1994–2001 (Nat. Chm., Friends of WNO, 1980–2000). Freeman, City of London, 1986; Liveryman, Founders' Co., 1986. *Recreations:* opera, gardening, fine weather sailing. *Address:* Rose Revived, Llantrithyd, Cowbridge, Vale of Glamorgan CF71 7UB. *T:* (01446) 781357. *Club:* Cardiff and County (Cardiff).

WILLIAMS, Prof. David Michael, PhD; FRCPath, FDSRCS; Professor of Oral Pathology, Bart's and The London, Queen Mary's School of Medicine and Dentistry (formerly St Bartholomew's and Royal London School of Medicine and Dentistry, Queen Mary and Westfield College), since 1994, and Vice-Principal, Queen Mary, since 2001, University of London; *b* 4 Nov. 1946; *s* of Reginald Albert Williams and Mary Williams (*née* Holland); *m* 1970, Gillian Elizabeth Regester; one *s* one *d. Educ:* Plymouth Coll.; London Hosp. Med. Coll., Univ. of London (BDS Hons 1969; MSc 1972; PhD 1976). FRCPath 1991; FDSRCS 1994. London Hospital Medical College: Sen. Lectr in Oral Pathology, 1982–89; Reader in Oral Pathology, 1989–93; Dean of Clinical Dentistry, 1994–98, Dep. Warden, 1998–2001, St Batholomew's and Royal London Sch. of Medicine and Dentistry, QMW, Univ. of London; Hon. Consultant, Bart's and the London NHS Trust (formerly Royal London Hosp., then Royal Hosps NHS Trust),

1982–. Mem., GDC, 1998– (Chm., Registration Sub-Cttee, 1999–). FRSocMed. Mem., several editl bds. *Publications:* (jtly) Pathology of Periodontal Disease, 1992; numerous articles in learned jls. *Recreations:* golf, scuba diving, hill walking, sailing. *Address:* Queen Mary, University of London, Mile End Road, E1 4NS. *T:* (020) 7882 3006. *Clubs:* Athenæum; Sundridge Park Golf, Bigbury Golf.

WILLIAMS, David Oliver; General Secretary, Confederation of Health Service Employees, 1983–87; *b* 12 March 1926; *m* 1949, Kathleen Eleanor Jones, Dinorwic; two *s* five *d* (and one *s* decd). *Educ:* Brynrefail Grammar Sch.; North Wales Hospital, Denbigh (RMN 1951). COHSE: full-time officer, Regional Secretary, Yorkshire Region, 1955; National Officer, Head Office, 1962; Sen. National Officer, 1969; Asst General Secretary, 1974. Chairman: Nurses and Midwives Whitley Council Staff Side, 1977–87; General Whitley Council Staff Side, 1974–87. Jubilee Medal, 1977. *Recreations:* walking, birdwatching, swimming, music. *Address:* 1 King's Court, Beddington Gardens, Wallington, Surrey SM6 0HR. *T:* (020) 8647 6412.

WILLIAMS, Air Vice-Marshal David Owen C.; *see* Crwys-Williams.

WILLIAMS, Prof. David Raymond, OBE 1993; Professor of Chemistry, Cardiff University; *b* 20 March 1941; *s* of Eric Thomas and Amy Gwendoline Williams; *m* 1964, Gillian Kirkpatrick Murray; two *d*. *Educ:* Grove Park Grammar Sch., Wrexham, Clwyd; Univ. of Wales, Bangor (BSc (1st Cl. Hons Chemistry); PhD); DSc St Andrews. CChem, FRSC, 1976; EurChem 1992. NATO Postdoctoral Fellowship, Univ. of Lund, 1965–66; Lectr in Chemistry, Univ. of St Andrews, 1966–77; Prof. of Applied Chemistry, UWIST, then Speciation and Analytical Chemistry, now Chemistry, UC, Cardiff, later UWCC, now Univ. of Wales, Cardiff, 1977–. Chm., Sci. Adv. Cttee, British Council, 1986–94; Member: Radioactive Waste Management Adv. Cttee, DoE, 1980–95; Cttee on Medical Aspects of Radiation in the Environment, DHSS, later Dept of Health, 1985–89; Adv. Cttee on Hazardous Substances, DETR, 2000–. FRSA 1978. Jeyes Silver Medal, RSC, 1987; Wolfson Foundn Res. Award, 1988. *Publications:* The Metals of Life, 1970; An Introduction to Bioinorganic Chemistry, 1976; The Principles of Bioinorganic Chemistry, 1977; Laboratory Introduction to Bioinorganic Chemistry, 1979; Analysis Using Glass Electrodes, 1984; Trace Metals in Medicine and Chelation Therapy, 1995; What is Safe?: the risks of living in a nuclear age, 1998; 450 res. papers. *Recreations:* cycling, swimming, other outdoor pursuits, public speaking. *Address:* Department of Chemistry, Cardiff University, PO Box 912, Cardiff CF10 3TB. *T:* (029) 2087 4778.

WILLIAMS, Sir David (Reeve), Kt 1999; CBE 1990; Member (Lib Dem) since 1974, Cabinet Member, since 2001, Richmond upon Thames Borough Council; *b* 8 June 1939; *s* of Edmund George Williams and May Williams (*née* Partridge); *m* 1964, Christine Margaret Rayson. *Educ:* St Cuthbert's Soc.; Univ. of Durham (BA Hons Politics and Econs). Computer systems analyst, 1961–95: IBM UK Ltd, 1961–70; Insurance Systems and Services, 1970–78; David Williams and Associates, 1978–91; Teleglobe Insce Systems Ltd, 1991–95. Leader of Opposition, 1978–83, Leader, 1983–2001, Richmond upon Thames BC. Dep. Chm., and Leader, Lib Dem Gp, LGA, 1996–. *Recreations:* collecting books, particularly about Lloyd George, listening to jazz, particularly Charlie Parker. *Address:* 8 Arlington Road, Petersham, Richmond, Surrey TW10 7BY. *T:* (020) 8940 9421.

WILLIAMS, David Wakelin, (Lyn), MSc, PhD; CBiol, FIBiol; retired as Director, Department of Agriculture and Fisheries for Scotland, Agricultural Scientific Services, 1963–73; *b* 2 Oct. 1913; *e s* of John Thomas Williams and Ethel (*née* Lock); *m* 1948, Margaret Mary Wills, BSc (*d* 1993), *d* of late Rev. R. H. Wills; one *s*. *Educ:* Rhondda Grammar School, Porth; University College, Cardiff. Demonstrator, Zoology Dept, Univ. Coll., Cardiff, 1937–38; Lectr in Zoology and Botany, Tech. Coll., Crumlin, Mon., 1938–39; research work on nematode physiology, etc. (MSc, PhD), 1937–41; biochemical work on enzymes (Industrial Estate, Treforest), 1942–43. Food Infestation Control Inspector (Min. of Food), Glasgow; Sen. Inspector, W Scotland, 1945; Scotland and N Ireland, 1946. Prin. Scientific Officer, Dept Agriculture for Scotland, 1948; Sen. Prin. Scientific Officer, 1961; Dep. Chief Scientific Officer (Director), 1963. Chairman, Potato Trials Advisory Cttee, 1963–; FIBiol 1966 (Council Mem. Scottish Br., 1966–69). MBIM, 1970–76. *Publications:* various papers, especially for the intelligent layman, on the environment, and on pest control and its side effects. *Recreations:* writing, music, Hi-Fi, photography, natural history. *Address:* 8 Hillview Road, Edinburgh EH12 8QN. *T:* (0131) 334 1108.

WILLIAMS, David Whittow; Chief Executive, Enodis (formerly Berisford) plc, 1999–2001; *b* 18 Aug. 1957; *s* of David Whittow Williams and Eileen Williams; *m* 1992, Helle Nordensgaard. *Educ:* Birkenhead Sch.; Mansfield Coll., Oxford (MA). Exec. Vice Pres., Melwire Inc., 1982–86; Mkting Dir, Vickers Healthcare, 1986–88; Eur. Business Develt Manager, Blue Circle Cement, 1988–90; Business Develt Dir, Blue Circle Home Products plc, 1991–94; Managing Director: Potterton/Myson, 1994–96; Magnet, 1996–99. *Recreations:* Rugby, tennis, cricket.

WILLIAMS, Dr David William; Social Security and Child Support Commissioner, since 1998; *b* 13 Feb. 1946; *s* of J. W. (Bill) Williams, DFC, and Joan Adair (*née* Wallis); *m* 1968, Elisabeth Jones Pierce; three *s*. *Educ:* Queen Elizabeth's Grammar Sch., Faversham; Univ. of Bristol (LLB; LLM; PhD 1979). ATII 1970. Admitted Solicitor, 1970; Lectr, Faculty of Law, Univ. of Bristol, 1969–76; Faculty of Law, University of Manchester: Lectr, then Sen. Lectr, 1976–86; Reader, 1986–87; Dean of Faculty, 1984–86; Queen Mary and Westfield College, University of London: Prof. of Tax Law, 1987–98; Vis. Prof., 1998–; Dean, Faculty of Laws, 1991–93. Vis. Lectr, Univ. of Liverpool, 1978–80; Visiting Professor: Univ. of Buckingham, 1992–93; Univ. of Sydney, 1997; Tech. Univ. of Vienna, 1997–2001; Sorbonne, Paris, 1998–99. Former Asst Ed., British Tax Rev. Consultant, OECD Fiscal Affairs Dept, 1993–97. Pt-time Chairman: Medical Appeal Tribunals, 1990–98; Social Security Appeal Tribunals, 1984–96; Dep. Social Security Comr, 1996–98. Member: Educn Cttee, Chartered Inst. Taxation, 1988–92; Revenue Law Cttee, Law Soc., 1992–97; Perm. Scientific Cttee, Internat. Fiscal Assoc., 1996–98; Tax Law Rewrite Consultative Cttee, 1997–. Governor: Didsbury C of E Sch., Manchester, 1984–87; Parrs Wood Sch., Manchester, 1985–87. Mem. Bd, Centre for Juridico-Economic Investigation, Univ. of Porto, 1997–. *Publications:* Maladministration: remedies for injustice, 1979; (with G. K. Morse) Profit Sharing, 1979; Running Your Own Business, 1979; Tax for the Self-Employed, 1980; Social Security Taxation, 1982; National Insurance Contributions Handbook, 1987; Trends in International Taxation, 1991; Taxation Principles and Practice, 1993; EC Tax Law, 1998; editor: (with G. K. Morse) Introduction to Revenue Law, 1985; Tax on International Transfers of Information, 1991; Principles of Tax Law, 1996, 2nd edn 2000; Practical Application of Double Tax Conventions, 1998; consulting editor: Reader's Digest Guide to the Law, 8th–10th edn, 1986–92; Reader's Digest Know Your Rights, 1997; contrib. articles to legal jls. *Address:* Yr Hen Rheithordy, Rhiw, Pwllheli, Gwynedd LL53 8AD; Harp House, 83–86 Farringdon Street, EC4A 4DH.

WILLIAMS, Delwyn; *see* Williams, D. J. D.

WILLIAMS, Sir Denys (Ambrose), KCMG 1993; Kt 1987; Gold Crown of Merit, Barbados, 1981; Chief Justice of Barbados, since 1987; *b* 12 Oct. 1929; *s* of George Cuthbert and Violet Irene Williams; *m* 1954, Carmel Mary Coleman; two *s* four *d*. *Educ:* Combermere and Harrison College, Barbados; Worcester College, Oxford (BCL, MA). Called to the Bar, Middle Temple, 1954. Asst Legal Draftsman, Barbados, 1957; Asst to Attorney General, 1959; Asst Legal Draftsman, Fedn of West Indies, 1959; Senior Parly Counsel, Barbados, 1963; Judge of the Supreme Court, 1967. *Recreations:* horse racing, tennis, walking. *Address:* No 9, Garrison, St Michael, Barbados. *T:* 4271164. *Clubs:* Carlton, Barbados Turf (Barbados).

WILLIAMS, Derrick; *see* Williams, R. D.

WILLIAMS, Sir Dillwyn; *see* Williams, Sir E. D.

WILLIAMS, Rev. Doiran George; Non-Stipendiary Minister, Greater Whitbourne, since 1993; *b* 27 June 1926; *s* of Rev. Dr Robert Richard Williams and Dilys Rachel Williams; *m* 1st, 1949, Flora Samitz (decd); one *s* one *d*; 2nd, 1977, Maureen Dorothy Baker; one *d*. *Educ:* Hereford Cathedral Sch.; Colwyn Bay Grammar Sch.; Liverpool Coll.; John F. Hughes Sch., Utica, NY. Served Army (Infantry), 1944–47. Called to the Bar, Gray's Inn, 1952; practised in Liverpool, 1952–58; Dept of Dir of Public Prosecutions, 1959, Asst Dir, 1977–82, Principal Asst Dir of Public Prosecutions, 1982–86; Chm., Med. Appeal Tribunals, 1987–98. Sec., Liverpool Fabian Soc., 1956–58. Reader: Liverpool Dio., 1953–58; London Dio., 1959–63; Southwark Dio., 1963–88; Hereford Dio., 1988–93; Mem., Southwark Readers' Bd, 1977–88. Ordained deacon, 1993, priest, 1994. *Recreations:* arts, mountains, sport, wine. *Address:* Howberry, Whitbourne, Worcester WR6 5RZ.

WILLIAMS, Sir Donald Mark, 10th Bt *cr* 1866; *b* 7 Nov. 1954; *s* of Sir Robert Ernest Williams, 9th Bt, and of Ruth Margaret, *d* of Charles Edwin Butcher, Hudson Bay, Saskatchewan, Canada; *S* father, 1976; *m* 1982, Denise, *o d* of Royston H. Cory; three *d* (one *s* decd). *Educ:* West Buckland School, Devon. *Heir:* *b* Barton Matthew Williams [*b* 21 Nov. 1956; *m* 1st, 1980, Karen Robinson (marr. diss.); one *s* one *d*; 2nd, 1985, Sarah (marr. diss.); one *d*]. *Address:* Upcott House, Barnstaple, N Devon EX31 4DR.

WILLIAMS, Douglas, CB 1977; CVO 1966; Deputy Secretary, Ministry of Overseas Development (later Overseas Development Administration), 1973–77, retired; *b* 14 May 1917; *s* of late James E. Williams and Elsie Williams; *m* 1948, Marie Jacquot; no *c*. *Educ:* Wolverhampton Sch.; Exeter Coll., Oxford. Served War, 1939–46 (despatches): Major, RA. Colonial Office, 1947; Principal, 1949; Colonial Attaché, Washington, 1956–60; Asst Sec., Colonial Office, 1961; transferred to ODM (later ODA), 1967, Under-Sec., 1968–73. Member: Bd, Crown Agents, 1978–84; EEC Econ. and Social Cttee, 1978–82; Governing Council, ODI, 1979–85. Trustee, Help the Aged and associated charities, 1984–92 (Chm. of Exec. Cttee, 1985–87, Chm., Overseas Cttee, 1987–88); Mem. Exec. Cttee, David Davies Meml Inst. of Internat. Studies, 1986–. *Publications:* The Specialized Agencies and the United Nations: the system in crisis, 1987; contrib. to United Kingdom—United Nations, 1990; articles on human rights and economic development, British colonial history. *Address:* 14 Gomshall Road, Cheam, Sutton, Surrey SM2 7JZ. *T:* (020) 8393 7306. *Club:* Oxford and Cambridge.

WILLIAMS, Prof. Dudley Howard, PhD, ScD; FRS 1983; Professor of Biological Chemistry, University of Cambridge, since 1996; Fellow of Churchill College, since 1964; *b* 25 May 1937; *s* of Lawrence Williams and Evelyn (*née* Hudson); *m* 1963, Lorna Patricia Phyllis, *d* of Anthony and Lorna Bedford; two *s*. *Educ:* Grammar Sch., Pudsey, Yorks; Univ. of Leeds (state schol.; BSc, PhD); MA, ScD Cantab. Fulbright Schol., Post-doctoral Fellow and Research Associate, Stanford Univ., Calif, 1961–64; University of Cambridge: Sen. Asst in Research, 1964–66; Asst Dir of Research, 1966–74; Reader in Organic Chemistry, 1974–96. Nuffield Vis. Lectr, Sydney Univ., 1973; Dist. Vis. Lectr, Texas A & M Univ., 1986; Lee Kuan Yew Dist. Visitor, Singapore, 2000; Visiting Professor: Univ. of California, Irvine, 1967, 1986, 1989 and 1997; Univ. of Cape Town, 1972; Univ. of Wisconsin, 1975; Univ. of Copenhagen, 1976; ANU, 1980. Lectures: Arun Guthikonda Meml Award, Columbia Univ., 1985; Rohrer, Ohio State Univ., 1989; Foundn, Univ. of Auckland, 1991; Pacific Coast, 1991; Steel, Univ. of Queensland, 1994. Mem. Acad. Europaea. Meldola Medal, RIC, 1966; Corday-Morgan Medal, 1968; Tilden Medal and Lectr, 1983; Structural Chemistry Award, 1984, Bader Award, 1991, RSC; Leo Friend Award, ACS, 1996. *Publications:* Applications of NMR in Organic Chemistry, 1964; Spectroscopic Methods in Organic Chemistry, 1966, 5th edn 1995; Mass Spectrometry of Organic Compounds, 1967; Mass Spectrometry—Principles and Applications, 1981; papers in chemical and biochemical jls, incl. co-discovery of human hormone (1,25-dihydroxyvitamin D) responsible for calcium absorption, and chemistry and action of antibiotics vancomycin and teicoplanin. *Recreations:* music, gardening. *Address:* 7 Balsham Road, Fulbourn, Cambridge CB1 5BZ. *T:* (01223) 740971.

WILLIAMS, Dr Dyfri John Roderick, FSA; Keeper, Department of Greek and Roman Antiquities, British Museum, since 1993; *b* 8 Feb. 1952; *s* of Roderick Trevor Williams and Eira Williams (*née* Evans); *m* 1980, Korinna Pilafidis; one *s* one *d*. *Educ:* Repton Sch.; University Coll. London (BA); Lincoln Coll., Oxford (DPhil). FSA 1987. Shuffrey Jun. Res. Fellow, Lincoln Coll., Oxford, 1976–79; Department of Greek and Roman Antiquities, British Museum, 1979–: Res. Asst, 1979–83; Asst Keeper, 1983–93. Corresp. Mem., German Archaeol Inst., 1984. *Publications:* Greek Vases, 1985, rev. and enlarged edn 1999; Corpus Vasorum Antiquorum, BM fasc. 9, 1993; Greek Gold: jewellery of the classical world, 1994; (ed) The Art of the Greek Goldsmith, 1998. *Recreations:* family, reading, music. *Address:* Department of Greek and Roman Antiquities, British Museum, Great Russell Street, WC1B 3DG. *T:* (020) 7323 8411.

WILLIAMS, Prof. Sir (Edward) Dillwyn, Kt 1990; FRCP; FRCPath; Professor of Histopathology, University of Cambridge, 1992–96, now Emeritus; *b* 1 April 1929; *s* of Edward Williams and Ceinwen Williams (*née* James); *m* 1st, 1954, Ruth Hill; one *s* two *d* (and one *s* decd); 2nd, 1976, Olwen Williams; one *s* one *d*. *Educ:* Christ's Coll., Cambridge (MA, MD; Hon. Fellow, 1991); London Hospital Med. Coll. Jun. appts, London Hosp. and RPMS; successively Lectr, Sen. Lectr, Reader, in Morbid Anatomy, RPMS; Prof. of Pathology, 1969–92, Vice-Provost, 1982–84, Univ. of Wales Coll. of Medicine. Consultant Pathologist, Cardiff, 1969–92. Res. Fellowship, Harvard Univ., 1962–63. President: RCPath, 1987–90; BMA, 1998–99; Hd and Prin. Investigator of WHO's Internat. Reference Centre for Endocrine Tumours, 1972–; Chm., Welsh Sci. Adv. Cttee, 1985–92; Mem., GMC, 1987–90. Corresp. Mem., Amer. Thyroid Assoc.; President: Thyroid Club of GB, 1987–90; European Thyroid Assoc., 1993–96. Founder FMedSci 1998. *Publications:* International Histological Classification of Tumours: histological typing of endocrine tumours, 1980; Pathology and Management of Thyroid Disease, 1981; Current Endocrine Concepts, 1982; numerous contribs to learned jls in field of endocrine pathology and carcinogenesis. *Recreations:* natural history in general, birdwatching in particular, mountain walking. *Address:* Burford House, Hildersham, Cambs CB1 6BU. *T:* (01223) 893316.

WILLIAMS, Air Cdre Edward Stanley, CBE 1975 (OBE 1968); defence consultant; *b* 27 Sept. 1924; *s* of late William Stanley Williams and Ethel Williams; *m* 1947, Maureen Donovan; two *d. Educ:* Wallasey Central Sch.; London Univ. Sch. of Slavonic and E European Studies; St John's Coll., Cambridge (MPhil (Internat. Relations), 1982). Joined RAF, 1942; trained in Canada; service in flying boats, 1944; seconded BOAC, 1944–48; 18 Sqdn, Transport Comd, 1949; Instr, Central Navigation Sch., RAF Shawbury, 1950–52; Russian Language Study, 1952–54; Flying Appts MEAF, A&AEE, 216 Sqdn Transport Comd, 1954–61; OC RAF Element, Army Intell. Centre, 1961–64; Asst Air Attaché, Moscow, 1964–67; first RAF Defence Fellow, UCL, 1967–68; comd Jt Wing, Sch. of Service Intell., 1968–71; Chief, Target Plans, HQ Second ATAF, 1971–73; Chief Intell. Officer, HQ British Forces Near East, 1973–75; comd Jt Air Reconn. Intell. Centre, 1976–77; Defence and Air Attaché, Moscow, 1978–81, retired RAF, 1981. Vice-Chm. (Air), NW Area, TAVRA, 1988–93. *Publications:* The Soviet Military, 1986; Soviet Air Power: prospects for the future, 1990; Cold War, Hot Seat, 2000; various articles in professional jls. *Recreations:* Russian studies, photography. *Address:* c/o HSBC, 2 Liscard Way, Wallasey, Merseyside CH44 5TR. *Club:* Royal Air Force.

WILLIAMS, Elizabeth, (Betty), (Mrs J. T. Perkins); working for peace, since 1976; *b* 22 May 1943; *m* 1st, 1961, Ralph Williams (marr. diss.); one *s* one *d*; 2nd, 1982, James T. Perkins. *Educ:* St Dominic's Grammar School. Office Receptionist. Leader, NI Peace Movement, 1976–78. Hon. LLD, Yale Univ., 1977; Hon. HLD, Coll. of Sienna Heights, Michigan, 1977. Nobel Peace Prize (jtly), 1976; Carl-von-Ossietsky Medal for Courage, 1976. *Recreation:* gardening. *Address:* PO Box 725, Valparaiso, FL 32580–0725, USA.

WILLIAMS, Evelyn Faithfull M.; *see* Monier-Williams.

WILLIAMS, Francis Julian, CBE 1986; JP; Vice Lord-Lieutenant, Cornwall, since 1998; Member of Prince of Wales' Council, Duchy of Cornwall, 1969–85; *b* 16 April 1927; 2nd *s* of late Alfred Martyn Williams, CBE, DSC; *m* Delia Fearne Marshall, *e d* of Captain and Mrs Campbell Marshall, St Mawes; two *s. Educ:* Eton; Trinity Coll., Cambridge (BA). RAF, 1945–48. Chm., Cambridge Univ. Conservative Assoc., 1950; Pres., Cambridge Union, 1951. Contested (C) All Saints Div. of Birmingham, 1955. Chm., Royal Instn of Cornwall, 1998–. Succeeded to Caerhays, 1955. Pres., Cornwall Cricket Club. Mem., Cornwall CC, 1967–89 (Vice-Chm., 1974; Chm., 1980–89). JP 1970, DL 1977, Cornwall. *Recreation:* gardening. *Address:* Caerhays Castle, Gorran, St Austell, Cornwall PL26 6LY. *T:* (01872) 501250. *Clubs:* Brooks's, White's.

WILLIAMS, Sir Francis Owen Garbett, (Sir Frank), Kt 1999; CBE 1987; Managing Director, Williams Grand Prix Engineering Ltd; *b* 16 April 1942; *s* of Owen Garbett Williams; *m* 1974, Virginia Jane, *d* of Raymond Berry; three *c. Educ:* St Joseph's Coll., Dumfries. Racing driver to 1966, competing first in Austin A40; grand prix team management, 1969–; Formula One with Brabham BT 26A; founded Frank Williams Racing Cars, 1975; first Grand Prix race, with FW07, Silverstone, 1979; won Constructors' Cup, 1980, 1981, 1986, 1987, 1992, 1993, 1994, 1996, 1997; introduced active ride system, 1988, semi-automatic 6-speed gear box, 1991. *Address:* Williams Grand Prix Engineering, Grove, Wantage, Oxon OX12 0DQ.

WILLIAMS, Frank Denry Clement, CMG 1956; *b* 3 May 1913; *s* of Frank Norris Williams and Joanna Esther Williams; *m* 1941, Traute Kahn; no *c. Educ:* Leighton Park School, Reading; London School of Economics (BSc Econ.). Cadet, Colonial Administrative Service, 1946; Asst Financial Sec., Nigeria, 1952, Financial Secretary: Jamaica, 1954; Federation of Nigeria, 1956; Economic Adviser, Federation of Nigeria, 1957–58; Permanent Secretary, Prime Minister's Dept, Fedn of The W Indies, 1958–62; Financial Sec., The Gambia, 1962–65. *Recreation:* languages. *Address:* 51 The Priory, London Road, Brighton, Sussex BN1 8QT.

WILLIAMS, Frank John; actor and playwright; *b* 2 July 1931; *s* of William Williams and Alice (*née* Myles). *Educ:* Ardingly Coll.; Hendon County Sch. *Theatre* includes: Stage Manager and actor, Gateway Theatre, London, 1951; *writer:* No Traveller, 1952; The TV Murders, 1960; The Substitute, 1961; Murder by Appointment, 1985; Alibi for Murder, 1989; Murder Weekend, 1993; Mask for Murder, 1993; *actor:* The Cresta Run, Royal Court, 1965; The Waiters, Watford, 1967; Dad's Army, Shaftesbury, and tour, 1975–76; The Editor Regrets, tour, 1978; Stage Struck, 1980, The Winslow Boy, 1982, Vienna; Lloyd George Knew My Father, tour, Middle East and Far East, 1993; A Midsummer Night's Dream, Almeida, and tour, 1996–97; *television* includes: The Call Up, 1952; The Queen came by, 1955; The Army Game, 1958–61; Anna Karenina, 1961; Diary of a Young Man, 1964; After Many a Summer, 1967; Dad's Army, 1969–77; How Many Miles to Babylon, 1981; Grey Granite, 1982; Love's Labour Lost, 1984; You Rang M'Lord, 1989–92; *films* include: Shield of Faith, 1954; The Extra Day, 1955; The Square Peg, 1958; The Bulldog Breed, 1960; Dad's Army, 1970; Jabberwocky, 1976; The Human Factor, 1979. Member: London Diocesan Synod and Bishop's Council; Gen. Synod, 1985–2000; Crown Appts Commn, 1992–97; Trustee, Annunciation Trust, 1995–. Mem., Equity Council, 1984–88, 1990–94, 1998–; Dir, Equity Trust Fund, 1992–. *Recreations:* theatre, cinema, collecting boys' school stories. *Address:* 31 Manor Park Crescent, Edgware, Middx HA8 7NE. *T:* (020) 8952 4871.

WILLIAMS, Prof. Gareth Howel; Professor of Chemistry, University of London, 1967–84 (Head of Department of Chemistry, Bedford College, 1967–84), now Emeritus Professor; *b* 17 June 1925; *s* of Morgan John and Miriam Williams, Treherbert, Glam; *m* 1955, Marie, BA, *yr d* of William and Jessie Mary Mitchell, Wanlockhead, Dumfriesshire; one *s* one *d. Educ:* Pentre Grammar Sch.; University Coll., London. BSc, PhD, DSc London; FRSC 1960. Asst Lectr, then Lectr in Chemistry, King's Coll., Univ of London, 1947–60; Research Fellow, Univ. of Chicago, 1953–54; Reader in Organic Chemistry, Birkbeck Coll., Univ. of London, 1960–67. Vis. Lectr, Univ. of Ife, Nigeria, 1965; Rose Morgan Vis. Prof., Univ. of Kansas, 1969–70; Vis. Prof., Univ. of Auckland, NZ, 1977. External Examr: Univ. of Rhodesia, 1967–70; Univ. of Khartoum, 1967–73, 1976–80; City Univ., 1968–74; Univ. of Surrey, 1974–76; Brunel Univ., 1980–85. Chm., London Welsh Assoc., 1987–90. JP Brent, 1979 (Dep. Chm., 1989–91). *Publications:* Homolytic Aromatic Substitution, 1960; Organic Chemistry: a conceptual approach, 1977; (Editor) Advances in Free-Radical Chemistry, Vol. I, 1965, Vol. II, 1967, Vol. III, 1969, Vol. IV, 1972, Vol. V, 1975, Vol. VI, 1980; numerous papers in Jl Chem. Soc. and other scientific jls. *Recreation:* music. *Address:* Hillside, 22 Watford Road, Northwood, Middx HA6 3NT. *T:* (01923) 825297. *Club:* Athenæum.

WILLIAMS, Prof. Gareth Lloyd; Professor of Educational Administration, Institute of Education, University of London, since 1984; *b* 19 Oct. 1935; *s* of Lloyd and Katherine Enid Williams; *m* 1960, Elizabeth Ann Peck; two *s* one *d. Educ:* Creeting St Mary; Framlingham; Cambridge Univ. (MA). Res. Officer, Agricl Econs Res. Inst., Oxford Univ., 1959–62; Res. Fellow, OECD, Athens, 1962–64; Principal Administrator, OECD, Paris, 1964–68; Associate Dir, Higher Educn Res. Unit, LSE, 1968–73; Prof. of Educnl Planning, Univ. of Lancaster, 1973–84. Visiting Professor: Melbourne Univ., 1981–82; Coll. of Europe, 1994–. Specialist Adviser to Arts and Educn Sub-Cttee to House of Commons Cttee on Expenditure, 1972–76; Consultant to OECD, ILO, UNESCO, and World Bank. Member: Council, Policy Studies Inst., 1979–85; Governing Council for Soc. for Res. into Higher Educn, 1970– (Chm., 1978–80, 1986–88). Mem. Bd, Red Rose Radio PLC, 1981–92. FRSA 1982. *Publications:* (with Greenaway) Patterns of Change in Graduate Employment, 1973; (with Blackstone and Metcalf) The Academic Labour Market in Britain, 1974; Towards Lifelong Learning, 1978; (with Zabalza and Turnbull) The Economics of Teacher Supply, 1979; (with Woodhall) Independent Further Education, 1979; (with Blackstone) Response to Adversity, 1983; Higher Education in Ireland, 1985; (with Woodhall and O'Brien) Overseas Students and their Place of Study, 1986; Changing Patterns of Finance in Higher Education, 1992. *Address:* 11 Thornfield, Ashton Road, Lancaster LA1 5AG. *T:* (01524) 66002.

WILLIAMS, Sir Gareth R.; *see* Rhys Williams, Sir A. G. L. E.

WILLIAMS, Geoffrey Guy; Public Works Loan Commissioner, 1990–98; *b* 12 July 1930; *s* of late Captain Guy Williams, OBE, and Mrs Margaret Williams (*née* Thomas). *Educ:* Blundell's Sch.; Christ's Coll., Cambridge (MA, LLM). Slaughter and May, Solicitors, 1952–66, Partner 1961; Dir, J. Henry Schroder Wagg & Co. Ltd, 1966–90, Vice-Chm. 1974, Dep. Chm., 1977–90. Chm., National Film Finance Corp., 1976–85 (Dir, 1970). Director: Bass plc, 1971–91; Schroders plc, 1976–90; John Brown plc, 1977–85; Standard Chartered plc, 1990–94. Chm., Issuing Houses Assoc., 1979–81. *Recreations:* reading, theatre, cinema. *Address:* 18G Eaton Square, SW1W 9DD. *T:* (020) 7235 5212. *Club:* Brooks's.

WILLIAMS, (George Haigh) Graeme; QC 1983; barrister; a Recorder of the Crown Court, 1981–2001; *b* 5 July 1935; *s* of Dr Leslie Graeme Williams and Joan Haigh Williams (*née* Iago); *m* 1963, Anna Maureen Worrall, *qv*; two *d. Educ:* Tonbridge Sch. (Scholar); Brasenose Coll., Oxford (MA). Nat. Service, RA, England and Hong Kong, 1953–55. Called to the Bar, Inner Temple, 1959 (Entrance Scholar; Bencher, 1996). Hd of Chambers, 1988–98. Mem., No 3 Legal Aid Area Cttee, 1980–; Legal Pres., Mental Health Review Tribunals, 1996–. Legal Assessor, GMC and GDC, 1998–. *Address:* 13 King's Bench Walk, Temple, EC4Y 7EN. *T:* (020) 7353 7204; King's Bench Chambers, 32 Beaumont Street, Oxford OX1 2NP. *T:* (01865) 311066. *Club:* Orford Sailing.

WILLIAMS, George Mervyn, CBE 1977; MC 1944; TD; Vice Lord-Lieutenant of Mid Glamorgan, 1986–94; *b* 30 Oct. 1918; *yr s* of late Owain Williams and late Mrs Williams; *m* 1st, 1940, Penelope (marr. diss. 1946), *d* of late Sir Frank Mitchell, KCVO; 2nd, 1950, Grizel Margaretta Cochrane, DStJ, *d* of late Major Walter Stewart, DSO; one *s. Educ:* Radley Coll. Served Royal Fusiliers, N Africa and Italy, 1939–46; Major, British Military Mission to Greece, 1945. Great Universal Stores, 1946–49; Christie-Tyler PLC: Sales Dir, 1949; Man. Dir, 1950–80; Chm., 1959–85; Director: Lloyds Bank plc, 1972–77; Lloyds Bank UK Management Ltd, 1975–85; Chm., S Wales Regl Bd, Lloyds Bank, 1977–87. Governor, United World Coll. of Atlantic, 1980–88. JP 1965–70, High Sheriff 1966, DL 1967–86, Glamorgan. CStJ. *Address:* 27 Broad Street, Ludlow, Shropshire SY8 1NJ. *T:* (01584) 872877; Llanharan House, Llanharan, Mid Glamorgan CF7 9A. *T:* (01443) 226253. *Clubs:* Brooks's; Cardiff and County (Cardiff).

WILLIAMS, Gethin A.; *see* Abraham-Williams.

WILLIAMS, Sir Glanmor, Kt 1995; CBE 1981; FBA 1986; Professor of History, University College of Swansea, 1957–82; Chairman, Ancient Monuments Board (Wales), 1983–95; *b* 5 May 1920; *s* of Daniel and Ceinwen Williams, Dowlais, Glam; *m* 1946, Margaret Fay Davies; one *s* one *d. Educ:* Cyfarthfa Grammar Sch., Merthyr Tydfil; Univ. Coll. of Wales, Aberystwyth. MA 1947; DLitt 1962. University College of Swansea: Asst Lectr in History, 1945; Sen. Lectr, 1952; a Vice-Principal, 1975–78; Hon. Fellow, 1988. Nat. Governor, BBC, for Wales, 1965–71; Chm., Royal Commn on Ancient and Historical Monuments in Wales, 1986–90 (Mem., 1962–90); Member: Historic Bldgs Council for Wales, 1962–; British Library Bd, 1973–80 (Chm., Adv. Council, 1981–85); Adv. Council on Public Records, 1974–82; Welsh Arts Council, 1978–81; Council, Nat. Museum of Wales, 1983–90; Chm., Welsh Folk-Museum Cttee, 1987–90. Vice-Pres., Univ. of Wales, Aberystwyth, 1986–96, and Hon. Fellow, 1993. Chm., Pantyfedwen Foundations, 1973–79; Pres., Cambrian Arch. Assoc., 1980. FRHistS 1954 (Vice-Pres., 1979–83); FSA 1978. Hon. LLD Wales, 1998. Medal of Hon. Soc. of Cymmrodorion, 1991. *Publications:* Yr Esgob Richard Davies, 1953; The Welsh Church, 1962; Owen Glendower, 1966; Welsh Reformation Essays, 1967; (ed) Glamorgan County History, vol. II 1984, vol. III 1971, vol. IV 1974, vol. V 1980, vol. VI 1988; Religion, Language and Nationality in Wales, 1979; Grym Tafodau Tân, 1984; Henry Tudor and Wales, 1985; Wales 1415–1642, 1987; (ed) Swansea: an illustrated history, 1990; (ed) The Celts and the Renaissance, 1990; The Welsh and their Religion, 1991; (ed) Social Policy, Crime and Punishment, 1994; Wales and the Reformation, 1997; Cymru a'r Gorffennol, 2000; contrib. to: History, Welsh History Review, etc. *Recreations:* music, camera. *Address:* 11 Grosvenor Road, Swansea SA2 0SP. *T:* (01792) 204113.

WILLIAMS, Glynn Anthony, FRBS, FRCA; sculptor; Professor of Sculpture, Royal College of Art, since 1990 (Head, School of Fine Art, 1995–99, and since 2001); *b* 30 March 1939; *s* of Idris Merion Williams and Muriel Elizabeth Purslow; *m* 1963, Heather Woodhall (marr. diss. 2001); two *d. Educ:* Wolverhampton Grammar Sch.; Wolverhampton Coll. of Art (NDD Sculpture Special Level); British Sch. in Rome (Rome Scholar). Head of Sculpture Departments: Leeds Coll. of Art, later Leeds Polytechnic, 1968–75; Wimbledon Sch. of Art, 1976–90. 24 one-man exhibns incl. retrospective, Margam Park, S Wales, 1992; numerous group exhibns incl. British Sculpture of 20th Century, Whitechapel Gall., 1981; rep. GB, Kotara Takamura Grand Prize Exhibn, Japan, 1984; work in collections: Arts Council of GB; Bottisham Village Coll., Cambridge; Bradford City Art Gall.; British Sch. in Rome; Grisedale Theatre in the Forest, Cumbria; Hakone Open Air Mus., Japan; Hampshire Sculpture Trust; Haroldwood Hosp., Essex; Hemel Hempstead Arts Trust; Henry Moore Centre for Sculpture, Leeds; Hove Mus. and Art Gall.; Hull City Art Gall.; Leeds City Council; Lincoln City Council; London Borough of Hounslow; Middlesbrough Council; Milton Keynes Develt Corp.; Nat. Portrait Gall.; Newport (Gwent) Educn Cttee; Northern Arts Assoc.; Peterborough Develt Corp.; Southern Arts Assoc.; Tate Gall.; V & A; Welsh Arts Council; Welsh Sculpture Trust; Wolverhampton Educn Cttee; Yorkshire Arts Assoc. Commissions: 14´ bronze meml to Henry Purcell, Flowering of the English Baroque, City of Westminster, 1995; Lloyd George Meml, Parliament Sq., 2001. FRCA 1991; FRBS 1992. FRSA 1996. Hon. Fellow, Wolverhampton Polytechnic, 1989. *Publications:* contribs to arts magazines, jls, TLS. *Recreations:* cooking, crosswords, music. *Address:* c/o Bernard Jacobson Gallery, 14A Clifford Sueet, W1X 1RF. *Club:* Chelsea Arts.

WILLIAMS, Gordon; *see* Williams, J. G.

WILLIAMS, Graeme; *see* Williams, George H. G.

WILLIAMS, Air Vice-Marshal Graham Charles, AFC 1970 and Bar 1975; FRAeS; Director, Lockheed Martin International (formerly Loral International Inc.), since 1993; Commandant General, RAF Regiment and Director General of Security (RAF),

1990–91; *b* 4 June 1937; *s* of Charles Francis Williams and Molly (*née* Chapman); *m* 1962, Judith Teresa Ann Walker; one *s* one *d*. *Educ:* Marlborough College; RAF College, Cranwell. FRAeS 1984. 54 Sqn, 229 OCU, 8 Sqn, Empire Test Pilots' School, A Sqn, A&AEE, 1958–70; RAF Staff Coll., 1971; OC 3 Sqn, Wildenrath, 1972–74; Junior Directing Staff (Air), RCDS, 1975–77; OC RAF Brüggen, 1978–79; Group Captain Ops, HQ RAF Germany, 1980–82; CO Experimental Flying Dept, RAE, 1983; Comdt, Aeroplane and Armament Exptl Estabt, 1983–85; Dir, Operational Requirements, MoD, 1986; ACDS, Operational Requirements (Air), 1986–89. Harmon Internat. Trophy for Aviators, USA, 1970. *Recreations:* old cars, golf. *Address:* Gate Cottage, Horsenden, Princes Risborough, Bucks HP27 9NF. *Club:* Royal Air Force.

WILLIAMS, Rev. Harry Abbott; Community of the Resurrection, since 1969; *b* 10 May 1919; *s* of late Captain Harry Williams, RN, and Annie Williams. *Educ:* Cranleigh Sch.; Trinity Coll., Cambridge; Cuddesdon Coll., Oxford. BA 1941; MA 1945. Deacon, 1943; Priest, 1944. Curate of St Barnabas, Pimlico, 1943–45; Curate of All Saints, Margaret Street, 1945–48; Chaplain and Tutor of Westcott House, Cambridge, 1948–51; Fellow of Trinity Coll., Cambridge, 1951–69; Dean of Chapel, 1958–69, and Tutor, 1958–68; Exam. Chaplain to Bishop of London, 1948–69. Mem., Anglican delegation to Russian Orthodox Church, Moscow, 1956; Select Preacher, Univ. of Cambridge, 1950, 1958, 1975; Hulsean Preacher, 1962, 1975; Select Preacher, Univ. of Oxford, 1974. Licensed to officiate in Dio. of Ely, 1948–, Dio. of Wakefield, 1979–. *Publications:* Jesus and the Resurrection, 1951; God's Wisdom in Christ's Cross, 1960; The Four Last Things, 1960; The True Wilderness, 1965; True Resurrection, 1972; Poverty, Chastity and Obedience: the true virtues, 1975; Tensions, 1976; Becoming What I Am, 1977; The Joy of God, 1979; Some Day I'll Find You (autobiog.), 1982; contribs to: Soundings, 1962; Objections to Christian Belief, 1963; The God I Want, 1967. *Recreations:* idleness and religion. *Address:* House of the Resurrection, Mirfield, West Yorks WF14 0BN.

WILLIAMS, Helen Elizabeth Webber, MA; Principal, RNIB New College, Worcester, since 1995; *b* 28 April 1938; *o d* of Alwyn and Eleanor Thomas; *m* 1962, Dr Peter Williams (marr. diss. 1974); one *s* one *d*. *Educ:* Redland High Sch., Bristol; Girton Coll., Cambridge (MA; DipEd). Assistant English Mistress: St Paul's Girls' Sch., 1962–63; St George's Sch., Edinburgh, 1963–64; Edinburgh University: Asst Lectr, Dept of English, 1964–67; Lectr in English and Dir of Studies, Faculty of Arts, 1967–78; Headmistress, Blackheath High Sch., 1978–89; High Mistress, St Paul's Girls' Sch., 1989–92; Trevelyan Fellow, Trevelyan Coll., Univ. of Durham, 1993; English teacher, The Brearley Sch., NY, 1993–94. Member: HMC, 1994–; Governing Body, SOAS, 1988–96; Council, City Univ., 1990–92; Governing Body, Stowe Sch., 1992–. *Publication:* (ed) T. S. Eliot: The Wasteland, 1968. *Recreations:* music, drama, cookery, gardening. *Address:* The Principal's House, RNIB New College, Worcester, Whittington Road, Worcester WR5 2JX; 4/2 Advocates Close, The Royal Mile, Edinburgh EH1 1PS.

WILLIAMS, Helen Mary, (Mrs D. M. Forrester); Director, School Organisation and Funding, Department for Education and Skills (formerly Education and Employment), since 1999; *b* 30 June 1950; *d* of Graham Myatt and Mary (*née* Harrison); *m* 1st, 1975, Ian Vaughan Williams (marr. diss. 1982); 2nd, 1993, David Michael Forrester, *qv*; one *s* one *d*. *Educ:* Allerton High Sch., Leeds; St Hilda's Coll., Oxford (BA Hons Mod. Hist.). Joined DES, 1972; Private Sec. to Joan Lester and to Margaret Jackson, 1975–76; Asst Sec., DES, subseq. DFE, 1984–93; Under-Sec., then Dir, OST, Cabinet Office, subseq. DTI, 1993–98. *Recreations:* family life, walking, bell-ringing. *Address:* Department for Education and Skills, Sanctuary Buildings, Great Smith Street, SW1P 3BT. *T:* (020) 7925 5938.

WILLIAMS, Ven. Henry Leslie; Archdeacon of Chester, 1975–88; *b* 26 Dec. 1919; *m* 1949, Elsie Marie; one *s*. *Educ:* Bethesda County Sch.; St David's Coll., Lampeter (BA); St Michael's Coll., Llandaff. Deacon 1943, priest 1944, Bangor; Curate of Aberdovey, 1943–45; St Mary's, Bangor, 1945–48; Chaplain, HMS Conway, 1948–49; Curate, St Mary-without-the-Walls, Chester, 1949–53; Vicar of Barnston, Wirral, 1953–84. RD of Wirral North, 1967–75; Hon. Canon of Chester Cathedral, 1972–75. Mem., General Synod, 1978–80, 1985–88. CF (TA), 1953–62. *Recreations:* fly-fishing, grandparenthood. *Address:* 1 Bartholomew Way, Westminster Park, Chester CH4 7RJ. *T:* (01244) 675296.

WILLIAMS, (Henry) Nigel, FRSL; author and broadcaster; *b* 20 Jan. 1948; *s* of late David Ffrancon Williams and of Sylvia Margaret Williams (*née* Hartley); *m* 1973, Susan Elizabeth Harrison; three *s*. *Educ:* Highgate Sch.; Oriel Coll., Oxford (MA Hist.). BBC: gen. trainee, 1969–73; Producer/Dir, Arts Dept, 1973–85; Editor: Bookmark, 1985–92; Omnibus, 1992–96; writer/presenter, 1997–2000. *Plays:* Class Enemy, Royal Court, 1978 (Most Promising Playwright Award, Plays and Players mag.); Sugar and Spice, Royal Court, 1980; Line 'Em, NT, 1980; Trial Run, Oxford Playhouse, 1980; My Brother's Keeper, Greenwich, 1985; Country Dancing, RSC, 1987; Lord of the Flies (adapted), RSC, 1996; *television plays* include: Charlie, 1980; Breaking Up, 1986; The Last Romantics, 1990; Skallagrig, 1994 (BAFTA Award). FRSL 1994. *Publications:* (novels): My Life Closed Twice, 1978 (Somerset Maugham Award); Jack Be Nimble, 1980; Star Turn, 1985; Witchcraft, 1987; Black Magic, 1988; The Wimbledon Poisoner, 1990; They Came from SW19, 1992; East of Wimbledon, 1993; 2½ Men in a Boat, 1993; Scenes from a Poisoner's Life, 1994; From Wimbledon to Waco, 1995; Stalking Fiona, 1997; Fortysomething, 1999. *Recreations:* swimming, drinking, walking, talking, family, dogs. *Address:* 18 Holmbush Road, Putney, SW15 3LE.

WILLIAMS, Sir (Henry) Sydney, Kt 1983; OBE 1978; company director; *b* 10 Jan. 1920; *s* of Edward Stratten Williams and Zilla Williams (*née* McHugh); *m* 1940, Joyce Veronica Meldon; four *s*. *Educ:* Mt Carmel Coll., Charters Towers, Qld, Aust. Served 7th Aust. Div. Cavalry Regt, ME and PNG, 1940–45; 51st Inf. Bn (Far North Qld Regt), 1947–57, Lt-Col Comd 1954–57. Chm., Air Queensland Ltd (formerly Bush Pilots Airways Ltd), 1960–86; Chairman: Willtrac Pty Ltd, 1964–; Lizard Island Pty Ltd, 1970–86; Director: Carlton & United Breweries (NQ) Ltd, 1964–90; Placer Pacific Ltd, 1986–90. Member: Queensland Art Gall., 1981–; Cairns Port Authority, 1982–; Life Mem., Cairns RSSAILA; Trustee, WWF, 1981–; Councillor, Enterprise Australia, 1980–; Pres., Far North Queensland Amateur Turf Club, 1959–; past Dep. Chm., Australian Tourist Commn; past Pres., Cairns Legacy Club. Hon. Col, 51st Infantry Bn (Far North Qld Regt), 1987–; Patron, Light Horse Assoc. Ltd, Qld, 1989–93. *Recreations:* fishing, bowls, golf. *Address:* 14 Bellevue Crescent, Edge Hill, Cairns, Qld 4870, Australia. *T:* (7) 40531489. *Clubs:* North Queensland (Townsville); United Services, Brisbane (Brisbane).

WILLIAMS, Hilary a'Beckett E.; *see* Eccles-Williams.

WILLIAMS, Hubert Glyn, AE 1944; a Recorder of the Crown Court, 1974–77; Senior Partner, Blake, Lapthorn, Rea & Williams, Solicitors, Portsmouth and District, 1973–83; *b* 18 Dec. 1912; *s* of John Christmas Williams and Florence Jane Williams (*née* Jones); *m* 1952, Audrey Elizabeth Righton; one *s* one *d*. *Educ:* Ruthin. Admitted solicitor, 1934 (2nd cl. Hons). Served War of 1939–45 (Sqdn Ldr; AE): AAF, 1939–41; RAFVR, 1941–45; UK, Egypt, E Africa, Palestine. Pres., Hampshire Inc. Law Soc., 1977–78. *Recreation:* cricket. *Address:* 29 The Avenue, Alverstoke, Gosport, Hants PO12 2JS. *T:* (023) 9258 3058. *Club:* MCC.

WILLIAMS, Hugo Mordaunt; writer; *b* 20 Feb. 1942; *s* of late Hugh Williams, actor and playwright, and Margaret Vyner; *m* 1965, Hermine Demoriane; one *d*. *Educ:* Eton College. Asst Editor, London Magazine, 1961–70; television critic, 1983–88, and poetry editor, 1984–93, New Statesman; theatre critic, The Sunday Correspondent, 1989–91; columnist, TLS, 1988–; film critic, Harpers & Queen, 1993–98. Henfield Writer's Fellowship, Univ. of East Anglia, 1981. Awards (for poetry): Eric Gregory, 1965; Cholmondeley, 1970; Geoffrey Faber Memorial Prize, 1979. *Publications:* *poems:* Symptoms of Loss, 1965; Sugar Daddy, 1970; Some Sweet Day, 1975; Love-Life, 1979; Writing Home, 1985; Selected Poems, 1989; Self-Portrait With A Slide, 1990; Dock Leaves, 1994; Billy's Rain (T. S. Eliot Prize), 1999; *travel:* All the Time in the World, 1966; No Particular Place to Go, 1981; *journalism:* Freelancing, 1995. *Address:* 3 Raleigh Street, N1 8NW. *T:* (020) 7226 1655.

WILLIAMS, Hywel; MP (Plaid Cymru) Caernarfon, since 2001; *b* 14 May 1953; *s* of late Robert Williams and of Jennie Page Williams; *m* 1977, Sian Davies (marr. diss. 1998); three *d*. *Educ:* Ysgol Glan y Mor, Pwllheli, Gwynedd; UC Cardiff (BSc Hons Psychol. 1974); UCNW, Bangor (CQSW 1980). Approved Social Worker (Mental Health), 1984. Social Worker: Child Care and Long Term Team, Social Services Dept, Mid Glam CC, 1974–76; Mental Health Team, Social Services Dept, Gwynedd CC, 1976–78 and 1980–84; Welsh Office funded project worker, 1985–91, Hd of Centre, 1991–93, N and W Wales Practice Centre, UCNW, Bangor; freelance lectr, consultant and author in social work and social policy, 1994–2001. CCETSW Cymru: Mem. Welsh Cttee and Chm., Welsh Lang. Sub-cttee, 1989–92; Mem., Welsh Lang. Pubns Adv. Panel, 1992–93. N and W Wales (Social Work) Training Consortium, 1991–93: Mem., Consortium and Mem., Post Qualifying Consortium; Chm., Practice Teaching Award Gp; Convenor, Bilingual Provision Gp; Member: Assessment Panel; Anti Oppressive Practice Planning Gp. *Publications:* (contrib.) Social Work in Action in the 1980s, 1985; (compiled and ed) A Social Work Vocabulary, 1988; (gen. ed.) Child Care Terms, 1993; (contrib. and ed jtly) Social Work and the Welsh Language, 1994; (compiled and ed) An Index of Trainers and Training, 1994; (contrib. and ed jtly) Gofal: a training and resource pack for community care in Wales, 1998. *Recreations:* walking, cinema, reading. *Address:* House of Commons, SW1A 0AA; 8 Stryd Y Castell, Caernarfon, Gwynedd LL15 1SE. *T:* (01286) 672076.

WILLIAMS, Prof. (James) Gordon, FRS 1994; FREng; Professor of Mechanical Engineering, Imperial College, London, since 1990 (Head, Department of Mechanical Engineering, 1990–2000); *b* 13 June 1938; *s* of John William and Eira Williams; *m* 1960, Ann Marie Joscelyne; two *s* one *d*. *Educ:* Imperial Coll. (BScEng, PhD, DScEng); FCGI; FREng (FEng 1982). RAE, Farnborough, 1956–61; Imperial College: Asst Lectr, 1962–64; Lectr, 1964–70; Reader, 1970–75; Prof. of Polymer Engrg, 1975–90. *Publications:* Stress Analysis of Polymers, 1973, 2nd edn 1981; Fracture Mechanics of Polymers, 1984. *Recreations:* gardening, mountains (walking and ski-ing), golf. *Address:* Mechanical Engineering Department, Imperial College, Exhibition Road, South Kensington, SW7 2BX. *T:* (020) 7594 7000.

WILLIAMS, (Jean) Adèle, (Mrs A. Patience); Her Honour Judge Williams; a Circuit Judge, since 2000; *b* 28 July 1950; *d* of David James Williams and Dorothy Williams; *m* 1975, Andrew Patience, *qv*; one *s* one *d*. *Educ:* Llanelli Girls' Grammar Sch.; University Coll. London (LLB). Called to the Bar, Gray's Inn, 1972; in practice on S Eastern Circuit, 1972–2000; a Recorder, 1995–2000. Sen., Kent Bar Mess, 1997–2000. *Recreations:* cinema, theatre, holidays, conversation. *Address:* Canterbury Crown Court, Chaucer Road, Canterbury, Kent CT1 1ZA. *T:* (01227) 819200.

WILLIAMS, Jennifer Mary, (Jenny); Director General, Judicial Group, and Secretary of Commisions, Lord Chancellor's Department, since 2001; *b* 26 Sept. 1948; *d* of Baron Donaldson of Lymington, *qv* and Dame Mary Donaldson, *qv*; *m* 1970, Michael Lodwig Williams, *qv*; three *s*. *Educ:* New Hall, Cambridge (BA 1970; MA 1971). Joined Home Office, 1973; Dir, PSA Privatisation and Strategy, DoE, 1990–93; Hd, Railways Privatisation and Regulation Directorate, Dept of Transport, 1993–97; Dir, Local Govt Finance Policy, DoE, later DETR, 1997–98; Dir, Company, later Business, Tax Div., Bd of Inland Revenue, 1998–2000. Non-exec. Dir, Morley Coll., 1993–2000. *Address:* Lord Chancellor's Department, Selborne House, 56/60 Victoria Street, SW1E 6QW.

WILLIAMS, John, AO 1987; OBE 1980; guitarist; *b* Melbourne, 24 April 1941. Studied with father, Segovia and at the Accademia Musicale Chigiana, Siena and RCM, London; since when has given recitals, concerts, and made TV and radio appearances worldwide. Mem., Sky, 1979–84. Artistic Dir, South Bank Summer Music, 1984 and 1985; Artistic Dir, Melbourne Arts Fest., 1987. Wide range of recordings with other musicians including Julian Bream, John Dankworth and Cleo Laine, NYJO, Itzhak Perlman, Inti Illimani, etc, and many orchestras. Hon. FRCM; Hon. FRNCM. *Recreations:* people, living, chess, table-tennis, music. *Address:* c/o Askonas Holt Ltd, Lonsdale Chambers, 27 Chancery Lane, WC2A 1PF.

WILLIAMS, John; Press Secretary, Foreign and Commonwealth Office, since 2000; *b* 20 Feb. 1954; *s* of Roy and Barbara Williams; *m* 1976, Pamela Blackburn; two *s* one *d*. *Educ:* Sir Roger Manwood's Sch., Sandwich. Reporter: Chatham News, 1973–77; Birmingham Evening Mail, 1977–80; Industrial Corresp., 1980–85, Political Corresp., 1985–93, London Evening Standard; political columnist, Daily Mirror, 1993–98; Dep. Hd, News Dept, FCO, 1998–2000. *Publication:* Victory, 1997. *Recreations:* gardening, guitar, books, family, walking. *Address:* Cherry Trees, Fore Street, Weston, Hitchin, Herts SG4 7AS. *T:* (01462) 790536.

WILLIAMS, John Brinley, OBE 1988; FCIT, FILT; Managing Director, Associated British Ports (formerly British Transport Docks Board), 1985–89 (Board Member, 1980–89; Joint Managing Director, 1982–85); *b* 18 Aug. 1927; *s* of late Leslie Williams and Alice Maud Williams; *m* 1951, Eileen (*née* Court) one *s* one *d*. *Educ:* Eveswell Sch., Newport. FCIT 1979; FILT 1998. Asst Manager, Cardiff Docks, 1963–65; Commercial and Development Asst to Chief Docks Manager, South Wales Ports, 1965–67; Docks Manager: Cardiff and Penarth Docks, 1968–72; Hull Docks, 1972–75; Port Director: South Wales Ports, 1976–78; Southampton, 1978–82. *Recreations:* Rugby, open air pursuits. *Address:* 34 Marine Drive, Barry, S Glamorgan CF6 6QP. *T:* (01446) 737477.

WILLIAMS, (John Bucknall) Kingsley; solicitor; *b* 28 July 1927; *s* of Charles Kingsley Williams and Margaret Elizabeth (*née* Bucknall); *m* 1961, Brenda (*née* Baldwin) (*d* 2001); two *s*; *m* 2001, Eleanor Marion Yates. *Educ:* Kingswood Sch., Bath; Trinity Hall, Cambridge (MA, LLB). Partner, Dutton Gregory & Williams, Solicitors, Winchester, 1956–91. Chm., Wessex RHA, 1975–82. Member: Winchester City Council, 1966–73; Hampshire CC, 1973–75; Assoc. of County Councils, 1973–75. Chairman: Exec. Cttee, NHS Supply Council, 1980–82; Adv. Cttee, Wessex Inst. of Public Health Medicine, 1991–96. Chm. Council, Southampton Univ., 1987–98 (Mem., 1977–98); Chm. of Governors, Winchester Sch. of Art, 1986–96. DUniv Southampton, 1999. *Address:* Danesacre, Worthy Road, Winchester, Hants SO23 7AD. *T:* (01962) 852594, *Fax:* (01962) 869883.

WILLIAMS, Ven. John Charles; Archdeacon of Worcester, 1975–80, now Archdeacon Emeritus; Residentiary Canon of Worcester Cathedral, 1975–80; *b* 17 July 1912; *s* of William and Edith Williams; *m* 1940, Agnes Mildred Hutchings, MA; one *s* one *d*. *Educ:* Cowbridge Sch.; St David's University Coll., Lampeter; University College, Oxford. Asst Curate, Christ Church, Summerfield, Birmingham, 1937–39; Asst Curate, Hales Owen, in charge of St Margaret's, Hasbury, 1939–43; Vicar: Cradley Heath, Staffs, 1943–48; Redditch, Worcs, 1948–59. Surrogate, 1951–71; Rural Dean of Bromsgrove, 1958–59; Rector, Hales Owen, 1959–70; Archdeacon of Dudley, 1968–75; Vicar of Dodderhill, 1970–75. Hon. Canon, Worcester Cathedral, 1965–75; Examng Chaplain to Bishop of Worcester, 1969–80; Dir, Worcester Diocesan Central Services, 1974–75; Director of Ordination Candidates, 1975–79. Substitute Chaplain, HM Prison Long Lartin, Evesham, 1982–87. *Publication:* One Hundred Years, 1847–1947; A History of Cradley Heath Parish. *Recreations:* history of architecture, sailing. *Address:* The Old Vicarage, Norton with Lenchwick, Evesham, Worcs WR11 4TL. *Clubs:* Oxford University Occasionals, Oxford and Cambridge.

WILLIAMS, John Charles, OBE 1997; PhD; FREng; Secretary and Chief Executive, Institution of Electrical Engineers, 1989–99; *b* 17 July 1938; *s* of Frank and Miriam Williams; *m* 1968, Susan Winifred Ellis; one *s* one *d*. *Educ:* High Wycombe Royal GS; Queen Mary Coll. (BScEng (1st Cl. Hons), 1960; PhD 1964; Fellow, 1995). Philips Research Labs, 1964–78; GEC Marconi Space and Defence Systems, Stanmore, 1978–80; GEC Central Res. Labs, Wembley, 1980–82; GEC Marconi Res. Centre, Gt Baddow, 1982–88. Freeman, City of London, 1996. FREng (FEng 1990). Hon. FIEE. *Recreations:* traditional jazz, contract bridge, walking his dog, gardening, listening to his family play classical music. *Address:* Beightons, Bassetts Lane, Little Baddow, Chelmsford, Essex CM3 4DA. *T:* (01245) 225092, *Fax:* (01245) 226314; *e-mail:* johnchaswilliams@btinternet.com.

WILLIAMS, Rt Rev. (John) Christopher (Richard); *see* Arctic, Bishop of The.

WILLIAMS, John Eirwyn F.; *see* Ffowcs Williams.

WILLIAMS, Prof. John Eryl Hall; Professor Emeritus of Criminology with Special Reference to Penology, London School of Economics, University of London; *b* 21 Sept. 1921; *s* of late Edward Hall Williams and Kitty Hall Williams; *m* 1951, Constance Mary Evans. *Educ:* Barry County Sch.; University Coll. of Wales, Aberystwyth (LLB 1942, LLM 1953). Called to the Bar, Middle Temple, 1949. Lectr, Dept of Law, University Coll. of Hull, 1946–50; LSE: Lectr, Law Dept, 1950–59; Reader in Criminology, 1959; Prof. of Criminology with Special Reference to Penology, 1984–86. Vis. Associate Prof., NY Univ. Sch. of Law, 1955–56; Senior Fellow and Vis. Lectr, Yale Law Sch., 1965–66. Mem., Parole Bd, 1970–72, 1976–78. Pres., British Soc. of Criminology, 1970–72; Sec.-Gen., Internat. Soc. for Criminology, 1974–79, Vice-Pres., 1985–94; Mem., Criminological Scientific Council, Council of Europe, 1985–89. Hon. LLD JFK Univ., Calif., 1981. Jt Editor, British Jl of Criminology, 1966–79. *Publications:* The English Penal System in Transition, 1970; Changing Prisons, 1975; (with L. H. Leigh) The Management of the Prosecution Process in Denmark, Sweden and The Netherlands, 1981; Criminology and Criminal Justice, 1982; (ed) The Role of the Prosecutor, 1988; (ed jtly) Punishment, Custody and the Community: reflections and comments on the Green Paper, 1989; A Page of History in Relief, 1993. *Recreations:* landscape painting, foreign travel. *Address:* Law Department, London School of Economics and Political Science, Houghton Street, Aldwych, WC2A 2AE. *T:* (020) 7405 7686.
See also R. H. Williams.

WILLIAMS, John G.; *see* Griffith Williams.

WILLIAMS, Rev. John Herbert, LVO 1989; Chaplain to the Royal Victorian Order and Chaplain of the Queen's Chapel of the Savoy, 1983–89; Chaplain to the Queen, 1988–89; *b* 15 Aug. 1919; *s* of Thomas and Mary Williams; *m* 1948, Joan Elizabeth (*née* Morgan); one *s*. *Educ:* St David's Coll., Lampeter (BA Hons); Salisbury Theological Coll. Deacon 1943; priest 1944; Curate: Blaenavon (Gwent), 1943–46; Llanishen, Cardiff, 1946–48; Priest in Charge, Rogerstone (Gwent), 1948–51; Asst Chaplain, HM Prison, Manchester, 1951; Chaplain, HM Prison: Holloway, 1952; Birmingham, 1957; Wormwood Scrubs, 1964; South East Regional Chaplain, 1971; Deputy Chaplain General, Home Office Prison Dept, 1974–83; Priest-in-Ordinary to the Queen, 1980–83. *Recreations:* Rugby, classical music/opera, Francophile. *Address:* 75 Monks Drive, W3 0ED. *T:* (020) 8992 5206.

WILLIAMS, Sir (John) Kyffin, Kt 1999; OBE 1982; DL; RA 1974 (ARA 1970); *b* 9 May 1918; *s* of Henry Inglis Wynne Williams and Essyllt Mary Williams (*née* Williams). *Educ:* Shrewsbury Sch.; Slade Sch. of Art. Sen. Art Master, Highgate Sch., 1944–73. One-man shows: Leicester Galleries, 1951, 1953, 1956, 1960, 1966, 1970; Colnaghi Galleries, 1948, 1949, 1965, 1970; Thackeray Gall., biennially 1975–; Albany Gall., Cardiff, 1997. Retrospective exhibn, Nat. Mus. of Wales, Mostyn Art Gall., Llandudno and Glynn Vivian Art Gall., Swansea, 1987. Pres., Royal Cambrian Acad., 1969–76 and 1992–. Winston Churchill Fellow, 1968; Hon. Fellow: University Coll. of Swansea, 1989; UCNW, 1991; UCW, Aberystwyth, 1992. DL Gwynedd 1985. Hon. MA Wales, 1973; Hon. DLitt Wales, 1993. Medal, Hon. Soc. of Cymmrodorion, 1991. *Publications:* Across the Straits (autobiog.), 1973; A Wider Sky (autobiog.), 1991; Portraits, 1996; Boyo Ballads, 1996; The Land and the Sea, 1998; Drawings, 2001. *Recreations:* the countryside, sport. *Address:* Pwllfanogl, Llanfairpwll, Gwynedd LL61 6PD. *T:* (01248) 714693.

WILLIAMS, John Leighton; QC 1986; a Recorder of the Crown Court, since 1985; a Deputy High Court Judge, since 1995; *b* 15 Aug. 1941; *s* of Reginald John Williams and Beatrice Beynon; *m* 1969, Sally Elizabeth Williams; two *s*. *Educ:* Neath Boys' Grammar School; King's College London (LLB); Trinity Hall, Cambridge (MA). Called to the Bar, Gray's Inn, 1964, Bencher, 1994. Mem., Criminal Injuries Compensation Bd, 1987–. Mem. Council, Med. Protection Soc., 1998–. *Address:* Farrar's Building, Temple, EC4Y 7BD. *T:* (020) 7583 9241.

WILLIAMS, John Llewellyn, CBE 1999; FRCS, FRCSE, FDSRCS, FDSRCSE, FRCA; Consultant Oral and Maxillofacial Surgeon, St Richard's Hospital, Chichester, Worthing and Southlands Hospitals, Worthing and St Luke's Hospital, Guildford, since 1973; Vice-President, Royal College of Surgeons of England, 1997–99; *b* 24 Jan. 1938; *s* of David John Williams and Anne Rosamund Williams (*née* White); *m* 1960, Gillian Joy Morgan; three *d*. *Educ:* Christ's Hosp.; Guy's Hosp. Med. Sch. (MB BS, BDS). FDSRCS 1966; FRCSE 1991; FRCS 1996; FRCA 2000. Registrar in Oral and Maxillo-Facial Surgery, Plymouth, 1970; Sen. Registrar, Westminster Hosp., UCH and Queen Mary's, Roehampton, 1970–73; Postgrad. Tutor, BMPF, 1973–95; Hon. Consultant: Queen Mary's, Roehampton, 1974–; King Edward VII Hosp., Midhurst, 1974–; Hon. Clinical Tutor, Guy's and St Thomas', now Guy's, King's and St Thomas' Hosps' Med. and Dental Sch. of KCL, 1976–. Hon. Consultant to Army, Cambridge Hosp., 1992–. Chairman: Nat. Cttee of Enquiry into Perio-operative Deaths, 1998–; Med. Adv. Cttee, Med. Devices Agency, DoH, 2001–. Dean, Faculty of Dental Surgery, RCS, 1996–99; Pres., Eur. Assoc. for Cranio-Maxillofacial Surgery, 1998–2000; Pres., BAOMS, 2000. Hon. Fellow, Amer. Assoc. Oral and Maxillofacial Surgeons, 1998. Evelyn Sprawson Prize, RCS, 1961; Down Surgical Prize, BAOMS, 1996; John Tomes Medallist, BDA, 1998; Colyer Gold Medallist, RCS, 2000. *Publications:* (with N. L. Rowe) Maxillofacial Injuries, Vols I and II, 1985, 2nd edn 1994; contribs to Brit. Dental Jl, RCS Annals. *Recreations:* gardening (garden open under Nat. Gardens Scheme), sailing (RYA Race Training Instructor). *Address:* Cookscroft, Bookers Lane, Earnley, Chichester, W Sussex PO20 7JG. *T:* (01243) 513671. *Clubs:* Oral Surgery of Great Britain; Hayling Island Sailing.

WILLIAMS, Prof. (John) Mark (Gruffydd), DSc; FBPsS; Director, Institute for Medical and Social Care Research (formerly Centre for Medical and Health Sciences), University of Wales, Bangor, since 1997; *b* 23 July 1952; *s* of John Howard Williams and Anna Barbara Mary Williams (*née* Wright); *m* 1973, Phyllis Patricia Simpson; one *s* two *d*. *Educ:* Stockton-on-Tees Grammar Sch.; St Peter's Coll., Oxford (BA 1973; MSc 1976; MA 1977; DPhil 1979; DSc 1998); E Anglian Ministerial Trng Course. FBPsS 1984. Lecturer in: Psychology, Magdalen Coll., Oxford, 1977–79; Applied Psychology, Univ. of Newcastle upon Tyne, 1979–82; Scientist, then Sen. Scientist, MRC Applied Psychol. Unit, Cambridge, 1983–91; Prof. of Clinical Psychology, UCNW (Bangor), then Univ. of Wales, Bangor, 1991–97; Pro Vice-Chancellor, Univ. of Wales, Bangor, 1997–2001. Member: Grants Cttee, Neuroscis Bd, MRC, 1992–96; Neuroscis & Mental Health Panel, Wellcome Trust, 1997–2001; Panel Mem. for Psychology, RAE 2001. Ordained deacon, Ely, 1989, priest 1990; Asst Curate (NSM), Girton, 1989–91; permission to officiate, dio. of Bangor, 1991–. Gov., NE Wales Inst. of Higher Educn, 1999–. *Publications:* Psychological Treatment of Depression, 1983, 2nd edn 1992; (jtly) Cognitive Psychology and Emotional Disorders, 1988, 2nd edn 1997; (with F. Watts) The Psychology of Religious Knowing, 1988; (jtly) Cognitive Therapy and Clinical Practice, 1989; Cry of Pain: understanding suicide and self-harm, 1997; (with Z. Segal and J. D. Teasdale) Mindfulness-based Cognitive Therapy for Depression: a new approach to preventing relapse, 2001; Suicide and Attempted Suicide, 2002; papers in scientific jls on psychological models and treatment of depression and suicidal behaviour. *Recreation:* piano and organ playing. *Address:* Institute for Medical and Social Care Research, University of Wales, Bangor LL57 2UW. *T:* (01248) 382628; *e-mail:* j.m.g.williams@bangor.ac.uk.

WILLIAMS, John Melville; QC 1977; a Recorder, 1986–94; *b* 20 June 1931; *o s* of late Baron Francis-Williams and late Lady (Jessie Melville) Francis-Williams; *m* 1955, Jean Margaret (*d* 1995), *d* of Harold and Hilda Lucas, Huddersfield; three *s* one *d*. *Educ:* St Christopher Sch., Letchworth; St John's Coll., Cambridge (BA). Called to the Bar, Inner Temple, 1955, Bencher, 1985. A legal assessor to GMC and GDC, 1983–; first Pres., Assoc. of Personal Injury Lawyers, 1990–94; Co-Chm., Internat. Practice Sect., Assoc. of Trial Lawyers of Amer., 1991–92; Mem., Indep. Review Body Under New Colliery Review Procedure, 1985–. Member: Criminal Injuries Compensation Bd, 1998–2000; Criminal Injuries Compensation Appeals Panel, 2000–. Chm., Y2K Lawyers Assoc., 1999. *Recreations:* mountain scrambling and walking (including climbing Munros), grandchildren and bird photography. *Address:* Deers Hill, Sutton Abinger, near Dorking, Surrey RH5 6PS. *T:* (01306) 730331, *Fax:* (01306) 730913; *e-mail:* jmwqc@dial.pipex.com; Cnoclochan, Scourie, by Lairg, Sutherland IV27 4TE; Old Square Chambers, 1 Verulam Buildings, Gray's Inn, WC1R 5LQ. *T:* (020) 7269 0315, *Fax:* (020) 7405 1387.

WILLIAMS, Very Rev. Monsignor John Noctor, CBE 1989; Prelate of Honour, 1985; Parish Priest, Our Lady and St John's, Heswall, since 1990; *b* 9 Aug. 1931; *s* of Thomas Williams and Anne Williams (*née* Noctor). *Educ:* St Anselm's Grammar School, Birkenhead; Ushaw College, Durham. Curate: St Laurence's, Birkenhead, 1956; St Joseph's, Sale, 1958; Sacred Heart, Moreton, 1958; Our Lady's, Birkenhead, 1959–66; Army, Chaplains' Dept, 1966–89: 7 Armd Bde, 1966; Singapore, 1969; 6 Armd Bde, 1971; UN, Cyprus, 1972; Senior Chaplain: Hong Kong, 1976; 1 Div., 1978; N Ireland, 1980; HQ BAOR, 1982; SE District, 1984; Prin. RC Chaplain, 1985–89, retd. VG 1986–89. *Recreations:* bridge, golf, motoring. *Clubs:* Delamere Forest Golf; Conwy (Caernarvonshire) Golf.

WILLIAMS, John Peter Rhys, MBE 1977; FRCSEd; Consultant in Trauma and Orthopaedic Surgery, Princess of Wales Hospital, Bridgend, since 1986; *b* 2 March 1949; *s* of Peter Williams, MB, BCh and Margaret Williams, MB, BCh; *m* 1973, Priscilla Parkin, MB, BS, DObst, RCOG, DA; one *s* three *d*. *Educ:* Bridgend Grammar School; Millfield; St Mary's Hosp. Med. School. MB, BS London 1973; LRCP, MRCS, 1973; Primary FRCS 1976; FRCSEd 1980. University Hosp., Cardiff, Battle Hosp., Reading, St Mary's Hosp., London, 1973–78; Surgical Registrar, 1978–80, Orthopaedic Registrar, 1980–82, Cardiff Gp of Hosps; Sen. Orthopaedic Registrar, St Mary's Hosp., London, 1982–86. Played Rugby for Bridgend, 1967–68, 1976–79 (Captain, 1978–79), 1980–81, for London Welsh, 1968–76; 1st cap for Wales, 1969 (Captain, 1978); British Lions tours, 1971, 1974; a record 55 caps for Wales, to 1981; won Wimbledon Lawn Tennis Junior Championship, 1966. *Publication:* JPR (autobiog.), 1979. *Recreations:* sport and music. *Address:* Llansannor Lodge, Llansannor, near Cowbridge, South Glamorgan CF71 7RX. *Clubs:* Wig and Pen; Lord's Taverners.

WILLIAMS, John Towner; composer of film scores; *b* 8 Feb. 1932. *Educ:* Juilliard Sch., NY. Conductor, Boston Pops Orchestra, 1980–84. Hon. DMus: Berklee Coll. of Music, Boston, 1980; St Anselm Coll., Manchester, NH, 1981; Boston Conservatory of Music, 1982; Hon. DHL S Carolina, 1981; Hon. Dr of Fine Arts Northeastern Univ. (Boston), 1981; Hon. DMus, William Woods Coll., USA, 1982. Awards include Oscars for: Fiddler on the Roof (filmscore arrangement), 1971; Jaws, 1976; Star Wars, 1978; E.T., 1983; 14 Grammies, 2 Emmys and many other awards; 16 Academy Award nominations. *Composer of film scores* including: The Secret Ways, 1961; Diamond Head, 1962; None but the Brave, 1965; How to Steal a Million, 1966; Valley of the Dolls, 1967; The Cowboys, 1972; The Poseidon Adventure, 1972; Tom Sawyer, 1973; Earthquake, 1974; The Towering Inferno, 1974; Jaws, 1975; Jaws 2, 1976; The Eiger Sanction, 1975; Family Plot, 1976; Midway, 1976; The Missouri Breaks, 1976; Raggedy Ann and Andy, 1977; Black Sunday, 1977; Star Wars, 1977; Close Encounters of the 3rd Kind, 1977; The Fury, 1978; Superman, 1978; Dracula, 1979; The Empire Strikes Back, 1980; Raiders of the Lost Ark, 1981; E. T. (The Extra Terrestial), 1982; Return of the Jedi, 1983; Indiana Jones and the Temple of Doom, 1984; Empire of the Sun, 1988; Jurassic Park, 1993; Schindler's List, 1994; Amistad, 1998; Saving Private Ryan, 1998; The Phantom Menace, 1999; AI, 2001; Harry Potter and the Philosopher's Stone, 2001; many TV films. *Address:* 20th Century Fox, Music Department, PO Box 900, Beverly Hills, CA 90213, USA.

WILLIAMS, Rev. John Tudno, PhD; Professor of Biblical Studies, since 1973, Principal, since 1998, United Theological College, Aberystwyth; Moderator of the Free Church Federal Council, March 1990–91; *b* 31 Dec. 1938; *s* of late Rev. Arthur Tudno Williams and Primrose (*née* Hughes Parry); *m* 1964, Ina Lloyd-Evans; one *s* one *d*. *Educ:* Liverpool Inst. High School; Colfe's GS, Lewisham; Jesus Coll., Oxford (MA); UCW, Aberystwyth (PhD); United Theol Coll., Aberystwyth. Ordained as Welsh Presbyterian Minister, 1963; Minister in Borth, Cards, 1963–73; Part-time Lecturer: United Theol Coll., 1966–73; UCW (Religious Studies), 1976–87; Tutor responsible for Religious Studies, external degree through medium of Welsh, UCW, 1984–; Dean, Aberystwyth and Lampeter Sch. of Theology, 1985–87, 1994–97. Vis. Prof., Acadia Divinity Coll., Nova Scotia, 1997. Secretary: Theology Section, Univ. of Wales Guild of Graduates, 1967–; Educn Cttee, Gen. Assembly of Presbyterian Church of Wales, 1979–2000; Bd of Trustees, Davies Lecture, 1983– (Lectr, 1993). External examnr, QUB and Sheffield Univ.; examiner in religious studies and member of various educn cttees. Mem., Aberystwyth Town Council, 1979–87. *Publications:* Cewri'r Ffydd (Heroes of the Faith), 1974, 2nd edn 1979; Problem Dioddefaint a Llyfr Job (The Problem of Suffering and the Book of Job), 1980; Yr Epistol Cyntaf at y Corinthiaid (Commentary on I Corinthians), 1991; Y Llythyran at y Galatiaid a'r Philipiaid (Commentary on the Letters to the Galatians and to the Philippians), 2001; contrib. to: Studia Biblica, 1978, Vol. ii 1980; C. H. Dodd, The Centenary Lectures, 1985; articles in Welsh jls. *Recreations:* music (singing), Welsh language and culture. *Address:* United Theological College, Aberystwyth, Dyfed SY23 2LT. *T:* (01970) 624574. *Club:* Penn.

WILLIAMS, Jonathan R.; *see* Rees-Williams.

WILLIAMS, Dame Judi; *see* Dench, Dame J. O.

WILLIAMS, Katrina Jane; Counsellor (Agriculture, Fisheries and Food), UK Permanent Representation to European Union, Brussels, since 1999; *b* 30 July 1962; *d* of Ian Clive Williams and June Elizabeth Williams (*née* Dedman). *Educ:* Cheadle Hulme Sch.; Lady Margaret Hall, Oxford (BA Hons English Lang. and Lit.). MAFF, London, 1983–93; First Sec. (Agriculture), UK Perm. Representation to EU, 1993–96; Hd of Br., EU Div., MAFF, 1996–98; Principal Private Sec. to Minister of Agriculture, Fisheries and Food, 1998–99. *Address:* c/o Foreign and Commonwealth Office, King Charles Street, SW1A 2AH. *T:* (Brussels) (2) 2878254.

WILLIAMS, Kevin Raymond; Group Managing Director, Distribution Services, Consignia (formerly The Post Office), since 1999; *b* 14 May 1948; *s* of Kenneth Williams and Betty (*née* Haskell); *m* 1972, Shionagh Mary Gee; two *s* one *d. Educ:* St Bartholomew's Grammar Sch., Newbury; Exeter Univ. (BA Hons). Head Postmaster: Aldershot, 1982–85; Portsmouth, 1985–86; Dist Head Postmaster, City of London, 1986–88; Royal Mail: Dir, Employee Relns, 1988–90; Dir, Business Develt, 1990–92; Ops Dir, 1992–93; Man. Dir, Parcelforce, 1993–99. Lt Col, Engr and Logistics Staff Corps. Trustee, Help the Aged, 1998–. Freeman, City of London, 1988. MILog 1998; FRSA. *Recreations:* cricket, travel, gardening, European twinning movement, supporting Aldershot Town FC. *Club:* Headley Cricket.

WILLIAMS, Kingsley; *see* Williams, J. B. K.

WILLIAMS, Kirsty; *see* Williams, V. K.

WILLIAMS, Sir Kyffin; *see* Williams, Sir J. K.

WILLIAMS, Laurence Glynn, CEng, FIMechE, FINucE; HM Chief Inspector of Nuclear Installations and Director, Nuclear Safety Directorate, Health and Safety Executive, since 1998; *b* 14 March 1946; *s* of Hugh Williams and Ruby Williams (*née* Lawrence); *m* 1976, Lorna Susan Rance (marr. diss. 1997); one *s* one *d. Educ:* Liverpool Poly. (BSc Hons Mech. Engrg); Univ. of Aston in Birmingham (MSc Nuclear Reactor Technol. 1972). CEng 1976; FIMechE 1991; FINucE 1998. Design engr, Nuclear Power Gp, 1970–71; nuclear engr, CEGB, 1973–76; Health and Safety Executive: Nuclear Installations Inspectorate: Inspector, 1976–78; Principal Inspector, 1978–86; Superintending Inspector, 1986–91; Dep. Chief Inspector, 1991–96; Div. Head, Safety Policy Directorate, 1996–98. Chm., UN/IAEA Comm on Safety Standards; Advr on Nuclear Safety, EBRD. Chm., Internat. Nuclear Regulators' Assoc., 1999–2001. *Recreations:* cycling, keeping fit, music, theatre, supporting Liverpool Football Club. *Address:* Health and Safety Executive, Nuclear Safety Directorate, Balliol Road, Bootle L20 3LZ. *T:* (0151) 951 4170.

WILLIAMS, Sir Lawrence (Hugh), 9th Bt *cr* 1798, of Bodelwyddan, Flintshire; farmer; *b* 25 Aug. 1929; *s* of Col Lawrence Williams, OBE, DL (*d* 1958) (*gs* of 1st Bt), and his 2nd wife, Elinor Henrietta (*d* 1980), *d* of Sir William Williams, 4th Bt of Bodelwyddan; *S* half-brother, 1995; *m* 1952, Sara Margaret Helen, 3rd *d* of Sir Harry Platt, 1st Bt; two *d. Educ:* Royal Naval Coll., Dartmouth. Commnd Royal Marines, 1947; served Korea 1951, Cyprus 1955, Near East 1956; Captain, 1959, retired 1964. Chm., Parciau Caravans Ltd, 1964–. Underwriting Mem., Lloyds, 1977–96. Lieut Comdr, RNXS, 1965–87. High Sheriff, Anglesey, 1970. *Recreations:* enjoying all aspects of country life, gentle sailing. *Heir:* none. *Address:* Old Parciau, Marianglas, Anglesey LL73 8PH. *Clubs:* Army and Navy; Royal Naval Sailing Association.
See also Baron Suffield.

WILLIAMS, Sir Leonard, KBE 1981; CB 1975; Director-General for Energy, Commission of the European Communities, 1976–81; *b* 19 Sept. 1919; *m* Anne Taylor Witherley; three *d. Educ:* St Olave's Grammar Sch.; King's Coll., London. Inland Revenue, 1938. War Service (RA), 1940–47. Ministry of Defence, 1948; NATO, 1951–54; Min. of Supply (later Aviation), 1954; Min. of Technology (later DTI), 1964; IDC 1966; Dep. Sec., 1973; Dept of Energy, 1974–76. *Address:* Blue Vines, Bramshott Vale, Liphook, Hants GU30 7PZ.

WILLIAMS, Leonard Edmund Henry, CBE 1981; DFC 1944; President, Nationwide Anglia Building Society, 1989–92 (Chairman, 1987–88); *b* 6 Dec. 1919; *s* of William Edmund Williams; *m* 1946, Marie Harries-Jones; four *s* one *d. Educ:* Acton County Grammar School. FCA, FCIB, IPFA; FRSA; CIMgt. RAF, 1939–46. Acton Borough Council, 1935–39, Chief Internal Auditor 1946–49; Asst Accountant, Gas Council, 1949–53; Nationwide Building Society: Finance Officer, 1954–61; Dep. Gen. Man., 1961–67; Chief Exec., 1967–81; Dir, 1975–87; Chm., 1982–87. Director: Y. J. Lovell (Hldgs) plc, 1982–89; Peachey Property Corp. plc, 1982–88; Dep. Chm., BUPA Ltd, 1988–90 (Governor, 1982–88); Mem., Housing Corp., 1976–82. Chm., Building Socs Assoc., 1979–81 (Dep. Chm., 1977–79); Pres., Metrop. Assoc. of Building Socs, 1989–92 (Chm., 1972–73). Pres., Chartered Building Socs Inst., 1969–70. Hon. Life Mem., Internat. Union of Housing Finance Instns. *Publication:* Building Society Accounts, 1966. *Recreation:* reading. *Address:* The Romanys, 11 Albury Road, Burwood Park, Walton-on-Thames, Surrey KT12 5DY. *T:* (01932) 242758. *Clubs:* Royal Air Force, City Livery.

WILLIAMS, Lyn; *see* Williams, D. W.

WILLIAMS, Marjorie Eileen; Director, Capital and Savings Tax Policy, Board of Inland Revenue, since 2000; *b* 18 Dec. 1946; *d* of Leslie Vernon Cuttle and Mary Fleming Cuttle (*née* Howie); *m* 1970, Graham Terence Williams. *Educ:* Reading Univ. (BSc Hons Geog. with Geol. 1968); Centre for W African Studies, Birmingham Univ. (postgrad. studies). Joined Inland Revenue, 1972; Regl Dir, SW Reg., 1994–96; Dir, Large Business Office, 1996–2000. *Publication:* Birdwatching in Lesbos, 1992. *Recreations:* birdwatching, gardening, Romanian needlework. *Address:* Board of Inland Revenue, Somerset House, WC2R 1LB. *T:* (020) 7438 6614.

WILLIAMS, Mark; *see* Williams, J. M. G.

WILLIAMS, Martin John, CVO 1983; OBE 1979; HM Diplomatic Service, retired; High Commissioner, New Zealand, Governor (non-resident) of Pitcairn, Henderson, Ducie and Oeno Islands, and High Commissioner (non-resident), Samoa, 1998–2001; *b* 3 Nov. 1941; *s* of John Henry Stroud Williams and Barbara (*née* Benington); *m* 1964, Susan Dent; two *s. Educ:* Manchester Grammar Sch.; Corpus Christi Coll., Oxford (BA). Joined Commonwealth Relations Office, 1963; Private Sec. to Permanent Under Secretary, 1964; Manila, 1966; Milan, 1970; Civil Service College, 1972; FCO, 1973; Tehran, 1977; FCO, 1980; New Delhi, 1982; Rome, 1986; Hd of S Asian Dept, FCO, 1990; on secondment to NI Office as Asst Under-Sec. of State (Political), Belfast, 1993; High Comr, Zimbabwe, 1995–98. *Recreations:* music, gardening. *Address:* c/o Foreign and Commonwealth Office, SW1A 2AH. *Clubs:* Royal Commonwealth Society, Royal Over-Seas League; Wellington (New Zealand).

WILLIAMS, Sir Max; *see* Williams, Sir W. M. H.

WILLIAMS, Prof. Michael, FBA 1989; Professor of Geography, since 1996, Sir Walter Ralegh Fellow of Oriel College, since 1993, and Lecturer, St Anne's College, since 1978, University of Oxford; *b* 24 June 1935; *s* of Benjamin Williams and Ethel (*née* Marshell); *m* 1955, Eleanore Lerch; two *d. Educ:* Emmanuel Grammar Sch.; Dynevor Grammar Sch., Swansea; Swansea UC (BA 1956; PhD 1960; DLitt 1991); St Catharine's Coll., Cambridge (DipEd 1960). Deptl Demonstrator in Geography, Swansea, 1957–60; University of Adelaide: Lectr in Geog., 1960–66; Sen. Lectr, 1966–69; Reader, 1970–77; Oxford University: Lectr in Geog., 1978–89; Reader, 1990–96; Dir, MSc course, Envmtl Change Unit, 1994–98; Fellow of Oriel Coll., 1978–. Visiting Professor: Univ. of Wisconsin-Madison, 1973 and 1994; Univ. of Chicago, 1989; UCLA, 1994; Vis. Lectr, UCL, 1966, 1973. Mem., State Commn on Uniform Regl Boundaries, SA, 1974–75; Chm., Histl Geog. Res. Gp, Inst. of British Geographers, 1983–86; Sec., Inst. of Aust. Geographers, 1969–72; Pres., SA Br., RGS, 1975–76 (Ed. of Procs, 1962–70). Mem. Council, British Acad., 1993–96 (Chm., Sect. N, Geog. and Social Anthropology, 1994–97). Editor: Trans of Inst. of British Geographers, 1983–88; Progress in Human Geography, 1991–; Global Environmental Change, 1993–97. John Lewis Gold Medal, RGS, SA, 1979; Lit. Prize, Adelaide Fest. of Arts, 1976; Hidy Award, Forest Hist. Soc., Durham, NC, 1987 (Hon. Fellow, 1990). *Publications:* South Australia from the Air, 1969; The Draining of the Somerset Levels, 1970; The Making of the South Australian Landscape, 1974; (ed jtly) Australian Space, Australian Time, 1975; The Changing Rural Landscape of South Australia, 1977, 2nd edn 1992; Americans and their Forests, 1989; (ed) Wetlands: a threatened landscape, 1991; (ed) Planet Management, 1992; edited vols of essays; contribs to geogl and histl jls. *Recreations:* walking, music. *Address:* Westgates, Vernon Avenue, Harcourt Hill, Oxford OX2 9AU. *T:* (01865) 243725.

WILLIAMS, Rev. Canon Michael Joseph; Vicar of Bolton, since 1999; *b* 26 Feb. 1942; *s* of James and Edith Williams; *m* 1971, Mary Miranda Bayley; one *s* one *d. Educ:* St John's College, Durham (BA in Philosophy 1968). Apprentice Mechanical Engineer, then Engineer, with W & T Avery, Birmingham, 1958–63 (HNC in Mech. Eng 1962). Deacon 1970, priest 1971; Curate, then Team Vicar, St Philemon, Toxteth, 1970–78; Director of Pastoral Studies, St John's Coll., Durham, 1978–88; Principal, Northern Ordination Course, 1989–99. Hon. Tutor in Pastoral Theology, Univ. of Manchester, 1990–. Hon. Canon: Liverpool Cathedral, 1992–99; Manchester Cathedral, 2000–. Pres., Northern Fedn for Trng in Ministry, 1991–93. *Publications:* The Power and the Kingdom, 1989; regular contribs to Anvil. *Address:* The Vicarage, Churchgate, Bolton BL1 1PS.

WILLIAMS, Michael Lodwig; Chief Executive, UK Debt Management Office, since 1998; *b* 22 Jan. 1948; *s* of John and Eileen Williams; *m* 1970, Jennifer Mary Donaldson (*see* J. M. Williams); three *s. Educ:* Wycliffe Coll., Stonehouse, Glos; Trinity Hall, Cambridge (BA 1969; MA); Nuffield Coll., Oxford. Min. of Finance, Lusaka, Zambia, 1969–71; HM Treasury, 1973–: on secondment to Price Waterhouse, 1980–81; Under Sec., then Dep. Dir, Industry, 1992–98. *Address:* UK Debt Management Office, Eastcheap Court, 11 Philpot Lane, EC3M 8UD. *T:* (020) 7862 6533.

WILLIAMS, Prof. Michael Maurice Rudolph; consultant engineer; Professor of Nuclear Engineering, University of Michigan, 1987–89; Professor of Nuclear Engineering, 1970–86, now Emeritus, and Head of Department, 1980–86, Queen Mary College, London University; *b* 1 Dec. 1935; *s* of late M. F. Williams and G. M. A. Williams (*née* Redington); *m* 1958, Ann Doreen Betty; one *s* one *d. Educ:* Ewell Castle Sch.; Croydon Polytechnic; King's Coll., London; Queen Mary Coll., London. BSc, PhD, DSc; CEng; FINucE (Vice-Pres., 1971); CPhys, FInstP. Engr with Central Electricity Generating Board, 1962; Research Associate at Brookhaven Nat. Lab., USA, 1962–63; Lectr, Dept of Physics, Univ. of Birmingham, 1963–65; Reader in Nuclear Engrg, 1965–70, Dir, Nuclear Reactor, 1980–83, QMC, London Univ.; Prin. Scientist, Electrowatt Engrg Services (UK) Ltd, 1989–95. Mem., Adv. Cttee on Safety of Nuclear Installations, 1983–86. UN Advr on Engrg Educn in Argentina, 1979–89. Mem., Electrical Engrg Coll., EPSRC, 1995–97. Chm. of Governors, Ewell Castle Sch., 1976–79; Mem., Academic Bd, RNC, Greenwich, 1975–86. Exec. Editor, Annals of Nuclear Energy. Fellow American Nuclear Soc. (Arthur Holly Compton Award, 1994). Eugene P. Wigner Award, 2000. *Publications:* The Slowing Down and Thermalization of Neutrons, 1966; Mathematical Methods in Particle Transport Theory, 1971; Random Processes in Nuclear Reactors, 1974; Aerosol Science, 1991; contribs to Proc. Camb. Phil. Soc., Nucl. Science and Engrg, Jl Nuclear Energy, Jl Physics. *Address:* 2A Lytchgate Close, South Croydon, Surrey CR2 0DX.

WILLIAMS, Sir Michael O.; *see* Williams, Sir Osmond.

WILLIAMS, Nicholas James Donald; *b* 21 Oct. 1925; *s* of late Nicholas Thomas Williams and Daisy Eustace (*née* Hollow); *m* 1st, 1947, Dawn Vyvyan (*née* Hill); one *s* one *d*; 2nd, 1955, Sheila Mary (*née* Dalgety); two *s* one *d. Educ:* St Erbyn's Sch., Penzance; Rugby Sch. (Scholar). Admitted Solicitor 1949. Served Royal Marines, 1943–47 (Captain). Partner, Nicholas Williams & Co., Solicitors, London, 1950; Senior Partner, Surridge & Beecheno, Solicitors, Karachi, 1955; Burmah Oil Co. Ltd: Legal Adviser, 1961; Co-ordinator for Eastern ops, 1963; Dir, 1965; Asst Man. Dir, 1967; Man. Dir and Chief Exec., 1969–75; Man. Dir and Chief Exec., Don Engineering, 1977–84. Director: Flarebay Ltd, 1978–85; EBC Gp PLC, 1986–90; Ranvet Ltd, 1986–92. *Recreation:* sailing. *Clubs:* Royal Ocean Racing; Royal Cornwall Yacht.

WILLIAMS, Nigel; *see* Williams, H. N.

WILLIAMS, Nigel Christopher Ransome, CMG 1985; HM Diplomatic Service, retired; UK Permanent Representative to the Office of the United Nations and other international organisations, Geneva, 1993–97; *b* 29 April 1937; *s* of Cecil Gwynne Ransome Williams and Corinne Belden (*née* Rudd). *Educ:* Merchant Taylors' Sch.; St

John's Coll., Oxford. Joined Foreign Service and posted to Tokyo, 1961; FO, 1966; Private Secretary: to Minister of State, 1968; to Chancellor of Duchy of Lancaster, 1969; UK Mission to UN, New York, 1970; FCO, 1973; Counsellor (Economic), Tokyo, 1976; Cabinet Office, 1980; Hd of UN Dept, FCO, 1980–84; Minister, Bonn, 1985–88; Ambassador to Denmark, 1989–93. *Address:* 58 Langham Road, Blakeney, Norfolk NR25 7PJ.

WILLIAMS, Noel Ignace B.; *see* Bond-Williams.

WILLIAMS, Norman; *see* Williams, R. N.

WILLIAMS, Prof. Norman Stanley, FRCS; Professor of Surgery and Director, Academic Department of Surgery, Bart's and The London, Queen Mary's School of Medicine and Dentistry (formerly London Hospital Medical College), London University, since 1986; *b* 15 March 1947; *s* of Jules Williams and Mabel Sundle; *m* 1977, Linda Feldman; one *s* one *d*. *Educ:* Roundhay Sch., Leeds; London Hosp. Med. Coll., Univ. of London (MB BS, MS). LRCP, MRCS. House and Registrar appts, London Hosp., 1970–76; Registrar, Bristol Royal Infirmary, 1976–78; Res. Fellow and Lectr, Leeds Gen. Infirmary, 1978–80; Res. Fellow, UCLA, 1980–82; Sen. Lectr, Leeds Gen. Infirmary, 1982–86. Fulbright Scholar, UCLA, 1980; Ethicon Foundn Fellow, RCS, 1980; Moynihan Fellow, Assoc. of Surgeons of GB and Ireland, 1985. President: Ileostomy and Internal Pouch Support Group, 1992–; European Digestive Surgery, 1997–98; Chm., UK Co-ordinating Cttee of Cancer Res. Sub-Cttee on Colorectal Cancer, 1996–. Vice-Chm., British Jl of Surgery, 1995–2001. Patey Prize, Surgical Res. Soc., 1978; Nessim Habif Prize, Univ. of Geneva, 1995. *Publications:* (jtly) Surgery of the Anus, Rectum and Colon, 1993 (BUPA and Soc. of Authors Med. Writer's Gp Prize), 2nd edn 1999; (ed jtly) Bailey and Love's Short Practice of Surgery, 22nd edn 1995, 23rd edn 2000; (ed) Colorectal Cancer, 1996; scientific papers. *Recreations:* long distance swimming, Rugby football, cinema, reading about crime, fact and fiction. *Address:* Academic Department of Surgery, Royal London Hospital, Whitechapel, E1 1BB. *T:* (020) 7377 7079. *Club:* Royal Society of Medicine.

WILLIAMS, Sir Osmond, 2nd Bt *cr* 1909; MC 1944; JP; *b* 22 April 1914; *s* of late Captain Osmond T. D. Williams, DSO, 2nd *s* of 1st Bt, and Lady Gladys Margaret Finch Hatton, *o d* of 13th Earl of Winchilsea; *S* grandfather, 1927; *m* 1947, Benita Mary, *yr d* of late G. Henry Booker, and late Mrs Michael Burn; two *d*. *Educ:* Eton; Freiburg Univ. Royal Scots Greys, 1935–37, and 1939–45; served Palestine, Africa, Italy and NW Europe. Chm., Quarry Tours Ltd (Llechwedd Slate Caverns), 1973–77. Vice-Chm., Amnesty Internat. (British Sect.), 1971–74. Mem., Merioneth Park Planning Cttee, 1971–74. Governor, Rainer Foundn Outdoor Pursuits Centre, 1964–76. MRI 1967. JP 1960 (Chairman of the Bench, Ardudwy-uwch-Artro, Gwynedd, 1974–84). Chevalier, Order of Leopold II with Palm; Croix de Guerre with Palm (Belgium), 1940. *Recreations:* music, travelling. *Heir:* none. *Address:* Borthwen, Penrhyndeudraeth, Gwynedd LL48 6EN. *Club:* Travellers.

WILLIAMS, Paul Glyn; Chairman and Managing Director, Mount Charlotte Investments, 1966–77; *b* 14 Nov. 1922; *s* of late Samuel O. Williams and Esmée I. Williams (*née* Cail); *m* 1947, Barbara Joan Hardy (marr. diss. 1964); two *d*; *m* 1964, Gillian Foote, *e d* of late A. G. Howland Jackson, Elstead, Surrey, and of Mrs E. J. Foote and step *d* of late E. J. Foote; one *d*. *Educ:* Marlborough; Trinity Hall, Cambridge (MA; athletics ½ blue, Mem. LX Club, 1942). MP (C) Sunderland South, (C 1953–57, Ind. C 1957–58, C 1958–64). Chairman, Monday Club, 1964–69. Chm., Backer Electric Co., 1978–87. Director: First South African Cordage, 1947–54; Transair, 1955–62; Hodgkinson Partners Ltd, PR consultants, 1956–64; Minster Executive, 1977–83; Henry Sykes, 1980–83; consultant: P-E Internat. plc, 1983–91; Hogg Robinson Career Services, 1991–95. FInstD; FIMgt. *Address:* The Mill House, New Mill, near Pewsey, Wilts SN9 5LD. *T:* (01672) 562545.

WILLIAMS, Paul H.; *see* Hodder-Williams.

WILLIAMS, Dr Paul Randall, CBE 1996; DL; FInstP; Chairman and Chief Executive, Council for Central Laboratory of Research Councils, 1995–98; *b* 21 March 1934; *s* of Fred and Eileen Westbrook Williams; *m* 1957, Marion Frances Lewis; one *s* one *d*. *Educ:* Baines' Grammar School; Loughborough College (BSc London external); Liverpool Univ. (PhD). DLC. ICI Research Fellow, Liverpool Univ., 1957; Research Physicist, British Nat. Bubble Chamber, 1958–62; Rutherford Lab., SRC, 1962–79 (Dep. Div. Head, Laser Div., 1976–79); Science and Engineering Research Council: Head, Astronomy, Space and Radio Div., 1979–81; Head, Engineering Div., 1981–83; Dep. Dir, 1983–87, Dir, 1987–94, Rutherford Appleton Lab.; Dir, Daresbury and Rutherford Appleton Lab., EPSRC, 1994–95. Chm., Abingdon Coll. Corp., 1993–95. Local Preacher, Methodist Church. DL Oxfordshire, 1998. Hon. DSc Keele, 1996. Glazebrook Medal, Inst. of Physics, 1994. *Recreations:* sailing, choral singing, ski-ing. *Address:* 5 Tatham Road, Abingdon, Oxon OX14 1QB. *T:* (01235) 524654.

WILLIAMS, Penry Herbert; Fellow and Tutor in Modern History, New College, Oxford, 1964–92, Hon. Fellow, 1998; *b* 25 Feb. 1925; *s* of late Douglas Williams and Dorothy Williams (*née* Murray); *m* 1952, June Carey Hobson (*d* 1991), *d* of late George and Kathleene Hobson; one *s* one *d*. *Educ:* Marlborough Coll.; New Coll., Oxford, 1947–50; St Antony's Coll., Oxford, 1950–51. MA, DPhil Oxon. Served Royal Artillery, 1943–45, Royal Indian Artillery, 1945–47. Asst Lecturer in History, 1951–54, Lectr, 1954–63, Sen. Lectr, 1963–64, Univ. of Manchester. Sexual Harrassment Officer and Dir, Graduate Studies, Faculty of Modern History, Univ. of Oxford, 1989–90. Fellow of Winchester Coll., 1978–93. Chairman: New Coll. Develt Cttee, 1992–97; Thomas Wall Trust, 1995–99. Jt Editor, English Historical Review, 1982–90; Editor, New College Record, 1993–. *Publications:* The Council in the Marches of Wales under Elizabeth I, 1958; Life in Tudor England, 1963; The Tudor Regime, 1979; (ed with John Buxton) New College, Oxford 1379–1979, 1979; The Later Tudors: England 1547–1603, 1995; contribs to learned jls. *Recreations:* hill-walking, travel, theatre. *Address:* New College, Oxford OX1 3BN; Green Corner, Wood Green, Witney, Oxon OX28 1DQ. *T:* (01993) 702545; *e-mail:* penry@beeb.net.

WILLIAMS, Peter F.; *see* Firmston-Williams.

WILLIAMS, Peter Keegan, CMG 1992; HM Diplomatic Service, retired; Chairman, Vietnam Enterprise Investments Ltd, since 1997; Senior Advisor: Prudential Corp. Ltd, since 1997; Tate & Lyle, since 1997; Scottish Enterprise, since 1997; *b* 3 April 1938; *s* of William Edward Williams and Lilian (*née* Spright); *m* 1969, Rosamund Mary de Worms; two *d*. *Educ:* Calday Grange Grammar Sch.; Collège de Marcq-en-Baroeul (Nord); Univ. de Lille; Pembroke Coll., Oxford (MA). Joined Diplomatic Service, 1962; language student, MECAS, Lebanon, 1962; Second Sec., Beirut, 1963, Jedda, 1964; Commonwealth Office, 1967; First Sec., FCO, 1969; Director, Policy and Reference Div., British Information Services, New York, 1970; First Sec., FCO, 1973; First Sec., Head of Chancery and Consul, Rabat, 1976 (Chargé d'Affaires, 1978 and 1979); Counsellor, GATT, UK Mission, Geneva, 1979–83 (Chm. Panel, USA/Canada, 1980–81; Chm., Cttee on Finance, 1981–83); Ambassador, People's Democratic Republic of Yemen, 1983–85; Hd of UN Dept, FCO, 1986–89; RCDS, 1989; Ambassador to Socialist Republic of Vietnam, 1990–97. Chm., Internat. Council, Christina Noble Children's Foundn, 1998–99. *Recreations:* wine, walking. *Address:* Lhoob Dhoo, Dalby, Isle of Man IM5 3BS. *Clubs:* Travellers, Oxford and Cambridge.

WILLIAMS, Sir Peter (Michael), Kt 1998; CBE 1992; PhD; FRS 1999; FREng; Master, St Catherine's College, Oxford, 2000–June 2002; Chairman, Engineering and Technology Board, since 2002; *b* 22 March 1945; *s* of Cyril Lewis and Gladys Williams; *m* 1970, Jennifer Margaret Cox; one *s*. *Educ:* Hymers College, Hull; Trinity College, Cambridge (MA, PhD). Mullard Research Fellow, Selwyn College, Cambridge, 1969–70; Lectr, Dept of Chemical Engineering and Chemical Technology, Imperial College, 1970–75; VG Instruments Group, 1975–82 (Dep. Man. Dir, 1979–82); Oxford Instruments Group plc, 1982–99: Man. Dir, 1983–85; Chief Exec., 1985–98; Chm., 1991–99. Chm., Isis Innovation Ltd, Oxford Univ., 1997–2001; non-exec. Dir, GKN plc, 2001–. Chairman: PPARC, 1994–99; Trustees, Science Mus., 1996–. Mem., Council for Sci. and Technology, 1993–98. Supernumerary Fellow, St John's Coll., Oxford, 1988–2000. FREng (FEng 1996). FIC 1997; Hon. Fellow: Selwyn Coll., Cambridge, 1997; UCL, 1997. Hon DSc: Leicester, 1995; Nottingham Trent, 1995; Loughborough, 1996; Brunel, 1997; Wales, 1999; Sheffield, 1999. Guardian Young Business Man of the Year, 1986. *Publications:* numerous contribs to jls relating to solid state physics. *Recreations:* ski-ing, walking. *Address:* (until June 2002) The Master's Lodgings, St Catherine's College, Oxford OX1 3UJ; 41 Plater Drive, Oxford OX2 6QU.

WILLIAMS, Dr Peter Orchard, CBE 1991; FRCP; Director: The Wellcome Trust, 1965–91; Wellcome Institute for the History of Medicine, 1981–83; *b* 23 Sept. 1925; *s* of Robert Orchard Williams, CBE, and Agnes Annie Birkinshaw; *m* 1949, Billie Innes Brown; two *d*. *Educ:* Caterham Sch.; Queen's Royal College, Trinidad; St John's Coll., Cambridge (MA); St Mary's Hospital Medical School. MB, BChir 1950; MRCP 1952; FRCP 1970. House Physician, St Mary's Hospital, 1950–51; Registrar, Royal Free Hospital, 1951–52; Medical Specialist, RAMC, BMH Iserlohn, 1954; Medical Officer, Headquarters, MRC, 1955–60; Wellcome Trust: Asst and Dep. Scientific Secretary, 1960–64; Scientific Secretary, 1964–65. Vice-Pres., Royal Soc. of Tropical Med. and Hygiene, 1975–77, Pres., 1991–93; Member: Nat. Council of Soc. Services Cttee of Enquiry into Charity Law and Practice, 1974–76; BBC, IBA Central Appeals Adv. Cttee, 1978–83; DHSS Jt Planning Adv. Cttee, 1986–; Chairman: Foundations Forum, 1977–79; Assoc. of Med. Res. Charities, 1974–76, 1979–83; Hague Club (European Foundns), 1981–83. Hon. Vis. Fellow, Green Coll., Oxford, 1993. Hon. Fellow, LSHTM, 1986. Hon. DSc: Birmingham, 1989; West Indies, 1991; Glasgow, 1992; Hon. DM: Nottingham, 1990; Oxford, 1993. Mary Kingsley Medal for Services to Tropical Medicine, Liverpool Sch. of Trop. Med., 1983. *Publications:* Careers in Medicine, 1952; papers in scientific journals. *Recreations:* garden, history of science. *Address:* Courtyard House, Bletchingdon, Kidlington, Oxon OX5 3DL.

WILLIAMS, Sir Philip; *see* Williams, Sir R. P. N.

WILLIAMS, Prof. Philip James Stradling, PhD; FRAS, FInstP; Professor of Physics, University of Wales, Aberystwyth (formerly University College of Wales, Aberystwyth), since 1991; Member (Plaid Cymru) South East Wales, National Assembly for Wales, since 1999; *b* 11 Jan. 1939; *s* of Glyndwr and Morfydd Williams; *m* 1962, Ann Green; one *s* one *d*. *Educ:* Lewis Sch., Pengam; Clare Coll., Cambridge (MA, PhD 1964). FRAS 1984; FInstP 1992. Fellow, Clare Coll., Cambridge, 1964–67; Lectr, then Sen. Lectr, 1967–86, Reader, 1986–91, UCW, Aberystwyth. Plaid Cymru spokesperson for Econ. Develt, Nat. Assembly for Wales, 1999–. Plaid Cymru: Nat. Chm., 1970–76; Co-ordinator, Campaign for Self-Govt, 1996–. Welsh Politician of the Year, Channel 4, 2000. *Publications:* (with D. Wigley) An Economic Plan for Wales, 1970; A Voice from the Valleys, 1981; The Welsh Budget, 1998; contrib. numerous papers to internat. refereed jls on radio astronomy, space and atmospheric physics. *Recreations:* jazz (alto sax), dancing, hill-walking, history, poetry. *Address:* National Assembly for Wales, Cardiff Bay, Cardiff CF99 1NA. *T:* (029) 2089 8286; Rhydyfirian, Aberystwyth, Ceredigion SY23 4LU. *T:* (01970) 612857. *Club:* Bryn Amlwg Sports and Social (Aberystwyth).

WILLIAMS, Raymond Lloyd, CBE 1987; DPhil, DSc; CChem, FRSC; Director, Metropolitan Police Laboratory, 1968–87; Visiting Professor in Chemistry, University of East Anglia, 1968–93; *b* Bournemouth, 27 Feb. 1927; *s* of late Walter Raymond Williams and Vera Mary Williams; *m* 1956, Sylvia Mary Lawson Whitaker; one *s* one *d*. *Educ:* Bournemouth Sch.; St John's Coll., Oxford (schol.). Gibbs Univ. Schol. 1948, BA 1st Cl. Hons Nat Sci-Chem, MA, DPhil, DSc Oxon. Research Fellow, Pressed Steel Co., 1951–53; Commonwealth Fund Fellow, Univ. of California, Berkeley, 1953–54; progressively, Sen. Res. Fellow, Sen. Scientific Officer, Principal Sci. Officer, Explosives R&D Estab., 1955–60; PSO, Admiralty Materials Lab., 1960–62; Explosives R&D Establishment: SPSO, 1962; Supt, Analytical Services Gp, 1962–65; Supt, Non-metallic Materials Gp, 1965–68. External Examiner: Univ. of Strathclyde, 1983–85; KCL, 1986–88. Vis. Lectr, Univ. of Lausanne, 1989; Lectures: Theophilus Redwood, RSC, 1984; Schools, RSC, 1988; Public, RSC, 1990; Dalton, RSC, 1995. Jt Editor: Forensic Science International, 1978–97; Forensic Science Progress, 1984–92. Pres., Forensic Science Soc., 1983–85; Hon. Mem., Assoc. of Police Surgeons of GB, 1980. Adelaide Medal, Internat. Assoc. of Forensic Scis, 1993. *Publications:* papers in scientific jls on spectroscopy, analytical chemistry, and forensic science. *Recreations:* lawn tennis (played for Civil Service and Oxfordshire: representative colours), carpentry. *Address:* 9 Meon Road, Bournemouth, Dorset BH7 6PN. *T:* (01202) 423446.

WILLIAMS, (Reginald) Norman, CB 1982; Assistant Registrar of Friendly Societies, 1984–93; *b* 23 Oct. 1917; *s* of Reginald Gardnar Williams and Janet Mary Williams; *m* 1956, Hilary Frances West; two *s*. *Educ:* Neath Grammar Sch.; Swansea Univ. Served War: Captain RA and later Staff Captain HQ 30 Corps, 1940–46. Solicitor in private practice, 1947–48. Dept of Health and Social Security (formerly Min. of Nat. Insurance): Legal Asst, 1948; Sen. Legal Asst, 1959; Asst Solicitor, 1966; Principal Asst Solicitor, 1974; Under Sec., 1977–82. Member of Law Society. *Recreations:* golf, photography, reading. *Address:* Brecon, 23 Castle Hill Avenue, Berkhamsted, Herts HP4 1HJ. *T:* (01442) 865291.

WILLIAMS, (Richard) Derrick, MA (Cantab); Principal, Gloucestershire College of Arts and Technology, 1981–89; *b* 30 March 1926; *s* of Richard Leslie Williams and Lizzie Paddington; *m* 1949, Beryl Newbury Stonebanks; four *s*. *Educ:* St John's Coll., Cambridge. Asst Master, Lawrence Sherrif Sch., Rugby, 1950–51; Lectr, University Coll., Ibadan, Nigeria, 1951–52; Adult Tutor, Ashby-de-la-Zouch Community Coll., Leicestershire, 1952–54; Further Educn Organising Tutor, Oxfordshire, 1954–60; Asst Educn Officer: West Suffolk, 1960–65; Bristol, 1965–67; Dep. Chief Educn Officer, Bristol, 1967–73; Chief Educn Officer, County of Avon, 1973–76; Dir, Glos Inst. of Higher Educn, 1977–80. *Recreations:* cricket, music. *Address:* Glan y Nant, Bryniau, Brithdir, Dolgellau, Gwynedd LL40 2TY.

WILLIAMS, Richard Hall; Under Secretary, Agriculture Department, Welsh Office, Cardiff, 1981–86; Deputy Chairman, Local Government Boundary Commission for Wales, 1989–96; *b* 21 Oct. 1926; *s* of late Edward Hall Williams and Kitty Hall Williams; *m* 1949, Nia Wynn (*née* Jones); two *s* two *d. Educ:* Barry Grammar Sch., Glamorgan; University College of Wales, Aberystwyth (BScEcon Hons). Career within Welsh Office included service in Health and Economic Planning Groups before entering Agriculture Dept, 1978. Treasurer, Ministerial Bd, Presbyterian Church of Wales, 1986–95. Vice Chm., Age Concern Wales, 1990–93. Moderator, E Glam Presbytery (Welsh), Presbyterian Ch of Wales, 2000–01. *Recreation:* enjoying all things Welsh. *Address:* Argoed, 17 West Orchard Crescent, Llandaff, Cardiff CF5 1AR. *T:* (029) 2056 2472.

See also J. E. H. Williams.

WILLIAMS, Sir Robert (Evan Owen), Kt 1976; MD, FRCP, FRCPath; FFPHM; Director, Public Health Laboratory Service, 1973–81; Chairman, Advisory Committee on Genetic Manipulation, Health and Safety Executive, 1984–86 (Chairman, Genetic Manipulation Advisory Group, 1981–84); *b* 30 June 1916; *s* of Gwynne Evan Owen Williams and Cicely Mary (*née* Innes); *m* 1944, Margaret (*née* Lumsden) (*d* 1990); one *s* two *d. Educ:* Sherborne Sch., Dorset; University College, London and University College Hospital. Assistant Pathologist, EMS, 1941–42; Pathologist, Medical Research Council Unit, Birmingham Accident Hospital, 1942–46; on staff Public Health Laboratory Service, 1946–60 (Director, Streptococcus, Staphylococcus and Air Hygiene Laboratory, 1949–60); Prof. of Bacteriology, Univ. of London, at St Mary's Hosp. Med. Sch., 1960–73, Dean 1967–73. Mem. MRC, 1969–73. Pres., RCPath, 1975–78. Fellow, UCL, 1968. Hon. FRCPA, 1977; Hon. MD Uppsala, 1972; Hon. DSc Bath, 1977; Dr *hc* Lisbon, 1992. *Publications:* (jt author) Hospital Infection, 1966; Microbiology for the Public Health, 1985; numerous publications in journals on bacteriological and epidemiological subjects. *Recreation:* horticulture. *Address:* Little Platt, Plush, Dorchester, Dorset DT2 7RQ. *T:* (01300) 348320. *Club:* Athenæum.

See also Sir D. I. Williams.

WILLIAMS, Prof. Robert Hughes, (Robin), FRS 1990; CPhys, FInstP; Vice-Chancellor and Principal, University of Wales, Swansea, since 1994; *b* 22 Dec. 1941; *s* of Emrys and Catherine Williams; *m* 1967, Gillian Mary Harrison; one *s* one *d. Educ:* Bala Boys' Grammar Sch.; University College of North Wales, Bangor (BSc, PhD, DSc). Res. Fellow, Univ. of Wales, 1966–68; Lectr, then Reader and Prof., New University of Ulster, 1968–83; Prof. and Hd of Dept of Physics, later Physics and Astronomy, 1984–94, Dep. Principal, 1993–94, Univ. of Wales Coll. of Cardiff. Visiting Professor: Max Planck Inst., Stuttgart, 1975; Xerox Res. Labs, Palo Alto, USA, 1979; IBM Res. Labs, Yorktown Heights, USA, 1982. Mott Lectr, Inst. of Physics, 1992. Silver Medal, British Vacuum Council, 1988; Max Born Medal and Prize, German Physics Soc. and Inst. of Physics, 1989. *Publications:* Metal-Semiconductor Contacts (with E. H. Rhoderick), 1988; over 300 pubns in field of solid state physics and semiconductor devices. *Recreations:* walking, fishing, soccer. *Address:* Dolwerdd, Trerhyngyll, Cowbridge, Vale of Glamorgan CF71 7TN. *T:* (01446) 773402; Danver House, 236 Gower Road, Sketty, Swansea, W Glam SA2 9JJ.

WILLIAMS, Prof. Robert Joseph Paton, DPhil; FRS 1972; Emeritus Fellow, Wadham College, Oxford, since 1995 (Fellow, 1955–95, Senior Research Fellow, 1991–95); Royal Society Napier Research Professor at Oxford, 1974–91; *b* 25 Feb. 1926; *m* 1952, Jelly Klara (*née* Büchli); two *s. Educ:* Wallasey Grammar Sch.; Merton Coll., Oxford (MA, DPhil; Hon. Fellow, 1991). FRSC. Rotary Foundn Fellow, Uppsala, 1950–51; Jun. Res. Fellow, Merton Coll., Oxford, 1951–55; Lectr, 1955–72, Reader in Inorganic Chemistry, 1972–74, Univ. of Oxford. Associate, Peter Bent Brigham Hosp., Boston, USA; Commonwealth Fellow, Mass, 1965–66; Vis. Prof., Royal Free Hosp., London Univ., 1991–. Lectures: Liversidge, Chem. Soc., 1979; Commem., Biochem. Inst., Univ. of Zurich, 1981; Bakerian, 1981, Rutherford, 1996, Royal Soc.; Cohn, Univ. of Philadelphia, 1997; Birchall, Univ. of Keele, 1999; Huxley, Univ. of Birmingham, 2000. President: Chem. Sect., BAAS, 1985–86; Dalton Div., RSC, 1991–93. Foreign Member: Acad. of Science, Portugal, 1981; Royal Soc. of Science, Liège, 1981; Royal Swedish Acad. of Sciences, 1983; Czechoslovak Acad. of Science, 1989. Hon. DSc: Liège, 1980; Leicester, 1985; East Anglia, 1992; Keele, 1993; Instituto Superior Tecnico, Lisbon, 1997. Tilden Medal, Chem. Soc., 1970; Keilin Medal, Biochem. Soc., 1972; Hughes Medal, Royal Soc., 1979; Claire Bruylants Medal, Louvain, 1980; Krebs Medal, Europ. Biochem. Soc., 1985; Linderstrøm-Lang Medal, Carlsberg Foundn, Copenhagen, 1986; Sigillum Magnum (Medal), Univ. of Bologna, 1987; Heyrovsky Medal, Internat. Union of Biochem., 1988; Frederick Gowland Hopkins Medal, Biochem. Soc., 1989; Royal Medal, Royal Soc., 1995; Longstaff Medal, Chem. Soc., 2002. *Publications:* (with C. S. G. Phillips) Inorganic Chemistry, 1965; (jtly) Nuclear Magnetic Resonance in Biology, 1977; (ed jtly) New Trends in Bio-Inorganic Chemistry, 1978; (with S. Mann and J. Webb) Biomineralization, 1989; (with J. J. R. Frausto da Silva) The Biological Chemistry of the Elements, 1991, 2nd edn 2001; (with J. J. R. Frausto da Silva) The Natural Selection of the Chemical Elements, 1996; (with J. J. R. Frausto da Silva) Bringing Chemistry to Life, 1999; papers in Jl Chem. Soc., biochemical jls, etc. *Recreation:* walking in the country. *Address:* Wadham College, Oxford OX1 3QR. *T:* (01865) 242564.

WILLIAMS, Robert Martin, CB 1981; CBE 1973; retired; Chairman, State Services Commission, New Zealand, 1975–81; *b* 30 March 1919; *s* of late Canon Henry Williams; *m* 1944, Mary Constance, *d* of late Rev. Francis H. Thorpe; one *s* two *d. Educ:* Christ's Coll., NZ; Canterbury University College, NZ; St John's Coll., Cambridge. MA. 1st Class Hons Mathematics, Univ. Sen. Schol., Shirtcliffe Fellow, NZ, 1940; BA, 1st Class Hons Mathematics Tripos, Cantab, 1947; PhD Math. Statistics, Cantab, 1949. Mathematician at Radar Development Laboratory, DSIR, NZ, 1941–44; Member UK Atomic Group in US, 1944–45; Member, 1949–53, Director, 1953–62, Applied Mathematics Laboratory, DSIR, NZ; Harkness Commonwealth Fellow and Vis. Fellow, at Princeton Univ., 1957–58; State Services Commissioner, NZ Public Service, 1963–67; Vice-Chancellor: Univ. of Otago, Dunedin, 1967–73; ANU, 1973–75. Mem., NZ Metric Adv. Bd, 1969–73. Mem., Internat. Statistical Inst., 1961–97. Chairman: Cttee of Inquiry into Educnl TV, 1970–72; Policy Cttee, Dictionary of NZ Biography, 1983–90. President: NZ Book Council, 1989–92; Nat. Liby Soc., 1992–95. Carnegie Travel Award, 1969. Hon. LLD Otago, 1972. *Publications:* papers mainly on mathematical statistics and related topics. *Address:* 21 Wadestown Road, Wellington, New Zealand. *Club:* Wellington (Wellington, NZ).

WILLIAMS, Sir (Robert) Philip (Nathaniel), 4th Bt *cr* 1915; JP; DL; *b* 3 May 1950; *s* of Sir David Philip Williams, 3rd Bt and of Elizabeth Mary Garneys, *d* of late William Ralph Garneys Bond; *S* father, 1970; *m* 1979, Catherine Margaret Godwin, *d* of Canon Cosmo Pouncey, Tewkesbury; one *s* three *d. Educ:* Marlborough; St Andrews Univ. MA Hons. JP W Dorset PSA (formerly Dorchester), 1992; DL Dorset, 1995. *Heir: s* David Robert Mark Williams, *b* 31 Oct. 1980. *Address:* Bridehead, Littlebredy, Dorchester, Dorset DT2 9JA. *T:* (01308) 482232. *Club:* MCC.

WILLIAMS, Robin; *see* Williams, Robert H.

WILLIAMS, Maj.-Gen. Robin Guy, CB 1983; MBE 1969; retired; Chief Executive Officer, Auckland Regional Trust Board, Order of St John, 1993–98; *b* 14 Aug. 1930; *s* of John Upham and Margaret Joan Williams; *m* 1953, Jill Rollo Tyrie; one *s* two *d. Educ:* Nelson Coll., New Zealand. psc(UK) 1963, jssc(AS) 1972, rcds(UK) 1976. Commissioned RMC, Duntroon, 1952; 1 Fiji Inf. Regt Malaya, 1953–54; Adjt/Coy Comd 2 NZ Regt Malaya, 1959–61 Chief Instructor Sch. of Inf. (NZ), 1964–65; BM 28 Comwel Inf. Bde, Malaysia, 1965–68; CO 1 Bn Depot (NZ), 1969; CO 1 RNZIR (Singapore), 1969–71; GSO1 Field Force Comd (NZ), 1972–73; CofS Field Force Comd (NZ), 1973–74; Col SD, Army GS, 1974–75; Comd Field Force, 1977–79; ACDS (Ops/Plans), 1979–81; DCGS 1981; CGS, 1981–84. Hon. Col 1 RNZIR, 1986–88; Col, RNZIR, 1988–90. Chm., Bell Helicopter (BH) Pacific, 1988–90. Vice-Chm., 1985–86, Chm., 1986–88, Operation Raleigh, NZ; Chief Executive: Order of St John (NZ), 1986–87; Auckland Div., Cancer Soc. of NZ, 1988–93. *Recreations:* golf, swimming, walking. *Address:* 14 Walton Street, Remuera, Auckland 5, New Zealand. *T:* (9) 5201547. *Clubs:* Northern (Auckland); Auckland Golf (Middlemore, NZ).

WILLIAMS, Sir Robin (Philip), 2nd Bt *cr* 1953; Insurance Broker, 1952–91; Lloyd's Underwriter, 1961; 2nd Lieut, retired, RA; *b* 27 May 1928; *s* of Sir Herbert Geraint Williams, 1st Bt, MP, MSc, MEngAssoc, MInstCE; *S* father, 1954; *m* 1955, Wendy Adèle Marguerite, *o d* of late Felix Joseph Alexander, London and Hong Kong; two *s. Educ:* Eton Coll.; St John's Coll., Cambridge (MA). 2nd Lieut, Royal Artillery, 1947. Vice-Chairman, Federation of Univ. Conservative and Unionist Assocs, 1951–52; Acting Chairman, 1952; Chairman of Bow Group (Conservative Research Society), 1954. Called to Bar, Middle Temple, 1954; Chm., Anti-Common Market League, 1969–84; Dir, Common Market Safeguards Campaign, 1973–76; Hon. Secretary: Safeguard Britain Campaign, 1976–89; Campaign for an Independent Britain, 1989–. Councillor, Haringey, 1968–74. *Publication:* Whose Public Schools?, 1957. *Heir: s* Anthony Geraint Williams [*b* 22 Dec. 1958; *m* 1990, Rachel Jane, *e d* of Norman Jennings; three *s* one *d*]. *Address:* 1 Broadlands Close, Highgate, N6 4AF.

WILLIAMS, Prof. Roger; Vice-Chancellor of The University of Reading, since 1993; *b* 21 March 1942; *s* of late M. O. Williams, MBE and W. Williams; *m* 1967, Rae Kirkbright; two *d. Educ:* Tredegar Grammar Sch.; Worcester Coll., Oxford (BA Nat. Scis (Physics); Hon. Fellow, 1999); Univ. of Manchester (MA). Nat. Coal Bd, 1963–64; Department of Government, University of Manchester: Res. Student, 1964–66; Asst Lectr, Lectr, Sen. Lectr, 1966–78; Prof. of Govt and Sci. Policy, 1979–93; Dean of Economic and Social Studies, 1989–92. NATO Envtl Fellowship, 1977–79; Aust. Univs Fellowship, 1984; Vis. Prof., Univ. of Montreal, 1981. Sci. Advr, Sci. Council of Canada (on secondment), 1974–75; Specialist Advr, H of L Select Cttees on Sci. and Technology, 1986–92, on European Communities, 1990. Chm., Jt SERC-ESRC Cttee, 1991–93; Member: ESRC, EPSRC and NERC Cttees; HEFCW, 1995–(Acting Chm., 2000–); Quality Assurance Agency for Higher Educn, 1997–. British Council Delegn to China, 1985. *Publications:* Politics and Technology, 1972; European Technology, 1973; The Nuclear Power Decisions, 1980; Public Acceptability of New Technology, 1986. *Address:* The University of Reading, Whiteknights, Reading, Berks RG6 6AH. *T:* (0118) 987 5123. *Club:* Athenæum.

WILLIAMS, Roger Hugh; MP (Lib Dem) Brecon Radnorshire, since 2001; farmer, since 1969; *b* 22 Jan. 1948; *s* of Morgan Glyn Williams and Eirlys Williams; *m* 1973, Penelope James; one *s* one *d. Educ:* Llanfilo Co. Primary Sch.; Christ Coll., Brecon; Selwyn Coll., Cambridge (BA). Mem. (Lib Dem) Powys CC, 1981–. Dir, Develt Bd for Rural Wales, 1989–97. Chm., Brecon Beacons Nat. Park, 1991–96. *Recreations:* sport, walking. *Address:* House of Commons, SW1A 0AA; Tredonium Court, Llanfilo, Brecon, Powys LD3 0RL.

WILLIAMS, Prof. Roger Stanley, CBE 1993; MD; FRCP, FRCS, FMedSci; Professor of Hepatology, University of London, since 1994; Director, Institute of Hepatology, University College London Medical School, and Hon. Consultant Physician, University College Hospitals NHS Trust, since 1996; *b* 28 Aug. 1931; *s* of Stanley George Williams and Doris Dagmar Clatworthy; *m* 1st, 1954, Lindsay Mary Elliott (marr. diss. 1977); two *s* three *d*; 2nd, 1978, Stephanie Gay de Laszlo; one *s* two *d. Educ:* St Mary's Coll., Southampton; London Hosp. Med. Coll., Univ. of London. MB, BS (Hons), MD; LRCP, MRCP, FRCP 1966; MRCS, FRCS 1988; FRCPE 1990; FRACP 1991. House appointments and Pathology Asst, London Hospital, 1953–56; Jun. Med. Specialist, Queen Alexandra Hospital, Millbank, 1956–58; Medical Registrar and Tutor, Royal Postgrad. Med. Sch., 1958–59; Lectr in Medicine, Royal Free Hospital, 1959–65; Consultant Physician, Royal South Hants and Southampton General Hospital, 1965–66; Consultant Physician, KCH, 1966–96; Dir, Liver Res. Unit, then Inst. of Liver Studies, KCH and Med Sch., then King's Coll. Sch. of Medicine and Dentistry, 1966–96. Hon. Consultant: Liver Res. Trust, 1974–; in medicine to the Army, 1988–. Member: Clinical Standards Adv. Gp, 1994–; Adv. Gp on Hepatitis, DHSS, 1980–; Transplant Adv. Panel, DHSS, 1974–83; WHO Scientific Gp on Viral Hepatitis, Geneva, 1972. Rockefeller Travelling Fellowship in Medicine, 1962; Legg Award, Royal Free Hosp. Med. Sch., 1964; Sir Ernest Finch Vis. Prof., Sheffield, 1974; Lectures: Melrose Meml, Glasgow, 1970; Goulstonian, RCP, 1970; Searle, Amer. Assoc. for the Study of Liver Diseases, 1972; Fleming, Glasgow Coll. of Physicians and Surgeons, 1975; Sir Arthur Hurst Meml, British Soc. of Gastroenterology, 1975; Skinner, Royal Coll. of Radiologists, 1978; Albert M. Snell Meml, Palo Alto Med. Foundn, 1981; Milford Rouse, Baylor Med. Center, Dallas, 1989; Norman Tanner Meml, St George's Hosp., 1992; Searle Special, St Bartholomew's Hosp., 1992; Datta Meml Oration, India, 1984; Quadrennial Review, World Congress of Gastroenterol., Sydney, 1990; Sir Jules Thorn, RCP, 1994. Vice-Pres., RCP, 1991–93; Pres., Internat. Med. Club, 1989–; Member: European Assoc. for the Study of the Liver, 1966– (Cttee Mem., 1966–70; Pres., 1983); Harveian Soc. of London (Sec., Councillor and Vice-Pres., 1963–70, Pres., 1974–75); British Assoc. for Study of Liver (formerly Liver Club) (Sec. and Treasurer, 1968–71; Pres., 1984–86); Royal Soc. of Medicine (Sec. of Section, 1969–71); British Soc. of Gastroenterology (Pres., 1989). FKC 1992; FMedSci 1999. Hon. FACP 1992; Hon. FRCPI 2001. Gold Medal, Canadian Liver Foundn, 1992. *Publications:* (ed) Fifth Symposium on Advanced Medicine, 1969; (ed) International Developments in Health Care, 1995; edited jointly: Immunology of the Liver, 1971; Artificial Liver Support, 1975; Immune Reactions in Liver Disease, 1978; Drug Reactions and the Liver, 1981; Variceal Bleeding, 1982; Antiviral Agents in Chronic Hepatitis B Virus Infection, 1985; The Practice of Liver Transplantation, 1995; International Developments in Health Care, 1995; Acute Liver Failure, 1996; author of over 2000 scientific papers, review articles and book chapters. *Recreations:* tennis, sailing, opera. *Address:* Brickworth Park, Whiteparish, Wilts SP5 2QE; 8 Eldon Road, W8 5PU. *T:* (020) 7937 5301; Institute of Hepatology, University College London Medical School, Chenies Mews, WC1E 6BT. *Clubs:* Carlton, Saints and Sinners, Royal Ocean Racing; Royal Yacht Squadron (Cowes).

WILLIAMS, Ronald; *see* Williams, A. R.

WILLIAMS, Rt Rev. Ronald John Chantler; Bishop of the Southern Region, and an Assistant Bishop, Diocese of Brisbane, since 1993; *b* 19 July 1938; *s* of Walter Chantler

Williams and Constance Bertha Williams (*née* Pool); *m* 1963, Kathryn Rohrsheim; two *s* one *d*. *Educ:* Prince Alfred Coll., Adelaide; St John's Coll., Morpeth (ThL); St Mark's Coll., Adelaide Univ. (BA); Bristol Univ. (MSc 1974); Australian Management Coll., Mt Eliza (AMP). Ordained deacon, 1963, priest, 1964; Curate, Toorak Gardens, 1963–64; Australian Bd of Missions, Sydney, 1965; Domestic Chaplain, Bishop of Polynesia, 1966–67; Priest, Labasa, Fiji, 1967–71; Hon. Priest, Bedminster, Bristol, 1972–74; Dean of Suva, Fiji, 1974–79; Rector, Campbelltown, Adelaide, 1979–84; Priest to City of Adelaide and founding Dir, St Paul's Centre, 1984–93; Hon. Canon, St Peter's Cathedral, Adelaide, 1986–93. *Recreation:* jazz musician—double bass. *Address:* GPO Box 421, Brisbane, Qld 4001, Australia. *T:* (office) (7) 38352213, (home) (7) 38431546; *e-mail:* rkwill@gil.com.au.

WILLIAMS, Ronald Millward, CBE 1990; DL; Member, Essex County Council, 1970–93 and since 1997 (Chairman, 1983–86); *b* 9 Dec. 1922; *s* of George and Gladys Williams; *m* 1943, Joyce; one *s* two *d*. *Educ:* Leeds College of Technology. Electrical Engineer, then Industrial Eng Superintendent, Mobil Oil Co. Ltd, 1954–82. Member: Benfleet Urban Dist Council, 1960–74 (Chm. 1963–66, 1972–74); Castle Point Dist Council, 1974–87 (Chm. 1980–81; Leader, 1981–87); Essex County Council: Leader Cons. Gp, 1977–83, 1986–87; Chairman: County Planning Cttee, 1981–83; County Highways Cttee, 1989–93; Envmtl Services Bd, 1998–2000; Exec. Mem., with strategic planning and transportation portfolio, 2000–. Chm., Southend Health Authority, 1982–90, Southend Health Care Services, NHS Trust, 1990–96. Chm., SE Essex Abbeyfield Soc., 1983–88. DL Essex 1983. *Recreations:* supporter, football, cricket, bowls, tennis; video filming of countryside. *Address:* 41 Poors Lane, Hadleigh, Benfleet, Essex SS7 2LA. *T:* (01702) 559565.

WILLIAMS, Ronald William; Senior Adviser, PricewaterhouseCoopers (formerly Coopers & Lybrand), 1986–2001; Director, Office of Manpower Economics, 1980–86 (on secondment); *b* 19 Dec. 1926; *yr s* of late Albert Williams and Katherine Teresa Williams (*née* Chilver). *Educ:* City of London Sch.; Downing Coll., Cambridge (BA, LLB). RN, 1945–48. Iraq Petroleum Co. Ltd, 1956–58; Philips Electrical Industries Ltd, 1958–64; Consultant, later Sen. Consultant, PA Management Consultants Ltd, 1964–69; Asst Sec., NBPI, 1969–71; Sen. Consultant, Office of Manpower Economics, 1971–73; Asst Sec., CSD, 1973–80 (UK Govt rep., ILO Tripartite Conf. on Public Servs, 1975); Under Sec. 1980; HM Treasury, 1982; Dept of Employment, 1986. *Publications:* reports on corporate governance and executive remuneration. *Recreations:* music, visual arts. *Address:* 10 Pine Park Mansions, Wilderton Road, Branksome Park, Poole, Dorset BH13 6EB. *T:* (01202) 769736.

WILLIAMS, Most Rev. Rowan Douglas; *see* Wales, Archbishop of.

WILLIAMS, Roy, CB 1989; Deputy Secretary, Department of Trade and Industry, 1984–94; *b* 31 Dec. 1934; *s* of Eric Williams and Ellen Williams; *m* 1959, Shirley, *d* of Captain and Mrs O. Warwick; one *s* one *d*. *Educ:* Liverpool Univ. (1st Cl. BA Econs). Asst Principal, Min. of Power, 1956; Principal, 1961; Harkness Commonwealth Fellow, Univs of Chicago and Berkeley, 1963–64; Principal Private Sec., Minister of Power and subseq. Paymaster Gen., 1969; Asst Sec., DTI, 1971; Principal Private Sec., Sec. of State for Industry, 1974; Under-Sec., DoI, later DTI, 1976–84. Dir, EIB, 1991–94. Chm., EU High Level Gp on Eureka prog., 1995–; Mem., Design Council, 1995–. Chm. Trustees, Nat. Centre for Young People with Epilepsy, St Pier's, Lingfield, 1995–. *Address:* Dail Oast, The Street, Ightham, Sevenoaks, Kent TN15 9HH. *T:* (01732) 883944.

WILLIAMS, Rev. Samuel Lewis; Minister, St Columba's United Reformed Church, Gosport, 1991–96; *b* 8 Jan. 1934; *s* of Thomas John Williams and Miriam Mary Williams (*née* West); *m* 1958, Mary Sansom (*née* Benjamin); one *s* one *d*. *Educ:* Pagefield College Public Day School, Newport, Gwent; Memorial Coll. (Congregational), Brecon. Local government officer, 1950–52; RAF, 1952–55; theol. training, 1955–58. Ordained Congregational (URC) Minister, 1958; Mill Street Congregational Church, Newport, Gwent, 1958–63; Bettws Congregational Church, 1963–68; Llanvaches Congregational Church, 1966–68; Free Churches Chaplain, St Woolas Hosp., Newport, 1964–68. Entered RN as Chaplain, 1968; served HMS: Seahawk, 1968–69; Hermes, 1969–70; Raleigh, 1970–71; Seahawk, 1971–73; Daedalus, 1973–74; served Malta, 1974–76; C-in-C Naval Home Comd staff, 1977–81; HMS Sultan, 1981–84; Flag Officer Scotland and NI staff, 1984–86; HMS Heron, 1986; Prin. Chaplain (Navy), Ch. of Scotland and Free Churches, 1986–91; RN retired, 1991. QHC, 1986–91. *Recreations:* oil painting, golf, hill walking, music, gardening, Rugby. *Address:* 18 Brodrick Avenue, Gosport, Hants PO12 2EN. *T:* (023) 9258 1114.

WILLIAMS, Rev. (Sidney) Austen, CVO 1980; Vicar of St Martin-in-the-Fields, 1956–84; Chaplain to the Queen's Household, 1961–82, Extra Chaplain since 1982; a Prebendary of St Paul's Cathedral, since 1973; *b* 23 Feb. 1912; *s* of Sidney Herbert and Dorothy Williams; *m* 1945, Daphne Joan McWilliam; one *s* one *d*. *Educ:* Bromsgrove School; St Catharine's College, Cambridge (MA); Westcott House, Cambridge. Curate of St Paul, Harringay, 1937–40. Chaplain, Toc H, France and Germany, 1940–48 (POW, 1940–44). Curate of: All Hallows, Barking by the Tower, 1945–46; St Martin-in-the-Fields, 1946–51; Vicar of St Albans, Westbury Park, Clifton, Bristol, 1951–56. Freeman of the City of London, 1977. *Recreations:* photography, ornithology. *Address:* 37 Tulsemere Road, SE27 9EH. *T:* (020) 8670 7945.

WILLIAMS, Susan Elizabeth, OBE 2000; Nurse Adviser to Greater Glasgow Health Board, since 1998; *b* 30 Oct. 1942; *d* of late Ernest George Fost and of Kathleen Beatrice Maud Fost; *m* 1st, 1964, Dennis Norman Carnevale (decd); one *s* one *d*; 2nd, 1977, Keith Edward Williams. *Educ:* Grammar School for Girls, Weston-super-Mare; Wolverhampton Polytechnic (Post-grad. DipPsych); Bristol Royal Hosps (RSCN, RGN, RNT); BEd (Hons), DipN London. Ward Sister, Royal Hosp. for Sick Children, Bristol, 1972–76; Nurse Tutor, Salop Area Sch. of Nursing, 1976–80; Sen. Tutor, Dudley AHA, 1980–83; Reg. Nurse (Educn and Res.), W Midlands RHA, 1983–87; Chief Nurse Advr/Dir of Nurse Educn, Bromsgrove and Redditch HA, 1987–88; Regl Dir of Nursing and Quality Assurance, W Midlands RHA, 1988–93; Dep. Dir of Nursing Management Exec., DoH, 1993–94; Dir of Nursing, Greater Glasgow Community and Mental Health NHS Trust, 1994–98. *Recreations:* hill walking, photography, reading, listening to music, foreign travel. *Address:* Greater Glasgow Health Board, Dalian House, PO Box 15329, 350 St Vincent Street, Glasgow G3 8YZ. *T:* (0141) 201 4610.

WILLIAMS, Mrs Susan Eva, MBE 1959; Lord-Lieutenant of South Glamorgan, 1985–90; *b* 17 Aug. 1915; *d* of Robert Henry Williams and Dorothy Marie Williams; *m* 1950, Charles Crofts Llewellyn Williams (*d* 1952). *Educ:* St James's, West Malvern. WAAF, 1939–45. JP 1961, High Sheriff 1968, DL 1973, Glamorgan; Lieut, S Glam, 1981–85. DStJ 1990. *Recreation:* National Hunt racing. *Address:* Caercady, Welsh St Donats, Cowbridge, Vale of Glamorgan CF71 7ST. *T:* (01446) 772346.

WILLIAMS, Sir Sydney; *see* Williams, Sir Henry S.

WILLIAMS, His Eminence Cardinal Thomas Stafford; *see* Wellington (NZ), Archbishop of, (RC).

WILLIAMS, Trevor; *see* Williams, A. T.

WILLIAMS, Victoria Kirstyn, (Kirsty); Member (Lib Dem) Brecon and Radnorshire, National Assembly for Wales, since 1999; *b* 19 March 1971; *d* of Edward G. Williams and Pamela M. Williams (*née* Hall); *m* 2000, Richard John Rees. *Educ:* St Michael's Sch., Llanelli; Univ. of Manchester (BA Hons Amer. Studies 1993); Univ. of Missouri. Marketing and PR Exec., 1994–97. Chm., Health and Social Service Cttee, Nat. Assembly for Wales, 1999–. Lib Dem Business Manager, 2000–. Dep. Pres., Welsh Liberal Democrats, 1997–99. *Recreations:* horse riding, sport, farming. *Address:* National Assembly for Wales, Crickhowell House, Cardiff CF99 1NA. *T:* (029) 2089 8358.

WILLIAMS, Prof. William David, MA, DPhil; Professor of German, Liverpool University, 1954–80; *b* 10 March 1917; *s* of William Williams and Winifred Ethel Williams (*née* Anstey); *m* 1946, Mary Hope Davis; one *s* one *d*. *Educ:* Merchant Taylors' School; St John's Coll., Oxford (MA, DPhil). Served War of 1939–45, with Sudan Defence Force, Middle East, and as Liaison Officer with Polish Army in Italy; Asst Lecturer in German, Leeds Univ., 1946; Lecturer in German, Oxford Univ., 1948–54; Pro-Vice-Chancellor, Liverpool Univ., 1965–68. *Publications:* Nietzsche and the French, 1952; The Stories of C. F. Meyer, 1962; reviews, etc, in Modern Language Review, and Erasmus. *Recreation:* gardening. *Address:* Strangers Corner, 5 Summerfield Rise, Goring-on-Thames, near Reading, Berks RG8 0DS. *T:* (01491) 872603.

WILLIAMS, Sir (William) Max (Harries), Kt 1983; solicitor; Senior Partner, Clifford Chance, 1989–91 (Joint Senior Partner, 1987–89); *b* 18 Feb. 1926; *s* of Llwyd and Hilary Williams; *m* 1951, Jenifer (*d* 1999), *d* of late Rt Hon. E. L. Burgin, LLD, and Mrs Burgin, JP; two *d*. *Educ:* Nautical Coll., Pangbourne. Served 178 Assault Field Regt RA, Far East (Captain), 1943–47. Admitted Solicitor, 1950. Sen. Partner, Clifford Turner, 1984–87. Mem. Council, 1962–85, Pres., 1982–83, Law Society. Mem., Crown Agents for Oversea Govts and Administration, 1982–86; Lay Mem., Stock Exchange Council, 1984–93; Mem., Stock Exchange Appeals Cttee, 1989–2000. Director: Royal Insurance plc, 1985–95 (Dep. Chm., 1992–95); 3i Group plc, 1988– (Dep. Chm., 1993–96; Chm. Audit Cttee, 1991–96); Garden Pension Trustees Ltd, 1990–; Royal Insurance Co. of Canada, 1991–95. Chairman: Review Bd for Govt Contracts, 1986–93; Police Appeals Tribunal, 1993–99. Member: Royal Commission on Legal Services, 1976–79; Cttee of Management of Inst. of Advanced Legal Studies, 1980–86; Council, Wildfowl Trust (Hon. Treasurer, 1974–80). Pres., City of London Law Soc., 1986–87. Mem., Amer. Law Inst., 1985–; Hon. Member: Amer. Bar Assoc.; Canadian Bar Assoc. Master, Solicitors' Co., 1986–87. Hon. LLD Birmingham, 1983. *Recreations:* golf, fishing, ornithology. *Address:* (office) 200 Aldersgate Street, EC1A 4JJ. *T:* (020) 7600 1000. *Clubs:* Garrick; Brocket Hall Golf.

WILLIAMS, Col William Trevor, FCIS; Director General, Engineering Industries Association, 1981–95; *b* 16 Oct. 1925; *s* of Francis Harold and Ellen Mabel Williams, Newton Manorbier; *m* 1951, Elizabeth, *d* of late Brig. Arthur Goldie; two *s* two *d*. *Educ:* Darwin Coll., Univ. of Kent (MA). FIMgt, MCIT. Commissioned in Infantry, 1945; regimental service, India and Malaya, to 1949; seconded to Guyanese Govt, 1964, 1965; Commander, Maritime Air Regt, Far East, 1967–69; Project Office, National Defence Coll., 1970–71; Adviser, Ethiopian Govt, 1971–72; Col Q BAOR, 1973–76 (Chm., Berlin Budget Cttee); Head of Secretariat, MoD, 1976–77; Director, SATRA, 1979–80. *Publications:* military. *Recreations:* golf, photography. *Address:* 15 Mill Lane, Lower Harbledown, Canterbury CT2 8NE. *T:* (01227) 768170.

WILLIAMS, Wyn Lewis; QC 1992; a Recorder, since 1992; *b* 31 March 1951; *s* of Ronald and Nellie Williams; *m* 1973, Carol Ann Bosley; one *s* one *d*. *Educ:* Rhondda County Grammar Sch.; Corpus Christi Coll., Oxford (MA). Called to the Bar, Inner Temple, 1974; in practice at the Bar, Cardiff, 1974–. *Recreations:* sport, particularly Rugby, music, reading. *Address:* 39 Essex Street, WC2R 3AT; Tall Trees, Caemawr Road, Porth, Mid Glamorgan CF39 9BY. *Clubs:* Cardiff and County; Tylorstown Rugby Football.

WILLIAMS-BULKELEY, Sir Richard (Thomas), 14th Bt *cr* 1661 of Penrhyn, Caernarvonshire; DL; *b* 25 May 1939; *s* of Sir Richard Harry David Williams-Bulkeley, 13th Bt, TD and Renée Arundell (*d* 1994), *yr d* of Sir Thomas Neave, 5th Bt; *S* father, 1992; *m* 1964, Sarah Susan, *er d* of Rt Hon. Sir Henry Josceline Phillimore, OBE; twin *s* one *d*. *Educ:* Eton. FRICS 1989. Captain, Welsh Guards, 1964. High Sheriff, Gwynedd, 1993; DL Gwynedd, 1998. *Recreation:* astronomy. *Heir: s* Major Richard Hugh Williams-Bulkeley, Welsh Guards [*b* 8 July 1968; *m* 1995, Jacqueline, *er d* of David Edwards; two *s*].

WILLIAMS-WYNN, Sir (David) Watkin, 11th Bt *cr* 1688, of Gray's Inn; DL; *b* 18 Feb. 1940; *s* of Sir Owen Watkin Williams-Wynn, 10th Bt, CBE and Margaret Jean (*d* 1961), *d* of late Col William Alleyne Macbean, RA; *S* father, 1988; *m* 1st, 1967, Harriet Veryan Elspeth (marr. diss. 1981), *d* of Gen. Sir Norman Tailyour, KCB, DSO; two *s* twin *d*; 2nd, 1983, Victoria Jane Dillon (marr. diss. 1998), *d* of late Lt-Col Ian Dudley De-Ath, DSO, MBE; twin *s*. *Educ:* Eton. Lt Royal Dragoons, 1958–63; Major Queen's Own Yeomanry, 1970–77. DL 1970, High Sheriff, 1990, Clwyd. *Recreations:* foxhunting and other field sports. *Heir: s* Charles Edward Watkin Williams-Wynn, *b* 17 Sept. 1970. *Address:* Plas-yn-Cefn, St Asaph, N Wales LL17 0EY. *T:* (01745) 582200. *Clubs:* Pratt's, Cavalry and Guards.

WILLIAMSON, family name of **Barons Forres** and **Williamson of Horton**.

WILLIAMSON OF HORTON, Baron *cr* 1999 (Life Peer), of Horton in the county of Somerset; **David Francis Williamson,** GCMG 1998; CB 1984; Secretary-General, Commission of the European Communities, 1987–97; *b* 8 May 1934; *s* of late Samuel Charles Wathen Williamson and Marie Eileen Williamson (*née* Denney); *m* 1961, Patricia Margaret Smith; two *s*. *Educ:* Tonbridge Sch.; Exeter Coll., Oxford (MA). Entered Min. of Agriculture, Fisheries and Food, 1958; Private Sec. to Permanent Sec. and to successive Parly Secs, 1960–62; HM Diplomatic Service, as First Sec. (Agric. and Food), Geneva, for Kennedy Round Trade Negotiations, 1965–67; Principal Private Sec. to successive Ministers of Agric., Fisheries and Food, 1967–70; Head of Milk and Milk Products Div., Marketing Policy Div. and Food Policy Div., 1970–74; Under-Sec., Gen. Agricultural Policy Gp, 1974–76, EEC Gp, 1976–77; Dep. Dir Gen., Agriculture, European Commn, 1977–83; Dep. Sec., Cabinet Office, 1983–87. Non-exec. Dir, Whitbread plc, 1998–. Vis. Prof., Univ. of Bath, 1997–2000. Hon. DEconSc Limerick, 1996; Hon. DCL Kent, 1998; Hon. Dr of Laws: Robert Gordon, 1999; Bath, 1999. Kt Commander's Cross, Order of Merit (Germany), 1991; Commander Grand Cross, Royal Order of Polar Star (Sweden), 1998; Commandeur, Légion d'Honneur (France), 1999. *Address:* Thatchcroft, Broadway, Ilminster, Somerset TA19 9QZ.

WILLIAMSON, Aldon Thompson; Head, Dame Alice Owen's School, since 1994; *b* 19 June 1944; *d* of Gordon Anderson Baxter and Margaret Sophia Baxter; *m* 1966, Prof. James Williamson; one *s* one *d*. *Educ:* Aberdeen Univ. (MA Hons); Inst. of Educn, Univ. of

London (PGCE). Maths teacher, S Hampstead High Sch. (GPDST), 1967–69, Head of Maths, 1969–71; Dep. Head, Dame Alice Owen's Sch., 1983–89; Head, Leventhorpe Sch., Herts, 1989–94. FRSA 1997. *Recreations:* opera, art, reading. *Address:* Dame Alice Owen's School, Dugdale Hill Lane, Potters Bar, Herts EN6 2DU.

WILLIAMSON, Andrew George, CBE 1999; Chairman, North and East Devon Health Authority, since 2000; *b* 29 Feb. 1948; *s* of Albert and Jocelyn Williamson; *m* 1972, Mary Eleanor White; one *s* one *d*. *Educ:* Southern Grammar Sch., Portsmouth; Oxford Poly. (Dip. in Social Work; CQSW); Birmingham Univ. (Advanced Management Develt Prog., 1982). Residential Child Care, Portsmouth, 1967; Child Care Officer, Hants, 1969; social work management positions in Northumberland and Wandsworth; Asst Dir of Social Services, East Sussex, 1983; Dep. Dir, West Sussex, 1986; Dir of Social Services, Devon CC, 1990–99. Member: Top Mgt Programme, 1992–; Criminal Justice Consultative Council, 1992–95; Sec. of State for the Home Dept's Youth Justice Task Force, 1997–. Hon. Sec., Assoc. of Dirs of Social Services, 1996–. Trustee, Michael Sieff Foundn, 1996–. FRSA 1995. *Recreations:* reading, cricket, music, theatre. *Address:* Randolls, Victoria Road, Topsham, Exeter EX3 0EU. *T:* (01392) 877458.

WILLIAMSON, Sir Brian; *see* Williamson, Sir R. B.

WILLIAMSON, Dame (Elsie) Marjorie, DBE 1973; MSc, PhD (London); Principal, Royal Holloway College, University of London, 1962–73; *b* 30 July 1913; *d* of late Leonard Claude Williamson and Hannah Elizabeth Cary. *Educ:* Wakefield Girls' High School; Royal Holloway College. Demonstrator in Physics, Royal Holloway College, University of London, 1936–39; Lecturer in Physics, University College of Wales, Aberystwyth, 1939–45; Lecturer in Physics, Bedford Coll., Univ. of London, 1945–55; Principal, St Mary's Coll., Univ. of Durham, 1955–62; Deputy Vice-Chancellor, Univ. of London, 1970–71, 1971–72. Fellow, Bedford Coll., Univ. of London, 1975. A Manager, The Royal Instn, 1967–70, 1971–74. Mem., Commonwealth Scholarship Commn, 1975–83. *Recreations:* music, gardening. *Address:* Priory Barn, Lower Raydon, Ipswich, Suffolk IP7 5QT. *T:* (01473) 824033.

WILLIAMSON, (George) Malcolm, FCIB; President and Chief Executive Officer, Visa International, San Francisco, since 1998; *b* 27 Feb. 1939; *s* of George and Margery Williamson; *m* Hang Thi Ngo; one *s* one *d*, and one *s* one *d* by a previous marriage. *Educ:* Bolton School. FIB. Barclays Bank: Local Director, 1980; Asst Gen. Manager, 1981; Regional Gen. Manager, 1983–85; Bd Mem., Post Office, and Man. Dir, Girobank plc, 1985–89; Gp Exec. Dir, Standard Chartered Bank, 1989–91; Gp Man. Dir, 1991–93, Gp Chief Exec., 1993–98, Standard Chartered PLC. Director: British Invisibles, 1996–98; (non-exec.) National Grid Group, 1995–99. UK Chm., British-Thai Business Gp, 1997–; Mem. Council, Industrial Soc., 1996–98. *Recreations:* mountaineering, golf, chess. *Address:* c/o Visa International, PO Box 8999, San Francisco, CA 94128–8999, USA. *Clubs:* Rucksack, Pedestrian (Manchester).

WILLIAMSON, Hazel Eleanor, (Mrs H. C. J. Marshall); QC 1988; a Deputy High Court Judge, since 1994; a Recorder, since 1996; *b* 14 Jan. 1947; *d* of Geoffrey Briddon and late Nancy Briddon; *m* 1st, 1969, Robert Hector Williamson (marr. diss. 1980); 2nd, 1983, Harvey Christopher John Marshall; one step *s*. *Educ:* Wimbledon High Sch; St Hilda's Coll., Oxford (MA Jurisprudence). FCIArb 1992. Atkin Scholar, Gray's Inn. Called to the Bar, Gray's Inn, 1972, Bencher, 1996; Asst Recorder, 1993–96. Acting Deemster, I of M, 1999–. Chm., Chancery Bar Assoc., 1994–97. Mem., DTLR (formerly DoE, then DETR) Property Adv. Gp, 1994–. *Publication:* (with Harvey Marshall) Law and Valuation of Leisure Property, 1994. *Recreations:* gardening, opera, occasional off-shore sailing. *Address:* Maitland Chambers, 7 Stone Buildings, Lincoln's Inn, WC2A 3SZ. *T:* (020) 7406 1200. *Club:* Reform.

WILLIAMSON, Prof. Hugh Godfrey Maturin, FBA 1993; Regius Professor of Hebrew, and Student of Christ Church, Oxford University, since 1992; *b* 15 July 1947; *s* of Thomas Broadwood Williamson and Margaret Frances (*née* Davy); *m* 1971, Julia Eiluned Morris; one *s* two *d*. *Educ:* Rugby Sch.; Trinity Coll., Cambridge (BA 1st cl. Hons Theol., 1969; MA); St John's Coll., Cambridge; PhD 1975, DD 1986, Cantab. Cambridge University: Asst Lectr in Hebrew and Aramaic, 1975–79; Lectr, 1979–89; Reader, 1989–92; Fellow of Clare Hall, 1985–92. Chm., Anglo-Israel Archaeol Soc., 1990–. *Publications:* Israel in the Books of Chronicles, 1977; 1 and 2 Chronicles, 1982; Ezra, Nehemiah, 1985; Ezra and Nehemiah, 1987; Annotated Key to Lambdin's Introduction to Biblical Hebrew, 1987; (ed jtly) The Future of Biblical Studies, 1987; (ed jtly) It is Written: essays in honour of Barnabas Lindars, 1988; The Book Called Isaiah, 1994; (ed jtly) Wisdom in Ancient Israel: essays in honour of J. A. Emerton, 1995; Variations on a Theme: King, Messiah and Servant in the Book of Isaiah, 1998; contrib. to learned jls incl. Vetus Testamentum, Jl of Theol Studies, Jl of Biblical Lit., Jl of Semitic Studies, Jl for Study of OT, Palestine Exploration Qly, Zeitschrift für die alttestamentliche Wissenschaft, Oudtestamentische Studiën. *Recreations:* sea angling, model yacht sailing. *Address:* 7 Chester Road, Southwold, Suffolk IP18 6LN. *T:* (01502) 722319; Christ Church, Oxford OX1 1DP.

WILLIAMSON, Prof. James, CBE 1985; FRCPE; Professor of Geriatric Medicine, University of Edinburgh, 1976–86, now Emeritus; *b* 22 Nov. 1920; *s* of James Mathewson Williamson and Jessie Reid; *m* 1945, Sheila Mary Blair; three *s* two *d*. *Educ:* Wishaw High Sch., Lanarkshire; Univ. of Glasgow (MB ChB 1943); FRCPE 1959 (MRCPE 1949). Training in general medicine, incl. two years in general practice, later specialising in respiratory diseases, then in medicine of old age; Consultant Physician, 1954–73; Prof. of Geriatric Medicine in newly established Chair, Univ. of Liverpool, 1973–76. Pres., British Geriatrics Soc., 1986–88; Chairman: Age Concern Scotland, 1987–90; Chest Heart Stroke Assoc., Scotland, 1993–98. Hon. DSc Rochester, USA, 1989. *Publications:* chapters in various textbooks; numerous articles in gen. med. jls and in jls devoted to subject of old age. *Recreations:* walking, reading. *Address:* 8 Chester Street, Edinburgh EH3 7RA. *T:* (0131) 477 0282.

WILLIAMSON, Marshal of the Royal Air Force Sir Keith (Alec), GCB 1982 (KCB 1979); AFC 1968; Chief of the Air Staff, 1982–85; Air ADC to the Queen, 1982–85; *b* 25 Feb. 1928; *s* of Percy and Gertrude Williamson; *m* 1953, Patricia Anne, *d* of W/Cdr F. M. N. Watts; two *s* twin *d*. *Educ:* Bancroft's Sch., Woodford Green; Market Harborough Grammar Sch.; RAF Coll., Cranwell. Commissioned, 1950; flew with Royal Australian Air Force in Korea, 1953; OC 23 Sqdn, 1966–68; Command, RAF Gütersloh, 1968–70; RCDS 1971; Dir, Air Staff Plans, 1972–75; Comdt, RAF Staff Coll., 1975–77; ACOS (Plans and Policy), SHAPE, 1977–78; AOC-in-C, RAF Support Comd, 1978–80; AOC-in-C, RAF Strike Command and C-in-C, UK Air Forces, 1980–82. *Recreation:* golf. *Address:* c/o National Westminster Bank, Fakenham, Norfolk NR21 9BA.

WILLIAMSON, Malcolm; *see* Williamson, G. M.

WILLIAMSON, Malcolm Benjamin Graham Christopher, CBE 1976; composer, pianist, organist; Master of the Queen's Music, since 1975; *b* 21 Nov. 1931; *s* of Rev. George Williamson, Sydney, Australia, and Bessie (*née* Wrigley); *m* 1960, Dolores Irene Daniel; one *s* two *d*. *Educ:* Barker Coll., Hornsby, NSW; Sydney Conservatorium. Asst Organist, Farm Street, London, 1955–58; Organist, St Peter's, Limehouse, 1958–60; Lectr in Music, Central Sch. of Speech and Drama, 1961–62; Composer-in-Residence: Westminster Choir Coll., Princeton, NJ, 1970–71 (Hon. Fellow, 1971); Florida State Univ., 1975; Creative Arts Fellow, ANU, 1974–81; Ramaciotti Medical Research Fellow, Univ. of NSW, 1982–83; Vis. Prof. of Music, Strathclyde Univ., 1983–86. Mem. Exec. Cttee, Composers' Guild of GB, 1964. President: Beauchamp Sinfonietta, 1972–; Birmingham Chamber Music Soc., 1975–; Univ. of London Choir, 1976–; Purbeck Festival of Music, 1976–; RPO, 1977–82; Sing for Pleasure, 1977–; British Soc. for Music Therapy, 1977–; Stevenage Music Soc., 1987–; Ditchling Choral Soc., 1989–; Finchley Children's Music Gp, 1991–; Vice President: Elgar Foundn; St Michael's Singers; Nat. Music Council of GB; NYO of GB; patron of orchestras, choirs, trusts, etc. Hon. DMus: Westminster Choir Coll., Princeton, NJ, 1970; Melbourne, 1982; Sydney, 1982; DUniv Open, 1983. Hon. AO 1987. *Compositions include: grand operas:* Our Man in Havana (also orchestral suite); The Violins of Saint-Jacques; Lucky Peter's Journey; *chamber operas:* English Eccentrics (also choral suite); The Happy Prince; Julius Caesar Jones; Dunstan and the Devil; The Growing Castle; The Red Sea; The Death of Cuchulain; The Musicians of Bremen; *operatic sequence:* The Brilliant and the Dark; *choral operas or cassations:* The Moonrakers; Knights in Shining Armour; The Snow Wolf; Genesis; The Stone Wall; The Winter Star; The Glitter Gang; The Terrain of the Kings; The Valley and the Hill; The Devil's Bridge; *ballets:* Sun into Darkness; Spectrum; Heritage; *orchestral:* seven symphonies; Santiago de Espada (overture); Sinfonia concertante (also ballet); The Display (concert suite; also ballet); Sinfonietta (also ballet); Concerto Grosso; Symphonic Variations; Serenade and Aubade; Epitaphs for Edith Sitwell (also organ arrangement); The Bridge that Van Gogh Painted; Perisynthion (also ballet); The House of Windsor (orchestral suite); Fiesta; Ochre; Fanfarade; Ode for Queen Elizabeth; In Thanksgiving—Sir Bernard Heinze; Cortège for a Warrior; Lento for Strings; Bicentennial Anthem; *concertos:* three piano concertos (ballet, Have Steps Will Travel, to Piano Concerto No 3); Concerto for Two Pianos and Strings; Organ Concerto; Violin Concerto; Lament in Memory of Lord Mountbatten of Burma (violin and strings); Au Tombeau du Martyr Juif Inconnu (harp and strings); *solo voice and orchestra:* Six English Lyrics (also arrangement for solo voice and piano); Hammarskjold Portrait; Les Olympiques; Tribute to a Hero; Next Year in Jerusalem; White Dawns (also arrangement for solo voice and piano); *solo voice and piano:* A Vision of Beasts and Gods; Celebration of Divine Love; Three Shakespeare Songs; A Christmas Carol; From a Child's Garden; The Fly; The Mower to the Glow-worm; The White Island or Place of the Blessed; Day that I Have Loved; Two Vocalises; *chorus and orchestra:* The Icy Mirror; Ode to Music; Jubilee Hymn; Mass of Christ the King (to celebrate the Queen's Silver Jubilee); Little Mass of Saint Bernadette; Now is the Singing Day; A Pilgrim Liturgy; Songs for a Royal Baby; The True Endeavour; The Dawn is at Hand; The Cradle of the Hope of Peace; *choral:* Two Motets; Adoremus; Dawn Carol; Ascendit Deus; Tu es Petrus; Agnus Dei; Dignus est Agnus; Procession of Psalms; Easter Carol; Jesu, Lover of My Soul; Symphony for Voices; Harvest Thanksgiving; Let Them Give Thanks; Wrestling Jacob; The Morning of the Day of Days; An Australian Carol; Epiphany Carol; Mass of Saint Andrew; A Young Girl; Sweet and Low; A Canon for Stravinsky; Sonnet; Cantate Domino—Psalm 98; In Place of Belief; Te Deum; Love, the Sentinel; Canticle of Fire; The World at the Manger; This Christmas Night; Kerygma; Mass of Saint Margaret of Scotland; Three Choric Hymns; Now is the Singing Day; Galilee; Easter in St Mary's Church; *unison voices:* Planctus; 12 New Hymn Tunes; 6 Christmas Songs for the Young; Mass of Saint Andrew; 6 Evening Hymns; A Psalm of Praise; Hallo Everybody; 5 Carols of King David; 6 Wesley Songs for the Young; Communion Hallelujahs; 16 Hymns and Processionals; Love Chorales (8 hymns); Dove Chorales (8 hymns); Above Chorales (8 hymns); Mass of Saint James; 20 Psalms of the Elements; Mass of the People of God; Our Church Lives; *chamber music:* Nonet; Variations for Violoncello and Piano; Concerto for Wind Quartet and Two Pianos; Serenade for Flute, Piano and String Trio; Pas de Quatre for Piano and Woodwind Quartet (also ballet as BigfellaTootsquoodgeandNora); Piano and String Quintet; Partita for Viola on Themes of Walton; Pietà; Piano Trio; The Feast of Eurydice; Champion Family Album; Channukkah Sketches for Flute and Guitar; *brass ensembles:* Canberra Fanfare; Adelaide Fanfare; Konstanz Fanfare; Richmond Fanfare; Fontainebleau Fanfare; Ceremony for Oodgeroo; Fanfares and Chorales; Bratsvo-Brotherhood; Music for a Quiet Day; Concertino for Charles; *piano solos:* 2 piano sonatas; Five Preludes for Piano; Ritual of Admiration; Himna Titu; Sonata for Two Pianos; Springtime on the River Moskva (piano duet); 7 books of travel diaries; 2 books of peace pieces; *organ:* Fons Amoris; Résurgence du Feu; Symphony for Organ; Vision of Christ Phœnix; Elegy—JFK; Little Carols of the Saints; Mass of a Medieval Saint; Organ Fantasies on This is my Father's World and O Paradise!; The Lion of Suffolk; Mass of the People of God; *musicals:* No Bed for Bacon; Trilby; also arrangements, film scores, music for television and radio. *Recreation:* literature. *Address:* c/o Campion Press, Sandon, Buntingford, Herts SG9 0QW.

WILLIAMSON, Dame Marjorie; *see* Williamson, Dame E. M.

WILLIAMSON, Nicol; actor; *b* Hamilton, Scotland, 14 Sept. 1938. Dundee Rep. Theatre, 1960–61; Royal Court: That's Us, Arden of Faversham, 1961; A Midsummer Night's Dream, Twelfth Night, 1962; Royal Shakespeare Company, 1962; Nil Carborundum, The Lower Depths, Women Beware Women; Spring Awakening, Royal Court, 1962; Kelly's Eye, The Ginger Man, Royal Court, 1963; Inadmissible Evidence, 1964, 1978, Royal Court, Wyndham's 1965 (Evening Standard Best Actor Award), NY 1965 (NY Drama Critics Award); A Cuckoo in the Nest, Waiting for Godot, Miniatures, 1964; Sweeney Agonistes, Globe, 1965; Diary of a Madman, Duchess, 1967; Plaza Suite, NY, 1968; Hamlet, Round House, 1969 (Evening Standard Best Actor Award), NY and US tour, 1969; Midwinter Spring, Queen's, 1972; Circle in the Square, Uncle Vanya, NY, 1973; Royal Shakespeare Company, 1973–75: Coriolanus, Midwinter Spring, Aldwych, 1973; Twelfth Night, Macbeth, Stratford 1974, Aldwych 1975; dir and title role, Uncle Vanya, Other Place, Stratford, 1974; Rex, NY, 1975; Inadmissible Evidence, NY, 1981; Macbeth, NY, 1983; The Entertainer, NY, 1983; The Lark, USA, 1983; The Real Thing, NY, 1985; Jack—A Night on the Town with John Barrymore, Criterion, 1994; King Lear, Clwyd Th. Cymru, 2001. *Films:* Inadmissible Evidence, 1967; The Bofors Gun, 1968; Laughter in the Dark, 1968; The Reckoning, 1969; Hamlet, 1970; The Jerusalem File, 1971; The Wilby Conspiracy, 1974; The Seven Per Cent Solution, 1975; The Cheap Detective, The Goodbye Girl, Robin and Marion, 1977; The Human Factor, 1979; Excalibur, Venom, 1980; I'm Dancing as Fast as I Can, 1981; Return to Oz, 1984; Black Widow, 1986; The Hour of the Pig, 1994. *Television:* The Word, 1977; Macbeth, BBC Shakespeare series, 1982; Christopher Columbus, 1983; Lord Mountbatten—the Last Viceroy, 1985; Passion Flower, 1985. *Publication:* Ming's Kingdom, 1996.

WILLIAMSON, Nigel; writer; *b* 4 July 1954; *s* of Neville Albert and Anne Maureen Williamson; *m* 1976, Magali Patricia Wild; two *s*. *Educ:* Chislehurst and Sidcup Grammar School; University College London. Tribune: Journalist, 1982–84; Literary Editor, 1984; Editor, 1984–87; Editor: Labour Party News, 1987–89; New Socialist, 1987–89; The Times: political reporter, 1989–90; Diary Editor, 1990–92; Home News Editor, 1992–95;

Whitehall correspondent, 1995–96; celebrity interviewer and music writer, 1996–; music news ed., Uncut mag., 1997–; weekly columnist, Billboard, 1999–. A Judge, Mercury Music Prize, 1999–. *Publications:* The SDP (ed), 1982; The New Right, 1984; (contrib.) Rough Guide to World Music. *Recreations:* world music, cricket, gardening. *Address:* High Beeches, 60 Sutherland Avenue, Biggin Hill, Westerham, Kent TN16 3H9. *T:* (01959) 571127. *Clubs:* St James's; Earlswood Strollers Cricket (Greenwich).

WILLIAMSON, Dr Paul, FSA; Chief Curator, Department of Sculpture, Victoria and Albert Museum, since 1989; *b* 4 Aug. 1954; *s* of Peter Williamson and Mary Teresa Williamson (*née* Meagher); *m* 1984, Emmeline Mary Clare Mandley; one s. *Educ:* Wimbledon Coll.; Univ. of East Anglia (BA Hons; MPhil; LittD). Res., British Sch. at Rome, 1978; Major State Student, DES, 1978–79; Department of Sculpture, Victoria and Albert Museum: Asst Keeper, 1979–89; acting Keeper, 1989; Sen. Chief Curator, 1995–98. Member: Wells Cathedral West Front Specialist Cttee, 1981–83; Wall Paintings Sub-Cttee, Council for the Care of Churches, 1987–90; Cttee, British Acad. Corpus of Romanesque Sculpture in Britain and Ireland, 1990–97; Lincoln Cathedral Fabric Adv. Council, 1990–; Cosmati Pavement Adv. Cttee, Westminster Abbey, 1996–99; Expert Advr on Sculpture, Reviewing Cttee on Export of Works of Art, 1989–. Lansdowne Vis. Prof., Univ. of Victoria, BC, 2001; Diskant Lectr, Philadelphia Mus. of Art, 2001. FSA 1983 (Mem. Council, 1997–; Vice-Pres., 1999–). *Publications:* An Introduction to Medieval Ivory Carvings, 1982 (trans. German); Catalogue of Romanesque Sculpture in the Victoria and Albert Museum, 1983; (ed) The Medieval Treasury: the art of the Middle Ages in the Victoria and Albert Museum, 1986, 3rd edn 1998; The Thyssen-Bornemisza Collection: medieval sculpture and works of art, 1987; Northern Gothic Sculpture 1200–1450, 1988; (ed jtly) Early Medieval Wall Painting and Painted Sculpture in England, 1990; Gothic Sculpture 1140–1300, 1995 (trans. Spanish 1997, trans. Portuguese, 1998); (ed) European Sculpture at the Victoria and Albert Museum, 1996; contribs to numerous exhibn catalogues; articles and book reviews in learned jls. *Recreation:* travel. *Address:* Department of Sculpture, Victoria and Albert Museum, SW7 2RL. *T:* (020) 7942 2611.

WILLIAMSON, Peter Roger; HM Diplomatic Service, retired; Consultant on Sub-Sahara Africa; *b* 20 April 1942; *s* of Frederick W. and Dulcie R. Williamson; *m* 1977, Greta Helen Clare Richards; one *s* one *d*. *Educ:* Bristol Grammar Sch.; St John's Coll., Oxford (MA). Journalist and teacher, Far East, 1965–66; joined FCO, 1966; Kuala Lumpur, 1970; 1st Sec., FCO, 1973; Hong Kong, 1975; FCO, 1979; Counsellor: Kuala Lumpur, 1985–88; FCO, 1988–92; on loan to Cabinet Office, 1992–94; Counsellor, Nairobi, 1994–97. *Recreations:* tennis, travel, theatre, cinema.

WILLIAMSON, Richard Arthur; Director, Midland Region, Crown Prosecution Service, 1987–89; *b* 9 Jan. 1932; *s* of George Arthur and Winifred Mary Williamson; *m* 1957, Christina Elizabeth, *d* of Harry Godley Saxton, Worksop, Notts, and Helena Saxton; two *s*. *Educ:* King Edward VI Grammar Sch., East Retford; Sheffield Univ. (statutory year). Solicitor, 1956. National Service, RN (Sub-Lieut), 1956–58. Asst Solicitor, Lancs CC, 1958–61; Sen. Asst Solicitor, Lincs (Lindsey) CC, 1961–65; private practice, Partner in Hetts, Solicitors, Scunthorpe, 1965–76; Prin. Prosecuting Solicitor, Greater Manchester, 1976–83; Chief Prosecuting Solicitor, Lincs, 1983–85; Asst Hd of Field Management, Crown Prosecution Service, 1985–87. Prosecuting Solicitors Soc. of England and Wales: Mem. Exec. Council, 1978–85; Treas., 1978–85; Chm., Hds of Office, 1984–85. Mem., S Yorks and the Humber War Pensions Cttee, 1997–. *Recreations:* family, theatre, gardening. *Address:* The Lookout, Back Street, Alkborough, near Scunthorpe, North Lincolnshire DN15 9JN. *T:* (01724) 720843.

WILLIAMSON, Prof. Robert, FRCP, FRCPath; FRS 1999; Director, Murdoch Childrens Research Institute (formerly Murdoch Research Institute), Royal Children's Hospital, Melbourne, since 1995; Research Professor of Medical Genetics, University of Melbourne School of Medicine, since 1995; *b* 14 May 1938; *s* of John and Mae Williamson; *m* 1st, 1962, Patricia Anne Sutherland (marr. diss. 1994); one *s* one *d*; 2nd, 1994, Robyn Elizabeth O'Hehir; one *s* one *d*. *Educ:* Bronx High School of Science, NY; Wandsworth Comprehensive School; University College London (BSc, MSc, PhD). FRCP 1990. Lectr, Univ. of Glasgow, 1963–67; Sen. Scientist (Molecular Biol.), Beatson Inst. for Cancer Research, Glasgow, 1967–76; Prof. of Biochem., St. Mary's Hosp. Med. Sch., London Univ., 1976–95. Sen. Fellow, Carnegie Instn of Washington, Baltimore,1972–73. External Examnr, Malaysia, Saudi Arabia. Member: UK Genetic Manipulation Adv. Cttee, 1976–91; Grants Cttees, MRC, Cancer Research Campaign, Action Research for Crippled Child, Cystic Fybrosis Research Trust. Francqui Hon. Prof., Belgian Univs, 1995. FAA. Hon. MRCP 1986. Hon. MD Turku, 1987. Wellcome Award, Biochem. Soc., 1983; King Faisal Internat. Prize for Medicine, 1994. *Publications:* (ed) Genetic Engineering, vol. 1, 1981, vol. 2, 1982, vol. 3, 1982, vol. 4, 1983; articles in Nature, Cell, Procs of US Nat. Acad. of Scis, Biochemistry, Nucleic Acids Research. *Recreations:* reading, sport. *Address:* Murdoch Childrens Research Institute, Royal Children's Hospital, Flemington Road, Parkville, Melbourne, Vic 3052, Australia. *T:* (3) 83416200, *Fax:* (3) 93481391; *e-mail:* williamb@cryptic.rch.unimelb.edu.au.

WILLIAMSON, Sir (Robert) Brian, Kt 2001; CBE 1989; Chairman: London International Financial Futures and Options Exchange, 1985–88, and since 1998 (Director, 1982–89); Electra Investment Trust plc, since 2000 (Director, since 1994); *b* 16 Feb. 1945; *m* 1986, Diane Marie Christine de Jacquier de Rosée. *Educ:* Trinity College, Dublin (MA). Personal Asst to Rt Hon. Maurice Macmillan (later Viscount Macmillan), 1967–71; Editor, International Currency Review, 1971; Man. Dir, Gerrard & National Hldgs, 1978–89; Chairman: GNI Ltd, 1985–89; Gerrard & Nat. Hldgs, later Gerrard Gp PLC, 1989–98; Fleming Worldwide Investment Trust, 1998 (Dep. Chm., 1996–98); Director: Fleming Internat. High Income Investment Trust plc, 1990–96; Court, Bank of Ireland, 1990–98; Barlows plc, 1997–98. Member: Bd, Bank of Ireland Britain Hldgs, 1986–90; Council, 1985–88, Council, Eur. Cttee, 1988–90, British Invisible Exports Council; FSA (formerly SIB), 1986–98. Mem., Adv. Council, 1998–, Dir, 1999–, Politeia. Gov. at Large, Nat. Assoc. of Securities Dealers, USA, 1995–98; Mem., Internat. Markets Adv. Bd, NASDAQ Stock Market, 1993– (Chm., 1996–99). Mem. Governing Council, Centre for Study of Financial Innovation, 2000–. Mem. HAC, commissioned 1975. Dir, Rowing Mus., Henley Foundn, 1992–94. Mem. Council, St George's House, 1996–, Dir, St George's House Trust (Windsor Castle), 1998–; Trustee, St Paul's Cathedral Foundn, 1999–. Contested (C) Sheffield Hillsborough, Feb. and Oct. 1974; prosp. parly cand., Truro, 1976–77. FRSA 1991. *Address:* 23 Paultons Square, SW3 5AP. *Clubs:* Pratt's, Flyfishers'; Kildare and University (Dublin); Brook (New York).

WILLIAMSON, Rt Rev. Robert Kerr, (Roy); Bishop of Southwark, 1991–98; *b* 18 Dec. 1932; *s* of James and Elizabeth Williamson; *m* 1956, Anne Boyd Smith; three *s* two *d*. *Educ:* Elmgrove School, Belfast; Oak Hill College, London. London City Missionary, 1955–61; Oak Hill Coll., 1961–63; Asst Curate, Crowborough Parish Church, 1963–66; Vicar: St Paul, Hyson Green, Nottingham, 1966–71; St Ann w. Emmanuel, Nottingham, 1971–76; St Michael and All Angels, Bramcote, 1976–79; Archdeacon of Nottingham, 1978–84; Bishop of Bradford, 1984–91. Chm., Central Religious Adv. Cttee to BBC and ITC, 1993–97; Co-Chm., Inter-Faith Network for the UK, 1994–99. *Publications:* Can You Spare a Minute?, 1991; Funny You Should Say That, 1992; For Such a Time as This, 1996; Joyful Uncertainty, 1999; Open Return, 2000; Not Least in the Kingdom, 2001. *Recreations:* walking, bird watching, reading, music. *Address:* 30 Sidney Road, Beeston, Nottingham NG9 1AN.

WILLIAMSON, Prof. Robin Charles Noel, FRCS; Associate Dean, Royal Society of Medicine; Consultant Surgeon, Hammersmith Hospital, since 1987; Professor of Surgery, Imperial College School of Medicine (formerly Professor and Head of Department of Surgery, Royal Postgraduate Medical School), University of London, since 1987; *b* 19 Dec. 1942; *s* of James Charles Frederick Lloyd Williamson and Helena Frances Williamson (*née* Madden); *m* 1967, Judith Marjorie (*née* Bull); three *s*. *Educ:* Rugby School; Emmanuel College, Cambridge; St Bartholomew's Hosp. Med. Coll. MA, MD, MChir (Cantab). Surgical Registrar, Reading, 1971–73; Sen. Surgical Registrar, Bristol, 1973–75; Res. Fellow, Harvard, 1975–76; Consultant Sen. Lectr, Bristol, 1977–79; Prof. of Surgery, Univ. of Bristol, 1979–87. Mem., Cell Biology and Disorders Bd, MRC, 1987–91. Fulbright-Hays Sen. Res. Scholar, USA, 1975; Sen. Penman Vis. Fellow, South Africa, 1985; Paul Grange Vis. Fellow, Univ. of Monash, 1986; Hunterian Prof., RCS, 1981–82; Raine Vis. Prof., Univ. of Western Australia, 1983; Richardson Prof., Mass Gen. Hosp., 1985; Visiting Professor: Univ. of Lund, Sweden, 1985; Univ. of Hong Kong, 1987; Univ. of Hamburg, 1999; Johnson and Johnson Vis. Prof., Univ. of Calif, San Francisco, 1989; Edwin Tooth Guest Prof., Royal Brisbane Hosp., Qld, 1989; Totalisator Bd Vis. Prof., Nat. Univ. of Singapore, 1994. Lectures: Arris and Gale, RCS, 1977–78; Finlayson Meml, RCPSG, 1985; Sir Gordon Bell Meml, RACS, NZ, 1988. Association of Surgeons of GB and Ireland: Moynihan Fellow, 1979; Mem. Council, 1993–99; Chm., Scientific Cttee, 1995–97; Vice Pres., 1997–98; Pres., 1998–99. President: Pancreatic Soc. of GB and Ireland, 1984–85; Internat. HepatoPancreatoBiliary Assoc., 1996–98 (Sec. Gen., 1994–96); Assoc. of Upper Gastrointestinal Surgeons, 1996–98; European Soc. of Surgery, 1998; Chm., Educn Cttee, British Soc. of Gastroenterology, 1981–87; Member: Med. Adv. Cttee, British Council, 1988–94; Clin. Res and Trng and Career Panel, MRC, 1997–; Internat. Adv. Bd, Nat. Univ. of Singapore, 1998–2000; Res. Cttee, Mason Med. Res. Foundn, 1999–; Sec. Gen., World Assoc. of HepatoPancreatoBiliary Surgery, 1990–94 (Treas., 1986–90). Examiner: Primary FRCS, 1981–87; Intercollegiate Bd in General Surgery, 1994– (Mem., Intercollegiate Examng Bd in Gen. Surg., 1998–). Hon. FRCS Thailand, 1992. Hon. PhD Mahidol Univ., Thailand, 1994. Hallett Prize, RCS, 1970; Research Medal, British Soc. of Gastroenterology, 1982; Bengt Ihre Medal, Swedish Soc. of Gastroenterology, 1998. Sen. Ed., British Jl of Surgery, 1991–96 (Co. Sec., 1983–91); Ed., HPB, 1999–. *Publications:* edited jointly: Colonic Carcinogenesis, 1982; General Surgical Operations, 2nd edn 1987; Emergency Abdominal Surgery, 1990; Surgical Management, 2nd edn 1991; Clinical Gastroenterology: gastrointestinal emergencies, 1991; Scott, An Aid to Clinical Surgery, 6th edn 1998; Hepatobiliary and Pancreatic Tumours, 1994; Upper Digestive Surgery: oesophagus, stomach and small intestine, 1999; Surgery, 2000; numerous papers in surgical and med. jls. *Recreations:* travel, military uniforms and history. *Address:* The Barn, 88 Lower Road, Gerrards Cross, Bucks SL9 8LB. *T:* (01753) 889816. *Clubs:* Oxford and Cambridge, Royal Society of Medicine.

WILLIAMSON, Rt Rev. Roy; *see* Williamson, Rt Rev. Robert K.

WILLIAMSON, Prof. Stephen, FREng; Professor of Electrical Engineering, University of Manchester Institute of Science and Technology, since 2000; *b* 15 Dec. 1948; *s* of Donald Williamson and Patricia K. M. Williamson (*née* Leyland); *m* 1970, Zita Mellor; one *s* two *d*. *Educ:* Burnage Grammar Sch., Manchester; Imperial Coll. of Science and Technology (scholarship, 1968; Sylvanus P. Thompson Prize, 1969; BScEng, ACGI, PhD, DIC; DScEng 1989). FIEEE 1995; FREng (FEng 1995). Lectr in Engineering, Univ. of Aberdeen, 1973–81; Sen. Lectr, 1981–85, Reader, 1985–89, Dept of Electrical Engineering, Imperial College; Prof. of Engineering, 1989–97, and Fellow, St John's Coll., 1990–97, Cambridge Univ.; Technical Dir, Brook Hansen, later Invensys Brook Crompton, 1997–2000. FCGI 1989. Institution of Electrical Engineers: John Hopkinson Premium, 1981; Crompton Premium, 1987, 1996, 1998; Swan Premium, 1989; Science, Educn and Technol. Div. Premium, 1991; Power Div. Premium, 1995; Achievement Medal, 2000; Nikola Tesla Award, IEEE, 2001. *Publications:* papers relating to induction machines. *Recreations:* reading, walking, gardening. *Address:* Department of Electrical Engineering and Electronics, University of Manchester Institute of Science and Technology, PO Box 88, Manchester, M60 1QD. *T:* (0161) 200 4683.

WILLIAMSON, Prof. Timothy, FRSE; FBA 1997; Wykeham Professor of Logic, and Fellow of New College, Oxford University, since 2000; *b* 6 Aug. 1955; *er s* of late Colin Fletcher Williamson and of Karina Williamson (*née* Side; she *m* 2nd, Prof. Angus McIntosh, *qv*); *m* 1984, Elisabetta Perosino; one *s* one *d*. *Educ:* Henley Grammar Sch.; Balliol Coll., Oxford; Christ Church, Oxford (MA 1981; DPhil 1981); MA *aeg* Dublin 1986. FRSE 1997. Sen. Scholar, Christ Church, Oxford, 1976–80; Lectr in Philosophy, TCD, 1980–88; Fellow and Praelector in Philosophy, University Coll., and CUF Lectr in Philosophy, Univ. of Oxford, 1988–94; Prof. of Logic and Metaphysics, Edinburgh Univ., 1995–2000. Visiting Professor: MIT, 1994; Princeton, 1998–99; Vis. Fellow, ANU, 1990, 1995; Vis. Erskine Fellow, Univ. of Canterbury, NZ, 1995. *Publications:* Identity and Discrimination, 1990; Vagueness, 1994; Knowledge and its Limits, 2000; articles in Jl of Phil., Phil Rev., Mind, Jl of Symbolic Logic, etc. *Recreation:* conventional behaviour. *Address:* New College, Oxford OX1 3BN. *T:* (01865) 279555.

WILLING, Maria Paula Figueiroa, (Mrs Victor Willing); *see* Rego, Paula.

WILLINK, Sir Charles (William), 2nd Bt *cr* 1957; *b* 10 Sept. 1929; *s* of Rt Hon. Sir Henry Urmston Willink, 1st Bt, MC, QC (*d* 1973), and Cynthia Frances (*d* 1959), *d* of H. Morley Fletcher, MD, FRCP; *S* father, 1973; *m* 1954, Elizabeth, *d* of Humfrey Andrewes, Highgate, London; one *s* one *d*. *Educ:* Eton College (scholar); Trinity College, Cambridge (scholar; MA, PhD). Assistant Master: Marlborough College, 1952–54; Eton College, 1954–85 (Housemaster, 1964–77). *Publications:* (ed) Euripides' Orestes, 1986; articles in Classical Quarterly. *Recreations:* bridge, field botany, music (bassoon). *Heir:* *s* Edward Daniel Willink, *b* 18 Feb. 1957. *Address:* 22 North Grove, Highgate, N6 4SL. *T:* (020) 8340 3996.

WILLIS, (George) Philip; MP (Lib Dem) Harrogate and Knaresborough, since 1997; *b* 30 Nov. 1941; *s* of George Willis and Hannah (*née* Gillespie); *m* 1974, Heather Elizabeth Sellars; one *s* one *d*. *Educ:* City of Leeds and Carnegie Coll.; Univ. of Leeds (Cert Ed 1963); Univ. of Birmingham (BPhil 1978). Asst teacher, Middleton Co. Secondary Boys' Sch., 1963–65; Head of History, Moor Grange Co. Secondary Boys' Sch., 1965–67; Sen. Master, Primrose Hill High Sch., Leeds, 1967–74; Dep. Hd, W Leeds Boys' GS, 1974–78; Head Teacher: Ormsby Sch., Cleveland, 1978–82; John Smeaton Community Sch., 1983–97. Front bench spokesman on further and higher educn, 1997–99, on educn and employment, 1999–2001, on educn and skills, 2001–. Mem., Educn and Employment Select Cttee, 1999–2001. *Recreations:* Leeds United season ticket holder, dance (ballet), current affairs, fishing. *Address:* House of Commons, SW1A 0AA. *T:* (020) 7219 5709. *Club:* National Liberal.

WILLIS, Vice-Adm. Sir (Guido) James, KBE 1981; AO 1976; Chief of Naval Staff, Australia, 1979–82, retired; *b* 18 Oct. 1923; *s* of late Dr Jack Rupert Law Willis and Théa Willis; *m* 1976, Marjorie J. Campbell-Smith, *d* of W. E. R. Rogers. *Educ:* Wesley Coll., Melbourne; Royal Australian Naval Coll. Imperial Defence Coll., 1967; Director General Operations and Plans, 1968–71; CO HMAS Melbourne, 1971–72; DDL Project Director, 1972–73; Chief of Naval Personnel, 1973–75; Chief of Naval Material, 1975–76; Asst Chief of Defence Force Staff, 1976–78; Flag Officer Commanding HMA Fleet, 1978–79. Commander 1956, Captain 1962, Rear-Adm. 1973, Vice-Adm. 1979. *Address:* 20 Wilsden Street, Walkerville, SA 5081, Australia.

WILLIS, Sir James; *see* Willis, Sir G. J.

WILLIS, Maj.-Gen. John Brooker, CB 1981; *b* 28 July 1926; *s* of late William Noel Willis and of Elaine Willis; *m* 1959, Yda Belinda Jane Firbank; two *s* two *d*. *Educ:* privately, until 1941; Redhill Technical Coll. ptsc, jssc. Enlisted in Royal Navy (Fleet Air Arm) as Trainee Pilot; basic training in USA, 1944; transf. to Indian Army, attended Armoured OTS Ahmed Nagar, 1945; commnd 1947, joined 10th Royal Hussars; attended 13 Technical Staff Course, RMCS, 1958–60; Bt Lt-Col 1965, in comd 10th Hussars Aden and BAOR; GSO1 (Armour) DS RMCS, 1968–69; Col GS MGO Secretariat, MoD, 1969–71; Dep. Comdt, RAC Centre, 1971–74; Sen. Officers' War Course, Greenwich, 1974; Dir, Projects (Fighting Vehicles), 1974–77; Dir Gen., Fighting Vehicles and Engr Equipment, 1977–81, retd. *Recreations:* golf, gardening, aviation, amateur dramatics.

WILLIS, John Edward; Managing Director, LWT and United Productions, since 2000; *b* 4 April 1946; *s* of Baron Willis and of Lady (Audrey Mary) Willis (*née* Hale); *m* 1972, Janet Ann Sperrin; one *s* one *d*. *Educ:* Eltham Coll.; Fitzwilliam Coll., Cambridge (MA); Bristol Univ. (PG Cert. in Film and TV). Yorkshire Television: journalist, 1970–75; Documentary Dir, 1975–82; Controller of Documentaries and Current Affairs, 1982–88; Channel Four Television: Controller of Factual Progs, 1988–89; Dep. Dir of Progs, 1990–92; Dir of Progs, 1993–97; Man. Dir, 1997–98, Chief Exec., 1998–2000, United (formerly United Film and Television) Productions. Member, Board: Channel 5 Broadcasting, 1998–2000; ITN, 1999–2000. Chairman: Broadcasting Support Services, 1997–; Edinburgh Internat. Television Fest., 1998–; Internat. Television Enterprises Ltd Distributors, 1999–2000; Granada Wild (formerly United Wildlife), 1999–; Cosgrove Hall Ltd, 1999–. Vis. Industrial Prof. in Television, Univ. of Bristol, 1999–; Hon. Prof., Univ. of Stirling, 1997–. Ombudsman, The Guardian, 1998–. FRTS 1993; FRSA 1997. Numerous prizes and awards. *Publications:* Johnny Go Home, 1976; Churchill's Few: the Battle of Britain remembered, 1985. *Recreations:* cycling, soccer, cinema, theatre. *Address:* London Television Centre, Upper Ground, SE1 9LT. *T:* (020) 7737 8455, *Fax:* (020) 7261 8445.

WILLIS, Air Chief Marshal Sir John (Frederick), GBE 1997 (CBE 1988); KCB 1993 (CB 1991); Vice Chief of the Defence Staff, 1995–97; *b* 27 Oct. 1937; *s* of F. A. and K. E. Willis; *m* 1959, Merrill Thewliss; three *s* two *d*. *Educ:* Dulwich Coll.; RAF Coll., Cranwell. Entered RAF, 1955; comnd, 1958; Pilot, 83/44/9/Sqdns (Vulcan), 1958–64; Flying Instr, 1964–67; Officer and Aircrew Selection Centre, 1967–69; Staff Coll., 1970; Chief Flying Instr, Vulcan OCU, Flt Comdr/Sqdn Comdr, 27 Sqdn, 1971–77; Policy Div., Air Force Dept, MoD, 1977–82; Stn Comdr, Akrotiri, Cyprus, 1982–84; Briefing Officer to CAS, 1984–85; SHAPE, 1985–88; ACDS (Policy and Nuclear), 1989–90; Dir Gen. of Trng, RAF, 1991–92; AOC-in-C, RAF Support Comd, 1992–94; COS, RAF Logistics Comd, 1994–95. FRAeS 1997. *Recreation:* making things. *Address:* c/o Lloyds TSB, Cox's and King's Branch, PO Box 1190, 7 Pall Mall, SW1Y 5NA. *Club:* Royal Air Force.

WILLIS, Prof. John Raymond, PhD; FRS 1992; FIMA; Professor of Theoretical Solid Mechanics, University of Cambridge, 1994–2000 and since 2001; *b* 27 March 1940; *s* of John V. G. and L. Gwendoline Willis; *m* 1964, Juliette Louise Ireland; three *d*. *Educ:* Imperial Coll., London (BSc, PhD). MA Cantab 1966. ARCS, DIC; FIMA 1966. Asst Lectr, Imperial Coll., 1962–64; Res. Associate, NY Univ., 1964–65; Cambridge University: Sen. Asst in Research, 1965–67; Asst Dir of Research, 1968–72; Fellow, 1966–72 and 1994–2000, Dir of Studies in Maths, 1966–72, Fitzwilliam Coll.; Bath University: Prof. of Applied Maths, 1972–94; Prof. of Maths, 2000–01. Editor-in-Chief, 1982–92, Jt Editor, 1992–, Jl Mechanics and Physics of Solids. Timoshenko Medal, ASME, 1997; Prager Medal, Soc. of Engrg Sci., 1998. *Publications:* papers on mechanics of solids in learned jls. *Recreations:* swimming, hiking, music. *Address:* Department of Applied Mathematics and Theoretical Physics, Silver Street, Cambridge CB3 9EW. *T:* (01223) 337900.

WILLIS, Norman David; General Secretary, Trades Union Congress, 1984–93; *b* 21 Jan. 1933; *s* of Victor J. M. and Kate E. Willis; *m* 1963, Maureen Kenning; one *s* one *d*. *Educ:* Ashford County Grammar Sch.; Ruskin and Oriel Colls, Oxford, 1955–59 (Hon. Fellow, Oriel Coll., 1984). Employed by TGWU, 1949; Nat. Service, 1951–53; PA to Gen. Sec., TGWU, 1959–70; Nat. Sec., Research and Educn, TGWU, 1970–74; TUC: Asst Gen. Sec., 1974–77, Dep. Gen. Sec., 1977–84. Councillor (Lab) Staines UDC, 1971–74. Member: NEDC, 1984–92; Council, ODI, 1985–93; Council, Motability, 1985–93; Employment Appeal Tribunal, 1995–; Chm., Nat. Pensioners' Convention Steering Cttee, 1979–93; Vice-President: IMS, 1985–93; ICFTU, 1984–93; WEA, 1985–93; Trades Union Adv. Cttee to OECD, 1986–93; Pres., ETUC, 1991–93 (Vice-Pres., 1984–91). Member: Exec. Bd, UNICEF, 1986–90; Council for Charitable Support, 1988–93; Trustee: Duke of Edinburgh's Commonwealth Study Conf., 1986–93; Anglo-German Foundn for the Study of Industrial Soc., 1986–95; Council, Prince of Wales Youth Business Trust, 1986–93; Patron, West Indian Welfare (UK) Trust, 1986–93. Vice-Pres., Poetry Soc.; Member: Norfolk Naturalist Trust; Wildfowl and Wetlands Trust; Nat. Trust; Spelthorne Natural History Soc.; Thames Valley Horticultural Soc.; The Arthur Ransome Soc. (Pres., 2000–); Cley Bird Club; New Chalet Club; Embroiderers' Guild; Cross Stitch Guild; Friends of Royal Sch. of Needlework; Dir and Trustee, Royal Sch. of Needlework, 1999–. Hon. Mem., Writers' Guild of GB. Fellow, RSPB. *Recreations:* painting, poetry, embroidery, birdwatching. *Address:* c/o Trades Union Congress, Congress House, Great Russell Street, WC1B 3LS.

WILLIS, Philip; *see* Willis, G. P.

WILLIS, Hon. Ralph; Chairman, C+BUS Industry Superannuation Fund, since 2000; Treasurer of Australia, Dec. 1990 and 1993–96; *b* 14 April 1938; *s* of S. Willis; *m* 1970, Carol Dawson; one *s* two *d*. *Educ:* Footscray Central Sch.; University High Sch.; Melbourne Univ. (BCom). Australian Council of Trade Unions: Research Officer, 1960–70; Industrial Advocate, 1970–72. MP (ALP) Gellibrand, Vic, 1972–98; instrumental in developing econ., finance and ind. relns policies for Opposition, 1976–83; Opposition spokesperson on: Ind. Relns, 1976–77; Econ. Affairs, 1977–83; Econ. Develt, Jan.–March 1983; Minister for Employment and Ind. Relns and Minister Assisting the Prime Minister for Public Service Matters, 1983–88; Minister for Transport and Communications, 1988–90; Minister of Finance, 1990–93. *Recreations:* tennis, reading, football. *Address:* 24 Gellibrand Street, Williamstown, Vic 3016, Australia.

WILLIS, Very Rev. Robert Andrew; Dean of Canterbury, since 2001; *b* 17 May 1947; *s* of Thomas Willis and Vera Rosina Willis (*née* Britton). *Educ:* Kingswood Grammar Sch.; Warwick Univ. (BA); Worcester Coll., Oxford (DipTheol); Cuddesdon Coll., Oxford. Ordained deacon, 1972, priest, 1973; Curate, St Chad's, Shrewsbury, 1972–75; Vicar Choral, Salisbury Cathedral and Chaplain to Cathedral Sch., 1975–78; Team Rector, Tisbury, Wilts, 1978–87; Chaplain, Cranborne Chase Sch. and RAF Chilmark, 1978–87; RD, Chalke, 1982–87; Vicar, Sherborne with Castleton and Lillington, 1987–92; Chaplain, Sherborne Sch. for Girls, 1987–92; RD, Sherborne, 1991–92; Dean of Hereford, 1992–2001; Priest-in-charge, St John the Baptist, Hereford, 1992–2001. Canon and Prebendary of Salisbury Cathedral, 1988–92; Proctor in Convocation, 1985–92, 1994–. Member: Council, Partnership for World Mission, 1990–; Cathedrals' Fabric Commn for England, 1994–; C of E Liturgical Commn, 1994–98; Chm., Deans' and Provosts' Conf., 1999–. Governor: Cranborne Chase Sch., 1985–87; Sherborne Sch., 1987–92; Chairman of Governors: Hereford Cathedral Sch., 1993–2001; King's Sch., Canterbury, 2001–. FRSA 1993. CStJ 2001 (Sub ChStJ 1991; Sub Dean, 1999). *Publications:* (contrib.) Hymns Ancient and Modern, New Standard edn, 1983; (jtly) The Chorister's Companion, 1989; (contrib.) Common Praise, 2000. *Recreations:* music, literature, travel. *Address:* The Deanery, The Precincts, Canterbury, Kent CT1 2EP. *T:* (01227) 762862, *Fax:* (01227) 865222. *Club:* Oxford and Cambridge.

WILLIS, His Honour Stephen Murrell; a Circuit Judge, 1986–95; *b* 21 June 1929; *s* of late John Henry Willis and late Eileen Marian (*née* Heard), Hadleigh, Suffolk; *m* 1st, 1953; one *s* three *d*; 2nd, 1975, Doris Florence Davies (*née* Redding); two step *d*. *Educ:* (chorister) Christ Church Cathedral, Oxford; Bloxham Sch. (scholar). Admitted solicitor, 1955; Partner: Chamberlin Talbot & Bracey, Lowestoft and Beccles, Suffolk, 1955–63; Pearless, de Rougemont & Co., East Grinstead, Sussex, 1964–85; a Recorder, 1980–85. Chm., Lord Chancellor's Adv. Cttee for SE London, 1987–95. Founded The Suffolk Singers, 1960; Founder and Director, The Prodigal Singers and Gallery Band, 1964–96. *Compositions:* mediaeval song settings for radio and theatre plays. *Recording:* (with The Prodigal Singers) Christmas Tree Carols. *Recreations:* performing early music, sailing, travel, walking. *Address:* Villa Callisto, 49 Melissovounou Avenue, Tala Paphos, 8577, Cyprus.

WILLISON, Lt-Gen. Sir David (John), KCB 1973; OBE 1958; MC 1945; Director General of Intelligence (Deputy Under-Secretary of State), Ministry of Defence, 1975–78; Chief Royal Engineer, 1977–82; *b* 25 Dec. 1919; *s* of Brig. A. C. Willison, DSO, MC; *m* 1st, 1941, Betty Vernon Bates (*d* 1989); one *s* two *d*; 2nd, 1994, Trisha Clitherow. *Educ:* Wellington; RMA Woolwich. 2/Lt RE, 1939; First Instructor, Bailey Bridge SME Ripon, 1942–43; OC 17 and 246 Field Cos, 1944–45; Staff Coll., Camberley 1945; Brigade Major, 1 Indian Inf. Brigade, Java, 1946; Malaya, 1947; WO, 1948–50; OC 16 Field Co., Egypt, 1950–52; GHQ MELF, 1952–53; OC, RE Troops, Berlin, 1953–55; Directing Staff, Staff Coll., Camberley, 1955–58; AQMG (Ops), HQ British Forces Aden, 1958–60; CO, 38 Engr Regt, 1960–63; Col GS MI/DI4, MoD, 1963–66; idc 1966; BGS (Intell.), MoD, 1967–70; BGS (Intell. and Security)/ACOS, G2, HQ NORTHAG, 1970–71; Dir of Service Intelligence, MoD, 1971–72; Dep. Chief Defence Staff (Int.), 1972–75. Col Comdt RE, 1973–82. Chm., RE Widows Soc., 1987–91. Consultant on Internat. Affairs, Nat. Westminster Bank Gp, 1980–84; Consultant: County Natwest Investment Bank, 1985–91; Pareto Partners, 1991–95. Pres., Western Area, Hants, St John's Ambulance, 1987–94; Freeman, City of London, 1981. *Recreations:* sailing, shooting, gardening, fishing. *Address:* The Old Coach House, 14 Fairfield Close, Lymington, Hants SO41 3NP. *Clubs:* Naval and Military; Royal Lymington Yacht.

WILLISON, Sir John (Alexander), Kt 1970; OBE 1964; QPM 1968; DL; *b* 3 Jan. 1914; *s* of John Willison Gow Willison and Mabel Willison, Dalry, Ayrshire; *m* 1947, Jess Morris Bruce (*d* 1996). *Educ:* Sedbergh School. Joined City of London Police, 1933; served with RNVR, 1943–46; Chief Constable: Berwick, Roxburgh and Selkirk, 1952–58; Worcestershire Constabulary, 1958–67; West Mercia Constabulary, 1967–74. DL Worcs 1968. KStJ 1973. *Address:* Ravenhills Green, Lulsley, near Worcester WR6 5QW.

WILLISON, Prof. Keith Robert, PhD; Head, Chester Beatty Laboratories, Institute of Cancer Research, since 1996; *b* 12 Oct. 1953; *s* of Dr Robin Gow Willison and Gillian Margaret Willison (*née* Caven-Irving); *m* 1979, Jennifer Anne Bardsley; two *s*. *Educ:* New College Sch., Oxford; St Edward's Sch., Oxford (Schol.); Univ. of Sussex (BSc Hons 1975); St John's Coll., Cambridge (PhD 1979). MRC Schol., MRC Lab. of Molecular Biol., Cambridge, 1975–78; Postdoctoral Fellow, Cold Spring Harbor Labs, NY, 1979–81; Res. Scientist, Inst. of Cancer Res., 1981–; Personal Chair in Molecular Cell Biol., Inst. of Cancer Res. (formerly at BPMF), Univ. of London, 1995–. Vis. Prof., Osaka Univ., 1990–91. Institute of Cancer Research: Member: Exec. Cttee, 1994–; Bd of Mgt, 1997–; Mem., Jt Res. Cttee, Royal Marsden Hosp. and Inst. Cancer Res., 2000–. *Publications:* contrib. papers to scientific jls on topics in genetics and protein biochem. *Recreations:* cricket (Mem., Presidents XI CC, Wimbledon, 1983–99), football, Japan, restaurants. *Address:* Chester Beatty Laboratories, Institute of Cancer Research, 237 Fulham Road, SW3 6JB. *T:* (020) 7352 8133.

WILLMAN, John; Banking Editor, Financial Times, since 2000; *b* 27 May 1949; *s* of late John Willman and Kate Willman (*née* Thornton); *m* 1978, Margaret Shanahan; one *s* two *d*. *Educ:* Bolton Sch.; Jesus Coll., Cambridge (MA); Westminster Coll., Oxford (CertEd). Teacher, Brentford Sch. for Girls, Brentford, Mddx, 1972–76; Financial Researcher, Money Which?, 1976–79; Editor, Taxes and Assessment (Inland Revenue Staff Fedn pubn), 1979–83; Pubns Manager, Peat, Marwick, Mitchell & Co., 1983–85; Gen. Sec., Fabian Soc., 1985–89; Jt Editor, New Socialist, 1989; Editor, Consumer Policy Review, 1990–91; Financial Times: Public Policy Editor, 1991–94; Features Editor, 1994–97; Consumer Industries Editor, 1997–2000. Visiting Research Fellow: IPPR, 1990–91; Social Market Foundn, 1997. Journalist of the Year, Financing Healthcare, Norwich Union, 1998; Financial Journalist of the Year, 2001. *Publications:* Lloyds Bank Tax Guide, annually, 1987–2000; Make Your Will, 1989; Labour's Electoral Challenge, 1989; Sorting Out Someone's Will, 1990; The Which? Guide to Planning and Conservation, 1990; Work for Yourself, 1991; A Better State of Health, 1998. *Address:* 143 Jerningham Road, SE14 5NJ. *T:* (020) 7639 3826.

WILLMAN, Prof. Paul William, DPhil; Ernest Butten Professor of Management Studies, Said Business School, University of Oxford, since 2000; Fellow, Balliol College, Oxford, since 2000; *b* 24 Aug. 1953; *s* of William and Marjorie Willman; *m* 1997, Kathleen Pickett. *Educ:* St Catharine's Coll., Cambridge (BA, MA); Trinity Coll., Oxford (DPhil 1979). Lectr in Industrial Sociol., Imperial Coll., London, 1979–83; Lectr, Sch. of Mgt, Cranfield Inst. of Technol., 1983–84; London Business School: Asst, 1984–88; Associate Prof., 1988–91; Prof. of Organisational Behaviour, 1991–2000. *Publications:* Fairness, Collective Bargaining and Incomes Policy, 1982; (jtly) Power Efficiency and Institutions, 1983; (ed jtly and contrib.) The Organisational Failures Framework and Industrial Sociology, 1983; (jtly) Innovation and Management Control, 1985; (jtly) The Car Industry: labour relations and industrial adjustment, 1985; Technological Change, Collective Bargaining and Industrial Efficiency, 1986; (jtly) The Limits to Self-Regulation, 1988; Union Business,

Trade Union Organisation and Financial Reform in the Thatcher Years, 1993; contrib. books and learned jls on industrial relations etc. *Recreations:* opera, parish churches, dogs. *Address:* Balliol College, Oxford OX1 3BJ. *T:* (01865) 277753.

WILLMER, John Franklin; QC 1967; Lloyd's Appeal Arbitrator in Salvage Cases, 1991–2000; *b* 30 May 1930; *s* of Rt Hon. Sir (Henry) Gordon Willmer, OBE, TD and Barbara, *d* of Sir Archibald Hurd; *m* 1st, 1958, Nicola Ann Dickinson (marr. diss. 1979); one *s* three *d*; 2nd, 1979, Margaret Lilian, *d* of Chester B. Berryman. *Educ:* Winchester; Corpus Christi Coll., Oxford. National Service, 2nd Lieut, Cheshire Regt, 1949–50; TA Cheshire Regt, 1950–51; Middlesex Regt, 1951–57 (Captain). Called to Bar, Inner Temple, 1955, Bencher, 1975. A Gen. Comr of Income Tax for Inner Temple, 1982. Member: panel of Lloyd's Arbitrators in Salvage Cases, 1967–91; panel from which Wreck Commissioners appointed, 1967–79, reapptd 1987–2000; Admiralty Court Cttee, 1980–95. Leader, Admiralty Bar, 1992–95. Retired from practice at Bar, 1995, from practice as Arbitrator, 2001. Freeman, Arbitrators' Co., 1992. *Recreations:* walking, visiting ancient sites and buildings, amateur dramatics. *Address:* Flat 4, 23 Lymington Road, NW6 1HZ. *T:* (020) 7435 9245. *Club:* Oxford and Cambridge.

WILLMORE, Prof. (Albert) Peter, FRAS; Professor of Space Research, University of Birmingham, 1972–97, now Emeritus; *b* 28 April 1930; *s* of Albert Mervyn Willmore and Kathleen Helen Willmore; *m* 1st, 1963, Geraldine Anne Smith; two *s*; 2nd, 1972, Stephanie Ruth Alden; one *s* one *d*. *Educ:* Holloway Sch.; University Coll. London (BSc, PhD). Research interests: fusion res., AERE, 1954–57; upper atmosphere, using sounding rockets and satellites, esp. Ariel I (launched 1962), UCL, 1957–70; X-ray astronomy, using sounding rockets and satellites, UCL, 1970–72, Univ. of Birmingham, 1972–. Academician, 1996, and Mem. Bd of Trustees, Internat. Acad. of Astronautics, 1998–. Tsiolkowski Medal, USSR, 1987. *Publications:* approx. 150 papers in learned jls, together with many other articles and reviews. *Recreations:* music, playing the violin (though this may not be music), literature, Bronze Age history, travel, sailing. *Address:* 38 Grove Avenue, Moseley, Birmingham B13 9RY. *T:* (0121) 449 2616.

WILLMOTT, Dennis James, CBE 1988; QFSM 1981; Group Contingency Manager, 1988–93, and Fire Safety Consultant, 1993–98, Avon Rubber plc; *b* 10 July 1932; *s* of James Arthur Willmott and Esther Winifred Maude Willmott (*née* Styles); *m* 1958, Mary Patricia Currey; three *s*. *Educ:* St Albans County Grammar School. MIFireE. Regular Army Service, East Surrey Regt, 1950–51, Royal Norfolk Regt, 1951–57. London, Bucks, Hants and Isle of Wight Fire Brigades, 1957–74; Dep. Chief Officer, Wilts Fire Brigade, 1974–76; Chief Staff Officer, 1976–81, Dep. Chief Officer, 1981–83, London Fire Brigade; Chief Fire Officer, Merseyside Fire Brigade, 1983–88. Member: Kennet DC, 1991– (Leader, 1999–); (C) Wilts CC, 1993–. Chm., Devizes Constituency Cons. Assoc., 1999–. *Recreation:* walking. *Address:* 27 Highlands, Potterne, Devizes, Wilts SN10 5NS. *T:* (01380) 725672; *e-mail:* djwillmott@btinternet.com. *Clubs:* Conservative (Devizes); Royal British Legion (Potterne).

WILLMOTT, Maj.-Gen. Edward George, CB 1990; OBE 1979; CEng, FICE; Chairman, Herefordshire Primary Care Trust, since 2000; *b* 18 Feb. 1936; *s* of late T. E. Willmott and E. R. Willmott (*née* Murphy); *m* 1960, Sally Penelope (*née* Banyard); two *s* one *d*. *Educ:* Gonville and Caius Coll., Cambridge (MA). FICE 1989; CEng 1990. Commissioned RE 1956; psc 1968; active service, N Borneo 1963, N Ireland 1971, 1972, 1977, comd 8 Field Sqdn, 1971–73; 23 Engr Regt, 1976; 2 Armd Div. Engr Regt, 1977–78; 30 Engr Bde, 1981–82; RCDS 1983; Dep. Comdt RMCS, 1984–85; Vice-Pres. (Army), Ordnance Bd, 1985–86; Pres., Ordnance Bd, 1986–88; Dir Gen., Weapons (Army), 1988–90. Chief Exec., CITB, 1991–98. Col Comdt, RE, 1987–97. Hon. Col 101 (London) Engr Regt (V), 1990–97. Pres., Instn of Royal Engrs, 1987–90. Warden, Engineers' Co., 2001–. Mem. Council, Roedean Sch., 1994–. MInstD 1988. *Recreation:* gardening.

WILLMOTT, Prof. John Charles, CBE 1983; PhD; Professor of Physics, University of Manchester, 1964–89 (Director of the Physical Laboratories, 1967–89; a Pro-Vice-Chancellor, 1982–85; Adviser to Vice-Chancellor on Research Exploitation, 1988–93); *b* 1 April 1922; *s* of Arthur George Willmott and Annie Elizabeth Willmott; *m* 1952, Sheila Madeleine Dumbell; two *s* one *d*. *Educ:* Bancroft's Sch., Woodford; Imperial Coll. of Science and Technol. (BSc, PhD). ARCS. Lectr in Physics, Liverpool Univ., 1948–58, Sen. Lectr, 1958–63, Reader, 1963–64. Member: SERC (formerly SRC), 1978–82; Science for Stability Cttee, NATO, 1981–97. *Publications:* Tables of Coefficients for the Analysis of Triple Angular Correlations of Gamma-rays from Aligned Nuclei, 1968; Atomic Physics, 1975; articles on nuclear structure in learned jls. *Address:* 37 Hall Moss Lane, Bramhall, Cheshire SK7 1RB. *T:* (0161) 439 4169.

WILLMOTT, Ven. Trevor; Archdeacon of Durham, since 1997; *b* 29 March 1950; *s* of Frederick and Phyllis Willmott; *m* 1973, Margaret Anne Hawkins; one *d*. *Educ:* St Peter's Coll., Oxford (MA); Fitzwilliam Coll., Cambridge (DipTh); Westcott House, Cambridge. Ordained deacon, 1974, priest, 1975; Asst Curate, St George's, Norton, 1974–78; Asst Chaplain, Oslo with Trondheim, 1978–79; Chaplain of Naples with Capri, Bari and Sorrento, 1979–83; Rector of Ecton, 1983–89; Diocesan Dir of Ordinands and Post Ordination Training, Peterborough, 1986–97; Canon Residentiary of Peterborough Cathedral, 1989–97. *Recreations:* travel, cooking, the appreciation of good wine, sport, music. *Address:* 15 The College, Durham DH1 3EQ. *T:* (0191) 384 7534.

WILLOTT, Brian; *see* Willott, W. B.

WILLOTT, (William) Brian, CB 1996; PhD; Chief Executive, Welsh Development Agency, 1997–2000; *b* 14 May 1940; *s* of late Dr William Harford Willott and Dr Beryl P. M. Willott; *m* 1970, Alison Leyland Pyke-Lees; two *s* two *d*. *Educ:* Trinity Coll., Cambridge (MA, PhD). Research Associate, Univ. of Maryland, USA, 1965–67; Asst Principal, Board of Trade, 1967–69; Principal: BoT, 1969–73; HM Treasury, 1973–75; Asst Sec., Dept of Industry, 1975–78; Secretary: Industrial Development Unit, DoI, 1978–80; NEB, 1980–81; Chief Exec., British Technology Gp (NEB and NRDC), 1981–84; Head of IT Div., DTI, 1984–87; Hd of Financial Services Div., DTI, 1987–92; Chief Exec., ECGD, 1992–97. Mem. Council, Nat. Museums and Galls of Wales, 2001–. Vis. Prof., Univ. of Glamorgan, 2000–. *Recreations:* music, reading, gardening. *Address:* Coed Cefn, Tregare, Monmouth NP25 4DT.

WILLOUGHBY, family name of **Baron Middleton**.

WILLOUGHBY DE BROKE, 21st Baron *cr* 1491; **Leopold David Verney;** DL; *b* 14 Sept. 1938; *s* of 20th Baron Willoughby de Broke, MC, AFC, AE and Rachel (*d* 1991), *d* of Sir Bourchier Wrey, 11th Bt; *S* father, 1986; *m* 1965, Petra (marr. diss. 1989), 2nd *d* of Sir John Aird, 3rd Bt, MVO, MC; three *s*. *Educ:* Le Rosey; New College, Oxford. Chairman: S. M. Theatre Co. Ltd, 1992–; Compton Verney Opera and Ballet Project, 1992–; St Martins Magazines plc, 1992–. Pres., Heart of England Tourist Bd, 1996–; Patron, Warwicks Assoc. of Boys' Clubs, 1991–. Mem. Council, Anglo-Hong Kong Trust, 1989–. Mem., H of L Select Cttee on EC, 1996–; elected Mem., H of L, 1999. DL Warwickshire, 1999. *Heir:* *s* Hon. Rupert Greville Verney, *b* 4 March 1966. *Address:* Ditchford Farm, Moreton-in-Marsh, Glos GL56 9RD.

WILLOUGHBY DE ERESBY, Baroness (27th in line), *cr* 1313; **Nancy Jane Marie Heathcote-Drummond-Willoughby;** DL; *b* 1 Dec. 1934; *d* of 3rd Earl of Ancaster, KCVO, TD, and Hon. Nancy Phyllis Louise Astor (*d* 1975), *d* of 2nd Viscount Astor; *S* to Barony of father, 1983. Trustee, Nat. Portrait Gall., 1994–. Mem. (Ind.), South Kesteven DC, 1969–82. DL Lincs, 1993. DStJ 2000. *Heir:* *co-heiresses:* Eloise Carola Philippi [*b* 26 Oct. 1938; *m* 1st, 1961, George Fillmore Miller III; one *s*; 2nd, 1974, Robert E. J. Philippi; one *s*]; Lady Priscilla Aird [*b* 29 Oct. 1909; *m* 1939, Col Sir John Renton Aird, 3rd Bt, MVO, MC; one *s* three *d*]. *Address:* Grimsthorpe, Bourne, Lincs PE10 0LZ.

WILLOUGHBY, Kenneth James; *b* 6 Nov. 1922; *y s* of late Frank Albert Willoughby and late Florence Rose (*née* Darbyshire); *m* 1943, Vera May Dickerson; one *s* one *d*. *Educ:* Hackney Downs (Grocers') Sch.; Selwyn Coll., Cambridge. Tax Officer, Inland Revenue, 1939; Royal Engineers, UK, Egypt, Italy, Austria, Greece, 1941–47 (despatches, Captain); Asst Auditor, Exchequer and Audit Dept, 1947; Asst Prin., Min. of Civil Aviation, 1949; Asst Private Sec. to Minister of Civil Aviation, 1950; Private Sec. to Perm. Sec., 1951; Principal, Min. of Transport (and later, Civil Aviation), 1951; Sec., Air Transport Adv. Council, 1957–61; Asst Sec., Min. of Aviation, 1962; Under-Secretary: Min. of Technology, 1968–70; DTI, 1970–74. *Recreations:* music, reading. *Address:* 84 Douglas Avenue, Exmouth, Devon EX8 2HG. *T:* (01395) 271175.

WILLOUGHBY, Rt Rev. Noel Vincent; Bishop of Cashel and Ossory, 1980–97; *b* 15 Dec. 1926; *s* of George and Mary Jane Willoughby; *m* 1959, Valerie Moore, Dungannon, Tyrone; two *s* one *d*. *Educ:* Tate School, Wexford; Trinity Coll., Dublin (Scholar, Moderator and Gold Medallist in Philosophy). Deacon 1950, priest 1951, Armagh Cathedral; Curate: Drumglass Parish, 1950–53; St Catherine's, Dublin, 1953–55; Bray Parish, 1955–59; Rector: Delgany Parish, 1959–69; Glenageary Parish, 1969–80; Hon. Sec., General Synod, 1976–80; Treasurer, St Patrick's Cathedral, Dublin, 1976–80; Archdeacon of Dublin, 1979–80. *Recreations:* gardening, golf, tennis, fishing. *Address:* Dromingle, Belmont, Newtown, Wexford, Ireland. *T:* (53) 20008.

WILLOUGHBY, Roger James; Registrar of Members' Interests, House of Commons, 1994–2000; *b* 30 Sept. 1939; *s* of late Hugh Lloyd Willoughby and Gerd Willoughby; *m* 1970, Veronica, *d* of Frank and Elisabeth Lepper. *Educ:* Shrewsbury Sch.; Balliol Coll., Oxford (BA). A Clerk in the House of Commons, 1962–2000: Dep. Principal Clerk, 1975; Sec. to UK Delegn to European Parlt, 1976; Clerk of Home Affairs Cttee, 1979; Clerk of Supply, Public Bill Office, 1984; Clerk of Private Bills, H of C, 1988–97. *Recreations:* literature, cricket, walking in solitary places, bonfires. *Address:* 35 Defoe Avenue, Kew, Richmond, Surrey TW9 4DS. *T:* (020) 8876 1718.

WILLS, family name of **Baron Dulverton**.

WILLS, Arthur William, OBE 1990; DMus (Dunelm), FRCO (CHM), ADCM; composer; Organist, Ely Cathedral, 1958–90; *b* 19 Sept. 1926; *s* of Violet Elizabeth and Archibald Wills; *m* 1953, Mary Elizabeth Titterton; one *s* one *d*. *Educ:* St John's Sch., Coventry. Sub. Organist, Ely Cathedral, 1949; Director of Music, King's School, Ely, 1953–65; Prof., Royal Academy of Music, 1964–92. Mem. Council, RCO, 1966–95; Examr to Royal Schs of Music, 1966–. Recital tours in Canada, Europe, USA, Australia and New Zealand; recording artist. Hon. RAM, Hon. FLCM, FRSCM. *Publications:* (contrib.) English Church Music, 1978; Organ, 1984, 2nd edn 1993; numerous musical compositions include: *organ:* Sonata, Trio Sonata, Christmas Meditations, Prelude and Fugue (Alkmaar), Tongues of Fire, Variations on Amazing Grace, Symphonia Eliensis, Concerto (organ, strings and timpani), The Fenlands (symphonic suite for brass band and organ), Etheldreda Rag (organ or piano); Wondrous Machine! A Young Person's Guide to the Organ; *brass band:* Overture: A Muse of Fire; *guitar:* Sonata, Pavane and Galliard, Hommage à Ravel, Four Elizabethan Love Songs (alto and guitar), Moods and Diversions, The Year of the Tiger, Suite Africana, Concerto Lirico for Guitar Quartet; Concerto for guitar and organ; *chamber:* Sacrae Symphoniae: Veni Creator Spiritus; A Toccata of Galuppi's (counter-tenor and string quartet); *piano:* Sonata; *choral:* Missa Eliensis, The Child for Today (carol sequence), The Light Invisible (double choir, organ and percussion), Missa in Memoriam Benjamin Britten, An English Requiem, Jerusalem Luminosa (choir and organ), Ely (part-song for treble voices), Caedmon: a children's cantata, The Gods of Music (choral concerto); *vocal:* When the Spirit Comes (four poems of Emily Brontë), The Dark Lady (eight Shakespeare Sonnets); Eternity's Sunrise (three poems of William Blake); *opera:* '1984'; *orchestra:* Symphony No 1 in A minor. *Recreations:* travel, antique collecting, Eastern philosophy. *Address:* Paradise House, 26 New Barns Road, Ely, Cambs CB7 4PN. *T:* (01353) 662084; *e-mail:* artwill@argonet.co.uk.

WILLS, Brian Alan, PhD; FRPharmS, CChem, FRSC; Chief Pharmacist, Department of Health (formerly of Health and Social Security), 1978–89, retired; *b* 17 Feb. 1927; *s* of late William Wills and Emily (*née* Hibbert); *m* 1955, Barbara Joan Oggelsby; one *d*. *Educ:* Univ. of Nottingham (BPharm); PhD London 1955; MA Leeds 1997. FRPharmS (MPS 1949; FPS 1972); FRSC (ARIC 1957; FRIC 1967); CChem 1975. Lecturer in Pharmaceutics, Sch. of Pharmacy, Univ. of London, 1951–57; Head of Research and Control Dept, Allen & Hanburys (Africa) Ltd, Durban, S Africa, 1957–62; Head of Control Div., Allen & Hanburys Ltd, London, E2, 1962–78. Member: British Pharmacopoeia Commn, 1973–94; UK delegn to European Pharmacopoeia Commn, 1975–94; UK delegn to Council of Europe Public Health Cttee (Partial Agreement) on Pharmaceutical Questions, 1979–89; WHO Expert Adv. Panel on Internat. Pharmacopoeia and Pharmaceutical Preparations, 1979–89. Vis. Professor: Univ. of Bath, 1979–83; Univ. of Bradford, 1984–. Member: Jt Formulary Cttee for British Nat. Formulary, 1979–89; Pharmacy Working Party, Nat. Adv. Body for Local Authy Higher Educn, 1982–89; Bd of Studies in Pharmacy, London Univ., 1979–87; Council, Sch. of Pharmacy, London Univ., 1981–89. Hon. Auditor, RPSGB, 1990–. Mem. Ct of Assts, Soc. of Apothecaries of London, 1987–98, Emeritus Asst, 1998–. *Publications:* papers on sterilisation and disinfection and on the preservation, stability and quality control of pharmaceutical preparations. *Address:* Arnisdale, Barrack Road, Comrie, Perthshire PH6 2EQ. *T:* (01764) 679910.

WILLS, Sir David James Vernon, 5th Bt *cr* 1923 of Blagdon, co. Somerset; *b* 2 Jan. 1955; *s* of Sir John Vernon Wills, 4th Bt, KCVO, TD and of Diana Veronica Cecil, (Jane), (*née* Baker); *S* father, 1998; *m* 1999, Mrs Paula Burke. *Heir:* *b* Anthony John Vernon Wills [*b* 10 Dec. 1956; *m* 1983, Katherine Wilks]. *Address:* Vale Cottage, Blagdon, Bristol BS40 7RQ.

WILLS, Sir (David) Seton, 5th Bt *cr* 1904, of Hazelwood and Clapton-in-Gordano; FRICS; *b* 29 Dec. 1939; *s* of Major George Seton Wills (*d* 1979) (*yr s* of 3rd Bt) and Lilah Mary, *y d* of Captain Percy Richard Hare; *S* uncle, 1983; *m* 1968, Gillian, twin *d* of A. P. Eastoe; one *s* three *d*. *Educ:* Eton. FRICS 1976. *Heir:* *s* James Seton Wills, *b* 24 Nov. 1970. *Address:* Eastridge House, Ramsbury, Marlborough, Wilts SN8 2HJ.

WILLS, Dean Robert, AO 1994 (AM 1986); Chairman, National Mutual Holdings Ltd, 1997–2000 (Deputy Chairman, 1995–97); *b* 10 July 1933; *s* of Walter William Wills and Violet Wills (*née* Kent); *m* 1955, Margaret Florence Williams, *d* of E. G. Williams; one *s* two *d*. *Educ:* Sacred Heart Coll., S. Aust.; SA Inst. of Technology. AASA. Dir, 1974, Man. Dir, 1977–83, Chm., 1983–86, W. D. & H. O. Wills (Australia) Ltd; Amatil Ltd, later Coca-Cola Amatil Ltd: Dir, 1975–99; Dep. Chm., 1983–84; Man. Dir, 1984–94; Chm., 1984–99; Chm., Australian Eagle Insurance Co., 1986–89. Chairman: Nat. Mutual Life Assoc., 1997–2000 (Dir, 1991; Vice Chm., 1992–97); Transfield Services Ltd, 2001–; Director: Australian Grand Prix Corp., 1994– (Dep. Chm., 1994–); Westfield Hldgs/ Westfield America Trust,1994–; John Fairfax Hldgs, 1994–. Member: Business Council of Aust., 1984–94 (Vice Pres., 1987–88, Pres., 1988–90); Bd of Aust. Graduate Sch. of Management, Univ. of NSW, 1985–. Pres., 1991, Gov., 1992–94, Med. Foundn; Trustee, Mus. of Applied Arts and Sciences (Powerhouse Mus.), NSW, 1986–90. *Recreations:* tennis, exotic cars. *Address:* 71 Macquarie Street, Sydney, NSW 2001, Australia.

WILLS, Michael David; MP (Lab) Swindon North, since 1997; Parliamentary Secretary, Lord Chancellor's Department, since 2001; *b* 20 May 1952; *s* of Stephen Wills and Elizabeth Wills (*née* McKeown); *m* 1984, Jill Freeman; three *s* two *d*. *Educ:* Haberdasher's Aske's Sch., Elstree; Clare Coll., Cambridge (BA 1st cl. Hons Hist.). HM Diplomatic Service, 1976–80; Researcher, 1980–82, Producer, 1982–84, LWT; Dir, Juniper Productions, 1985–97. Parliamentary Under-Secretary of State: DTI, 1999; DFEE, 1999–2001. *Address:* House of Commons, SW1A 0AA. *T:* (020) 7219 3000.

WILLS, Nicholas Kenneth Spencer, FCA; international consultant and company director; *b* 18 May 1941; *s* of Sir John Spencer Wills, and Elizabeth Drusilla Alice Clare Garcke; *m* 1st, 1973, Hilary Ann (marr. diss. 1983); two *s* two *d*; 2nd, 1985, Philippa Trench Casson, *d* of Rev. D. Casson; one *d*. *Educ:* Rugby Sch.; Queens' Coll., Cambridge (MA; Hon. Fellow, 1990). Binder Hamlyn & Co., 1963–67; Morgan Grenfell, 1967–70; BET plc, 1970–92 (Director, 1975–92; Man. Dir, 1982–91; Chief Exec., 1985–91; Chm., 1991–92). Managing Director: Birmingham & Dist Investment Trust, 1970–91; Electrical & Industrial Investment, 1970–91; National Electric Construction, 1971–91; Chairman: Argus Press Hldgs, 1974–83; Electrical Press, 1974–83; Boulton & Paul plc, 1979–84; Initial plc, 1979–87; BET Building Services Ltd, 1984–87; Dep. Chm., Nat. Mutual Home Loans, 1994–96; Director: Bradbury, Agnew & Co. Ltd, 1974–83; National Mutual Life Assce Soc., 1974–85, 1991– (Dep. Chm., 1992–99; Chm., 1999–); St George Assce Co. Ltd, 1974–81; Colonial Securities Trust Co. Ltd, 1976–82; Cable Trust Ltd, 1976–77; Globe Investment Trust plc, 1977–90; Drayton Consolidated, 1982–92; Tribune (formerly Barings Tribune) Investment Trust, 1992–; Hitchin Priory Ltd, 1992– (Dep. Chm., 1994–99; Chm., 1999–); Onslow Trading and Commercial, 1994–99; Manchester Trading and Commercial, 1995–2000; Toye & Co., 1996–; SMC Gp plc, 1999–; American Chamber of Commerce (UK), 1985–2000 (Vice-Pres., 1988–2000; Mem., Transatlantic Council, British Amer. Business Inc.; United World Colls (Internat.) Ltd, 1987–95; IQ-Ludorum plc, 2000–; Solid Terrain Modeling Inc., 2000–; Advr, City and West End, National Westminster Bank, 1982–91; Adv. Bd, Charterhouse Buy-Out Funds, 1990–98. Member: Council, CBI, 1987–92 (Member: Overseas Cttee, 1987–90; Public Expenditure Task Force, 1988; Economic Affairs Cttee, 1991–96); Council, Business in the Community, 1987–92; Advisory Board: Fishman-Davidson Center for Study of Service Sector, Wharton Sch., Univ. of Pennsylvania, 1988–92; Centre of Internat. Studies, Cambridge Univ., 1999– (Hon. Fellow, 2000). Mem. Adv. Council, Prince's Youth Business Trust, 1988– (Hon. Treas., 1989–92; Mem., Investment Cttee, 1992–98); Chm., Internat. Trustees, Internat. Fedn of Keystone Youth Orgns, 1990–. Chm., Involvement & Participation Assoc., 1991–96. Chm., Mgt Cttee, Cambridge Rev. of Internat. Affairs, 1998–. Treasurer and Churchwarden, Church of St Bride, Fleet Street, 1978–2001; Asst, Co. of Haberdashers, 1981– (Master, 1997–98); Gov., Haberdashers' Aske's Schs, Elstree, 1989–98 (Chm., Girls' Sch. Cttee, 1994–97). Hon. Mem., Clan McEwan. CIMgt; FCIM; FCT; FRSA. *Recreations:* ski-ing on blue runs, extremely bad tennis, shooting, trying to farm in the Highlands. *Address:* 33 Davies Street, W1K 4LR. *T:* (020) 7495 8919. *Clubs:* White's, Royal Automobile, City Livery; Clyde Cruising; Beaver Creek (Colorado, USA).

WILLS, Peter Gordon Bethune, TD 1967; Director: Hambro Clearing Ltd (formerly Sheppards and Chase Options Ltd), 1977–93 (Chairman, 1977–92); BCW Stock Lending Consultants Ltd, 1992–93; *b* 25 Oct. 1931; *s* of P. L. B. Wills and E. W. Wills (*née* Stapleton); *m* 1st, Linda Hutton; two *s* one *d*; 2nd, Gloria Hart; 3rd, Faith Hines. *Educ:* Malvern Coll.; Corpus Christi Coll., Cambridge, 1952–55 (MA). National Service with Royal Inniskilling Fusiliers, N Ireland and Korea, 1950–52; TA, London Irish Rifles, 1952–67. Joined Sheppards & Co. (later Sheppards and Chase), 1955, Partner, 1960–85; Chairman, Sheppards Moneybrokers Ltd, 1985–89. Member, Stock Exchange Council, 1973–87 (Dep. Chm., 1979–82; Chm., Money Brokers' Cttee, 1985–89). Director: Wills Group plc, 1969–87 (Vice Chm.); LIFFE, 1982; BAII Holding, 1986–89; The Securities Assoc., 1986–89 (Chm., Membership Cttee); London Clear, 1986–89; The Securities Inst., 1992–93 (Chm., Membership Cttee; Fellow, 1993). Specialist Advr to Social Security Cttee, H of C, 1993. *Address:* 2 Wellswood Park, Torquay TQ1 2QB.

WILLS, Sir Seton; *see* Wills, Sir D. S.

WILLSON, Prof. (Francis Michael) Glenn; Vice-Chancellor, 1978–84, Emeritus Professor, since 1985, Murdoch University, Western Australia; *b* 29 Sept. 1924; *s* of late Christopher Glenn Willson and late Elsie Katrine (*née* Mattick); *m* 1945, Jean (*née* Carlyle); two *d*. *Educ:* Carlisle Grammar Sch.; Manchester Univ. (BA Admin); Balliol and Nuffield Colls, Oxford (DPhil, MA). Merchant Navy, 1941–42; RAF, 1943–46; BOAC 1946–47. Research Officer, Royal Inst. of Public Admin, 1953–60; Res. Fellow, Nuffield Coll., Oxford, 1955–60; Lectr in Politics, St Edmund Hall, Oxford, 1958–60; Prof. of Govt, UC Rhodesia and Nyasaland, 1960–64; Dean, Faculty of Social Studies, UC Rhodesia and Nyasaland, 1962–64; University of California, Santa Cruz: Prof. of Govt/Politics, 1965–74; Provost of Stevenson Coll., 1967–74; Vice-Chancellor, College and Student Affairs, 1973–74; Vis. Prof., 1985–92; Warden, Goldsmiths' Coll., London, 1974–75; Principal of Univ. of London, 1975–78. *Publications:* (with D.N. Chester) The Organization of British Central Government 1914–56, 2nd edn 1914–64, 1968; Administrators in Action, 1961; A Strong Supporting Cast: the Shaw Lefevres 1789–1936, 1993; Our Minerva: the men and politics of the University of London 1836–1858, 1995; In Just Order Move: the progress of the Laban Centre for Movement and Dance, 1997; contrib. Public Admin, Polit. Studies, Parly Affairs, etc. *Address:* 32 Digby Mansions, Hammersmith Bridge Road, W6 9DF.

WILLSON, John Michael, CMG 1988; HM Diplomatic Service, retired; High Commissioner in Zambia, 1988–90; *b* 15 July 1931; *e s* of late Richard and Kathleen Willson; *m* 1954, Phyllis Marian Dawn, *o c* of late William and Phyllis Holman Richards, OBE; two *s* two *d*. *Educ:* Wimbledon Coll.; University Coll., Oxford (MA); Trinity Hall, Cambridge. National Service, 1949–51. HM Colonial Service, N Rhodesia, 1955–64; Min. of Overseas Development, 1965–70 (seconded to British High Commn, Malta, 1967–70); joined HM Diplomatic Service, 1970; British Consulate-General, Johannesburg, 1972–75; FCO (W Indian and N American Depts), 1975–78; Special Counsellor for African Affairs, 1978; Secretary-General, Rhodesian Independence Conf., 1979; Salisbury (on staff of Governor of Rhodesia), 1979–80; Counsellor, Bucharest, 1980–82; Ambassador to Ivory Coast, Burkina (formerly Upper Volta) and Niger, 1983–87; seconded to RCDS, 1987. *Recreations:* gardening, photography, music. *Address:* c/o C. Hoare & Co., 37 Fleet Street, EC4P 4DQ. *Club:* Royal Commonwealth Society.

WILMERS, Mary-Kay; Editor, London Review of Books, since 1992; *b* 19 July 1938; *d* of Charles Wilmers and Cesia (*née* Eitingon); *m* 1968, Stephen Frears, *qv* (marr. diss. 1975); two *s*. *Educ:* Athénée Royal d'Uccle, Brussels; Badminton Sch., Bristol; St Hugh's Coll., Oxford (BA). Editor, Faber & Faber, 1961–68; Dep. Ed., The Listener, 1968–73; Fiction Ed., TLS, 1974–79; Dep. Ed., then Co-Ed., London Rev. of Books, 1979–92. *Recreation:* thinking about writing a book. *Address:* c/o London Review of Books, 28 Little Russell Street, WC1A 2HN. *T:* (020) 7209 1101.

WILMOT, David, QPM 1989; DL; Chief Constable, Greater Manchester Police, since 1991; *b* 12 March 1943; *m* Ann Marilyn (*née* Doyle). *Educ:* Southampton Univ. (BSc). Lancashire Constabulary, 1962; Merseyside Police, 1974; W Yorkshire Police, 1983; Deputy Chief Constable, Greater Manchester Police, 1987. DL Greater Manchester, 1996. Hon. DSc Salford, 2000. *Address:* Greater Manchester Police, PO Box 22 (S West PDO), Chester House, Boyer Street, Manchester M16 0RE. *T:* (0161) 872 5050.

WILMOT, Sir Henry Robert, 9th Bt *cr* 1759; *b* 10 April 1967; *s* of Sir Robert Arthur Wilmot, 8th Bt, and of Juliet Elvira, *e d* of Captain M. N. Tufnell, RN; *S* father, 1974; *m* 1995, Susan Clare, *er d* of John Malvern, *qv*; one *s*. Mem., TGWU. *Heir: s* Oliver Charles Wilmot, *b* 12 July 1999. *Address:* Beck House, Great Broughton, N Yorks.

WILMOT, Sir Michael John Assheton E.; *see* Eardley-Wilmot.

WILMOT, Robert William, (Robb Wilmot), CBE 1985; Founder and Chairman: Wilmot Consulting Inc., since 1994; WAM Communications Inc., since 1994; Poqet Computer Inc., since 1987; Voicewaves Inc., since 1993; *b* 2 Jan. 1945; *s* of Thomas Arthur William Wilmot and Frances Mary Hull; *m* 1969, Mary Josephine Sharkey; two *s*. *Educ:* Royal Grammar Sch., Worcester; Nottingham Univ. (BSc (1st cl. Hons) Electrical Engrg). Texas Instruments, 1966–81: European Technical Dir, France, 1973–74; Div. Dir, USA, 1974–78; Man. Dir, 1978–81; Asst Vice Pres., 1980; International Computers (ICL): Man. Dir, 1981–83; Chief Exec., 1983–84; Chm., 1985. Chairman: Virtual Vineyards Inc., 1995–; Euroventures BV, 1993–; Founder Dir, Movid Technology Inc., 1986–; Director: Sequent Inc., 1990–; Com 21 Inc., 1995–; First Virtual Communications, 1998–. Hon. DSc: Nottingham, 1983; City, 1984; Cranfield, 1988. *Recreations:* music, theatre, walking, vintage boats.

WILMOT-SITWELL, Peter Sacheverell; Joint Chairman, 1986–90, Chairman, 1990–94, Consultant, 1995–98, S. G. Warburg (formerly S. G. Warburg, Akroyd, Rowe & Pitman, Mullens) Securities Ltd; *b* 28 March 1935; *s* of late Robert Bradshaw Wilmot-Sitwell and Barbara Elizabeth Fisher; *m* 1960, Clare Veronica Cobbold (LVO 1991); two *s* one *d*. *Educ:* Eton Coll.; Oxford Univ., 1955–58 (BA, MA). Commnd Coldstream Guards, 1953–55. Trainee, Hambros Bank Ltd, 1958–59; Partner 1959–82, Sen. Partner 1982–86, Rowe & Pitman; Vice-Chm., S. G. Warburg Gp, 1987–94. Chm., Mercury World Mining Trust, 1993–; non-executive Director: W. H. Smith Ltd, 1987–96; Stock Exchange Bd, 1991–94; Minorco, 1993–99; Foreign & Colonial Income Growth Investment Trust, 1994–; Close Bros, 1995–; Southern Africa Investors, 1996–98; Anglo American plc, 1999–. *Recreations:* shooting, golf, tennis. *Address:* Portman House, Dummer, near Basingstoke, Hants RG25 2AD. *Clubs:* White's; Swinley Forest (Ascot).

WILMOT-SMITH, Richard James Crosbie; QC 1994; a Recorder, since 2000; *b* 12 May 1952; *s* of late John Patrick Wilmot-Smith and of Rosalys Wilmot-Smith (*née* Massy); *m* 1978, Jenny, *d* of late R. W. Castle and L. M. Castle; one *s* two *d*. *Educ:* Charterhouse; Univ. of N Carolina (Morehead Schol.; AB 1975). Called to the Bar, Middle Temple, 1978 (Benefactors Law Schol.). Trustee, Free Representation Unit, 1997–. *Publications:* Encyclopedia of Forms and Precedents, 5th edn: (contrib. and ed) Vol. 5, Building and Engineering Contracts, 1986; (contrib.) Vol. 12, Contracts for Services, 1994; (ed jtly) Human Rights in the United Kingdom, 1996. *Recreations:* music, theatre, cinema, cricket. *Address:* 39 Essex Street, WC2R 3AT. *T:* (020) 7832 1111. *Club:* Kent CC.

WILMOTT, Peter Graham, CMG 1996; consultant on European and governmental affairs, since 1996; Président, Office de Développement par l'Automatisation et la Simplification du Commerce Extérieur, Paris, since 2000; *b* 6 Jan. 1947; *s* of John Joseph Wilmott and Violet Ena Wilmott; *m* 1969, Jennifer Carolyn Plummer; two *d*. *Educ:* Hove Grammar Sch.; Trinity Coll., Cambridge (MA). Asst Principal, Customs and Excise, 1968; Second Sec., UK Delegn to EEC, Brussels, 1971; Principal, Customs and Excise, 1973; First Sec., UK Perm. Rep's Office to EEC, Brussels, 1977; Asst to UK Mem., European Ct of Auditors, Luxembourg, 1980; Asst Sec., Customs and Excise, 1983; a Comr of Customs and Excise, 1988; Dir-Gen. (Customs and Indirect Taxation), Commn of the EC, 1990–96; Partner, Prisma Consulting Gp SA, 1996–2000. Dir, Ad Valorem Internat. Ltd, 2000–. Chm., Internat. VAT Assoc., 1998–2000. *Recreations:* travelling, building and mending things. *Address:* 31 Wilbury Avenue, Hove, East Sussex BN3 6HS.

WILMSHURST, Elizabeth Susan, CMG 1999; HM Diplomatic Service; Deputy Legal Adviser, Foreign and Commonwealth Office, since 1999; *b* 28 Aug. 1948; *d* of Owen David Wilmshurst and Constance Hope Wilmshurst (*née* Brand). *Educ:* Clarendon Sch., N Wales; King's Coll., London (LLB 1969, AKC 1969). Admitted Solicitor, 1972. Asst Lectr, Bristol Univ., 1973–74; joined FCO, 1974; Asst Legal Advr, FCO, 1974–86; Legal Counsellor: Attorney-Gen.'s Chambers, 1986–91; FCO, 1991–94, 1997–99; Legal Advr, UKMIS to UN, NY, 1994–97. *Address:* c/o Foreign and Commonwealth Office, King Charles Street, SW1A 2AH.

WILMSHURST, Jon Barry; Under Secretary, Economic and Social Division, and Chief Economist, Overseas Development Administration, 1990–96; *b* 25 Oct. 1936; *s* of Edwin and Sylvia Wilmshurst (*née* Munson); *m* 1960, June Taylor; four *d*. *Educ:* Beckenham and Penge Grammar Sch.; Manchester Univ. (BA Econ.). Statistician, Fedn of Rhodesia and Nyasaland, 1960–63; Inst. of Economic and Social Research, 1964; Statistician and Economic Adviser, ODA, 1964–71; Senior Economic Adviser: ODA, 1971–79; Dept of Transport, 1979–83; Monopolies and Mergers Commn, 1983–85; ODA, 1985–90. *Recreations:* golf, gardening. *Address:* 58 Wickham Way, Beckenham, Kent BR3 3AF. *Club:* Langley Park Golf.

WILMSHURST, Michael Joseph; HM Diplomatic Service, retired; *b* 14 Sept. 1934; *s* of Mr and Mrs E. J. Wilmshurst; *m* 1958, Mary Elizabeth Kemp; one *s* one *d*. *Educ:* Latymer Upper Sch.; Christ's Coll., Cambridge. BA 1959. Entered Foreign Service, 1953. 2nd Lieut, Royal Signals, 1953–55. Asst Private Sec. to Foreign Secretary, 1960–62; 2nd Sec., The Hague, 1962–65; 1st Sec. (Commercial), Bogota, 1965–67; Western European Dept, FCO, 1968–70; 1st Sec. (Commercial), Cairo, 1970–73; Asst Head of Energy Dept, FCO, 1974–75; Asst Head of Energy and Arms Control and Disarmament Depts, 1975–77;

Counsellor and Head of Joint Nuclear Unit, FCO, 1977–78; Consul, Guatemala City, 1978–81; Sabbatical, Stiftung Wissenschaft und Politik, Ebenhausen, 1982; UK Permanent Rep. to IAEA, UNIDO and UN, Vienna, 1982–87; seconded to IAEA, Vienna as Dir of External Relns, 1987; retd from HM Diplomatic Service, 1989, from IAEA, 1991. *Publications:* Nuclear Non-Proliferation: can the policies of the Eighties prove more successful than those of the Seventies?, 1982; (contrib.) The International Nuclear Non-Proliferation System: challenges and choices, 1984. *Recreations:* reading, bird-watching. *Address:* 7 East Street, Southwold, Suffolk IP18 6EH.

WILMUT, Ian, OBE 1999; PhD; Head of Department of Gene Expression and Development, BBSRC Roslin Institute, since 2000 (Principal Investigator, 1981–2000); *b* 7 July 1944; *s* of Leonard (Jack) and Eileen Mary Wilmut; *m* 1967, Vivienne Mary Craven; two *d*, one adopted *s*. *Educ:* Nottingham Univ. (BSc 1967); Darwin Coll., Cambridge (PhD 1971). Post-doctoral Fellow, Unit of Reproductive Physiol. and Biochem., Cambridge, 1971–73; res. posts at Animal Breeding Res. Orgn, ARC, now BBSRC Roslin Inst., 1973–. Hon. Prof., Edinburgh Univ., 1998–. Hon. DSc Nottingham, 1998. FRSE 2000. *Publications:* (jtly) The Second Creation, 2000; contrib. papers to Nature and Science on cloning of Dolly the sheep, first animal produced from an adult cell, using procedure developed at Roslin Inst. and use of this procedure to introduce genetic changes in sheep. *Recreations:* walking in countryside, photography, music, curling, gardening. *Address:* Roslin Institute, Roslin, Midlothian EH25 9PS. *T:* (0131) 527 4219.

WILSEY, Gen. Sir John (Finlay Willasey), GCB 1996 (KCB 1991); CBE 1985 (OBE 1982); DL; Chairman, Western Provident Association, since 1996; *b* 18 Feb. 1939; *s* of Maj.-Gen. John Harold Owen Wilsey, CB, CBE, DSO and of Beatrice Sarah Finlay Wilsey; *m* 1975, Elizabeth Patricia Nottingham; one *s* one *d*. *Educ:* Sherborne Sch.; RMA Sandhurst. Commissioned, Devonshire and Dorset Regt, 1959; regtl service in Cyprus, Libya, British Guyana, Germany, Malta, UK; Instructor, RMA, 1967–68; Great Abbai (Blue Nile) Expedition, 1968; Staff Coll., 1973, Defence Policy Staff, MoD, 1974–75; Co. Comdr, 1976–77, BAOR and NI (despatches 1976); Directing Staff, Staff Coll., 1978–79; Comd 1st Bn Devonshire and Dorset Regt, 1979–82 (despatches 1981); COS, HQ NI, 1982–84; Comdr 1st Inf. Brigade, 1984–86; RCDS 1987; COS, HQ UKLF, 1988–90; GOC NI, 1990–93; C-in-C, UK Land Forces then Land Comd, 1993–96; Jt Comdr, British Forces in Former Republic of Yugoslavia, 1993–96; ADC Gen. to the Queen, 1994–96. Col, Devonshire and Dorset Regt, 1990–97; Col Comdt, POW Div., 1991–94. Hon. Col, Royal Jersey Militia Sqdn, RE, 1993–. Mem., Commonwealth War Graves Commn, 1998– (Vice Chm., 2001–). President: Army Winter Sports Assoc., 1993–97; Army Catering Corps Assoc., 1996–. Governor: Sherborne Sch., 1994–2001 (Vice-Chm., 1996–); Sherborne Sch. for Girls, 1996–2001; Sutton's Hosp., Charterhouse, 1996–2001; Comr, Royal Hosp. Chelsea, 1996–. Patron: Hope and Home for Children, 1996–; Youth for Britain, 1996–. Mem., Scientific Exploration Soc. DL Wilts, 1996. *Publications:* Service for the Nation: Seaford papers, 1987; Biography of Lt-Col H. Jones, VC, OBE, 2002. *Recreations:* ski-ing, fishing, breeding alpacas. *Address:* c/o Lloyds TSB, 9 Broad Street, St Helier, Jersey, CI. *Clubs:* Army and Navy; Royal Channel Islands Yacht; St Moritz Tobogganing.

WILSEY, Timothy Andrew W.; *see* Willasey-Wilsey.

WILSHAW, Sir Michael (Norman), Kt 2000; Headteacher, St Bonaventure's Roman Catholic Comprehensive School, since 1985; *b* 3 Aug. 1946; *s* of Norman and Verna Wilshaw; *m*; one *s* two *d*. *Educ:* Birkbeck Coll., London Univ. (BA Hons). Teacher, later Head of Department, Inner London comprehensive schools, 1968–81: St Michael's, Bermondsey; Edith Cavell, Hackney; St Thomas the Apostle, Peckham; Dep. Headteacher, Trinity High Sch., Redbridge, 1981–85. *Recreations:* sport of all kinds, reading, theatre and cinema. *Address:* 24 Brand Street, Greenwich, SE10 8SR. *T:* (020) 8293 8550.

WILSHIRE, David; MP (C) Spelthorne, since 1987; *b* 16 Sept. 1943; *m* 1967, Margaret Weeks; one *s* (one *d* decd). *Educ:* Kingswood School, Bath; Fitzwilliam College, Cambridge. Partner, Western Political Research Services, 1979–2000; Co-Director, Political Management Programme, Brunel Univ., 1986–91. Mem., Avon CC, 1977–81; Leader, Wansdyke DC, 1981–87. Parliamentary Private Secretary: to Minister for Defence Procurement, 1991–92; to Minister of State, Home Office, 1992–94. *Recreations:* gardening, grape growing, wine making. *Address:* 55 Cherry Orchard, Staines, Middx TW18 2DQ. *T:* (01784) 450822.

WILSON; *see* Marslen-Wilson.

WILSON, family name of **Barons Moran, Nunburnholme, Wilson** and **Wilson of Tillyorn**.

WILSON, 2nd Baron *cr* 1946, of Libya and of Stowlangtoft; **Patrick Maitland Wilson;** *b* 14 Sept. 1915; *s* of Field-Marshal 1st Baron Wilson, GCB, GBE, DSO, and Hester Mary (*d* 1979), *d* of Philip James Digby Wykeham, Tythrop House, Oxon; *S* father, 1964; *m* 1945, Violet Storeen (*d* 1990), *d* of late Major James Hamilton Douglas Campbell, OBE. *Educ:* Eton; King's College, Cambridge. Served War of 1939–45 (despatches). *Heir:* none. *Address:* c/o Barclays Bank, Cambridge CB2 3PZ.

WILSON OF TILLYORN, Baron *cr* 1992 (Life Peer), of Finzean in the District of Kincardine and Deeside and of Fanling in Hong Kong; **David Clive Wilson,** KT 2000; GCMG 1991 (KCMG 1987 CMG 1985); PhD; FRSE; Registrar, Order of Saint Michael and Saint George, since 2001; *b* 14 Feb. 1935; *s* of Rev. William Skinner Wilson and Enid Wilson; *m* 1967, Natasha Helen Mary Alexander; two *s*. *Educ:* Trinity Coll., Glenalmond; Keble Coll., Oxford (schol., MA); PhD London 1973. FRSE 2000. National Service, The Black Watch, 1953–55; entered Foreign Service, 1958; Third Secretary, Vientiane, 1959–60; Language Student, Hong Kong, 1960–62; Second, later First Secretary, Peking, 1963–65; FCO, 1965–68; resigned, 1968; Editor, China Quarterly, 1968–74; Vis. Scholar, Columbia Univ., New York, 1972; rejoined Diplomatic Service, 1974; Cabinet Office, 1974–77; Political Adviser, Hong Kong, 1977–81; Hd, S European Dept, FCO, 1981–84; Asst Under-Sec. of State, FCO, 1984–87; Governor and C-in-C, Hong Kong, 1987–92. Chm., Scottish Hydro-Electric, then Scottish and Southern Energy, 1993–2000; Dir, Martin Currie Pacific Trust plc, 1993–. Mem. Board, British Council, 1993– (Chm., Scottish Cttee, 1993–). Chm., Scottish Peers Assoc., 2000– (Vice Chm., 1998–2000). Trustee: Museums of Scotland, 1999–; Scotland's Churches Scheme, 1999–; Carnegie Trust for the Univs of Scotland, 2000–. Member: Council, CBI Scotland, 1993–; Prime Minister's Adv. Cttee on Business Appts, 2000–. Chancellor's Assessor, Court, Univ. of Aberdeen, 1993–97; Chancellor, Univ. of Aberdeen, 1997–; Member: Governing Body, SOAS, 1992–97; Council, Glenalmond Coll., 1994– (Chm. Council, 2000–). Oxford Univ. Somaliland Expedn, 1957; British Mt Kongur Expedn (NW China), 1981. President: Bhutan Soc. of UK, 1993–; Hong Kong Assoc., 1994–; Hong Kong Soc., 1994–; Vice Pres., RSGS, 1996–. Hon. LLD: Aberdeen, 1990; Chinese Univ. of Hong Kong, 1996. Hon. DLitt: Sydney, 1991; Abertay Dundee, 1994. KStJ 1987. *Recreations:* hill-walking, theatre, reading. *Address:* c/o House of Lords, SW1A 0PW. *Clubs:* Alpine; New (Edinburgh); Royal Northern and University (Aberdeen).

WILSON, Sir Alan (Geoffrey), Kt 2001; FBA 1994; Professor of Urban and Regional Geography, since 1970, Vice-Chancellor, since 1991, University of Leeds (Pro-Vice-Chancellor, 1989–91); *b* 8 Jan. 1939; *s* of Harry Wilson and Gladys (*née* Naylor); *m* 1987, Sarah Caroline Fildes. *Educ:* Corpus Christi Coll., Cambridge (MA). Scientific Officer, Rutherford High Energy Lab., 1961–64; Res. Officer, Inst. of Econs and Statistics, Univ. of Oxford, 1964–66; Math. Adviser, MoT, 1966–68; Asst Dir, Centre for Environmental Studies, London, 1968–70. Mem., Kirklees AHA, 1979–82; Vice-Chm., Dewsbury HA, 1982–85; non-exec. Mem., Northern and Yorks RHA, 1994–96. Mem., ESRC, 2000– (Vice-Chm. Environment and Planning Cttee, 1986–88). Dir, GMAP Ltd, 1991–2001. MAE 1991; AcSS 2000. FCGI 1997. Gill Meml Award, RGS, 1978; Honours Award, Assoc. of Amer. Geographers, 1987; Founder's Medal, RGS, 1992. *Publications:* Entropy in Urban and Regional Modelling, 1970; Papers in Urban and Regional Analysis, 1972; Urban and Regional Models in Geography and Planning, 1974; (with M. J. Kirkby) Mathematics for Geographers and Planners, 1975, 2nd edn 1980; (with P. H. Rees) Spatial Population Analysis, 1977; (ed with P. H. Rees and C. M. Leigh) Models of Cities and Regions, 1977; Catastrophe Theory and Bifurcation: applications to urban and regional systems, 1981; (jtly) Optimization in Locational and Transport Analysis, 1981; Geography and the Environment: Systems Analytical Methods, 1981; (with R. J. Bennett) Mathematical Methods in Geography and Planning, 1985; (ed jtly) Urban Systems, 1987; (ed jtly) Urban Dynamics, 1990; (ed jtly) Modelling the City, 1994; (jtly) Intelligent Geographical Information Systems, 1996; Complex Spatial Systems, 2000. *Recreation:* writing. *Address:* Vice-Chancellor's Office, University of Leeds, Leeds LS2 9JT. *T:* (0113) 233 3000. *Club:* Athenæum.

WILSON, (Alan) Martin; QC 1982; a Recorder of the Crown Court, since 1979; *b* 12 Feb. 1940; *s* of late Joseph Norris Wilson and Kate Wilson; *m* 1st, 1966, Pauline Frances Kibart (marr. diss. 1975); two *d*; 2nd, 1976, Julia Mary Carter; one *d*. *Educ:* Kilburn Grammar Sch.; Nottingham Univ. (LLB Hons). Called to the Bar, Gray's Inn, 1963. Occasional Mem., Hong Kong Bar, 1988–; admitted to Malaysian Bar, 1995. *Recreations:* shooting, sailing, poetry. *Address:* 7 Bedford Row, WC1R 4BU. *Clubs:* Sloane; Bar Yacht.

WILSON, Alastair James Drysdale; QC 1987; a Recorder, since 1996; *b* 26 May 1946; *s* of late A. Robin Wilson and of Mary Damaris Wilson; *m* (marr. diss.); one *s* two *d*. *Educ:* Wellington College; Pembroke College, Cambridge. Called to the Bar, Middle Temple, 1968. *Recreations:* gardening, restoring old buildings. *Address:* 19 Old Buildings, Lincoln's Inn, WC2A 3UP. *T:* (020) 7405 2001, *Fax:* (020) 7405 0001; Rainthorpe Hall, Tasburgh, Norfolk NR15 1RQ.

WILSON, Alexander, CBE 1986; FLA; Director General, British Library Reference Division, 1980–86; *b* 12 Feb. 1921; *s* of late William Wilson and Amelia Wilson; *m* 1949, Mary Catherin Traynor; two *s*. *Educ:* Bolton County Grammar Sch. FLA 1950; Hon. FLA 1984. Served War, RAF, 1941–46. Librarian at Bolton, Harrogate, Taunton, and Swindon, 1946–52; Dir of Library and Cultural Services, Dudley and later Coventry, 1952–72; Dir, Cheshire Libraries and Museums Service, 1972–79. Member: Library Adv. Council (England), 1971–74; British Library Bd, 1974–86. Pres., LA, 1986. Fellow, Birmingham Polytechnic, 1989. Hon. DLit Sheffield, 1989. *Publications:* contrib. books and periodicals on libraries and other cultural services. *Recreations:* walking, listening to music. *Address:* 1 Brockway West, Tattenhall, Chester CH3 9EZ.

WILSON, Lt-Gen. Sir (Alexander) James, KBE 1974 (CBE 1966; MBE 1948); MC 1945; DL; Chief Executive, Tobacco Advisory Council, 1983–85 (Chairman, 1977–83); *b* 13 April 1921; *s* of Maj.-Gen. Bevil Thomson Wilson, CB, DSO, and of Florence Erica, *d* of Sir John Starkey, 1st Bt; *m* 1958, Hon. Jean Margaret Paul, 2nd *d* of 2nd Baron Rankeillour; two *s*. *Educ:* Winchester Coll.; New Coll., Oxford (BA Law, MA). Served War of 1939–45, North Africa and Italy, Rifle Bde (despatches); Adjt, IMA Dehra Dun, 1945–47; PS to C-in-C Pakistan, 1948–49; Co. Comdr, 1st Bn Rifle Bde, BAOR 1949 and 1951–52, Kenya 1954–55 (despatches); psc 1950; Bde Major 11th Armd Div., BAOR, 1952–54; Instr, Staff Coll. Camberley, 1955–58; 2nd in comd 3rd Green Jackets, BAOR, 1959–60; GSO1 Sandhurst, 1960–62; CO 1st Bn XX Lancs Fus, 1962–64; Chief of Staff, UN Force in Cyprus, 1964–66 (Actg Force Comdr, 1965–66); Comdr, 147 Inf. Bde TA, 1966–67; Dir of Army Recruiting, MoD, 1967–70; GOC NW District, 1970–72; Vice Adjutant General, MoD, 1972–74; GOC SE District, 1974–77. Dep. Col (Lancashire), RRF, 1973–77, Col, 1977–82; Hon. Col, Oxford Univ. OTC, 1978–82. Col Commandant: Queen's Division, 1974–77; RAEC, 1975–79; Royal Green Jackets, 1977–81. Director: Standard Commercial Corp., 1983–92; Standard Wool, 1987–92; Mem., Marketing Council, 1990–92, and Adv. Consultant, 1992–94, Drake Beam Morin (UK); adviser in politics and economics, Standard Commercial Corp., 1992–2000. Chm., Council, RUSI, 1973–75. Member: Sports Council, 1973–82; Council, CBI, 1977–85; Pres., Army Cricket Assoc., 1973–76; Vice-Pres., Army Football Assoc., 1973–76, Chm., 1976–77, Pres., 1977–82; Hon. Vice-Pres., FA, 1976–82; Pres., British Assoc. for Physical Trng, 1998–2000. Chm., Crown and Manor Club, Hoxton, 1977–95 (Pres., 1995–); Vice Pres., NABC Clubs for Young People, 1990– (Vice Chm., 1977–90); President: Notts Clubs for Young People, 1986–98; Broadway Lodge (formerly Broadway Foundn), 1989–99. Association Football Correspondent, Sunday Times, 1957–90; Review Editor, Army Quarterly, 1985–2000. DL Notts, 1993. *Publications:* articles and book reviews on mil. subjects. *Recreations:* cricket, Association football. *Address:* 151 Rivermead Court, SW6 3SF. *T:* (020) 7736 7228. *Clubs:* Travellers, MCC; Notts CC.

WILSON, Allan; Member (Lab) Cunninghame North, Scottish Parliament, since 1999; *b* 5 Aug. 1954; *s* of Andrew Wilson and Elizabeth (*née* Lauchlan); *m* 1981, Alison Isabel Melville Liddell; two *s*. *Educ:* Spiers Sch., Beith. Trainee Officer, 1972–75, Area Officer, 1975–93, NUPE; Sen. Regl Officer, UNISON, 1993–94; Head of Higher Educn, UNISON (Scotland), 1994–99. Dep. Minister for Sport, the Arts and Culture, Scottish Exec., 2001–. *Recreations:* football, reading, golf. *Address:* 44 Stoneyholm Road, Kilbirnie, Ayrshire KA25 7JS. *Clubs:* Garnock Labour, Place Golf (Kilbirnie).

WILSON, Air Chief Marshal Sir Andrew; *see* Wilson, Air Chief Marshal Sir R. A. F.

WILSON, Andrew James; *see* Wilson, Snoo.

WILSON, Andrew John; Member (SNP) Central Scotland, Scottish Parliament, since 1999; *b* Lanark, 27 Dec. 1970; *s* of Harry Arthur Wilson and Dorothy Wilson (*née* Bunting). *Educ:* Coltness High Sch., Wishaw; Univ. of St Andrews; Univ. of Strathclyde (BA Hons Econs and Politics). Economist, Government Economic Service: Forestry Commn, 1993–95; Scottish Office, 1995–96; Economist: and Sen. Researcher, SNP, 1996–97; Royal Bank of Scotland, 1997–98. Shadow Minister of Finance, Scottish Parlt, 1999–. Columnist, Sunday Mail. *Publications:* contribs to various jl and conf. papers. *Recreations:* football, swimming, carousing, reading, films. *Address:* Scottish Parliament, Edinburgh EH99 1SP. *T:* (0131) 348 5674. *Club:* Motherwell Football and Athletic.

WILSON, Andrew N.; author; *b* 27 Oct. 1950; *s* of late N. Wilson and of Jean Dorothy Wilson (*née* Crowder); *m* Katherine Duncan-Jones, *qv*; two *d*; *m* 1991, Ruth Alexandra Guilding; one *d*. *Educ:* Rugby; New College, Oxford (MA). Chancellor's Essay Prize, 1971, and Ellerton Theological Prize, 1975. Asst Master, Merchant Taylors' Sch., 1975–76; Lectr, St Hugh's Coll. and New Coll., Oxford, 1976–81; Literary Editor: Spectator, 1981–83; Evening Standard, 1990–97. Mem., AAIL, 1988. FRSL 1981. *Publications: novels:* The Sweets of Pimlico, 1977 (John Llewellyn Rhys Memorial Prize, 1978); Unguarded Hours, 1978; Kindly Light, 1979; The Healing Art, 1980 (Somerset Maugham Award, 1981; Arts Council National Book Award, 1981; Southern Arts Prize, 1981); Who was Oswald Fish?, 1981; Wise Virgin, 1982 (W. H. Smith Literary Award, 1983); Scandal, 1983; Gentlemen in England, 1985; Love Unknown, 1986; Stray, 1987; Incline Our Hearts, 1988; A Bottle in the Smoke, 1990; Daughters of Albion, 1991; The Vicar of Sorrows, 1993; Hearing Voices, 1995; A Watch in the Night, 1996; (for children) Hazel the Guinea-pig, 1997; Dream Children, 1998; *non fiction:* The Laird of Abbotsford, 1980 (John Llewellyn Rhys Memorial Prize, 1981); A Life of John Milton, 1983; Hilaire Belloc, 1984; How Can We Know?, 1985; (jtly) The Church in Crisis, 1986; The Lion and the Honeycomb, 1987; Penfriends from Porlock, 1988; Tolstoy, 1988 (Whitbread Biography Award); Eminent Victorians, 1989; C. S. Lewis, a biography, 1990; Against Religion, 1991; Jesus, 1992; (ed) The Faber Book of Church and Clergy, 1992; The Rise and Fall of the House of Windsor, 1993; (ed) The Faber Book of London, 1993; Paul: the mind of the apostle, 1997; God's Funeral, 1999. *Address:* 5 Regent's Park Terrace, NW1 7EE. *Clubs:* Travellers, Beefsteak, Academy.
See also Viscount Runciman of Doxford.

WILSON, Andrew Thomas, CMG 1982; Consultant, Agricultural Sciences Division, Rockefeller Foundation, 1987–98; Chief Natural Resources Adviser, Overseas Development Administration, 1983–87, retired; *b* 21 June 1926; *s* of John Wilson, farmer, and Gertrude (*née* Lucas); *m* 1954, Hilda Mary (*née* Williams) (*d* 1996); two *d*. *Educ:* Cowley Sch.; Leeds Univ. (BSc); St John's Coll., Cambridge (DipAg); Imperial College of Tropical Agriculture (DTA). Colonial Service/HMOCS, Northern Rhodesia/Zambia, 1949–66: Agricultural Officer, 1949; Chief Agricl Officer, 1959; Chief Agricl Research Officer, 1961; Dep. Director of Agriculture, 1963; ODM/ODA: Agricl Adviser, British Development Div. in the Caribbean, 1967; FCO: Agricl Adviser, Nairobi and Kampala, 1969; ODM/ODA: Agricl Adviser, E Africa Development Div., 1974; Agricl Adviser, Middle East Development Div., 1976; Head of British Develt Div. in S Africa, 1979. *Recreations:* sport, gardening. *Address:* 16 Henley Court, Henley Road, Brighton, East Sussex BN2 5NA. *Clubs:* Farmers'; Nairobi (Kenya).

WILSON, Sir Anthony, Kt 1988; FCA; Head of Government Accountancy Service and Chief Accounting Adviser to HM Treasury, 1984–88; *b* 17 Feb. 1928; *s* of late Charles Ernest Wilson and Martha Clarice Wilson (*née* Mee); *m* 1955, Margaret Josephine Hudson; two *s* one *d*. *Educ:* Giggleswick School. Royal Navy, 1946–49. John Gordon Walton & Co., 1945–46 and 1949–52; Price Waterhouse, 1952, Partner, 1961–84; HM Treasury, 1984–88. Non-exec. Dir, Capita Gp plc, 1989–92. Chm., Jt Disciplinary Scheme of UK Accountancy Profession, 1990–93; Member: UK Govt Production Statistics Adv. Cttee, 1972–84; Accounting Standards Cttee, 1984–88; Auditing Practices Cttee, 1987–88; Rev. Body on Sen. Salaries, 1989–98; Council, Inst. of Chartered Accountants in England and Wales, 1985–88. Mem. Management Cttee, SW Regl Arts Assoc., 1983–91 (Chm., 1988–91); Member: English Ceramic Circle, 1983–; Northern Ceramic Soc., 1976–89. Pres., Chandos Chamber Choir, 1986–88; Chairman: Dorset Opera, 1988–93; Dorset Musical Instruments Trust, 1994–; Vice Chm., Sherborne House Trust, 1995–2000; Dir, Opera-80 Ltd, 1989–91. Liveryman, Chartered Accountants' Co., 1977–; Master, Needlemakers' Co., 1999–2000. FRSA 1983. *Recreations:* fishing, gardening, golf, collecting pottery. *Address:* The Barn House, 89 Newland, Sherborne, Dorset DT9 3AG. *T:* (01935) 815674. *Club:* Reform.

WILSON, Anthony Joseph, (Joe); Member (Lab) North Wales, European Parliament, 1989–99; *b* 6 July 1937; *s* of Joseph Samuel Wilson and Eleanor Annie (*née* Jones); *m* 1st, 1959, June Mary Sockett (marr. diss. 1987); one *s* two *d*; 2nd, 1998, Sue Bentley. *Educ:* Birkenhead Sch.; Loughborough Coll. (DLC); Univ. of Wales (BEd Hons). National Service, RAPC, 1955–57. Teacher: Vauvert Sec. Mod. Sch., Guernsey, 1960–64; Les Beaucamps Sec. Mod. Sch., Guernsey, 1964–66; Man., St Mary's Bay Sch. Journey Centre, Kent, 1966–69; Lectr in PE, Wrexham Tech. Coll., subseq. NE Wales Inst. of Higher Educn, 1969–89. Contested (Lab) Wales, EP elecn, 1999. *Recreations:* basketball, camping. *Address:* 79 Ruabon Road, Wrexham, North Wales LL13 7PU. *T:* (01978) 352808.

WILSON, Anthony Keith; Chief Executive of the Press, University Printer and Secretary, Press Syndicate, Cambridge University Press, 1992–99; Fellow of Wolfson College, Cambridge, since 1994; *b* 28 Sept. 1939; *s* of late Sidney Walter Wilson and Doris Jessie Wilson (*née* Garlick), Streatham; *m* 1963, Christina Helen, *d* of late Ivor Gray Nixon and Margaret Joan (*née* Smith); two *s* one *d*. *Educ:* Lexden House Sch.; Dulwich Coll.; Corpus Christi Coll., Cambridge (Maj. Scholar; BA Hons Modern and Medieval Langs 1961; MA 1966). Longmans Green & Co. Ltd, 1961–64; Thomas Nelson & Sons Ltd, 1964–68; George Allen & Unwin Ltd, 1968–72; Cambridge University Press, 1972–99: Sen. Editor, R&D, 1972–73; Publishing Ops Dir, 1973–82; Dep. Sec., Press Syndicate, 1979–92; Actg Man. Dir, 1982–83, Man. Dir, 1983–92, Publishing Div.; Dep. Chief Exec., 1991–92. Royal Shakespeare Company: Gov., 1983–; Mem. Council, 1991–2000; Mem., Exec. Cttee, 1991–2000; Mem. Bd, 2001–; Chm., Budget Cttee, 1991–96; Chm., Budget and Audit Cttee, 1996–2000; Chm., Audit Cttee, 2000–. Gov., Perse Sch. for Girls, Cambridge, 1979–99 (Chm. Govs, 1988–99); Hon. Treas., Westcott House, Cambridge, 2000–. FInstD 1978 (Life-Mem.); FRSA 1985. *Recreations:* walking, talking, walking and talking. *Address:* Wolfson College, Cambridge CB3 9BB.

WILSON, Arthur Andrew; Programme Director, Avon Health Authority, since 2000; *b* 23 July 1946; *s* of Arthur James Wilson and late Hilda Mellor Wilson (*née* Kennedy); *m* 1968, Susan Ann Faulkner; one *s* one *d*. *Educ:* Moulton Sch., Northampton. CIPFA; IHSM. W. H. Grigg & Co., 1963; Calne and Chippenham RDC, 1963–66; Berkshire CC, 1966–67; Bath City Council, 1967–73; Chief Accountant, Avon CC, 1973–76; Principal Asst Regl Treasurer, SW RHA, 1976–82; Dist Treasurer, Plymouth HA, 1982–84; South Western RHA: Regl Treasurer, 1984–91; Dep. Regl Gen. Manager, 1991–93; Chief Exec., Plymouth Hosps NHS Trust, 1993–2000. Mem. Mgt Council, 1997–, Chm. Exec. Cttee, 1998–, UC of St Mark and St John, Plymouth. *Recreations:* golf, reading, listening to music, musical theatre, first editions of modern novels. *Address:* Heathfield, Sowton Road, Yelverton, Plymouth PL20 6DD. *T:* (01822) 853309.

WILSON, Austin Peter; Assistant Under Secretary of State, 1981–96; Member, Criminal Injuries Compensation Appeals Panel, since 1997; *b* 31 March 1938; *s* of Joseph and Irene Wilson; *m* 1962, Norma Louise, *y d* of D. R. Mill; one *s* two *d*. *Educ:* Leeds Grammar Sch.; St Edmund Hall, Oxford (BA). Entered Home Office, 1961; Private Secretary to Minister of State, 1964–66; Principal, 1966; Secretary, Deptl Cttee on Death Certification and Coroners (Brodrick Cttee), 1968–71; Asst Sec., 1974, Prison Dept; seconded to N Ireland Office, 1977–80; Asst Under Secretary of State, Criminal Justice Dept, 1981; Hd of Community Progs and Equal Opportunities Dept, 1982–86, Equal Opportunities and Gen. Dept, 1986–87, Police Dept, 1987–88, Home Office; NI Office, 1988–92; Criminal Policy Dept, 1992–94, Fire and Emergency Planning Dept, 1994–96, Home Office. *Recreations:* theatre, reading, walking, travel. *Address:* 2 Stocks Hill Garth, Main Street, Menston, W Yorks LS29 6EG. *T:* (01943) 877691.

WILSON, Barbara Jocanta Maria, PhD; Director of Research and Development, National Assembly for Wales, since 2000; *b* 26 June 1947; *d* of Edward Szczepanik and late Anne Szczepanik (*née* Janikowska); *m* 1971, Peter Brian Wilson (*d* 1996); one *s* one *d*. *Educ:* King George V Sch., Hong Kong; Convent of Sacred Heart, Tunbridge Wells; St Anne's Coll., Oxford (MA Maths); Keele Univ. (PhD 1975). Statistical Res. Unit in Sociol., Keele Univ., 1969–73; Welsh Office, 1974–99: Sen. Asst Statistician, 1974–76; Statistician, 1976–84; Principal, Local Govt Finance, 1984–86; Educn Dept, 1986–89; Head of: Resource and Quality Mgt Div., 1989–92; Community Care Div., 1992–96; Personnel, 1996–99; Principal Estabts Officer, April–Aug. 1999; Dep. Clerk, Nat. Assembly for Wales, 1999–2000. Founder Trustee and Treas., WAY (Widowed and Young) Foundn. *Recreations:* walking, music, cooking. *Address:* National Assembly for Wales, Cathays Park, Cardiff CF10 3NQ. *T:* (029) 2082 5111.

WILSON, Vice-Adm. Sir Barry (Nigel), KCB 1990; Deputy Chief of Defence Staff (Programmes and Personnel), 1989–92; *b* 5 June 1936; *s* of Rear-Adm. G. A. M. Wilson, CB, and of Dorothy Wilson; *m* 1961, Elizabeth Ann (*née* Hardy); one *s* one *d*. *Educ:* St Edward's Sch., Oxford; Britannia Royal Naval Coll. Commanded: HMS Mohawk, 1973–74; HMS Cardiff, 1978–80; RCDS 1982; Dir Navy Plans, 1983–85; Flag Officer Sea Training, 1986–87; ACDS (Progs), 1987–89. Chairman: SSAFA Forces Help (formerly SSAFA), 1994–2000; Royal Naval Mus., Portsmouth, 1994–. Chm. Bd of Visitors, Guys Marsh HMP/YOI, 1997–99. *Recreations:* campanology, gardening. *Address:* Green Bough, Child Okeford, Blandford Forum, Dorset DT11 8HD.

WILSON, Lt-Col Sir Blair Aubyn S.; *see* Stewart-Wilson.

WILSON, Brian David Henderson; MP (Lab) Cunninghame North, since 1987; Minister of State (Minister for Industry and Energy), Department of Trade and Industry, since 2001; *b* 13 Dec. 1948; *s* of late John Forrest Wilson and Marion MacIntyre; *m* 1981, Joni Buchanan; two *s* one *d*. *Educ:* Dunoon Grammar School; Dundee Univ. (MA Hons); University College Cardiff (Dip. Journalism Studies). Publisher and founding editor, West Highland Free Press, 1972–97. Opposition front bench spokesman on Scottish affairs, 1988–92, on transport, 1992–94 and 1995–96, on trade and industry, 1994–95, on election planning, 1996–97; Minister of State: Scottish Office, 1997–98 and 1999–2001; (Minister for Trade), DTI, 1998–99; FCO, Jan.–June 2001. First winner, Nicholas Tomalin Meml Award, 1975. *Publications:* Celtic: a century with honour, 1988; contribs to Guardian, Glasgow Herald, New Statesman, etc. *Address:* House of Commons, SW1A 0AA; 37 Main Street, Kilbirnie, Ayrshire. *T:* (office) (01505) 682847; 219 Queen Victoria Drive, Glasgow G13 1UU. *T:* (0141) 959 1758; Miavaig House, Isle of Lewis. *T:* (01851) 672357. *Clubs:* Garnock Labour; Kilbirnie Place Golf.

WILSON, Prof. Brian Graham, AO 1995; Vice-Chancellor, University of Queensland, 1979–95; *b* 9 April 1930; *s* of Charles Wesley Wilson and Isobel Christie (*née* Ferguson); *m* 1st, 1959, Barbara Elizabeth Wilkie; two *s* one *d*; 2nd, 1978, Margaret Jeanne Henry; 3rd, 1988, Joan Patricia Opdebeeck; three *s* (incl. twins). *Educ:* Queen's Univ., Belfast (BSc Hons); National Univ. of Ireland (PhD Cosmic Radiation). Post-doctoral Fellow, National Research Council, Canada, 1955–57; Officer in Charge, Sulphur Mt Lab., Banff, 1957–60, Associate Res. Officer, 1959–60; Associate Prof. of Physics, Univ. of Calgary, 1960–65, Prof., 1965–70, Dean of Arts and Science, 1967–70; Prof. of Astronomy and Academic Vice-Pres., Simon Fraser Univ., 1970–78. Pres., Internat. Develt Program of Australian Univs and Colls, 1991–93; Chairman: Australian Vice-Chancellors' Cttee, 1989–90 (Dep. Chm., 1987–88); Quality Assurance in Higher Educn, 1993–95. Member: Council, Northern Territory Univ., 1988–93; Council, Univ. of South Pacific, 1991–95. FTS 1990. Hon. LLD Calgary, 1984; DUniv Queensland Univ. Tech., 1995; Hon. DSc Queensland, 1995. *Publications:* numerous, on astrophysics and on higher educn issues, in learned jls. *Recreations:* golf, swimming. *Address:* Les Tisseyres, Fanjeaux 11270, France.

WILSON, Brian William John Gregg, MA; Deputy Head, St Mary's School, Wantage, 1989–97; *b* 16 June 1937; *s* of late Cecil S. and Margaret D. Wilson; *m* 1969, Sara Remington (*née* Hollins); two *d*. *Educ:* Sedbergh Sch., Yorks; Christ's Coll., Cambridge (MA). NI short service commn, RIrF, 1955–57; Flt Lt, RAFVR (T), 1964–71. Asst Master, Radley Coll., 1960–65; Housemaster, King's Sch., Canterbury, 1965–73; Dir of Studies, Eastbourne Coll., 1973–76; Headmaster, Campbell Coll., Belfast, 1977–87. Project Manager, Navan Fort Initative Gp, 1987–88. Mem., and Chm. Planning Cttee, Wantage Town Council, 1999–2000. Member: Central Religious Adv. Cttee, BBC/ITV, 1982–86; Management Cttee, NISTRO, 1980–87. Hon. Sec., Ancient History Cttee, JACT, 1967–77; Treas., JACT Ancient History Bureau, 1998–2000. Secretary: Wantage PCC, 1999–2000; Cleeve PCC, 2001–. *Publications:* (with W. K. Lacey) Res Publica, 1970; (with D. J. Miller) Stories from Herodotus, 1973; (with J. W. Rich) Augustus, 2000. *Recreations:* fives, squash, golf, cricket, hockey, etc; translating, theology, stock market, drama, walking, birds, trees. *Address:* 30 Warner Close, Cleeve, Bristol BS49 4TA.

WILSON, Rt Rev. Bruce Winston; Bishop of Bathurst (NSW), 1989–2000; *b* 23 Aug. 1942; *s* of Alick Bruce Wilson and Maisie Catherine (*née* Pye); *m* 1966, Zandra Robyn Parkes; one *s* one *d*. *Educ:* Canterbury Boys' High School; Univ. of Sydney (MA); London Univ. (BD); Univ. of NSW (BA); Australian Coll. of Theology (ThL). Curacies, Darling Point and Beverly Hills, Sydney, 1966–69; Anglican Chaplain, Univ. of NSW, 1970–75; Rector of St George's, Paddington, Sydney, 1975–83; Director, St Mark's Theol Coll., Canberra, 1984–89; Asst Bishop, Diocese of Canberra and Goulburn, 1984–89. Exec., Nat. Council of Churches in Australia, 1994–97. *Publications:* The Human Journey: Christianity and Modern Consciousness, 1981; Can God Survive in Australia?, 1983; Reasons of the Heart, 1998. *Recreations:* jogging, motor car restoration, reading, cooking. *Address:* 48 Mount Piddington Road, Mount Victoria, NSW 2786, Australia.

WILSON, Bryan Ronald, PhD, DLitt; FBA 1994; Reader in Sociology, University of Oxford, 1962–93; Fellow, 1963–93, and Domestic Bursar, 1989–93, All Souls College, Oxford (Sub-Warden, 1988–90); *b* 25 June 1926. *Educ:* University Coll., Leicester (BSc Econ London); London Sch. of Economics (PhD); MA, DLitt Oxon. Lectr in Sociology, Univ. of Leeds, 1955–62. Commonwealth Fund Fellow (Harkness), 1957–58; Fellow, Amer. Council of Learned Socs, 1966–67; Visiting Professor or Fellow, Universities of: Louvain, 1976, 1982, 1986, 1993; Toronto, 1978; Melbourne (Ormond Coll.), 1981; Queensland, 1986; California, Santa Barbara, 1987. Pres., Conf. Internat. de sociologie religieuse, 1971–75. Sen. Treasurer, Oxford Union Soc., 1983–91. Hon. DLitt Soka Univ., Japan, 1985; Dr *hc* Louvain, 1992. *Publications:* Sects and Society, 1961; Religion in Secular Society, 1966; (ed) Patterns of Sectarianism, 1967; The Youth Culture and the Universities, 1970; (ed) Rationality, 1970; Religious Sects, 1970; Magic and the Millennium, 1973; (ed) Education, Equality and Society, 1975; The Noble Savages, 1975;

Contemporary Transformations of Religion, 1976; (ed) The Social Impact of New Religious Movements, 1981; Religion in Sociological Perspective, 1982; (with Daisaku Ikeda) Human Values in a Changing World, 1984; (ed with Brenda Almond) Values: a symposium, 1988; The Social Dimensions of Sectarianism, 1990; (ed) Religion: contemporary issues, 1992; (with K. Dobbelaere) A Time to Chant, 1994; (ed with Jamie Cresswell) New Religious Movements: challenge and response, 1999; (ed with D. Machacek) Global Citizens: the Soka Gakkai Buddhist movement in the world, 2000; contribs to learned jls. *Address:* 12 Victoria Court, London Road, Headington, Oxford OX3 7SP.

WILSON, Catherine Mary, (Mrs P. J. Wilson), OBE 1996; FMA, FSA; Director, Norfolk Museums Service, 1991–98; *b* 10 April 1945; *d* of Arthur Thomas Bowyer and Kathleen May (*née* Hawes); *m* 1968, Peter John Wilson. *Educ:* Windsor County Grammar Sch. FMA 1984 (AMA 1972); FSA 1990. Museum Asst, Lincoln City Museums, 1964; Curator, Museum of Lincolnshire Life, 1972; Asst Dir (Museums), Lincs CC, 1983. Member: Museums and Galleries Commn, 1996–2000; Railway Heritage Cttee, 2000–. Pres., Soc. for Folklife Studies, 2000–. *Recreations:* industrial archaeology, vernacular architecture, all local history. *Address:* Penates et Lares, 5 Station Road, Reepham, Lincoln LN3 4DN.

WILSON, Cedric Gordon; Member, Strangford, Northern Ireland Assembly (UKU 1998–99, NIU since 1999); Leader, Northern Ireland Unionist Party, since 1999; *b* 6 June 1948; *s* of Samuel Wilson and Elizabeth Wilson; *m* 1975, Eva Kverneland; one *s* two *d*. *Educ:* Hillcrest Prep. Sch.; Belmont Primary Sch.; Orangefield High Sch. Dir, Hollymount Develts Ltd, 1988–. Mem., 1981–89, Dep. Mayor, 1982–83, Mayor, 1983–84, Castlereagh BC. *Recreations:* art, music, photography. *Address:* Parliament Buildings, Stormont, Belfast, Northern Ireland BT4 3SW. *T:* (028) 9052 1481; 22 Shore Road, Ballyhalbert, Co. Down BT22 1BJ.

WILSON, Sir Charles Haynes, Kt 1965; MA; Principal and Vice-Chancellor of University of Glasgow, 1961–76; *b* 16 May 1909; 2nd *s* of late George Wilson and Florence Margaret Hannay; *m* 1935, Jessie Gilmour Wilson; one *s* two *d*. *Educ:* Hillhead High School; Glasgow Univ. (MA). Glasgow University Faulds Fellow in Political Philosophy, 1932–34. Lecturer in Political Science, London School of Economics, 1934–39; Fellow and Tutor in Modern History, Corpus Christi College, Oxford, 1939–52. Junior Proctor, 1945; Faculty Fellow, Nuffield College. Visiting Professor in Comparative Government at Ohio State Univ., 1950; Principal, The University College of Leicester, 1952–57; Vice-Chancellor, Univ. of Leicester, 1957–61. Chairman: Commn on Fourah Bay Coll., Sierra Leone, 1957; Acad. Planning Bd for Univ. of E Anglia, 1960; Member: Academic Planning Cttee and Council of UC of Sussex, 1958; Acad. Adv. Cttee, Royal Coll. of Science and Technology, Glasgow (now Univ. of Strathclyde), 1962; Acad. Planning Bd, Univ. of Stirling, 1964; Chairman, Cttee of Vice-Chancellors and Principals, 1964–67; Chm., Assoc. of Commonwealth Univs, 1966–67 and 1972–74. Hon. Fellow: Corpus Christi Coll., Oxford, 1963; LSE, 1965. Hon. LLD: Glasgow, 1957; Leicester, 1961; Rhodes Univ., 1964; Queen's Univ., Kingston, Ont, 1967; Ohio State Univ., 1969; Pennsylvania, 1975; Hon. DLitt: Strathclyde, 1966; NUU, 1976; Heriot-Watt, 1977; Hon. DCL East Anglia, 1966. Comdr, St Olav (Norway), 1966; Chevalier, Legion of Honour, 1976. *Address:* Whinnymuir, Dalry, Castle Douglas DG7 3TT. *T:* (01644) 430218.

WILSON, Charles Martin; Managing Director, Mirror Group (formerly Mirror Group Newspapers) plc, 1992–98 (Editorial Director, 1991–92); Managing Director and Editor-in-chief, The Sporting Life, 1990–98; *b* 18 Aug. 1935; *s* of Adam and Ruth Wilson; *m* 1st, 1968, Anne Robinson, *qv* (marr. diss. 1973); one *d*; 2nd, 1980, Sally Angela O'Sullivan, *qv* (marr. diss. 2001); one *s* one *d*; 3rd, 2001, Rachel, *d* of Baroness Pitkeathley, *qv*. *Educ:* Eastbank Academy, Glasgow. News Chronicle, 1959–60; Daily Mail, 1960–71; Dep. Northern Editor, Daily Mail, 1971–74; Asst Editor, London Evening News, 1974–76; Editor, Glasgow Evening Times, Glasgow Herald, Scottish Sunday Standard, 1976–82; The Times: Exec. Editor, 1982; Dep. Editor, 1983; Editor, 1985–90; Internat. Develts Dir, News Internat. plc, 1990. Non-exec. Dir, Chelsea and Westminster NHS Trust, 2000–. Mem., Newspaper Panel, Competition Commn, 1999–; Board Member: Youth Justice, 1998–; Countryside Alliance, 1998–. Mem., Jockey Club, 1993–. Trustee: WWF-UK, 1996–; Royal Naval Mus., 1999–. *Recreations:* reading, riding, horse racing, countryside. *Address:* 23 Campden Hill Square, W8 7JY. *T:* (020) 7727 3366.

WILSON, (Christopher) David, CBE 1968; MC 1945; Chairman: Southern Television Ltd, 1976–81 (Managing Director, 1959–76); Southstar Television International, 1976–81; Beaumont (UK) Ltd, 1979–81; *b* 17 Dec. 1916; *s* of late James Anthony Wilson, Highclere, Worplesdon, Surrey; *m* 1947, Jean Barbara Morton Smith (*d* 1997); no *c*. *Educ:* St George's Sch., Windsor; Aldenham. Served War of 1939–45: Captain RA, in India, Middle East and Italy. Business Manager, Associated Newspapers Ltd, 1955–57; Dir, Associated Rediffusion Ltd, 1956–57; Gen. Manager, Southern Television Ltd, 1957–59; Chm., ITN Ltd, 1969–71. Mem. Council, Southampton Univ., 1980–89; Trustee, Chichester Festival Theatre Trust Ltd. FCA 1947. *Recreations:* sailing, music. *Address:* 1 Hamble Manor, The Green, Hamble, Southampton SO31 4GB. *T:* (023) 8045 5824. *Clubs:* MCC; Royal Southern Yacht.

WILSON, Christopher G.; *see* Grey-Wilson.

WILSON, Clive Hebden; Independent Complaints Reviewer: Community Fund (formerly National Lottery Charities Board), since 1998; New Opportunities Fund, since 2000; Awards for All Scheme, since 2000; *b* 1 Feb. 1940; *s* of Joseph and Irene Wilson; *m* 1976, Jill Garland Evans; two *d*. *Educ:* Leeds Grammar Sch.; Corpus Christi Coll., Oxford. Joined Civil Service, 1962; Ministry of Health: Asst Principal, 1962–67; Asst Private Sec. to Minister of Health, 1965–66; Principal, 1967–73; Assistant Secretary: DHSS, 1973–77; Cabinet Office, 1977–79; DHSS, 1979–82; Under Sec., DHSS, later DoH, 1982–98: Dir of Estabs (HQ), 1982–84; Child Care Div., 1984–86; Children, Maternity, Prevention Div., 1986–87; Medicines Div., 1987–90; Priority Health Services Div., subseq. Health Care (A) Div., 1990–92; on secondment from Department of Health: Hd of Health and Community Care Gp, NCVO, 1992–95; Dir, Office of Health Service Comr, 1995–96; Dep. Health Service Comr, 1996–98; Clerk Advr, H of C, 1998–2001. *Recreations:* walking, gardening, tennis.

WILSON, Colin Alexander Megaw; Scottish Parliamentary Counsel, since 1993; *b* 4 Jan. 1952; *s* of James Thompson Wilson and Sarah Elizabeth Howard Wilson (*née* Megaw); *m* 1987, Mandy Esca Clay; one *s* one *d*. *Educ:* Glasgow High Sch.; Edinburgh Univ. (LLB Hons 1973). Admitted solicitor, Scotland, 1975; Asst Solicitor, then Partner, Archibald Campbell & Harley, WS, Edinburgh, 1975–79; Asst, later Depute, Parly Draftsman for Scotland, 1979–93; Asst Legal Sec. to Lord Advocate, 1979–99. *Recreations:* choral singing, cycling, walking, reading. *Address:* Office of the Scottish Parliamentary Counsel, Victoria Quay, Edinburgh EH6 6QQ. *T:* (0131) 244 1670.

WILSON, Sir Colin (Alexander) St John, Kt 1998; RA 1991 (ARA 1990); FRIBA; Professor of Architecture, Cambridge University, 1975–89, now Emeritus Professor; Fellow, Pembroke College, Cambridge, since 1977; Architect (own private practice); *b* 14 March 1922; *yr s* of late Rt Rev. Henry A. Wilson, CBE, DD; *m* 1st, 1955, Muriel Lavender (marr. diss. 1971); 2nd, 1972, Mary Jane Long; one *s* one *d*. *Educ:* Felsted Sch.; Corpus Christi Coll., Cambridge, 1940–42 (MA; Hon. Fellow, 1998); Sch. of Architecture, London Univ., 1946–49 (Dip. Lond.). Served War, RNVR, 1942–46. Asst in Housing Div., Architects Dept, LCC, 1950–55; Lectr at Sch. of Architecture, Univ. of Cambridge, 1955–69; Fellow, Churchill Coll., Cambridge, 1962–71, Hon. Fellow 1998. Practised in assoc. with Sir Leslie Martin, 1956–64: on bldgs in Cambridge (Harvey Court, Gonville and Caius Coll.; Stone Building, Peterhouse); Univ. of Oxford, Law Library; Univ. of Leicester, Science Campus; Univ. of London, Royal Holloway Coll. In own practice, buildings include: Extension to Sch. of Architecture, Cambridge; Research Laboratory, Babraham; Extension to British Museum; Library for QMC, Univ. of London (SCONUL award for design excellence); Meml Library for Bishop Wilson Sch., Spring Field; The British Library, St Pancras; various residences; Projects for Liverpool Civic and Social Centre, and Group Headquarters and Research Campus for Lucas Industries Ltd. Exhibitions: Venice Biennale, 1996; retrospective, RIBA, 1997, Bristol, and Glasgow, 1998; architecture of British Liby exhibition, tour, USA, 2000. Vis. Critic, 1960, 1964 and 1983, Bishop Vis. Prof., 2000, Yale Sch. of Architecture, USA; Bemis Prof. of Architecture, MIT, USA, 1970–72. Consultant, Chicago City Library. Member: Fitzwilliam Mus. Syndicate, 1985–89; Arts Council of GB, 1990–94 (Chair, Architecture Unit, 1992–94); Bd of Advisors, MAArch, Helsinki Univ. of Technology, Finland, 1994–. Trustee: Tate Gall., 1973–80; Nat. Gall., 1977–80. FRSA. DUniv Essex, 1998; Hon. LittD Cambridge, 1999; Hon. LLD Sheffield, 1999. Commander, Order of the Lion (Finland), 1992. *Publications:* Architectural Reflections, 1992; The Other Tradition of Modern Architecture, 1995; The Design and Construction of the British Library, 1998; The Artist at Work, 1999; articles in: The Observer; professional jls in UK, USA, France, Spain, Japan, Germany, Norway, Italy, Switzerland, Finland, etc. *Address:* 31A Grove End Road, NW8. *T:* (020) 7286 8306; (office) Colin St John Wilson & Associates, Clarendon Buildings, 27 Horsell Road, N5 1XL. *T:* (020) 7607 3084.

WILSON, Colin Henry; author; *b* Leicester, 26 June 1931; *s* of Arthur Wilson and Annetta Jones; *m* Dorothy Betty Troop; one *s*; *m* Joy Stewart; two *s* one *d*. *Educ:* The Gateway Secondary Technical School, Leicester. Left school at 16. Laboratory Asst (Gateway School), 1948–49; Civil Servant (collector of taxes), Leicester and Rugby, 1949–50; national service with RAF, AC2, 1949–50. Various jobs, and a period spent in Paris and Strasbourg, 1950; came to London, 1951; various labouring jobs, long period in plastic factory; returned to Paris, 1953; labouring jobs in London until Dec. 1954, when began writing The Outsider: has since made a living at writing. Visiting Professor: Hollins Coll., Va, 1966–67; Univ. of Washington, Seattle, 1967; Dowling Coll., Majorca, 1969; Rutgers Univ., NJ, 1974. Plays produced: Viennese Interlude; The Metal Flower Blossom; Strindberg. *Publications:* The Outsider, 1956; Religion and the Rebel, 1957; The Age of Defeat, 1959; Ritual in the Dark, 1960; Adrift in Soho, 1961; An Encyclopædia of Murder, 1961; The Strength to Dream, 1962; Origins of the Sexual Impulse, 1963; The Man without a Shadow, 1963; The World of Violence, 1963; Rasputin and the Fall of the Romanovs, 1964; The Brandy of the Damned (musical essays), 1964; Necessary Doubt, 1964; Beyond the Outsider, 1965; Eagle and Earwig, 1965; The Mind Parasites, 1966; Introduction to The New Existentialism, 1966; The Glass Cage, 1966; Sex and the Intelligent Teenager, 1966; The Philosopher's Stone, 1968; Strindberg (play), 1968; Bernard Shaw: A Reassessment, 1969; Voyage to a Beginning, 1969; Poetry and Mysticism, 1970; The Black Room, 1970; A Casebook of Murder, 1970; The God of the Labyrinth, 1970; Lingard, 1970; (jtly) The Strange Genius of David Lindsay, 1970; The Occult, 1971; New Pathways in Psychology, 1972; Order of Assassins, 1971; Tree by Tolkien, 1973; Hermann Hesse, 1973; Strange Powers, 1973; The Schoolgirl Murder Case, 1974; Return of the Lloigor, 1974; A Book of Booze, 1974; The Craft of the Novel, 1975; The Space Vampires, 1976 (filmed as Lifeforce, 1985); Men of Strange Powers, 1976; Enigmas and Mysteries, 1977; The Geller Phenomenon, 1977; Mysteries, 1978; Mysteries (play), 1979; The Quest for Wilhelm Reich, 1979; The War Against Sleep: the philosophy of Gurdjieff, 1980; Starseekers, 1980; Frankenstein's Castle, 1981; (ed with John Grant) The Directory of Possibilities, 1981; Poltergeist!, 1981; Access to Inner Worlds, 1982; The Criminal History of Mankind, 1983; (with Donald Seaman) Encyclopaedia of Modern Murder, 1983; Psychic Detectives, 1983; The Janus Murder Case, 1984; The Essential Colin Wilson, 1984; The Personality Surgeon, 1985; Spider World: the tower, 1987; (with Damon Wilson) Encyclopedia of Unsolved Mysteries, 1987; Spider World: the delta, 1987; (ed with Ronald Duncan) Marx Refuted, 1987; Aleister Crowley: the nature of the beast, 1987; (with Robin Odell) Jack the Ripper: summing up and verdict, 1987; The Magician from Siberia, 1988; The Misfits: a study of sexual outsiders, 1988; Beyond the Occult, 1988; Written in Blood, 1989; (with Donald Seaman) The Serial Killers, 1990; Mozart's Journey to Prague (play), 1991; Spider World: the magician, 1992; The Strange Life of P. D. Ouspensky, 1993; From Atlantis to the Sphinx, 1996; Atlas of Sacred Sites and Holy Places, 1996; Alien Dawn, 1998; The Devil's Party, 2000; (with Rand Fle'math) Atlantis Blueprint, 2000; contribs to: The Times, Literary Review, Audio, Daily Mail, Spectator, etc. *Recreations:* collecting gramophone records, mainly opera; mathematics. *Address:* Tetherdown, Trewallock Lane, Gorran Haven, Cornwall PL26 6NT. *Club:* Savage.

WILSON, Maj.-Gen. Dare; *see* Wilson, Maj.-Gen. R. D.

WILSON, David; *see* Wilson, C. D.

WILSON, Sir David, 3rd Bt *cr* 1920; *b* 30 Oct. 1928; *s* of Sir John Mitchell Harvey Wilson, 2nd Bt, KCVO, and Mary Elizabeth (*d* 1979), *d* of late William Richards, CBE; *S* father, 1975; *m* 1955, Eva Margareta, *e d* of Tore Lindell, Malmö, Sweden; two *s* one *d*. *Educ:* Deerfield Acad., Mass., USA; Harrow School; Oriel Coll., Oxford (Brisco Owen Schol.). Barrister, Lincoln's Inn, 1954–61; admitted Solicitor, 1962; Partner, Simmons & Simmons, EC2, 1963–92. *Heir:* *s* Thomas David Wilson [*b* 6 Jan. 1959; *m* 1984, Valerie, *er d* of Vivian Stogdale, Shotover, Oxford; two *s*]. *Address:* Tandem House, Queen's Drive, Oxshott, Leatherhead, Surrey KT22 0PH. *Club:* Royal Southern Yacht.

WILSON, Sir David (Mackenzie), Kt 1984; FBA 1981; Director of the British Museum, 1977–92; *b* 30 Oct. 1931; *e s* of Rev. Joseph Wilson; *m* 1955, Eva, *o d* of Dr Gunnar Sjögren, Stockholm; one *s* one *d*. *Educ:* Kingswood Sch.; St John's Coll., Cambridge (LittD; Hon. Fellow, 1985); Lund Univ., Sweden. Research Asst, Cambridge Univ., 1954; Asst Keeper, British Museum, 1954–64; Reader in Archaeology of Anglo-Saxon Period, London Univ., 1964–71; Prof. of Medieval Archaeology, Univ. of London, 1971–76; Jt Head of Dept of Scandinavian Studies, UCL, 1973–76 (Hon. Fellow, 1988). Slade Prof., Cambridge, 1985–86. Member: Ancient Monuments Bd for England, 1976–84; Historic Bldgs and Monuments Commn, 1990–97. Governor, Museum of London, 1976–81; Trustee: Nat. Museums of Scotland, 1985–87; Nat. Museums of Merseyside, 1986–2001. Crabtree Orator 1966. Member: Royal Swedish Acad. of Sci.; Royal Acad. of Letters, History and Antiquities, Sweden; Norwegian Acad. of Science and

Letters; German Archaeological Inst.; Royal Gustav Adolf's Acad. of Sweden; Royal Soc. of Letters of Lund; Vetenskapssocieteten, Lund; Royal Soc. of Sci. and Letters, Gothenburg; Royal Soc. of Sci., Uppsala; Royal Norwegian Soc. of Sci. and Letters; FSA; MAE; Hon. MRIA; Hon. Mem., Polish Archaeological and Numismatic Soc.; Hon. FMA. Sec., Soc. for Medieval Archaeology, 1957–77; Pres., Viking Soc., 1968–70; Pres., Brit. Archaeological Assoc., 1962–68. Mem. Council, Nottingham Univ., 1988–94. Hon. Fil.Dr Stockholm; Hon. Dr Phil: Aarhus; Oslo; Hon. DLitt: Liverpool; Birmingham; Nottingham; Leicester; Hon LLD Pennsylvania. Félix Neuburgh Prize, Gothenburg Univ., 1978; Gold Medal, Soc. of Antiquaries, 1995. Order of Polar Star, 1st cl. (Sweden), 1977. *Publications:* The Anglo-Saxons, 1960, 3rd edn 1981; Anglo-Saxon Metalwork 700–1100 in British Museum, 1964; (with O. Klindt-Jensen) Viking Art, 1966; (with G. Bersu) Three Viking Graves in the Isle of Man, 1969; The Vikings and their Origins, 1970, 2nd edn 1980; (with P. G. Foote) The Viking Achievement, 1970; (with A. Small and C. Thomas) St Ninian's Isle and its Treasure, 1973; The Viking Age in the Isle of Man, 1974; (ed) Anglo-Saxon Archaeology, 1976; (ed) The Northern World, 1980; The Forgotten Collector, 1984; Anglo-Saxon Art, 1984; The Bayeux Tapestry, 1985; The British Museum: purpose and politics, 1989; Awful Ends, 1992; Showing the Flag, 1992; Vikingatidens Konst, 1995; Vikings and Gods in European Art, 1997. *Address:* The Lifeboat House, Castletown, Isle of Man IM9 1LD. *T:* (01624) 822800. *Club:* Athenæum.

WILSON, David William; Chairman, Wilson Bowden PLC, since 1987; *b* 5 Dec. 1941; *s* of Albert Henry Wilson and Kathleen May Wilson; *m* 1st, 1964, Ann Taberner; one *s* one *d*; 2nd, 1985, Laura Isobel Knifton; two *s*. *Educ:* Ashby Boys' Grammar Sch.; Leicester Polytechnic. Created from scratch what is now Wilson Bowden PLC. *Recreation:* farming. *Address:* Lowesby Hall, Lowesby, Leics LE7 9DD. *T:* (0116) 259 5321.

WILSON, Prof. Deirdre Susan Moir, PhD; FBA 1990; Professor of Linguistics, University College London, since 1991; *b* 1941; *m* 1975, Dr Theodore Zeldin, *qv*. *Educ:* Somerville Coll., Oxford (BA 1964); BPhil Oxon 1967; PhD 1973. Lectr in Philosophy, Somerville Coll., Oxford, 1967–68; Harkness Fellow, MIT, 1968–70; University College London: Lectr in Linguistics, 1970–85; Reader, 1985–91; British Acad. Res. Reader, 1988. *Publications:* Presuppositions and Non-truth Conditional Semantics, 1975; (with Neil Smith) Modern Linguistics: the result of Chomsky's Revolution, 1979; (with Dan Sperber) Relevance: communication and cognition, 1995; contrib. to learned jls. *Address:* Department of Phonetics and Linguistics, University College London, Gower Street, WC1E 6BT.

WILSON, Derek Robert; Chief Executive, Slough Estates, since 1996; *b* 10 Oct. 1944; *m* 1972, Maureen Thorpe; one *s* one *d*. *Educ:* Bristol Univ. (BA Econs and Accounting). FCA 1970. Deloitte Haskins & Sells, London and Geneva, 1966–72; Cavenham, 1973–78; Wilkinson Match, 1978–83; Dir of Finance, Cadbury Schweppes, 1983–86; Finance Dir, 1986, Group Managing Dir, 1992–96, Slough Estates. Director: Candover Investments, 1994–; Westbury, 1996–. *Recreation:* golf. *Address:* c/o Slough Estates, 234 Bath Road, Slough, Berks SL1 4EE.

WILSON, Des; Special Adviser, BAA plc, since 2000 (Director of Corporate and Public Affairs, 1994–2000); *b* 5 March 1941; *s* of Albert H. Wilson, Oamaru, New Zealand; *m* 1985, Jane Dunmore; one *s* one *d* by a previous marriage. *Educ:* Waitaki Boys' High Sch., New Zealand. Journalist-Broadcaster, 1957–67; Director, Shelter, Nat. Campaign for the Homeless, 1967–71; Head of Public Affairs, RSC, 1974–76; Editor, Social Work Today, 1976–79; Dep. Editor, Illustrated London News, 1979–81; Chm., 1981–85, Project Advr, 1985–89, CLEAR (Campaign for Lead-Free Air); Dir of Public Affairs, 1993–94, World Wide Vice Chm., Public Affairs, 1994, Burson-Marsteller. Non-executive Director: Carphone Warehouse plc, 2000–; Ingenious Media plc, 2000–. Chairman: Friends of the Earth (UK), 1982–86; Campaign for Freedom of Information, 1984–91; Citizen Action, 1983–91; Parents Against Tobacco, 1990. Member: Nat. Exec., Nat. Council for Civil Liberties, 1971–73; Cttee for City Poverty, 1972–73; Bd, Shelter, 1982– (Trustee, 1982–86); Council, Nat. Trust, 2001–; Trustee, Internat. Year of Shelter for the Homeless (UK), 1985–87. Mem. Bd, BTA, 1997–; Sen. Vice Chm., Sport England, 1999– (Chm., Lottery Panel, 1999–); Mem., UK Sports Council, 2000–. Columnist: The Guardian, 1968–70; The Observer, 1971–75; New Statesman, 1997–; regular contributor, Illustrated London News, 1972–85. Contested (L) Hove, 1973, 1974; Liberal Party: Mem. Council, 1973–74 and 1984–85; Mem., Nat. Exec., 1984–85; Pres., 1986–87; Pres., NLYL, 1984–85; Mem. Federal Exec., SLD, 1988; Gen. Election Campaign Dir, Lib Dems, 1990–92. *Publications:* I Know It Was the Place's Fault, 1970; Des Wilson's Minority Report (a diary of protest), 1973; So you want to be Prime Minister: a personal view of British politics, 1979; The Lead Scandal, 1982; Pressure, the A to Z of Campaigning in Britain, 1984; (ed) The Environmental Crisis, 1984; (ed) The Secrets File, 1984; The Citizen Action Handbook, 1986; Battle for Power — Inside the Alliance General Election Campaign, 1987; Costa Del Sol (novel), 1990; Campaign (novel), 1992; Campaigning, 1993. *Address:* 48 Stapleton Hall Road, Stroud Green, N4 3QG.

WILSON, Prof. Edward Osborne, PhD; Pellegrino University Research Professor, and Hon. Curator in Entomology, Harvard University, since 1997 (Curator in Entomology, 1972–97); *b* 10 June 1929; *s* of Edward O. Wilson, Sen. and Inez Freeman; *m* 1955, Irene Kelley; one *d*. *Educ:* Univ. of Alabama (BS 1949; MS 1950); Harvard Univ. (PhD 1955). Harvard University: Jun. Fellow, Soc. of Fellows, 1953–56; Asst Prof. of Biology, 1956–58; Assoc. Prof. of Zoology, 1958–64; Prof. of Zoology, 1964–76; Baird Prof. of Sci., 1976–94; Mellon Prof. of the Scis, 1990–93; Pellegrino University Prof., 1994–97. Hon. DSc Oxon, 1993; 23 other hon. doctorates. Nat. Medal of Sci., USA, 1978; Pulitzer Prize for General Non-Fiction, 1978 and 1991; Tyler Prize for Envmtl Achievement, 1984; Crafoord Prize, Swedish Royal Acad. of Sci., 1990; Internat. Prize for Biol., Japan, 1994; King Faisal Internat. Prize for Sci., 2000. *Publications:* (with R. H. MacArthur) The Theory of Island Biogeography, 1967; The Insect Societies, 1971; Sociobiology: the new synthesis, 1975; On Human Nature, 1978; Biophilia, 1984; (with B. Holldobler) The Ants, 1990; The Diversity of Life, 1992; Naturalist (autobiog.), 1995; In Search of Nature, 1997; Consilience, 1998. *Address:* Museum of Comparative Zoology, Harvard University, 26 Oxford Street, Cambridge, MA 02138–2902, USA. *T:* (617) 4952315.

WILSON, Elizabeth Alice, (Mrs W. I. Wilson), OBE 1995; Chairman, Dumfries and Galloway Community NHS Trust, 1995–97; *b* 26 May 1937; *m* 1996, William Iain Wilson, MBE. *Educ:* Coleraine High Sch.; Univ. of Edinburgh (BSc Soc. Sci.); SRN, SCM. Staff Nurse, Midwife, Ward Sister and nurse management posts, 1958–72; Principal Nursing Officer, Edinburgh Northern Hosps Gp, 1972–74; Dist Nursing Officer, N Lothian, Lothian Health Bd, 1974–80; Chief Area Nursing Officer: Dumfries and Galloway Health Bd, 1980–88; Tayside Health Bd, 1988–94. Mem., Nat. Bd for Nursing, Midwifery and Health Visiting, Scotland, 1983–93 (Dep. Chm., 1985–93). Chm., Stranraer Cancer Drop In Centre Assoc., 1998–. Hon. Sen. Lectr, Univ. of Dundee, 1988–94. *Publications:* papers on nursing. *Address:* 32 Ryanview Crescent, Stranraer DG9 0JL.

WILSON, Lt-Col Eric Charles Twelves, VC 1940; *b* 2 October 1912; *s* of Rev. C. C. C. Wilson; *m* 1943, Ann (from whom he obtained a divorce, 1953), *d* of Major Humphrey Pleydell-Bouverie, MBE; two *s*; *m* 1953, Angela Joy, *d* of Lt-Col J. McK. Gordon, MC; one *s*. *Educ:* Marlborough; RMC, Sandhurst. Commissioned in East Surrey Regt, 1933; seconded to King's African Rifles, 1937; seconded to Somaliland Camel Corps, 1939; Long Range Desert Gp, 1941–42; Burma, 1944; seconded to N Rhodesia Regt, 1946; retd from Regular Army, 1949; Admin Officer, HM Overseas Civil Service, Tanganyika, 1949–61; Dep. Warden, London House, 1962, Warden, 1966–77. Hon. Sec., Anglo-Somali Soc., 1972–77 and 1988–90. *Publication:* Stowell in the Blackmore Vale, 1986. *Recreation:* country life. *T:* (01963) 370264.

WILSON, Frank Richard, CMG 1963; OBE 1946; Controller of Administration, Commonwealth Development Corporation, 1976–80; retired HMOCS Oct. 1963; *b* 26 Oct. 1920; *er s* of late Sir Leonard Wilson, KCIE and the late Muriel Wilson; *m* 1947, Alexandra Dorothy Mary (*née* Haigh); two *s*. *Educ:* Oundle Sch.; Trinity Hall, Cambridge (1939–40 only). Commnd Indian Army, 1941; retired as Lieut-Col, 1946. Joined Colonial Administrative Service (later HMOCS) in Kenya, 1947; District Comr, 1950–56; Private Sec. to the Governor, 1956–59; Provincial Comr, Central Province, 1959–63; Civil Sec., Central Region, 1963. With Commonwealth Develt Corp., 1964–80. *Address:* Chelsea House, Mickleton, Chipping Campden, Glos GL55 6SD.

WILSON, Fraser Andrew, MBE 1980; HM Diplomatic Service; Ambassador to Turkmenistan, 1998–2002; High Commissioner designate to the Seychelles; *b* 6 May 1949; *s* of William McStravick Wilson and Mary McFadyen Wilson (*née* Fraser); *m* 1981, Janet Phillips; two *s*. *Educ:* Bellahouston Acad.; Surrey Univ. (Dip. Russian Studies). Joined Diplomatic Service, 1967; served: FCO, 1967–70; Havana, 1970–71; SE Asia, 1971–73; Seoul, 1973–77; Salisbury, 1977–80; FCO, 1980–84; Moscow, 1984–85; First Sec. (Commercial), Rangoon, 1986–90; FCO, 1990–94; Dep. Consul Gen., São Paulo, 1994–98. *Recreations:* travelling, reading. *Address:* c/o Foreign and Commonwealth Office, King Charles Street, SW1A 2AH.

WILSON, Geoffrey; Chairman, Wells, O'Brien & Co., 1972–82; *b* 11 July 1929; *m* 1962, Philomena Mary Kavanagh; one *s* one *d*. *Educ:* Bolton County Grammar Sch.; Univ. of Birmingham; Linacre Coll., Oxford. PE Consulting Group, 1958–63; British Railways, 1963–71; Mem., BR Bd, 1968–71, Chief Exec. (Railways), 1971. Member: Council, Royal Inst. of Public Admin, 1970–71; Council, Inst. of Transport, 1970–71. *Recreations:* golf, gardening, painting. *Address:* 10 Montpellier Grove, Cheltenham, Glos GL50 2XB.

WILSON, Geoffrey Alan; Chairman, Equity Land Ltd, since 1994; *b* 19 Feb. 1934; *s* of Lewis Wilson and Doris Wilson (*née* Shrier); *m* 1963, Marilyn Helen Freedman; one *s* two *d*. *Educ:* Haberdashers' Aske's School; College of Estate Management. FRICS. 2nd Lieut RA, 1955–56. Private practice, 1957–60; Director: Amalgamated Investment & Property Co., 1961–70; Sterling Land Co., 1971–73 (and co-founder); Greycoat, 1976–94 (Chm., 1985–94, and co-founder); Perspectives on Architecture (formerly Perfect Harmony) Ltd, 1993–98. Member: W Metropolitan Conciliation Cttee, Race Relations Bd, 1969–71; Council, Central British Fund for World Jewish Relief, 1993–97. Trustee: ORT Trust, 1980–; Public Art Develt Trust, 1990–95; British Architectural Liby Trust, 1996–2000; AA Foundn, 1998–; Buildings at Risk Trust, 1998–. English Heritage: Comr, 1992–98; Chm., London Adv. Cttee, 1995–98; Chm., Urban Panel, 2000–. Mem., Governing Council, UCS, 1991–95. Governor: Peabody Trust, 1998–; City Literary Inst., 1998–; Mus. of London, 2000–. Hon. FRIBA 1995. *Recreations:* reading, architecture, art, film. *Address:* 2 Bentinck Street, W1U 2FA. *T:* (020) 7009 0220. *Club:* Reform.

WILSON, Hon. Geoffrey Hazlitt, CVO 1989; FCA, FCMA; Chairman, Southern Electric plc, 1993–96 (Director, 1989–96); *b* 28 Dec. 1929; *yr s* of 1st Baron Moran, MC, MD, FRCP, and Lady Moran, MBE; *m* 1955, Barbara Jane Hebblethwaite; two *s* two *d*. *Educ:* Eton; King's Coll., Cambridge (BA Hons). JDipMA. Articled to Barton Mayhew (now Ernst & Young), 1952; Chartered Accountant 1955; joined English Electric, 1956; Dep. Comptroller, 1965; Financial Controller (Overseas), GEC, 1968; joined Delta Group as Financial Dir, Cables Div., 1969; elected to Main Board as Gp Financial Dir, 1972; Jt Man. Dir, 1977; Dep. Chief Executive, 1980; Chief Exec., 1981–88; Chm., 1982–94. Director: Blue Circle Industries plc, 1980–97; Drayton English & International Trust, 1978–95; W Midlands and Wales Regl Bd, Nat. Westminster Bank PLC, 1985–92 (Chm., 1990–92); Johnson Matthey plc, 1990–97 (Dep. Chm., 1994–97); UK Adv. Bd, National Westminster Bank, 1990–92. Member: Council, Inst. of Cost and Management Accountants, 1972–78; Accounting Standards Cttee, 1978–79; Financial Reporting Council, 1990–93; London Metal Exchange, 1982–94; Chm., 100 Gp of Chartered Accountants, 1979–80 (Hon. Mem., 1985). Mem. Management Bd, Engineering Employers Fedn, 1979–83 (Vice-Pres., 1983–86 and 1990–94; Dep. Pres., 1986–90); Chm., EEF Cttee on Future of Wage Bargaining, 1980; Dep. Pres., 1986–87, Pres., 1987–88, Counsellor, 1989–94, BEAMA; Member: Administrative Council, Royal Jubilee Trusts, 1979–88, Hon. Treas., 1980–89; Council, Winchester Cathedral Trust, 1985–93; Council, St Mary's Hosp. Med. Sch., 1985–88. Vice-Chm., Campaign Appeal, 1994–97, Fellow Commoner, 1996–, King's Coll., Cambridge. CIMgt. Mem. Ct of Assistants, Chartered Accountants' Co., 1982–95 (Master, 1988–89). OStJ 1996. *Recreations:* family, reading, walking, ski-ing, vintage cars. *Clubs:* Boodle's, Royal Automobile.

WILSON, Sir Geoffrey Masterman, KCB 1969 (CB 1968); CMG 1962; Chairman, Oxfam, 1977–83; *b* 7 April 1910; 3rd *s* of late Alexander Cowan Wilson and Edith Jane Brayshaw; *m* 1st, 1946, Julie Stafford Trowbridge (marr. diss. 1979); two *s* two *d*; 2nd; 1989, Stephanie Stainsby (*née* Ross). *Educ:* Manchester Grammar School; Oriel College, Oxford. Chairman, Oxford Univ. Labour Club, 1930; Pres., Oxford Union, 1931. Harmsworth Law Scholar, Middle Temple, 1931; called to Bar, Middle Temple, 1934. Served in HM Embassy, Moscow, and Russian Dept of Foreign Office, 1940–45. Cabinet Office, 1947; Treasury, 1948; Director, Colombo Plan Technical Co-operation Bureau, 1951–53; Under-Secretary, Treasury, 1956–58; Deputy Head of UK Treasury Delegn and Alternate Exec. Dir for UK, Internat. Bank, Washington, 1958; Vice-President, International Bank, Washington, 1961–66; Deputy Secretary, ODM, 1966–68, Permanent Secretary, 1968–70; Dep. Sec.-Gen. (Economic), Commonwealth Secretariat, 1971. Chm., Race Relations Bd, 1971–77. Hon. Fellow: Wolfson Coll., Cambridge, 1971; Inst. of Develt Studies, Brighton, 1981; Oriel Coll., Oxford, 1992. *Address:* 1 Rawlinson Road, Oxford OX2 6UE.

WILSON, Geoffrey Studholme, CMG 1961; Commissioner of Police, Tanganyika Police Force, 1958–62; *b* 5 June 1913; *s* of late J. E. S. Wilson; *m* 1936, Joy Noel, *d* of Capt. C. St G. Harris-Walker; two *s*. *Educ:* Radley College. Joined Hong Kong Police, 1933; Commissioner of Police, Sarawak Constabulary, 1953–58. King's Police Medal, 1950. OStJ 1961. *Recreations:* golf, fishing, sailing. *Address:* British Bank of the Middle East, 29 Hill Street, W1X 7FD. *Club:* Hong Kong (Hong Kong).

WILSON, Prof. Geoffrey Victor Herbert, AM 1998; PhD; Vice Chancellor and President, Deakin University, since 1996; *b* 23 Sept. 1938; *s* of Victor Hawthorne Wilson and Dorothy Eleanor Wilson (*née* Spooner); *m* 1961, Beverley Wigley; two *s* two *d*. *Educ:* Univ. of Melbourne (BSc 1958; MSc 1960; DSc 1977); PhD Monash Univ. 1964. FAIP,

MACE, FTSE, FAIM. Postgrad. Schol., Univ. of Melbourne, 1958–60; Teaching Fellow, Monash Univ., 1960–63; Nuffield Foundn Travelling Fellow, Oxford Univ., 1963–65; Sen. Lectr in Physics, Monash Univ., 1965–71; University of New South Wales: Prof. of Physics, 1971–85, Dean, Faculty of Mil. Studies, 1978–86, Royal Mil. Coll.; Rector of University Coll., Aust. Defence Acad., 1984–91; Vice Chancellor, Central Queensland Univ., 1991–96. Vis. Prof., Free Univ. of Berlin, 1977–78. *Recreations:* gardening, theatre, physical recreation. *Address:* Deakin University, Geelong Waterfront Campus, Geelong, Vic 3217, Australia. *T:* (3) 52278503.

WILSON, George; *see* Wilson, W. G.

WILSON, George Pritchard Harvey, CMG 1966; JP; Chairman, Victorian Inland Meat Authority, 1973–77 (Deputy Chairman, 1970–73); *b* 10 March 1918; *s* of late G. L. Wilson; *m* 1945, Fay Hobart Duff; two *s* one *d*. *Educ:* Geelong Grammar School. Nuffield Scholar (Farming), 1952. Council Member, Monash University, 1961–69; Royal Agricultural Society of Victoria: Councillor, 1950; President, 1964–73; Trustee, 1968–. Member: Victoria Promotion Cttee, 1968–81; Victoria Economic Develt Corp., 1981–82. Chm., Australian Nuffield Farming Scholars Assoc., 1973–89; Hon. Trustee, UK Nuffield Farming Scholarship Trust, 1989–. JP 1957. *Recreation:* fishing. *Address:* Wilson House, Berwick, Victoria 3806, Australia. *T:* (3) 97071271. *Clubs:* Melbourne, Royal Automobile of Victoria (Melbourne); Melbourne Cricket.

WILSON, Gerald Robertson, CB 1991; FRSE; Chairman, Scottish Biomedical Research Trust, since 1999; Director (non-executive), ICL (Scotland) Ltd, since 2000; Special Adviser, Royal Bank of Scotland, since 2000; *b* 7 Sept. 1939; *s* of late Charles Robertson Wilson and Margaret Wilson (*née* Early); *m* 1963, Margaret Anne, *d* of late John S. and Agnes Wight; one *s* one *d*. *Educ:* Holy Cross Academy, Edinburgh; University of Edinburgh. (MA). FRSE 1999. Asst Principal, Scottish Home and Health Dept, 1961–65; Private Sec. to Minister of State for Scotland, 1965–66; Principal, Scottish Home and Health Dept, 1966–72; Private Sec. to Lord Privy Seal, 1972–74, to Minister of State, Civil Service Dept, 1974; Asst Sec., Scottish Economic Planning Dept, 1974–77; Counsellor, Office of the UK Perm. Rep. to the European Communities, Brussels, 1977–82; Asst Sec., Scottish Office, 1982–84; Under Sec., Industry Dept for Scotland, 1984–88; Sec., Scottish Office Educn, later Educn and Industry, Dept, 1988–99. Chm., E Scotland, RIPA, 1990–92. Bd Mem., Royal Scottish Nat. Orchestra, 1999–. Mem. Ct, Strathclyde Univ., 1999–; Gov., George Watson's Coll., Edinburgh, 2000–. Mem. Council, Fairbridge in Scotland, 2000–. DUniv Stirling, 1999. *Recreation:* music. *Address:* 4 Inverleith Avenue South, Edinburgh EH3 5QA. *Club:* New (Edinburgh).

WILSON, Gillian Brenda, (Mrs Kenneth Wilson); *see* Babington-Browne, G. B.

WILSON, Gordon; *see* Wilson, Robert G.

WILSON, Guy Murray, MA; FSA; Master of the Armouries, since 1988; *b* 18 Feb. 1950; *s* of late Rowland George Wilson and Mollie (*née* Munson; later Mrs Youngs); *m* 1972, Pamela Ruth McCredie; two *s* two *d*. *Educ:* New Coll., Oxford (MA); Manchester Univ. (Dip. Art, Gallery and Museum Studies). FSA 1984. Joined Royal Armouries, 1972; Keeper of Edged Weapons, 1978; Dep. Master of the Armouries, 1981. Member: British Commn for Military History, 1978–; Adv. Cttee on History Wreck Sites, 1981–99; Arms and Armour Soc. of GB, 1973–; Arms and Armour Soc. of Denmark, 1978–; Meyrick Soc., 1980–. FRSA 1992. *Publications:* Treasures of the Tower: Crossbows, 1975; (with A. V. B. Norman) Treasures from the Tower of London, 1982; (with D. Walker) The Royal Armouries in Leeds: the making of a museum, 1996; contribs to museum and exhibn catalogues and to Jl of Arms and Armour Soc., Internat. Jl of Nautical Archaeol., Connoisseur, Burlington, Country Life, Museums Jl, Guns Rev., etc. *Recreations:* theatre, music, reading, walking. *Address:* Tang Croft, Tang Road, High Birstwith, Harrogate, North Yorks HG3 2JU; Royal Armouries Museum, Armouries Drive, Leeds LS10 1LT.

WILSON, His Honour Harold; a Circuit Judge, 1981–2000 (Midland and Oxford Circuit); a Deputy High Court Judge, 2001; *b* 19 Sept. 1931; *s* of late Edward Simpson Wilson; *m* 1st, Diana Marion (marr. diss.), *d* of late (Philip) Guy (Dudley) Sixsmith; three *s* one *d*; 2nd, Jill Ginever, *d* of late Charles Edward Walter Barlow; one step *s* one step *d*. *Educ:* St Albans Sch.; Sidney Sussex Coll., Cambridge (State Scholar; MA). Commnd service, RAF, RAFVR, RAuxAF, 1950–disbandment. Administrative Trainee, KCH, 1954–56; Schoolmaster, 1957–59. Called to the Bar, Gray's Inn, 1958 (Holker Exhbr; runner-up, Lee Essay Prize, 1959), Bencher, 1998; Oxford Circuit, 1960–70 (Circuit Junior, 1964–65); Midland and Oxford Circuit, 1971–75; Dep. Chm., Monmouthshire Quarter Sessions, 1969–70; a Recorder, Midland and Oxford Circuit, 1971–75; Chm. of Industrial Tribunals, Birmingham, 1976–81; Resident Judge, Coventry Crown Ct, 1983–92; Liaison Judge, 1986–92; Hon. Recorder of Coventry, 1986–93; designated Care Centre Judge, Coventry, 1991–92, Oxford, 1993–2000; Resident Judge, Oxford Crown Ct, 1993–2000; Liaison Judge to Oxfordshire Magistrates, 1993–96; Hon. Recorder of Oxford, 1999–2001; a Judge of the Employment Appeal Tribunal, 1999–2000. Pres., Transport Tribunal, 1991–96; Chairman: Coventry Reparation Unit Adv. Cttee, 1991–92; Thames Valley Area Criminal Justice Strategy (formerly Liaison) Cttee, 1996–2000. Member: Matrimonial Causes Rules Cttee, 1984–88; W Midlands Probation Cttee, 1985–92. *Recreations:* watching rugby football, reading and listening to music. *Address:* 2 Harcourt Buildings, Temple, EC4Y 9DB. *T:* (020) 7353 6961. *Club:* Royal Air Force.

WILSON, Prof. Henry Wallace, PhD; CPhys, FInstP; FRSE; physicist; Director, Scottish Universities' Research and Reactor Centre, 1962–85; Personal Professor of Physics, Strathclyde University, 1966–85, now Emeritus; *b* 30 Aug. 1923; *s* of Frank Binnington Wilson and Janet (*née* Wilson); *m* 1955, Fiona McPherson Martin, *d* of Alfred Charles Steinmetz Martin and Agnes Mary (*née* McPherson); three *s*. *Educ:* Allan Glen's Sch., Glasgow; Glasgow Univ. (BSc, PhD Physics). AInstP 1949, FInstP 1962; FRSE 1963. Wartime work as Physicist, Explosives Res. Div., ICI, Ardeer. Asst Lectr, Natural Philosophy Dept, Glasgow Univ., 1947–51; post-doctoral Res. Fellow, Univ. of Calif, Berkeley, 1951–52; Lectr, Nat. Phil. Dept, Glasgow Univ., 1952–55; Leader of Physical Measurements Gp, UKAEA, Aldermaston, 1955–62 (Sen. Principal Scientific Officer, 1958). Hon. Scientific Advr, Nat. Mus. of Antiquities of Scotland, 1969; Scientific Advr, Scottish Office, 1975–93. Mem., Nuclear Safety Cttee, 1964–89, and Consultant, SSEB; Mem., Radioactive Substances Adv. Cttee, 1966–70. Inst. of Physics: Mem. Council, 1970–71; Chm., Scottish Br., 1969–71; mem. several cttees; Royal Soc. of Edinburgh: Mem. Council, 1966–69, 1976–79; Vice Pres., 1979–81. Member: Brit. Nuclear Energy Soc.; British Mass Spectrometry Soc. (Chm., 1977–79). FRSA 1996. *Publications:* contributions to: Alpha, Beta and Gamma-ray Spectroscopy, ed K. Siegbahn, 1965; Activation Analysis, ed Lenihan and Thomson, 1965; Modern Aspects of Mass Spectrometry, ed R. I. Reed, 1968; Encyclopaedic Dictionary of Physics, ed J. Thewlis, 1973; (ed) Nuclear Engineering sect., Chambers' Science and Technology Dictionary, gen. ed. P. M. B. Walker, 1988; papers on radioactivity, low energy nuclear physics, meson physics, mass spectrometry, isotope separation, effects of radiation, and reactor physics, in scientific jls. *Recreations:* hill-walking, sailing, industrial archaeology, photography. *Address:* Ashgrove, The Crescent, Busby, Glasgow G76 8HT. *T:* (0141) 644 3107. *Club:* Royal Scottish Automobile (Glasgow).

WILSON, Ven. Hewitt; *see* Wilson, Ven. J. H.

WILSON, (Iain) Richard, OBE 1994; actor and director; *b* 9 July 1936; *s* of John Boyd Wilson and Euphemia (*née* Colquhoun). *Educ:* Greenock High Sch.; Royal Acad. of Dramatic Art. Associate Director, Royal Court, 2000–. *Theatre* includes: Normal Service, Hampstead, 1979; Operation Bad Apple, 1982, An Honourable Trade, 1984, May Days, 1990, Royal Court; The Weekend, Strand, 1994; Waiting for Godot, Manchester Royal Exchange, 1999; *plays directed:* Heaven and Hell, 1981, Other Worlds, 1983, Royal Court; An Inspector Calls, Manchester Royal Exchange, 1986; A Wholly Healthy Glasgow, Manchester Royal Exchange, Royal Court and Edinburgh Fest., 1987, 1988; Prin, Lyric, Hammersmith, 1989; Imagine Drowning, Hampstead, 1991; Women Laughing, Manchester Royal Exchange, transf. Royal Court, 1992; Simply Disconnected, Chichester, 1996; Tom and Clem, Aldwych, 1997; Royal Court: Four, 1998; Toast, 1999; Mr Kolpert, I Just Stopped By to See the Man, 2000; *television series* include: My Good Woman, 1972; Crown Court, 1973–84; A Sharp Intake of Breath, 1979–81; Only When I Laugh, 1979–82; High and Dry, 1987; Tutti Frutti, 1987; One Foot in the Grave, six series, 1989–2000; High Stakes, 2001; Life – As We Know It, 2001; *films* include: A Passage to India, 1984; Whoops Apocalypse, 1986; Prick Up Your Ears, 1987; How to Get Ahead in Advertising, 1989; Fellow Traveller, 1990; Carry on Columbus, 1992; The Man Who Knew Too Little, 1998. Rector, Glasgow Univ., 1996–99. Hon. DLitt Glasgow Caledonian, 1995. Top TV Comedy Actor, British Comedy Awards, 1991; Light Entertainment Award, BAFTA, 1991 and 1993. *Recreations:* squash, collecting work of living Scottish painters. *Address:* c/o Conway van Gelder Robinson Ltd, 18–21 Jermyn Street, SW1Y 6HP. *T:* (020) 7287 0077. *Clubs:* Royal Automobile, Groucho.

WILSON, Prof. Ian Andrew, DPhil, DSc; FRS 2000; Professor of Molecular Biology and Skaggs Institute for Chemical Biology, Scripps Research Institute, since 1982; *b* 22 March 1949; *s* of George Alexander Wilson and Margaret Stewart Wilson (*née* McKillop). *Educ:* Perth Acad.; Univ. of Edinburgh (BSc 1st Cl. Hons 1971); Corpus Christi Coll., Oxford (DPhil 1976; DSc 2000). Jun. Res. Fellow, Corpus Christi Coll., Oxford, 1975–77; Res. Fellow in Biochem., 1977–80, Res. Associate, 1980–82, Harvard Univ.; Asst Mem., 1982–84, Associate Mem., 1984–90, Scripps Clinic and Res. Foundn. Adjunct Prof., UCSD, 1998–. *Recreations:* scuba diving, tennis, golf, opera. *Address:* Department of Molecular Biology, BCC206, Scripps Research Institute, 10550 North Torrey Pines Road, La Jolla, CA 92037, USA. *T:* (858) 7849706. *Club:* La Jolla Beach and Tennis.

WILSON, Ian D.; *see* Douglas-Wilson.

WILSON, Ian Matthew, CB 1985; Under Secretary, Scottish Education Department, 1977–86; *b* 12 Dec. 1926; *s* of Matthew Thomson Wilson and Mary Lily Barnett; *m* 1st, 1953, Anne Chalmers (*d* 1991); three *s*; 2nd, 1996, Joyce Town. *Educ:* George Watson's Coll.; Edinburgh Univ. (MA). Asst Principal, Scottish Home Dept, 1950; Private Sec. to Perm. Under-Sec. of State, Scottish Office, 1953–55; Principal, Scottish Home Dept, 1955; Asst Secretary: Scottish Educn Dept, 1963; SHHD, 1971; Asst Under-Sec. of State, Scottish Office, 1974–77. Sec. of Commns for Scotland, 1987–92. Dir, Scottish Internat. Piano Competition, 1997–. Mem., Bd of Govs, RSAMD, 1992–2000. Pres., Univ. of Edinburgh Graduates' Assoc., 1995–97. *Address:* 1 Bonaly Drive, Edinburgh EH13 0EJ. *T:* (0131) 441 2541. *Club:* New (Edinburgh).

WILSON, Ivan Patrick; Partnership Secretary, Freshfields, 1998–99; *b* 24 Aug. 1941; *s* of William Wilson and Jessie (*née* Bateson); *m* 1966, Kathleen Mary Price; three *s*. *Educ:* Royal Sch., Dungannon; Academy, Omagh; Queen's Univ., Belfast. HM Treasury, 1965–95; Private Sec. to Perm. Sec., Overseas Finance, 1971–73; Press Office, 1973–76; Defence Policy and Budget Div., 1981–84; RCDS 1985; Information Systems, 1986–89; Under-Sec., Industry and Employment Gp, 1989–90; Dir, Govt Centre for Information Systems, 1990–93; Under Sec., Public Enterprises Gp, HM Treasury, 1993–95; Exec. Advr, ICL Enterprises, 1995–98. *Recreations:* foreign travel, sport, walking. *Address:* 88 Redhill Wood, New Ash Green, Longfield, Kent DA3 8QP. *T:* (01474) 874740.

WILSON, Jacqueline; author; *b* 17 Dec. 1945; *d* of Harry Aitken and Margaret Aitken (*née* Clibbons); *m* 1965, William Millar Wilson (separated); one *d*. *Educ:* Coombe Girls' Sch. Journalist, D. C. Thomsons, 1963–65. Ambassador, Reading is Fundamental, UK, 1998–; Cttee Mem., Children's Writers and Illustrators Gp, Soc. of Authors, 1997–; Adv. Mem., Whitbread Book Awards Panel, 1997–; Judge, Rhône-Poulenc Prizes for Jun. Sci. Books, 1999; Bd Mem., Children's Film and TV Foundn, 2000. Hon. Dr Kingston, 2001. *Publications* include: *fiction:* Hide and Seek, 1972; Truth or Dare, 1973; Snap, 1974; Let's Pretend, 1975; Making Hate, 1977; *for children:* Nobody's Perfect, 1982; Waiting for the Sky to Fall, 1985; Other Side, 1990; Take a Good Look, 1990; The Story of Tracy Beaker, 1991; The Suitcase Kid, 1992 (Children's Book of the Year Award, 1993); Video Rose, 1992; The Mum-minder, 1993; The Werepuppy, 1993; The Bed and Breakfast Star, 1994; Mark Spark in the Dark, 1994; Twin Trouble, 1995; Glubbslyme, 1995; Jimmy Jelly, 1995; Dinosaur's Packed Lunch, 1995; Cliffhanger, 1995; Double Act, 1995 (Children's Book of the Year Award; Smarties Prize); My Brother Bernadette, 1995; Werepuppy on Holiday, 1995; Bad Girls, 1996; Mr Cool, 1996; Monster Story-teller, 1997; The Lottie Project, 1997; Girls in Love, 1997; Connie and the Water Babies, 1997; Buried Alive!, 1998; Girls Under Pressure, 1998; The Illustrated Mum, 1999; Girls Out Late, 1999; The Dare Game, 2000; Vicky Angel, 2000; The Cat Mummy, 2001; Sleepovers, 2001; Dustbin Baby, 2001. *Recreations:* talking to my daughter, reading, swimming, going to art galleries and films … and line dancing. *Address:* 1[B] Beaufort Road, Kingston upon Thames, Surrey KT1 2TH. *T:* (020) 8549 3428.

WILSON, Sir James; *see* Wilson, Sir A. J.

WILSON, Brig. James, CBE 1986; Director, Edinburgh Old Town Trust, 1987–90; Chief Executive, Livingston Development Corporation, 1977–87; *b* 12 March 1922; *s* of late Alexander Robertson Wilson and Elizabeth Wylie Wilson (*née* Murray); *m* 1949, Audrie Veronica, *er d* of late A. W. and O. V. Haines; three *d*. *Educ:* Irvine Royal Academy; Edinburgh Academy; Aberdeen Univ. Commissioned RA, 1941; served War with 71 (West Riding) Field Regt, N Africa and Italy, 1941–45; Instructor, Sch. of Artillery, India, 1945–47; Adjt, Sussex Yeo., 1948–49; active service in Malaya and ME, 1950–53; psc 1954; DAQMG, War Office, 1955–57; Instructor, Staff Coll., 1959–61; CO, 439 (Tyne) Light Air Defence Regt, 1964–67; AQMG, Northern Comd, 1967–68; Col GS SD, HQ BAOR, 1969–71; AMA and DCBAS, Washington, 1972–73; DQMG, HQ UKLF, 1974–77. Member: Executive Council, TCPA (Scotland), 1977–87; Edin. Univ. Careers Adv. Cttee, 1982–86; Scottish Cttee, Inst. of Dirs, 1983–86; Dir, Edinburgh Chamber of Commerce, 1979–82. Mem., Royal Artillery Council for Scotland, 1979–93; Chairman: W Lothian SSAFA, 1983–93; E Scotland SSAFA Cttee, 1986–93; RA Assoc. (Scotland), 1987–91 (Pres., 1991–94); Vice Pres. Tetbury Br., RBL, 1996–; Chm., Tetbury Civic Soc., 1999–. FIMgt (FBIM 1980). *Recreations:* golf, gardening, bridge. *Address:* The Stables, The Green, Tetbury, Glos GL8 8DN. *T:* (01666) 503030. *Clubs:* Army and Navy; Hon. Co. of Edinburgh Golfers.

WILSON, James Elliott, OBE 1978; JP; Lord-Lieutenant, County Borough of Belfast, 1991–2000; *b* 3 May 1925; *s* of Samuel Robinson Wilson and Clarice Evelyn (*née* Duckham); *m* 1954, Rosemary Clarke; three *d. Educ:* Clifton Coll., Bristol. Served Royal Inniskilling Fusiliers, 1943–48. Ormeau Bakery Ltd, Belfast, 1948–80. Chm., Trustee Savings Bank of NI, 1974–82; Dir, First Trust Bank, NI, 1994–96. Chm., Assoc. Citizens' Advice Bureaux, NI, 1985–88. Member, Board of Management: Somme Hosp., Belfast, 1965–98; NI Fever Hosp., 1968–73; Chm., Glendhu Children's Hostel, Belfast, 1981–85. DL 1982, JP 1991, Belfast. Hon. Col, 40th Ulster Signal Regt (V), 1982–90. CStJ 1993. *Recreations:* golf, gardening, travel. *Address:* White Lodge, The Temple, Boardmills, Lisburn, Co. Antrim BT27 6UQ. *T:* (028) 9263 8413. *Club:* Royal County Down Golf (Newcastle, Co. Down).

WILSON, Dr James Maxwell Glover, FRCP, FRCPE, FFPHM; Senior Principal Medical Officer, Department of Health and Social Security, 1972–76; *b* 31 Aug. 1913; *s* of late James Thomas Wilson and Mabel Salomons; *m* Lallie Methley; three *s. Educ:* King's College Choir Sch., Cambridge; Oundle Sch.; St John's Coll., Cambridge; University College Hosp., London. MA, MB, BChir (Cantab). Clinical appts, London and Cambridge, 1937–39. Served War, RAMC (Major, 6th Airborne Div.), 1939–45. Hospital appts, London and Edinburgh, 1945–54; medical work on tea estates in India, 1954–57; Medical Staff, Min. of Health (later DHSS), concerned with the centrally financed research programme, 1957–76; Sen. Res. Fellow, Inf. Services Div., Common Services Agency, Scottish Health Service, 1976–81. Lectr (part-time), Public Health Dept, London Sch. of Hygiene and Tropical Med., 1968–72. *Publications:* (with G. Jungner) Principles and Practice of Screening for Disease (WHO), 1968; contribs to med. jls, mainly on screening for disease. *Recreations:* reading, conservation. *Address:* Millhill House, 77 Millhill, Musselburgh, Midlothian EH21 7RP. *T:* (0131) 665 5829.

WILSON, James Millar; Member (UU) Antrim South, Northern Ireland Assembly, since 1998; *b* 15 Dec. 1941; *s* of James Millar Wilson and Isobel Wilson; *m* 1965, Muriel Smyth; one *s* one *d. Educ:* Ballyclare High Sch.; Belfast Coll. of Technol. Engineer: Port Line Ltd, Merchant Navy, 1962–64; British Enkalon Ltd, 1964–73; partner, retail grocery business, 1972–88. Chief Exec., UU Party, 1987–98. Chief UUP Whip, NI Assembly, 1998–. Mem., UU Council, 1982–87 and 1998– (Mem. Exec. Cttee, 1985–87 and 1998–); Vice Pres., S Antrim UU Assoc., 1996–. *Recreations:* gardening, angling. *Address:* 83 Clare Heights, Ballyclare, Co. Antrim BT39 9SB. *T:* (028) 9332 4477; (office) 3A Rashee Road, Ballyclare, Co. Antrim BT39 9HJ. *T:* (028) 9332 4461; *e-mail:* jim.wilson@niassembly.gov.uk.

WILSON, James Noel, OBE 1996; ChM, FRCS; retired; Consultant Orthopædic Surgeon: Royal National Orthopædic Hospital, London (Surgeon i/c Accident Unit, RNOH Stanmore), 1955–84; National Hospitals for Nervous Diseases, Queen Square and Maida Vale, 1962–84; Teacher of Orthopædics, Institute of Orthopædics, University of London; retired; *b* Coventry, 25 Dec. 1919; *s* of Alexander Wilson and Isobel Barbara Wilson (*née* Fairweather); *m* 1945, Patricia Norah McCullough; two *s* two *d. Educ:* King Henry VIII Sch., Coventry; University of Birmingham. Peter Thompson Prize in Anatomy, 1940; Sen. Surgical Prize, 1942; Arthur Foxwell Prize in Clinical Medicine, 1943; MB, ChB 1943; MRCS, LRCP, 1943; FRCS 1948; ChM (Birmingham) 1949; House Surgeon, Birmingham General Hospital, 1943; Heaton Award as Best Resident for 1943. Service in RAMC, Nov. 1943–Oct. 1946, discharged as Captain; qualified as Parachutist and served with 1st Airborne Division. Resident surgical posts, Birmingham General Hospital and Coventry and Warwickshire Hospital, 1947–49; Resident Surgical Officer, Robert Jones and Agnes Hunt Orthopædic Hospital, Oswestry, 1949–52; Consultant Orthopædic Surgeon to Cardiff Royal Infirmary and Welsh Regional Hospital Board, 1952–55. Prof. of Orthopaedics, Addis Ababa Univ., 1989. Watson-Jones Lectr, RCS, 1988; Duraiswami Meml Oration, Delhi Orthopaedic Assoc., 1989; Jackson Burrows Medal Lectr, Inst. of Orthopaedics, 1991. World Orthopaedic Concern: Pres., 1979–84; Chm., UK Region, 1984–90; Editor, News-Letter, 1988–2000. Vice-Chm., Impact (UK) Foundn, 1988–2000; Pres., Orthopaedic Section, RSocMed, 1982–83; former Mem. Brit. Editorial Bd, Jl of Bone and Joint Surgery; Sen. Fellow, and formerly Editorial Sec., British Orthopædic Assoc. (BOA Travelling Fellowship to USA, 1954); FRSocMed 1959, Hon. FRSocMed 1998. Life Mem., Bangladesh Orthopaedic Soc.; Hon. Mem., Egyptian Orthopaedic Assoc. *Publications:* (ed) Watson Jones Fractures and Joint Injuries, 6th edn 1982; former contributor, Butterworth's Operative Surgery; chapters and articles on orthopædic subjects to various books and journals. *Recreations:* golf, reluctant gardening, photography. *Address:* The Chequers, Waterdell, Watford, Herts WD25 0GP. *T:* (01923) 672364. *Club:* Royal Society of Medicine.

WILSON, Sir James (William Douglas), 5th Bt *cr* 1906; farmer; *b* 8 Oct. 1960; *s* of Captain Sir Thomas Douglas Wilson, 4th Bt, MC, and of Pamela Aileen, *d* of Sir Edward Hanmer, 7th Bt; *S* father, 1984; *m* 1985, Julia Margaret Louise, fourth *d* of J. C. F. Mutty, Mulberry Hall, Melbourn, Cambs; two *s* two *d. Educ:* London Univ. (BA Hons French). *Heir: s* Thomas Edward Douglas Wilson, *b* 15 April 1990. *Address:* Lillingstone Lovell Manor, Buckingham MK18 5BQ. *T:* (01280) 860643.

WILSON, Joe; *see* Wilson, A. J.

WILSON, Ven. (John) Hewitt, CB 1977; Chaplain-in-Chief, Royal Air Force, 1973–80, Archdeacon Emeritus, since 1980; Canon and Prebendary of Lincoln Cathedral, 1974–80, Canon Emeritus, since 1980; *b* 14 Feb. 1924; 2nd *s* of John Joseph and Marion Wilson; *m* 1951, Gertrude Elsie Joan Weir; three *s* two *d. Educ:* Kilkenny Coll., Kilkenny; Mountjoy Sch., Dublin; Trinity Coll., Dublin (BA 1946; MA 1956). Curate, St George's Church, Dublin, 1947–50; entered RAF, 1950: RAF Coll., Cranwell, 1950–52; Aden, 1952–55; RAF Wittering, 1955–57; RAF Cottesmore, 1957–58; RAF Germany, 1958–61; Staff Chaplain, Air Ministry, 1961–63; RAF Coll., Cranwell, 1963–66; Asst Chaplain-in-Chief: Far East Air Force, 1966–69; Strike command, 1969–73; Rector of The Heyfords with Rousham and Somerton, diocese of Oxford, 1981–93. QHC 1972–80. Liveryman, Coachmakers' and Coach-Harness Makers' Co., 1994– (Hon. Chaplain, 1977–). *Recreations:* Rugby football, golf, tennis, gardening, theatre. *Address:* Glencree, Philcote Street, Deddington, Banbury, Oxon OX15 0TB. *T:* and *Fax:* (01869) 338903; *e-mail:* glencree@freecall-uk.co.uk. *Club:* Royal Air Force.

WILSON, Dr John Murray, MBE 1964; Controller, Home Division, British Council, 1985–86; *b* 25 July 1926; *s* of Maurice John and Mary Ellen Wilson (*née* Murray); *m* 1957, Audrey Miriam Simmons; one *s* one *d. Educ:* Selwyn Avenue Junior, Highams Park; Bancroft's School, Essex; St John's College, Oxford (MA Botany 1952; DPhil 1957; *prox. acc.* Christopher Welch Scholarship 1951). Served RAF, 1945–48. British Council, 1955–86: Science Dept, 1955–58; Chile, 1958–62; Brazil, 1962–66; India, 1966–71; Dep. Rep./Sci. Officer, Italy, 1971–74; Sci. Officer, Germany, 1974–79; Dep. Rep., Germany, 1979–81; Dep. Controller, Home Div., 1981–85. *Publications:* (with J. L. Harley) papers in New Phytologist. *Recreations:* gardening, photography, messing about.

WILSON, John Richard; Chief Executive, Defence Housing Executive, since 1999; *b* 8 March 1946; *s* of Kenneth Charles Wilson and Mary Edith Wilson (*née* Dalladay); *m* 1968, Anne Margaret Saville; two *s. Educ:* Lewes Co. Grammar Sch. for Boys. Ministry of Defence: Exec. Officer, Navy Dept, 1965–68; Secretariat Divs, 1968–85; Directing Staff, JSDC, 1985–87; Hd, Br. Personnel and Logistics Div., 1987–89; Project Manager, Quality Assce Relocation, 1989–92; Hd, Plans and Budgets, for Dir Gen. Support Systems (RAF), 1992–94; Hd, Plans and Budgets, for AO CIS, HQ RAF Logistics Comd, 1994–95; Dir, Finance and Secretariat, Defence Housing Exec., 1995–99. *Recreations:* walking, DIY, classic cars. *Address:* Ministry of Defence, Defence Housing Executive, St Christopher House, Southwark Street, SE1 0TD. *T:* (020) 7305 2777.

WILSON, John Veitch D.; *see* Drysdale Wilson.

WILSON, His Honour John Warley; a Circuit Judge, 1982–2001; *b* 13 April 1936; *s* of late John Pearson Wilson and Nancy Wade Wilson (*née* Harston); *m* 1962, Rosalind Mary Pulford. *Educ:* Warwick Sch.; St Catharine's Coll., Cambridge (MA). Called to the Bar, Lincoln's Inn, 1960, in practice, 1960–82; a Recorder of the Crown Court, 1979–82. Dep. Chairman, West Midlands Agricultural Land Tribunal, 1978–82. *Recreations:* gardening, National Hunt racing. *Address:* Victoria House, Farm Street, Harbury, Leamington Spa CV33 9LR. *T:* (01926) 612572.

WILSON, Rt Rev. Dr John Warwick; Bishop of the Southern Region (Assistant Bishop, Diocese of Melbourne), since 1985; *b* 12 July 1937; *s* of Walter and Norma Wilson; *m* 1963, Jill Brady; two *d. Educ:* Bathurst Coll., NSW; Ridley Coll., Parkville, Victoria (ThL, ThSchol); London Univ. (BD (Hons)); Yale Univ. (STM); Duke Univ. (PhD). Educn Officer, Papua New Guinea, 1957–59. Ordained deacon and priest, 1964; Asst, St Cyprian's, Narrabri, 1964–67; Vicar, St Andrew, Tingha, 1967–68; Priest in charge, St John's Henderson, North Carolina, USA, 1969–72; Lectr in OT, Ridley Coll., 1973–85. *Publications:* The Old Testament and Christian Living, 1981, 2nd edn 1985; Ezekiel: God's Communicator, 1990; The Old Testament on the Way to the Cross, 1994. *Recreations:* reading, music, cinema. *Address:* Anglican Centre, 209 Flinders Lane, Melbourne, Vic 3000, Australia. *T:* (3) 96534220, *Fax:* (3) 96502184.

WILSON, John Willoughby; QC (NI) 1988; Master, Queen's Bench and Appeals, Supreme Court of Northern Ireland, since 1993; Clerk of the Crown for Northern Ireland, since 1993; *b* 4 Sept. 1933; *s* of late Willoughby Wilson and Martha (*née* Wood); *m* 1963, Rosemary Frances Turner (*d* 1999); one *s* two *d. Educ:* Leys Sch.; Magdalene Coll., Cambridge (MA); Queen's Univ., Belfast (LLB). Called to the Bar, NI, 1960; in practice, 1960–66; Private Sec., 1966–79, Legal Sec., 1979–80, to Lord Chief Justice of NI; Asst Dir, NI Court Service, 1980–85; Master, High Court, Supreme Court of NI, 1985–93. Under Treas., Inn of Court of NI, 1997–. Gov., Victoria Coll., Belfast, 1970– (Chm., 1990–95). Chancellor, Dio. Connor, 1982–. *Recreations:* music, reading, cycling. *Address:* Royal Courts of Justice, Belfast BT1 3JF. *T:* (028) 9072 4699.

WILSON, Joseph Albert; Secretary to the Cabinet, Sierra Leone Government, 1968–69; Barrister-at-Law; Solicitor of High Court of Sierra Leone; Notary Public; Commissioner for Oaths; *b* 22 Jan. 1922; *e s* of late George Wilson; *m* 1947, Esther Massaquoi; two *s* four *d* (and one *s* decd). *Educ:* St Edward's Secondary Sch., Freetown, Sierra Leone; University of Exeter, (DPA); Middle Temple. Graded Clerical Service, Sierra Leone Government, 1941–47; family business, 1948–51; Secretary, Bonthe District Council, 1951–59; Administrative Officer, Sierra Leone Government, rising to rank of Cabinet Secretary, 1959; High Comr from Sierra Leone to UK, 1967–68. Manager (Special Duties), SLST Ltd, 1959. Comdr of the Republic, CR. *Recreations:* tennis, golf.

WILSON, Julian David Bonhôte; freelance journalist and broadcaster; Racing Correspondent, BBC Television, 1966–97; *b* 21 June 1940; *s* of Peter Jardine Bonhôte Wilson, OBE and Helen Angela Josephine Mann; *m* 1st, 1970, Carolyn Anne Michael (marr. diss. 1980); one *s*; 2nd, 1981, Alison Christian Findlay Ramsay. *Educ:* Harrow. Writer and reporter, Mirror Group Newspapers, 1958–64; Editor, Tote Racing Annual, 1965. *Publications:* Lester Piggott: the pictorial biography, 1985; 100 Greatest Racehorses, 1987; The Racing World, 1991; Some You Win (autobiog.), 1998. *Recreation:* cricket. *Address:* Home Farm Cottage, Burrough Green, Newmarket, Suffolk CB8 9LY; 10 Windsor Lane, Tokai 7945, Cape Town, South Africa. *Clubs:* Turf, St Moritz Tobogganing.

WILSON, Mrs (Katherine) Muriel (Irwin), OBE 1985; Chairman and Chief Executive, Equal Opportunities Commission for Northern Ireland, 1981–84; *b* 3 Dec. 1920; *d* of Francis Hosford and Martha Evelyn (*née* Irwin); *m* 1949, William George Wilson; one *s. Educ:* Methodist Coll., Belfast; The Queen's University of Belfast (DPA); MIMgt. Northern Ireland Civil Service, 1939–49; N Ireland Health Service, 1949–73: Eastern Special Care Management Cttee (Services for the Mentally Handicapped): Asst Sec., 1963–71; Gp Sec. and Chief Admin. Officer, 1971–73; Asst Chief Admin. Officer (Personnel and Management Services), Northern Health and Social Services Board, 1973–81. Chm. NI Div., 1977–79, National Vice-Pres. 1979–81, United Kingdom Fedn of Business and Professional Women; Member: Bd, Labour Relations Agency (NI), 1976–81; Fair Employment Agency for NI, 1981–84; NI Adv. Cttee, IBA, 1978–83; NI Council, RIPA, 1985–88; Women's Forum, NI, 1990–. Dir, Ulster Telethon Trust, 1989–2000. Chairman, Board of Governors: Glenravel Special Sch., Belfast, 1987–93; Hill Croft Sch., Newtownabbey, 1987–89; Glenveagh Sch., Belfast, 1993–97; Chm., Whiteabbey Hosp. League of Friends, 1989–92. *Recreations:* swimming, reading.

WILSON, Rev. Dr Kenneth Brian, OBE 1993; Director of Research, The Queen's Foundation, Birmingham, since 1996; *b* 10 April 1937; *s* of Norman Harold Wilson and Violet Frances Sarah Wilson; *m* 1962, Jennifer Rosemary Floyd; one *s* two *d. Educ:* Kingswood Sch., Bath; Trinity Hall, Cambridge (BA 1961; MA); Univ. of Bristol (MLitt; PhD); MA Oxon. Ordained Minister in Methodist Church; Asst Minister, Hinde St Methodist Church, London, 1964–66; Asst Chaplain, 1966–69, Chaplain, 1969–73, Kingswood Sch., Bath; Rowbotham Prof. of Philosophy and Ethics, Wesley Coll., Bristol, 1973–80; Principal, Westminster Coll., Oxford, 1981–96. Fernley Hartley Lectr, 1973. Dir, Methodist Newspaper Co., 1991–. Director: Hinksey Network, 1981–; Ammerdown Christian Study Centre, Radstock, 1986–. Chairman: Science and Religion Forum, 1979–81; Nat. Primary Centre, Oxford, 1987–93; Christian Educn Movt, 1995–; Member: Council, CNAA, 1982–92; Cttee, Ian Ramsey Centre, Oxford, 1985–99; Council, Inst. of Educn, Univ. of London, 1991–96 (Chm., 1993–95); CATE, 1992–94. Trustee, Higher Educn Foundn, 1985–96. Gov., The Leys Sch., Cambridge, 1990–. FRSA. Hon. DTh Lycoming, 1994; Hon. DLL High Point Univ., 1995. *Publications:* Making Sense of It, 1973; Living it Out, 1975; (ed) Experience of Ordination, 1979; (with F. Young) Focus on God, 1986. *Recreations:* books, poetry, art, religion. *Address:* Knapp Cottage, West Bradley, Glastonbury, Som BA6 8LT. *Club:* Oxford and Cambridge.

WILSON, Prof. Kenneth Geddes, PhD; Professor of Physics, Ohio State University, since 1988; *b* 8 June 1936; *s* of Edgar Bright Wilson and Emily Fisher Buckingham; *m* 1982, Alison Brown. *Educ:* Harvard Univ. (AB); Calif Inst. of Technol. (PhD). Cornell

University: Asst Prof. of Physics, 1963; Prof. of Physics, 1963–88; Dir, Center for Theory and Simulation in Sci. and Engrg, 1985–88. Co-Prin. Investigator, Nat. Sci. Foundn Statewide Systematic Initiative, Project Discovery, Ohio, to reform sci. and math. educn, 1991–96. Hon. PhD: Harvard, 1981; Chicago, 1976. Nobel Prize for Physics, 1982. *Publications:* (ed jtly) Broken Scale Invariance and the Light Cone, 1971; Quarks and Strings on a Lattice, 1975; (contrib.) New Pathways in High Energy Physics, Vol. II 1976; (contrib.) New Developments in Quantum Field Theory and Statistical Mechanics, 1977; (contrib.) Recent Developments in Gauge Theories, 1980; (with Bennett Daviss) Redesigning Education, 1994; contrib. Jl of Math. Phys, Nuovo Cimento, Acta Phys. Austriaca, Phys Rev., Jl of Chem. Phys, Comm. Math. Phys, Phys Reports, Advances in Maths, Rev. of Mod. Phys, Scientific American; symposia and conf. papers. *Address:* Department of Physics, Ohio State University, 174 West 18th Avenue, Columbus, OH 43210–1106, USA. *T:* (614) 2929396.

WILSON, Leslie William; JP; Director-General, Association of Special Libraries and Information Bureaux (Aslib), 1950–78, retired; *b* 26 Sept. 1918; *s* of Harry Wilson and Ada Jane Wilson; *m* 1942, Valerie Jones; one *s* two *d.* *Educ:* Cambridgeshire High Sch.; Trinity Hall, Cambridge (Open Scholar, MA Mod. Langs). Army Service, India, 1940–46. Foreign Editor, Times Educnl Supplement, 1946–50. Mem., Parly and Scientific Cttee, 1965–78. Hon. Fellow, Internat. Fedn for Documentation, 1978; Hon. Member: Inst. of Information Scientists, 1977; US Special Libraries Assoc., 1978; Aslib, 1978. Chm., Richmond Assoc. for Nat. Trust, 1997–2001. JP Middx, 1971. Dep. Grand Master, Masonic Province of Middx, 1989–93. *Address:* 6 Queensberry House, Friars Lane, Richmond, Surrey TW9 1NT. *T:* (020) 8948 0421.

WILSON, Lynn Anthony; Deputy Chairman, Wilson Connolly Holdings PLC, since 2001 (Chairman, 1982–2001); Director of 24 subsidiary companies; *b* 8 Dec. 1939; *s* of Connolly Thomas Wilson and Frances (*née* Chapman); *m* 1964, Judith Helen Mann; two *s.* *Educ:* Oakham Sch., Rutland. FCIOB; CBIM. Wilson Builders (N'pton) Ltd, 1957; Man. Dir, Wilson (Connolly) Holdings, on flotation, 1966. Nat. Pres., House Builders Fedn, 1981. Pres., Old Oakhamian Club, 1988; Trustee, Oakham Sch., 1983–96. Pres., Northants CCC, 2000– (Chm., 1990–2000; Mem. Cttee, 1971–80; Treas., 1974–79). *Recreations:* cricket, golf, horseracing, shooting. *Address:* c/o Wilson Connolly Holdings PLC, Thomas Wilson House, Tenter Road, Moulton Park, Northampton NN3 6QJ. *T:* (01604) 790909. *Clubs:* East India, MCC; Northants CC.

WILSON, Lynton Ronald, OC 1997; Chairman: CAE Inc.; Nortel Networks Corp.; *b* Port Colborne, Canada, 3 April 1940; *s* of Ronald Alfred and Blanche Evelyn Wilson; *m* 1968, Brenda Jean Black; one *s* two *d.* *Educ:* Port Colborne High Sch.; McMaster Univ. (BA Hons 1962); Cornell Univ. (MA 1967). Dep. Minister, Min. of Industry and Tourism, Govt of Ontario, 1978–81; Pres. and CEO, 1981–88, Chm., 1988–89, Redpath Industries Ltd, Toronto; Man. Dir, North America, Tate & Lyle plc, 1986–89; Vice-Chm., Bank of Nova Scotia, Toronto, 1989–90; BCE Inc.: Chief Operating Officer, 1990–92; Pres., 1990–96; CEO, 1992–98; Chm., 1993–2000. Director: DaimlerChrysler Canada Inc.; Supervisory Bd, DaimlerChrysler AG, 1998– (Mem. Chm.'s Council, 2000–); Imperial Oil Ltd; Ontario Power Generation Inc. Mem., Internat. Council, J. P. Morgan & Co., subseq. J. P. Morgan Chase & Co., NY. Hon. *Dhc* Montreal, 1995; Hon. LLD: McMaster, 1995; UC of Cape Breton, 1998; Mount Allison, 2000; Hon. DCL Bishop's Univ., 1997. *Recreations:* golf, ski-ing. *Address:* BCE Inc., 181 Bay Street, Suite 4700, Toronto, ON M5J 2T3, Canada. *T:* (416) 3644789. *Clubs:* York, Toronto (Toronto); Rideau (Ottawa); Toronto Golf, Mount Royal, Mount Bruno Golf.

WILSON, Ven. Mark John Crichton; Archdeacon of Dorking, since 1996; *b* 14 Jan. 1946; *s* of Rev. William Hubert Wilson and Gladys Margaret Wilson; *m* 1970, Rev. Canon Mavis Kirby Wilson; one *s* three *d.* *Educ:* St Paul's Cathedral Choir Sch.; St John's Sch., Leatherhead; Clare Coll., Cambridge (BA, MA 1970); Ridley Hall, Cambridge. Ordained deacon, 1969, priest, 1970; Assistant Curate: Luton with East Hyde, 1969–72; Ashtead, Surrey, 1972–77; Chaplain, Epsom Coll., 1977–81; Vicar, Christ Church, Epsom Common, 1981–96. Rural Dean of Epsom, 1987–92. *Recreations:* golf, gardening (growing fuchsias). *Address:* Littlecroft, Heathside Road, Woking, Surrey GU22 7EZ. *T:* (01483) 772713, *Fax:* (01483) 757353; *e-mail:* mark.wilson@cofeguildford.org.uk.

WILSON, Martin; *see* Wilson, A. M.

WILSON, Martin Joseph, FCA; Group Chief Executive, Ulster Bank, since 1998; *b* 13 March 1950; *s* of Michael and Elizabeth Wilson; *m* Paulette Palmer; one *s* two *d.* *Educ:* Oatlands Coll., Dublin. ACA 1975, FCA 1985; FIBI 1991. Articled Clerk, Fay McMahon & Co., Chartered Accountants, 1969–75; Sen. Audit Manager, KPMG, 1975–78; Chief Accountant, Bell Lines Ltd, 1978–80; Financial Controller, 1980–89, Head of Treasury, 1984–89, Ulster Investment Bank; Ulster Bank: Gp Treas., 1989–95; Dir, 1991–; Dep. Gp Chief Exec., 1997–98; Chief Exec., Ulster Bank Mkts, 1995–97. *Recreations:* golf, reading, music. *Address:* Ulster Bank Ltd, Group Head Office, Donegall Square East, Belfast BT1 5UB. *T:* (028) 9027 6000.

WILSON, Sir Mathew John Anthony, 6th Bt *cr* 1874, of Eshton Hall, Co. York; OBE 1979 (MBE 1971); MC 1972; President, Dolphin Voyaging Inc., since 1995; *b* 2 Oct. 1935; *s* of Anthony Thomas Wilson (*d* 1979; 2nd *s* of Sir Mathew Richard Henry Wilson, 4th Bt) and Margaret (*d* 1980), *d* of late Alfred Holden; *S* uncle, 1991; *m* 1962, Janet Mary, *e d* of late E. W. Mowll, JP; one *s* one *d.* *Educ:* Trinity Coll. Sch., Ontario. Brig. KOYLI, retired 1983. Exec. Dir, Wilderness Foundn (UK), 1983–85. Former Vice-Pres., Internat. Wilderness Leadership Foundn. *Heir:* *s* Mathew Edward Amcotts Wilson, *b* 13 Oct. 1966. *Publications:* Taking Terrapin Home: a Love Affair with a Small Catamaran, 1994; The Bahamas Cruising Guide, 1998.

WILSON, Michael; *see* Wilson, T. M. A.

WILSON, Michael Anthony, FRCGP; general practitioner; *b* 2 June 1936; *s* of late Charles Kenneth Wilson and Bertha Wilson; *m* 1959, Marlene (*née* Wilson); two *s.* *Educ:* Roundhay Grammar Sch., Leeds; Medical Sch., Univ. of Leeds (MB ChB 1958). DObst RCOG 1961; MRCGP 1965, FRCGP 1980. British Medical Association: Chm., Gen. Med. Services Cttee, 1984–90 (Dep. Chm., 1979–84); Pres., Yorkshire Regional Council, 1975–79; Mem. Council, 1977–90, 1992–2000; Vice-Pres.; Fellow, 1979. Member: GMC, 1989–; Standing Med. Adv. Cttee to DHSS, 1967–69, 1978–90 (Dep. Chm., 1986–90); NHS Clinical Standards Adv. Gp, 1990–93; Code of Practice Authy, Assoc. of British Pharmaceutical Industry, 1990–; Jt Consultants Cttee, 1991–97. Chm., BMA Pension Trustees Ltd, 1994–2000; Dir, Professional Affinity Group Services Ltd, 1987–2000. Sec., Ampleforth Coll. Golf Club. *Recreations:* golf, Rotary. *Address:* Longueville, Mill Hill, Huntington, York YO32 9PY. *T:* (01904) 768861. *Clubs:* East India; York Golf.

WILSON, Michael Anthony; Chief Executive, Waltham Forest Housing Action Trust, since 1992; *b* 19 Feb. 1948; *s* of Alan Wilson and Christina Wilson (*née* McFarlane); *m* 1972, Aileen Athey (marr. diss. 1991); one *s* two *d.* *Educ:* Aston Univ. (BSc Hons Behavioural Sci. 1972); DipTP 1977. MRTPI 1979; AIH 1984. Planning Asst, London Borough of Barnet, 1972–74; Res. and Inf. Officer, Harlow Develt Corp., 1974–80; Housing Manager, City of Glasgow, 1980–84; Dir of Housing and Envmtl Services, London Borough of Brent, 1984–92. MIMgt 1978. *Recreations:* watching football (Spurs), cinema, theatre, good food and wine, the children. *Address:* 40 Salters Road, E17 3PQ. *Club:* Tottenham Hotspur Football.

WILSON, Maj.-Gen. Michael Peter Bruce Grant; Chief Executive, Defence Vetting Agency, since 1996; *b* 19 Aug. 1943; *s* of Ian Henry Wilson and Catherine Collingwood Wilson; *m* 1967, Margaret Ritchie; two *s* one *d.* *Educ:* Duke of York's Sch., Nairobi; Dip. Photogrammetry, UCL. FRICS 1995 (ARICS 1988); FRGS 1990. Commnd RE, 1966; served UK, Kenya, Uganda, Nigeria, BAOR, MoD; UK Exchange Officer, US Defense Mapping Agency, 1978; Sen. Instructor in Air Survey and Cartography, Sch. of Mil. Survey, 1981; Asst Dir, Mil. Survey Systems and Techniques Unit, 1983; CO 512 Special Team RE and Comdr, Geographic Staff, Washington, 1986; Comdr, 42 Survey Engr Gp, 1987; Dir, Geographic Ops, MoD, 1990; Dir-Gen., Mil. Survey and Chief Exec., Mil. Survey Defence Agency, 1993; Dir-Gen. Intelligence and Geographic Resources, MoD, 1995–96. Col Comdt RE, 1997–. FIMgt. *Recreations:* mountaineering, rock climbing, shooting, stalking, fishing, golf, cricket. *Clubs:* Geographical; Pyrford Cricket; British Sporting Rifle.

WILSON, Michael Sumner; Chief Executive, St James's Place, since 1992; *b* 5 Dec. 1943; *s* of late Peter and Margaret Wilson; *m* 1975, Mary Drysdale (marr. diss. 1997); one *d.* *Educ:* St Edward's School, Oxford. Equity & Law, 1963–68; Abbey Life, 1968–71; Allied Dunbar (Hambro Life until 1985, when name was changed), 1971–91: Exec. Dir, 1973; Board Dir, 1976; Dep. Man. Dir, 1982; Man. Dir, 1984; Gp Chief Exec., 1988–91; Dir, St James's Place Capital, 1997–. Director: BAT Industries, 1989–91; Vendôme Luxury Gp, 1993–98. *Recreations:* tennis, racing. *Clubs:* Raffles, Annabel's.

WILSON, Muriel; *see* Wilson, K. M. I.

WILSON, Prof. Nairn Hutchison Fulton, PhD; FDS; Professor of Restorative Dentistry and Head, Unit of Operative Dentistry and Endodontology (formerly of Conservative Dentistry), University Dental Hospital, Manchester, since 1986; *b* 26 April 1950; *s* of William Fulton Wilson and Anne Hutchison Wilson (*née* Stratton); *m* 1st, 1971, Madeleine Christina Munro (marr. diss. 1981); two *d*; 2nd, 1982, Margaret Alexandra Jones; one *s* one *d.* *Educ:* Strathallan Sch.; Univ. of Edinburgh (BDS 1973); Univ. of Manchester (MSc 1979; PhD 1985); Royal Coll. of Surgeons of Edinburgh (FDS 1977; DRD 1980). FACD 1990; FADM 1991; FDS RCS (*ad eundem*), 1994. Lectr in Restorative Dentistry (Prosthetics), Univ. of Edinburgh, 1974–75; University of Manchester: Lectr in Conservative Dentistry, 1975–81; Sen. Lectr, 1981–86; Head, Dept of Conservative Dentistry, 1986–88, Dept of Restorative Dentistry, 1988–92; Dep. Dean, 1991–92, Dean and Clin. Dir, 1992–95, Univ. Dental Hosp.; Pro Vice-Chancellor, 1997–99. Hon. Consultant in Restorative Dentistry, Central Manchester Healthcare NHS Trust (formerly Central Manchester HA), 1982–. Non-exec. Dir, N Manchester Healthcare NHS Trust, 1994–97. Dean, Faculty of Dental Surgery, RCSE, 1995–98. President: British Assoc. of Teachers of Conservative Dentistry, 1992; Sect. of Odontology, Manchester Med. Soc., 1993–94; British Soc. for Restorative Dentistry, 1994–95; Eur. Sect., Acad. of Operative Dentistry, 1998–2000; Educn Res. Gp, IADR, 1998–2000; GDC, 1999–. Hon. Fellow, Coll. of Dental Surgeons of HK, 1999. Editor, Jl of Dentistry, 1986–. *Publications:* contrib. chaps in contemporary texts and numerous papers in jls. *Recreations:* D-I-Y, gardening, ski-ing. *Address:* Turner Dental School, University Dental Hospital of Manchester, Higher Cambridge Street, Manchester M15 6FH. *T:* (0161) 275 6660. *Club:* Strathallan.

WILSON, Hon. Sir Nicholas (Allan Roy), Kt 1993; **Hon. Mr Justice Wilson;** a Judge of the High Court of Justice, Family Division, since 1993; *b* 9 May 1945; *s* of late Roderick Peter Garratt Wilson and of Dorothy Anne Wilson (*née* Chenevix-Trench); *m* 1974, Margaret (*née* Higgins); one *s* one *d.* *Educ:* Bryanston School; Worcester College, Oxford (BA 1st cl. hons Jurisp. 1966). Eldon Scholar, 1967. Called to the Bar, Inner Temple, 1967, Bencher, 1993; QC 1987; a Recorder, 1987–93. Pres., Family Mediators Assoc., 1998–. *Address:* Royal Courts of Justice, Strand, WC2A 2LL.

WILSON, Nigel Guy, FBA 1980; Fellow and Tutor in Classics, Lincoln College, Oxford, since 1962; *b* 23 July 1935; *s* of Noel Wilson and Joan Lovibond; *m* 1996, Hanneke Marion Wirtjes. *Educ:* University Coll. Sch.; Corpus Christi Coll., Oxford (1st Cl. Classics (Mods) 1955; 1st Cl. Lit. Hum. 1957; Hertford Scholar 1955; Ireland and Craven Scholar 1955; Derby Scholar 1957). Lectr, Merton Coll., Oxford, 1957–62. Jt Editor, Classical Rev., 1975–87. Ospite Linceo, Scuola normale superiore, Pisa, 1977; Visiting Professor: Univ. of Padua, 1985; Ecole Normale Supérieure, Paris, 1986. Gaisford Lectr, 1983. Hon. DLitt Uppsala, 2001. Gordon Duff Prize, 1968; Premio Anassilao, Reggio Calabria, 1999. *Publications:* (with L. D. Reynolds) Scribes and Scholars, 1968, 3rd edn 1991; An Anthology of Byzantine Prose, 1971; Medieval Greek Bookhands, 1973; St Basil on the Value of Greek Literature, 1975; Scholia in Aristophanis Acharnenses, 1975; (with D. A. Russell) Menander Rhetor, 1981; Scholars of Byzantium, 1983; (with Sir Hugh Lloyd-Jones) Sophoclea, 1990; (ed with Sir Hugh Lloyd-Jones) Sophocles: Fabulae, 1990; From Byzantium to Italy, 1992; Photius: the Bibliotheca, 1994; Aelian: Historical Miscellany, 1997; articles and reviews in various learned jls. *Recreations:* bridge, real tennis. *Address:* Lincoln College, Oxford OX1 3DR. *T:* (01865) 279794, *Fax:* 279802.

WILSON, Sir Patrick Michael Ernest David McN.; *see* McNair-Wilson.

WILSON, Pete; Managing Director, Pacific Capital Group Inc.; Governor of California, 1991–98; *b* 23 Aug. 1933; *m* Betty Robertson (marr. diss.); *m* 1983, Gayle Edlund. *Educ:* Yale Univ. (BA); Univ. of California at Berkeley (JD). Admitted to California Bar, 1962. Mayor of San Diego, 1971–73; US Senator (Republican) from California, 1983–91. *Address:* Pacific Capital Group Inc., 360 N Crescent Drive, Beverly Hills, CA 90210, USA.

WILSON, Peter Michael; Chairman, Gallaher Group Plc, since 1997 (Chief Executive, 1997–99); Chairman, Gallaher Ltd, since 1994 (Deputy Chairman, 1987–94; Chief Executive, 1994–99); *b* 9 June 1941; *s* of Michael Wilson and late Mary Wilson; *m* 1964, Lissa Trab; one *s* one *d.* *Educ:* Downside Sch.; Oriel Coll., Oxford (MA Hons Law). Marketing appts, Reckitt & Colman and Beecham Gp, 1963–69; joined Gallaher Ltd, 1969: Gen. Manager, Cigarette Marketing, 1974–79; Man. Dir, Gallaher (Dublin), 1979–81; Marketing Dir, Gallaher Tobacco Ltd, 1981–84; Jt Man. Dir, 1984–85, Dep. Chm., 1986, Gallaher Tobacco (UK) Ltd. Non-exec. Dir, Fortune (formerly American) Brands Inc., 1994–. *Address:* Gallaher Group Plc, Members Hill, Brooklands Road, Weybridge, Surrey KT13 0QU. *T:* (01932) 859777.

WILSON, Prof. Peter Northcote, CBE 1987; FRSE; General Secretary, Royal Society of Edinburgh, since 1996; *b* 4 April 1928; *s* of Llewellyn W. C. M. Wilson and F. Louise Wilson; *m* 1950, Maud Ethel (*née* Bunn); two *s* one *d.* *Educ:* Whitgift School; Wye

College, Univ. of London (BSc (Agric), MSc, PhD); Univ. of Edinburgh (Dip. Animal Genetics). CBiol, FIBiol; FRSE 1987. Lectr in Agriculture, Makerere Coll., UC of E Africa, 1951–57; Sen. Lectr in Animal Production, Imperial Coll. of Tropical Agriculture, 1957–61; Prof. of Agriculture, Univ. of W Indies, 1961–64; Senior Scientist, Unilever Res. Lab., 1964–68; Agricl Dir, SLF Ltd (Unilever), 1968–71; Chief Agricl Advr, BOCM Silcock Ltd (Unilever), 1971–83; Prof. of Agric. and Rural Economy and Hd of Sch. of Agric., Univ. of Edinburgh, 1984–90; Principal, East of Scotland Coll. of Agric., 1984–90; Scientific Dir, Edinburgh Centre for Rural Res., 1990–97. Vis. Prof. Univ. of Reading, 1975–83. President: Brit. Soc. of Animal Production, 1977 (Vice-Pres., 1976); Edin. Agricl Soc., 1992–93 (Vice-Pres., 1991–92); Scotia Club, 1992–93 (Vice Pres., 1990–92); Hon. Sec., Inst. of Biol., 1992–96 (Vice-Pres., 1977–79, 1991–92); Mem. Council, Scottish Agricl Colls, 1995– (Sec.-Gen., 1985–86; Mem. Exec. Bd, 1987–90); Vice Convener Business Cttee, Gen. Council, Univ. of Edinburgh, 1997–2000. Chm., Frank Parkinson Agricl Trust, 1980–99; Trustee, Frank Parkinson Yorks Trust, 1992–. FRAgS 2001. DUniv Stirling, 2000. *Publications:* Agriculture in the Tropics, 1965, 3rd edn 1998; Improved Feeding of Cattle and Sheep, 1981; A Tale of Two Trusts, 2000; Purchase Two Kilts, 2001; numerous papers in learned jls. *Recreations:* hill walking, ornithology, curling, photography, foreign travel, philately. *Address:* 8 St Thomas' Road, Edinburgh EH9 2LQ. *T:* (0131) 667 3182. *Clubs:* Farmers'; New (Edinburgh).

WILSON, Philip Alexander P.; *see* Poole-Wilson.

WILSON, Quintin Campbell, OBE 1975; HM Inspector of Constabulary for Scotland, 1975–79; *b* 19 Nov. 1913; *s* of William Wilson and Mary (*née* Cowan); *m* 1939, Adelia Campbell Scott; two *s*. *Educ:* Barr Primary Sch.; Girvan High Sch. Halifax Borough Police, April 1936; Ayrshire Constabulary, Nov. 1936; Chief Supt, Police Research and Planning Branch, Home Office, London, 1965; Dep. Chief Constable, Ayrshire, 1966; Chief Constable, Ayrshire, 1968–75. *Recreation:* golf. *Address:* 15 Portmark Avenue, Alloway, Ayr KA7 4DN. *T:* (01292) 443034.

WILSON, Richard; *see* Wilson, I. R.

WILSON, Sir Richard (Thomas James), GCB 2001 (KCB 1997; CB 1991); Secretary of the Cabinet and Head of the Home Civil Service, 1998–Oct. 2002; *b* 11 Oct. 1942; *s* of late Richard Ridley Wilson and Frieda Bell Wilson (*née* Finlay); *m* 1972, Caroline Margaret, *y d* of Rt Hon. Sir Frank Lee, GCMG, KCB and of Lady Lee; one *s* one *d*. *Educ:* Radley Coll.; Clare Coll., Cambridge (Exhibnr; BA 1964, LLB 1965). Called to the Bar, Middle Temple, 1965. Joined BoT as Asst Principal, 1966; Private Sec. to Minister of State, BoT, 1969–71; Principal: Cabinet Office, 1971–73; Dept of Energy, 1974; Asst Sec., 1977–82; Under Sec., 1982; Prin. Estabt and Finance Officer, Dept of Energy, 1982–86; on loan to Cabinet Office (MPO), 1986–87; Dep. Sec., Cabinet Office, 1987–90; Dep. Sec. (Industry), HM Treasury, 1990–92; Perm. Sec., DoE, 1992–94; Perm. Under-Sec. of State, Home Office, 1994–97. *Address:* Cabinet Office, 70 Whitehall, SW1A 2AS.

WILSON, Sir Robert, Kt 1989; CBE 1978; FRS 1975; Perren Professor of Astronomy, University College London, 1972–94, now Emeritus; *b* 16 April 1927; *s* of Robert Graham Wilson and Anne Wilson; *m* 1986, Fiona (*née* Nicholson). *Educ:* King's Coll., Univ. of Durham; Univ. of Edinburgh. BSc (Physics) Dunelm, 1948; PhD (Astrophysics), Edin., 1952. SSO, Royal Observatory, Edinburgh, 1952–57; Research Fellow, Dominion Astrophysical Observatory, Canada, 1957–58; Leader of Plasma Spectroscopy Gp, CTR Div., Harwell, 1959–61; Head of Spectroscopy Div., Culham Laboratory, 1962–68; Dir, Science Research Council's Astrophysics Research Unit, Culham, 1968–72; Dean, Faculty Sci., 1982–85, Head, Dept of Physics and Astronomy, 1987–93, UCL. Member: SERC, 1985–89; NERC, 1985–88; Chairman: British National Cttee for Space Res., 1983–88; Anglo-Australian Telescope Bd, 1986–89; James Clerk Maxwell Telescope Bd, 1987–91; Council, Royal Instn, 1992–93. Foreign Member: Société Royale des Sciences, Liège; Amer. Philosophical Soc., 1996; Vice-Pres., Internat. Astronomical Union, 1979–85; Trustee, Internat. Acad. of Astronautics, 1985; Mem., COSPAR Bureau, 1986–90. Hon. Fellow, UCL, 1990. Hon. DSc QUB, 1995. (Jtly) Herschel Medal, RAS, 1986; Science Award, Internat. Acad. of Astronautics, 1987; President Reagan's Award for design excellence (on behalf of UK team on the Internat. Ultraviolet Explorer), 1988; Royal Soc./COSPAR Massey Award, 1994. *Publications:* Astronomy Through the Ages, 1998; papers in many jls on: optical astronomy, plasma spectroscopy, solar physics, ultraviolet astronomy. *Address:* Department of Physics and Astronomy, University College London, Gower Street, WC1E 6BT. *T:* (020) 7380 7154.

WILSON, Robert; Presenter, ITV football, since 1994; *b* 30 Oct. 1941; *s* of William Smith Wilson and Catherine Wingate (*née* Primrose); *m* 1964, Margaret Vera Miles; two *s* (one *d* decd). *Educ:* Tapton House Grammar Sch.; Chesterfield Grammar Sch.; Loughborough Coll. (DipPE). PE teacher, 1963–64; represented England Schoolboys, 1957, Derbyshire Schs, 1957–60, and British Univs, 1960–63, at football; Mem., England Amateur Squad, 1960–63; professional footballer (goalkeeper), Arsenal FC, 1964–74 (winner: Euro Fairs Cup, 1970; League and Cup Double, 1971); internat. appearances for Scotland, 1971–72. BBC presenter, 1974–94. Chm., London Football Coaches Assoc., 1990–. Co-founder, Willow Foundn Charity, 1999–. Gov., Univ. of Hertfordshire, 1997–. Hon. DLitt Loughborough, 1989; Hon. Dr Derby, 2001. *Publications:* Goalkeeping, 1970; The Art of Goalkeeping, 1973; You've Got to be Crazy, 1989. *Recreations:* reading, golf, boating, theatre. *Address:* c/o Threepwood Leisure Ltd, 27 Great North Road, Brookmans Park, Hatfield, Herts AL9 6LB. *T:* (01707) 654698.

WILSON, (Robert) Gordon; solicitor in private practice, with Gordon Wilson; *b* 16 April 1938; *s* of R. G. Wilson; *m* 1965, Edith M. Hassall; two *d*. *Educ:* Douglas High Sch.; Edinburgh Univ. (BL). Scottish National Party: Nat. Sec., 1963–71; Exec. Vice-Chm., 1972–73; Sen. Vice-Chm., 1973–74; Dep Leader, 1974–79; Nat. Convener (formerly Chm.), 1979–90; Vice-Pres., 1992–. Contested (SNP) Dundee E, 1987. MP (SNP) Dundee E, Feb. 1974–1987. Parly Spokesman: on Energy, 1974–79; on Home Affairs, 1975–76; on Devolution (jt responsibility), 1976–79; SNP spokesman: on energy, 1992–93; on Treasury affairs, 1993–94. Rector, Dundee Univ., 1983–86. Chm., Marriage Counselling (Tayside) (formerly Dundee Marriage Guidance Council), 1989–92. Mem., Church and Nation Cttee, C of S, 2000–. Gov., Dundee Inst. of Technology, subseq. Univ. of Abertay, 1991–97. Hon. LLD Dundee, 1986. *Recreations:* reading, walking, photography, sailing. *Address:* 48 Monifieth Road, Broughty Ferry, Dundee DD5 2RX. *T:* (01382) 79009; Gordon Wilson, 26 Castle Street, Dundee DD1 3AF.

WILSON, Robert Julian, (Robin), MA; Headmaster, Trinity School of John Whitgift, Croydon, 1972–94; *b* 6 July 1933; *s* of late Prof. Frank Percy Wilson, FBA, and Joanna Wilson (*née* Perry-Keene); *m* 1957, Caroline Anne (*née* Maher); two *d* (and one *s* one *d* decd). *Educ:* St Edward's Sch., Oxford; Trinity Coll., Cambridge (MA). Lektor, Univ. of Münster, Westphalia, 1955–58; Assistant Master: St Peter's, York, 1958–62; Nottingham High Sch. (Hd of English), 1962–72. Mem. Cttee, HMC, 1987–94 (Chm., 1993); Vice-Chm., Academic Policy Cttee, 1990–92; Member: Council, GPDST, 1994–; Cttee, GBA, 1999–. Governor: Brentwood Sch., 1995–; St Peter's Sch., York, 1996–. FRSA 1982. *Publications:* Bertelsmann Sprachkursus English (jtly), 1959; (ed) The Merchant of Venice, 1971; articles on the teaching of English. *Recreations:* drama, travel, ski-ing, golf. *Address:* 22 Beech House Road, Croydon, Surrey CR0 1JP. *T:* (020) 8686 1915. *Clubs:* East India, Devonshire, Sports and Public Schools; Addington Golf.

WILSON, Prof. Robert McLachlan, FBA 1977; Professor of Biblical Criticism, University of St Andrews, 1978–83; *b* 13 Feb. 1916; *er s* of Hugh McL. Wilson and Janet N. (*née* Struthers); *m* 1945, Enid Mary, *d* of Rev. and Mrs F. J. Bomford, Bournemouth, Hants; two *s*. *Educ:* Greenock Acad.; Royal High Sch., Edinburgh; Univ. of Edinburgh (MA 1939, BD 1942); Univ. of Cambridge (PhD 1945). Minister of Rankin Church, Strathaven, Lanarkshire, 1946–54; Lectr in New Testament Language and Literature, St Mary's Coll., Univ. of St Andrews, 1954, Sen. Lectr, 1964, Prof., 1969–78. Vis. Prof., Vanderbilt Divinity Sch., Nashville, Tenn, 1964–65. Pres., Studiorum Novi Testamenti Societas, 1981–82. Hon. Mem., Soc. of Biblical Literature, 1972–. Associate Editor, New Testament Studies, 1967–77, Editor 1977–83; Mem., Internat. Cttee for publication of Nag Hammadi Codices, and of Editorial Bd of Nag Hammadi Studies monograph series. Hon. DD Aberdeen, 1982. Burkitt Medal for Biblical Studies, British Academy, 1990. *Publications:* The Gnostic Problem, 1958; Studies in the Gospel of Thomas, 1960; The Gospel of Philip, 1962; Gnosis and the New Testament, 1968; (ed) English trans., Hennecke-Schneemelcher, NT Apocrypha: vol. 1, 1963 (3rd edn, completely revised, 1991); vol. 2, 1965 (3rd edn 1993); (ed) English trans., Haenchen, The Acts of the Apostles, 1971; (ed) English trans., Foerster, Gnosis: vol. 1, 1972; vol. 2, 1974; (ed and trans., jtly) Jung Codex treatises: De Resurrectione, 1963, Epistula Jacobi Apocrypha, 1968, Tractatus Tripartitus, pars I, 1973, partes II et III, 1975; (ed) Nag Hammadi and Gnosis, 1978; (ed) The Future of Coptology, 1978; (ed jtly) Text and Interpretation, 1979; (ed) English trans., Rudolph, Gnosis, 1983; Commentary on Hebrews, 1987; articles in British, Amer. and continental jls. *Recreation:* golf. *Address:* 10 Murrayfield Road, St Andrews, Fife KY16 9NB. *T:* (01334) 474331.

WILSON, Sir Robert (Peter), KCMG 2000; Chairman: Rio Tinto plc, since 1997; Rio Tinto Ltd, since 1999; *b* 2 Sept. 1943; *s* of late Alfred Wilson and Dorothy (*née* Mathews); *m* 1975, Shirley Elisabeth Robson; one *s* one *d*. *Educ:* Epsom Coll.; Sussex Univ. (BA); Harvard Business Sch. (AMP). With Dunlop Ltd, 1966–67; Mobil Oil Co. Ltd, 1967–70; RTZ Corporation plc, later Rio Tinto plc, 1970–: Dir, Main Bd, 1987–; Dir, Planning and Develt, 1987–89, Mining and Metals, 1989–91; Chief Exec., 1991–97. Non-executive Director: The Boots Co. PLC, 1991–98; Diageo plc, 1998–; BP Amoco (formerly British Petroleum) plc, 1998–. Trustee, Camborne Sch. of Mines, 1993–99. CIMgt; FRSA. Hon. DSc Exeter, 1993; Hon. LLD Dundee, 2001. *Recreations:* theatre, opera. *Address:* 6 St James's Square, SW1Y 4LD. *T:* (020) 7930 2399.

WILSON, Dr Robert Woodrow; Senior Scientist, Harvard–Smithsonian Center for Astrophysics, since 1994; *b* 10 Jan. 1936; *s* of Ralph Woodrow Wilson and Fannie May Willis; *m* 1958, Elizabeth Rhoads Sawin; two *s* one *d*. *Educ:* Rice Univ. (BA Physics, 1957); Calif Inst. of Technol. (PhD 1962). Post-doctoral Fellowship, Calif Inst. of Technol., 1962–63; Mem. Technical Staff, Bell Labs, Holmdel, NJ, 1963–76; Head, Radio Physics Res. Dept, Bell Telephone Labs, Inc., later AT&T Bell Labs, 1976–94. Member: Phi Beta Kappa; Amer. Acad. of Arts and Sciences, 1978; US Nat. Acad. of Science, 1979. Hon. degrees: Monmouth Coll., 1979; Jersey City State Coll., 1979; Thiel Coll., 1980. Henry Draper Award, 1977; Herschel Award, RAS, 1977; (jtly) Nobel Prize for Physics, 1978. *Publications:* contrib. to Astrophys. Jl. *Recreations:* running, ski-ing. *Address:* 9 Valley Point Drive, Holmdel, NJ 07733–1320, USA. *T:* (201) 6717807; Harvard–Smithsonian Center for Astrophysics, 60 Garden Street #42, Cambridge, MA 02138–1516, USA.

WILSON, Robin; *see* Wilson, R. J.

WILSON, Robin Lee, CBE 1992; FREng; consulting engineer; *b* 4 March 1933; *s* of late Henry Eric Wilson, OBE and Catherine Margaret Wilson; *m* 1956, Gillian Margaret, *d* of late L. J. N. Kirkby and Margaret Kirkby; one *s* two *d*. *Educ:* Glenalmond College; Univ. of Glasgow (BSc Eng. 1955). FICE 1966; FIHT 1966; MConsE 1966; FCIT 1992. Joined R. Travers Morgan & Partners, 1956, Partner, 1966, Sen. Partner, 1985; Dir and Gp Chm., Travers Morgan Ltd, Consulting Engineers, 1988–91; Chairman: New Builder Publications Ltd, 1989–94; Thomas Telford Ltd, publishers, 1990–94. Dir, Mid Kent Hldgs, 1994–97. Member Council: ICE, 1977–80, 1983–86, 1987–93 (Pres., 1991–92); ACE, 1985–88; Construction Industry Council, 1990–97 (Chm., 1994–96); Engrg Council, 1991–99 (Chm., Bd for Engineers' Regulation, 1994–99); Glenalmond Coll., 1985–2001 (Chm. Cttee, 1995–2001). Minister's nominee, SE Council for Sport and Recreation, 1987–90. DSc *hc* City Univ., 1991. Coopers Hill Meml Prize, ICE, 1989; Instn of Highways and Transportation Award, 1990. *Publications:* papers in learned jls on highway engineering and related subjects. *Recreations:* sailing, golf. *Address:* The Grove House, Little Bognor, Pulborough, Sussex RH20 1JT. *T:* (01798) 865569. *Clubs:* Royal Thames Yacht; Itchenor Sailing, West Sussex Golf.

WILSON, Rodney Herbert William; Director, Department of Film, Video and Broadcasting, Arts Council of England, 1986–98; *b* 21 June 1942; *s* of Herbert Herman Wilson and Vera Anne Faulkner. *Educ:* Windsor Grammar Sch. for Boys; Berkshire Coll. of Art (Intermediate Diploma); Camberwell Sch. of Art (NDD); Hornsey Coll. of Art (ATD). Asst Lectr, Loughborough Coll. of Art, 1965–69; Film Officer, 1970, Head of Film Section, 1980, Arts Council of GB. Member: Film, Video and Television Adv. Cttee, British Council, 1983; Council, Edinburgh Film Festival, 1984–94; Festival Council, Art Film Fest., Slovakia, 1995–; RTS, 1994. Exec. Producer for Arts Council Films, 1970–, including: Lautrec (Palm d'Or, Cannes, 1975); Monet in London (BAFTA Best Factual Film, 1975); Tom Philips (Grierson Award, 1977); Ubu (Golden Bear, Berlin, 1979); Give Us This Day (Grierson Award, 1983); Shadows from Light (Best Film, Montreal, 1984); Steve Reich: a new musical language (Best TV Arts Film, Rio de Janeiro, 1987); Jacob Epstein: rebel angel (Best TV Arts Film, Montreal, 1988); Dance (8 short films for Camera series, and Sound on Film series). BFI Award for Ind. Film, 1984. *Recreations:* walking, doodling, photography. *Address:* c/o The Arts Council of England, 14 Great Peter Street, SW1P 3NQ.

WILSON, Rt Rev. Roger Plumpton, KCVO 1974; DD (Lambeth), 1949; Clerk of the Closet to the Queen, 1963–75; Hon. Assistant Bishop, Diocese of Bath and Wells, since 1974; *b* 3 Aug. 1905; *s* of Canon Clifford Plumpton Wilson, Bristol, and Hester Marion Wansey; *m* 1935, Mabel Joyce Avery (*d* 1995), Leigh Woods, Bristol; two *s* one *d*. *Educ:* Winchester Coll. (Exhibitioner); Keble Coll., Oxford (Classical Scholar). Hon. Mods in Classics 1st Class, Lit. Hum. 2nd Class, BA 1928; MA 1932. Classical Master, Shrewsbury Sch., 1928–30, 1932–34; Classical Master, St Andrew's Coll., Grahamstown, S Africa, 1930–32. Deacon, 1935; Priest, 1936; Curacies: St Paul's, Prince's Park, Liverpool, 1935–38; St John's, Smith Square, SW1, 1938–39; Vicar of South Shore, Blackpool, 1939–45; Archdeacon of Nottingham and Vicar of Radcliffe on Trent, 1945–49; also Vicar of Shelford (in plurality), 1946–49; Bishop of Wakefield, 1949–58; Bishop of Chichester, 1958–74. Chm., Church of England Schools Council, 1957–71; Mem., Presidium, Conf. of European Churches, 1967–74. *Recreations:* Oxford University

Authentics Cricket Club, Oxford University Centaurs Football Club, golf. *Clubs:* Athenæum, Royal Commonwealth Society.

WILSON, Air Chief Marshal Sir (Ronald) Andrew (Fellowes), (Sir Sandy), KCB 1991 (CB 1990); AFC 1978; Air Member for Personnel and Air Aide-de-Camp to the Queen, 1993–95; *b* 27 Feb. 1941; *s* of late Ronald Denis Wilson and Gladys Vera Groombridge; *m* 1979, Mary Christine Anderson; one *d* and one step *s* one step *d*. *Educ:* Tonbridge Sch.; RAF Coll., Cranwell. Flying Instr, 1963–65; No 2 Sqn, 1966–68; ADC to C-in-C, RAF Germany, 1967–68; Flt Comdr No 2 Sqn, 1968–72; RAF Staff Coll., 1973; HQ STC, 1974–75; CO No 2 Sqn, 1975–77; Air Plans, MoD, 1977–79; CO RAF Lossiemouth, 1980–82; Air Cdre Falkland Islands, 1982–83; Central Staff, MoD, 1983–85; Dir Ops Strike, MoD, 1985; Dir Air Offensive, MoD, 1986–87; SASO, HQ, RAF Strike Comd, 1987–89; AOC No 1 Group, 1989–91; Comdr, British Forces during Op. Granby, ME, Aug.–Dec. 1990; C-in-C, RAF Germany and Comdr Second ATAF, 1991–93. Pres., Aircrew Assoc., 1997–. Mem. Council, Air League, 1997–. Mem. Council, Lord Kitchener Meml Fund, 1998–. Freeman, City of London, 1966; Liveryman, 1970, Mem. Court, 1984–87, 1994–, Master, 1999–2000, Worshipful Co. of Skinners. CIMgt 1993; FRAeS 1994. *Recreations:* painting, antique restoration, genealogy, golf. *Club:* Royal Air Force.

WILSON, Maj.-Gen. (Ronald) Dare, CBE 1968 (MBE 1949); MC 1945; MA Cantab; DL; retired; current interests farming and forestry; *b* 3 Aug. 1919; *s* of Sydney E. D. Wilson and Dorothea, *d* of George Burgess; *m* 1973, Sarah, *d* of Sir Peter Stallard, KCMG, CVO, MBE; two *s*. *Educ:* Shrewsbury Sch.; St John's Coll. Cambridge (Part I 1939, BA 1972). Commissioned into Royal Northumberland Fusiliers, 1939; served War, 1939–45: BEF 1940, ME and NW Europe (MC, despatches 1946); 6th Airborne Div., 1945–48; 1st Bn Parachute Regt, 1949; MoD, 1950; Royal Northumberland Fusiliers: Korea, 1951; Kenya, 1953; GSO2, Staff Coll., Camberley, 1954–56; Brevet Lt-Col 1958; AA&QMG, 3rd Div., 1958–59; comd 22 Special Air Service Regt, 1960–62; Canadian Nat. Defence Coll., 1962–63; Col GS 1(BR) Corps BAOR, 1963–65; comd 149 Infantry Bde (TA), 1966–67; Brig. 1966; Brig., AQ ME Comd, 1967; Maj.-Gen. 1968; Dir, Land/Air Warfare, MoD, 1968–69; Dir, Army Aviation, MoD, 1970–71. Exmoor Nat. Park Officer, 1974–78. Formerly Consultant to Fedn of Nature and Nat. Parks of Europe. Speaker for E-SU in USA. Church Warden, Church of St George, Morebath, Devon, 1980–93. Helicopter and light aircraft pilot; Mem., Army Cresta Run Team and Army Rifle VIII; captained British Free-Fall Parachute Team, 1962–65; Chm., British Parachute Assoc., 1962–65. Mem. Council, Cambridge Soc., 1989–. FRGS. DL Somerset, 1979. Royal Humane Soc. Award, 1953; Royal Aero Club Silver Medal, 1967. *Publications:* Cordon and Search, 1948, reissued USA, 1984; contribs to military jls. *Recreations:* country pursuits, music, travelling, writing. *Address:* Combeland, Dulverton, Somerset TA22 9LJ. *Club:* Flyfishers'.

WILSON, Hon. Sir Ronald (Darling), AC 1988; KBE 1979; CMG 1978; Justice of the High Court of Australia, 1979–89; President: Uniting Church in Australia, 1988–91; Human Rights and Equal Opportunity Commission, 1990–97; *b* 23 Aug. 1922; *s* of Harold Wilson and Jean Ferguson Wilson (*née* Darling); *m* 1950, Leila Amy Gibson Smith; three *s* two *d*. *Educ:* Geraldton State School; Univ. of Western Australia (LLB Hons; Hon. LLD 1980); Univ. of Pennsylvania (LLM). Assistant Crown Prosecutor, Western Australia, 1954–59; Chief Crown Prosecutor, WA, 1959–61; Crown Counsel, WA, 1961–69; QC 1963; Solicitor General, WA, 1969–79. Moderator, Presbyterian Church in Western Australia, 1965; Moderator, WA Synod, Uniting Church in Australia, 1977–79. Chancellor, Murdoch Univ., 1980–95. Hon. Pres., Australian Council for Overseas Aid, 1997–2001. Hon. DEd Keimyung Univ., Korea, 1989; DUniv Murdoch, 1995; Hon. DLitt Univ. of Technology, Sydney, 1998; Hon. LLD WA. *Address:* 6B Atkins Road, Applecross, WA 6153, Australia.

WILSON, Ronald Marshall, CBE 1982; sole proprietor, Ronnie Wilson, Chartered Surveyors, since 1983; Chairman, Nightingale Secretariat PLC, 1985–92; *b* 6 March 1923; *s* of Marshall Lang Wilson and Margaret Wilson Wilson; *m* 1948, Marion Robertson Scobie (marr. diss. 1985); two *s*. *Educ:* Sedbergh; London Univ. (BSc Estate Management 1950). Served War of 1939–45; North Irish Horse; Court Orderly Officer, Wüppertal War Crimes Trial, 1946. Partner, Bell-Ingram, Chartered Surveyors, 1957–83. Director: Central Farmers Ltd, 1972–86; Control Securities plc, 1986–92. Royal Institution of Chartered Surveyors: Mem. General Council, 1973–; President, 1979–80; Mem. Land Agency and Agricl Divisional Council, 1970–77 (Chm., 1974–75); Chm., Internat. Cttee, 1976–78. *Publications:* articles on technical and professional subjects, incl. Planning in the Countryside. *Recreations:* golf, fishing, shooting. *Address:* 6 Acreman Court, Sherborne, Dorset DT9 3PW. *T:* (01935) 814171. *Club:* Farmers'.

WILSON, Roy Vernon, CEng, MICE; Director, Eastern Region, Property Services Agency, Department of the Environment, 1980–82; *b* 23 July 1922; *s* of late Alfred Vincent Wilson and Theresa Elsie Wilson; *m* 1951, Elsie Hannah Barrett; three *s*. *Educ:* Cheadle Hulme Sch.; Manchester Univ. (BScTech Hons). Served Royal Engineers, 1942–44. Civil Engineer, local govt, 1945–51; Harlow Develt Corp., 1951–54; Air Ministry Works Directorate: Warrington, 1954–59; Newmarket, 1959–62; Germany, 1962–65; District Works Officer: Wethersfield, 1965–67; Mildenhall, 1967–72; Area Officer, Letchworth (PSA), 1972–76; Regional Director, Cyprus (PSA), 1976–79; Chief Works Officer, Ruislip, 1979. *Recreations:* lacrosse (earlier years), golf, tennis. *Address:* 12 Diomed Drive, Great Barton, Bury St Edmunds, Suffolk IP31 2TD. *Club:* Civil Service.

WILSON, Samuel; Member (DemU) Belfast East, Northern Ireland Assembly, since 1998; *b* 4 April 1953; *s* of Alexander and Mary Wilson. *Educ:* Methodist Coll., Belfast; The Queen's Univ., Belfast (BScEcon; PGCE). Teacher of Economics, 1975–83; Researcher in N Ireland Assembly, 1983–86. Councillor, Belfast CC, 1981–; Lord Mayor of Belfast, 1986–87 and 2000–01. Press Officer for Democratic Unionist Party, 1982–96. Contested (DemU) Antrim E, 2001. *Publications:* The Carson Trail, 1982; The Unionist Case—The Forum Report Answered, 1984; Data Response Questions in Economics, 1995. *Recreations:* reading, motor cycling, windsurfing. *Address:* Parliament Buildings, Stormont, Belfast BT4 3SW; 19 Jocelyn Gardens, Belfast BT6 9BA. *T:* (028) 9045 9934.

WILSON, Air Chief Marshal Sir Sandy; *see* Wilson, Air Chief Marshal Sir R. A. F.

WILSON, Sandy; composer, lyric writer, playwright; *b* 19 May 1924; *s* of George Walter Wilson and Caroline Elsie (*née* Humphrey). *Educ:* Elstree Preparatory School; Harrow School; Oriel College, Oxford (BA Eng. Lit.). Contributed material to Oranges and Lemons, Slings and Arrows, 1948; wrote lyrics for touring musical play Caprice, 1950; words and music for two revues at Watergate Theatre, 1951 and 1952; (musical comedy) The Boy Friend for Players' Theatre, 1953, later produced in West End and on Broadway, 1954, revival, Comedy, 1967 (also directed), revival, Old Vic, 1984, 40th anniv. production, Players' Theatre, 1994; (musical play) The Buccaneer, 1955; Valmouth (musical play, based on Firbank's novel), Lyric, Hammersmith and Savile Theatre, 1959, New York, 1960, revival, Chichester, 1982; songs for Call It Love, Wyndham's Theatre, 1960; Divorce Me, Darling! (musical comedy), Players' Theatre, 1964, Globe, 1965, revival, Chichester, 1997; music for TV series, The World of Wooster, 1965–66; music for As Dorothy Parker Once Said, Fortune, 1969; songs for Danny la Rue's Charley's Aunt (TV), 1969; wrote and performed in Sandy Wilson Thanks the Ladies, Hampstead Theatre Club, 1971; His Monkey Wife, Hampstead, 1971; The Clapham Wonder, Canterbury, 1978; Aladdin, Lyric, Hammersmith, 1979. *Publications:* This is Sylvia (with own illustrs), 1954; The Boy Friend (with own illustrs), 1955; Who's Who for Beginners (with photographs by Jon Rose), 1957; Prince What Shall I Do (illustrations, with Rhoda Levine), 1961; The Poodle from Rome, 1962; I Could Be Happy (autobiog.), 1975; Ivor, 1975; Caught in the Act, 1976; The Roaring Twenties, 1977. *Recreations:* cinema, travel, reminiscing. *Address:* 2 Southwell Gardens, SW7 4SB. *T:* (020) 7373 6172. *Club:* Players' Theatre.

WILSON, Snoo; writer, since 1969; *b* 2 Aug. 1948; *s* of Leslie Wilson and Pamela Mary Wilson; *m* 1976, Ann McFerran; two *s* one *d*. *Educ:* Bradfield Coll.; Univ. of East Anglia (BA English and American Studies). Associate Director, Portable Theatre, 1970–75; Dramaturge, Royal Shakespeare Co., 1975–76; Script Editor, Play for Today, 1976; Associate Prof. of Theatre, Univ. of Calif at San Diego, 1987. Henfield Fellow, Univ. of E Anglia, 1978; US Bicentennial Fellow in Playwriting, 1981–82. Hon. Texan, 1992. *Filmscripts:* Shadey, 1986; The Touch, 1989; *opera:* (adapted) Gounod's La Colombe, 1983; *radio plays:* Poonsh, 1993; The Good Doctor, 1994; Johnson's Xmas Interlude, 1994; I'll be George, 2001. *Publications: plays:* Layby (jtly), 1972; Pignight, 1972; The Pleasure Principle, 1973; Blowjob, 1974; Soul of the White Ant, 1976; England England, 1978; Vampire, 1978; The Glad Hand, 1978; A Greenish Man, 1978; The Number of the Beast, 1982; Flaming Bodies, 1982; Grass Widow, 1983; Loving Reno, 1983; Hamlyn, 1984; More Light, 1987; Lynchville, 1989; Callas, 1990; Erofeyev's Walpurgis Night (adaptation), 1991; HRH, 1994; Darwin's Flood, 1994; Bedbug (adaptation, after Mayakovsky), 1995; Framing Faust (adaptation, after Ernst), 1996; Sabina, 1998; Moonshine, 1999; *novels:* Spaceache, 1984 (adapted for radio, 1990); Inside Babel, 1985; I, Crowley, 1997; *opera:* Orpheus in the Underworld (new version), 1984; *musical:* 80 Days, 1988. *Recreations:* beekeeping, space travel. *Address:* 41 The Chase, SW4 0NP.

WILSON, Stanley John, CBE 1981; FCIS; Chairman, Burmah Oil (South Africa) (Pty) Ltd, 1982–87; Managing Director, 1975–82 and Chief Executive, 1980–82, The Burmah Oil Co. Ltd; *b* 23 Oct. 1921; *s* of Joseph Wilson and Jessie Cormack; *m* 1952, Molly Ann (*née* Clarkson); two *s*. *Educ:* King Edward VII Sch., Johannesburg Witwatersrand Univ. CA (SA); ASAA, ACMA; FCIS 1945; CIMgt 1976; FInst Pet 1977. 1948–75: Chartered Accountant, Savory & Dickinson; Sec. and Sales Man., Rhodesian Timber Hldgs; Chm. and Chief Exec. for S Africa, Vacuum Oil Co.; Reg. Vice Pres. for S and E Asia, Mobil Petroleum; Pres., Mobil Sekiyu; Pres., subseq. Reg. Vice Pres. for Europe, Mobil Europe Inc.; Pres., Mobil East Inc., and Reg. Vice Pres. for Far East, S and SE Asia, Australia, Indian Sub-Continent; Reg. Pres. for Africa, etc. Freeman, City of London; Liveryman, Basketmakers' Co. FRSA. *Recreations:* golf, shooting, fishing. *Address:* The Jetty, PO Box 751, Plettenberg Bay, Cape Province, 6600, South Africa. *T:* (44) 5359624, *Fax:* (44) 5359655. *Clubs:* Royal Automobile; Royal & Ancient Golf; Plettenberg Bay Country (Cape Province); Kelvin Grove (Cape Town); Johannesburg Country (Johannesburg).

WILSON, Prof. Thomas Michael Aubrey, PhD; CBiol, FIBiol; FIHort; FRSE; Chief Executive, Horticulture Research International, Wellesbourne, since 1999 (Science Director, April–Aug. 1999); *b* 10 Oct. 1951; *s* of Basil Francis Aubrey Wilson and Elisabeth Mathew Wilson (*née* Hogg); *m* 1975, Judith Lindsey Dring; two *s* one *d*. *Educ:* Univ. of Edinburgh (BSc 1st Cl. Hons Biol Scis 1973); St John's Coll., Cambridge (PhD Biochem. 1976). CBiol 1995; FIBiol 1998; FIHort 1999; FRSE 1999. MRC Res. Fellow, Univ. of Nottingham, 1976–78; Lectr in Biochem., Univ. of Liverpool, 1979–83; SSO, 1983–86, PSO, 1986–89, John Innes Inst., Norwich; Prof., Rutgers Univ., NJ, 1989–92; Head of Virology, 1992–95, Dep. Dir, 1995–99, Scottish Crop Res. Inst., Dundee. Hon. Lectr, UEA, 1985–92; Hon. Professor: Univ. of Dundee, 1993–99; Zhejiang Acad. Agricl Scis, China, 1993–; Univ. of Birmingham, 1999–; Univ. of Warwick, 1999–. *Publications:* (with J. W. Davies) Genetic Engineering with Plant Viruses, 1992; Engineering Genesis, 1998; contrib. numerous papers in specialist jls; also abstracts, proceedings and invited seminars. *Recreations:* family travel, DIY (mild), walking in the hills! *Address:* Horticulture Research International, Wellesbourne, Warwick CV35 9EF. *T:* (01789) 470382, *Fax:* (01789) 470363; *e-mail:* michael.wilson@hri.ac.uk.

WILSON, Timothy Hugh, FSA; Keeper of Western Art, Ashmolean Museum, Oxford, since 1990; Professorial Fellow, Balliol College, Oxford, since 1990; *b* 8 April 1950; *s* of late Col Hugh Walker Wilson and of Lilian Rosemary (*née* Kirke); *m* 1984, Jane Lott; two *s* one *d*. *Educ:* Winchester Coll.; Mercersburg Acad., USA; Corpus Christi Coll., Oxford (BA 1973; MA); Warburg Inst., London Univ. (MPhil 1976); Dept of Museum Studies, Leicester Univ. FSA 1989. Res. Asst, Dept of Weapons and Antiquities, Nat. Maritime Mus., Greenwich, 1977–79; Asst Keeper (Renaissance collections), Dept of Medieval and Later Antiquities, BM, 1979–90. Trustee, Ruskin Foundn, 1994—2000. Fellow, Harvard Univ. Center for Renaissance Studies, Villa I Tatti, Florence, 1984; Hon. Fellow, Royal Soc. Painter-Printmakers, 1991. *Publications:* (jtly) The Art of the Jeweller, 1984; Flags at Sea, 1986, 2nd edn 1999; Ceramic Art of the Italian Renaissance, 1987; Maiolica, 1989; (ed) Italian Renaissance Pottery, 1991; (jtly) Systematic Catalogue of the National Gallery of Art: Western Decorative Arts, Part 1, 1993; (ed jtly) C. D. E. Fortnum and the Collecting and Study of Applied Arts and Sculpture in Victorian England, 1999; articles in Apollo, Burlington Mag., Faenza, Jl Warburg and Courtauld Insts, etc; contribs exhibition catalogues. *Recreations:* cycling, second-hand bookshops. *Address:* Balliol College, Oxford OX1 3BJ; 6 Longworth Road, Oxford OX2 6RA. *T:* (01865) 511029.

WILSON, William; DL; *b* 28 June 1913; *s* of Charles and Charlotte Wilson; *m* 1939, Bernice Wilson; one *s*. *Educ:* Wheatley St Sch.; Cheylesmore Sch.; Coventry Jun. Technical School. Qual. as solicitor, 1939, retired 1999. Entered Army, 1941; served in N Africa, Italy and Greece; demobilised, 1946 (Sergeant). Contested (Lab) Warwick and Leamington, 1951, 1955, March 1957, 1959. MP (Lab) Coventry S, 1964–74, Coventry SE, 1974–83; Mem., Commons Select Cttee on Race Relations and Immigration, 1970–79. Mem., Warwicks CC, 1958–70 (Leader Labour Group), 1972–93. DL County of Warwick, 1967. *Recreations:* gardening, theatre, watching Association football. *Address:* Avonside House, High Street, Barford, Warwickshire CV35 8BU. *T:* (01926) 624278.

WILSON, William Desmond, OBE 1964 (MBE 1954); MC 1945; DSC (USA) 1945; HM Diplomatic Service, retired; Deputy High Commissioner, Kaduna, Nigeria, 1975–81; *b* 2 Jan. 1922; *s* of late Crozier Irvine Wilson and Mabel Evelyn (*née* Richardson); *m* 1949, Lucy Bride; two *s*. *Educ:* Royal Belfast Acad. Instn; QUB; Trinity Coll., Cambridge. Joined Indian Army, 1941; served with 10 Gurkha Rifles, India and Italy, 1942–46 (Major). Colonial Admin. Service: Northern Nigeria, 1948–63 (MBE for Gallantry, 1954); retd as Permanent Sec.; joined Foreign (subseq. Diplomatic) Service, 1963; First Sec., Ankara, 1963–67; UN (Polit.) Dept, FO, 1967; First Sec. and Head of Chancery, Kathmandu, 1969–74; Counsellor, 1975; Sen. Officers' War Course, RNC Greenwich, 1975. *Recreations:* shooting, riding. *Address:* 19 The Haven, Hythe, Kent CT21 4PJ. *T:* (01303) 260767. *Club:* East India.

WILSON, (William) George, OBE 1960; Associate Director, PA Consulting Group, 1989–92; *b* 19 Feb. 1921; *s* of late William James Wilson and late Susannah Wilson; *m* 1948, Freda Huddleston; three *s.* Min. of Health, 1939. Served War, Army, in India and Ceylon, 1940–46. Min. of Nat. Insurance, 1947; Asst Principal, Colonial Office, 1947; Principal, CO, 1950–57 (Adviser, UK Delegn to UN Gen. Assembly, 1951); Financial Sec., Mauritius, 1957–60; Asst Sec., MoH, 1962; Consultant, Hosp. Design and Construction, Middle East and Africa, 1968–70; Asst Sec., DHSS, 1971; Under-Sec., DHSS, 1972–81. Chm., Paul James & George Wilson Ltd, Health Service Develt Advrs, 1986–89 (Dir, 1983–86). *Recreations:* Border history and genealogy. *Address:* Clarghyll Hall, Alston, Cumbria CA9 3NF. *Club:* Royal Commonwealth Society.

WILSON, William Moore; Director, Royal Bank of Scotland Group, since 1993; *b* 21 May 1937; *s* of late Thomas Martin Wilson and of Mary Wilson (*née* Moore); *m* 1966, Margaret Roan Spalding; one *s* two *d. Educ:* Belmont House Prep. Sch., Glasgow; Merchiston Castle Sch., Edinburgh. CA. CA apprenticeship, Deloittes, Glasgow, 1955–60; Peat Marwick Mitchell, 1960–61; Stenhouse Holdings, Glasgow, 1961–73; Reed Stenhouse Companies, Toronto: Dir, 1973–95 (Pres. and CEO, 1979–89); Alexander & Alexander: Chm. and CEO, NY, 1985–88; Chm. and CEO, Europe, 1988–92, Chm., Europe, 1993–97. Dir, Soc. Gen. de Courtages d'Assurances, Paris, 1989–97 (Vice-Chm., 1993–97). Director of numerous organisations, incl. Scottish Rugby Union plc. *Recreations:* yachting, shooting, Rugby. *Address:* Silverton Farmhouse, Braco, by Dunblane, Perthshire FK15 9QZ. *T:* (01786) 880688. *Clubs:* Caledonian; London Scottish Football, Royal Scottish Automobile; Toronto, Royal Canadian Yacht.

WILSON, William Napier M.; *see* Menzies-Wilson.

WILSON-BARNETT, Prof. Jenifer, (Mrs M. R. Trimble); Professor of Nursing, since 1986, and Head of Florence Nightingale School of Nursing and Midwifery, since 1999, King's College, London (Head of Division of Nursing and Midwifery, 1994–99); *b* 10 Aug. 1944; adopted by Edith M. Barnett and Barbara M. Wilson; *m* 1975, Michael Robert Trimble. *Educ:* Chichester High School for Girls; St George's Hosp., London (student nurse), 1963–66; Univ. of Leicester, 1967–70 (BA Politics); Edinburgh Univ., 1970–72 (MSc); Guy's Hosp. Med. Sch., London (PhD 1977). FRCN 1984; FKC 1995. Staff Nurse, 1966, Nursing Sister, 1972–74, St George's Hosp.; Researcher, Guy's Hosp., 1974–77; Chelsea College: Lectr in Nursing, 1977; Sen. Lectr, 1983; Reader and Hd of Dept, 1984. *Publications:* Stress in Hospital: patients' psychological reactions to illness and health care, 1979; (with Morva Fordham) Recovery from Illness, 1982; Patient Teaching, 1983; Nursing Research: ten studies in patient care, 1983; Nursing Issues and Research in Terminal Care, 1988; Patient Problems: a research base for nursing care, 1988; (with Sarah Robinson) Direction in Nursing Research, 1989; (with Jill Macleod Clark) Health Promotion and Nursing Research, 1993; (with Alison Richardson) Nursing Research in Cancer Care, 1996. *Recreations:* ski-ing, music, clothes-shopping, writing, 'singing'. *Address:* Florence Nightingale School of Nursing and Midwifery, King's College London, James Clerk Maxwell Building, 57 Waterloo Road, SE1 8WA. *Clubs:* Royal Automobile, Royal College of Nursing, Royal Society of Medicine.

WILSON-JOHNSON, David Robert; baritone; *b* 16 Nov. 1950; *s* of Sylvia Constance Wilson and Harry Kenneth Johnson. *Educ:* Wellingborough School; British Institute, Florence; St Catharine's College, Cambridge (BA Hons 1973); Royal Acad. of Music. NFMS Award, 1977; Gulbenkian Fellowship, 1978–81. Royal Opera House, Covent Garden: We Come to the River (début), 1976; Billy Budd, 1982; L'Enfant et les Sortilèges, 1983; Le Rossignol, 1983; Les Noces, Boris Godunov, 1984; Die Zauberflöte, 1985; Werther, Turandot, 1987; Madam Butterfly, 1988; title rôle, St François d'Assise (Messiaen), 1988–89; Wigmore Hall recital début, 1977; BBC Proms début, 1981; Paris Opera début (Die Meistersinger), 1989; US début, Cleveland Orch., 1990; appearances at Netherlands Opera, Geneva, Houston, New York, Turin, Salzburg, etc; numerous recordings, including works by Bach, Schönberg and Schubert. FRAM 1988 (ARAM 1982). *Recreations:* swimming, slimming, gardening and growing walnuts at Dordogne house. *Address:* 28 Englefield Road, N1 4ET. *T:* (020) 7254 0941.

WILSON JONES, Prof. Edward, FRCP, FRCPath; Professor of Dermatopathology, Institute of Dermatology, University of London, 1974–91, now Emeritus (Dean, 1980–89); *b* 26 July 1926; *s* of Percy George Jones and Margaret Louisa Wilson; *m* 1952, Hilda Mary Rees; one *s* one *d. Educ:* Oundle Sch.; Trinity Hall, Cambridge (MB, BChir 1951); St Thomas' Hosp., London. FRCP 1970; FRCPath 1975. National Service, Army, 1953–54. House Surgeon (Ophthalmic), St Thomas' Hosp., 1951; House Physician (Gen. Medicine), St Helier Hosp., Carshalton, 1951–52; House Physician (Neurology and Chest Diseases), St Thomas' Hosp., 1955; Registrar (Gen. Medicine), Watford Peace Meml Hosp., 1955–57; Registrar (Derm.), St Thomas' Hosp., 1957–60; Inst. of Dermatology, St John's Hosp. for Diseases of the Skin: Sen. Registrar (Derm.), 1960–62; Sen. Registrar (Dermatopath.), 1962–63; Sen. Lectr (Dermatopath.), 1963–74; Hon. Consultant, St John's Hosp. for Diseases of Skin, 1974–. *Publications:* (contrib.) Textbook of Dermatology, ed Rook, Wilkinson and Ebling, 3rd edn 1979; articles on dermatopath. subjects in British Jl of Derm., Arch. of Derm., Acta Dermatovenereologica, Dermatologica, Clin. and Exptl Derm., Histopath., and in Human Path. *Recreation:* art history. *Address:* 80 Harley Street, W1N 1AE. *T:* (020) 7580 8356.

WILTON, 8th Earl of, *cr* 1801; **Francis Egerton Grosvenor;** Viscount Grey de Wilton 1801; Baron Ebury 1857; *b* 8 Feb. 1934; *s* of 5th Baron Ebury, DSO and Ann Acland-Troyte; *S* to Barony of father, 1957; *S* to Earldom of kinsman, 1999; *m* 1st, 1957, Gillian Elfrida (Elfin) (marr. diss. 1962), *d* of Martin Soames, London; one *s*; 2nd, 1963, Kyra (marr. diss. 1973), *d* of late L. L. Aslin; 3rd, 1974, Suzanne Jean, PhD, *d* of Graham Suckling, Christchurch, NZ; one *d. Educ:* Eton; Univ. of Melbourne. *Recreation:* ornithology. *Heir: s* Viscount Grey de Wilton, *qv. Address:* PO Box 466, Mt Macedon, Vic 3441, Australia. *Clubs:* Oriental; Melbourne, Melbourne Savage (Melbourne); Hong Kong.

WILTON, Andrew; *see* Wilton, J. A. R.

WILTON, Sir (Arthur) John, KCMG 1979 (CMG 1967); KCVO 1979; MC 1945; MA; HM Diplomatic Service, retired; *b* 21 Oct. 1921; *s* of Walter Wilton and Annetta Irene Wilton (*née* Perman); *m* 1950, Maureen Elizabeth Alison Meaker; four *s* one *d. Educ:* Wanstead High School; Open Schol., St John's Coll., Oxford, 1940. Commissioned, Royal Ulster Rifles, 1942; served with Irish Brigade, N Africa, Italy and Austria, 1943–46 (despatches). Entered HM Diplomatic Service, 1947; served Lebanon, Egypt, Gulf Shaikhdoms, Roumania, Aden, and Yugoslavia; Dir, Middle East Centre for Arabic Studies, Shemlan, 1960–65; Ambassador to Kuwait, 1970–74; Asst Under-Sec. of State, FCO, 1974–76; Ambassador to Saudi Arabia, 1976–79. Dir, London House for Overseas Graduates, 1979–86. Chm., Arab-British Centre, 1981–86; Pres., Plymouth Br., ESU, 1991– (Vice-Pres., 1988–91); Trustee, Arab-British Chamber Charitable Foundn, 1989–. Gov., Hele Sch., Plympton, 1988–92. Churchwarden, St Maurice, Plympton, 1992–. Hon. LLD New England Coll., NH, 1986. *Recreations:* reading, gardening. *Address:* Legassick House, 69 Fore Street, Plympton St Maurice, Plymouth PL7 3NA.
See also C. E. J. Wilton.

WILTON, Christopher Edward John; HM Diplomatic Service; Counsellor, Foreign and Commonwealth Office, since 2001; *b* 16 Dec. 1951; *s* of Sir (Arthur) John Wilton, *qv*; *m* 1975, Dianne Hodgkinson; one *s* one *d. Educ:* Tonbridge Sch.; Manchester Univ. (Hons Near Eastern Studies). Production Supervisor, Esso Petroleum, 1975–77; HM Diplomatic Service, 1977–98: FCO, 1977; Bahrain, 1978–81; FCO, 1981–84; Tokyo, 1984–88; on loan to Cabinet Office, 1988–90; Commercial Counsellor, Riyadh, 1990–94; Consul Gen., Dubai, 1994–97; Counsellor, FCO, and Comr (non-resident), British Indian Ocean Territories, 1998; Regl Man. Dir, GEC, later BAE Systems, 1999–2001. *Recreations:* squash, tennis, golf, piano. *Address:* c/o Foreign and Commonwealth Office, SW1A 2AH. *Club:* Athenæum.

WILTON, (James) Andrew (Rutley), FSA; Keeper and Senior Research Fellow, Tate Gallery, since 1998; *b* 7 Feb. 1942; *s* of Herbert Rutley Wilton and Mary Cecilia Morris (*née* Buckerfield); *m* 1976, Christina Frances Benn (marr. diss.); one *s. Educ:* Dulwich Coll.; Trinity Coll., Cambridge (MA). Assistant Keeper: Walker Art Gallery, Liverpool, 1965; Dept of Prints and Drawings, BM, 1967; Curator of Prints and Drawings, Yale Center for British Art, 1976; Asst Keeper, Turner Collection, BM, 1981; Curator, Turner Collection, 1985–89, Keeper of British Art, 1989–98, Tate Gallery. FRSA 1973; FSA 2000. Hon. RWS 1985. *Publications:* Turner in Switzerland (with John Russell), 1976; British Watercolours 1750–1850, 1977; The Wood Engravings of William Blake, 1977; The Life and Work of J. M. W. Turner, 1979; The Art of Alexander and John Robert Cozens, 1979; William Pars: journey through the Alps, 1979; Turner and the Sublime, 1980; Turner Abroad, 1982; Turner in his Time, 1987; Painting and Poetry, 1990; The Swagger Portrait, 1992; The Great Age of British Watercolour, 1992; (ed jtly) Grand Tour, 1996; (ed jtly) Pictures in the Garrick Club: a catalogue, 1997; (ed jtly) The Age of Rossetti, Burne-Jones and Watts: symbolism in Britain, 1997; contribs to arts magazines. *Recreations:* people, nature, the arts. *Address:* Tate Gallery, SW1P 4RG. *Club:* Athenæum.

WILTON, Sir John; *see* Wilton, Sir A. J.

WILTON, Maxwell William M.; *see* Moore-Wilton.

WILTON, Penelope Alice; actress; *b* 3 June 1946; *m* 1st, Daniel Massey, actor (marr. diss.; he *d* 1998); one *d*; 2nd, 1991, Sir Ian Holm, *qv. Educ:* Drama Centre. *Theatre* includes: National Theatre, later Royal National Theatre: the Philanderer; Betrayal; Much Ado About Nothing; Man and Superman; Major Barbara, 1982; The Secret Rapture, 1988; Piano, 1990; Landscape, 1994; Greenwich Theatre: Measure for Measure; All's Well That Ends Well; The Norman Conquests; King Lear, Nottingham Playhouse; The Deep Blue Sea, Almeida, 1992, transf. Apollo, 1993; Vita and Virginia, Chichester, 1992, transf. Ambassadors, 1993; The Cherry Orchard, RSC, 1995; Long Day's Journey into Night, Young Vic, 1996; A Kind of Alaska, Dublin, 1997, Donmar Warehouse, 1998; The Seagull, RSC, 2000; The Little Foxes, Donmar, 2001; *television* includes: Othello; King Lear; Country; The Norman Conquests, 1977; The Tale of Beatrix Potter, 1983; Ever Decreasing Circles; Screaming; The Borrowers, 1992; The Deep Blue Sea, 1994; Landscapes, 1995; Talking Heads (Nights in the Gardens of Spain), 1998; Wives and Daughters, 1999; Victoria and Albert, 2001; Bob and Rose, 2001; *radio* includes: Jane and Prudence, 1994; *films* include: The French Lieutenant's Woman, 1981; Clockwise, 1986; Cry Freedom, 1987; The Secret Rapture, 1993; Carrington, 1995. *Address:* c/o ICM Ltd, 76 Oxford Street, W1N 0AX.

WILTS, Archdeacon of; *see* Hopkinson, Ven. B. J.

WILTSHAW, Eve, OBE 1992; MD; FRCP, FRCOG; Medical Director, Royal Marsden Hospital, 1986–94; *b* 23 Jan. 1927. *Educ:* Univ. of Wales Med. Sch. (MB BCh, MD). Jun. med. posts, 1951–52; jun. post in clin. haematol., Tufts Med. Sch., Boston, 1953–55; Inst. of Cancer Res., 1955–74; Consultant in Cancer Medicine, Royal Marsden Hosp., 1974–92. *Publication:* A History of the Royal Marsden Hospital, 1998.

WILTSHIRE, Earl of; Christopher John Hilton Paulet; *b* 30 July 1969; *s* and *heir* of Marquess of Winchester, *qv*; *m* 1992, Christine, *d* of Peter Town; one *d.*

WILTSHIRE, Edward Parr, CBE 1965; HM Diplomatic Service, retired; *b* 18 Feb. 1910; 2nd *s* of late Major Percy Wiltshire and Kathleen Olivier Lefroy Parr Wiltshire, Great Yarmouth; *m* 1942, Gladys Mabel Stevens; one *d. Educ:* Cheltenham College; Jesus College, Cambridge. Entered Foreign Service, 1932. Served in: Beirut, Mosul, Baghdad, Tehran, Basra, New York (one of HM Vice-Consuls, 1944); promoted Consul, 1945; transf. Cairo, 1946 (Actg Consul-Gen., 1947, 1948); transf. Shiraz (having qual. in Arabic, and subseq. in Persian); Consul, Port Said, 1952; 1st Sec. and Consul: Baghdad, 1952, Rio de Janeiro, 1957; promoted Counsellor, 1959; Political Agent, Bahrain, 1959–63; Consul-General, Geneva, 1963–67; Dir, Diplomatic Service Language Centre, London, 1967–68; worked for Council for Nature (Editor, Habitat), 1968–69; Consul, Le Havre, 1969–75. Hon. Associate, BM (Nat. Hist.), 1980. *Publications:* The Lepidoptera of Iraq, 1957; A Revision of the Armadini, 1979. *Recreations:* music, entomology. *Address:* Wychwood, High Road, Cookham, Berks SL6 9JS.

WIMBORNE, 4th Viscount *cr* 1918; **Ivor Mervyn Vigors Guest;** Baron Wimborne 1880; Baron Ashby St Ledgers 1910; Bt 1838; *b* 19 Sept. 1968; *o s* of 3rd Viscount Wimborne and of his 1st wife, Victoria Ann, *o d* of Col Mervyn Vigors, DSO, MC; *S* father, 1993. *Educ:* Eton. *Heir: uncle* Hon. Julian John Guest [*b* 12 Oct. 1945; *m* 1st, 1970, Emma Jane Arlette (marr. diss. 1978), *e d* of Cdre Archibald Gray, RN; 2nd, 1983, Jillian, *d* of late N. S. G. Bannatine]. *e-mail:* ivor@easynet.co.uk.

WINCH, Prof. Donald Norman, FBA 1986; FRHistS; Emeritus Research Professor, University of Sussex, since 2000 (Professor of History of Economics, 1969–2000); *b* 15 April 1935; *s* of Sidney and Iris Winch; *m* 1983, Doreen Lidster. *Educ:* Sutton Grammar Sch.; LSE (BSc Econ 1956); Princeton Univ. (PhD 1960). Vis. Lectr, Univ. of California, 1959–60; Lectr in Economics, Univ. of Edinburgh, 1960–63; University of Sussex: Lectr, 1963–66; Reader, 1966–69; Dean, Sch. of Social Scis, 1968–74; Pro-Vice-Chancellor (Arts and Social Studies), 1986–89. Visiting Fellow: Sch. of Social Sci., Inst. for Advanced Study, Princeton, 1974–75; King's Coll., Cambridge, 1983; History of Ideas Unit, ANU, 1983; St Catharine's Coll., Cambridge, 1989; All Souls Coll., Oxford, 1994; British Council Distinguished Vis. Fellow, Kyoto Univ., 1992. Carlyle Lectr, Oxford Univ., 1995. Vice-Pres., British Acad., 1993–94. Publications Sec., Royal Economic Soc., 1971–; Review Editor, Economic Jl, 1976–83. *Publications:* Classical Political Economy and Colonies, 1965; James Mill: selected economic writings, 1966; Economics and Policy, 1969; (with S. K. Howson) The Economic Advisory Council 1930–1939, 1976; Adam Smith's Politics, 1978; (with S. Collini and J. W. Burrow) That Noble Science of Politics, 1983; Malthus, 1987; Riches and Poverty, 1996. *Address:* Arts B, University of Sussex, Brighton BN1 9QN. *T:* (01273) 678634.

WINCHESTER, 18th Marquess of, *cr* 1551; **Nigel George Paulet;** Baron St John of Basing, 1539; Earl of Wiltshire, 1550; Premier Marquess of England; *b* 23 Dec. 1941; *s* of George Cecil Paulet (*g g g s* of 13th Marquess) (*d* 1961), and Hazel Margaret (*d* 1976), *o d* of late Major Danvers Wheeler, RA, Salisbury, Rhodesia; *S* kinsman, 1968; *m* 1967, Rosemary Anne, *d* of Major Aubrey John Hilton; two *s* one *d*. *Heir: s* Earl of Wiltshire, *qv*. *Address:* 6A Main Road, Irene 1675, Transvaal, South Africa.

WINCHESTER, Bishop of, since 1995; **Rt Rev. Michael Charles Scott-Joynt;** *b* 1943; *m* 1965, Louise White; two *s* one *d*. *Educ:* King's College, Cambridge (BA 1965, MA 1968); Cuddesdon Theological College. Deacon 1967, priest 1968; Curate, Cuddesdon, 1967–70; Tutor, Cuddesdon Coll., 1967–71, Chaplain 1971–72; Team Vicar, Newbury, 1972–75; Priest-in-charge: Caversfield, 1975–79; Bicester, 1975–79; Bucknell, 1976–79; Rector, Bicester Area Team Ministry, 1979–81; RD of Bicester and Islip, 1976–81; Canon Residentiary of St Albans, 1982–87; Dir of Ordinands and In-Service Training, Diocese of St Albans, 1982–87; Suffragan Bishop of Stafford, 1987–95. *Address:* Wolvesey, Winchester, Hants SO23 9ND. *T:* (01962) 854050.

WINCHESTER, Dean of; *see* Till, Very Rev. M. S.

WINCHESTER, Archdeacon of; *see* Guille, Ven. J. A.

WINCHILSEA, 17th Earl of, *cr* 1628, **AND NOTTINGHAM,** 12th Earl of, *cr* 1681; **Daniel James Hatfield Finch Hatton;** Bt 1611; Viscount Maidstone 1623; Bt 1660; Baron Finch, 1674; Custodian of the Royal Manor of Wye; *b* 7 Oct. 1967; *s* of 16th Earl of Winchilsea and 11th Earl of Nottingham, and of Shirley (*née* Hatfield); *S* father, 1999; *m* 1994, Shelley Amanda, *d* of Gordon Gillard; one *s*. *Educ:* Univ. of the West of England, Bristol. *Recreations:* interior design, motor racing, swimming, cycling. *Heir: s* Viscount Maidstone, *qv*.

WINCKLER, Andrew Stuart; Chairman, UK Financial Services Regulatory Group, Ernst & Young, since 1998; *b* 8 Jan. 1949; *s* of Aubrey Norman Toussaint Winckler and Pamela Elizabeth Essie (*née* Webb); *m* 1971, Marie Estelle Sigwart; three *s*. *Educ:* Bedford Modern Sch.; Christ's Coll., Cambridge (Open Exhibn; BA Hist. 1970; Dip Econ. 1975). MSI. HM Treasury, 1970–82, seconded to HM Diplomatic Service as First Sec. (Finance), British Embassy, Washington, 1978–81; Lloyds Bank, 1982–87: Syndicates Manager, Internat. Bank, 1982–85; Dir, Merchant Bank, 1985–87; Dir, Security Pacific Hoare Govett, 1987–90; Dep. Chm., European Capital Co., 1990–94; Exec. Dir, Head of Supervision, SIB, 1994–95; Chief Exec., SIB, 1996–97, FSA, 1997–98. Sen. Independent Dir, CrestCo Ltd, 1998–. Member: Bd, Housing Corp.; Jersey Financial Services Commn, 1998–. Trustee, Kennedy Meml Trust, 1998–. Mem. Council, QMW, 2000–. FRGS 1995. *Recreations:* reading, gardening, opera, bridge. *Address:* Rolls House, 7 Rolls Buildings, Fetter Lane, EC4A 1NH. *Club:* Oxford and Cambridge.

WINDEATT, Dr Barry Alexander Corelli; Reader in Medieval Literature, University of Cambridge, since 1995; Fellow of Emmanuel College, Cambridge, since 1978; *b* 5 April 1950; *s* of Edwin Peter Windeatt and Queenie Gladys Windeatt (*née* Rusbridge). *Educ:* Sutton County GS, Surrey; St Catharine's Coll., Cambridge (BA 1971; MA 1975; PhD 1975; LittD 1996). Cambridge University: Res. Fellow, Gonville and Caius Coll., 1974–78; Asst Lectr in English, 1983–87; Lectr in English, 1987–95; Tutor, 1982–95, Dir of Studies in English, 1979–98, Emmanuel Coll. *Publications:* (ed and trans.) Chaucer's Dream Poetry: sources and analogues, 1982; (ed) Geoffrey Chaucer, Troilus and Criseyde: A New Edition of The Book of Troilus, 1984, 2nd edn 1990; (trans.) The Book of Margery Kempe, 1985, new edn 2000; (ed with Ruth Morse) Chaucer Traditions, 1990; Troilus and Criseyde, 1992, 2nd edn 1995; (ed) English Mystics of the Middle Ages, 1994; articles on medieval English, French and Italian lit. *Recreations:* opera, gardens, visual arts. *Address:* Emmanuel College, Cambridge CB2 3AP. *T:* (01223) 334200.

WINDELER, John Robert; Chairman, Alliance & Leicester plc, since 1999; *b* 21 March 1943; *s* of Alfred Stewart Windeler and Ethela Windeler (*née* Boremuth); *m* 1965, Judith Lynn Taylor; two *s*. *Educ:* Ohio State Univ. (BA, MBA). Exec. Vice Pres., Irving Trust Co., 1969–89; Chief Financial Officer, Nat. Australia Bank, 1989–94; Dir, Alliance & Leicester Building Soc., subseq. Alliance & Leicester plc, 1995–, Dep. Chm., 1998–99. *Recreations:* tennis, ski-ing, antiques. *Address:* (office) 49 Park Lane, W1Y 4EQ. *T:* (020) 7629 6661. *Club:* Hurlingham.

WINDER, Robert James; Section Editor, Independent on Sunday, since 1998; *b* 26 Sept. 1959; *s* of Herbert James Winder and Mary Nina (*née* Dalby); *m* 1989, Hermione Davies; two *s*. *Educ:* Bradfield Coll.; St Catherine's Coll., Oxford (BA English). Euromoney Publications, 1982–86; Dep. Lit. Ed., 1986–89, Lit. Ed., 1989–95, The Independent; Dep. Ed., Granta Publications, 1996–98. *Publications:* No Admission, 1988; The Marriage of Time and Convenience, 1994; Hell for Leather, 1996. *Recreations:* reading, writing, walking, talking, etc.

WINDHAM, William Ashe Dymoke; Chairman, Skelmersdale Development Corporation, 1979–85; (Deputy Chairman, 1977); *b* 2 April 1926; *s* of late Lt-Col Henry Steuart Windham and Marjory Russell Dymock; *m* 1956, Alison Audrey, *d* of late Maj. P. P. Curtis, MC and Ellinor Kidston; two *s* one *d*. *Educ:* Bedford; Christ's Coll., Cambridge (schol.; University prize; MA). Gen. Manager, Runcorn Div., Arthur Guinness Son & Co. (GB), 1972–84. Mem., Runcorn Develt Corp., 1975–77. Steward, Henley Royal Regatta, 1953– (Mem. Cttee of Mgt, 1972–94); rowed for: Cambridge, 1947 and 1951; England, Empire Games, 1950; GB, European Championships, 1950 and 1951 (Gold Medal); Olympic Games, 1952. High Sheriff, Powys, 1996. *Recreations:* shooting, fishing. *Clubs:* Hawks (Cambridge); Leander (Henley) (Pres., 1993–98).

WINDLE, Prof. Alan Hardwick, FRS 1997; FIM, FInstP; Professor of Materials Science, University of Cambridge, since 1992; Fellow, Trinity College, Cambridge, since 1978; *b* 20 June 1942; *s* of Stuart George Windle and Myrtle Lillian (*née* Povey); *m* 1968, Janet Susan Carr; one *s* three *d*. *Educ:* Whitgift Sch.; Imperial Coll., London (BSc Eng. 1963; ARSM 1963); Trinity Coll., Cambridge (PhD 1966). FIM 1992; FInstP 1997. Imperial College, University of London: ICI Res. Fellow, 1966–67; Lectr in Metallurgy, 1967–75; Cambridge University: Lectr in Metallurgy and Materials Sci., 1975–92; Hd of Dept of Materials Sci. and Metallurgy, 1996–2001; Trinity College, Cambridge: Lectr and Dir of Studies in Natural Scis, 1978–92; Tutor, 1983–91. Exec. Dir, Cambridge-MIT Inst., 2000–. Vis. Prof., N Carolina State Univ., 1980. Vice-Pres., Inst. of Materials, 2001–. Comr, Royal Commn for Exhibition of 1851, 2001–. Chm. Trustees, Mission Aviation Fellowship Europe, 2001–. Gov., Whitgift Foundn, 1997–. Fellow, APS, 2001. Bessemer Medal, Imperial Coll., 1963; Silver Medal, RSA, 1963; Rosenhain Medal and Prize, Inst. Metals, 1987; Swinburne Medal and Prize, PRI, 1992. *Publications:* A First Course in Crystallography, 1978; (with A. M. Donald) Liquid Crystalline Polymers, 1992; contribs to learned jls mainly on polymer morphology, polymer glasses, polymer diffusion, liquid crystalline polymers and polymer modelling. *Recreation:* flying light aircraft. *Address:* Department of Materials Science and Metallurgy, Pembroke Street, Cambridge CB2 3QZ. *T:* (01223) 334321.

WINDLE, Terence Leslie William, CBE 1991; Director, Directorate General for Agriculture, European Commission, 1980–91; *b* 15 Jan. 1926; *s* of Joseph William Windle and Dorothy Windle (*née* Haigh); *m* 1957, Joy Winifred Shield; one *s* two *d*. *Educ:* Gonville and Caius College, Cambridge (MA); London University (Colonial Course). Colonial/HMOCS: Nigeria, 1951–59; Zambia, 1959–69 (Under Sec., Min. of Natural Resources and Tourism); Home Civil Service, MAFF, 1969–73; Commn of EC, 1973–91. *Address:* rue du Fond Agny 20, 1380 Lasne, Belgium. *T:* (2) 6334410.

WINDLESHAM, 3rd Baron *cr* 1937; **David James George Hennessy,** CVO 1981; PC 1973; Bt 1927; DLitt; Baron Hennessy (Life Peer), 1999; Principal, Brasenose College, Oxford, 1989–July 2002; Chairman, Trustees of the British Museum, 1986–96 (Trustee, 1981–96); *b* 28 Jan. 1932; *s* of 2nd Baron Windlesham; *S* father, 1962; *m* 1965, Prudence Glynn (*d* 1986); one *s* one *d*. *Educ:* Ampleforth; Trinity Coll., Oxford (MA; DLitt 1995; Hon. Fellow 1982). Chairman, Bow Group, 1959–60, 1962–63; Member, Westminster City Council, 1958–62. Minister of State, Home Office, 1970–72; Minister of State for Northern Ireland, 1972–73; Lord Privy Seal and Leader of the House of Lords, 1973–74. Mem., Cttee of Privy Counsellors on Ministerial Memoirs, 1975. Man. Dir, Grampian Television, 1967–70; Jt Man. Dir, 1974–75, Man. Dir, 1975–81, Chm., 1981, ATV Network; Director: The Observer, 1981–89; W. H. Smith Gp, plc, 1986–95. Vis. Fellow, All Souls Coll., Oxford, 1986; Weinberg/Goldman Sachs Vis. Prof., Princeton Univ., 1997. Chm., The Parole Bd, 1982–88. Pres., Victim Support, 1992–2001; Vice-Pres., Royal Television Soc., 1977–82; Jt Dep. Chm., Queen's Silver Jubilee Appeal, 1977; Dep. Chm., The Royal Jubilee Trusts, 1977–80; Chairman: Oxford Preservation Trust, 1979–89; Oxford Society, 1985–88; Mem, Museums and Galleries Commn, 1984–86. Ditchley Foundation: Governor and Mem., Council of Management, 1983–; Vice-Chm., 1987–; Trustee: Charities Aid Foundn, 1977–81; Community Service Volunteers, 1981–2000; Royal Collection Trust, 1993–2000. Hon. Bencher, Inner Temple, 1999. *Publications:* Communication and Political Power, 1966; Politics in Practice, 1975; Broadcasting in a Free Society, 1980; Responses to Crime, Vol. 1 1987, Vol. 2 1993, Vol. 3 1996, Vol. 4 2001; (with Richard Rampton) The Windlesham/Rampton Report on Death on the Rock, 1989; Politics, Punishment, and Populism, 1998. *Heir: s* Hon. James Hennessy, *b* 9 Nov. 1968. *Address:* c/o House of Lords, SW1A 0PW.

WINDSOR, Viscount; Ivor Edward Other Windsor-Clive; *b* 19 Nov. 1951; *s* and *heir* of 3rd Earl of Plymouth, *qv*; *m* 1979, Caroline, *d* of Frederick Nettlefold and Hon. Mrs Juliana Roberts; three *s* one *d*. *Educ:* Harrow; Royal Agricl Coll., Cirencester. Co-founder, and Dir, Centre for the Study of Modern Art, 1973. Chm., Heart of England Reg., HHA, 1996–. *Recreation:* cricket. *Heir: s* Hon. Robert Other Ivor Windsor-Clive, *b* 25 March 1981. *Address:* Oakly Park, Ludlow, Shropshire SY8 2JW; Flat 3, 6 Oakley Street, SW3 5NN.

WINDSOR, Dean of; *see* Conner, Rt Rev. D. J.

WINDSOR, Barbara Anne, MBE 2000; actress; *b* 6 Aug. 1937; *d* of John Deeks and Rose Deeks (*née* Ellis). *Educ:* Our Lady's Convent, London; Aida Foster Stage Sch. *Theatre includes:* Love from Judy, Palace; Fings Ain't Wot They Used T' Be, Garrick, 1959; Oh What a Lovely War, NY; Come Spy with Me, Whitehall; Sing a Rude Song, Garrick; The Threepenny Opera, Prince of Wales, 1972; The Owl and the Pussycat; Carry on London, Victoria Palace; A Merry Whiff of Windsor (one women show, UK and world tour), Twelfth Night, Chichester; Calamity Jane (UK tour); Entertaining Mr Sloane, Lyric, Hammersmith, 1981; The Mating Game; Guys and Dolls (tour). *Television includes:* The Rag Trade, 1961–63; Carry on Laughing, 1975; Worzel Gummidge, 1979; Peggy Mitchell in EastEnders, 1994–. *Films include:* Lost, 1956; Too Hot to Handle, 1959; Flame in the Street, 1961; On the Fiddle, 1961; Sparrers Can't Sing, 1963; Crooks in Cloisters, 1963; Carry on Spying, 1964; A Study in Terror, 1965; Carry on Doctor, 1968; Carry on Camping, Hair of the Dog, Chitty Chitty Bang Bang, 1969; Carry on Girls, 1971; The Boyfriend, 1971; Carry on Dick, 1974; Comrades, 1987; Double Vision. Numerous albums and radio performances. Variety Club of GB Award; Best Actress, Nat. Soap Awards; Best Actress, Manchester Evening News Awards; RADAR People of the Year Award, 1999. *Publications:* Laughter and Tears of a Cockney Sparrow; (with Robin McGibbon) All of Me: my extraordinary life (autobiog.), 2000. *Address:* c/o Burnett Granger Associates Ltd, Prince of Wales Theatre, 31 Coventry Street, W1D 6AS.

WINDSOR, Dr Colin George, FRS 1995; FInstP, FInstNDT; Consultant, United Kingdom Atomic Energy Authority, Fusion, since 1998; Senior Consultant, Penop, since 1998; *b* 28 June 1938; *s* of late George Thomas Macdonald Windsor and Mabel (*née* Rayment); *m* 1963, Margaret Lee; one *s* two *d*. *Educ:* Beckenham Grammar Sch.; Magdalen Coll., Oxford (BA 1st Cl. Hons Physics; DPhil 1963). FInstP 1975; FInstNDT 1993. Magnetic resonance research, Clarendon Lab., Oxford, 1963; Res. Fellow, Yale Univ., 1964; Neutron scattering research, Harwell, 1964–96; Sen. Scientist, Nat. Non-Destructive Testing Centre, AEA Technology, 1988–96; Programme Area Manager, UKAEA, Fusion, 1996–98. Fellow: Japanese Soc. for Promotion of Sci., 1980; Neural Network Applications, 1987–. Hon. Prof. of Physics, Birmingham Univ., 1990. *Publications:* Pulsed Neutron Scattering, 1981; Four Computer Models, 1982; (ed jtly) Solid State Science, Past, Present and Predicted, 1987; contrib. to learned jls. *Recreations:* cycling to work, tennis, sketching, singing, piano, composing. *Address:* D3, Culham Laboratory, Abingdon, Oxon OX14 3DB. *T:* (01235) 463652, *Fax:* (01235) 463414; *e-mail:* colin.windsor@ukaea.org.uk; (home) 21 Blackwater Way, Didcot OX11 7RL. *T:* (01235) 512036.

WINDSOR-CLIVE, family name of **Earl of Plymouth**.

WINDWARD ISLANDS, Bishop of, since 1994; **Rt Rev. Sehon Sylvester Goodridge;** *b* Barbados, 9 Oct. 1937; *s* of late Simeon Goodridge and Vernese (*née* Burrows); *m* 1966, Janet Rosalind Thomas; one *s* two *d*. *Educ:* Harrison Coll., Barbados; Codrington Coll., Barbados; King's Coll. London (BD 1966, AKC 1991). Asst Master, Grenada Boys' Sec. Sch., 1957–58. Deacon 1963, priest 1964, Windward Is; Curate, Holy Trinity, St Lucia, 1964–66; Anglican Chaplain, Univ. of W Indies and part-time Teacher, Kingston Coll., 1967–69; Anglican Tutor, United Theol Coll. of W Indies, Mona, Jamaica, 1969–71; Principal, Codrington Coll., Barbados, 1971–82; Warden/Student Counsellor, Univ. of W Indies, Cave Hill Campus, Barbados, 1983–89; Mem., Synod Council, Dio. Barbados, 1973–87; Hon. Canon, Dio. Barbados, 1976–; Principal, Simon of Cyrene Theol Inst., 1989–94. Chaplain to the Queen, 1993–94. Univ. Preacher, Univ. of St Andrews, 1997. Member: Inter-Anglican Theol and Doctrinal Commn, 1981–85; Bd of Govs, Coll. of Ascension, Birmingham, 1989–94; Standing Cttee on Theol Educn, CCBI, 1989–94; Bd for Social Responsibility, Gen. Synod, C of E, 1990–94; Council of Southwark Ordination Course, 1990–94; Partnership Adv. Gp, USPG, 1990–94; URC Trng Cttee, 1991–94; Initial Ministerial Educn Cttee, ABM, 1991–94; Gov. Body, SPCK, 1991–94; Bd, William Temple Foundn, 1992–94. Chm. Adv. Cttee, Sch. of Continuing Studies, Univ. of W Indies, St Vincent and the Grenadines, 1998–. Exam. Chaplain to Bishop of Southwark, 1990–94. Vis. Prof., Gen. Theol Seminary, NY, 1986. Hon. DD: Huron Coll., Univ. of W Ont, 1977; Gen. Theol Seminary, NY, 1995. Mem. of Privy Council, Barbados, 1986–91. *Publications:* St Mary's: 1827–1977, 1977; Facing the

Challenge of Emancipation, 1981; A Companion to Liberation Theology, 1984; (ed jtly) Facing the Challenge of Racism, 1994; (contrib.) Window on Salvation, 1994; (contrib.) The Terrible Alternative, 1998; *monographs:* Politics and the Caribbean Church, 1971; The Church Amidst Politics and Revolution, 1977; The Abortion Question, 1977; articles in Bull. E Caribbean Affairs, The Bajan, Caribbean Contact, Christian Action Jl, The Month, Crucible. *Recreations:* reading, cricket, gardening. *Address:* PO Box 502, Bishop's Court, Kingstown, St Vincent, WI.

WINEGARTEN, Jonathan Isaac; Chief Master of the Supreme Court, Chancery Division, since 1998 (a Master, since 1991); *b* 10 Dec. 1944; *s* of Moshe Winegarten and Hannah Deborah Winegarten (*née* Cohen). *Educ:* Hasmonean Grammar Sch., Hendon; Gateshead Yeshiva; University Coll. London (LLB Hons 1967); Slabodka Yeshiva, Israel. Chm., Yavneh, 1966. Winston Churchill Award and called to the Bar, Middle Temple, 1969, *ad eundem* Lincoln's Inn, 1972 (Bencher, 1990); in practice, Chancery Bar, 1970–91. Member: Chancery Bar Assoc. Cttee, 1982, 1983; Supreme Court Procedure Cttee, 1992–. Member: Bd of Deputies, 1973–79; Council, Jews' Coll., 1989–2000; Vice Pres., Fedn of Synagogues, 1989–2001. Pres., Shomrei Hadath Synagogue, 1983–. Freeman, City of London, 1992. Adv. Editor, Atkin's Court Forms, 1993–; Editor: Tristram and Coote's Probate Practice, 1995–; Civil Procedure (The White Book), 1999–. *Publications:* (ed) Collected works of Rabbi Z. H. Ferber (11 vols), 1983–92. *Recreations:* violin playing, painting, esp. glass painting and etching, music, reading, publishing. *Address:* Thomas More Building, Royal Courts of Justice, Strand, WC2A 2LL.

WINFIELD, Dr Graham, CBE 1991; Chairman: Booker Tate Ltd, 1993–98; Zinc Corporation PLC, 1997–98; *b* 28 May 1931; *s* of Josiah and Gladys Winfield; *m* 1959, Olive Johnson; three *s* one *d.* *Educ:* Univ. of Liverpool (BSc, PhD Chemistry). Chemist, Min. of Supply, 1956–57; Lectr, Univ. of Liverpool, 1957–58; Chief Chemist, later Develt Manager, Ciba ARL, 1958–62; Develt Manager, MaxMeyer Co., Milan, 1962–63; BOC Group, 1963–89: R&D, marketing, gen. management; Chief Executive: Metals Div. UK, 1969–74; Gases Div. UK, 1974–79; Overseas Gp, 1979–89. Non-exec. Dir., Baker Perkins Group, 1984–87. Mem., ESRC, 1985–90; Chairman: Post Grad. Trng Bd, 1987–90; Retail and Distbn Panel, Technol. Foresight, Cabinet Office, 1994–97. *Publications:* numerous papers in pure and applied chemistry. *Recreations:* golf, bridge, music, reading. *Address:* Tawelfan, Crossing Lane, Claydon, Banbury, Oxon OX17 1EX.

WINFIELD, William Richard, MA; Headmaster, Mill Hill School, since 1995; *b* 19 March 1947; *s* of William Arthur and Paula Constance Winfield; *m* 1986, Margaret Ruth Richards; one *s* one *d.* *Educ:* William Ellis Sch.; Royal Acad. of Music (Jun. Exhibnr); Clare Coll., Cambridge (BA Mod. and Med. Langs 1968; PGCE 1970; MA 1972). Lectr, Maison de l'Europe, Bordeaux, 1968–69; Mill Hill School: Asst Master, 1970–75; Head of Modern Langs, 1975–87; Dir of Studies, 1982–92; Dep. Headmaster, 1992–95. Chief Examr, French Studies, JMB, 1980–87. Gov., Keble Sch., 1999–. *Publications:* (jtly) Vocational French, 1985; contribs to jls on Section Bilingue and intensive language teaching. *Recreations:* playing chamber music, hill walking. *Address:* Mill Hill School, Mill Hill Village, NW7 1QS. *T:* (020) 8959 1176.

WING, Prof. John Kenneth, CBE 1990; MD, PhD; DPM; FRCPsych; Director of Research Unit, Royal College of Psychiatrists, 1989–94; Professor of Social Psychiatry, Institute of Psychiatry and London School of Hygiene and Tropical Medicine, 1970–89, now Emeritus Professor, University of London; *b* 22 Oct. 1923; *m* 1950, Lorna Gladys Tolchard (*see* L. G. Wing); one *d.* *Educ:* Strand Sch.; University College London (MB, BS, MD, PhD). Served RNVR, 1942–46, Lieut (A). Dir, MRC Social Psychiatry Unit, 1965–89. Mem., MRC, 1985–89 (Chm., Neurosciences Bd, 1985–87; Chm., Health Services Res. Cttee, 1987–89). Hon. Consultant Psychiatrist, Maudsley and Bethlem Royal Hosp., 1960–89. Advr to H of C Social Services Cttee, 1984–85 and 1990. Founder FMedSci 1998. Hon. MD Heidelberg, 1977. *Publications:* (ed) Early Childhood Autism, 1966, 2nd edn 1975 (trans. Italian 1970, German 1973); (with G. W. Brown) Institutionalism and Schizophrenia, 1970; (with J. E. Cooper and N. Sartorius) Description and Classification of Psychiatric Symptoms, 1974 (trans. German 1978, French 1980, Japanese 1981); Reasoning about Madness, 1978 (trans. Portuguese 1978, German 1982, Italian 1983); ed, Schizophrenia: towards a new synthesis, 1978; ed (with R. Olsen), Community Care for the Mentally Disabled, 1979; (with J. Leach) Helping Destitute Men, 1979; (ed jtly) What is a Case?, 1981; (ed jtly) Handbook of Psychiatric Rehabilitation, 1981; (with L. G. Wing) Psychoses of Uncertain Aetiology, vol. III of Cambridge Handbook of Psychiatry, 1982; (ed) Contributions to Health Services Planning and Research, 1989; (ed) Measurement for Mental Health, 1995; (jtly) Diagnosis and Clinical Measurement in Psychiatry, 1998; (with P. Lelliott) Progress on Health of the Nation Outcome Scales, 2000; Epidemiological Needs Assessment: severe mental illness, 2000.

WING, Dr Lorna Gladys, OBE 1995; FRCPsych; Consultant Psychiatrist to National Autistic Society, since 1990; *b* 7 Oct. 1928; *d* of Bernard Newbury Tolchard and Gladys Ethel Tolchard (*née* Whittell); *m* 1950, John Kenneth Wing, *qv*; one *d.* *Educ:* Chatham Grammar Sch.; University Coll. Hosp. (MD). Scientific Staff, MRC Social Psychiatry Unit, 1964–90; Hon. Consultant Psychiatrist, Maudsley Hosp., 1972–90; Hon. Sen. Lectr, Inst. of Psychiatry, 1974–90. *Publications:* Autistic Children, 1971, 2nd edn 1980; (ed) Early Childhood Autism, 1976; (ed) Aspects of Autism, 1988; Hospital Closure and the Resettlement of Residents, 1989; The Autistic Spectrum, 1996; papers in sci. jls. *Recreations:* reading, gardening, walking. *Address:* Elliot House, 113 Masons Hill, Bromley, Kent BR2 9HT. *T:* (020) 8466 0098.

WINGATE, Rev. Canon Andrew David Carlile, PhD; Diocesan Director of Ministry and Training, Leicester, Bishop's Inter-Faith Consultant, and Canon Theologian of Leicester Cathedral, since 2000; *b* 2 Aug. 1944; *s* of Rev. Canon David Wingate and late Olga Wingate; *m* 1967, Angela Beever; one *s* two *d.* *Educ:* Worcester Coll., Oxford (BA 1st class, MA, MPhil); Lincoln Theol Coll.; Univ. of Birmingham (PhD 1995). Asst Master, King Edward's Sch., Birmingham, 1968–70; ordained deacon, 1972, priest, 1973; Asst Curate, Halesowen Parish Church, 1972–75; Lectr, Tamil Nadu Theol Seminary, Madurai, S India, 1975–82; Principal: W Midlands Ministerial Training Course, Queen's Coll., Birmingham, 1982–90; United Coll. of the Ascension, Selly Oak, Birmingham, 1990–2000. Chm., British Assoc. of Mission Studies, 2001–. Hon. Lectr in Theol, Univ. of Birmingham, 1998–. *Publications:* Encounter in the Spirit: Muslim Christian dialogue in practice, 1988, 2nd edn 1991; The Church and Conversion, 1997; (ed) Anglicanism: a global communion, 1998; Does Theological Education Make a Difference?, 1999; articles in theol jls. *Recreations:* tennis, swimming, golf, painting, mountain walking. *Address:* 23 Roundhill Road, Evington, Leicester LE5 5RJ.

WINGATE, Captain Sir Miles (Buckley), KCVO 1982; FNI; Deputy Master and Chairman of the Board of Trinity House, London, 1976–88, retired; *b* 17 May 1923; *s* of Terrence Wingate and Edith Wingate; *m* 1947, Alicia Forbes Philip; three *d.* *Educ:* Taunton Grammar Sch.; Southampton and Prior Park Coll., Somerset. Master Mariner. Apprenticed to Royal Mail Lines Ltd, 1939; first Comd, 1957; elected to Bd of Trinity House, 1968. Commonwealth War Graves Comr, 1986–91. Vice-President: Seamen's Hosp. Soc., 1980–; Royal Alfred Seafarers Soc., 1980–; British Maritime Charitable Foundn, 1983–; Pres., Internat. Assoc. of Lighthouse Authorities, 1985–88 (Vice-Pres., 1980–85); Dep. Chm., Gen. Council, King George's Fund for Sailors, 1983–93; Mem., Cttee of Management, RNLI, 1976–98; Council, Missions to Seamen, 1982–93. Liveryman: Hon. Co. of Master Mariners, 1970–; Shipwrights' Co., 1977–90; Freeman, Watermen and Lightermen's Co., 1984. Governor, Pangbourne Coll., 1982–91. *Recreation:* golf. *Address:* Trinity House, Tower Hill, EC3N 4DH. *T:* (020) 7480 6601.

WINGFIELD, family name of **Viscount Powerscourt.**

WINGFIELD DIGBY, Very Rev. Richard Shuttleworth, MA; Dean of Peterborough, 1966–80, Dean Emeritus since 1980; *b* 19 Aug. 1911; *s* of late Everard George Wingfield Digby and Dorothy (*née* Loughnan); *m* 1936, Rosamond Frances, *d* of late Col W. T. Digby, RE; two *s* one *d.* *Educ:* Nautical Coll., Pangbourne; Royal Navy; Christ's Coll., Cambridge; Westcott House, Cambridge. BA 1935; MA 1939. Asst Curate of St Andrew's, Rugby, 1936–46. Chaplain to the Forces (4th Cl. Emergency Commn), 1940–45; POW, 1940–45. Vicar of All Saints, Newmarket, 1946–53; Rector of Bury, Lancs, 1953–66; Rural Dean of Bury, 1962–66. Pres. and Chm., Bury Trustee Savings Bank, 1953–66; Dep. Chm., Trustee Savings Bank Assoc., North-West Area, 1965–66. Hon. Canon of Manchester Cathedral, 1965; Hon. Chaplain to Regt XX, The Lancs Fusiliers, 1965. Chm. C of E Council for Places of Worship, 1976–81. *Recreations:* walking, dry stone walling. *Address:* Byways, Higher Holton, near Wincanton, Somerset BA9 8AP. *T:* (01963) 32137. *Club:* Army and Navy.

WINKELMAN, Joseph William, PPRE (RE 1982; ARE 1979); RWA 1990 (ARWA 1983); free-lance painter-printmaker, since 1971; President, Royal Society of Painter-Printmakers (formerly Royal Society of Painter-Etchers and Engravers), 1989–95; *b* 20 Sept. 1941; *s* of George William Winkelman and Cleo Lucretia (*née* Harness); *m* 1969, Harriet Lowell Belin; two *d.* *Educ:* Univ. of the South, Sewanee, Tenn (BA English 1964); Wharton School of Finance, Univ. of Pennsylvania; Ruskin Sch. of Drawing; Univ. of Oxford (Cert. of Fine Art 1971). Royal Society of Painter-Etchers and Engravers: Hon. Sec., 1982; Vice-Pres., 1986; Fellow, Printmakers' Council of GB, 1978 (Hon. Fellow, 1988). Former tutor for: Sch. of Architecture, Oxford Polytechnic; Ruskin Sch. of Drawing, Oxford Univ.; Dept for External Studies, Oxford Univ. Chm., Oxford Art Soc., 1987–93 (Vice Pres., 1994–). Chm., Nat. Assoc. of Blood Donors, 1994–95. Gov., Windmill First Sch., Headington, Oxford, 1994–98. Hon. RWS 1997. *Recreations:* gardening, theatre, hill walking. *Address:* The Hermitage, 69 Old High Street, Headington, Oxford OX3 9HT. *T:* (01865) 762839; *e-mail:* Winkelman@ukgateway.net.

WINKLEY, Sir David (Ross), Kt 1999; DPhil; Founder and President, National Primary Trust; *b* 30 Nov. 1941; *s* of late Donald Joseph Winkley and Winifred Mary Winkley; *m* 1967, Dr Linda Mary Holland; one *s* one *d.* *Educ:* King Edward's Sch., Birmingham; Selwyn Coll., Cambridge (MA); Wadham Coll., Oxford (DPhil 1975); DLitt Birmingham 1999. Mem., Centre for Contemporary Cultural Studies, Univ. of Birmingham, 1965; Dep. Head, Perry Common Sch., 1968–71; Head, Grove Primary Sch., 1974–97. Fellow, Nuffield Coll., Oxford, 1981–82. Hon. Prof., Univ. of Birmingham, 1999–. Member: CATE, 1985–90; Stevenson Cttee on Information and Communication Technol., 1996; Standards Task Force, 1998–. Founder and Chm., Birmingham Children's Community Venture, 1967–. DLitt Birmingham, 1999; DUniv UCE, 2000. *Publications:* Diplomats and Detectives, 1986; numerous academic articles on educational and philosophical issues. *Recreations:* reading, music, piano playing, writing fiction. *Address:* 68 Butlers Road, Handsworth Wood, Birmingham B20 2PA.

WINKLEY, Dr Stephen Charles, MA; Headmaster, Uppingham School, since 1991; *b* 9 July 1944; *e s* of late George Winkley and Eunice Winkley (*née* Golding); *m* 1st, 1968, Georgina Smart; two *s*; 2nd, 1983, Jennifer Burt; two *d.* *Educ:* St Edward's School, Oxford; Brasenose College, Oxford (MA 1967; DPhil 1973). Asst Master, Cranleigh Sch., 1969–85; Second Master, Winchester College, 1985–91. *Recreations:* music, water colours. *Address:* Headmaster's House, Spring Back Way, Uppingham, Rutland LE15 9QE. *T:* (01572) 822688.

WINKS, Prof. Robin W(illiam Evert), MA, PhD; Randolph W. Townsend Professor of History, Yale University, since 1957; *b* 5 Dec. 1930; *s* of Evert McKinley Winks and Jewell Sampson; *m* 1952, Avril Flockton, Wellington, NZ; one *s* one *d.* *Educ:* Univ. of Colorado (BA Hons 1952, MA 1953); Victoria Univ., NZ (Cert. 1952); Johns Hopkins Univ. (PhD 1957). Yale University: Dir, Office of Special Projects and Foundns, 1974–76; Master of Berkeley Coll., 1977–90; Chairman: Council of Masters, 1978–84, 1986–88; Studies in the Envmt, 1993–96; Dept of History, 1996–99. Smith-Mundt Prof., Univ. of Malaya, 1962; Vis. Prof., Univ. of Sydney, 1963; Vis. Fellow, Inst. of Commonwealth Studies, 1966–67; Guggenheim Fellow, 1976–77; Vis. Prof. of Economics, Univ. of Stellenbosch, 1983; Fellow, Amer. Sch. for Research, 1985 and 1991; George Eastman Vis. Prof., 1992–93, Harmsworth Vis. Prof., 1999–2000, Oxford Univ. Cultural Attaché, Amer. Embassy, London, 1969–71; Advisor to Dept of State, 1971–. Chm., Nat. Park Service Adv. Bd, 1981–83; Trustee, Nat. Parks and Conservation Assoc., 1985–. Mem. Council on For. Relations. FRHistS; Fellow, Explorers' Club, 1986. Hon. MA: Yale 1967; Oxon, 1992; Hon. DLitt: Nebraska, 1976; Colorado, 1987; Westminster Coll., 1995. *Publications:* Canada and the United States, 1960, 4th edn 1998; The Cold War, 1964, 2nd edn 1977; Historiography of the British Empire-Commonwealth, 1966, 2nd edn 1994; Malaysia, 1966, 2nd edn 1979; Age of Imperialism, 1969; Pastmasters, 1969; The Historian as Detective, 1969; The Blacks in Canada, 1971, 2nd edn 1997; Slavery, 1972; An American's Guide to Britain, 1977, 3rd edn 1987; Other Voices, Other Views, 1978; The Relevance of Canadian History, 1979, 2nd edn 1988; World Civilization, 1979, 3rd edn 1993; Detective Fiction, 1980; The British Empire, 1981; Modus Operandi, 1982; History of Civilization, 1984, 9th edn 1995; Cloak and Gown, 1987, 2nd edn 1996; Asia in Western Language Fiction, 1990; Frederick Billings: a life, 1991, 2nd edn 1998; Laurance S. Rockefeller: catalyst for conservation, 1997; (ed) The Oxford History of the British Empire, vol. V: historiography, 1999; articles in Amer. Hist. Rev. *Recreations:* travel, conservation, detective fiction. *Address:* Box 208324 Yale Station, New Haven, CT 06520, USA. *Clubs:* Athenæum, Royal Commonwealth Society, Special Forces; Yale, Explorers' (NY).

WINKWORTH-SMITH, (Michael) John; mediator; Regional Managing Partner, Leeds Office, Dibb Lupton Alsop (formerly Dibb Lupton Broomhead), 1995–99; *b* 4 May 1944; *s* of late Frank Winkworth-Smith and of Marjorie Beaumont Winkworth-Smith (*née* Smith); *m* 1974, Sarah Elisabeth Jackson; two *s* (one *d* decd). *Educ:* Ermysted's Grammar Sch., Skipton. Admitted solicitor, 1970; Partner, Broomhead Wightman & Reed, later Dibb Lupton Broomhead, then Dibb Lupton Alsop, 1972–99; Man. Partner, Birmingham Office, 1993–95. Treas., Royal Sheffield Instn for the Blind, 1972–78; Mem., Sheffield CVS, 1978–90; Dir, Broomgrove Trust, 1980–; Chairman: Taptonholme Ltd, 1984–2000; Champion Hse, Derby Diocesan Youth Centre, 1988–93. Director: CEDR, 1991–99; Japan Adv. Services Ltd, 1991–97. FRSA 1997. *Recreations:* family, farming, shooting. *Address:* Churchdale Farm, Ashford-in-the-Water, Bakewell, Derbys DE45 1NX. *T:* (01629) 640269.

WINN, family name of **Baron St Oswald.**

WINN, Allan Kendal, FRAeS, FCIT; Publisher, Reed Aerospace, since 1998; (Editor-in-Chief, 1977–98); *b* 19 March 1950; *s* of Atkinson Winn and Janet Winn; *m* 1994, Jacqueline Christina Worsley; one step *s* one step *d. Educ:* Nelson Coll., NZ; Univ. of Canterbury, Christchurch, NZ (BEng, Diploma in Journalism). FCIT 1992; FRAeS 1996. Technical Editor, Consulting Engineer, 1975–77; Technical Editor, Editor, Man. Editor, Engineering Today, later New Technology, 1977–85; Editor: Commercial Motor, 1985–88; Flight International, 1989–98. Chm., Assoc. of Friends of Brooklands Mus., 1995–. Liveryman, GAPAN, 1999–. *Recreation:* vintage motor vehicles. *Address:* Reed Aerospace, Quadrant House, The Quadrant, Sutton, Surrey SM2 5AS. *T:* (020) 8652 3882; 39 Heathcote, Tadworth, Surrey KT20 5TH. *T:* (01737) 362760. *Clubs:* Aviation of UK (Chm., 1991–97), Vintage Sports Car, Bentley Drivers'.

WINNER, Michael Robert; Chairman: Scimitar Films Ltd, Michael Winner Ltd, Motion Picture and Theatrical Investments Ltd, since 1957; *b* 30 Oct. 1935; *s* of late George Joseph and Helen Winner. *Educ:* St Christopher's Sch., Letchworth; Downing Coll., Cambridge Univ. (MA). Film critic and Fleet Street journalist and contributor to: The Spectator, Daily Express, London Evening Standard, etc; columnist, Sunday Times and News of the World. Panellist, Any Questions, BBC radio; presenter, Michael Winner's True Crimes, LWT. Entered Motion Pictures, 1956, as Screen Writer, Asst Director, Editor. Sen. Mem. Council, Directors' Guild of Great Britain, 1991– (Mem. Council, Chief Censorship Officer, and Trustee, 1983–). Films include: Play It Cool (Dir), 1962; The Cool Mikado (Dir and Writer), 1962; West Eleven (Dir), 1963; The System (Prod. and Dir), 1963; You Must Be Joking (Prod., Dir, Writer), 1965; The Jokers (Prod., Dir, Writer), 1966; I'll Never Forget What's 'isname (Prod. and Dir), 1967; Hannibal Brooks (Prod., Dir, Writer), 1968; The Games (Prod. and Dir), 1969; Lawman (Prod. and Dir), 1970; The Nightcomers (Prod. and Dir), 1971; Chato's Land (Prod. and Dir), 1971; The Mechanic (Dir), 1972; Scorpio (Prod. and Dir), 1972; The Stone Killer (Prod. and Dir), 1973; Death Wish (Prod. and Dir), 1974; Won Ton Ton The Dog That Saved Hollywood (Prod. and Dir), 1975; The Sentinel (Prod., Dir, Writer), 1976; The Big Sleep (Prod., Dir, Writer), 1977; Firepower (Prod., Dir), 1978; Death Wish Two (Prod., Dir, Writer), 1981; The Wicked Lady (Prod., Dir, Writer), 1982; Scream for Help (Prod., Dir), 1984; Death Wish Three (Prod. and Dir), 1985; Appointment with Death (Prod., Dir, Writer), 1988; A Chorus of Disapproval (Prod., Dir, Jt screenplay writer), 1989; Bullseye! (Prod., Dir, jt screenplay writer), 1990; Dirty Weekend (Prod., Dir, jt screenplay writer), 1993; Parting Shots (Prod., Dir, Writer), 1997; actor: For the Greater Good, 1990; Decadence, 1993; radio play: The Flump, 2000. Theatre productions: The Tempest, Wyndhams, 1974; A Day in Hollywood A Night in the Ukraine, 1978. Founder and Chm., Police Meml Trust, 1984–. *Publication:* Winner's Dinners, 1999, rev. edn 2000. *Recreations:* walking around art galleries, museums, antique shops, eating, being difficult, making table mats. *Address:* 219 Kensington High Street, W8 6BD. *T:* (020) 7734 8385.

WINNICK, David Julian; MP (Lab) Walsall North, since 1979; *b* Brighton, 26 June 1933; *s* of late Eugene and Rose Winnick; one *s*; *m* 1968, Bengi Rona (marr. diss.), *d* of Tarik and Zeynep Rona. *Educ:* secondary school; London Sch. of Economics (Dip. in Social Admin). Army National Service, 1951–53. Branch Secretary, Clerical and Administrative Workers' Union, 1956–62 (later APEX GMB; Mem. Exec. Council, 1978–88, Vice-Pres., 1983–88); Advertisement Manager, Tribune, 1963–66; employed by UKIAS, 1970–79 (Chm., 1984–90). Member: Willesden Borough Council, 1959–64; London Borough of Brent Council, 1964–66 (Chairman, Children Cttee, 1965–66). Contested (Lab) Harwich, 1964; MP (Lab) Croydon South, 1966–70; contested (Lab): Croydon Central, Oct. 1974; Walsall N, Nov. 1976. Member: Select Cttee on the Environment, 1979–83; Home Affairs Cttee, 1983–87, 1997–; Select Cttee on Procedure, 1989–97; Co-Chm., British-Irish Inter-Parly Body, 1997 (Vice-Chm., 1993–97). *Recreations:* walking, cinema, theatre, reading. *Address:* House of Commons, SW1A 0AA.

WINNIFRITH, Charles Boniface, CB 1998; Clerk of Committees, House of Commons, 1995–2001; *b* 12 May 1936; *s* of Sir John Winnifrith, KCB and late Lesbia Margaret Winnifrith; *m* 1st, 1962, Josephine Poile, MBE (*d* 1991); one *s* two *d*; 2nd, 1993, Sandra (*née* Stewart). *Educ:* Tonbridge Sch.; Christ Church, Oxford (MA). 2nd Lieut, RAEC, 1958–60. Joined Dept of the Clerk of the House of Commons, 1960; Second Clerk of Select Cttees, 1983; Clerk of Select Cttees, 1987; Principal Clerk of the Table Office, 1989. Mem., General Synod of C of E, 1970–90. Governor, Ashford Sch., Kent, 1973–93. *Recreations:* cricket, American soap opera. *Address:* Gale Lodge Farm, Long Buckby, Northants NN6 7PH. *T:* (01604) 770396; Cliffe Cottage, St Margaret's-at-Cliffe, Kent CT15 6BJ. *T:* (01304) 853280. *Club:* MCC.

WINNINGTON, Sir Francis Salwey William, 6th Bt *cr* 1755; Lieut, late Welsh Guards; *b* 24 June 1907; *er s* of late Francis Salwey Winnington, *e s* of 5th Bt and Blanch, *d* of Commander William John Casberd-Boteler, RN; *S* grandfather, 1931; *m* 1944, Anne, *o d* of late Captain Lawrence Drury-Lowe; one *d. Educ:* Eton. Served War of 1939–45 (wounded, prisoner). Owns 4700 acres. *Heir: nephew* Anthony Edward Winnington [*b* 13 May 1948; *m* 1978, Karyn Kathryn, *d* of F. H. Kettles; one *s* two *d*].
See also Viscount Campden.

WINNINGTON-INGRAM, Edward John; Managing Director, Mail Newspapers Plc (formerly Associated Newspapers Group), 1986–89, retired; *b* 20 April 1926; *s* of Rev. Preb. Edward Francis and Gladys Winnington-Ingram; *m* 1st, 1953, Shirley Lamotte (marr. diss. 1968); two *s*; 2nd, 1973, Elizabeth Linda Few Brown. *Educ:* Shrewsbury; Keble Coll., Oxford (BA). Served RN (Sub-Lieut), 1944–47. Joined Associated Newspapers, 1949; Circulation Manager, Daily Mail, 1960–65; Gen. Manager, Daily Mail Manchester, 1965–70; helped create Northprint Manchester Ltd, a jt printing consortium with Manchester Guardian and Evening News and Associated, 1969; Dir, Associated Newspapers, 1971; Managing Director: Harmsworth Publishing, 1973; Mail on Sunday, 1982; Dir, Associated Newspapers Holdings, 1983; non-executive Director: NAAFI, 1987–93; Burlington Gp, 1988–92. *Recreations:* tennis, shooting, beagling, gardening, music, defending the 1662 Prayer Book. *Address:* Old Manor Farm, Cottisford, Brackley, Northants NN13 5SW. *T:* (01280) 848367. *Clubs:* Buck's, Roehampton.

WINSHIP, Peter James Joseph, CBE 1998; QPM 1990; HM Inspector of Constabulary, since 1995; *b* 21 July 1943; *s* of late Francis Edward Winship and Iris May (*née* Adams); *m* 1st, 1963, Carol Ann McNaughton; two *s* one *d*; 2nd, 1989, Janet Mary Bird; one *d. Educ:* Bicester Grammar Sch.; St John's Coll., Oxford (BA Eng. Lang. and Lit.; MA). Oxfordshire Constabulary, 1962; Sergeant to Supt, Thames Valley Police, 1968–79; Graduate, FBI Acad., 1980; Chief Supt, Metropolitan Police, 1982; Asst Chief Constable, Thames Valley Police, 1984; Metropolitan Police: Dep. Asst Comr, Policy & Planning, 1987, No 1 Area HQ, 1988; Asst Comr, 1989–95; Management Support and Strategy Dept, 1989–91; Inspection and Review Dept, 1992–95. Dir, Police Extended Interviews, 1993–95. Chm., Technical and Res. Cttee, ACPO, 1992–95. Member: Exec. Council, London Fedn of Boys' Clubs, 1988–95; Exec. Cttee, Royal Humane Soc., 1989–95; Governing Bd, Revolving Doors Agency, 1993–95. FIMgt. *Publications:* articles in police jls and other periodicals on professionally related subjects, travel, and treatment of police in literature; essay on delinquency and social policy (Queen's Police Gold Medal, Essay Competition, 1969). *Recreations:* reading, riding, gardening, music. *Address:* (office) White Rose Court, Oriental Road, Woking, Surrey GU22 7LG.

WINSKEL, Prof. Glynn, ScD, PhD; Professor of Computer Science, University of Cambridge, since 2000; Fellow, Emmanuel College, Cambridge, since 2000; *b* 23 May 1953; *s* of Thomas Francis Winskel and Helen Juanita Winskel (*née* McCall); *m* 1982, Kirsten Krog Jensen; two *d. Educ:* Emmanuel Coll., Cambridge (BA, MA Maths, ScD Computer Sci. 1995); St Catherine's Coll., Oxford (MSc Maths); Univ. of Edinburgh (PhD Computer Sci. 1980). Res. Scientist, Carnegie-Mellon Univ., Pittsburgh, 1982–83; University of Cambridge: Lectr in Computer Sci., 1984–87; Reader, 1987–88; Fellow, King's Coll., 1985–88; Prof. of Computer Sci., 1988–2000, Dir, Basic Res. in Computer Sci., 1994–2000, Aarhus Univ., Denmark. Ed., Jl of Mathematical Structures in Computer Science. *Publications:* Formal Semantics of Programming Languages: an introduction, 1993; (contrib.) Handbook of Logic in Computer Science, 1994. *Recreations:* music, art, theatre, running, swimming, reading. *Address:* Computer Laboratory, University of Cambridge, New Museums Site, Cambridge CB2 3QG.

WINSKILL, Air Commodore Sir Archibald (Little), KCVO 1980 (CVO 1973); CBE 1960; DFC 1941 and Bar 1943; AE 1944; Extra Equerry to The Queen; *b* 24 Jan. 1917; *s* of late James Winskill; *m* 1947, Christiane Amilie Pauline, *d* of M. Bailleux, Calais, France; one *d* (one *s* decd). War of 1939–45: Fighter Pilot: Battle of Britain; European and North African Theatres; evaded capture in enemy territory, in occupied France, 1941, and in Tunisia, 1943; Post War: graduate, Army Staff Coll., Flying Coll., JSSC; Air Adviser to Belgian Govt; Station Cmdr, RAF Turnhouse and Duxford; Gp Capt. Ops Germany; Air Attaché, Paris; Dir of Public Relations, MoD (RAF); Captain of the Queen's Flight, 1968–82. Pres., Queen's Flight Assoc., 1982–. Freedom of City of London, 1978. *Recreations:* golf, bridge. *Address:* 28 Swinnerton House, Phyllis Court Drive, Henley-on-Thames, Oxon RG9 2HU. *T:* (01491) 578069. *Clubs:* Royal Air Force; Phyllis Court (Henley); Huntercombe Golf.

WINSOR, Thomas Philip; Rail Regulator and International Rail Regulator, since 1999; *b* 7 Dec. 1957; twin *s* of Thomas Valentine Marrs Winsor and Phyllis Margaret Winsor (*née* Bonsor); *m* 1989, Sonya Elizabeth Field; one *d. Educ:* Grove Acad., Broughty Ferry; Univ. of Edinburgh (LLB Scots Law 1979); Univ of Dundee (Postgrad. Dip. Petroleum Law 1983). Admitted solicitor, 1981, NP 1981, WS 1984, Scotland; admitted solicitor, England and Wales, 1991; in general practice, Dundee, 1981–83; Assistant Solicitor: Dundas & Wilson, CS, 1983–84; Norton Rose, 1984–91; Partner, Denton Hall, 1991–99; Chief Legal Advr and Gen. Counsel, Office of Rail Regulator, 1993–95. Hon. Lectr, Centre for Energy, Petroleum and Mineral Law and Policy, Univ. of Dundee, 1993–. Member: Law Soc. of Scotland, 1981–; Internat. Bar Assoc., 1983–; Univ. of Dundee Petroleum and Mineral Law Soc., 1987– (Pres., 1987–89); Soc. of Scottish Lawyers in London, 1987– (Pres., 1987–89); Law Soc. of England and Wales, 1991–. Mem., Labour Party. *Publications:* (with M. P. G. Taylor) Taylor and Winsor on Joint Operating Agreements, 1989; contrib. Legal Lines, articles in Modern Railways mag., 1996–99; contrib. articles in books and learned jls on oil and gas, electricity and railways law and regulation. *Recreations:* literature, theatre, opera, music, hill-walking, gardening, cycling, Scottish constitutional history, law. *Address:* Office of the Rail Regulator, 1 Waterhouse Square, 138–142 Holborn, EC1N 2TQ. *T:* (020) 7282 2000; *e-mail:* twinsor.orr@gtnet.gov.uk.

WINSTANLEY, Rt Rev. Alan Leslie; Vicar of Eastham, and Assistant Bishop, diocese of Chester, since 1994; *b* 7 May 1949; *s* of John Leslie Winstanley and Eva Winstanley; *m* 1972, Vivien Mary Parkinson; two *s* one *d. Educ:* St John's College, Nottingham (BTh, ALCD). Deacon 1972, priest 1973, Blackburn; Curate: St Andrew's, Livesey, Blackburn, 1972–75; St Mary's, Great Sankey, dio. Liverpool, with responsibility for St Paul's, Penketh, 1975–77; Vicar of Penketh, 1978–81; SAMS Missionary in Peru: Lima, 1981–85; Arequipa, 1986–87; Bishop of Peru and Bolivia, 1988–93. *Recreations:* caravanning, steam locomotives. *Address:* The Vicarage, Ferry Road, Eastham, Wirral, Merseyside CH62 0AJ. *T:* (0151) 327 2182.

WINSTANLEY, John, MC 1944; TD 1951; FRCS, FRCOphth; Hon. Consultant Ophthalmic Surgeon, St Thomas' Hospital, since 1983 (Ophthalmic Surgeon, 1960–83); *b* 11 May 1919; 3rd *s* of late Captain Bernard Joseph Winstanley and Grace Taunton; *m* 1959, Jane Frost; one *s* two *d. Educ:* Wellington Coll., Berks; St Thomas's Hosp. Med. Sch. (MB, BS 1951). FRCS 1957; FRCOphth (FCOphth 1988). Served 4th Bn Queen's Own Royal West Kent Regt, 1937–46 (despatches BEF, 1940). Resident med. appts, St Thomas' and Moorfields Eye Hosps, 1951–56; Chief Clin. Asst, Moorfields Eye Hosp., 1956–60; Sen. Registrar, St Thomas' Hosp., 1956–60; recog. teacher of ophthalmol., St Thomas' Hosp., 1960–83; Ophth. Surg., Lewisham and Greenwich Health Dists, 1959–70; Hon. Ophthalmic Surgeon: Royal Hosp., Chelsea, 1963–85; Queen Alexandra's Mil. Hosp., Millbank,1966–72; Queen Elizabeth Mil. Hosp., Woolwich, 1972–83. Hon. Civilian Consultant in Ophthalmol. to MOD (Army), 1971–83. Examiner in Ophthalmology (DipOphth of Examining Bd of RCP and RCS, 1968–72; Mem. Court of Examiners, RCS, 1972–78). FRSocMed 1963 (Vice-Pres., Sect. of Ophth., 1979); Member: Ophthal. Soc. UK, 1958–88 (Hon. Sec. 1966–68, Vice-Pres. 1980–83); Faculty of Ophthalmologists, 1958–88, Mem. Council, 1973–85, Vice-Pres., 1979–85; Mem. Council, Medical Protection Soc., 1979–90. Liveryman, Soc. of Apothecaries, 1965 (Mem. Livery Cttee, 1982). *Publications:* chapter, Rose's Medical Ophthalmology, 1983; papers on ophthalmic topics and med. hist. in med. jls. *Recreations:* fishing, medical history. *Address:* 10 Pembroke Villas, The Green, Richmond, Surrey TW9 1QF. *T:* (020) 8940 6247. *Clubs:* Army and Navy, Flyfishers'.

WINSTANLEY, Robert James; His Honour Judge Winstanley; a Circuit Judge, since 1996; *b* 4 Nov. 1948; *s* of late Morgan James Winstanley and of Joan Martha Winstanley; *m* 1972, Josephine Langhorne; two *s. Educ:* St Catharine's Coll., Cambridge (MA 1970). Admitted Solicitor, 1973; Asst Solicitor, Dawson & Co., 1973–75; Partner, Winstanley-Burgess, Solicitors, 1975–96. Mem. Council, Law Soc., 1985–96. *Recreations:* golf, cricket, motorcycling, bridge. *Address:* c/o The Court Service, South Eastern Circuit, New Cavendish House, 18 Maltravers Street, WC2R 3EU. *T:* (020) 7936 7271. *Clubs:* Oxford and Cambridge, MCC.

WINSTON, family name of **Baron Winston.**

WINSTON, Baron *cr* 1995 (Life Peer), of Hammersmith in the London Borough of Hammersmith and Fulham; **Robert Maurice Lipson Winston,** FRCOG; Professor of Fertility Studies, University of London at Imperial College School of Medicine (formerly at the Institute of Obstetrics and Gynaecology, Royal Postgraduate Medical School), since 1987; Consultant Obstetrician and Gynaecologist: Hammersmith Hospital, since 1978; Director of NHS Research and Development, Hammersmith Hospitals NHS Trust; *b* 15 July 1940; *s* of late Laurence Winston and of Ruth Winston-Fox, *qv*; *m* 1973, Lira Helen Feigenbaum; two *s* one *d. Educ:* St Paul's Sch., London; London Hosp. Med. Coll., London Univ. (MB, BS 1964). MRCS, LRCP 1964; FRCOG 1983 (MRCOG 1971).

Jun. posts, London Hosp., 1964–66; Registrar and Sen. Registrar, Hammersmith Hosp., 1970–74; Wellcome Res. Sen. Lectr, Inst. of Obs and Gyn., 1974–78; Sen. Lectr, Hammersmith Hosp., 1978–81; Reader in Fertility Studies, RPMS, 1982–86. Vis. Prof., Univ. of Leuven, Belgium, 1976–77; Prof. of Gyn., Univ. of Texas at San Antonio, 1980–81; Clyman Vis. Prof., Mt Sinai Hosp., New York, 1985. Member, Steering Cttee, WHO: on Tubal Occlusion, 1975–77; on Ovum Transport, 1977–78. Pres., Internat. Fallopius Soc., 1987–88. Mem. Council, ICRF, 1998–. Vice Pres., Progress (all-party parly campaign for res. into human reprodn), 1992 (Chm., 1988–91). Mem. Bd, OST, 1998–; Mem., 1997, Chm., 1998–2001, Select Cttee on Sci. and Technol., H of L. Founder Mem., British Fertility Soc., 1975–; Hon. Member: Georgian Obs Soc., 1983–; Pacific Fertility Soc., 1983–; Spanish Fertility Soc., 1985–. Mem. Council, RPMS, 1992–97. Chancellor, Sheffield Hallam Univ., 2001–. Presenter: Your Life in their Hands, BBC TV, 1979–87; The Human Body, BBC TV, 1998; The Secret Life of Twins, BBC TV, 1999; A Child of Our Time, 2000; Superhuman, 2000. Member, Editorial Board: Internat. Jl of Microsurgery, 1981–; Clinical Reproduction and Fertility, 1985–. Founder FMedSci 1998. Hon. Fellow, QMW, 1996. Hon. DSc: Cranfield, 2001; UMIST, 2001; Oxford Brookes, 2001. Chief Rabbinate Award for Contribn to Society, 1992–93; Victor Bonney Prize, RCS, 1991–93; Cedric Carter Medal, Clinical Genetics Soc., 1993; Michael Faraday Gold Medal, Royal Soc., 1999; Gold Medal, RSH, 1999; Gold Medal for Medicine in the Media, BMA, 1999; Wellcome Award for Sci. in the Media, 2001. *Publications:* Reversibility of Sterilization, 1978; (jtly) Tubal Infertility, 1981; Infertility, a Sympathetic Approach, 1987; scientific pubns on human and experimental reproduction. *Recreations:* theatre (directed award-winning Pirandello production, Each in his Own Way, Edinburgh Fest., 1969), broadcasting, music, wine. *Address:* 11 Denman Drive, NW11 6RE. *T:* (020) 8455 7475.

WINSTON, Prof. Brian Norman; Head, Department of Communication, Media and Design, University of Westminster, since 1997; *b* 7 Nov. 1941; *s* of Reuben and Anita Winston; *m* 1978, Adèle Paul; one *s* one *d*. *Educ:* Kilburn Grammar Sch.; Merton Coll., Oxford (BA Laws; MA). Researcher, 1963–66, Prod. and Dir, 1963–66, 1969–71, Granada TV; Prod. and Dir, BBC TV, 1966–69; Lectr, Bradford Coll. of Art, 1972–73; Head of Gen. Studies, Nat. Film Sch., 1973–79; Res. Dir, Dept of Sociology, Glasgow Univ., 1974–76; Vis. Prof., 1976–77, Prof., 1979–86, Sch. of the Arts, NY Univ.; writer, WNET-TV, NY, 1984–85; Dean, Coll. of Communications, Pennsylvania State Univ., 1986–92; Head of Mass Communications, and Dir, Centre for Journalism Studies, UWCC, then Univ. of Wales, Cardiff, 1992–97. Gov., BFI, 1995–. Emmy Award for documentary script writing, 1985. *Publications:* Dangling Conversations, vol. 1, the image of the media, 1973, vol. 2, hardware/software, 1974; (jtly) Bad News, 1976; (jtly) More Bad News, 1980; Misunderstanding Media, 1986; (jtly) Working with Video, 1986; Claiming the Real, 1995; Technologies of Seeing, 1996; Media, Technology and Society: a history, 1998; Fires Were Started, 1999; Lies, Damn Lies and Documentaries. *Recreations:* cooking, theatre. *Address:* 141 Wood Street, Barnet, Herts EN5 4BX; University of Westminster, 309 Regent Street, W1B 2UW.

WINSTON, Clive Noel; Assistant Director, Federation Against Copyright Theft Ltd, 1985–88; *b* 20 April 1925; *s* of George and Alida Winston; *m* 1952, Beatrice Jeanette; two *d*. *Educ:* Highgate Sch.; Trinity Hall, Cambridge (BA). Admitted solicitor, 1951. Joined Metropolitan Police, 1951; Dep. Solicitor, Metropolitan Police, 1982–85. Chairman, Union of Liberal and Progressive Synagogues, 1981–85 (Vice-Pres., 1985–); Treas., Eur. Bd, World Union of Progressive Judaism, 1990–95. *Recreations:* golf, gardening.

WINSTON-FOX, Mrs Ruth, MBE 1996; JP; Co-Chairman, Women's National Commission, 1979–81 (Member, since 1971); *b* 12 Sept. 1912; *d* of Major the Rev. Solomon Lipson, Hon. SCF, and Tilly Lipson (*née* Shandel); *m* 1st, 1938, Laurence Winston (*d* 1949); two *s* one *d*; 2nd, 1960, Goodwin Fox (*d* 1974). *Educ:* St Paul's Girls' Sch.; London Univ. BSc Household and Social Sci.; Home Office Child Care Cert. Mental Hosps Dept and Child Care Dept, LCC, 1936–39; Dep. Centre Organiser, WVS, Southgate, 1941–45; Southgate Borough Council: Member, 1945–65; Alderman, 1955–65; Mayor of Southgate, 1958–59, Dep. Mayor, 1959–61; Sen. Officer, Adoptions Consultant, Social Services Dept, Herts CC, 1949–77. Member: London Rent Assessment Panel and Tribunals, 1975–; Review Cttee for Secure Accommodation, London Borough of Enfield, 1982–; Bd of Deputies of British Jews, 1960– (Chm. Educn Cttee, 1974–80; voluntary nat. organiser, exhibn Jewish Way of Life, 1978–, which visited 44 communities in Britain); Vice-Pres., Internat. Council of Jewish Women, 1974– (Chairman: Status of Women Cttee, 1966–75; Inter-Affiliate Travel Cttee, 1975–81); Mem. Governing Body, World Jewish Congress, 1981–; Co-Chm., Jewish Community Exhibn Centre, 1984–. Founder, one of first Day Centres for the Elderly in GB, Ruth Winston House, Southgate Old People's Centre, opened by Princess Alexandra, 1961, and again, 1972; Vice-President: Southgate Old People's Welfare Cttee, 1974–; Southgate Horticultural Soc.; President: League of Jewish Women, 1969–72; First Women's Lodge, England, 1972–74; Enfield Relate (formerly Enfield Marriage Guidance Council), 1984–. JP Mddx Area GLC, 1954. *Publications:* articles only. *Recreations:* five grandchildren, travel, voluntary service. *Address:* 4 Morton Crescent, Southgate, N14 7AH. *T:* (020) 8886 5056. *Clubs:* University Women's, Bnai Brith.

See also Baron Winston.

WINSTONE, Dame Dorothy (Gertrude), DBE 1990; CMG 1976; *b* 23 Jan. 1919; *d* of Stanley Fowler and Constance May Fowler (*née* Sherwin); *m* 1941, Wilfrid Frank Winstone; three *s* one *d*. *Educ:* Auckland Girls' Grammar Sch.; Auckland Teachers' Coll.; Auckland University Coll. (BA, DipEd 1940, BTh 1998). Primary School Teacher, 1938; Asst Mistress, Seddon Memorial Tech. Coll., 1939–45; voluntary community worker, 1945–. Mem., Royal Commn on Contraception, Sterilisation and Abortion, 1975–77. Foundn Mem., NZ Envmtl Council, 1970–81. Dir, Virginia Gildersleeve Fund, Internat. Fedn of Univ. Women, 1993–. Member Emerita, NZ Fedn of Univ. Women, 1973; Life Mem., Nat. Council of Women of NZ, 1980. Hon. LLD Univ. of Auckland, 1983. Adelaide Ristori Medal, Centro Culturale Italiano, 1975; New Zealand Suffrage Centennial Medal, 1993. *Publications:* Everyday Words and Phrases, 1975; A Century of Service, 1985; Wesley Methodist Church 1938–1993, 1996. *Recreations:* reading, gardening, 13 grandchildren. *Address:* 17 Tuhaere Street, Auckland 5, New Zealand. *T:* (9) 5203407.

WINTER, Rev. Canon David Brian; Team Minister, Hermitage Team Ministry, 1995–2000; Hon. Canon, Christ Church Cathedral, Oxford, 1995–2000, now Canon Emeritus; *b* 19 Nov. 1929; *s* of Walter George Winter and Winifred Ella Winter; *m* 1961, Christine Ellen Martin; two *s* one *d*. *Educ:* Machynlleth County Sch.; Trinity County Grammar Sch., Wood Green; King's Coll., Univ. of London (BA, PGCE). Nat. Service, RAF, 1948–50. Teacher: Ware CE Secondary Sch., 1954–58; Tottenham County Grammar Sch., 1958–59; Editor, Crusade, 1959–70; freelance writer and broadcaster, 1970–71; BBC: Producer, Religious Broadcasting, 1971–75, Sen. Producer, 1975–82; Hd of Religious Progs, Radio, and Dep. Hd, Religious Broadcasting, 1982–87; Hd of Religious Broadcasting, 1987–89. Chm., Arts Centre Gp, 1976–82. Oak Hill Ministerial Trng Course, 1985–87. Deacon, 1987, priest, 1988. Hon. Asst Curate, St Paul and St Luke, Finchley, 1987–89; Priest-in-Charge, Ducklington, 1989–95; Bishop's Officer for Evangelism, Dio. of Oxford, 1989–95. Editor, Bible Reading Fellowship, 1997–2001. *Publications:* Ground of Truth, 1964; New Singer, New Song (biog. of Cliff Richard), 1967; (with S. Linden) Two a Penny, 1968; Closer than a Brother, 1971; Hereafter, 1972; (ed) Matthew Henry's Commentary on the New Testament, 1974; After the Gospels, 1977; But this I can believe, 1980; The Search for the Real Jesus, 1982; Truth in the Son, 1985; Living through Loss, 1985; Walking in the Light (confessions of St Augustine), 1986; Believing the Bible, 1987; Battered Bride, 1988; What happens after Death?, 1992; You Can Pray, 1993; What's in a Word, 1994; Mark for Starters, 1995; Where do we go from here?, 1996; Forty Days with the 'Messiah', 1996; Message for the Millennium, 1998; (ed) The Poets' Christ (anthology), 1998; Winter's Tale (autobiog.), 2001; The Upper Room, 2001. *Recreations:* watching cricket, fish-keeping, talking. *Address:* 6 Courtiers Green, Clifton Hampden, Abingdon, Oxon OX14 3EN. *T:* (01865) 407237.

WINTER, Frederick Thomas, CBE 1963; racehorse trainer, 1964–87, retired; *b* 20 Sept. 1926; *s* of late Frederick Neville Winter and Ann (*née* Flanagan); *m* 1956, Diana Pearson; three *d* (incl. twins). *Educ:* Ewell Castle. Served as Lieut, 6th Bn Para. Regt, 1944–47. Jockey, Flat, 1939–42; National Hunt jockey, 1947–64. *Recreations:* golf, gardening. *Address:* Montague House, Eastbury, Newbury, Berks RG17 7JN. *T:* (01488) 71438.

WINTER, Prof. Gerald Bernard, FDSRCS; Professor and Head of Department of Children's Dentistry, 1966–94, now Emeritus Professor, Dean and Director of Studies, 1983–93, Institute of Dental Surgery, University of London; *b* 24 Nov. 1928; *s* of Morris Winter and Edith (*née* Malter); *m* 1960, Brigitte Eva Fleischhacker; one *s* one *d*. *Educ:* Coopers' Company's Sch.; London Hospital Med. Coll. (BDS, MB BS); DCH London. Ho. Surg./Ho. Phys., London Hosp. Med. Coll., 1955–59; Lectr in Children's Dentistry, Royal Dental Hosp., London, 1959–62; Cons. Dent. Surg., Eastman Dental Hosp., 1962–94 (Hon. Cons. Dent. Surg., 1994–). Hon. Sec. 1962–65, Pres. 1970–71 and 1993–94, Brit. Paedodontic Soc., subseq. British Soc. for Paediatric Dentistry; Hon. Gen. Sec., Internat. Assoc. of Dentistry for Children, 1971–79; Founder Chm., Brit. Soc. of Dentistry for the Handicapped, 1976–77; Hon. Dir, Oral and Dental Res. Trust, 1996–. FRSA 1996. *Publications:* A Colour Atlas of Clinical Conditions in Paedodontics (with R. Rapp), 1979; many chapters and sci. papers. *Recreations:* theatre, music, gardening. *Address:* 1 Hartfield Close, Elstree, Herts WD6 3JD. *T:* (020) 8953 3403.

WINTER, Dr Gregory Paul, CBE 1997; FRS 1990; Joint Head, Division of Protein and Nucleic Acid Chemistry, Medical Research Council Laboratory of Molecular Biology, since 1994 and Deputy Director, Centre for Protein Engineering, since 1990; Senior Research Fellow, Trinity College, Cambridge, since 1991; *b* 14 April 1951; *m* Fiona Jane Winter. *Educ:* Royal Grammar Sch., Newcastle-upon-Tyne; Trinity College, Cambridge (BA Natural Scis 1973; MA; PhD 1976). Postgrad. studies in protein chem., Cambridge, 1973–76; Fellow, Trinity College, Cambridge (structure of genes and influenza virus), 1976–80; MRC–LMB (protein and antibody engineering), 1981–. Novo Biotechnology Award, Denmark, 1986; Colworth Medal, Biochem. Soc., 1986; Behring Prize, FRG, 1989; Louis Jeantet Foundn Award for Medicine, Switzerland, 1989; Pfizer Award, 1989; Milano Award, Italy, 1990; Scheele Award, Swedish Acad. of Pharmaceutical Scis, 1994; Biochemical Analysis Prize, German Soc. for Clin. Chem., 1995; King Faisal Internat. Prize in Medicine, 1995; William B. Coley Award, Cancer Res. Inst., USA, 1999. *Publications:* articles in learned jls on protein and gene structure, enzymes, viral proteins and antibodies. *Address:* Medical Research Council Laboratory of Molecular Biology, Hills Road, Cambridge CB2 2QH.

WINTERBOTTOM, Prof. Michael, MA, DPhil; FBA 1978; Corpus Christi Professor of Latin, University of Oxford, 1993–2001; Fellow, Corpus Christi College, Oxford, 1993–2001, now Emeritus; *b* 22 Sept. 1934; *s* of Allan Winterbottom and Kathleen Mary (*née* Wallis); *m* 1st, 1963, Helen Spencer (marr. diss. 1983); two *s*; 2nd, 1986, Nicolette Janet Streatfeild Bergel. *Educ:* Dulwich Coll.; Pembroke Coll., Oxford. 1st Cl. Hon. Mods and Craven Schol., 1954; 1st Cl. Lit. Hum. and Derby Schol., 1956; Domus Sen. Schol., Merton Coll., 1958–59; Research Lectr, Christ Church, 1959–62. MA 1959, DPhil 1964 (Oxon). Lectr in Latin and Greek, University Coll. London, 1962–67; Fellow and Tutor in Classics, Worcester Coll., Oxford, 1967–92; Reader in Classical Langs, Univ. of Oxford, 1990–92. Dhc Besançon, 1985. *Publications:* (ed) Quintilian, 1970; (with D. A. Russell) Ancient Literary Criticism, 1972; Three Lives of English Saints, 1972; (ed and trans.) The Elder Seneca, 1974; (ed with R. M. Ogilvie) Tacitus, *Opera Minora*, 1975; (ed and trans.) Gildas, 1978; Roman Declamation, 1980; (ed with commentary) The Minor Declamations ascribed to Quintilian, 1984; (with D. C. Innes) Sopatros the Rhetor, 1988; (with M. Brett and C. N. L. Brooke) rev. edn of Charles Johnson (ed), Hugh the Chanter, 1990; (ed) Cicero, *De Officiis*, 1994; (ed with R. A. B. Mynors and R. M. Thomson) William of Malmesbury, *Gesta Regum Anglorum*, 1998; articles and reviews in jls. *Recreations:* travel and plans for travel, hill walking, under-gardening. *Address:* 53 Thorncliffe Road, Oxford OX2 7BA. *T:* (01865) 513066.

WINTERBOTTOM, Sir Walter, Kt 1978; CBE 1972 (OBE 1963); retired; *b* 31 March 1913; *s* of James Winterbottom and Frances Holt; *m* 1942, Ann Richards; two *d* (one *s* decd). *Educ:* Chester Coll. of Educn; Carnegie Coll. of Physical Educn. Schoolmaster, Oldham; Lectr, Carnegie Coll. of Phys. Educn; Wing Comdr, RAF, 1939–45; Dir of Coaching and Manager of England Team, Football Assoc., 1946–62; Gen. Sec., Central Council of Physical Recreation, 1963–72; Dir, The Sports Council, 1965–78. *Publications:* technical, on association football. *Recreations:* golf, bowls. *Address:* 15 Orchard Gardens, Cranleigh, Surrey GU6 7LG. *T:* (01483) 271593.

WINTERFLOOD, Brian Martin; Founder, 1988, and Chairman, since 2002, Winterflood Securities Ltd (Managing Director, 1988–99; Chief Executive Officer, 1999–2002); Chief Executive Officer, Winterflood Gilts, 1999–2002 (Managing Director, 1994–99); Chairman, Gilts and Securities, since 2001; *b* 31 Jan. 1937; *s* of late Thomas G. Winterflood and of Doris M. Winterflood; *m* 1966, Doreen Stella McCartney; two *s* one *d*. *Educ:* Fray's Coll., Uxbridge. National Service, 1955–57. Greener Dreyfus & Co., 1953–55; Bisgood Bishop & Co. Ltd, 1957–85: Partner, 1967–71; Dir, 1971–81; Man. Dir, 1981–85; Man. Dir, County Bisgood, 1985–86; County NatWest Securities Ltd: Dir, 1986–87; Exec. Dir, 1986–88, resigned, 1988. Founder, Winterflood Gilt-Edged Market-Making, 1994. Director: Union Discount Co. of London, 1991–93; Close Brothers Group, 1993–; PROSHARE, 1998–. Jt Chm., Cttee of USM Initiative, Prince's Youth Bus. Trust, 1989. Member: City Gp for Smaller Cos, now Quoted Cos Alliance, 1992– (Mem. Exec. Cttee, 1992–96); City Disputes Practitioners Panel, 1994–; AIM Adv. Cttee, 1995–; AIM Appeals Cttee, 1995–98; Non FTSE 100 Wkg Party Cttee, 1996–; Secondary Markets Cttee, 1996–; UK Adv. Bd, EASD, 2000–; Market Adv. Cttee, EASD, 2000–. Mem. Cttee, October Club, 1993–; Trustee, Stock Exchange Benevolent Fund, 1995–. President: Rehabilitation and Med. Res. Trust, 1998–; Reeds Sch. Appeal, 1997–98. FSI 1997. PLC Achievement Award, 1994. *Recreations:* family, work, travel. *Address:* Winterflood Securities Ltd, Walbrook House, 23–29 Walbrook, EC4N 8LA. *T:* (020) 7621 0004. *Club:* City of London.

WINTERSGILL, Dr William, FFPHM; Examining Medical Officer (part-time), Department of Health, since 1989; Member, Research and Advisory Committee, Cambridge Applied Nutrition, Toxicology and Biosciences Ltd, since 1984; *b* 20 Dec. 1922; *s* of Fred Wintersgill and May Wintersgill; *m* 1952, Iris May Holland; three *d. Educ:* Barnsley Holgate Grammar Sch.; Leeds Medical Sch., Univ. of Leeds (MB, ChB). MRCGP, MFCM; FFCM 1983. House Surgeon, 1948, and Registrar, 1948–49, Pontefract Infirmary; Principal, Gen. Practice, Snaith, Yorks, 1950–66; Dept of Health and Social Security (formerly Min. of Health): Reg. MO, 1967–70; SMO, 1970–72; PMO, 1972–76; SPMO, 1976–83. Specialist in Community Medicine, York HA, 1983–89. Pt-time MO, Cttee on Safety of Medicines, 1987–; Mem., Health Adv. Service Vis. Team, 1987–90; Dist Med. Advr, 1987–88. Chm., British Assoc. of Community Physicians, 1985–89. *Recreations:* gardening, antique collecting, playing the piano, choral singing, painting, old buildings. *Address:* The Latchetts, Eardisland, Leominster HR6 9BE.

WINTERSON, Jeanette; writer; *b* 27 Aug. 1959; partner, Dr M. Reynolds. *Educ:* St Catherine's Coll., Oxford (BA Hons English). Internat. Fiction Award, Fest. Letteratura, Italy, 1999. *Publications:* Oranges are not the only fruit, 1985 (Whitbread Prize, 1st Novel; numerous awards for screenplay, televised 1990); The Passion, 1987 (John Llewellyn Rhys Prize); Sexing the Cherry, 1989 (E. M. Forster Award, Amer. Acad. and Inst. of Arts and Letters); Written on the Body, 1992; Art and Lies, 1994; Great Moments in Aviation (screenplay), 1994; Art Objects: essays on ecstasy and effrontery, 1995; Gut Symmetries, 1997; The World and Other Places (short stories), 1998; The Powerbook, 2000; The King of Capri (for children), 2002. *Recreations:* opera, ballet, champagne. *Address:* c/o ICM, 40 West 57th Street, New York, NY 10019, USA; *e-mail:* info@jeanettewinterson.com.

WINTERTON, 8th Earl *cr* 1766 (Ire.); **Donald David Turnour;** Baron Winterton 1761 (Ire.); Viscount Turnour 1766 (Ire.); *b* 13 Oct. 1943; *s* of Cecil Noel Turnour, DFM, CD (*d* 1987), *yr b* of 7th Earl Winterton and of Evelyn Isabel, *d* of Dr C. A. Oulton; *S* uncle, 1991; *m* 1968, Jill Pauline, *d* of late John Geddes Esplen; two *d. Educ:* Waterloo Lutheran Univ., Ontario (BA). *Heir: b* Robert Charles Turnour [*b* 30 Jan. 1950; *m* 1st, 1974, Sheila (marr. diss. 1976), *d* of G. H. Stocking; 2nd, 1983, Patricia Ann, *d* of William Avery; two *d*].

WINTERTON, (Jane) Ann; MP (C) Congleton, since 1983; *b* 6 March 1941; *d* of late Joseph Robert Hodgson and of Ellen Jane Hodgson; *m* 1960, Nicholas R. Winterton, *qv*; two *s* one *d. Educ:* Erdington Grammar Sch. for Girls. Opposition spokesman on nat. drug strategy, 1998–2001; Shadow Agriculture Minister, 2001–. Mem., Chairmen's Panel, 1992–98; Chm., All Party Parly Pro-Life Gp, 1992–. Fellow, Industry and Parlt Trust, 1987–. Pres., Congleton Div., St John Ambulance, 1984–; Vice Pres., Townswomen's Guilds, 1994–. *Recreations:* music, theatre, tennis, ski-ing. *Address:* House of Commons, SW1A 0AA.

WINTERTON, Nicholas Hugh; Executive Director (formerly Administrative Secretary), Medical Research Council, since 1995; *b* 1 May 1947; *s* of Deryck Winterton and Margaret Winterton (*née* Simms). *Educ:* Chislehurst and Sidcup GS for Boys; Sidney Sussex Coll., Cambridge (BA 1968, MA 1971; DipEcon 1969). Medical Research Council: various admin. posts, 1969–81; Head of Personnel, 1981–88; on secondment to Wellcome Foundn, Dartford, 1988–89; Director: Corporate Affairs, 1989–94; Finance, 1994–95. Director: UK Med. Ventures Mgt Ltd, 1996–; Imaging Research Solutions Ltd, 2001–; Chm. Bd, MRC Technol., 2000–. Non-exec. Dir, Royal Free Hampstead NHS Trust, 1998–. Chairman, Trustees: Bridge Theatre Trng Co., 1995–; Vinjeru (Educn Concern Malawi North), 1999–. *Recreations:* gardening, travel, walking, theatre. *Address:* Medical Research Council, 20 Park Crescent, W1N 4AL. *T:* (020) 7637 6016.

WINTERTON, Nicholas Raymond; MP (C) Macclesfield, since Sept. 1971; *b* 31 March 1938; *o s* of late N. H. Winterton, Lysways House, Longdon Green, near Rugeley, Staffs; *m* 1960, Jane Ann Hodgson (*see* J. A. Winterton); two *s* one *d. Educ:* Bilton Grange Prep. Sch.; Rugby Sch. Commnd 14th/20th King's Hussars, 1957–59. Sales Exec. Trainee, Shell-Mex and BP Ltd, 1959–60; Sales and Gen. Manager, Stevens and Hodgson Ltd, Birmingham (Co. engaged in sale and hire of construction equipment), 1960–71. Chairman: CPC Cttee, Meriden Cons. Assoc., 1966–68; Midland Branch, Contractors Mech. Plant Engrs Assoc., 1968–69. Member: W Midlands Cons. Council, 1966–69, 1971–72; Central Council, Nat. Union of Cons. and Unionist Assocs, 1971–72. Contested (C) Newcastle-under-Lyme, Oct. 1969, 1970. Chairman: Select Cttee on Health, 1991–92; Select Cttee on Procedure, 1997–; Member: Social Services Select Cttee, 1980–90; Select Cttee on Modernisation of H of C, 1997–; Liaison Select Cttee, 1997–; Chairmen's Panel, 1987–. Chairman, All Party Parliamentary: Gp for Cotton and Allied Textiles, 1979–97; Gp for Media, 1992–2000; British Danish Gp, 1992–; British Falklands Is Gp, 1997–; British Bahamas Gp, 1997–; British Austria Gp, 1999–; Joint Chairman: All Party Parly British Taiwan Gp, 1997–; W Coast Mainline Gp, 2001–; Vice Chairman, All Party Parliamentary: British Swedish Gp, 1992–; British Indonesian Gp, 1992–2000; Anglo S Pacific Gp, 1997–; Road Transport Study Gp, 1997–2001; Clothing and Textiles Gp, 1997–. Member Executive: 1922 Cttee, 1997–2001 (Vice-Chm., 2001–); UK Br., CPA, 1997–. Member: Exec. Cttee, Anglo-Austrian Soc., 1987– (Chm., 1998–2000); Nat. Adv. Cttee, Duke of Edinburgh Award Scheme, 1973–99. County Councillor, Atherstone Div. Warwickshire CC, 1967–72. President: Macclesfield Fermain Club, 1973–; Poynton Youth and Community Centre, 1971–; Upton Priory Youth Club, Macclesfield, 1992–2001; Vice-President: Macclesfield and Congleton District Scout Council; Cheshire Scout Assoc.; E Cheshire Hospice; Nat. Assoc. of Local Councils; Royal Coll. of Midwives; Nat. Assoc. of Master Bakers, Confectioners and Caterers. Hon. Mem., Macclesfield Lions Club; Hon. Life Mem., Macclesfield Rugby Union Football Club; Pres., Macclesfield Hockey Club; Patron: Macclesfield and District Sheep Dog Trials Assoc., 1972–; Internat. Centre for Child Care Studies, 1980–94; Civit Hills Open Air Theatre, 1996–; Elizabeth Trust, 1983–94. President, Macclesfield Branch: Riding for the Disabled, 1987–; Multiple Sclerosis Soc., 1987–. Founder Pres., Bollington Light Opera Gp, 1978–. Life Mem., Poynton Gilbert and Sullivan Soc. Liveryman, Past Upper Bailiff and Mem. of Court, Weavers' Co.; Freeman of the City of London. *Recreations:* Rugby football, squash, hockey, tennis, swimming, horse riding. *Address:* Whitehall Farm, Mow Lane, Newbold Astbury, Congleton, Cheshire CW12 3NH. *Clubs:* Cavalry and Guards, Lighthouse; Lords and Commons Tennis; Old Boys and Park Green (Macclesfield).

WINTERTON, Rosalie, (Rosie); MP (Lab) Doncaster Central, since 1997; Parliamentary Secretary, Lord Chancellor's Department, since 2001; *b* 10 Aug. 1958; *d* of Gordon and Valerie Winterton. *Educ:* Doncaster Grammar Sch.; Hull Univ. (BA Hons Hist.). Asst to John Prescott, MP, 1980–86; Parliamentary Officer: London Borough of Southwark, 1986–88; RCN, 1988–90; Man. Dir, Connect Public Affairs, 1990–94; Hd, private office of John Prescott, MP, 1994–97. *Recreations:* sailing, reading. *Address:* House of Commons, SW1A 0AA; 25 Town Moor Avenue, Doncaster DN2 6BW.

WINTLE, Rev. Canon Ruth Elizabeth; Bishop's Adviser on Women's Ministry, Worcester, 1995–97; Canon Emeritus, Worcester Cathedral, since 1998 (Hon. Canon, 1987–97); *b* 30 Sept. 1931; *d* of John Wintle and Vera (*née* Lane). *Educ:* Clarendon Sch., Malvern, and Abergele, Wales; Westfield Coll., London (BA Hons French 1953); St Hugh's Coll., Oxford (MA Theol. 1972); St Michael's House, Oxford (IDC 1966). Teacher, St Hilda's Sch., Jamaica, 1953–60; Travelling Sec., Inter-Varsity Fellowship and Technical Colls Christian Fellowship, 1960–63; Accredited Lay Worker, St Andrew's Church, N Oxford, 1967–69; Tutor, St John's Coll., Durham, 1969–74; Deaconess (C of E), 1972; Selection Sec., ACCM, 1974–83; Organiser, Internat. Diakonia Conf., Coventry, 1983; Diocesan Dir of Ordinands, Worcester, 1984–92; ordained Deacon, 1987, priest 1994; Mem., Third Order, SSF, 1990–; Parish Deacon, St John-in-Bedwardine, 1984–94. Mem., Bishop's Staff Meeting, Worcs, 1993–97. Member: Church Army Bd, 1985–2000; Crown Appointments Commn, 1990–95; Gen. Synod of C of E, 1990–95. Mem. Council, Malvern Coll., 1991–2000. Chm., Li Tim-Oi Foundn, 1993–. *Recreations:* reading, driving, ornithology. *Address:* Westwood, Claphill Lane, Rushwick, Worcester WR2 5TP. *T:* (01905) 422841.

WINTON, Alexander, CBE 1993; QFSM 1987; HM Chief Inspector of Fire Services for Scotland, 1990–93; *b* 13 July 1932; *s* of Alexander and Jean Winton; *m* 1957, Jean Dowie; two *s.* MIFireE. Fireman, Perth, 1958–64; Station Officer: Perth, 1964–67; Lancashire, 1967–69; Assistant Divisional Officer: E Riding, 1969–72; Angus, 1972–73; Divisional Officer III: Angus, 1973–75; Tayside, 1975–76; Divl Comdr (DOI), Tayside, 1976–80; Temp. Sen. Divl Officer, 1980–81; Dep. Firemaster, 1981–85; Firemaster, Tayside Fire Bde, 1985–89. *Recreations:* golf, curling, reading. *Address:* 5 Ferndale Drive, Broughty Ferry, Dundee DD5 3DB. *T:* (01382) 778156.

WINTON, Walter; Keeper, Department of Electrical Engineering, Telecommunications and Loan Circulation, Science Museum, 1976–80; *b* 15 May 1917; *m* 1942, Dorothy Rickard; two *s* one *d. Educ:* Glossop Grammar Sch.; Manchester Univ. (BSc and Teacher's Diploma). Royal Ordnance Factories, Chemist, 1940–45. Taught Science, Harrow County and Greenford, 1945–50; Assistant and Deputy Keeper, Science Museum, 1950–67; Keeper: Dept of Loan Circulation, Mining and Marine Technol., 1968–73; Dept of Museum Services, 1973; Dept of Mechanical and Civil Engrg and Loan Circulation, 1973–76. *Publications:* contrib. to journals. *Recreations:* Scottish dancing, sailing, fell-walking. *Address:* Lantern Lodge, Village Road, Denham, Bucks UB9 5BN. *T:* (01895) 832692.

WINTOUR, Anna, (Mrs David Shaffer); Editor, US Vogue, since 1988; *b* 3 Nov. 1949; *d* of late Charles Wintour, CBE; *m* 1984, Dr David Shaffer; one *s* one *d. Educ:* Queen's College Sch., London; North London Collegiate Sch. Dep. Fashion Editor, Harpers and Queen Magazine, 1970–76; Fashion Editor, Harpers Bazaar, NY, 1976–77; Fashion and Beauty Editor, Viva Mag., 1977–78; Contributing Editor for Fashion and Style, Savvy Mag., 1980–81; Sen. Editor, New York Mag., NY, 1981–83; Creative Dir, US Vogue, 1983–86; Editor-in-Chief, Vogue, 1986–87; Editor, House and Garden, New York, 1987–88.

WINTOUR, Audrey Cecelia; *see* Slaughter, A. C.

WINYARD, Dr Graham Peter Arthur, CBE 1999; FRCP; FFPHM; Regional Postgraduate Dean, Wessex Deanery, South East Regional Office, NHS Executive, Department of Health, since 1999; *b* 19 Jan. 1947; *s* of Lyonel Arthur Winyard and Dorothy Elizabeth Payne; *m* 1979, Sandra Catherine Bent; one *s* two *d. Educ:* Southend High Sch.; Hertford Coll., Oxford (MA); Middlesex Hosp. (BM, BCh). Sen. House Officer, United Oxford Hosps, 1973–75; Registrar in Community Medicine, 1975–77; Provincial Health Officer, Madang, PNG, 1977–79; Sen. Registrar in Community Medicine, Oxford RHA, and Lectr, LSHTM, 1979–82; Dist MO, Lewisham and N Southwark HA, 1982–87; SPMO, DHSS, later Dept of Health, 1987–90; Regl Med. Dir and Dir of Public Health, Wessex RHA, 1990–93; Dep. CMO and Dir Health Services, NHS Exec., DoH, 1993–98. Hon. Prof. of Public Health Mgt, Univ. of Southampton. *Publications:* various on med. care in med. jls. *Recreations:* gardening, DIY, music.

WISBECH, Archdeacon of; *see* Rone, Ven. J.

WISDOM, Sir Norman, Kt 2000; OBE 1995; actor/comedian; *b* 4 Feb. 1915. Has starred regularly on stage and screen, since 1952. First film Trouble in Store, in 1953 (winning an Academy Award) since which has starred in 19 major films in both England and America; two Broadway awards for stage musical, Walking Happy; numerous Royal Performances, both film and stage. Freeman: Tirana, Albania, 1995; City of London, 1995. Lifetime Achievement Award for Comedy, British Comedy Awards, 1991. *Publication:* (with William Hall) Don't Laugh at Me, 1992. *Recreations:* all sports. *Address:* c/o Johnny Mans, Johnny Mans Productions Ltd, The Maltings, Brewery Road, Hoddesdon, Herts EN11 8HF.

WISE, family name of **Baron Wise**.

WISE, 2nd Baron *cr* 1951, of King's Lynn; **John Clayton Wise;** farmer; *b* 11 June 1923; *s* of 1st Baron Wise and of Kate Elizabeth (*d* 1987), *e d* of late John Michael Sturgeon; *S* father, 1968; *m* 1st, 1946, Margaret Annie (marr. diss. 1986), *d* of Frederick Victor Snead, Banbury; two *s*; 2nd, 1993, Janice Harman Thompson (marr. diss. 1998). *Heir: s* Hon. Christopher John Clayton Wise, PhD, BSc Hons [*b* 19 March 1949. *Educ:* Norwich School; Univ. of Southampton. Plant Scientist].

WISE, Prof. Christopher, RDI 1998; Professor of Civil Engineering Design, Imperial College of Science, Technology and Medicine, since 1998; Co-founder, Expedition, 1999; *b* 2 Nov. 1956; *s* of Jeffery and Jean Wise; one *s* by Elspeth Beard. *Educ:* Reigate Grammar Sch.; Univ. of Southampton (BSc Hons 1979). MIStructE 1985. Joined Ove Arup and Partners, Consulting Engrs, 1979; Dir, Ove Arup Partnership, 1993–99; *projects* include: Torre de Collserola, Barcelona, 1992; Channel 4 HQ, 1995; Commerzbank HQ, Frankfurt, 1996; American Air Mus., Duxford, 1997; Millennium Bridge, London, 2000. Reconstructions of Roman technology, for Secrets of Lost Empires series, BBC2: Colosseum, 1996; Caesar's Bridge, 1999. FRSA 1995. Guthrie Brown Award, 1993, Oscar Faber Medal, 1996, IStructE. *Publications:* papers on engrg educn projects in IStructE jl. *Recreations:* abstract painting, guitar, rock and ice climbing, soccer.

WISE, Derek; *see* Wise, R. D.

WISE, Prof. Douglass, OBE 1980; FRIBA; Principal, Douglass Wise & Partners, Architects, since 1959, Director, Institute of Advanced Architectural Studies, University of York, 1975–92; *b* 6 Nov. 1927; *s* of Horace Watson Wise and Doris Wise; *m* 1958, Yvonne Jeannine Czeiler (marr. diss. 1985); one *s* one *d. Educ:* King's Coll., Newcastle, Durham Univ. (BArch; DipTP). Lecturer in Architecture, 1959–65, Prof. of Architecture, 1965–69, Head of Dept of Architecture, 1969–75, Newcastle Univ. RIBA: Chm., Moderators, 1969–75; Chm., Examinations Cttee, 1969–75; Mem. Council, 1976–79; Chm., Heads of Schools Cttee, 1971–73; Mem. Bd of Management, North Eastern Housing Assoc., 1967–76 (Vice-Chm., 1974–76); Mem. Council, Newcastle Polytechnic, 1974–77; past Mem. Council, Senate and Court, Newcastle Univ.; Governor, Building Centre Trust, London, 1976–92; Chairman: NE Civic Trust, 1993–; Northern Regl

Centre for the Built Envmt, 1994–98. Hon. LittD Sheffield, 1992. *Publications:* contribs to various technical jls on housing, continuing educn and architectural theory. *Recreations:* painting, natural history. *Address:* Welburn, Kirkwhelpington, Newcastle upon Tyne NE19 2SA. *T:* (01830) 540219.

WISE, Prof. Michael John, CBE 1979; MC 1945; PhD; FRGS; Emeritus Professor of Geography, University of London; *b* Stafford, 17 August 1918; *s* of Harry Cuthbert and Sarah Evelyn Wise; *m* 1942, Barbara Mary, *d* of C. L. Hodgetts, Wolverhampton; one *d* one *s*. *Educ:* Saltley Secondary School, Birmingham; University of Birmingham (BA (Hons Geography) and Mercator Prize in Geography, 1939; DipEd 1940; PhD 1951). Served War, Royal Artillery, 80th LAA Regt, 1941–44, 5th Bn The Northamptonshire Regt, 1944–46, in Middle East and Italy; commissioned, 1941, Major, 1944. Assistant Lecturer, Univ. of Birmingham, 1946–48, Lecturer in Geography, 1948–51; London School of Economics: Lecturer in Geography, 1951–54; Sir Ernest Cassel Reader in Economic Geography, 1954–58; Prof. of Geography, 1958–83; Pro-Director, 1983–85; Hon. Fellow, 1988. Chm., Departmental Cttee of Inquiry into Statutory Smallholdings, 1963–67; Mem., Dept of Transport Adv. Cttee on Landscape Treatment of Trunk Roads, 1971–90 (Chm., 1981–90). Mem., UGC for Hong Kong, 1966–73. Recorder, Sect. E, Brit. Assoc. for Advancement of Science, 1955–60 (Pres., 1965); Founder Pres., Transport Studies Soc., 1962; President: Inst. of British Geographers, 1974 (Hon. Mem., 1989); IGU, 1976–80 (Vice-Pres., 1968–76); Geographical Assoc., 1976–77 (Hon. Treasurer, 1967–76, Hon. Mem., 1983); Vice-Pres., Nat. Assoc. for Envmtl Educn, 1977–; Mem., SSRC, 1976–82; Chm., Council for Extra-Mural Studies, Univ. of London, 1976–83; Chm., Exec. Cttee, Assoc. of Agriculture, 1972–83 (Vice-Pres., 1983–93); Mem. Adv. Cttees, UN Univ., 1976–82; Hon. Sec., RGS, 1963–73, Vice-Pres., 1975–78, Hon. Vice-Pres., 1978–80, 1983–, Pres., 1980–82. Chm., Birkbeck Coll., 1983–89 (Governor, 1968–89; Fellow, 1989); Mem. Delegacy, Goldsmiths' Coll., 1984–88. Chm., Dudley Stamp Meml Trust, 1988– (Hon. Sec., 1966–88). Erskine Fellow, Univ. of Canterbury, NZ, 1970. Hon. Life Mem., Univ. of London Union, 1977. Hon. Member: Geog. Soc. of Russia, 1975; Assoc. of Japanese Geographers, 1980; Geog. Soc. of Mexico, 1984; Geog. Soc. of Poland, 1986; Membre d'Honneur, Société de Géographie, 1983. FInstEnvSci 1980; FRSA 1983. Hon. FLI 1991. DUniv Open, 1978; Hon. DSc Birmingham, 1982. Received Gill Memorial award of RGS, 1958; RGS Founder's Medal, 1977; Alexander Kőrösi Csoma Medal, Hungarian Geographical Soc., 1980; Tokyo Geographical Soc. Medal, 1981; Lauréat d'Honneur, IGU, 1984. *Publications:* Hon. Editor, Birmingham and its Regional Setting, 1951; A Pictorial Geography of the West Midlands, 1958; General Consultant, An Atlas of Earth Resources, 1979; General Consultant, The Great Geographical Atlas, 1982; (consultant and contrib.) The Ordnance Survey Atlas of Great Britain, 1982; numerous articles on economic and urban geography. *Recreations:* music, gardening. *Address:* 45 Oakleigh Avenue, N20 9JE. *T:* (020) 8445 6057. *Clubs:* Athenæum, Geographical.

WISE, Peter Anthony Surtees, MBE 1993; Director, Wise Consultancy Ltd; *b* 26 June 1934; *s* of late J. A. S. (Tony) Wise and Lenore Dugdale; *m* 1st, 1956, Elizabeth Muirhead Odhams (*d* 1995); two *s*; 2nd, 1998, Jill Fountain-Barber. *Educ:* Royal Naval College, Dartmouth. Served Royal Navy, 1948–56 (invalided). Marconi Instruments Ltd, 1956–60; Vickers Ltd, 1961–74; First Secretary, later Counsellor (Hong Kong Affairs), UK Mission, Geneva, 1974–78; Head of Commercial Div. (formerly Asst Comr (Commercial)), Hong Kong Govt Office, London, 1978–93; also Rep. for Commercial Relns with Austria and the Nordic Countries, 1980–93 (formerly non-resident Counsellor (HK Trade Affairs), Helsinki, Oslo, Stockholm, Vienna). *Address:* Lennoxdale House, Goatacre Road, Medstead, Alton, Hants GU34 5PU. *T:* (01420) 562915. *Club:* Hong Kong (Hong Kong).

WISE, (Reginald) Derek, CBE 1977; Partner, Wise & Mercer, Paris, 1983–96; avocat honoraire; *b* 29 July 1917; *s* of Reginald and Rita Wise; *m* 1957, Nancy Brenta Scialoya; two *s* one *d*. *Educ:* St Paul's Sch. Admitted solicitor, 1947. Served War of 1939–45, RA and Intell. Partner, Theodore Goddard, Paris, 1957–82. Legal Adviser, British Embassy, Paris, 1962–96. *Address:* 203 bis Boulevard St Germain, 75007 Paris, France. *T:* 142220794. *Club:* Travellers (Paris).

WISE, Dr Richard; Consultant Medical Microbiologist, City Hospital, Birmingham, since 1974; *b* 7 July 1942; s of late James Wise and of Joan Wise; *m* 1979, Jane M. Symonds; one *d* (one *s* decd). *Educ:* Univ. of Manchester (MB ChB; MD 1980). Hon. Prof. of Clin. Microbiol., Univ. of Birmingham, 1995–. Advr, Sci. and Technol. Cttee, H of L, 1997–. Chm., Expert Adv. Cttee on Antimicrobial Resistance, 2001–. Non-exec. Dir, Centre for Applied Microbiol Res., Porton Down, 1999–. Pres., British Soc. Antimicrobial Chemotherapy, 1997–2000. Hon. FRCP, 1997. *Publications:* numerous contribs on antibiotic therapy. *Recreations:* gardening, wine and food, walking. *Address:* Department of Medical Microbiology, City Hospital, Birmingham B18 7QH. *T:* (0121) 507 4255. *Club:* East India.

WISEMAN, Prof. Donald John, OBE 1943; DLit; FBA 1966; FSA; Professor of Assyriology in the University of London, 1961–82, Emeritus 1982; *b* 25 Oct. 1918; *s* of Air Cdre Percy John Wiseman, CBE, RAF; *m* 1948, Mary Catherine, *d* of P. O. Ruoff; three *d*. *Educ:* Dulwich College; King's College, London. BA (London); AKC, McCaul Hebrew Prize, 1939; FKC 1982. Served War of 1939–45, in RAFVR. Ops, 11 Fighter Group, 1939–41; Chief Intelligence Officer, Mediterranean Allied Tactical Air Forces with Rank of Group Capt., 1942–45. Heap Exhibitioner in Oriental Languages, Wadham Coll., Oxford, 1945–47; MA 1949. Asst Keeper, Dept of Egyptian and Assyrian, later Western Asiatic, Antiquities, British Museum, 1948–61. Epigraphist on archæological excavations at Nimrud, Harran, Rimah; Jt Dir of British School of Archæology in Iraq, 1961–65, Chm. 1970–88, Vice-Pres., 1988–93, Pres., 1993–2001. Trustee, British Sch. of Archæology in Jerusalem, 1984–. Pres., Soc. for Old Testament Studies, 1980; Chm., Tyndale House for Biblical Research, Cambridge, 1957–86. Corresp. Mem., German Archæological Inst., 1961. Editor, Journal IRAQ, 1953–78; Joint Editor, Reallexion der Assyriologie, 1959–83. Bronze Star (USA), 1944. *Publications:* The Alalakh Tablets, 1953; Chronicles of Chaldaean Kings, 1956; Cuneiform Texts from Cappadocian Tablets in the British Museum, V, 1956; Cylinder-Seals of Western Asia, 1958; Vassal-Treaties of Esarhaddon, 1958; Illustrations from Biblical Archæology, 1958; Catalogue of Western Asiatic Seals in the British Museum, 1963; Peoples of Old Testament Times, 1973; Archaeology and the Bible, 1979; Essays on the Patriarchal Narratives, 1980; Nebuchadrezzar and Babylon, 1985; I and II Kings (commentary), 1993; Nimrud Literary Texts, 1996; contrib. to journals. *Address:* Low Barn, 26 Downs Way, Tadworth, Surrey KT20 5DZ. *T:* (01737) 813536.

WISEMAN, Sir John William, 11th Bt *cr* 1628; *b* 16 March 1957; *o s* of Sir William George Eden Wiseman, 10th Bt, CB, and of Joan Mary, *d* of late Arthur Phelps, Harrow; *S* father, 1962; *m* 1980, Nancy, *d* of Casimer Zyla, New Britain, Conn; two *d*. *Educ:* Millfield Sch.; Univ. of Hartford, Conn, USA. *Heir: kinsman* Thomas Alan Wiseman [*b* 8 July 1921; *m* 1946, Hildemarie Domnik (*d* 1991); (one *s* one *d* decd)].

WISEMAN, Julian Paul Geoffrey, CMG 2000; Director, Retainagroup Ltd, since 1999; *b* 3 Oct. 1944; *s* of Norman William Thomas Wiseman and Joan Marion Allen Wiseman; *m* 1973, Diana Christine Spooner; two *d*. *Educ:* Cranleigh Sch.; Australian Nat. Univ. (Dip. in Mod. Langs, 1969). Royal Marines, 1963–75: Troop Comdr, 40 Cdo; ADC to Gov. of Qld, 1967–69; Adjt, 42 Cdo, 1972–74; Bde Signal Officer, 3 Cdo Bde, 1975; HM Diplomatic Service, 1976–99: First Secretary: FCO, 1976–78; UKMIS to UN, Geneva, 1978–82; SOAS, 1982–83; FCO, 1982–84; Dhaka, 1984–87; FCO, 1987–90; Counsellor: Islamabad, 1990–92; FCO, 1992–99. Mem., Sussex Cttee and London Reg. Adv. Cttee, Duke of Edinburgh's Award. FRGS. *Recreations:* ski-ing, fishing, golf, music, travel. *Address:* Retainagroup Ltd, 134 Buckingham Palace Road, SW1W 9SA. *Clubs:* Flyfishers', Army and Navy; Piscatorial Society.

WISEMAN, Prof. Timothy Peter, DPhil; FSA; FBA 1986; Professor of Classics, University of Exeter, 1977–2001, now Emeritus; *b* 3 Feb. 1940; *s* of Stephen Wiseman and Winifred Agnes Wiseman (*née* Rigby); *m* 1962, Doreen Anne Williams. *Educ:* Manchester Grammar Sch.; Balliol Coll., Oxford (MA 1964; DPhil 1967). FSA 1977. Rome Schol. in Classical Studies, British Sch. at Rome, 1962–63; University of Leicester: Asst Lectr in Classics, 1963–65; Lectr, 1965–73; Reader in Roman History, 1973–76. Vice-Pres., British Acad., 1992–94; President: Roman Soc., 1992–95; Jt Assoc. of Classical Teachers, 1998–99; Classical Assoc., 2000–01. Vis. Associate Prof., Univ. of Toronto, 1970–71; Lansdowne Lectr, Univ. of Victoria (BC), 1987; Whitney J. Oates Fellow, Princeton, 1988; Webster Lectr, Stanford, 1993. Hon. DLitt Durham, 1988. *Publications:* Catullan Questions, 1969; New Men in the Roman Senate, 1971; Cinna the Poet, 1974; Clio's Cosmetics, 1979; (with Anne Wiseman) Julius Caesar: The Battle for Gaul, 1980; (ed) Roman Political Life, 1985; Catullus and his World, 1985; Roman Studies Literary and Historical, 1987; trans., Flavius Josephus, Death of an Emperor, 1991; Talking to Virgil, 1992; Historiography and Imagination, 1994; Remus: a Roman myth, 1995; Roman Drama and Roman History, 1998. *Address:* Classics Department, The University, Exeter EX4 4QH. *T:* (01392) 264201.

WISHART, Maureen; *see* Lehane, M.

WISHART, Peter; MP (SNP) Tayside North, since 2001; *b* 9 March 1962; *s* of Alex and Nan Wishart; *m* 1990, Carrie Lindsay; one *s*. *Educ:* Moray House Coll. of Educn. Community worker, 1984–85; musician with rock band, Runrig, 1985–2001. *Recreations:* music, hillwalking. *Address:* 35 Perth Street, Blairgowrie PH10 6DL.

WISTRICH, Enid Barbara, PhD; Visiting Professor, School of Humanities, Middlesex University, since 1997; *b* 4 Sept. 1928; *d* of Zadik Heiber and Bertha Brown; *m* 1950, Ernest Wistrich, *qv*; two *c* (and one *c* decd). *Educ:* Froebel Institute Sch.; Brackley High Sch.; St Paul's Girls' Sch.; London School of Economics (BScEcon, PhD). Research Asst, LSE, 1950–52; Instructor, Mt Holyoke Coll., Mass, USA, 1952–53; Research Officer, Royal Inst. of Public Administration, 1954–56; Sen. Res. Officer, LSE, 1969–72; NEDO, 1977–79; Prin. Lectr, 1979–91, Reader in Politics and Public Admin, 1991–94, Middlesex Poly., subseq. Middlesex Univ. Vis. Lectr, Univ. of Waikato, NZ, 1989. Councillor (Lab): Hampstead Metropolitan Bor. Council, 1962–65; London Bor. of Camden, 1964–68 and 1971–74; GLC, ILEA, 1973–77. Mem., Hampstead Community Health Council, 1984–92 (Chm., 1986–88). Governor: British Film Inst., 1974–81 (also Actg Chm., 1977–78); National Film Sch., 1978–82. Chm. of Governors, Heathlands Sch. for Autistic Children, 1976–86. *Publications:* Local Government Reorganisation: the first years of Camden, 1972; I Don't Mind the Sex, It's the Violence: film censorship explored, 1978; The Politics of Transport, 1983; (jtly) The Migrants' Voice in Europe, 1999; chapters and articles in various books and jls. *Recreations:* experiencing the arts, admiring nature, fussing round the family. *Address:* 37B Gayton Road, NW3 1UB. *T:* (020) 7419 1742.

WISTRICH, Ernest, CBE 1973; Director, European Movement (British Council), 1969–86; *b* 22 May 1923; *s* of Dr Arthur and Mrs Eva Wistrich; *m* 1950, Enid Barbara (*née* Heiber), *qv*; two *c* (and one *c* decd). *Educ:* Poland; University Tutorial Coll., London. Served in RAF, 1942–46; Timber Merchant, 1946–67; Dir, Britain in Europe, 1967–69; Councillor, Hampstead Borough Council, 1959–65; Camden Borough Council, Alderman 1964–71, Councillor 1971–74; Chm., Camden Cttee for Community Relations, 1964–68; Mem., Skeffington Cttee on Public Participation in Planning, 1968–69. Contested (Lab): Isle of Thanet, 1964; Hendon North, 1966; Cleveland, 1979; contested (SDP) London Central, 1984, European Parly elections. Editor of various jls, incl. The European, 1986–88. *Publications:* After 1992, 1989; The United States of Europe, 1994; contrib. Into Europe, Facts, New Europe and other jls. *Recreations:* music, walking. *Address:* 37B Gayton Road, NW3 1UB. *T:* (020) 7419 1686.

WITCHELL, Nicholas Newton Henshall; Diplomatic Correspondent, since 1995, Royal Correspondent, since 1998, BBC News; *b* 23 Sept. 1953; *s* of William Joseph Henshall Witchell and late Barbara Sybil Mary Witchell (*née* Macdonald); two *d*. *Educ:* Epsom Coll.; Leeds Univ. (LLB). Joined BBC, 1976: grad. news trainee, 1976–78; reporter: TV and radio, NI, 1978–82; TV Network News, 1982–83; Ireland Corresp., 1983–84; Presenter: Six O'Clock News, 1984–89; BBC Breakfast News, 1989–94; Associate Producer: News '39, 1989; News '44, 1994; News '45, 1995; Corresp., Panorama, 1994–95; Presenter, BBC News, 1995–98. Gov., Queen Elizabeth's Foundn for Disabled People, 1992–. FRGS 1990. OStJ 1995. *Publication:* The Loch Ness Story, 1974. *Address:* BBC News, BBC TV Centre, W12 7RJ. *T:* (020) 8743 8000. *Club:* Reform.

WITCHER, Sally Anne; freelance management and social policy consultant, since 1998; *b* 11 July 1960; *d* of Michael James Witcher and Janet Mary Witcher (*née* Ashford). *Educ:* Slade Sch. of Fine Art (BA Hons); University Coll. London; Edinburgh Univ. (MSc Policy Studies). Teacher, English as a Foreign Language, British Inst., Lisbon, 1984–85; freelance sculptor, 1985–87; Homeless Families Liaison Worker, Earls Court Homelessness Project, 1987–89; Campaign Worker, Disability Alliance, 1989–93; Dir, CPAG, 1993–98. *Publications:* (jtly) A Way out of Poverty and Disability, 1991; (jtly) Letters, Lobbies, Legislation: a guide to Parliamentary campaigning in Scotland, 1999; (jtly) Direct Payments: the impact on choice and control for disabled people, 2000. *Address:* 2 Montague Street, Edinburgh EH8 9QU. *T:* (0131) 662 8855.

WITHALL, Maj.-Gen. William Nigel James, CB 1982; Marketing Director, and Member, Board of Directors, Link-Miles Ltd, 1985–93 (Consultant, 1984); *b* 14 Oct. 1928; *s* of late Bernard Withall and Enid (*née* Hill); *m* 1952, Pamela Hickman; one *s* one *d*. *Educ:* St Benedict's. Army Engr Cadet, 1947–50; Mons OCS, 1950; Commnd RE, 1950; served in Hong Kong, Gulf States, Aden, Germany and India; Staff Coll., 1961; Sqdn Comd, 73 Fd Sqdn, 1964–66; Jt Services Staff Coll., Latimer, 1967; Mil. Asst to MGO, 1968–70; CO 26 Engr Regt, BAOR, 1970–72; Bde Comd, 11 Engr Bde, 1974–76; NDC, India, 1977; No 259 Army Pilots Course, 1978; Dir, Army Air Corps, 1979–83. Col Comdt RE, 1984–97. Chm., Army Football Assoc., 1980–81; Pres., Army Cricket Assoc., 1981–83; Hon. Life Vice Pres., Aircrew Assoc., 1986; Chm., RE Assoc., 1993–97. Freeman, City of London, 1981; Liveryman, GAPAN, 1981. *Recreations:* cricket, squash, all games, reading, walking. *Address:* c/o Barclays Bank, High Street,

Andover, Hants SP10 1LN. *Clubs:* MCC, I Zingari, Band of Brothers, Free Foresters, Stragglers of Asia.

WITHERIDGE, Rev. John Stephen, MA; Headmaster of Charterhouse, since 1996; *b* 14 Nov. 1953; *s* of late Francis Edward Witheridge and Joan Elizabeth Witheridge (*née* Exell); *m* 1975, Sarah Caroline, *d* of Rev. Peter Phillips; two *s* two *d. Educ:* St Albans Sch.; Univ. of Kent at Canterbury (BA 1st cl. Eng. and Theol.); Christ's Coll., Cambridge (BA 2nd cl. Theol Tripos; MA); Ridley Hall, Cambridge. Ordained deacon, 1979, priest, 1980; Curate, Luton Parish Church, 1979–82; Head of Religious Studies and Asst Chaplain, Marlborough Coll., 1982–84; Chaplain to Archbishop of Canterbury, 1984–87; Conduct (Sen. Chaplain), Eton Coll., 1987–96. FRSA 1998. *Publications:* articles and reviews. *Recreations:* family, history, travel, gardening, running. *Address:* Charterhouse, Godalming, Surrey GU7 2DJ. *T:* (01483) 291600. *Club:* East India.

WITHEROW, David Michael Lindley; Deputy Chair, Radio Authority, since 2000 (Member, since 1998); *b* 19 July 1937; *s* of Dr James Witherow and Greta (*née* Roberts); *m* 1st, 1960, Ragnhild Kadow (marr. diss. 1994); two *d*; 2nd, 1994, Elizabeth Anne Wright. *Educ:* King Edward's Sch., Birmingham (Foundn Schol.); Pembroke Coll., Cambridge (BA Hons 1960). Nat. service, RCS, 1955–57. Press Assoc., 1960–63; BBC, 1963–96: Ext. Services News, 1963–77, Editor, 1973–77; Editor, Weekly Progs, TV News, 1977–79; Chief Assistant, Regions, 1980; Head, then Gen. Manager, Monitoring Service, Caversham, 1980–85; Controller, Resources and Admin, Ext. Services, 1985–89; Dep. Man. Dir, 1989–94, Policy Consultant, 1994–96, World Service; Project Dir, Digital Audio Broadcasting Services, 1994–96. Pres., World (formerly Europ.) DAB Forum, 1995–97. FRSA 1992. *Recreations:* travel, music, crime fiction. *Address:* 6 Northfield Hall, 59 North Road, N6 4BJ.

WITHEROW, John Moore; Editor, The Sunday Times, since 1995; *b* Johannesburg, 20 Jan. 1952; *s* of Cecil and Millicent Witherow; *m* 1985, Sarah Jane Linton; two *s* one *d. Educ:* Bedford Sch.; York Univ. (BA Hons Hist.). Reuters trainee, London and Madrid, 1977–80; home and foreign corresp., The Times, 1980–83; Sunday Times: Defence corresp., 1984–85; Diplomatic Corresp., 1985–87; Focus Ed., 1987–89; Foreign Ed., 1989–92; Man. Ed. (News), 1992–94; Actg Ed., 1994. *Publications:* (with Patrick Bishop) The Winter War: the Falklands, 1982; The Gulf War, 1993. *Recreations:* tennis, sailing. *Address:* The Sunday Times, 1 Pennington Street, E98 1ST. *T:* (020) 7782 5640. *Club:* Royal Automobile.

WITHERS, Googie, (Mrs John McCallum), AO 1980; CBE 2001; actress, since 1932; *b* Karachi, India, 12 March 1917; *d* of late Captain E. C. Withers, CBE, CIE, RIM, and late Lizette Catherine Wilhelmina van Wageningen; *m* 1948, John Neil McCallum, *qv*; one *s* two *d. Educ:* Fredville Park, Nonnington, Kent; Convent of the Holy Family, Kensington. Started as dancer in Musical Comedy. First film contract at age of 17; has acted in over 50 pictures, starring in 30. *Films include:* One of our Aircraft is Missing, 1941; The Silver Fleet, 1941; On Approval, 1942; Loves of Joanna Godden, 1946; It Always Rains on Sunday, 1947; White Corridors, 1950; Nickel Queen, 1970; Country Life, 1994; Shine, 1995. *Plays include:* They Came to a City; Private Lives; Winter Journey; The Deep Blue Sea; Waiting for Gillian; Janus; Stratford on Avon Season, 1958: Beatrice in Much Ado About Nothing; Gertrude in Hamlet; The Complaisant Lover, New York, 1962; Exit the King, London, 1963; Getting Married, Strand, 1967; Madame Renevsky in The Cherry Orchard, Mrs Cheveley in An Ideal Husband, 1972; Lady Kitty in The Circle, Chichester Festival Theatre, 1976, Haymarket, 1977 (nominated for SWET best actress award), Toronto, 1978; Lady Bracknell in The Importance of Being Earnest, Chichester, 1979; Time and the Conways, Chichester, 1983; Lady Sneerwell in The School for Scandal, Duke of York's, 1984 (also European tour); The Chalk Garden, Chichester, 1986; Hay Fever, Ring Round the Moon, Chichester, 1988; An Ideal Husband, Old Vic, 1995–96, Australia, 1997–98; Lady Windermere's Fan, Chichester, 1997. Tours: Roar Like a Dove, The Constant Wife and Woman in a Dressing Gown, Australia and NZ, 1959; excerpts Shakespeare (Kate, Margaret of Anjou, Beatrice, Portia, Rosalind, Cleopatra), 1964; Beekman Place, Australia and NZ, 1965; Relatively Speaking, Australia, 1968; Plaza Suite, Australia and NZ, 1969–70; The Kingfisher, Australia, NZ and Far East, 1978–80, FE, ME and Gulf, 1987; The Cherry Orchard, The Skin Game, Dandy Dick, UK, 1981; Stardust, UK and Australia, 1984–85; The Cocktail Hour, Australia and UK, 1989–90; High Spirits, Australia, 1991, 1993; On Golden Pond, UK, 1992; The Chalk Garden, Australia, 1995. *Television* appearances in drama including The Public Prosecutor; Amphitryon 38; The Deep Blue Sea (Best Actress, 1954); Last Year's Confetti, Court Circular, 1971; Knightsbridge, 1972; The Cherry Orchard, 1973; series Within These Walls, 1974–76 (Best Actress of the Year, 1974); Time after Time (TV film), 1985 (Best Actress ACE Award, USA, 1988); Hotel du Lac (TV film), 1985; Northanger Abbey (TV film), 1986; Ending Up, 1989. *Recreations:* music, travel, reading, interior decorating. *Address:* 1740 Pittwater Road, Bay View, NSW 2104, Australia; c/o Coutts & Co., 440 Strand, WC2R 0QS.

WITHERS, Rt Hon. Reginald (Greive); PC 1977; Senator (L) for Western Australia, 1966–87; Lord Mayor of Perth, Western Australia, 1991–93; *b* 26 Oct. 1924; *s* of late F. J. Withers and I. L. Greive; *m* 1953, Shirley Lloyd-Jones; two *s* one *d. Educ:* Bunbury; Univ. of WA (LLB). Barrister-at-law 1953. Served War, RAN, 1942–46. Councillor, Bunbury Municipal Council, 1954–56; Mem., Bunbury Diocesan Council, 1958–59, Treasurer, 1961–68. State Vice-Pres., Liberal and Country League of WA, 1958–61, State Pres., 1961–65; Mem., Federal Exec. of Liberal Party, 1961–65; Fed. Vice-Pres., Liberal Party, 1962–65. Govt Whip in Senate, 1969–71; Leader of Opposition in Senate, 1972–75; Special Minister of State, Minister for Capital Territory, Minister for Media, and Minister for Tourism and Recreation, Nov.–Dec. 1975; Vice-Pres. of Exec. Council, Leader of Govt in Senate, and Minister for Admin. Services, 1975–78. Sec., SW Law Soc., 1955–68. *Recreations:* swimming, reading, painting. *Address:* 23 Malcolm Street, West Perth, WA 6005, Australia. *T:* (8) 93241322, *Fax:* (8) 93241426.

WITHERS, Roy Joseph, CBE 1983; FREng; Director, Vosper Thornycroft (Holdings), 1985–96 (Chairman, 1985–90); *b* 18 June 1924; *s* of Joseph Withers and Irene Ada Withers (*née* Jones); *m* 1947, Pauline M. G. Johnston; four *s. Educ:* Tiffin School, Kingston upon Thames; Trinity College, Cambridge (1st. cl. Hons Mech. Scis Tripos). ICI, 1948–55; Humphreys & Glasgow, 1955–63; Engineering Dir, then Man. Dir, Power-Gas Corp. (subsid. of Davy Corp.), 1963–71; Chief Exec., Davy Powergas International, 1972–73; Man. Dir, Davy Corp., 1973–83; Vice-Chm., Davy Corp, 1983–91. Director: A. Monk & Co., 1983–88; Transmark, 1987–95 (Chm., 1991–95). Mem., BOTB, 1983–86; Chm., Overseas Projects Board, 1983–86. FIMechE 1972; FREng (FEng 1983). Hon. FIChemE 1983. *Recreations:* painting, golf, walking. *Address:* Wheelwrights Cottage, Bramshaw, Lyndhurst, Hants SO4 7JB. *T:* (023) 8081 2543. *Clubs:* Carlton; Hampstead Golf, Bramshaw Golf.

WITHEY, Anthony George Hurst, CBE 1997; FCMA; Chief Executive, Remploy Ltd, 1988–2000; *b* 4 Oct. 1942; *s* of Walter Ronald Withey and Laura Maria Withey (*née* Thomas); *m* 1967, Yvonne Jeanette Price Thomas; one *s* one *d. Educ:* Bishop Gore Grammar Sch., Swansea; Wadham Coll., Oxford (BA Hons Modern Hist.). FCMA 1986. Gen. Manager, BXL Plastics Ltd, various divs, and Dir, various subsids, 1976–83; Gp Exec., Tarmac Bldg Products Ltd, 1983–85; Chief Exec., Polymers Div., Evered Holdings PLC, 1985–88. Director: Pan Graphics Industries Ltd, 1991–94; Linx Printing Technologies PLC, 1994–; GCE (UK) Ltd, 2000–. Director: Morriston Hosp. NHS Trust, 1997–99; Swansea NHS Trust, 1999–. Dir, Internat. Orgn for Provision of Work to Disabled People, 1993–. Mem., S Wales Police Selection Panel, 1998–. Mem. Council, Industrial Soc., 1989–2000. *Recreations:* squash, gardening, antiques, theatre. *Address:* Westwoods, Caswell Bay, Swansea SA3 3BS. *T:* (01792) 363068. *Club:* Swansea Lawn Tennis and Squash Racquets.

WITNEY, Nicholas Kenneth James; Director-General, Equipment, Ministry of Defence, since 1999; *b* 14 Dec. 1950; *s* of Kenneth Witney and Joan Witney (*née* Tait); *m* 1977, Ann Margaret Russell; one *s* one *d. Educ:* Tonbridge Sch.; Corpus Christi Coll., Oxford (MA Lit Hum). Joined Foreign and Commonwealth Office, 1973: E European and Soviet Dept, 1973; Arabic lang. trng, Lebanon and Jordan, 1974–76; Third, later Second, Sec., Baghdad, 1976–78; Second, later First, Sec. and Private Sec. to Ambassador, Washington, 1978–82; EC Dept, FCO, 1982–83; on secondment, later perm. transfer, to MoD, 1983–; Principal: defence policy Africa/Asia, 1983–85; Army budget and plans, 1985–87; Director: (Ops), Saudi Armed Forces Project, 1987–90; Nuclear Policy and Security, 1990–93; sabbatical at Rand Corp., Santa Monica, 1993–94; Hd, Housing Project Team, 1994–96; Dir-Gen., Mgt and Orgn, 1996–98; Asst Under-Sec. of State, Systems, 1998–99. *Publication:* (jtly) Western European Nuclear Forces, 1995. *Recreations:* Rugby, sailing, modern fiction. *Address:* Ministry of Defence, Whitehall, SW1A 2HB.

WITT, Karsten; Chief Executive Officer, South Bank Centre, London, 1999–2002; *b* Hamburg, 5 March 1952; *s* of Reimer Witt and Hilde Witt (*née* Vöge); *m* 1st, 1982, Anna Zeijl; three *s*; 2nd, 1996, Marie-Annick Le Blanc. *Educ:* Univ. of Hamburg (BA Philosophy of Sci.); Univ. of Constance (MA). Founder: Junge Deutsche Philharmonie (Nat. Student Orch.), 1974 (Manager, 1974–87); Deutsche Kammerphilharmonie, 1980 (Manager, 1980–89); Ensemble Modern, 1980 (Manager, 1980–91); Manager, ISCM (German Br.), 1986–90; Gen. Sec., Vienna Konzerthaus, 1991–96; Pres., Deutsche Grammophon, 1996–99. Ehrenkreuz für Wissenschaft und Kunst (Austria), 1996; Silbernes Ehrenzeichen für Verdienste um das Land Wien, 1997. *Address:* c/o Royal Festival Hall, SE1 8XX. *T:* (020) 7921 0600.

WITTEVEEN, Dr (Hendrikus) Johannes, Commander, Order of Netherlands Lion; Commander, Order of Orange Nassau; Chairman, Internationale Nederlanden Group, 1991–93 (Mem. Supervisory Board, 1979–90); Board Member: Royal Dutch Petroleum Co., 1971–73 and 1978–89; Robeco, 1971–73 and 1979–91 (Adviser, 1971–73); *b* Zeist, Netherlands, 12 June 1921; *m* 1949, Liesbeth de Vries Feyens; two *s* one *d. Educ:* Univ. Rotterdam (DrEcons). Central Planning Bureau, 1947–48; Prof., Univ. Rotterdam, 1948–63; Mem. Netherlands Parlt, First Chamber, 1959–63 and 1971–73, and Second Chamber, 1965–67; Minister of Finance, Netherlands, 1963–65 and 1967–71; First Deputy Prime Minister, 1967–71; Managing Director, IMF, 1973–78. Chm., Group of Thirty, 1979–85, Hon. Chm., 1985–; Member: Internat. Council, Morgan Guaranty Trust Co. of NY, 1978–85; European Adv. Council, General Motors, 1978–91; Bd Mem., Thyssen-Bornemisza NV, 1978–86; Advr for Internat. Affairs, Amro Bank, Amsterdam, 1979–90. Grand Cross, Order of Crown (Belgium); Order of Oak Wreath (Luxemburg); Order of Merit (Fed. Republic Germany). *Publications:* Loonshoogte en Werkgelegenheid, 1947; Growth and Business Cycles, 1954; articles in Economische Statistische Berichten, Euromoney. *Recreation:* hiking. *Address:* 2243 HL Wassenaar, Waldeck Pyrmontlaan 15, The Netherlands.

WITTS, Canon Diana Katharine, OBE 2000; General Secretary, Church Mission Society, 1995–2000; *b* 14 May 1936; *d* of Maj.-Gen. Frederick Vavasour Broome Witts, CB, CBE, DSO, MC and Alice Mary Witts (*née* Wrigley). *Educ:* Bristol Univ. (BSc Physics). Hospital Physicist: Charing Cross Hosp., 1958–59; Royal Victoria Hosp., Montreal, 1959–61; Teacher of Maths and Physics: Parliament Hill Sch., 1961–63; Highlands Sch., Eldoret, Kenya, 1963–65; Mem., Lee Abbey Community, Devon, 1966; Teacher of Maths and Physics, Alliance Girls' High Sch., Kenya, 1966–70; Sen. Mistress, introducing co-educn, Gordonstoun Sch., 1970–75; educnl work with Maasai girls in Kenya, 1976–79; Tutor, Crowther Hall, Birmingham, 1980; CMS Rep. in E Africa, 1981–83; theol educn by extension, Zaïre, 1983–84; CMS Regl Sec. for W Africa, Sudan and Zaïre, 1985–95. Reader, Southwark Dio., 1991–; Lay Canon, Salisbury Cathedral, 1998–. Cross of St Augustine, 1994. *Recreation:* hill-walking. *Address:* 47 Gloucester Court, Kew Road, Richmond, Surrey TW9 3EA.

WITTY, (John) David, CBE 1985; Director, Great Portland Estates PLC, 1987–97; *b* 1 Oct. 1924; *s* of late Harold Witty and Olive Witty, Beverley; *m* 1955, Doreen Hanlan; one *s. Educ:* Beverley Grammar Sch.; Balliol Coll., Oxford (MA). Served War, RN, 1943–46. Asst Town Clerk, Beverley, 1951–53; Asst Solicitor: Essex CC, 1953–54; Hornsey, 1954–60; Dep. Town Clerk: Kingston upon Thames, 1960–65; Merton, 1965–67; Asst Chief Exec., Westminster, 1967–77, Chief Exec., 1977–84. Hon. Sec., London Boroughs Assoc., 1978–84. Chm., London Enterprise Property Co., 1984–85. Lawyer Mem., London Rent Assessment Panel, 1984–92. Order of Infante D. Henrique (Portugal), 1978; Order of Right Hand (Nepal), 1980; Order of King Abdul Aziz (Saudi Arabia), 1981; Order of Oman, 1982; Order of Orange-Nassau, 1982. *Recreation:* golf. *Address:* 14 River House, 23–24 The Terrace, Barnes, SW13 0NR.

WIX, Ethel Rose; Special Commissioner of Income Tax, 1977–86; *b* 1 Nov. 1921; *d* of Michael Wix and Anna Wix (*née* Snyder). *Educ:* Henrietta Barnett Sch.; Cheltenham Ladies' Coll.; University Coll. London (BA Hons 1942); Hull University Coll. (Cert Ed 1943). Special Operations Executive, 1944–45; lived in S Africa, 1948–54; work for S African Inst. of Race Relations, 1950–54; Africa Bureau, London, 1955–56; Solicitor of Supreme Court, 1960; Partner, Herbert Oppenheimer, Nathan & Vandyk, 1960–75; General Commissioner of Income Tax, 1976–78. Mem., Arbitrators Panel, The Securities and Futures Authy Consumer Arbitration Scheme, 1988–94. Member: Exec. Cttee, Jewish Mus., 1987–93 (Hon. Treas., 1987–89); Exec. Cttee, Inst. of Jewish Affairs, 1990–92; Liby Cttee, Oxford Centre for Postgrad. Hebrew Studies, 1990–94. Mem. Council: Richmond Fellowship, 1975–85; Trinity Hospice, Clapham, 1981–90; Cheltenham Ladies' Coll., 1983–93 (Vice-Chm., 1990–92); St Christopher's Hospice, 1985–95; Clifton Coll., 1987–91; Governor, Warwick Schs Foundn, 1988–90, and 1992–96 (Vice-Chm., 1994–96). *Publications:* papers on Cost of Living, 1951, and Industrial Feeding Facilities, 1953, for S African Inst. of Race Relations; summary of Royal Commn Report on E Africa, 1956, for Africa Bureau. *Recreations:* reading, cooking, theatre. *Address:* 5 Phillimore Gardens, W8 7QG. *T:* (020) 7937 8899. *Club:* Special Forces.

WODEHOUSE, family name of **Earl of Kimberley**.

WODEHOUSE, Lord; John Armine Wodehouse, CEng; Advanced Informatics and Technology Specialist, GlaxoSmithKline (formerly Glaxo Wellcome), since 1996; *b* 15 Jan. 1951; *s* and *heir* of 4th Earl of Kimberley, *qv*; *m* 1973, Hon. Carol Palmer, (Rev. Lady

Wodehouse), MA (Oxon), PGCE, *er d* of 3rd Baron Palmer, OBE; one *s* one *d*. *Educ:* Eton; Univ. of East Anglia. BSc (Chemistry) 1973; MSc (Physical Organic Chemistry) 1974. CEng 1993. FRSA. Glaxo, subseq. Glaxo Wellcome: Research Chemist, 1974–79; Systems Programmer, 1979–86, Prin. Systems Programmer, 1987–95. Chm., UK Info Users Gp, 1981–83. Fellow, British Interplanetary Soc., 1984 (Associate Fellow, 1981–83). MBCS 1988. *Recreations:* interest in spaceflight, photography, computing, fantasy role playing games. *Heir: s* David Simon John Wodehouse, *b* 10 Oct. 1978. *Address:* Kingswood, Henley Road, Medmenham, Marlow, Bucks SL7 2EU.

WOGAN, Michael Terence, (Terry), Hon. OBE 1997; jobbing broadcaster; *b* 3 Aug. 1938; *s* of late Michael Thomas and Rose Wogan; *m* 1965, Helen Joyce; two *s* one *d*. *Educ:* Crescent Coll., Limerick, Ireland; Belvedere Coll., Dublin. Joined RTE as Announcer, 1963, Sen. Announcer, 1964–66; various programmes for BBC Radio, 1965–67; Late Night Extra, BBC Radio, 1967–69; The Terry Wogan Show, BBC Radio One, 1969–72, BBC Radio Two, 1972–84 and 1993–95; television shows include: Lunchtime with Wogan, ATV; BBC: Come Dancing; Song for Europe; The Eurovision Song Contest; Children in Need; Wogan's Guide to the BBC; Blankety-Blank; Wogan; Terry Wogan's Friday Night; Auntie's Bloomers; Do the Right Thing; Auntie's Sporting Bloomers; Wogan's Island; Points of View, 2000–01; Awards include: Pye Radio Award, 1980; Radio Industries Award (Radio Personality 3 times; TV Personality, 1982, 1984, 1985, 1987); TV Times TV Personality of the Year (10 times); Daily Express Award (twice); Carl Alan Award (3 times); Variety Club of GB: Special Award, 1982; Showbusiness Personality, 1984; Radio Personality of last 21 yrs, Daily Mail Nat. Radio Awards, 1988; Sony Radio Award, 1993, 1994; Radio Prog. of the Year, TRIC Award, 1997. *Publications:* Banjaxed, 1979; The Day Job, 1981; To Horse, To Horse, 1982; Wogan on Wogan, 1987; Wogan's Ireland, 1988; Is it Me? (autobiog.), 2000. *Recreations:* tennis, golf, swimming, reading, writing. *Address:* c/o Jo Gurnett, 2 New Kings Road, SW6 4SA. *Clubs:* Garrick, Lord's Taverners, Saints and Sinners; London Irish Rugby Football; Temple Golf (Henley-on-Thames); Stoke Poges Golf.

WOGAN, Patrick Francis Michael, CMG 1991; HM Diplomatic Service, retired; Officer of the House of Lords, 1999. Joined FO, subseq. FCO, 1959; Second Sec., Bahrain, 1970; Second, then First, Sec., FCO, 1972; Brussels, 1976; FCO, 1981; Counsellor, FCO, 1983, Tehran, 1984; RCDS, 1987; Consul-Gen., Karachi, 1988; Ambassador to Iceland, 1991–93; Ambassador and Consul-Gen., Qatar, 1993–97. *Address:* c/o Foreign and Commonwealth Office, SW1A 2AH.

WOHL, Maurice, CBE 1992; Founder, Maurice Wohl Charitable Foundation and Maurice Wohl Charitable Trust, since 1965; *s* of Max Wohl and Miriam Rachel Wohl; *m* 1966, Vivienne Susan Monica Horowitz. *Educ:* Grocers' Co. Sch.; City of London Sch. Chm., United Real Property Trust, 1960–74. Pres., Jerusalem Great Synagogue, 1987–. Fellow: RPMS, 1991; ICSM, 1999; Presentation Fellow, KCL, 1992. Hon. FRCSE 2000; Hon. Fellow: City of Jerusalem, 1998; UCL, 2000. Hon. PhD Bar-Ilan, 2001. Médaille de la Ville de Paris, 1988. *Recreations:* reading, walking, art collecting. *Address:* c/o Maurice Wohl Charitable Foundation, 7/8 Conduit Street, W1S 2XF.

WOLEDGE, Brian, FBA 1989; Emeritus Professor of French Language and Literature, University of London; Fielden Professor of French, University College, London, 1939–71; Hon. Research Fellow, University College London; *b* 16 Aug. 1904; *m* 1933, Christine Mary Craven; one *s* one *d*. *Educ:* Leeds Boys' Modern School; University of Leeds. BA (Leeds) 1926; MA (Leeds) 1928; Docteur de l'Université de Paris, 1930; Asst Lecturer in French, University College, Hull, 1930–32; Lecturer in French, University of Aberdeen, 1932–39. Visiting Andrew Mellon Professor of French, University of Pittsburg, 1967. Docteur *hc* de l'Université d'Aix-Marseille, 1970. *Publications:* L'Atre périlleux; études sur les manuscrits, la langue et l'importance littéraire du poème, 1930; L'Atre périlleux, roman de la Table ronde (Les Classiques français du moyen âge 76), 1935; Bibliographie des romans et nouvelles en prose française antérieurs à 1500, 1954, repr. 1975, Supplement 1975; The Penguin Book of French Verse, Vol. 1, To the Fifteenth Century, 1961; Répertoire des premiers textes en prose française, 842–1210 (with H. P. Clive), 1964; La Syntaxe des substantifs chez Chrétien de Troyes, 1979; Commentaire sur Yvain (Le Chevalier au Lion) de Chrétien de Troyes, Vol. 1, 1986, Vol. 2, 1988. *Address:* 28a Dobbins Lane, Wendover, Aylesbury, Bucks HP22 6DH. *T:* (01296) 622188.

WOLF, Prof. (Charles) Roland, PhD; FMedSci; FRSE; FSA; Director, University of Dundee Biomedical Research Centre and Hon. Director, ICRF Molecular Pharmacology Unit, since 1992; *b* 26 Feb. 1949; *s* of Werner Max Wolf and Elizabeth Wolf; *m* 1975, Helga Loth; one *s* one *d*. *Educ:* Univ. of Surrey (BSc Chem.; PhD Biochem. 1975). Vis. Fellow, Nat. Inst. of Envmtl Health Scis, N Carolina, 1977–80; Vis. Scientist, ICI Central Toxicology Labs, Macclesfield, 1980–81; Hd of Biochemistry, Inst. of Toxicology, Univ. of Mainz, W Germany, 1981–82; Sen. Scientist, ICRF Med. Oncology Unit, Western Gen. Hosp., Edinburgh, 1982–86; Head, ICRF Molecular Pharmacology Gp, Univ. of Edinburgh, 1986–92. FRSE 1995; FMedSci 2000. *Publications:* (ed jtly) Molecular Genetics of Drug Resistance, 1997; numerous scientific papers. *Recreations:* weaving, piano playing, gardening, poetry, hiking. *Address:* University of Dundee Biomedical Research Centre, Level 5, Ninewells Hospital and Medical School, Dundee DD1 9SY. *T:* (01382) 632621.

WOLF, Martin Harry, CBE 2000; Associate Editor, since 1990, and Chief Economics Commentator, since 1996, Financial Times; *b* 16 Aug. 1946; *s* of Edmund Wolf and Rebecca Wolf (*née* Wijnschenk); *m* 1970, Alison Margaret Potter; two *s* one *d*. *Educ:* University College Sch.; Corpus Christi Coll., Oxford (MA 1st cl. Hons Mods 1967; 1st cl. Hons PPE 1969); Nuffield Coll., Oxford (MPhil (BPhil Econs 1971)). World Bank: Young Professional, 1971; Sen. Economist, India Div., 1974–77, Internat. Trade Div., 1979–81; Dir of Studies, Trade Policy Res. Centre, 1981–87; Chief Economics Leader Writer, Financial Times, 1987–96. Special Prof., Economics Dept, Univ. of Nottingham, 1993–; Vis. Fellow, Nuffield Coll., Oxford, 1999–. Member: NCC, 1967–73; Council, REconS, 1991–96; Adv. Bd on European Economic Integration, Erasmus Univ., 1992–. Advr and Rapporteur, Eminent Persons Gp on World Trade, 1990. (Jtly) Sen. Prize, Wincott Foundn, 1989 and 1997; RTZ David Watt Meml Prize, 1994. Commemoration Medal (NZ), 1990. *Publications:* India's Exports, 1982; numerous articles, mainly on commercial policy. *Recreations:* ski-ing, opera, theatre. *Address:* 27 Court Lane, SE21 7DH. *T:* (020) 8299 0199. *Club:* Reform.

WOLF, Prof. Peter Otto, FREng, FICE, FCIWEM; FRMetS; FASCE; consultant; Director, Pell Frischmann Consulting Engineers Ltd, since 1993; Professor and Head of Department of Civil Engineering, 1966–82, The City University, London, now Professor Emeritus; *b* 9 May 1918; *s* of Richard Wolf and Dora (*née* Bondy); *m* 1st, 1944, Jennie Robinson; two *s* one *d*; 2nd, 1977, Janet Elizabeth Robertson. *Educ:* University of London (BScEng). Assistant under agreement to C. E. Farren, Cons. Engr, 1941–44; Civilian Asst, a Dept of the War Office, 1944–45; Engineer (Chief Designer, Loch Sloy Project), under James Williamson, Cons. Engr, 1945–47; Engineer for Mullardoch Dam (Affric Project), John Cochrane & Sons Ltd, 1947–49; Imperial College of Science and Technology: Lectr in Fluid Mechanics and Hydraulic Engrg, 1949–55; Reader in Hydrology in Univ. of London, 1955–66. Private consultancy, London, 1950–. Chairman: Cttee on Flood Protection Res., MAFF, 1984–85; Standing Cttee on Natural Hazards, Hazards Forum, 1991–94 (Trustee, 1994–99); Mem., UK Co-ordination Cttee, UN Internat. Decade of Natural Disaster Reduction, 1993–97. Visiting Professor: Stanford Univ., Calif, 1959–60, 1961–64; Cornell Univ., 1963. Mem. Ct, Brunel Univ., 1999–. Hon. Member: BHRA, 1984–; British Hydrol Soc., 1994– (Pres., 1987–89). Hon. DrIng Technological Univ. of Dresden, 1986. *Publications:* trans. and ed, Engineering Fluid Mechanics, by Charles Jaeger, 1956; papers in Proc. ICE, Jl IWE, UNESCO Reports, UNESCO Nature and Resources, Proc. Internat. Water Resources Assoc., etc. *Recreations:* classical music, reading, ski-ing, walking. *Address:* 69 Shepherds Hill, N6 5RE. *T:* and *Fax:* (020) 8340 6638. *Club:* Athenæum.

WOLF, Roland; *see* Wolf, C. R.

WOLFE, Hon. Justice Lensley Hugh, OJ 1996; Chief Justice of Jamaica, since 1996; *b* 19 June 1938; *s* of Ernest Wolfe and Lucille Wolfe (*née* Hewitt); *m* 1965, Audrey Yvonne Pink; three *d*. *Educ:* St Jago High Sch.; Univ. of West Indies (DMS); Council of Legal Educn Law Sch. Called to the Bar, Lincoln's Inn, 1967. Asst Clerk of Courts, Jamaica, 1958–66; Dep. Clerk of Courts, 1966–67; Clerk of Courts, 1967–70; Crown Counsel, DPP's Office, 1970–71; practised at private Bar, 1971–77; Resident Magistrate, 1977–81; Judge of Supreme Court, 1981–93; Judge of Appeal, 1993–96; Chancellor, Dio. Jamaica, 1996–. Chm., Nat. Task Force on Crime, 1992–93. *Recreations:* walking, music, browsing on the Internet. *Address:* Supreme Court of Jamaica, Public Buildings (East), King Street, Kingston, Jamaica. *T:* 9228300, 9222933.

WOLFE, Thomas Kennerly, PhD; author and journalist; *b* 2 March 1931; *m* Sheila; one *s* one *d*. *Educ:* Washington and Lee Univ.; Yale Univ. (PhD 1957). Reporter, Springfield (Mass) Union, 1956–59; Reporter and Latin America correspondent, Washington Post, 1959–62; Reporter and magazine writer, New York Herald Tribune, 1962–66; magazine writer, New York World Journal Tribune, 1966–67; Contributing Editor: New York, magazine, 1968–76; Esquire, 1977–. Contributing artist, Harper's, 1978–81; one-man exhibns of drawings, Maynard Walker Gall., NY, 1965, Tunnel Gall., NY, 1974. *Publications:* The Kandy-Kolored Tangerine-Flake Streamline Baby, 1965; The Electric Kool-Aid Acid Test, 1968; The Pump House Gang, 1968; Radical Chic and Mau-mauing the Flak Catchers, 1970; The New Journalism, 1973; The Painted Word, 1975; Mauve Gloves and Madmen, Clutter and Vine, 1976; The Right Stuff, 1979; In Our Time, 1980; From Bauhaus to Our House, 1981; Bonfire of the Vanities, 1987; The New America, 1989; A Man in Full, 1998; Hooking Up (essays), 2000. *Address:* c/o Farrar, Straus and Giroux, 19 Union Square West, New York, NY 10003, USA.

WOLFE, William Cuthbertson; Member, National Council, since 1991, National Executive Committee, since 1998, Scottish National Party; *b* 22 Feb. 1924; *s* of late Major Tom Wolfe, TD, and Katie Cuthbertson; *m* 1st, 1953, Arna Mary (marr. diss. 1989), *d* of late Dr Melville Dinwiddie, CBE, DSO, MC; two *s* two *d*; 2nd, 1993, Catherine Margaret, *d* of late James Parker, and *widow* of John McAteer. *Educ:* Bathgate Academy; George Watson's Coll., Edinburgh. CA. Army service, 1942–47, NW Europe and Far East; Air OP Pilot. Hon. Publications Treas., Saltire Society, 1953–60; Scout County Comr, West Lothian, 1960–64; Hon. Pres. (Rector), Students' Assoc., Heriot-Watt Univ., 1966–69. Contested (SNP): West Lothian, 1962, 1964, 1966, 1970, Feb. and Oct. 1974, 1979; North Edinburgh, Nov. 1973; Chm., SNP, 1969–79, Pres., 1980–82. Treas., Scottish CND, 1982–85; Sec., Scottish Poetry Liby, 1985–91. Mem., Forestry Commn Nat. Cttee for Scotland, 1974–87. *Publication:* Scotland Lives, 1973. *Address:* 17 Limekilnburn Road, Quarter, Hamilton ML3 7XA. *T:* (01698) 281072.

WOLFENDALE, Sir Arnold (Whittaker), Kt 1995; PhD, DSc; FRS 1977; FInstP, FRAS; Professor of Physics, University of Durham, 1965–92, now Emeritus; Astronomer Royal, 1991–95; *b* 25 June 1927; *s* of Arnold Wolfendale and Doris Wolfendale; *m* 1951, Audrey Darby; twin *s*. *Educ:* Univ. of Manchester (BSc Physics 1st Cl. Hons 1948, PhD 1953, DSc 1970). FInstP 1958; FRAS 1973. Asst Lectr, Univ. of Manchester, 1951, Lectr, 1954; University of Durham: Lectr, 1956; Sen. Lectr, 1959; Reader in Physics, 1963; Head of Dept, 1973–77, 1980–83, 1986–89. Vis. Lectr, Univ. of Ceylon, 1952; Vis. Prof., Univ. of Hong Kong, 1977–78; Kan Tong Po Vis. Prof. of Physics, City Univ. of Hong Kong, 1995; Prof. of Experimental Physics, Royal Instn of GB, 1996–Jan. 2002. Lectures: H. C. Bhuyan Meml, Gauhati Univ., 1978 and 1993; B. B. Roy Meml, Calcutta Univ., 1978; Norman Lockyer, Exeter Univ., 1978; E. A. Milne, Oxford Univ., 1982; Rochester, Durham Univ., 1990; A. W. Mailvaganam Meml, Colombo Univ., 1990; Perren, QMW, 1991; O'Neill, Glasgow, 1991; Durham Observatory Anniversary, 1992; Cormack, RSE, 1992; Robinson, Armagh, 1992; David Martin, Royal Soc./British Acad., 1992; Preston Guild, Univ. of Central Lancs, 1992; J. H. Holmes Meml, Newcastle Univ., 1993; Irvine Meml, Stirling, 1993; Tompion, Clockmakers' Co., 1993; Courtauld, Manchester Lit. and Phil., 1993; Minerva, Scientific Instrument Makers' Co., 1993; Hess, IUPAP Cosmic Ray Commn, 1993; Poynting, Univ. of Birmingham, 1994; Mme Curie, Inst. of Physics, 1995; Dee, Glasgow Univ., 1995; Harland, Univ. of Exeter, 1996; Temple Chevallier, Univ. of Durham, 1996; Carter Meml, Nat. Observatory of NZ, 1997; Charter, Inst. of Biology, 1997; Manley Meml, Univ. of Durham, 1997; Cockroft & Walton, Inst. of Physics, India, 1998; Wdowczyk Meml, Univ. of Lodz, Poland, 1998. Home Office, Civil Defence, later Regl Scientific Advr, 1956–84. Chm., Northern Reg. Action Cttee, Manpower Services Commn's Job Creation Prog., 1975–78; Mem., SERC, 1988–94 (Chm., Astronomy and Planetary Sci. Bd, 1988–93; Chm., Particles, Space and Astronomy Bd, 1993–94). Chm., Cosmic Ray Commn, IUPAP, 1982–84. President: RAS, 1981–83; Antiquarian Horological Soc., 1993–; Inst. of Physics, 1994–96; European Physical Soc., 1999–2001. Pres., Durham Univ. Soc. of Fellows, 1988–94. Freeman: Clockmakers' Co., 1991; Sci. Instrument Makers' Co., 1993. MAE 1998. Foreign Fellow: INSA, 1990; Indian Nat. Acad. Scis; For. Associate, RSSAf, 1995; Hon. Fellow, Lancashire Poly., 1991; Hon. Professor: Univ. of Yunnan, China, 1995; Univ. of Sci. and Technology, Hefei, China, 1995. Hon. DSc: Univ. of Potchefstroom for Christian Higher Educn, 1989; Lodz, 1989; Teeside, 1993; Newcastle upon Tyne, 1994; Paisley, 1996; Lancaster, 1996; Bucharest, 2000; DUniv: Open, 1995; Durham, 2001; Dip. *hc* Romanian Acad., 2000. Univ. of Turku Medal, 1987; Armagh Observatory Medal, 1992; Marian Smoluchowski Medal, Polish Phys. Soc., 1993; Powell Meml Medal, EPS, 1996. Silver Jubilee Medal, 1977. *Publications:* Cosmic Rays, 1963; (ed) Cosmic Rays at Ground Level, 1973; (ed) Origin of Cosmic Rays, 1974; (ed jtly and contrib.) Origin of Cosmic Rays, 1981; (ed) Gamma Ray Astronomy, 1981; (ed) Progress in Cosmology, 1982; (with P. V. Ramana Murthy) Gamma Ray Astronomy, 1986, 2nd edn 1993; (with F. R. Stephenson) Secular Solar and Geomagnetic Variations in the last 1,000 years, 1988; (ed jtly) Observational Tests of Cosmological Inflation, 1991; original papers on studies of cosmic radiation and aspects of astrophysics. *Recreations:* walking, gardening, foreign travel. *Address:* Ansford, Potters Bank, Durham DH1 3RR. *T:* (0191) 384 5642.

WOLFENSOHN, James David, Hon. KBE 1995; President, International Bank for Reconstruction and Development, since 1995; *b* Sydney, 1 Dec. 1933; *s* of Hyman Wolfensohn and Dora Weinbaum; *m* 1961, Elaine Botwinick; one *s* two *d*. *Educ:* Univ.

of Sydney (BA, LLB); Harvard Business Sch. (MBA). Lawyer, Allen Allen & Hemsley; Officer, RAAF; former Exec. Dep. Chm. and Man. Dir, Schroders Ltd, London; former Man. Dir, Darling & Co., Australia; Pres., J. Henry Schroder Banking Corp., 1970–76; Chm., Salomon Brothers Internat., 1977–81; Pres., James D. Wolfensohn Inc., 1981–95. Mem. Bd, Carnegie Hall, NY, 1970 (Chm. Bd, 1980–91, now Chm. Emeritus); Chm., Kennedy Center for the Performing Arts, 1990–95, now Chm. Emeritus. Trustee, Rockefeller Univ., 1985–94; Chm. Bd, Inst. for Advanced Study, Princeton Univ. Fellow: American Acad. of Arts and Scis; American Philosophical Soc. David Rockefeller Prize, Mus. of Modern Art, NY. *Address:* World Bank, 1818 H Street NW, Washington, DC 20433, USA.

WOLFF, Prof. Heinz Siegfried, FIBiol; FIEE; Director, Brunel Institute for Bioengineering, Brunel University, 1983–95, Emeritus Professor, since 1995; *b* 29 April 1928; *s* of Oswald Wolff and Margot (*née* Saalfeld); *m* 1953, Joan Eleanor Stephenson; two *s. Educ:* City of Oxford Sch.; University Coll. London (BSc(Hons)Physiology) (Fellow, 1987). FIEE 1993; FIPEMB (FBES 1994). National Institute for Medical Research: Div. of Human Physiology, 1954–62; Hd, Div. of Biomedical Engrg, 1962–70; Hd, Bioengrg Div., Clinical Res. Centre of MRC, 1970–83. European Space Agency: Chm., Life Science Working Gp, 1976–82; Mem., Sci. Adv. Cttee, 1978–82; Chm., Microgravity Adv. Cttee, 1982–91. Chm., Microgravity Panel, Brit. Nat. Space Centre, 1986–87. Bd Dir, Edinburgh Internat. Science Fest., 1995–. Vice-President: Coll. of Occupational Therapy, 1990–; Rehabilitation Engrg Movt Adv. Panel, 1995–; Disabled Living Foundn, 1997–. FRSA; Hon. Fellow, Ergonomics Soc., 1991. *Television series:* BBC TV Young Scientist of the Year (contributor), 1968–81; BBC2: Royal Instn Christmas Lectures, 1975; Great Egg Race, 1978–; Great Experiments, 1985–86. Hon. FRCP 1999. DUniv: Open, 1993; De Montfort, 1995; Oxford Brookes, 1999; Hon. Dr Middlesex, 1999. Harding Award, Action Res. for the Crippled Child/RADAR, 1989; Edinburgh Medal, Edinburgh Internat. Sci. Fest., 1992; Donald Julius Groen Prize, IMechE, 1994; Medal, 1996, Keith Medal for Innovation, 2001, Royal Scottish Soc. of Arts. *Publications:* Biomedical Engineering, 1969 (German, French, Japanese and Spanish trans, 1970–72); about 120 papers in sci. jls and contribs to books. *Recreations:* working, lecturing to children, dignified practical joking. *Address:* Brunel Institute for Bioengineering, Brunel University, Uxbridge, Middx UB8 3PH.

WOLFF, Michael, PPCSD; FRSA; President, Newhouse Associates, since 1993; Member, Board of Trustees, the Hunger Project, since 1979; *b* 12 Nov. 1933; *s* of Serge Wolff and Mary (*née* Gordon); *m* 1st, 1976, Susan Kent (marr. diss.); one *d*; 2nd, 1989, Martha Newhouse. *Educ:* Gresham's Sch., Holt, Norfolk; Architectural Association Sch. of Architecture. Designer: Sir William Crawford & Partners, 1957–61; BBC Television, 1961–62; Main Wolff & Partners, 1964–65; with Wolff Olins Ltd as a founder and Creative Director, 1965–83; Chm., Addison Design Consultants, 1987–92. Design Consultant, W. H. Smith Gp, 1990–98. Non-exec. Dir, Newell & Sorrell, 1995–98. Founding Partner, Fourth Room, 1998. President: D&AD, 1971; SIAD, then CSD, 1985–87. *Recreations:* enjoying a family, seeing. *Address:* 9 Cumberland Gardens, WC1X 9AG. *T:* (020) 7833 0007; (office) (020) 7430 5900.

WOLFF, Prof. Otto Herbert, CBE 1985; MD, FRCP; Nuffield Professor of Child Health, University of London, 1965–85, now Emeritus Professor; Dean of the Institute of Child Health, 1982–85; *b* 10 Jan. 1920; *s* of Dr H. A. J. Wolff; *m* 1952, Dr Jill Freeborough; one *s* one *d. Educ:* Peterhouse, Cambridge; University College Hospital, London. Lieut and Capt. RAMC, 1944–47. Resident Medical Officer, Registrar and Sen. Med. Registrar, Birmingham Children's Hospital, 1948–51; Lecturer, Sen. Lectr, Reader, Dept of Pædiatrics and Child Health, Univ. of Birmingham, 1951–64. Senator, London Univ.; Representative of London Univ. on GMC. Past Pres., British Pædiatric Assoc.; Member: Royal Society of Medicine; American Pædiatric Society; New York Academy of Sciences; Amer. Academy of Pediatrics; European Soc. for Paediatric Research; European Soc. for Paediatric Gastroenterology; Deutsche Akad. der Naturforscher Leopoldina. Corresp. Member: Société Française de Pédiatrie; Société Suisse de Pédiatrie; Österreichische Gesellschaft für Kinderheilkunde; Società Italiana di Pediatria; Deutsche Gesellschaft für Kinderheilkunde; Fellow, Indian Acad. of Pediatrics. Chm. of Trustees, Child-to-Child Charity, 1989–93. Dawson Williams Meml Prize, BMA, 1984; Medal, Assoc. Française pour le Dépistage et la Prévention des Maladies Métaboliques et des Handicaps de l'Enfant, 1986; Harding Award, Action Res. for Crippled Child, 1987; James Spence Medal, BPA, 1988. *Publications:* chapter on Disturbances of Serum Lipoproteins in Endocrine and Genetic Diseases of Childhood (ed L. I. Gardner); chapter on Obesity in Recent Advances in Paediatrics (ed David Hull); articles in Lancet, British Medical Journal, Archives of Disease in Childhood, Quarterly Jl of Medicine, etc. *Recreation:* music. *Address:* 53 Danbury Street, N1 8LE. *T:* (020) 7226 0748.

WOLFF, Rosemary Langley; Member, Police Complaints Authority, 1985–92 (Member, Police Complaints Board, 1977–85); *b* 10 July 1926; *er d* of late A. C. V. Clarkson; *m* 1956, Michael Wolff, JP (*d* 1976); two *d. Educ:* Haberdashers' Aske's Sch. Mem., Community Relations Commn, 1973–77. Manager of various primary schs in North Kensington and Tower Hamlets, 1963–; Governor, City College; Chm., Conservative Contact Group, 1973–77; Mem., Managing Cttee, Working Ladies' Guild. Assoc. Mem., Kensington, Chelsea and Westminster FHSA, 1994–96. *Address:* 38 Finstock Road, W10 6LU. *T:* (020) 8964 0690.

WOLFSON, family name of **Barons Wolfson** and **Wolfson of Sunningdale**.

WOLFSON, Baron *cr* 1985 (Life Peer), of Marylebone in the City of Westminster; **Leonard Gordon Wolfson,** Bt 1962; Kt 1977; Chairman, since 1972, and Founder Trustee, since 1955, Wolfson Foundation; Chairman: Great Universal Stores, 1981–96 (Managing Director, 1962–81; Director, 1952); Burberrys Ltd, 1978–96; *b* London, 11 Nov. 1927; *s* of Sir Isaac Wolfson, 1st Bt, FRS (*d* 1991) and Lady (Edith) Wolfson (*d* 1981); *m* 1st, 1949 (marr. diss. 1991); four *d*; 2nd, 1991, Estelle (*née* Feldman), *widow* of Michael Jackson, FCA; one step *s* one step *d. Educ:* King's School, Worcester. Pres., Jewish Welfare Bd, 1972–82. Trustee, Imperial War Mus., 1988–94. Hon. Fellow: St Catherine's Coll., Oxford; Wolfson Coll., Cambridge; Wolfson Coll., Oxford; Worcester Coll., Oxford; UCL; LSHTM 1985; QMC 1985; Poly. of Central London, 1991; Imperial Coll., 1991; LSE, 1999; Somerville Coll., Oxford, 1999; Hon. Mem., Emmanuel Coll., Cambridge, 1996. Hon. FRCP 1977; Hon. FRCS 1988; Hon. FBA 1986; Hon. FREng (Hon. FEng 1997); Hon. MRCSEd 1997. Hon. DCL: Oxon, 1972; East Anglia, 1986; Hon. LLD: Strathclyde, 1972; Dundee, 1979, Cantab, 1982; London, 1982; Hon. DSc: Hull, 1977; Wales, 1984; Hon. PhD: Tel Aviv, 1971; Hebrew Univ., 1978; Weizmann Inst., 1988; Hon. DHL Bar Ilan Univ., 1983; DUniv: Surrey, 1990; Glasgow, 1997; Hon. MD Birmingham, 1992; Dr *hc:* Technion, 1995; Edinburgh, 1996. Sir Winston Churchill Award, British Technion Soc., 1989. *Address:* 8 Queen Anne Street, W1M 9LD.

See also Hon. J. F. W. de Botton.

WOLFSON OF SUNNINGDALE, Baron *cr* 1991 (Life Peer), of Trevose in the County of Cornwall; **David Wolfson,** Kt 1984; Chairman: Next plc, 1990–98; Great Universal Stores, 1996–2000; *b* 9 Nov. 1935; *s* of Charles Wolfson and Hylda Wolfson; *m* 1st, 1962, Patricia E. Rawlings (*see* Baroness Rawlings) (marr. diss. 1967); 2nd, 1967, Susan E. Davis; two *s* one *d. Educ:* Clifton Coll.; Trinity Coll., Cambridge (MA); Stanford Univ., California (MBA). Great Universal Stores, 1960–78, 1993–2000, Director, 1973–78 and 1993–2000; Secretary to Shadow Cabinet, 1978–79; Chief of Staff, Political Office, 10 Downing Street, 1979–85. Chm., Alexon Group PLC (formerly Steinberg Group PLC), 1982–86; non-executive Director: Stewart Wrightson Holdings PLC, 1985–87; Next, 1989–90; Director: Compco Hldgs plc, 1995–; Fibernet Gp plc, 2001– (Chm., 2002–). Hon. Fellow, Hughes Hall, Cambridge, 1989. Hon. FRCR 1978; Hon. FRCOG 1989. *Recreations:* golf, bridge. *Clubs:* Portland; Sunningdale; Woburn Golf; Trevose Golf (N Cornwall).

See also S. A. Wolfson.

WOLFSON, Sir Brian (Gordon), Kt 1990; Chairman: PST (International) Ltd, since 1997; Kepner Tregoe Inc., USA, since 2000 (Director, since 1980); Fruit of the Loom Inc., Chicago, since 2000 (Director, since 1992); *b* 2 Aug. 1935; *s* of Gabriel and Eve Wolfson; *m* 1958, Helen, *d* of late Lewis Grodner; one *s* one *d. Educ:* Liverpool Coll.; Liverpool Univ. Joined Granada Group, 1961, Jt Man. Dir, 1967–70; Chairman: Anglo Nordic Holdings, 1976–87; Wembley Stadium Ltd, 1986–95; Dir, Charles Ede Ltd, London, 1971–. Chairman: Trng Commn, later Trng Agency, then Nat. Trng Task Force, 1988–92; Investors in People (UK), 1992–99. First non-North American World Pres., Young Presidents' Orgn, 1979–80; Mem., NEDC, 1989–92 (Chm., Cttee on leisure, 1986–92). University of Pennsylvania: Mem. Adv. Bd, Wharton Center for Internat. Management Studies, 1980–; Bd, Joseph H. Lauder Inst., 1983–. Governor: Ashridge Management Coll., 1991– (Chm., Ashridge MBA Prog., 1988–93); NIESR, 1993–95. CIMgt (FBIM 1969, CBIM 1970; Chm., 1986–88; Vice-Pres., 1988; Verulam Medal, 1995); Fellow, Inst BE. Hon. DBA Liverpool Poly., 1989. *Recreations:* archaeological digs, making wildlife films. *Address:* 117 Chiltern Court, Baker Street, NW1 5SN.

WOLFSON, (Geoffrey) Mark; *b* 7 April 1934; *s* of late Captain V. Wolfson, OBE, VRD, RNR, and Dorothy Mary Wolfson; *m* 1965, Edna Webb (*née* Hardman); two *s. Educ:* Eton Coll.; Pembroke Coll., Cambridge (MA). Served Royal Navy, 1952–54; Cambridge, 1954–57; Teacher in Canada, 1958–59; Warden, Brathay Hall Centre, Westmorland, 1962–66; Head of Youth Services, Industrial Soc., 1966–69; Hd of Personnel, 1970–85, Dir, 1973–88, Hambros Bank. MP (C) Sevenoaks, 1979–97. PPS to Minister of State for NI, 1983–84, to Minister of State for Defence Procurement, 1984–85, to Minister of State for Armed Forces, 1987–88. Mem., NI Select Cttee, 1994–97. Officer, Cons. Backbench Employment Cttee, 1981–83. Mem., Parly Human Rights Delegn to Nicaragua, 1982, El Salvador and Baltic States, 1990. Associate Advr, Industrial Soc., 1997–98. Chm., Brathay Hall Trust, 1991–2000. *Address:* 6 Fynes Street, Westminster, SW1P 4NH.

WOLFSON, Mark; *see* Wolfson, G. M.

WOLFSON, Hon. Simon Adam; Chief Executive, Next plc, since 2001; *b* 27 Oct. 1967; *e s* of Lord Wolfson of Sunningdale, *qv. Educ:* Radley Coll.; Trinity Coll., Cambridge. Dir, 1997–, Man. Dir, 1999–2001, Next plc. *Address:* Next plc, Desford Road, Enderby, Leicester LE9 5AT. *T:* (0116) 284 2308.

WOLLHEIM, Prof. Richard Arthur, FBA 1972; Professor of Philosophy, University of California, Berkeley, since 1985; Emeritus Grote Professor in the University of London; *b* 5 May 1923; *s* of Eric Wollheim; *m* 1st, 1950, Anne, *yr d* of Lieutenant-Colonel E. G. H. Powell (marr. diss. 1967); two *s*; 2nd, 1969, Mary Day, *er d* of Robert S. Lanier, NYC; one *d. Educ:* Westminster School; Balliol College, Oxford (MA). Served in the Army, N Europe, 1942–45 (POW during Aug. 1944). University College London: Asst Lectr in Philosophy, 1949; Lectr, 1951; Reader, 1960; Hon. Fellow, 1994; Grote Prof. of Philosophy of Mind and Logic in Univ. of London, 1963–82; Prof. of Philosophy, Columbia Univ., 1982–85; Prof. of Philosophy and the Humanities, Univ. of Calif., Davis, 1989–96. Visiting Professor: Columbia Univ., 1959–60, 1970; Visva-Bharati Univ., Santiniketan, India, 1968; Univ. of Minnesota, 1972; Graduate Centre, City Univ. of NY, 1975; Univ. of California, Berkeley, 1981; Harvard Univ., 1982; Sarah Lawrence Coll., 1987; Univ. of Guelph, 1988; Washington Univ., St Louis, 1989; Claremont Coll., 1995–96; Univ. of New Mexico, 1996. Lectures: Ernest Jones, British Psychoanalytical Soc., 1969; Power, Univ. of Sydney, 1972; Leslie Stephen, Univ. of Cambridge, 1979; William James, Harvard Univ., 1982; Andrew W. Mellon, Nat. Gall., Washington, 1984; Lewin, Washington Univ., 1989; Tamblyn, Univ. of W Ontario, 1989; Cassirer, Yale Univ., 1991; Hoffmann, Dallas Mus., 1992; David A. Jones, Claremont Coll., 1995–96; Gareth Evans, Univ. of Oxford, 1996; Penrose, Tate Gallery, 1998; Werner Heisenberg, Bavarian Acad., 2001; Lindley, Univ. of Kansas, 2001. President: Aristotelian Soc., 1967–68; British Soc. of Aesthetics, 1993– (Vice-Pres., 1969–93). Mem., American Acad. of Arts and Scis, 1986. Hon. Affiliate, British Psychoanalytical Soc., 1982; Hon. Mem., San Francisco Psychoanalytic Inst., 1994. Award for Dist. Services to Psychoanalysis, Internat. Psychoanalytic Soc., 1991. *Publications:* F. H. Bradley, 1959, rev. edn 1969; Socialism and Culture, 1961; On Drawing an Object (Inaugural Lecture), 1965; Art and its Objects, 1968, 2nd edn with suppl. essays, 1980; A Family Romance (fiction), 1969; Freud, 1971; On Art and the Mind (essays and lectures), 1973; The Good Self and the Bad Self (Dawes Hicks lecture), 1976; The Sheep and the Ceremony (Leslie Stephen lecture), 1979; The Thread of Life, 1984; Painting as an Art, 1987; The Mind and its Depths (essays and lectures), 1993; On the Emotions, 1999; edited: F. H. Bradley, Ethical Studies, 1961; Hume on Religion, 1963; F. H. Bradley, Appearance and Reality, 1968; Adrian Stokes, selected writings, 1972; Freud, a collection of critical essays, 1974; J. S. Mill, Three Essays, 1975; (with Jim Hopkins) Philosophical Essays on Freud, 1982; articles in anthologies, philosophical and literary jls. *Address:* 1814 Marin Avenue, Berkeley, CA 94707, USA; 20 Ashchurch Park Villas, W12 9SP.

WOLLONGONG, Bishop of; *see* Piper, Rt Rev. R. J.

WOLMER, Viscount; William Lewis Palmer; *b* 1 Sept. 1971; *s* and *heir* of 4th Earl of Selborne, *qv. Educ:* Eton Coll.; Christ Church, Oxford. *Address:* Temple Manor, Selborne, Alton, Hants GU34 3LR.

WOLPERT, Prof. Lewis, CBE 1990; DIC, PhD; FRS 1980; FRSL; Professor of Biology as Applied to Medicine, London University, at University College London Medical School (formerly at Middlesex Hospital Medical School), since 1966; *b* 19 Oct. 1929; *s* of William and Sarah Wolpert; *m* 1961; two *s* two *d. Educ:* King Edward's Sch., Johannesburg; Univ. of Witwatersrand (BScEng); Imperial Coll., London (DIC; FIC 1996); King's Coll., London (PhD; FKC 2001). Personal Asst to Director of Building Research Inst., S African Council for Scientific and Industrial Research, 1951–52; Engineer, Israel Water Planning Dept, 1953–54; King's College, London: Asst Lectr in Zoology, 1958–60; Lectr in Zoology, 1960–64; Reader in Zoology, 1964–66; Hd of Dept of Biology as Applied to Medicine, later Dept of Anatomy and Biology as Applied to Medicine, Middlesex Hosp. Med. Sch., 1966–87. MRC: Mem. Council, 1984–88; Mem., 1982–88, Chm., 1984–88, Cell Bd; Chairman: Scientific Inf. Cttee, Royal Soc.,

1983–88; COPUS, 1994–98; Biology Concerted Action Cttee, EEC, 1988–91. President: British Soc. for Cell Biology, 1985–91; Inst. of Information Scientists, 1986–87. Lectures: Steinhaus, Univ. of California at Irvine, 1980; van der Horst, Univ. of Witwatersrand, Johannesburg, 1981; Bidder, Soc. for Experimental Biology, Leicester, 1982; Swirling, Dana-Faber, Boston, 1985; Lloyd-Roberts, RCP, 1986; Royal Instn Christmas Lectures, 1986; R. G. Williams, Univ. of Pennsylvania, 1988; Bernal, Birkbeck Coll., 1989; Radcliffe, Warwick Univ., 1990; Redfearn, Leicester, 1991; Wade, Southampton, 1991; Robb, Univ. of Auckland, 1994; Samuel Gee, RCP, 1995; Hunterian Oration, 1996; Gerald Walters Meml, Bath Univ., 1997; Medawar, Royal Soc., 1998. Presenter: Antenna, BBC2, 1987–88; A Living Hell, BBC2, 1999; interviews with scientists, Radio 3, 1981–; radio documentaries: The Dark Lady of DNA, 1989; The Virgin Fathers of the Calculus, 1991. FRSL 1999. For. Mem., Polish Acad. of Arts and Scis, 1998. Hon. MRCP, 1986. Hon. Fellow, UCL, 1995. Hon. DSc: CNAA, 1992; Leicester, 1996; Westminster, 1996; Bath, 1997. Scientific Medal, Zoological Soc., 1968; Michael Faraday Award, Royal Soc., 2000. *Publications:* A Passion for Science (with A. Richards), 1988; Triumph of the Embryo, 1991; The Unnatural Nature of Science, 1992; (with A. Richards) Passionate Minds, 1997; Principles of Development, 1998; Malignant Sadness: the anatomy of depression, 1999; articles on cell and developmental biology in scientific jls. *Recreation:* tennis. *Address:* Department of Anatomy and Developmental Biology, University College London, Gower Street, WC1E 6BT.

WOLRIGE-GORDON, Patrick; *b* 10 Aug. 1935; *s* of late Captain Robert Wolrige-Gordon, MC and Joan Wolrige-Gordon; *m* 1962, Anne, *o d* of late Peter D. Howard and Mrs Howard; one *s* two *d*. *Educ:* Eton; New College, Oxford. MP (C) Aberdeenshire East, Nov. 1958–Feb. 1974. Liveryman Worshipful Company of Wheelwrights, 1966. *Recreations:* reading, golf, music. *Address:* Ythan Lodge, Newburgh, Aberdeenshire AB41 6AD. *Club:* Royal Over-Seas League.

See also John MacLeod of MacLeod.

WOLSELEY, Sir Charles Garnet Richard Mark, 11th Bt *cr* 1628; Partner, Smiths Gore, Chartered Surveyors, 1979–87 (Associate Partner, 1974); *b* 16 June 1944; *s* of Capt. Stephen Garnet Hubert Francis Wolseley, Royal Artillery (*d* 1944, of wounds received in action), and of Pamela, *yr d* of late Capt. F. Barry and Mrs Lavinia Power, Wolseley Park, Rugeley, Staffs; *S* grandfather, Sir Edric Charles Joseph Wolseley, 10th Bt, 1954; *m* 1st, 1968, Anita Maria (marr. diss. 1984), *er d* of late H. J. Fried, Epsom, Surrey; one *s* three *d*; 2nd, 1984, Mrs Imogene Brown. *Educ:* St Bede's School, near Stafford; Ampleforth College, York. FRICS. *Recreations:* shooting, fishing, gardening, painting. *Heir: s* Stephen Garnet Hugo Charles Wolseley, *b* 2 May 1980. *Address:* Wolseley Park House, Rugeley, Staffs WS15 2TU. *T:* (01889) 582346. *Club:* Shikar.

WOLSELEY, Sir James Douglas, 13th Bt *cr* 1745 (Ire.), of Mount Wolseley, Co. Carlow; *b* 17 Sept. 1937; *s* of James Douglas Wolseley (*d* 1960), and of Olive, *d* of Carroll Walter Wofford; *S* kinsman, Sir Garnet Wolseley, 12th Bt, 1991; *m* 1st, 1965, Patricia Lynn (marr. diss. 1971), *d* of William R. Hunter; 2nd, 1984, Mary Anne, *d* of Thomas G. Brown. *Heir: kinsman* John Walter Wolseley [*b* 21 April 1938; *m* 1964, Patricia Ann Newland (marr. diss. 1978); two *s*].

WOLSTENCROFT, Alan, CB 1961; Director, 1974–87, and Chairman, 1979–84, National Counties Building Society; *b* 18 Oct. 1914; *yr s* of late Walter and Bertha Wolstencroft; *m* 1951, Ellen, *d* of late W. Tomlinson. *Educ:* Lancaster Royal Grammar Sch.; Caius Coll., Cambridge (MA 1st Cl. Classical Tripos). Assistant Principal, GPO, 1936. Served War of 1939–45: Royal Engineers (Postal Section), France and Middle East. Principal GPO, 1945; Assistant Secretary, GPO, 1949; Secretary, Independent Television Authority, 1954; General Post Office: Director of Personnel, 1955; Director of Postal Services, 1957; Director of Radio Services, 1960–64; Deputy Director General, 1964–67; Man. Dir Posts, 1967, Posts and GIRO, 1968; Adviser on Special Projects to Chm. of Post Office Corporation, 1969–70; Sec. to Post Office, 1970–73; retired. *Address:* Green Court, 161 Long Lane, Tilehurst, Reading RG3 6YW.

WOLSTENCROFT, Ven. Alan; Archdeacon of Manchester, Canon Residentiary of Manchester Cathedral, and Fellow of the College, since 1998; *b* 16 July 1937; *s* of John Wolstencroft and Jean (*née* Miller); *m* 1968, Christine Mary Hall; one *s* one *d*. *Educ:* Wellington Tech. Sch., Altrincham; St John's Coll. of Further Educn, Manchester; Cuddesdon Coll., Oxford. Nat. Service, RAF, Nat. Mountain Rescue Team, 1955–57. Trainee Manager, W. H. Smith & Co., 1957–59; Regl Wine and Spirit Manager, Bass/Charrington Co., 1959–67; ordained deacon, 1969, priest, 1970; Assistant Curate: St Thomas, Halliwell, 1969–71; All Saints, Stand, 1971–73; Vicar, St Martin, Wythenshawe, 1973–80; Asst Chaplain, Wythenshawe Hosp., 1973–91; Rural, then Area, Dean of Withington, 1978–91; Vicar: St John the Divine, Brooklands, 1980–91; St Peter, Bolton, 1991–98. Theatre Chaplain, Actors' Church Union, 1975–. *Recreations:* squash, watching football, sport, theatre, reading, wines, beers, walking. *Address:* 2 The Walled Garden, Swinton, Manchester M27 0FR. *T:* (0161) 794 2401, *Fax:* (0161) 794 2411. *Clubs:* Concord (Manchester); Bolton Wanderers FC.

WOLSTENHOLME, Sir Gordon (Ethelbert Ward), Kt 1976; OBE (mil.) 1944; MA, MB, BChir; MRCS, FRCP, FIBiol; Founder, 1988, and Life President, 1995–2001, Action in International Medicine (Chairman, 1988–95); *b* Sheffield, 28 May 1913; *m* 1st; one *s* two *d*; 2nd; two *d*. *Educ:* Repton; Corpus Christi Coll., Cambridge (Hon. Fellow, 1998); Middlesex Hosp. Med. Sch. Served with RAMC, 1940–47 (OBE); France, UK, ME and Central Mediterranean; specialist and advr in transfusion and resuscitation; OC Gen. Hosp. in Udine and Trieste; Dir, Ciba Foundn, 1949–78; Harveian Librarian, RCP, 1979–89; Fellow, Green Coll., Oxford, 1986–90. Mem., GMC, 1973–83; Chm., Genetic Manipulation Adv. Gp, 1976–78. Founder Mem. 1954, Treasurer 1955–61, Mem. Exec. Bd 1961–70, UK Cttee for WHO; Organizer and Advr, Haile Selassie I Prize Trust, 1963–74; Advr, La Trinidad Med. Centre, Caracas, 1969–78. Royal Society of Medicine: Hon. Sec. 1964–70; Pres. Library (Sci. Res) Sect., 1968–70; Chm. Working Party on Soc's Future, 1972–73; Pres., 1975–77, 1978; Zoological Society: Scientific Fellow and Vice-Pres.; Member: Finance Cttee, 1962–69; Council, 1962–66, 1967–70, 1976–80; Chm., Nuffield Inst. for Comparative Medicine, 1969–70; Chm. Governors, Inst. for Res. into Mental and Multiple Handicap, 1973–77. Founder Mem. 1950, Hon. Treasurer 1956–69, Renal Assoc. of GB; Chm. Congress Prog. Cttee, 1962–64, Mem. Finance Cttee 1968–72, Internat. Soc. for Endocrinology; Trustee and Mem. Res. Bd, Spastics' Soc., 1963–67; Founder Chm., European Soc. for Clinical Investigation, 1966–67 (Boerhaave Lectr, 1976); Mem. Council 1969–75, Sponsor 1976–, Inst. for Study of Drug Dependence; Dir, Nuffield Foundn Inquiry into Dental Educn, 1978–80; Chairman: Dental Res. Strategy Gp, 1986–89; Oral and Dental Res. Trust, 1989–96. Member: Council, Westfield Coll., London Univ., 1965–73; Planning Bd, University College at Buckingham, 1969. Chm., Anglo-Ethiopian Soc., 1967–70. Emeritus Mem. Ct of Assistants, Soc. of Apothecaries, 1988– (Mem., 1969–88; Master, 1979–80; Chm., Faculty of Hist. and Philosophy of Med. and Pharmacy, 1973–75; Visitor, 1975–78); Chm., Skin Diseases Res. Fund, 1980–85. Vis. Prof., UCSD, 1982, 1983, 1984. Dir, IRL Press Ltd, 1980–88. Trustee, Foulkes Foundn; Trustee, 1978–90, Chm. Acad. Bd, 1978–88, St George's Univ. Sch. of Med., Grenada. Mem. Bd, Dahlem Konferenzen, 1978–90. Vice-Pres., ASLIB, 1979–82. Pres., Brit. Soc. Hist. Medicine, 1983–85. Patron, FRAME, 1977–. Member, Advisory Board: Neem Nagar, India, 1997–99; Imperial Coll. Press, 1997–2000. Hon. Life Governor, Middlesex Hosp., 1938. Fellow UCL, 1991; FRSA 1979. Hon. FACP, 1975; Hon. FDSRCS 1991; Hon. Fellow: Hunterian Soc., 1975 (Orator 1976); Royal Acad. of Med. in Ireland, 1976; European Soc. for Clinical Investigation, 1979; RSocMed, 1982; Faculty of Hist. Med. Pharm., 1982. Hon. Member: Swedish Soc. of Endocrinology, 1955; Soc. of Endocrinology, 1959; Swiss Acad. of Med. Sciences, 1975; Assoc. Med. Argentina, 1977; Internat. Assoc. for Dental Res., 1984; Osler Club, 1986 (Orator, 1986); Foreign Mem., Swedish Med. Soc., 1959; Hon. For. Mem., Amer. Acad. of Arts and Scis, 1981. Hon. LLD Cambridge, 1968; Hon. DTech Brunel, 1981; Hon. MD Grenada, 1982. Linnaeus Medal, Royal Swedish Acad. Sci., 1977; Pasteur Medal, Paris, 1982; Gold Medal: Perugia Univ., 1961; (class 1A) Italian Min. of Educn, 1961. Tito Lik, 1945; Chevalier, Légion d'Honneur, 1959; Star of Ethiopia, 1966. *Publications:* (ed) Ciba Foundation vols, 1950–78; Royal College of Physicians: Portraits, vol. I (ed with David Piper), 1964, vol. II (ed with John Kerslake), 1977; (ed with Valerie Luniewska) Munk's Roll, vol. VI, 1982, vol. VII, 1984, vol. VIII, 1989; (jtly) Portrait of Irish Medicine, 1984. *Recreations:* walking, photography. *Address:* La Villiaze Lodge, Rue de la Villiaze, Forest, Guernsey GY8 0HQ. *T:* (01481) 263034.

WOLSTENHOLME, (John) Scott; His Honour Judge Wolstenholme; a Circuit Judge, since 1995; *b* 28 Nov. 1947; *s* of Donald Arthur Wolstenholme and Kaye (*née* Humphrys); *m* 1972, Lynne Harrison; three *s* one *d*. *Educ:* Roundhay Sch., Leeds; University Coll., Oxford (MA). Called to the Bar, Middle Temple, 1971; practised North Eastern Circuit, 1971–92; Chm., Industrial Tribunals, Leeds Region, 1992–95; a Recorder, 1992–95. *Recreations:* playing the drums, walking, golf, photography. *Address:* Leeds Combined Court Centre, Oxford Row, Leeds LS1 3BG.

WOLSTENHOLME, Roy; Investment Consultant, Mercury Asset Management, since 1994; *b* 1 Jan. 1936; *m* 1959, Mary R. Wolstenholme; one *s* two *d*. *Educ:* Stretford Grammar Sch.; Manchester College of Commerce. Stretford Bor. Council, 1952–61; Worcs CC, 1961–63; Worthing Bor. Council, 1963–65; Glos CC, 1965–68; Holland (Lincs) CC, 1968–74; Lincs CC, 1974–77; County Treasurer: Northumberland CC, 1977–88; Surrey CC, 1988–94. *Recreations:* music, walking, gardening. *Address:* 39 Foxhill Crescent, Camberley, Surrey GU15 1PR. *Club:* Royal Over-Seas League.

WOLSTENHOLME, Scott; *see* Wolstenholme, J. S.

WOLTERS, Gwyneth Eleanor Mary; a Commissioner of Inland Revenue, 1971–78; *b* 21 Nov. 1918; *d* of late Prof. and Mrs A. W. Wolters. *Educ:* Abbey Sch., Reading; Reading Univ.; Newnham Coll., Cambridge (Class. Tripos; Hilda Richardson Prize). Temp. Admin. Asst, Min. of Works, 1941–47; Asst Principal, 1947–49, Principal, 1949–57, Asst Sec., 1957–71, Inland Revenue. *Address:* 45 Albert Road, Caversham, Reading RG4 7AW. *T:* (0118) 947 2605.

WOLTON, Harry; QC 1982; a Recorder, since 1985; *b* 1 Jan. 1938; *s* of late Harry William Wolton and Dorothy Beatrice Wolton; *m* 1971, Julie Rosina Josephine Lovell (*née* Mason); three *s*. *Educ:* King Edward's Sch., Birmingham (Foundn Scholar); Univ. of Birmingham. Called to the Bar, Gray's Inn, 1969; authorised to sit as a Dep. High Court Judge, 1990–. Dir, Bar Mutual Insurance Fund, 1997–. *Recreations:* cattle breeding, dendrology. *Address:* The Black Venn, Edwyn Ralph, Bromyard, Herefordshire HR7 4LU. *T:* (01885) 483302; 1781 Parrott's Pointe Road, Greensboro, GA 30642, USA.

WOLTZ, Alan Edward; Chairman, London International Group, 1985–93 (Chief Executive, 1985–91); *b* 29 Feb. 1932; *s* of Robert Woltz and Rose Woltz Katz; *m* 1977, Barbara Howell; three *s* one *d*. *Educ:* Dwight Morrow High Sch., Eaglewood, NJ; Wagner Coll., Staten Is, NY. Served US Army, Korea, 1952–54. Schmid Laboratories Inc.: Exec. Vice-Pres., 1971–74; Pres., 1974–78; Pres., LRC N America, 1978–79; Man. Dir and Chief Exec., London Internat. Gp, 1979–85. *Recreations:* golf, swimming. *Address:* c/o London International Group, 35 New Bridge Street, EC4V 6BJ. *T:* (020) 7489 1977. *Club:* Metropolitan (NY).

WOLVERHAMPTON, Bishop Suffragan of, since 1993; **Rt Rev. Michael Bourke;** *b* 28 Nov. 1941; *s* of Gordon and Hilda Bourke; *m* 1968, Elizabeth Bieler; one *s* one *d*. *Educ:* Hamond's Grammar Sch., Swaffham, Norfolk; Corpus Christi Coll., Cambridge (Mod. Langs, MA); Univ. of Tübingen (Theology); Cuddesdon Theological Coll. Curate, St James', Grimsby, 1967–71; Priest-in-charge, Panshanger Conventional Dist (Local Ecumenical Project), Welwyn Garden City, 1971–78; Vicar, All Saints', Southill, Beds, 1978–86; Archdeacon of Bedford, 1986–93. Course Dir, St Albans Diocese Ministerial Trng Scheme, 1975–87. Hon. Canon, Lichfield Cathedral, 1993–. *Recreations:* astronomy, railways, European history. *Address:* 61 Richmond Road, Merridale, Wolverhampton WV3 9JH. *T:* (01902) 824503.

WOLVERTON, 7th Baron *cr* 1869; **Christopher Richard Glyn,** FRICS; *b* 5 Oct. 1938; *s* of 6th Baron Wolverton, CBE and of Audrey Margaret, *d* of late Richard Stubbs; *S* father, 1988; *m* 1st, 1961, Carolyn Jane (marr. diss. 1967), *yr d* of late Antony N. Hunter; two *d*; 2nd, 1975, Mrs Frances S. E. Stuart Black (marr. diss. 1989); 3rd, 1990, Gillian Konig (marr. diss. 1994). *Educ:* Eton. Mem., Jockey Club. *Heir: b* Hon. Andrew John Glyn [*b* 30 June 1943; *m* 1st, 1965, Celia Laws (marr. diss. 1986); one *s* one *d*; 2nd, 1986, Wendy Carlin; one *s* one *d*]. *Address:* 97 Hurlingham Road, SW6 3NL.

WOMACK, Joanna Mary; Treasurer, Cambridge University, since 1993; Fellow, Trinity Hall, Cambridge, since 1990; *b* 12 Sept. 1947; *d* of Laurence Paul Hodges and Mary Elizabeth Hodges (*née* Lyon); *m* 1971, Michael Thomas Womack; three *s*. *Educ:* James Allen's Girls' Sch., Dulwich; New Hall, Cambridge (MA 1st Cl. Hons Law). Admitted solicitor, 1972; solicitor, Herbert Smith & Co., 1972–75; New Hall, Cambridge: Coll. Lectr in Law, 1975–83; Fellow, 1975–90; Bursar, 1983–90; Emeritus Fellow, 1996; Bursar and Steward, Trinity Hall, Cambridge, 1990–93. Gen. Comr of Tax, 1987–. Dir, Cambridge Building Soc., 1994–. Gov., Long Road VI Form Coll., Cambridge, 1992–2001. *Recreations:* family life, photography, music, hill-walking. *Address:* The Old Schools, Cambridge CB2 1TS. *T:* (01223) 332209.

WOMBELL, Paul David; Director, The Photographers' Gallery, London, since 1994; *b* 8 Oct. 1948; *s* of Clifford and Katherine Wombell; *m* 1995, Tricia Coral Buckley. *Educ:* St Martin's Sch. of Art, London (BA Fine Art). Midland Gp Art Centre, 1983–86; Dir, Impressions Gall., York, 1986–94. *Publications:* Battle, Passchendale 1917, 1981; Photo Video Photography in the Age of the Computer, 1991; Sportscape, the evolution of sport photography, 2000. *Recreation:* creating a contemporary building in London appropriate for one of the most significant mediums of this century, photography. *Address:* The Photographers' Gallery, 5 Great Newport Street, WC2H 7HY. *T:* (020) 7831 1772.

WOMBWELL, Sir George (Philip Frederick), 7th Bt *cr* 1778; *b* 21 May 1949; *s* of Sir (Frederick) Philip (Alfred William) Wombwell, 6th Bt, MBE, and late Ida Elizabeth, *er d* of Frederick J. Leitch; *S* father, 1977; *m* 1974, (Hermione) Jane, *e d* of T. S. Wrightson;

one *s* one *d.* *Educ:* Repton. *Heir:* *s* Stephen Philip Henry Wombwell, *b* 12 May 1977. *Address:* Newburgh Priory, Coxwold, York YO6 4AS.

WOMERSLEY, (Denis) Keith, CBE 1974; HM Diplomatic Service, retired; *b* 21 March 1920; *s* of late Alfred Womersley, Bradford, Yorks, and late Agnes (*née* Keighley); *m* 1st, 1955, Eileen Georgina (*d* 1990), *d* of late George and Margaret Howe; 2nd, 1992, Gillian Anne, *widow* of Dr Gerard O'Donnell; three step *s* one step *d.* *Educ:* Christ's Hospital; Caius Coll., Cambridge (Hons, MA). Served War, HM Forces, 1940–46. Entered Foreign (later Diplomatic) Service, 1946; Foreign Office, 1948, Control Commn Germany, 1952; Vienna, 1955; Hong Kong, 1957, FO, 1960; Baghdad, 1962; FO, 1963; Aden, 1966; Beirut, 1967; FCO, 1969–71; Bonn, 1971–74; Counsellor, FCO, 1974–77. FRSA 1976. Gov., Christ's Hosp., 1991–. *Recreations:* violin-playing, Abbeyfield Soc. work. *Club:* Christ's Hospital (Horsham).
See also J. A. O'Donnell.

WOMERSLEY, Keith; *see* Womersley, D. K.

WOMERSLEY, Sir Peter (John Walter), 2nd Bt *cr* 1945; JP; human resources consultant; *b* 10 Nov. 1941; *s* of Capt. John Womersley (*o s* of 1st Bt; killed in action in Italy, 1944), and of Betty, *d* of Cyril Williams, Elstead, Surrey; *S* grandfather, 1961; *m* 1968, Janet Margaret Grant; two *s* two *d.* *Educ:* Aldro; Charterhouse; RMA, Sandhurst. Entered Royal Military Academy (Regular Army), 1960; Lt, King's Own Royal Border Regt, 1964, retd 1968; Personnel, then Human Resources, Manager, later Evaluation Project Manager, Human Resources, SmithKline Beecham, 1972–97. JP Steyning, 1991, Worthing and Dist, 1996. *Publication:* (with Neil Grant) Collecting Stamps, 1980. *Heir:* *s* John Gavin Grant Womersley, *b* 7 Dec. 1971. *Address:* Broomfields, 23 Goring Road, Steyning, W Sussex BN44 3GF.

WONDRAUSCH, Mary, OBE 2000; potter, since 1975; painter; *b* 17 Dec. 1923; *d* of Harold Lambert and Margaret (*née* Montgomery); *m* 1st, 1943, Kenneth Fyfe (marr. annulled); 2nd, 1946, Basil Harthan (marr. diss.); 3rd, 1954, Witold Wondrausch (marr. diss.); one *s* two *d.* *Educ:* Convent IBVM, St Mary's, Ascot; Convent FCJ, Ware, Herts; Kingston Sch. of Art. WAAF (invalided out), 1943. Flibertygibbet, waitress, cook; professional painter, exhibited, Women's Internat. Art Club, FBA, etc; art teacher, Barrow Hills Sch., 1960–75; set up pottery, Godalming, 1975, later Farncombe, then stables at Brickfields, 1984. Lectures on Continental slipware to BM, Fitzwilliam Mus., Cambridge, and Nat. Ethnographic Mus., Budapest. Pots in private and public collections incl. V&A Mus.; pottery exhibitions: Heidelberg Gall.; Craftsman Potters' Assoc.; British Craft Centre; Farnham Gall.; Amalgam; Univ. of Aberystwyth; Stoke-on-Trent Mus.; BM; Abbots Hall, Kendall; Primavera, Cambridge; Haslemere Mus. *Publications:* Mary Wondrausch on Slipware, 1986, 2nd edn 2001; contrib. articles on Continental slipware to Ceramic Rev., Antique Collector; contribs on history of food to Oxford Encyclopaedia of Food, Petits Propos Culinaires, New DNB, Oxford Symposium of Food. *Recreations:* reading, eating and drinking good food and wine, making wacky fountains from found materials, wild mushroom gathering. *Address:* The Pottery, Brickfields, Compton, Guildford, Surrey GU3 1HZ. *T:* (01483) 414097.

WONFOR, Andrea Jean; Executive Chair, Granada Creative, since 2000; *b* 31 July 1944; *d* of George Duncan and Audrey Joan Player; *m* 1st, 1967, Patrick Masefield (marr. diss. 1973); one *d*; 2nd, 1974, Geoffrey Wonfor; one *d.* *Educ:* Simon Langton Girls School, Canterbury; New Hall, Cambridge (BA). Graduate trainee, Granada Television, 1966–67; Tyne Tees Television: Researcher, 1969; Director, 1973; Head of Children's and Young People's Programmes, 1976; Dir of Progs, 1983–87; Channel Four Television: Controller, Arts and Entertainment, 1990–93; Dep. Dir of Progs, 1993; Dir of Progs, Granada TV, 1993–94; Jt Man. Dir, Granada TV, then Granada Productions, 1994–99. Man. Dir, Zenith North, 1988–90. Mem., Bd of Govs, BFI, 1989–94. FRTS 1991 (Chm., 1996–98). *Recreations:* reading, music. *Address:* Fell Pasture, Ingoe, Matfen, Northumberland NE20 0SP. *T:* (01661) 886487.

WONG Kin Chow, Michael; Hon. Mr Justice Wong; a Justice of Appeal of the High Court of Hong Kong, since 1999; *b* 16 Aug. 1936; *s* of late Wong Chong and Au Ting; *m* 1963, Mae (*née* Fong); two *s* two *d.* *Educ:* Univ. of Liverpool (LLB Hons 1961). Called to the Bar, Middle Temple, 1962; private practice, Hong Kong, 1962–65; Hong Kong Government: Crown Counsel, Legal Dept, 1966–69; Senior Crown Counsel, 1969–72; Asst Principal Crown Counsel, 1973; Presiding Officer, Labour Tribunal, 1973–75; Asst Registrar, Supreme Court, 1975–77; District Judge, 1977; a Judge of the High Court, then of the Court of First Instance of the High Court, Hong Kong, 1985–99. Chm., Release Under Supervision Bd, 1988–94. *Address:* High Court, Hong Kong. *T:* 28254429. *Clubs:* Chinese, Hong Kong, Hong Kong Jockey, Kowloon Cricket (Hong Kong).

WOO, Kwok-Hing, CBE 1996; **Hon. Mr Justice Woo;** a Justice of Appeal, Hong Kong, since 2000; *b* 13 Jan. 1946; *s* of late Woo Leung and Leung Yuk-Ling; *m* 1973, Rowena Tang; two *s* two *d.* *Educ:* Univ. of Birmingham (LLB); University College, London (LLM). Called to the Bar, Gray's Inn, 1969; QC (Hong Kong), 1987; in private practice, Hong Kong, 1970–92; a High Court Judge, then Judge of the Ct of First Instance, High Ct, 1992–2000. Chairman: Boundary and Election Commn, Hong Kong, 1993–97; Electoral Affairs Commn, 1997–2000; Commn of Inquiry on New Airport, 1998–99; Comr of Inquiry into Garley Bldg Fire, 1997. *Address:* High Court, 38 Queensway, Hong Kong. *Clubs:* Hong Kong Jockey, Hong Kong, Hong Kong Country.

WOO, Sir Leo (Joseph), Kt 1993; MBE 1984; Chairman and Chief Executive, Woo Holdings Group, since 1984; *b* 17 Oct. 1952; *s* of Gabriel Bernard Woo and Molly Woo; *m* 1973, Emilyn Cha; one *s* two *d.* *Educ:* De La Salle Oakhill Coll., Sydney. *Address:* PO Box 659, Boroko, NCD, Papua New Guinea. *T:* 3201183, *Fax:* 3201162.

WOO, Sir Po-Shing, Kt 1999; FCIArb; Founder and Consultant, Woo Kwan Lee & Lo, Solicitors & Notaries, Hong Kong, since 1973; *b* 19 April 1929; *s* of late Seaward Woo, JP, and of Ng Chiu Man; *m* 1956, Helen Woo Fong Shuet Fun; four *s* one *d.* *Educ:* La Salle Coll., Hong Kong; King's Coll., London (LLB 1956; FKC 1995). Admitted Solicitor, England and Hong Kong, 1960; Founder, Woo & Kwan, Solicitors, Hong Kong, 1963; NP 1966; merged Woo & Kwan with Lee & Lo to form Woo Kwan Lee & Lo, Solicitors & Notaries, Hong Kong, 1973; admitted as Barrister and Solicitor, Supreme Court of Victoria, Australia, 1983. Hon. Prof., Nankai Univ. of Tianjin, China, 1995. Dir of numerous companies in Hong Kong. Member: Inst. Admin. Mgt, 1975; Inst. Trade Mark Agents, 1978. Founder, Po-Shing Woo Charitable Foundn, 1994. Patron: Woo Po-Shing Gall. of Chinese Bronze, Shanghai Mus., 1996–; Sir Po-Shing Woo Auckland Observatory Bldg, 1998–. Fellow, Hong Kong Mgt Assoc., 2000. FCIArb 1966; FIMgt 1975; FInstD 1975; World Fellow, Duke of Edinburgh's Award, 1994. Hon. LLD City Univ. of Hong Kong, 1995. *Recreations:* travelling, antiques (incl. Chinese paintings, bronze and ceramic), race-horse owner (incl. Derby winner, Helene Star, 1993). *Clubs:* Royal Automobile; Hong Kong Jockey, Hong Kong, China, Aberdeen Marina (Hong Kong).

WOOD; *see* Muir Wood.

WOOD, family name of **Earl of Halifax** and **Baron Holderness.**

WOOD, Adrian John Bickersteth; Chief Economist, Department for International Development, since 2000; *b* 25 Jan. 1946; *s* of John Henry Francis Wood and Mary Eva Bickersteth Wood (*née* Ottley, now Brain); *m* 1971, Joyce Miriam Teite; two *d.* *Educ:* King's Coll., Cambridge (BA, PhD 1973); Harvard Univ. (MPA). Fellow, King's College, Cambridge, 1969–77; Asst Lectr, then Lectr, Cambridge Univ., 1973–77; Economist, then Sen. Economist, World Bank, 1977–85; Professorial Fellow, Inst. Develt Studies, Univ. of Sussex, 1985–2000. *Publications:* A Theory of Profits, 1977; A Theory of Pay, 1979; (jtly) China: long-term development issues and options, 1985; North-South Trade, Employment and Inequality, 1994; contrib. articles to learned jls. *Recreations:* music, tennis. *Address:* Department for International Development, 1 Palace Street, SW1E 5HE.

WOOD, Alan John, CBE 1971; Tan Sri (Malaysia) 1972; Executive Vice President, Malwood Global, Inc., Aiken, since 1993; *b* 16 Feb. 1925; *s* of late Lt-Col Maurice Taylor Wood, MBE; *m* 1950 (marr. diss.); one *s* one *d*; *m* 1978, Marjorie Anne (*née* Bennett). *Educ:* King Edward VI Royal Grammar Sch., Guildford, Surrey, UK; Indian Mil. Acad., Dehra Dun (grad 1945). Served Army, 1943–47; demobilised rank Captain. Various exec. and managerial positions with Borneo Motors Ltd, Singapore and Malaya, 1947–64 (Dir, 1964); Dir, Inchcape Bhd, 1968–73, Exec. Dep. Chm. 1973–74; Exec. Vice Pres., Sowers, Lewis, Wood Inc., Old Greenwich, Conn, 1975–78; Gen. Man., India, Singer Sewing Machine Co., 1979–82; Asst Dir, Delaware River Port Authority, World Trade Div., then World Trade and Econ. Develt Div., 1983–93. Pres., Malaysian Internat. Chamber of Commerce, 1968–72; Chairman: Nat. Chambers of Commerce of Malaysia, 1968 and 1972; Internat. Trade Cttee, Chamber of Commerce of Southern NJ, 1990–93. Panglima Setia Mahkota (Hon.), 1972. *Recreation:* tennis. *Address:* 806 Oak Place, Aiken, SC 29801, USA. *Clubs:* Oriental; Lake (Kuala Lumpur); Penang (Penang); Houndslake (Aiken).

WOOD, Alan John; Chief Executive, Siemens plc, since 1998; *b* 20 March 1947; *s* of Joseph Wood and Ivy Wood (*née* Larcombe); *m* 1973, Jennifer Margaret Lynn; two *d.* *Educ:* King Edward VII Sch., Sheffield; Manchester Univ. (BSc 1st Cl. Hons 1968); Harvard Univ. (MBA 1975). MIMechE 1973. Unilever plc, 1968–73; Head of Production, Crittall Construction, 1975–78; Man. Dir, Small Electric Motors, 1978–81; joined Siemens, 1981: Siemens AG, 1981–82; Production Dir, 1982–84, Man. Dir, 1984–87, Siemens Measurements Ltd; Managing Director: Electronic Components & Telecom Networks, 1987–91; Energy & Industry, 1991–98. Chairman: North West Reg., CBI, 1996–98; Nat. Mfg Council, CBI, 2000–. *Recreations:* family, swimming, opera, tennis, gardening. *Address:* Siemens plc, Oldbury RG12 8FZ. *T:* (01344) 396100.

WOOD, Sir Andrew (Marley), GCMG 2000 (KCMG 1995 CMG 1986); HM Diplomatic Service, retired; Senior Adviser, since 2000: Ernst & Young; Glaxo SmithKline; Guinness UDV; Unilever; *b* 2 Jan. 1940; *s* of Robert George Wood; *m* 1st, 1972, Melanie LeRoy Masset (*d* 1977); one *s*; 2nd, 1978, Stephanie Lee Masset; one *s* one *d.* *Educ:* Ardingly Coll.; King's Coll., Cambridge (MA 1965). Foreign Office, 1961; Moscow, 1964; Washington, 1967; FCO, 1970; seconded to Cabinet Office, 1971; First Sec., FCO, 1973; First Sec. and Hd of Chancery, Belgrade, 1976; Counsellor, 1978; Hd of Chancery, Moscow, 1979; Hd of W European Dept, 1982, Hd of Personnel Operations Dept, 1983, FCO; Ambassador to Yugoslavia, 1985–89; Minister, Washington, 1989–92; Chief Clerk, FCO, 1992–95; Ambassador to Russian Fedn and to Moldova, 1995–2000. Dir, Foreign and Colonial Trust. Chm., Britain Russia Centre; Member: Exec. Council, Russo British Chamber of Commerce; Adv. Council, British Consultants Bureau.

WOOD, Anne, CBE 2000; Founder, and Creative Director, Ragdoll Ltd, since 1984; *b* 18 Dec. 1937; *d* of Jack Savage and Eleanor Savage (*née* Thomson); *m* 1959, Barrie Wood; one *s* one *d.* *Educ:* Tudhoe Colliery Primary Sch.; Alderman Wraith Grammar Sch.; Bingley Teachers' Trng Coll. Teacher, Spennymoor Secondary Modern Sch., 1959–65; Founder: Books for Your Children mag., 1965, Ed. and publisher, 1965–95; Fedn of Children's Book Gps, 1969; Consultant, Tyne Tees TV, 1977–79; Children's Producer, Yorkshire TV (The Book Tower, Ragdolly Anna), 1979–82; Hd, Children's Progs, TV-am (originator of Rub a dub tub, Roland Rat), 1982–84. FRTS 1998. Eleanor Farjeon Award, 1969; Ronald Politzer Award, 1974; BAFTA Awards, 1979 and 1982, Prix Jeunesse, 1980, for The Book Tower; BAFTA Awards, 1996 and 1997, for Tots TV; Japon Prize, 1997 and BAFTA Award, 1998, for Teletubbies; Veuve Clicquot Business Woman of Year Award, 1998. *Recreations:* reading, gardening. *Address:* Ragdoll Ltd, Russell House, Ely Street, Stratford upon Avon, Warwickshire CV37 6LW. *T:* (01789) 404100.

WOOD, Sir Anthony John P.; *see* Page Wood.

WOOD, Anthony Richard; HM Diplomatic Service, retired; *b* 13 Feb. 1932; *s* of late Rev. T. J. Wood and of Phyllis Margaret (*née* Bold); *m* 1966, Sarah Drew (marr. diss. 1973); one *s* one *d.* *Educ:* St Edward's Sch.; Worcester Coll., Oxford (BA). HM Forces, 1950–52. British Sch. of Archaeology in Iraq, Nimrud, 1956; joined HM Foreign Service, 1957; served: Beirut, 1957; Bahrain, 1958; Paris, 1959; Benghazi, 1962; Aden, 1963; Basra, 1966; Tehran, 1970; Muscat, 1980; Counsellor, FCO, 1984–87. *Recreations:* walking, singing. *Clubs:* Army and Navy, Royal Green Jackets.

WOOD, Ven. Arnold; Warden, Community of the Epiphany, 1985–2000; Archdeacon of Cornwall and Canon Residentiary (Librarian), Truro Cathedral, 1981–88; Archdeacon and Canon Emeritus, 1988; *b* 24 Oct. 1918; *s* of Harry and Annie Wood; *m* 1945, Dorothy Charlotte Tapper (*d* 1998); two *d.* *Educ:* Holy Trinity School, Halifax; London Univ. (Dip. Economics); Open Univ. (Dip.Eur.Hum.). Commissioned, RASC, 1939–49. Legal Adviser and Man. Director, CMI Engineering Co. Ltd, 1949–63; student, Clifton Theological Coll., 1963–65; Curate, Kirkheaton, W Yorks, 1965–67; Vicar, Mount Pellon, W Yorks, 1967–73; Rector of Lanreath and Vicar of Pelynt, 1973–81; Rural Dean, West Wivelshire, dio. Truro, 1976–81. Mem., General Synod, 1985–88. Gen. Comr of Income Tax, 1977–93. *Recreations:* walking, bowls, music. *Address:* Cobblers, Quethiock, Liskeard, Cornwall PL14 3SQ. *T:* (01579) 344788. *Club:* Royal Commonwealth Society.

WOOD, Prof. Bernard Anthony, PhD, DSc; Henry R. Luce Professor of Human Origins, and Professor of Human Evolutionary Anatomy, George Washington University, since 1997; Hon. Senior Scientist, Smithsonian Institution, since 1997; *b* 17 April 1945; *s* of Anthony Wood and Joan Wood (*née* Slocombe); *m* 1st, 1965, Hazel Francis (marr. diss. 1980); one *s* one *d*; 2nd, 1982, Alison Richards; one *d.* *Educ:* King's Sch., Gloucester; Middlesex Hosp. Med. Sch., Univ. of London (BSc 1966; MB BS 1969; PhD 1975; DSc 1996). Lectr, Charing Cross Hosp. Med. Sch., 1973–74; Middlesex Hospital Medical School: Asst Lectr, 1971–73; Lectr, subseq. Sen. Lectr, 1974–78; Reader in Anatomy, 1978–82; S. A. Courtauld Prof. of Anatomy, 1982–85; Derby Prof. of Anatomy, 1985–97, and Dean, Faculty of Medicine, 1996–97, Univ. of Liverpool. Non-executive Director: Royal Liverpool and Broad Green NHS Trust, 1994–96; Liverpool HA, 1996–97. West

Meml Lecture, Univ. of Wales, Cardiff, 1996. Chairman: Science-based Archaeol. Cttee, SERC, 1992–95; Science-based Archaeol. Strategy Gp, NERC, 1995–96; President: Primate Soc., 1986–89; Anatomical Soc. of GB and Ireland, 1996–97; Vice-Pres., Royal Anthropological Inst., 1989–92. *Publications:* (ed) Food Acquisition and Processing in Primates, 1984; (ed) Major Topics in Primate and Human Evolution, 1986; Koobi Fora Research Project: hominid cranial remains, 1991; articles on palaeoanthropology, hominid palaeobiology, and human morphology in scientific jls. *Recreations:* listening to music, wood-chopping. *Address:* Department of Anthropology, George Washington University, 2110 G Street NW, Washington, DC 20052, USA. *T:* (202) 9946077.

WOOD, Prof. Bernard John, PhD; FRS 1998; Professor of Earth Sciences, University of Bristol, since 1989; *b* 10 May 1946; *s* of Sidney James Wood and Marjorie Ethel Wood; *m* 1st, 1968, Susan Brightmore (marr. diss.); two *d*; 2nd, 1982, Kristin Vala Ragnarsdottir; one *s* one *d*. *Educ:* Northern Poly. (BSc London); Univ. of Leeds (MSc); Univ. of Newcastle upon Tyne (PhD 1971). Lectr in Geol., 1973–78, Reader, 1978–79, Univ. of Manchester; Principal Scientist, Rockwell Hanford Ops, Richland, Washington, 1980–81; Prof., Northwestern Univ., 1982–89. Vis. Prof., Univ. of Chicago, 1979–80. Award, Mineralogical Soc. of America, 1984; Schlumberger Medal, Mineralogical Soc. of GB, 1991; Holmes Medal, Eur. Union of Geoscis, 1997; Murchison Medal, Geol. Soc., 1997. *Publications:* (with D. G. Fraser) Elementary Thermodynamics for Geologists, 1976; (with J. R. Holloway) Simulating the Earth, 1988. *Address:* Department of Earth Sciences, University of Bristol, Bristol BS8 1RJ. *T:* (0117) 954 5422.

WOOD, Charles; Chief Executive, London Borough of Brent, 1986–95; *b* 16 May 1950; *s* of Sir Frank Wood, KBE, CB and Lady (Olive May) Wood (*née* Wilson); *m* Carolyn Hall; three *s* two *d*. *Educ:* King's College London (BSc Hons); Polytechnic of Central London (DipTP). Engineer, GLC, 1971–76; Planner, and Dep. Dir of Housing, London Borough of Hammersmith and Fulham, 1976–82; Dir of Develt, London Borough of Brent, 1982–86. *Recreations:* walking, tennis. *Address:* Aux Deux Soeurs, St Etienne du Grès, France.

See also W. J. Wood.

WOOD, Charles Gerald, FRSL 1984; writer for films, television and the theatre, since 1962; *b* 6 Aug. 1932; *s* of John Edward Wood, actor and Catherine Mae (*née* Harris), actress; *m* 1954, Valerie Elizabeth Newman, actress; one *s* one *d*. *Educ:* King Charles I Sch., Kidderminster; Birmingham Coll. of Art. Corp., 17/21st Lancers, 1950–55; Factory worker, 1955–57; Stage Manager, advertising artist, cartoonist, scenic artist, 1957–59; Bristol Evening Post, 1959–62. Member: Drama Adv. Panel, South Western Arts, 1972–73; Council, BAFTA, 1991–93. Consultant to Nat. Film Develt Fund, 1980–82. *Wrote plays:* Prisoner and Escort, John Thomas, Spare, (Cockade), Arts Theatre, 1963; Meals on Wheels, Royal Court, 1965; Don't Make Me Laugh, Aldwych, 1966; Fill the Stage with Happy Hours, Nottingham Playhouse, Vaudeville Theatre, 1967; Dingo, Bristol Arts Centre, Royal Court, 1967; H, National Theatre, 1969; Welfare, Liverpool Everyman, 1971; Veterans, Lyceum, Edinburgh, Royal Court, 1972; Jingo, RSC, 1975; Has 'Washington' Legs?, Nat. Theatre, 1978; Red Star, RSC, 1984; Across from the Garden of Allah, Comedy, 1986; adapted Pirandello's Man, Beast and Virtue, Nat. Theatre, 1989 and The Mountain Giants, Nat. Theatre, 1993; Dumas's The Tower, Almeida, 1995. *Screenplays include:* The Knack, 1965 (Grand Prix, Cannes; Writers Guild Award for Best Comedy); Help!, 1965; How I Won the War, 1967; The Charge of the Light Brigade, 1968; The Long Day's Dying, 1969; Cuba, 1980; Wagner, 1983; Red Monarch, 1983; Puccini, 1984; Tumbledown, 1988 (Prix Italia, RAI Prize, 1988; BAFTA, Broadcasting Press Guild and RTS awards, 1989); Shooting the Hero, 1991; An Awfully Big Adventure, 1995; (with Richard Eyre) Iris, 2001; *adapted:* Bed Sitting Room, 1973. Numerous *television* plays incl. Prisoner and Escort, Drums Along the Avon, Drill Pig, A Bit of a Holiday, A Bit of an Adventure, Do As I Say, Love Lies Bleeding, Dust to Dust; creator of Gordon Maple in series, Don't Forget to Write; Company of Adventurers (series for CBC), 1986; My Family and Other Animals (series for BBC), 1987; The Settling of the Sun, 1987; Sharpe's Company, 1994; A Breed of Heroes, 1994; (with John Osborne) England My England, 1996; Sharpe's Regiment, 1996; Sharpe's Waterloo, 1997; Mute of Malice, 1997; Briefs Trooping Gaily, 1998; Monsignor Renard, 2000. Evening Standard Awards, 1963, 1973. *Publications:* plays: Cockade, 1965; Fill the Stage with Happy Hours, 1967; Dingo, 1967; H, 1970; Veterans, 1972; Has 'Washington' Legs?, 1978; Tumbledown, 1987; Man, Beast and Virtue, 1990; The Mountain Giants, 1993; (trans.) Dumas, The Tower, or Marguerite of Bourgogne, 1995. *Recreations:* military and theatrical studies; gardening. *Address:* c/o Sue Rodgers, ICM Ltd, Oxford House, 76 Oxford Street, W1D 1BS. *T:* (020) 7636 6565; *e-mail:* 101641.210@compuserve.com. *Clubs:* Royal Over-Seas League, British Playwrights' Mafia.

WOOD, Rear Adm. Christopher Lainson, CB 1991; voluntary service, London Ambulance, since 1998; *b* 9 Feb. 1936; *s* of Gordon and Eileen Wood; *m* 1962, Margot Price; two *s* one *d*. *Educ:* Pangbourne College. Seaman Officer, RN, 1954; joined submarine service, 1958; CO's qualifying course, 1966; in comd, HMS Ambush, 1966–68; JSSC, 1970; nuclear submarine training, 1971; in comd, HMS Warspite, 1971–73; Staff of FO Submarines, 1973–75; Staff of Dir, Naval Op. Requirements, 1975–77; Underwater Weapons Acceptance, 1978–81; Dep. Dir, Naval Op. Requirements, 1981–83; Dir Gen., Underwater Weapons, 1983–85; Dir Gen., Fleet Support, 1986–88; ACDS, Operational Requirements (Sea Systems), 1988–91. Dir, ALVA, 1992–96. *Recreations:* reading, fishing, sporting interests.

WOOD, Rt Rev. Clyde Maurice; *see* Queensland, North, Bishop of.

WOOD, David; actor, playwright, composer, theatrical producer and director; *b* 21 Feb. 1944; *s* of Richard Edwin Wood and Audrey Adele Wood (*née* Fincham); *m* 1975, Jacqueline Stanbury; two *d*. *Educ:* Chichester High Sch. for Boys; Worcester Coll., Oxford. BA (Hons). Acted with OUDS and ETC at Oxford; first London appearance in ETC prodn, Hang Down Your Head and Die (also co-writer), Comedy, 1964; later performances include: A Spring Song, Mermaid, 1964; Dr Faustus (OUDS), 1966; Four Degrees Over, Edinburgh Festival and Fortune, 1966 (also contrib. lyrics and sketches); repertory, 1966–69; RSC's After Haggerty, Aldwych 1970, and Criterion 1971; A Voyage Round My Father, Greenwich, 1970, Toronto, 1972; Me Times Me, tour, 1971; Mrs Warren's Profession, 1972, and revue Just the Ticket, 1973, Thorndike, Leatherhead; The Provok'd Wife, Greenwich, 1973; Jeeves, Her Majesty's, 1975; Terra Nova, Chichester, 1980. *Films include:* If . . . , 1968; Aces High, 1975; Sweet William, 1978; North Sea Hijack, 1979. *TV plays and series include:* Mad Jack, Fathers and Sons, Cheri, The Vamp, Sporting Scenes, Disraeli, The Avengers, Van der Valk, Danger UXB, Huntingtower, Enemy at the Door, Jackanory, Jim'll Fix It, When the Boat Comes In, The Brack Report, Tricky Business, Watch, Longitude. Wrote various theatre revues in collaboration with John Gould; music and lyrics, The Stiffkey Scandals of 1932, Queen's, 1967 (revived as The Prostitutes' Padre, Norwich Playhouse, 1997); with John Gould formed Whirligig Theatre, touring children's theatre company, 1979; has directed one of own plays on tour and at Sadler's Wells Theatre, annually 1979–, also nat. tours and West End productions for Clarion Productions, including The BFG, 1991–92 and 1993–94, The Witches, 1992–93 and 1996–97, Noddy, 1993–94, and More Adventures of Noddy, 1995–96; has performed David Wood Magic and Music Show in theatres all over UK, incl. Polka Theatre, Arts Theatre and Purcell Room, 1983–. Chm., Action for Children's Arts, 1998–. Formed, jointly: Verronmead Ltd, indep. TV producing co., 1983; Westwood Theatrical Productions Ltd, 1986; W2 Productions Ltd, 1995. *TV series scripts:* Chips' Comic; Chish 'n' Fips; Seeing and Doing; The Gingerbread Man; Watch; *screenplays:* Swallows and Amazons, 1974; Back Home, 1989; Tide Race, 1989; *radio play:* Swallows and Amazons, 1999. *Publications: musical plays for children:* (with Sheila Ruskin) The Owl and the Pussycat went to see . . . , 1968; (with Sheila Ruskin) Larry the Lamb in Toytown, 1969; The Plotters of Cabbage Patch Corner, 1970; Flibberty and the Penguin, 1971; The Papertown Paperchase, 1972; Hijack over Hygenia, 1973; Old Mother Hubbard, 1975; The Gingerbread Man, 1976; Old Father Time, 1976; (with Tony Hatch and Jackie Trent) Rock Nativity, 1976; Nutcracker Sweet, 1977; Mother Goose's Golden Christmas, 1977; Tickle, 1978; Babes in the Magic Wood, 1978; There Was an Old Woman . . . , 1979; Cinderella, 1979; Aladdin, 1981; (with Dave and Toni Arthur) Robin Hood, 1981; Dick Whittington and Wondercat, 1981; Meg and Mog Show, 1981; The Ideal Gnome Expedition, 1982; Jack and the Giant, 1982; The Selfish Shellfish, 1983; (with ABBA and Don Black) Abbacadabra, 1984; (with Dave and Toni Arthur) Jack the Lad, 1984; (with Peter Pontzen) Dinosaurs and all that Rubbish, 1985; The Seesaw Tree, 1986; The Old Man of Lochnagar (based on book by HRH the Prince of Wales), 1986; (with Dave and Toni Arthur) The Pied Piper, 1988; Save the Human, 1990; The BFG (based on book by Roald Dahl), 1991; The Witches (based on book by Roald Dahl), 1992; Rupert and the Green Dragon, 1993; Noddy (based on books by Enid Blyton), 1994; More Adventures of Noddy, 1995; Babe, the Sheep-Pig, 1998; The Forest Child (children's opera based on book by Richard Edwards), 1998; The Twits (based on book by Roald Dahl), 1999; David Wood Plays 1, 1999; David Wood Plays 2, 1999; Spot's Birthday Party (based on books by Eric Hill), 2000; The Lighthouse Keeper's Lunch (based on book by Ronda and David Armitage), 2000; Tom's Midnight Garden (based on book by Philippa Pearce), 2000; Fantastic Mr Fox (based on book by Roald Dahl), 2001; James and the Giant Peach (based on book by Roald Dahl), 2001; *books for children:* The Gingerbread Man, 1985; (with Geoffrey Beitz) The Operats of Rodent Garden, 1984; (with Geoffrey Beitz) The Discorats, 1985; Chish 'n' Fips, 1987; Sidney the Monster, 1988; Save the Human, 1991; The BFG: plays for children, 1993; Meg and Mog: plays for children, 1994; The Christmas Story, 1996; (with Peters Day) The Phantom Cat of the Opera, 2000; The Witches: plays for children, 2001; with Richard Fowler: Play-Theatres, 1987; Happy Birthday, Mouse, 1991 (USA 1990); Baby Bear's Buggy Ride, 1993; Pop-up Theatre (Cinderella), 1994; Bedtime Story, 1995; The Magic Show, 1995; Mole's Summer Story, 1997; Silly Spider, 1998; Mole's Winter Story, 1998; Funny Bunny, 2000; The Toy Cupboard, 2000; *book for adults:* (with Janet Grant) Theatre for Children: guide to writing, adapting, directing and acting, 1997; articles in Drama, London Drama, Stage, ArtsBusiness. *Recreations:* writing, conjuring (Assoc. Mem. of the Inner Magic Circle with Silver Star), collecting old books. *Address:* c/o Casarotto Co. Ltd, National House, 60–66 Wardour Street, W1V 4ND. *T:* (020) 7287 4450, *Fax:* (020) 7287 9128.

WOOD, Sir David (Basil) H.; *see* Hill-Wood.

WOOD, Rear-Adm. David John, CB 1998; CEng, FRAeS; defence aviation consultant; *b* 12 June 1942; *s* of John Herbert Wood and Nesta (*née* Jones); *m* 1966, Hilary Jolly; two *s* one *d*. *Educ:* St Paul's Sch.; BRNC Dartmouth; RNEC Manadon (BScEng 1965). Joined BRNC 1960; service in 892, 846, 707 Sqdns and HMS Ark Royal, 1967–73; Aircraft Dept (Navy), 1973–76; Air Engineer Officer, Lynx IFTU, 1976–77; Army Staff Course, 1978; Helicopter Procurement, MoD (PE), 1979–81; Naval Sec's Dept, MoD, 1981–84; Staff of FONAC, 1984–86; NATO Defence Coll., 1986–87; Asst Dir, EH101, MoD (PE), 1987–89; Dir, Aircraft Support Policy (Navy), 1989–91; Dir, Maritime Projects, MoD (PE), 1991–95; DG Aircraft (Navy), MoD, 1995–98. Mem. Council, RAeS, 1996–. FIMgt 1995. *Recreations:* cross-country and long distance running, choral singing. *Club:* Army and Navy.

WOOD, David Russell; His Honour Judge David Wood; a Circuit Judge, since 1995; *b* 13 Dec. 1948; *s* of Christopher Russell Wood and Muriel Wynn Wood (*née* Richardson); *m* 1979, Georgina Susan Buckle; two *s* one *d*. *Educ:* Sedbergh Sch.; Univ. of East Anglia (BA). Called to the Bar, Gray's Inn, 1973; Recorder, 1989–95. *Recreations:* country pursuits, tennis, golf, music. *Address:* Newcastle upon Tyne Crown Court, Quayside, Newcastle upon Tyne NE1 3LA. *Club:* Northern Counties (Newcastle upon Tyne).

WOOD, Maj.-Gen. Denys Broomfield, CB 1978; Independent Inquiry Inspector, 1984–93; General Commissioner for Taxes, 1986–98; *b* 2 Nov. 1923; *s* of late Percy Neville Wood and Meryl Broomfield; *m* 1948, Jennifer Nora Page (*d* 1999), *d* of late Air Cdre William Morton Page, CBE; one *s* two *d*. *Educ:* Radley; Pembroke Coll., Cambridge (MA). CEng, FIMechE. Commissioned into REME, 1944; war service in UK and Far East, 1944–47; Staff Captain, WO, 1948–49; Instructor, RMA, Sandhurst, 1949–52; Staff Coll., 1953; DAA&QMG, 11 Infantry Bde, 1955–57; OC, 10 Infantry Workshop, Malaya, 1958–60; jssc 1960; Directing Staff, Staff Coll., 1961–63; Comdr, REME, 3rd Div., 1963–65; Operational Observer, Viet Nam, 1966–67; Col GS, Staff Coll., 1967–69; idc 1970; Dir, Administrative Planning, 1971–73; Dep. Military Sec. (2), 1973–75; Dir of Army Quartering, 1975–78. Exec. Sec., 1978–82, Sec., 1982–84, CEI. Col Comdt, REME, 1978–84. Lay Mem., Law Soc. Adjudication Cttee, 1986–92. FRSA. *Recreations:* walking, gardening, reading. *Address:* Elmtree House, Hurtmore, Godalming, Surrey GU7 2RA. *T:* (01483) 416936. *Club:* Army and Navy.

WOOD, Derek Alexander, CBE 1995; QC 1978; a Recorder, since 1985; Principal, St Hugh's College, Oxford, 1991–July 2002; *b* 14 Oct. 1937; *s* of Alexander Cecil Wood and Rosetta (*née* Lelyveld); *m* 1961, Sally Teresa Clarke (marr. diss. 2001), *d* of Lady Elliott and step *d* of Sir Norman Elliott, CBE; two *d*; *m* 2001, Barbara Kaplan (*née* Spector). *Educ:* Tiffin Boys' Sch., Kingston-upon-Thames; University Coll., Oxford (MA, BCL). Called to the Bar, Middle Temple, 1964, Bencher, 1986. Department of the Environment: Mem., Adv. Gp on Commercial Property Develt, 1975–78; Mem., Property Adv. Gp, 1978–94; Mem., Working Party on New Forms of Social Ownership and Tenure in Housing, 1976; Chairman: Review of Rating of Plant and Machinery, 1991, 1997–98; Property Industry's Working Gp on Code of Practice for Commercial Leases, 1995; Standing Adv. Cttee on Trunk Road Assessment, Dept of Transport, 1987–94. Dep. Chm., Soc. of Labour Lawyers, 1978–90. Chm., Chislehurst Constituency Labour Party, 1972–76, 1979–84. Chm., Oxfordshire Community Foundn, 1995–. Mem. Council, London Bor. of Bromley, 1975–78. Fellow, CAAV, 1988; FCIArb 1993. FRSA 1992. Hon. MRICS (Hon. ARICS 1991). *Publication:* (jtly) Handbook of Arbitration Practice, 2nd edn 1993, 3rd edn 1997. *Recreation:* music. *Address:* (until July 2002) St Hugh's College, Oxford OX2 6LE; (from Aug. 2002) Falcon Chambers, Falcon Court, EC4Y 1AA. *Clubs:* Athenæum, Royal Automobile, Architecture; Kent Valuers' (Hon. Mem.).

WOOD, Dudley Ernest, CBE 1995; Secretary, Rugby Football Union, 1986–95; *b* 18 May 1930; *s* of Ernest Edward and Ethel Louise Wood; *m* 1955, Mary Christina Blake;

two *s*. *Educ:* Luton Grammar School; St Edmund Hall, Oxford (MA Modern Languages). Sen. Manager, ICI, 1954–86. Rugby Football: Oxford Blue, 1952, 1953; played for Bedford, Rosslyn Park, Waterloo, Streatham-Croydon, East Midlands; Pres., Surrey County RFU, 1983–85; Sen. Trustee, Oxford Univ. RFC, 1995–. Pres., St Edmund Hall Assoc., 1996–99. Pres., Bedfordshire CCC, 1998–; Hon. Life Mem., Squash Rackets Assoc., 1984. Hon. DArts De Montfort, 1999. *Recreations:* walking with dogs, watching cricket, after-dinner speaking and socializing. *Address:* Mead Hall, Little Walden, Saffron Walden, Essex CB10 1UX. *Clubs:* East India, Lord's Taverners.

WOOD, Eric; Finance Director (formerly Finance Officer), University of Bristol, 1979–91; *b* 22 Sept. 1931; *s* of late Herbert Francis and Eva Wood; *m* 1955, Erica Twist; three *d*. *Educ:* West Hartlepool Grammar Sch.; Blandford Grammar Sch.; St Peter's Coll., Oxford (MA). CPFA. National Service, Army, 1950–51. Finance Depts, Cheshire, Durham and Notts County Councils, 1954–65; Finance Dept, London Transport, 1965–67; Asst Treasurer, GLC, 1967–73; Dir, CIPFA, 1973–79. *Publications:* articles in prof. accountancy press. *Recreations:* skiing, squash, hill-walking, bridge. *Address:* 6 Royal York Mews, Royal York Crescent, Clifton, Bristol BS8 4LF. *T:* (0117) 946 6311.

WOOD, Francis Gordon, FIA; Deputy Chief General Manager, Prudential Assurance Co. Ltd, 1982–85; non-Executive Director, Prudential Corporation, 1985–90 (Director, 1984); *b* 30 Oct. 1924; *s* of Francis R. and Florence A. Wood; *m* 1950, Margaret Parr; two *d*. *Educ:* Alleyne's Grammar School, Stone, Staffs. ACII. Prudential Assurance Co. Ltd, 1941–85; Dir, 1981. *Recreation:* golf. *Address:* 6 Matching Lane, Bishop's Stortford, Herts CM23 2PP. *T:* (01279) 315536.

WOOD, Frank; His Honour Judge Wood; Deputy Senior Judge, Sovereign Base Areas of Akrotiri and Dhekelia, since 1995 (Resident Judge, 1986–95); *b* 10 June 1929; *s* of late Robert Wood and Marjorie Edith Park Wood (*née* Senior); *m* 1951, Diana Mae Shenton; two *s* one *d*. *Educ:* Berkhamsted; RMA Sandhurst. Called to the Bar, Lincoln's Inn, 1969. Commissioned RASC, 1949–52. Bechuanaland Protectorate Police, 1953–65 (Supt 1965), Acting Dist Comr, 1957–58, 1959–60; Crown Counsel, Bechuanaland, 1965–66, State Counsel, 1966–67; Magistrate, Seychelles, 1970, Sen. Magistrate, 1974; Puisne Judge and Justice of Appeal, Seychelles, 1977–85, Acting Chief Justice, 1982–84; Chief Justice and Justice of Appeal, Solomon Islands, 1985–86; Justice of Appeal, Vanuatu, 1985–87. Chancellor, Dio. of Seychelles, 1973–84. Mem. Council, Commonwealth Magistrates' Assoc., 1973–77. *Publication:* Sovereign Base Areas Law Reports 1960–87, 1988. *Recreations:* reading, philately. *Address:* Pooh Corner, 2 Erimi Gardens, Erimi 4630, Limassol, Cyprus; The Barn, Ewyas Harold, Hereford HR2 0JF. *Clubs:* Royal Commonwealth Society, Civil Service.

WOOD, Sir Frederick (Ambrose Stuart), Kt 1977; Hon. Life President, Croda International Ltd, since 1987 (Managing Director, 1953–85, Executive Chairman, 1960–85, non-executive Chairman, 1985–86); *b* 30 May 1926; *s* of Alfred Phillip Wood, Goole, Yorkshire, and Patras, Greece, and Charlotte Wood (*née* Barnes), Goole, Yorkshire, and Athens, Greece; *m* 1947, J. R. (Su) King; two *s* one *d*. *Educ:* Felsted Sch., Essex; Clare Coll., Cambridge. Served War, Sub-Lt (A) Observer, Fleet Air Arm, 1944–47. Trainee Manager, Croda Ltd, 1947–50; Pres., Croda Inc., New York, 1950–53. Chm., Nat. Bus Co., 1972–78. Mem., 1973–78, Chm., 1979–83, NRDC; Chm. NEB, 1981–83; Chm., British Technology Gp, 1981–83. Mem., Nationalised Industries Chms' Gp, 1976–78; Chm., British Sect., Centre Européen d'Entreprise Publique, 1976–78. Hon. LLD Hull, 1983. *Address:* Hearn Wood, The Mount, Headley, Hants GU35 8AG. *T:* (01428) 712134.

WOOD, Gillian, (Mrs R. Wood); *see* Tishler, G.

WOOD, Prof. Graham Charles, FRS 1997; FREng; Professor of Corrosion Science and Engineering, University of Manchester Institute of Science and Technology, 1972–97, now Emeritus and Visiting Professor; *b* 6 Feb. 1934; *s* of Cyril Wood and Doris Hilda Wood (*née* Strange); *m* 1959, Freda Nancy Waithman; one *s* one *d*. *Educ:* Bromley Grammar Sch., Kent; Christ's Coll., Cambridge (MA 1960, PhD 1959, ScD 1972). CChem 1969; FRSC 1969; FIM 1969; FICorr (FICorrST 1968); FIMF 1972; FREng (FEng 1990). University of Manchester Institute of Science and Technology: Lectr, 1961, Sen. Lectr, 1966; Reader in Corrosion Sci., 1970–72; Hd, Corrosion and Protection Centre, 1972–82; Vice-Principal for Acad. Develt, 1982–84; Dep. Principal, 1983; Dean, Faculty of Technol., 1987–89; Pro-Vice-Chancellor, 1992–97. Pres., ICorrST, 1978–80. Chm., Internat. Corrosion Council, 1993–96. Mem., Manchester Literary and Philosophical Soc., 1994–. Hon. DSc UMIST, 2001. Sir George Beilby Medal and Prize, Inst. of Metals, SCI and RIC, 1973; U. R. Evans Award, Instn of Corrosion Sci. and Technol., 1983; Carl Wagner Meml Award, Electrochem. Soc., 1983; Cavallaro Medal, Eur. Fedn of Corrosion, 1987; Hothersall Medal, Inst. of Metal Finishing, 1989; Griffith Medal and Prize, Inst. of Materials, 1997; Eur. Corrosion Medal, Eur. Fedn of Corrosion, 1999. *Publications:* numerous papers in Phil Trans Royal Soc., Proc. Royal Soc., Nature, Phil Mag., Corrosion Sci., Oxidation of Metals, Jl Electrochem. Soc. and Trans Inst. Metal Finishing. *Recreations:* travel, cricket, walking, reading about history of art, science and politics. *Address:* University of Manchester Institute of Science and Technology, Corrosion and Protection Centre, PO Box 88, Manchester M60 1QD. *T:* (0161) 200 4850/4851.

WOOD, (Gregory) Mark, FCA; Executive Director, Prudential PLC, since 2001; *b* 26 July 1953; *s* of William and Anne Wood; *m* 1975, Susan Dorothy Twycross-Raines; one *s* two *d*. *Educ:* Univ. of East Anglia (BA Econ). FCA 1979. Work with Price Waterhouse, Commercial Union, Barclays, BZW, British & Commonwealth; Chairman: Wagon Finance Ltd, 1991–94; Safeguard Insce Services, 1991–94; Divl Chief Exec., UK Retail Financial Services, MAI plc, 1991–94; Man. Dir, AA Insce, Financial Services and Retail, 1994–96; Chief Exec., AXA Equity & Law, 1997; Gp Chief Exec., AXA in the UK (formerly Sun Life & Provincial Hldgs), 1997–2001. Dep. Chm., ABI (Chm., Gen. Insce Cttee); Chm., Govt's Property Crime Reduction Action Team, 2000–. Trustee, NSPCC, 1999–. MSI 1986. *Recreations:* tennis, ski-ing. *Address:* Prudential PLC, Laurence Pountney Hill, EC4R 0HH. *Club:* Royal Automobile.

WOOD, Maj.-Gen. Harry Stewart, CB 1967; TD 1950; *b* 16 Sept. 1913; *e s* of late Roland and Eva M. Wood; *m* 1939, Joan Gordon, *d* of Gordon S. King; two *s* (and one *s* decd). *Educ:* Nautical Coll., Pangbourne. Civil Engineer (inc. articled trg), 1931–39. Commnd RA (TA), 1937. Served War of 1939–45: Regimental Service, Sept. 1939–June 1944; subseq. Technical Staff. Dep. Dir of Artillery, Min. of Supply (Col), 1958–60; Dep. Dir, Inspectorate of Armaments (Brig.), 1960–62; Sen. Mil. Officer, Royal Armament Research and Development Estab. (Brig.), 1962–64; Vice-President, Ordnance Board, 1964–66, President, 1966–67. Maj.-Gen. 1964; retd, 1967. Legion of Merit, degree of Legionnaire (USA), 1947. *Recreations:* home and garden, motor sport. *Address:* Brook House, Faygate, near Horsham, Sussex RH12 4SS. *T:* (01293) 851342.

WOOD, Hugh Bradshaw; composer; University Lecturer in Music, Cambridge University, and Fellow of Churchill College, Cambridge, 1977–99; *b* 27 June 1932; *s* of James Bonar Wood and Winifred Bradshaw Wood; *m* 1960, Susan McGaw; one *s* one *d* (and one *d* decd). *Educ:* Oundle Sch.; New Coll., Oxford (Major Scholar; 2nd Cl. Hons Modern History, 1954). ARCM (private study with Dr W. S. Lloyd Webber), 1955. Studied: composition with Iain Hamilton, and harmony and counterpoint with Anthony Milner, 1956–58; composition with Mátyás Seiber, 1958–60; taught at: Morley Coll., 1958–67; Royal Acad. of Music, 1962–65; Univ. of Glasgow (Cramb Res. Fellow), 1966–70; Univ. of Liverpool, 1971–75; Univ. of Leeds, 1975–76; teacher, Dartington Summer Sch. of Music, 1959–74. *Main compositions: for orchestra:* Scenes from Comus (with soprano and tenor), 1965; Concerto for Cello, 1969; Chamber Concerto, 1971; Concerto for Violin, 1972; Symphony, 1982; Concerto for Piano, 1991; Variations for Orchestra, 1997; Serenade and Elegy (for string quartet and string orch.), 1999; *chamber music:* Variations for Viola and Piano, 1958; String Quartet No 1, 1962, No 2, 1970, No 3, 1976, No 4, 1993; Piano Trio, 1984; Horn Trio, 1989; Clarinet Trio, 1997; *for voice(s) and ensembles:* Logue Songs, 1961; Song Cycle to Poems of Pablo Neruda, 1974; Cantata, 1989; *songs:* Robert Graves Songs, set no 1, 1976, set no 2, 1983, set no 3, 1985. *Recreation:* thinking about going to Greece. *Address:* 32 Woodsome Road, NW5 1RZ. *T:* (020) 7267 0318.

WOOD, Humphrey; *see* Wood, J. H. A.

WOOD, Sir Ian (Clark), Kt 1994; CBE 1982; FRSE; Chairman since 1981, and Managing Director since 1967, John Wood Group plc; Chairman, J. W. Holdings Ltd, since 1981; *b* 21 July 1942; *s* of John Wood and Margaret (*née* Clark); *m* 1970, Helen Macrae; three *s*. *Educ:* Aberdeen Univ. (BSc Psychology, First Cl. Hons 1964). Joined John Wood Group, 1964. Dir, Royal Bank of Scotland, 1988–97. Chairman: Aberdeen Beyond 2000, 1986–90; Grampian Enterprise, 1990–95. Member: Aberdeen Harbour Bd, 1972–90; Sea Fish Industry Authority, 1981–87; Offshore Industry Adv. Bd, 1988–93; Offshore Industry Export Adv. Gp, 1989–93; Bd, Oil, Gas & Petrochemical Supplies Office (formerly Oil & Gas Projects & Supplies Office), 1994– (Chm., 1997–); Bd, Scottish Develt Agency, 1984–90; Scottish Econ. Council, 1987–98; Scottish Enterprise Bd, 1995–2000 (Chm., 1997–2000); Bd, Scottish Business Forum, 1998–; Scottish Sub-Cttee, UGC, subseq. UFC, 1988–91; SHEFC, 1992–97; Nat. Trng Task Force, 1988–92; PILOT, 2000–. CIMgt (CBIM 1983); FCIB 1998; FRSE 2000. Hon. LLD Aberdeen, 1984; Hon. DBA Robert Gordon, 1998. Scottish Free Enterprise Award, 1985; (jtly) Scottish Business Achievement Award Trust Award, 1992; Corporate Elite Leadership Award, 1992; Corporate Elite World Player Award, 1996. Silver Jubilee Medal, 1977. *Recreations:* family, squash, hill walking, reading, art. *Address:* Marchmont, 42 Rubislaw Den South, Aberdeen AB15 4BB. *T:* (01224) 313625.

WOOD, James Alexander Douglas; QC 1999; a Recorder, since 2000; *b* 25 June 1952; *s* of Alexander Blyth Wood and Cynthia Mary Wood (*née* Boot); two *s* by Ros Carne; *m* 1999, Janet Allbeson. *Educ:* Haileybury Coll.; Warwick Univ. (LLB 1974). Called to the Bar, Middle Temple, 1975; criminal defence barrister specialising in civil liberties and human rights; has appeared in many leading miscarriage of justice cases, incl. both appeals of Birmingham 6, and Carl Bridgwater case; Asst Recorder, 1998–2000. *Publications:* The Right to Silence, 1989; Justice in Error, 1993; reports. *Recreations:* travel, gardening, cycling, painting. *Address:* Doughty Street Chambers, 11 Doughty Street, WC1N 2PG. *T:* (020) 7404 1313. *Club:* Blacks.

WOOD, John; actor. *Educ:* Bedford Sch.; Jesus Coll., Oxford (Pres. OUDS). Old Vic Co., 1954–56; Camino Real, Phoenix, 1957; The Making of Moo, Royal Court, 1957; Brouhaha, Aldwych, 1958; The Fantasticks, Apollo, 1961; Rosencrantz and Guildenstern are Dead, NY, 1967; Exiles, Mermaid, 1970; joined Royal Shakespeare Company, 1971; Enemies, The Man of Mode, Exiles, The Balcony, Aldwych, 1971; The Comedy of Errors, Stratford, 1972; Julius Caesar, Titus Andronicus, Stratford, 1972, Aldwych, 1973; Collaborators, Duchess, 1973; A Lesson in Blood and Roses, The Place, 1973; Sherlock Holmes, Travesties (Evening Standard Best Actor Award, 1974; Tony Award, 1976), Aldwych, 1974, NY, 1974; The Devil's Disciple, Ivanov, Aldwych, 1976; Death Trap, NY, 1978; Undiscovered Country, Richard III, Nat. Theatre, 1979; Piaf, Wyndham's, 1980; The Provok'd Wife, Nat. Theatre, 1980; Royal Shakespeare Co.: The Tempest, 1988; The Man Who Came to Dinner, The Master Builder, 1989; King Lear, 1990 (Evening Standard Best Actor Award, 1991); Love's Labours Lost, 1990; The Invention of Love, RNT, 1997, transf. Haymarket, 1998. *Television:* A Tale of Two Cities, Barnaby Rudge, 1964–65; The Victorians, 1965; The Duel, 1966. *Films:* Nicholas and Alexandra, 1971; Slaughterhouse Five, 1972; War Games, 1983; The Madness of King George, 1994; Sabrina, Richard III, Jane Eyre, 1996; The Gambler, 1997; Chocolat, 2001.

WOOD, John, CB 1989; Solicitor, Morgan Lewis & Bockius, 1997–99; *b* 11 Jan. 1931; *s* of Thomas John Wood and Rebecca Grand; *m* 1958, Jean Iris Wood; two *s*. *Educ:* King's College Sch., Wimbledon. Admitted Solicitor, 1955. Director of Public Prosecutions: Legal Assistant, 1958; Sen. Legal Asst, 1963; Asst Solicitor, 1971; Asst Director, 1977; Principal Asst Dir, 1981; Dep. Dir., 1985–87; Head of Legal Services, Crown Prosecution Service, 1986–87; Dir of Serious Fraud Office, 1987–90; DPP, Hong Kong, 1990–94; Consultant Solicitor, Denton Hall, 1995–97. Pres., Video Appeals Cttee, 1996–. *Recreations:* cricket, Rugby football, music, theatre.

WOOD, John Edwin, PhD; consultant in underwater technology, since 1990; *b* 24 July 1928; *s* of late John Stanley Wood and Alice (*née* Hardy); *m* 1953, Patricia Edith Wilson Sheppard (marr. diss. 1978); two *s* two *d*. *Educ:* Darlington Grammar Sch.; Univ. of Leeds (BSc, PhD). Joined Royal Naval Scientific Service at HM Underwater Countermeasures and Weapons Estabt, 1951; Admiralty Underwater Weapons Estabt, 1959; Head of Acoustic Research Div., 1968; Head of Sonar Dept, 1972; Admiralty Surface Weapons Establishment: Head of Weapons Dept, 1976; Head of Communications, Command and Control Dept, 1979; Chief Scientist (Royal Navy), and Director General Research (A), 1980; joined Sperry Gyroscope (subseq. British Aerospace), Bracknell, 1981; Exec. Dir, BAe, Bristol, 1984–88; Dir of Underwater Engrg, BAe Dynamics Div., 1988–90. Pres., Gp 12, Council of British Archaeology, 1984–93. *Publications:* Sun, Moon and Standing Stones, 1978, 2nd edn 1980; papers and book reviews in technical and archaeological jls. *Recreations:* archaeology, fell-walking. *Address:* 7 Pennant Hills, Bedhampton, Havant, Hants PO9 3JZ. *T:* (023) 9247 1411.

WOOD, (John) Humphrey (Askey); a Managing Director, Consolidated Gold Fields plc, 1979–89; Chairman, Vitec (formerly Vinten) Group plc, 1991–99; *b* 26 Nov. 1932; *s* of late Lt-Col Edward Askey Wood and Irene Jeanne Askey Wood; *m* 1st, 1965, Jane Holland; one *s*; 2nd, 1981, Katherine Ruth Stewart Reardon (*née* Peverley); one step *s* one step *d*. *Educ:* Abberley Hall; Winchester College; Corpus Christi College, Cambridge. MA (Mech. Scis). De Havilland Aircraft Co. Ltd, 1956; Hawker Siddeley Aviation Ltd, 1964, Dir and Gen. Manager, Manchester, 1969–76; Man. Dir, Industrial and Marine Div., Rolls-Royce Ltd, 1976–79; Chm., Amey Roadstone Corp., 1979–86. Director: Gold Fields of South Africa Ltd, 1986–89; Blue Tee Corp., 1986–89; Non-Exec. Director: Birse Gp plc, 1989–95; Albrighton plc, 1990–96 (Chm., 1993–96); Ennstone plc, 1996–98. Butten Trustee, PA Consulting Gp, 1991–97. Vice-Pres., Nat. Council of Building Material Producers, 1985–89. Mem. Council, CBI, 1983–89. *Recreations:* fly fishing, sailing, painting, gardening. *Address:* Albyn House, 239 New King's Road, SW6 4XG. *T:* (020) 7371 0042.

WOOD, Sir John (Kember), Kt 1977; MC 1944; a Judge of the High Court of Justice, Family Division, 1977–93; President, Employment Appeal Tribunal, 1988–93 (Judge, 1985–88); *b* Hong Kong, 8 Aug. 1922; *s* of John Roskruge Wood and Gladys Frances (*née* Kember); *m* 1952, Kathleen Ann Lowe; one *s* one *d*. *Educ:* Shrewsbury Sch.; Magdalene Coll., Cambridge. Served War of 1939–45: Rifle Brigade, 1941–46; ME and Italy; PoW, 1944. Magdalene Coll., 1946–48. Barrister (Lincoln's Inn), 1949, Bencher, 1977; QC 1969; a Recorder of the Crown Court, 1975–77. Vice-Chm., Parole Bd, 1987–89 (Mem. 1986–89). *Recreations:* sport, travel. *Address:* 22 Addison Avenue, Holland Park, W11 4QR. *Clubs:* Garrick, MCC; Hawks (Cambridge).

WOOD, J(ohn) Laurence; Keeper, Department of Printed Books, British Library, 1966–76; retired; *b* 27 Nov. 1911; *s* of J. A. Wood and Clara Josephine (*née* Ryan); *m* 1947, Rowena Beatrice Ross; one *s* one *d*. *Educ:* Bishop Auckland; Merton Coll., Oxford (BA); Besançon; Paris. Lecteur, Univ. of Besançon, 1934; Asst Cataloguer, British Museum, 1936; seconded to Foreign Office, 1941; Asst Keeper, British Museum, 1946; Deputy Keeper, 1959. Editor, Factotum, 1978–95. *Publications:* (trans.) The French Prisoner, Garneray, 1957; (trans.) Contours of the Middle Ages, Genicot, 1967. *Recreation:* bookbinding. *Address:* 88 Hampstead Way, NW11 7XY. *T:* (020) 8455 4395.

WOOD, John Peter; freelance gardening journalist and broadcaster; Editor, The Rose, since 1996; *b* 27 March 1925; *s* of Walter Ralph Wood and Henrietta Martin; *m* 1956, Susan Maye White; one *s* one *d*. *Educ:* Grove Park Grammar Sch.; Seale Hayne Agricultural Coll. (NDH and Dip. in Hort., of College). FIHort 1986. Served War, 1943–46. Horticultural studies, 1946–52; Amateur Gardening: Asst Editor, 1952–66; Dep. Editor, 1966–71; Editor, 1971–86; Cons. Editor, 1986–89. *Publications:* Amateur Gardening Handbook—Bulbs, 1957; Amateur Gardening Picture Book—Greenhouse Management, 1959; (jtly) The Complete Book of Roses, 1993. *Recreations:* gardening, choral singing. *Address:* 1 Charlton House Court, Charlton Marshall, Blandford, Dorset DT11 9NT. *T:* (01258) 454653.

WOOD, Joseph Neville, (Johnnie), CBE 1978; Director General, The General Council of British Shipping, 1975–78; *b* 25 October 1916; *o s* of late Robert Hind Wood and Emily Wood, Durham; *m* 1st, 1944, Elizabeth May (*d* 1959); three *d*; 2nd, 1965, Josephine Samuel (*née* Dane) (*d* 1985); 3rd, 1986, Frances Howarth (*née* Skeer). *Educ:* Johnston School, Durham; London School of Economics. Entered Civil Service (Board of Trade), 1935; Ministry of War Transport, 1940; jssc 1950; Ministry of Transport: Asst Sec., 1951; Far East Representative, 1952–55; Under-Sec., 1961; Chief of Highway Administration, 1967–68. Joined Chamber of Shipping of the UK, 1968, Dep. Dir, 1970, Dir, 1972–78. Mem., Baltic Exchange, 1968–96; Director: Finance for Shipping Ltd, 1978–82; Ship Mortgage Finance Co. Ltd, 1978–83. Mem. Chichester DC, 1979–91. Vice Pres., Shipwrecked Fishermen and Mariners Royal Benevolent Soc., 1989–2001 (Dep. Chm., 1983–89). FCIT 1976. Freeman, City of London, 1978. Officier, Ordre de Mérite Maritime, 1950. *Recreation:* gardening. *Address:* Barbers Cottage, Heyshott, Midhurst, Sussex GU29 0DE. *T:* (01730) 814282.

See also P. J. Torry.

WOOD, Leslie Walter; General Secretary, Union of Construction, Allied Trades and Technicians, 1978–85, retired; Member, TUC General Council, 1979–85; *b* 27 Nov. 1920; *s* of Walter William Wood and Alice Bertha Wood (*née* Clark); *m* 1945 Irene Gladys Emery; two *d*. *Educ:* Birmingham Central Technical Coll.; Ruskin Coll., Oxford. Apprenticed carpenter and joiner, 1935; RAF, 1939–45; Asst Workers' Sec., Cadbury's Works Council, 1948–49; full time employment in Union, 1953–85; Asst Gen. Sec., Amalgamated Soc. of Woodworkers, 1962. Mem. Council, ACAS, 1980–85. *Publication:* A Union to Build (history of Building Trades Unionism), 1979. *Recreations:* golf, swimming, bridge. *Address:* 67 Chestnut Grove, South Croydon, Surrey CR2 7LL. *T:* (020) 8657 7852.

WOOD, Mark; *see* Wood, G. M.

WOOD, Rt Rev. Mark; *see* Wood, Rt Rev. S. M.

WOOD, Mark William; Editor-in-Chief, Reuters, since 1989; *b* 28 March 1952; *s* of Joseph Hatton Drew Wood and Joyce Wood; *m* 1986, Helen Lanzer; one *s* one *d*. *Educ:* Univs of Leeds (BA Hons), Warwick (MA) and Oxford. Joined Reuters, 1976; corresp. in Vienna, 1977–78, East Berlin, 1978–81, Moscow, 1981–85; Chief Corresp., West Germany, 1985–87; Editor, Europe, 1987–89. Director: Reuters Hldgs, 1990–96; ITN, 1993– (Chm., 1998–); Chm., Reuters Television, 1992–. Chm., Library and Inf. Commn, 1999– (Mem., 1995–; Vice Chm., 1998–99); Member: Bd, Re:source, 2000–; Commonwealth Press Union, 1996– (Exec. Dir, 1998–); Carl Bertelsmann Prize Commn, 1997–. *Recreations:* opera, ski-ing. *Address:* c/o Reuters, 85 Fleet Street, EC4P 4AJ. *T:* (020) 7250 1122.

WOOD, Sir Martin (Francis), Kt 1986; OBE 1982; FRS 1987; DL; Deputy Chairman, Oxford Instruments Group plc, since 1983; Fellow, Wolfson College, Oxford, 1967–94, Hon. Fellow, 1994; *b* 19 April 1927; *s* of late Arthur Henry Wood and Katharine Mary (*née* Altham); *m* 1955, (Kathleen) Audrey, *d* of Rev. John Howard Stanfield; one *s* one *d* and one step *s* one step *d*. *Educ:* Gresham's; Trinity Coll., Cambridge (BA Engrg, MA); Imperial Coll. (RSM) (BSc); Christ Church, Oxford (MA). Nat. Service, Bevin Boy, S Wales and Derbyshire coalfields, 1945–48. Mgt Trainee, NCB, 1954–55; Sen. Res. Officer, Clarendon Lab., Oxford Univ., 1955–69; Founder, Oxford Instruments Ltd, 1959 (co. floated, 1983). Chm., Synaptica Ltd. Chm., Nat. Cttee for Superconductivity, SERC/DTI, 1987–92; Member: ABRC, 1983–89; ACOST, 1990–93; NRPB, 1991–; Council, Central Lab. of the Res. Councils, 1995–98. Co-Founder, CONECTUS, 1994. Vice-Chm. Council, FARM/Africa Ltd, 1985–; Mem. Council, Royal Soc., 1995–. Founder Trustee, Northmoor Trust (for nature conservation); Founder, Oxford Trust (for encouragement of study and application of science and technol.); Chm., Oxford Econ. Partnership. Hon. FREng (Hon. FEng 1994). Hon. Fellow UMIST, 1989. Hon. DSc: Cranfield Inst. of Technol., 1983; Nottingham, 1996; Hon. DTech Loughborough Univ. of Technol., 1985; Hon. DEng Birmingham, 1997; DUniv Open, 1999. Mullard Medal (jtly), Royal Soc., 1982. DL Oxon, 1985. Lectr, UK and abroad. *Publications:* articles in prof. jls. *Address:* c/o Oxford Instruments Group plc, Old Station Way, Eynsham, Witney, Oxon OX8 1TL.

WOOD, Rt Rev. Maurice Arthur Ponsonby, DSC 1944; MA; RNR; an Hon. Assistant Bishop, Diocese of London, since 1985; *b* 26 Aug. 1916; *o s* of late Arthur Sheppard Wood and of Jane Elspeth Dalzell Wood (*née* Piper); *m* 1st, 1947, Marjorie (*née* Pennell) (*d* 1954); two *s* one *d*; 2nd, 1955, M. Margaret (*née* Sandford); two *s* one *d*. *Educ:* Monkton Combe Sch.; Queens' Coll., Cambridge (MA); Ridley Hall, Cambridge. Deacon, 1940; priest, 1941; Curate, St Paul's, Portman Square, 1940–43. Royal Naval Chaplain, 1943–47 (still Chap. to Commando Assoc.); attached RM Commandos, 1944–46 (landed on D-Day, June 1944); Chaplain, RNR, 1971–. Rector, St Ebbe's, Oxford, 1947–52; Vicar and RD of Islington, and Pres. Islington Clerical Conf., 1952–61; Principal, Oak Hill Theological Coll., Southgate, N14, 1961–71; Prebendary of St Paul's Cathedral, 1969–71; Bishop of Norwich, 1971–85; introduced to House of Lords, 1975; Abbot of St Benet's, 1971–85; Resident Priest of Englefield, 1987–94; Hon. Asst Bishop, dio. of Oxford, 1989–95. Proctor in Convocation of Canterbury and Mem. House of Clergy and Gen. Synod of Church of England (formerly Church Assembly), 1954–85 (House of Bishops, 1971–85); Member: Archbishops' Council on Evangelism, 1972–85; Church Comrs' Houses Cttee, 1980–85; Lords and Commons Family and Child Protection Gp, 1980–. Chairman: Theological Colls Principals' Conf., 1970–71; Norfolk Water Safety Assoc, 1966–71; Norwich RSPCA, 1971–85; The Mansion Trust (India), 1984–2001; Order of Christian Unity, 1986–96 (Pres., 1996–); President: Hildenborough Hall Christian Conf. Centre, 1970–85; Christian Communications Council, 1997–; Vice-President: Crosslinks Soc.; Boys' Brigade, 1986– (Chm., Anglican Council); Trustee: Mary Whitehouse Trust, 1986–90; Riding Lights Theatre Co., 1986–; Parly Christian Fellowship Trust, 1989–; Council Member: Wycliffe Hall, Oxford, 1981–94; British Atlantic Council, 1985–88; Commonwealth Human Ecology Council, 1986–2001. Patron, Friends of St Catherine's Church, Ludham, 1994–. Governor: Monkton Combe Sch., Bath; Gresham's Sch., Holt, 1971–85; St Helen's Sch., Abingdon, 1989–; Visitor: Langley Sch., Norfolk, 1980–89; Luckley-Oakfield Sch., 1990–. Chaplain, Weavers' Co., 1986–93, Hon. Freeman, 1993. Mission work with Dr Billy Graham in Tokyo, Toronto, Virginia, Osaka, Boston, Amsterdam. Mem., House of Lords, 1975–85. *Publications:* Like a Mighty Army, 1956; Comfort in Sorrow, 1957; Your Suffering, 1959; Christian Stability, 1968; To Everyman's Door, 1968; Into the Way of Peace, 1982; This is our Faith, 1985. *Recreations:* swimming, painting, (still) supporting Norwich City FC. *Address:* Stuart Court, High Street, Kibworth Beauchamp, Leicester LE8 0LR. *T:* (0116) 279 6266; Abbot's Cottage, Horning, Norfolk NR12 8NE. *Club:* Royal Commonwealth Society.

WOOD, Michael Charles, CMG 1995; HM Diplomatic Service; Legal Adviser, Foreign and Commonwealth Office, since 1999 (Deputy Legal Adviser, 1996–99); *b* 5 Feb. 1947; *s* of late Walter Wood and of Hilda Maude Wood (*née* Forrester). *Educ:* Solihull Sch.; Trinity Hall, Cambridge (MA, LLM); Free Univ., Brussels. Called to the Bar, Gray's Inn, 1968. HM Diplomatic Service, 1970; Asst Legal Advr, FCO, 1970–81; Legal Advr, Bonn, 1981–84; Legal Counsellor, FCO, 1986–91 and 1994–96; Counsellor (Legal Advr), UK Mission to UN, NY, 1991–94. *Publications:* The Legal Status of Berlin, 1987; articles on internat. law. *Recreations:* walking, music, travel. *Address:* c/o Foreign and Commonwealth Office, King Charles Street, SW1A 2AH. *T:* (020) 7270 3052.

WOOD, Michael David; film maker, broadcaster and historian; Director, Maya Vision Ltd, since 1989; *b* Manchester, 23 July 1948; *s* of George Wood and Elsie Bell; *m* 1988, Rebecca Ysabel Dobbs; two *d*. *Educ:* Manchester GS (Foundn Scholar); Oriel Coll., Oxford (Open Scholar; BA Hons; Postgrad. Scholar). Journalist: ITV, 1973–76; BBC, 1976–79; documentary film maker: BBC, 1979–86; Central TV, 1987–91. Has made 75 documentaries for British and US TV. FRHistS 2001. Numerous awards. *Publications:* In Search of the Dark Ages, 1981, 5th edn 2001; In Search of the Trojan War, 1985, 5th edn 2001; Domesday, 1986, 4th edn 1999; Legacy, 1992, 2nd edn 1999; The Smile of Murugan, 1995, new edn 2002; In the Footsteps of Alexander the Great, 1997, 2nd edn 2001; In Search of England, 1999; Conquistadors, 2000. *Recreations:* theatre, music, reading history, walking in Greece. *Address:* Maya Vision Ltd, 43 New Oxford Street, WC1A 1BH. *T:* (020) 7836 1113.

WOOD, Rear Adm. Michael George, CBE 1995; Director General Defence Logistics (Operations and Business Development), Ministry of Defence, since 2000; Chief Naval Engineer Officer, since 2001; *b* 8 June 1948; *s* of George William Wood and late Margaret Jean Wood (*née* Cottier); *m* 1972, Judith Vivienne Tickle; one *s* two *d*. *Educ:* Plymouth Coll.; BRNC Dartmouth; RNEC Manadon. BSc, CNAA; CEng, FIMechE. Joined RN, 1968; served HM Ships Tenby, Torquay, Hermes, HM Yacht Britannia, Minerva, and ashore at RNC Greenwich, Raleigh, RNEC and staff of Flag Officer Sea Training, 1968–85; exchange with US Navy, 1986–88; SMEO to Captain Seventh Frigate Sqn, 1988–90; jsdc 1990; Naval Asst to First Sea Lord, 1991–92; rcds 1993; staff of FO Portsmouth, 1994; Captain Fleet Maintenance, Devonport, 1994–96; Sec. to Chiefs of Staff Cttee, 1996–98; Dir Naval Logistic Policy, MoD, 1998–99; Dir Gen. Fleet Support (Ops and Plans), MoD, 1999–2000. *Recreations:* family, sailing, windsurfing, ski-ing, tennis. *Address:* c/o Naval Secretary, Victory Building, HM Naval Base, Portsmouth PO1 3LS. *Club:* Army and Navy.

WOOD, Michael Mure; QC 1999; a Recorder, since 1999; *b* 22 Oct. 1953; *o s* of John Craig Mure Wood and Jean Margaret Wood; *m* 1978, Marianne Smith; one *d*. *Educ:* Rugby Sch.; Southampton Univ. (LLB Hons). Called to the Bar, Middle Temple, 1976; an Asst Recorder, 1994–99. Member: Criminal Bar Assoc. Cttee, 1992–94; Bar Human Rights Cttee, 1995–2000. *Publications:* articles for Criminal Bar Assoc. and Law Commn. *Recreations:* food, wine, travel, shooting, horses. *Address:* 23 Essex Street, WC2R 3AS. *T:* (020) 7413 0353.

WOOD, Michael Roy; MP (Lab) Batley and Spen, since 1997; *b* 3 March 1946; *s* of late Rowland W. Wood and of Laura M. Wood; *m* 1999, Christine O'Leary; two step *d*; one *s* one *d* by a previous marr. *Educ:* Nantwich and Acton Grammar Sch.; Salisbury and Wells Theol Coll. (CertTheol); Leeds Univ. (CQSW); Leeds Metropolitan Univ. (BA). Probation officer. Contested (Lab) Hexham, 1987. *Address:* (office) 9 Cross Crown Street, Cleckheaton, W Yorks BD19 3HW; House of Commons, SW1A 0AA.

WOOD, Norman, CBE 1965; Director: Manchester Ship Canal Co., 1954–64; Associated British Foods Ltd, 1964–75, retired; *b* 2 Oct. 1905; *m* 1st, 1933, Ada Entwisle (*d* 1974); two *s* (one *d* decd); 2nd, 1976, Nita Miller. *Educ:* Bolton Co. Grammar Sch.; Co-operative Coll. Mem. Cttee, Nat. Exec. Co-operative Party, and Central Board of Co-operative Union, 1934; served in Ministry of Information, NW England, 1939; Cttee Mem., Chocolate and Sugar Confectionery War-time Assoc., 1942; elected Dir, CWS, 1942–64, resigned; Mem., British Tourist and Holidays Board (later BTA), 1947–70 (Dep. Chm., 1964–67; sometime Chm., Finance and Exec. Cttee); Trustee, Plunkett Foundation, 1948 (sometime Chm., Exec. Cttee; (Vice-Pres. 1972–; Hon. Life Mem., 1994); served on: Cake and Biscuit Alliance, 1948; Wheat Commission, 1950; Mem. Nat. Cttee, Domestic Coal Consumers Council, 1950; Coronation Accommodation Cttee, 1952. Member: British and Irish Millers, 1950–64; White Fish Authority, 1959–63; Food Res. Adv. Cttee, 1961–65; DTI Japan Trade Adv. Cttee, 1971–; Exec. Mem., British Food Export Council, 1970–75. Chairman: Food and Drink Cttee, British Week, Toronto, 1967, Tokyo, 1969; Chm., ten Food and Drink Missions to Hong Kong and Japan, 1968–76; Dir, Fedn of Agricl Co-ops (UK) Ltd, 1975–; Mem., Lab Party Study Gp on Export Services and Organisation, 1974; Founder Mem., SDP, 1981; Chm., SDP Surrey Forum, 1988–92 (the last expression of the SDP); rejoined Lab. Pty. *Recreations:* walking, music. *Address:* 17 Wallace Fields, Epsom, Surrey KT17 3AX. *T:* (020) 8393 9052. *Club:* Oriental.

WOOD, Peter Anthony; Finance Director, Standard Chartered Bank, 1993–2000; *b* 4 Feb. 1943; *s* of Roger Sydney Wood and Winifred May (*née* Hine); *m* 1965, Janet

Catherine Brown; one *s* one *d. Educ:* Oldershaw Grammar Sch.; Manchester Univ. (BSc Hons Maths); Birkbeck Coll., London Univ. (MSc Stats). ACIB; FCT; FSS. NCB, 1964–66; Barclays Bank, 1966–93: Treas., 1985–91; Finance Dir, 1991–93. *Recreations:* golf, birdwatching. *Address:* Nilgiris, Mill Lane, Hildenborough, Kent TN11 9LU. *Club:* Wildernesse (Sevenoaks).

WOOD, Prof. Peter Anthony, PhD; Professor of Geography, since 1996, and Head, Department of Geography, since 1997, University College London; *b* 24 Aug. 1940; *s* of Peter Barron Wood and Mary Theresa Wood. *Educ:* Univ. of Birmingham (BSc 1961; PhD 1966). University College London: Asst Lectr, 1965–68; Lectr, 1968–82; Sen. Lectr, 1982–92; Reader, 1992–96. *Publications:* (with G. M. Lomas) Employment Location in Regional Economic Planning, 1970; (with K. E. Rosing) Character of a Conurbation: a computer atlas of the West Midlands Conurbation, 1971; (jtly) Housing and Labour Migration in England and Wales, 1974; Industrial Britain: the West Midlands, 1974; (ed with H. D. Clout) London: problems of change, 1986; (ed with P. Damesick) Regional Problems, Problem Regions and Public Policy in the United Kingdom, 1987; (with J. N. Marshall) Services and Space: aspects of urban and regional development, 1995; numerous contribs to Trans of IBG, Progress in Human Geog., Geog., Regl Studies, Envmt and Planning A, Internat. Small Business Jl, Entrepreneurship and Regl Develt, L'Espace Géographique, Tijdschrift voor Econ. En Sociaale Geografie, Papers in Regl Sci., Economia Industrial. *Recreations:* music, opera, golf. *Address:* Department of Geography, University College London, 26 Bedford Way, WC1H 0AP. *T:* (020) 7679 7562.

WOOD, Peter Edric, OBE 1994; Chairman (part-time), West Yorkshire (formerly Huddersfield), Health Authority, 1982–96; Member, Audit Commission, 1990–96; *b* 17 July 1929; *s* of Edric Wood and Ruby (*née* Revill); *m* 1952, Barbara Evans; one *s* three *d. Educ:* RAF Coll.; Bradford Univ. (MSc); Open Univ. (BA). DipEE. RAF, 1946–61. With ICI, 1961–82; Lectr (part-time), Manchester Univ., 1982–84; Sen. Teaching Fellow (part-time), Leeds Univ., 1984–89. Hon. Prof. of Mgt Scis, Lancaster Univ., 1996–. Mem. Council, Huddersfield Univ., 1996–. Chm. Trustees, Nat. Children's Centre, 1993–; Trustee, Safe Anchor Trust, 1996–. *Recreations:* reading, walking, golf. *Address:* 9 Abbey Close, Hade Edge, Holmfirth, Huddersfield HD7 1RT. *T:* (01484) 686977.

WOOD, Peter John, CBE 1996; Chairman, Esure, since 2000; Vice-Chairman: Direct Response Corporation, USA; Homesite Group Incorporated, USA; *m* (marr. diss.); five *d.* Founder, 1985, Chief Exec., 1985–96, Chm., 1996–97, Direct Line Insurance. Non-exec. Dir, The Economist Newspaper Ltd, 1998–. *Address:* Esure, The Observatory, Castlefield Road, Reigate, Surrey RH2 0SG.

WOOD, Peter (Lawrence); theatrical and television director; *b* 8 Oct. 1925; *s* of Frank Wood and Lucy Eleanor (*née* Meeson). *Educ:* Taunton School; Downing College, Cambridge. Resident Director, Arts Theatre, 1956–57; Associate Dir, NT, 1978–89. Director: The Iceman Cometh, Arts, 1958; The Birthday Party, Lyric, Hammersmith, 1958; Maria Stuart, Old Vic, 1958; As You Like It, Stratford, Canada, 1959; The Private Ear and The Public Eye, Globe, 1962, Morosco, New York, 1963; Carving a Statue, Haymarket, 1964; Poor Richard, Helen Hayes Theatre, New York, 1964; Incident at Vichy, Phœnix, 1966; The Prime of Miss Jean Brodie, Wyndham's, 1966; White Liars, and Black Comedy, 1968; In Search of Gregory (film), 1968–69; Design for Living, Los Angeles, 1971; Jumpers, Burgtheater, Vienna, 1973, Billy Rose Theatre, NY, 1974; Dear Love, Comedy, 1973; Macbeth, LA, 1975; The Mother of Us All (opera), Santa Fe, 1976; Long Day's Journey into Night, LA, 1977; Cosi Fan Tutte, Santa Fé, 1977; She Stoops to Conquer, Burgtheater, Vienna, 1978; Night and Day, Phoenix, 1978, NY, 1979; Il Seraglio, Glyndebourne, 1980, 1988; Don Giovanni, Covent Garden, 1981; Macbeth, Staatsoper, Vienna, 1982; The Real Thing, Strand, 1982; Orione (opera), Santa Fé, 1983; Orion, King's Theatre, Edinburgh, 1984; Jumpers, Aldwych, 1985; Wildfire, Phoenix, 1986; Otello, Staatsoper, Vienna, 1987; Les Liaisons Dangereuses, LA, 1988; Hapgood, Aldwych, 1988, LA, 1989; Map of the Heart, Globe, 1991; Midsummer Night's Dream, Zurich, 1992; Arcadia, Zurich, 1993; The Bed Before Yesterday, Almeida, 1994; Indian Ink, Aldwych, 1995; *Chichester:* The Silver King, 1990; Preserving Mr Panmure, 1991; She Stoops to Conquer, 1992; Arcadia, 2000; On the Razzle, 2001; *Royal Shakespeare Company:* Winter's Tale, 1960; The Devils, 1961; Hamlet, 1961; The Beggar's Opera, 1963; Co-Dir, History Cycle, 1964; Travesties, 1974 (NY, 1975); Dr Jekyll and Mr Hyde, 1991; *National Theatre:* The Master Builder, 1964; Love for Love, 1965 (also Moscow); Jumpers, 1972; The Guardsman, The Double Dealer, 1978; Undiscovered Country, 1979; The Provok'd Wife, 1980; On the Razzle, 1981; The Rivals, 1983; Rough Crossing, 1984; Love for Love, 1985; Dalliance, 1986; The Threepenny Opera, 1986; The American Clock, 1986; The Beaux Strategem, 1989; The School for Scandal, 1990; *television:* Hamlet, USA, 1970; Long Day's Journey Into Night, USA, 1973; Shakespeare, episode I, 1976; Double Dealer, 1980; The Dog it was that Died, 1988. *Recreation:* gastronomy. *Address:* The Old Barn, Batcombe, Somerset BA4 6HD.

WOOD, Philip, CB 1997; OBE 1979; Director General, Department for Transport, Local Government and the Regions (formerly Department of the Environment, Transport and the Regions), since 1997; *b* 30 June 1946; *s* of late Frank and Eleanor Wood; *m* 1971, Dilys Traylen Smith; one *s. Educ:* Queen Elizabeth Grammar Sch., Wakefield; Queen's Coll., Oxford. Entered Civil Service, 1967; Min. of Transport, 1967–70; DoE, 1970–75; a Private Sec. to the Prime Minister, 1975–79; Dept of Transport, 1979–97: Sec. to Armitage Inquiry into Lorries and the Envmt, 1980; Under Sec., 1986–95; seconded to BRB, 1986–88; Dep. Sec., 1995–97. *Address:* Department for Transport, Local Government and the Regions, Eland House, Bressenden Place, SW1E 5DU.

WOOD, (René) Victor; Director: Sun Life Corp. plc, 1986–96; Wemyss Development Co. Ltd, since 1982; *b* 4 Oct. 1925; *e s* of late Frederick Wood and Jeanne Wood (*née* Raskin); *m* 1950, Helen Morag, *o d* of late Dr David S. Stewart. *Educ:* Jesus Coll., Oxford (BA). FFA. Chief Exec., 1969–79, Chm. 1974–79, Hill Samuel Insurance and Shipping Holdings Ltd; Chm., Lifeguard Assurance, 1976–84. Director: Haslemere Estates, 1976–86; Coalite Gp, 1977–89; Chandros Insce Co., 1979–89; Colbourne Insce Co., 1980–90; Criterion Insce Co., 1984–90; Scottinvest SA, 1985–95; Wemyss Hotels France SA, 1985–95; Les Résidences du Colombier SA, 1985–93; Domaine de Rimauresq SARL, 1985–; Worldwide and General Investment Co., 1992–. Vice-Pres., British Insurance Brokers' Assoc., 1981–84. *Publications:* (with Michael Pilch): Pension Schemes, 1960; New Trends in Pensions, 1964; Pension Scheme Practice, 1967; Company Pension Schemes, 1971; Managing Pension Schemes, 1974; Pension Schemes, 1979. *Address:* Little Woodbury, Newchapel, near Lingfield, Surrey RH7 6HR. *T:* (01342) 832054.

WOOD, Prof. Richard Dean, PhD; FRS 1997; Richard Cyert Professor of Molecular Oncology and Director, Molecular and Cellular Oncology Program, University of Pittsburgh Cancer Institute, since 2001; *b* 3 June 1955; *s* of Robert Dean Wood and Maxine Louise (*née* Hargis); *m* 1975, Enid Alison Vaag. *Educ:* Farmington High Sch., New Mexico; Westminster Coll., Salt Lake City (BS 1977); Univ. of Calif, Berkeley (PhD 1981). Grad. Fellow, NSF, 1977–80; Postdoctoral Fellow, Yale Univ., 1982–85; Imperial Cancer Research Fund: Postdoctoral Fellow, 1985–88; Res. Scientist, 1988–92; Sen. Scientist, 1992–95; Principal Scientist, 1995–2001. Hon. Prof., UCL, 1998. Mem., EMBO, 1998. Trustee, Marie Curie Cancer Care, 2000–01 (Chm., Scientific Cttee, 2000–01). Meyenburg Award for Cancer Res., 1998; Westminster Coll. Alumni Award, 1999. *Publications:* papers in scientific res. jls. *Recreations:* playing bass, jazz, gramophone recordings. *Address:* University of Pittsburgh Cancer Institute, S-867 Scaife Hall, Box 100, 3550 Terrace Street, Pittsburgh, PA 15261, USA.

WOOD, Prof. Richard Frederick Marshall, RD 1976; MD; FRCSG, FRCS, FRCSE, FMedSci; Professor of Surgery, University of Sheffield, and Hon. Consultant Surgeon, Sheffield Teaching Hospitals (formerly Northern General Hospital) NHS Trust, since 1994; *b* 6 Jan. 1943; *s* of Sir Henry Peart Wood, CBE; *m* 1968, Christine Crawford Smith Jamieson; two *s. Educ:* Glasgow Acad.; Univ. of Glasgow (MB ChB 1967; MD 1976); MA Oxon 1981. FRCS 1972; FRCSG 1972; FRCSE 2001. Surgeon Lt-Comdr, RNR, 1973–87. Jun. surgical appts at Western Infirmary, Glasgow, 1967–74; Lectr and Sen. Lectr in Surgery, Univ. of Leicester, 1974–81; Hon. Consultant Surgeon, Leics AHA, 1977–81; Clinical Reader in Surgery and Fellow of Green Coll., Oxford Univ., and Hon. Consultant Surgeon, Oxford AHA, 1981–84; Prof. of Surgery, St Bartholomew's Hosp. Med. Coll., Univ. of London, and Hon. Consultant Surgeon, City and Hackney Health Dist, 1984–94. Vis. Fellow, Peter Bent Brigham Hosp., Boston, 1980; Hunterian Prof., RCS, 1985. Mem., Management Cttee, UK Transplant Service, 1980–89. Sec., Surgical Res. Soc., 1987–90; Vice-Pres., Transplantation Soc., 1998–2000 (Sec. and Cllr, 1986–96); Founding Pres., Sect. of Transplantation, RSM, 1993–95. Fellow, Assoc. of Surgeons of GB; Mem., European Surgical Assoc., 1998; Founder FMedSci 1998. Member Editorial Board: British Jl of Surgery, 1984–89; Transplantation, 1982–; Transplant International, 1998. *Publications:* Renal Transplantation: a clinical handbook, 1983; Surgical Aspects of Haemodialysis, 1983; Fundamental Anatomy for Operative General Surgery, 1989; (jtly) Small Bowel Transplantation, 1994; papers and chapters in textbooks on transplantation, and vascular surgery. *Recreations:* music, sailing. *Address:* Clinical Sciences Building, Northern General Hospital, Herries Road, Sheffield S5 7AU.

WOOD, Rt Rev. Richard James; Hon. Assistant Bishop of York, 1985–99; *b* 25 Aug. 1920; *s* of Alexander and Irene Wood; *m* 1st, 1946, Elsa Magdalena de Beer (*d* 1969); one *s* one *d* (twins); 2nd, 1972, Cathleen Anne Roark; two *d. Educ:* Oldham Hulme Grammar School; Regent St Polytechnic; Wells Theological Coll. Electrical Officer, RAF, then with Ceylon Fire Insurance Assoc. Curate, St Mary's, Calne, 1952–55; Curate, St Mark's Cathedral, George, S Africa, 1955–58; Rector, Christ Church, Beaufort West, 1958–62; Vicar of St Andrew's, Riversdale, 1962–65; Chaplain, S African Defence Force, 1965–68; Asst, St Alban's, E London, 1968; Rector of St John's, Fort Beaufort, 1969–71; Rector of Keetmanshoop, dio. Damaraland, 1971; Priest-in-Charge of Grace Church and St Michael's, Windhoek and Canon of St George's Cathedral, 1972; Vicar Gen. and Suffragan Bishop of Damaraland, 1973–75; expelled by S Africa, 1975; Hon. Asst Bishop of Damaraland, 1976–; Sec. to The Africa Bureau, 1977; Priest-in-Charge of St Mary, Lowgate, Hull, Chaplain to Hull Coll. of Higher Education and Hon. Asst Bishop of York, 1978–79; at St Mark's Theolog. Coll., Dar es Salaam, 1979–83; Interim Rector: St Matthew's, Wheeling, W Virginia, 1983–84; Trinity, Martinsburg, W Virginia, 1984–85. Hon. Life Mem., Hull Univ. Student Union. *Recreations:* general home interests. *Address:* 3 Plough Steep, Itchen Abbas, Winchester SO21 1BQ. *T:* (01962) 779400.

WOOD, Prof. Robert Anderson, FRCSE, FRCPE, FRCPGlas, FRCPsych; Postgraduate Dean, and Professor in Clinical Medicine, University of Aberdeen Medical School, 1992–99; *b* 26 May 1939; *s* of late Dr John Fraser Anderson Wood and Janet Meikle Wood (*née* Hall); *m* 1966, Dr Sheila Margaret Pirie; one *s* three *d. Educ:* Edinburgh Academy; Univ. of Edinburgh (BSc Hons, MB ChB). FRCPE 1976; FRCSE 1994; FRCPGlas 1997; FRCPsych 1999. House Officer, Royal Infirmary, Edinburgh, 1963–64, Asst Lectr, Univ. of Edinburgh, 1964–65; Registrar and Sen. Registrar in Medicine, Dundee Teaching Hosps, 1965–69; Lectr in Therapeutics, Univ. of Aberdeen, 1969–72; Sen. Lectr in Therapeutics, 1972–92, Dep. Dir, Postgrad. Med. Educn, 1986–92, Univ. of Dundee; Consultant Physician, Perth Royal Infirmary, 1972–92. Mem., Criminal Injuries Compensation Appeals Panel, 2000–. Mem. Council, 1990–92, Dean, 1992–95, Treas., 1999–, RCPE. Mem. Council, Med. and Dental Defence Union of Scotland, 1992– (Mem. Mgt Cttee, 1997–). *Publications:* papers on clinical pharmacology and medical education. *Recreations:* golf, sheep-husbandry. *Address:* Ballomill House, Abernethy, Perthshire PH2 9LD. *T:* (01738) 850201. *Clubs:* Royal & Ancient Golf (St Andrews); Craigie Hill Golf (Captain, 1999–2001) (Perth).

WOOD, Air Vice-Marshal Robert Henry, OBE 1977; *b* 24 Jan. 1936; *s* of Jack Cyril Wood and May Doris Wood; *m* 1957, Amy Cameron Wright; one *s* two *d. Educ:* Maldon Grammar School; cfs, psc, ndc, rcds. Commnd RAF, 1956; served Nos 617 and 88 Sqns, 1957–63; CFS, 1965–67; No 44 Sqn, 1967–69; attended Indian Staff Coll., 1970; MA to COS Far East Command, Singapore, 1970–71; PSO to Air Sec., 1972; NDC, Latimer, 1973; OC 51 Sqn, 1974; MoD Policy and Plans Dept, 1977; OC RAF Cranwell, 1978; OC RAF Linton-on-Ouse, 1979; Gp Capt. Flying Trng, HQ RAFSC, 1981–83; Dir Personal Services 1 (RAF), 1983–85; RCDS, 1985; Dep. Comdt, RAF Staff Coll., Bracknell, 1986; AOC and Comdt, RAF Coll., Cranwell, 1987–89; retd 1990. Director: Airways Flight Trng, 1992; British Red Cross, Leicestershire, 1993–96. *Recreations:* golf, music. *Clubs:* Royal Air Force; Luffenham Heath Golf.

WOOD, Robert Noel; psychotherapist; *b* 24 Dec. 1934; *s* of Ernest Clement Wood, CIE and Lucy Eileen Wood; *m* 1962, Sarah Child (marr. diss. 1981); one *s* one *d. Educ:* Sherborne Sch.; New Coll., Oxford (BA Hons PPE); LSE (Rockefeller Student; Certif. in Internat. Studies). Nat. Service Commn, RHA, 1953–55 (Best Cadet, Mons OCS). Dep. Res. Dir, Internat. Div., Economist Intelligence Unit Ltd, 1959–65; Inst. of Econs and Statistics, Oxford, 1965–70; Sen. Economist, Min. of Econ. Affairs and Develt Planning, Tanzania, 1966–69; Econ. Advr, ODM, 1970; Dir of Studies, Overseas Develt Inst., 1970–74; Adviser to House of Commons Select Cttee on Overseas Develt, 1973–74; Dir, Overseas Develt Inst., 1974–82. Jungian analysis, 1982–90; full Mem., Foundn for Psychotherapy and Counselling. Chm., Friends of the Union Chapel, 1983–87; Mem., Religious Soc. of Friends (Quakers), 1982–. Gov., Quintin Kynaston Sch., 1974–86. *Publications:* contrib. Bull. Oxford Inst. of Econs and Statistics, ODI Rev. *Recreations:* Victorian artists, listening to music, singing, swimming, walking, Arsenal football club, poetry, Jung. *Address:* 19 Baalbec Road, N5 1QN. *T:* (020) 7226 4775.

WOOD, Roderic Lionel James; QC 1993; a Recorder, since 1997; *b* 8 March 1951; *s* of Lionel James Wood and Marjorie Wood (*née* Thompson). *Educ:* Nottingham High Sch.; Lincoln Coll., Oxford. Called to the Bar, Middle Temple, 1974. Member: Cttee, Family Law Bar Assoc., 1988–; Family Div. Sub-Cttee, Supreme Court Rules Cttee, 1989–95; Bar Council, 1993–95; Professional Conduct Cttee of the Bar, 1993–2000 (Vice-Chm., 1997–98; Chm., 1999–2000); Legal Aid and Fees Cttee, Gen. Council of the Bar, 1995–98 (Vice-Chm., Family, 1998); Court of Appeal (Civil Div.) User Cttee, 1995–. Jt Chm., Barristers/Clerks Liaison Cttee, 1994–95. Mem., Editl Bd, Longman Practitioner's Child Law Bull., 1993–94. *Recreations:* music, theatre, travel. *Address:* 1 King's Bench Walk, Temple, EC4Y 7DB. *T:* (020) 7583 6266.

WOOD, Roger Nicholas Brownlow; Director, Centrica plc, since 1996; Managing Director: British Gas Services Ltd, since 1996; Automobile Association, since 2001; *b* 21 July 1942; *s* of Reginald Laurence Charles Wood and Jean Olive Wood; *m* 1966, Julia Ellen Mallows; two *d*. *Educ:* Sherborne Sch.; Grad. Sch. of Management, Northwestern Univ., USA. With ICL, 1962–89 (Dir, ICL (UK) Ltd, 1987–89); Man. Dir, STC Telecoms Ltd, 1989–91; Gp Vice Pres., NT Europe SA, 1991–93; Man. Dir, Matra Marconi Space UK Ltd, 1993–96. Director: Northern Telecom UK Ltd, 1991–93; Radiotronica Espagna Spa, 1991–93; MMS NV, 1993–96. Member: Parly Space Cttee, 1993–96; UK Industry Space Cttee, 1993–96. FBCS 1991; FIMgt 1984; FInstD 1990. *Recreations:* music, Provence, aviation, ski-ing. *Address:* 20 Whitfield Place, W1P 5SB. *Club:* Molesey Boat.

WOOD, Rt Rev. Roland Arthur; Rector, St James' Cathedral, and Dean of the Diocese of Athabasca, 1993–98; Bishop of Saskatoon, 1981–93; *b* 1 Jan. 1933; *s* of Cyril Arthur Wood and Evelyn Mae Wood (*née* Cave); *m* 1959, Elizabeth Nora (*née* Deacon); one *s* two *d*. *Educ:* Bishop's Univ., Lennoxville, Quebec (BA 1956, LST 1958). Deacon, May 1958, priest. Dec. 1958; Asst Curate, St Matthew's, Winnipeg, 1958–60; Rector, Christ Church, Selkirk, 1960–64; Assistant Priest, St John's Cathedral, Saskatoon, 1964–67; Rector, Holy Trinity Church, Yorkton, 1967–71; Dean, St John's Cathedral, Saskatoon, 1971–81. Hon. DD, Coll. of Emmanuel and St Chad, Saskatoon, 1979. *Recreations:* model railroading, camping, painting, refurbishing old furniture.

WOOD, Prof. Ronald Karslake Starr, FRS 1976; Senior Research Fellow, and Emeritus Professor, Imperial College, University of London, since 1986 (Professor of Plant Pathology, 1964–86); *b* 8 April 1919; *s* of Percival Thomas Evans Wood and Florence Dix Starr; *m* 1947, Marjorie Schofield; one *s* one *d*. *Educ:* Ferndale Grammar Sch.; Imperial College. Royal Scholar, 1937; Forbes Medal, 1941; Huxley Medal, 1950. Research Asst to Prof. W. Brown, 1941; Directorate of Aircraft Equipment, Min. of Aircraft Production, 1942; London University: Lectr, Imperial Coll., 1947; Reader in Plant Pathology, 1955; Head of Dept of Pure and Applied Biol., Imperial Coll., 1981–84. Commonwealth Fund Fellow, 1950; Research Fellow, Connecticut Agric. Experiment Stn, 1957. Mem. Council, British Mycological Soc., 1948; Sec., Assoc. of Applied Biologists; Mem., 1949, Chm., 1987–91, Biological Council; Mem., Parly and Scientific Cttee; Consultant, Nat. Fedn of Fruit and Potato Trades, 1955; Mem. Council, Inst. of Biology, 1956 (Vice-Pres., 1991–); Chm., Plant Pathology Cttee, British Mycological Soc.; Mem. Governing Body, Nat. Fruit and Cider Inst., Barnes Memorial Lectr, 1962; Sec., First Internat. Congress of Plant Pathology, 1965; Hon. Pres., 7th Internat. Congress of Plant Pathology, 1998. Mem. Governing Body: East Malling Research Stn, 1966 (Vice-Chm.); Inst. for Horticultural Res., 1987; Pres., Internat. Soc. for Plant Pathology, 1968 (Hon. Mem., 1988); Mem., Nat. Cttee for Biology, 1978; Chm., British Nat. Sub-Cttee for Botany, 1978; Dean, RCS, 1975–78; Founder Pres. and Hon. Mem., British Soc. for Plant Pathol., 1987. Scientific Dir, NATO Advanced Study Institute, Pugnochiuso, 1970, Sardinia, 1975, Cape Sounion, 1980; Consultant, FAO/UNDP, India, 1976. Fellow, Amer. Phytopathological Soc., 1972; Corres. Mem., Deutsche Phytomedizinische Gesellschaft, 1973. Otto-Appel-Denkmünster, 1978. Thurburn Fellow, Univ. of Sydney, 1979; Sir C. V. Raman Prof., Univ. of Madras, 1980; Regents' Lectr, Univ. of California, 1981. *Publications:* Physiological Plant Pathology, 1967; (ed) Phytotoxins in Plant Diseases, 1972; (ed) Specifity in Plant Diseases, 1976; (ed) Active Defence Mechanisms in Plants, 1981; (ed) Plant Diseases: infection, damage and loss, 1984; numerous papers in Annals of Applied Biology, Annals of Botany, Phytopathology, Trans British Mycological Soc. *Recreation:* gardening. *Address:* Pyrford Woods, Pyrford, near Woking, Surrey GU22 8QL. *T:* (01932) 343827, *Fax:* (020) 7584 2056; *e-mail:* r.carpenter@ic.ac.uk.

WOOD, Maj.-Gen. Roy; Chairman, Geo-UK Ltd, since 1995; *b* 14 May 1940; *s* of Alec and Lucy Maud Wood; *m* 1963, Susan Margaret Croxford; two *s*. *Educ:* Farnham Grammar Sch.; Welbeck College; RMA; Cambridge Univ. (MA); University College London (MSc 1971). FRICS; FRGS. Commissioned RE 1960; Mapping Surveys, Sarawak, Sierra Leone and Sabah, 1964–70; Instructor, Sch. of Military Survey, 1972–75; MoD, 1975–77; OC 14 Topo. Sqn, BAOR, 1977–79; CO Mapping and Charting Estabt, 1979–81; Defense Mapping Agency, USA, 1981–83; MoD, 1984; Comdr, 42 Survey Engr Gp, 1985–87; Dir, Military Survey, 1987–90; Dir Gen., Military Survey, MoD, 1990–94. Col Comdt, RE, 1994–; Hon. Col, 135 Indep. Topographic Sqn RE (V), 1994–99. Pres., Photogrammetric Soc., 1993–95; Chairman: Assoc. for Geographic Information, 1996–97; RE Assoc., 2000–. *Publications:* articles on surveying and mapping in professional and technical jls. *Recreations:* orienteering, hill walking, travel. *Club:* Geographical.

WOOD, Sir Russell (Dillon), KCVO 1985 (CVO 1979; MVO 1975); VRD 1964; Lt-Comdr, RNR; Deputy Treasurer to the Queen, 1969–85; an Extra Gentleman Usher to the Queen, since 1986; *b* 16 May 1922; *s* of William G. S. Wood, Whitstable, Kent, and Alice Wood; *m* 1948, Jean Violet Yelwa Davidson, *d* of late Alan S. Davidson, Lenham, Kent; one *s* three *d*. *Educ:* King's Sch., Canterbury. Fleet Air Arm Pilot, 1940–46 (despatches twice). Qual. as Chartered Accountant, 1951; financial management career with major public companies, 1951–68. *Recreations:* private flying, sailing, shooting. *Address:* The Old Forge, Dunwich, Suffolk IP17 3DU. *T:* (01728) 648595. *Clubs:* Army and Navy; East Anglian Flying, Aldeburgh Yacht.

WOOD, Rt Rev. (Stanley) Mark; Bishop Suffragan of Ludlow, 1981–87; *b* 21 May 1919; *s* of Arthur Mark and Jane Wood; *m* 1947, Winifred Ruth, *d* of Edward James Toase; three *s* two *d*. *Educ:* Pontypridd County School; University College, Cardiff (BA 2nd cl. Greek and Latin); College of the Resurrection, Mirfield. Curate at St Mary's, Cardiff Docks, 1942–45; Curate, Sophiatown Mission, Johannesburg, 1945–47; Rector of Bloemhof, Transvaal, 1947–50; Priest in charge of St Cyprian's Mission, Johannesburg, 1950–55; Rector of Marandellas, Rhodesia, 1955–65; Dean of Salisbury, Rhodesia, 1965–70; Bishop of Matabeleland, 1971–77; Asst Bishop of Hereford, 1977–81; Archdeacon of Ludlow, 1982–83. *Address:* College of St Barnabas, Lingfield, Surrey RH7 6NJ. *T:* (01342) 871556; *e-mail:* markwood@talk21.com.

WOOD, Terence Courtney, CMG 1989; HM Diplomatic Service, retired; Ambassador to Austria, 1992–96; *b* 6 Sept. 1936; *s* of Courtney and Alice Wood; *m* 1st, 1962, Kathleen Mary Jones (marr. diss. 1981); one *s* one *d*; 2nd, 1982, Diana Humphreys-Roberts. *Educ:* King Edward VI Sch., Chelmsford; Trinity Coll., Cambridge. BA Hons 1960. RA, 1955–57 (2nd Lieut). Information Officer, FBI (later CBI), 1963–67; entered HM Diplomatic Service, 1968; Foreign Office, 1968–69; 1st Sec., Rome, 1969–73; FCO, 1973–77; Counsellor (Economic and Commercial), New Delhi, 1977–81; Political Advr and Hd of Chancery, Brit. Mil. Govt, Berlin, 1981–84; Hd of S Asian Dept, FCO, 1984–86; Vis. Fellow, Center for Internat. Affairs, Harvard Univ., 1986–87; Minister, Rome, 1987–92; Head, UK Delegn to Negotiations on Conventional Arms Control in Europe, Vienna, 1992–93. sowc, Royal Naval Coll., Greenwich, 1977. Gov., Bruton Sch. for Girls, 1999–. Grosses Goldenes Ehrenzeichen: Styria, 1996; Carinthia, 1996. *Recreations:* music, painting. *Address:* Knapp Cottage, Charlton Horethorne, Sherborne, Dorset DT9 4PQ. *Club:* Travellers.

WOOD, Timothy John Rogerson; Chairman, Autotronics plc, 1998–2000; *b* 13 Aug. 1940; *s* of Thomas Geoffrey Wood and Norah Margaret Annie (*née* Rogerson); *m* 1969, Elizabeth Mary Spencer; one *s* one *d*. *Educ:* King James's Grammar Sch., Knaresborough, Yorks; Manchester Univ. (BSc Maths). Joined Ferranti Ltd as Lectr in Computer Programming, 1962; joined ICT Ltd (later ICL), 1963; subseq. involved in develt of ICL systems software; Sen. Proj. Management Consultant advising on introdn of large computer systems, 1977; Sen. Proj. Manager on application systems, 1981; resigned from ICL, 1983. MP (C) Stevenage, 1983–97; contested (C) same seat, 1997. PPS to: Minister for Armed Forces, 1986–87; Minister of State, 1987–89, Sec. of State, 1989–90, Northern Ireland; Asst Govt Whip, 1990–92; Lord Comr of HM Treasury (Govt Whip), 1992–95; Comptroller of HM Household, 1995–97. Chm., Wokingham Cons. Assoc., 1980–83; Pres., Bracknell Cons. Assoc., 1998–; Vice Chairman: National Assoc. of Cons. Graduates, 1975–76; Thames Valley Euro Constituency Council, 1979–83; Member: Bow Gp, 1962– (Mem. Council, 1968–71); Bracknell DC, 1975–83 (Leader, 1976–78); Bd, Bracknell Develt Corp., 1977–82. Gov., Princess Helena Coll., 2000–. *Publications:* Bow Group pamphlets on educn, computers in Britain, and the Post Office. *Recreations:* gardening, chess, reading. *Club:* Carlton.

WOOD, Victor; *see* Wood, R. V.

WOOD, Victoria, OBE 1997; writer and comedienne; *b* 19 May 1953; *d* of late Stanley and of Helen Wood; *m* 1980, Geoffrey Durham; one *s* one *d*. *Educ:* Bury Grammar School for Girls; Univ. of Birmingham (BA Drama, Theatre Arts). Performed regularly on television and radio as singer/songwriter, 1974–78. First stage play, Talent, performed at Crucible Th., Sheffield, 1978; TV production of this, broadcast, 1979 (3 National Drama awards, 1980); wrote Good Fun, stage musical, 1980; wrote and performed, TV comedy series: Wood and Walters, 1981–82; Victoria Wood As Seen On TV, 1st series 1985 (Broadcasting Press Guilds Award; BAFTA Awards, Best Light Entertainment Prog., Best Light Entertainment Perf.), 2nd series 1986 (BAFTA Award, Best Light Entertainment Prog.), Special, 1987 (BAFTA Best Light Entertainment Prog.); An Audience with Victoria Wood, 1988 (BAFTA Best Light Entertainment Prog., BAFTA Best Light Entertainment Perf.); Victoria Wood, 1989; Victoria Wood's All Day Breakfast, 1992 (Writers' Guild Award); Victoria Wood Live in Your Own Home, 1994; Dinnerladies, 1998–2000 (Best TV Comedy); Still Standing (Special), 1998; Christmas Special, 2000; Victoria Wood's Sketch Show Story, 2001. Appeared in stage revues, Funny Turns, Duchess Th., 1982, Lucky Bag, Ambassadors, 1984; own shows include: Victoria Wood, Palladium, 1987; Victoria Wood Up West, 1990; Victoria Wood - At It Again, Royal Albert Hall, 2001. Variety Club BBC Personality of the Year, 1987; British Comedy Awards: Top Female Comedy Performer, 1996; Writer of the Year. Hon. DLitt: Lancaster, 1989; Sunderland, 1994; Bolton, 1995; Birmingham, 1996. *Screenplay:* Pat and Margaret, 1994 (BPG Award, Best Single Drama Critic's Award, Monte Carlo, and Nymphe d'Or). *Publications:* Victoria Wood Song Book, 1984; Up to you, Porky, 1985; Barmy, 1987; Mens Sana in Thingummy Doodah, 1990; Chunky, 1996. *Recreation:* Pokémon. *Address:* c/o Phil McIntyre, 35 Soho Square, W1V 5DG. *T:* (020) 7439 2270.

WOOD, Rt Rev. Wilfred Denniston; *see* Croydon, Area Bishop of.

WOOD, Sir William (Alan), KCVO 1978; CB 1970; Second Crown Estate Commissioner, 1968–78; Ombudsman, Mirror Group Newspapers, 1985–89; Chairman, London and Quadrant Housing Trust, 1980–89; *b* 8 Dec. 1916; *m* 1st, 1943, Zoë (*d* 1985), *d* of Rev. Dr D. Frazer-Hurst; two *s* two *d*; 2nd, 1985, Mrs Mary Hall (*née* Cowper). *Educ:* Dulwich Coll.; Corpus Christi Coll., Cambridge (Scholar). Ministry of Home Affairs, N. Ireland, 1939. Lieut, RNVR, 1942–46. Ministry of Town and Country Planning, 1946; Minister's Private Secretary, 1951; Principal Regional Officer (West Midlands), Ministry of Housing and Local Government, 1954; Asst Secretary, 1956; Under-Secretary, 1964–68. Chm. Council, King Alfred Sch., 1966–78, Pres. 1978–2000. *Address:* 26 Fitzharry's Road, Abingdon, Oxon OX14 1EJ. *T:* (01235) 520515. *Club:* Athenæum.

WOOD, William James; QC 1998; *b* 10 July 1955; *s* of Sir Frank Wood, KBE, CB, and Lady (Olive May) Wood (*née* Wilson); *m* 1986, Tonya Mary Pinsent; one *s* one *d*. *Educ:* Dulwich Coll.; Worcester Coll., Oxford (BA, BCL); Harvard Law Sch. (LLM). Called to the Bar, Middle Temple, 1980. *Recreations:* fishing, ski-ing, tennis. *Address:* The Old Rectory, Charlbury, Oxon OX7 3PX.

See also C. Wood.

WOOD, William Rowley; QC 1997; a Recorder, since 1990; *b* 22 March 1948; *s* of Dr B. S. B. Wood and Elizabeth Wood; *m* 1973, Angela Beatson-Hird; one *s* two *d*. *Educ:* Bradfield Coll., Berks; Magdalen Coll., Oxford (MA). Called to the Bar, Gray's Inn, 1970. Chm., Birmingham DAC. *Recreations:* sailing, tennis, theatre. *Address:* Ashmead House, 49 Carpenter Road, Edgbaston B15 2JP. *T:* (0121) 455 6226. *Clubs:* Buckland (Birmingham); Edgbaston Priory Lawn Tennis.

WOODALL, Alec; *b* 20 Sept. 1918; *m* 1950; one *s* one *d*. *Educ:* South Road Elementary School. Colliery official. MP (Lab) Hemsworth, Feb. 1974–1987. PPS to Sec. of State for Trade, 1976–78. Mem. Nat. Council, 1975–87, case worker, 1987–, SSAFA. *Address:* 2 Grove Terrace, Hemsworth, West Yorkshire WF9 4BQ. *T:* (01977) 613897.

WOODARD, Rear-Adm. Sir Robert (Nathaniel), KCVO 1995; DL; Flag Officer Royal Yachts, 1990–95; an Extra Equerry to the Queen, since 1992; *b* 13 Jan. 1939; *s* of Francis Alwyne Woodard and Catherine Mary Woodard (*née* Hayes); *m* 1963, Rosamund Lucia, *d* of Lt-Col D. L. A. Gibbs, DSO and Lady Hilaria Gibbs (*née* Edgcumbe); two *s* one *d*. *Educ:* Lancing College. Joined Royal Navy as Cadet, 1958; specialised in flying; served HM Ships Ark Royal, Eagle, Victorious, Bulwark in 800, 801, 845, 846 and 848 Sqns (active service Malaya, Borneo); Commands: 771 Sqn, 1973–74; 848 Sqn, 1974–75; HMS Amazon, 1978–80; HMS Glasgow, 1983–84; HMS Osprey, 1984–86; MoD Op. Requirements, 1986–88; comd Clyde Submarine Base, 1989–90. Dir, Crownhill Estates, 1996–. Dir, Woodard (Western Div.) plc; Fellow Western Div., and Trustee, 2001–, Woodard Corp. Vice-Pres., Falmouth Br., Royal Naval Assoc. Pres., SSAFA, Cornwall, 1995. Chm., Regl Cttee, Devon and Cornwall, NT, 1997–. Chairman of Governors: King's Coll., Taunton, 2000–; King's Hall, Pyrland, 2000–; Gov., Bolitho Sch., Penzance, 1994–. Younger Brother, Trinity House, 1994–. DL Cornwall, 1999. FIMgt (FBIM 1979); MInstD 1995. *Recreations:* shooting, fishing, painting, sailing. *Clubs:* Naval and Military; Royal Yacht Squadron, Port Navas Yacht, Royal Fowey Yacht.

WOODBURN, Christopher Hugh, FCA; Chief Executive, General Insurance Standards Council, since 1999; *b* 6 Nov. 1947; *s* of Leonard Arthur and Phyllis Lydia Woodburn; *m* 1972, Lesley Avril Mohan; two *d*. *Educ:* St John's Sch., Leatherhead. FCA 1972. Articled Clerk and Audit Senior, Deloitte & Co., 1966–72; London Stock Exchange, 1972–88 (Hd, Financial Regulation, 1987–88); Securities Assoc., 1988–91 (Dep. Chief Exec., 1990–91); SFA, 1991–99 (Chief Exec., 1997–99). *Recreations:* sailing, history. *Address:* 61 Springwood Road, Heathfield, E Sussex TN21 8JX. *T:* (01435) 865501.

WOODCOCK, Gordon, FCA, CPFA; County Treasurer of Staffordshire, 1973–83. Served War, Royal Navy, 1942–46; Lieut RNVR. City Treasurer's Dept: Birmingham, 1937–42 and 1946–54; Stoke-on-Trent, 1954–73; City Treasurer of Stoke-on-Trent, 1971–73.

WOODCOCK, Sir John, Kt 1989; CBE 1983; QPM 1976; HM Chief Inspector of Constabulary, 1990–93; *b* 14 Jan. 1932; *s* of late Joseph Woodcock and of Elizabeth May Woodcock (*née* Whiteside); *m* 1953, Kathleen Margaret Abbott; two *s* one *d*. *Educ:* Preston, Lancs, elementary schs; Preston Technical Coll. Police cadet, Lancashire Constabulary, 1947–50; Army Special Investigation Branch, 1950–52; Constable to Chief Inspector, Lancashire Constabulary, 1952–65; Supt and Chief Supt, Bedfordshire and Luton Constabulary, 1965–68; Asst Chief Constable, 1968–70, Dep. Chief Constable, 1970–74, Gwent Constabulary; Dep. Chief Constable, Devon and Cornwall Constabulary, 1974–78; Chief Constable: N Yorkshire Police, 1978–79; S Wales Constabulary, 1979–83; HM Inspector of Constabulary, Wales and Midlands, 1983–90. Conducted inquiry into escapes from Whitemoor Prison, reported 1994. Intermed. Comd Course, Police Coll., 1965, Sen. Comd Course, 1968; Study, Bavarian Police, 1977; European Discussion Centre, 1977; Internat. Police Course (Lectr), Sicily, Rome, 1978; FBI, Nat. Exec., Washington, 1981; Lectr, Denmark, 1983, Holland, 1990; Study, Royal Hong Kong Police, 1989. Adviser and Member: UK Atomic Energy Police Authy, 1993–99; MoD Police Cttee, 1995–2000. Dir, Capital Corp. plc, 1994–99; Advr, Control Risks Group Ltd, 1995–. Vice-Pres., Welsh Assoc. of Youth Clubs, 1981–87; Chm., South Wales Cttee, Royal Jubilee and Prince's Trusts, 1983–85; Member: Admin. Council, Royal Jubilee Trusts, 1981–85; Prince's Trust Cttee for Wales, 1981–85; Mem., Governing Body, World College of the Atlantic, 1980–85. Pres., Police Mutual Assurance Soc., 1990–94. St John Council, N Yorks, S Glam, Mid Glam (Chm.), Hereford and Worcs, 1979–90. CIMgt 1980. FRCA 1995. CStJ 1992; KSG 1984. *Recreation:* golf. *Address:* c/o Home Office, Queen Anne's Gate, SW1H 9AT. *Clubs:* Swansea Lions (Hon. Mem.); Droitwich Golf (Worcs); Merlin Golf (Cornwall).

WOODCOCK, John Charles, OBE 1996; cricket writer; *b* 7 Aug. 1926; *s* of late Rev. Parry John Woodcock and Norah Mabel Woodcock (*née* Hutchinson). *Educ:* Dragon Sch.; St Edward's Sch., Oxford; Trinity Coll., Oxford (MA; OUHC *v* Cambridge, 1946, 1947). Manchester Guardian, 1952–54; Cricket Correspondent to The Times, 1954–, and to Country Life, 1962–91; Editor, Wisden Cricketers' Almanack, 1980–86; has covered over 40 Test tours, 1950–98, to Australia, 18 times, S Africa, W Indies, New Zealand, India, Pakistan and Sri Lanka. Mem., MCC Cttee, 1988–91 and 1992–95 (Trustee, 1996–99). Pres., Cricket Writers' Club, 1986–. Patron of the living of Longparish. Sports Journalist of the Year, British Press Awards, 1987. *Publications:* The Ashes, 1956; (with E. W. Swanton) Barclay's World of Cricket, 1980 (Associate Editor, 2nd edn 1986, Consultant Editor, 3rd edn, 1986); The Times One Hundred Greatest Cricketers, 1998. *Recreations:* the countryside, golf. *Address:* The Old Curacy, Longparish, Andover, Hants SP11 6PB. *T:* (01264) 720259. *Clubs:* MCC, Flyfishers'; Vincent's (Oxford); St Enodoc Golf.

WOODCOCK, Michael, (Mike); JP; company director, consultant, researcher and writer; *b* 10 April 1943; *s* of Herbert Eric Woodcock and Violet Irene Woodcock; *m* 1969, Carole Ann (*née* Berry); one *s* one *d*. *Educ:* Queen Elizabeth's Grammar Sch., Mansfield, Notts; DLitt IMCB, 1988. Successively: Accountant, Personnel Officer, Management Development Adviser, Head of Small Business Development Unit, Consultant, Vice-Pres. of US Corp., Founder of six UK companies. Underwriting Mem. of Lloyd's, 1984–. Proprietor of Estates in Scotland: Glenrinnes; Rigg; Carron Bridge; Corbiewells. MP (C) Ellesmere Port and Neston, 1983–92. Member: Trade and Industry Select Cttee, 1984–87; Home Affairs Select Cttee, 1987–92; Secretary: Cons. Smaller Business Cttee, 1990–92; All Party Transpennine Gp of MPs, 1990–92. Parly Advr, Chamber of Coal Traders, 1985–93. Nat. Vice Pres., Ramblers' Assoc., 1993–. Vis. Prof., Univ. of Lancaster Mgt Sch., 1992–96; Vis. Fellow, Leeds Business Sch., 1994–97. Companion, IMCB, 1990. JP Mansfield, Notts, 1971. *Publications:* People at Work, 1975; Unblocking Your Organisation, 1978 (UK, USA and Holland); Team Development Manual, 1979 (UK, USA and Indonesia); Organisation Development Through Teambuilding, 1981 (UK and USA); The Unblocked Manager, 1982 (UK, USA and four foreign edns); 50 Activities for Self Development, 1982 (UK, USA and eight foreign edns); Manual of Management Development, 1985; 50 Activities for Teambuilding, 1989 (UK, USA and 11 foreign edns); (jtly) Clarifying Organisational Values, 1989 (UK and Sweden); 50 Activities for Unblocking Your Organisation, vol. 1, 1990, vol. 2, 1991; The Self Made Leader, 1990; Unblocking Organisational Values, 1990; Change: a collection of activities and exercises, 1992; The Woodcock Francis series of Management Audits, 1994; Teambuilding Strategy, 1994 (UK and India); The Teambuilders Toolkit, 1996; The Problem Solvers Toolkit, 1996; The New Unblocked Manager, 1996; 25 Interventions for Improving Team Performance, 1997; Developing Your People, 1998; Interventions for Developing Managerial Competencies, 1998; Management Skills Assessment, 1999; The Agile Organisation, 1999. *Recreation:* walking. *Address:* Inkersall Farm, Bilsthorpe, Newark, Notts NG22 8TL; 13 Denny Street, SE11 4UX; Cuilangortan, Old Manse, Glenrinnes, by Dufftown, Moray AB55 4DE. *Clubs:* Carlton, Farmers'.

WOODCOCK, Thomas, LVO 1996; FSA; Norroy and Ulster King of Arms, since 1997; *b* 20 May 1951; *s* of late Thomas Woodcock, Hurst Green, Lancs, and of Mary, *d* of William Woodcock, Holcombe, Lancs; *m* 1998, Lucinda Mary Harmsworth, *d* of late Lucas Michael Harmsworth King. *Educ:* Eton; University Coll., Durham (BA); Darwin Coll., Cambridge (LLB). FSA 1990. Called to Bar, Inner Temple, 1975. Research Assistant to Sir Anthony Wagner, Garter King of Arms, 1975–78; Rouge Croix Pursuivant, 1978–82; Somerset Herald, 1982–97; Advr on Naval Heraldry, 1996–. *Publications:* (with John Martin Robinson) The Oxford Guide to Heraldry, 1988; (ed with D. H. B. Chesshyre) Dictionary of British Arms: Medieval Ordinary, vol. 1, 1992, vol. 2 (ed with Hon. J. Grant and I. Graham), 1996; (with John Martin Robinson) Heraldry in National Trust Houses, 2000. *Address:* College of Arms, Queen Victoria Street, EC4V 4BT. *T:* (020) 7236 3634. *Club:* Travellers.

WOODFORD, Air Vice-Marshal Anthony Arthur George, CB 1989; Home Bursar and Fellow, Magdalen College, Oxford, 1992–2001; *b* 6 Jan. 1939; *s* of Arthur and May Woodford; *m* 1965, Christine Barbara Tripp; one *s* two *d*. *Educ:* Haberdashers' Aske's Hampstead School; RAF College, Cranwell. BA Hons Open Univ. 1978; MA Oxon 1992. Commissioned pilot, 1959; served Nos 12, 44, 53, 101 Sqns and 4017th CCTS USAF; Asst Air Attaché, British Embassy, Washington, 1978–81; Comdr RAF St Mawgan, 1982–83; Comdr British Forces Ascension Island, 1982; ADC to the Queen, 1982–83; RCDS 1984; HQ Strike Command: Air Cdre Plans, 1985–87; AOA, 1987–89; ACOS Policy, SHAPE, 1989–92, retd. *Address:* Filkins Moor, Filkins, Lechlade, Glos GL7 3JJ. *Club:* Royal Air Force.

WOODFORD, Maj.-Gen. David Milner, CBE 1975; retired; Member, Lord Chancellor's Panel of Independent Inspectors, 1988–2000; *b* 26 May 1930; *s* of late Major R. M. Woodford, MC, and Marion Rosa Woodford (*née* Gregory); *m* 1st, 1959, Mary E. Jones (marr. diss. 1987); 2nd, 1995, Carole M. Westoby. *Educ:* Prince of Wales Sch., Nairobi; Wadham Coll., Oxford. psc, jsdc, rcds. National Service, then Regular, 1st Royal Fusiliers, Korea, 1953, then Regtl service, Egypt, Sudan, UK, 1953–55; ADC/GOC Berlin, 1956–58; Adjt and Co. Comd 1RF, Gulf, Kenya, Malta, Cyprus, Libya, UK, 1958–61; GSO3 Div./Dist, UK, 1962; sc Camberley, 1963; GSO2 MO 1, then MA/VCGS, 1964–66; Co. Comd 1RF, BAOR, UK, Gulf and Oman, 1966–68; GSO1 (DS) Staff Coll., 1968–70; CO 3 RRF, Gibraltar, UK, N Ireland, 1970–72; Col GS NEARELF (Cyprus), 1972–75; Comd 3 Inf. Bde (N Ireland), 1976–77; Dep. Col, RRF, 1976–81; RCDS 1978; D Comd and COS SE Dist, UK, 1979–80; Dir Army Training, 1981–82; Sen. Army Mem., RCDS, 1982–84; Comdt, JSDC, 1984–86. Col RRF, 1982–86. *Recreations:* literary, historical; passionate golfer. *Address:* c/o Regimental Headquarters, The Royal Regiment of Fusiliers, HM Tower of London, EC3N 4AB. *Clubs:* Army and Navy, New Zealand Golf.

WOODFORD, F(rederick) Peter, PhD; FRCPath; CChem, FRSC; FIPEM; Chief Scientific Officer, Department of Health (formerly of Health and Social Security), 1984–93; *b* 8 Nov. 1930; *s* of Wilfrid Charles Woodford and Mabel Rose (*née* Scarff); *m* 1964, Susan Silberman, NY; one *d*. *Educ:* Lewis Sch., Pengam, Glam; Balliol Coll., Oxford (Domus Exhibnr; BA (Hons Chem.) 1952; MA 1955); PhD Leeds 1955. FRCPath 1984; CChem, FRSC 1990; FIPEM (FBES 1993; MBES 1991). Res. Fellow, Leiden Univ., 1958–62; Vis. Scientist/Lectr, Univ. of Tennessee Med. Sch. and NIH, USA, 1962–63; Guest Investigator, Rockefeller Univ., NY, 1963–71; Scientific Historian, Ciba Foundn, and Scientific Associate, Wellcome Trust, 1971–74; Exec. Dir, Inst. for Res. into Mental and Multiple Handicap, 1974–77; PSO (Clin. Chem.), DHSS, 1977–84. Distinguished Visitor, Royal Free Hosp. Sch. of Med., 1994–. Consultant: Clin. Res. Inst., Montreal, 1970–90; Inst. of Pharmacology, Milan Univ., 1995–. Chm., Council of Biology Editors (USA), 1969–70; Managing/Executive Editor: Jl of Atherosclerosis Res., 1960–62; Jl of Lipid Res., 1963–69; Procs of Nat. Acad. of Scis, USA, 1970–71; Editl Consultant, King's Fund Centre for Health Service Devlt, 1990–93; Editor, Camden History Review, 1995–. Student Gov., City Lit. Inst., 1999–2001. Chm., Hampstead Music Club, 1996–99; Patron, Cavatina Chamber Music Trust, 2000–. First non-med. Affiliate, RCP, 2000. Hon. DSc Salford, 1993. Waverley Gold Medal for scientific writing, 1955; Meritorious Award, Council of Biology Editors, USA, 1984. *Publications:* Scientific Writing for Graduate Students, 1969, 4th edn 1986; Medical Research Systems in Europe, 1973; The Ciba Foundation: an analytic history 1949–1974, 1974; Writing Scientific Papers in English, 1975; In-Service Training series: of Physiological Measurement Technicians, 1988; of Medical Physics Technicians, 1989; of Medical Laboratory Assistants, 1991; of Rehabilitation Engineering Technicians, 1992; (ed) From Primrose Hill to Euston Road, 1995; Atherosclerosis X, 1995; A Constant Vigil, 1997; (ed) Streets of Bloomsbury and Fitzrovia (a historical survey), 1997; (ed) East of Bloomsbury, 1998; How to Teach Scientific Communication, 1999; (ed) Streets of Old Holborn, 1999; (ed) The Streets of Hampstead, 3rd edn, 2000; (ed) The Good Grave Guide to Hampstead Cemetary, Fortune Green, 2000; (ed) Streets of St Giles, 2000; (ed) Victorian St Giles, 2001; (ed) 200 Years of Local Justice in Hampstead and Clerkenwell, 2001; articles on scientific writing, lipids of the arterial wall, editing of biomed. jls, prevention and treatment of handicapping disorders, screening for spina bifida, quality in pathology labs, costing and ethics in clin. chem., history of Heath and Old Hampstead Soc., clinical significance of antioxidants. *Recreations:* chamber music (pianist), local history. *Address:* 1 Akenside Road, NW3 5BS.

WOODGATE, Joan Mary, CBE 1964; RRC 1959; Matron-in-Chief, Queen Alexandra's RN Nursing Service, 1962–66, retired; *b* 30 Aug. 1912; *d* of Sir Alfred Woodgate, CBE, and Louisa Alice (*née* Digby). *Educ:* Surbiton High Sch., Surrey. Trained at St George's Hospital, 1932–36, Sister, 1937–38; Queen Charlotte's Hospital, 1936. Joined QARNNS, 1938; served Middle East and Far East; HM Hospital Ship, Empire Clyde, 1945–47; HM Hospital Ship, Maine, 1953–54; Principal Matron: RNH Haslar, 1959–61; RNH Malta, 1961–62. OStJ 1959; QHNS, 1962–64. Member, Commonwealth War Graves Commn, 1966–83. *Recreations:* gardening, country pursuits. *Address:* Laurel Cottage, Northover Lane, Tiptoe, near Lymington, Hants SO41 6FS. *Club:* English-Speaking Union.

WOODHALL, David Massey, CBE 1992; Chief Executive, Commission for New Towns, 1982–92; *b* 25 Aug. 1934; *s* of Douglas J. D. and Esme Dorothy Woodhall; *m* 1954, Margaret A. Howarth; two *s*. *Educ:* Bishop Holgate's Sch., Barnsley; Royds Hall, Huddersfield; Henley Administrative Staff Coll. Dip. Leeds Sch. of Architecture and Town Planning. West Riding CC, 1951–60; Cumberland CC, 1960–63; Northamptonshire CC, 1963–82: County Planning Officer, 1971–80; Asst Chief Executive, 1980–82. Dir, Adnams Co. plc, 1986–; Partner, The Woodhall Consultancy; Consultant, Caws and Morris, Chartered Surveyors. A Countryside Comr, 1996–99; Mem., Countryside Agency, 1999–2001. *Recreations:* National Hunt racing, landscape, food and wine. *Address:* 2 Hardingstone Lane, Hardingstone, Northampton NN4 6DE. *T:* (01604) 764654.

WOODHEAD, Vice-Adm. Sir (Anthony) Peter, KCB 1992; Prisons' Ombudsman, 1994–99; *b* 30 July 1939; *s* of Leslie and Nancy Woodhead; *m* 1964, Carol; one *s* one *d*. *Educ:* Leeds Grammar Sch.; Conway; BRNC Dartmouth. Seaman Officer; Pilot, 1962; Aircraft Carriers, Borneo Campaign; CO, HM Ships Jupiter, 1974, Rhyl, 1975; NDC 1976; Naval Plans Div., MoD, 1977; CSO to Flag Officer, Third Flotilla, 1980; COS to FO Comdg Falklands Task Force, 1982; Captain, Fourth Frigate Sqdn, 1983; RCDS 1984; Dir, Naval Ops, 1985; CO HMS Illustrious, 1986; Flag Officer: Flotilla Two, 1988; Flotilla One, 1989. Dep. SACLANT, 1991–93. Lay Reader: Guildford, 1991; Chichester, 1997. Pres., Marriage Resource, 1995–. Non-exec. Dir, BMT, 1996–. Chm., Crime Reduction Initiatives, 2001. Gov., Aldro Sch., 1996–. *Recreations:* ball games, antique restoration. *Club:* Royal Navy of 1765 and 1785.

WOODHEAD, Christopher Anthony; HM Chief Inspector of Schools, 1994–2000; *b* 20 Oct. 1946; one *d* from former marriage. *Educ:* Bristol Univ. (BA Sp. Hons English, PGCE); Univ. of Keele (MA). English Teacher, Priory Sch., Shrewsbury, 1969–72; Dep. Head of English, Newent Sch., Gloucester, 1972–74; Head of English, Gordano Sch., Avon, 1974–76; Tutor for English, Oxford Univ., 1976–82; English Advr, 1982–84, Chief Advr, 1984–88, Shropshire LEA; Dep. Chief Educn Officer, Devon LEA, 1988–90, Cornwall LEA, 1990–91; Dep. Chief Exec., 1991, Chief Exec., 1991–93, Nat. Curriculum Council; Chief Exec., SCAA, 1993–94. Special Prof., Univ. of Nottingham, 1993–95. *Recreations:* rock climbing, running. *Address:* Hendre Gwenllian, Llanfrothen, Penrhyndeudraeth, Gwynedd LL48 6DJ.

WOODHEAD, David James; National Director, Independent Schools Information Service, since 1985; Deputy General Secretary, Independent Schools Council, since 1998; *b* 9 Nov. 1943; *s* of Frank and Polly Woodhead; *m* 1974, Carole Underwood; two *s*. *Educ:* Queen Elizabeth Grammar Sch., Wakefield; Univ. of Leicester (BA Hons history, politics and English; Chm., Univ. Conservative Assoc., 1964–65). Journalist: Cambridge Evening News (educn corresp.), 1965; Sunday Telegraph, 1968; ILEA Press Office: Press Officer,

1975; Chief Press Officer, 1978; Press Officer, London Schs Symphony Orch., 1975–84. Editor, ISIS News, 1985–89; Editl Dir, The ISIS Magazine, 1990–. Rep. UK at internat. conf. on private schs, Beijing, 1999. Trustee: Jt Educnl Trust, 1988–; Oratory Gp, 1995–98; Founder-Trustee, Nat. ISIS Strings Acad., 1996–. Mem., Dresden Trust, 1995– (Founder, Dresden Scholars' Scheme, 2001). Member: Court and Council, Leicester Univ., 2000–; Adv. Develt Bd, Rudolf Kempe Soc., 2000–. Governor: Battle Abbey Sch., 1988–91; St John's Sch., Leatherhead, 1994–; Feltonfleet Prep. Sch., Cobham, 1998–2001. FRSA 1990. *Publications:* Choosing Your Independent School, annually, 1985–99; (ed) Good Communications Guide, 1986, 2nd edn 1989; The ISIS Guide to Accredited Independent Schools, annually, 2000–; numerous newspaper and magazine articles. *Recreations:* family, opera, classical music, enjoying being a Wagner fanatic, books, German and Austrian history, travel. *Address:* ISC/Independent Schools Information Service, Grosvenor Gardens House, 35–37 Grosvenor Gardens, SW1W 0BS. *T:* (020) 7798 1500. *Club:* Royal Over-Seas League.

WOODHEAD, Vice-Adm. Sir Peter; *see* Woodhead, Vice-Adm. Sir A. P.

WOODHEAD, Robin George; Chief Executive, Sotheby's Europe and Asia, since 2000; *b* 28 April 1951; *s* of Walter Henry Woodhead and Gladys Catherine (*née* Ferguson); *m* 1980, Mary Fitzgerald Allen (marr. diss. 1991), *qv*. *Educ:* Mt Pleasant Sch., Salisbury, Rhodesia; UC of Rhodesia and Nyasaland (LLB Hons London ext.). Admitted Solicitor, 1978; Man. Dir, Premier Man Ltd, 1980–86; Chief Executive: Nat. Investment Gp, 1986–90; London Commodity Exchange, 1991–97; Man. Dir, 1998–99, Chief Exec., 1999–2000, Sotheby's Europe. Chm., Internat. Petroleum Exchange, 1980–86. Chairman: Rambert Dance Co., 1995–2000; Music Research Inst., 1997–2000. *Recreations:* game reserve development in Zululand, ski-ing, riding, tennis, music, visual arts, performing arts. *Address:* Sotheby's, 34–35 New Bond Street, W1A 2AA. *T:* (020) 7293 6066. *Club:* City of London.

WOODHOUSE, family name of **Baron Terrington.**

WOODHOUSE, Ven. Andrew Henry, DSC 1945; MA; Archdeacon of Hereford and Canon Residentiary, Hereford Cathedral, 1982–91, now Archdeacon Emeritus; *b* 30 Jan. 1923; *s* of H. A. Woodhouse, Dental Surgeon, Hanover Square, W1, and Woking, Surrey, and Mrs P. Woodhouse; unmarried. *Educ:* Lancing Coll.; The Queen's Coll., Oxford. MA 1949. Served War, RNVR, 1942–46 (Lieut). Oxford, 1941–42 and 1946–47; Lincoln Theological Coll., 1948–50. Deacon, 1950; Priest, 1951; Curate of All Saints, Poplar, 1950–56; Vicar of St Martin, West Drayton, 1956–70; Rural Dean of Hillingdon, 1967–70; Archdeacon of Ludlow and Rector of Wistanstow, 1970–82. *Recreations:* photography, walking. *Address:* Orchard Cottage, Bracken Close, Woking, Surrey GU22 7HD. *T:* (01483) 760671. *Club:* Naval.
See also R. M. Woodhouse.

WOODHOUSE, Rt Hon. Sir (Arthur) Owen, KBE 1981; Kt 1974; DSC 1944; PC 1974; Founding President, Law Commission, New Zealand, 1986–91; a Judge of the Supreme Court, New Zealand, 1961–86; a Judge of the Court of Appeal, 1974–86, President of the Court of Appeal, 1981–86; *b* Napier, 18 July 1916; *s* of A. J. Woodhouse and W. J. C. Woodhouse (*née* Allen); *m* 1940, Margaret Leah Thorp; four *s* two *d*. *Educ:* Napier Boys' High Sch.; Auckland Univ. (LLB). Served War of 1939–45, Lt-Comdr in RNZNVR on secondment to RN; service in MTBs; liaison officer with Yugoslav Partisans, 1943; Asst to Naval Attaché, HM Embassy Belgrade, 1945. Joined Lusk, Willis & Sproule, barristers and solicitors, 1946; Crown Solicitor, Napier, 1953; appointed Judge of Supreme Court, 1961. Chm., Royal Commn on Compensation and Rehabilitation in respect of Personal Injury in NZ, 1966–67, and of inquiry into similar questions in Australia, 1973–74; Pres., NZ Sect., Internat. Commn of Jurists, 1986–93. Hon. LLD: Victoria Univ. of Wellington, 1978; Univ. of York, Toronto, 1981. *Recreations:* music, golf. *Address:* 244 Remuera Road, Auckland 1005, New Zealand. *Clubs:* Northern (Auckland); Hawkes Bay (Napier); Wellesley, Wellington (Wellington).

WOODHOUSE, Ven. (Charles) David (Stewart); Archdeacon of Warrington, 1981–2001, now Emeritus; Vicar of St Peter's, Hindley, 1981–92; *b* 23 Dec. 1934; *s* of Rev. Hector and Elsie Woodhouse. *Educ:* Silcoates School, Wakefield; Kelham Theological College; Lancaster Univ. (MA 1995). Curate of St Wilfrid's, Halton, Leeds, 1959–63; Youth Chaplain, Kirkby Team Ministry, Diocese of Liverpool, 1963–66; Curate of St John's, Pembroke, Bermuda, 1966–69; Asst Gen. Secretary, CEMS, 1969–70; Gen. Sec., 1970–76; Rector of Ideford, Ashcombe and Luton and Domestic Chaplain to Bishop of Exeter, 1976–81. Hon. Canon, Liverpool Cathedral, 1983. *Address:* 9 Rob Lane, Newton-le-Willows WA12 0DR.

WOODHOUSE, Charles Frederick, CVO 1998; Partner, Farrer and Co., Solicitors, 1969–99 (Consultant, 1999–2001); Solicitor to the Duke of Edinburgh, 1983–2001; *b* 6 June 1941; *s* of late Wilfrid Meynell Woodhouse and Peggy Woodhouse (*née* Kahl); *m* 1969, Margaret Joan Cooper; one *s* two *d*. *Educ:* Marlborough; McGill Univ.; Peterhouse, Cambridge (BA Hons). Hon. Legal Advr, Commonwealth Games Council for England, 1983–; Legal Advr, CCPR, 1971–99 (Mem., Inquiry on Amateur Status, 1986–88). Pres., British Assoc. for Sport and Law, 1997–2000; Chm., Sports Dispute Resolution Panel, 1998–. Dir, Santos USA Corp., 1992–. Mem., Royal Parks Rev. Gp, 1992–96. Chairman: Cheviot Trust, 1991–97; Rank Pension Plan Trustee Ltd, 1992–; Trustee: LSA Charitable Trust, 1991–; Brian Johnston Meml Trust, 1996–99; Yehudi Menuhin Meml Trust, 1999–2001. Mem., Guild of Sports Internationalists, 1999–. *Publications:* articles on sports law, incl. The Law and Sport, 1972; The Role of the Lawyer in Sport, 1993; contrib. to Jl British Assoc. for Sport and Law. *Recreations:* cricket, golf, canal boating. *Address:* Quarry Hill House, Mealsgate, Cumbria CA7 1AE. *Clubs:* Oxford and Cambridge, MCC; Worplesdon Golf; Silloth-on-Solway Golf; Free Foresters; Guildford Cricket (Pres., 1991–), Surrey County Cricket.

WOODHOUSE, Ven. David; *see* Woodhouse, Ven. C. D. S.

WOODHOUSE, Dr Frank, OBE 1998; Director, British Institute of Florence, 1988–97; *b* 29 April 1943; *s* of Samuel Woodhouse and Clarice (*née* Bache); *m* 1966, Melba Sterry; two *s*. *Educ:* King Edward VI Grammar Sch., Stourbridge; Birmingham Univ. (BCom); Trinity Hall, Cambridge (MA, PhD). Asst Lectr, later Lectr in Italian, Hull Univ., 1972–81; Lectr in Italian, Cambridge Univ., 1981–92; Fellow, 1983–92, Associate Dean, 1986–87, Darwin Coll., Cambridge. *Publications:* Language and Style in a Renaissance Epic, 1982; articles on Italian subjects. *Recreations:* reading, travel, Italy. *Address:* Largo Bargellini 10, 50122 Firenze, Italy. *Club:* Travellers.

WOODHOUSE, James Stephen; Director, ISIS East, 1994–2000; *b* 21 May 1933; *s* of late Rt Rev. J. W. Woodhouse, sometime Bishop of Thetford, and late Mrs K. M. Woodhouse; *m* 1957, Sarah, *d* of late Col Hubert Blount, Cley, Norfolk; three *s* one *d*. *Educ:* St Edward's Sch.; St Catharine's Coll., Cambridge. BA (English) Cantab, 1957; MA 1961. Nat. Service, 14th Field Regt RA, 1953. Asst Master, Westminster Sch., 1957; Under Master and Master of the Queen's Scholars, 1963; Headmaster, Rugby Sch., 1967–81; Headmaster, Lancing Coll., 1981–93. Chairman: NABC Religious Adv. Cttee, 1971–93; Bloxham Project, 1972–77; Head Masters' Conf., 1979; Joint Standing Cttee of HMC, IAPS and GSA, 1981–86; Vice-Chm., E-SU Schoolboy Scholarship Cttee, 1973–77. Director: The Norfolk Boat, 1993–; Holkham Pageant, 1994. Mem. Cttee of Mgt, RNLI, 1994–. *Recreations:* sailing, music, hill walking. *Address:* Welcome Cottage, Wiveton, Holt, Norfolk NR25 7TH.

WOODHOUSE, Prof. John Henry, PhD; FRS 2000; Professor of Geophysics, since 1990, and Head of Department of Earth Sciences, since 2000, University of Oxford; Fellow of Worcester College, Oxford, since 1990; *b* 15 April 1949; *s* of G. B. Woodhouse. *Educ:* Southall Grammar Sch.; Bristol Univ. (BSc 1970); King's Coll., Cambridge (MA, PhD 1975). Fellow, King's Coll., Cambridge, 1974–78; Vis. Asst Res. Geophysicist, Inst. of Geophysics and Planetary Physics, Univ. of Calif., San Diego, 1976–77; Asst Prof., 1978–80, Associate Prof., 1980–83, Prof. of Geophysics, 1983–90, Harvard Univ. Chm., Commn on Seismological Theory, Internat. Assoc. of Seismol. and Physics of Earth's Interior, 1983–87. Fellow, Amer. Geophys. Union (Macelwane Award, 1984; Inge Lehmann Medal, 2001). *Publications:* many contribs to learned jls. *Address:* Department of Earth Sciences, Parks Road, Oxford OX1 3PR; Worcester College, Oxford OX1 2HB.

WOODHOUSE, Prof. John Robert, FBA 1995; Fiat Serena Professor of Italian Studies, Oxford, 1990–2001; Fellow, Magdalen College, Oxford, 1990–2001, now Emeritus; *b* 17 June 1937; *s* of Horace Woodhouse and Iris Evelyn Pewton; *m* 1967, Gaynor Mathias. *Educ:* King Edward VI Grammar School, Stourbridge; Hertford College, Oxford (MA, DLitt); Univ. of Pisa; PhD Wales. Asst Lectr in Italian, Univ. of Aberdeen, 1961–62; British Council Scholar, Scuola Normale Superiore, Pisa, 1962–63; Asst Lectr and Lectr, UCNW, Bangor, 1963–66; Lectr and Sen. Lectr, Univ. of Hull, 1966–73; Oxford University: Univ. Lectr in Italian and Fellow of St Cross Coll., 1973–84; Lectr at Jesus Coll., 1973, St Edmund Hall, 1975, Brasenose Coll., 1976; Fellow, 1984–89, Supernumerary Fellow, 1991, Pembroke Coll. Mem., Exec. Cttee, Soc. for Italian Studies, 1979–85 and 1989–95. Gov., British Inst. of Florence, 1991–2001. Harvard Old Dominion Foundn Fellow, Villa I Tatti, 1969; Founding Fellow, Centro Studi Dannunziani, Pescara, 1979; Fellow: Accad. lett. ital. dell'Arcadia, 1980; Accademia della Crusca, 1991; Corresp. Fellow, Commissione per i Testi di Lingua, Bologna, 1993; Sen. Res. Fellow, Center for Medieval and Renaissance Studies, UCLA, 1985; Fellow: Huntington Liby, Calif., 1986; Newberry Liby, Chicago, 1988. Editor (Italian), Modern Language Review, 1984–94; Mem., Editl Bd, Italian Studies, 1987–91. Premio D'Annunzio, Centro Nazionale Studi Dannunziani, 2000. Cavaliere Ufficiale, Order of Merit (Italy), 1991. *Publications:* Italo Calvino: a reappraisal and an appreciation of the trilogy, 1968; (ed) Italo Calvino, Il barone rampante, 1970; (ed) V. Borghini, Scritti inediti o rari sulla lingua, 1971; (ed) V. Borghini, Storia della nobiltà fiorentina, 1974; Baldesar Castiglione, a reassessment of the Cortegiano, 1978; (ed) G. D'Annunzio, Alcyone, 1978; (ed with P. R. Horne) G. Rossetti, Lettere familiari, 1983; (ed jtly) G. Rossetti, Carteggi, I, 1984, II, 1988, III, 1992, IV, 1996; (ed jtly) The Languages of Literature in Renaissance Italy, 1988; From Castiglione to Chesterfield: the decline in the courtier's manual, 1991; (ed) Dante and Governance, 1997; Gabriele D'Annunzio: defiant archangel, 1998 (trans. Italian, 1999); articles in learned jls. *Recreations:* gardening, hill walking. *Address:* Magdalen College, Oxford OX1 4AU.

WOODHOUSE, Michael; *see* Woodhouse, R. M.

WOODHOUSE, Rt Hon. Sir Owen; *see* Woodhouse, Rt Hon. Sir A. O.

WOODHOUSE, (Ronald) Michael, CVO 2000; Chairman, Rexam PLC (formerly Bowater), 1993–96 (Director, 1988–96); Chairman, Prince's Trust Volunteers, 1991–2000; *b* 19 Aug. 1927; *s* of Henry Alfred Woodhouse and Phyllis Woodhouse (*née* Gemmell); *m* 1955, Quenilda Mary (*d* 1997), *d* of Rt Rev. Neville Vincent Gorton; one *s* three *d*. *Educ:* Lancing Coll.; Queen's Coll., Oxford (BA Mod. History). Courtaulds plc, 1951–91: Dir, 1976–91; Dep. Chm., 1986–91; Man. Dir, 1972–79, Chm., 1979–84, Internat. Paint Co.; Chm., British Cellophane Ltd, 1979–86. A Director: RSA Exam. Board, 1991–95; RSA Exams and Assessment Foundn, 1995–97; Mem., Prince's Trust Council, 1995–2000. Dir, London Mozart Players, 1990–97; Mem. Council of Mgt, Friends of Royal Acad., 1996–; Trustee, Royal Acad. Pension Fund, 1997–. CIMgt (CBIM 1978); FRSA 1979. *Recreations:* walking in Lake District, watching Rugby and cricket, opera, music, gardening, art, reading. *Address:* Tankards, Wonersh, Guildford, Surrey GU5 0PF. *T:* (01483) 892078; Dalehead, Hartsop, Patterdale, Cumbria CA11 0NZ. *Club:* Carlton.
See also Ven. A. H. Woodhouse.

WOODING, Sir Norman (Samuel), Kt 1992; CBE 1986; PhD; Chairman, BEARR Trust, since 1993; *b* 20 April 1927; *s* of Samuel and Nellie Gertrude Wooding; *m* 1949, Dorothy Elizabeth Smith; one *s* two *d*. *Educ:* Lawrence Sheriff Sch., Rugby; Univ. of London (BSc); Univ. of Leeds (PhD); Univ. of Manchester. Joined Courtaulds, 1944; Main Board Dir, 1973; Dep. Chm., 1976–87; retd. Earlys of Witney: Dir, 1971–84; Chm., 1978–83. Chairman: Agricl Genetics Co. Ltd, 1988–93; E Europ. Trade Council, 1990–96; British Textile Technol. Gp, 1991–94; EIS Group, 1994–98; non-exec. Dep. Chm., Royal London Mutual Insce Soc. Ltd, 1988–96; non-exec. Dir, British Nuclear Fuels plc, 1987–98. Pres., Russo-British (formerly Brit. Soviet) Chamber of Commerce, 1988–; Chm. Council, SSEES, Univ. of London, 1992–99; Member: Governing Body, Brit. Assoc. for Central and Eastern Europe, 1988–; Adv. Bd, British Know How Fund, 1989–99. Sen. Associate Mem., St Antony's Coll., Oxford, 1987–. CIMgt (CBIM 1983); FRSA 1992. *Publications:* papers in scientific journals, E European trade jls, etc. *Recreations:* mountain walking, gardening, fast cars. *Address:* BEARR Trust, 24 Greville Street, EC1N 8SS. *Club:* Reform.

WOODLEY, Keith Spencer, FCA; chartered accountant; *b* 23 Oct. 1939; *s* of Charles Spencer Woodley and Hilda Mary Woodley (*née* Brown); *m* 1962, Joyce Madeleine Toon; one *s* two *d*. *Educ:* Stationers' Co. Sch. Articled Clerk, Senior Deloitte Plender Griffiths & Co., 1959–69; Partner, Deloitte Haskins & Sells, 1969–90: Nat. Personnel Partner, 1978–82; Mem., Partnership Bd, 1985–90. Complaints Commissioner: SIB, 1990–94; SFA, 1990–91; FIMBRA, 1990–91; PIA, 1991; LSE, 1994–; Indep. Investigator, Investors' Compensation Scheme, 1991–. Director: Royscot Trust, 1990–96; National & Provincial Building Soc., 1991–96; Abbey National Plc, 1996– (Dep. Chm., 1999–); Abbey National Treasury Service Plc, 1998–. Member Council: ICAEW, 1988–98 (Pres., 1995–96); NACAB, 1991–94 and 1997–99 (Hon. Treas., 1991–94); Univ. of Bath, 1996–. Trustee, Methodist Ministers' Pension Scheme, 1998–. *Recreations:* theatre, music, hill walking. *Address:* 11 Sion Hill, Bath BA1 2UH; (office) 2 Gay Street, Bath BA1 2PH.

WOODLEY, Leonard Gaston; QC 1988. *Educ:* Univ. of London (Dip. Internat. Affairs). Called to the Bar, Inner Temple, 1963, now Bencher; a Recorder. Called to Trinidad and Tobago Bar. Mem., Royal Commn on Care of the Elderly, 1997–99. Chm., Landat Enquiry under Mental Health Act; Mem., internat. enquiry into illegal hanging in Trinidad. First black person to be appointed QC and Recorder. Patron, Plan Internat. UK. *Recreations:* sports, music. *Address:* (office) 8 King's Bench Walk, Temple, EC4Y 7DU.

WOODLEY, Ven. Ronald John; Archdeacon of Cleveland, 1985–91, Emeritus, since 1991; *b* 28 Dec. 1925; *s* of John Owen Woodley and Maggie Woodley; *m* 1959, Patricia Kneeshaw; one *s* two *d*. *Educ:* Montagu Road School, Edmonton; St Augustine's Coll., Canterbury; Bishops' Coll., Cheshunt. Deacon 1953, priest 1954; Curate: St Martin, Middlesbrough, 1953–58; Whitby, 1958–61; Curate in Charge 1961–66, and Vicar 1966–71, The Ascension, Middlesbrough; Rector of Stokesley, 1971–85; RD of Stokesley, 1977–84. Canon of York, 1982–2000, Emeritus, 2001–. *Address:* 2A Minster Court, York YO1 7JJ. *T:* (01904) 679675.

WOODLEY, Sonia; QC 1996; a Recorder, since 1985; *b* 8 Oct. 1946; *d* of Stanley and Mabel Woodley; *m* 1973, Stuart McDonald (marr. diss. 1986); two *s* one *d*. *Educ:* Convent High Sch., Southampton. Called to the Bar, Gray's Inn, 1968. *Recreations:* fishing, gardening. *Address:* 9–12 Bell Yard, WC2A 2LF.

WOODROFFE, Most Rev. George Cuthbert Manning, KBE 1980 (CBE 1973); MA, LTh; Archbishop of West Indies, 1980–86; Bishop of Windward Islands, 1969–86, retired; *b* 17 May 1918; *s* of James Manning Woodroffe and Evelyn Agatha (*née* Norton); *m* 1947, Aileen Alice Connell; one *s* one *d* (and one *s* decd). *Educ:* Grenada Boys' Secondary School; Codrington Coll., Barbados. Clerk in Civil Service, Grenada, 1936–41; Codrington Coll. (Univ. of Durham), 1941–44; Deacon 1944; Priest 1945; Asst Priest, St George's Cath., St Vincent, 1944–47; Vicar of St Simon's, Barbados, 1947–50; Rector: St Andrew, 1950–57; St Joseph, 1957–62; St John, 1962–67; Rural Dean of St John, Barbados, 1965–67; Sub-Dean and Rector of St George's Cathedral, St Vincent, Windward Islands, 1967–69. Vice-Chm., Anglican Consultative Council, 1974. Chm., Vis. Justices St Vincent Prisons, 1968–76. Mem., Prerogative of Mercy Cttee, St Vincent, 1969–86. Member: Bd of Educn, Barbados, 1964–67; National Trust of St Vincent, 1967–86 (Chm., 1972–82); Council, Univ. of the West Indies, 1980–83; Chm., Bd of Governors, Alleyne Sch., Barbados, 1951–57. Hon. DD Nashotah House, USA, 1980; Hon. LLD Univ. of the West Indies, 1981. *Recreations:* music, driving, detective tales and novels, military band music. *Address:* PO Box 919, Murray Road, St Vincent and the Grenadines, West Indies. *T:* 4561277. *Club:* Royal Commonwealth Society.

WOODROFFE, Jean Frances, (Mrs J. W. R. Woodroffe), CVO 1953; *b* 22 Feb. 1923; *d* of late Capt. A. V. Hambro; *m* 1st, 1942, Capt. Hon. Vicary Paul Gibbs, Grenadier Guards (killed in action, 1944), *er s* of 4th Baron Aldenham; one *d* (and one *d* decd); 2nd, 1946, Rev. Hon. Andrew Charles Victor Elphinstone (*d* 1975), 2nd *s* of 16th Lord Elphinstone, KT; one *d* (one *s* decd); 3rd, 1980, Lt-Col John William Richard Woodroffe (*d* 1990). Lady-in-Waiting to the Queen as Princess Elizabeth, 1945; Extra Woman of the Bedchamber to the Queen, 1952–. *Address:* Maryland, Worplesdon, Guildford, Surrey GU3 3RB. *T:* (01483) 232629.

WOODROOFE, Sir Ernest (George), Kt 1973; PhD, FInstP, FIChemE; *b* 6 Jan. 1912; *s* of late Ernest George Woodroofe and Ada (*née* Dickinson); *m* 1st, 1938, Margaret Downes (*d* 1961); one *d*; 2nd, 1962, Enid Grace Hutchinson Arnold. *Educ:* Cockburn High Sch.; Leeds Univ. Staff of Loders & Nucoline Ltd, 1935–44; Staff of British Oil & Cake Mills Ltd, 1944–50; Mem., Oil Mills Executive of Unilever Ltd, 1951–55; Director of British Oil & Cake Mills Ltd, 1951–55; Head of Research Division of Unilever Ltd, 1955–61; Director: United Africa Co. Ltd, 1961–63; Unilever NV, 1956–74; Chm., Unilever Ltd, 1970–74 (Dir, 1956–74; Vice-Chm., 1961–70); Trustee, Leverhulme Trust, 1962–82 (Chm., 1974–82). President, International Society for Fat Research, 1962. Member Cttee of Enquiry into the Organisation of Civil Science, 1962–63; A Vice-Pres., Soc. of Chemical Industry, 1963–66; Member: Tropical Products Inst. Cttee, 1964–69; Council for Nat. Academic Awards, 1964–67; Cttee of Award of the Commonwealth Fund, 1965–70; Royal Commn for the Exhibn of 1851, 1968–84; British Gas Corp., 1973–81. Director: Schroders Ltd, 1974–89; Burton Group Ltd, 1974–83; Guthrie Corp. Ltd, 1974–82. Chairman: Review Body on Doctors' and Dentists' Remuneration, 1975–79; CBI Research Cttee, 1966–69. Governor, London Business Sch., 1970–75 (Dep. Chm., 1973–75). Hon. ACT Liverpool, 1963; Hon. Fellow, University of Manchester Inst. of Science and Technology, 1968; Hon. LLD Leeds, 1968; DUniv Surrey, 1970; Hon. DSc: Cranfield, 1974; Liverpool, 1980. Vis. Fellow, Nuffield Coll., Oxford, 1972–80. Comdr, Order of Orange Nassau (Netherlands), 1972. *Recreation:* fishing. *Address:* 44 The Street, Puttenham, Surrey GU3 1AR. *T:* (01483) 810977.

WOODROW, Bill; *see* Woodrow, W. R.

WOODROW, William Robert, (Bill); sculptor; *b* 1 Nov. 1948; *s* of Geoffrey W. Woodrow and Doreen M. (*née* Fasken); *m* 1970, Pauline Rowley; one *s* one *d*. *Educ:* Barton Peveril GS, Eastleigh; Winchester Sch. of Art; St Martin's Sch. of Art (DipAD); Chelsea Sch. of Art. Trustee, Tate Gall., 1996–. Solo exhibns in UK, Europe, Australia, USA and Canada, 1972–, including: Fools' Gold, Tate Gall., London, 1996; Regardless of History, for Fourth Plinth, Trafalgar Square, 2000; The Beekeeper, S London Gall. and Mappin Art Gall., Sheffield, 2001; work in group exhibitions worldwide, including: British Sculpture in the 20th Century, Whitechapel Art Gall., 1981; An International Survey of Recent Painting and Sculpture, Mus. of Modern Art, NY, 1984; Skulptur Im 20. Jahrhundert, Basle, Switzerland, 1984; Carnegie Internat. Mus. of Art, Pittsburgh, 1985; British Sculpture since 1965, USA tour, 1987; Great Britain–USSR, Kiev and Moscow, 1990; Metropolis, Berlin, 1991; Arte Amazonas, Rio de Janeiro, Brasilia, Berlin, Dresden and Aachen, 1992–94; Ripple across the Water, Tokyo, 1995; Un Siècle de Sculpture Anglaise, Jeu de Paume, Paris, 1996; Forjar el Espacio, Las Palmas, Valencia and Calais, 1998–99; Bronze, Holland Park, 2000–01; Field Day, Taipei Fine Arts Mus., Taiwan, 2001. Represented GB at Biennales of Sydney, 1982, Paris, 1982 and 1985, São Paulo, 1983 and 1991, Havana, 1997. Anne Gerber Award, Seattle Mus. of Art, USA, 1988. *Address:* 14 Cormont Road, SE5 9RA. *T:* (020) 7733 2435, *Fax:* (020) 7733 9585; *e-mail:* bill@billwoodrow.com.

WOODRUFF, William Charles, CBE 1985; FRAeS; *b* 14 Aug. 1921; *s* of late Thomas and Caroline Woodruff; *m* 1st, 1946, Ethel May Miles (*d* 1981); one *s* one *d*; 2nd, 1987, Olivia Minerva Henson. *Educ:* St George's, Ramsgate. RAF, 1941–46: Navigator/ Observer, 1409 Flight; POW Germany, 1943–45. Seconded Air Min., 1945, and later Min. of Civil Aviation for Air Traffic Control planning; various air traffic control appts at Hurn, Northolt, Southern Centre, Heston and MTCA Hdqrs, 1946–56; Air Traffic Control Officer i/c Heathrow, 1956–62; Sec. of Patch Long-term Air Traffic Control Planning Group, 1960–61; Dep. Dir, 1962–67, Dir, 1967–69, Civil Air Traffic Ops; National Air Traffic Services: Jt Field Comdr, 1969–74; Dep. Controller, 1974–77; Controller, 1977–81. Assessor, Stanstead/Heathrow Airports Public Inquiries, 1981–84; Specialist Advr, H of C Transport Select Cttee on Air Safety, 1988–89. Guild of Air Traffic Control Officers: Clerk, 1952–56; Master, 1956. *Publications:* articles on aviation subjects. *Address:* 21 Atwater Court, Lenham, Kent ME17 2PW. *T:* (01622) 850560.

WOODS, Prof. Andrew William, PhD; BP Professor of Petroleum Science, BP Institute, University of Cambridge, since 2000; Fellow, St John's Coll., Cambridge, since 2000; *b* 2 Dec. 1964; *s* of Prof. William Alfred Woods and Dorothy Elizabeth Woods; *m* 1996, Dr Sharon Jane Casey; three *s*. *Educ:* St John's Coll., Cambridge (BA 1st Cl. Maths 1985, Part III Maths 1986, MA 1988; PhD Applied Maths 1989). Green Scholar, Scripps Instn of Oceanography, UCSD, 1989–90; University of Cambridge: Res. Fellow, 1988–90, Teaching Fellow, 1991–96, St John's College; Lectr, Inst. of Theoretical Geophysics, 1991–96; Prof. of Applied Maths, Univ. of Bristol, 1996–99. Italgas Prize, Turin, 1997; Marcello Carapezza Prize, Gp. Nat. per la Volcanologia, Rome, 1997. *Publication:* (jtly) Volcanic Plumes, 1997. *Address:* BP Institute, Madingley Rise, Madingley Road, University of Cambridge, Cambridge CB3 0EZ. *T:* (01223) 765702.

WOODS, His Honour Brian; DL; a Circuit Judge, 1975–94; *b* 5 Nov. 1928; *yr s* of late E. P. Woods, Woodmancote, Cheltenham; *m* 1957, Margaret, *d* of late F. J. Griffiths, Parkgate, Wirral; three *d*. *Educ:* City of Leicester Boys' Sch.; Nottingham Univ. (LLB 1952). National Service, RAF, 1947–49. Called to the Bar, Gray's Inn, 1955; Midland Circuit; Dep. Chm., Lincs (Lindsey) QS, 1968. Chancellor, Diocese of Leicester, 1977–79; Reader, dio. of Leicester, 1970–79, dio. of Lichfield, 1978–. Member Council: S Mary and S Anne's Sch., Abbots Bromley, 1977–92; Ellesmere Coll., 1983–84. Mem., Law Adv. Cttee, Nottingham Univ., 1979–94; a Legal Mem., Mental Health Review Tribunals for Trent, W Midlands, Yorkshire, N and SW Thames Region, 1983–99. Fellow, Midland Div., Woodard Corp., 1979–92. DL Derbys, 1994. *Recreations:* daughters, musical music, taking photographs.

WOODS, Christopher Matthew, CMG 1979; MC 1945; HM Diplomatic Service, retired; Special Operations Executive Adviser, Foreign and Commonwealth Office, 1982–88; *b* 26 May 1923; *s* of Matthew Grosvenor Woods; *m* 1st, 1954, Gillian Sara Rudd (*d* 1985); four *s* one *d*; 2nd, 1992, Mrs Patricia Temple Muir. *Educ:* Bradfield Coll.; Trinity Coll., Cambridge. HM Forces, KRRC and SOE, 1942–47; Foreign Office, 1948; served Cairo, Tehran, Milan, Warsaw, Rome; FO, later FCO, 1967. *Recreations:* birds, churches, music, books. *Address:* Old Bank House, 12 Market Hill, Framlingham, Suffolk IP13 9AN. *T:* (01728) 621057. *Club:* Special Forces.

WOODS, Dr David Randle, DPhil; FRSSAf; Vice-Chancellor, Rhodes University, South Africa, since 1996; *b* Pietermaritzburg, 18 July 1940; *s* of Arthur Phillips Woods and Katherine Isabella Woods (*née* Straffen); *m* 1965, Anne Charlotte Abbott; one *s* one *d*. *Educ:* Michaelhouse Sch.; Rhodes Univ. (BSc Dist. Botany; BSc Hons Dist. Botany); University Coll., Oxford (DPhil 1966). Rhodes Schol., Natal, 1963–66; Asst Lectr in Microbiol., Dept of Botany and Microbiol., QMC, 1966–67; Rhodes University: Sen. Lectr in Microbiol., 1967–71; Prof. and Head of Microbiol., 1972–79; University of Cape Town: Dir, Microbial Genetics and Industrial Microbiol. Res. Unit, 1975–96; Prof. and Head of Dept of Microbiol., 1980–87; Fellow, 1985; Dep. Vice-Chancellor, 1988–96; Dir, Foundn for Res. Develt/Univ. of Cape Town Microbial Genetics Res. Unit, 1980–96. Research Fellow: Institut Pasteur, Paris, 1973–74; Dept. of Biochem., Trondheim Univ., Norway, 1974–75. Member, Editorial Board: Jl Bacteriol., 1987–89; Anaerobe Microbiol., 1994–98. Chm., Bacteriol. and Applied Microbiol. Div., and Mem., Exec. Bd, Internat. Union of Microbiol Socs, 1995–99. Member: S African Soc. for Microbiol., 1970 (Pres., 1982–84); S African Soc. for Biochem., 1970–96; Amer. Soc. for Microbiol., 1980; S African Acad. of Sci., 1995–. FRSSAf 1987; Fellow, Amer. Acad. Microbiol., 1995. *Publications:* (ed) The Clostridia and Biotechnology (series), 1993; jt author numerous res. papers. *Recreations:* squash, reading, music, hiking. *Address:* Rhodes University, PO Box 94, Grahamstown 6140, South Africa. *T:* (46) 6038148.

See also T. P. Woods.

WOODS, Eldrick, (Tiger); golfer; *b* 30 Dec. 1975; s of Lt-Col Earl and Kultida Woods. *Educ:* Western High Sch., Anaheim, Calif; Stanford Univ. Professional golfer, 1996–; wins include: US Masters, 1997 (youngest winner), 2001 (first player ever to hold all four major professional titles concurrently); US PGA Championship, 1999, 2000, 2001; US Open, 2000; The Open, St Andrews, 2000; numerous other tournaments. *Address:* PGA, PO Box 109601, 100 Avenue of the Champions, Palm Beach Gardens, FL 33418, USA.

WOODS, Elisabeth Ann; part-time consultant on management and policy issues for UK and overseas government departments and other organisations, since 1998; *b* 27 Oct. 1940; *d* of Norman Singleton, *qv*; *m* 1976, James Maurice Woods. *Educ:* South Hampstead High Sch.; Girton Coll., Cambridge (BA Hons Cl. 1 Modern Languages, 1963). Asst Principal, Min. of Pensions and Nat. Insurance, 1963–69 (Asst Private Sec. to the Minister, and Private Sec. to Permanent Sec.); Principal, DHSS, 1969–76 (Sec. to Cttees on Nursing and on Allocation of Resources to Health Authorities); Asst Sec., DHSS, 1976–88 (responsible for mental handicap policy, later for liaison with RHAs, finally for aspects of supplementary benefit); seconded to HM Treasury, 1980–82; Grade 3, DHSS Central Resource Management, 1988; Hd of Finance, DSS, 1988–91; HM Customs and Excise: a Comr, 1991–97; Dir, VAT Control, 1991–94; Dir, Ops (Compliance), 1994–97. Mem., HFEA, 1999– (Chm., Audit Cttee). Volunteer advr, Salisbury CAB, 1999–. *Recreations:* cycling, reading, cooking, being with friends. *Address:* West Wing, 43 Church Lane, Lower Bemerton, Salisbury SP2 9NR; *e-mail:* liswoods@cs.com.

WOODS, Maj.-Gen. Henry Gabriel, CB 1979; MBE 1965; MC 1945; Vice Lord-Lieutenant, North Yorkshire, 1985–99; Vice-President, St William's Foundation, since 1998 (Secretary, then Director, 1984–98); *b* 7 May 1924; *s* of late G. S. Woods and F. C. F. Woods (*née* McNevin); *m* 1953, Imogen Elizabeth Birchenough Dodd; two *d*. *Educ:* Highgate Sch.; Trinity Coll., Oxford (MA 1st Cl. Hons Mod. History). FIMgt. psc, jssc, rcds. Commnd 5th Royal Inniskilling Dragoon Guards, 1944; served NW Europe, 1944–45; Korea, 1951–52; Adjt, 1952–53; Sqdn Leader, 1954–55 and 1960–62; Army Staff Coll., 1956; Jt Services Staff Coll., 1960; Mil. Asst to Vice CDS, MoD, 1962–64; comd 5th Royal Inniskilling Dragoon Gds, 1965–67; Asst Mil. Sec. to C-in-C BAOR, 1968–69; Comdt, RAC Centre, 1969–71; RCDS, 1972; Mil. Attaché, Brit. Embassy, Washington, 1973–75; GOC NE Dist, 1976–80, retd. Head, Centre for Industrial and Educnl Liaison (W and N Yorks), 1980–87. Chairman: SATRO Panel, 1982–83; W and N Yorks Regl Microelectronics Educn Programme, 1982–86; Yorks and Humberside Industry/Educn Council, 1982–87; Bradford and W Yorks Br., BIM, 1982–84; N Yorks Scouts, 1982–2000; Yorks Region, Royal Soc. of Arts, 1982–92 (Mem. Council); Vice Chm., W Yorks Br. Exec. Cttee, Inst. of Dirs, 1985–91; Mem., Yorks Br. Exec. Cttee, BAAS, 1982–87. Mem. Court, Univ. of Leeds, 1980–2001 (Mem. Council, 1980–91). Chm., 5th Royal Inniskilling Dragoon Guards Regtl Assoc., 1979–92 (Pres., 1992–). Pres., York and Humberside Br., Royal Soc. of St George, 1986–88; Member: Trinity Soc., 1947–; Oxford Soc., 1987– (Pres., York Br., 1997–). FRSA; MInstD; MIMgt. Hon. Mem., Yorks Reg., RIBA, 1994. Mayor, Co. of Merchants of Staple of England, 1991–92; Mem., Merchant Adventurers of the City of York. DL N Yorks, 1984. Hon. DLitt Bradford, 1988. Officier, Ordre de Léopold, Belgium, 1965. *Publication:* Change and Challenge: the story of 5th Royal Inniskilling Dragoon Guards, 1978. *Recreations:* hunting (foot follower), fencing, sailing, military history. *Address:* Grafton House, Tockwith, York YO26 7PY. *T:* (01423) 358735. *Club:* Ends of the Earth (UK section).

WOODS, Prof. Hubert Frank, CBE 2001; FRCP, FRCPE; Sir George Franklin Professor of Medicine, University of Sheffield, since 1990 (Dean, Faculty of Medicine, 1989–98); *b* 18 Nov. 1937; *s* of Hubert George Woods and Julia Augusta Woods; *m* 1966, Hilary Sheila Cox (*d* 1999); one *s* two *d*. *Educ:* St Bees Sch., Cumbria; Leeds Univ. (BSc

1962); Pembroke Coll., Oxford (BM BCh 1965; DPhil 1970). MRCP 1968, FRCP 1978; FFPM 1989; FRCPE 1991. House appts, Radcliffe Infirmary and Hammersmith Hosp., 1965–67; Lectr in Medicine, Oxford Univ., 1967–72; Mem., MRC Ext. Clinical Scientific Staff and Hon. Sen. Registrar, MRC Clinical Pharmacology Unit, Radcliffe Infirmary, 1972–76; Prof. of Clinical Pharmacology and Therapeutics, Univ. of Sheffield, 1976–90; Hon. Consultant Physician, Royal Hallamshire Hosp., 1976–. Visiting Professor: Maryland Med. Center, 1999; Meml Sloan Kettering Cancer Center, 1999. Non-executive Member: Sheffield HA, 1990–96; Rampton Hosp. Authy, 1996–99. Chairman: Adv. Cttee on Toxicity of Food, Consumer Products and the Environment, DoH, 1992–April 2002; Department of Health Working Group: on Peanut Allergy, 1997–98; on Organophosphates, 1998–99; on Phyto-oestrogens, 1999–; Member: Adv. Cttee on Novel Foods and Processes, MAFF, 1992–April 2002; Food Adv. Cttee, MAFF, 1992–April 2002. Mem., GMC, 1994– (Mem., 1994–, Dep. Chm., 1996–99, Chm., 1999–, Health Cttee; Mem., Review Bd for Overseas Practitioners, 1997–). Special Trustee, Former United Sheffield Hosps, 1989–2000; Trustee, Harry Bottom Charitable Trust, 1989–. Founder FMedSci 1998. FIFST 1996. Hon. FFOM 1995. *Publications:* (with R. D. Cohen) Lactic Acidosis, 1976; papers on metabolism and pharmacogenetics in med. and sci. jls. *Recreations:* gardening, fly fishing, works of Raymond Chandler. *Address:* Edge Farm, Aston Lane, Hope, Hope Valley, Derbys S33 6RA. *T:* (0114) 271 2475. *Club:* Athenæum.

WOODS, Ivan; *see* Woods, W. I.

WOODS, Prof. John David, CBE 1991; PhD; Professor of Oceanography, T. H. Huxley School of the Environment, Earth Sciences and Engineering (formerly Department of Earth Resources Engineering), Imperial College, University of London, since 1994; Adjunct Fellow, Linacre College, Oxford, since 1991; *b* 26 Oct. 1939; *s* of late Ronald Ernest Goff Woods and Ethel Marjorie Woods; *m* 1971, Irina (marr. diss. 1996), *y d* of Bernd von Arnim and Elizabeth Gräfin Platen-Hallermund; one *s* one *d*. *Educ:* Imperial College, Univ. of London. BSc Physics 1961, PhD 1965. Research Asst, Imperial Coll., 1964–66; Sen., later Principal, Research Fellow, Meteorol Office, 1966–72; Prof. of Physical Oceanography, Southampton Univ., 1972–77; Ordinarius für Ozeanographie, Christian Albrechts Universität und Direktor Regionale Ozeanographie, Kiel Institut für Meereskunde, Schleswig-Holstein, 1977–86; Dir, Marine and Atmospheric Sci., NERC, 1986–94; Imperial College, London: Hd, Dept of Earth Resources Engrg, 1994–97; Dean, Graduate Sch. of the Envmt, 1994–97. Vis. Prof. Atmospheric Scis, Miami Univ., 1969; Hon. Prof. of Oceanography, Southampton Univ., 1994–. Member: NERC, 1979–82; Meteorol Res. Cttee, Meteorol Office, 1976–77, 1987–96; OST Foresight Marine Panel, 1996–. Council Member: Underwater Assoc., 1967–72 (Hon. life mem., 1987); RMetS, 1972–75; RGS, 1975–77, 1987–92 (Vice-Pres., 1989–91; Patron's Medal, 1996); Member, international scientific committees for: Global Atmospheric Research Prog., 1976–79; Climate Change and the Ocean, 1979–84; World Climate Research Prog., 1980–86; World Ocean Circulation Experiment, 1983–89 (Chm., 1984–86); Internat. Geosphere Biosphere Prog., 1987–91; Global Ocean Observing System, 1994– (Chm., Europ. Consortium, 1994–); Global Envmt Facility, 1996–. Mem., Academia Europaea, 1988. Lectures: Iselin, Harvard, 1989; Linacre, Oxford, 1991; Adye, Fellowship of Engrg, 1991; European Geophys. Soc., Edinburgh, 1992; Bruun, Unesco, 1993, 1999. Hon. DSc: Liège, 1980; Plymouth, 1991. L. G. Groves Prize, MoD, 1968; Medal of Helsinki Univ., 1982. *Publications:* (with J. Lythgoe) Underwater Science, 1971; (with E. Drew and J. Lythgoe) Underwater Research, 1976; papers on atmospheric physics and oceanography in learned jls. *Recreation:* history. *Address:* T. H. Huxley School of the Environment, Imperial College, SW7 2AZ. *T:* (020) 7594 7414. *Club:* Athenæum.

WOODS, Rev. Canon John Mawhinney; *b* 16 Dec. 1919; *s* of Robert and Sarah Hannah Woods. *Educ:* Edinburgh Theological College. Deacon 1958, for St Peter's, Kirkcaldy, Fife; priest, 1959; Rector of Walpole St Peter, Norfolk, 1960–75; Provost, St Andrew's Cathedral, Inverness, 1975–80; Rector of The Suttons with Tydd, 1980–85; Canon of Inverness, 1980–. *Address:* 4 Trenowath Place, King Street, King's Lynn, Norfolk PE30 1EN.

WOODS, Prof. Kent Linton, MD, FRCP; Professor of Therapeutics, University of Leicester, since 1996; *b* 5 June 1948; *s* of Stephen and Mary Woods; *m* 1970, Rose Whitmarsh; three *s* (one *d* decd). *Educ:* Lawrence Sheriff Sch., Rugby; Clare Coll., Cambridge (MA, MB BChir 1972; MD 1980 (Horton Smith Prize)); Birmingham Univ.; Harvard Sch. of Public Health (SM Epidemiology 1983). MRCP 1974, FRCP 1988. Clinical trng posts, Birmingham, 1972–75; Sheldon Res. Fellow and MRC Trng Fellow, 1975–78; Lectr in Clinical Pharmacology, Birmingham Univ., 1978–84; MRC Travelling Fellow, Harvard, 1982–83; Sen. Lectr in Clinical Pharmacology, 1984–94, Reader, 1994–96, Univ. of Leicester. Regl Dir of R&D, Trent, NHS Exec., DoH, 1995–99; Dep. Dir, 1998, Dir, 1999–, NHS Health Technol. Assessment Programme. Hon. Consultant Physician, Leicester Royal Infirmary, 1984–. *Publications:* contrib. numerous papers to med. and scientific jls, mainly on cardiovascular topics. *Recreations:* travel, books. *Address:* Division of Medicine and Therapeutics, Robert Kilpatrick Clinical Sciences Building, Leicester Royal Infirmary, Leicester LE2 7LX. *T:* (0116) 252 3126.

WOODS, Prof. Leslie Colin, BE, MA, DPhil, DSc; Professor of Mathematics (Theory of Plasma), University of Oxford, 1970–90, now Emeritus Professor; Fellow of Balliol College, Oxford, 1970–90, Emeritus Fellow, since 1991; *b* Reporoa, NZ, 6 Dec. 1922; *s* of A. B. Woodhead, Sandringham, NZ; *m* 1st, 1943; five *d*; 2nd, 1977; 3rd, 1990. *Educ:* Auckland Univ. Coll.; Merton Coll., Oxford. Fighter pilot, RNZAF, Pacific Area, 1942–45. Rhodes Schol., Merton Coll., Oxford, 1948–51; Scientist (NZ Scientific Defense Corps) with Aerodynamics Div., NPL Mddx, 1951–54; Senior Lectr in Applied Maths, Sydney Univ., 1954–56; Nuffield Research Prof. of Engineering, Univ. of New South Wales, 1956–60; Fellow and Tutor in Engrg Science, Balliol Coll., Oxford, 1960–70; Reader in Applied Maths, Oxford, 1964–70. Chm., Mathematical Inst., Oxford, 1984–89. Hon. DSc Auckland, 1983. *Publications:* The Theory of Subsonic Plane Flow, 1961; Introduction to Neutron Distribution Theory, 1964; The Thermodynamics of Fluid Systems, 1975; Principles of Magnetoplasma Dynamics, 1987; Kinetic Theory of Gases and Magnetoplasmas, 1993; Thermodynamic Inequalities in Gases and Magnetoplasmas, 1996; Against the Tide: an autobiographical account of a professional outsider, 2000; many research papers in aerodynamics and plasma physics in Proc. Royal Soc., Physics of Fluids, etc. *Recreations:* music, gliding. *Address:* Balliol College, Oxford OX1 3BJ.

WOODS, Maurice Eric; Part-time Chairman, Employment (formerly Industrial) Tribunals (Bristol), since 1998 (Regional Chairman, 1990–98); *b* 28 June 1933; *s* of late Leslie Eric Woods and of Winifred Rose Woods (*née* Boniface); *m* 1956, Freda Pauline Schlosser; two *s* two *d*. *Educ:* Moulsham Secondary Modern Sch., Chelmsford. LLB London. National Service (Army), 1951–53. Clerk with Essex CC, 1948–51; Police Constable, Essex Police Force, 1954–59; Claims Assistant, Cornhill Insce, 1959–61; Solicitors' Clerk and Articled Clerk, Barlow Lyde and Gilbert, 1961–65; admitted Solicitor, 1965; private practice, 1965–84; Dep. County Court Registrar, 1977–84; Chairman: Suppl. Benefit Appeal Tribunals and Social Security Appeal Tribunals, 1981–84; Industrial Tribunals, Bristol, 1984–90. *Recreations:* music, travel. *Address:* Regional Office of Employment Tribunals, 1st Floor, The Crescent Centre, Temple Back, Bristol BS1 6EZ. *T:* (0117) 929 8261.

WOODS, Nigel Dermot, FRICS; Chief Executive and Commissioner of Valuation for Northern Ireland, Valuation and Lands Agency, since 1998; *b* 21 Feb. 1947; *s* of Victor and Sheila Woods; *m* 1974, Alison Grant; one *s* two *d*. *Educ:* Bangor Grammar Sch. FRICS 1983 (ARICS 1970). Worked in estate agency, Belfast, 1964–67; with Valuation Office, subseq. Valuation and Lands Agency, 1967–. *Recreations:* golf, bridge. *Address:* Valuation and Lands Agency, Queen's Court, 56–66 Upper Queen Street, Belfast BT1 6FD. *Club:* Bangor Golf.

WOODS, Justice Sir Robert (Kynnersley), Kt 2000; CBE 1986; Judge, District Court of New South Wales, since 2000; *b* 12 Nov. 1939; *s* of Frederick Kynnersley Smythies Woods, OBE and Ruth Cecilia Woods (*née* Shaw). *Educ:* Univ. of Sydney (LLB). Solicitor, NSW, 1966–69; Legal Officer, PNG Govt, 1969–81; Justice, Nat. and Supreme Courts of PNG, 1982–99. *Address:* Parkes Road, Wellington, NSW 2820, Australia. *T:* (2) 68453707.

WOODS, Prof. Robert Thomas, FBPsS; Professor of Clinical Psychology of the Elderly, since 1996, and Co-Director, Dementia Services Development Centre, since 1999, University of Wales, Bangor; *b* 9 April 1952; *s* of Walter T. W. Woods and Kathleen Ellen Woods (*née* Brooks); *m* 1972, Joan Doreen Foster; one *s* one *d*. *Educ:* Gravesend Sch. for Boys; Churchill Coll., Cambridge (BA 1973; MA 1977); Univ. of Newcastle-upon-Tyne (MSc 1975). CPsychol 1988; FBPsS 1992. Clinical psychologist, Newcastle Gen. Hosp., 1975–80; Lectr, then Sen. Lectr, Inst. of Psychiatry, Univ. of London and Hon. Clinical Psychologist, Maudsley and Bethlem Royal Hosps, 1980–92; Head, Psychol. Services for Older People, Camden and Islington Community Health Services NHS Trust, 1992–96; Hon. Sen. Lectr in Psychol., UCL, 1992–96; Hon. Clinical Psychologist, NW Wales (formerly Gwynedd Community Health) NHS Trust, 1996–. Mem., Med. and Scientific Adv. Panel, Alzheimer's Disease Soc., 1987–, and Alzheimer's Disease Internat., 1997–. Associate Specialist Advr, Health Adv. Service 2000, 1998–. Associate Editor, Aging and Mental Health, 1997–. *Publications:* (with U. Holden) Reality Orientation, 1982, 3rd edn as Positive Approaches to Dementia Care, 1995; (with C. Lay) Caring for the Person with Dementia: a guide for families and other carers, 1982, 3rd edn 1994; (with P. Britton) Clinical Psychology with the Elderly, 1985; Alzheimer's Disease: coping with a living death, 1989; (ed) Handbook of the Clinical Psychology of Ageing, 1996; (ed) Psychological Problems of Ageing, 1999. *Recreations:* football, cooking. *Address:* Dementia Services Development Centre, Neuadd Ardudwy, University of Wales, Bangor, Holyhead Road, Bangor, Gwynedd LL57 2PX. *T:* (01248) 383719.

WOODS, Hon. Ronald Earl; Professor of United States Foreign Policy, University of Washington, since 1996; *b* 10 Oct. 1938; *s* of Earl L. Woods and Marie C. Woods; *m* 1959, Judith M. Wishner; two *d*. *Educ:* Georgetown Univ.; School of Foreign Service (BSFS 1961). Joined US Foreign Service, 1961; served: Cairo, 1962; Washington, 1963; Rome, 1966; Paris, 1969; Strasbourg, 1971; Washington, 1974; Madrid, 1979; Oslo, 1982; Brussels, 1985; Minister, London, 1989–93; Exec. Dir, World Affairs Council, 1993–96. *Recreations:* tennis, ski-ing, walking. *Address:* 4527 52 Avenue South, Seattle, WA 98118, USA. *T:* (206) 7230405; *e-mail:* rewoods&u.washington.edu.

WOODS, Tiger; *see* Woods, E.

WOODS, Timothy Phillips, MA, DPhil; Head of History, Trent College, since 1985; *b* 24 Dec. 1943; *s* of late Arthur Phillips Woods and of Katherine Isabella Woods; *m* 1969, Erica Lobb. *Educ:* Cordwalles Prep. Sch., Natal; Michaelhouse Sch., Natal; Rhodes Univ. (BA Hons, MA; UED); Oxford Univ. (DPhil). Cape Province Rhodes Scholar, 1968; Felsted School: Asst Master, 1971; Head of History, 1975; Headmaster, Gresham's Sch. 1982–85. *Recreations:* cricket, hockey, squash, gardening, music, history and architecture of cathedrals. *Address:* 63 Curzon Street, Long Eaton, Nottingham NG10 4FG. *T:* (0115) 972 0927. *Club:* Vincent's (Oxford).
See also D. R. Woods.

WOODS, Victoria Patricia Ann, (Vicki), (Mrs F. A. Woods Walker); Contributing Editor, Vogue (USA), since 1994; *b* 25 Sept. 1947; *d* of Frederick Woods and Barbara Joan (*née* Hinchliffe); *m* 1980, Frank A. Walker; one *s* one *d*. *Educ:* Lancaster Girls' Grammar Sch.; Univ. of Lancaster (BA). Sub-editor, Harpers & Queen, 1970–73; Chief sub-editor, Radio Times, 1973–75; Exec. Editor, Harpers & Queen, 1975–79; Associate Editor, then Dep. Editor, Tatler, 1982–87; Femail Editor, Daily Mail, 1987–89; Contributing Editor, Vogue (USA) and Associate Editor, Spectator, 1989–91; Editor, Harpers & Queen, 1991–94.

WOODS, (William) Ivan; 3rd *s* of late William and Anna Woods, Annaghmore, Co. Armagh; *m* (1st wife *d* 1965); one *s* one *d*; 2nd, 1966, Florence Margaret, *o d* of late William and Florence Sloan, Ach-na-mara, Donaghadee, Co. Down; one *s* two *d*. *Educ:* Ranelagh Sch., Athlone; Mountjoy Sch., Dublin. Accountant, Min. of Finance for N Ire., 1962; N Ire. Govt Liaison Officer in London, 1963; Dir of Office of Parliamentary Commissioner for Administration, NI, 1969; Dir of Office of Commissioner for Complaints, NI, 1969; Dep. Sec., Dept of Finance for NI, 1973–76. Sec., Milibern Trust, 1976–79. *Address:* 112 Warren Road, Donaghadee, Co. Down BT21 0PQ. *T:* (028) 9188 3568. *Club:* Portaferry Sailing (Co. Down).

WOODS WALKER, Victoria Patricia Ann, (Mrs F. A. Woods Walker); *see* Woods, V. P. A.

WOODSTOCK, Viscount; William Jack Henry Bentinck; Count of the Holy Roman Empire; *b* 19 May 1984; *s* and *heir* of Earl of Portland, *qv*. *Heir:* *b* Hon. Jasper James Mellowes Bentinck, *b* 1988.

WOODWARD, Hon. Sir (Albert) Edward, AC 2001; Kt 1982; OBE 1969; Chairman, Australian Banking Industry Ombudsman Council, since 1997; *b* 6 Aug. 1928; *s* of Lt-Gen. Sir Eric Winslow Woodward, KCMG, KCVO, CB, CBE, DSO, and Amy Freame Woodward (*née* Weller); *m* 1950, Lois Thorpe; one *s* six *d*. *Educ:* Melbourne C of E Grammar Sch.; Melbourne Univ. (LLM). Practising barrister, 1953–72; QC 1965; Judge: Australian Industrial Court and Supreme Court of Australian Capital Territory, 1972–90; Federal Ct of Australia, 1977–90. Chairman, Armed Services Pay Inquiry, 1972; Royal Commissioner: Aboriginal Land Rights, 1973–75; into Australian Meat Industry, 1981–82; into Tricontinental Gp Cos, 1991–92; President: Trade Practices Tribunal, 1974–76; Defence Force Discipline Appeal Tribunal, 1988–90; Director-General of Security, 1976–81. Chairman: Victorian Dried Fruits Bd, 1963–72; Nat. Stevedoring Industry Conf. and Stevedoring Industry Council, 1965–72; Australian Defence Force Academy Council, 1982–99; Schizophrenia Australia Foundn, 1985–97. Mem. Council, Melbourne Univ., 1973–76, 1986–, Chancellor, 1990–2001; Chm. Council, Camberwell Grammar Sch., 1983–87. Hon. LLD: New South Wales, 1986; Melbourne, 2001; Hon.

DLitt Ballarat, 1998. *Address:* 63 Tivoli Road, South Yarra, Victoria 3141, Australia. *T:* (3) 98268404.

WOODWARD, Barry; His Honour Judge Woodward; a Circuit Judge, since 1990; *s* of Wilfred and Mary Hannah Woodward; *m* 1963, Patricia Holland; two *d. Educ:* Sheffield Univ. (LLM). Called to the Bar, Gray's Inn, 1970. Teaching positions, 1961–70; practice on Northern Circuit, 1970–84; Chm., Industrial Tribunals, Manchester Region, 1984; a Recorder, 1988. *Recreations:* ski-ing, windsurfing, motorcycling, any other sporting activity that time and fitness permits, messing with classic motor cars. *Address:* Minshull Street Crown Court, Manchester M1 3FS. *T:* (0161) 954 7500.

WOODWARD, Clive; Manager, England Rugby Football Union team, since 2000 (Coach, 1997–2000); *b* 6 Jan. 1956. *Educ:* HMS Conway; Loughborough Coll. Rugby Football Union player: début for England U-23, 1976; 21 England caps, 1980–84; Leicester RFC, 1979; Manly, Australia, 1985; Coach: Henley RFC, 1993–95; London Irish RFC, 1995; Bath RFC, 1996–97. *Address:* Rugby Football Union, Twickenham TW1 1DZ.

WOODWARD, David John, CMG 2000; on secondment from National Audit Office to Cour des Comptes, France, since 2001; *b* 12 Dec. 1949; *s* of Lionel John Innes Woodward and Ethel Woodward; *m* 1st, 1973, Agnes Kane (marr. diss. 1985); 2nd, 1985, Yvonne Yee Fun Wong; one *s. Educ:* Reigate Grammar Sch.; Woolwich Poly.; City of London Poly. (Dip. Auditing and Accounting). With BR, 1969–75; Nat. Audit Office, 1975–: Associate Dir, 1987–93, Dir, 1993–; Director: Internat., London, 1993–94; Audit Ops, UN HQ, NY, 1995–2001. *Recreation:* English history. *Address:* Cour des Comptes, 13 rue Cambon, 75100 Paris RP, France.

WOODWARD, Hon. Sir Edward; *see* Woodward, Hon. Sir A. E.

WOODWARD, Edward, OBE 1978; actor and singer, since 1946; *b* 1 June 1930; *s* of Edward Oliver Woodward and Violet Edith Woodward; *m* 1st, 1952, Venetia Mary Collett; two *s* one *d*; 2nd, 1987, Michele Dotrice; one *d. Educ:* Kingston Coll.; RADA. *Stage:* Castle Theatre, Farnham, 1946; appeared for some years in rep. cos throughout England and Scotland; first appearance on London stage, Where There's a Will, Garrick, 1955; Mercutio in Romeo and Juliet, and Laertes in Hamlet, Stratford, 1958; Rattle of a Simple Man, Garrick, 1962; Two Cities (musical), 1968; Cyrano in Cyrano de Bergerac, and Flamineo in The White Devil, Nat. Theatre Co., 1971; The Wolf, Apollo, 1973; Male of the Species, Piccadilly, 1975; On Approval, Theatre Royal Haymarket, 1976; The Dark Horse, Comedy, 1978; starred in and directed Beggar's Opera, 1980; Private Lives, Australia, 1980; The Assassin, Greenwich, 1982; Richard III, Ludlow Fest., 1982; The Dead Secret, Plymouth and Richmond, 1992; has appeared in 3 prodns in NY (Rattle of a Simple Man, High Spirits, and Best Laid Plans); *films:* Becket, 1966; File on the Golden Goose, 1968; Hunted, 1973; Sitting Target, Young Winston, The Wicker Man, 1974; Stand Up Virgin Soldiers, 1977; Breaker Morant, 1980; The Appointment, 1981; Who Dares Wins, Forever Love, Merlin and the Sword, 1982; Champions, 1983; Christmas Carol, 1984; King David, Uncle Tom's Cabin, 1986; Mister Johnson, 1990; Deadly Advice, 1993; A Christmas Reunion, 1994; Gulliver's Travels, 1995; The Abduction Club, 2000; *television:* over 2000 prodns, inc. Callan (series and film, and in Wet Job, 1981), The Trial of Lady Chatterley, Blunt Instrument, 1980; Churchill: The Wilderness Years, 1981; The Equalizer (series), 1985–89; Codename Kyril, 1987; Hunted, 1988; The Man in the Brown Suit, 1988; Hands of a Murderer, or The Napoleon of Crime, 1990; Over My Dead Body (series), 1990; In Suspicious Circumstances (series), 1991–95; In My Defence, 1991; America at Risk (series), 1991–92; Harrison, 1994; Common as Muck (series), 1994, 1996; Cry of the City, 1995; The Woodward File, 1995; The House of Angelo, 1997; The New Professionals (series), 1998–99; Emma's Boy, 2000; Nikita (series), 2000; Night and Day, 2001; Messiah, 2001; 12 long-playing records (singing), 3 records (poetry) and 14 talking book recordings. Over 20 national and internat. acting awards incl. BAFTA best actor award and an Emmy. *Recreations:* boating, geology. *Address:* c/o Janet Glass, Eric Glass Ltd, 28 Berkeley Square, W1X 6HD. *T:* (020) 7629 7162, *Fax:* (020) 7499 6980. *Clubs:* Garrick, Green Room.

WOODWARD, Prof. (Frank) Ian, PhD; Professor of Plant Ecology, Department of Animal and Plant Sciences, University of Sheffield, since 1991; *b* 15 Dec. 1948; *s* of Frank Clement Woodward and Gwenda Agnes Woodward (*née* Allen); *m* 1972, Pearl May Chambers; one *s* one *d. Educ:* Mansfield Coll., Oxford (BA Hons Botany 1970); Univ. of Lancaster (PhD 1973); MA Cantab 1979. NERC Res. Fellow, Univ. of Lancaster, 1973–75; Higher Scientific Officer, Grassland Res. Inst., 1975–76; Lectr, Dept of Plant Scis, UWCC, 1976–79; Lectr, Dept of Botany, 1979–91, Fellow, Trinity Hall, 1981–91, Univ. of Cambridge. Henry J. Oosting Lectr, Duke Univ., USA, 1996. FLS 1990. W. S. Cooper Award, Ecological Soc. of America, 1991. *Publications:* Principles and Measurements in Environmental Biology, 1983; Climate and Plant Distribution, 1987 (trans. Japanese 1993); numerous articles in jls on influences of climate and carbon dioxide on plants and vegetation. *Recreations:* wood turning, music. *Address:* 16 Ecclesall Road South, Ecclesall, Sheffield S11 9PE. *T:* (0114) 266 0399.

WOODWARD, John Collin; Chief Executive Officer, Film Council, since 1999; *b* 18 Feb. 1961; *s* of Anthony and Anne Woodward. *Educ:* Shiplake Coll.; Poly. of Central London. (BA Hons Media Studies). Co-ordinator, 25% Campaign, 1986–87; Dir, Independent Access Steering Cttee, 1987–88; Dep. Dir, Independent Producers Programme Assoc., 1988–90; Chief Executive: Producers Assocs, 1990–92; Producers Alliance for Cinema and Television, 1992–98; Dir, BFI, 1998–99. Member: Govt Film Policy Rev. Gp, 1997; Film Policy Rev. Action Cttee, 1998; Video Consultative Council, BBFC; British Screen Adv. Council. FRTS. *Recreations:* cinema, television, reading. *Address:* Film Council, 10 Little Portland Street, W1W 7JG. *T:* (020) 7861 7861, *Fax:* (020) 7861 7863. *Club:* Union.

WOODWARD, Adm. Sir John (Forster), GBE 1989; KCB 1982; *b* Penzance, Cornwall, 1 May 1932; *s* of late T. Woodward and M. B. M. Woodward; *m* 1960, Charlotte Mary McMurtrie; one *s* one *d. Educ:* Royal Naval College, Dartmouth. Under training, Home Fleet, until 1953; Submarine Specialist, serving in HMS Sanguine, Porpoise, Valiant, and commanding HMS Tireless, Grampus and Warspite, from 1953; Min. of Defence and senior training posts, from 1971, plus comd HMS Sheffield, 1976–77; Director of Naval Plans, 1978–81; Flag Officer, First Flotilla, 1981–83, Sen. Task Gp Comdr, S Atlantic, during Falklands Campaign, Apr.-July 1982; Flag Officer, Submarines, and Comdr, Submarines Eastern Atlantic, 1983–84; Dep. Chief of Defence Staff (Commitments), 1985–87; C-in-C, Naval Home Command, 1987–89; Flag ADC to the Queen, 1987–89. Ind. Inspector, Lord Chancellor's Panel, 1994–96. Chm., Falklands Is Meml Chapel Trust, 1994–2000. Hon. Liveryman, Glass Sellers' Co., 1982. *Publication:* One Hundred Days: the memoirs of the Falklands Battle Group Commander, 1992. *Recreations:* sailing, golf, bridge. *Address:* c/o The Naval Secretary, Victory Building, HM Naval Base, Portsmouth PO1 3LS.

WOODWARD, Nicholas Frederick; His Honour Judge Nicholas Woodward; a Circuit Judge, since 2001; *b* 12 March 1952; *s* of Frederick Cyril Woodward and Joan Woodward; *m* 1982, Denise Harding; one *s. Educ:* Trent Poly., Nottingham (BA). Called to the Bar, Lincoln's Inn, 1975; in practice as barrister, Chester, 1977–2001. *Address:* Wales & Chester Circuit Secretariat, 2nd Floor, Churchill House, Churchill Way, Cardiff CF1 4HH. *Club:* City (Chester).

WOODWARD, Prof. Roger Robert, AC 1992; OBE 1980; Australian pianist, conductor, composer; Prof. of Music, University of New England, and Chief Executive Officer and Head, New England Conservatorium of Music, since 2000; *b* 20 Dec. 1942; *s* of Francis William Woodward and Gladys A. Woodward. *Educ:* NSW State Conservatorium of Music; Polish State Acad. of Music, Warsaw. Début at RFH, London, 1970; since then has appeared with major orchestras throughout the world. Artistic Dir, Alpha Centaur Chamber Emsemble, 1989. Prof., Sch. of Music, Sydney Univ., 1999. Has made numerous recordings. *Address:* School of Music, University of New England, C.B. Newling Building, Mossman Street, Armidale, NSW 2350, Australia. *T:* (612) 67736514, *Fax:* (612) 67736450; *e-mail:* woodward@metz.une.edu.au.

WOODWARD, Shaun Anthony; MP (Lab) St Helens South, since 2001; *b* 26 Oct. 1958; *s* of Dennis George Woodward and late Joan Lillian (*née* Nunn); *m* 1987, Camilla Davan, *e d* of Rt Hon. Sir Timothy Sainsbury, *qv*; one *s* three *d. Educ:* Bristol Grammar Sch.; Jesus Coll., Cambridge (first class double MA). Parly Lobbyist, Nat. Consumer Council, 1981–82; BBC TV: Researcher, That's Life!, 1982–85; Producer: Newsnight, 1985–87; Panorama, 1988–89; Editor, That's Life!, 1989–91; Researcher, Lost Babies, 1983; Producer: Drugwatch, 1985; The Gift of Life!, 1987; Dir of Communications, Cons. Party, 1991–92; Vis. Professorial Fellow, QMW, 1992–96; Fellow, Inst. of Politics at Kennedy Sch., Harvard Univ., 1994–95. MP Witney, 1997–2001 (C, 1997–99, Lab, 1999–2001). Opposition front bench spokesman for London, 1999. Member, Select Committees: EU, 1997–99; Foreign Affairs, 1999. Broadcasting Dir and Chm., Redevelt Campaign, ENO, 1994–; Dir, Jerusalem Productions, 1989–96. Chairman: Understanding Industry, 1995–97; Oxford Student Radio, 1995–97. Chm., Ben Hardwick Meml Fund, 1984–93; Trustee, 1993–, Dep. Chm., 1993–97, Childline. Mem., Foundn Bd, RSC, 1998–; Dir, Marine Stewardship Council, 1998–. *Publications:* (with Ron Lacey) Tranquillisers, 1983; (with Esther Rantzen) Ben: the story of Ben Hardwick, 1985; (with Sarah Caplin) Drugwatch, 1986. *Recreations:* opera, architecture, gardening, reading, travel. *Address:* c/o House of Commons, SW1A 0AA.

WOODWARD, Thomas Jones, (Tom Jones), OBE 1999; entertainer; *b* 7 June 1940; *s* of Thomas Woodward and Freda (*née* Jones); *m* 1956, Melinda Trenchard; one *s.* Singing début at age of 3; sang in clubs and dance halls; first hit record, It's Not Unusual, 1964; toured US, 1965; many internat. hit records, incl. Reload, 2000 (most successful album in career); radio and TV appearances, incl. series, This is Tom Jones, 1969–71; has toured worldwide. Score for musical play, Matador, 1987. *Films:* Mars Attacks, 1997; Agnes Brown, 1999. Appeared as character in Disney animated feature, Emperor's New Groove, 2000. Silver Clef Award, Nordoff Robbins Music Therapy, 2001. Hon. FWCMD 1994. MTV Video Award, 1988. *Recreations:* music, history. *Address:* Tom Jones Enterprises, 10100 Santa Monica Boulevard, Suite 225, Los Angeles, CA 90067, USA. *T:* (310) 5520044. *Club:* Friars (Los Angeles and New York).

WOODWARD, William Charles; QC 1985; a Recorder, since 1989; a Deputy High Court Judge, since 1997; *b* 27 May 1940; *s* of Wilfred Charles Woodward and Annie Stewart Woodward (*née* Young); *m* 1965, Carolyn Edna Johns; two *s* one *d. Educ:* South County Junior Sch.; Nottingham High Sch.; St John's Coll., Oxford (BA Jurisp). Marshall to Sir Donald Finnemore, Michaelmas 1962. Called to the Bar, Inner Temple, 1964; pupillage with Brian J. Appleby, QC; Midland and Oxford Circuit, 1964–; Head of Ropewalk Chambers, Nottingham, 1986–94. Pres., Mental Health Review Tribunal, 2000–. Member: E Midlands Area Cttee, Law Soc., 1972–; Bar Eur. Gp, 1998–; Founder Member: Notts Medico-Legal Soc., 1985–; E Midlands Business and Property Bar Assoc., 1994–. Special Prof., Univ. of Nottingham Sch. of Law, 1998–. *Recreations:* family, friends, holidays. *Address:* (chambers): 24 The Ropewalk, Nottingham NG1 5EF. *T:* (0115) 947 2581, *Fax:* (0115) 947 6532. *Clubs:* Pre War Austin Seven; Nottingham and Notts United Services.

WOOF, Robert Samuel, CBE 1998; PhD; Director, Wordsworth Trust, Dove Cottage, Grasmere, since 1989; *b* 20 April 1931; *s* of late William Woof and Annie (*née* Mason); *m* 1958, Pamela Shirley Moore; two *s* two *d. Educ:* Lancaster Royal Grammar School; Pembroke College, Oxford (MA); University of Toronto (PhD). Goldsmith Travelling Fellow, 1953–55; Lectr, Univ. of Toronto, 1958–61; University of Newcastle: Lord Adams of Ennerdale Fellow, 1961–62; Lectr, 1962; Reader in Eng. Lit., 1971–92; Leverhulme Fellow, 1983–84. Vice-Chm., Northern Arts Assoc., 1974–81; Hon. Keeper of Collections, Trustees of Dove Cottage, Grasmere, 1974–89, Hon. Sec. and Treasurer, 1978–95. Mem., 1982–88, Rep., 1988–, Arts Council: Vice-Chm., 1982–88, acting Chm, 1985–86, Drama Panel; Chm., Literature Panel, 1984–88 (Vice-Chm., 1983–84). Chairman: Century Theatre, 1991–92; English Touring Theatre, 1993–2000. FRSL 2000. Hon. DLitt: Lancaster, 1994; Newcastle upon Tyne, 2001. Creative Briton Award, Arts & Business, 1999. *Publications:* (ed) T. W. Thompson, Wordsworth's Hawkshead, 1970; The Wordsworth Circle, 1979; (with Peter Bicknell) The Discovery of the Lake District 1750–1810, 1982; (with Peter Bicknell) The Lake District Discovered 1810–50, 1983; Thomas De Quincey: an English opium-eater 1785–1859, 1985; (with David Thomason) Derwentwater, the Vale of Elysium, 1986; The Artist as Evacuee, 1987; (with Jonathan Wordsworth and Michael C. Jaye) William Wordsworth and the Age of English Romanticism, 1987; Matthew Arnold, a Centennial Exhibition, 1988; Byron: a dangerous romantic?, 1989; Tennyson: a bicentenary tribute, 1992; Shelley: an ineffectual angel?, 1992; (with Stephen Hebron) John Keats 1795–1995, 1995; (with David Brown and Stephen Hebron) Benjamin Robert Haydon: painter and writer, friend of Wordsworth and Keats, 1996; (with Fay Godwin) A Perfect Republic of Shepherds, 1997; (with Stephen Hebron) The Ancient Mariner, 1997; (with Stephen Hebron, Claire Tomalin and Pamela Woof) Hyenas in Petticoats, 1997; (with Stephen Hebron) Towards Tintern Abbey, 1998; (with Stephen Hebron) Romantic Icons, 1999; (with Stephen Hebron and Pamela Woof) English Poetry, 850–1850: the first thousand years, 2000; Wordsworth: the critical heritage, 2 vols, 2001. *Recreations:* the arts, the Lake District. *Address:* 4 Burdon Terrace, Jesmond, Newcastle upon Tyne NE2 3AE. *T:* (0191) 281 2680; The Wordsworth Trust, Dove Cottage, Grasmere, Cumbria LA22 9SH. *T:* (015394) 63500/35544.

WOOL, Dr Rosemary Jane, CB 1995; FRCPsych; Independent Consultant in Health Care in a Secure Environment, since 1996; Specialist in Psychiatry, specialising in drug and alcohol misuse, West Hertfordshire Health Care Trust, since 1998. *Educ:* University of London (Charing Cross Hospital Medical School). MB BS, DPM, DRCOG. Dir of Health Care, Prison Medical Service, later Prison Service, 1989–96; Hd of Educn and Trng Unit, Dept of Psychiatry of Addictive Behaviour, St George's Hosp. Med. Sch., 1996–98. Sec. Gen., 1995–2001, Vice-Pres., Internat. Relations, 2001–, Internat. Council of Prison Med. Services. *Address:* Wicken House, 105 Weston Road, Aston Clinton, Bucks HP22 5EP.

WOOLARD, Edgar Smith; Chairman, 1989–97, and Chief Executive Officer, 1989–96, Du Pont; *b* 15 April 1934; *s* of Edgar S. Woolard and Mamie (Boone) Woolard; *m* 1956, Peggy Harrell; two *d*. *Educ:* North Carolina State Univ. (BSc Indust. Eng. 1956). Joined Du Pont 1957; industrial engineer, Kinston, NC, 1957–59; group supervisor, industrial engrg, 1959–62; supervisor, manufg sect., 1962–64; planning supervisor, 1964–65; staff asst to Prodn Manager, Wilmington, 1965–66; product supt, Old Hickory, Tenn, 1966–69; engrg supt, 1969–70; Asst Plant Manager, Camden, SC, 1970–71; Plant Manager, 1971–73; Dir of products marketing div., Wilmington, 1973–75; Man. Dir, textile marketing div., 1975–76; Manager, corp. plans dept, 1976–77; Gen. Dir, products and planning div., 1977–78; Gen. Manager, textile fibers, 1978–81; Vice-Pres., textile fibers, 1981–83; Exec. Vice President, 1983–85; Vice Chm., 1985–87; Pres. and Chief Operating Officer, 1987–89. Director: Citicorp; N Carolina Textile Foundn; Member: Bd of Trustees, Winterthur Mus.; Bd of Trustees, N Carolina State Univ.; Med. Center of Delaware; Protestant Episcopal Theol Seminary, Virginia; Exec. Cttee, Delaware Roundtable; Bretton Woods Cttee; World Affairs Council; Business Roundtable. *Address:* c/o Du Pont, 1007 Market Street, Wilmington, DE 19898, USA.

WOOLAS, Philip James; MP (Lab) Oldham East and Saddleworth, since 1997; an Assistant Government Whip, since 2001; *b* 11 Dec. 1959; *s* of Dennis Woolas and Maureen Woolas (*née* White); *m* 1988, Tracey Jane Allen; one *s*. *Educ:* Univ. of Manchester (BA Hons Philosophy 1981). Treas., 1983–84, Pres., 1984–86, NUS; journalist, Television South, 1987; Asst Prod., BBC Newsnight, 1988–90; Prod., Channel Four News, 1990–91; Head of Communications, GMB, 1991–97. PPS to Minister for Transport, 1999–2001. Chm., All Party Parly Clothing and Textile Gp, 1998–2001; Mem., PLP Leadership Campaign Team, 1997–99 (Dep. Chm., 1998–99). Chm., Tribune Publications Ltd, 1997–2001. *Recreations:* photography, reading, cricket, Manchester United supporter. *Address:* 1 Hopkin Mill Cottage, Sunnybank, Lees, Oldham OL4 5DD. *T:* (0161) 624 7671; House of Commons, SW1A 0AA. *Clubs:* Groucho; Lancashire County Cricket.

WOOLDRIDGE, Ian Edmund, OBE 1991; Sports Columnist, Daily Mail, since 1972; BBC Television documentary reporter and writer; *b* 14 Jan. 1932; *s* of late Edmund and Bertha Wooldridge; *m* 1st, Veronica Ann Churcher; three *s*; 2nd, Sarah Margaret Chappell Lourenço. *Educ:* Brockenhurst Grammar School. New Milton Advertiser, 1948; Bournemouth Times, 1953; News Chronicle, 1956; Sunday Dispatch, 1960; Daily Mail, 1961. Columnist of Year, 1975 and 1976; Sportswriter of Year, 1972, 1974, 1981, 1989, in British Press Awards; Sports Council Awards: Sportswriter of the Year, 1987, 1988, 1996; Sports Feature Writer of the Year, 1991, 1997. *Publications:* Cricket, Lovely Cricket, 1963; (with Mary Peters) Mary P, 1974; (with Colin Cowdrey) MCC: The Autobiography of a Cricketer, 1976; The Best of Wooldridge, 1978; Travelling Reserve, 1982; Sport in the Eighties, 1989. *Recreations:* travel, golf, Beethoven and dry Martinis. *Address:* 22 Gloucester Walk, W8 4HZ. *Club:* Reform.

WOOLER, Stephen John; HM Chief Inspector, Crown Prosecution Service, since 1999 (became statutory independent inspectorate, 2001); *b* 16 March 1948; *s* of Herbert George Wooler and Mabel Wooler; *m* 1974, Jonquil Elizabeth Wilmshurst-Smith; one *s* one *d*. *Educ:* Bedford Modern Sch.; University Coll. London (LLB Hons 1969). Called to the Bar, Gray's Inn, 1969; in practice at Common Law Bar, 1970–73; joined Office of Director of Public Prosecutions, 1973: Legal Asst, 1973–76; Sen. Legal Asst, 1976–82; Asst DPP, 1982–83; on secondment to Law Officers' Dept, 1983–87; Chief Crown Prosecutor (London North), 1987–89; on secondment to Law Officers' Dept, 1989–99: Dep. Legal Sec. to Law Officers, 1992–99. *Recreations:* campanology, Rugby, walking, gardening. *Address:* HM Crown Prosecution Service Inspectorate, 26 Old Queen Street, SW1H 9HP. *T:* (020) 7210 1197.

WOOLF, family name of **Baron Woolf**.

WOOLF, Baron *cr* 1992 (Life Peer), of Barnes in the London Borough of Richmond; **Harry Kenneth Woolf,** Kt 1979; PC 1986; Lord Chief Justice of England and Wales, since 2000; *b* 2 May 1933; *s* of late Alexander Woolf and Leah Woolf (*née* Cussins); *m* 1961, Marguerite Sassoon, *d* of late George Sassoon; three *s*. *Educ:* Fettes Coll.; University Coll., London (LLB; Fellow, 1981). Called to Bar, Inner Temple, 1954; Bencher, 1976. Commnd (Nat. Service), 15/19th Royal Hussars, 1954; seconded Army Legal Services, 1955; Captain 1955. Started practice at Bar, 1956. A Recorder of the Crown Court, 1972–79; Jun. Counsel, Inland Revenue, 1973–74; First Treasury Junior Counsel (Common Law), 1974–79; a Judge of the High Court of Justice, Queen's Bench Div., 1979–86; Presiding Judge, SE Circuit, 1981–84; a Lord Justice of Appeal, 1986–92; a Lord of Appeal in Ordinary, 1992–96; Master of the Rolls, 1996–2000. Held inquiry into prison disturbances, 1990, Part II with Judge Tumin, report 1991; conducted inquiry, Access to Justice, 1994–96. Member: Senate, Inns of Court and Bar, 1981–85; Bd of Management, Inst. of Advanced Legal Studies, 1985–94 (Chm., 1986–94); World Bank Internat. Adv. Council on Law and Justice; Chairman: Lord Chancellor's Adv. Cttee on Legal Educn., 1986–91; Mddx Adv. Cttee on Justices of the Peace, 1986–90; Lord Chancellor's Adv. Cttee on Public Records, 1996–2000; Council of Civil Justice, 1998–2000; Rules Cttee, 1998–2000; President: Assoc. of Law Teachers, 1985–89; Central Council of Jewish Social Services, 1987–2000; SW London Magistrates Assoc., 1987–93; Assoc. of Mems of Bds of Visitors, 1994–; Public Records Soc., 1996–2000. Vice-Pres., Royal Over-Seas League, 2001. Pro-Chancellor, London Univ., 1994–. Chairman: Trustees, Butler Trust, 1992–96 (Trustee, 1991–96; Pres., 1996–); Special Trustees, St Mary's Hosp., Paddington, 1993–97; Magna Carta Trust, 1996–2000. Visitor: Nuffield Coll., Oxford, 1996–2000; UCL, 1996–2000. Gov., Oxford Centre for Postgrad. Hebrew Studies, 1989–93. Hon. Mem., SPTL, 1988. Hon. FBA 2000. Hon. Fellow, Leeds Poly., 1990. Hon. LLD: Buckingham, 1992; Bristol, 1992; London, 1993; Anglia Poly. Univ., 1994; Manchester Metropolitan, 1994; Hull, 2001; Cranfield, 2001. Hon. Freeman, Drapers' Co., 1999. *Publications:* Protecting the Public: the new challenge (Hamlyn Lecture), 1990; (ed with J. Woolf) Declaratory Judgement, 2nd edn, 1993; (ed jtly) De Smith, Judicial Review of Administrative Action, 5th edn, 1995; (jtly) Principles of Judicial Review, 1999. *Address:* Royal Courts of Justice, WC2A 2LL. *Clubs:* Athenæum, Garrick, Royal Automobile.

WOOLF, Prof. Clifford John; Richard Kitz Professor of Anaesthesia Research, Harvard Medical School, since 1997; *b* 30 Jan. 1952; *s* of Jeffery Woolf and Lorna Woolf (*née* Lusman); *m* 1976, Fredia Maltz; two *s*. *Educ:* Univ. of the Witwatersrand, Johannesburg (MB, BCh, PhD). MRCP. Lectr, Middlesex Hosp. Med. Sch., London, 1979–81; Lectr, 1981–88, Reader, 1988–92, Prof. of Neurobiology, 1992–97, UCL, now Vis. Prof. Hon. Consultant, UCH NHS Trust, 1996–. *Publications:* numerous articles in scientific jls on the pathophysiology of pain and the regeneration of the nervous system. *Recreation:* mind surfing. *Address:* Department of Anaesthesia, Massachusetts General Hospital and Harvard Medical School, Boston, MA 02114, USA. *Club:* Stormont Lawn Tennis.

WOOLF, Geoffrey David; Organiser, Institution of Professionals, Managers and Specialists, since 1997; *b* 15 April 1944. *Educ:* Polytechnic of Central London (BSc Econ). Lecturer in History, Southgate Technical College, 1974–89; Gen. Sec., NATFHE, 1989–94; Trade Union Manager, LV Gp, 1996–97. *Recreation:* politics. *Address:* 8 Russell Court, Woburn Place, WC1H 0LL. *T:* (020) 7278 7829; *e-mail:* geoffwoolf@tesco.net.

WOOLF, Harry, PhD; Professor-at-Large, Institute for Advanced Study, Princeton, USA, 1987–94, now Emeritus (Director, 1976–87); *b* 12 Aug. 1923; *s* of Abraham Woolf and Anna (*née* Frankman); *m* (marr. diss.); two *s* two *d*. *Educ:* Univ. of Chicago (BS Physics and Maths 1948; MA Physics and History 1949); Cornell Univ. (PhD Hist. of Science 1955). Served US Army, 1943–46. Instructor: Boston Univ., Mass, 1953–55; Brandeis Univ., Waltham, Mass, 1954–55; Univ. of Washington, Seattle: Asst Prof., Associate Prof., and Prof., 1955–61; Johns Hopkins University: Prof., Hist. of Science Dept, 1961–76 (Chm. of Dept, 1961–72); Provost, 1972–76; Princeton University: Mem. Adv. Council, Depts of Philosophy, 1980–84, and of Comparative Lit., 1982–86. Pres., Chm. of Bd, Johns Hopkins Program for Internat. Educn in Gynecology and Obstetrics, Inc., 1973–76, Trustee 1976–; Mem. Adv. Bd, Smithsonian Research Awards, 1975–79; Member: Vis. Cttee Student Affairs, MIT, 1973–77; Corporation Vis. Cttee, Dept of Linguistics and Philosophy, MIT, 1977–83; Nat. Adv. Child Health and Human Develt Council, NIH, 1977–80; Mem. Vis. Cttee, Research Center for Language Sciences, Indiana Univ., 1977–80; Trustee: Associated Universities Inc., Brookhaven Nat. Laboratories, Nat. Radio Astronomy Observatory, 1972–82; Hampshire Coll., Amherst, Mass, 1977–81; Merrill Lynch Cluster C Funds, 1982–95; Reed Coll., 1992–97; Dibner Inst. for the Hist. of Science, 1992–98; Trustee-at-Large, Univs Research Assoc. Inc., Washington, DC (Fermi Nat. Accelerator Lab.), 1978–91, Chm. Bd 1979–89. Member: Corp. Visiting Cttee for Dept. of Physics, MIT, 1979–85; Council on Foreign Relations Inc., 1979–; Adv. Panel, WGBH, NOVA, 1979–; Internat. Research and Exchanges Bd, NY, 1980–94; Scientific Adv. Bd, Wissenschaftskolleg zu Berlin, 1981–87; Board of Directors: Alex. Brown Mutual Funds, Inc., Baltimore, 1981–96; W. Alton Jones Cell Science Center, 1982–86; Westmark Corp., 1987–92; Family Health Internat., 1992–; Advanced Technology Labs, 1992–99; Spacelabs Medical, 1992–98; Pres., Bankers Trust/Alex. Brown Funds Inc., 1997–99. Member: Adv. Council, Dept of Comparative Literature, Princeton Univ., 1982–94; Adv. Council, Nat. Science Foundn, 1984–89; Bd of Trustees, Rockefeller Foundn, 1984–94; Dir-at-large, Amer. Cancer Soc., 1982–86. Member: Académie Internat. d'Histoire des Sciences; Amer. Philosoph. Soc.; Phi Beta Kappa; Sigma Xi (also Bicentennial Lectr, 1976). Editor, ISIS Internat. Review, 1958–64; Associate Editor, Dictionary of Scientific Biog., 1970–80; Mem. Editl Bd, Interdisciplinary Science Revs, 1975–; Mem. Editl Adv. Bd, The Writings of Albert Einstein, 1977–. Fellow, Amer. Acad. of Arts and Scis; FAAAS. Hon. DSc: Whitman Coll., 1979; Amer. Univ., Washington DC, 1982; Hon. LHD: Johns Hopkins Univ., 1983; St Lawrence Univ., 1986. *Publications:* The Transits of Venus: a study in eighteenth-century science, 1959, repr. 1981; (ed) Quantification: essays in the history of measurement in the natural and social sciences, 1961; (ed) Science as a Cultural Force, 1964; (ed and contrib.) Some Strangeness in the Proportion: a centennial symposium to celebrate the achievements of Albert Einstein, 1980; (ed) The Analytic Spirit: essays in the history of science, 1981. *Address:* Institute for Advanced Study, Princeton, NJ 08540, USA. *T:* (609) 7348018.

WOOLF, John Moss, CB 1975; Deputy Chairman of the Board of Customs and Excise, and Director-General (Customs and Establishments), 1973–78; *b* 5 June 1918; *o s* of Alfred and Maud Woolf; *m* 1940, Phyllis Ada Mary Johnson (*d* 1990); one *d*. *Educ:* Drayton Manor Sch.; Honourable Society of Lincoln's Inn. Barrister-at-law, 1948. War Service, 1939–46 (Captain, RA). Inland Revenue, 1937. Asst Principal, Min. of Fuel and Power, 1948; HM Customs and Excise, 1950: Principal, 1951; Asst Sec., 1960; Chm., Valuation Cttee, Customs Cooperation Council, Brussels, 1964–65; National Bd for Prices and Incomes, 1965; Under-Secretary, 1967; Asst Under-Sec. of State, Dept of Employment and Productivity, 1968–70; HM Customs and Excise: Comr, 1970; Dir of Establishments and Organisation, 1971–73. Advr on Price Problems, Govt of Trinidad & Tobago, 1968. Assoc. of First Div. Civil Servants: Mem. of Exec. Cttee, 1950–58 and 1961–65; Hon. Sec., 1952–55; Chm., 1955–58 and 1964–65; Mem., Civil Service National Whitley Council (Staff Side), 1953–55. Leader of Review Team to examine responsibilities of the Directors of the Nat. Museums and Galleries, 1978–79; Review of Organisation and Procedures of Chancery Div. of High Court, 1979–81; Overseas Adviser to CEGB, 1979–82. Commandeur d'Honneur, Ordre du Bontemps de Médoc et des Graves, 1973; Hon. Borgenerális (Hungary), 1974. *Publications:* Report on Control of Prices in Trinidad and Tobago (with M. M. Eccleshall), 1968; Report of the Review Body on the Chancery Division of the High Court (with Lord Oliver of Aylmerton and R. H. H. White), 1981. *Recreation:* reading. *Address:* 20 Bushey Park, High Street, Bushey, Herts WD23 1BJ. *T:* (020) 8950 4918. *Club:* Civil Service.

WOOLFSON, Prof. Michael Mark, FRS 1984; FRAS; FInstP; Professor of Theoretical Physics, University of York, 1965–94, now Emeritus; *b* 9 Jan. 1927; *s* of Morris and Rose Woolfson; *m* 1951, Margaret (*née* Frohlich); two *s* one *d*. *Educ:* Jesus College, Oxford (MA; Hon. Fellow, 1999); UMIST (PhD, DSc). Royal Engineers, 1947–49. Research Assistant: UMIST, 1950–52; Cavendish Lab., Cambridge, 1952–54; ICI Fellow, Univ. of Cambridge, 1954–55; Lectr, 1955–61, Reader, 1961–65, UMIST; Head of Dept. of Physics, 1982–87, Univ. of York. Hughes Medal, Royal Soc., 1986; Patterson Award, Amer. Crystallographic Assoc., 1990; Aminoff Medal, Royal Swedish Acad. of Scis, 1992; Dorothy Hodgkin Prize, British Crystallographic Assoc., 1997. *Publications:* Direct Methods in Crystallography, 1961; An Introduction to X-Ray Crystallography, 1970, 2nd edn 1997; The Origin of the Solar System, 1989; Physical and Non-Physical Methods of Solving Crystal Structures, 1995; An Introduction to Computer Simulation, 1999; The Origin and Evolution of the Solar System, 2000; Planetary Science, 2001; papers in learned jls. *Recreation:* wine making. *Address:* 24 Sandmoor Green, Leeds LS17 7SB. *T:* (0113) 266 2166.

WOOLGAR, Prof. Stephen William, PhD; Professor of Sociology and Marketing, University of Oxford, since 2000; Fellow, Green College, Oxford, since 2000; *b* 14 Feb. 1950; *s* of William Thomas Woolgar, III, and Constance Lillian Stuart Woolgar (*née* Hinkes); *m* 1983, Jacqueline Stokes; three *d*. *Educ:* Brentwood Sch.; Emmanuel Coll., Cambridge (BA 1st Cl. Hons 1972; MA 1976; PhD 1978). Brunel University: Lectr in Sociol., 1975–88; Reader 1988–92; Prof. of Sociol., 1992–2000; Dir, Centre for Res. into Innovation, Culture and Technol., 1991–98; Hd, Dept of Human Scis, 1996–98; Dir, ESRC prog. Virtual Society? the social sci. of electronic technologies, Univ of Oxford, 1997–. Vis. Prof., McGill Univ., Canada, 1979–81; Exxon Fellow, MIT, 1983–84; Maître de Recherche Associé, Ecole Nationale Supérieure des Mines, Paris, 1988–89; ESRC Sen. Res. Fellow, 1994–95; Fulbright Sen. Schol., Dept of Sociol., UC San Diego, 1995–96. OST Technology Foresight Panel: Leisure and Learning, 1994–96; IT, Electronics and Communications, 1996–99; Member: Sociol. Panel, HEFCE RAE 1996 and 2001; Council Consumers' Assoc., 2000–. *Publications:* (with B. Latour) Laboratory Life: the construction of scientific facts, 1979, 2nd edn 1986; (ed) Knowledge and Reflexivity, 1988; Science: the very idea, 1988; (ed jtly) The Cognitive Turn: sociological and psychological perspectives on science, 1989; (ed with M. Lynch) Representation in Scientific Practice, 1990; (with K. Grint) The Machine at Work: technology, work and organisation, 1997; Virtual Society? Get Real!—the social science of electronic technologies, 2002; numerous articles. *Address:* Said Business School, University of Oxford, Park End Street, Oxford OX1 1HP. *T:* (01865) 288934; *e-mail:* steve.woolgar@sbs.ox.ac.uk.

WOOLHOUSE, Prof. John George, CBE 1988; Professor of Education and Industry, and Director of Centre for Education and Industry, University of Warwick, 1988–97, now Emeritus; *b* 17 June 1931; *s* of George Francis Woolhouse and Doris May Woolhouse (*née* Webber); *m* 1958, Ruth Carolyn Harrison; two *s* one *d*. *Educ:* Chichester High Sch. for Boys; Ardingly Coll; Brasenose Coll., Univ. of Oxford (MA). Rolls-Royce Ltd, 1954–72: Dir, Rolls-Royce and Associates, 1965–68; Co. Educn and Trng Officer, 1968–72; Asst Dir, Kingston Polytechnic and Dir, Kingston Regl Management Centre, 1972–78; Dir Atkins Planning, W. S. Atkins Gp Consultants, and Hd of Human Resources Develt, 1978–82; Dir, Technical and Vocational Educn Initiative, MSC, 1983–86; Dir of Educn Progs, MSC, 1986–87. Chm., Assoc. of Regional Management Centres, 1977–78. *Publications:* chapters in: The Training of Youth in Industry, 1966; The Management Development Handbook, 1973; Gower Handbook of Management, 1983; Reform of Post-16 Education and Training in England and Wales, 1993. *Recreations:* travel, music, boating, fishing. *Address:* Ivy Farmhouse, Ivy Farm Lane, Coventry CV4 7BW. *Club:* Royal Air Force.

WOOLLAM, John Victor; Barrister-at-Law; *b* 14 Aug. 1927; *s* of Thomas Alfred and Edie Moss Woollam; *m* 1964, Lavinia Rosamond Ela, *d* of S. R. E. Snow; two *s*. *Educ:* Liverpool Univ. Called to the Bar, Inner Temple. Contested (C) Scotland Div. of Liverpool, 1950; MP (C) W Derby Div. of Liverpool, Nov. 1954–Sept. 1964; Parliamentary Private Sec. to Minister of Labour, 1960–62. *Recreation:* philately. *Address:* Old Ruggs Cottage, The Street, Kilmington, Devon EX13 7RW. *T:* (01297) 33336.

WOOLLAM, Suzanna Elizabeth; Her Honour Judge Woollam; a Circuit Judge, since 2001; *b* 6 Dec. 1946; *d* of John Martin Woollam and Elizabeth Mary Woollam (*née* Brennan). *Educ:* various convents; Trinity Coll., Dublin (MA Philosophy 1969). Called to the Bar, Gray's Inn, 1975; law reporting for the Weekly Law Reports and Times Law Reports, 1975–77; Army Legal Service, 1977–79; Solicitor to Scotland Yard, 1980–88; Sen. Legal Asst, office of JAG, 1988–90; Asst JAG, 1990–2001. *Recreations:* walking, gardening, reading, films, theatre. *Address:* Snaresbrook Crown Court, 75 Hollybush Hill, E11 1QW.

WOOLLARD, John Ian; a District Judge (Magistrates' Courts) (formerly Stipendiary Magistrate), Hampshire, since 1998; *b* 13 July 1954; *s* of Charles and Joy Woollard; *m* 1981, Angela Margaret Lee; one *s* one *d*. *Educ:* Brentwood Sch. Admitted Solicitor, 1977; Asst Solicitor, T. V. Edwards & Co., 1977–78; County Prosecuting Solicitors' Office, Essex, 1978–82; Partner, Mitchell Maudsley & Wright, Basildon, 1982–87; freelance solicitor advocate, 1987–98. *Recreations:* music, reading, tennis, psephology. *Address:* c/o Law Courts, Winston Churchill Avenue, Portsmouth PO1 2DQ.

WOOLLCOMBE, Rt Rev. Kenneth John; an Assistant Bishop, Diocese of Worcester, since 1989; *b* 2 Jan. 1924; *s* of late Rev. E. P. Woollcombe, OBE, and Elsie Ockenden Woollcombe; *m* 1st, 1950, Gwendoline Rhona Vyvien Hodges (*d* 1976); three *d*; 2nd, 1980, Rev. Juliet Dearmer; one *d*. *Educ:* Haileybury Coll., Hertford; St John's Coll., Oxford; Westcott House, Cambridge. Sub-Lieut (E) RNVR, 1945. Curate, St James, Grimsby, 1951; Fellow, Chaplain and Tutor, St John's Coll., Oxford, 1953, Hon. Fellow, 1971; Professor of Dogmatic Theology, General Theological Seminary, New York, 1960; Principal of Episcopal Theological Coll., Edinburgh, 1963; Bishop of Oxford, 1971–78; Asst Bishop, Diocese of London, 1978–81; Canon Residentiary of St Paul's, 1981–89, Precentor 1982–89. Chm., SPCK, 1973–79; Mem., Central Cttee, World Council of Churches, 1975–83; Chm., Churches' Council for Covenanting, 1978–82; Co-Chm., English Anglican-RC Cttee, 1985–88; Judge in Court of Ecclesiastical Causes Reserved, 1984–89. Hon. Chaplain, 1978–87, Hon. Liveryman, 1986, Glass Sellers' Co. STD Univ. of the South, Sewanee, USA, 1963; Hon. DD Hartford, Conn, 1975. *Publications:* (contrib.) The Historic Episcopate, 1954; (jointly) Essays on Typology, 1957. *Address:* 19 Ashdale Avenue, Pershore, Worcs WR10 1PL.

WOOLLETT, Maj.-Gen. John Castle, CBE 1957 (OBE 1955); MC 1945; MA Cantab; FICE; Principal Planning Inspector, Department of the Environment, 1971–81; *b* 5 Nov. 1915; *o s* of John Castle Woollett and Lily Bradley Woollett, Bredgar, Kent; *m* 1st, 1941, Joan Eileen Stranks (marr. diss., 1957); two *s* (and one *s* decd); 2nd, 1959, Helen Wendy Willis; two step *s*. *Educ:* St Benedict's Sch.; RMA Woolwich; St John's Coll., Cambridge. Joined RE, 1935; 23 Field Co., 1938–40 (BEF, 1939–40); 6 Commando, 1940–42; Major Comdg 16 Field Sqdn and 16 Assault Sqdn RE, 1942–45 (BLA, 1944–45); Student, Staff Coll., Camberley, 1946; DAAG and GSO2, Brit. Service Mission to Burma, 1947–50; Major Comdg 51 Port Sqdn RE, 1950; Instructor, Staff Coll., Camberley, 1950–53; Lt-Col Comdg 28 Field Engr Regt, 1954–55 (Korea); Bt Lt-Col 1955; Comdr Christmas Is, 1956–57; GSO1, Northern Army Gp, 1957–59; Col GS, US Army Staff Coll., Fort Leavenworth, 1959–61; DQMG (Movements), BAOR, 1962–64; Brig. Comdg Hants Sub District and Transportation Centre, RE, 1964–65; Sch. of Transport, 1965–66; Dep. Engr-in-Chief, 1966–67; Maj.-Gen., Chief Engineer, BAOR, 1967–70, retired. Col Comdt, RE, 1973–78. Pres., Instn of RE, 1974–79. *Address:* 42 Rhinefield Close, Brockenhurst, Hants SO42 7SU. *Clubs:* Army and Navy, Royal Ocean Racing, Royal Cruising; Island Sailing (Cowes), Royal Lymington Yacht.

WOOLLEY, David Rorie; QC 1980; barrister-at-law; a Recorder of the Crown Court, 1982–94; *b* 9 June 1939; *s* of Albert and Ethel Woolley; *m* 1988, Mandy, *d* of Donald and Barbara Hutchison, Upper Dicker, Sussex. *Educ:* Winchester Coll.; Trinity Hall, Cambridge (BA Hons Law). Called to the Bar, Middle Temple, 1962, Bencher, 1988. Vis. Scholar, Wolfson Coll., Cambridge, 1982–87. Inspector, DoE inquiry into Nat. Gall. extension, 1984. *Publications:* Town Hall and the Property Owner, 1965; (jtly) Environmental Law, 2000; contribs to various legal jls. *Recreations:* opera, mountaineering, Real tennis. *Address:* 1 Sergeants' Inn, EC4Y 1NH. *T:* (020) 7583 1355. *Clubs:* MCC; Swiss Alpine.

WOOLLEY, John Maxwell, MBE 1945; TD 1946; Clerk, Merchant Taylors' Company, and Clerk to The Governors, Merchant Taylors' School, 1962–80; *b* 22 March 1917; *s* of Lt-Col Jasper Maxwell Woolley, IMS (Retd) and Kathleen Mary Woolley (*née* Waller); *m* 1952, Esme Adela Hamilton-Cole; two *s*. *Educ:* Cheltenham College; Trinity College, Oxford. BA (Oxon) 1938, MA (Oxon) 1962. Practising Solicitor, 1950–55; Asst Clerk, Merchant Taylors' Company, 1955–62. Hon. Mem. CGLI, 1991. *Address:* Flat 27, 15 Grand Avenue, Hove, E Sussex BN3 2NG. *T:* (01273) 733200.

WOOLLEY, (John) Moger; DL; Chairman: Bristol Water Holdings, since 1998; API plc, since 1992; Brunel (Holdings) plc (formerly BM Group), since 1992; *b* 1 May 1935; *s* of Cyril Herbert Steele Woolley and Eveline Mary May Woolley; *m* 1960, Gillian Edith Millar; one *s* one *d*. *Educ:* Taunton Sch.; Bristol Univ., 1956–59 (BSc). National Service, 1954–56. Various management positions, DRG plc, 1959–89, Chief Exec., 1985–89; Chm., Dolphin Packaging, 1990–95. Non-executive Director: Staveley Industries, 1990–; United Bristol Hosp. Trust, 1991–93; Avon Rubber, 1992–96. Chm. Council, Univ. of Bristol, 1997–. DL Glos, 2000. *Recreations:* cricket, hockey, golf, gardening. *Address:* Matford House, Northwoods, Winterbourne, Bristol BS36 1RS. *T:* (01454) 772180. *Clubs:* MCC; Merchant Venturers' (Bristol).

WOOLLEY, His Honour Roy Gilbert; a Circuit Judge, 1976–93; *b* 28 Nov. 1922; *s* of John Woolley and Edith Mary Woolley; *m* 1953, Doreen, *d* of Humphrey and Kathleen Morris; two *s* two *d*. *Educ:* Overton and Marchwiel Primary Schs; Deeside Secondary Sch.; UCL (LLB Hons 1949). Served War, 1939–45, Air Gunner, RAF. Christopher Tancred Student, Lincoln's Inn, 1948; called to the Bar, 1951; Wales and Chester Circuit; Recorder, 1975. Reader: Diocese of Chester, 1955–77; Diocese of Lichfield, 1977–95. Member: Lichfield Diocesan Synod, 1988–; General Synod of C of E, 1990–95; Legal Adv. Commn of C of E, 1991–96. *Recreations:* outdoor pursuits, incl. horse riding, gardening; interested in music, poetry, art and antique furniture. *Address:* Henlle Hall, St Martins, Oswestry, Salop SY10 7AX. *T:* (01691) 661257.

WOOLLEY, Trevor Adrian; Director General, Resources and Plans, Ministry of Defence, since 1998; *b* 9 Aug. 1954; *s* of late Harry George Woolley and Doreen Vera Woolley (*née* O'Hale). *Educ:* Latymer Upper Sch., Hammersmith; Peterhouse, Cambridge (MA Hist.). Ministry of Defence, 1975–: Private Sec. to Sec. of Cabinet, 1986–90 (on secondment); Dir, Procurement Policy, 1990–93; Head, Resources and Progs (Army), 1993–97; Asst Under Sec. of State (Systems), 1997–98. *Recreations:* cricket, golf, travel, trekking. *Address:* c/o Ministry of Defence, Whitehall, SW1A 2HB. *T:* (020) 7218 2605. *Club:* Chiswick and Latymer Cricket.

WOOLMAN, (Joseph) Roger, CB 1997; Deputy Secretary, and Legal Adviser and Solicitor to Ministry of Agriculture, Fisheries and Food, Forestry Commission and Intervention Board for Agricultural Produce, 1993–97; *b* 13 Feb. 1937; *s* of late Maurice Wollman and Hilda Wollman; *m* 1st, 1973, Elizabeth (marr. diss. 1999); one *s* one *d*; 2nd, 2000, Dr Judith E. Bronkhurst, art historian. *Educ:* Perse School, Cambridge; Trinity Hall, Cambridge (Exhibnr; MA). Solicitor, 1974. DTI and OFT Legal Departments, 1976–93: Under Sec., DTI, 1985–88 and 1991–93; Legal Dir, OFT, 1988–91. *Address:* 146 Willifield Way, NW11 6YD. *Clubs:* Reform; Hampstead Golf.

WOOLMAN, Stephen Errol; QC (Scot.) 1998; *b* 16 May 1953; *s* of Errol Woolman, architect, and Frances Woolman (*née* Porter); *m* 1977, Dr Helen Mackinnon; two *d*. *Educ:* George Heriot's Sch., Edinburgh; Aberdeen Univ. (LLB). Lectr, 1978–87, Associate Dean, Faculty of Law, 1981–84, Edinburgh Univ.; admitted to Faculty of Advocates, 1987; Standing Junior Counsel in Scotland: Office of Fair Trading, 1991–95; MoD (Procurement Exec.), 1995–96; Inland Revenue, 1996–98; Advocate Depute, 1999–. *Publications:* An Introduction to the Scots Law of Contract, 1987, 2nd edn 1994. *Recreation:* cinema. *Address:* 16 Garscube Terrace, Edinburgh EH12 6BQ. *T:* (0131) 313 1213. *Club:* New (Edinburgh).

WOOLMER, family name of **Baron Woolmer of Leeds**.

WOOLMER OF LEEDS, Baron *cr* 1999 (Life Peer), of Leeds in the county of West Yorkshire; **Kenneth John Woolmer;** Partner and Director: Halton Gill Associates, consultants on central and local government relations, since 1999 (Principal, 1979–97); Anderson McGraw, since 2001; *b* 25 April 1940; *s* of Joseph William and Gertrude May Woolmer; *m* 1961, Janice Chambers; three *s*. *Educ:* Gladstone Street County Primary, Rothwell, Northants; Kettering Grammar Sch.; Leeds Univ. (BA Econs). Research Fellow, Univ. of West Indies, 1961–62; Teacher, Friern Rd Sec. Mod. Sch., London, 1963; Lecturer: Univ. of Leeds (Economics), 1963–66; Univ. of Ahmadu Bello, Nigeria, 1966–68; Univ. of Leeds, 1968–79; Dir, MBA Progs, 1991–97, Dean of Ext. Relns, 1997, Chm., subseq. Dean, 1997–2000, Sch. of Business and Econ. Studies, Leeds Univ., later Leeds Univ. Business Sch. Councillor: Leeds CC, 1970–78; West Yorkshire MCC, 1973–80 (Leader, 1975–77; Leader of Opposition, 1977–79). Chairman, Planning and Transportation Cttee, Assoc. of Metropolitan Authorities, 1974–77. Contested (Lab) Batley and Spen, 1983, 1987. MP (Lab) Batley and Morley, 1979–83; Opposition spokesman on trade, shipping and aviation, 1981–83; Mem., Select Cttee on Treasury and Civil Service, 1980–81; Chm., 1981, Vice-Chm., 1982, PLP Economics and Finance Gp. Dir, Leeds United AFC, 1991–96. Non-executive Director: Thornfield Properties plc, 2000–; Saiinfo plc, 2000–; Courtcom Ltd, 2001–.

WOOLRICH, John; composer; *b* 3 Jan. 1954; *s* of Derek Holland Woolrich and Una Woolrich (*née* MacDougall). *Educ:* Manchester Univ. (BA); Lancaster Univ. (MLitt). Northern Arts Fellow, Durham Univ., 1982–85; Composer in Residence, Nat. Centre for Orchestral Studies, 1985–86; Artistic Dir, Composers' Ensemble, 1989–; Composer in Association, Orch. of St John's, Smith Square, 1994–95; Dir of Concerts, Almeida Opera, 1999–. Lectr in Music, RHBNC, 1994–98. Vis. Fellow, Clare Hall, Cambridge, 1999–2001. Hon. FTCL 1996. *Compositions* include: orchestral: The Barber's Timepiece, 1986; The Ghost in the Machine, 1990; The Theatre Represents a Garden: Night, 1991; Concerto for Viola, 1993; Concerto for Oboe, 1996; Cello Concerto, 1998; Concerto for Orchestra, 1999; chamber music: Ulysses Awakes, 1989; Lending Wings, 1989; The Death of King Renaud, 1991; It is Midnight, Dr Schweitzer, 1992; A Farewell, 1992. *Address:* c/o Faber Music, 3 Queen Square, WC1N 3AU. *T:* (020) 7278 7436.

WOOLRYCH, Prof. Austin Herbert, FBA 1988; Professor of History, University of Lancaster, 1964–85, now Emeritus; *b* 18 May 1918; *s* of Stanley Herbert Cunliffe Woolrych and May Gertrude (*née* Wood); *m* 1941, Muriel Edith Rolfe (*d* 1991); one *s* one *d*. *Educ:* Westminster Sch.; Pembroke Coll., Oxford (BLitt, MA). Served War, RAC, 1939–46: commnd RTR, 1940; Captain 1943. Lectr in History, subseq. Sen. Lectr, Univ. of Leeds, 1949–64; Pro-Vice-Chancellor, Univ. of Lancaster, 1971–75. Vis. Fellow, All Souls Coll., Oxford, 1981–82; Commonwealth Vis. Fellow to univs in Australia and NZ, 1983. Hon. DLitt Lancaster, 1986. *Publications:* Battles of the English Civil War, 1961, rev. edn 2000; Oliver Cromwell, 1964; (introd) Complete Prose Works of John Milton, vol. 7, 1980; Commonwealth to Protectorate, 1982; England without a King, 1983; Soldiers and Statesmen, 1987; articles and reviews in jls and symposia. *Recreations:* walking, travel, opera. *Address:* 9 Hollowrayne, Burton-in-Kendal, Carnforth LA6 1NS. *T:* (01524) 782471.

WOOLSEY, Rt Rev. Gary Frederick; Assistant Bishop of Calgary, since 1992, and Rector of St Peter's, Calgary, since 1991; *b* 16 March 1942; *s* of William and Doreen Woolsey; *m* 1967, Marie Elaine Tooker; two *s* two *d*. *Educ:* Univ. of Western Ontario (BA); Huron Coll., London, Ont. (BTh); Univ. of Manitoba (Teacher's Cert.). Deacon, 1967; Priest-pilot, Diocese of Keewatin, 1967–68; Rector: St Peter's, Big Trout Lake, Ont., 1968–72; St Mark's, Norway House, Manitoba, 1972–76; St Paul's, Churchill, Man., 1976–80; Program Director and Archdeacon of Keewatin, 1980–83; Bishop of Athabasca, 1983–91. *Recreations:* fishing, hunting, boating, camping, photography, flying.

Address: 184 Cedar Ridge Crescent SW, Calgary, AB T2W 1X8, Canada. *T:* (home) (403) 2519569, (office) (403) 2520393.

WOOLTON, 3rd Earl of, *cr* 1956; **Simon Frederick Marquis;** Baron Woolton, 1939; Viscount Woolton, 1953; Viscount Walberton, 1956; *b* 24 May 1958; *s* of 2nd Earl of Woolton and of Cecily Josephine (now Countess Lloyd George of Dwyfor), *e d* of Sir Alexander Gordon Cumming, 5th Bt; *S* father, 1969; *m* 1st, 1987, Hon. Sophie Frederika (marr. diss. 1997), *o c* of Baron Birdwood, *qv*; three *d*; 2nd, 1999, Mrs Carol Chapman (*née* Davidson). *Educ:* Eton College; St Andrews Univ. (MA Hons). Landowner and company director. Merchant banker, S. G. Warburg & Co. Ltd, 1982–88; Woolton Elwes Ltd, 1994–2000; New Boathouse Capital Ltd, 2000–. Trustee, Woolton Charitable Trust. Freeman, Skinners' Co. *Recreations:* gardening, golf. *Address:* Auchnacree House, Glenogil, by Forfar, Angus DD8 3SX; Avenue Lodge, 51 Ham Common, Richmond, Surrey TW10 7JG. *Clubs:* White's, Brooks's, Pratt's, MCC; Royal and Ancient; Swinley Forest Golf.

WOOLVERTON, Kenneth Arthur; Head of Latin America, Caribbean and Pacific Department, Overseas Development Administration of the Foreign and Commonwealth Office, 1985–86; *b* 4 Aug. 1926; *s* of Arthur Eliott Woolverton and Lilian Woolverton; *m* 1957, Kathleen West; one *s*. *Educ:* Orange Hill Grammar Sch. Colonial Office, 1950–61; CRO, 1961–66 (2nd Sec., Jamaica); Min. of Overseas Development, 1966–79; Hd of Middle East Develt Div., ODA, 1979–81; Hd of British Develt Div. in the Caribbean, ODA, 1981–84. ARPS 1992. *Recreations:* photography, archaeology, sailing. *Address:* 47 Durleston Park Drive, Great Bookham, Surrey KT23 4AJ. *T:* (01372) 454055.

WOOLWICH, Area Bishop of, since 1996; **Rt Rev. Colin Ogilvie Buchanan;** *b* 9 Aug. 1934; *s* of late Prof. Robert Ogilvie Buchanan and of Kathleen Mary (*née* Parnell); *m* 1963; two *d*. *Educ:* Whitgift Sch., S Croydon; Lincoln Coll., Oxford (BA, 2nd Cl. Lit. Hum., MA). Theological training at Tyndale Hall, Bristol, 1959–61; deacon, 1961; priest, 1962; Curate, Cheadle, Cheshire, 1961–64; joined staff of London Coll. of Divinity (now St John's Coll., Nottingham), 1964; posts held: Librarian, 1964–69; Registrar, 1969–74; Director of Studies, 1974–75; Vice-Principal, 1975–78; Principal, 1979–85; Hon. Canon of Southwell Minster, 1982–85; Bishop Suffragan of Aston, 1985–89; Hon. Asst Bishop, dio. of Rochester, 1989–96; Vicar, St Mark's, Gillingham, Kent, 1991–96. Member: Church of England Liturgical Commn, 1964–86; Doctrinal Commn, 1986–91; General Synod of C of E, 1970–85, 1990–; Assembly of British Council of Churches, 1971–80; Steering Cttee, CCBI, 1990–92; Council for Christian Unity, 1991–2001; Steering Gp, Internat. Anglican Liturgical Consultations, 1995–2001. Mem., Lambeth Conf., 1988, 1998 (Mem., Chaplaincy Team, 1998). Chm., Millennium Dome Chaplaincy Gp, 1999–2000. Pres., Movt for Reform of Infant Baptism, 1988–. Vice-Pres., Electoral Reform Soc., 1987–. Grove Books: Proprietor, 1970–85; Hon. Manager, 1985–93; Editorial Consultant, 1993–. DD Lambeth, 1993. *Publications:* (ed) Modern Anglican Liturgies 1958–1968, 1968; (ed) Further Anglican Liturgies 1968–1975, 1975; (jtly) Growing into Union, 1970; (ed jtly) Anglican Worship Today, 1980; (ed) Latest Anglican Liturgies 1976–1984, 1985; (jtly) Reforming Infant Baptism, 1990; Open to Others, 1992; Infant Baptism and the Gospel, 1993; Cut the Connection, 1994; Is the Church of England Biblical?, 1998; (ed) Michael Vasey—Liturgist and Friend, 1999; editor: Grove Booklets on Ministry and Worship, 1972–; Grove Liturgical Studies, 1975–86; Alcuin/GROW Joint Liturgical Studies, 1987– (regular author in these series); News of Liturgy, 1975–; contrib. learned jls. *Recreations:* interested in electoral reform, sport, etc. *Address:* 37 South Road, Forest Hill, SE23 2UJ.

WOON, Peter William; Editor, BBC TV News, 1980–85; *b* 12 Dec. 1931; *s* of Henry William Woon and Gwendoline Constance Woon; *m* 1st, 1956, Elizabeth Hird (marr. diss. 1974); one *s*; 2nd, 1974, Diana Ward (marr. diss. 1993). *Educ:* Christ's Hospital. 2nd Lieut Royal Signals, 1954–56; Reporter, Bristol Evening Post, 1949–54 and 1956–58; air corresp., Daily Express, 1958–61; BBC: reporter, 1961–66; Asst Editor, TV News, 1966–69; Editor, Radio News, 1969–75; Head of Information, 1975–77; Editor, News and Current Affairs, radio, 1977–80; Head, Ops, N America, 1985–88. *Address:* 8 Mulberry Close, Rosslyn Hill, Hampstead, NW3 5UP. *T:* (020) 7794 1454.

WOOSNAM, Charles Richard, CBE 1993; a Forestry Commissioner, 1986–94; *b* 4 Aug. 1925; *s* of late Ralph William Woosnam and Kathleen Mary Woosnam (*née* Evan-Thomas); *m* 1950, Patricia Rodney Carruthers; two *s* two *d*. *Educ:* Winchester; Pembroke Coll., Cambridge. BA Estate Management. FRICS. Commissioned 15th/19th The King's Royal Hussars, 1943–47, served Europe and Palestine; with Land Agents Strutt & Parker, Builth Wells office, 1950–63; set up own Land Agency partnership, Woosnam & Tyler, 1964, merged with Strutt & Parker, 1996, Consultant, 1988–98. Member: Welsh Water Authy, 1973–76 (Chm., Fisheries Adv. Cttee); Exec. Cttee, Timber Growers UK (formerly Timber Growers England & Wales), 1976–86 (Dep. Chm., England and Wales; Chm., Finance Cttee); Chm., CLA Game Fair Local Cttee, 1976; Pres., Royal Forestry Soc. of England, Wales and NI, 1995–97. High Sheriff, Powys, 1985–86. *Recreations:* shooting, fishing. *Address:* Cefnllysgwynne, Builth Wells, Powys LD2 3HN. *T:* (01982) 552237. *Club:* Army and Navy.

WOOSNAM, Ian Harold, MBE 1992; professional golfer since 1976; *b* 2 March 1958; *s* of Harold and Joan Woosnam; *m* 1983, Glendryth Mervyn Pugh; one *s* two *d*. *Educ:* St Martin's Modern Sch. Numerous championship wins, 1987–, including: World Cup (individual), 1987 and 1991; World Match Play, 1987, 1990 and 2001; PGA, 1988 and 1997; PGA Grand Slam of Golf, 1991; US Masters, 1991; British Masters, 1994. Hon. Mem., PGA European tour. Pres., World Snooker Assoc., 1999–. *Publications:* Ian Woosnam's Golf Masterpieces, 1988; Power Golf, 1989, new edn 1991; Golf Made Simple: the Woosie Way, 1997. *Recreations:* snooker, water-skiing, shooting. *Address:* c/o IMG, Pier House, Strand on the Green, W4 3NN. *Clubs:* Oswestry Golf; Wentworth Golf; La Moye Golf; Dale Hill Golf.

WOOTTON, Adrian; Head of BFI Exhibition (including Executive Head of National Film Theatre and Director, London Film Festival, since 1993); *b* 18 May 1962; *s* of Ronald Oliver Wootton and Unity Wootton; *m* 1986, Karen Sarah Goodman; one *d*. *Educ:* Univ. of East Anglia (BA Hons English and Amer. Studies, MA Film Studies). Director: Bradford Playhouse and Film Theatre, 1986–89; Nottingham Media Centre Ltd, 1989–93; Shots in the Dark, Internat. Crime, Mystery and Thriller Fest., Nottingham, 1991–; Crime Scene, fest. of crime and mystery genre, 2000–; Co-Curator, Soundtracking, Fest. of Popular Music and Cinema, Sheffield, 1999–. Foreign Consultant, Noir in Fest., Italy, 1999–. *Publications:* (contrib.) 100 Great Detectives, 1992; (ed jtly) Celluloid Jukebox, 1995; contribs to arts magazines. *Recreations:* film, literature, music, theatre. *Address:* National Film Theatre, Waterloo, SE1 8XT. *T:* (020) 7815 1300. *Clubs:* Groucho, Soho House.

WOOTTON, Godfrey; *see* Wootton, N. G.

WOOTTON, Prof. (Harold) John, CBE 1997; FREng; FCIT; FICE; FIHT; FILT; Rees Jeffreys Professor of Transport Planning, University of Southampton, since 1997; *b* 17 Nov. 1936; *s* of Harold Wootton and Hilda Mary (*née* Somerfield); *m* 1960, Patricia Ann Riley; two *s*. *Educ:* Queen Mary's Grammar Sch., Walsall; QMC, Univ. of London; Univ. of Calif, Berkeley. FIHT 1980; FCIT 1987; CEng 1990, FREng 2000; FICE 1996; FILT 1999. Lectr, Dept of Civil Engrg, Univ. of Leeds, 1959–62; Technical Dir, Freeman Fox Wilbur Smith, 1963–67; Jt Man. Dir, SIA Ltd, 1967–71; Chm., Wootton Jeffreys Consultants Ltd, 1971–91; Chief Exec., Transport and Road, subseq. Transport, Res. Lab., 1991–97. Visiting Professor in: Computing, KCL, 1987–89; Transport Studies, UCL, 1989–92. Pres., Instn of Highways and Transportation, 1997–98. *Publications:* numerous papers on transport, planning and computer topics. *Recreations:* cricket, golf, Rotary, photography, travel. *Address:* Transportation Research Group, Department of Civil and Environmental Engineering, University of Southampton, Highfield, Southampton SO17 1BJ. *T:* (023) 8059 3148. *Club:* Royal Automobile.

WOOTTON, Ian David Phimester, MA, MB, BChir, PhD, FRSC, FRCPath, FRCP; Professor of Chemical Pathology, Royal Postgraduate Medical School, University of London, 1963–82; *b* 5 March 1921; *s* of D. Wootton and Charlotte (*née* Phimester); *m* 1946, Veryan Mary Walshe; two *s* two *d*. *Educ:* Weymouth Grammar School; St John's College, Cambridge; St Mary's Hospital, London. Research Assistant, Postgraduate Med. School, 1945; Lecturer, 1949; Sen. Lecturer, 1959; Reader, 1961. Consultant Pathologist to Hammersmith Hospital, 1952. Member of Medical Research Council Unit, Cairo, 1947–48; Major, RAMC, 1949; Smith-Mundt Fellow, Memorial Hosp., New York, 1951. Chief Scientist (Hosp. Scientific and Technical Services), DHSS, 1972–73. *Publications:* Microanalysis in Medical Biochemistry, 1964, ed 6th edn, 1982; Biochemical Disorders in Human Disease, 1970; papers in medical and scientific journals on biochemistry and pathology. *Recreations:* carpentry, boating, beekeeping. *Address:* Cariad Cottage, Cleeve Road, Goring, Oxon RG8 9DB. *T:* (01491) 873050.

WOOTTON, John; *see* Wootton, H. J.

WOOTTON, (Norman) Godfrey; Stipendiary Magistrate for Merseyside, 1976–94; *b* 10 April 1926; *s* of H. N. and E. Wootton, Crewe, Cheshire. *Educ:* The Grammar Sch., Crewe; Liverpool Univ. (LLB). Called to Bar, Gray's Inn, 1951. Joined Northern Circuit, 1951. A Recorder of the Crown Court, 1972–96. *Recreations:* travel, photography. *Club:* Athenæum (Liverpool).

WOOTTON, Ronald William, CBE 1991; Head of West and North Africa and Mediterranean Department, Overseas Development Administration, 1986–91; *b* 7 April 1931; *s* of William George and late Lilian Wootton; *m* 1954, Elvira Mary Gillian Lakeman; one *s* one *d*. *Educ:* Christ's College, Finchley. Served Royal Signals, 1950–52. Colonial Office, 1952–63; Commonwealth Relations Office, 1963–65; ODM/ODA, 1965–91: Head of Overseas Manpower and Consultancies Dept, 1976–79; Head of UN Dept, 1979–82; Head of British Develt Div. in the Pacific, 1982–85. Mem., Internat. Cttee, Leonard Cheshire Foundn, 1992–98. *Address:* 16 The Heath, Chaldon, Surrey CR3 5DG. *T:* (01883) 344903.

WOOZLEY, Prof. Anthony Douglas, MA; University Professor Emeritus of Philosophy and Law, University of Virginia, since 1983; *b* 14 Aug. 1912; *o s* of David Adams Woozley and Kathleen Lucy Moore; *m* 1st, 1937, Thelma Suffield (marr. diss. 1978), *e d* of late Frank Townshend, Worcester; one *d*; 2nd, 1995, Cora, *e d* of late Abraham Diamond, New York. *Educ:* Haileybury College; Queen's College, Oxford. Open Scholar, Queen's College, 1931–35; 1st Cl. Class. Hon. Mods, 1933; 1st Cl. Lit. Hum., 1935; John Locke Schol., 1935. Served War, 1940–46 (despatches); commissioned King's Dragoon Guards, 1941; served N Africa, Italy, Greece, Egypt, Syria, Palestine; Major. Fellow of All Souls College, 1935–37; Fellow and Praelector in Philosophy, Queen's Coll., 1937–54; Librarian, 1938–54; Tutor, Queen's College, 1946–54; University Lecturer in Philosophy, 1947–54; Senior Proctor, 1953–54; Prof. of Moral Philosophy, Univ. of St Andrews, 1954–67; University of Virginia: Prof. of Philosophy, 1966; Commonwealth Prof. of Philosophy, 1974–77; Commonwealth Prof. and Univ. Prof. of Philosophy and Law, 1977–83. Editor of The Philosophical Quarterly, 1957–62; Editor, Home University Library, 1962–68. Visiting Professor of Philosophy: Univ. of Rochester, USA, 1965; Univ. of Arizona, 1972. *Publications:* (ed) Thomas Reid's Essays on the Intellectual Powers of Man, 1941; Theory of Knowledge, 1949; (with R. C. Cross) Plato's Republic: a Philosophical Commentary, 1964; (ed) John Locke's Essay Concerning Human Understanding, 1964; Law and Obedience, 1979; articles and reviews in Mind, etc. *Address:* 655 Kearsarge Circle, Charlottesville, VA 22903, USA.

WORCESTER, Marquess of; Henry John Fitzroy Somerset, FRICS; *b* 22 May 1952; *s* and *heir* of 11th Duke of Beaufort, *qv*; *m* 1987, Tracy Louise, *yr d* of Hon. Peter Ward and Hon. Mrs Claire Ward; two *s* one *d*. *Educ:* Eton; Cirencester Agricultural College. With Morgan Grenfell Laurie Ltd (formerly Michael Laurie & Partners), London, 1977; subseq. with Franc Warwick. *Recreations:* hunting, shooting, golf, tennis, skiing, rock music. *Heir:* *s* Earl of Glamorgan, *qv*. *Club:* Turf.

WORCESTER, Bishop of, since 1997; **Rt Rev. Peter Stephen Maurice Selby,** PhD; *b* 7 Dec. 1941. *Educ:* St John's Coll., Oxford (BA 1964; MA 1967); Episcopal Theol Sch., Cambridge, Mass (BD 1966); Bishops' Coll., Cheshunt; PhD London, 1975. Asst Curate, Queensbury, 1966–68; Associate Dir of Training, Southwark, 1969–73; Asst Curate, Limpsfield with Titsey, 1969–77; Vice-Principal, Southwark Ordination Course, 1970–72; Asst Missioner, Dio. Southwark, 1973–77; Canon Residentiary, Newcastle Cathedral, 1977–84; Diocesan Missioner, Dio. Newcastle, 1977–84; Suffragan Bishop, 1984–91, Area Bishop, 1991–92, of Kingston-upon-Thames; William Leech Professorial Fellow in Applied Christian Theol., Univ. of Durham, 1992–97; Hon. Asst Bishop, dios of Durham and Newcastle, 1992–97; Bishop to HM Prisons, 2001–. *Publications:* Look for the Living, 1976; Liberating God, 1983; BeLonging, 1991; Rescue, 1995; Grace and Mortgage, 1997. *Address:* The Bishop's House, Hartlebury Castle, Kidderminster, Worcs DY11 7XX.

WORCESTER, Dean of; *see* Marshall, Very Rev. P. J.

WORCESTER, Archdeacon of; *see* Tetley, Ven. J. D.

WORCESTER, Robert Milton; Chairman, Market & Opinion Research International (MORI) Ltd, since 1973 (Managing Director, 1969–94); *b* 21 Dec. 1933; *s* of late C. M. and Violet Ruth Worcester, of Kansas City, Mo, USA; *m* 1st, 1958, Joann (*née* Ransdell) (decd); two *s*; 2nd, 1982, Margaret Noel (*née* Smallbone). *Educ:* Univ. of Kansas (BSc). Consultant, McKinsey & Co., 1962–65; Controller and Asst to Chm., Opinion Research Corp., 1965–68. Past Pres., World Assoc. for Public Opinion Research. Vice President: Internat., Social Science Council, UNESCO, 1989–94; UNA, 1999–. Visiting Professor: City Univ., 1990–; LSE, 1992– (Gov., 1995–); Strathclyde Univ., 1996–. Member: Pilgrims' Soc. of GB (Chm., Exec. Cttee, 1993–); Ditchley Foundn. Comr, US-UK Fulbright Commn, 1995–. Vice-Pres., RSNC, 1995–; Trustee, Magna Carta Trust, 1995–. Consultant: The Times; Economist. Frequent broadcaster and speaker on British and Amer. politics. Freeman, City of London, 2001. FRSA; Fellow, Market Res. Soc., 1997. Co-Editor, Internat. Jl of Public Opinion Research. Hon. DSc Buckingham, 1999;

Hon. DLitt Bradford, 2001; DUniv Middlesex, 2001. *Publications:* (ed) Consumer Market Research Handbook, 1971, 3rd edn 1986; (with M Harrop) Political Communications, 1982; (ed) Political Opinion Polling: an international review, 1983; (with Lesley Watkins) Private Opinions, Public Polls, 1986; (with Eric Jacobs) We British, 1990; British Public Opinion: history and methodology of political opinion polling in Great Britain, 1991; (with Eric Jacobs) Typically British, 1991; (with Samuel Barnes) Dynamics of Societal Learning about Global Environmental Change, 1992; (with Roger Mortimore) Explaining Labour's Landslide, 1999; contrib. The Times; papers in tech. and prof. jls. *Recreations:* choral music, gardening. *Address:* 32 Old Queen Street, SW1H 9HP. *T:* (020) 7222 0232. *Clubs:* Beefsteak, Reform.

WORDEN, Prof. (Alastair) Blair, FBA 1997; Professor of Early Modern History, University of Sussex, since 1996; *b* 12 Jan. 1945; *s* of late Prof. Alastair Norman Worden and of Agnes Marshall Scutt. *Educ:* St Edward's Sch., Oxford; Pembroke Coll., Oxford (BA 1966; MA 1971). Res. Fellow, Pembroke Coll., Cambridge, 1969–71; Fellow, and Dir of Studies in History, Selwyn Coll., Cambridge, 1972–74; Fellow, and Tutor in Modern History, St Edmund Hall, Oxford, 1974–95. *Publications:* The Rump Parliament, 1974; (ed) Edmund Ludlow, A Voyce from the Watch Tower, 1978; (ed) David Wootton, Republicanism, Liberty and Commercial Society, part I, 1994; The Sound of Virtue: politics in Philip Sidney's 'Arcadia', 1996; articles on early modern English history and lit. *Address:* School of English and American Studies, University of Sussex, Falmer, Brighton BN1 9QN. *T:* (01273) 606755.

WORDLEY, Ronald William; Chairman, The Buckingham Group (Winslow Press) Ltd, 1987–93; Director, BCS Developments Ltd, since 1989; Managing Director, 1978–87, Chairman, 1985–86, HTV Ltd; *b* 16 June 1928; *s* of William Wordley and Elizabeth Anne Hackett; *m* 1953, Pamela Mary Offord; two *s* one *d* (and one *s* decd). *Educ:* Barnet Grammar Sch.; City of London Coll.; RMA, Sandhurst. Regular Army Officer: 2/Lieut RA, 1948; regtl duty, UK, Far East and Europe; Liaison Officer, RM Commando Bde, 1951, Captain; Air OP Pilot, 1953; Army Light Aircraft Sch., 1955; seconded Army Air Corps Cadre, 1957; resigned commn, 1958. Unilever (United Africa Co.), 1958–59; Anglia Television Ltd: Sales Exec., 1959; Gen. Sales Manager, 1962; Dep. Sales Controller, 1964; joined Harlech Consortium as Sales Controller, 1967; Sales Dir on bd of HTV Ltd, 1971. Director: Instock Ltd; Independent Television Publications Ltd; (also Mem. Council), Independent Television Cos Assoc. Ltd; HTV Gp plc; HTV Equipment Ltd; HTV Property Ltd., 1971–87. Hon. Patron, Royal Regt of Wales, 1986–91. Mem., Inst. of Marketing; FRSA 1983; FInstD 1986. *Recreations:* music, travel, golf, swimming. *Address:* 6 Spring Leigh, Leigh Woods, Bristol, Avon BS8 3PG. *T:* (0117) 973 9256; TSDY Tirion II, Quay 11, Berth 14, Port de La Rague, Theoule-sur-Mer 06590, France. *Clubs:* Clifton (Bristol); Bristol and Clifton Golf.

WORDSWORTH, Barry; conductor; Music Director, Birmingham Royal Ballet, since 1990; *b* 20 Feb. 1948; *s* of Ronald and Kathleen Wordsworth; *m* 1970, Ann Barber; one *s*. *Educ:* Royal College of Music. Conductor, Royal Ballet, 1974–84; Music Dir, New Sadler's Wells Opera, 1982–84; Musical Dir and Prin. Conductor, Brighton Philharmonic Orch., 1989–; Prin. Conductor, BBC Concert Orch., 1989–; Music Dir, Covent Garden Royal Ballet, 1990–94. Joint winner, Sargent Conductor's Prize, 1970; Tagore Gold Medal, RCM, 1970. *Recreations:* swimming, photography, cooking. *Address:* c/o ICM, 76 Oxford Street, W1N 0AX.

WORDSWORTH, Prof. (Bryan) Paul, FRCP; Clinical Reader in Rheumatology, since 1992, and Titular Professor of Rheumatology, since 1998, University of Oxford; Fellow, Green College, Oxford, since 1992; *b* 4 April 1952; *s* of Victor Pargiter Wordsworth and Dora Mary Wordsworth; *m* 1981, Christine Brow; two *s* one *d*. *Educ:* Whitgift Sch.; Westminster Med. Sch., London Univ. (MB BS 1975); MA Oxon 1992. MRCP 1978, FRCP 1996. Registrar in Rheumatology, Middx Hosp., 1978–80; Sen. Registrar in Rheumatology, Oxford Hosps, 1980–87; University of Oxford: Res. Fellow, Nuffield Depts of Pathology and Medicine, 1983–85 and 1987–92; Sen. Tutor, Green Coll., 1997–2000. Michael Mason Prize, British Soc. for Rheumatology, 1992. *Publications:* contribs to books and learned jls on genetics of disorders of the musculo skeletal system and inflammatory arthritis. *Recreation:* cricket. *Address:* Nuffield Orthopaedic Centre, Headington, Oxford OX3 7LD. *T:* (01865) 227526.

WORDSWORTH, Paul; *see* Wordsworth, B. P.

WORDSWORTH, Stephen John, LVO 1992; HM Diplomatic Service; Head, Eastern Adriatic Department, Foreign and Commonwealth Office, since 1999; *b* 17 May 1955; *s* of Christopher Wordsworth and Ruth Wordsworth (*née* Parrington); *m* 1981, Nichole Mingins; one *s*. *Educ:* St John's Sch., Porthcawl; Epsom Coll.; Downing Coll., Cambridge (MA). Joined FCO, 1977; Third, later Second Sec., Moscow, 1979–81; FCO, 1981–83; First Sec. (Econ. and Commercial), Lagos, 1983–86; on loan to Cabinet Office, 1986–88; First Secretary: FCO, 1988–90; (Political), Bonn, 1990–94; Counsellor (Dep. Internat. Affairs Advr), SHAPE, Mons, 1994–98; FCO, 1998–. Bundesverdienstkreuz (FRG), 1992. *Recreations:* travel, walking the dog, family history research, good food and drink. *Address:* Foreign and Commonwealth Office, King Charles Street, SW1A 2AH.

WORKMAN, Charles Joseph, TD 1966; Part-time Chairman: Industrial Tribunals for Scotland, 1986–92; Social Security Appeal Tribunals, 1986–94; Disability Appeal Tribunals, 1992–94; *b* 25 Aug. 1920; *s* of Hugh William O'Brien Workman and Annie Shields; *m* 1949, Margaret Jean Mason; one *s* two *d*. *Educ:* St Mungo's Acad., Glasgow; Univ. of Glasgow (MA 1950, LLB 1952). Admitted solicitor, 1952. Served War, 1939–45: France, Belgium, Holland, Germany; commnd Second Fife and Forfar Yeomanry, RAC, 1942; Captain, 1945; served Intell. Corps TA and TAVR, 1954–69; Bt Lt-Col 1969; Hon. Col, Intell. and Security Gp (V), 1977–86. Entered Office of Solicitor to Sec. of State for Scotland as Legal Asst, 1955; Sen. Legal Asst, 1961; Asst Solicitor, 1966; Dep. Solicitor to Sec. of State, 1976; Dir, Scottish Courts Administration, 1978–82; Senior Dep. Sec. (Legal Aid), Law Soc. of Scotland, 1982–86. Chm., Public Service and Commerce Gp, Law Soc. of Scotland, 1977–78. Founder Mem., Edinburgh Chamber Music Trust, 1977–. *Publication:* (contrib.) The Laws of Scotland: Stair Memorial Encyclopaedia, vol. 2, 1987. *Recreations:* hill walking, swimming, music. *Address:* Ravenswood, 6 Lower Broomieknowe, Lasswade, Midlothian EH18 1LW. *Club:* New (Edinburgh).

WORKMAN, Timothy (Henry); a District Judge (Magistrates' Courts) (formerly Metropolitan Stipendiary Magistrate), since 1986; Deputy Chief Magistrate and Deputy Senior District Judge (Magistrates' Courts), since 2000; a Chairman, Inner London Youth Court, since 1989, and Family Proceeding Court, since 1992; a Recorder, since 1994; *b* 18 Oct. 1943; *s* of late Gordon and Eileen Workman; *m* 1971, Felicity Ann Caroline Western; one *s* one *d*. *Educ:* Ruskin Grammar Sch., Croydon. Probation Officer, Inner London, 1967–69; admitted Solicitor, 1969; Solicitor, subseq. Partner, C. R. Thomas & Son, later Lloyd Howorth & Partners, Maidenhead, 1969–85. *Recreations:* ski-ing, pottery. *Address:* Bow Street Magistrates' Court, WC2E 7AS. *T:* (020) 7853 9264. *Club:* Medico-Legal.

WORMALD, Brian; *see* Wormald, T. B. H. G.

WORMALD, Peter John, CB 1990; Director, Office of Population Censuses and Surveys, and Registrar General for England and Wales, 1990–96; *b* 10 March 1936; *s* of late H. R. and G. A. Wormald; *m* 1962, Elizabeth North; three *s*. *Educ:* Doncaster Grammar Sch.; The Queen's Coll., Oxford (MA). Assistant Principal, Min. of Health, 1958, Principal, 1963; HM Treasury, 1965–67, Asst Sec., 1970; Under Sec., DHSS, 1978; Dep. Sec., Dept of Health (formerly DHSS), 1987. *Recreations:* music, golf, contract bridge. *Club:* Oxford and Cambridge.

WORMALD, (Thomas) Brian (Harvey Goodwin), MA; University Lecturer in History, Cambridge, 1948–79; Fellow of Peterhouse, 1938–79; *b* 24 July 1912; *s* of late Rev. C. O. R. Wormald and Mrs A. W. C. Wormald (*née* Brooks); *m* 1946, Rosemary, *d* of E. J. B. Lloyd; four *s*. *Educ:* Harrow; Peterhouse, Cambridge (Scholar). BA 1934 (1st Class Hons Hist. Tripos, Parts I and II); Members Prize (English Essay), 1935; Strathcona Research Student, St John's College, 1936–38; Prince Consort Prize, 1938; MA 1938. Chaplain and Catechist, Peterhouse, 1940–48; Dean, 1941–44; Tutor, 1952–62. Select Preacher, Cambridge, 1945 and 1954. Junior Proctor, 1951–52. Received into Catholic Church, 1955. *Publications:* Clarendon: Politics, History and Religion, 1951; Francis Bacon: History, Politics, Science, 1993. *Address:* c/o Peterhouse, Cambridge CB2 1RD. *Club:* Travellers.

WORRALL, Anna Maureen, (Mrs G. H. G. Williams); QC 1989; a Recorder, since 1987; *m* 1964, G. H. Graeme Williams, *qv*; two *d*. *Educ:* Hillcrest Sch., Bramhall; Loreto Coll., Llandudno; Manchester Univ. Called to the Bar, Middle Temple, 1959, Bencher, 1996; in practice, 1959–63 and 1971–; Lectr in Law, Holborn Coll. of Law, Language and Commerce, 1964–69; Dir, ILEA Educnl Television Service, 1969–71. Pres., Mental Health Review Tribunals, 1995–. *Recreations:* theatre, music, cooking, walking, travel. *Address:* Lamb Building, Ground Floor, Temple, EC4Y 7AS. *T:* (020) 7797 7788, *Fax:* (020) 7353 0535. *Club:* Reform.

WORRALL, Denis John, PhD; Chief Executive, Omega Investment Research Ltd, since 1990; Senior Counsellor, A. T. Kearney; *b* 29 May 1935; *s* of Cecil John Worrall and Hazel Worrall; *m* 1965, Anita Ianco; three *s*. *Educ:* Univ. of Cape Town (BA Hons, MA); Univ. of South Africa (LLB); Cornell Univ. (PhD). Teaching and research positions, Univs of Natal, S Africa, Ibadan, Witwatersrand, California, Cornell; Rearch Prof. and Dir, Inst. of Social and Economic Research, Rhodes Univ., 1973. Senator, 1974; elected to Parlt, 1977; Chm., Constitutional Cttee, President's Council, 1981; Ambassador: to Australia, 1983–84; to the UK, 1984–87; Co-Leader, Democratic Party, 1988–90; MP (Democratic Party) Berea (Durban), South Africa, 1989–94. Advocate of Supreme Court of S Africa. *Publication:* South Africa: government and politics, 1970. *Recreations:* tennis, reading, music. *Address:* PO Box 5455, Cape Town, 8000, South Africa.

WORRALL THOMPSON, (Henry) Antony (Cardew); TV chef; restaurateur; *b* 1 May 1951; *s* of late Michael Worrall Thompson and Joanna Duncan; *m* 1st, 1974, Jill Thompson (marr. diss.); 2nd, 1983, Militza Millar (marr. diss.); two *s*; 3rd, 1996, Jacinta Shiel; one *s* one *d*. *Educ:* King's Sch., Canterbury; Westminster Hotel Sch. (HND). Sous chef, Brinkley's Restaurant, Fulham Rd, Sept.–Oct. 1978, head chef, Oct. 1978–1980; head chef, Dan's Restaurant, Chelsea, 1980–81; opened Ménage à Trois, Knightsbridge, 1981; first chef/patron, restaurant at One Ninety, Queen's Gate, 1989 (Best New Restaurant, Time Out, 1990); restaurants opened: Managing Director: Bistrot 190, 1990; dell 'Ugo, Frith St, 1992; Palio, Notting Hill Gate, 1992; Zoe, St Christopher's Place, 1993; Cafe dell 'Ugo, City of London, 1993; The Atrium, Westminster, 1994; Drones, Belgravia, 1995; De Cecco, Parsons Gn, 1995; chef/proprietor: Woz, N Kensington, 1997–; Wiz, Holland Park, 1998–; Bistrorganic, N Kensington, 1999. Restaurant consultant, Bombay, Melbourne, Stockholm and NY, 1981–88. Man. Dir, Simpson's of Cornhill Gp, 1996–97. Numerous TV appearances, incl. Ready, Steady, Cook, 1994–; Food and Drink prog., 1997–. FHCIMA 1989. Meilleur Ouvrier de GB, 1987. *Publications:* The Small and Beautiful Cookbook, 1984; (with M. Gluck) Supernosh, 1993; Modern Bistrot Cookery, 1994; 30 Minute Menus, 1995; Simply Antony, 1998; The ABC of AWT, 1998. *Recreations:* gardening, antiques, interior design, eating, cooking. *Address:* Wiz Restaurant, 123A Clarendon Road, W11 4JG. *T:* (020) 7229 1500. *Clubs:* Groucho, Chelsea Arts.

WORSFOLD, Reginald Lewis, CBE 1979; Member for Personnel, British Gas Corporation (formerly Gas Council), 1973–80, retired; *b* 18 Dec. 1925; *s* of Charles S. and Doris Worsfold; *m* 1st, 1952, Margot Kempell (marr. diss. 1974); one *s* one *d*; 2nd, 1982, Christine McKeown. *Educ:* School of Technology, Art and Commerce, Oxford; London Sch. of Economics. MIPM. Served War of 1939–45: Lieut 44 Royal Marine Commandos, 1943–46. Organising Commissioner, Scout Council of Nigeria, 1947–49; Personnel Manager: British European Airways, 1953–65; W Midlands Gas Bd, 1965–69; Gas Council: Dep. Personnel Dir, 1969–70; Personnel Dir, 1970–72. *Recreations:* sailing, camping, music. *Address:* Beck House, 43 Wychwood Grove, Chandler's Ford, Hants SO53 1FQ. *T:* (023) 8026 9873.

WORSKETT, Prof. Roy, RIBA; MRTPI; consultant architect and town planner; Partner, Architectural Planning Partnership, Horsham, 1982–85; *b* 3 Sept. 1932; *s* of Archibald Ellwood Worskett and Dorothy Alice Roffey; two *s* one *d*. *Educ:* Collyer's Sch., Horsham; Portsmouth Sch. of Architecture. MRTPI 1975; RIBA 1955. Architect's Dept, LCC, 1957–60; Architect, Civic Trust, London, 1960–63; Historic Areas Div., DoE (formerly MPBW), 1963–74; City Architect and Planning Officer, Bath City Council, and Prof. of Urban Conservation, Sch. of Architecture, Bath Univ., 1974–79; Consultant Head, Conservation Section, Crafts Council, 1979–82. Consultant Architect: Bath CC, 1979–83; Salisbury DC, 1980–; Brighton Palace Pier, 1987–; London borough of Greenwich, 1988–99; London boroughs of Lambeth, Kensington and Chelsea, and Richmond, 1988–; Consultant: Ford Foundn in India, 1982–; Council of Europe, 1984–; Nat. Audit Office, 1987; evidence to Public Inquiries at: Mansion House, for City of London; County Hall, London, 1984–; Thameslink, 2000; Advr, Urban Redevelt Authority, Singapore, 1992–; Conservation Advr, Union Rlys and British Land, 1993–; Advisor: Historic Royal Palaces, Tower of London Environs Scheme, 1996–98; King's Cross Station Proposals, London Borough of Camden, 1997–99; Cambridge City Centre, 1997–98; Nat. Film and TV Sch., 2001. Chairman: Conservation Cttees, Crafts Adv. Cttee, 1974–79; Design Panel, Spitalfields Develt Gp, 1990–96; Member: Heritage Educn Group, 1976–88; Council for Urban Study Centres, TCPA, 1977–80; Council of Management, Architectural Heritage Fund, 1977–2000. Pres., Urban Design Gp, 1983–84. Vis. Prof., Internat. Centre for Conservation, Rome, 1972–97. *Publications:* The Character of Towns, 1968; articles in architect. and planning magazines. *Recreation:* looking and listening in disbelief. *Address:* 1 Hampers Lane, Horsham, West Sussex RH13 6HB. *T:* (01403) 254208.

WORSLEY, Lord; George John Sackville Pelham; *b* 9 Aug. 1990; *s* and *heir* of 8th Earl of Yarborough, *qv*.

WORSLEY, Daniel; His Honour Judge Worsley; a Circuit Judge, since 1999; *b* 27 March 1948; *s* of Francis Arthur Worsley and Mary Worsley; *m* 1971, Virginia Caroline Wilkinson; one *s* one *d*. *Educ:* Ampleforth Coll.; Emmanuel Coll., Cambridge (BA). Called to the Bar, Gray's Inn, 1971; Barrister, 1971–99. *Publications:* Contrib. Ed., Halsbury's Laws of England, 4th edn, 1998; contrib. to legal textbooks. *Recreations:* East Anglia, sailing, trout streams, wine, early music, fruit growing, France. *Club:* Norfolk (Norwich).

WORSLEY, Francis Edward, (Jock); Complaints Commissioner, Financial Services Authority (formerly Securities and Investment Board), since 1994; *b* 15 Feb. 1941; *s* of late Francis Arthur Worsley and Mary Worsley; *m* 1962, Caroline Violet (*née* Hatherell); two *s* two *d*. *Educ:* Stonyhurst College. FCA. Articled, Barton, Mayhew & Co., 1959–64; with Anderson Thomas Frankel, Chartered Accountants, 1964–69; Financial Training Co., 1969–93 (Chm., 1972–92). Dir, 1990–94, Dep. Chm., 1992–94, Lautro. Non-executive Director: Cleveland Trust PLC, 1993–99; Reece Plc, 1994–98; non-exec. Chm., Lloyds Members Agency Services Ltd, 1994–. Pres., Inst. of Chartered Accountants in England and Wales, 1988–89. Mem., Building Socs Commn, 1991–. Chm., Cancer Res. Campaign, 1998–. *Recreations:* tennis, wine, travel, cooking.

WORSLEY, Giles Arthington, PhD; FSA; Architecture Correspondent, The Daily Telegraph, since 1998; Member, Royal Fine Art Commission, 1994–99; *b* 22 March 1961; *s* of Sir (William) Marcus (John) Worsley, *qv* and Hon. Bridget Assheton, *d* of 1st Baron Clitheroe, PC, KCVO; *m* 1996, Joanna Pitman; two *d*. *Educ:* Eton; New Coll., Oxford; Courtauld Inst., Univ. of London (PhD 1989). Country Life: architectural writer, 1985–88; Architectural Editor, 1989–94; Editor: Georgian Group Jl, 1991–94; Perspectives on Architecture, 1994–98. Member: Historic Buildings and Areas Adv. Cttee, English Heritage, 1995–98; Exec. Cttee, Save Britain's Heritage, 1985–; Exec. Cttee, Georgian Gp, 1990–; Somerset House Trust, 1997–; Bldg Cttee, Nat. Gall. Trustees, 1998–. Prizes incl. Alexander Prize, RHistS, 1992. *Publications:* Architectural Drawings of the Regency Period, 1991; Classical Architecture in Britain: the heroic age, 1995; (ed) Brian Wragg, The Life and Works of John Carr, 2000. *Recreations:* walking, reading, buildings. *Address:* The Daily Telegraph, 1 Canada Square, Canary Wharf, E14 5DT. *T:* (020) 8962 6371, *Fax:* (020) 8968 0693.

WORSLEY, Jock; *see* Worsley, F. E.

WORSLEY, Sir Marcus; *see* Worsley, Sir W. M. J.

WORSLEY, Michael Dominic Laurence; QC 1985; *b* 9 Feb. 1926; *s* of Paul Worsley and Magdalen Teresa Worsley; *m* 1962, Pamela (*née* Philpot) (*d* 1980); one *s* (and one *s* decd); *m* 1986, Jane, *d* of Percival and Mary Sharpe. *Educ:* Bedford School; Inns of Court School of Law. RN 1944–45. Lived in Africa, 1946–52; called to the Bar, Inner Temple, 1955, Bencher, 1980; Standing Prosecuting Counsel to Inland Revenue, 1968–69; Treasury Counsel at Inner London Sessions, 1969–71; Junior Treasury Counsel, 1971–74, Senior Treasury Counsel, 1974–84, CCC. *Recreations:* music, travelling. *Address:* 6 King's Bench Walk, Temple, EC4Y 7DR. *T:* (020) 7583 0410. *Clubs:* Garrick, Lansdowne; Thomas More Society.

WORSLEY, Nicholas Jarvis; QC 1993; a Recorder, since 1985; *b* 21 July 1943; *s* of Edgar Taylor Worsley and Vida Worsley (*née* McCormick); *m* 1967, Anna Maxine Bekenn; two *d*. *Educ:* Clifton Coll., Bristol; Fitzwilliam House, Cambridge. Called to the Bar, Inner Temple, 1966. Chm., Agricl Lands Tribunal, 1976–. *Recreations:* contemporary art and design, architecture. *Address:* Lansdowne Crescent, Worcester.

WORSLEY, Paul Frederick; QC 1990; a Recorder, since 1987; *b* 17 Dec. 1947; *s* of Eric Worsley, MBE, GM and Sheila Mary Worsley (*née* Hoskin); *m* 1974, Jennifer Ann, JP, *d* of late Ernest Avery; one *s* one *d*. *Educ:* Hymers College, Hull; Mansfield College, Oxford (MA). Called to the Bar, Middle Temple, 1970 (Astbury Scholar), Bencher, 1999; practised NE Circuit, 1970–; Mem. Exec., NE Circuit, 1997–. Mem., Advocacy Studies Bd, 1996–. Gov., Scarborough Coll., 1996–. *Recreations:* Spy prints, opera, sailing, croquet. *Address:* Park Court Chambers, 16 Park Place, Leeds LS1 1SJ. *T:* (0113) 244 3277; 2 Hare Court, EC4Y 7BH. *T:* (020) 7353 5324. *Club:* Yorkshire (York).

WORSLEY, Gen. Sir Richard (Edward), GCB 1982 (KCB 1976); OBE 1964; Chairman: Western Provident Assoc., 1989–96; Electro-Optical Division, Pilkington Brothers, 1984–86 (Chief Executive, 1982–86); Barr and Stroud, 1982–86; Pilkington PE, 1982–86; *b* 29 May 1923; *s* of H. H. K. Worsley, Grey Abbey, Co. Down; *m* 1st, 1959, Sarah Anne Mitchell; one *s* one *d*; 2nd, 1980, Caroline, Duchess of Fife, *er d* of 3rd Baron Forteviot, MBE. *Educ:* Radley Coll. Served War: commissioned into Rifle Bde, 1942, Middle East and Italian Campaigns, 1942–45. Instr, RMA Sandhurst, 1948–51; Malayan Emergency, 1956–57; Instr, Staff Coll., Camberley, 1958–61; CO, The Royal Dragoons, 1962–65; Comdr, 7th Armoured Bde, 1965–67; Imperial Defence Coll., 1968; Chief of Staff, Far East Land Forces, 1969–71; GOC 3rd Div., 1972–74; Vice-QMG, MoD, 1974–76; GOC 1 (Br) Corps, 1976–78; QMG, 1979–82. Freeman, City of London, 1983. *Recreations:* shooting, ornithology. *Club:* Cavalry and Guards.

WORSLEY, Sir (William) Marcus (John), 5th Bt *cr* 1838; JP; Lord-Lieutenant of North Yorkshire, 1987–99; *b* 6 April 1925; *s* of Colonel Sir William Arthington Worsley, 4th Bt, and Joyce Morgan (*d* 1979), *d* of Sir John Fowler Brunner, 2nd Bt; *S* father, 1973; *m* 1955, Hon. Bridget Assheton, *d* of 1st Baron Clitheroe, PC, KCVO; three *s* one *d*. *Educ:* Eton; New Coll., Oxford. Green Howards, 1943–47 (Lieut seconded to Royal West African Frontier Force). BA Hons (Oxford) Modern History, 1949. Programme Assistant, BBC European Service, 1950–53. Contested (C) Keighley, 1955; MP (C) Keighley, 1959–64, Chelsea, 1966–Sept. 1974; Parliamentary Private Secretary: to Minister of Health, 1960–61; to Minister without Portfolio, 1962–64; to Lord President of the Council, 1970–72. Second Church Estates Commissioner, 1970–74; a Church Commissioner, 1976–84. Pres., Royal Forestry Soc. of England, Wales and N Ireland, 1980–82 (Vice-Pres., 1976–80); National Trust: Dep. Chm., 1986–92; Chm., Yorks Reg. Cttee, 1969–80; Chm., Properties Cttee, 1980–90. Hon. Col, 2nd Bn, Yorkshire Volunteers, 1988–93. JP 1957 (Chm., Malton Bench, 1983–90), DL 1978, North Yorks; High Sheriff of North Yorks, 1982. KStJ 1987. *Recreations:* walking, reading. *Heir:* *s* William Ralph Worsley, FRICS [*b* 12 Sept. 1956; *m* 1987, Marie-Noëlle, *yr d* of Bernard H. Dreesmann; one *s* two *d*]. *Address:* Hovingham Hall, York YO62 4LU. *T:* (01653) 628206. *Club:* Boodle's.

WORSTHORNE, Sir Peregrine (Gerard), Kt 1991; writer; Editor, Comment Section, Sunday Telegraph, 1989–91; *b* 22 Dec. 1923; *s* of Col Koch de Gooreynd, OBE (who assumed surname of Worsthorne by deed poll, 1921), and Baroness Norman, CBE; *m* 1st, 1950, Claude Bertrand de Colasse (*d* 1990); one *d*; 2nd, 1991, Lady Lucinda, *d* of Viscount Lambton (*see* L. Lambton). *Educ:* Stowe; Peterhouse, Cambridge (BA); Magdalen Coll., Oxford. Commnd Oxf. and Bucks LI, 1942; attached Phantom, GHQ Liaison Regt, 1944–45. Sub-editor, Glasgow Herald, 1946; Editorial staff: Times, 1948–53; Daily Telegraph, 1953–61; Deputy Editor, Sunday Telegraph, 1961–76, Associate Editor, 1976–86, Editor, 1986–89. *Publications:* The Socialist Myth, 1972; Peregrinations: selected pieces, 1980; By the Right, 1987; Tricks of Memory (autobiog.), 1993. *Recreations:* swimming, reading. *Address:* The Old Rectory, Hedgerley, Bucks SL2 3UY. *T:* (01753) 646167. *Clubs:* Beefsteak, Garrick, Pratt's.

See also Sir S. P. E. C. W. Towneley.

WORSWICK, Dr Richard David, CChem, FRSC; Government Chemist, since 1991; Chief Executive, LGC (Holdings) Ltd, since 1996; *b* 22 July 1946; *s* of (George) David (Norman) Worswick, CBE, FBA; *m* 1970, Jacqueline Brigit Isobel Adcock; three *d*. *Educ:* New College, Oxford (BA Hons Nat. Sci. 1969; MA 1972; DPhil 1972). CChem, FRSC 1991. SRC post-doctorate res. asst, Inorganic Chem. Lab., Oxford, 1972–73; Res. Admin, Boots Co., Nottingham, 1973–76; Harwell Lab., UKAEA, 1976–91: marketing and planning, 1976–85; Head, Res. Planning and Inf. Services, 1985–87; Head, Safety Branch, 1988; Head, Envtl and Med. Scis Div., 1988–90; Dir, Process Technology and Instrumentation, AEA Industrial Technology, 1990–91; Chief Exec., Lab. of Govt Chemist, DTI, 1991–96. *Publications:* research papers in sci. jls. *Recreations:* listening to music, playing the violin, gardening. *Address:* LGC, Queen's Road, Teddington, Middx TW11 0LY. *T:* (020) 8943 7300.

WORTH, Irene, Hon. CBE 1975; actress; *b* 23 June 1916. *Educ:* University of California, Los Angeles (BE). Antoinette Perry Award for distinguished achievement in the Theatre, 1965. First appeared as Fenella in Escape Me Never, New York, 1942; debut on Broadway as Cecily Harden in The Two Mrs Carrolls, Booth Theatre, 1943. Studied for six months with Elsie Fogerty, 1944–45. Subsequently appeared frequently at Mercury, Bolton's, Q, Embassy, etc. Parts include: Anabelle Jones in Love Goes to Press, Duchess Theatre, 1946 (after Embassy); Ilona Szabo in The Play's the Thing, St James's, 1947 (after tour and Lyric, Hammersmith); Eileen Perry in Edward my Son, Lyric, 1948; Lady Fortrose in Home is Tomorrow, Cambridge Theatre, 1948; Olivia Raines in Champagne for Delilah, New, 1949; Celia Coplestone in The Cocktail Party, New, 1950 (after Edinburgh Festival, 1949; Henry Miller Theatre, New York, 1950); Desdemona in Othello, Old Vic, 1951; Helena in Midsummer Night's Dream, Old Vic, 1952; Catherine de Vausselles in The Other Heart, Old Vic, 1952; Lady Macbeth in Macbeth, Desdemona in Othello, Helena in Midsummer Night's Dream, Catherine de Vausselles in The Other Heart, Old Vic tour of S Africa, 1952; Portia in The Merchant of Venice, Old Vic, 1953; Helena in All's Well That Ends Well and Queen Margaret in Richard III, First Season Shakespeare Festival Theatre, Stratford, Ont, Canada, 1953; Frances Farrar in A Day By The Sea, Haymarket, 1953–54; Alcestis in A Life in the Sun, Edinburgh Festival, 1955; leading rôles in: The Queen and the Rebels, Haymarket, 1955; Hotel Paradiso, Winter Garden, 1956; Mary Stuart, Phœnix Theatre, NY, 1957, Old Vic, 1958; The Potting Shed, Globe Theatre, London, 1958; Rosalind in As You Like It, Shakespeare Festival Theatre, Stratford, Ont, 1959; Albertine Prine in Toys in the Attic, Hudson Theatre, New York, 1960 (NY Newspaper Guild Page One Award); Season at Royal Shakespeare Theatre, Stratford, 1962; Goneril in King Lear, Aldwych, 1962; Doctor Mathilde von Zahnd in The Physicists, Aldwych, 1963; Clodia Pulcher in The Ides of March, Haymarket, 1963; World tour of King Lear for Royal Shakespeare Company, 1964; Alice in Tiny Alice, Billy Rose Theatre, New York, 1965 (Tony award 1965), Aldwych, 1970; Hilde in A Song at Twilight, Anne in Shadows of the Evening, Anna-Mary in Come into the Garden Maud (Noël Coward Trilogy), Queen's, 1966 (Evening Standard Award); Hesione Hushabye in Heartbreak House, Chichester and Lyric, 1967 (Variety Club of GB Award, 1967); Jocasta in Seneca's Oedipus, National Theatre, 1968; Hedda in Hedda Gabler, Stratford, Ont, 1970; worked with internat. Co. for Theatre Res., Paris and Iran, 1971; Notes on a Love Affair, Globe, 1972; Madame Arkadina, The Seagull, Chichester, 1973; Hamlet, Ghosts, The Seagull, Greenwich, 1974; Sweet Bird of Youth, Lake Forest, Washington, NY (Tony Award, Jefferson Award), 1975; Misalliance, 1976, Old Times, 1977, After the Season, 1978, Lake Forest, Ill; The Cherry Orchard, NY, 1977 (Drama Desk Award, 1977); Happy Days, NY, 1979; The Lady from Dubuque, NY, 1980; L'Olimpiade, Edinburgh Fest., 1982; The Chalk Garden, NY, 1982; The Physicists, Washington, 1983; The Golden Age, NY, 1984; Coriolanus, Nat. Theatre, 1984; The Bay at Nice, Nat. Theatre, 1986; You Never Can Tell, Haymarket, 1987; Volumnia in Coriolanus, Public Theatre, NY, 1988–89; Lost in Yonkers, NY (Tony Award), 1991; A Week's Worth, Almeida, 1996; Irene Worth's Portrait of Edith Wharton; The Gypsy and the Yellow Canary, 1997; Chère Maître, Almeida, 1999. *Films:* Orders to Kill, 1957 (British Film Academy Award for Best Woman's Performance, 1958); The Scapegoat, 1958; King Lear (Goneril), 1970; Nicholas and Alexandra, 1971; Eye Witness, 1980; Deathtrap, 1982; Fast Forward, 1985; Lost in Yonkers, 1993; A Piece of Cake, 1997. *Television:* The Lady from the Sea, BBC, 1953; The Lake, BBC, 1953 (Daily Mail National Television Award, 1953–54), and has subseq. appeared on television and acted with CBC Television in NY and Canada; Coriolanus (BBC Shakespeare series), 1984. Hon. Dr Arts Tufts Univ., 1980; Hon. DFA Queen's Coll., NY, 1986. Whitbread Anglo-American Award for Outstanding Actress, 1967; NY Theatre Hall of Fame, 1979; Obie Award for outstanding achievement in the theatre, 1989. *Recreation:* music. *Address:* c/o ICM, Sam Cohn, 40 West 57th Street, New York, NY 10019, USA.

WORTH, Prof. Katharine Joyce; Professor of Drama and Theatre Studies in the University of London at Royal Holloway and Bedford New College, 1985–87, now Emeritus (at Royal Holloway College, 1978–85); *b* 4 Aug. 1922; *d* of George and Elizabeth Lorimer; *m* 1947, George Worth; two *s* one *d*. *Educ:* Bedford Coll., Univ. of London (BA English, MA res. degree, PhD). Lectr in drama and theatre history (pt-time), Central Sch. of Speech and Drama and for Univ. of London Dept of Extra-Mural Studies, 1948 intermittently until 1963; Lectr 1964–74, Reader 1974–78, in English Lit., RHC; Hon. Fellow, RHBNC, 1990. Leverhulme Professorial Fellowship, 1987–89. Vis. Prof., KCL, 1987–96. Chm., Boilerhouse Fund-raising Cttee, Royal Holloway, 1999–. Hon. Pres., Consortium for Drama and Media in Higher Educn, 1987–; Co-editor, Theatre Notebook, 1987–97; Member, Editorial Board: Yeats Annual, 1985–; Modern Drama, 1985–2000; Univ. of Michigan Press, 1988–. Hon. Life Mem., Soc. for Theatre Res., 1997. Prodns of Beckett's TV play, Eh Joe, and his radio plays, Words and Music, Embers and Cascando, 1972–84 (music for Words and Music and Cascando by Humphrey Searle); stage adaptation of Samuel Beckett's Company, perf. Edinburgh, Belfast, London and NY, 1987–88, Dublin, 1991; Dir, staged readings of the play behind the opera, Verdi Fest., Royal Opera House, 1995–99. *Publications:* Revolutions in Modern English Drama, 1973; (ed) Beckett the Shape Changer, 1975; The Irish Drama of Europe: from Yeats to Beckett, 1978; Oscar Wilde, 1983; Maeterlinck's Plays in Performance, 1985; (critical edn): W. B. Yeats: Where There is Nothing, and, W. B. Yeats and Lady Gregory: The Unicorn from the Stars, 1987; Waiting for Godot and Happy Days: text and performance, 1990; Sheridan and Goldsmith, 1992; Samuel Beckett's Theatre: life journeys, 1999; many articles and reviews on modern drama in symposia and in English, Irish and Amer. jls, incl. Modern Drama, TLS, Irish Univ. Rev., Th. Notebook, etc. *Recreations:* foreign travel, theatre, art galleries, walking in the country. *Address:* 48 Elmfield Avenue, Teddington, Mddx TW11 8BT. *T:* (020) 8977 5778.

WORTHINGTON, Anthony, (Tony); MP (Lab) Clydebank and Milngavie, since 1987; *b* 11 Oct. 1941; *s* of late Malcolm and Monica Worthington; *m* 1966, Angela Oliver;

one *s* one *d*. *Educ:* LSE (BA Hons); Univ. of Glasgow (MEd). Lecturer, Social Policy and Sociology: HM Borstal, Dover, 1962–66; Monkwearmouth Coll. of Further Educn, Sunderland, 1967–71; Jordanhill Coll. of Educn, Glasgow, 1971–87. Councillor, Strathclyde Region, 1974–87 (Chm., Finance Cttee, 1986–87). Opposition front bench spokesman: on educn and employment in Scotland, 1989–92; on overseas develt, 1992–93; on foreign affairs, 1993–94; on Northern Ireland, 1995–97; Parly Under-Sec. of State, NI Office, 1997–98. Member: Home Affairs Select Cttee, 1987–89; Internat. Develt Select Cttee, 1999–; Sec., All Party Population and Develt Gp, 1989–97; Chm., All Party Gp on Overseas Develt, 2000–. Chm., Labour Campaign for Criminal Justice, 1987–89. *Recreation:* gardening. *Address:* House of Commons, SW1A 0AA; 24 Cleddans Crescent, Hardgate, Clydebank G81 5NW. *T:* (01389) 873195. *Club:* Radnor Park Bowling.

WORTHINGTON, Prof. Brian Stewart, FRCR, FMedSci; FRS 1998; Professor of Diagnostic Radiology, University of Nottingham, 1981–98, now Professor Emeritus; *b* 9 June 1938; *s* of Eric Worthington and Jessie Worthington (*née* Dibb); *m* 1961, Margaret Ann Mayne; two *s*. *Educ:* Hulme Grammar Sch., Oldham; Guy's Hosp., London (Ken Clifford Scholar; BSc Physiol. 1960; MB BS 1963). LRCP 1963; MRCS 1963; DMRD 1967; FRCR (Rohan Williams Medal) 1969; LIMA 1979; FInstP 1998. Registrar, London Hosp., 1965–70; Consultant Radiologist, Nottingham Hosps, 1970–71; Consultant Neuroradiologist, Nottingham Hosps and Derby Royal Infirmary, 1971–75; Reader, Dept of Radiology, Univ. of Nottingham, 1975–81. Kodak Vis. Prof., Univ. of Dublin, 1987; Visiting Professor: Univs of Turku and Helsinki, 1992; Univ. of Vancouver, 1994. Lectures: George Simon Meml, Nottingham, 1982; Malthé Meml, Oslo, 1983; Grout Meml, Sheffield, 1983; W. S. Moore Meml, London, 1996. Examiner: RCR, 1977–82; Coll. of Radiographers, 1977–87; Univ. of Liverpool, 1987–91. Pres., BIR, 1988–89. Member: Radiol Adv. Cttee, DHSS, 1987–90; MRC Molecular and Cellular Medicine Bd, 1996–2000. Fellow, Soc. of Magnetic Resonance in Medicine, 1997 (Mem. Bd of Trustees, 1987–90). Founder FMedSci 1998. Hon. Mem., Radiol Socs of Iceland, 1986, and Finland, 1993. Mem., Radiological Visiting Club, 1974–. Gold Medal: Back Pain Assoc., 1985; Soc. of Magnetic Resonance in Medicine, 1990; RCR, 1998; Barclay Medal, BIR, 1992; Trent Medal, NHS Exec., 1997. *Publications:* (with G. Whitehouse) Techniques in Diagnostic Imaging, 1983, 3rd edn 1996; contrib. papers in learned jls on neuroradiology, magnetic resonance imaging and cognitive aspects of diagnostic radiology. *Recreations:* Icelandic language and culture, classical music, archaeology. *Address:* Cliff Cottage, Belper Road, Shirland, Alfreton, Derbys DE55 6AG. *T:* (01773) 834096.

WORTHINGTON, Edgar Barton, CBE 1967; MA, PhD; environmental consultant; *b* 13 Jan. 1905; *s* of Edgar Worthington and Amy E. Beale; *m* 1st, 1930, Stella Desmond Johnson (*d* 1978); three *d*; 2nd, 1980, Harriett Stockton, Cape Cod. *Educ:* Rugby; Gonville and Caius Coll., Cambridge. Expeditions to African Lakes, 1927–31; Balfour Student, 1930–33, and Demonstrator in Zoology, Cambridge Univ., 1933–37; Scientist for the African Research Survey, 1934–37; Mungo Park Medal, RSGS, 1939; Director of Laboratories and Secretary of Freshwater Biological Assoc., Windermere, 1937–46; Scientific Adviser to Middle East Supply Centre, 1943–45; Development Adviser, Uganda, 1946; Scientific Secretary to Colonial Research Council, 1946–49, to E Africa High Commission, 1950–51; Secretary-General to Scientific Council for Africa South of the Sahara, 1951–55; Deputy Director-General (Scientific) Nature Conservancy, 1957–65; Scientific Dir, Internat. Biological Programme, 1964–74; Pres., Cttee on Water Res., ICSU, 1973–77. Mem. of Honour, IUCN, 1978; Mem. (*hc*), Linnean Soc., 1991. Gill Meml award, RGS, 1932; Mungo Park Medal, RSGS, 1938; Avicenne Medal, UNESCO, 1993. Order of Golden Ark (Netherlands), 1976. *Publications:* (with Stella Worthington) Inland Waters of Africa, 1933; Science in Africa, 1938; Middle East Science, 1946; Development Plan for Uganda, 1947; (with T. T. Macan) Life in Lakes and Rivers, 1951, rev. edn 1973; Science in the Development of Africa, 1958 (trans. French, 1960); (ed) Man-made Lakes: problems and environmental effects, 1973; Evolution of the IBP, 1975; (ed) Arid Land Irrigation: problems and environmental effects, 1976; The Nile, 1978; The Ecological Century, 1983; official reports and papers in scientific journals. *Recreations:* nature conservation, field sports and farming. *Address:* Colin Godmans, Furner's Green, Uckfield, East Sussex TN22 3RR. *T:* (01825) 740322.

WORTHINGTON, His Honour George Noel; a Circuit Judge, 1979–94; *b* 22 June 1923; *s* of late George Errol Worthington and Edith Margaret Boys Worthington; *m* 1954, Jacqueline Kemble Lightfoot, 2nd *d* of late G. L. S. Lightfoot and Mrs Lightfoot; one *s* one *d* (and one *s* decd). *Educ:* Rossall Sch., Lancashire. Served War of 1939–45 in Royal Armoured Corps, 1941–46. Admitted a solicitor, 1949; a Recorder of the Crown Court, 1972–79. Liveryman, Wax Chandlers' Co. *Recreations:* gardening, theatre. *Clubs:* Athenæum, Hurlingham.

WORTHINGTON, Prof. Michael Hugh, PhD; Professor of Geophysics, Imperial College of Science, Technology and Medicine, since 1985 (Head, Department of Geology, 1993–97); *b* 16 June 1946; *s* of Air Vice-Marshal Sir Geoffrey Worthington, KBE, CB, and late Margaret Joan (*née* Stevenson); *m* 1975, Mary Archange Mackintosh; one *s* one *d*. *Educ:* Wellington Coll.; Durham Univ. (BSc 1968; MSc 1969); ANU (PhD 1973). Univ. Lectr in Geophysics, and Fellow of Exeter Coll., Oxford, 1973–85. Vis. Prof., Dept of Applied and Engrg Physics, Cornell Univ., 1978. Member: Soc. of Exploration Geophysicists; European Assoc. of Geoscientists and Engineers; FGS. *Publications:* (jtly) Seismic Data Processing, 1986; contribs to professional jls. *Recreations:* sailing, cross-country running, painting. *Address:* T. H. Huxley School of the Environment, Earth Sciences and Engineering, Imperial College of Science, Technology and Medicine, Prince Consort Road, SW7 2BP. *T:* (020) 7594 6400.

WÖSSNER, Dr Mark Matthias; Chairman and Chief Executive Officer, Bertelsmann Foundation, 1998–2000; Chairman, Supervisory Board, Bertelsmann AG, 1998–2000. *Educ:* Karlsruhe Technical University (DrIng). Management Asst, Bertelsmann AG, Gütersloh, 1968; Mohndruck (Bertelsmann largest printing operation): Production Manager, 1970; Technical Dir, 1972; Gen. Manager, 1974; Mem. Exec. Bd, Bertelsmann, 1976; Dep. Chm. of Bd, 1981, Chm. and CEO, 1983–98. *Address:* c/o Bertelsmann AG, Carl Bertelsmann Strasse 270, 33311 Gütersloh, Germany. *T:* 05241800.

WOUK, Herman; author, US; *b* New York, 27 May 1915; *s* of Abraham Isaac Wouk and Esther Wouk (*née* Levine); *m* 1945, Betty Sarah Brown; two *s* (and one *s* decd). *Educ:* Townsend Harris High Sch.; Columbia Univ. (AB). Radio script writer, 1935–41; Vis. Professor of English, Yeshiva Univ., 1952–57; Presidential consultative expert to the United States Treasury, 1941. Served United States Naval Reserve, 1942–46, Deck Officer (four campaign stars). Member Officers' Reserve Naval Services. Trustee, College of the Virgin Islands, 1961–69. Hon. LHD Yeshiva Univ., New York City, 1954; Hon. DLit: Clark Univ., 1960; American Internat. Coll., 1979; Trinity Coll., Hartford, Conn, 1998; George Washington Univ., Washington; Hon. PhD: Bar-Ilan, 1990; Hebrew, 1997. Columbia University Medal for excellence, 1952; Alexander Hamilton Medal, Columbia Univ., 1980; Berkeley Medal, Univ. of Calif, 1984; Golden Plate Award, Amer. Acad. of Achievement, 1986; Lone Sailor Award, US Navy Meml Foundn, 1987; Kazetnik Award, Yad Vashem, 1990; Guardian of Zion Award, Bar Ilan Univ., 1998; UCSD Medal, Univ. of Calif, San Diego, 1998. *Publications: novels:* Aurora Dawn, 1947; The City Boy, 1948; The Caine Mutiny (Pulitzer Prize), 1951; Marjorie Morningstar, 1955; Youngblood Hawke, 1962; Don't Stop The Carnival, 1965; The Winds of War, 1971 (televised 1983); War and Remembrance, 1978 (televised 1989); Inside, Outside (Washingtonian Book Award), 1985; The Hope, 1993; The Glory, 1994; *plays:* The Traitor, 1949; The Caine Mutiny Court-Martial, 1953; Nature's Way, 1957; *non-fiction:* This Is My God, 1959; The Will to Live On, 2000. *Address:* c/o BSW Literary Agency, 303 Crestview Drive, Palm Springs, CA 92264, USA. *Clubs:* Cosmos, Metropolitan (Washington); Bohemian (San Francisco); Century (New York).

WRAGG, Prof. Edward Conrad; Professor of Education, Exeter University, since 1978 (Director, School of Education, 1978–94); *b* 26 June 1938; *s* of George William and Maria Wragg; *m* 1960, Judith (*née* King); one *s* two *d*. *Educ:* King Edward VII Grammar Sch., Sheffield; Durham Univ. (BA Hons German Cl. 1; Postgrad. CertEd, Cl. 1); Leicester Univ. (MEd); Exeter Univ. (PhD). Asst Master, Queen Elizabeth Grammar Sch., Wakefield, 1960–64; Head of German, Wyggeston Boys' Sch., Leicester, 1964–66; Lectr in Education, Exeter Univ., 1966–73; Prof. of Educn, Nottingham Univ., 1973–78. Pres., British Educnl Research Assoc., 1981–82; Specialist Adviser, Parliamentary Select Cttee, 1976–77; Chairman: School Broadcasting Council for UK, 1981–86; Educnl Broadcasting Council for UK, 1986–87; BBC Regl Adv. Council for South and West, 1989–92, for South, 1992–96; Member: Educnl Res. Bd, SSRC, 1974–78; Educn Sub-Cttee, UGC, 1981–89; Bd, Qualifications and Curriculum Authty, 1997–. Specialist Advr in Educn, UFC, 1989–92. Presenter of radio and TV series and items on education, including Chalkface (Granada), Crisis in Education (BBC), The Education Roadshow (BBC), The Education Programme (BBC), Pebble Mill at One (BBC), Teaching Today (BBC). Editor, Research Papers in Education, 1986–. FCP 1988. DUniv: Open, 1989; Strathclyde, 1993; Hon. DCL Northumbria, 1999. *Publications:* Teaching Teaching, 1974; Teaching Mixed Ability Groups, 1976; Classroom Interaction, 1976; A Handbook for School Governors, 1980; Class Management and Control, 1981; A Review of Teacher Education, 1982; Swineshead Revisited, 1982; Classroom Teaching Skills, 1984; Pearls from Swineshire, 1984; The Domesday Project, 1985; Education: an action guide for parents, 1986; Teacher Appraisal, 1987; Education in the Market Place, 1988; The Wragged Edge, 1988; Parents and Schools, 1989; Riches from Wragg, 1990; Mad Curriculum Disease, 1991; Class Management, 1993; Questioning, 1993; Explaining, 1993; Primary Teaching Skills, 1993; The Parents' File, 1993; No, Minister!, 1993; An Introduction to Classroom Observation, 1994; Flying Boot, 1994; Effective Teaching, 1994; A Parent's Guide to the National Curriculum, 1995; The Ted Wragg Guide to Education, 1995; Teacher Appraisal Observed, 1996; (jtly) The Longman Parent's and Students' Guides, 1996; The Last Quango, 1996; Assessment and Learning, 1997; The Cubic Curriculum, 1997; Teach Your Child French, 1997; The Prince of Darkness, 1998; Improving Literacy in the Primary School, 1998; Failing Teachers?, 2000; frequent contributor to Guardian, Times Educnl Supp. (regular columnist), Times Higher Educn Supp., Observer, Independent, Good Housekeeping. *Recreations:* football playing, watching and coaching; cooking, running, writing, music. *Address:* Higher Duryard House, Pennsylvania Road, Exeter EX4 5BQ. *T:* (01392) 491052.

WRAGG, John, RA 1991 (ARA 1983); FRBS 1996; sculptor; *b* 20 Oct. 1937; *s* of Arthur and Ethel Wragg. *Educ.* York Sch. of Art; Royal Coll. of Art. *Work in public collections:* Israel Mus., Jerusalem; Tate Gall.; Arts Council of GB; Arts Council of NI; Contemp. Art Soc.; Wellington Art Gall., NZ; work in private collections in GB, America, Canada, France and Holland. *One-man exhibitions:* Hanover Gall., 1963, 1966 and 1970; Galerie Alexandre Iolas, Paris, 1968; York Fest., 1969; Bridge Street Gall., Bath, 1982; Katherine House Gall., Marlborough, 1984; Quinton Green Fine Art, London, 1985; Devizes Mus. Gall., 1994; England & Co., London, 1994; L'Art Abstrait, London, 1995; Handel House Gall., Devizes, 2000; Bruton Gall., Leeds, 2000; *exhibitions:* Lord's Gall., 1959; L'Art Vivant, 1965–68; Arts Council Gall., Belfast, 1966; Pittsburgh Internat., 1967; Britische Kunst heute, Hamburg, Fondn Maeght, and Contemp. Art Fair, Florence, 1968; Bath Fest. Gall., 1977 and 1984; Artists Market, 1978; Biennale di Scultura di Arese, Milan, and King Street Gall., Bristol, 1980; Galerie Bollhagen Worpswede, N Germany, 1981 and 1983; Quinton Green Fine Art, London, 1984, 1985, 1986 and 1987; Best of British, Simpsons, 1993; Connought Brown, London, 1993; Monumental '96, Belgium, 1996; Courcoux & Courcoux, 1997; Bruton Gall., Leeds, 1999; Bruton St Gall., London, 1999. Sainsbury Award, 1960; Winner of Sainsbury Sculpture Comp., King's Road, Chelsea, 1966; Arts Council Major Award, 1977; Chantry Bequest, 1981. *Relevant publications:* chapters and articles about his work in: Neue Dimensionen der Plastic, 1964; Contemporary British Artists, 1979; British Sculpture in the Twentieth Century, 1981; Studio Internat., Art & Artiste, Sculpture Internat., Arts Rev., and The Artist. *Recreation:* walking. *Address:* 6 Castle Lane, Devizes, Wilts SN10 1HJ. *T:* (01380) 727087.

WRAIGHT, Margaret Joan; *see* Hustler, M. J.

WRAN, Hon. Neville Kenneth, AC 1988; QC (NSW) 1968; Premier of New South Wales, 1976–86. *Educ:* Fort Street Boys' High Sch., Sydney; Sydney Univ. (LLB). Solicitor before admission to Bar of NSW, 1957. Joined Australian Labor Party, 1954, Nat. Pres., 1980–86. Elected to Legislative Council, 1970; Dep. Leader of Opposition, 1971; Leader of Opposition, Legislative Council, 1972; MLA for Bass Hill, Nov. 1973–1986; Leader of Opposition, Dec. 1973–76. Chm., CSIRO, 1986–91. Is especially interested in law reform, civil liberties, industrial relations, conservation and cultural matters. Exec. Chm., Wran Partners Pty Ltd; Director: Powerlan Ltd; Cabcharge Australia Ltd. Chm., Victor Chang Cardiac Res. Inst. Australian Mem., Eminent Persons' Gp, Asia-Pacific Econ. Co-operation, 1993–95. FRSA 1990. Hon. LLD Sydney, 1995. *Recreations:* reading, walking, swimming, tennis. *Address:* GPO Box 4545, Sydney, NSW 2001, Australia. *T:* (2) 92235151. *Club:* Sydney Labor (Hon. Life Mem.).

WRATTEN, Donald Peter; Director, National Counties Building Society, 1985–96; *b* 8 July 1925; *er s* of late Frederick George and Marjorie Wratten; *m* 1947, Margaret Kathleen (*née* Marsh); one *s* one *d*. *Educ:* Morehall Elem. Sch. and Harvey Grammar Sch., Folkestone; London Sch. of Economics. Storehand, temp. clerk, meteorological asst (Air Min.), 1940–43; service with RAF Meteorological Wing, 1943–47. LSE, 1947–50. Joined Post Office, 1950; Private Sec. to Asst Postmaster Gen., 1955–56; seconded to Unilever Ltd, 1959; Private Sec. to Postmaster Gen., 1965–66; Head of Telecommunications Marketing Div., 1966–67; Director: Eastern Telecommunications Region, 1967–69; Exec. Dir, Giro and Remittance Services, 1969–74 (Sen. Dir, 1970–74); Sen. Dir, Data Processing Service, 1974–75; Sen. Dir, Telecom Personnel, 1975–81. Member: Industrial Adv. Panel, City Univ. Business Sch., 1974–81 (Chm., 1977–81); Court, Cranfield Inst. of Technology, 1976–81; Business Educn Council, 1977–83; Council: Intermediate Technology Develt Gp, 1982–85; Internat. Stereoscopic Union, 1987–; Pres., Stereoscopic Soc., 1996–98 (Vice-Chm., 1990–92; Chm., 1993–95). Pres., Radlett Soc. & Green Belt Assoc., 1996– (Chm., 1989–96). *Publication:* The Book of Radlett and Aldenham, 1990. *Recreations:* 3-D photography, social history. *Address:* 10 Homefield Road, Radlett, Herts WD7 8PY. *T:* (01923) 854500.

WRATTEN, Air Chief Marshal Sir William (John), GBE 1998 (KBE 1991; CBE 1982); CB 1991; AFC 1973; Chief Military Adviser, Rolls-Royce Defence (Europe), 1998–2000; *b* 15 Aug. 1939; *s* of William Wellesley Wratten and Gwenneth Joan (*née* Bourne); *m* 1963, Susan Jane Underwood; two *s* two *d*. *Educ:* Chatham House Grammar Sch., Ramsgate; RAF Coll., Cranwell. OC, RAF Coningsby, 1980–82; Sen. RAF Officer, Falkland Is, 1982; RCDS, 1983; Dir, Operational Requirements (RAF), MoD, 1984–86; SASO, HQ 1 Gp, 1986–89; AOC No 11 Gp, 1989–91; Air Comdr British Forces ME, and Dep. to Comdr (on attachment), Nov. 1990–March 1991; Dir Gen., Saudi Armed Forces Project, 1992–94. AOC-in-C Strike Comd, and Comdr Allied Air Forces Northwestern Europe, 1994–97; Air ADC to the Queen, 1995–97. CIMgt 1996. Legionnaire, Legion of Merit (USA), 1993. *Recreation:* photography. *Address:* 14 College Road, Cheltenham GL53 7HX. *Club:* Royal Air Force.

WRAXALL, 3rd Baron *cr* 1928, of Clyst St George, co. Devon; **Eustace Hubert Beilby Gibbs,** KCVO 1986; CMG 1982; HM Diplomatic Service, retired; Vice Marshal of the Diplomatic Corps, 1982–86; *b* 3 July 1929; *s* of 1st Baron Wraxall, PC; *S* brother, 2001; *m* 1957, Evelyn Veronica Scott; three *s* two *d*. *Educ:* Eton College; Christ Church, Oxford (MA). ARCM 1953. Entered HM Diplomatic Service, 1954; served in Bangkok, Rio de Janeiro, Berlin, Vienna, Caracas, Paris. *Recreations:* music, golf. *Heir:* *s* Hon. Antony Hubert Gibbs [*b* 19 Aug. 1958; *m* 1st, 1988, Caroline Jane Gould (marr. diss. 1994); two *d*; 2nd, 1995, Virginia, *d* of Colin Gilchrist; two *s*]. *Address:* Coddenham House, Coddenham, Ipswich, Suffolk IP6 9TY. *T:* (01449) 760332, *Fax:* (01449) 761729. *Clubs:* Brooks's, Pratt's.

WRAXALL, Sir Charles (Frederick Lascelles), 9th Bt *cr* 1813; Assistant Accountant, Morgan Stanley International, since 1987; *b* 17 Sept. 1961; *s* of Sir Morville William Lascelles Wraxall, 8th Bt, and of Lady (Irmgard Wilhelmina) Wraxall; *S* father, 1978; *m* 1983, Lesley Linda, *d* of late William Albert and Molly Jean Allan; one *s* one *d*. *Educ:* Archbishop Tenison's Grammar School, Croydon. *Recreations:* stamp collection, watching football. *Heir:* *s* William Nathaniel Lascelles Wraxall, *b* 3 April 1987.

WRAY, Prof. David; Professor of Oral Medicine, since 1993, and Dean of Dental School, since 2000, Glasgow University; Hon. Consultant in Oral Medicine, North Glasgow NHS Trust, since 1993; *b* 3 Jan. 1951; *s* of Arthur Wray and Margaret Wray (*née* Craig); *m* 1st, 1974, Alison Young (marr. diss. 1997); two *s*; 2nd, 1997, Alyson Urquhart; two *s*. *Educ:* Uddingston Grammar Sch.; Glasgow Univ. (BDS 1972; MBChB 1976; MD 1982). FDSRCPSGlas 1979; FDSRCSE 1987. Fogarty Vis. Associate, NIH, Bethesda, 1979–81; Wellcome Res. Fellow, Royal Dental Sch., Univ. of London, 1982; Sen. Lectr, Dept of Oral Medicine and Pathology, Univ. of Edinburgh, 1983–93; Associate Dean for Res., Dental Sch., Glasgow Univ., 1995–2000. Founder FMedSci, 1998. *Publications:* Oral Medicine, 1997; Oral Candidosis, 1997; Textbook of General and Oral Medicine, 1999. *Recreations:* golf, wine, cooking. *Address:* Glasgow Dental Hospital and School, 378 Sauchiehall Street, Glasgow G2 3JZ;125 Dowanhill Street, Glasgow G12 9DN. *T:* (0141) 334 0021.

WRAY, Prof. Gordon Richard, FRS 1986; FREng; Eur Ing; Royal Academy of Engineering Professor in Principles of Engineering Design, Engineering Design Institute, Loughborough University of Technology, 1988–93, now Professor Emeritus; *b* 30 Jan. 1928; *s* of Joseph and Letitia Wray (*née* Jones); *m* 1954, Kathleen Senior; one *s* one *d*. *Educ:* Bolton Tech. Coll., Univ. of Manchester (BScTech, MScTech, PhD); DSc Loughborough; FTI 1963; FIMechE 1973; FREng (FEng 1980). Engineering apprentice, Bennis Combustion, Bolton, 1943; Design draughtsman, Dobson & Barlow, Bolton, 1946; Sir Walter Preston Scholar, Univ. of Manchester, 1949; Develt Engineer, Platts (Barton), 1952; Lectr in Mech. Engrg, Bolton Tech. Coll., 1953; Lectr in Textile Engrg, UMIST, 1955; Loughborough University of Technology: Reader, 1966–70, Prof. and Hd of Dept, 1970–88, Dept of Mech. Engrg; Dir, Engrg Design Inst., 1988–91. Springer Vis. Prof., Univ. of California, Berkeley, 1977; Royal Soc./Royal Acad. of Engrg Vis. Lectr, Australia and NZ, 1992; Lectures: Brunel, BAAS, 1980; Thomas Hawksley Meml, IMechE, 1989; Bill Aldridge Meml, Textile Inst., Auckland, NZ, 1994. Member: DoI Chief Scientist's Requirements Bd, 1974–75; CEI/CSTI Interdisciplinary Bd, 1978–83; SEFI Cttee on Innovation, Brussels, 1980–82; Royal Soc. Working Gp on Agricl Engrg, 1981–82; SERC Applied Mechanics Cttee, 1982–85; Fellowship of Engrg Working Party on DoI Requirements Bds, 1982; SERC Working Party on Engrg Design, 1983; Royal Soc. Sectional Cttee 4 (i), 1986–89; Cttee, Engrg Profs Conf., 1986–88; Royal Soc. Mullard Award Cttee, 1986–92; Royal Soc./SERC Industrial Fellowships Panel, 1986–89; Royal Soc. Technology Activities Cttee, 1989–93; Chm., Engrg Council/Design Council Wkg Party on Attaining Competences in Engrg Design, 1989–91. First recipient of title European Engineer (Eur Ing), Paris, 1987. Mem. Council, IMechE, 1964–67 (Chm., Manip. and Mech. Handling Machinery Gp, 1969–71). Chm., Judging Panel, William Lee Quatercentenary Technology Prize, 1989. FRSA 1974. Hon. FIED 2001 (Hon. MIED 1990). IMechE Prizes: Viscount Weir, 1959; Water Arbitration, 1972; James Clayton, 1975; Warner Medal, Textile Inst., 1976; S. G. Brown Award and Medal, Royal Soc., 1978; Engrg Merit Award, ASME, 1977. Mem., East Leake Summer Wine Club. *Publications:* (contrib.) Textile Engineering Processes, ed Nissan, 1959; Modern Yarn Production from Man-made Fibres, 1960; Modern Developments in Weaving Machinery, 1961; An Introduction to the Study of Spinning, 3rd edn 1962; (contrib.) Contemporary Textile Engineering, ed Happey, 1982; State/Industry Linkages, 1993; (contrib.) Mechatronic Design in Textile Engineering, ed Acar, 1995; numerous papers to learned jls. *Recreations:* fell-walking, photography, steam traction engines, theatre, music, gardening, DIY. *Address:* Stonestack, Rempstone, Loughborough, Leics LE12 6RH. *T:* (01509) 880043.

WRAY, James; MP (Lab) Glasgow Baillieston, since 1997 (Glasgow, Provan, 1987–97); *b* 28 April 1938; *m*; one *s* two *d*; *m* 3rd, 1999, Laura Walker; one *s*. Heavy goods vehicle driver. Mem., Strathclyde Regl Council, 1976. President: Scottish Fedn of the Blind, 1987 (Vice Pres., 1986); St Enoch's Drug Centre; Scottish Ex-Boxers' Assoc.; Gorbals United FC. Mem., TGWU. *Address:* House of Commons, SW1A 0AA.

WRAY, (Karen) Prudence Patricia, (Mrs B. H. Wray); *see* Skene, K. P. P.

WRAY, Nigel William; non-executive Chairman, WILink.com (formerly Knutsford) plc, since 1999; *b* 9 April 1948. *Educ:* Mill Hill Sch.; Univ. of Bristol (BSc). Chairman: Fleet Street Letter plc, 1976–90; Burford Hldgs plc, 1988–2001; Nottingham Forest plc, 1997–99; Dir, Saracens Ltd, 1995–; non-executive Director: Carlton Communications plc, 1976–97; Singer and Friedlander Gp plc, 1986–2001; Peoples Phone, 1989–96; Columbus Gp, 1991–2000; Chorion (formerly Trocadero) plc, 1995–; SkyePharma plc, 1995–2000; Domino's Pizza Gp, 1997–; Carlisle Hldgs, 1998–; Hartford Gp, 1998–2000; Safestore plc, 1999–; Seymour Pierce Gp (formerly Talisman House) plc, 2000–; Electric Word plc, 2000–; Printpotato.com plc, 2000–. *Address:* 20 Thayer Street, W1M 6DD. *T:* (020) 7224 2240.

WRENBURY, 3rd Baron *cr* 1915; **Rev. John Burton Buckley;** Non-Stipendiary Minister, Brightling, Dallington, Mountfield and Netherfield, diocese of Chichester, since 1990; *b* 18 June 1927; *s* of 2nd Baron Wrenbury and Helen Malise (*d* 1981), 2nd *d* of late His Honour John Cameron Graham of Ballewan, Stirlingshire; *S* father, 1940; *m* 1st, 1956, Carolyn Joan Maule (marr. diss., 1961), *o d* of Lt-Col Ian Burn-Murdoch, OBE, of Gartincaber, Doune, Perthshire; 2nd, 1961, Penelope Sara Frances, *o d* of Edward D. Fort, The White House, Sixpenny Handley, Dorset; one *s* two *d*. *Educ:* Eton Coll.; King's Coll., Cambridge. Deputy Legal Adviser to the National Trust, 1955–56; Partner: Freshfield's, Solicitors, 1956–74; Thomson Snell and Passmore, 1974–90. Ordained deacon in Church of England, 1990, priest, 1991. *Recreations:* golf, campanology, bagpipes. *Heir:* *s* Hon. William Edward Buckley [*b* 19 June 1966; *m* 1996, Emma, *o d* of Peter Clementson]. *Address:* Oldcastle, Dallington, near Heathfield, East Sussex TN21 9JP. *T:* (01435) 830400. *Club:* Oriental.

WRENCH, Peter Nicholas; Deputy Director General, Immigration and Nationality Directorate, Home Office, since 2000; *b* 5 April 1957; *s* of late Cyril Wrench and of Edna Mary Wrench; *m* 1978, Pauline Jordan; two *d*. *Educ:* Clitheroe Royal Grammar Sch.; Royal Holloway Coll., London (BA). Home Office, 1980–: Private Sec. to Perm. Sec., 1987–88; Immigration and Nationality Dept, 1988–93; Organised and Internat. Crime Directorate, 1993–2000. *Recreations:* obscure music, hard liquor, family, friends, dog. *Address:* Home Office, Apollo House, 36 Wellesley Road, Croydon, Surrey CR9 3RR.

WREXHAM, Bishop of, (RC), since 1994; **Rt Rev. Edwin Regan;** *b* 31 Dec. 1935; *s* of James Regan and Elizabeth Ellen Regan (*née* Hoskins). *Educ:* St Joseph's RC Primary Sch., Aberavon; Port Talbot County Grammar Sch.; St John's Coll., Waterford, Eire; Corpus Christi Coll., London. Priest, 1959; Curate, Neath, 1959–66; Adviser in RE, Archdio. Cardiff, 1967–87; Chaplain, St Clare's Convent, Porthcawl, 1967–71; Administrator, St David's Cathedral, Cardiff, 1971–84; Parish Priest: St Helen's, Barry, 1984–89; St Mary's, Bridgend, 1989–94. *Recreation:* hill-walking. *Address:* Bishop's House, Sontley Road, Wrexham LL13 7EW. *T:* (01978) 262726.

WREY, Benjamin Harold Bourchier; Chairman, Henderson Global Investors (formerly Henderson Administration Group and Henderson Investors), since 1992; *b* 6 May 1940; *s* of Christopher B. Wrey and Ruth Wrey (*née* Bowden); *m* 1970, (Anne) Christine (Aubrey) Cherry; one *d*. *Educ:* Blundell's Sch.; Clare Coll., Cambridge (Hons in Econs; MA). Legal and General Assurance Soc., 1963–66; Investment Dept, Hambros Bank, 1966–69; joined Henderson Administration, 1969; Director, 1971; Jt Man. Dir/Dep. Chm., 1982; Director: Henderson Electric and General Investment Trust plc (formerly Electric and General Investment Co.), 1977–2000; Henderson American Capital and Income Trust plc, 1996–99. Chm., Institutional Fund Managers' Assoc., 1996–98 (Dep. Chm., 1994–96); Member: Institutional Investors Adv. Cttee, London Stock Exchange, 1994–2000; Exec. Cttee, Assoc. of Investment Trust Cos, 1997–. Trustee, Charities Official Investment Funds, 1999–. Mem., Adv. Council, Nat. Opera Studio, 1996–. *Publications:* articles on investment. *Recreations:* shooting, fishing, travel, ballet, photography. *Address:* Henderson Global Investors, 4 Broadgate, EC2M 2DA. *T:* (020) 7638 5757. *Clubs:* Boodle's, City of London; Hurlingham.

WREY, Sir (George Richard) Bourchier, 15th Bt *cr* 1628, of Trebitch, Cornwall; *b* 2 Oct. 1948; *s* of Sir Bourchier Wrey, 14th Bt and of Sybil Mabel Alice Wrey, *d* of Dr George Lubke, S Africa; *S* father, 1991; *m* 1981, Lady Caroline Lindesay-Bethune, *d* of 15th Earl of Lindsay; two *s* one *d*. *Educ:* Eton. *Recreation:* shooting. *Heir:* *s* Harry David Bourchier Wrey, *b* 3 Oct. 1984. *Address:* Hollamoor Farm, Tawstock, Barnstaple, Devon EX31 3NY. *T:* (01271) 373466.

WRIGGLESWORTH, Sir Ian (William), Kt 1991; Chairman, UK Land Estates Ltd, since 1995; *b* Dec. 1939; *s* of Edward and Elsie Wrigglesworth; *m* 1967, Patricia Truscott; two *s* one *d*. *Educ:* Stockton Grammar Sch.; Stockton-Billingham Technical Coll; Coll. of St Mark and St John, Chelsea. Formerly: Personal Assistant to Gen. Sec., NUT; Head of Research and Information Dept of Co-operative Party; Press and Public Affairs Manager of National Giro. Chm., Govt Policy Consultants Ltd, 1998–2000; Dep. Chm., John Livingston & Sons Ltd, 1987–; Dir, CIT Hldgs Ltd, 1987–; Divl Dir, Smiths Industries PLC, 1976–2000. Contested (SDP/Alliance) Stockton South, 1987. MP (Lab and Co-op, 1974–81, SDP, 1981–87) Teesside, Thornaby, Feb. 1974–1983, Stockton South, 1983–87. PPS to Mr Alec Lyon, Minister of State, Home Office, 1974; PPS to Rt Hon. Roy Jenkins, Home Secretary, 1974–76; Opposition spokesman on Civil Service, 1979–80; SDP spokesman on industry, 1981, on industry and economic affairs, 1983–87. Pres., Liberal Democrats, 1988–90. Chairman: Northern Reg., CBI, 1992–94; Newcastle-Gateshead Initiative, 1999–. Gov., 1993–, Dep. Chm. Govs, 1997–, Univ. of Teesside. Freeman, City of London, 1995; Liveryman, Co. of Founders, 1994. *Address:* UK Land Estates Ltd, Avalon House, Princes Park, Princesway, Team Valley, Tyne and Wear NE11 0NF. *Clubs:* Reform, Groucho.

WRIGHT, family name of **Baron Wright of Richmond.**

WRIGHT OF RICHMOND, Baron *cr* 1994 (Life Peer), of Richmond-upon-Thames in the London Borough of Richmond-upon-Thames; **Patrick Richard Henry Wright,** GCMG 1989 (KCMG 1984 CMG 1978); HM Diplomatic Service, retired; *b* 28 June 1931; *s* of late Herbert H. S. Wright and Rachel Wright (*née* Green); *m* 1958, Virginia Anne Gaffney; two *s* one *d*. *Educ:* Marlborough; Merton Coll. (Postmaster), Oxford (MA; Hon. Fellow, 1987). Served Royal Artillery, 1950–51; joined Diplomatic Service, 1955; Middle East Centre for Arabic Studies, 1956–57; Third Secretary, British Embassy, Beirut, 1958–60; Private Sec. to Ambassador and later First Sec., British Embassy, Washington, 1960–65; Private Sec. to Permanent Under-Sec., FO, 1965–67; First Sec. and Head of Chancery, Cairo, 1967–70; Dep. Political Resident, Bahrain, 1971–72; Head of Middle East Dept, FCO, 1972–74; Private Sec. (Overseas Affairs) to Prime Minister, 1974–77; Ambassador to: Luxembourg, 1977–79; Syria, 1979–81; Dep. Under-Sec. of State, FCO, 1982–84; Ambassador to Saudi Arabia, 1984–86; Permanent Under-Sec. of State and Head of Diplomatic Service, 1986–91. Mem., Security Commn, 1993–. Director: Barclays Bank plc, 1991–96; BP Amoco (formerly British Petroleum Co.), 1991–2001; De La Rue, 1991–2000; Unilever, 1991–99; BAA, 1992–98. Vice Pres., Home Start, 1991–. Chm., RIIA, 1995–99 (Mem. Council, 1992–99); Member: Council, RCM, 1991–2001 (FRCM 1994); Atlantic Coll., 1993–2000; ICRC Consultative Gp of Internat. Experts, 1992–95. Governor: Ditchley Foundn, 1986–; Wellington Coll., 1991–2001. KStJ 1990; Registrar, 1991–95, Dir of Overseas Relations, 1995–97, Order of St John of Jerusalem. *Recreations:* music, philately, travel. *Address:* c/o House of Lords, Westminster, SW1A 0PW. *Club:* Oxford and Cambridge.

See also S. G. McDonald.

WRIGHT, Alan John; a Master of the Supreme Court, Supreme Court Taxing Office, 1972–91; *b* 21 April 1925; *s* of late Rev. Henry George Wright, MA and Winifred Annie Wright; *m* 1952, Alma Beatrice Ridding; two *s* one *d*. *Educ:* St Olave's and St Saviour's Grammar Sch., Southwark; Keble Coll., Oxford. BA 1949, MA 1964. Served with RAF, India, Burma and China, 1943–46. Solicitor 1952; in private practice with Shaen Roscoe & Co., 1952–71; Legal Adviser to Trades Union Congress, 1955–71. Lay Reader,

Southwark dio., 1989–. *Recreations:* Germanic studies, walking, travel, youth work, foreign languages. *Address:* 21 Brockley Park, Forest Hill, SE23 1PT.

WRIGHT, Alec Michael John, CMG 1967; *b* Hong Kong, 19 Sept. 1912; *s* of Arthur Edgar Wright and Margery Hepworth Chapman; *m* 1948, Ethel Surtees; one *d. Educ:* Brentwood Sch. ARICS 1934; ARIBA 1937. Articled pupil followed by private practice in London. Joined Colonial Service, 1938; appointed Architect in Hong Kong, 1938. Commissioned Hong Kong Volunteer Defence Force, 1941; POW in Hong Kong, 1941–45. Chief Architect, Public Works Dept, Hong Kong, 1950; Asst Director of Public Works, 1956; Dep. Director, 1959; Director, 1963–69; Commissioner for Hong Kong in London, 1969–73. *Address:* 13 Montrose Court, Princes Gate, SW7 2QQ. *T:* (020) 7584 4293. *Club:* Hong Kong (Hong Kong).
See also Sir Denis Wright.

WRIGHT, Sir Allan Frederick, KBE 1982; farmer; Chairman: R. G. Robinson Ltd; Lincoln Holdings Ltd; Richina Pacific Ltd; Medway River Vineyard; *b* Darfield, 25 March 1929; *s* of Quentin A. Wright; *m* 1953, Dorothy June Netting; three *s* two *d. Educ:* Christ's Coll., Christchurch. Nat. Pres., Young Farmers' Clubs, 1957–58; President: N Canterbury Federated Farmers, 1971–74; Federated Farmers of NZ, 1977–81 (formerly Sen. Nat. Vice-Pres.). Mem., NZ Cricket Bd of Control, 1967–90; Manager, NZ Cricket Team to England, 1983; Pres., NZ Cricket, 1993–94. Director: Orion Ltd; Earnscleugh Orchards. Chancellor, Lincoln Univ., 1990–94 (Chm. Council, Lincoln Coll., 1985–89, Mem., 1974–89). Hon. DCom Lincoln, 1997. *Recreations:* cricket (played for N Canterbury), Rugby, golf. *Address:* Annat, RD Sheffield, Canterbury, New Zealand.

WRIGHT, Andrew Paul Kilding, OBE 2001; PPRIAS, RIBA; Partner, 1981–2001, and Chairman, 1999–2001, Law & Dunbar-Nasmith (architects); Commissioner, Royal Fine Art Commission for Scotland, since 1997; *b* 11 Feb. 1947; *s* of Harold Maurice Wright, ARIBA and Eileen May Wright; *m* 1970, Jean Patricia Cross; one *s* two *d. Educ:* Queen Mary's Grammar Sch., Walsall; Univ. of Liverpool (BArch Hons). RIBA 1973; ARIAS 1976, FRIAS 1987; FSAScot 1998. Weightman & Bullen, Liverpool, 1970–72; Rowand Anderson Kininmonth & Paul, Edinburgh, 1972–73; Sir Basil Spence, Glover & Ferguson, Edinburgh, 1973–78; Law & Dunbar-Nasmith, 1978–2001. Dir, Exec. Bd, UK City of Architecture and Design, Glasgow 1999 Festival Co. Ltd, 1995–. Archt, dio. of Moray, Ross and Caithness, 1988–98; Cons. Archt, Mar Lodge Estate, NT for Scotland, 1996–99; Hon. Archtl Advr, Scottish Redundant Churches Trust, 1996–; Archtl Advr, Holyrood Progress Gp, Scottish Parlt, 2000–. Mem., Ancient Monuments Bd for Scotland, 1996–. Member Council: Inverness Archtl Assoc., 1981–90 (Pres., 1986–88); RIAS, 1986–94, 1995–99 (Vice-Pres., 1986–88; Convener, Memship Cttee, 1992–94; Pres., 1995–97); RIBA, 1992–94, 1995–97. Member: Ecclesiastical Archts and Surveyors Assoc., 1989; Conservation Adv. Panel, Hopetoun Hse Preservation Trust, 1997–; C of S Adv. Cttee on Artistic Matters, 2000–; Arts and Crafts in Architecture Award Panel, Saltire Soc., 2001–. Mem. Estates Cttee, Gordonstoun Sch., 2000–. Trustee, Clan Mackenzie Charitable Trust, 1998–. FRSA. *Recreations:* cycling, fishing, railway history, music of Hector Berlioz. *Address:* Andrew P. K. Wright, Chartered Architect, Craiglen, Sanquhar Road, Forres, Moray IV36 1DG. *T:* (01309) 672749.

WRIGHT, Dr Anne Margaret, CBE 1997; DL; Chief Executive, UFI Ltd, since 1998; *b* 26 July 1946; *d* of Herbert and Florence Holden; *m* 1970, Martin Wright; one *d. Educ:* Holy Trinity Indep. Grammar Sch., Bromley; King's Coll., London (BA Hons English I, 1967; Inglis Teaching Studentship, 1967–68; PhD 1970). Lectr in English, Lancaster Univ., 1969–71; Lectr, then Sen. Lectr, Principal Lectr and Reader in Modern English Studies, Hatfield Poly., 1971–84; British Acad. Res. Award, Univ. of Texas at Austin, 1979; Registrar for Arts and Humanities, CNAA, 1984–86; Dep. Rector (Academic), Liverpool Poly, 1986–90; Rector and Chief Exec., Sunderland Poly., 1990–92, Vice Chancellor and Chief Exec., Univ. of Sunderland, 1992–98. Member: English Studies Bd, 1978–84, Arts and Humanities Res. Sub-Cttee, 1979–84, CNAA; Cttee I of Cttee for Internat. Co-op. in Higher Educn, British Council, 1990–; Council for Industry and Higher Educn, 1994–; Director: FEFC, 1992–97; Hong Kong UPGC, 1992–; HEQC, 1993–97. Mem., EOC, 1997–98. Chairman: City of Sunderland (formerly Wearside) Common Purpose, 1990–97; Nat. Glass Centre, 1997–98; Director: Everyman Theatre, Liverpool, 1988–90; The Wearside Opportunity, 1990–93; Northern Sinfonia, 1990–96; Northern Arts, 1991–95; Wearside TEC, 1992–98. CIMgt 1994 (Mem. Bd of Companions, 1999–); FRSA 1992. DL Tyne and Wear, 1997. *Publications:* (ed jtly) Heartbreak House: a facsimile of the revised typescript, 1981; Literature of Crisis 1910–1922, 1984; Bernard Shaw's Saint Joan, 1984; articles in jls and entries in dictionaries of lit. biog. *Recreations:* singing, theatre, opera, the arts. *Address:* UFI Ltd, Innovation Centre, 217 Portobello Street, Sheffield S1 4DR.

WRIGHT, Prof. Anthony, DM; FRCS; Professor of Otorhinolaryngology, and Director, Institute of Laryngology and Otology, University College London, since 1991; *b* 21 Nov. 1949; *s* of Arthur Donald and Hilda Wright; *m* 1989, Linda Steele; two *d. Educ:* Mill Hill Sch.; Emmanuel Coll., Cambridge (Sen. Schol.; Captain, Univ. Boxing Team, 1970); Lincoln Coll., Oxford (Full Blue, Boxing, 1972). DM Oxon 1986; LLM UWC Cardiff, 1995; FRCSE 1979; FRCS *ad eundem* 1995. Sen. Lectr in ENT Surgery, Inst. of Laryngology and Otology, 1984–89; Consultant ENT Surgeon, Royal Free Hosp., 1989–91. *Publications:* Dizziness: a guide to disorders of balance, 1988; (with Harold Ludman) Diseases of the Ear, 1998; scientific articles on the structure and function of the inner ear. *Recreation:* attempting to make coffee that tastes as good as it smells. *Address:* 4 Grange Road, Highgate, N6 4AP. *T:* (020) 8340 5593. *Clubs:* Athenæum; Hawks (Cambridge).

WRIGHT, Anthony David; MP (Lab) Great Yarmouth, since 1997; *b* 12 Aug. 1954; *s* of late Arthur Wright and of Jean Wright; *m* 1988, Barbara Fleming; one *s* one *d*, and one step *d. Educ:* secondary modern sch. Engineer. Mem. (Lab) Great Yarmouth BC, 1980–82, 1986–98. Dir, Great Yarmouth Tourist Authority, 1994–97; Mem., Great Yarmouth Marketing Initiative, 1992–97 (Chm., 1996–97). Mem., Public Admin Select Cttee, 2000–. *Address:* House of Commons, SW1A 0AA.

WRIGHT, Rev. Canon (Anthony) Robert; Canon of Westminster Abbey, Rector of St Margaret's, Westminster, and Chaplain to the Speaker of the House of Commons, since 1998; *b* 24 April 1949; *s* of Kenneth William Wright and Christabel Annie Wright (*née* Flett); *m* 1970, Leah Helen Flower; one *s* one *d. Educ:* Lanchester Poly. (BA Hons Modern Studies); St Stephen's House, Oxford (CertTheol Oxon). Ordained deacon, 1973, priest, 1974; Curate: St Michael, Amersham, 1973–76; St Giles-in-Reading, 1976–78; Vicar: Prestwood, 1978–84; Wantage, 1984–92; RD of Wantage, 1984–92; Vicar of Portsea, 1992–98. *Recreations:* gardening (old fashioned roses), walking, reading. *Address:* c/o Chapter Office, Dean's Yard, Westminster Abbey, SW1P 3PA. *T:* (020) 7654 4806.

WRIGHT, Dr Anthony Wayland; MP (Lab) Cannock Chase, since 1997 (Cannock and Burntwood, 1992–97); *b* 11 March 1948; *s* of Frank and Maud Wright; *m* 1973, Moira Elynwy Phillips; three *s* (and one *s* decd). *Educ:* Desborough County Primary Sch.; Kettering Grammar Sch.; LSE (BSc Econ 1st Cl. Hons); Harvard Univ. (Kennedy Schol.); Balliol Coll., Oxford (DPhil). Lectr in Politics, UCNW, Bangor, 1973–75; Lectr 1975, Sen. Lectr 1987, Reader 1989, in Politics, Sch. of Continuing Studies, Univ. of Birmingham. Educnl Fellowship, IBA, 1979–80; Chm., S Birmingham CHC, 1983–85. PPS to the Lord Chancellor, 1997–98. Chm., Public Admin Select Cttee, 1999–. Hon. Prof., Univ. of Birmingham, 1999–. Jt Editor, Political Qly, 1994–. *Publications:* G. D. H. Cole and Socialist Democracy, 1979; Local Radio and Local Democracy, 1982; British Socialism, 1983; Socialisms: theories and practices, 1986; R. H. Tawney, 1987; (ed jtly) Party Ideology in Britain, 1989; (ed jtly) The Alternative, 1990; (ed jtly) Consuming Public Services, 1990; (ed jtly) Political Thought since 1945, 1992; Citizens and Subjects, 1993; (ed with G. Brown) Values, Visions and Voices, 1995; Socialisms: old and new, 1996; Who Do I Complain to?, 1997; Why Vote Labour?, 1997; (jtly) The People's Party, 1997; The British Political Process, 2000; contribs to learned jls. *Recreations:* tennis, walking, gardening. *Address:* House of Commons, SW1A 0AA. *T:* (020) 7219 5029.

WRIGHT, (Arthur Robert) Donald, OBE 1984; *b* 20 June 1923; *s* of late Charles North Wright and Beatrice May Wright; *m* 1948, Helen Muryell Buxton; two *s* three *d. Educ:* Bryanston Sch.; Queens' Coll., Cambridge. War Service (commnd 1943), NW Europe (despatches) and India, 1942–46. Taught at: University Coll. Sch., 1948–50; The Hill School, Pennsylvania, 1950; Leighton Park School, 1951–52; Marlborough College (Housemaster), 1953–63; Headmaster, Shrewsbury Sch., 1963–75. Chm., HMC, 1971. Appointments' Sec. to Archbishops of Canterbury and York, 1975–84 and Sec., Crown Appointments Commn, 1977–84. A Chm., Civil Service Comrs' Interview Panels, 1984–91. Chm., William Temple Foundn, 1976–85. Chm., Council, Benenden Sch., 1976–86; Governor, King's Coll. Sch., Wimbledon, 1981–93. *Publications:* (ed) Neville Cardus on Music: a centenary collection, 1988; (ed and contrib.) Walter Hamilton: a portrait, 1991. *Recreations:* musical, defending the rural environment and counting my blessings. *Address:* Mill Barn, Coulston, near Westbury, Wilts BA13 4NY.

WRIGHT, Beatrice Frederika, (Lady Wright), MBE 1996; Vice-President, Royal National Institute for the Deaf, since 1978; Co-Founder, Hearing Dogs for Deaf People, 1982 (President, 1983–88; Life Vice President); *b* New Haven, Connecticut, 17 June 1910; *d* of Mr and Mrs F. Roland Clough; *m* 1st, 1932, John Rankin Rathbone (Flight Lieut, RAFVR, MP, killed in action, 1940); one *s* one *d*; 2nd, 1942, Paul Hervé Giraud Wright (*see* Sir Paul Wright); one *d. Educ:* Ethel Walker School, Simsbury, Conn; Radcliffe College, Oxford. MP (U) Bodmin Div. of Cornwall, 1941–45. *Address:* 62 Westminster Gardens, Marsham Street, SW1P 4JG.
See also J. R. Rathbone.

WRIGHT, Rt Rev. Benjamen; Priest in charge, Heathridge, Western Australia; *b* 15 March 1942; *s* of Clarice and Herbert Wright; *m* 1966, Annette Jennifer Dunne; two *s* one *d. Educ:* Slade Sch., Warwick, Qld; Murdoch Univ., Perth (ThL, BA). Ordained deacon, 1964, priest, 1965; Asst Curate, Applecross, 1964–67; Priest-in-charge, 1967–69, Rector, 1969–71, Narembeen; Army Reserve Chaplain, 1971–76; Rector, Alice Springs and Chaplain, St Mary's Child and Welfare Services, dio. of NT, 1976–80; Rector, Scarborough, 1980–88; Archdeacon of Stirling, 1986–88; Rector, Kalgoorlie, Boulder, 1988; Asst Bishop, dio. of Perth (Goldfields Region), 1988–91; Archdeacon of Goldfields, 1988–89; Archdeacon of O'Connor, 1990; Bishop of Bendigo, 1992–93; Rector of Busselton, WA, 1993. Hon. Canon of Christ Church Cathedral, Darwin, 1979–80. *Recreations:* fishing, gardening. *Address:* PO Box 785, Joondalup, WA 6919, Australia.

WRIGHT, Brian; *see* Wright, G. B.

WRIGHT, (Charles) Christopher; Master of Supreme Court Costs (formerly Taxing) Office, since 1992; *b* 15 July 1938; *s* of late Charles Gordon Wright, LDS RCS and Gwendoline Margaret Wright; *m* 1969, Angela Whitford. *Educ:* Emscote Lawn, Warwick; Rugby Sch.; New Coll., Oxford (MA 2nd Cl. Hons Jurisp. 1961). Solicitor of the Supreme Court, 1965; Partner, Lee & Pembertons, 1967–92. Sen. Vice-Pres., West London Law Society, 1991–92. Editor, Civil Legal Aid sect., Butterworths Costs Service, 1996–. *Recreations:* walking, swimming, holiday golf, reading. *Address:* Supreme Court Costs Office, Cliffords Inn, Fetter Lane, EC4A 1DQ. *Club:* Royal Automobile.

WRIGHT, Christopher John; Fellow, Center for International Affairs, Harvard University, 2001–June 2002; *b* 22 March 1953; *s* of James Wright and Ruby Wright (*née* Galbraith); *m* 1995, Barbara Ann Spells. *Educ:* Royal Grammar Sch., Newcastle upon Tyne; Univ. of York (BA). Joined MoD, 1974; Private Sec. to Air Mem. for Supply and Orgn, 1981; Office of Manpower Econs, 1982–85; Private Sec. to Perm. Under-Sec. of State, 1987–90; Asst Sec., 1990; Head: Central Services, 1990–93; NATO and European Policy Secretariat, 1993–94; Cost Review Secretariat, 1994–95; Dir of Orgn and Mgt Devlt, 1995–98; Comd Sec., RAF Strike Comd, 1998–2001. *Recreations:* reading, cinema, modern art, house refurbishment.

WRIGHT, Christopher Norman; Chairman: Chrysalis Group plc (formerly Chrysalis), since 1969; Loftus Road PLC (incorporating Queen's Park Rangers Football and Athletic Club and Wasps Rugby Football Club), since 1996; non-executive Chairman, CVI Media Group Europe, BV, since 1997; *b* 7 Sept. 1944; *s* of Walter Reginald Wright and Edna May (*née* Corden); *m* 1972, Carolyn Rochelle Nelson (marr. diss. 1999); two *s* one *d*; one *d. Educ:* King Edward VI Grammar Sch., Louth; Manchester Univ. (BA Hons 1966); Manchester Business Sch. Co-Founder, Ellis Wright Agency, 1967; name changed to: Chrysalis, 1968; Chrysalis Gp plc, 1985. Chm., British Phonographic Industry, 1980–83; Director: Phonographic Performance Ltd, 1980–94; Internat. Fedn of Phonographic Industry, 1981–95 (Vice-Pres., 1981–91). *Recreations:* playing tennis, breeding race horses, music, watching sport of all kinds. *Address:* c/o Chrysalis Group plc, 13 Bramley Road, W10 6SP. *T:* (020) 7221 2213. *Club:* Turf.

WRIGHT, Claud William, CB 1969; Deputy Secretary, Department of Education and Science, 1971–76; *b* 9 Jan. 1917; *s* of Horace Vipan Wright and Catherine Margaret Sales; *m* 1947, Alison Violet Readman; one *s* four *d. Educ:* Charterhouse; Christ Church, Oxford (MA). Assistant Principal, War Office, 1939; Private, Essex Regiment, 1940; 2nd Lieut, KRRC, 1940; War Office, rising to GSO2, 1942–45; Principal, War Office, 1944; Min. of Defence: Principal, 1947; Asst Sec., 1951; Asst Under-Sec. of State, 1961–68; Dep. Under-Sec. of State, 1968–71. Chm., Cttee on Provincial Museums and Galleries, 1971–73. Research Fellow, Wolfson Coll., Oxford, 1977–83. President, Geologists Assoc., 1956–58. Lyell Fund, 1947, R. H. Worth Prize, 1958, Prestwich Medal, 1987, Geological Society of London; Foulerton Award, Geologists Association, 1955; Stamford Raffles Award, Zoological Society of London, 1965; Phillips Medal, Yorks Geol. Soc., 1976; Strimple Award, Paleontol Soc., USA, 1988; H. H. Bloomer Award for Zoology, Linnean Soc., 1998. Hon. Associate, British Museum (Nat. Hist.), 1973; fil.Dr *hc* Uppsala, 1979; Hon. DSc Hull, 1987. *Publications:* (with W. J. Arkell *et al*) vol. on Ammonites, 1957, 2nd edn 1996, (with W. K. Spencer) on Starfish, 1966, in Treatise on Invertebrate Palaeontology; (with J. S. H. Collins) British Cretaceous Crabs, 1972; (with W. J. Kennedy) Ammonites of the Middle Chalk, 1981; (with W. J. Kennedy) Ammonites of the Lower Chalk, pt I, 1984, pt II, 1987, pt III, 1990, pt IV, 1995, pt V, 1996; (with A. B. Smith) British Cretaceous Echinoidea, pt I, 1988, pt II, 1990, pt III, 1993, pt IV, 1996, pt V, 1999, pt VI, 2000; papers in geological, palaeontological and archaeological journals. *Recreations:* palaeontology, natural history, gardening, archæology. *Address:* The Cotswold Home, Woodside Drive, Bradwell Village, Burford, Oxfordshire OX18 4XA. *T:* (01993) 824430.

WRIGHT, Prof. Crispin James Garth, PhD, DLitt; FBA 1992; FRSE; Professor of Logic and Metaphysics, since 1978, Wardlaw Professor, since 1997, University of St Andrews; *b* 21 Dec. 1942; *s* of Geoffrey Joseph Wright and Jean Valerie Holford; *m* 1985, Catherine Steedman (*née* Pain); two *s*, and one step *s* one step *d*. *Educ:* Birkenhead Sch.; Trinity Coll., Cambridge (BA Hons 1964; MA, PhD 1968); BPhil 1969, DLitt 1988, Oxon. Oxford University: Jun. Res. Fellow, Trinity Coll., 1967–69; Prize Fellow, All Souls Coll., 1969–71; Lectr, Balliol Coll., 1969–70; Lectr, UCL, 1970–71; Res. Fellow, All Souls Coll., Oxford, 1971–78; Prof. of Phil., 1987–92, Nelson Prof. of Phil., 1992–94, Univ. of Michigan, Ann Arbor. Leverhulme Res. Prof., 1998–. FRSE 1996. *Publications:* Wittgenstein on the Foundations of Mathematics, 1980; Frege's Conception of Numbers as Objects, 1983; Realism, Meaning and Truth, 1986; Truth and Objectivity, 1993; (with Bob Hale) The Reason's Proper Study, 2001; Rails to Infinity, 2001. *Recreations:* gardening, mountain-walking, running, P. G. Wodehouse, Liverpool FC. *Address:* Department of Logic and Metaphysics, University of St Andrews, Fife KY16 9AL. *T:* (01334) 462467.

WRIGHT, David; MP (Lab) Telford, since 2001; *b* 22 Dec. 1966; *s* of Kenneth William Wright and Heather Wright; *m* 1996, Lesley Insole. *Educ:* Wolverhampton Poly. (BA Hons Humanities). MCIH 1994. With Sandwell MBC, 1988–2001 (Housing Strategy Manager, 1995–2001). *Recreations:* football fanatic, visiting old towns and cities. *Address:* House of Commons, SW1A 0AA. *T:* (020) 7219 8331. *Clubs:* Wrockwardine Wood and Trench Labour, Dawley Social.

WRIGHT, David Alan, OBE 1983; HM Diplomatic Service; Ambassador and Consul General, Qatar, since 1997; *b* 27 May 1942; *s* of Herbert Ernest Wright and Ivy Florence (*née* Welch); *m* 1966, Gail Karol Mesling; four *s* one *d*. *Educ:* Surbiton Grammar Sch.; Univ. of Birmingham (BSocSc 1963). VSO, Chad, 1963; Inf. Officer, BoT, 1964; entered Foreign Office, 1965: Asst Private Sec. to Minister of State, FO, 1966–68; MECAS, 1968–70; Baghdad, 1970–73; Doha, 1973–76; on secondment to DHSS, 1976–78; FCO, 1978–80; Durban, 1980–83; Baghdad, 1983–87; FCO, 1987–92 (Head: Communications Dept, 1988–90; Inf. Systems Div. (Resources), 1990–92); Consul Gen., Atlanta, 1992–97. *Recreations:* jogging, sailing, pottery, travel, music. *Address:* c/o Foreign and Commonwealth Office, King Charles Street, SW1A 2AH. *Clubs:* Royal Over-Seas League, Royal Commonwealth Society.

WRIGHT, David Arthur, FRCS; Consultant Otolaryngologist, Royal Surrey County Hospital, 1970–99, now Hon. Consultant; President, British Association of Otorhinolaryngologists and Head and Neck Surgeons, 1997–99; *b* 13 April 1935; *s* of Arthur Albert Wright and Ena May (*née* Caxton); *m* 1969, Hillery Drina Seex; one *s* one *d*. *Educ:* Repton; Jesus Coll., Cambridge (MB BChir, MA 1960); Guy's Hosp. LRCP 1959; MRCS 1959, FRCS 1966. Hon. Consultant Otolaryngologist: Cambridge Mil. Hosp., 1981–96; King Edward VII Hosp., Midhurst, 1995–. Ear, Nose and Throat Adviser: British Airways, 1987–97; CAA, 1994–; Army, 1999–. Asst Ed., Jl Laryngology and Otology, 1981–88. Chm., Thomas Wickham-Jones Med. Res. Foundn, 1974–. Sec. Gen., Eur. Bd Otolaryngology, 1998–2000. Member: BMA, 1960–; Council, RCS, 1995–; Pres., Section of Otology, RSocMed, 1992. Examr, Intercollegiate Bd Otolaryngology, 1990–94. Mem. Senate, Royal Surgical Colls, 1997– (Chm., Specialist Adv. Cttee, 1988–94). Patron, British Soc. of Hearing Therapists, 1999–. George Davey Howells Meml Prize, RSocMed, 1989; Walker Jobson Horne Prize, BMA, 1997; Gold Medal, British Assoc. of Otorhinolaryngologists, 1999. *Publications:* (ed) Scott-Brown's Otolaryngology, vol. 1, Basic Sciences, 5th edn 1988; chapters in text books; contrib. articles in med. jls on noise induced hearing loss, multi-channel hearing aids and functional endoscopic sinus surgery. *Recreations:* off-shore sailing, ski-ing, golf, weather forecasting, lawns. *Address:* Eastbury Farmhouse, Compton, Guildford, Surrey GU3 1EE. *T:* (01483) 810343. *Clubs:* Royal Society of Medicine, McKenzie; Royal Southern Yacht (Hamble); Milford Golf (Surrey); Royal Cork Yacht.

WRIGHT, Sir David (John), KCMG 1996 (CMG 1992); LVO 1990; HM Diplomatic Service; Group Chief Executive (Permanent Secretary), British Trade International, since 1999; *b* 16 June 1944; *s* of J. F. Wright; *m* 1968, Sally Ann Dodkin; one *s* one *d*. *Educ:* Wolverhampton Grammar Sch.; Peterhouse, Cambridge (MA). Third Secretary, FO, 1966; Third Sec., later Second Sec., Tokyo, 1966–72; FCO, 1972–75; Ecole Nationale d'Administration, Paris, 1975–76; First Sec., Paris, 1976–80; Private Sec. to Secretary of the Cabinet, 1980–82; Counsellor (Economic), Tokyo, 1982–85; Head of Personnel Services Dept, FCO, 1985–88; Dep. Private Sec. to HRH the Prince of Wales, 1988–90 (on secondment); Ambassador to Republic of Korea, 1990–94; Dep. Under-Sec. of State, FCO, 1994–96; Ambassador to Japan, 1996–99. Chm. and Trustee, Daiwa Anglo-Japanese Foundn, 2001–. Hon. LLD: Wolverhampton, 1997; Birmingham, 2000. Grand Cordon, Order of the Rising Sun (Japan), 1998. *Recreations:* running, golf, cooking, military history. *Address:* c/o Foreign and Commonwealth Office, SW1A 2AH; British Trade International, Kingsgate House, 66–74 Victoria Street, SW1E 6SW. *Club:* Travellers.

WRIGHT, David Stephen, OBE 1995; FRCP, FFOM; consultant occupational physician; Chief Medical Officer, British Petroleum Co. plc, 1989–95; *b* 4 Aug. 1935; *s* of Edward Alfred Wright and Winifred May Wright (*née* Oliver); *m* 1966, Caroline Auza; two *s* one *d*. *Educ:* Epsom Coll.; St Bartholomew's Hosp. Med. Coll. (MB BS 1959); MSc Salford 1973; DPH, DIH. FFOM 1983; FRCP 1989. MO, RN, 1960–85; Prof. of Naval Occupational Medicine, 1982–85; Head, BP Gp Occupational Health Centre, 1985–91. Vice-Dean, 1988–91, Dean, 1991–94, Faculty of Occupational Medicine. British Medical Association: Member: Armed Forces Cttee, 1966–88 (Chm., 1985–88); Council, 1985–88. OStJ 1984. *Publications:* (ed) 5th edn, Guidance on Ethics for Occupational Physicians, 1999; (contrib.) Fitness for Work, 2000; contribs on asbestos and noise to learned jls. *Recreations:* gardening, walking, golf. *Address:* 9 Ashburton Road, Alverstoke, Gosport, Hants PO12 2LH. *T:* (023) 9258 2459.

WRIGHT, Sir Denis (Arthur Hepworth), GCMG 1971 (KCMG 1961 CMG 1954); HM Diplomatic Service, retired; *b* 23 March 1911; *s* of late A. E. Wright, Hong Kong, and Margery Hepworth Chapman, York; *m* 1939, Iona Craig, Bolney, Sussex; no *c*. *Educ:* Brentwood School; St Edmund Hall, Oxford, Hon. Fellow 1972. Asst Advertising Manager to Gallaher & Co. (Tobacco Manufacturers), 1935–39. Employed from outbreak of war as Vice-Consul on economic warfare work at HM Consulate at Constantza (Roumania), 1939–41. Vice-Consul-in-charge of HM Consulate at Trebizond (Turkey), 1941–43; Acting-Consul-in-charge of HM Consulate, Mersin (Turkey), 1943–45; First Secretary (Commercial) to HM Embassy, Belgrade, 1946–48; Superintending Trade Consul at Chicago for Middle-Western Region of USA, 1949–51; Head of Economic Relations Department in the Foreign Office, 1951–53; appointed Chargé d'Affaires, Tehran, on resumption of diplomatic relations with Persia, Dec. 1953; Counsellor, HM Embassy, Tehran, 1954–55; Asst Under-Sec., FO, 1955–59; Ambassador to Ethiopia, 1959–62; Asst Under-Sec., FO, 1962; Ambassador to Iran, 1963–71. Dir, Shell Transport & Trading Co., Standard Chartered Bank, and Mitchell Cotts Gp, 1971–81. Governor, Oversea Service, Farnham Castle, 1972–86; Mem. Council, British Inst. of Persian Studies, 1973– (Pres., 1978–87); Pres., Iran Soc., 1989–95 (Chm., 1976–79). Hon. Fellow St Antony's Coll., Oxford, 1976. Sir Percy Sykes Meml Medal, RSAA, 1990. *Publications:* Persia (with James Morris and Roger Wood), 1969; The English Amongst the Persians, 1977; The Persians Amongst the English, 1985. *Address:* Duck Bottom, 15 Flint Street, Haddenham, Aylesbury, Bucks HP17 8AL. *Club:* Travellers.

See also A. M. J. Wright.

WRIGHT, Desmond Garforth; QC 1974; *b* 13 July 1923; *s* of late Arthur Victor Wright and Doris Greensill; *m* 1952, Elizabeth Anna Bacon; one *s* one *d*. *Educ:* Giggleswick; Royal Naval Coll., Greenwich; Worcester Coll., Oxford (MA). Cholmondley Scholar of Lincoln's Inn. Served War of 1939–45: RNVR, 1942–46. Staff of Flag Officer Malaya Forward Area, 1946. Called to Bar, Lincoln's Inn, 1950, Bencher, 1981. *Publication:* Wright on Walls, 1954. *Recreations:* cartology, conversation. *Address:* 1 Atkin Building, Gray's Inn, WC1R 5BQ. *T:* (020) 7404 0102.

WRIGHT, Donald; *see* Wright, A. R. D.

WRIGHT, Sir Edward (Maitland), Kt 1977; MA, DPhil, LLD, DSc; FRSE; Research Fellow, University of Aberdeen, 1976–83; *b* 1906; *s* of M. T. Wright, Farnley, Leeds; *m* 1934, Elizabeth Phyllis (*d* 1987), *d* of H. P. Harris, Bryn Mally Hall, N Wales; one *s*. *Educ:* Jesus Coll. and Christ Church, Oxford; Univ. of Göttingen. Master, Chard School, Somerset, 1923–26; Scholar, Jesus College, Oxford, 1926–30; Senior Scholar, Christ Church, 1930–33; Lecturer, King's College, London, 1932–33; Lecturer, Christ Church, 1933–35; Flt Lieut, RAFVR, 1941–43; Principal Scientific Officer, Air Ministry, 1943–45; Prof. of Mathematics, 1935–62, Vice-Principal, 1961–62, Principal and Vice-Chancellor, 1962–76, Univ. of Aberdeen. Member: Anderson Cttee on Grants to Students, 1958–60; Hale Cttee on Univ. Teaching Methods, 1961–64; Scottish Universities Entrance Bd, 1948–62 (Chm. 1955–62); Royal Commission on Medical Education, 1965–67. Vice-Pres., RUSI, 1969–72. Hon. Editor: Zentralblatt Math., 1950–; Jl Graph Theory, 1983–. Hon. LLD: St Andrews, 1963; Pennsylvania, 1975; Aberdeen, 1978; Hon. DSc Strathclyde, 1974. Hon. Fellow, Jesus College, Oxford, 1963. Macdougall-Brisbane Prize, RSE, 1952; Sen. Berwick Prize, London Math. Soc., 1978. Gold Medal of the Order of Polonia Restituta of the Polish People's Republic, 1978. *Publications:* Introduction to the Theory of Numbers (with Professor G. H. Hardy), 1938, 5th edn 1979; 170 mathematical papers in scientific journals. *Club:* Caledonian.

WRIGHT, Eric; Chairman, Yorkshire and Humberside Development Agency (formerly Association), 1993–99; *b* 17 Nov. 1933; *s* of Alec Wright and Elsie (*née* Worthington); *m* 1st, 1955, Pauline Sutton (marr. diss. 1993); three *s* (and one *s* decd); 2nd, 1993, Hazel Elizabeth Story. *Educ:* Wolstanton Grammar Sch.; Keble Coll., Oxford (BA 1st Cl. Hons Mod. Hist.). 2nd Lieut RASC, 1955–57. Ministry of Fuel and Power, 1957–65; Civil Service Commission, 1965–67; Min. of Technology, 1968–70; Sloan Fellow, London Business Sch., 1970–71; Principal Private Sec. to Secretary of State, DTI, 1971–72; Dept of Trade, 1972–77; Dept of Industry, 1977–83; Under-Sec., 1979–; DTI, 1983–93 (Regl Dir, Yorks and Humberside, 1985–93). *Recreations:* music, tennis, chess. *Address:* 17 Foxhill Crescent, Leeds LS16 5PD. *T:* (0113) 275 4309.

WRIGHT, Eric David, CB 1975; Deputy Under-Secretary of State, Home Office, and Director-General, Prison Service, 1973–77; *b* 12 June 1917; *s* of Charles Henry and Cecelia Wright; *m* 1944, Doris (*née* Nicholls); one *s*. *Educ:* Ealing County Grammar School. Joined War Office, 1935; Principal, 1945; seconded to Dept of the Army, Australia, 1951; Asst Secretary, 1955; Command Secretary, BAOR, 1955–58; Imperial Defence College, 1964; Asst Under-Sec. of State, MoD, 1965; on loan to Home Office, Police Dept, 1970–73. Mem., Parole Bd, 1978–83. Chm., Hillingdon CHC, 1988–90. *Address:* 32 Valley Road, Rickmansworth, Herts WD3 4DS.

WRIGHT, Prof. Esmond; Emeritus Professor of American History, University of London, since 1983; Vice-President, Automobile Association, since 1985 (Vice-Chairman and Hon. Treasurer, 1971–85; Chairman, Drive Publications, 1980–85); *b* 5 Nov. 1915; *m* 1945, Olive Adamson. *Educ:* University of Durham (Open Entrance Schol.); Univ. of Virginia (Commonwealth Fund Fellow). War Service, 1940–46, demobilised as Lt-Col, 1946. Glasgow Univ., 1946–67; Prof. of Modern History, 1957–67. MP (C) Glasgow, Pollok, March 1967–1970; Dir, Inst. of US Studies and Prof. of American History, Univ. of London, 1971–83; Principal, Swinton Cons. Coll., 1972–76. Chm., Border TV, 1981–85 (Vice-Chm., 1976–81). Founder-Mem., British Association for American Studies (Chm., 1965–68). Mem., Marshall Aid Commemoration Commn, 1966–83; Vice-Chm., British Road Fedn, 1981–85. For. Mem., Amer. Philosophical Soc., 1990–. FRHistS; FRSA (Franklin Medal, 1988). Hon. LHD Pennsylvania, 1983; Hon. DLitt New Brunswick, 1984. *Publications:* A Short History of our own Times, 1951; George Washington and the American Revolution, 1957; The World Today, 1961, 4th edn 1978; Fabric of Freedom, 1961, 2nd edn 1978; (ed) Illustrated World History, 1964; Benjamin Franklin and American Independence, 1966; (ed) Causes and Consequences of the American Revolution, 1966; (ed) American Themes, 1967; American Profiles, 1967; (ed) Benjamin Franklin, a profile, 1970; A Time for Courage, 1971; A Tug of Loyalties, 1974; Red, White and True Blue, 1976; (with A. G. Nicolson) Europe Today, 1979; The Great Little Madison (British Academy Lecture), 1981; The Fire of Liberty, 1983; (ed) History of the World: Pre-History to Renaissance, 1985, The Last Five Hundred Years, 1986; Franklin of Philadelphia, 1986; Franklin: his life as he wrote it, 1989; The Sayings of Benjamin Franklin, 1995; The Search for Liberty, 1995; An Empire for Liberty, 1995; The American Dream, 1995; articles in periodicals. *Address:* Radleigh House, Masham, N Yorks HG4 4EF. *Club:* Athenæum.

WRIGHT, Georg Henrik von, Hon. GCVO 1976; MA; Research Professor in the Academy of Finland, 1961–86; *b* Helsingfors, 14 June 1916; *s* of Tor von Wright and Ragni Elisabeth Alfthan; *m* 1941, Maria Elisabeth von Troil, Hon. CVO; one *s* one *d*. *Educ:* Svenska Normallyceum, Helsingfors; Helsingfors Univ. Helsingfors University: Lectr and Acting Prof. of Philosophy, 1943–46; Prof. of Philosophy, 1946–61 (also in Univ. of Cambridge, 1948–51); Prof. at Large, Cornell Univ., 1965–77; Chancellor of Abo Academy, 1968–77; Visiting Professor: Cornell Univ., 1954 and 1958; Univ. Calif, Los Angeles, 1963; Univ. Pittsburg, 1966; Univ. Karlsruhe, 1975; Univ. Leipzig, 1994–95; Lectures: Shearman Meml, University Coll., London, 1956; Gifford, Univ. of St Andrews, 1959–60; Tarner, Trinity Coll., Cambridge, 1969; Woodbridge, Columbia Univ., 1972; Nellie Wallace, Univ. of Oxford, 1978; Tanner, Helsingfors Univ., 1984. President: Internat. Union of History and Philosophy of Science, 1963–65; Acad. of Finland, 1968–69; Philosophical Soc. of Finland, 1962–73; Institut International de Philosophie, 1975–78. Fellow: Finnish Soc. of Sciences (Pres., 1966–67, Hon. Fellow 1978); New Soc. of Letters, Lund; Royal Swedish Academy of Sciences; Royal Soc. of Letters, Lund; British Academy; Royal Swedish Academy of Letters, History and Antiquities; Finnish Acad. of Sciences; Royal Danish Acad. of Sciences and Letters; Royal

Acad. of Arts and Sciences, Uppsala; Norwegian Acad. of Science and Letters; Royal Acad. of Science, Trondheim; European Acad. of Arts, Sciences and Humanities; World Acad. of Arts and Scis; Serbian Acad. of Scis and Arts; Hon. Foreign Mem., Amer. Acad. of Arts and Sciences. Sometime Fellow, Trinity College, Cambridge, Hon. Fellow 1983. Hon. degrees: Helsingfors Univ. (doctor of pol. sci.); Univ. of Liverpool (DLitt); doctor of philosophy: Univ. of Lund; Univ. of Bologna; Abo Acad.; Univ. of Tromsø; Univ. of Leipzig; Univ. of Innsbruck; Turku Univ. (doctor of philosophy, doctor of law); Saint Olaf Coll., Northfield, Minn. (doctor of humane letters); Tampere Univ. (doctor of soc. sci.); Univ. of Stockholm (doctor of law); Univ. of Buenos Aires; Univ. of Salta. Wilhuri Foundn Internat. Prize, 1976; Alexander von Humboldt Foundn Forschungspreis, 1986; Gold Medal, Swedish Acad., 1986; Selma Lagerlöf Foundn Literature Prize, 1993; Tage Danielsson Humanist Prize, Linköping, 1998. *Publications:* The Logical Problem of Induction, 1941, rev. edn 1957; Den logiska Empirismen, 1943; Über Wahrscheinlichkeit, 1945; A Treatise on Induction and Probability, 1951; An Essay in Modal Logic, 1951; Logical Studies, 1957; The Varieties of Goodness, 1963; The Logic of Preference, 1963; Norm and Action, 1963; An Essay in Deontic Logic, 1968; Time, Change, and Contradiction, 1969; Explanation and Understanding, 1971; Causality and Determinism, 1974; Freedom and Determination, 1980; Wittgenstein, 1982; Philosophical Papers I-III, 1983–84; Vetenskapen och förnuftet, 1986; (contrib.) The Philosophy of Georg Henrik von Wright, 1989; The Tree of Knowledge, 1993; Normen, Werte und Handlungen, 1994; Six Essays in Philosophical Logic, 1996; In the Shadow of Descartes, 1998; Mitt Liv (autobiog.), 2001. *Address:* 4 Skepparegatan, Helsingfors, Finland.

WRIGHT, (George) Brian; JP; Head of Educational Broadcasting Services, BBC, 1989–93; *b* 9 April 1939; *s* of George Wright and Martha Blair Wright (*née* Dundee); *m* 1963, Joyce Avril Frances Camier; two *s*. *Educ:* Trinity Coll., Dublin (MA, HDipEd). Schoolmaster, 1961–67; Local Govt Administrator, 1967–69; BBC Educn Officer, Belfast, Nottingham, Birmingham, 1969–81; Chief Educn Officer, BBC, 1981–89. Occasional Lectr, Henley Management Coll., 1994–95. Mem., Lord Chancellor's Nottingham Div. Adv. Cttee, 1997–2001. Mem., City and Co. of Notts Adv. Bd, Salvation Army, 1999–2001. JP Ealing, 1992–93, Nottingham, 1993. *Publications:* How Britain Earns Its Living, 1980; (with John Cain) In a Different Class, 1994. *Recreations:* reading, crosswords, watching Rugby, dabbling at being a writer. *Address:* 56 Lyndhurst Road, Chichester, W Sussex PO19 2LE. *T:* (01243) 773432; *e-mail:* brian@gbwright.freeserve.co.uk.

WRIGHT, George Henry, MBE 1977; Regional Secretary, Wales, Transport and General Workers Union, 1972–99; Vice-Chairman, Wales Co-operative Development Centre, since 1985 (Chairman, 1983–85); *b* 11 July 1935; *s* of William Henry and Annie Louisa Wright; *m* 1956, Margaret Wright; two *d*. *Educ:* Tinkers Farm Sch., Birmingham. Car worker, 1954–65. T&GWU: District Officer, West Bromwich, 1966–68; District Secretary, Birmingham, 1968–72. Gen. Sec., Wales TUC, 1974–84 (Chm., 1989–90). Member: MSC Wales, 1976–88; Employment Appeal Tribunal, 1985–; Welsh Trng Adv. Gp, 1989–; Bd, Welsh Develt Agency, 1994–; Central Arbitration Cttee, Dept of Employment, 1994–; Econ. and Social Cttee, EC, 1994–; S Wales Police Authority, 1994–. *Recreations:* fishing, gardening. *Address:* 5 Kidwelly Court, Caerphilly CF8 2TY. *T:* (029) 2088 5434.

WRIGHT, George Paul; Chief Superintendent, Royal Signals and Radar Establishment, Ministry of Defence, Baldock, 1976–80; *b* 27 April 1919; *s* of late George Maurice Wright, CBE, and of late Lois Dorothy Wright (*née* Norburn); *m* 1957, Jean Margaret Reid, *d* of Lt-Col Charles Alexander Reid Scott, DSO and Marjorie Reid Scott (*née* Mackintosh); one *s* one *d*. *Educ:* Bishops Stortford Coll.; Magdalen Coll., Oxford. BA 1948, MA 1951; FInstP. Admty Signal Estabt, 1939–45; Services Electronics Research Lab., 1945–57; Dept of Physical Research, Admty, 1957–63; Services Electronics Research Lab., 1963–76 (Dir, 1972–76). *Recreations:* music, sailing, gardening. *Address:* Tullom Grange, 11 Elwin Road, Tiptree, Essex CO5 0HL. *T:* (01621) 815239. *Clubs:* Oxford and Cambridge, Civil Service; Blackwater Sailing (Maldon).

WRIGHT, Gerard; QC 1973; *b* 23 July 1929; *s* of Leo Henry and Catherine M. F. Wright; *m* 1950, Betty Mary Fenn (*d* 2001); one *s* two *d*. *Educ:* Stonyhurst Coll.; Lincoln Coll., Oxford (BA, BCL). Served in Army, 1947–49, rank T/Captain. Called to Bar, Gray's Inn, 1954 (Arden Scholar, Barstow Scholar); Northern Circuit. KHS 1974; KCHS 1979; KCSHS 1992; Auxiliaire de l'Hospitalité de Notre Dame de Lourdes, 1982, Titulaire 1985. *Publication:* Test Tube Babies—a Christian view (with others), 1984. *Recreations:* skiing, sailing. *Address:* 1 King's Court, Hoylake, Wirral CH47 1JE. *T:* (0151) 632 5566; 25–27 Castle Street, First Floor, Liverpool L2 4TA.

WRIGHT, Graeme Alexander; Editor, Wisden Cricketers' Almanack, 1986–92 and since 2000; cricket writer, Independent on Sunday, since 1990; *b* 23 April 1943; *s* of Alexander John Wright and Eileen Margaret Wright. *Educ:* St Patrick's Coll., Wellington, NZ; St Patrick's High Sch., Timaru, NZ; Univ. of Canterbury, Christchurch, NZ. Copywriter, NZ Broadcasting Corp., 1965–67; Sub-editor, BSI, 1968–69; Editor and writer, Publicare Ltd, 1969–72; Managing Editor, Queen Anne Press, 1973–74; freelance editor and writer, 1974–; Dir, John Wisden & Co. Ltd, 1983–86. *Publications:* (with Phil Read) Phil Read, 1977; The Illustrated Handbook of Sporting Terms, 1978; Olympic Greats, 1980; (with George Best) Where do I go from here?, 1981; (with Patrick Eagar): Test Decade 1972–1982, 1982; Botham, 1985; (with Joe Brown) Brown Sauce, 1986; Merrydown: forty vintage years, 1988; Betrayal: the struggle for cricket's soul, 1993; Chelton: the first 50 years, 1997; (ed) Wisden on Bradman, 90th Birthday Edition, 1998. *Recreations:* reading, music, letter-writing. *Address:* 14 Field End Road, Eastcote, Pinner, Middx HA5 2QL. *Club:* MCC.

WRIGHT, Hannah Margaret, (Mrs E. G. Wright); *see* Cross, H. M.

WRIGHT, Prof. H(enry) Myles, RIBA; RTPI; Lever Professor of Civic Design, University of Liverpool, 1954–75; now Emeritus Professor; University Planning Consultant, 1957–77; *b* 9 June 1908; *s* of H. T. Wright, Gosforth, Newcastle upon Tyne; *m* 1939, Catharine Noble (*d* 1981), *y d* of Very Rev. H. N. Craig, Dean of Kildare; two *d*. *Educ:* Fettes College, Edinburgh (Foundationer); King's College, Newcastle upon Tyne; St John's College, Cambridge. Assistant in various private offices, 1930–35; Asst Editor, The Architects' Journal, and in private practice, 1935–40; Partner in firm of Sir William Holford, 1948–54; principally engaged on planning proposals for Cambridge and Corby New Town. Member British Caribbean Federal Capital Commn, 1956. *Publications:* The Planner's Notebook, 1948; Cambridge Planning Proposals, 1950, and Corby New Town (with Lord Holford), 1952; Land Use in an Urban Environment (Editor and contributor), 1961; The Dublin Region: Preliminary and Final Reports, 1965 and 1967; Lord Leverhulme's Unknown Venture, 1982; other technical publications. *Recreations:* gardening, reading. *Address:* 9 Pine Hey, Neston, S Wirral, Cheshire CH64 3TJ.

WRIGHT, Hugh Raymond, MA; Chief Master, King Edward's School, Birmingham, 1991–98; *b* 24 Aug. 1938; *s* of Rev. Raymond Blayney Wright and Alice Mary Wright (*née* Hawksworth); *m* 1962, Jillian Mary McIldowie Meiklejohn; three *s*. *Educ:* Kingswood Sch., Bath; The Queen's Coll., Oxford (Bible Clerk; MA Lit. Hum.). Asst Master, Brentwood Sch., 1961–64; Cheltenham Coll., 1964–79: Hd of Classics, 1967–72; Housemaster, Boyne House, 1971–79; Headmaster: Stockport Grammar Sch., 1979–85; Gresham's School, Holt, 1985–91. Headmasters' Conference: Chm., 1995; Chm., NW Dist, 1983; Chm., Community Service Sub-Cttee, 1985–90 (Mem., 1980–90); Rep. on ISC (formerly ISJC) Europe Cttee, 1997–2001; Mem., Assisted Places Wking Pty, 1992–97. Mem., Chaplaincy Team, Shepton Mallet Prison, 2001–. Member: Bloxham Project Cttee, 1993–98 (Trustee, 1998–); Admty Interview Bd Panel, 1982–; ABM (formerly ACCM), C of E, 1982–; GBA Cttee, 2000-. Chairman: Nat. Steering Cttee, Children's Univ., 1998–2001; Governors, Kingswood Sch., Bath. *Publication:* film strips and notes on The Origins of Christianity and the Medieval Church, 1980. *Recreations:* music, theatre, hill walking, wildfowl, gardening, Rugby football. *Address:* Halfway House, 10 Woods Hill, Limpley Stoke, Bath BA2 7EZ. *Club:* East India.

WRIGHT, Prof. Jack Clifford, MA, BA; Professor of Sanskrit, 1964–96, Research Fellow, 1996–99, Research Associate, since 1999, and Professor Emeritus, since 2000, School of Oriental and African Studies, University of London; *b* 5 Dec. 1933; *s* of late Jack and Dorothy Wright, Aberdeen; *m* 1958, Hazel Chisholm (*née* Strachan), Crathes, Banchory; one *s*. *Educ:* Robert Gordon's Coll., Aberdeen; Univ. of Aberdeen (MA Hons in French and German, 1955); University of Zürich; Univ. of London (BA Hons in Sanskrit, 1959). Lectr in Sanskrit, 1959–64, Head, Dept of Indology and Mod. Langs and Lits of S Asia, 1970–83, SOAS, Univ. of London. *Address:* c/o South Asia Department, School of Oriental and African Studies, University of London, Thornhaugh Street, Russell Square, WC1H 0XG.

WRIGHT, Hon. James Claude, Jr; Speaker, US House of Representatives, 1987–89; Senior Political Consultant, American Income Life Insurance Co., since 1989; *b* 22 Dec. 1922; *s* of James C. Wright and Marie Wright (*née* Lyster); *m* 1972, Betty Hay; one *s* three *d* by former marr. *Educ:* Weatherford College, Univ. of Texas. Served US Army Air Force, 1941–45 (DFC, Legion of Merit). Mem., Texas Legislature, 1947–49; Mayor of Weatherford, Texas, 1950–54; Mem., US House of Representatives for Fort Worth, 1955–89; Dep. Democratic Whip to 1976; Majority Leader, 1976–87; former Mem. of Committees: Budget, Public Works and Transportation; Govt Operations; Highway Beautification (Chm.). Vis. Prof., Texas Christian Univ., 1991–. Former lay minister, Presbyterian Church. Columnist, Fort Worth Star-Telegram, 1992–. *Publications:* You and Your Congressman, 1965; The Coming Water Famine, 1966; Of Swords and Plowshares, 1968; (jtly) Congress and Conscience, 1970; Reflections of a Public Man, 1984; Worth It All, 1993; Balance of Power, 1996.

WRIGHT, James Robertson Graeme, CBE 2001; DL; Vice-Chancellor, University of Newcastle upon Tyne, 1992–2000; *b* 14 June 1939; *s* of John Wright and Elizabeth Calder (*née* Coghill); *m* 1966, Jennifer Susan Greenberg; two *d*. *Educ:* Inverness Royal Acad.; Dundee High Sch.; Univ. of Edinburgh (MA 1st cl. Hons Classics 1961, Guthrie Fellowship in Classical Lit., C. B. Black Scholarship in New Testament Greek); St John's Coll., Cambridge (Major Scholar, BA 1st cl. Classical Tripos Pt II 1963, MA 1968, Henry Arthur Thomas Studentship, Denney Studentship, Ferguson Scholarship in Classics, 1962). University of Edinburgh: Asst Lectr in Humanity (Latin), 1965; Lectr, 1966–78; Sen. Warden, Pollock Halls of Residence, 1973–78; Mem., Univ. Court, 1975–78; St Catharine's College, Cambridge: Fellow, 1978–87; Professorial Fellow, 1987–91; Hon. Fellow, 1992–; Dir, Studies in Classics, 1978–87; Bursar, 1979–87; Cambridge Bursar's Committee: Sec., 1983–86; Chm., 1986–87; Sec.-Gen. of Faculties, Univ. of Cambridge, 1987–91. Non-executive Member: Cambridge Dist HA, 1990–91; Northern and Yorks RHA, 1994–96. Mem. Council, CVCP, 1996–2000. Chm., Higher Educn Management Statistics Gp, 1995–2000; Mem., SHEFC, 1992–99; Associate Comr, Hamlyn Nat. Commn on Educn, 1992–93; Dir, UCAS, 1997–2000; Chm. Exec. Cttee, UKCOSA: Council for Internat. Educn, 1998–. British Council: Mem., CICHE, 1993–2000; Mem., CICHE Cttee 2 (Asia and Oceans Reg.), 1992–94. Dir, Newcastle Initiative, 1993–2000. Mem., Governing Body, Shrewsbury Sch., 1986–2000. Trustee, Nat. Heritage Meml Fund, 2000–. DL Tyne and Wear, 1995. Hon. LLD Abertay Dundee, 1999; Hon. DEd Naresuan, Thailand, 2000; Hon. DCL Newcastle upon Tyne, 2001. *Publications:* articles and reviews in classical jls. *Recreations:* walking, travel in France, food, wine. *Address:* 10 Montagu Avenue, Newcastle upon Tyne NE1 7RU. *Clubs:* Athenæum; Northern Counties (Newcastle upon Tyne).

WRIGHT, Joe Booth, CMG 1979; HM Diplomatic Service, retired; Ambassador to Ivory Coast, Upper Volta and Niger, 1975–78; *b* 24 Aug. 1920; *s* of Joe Booth Wright and Annie Elizabeth Wright; *m* 1st, 1945, Pat (*née* Beaumont); one *s* two *d*; 2nd, 1967, Patricia Maxine (*née* Nicholls). *Educ:* King Edward VI Grammar Sch., Retford; Univ. of London. BA Hons, French. GPO, 1939–47. Served War, HM Forces: RAOC, Intelligence Corps, 1941–46. Entered Foreign Office, 1947; FO, 1947–51; Vice-Consul, Jerusalem, 1951; Consul, Munich, 1952, and Basra, 1954; Dep. Consul, Tamsui, 1956; FO, 1959–64; Consul, Surabaya, 1964; Consul, Medan, 1965–67; First Sec. (Information), Nicosia, 1968; Head of Chancery and Consul, Tunis, 1968–71; Consul-General: Hanoi, 1971–72; Geneva, 1973–75. Mem., Inst. of Linguists and Translators' Guild, 1982–. FRSA 1987. *Publications:* Francophone Black Africa Since Independence, 1981; Zaire Since Independence, 1983; Paris As It Was, 1985; Who Was the Enemy?, 1993; Security and Cooperation in Europe: the view from the East, 1993; Enlarging the European Union: risks and benefits, 1998. *Recreations:* cricket, film-going, music, Chinese painting. *Address:* 29 Brittany Road, St Leonards-on-Sea, East Sussex TN38 0RB; *e-mail:* wright29@onetel.net.uk. *Club:* Royal Over-Seas League.

WRIGHT, Captain John, DSC 1944; RN (retd); General Manager, HM Dockyard, Devonport, 1972–77; *b* 30 April 1921; *s* of Percy Robert and Lucy Ada Wright; *m* 1946, Ethel Lumley Sunderland; one *s* two *d*. *Educ:* Liverpool Univ. (Part I for BSc). MIEE; Silver Medal, City and Guilds. Served War: RNVR, 1942; 16th Destroyer Flotilla, 1942; HMS Birmingham, 1943; HMS Diadem, 1943. Devonport Gunnery Sch., 1946; HMS Collingwood, 1948; BJSM, USA, 1951; Admiralty Surface Weapons Estabt, 1952; HMS Cumberland, 1956; Naval Ordnance Div., 1958; British Naval Staff, USA, 1960; Polaris Technical Dept, 1964; HM Dockyard, Chatham, 1968; RN retd 1972. Gen. Manager, Marconi Space and Defence Systems Ltd, Portsmouth, 1981–82; Asst Man. Dir and Gen. Manager, Marconi Underwater Systems, 1982–84. *Recreations:* fishing, gardening, golf. *Address:* The Ferns, 15 Brook Meadow, Fareham, Hants PO15 5JH. *T:* (01329) 280512.

WRIGHT, John Hurrell C.; *see* Collier-Wright.

WRIGHT, Hon. Sir (John) Michael, Kt 1990; **Hon. Mr Justice Wright;** a Judge of the High Court of Justice, Queen's Bench Division, since 1990; Presiding Judge, South Eastern Circuit, 1995–98; *b* 26 Oct. 1932; *s* of Prof. John George Wright, DSc, MVSc, FRCVS, and Elsie Lloyd Razey; *m* 1959, Kathleen, *er d* of F. A. Meanwell; one *s* two *d*. *Educ:* King's Sch., Chester; Oriel Coll., Oxford (BA Jurisprudence 1956; MA 1978; Hon. Fellow, 2000). Served Royal Artillery, 1951–53; TA, 1953–57. Called to Bar, Lincoln's Inn (Tancred Student), 1957, Bencher 1983; QC 1974; a Recorder, 1974–90; Leader, SE

Circuit, 1981–83; Chm. of the Bar, 1983–84 (Vice-Chm., 1982–83). Member: Bar Council, 1972–73; Senate of the Four Inns of Court, 1973–74; Senate of the Inns of Court and the Bar, 1975–84. Mem. Supreme Court Rules Cttee, 1973–74. Legal Assessor to the Disciplinary Cttee, RCVS, 1983–90; Vice-Chm., Appeal Cttee, ICA, 1989–90. Hon. Member: American Bar Assoc.; Canadian Bar Assoc. Trustee, Thalidomide Trust, 1997–. *Recreations:* books, music. *Address:* c/o Royal Courts of Justice, Strand, WC2A 2LL.

WRIGHT, Sir (John) Oliver, GCMG 1981 (KCMG 1974; CMG 1964); GCVO 1978; DSC 1944; HM Diplomatic Service, retired; King of Arms, Most Distinguished Order of St Michael and St George, 1987–96; *b* 6 March 1921; *m* 1942, Lillian Marjory Osborne; three *s. Educ:* Solihull School; Christ's College, Cambridge (MA; Hon. Fellow 1981; pre-elected Master, May 1982, resigned July 1982). Served in RNVR, 1941–45. Joined HM Diplomatic Service, Nov. 1945; served: New York, 1946–47; Bucharest, 1948–50; Singapore, 1950–51; Foreign Office, 1952–54; Berlin, 1954–56; Pretoria, 1957–58. Imperial Defence College, 1959. Asst Private Sec. to Sec. of State for Foreign Affairs, 1960; Counsellor and Private Sec., 1963; Private Sec. to the Prime Minister, 1964–66 (to Rt Hon. Sir Alec Douglas-Home, and subseq. to Rt Hon. Harold Wilson); Ambassador to Denmark, 1966–69; seconded to Home Office as UK Rep. to NI Govt, Aug. 1969–March 1970; Chief Clerk, HM Diplomatic Service, 1970–72; Dep. Under-Sec. of State, FCO, 1972–75; Ambassador to Federal Republic of Germany, 1975–81; retired, then re-apptd, Ambassador to Washington, 1982–86. Director: Siemens Ltd, 1981–82; Amalgamated Metal Corp., April-July 1982; Savoy Hotel plc, 1987–94; Berkeley Hotel, 1994–96; General Technology Systems Inc., 1990–95; Enviromed plc, 1993–97. Distinguished Vis. Prof., Univ. of S Carolina, 1986–90; Clark Fellow, Cornell Univ., 1987; Lewin Vis. Prof., Washington Univ., St Louis, 1988. Pres., German Chamber of Industry and Commerce, London, 1989–92. Bd Mem., British Council, 1981–82, 1986–90. Trustee: British Museum, 1986–91; Internat. Shakespeare Globe Centre, 1986–; Chm., British Königswinter Conf. Steering Cttee, 1987–97; Co-Chm., Anglo-Irish Encounter, 1986–91. Gov., Reigate Grammar Sch., 1987–97 (Chm., 1990–97). Hon. DHL Univ. of Nebraska, 1983; Hon. DL Rockford Coll., Ill, 1985. Grand Cross, German Order of Merit, 1978. *Recreations:* theatre, gardening. *Address:* Burstow Hall, near Horley, Surrey RH6 9SR. *T:* (01293) 783494. *Club:* Travellers.

WRIGHT, John Robertson; Chief Executive, Clydesdale Bank plc and Yorkshire Bank, since 1998; *b* 10 Sept. 1941; *s* of George Alexander Wright and Jean Robertson Wright (*née* Buchanan); *m* 1971, Christine; one *s* one *d. Educ:* Daniel Stewart's Coll., Edinburgh. ACIBS; FIBI. Posts with Bank of Montreal, Canada and Hong Kong, Bank of North Lagos, Nigeria, Grindlays Bank Ltd, London, Calcutta and Colombo, Clydesdale Bank Ltd, 1958–74; Vice Pres., First Interstate Bank of California, 1974–79; Asst Gen. Manager, Internat. Div., Bank of Scotland, 1979–86; Dir and CEO, Oman International Bank, 1986–93; Chief Executive and Director: Northern Bank Ltd 1993–96; Northern & National Irish Banks, 1996–97; Chief Exec. and Chief Gen. Manager, Gulf Bank KSC, Kuwait, 1997–98. *Recreations:* jogging, watching Rugby. *Address:* Clydesdale Bank plc, 30 St Vincent Place, Glasgow G1 2HL. *T:* (0141) 248 7070. *Clubs:* Royal Scots (Edinburgh); Hong Kong; Edinburgh Academicals Sports, Hong Kong Football.

WRIGHT, (John) Stephen; Managing Director and Senior International Vice-President, IMG Artists (formerly IMG Artists Europe), since 1991; *b* 12 Feb. 1946; *s* of Eustace McDonald Wright and Hilde Wright; *m* 1977, Jadwiga Maria Rapf; two *s* one *d. Educ:* Dragon Sch., Oxford; Westminster; Magdalene Coll., Cambridge (Hons Mod. Langs and Law). Co-founder and Dir, Oxford and Cambridge Shakespeare Co., 1969–71; Dir, Shawconcerts Ltd, 1971–75; Dir, later Jt Man. Dir, Harold Holt, 1975–90. *Recreations:* cricket, wine, classic cars. *Address:* 19 Shaa Road, W3 7LW. *Club:* Garrick.

WRIGHT, Joseph, OBE 1978; FRPharmS; FCIS; Secretary (Chief Executive), National Pharmaceutical Association (formerly National Pharmaceutical Union), 1961–81; *b* 7 Jan. 1917; *s* of late Thomas Wright and Margaret (*née* Cardwell); *m* 1942, Margaretta May Hart Talbot, BA, MRPharmS; two *s* two *d. Educ:* Blackpool Boys' Grammar Sch.; Chelsea Polytechnic. Dip., Chem. and Druggist and PhC examinations. Called to the Bar, Middle Temple, 1952. In retail pharmacy, 1933–47, incl. 4 years apprenticeship in Blackpool, with subseq. experience in London. Served war, RAF, commnd wireless navigator, Coastal Comd. On staff, Pharm. Section, Min. of Health, 1947–48; joined NPU, 1948: Asst Sec., 1949, Dep. Sec., 1955, Sec. and Manager, 1961; Dir, NPA Gp, 1971 (Gp comprises Nat. Pharm. Assoc. Ltd, Chemists' Def. Assoc. Ltd, Pharmacy Mutual Insce Co. Ltd, Pharm. and Gen. Prov. Soc., NPU Ltd (t/a NPA Sces), NPU Holdings Ltd). Director: NPU Holdings Ltd, 1965–81; NPU Ltd, 1971–81; Indep. Chemists Marketing Ltd, 1972–81; NPU Marketing Ltd, 1966–81; Member: Standing Pharm. Adv. Cttee, 1964–82; Poisons Bd, 1963–84; Panel of Fellows of Pharm. Soc., 1965–82; Gen. Practice Sub-Cttee, PSGB, 1963–81; Bd, Nat. Chamber of Trade, 1973–82; Trade & Professional Alliance, 1975–81; Legislation & Taxation Cttee, Nat. Ch. of Trade, 1964–81; Adviser to Pharm. Services Negotiating Cttee, 1977–81. Hon. Life Mem., S African Retail Chem. and Druggists Assoc., 1974; Distinguished Service Award, Pharmacy Guild of Aust., 1978. Charter Gold Medal of Pharmaceutical Soc. of GB, 1980. Liveryman, Worshipful Soc. of Apoth. of London, 1978–. Freedom of City of London. *Recreations:* reading, travel and—intermittently—grandchildren. *Address:* 116 Wynchgate, Winchmore Hill, N21 1QU. *T:* (020) 8886 1645.

WRIGHT, Kenneth Campbell, CMG 1987; OBE 1973; PhD; HM Diplomatic Service, retired; Political Affairs Adviser, Saferworld Foundation, since 1992; with Research Department, The Economist, since 1992; *b* 31 May 1932; *s* of James Edwin Wright and Eva Rebecca Wright (*née* Sayers); *m* 1958, Diana Yolande Binnie; one *s* two *d. Educ:* George Heriot's Sch., Edinburgh; Univs of Edinburgh (MA 1st Cl. Hons Mod Langs, PhD) and Paris (LèsL). Short-service commission, Royal Air Force, 1957–60. Lecturer, Inst. Politique Congolais and Lovanium Univ., Congo (Zaire), 1960–63; Lectr, later Sen. Lectr, Dept of Modern Languages, Univ. of Ghana, 1963–65; entered HM Diplomatic Service, 1965; FO, 1965–68; First Sec., Bonn, 1968–72; FCO, 1972–75; First Sec., later Counsellor, UK Permanent Representation to the European Communities, Brussels, 1975–79; FCO, 1979–82; Counsellor, Paris, 1982–85; Asst Under-Sec. of State, FCO, 1985–89. Dir, BIEC, subseq. BI, 1989–91. *Recreations:* people, places, books. *Address:* Leven House, 2 The Meadway, Heath Lane, SE3 0UP. *T:* (020) 8852 3650. *Clubs:* Athenæum, Special Forces.

WRIGHT, Lance Armitage, RIBA; Associate Director, International Committee of Architectural Critics, since 1978; *b* 25 Dec. 1915; *s* of Edmund Lancelot Wright and Elizabeth Helen (*née* Bonser); *m* 1942, Susan Melville Foster; two *s* two *d. Educ:* Haileybury; University Coll. London; Architectural Assoc. Sch. Architect in private practice, 1946–73; Registrar, Royal West of England Academy Sch. of Architecture, 1950–53; Technical Editor, The Architects Journal, 1954; Editor, The Architectural Review, 1973–80. Exhibn of drawings, Hot Bath Gall., Bath, 1995. Chevalier, Order of St Gregory the Great, 1971. *Publication:* (with D. A. C. A. Boyne) Architects Working Details, vols 4–15, 1953–69. *Address:* The White House, Summerside, Buckland, near Faringdon, Oxon, OX7 8RA.

WRIGHT, Lester Paul; Under Secretary, Department for Culture, Media and Sport (formerly of National Heritage), 1992–99; *b* 2 July 1946; *s* of late Christopher Percy Wright and of Mary Wright (*née* Sutton); *m* 1969, Jill Wildman; one *s* (and one *s* decd). *Educ:* Bedford Sch.; Gonville and Caius Coll., Cambridge (MA, PhD); Harvard Univ. Lectr in History, Univ. of Reading, 1970–71; Home Office, 1971; Asst Private Sec. to Home Sec., 1972; Harkness Fellow, Harvard Univ. and Univ. of California at Berkeley, 1976–77; Private Sec. to Perm. Under Sec., 1980–82; Asst Sec., 1983–92. *Recreations:* music, walking, looking at pictures. *Address:* Pedn Brose, Mousehole Lane, Paul, Penzance, Cornwall TR19 6TY. *T:* (01736) 731789.

WRIGHT, Margaret; Development Executive, The Law Society, 1988–91; *b* 18 Oct. 1931; *d* of Harry Platt and Edith Baxter; *m* 1991, Bill Wright (*d* 1999). *Educ:* Bedford College, Univ. of London (BA Hons 1st Cl., History). Called to the Bar, Gray's Inn, 1956. Estate Duty Officer, Inland Revenue, 1952–63; Inst. of Professional Civil Servants, 1963–87 (Dep. Gen. Sec., 1980–87); Gen. Sec., Clearing Bank Union, 1987–88. Mem., Industrial Disputes Panel, Jersey, 1989–. *Recreations:* renovating old houses, travel, reading. *Address:* Brickwall Barn, Broad Road, Bacton, Stowmarket, Suffolk IP14 4HP. *T:* (01449) 780197.

WRIGHT, Prof. Margaret S.; *see* Scott Wright.

WRIGHT, Martin; Visiting Research Fellow, School of (formerly Centre for) Legal Studies, University of Sussex, since 1995; *b* 24 April 1930; *s* of late Clifford Kent Wright and Rosalie Wright, Stoke Newington; *m* 1957, Louisa Mary Nicholls; three *s* one *d* (and one *d* decd). *Educ:* Repton; Jesus Coll., Oxford; PhD LSE, 1992. Librarian, Inst. of Criminology, Cambridge, 1964–71; Dir, Howard League for Penal Reform, 1971–81; NAVSS, later Victim Support, 1985–94: Information Officer, 1985–88; Policy Officer, 1988–94. Vis. Scholar, Centre for Criminological and Legal Res., Univ. of Sheffield, 1994–95. Chm., Lambeth Mediation Service, 1989–92; Mem. Exec. Cttee, Mediation UK (formerly Forum for Initiatives in Reparation and Mediation), 1984–99; Bd Mem., European Forum for Victim/Offender Mediation and Restorative Justice, 2000–; Vice-Chm., Restorative Justice Consortium, 2001–. ALA 1960. *Publications:* (ed) The Use of Criminological Literature, 1974; Making Good: Prisons, Punishment and Beyond, 1982; (ed jtly) Mediation and Criminal Justice, 1988; Justice for Victims and Offenders: a restorative response to crime, 1991, 2nd edn 1996; Restoring Respect for Justice, 1999. *Recreation:* suggesting improvements. *Address:* 19 Hillside Road, SW2 3HL. *T:* (020) 8671 8037, *Fax:* (020) 8671 5697.

WRIGHT, Hon. Sir Michael; *see* Wright, Hon. Sir J. M.

WRIGHT, Michael Thomas, FSA; writer and lecturer on architecture, fine arts and conservation; *b* 10 Dec. 1936; *o c* of Thomas Manning Wright and Hilda Evelyn Wright (*née* Whiting); *m* 1st, 1964, Jennifer Olga Angus (marr. diss. 1990), 2nd *d* of C. B. Angus, Singapore; two *s*; 2nd, 1990, Wendelina Elisabeth Pascall (*née* van Manen). *Educ:* Bristol Grammar Sch.; Gonville and Caius Coll., Cambridge (MA); Trinity Coll., Dublin. FSA 1998. Formerly: Financial Analyst, Ford Motor Co. Asst Sec., Town Planning Inst.; Editor, Town Planning Inst. Jl; Asst Editor, Country Life; Managing Editor, Journal of Royal Inst. of British Architects; Dep. Editor, Country Life; Publisher: Country Life, 1984–87 (Editor, 1973–84, Editor in Chief, 1980–84); Practical Woodworking, 1985–87; Television, 1985–87; Editor in Chief and Publisher, Antique Dealer and Collectors' Guide, 1982–87; Dir, Nat. Heritage Meml Fund, 1987–88; Editorial Consultant, Country Life Books, 1978–86. Vis. Lectr in British Architecture, Roger Williams Univ., USA, 1995–99. Member, Honourable Society of Gray's Inn. Churchwarden, St Michael's Parish Church, Highgate, 1974–79; Chm., Highgate Soc., 1985–87. Judge, RICS (formerly RICS/The Times) Conservation Awards, 1976–89, 1991–2001. Lectr, NADFAS, 1989–; Tutor, Dept of Continuing Educn, Univ. of Cambridge. Chairman: Lutyens Trust, 1993–95 (Trustee, 1986–95); Friends of Bristol Art Gall., 1993–97; Member: DoE Working Party on Rural Settlements; Cttee, SPAB, 1987–96. FRSA 1980. JP Haringey, 1986–89. *Publications:* Explore Britain's Country Gardens, 1993; contrib. articles to: TPI Jl; RIBA Jl; Water Space; Country Life; Homes and Gardens. *Recreations:* music, tennis, walking; participation in local amenity society work. *Address:* Vyne Cottage, Church Road, Bruisyard, Suffolk IP17 2EG. *T:* (01728) 638090. *Club:* Royal Over-Seas League.

WRIGHT, Prof. Michael Thomas, FREng; Professor of Mechanical Engineering, since 1990, and Vice Chancellor, since 1996, Aston University; *b* 11 April 1947; *s* of William George and Lilly May Wright; *m* 1970, Patricia Eunice Cox; one *d. Educ:* Sheldon Heath Sch., Birmingham; Aston Univ. (BSc 1st Cl. Hons, PhD). Sen. Mem., IEEE 1980; FIEE 1981; FREng (FEng 1988); FIMechE 1989; FIMA 1994. Apprentice, Electrical Power Engineering Co.; 1969–82: Redman Heenan Froude, Heenan Drives, Linear Motors, Parsons Peebles Motors and Generators, NEI Peebles, Scottish Engineering Training Scheme; Engrg Dir, GEC Large Machines, 1982–85; Man. Dir, Molins Tobacco Machinery, 1985–87; Man. Dir, 1988–90, non-Exec. Dir, 1990–97, Molins; Aston University: Vis. Prof. of Electrical Engrg, 1986–90; Head, Dept of Mech. and Elect. Engrg, 1990–92; Sen. Pro-Vice-Chancellor, 1994–96. Chairman: Aston Business Sch., 1992–93; 600 Group plc, 1993–. Non-executive Director: ERA Technology Ltd, 1995–; Birmingham Technology Ltd, 1996–; Aston Science Park Ltd, 1996–; ERA Foundn, 2001–; Dir, West Midlands Develt Agency, 1997–. CIMgt 1997. *Publications:* numerous papers on electrical machines and drives in learned jls; articles on shooting and ballistics. *Recreations:* shooting, history of film, travelling, reading, classic motorcycles. *Address:* Aston University, Aston Triangle, Birmingham B4 7ET. *T:* (0121) 359 3611.

WRIGHT, Prof. Nicholas Alcwyn, MD, PhD, DSc; FRCS, FRCPath; Warden, Bart's and The London, Queen Mary's School of Medicine and Dentistry, London University, since 2001; Director, Histopathology Unit, Imperial Cancer Research Fund, since 1988; *b* 24 Feb. 1943; *s* of late Glyndwr Alcwyn Wright and Hilda Lilian (*née* Jones); *m* 1966, Vera, (Ned), Matthewson; one *s* one *d. Educ:* Bristol Grammar Sch.; Durham Univ. (MB BS 1965); Newcastle Univ. (MD 1974; PhD 1975; DSc 1984); MA (Oxon) 1979. *T:* and *Fax:* FRCPath 1986; MRCP 1998; FRCS 1999. University of Newcastle upon Tyne: Demonstrator in Pathology, 1966–71; Res. Fellow, 1971–74; Lectr in Pathology, 1974–76; Sen. Lectr, 1976–77; Clinical Reader in Pathology, Univ. of Oxford, 1977, Nuffield Reader, 1978; Fellow, Green Coll., Oxford, 1979–80; Prof. of Histopathology, RPMS, 1980–96; Dir of Histopathology, Hammersmith Hosp., 1980–96; Dean, RPMS, 1996–97; Clin. Dir of Path., Hammersmith Hosps NHS Trust, 1994–96; Vice Principal for Res., 1996–2001, Dep. Principal, 1997–2001, ICSM, Univ. of London; Imperial Cancer Research Fund: Asst Dir, 1988; Associate Dir, 1989; Dep. Dir, 1990; Dir of Clinical Res., 1991–96. Chm., Research for Health Charities Gp, 1994–96. Mem. Council: RCPath, 1982, 1986, 1990; British Soc. for Gastroenterology, 1986, 1990. Editor, Cell and Tissue Kinetics, 1980–87. Lectures: Avery Jones, Central Middx Hosp., 1989; Kettle, RCPath, 1990; Showering, Southmead Hosp., 1991; Morson, 1991, Sir Arthur Hurst, 1997, British Soc. of Gastroenterology; Burroughs Wellcome, Yale Univ., 1993; Watson Smith, RCP, 1998; Sidney Truelove, Internat. Soc. for Inflammatory Bowel Disease, 1999. Founder FMedSci 1998. *Publications:* Introduction to Cell Population Kinetics, 1977; (ed) Psoriasis: cell proliferation, 1982; The Biology of

Epithelial Cell Populations, 1984; (ed) Colorectal Cancer, 1989; (ed) Oxford Textbook of Pathology, 1991; (ed) Clinical Aspects of Cell Proliferation, 1991; (ed) Molecular Pathology of Cancer, 1993; (ed) Growth Factors and Cytokines of the Gut, 1996; (ed) The Gut as a Model for Cell Molecular Biology, 1997; papers on cell proliferation and differentiation in the gut. *Recreations:* Rugby football, cricket, squash, military history, cooking. *Address:* Queen Mary's School of Medicine and Dentistry, Turner Street, E1 2AD. *T:* (020) 7377 7600; Imperial Cancer Research Fund, Lincoln's Inn Fields, WC2A 3PX. *T:* (020) 7242 0200. *Club:* Athenæum.

WRIGHT, Rev. Canon (Nicholas) Thomas, DPhil, DD; Canon of Westminster, since 2000; *b* 1 Dec. 1948; *s* of Nicholas Irwin Wright and Rosemary (*née* Forman); *m* 1971, Margaret Elizabeth Anne Fiske; two *s* two *d. Educ:* Sedbergh Sch.; Exeter Coll., Oxford (BA 1st cl. Hons LitHum 1971; MA 1975; DPhil 1981; DD 2000); Wycliffe Hall, Oxford (BA 1st cl. Hons Theology 1973). Ordained deacon, 1975, priest 1976; Jun. Res. Fellow, 1975–78, Jun. Chaplain, 1976–78, Merton Coll., Oxford; Fellow and Chaplain, Downing Coll., Cambridge, 1978–81; Asst Prof. of New Testament Studies, McGill Univ., Montreal, and Hon. Prof., Montreal Dio. Theol Coll., 1981–86; Lectr in Theology, Oxford Univ., and Fellow, Tutor and Chaplain, Worcester Coll., Oxford, 1986–93; Dean of Lichfield, 1994–99. Fellow, Inst. for Christian Studies, Toronto, 1992–; Canon Theologian, Coventry Cathedral, 1992–99. Mem., Doctrine Comn of C of E, 1979–81, 1989–95. DD Aberdeen, 2001. *Publications:* Small Faith, Great God, 1978; The Work of John Frith, 1983; The Epistles of Paul to the Colossians and to Philemon, 1987; The Glory of Christ in the New Testament, 1987; The Interpretation of the New Testament 1861–1986, 1988; The Climax of the Covenant, 1991; New Tasks for a Renewed Church, 1992; The Crown and the Fire, 1992; The New Testament and the People of God, 1992; Who Was Jesus?, 1992; Following Jesus, 1994; Jesus and the Victory of God, 1996; The Lord and His Prayer, 1996; What Saint Paul Really Said, 1997; For All God's Worth, 1997; Reflecting the Glory, 1998; (with M. Borg) The Meaning of Jesus, 1999; The Myth of the Millennium, 1999; (ed jtly) Romans and the People of God, 1999; Holy Communion for Amateurs, 1999; The Challenge of Jesus, 2000; Twelve Months of Sundays, Year C, 2000; (with Paul Spicer) Easter Oratorio, 2000; Twelve Months of Sundays, Year A, 2001; Luke for Everyone, 2001; Mark for Everyone, 2001. *Recreations:* music, hill walking, poetry, cricket, golf. *Address:* 3 Little Cloister, Westminster Abbey, SW1P 3PL. *T:* (020) 7654 4808, *Fax:* (020) 7654 4809; 14 High Newton Farm, Alnwick, Northumberland NE66 3ED. *T:* (01665) 576140, *Fax:* (01665) 576956; *e-mail:* tom.wright@westminster-abbey.org.

WRIGHT, Sir Oliver; *see* Wright, Sir J. O.

WRIGHT, Sir Paul (Hervé Giraud), KCMG 1975 (CMG 1960); OBE 1952; HM Diplomatic Service, retired; Chairman: Irvin Great Britain Ltd, 1979–88; British American Arts Association, 1983–88; Member Council, Forte plc (formerly Trusthouse Forte), 1987–97; *b* 12 May 1915; *o s* of late Richard Hervé Giraud Wright; *m* 1942, Beatrice Frederika Rathbone (*see* Beatrice Wright), *widow* of Flt-Lt J. R. Rathbone, MP; one *d. Educ:* Westminster Sch. (Hon. Fellow, 1992). Employed by John Lewis Partnership Ltd, 1933–39. Served HM Forces, War of 1939–45; Major, KRRC; HQ 21 Army Group, 1944–45 (despatches). Contested (L) NE Bethnal Green, 1945. Asst Dir, Public Relations, National Coal Bd, 1946–48; Dir, Public Relations, Festival of Britain, 1948–51. HM Foreign Service: Paris and New York, 1951–54; Foreign Office, 1954–56; The Hague, 1956–57; Head of Information, Policy Dept in FO, 1957–60; Cairo, 1960–61; UK Delegn to N Atlantic Council, 1961–64; Minister (Information), Washington, 1965–68, and Dir-Gen., British Inf. Services, NY, 1964–68; Ambassador to Congo (Kinshasa) and to Republic of Burundi, 1969–71; Ambassador to the Lebanon, 1971–75. Special Rep. of Sec. of State for Foreign and Commonwealth Affairs, 1975–78. Chm., British Lebanese Assoc., 1987–90. Hon. Sec. Gen., London Celebrations Cttee for Queen's Silver Jubilee, 1977; Vice-Chm., The American Fest., 1985; Pres., Elizabethan Club, 1988–95; Governor, Westminster Cathedral Choir School, 1981–2000 (Chm., 1993–2000); Chm., Westminster Sch. Develt Council, 1994–97. Trustee, Trusthouse Charitable Foundn, 1996–2000; Life Vice-Pres., Hearing Dogs for Deaf People. Hon. RCM 1990. GCSG 2000 (KCSG 1996). Kt of the Order of the Cedar of Lebanon, 1990. *Publication:* A Brittle Glory (autobiog.), 1986. *Address:* 62 Westminster Gardens, Marsham Street, SW1P 4JG. *Club:* Garrick.

WRIGHT, Penelope Ann, (Mrs D. C. H. Wright); *see* Boys, P. A.

WRIGHT, Peter, CBE 1988 (OBE 1982); Chief Constable, South Yorkshire Police, 1983–90; *b* Stockport, 21 July 1929; *s* of late Henry Wright and Elizabeth (*née* Burton); *m* 1950, Mary Dorothea (*née* Stanway); one *s. Educ:* Edgeley Roman Catholic Sch.; Stockport Technical School. RN, 1947–49. Manchester City Police, 1954, to Chief Superintendent, Greater Manchester, 1975; Asst Chief Constable, 1975–79, Dep. Chief Constable, 1979–82, Merseyside. Police Advr, MoD, 1990–93. Mem., Parole Review Cttee, 1987–88. Pres., ACPO, 1988–89. Freeman, City of London, 1992. *Recreations:* walking, gardening. *Address:* c/o South Yorkshire Police, Snig Hill, Sheffield S3 8LY.

WRIGHT, Peter, FRCP, FRCS, FRCOphth; Consultant Ophthalmic Surgeon, Moorfields Eye Hospital, 1973–94, Consulting Ophthalmic Surgeon, 1994; President, Royal College of Ophthalmologists, 1991–94; *b* 7 Sept. 1932; *s* of late William Victor Wright and Ada Amelie (*née* Craze); *m* 1960, Elaine Catherine Donoghue (marr. diss. 1992); two *d* (one *s* decd). *Educ:* St Clement Danes; King's Coll. London; King's Coll. Hosp. (MB BS 1955). AKC 1955; MRCS, LRCP 1955; FRCS 1964; DO 1959; FCOphth 1988 (Hon. FRCOphth 1998); FRCP 1994. Resident appts, KCH and Guy's Hosp., 1955–57; ophthalmic specialist, RAF Med. Br., 1957–59; Lectr in Anatomy and Physiology, Guy's Hosp. Med. Sch., 1959–61; House Surgeon and Sen. Resident, Moorfields Eye Hosp., 1961–65; Lectr in Physiology, Inst. of Ophthalmology, 1965–68; Consultant Ophthalmic Surgeon: KCH, 1966–78; Sydenham Children's Hosp., 1967–73; Clinical Sub-Dean, Inst. Ophthalmology, 1980–86; Surgical Tutor, Moorfields Eye Hosp., 1981–86; Cons. Advr in Ophthalmology, DoH, 1988–. Cons. Advr, Royal Soc. of Musicians, 1986–. Examiner: Dip. in Ophthalmology, 1967–73; Ophthalmic Nursing Bd, 1973–78 (Mem., 1974–87); Mem., Court of Examnrs, RCS, 1977–83. Ophthalmic Section, Royal Society of Medicine: Mem. Council and Vice-Pres., 1968–75; Pres., 1988–90; Ophthalmological Society of UK: Sec., 1968–70; Mem. Council, 1970–74; Vice-Pres., 1985–87; Pres., 1987–88, Southern Ophthalmic Society: Mem. Council, 1970–74; Pres., 1984–85; Sen. Vice-Pres., Coll. of Ophthalmologists, 1988–92; Mem. Council, RCS, 1992–; Trustee and Mem. Council, Assoc. for Eye Res., 1966– (Treas. 1966–82). Lectures: Charnwood, 1977; Doyne (and Medal), 1986; Mauerberger Meml, 1987. Hon. Mem., NZ Ophthalmol Soc.; Mem., French and German Ophthalmol Socs; Internat. Mem., Amer. Acad. Ophthal. Freeman, City of London; Liveryman, Soc. of Apothecaries. *Publications:* chapters in: Clinical Aspects of Immunology, 1981; Clinical Ophthalmology, 1987; Relationships in Dermatology, 1988; contribs on external eye disease and immunology to med. jls. *Recreations:* playing the piano, gardening. *Address:* Southbrook Court, Southbrook Lane, Bovey Tracey, Devon TQ13 9NB.

WRIGHT, Peter; Editor, Mail on Sunday, since 1998; *b* 13 Aug. 1953; *s* of Nigel and June Wright; *m* 1974, Dorothy Manders; three *s* one *d. Educ:* Marlborough Coll.; Clare Coll., Cambridge (MA History). Reporter, Evening Echo, Hemel Hempstead, 1976–79; Daily Mail: Reporter, 1979; Asst News Editor, 1980–85; Associate News Editor (Foreign), 1985; Asst Features Editor, 1986–88; Femail Editor, 1988–91; Asst Editor (Features), 1991; Associate Editor, 1992–95; Dep. Editor, 1995–98. *Address:* Mail on Sunday, 2 Derry Street, W8 5TS. *Club:* Keyhaven Yacht.

WRIGHT, Peter Duncan; QC 1999; a Recorder, since 2001; *b* 2 Nov. 1957; *s* of Harvey Wright and Margaret Wright; *m* 1982, Stephanie Maria Mandziuk; one *s* two *d. Educ:* Hull Univ. (LLB Hons). Called to the Bar, Inner Temple, 1981. *Recreations:* Rugby, travel. *Address:* Lincoln House, 1 Brazennose Street, Manchester M2 5EL. *T:* (0161) 832 5701.

WRIGHT, Peter Michael, FRCO(CHM); Organist and Director of Music, Southwark Cathedral, since 1989; *b* 6 March 1954; *s* of Dudley Cyril Brazier Wright and Pamela Deirdre (*née* Peacock). *Educ:* Highgate Sch. (Music Schol.); Royal Coll. of Music (Exhibnr; ARCM); Emmanuel Coll., Cambridge (Organ Schol.; MA). LRAM. Sub-Organist, Guildford Cathedral, and Music Master, Royal Grammar Sch., Guildford, 1977–89. Conductor: Guildford Chamber Choir, 1984–94; Surrey Festival Choir, 1987–2001. Freelance conductor, recitalist (organ), adjudicator and broadcaster. Mem. Council, 1990–, Hon. Sec., 1997–, RCO; Mem. Council, Friends of Cathedral Music, 2001–. Hon. FGCM 2000. *Recreations:* travel, theatre, reading, good food. *Address:* 52 Bankside, SE1 9JE. *T:* (020) 7261 1291.

WRIGHT, Sir Peter (Robert), Kt 1993; CBE 1985; Director Laureate, The Birmingham (formerly Sadler's Wells) Royal Ballet, since 1995 (Director, 1977–95); *b* 25 Nov. 1926; *s* of Bernard and Hilda Mary Wright; *m* 1954, Sonya Hana; one *s* one *d. Educ:* Bedales School; Leighton Park Sch. Dancer: Ballets Jooss, 1945–47, 1951–52; Metropolitan Ballet, 1947–49; Sadler's Wells Theatre Ballet, 1949–51, 1952–56; Ballet Master, Sadler's Wells Opera, and Teacher, Royal Ballet Sch., 1956–58; freelance choreographer and teacher, 1958–61; Ballet Master and Asst Dir, Stuttgart Ballet, 1961–63; BBC Television Producer, 1963–65; freelance choreographer, 1965–69; Associate Dir, Royal Ballet, 1969–77. Special Prof., Sch. of Performance Studies, Birmingham Univ., 1990–. Governor: Royal Ballet Sch., 1976–; Sadler's Wells Theatre, 1987–. President: Benesh Inst., 1993–; Friends of Sadler's Wells Theatre, 1994–; Council for Dance Educn and Trng, 1995–2000; Vice Pres., Royal Acad. of Dancing, 1995–. *Creative Works:* Ballets: A Blue Rose, 1957; The Great Peacock, 1958; Musical Chairs, 1959; The Mirror Walkers, 1962; Quintet, 1962; Namouna, 1963; Designs for Dancers, 1963; Summer's Night, 1964; Danse Macabre, 1964; Variations, 1964; Concerto, 1965; Arpege, 1974; El Amor Brujo, 1975; Summertide, 1976; own productions of classics: Giselle: Stuttgart, 1966; Cologne, 1967; Royal Ballet, 1968 and 1985; Canadian National Ballet, 1970; Munich, 1976; Dutch National Ballet, 1977; Houston, Texas, 1979; Frankfurt, 1980; Rio de Janeiro, Brazil, 1982; Winnipeg, 1982; Tokyo, 1989; The Sleeping Beauty: Cologne, 1968; Royal Ballet, 1968; Munich, 1974; Dutch National Ballet, 1981; Sadler's Wells Royal Ballet, 1984; Vienna State Opera Ballet, 1995; Coppelia: Royal Ballet Touring Co., 1976; Sadler's Wells Royal Ballet, 1979; Scottish Ballet, 1992; Birmingham Royal Ballet, 1995; Tokyo, 1997; Swan Lake: Sadler's Wells Royal Ballet, 1981; Munich, 1984; Birmingham Royal Ballet, 1991; Nutcracker: Royal Ballet, 1984–94, revised 1990; Birmingham Royal Ballet, 1990; Tokyo, 1998. FBSM (Conservatoire Fellow), 1991; Fellow, Birmingham Soc., 1995. Hon. DMus London, 1990; Hon. DLitt Birmingham, 1994. Evening Standard Award for Ballet, 1982; Queen Elizabeth II Coronation Award, Royal Acad. of Dancing, 1990; Digital Premier Award, 1991; Critics Circle Award, 1995. *Recreations:* 'cello, ceramics, gardening. *Address:* 10 Chiswick Wharf, W4 2SR.

WRIGHT, Maj.-Gen. Richard Eustace John G.; *see* Gerrard-Wright.

WRIGHT, Richard Irwin V.; *see* Vane-Wright.

WRIGHT, Sir Richard (Michael) C.; *see* Cory-Wright.

WRIGHT, Rev. Canon Robert; *see* Wright, Rev. Canon A. R.

WRIGHT, Air Vice-Marshal Robert Alfred, AFC 1982; FRAeS; Assistant Chief of Staff (Policy and Requirements), Supreme HQ Allied Powers in Europe, since 2000; *b* 10 June 1947; *s* of Leslie Dominic Wright and Marjorie Wright; *m* 1970, Maggie Courtliff; one *s* one *d. Educ:* Maidstone Grammar Sch. FRAeS 1997. No 8 (Day Fighter Ground Attack) Sqn (Hunters), 1969–71; No 17(F) Sqn (Phantoms), 1971–74; No 1 Tactical Weapons Unit (Hunters), 1974–76; Exchange Duty, USN (Phantoms), 1976–79; No 208 Sqn (Buccaneers), 1979–82; RAF Staff Coll., 1982; Operational Requirements Div., MoD, 1982–84; Directing Staff, RAF Staff Coll., 1984–87; OC, No 9 Sqn (Tornadoes), Bruggen, 1987–89; PSO to CAS, 1989–91; OC, RAF Bruggen, 1992–94; Asst COS, Policy and Plans, HQ AirNorthWest, 1994–95; Air Cdre Ops, and Dep. Dir Franco British Air Gp, HQ STC, 1995–97; MA to High Rep., Sarajevo, 1997–98; COS to Air Mem. for Personnel, and Dep. C-in-C, HQ PTC, 1998–2000. Pres., RAF Athletics Assoc, 1998–. *Publications:* contrib. articles to RUSI Jl. *Recreations:* golf, tennis, ski-ing, walking. *Address:* SHAPE, 7010 Mons, Belgium. *Club:* Royal Air Force.

WRIGHT, Robert Anthony Kent; QC 1973; *b* 7 Jan. 1922; *s* of Robert and Eva Wright; *m* 1956, Gillian Elizabeth Drummond Hancock. *Educ:* Hilton Coll., Natal, S Africa; St Paul's Sch., London; The Queen's Coll., Oxford (MA). Indian Army, 1942–46, Major. Oxford, 1946–48. Called to Bar, Lincoln's Inn, 1949, Bencher 1979; retired from practice, 1999. Hon. Fellow, Univ. of Central England. *Recreations:* music, golf, walking. *Address:* 18 Parkside Avenue, SW19 5ES. *T:* (020) 8946 5978. *Clubs:* National Liberal; Bosham Sailing (Bosham); Island Sailing (Cowes); Royal Wimbledon Golf (Wimbledon).

WRIGHT, Robert Douglas John; Director, Coal Policy, Department of Trade and Industry, since 2001; *b* 2 March 1951; *s* of Douglas Norman Wright and Nora Hermione Wright (*née* Hatton-Jones); *m* 1983, Jane Clare Augier; one *s* two *d. Educ:* Canford Sch.; Southampton Univ. (BSc Psychol. 1973). CSD, 1975–81; attachment to Canadian Govt, Ottawa, 1981–82; Cabinet Office (Mgt and Personnel Office), 1982–85; on secondment to Hong Kong Govt, Hong Kong, 1985–88; Cabinet Office (OPSS), 1988–94; Director: Internat. Affairs, OST, 1994–98; Personnel Ops, DTI, 1999–2001. *Recreations:* family, walking (Nat. Deaf Children's Soc. Cuba Trek, 2001), theatre, tennis. *Address:* c/o Department of Trade and Industry, 1 Victoria Street, SW1H 0ET. *T:* (020) 7215 3991. *Club:* Liphook United Football.

WRIGHT, Rt Rev. Roderick; Bishop (RC) of Argyll and the Isles, 1991–96; *b* 28 June 1940; *m* 1998, Kathleen McPhee. *Educ:* St Mary's Coll., Blairs, Grampian; St Peter's Coll., Cardross, Strathclyde. Ordained 1964; Assistant Priest: St Laurence's, Drumchapel, 1964–66; St Jude's, Barlanark, 1966–69; Procurator, Blairs Coll., Grampian, 1969–74; Assistant Priest: Dunoon, Argyll, 1974–76; Fort William, 1976–80; Parish priest: Ardkenneth, South Uist, 1980–87; St Anne's Corpach and St John the Evangelist, Caol, 1987–91. Mem., Cttee on local and regl ecumenism of Action of Churches Together in Scotland. *Publication:* Feet of Clay (autobiog.), 1999.

WRIGHT, Roger; Controller, BBC Radio 3, since 1998; *b* 1956; *m*; two *c*. *Educ:* Chetham's Sch., Manchester; Royal Holloway College, London Univ. (BMus 1977; Pres., Students' Union, 1977–78). Manager, then Dir, British Music Inf. Centre, 1978–87; Sen. Producer, BBC SO, 1987–89; Artistic Administrator, Cleveland Orch., 1989–92; Exec. Producer, then Vice-Pres., Deutsche Grammophon, 1992–97; Head of Classical Music, BBC, 1997–98. *Publications* include: (with M. Finnissy) New Music 1989, 1989. *Address:* BBC, Broadcasting House, W1A 1AA.

WRIGHT, Rosalind, CB 2001; Director, Serious Fraud Office, since 1997; *b* 2 Nov. 1942; *d* of late Alfred Kerstein and of Felicie Kerstein (*née* Margulin); *m* 1966, Dr David Julian Maurice Wright; three *d*. *Educ:* University College London (LLB Hons). Called to the Bar, Middle Temple, 1964, Bencher, 2001; in practice at the Bar, 1965–69; Department of the Director of Public Prosecutions, then Crown Prosecution Service: Legal Asst, 1969–72; Sen. Legal Asst, 1972–81; Asst Dir, 1981–87 and Head of Fraud Investigation Gp (London), 1984–87; Head of Prosecutions, Securities Assoc., later SFA, 1987–94; Exec. Dir (Legal and Investor Protection Policy) and Gen. Counsel, SFA, 1994–97. Mem. of the Bar, NI, 1999–. Mem., Gen. Council of the Bar, 1998–. Trustee, Jewish Assoc. for Business Ethics, 1999–. *Recreations:* music, theatre, visiting garden centres. *Address:* Serious Fraud Office, 10–16 Elm Street, WC1X 0BJ. *T:* (020) 7239 7272. *Club:* Arts.

WRIGHT, Roy Kilner; Deputy Editor, The London Standard (formerly Evening Standard), 1979–88; *b* 12 March 1926; *s* of Ernest Wright and Louise Wright; *m* 1st (marr. diss.); two *d*; 2nd, 1969, Jane Barnicoat (*née* Selby). *Educ:* elementary sch., St Helens, Lancs. Jun. Reporter, St Helens Reporter, 1941; Army Service; Sub-Editor: Middlesbrough Gazette, 1947; Daily Express, Manchester, 1951; Daily Mirror, London, 1952; Features Editor, Daily Express, London; Dep. Editor, Daily Express, 1976, Editor, 1976–77; Dir, Beaverbrook Newspapers, 1976–77; Senior Asst Editor, Daily Mail, 1977. *Address:* 3 The Square, Cranebridge Road, Salisbury, Wilts SP2 7TW. *T:* (01722) 414464.

WRIGHT, Rt Rev. Royston Clifford; Bishop of Monmouth, 1986–91; *b* 4 July 1922; *s* of James and Ellen Wright; *m* 1945, Barbara Joyce Nowell; one *s* one *d*. *Educ:* Univ. of Wales, Cardiff (BA 1942); St Stephen's House, Oxford. Deacon 1945, priest 1946; Curate: Bedwas, 1945–47; St John Baptist, Newport, 1947–49; Walton-on-the-Hill, Liverpool, 1949–51; Chaplain RNVR, 1950; Chaplain RN, 1951–68; Vicar of Blaenavon, Gwent, 1968–74; RD of Pontypool, 1973–74; Canon of Monmouth, 1974–77; Rector of Ebbw Vale, Gwent, 1974–77; Archdeacon of Monmouth, 1977; Archdeacon of Newport, 1977–86. *Recreations:* four grandchildren; listening to Baroque music. *Address:* 23 Rupert Brooke Drive, Newport, South Wales NP20 3HP. *T:* (01633) 250770.

WRIGHT, Hon. Ruth Margaret; *see* Richardson, Hon. R. M.

WRIGHT, Sheila Rosemary Rivers; *b* 22 March 1925; *d* of Daniel Rivers Wright and Frances Grace Wright; *m* 1949, Ronald A. Gregory; two *c*. Social Science Cert. 1951; BScSoc London External 1956. Personnel Officer, 1951–57; Social Worker, 1957–74. Councillor: Birmingham CC, 1956–78; West Midlands CC, 1973–81. MP (Lab) Birmingham, Handsworth, 1979–83. Member, Birmingham Reg. Hosp. Bd and W Midlands RHA, 1966–80. *Address:* 249 Vicarage Road, Birmingham B14 7LZ. *T:* (0121) 444 3427.

WRIGHT, Shirley Edwin McEwan; corporate consultant; *b* 4 May 1915; *s* of Alfred Coningsby Wright and Elsie Derbyshire; *m* 1939, Dora Fentem; one *s* three *d*. *Educ:* Herbert Strutt Sch., Belper; Coll. of Technology, Manchester; Univ. of Sheffield. BEng, CEng, FIMechE. Metropolitan Vickers, 1932, ICI Explosives Div., 1938; Asst Chief Engr, ICI Nobel Div., 1955; Dir, Irvine Harbour Bd, 1962; Engrg and Techn Dir, ICI Nobel Div., 1965; Pres., Philippine Explosives Corp., 1970; Chief Exec., Livingston Develt Corp., 1972–77; Dir, Premix-Fibreglass, 1978–80. *Recreations:* cricket, golf. *Address:* 33 St Juliens Way, Cawthorne, near Barnsley S75 4ES. *T:* (01226) 792030.

WRIGHT, Stanley Harris; *b* 9 April 1930; *er s* of John Charles Wright and Doris Wright; *m* 1st, 1957, Angela Vivien Smith (marr. diss. 1973); one *s*; 2nd, 1973, Hon. Alison Elizabeth Franks (*d* 2000), *d* of Baron Franks, OM, GCMG, KCB, KCVO, CBE, FBA. *Educ:* Bolton Sch.; Merton Coll., Oxford (Postmaster); 1st cl. hons PPE. Nat. Service, Manchester Regt, 1948–49. Asst Principal, BoT, 1952–55; 2nd Sec., UK Delegn to OEEC, Paris, 1955–57; Principal, HM Treasury, 1958–64; 1st Sec. (Financial), British Embassy, Washington, 1964–66; Asst Sec., HM Treasury, 1966–68; Lazard Bros & Co. Ltd, 1969 and 1970 (Dir 1969); Under-Sec., HM Treasury, 1970–72. Exec. Dir, Lazard Bros & Co. Ltd, 1972–81; Exec. Chm., International Commercial Bank Plc, 1981–83; Non-executive Director: Wilkinson Match Ltd, 1974–81; Scripto Inc., 1977–81; Law Land Co., 1979–81; Wolstenholme Rink, 1980–93 (Chm., 1982–91); Royal Trust Bank, 1984–88; Royal Trust Asset Management (UK Holdings) Ltd, 1987–88 (Chm.); James Ferguson Holdings Plc, 1987–88; Stadium Group plc, 1989–96; Partner, Price Waterhouse and Partners, 1985–88. Business consultant, 1989–93. Chm., British Bankers Assoc. Fiscal Cttee, 1974–80; Member: Layfield Cttee on Local Government Finance, 1974–76; Armstrong Cttee on Budgetary Reform, 1979–80; (and Dir of Studies), CBI Wkg Pty on Tax Reform, 1984–85; CS Commn Final Selection Bd, 1986–; Panel for Financial Services Tribunal, 1988–91. Mem. Council, 1977–89, Hon. Treas., 1987–89, Westfield Coll, Univ. of London; Mem. Council, 1989–2000, Treas., 1989–99, QMW. *Publications:* Two Cheers for the Institutions, 1994; articles on financial and fiscal matters. *Recreations:* various. *Address:* 6 Holly Place, NW3 6QU. *Clubs:* Reform, Capital, MCC.

WRIGHT, Stephen; *see* Wright, J. S.

WRIGHT, Stephen John Leadbetter, CMG 1997; HM Diplomatic Service; Deputy Under-Secretary of State, Foreign and Commonwealth Office, since 2000; *b* 7 Dec. 1946; *s* of late J. H. Wright, CBE and Joan Wright; *m* 1970, Georgina Susan Butler (marr. diss. 2000); one *s* one *d*. *Educ:* Shrewsbury Sch.; The Queen's Coll., Oxford (BA Mod. History, 1968). HM Diplomatic Service, 1968; Havana, 1969–71; CS Coll., 1971–72; FCO, 1972–75; British Information Services, NY, 1975–80; UK Permanent Repn to EC, Brussels, 1980–84; FCO, 1984–85; seconded to Cabinet Office, 1985–87; Counsellor and Hd of Chancery, New Delhi, 1988–91; Counsellor (Ext. Relations), UK Perm. Repn to EC, Brussels, 1991–94; Asst Under Sec. of State, later Dir, EU affairs, FCO, 1994–97; Minister, Washington, 1997–99; Dir, Wider Europe, FCO, 1999–2000. *Recreations:* photography, rowing, books. *Address:* c/o Foreign and Commonwealth Office, King Charles Street, SW1A 2AH.

WRIGHT, Rev. Canon Thomas; *see* Wright, Rev. Canon N. T.

WRIGHT, Rt Rev. Dom Timothy Martin, OSB; Abbot of Ampleforth, since 1997; *b* 13 April 1942; *s* of Monty Wright and Marjorie (*née* Brook). *Educ:* Ampleforth Coll.; St Benet's Hall, Oxford (MA); London Univ. (BD (ext.) 1972). Ordained priest, 1972; Master of Ceremonies, 1971–80, Jun. Master, 1985–88, Ampleforth Abbey; Appeal Dir, Ampleforth Abbey Trust, 1994–97. Ampleforth College: Head of Religious Studies, 1977–91; Housemaster, 1980–97; Dep. Head, 1988–97. Member, Religious Studies Panel: Midland Examining Gp, 1984–96; Univ. of Cambridge Local Exams Syndicate, 1988–94; SEAC, 1988–93. Mem., Abbey Farm Bd, 1985–97. Governor: Bar Convent Direct Grant Sch., York, 1980–85; All Saints RC Comprehensive Sch., York, 1985–96; Westminster Cathedral Choir Sch., 1995–. *Publications:* The Eucharist, 1988; Jesus Christ, the Way, the Truth and the Life, 1994. *Recreations:* sport, travel, cycling. *Address:* Ampleforth Abbey, York YO62 4EN. *T:* (01439) 766700.

WRIGHTSON, Sir (Charles) Mark (Garmondsway), 4th Bt *cr* 1900; Chairman, Close Brothers Corporate Finance Ltd, since 1999 (Managing Director, 1996–99); *b* 18 Feb. 1951; *s* of Sir John Garmondsway Wrightson, 3rd Bt, TD, and Hon. Rosemary (*d* 1998), *y d* of 1st Viscount Dawson of Penn, GCVO, KCB, KCMG, PC; *S* father, 1983; *m* 1975, Stella Virginia, *d* of late George Dean; three *s*. *Educ:* Eton; Queens' Coll., Cambridge (BA 1972). Called to the Bar, Middle Temple, 1974. Hill Samuel & Co. Ltd, 1977–96 (Dir, 1984–96). *Heir: s* Barnaby Thomas Garmondsway Wrightson, *b* 5 Aug. 1979. *Address:* 39 Westbourne Park Road, W2 5QD.

WRIGHTSON, Prof. Keith Edwin, PhD; FRHistS; FBA 1996; Professor of History, Yale University, since 1999; *b* 22 March 1948; *s* of Robert Wrightson and Evelyn Wrightson (*née* Atkinson); *m* 1972, Eva Mikušová; one *s* one *d*. *Educ:* Dame Allan's Boys' Sch., Newcastle upon Tyne; Fitzwilliam Coll., Cambridge (BA 1970; MA 1974; PhD 1974). FRHistS 1986. Research Fellow in Hist., Fitzwilliam Coll., Cambridge, 1972–75; Lectr in Modern Hist., Univ. of St Andrews, 1975–84; University of Cambridge: Univ. Lectr in Hist., 1984–93; Reader in English Social Hist., 1993–98; Prof. of Social Hist., 1998–99; Fellow, Jesus Coll., 1984–99. Visiting Professor: Univ. of Toronto, 1984, 1992; Univ. of Alberta, 1988. *Publications:* (with D. Levine) Poverty and Piety in an English Village, 1979, 2nd edn 1995; English Society 1580–1680, 1982; (ed jtly) The World We Have Gained, 1986; (with D. Levine) The Making of an Industrial Society, 1992; Earthly Necessities: economic lives in early modern Britain, 2000; numerous essays and articles on English social history. *Recreation:* modern jazz. *Address:* Department of History, Yale University, PO Box 208324, New Haven, CT 06520–8324, USA.

WRIGHTSON, Sir Mark; *see* Wrightson, Sir C. M. G.

WRIGLEY, Prof. Christopher John, PhD; Professor of Modern British History, since 1991, and Head of the School of History and Art History, since 2000, Nottingham University; *b* 18 Aug. 1947; *s* of late Arthur Wrigley and of Eileen Sylvia Wrigley; *m* 1987, Margaret Walsh. *Educ:* Goldsworth Primary Sch., Woking; Kingston Grammar Sch.; Univ. of E Anglia (BA 1968); Birkbeck Coll., London (PhD 1973). Lecturer in Econ. Hist., QUB, 1971–72; Loughborough University: Lectr in Econ. Hist., 1972–78; Sen. Lectr, 1978–84; Reader, 1984–88; Reader in Econ. Hist., Nottingham Univ., 1988–91. Ed., The Historian, 1993–98. Member of Council: Historical Assoc., 1980– (Pres., 1996–99); Econ. Hist. Soc., 1983–92 and 1994–2000; a Vice-Pres., RHistS, 1997–2001; Exec. Mem., Soc. for Study of Labour, 1983– (Vice Chm., 1993–97; Chm., 1997–2001). Mem. (Lab) Leics CC, 1981–89 (Labour Chief Whip, 1985–86; Leader, Labour Gp, 1986–89); Mem. (Lab) Charnwood BC, 1983–87 (Dep. Leader, Labour Gp). Contested: (Lab) Blaby, 1983; (Lab and Co-op) Loughborough, 1987. Hon. LittD E Anglia, 1998. *Publications:* David Lloyd George and the British Labour Movement, 1976, 2nd edn 1992; A. J. P. Taylor: a complete bibliography, 1980; (ed) A History of British Industrial Relations: Vol. 1: 1875–1914, 1982; Vol. 2: 1914–1939, 1986, 2nd edn 1992; Vol. 3: 1939–1979, 1996; (ed) William Barnes: the Dorset poet, 1984; (ed) Warfare, Diplomacy and Politics, 1986; Arthur Henderson, 1990; Lloyd George and the Challenge of Labour, 1990; (ed jtly) On the Move, 1991; Lloyd George, 1992; (ed) Challenges of Labour, 1993; (ed) British Trade Unionism 1945–95, 1997; (ed) The Impact of the First World War on the International Economy, 2000. *Recreations:* swimming, music, visiting art galleries, reading even more history. *Address:* Department of History, Nottingham University, Nottingham NG7 2RD. *T:* (0115) 951 5945, *Fax:* (0115) 951 5948; *e-mail:* chris.wrigley@nottingham.ac.uk; (home) 124 Musters Road, West Bridgford, Nottingham NG2 7PW.

WRIGLEY, Sir Edward Anthony, (Sir Tony), Kt 1996; PhD; FBA 1980; Master of Corpus Christi College, Cambridge, 1994–2000; President, British Academy, 1997–2001; *b* 17 Aug. 1931; *s* of Edward Ernest Wrigley and Jessie Elizabeth Wrigley; *m* 1960, Maria Laura Spelberg; one *s* three *d*. *Educ:* King's Sch., Macclesfield; Peterhouse, Cambridge (MA, PhD). William Volker Res. Fellow, Univ. of Chicago, 1953–54; Lectr in Geography, Cambridge, 1958–74; Peterhouse, Cambridge: Fellow, 1958–74, Hon. Fellow, 1997; Tutor, 1962–64; Sen. Bursar, 1964–74; Co-Dir, Cambridge Gp for History of Population and Social Structure, 1974–94; Prof. of Population Studies, LSE, 1979–88; Sen. Res. Fellow, 1988–94, Academic Sec., 1992–94, All Souls Coll., Oxford; Prof. of Econ. History, Univ. of Cambridge, 1994–97. Pres., Manchester Coll., Oxford, 1987–96. Mem., Inst. for Advanced Study, Princeton, 1970–71; Hinkley Vis. Prof., Johns Hopkins Univ., 1975; Tinbergen Vis. Prof., Erasmus Univ., Rotterdam, 1979. President: British Soc. for Population Studies, 1977–79; Econ. History Soc., 1995–98; Chm., Population Investigation Cttee, 1984–90; Treas., British Acad., 1989–95. Editor, Economic History Review, 1986–92. Mem., Amer. Philosophical Soc., 2001; Hon. Foreign Mem., Amer. Acad. of Arts and Scis, 2001. Hon. LittD: Manchester, 1997; Sheffield, 1997; Bristol, 1998; Hon. DLitt: Oxford, 1999; Leicester, 1999; Hon. DSc Edinburgh, 1998. IUSSP Laureate, 1993; Founder's Medal, RGS, 1997. *Publications:* Industrial Growth and Population Change, 1961; (ed) English Historical Demography, 1966; Population and History, 1969; (ed) Nineteenth Century Society, 1972; (ed) Identifying People in the Past, 1973; (ed with P. Abrams) Towns in Societies, 1978; (with R. S. Schofield) Population History of England, 1981; (ed jtly) The Works of Thomas Robert Malthus, 1986; People, Cities and Wealth, 1987; Continuity, Chance and Change, 1988; (ed with R. A. Church) The Industrial Revolutions, 1994; (jtly) English Population History from Family Reconstitution, 1997. *Recreation:* gardening. *Address:* 13 Sedley Taylor Road, Cambridge CB2 2PW. *T:* (01223) 247614.

WRIGLEY, Prof. Jack, CBE 1977; Professor of Education, 1967–88, and Deputy Vice-Chancellor, 1982–88, University of Reading, now Professor Emeritus; *b* 8 March 1923; *s* of Harry and Ethel Wrigley; *m* 1946, Edith Baron; two *s*. *Educ:* Oldham High Sch.; Manchester Univ. BSc, MEd (Manch.); PhD (Queen's, Belfast). Asst Mathematics Teacher: Stretford Grammar Sch., 1946–47; Chadderton Grammar Sch., 1948–50; Research Asst, Manchester Univ., 1950–51; Lectr in Educn: Queen's Univ., Belfast, 1951–57; Univ. of London Inst. of Educn, 1957–62; Research Adviser, Curriculum Study Gp in Min. of Educn, 1962–63; Prof. of Educn, Univ. of Southampton, 1963–67; Dir of Studies, Schools Council, 1967–75. Member: Bullock Cttee on Teaching of Reading and other uses of English, 1972–74; SSRC, Mem. Council and Chm. Educnl Res. Bd, 1976–81. Specialist Adviser, H of C Select Cttee on Educn, Sci., and Arts, 1989–90. *Publications:* (ed) The Dissemination of Curriculum Development, 1976; Values and Evaluation in Education, 1980; contrib. learned jls. *Recreations:* chess (Ulster Chess Champion, 1957), theatre, foreign travel. *Address:* Valley Crest, Thrushwood, Keswick, Cumbria CA12 4PG. *T:* (017687) 71146.

WRIGLEY, Sir Tony; *see* Wrigley, Sir E. A.

WRINTMORE, His Honour Eric George; a Circuit Judge, 1984–2000; *b* 11 June 1928; *s* of Rev. F. H. and Muriel Wrintmore; *m* 1951, Jean Blackburn; two *s* one *d*. *Educ:* Stationers' Company's Sch.; King's Coll. London (LLB Hons). Called to Bar, Gray's Inn, 1955; full-time Chm., Industrial Tribunals, 1971; Regional Chm., Industrial Tribunals, 1976–84; a Dep. Circuit Judge, 1980–83; a Recorder, 1983–84. *Recreations:* sailing, golf. *Club:* Chichester Yacht.

WRIXON-BECHER, Sir John William Michael; *see* Becher.

WROATH, His Honour John Herbert; a Circuit Judge, 1984–97; *b* 24 July 1932; *s* of Stanley Wroath and Ruth Ellen Wroath; *m* 1959, Mary Bridget Byrne; two *s* one *d*. *Educ:* Ryde Sch., Ryde, IoW. Admitted Solicitor, 1956; private practice, 1958–66; Registrar, Isle of Wight County Court, 1965; County Prosecuting Solicitor, 1966; full-time County Court Registrar, 1972; a Recorder of the Crown Court, 1978–84. *Recreations:* sailing, bowling, reading, painting. *Address:* 8 Tides Reach, Birmingham Road, Cowes, Isle of Wight PO31 7NU. *T:* (01983) 293072. *Clubs:* Royal London Yacht, Island Sailing (Cowes).

WROE, David Charles Lynn, CB 1995; consultant; Special Adviser to the European Commission, 1998–99; *b* 20 Feb. 1942; *m* 1966, Susan Higgitt; three *d*. *Educ:* Reigate Grammar Sch.; Trinity Coll., Cambridge (MA); Trinity Coll., Oxford (Cert. Statistics); Birkbeck Coll., London (MSc). Min. of Pensions and National Insurance, 1965–68; Central Statistical Office, 1968–70, 1973–75, 1976–82; secondment to Zambian Govt, 1971–72; Secretariat of Royal Commission on Distribution of Income and Wealth, 1975–76; Under Sec., Regional Policy Directorate, 1982–86, Dir of Stats, 1982–91, Under Sec., Housing Monitoring and Analysis, 1986–91, DoE; Dep. Dir, CSO, 1991–96 (Actg Dir, April–June 1996). Non-exec. Dir, John Laing Construction Ltd, 1994–96. Vice Pres., Royal Statistical Soc., 1995–98 (Mem. Council, 1993–98). Trustee: Community Links Bromley, 1999–; Bromley Voluntary Sector Trust, 2000–. *Recreation:* sailing.

WRONG, Henry Lewellys Barker, CBE 1986; Director, Barbican Centre, 1970–90; *b* Toronto, Canada, 20 April 1930; *s* of Henry Arkel Wrong and Jean Barker Wrong; *m* 1966, Penelope Hamilton Norman; two *s* one *d*. *Educ:* Trinity Coll., Univ. of Toronto (BA). Stage and business administration, Metropolitan Opera Assoc., New York, 1952–64; Director Programming, National Arts Center, Ottawa, 1964–68; Dir, Festival Canada Centennial Programme, 1967; Chm., Spencer House (St James's) Ltd, 1989–92; Dir, European Arts Foundn, 1990–95. Member: Royal Opera House Trust, 1989–95; Adv. Cttee, ADAPT (Access for Disabled People to Arts Premises Today). Trustee: Henry Moore Foundn, 1990–; LSO, 1990–; Royal Fine Art Commn, 1995–; Governor, Compton Verney House Trust, 1995–. Liveryman, Fishmongers' Co., 1987. FRSA 1988. Hon. DLitt City, 1985. Pro cultura Hungarica, 1989. Centennial Medal, Govt of Canada, 1967; Officier, Ordre Nat. du Mérite (France), 1985. *Address:* Yew Tree House, Much Hadham, Herts SG10 6AJ. *T:* (01279) 842106. *Clubs:* White's; Badminton and Rackets (Toronto).

WRONG, Prof. Oliver Murray, DM; FRCP, FRCPE; Professor of Medicine, University College London, 1972–90, now Emeritus Professor; *b* 7 Feb. 1925; *s* of Edward Murray Wrong and Rosalind Grace Wrong (*née* Smith); *m* 1956, Marilda Musacchio; two *d* (and one *d* decd). *Educ:* Upper Canada Coll., Toronto; Edinburgh Acad.; Magdalen Coll., Oxford (Demy; BM BCh 1947, DM 1964). FRCP 1968; FRCPE 1970. Junior hosp appts, Oxford, 1947–51; RAMC, MO Singapore and Malaya, 1948–50; Toronto Gen. Hosp., 1951–52; Mass. Gen. Hosp., Boston, 1952–53; Univ. Tutor in Medicine, Manchester, 1954–58; Lectr and Sen. Lectr in Medicine, RPMS, 1961–69; Prof. of Medicine, Univ. of Dundee, 1969–72; Dir, Dept of Medicine, UCL, 1972–82. Teale Lectr, RCP, 1971; James Howard Means Vis. Physician, Mass. Gen. Hosp., 1974; Vis. Prof., Harvard and Sherbrooke Med. Schs, 1974; Toronto and McGill Med. Schs, 1976. Chm., Nat. Kidney Res. Fund, 1976–80. *Publications:* (with C. J. Edmonds and V. S. Chadwick) The Large Intestine: its role in mammalian nutrition and homeostasis, 1981; articles in med. jls on salt and water metabolism, kidney function, the large intestine. *Recreations:* nature, travel, music (esp. baroque). *Address:* Flat 8, 96–100 New Cavendish Street, W1W 6XN. *T:* (020) 7637 4740; School House, West Dean, Salisbury, Wilts SP5 1JQ.

WROTTESLEY, family name of **Baron Wrottesley**.

WROTTESLEY, 6th Baron *cr* 1838; **Clifton Hugh Lancelot de Verdon Wrottesley;** Bt 1642; Director, Titan Hyde Torrance Yacht Brokerage, since 1999; *b* 10 Aug. 1968; *s* of Hon. Richard Francis Gerard Wrottesley (*d* 1970) (2nd *s* of 5th Baron) and of Georgina Anne (who *m* 1982, Lt-Col Jonathan L. Seddon-Brown), *er d* of Lt-Col Peter Thomas Clifton, CVO, DSO; *S* grandfather, 1977; *m* 2001, Sascha, *d* of Urs Schwarzenbach. *Educ:* Eton; Edinburgh Univ. Commnd 1st Bn Grenadier Guards, 1990; Lieut, 1993, Capt. 1994; retd, 1995. *Heir:* half-uncle Hon. Stephen John Wrottesley [*b* 21 Dec. 1955; *m* 1982, Mrs Roz Fletcher (*née* Taylor); two *d*]. *Address:* C. Hoare & Co., 32 Lowndes Street, SW1X 9HZ. *Clubs:* Cavalry and Guards; St Moritz Tobogganing.

WROUGHTON, Philip Lavallin; Lord-Lieutenant of Berkshire, since 1995; Chairman and Chief Executive, C. T. Bowring & Co. Ltd, 1988–96; *b* 19 April 1933; *s* of Michael Lavallin Wroughton and Elizabeth Angela Wroughton (*née* Rate); *m* 1957, Catriona Henrietta Ishbel MacLeod; two *d*. *Educ:* Eton Coll. Nat. Service, 1951–53, 2nd Lieut KRRC. Price Forbes & Co. Ltd, 1954–61; C. T. Bowring & Co. Ltd, 1961–96; Dir, Marsh & McLennan Cos, Inc., 1988–96 (Vice Chm., 1994–96); Chm., Venton Underwriting Agencies Ltd, 1996–99; Dir, Newmarket Underwriting Ltd, 1999–. Mem., Council of Lloyds, 1992–95. High Sheriff, Berks, 1977; DL Berks, 1994. *Recreations:* shooting, racing. *Address:* Woolley Park, Wantage OX12 8NJ. *T:* (01488) 638214. *Club:* White's.

WU, Sir Gordon (Ying Sheung), KCMG 1997; Managing Director, Hopewell Holdings Group; *b* Hong Kong, 3 Dec. 1935; *s* of Chung Wu and Sum Wu (*née* Chang); *m* 1970, Kwok, (Ivy), San-Ping; two *s* two *d*. *Educ:* Princeton Univ. (BS Civil Engrg 1958). Architect; civil engr. Founder: Central Enterprises Co. Ltd, 1962; Gordon Wu and Associates, 1962; Hopewell Construction Co. Ltd, 1963; Hopewell Hldgs Ltd, 1972; Consolidated Electric Power Asia Ltd, 1993. *Projects* include: Hopewell Centre, Hong Kong (66 storey building); China Hotel, Guangdon, China; Shajiao B and C (coal-fired power stations), Guangdon, China; G-S-Z Superhighway (motorway linking Hong Kong and China), 1994–. Vice Pres., Hong Kong Real Estate Developer's Assoc., 1970–; Mem., Chinese People's Political Consultative Conf., 1984–. *Address:* Hopewell Holdings Ltd, 64th Floor, Hopewell Centre, 183 Queen's Road East, Hong Kong.

WU Shu-Chih, Hon. Alex, CBE 1983 (OBE 1973); JP; company director; Chairman, Fidelity Management Ltd, since 1965; Vice-Chairman, Dai Nippon Printing Co. (HK) Ltd, since 1973 (Managing Director, 1964–73); *b* 14 Sept. 1920; *s* of Wu Chao-Ming and Yeh Huei-Cheng; *m* 1946; three *s* three *d*. *Educ:* National South West Associated Univ., Kunming, China. Director: Hong Kong Ferry Co. Ltd, 1976–; Hong Kong Aircraft Engineering Co. Ltd, 1983–; Longman China Ltd (formerly Longman Group (Far East) Ltd), 1984–; Nat. Electronics (Consolidated) Ltd, 1984–; K. Wah Stones (Holdings) Ltd, 1986–; Hung Hing Printing Group Ltd, 1992–; Dransfield Hldgs Ltd, 1993–2000; Paliburg Hldgs Ltd, 1995–; Alpha General (Hldgs) Ltd, 1997–; Consultant: Austdairy Ltd, 1987– (Dir, 1983–87); China Daily, 1988–; Proprietor, Sino-Scottish Trading Co., 1960–2000; Publisher, Sino-American Publishing Co., 1960–. Chairman: Supplementary Med. Professions Council, 1981–89; Printing Industry Trng Bd, 1967–89; Council for the Performing Arts, 1982–89; Council, Hongkong Acad. for Performing, 1982–86; Vice-Chairman: Hong Kong Trade Develt Council, 1974–83; Vocational Trng Council, 1982–89; Nominating Cttee, Stock Exchange of Hong Kong Ltd, 1992– (Chm., 1989–91; Vice-Chm., 1991–92); Member: Hong Kong Heart Foundn Ltd, 1975–; Aviation Adv. Bd, 1980–89; Med. Sub-Cttee, Univ. and Polytechnic Grants Cttee, 1983–89; Hong Kong Indust. Estates Corp., 1984–89; Adv. Cttee on China–Hong Kong Trade Develt Council, 1985–; Hong Kong Inst. for Promotion of Chinese Culture, 1985–; Securities and Futures Commn Adv. Cttee, 1993–; Hong Kong Affairs Advrs, 1995–; Selection Cttee for first Govt of HKSAR, 1996–. Mem., Bd of Governors, Hong Kong Philharmonic Soc. Ltd, 1978–. Pres., Hongkong Jun. Chamber of Commerce, 1960; Hon. Pres., Hong Kong Printers Assoc., 1983–. MLC Hong Kong, 1975–85. JP Hong Kong, 1973. Fellow, Hong Kong Management Assoc., 1983; FIMgt (FBIM 1979); FInstD 1980; FIOP 1984. Hon. LLD Hong Kong, 1992. *Recreations:* classical music, Western and Peking opera, tennis, soccer, swimming, contract bridge. *Address:* 14/F, Hart House, 12–14 Hart Avenue, Tsimshatsui, Kowloon, Hong Kong. *T:* 668789. *Clubs:* Hong Kong, Rotary of Hong Kong; Hong Kong Jockey; Hong Kong Golf.

WULF-MATHIES, Dr Monika; Member, European Commission, 1995–99; *b* 17 March 1942; *d* of Carl-Hermann Baier and Margott Heisser; *m* 1968, Dr Carsten Wulf-Mathies. *Educ:* Univ. of Hamburg (DrPhil 1968). Br. Asst, Federal Ministry of Econs, Germany, 1968–71; Hd, Dept for Social Policy, Federal Chancellery, 1971–76; joined Gewerkschaft Öffentliche Dienste, Transport und Verkehr (Public Services and Transport Workers' Union), 1971; Mem., Man. Exec, Cttee, 1976–95; Chm., 1982–95. *Recreation:* garden.

WULSTAN, Prof. David; Research Professor, University of Wales, Aberystwyth, since 1990; *b* 18 Jan. 1937; *s* of Rev. Norman and (Sarah) Margaret Jones; *m* 1965, Susan Nelson Graham; one *s*. *Educ:* Royal Masonic Sch., Bushey; Coll. of Technology, Birmingham; Magdalen Coll., Oxford (Academical Clerk, 1960; Burrowes Exhibr, 1961; Mackinnon Sen. Schol., 1963; Fellow by examination, 1964). MA, BSc, BLitt; ARCM. Lectr in History of Music, Magdalen Coll., Oxford, 1968–78; also at St Hilda's and St Catherine's Colls; Vis. Prof., Depts of Near Eastern Studies and Music, Univ. of California, Berkeley, 1977; Statutory (Sen. Lectr), University Coll., Cork, 1979, Prof. of Music, 1980–83; Gregynog Prof. of Music, UCW, Aberystwyth, 1983–90. Mem. Council, Plainsong and Mediaeval Music Soc. Dir, Clerkes of Oxenford (founded 1961); appearances at Cheltenham, Aldeburgh, York, Bath, Flanders, Holland, Krakow, Zagreb, Belgrade Fests, BBC Proms; many broadcasts and TV appearances, gramophone recordings; also broadcast talks, BBC and abroad. Consulting Ed., Spanish Academic Press. *Publications:* Septem Discrimina Vocum, 1983; Tudor Music, 1985; Musical Language, 1992; The Emperor's Old Clothes, 1994, 2nd edn 2001; editor: Gibbons, Church Music, Early English Church Music, vol. 3, 1964, vol. 27, 1979; Anthology of Carols, 1968; Anthology of English Church Music, 1971; Play of Daniel, 1976, 2nd edn 2000; Victoria, Requiem, 1977; Tallis, Puer Natus Mass, 1977; Coverdale Chant Book, 1978, Sheppard, Complete Works, 1979–; Weelkes, Ninth Service, 1980; many edns of anthems, services etc; entries in Encyclopédie de Musique Sacrée, 1970; chapter in A History of Western Music, ed Sternfeld, 1970; chapters in Cobras e Som, 2001; articles and reviews in learned jls incl. Plainsong and Medieval Music, contrib. Bull. of Cantigueiros of Santa Maria. *Recreations:* badminton, tennis, cooking, eating, aikido, self-defence (instructor). *Address:* Tŷ Isaf, Llanilar, Aberystwyth, Cardiganshire SY23 4NP. *T:* (01974) 241229; *e-mail:* dww@aber.ac.uk.

WYAND, Roger Nicholas Lewes; QC 1997; a Recorder, since 2000; *b* 31 Oct. 1947; *s* of John Blake Wyand and Diana Wyand (*née* Williams); *m* 1973, Mary Elizabeth Varley; three *s*. *Educ:* Lakefield Coll. Sch., Canada; Rugby Sch.; Downing Coll., Cambridge (MA Nat. Sci.). Called to the Bar, Middle Temple, 1973; Asst Recorder (Patents County Court), 1994–2000. Vice-Chm., Intellectual Property Bar Assoc. *Recreations:* theatre, golf, Arsenal FC. *Address:* Hogarth Chambers, 5 New Square, Lincoln's Inn, WC2A 3RJ. *T:* (020) 7404 0404.

WYATT, (Alan) Will, CBE 2000; Chairman, Human Capital Ltd; Director, Coral Eurobet, since 2000; *b* 7 Jan. 1942; *s* of Basil Wyatt and Hettie Evelyn (*née* Hooper); *m* 1966, Jane Bridgit Bagenal; two *d*. *Educ:* Magdalen College Sch., Oxford; Emmanuel Coll., Cambridge. Trainee reporter, Sheffield Telegraph, 1964; Sub-Editor, BBC Radio News, 1965; moved to BBC television, 1968; Producer: Late Night Line Up, In Vision, The Book Programme, B. Traven—a mystery solved, *et al*, 1970–77; Asst Hd of Presentation (Programmes), 1977; Hd of Documentary Features, 1981; Hd of Features and Documentaries Gp, 1987; Asst Man. Dir, 1988–91, Man. Dir, 1991–96, BBC Network Television; Chief Exec., BBC Broadcast, 1996–99. Chm., BBC Guidelines on Violence, 1983, 1987; Director: BARB, 1989–91; BBC Subscription TV, 1990–93; BBC Enterprises, 1991–94; BBC Worldwide Television, 1994–96; UKTV, 1997–99. Governor: London Inst., 1990– (Chm., 1999–); Nat. Film and TV Sch., 1991–97; Magdalen Coll. Sch., Oxford, 2000–. Vice-Pres., EBU, 1998–99. FRTS 1992 (Vice-Pres., 1997; Pres., 2000–). *Publications:* The Man Who Was B. Traven, 1980; numerous articles on broadcasting. *Recreations:* fell walking, horse racing, opera. *Address:* c/o London Institute, 65 Davies Street, W1Y 2DA. *Clubs:* Garrick; Century.

WYATT, Arthur Hope, CMG 1980; HM Diplomatic Service, retired; re-employed in Foreign and Commonwealth Office, 1990–95; *b* 12 Oct. 1929; *s* of Frank and Maggie Wyatt, Anderton, Lancs; *m* 1957, Barbara Yvonne, *d* of Major J. P. Flynn, late Indian Army; one *d* (and one *d* decd). *Educ:* Bolton School. Army, 1947–50; FO, 1950–52; 3rd Sec., Ankara, 1952–56; 2nd Sec., Phnom Penh, 1956–58; 2nd Sec., Ankara, 1958–61; FO, 1962–66; 1st Sec., Bonn, 1966–70; FCO, 1970–72; Counsellor and Head of Chancery, Lagos, 1972–75; Dep. High Comr, Valletta, 1975–76; Diplomatic Service Inspector, 1977–79; Counsellor (Econ. and Comm.) and Consul-Gen., Tehran, 1979–80; Counsellor, Ankara, 1981–84; Minister, Lagos, 1984–86; High Comr to Ghana and Ambassador (non-resident) to Togo, 1986–89. *Recreations:* golf, football, bridge, stamp collecting. *Address:* 44 Baronsmede, W5 4LT. *T:* (020) 8579 0782.

WYATT, (Christopher) Terrel, FREng, FICE, FIStructE; Chairman, W. S. Atkins plc, 1987–98; *b* 17 July 1927; *s* of Lionel Harry Wyatt and Audrey Vere Wyatt; *m*; four *s*; *m* 1990, Patricia Perkins. *Educ:* Kingston Grammar Sch.; Battersea Polytechnic (BScEng); Imperial Coll. (DIC). FICE 1963; FIStructE 1963; FREng (FEng 1980). Served RE, 1946–48. Charles Brand & Son Ltd, 1948–54; Richard Costain Ltd, 1955–87: Dir, 1970–87; Gp Chief Exec., 1975–80; Dep. Chm., 1979–80; Chm., Costain Group PLC, 1980–87. *Recreation:* sailing. *Address:* The White House, St Martin's Avenue, Epsom, Surrey KT18 5HS.

WYATT, David Joseph, CBE 1977; Adviser on International Relations, British Red Cross Society, 1992–99; HM Diplomatic Service, 1949–85; *b* 12 Aug. 1931; *s* of late Frederick Wyatt and Lena (*née* Parr); *m* 1st, 1957, Annemarie Angst (*d* 1978); two *s* one *d*; 2nd, 1990, Dr Wendy Baron, *qv*. *Educ:* Leigh Grammar Sch. National Service, RAF, 1950–52. Entered Foreign Service, 1949; Berne, 1954; FO, 1957–61; Second Sec., Vienna, 1961; First Sec., Canberra, 1965; FCO, 1969–71; First Sec., Ottawa, 1971; Counsellor, 1974; seconded Northern Ireland Office, Belfast, 1974–76; Counsellor and Head of Chancery, Stockholm, 1976–79; Under Sec. on loan to Home Civil Service, 1979–82; UK Mission to UN during 1982 General Assembly (personal rank of Ambassador); Minister and Dep. Comdt, British Mil. Govt, Berlin, 1983–85. Acting Dir Gen, Jan.–July 1990, Dir, Internat. Div., 1985–92, BRCS; Chm., Internat. Red Cross/Red Crescent Adv. Commn, 1996–97. FRSA 1991.

WYATT, Derek Murray; MP (Lab) Sittingbourne and Sheppey, since 1997; *b* 4 Dec. 1949; *s* of late Reginald Swythn Wyatt and of Margaret Eira (*née* Holmden); *m* 1987, Joanna Willett; one *d* one *s*. *Educ:* St Luke's Coll., Exeter; Open Univ. (BA Hons); St Catherine's Coll., Oxford. History teacher, 1972–81; journalist and writer, 1982–84; editor, George Allen & Unwin Ltd, 1984–85; Dir and Publisher, William Heinemann Ltd, 1986–88; Dir, TSL Ltd, 1988–91; consultant, writer and journalist, 1992–94; Head of Programmes, Wire TV, 1994–95; Dir, Computer Channel, BSkyB, 1995–97. Non-executive Chairman: Einstein TV plc, 2000–; Spafax, 2001–. Mem., Select Cttee on Culture, Media and Sport, 1997–. Chairman: All Party Parly Internet Cttee (founder), 1997–; All Party Parly Rugby Union Cttee, 1997–; All Party Parly British Council, 2000–. Chm., Clicksure Council, 1999–2001. Founder: Women's Sports Foundn (UK), 1985; World Internet Forum, 1999; Oxford Internet Inst., 2000. Trustee: PIN (Parents Information Network), 1999–; Major Stanley's (Trustee Gp for OURFC). Freeman, City of London, 2001; Mem., Co. of Information Technologists, 2001–. Commendation for work on sport and apartheid, UNO, 1987. *Publications:* Wisecracks from the Movies, 1987; The International Rugby Almanack 1994, 1993; The International Rugby Almanack 1995, 1994; Rugby Disunion, 1995. *Recreations:* Rugby (played for Oxford University, Barbarians, England), film, reading, software. *e-mail:* wyattd@parliament.uk. *Clubs:* Royal Automobile; Vincent's (Oxford).

WYATT, Prof. Derrick Arthur; QC 1993; Professor of Law, University of Oxford, since 1996; Fellow, St Edmund Hall, Oxford, since 1978; *b* 25 Feb. 1948; *s* of Iris Ross (formerly Wyatt, *née* Thompson) and step *s* of Alexander Ross; *m* 1970, (Margaret) Joan Cunnington; one *s* one *d*. *Educ:* Alsop High Sch.; Emmanuel Coll., Cambridge (MA, LLB); Univ. of Chicago Law Sch. (JD). Lectr in law, Univ. of Liverpool, 1971–75; called to the Bar, Lincoln's Inn, 1972; Fellow, Emmanuel Coll., Cambridge, 1975–78; CUF Lectr in Law, Oxford Univ., 1978–96. Vis. Prof., Florida State Univ., 1987. Consultant, Oxford Inst. of Legal Practice, 1993–97. Gave evidence to Bundestag and Bundesrat on subsidiarity in EU, 1996. Member: Vale of White Horse DC, 1983–87; Abingdon Town Council, 1983–87. Mem. Editl Cttee, British Yearbook of Internat. Law, 1992–. *Publications:* Wyatt and Dashwood's European Union Law, 1980, 4th edn 2000; (with B. Rudden) Basic Community Laws, 1980, 7th edn 1999; (ed with A. Barav) Yearbook of European Law, 1988–97; articles and reviews in learned jls. *Recreations:* walking, reading. *Address:* St Edmund Hall, Oxford OX1 4AR. *T:* (01865) 279000.

WYATT, Hugh Rowland; Lord-Lieutenant of West Sussex, since 1999; *b* 18 Nov. 1933; *s* of late Brig. Richard John Penfold Wyatt, MC, TD and Hon. Margaret Agnes, *d* of 1st Baron Ebbisham, GBE; *m* 1959, Jane Ann Elizabeth Eden; one *s* two *d*. *Educ:* Winchester. 2nd Lieut, The Royal Sussex Regt, 1952–54; Captain, TA, 1954–61. Dir, McCorquodale plc, 1964–85; farmer. Chairman: Chichester Cathedral Trust, 1991–98; Chichester Dio. Bd of Finance, 1997–. High Sheriff of West Sussex, 1995–96. Pres., Royal Sussex Regtl Assoc., 1997–. *Recreations:* travel, opera. *Address:* Cissbury, Findon, West Sussex BN14 0SR. *T:* (01903) 873328. *Club:* Sussex.

WYATT, Terrel; *see* Wyatt, C. T.

WYATT, Wendy, (Mrs D. J. Wyatt); *see* Baron, O. W.

WYATT, Will; *see* Wyatt, A. W.

WYETH, Andrew Newell; artist; landscape painter; *b* 12 July 1917; *s* of Newell and Carolyn Wyeth; *m* 1940, Betsy Merle James; two *s*. *Educ.* privately. First one man exhibn, William Macbeth Gall., NY, 1937; subsequent exhibitions include: Doll & Richards, Boston, 1938, 1940, 1942, 1944; Cornell Univ., 1938; Macbeth Gall., 1938, 1941, 1943, 1945; Art Inst. of Chicago, 1941; Museum of Modern Art, NYC, 1943; M. Knoedler & Co., NYC, 1953, 1958; Dunn Internat. Exhibn, London, 1963; MIT, Cambridge, 1966; The White House, Washington, 1970; Tokyo, 1974, 1979; Metropolitan Museum, NY, 1976; RA, 1980 (first by living American artist); Arnot Museum, Elmira, NY, 1985; Seibu-Pisa, Tokyo, 1986; Moscow, Leningrad, 1987; Nat. Gall. of Art, Corcoran Gall. of Art, Washington, 1987; Milan, 1987; Fitzwilliam Mus., Cambridge, 1988. Member: Nat. Inst. of Arts and Letters (Gold Medal, 1965); Amer. Acad. of Arts and Sciences; Amer. Acad. of Arts and Letters (Medal of Merit, 1947); Académie des Beaux-Arts, 1977; Hon. Mem., Soviet Acad. of the Arts, 1978. Presidential Medal of Freedom, 1963; Einstein Award, 1967; Congressional Medal, USA, 1988. Hon. AFD: Colby Coll., Maine, 1954; Harvard, 1955; Dickinson, 1958; Swarthmore, 1958; Nasson Coll., Maine, 1963; Temple Univ., 1963; Maryland, 1964; Delaware, 1964; Northwestern Univ., 1964; Hon. LHD Tufts, 1963. *Publications:* The Helga Paintings, 1987; Andrew Wyeth: autobiography, 1995. *Address:* c/o Frank E. Fowler, PO Box 247, Lookout Mountain, TN 37350, USA.

WYKE, Prof. John Anthony, PhD; Director, Beatson Institute for Cancer Research, since 1987; Professor of Medicine, University of Glasgow, since 1991; *b* 5 April 1942; *s* of late Eric John Edward Wyke and Daisy Anne Wyke (*née* Dormer); *m* 1968, Anne Wynne Mitchell; one *s*. *Educ:* Dulwich Coll.; St John's Coll., Cambridge (Schol.; VetMB, MA); Univ. of Glasgow; UCL (PhD). MRCVS. FRSE 1989. Postdoctoral res., Univ. of Washington and Univ. of Southern California, 1970–72; Imperial Cancer Research Fund: scientific staff, London, 1972–83; Head, ICRF Labs at St Bartholomew's Hosp., 1983–87; Asst Dir, 1985–87. Founder FMedSci 1998. Hon. FRCVS 1999. *Publications:* more than 100 scientific articles. *Recreations:* hill walking, ski touring, gardening. *Address:* Beatson Institute for Cancer Research, Garscube Estate, Switchback Road, Bearsden, Glasgow G61 1BD. *T:* (0141) 330 3950; *e-mail:* j.wyke@beatson.gla.ac.uk.

WYKES, Dr David Lewis; Director, Dr Williams's Trust and Library, since 1998; *b* 29 June 1954; *s* of Christopher Lewis Wykes, FCA and Joan Margaret Wykes; *m* 1997, Dr Elizabeth Jane Clapp. *Educ:* Univ. of Durham (BSc); Univ. of Leicester (PhD 1987). *Publications:* numerous articles in acad. and learned jls. *Recreations:* chamber music, walking, history. *Address:* Dr Williams's Library, 14 Gordon Square, WC1H 0AR. *T:* (020) 7387 3727.

WYLD, Martin Hugh, CBE 1997; Chief Restorer, National Gallery, since 1979; *b* 14 Sept. 1944; *s* of John Wyld and Helen Leslie Melville; one *s* one *d*. *Educ:* Harrow School. Assistant Restorer, National Gallery, 1966. *Recreation:* travel. *Address:* 21 Grafton Square, SW4 0DA. *T:* (020) 7720 2627. *Clubs:* Colony Room, MCC.

WYLDBORE-SMITH, Maj.-Gen. Sir (Francis) Brian, Kt 1980; CB 1965; DSO 1943; OBE 1944; General Officer Commanding, 44th Division (TA) and Home Counties District, 1965–68; Director, Conservative Board of Finance, 1970–92; *b* 10 July 1913; *s* of Rev. W. R. Wyldbore-Smith and Mrs D. Wyldbore-Smith; *m* 1944, Hon. Molly Angela Cayzer (*d* 2001), *d* of 1st Baron Rotherwick; three *d* (and one *s* one *d* decd). *Educ:* Wellington Coll.; RMA, Woolwich. Served Middle East, Italy, France and Germany, 1941–45; Military Adviser to CIGS, 1947–49; GSO1, 7 Armoured Div., 1951–53; Comd 15/19 King's Royal Hussars, 1954–56; IDC 1959; BGS Combat Development, 1959–62; Chief of Staff to Commander-in-Chief, Far East Command, 1962–64. Col, 15/19 Hussars, 1970–77. *Recreations:* hunting, shooting. *Address:* Grantham House, Grantham, Lincs NG31 6SS. *T:* (01476) 564705. *Club:* Buck's.

WYLIE, Rt Hon. Lord; Norman Russell Wylie; PC 1970; VRD 1961; a Senator of the College of Justice in Scotland, 1974–90; *b* 26 Oct. 1923; *o s* of late William Galloway Wylie and late Mrs Nellie Smart Wylie (*née* Russell), Elderslie, Renfrewshire; *m* 1963, Gillian Mary, *yr d* of late Dr R. E. Verney, Edinburgh; three *s*. *Educ:* Paisley Grammar Sch.; St Edmund Hall, Oxford (Hon. Fellow, 1975); Univs of Glasgow and Edinburgh. BA (Oxon) 1948; LLB (Glasgow) 1951. Admitted to Faculty of Advocates, 1952; QC (Scotland) 1964. Appointed Counsel to Air Ministry in Scotland, 1956; Advocate-Depute, 1959; Solicitor-General for Scotland, April-Oct. 1964. MP (C) Pentlands Div., Edinburgh, Oct. 1964–Feb. 1974; Lord Advocate, 1970–74. Mem., Parole Bd for Scotland, 1991–93. Justice of Appeal, Republic of Botswana, 1994–96. Trustee, Carnegie Trust for Univs of Scotland, 1976–96; Chm., Scottish Nat. Cttee, English-Speaking Union of the Commonwealth, 1978–84. Served in Fleet Air Arm, 1942–46; subseq. RNR; Lt-Comdr, 1954. *Address:* 30 Lauder Road, Edinburgh EH9 2JF. *T:* (0131) 667 8377. *Club:* New (Edinburgh).

WYLIE, Alexander Featherstonhaugh; QC (Scot) 1991; *b* 2 June 1951; *s* of Ian Hamilton Wylie and Helen Jane Mearns or Wylie; *m* 1975, Gail Elizabeth Watson Duncan; two *d*. *Educ:* Edinburgh Univ. (LLB Hons). ACIArb 1977, FCIArb 1991. Qualified Solicitor in Scotland, 1976; called to the Scottish Bar, 1978; called to the Bar, Lincoln's Inn, 1990. Standing Junior Counsel in Scotland to Accountant of Court, 1986; Advocate Depute, 1989–92; part-time Sheriff, 2000–. Jt Chm., Discipline Cttee, Inst. of Chartered Accountants of Scotland, 1994–; Mem. (part-time), Scottish Legal Aid Bd, 1994–. *Address:* Advocates' Library, Parliament House, Parliament Square, Edinburgh EH1 1RF. *T:* (clerk) 0131–226 2881.

WYLIE, Andrew; President, The Wylie Agency, since 1980; *b* 4 Nov. 1947; *s* of Craig and Angela Fowler Wylie; *m* 1969, Christina Meyer; one *s*; *m* 1980, Camilla Carlini; two *d*. *Educ:* St Paul's Sch.; Harvard Coll. (BA 1970). Established: Wylie Agency, NY, 1980; London office, 1996; Madrid office, 1999. *Recreations:* running, bicycling. *Address:* The Wylie Agency Inc., 250 West 57th Street, Suite 2114, New York, NY 10107, USA. *T:* (212) 2460069. *Clubs:* Knickerbocker, Harvard, River (New York); Bathing Corporation (Southampton).

WYLIE, Prof. Christopher Craig; William Schubert Professor of Developmental Biology, and Director Developmental Biology Division, Children's Hospital Medical Centre, Cincinnati, since 2000; *b* 15 Sept. 1945; *s* of Joseph and Edna Wylie; *m* 1st, 1969, Christine Margaret Hall; 2nd, 1976, Janet Heasman; three *s* one *d*. *Educ:* Chislehurst and Sidcup County Grammar School for Boys; University College London (BSc, 1st cl. Hons Anatomy 1966; PhD 1971). Lectr in Anatomy, University College London, 1969; St George's Hospital Medical School: Sen. Lectr in Anatomy, 1975; Reader, 1983; Prof., 1985; F. J. Quick Prof. of Biol., Cambridge Univ., 1988–94, now Prof. Emeritus; Fellow, Darwin Coll., Cambridge, 1989–94; University of Minnesota: Martin Lenz Harrison Prof. of Develtl Biol. and Genetics, 1994–2000; Dir, Develtl Biol. Centre, 1994–2000; Dir, Develtl Genetics Prog., Sch. of Med., 1994–2000. Vis. Asst Prof. in Biology, Dartmouth Coll., 1975; Vis. Associate Prof. of Anatomy, Harvard Med. Sch., 1981. Editor in Chief, Development (internat. jl of develt biol.), 1987–. *Publications:* numerous research articles in sci. jls of biology. *Recreations:* relaxing with the family, racket sports. *Address:* 411 Bishopsbridge Drive, Cincinnati, OH 45255, USA. *T:* (513) 2339735.

WYLIE, Rt Hon. Norman Russell; *see* Wylie, Rt Hon. Lord.

WYLIE, Sian Meryl, (Mrs Ian Wylie); *see* Griffiths, S. M.

WYLLIE, Prof. Andrew David Hamilton, FRS 1995; Professor of Pathology and Fellow of St John's College, Cambridge University, since 1998. *Educ:* Aberdeen Univ. (BSc 1964; MB ChB 1967; PhD 1975). MRCP 1971; MRCPath 1975, FRCPath 1987; FRCPE 1993. Res. Fellow, Hammersmith Hosp., 1969; Res. Fellow, then Lectr in Pathol., Aberdeen Univ., 1970–72; Edinburgh University: Lectr, 1972–77; Sen. Lectr, 1977–85; Reader, 1985–92; Prof. of Experimental Pathology, and Co-Dir CRC Labs, 1992–98, and Head, 1995–98, Dept of Pathol. FRSE 1991. Hon. DSc Aberdeen, 1998. *Address:* Department of Pathology, University of Cambridge, Tennis Court Road, Cambridge CB2 1QP. *T:* (01223) 333692, *Fax:* (01223) 339067.

WYLLIE, Very Rev. Hugh Rutherford; Moderator of the General Assembly of the Church of Scotland, 1992–93; Minister at the Old Parish Church of Hamilton, 1981–2000; *b* 11 Oct. 1934; *s* of late Hugh McPhee Wyllie and Elizabeth Buchanan; *m* 1962, Eileen Elizabeth Cameron, MA; two *d*. *Educ:* Shawlands Acad., Glasgow; Hutchesons' Grammar Sch., Glasgow; Univ. of Glasgow (MA; Pitcairn Miller Frame Awards, 1961, 1962). The Union Bank of Scotland, 1951–53 (MCIBS). RAF Nat. Service, 1953–55. Licensed and ordained by Presbytery of Glasgow, 1962; Asst Minister, Glasgow Cathedral, 1962–65; Minister: Dunbeth Church, Coatbridge, 1965–72; Cathcart South Church, Glasgow, 1972–81; Convener, General Assembly: Stewardship and Budget Cttee, 1978–83; Stewardship and Finance Bd, 1983–86; Assembly Council, 1987–91; Member, General Assembly: Bd of Nomination to Church Chairs, 1985–91, 1993–99; Bd of Practice and Procedure, 1991–95; Moderator of the Presbytery of Hamilton, 1989–90; Convener, Business Cttee, 1991–95; Chaplain: Royal British Legion (Hamilton Br.), 1981–; Lanarks Burma Star Assoc., 1983–; Strathclyde Police 'Q' Div., 1983–. Master, Hamilton Hosp., 1982–2001; Vice-Chm., Lanarkshire Healthcare NHS Trust, 1996–99 (non-exec. Dir, 1995–99); Trustee, Lanarkshire Primary Care NHS Trust, 1999–2001. Established Centre for Information for the Unemployed, Hamilton, 1983; introduced Dial-a-Fact on drugs and alcohol, 1986; established Hamilton Church History Project, 1984–87; Pres., Glasgow Univ. SCM, 1958; Chm., SCM Scottish Council, 1958. Mem. Council, Scout Assoc., 1993–. Pres., Hamilton Burns Club, 1990. Hon. Freeman, District of Hamilton, 1992. Dr William Barclay Meml Fund Lectr, 1994. Hon. FCIBS 1997. Hon. DD Aberdeen, 1993. *Recreations:* gardening, DIY, yellow Labrador. *Address:* 18 Chantinghall Road, Hamilton ML3 8NP.

WYLLIE, Prof. Peter John, PhD; FRS 1984; Professor of Geology, California Institute of Technology, 1983–99, now Emeritus (Chairman, Division of Geological and Planetary Sciences, 1983–87); *b* 8 Feb. 1930; *s* of George William and Beatrice Gladys Wyllie (*née* Weaver); *m* 1956, Frances Rosemary Blair; two *s* one *d* (and one *d* decd). *Educ:* Univ. of St Andrews. BSc 1952 (Geology and Physics); BSc 1955 (1st cl. hons Geology); PhD 1958 (Geology). Nat. Service, 1948–49: Aircraftsman First Cl. (Best Recruit, Basic Trng, Padgate, 1948). Heavyweight boxing champion, RAF, Scotland, 1949. Glaciologist, British W Greenland Expdn, 1950; Geologist, British N Greenland Expdn, 1952–54; Asst Lectr in Geology, Univ. of St Andrews, 1955–56; Research Asst, 1956–58, Asst Prof. of Geochemistry, 1958–59, Pennsylvania State Univ.; Research Fellow in Chemistry, 1959–60, Lectr in Exptl Petrology, 1960–61, Leeds Univ.; Associate Prof. of Petrology, Pennsylvania State Univ., 1961–65 (Acting Head, Dept Geochem. and Mineralogy, 1962–63); University of Chicago: Prof. of Petrology and Geochem., 1965–77; Master Phys. Scis, Collegiate Div., Associate Dean of Coll. and of Phys. Scis Div., 1972–73; Homer J. Livingston Prof., 1978–83; Chm., Dept of Geophysical Scis, 1979–82. Louis Murray Vis. Fellow, Univ. of Cape Town, 1987; Hon. Prof., Chinese Univ. of Geosciences, Beijing, 1996. President: Internat. Mineralogical Assoc., 1986–90 (Vice Pres., 1978–86); Internat. Union of Geodesy and Geophysics, 1995–99 (Vice Pres., 1991–95). MAE 1996. Foreign Associate, US Nat. Acad. of Scis, 1981 (Chm. Cttee on Solid-Earth Sciences and Society, report published 1993); Fellow: Amer. Acad. of Arts and Scis, 1982; Amer. Geophys. Union; Geol Soc. Amer.; Mineral Soc. Amer., 1965; Corresponding Fellow, Edin. Geol Soc., 1985–; Foreign Fellow: Indian Geophys. Union, 1987; Indian Nat. Sci. Acad., 1991; Nat. Acad. of Scis, India, 1992; Foreign Member: Russian (formerly USSR) Acad. of Scis, 1988; Chinese Acad. of Scis, 1996; Academia Europaea, 1996. Hon. Member: Mineralogical Soc. of GB and Ireland, 1986–; Mineralogical Soc. of Russia, 1986–. Hon. DSc St Andrews, 1974. Polar Medal, 1954; Wollaston Medal, Geol Soc. of London, 1982; Abraham-Gottlob-Werner Medal, German Mineral Soc., 1987; Roebling Medal, Mineralogical Soc. of America, 2001; Leopold von Buch Medal, Deutschen Geologischen Ges., 2001. *Publications:* Ultramafic and Related Rocks, 1967; The Dynamic Earth, 1971; The Way the Earth Works, 1976; (ed) Solid-Earth Sciences and Society, 1993; numerous papers in sci. jls. *T:* (626) 395–6461.

WYLLIE, William Robert Alexander, AM 1993; Chairman, Wyllie Group (formerly Asia Securities) Pty Ltd, since 1973; *b* 9 Oct. 1932; *s* of Robert Wyllie and Marion Margaret Rae (*née* McDonald); *m* 1988, Rhonda Noreen (*née* McGrath); one *s* one *d*, and two *s* one *d* from previous marr. *Educ:* Scarborough State Sch., Perth, W Australia; Perth Technical Coll. (qual. Automobile and Aeronautical Engrg). MIRTE. Sen. Exec./Br. Manager, Wearne Bros Ltd, Malaysia/Singapore, 1953–64; Man. Dir, Harpers Internat. Ltd, Hong Kong, 1964–73; Chm. and Chief Exec., China Engineers Holdings Ltd, Hong Kong, 1973–75; Deputy Chairman and Chief Executive: Hutchison Internat. Ltd, Hong Kong, 1975–Dec. 1977; Hutchison Whampoa Ltd, Hong Kong, Jan. 1978–June 1979 (Chm. and Chief Exec., 1979–80); Chm. and Chief Exec., Asia Securities Ltd, Hong Kong, 1971–90; Chm., Asia Securities International Ltd, 1987–90. *Recreations:* power boating, water skiing, Scuba diving, restoration of vintage cars and planes. *Address:* c/o Wyllie Group Pty Ltd, PO Box 7751, Cloisters Square, Perth, WA 6850, Australia. *Clubs:* Royal Aero, Royal Perth Yacht, Pearce Flying, Fremantle Sailing (Perth); Hong Kong, American, Shek O Country, Hong Kong Jockey, Royal Hong Kong Yacht (Hong Kong).

WYMAN, Peter Lewis, FCA; Partner, PricewaterhouseCoopers, since 1978; Deputy President, 2001–02, President, from June 2002, Institute of Chartered Accountants in England and Wales; *b* 26 Feb. 1950; *s* of late John Bernard Wyman and of Joan Dorethea Wyman (*née* Beighton); *m* 1978, Joy Alison Foster; one *s* one *d*. *Educ:* Epsom Coll. ACA 1973, FCA 1978. Chartered Accountant; articled clerk, Ogden Parsons & Co. and Harmood Banner, 1968–73; Deloitte Haskins & Sells, then Coopers & Lybrand, now PricewaterhouseCoopers: Manager, 1973–78; Partner, 1978–; Hd of Tax, 1993–98; Hd of External Relations, 1998–2000. Mem. Cttee, London Soc. of Chartered Accountants, 1981–90 (Chm., 1987–88); Institute of Chartered Accountants in England and Wales: Mem. Council, 1991–; Chm., Faculty of Taxation, 1991–95; Chm., Educn and Trng Directorate, 1995–99; Chm., Professional Standards Office, 1999–2000; Mem., Exec. Cttee, 1996–; Vice Pres., 2000–01. Special Advr on Deregulation and Taxation to Parly Under-Sec. of State for Corporate Affairs, 1993–94; Mem., Deregulation Task Force, 1994–97; External Overseer, Contributions Agency/IR Jt Working Prog., 1995–97; Mem., Regulation of Accounting Profession Implementation Working Party, 1999–2001. FIMgt (FBIM 1974); FRSA. Freeman: Worshipful Co. of Chartered Accountants, 1988; City of London, 1988. Gov., Aylwin Girls' Sch., Southwark, 2001–. *Publications:* various professional jls on taxation and accountancy matters. *Recreations:* twentieth century history, family history, equestrian sports, gardening. *Address:* Plainsfield Court, Plainsfield, Over Stowey, Somerset TA5 1HH. *T:* (01278) 671292.

WYMER, Dr John James, FSA; FBA 1996; Director of English Rivers Palaeolithic Survey for English Heritage, 1991–99; *b* 5 March 1928; *s* of Bertram Osborne Wymer and Leah Wymer (*née* Vidal); *m* 1st, 1948, Pauline May (marr. diss. 1972); two *s* three *d*; 2nd, 1976, Eunice Mollie (*née* Spurling) (*d* 1999). *Educ:* Richmond and East Sheen County Sch.; Shoreditch Training Coll. FSA 1963. Archaeologist, Reading Museum, 1956–65; Res. Associate, Univ. of Chicago and UEA, 1965–80; Field Officer: Essex Archaeol. Unit, 1981–82; Norfolk Archaeol. Unit, 1983–90; directed excavations at numerous sites, mainly of Palaeolithic or later prehistoric periods. Pres., Quaternary Res. Assoc., 1975–77; Vice-President: Suffolk Inst. of Archaeol. and History, 1985–; Norfolk and Norwich Archaeol. Soc., 1994–; Berkshire Archaeol. Soc., 1995–; former exec. mem., other learned socs. Hon. MA Durham 1969; Hon. DSc Reading 1993. Stopes Meml Medal, 1972. *Publications:* Lower Palaeolithic Archaeology in Britain, 1968; Gazetteer of Mesolithic Sites, 1977; The Palaeolithic Age, 1982; (with R. Singer) The Middle Stone Age at Klasies River Mouth in South Africa, 1982; The Palaeolithic Sites of East Anglia, 1985; (with R. Singer and B. G. Gladfelter) The Lower Palaeolithic Site at Hoxne, England, 1993. *Recreations:* travelling, reading, gardening, carpentry, drinking good beer in congenial company. *Address:* 17 Duke Street, Bildeston, Ipswich, Suffolk IP7 7EW. *T:* (01449) 741691.

WYN, Eurig; Member (Plaid Cymru) Wales, European Parliament, since 1999; *b* 10 Oct. 1944; *s* of Albert and Alvira Davies; *m* 1972, Gillian; one *s* one *d*. *Educ:* Univ. of Wales, Aberystwyth. Journalist/presenter, BBC Wales, 1970–75; Organiser, Plaid Cymru Party, 1975–78; Develt Officer, Community Co-operative Movt, 1978–82; freelance journalist, newspapers and BBC radio, 1982–85. Mem. (Plaid Cymru) Gwynedd CC, 1990–99. Mem., Cttee of the Regions, EU, 1994–99. *Address:* Y Freni, Waunfawr, Caernarfon, Gwynedd LL55 4YY. *T:* (01286) 650512; (office) 29 Lloyd Street, Llandudno, Conwy LL30 2UU. *T:* (01492) 871700.

WYNDHAM, family name of **Baron Egremont and Leconfield**.

WYNDHAM-QUIN, family name of **Earl of Dunraven**.

WYNESS, James Alexander Davidson; Chairman, Saracens Ltd, since 1996; non-executive Director, Spirent (formerly Bowthorpe) plc, since 1979; *b* 27 Aug. 1937; *s* of late Dr James Alexander Davidson Wyness and Millicent Margaret (*née* Beaton); *m* 1966, Josephine Margaret Worsdell; three *d*. *Educ:* Stockport Grammar Sch.; Emmanuel Coll., Cambridge (MA, LLB). National Service, 2 Lieut, RA. Articled Clerk, A. F. & R. W. Tweedie, 1964–66 (qualified 1965); Linklaters & Paines, 1966–97: Partner, 1970–97; Managing Partner, 1987–91; Jt Sen. Partner, 1991–93; Sen. Partner, 1994–96. Mem., Law Soc. Mem., Co. of City of London Solicitors. Life Mem., Saracens FC (RFU) (Captain, 1962–65); Mddx RFU; London Div. RFU. *Recreations:* visiting France, growing vegetables, Rugby football, reading. *Address:* c/o Linklaters & Paines, One Silk Street, EC2Y 8HQ.

WYNFORD, 8th Baron *cr* 1829; **Robert Samuel Best,** MBE 1953; DL; Lt-Col Royal Welch Fusiliers; *b* 5 Jan. 1917; *e s* of 7th Baron Wynford and Evelyn (*d* 1929), *d* of late Maj.-Gen. Sir Edward S. May, KCB, CMG; *S* father, 1943; *m* 1941, Anne Daphne Mametz, *d* of late Maj.-Gen. J. R. Minshull Ford, CB, DSO, MC; one *s* two *d*. *Educ:* Eton; RMC, Sandhurst. 2nd Lieut, RWF, 1937; served BEF; GHQ Home Forces; North Africa (Croix de Guerre); Egypt; Italy; wounded, 1944; Instructor, Staff College, 1945–46; War Office, 1947–49; OC Depot, RWF, 1955–57; Instructor Joint Service Staff Coll., 1957–60; RARO 1960. DL Dorset, 1970. *Heir:* *s* Hon. John Philip Robert Best [*b* 23 Nov. 1950; *m* 1981, Fenella Christian Mary, *o d* of Arthur Reginald Danks; one *s* one *d*]. *Club:* Army and Navy.

WYNGAARDEN, James Barnes, MD; FRCP; Principal, Washington Advisory Group, since 1995; Foreign Secretary, National Academy of Sciences, Washington, 1990–94; *b* 19 Oct. 1924; *s* of Martin Jacob Wyngaarden and Johanna Kempers Wyngaarden; *m* 1946, Ethel Dean Vredevoogd (marr. diss. 1976); one *s* four *d*. *Educ:* Calvin College; Western Michigan University; University of Michigan. MD 1948; FRCP 1984. Investigator, NIH, 1953–56; Associate Prof. of Medicine, Duke Univ. Med. Center, 1956–61; Prof. of Medicine, Duke Univ. Med. Sch., 1961–65; Chairman, Dept of Medicine: Univ. of Pennsylvania Med. Sch., 1965–67; Duke Univ. Med. Sch., 1967–82; Dir, NIH, 1982–89; Assoc. Dir, Life Scis, Exec. Office of the President of USA, 1989–90. Hon. DSc: Michigan, 1980; Ohio, 1984; Illinois, 1985; George Washington, 1986; S Carolina, 1989; Western Michigan, 1989; Hon. PhD Tel Aviv, 1987. *Publications:* (ed jtly) The Metabolic Basis of Inherited Disease, 1960, 5th edn 1983; (with O. Sperling and A. DeVries) Purine Metabolism in Man, 1974; (with W. N. Kelley) Gout and Hyperuricemia, 1976; (with L. H. Smith) Review of Internal Medicine; a self-assessment guide, 1979, 3rd edn 1985; (ed jtly) Cecil Textbook of Medicine, 15th edn 1979 to 19th edn 1992. *Recreations:* tennis, skiing, painting. *Address:* 3504 Stoneybrook Drive, Durham, NC 27705–2427, USA.

WYNN, family name of **Baron Newborough**.

WYNN, Sir (David) Watkin W.; *see* Williams-Wynn.

WYNN, Terence; Member (Lab) North West Region, England, European Parliament, since 1999 (Merseyside East, 1989–94, Merseyside East and Wigan, 1994–99); *b* 27 June 1946; *s* of Ernest Wynn and Lily (*née* Hitchen); *m* 1967, Doris Ogden; one *s* one *d*. *Educ:* Leigh Technical Coll.; Riversdale Technical Coll., Liverpool (OND); Liverpool Polytechnic (Combined Chief Engrs Cert); Salford Univ. (MSc Manpower Studies and Industrial Relns 1984). Seagoing Marine Engr Officer, MN, 1962–74; Engr Surveyor, ICI, Runcorn, 1975–76; Ship Repair Man., Manchester Dry Docks, 1976–78; Trng Advr, Shipbuilding ITB, 1978–82; Sen. Trng Exec., Marine Trng Assoc., 1982–99. Methodist local preacher, 1978–. *Publication:* Onward Christian Socialist, 1996. *Recreation:* Rugby League supporter. *Address:* Alexandra Park, Prescot Road, St Helens WA10 3TT. *Club:* Leigh Labour.

WYNN, Terence Bryan; freelance journalist and writer; Editor, Brentwood News, since 1990; *b* 20 Nov. 1928; *o s* of late Bernard Wynn and Elsie Wynn (*née* Manges); unmarried. *Educ:* St Cuthbert's Grammar Sch., Newcastle upon Tyne. Started as jun. reporter with Hexham Courant, Northumberland, 1945; Blyth News, 1947–48; Shields Evening News, 1948–50; Sunderland Echo, 1950–53; Reporter with Daily Sketch, 1953–58; News Editor, Tyne Tees Television, 1958, then Head of News and Current Affairs, 1960–66; Editorial Planning, BBC Television News, 1966–67; Sen. Press and Information Officer with Land Commn, 1967–71; Sen. Inf. Officer, HM Customs and Excise, 1971–72; Editor, The Universe, 1972–77; Editor, Liberal News, and Head of Liberal Party Orgn's Press Office, 1977–83; Regl Press Officer, MSC, COI, London and SE Region, 1983–85; Editor, Your Court (house jl of Lord Chancellor's Dept), 1985–88. Helped to found and first Editor of Roman Catholic monthly newspaper, Northern Cross. Chm., Catholic Writers' Guild, 1967–70 (Hon. Vice-Pres., 1970); Judge for British Television News Film of the Year Awards, 1961–64; Mem. Mass Media Commn, RC Bishops' Conf. of England and Wales, 1972–83. Chm., Editors' Forum (diocesan newspapers), 1999–. KSG 2001. *Publication:* Walsingham, a modern mystery play, 1975. *Recreations:* reading, writing, talking. *Address:* Bosco Villa, 30 Queen's Road, South Benfleet, Essex SS7 1JW. *T:* (01268) 792033.

WYNN OWEN, Philip; Director, Regulatory Impact Unit, Cabinet Office, since 1999; *b* 10 June 1960; *s* of Emrys and Ruth Wynn Owen; *m* 1989, Elizabeth Mary Fahey; three *s*. *Educ:* Maidstone Grammar Sch.; University Coll., Oxford (MA Mod. Hist.); London Business Sch. (MBA Dist.). HM Treasury, 1981–99: Asst Private Sec. to Chancellor of Exchequer, 1984–86; Private Sec. to Perm. Sec., 1991–93; Team Leader: Transport Team, 1993–96; Tax and Budget Team, 1996; Tax Policy Team, 1997–99. Alternate Dir, EIB, 1994–96. *Recreations:* family, cricket, gym, swimming. *Address:* Cabinet Office, Regulatory Impact Unit, 2nd Floor, 35 Great Smith Street, SW1P 3BQ. *T:* (020) 7276 2150. *Clubs:* MCC; Leigh Cricket (Kent).

WYNNE, David, OBE 1994; sculptor, since 1949; *b* Lyndhurst, Hants, 25 May 1926; *s* of Comdr Charles Edward Wynne and Millicent (*née* Beyts); *m* 1959, Gillian Mary Leslie Bennett (*née* Grant) (*d* 1990); one *s* (and one *s* decd), and one step *s* one step *d*. *Educ:* Stowe Sch.; Trinity Coll., Cambridge. FZS; FRSA. Served RN, 1944–47: minesweepers and aircraft carriers (Sub-Lieut RNVR). No formal art training. First exhibited at Leicester Galls, 1950, and at Royal Acad., 1952. One-man Exhibitions: Leicester Galls, 1955, 1959; Tooth's Gall., 1964, 1966; Temple Gall., 1964; Findlay Galls, New York, 1967, 1970, 1973; Covent Garden Gall., 1970, 1971; Fitzwilliam Museum, Cambridge, 1972; Pepsico World HQ, New York, 1976; Agnew's Gall., 1983; retrospective, Cannizaro House, 1980; also various mixed exhibns. Large works in public places: Magdalen Coll., Oxford; Malvern Girls' Coll.; Civic Centre, Newcastle upon Tyne; Lewis's, Hanley; Ely Cathedral; Birmingham Cath.; Church of St Paul, Ashford Hill, Berks; Ch. of St Thomas More, Bradford-on-Avon; Mission Ch., Portsmouth; Fountain Precinct, Sheffield; Bowood House, Wilts; Risen Christ and 2 seraphim, west front of Wells Cathedral, 1985; Abbey Gdns, Tresco, Isles of Scilly; Highgrove, Glos; London and environs: Albert Bridge; British Oxygen Co., Guildford; Cadogan Place Gardens and Cadogan Sq.; Crystal Palace Park; Guildhall; Longbow House; St Katharine-by-the-Tower; Taylor Woodrow; Wates Ltd, Norbury; also London Road, Kingston-upon-Thames; Elmsleigh Centre, Staines; IPC HQ, Sutton; St Raphael's Hospice, Cheam, Surrey; Central Park, Watford; Queen Elizabeth Gates, Hyde Park Corner; Hurlingham Club; Highgrove Gardens; USA:

Ambassador Coll., Texas, and Ambassador Coll., Calif; Atlantic Richfield Oil Co., New Mexico; Lakeland Meml Hosp., Wis; First Fed. Savings, Mass; Pepsico World HQ, Purchase, NY; Playboy Hotel and Casino, Atlantic City, NJ; Sarasota, Fla; Mayo Foundation, Minn; Sherman, Texas; Ritz Carlton, Rancho Mirage, Calif; Mayo Clinic, Rochester, Minn; Grayson Bank, Sherman, Texas; also Perth, WA, and Place Camelotti, Geneva, 1988. Bronze portraits include: Sir Thomas Beecham, 1956; Sir John Gielgud, 1962; Yehudi Menuhin, 1963; The Beatles, 1964; Kokoschka, 1965; Sir Alec Douglas-Home, 1966; Robert, Marquess of Salisbury, 1967; The Prince of Wales, 1969; Lord Baden-Powell, 1971; Virginia Wade, 1972; The Queen, 1973; King Hassan of Morocco, 1973; Air Chief Marshal Lord Dowding, 1974; The Begum Aga Khan, 1975; Pele, 1976; Lord Hailsham, 1977; Prince Michael of Kent, 1977; Earl Mountbatten of Burma, 1981; Paul Daniels, 1982; Jackie Stewart, 1982; Elvis Presley; Victor Ubogu; Portrait Figures: Arnold Palmer, 1983; Björn Borg, 1984; Leonard Cheshire, for Stowe Sch., 1995; Bernard Gallacher, Wentworth Club, 1998; other sculptures: Fred Perry, AELTC, 1984; Shergar and jockey, 1981; Shareef Dancer and groom, 1984; Cresta Rider, St Moritz, 1985; Two Dolphins, Provence, France, 1986. Designed: Common Market 50 pence piece of clasped hands, 1973; King Hassan, for Moroccan coinage, 1973; the Queen's Silver Jubilee Medal, 1977 (with new effigy of the Queen wearing St Edward's Crown). *Publication:* The Messenger, a sculpture by David Wynne, 1982; *relevant publications:* T. S. R. Boase, The Sculpture of David Wynne 1949–1967, 1968; Graham Hughes, The Sculpture of David Wynne 1968–1974, 1974; Jonathan Stone (ed), The Sculpture of David Wynne 1974–92, 1993. *Recreations:* active sports, poetry, music. *Address:* 5 Burlington Lodge Studios, Buer Road, SW6 4LA. *T:* (020) 7731 1071. *Clubs:* Garrick, Queen's, Hurlingham; Village (Wimbledon); Leander (Henley-on-Thames); 1st and 3rd Trinity Boat; St Moritz Tobogganing; The Royal Tennis Court (Hampton Court Palace).

WYRKO, David John, QPM 1995; Chief Constable of Leicestershire, since 1997; *b* 15 July 1948; *s* of late Wasyl John Wyrko and of Stella Doreen Wyrko (*née* Witts); *m* 1973, Beryl Case; one *s* one *d*. *Educ:* City of Bath Technical Sch.; Univ. of Surrey (BSc Electrical, Electronic and Control Engineering 1969). Police Constable to Chief Superintendent, Northants, 1972–91; Asst Chief Constable, Northants, 1991–93; Dep. Chief Constable, Leics, 1993–97. Co-Dir, Police Extended Interviews, 1999–. FBI Nat. Acad., Quantico, 1984; Cabinet Office Top Mgt Prog., 1995. Hon. Treas., 1994–98, Chm., Inf. Mgt Cttee, 1997–2000, ACPO; Mem., PITO Bd, 1997–. *Recreations:* cabinet making, golf, cycling. *Address:* Leicestershire Constabulary HQ, St John's, Narborough, Leics LE9 5BX. *T:* (0116) 222 2222.

Y

YACOUB, Sir Magdi (Habib), Kt 1992; FRCS; FRS 1999; British Heart Foundation Professor of Cardiothoracic Surgery, National Heart and Lung Institute (formerly Cardiothoracic Institute), Imperial College School of Medicine (formerly British Postgraduate Medical Federation), London University, since 1986; Consultant Cardiothoracic Surgeon: Royal Brompton Hospital; Harefield Hospital, Middlesex, since 1969; *b* Cairo, 16 Nov. 1935; *m*; one *s* two *d*. *Educ:* Cairo University. FRCS, FRCSE, FRCSGlas, 1962; LRCP 1966, MRCP 1986, Hon. FRCP 1990. Rotating House Officer, Cairo Univ. Hosp., 1958–59; Surgical Registrar, Postgrad. Surgical Unit, Cairo Univ., 1959–61; Resident Surgical Officer, 1962–63, Surgical Registrar, 1963–64, London Chest Hosp.; Rotating Sen. Surgical Registrar, Nat. Heart and Chest Hosps, 1964–68; Asst Prof. of Cardiothoracic Surgery, Chicago Univ., 1968–69; Consultant Cardiac Surgeon, Nat. Heart Hosp., 1973–89. Hon. Consultant: Royal Free Hosp. Med. Sch.; King Edward's Coll. of Medicine, Lahore, Pakistan; Hon. Prof. of Surgery, Univ. of Sienna; Hon. Prof. of Cardiac Surgery, Charing Cross and Westminster Hosp. Med. Schs. Has developed innovations in heart and heart-lung transplants. Mem., Soc. Thoracic Surgeons; FRSocMed; Founder FMedSci 1998. Hon. DSc: Brunel, 1985; Amer. Univ. at Cairo, 1989; Loughborough, 1990; Hon. MCh Cardiff, 1986; Hon. PhD Lund, 1988. Editor: Annual in Cardiac Surgery; Current Opinion in Cardiology: coronary artery surgery. *Publications:* papers on pulmonary osteoarthropath, aortic valve homografts, surgical treatment of ischaemic heart disease, valve repairs, and related subjects. *Address:* National Heart and Lung Institute, Dovehouse Street, SW3 6LY.

YALE, David Eryl Corbet, FBA 1980; Reader in English Legal History, Cambridge University, 1969–93, now Emeritus; Fellow, Christ's College, Cambridge, since 1950; *b* 31 March 1928; *s* of Lt-Col J. C. L. Yale and Mrs Beatrice Yale (*née* Breese); *m* 1959, Elizabeth Ann, *d* of C. A. B. Brett, Belfast; two *s*. *Educ:* Malvern Coll., Worcs; Queens' Coll., Cambridge (BA 1949, LLB 1950, MA 1953). Called to the Bar, Inner Temple, 1951; Asst Lectr and Lectr in Law, Cambridge Univ., 1952–69. Pres., Selden Soc., 1994–97. Hon. QC 2000. *Publications:* various, mainly in field of legal history. *Recreation:* fishing. *Address:* Christ's College, Cambridge CB2 3BU. *T:* (01223) 334900; Saethon, Porthmadog, Gwynedd LL49 9UR. *T:* (01766) 512129.

YALOW, Rosalyn Sussman, PhD; Senior Medical Investigator, Veterans Administration, later Veterans Affairs, 1972–92, Senior Medical Investigator Emeritus, since 1992; *b* 19 July 1921; *d* of Simon Sussman and Clara (*née* Zipper); *m* 1943, Aaron Yalow; one *s* one *d*. *Educ:* Hunter Coll., NYC (AB Physics and Chemistry, 1941); Univ. of Ill, Urbana (MS Phys. 1942, PhD Phys. 1945). Diplomate, Amer. Bd of Radiol., 1951. Asst in Phys., Univ. of Ill, 1941–43, Instr, 1944–45; Lectr and Temp. Asst Prof. in Phys., Hunter Coll., 1946–50. Veterans Admin Hospital, Bronx, NY: Consultant, Radioisotope Unit, 1947–50; Physicist and Asst Chief, Radioisotope Service, 1950–70 (Actg Chief, 1968–70); Chief, Nuclear Medicine Service, 1970–80; Dir, Solomon A. Berson Res. Lab., 1973–; Chm., Dept of Clin. Scis, Montefiore Hosp. and Med. Center, Bronx, NY, 1980–85; Chief, VA Radioimmunoassay Ref. Lab., 1969–. Consultant, Lenox Hill Hosp., NYC, 1952–62. Res. Prof., Dept of Med., Mt Sinai Sch. of Med., 1968–74, Distinguished Service Prof., 1974–79; Distinguished Prof.-at-Large, Albert Einstein Coll. of Med., Yeshiva Univ., NY, 1979–85, Prof. Emeritus, 1985–; Solomon A. Berson Distinguished Prof.-at-Large, Mt Sinai Sch. of Medicine, City Univ. of NY, 1986–. IAEA Expert, Instituto Energia Atomica, Brazil, 1970; WHO Consultant, Radiation Med. Centre, India, 1978; Sec., US Nat. Cttee on Med. Physics, 1963–67. Member: President's Study Gp on Careers for Women, 1966–67; Med. Adv. Bd, Nat. Pituitary Agency, 1968–71; Endocrinol. Study Sect., Nat. Insts of Health, 1969–72; Cttee for Evaluation of NPA, Nat. Res. Council, 1973–74; Council, Endocrine Soc., 1974–80 (Koch Award, 1972; Pres., 1978); Bd of Dirs, NY Diabetes Assoc., 1974–77. Member: Editorial Adv. Council, Acta Diabetologica Latina, 1975–77; Ed. Adv. Bd, Encyclopaedia Universalis, 1978–; Ed. Bd, Mt Sinai Jl of Medicine, 1976–79; Ed. Bd, Diabetes, 1976–79. Fellow: NY Acad. of Sciences (Chm., Biophys. Div., 1964–65; A. Cressy Morrison Award in Nat. Sci., 1975); Radiation Res. Soc.; Amer. Assoc. of Physicists in Med.; Biophys. Soc.; Amer. Diabetes Assoc. (Eli Lilly Award, 1961; Commemorative Medallion, 1972; Banting Medal, 1978; Rosalyn S. Yalow Res. and Develt Award estabd 1978); Amer. Physiol Soc.; Soc. of Nuclear Med. Associate Fellow in Phys., Amer. Coll. of Radiol. Member: Nat. Acad. of Sciences; Amer. Acad. Arts and Sciences; Foreign Associate, French Acad. of Medicine. Hon. DSc and Hon. DHumLett from univs and med. colls in the US, France, Argentina, Canada. Nobel Prize in Physiology or Medicine, 1977; VA Exceptional Service Award, 1975 and 1978; Nat. Medal of Sci., 1988. Has given many distinguished lectures and received many awards and prizes from univs and med. socs and assocs. *Publications:* over 500 papers and contribns to books, research reports, proceedings of conferences and symposia on radioimmunoassay of peptide hormones and related subjects, since 1950. *Address:* VA Medical Center, 130 West Kingsbridge Road, Bronx, NY 10468, USA. *T:* (718) 579 1644.

YAM Yee-Kwan, David; Hon. Mr Justice Yam; a Judge of the Court of First Instance of the High Court (formerly Judge of the High Court), Hong Kong, since 1994; *b* 4 Oct. 1948; *s* of Yam Fat-Shing Frank and Ng Yuet-Hing Nora; *m* 1977, Dr Stella T. P. Wong; two *s*. *Educ:* Hong Kong Univ. (BSc 1971; LLB 1975); Inns of Court Sch. of Law. Called to the Bar, Middle Temple, and to Hong Kong Bar, 1976; in practice, 1977–87; District Court Judge, 1987–94. Chm., Insider Dealing Tribunal, 1995–97. *Recreations:* golf, music, travelling. *Address:* High Court, 38 Queensway, Hong Kong. *T:* 28254427. *Clubs:* Hong Kong Jockey, Shek O Golf and Country (Hong Kong).

YAMAZAKI, Toshio, Hon. KBE 1996; Adviser, Saison Foundation, since 1991; Japanese Ambassador to the Court of St James's, 1985–88; retired; *b* 13 Aug. 1922; *s* of Takamaro Yamazaki and Konoe Yamazaki; *m* 1955, Yasuko Arakawa; one *s* one *d*. *Educ:* Tokyo University (Faculty of Law). 2nd Sec., Japanese Embassy, London, 1955–59; Dir, British Commonwealth Div., European and Oceanic Affairs Bureau, Min. of Foreign Affairs, 1962–64; Counsellor, Permt Mission to UN, New York; 1964–67; Dir, Financial Affairs Div., Minister's Secretariat, Min. of Foreign Affairs, 1967–70; Dep. Dir-Gen., Treaties Bureau, 1970; Minister, Washington, 1971–74; Dir-Gen., Amer. Affairs Bureau, Min. of Foreign Affairs, 1974–77; Dep. Vice-Minister for Admin, 1978–80; Ambassador to Egypt, 1980–82, to Indonesia, 1982–84. Chm., Japan-British Soc., Tokyo, 1988–94. Pres., Temple Univ., Japan, 1991–96. Grand Cordon, Order of Sacred Treasure (Japan), 1994; Order of Republic, 1st cl. (Egypt), 1982; Banda 2nd cl., Orden del Aguila Azteca (Mexico), 1978; Grosses Verdienstkreuz mit Stern (FRG), 1979. *Recreations:* theatre-going, golf. *Address:* 9-1-506 Sanban-cho, Chiyoda-ku, Tokyo 102, Japan. *T:* (3) 32881458. *Clubs:* Tokyo (Tokyo); Tokyo Golf.

YAMEY, Prof. Basil Selig, CBE 1972; FBA 1977; Professor of Economics, University of London, 1960–84, now Emeritus; Member (part-time), Monopolies and Mergers Commission, 1966–78; *b* 4 May 1919; *s* of Solomon and Leah Yamey; *m* 1st, 1948, Helen Bloch (*d* 1980); one *s* one *d*; 2nd, 1991, Demetra Georgakopoulou. *Educ:* Tulbagh High Sch.; Univ. of Cape Town; LSE. Lectr in Commerce, Rhodes Univ., 1945; Senior Lectr in Commerce, Univ. of Cape Town, 1946; Lectr in Commerce, LSE, 1948; Associate Prof. of Commerce, McGill Univ., 1949; Reader in Economics, Univ. of London, 1950. Dir, Private Bank and Trust Co. Ltd, 1989–94. Managing Trustee, IEA, 1986–91. Trustee: National Gall., 1974–81; Tate Gall., 1979–81; Member: Council, National Trust, 1979–81; Museums and Galls Commn, 1983–84; Cinematograph Films Council, 1969–73. Mem. Committee of Management: Courtauld Inst., 1981–84; Warburg Inst., 1981–84; Mem., Governing Body, London Business Sch., 1965–84. *Publications:* Economics of Resale Price Maintenance, 1954; (jt editor) Studies in History of Accounting, 1956; (with P. T. Bauer) Economics of Under-developed Countries, 1957; (jt editor) Capital, Saving and Credit in Peasant Societies, 1963; (with H. C. Edey and H. Thomson) Accounting in England and Scotland, 1543–1800, 1963; (with R. B. Stevens) The Restrictive Practices Court, 1965; (ed) Resale Price Maintenance, 1966; (with P. T. Bauer) Markets, Market Control and Marketing Reform: Selected Papers, 1968; (ed) Economics of Industrial Structure, 1973; (jt editor) Economics of Retailing, 1973; (jt editor) Debits, Credits, Finance and Profits, 1974; (with B. A. Goss) Economics of Futures Trading, 1976; Essays on the History of Accounting, 1978; (jt editor) Stato e Industria in Europa: Il Regno Unito, 1979; Further Essays on the History of Accounting, 1983; Arte e Contabilità, 1986; Análisis Económico de los Mercados, 1987; Art and Accounting, 1989; (ed) Luca Pacioli, Exposition of Double Entry Book-keeping, Venice 1494, 1994; (jt editor) Accounting History: some British contributions, 1994; articles on economics, economic history and law in learned journals. *Address:* 27B Elsworthy Road, NW3 3BT. *T:* (020) 7405 7686.

YANG, Chen Ning, FInstP; physicist, educator; Einstein Professor and Director, Institute for Theoretical Physics, State University of New York at Stony Brook, New York, 1966, now Emeritus Professor and Director; *b* Hofei, China, 22 Sept. 1922; *s* of Ke Chuen Yang and Meng Hwa Lo; *m* 1950, Chih Li Tu; two *s* one *d*. Naturalized 1964. *Educ:* National Southwest Associated Univ., Kunming, China (BSc), 1942; University of Chicago (PhD), 1948. FInstP 1998. Institute for Advanced Study, Princeton, NJ: Member, 1949–55; Prof. of Physics, 1955–66; several DSc's from universities. Member of Board: Rockefeller Univ., 1970–76; AAAS, 1976–80; Salk Inst., 1978–; Ben Gurion Univ.; Member: Amer. Phys. Soc.; Nat. Acad. Sci.; Amer. Philos. Soc., Sigma Xi; Brazilian, Venezuelan, Royal Spanish and Chinese Acads of Sci; Academia Sinica; Foreign Member: Royal Soc., 1992; Russian Acad. of Sciences, 1994. Nobel Prize in Physics, 1957; Rumford Prize, 1980; Nat. Medal of Science, 1986; Benjamin Franklin Medal, Amer. Phil Soc., 1993; Bower Prize, Franklin Inst., 1994; King Faisal Internat. Prize, 2001. *Publications:* contrib. to Physical Review, Reviews of Modern Physics. *Address:* State University of New York at Stony Brook, NY 11794-3840, USA.

YANG, Sir Ti Liang, Kt 1988; Member Executive Council, Hong Kong Special Administrative Region, since 1997; Chairman, Exchange Fund Investment Ltd, since 1998; Chief Justice of Hong Kong, 1988–96; *b* 30 June 1929; *s* of late Shao-nan Yang and Elsie (*née* Chun); *m* 1954, Eileen Barbara (*née* Tam); two *s*. *Educ:* The Comparative Law Sch. of China; Soochow Univ., Shanghai; UCL (LLB Hons 1953; Fellow 1989). FCIArb 1990. Called to the Bar (with honours), Gray's Inn, 1954, Hon. Bencher, 1988. Magistrate, Hong Kong, 1956; Sen. Magistrate, 1963; Rockefeller Fellow, London Univ., 1963–64; District Judge, Dist Court, 1968; Judge of the High Court, Hong Kong, 1975; Justice of Appeal, Hong Kong, 1980; Pres., Court of Appeal of Negara Brunei Darussalam, 1988–92. Candidate for selection of Chief Exec., HKSAR, 1996. Chairman: Kowloon Disturbances Claims Assessment Bd, 1966, Compensation Bd, 1967; Commn of Inquiry into the Rainstorm Disasters, 1972; Commn of Inquiry into the Leung Wing-sang Case, 1976; Commn of Inquiry into the MacLennan Case, 1980; Mem., Law Reform Commn, 1980–96 (Chm., Sub-cttee on law relating to homosexuality, 1980). Mem., Chinese Lang. Cttee (Chm. Legal Sub-cttee), 1970. Chairman: University and Polytechnic Grants Cttee, 1981–84; Hong Kong Univ. Council, 1987–; Pro-Chancellor, Hong Kong Univ., 1994–. Chm., Hong Kong Red Cross, 1998–. Pres., Bentham Club. Hon. LLD: Chinese Univ. of Hong Kong, 1984; Hong Kong Poly., 1992; Hon. DLitt Hong Kong Univ., 1991. Order of Chivalry, First Class, SPMB, Negara Brunei Darussalam, 1990; Grand Bauhinia Medal (Hong Kong), 1999. *Publications:* (trans.) General Yue Fei, by Qian Cai (Qing Dynasty novel), 1995; (trans.) Peach Blossom Fan, (novel by Gu Shifan, 1948), 1998. *Recreations:* philately, reading, walking, oriental ceramics, travelling, music. *Address:* Executive Council, Hong Kong Special Administrative Region, Central Government Offices, Lower Albert Road, Hong Kong. *Fax:* 28498099; Flat 8, Duchess of Bedford

House, Duchess of Bedford's Walk, W8 7QL. *Clubs:* Athenæum; Hong Kong, Hong Kong Country, Hong Kong Jockey (Hong Kong).

YAPP, John William; HM Diplomatic Service; High Commissioner, Seychelles, since 1998; *b* 14 Jan. 1951; *s* of late William Yapp and Pamela Yapp (*née* Clarke); *m* 1997, Petra Jodelis; one *d*, and one *s* three *d* from previous marriages. *Educ:* St Augustine's Coll., Ramsgate. Joined HM Diplomatic Service, 1971: Islamabad, 1973–75; Third Sec. (Consular), Kuala Lumpur, 1976–77; Asst Private Sec. to Ministers of State, FCO, 1978–80; Second Sec. (Commercial), Dubai, 1980–84; Second Sec. (Economic), The Hague, 1984–88; Jt Export Promotion Directorate, FCO/DTI, 1988–91; First Sec. (Political/PR), Wellington, NZ, 1992–95 (concurrently Dep. Governor, Pitcairn Is); Dep. Head, N American Dept, FCO, 1995–97. *Recreations:* reading, cooking, Rugby Union (now as a spectator). *Address:* c/o Foreign and Commonwealth Office, King Charles Street, SW1A 2AH.

YAPP, Sir Stanley Graham, Kt 1975; Chairman, Birmingham International Airport, 1988–94; Chairman, West Midlands County Council, 1983–84 (Leader, 1973–77; Vice-Chairman, 1982–83); Member, Birmingham City Council, later Birmingham District Council, 1961–77 (Leader, 1972–74); *s* of late William and of Elsie Yapp; *m* 1961, Elisbeth Wise (marr. diss.); one *d*; *m* 1974, Carol Matheson (marr. diss.); one *s*; *m* 1983, Christine Horton. Member, West Midlands Economic Planning Council (Chm., Transport Cttee); Member many bodies both local and national, inc.: Vice-Chm. LAMSAC; Member: Local Govt Trng Board; Nat. Jt Councils on pay and conditions; AMA; BR Adv. Bd, Midlands and N Western Reg., 1977–79; Chm., West Midlands Planning Authorities Conf., 1973–75, Vice-Chm. 1975–77. Governor, BFI, 1977–79. FIMgt. *Publications:* contribs to Local Government Chronicle, Municipal Journal, Rating and Valuation. *Recreations:* astronomy, reading, walking. *Address:* 134 Bushmore Road, Hall Green, Birmingham B28 9QZ.

YARBOROUGH, 8th Earl of, *cr* 1837; **Charles John Pelham;** Baron Yarborough, 1794; Baron Worsley, 1837; *b* 5 Nov. 1963; *o s* of 7th Earl of Yarborough and Ann, *d* of late John Herbert Upton; *S* father, 1991; *m* 1990, Anna-Karin Zecevic, *d* of George Zecevic; three *s* one *d*. *Heir: s* Lord Worsley, *qv*. *Address:* Brocklesby Park, Habrough, Lincs DN41 8FB.

YARBURGH-BATESON; *see* de Yarburgh-Bateson, family name of Baron Deramore.

YARD, John Ernest, CBE 2000; Director, Business Services Division (formerly Business Services (Information Technology) Office), Inland Revenue, since 1993; *b* 29 July 1944; *s* of Ernest Alfred and Kathleen Lilian Yard; *m* Jean Pamela Murray; three *s* two *d*. *Educ:* St Marylebone Grammar Sch. Inland Revenue: Exec. Officer and PAYE Auditor, 1963–71; Inspector of Taxes, 1971–84; Dep. Dir (Systems and Policy), 1984–91; Dir of Change Mgt, 1992. *Recreations:* holidays, gardening. *Address:* Business Services Division, Inland Revenue, 3rd Floor, South West Wing, Bush House, Strand, WC2B 4RD.

YARDE-BULLER, family name of **Baron Churston.**

YARDLEY, Sir David (Charles Miller), Kt 1994; Chairman, Commission for Local Administration in England, 1982–94; a Complaints Commissioner, Financial Services Authority (formerly Securities and Investments Board), since 1994; *b* 4 June 1929; *s* of late Geoffrey Miller Yardley and Doris Woodward Yardley (*née* Jones); *m* 1954, Patricia Anne Tempest Olver; two *s* two *d*. *Educ:* The Old Hall Sch., Wellington; Ellesmere Coll., Shropshire; Univ. of Birmingham (LLB, LLD); Univ. of Oxford (MA, DPhil). Called to Bar, Gray's Inn, 1952. RAF Flying Officer (nat. service), 1949–51. Bigelow Teaching Fellow, Univ. of Chicago, 1953–54; Fellow and Tutor in Jurisprudence, St Edmund Hall, Oxford, 1953–74, Emeritus Fellow, 1974–; CUF Lectr, Univ. of Oxford, 1954–74; Sen. Proctor, Univ. of Oxford, 1965–66; Barber Prof. of Law, Univ. of Birmingham, 1974–78; Head of Dept of Law, Politics and Economics, Oxford Poly., 1978–80; Rank Foundn Prof. of Law, University Coll. at Buckingham, 1980–82. Visiting Prof. of Law, Univ. of Sydney, 1971; Hon. Prof. of Law, Univ. of Buckingham, 1994; Vis. Prof., Oxford Brookes Univ., 1995–2001. Constitutional Consultant, Govt of W Nigeria, 1956. Chm., Thames Valley Rent Tribunal, 1963–82; Vice-Pres., Cambs Chilterns and Thames Rent Assessment Panel, subseq. Chilterns Thames and Eastern Rent Assessment Panel, 1966–82, 1995–99; Oxford City Councillor, 1966–74; Chairman: Oxford Area Nat. Ins. Local Appeal Tribunal, 1969–82; Oxford Preservation Trust, 1989–; Examining Bd and Awards Panel, IRRV, 1994–; Ind. Adjudicator, W Bromwich Building Soc., 1996–. Chm. of Governors, St Helen's Sch., Abingdon, 1967–81. FRSA 1991. Freeman, City of Oxford, 1989. *Publications:* Introduction to British Constitutional Law, 1960, 8th edn (as Introduction to Constitutional and Administrative Law), 1995; A Source Book of English Administrative Law, 1963, 2nd edn, 1970; The Future of the Law, 1964; Geldart's Elements of English Law, 7th edn, 1966–10th edn (as Geldart's Introduction to English Law), 1991, 11th edn 1995; Hanbury's English Courts of Law, 4th edn, 1967; Hanbury and Yardley, English Courts of Law, 5th edn, 1979; Principles of Administrative Law, 1981, 2nd edn, 1986; (with I. N. Stevens) The Protection of Liberty, 1982; contrib. Halsbury's Laws of England, and Atkin's Court Forms. *Recreations:* lawn tennis, opera, cats. *Address:* 9 Belbroughton Road, Oxford OX2 6UZ. *T:* (01865) 554831. *Club:* Royal Air Force.

YARMOUTH, Earl of; William Francis Seymour; *b* 2 Nov. 1993; *s* and *heir* of Marquess of Hertford, *qv*.

YARNOLD, Rev. Edward John, SJ; DD; Tutor in Theology, Campion Hall, Oxford, since 1964 (Master, 1965–72; Senior Tutor, 1972–74); *b* 14 Jan. 1926; *s* of Edward Cabré Yarnold and Agnes (*née* Deakin). *Educ:* St Michael's Coll., Leeds; Campion Hall, Oxford (MA); Heythrop College (STL). Taught classics at St Francis Xavier's Coll., Liverpool, 1954–57; ordained, 1960; taught classics at St Michael's Coll., Leeds, 1962–64; Res. Lectr, Oxford Univ., 1991–. Sarum Lectr, Univ. of Oxford, 1972–73; Lectr (part-time), Heythrop Coll., London, 1978–80; Vis. Prof., Univ. of Notre Dame, 1982–; Murray Vis. Prof. of Catholic Thought, Univ. of Toledo, Ohio, 1995; Francis P. Wade Vis. Prof. in Theology, Marquette Univ., 1997; Vis. Scholar, Seton Hall Univ., NJ, 1999. Gen. Sec., Ecumenical Soc. of Blessed Virgin Mary, 1994–97 (Associate Gen. Sec., 1975–94); Mem., Anglican-Roman Catholic Internat. Commn, 1970–81 and 1983–91; Pres., Catholic Theol. Assoc. of GB, 1986–88. Order of St Augustine, 1981. *Publications:* The Theology of Original Sin, 1971; The Awe-Inspiring Rites of Initiation, 1972; The Second Gift, 1974; (with H. Chadwick) Truth and Authority, 1977; (ed jtly and contrib.) The Study of Liturgy, 1978; They are in Earnest, 1982; Eight Days with the Lord, 1984; (ed jtly and contrib.) The Study of Spirituality, 1986; In Search of Unity, 1989; Time for God, 1991; (ed jtly and contrib.) Anglicans and Roman Catholics: the search for unity, 1994; (ed jtly and contrib.) Anglican Orders: the documents in the debate, 1997; Cyril of Jerusalem, 2000; (ed jtly and contrib.) Studia Patristica, vols xxxiv–xxxviii, 2001; articles in learned jls. *Recreations:* opera, cricket. *Address:* Campion Hall, Oxford OX1 1QS. *T:* (01865) 286111, *Fax:* (01865) 286148; *e-mail:* edward.yarnold@campion.ox.ac.uk.

YARNOLD, Patrick; HM Diplomatic Service, retired; professional genealogist; *b* 21 March 1937; *s* of late Leonard Francis Yarnold and Gladys Blanche Yarnold (*née* Merry); *m* 1961, Caroline, *er d* of late Andrew J. Martin; two *d*. *Educ:* Bancroft's School. HM Forces, 1955–57. Joined HM Foreign (now Diplomatic) Service, 1957; served: FO, 1957–60; Addis Ababa, 1961–64; Belgrade, 1964–66; FO (later FCO), 1966–70; 1st Sec., Head of Chancery, Bucharest, 1970–73; 1st Sec. (Commercial), Bonn, 1973–76; FCO, 1976–79; Counsellor (Economic and Commercial), Brussels, 1980–83; Consul-Gen., Zagreb, 1983–85; Counsellor and Head of Chancery, Belgrade, 1985–87; Hd of Defence Dept, FCO, 1987–90; Consul-Gen., Hamburg, 1990–94; Consul-Gen., Marseilles, 1995–97. *Recreations:* travel, photography, walking, local history, Chinese cooking, etc. *Address:* Cherry Cottage, The Street, Puttenham, Guildford, Surrey GU3 1AT.

YARRANTON, Sir Peter (George), Kt 1992; Chairman: Sports Council, 1989–94; Sports Partner Ltd, 1990–95; *b* 30 Sept. 1924; *s* of late Edward John Yarranton and Norah Ellen (*née* Atkins); *m* 1947, Mary Avena (*née* Flowitt); one *s* one *d*. *Educ:* Willesden Technical Coll. Prelim. ARIBA. Joined RAF, 1942; commnd 1944; Flying Officer, 1945; Flt Lieut, 1949; voluntarily retd, 1957. Shell Mex & BP Ltd: management trainee, 1957–58; Ops Officer, Reading, 1958–61; UK Indust. Relations Officer, 1961–63; i/c Indust. Relations, 1963–66; Manager, Indust. Relations, 1966–69; Regional Ops Manager, SE Region, 1969–75; Manager, Plant and Engrg, Distbn Div., Shell UK Oil, 1975–77; Gen. Manager, Lensbury Club, 1978–92. Founder Dir, London Docklands Arena Ltd, 1984–93; non-exec. Dir, Drug Check UK Ltd, 1995–. Consultant: Jet Heritage, 1994–96; Stuart Canvas Products, 1996–. Governor: Sports Aid Foundn, 1989–; London Marathon Ltd, 1989–94; Trustee, Golden Globe Charity Trust, 1990–93; Vice Pres., Comet Foundn, 1996–98. Fellow, 1979–, and Patron, 1998–, Recreation Managers Assoc.; President: Rugby Football Union, 1991–92 (Public Relations Advr to the Union, 1983–94); Lensbury RFC, 1978–; Wasps FC, 1982–85; Middx County RFU, 1986–88; England Internat. (5 caps), Rugby Union Football: *v* Ireland, New Zealand and Wales, 1954, Scotland and France 1955; played for and captained Barbarians, London, Mddx, Wasps, British Combined Services, and RAF Rugby Clubs; formerly: Mem., London and Mddx Premier Swimming and Water Polo Teams; Captain, RAF Swimming and Water Polo Teams. Patron: Royal Canoe Club Trust, 1993–; Cottesloe W Australia Veterans Surf Life Saving Assoc., 1999–; Trustee, Richmond Boat Project, 1992–97; Pres., The Great River Race, 1993–99. Chm., Sport Supports St John Ambulance Cttee, 1999–. Gov., Queen's Coll., Taunton, 1993–2000. Freeman, City of London, 1977; Liveryman, Worshipful Co. of Gold and Silver Wyre Drawers, 1977 (Mem., Court of Assts, 1987; Master, 2001). FIMgt (FBIM 1980); FIPD (FIPM 1975). Hon. DArts De Montfort, 1993. *Recreations:* all sports, indoor and outdoor, particularly Rugby, soccer, cricket, swimming, water polo and sub-aqua diving. *Address:* Broom Point, Broom Water West, Teddington, Middx TW11 9QH; 2 Sunnydale Villas, Durlston Road, Swanage, Dorset BH19 2HY. *Clubs:* East India, Royal Air Force.

YARROW, Dr Alfred, FFPHM; Honorary Member, Epidemiology Unit, Ministry of Health, Jerusalem, 1987–96; *b* 25 May 1924; *s* of Leah and step *s* of Philip Yarrow; *m* 1953, Sheila Kaufman; two *d*. *Educ:* Hackney Downs Grammar Sch.; Edinburgh Univ. (MB, ChB); London Sch. of Hygiene and Trop. Medicine (Hons DPH). Foundn FFCM (now FFPHM) 1972. Dep. Area MO, Tottenham and Hornsey, 1955–60; Area MO, SE Essex, 1960–65; MOH, Gateshead, 1965–68; Dir, Scottish Health Educn Unit, 1968–73; SMO, 1973–77, SPMO, 1977–84, DHSS. Temp. Consultant, WHO, 1975–76. Brit. Council Lectr, 1975; Council of Europe Fellow, 1978. *Publications:* So Now You Know About Smoking, 1975; Politics, Society and Preventive Medicine, 1986; scientific papers on demography, epidemiology, preventive medicine and health educn. *Recreations:* lawn bowls, travelling, reading. *Address:* 9/4 Nof Harim, Jerusalem 96190, Israel. *T:* 6438792.

YARROW, Sir Eric Grant, 3rd Bt *cr* 1916; MBE (mil.) 1946; DL; Chairman, Clydesdale Bank PLC, 1985–91 (Director 1962–91, Deputy Chairman, 1975–85); Director: Standard Life Assurance Co., 1958–91; National Australia Bank Ltd, 1987–91; *b* 23 April 1920; *o s* of Sir Harold Yarrow, 2nd Bt and 1st wife, Eleanor Etheldreda (*d* 1934); *S* father, 1962; *m* 1st, 1951, Rosemary Ann (*d* 1957), *yr d* of late H. T. Young, Roehampton, SW15; (one *s* decd); 2nd, 1959, Annette Elizabeth Françoise (marr. diss. 1975), *d* of late A. J. E. Steven, Ardgay; three *s* (including twin *s*); 3rd, 1982, Mrs Joan Botting, *d* of late R. F. Masters, Piddinghoe, Sussex. *Educ:* Marlborough Coll.; Glasgow Univ. Served apprenticeship, G. & J. Weir Ltd. Served Burma, 1942–45; Major RE, 1945. Asst Manager Yarrow & Co., 1946; Dir, 1948; Man. Dir, 1958–67; Chm., 1962–85; Pres., Yarrow PLC, 1985–87. Mem. Council, RINA, 1957–; Vice-Pres., 1965; Hon. Vice-Pres., 1972. Mem., General Cttee, Lloyd's Register of Shipping, 1960–87; Prime Warden, Worshipful Co. of Shipwrights, 1970; Deacon, Incorporation of Hammermen of Glasgow, 1961–62; Retired Mem. Council, Institution of Engineers & Shipbuilders in Scotland; Mem. Council, Inst. of Directors, 1983–90; Mem., Glasgow Action, 1985–91. Pres., Scottish Convalescent Home for Children, 1957–70; Hon. Pres., Princess Louise Scottish Hospital at Erskine, 1986– (Chm., 1980–86). President: British Naval Equipment Assoc., 1982–90; Smeatonian Soc. of Civil Engineers, 1983; Marlburian Club, 1984; Scottish Area, Burma Star Assoc., 1990–; Vice President: RHAS, 1990–91; Glasgow Br., RNLI, 1988–96; Chm., Blythe Sappers, 1989. DL Renfrewshire, 1970. OStJ. *Recreations:* golf, family life. *Heir: g s* Ross William Grant Yarrow, *b* 14 Jan. 1985. *Address:* Cloak, Kilmacolm, Renfrewshire PA13 4SD. *T:* (01505) 872067. *Clubs:* Army and Navy; Royal & Ancient Golf (St Andrews).

YARWOOD, Michael Edward, OBE 1976; entertainer, since 1962; *b* 14 June 1941; *s* of Wilfred and Bridget Yarwood; *m* 1969, Sandra Burville (marr. diss. 1987); two *d*. *Educ:* Bredbury Secondary Modern Sch., Cheshire. First television appearance, 1963; *BBC TV:* Three of a Kind, 1967; Look—Mike Yarwood, and Mike Yarwood in Persons (series), 1971–82; *ATV:* Will the Real Mike Yarwood Stand Up? (series), 1968; *Thames:* Mike Yarwood in Persons, 1983–84; Yarwood's Royal Variety Show, the Yarwood Chat Show, and Mike Yarwood in Persons, 1986; *stage:* Royal Variety performances, 1968, 1972, 1976, 1981, 1987, 1993; One for the Pot, UK tour, 1988. Variety Club of Gt Britain award for BBC TV Personality of 1973; Royal Television Society award for outstanding creative achievement in front of camera, 1978. Mem., Grand Order of Water Rats, 1968. *Publications:* And This Is Me, 1974; Impressions of my life (autobiog.), 1986. *Recreations:* golf, tennis. *Address:* c/o International Artistes Ltd, 235 Regent Street, W1R 8AX. *Club:* Lord's Taverners.

YASS, Irving, CB 1993; Director, Policy and Transport, London First, since 1999 (Director, Transport and Planning, 1995–99); *b* 20 Dec. 1935; *s* of late Abraham and Fanny Yass; *m* 1962, Marion Leighton; two *s* one *d*. *Educ:* Harrow County Grammar School for Boys; Balliol Coll., Oxford (Brackenbury Schol.; BA). Assistant Principal, Min. of Transport and Civil Aviation, 1958; Private Sec. to Joint Parliamentary Secretary, 1960; HM Treasury, 1967–70; Asst Secretary, Dept of the Environment, 1971; Secretary, Cttee of Inquiry into Local Govt Finance, 1974–76; Dept of Transport, 1976–94 (Under Sec., 1982); Dir, Planning and Transport, Govt Office for London, 1994–95. *Address:* London First, 1 Hobhouse Court, Suffolk Street, SW1Y 4HH. *T:* (020) 7665 1589.

YASSUKOVICH, Stanislas Michael, CBE 1991; Chairman, Easdaq, since 1997; *b* 5 Feb. 1935; adopted British nationality, 1993; *s* of Dimitri and Denise Yassukovich; *m* 1961, Diana (*née* Townsend); two *s* one *d*. *Educ:* Deerfield Academy; Harvard University. US Marine Corps, 1957–61. Joined White, Weld & Co., 1961: posted to London, 1962; Branch Manager, 1967; General Partner, 1969; Managing Director, 1969; European Banking Co. Ltd: Managing Director, 1973; Group Dep. Chm., 1983. Sen. Advr, Merrill Lynch & Co., 1989–90; Dir, Merrill Lynch Europe Ltd, 1985–90 (Chm., 1985–90); Chairman: Park Place Capital, 1991–; Henderson Euro Trust PLC, 1992–; Hemingway Properties, 1993–; Gallo & Co., 1995–; Manek Investment Management, 1998–; Vice-Chm., Bristol & West plc, 1991–; Deputy Chairman: ABC Internat. Bank, 1993–; Flextech, 1997– (Chm., 1989–97); Director: Mossiman's Ltd, 1989–; Henderson plc, 1991–98; SW Water, 1992– (Dep. Chm., 1997–); Tradepoint Financial Network, 1997–. Jt Dep. Chm., Internat. Stock Exchange, 1986–89; Chm., Securities Assoc., 1988–91. Chairman: City Res. Project, 1991–95; City Disputes Panel, 1994–. *Publications:* articles in financial press. *Recreations:* hunting, shooting, polo. *Address:* S. M. Yassukovich & Co. Ltd, 42 Berkeley Square, W1X 5DB. *T:* (020) 7318 0825. *Clubs:* Buck's, White's, Turf; Travellers (Paris); Brook (New York).

YATES, Alfred, CBE 1983; FBPsS; Director, National Foundation for Educational Research in England and Wales, 1972–83; *b* 17 Nov. 1917; *s* of William Oliver Yates and Frances Yates; *m* 1st, 1943, Joan Mary Lawrence-Fellows (*d* 1987); one *s* one *d*; 2nd, 1989, Elsie Roberts. *Educ:* Farnworth Grammar Sch.; Sheffield Univ. (BA); Oxford Univ. (MA); QUB (MEd). FBPsS 1957. Served War, Army, 1940–46: Captain, REME. Schoolmaster, Launceston Coll., Cornwall, 1939–40; Lectr, QUB, 1946–51; Sen. Res. Officer, NFER, 1951–59; Sen. Tutor, Dept of Educnl Studies, Oxford Univ., 1959–72. FCP 1981. *Publications:* Admission to Grammar Schools, 1957; Grouping in Education, 1966; An Introduction to Educational Measurement, 1968; The Role of Research in Educational Change, 1971; The Organisation of Schooling, 1971. *Recreations:* reading, theatre, watching Association football and cricket. *Address:* 12 Sharples Hall Fold, Sharples, Bolton BL1 7EH. *T:* (01204) 595642.

YATES, Anne; *see* Yates, E. A.

YATES, Anthony David; Warden, Robinson College, Cambridge, since 2001; *b* 5 May 1946; *s* of Cyril Yates and Violet Ethel Yates (*née* Mann); *m* 1st, 1974, Carolyn Paula Hamilton (marr. diss. 1988); 2nd, 1992, Susanna Margaret McGarry. *Educ:* Bromley Grammar Sch. for Boys; St Catherine's Coll., Oxford (Exhibnr; BA 1967, MA 1971). Admitted solicitor, 1972; Lecturer in Law: Univ. of Hull, 1969–72; Univ. of Bristol, 1972–74; University of Manchester: Lectr in Law, 1974–76; Sen. Lectr, 1976–78; Principal, Dalton Hall, 1975–80; Foundn Prof. of Law, 1979–87, Dean, Sch. of Law, 1979–84, and Pro-Vice-Chancellor, 1985–87, Univ. of Essex; Dir, Professional Develt, 1987–93, Dir of Strategy, 1993–97, Partner, 1993–2001, and Chief Operating Officer, 1997–2001, Baker & McKenzie. Visiting Professor: Univ. of Manchester, 1979; Univ. of NSW, 1995; Parsons Vis. Fellow, Univ. of Sydney, 1995. Mem. Council, Law Soc., 1992–97. *Publications:* Exclusion Clauses in Contracts, 1978, 2nd edn 1982; Leases of Business Premises, 1979; (with A. J. Hawkins) Landlord and Tenant Law, 1981, 2nd edn 1986; (with A. J. Hawkins) Standard Business Contracts, 1986; (Ed. in Chief) The Carriage of Goods by Land, Sea and Air, annually 1993–. *Recreations:* opera, food, wine, Rugby football. *Address:* Warden's Lodge, Robinson College, Cambridge CB3 9AF. *Clubs:* Oxford and Cambridge, Royal Commonwealth Society.

YATES, Brian Douglas; Chairman, Consumers' Association, since 1994; *b* 1 May 1944; *s* of Bertram Yates and Barbara (*née* Wenham); *m* 1971, Patricia, *d* of Arthur Hutchinson, DFC; one *s*. *Educ:* Uppingham Sch.; Clare Coll., Cambridge (MA); London Business Sch. (MBA). CEng; Eur Ing. RHP Bearings, 1973–81; Thorn EMI, 1981–85; Dexion, 1985–88; Morris Material (formerly Morris Mechanical) Handling, 1988–. Member: Northampton BC, 1979–83; Hampshire CC, 1985–89. Member: Council, Consumers' Assoc., 1986–; Professional Conduct Cttee, GMC, 2001–. Mem., Lunar Soc., Birmingham. FRSA. *Recreations:* tennis, cross country ski-ing. *Address:* 19 Park Avenue, Harpenden AL5 2DZ. *T:* (01582) 768484. *Clubs:* Royal Over-Seas League; Hatfield House Tennis, Harpenden Lawn Tennis.

YATES, Prof. David William, FRCS; Professor of Emergency Medicine, University of Manchester, since 1990; *b* 19 Nov. 1941; *o s* of Bill and Lena Yates; *m* 1977, Veronica Mary Henderson; two *s*. *Educ:* Bradford Grammar Sch.; Emmanuel Coll., Cambridge (MB BChir 1967; MD 1990); St Thomas's Hosp., London. FRCS 1972. Med. posts in orthopaedic surgery; first Prof. of Emergency Medicine in UK, 1990. Dean, Faculty of A&E Medicine, RCS. *Address:* Hope Hospital, Salford M6 8HD. *T:* (0161) 787 4842.

YATES, Edgar; *see* Yates, W. E.

YATES, (Edith) Anne, (Mrs S. J. Yates), CBE 1972; *b* 21 Dec. 1912; *d* of William Blakeman and Frances Dorothea (*née* Thacker); *m* 1935, Stanley James Yates (*d* 1990); one *s* one *d* (and one *s* decd). *Educ:* Barrs' Hill Girls' Sch., Coventry. Nottinghamshire County Council: Mem., 1955–93; Alderman, 1966; Chm., 1968–74; Leader, Cons. Gp, 1991–92. Mem., BTEC Bd for Distribution, Hotel and Catering and Leisure Services, 1984–88. Chairman: E Midlands Tourist Bd, 1971–76; E Midlands Sports Council, 1972–77; Indep. Chm., Nat. Cttee on Recreation Management Trng, 1976–82 (Yates Report, 1984); Member: Sports Council, 1971–74; E Midlands Council of Sport and Recreation, 1977–82; MSC, 1974–76; E Midlands Regional MSC, 1977–82; English Tourist Bd, 1975–81; Nat. Water Council, 1973–79 (Chm., Water Training Cttee, 1973–79). Life Vice Pres., Inst. of Trading Standards Admin, 1965. Chm., Notts Internat. Rowing Regatta, 1987–90; Mem., Sports Aid Foundn, 1984–94; Chm., Sports Aid Foundn (E Midlands), 1990–94. *Recreations:* reading, music, theatre. *Address:* Manor Court, Rolleston, Newark, Notts NG23 5SE. *T:* (01636) 813362.

YATES, Ian Humphrey Nelson, CBE 1991; Director, 1989–90, Chief Executive, 1975–90, The Press Association Ltd; *b* 24 Jan. 1931; *s* of James Nelson Yates and Martha (*née* Nutter); *m* 1956, Daphne J. Hudson, MCSP; three *s*. *Educ:* Lancaster Royal Grammar Sch.; Canford Sch., Wimborne. Royal Scots Greys, Germany and ME (National Service Commn), 1951–53. Management Trainee, Westminster Press Ltd, 1953–58 (Westmorland Gazette, and Telegraph & Argus, Bradford); Asst to Man. Dir, King & Hutchings Ltd, Uxbridge, 1958–60; Bradford and District Newspapers: Asst Gen. Man., 1960; Gen. Man., 1964; Man. Dir, 1969–75; Dir, Westminster Press Planning Div., 1969–75. Chairman: Universal News Services Ltd, 1988–90; Tellex Monitors Ltd, 1988–90; CRG Communications Gp Ltd, 1990–. President: Young Newspapermen's Assoc., 1966; Yorks Newspaper Soc., 1968. Member: Council, Newspaper Soc., 1970–75; Council, Commonwealth Press Union, 1977–90; Pres., Alliance of European News Agencies, 1987–88 (Chm., New Media Cttee, 1984–89). FRSA 1989. *Recreations:* walking, reading, theatre.

YATES, Ivan R., CBE 1982; FREng; independent consultant; Deputy Chief Executive, 1986–90, Director, 1981–90, British Aerospace PLC; *b* 22 April 1929; *m* 1967, Jennifer Mary Holcombe; one *s* one *d*. *Educ:* Liverpool Collegiate Sch.; Liverpool Univ. (BEng 1st Class Hons). FIMechE; FRAeS 1968; FREng (FEng 1983); FAIAA 1984. Graduate Apprentice, English Electric, Preston, 1950; Chief Project Engr, TSR-2, 1959; Project Manager, Jaguar, 1966; British Aircraft Corporation: Special Dir, Preston Div., 1970; Dir, Preston, Warton Div., 1973; Dir, Aircraft Projects, 1974; Director: SEPECAT SA, 1976; Panavia GmbH, 1977; Eurofighter GmbH, 1986–90; British Aerospace: Man. Dir, Warton, 1978; Dir of Engrg and Project Assessment, Aircraft Gp, 1981; Chief Exec., Aircraft Gp, 1982–85; Dep. Man. Dir (Aircraft), 1985–86. Vis. Prof. in Design, Cambridge Univ., 1991–; By-Fellow, Churchill Coll., Cambridge, 1992–. Mem., Technology Requirements Bd, 1985–; Advr, H of C Sci. and Technol. Cttee, 1993–94. Pres., 1988–89, Dep. Pres., 1989–90, SBAC; Mem. Council, RAeS, 1986–91. Member: Design Council, 1990–99; Council, RUSI, 1989–93. Commissioner, Royal Commn for Exhibn of 1851, 1990–99. Mem. Council, Imperial Coll., 1991–99. CIMgt; FRSA 1985. Foreign Mem., Royal Swedish Acad. of Engrg Scis, 1990. Hon. DSc: Loughborough, 1989; City, 1991. British Silver Medal, 1979, Gold Medal, 1985, RAeS. *Publications:* Innovation, Investment and Survival of UK Economy, 1993; numerous papers and lectures. *Recreations:* walking, ski-ing, painting, music. *Fax:* (office) (01273) 480695; *e-mail:* associates@iryates.globalnet.co.uk. *Club:* Athenæum.

YATES, Rt Rev. John; Bishop of Gloucester, 1975–91; *b* 17 April 1925; *s* of late Frank and Edith Ethel Yates; *m* 1st, 1954, Jean Kathleen Dover (*d* 1995); one *s* two *d*; 2nd, 1998, Rev. Mrs Beryl Kathleen Wensley. *Educ:* Battersea Grammar School; Blackpool Grammar School; Jesus College, Cambridge (MA). RAFVR (Aircrew), 1943–47; University of Cambridge, 1947–49; Lincoln Theological College, 1949–51. Curate, Christ Church, Southgate, 1951–54; Tutor and Chaplain, Lincoln Theological College, 1954–59; Vicar, Bottesford-with-Ashby, 1959–65; Principal, Lichfield Theological College, 1966–72; Bishop Suffragan of Whitby, 1972–75; Head, Archbp of Canterbury's staff (with title of Bp at Lambeth), 1991–94. Chm., Gen. Synod Bd for Social Responsibility, 1987–91. Hon. DLitt CNAA, 1992. *Address:* 15 Abbotts Ann Road, Winchester, Hants SO22 6ND.

YATES, Peter (James); film director/producer and theatre director; *b* 24 July 1929; *s* of Col Robert L. Yates and Constance Yates; *m* 1960, Virginia Pope; two *s* one *d* (and one *d* decd). *Educ:* Charterhouse; Royal Academy of Dramatic Art. Entered film industry, 1956. *Films directed:* Summer Holiday, 1962; One Way Pendulum, 1964; Robbery, 1966; Bullitt, 1968; John and Mary, 1969; Murphy's War, 1970; The Hot Rock, 1971; The Friends of Eddie Coyle, 1972; For Pete's Sake, 1973; Mother, Jugs and Speed, 1975; The Deep, 1976; Breaking Away (dir and prod.), 1979 (nominated 1980 Academy Awards, Director and Producer); The Janitor (dir and prod.), 1980; Krull, 1982; The Dresser (dir and prod.), 1983 (nominated 1984 Academy Awards, Dir and Producer); Eleni, 1985; The House on Carroll Street (dir and prod.), 1986; Suspect, 1987; An Innocent Man, 1989; Year of the Comet, 1991; Roommates, 1993; The Run of the Country, 1996; Curtain Call, 1997. *Theatre directed:* The American Dream, Royal Court, 1961; The Death of Bessie Smith, (London) 1961; Passing Game, (New York) 1977; Interpreters, (London) 1985. *Recreations:* tennis, sailing, skiing. *Address:* c/o William Morris Agency, 151 El Camino Drive, Beverley Hills, CA 90212, USA. *Club:* Garrick.

YATES, William; The Administrator of Christmas Island, Indian Ocean, 1982–83; *b* 15 September 1921; *er s* of late William Yates and of Mrs John T. Renshaw, Burrells, Appleby, Westmorland; *m* 1st, 1946, Hon. Rosemary (marr. diss. 1955), *yr d* of 1st Baron Elton; two *d* (one *s* decd); 2nd, 1957, Camilla, *d* of late E. W. D. Tennant, Orford House, Ugley, Bishop's Stortford; four *s*. *Educ:* Uppingham; Hertford Coll., Oxford. Served War, 1940–45, North Africa and Italy; Captain The Bays, 1945. Shropshire Yeomanry, 1956–67. Appointed Legal Officer to report on State lands in Department of Custodian's Office in Tripoli, Libya, 1951. MP (C) The Wrekin Division of Shropshire, 1955–66. Myron Taylor Lectures in International Affairs, Cornell Univ., USA, 1958 and 1966. MP (L) Holt, Vic, Aust. Commonwealth, 1975–80; Mem. Liberal Party Parly Cttee for Defence and Foreign Affairs, 1975–80; Mem., Cttee of Privileges, House of Representatives, 1977–80. Mem., Inst. of Internat. Affairs, Victoria. *Address:* The Old House, Old Tallangatta, Vic 3700, Australia. *Clubs:* Cavalry and Guards; Commonwealth (Canberra).

YATES, Prof. (William) Edgar, MA, PhD; Professor of German, University of Exeter, since 1972; *b* 30 April 1938; *s* of Douglas Yates and Doris Yates (*née* Goode); *m* 1963, Barbara Anne Fellowes; two *s*. *Educ:* Fettes Coll. (Foundn Schol.); Emmanuel Coll., Cambridge (Minor Open Schol.; MA, PhD). 2nd Lieut, RASC, 1957–58. Lectr in German, Univ. of Durham, 1963–72; University of Exeter: Hd of Dept of German, 1972–86; Dep. Vice-Chancellor, 1986–89. Vice-Chm., Conf. of Univ. Teachers of German, 1991–93. Lewis Fry Meml Lectr, Univ. of Bristol, 1994. Vice Pres., Wiener Shakespeare-Ges., 1992–; Member: Cttee, MHRA, 1980–; Council, English Goethe Soc., 1984–; Council, Internat. Nestroy-Ges., 1986– (Vice-Pres., 1997–). Germanic Editor, MLR, 1981–88; Editor, Nestroyana, 1992–; Co-ordinating Gen. Editor, historisch-kritische Nestroy-Ausgabe, 1992–. Corresp. Mem., Austrian Acad. of Scis, 1995. Gov., Exeter Sch., 1986– (Vice Chm., 1992–94, Chm., 1994–). J. G. Robertson Prize, Univ. of London, 1975. *Publications:* Grillparzer: a critical introduction, 1972; Nestroy: satire and parody in Viennese popular comedy, 1972; Humanity in Weimar and Vienna: the continuity of an ideal, 1973; Tradition in the German Sonnet, 1981; Schnitzler, Hofmannsthal, and the Austrian Theatre, 1992; Nestroy and the Critics, 1994; Theatre in Vienna 1776–1995: a critical history, 1996; (with B. Pargner) Nestroy in München, 2001; *edited:* Hofmannsthal: Der Schwierige, 1966; Grillparzer: Der Traum ein Leben, 1968; Nestroy: Stücke 12-14 (Hist.-krit. Ausgabe), 1981–82, Stücke 34, 1989, Stücke 18/1, 1991, Stücke 22, 1996, Stücke 17/2, 1998, (jtly) Stücke 2, 2000; (jtly) Viennese Popular Theatre, 1985; (jtly) Grillparzer und die europäische Tradition, 1987; Vom schaffenden zum edierten Nestroy, 1994; Nestroys Reserve und andere Notizen, 2000; (jtly) From Perinet to Jelinek, 2001; numerous articles on Austrian literary and cultural history, on German literature of the Biedermeier period, and on German lyric poetry; *festschrift:* The Austrian Comic Tradition, 1998. *Recreations:* music, theatre. *Address:* 7 Clifton Hill, Exeter EX1 2DL. *T:* (01392) 254713.

YATES, William Hugh; Senior Partner, Knight Frank (formerly Knight Frank & Rutley), 1992–96; *b* 18 Dec. 1935; *s* of late Brig. Morris Yates, DSO, OBE and Kathleen Rosanna Yates (*née* Sherbrooke, later Mrs Hugh Cowan); *m* 1st, 1963, Celia Geraldine Pitman (marr. diss. 1972); one *s*; 2nd, 1979, Elizabeth Susan Mansel-Pleydell (*née* Luard); four step *s*. *Educ:* Lancing Coll.; RMA Sandhurst. FRICS. Commissioned, Royal Dragoons, 1955; ADC to Governor of Aden, 1959. Articled surveyor, Rylands & Co., 1961; Knight Frank & Rutley, 1964–96: Man. Dir, Geneva, 1968–72; Partner, 1972; Man. Partner, 1978–82; Head of Residential Div., 1982–92. Director: INCAS SA, 1970–78; European Property Investment Co. NV, 1973–81; Ecclesiastical Insurance Group, 1985– (Dep. Chm., 1995–); Woolwich plc (formerly Woolwich Building Soc.), 1990–2000 (Dep. Chm., 1996–2000). Save the Children Fund: Chm., Fund Raising Cttee, 1980–86; Hon. Treasurer, 1986–92. *Recreations:* riding, gardening, golf, music. *Address:* Upper Farm, Milton Lilbourne, Pewsey, Wilts SN9 5LQ. *T:* (01672) 563438. *Clubs:* Turf; Wentworth Golf.

YATIM, Datuk Dr Rais, DSNS (Malaysia) 1978; Advocate and Solicitor of the High Court of Malaya; *b* 15 April 1942; *s* of Yatim Tahir and Siandam Boloh; *m* 1975, Datin Masnah; three *s* one *d*. *Educ:* Language Inst., Kuala Lumpur (DipEd 1964; DipPsych); Univ. of Singapore (LLB (Hons) 1973); PhD London, 1994. Specialist language teacher, Northern Illinois Univ., 1964–66. Parly Sec., Min. of Youth, 1974; Dep. Law Minister, 1976; Dep. Home Minister, 1977; Chief Minister, State of Negeri Sembilan, 1978–82; Minister of Land Regl Develt, Malaysia, 1982–84; Minister of Information, 1984–86; Foreign Minister, 1986–87. Dep. Pres., Parti Melayu, 1989–96. Returned to law practice in Kuala Lumpur, 1987–. Founder Pres., PEMADAM, Malaysia's Anti-Drug Assoc., 1976–87. Member: Civil Liberty Cttee, Bar Council, Kuala Lumpur, 1996–; Internet Soc., Washington. *Publications:* Faces in the Corridors of Power: a pictorial depiction of Malaysians in power and authority, 1987; Freedom Under Executive Power in Malaysia, 1995. *Recreations:* photography, jogging, travel, writing. *Address:* (residence) 41 Road 12, Taman Grandview, Ampang Jaya, 68000 Ampang, Selangor Darul Ehsan, Malaysia. *T:* (3) 4569621. *Club:* Darul Ehsan Recreational (Kuala Lumpur).

YAXLEY, John Francis, CBE 1990; HM Overseas Civil Service, 1961–94, retired; *b* 13 Nov. 1936; *s* of late Rev. Canon R. W. and of Dorothy Yaxley; *m* 1960, Patricia Anne Scott; one *s*. *Educ:* Hatfield Coll., Durham Univ. National Service, 1958–60. Joined HMOCS, 1961; posts in New Hebrides and Solomon Islands, 1961–75; seconded FCO, 1975–77; Hong Kong, 1977–89: posts included Dir of Industry, Sec. for Econ. Services, and Dep. Financial Sec.; Comr, Hong Kong Govt, London, 1989–93. Mem., Salvation Army Nat. Adv. Bd, 1990–98; Chm., Oxford Diocesan Bd of Finance, 1996–2001. Mem. Council, Durham Univ., 1995–2001; Mem. Governing Body, Hatfield Coll., Durham, 1997–. Treasurer: W Mercia NADFAS, 1995–2000; Northleach DFAS, 2001–. Trustee, Triumph over Phobia UK, 1995–2000. *Publications:* The Population of the New Hebrides (with Dr Norma McArthur), 1968; (ed) Public Sector Reform in the Hong Kong Government, 1989. *Recreations:* walking, birdwatching, history, gardening. *Address:* Old Housing, Fifield, Oxon OX7 6HF. *Club:* Royal Over-Seas League.

YELLAND, David Ian; Editor, The Sun, since 1998; *b* Harrogate, 14 May 1963; *s* of John Michael Yelland and Patricia Ann (*née* McIntosh); *m* 1996, Tania Farrell; one *s*. *Educ:* Brigg Grammar Sch., Lincs; Coventry Univ. (BA Hons Econs 1984). Grad. trainee, Westminster Press, 1985; trainee reporter, Buckinghamshire Advertiser, 1985–87; industrial reporter, Northern Echo, 1987–88; gen. news and business reporter, North West Times and Sunday Times, 1988–89; city reporter, Thomson Regl Newspapers, 1989–90; joined News Corporation, 1990: city reporter, city editor and NY corresp., The Sun, 1990–93; Dep. Business Ed., Business Ed., Dep. Ed., New York Post, 1993–98. *Address:* The Sun, 1 Virginia Street, E1 1XY. *T:* (020) 7782 4000. *Club:* Royal Automobile.

YELLOWLEES, Sir Henry, KCB 1975 (CB 1971); Chief Medical Officer, Department of Health and Social Security, Department of Education and Science and Home Office, 1973–83; *b* 1919; *s* of late Henry Yellowlees, OBE, Psychiatrist of Bath; *m* 1st, 1948, Gwyneth (Sally) Comber (*née* Maddox); one *s* two *d*; 2nd, 2001, Mary Porter (*née* McGowan). *Educ:* Stowe Sch.; University Coll., Oxford (MA, BM, BCh 1950). FRCP 1971 (MRCP 1966, LRCP 1950); FFCM 1972; FRCS 1983 (MRCS 1950); FRCPE 1993. Pilot, RAF, 1941–45. Resident Med. Officer, Mddx Hosp., London, 1951–54; Asst Senior Med. Officer, South West Regional Hosp. Bd, 1954–59; Dep. Sen. Admin. Med. Officer, North West Metropolitan Regional Hosp. Bd, 1959–63; Principal Med. Officer, Min. of Health, 1963–65 (seconded); Senior Principal Med. Officer, 1965–67 (established); Dep. Chief Med. Officer, 1967–72, 2nd Chief Med. Officer, 1972–73, Dept of Health and Social Security. Consultant, MoD, 1985; Occasional Consultant, European Reg., WHO, 1985–95. Chm., WHO Commn to investigate health care of Bulgarian citizens arriving in Turkey, 1989. Member: Medical Research Council, 1974–83; Gen. Medical Council, 1979–89; Health Services Supervisory Bd, 1983; Council, BMA, 1986–90; Council, British Nutrition Foundn, 1973–95. Hon. FRCP Glasgow, 1974; Hon. FRCPsych, 1977; Fellow Brit. Inst. of Management, 1974–83; Vice-Pres., Mental After-Care Assoc.; Hon. Mem., Nat. Assoc. of Clinical Tutors. *Address:* 33 Lea Road, Harpenden, Herts AL5 4PQ.

YELTON, Michael Paul; His Honour Judge Yelton; a Circuit Judge, since 1998; *b* 21 April 1950; *s* of Joseph William Yelton and Enid Hazel Yelton; *m* 1973, Judith Sara Chaplin; two *s* one *d*. *Educ:* Colchester Royal Grammar Sch.; Corpus Christi Coll., Cambridge (BA 1971; MA 1973). Called to the Bar, Middle Temple, 1972; in practice at the Bar, 1973–98; Fellow and Dir of Studies in Law, Corpus Christi Coll., Cambridge, 1977–81. *Publication:* Fatal Accidents: a practical guide to compensation, 1998. *Recreations:* ecclesiology, history of road passenger transport, Association football. *Address:* Southend County Court, Tylers Avenue, Southend-on-Sea SS1 2AW. *T:* (01702) 601991.

YELTSIN, Boris Nikolayevich; President, Russian Federation, 1991–99, and Supreme Commander-in-Chief of the Armed Forces, 1992–99; *b* Sverdlovsk, 1 Feb. 1931; *m* Naina Iosifovna (*née* Grinyova); two *d*. *Educ:* Urals Polytechnic Inst. (Construction Engr Dip., 1955). Foreman, then chief of works, chief engr, head of construction admin, Yushgorstvoy trust, 1955–63; chief engr, dir, Sverdlovsk house building complex, 1963–68. Mem., CPSU, 1961–90: Sec., Sverdlovsk regl cttee, 1968–76; First Sec., Dist Central Cttee, Sverdlosk, 1976–85; Mem., Party Central Cttee, 1981; Sec., Central Cttee, 1985–86 (Hd, Construction Dept); First Sec., Moscow Party Cttee, 1985–87; Candidate Mem., Politburo, 1986–88; First Dep. Chm., State Cttee for Construction, 1987–89; Chm., Cttee for Construction and Architecture, 1989–90; Mem., Congress of People's Deputies, 1989–91. Chairman: Supreme Soviet, RSFSR, 1990–91; Russian Fedn, 1991–92; Commonwealth of Ind. States, 1993–99. *Publications:* Against the Grain (autobiog.), 1990; Three Days, 1992; The View from the Kremlin (memoirs), 1994; Midnight Diaries (memoirs), 2000. *Address:* c/o The Kremlin, Moscow, Russia.

YENTOB, Alan; Director of Drama, Entertainment and Children's Programmes, BBC, since 2000; *b* 11 March 1947; *s* of Isaac Yentob and Flora Yentob (*née* Khazam); one *s* one *d* by Philippa Walker. *Educ:* King's School, Ely; Univ. of Grenoble; Univ. of Leeds (LLB). BBC general trainee, 1968; producer/director, 1970–; arts features, incl. Omnibus, and Arena (Best Arts Series, British Acad. Awards, 1982, 1983, 1984, BPG Awards, 1985); Editor, Arena, 1978–85; Co-Editor, Omnibus, 1985; Hd of Music and Arts, BBC TV, 1985–88; Controller: BBC2, 1988–93, responsible for progs incl. The Late Show, Have I Got News For You, Absolutely Fabulous, Rab C. Nesbitt; BBC1, 1993–96; Dir of Progs, BBC TV, 1996–97; Dir of Television, BBC, 1997–2000. Member: Bd of Directors, Riverside Studios, 1984–91; BFI Production Board, 1985–93; Council, English Stage Co., 1990–. Governor: Nat. Film School, 1988–; S Bank Bd, 1999–; Trustee: Architecture Foundn, 1992–; Timebank, 2001–; Kids Co. FRTS; Fellow, BFI, 1997. Hon. Fellow: RCA, 1987; RIBA, 1991. Programming Supremo of Year, Broadcast Prodn Awards, 1997. *Recreations:* swimming, books.

YEO, Rt Rev. (Christopher) Richard, JCD; OSB; Abbot of Downside, since 1998; *b* 7 July 1948; *s* of Peter and Patricia Yeo. *Educ:* Downside Sch.; Lincoln Coll., Oxford (MA); St Benet's Hall, Oxford; Pontifical Gregorian Univ., Rome (JCD). Entered monastery, 1970; ordained priest, 1976; Sec. of Abbot Primate of the Benedictines, 1980–86; Parish Priest, Bungay, 1986–93; Official, Congregation for Consecrated Life, 1993–98. *Publication:* The Structure and Content of Monastic Profession, 1982. *Address:* Downside Abbey, Stratton-on-the-Fosse, Radstock, Somerset BA3 4RH.

YEO, Diane Helen; Chief Executive, Sargent Cancer Care for Children (formerly Malcolm Sargent Cancer Fund for Children), since 1995; *b* 22 July 1945; *d* of Brian Harold Pickard, FRCS and Joan Daisy Pickard; *m* 1970, Timothy Stephen Kenneth Yeo, *qv*; one *s* one *d*. *Educ:* Blackheath High Sch.; London Univ.; Institut Français de Presse. BBC Radio, 1968–74; Africa Educnl Trust, 1974–79; Girl Guides' Assoc., 1979–82; YWCA, 1982–85; Dir, Inst. of Charity Fundraising Managers, 1985–88; Charity Comr, 1989–95. Consultant: Centre for Voluntary Organisation, LSE, 1988–; Centre for Charity and Trust Research, South Bank Univ., 1995–; Chm., Charity Standards Cttee, 1991–95; Member: Nathan Cttee on Effectiveness and the Voluntary Sector, 1989–90; Council and Audit Cttee, Advertising Standards Authy, 1997–; Adv. Council, NCVO, 1994–; Adv. Council, Voluntary Sector TV, 1995–. A Dir, Charity Appointments, 1985–96. Vice-Chm., NCVO/Charity Commn Cttee on Trng of Trustees, 1989– (report, On Trust, 1990). FICFM; FRSA. Paul Harris Fellow, Rotary Internat., 2000. *Publications:* contribs to professional jls. *Recreations:* tennis, photography, piano. *Address:* Sargent Cancer Care for Children, Griffin House, 161 Hammersmith Road, W6 8SG. *T:* (020) 8752 2800, *Fax:* (020) 8752 2806; *e-mail:* dianeyeo@sargent.org.

YEO, Douglas; Director, Shell Research Ltd, Thornton Research Centre, 1980–85; *b* 13 June 1925; *s* of Sydney and Hylda Yeo; *m* 1947, Joan Elisabeth Chell; two *d*. *Educ:* Secondary Sch., St Austell; University Coll., Exeter (BSc London). Expedn on locust control, Kenya, 1945. HMOCS, 1948–63; Tropical Pesticides Research Inst., Uganda and Tanzania, 1948–61 (Scientific Officer, 1948–51, Sen. Scientific Officer, 1951–57, Prin. Scientific Officer, 1957–61). Internat. African Migratory Locust Control Organisation, Mali: on secondment, 1958, 1960; Dir and Sec. Gen., 1961–63. Shell Research Ltd: Research Dir, Woodstock Agricultural Research Centre, 1963–69, Dir, 1969–76; Dir, Biosciences Lab., Sittingbourne, 1976–80. Mem. Council, RHBNC, London Univ., 1985–90. FIBiol. *Publications:* papers in Bulletin Ent. Res., Bull. WHO, Anti-Locust Bull., Qly Jl Royal Met. Soc., Jl Sci. Fd. Agric., Plant Protection Confs, etc. *Recreations:* sailing, hill walking, fishing. *Address:* Tremarne, Tremarne Close, Feock, Truro TR3 6SB.

YEO, Kok Cheang, CMG 1956; MD; MB; BS; DPH; DTM&H; *b* 1 April 1903; *s* of Yeo Kim Hong; *m* Florence, *d* of late Sir Robert Ho-tung, KBE; one *s* two *d*. *Educ:* Hong Kong University; Cambridge University; London School of Hygiene and Tropical Medicine. MB, BS, Hong Kong, 1925, MD, 1930; DTM&H (England) 1927; DPH, Cambridge, 1928. Assistant Medical Officer of Health, Hong Kong, 1928; Lecturer and Examiner in public health, Hong Kong University, 1936–37; Official JP 1938; Chinese Health Officer, senior grade, 1939–47; Deputy Director of Health Services, and Vice-Chairman of Urban Council, 1947–50; Deputy Director of Medical and Health Services, 1950–52; member of Legislative Council, Hong Kong, 1951–57; Director of Medical and Health Services, Hong Kong, 1952–58; part-time Professor of Social Medicine, Hong Kong University, 1952–58; retd 1958. *Address:* 10 Rowbarns, Battle, East Sussex TN33 0JQ.

YEO, Rt Rev. Richard; *see* Yeo, Rt Rev. C. R.

YEO, Timothy Stephen Kenneth; MP (C) Suffolk South, since 1983; *b* 20 March 1945; *s* of late Dr Kenneth John Yeo and Norah Margaret Yeo; *m* 1970, Diane Helen Pickard (*see* D. H. Yeo); one *s* one *d*. *Educ:* Charterhouse; Emmanuel Coll., Cambridge (Open Exhibnr 1962; MA 1971). Asst Treas., Bankers Trust Co., 1970–73; Director, Worcester Engineering Co. Ltd, 1975–86. Dir, Spastics Soc., 1980–83, Mem., Exec. Council, 1984–86. PPS to Sec. of State for Home Dept, 1988–89, to Sec. of State for Foreign Affairs, 1989–90; Parly Under Sec. of State, DoE, 1990–92, DoH, 1992–93; Minister of State, DoE, 1993–94. Opposition spokesman on local govt and envmt, 1997–98, on agric., 1998–2001; Shadow Culture, Media and Sport Sec., 2001–. Member: Social Services Select Cttee, 1985–88; Employment Select Cttee, 1994–96; Treasury Select Cttee, 1996–97; Jt Sec., Cons. Pty Finance Cttee, 1984–87. Captain, Parly Golfing Soc., 1991–95. Hon. Treasurer, International Voluntary Service, 1975–78. Trustee: African Palms, 1970–85; Tanzania Development Trust, 1980–97; Chm., Tadworth Court Trust, 1983–90. *Publication:* Public Accountability and Regulation of Charities, 1983. *Recreation:* skiing. *Address:* House of Commons, SW1A 0AA. *T:* (020) 7219 3000. *Clubs:* Sudbury Conservative (Sudbury); Royal St George's (Sandwich).

YEOMAN, Maj.-Gen. Alan, CB 1987; Director, Army Sport Control Board, 1988–95; *b* 17 Nov. 1933; *s* of George Smith Patterson Yeoman and Wilhelmina Tromans Elwell; *m* 1960, Barbara Joan Davies; two *s* (one *d* decd). *Educ:* Dame Allan's School, Newcastle upon Tyne. Officer Cadet, RMA Sandhurst, 1952; commnd Royal Signals, 1954; served Korea, Malaysia, Singapore, Cyprus, UK, BAOR and Canada, 1954–70 (Staff Coll., 1963); CO 2 Div. Sig. Regt, BAOR, 1970–73; HQ 1 (BR) Corps, BAOR, 1973–74; MoD, 1974–77; Col AQ, HQLF Cyprus, 1978–79; Comd Trng Gp, Royal Signals and Catterick Garrison, 1979–82; Brig. AQ, HQ 1 (BR) Corps, BAOR, 1982–84; Comd Communications, BAOR, 1984–87; retd 1988. Col Comdt, Royal Corps of Signals, 1987–93. Hon. Col, 37th (Wessex and Welsh) Signal Regt, T&AVR, 1987–95. Chm., Royal Signals Assoc., 1995–. *Recreations:* golf, cricket, ski-ing. *Address:* c/o Lloyds TSB, 3 South Street, Wareham, Dorset BH40 4LX.

YEOMAN, Prof. Michael Magson, PhD; FRSE; Regius Professor of Botany, 1978–93, now Emeritus, and Curator of Patronage, 1988–93, University of Edinburgh; *b* 16 May 1931; *s* of Gordon Yeoman and Mabel Ellen (*née* Magson), Newcastle upon Tyne; *m* 1962, Erica Mary Lines; two *d*. *Educ:* Gosforth Grammar Sch.; King's Coll., Univ. of Durham (BSc 1952, MSc 1954, PhD 1960); FRSE 1980. National Service, Royal Corps of Signals, 1954–56. Demonstrator in Botany, King's Coll., Newcastle upon Tyne, 1957–59; Edinburgh University: Lectr in Botany, 1960; Sen. Lectr, 1968; Reader, 1973; Dean, Fac. of Science, 1981–84; Vice-Principal, 1988–91. Vis. Prof., NENU, Changchun, China, 1986–. Chm., Univs Council for Adult and Continuing Educn (Scotland), 1989–91. Member: Governing Bodies, Nat. Vegetable Res. Stn and Scottish Plant Breeding Stn, 1978–82; SERC Biological Scis Cttee, 1982–85; SERC Biotechnology Management Cttee, 1983–85; British Nat. Cttee for Biology, 1981–89. Chm., Edinburgh Centre for Rural Res., 1989–93; Governor: East of Scotland Coll. of Agriculture, 1984–93; Scottish Crops Res. Inst., 1986–89. Chm. Trustees, Edinburgh Botanic Gdn (Sibbald) Trust, 1996– (Trustee, 1986); Trustee, Royal Botanic Gdn, Edinburgh, 1992–98 (Chm., Scientific Adv. Bd, 1995–98). Mem. Council, RSE, 1985–91 (Fellowship Sec., 1986–91). Gov. and Chm., Ellingham C of E First Sch., 1993–99; Churchwarden, St Maurice, Ellingham, 1996–2000. Member Editorial Board: Jl of Experimental Botany, 1981–85; Plant Science Letters, 1974–83; New Phytologist, 1977–93 (Trustee); Botanical Jl of Scotland, 1992–99. *Publications:* (ed) Cell Division in Higher Plants, 1976; (jtly) Laboratory Manual of Plant Cell and Tissue Culture, 1982; (ed) Plant Cell Technology, 1986; contrib. scientific jls; chapters, articles and revs in books. *Recreations:* military history, photography, gardening, walking. *Address:* 116 Allerburn Lea, Alnwick, Northumberland NE66 2QP. *T:* (01665) 605822.

YEOMANS, Lucy; Editor, Harpers & Queen, since 2000; *b* 1 Nov. 1970; *d* of Harry Hammond Light Yeomans and Margaret (*née* Boyle). *Educ:* Univ. of St Andrews (MA Hons Hist. of Art 1992). Ed., Boulevard mag., Paris, 1993–95; Lit. Ed. and Features Ed., The European, 1995–98; Features Ed., Dep. Ed. and Actg Ed., Tatler, 1998–2000. *Recreations:* theatre, horse-riding, music, poetry. *Address:* Harpers & Queen, National Magazine House, 72 Broadwick Street, W1V 2BP. *T:* (020) 7439 5000. *Club:* Soho House.

YEOMANS, Richard Millett, CEng, FIEE; FIMechE; Chief Executive, Scottish Nuclear Ltd, 1989–91; *b* 19 July 1932; *s* of late Maj. Richard J. Yeomans and Lillian (*née* Spray); *m* 1957, Jennifer Margaret Wingfield Pert; three *s* one *d*. *Educ:* Durban, SA; Cornwall Tech. Coll. CEng; FIEE; FIMechE. Student apprentice, CEGB, 1948. Lt, REME, 1953–55. CEGB power stations, 1955–67; South of Scotland Electricity Board: Dep. Manager, Longannet Power Stn, 1971–75; Manager, Inverkip Power Stn, 1975–77; Manager, Hunterston A&B Nuclear Power Stns, 1977–80; Generation Engineer (Nuclear), 1980–87; Chief Engineer, 1987–89. *Recreations:* sailing, golf, gardening. *Address:* Ashcraig, Skelmorlie, Ayrshire PA17 5HB. *T:* (01475) 520298.

YERBURGH, family name of **Baron Alvingham.**

YERBURGH, John Maurice Armstrong; Vice Lord-Lieutenant of Dumfries and Galloway (District of Stewartry), 1990–98; President, Daniel Thwaites PLC, since 1993 (Director, since 1947; Chairman, 1966–93); *b* 23 May 1923; *e s* of late Major Guy Yerburgh (*d* 1926), OBE, Belgian Croix de Guerre, Italian Croce di Guerra and Lady (Hilda Violet Helena) Salisbury-Jones, *e d* of Rt Hon. Sir Maurice de Bunsen, Bt, GCMG, GCVO, CB; *m* 1973, Ann Jean Mary, *d* of N. P. Maclaren, Brooklands, Crocketford, Dumfries; one *s* four *d*. *Educ:* Eton; Magdalene College, Cambridge (BA). Commissioned Irish Guards 1943; served with 2nd Bn, France, Holland, Belgium, Germany; retired 1947 with rank of Captain. Contested (C) Blackburn, 1959 and 1963. Chm., S of Scotland Regional Adv. Cttee, Forestry Commn, 1972–87; Governor, Cumbria College of Agriculture and Forestry, 1975–89; Shire Horse Society: Pres., 1983–84; Dep. Pres., 1988. DL Dumfries and Galloway (Dist of Stewartry), 1989. *Recreations:* shooting, fishing, trees. *Address:* Barwhillanty, Parton, Castle Douglas, Kirkcudbrightshire DG7 3NS. *T:* (01644) 470237.

YEUNG, Kai-yin, CBE 1993; JP; Chairman and Chief Executive, Kowloon-Canton Railway Corporation, since 1996; *b* 6 Jan. 1941; *s* of late K. F. Yeung and C. H. Lai; *m* 1964, Anna Lau; one *s* one *d*. *Educ:* Univ. of Hong Kong (BA Hons 1962). Joined Hong Kong Civil Service, 1962: staff appts, Hong Kong Admin. Service, 1962–73; Directorate rank, 1973–93; various appts at Asst and Dep. Head of Dept level, in trade, econ. develt and public finance, 1973–84; Comr, Hong Kong Export Credit Insce Corp., 1984–86; Dir Gen. of Industry, 1986–89; Sec. for Educn and Manpower, 1989–91; Sec. for the Treasury, 1991–93; Sec. for Transport, 1993, retd; Exec. Dir, Sino Land Co. Ltd, 1993–96. Dir, Hong Kong Community Chest, 1997–. Chm., Vocational Trng Council, 1998–; Mem. Long Term Housing Strategy Adv. Cttee, 1999–. Advr to govt of China on Hong Kong affairs, 1995–97. JP Hong Kong, 1976. *Recreations:* serious music, racing, golf. *Address:* Kowloon-Canton Railway Corporation, KCRC House, No 9 Lok King Street, Fo Tan, New Territories, Hong Kong. *Clubs:* Hong Kong, Hong Kong Jockey (Voting Mem.).

YEVTUSHENKO, Yevgeny Aleksandrovich; poet, novelist, film director, film actor, photographer; *b* 18 July 1933; *m*; five *s*; *m* 4th, 1986, Maria Novikova. *Educ:* Moscow Literary Inst., 1952–56 (expelled). Elected Mem., Congress of People's Deputies of USSR, 1989. Distinguished Professor: Queen's College, New York; University of Tulsa. Has visited 94 countries; Vice-Pres., Russian PEN, 1990–93; Hon. Mem., Amer. Acad. of Arts and Letters, 1987; Mem., European Acad. of Scis and Arts; hon. degrees from numerous Univs. Film actor: Take Off, 1979 (silver prize, Moscow Internat. film fest.); film director: Kindergarten, 1984; Stalin's Funeral, 1990. *Publications: in Russian:* Scouts of the Future, 1952; The Third Snow, 1955; The Highway of Enthusiasts, 1956; The Promise, 1959; The Apple, 1960; A Sweep of the Arm, 1962; Tenderness, 1962; Mail Boat, 1966; Bratsk Power Station, 1967; Kazan's University, 1971; A Father's Hearing, 1975; Morning People, 1978; Talent is not a Miracle by Chance (essays), 1980; Wild Berries Places (novel), 1981; Mother and Neutron Bomb and other poems, 1983; Almost at the End, 1986; A Wind of Tomorrow (essays), 1987; Selected Poetry, 3 vols, 1987; Don't Die Before You're Dead (novel), 1993; Late Tears (poetry), 1995; The Best from the Best (poetry), 1995; Strophes of the Century (anthology), 1995; God Could be Each of Us, 1996; If All Danes were Jews (play), 1996; Wolf's Passport (memoirs), 1998; words to Shostakovich's 13th Symphony and Execution of Stepan Razin Oratorio; *in English:* Zima Junction, 1961; A Precocious Autobiography, 1963; Bratsk Power Station, 1966; Stolen Apples, 1972; From Desire to Desire, 1976; The Face Behind the Face, 1979; Dove in Santiago, 1982; Invisible Threads (photography), 1981; Wild Berries (novel), 1984; Ardabiola (novel), 1985; Almost at the End, 1987; Divided Twins (photography), 1987; Last Attempt, 1988; Politics—everybody's privilege (essays), 1990; Collected Poems 1952–90, 1991; Fatal Half Measures, 1991; (ed) Twentieth-Century Russian Poetry, 1993; Pre-morning (poetry), 1995; Collected Works, vols 1–2, 1997; The Thirteen, 1997; The Evening Rainbow, 1999; Selected Prose, 1999. *Address:* 2256 South Troost Avenue, Tulsa, OK 74114–1348, USA.

YIP, Prof. George Stephen, DBA; Professor of Strategic and International Management, London Business School, since 2001; *b* 24 Sept. 1947; *s* of Teddy Yip and Susie (*née* Ho); *m* 1970, Moira Winsland; one *s* one *d*. *Educ:* Peak Sch., Hong Kong; East Grinstead County Grammar Sch.; Dover Coll.; Magdalene Coll., Cambridge (BA Hons 1970; MA 1973); Cranfield Univ. (MBA 1976); Harvard Business Sch. (MBA 1976; DBA 1980). Account Executive, 1970–72, Account Supervisor, 1973–74, Lintas London; Product Manager, Birds Eye Foods, 1972–73; Business Manager, Data Resources Inc., 1976–78; Asst Prof., Harvard Business Sch., 1980–83; Sen. Associate, MAC Gp, 1983–86; Sen. Manager, Price Waterhouse, 1986–87; Vis. Associate Prof., Georgetown Univ., 1987–91; Adjunct Prof., UCLA, 1991–99; Beckwith Prof. of Mgt Studies, Judge Inst. and Fellow, Magdalene Coll., Univ. of Cambridge, 1998–2000. Jt Chm., Perseus Consulting, 1998–. Vis. Prof., Stanford Business Sch., 1997; Vis. Fellow, Templeton Coll., Oxford, 1998. Fellow, World Economic Forum, 1998–; Mem. Supervisory Bd, Glunz AG, 1999–. *Publications:* Barriers to Entry, 1982; Total Global Strategy, 1992; Asian Advantage, 1998; Strategies for Central and Eastern Europe, 2000; articles in internat. mgt and mkting jls. *Recreations:* theatre, opera, classical music, tennis, sailing, rural Maine. *Address:* London Business School, Regent's Park, NW1 4SA. *T:* (020) 7262 5050. *Club:* Harbour.

YOCKLUNN, Sir John (Soong Chung), KCVO 1977; Kt 1975; Associate University Librarian (Gippsland), Monash University Library, 1993–98 (Chief Librarian, Gippsland Institute of Advanced Education, then Monash University College, 1983–92); *b* Canton, China, 5 May 1933; *s* of late Charles Soong Yocklunn and Wui Sin Yocklunn, formerly of W Australia; *m* 1981, Patricia Ann Mehegan. *Educ:* Perth Modern Sch.; Northam High Sch., W Australia; Univ. of W Australia (BA); Aust. Nat. Univ. (BA); Univ. of Sheffield (MA). ALA; ALAA. Dept of the Treasury, Canberra, 1959–63; Nat. Library of Australia, Canberra, 1964–67; Librarian-in-Charge, Admin Coll. of Papua New Guinea, Port Moresby, 1967–69; Exec. Officer, Public Service Board of Papua New Guinea, 1969–70; Librarian, Admin Coll., 1970–72; Principal Private Sec. to Chief Minister, 1972–73; study in UK, under James Cook Bicentenary Schol., 1973–74; on return, given task of organising a national library; Sen. Investigation Officer, Public Services Commn, 1974–77; Asst Sec. (Library Services), Dept of Educn (National Librarian of PNG), 1978–83. Chm., PNG Honours and Awards Cttee, 1975–83; Advr on Honours to PNG Govt, 1984–85; Consultant on estabt of new honours system, 1985–86. Vice-Pres., Pangu Pati, 1968–72; Nat. Campaign Manager for Pangu Pati for 1972 general elections in Papua New Guinea; Treasurer, Pangu Pati, 1973–80. Asst Dir, Visit of Prince of Wales to PNG, 1975; Dir, Visits of the Queen and Prince Philip to PNG, 1977 and 1982. Mem. Nat. Adv. Council, Aust. Broadcasting Corp., 2001–. Australian Library and Information Association: Chm., Gippsland Regional Gp, 1984–94; Mem., Vict. Br. Council, 1986–94; rep. on Commonwealth Library Assoc., 1988–91; Mem. Exec. Cttee, Vict. Div., Aust. Council for Library and Inf. Servs, 1989–94; Vice Pres., University Liby Soc. of Rockhampton, 1999–. Vice Pres., Regl Arts Develt Fund Council, Rockhampton, 1999–; Mem. Adv. Council, CARE Aust., 1988–92. Trustee, 1986–98, Chm. of Friends, 1985–88, Vice-Chm., 1992–98, Mus. of Chinese Australian Hist.; Pres., Rockhampton Chinese Assoc., 2001– (Vice Pres., 1999–2000). *Publications:* The Charles Barrett Collection of Books relating to Papua New Guinea, 1967, 2nd edn 1969; articles on librarianship, etc., in various jls. *Recreations:* orders and medals research, heraldry, languages. *Address:* 11 Melbourne Street, Rockhampton, Qld 4700, Australia. *T:* (7) 49273960.

YONG, Most Rev. Datuk Ping Chung; *see* South East Asia, Archbishop of.

YONG NYUK LIN; Member, Presidential Council for Minority Rights, Singapore, 1979–91; *b* Seremban, Malaya, 24 June 1918; *s* of late Yong Thean Yong and Chen Shak Moi; *m* 1939, Kwa Geok Lan; two *d*. *Educ:* Raffles Coll., Singapore. Science Master, King George V Sch., Seremban, Malaya, 1938–41; with Overseas Assurance Corp., Singapore, 1941 (resigned, as Gen. Manager, 1958). Legislative Assemblyman, Singapore, 1959–65, MP 1965–79; Minister for Educn, 1959–63; Chm., Singapore Harbour Bd, 1961–62; Minister for: Health, 1963–68; Communications, 1968–75; Minister without Portfolio, 1975–76; High Comr in London, 1975–76. Chm., Singapore Land/Marina Centre Development Private Ltd, 1980–86. *Address:* 50 Oei Tiong Ham Park, Singapore 267055.

YONG PUNG HOW, Hon.; Chief Justice of the Supreme Court, Singapore, since 1990; *b* 11 April 1926; *o s* of Yong Shook Lin, advocate and solicitor, and Yu Tak Fong; *m* 1955, Cheang Wei-woo; one *d*. *Educ:* Victoria Instn, Kuala Lumpur (Treacher Schol., Rodger Schol.); Downing Coll., Cambridge (Exhibnr; MA; LLB; Associate Fellow); Harvard Business Sch. (AMP). Called to the Bar, Inner Temple, 1951, Hon. Bencher, 1997; admitted Advocate and Solicitor, Fedn of Malaya, 1952, Singapore, 1964; practised law as Partner, Shook Lin & Bok, 1952–70; sole arbitrator in strike by govt clerical services and telecoms workers, Singapore, 1953; Chm., Malayan Public Services Arbitration Tribunal, 1955–60; Mem., Chm.'s Panel, Malayan Industrial Court, 1961–67; Chm. and Man. Dir, Singapore Internat. Merchant Bankers Ltd, 1971–81; Chm. and CEO, Oversea-Chinese Banking Corp., 1983–89 (Dir, 1972, Vice-Chm., 1977–80); on secondment to Govt of Singapore, 1981–83, as: Man. Dir, Singapore Investment Corp. (GIC), 1981–83 (Dir, 1983–89); Man. Dir, Monetary Authy of Singapore, 1982–83; Dep. Chm., Bd of Comrs of Currency, 1982–83; alternate Gov. for Singapore, IMF, 1982–83; Judge, Supreme Court of Singapore, 1989–90; Actg Pres. of Singapore, July, Sept. and Nov. 1991. Chm., Presidential Council for Minority Rights, 1990–; Pres., Legal Services Commn, 1990–. Member: Securities Industry Council, 1974–81; Provisional Mass Rapid Transit Authy, 1980–83; Dir, Mass Rapid Transit Corp., 1983–86. Chairman: Malayan Airways Ltd and Malaysia-Singapore Airlines Ltd, 1964–69; Singapore Broadcasting Corp., 1985–89; Deputy Chairman: Malayan Banking Bd, 1966–70; Singapore Press Hldgs, 1984–89; Dir, Temasek Hldgs, 1985–89. Founder Chm., Singapore Inst. Policy Studies, 1987–89; Pres., Singapore Acad. Law, 1990–. Dir, Singapore SO, 1987–89. Fellow, Malaysian Inst. of Mgt, 1975. DSO (Singapore), 1989; Order of Temasek (First Class) (Singapore), 1999. *Address:* Supreme Court, 1 St Andrew's Road, Singapore 178957. *Clubs:* Pyramid, Singapore Cricket (Hon. Mem.), Warren Golf (Hon. Mem.) (Singapore).

YORK, Archbishop of, since 1995; **Most Rev. and Rt Hon. David Michael Hope,** KCVO 1995; PC 1991; DPhil; *b* 14 April 1940. *Educ:* Nottingham Univ. (BA Hons Theol); Linacre Coll., Oxford (DPhil; Hon. Fellow, 1993). Curate of St John, Tuebrook, Liverpool, 1965–70; Chaplain, Church of Resurrection, Bucharest, 1967–68; Vicar, St Andrew, Warrington, 1970–74; Principal, St Stephen's House, Oxford, 1974–82; Warden, Community of St Mary the Virgin, Wantage, 1980–87; Vicar of All Saints', Margaret Street, 1982–85; Bishop of Wakefield, 1985–91; Bishop of London, 1991–95. Prelate, Order of British Empire, 1991–95; Dean of the Chapels Royal, 1991–95. *Publications:* The Leonine Sacramentary, 1971; Living the Gospel, 1993. *Address:* Bishopthorpe, York YO23 2GE. *T:* (01904) 707021.

YORK, Dean of; *see* Furnell, Very Rev. R.

YORK, Archdeacon of; *see* Seed, Ven. R. M. C.

YORK, David; Operations Director, Highways Agency, since 2001; *b* 20 April 1950; *s* of George William York and Ann (*née* Morgan); *m* 1982, Lindsey Anne Murgatroyd. *Educ:* Manor Park Sch., Newcastle upon Tyne; Salford Univ. (BSc 1973). MICE 1976. Joined Dept of Transport, 1970; Project Engr, 1977–83; Principal Engr, 1983–87; Superintending Engr, 1987–90; Director: NW Network Mgt, 1990; Yorks and Humberside Construction Prog., 1990–93; Motorway Widening Unit, 1993–95; Dep. Road Prog. Dir, 1995–96, Road Prog. Dir, 1996; Project Services Dir, Highways Agency, 1996–2001. *Recreations:* flying, scuba diving, golf. *Address:* Highways Agency, Broadway, Broad Street, Birmingham B15 1BL. *T:* (0121) 678 8403.

YORK, Col Edward Christopher, TD 1978; Vice Lord-Lieutenant of North Yorkshire, since 1999; Managing Director, Hutton Wandesley Farms Co., since 1986; *b* 22 Feb. 1939; *o s* of late Christopher York and of Pauline Rosemary York (*née* Fletcher); *m* 1965, Sarah Ann, *d* of late Major James Kennedy Maxwell, MC; one *s* one *d*. *Educ:* Eton Coll. 1st Royal Dragoons, retd 1964. Chm., Thirsk Racecourse Co., 1995–. Vice Pres., Northern Assoc. of Building Socs, 1987; Pres., Yorks Agricl Soc., 1989; Hon. Show Dir, 1992–96, Pres., 1997, Chm. of Council, 1998–, RASE; Chm., Royal Armouries Develt Trust (Leeds), 1995–99. CO, Queen's Own Yeomanry, 1979–81 (Hon. Col, 1998–); ADC to the Queen, 1982–86; Col Comdt, Yeomanry, 1994–99. Chm., Yorks and Humberside TAVRA, 1998–. FRAgS 1998. DL 1988, High Sheriff, 1988, N Yorks. *Publications:* contribs to trade magazines. *Recreations:* racing, field sports. *Address:* Hutton Wandesley Hall, York YO26 7NA. *T:* (home) (01904) 738240; (office) (01904) 738755, *Fax:* (01904) 738468; *e-mail:* ecy@hwfarmsco.u-net.com. *Clubs:* Boodle's, Pratt's.

YORK, Michael, (Michael York-Johnson), OBE 1996; actor; *b* 27 March 1942; *s* of Joseph Johnson and Florence Chown; *m* 1968, Patricia Frances McCallum. *Educ:* Hurstpierpoint College; Bromley Grammar School; University College, Oxford (BA). *Stage:* Dundee Repertory Theatre, 1964; National Theatre Co., 1965; Outcry, NY, 1973; Bent, NY, 1980; Cyrano de Bergerac, Santa Fe, 1981; Whisper in the Mind, 1991; The Crucible, NY, 1992; Someone Who'll Watch Over Me, NY, 1993; *films:* The Taming of the Shrew, Accident, 1966; Romeo and Juliet, 1967; Cabaret, England Made Me, 1971; The Three Musketeers, 1973; Murder on the Orient Express, 1974; Logan's Run, 1975; The Riddle of the Sands, 1978; Success is the Best Revenge, 1984; Dawn, 1985; Vengeance, 1986; The Secret of the Sahara, Imbalances, 1987; The Joker, Midnight Blue, The Return of the Musketeers, 1988; The Long Shadow, 1992; Rochade, 1992; Eline Vere, 1992; Wide Sargasso Sea, 1993; Discretion Assured, 1993; The Shadow of a Kiss, 1994; Gospa, 1995; Austin Powers, 1997; Wrongfully Accused, 1998; Lovers and Liars, The Omega Code, 1999; Borstal Boy, 2000; Megiddo, 2001; *television* includes: Jesus of Nazareth, 1976; A Man Called Intrepid, 1978; For Those I Loved, 1981; The Weather in the Streets, The Master of Ballantrae, 1983; Space, 1984; The Far Country, 1985; The Four Minute Mile, The Heat of the Day, 1988; Till We Meet Again, 1989; The Night of the Fox, 1990; Fall from Grace, 1994; September, 1995; Not of This Earth, 1996; The Ring, 1996; True Women, Dark Planet, The Ripper, 1997; The Search for Nazi Gold, A Knight in Camelot, 1998; Perfect Little Angels, 1999; The Haunting of Hell House, 2000; The Lot, 2001. Chm., Calif Youth Theatre, 1987–. Hon. DFA S Carolina, 1988. *Publications:* (contrib.) The Courage of Conviction, 1986; (contrib.) Voices of Survival, 1987; Travelling Player (autobiog.), 1991; A Shakespearean Actor Prepares, 2000. *Recreations:* travel, music, collecting theatrical memorabilia.

YORK, Susannah; actress and writer; *b* 9 Jan. 1942; *d* of William Fletcher and Joan Bowring; *m* 1960, Michael Wells (marr. diss. 1976); one *s* one *d*. *Educ:* Marr Coll., Troon, Scotland; RADA, London. *Films* include: The Greengage Summer, 1961; Freud, 1962; Tom Jones, 1963; A Man for All Seasons, 1966; The Killing of Sister George, 1968; They Shoot Horses, Don't They, 1969; X, Y and Zee, 1971; Images, 1972; Superman, 1978; Golden Gate Murders, 1979; Alice, 1980; Superman 2, 1984; A Christmas Carol, Mio My Mio, 1986; Bluebeard; Just Ask for Diamonds, 1988; Melancholia, 1989; Barbarblu Barbarblu; Little Women. *Theatre* includes: Wings of a Dove, 1964; A Singular Man, 1965; The Maids, 1974; Peter Pan, 1977; The Singular Life of Albert Nobbs, 1978; Hedda Gabler, New York 1981, London 1982; Agnes of God, 1983; The Human Voice (own trans. of Cocteau), 1984; Fatal Attraction, Haymarket, 1985; The Apple Cart, Haymarket, 1986; The Women, Old Vic, 1986; The Glass Menagerie (tour), 1989; A Streetcar Named Desire, Octagon, Bolton, 1990; Noonbreak (own trans. of Claudel), London and Manchester, 1991; September Tide, London, 1993; The Merry Wives of Windsor, 1996, Hamlet, 1997, RSC; Camino Real, RSC, 1997. TV series: Second Chance, 1981; We'll Meet Again, 1982; The Prince Regent, 1983; Devices and Desires, 1990; Trainer, 1991, 1992. *Publications:* In Search of Unicorns, 1973, rev. edn 1984; Larks Castle, 1975, rev. edn, 1985; (ed) The Big One, 1984. *Recreations:* family, writing, gardening, reading, houses, riding, languages, travelling, theatre, cinema, walking. *Address:* c/o Peters Fraser & Dunlop, Drury House, 34–43 Russell Street, WC2B 5HA.

YORK-JOHNSON, Michael; *see* York, M.

YORKE, family name of **Earl of Hardwicke.**

YORKE, David Harry Robert, CBE 1993; FRICS; Senior Partner, Weatherall Green & Smith, Chartered Surveyors, 1984–89 (Partner, 1961–92; Group Chairman, 1989–92; Consultant, 1992–97); *b* 5 Dec. 1931; *s* of late Harry Yorke and Marie Yorke, Minera, N Wales; *m* 1955, Patricia Gwynneth Fowler-Tutt; one *d*. *Educ:* Dean Close Sch., Cheltenham; College of Estate Management. FRICS 1966 (ARICS 1956); FCIArb 1994. Articled to Tregear & Sons, 1948–54. 2nd Lieut RA, 1955–56. Weatherall Green & Smith, 1960–97. Dir, London Auction Mart, 1981–92; Chm., Belgravia Property Co. Ltd, 1993–95. Mem., Bristol Develt Corp., 1988–96; Dir, British Waterways Bd, 1988–2000 (Vice-Chm., 1998–2000). Royal Institution of Chartered Surveyors: Mem., Gen. Council, 1978–92; Pres., Gen. Practice Div., 1981–82; Pres., 1988–89; Chm., RICS Insurance Services, 1991–96. Mem. Council, British Property Fedn, 1990–94. Pres., British Chapter, Internat. Real Estate Fedn, 1974. Mem., Truro Conservation Area Adv. Cttee, 1998– (Chm., 1999–). Chm., St Mawes and St Just-in-Roseland Soc., 1987–. Freeman, City of London, 1979; Liveryman, Co. of Chartered Surveyors, 1979. *Publication:* (Consultant Ed.) Essentials of Rent Review, 1996. *Recreations:* crosswords, boats, swimming, occasional cookery. *Address:* Penolva, St Mawes, Truro, Cornwall TR2 5DR. *T:* (01326) 270235; 2 Chester Cottages, Bourne Street, SW1W 8HG. *T:* (020) 7823 4015. *Clubs:* Buck's; St Mawes Sailing.

YORKE, Margaret, (Margaret Beda Nicholson); writer; *b* 30 Jan. 1924; *d* of John Peel Alexander Larminie and Alison Yorke (*née* Lyle); *m* 1945, Basil Nicholson (marr. diss. 1957, he *d* 1987); one *s* one *d*. *Educ:* Prior's Field, Surrey. WRNS, 1942–45. Bookseller; School Sec.; Asst Librarian, St Hilda's Coll., Oxford, 1959–60; Library Asst (cataloguer), Christ Church, Oxford, 1963–65. Chm., Crime Writers' Assoc., 1979–80. CWA Cartier Diamond Dagger Award, 1999. *Publications:* Summer Flight, 1957; Pray Love Remember, 1958; Christopher, 1959; Deceiving Mirror, 1960; The China Doll, 1961; Once a Stranger, 1962; The Birthday, 1963; Full Circle, 1965; No Fury, 1967; The Apricot Bed, 1968; The Limbo Ladies, 1969; Dead in the Morning, 1970; Silent Witness, 1972; Grave Matters, 1973; Mortal Remains, 1974; No Medals for the Major, 1974; The Small Hours of the Morning, 1975; The Cost of Silence, 1977; The Point of Murder, 1978; Death on Account, 1979; The Scent of Fear, 1980 (Swedish Acad. of Detection Award, 1982); The Hand of Death, 1981; Devil's Work, 1982; Find Me a Villain, 1983; The Smooth Face of Evil, 1984; Intimate Kill, 1985; Safely to the Grave, 1986; Evidence to Destroy, 1987; Speak for the Dead, 1988; Crime in Question, 1989; Admit to Murder, 1990; A Small Deceit, 1991; Criminal Damage, 1992; Dangerous to Know, 1993; Almost the Truth, 1994; Pieces of Justice (short stories), 1994; Serious Intent, 1995; A Question of Belief, 1996; Act of Violence, 1997; False Pretences, 1998; The Price of Guilt, 1999; A Case to Answer, 2000; Cause for Concern, 2001. *Recreations:* theatre, reading, swimming, gardening, travel. *Address:* c/o Curtis Brown, 28/29 Haymarket, SW1Y 4SP. *Clubs:* Royal Over-Seas League, Detection, PEN.

YORKE, Very Rev. Michael Leslie; Dean of Lichfield, since 1999; *b* 25 March 1939; *s* of late Leslie Henry and Brenda Emma Yorke; *m* 1st, 1964, Michal Sara Dadd (*d* 1987); one *s* one *d*; 2nd, 1988, Frances Grace Archer. *Educ:* Midhurst Grammar Sch.; Brighton Coll.; Magdalene Coll., Cambridge (BA 1962; MA 1966); Cuddesdon Theol Coll., Oxford. Ordained deacon, 1964, priest, 1965; Curate, Croydon Parish Church, 1964–68; Precentor and Chaplain, 1968–73, Dep. Dir of Res. and Trng, 1972–74, Chelmsford Cathedral; Rector, Ashdon with Hadstock, 1974–78; Canon Residentiary, 1978–88, Vice Provost, 1984–88, Chelmsford Cathedral; Vicar, St Margaret's with St Nicholas, King's Lynn, 1988–94; Provost of Portsmouth, 1994–99. *Recreations:* opera, 20th century military history, long country walks, contemporary art. *Address:* The Deanery, Lichfield, Staffs WS13 7LD. *T:* (01543) 306145; Westgate House, The Green, Burnham Market, Norfolk PE31 8HD.

YORKE, Robert Anthony; management consultant, since 1981; *b* 27 June 1944; *s* of late Patrick Langdon Yorke and of Pamela Mary (*née* Rudgard; now Mrs Robert Michael Clive); *m* 1975, Morag, *d* of late J. S. M. Dow; one *s* one *d*. *Educ:* Marlborough Coll.; Clare Coll., Cambridge (MA); London Business Sch. (MSc). Financial Controller, Bowater Corp., 1975–77; Chief Exec., Ridham Freight Services, 1977–81; Dir, London and Devonshire Trust Ltd, 1987–. Comr, RCHME, 1991–99; Mem., Ancient Monuments Adv. Cttee, English Heritage, 1998–. Chairman: Nautical Archaeol. Soc., 1987–91; Jt Nautical Archaeol. Policy Cttee, 1995– (Vice-Chm., 1988–95). *Publications:* contribs to learned jls. *Recreations:* nautical archaeology, tennis, ski-ing. *Address:* Silver Birches, Bashurst Hill, Itchingfield, Horsham, W Sussex RH13 7NY. *T:* (01403) 790311.

YOSHIDA, Miyako; Principal Dancer, Royal Ballet, since 1995; *b* 28 Oct. 1965; *d* of Eiji Yoshida and Etsuko (*née* Fukuda). *Educ:* Royal Ballet Sch. Joined Sadler's Wells Royal Ballet, later Birmingham Royal Ballet, 1984; soloist, 1987; Principal, 1988; transf. to Royal Ballet, 1995. *Performances* include leading rôles in: Swan Lake, Sleeping Beauty, The Nutcracker, Giselle, Elite Syncopations, La Fille Mal Gardée, Hobson's Choice, The Dream, Don Quixote, Paquita, Allegri Diversi, Theme and Variations, Concerto Barroco, Les Sylphides, Divertimento No 15, Dances Concertantes, Les Patineurs, Romeo and Juliet, The Firebird, Coppélia. Prix de Lausanne, 1983; Global Award, 1989; Nakagawa Einosuke Award, 1995; Tachibana Akiko Award, 1996; Arts Encouragement Prize for New Artists, Min. of Educn, Sci., Sports and Culture, 1997; Hattori Chieko Award, 1998. *Recreations:* reading, watching films. *Address:* c/o Royal Ballet, Covent Garden, WC2E 9DD.

YOUARD, Richard Geoffrey Atkin; The Investment Ombudsman (formerly Investment Referee), 1989–96; *b* 27 Jan. 1933; *s* of Geoffrey Bernard Youard, MBE and Hon. Rosaline Joan Youard (*née* Atkin); *m* 1960, Felicity Ann Morton; one *s* two *d*. *Educ:* Bradfield Coll., Berks; Magdalen Coll., Oxford (BA Jurisprudence; MA 1998). Admitted Solicitor, 1959. Commnd (2nd Lieut) RA, 1952 (Nat. Service); Lieut TA, 1954. Slaughter and May, London: Articled Clerk, 1956–59; Asst Solicitor, 1959–68; Partner, 1968–89. Inspector, DTI, 1987. Ind. Investigator, SIB, 1994–97. Hon. Sen. Res. Fellow, KCL, 1988–. Chairman: Nat. Fedn of Consumers Groups, 1968; Cttee of Inquiry, Accountants Jt Disciplinary Scheme, 1989; Mem., Home Office Cttee on London Taxicab and Car Hire Trade, 1967. Clerk to Governors, Bradfield Coll., 1968–89, Governor, 1989–95. Mem., Chancellor's Court of Benefactors, Oxford Univ., 1995–2000. Mem. Council, Pali Text Soc., 1991–2000. *Publications:* (contrib.) Sovereign Borrowers, 1984; (contrib.) Current Issues of International Financial Law, 1985; (jtly) Butterworths Banking Documents, 1986; (contrib.) Butterworths Banking and Financial Law Review, 1987; contribs on legal aspects of internat. finance to Jl of Business Law, Euromoney and Internat. Financial Law Review. *Recreations:* gardening, electronics (holder of Amateur Transmitting Licence), beekeeping, map collecting, reading, jazz, Welsh language/history. *Address:* 12 Northampton Park, N1 2PJ. *T:* (020) 7226 8055; Cwm Mynach Ganol, Bontddu, Dolgellau, Gwynedd LL40 2TU. *Club:* Garrick.

YOUD, Samuel; writer, since 1958; *b* 16 April 1922; *s* of Sam and Harriet Youd; *m* 1st, 1946, Joyce Fairbairn (marr. diss. 1978); one *s* four *d*; 2nd, 1980, Jessica Ball (*d* 2001). *Educ:* Peter Symonds Sch., Winchester. Manager, Industrial Diamond Inf. Bureau, London, 1956–58. Chm., Children's Writers' Gp, Soc. of Authors, 1983–85. Atlantic Award in Literature, Rockefeller Foundn, 1947; George Stone Award, 1977. *Publications* include: as John Christopher: The Twenty Second Century (short stories), 1954; The Year of the Comet, 1955; The Death of Grass, 1956; The Caves of Night, 1958; A Scent of White Poppies, 1959; The Long Voyage, 1960; The World in Winter, 1962; Cloud on Silver, 1964; The Possessors, 1965; A Wrinkle in the Skin, 1965; The Little People, 1966; Pendulum, 1968; Bad Dream, 2000; for young adults: The Tripods trilogy (The White Mountains, 1967; The City of Gold and Lead, 1967; The Pool of Fire, 1968); The Lotus Caves, 1969; The Guardians, 1970 (Guardian Prize, and Christopher Medal, 1971; Jugendbuchpreis, 1976); The Sword trilogy (The Prince in Waiting, 1970; Beyond the Burning Lands, 1971; The Sword of the Spirits, 1972); Dom and Va, 1973; Wild Jack, 1974; Empty World, 1977; The Fireball trilogy (Fireball, 1981; New Found Land, 1983; Dragon Dance, 1986); When the Tripods Came, 1988; A Dusk of Demons, 1993; has also written as Hilary Ford, William Godfrey, Peter Graaf, Anthony Rye, Stanley Winchester, and Samuel Youd. *Recreation:* walking, with wireless. *Address:* One Whitefriars, Conduit Hill, Rye, E Sussex TN31 7LE. *T:* (01797) 224557; *e-mail:* samyoud@bigfoot.com. *Clubs:* Academy; United, Royal Channel Islands Yacht (Guernsey).

YOUDS, His Honour Edward Ernest; a Circuit Judge, Bedford, 1972–85; *b* 21 Nov. 1910; *s* of late Edward Youds. *Educ:* Birkenhead Sch.; Magdalene Coll., Cambridge. BA, LLB (Hons) Cantab. Called to Bar, Gray's Inn, 1936. Practised on Northern Circuit as Barrister-at-law. Served 1940–45, France and Germany (despatches, 1945). Dep. Chm., Lancs County Sessions, 1961–66; County Court Judge, 1966–69; Puisne Judge, High Court, Uganda, 1969–72.

YOUNG, family name of **Baron Kennet, Baroness Young** and **Barons Young of Dartington** and **Young of Graffham.**

YOUNG; *see* Hughes-Young, family name of Baron St Helens.

YOUNG, Baroness *cr* 1971 (Life Peer), of Farnworth in the County Palatine of Lancaster; **Janet Mary Young;** PC 1981; DL; *b* 23 Oct. 1926; *d* of John Norman Leonard Baker and Phyllis Marguerite Baker (*née* Hancock); *m* 1950, Geoffrey Tyndale Young; three *d*. *Educ:* Dragon School Oxford, Headington School, and in America; St Anne's Coll., Oxford; MA (Politics, Philosophy and Economics); Hon. Fellow, 1978. Baroness in Waiting (Govt Whip), 1972–73; Parly Under-Sec. of State, DoE, 1973–74; Minister of State, DES, 1979–81; Chancellor, Duchy of Lancaster, 1981–82; Leader of House of Lords, 1981–83; Lord Privy Seal, 1982–83; Minister of State, FCO, 1983–87. A Vice-Chm., Cons. Party Organisation, 1975–83, Dep. Chm., 1977–79; Pres., Assoc. of Cons. Peers, 2000– (Chm., 1995–2000). Co-Chm., Women's Nat. Commn, 1979–83. Councillor, Oxford City Council, 1957; Alderman, 1967–72; Leader of Conservative Group, 1967–72. A Vice-Pres., Assoc. of Dist Councils, 1990–; Pres., West India Cttee, 1995– (a Vice-Pres., 1987–95). Director: UK Provident Instn, 1975–79; Nat. Westminster Bank, 1987–96; Marks and Spencer Plc, 1987–97. Mem., BR Adv. Bd, Western Reg., 1977–79. Chairman: ISJC, 1989–92, 1994–97; GBGSA, 1989–94. Patron, Family and Youth Concern, 1997–2000. Chancellor, Univ. of Greenwich, 1993–98. Member: Council of Management, Ditchley Foundn, 1990–; Court, Cranfield Univ. (formerly Inst. of Technology), 1991–; Chm. Council, Headington Sch., Oxford, 1993–2001. DL Oxon, 1989. Hon. FICE. Hon. DCL Mt Holyoke Coll., 1982; DUniv Greenwich, 1998. Max Beloff Award, 2001; Parliamentarian of the Year Award, The Spectator, 2001; Peer of the Year, Channel 4 Political Awards, 2001. *Recreation:* music. *Address:* House of Lords, SW1A 0PW.

YOUNG OF DARTINGTON, Baron *cr* 1978 (Life Peer), of Dartington in the County of Devon; **Michael Young,** BSc (Econ), MA, PhD; Director, Institute of Community Studies since 1953; Trustee, Dartington Hall, 1942–92; *b* 9 Aug. 1915; father a musician, mother a writer; *m* 1st, 1945, Joan Lawson (*d* 1989); two *s* one *d*; 2nd, 1960, Sasha Moorsom (*d* 1993); one *s* one *d*; 3rd, 1995, Dorit Uhlemann; one *d*. *Educ:* Dartington Hall Sch.; London Univ. Barrister, Gray's Inn. Dir of Political and Economic Planning, 1941–45; Sec., Research Dept, Lab. Party, 1945–51. Chairman: Social Science Research Council, 1965–68; Dartington Amenity Research Trust, 1967–; Internat. Extension Coll., 1970–; Nat. Consumer Council, 1975–77; Mutual Aid Centre, 1977–; Coll. of Health, 1983–90; Health Information Trust, 1987–; Argo Venture, 1984–; Open Coll. of the Arts, 1987–90; Open Sch., 1989–; Language Line, 1989–; Educn Extra, 1990–; Sch. for Social Entrepreneurs, 1997–; Dir, Mauritius Coll. of the Air, 1972; Member: Central Adv. Council for Education, 1963–66; NEDC, 1975–78; Policy Cttee, SDP, 1981–83; President: Consumer's Assoc., 1965– (Chm., 1956–65); National Extension Coll., 1971– (Chm., 1962–71); Adv. Centre for Educn, 1976– (Chm., 1959–76); Birkbeck Coll., London Univ., 1989–92. Chm., Tawney Soc., 1982–84. Fellow, Churchill Coll., Cambridge, 1961–66 (Hon. Fellow, 1995); Vis. Prof. of Extension Educn, Ahmadu Bello Univ., Nigeria, 1974; Regents' Lectr, UCLA, 1985. Hon. FBA 1995. Hon. Fellow: LSE, 1978; Plymouth Polytechnic, 1980; QMC, 1983. Hon. LittD Sheffield, 1965; DUniv Open, 1973; Hon. DLitt: Adelaide, 1974; Keele, 1991; Hon. LLD Exeter, 1982. *Publications:* Family and Kinship in East London (with Peter Willmott), 1957; The Rise of the Meritocracy, 1958; (with Peter Willmott) Family and Class in a London Suburb, 1960; Innovation and Research in Education, 1965; (with Patrick McGeeney) Learning Begins at Home, 1968; (ed) Forecasting and the Social Sciences, 1968; (with Peter Willmott) The Symmetrical Family, 1973; (ed) The Poverty Report, 1974 and 1975; (with Marianne Rigge) Mutual Aid in a Selfish Society, 1979; (with others) Distance Teaching for the Third World, 1980; The Elmhirsts of Dartington—the creation of an Utopian Community, 1982; (with Marianne Rigge) Revolution From Within: co-operatives and co-operation in British industry, 1983; Social Scientist as Innovator, 1984; The Metronomic Society, 1988; (ed with Tom Schuller) The Rhythms of Society, 1988; (with Tom Schuller) Life After Work—the arrival of the ageless society, 1991; Your Head in Mine (poetry), 1994; (with Lesley Cullen) A Good Death, 1996; (with G. Lemos) Communities We Have Lost and Can Regain, 1997. *Recreation:* painting. *Address:* 18 Victoria Park Square, E2 9PF.

YOUNG OF GRAFFHAM, Baron *cr* 1984 (Life Peer), of Graffham in the County of W Sussex; **David Ivor Young;** PC 1984; DL; Chairman, Young Associates Ltd, since 1996; *b* 27 Feb. 1932; *s* of late Joseph and of Rebecca Young; *m* 1956, Lita Marianne Shaw; two *d*. *Educ:* Christ's Coll., Finchley; University Coll., London (LLB Hons; Fellow, 1988). Admitted solicitor, 1956. Exec., Great Universal Stores Ltd, 1956–61; Chairman: Eldonwall Ltd, 1961–74; Manufacturers Hanover Property Services Ltd, 1974–84; Cable and Wireless, 1990–95; Neoscorp Ltd (formerly Inter Digital Networks), 1997–; CDT Holdings plc, 1997–99; Pixology Ltd, 1997–; Autohit plc, 2000–; Director: Town & City Properties Ltd, 1971–74; Salomon Inc., 1990–94; Business for Sterling. Chm., British ORT, 1975–80 (Pres., 1980–82); Pres., World ORT Union, 1990–93 (Chm., Admin. Cttee, 1980–84). Dir, Centre for Policy Studies, 1979–82 (Mem., Management Bd, 1977); Mem., English Industrial Estates Corp., 1980–82; Chm., Manpower Services Commn, 1982–84; Mem., NEDC, 1982–89. Industrial Adviser, 1979–80, Special Adviser, 1980–82, DoI; Minister without Portfolio, 1984–85; Sec. of State for Employment, 1985–87; Sec. of State for Trade and Industry, 1987–89; Dep. Chm., Cons. Party, 1989–90. Pres., Inst. of Directors, 1993–; Chairman: EU-Japan Business Forum (formerly EU-Japan Assoc.), 1991–97; W Sussex Econ. Forum, 1996–; formerly Dir, Prince of Wales Business Leaders Forum. Pres., Jewish Care, 1990–97 (formerly Mem., Community Foundn); Chairman: Internat. Council of Jewish Social and Welfare Services, 1981–84; Central Council for Jewish Community Services, 1993–; Bd of Govs, Oxford Centre for Postgrad. Hebrew Studies, 1989–93. Chm., Chichester Festival Theatre Ltd, 1997–; Director: Royal Opera House Trust, 1990–95; South Bank Foundn Ltd; formerly Dir, Centre for Performing Arts; Chairman: London Philharmonic Trust, 1995–98; Develt Bd, 1994–, Council, 1995–, UCL. Hon. FRPS 1981. DL West Sussex, 1999. *Publication:* The Enterprise Years: a businessman in the Cabinet, 1990. *Recreations:* music, book-collecting, photography. *Address:* Young Associates Ltd, Harcourt House, 19 Cavendish Square, W1G 0PL. *T:* (020) 7447 8800, *Fax:* (020) 7447 8849. *Club:* Savile.
See also B. A. Rix.

YOUNG OF OLD SCONE, Baroness *cr* 1997 (Life Peer), of Old Scone, in Perth and Kinross; **Barbara Scott Young;** Chief Executive, Environment Agency, since 2000; *b* 8 April 1948; *d* of George Young and Mary (*née* Scott). *Educ:* Perth Acad.; Edinburgh Univ. (MA Classics); Strathclyde Univ. (Diploma Sec. Sci.); DipHSM, 1971. Various posts, finally Sector Administrator, Greater Glasgow Health Bd, 1973–78; Dir of Planning and Develt, St Thomas' Health Dist, 1978–79; Dist Gen. Administrator, NW Dist, Kensington and Chelsea and Westminster AHA, 1979–82; Dist Administrator, Haringey HA, 1982–85; District General Manager: Paddington and N Kensington HA, 1985–88; Parkside HA, 1988–91; Chief Exec., RSPB, 1991–98; Chm., English Nature, 1998–2000; Vice-Chm., Bd of Govs, BBC, 1998–2000. Member: BBC Gen. Adv. Council, 1985–88; Cttee, King's Fund Inst., 1986–90; Delegacy, St Mary's Hosp. Med. Sch., 1991–94; Cttee, Sec. of State for the Envmt's Going for Green initiative, 1994–96, UK Round Table on Sustainability, 1995–2000; Commn on Future of Voluntary Sector, 1995–96; Exec. Cttee, NCVO, 1997 (Mem., Trustee Bd, 1993–97); COPUS, 1996–97; Minister for Agriculture's Adv. Gp, 1997–98; EU Envmtl Adv. Forum, 1999–2001. Pres., Inst. of Health Services Management, 1987–88. Internat. Fellow, King Edward VII Hosp. Fund Coll., 1985–87 and 1990. Member: World Council, Birdlife Internat., 1994–98; Green Globe Task Force, 1997–98. Patron, Inst. of Ecol and Envmt Management, 1993–; Vice President: Flora & Fauna Internat., 1998–; Birdlife Internat., 1999–; RSPB, 2000–. Trustee, IPPR, 1999–. Hon. RICS 2000; Hon. Fellow, Geologists Assoc., 2000; Hon. FCIWEM 2001. DUniv: Stirling, 1995; York, St Andrews, Aberdeen, 2000; Open, 2001; Hon. DSc: Hertfordshire, 1997; Cranfield, 1998. *Publications:* (contrib.) What Women Want, 1990; (contrib.) Medical Negligence, 1990; articles in Hosp. Doctor. *Recreations:* obsessive cinema going, gardening. *Address:* Environment Agency, 25th floor, Millbank Tower, 21–24 Millbank, SW1P 4XL.

YOUNG, Prof. Alec David, OBE 1964; MA; FRS 1973; FREng; Professor and Head of the Department of Aeronautical Engineering, Queen Mary College, London University, 1954–78, now Emeritus; Vice-Principal, Queen Mary College, 1966–78; *b* 15 Aug. 1913; *s* of Isaac Young and Katherine (*née* Freeman); *m* 1st, 1937, Dora Caplan (*d* 1970); two *s* one *d*; 2nd, 1971, Rena Waldmann (*née* Szafer). *Educ:* Caius Coll., Cambridge (Wrangler, Mathematical Tripos, 1935). Research Student in Aeronautics, Cambridge, 1935–36; Mem. of staff, Aerodynamics Dept, Royal Aircraft Estab., 1936–46; College of Aeronautics: Senior Lectr and Dep. Head of Dept of Aerodynamics, 1946–50; Prof. and Head of Dept of Aerodynamics, 1950–54. Dean, Faculty of Engineering, Univ. of London, 1962–66; Mem. Senate, Univ. of London, 1970–78. Member: Fluid Dynamics Panel, AGARD, 1965–90; various Cttees of Aeronautical Research Council (Chm. of Council, 1968–71). Exec. Sec., Internat. Council of Aeronautical Scis, 1987–90. Chm., Bd of Direction, Von Karman Institute for Fluid Dynamics, 1964–93; Mem., Advisory Bd, RAF Coll., Cranwell, 1966. FRAeS 1951 (Hon. FRAeS 1984; Past Chm., Aerodynamics Data Sheets Cttee; Gold Medal, 1972); FREng (FEng 1976). Fellow: QMC, 1980; AIAA, 1987. Editor, Progress in Aerospace Sciences, 1983–93. Ludwig Prandtl Ring, Deutsche Gesellschaft für Luft-und Raumfahrt, 1976; Von Karman Medal, AGARD, 1979. Commandeur de l'Ordre de Leopold, 1976. *Publications:* (jtly) An Elementary Treatise on the Mechanics of Fluids, 1960, 2nd edn 1970; (jtly) Aircraft Excrescence Drag, 1981; Boundary Layers, 1989; various, of Aeronautical Research Council, Coll. of Aeronautics Reports series, and in Proc. and Reports of AGARD; articles in Aeronautical Quarterly and Jl of Royal Aeronautical Soc., Quarterly Jl of Mechanics and Applied Mathematics, and Aircraft Engineering. *Recreations:* drama, sketching, etching. *Address:* 70 Gilbert Road, Cambridge CB4 3PD. *T:* (01223) 354625.

YOUNG, Andrew; Vice Chairman, Law Companies Group, Inc., since 1993; President, National Council of the Churches of Christ, 2000–01; *b* New Orleans, La, 12 March 1932; *s* of Andrew J. Young and Daisy Fuller; *m* 1954, Jean Childs (*d* 1994); one *s* three *d*; *m* 1996, Carolyn Watson. *Educ:* Howard Univ., USA; Hartford Theological Seminary. Ordained, United Church of Christ, 1955; Pastor, Thomasville, Ga, 1955–57; Associate Dir for Youth Work, Nat. Council of Churches, 1957–61; Admin. Christian Educn Programme, United Church of Christ, 1961–64; Mem. Staff, Southern Christian Leadership Conf., 1961–70, Exec. Dir, 1964–70, Exec. Vice-Pres., 1967–70; elected to US House of Representatives from 5th District of Georgia, 1972 (first Black Congressman from Georgia in 101 years); re-elected 1974 and 1976; US Ambassador to UN, 1977–79; Mayor of Atlanta, 1982–89. Co-Chm., Atlanta Cttee for Olympic Games 1996. Formerly Chm., Law Internat., Inc. Chairman: Atlanta Community Relations Commn, 1970–72; National Democratic voter registration drive, 1976; during 1960s organized voter registration and community develt programmes. Mem. Bd of Dirs, Martin Luther King, Jr Center. Holds numerous hon. degrees and awards, including: Presidential Medal of Freedom, 1980; Légion d'Honneur (France). *Publication:* An Easy Burden, 1996.

YOUNG, Dr Andrew Buchanan, FRCPE, FFPHM; Deputy Chief Medical Officer, Scottish Office Department of Health (formerly Scottish Office Home and Health Department), 1989–97; *b* 11 Aug. 1937; *s* of Alexander and Elizabeth Young; *m* 1965, Lois Lilian Howarth; one *s* one *d*. *Educ:* Falkirk High School; Edinburgh Univ. (MB ChB). DTM&H. Supt, Presbyterian Church of E Africa Hosps, Kenya, 1965–72; Fellow in Community Medicine, Scottish Health Service, 1972–75; Scottish Home and Health Department: MO 1975; SMO 1978; PMO 1985. Pres., Edinburgh Medical Missionary Soc., 1992–97. QHP, 1993–96. *Recreations:* trying to learn computing, rambling, reading. *Address:* c/o 4241 Great North Road, Auckland, New Zealand.

YOUNG, Andrew George; Directing Actuary, Government Actuary's Department, since 1995; *b* 15 June 1949; *s* of James Cameron Young and Agnes Young; *m* 1975, Victoria Leslie; one *s* three *d*. *Educ:* Univ. of Glasgow (BSc 1st Cl. Hons Maths, Natural Philosophy). Government Actuary's Dept, 1973–. *Recreations:* music, theatre, travel. *Address:* 4 Ingleside Grove, SE3 7PH. *T:* (020) 8858 3044.

YOUNG, Prof. Andrew William, DSc; FBA 2001; Professor of Neuropsychology, University of York, since 1997; *b* 14 March 1950; *s* of Alexander Young and Winnifred Doris Young; *m* 1976, Mavis Langham; one *s* two *d*. *Educ:* Bedford Coll., London (BSc 1971); Warwick Univ. (PhD 1974). Lectr in Psychol., Univ. of Aberdeen, 1974–76; Lectr, then Reader in Psychol., Univ. of Lancaster, 1976–89; Prof. of Psychol., Univ. of Durham, 1989–93; Special Appt, MRC Scientific Staff, Applied Psychol. Unit, Cambridge, 1993–97. Dr *hc* Liège, 2000. Cognitive Psychol. Award, 1994, President's Award, 1995, Book Award, 2001, BPsS. *Publications:* (with A. W. Ellis) Human Cognitive Neuropsychology, 1996; (with V. Bruce) In the Eye of the Beholder: the science of face perception, 1998. *Recreations:* popular music, jukebox enthusiast, opera, partially reformed trainspotter. *Address:* Department of Psychology, University of York, Heslington, York YO10 5DD. *T:* (01904) 433159.

YOUNG, Anthony Ian; Senior Deputy General Secretary, Communication Workers' Union, since 1998; a Governor, BBC, since 1998; *b* 16 April 1942; *m* 1st, 1962, Doreen Goodman (marr. diss. 1984); one *s* two *d*; 2nd, 1985, Margaret Newnham; one *s* one *d*. *Educ:* Kenmore Park Primary Sch.; Harrow County GS. Joined GPO as telecommunications apprentice, 1958; Union Br. Officer, 1967, Mem. NEC, 1978–89, PO Engrg Union; Gen. Sec., Nat. Communications Union, 1989–95; Jt Gen. Sec., Communication Workers' Union, 1995–98. Mem., Gen. Council, TUC, 1989– (Pres., 2001–Sept. 2002); Eur. Co-Pres., Union Network Internat. *Recreations:* reading, music, cycling, tennis, skating, walking, spasmodic gardening and cooking. *Address:* 155 Tentelow Lane, Southall, Middx UB2 4LW; Communication Workers' Union, 150 The Broadway, Wimbledon, SW19 1RX. *T:* (020) 8971 7232.

YOUNG, Prof. Archibald, MD; FRCP, FRCPGlas, FRCPE; Professor of Geriatric Medicine, Edinburgh University, since 1998; *b* 19 Sept. 1946; *s* of Dr Archibald Young and Mary Downie Young (*née* Fleming); *m* 1973, Alexandra Mary Clark (marr. diss. 1995); one *s* one *d*. *Educ:* Glasgow Univ. (BSc 1st Cl. Hons 1969; MBChB 1971; MD 1983). MRCP 1973, FRCP 1989; FRCPGlas 1985; FRCPE 1999. Hon. Consultant Physician in Rehabilitation Medicine, Nuffield Dept of Orthopaedic Surgery, Oxford Univ., 1981–85; Consultant Physician in Geriatric Medicine, Royal Free Hosp., 1985–87; Royal Free Hospital School of Medicine: Hon. Sen. Lectr, 1985–87, Sen. Lectr, 1987–88, in Geriatric Medicine; Prof. and Head, Univ. Dept of Geriatric Medicine and Hon. Consultant Physician, 1988–98. *Publications:* contribs to learned jls on effects of ageing, use and disuse of muscle and exercise physiology. *Recreations:* physical. *Address:* Geriatric Medicine, 21 Chalmers Street, Edinburgh EH3 9EW. *T:* (0131) 536 4535. *Club:* Junior Mountaineering of Scotland.

YOUNG, Sir Brian (Walter Mark), Kt 1976; MA; Director General, Independent Broadcasting Authority (formerly Independent Television Authority), 1970–82; *b* 23 Aug. 1922; *er s* of late Sir Mark Young, GCMG and Josephine (*née* Price); *m* 1947, Fiona Marjorie (*d* 1997), *o d* of late Allan, 16th Stewart of Appin, and Marjorie (*née* Ballance); one *s* two *d*. *Educ:* Eton (King's Schol.); King's College, Cambridge (Schol.). FSA 1994. Served in RNVR, mainly in destroyers, 1941–45. First class hons in Part I, 1946, and Part II, 1947, of Classical Tripos; Porson Prize, 1946; Winchester Reading Prize, 1947; BA 1947; MA 1952. Assistant Master at Eton, 1947–52; Headmaster of Charterhouse, 1952–64; Dir, Nuffield Foundn, 1964–70. Chm., Christian Aid, 1983–90. Member: Central Advisory Council for Education, 1956–59 (Crowther Report); Central Religious Adv. Cttee of BBC and ITA, 1960–64; Bd of Centre for Educn Develt Overseas, 1969–72; Arts Council of GB, 1983–88; Exec. Cttee, British Council of Churches, 1983–90; Chm., Associated Bd of the Royal Schs of Music, 1984–87. Pres., British and Foreign Sch. Soc., 1991–. A Managing Trustee, Nuffield Foundn, 1978–90; Trustee: Lambeth Palace Liby, 1984–97; Imperial War Mus., 1985–92. Hon. RNCM, 1987. Hon. DLitt Heriot-Watt, 1980. *Publications:* Via Vertendi, 1952; Intelligent Reading (with P. D. R. Gardiner), 1964; The Villein's Bible: stories in Romanesque carving, 1990. *Recreations:*

music, travel, history, problems. *Address:* Hill End, Woodhill Avenue, Gerrards Cross, Bucks SL9 8DJ. *T:* (01753) 887793.

See also Maj.-Gen. A. P. Grant Peterkin, T. M. S. Young.

YOUNG, His Honour Christopher Godfrey; a Circuit Judge, 1980–97; *b* 9 Sept. 1932; *s* of late Harold Godfrey Young, MB, ChB, and Gladys Mary Young; *m* 1969, Jeanetta Margaret (*d* 1984), *d* of Halford and Dorothy Vaughan; one *s.* *Educ:* Bedford Sch.; King's Coll., Univ. of London (LLB Hons 1954; MA 1999). Called to the Bar, Gray's Inn, 1957; Midland and Oxford Circuit, 1959; a Recorder of the Crown Court, 1975–79; Resident Judge: Peterborough Crown Court, 1980–87; Leicester Crown Court, 1987–97. Mem., Parole Bd, 1990–93, 1997–; Pt time Chm., Immigration Appeal Tribunal, 1997–98. Hon. Pres., De Montfort Univ. Sch. of Law, 1996–98. Postgrad. res. in Byzantine Studies, RHC, 1999–. Chm., Maidwell with Draughton Parish Council, 1973–76. *Recreations:* music, travel, Byzantium. *Address:* Stockshill House, Duddington, Stamford, Lincs PE9 3QQ. *T:* (01780) 444658. *Club:* Athenæum.

YOUNG, Rt Rev. Clive; *see* Dunwich, Bishop Suffragan of.

YOUNG, Colin, CBE 1994 (OBE 1976); Senior Consultant, Ateliers du Cinéma Européen, since 1996 (Director, 1993–96); Director, National Film and Television School of Great Britain, 1970–92; *b* 5 April 1927; *s* of Colin Young and Agnes Holmes Kerr Young; *m* 1st, 1960, Kristin Ohman; two *s*; 2nd, 1987, Constance Yvonne Templeman; one *s* one *d.* *Educ:* Bellahouston Academy, Glasgow; Univs of Glasgow, St Andrews and California (Los Angeles). Theatre and film critic, Bon Accord, Aberdeen, 1951; cameraman, editor, writer, director, 1953–; producer, 1967–; UCLA (Motion Pictures): Instructor, 1956–59; Asst Prof., 1959–64; Assoc. Prof., 1964–68; Prof., 1968–70, Head, Motion Picture Div., Theater Arts Dept, UCLA, 1964–65; Chm., Dept of Theater Arts, 1965–70. Res. Associate, Centre Nat. de Recherche Scientifique, Paris, 1984 and 1987; Andrew W. Mellon Vis. Prof. in Humanities, Rice Univ., Houston, Texas, 1985–86. Tutor, Arista Story Editing Workshops, 1996–. Vice-Chm., 1972–76, Chm., 1976–91, Edinburgh Film Festival; Chm., Edinburgh Internat. Film and Television Council; Governor, BFI, 1974–80. Member: Arts Council Film Cttee, 1972–76; Public Media Panel, Nat. Endowment for Arts, Washington, 1972–77; Gen. Adv. Council, BBC, 1973–78; Council of Management, BAFTA, 1974–81; Exec. Cttee, Centre International de Liaison des Ecoles de Cinéma et de Télévision, 1974–94 (Pres., 1980–94); Nat. Film Finance Corp., 1979–85; British Screen Adv. Council, 1990–; Bd, Moonstone Film Labs Internat., 1997–; Lottery Film Prodn Cttee, Scottish Arts Council, 1998–2000; Lottery Film Prodn Cttee, Scottish Screen, 2000–. Consultant, Goldcrest Films & Television Ltd, 1985–86. FBKS 1975. Chm., Cttee on Educational Policy, UCLA, 1968–69. London Editor, Film Quarterly, 1970–91 (Los Angeles Editor, 1958–68). Michael Balcon Award, 1983, Fellow, 1993, BAFTA; Lifetime Achievement Award, British Indep. Film Awards, 2000. Chevalier de l'Ordre des Arts et des Lettres (France), 1987. *Publications:* various articles in collections of film essays including Principles of Visual Anthropology, 1975; experimental film essay for Unesco, 1963; ethnographic film essay for Unesco, 1966; contribs to Film Quarterly, Sight and Sound, Jl of Aesthetic Education, Jl of the Producers Guild of America, Kosmorama (Copenhagen), etc. *Address:* Ateliers du Cinéma Européen, 68 rue de Rivoli, 75004 Paris, France; Turret House, Ivy Hatch Court, Ivy Hatch, Sevenoaks, Kent TN15 0PQ.

YOUNG, Sir Colville (Norbert), GCMG 1994; MBE 1986; JP; DPhil; Governor-General of Belize, since 1993; *b* 20 Nov. 1932; *s* of Henry Oswald Young and Adney Wilhelmina (*née* Waite); *m* 1956, Norma Eleanor Trapp; three *s* one *d.* *Educ:* Univ. of West Indies (BA 1961); Univ. of York (DPhil 1971). Principal, St Michael's Coll., Belize, 1974–76; Lectr in English and Gen. Studies, Belize Tech. Coll., 1976–86; University College of Belize: Pres., 1986–90; Lectr, 1990–93. JP Belize, 1985. *Publications:* Creole Proverbs of Belize, 1980, rev. edn 1988; From One Caribbean Corner (poetry), 1983; Caribbean Corner Calling, 1988; Language and Education in Belize, 1989; Pataki Full, 1990; contrib. poetry and drama in various anthologies; articles in Belizean Affairs, Jl Belizean Affairs, Belcast Jl, Caribbean Dialogue, Handbook on World Educn. *Recreations:* creative writing, playing and arranging steelband music. *Address:* Belize House, Belmopan, Belize, Central America. *T:* (8) 22521.

YOUNG, David Edward Michael; QC 1980; a Recorder, since 1987; *b* 30 Sept. 1940; *s* of George Henry Edward Young and Audrey Young; *m* 1968, Ann de Bromhead; two *d.* *Educ:* Monkton Combe Sch.; Hertford Coll., Oxford (MA). Called to the Bar, Lincoln's Inn, 1966, Bencher, 1989; practising at Chancery Bar, specialising in intellectual property work. Dep. Judge, Patent County Court, 1990–; a Dep. High Court Judge, 1993–. Chm., Plant Varieties and Seeds Tribunal, 1987–. *Publications:* (co-ed) Terrell on the Law of Patents, 12th edn 1971 to 14th edn 1994; Passing Off, 1985, 3rd edn 1994. *Recreations:* tennis, country pursuits, ski-ing. *Address:* 3 New Square, Lincoln's Inn, WC2A 3RS. *T:* (020) 7405 1111.

YOUNG, (David) Junor; HM Diplomatic Service, retired; *b* 23 April 1934; *m* 1954, Kathleen Brooks; two *s* two *d.* *Educ:* Robert Gordon's College. Joined Foreign Office, 1951; served Berlin, Ankara, South Africa, DSAO, Port Louis, Belgrade, 1951–75; Consul (Comm.), Stuttgart, 1978–81; First Sec., Kampala, 1981–84; Consul Gen., Hamburg, 1984–86; Counsellor (Commercial), Bonn, 1986–88; High Comr, Solomon Is, 1988–90; Dep. High Comr, Karachi, 1991–94. *Recreations:* golf, gardening. *Address:* Pine Cottage, Hintlesham, Suffolk IP8 3NH.

YOUNG, Rt Rev. David Nigel de Lorentz, CBE 2000; Bishop of Ripon, 1977–99; *b* 2 Sept. 1931; *s* of late Brig. K. de L. Young, CIE, MC and Ada Lilian Young (*née* Tollinton); *m* 1962, Rachel Melverley Lewis (*d* 1966); one *s* one *d*; *m* 1967, Jane Havill, *y d* of late L. H. and E. M. Collison; three *s.* *Educ:* Wellington Coll.; Balliol Coll., Oxford (MA 1st. cl. Maths). 2nd Lt RE, Sch. of Military Survey, 1950–51; Wycliffe Hall, Oxford (BD qualifying exam 1959). Res. mathematician, Plessey Co., 1955–56. Ordained deacon, 1959, priest, 1960; Curate: All Hallows, Allerton, 1959–62; St Mark's, St John's Wood, 1962–63; studied Sanskrit and Pali, SOAS, 1962–63; CMS Missionary, Sri Lanka, 1964–67; Director, Dept of Buddhist Studies, Theological Coll. of Lanka, 1965–67; Lecturer in Buddhist Studies, Manchester Univ., 1967–70; Vicar of Burwell, Cambridge, 1970–75; Lectr, Faculty of Divinity, Univ. of Cambridge, 1970–75; Archdeacon of Huntingdon, 1975–77; Vicar of Great with Little and Steeple Gidding, 1975–77; Rector of Hemingford Abbots, 1977; Hon. Canon of Ely Cathedral, 1975–77. Entered H of L, 1984. Mem., Doctrine Commn, 1978–81; Chairman: Partnership for World Mission, 1978–86; Governing Body, SPCK, 1979–88; Anglican Interfaith Consultants, 1981–91; Scargill Council, 1984–90; Leeds Educn 2000, 1990–99; C of E Bd of Educn, 1994–99; Standing Cttee, Nat. Soc., 1994–99; Govs, UC of Ripon and York St John, 1995–97. *Publications:* contribs to Religious Studies. *Recreations:* walking, tennis, sailing. *Address:* Chapel House, Lawkland, Austwick, Lancaster LA2 8AT.

YOUNG, David Tyrrell; Chairman, City and Guilds of London Institute, since 1999; *b* 6 Jan. 1938; *s* of late Tyrrell F. Young and Patricia M. Young (*née* Spicer); *m* 1965, Madeline Helen Celia Philips; three *d.* *Educ:* Charterhouse. Trained as Chartered Accountant; joined Spicer & Pegler, later Spicer & Oppenheim, 1965 (merged with Touche Ross, 1990): Partner 1968; Managing Partner, 1982; Sen. Partner, 1988–90; Dep. Chm., 1990–93. Chm., N Herts NHS Trust, 1995–2000. Director: Lombard Ins. Gp, 1993–2000; Asprey, then Asprey & Garrard, 1993–2000; Wates City of London Properties, 1994–2000; Nomura Bank Internat., 1996–. Mem. Council, ICAEW, 1979–82. Mem. Court, Fishmongers' Co., 1981–. FRSA 1992. Hon. FCGI 1995. *Recreations:* golf, limited gardening. *Address:* Overhall, Ashdon, Saffron Walden, Essex CB10 2JH. *T:* (01799) 584556. *Clubs:* City of London, Honourable Artillery Company; Royal St George's Golf, Royal Worlington Golf.

YOUNG, David Wright; teacher; *b* Greenock, Scotland. *Educ:* Greenock Academy; Glasgow Univ.; St Paul's Coll., Cheltenham. Head of History Dept; subseq. insurance executive. Joined Labour Party, 1955; contested (Lab): South Worcestershire, 1959; Banbury, 1966; Bath, 1970. MP (Lab) Bolton E, 1974–1983, Bolton SE, 1983–97. PPS to Sec. of State for Defence, 1977–79. Mem., Select Cttee on Employment, 1982–97. Formerly Alderman, Nuneaton Borough Council; Councillor, Nuneaton District Council. Chm., Coventry East Labour Party, 1964–68. Member: TGWU; Co-operative Party. Is especially interested in comprehensive educn, defence, pensions, economics. *Recreations:* reading, motoring.

YOUNG, Donald Anthony, CEng, FIGasE; Managing Director, National Transmission, British Gas plc, 1991–93, retired; *b* 23 June 1933; *s* of Cyril Charles Young and Sarah Young; *m* 1960, June (*née* Morrey); two *d.* *Educ:* Stockport Secondary Sch. FIGasE 1969. National Service, 2nd Lieut REME, 1953–55. North Western Gas Bd, 1949–60; E Midlands Gas Bd, 1960–68; Gas Council Terminal Manager, Bacton Natural Gas Reception Terminal, 1968–70; Gas Council Plant Ops Engr, 1970–73; Asst Dir (Ops), Prodn & Supply Div., British Gas HQ, 1973–77; Regional Dep. Chm., N Thames Gas, 1977–79; Dir (Operations), Prodn & Supply Div., British Gas HQ, 1979–83; Regional Chairman: Southern Reg., British Gas Corp., subseq. British Gas plc Southern, 1983–89; British Gas plc West Midlands, 1989–91. CIMgt (CBIM 1986). *Recreations:* gardening, walking. *Address:* Georgian House, Penn Lane, Tanworth in Arden, Warwickshire B94 5HH.

YOUNG, Rt Rev. Donald Arthur; *see* Newfoundland, Central, Bishop of.

YOUNG, Edward Preston, DSO 1944; DSC 1943; writer and retired book designer; *b* 17 Nov. 1913; *m* 1st, 1945, Diana Lilian Graves (marr. diss.); two *d*; 2nd, 1956, Mary Reoch Cressall (*d* 2001). *Educ:* Highgate Sch. Served War, 1940–45: RNVR; entered submarine service 1940 (despatches, DSC); first RNVR officer to command operational submarine, 1943 (DSO, Bar to DSC); temp. Commander RNVR, 1945. Man. Dir, Rainbird Publishing Gp Ltd, 1970–73. *Publications:* One of Our Submarines, 1952; Look at Lighthouses, 1961; The Fifth Passenger, 1962; Look at Submarines, 1964. *Address:* 15 Maple Walk, Rustington, W Sussex BN16 3QP.

YOUNG, Eric, OBE 1976; HM Diplomatic Service, retired; Editor, Control Risks Information Services, 1984–93; *b* 16 Nov. 1924; *s* of late Robert Young, MBE, MIMinE and Emily Florence Young, Doncaster; *m* 1949, Sheila Hutchinson; three *s* one *d.* *Educ:* Maltby Grammar Sch.; Sheffield Univ. (BA 1948). Served War, RN, 1943–46. Editorial staff: Sheffield Telegraph, 1948; Western Morning News, 1951; Daily Dispatch, 1952; Manchester Guardian, 1953; PRO, NCB, Manchester, 1958; Dep. Dir, UK Inf. Office, Tanganyika and Zanzibar, 1960; First Secretary: (Inf.), Dar es Salaam, 1961; (Aid), Kaduna, 1963; Commonwealth Office (later FCO), 1967; Madras, 1969; Head of Chancery, Reykjavik, 1973 (Hd of Brit. Interests Section, French Embassy, during breach of diplomatic relations, 1976); Dep. High Comr, Bombay, 1977; High Comr, Seychelles, 1980–83. *Recreations:* music, books, walking. *Address:* 3 West Hall, Sudbourne Park, Orford, Woodbridge, Suffolk IP12 2AJ.

YOUNG, Rev. Prof. Frances Margaret, OBE 1998; PhD; Edward Cadbury Professor of Theology, since 1986, and Pro-Vice-Chancellor, since 1997, University of Birmingham; Methodist minister, since 1984; *b* 25 Nov. 1939; *d* of A. Stanley Worrall and Mary F. Worrall (*née* Marshall); *m* 1964, Robert Charles Young; three *s.* *Educ:* Bedford Coll., Univ. of London (BA); Girton Coll., Univ. of Cambridge (MA, PhD). Research Fellow, Clare Hall, Cambridge, 1967–68; University of Birmingham: Temp. Lectr, 1971–73; Lectr, 1973–82; Sen. Lectr, 1982–86; Hd, Dept of Theol., 1986–95; Dean, Faculty of Arts, 1995–97. Hon. DD Aberdeen, 1994. *Publications:* Sacrifice and the Death of Christ, 1975; (contrib.) The Myth of God Incarnate, 1977; From Nicaea to Chalcedon, 1983; Face to Face, 1985, 2nd edn 1990; (with David Ford) Meaning and Truth in 2 Corinthians, 1987; The Art of Performance, 1990; The Theology of the Pastoral Epistles, 1994; Biblical Exegesis and the Formation of Christian Culture, 1997; (ed) Encounter with Mystery, 1997; numerous articles, etc. *Recreations:* outdoor pursuits, music. *Address:* Pro-Vice-Chancellors' Office, University of Birmingham, Birmingham B15 2TT. *T:* (0121) 414 5940; 142 Selly Park Road, Birmingham B29 7LH. *T:* (0121) 472 4841.

YOUNG, Gavin Neil B.; *see* Barr Young.

YOUNG, George Bell, CBE 1976; Managing Director, East Kilbride Development Corporation, 1973–90 (and Stonehouse, 1973–77); *b* 17 June 1924; *s* of late George Bell Young and late Jemima Mackinlay; *m* 1946, Margaret Wylie Boyd (decd); one *s*; *m* 1979, Joyce Marguerite McAteer. *Educ:* Queens Park, Glasgow. MIEx 1958; FInstM 1984 (MInstM 1969); CBIM 1988 (FBIM 1982). RNVR, 1942–45, Lieut (destroyers and mine-sweepers). Journalist and Feature Writer, Glasgow Herald, 1945–48; North of Scotland Hydro-Electric Board, 1948–52; Chief Exec. (London), Scottish Council (Development and Industry), 1952–68 (Founder Fellow, 1986); Gen. Man., E Kilbride Develt Corp., 1968–73. Pres., Lanarks Br., BIM, 1985; Chm., BIM Scotland, 1988–91. Mem. Council, Nat. Trust for Scotland, 1974–79; Dir, Royal Caledonian Schools, 1957–85; Chm., East Kilbride and District National Savings Cttee, 1968–78; Trustee, Strathclyde Scanner Campaign; Scottish Chm., British Heart Foundn, 1975–79 (Mem., East Kilbride Cttee, 1970–97; Pres., Scottish Appeal, 1980–97). Hon. Vice-Pres., East Kilbride Dist Sports Council, 1984. Chm., E Kilbride Cttee, Order of St John, 1972–88 (CStJ 1979). Mem., Amer. Inst. of Corporate Asset Managers, 1985. Member: Saints and Sinners Club of Scotland (Hon. Sec., 1982–89; Chm., 1990; Hon. Mem., 1998); Royal Glasgow Inst. of the Fine Arts; The Merchants House of Glasgow; Mem. Scotland Cttee, Nat. Children's Homes, 1980–88. FRSA 1968. Freeman, East Kilbride, 1990. *Recreations:* reading, travel, watching the sunsets on the Firth of Clyde. *Address:* 30 Bowen Craig, Largs, Ayrshire KA30 8TB.

YOUNG, Rt Hon. Sir George (Samuel Knatchbull), 6th Bt *cr* 1813; PC 1993; MP (C) North West Hampshire, since 1997 (Ealing, Acton, Feb. 1974–1997); *b* 16 July 1941; *s* of Sir George Young, 5th Bt, CMG, and Elisabeth (*née* Knatchbull-Hugessen); *S* father, 1960; *m* 1964, Aurelia Nemon-Stuart, *er d* of late Oscar Nemon, and of Mrs Nemon-Stuart, Boar's Hill, Oxford; two *s* two *d.* *Educ:* Eton; Christ Church, Oxford (Open Exhibitioner); MA Oxon, MPhil Surrey. Economist, NEDO, 1966–67; Kobler Research Fellow, University of Surrey, 1967–69; Economic Adviser, PO Corp., 1969–74.

Councillor, London Borough of Lambeth, 1968–71; Mem., GLC, for London Borough of Ealing, 1970–73. An Opposition Whip, 1976–79; Parly Under Sec. of State, DHSS, 1979–81, DoE, 1981–86; Comptroller of HM Household, 1990; Minister of State, DoE, 1990–94; Financial Sec. to HM Treasury, 1994–95; Sec. of State for Transport, 1995–97; Shadow Leader, H of C, 1998–2000. Chm., Acton Housing Assoc., 1972–79. Dir, Lovell Partnerships Ltd, 1987–90. Trustee, Guinness Trust, 1986–90. *Publications:* Accommodation Services in the UK 1970–1980, 1970; Tourism, Blessing or Blight?, 1973. *Recreation:* bicycling. *Heir:* *s* George Horatio Young [*b* 11 Oct. 1966; *m* 1999, Marianne, *e d* of Dr Peter Toghill]. *Address:* House of Commons, SW1A 0AA.

YOUNG, Gerard Francis, CBE 1967; DL; CEng, FIMechE; HM Lord-Lieutenant and Custos Rotolurum, for South Yorkshire, 1974–85; *b* 5 May 1910; *s* of Smelter J. Young, MICE, and Edith, *d* of Sir John Aspinall, Pres. ICE and Pres. IMechE; *m* 1937, Diana Graham Murray, MA, BSc, JP, *d* of Charles Graham Murray, MD; two *s* three *d*. *Educ:* Ampleforth College. Engrg Apprentice, LNER, Doncaster. Entered family firm, The Tempered Spring Co. Ltd (later Tempered Group Ltd), 1930; Dir, 1936; Man. Dir, 1942; Chm., 1954–78. Dir, 1958, Chm., 1967–80, Sheffield Area Board, Sun Alliance & London Insurance Group; Dir, National Vulcan Engineering Insce Group, 1962–79. Member: Nat. Bd for Prices and Incomes, 1968–71; Top Salaries Review Body, 1971–74; Armed Forces Pay Review Body, 1971–74; Gen. Comr of Income Tax, 1947–74 (Chm., Don Div., 1968–74). Dir, Crucible Theatre Trust Ltd, 1967–75; Sec., Assoc. of Christian Communities in Sheffield, 1940–46; Chm., Radio Hallam Ltd, 1973–79; Trustee: Sheffield Town Trust (Town Collector, 1978–81); J. G. Graves Charitable Fund, 1974– (Chm., 1974–85); Freshgate Foundn, 1974–96 (Chm., 1979–86); Mem., Finance Bd, RC Dio. of Hallam, 1981–95. President: Council of St John, South and West Yorks, 1979–85; Yorks Volunteers Council, 1980–81; TAVRA Yorks & Humberside, 1983–85 (Vice-Pres., 1974–82). Univ. of Sheffield: Mem. Council, 1943; Treas., 1947–51; Pro-Chancellor, 1951–67; Chm., 1956–67; Life Mem. of Court, 1983. Mem. Bd of Govs, United Sheffield Hosps, 1948–53 (Chm. of Finance Cttee, 1948–50); Chm., Royal Hosp., 1951–53. Master, Company of Cutlers in Hallamshire, 1961–62. JP Sheffield, 1950–85. (Last) High Sheriff of Hallamshire, 1973–74; DL West Riding of Yorks, 1974. Hon. LLD Sheffield, 1962. KStJ 1976; GCSG 1974. *Recreations:* gardening, 13 grandchildren. *Address:* 69 Carsick Hill Crescent, Sheffield S10 3LS. *T:* (0114) 230 2834.
See also H. J. S. Young.

YOUNG, Hon. Sir Harold (William), KCMG 1983; Senator for South Australia, 1967–83, President of the Senate, 1981–83, retired; *b* 30 June 1923; *s* of Frederick James Garfield Young and Edith Mabel Scott; *m* 1952, Eileen Margaret Downing; two *s* two *d*. *Educ:* Prince Alfred Coll., Adelaide. Farmer and grazier prior to entering Parliament; former Vice Pres., United Farmers' and Graziers' Assoc. of SA; served on SA Wheat Res. Cttee, and Federal Exporters and Overseas Transport Shipping Freight Negotiating Cttee; Mem., Australian Wool Industry Council. Government Whip in the Senate, 1971–72; Opposition Whip, 1972 75; Shadow Spokesman on the Media, 1975; Chm., Govt Members' Cttee on National Resources, Energy and Trade, 1976–81; Senate: Temp. Chm. of Cttees, 1976–81; Chm., Select Cttee on Offshore Petroleum Resources, 1971 (Mem., 1968); Member: Industry and Trade Cttee, 1970–75; Estimates Cttee, 1970–81; Parlt Publications Cttee; Standing Orders Cttee; Broadcasting of Parlt Proceedings; Jt Foreign Affairs and Defence Cttee; Library Cttee; Jt Statutory Cttee on Public Works; Jt House Cttee; Jt Chm., New Parlt House Cttee, 1981–83 (Mem., 1976–83); Leader Delegn to S America and Africa. International Parliamentary Union: Leader, Delegn to Madrid and Sofia, 1976–77, to European Parlt, 1977; Mem., Internat. Exec., 1976–77. Order of Diplomatic Service Merit (Korea), 1982. *Address:* 1C Kingsley Avenue, Glenunga, SA 5064, Australia.

YOUNG, Hugo John Smelter; journalist; *b* 13 Oct. 1938; *s* of Gerard Francis Young, *qv*; *m* 1st, 1966, Helen Mason (*d* 1989); one *s* three *d*; 2nd, 1990, Lucy Waring. *Educ:* Ampleforth Coll.; Balliol Coll., Oxford (MA Jurisprudence). Yorkshire Post, 1961; Harkness Fellow, 1963; Congressional Fellow, US Congress, 1964; The Sunday Times, 1965–84: Chief Leader Writer, 1966–77; Political Editor, 1973–84; Jt Dep. Editor, 1981–84. Political Columnist, The Guardian, 1984–; Dir, The Tablet, 1985–. Chairman: Scott Trust, 1989–; UK Adv. Cttee, Harkness Fellowships, 1993–95. Hon. DLitt Sheffield, 1993. Columnist of the Year: British Press Awards, 1980, 1983, 1985; Granada TV What the Papers Say Awards, 1985. *Publications:* (jtly) The Zinoviev Letter, 1966; (jtly) Journey to Tranquillity, 1969; The Crossman Affair, 1974; (jtly) No, Minister, 1982; (jtly) But, Chancellor, 1984; (jtly) The Thatcher Phenomenon, 1986; One of Us, 1989, rev. edn 1991; This Blessed Plot: Britain and Europe from Churchill to Blair, 1998, rev. edn 1999. *Address:* c/o The Guardian, 119 Farringdon Road, EC1R 3ER; *e-mail:* hugoyoung@compuserve.com.

YOUNG, Ian Robert, OBE 1985; PhD; FRS 1989; FREng; consultant; *b* 11 Jan. 1932; *s* of John Stirling Young and Ruth Muir Young (*née* Whipple); *m* 1956, Sylvia Marianne Whewell Ralph; two *s* one *d*. *Educ:* Sedbergh Sch., Yorkshire; Aberdeen Univ. (BSc, PhD). FIEE; FREng (FEng 1988). Hilger & Watts Ltd, 1955–59; Evershed & Vignoles Ltd (and affiliates), 1959–76; EMI Ltd, 1976–81; GEC plc, 1981–97. Vis. Prof. of Radiology, RPMS, 1986. Hon. FRCR 1990; Hon. Mem., Amer. Soc. of Neuroradiology, 1995. Hon. DSc Aberdeen, 1992. *Publications:* over 100 papers in Proc. IEE, Magnetic Resonance in Medicine, Magnetic Resonance Imaging, Jl Magnetic Resonance, Computer Assisted Tomography, etc; 50 separate patents. *Recreations:* bird watching, hill walking, brick laying. *Address:* High Kingsbury, Kingsbury Street, Marlborough, Wilts SN8 1HZ. *T:* (01672) 516126.

YOUNG, James Edward D.; *see* Drummond Young.

YOUNG, Jimmy; *see* Young, L. R.

YOUNG, John Adrian Emile; Partner, Markby, Stewart & Wadesons, subseq. Cameron Markby Hewitt, 1965–95; *b* 28 July 1934; *s* of John Archibald Campbell Young and Irene Eugenie Young (*née* Bouvier); *m* 1959, Yvonne Lalage Elizabeth Bankes; three *s* one *d*. *Educ:* Cranbrook Sch., Kent; London Univ. (LLB). Admitted solicitor, 1958; Asst Sec., Law Soc., 1958–64. Adjudicator (formerly Legal Officer), Office of the Banking Ombudsman, 1996–98. Nat Chm., Young Solicitors Gp, 1965–66; Pres., Assoc. Internat. des Jeunes Avocats, 1968–69; Law Society: Mem. Council, 1971–95; Dep. Vice-Pres., 1993–94; Vice-Pres., 1994–95; Mem. Council, Internat. Bar Assoc., 1983–94. FRSA 1989. Master, City of London Solicitors' Co., 1989–90. *Publications:* sundry legal articles. *Recreations:* music (runs local church choir), gardening, family! *Address:* Stonewold House, The Street, Plaxtol, Sevenoaks, Kent TN15 0QH. *T:* (01732) 810289.

YOUNG, John Allen, CBE 1975; Chairman, Young & Co.'s Brewery, since 1962 (Chief Executive, 1989–99); *b* 7 Aug. 1921; *e s* of late William Allen Young and of Joan Barrow Simonds; *m* 1951, Yvonne Lieutenant, Liège; one *s*. *Educ:* Nautical Coll., Pangbourne; Corpus Christi Coll., Cambridge (BA Hons Econs). Served War, 1939–45: Lt-Comdr (A) RNVR; comd 888 Naval Air Sqdn (despatches). Runciman Ltd, 1947; Moor Line, 1949; Young & Co.'s Brewery, 1954–, Man. Dir, 1955–62. Chairman: Foster-Probyn Ltd; Cockburn & Campbell; RI Shipping Ltd. Gen. Comr of Taxes, 1965–91. President: London Carthorse Parade Soc., 1957–62; Shire Horse Soc., 1963–64 (Treas., 1962–73); Greater London Horse Show, 1972–74; Battersea Scouts, 1974–86; London Harness Horse Parade Soc., 1992–. Chm. Bd of Governors, Nat. Hosps for Nervous Diseases, 1982–86 (Mem. Bd, 1972–86; Chm. Finance, 1974–82); Dep. Chm., Inst. of Neurology, 1982–86 (Chm., Jt Res. Adv. Cttee, 1973–82); Pres., Nat. Hosps Develt Foundn, 1993– (Chm., 1984–93); Vice Pres., Chalfont Centre for Epilepsy, 1995– (Governor, 1983–95); Mem. Bd of Management, Royal Hosp. and Home, Putney, 1990–95. Trustee: Licensed Trade Charities Trust, 1984–91; Clapham Junction Disaster Fund, 1989–. Freeman: City of London, 1986; Borough of Wandsworth, 1992. *Recreations:* music, sailing. *Address:* Moonsbrook Cottage, Wisborough Green, West Sussex RH14 0EG. *Club:* Royal Yacht Squadron (Cowes).

YOUNG, John Henderson, OBE 1980; JP, DL; Member (C) West of Scotland, Scottish Parliament, since 1999; *b* 21 Dec. 1930; *s* of late William W. Young and Jeannie Young (*née* Henderson); *m* 1956, Doris Paterson (*d* 2001); one *s*. *Educ:* Hillhead High Sch., Glasgow; Scottish Coll. of Commerce. Served RAF, 1949–51. Shipping Manager/Dep. Contracts Manager, Kelvin-Diesel Engines, 1959–77; Export Admin Sales Manager, Teachers Whisky, 1977–88; Chm., Allied-Lyons Shipping & Marine Insce Cttee, 1987–88; Public Relns Consultant, Proscot Ltd, 1989–92. Newspaper columnist, The Extra, 1997–. Mem., Local Govt Commn, 1998. Mem. (C) Glasgow City Council, 1964–99: Leader, 1977–79; Opposition Leader, 1979–80, 1988–92, 1996–98; Police Judge, 1970–72; Bailie, 1968–71, 1977–80, 1984–88, 1988–92; Vice-Chm., Glasgow Corp. Airport Cttee, 1968–71; Mem., Strathclyde PTA, 1995–99. Chm., Assoc. Scottish Cons. Councillors, 1991–94. Tspt spokesman, Scottish Cons. Party, 1998–99. Mem., Scottish Parly Corporate Body, 1999–. Vice-Chm., Scottish Pakistani Assoc., 1981–84; Sec., Scottish/S African Soc., 1986–88. FIMgt 2001. Contested (C): Rutherglen, 1966; Cathcart, 1992; Eastwood, Scottish Parlt, 1999. Life Mem., Cathcart Conservatives. JP Glasgow, 1968; DL Glasgow, 1981. Gov., Hutcheson's Educnl Trust, 1991–97. KSJ. Life Mem., Merchants' House of Glasgow. *Publications:* A History of Cathcart Conservative Association 1918–93, 1993; contrib. articles to newspapers and magazines. *Recreations:* meeting people, history, writing, reading, animal welfare. *Address:* Scottish Parliament, George IV Bridge, Edinburgh EH99 1SP. *T:* (0131) 348 5000; Eastwood Conservative Office, 69 Ayr Road, Newton Mearns G77 6SP. *T:* (0141) 639 2686.

YOUNG, Sir John (Kenyon Roe), 6th Bt *cr* 1821; Purchasing Manager; *b* 23 April 1947; *s* of Sir John William Roe Young, 5th Bt, and Joan Minnie Agnes (*d* 1958), *d* of M. M. Aldous; *S* father, 1981; *m* 1977, Frances Elise, *o d* of W. R. Thompson; one *s* one *d*. *Educ:* Hurn Court; Napier College. Joined RN, 1963; transferred to Hydrographic Branch, 1970; qualified Hydrographic Surveyor, 1977; retired from RN, 1979; attended Napier Coll., 1979–80. Member: Hydrographic Soc.; Inst. of Purchasing Mgt. *Recreations:* Rugby, golf. *Heir:* *s* Richard Christopher Roe Young, *b* 14 June 1983. *Address:* Bolingey, 159 Chatham Road, Maidstone, Kent ME14 2ND.

YOUNG, Hon. Sir John (McIntosh), AC 1989; KCMG 1975. Lieutenant-Governor of Victoria, Australia, 1974–95; Chief Justice, Supreme Court of Victoria, 1974–91; *b* Melbourne, 17 Dec. 1919; *s* of George David Young, Glasgow, and Kathleen Mildred Young, Melbourne; *m* 1951, Elisabeth Mary, *yr d* of late Dr Edward Wing Twining, Manchester; one *s* two *d*. *Educ:* Geelong Grammar Sch.; Brasenose Coll., Oxford (MA; Hon. Fellow, 1991); Inner Temple; Univ. of Melbourne (LLB). Served War: Scots Guards, 1940–46 (Captain 1943); NW Europe (despatches), 1945. Admitted Victorian Bar, 1948; Associate to Mr Justice Dixon, High Court of Australia, 1948; practice as barrister, 1949–74; Hon. Sec., Victorian Bar Council, 1950–60; Lectr in Company Law, Univ. of Melbourne, 1957–61; Hon. Treas., Medico Legal Soc. of Vic., 1955–65 (Vice-Pres., 1966–68; Pres., 1968–69). QC (Vic) 1961; admitted Tasmanian Bar, 1964, QC 1964; NSW Bar, 1968, QC 1968; Consultant, Faculty of Law, Monash Univ., 1968–74. Mem., Bd of Examiners for Barristers and Solicitors, 1969–72; Pres.,Victorian Council of Legal Educn and Victoria Law Foundn, 1974–91; Chm., Police Board of Vic, 1992–98. Pres., Scout Assoc. of Australia, 1986–89, 1996–97 (Vice-Pres., 1985; Pres., Victorian Br., 1974–87); Chief Scout of Australia, 1989–96; Pres., St John Council for Victoria, 1975–82; GCStJ 1991 (KStJ 1977); Chancellor, Order of St John in Australia, 1982–91. Hon. Colonel: 4th/19th Prince of Wales's Light Horse, 1978–97; Royal Victoria Regt, 1994–99; Rep. Hon. Col, RAAC, 1986–97; Hon. Air Cdre, No 21 (City of Melbourne) Sqn, RAAF, 1986–98. Mem. Council, Geelong GS, 1974. Hon. LLD: Monash, 1986; Melbourne, 1989. *Publications:* (co-author) Australian Company Law and Practice, 1965; articles in legal jls. *Recreation:* reading. *Address:* 2/18 Huntingtower Road, Armadale, Victoria 3143, Australia. *T:* (3) 98226259. *Clubs:* Cavalry and Guards; Melbourne, Australian (Melbourne).

YOUNG, John Richard Dendy; Attorney of Supreme Court, South Africa, 1984; *b* 4 Sept. 1907; 5th *s* of James Young and Evelyn Maud Hammond; *m* 1946, Patricia Maureen Mount; four *s* two *d*. *Educ:* Hankey, Cape Province, SA; Humansdorp, CP, SA; University, South Africa (External). Joined Public Service, S Rhodesia, 1926; resigned to practise at Bar, 1934; joined Military Forces, 1940; active service, North Africa, Sicily and Italy; commissioned in the field; demobilised, 1945. QC 1948; MP Southern Rhodesia, 1948–53; Member Federal Assembly, 1953–56; Judge of the High Court of Rhodesia, 1956–68; Chief Justice, Botswana, 1968–71; Advocate of Supreme Court of SA, 1971–84; Sen. Counsel, 1979–84; Judge of Appeal, Lesotho, Swaziland, Botswana, 1979–84. *Recreations:* swimming, walking. *Address:* 8 Tulani Gardens, Greenfield Road, Kenilworth, Cape, 7700, South Africa.

YOUNG, John Robert Chester, CBE 1992; Nominated Member, since 1996, and Deputy Chairman, since 1997, Council of Lloyd's; Chairman, Lloyd's Regulatory Board, since 1997 (Member, since 1996); *b* 6 Sept. 1937; *s* of Robert Nisbet Young and Edith Mary (*née* Roberts); *m* 1963, Pauline Joyce (*d* 1997); one *s* one *d* (and one *s* decd). *Educ:* Bishop Vesey's Grammar Sch.; St Edmund Hall, Oxford Univ. (MA); Gray's Inn, London. Joined Simon & Coates, members of the Stock Exchange, 1961; Partner, 1965; Dep. Sen. Partner, 1976; London Stock Exchange (formerly Stock Exchange, subseq. Internat. Stock Exchange): Mem. Council, 1978–82; Dir of Policy and Planning, 1982–87; Vice-Chm. (non-exec.), Managing Bd, 1987–90. Chief Exec. and Dir, SFA (formerly Securities Assoc.), 1987–93; Dir, 1993–97, Chief Exec., 1993–95, SIB. Non-executive Director: Darby Gp plc, 1996–97; Elderstreet Millennium (formerly Gartmore) Venture Capital Trust, 1996–; E Surrey Healthcare (formerly E Surrey Hosp. and Community Healthcare) NHS Trust, 1992–96. Public Interest Dir, Financial Services Compensation Scheme Ltd, 2000–. Mem. Ethics Cttee, Securities Inst., 1995–. Advr, Royal Sch. for the Blind, 1997–. Formerly internat. athlete, Rugby player (England and British Lions) and England Rugby selector. FRSA 1995. *Recreations:* cooking, grandsons, Rugby football. *Address:* Richmond House, Falkland Grove, Dorking, Surrey RH4 3DL. *Clubs:* City of London; Vincent's (Oxford); Harlequins, Achilles.
See also L. Botting.

YOUNG, Sir John Robertson, (Sir Rob), KCMG 1999 (CMG 1991); HM Diplomatic Service; High Commissioner, New Delhi, since 1999; *b* 21 Feb. 1945; *s* of late Francis John Young and of Marjorie Elizabeth Young; *m* 1967, Catherine Suzanne Françoise Houssait; one *s* two *d*. *Educ:* King Edward VI Sch., Norwich; Leicester Univ. (BA 1st Cl. Hons, French). Entered FCO, 1967; MECAS, Lebanon, 1968; Third Sec., Cairo, 1970; Second Sec., FCO, 1972; Private Sec. to Minister of State, 1975; First Sec., Paris, 1977; Asst Head, Western European Dept, FCO, 1982; Counsellor, Damascus, 1984; Head of Middle East Dept, FCO, 1987; Minister, Paris, 1991; Dep. Under-Sec. of State, 1994–98, and Chief Clerk, 1995–98, FCO. *Recreations:* music, sailing, theatre. *Address:* c/o Foreign and Commonwealth Office, SW1A 2AH. *Clubs:* Beefsteak, Cruising Association.

YOUNG, John William Garne; Group Chief Executive, Wolseley plc, 1996–2000; *b* 6 Jan. 1945; *s* of David Richard Young and Pamela Mary Young (*née* Garne); *m* 1971, Eleanor Louise Walsh; three *s*. *Educ:* Shaftesbury Grammar Sch. Apprentice, Tube Investment Gp, 1962–67; Man. Dir, P. J. Parmiter & Sons Ltd, 1967–85; Wolseley plc: Chief Exec., Agricl Div., 1982–90, Agricl, Photographic & Technical Services Div., 1990–95; Dep. Chief Exec., 1994–96. *Recreations:* fishing, golf. *Address:* The Gables, Hindon Lane, Tisbury, Salisbury, Wilts SP3 6QF.

YOUNG, Jonathan Piers; Editor, The Field, since 1991; *b* 23 Sept. 1959; *s* of Peter and Mavis Young; *m* 1993, Caroline Bankes; one *s* one *d*. *Educ:* Blundell's; Univ. of Leicester (BA). Ed., Shooting Times and Country Magazine, 1986–90. *Publication:* A Pattern of Wings, 1989. *Recreations:* shooting, fishing, sloe-ginning. *Address:* The Field, King's Reach Tower, Stamford Street, SE1 9LS. *T:* (020) 7261 5198. *Clubs:* Flyfishers'; Tyburn Angling Society.

YOUNG, Joyce Jean, RGN, RMN; independent consultant and advisor to health services, since 1993; *b* 16 Nov. 1936; *d* of Leslie Cyril and Frances May Lyons. *Educ:* Cowes High School, Isle of Wight. General Nurse training, Essex County Hosp., Colchester, 1955–58; Mental Nurse training, Severalls Hosp., Colchester, 1959–60; Ward Sister posts, gen. and psych. hosps, 1960–70; Clinical Nurse Advr, Hosp. Adv. Service, 1970–72; Regl Nurse Advr, SE Metrop. Hosp. Bd for Mental Illness, Mental Handicap and Elderly Services, 1972–74; Dist Nursing Officer, Tunbridge Wells Health Dist., 1974–80; Chief Nursing Officer, Brighton HA, 1980–84; Regl Nursing Officer, Oxford, 1984–92. Dir and Chief Exec., Blenheim House Ltd, 1996. Nursing Advisor to Social Services Select Cttee, 1985; Mem., Broadmoor Hosp. Management Bd, 1987; Dir, NSQT, 1992–94; Member: Prison Health Adv. Cttee, 1992; (non-exec.), Bd, Special Hosps Service Authy, 1993. *Publications:* (contrib.) Impending Crisis of Old Age (Nuffield Provincial Trust), 1981; articles in Nursing Times and Nursing Mirror. *Recreations:* gardening, wild life.

YOUNG, Junor; *see* Young, D. J.

YOUNG, Kenneth Middleton, CBE 1977; Chairman, Further Education Funding Council for Wales, 1999–2001 (Member, Council, and Quality Assurance Committee, 1998–2001); *b* 1 Aug. 1931; *s* of Cyril W. D. Young and Gwladys Middleton Young; *m* 1958, Brenda May Thomas; one *s* one *d*. *Educ:* Neath Grammar Sch.; University Coll. of Wales, Aberystwyth (Hon. Fellow, 1991); Coll. of Science and Technology, Univ. of Manchester. BA (Hons) 1952; Diploma in Personnel Management, 1954. Pilot Officer/Navigator, General Duties (Aircrew), RAF, 1952–54. Asst Personnel Manager, Elliott-Automation Ltd, 1955–59; Collective Agreements Manager, later Salary Administration Manager, Massey-Ferguson (UK) Ltd, 1959–64; Personnel Adviser, Aviation Div., Smiths Industries Ltd, 1964–66; Group Personnel Manager, General Electric Company Ltd, and Dir, GEC (Management) Ltd, 1966–71; Post Office Corporation, 1972–92: Bd Mem. for Personnel, 1972–84, for Personnel and Corporate Resources, 1984–90; Man. Dir, Royal Mail Parcels, 1987; Vice-Chm., 1986–90; Actg Chm., 1989; Dep. Chm., 1990–92; Chairman: Subscription Services, 1988–92; Girobank PLC, 1989–90; Post Office Counters, 1990–92. Chm., Student Loans Co. Ltd, 1992–96; Director: Courage (formerly FBG) Pensions Ltd, 1993–; Courage (formerly FBG) Pensions Investments Ltd, 1993–. Member: Management Bd, Engineering Employers Fedn, 1971; CBI Employment Policy Cttee, 1978–84; Employment Appeal Tribunal, 1985–; BIC Target Team on Business/Educn Partnerships, 1988–89; Trustee, Post Office Pension Funds, 1989–95. Chairman: Rev. Gp, Further Educn Funding Councils for England and Wales, 1993; Further Educn Develt Assoc., subseq. Agency, 1994–97. Member: Council, Inst. of Manpower Studies, 1980–86; London Business Sch. Liaison Cttee, 1982–89; Chairman: Bd of Govs, SW London Coll., 1991; Roehampton Inst., 1992–95; Vice-Pres., Univ. of Wales (formerly St David's UC), Lampeter, 1993–99; Member: Council, Univ. of Wales, Aberystwyth, 1994–97 (Pres., Old Students Assoc., 1998–2000); Ct of Govs, 1998–2000, Council, 1999–2000, Univ. of Wales. CIMgt; FIPM. *Recreations:* photography, Wales Rugby, theatre. *Address:* Bryn Aber, Northcliffe Drive, Penarth, South Glamorgan CF64 1DQ.

YOUNG, Sir Leslie (Clarence), Kt 1984; CBE 1980; DL; Chairman, Enterprise plc, 1999–2000 (Director, Lancashire Enterprises, later Enterprise, plc, 1992–99); *b* 5 Feb. 1925; *s* of late Clarence James Young and of Ivy Isabel Young; *m* 1st, 1949, Muriel Howard Pearson (*d* 1998); one *s* one *d*; 2nd, 1999, Margaret Gittens. *Educ:* London School of Economics (BScEcon). Courtaulds Ltd: held range of senior executive appts, incl. chairmanship of number of gp companies, 1948–68; J. Bibby & Sons Ltd, 1968–86: Managing Director, J. Bibby Agriculture Ltd, 1968; Chm. and Man. Dir, J. Bibby Food Products Ltd, 1970; Gp Man. Dir, 1970, Dep. Chm. and Man. Dir, 1977, Chm., 1979–86, J. Bibby & Sons Ltd. Director: Bank of England, 1986–90; National Westminster Bank, 1986–90 (Regl Dir, 1979–90, Chm., 1986–90, Northern Regl Bd); Swiss Pioneer Life (formerly Pioneer Mutual Insce Co.), 1986–92; Sibec Developments PLC, 1988–91; Britannia Cable Systems Wirral plc, 1990–92. Chairman: NW Regional Council, CBI, 1976–78; NW Industrial Development Board, 1978–81; Merseyside Develt Corp., 1980–84; British Waterways Bd, 1984–87. Trustee, Civic Trust for the North West, 1978–83. Non-Exec. Dir, Granada Television Ltd, 1979–84. Chm. Trustees, Nat. Museums and Galls on Merseyside, 1986–95. Member Council: N of England Zoological Soc., 1979–85; Royal Liverpool Philharmonic Soc., 1980–. DL Merseyside, 1983. Hon. Col, Liverpool Univ. OTC, 1989–94. Hon. LLD Liverpool, 1988. *Recreations:* fly-fishing, walking. *Address:* Gloverstone Court, Castle Street, Chester CH1 2DS. *T:* (01244) 401276.

YOUNG, Leslie Ronald, (Jimmy Young), CBE 1993 (OBE 1979); Presenter, Jimmy Young Programme, BBC Radio Two, since 1973 (Radio One, 1967–73); *b* 21 Sept.; *s* of Frederick George Young and Gertrude Woolford; *m* 1st, 1946, Wendy Wilkinson (marr. diss.); one *d*; 2nd, 1950, Sally Douglas (marr. diss.); 3rd, 1996, Alicia Plastow. *Educ:* East Dean Grammar Sch., Cinderford, Glos. RAF, 1939–46. First BBC radio broadcast, songs at piano, 1949; pianist, singer, bandleader, West End, London, 1950–51; first theatre appearance, Empire Theatre, Croydon, 1952; regular theatre appearances, 1952–; first radio broadcast introd. records, Flat Spin, 1953; BBC TV Bristol, Pocket Edition series, 1955; first introd. radio Housewives' Choice, 1955; BBC radio series, incl.: The Night is Young, 12 o'clock Spin, Younger Than Springtime, Saturday Special, Keep Young, Through Till Two, 1959–65; presented progs, Radio Luxembourg, 1960–68. BBC TV: series, Jimmy Young Asks, 1972; The World of Jimmy Young, 1973. First live direct BBC broadcasts to Europe from Soviet Union, Jimmy Young Programme, 16 and 17 May 1977; Jimmy Young Programmes broadcast live from Egypt and Israel, 9 and 12 June 1978, from Zimbabwe-Rhodesia, 9 and 10 Aug. 1979; Host for Thames TV of first British Telethon, 2nd and 3rd Oct. 1980; Jimmy Young Programmes live from Tokyo, 26th, 27th and 28th May 1981, from Sydney, 4–8 Oct. 1982, from Washington DC, 3–7 Oct. 1983. ITV series: Whose Baby?, 1973; Jim's World, 1974; The Jimmy Young Television Programme, 1984–87. Hit Records: 1st, Too Young, 1951; Unchained Melody, The Man From Laramie, 1955 (1st Brit. singer to have 2 consec. no 1 hit records); Chain Gang, More, 1956; Miss You, 1963. Weekly Column, Daily Sketch, 1968–71. Hon. Mem. Council, NSPCC, 1981–. Freeman, City of London, 1969. Variety Club of GB Award, Radio Personality of the Year, 1968; Sony Award, Radio Personality of the Year, 1985; Sony Radio Awards Roll of Honour, 1988; Radio Broadcaster of the Year, BPG Radio Awards, 1994; Sony Gold Award, for Service to the Community, 1995, for Outstanding Service to Radio, 1997; Jimmy Young Programme: Radio Industries Award, Prog. of the Year, 1979; BBC Current Affairs Prog. of the Year, Daily Mail Nat. Radio Awards, 1988; Radio Prog. of the Year, TV and Radio Inds Club Award, 1989. Silver Jubilee Medal, 1977. *Publications:* Jimmy Young Cookbook: No 1, 1968; No 2, 1969; No 3, 1970; No 4, 1972; (autobiogs) JY, 1973, Jimmy Young, 1982; contrib. magazines, incl. Punch, Woman's Own. *Address:* c/o Broadcasting House, Portland Place, W1A 1AA. *Club:* Wigan Rugby League Social.

YOUNG, Prof. Lola, OBE 2001; PhD; Professor of Cultural Studies, Middlesex University, since 1997; *b* 1 June 1951; *d* of Maxwell Fela Young and Yele Santos; *m* 1984, Barrie Birch; one *s*. *Educ:* Middlesex Univ. (BA Hons; PhD 1995). Social worker, 1971–73; actor, 1976–85; Arts Develt Officer, Haringey Arts Council, 1985–89; freelance arts consultant, 1989–90; Lecturer: (pt-time) in Media Studies, 1989–90; Thames Valley Univ., 1990–92; Middx Univ., 1992–97. Advr to Arts Council, 2000–. Member: RCHME, 2000–; Board: inIVA, 1994; RNT, 2000–; Resource: Council for Museums, Archives & Libraries, 2000–. FRSA 1986. *Publications:* Fear of the Dark: race, gender and sexuality in cinema, 1996; contrib. articles and chapters in edited books; contrib. articles to acad. jls, incl. Women: A Cultural Rev., Cultural Studies from Birmingham, Oxford Art Jl, Parallax. *Recreations:* hiking, cinema, theatre, reading. *Address:* Middlesex University, White Hart Lane, N17 8HR. *T:* (020) 8411 6036. *Club:* Royal Commonwealth Society.

YOUNG, Hon. M. Douglas; PC (Canada) 1993; Chairman, Summa Strategies Canada, Inc., since 1997; *b* 20 Sept. 1940; *s* of Douglas Young and Annie Young (*née* Wishart); *m* 1979, Jacqueline David; one *s* two *d*. *Educ:* St Thomas Univ., USA (BA 1972); Univ. of New Brunswick (LLB 1975); New Brunswick Teachers' Coll. Cert., 1957. Lawyer and businessman; Counsel to Atlantic Canada Lawyers, Patterson Palmer Hunt Murphy. MLA for Tracadie, New Brunswick, 1978–88; Leader, New Brunswick Liberal Party, 1981–83; Provincial Minister of Fisheries and Aquaculture, 1987–88; MP (L) Gloucester, renamed Acadie-Bathurst, 1988–97; Canadian Minister: of Transport, 1993–96; of Human Resources, 1996; of Nat. Defence and of Veteran Affairs, 1996–97. Chairman: Canada–Taiwan Business Council; Maritime Road Develt Corp.; Sisters of Charity of Ottawa Health Service Foundn; Director: Magellan Aerospace Corp.; Genesee & Wyoming Inc.; CPCS Transcom Ltd; GRO Inc. Mem., Council for Canadian Unity. *Recreations:* ski-ing, reading, travelling. *Address:* (office) 100 Sparks Street, Suite 1000, Ottawa, ON K1P 5B7, Canada.

YOUNG, Malcolm, (Mal); Controller of Continuing Drama Series, BBC, since 2001; *b* 26 Jan. 1957; *s* of Charles Young, Liverpool, and Maria (*née* Williams). *Educ:* Liverpool Sch. of Art (DipAD). Design Manager, Littlewoods Orgn, 1975–81; actor/singer, 1981–84; Mersey Television, 1984–96: Design Asst on Brookside, then Asst Floor Manager and Floor Manager, 1986–91; Producer, Brookside and Dir, Brookside Prodns, 1991–95; Series Producer, Brookside, 1995–96 (also devised and produced And The Beat Goes On, Channel 4); Hd of Drama, Pearson TV, 1996–97; Hd of BBC Drama Series, 1997–2001, responsible for: EastEnders, Casualty, Holby City, Silent Witness, Waking the Dead, Doctors, Murder in Mind, In Deep, Judge John Deed, Mersey Beat, Down to Earth, etc. Huw Wheldon Meml Lecture, RTS, 1999. *Publication:* Sinbad's Scrapbook, 1996. *Recreations:* big music fan, musician, travelling in USA, telly addict from an early age. *Address:* BBC Centre House, Wood Lane, W12 7SB. *T:* (020) 8576 9460.

YOUNG, Neil; *see* Young, R. N.

YOUNG, Sir Nicholas (Charles), Kt 2000; Chief Executive, British Red Cross, since 2001; *b* 16 April 1952; *s* of late Leslie Charles Young and Mary Margaret Young (*née* Rudman); *m* 1978, Helen Mary Ferrier Hamilton; three *s*. *Educ:* Wimbledon Coll.; Birmingham Univ. (Hons LLB 2.1). Qualified Solicitor, 1977; Articled Clerk and Solicitor, Freshfields, 1975–78; Solicitor, later Partner, Turner, Martin & Symes, 1979–85; Sec. for Develt, Sue Ryder Foundn, 1985–90; Dir, UK Ops, BRCS, 1990–95; Chief Exec., 1995–2001 and Vice-Pres., 2001–, Macmillan Cancer Relief (formerly Cancer Relief Macmillan Fund). Vice Chm., Nat. Council for Hospice and Specialist Palliative Care Services, 1996–99; Member: Exec. Cttee, Healthwork UK, 1998–; NCVO Charity Law Reform Gp, 1998–; NHS Modernisation Bd, 2000–; Trustee, and Chm. Finance Cttee, Monte San Martino Trust, 2000–; Steering Cttee, The Giving Campaign, 2000–. Mem., Stumblers Assoc, 1978–. Gov., Wimbledon Coll, 1998–2000. *Recreations:* reading, theatre, walking, amateur dramatics, travel. *Address:* British Red Cross, 9 Grosvenor Crescent, SW1X 7EJ. *T:* (020) 7235 5454.

YOUNG, Peter Lance; Group Chief Executive, RMC Group, 1996–2000; *b* 26 June 1938; *s* of Harry Aubrey Young and Ethel Freda Young; *m* 1962, Susan Mary Wilkes; three *s* one *d*. *Educ:* Chippenham Grammar Sch. Joined RMC Group, 1961; Dir, 1977; Dep. Man. Dir, 1992; Man. Dir, 1993. *Recreations:* tennis, gardening. *Address:* RMC House, Coldharbour Lane, Thorpe, Egham, Surrey TW20 8TD.

YOUNG, Peter Michael Heppell, OBE 1995; HM Diplomatic Service, retired; *b* 23 April 1939; *s* of Denis Stanley Young and late Constance Young; *m* 1st, 1969, Maria Laura Aragon; 2nd, Verona Buchan; two step *s*. *Educ:* Haileybury Coll.; Williston Acad., USA (ESU Scholarship); Emmanuel Coll., Cambridge (MA). FCIPD. Royal Marines and Royal West Africa Frontier Force (2nd Lieut), 1958–60; FCO, 1964; served: Sofia, 1967–70; Geneva, 1970–72; Pretoria/Capetown, 1972–74; FCO 1974–77; First Sec., Lagos, 1977–79; Dep. High Comr, Ibadan, 1979–80; Consul (Commercial), Lyon, 1981–84; FCO, 1985–89; Counsellor, Lagos, 1989–93; seconded to Dept of National Heritage (Events Director, D-Day and VE-Day 50th Annivs), 1993–95; High Comr, Bahamas, 1996–99. *Recreations:* tennis, golf, African history. *Address:* PO Box EE, 16944 Nassau, Bahamas. *Clubs:* Oxford and Cambridge, MCC; Lyford Cay.

YOUNG, Priscilla Helen Ferguson, CBE 1982; Director, Central Council for Education and Training in Social Work, 1971–86; retired; *b* 25 Nov. 1925; *d* of Fergus Ferguson Young and Helen Frances Graham (*née* Murphy). *Educ:* Kingsley Sch., Leamington Spa; Univ. of Edinburgh (MA). Social Worker: London Family Welfare

Assoc., 1947–51; Somerset CC Children's Dept, 1951–53; Oxford City Children's Dept, 1953–58 (Dep. Children's Officer); Child and Family Services, Portland, Me, USA, 1958–61; Lectr/Sen. Lectr, Sch. of Social Work, Univ. of Leicester, 1961–71. Nat. Chairperson, Family Service Units, 1987–93. Hon. Fellow, Sheffield City Polytechnic, 1977. Hon. DLitt Ulster, 1987.

YOUNG, Sir Richard (Dilworth), Kt 1970; BSc, FIMechE; Chairman, Boosey & Hawkes Ltd, 1979–84 (Deputy Chairman, 1978–79); Director: The Rugby Group PLC (formerly Rugby Portland Cement Co.), 1968–89; Commonwealth Finance Development Corp. Ltd, 1968–86; *b* 9 April 1914; *s* of Philip Young and Constance Maria Lloyd; *m* 1951, Jean Barbara Paterson Lockwood, *d* of F. G. Lockwood; four *s*. *Educ:* Bromsgrove; Bristol Univ. Joined Weldless Steel Tube Co. Ltd, 1934; served with Tube Investments companies in engineering capacities until 1944; Man. Dir of Tubos Britanicos (Argentina) Ltda, 1945–50; Man. Dir of TI (Export) Ltd, 1950–53; Sales Dir of TI Aluminium Ltd, 1953–56; Asst to Chm. of Tube Investments Ltd, 1957–60; Dir, 1958; Asst Man. Dir, 1959; Man. Dir, 1961–64; Chairman: Park Gate Iron & Steel Co., 1959–64; Raleigh Industries Ltd, 1960–64; Alfred Herbert Ltd: Dep. Chm., 1965–66; Chm., 1966–74; Director: Ingersoll Milling Machine Co., USA, 1967–71; Ingersoll Engineers Inc., 1976–86; Retirement Securities Ltd, 1983–94. Member: Council BIM, 1960–65; Council, CBI, 1967–74; Council, IMechE, 1969–76; Adv. Cttee on Scientific Manpower, 1962–65; SSRC, 1973–75; Council, Warwick Univ., 1966–89; Central Adv. Council on Science and Technol., 1967–70; SRC Engineering Bd, 1974–76. Freeman, City of London, 1987. CIMgt. Hon. DSc Warwick, 1987. *Club:* Athenæum.

YOUNG, Sir Rob; *see* Young, Sir J. R.

YOUNG, Robert; Principal, since 2000, and Director, since 2001, LECG Ltd; *b* 27 March 1944; *s* of Walter Horace Young and Evelyn Joan Young; *m* 1965, Patricia Anne Cowin; one *s* one *d* (and one *s* decd). *Educ:* Magdalen College, Oxford (BA Hons 1965; MA). Graduate apprentice, Rolls-Royce, 1965; IBM UK, 1969–71; Rolls-Royce Motors, 1971–81: Man. Dir, Military Engine Div., 1977–79; Dir and Gen. Manager, Diesel Div., 1979–81; Vickers, 1981–85 (Group Commercial Dir, 1981–83); Man. Dir, Crane Ltd, 1985–88; Chief Exec., Plastics Div., McKechnie plc, 1989–90; Dir, Beauford plc, 1990–92; Competition Policy Consultant, Coopers & Lybrand, 1993–98; Dir, PricewaterhouseCoopers, 1998–2000. Member: Central Policy Review Staff, 1983; No 10 Policy Unit, 1983–84; CBI W Midlands Regional Council, 1980–81 (Chm., CBI Shropshire, 1981); Monopolies and Mergers Commn, 1986–92; Fulbright Commn, 1994–. FInstD. *Recreations:* Mozart, railways, cats, photography. *Address:* 12 Beechcroft Road, SW14 7JJ.

YOUNG, Prof. Robert Joseph, PhD; CEng; FIM; FInstP; Professor of Polymer Science and Technology, University of Manchester Institute of Science and Technology, since 1986; *b* 29 May 1948; *s* of Joseph and Florence Young; *m* 1971, Sheila Winifred Wilson; two *d*. *Educ:* St John's Coll., Cambridge (MA, PhD). Res. Fellow, St John's Coll., Cambridge, 1973–75; Lectr in Materials, QMC, 1975–86. Wolfson Res. Prof. in Materials Science, Royal Soc., 1992–97. Zeneca Lect., 1996, BAAS Public Lect., 1997, Royal Soc. Panel Chm., HEFCE RAE, 2001. *Publications:* Introduction to Polymers, 1981, 2nd edn (jtly), 1991; (jtly) Fracture Behaviour of Polymers, 1983; more than 200 papers in learned jls. *Recreations:* tennis, piano, gardening; former athlete (four blues, 1967–70; British Univs' Sports Fedn 110m Hurdles Champion, 1970). *Address:* Manchester Materials Science Centre, UMIST/University of Manchester, Grosvenor Street, Manchester M1 7HS. *T:* (0161) 200 3551.

YOUNG, Robin Urquhart; Permanent Secretary, Department of Trade and Industry, since 2001; *b* 7 Sept. 1948; *s* of late Col Ian U. Young and of Mary Young; *m* 1998, Madeleine Arnot. *Educ:* Fettes Coll., Edinburgh; University Coll., Oxford (BA 1971). Joined DoE, 1973; Private Sec. to Parly Sec., Planning and Local Govt, 1976; Private Sec. to Minister of Housing, 1980–81; Local Govt Finance, 1981–85; Private Sec. to successive Secs of State, 1985–88; Under Secretary: Housing, 1988–89; Envmt Policy, 1989–91; Local Govt Review, 1991–92; Local Govt, DoE, 1992–94; Dep. Sec., 1994–98; Regl Dir, Govt Office for London, 1994–97; Hd of Econ. and Domestic Affairs Secretariat, Cabinet Office, 1997–98; Permanent Sec., DCMS, 1998–2001. Dir (non-exec.), Bovis Construction Ltd, 1989–94. *Recreations:* squash, tennis, cinema. *Address:* Department of Trade and Industry, 1 Victoria Street, SW1H 0ET.

YOUNG, (Roderic) Neil; Investment Consultant, since 1989; *b* 29 May 1933; *s* of late Dr F. H. Young and of S. M. Young (*née* Robinson); *m* 1962, Gillian Margaret Salmon; two *s* one *d*. *Educ:* Eton; Trinity College, Cambridge (MA). FCA. 2nd Lieut Queen's Own Royal West Kent Regt, 1952–53. Howard Howes & Co., 1956–59; Fenn & Crosthwaite, 1960–63; Brown Fleming & Murray, 1964–68; Director: Murray Johnstone, 1969–70; Kleinwort Benson, 1971–88. Director: Malvern UK Index Trust, 1990–98; London and SE Bd, Bradford and Bingley Bldg Soc., 1990–97. City of London: Mem., Court of Common Council, 1980; Alderman, Ward of Bread Street, 1982–94; Sheriff, 1991–92; Master, Gunmakers' Co., 1994–95. Adv. Cttee, Greenwich Hosp., 1983–. *Recreations:* gardening, shooting, DIY, golf. *Address:* Pembury Hall, Pembury, Kent TN2 4AT. *T:* (01892) 822971. *Club:* Rye Golf.

YOUNG, Roger; President, FPL Group Inc., 1999–2000; *b* 14 Jan. 1944; *s* of Arnold and Margaret Young; *m* 1970, Sue Neilson; one *s* two *d*. *Educ:* Gordonstoun Sch.; Edinburgh Univ. (BSc Engrg); Cranfield Business Sch. (MBA). Rolls-Royce Ltd, 1961–72; Alidair Ltd, 1972–73; Wavin Plastics Ltd, 1973–76; Aurora Holdings Ltd, 1976–80; Low & Bonar plc, 1980–88; Chief Exec., Scottish Hydro-Electric plc, 1988–98. Non-executive Director: Friends Ivory & Sime (formerly Ivory & Sime) plc, 1993–99; Bank of Scotland, 1994–99. *Recreations:* family, hill walking, aviation.

YOUNG, Roger Dudley; Director General, Institute of Enterprise, since 1998; *b* 7 Jan. 1940; *s* of Henry G. Young and Winifred G. Young; *m* 1965, Jennifer J. Drayton; one *s* two *d*. *Educ:* Dulwich Coll. Drayton Group, 1958–69; Imperial Group, 1969–73; Robert Fleming, 1971–73; Director: Henry Ansbacher Group, 1973–82; Touche Remnant Group, 1982–85; Chief Executive: Bank Julius Baer (London), 1985–89; March Group, 1989–91; Dir Gen., Inst. of Mgt, 1992–98. Chairman: Clex Developments, 1976–; Winsade Finance, 1967–; Acorn Business Services (Anglia), 1996–; ASA Communicate Ltd, 1998–; Axcel Ltd, 1998–; Andrews and Partners Ltd; Andrews Estate Agents Ltd; World in Need; Bicon Marketing Ltd, 2000–; PMP Plus Ltd, 2000–. Director: Ipswich Hosp. NHS Trust, 1992–99; non-exec. appts. CIMgt; FRSA. *Recreations:* small businesses, tennis, sculpture. *Address:* Institute of Enterprise, Ashbrook House, Layham Road, Layham, Ipswich IP7 5NB. *T:* and *Fax:* (01473) 828878. *Club:* Honourable Artillery Company.

YOUNG, Sir Roger (William), Kt 1983; MA; STh, LHD, FRSE; Principal of George Watson's College, Edinburgh, 1958–85; *b* 15 Nov. 1923; *yr s* of late Charles Bowden Young and Dr Ruth Young, CBE; *m* 1950, Caroline Mary Christie; two *s* two *d*. *Educ:* Dragon Sch., Oxford; Westminster Sch. (King's Scholar); Christ Church, Oxford (Scholar). Served War of 1939–45, RNVR, 1942–45. Classical Mods, 1946, Lit Hum 1948. Resident Tutor, St Catharine's, Cumberland Lodge, Windsor, 1949–51; Asst Master, The Manchester Grammar Sch., 1951–58. 1st Class in Archbishop's examination in Theology (Lambeth Diploma), 1957. Participant, US State Dept Foreign Leader Program, 1964. Scottish Governor, BBC, 1979–84. Member: Edinburgh Marriage Guidance Council, 1960–75; Scottish Council of Christian Educn Movement, 1960–81 (Chm., 1961–67; Hon. Vice-Pres., 1981–85); Gen. Council of Christian Educn Movement, 1985–94 (Vice-Pres., 1989–); Management Assoc., SE Scotland, 1965–85; Educational Research Bd of SSRC, 1966–70; Court, Edinburgh Univ., 1967–76; Public Schools Commn, 1968–70; Consultative Cttee on the Curriculum, 1972–75; Adv. Cttee, Scottish Centre for Studies in Sch. Administration, 1972–75; Royal Soc. of Edinburgh Dining Club, 1972–; Scottish Adv. Cttee, Community Service Volunteers, 1973–78; Edinburgh Festival Council, 1970–76; Independent Schs Panel of Wolfson Foundn, 1978–82; Gen. Adv. Council of BBC, 1978–79; Scottish Council of Independent Schs, 1978–85; Royal Observatory Trust, Edin., 1981–93; Council, RSE, 1982–85; ISJC, 1988–94. Hon. Sec., Headmasters' Assoc. of Scotland, 1968–72, Pres., 1972–74; Chairman: HMC, 1976; BBC Consult. Gp on Social Effects of TV, 1978–79; Bursary Bd, Dawson International Ltd, 1977–85; Bath Film Soc., 1990–93; Catch-up Prog. for World in Need, 1996–2000; Caxton Trust, 1998–2000; Dep. Chm., GBA, 1988–94. Trustee: Campion Sch., Athens, 1984–91; Wells Cathedral Sch., 1987–; Chm. Council, Cheltenham Ladies' Coll., 1986–93; Member, Governing Body: Westminster Sch., 1986–97; Royal Sch., Bath, 1987–99; Mem. Council, Bath Univ., 1993–96, 1997–2001. Conducted Enquiry on Stirling Univ., 1973. Hon. LHD, Hamilton Coll., Clinton, NY, 1978. *Publications:* Lines of Thought, 1958; Everybody's Business, 1968; Everybody's World, 1970; Report on the Policies and Running of Stirling University 1966–1973, 1973. *Recreations:* gardening, films, photography, climbing, music, knitting. *Address:* 11 Belgrave Terrace, Bath BA1 5JR. *T:* (01225) 336940. *Club:* East India.

YOUNG, Prof. Stephen John, PhD; Professor of Information Engineering, Cambridge University, since 1995; Fellow of Emmanuel College, Cambridge, since 1985; *b* 23 Jan. 1951; *s* of John Leonard Young and Joan Young (*née* Shaw); *m* 1976 (marr. diss. 1996); two *d*; *m* 1999, Sybille Wiesmann. *Educ:* Maghull GS; Jesus Coll., Cambridge (MA, PhD). FIOA, FIEE, MBCS, CEng. Res. Engr, GEC Hirst Res. Centre, 1973–74; Univ. Lectr in Computation, UMIST, 1977–84; Lectr in Engrg, 1984–95, Reader, 1995, Cambridge Univ.; Tech. Dir, Entropic Cambridge Res. Lab., 1996–99; Architect, Microsoft Corp., 1999–2001. Editor, Computer Speech and Language, 1993–. *Publications:* Real Time Languages, 1982; An Introduction to Ada, 1985; (ed) Corpus-based Methods, 1997; articles in jls. *Recreations:* film, music, ski-ing. *Address:* Engineering Department, Trumpington Street, Cambridge CB2 1PZ. *T:* (01223) 332654.

YOUNG, Sir Stephen Stewart Templeton, 3rd Bt *cr* 1945; Sheriff Principal of Grampian, Highland and Islands, since 2001; advocate; *b* 24 May 1947; *s* of Sir Alastair Young, 2nd Bt, and Dorothy Constance Marcelle (*d* 1964), *d* of late Lt-Col Charles Ernest Chambers, and *widow* of Lt J. H. Grayburn, VC, Parachute Regt; *S* father, 1963; *m* 1974, Viola Margaret Nowell-Smith, *d* of Prof. P. H. Nowell-Smith, *qv* and Perilla Thyme (she *m* 2nd, Lord Roberthall, KCMG, CB); two *s*. *Educ:* Rugby; Trinity Coll., Oxford; Edinburgh Univ. Voluntary Service Overseas, Sudan, 1968–69. Sheriff: of Glasgow and Strathkelvin, March–June 1984; of N Strathclyde at Greenock, 1984–2001. *Heir:* *s* Charles Alastair Stephen Young, *b* 21 July 1979. *Address:* Glen Rowan, Shore Road, Cove, Dunbartonshire G84 0NU.

YOUNG, Thomas Nesbitt; HM Diplomatic Service; High Commissioner, Zambia, since 1998; *b* 24 July 1943; *s* of Sir Frank Young, FRS and Lady (Ruth) Young, DPM; *m* 1971, Elisabeth Ann Shepherdson (*née* Hick) (MBE 1998); one *s* one *d*. *Educ:* The Leys Sch., Cambridge; Pembroke Coll., Oxford (BA Hons Chem., MA). Teaching, Kigezi Coll., Kabale, Uganda, 1962; joined HM Diplomatic Service, 1966; Ankara, 1969–71; Madrid, 1972–76; Head of Chancery, Ankara, 1979–80; Dep. Dir of Trade Develt, NY, 1981; First Sec., Washington, 1981–84; Asst Head, Nuclear Energy Dept, FCO, 1984–86; Dep. High Comr, Accra, 1987–90; Dir of Trade Promotion, British High Commn, Canberra, 1990–93; Ambassador to Azerbaijan, 1993–97. *Recreations:* hill-walking, sailing, Renaissance music, reaching inaccessible places. *Address:* c/o Foreign and Commonwealth Office, King Charles Street, SW1A 2AH.

YOUNG, Timothy Mark Stewart; Headmaster, Royal Grammar School, Guildford, since 1992; *b* 6 Oct. 1951; *s* of Sir Brian Walter Mark Young, *qv*; *m* 1990, Dr Alison Mary Keightley, MRCP, FRCR; two *s*. *Educ:* Eton (King's Schol.); Magdalene Coll., Cambridge (BA 1974; MA 1978); Bristol Univ. (PGCE 1975). Asst Master, Eton, 1975–83 and 1985–87; Asst Master, Wanganui Collegiate Sch., NZ, 1984; Teacher, Harvard Sch., Los Angeles, 1987–88; Housemaster, Eton, 1988–92. Hon. Treas., HMC, 1999–. FRSA. *Recreations:* music, cinema, travel, Watford FC. *Address:* Cobbetts, Mavins Road, Farnham, Surrey GU9 8JS. *Club:* East India, Devonshire, Sports and Public Schools.

YOUNG, Timothy Nicholas; QC 1996; barrister; *b* 1 Dec. 1953; *s* of William Ritchie Young and Patricia Eileen Young; *m* 1981, Susan Jane Kenny; two *s* one *d*. *Educ:* Malvern Coll.; Magdalen Coll., Oxford (BA, BCL). Called to the Bar, Gray's Inn, 1977; in practice at the Commercial Bar, 1977–. Vis. Lectr, St Edmund Hall, Oxford, 1977–80. *Publication:* Voyage Charters, 1993. *Recreations:* watercolours, drawing, cricket, music, theatre, television. *Clubs:* Royal Automobile; Thebertons Cricket.

YOUNG, Wayland; *see* Kennet, Baron.

YOUNG, William Hilary, CMG 1957; HM Diplomatic Service, retired; Ambassador to Colombia 1966–70; *b* 14 Jan. 1913; *s* of late Rev. Arthur John Christopher Young and Ethel Margaret (*née* Goodwin); *m* 1st, 1946, Barbara Gordon Richmond, *d* of late Gordon Park Richmond; one *s* one *d*; 2nd, 1986, Virginia, *widow* of Sir Ivo Stourton, CMG, OBE, KPM. *Educ:* Marlborough Coll.; Emmanuel Coll., Cambridge. Entered Consular Service, 1935; served HM Legation, Tehran, 1938–41; Foreign Office, 1941–45; 1st Secretary, 1945; Berlin (Political Division, Control Commission), 1945–48; HM Legation, Budapest, 1948–50; attached to IDC, 1951; Counsellor: UK High Commn, New Delhi, 1952–54; Foreign Office, 1954–57; Minister, Moscow, 1957–60; Senior Civilian Instructor, IDC, 1960–62; Minister, British Embassy, Pretoria and Cape Town, 1962–65; Fellow, Harvard University Center for Internat. Affairs, 1965–66. *Address:* 2 Sutton Manor Mews, Sutton Scotney, Winchester, Hants SO21 3JX.

YOUNG, Hon. William Lambert, CMG 1992; JP; High Commissioner for New Zealand in UK, 1982–85; concurrently Ambassador to Ireland and High Commissioner in Nigeria, 1982–85; *b* 13 Nov. 1913; *s* of James Young and Alice Gertrude Annie Young; *m* 1946, Isobel Joan Luke; one *s* four *d*. *Educ:* Wellington Coll. Commenced work, 1930; spent first 16 yrs with farm servicing co., interrupted by War Service, N Africa with Eighth Army, 1940–43; took over management of wholesale distributing co. handling imported and NZ manufactured goods; Gen. Man. of co. manufg and distributing radios, records, electronic equipment and owning 32 retail stores, 1956; purchased substantial interest in importing and distributing business, 1962. MP (National) Miramar, 1966–81; Minister of Works and Develt, 1975–81; introduced Women's Rights of Employment Bill, 1975; Pres., Assoc. of Former MPs of NZ, 1993–95. Formerly Chairman: National Roads Bd; National Water and Soil Authority; NZ Fishing Licensing Authority. Formerly Director: Johnsons Wax of NZ Ltd (subsid. of USA Co.); Howard Rotovator Co. Ltd; AA Mutual Insurance Co.; J. J. Niven Ltd; NZ Motor Bodies Ltd; Trustee, Wellington Savings Bank. Patron, Star Boating Club, 1997– (Pres., 1981–97); Mem. Council, NZ Amateur Rowing Assoc., 1984–87. Life Mem., AA of Wellington (Mem. Council, 1976–81). JP 1962. *Address:* 3/28 Oriental Terrace, Oriental Bay, Wellington 6001, New Zealand. *T:* (4) 8018030. *Club:* Wellington (Wellington, NZ).

YOUNG, Sir William Neil, 10th Bt *cr* 1769; Chairman, New World Trust, since 2000; Director: Newgate Stud Co., since 2000; New Providence Fund, since 2000; *b* 22 Jan. 1941; *s* of Captain William Elliot Young, RAMC (killed in action 27 May 1942), and Mary (*d* 1997), *d* of late Rev. John Macdonald; *S* grandfather, 1944; *m* 1965, Christine Veronica Morley, *o d* of late R. B. Morley, Buenos Aires; one *s* one *d. Educ:* Wellington Coll.; Sandhurst. Captain, 16th/5th The Queen's Royal Lancers, retired 1970. Dir, Kleinwort Benson International Investment Ltd, 1982–87; Head: Investment Management, Saudi Internat. Bank, 1987–91; ME Dept, Coutts & Co., 1991–94; Dir, Barclays Private Bank Ltd, 1994–99. *Recreations:* ski-ing, sailing, tennis, shooting. *Heir: s* William Lawrence Elliot Young [*b* 26 May 1970; *m* 2001, Astrid Bartsch, Vienna]. *Clubs:* Woodroffe's, Caledonian.

YOUNGER, family name of **Viscount Younger of Leckie**.

YOUNGER OF LECKIE, 4th Viscount *cr* 1923, of Alloa, Clackmannanshire; **George Kenneth Hotson Younger;** Baron Younger of Prestwick (Life Peer), 1992; Bt 1911; KT 1995; KCVO 1993; TD 1964; PC 1979; DL; FRSE; Lord High Commissioner, General Assembly, Church of Scotland, 2001; *b* 22 Sept. 1931; *e s* of 3rd Viscount Younger of Leckie, OBE and Evelyn Margaret, MBE (*d* 1983), *e d* of Alexander Logan McClure, KC; *S* father, 1997; *m* 1954, Diana Rhona, *er d* of Captain G. S. Tuck, RN, Little London, Chichester, Sussex; three *s* one *d. Educ:* Cargilfield Sch., Edinburgh; Winchester Coll. (Fellow, 1992–); New Coll., Oxford (Hon. Fellow, 1997). Commnd in Argyll and Sutherland Highlanders, 1950; served BAOR and Korea, 1951; 7th Bn Argyll and Sutherland Highlanders (TA), 1951–65; Hon. Col, 154 (Lowland) Transport Regt, RCT, 1977–85. Chairman: Siemens Plessey Electronic Systems, 1990–97; Royal Bank of Scotland, 1990–2001 (Dir, 1989–2001; Dep. Chm., 1990); Royal Bank of Scotland Gp, 1991–2001; SPEED plc, 1992–98; Murray Johnstone Trusts, 1993–; Director: George Younger & Son Ltd, 1958–68; J. G. Thomson & Co. Ltd, Leith, 1962–66; Maclachlans Ltd, 1968–70; Tennant Caledonian Breweries Ltd, 1977–79; Scottish Equitable Life Assurance Soc., 1990–94; Prestwick Hldgs (formerly Ayrshire Community Airport Project, then PIK Ltd), 1991–98. Contested (U) North Lanarkshire, 1959; Unionist Candidate for Kinross and West Perthshire, 1963, but stood down in favour of Sir A. Douglas-Home. MP (C) Ayr, 1964–92; Scottish Conservative Whip, 1965–67; Parly Under-Sec. of State for Develt, Scottish Office, 1970–74; Minister of State for Defence, 1974; Sec. of State for Scotland, 1979–86; Sec. of State for Defence, 1986–89. Chm., Conservative Party in Scotland, 1974–75 (Dep. Chm., 1967–70); Pres., Nat. Union of Cons. and Unionist Assocs, 1987–88. Chancellor, Napier Univ., 1993–; Warden, Winchester Coll., 1997–. President: Royal Highland and Agricl Soc., 1990; Council, TA&VRAs, 1993; RSGS, 1993–99; Chairman: Royal Anniversary Trust, 1990–; Romanian Orphanage Trust, 1990; Festival City (formerly Empire, then Edinburgh Fest.) Theatre Trust, 1991–; Royal Armouries, 1994–; Trustees, The Former Royal Yacht Britannia Trust, 1998–. Brig., Queen's Body Guard for Scotland (Royal Company of Archers). DL Stirlingshire, 1968. Hon. LLD Glasgow, 1992; Dr *hc* Edinburgh, 1992; Hon. DLitt Napier, 1992; DUniv Paisley, 1994. *Recreations:* music, tennis, sailing, golf. *Heir: s* Hon. James Edward George Younger [*b* 11 Nov. 1955; *m* 1988, Jennie Veronica, *d* of William Wootton; one *s* two *d*]. *Address:* c/o Chairman's Office, Royal Bank of Scotland, 42 St Andrew Square, Edinburgh EH2 2YE. *T:* (0131) 523 2123. *Clubs:* Caledonian; Highland Brigade.

See also Hon. R. E. G. Younger.

YOUNGER, Maj.-Gen. Allan Elton, DSO 1944; OBE 1962; MA; Director-General, Royal United Services Institute for Defence Studies, 1976–78; *b* 4 May 1919; *s* of late Brig. Arthur Allan Shakespear Younger, DSO, and late Marjorie Rhoda Younger (*née* Halliley); *m* 1942, Diana Lanyon; three *d. Educ:* Gresham's; RMA Woolwich; Christ's Coll., Cambridge. Commnd RE, 1939; France and Belgium, 1940; France, Holland and Germany, 1944–45; Burma, 1946–47; Malaya, 1948; Korea, 1950–51; RMA Sandhurst, 1954–57; Bt Lt-Col 1959; comd 36 Corps Engineer Regt in UK and Kenya, 1960–62; Instructor US Army Comd and Gen. Staff Coll., Fort Leavenworth, 1963–66; Programme Evaluation Gp, 1966–68; Chief Engr, Army Strategic Comd, 1968–69; COS, HQ Allied Forces Northern Europe, Oslo, 1970–72; Sen. Army Mem., Directing Staff, RCDS, 1972–75. Col Comdt, RE, 1974–79. Silver Star (US), 1951. *Publications:* contribs to RUSI Jl, Military Review (USA). *Recreation:* gardening.

YOUNGER, David; *see* Younger, J. D. B.

YOUNGER, (James) Samuel; Chairman, Electoral Commission, since 2001; *b* 5 Oct. 1951; *s* of Rt Hon. Sir Kenneth Gilmour Younger, KBE, PC and Elisabeth Kirsteen (*née* Stewart); *m* 1984, Katherine Anne Spencer; one *s. Educ:* Westminster Sch.; New Coll., Oxford (BA Hons). Asst Editor, Middle East International, 1972–78; BBC World Service: Sen. Asst, Central Current Affairs Talks, 1979–84; Sen. Producer and Exec. Producer, Current Affairs, 1984–86; Asst Head, Arabic Service, 1986–87; Head, Current Affairs, 1987–89; Head, Arabic Service, 1989–92; Controller, Overseas Services, 1992–94; Director of Broadcasting, 1994; Man. Dir, 1994–98; Dir-Gen., BRCS, 1999–2000. Mem. Council, Univ. of Sussex, 1998–. Dir, English Touring Opera, 1999–. Gov., Commonwealth Inst., 1998–. Patron, Windsor Leadership Trust, 1998–. *Recreations:* sport, choral singing. *Address:* 28 Rylett Crescent, W12 9RL. *T:* (020) 8743 4449.

YOUNGER, Captain (John) David (Bingham); Lord-Lieutenant of Tweeddale, since 1994 (Vice Lord-Lieutenant, 1992–94); Managing Director, Broughton Brewery, 1979–95; *b* 20 May 1939; *s* of Major Oswald Bingham Younger, MC, A and SH, and Dorothea Elizabeth Younger (*née* Hobbs); *m* 1962, Anne Rosaleen Logan; one *s* two *d. Educ:* Eton Coll.; RMA Sandhurst. Regular Army, Argyll and Sutherland Highlanders, 1957–69; Scottish and Newcastle Breweries, 1969–79. Chairman: Belhaven Hill Trust, 1986–94; Scottish Borders Tourist Board, 1989–91; Dir, Queen's Hall (Edinburgh) Ltd, 1992–. Vice Pres., RHASS, 1994. Mem., Queen's Body Guard for Scotland, Royal Company of Archers, 1969– (Sec., 1993–). DL Borders, 1988. *Recreation:* the countryside. *Address:* Kirkurd House, Blyth Bridge, Peeblesshire EH46 7AH. *T:* and *Fax:* (01721) 752223.

YOUNGER, Maj.-Gen. Sir John William, 3rd Bt *cr* 1911; CBE 1969 (MBE 1945); Commissioner-in-Chief, St John Ambulance Brigade, 1980–85; *b* 18 Nov. 1920; *s* of Sir William Robert Younger, 2nd Bt, and of Joan Gwendoline Johnstone (later Mrs Dennis Wheatley; she *d* 1982); *S* father, 1973; *m* 1st, 1948, Mrs Stella Jane Dodd (marr. diss. 1952), *d* of Rev. John George Lister; one *s* one *d*; 2nd, 1953, Marcella Granito, Princess Pignatelli Di Belmonte (*d* 1989), *d* of Prof. Avv. R. Scheggi; 3rd, 1991, Anne Henrietta Maria St Paul Seely (*d* 1996), *o d* of Horace George St Paul Butler. *Educ:* Canford Sch.; RMC Sandhurst. Served War 1939–45, Middle East (PoW) (MBE); 2nd Lt, Coldstream Gds, 1939; staff coll., Camberley, 1949; Lt Col 1959; Comd, 1st Bn Coldstream Guards; AQMG, HQ London Dist, 1961–63; Col 1963; AAG, War Office, 1963–65; NDC, New Delhi, 1966; Brig. 1967; Dep. Dir, Army Staff Duties, MoD, 1967–70; Dir of Quartering (A), MoD, 1970–73; Maj.-Gen. 1971; Dir, Management and Support of Intelligence, 1973–76. Chm. or Mem., various Civil Service Commn and Home Office Interview Bds. Dep. Comr, St John Ambulance Bde, London (Prince of Wales's) Dist, 1978. KStJ 1980. *Recreations:* reading, photography, travel. *Heir: s* Julian William Richard Younger, [*b* 10 Feb. 1950; *m* 1981, Deborah Ann Wood; one *s*]. *Address:* Flat 4, 10 Wilbraham Place, SW1X 9AA. *Club:* Boodle's.

YOUNGER, Hon. Robert Edward Gilmour; Sheriff of Tayside, Central and Fife, since 1982; *b* 25 Sept. 1940; third *s* of 3rd Viscount Younger of Leckie, OBE and Evelyn Margaret, MBE, *e d* of Alexander Logan McClure, KC; *m* 1972, Helen Jane Hayes; one *s* one *d. Educ:* Cargilfield Sch., Edinburgh; Winchester Coll.; New Coll., Oxford (MA); Edinburgh Univ. (LLB); Glasgow Univ. Advocate, 1968; Sheriff of Glasgow and Strathkelvin, 1979–82. *Recreation:* wondering. *Address:* Old Leckie, Gargunnock, Stirling, Scotland FK8 3BN. *T:* (01786) 860213.

YOUNGER, Samuel; *see* Younger, J. S.

YOUNGER-ROSS, Richard; MP (Lib Dem) Teignbridge, since 2001; *b* 29 Jan. 1953; *m* 1982, Susan. *Educ:* Walton-on-Thames Secondary Modern Sch.; Ewell Tech. Coll. (HNC); Oxford Poly. Former architectural consultant; design consultant, 1990–. Joined Liberal Party, 1970 (Mem. Council, 1972–82). Contested (Lib Dem): Chislehurst, 1987; Teignbridge, 1992, 1997. *Address:* 2a Queen Street, Newton Abbot, Devon TQ12 2ET; (office) 41 Higher Brimley Road, Teignmouth, Devon TQ14 8JU; c/o House of Commons, SW1A 0AA.

YOUNGSON, Prof. Alexander John, CBE 1987; Emeritus Professor, Australian National University, since 1980; *b* 28 Sept. 1918; *s* of Alexander Brown, MA, MB, ChB and Helen Youngson; *m* 1948, Elizabeth Gisborne Naylor; one *s* one *d. Educ:* Aberdeen Grammar Sch.; Aberdeen Univ. Pilot, Fleet Air Arm, 1940–45. MA Aberdeen Univ., 1947; Commonwealth Fellow, 1947–48. Lecturer, University of St Andrews, 1948–50; Lecturer, University of Cambridge, 1950–58; Prof. of Political Economy 1963–74, and Vice-Principal, 1971–74, Univ. of Edinburgh; Dir, Res. Sch. of Social Scis, ANU, 1974–80; Prof. of Econs, Univ. of Hong Kong, 1980–82. Chm., Royal Fine Art Commn for Scotland, 1983–90 (Mem., 1972–74). Hon. FRIAS 1984. DLitt Aberdeen, 1952; DUniv York, 1993. *Publications:* The American Economy, 1860–1940, 1951; Possibilities of Economic Progress, 1959; The British Economy, 1920–1957, 1960; The Making of Classical Edinburgh, 1966; Overhead Capital, 1967; After the Forty-Five, 1973; Beyond the Highland Line, 1974; Scientific Revolution in Victorian Medicine, 1979; (ed) China and Hong Kong: the economic nexus, 1983; The Prince and the Pretender, 1985; Urban Development and the Royal Fine Art Commission, 1990; Edinburgh and the Border Country, 1993, enlarged edn as Edinburgh and the Borders, 2001; (contrib.) The Dictionary of Art, 1997; contrib. to various journals devoted to economics and economic history. *Recreation:* gardening. *Address:* 17 The Horseshoe, York YO24 1LY.

YOUNIE, Edward Milne, OBE 1978; HM Diplomatic Service, retired; Consultant, Trefoil Associates, since 1983; *b* 9 Feb. 1926; *s* of John Milne and Mary Dickie Younie; *m* 1st, 1952, Mary Groves (*d* 1976); 2nd, 1979, Mimi Barkley (marr. annulled 1991); 3rd, 1994, Mrs Alyn Denholm. *Educ:* Fettes Coll. (Scholar); Gonville and Caius Coll., Cambridge (Scholar) (BA Hons). RN, 1944–46. HM Colonial Service, Tanganyika, 1950–62; FCO, 1963; Johannesburg, 1964–67; Blantyre, 1967–69; First Secretary: Lagos, 1972–76; Nairobi, 1977–79; Salisbury, 1979–81 (Counsellor, 1980); FCO, 1981–82. Dir, Fairbridge (Scotland), 1996–. *Recreations:* golf, tennis, music. *Address:* Wester Corsehill, Thornhill, Stirling FK8 3QD. *Club:* Brooks's.

YOUNSON, Maj.-Gen. Eric John, OBE 1952; Eur Ing; CEng, FRAeS, FIMgt; *b* 1 March 1919; *o s* of late Ernest M. Younson, MLitt, BCom, Jarrow; *m* 1946, Jean Beaumont Carter, BA; three *d. Educ:* Jarrow Grammar Sch.; Univ. of Durham (BSc); Royal Military Coll. of Science. Served War of 1939–45: commissioned, RA, 1940; UK and NW Europe (despatches). Directing Staff, RMCS, 1953–55; Atomic Weapons Research Estab., 1957–58; Attaché (Washington) as rep. of Chief Scientific Adviser, 1958–61; Head of Defence Science 3, MoD, 1961–63; Dep. Dir of Artillery, 1964–66; Dir of Guided Weapons Trials and Ranges, Min. of Technology, 1967–69; Vice-Pres., Ordnance Board, 1970–72, Pres., 1972–73, retired 1973; Sen. Asst Dir, Central Bureau for Educnl Visits and Exchanges, 1973–74; Dep. Dir, SIMA, 1974–78; Sec.-Gen., EUROM, 1975–77; Clerk to Worshipful Co. of Scientific Instrument Makers, 1976–87 (Hon. Liveryman and Clerk Emeritus, 1987). FRSA. Freeman, City of London, 1981. *Publications:* The Worshipful Company of Scientific Instrument Makers: history, 1988; articles on gunnery and scientific subjects in Service jls. *Recreations:* photography, electronics, Talking Newspapers for the Blind. *Address:* 7 Pondwick Road, Harpenden, Herts AL5 2HG. *T:* (01582) 621691.

YUKON, Bishop of, since 1995; **Rt Rev. Terrence Owen Buckle;** *b* 24 Aug. 1940; *m* 1963, Moyra Blanche Cooke; two *s* two *d. Educ:* Church Army Training Coll., Canada; Wycliffe Coll., Toronto. Commnd as Church Army Evangelist, 1962; Parish Assistant, St Philip's, Etobicoke, Ont, 1962–64; Dir of Inner Parish, Little Trinity, Toronto, 1964–66; Church Army Incumbent: Ch of the Resurrection, Holman, 1966–70; St George's Anglican Mission, Cambridge Bay, 1970–72; Incumbent, St David's Anglican Mission, Fort Simpson, 1972–75; ordained deacon, May 1973, priest, Nov. 1973; Priest i/c, Ch of the Ascension, Inuvik, and Regl Dean, Lower Mackenzie, 1975–82; Archdeacon of Liard, dio. of Yukon, 1982–88; Rector: St Mary Magdalene, Fort Nelson, 1982–88; Holy Trinity, Yellowknife, 1988–93; Co-Founder and Evangelist, New Life Evangelism Ministries, 1984–94; Bishop Suffragan, dio. of the Arctic, 1993–95. Hon. Canon, St Jude's Cathedral, Iqaluit, 1978. *Recreations:* out-of-door activities, canoeing, camping, hiking. *Address:* PO Box 31136, Whitehorse, YT Y1A 5P7, Canada. *T:* (867) 6677746.

YURKO, Allen Michael; Chief Executive, Invensys plc, 1999–2001; *b* 25 Sept. 1951; *s* of Mike Yurko and Catherine (*née* Ewanishan); *m* 1991, Gayle Marie Skelley. *Educ:* Lehigh Univ. (BA Bus. and Econs); Baldwin-Wallace Coll., USA (MBA). Divl Controller, Joy Mfg, 1978–81; Gp Controller, Eaton Corp., 1981–83; Chief Financial Officer and Gp Vice-Pres., Mueller Hldgs, 1983–89; Robertshaw Controls: Vice-Pres. of Finance, 1989–90; Pres., 1990–91; Pres. and Chief Operating Officer, Siebe T. & A. Controls, 1991–92; Siebe plc: Chief Operating Officer, 1992–93; CEO, 1994–99. Non-exec. Dir, Tate & Lyle plc, 1996–. *Recreations:* boating, golf, sports cars, theatre. *Address:* c/o Invensys plc, Carlisle Place, SW1P 1BX. *T:* (020) 7834 3848. *Clubs:* Annabel's; Sunningdale Golf, Wentworth.

YUWI, Sir Matiabe, KBE 1997 (OBE); Member, National Citizenship Committee, Papua New Guinea, since 1982; Commissioner for Law and Order, Peace and Good Order Commission, Southern Highlands Province, since 1998; *b* 1935; *s* of Labe Yuwi and Colin Hongai; *m* 1st, 1961, Pulume Labe; five *s* one *d*; 2nd, 1975, Gamiabi Kamia; two *s*. *Educ:* Lake Kutubu sch.; Mt Hagen Hosp. (medical and Aid Post Orderly trng); Lae Health Educnl Instn. Pi-Nagia Aid Post, 1956–60; Health Educn Officer, Tari Dist, Southern Highlands, PNG, 1965–68. Elected Mem. and Pres., Tari Local Govt Council, 1964; MP for Tari, PNG, 1968–82; Mem., Constitutional Cttee, 1971–72, Constitutional Planning Cttee, 1974–75, for PNG self govt and independence; Minister for Media Services, 1981–82. *Recreations:* farming, political reviewing. *Address:* PO Box 173, Mendi, Southern Highlands Province, Papua New Guinea. *T:* and *Fax:* 5491387. *Club:* Mendi Valley.

Z

ZACHARIAH, Joyce Margaret; Secretary of the Post Office, 1975–77; *b* 11 Aug. 1932; *d* of Robert Paton Emery and Nellie Nicol (*née* Wilson); *m* 1978, George Zachariah. *Educ:* Earl Grey Sch., Calgary, Canada; Hillhead High Sch., Glasgow; Glasgow Univ. (MA 1st cl. Hons French and German, 1956). Post Office: Asst Principal, 1956; Private Sec. to Dir Gen., 1960; Principal, 1961; Asst Sec., 1967; Dir, Chairman's Office, 1970. *Address:* Kelvinbrae, Wisborough Lane, Storrington, W Sussex RH20 4ND.
See also E. J. Emery.

ZACHAROV, Prof. Vasilii, (Basil), PhD, DSc; consultant; Director of Information Processing, International Organization for Standardization, Geneva, 1990–95 (Head of Information Processing, 1989–90); *b* 2 Jan. 1931; *s* of Viktor Nikiforovich Zakharov and Varvara Semyenovna (*née* Krzak); *m* 1959, Jeanne (*née* Hopper) one *s* one *d*. *Educ:* Latymer Upper Sch.; Univ. of London (BSc: Maths 1951, Phys 1952; MSc 1958; PhD 1960; DIC 1960; DSc 1977). Research in Computer systems and applications, Birkbeck Coll., 1953–56; digital systems development, Rank Precision Instruments, 1956–57; Research Fellow, Imperial Coll., 1957–60; Physicist, European Organisation for Nuclear Res. (CERN), Geneva, 1960–65; Reader in Experimental Physics, Queen Mary Coll., London, 1965–66; Head of Computer Systems and Electronics Div., as Sen. Principal Sci. Officer, SRC Daresbury Laboratory, 1966–69, Dep. Chief Sci. Officer, 1970–78; Dir, London Univ. Computing Centre, 1978–80, and Prof. of Computing Systems, 1979–80; Sen. Associate, CERN, Geneva, 1981–83; Invited Prof., Univ. of Geneva, 1984–87. Vis Scientist: JINR Dubna, USSR, 1965; CERN, 1971–72; Consultant to AERE Harwell, 1965; Vis. Prof. of Physics, QMC London, 1968; Vis. Prof., Westfield Coll., 1974–78. Member, SRC Comp. Sci. Cttee, 1974–77. *Publications:* Digital Systems Logic, 1968, and other books; scientific papers in professional jls on photoelectronics, computer systems, elementary particle physics and computer applications. *Recreations:* collecting Russian miscellanea, skiing, shooting, amateur radio; grape growing, wine making, wine drinking. *Address:* The Firs, Oldcastle, Cheshire SY14 7NE.

ZAFIROPOULOS, Vassilis; Ambassador of Greece to the Court of St James's, 1996–99, retired; *b* Corfu, 24 Jan. 1934; *s* of Sarantis and Helen Zafiropoulos; *m* 1963; one *s*. *Educ:* Univ. of Athens. Joined Greek Civil Service, 1962; Min. of Finance, 1962–67; Head of Press Affairs, UN Information Centre for Greece, Israel, Turkey and Cyprus, 1967–71 (on secondment); joined Greek Diplomatic Service, 1971; Third Sec., Central Service, Min. of Foreign Affairs, 1971–73; Second Sec., Liège, 1973–76; First Sec., Nicosia, and Dir, Greek Press Office in Cyprus, 1976–78; Counsellor, Nicosia, 1978–80; Counsellor (Political), London, 1980–84; Head of Cyprus Affairs, Min. of Foreign Affairs, 1984–86; Minister and Dep. Permt Rep. to NATO, Brussels, 1986–90; Ambassador to Australia and New Zealand, 1991–93; Permt Rep. to NATO, 1993–96. DUniv N London. Higher Comdr, Order of Phoenix (Greece). *Recreation:* tennis. *Address:* 20B Sirinon Street, Athens 175 61, Greece.

ZAHIRUDDIN bin Syed Hassan, Tun Syed, SPCM 1987; SMN, PSM, DUNM; SPMP 1970; JMN, PJK; Hon. GCVO 1974; Orang Besat Empat, Perak, since 1984; a Pro-Chancellor, University of Malaya, since 1987; *b* 11 Oct. 1918; *m* 1949, Toh Puan Halimah, *d* of Haji Mohamed Noh; five *s* five *d*. *Educ:* Malay Coll., Kuala Kangsar; Raffles Coll., Singapore (Dip.Arts). Passed Cambridge Sch. Cert. Malay Officer, Tanjong Malim, etc, 1945–47; Dep. Asst Dist Officer, 1948; Asst Dist Officer, 1951–54; 2nd Asst State Sec., Perak, 1955; Registrar of Titles and Asst State Sec. (Lands), Perak, 1956; Dist Officer, Batang Padang, Tapah, 1957; Dep. Sec., Public Services Commn, 1958; Principal Asst Sec. (Service), Fedn Estabt Office, Kuala Lumpur, 1960; State Sec., Perak, 1961; Permanent Sec.: Min. of Agric. and Co-operatives, Kuala Lumpur, 1963; Min. of Educn, Kuala Lumpur, 1966; Dir-Gen., Public Services Dept, Kuala Lumpur, 1969; retd, 1972. Chm., Railway Services Commn, Kuala Lumpur, 1972–73. High Comr for Malaysia in London, 1974–75; Governor of Malacca, 1975–84. Chairman: Special Cttee on Superannuation in the Public Services, 1972, and Statutory Bodies; Bd of Governors, Malay Coll., Kuala Kangsar; Interim Council of Nat. Inst. of Technology; Central Bd. Vice-Pres., Subang Nat. Golf Club, 1972–74. *Recreation:* golf. *Address:* Rumah Keledong, No 10 Jalan Tun Dr Ismail, 30350 Ipoh, Malaysia.

ZAMBONI, Richard Frederick Charles, FCA; Managing Director, 1979–89 and a Vice-Chairman, 1986–89, Sun Life Assurance Society plc; Chairman, AIM Distribution Trust PLC, 1996–2000; *b* 28 July 1930; *s* of Alfred Charles Zamboni and Frances Hosler; *m* 1st, 1960, Pamela Joan Marshall (*d* 1993); two *s* one *d*; 2nd 1996, Deirdre Olive Baker (*née* Kingham). *Educ:* Monkton House Sch., Cardiff. Gordon Thomas & Pickard, Chartered Accountants, 1948–54; served Royal Air Force, 1954–56; Peat Marwick Mitchell & Co., 1956–58; British Egg Marketing Board, 1959–70, Chief Accountant, from 1965; Sun Life Assurance Society plc, 1971–89, Director, 1975–89; Chairman: Sun Life Investment Management Services, 1985–89; Sun Life Trust Management, 1985–89. Deputy Chairman: Life Offices' Assoc., 1985 (Mem., Management Cttee, 1981–85); Assoc. of British Insurers, 1986–88 (Dep. Chm., 1985–86, Chm., 1986–88, Life Insurance Council); Member: Council, Chartered Insurance Inst., 1983–85; Lautro's steering gp, 1985–86; Hon. Treasurer, Insurance Institute of London, 1982–85. Dir, 1984–97, and Chm., 1990–97, Avon Enterprise Fund Ltd. Member, Management Cttee, Effingham Housing Assoc. Ltd, 1980–86; Chairman: Council of Management, Grange Centre for People with Disabilities, 1991–96; Governing Body, Little Bookham Manor House Sch. Educnl Trust Ltd, 1999–. Pres., Insurance Offices RFU, 1985–87. *Recreations:* ornithology, gardening, golf. *Address:* The Old Vicarage, 80 Church Street, Leatherhead, Surrey KT22 8ER. *T:* (01372) 812398. *Club:* Royal Automobile.

ZAMYATIN, Leonid Mitrofanovich; Soviet Ambassador to the Court of St James's, 1986–91; *b* Nizhni Devitsk, 9 March 1922; *m* 1946; one *d*. *Educ:* Moscow Aviation Inst.; Higher Diplomatic School. Mem., CPSU, 1944–91 (apptd Mem. Central Cttee, 1976); Min. of Foreign Affairs, 1946; First Sec., Counsellor on Political Questions, USSR Mission to UN, 1953–57; Soviet Dep. Rep., Preparatory Cttee, later Bd of Governors, IAEA, 1957–59; Soviet Rep., IAEA, 1959–60; Dep. Head, American Countries Dept, Min. of Foreign Affairs, 1960–62; Head of Press Dept, 1962–70; Mem., Collegium of Ministry, 1962–70; Dir-Gen., TASS News Agency, 1970–78, Govt Minister, 1972; Dep. to USSR Supreme Soviet, 1970–89; Chief, Dept of Internat. Inf., Central Cttee, CPSU, 1978–86. Mem., Commn for Foreign Relations, Soviet of Nationalities, 1974. Lenin Prize 1978; USSR Orders and medals incl. Order of Lenin (twice). *Publication:* Gorby and Maggie (memoirs), 1995.

ZANDER, Prof. Michael; Professor of Law, London School of Economics, 1977–98, now Emeritus; *b* 16 Nov. 1932; *s* of late Dr Walter Zander and Margaret Magnus; *m* 1965, Betsy Treeger; one *d* one *s*. *Educ:* Royal Grammar Sch., High Wycombe; Jesus Coll., Cambridge (BA Law, double 1st Cl. Hons; LLB 1st Cl. Hons; Whewell Scholar in Internat. Law); Harvard Law Sch. (LLM). Solicitor of the Supreme Court. National Service, RA, 1950–52, 2nd Lieut. Cassel Scholar, Lincoln's Inn, 1957, resigned 1959; New York law firm, 1958–59; articled with City solicitors, 1959–62; Asst Solicitor with City firm, 1962–63; London Sch. of Economics: Asst Lectr, 1963; Lectr, 1965; Sen. Lectr, 1970; Reader, 1970; Convener, Law Dept, 1984–88, 1997–98. Legal Correspondent, The Guardian, 1963–87. Mem., Royal Commn on Criminal Justice, 1991–93. Hon. QC 1997. *Publications:* Lawyers and the Public Interest, 1968; (ed) What's Wrong with the Law?, 1970; (ed) Family Guide to the Law, 1971 (2nd edn 1972); Cases and Materials on the English Legal System, 1973 (8th edn 1999); (with B. Abel-Smith and R. Brooke) Legal Problems and the Citizen, 1973; Social Workers, their Clients and the Law, 1974 (3rd edn 1981); A Bill of Rights?, 1975 (4th edn 1996); Legal Services for the Community, 1978; (ed) Pears Guide to the Law, 1979; The Law-Making Process, 1980 (5th edn 1999); The State of Knowledge about the English Legal Profession, 1980; The Police and Criminal Evidence Act 1984, 1985 (4th edn 2002); A Matter of Justice: the legal system in ferment, 1988 (rev. edn 1989); The State of Justice, 2000; articles in Criminal Law Rev., Mod. Law Rev., Law Soc.'s Gazette, New Law Jl, Solicitors' Jl, Amer. Bar Assoc. Jl, New Society, etc. *Recreations:* swimming, the cello. *Address:* 12 Woodside Avenue, N6 4SS. *T:* (020) 8883 6257, *Fax:* (020) 8444 3348.

ZANI, John Andrew; District Judge (Magistrates' Courts), Inner London, since 2001; *b* 14 Feb. 1953; *s* of Primo and Alda Zani; *m* 1978, Cinthia Gallian. *Educ:* Highgate Sch.; Coll. of Law. Admitted solicitor, 1977; Partner, 1979, Sen. Partner, 1986–2000, Whitelock & Storr. Chm., Professional Matters Sub-Cttee, Holborn Law Soc., 1994–96. Mem. Founder Cttee, British Italian Law Assoc., 1982. Trustee, Friends of Highgate Sch., 1996–; Mem. Cttee, Old Cholmeleian Soc., 1994–. *Recreations:* cricket, football, the arts. *Address:* c/o Tower Bridge Magistrates' Court, 211 Tooley Street, SE1 2JY. *T:* (020) 7805 6703.

ZANZIBAR, Bishop of, since 2000; **Rt Rev. John Acland Ramadhani;** *b* 1 Aug. 1932. *Educ:* Univ. of Birmingham (DipTh 1975); Univ. of Dar-es-Salaam (BA 1967); Queen's Coll., Birmingham. Deacon 1975, Birmingham; priest 1976, Dar-es-Salaam; Asst Chaplain, Queen's Coll., Birmingham, 1975–76; Warden, St Mark's Theol Coll., Dar-es-Salaam, 1976–80; Bishop of Zanzibar and Tanga, 1980–2000; Archbishop of Tanzania, 1984–98. *Address:* PO Box 5, Zanzibar, Tanzania.

ZAPF, Hermann; freelance book and type designer, since 1938; *b* Nuremburg, 8 Nov. 1918; *s* of Hermann Zapf and Magdalene Zapf (*née* Schlamp); *m* 1951, Gudrun von Hesse; one *s*. Type dir, D. Stempel AG, type foundry, Frankfurt, 1947–56; design consultant, Mergenthaler Linotype Co., NYC and Frankfurt, 1957–74; Consultant, Hallmark Internat., Kansas City, 1966–73; Vice-Pres., Design Processing Internat. Inc., NYC, 1977–86; Prof., Typographic Computer Programs, Rochester Inst. Technol., NY, 1977–87; Chm., Zapf, Burns & Co., NYC, 1987–91. Designer of types: Palatino, Melior, Optima, ITC Zapf Chancery, ITC Zapf Internat., Digiset-Marconi, Digiset-Edison, Digiset-Aurelia, Pan-Nigerian, URW (Roman and San Serif), Renaissance Roman, Zapfino Script. Mem., RSA. Hon. Mem., Soc. of Scribes and Illuminators. Hon. RDI 1985. Frederic W. Goudy Award, Rochester Inst. Technol., Rochester, NY, 1969; Gutenberg Prize, City of Mainz, 1974; Robert H. Middleton Award, Soc. Typographic Arts, Chicago, 1987; Euro Design Award, Design Biennial Oostende, 1994; Wadim Lazursky Award, Acad. Design, Moscow, 1996. *Publications:* William Morris, 1948; Pen and Graver, 1952; Manual Typographicum, 1954, 2nd edn 1968; About Alphabets, 1960, 2nd edn 1970; Typographic Variations, 1964; Orbis Typographicus, 1980; Hora fugit/Carpe diem, 1984; Hermann Zapf and his Design Philosophy, 1987; ABC-XYZapf, 1989; Poetry Through Typography, 1993; August Rosenberger, 1996. *Address:* Seitersweg 35, 64287 Darmstadt, Germany. *T:* (6151) 76825, *Fax:* (6151) 717204. *Clubs:* Double Crown (Hon. Mem.), Wynkyn de Worde (Hon. Mem.); Directors (NY) (Hon. Mem.).

ZARNECKI, Prof. George, CBE 1970; MA, PhD; FSA; FBA 1968; Professor of History of Art, University of London, 1963–82, now Emeritus Professor (Reader, 1959–63); Deputy Director, Courtauld Institute of Art, 1961–74; *b* 12 Sept. 1915; *m* 1945, Anne Leslie Frith; one *s* one *d*. *Educ:* Cracow Univ. MA Cracow Univ., 1938; PhD Univ. of London, 1950. Junior Asst, Inst. of History of Art, Cracow Univ., 1936–39. Served war of 1939–45 as lance-corporal in Polish Army; in France, 1939–40 (Polish Cross of Valour and Croix de Guerre, 1940); prisoner of war, 1940–42; interned in Spain, 1942–43; in Polish Army in UK, 1943–45. On staff of Courtauld Institute of Art, Univ. of London, 1945–82, Hon. Fellow, 1986. Slade Professor of Fine Art, Univ. of Oxford, 1960–61. Vice-President: Soc. of Antiquaries of London, 1968–72; British Soc. of Master Glass Painters, 1976–90; British Archaeol Assoc., 1979–; British Academy: Member: Corpus Vitrearum Medii Aevi Cttee, 1956–85; Publications Cttee, 1978–84; Corpus of Romanesque Sculpture in Britain and Ireland, 1988–; Chm., Corpus of Anglo-Saxon

Sculpture Cttee, 1979–84. Member: Conservation Cttee, Council for Places of Worship, 1969–75; Royal Commn on Historical Monuments, 1971–84; Arts Sub-Cttee of UGC, 1972–77; Sub-Cttee for Higher Doctorates, CNAA, 1978–82; Chm., Working Cttee organizing Arts Council exhibition, English Romanesque Art 1066–1200, 1984. Mem., Inst. for Advanced Study, Princeton, 1966; Foreign Member: Polish Acad. of Learning, 1992; Polish Acad. of Scis, 1994. Hon. Mem., Royal Archaeol Inst., 1985. Hon. DLitt: Warwick, 1978; East Anglia, 1981; Hon. LittD Dublin, 1984. Gold Medal, Soc. of Antiquaries, 1986. Gold Medal of Merit (Poland), 1978. Order of Isabel la Católica (Spain), 1997. *Publications:* English Romanesque Sculpture 1066–1140, 1951; Later English Romanesque Sculpture 1140–1210, 1953; English Romanesque Lead Sculpture, 1957; Early Sculpture of Ely Cathedral, 1958; Gislebertus, sculpteur d'Autun, 1960 (English edn, 1961); Romanesque Sculpture at Lincoln Cathedral, 1964; La sculpture à Payerne, Lausanne, 1966; 1066 and Architectural Sculpture (Proceedings of Brit. Acad.), 1966; Romanik (Belser Stilgeschichte, VI), 1970 (English edn, Romanesque Art, 1971); The Monastic Achievement, 1972; (contrib.) Westminster Abbey, 1972; Art of the Medieval World, 1975 (trans. Chinese, 1991); Studies in Romanesque Sculpture, 1979; Romanesque Lincoln, 1988; Further Studies in Romanesque Sculpture, 1992; articles in archaeological journals. *Address:* 22 Essex Park, N3 1NE. *T:* (020) 8346 6497.

ZEALLEY, Christopher Bennett; trustee and company director; *b* 5 May 1931; *s* of Sir Alec Zealley and Lady Zealley (*née* King); *m* 1966, Ann Elizabeth Sandwith; one *s* one *d.* *Educ:* Sherborne Sch.; King's Coll., Cambridge (MA Law). Commnd RNVR, 1953; ICI Ltd, 1955–66; IRC, 1967–70; Chairman: Public Interest Res. Centre, 1972–; Social Audit Ltd, 1972–; Accreditation Bureau for Fundraising Orgns, 1997–; Director and Trustee: Dartington Hall Trust, 1970–88; Charity Appointments, 1988– (Chm., 1988–92). Association for Consumer Research (formerly Consumers' Association): Chm., 1991–92; Mem. Council, 1976–92, 1994– (Chm., 1977–82). Trustee: Charities Aid Foundn, 1982–90; Res. Inst. for Consumer Affairs, 1989–. Director: JT Group Ltd; Grant Instruments Ltd; Good Food Club Ltd. Chairman: Dartington Coll. of Art, 1973–91; Dartington Summer Sch. of Music, 1980–97. *Publication:* Creating a Charitable Trust, 1994. *Recreations:* rural affairs, music. *Address:* Sneydhurst, Broadhempston, Totnes, Devon TQ9 6AX. *Clubs:* Lansdowne, Naval.

ZEALLEY, Dr Helen Elizabeth, OBE 1998; MD; FRCPEd, FFPHM; Director of Public Health and Chief Administrative Medical Officer, 1988–2000, Executive Director, 1991–2000, Lothian Health Board; *b* 10 June 1940; *d* of late Sir John Howie Flint Brotherston and of Lady Brotherston; *m* 1965, Dr Andrew King Zealley; one *s* one *d.* *Educ:* St Albans High Sch. for Girls; Edinburgh Univ. (MB, ChB 1964; MD 1968). FRCPEd 1987; FFPHM 1980. Virologist, City Hosp., Edinburgh, 1965–70; Consultant in Public Health Medicine, Lothian Health Bd, 1974–88, with a special interest in the health of children. Mem. Court, Edinburgh Univ., 1992–98. QHP 1996–2000. Kentucky Colonel, 1961. Hon. DCCH 1993. *Recreations:* family, sailing, ski-ing, WHO Health for All movement. *Address:* Viewfield House, 12 Tipperlinn Road, Edinburgh EH10 5ET. *T:* (0131) 447 5545.

ZEEMAN, Sir (Erik) Christopher, Kt 1991; PhD; FRS 1975; Principal, Hertford College, Oxford, 1988–95; *b* 4 Feb. 1925; *s* of Christian Zeeman and Christine Zeeman (*née* Bushell); *m* 1960, Rosemary Gledhill; three *s* two *d.* *Educ:* Christ's Hospital; Christ's Coll., Cambridge (MA, PhD; Hon. Fellow, 1989). Commonwealth Fellow, 1954; Fellow of Gonville and Caius Coll., Cambridge, 1953–64; Lectr, Cambridge Univ., 1955–64; Prof., and Dir of Maths Res. Centre, Warwick Univ., 1964–88. Sen. Fellow, SRC, 1976–81. Visiting Prof. at various institutes, incl.: IAS; Princeton; IHES, Paris; IMPA, Rio; Royal Instn; also at various univs, incl.: California, Florida, Pisa. Hon. Dr, Strasbourg. *Publications:* numerous research papers on topology, dynamical systems, and applications to biology and the social sciences, in various mathematical and other jls. *Recreation:* family. *Address:* 23 High Street, Woodstock, Oxon OX20 1TE. *T:* (01993) 813402.

ZEFFIRELLI, G. Franco (Corsi); opera, film and theatrical producer and designer since 1949; *b* 12 February 1923. *Educ:* Florence. Designer: (in Italy): A Streetcar Named Desire; Troilus and Cressida; Three Sisters. Has produced and designed numerous operas at La Scala, Milan, 1952–, and in all the great cities of Italy, at world-famous festivals, and in UK and USA; *operas include:* Covent Garden: Lucia di Lammermoor, Cavalleria Rusticana and Pagliacci, 1959; Falstaff, 1961; Don Giovanni, Alcina, 1962; Tosca, Rigoletto, 1964; Metropolitan Opera, NY: Otello, 1972; Antony and Cleopatra, 1973; La Bohème, 1981; Tosca, Rigoletto, 1985; Turandot, 1987; Carmen, 1996; La Traviata, 1998; La Scala: Otello, 1976; Turandot, 1983; Don Carlos, 1992; Verona: Carmen, 1995; Il Trovatore, 2001; L'Elisir d'Amore, Glyndebourne, 1961; Don Giovanni, Vienna, 1972; Aida, Tokyo, 1997; Tosca, Rome, 2000; Aida, Busseto, 2001; *stage:* Romeo and Juliet , Old Vic, 1960; Othello, Stratford-on-Avon, 1961; Amleto, Nat. Theatre, 1964; After the Fall, Rome, 1964; Who's Afraid of Virginia Woolf, Paris, 1964, Milan, 1965; La Lupa, Rome, 1965; Much Ado About Nothing, Nat. Theatre, 1966; Black Comedy, Rome, 1967; A Delicate Balance, Rome, 1967; Saturday, Sunday, Monday, Nat. Theatre, 1973; Filumena, Lyric, 1977; Six Characters in Search of an Author, RNT, 1992; *films:* The Taming of the Shrew, 1965–66; Florence, Days of Destruction, 1966; Romeo and Juliet, 1967; Brother Sun, Sister Moon, 1973; Jesus of Nazareth, 1977; The Champ, 1979; Endless Love, 1981; La Traviata, 1983; Cavalleria Rusticana, 1983; Otello, 1986; The Young Toscanini, 1988; Hamlet, 1991; The Sparrow, 1993; Jane Eyre, 1996; Tea with Mussolini, 1999. Produced Beethoven's Missa Solemnis, San Pietro, Rome, 1971. *Publication:* Zeffirelli (autobiog.), 1986. *Address:* Via Lucio Volumnio 37, Rome 00178, Italy.

ZEHETMAYR, John Walter Lloyd, OBE 1991; VRD 1963; FICFor; Senior Officer for Wales and Conservator South Wales, Forestry Commission, 1966–81, retired; *b* 24 Dec. 1921; *s* of late Walter Zehetmayr and late Gladys Zehetmayr; *m* 1945, Isabell (Betty) Neill-Kennedy; two *s* one *d.* *Educ:* St Paul's, Kensington; Keble Coll., Oxford (BA). Served RNVR, 1942–46 (despatches); now Lt Cdr RNR retired. Forestry Commission: Silviculturist, 1948–56; Chief Work Study Officer, 1956–64; Conservator West Scotland, 1964–66. Chm., Forestry Safety Council, 1986–92. Member: Prince of Wales' Cttee, 1970–89; Brecon Beacons Nat. Park Cttee, 1982–91. Vice-Pres., Glamorgan Wildlife Trust, 1992–97. *Publications:* Experiments in Tree Planting on Peat, 1954; Afforestation of Upland Heaths, 1960; The Gwent Small Woods Project 1979–84, 1985; Forestry in Wales, 1985; The Effectiveness of Health and Safety Measures in Forestry, 1992. *Recreations:* garden, conservation, butterfly recording, ski-ing (club coach on plastic, 1996–). *Address:* 2 Highfields, Bradford Place, Penarth, Vale of Glam CF64 1AF.

ZEIDMAN, Martyn Keith; QC 1998; **His Honour Judge Zeidman;** a Circuit Judge, since 2001; *b* Cardiff, 30 May 1952; *s* of Abe and Jennie Zeidman; *m* 1977, Verity Owen; one *s* one *d.* *Educ:* Univ. of London (LLB Hons ext.). Called to the Bar, Middle Temple, 1974; Asst Recorder, 1995–99; a Recorder, 1999–2001. Pres., Mental Health Review Tribunal (Restricted Cases), 2000–. *Publications:* A Short Guide to The Landlord & Tenant Act 1987, 1987; A Short Guide to The Housing Act 1988, 1988; Steps to Possession, 1989; A Short Guide to The Courts and Legal Services Act 1990, 1990; A Short Guide to The Road Traffic Act 1991, 1991; Making Sense of The Leasehold Reform Housing & Urban Development Act 1993, 1994; Archbold Practical Research Papers on: Law of Mistake, 1997; Law of Self Defence, 1997; Intoxication, 1998. *Recreations:* family, studying Jewish religious texts, cycling. *Address:* Snaresbrook Crown Court, The Court House, Hollybush Hill, E11 1QW.

ZEIGERMAN, Dror, PhD; Ambassador of Israel to the Court of St James's, 1998–2000; *b* Israel, 15 May 1948; *s* of Itzchak Zeigerman; *m* Asi Sherf; two *s* one *d.* *Educ:* Hebrew Univ., Jerusalem (BA Hist. 1977; MA Hist. and Internat. Relns 1978); George Washington Univ. (PhD Internat. Relns 1986). Mem., Knesset (Likud Party), 1981–84; Leader, Delegn to Ethiopia, 1982; Member, Knesset Committees: Foreign Affairs; Security; Immigration and Absorption. Hd, Students' Dept, Zionist Orgn in Israel, 1987–88; Gen. Man., Israel Sch. of Tourism, 1988–92; Consul Gen., Toronto, 1992–95; rep., various internat. corps, 1996–97. *Recreation:* golf. *Address:* c/o Ministry of Foreign Affairs, Hakirya, Romema, Jerusalem 91950, Israel. *Clubs:* Athenæum, Travellers.

ZEKI, Prof. Semir, FRS 1990; Professor of Neurobiology, since 1981, and Co-head, Wellcome Department of Cognitive Neurology, since 1996, University College London (Fellow, 2000); *b* 8 Nov. 1940; *m* 1967, Anne-Marie Claire Blestel; one *d* one *s.* *Educ:* University College London (BSc Anat. 1964; PhD 1967). Asst Lectr, UCL, 1966–67; Res. Associate, St Elizabeth's Hosp., Washington DC, 1967–68; Asst Prof., Univ. of Wisconsin, 1968–69; Lectr in Anatomy, UCL, 1969–75; Henry Head Res. Fellow, Royal Soc., 1975–80; Reader in Neurobiology, UCL, 1980–81. Vis. Professorial Fellow, RPMS, Hammersmith Hosp., 1991–96. Visiting Professor: Duke Univ., 1977; Ludwig Maximillians Univ., Munich, 1982–87; Univ. of California, Berkeley, 1984; St Andrews, 1985; Vis. Upjohn Prof., Erasmus Univ., Brussels, 1997–98; Vis. Schol., J. Paul Getty Mus., 1996. Lectures include: David Marr, Cambridge Univ., 1989; Philip Bard, Johns Hopkins Univ., 1992; Ferrier, Royal Soc., 1995; Woodhull, Royal Instn, 1995; Royal Soc. Humphry Davy, Acad. des Scis, Paris, 1996; Carl Gustave Bernhard, Royal Swedish Acad., 1998. Member: Neuroscience Res. Program and Neurosci. Inst., NY, 1985–; Wellcome Trust Vision Panel, 1985–93 (Chm., 1987–93); Bd of Scientific Govs, Scripps Res. Inst., Calif., 1992–; Nat. Sci. Council of France, 1998–. Trustee, Fight for Sight, 1992–97; Guarantor, Brain, 1994–. Mem., Cttee of Honour, Paris DFAS, 1996–. Ed., Philosophical Trans of Royal Soc., series B, 1997–. Founder FMedSci 1998; MRI, 1985; Member: Academia Europaea, 1990; Eur. Acad. of Scis and Arts, 1992; Amer. Phil Soc., 1998; Hon. Mem., Italian Primatological Assoc., 1988. Hon. DSc Aston, 1994. Minerva Foundn Prize, USA, 1985; Prix Science pour l'Art, LVMH, Paris, 1991; Rank Prize, 1992; Zotterman Prize, Swedish Physiol Soc., 1993. *Publications:* A Vision of the Brain, 1993; (with Balthus) La Quête de l'Essential, Paris, 1995; Inner Vision: an exploration of art and the brain, 1999; articles on vision and the brain in professional jls. *Recreations:* reading (esp. about the darker side of man), music, deep sleep. *Address:* Wellcome Department of Cognitive Neurology, University College London, WC1E 6BT. *T:* (020) 7679 7316. *Clubs:* Athenæum, Garrick.

ZELDIN, Dr Theodore, CBE 2001; FBA 1995; FRSL, FRHistS; President, Oxford Muse, since 2001; Fellow, St Antony's College, Oxford, 1957-2001; *b* 22 Aug. 1933; *s* of Jacob Zeldin, civil engr and Emma Zeldin, dentist; *m* 1975, Deirdre Wilson, *qv.* *Educ:* Aylesbury Grammar Sch.; Birkbeck Coll., London (BA 1951); Christ Church, Oxford (schol.; BA 1954; MA); St Antony's Coll., Oxford (DPhil 1957). Oxford University: Lectr, Christ Church, and Univ. Lectr in Modern Hist., 1959–76; Dean, Sen. Tutor, and Tutor for Admissions, St Antony's Coll., 1963–76; Dir, Future of Work Project, 1997–2000. Res. Fellow, CNRS, Paris, 1952–53; Visiting Professor: Harvard Univ., 1969–70; Univ. of Southern Calif, 1980–83. Mem., EC Cttee for Eur. Voluntary Service, 1997–99; Vice-Pres., Culture Europe, 2000–. Pres., Planning Commn, Nord-Pas-de-Calais, 1993–95; Advr, French Millennium Commn, 1999; Hon. President: Centre du Paysage, France, 2000; Maison du Temps et de la Mobilité, Belfort, 2001. Pres., Internat. Fest. of Geography, 1999; Chm., Oxford Food Symposium; Member: Council, Vivendi-Universal Inst de Prospective; Adv. Council, Demos; Mgt Cttee, Soc. of Authors. Trustee: Wytham Hall Med. Charity for the Homeless; Amar Internat. Appeal for Refugees. MAE 1993. Wolfson Prize for History. Comdr, Ordre des Arts et des Lettres (France). *Publications:* The Political System of Napoleon III, 1958; (ed) Journal d'Emile Ollivier, 1961; Emile Ollivier and the Liberal Empire of Napoleon III, 1963; Conflicts in French Society, 1971; France 1848–1945: vol. 1, Ambition, Love and Politics, 1973, vol. 2, Intellect, Taste and Anxiety, 1977, both vols re-issued 1993 as History of French Passions; The French, 1983; Happiness (novel), 1987; An Intimate History of Humanity, 1994; Flirtations (filmscript), 1994; Conversation, 1998; contrib. nat. press and learned jls. *Recreations:* painting, gardening, mending things. *Address:* Tumbledown House, Cumnor, Oxford OX2 9QE.

ZELLICK, Prof. Graham John; Vice-Chancellor, since 1997, and President, University of London (Deputy Vice-Chancellor, 1994–97); *b* 12 Aug. 1948; *s* of R. H. and B. Zellick; *m* 1975, Jennifer Temkin, *qv*; one *s* one *d.* *Educ:* Christ's Coll., Finchley; Gonville and Caius Coll., Cambridge (MA, PhD); Stanford Univ. Called to the Bar, Middle Temple, 1992, Bencher, 2001. Ford Foundn Fellow, Stanford Law Sch., 1970–71; Queen Mary College, later Queen Mary and Westfield College, London: Lectr, 1971–78; Reader in Law, 1978–82; Prof. of Public Law, 1982–88; Dean of Faculty of Laws, 1984–88; Head, Dept of Law, 1984–90; Drapers' Prof. of Law, 1988–91; Prof. of Law, 1991–98, now Emeritus; Sen. Vice-Principal and Acting Principal, 1990–91; Principal, 1991–98; University of London: Dean, Faculty of Laws, 1986–88; Dep. Chm., Academic Council, 1987–89. Vis. Fellow, Centre of Criminology, 1978–79, and Vis. Prof. of Law, 1975, 1978–79, Toronto Univ.; Vis. Scholar, St John's Coll., Oxford, 1989. Lectures: Noel Buxton, NACRO, 1983; Webber, Jews' Coll., London, 1986; Sir Gwilym Morris, UWIST, Cardiff, 1986; Wythe, Coll. of William and Mary, Va, 1989; Atkin, Reform Club, 2000. Editor: European Human Rights Reports, 1978–82; Public Law, 1981–86; Member of Editorial Board: British Jl of Criminology, 1980–90; Public Law, 1981–91; Howard Jl of Criminal Justice, 1984–87; Civil Law Library, 1987–91. Member: Council and Exec. Cttee, Howard League for Penal Reform, 1973–82; Jellicoe Cttee on Bds of Visitors of Prisons, 1973–75; Sub Cttee on Crime and Criminal Justice, 1984–88, and Sub Cttee on Police Powers and the Prosecution Process, 1985–88, ESRC; Lord Chancellor's Legal Aid Adv. Cttee, 1985–88; Newham Dist Ethics Cttee, 1985–86; Data Protection Tribunal, 1985–96; Lord Chancellor's Adv. Cttee on Legal Educn, 1988–90; S Thames RHA, 1994–95; E London and the City HA, 1995–97; Criminal Injuries Compensation Appeals Panel, 2000–; Competition Commn Appeal Tribunals, 2000–; Electoral Commn, 2001–; Chairman: Prisoners' Advice and Law Service, 1984–89; Legal Cttee, All-Party Parly War Crimes Gp, 1988–91; Dep. Chm., Justice Cttee on Prisoners' Rights, 1981–83. Dir, UCAS, 1994–97. Chairman: Cttee of Heads of Univ. Law Schs, 1988–90; E London Strategic Forum for Nat. Educn and Trng Targets, 1993–95; Vice-Chm., Acad. Study Gp for Israel and ME, 1995–; Mem. Council, CVCP, 1993–97. Pres., West London Synagogue, 2000– (Mem. Council and Chm., Educn Cttee, 1990–93); Member: Council: UCS, 1983–92; City and East London Confedn for Medicine and Dentistry, 1991–95; St Bartholomew's Hosp. Med. Coll., 1991–95; Council of Govs, London Hosp. Med. Coll., 1991–95; Court of Governors: Polytechnic of Central London, 1973–77; Polytechnic of

N London, 1986–89; Univ. of Greenwich, 1994–97; Bd of Academic Govs, Richmond, Amer. Internat. Univ. in London, 1999–; Governor: Pimlico Sch., 1973–77; Tel Aviv Univ., 2000– (Chm., Lawyers' Gp, 1984–89, and Trustee, 1985–87, Tel Aviv Univ. Trust); Mem. Council, Spitalfields Heritage Centre, 1992–98; Patron: Redress Trust, 1993–; London Jewish Cultural Centre, 2001–; Trustee: William Harvey Res. Inst., 1995–2000; Samuel Courtauld Trust, 1997–; Gov., William Goodenough Trust, 1997–. JP Inner London (N Westminster), 1981–85. Freeman, City of London, 1992; Liveryman, Drapers' Co., 1995 (Freeman, 1992; Mem. Ct, 2000–; Jun. Warden, 2000–01). CIMgt 1997 (FBIM 1991); FRSA 1991; FRSocMed 1996; FInstD 1996; Founding FICPD, 1998; AcSS 2000. Hon. Fellow: Soc. of Advanced Legal Studies, 1997; Burgon Soc., 2001. Hon. LHD New York, 2001. *Publications:* Justice in Prison (with Sir Brian MacKenna), 1983; (ed) The Law Commission and Law Reform, 1988; (contrib.) Halsbury's Laws of England, 4th edn 1982; contribs to collections of essays, pamphlets, the national press, and professional and learned periodicals incl. British Jl of Criminology, Civil Justice Quarterly, Criminal Law Rev., Modern Law Rev., Public Law, Univ. of Toronto Law Jl, William and Mary Law Rev. *Address:* University of London, Senate House, WC1E 7HU. *T:* (020) 7862 8004, *Fax:* (020) 7862 8008; *e-mail:* vice-chancellor@lon.ac.uk; (chambers) 3 Verulam Buildings, Gray's Inn, WC1R 5NT; Burton House, Burton Park, W Sussex GU28 0QU. *Club:* Reform.

ZELLICK, Jennifer, (Mrs G. J. Zellick); *see* Temkin, J.

ZEMAN, Prof. Zbyněk Anthony Bohuslav; Research Professor in European History, 1982–96, now Emeritus, and Professorial Fellow of St Edmund Hall, 1983–96, Oxford University; *b* Prague, 18 Oct. 1928; *s* of late Jaroslav and Růžena Zeman; *m* 1st, 1956, Sarah Anthea Collins (*d* 1998); two *s* one *d*; 2nd, 1998, Dagmar Hájková. *Educ:* London and Oxford Universities. BA (Hons) London, DPhil Oxon. Research Fellow, St Antony's Coll., Oxford, 1958–61, and Mem. editorial staff, The Economist, 1959–62; Lectr in Modern History, Univ. of St Andrews, 1962–70; Head of Research, Amnesty International, 1970–73; Director, East-West SPRL (Brussels) and European Co-operation Research Gp, 1974–76; Prof. of Central and SE European Studies and Dir, Comenius Centre, Lancaster Univ., 1976–82. Vis. Prof. of Hist., Charles University, Prague, 1990–91. Hon. Fellow: Österreichisches Ost-und Südosteuropa-Institut, 1988–89; Inst. of History of Czech Army, Prague, 1994–95. *Publications* include: The Break-up of the Habsburg Empire 1914–1918, 1961; Nazi Propaganda, 1964; (with W. B. Scharlau) The Merchant of Revolution, A Life of Alexander Helphand (Parvus), 1965; Prague Spring, 1969; A Diplomatic History of the First World War, 1971; (ed jtly) International Yearbook of East West Trade, 1975; The Masaryks, 1976; (jtly) Comecon Oil and Gas, 1977; Selling the War: art and propaganda in the Second World War, 1978; Heckling Hitler: caricatures of the Third Reich, 1984; Pursued by a Bear: the making of Eastern Europe, 1989; The Making and Breaking of Communist Europe, 1991; (with A. Klimek) The Life of Edvard Beneš 1884–1948: Czechoslovakia in peace and war, 1997. *Address:* 28509 Kácov–Račiněves 35, Czech Republic.

ZENINED, Abdesselam, Hon. GCVO 1987; Minister-delegate in charge of Maghreb, Arab and Islamic Affairs, Morocco, since 1998; *b* 15 Dec. 1934; *m* 1960; one *s* two *d*. *Educ:* Bordeaux Univ.; Sorbonne. Carnegie scholarship, Inst. des Hautes Etudes Internat., Geneva, 1962. Ministry of Foreign Affairs, Morocco, 1959; Min. of Information, 1967; Under-Sec., Prime Minister's Office, 1974–77; MP 1977–80; Minister of Tourism, 1979–80; Ambassador: to Iraq, 1980–85; to UK, 1987–91; to USSR, later Russia, 1991–96. *Address:* Ministry of Foreign Affairs and Co-operation, avenue Franklin Roosevelt, Rabat, Morocco. *Club:* Ambassadors'.

ZEPHANIAH, Benjamin Obadiah Iqbal; writer and poet; *b* 15 April 1958; *s* of Oswald Springer and Leneve Faleta Wright; *m* 1990, Amina Iqbal. *Educ:* Broadway Comprehensive Sch., Birmingham; Glen-Parva Borstal, Leicester. Poet, 1977–. DUniv: N London, 1998; Staffordshire, 2001; Hon. DLitt W England, 1999. *Publications: poetry:* Pen Rhythm, 1980; The Dread Affair, 1985; Inna Liverpool, 1988; City Psalms, 1992; Propa Propaganda, 1996; School's Out, 1997; (ed) Bloomsbury Book of Love Poems, 1999; Too Black Too Strong, 2001; *prose:* Rasta Time in Palestine, 1990; *for children:* Talking Turkeys, 1994; Funky Chickens, 1996; Wicked World, 2000; A Little Book of Vegan Poems, 2000; (with Prodeepta Das) We Are Britain, 2002; *novels:* Face, 1999; Refugee Boy, 2001. *Recreation:* collecting money. *Address:* PO Box 673, East Ham, E6 3QD. *T:* (020) 7923 0606.

ZETLAND, 4th Marquess of, *cr* 1892; **Lawrence Mark Dundas;** Bt 1762; Baron Dundas, 1794; Earl of Zetland, 1838; Earl of Ronaldshay (UK), 1892; DL; *b* 28 Dec. 1937; *e s* of 3rd Marquess of Zetland, DL and of Penelope, *d* of late Col Ebenezer Pike, CBE, MC; S father, 1989; *m* 1964, Susan, 2nd *d* of late Guy Chamberlin, Oatlands, Wrington Hill, Wrington, Bristol, and late Mrs Chamberlin; two *s* two *d*. *Educ:* Harrow School; Christ's College, Cambridge. Late 2nd Lieut, Grenadier Guards. Founding Dir, British Horseracing Bd, 1993–97. DL N Yorks, 1994. *Heir: s* Earl of Ronaldshay, *qv*. *Address:* Aske, Richmond, N Yorks DL10 5HJ. *T:* (01748) 823222. *Clubs:* All England Lawn Tennis and Croquet, Jockey (Steward, 1992–94).

ZETTER, Paul Isaac, CBE 1981; President, Zetters Group Ltd (Chairman, 1972–2000); *b* 9 July 1923; *s* of late Simon and Esther Zetter; *m* 1954, Helen Lore Morgenstern; one *s* one *d*. *Educ:* City of London Sch. Army, 1941–46. Family business, 1946–2000; became public co., 1965. Chm., Southern Council for Sport and Recreation, 1985–87; Member: Sports Council, 1985–87; National Centres Bd, Sports Council, 1987–88; Governor, 1975–, and Hon. Vice-Pres., 1985–, Sports Aid Foundation (Chm., 1976–85); Vice-Chm., World Ice Skating Championships, 1994–95. Trustee: Thames Salmon Trust, 1988–92; Foundn for Sports and Arts, 1991–96 (Chm., Sports Working Party, 1991–94). President: John Carpenter Club, 1987–88; Restricted Growth Assoc., 1993–96. Liveryman, Glovers' Co., 1981–; Freeman, City of London, 1981. *Publications:* It Could Be Verse, 1976; Bow Jest, 1992; Zero Risk, 2000; Global Warming, 2001. *Recreations:* varied water sports, walking, writing. *Address:* Tarside, Pallingham Manor Farm, Billingshurst, W Sussex RH14 0EZ.

ZETTERBERG, Christer; Chairman, IDI AB (Industrial Development and Investment), since 1996; *b* 2 Nov. 1941; *m* 1966, Inger Mathson; three *d*. MBA 1967. Officer, Royal Swedish Navy Reserve, 1964. Svenska Cellulosa AB, 1968–76 (Manager, Pulp Sales and Head, Pulp Div.); President and Chief Executive Officer: Calor-Celsius, 1976–80; Tibnor, 1980–83; Holmens Bruk, 1983–88; PKBanken, 1988–90; AB Volvo, 1990–92. Chm., Carnegie AB. Board Member: Micronic Laser Systems, 1999–; LE Lundberggroup; Holmen AB; Camfil AB. Member: Royal Swedish Acad. of Engrg Scis, 1990; Royal Acad. of Naval Scis, 1991. *Address:* IDI AB, Hovslagargatan 5B, 11148 Stockholm, Sweden; Granneberg, 61075 Västerljung, Sweden.

ZEWAIL, Prof. Ahmed H., PhD; Linus Pauling Professor of Physics, since 1995, Director, NSF Laboratory of Molecular Sciences, since 1996, California Institute of Technology; *b* 26 Feb. 1946; *s* of Hassan A. Zewail and Rawhia Dar; *m* Dema; two *s* two *d*. *Educ:* Alexandria Univ., Egypt (BSc 1st Cl. Hons 1967; MS 1969); Univ. of Pennsylvania (PhD 1974). IBM Postdoctoral Fellow, Univ. of Calif, Berkeley, 1974–76; California Institute of Technology: Asst Prof. of Chemical Physics, 1976–78; Associate Prof., 1978–82; Prof. of Chemical Physics, 1982–89; Linus Pauling Prof. of Chemical Physics, 1990–94. Jtly, patent, Solar Energy Concentrator Devices, 1980. Foreign Mem., Royal Soc., 2001. Awards include: King Faisal Internat. Prize in Sci., 1989; Wolf Prize in Chem., 1993; Robert A. Welch Award in Chem., 1997; Benjamin Franklin Medal, Franklin Inst., USA, 1998; Nobel Prize in Chemistry, 1999. OM 1st Cl. (Scis and Arts) (Egypt), 1995; Grand Collar of the Nile (Egypt), 1999; Order of Zayed (UEA), 2000; OM (Tunisia), 2000; Order of Cedar (Lebanon), 2000; Order of ISESCO 1st Cl. (Saudi Arabia), 2000. *Publications:* Femtochemistry: ultrafast dynamics of the chemical bond, Vols I and II, 1994; numerous contribs to scientific jls incl. Science (USA), Nature and other professional jls. *Recreations:* reading, music, family-time travel. *Address:* California Institute of Technology, Mail Code 127-72, Pasadena, CA 91125, USA. *T:* (626) 3956536. *Clubs:* Hon. Life Member: Athenaeum Faculty (Pasadena); Gezira, Automobile, Cairo Capital (Cairo); Alexandria Sporting (Egypt).

ZHAO ZIYANG; General Secretary, Central Committee, Chinese Communist Party, 1987–89; *b* Huaxian County, Henan Prov., 1919; *m*; four *s* one *d*. Joined Chinese Communist Youth League, 1932, Chinese Communist Party, 1938; held various posts, S China Sub-Bureau of Central Cttee, Guangdong Provincial Cttee, and Cttee of Inner Mongolia Autonomous Reg., 1950–74; First Sec. of Provincial Cttee and Chm. of Revolutionary Cttee, Guangdong, 1974, Sichuan, 1975–80; First Political Commissar, Chengdu Mil. Reg., Chinese People's Liberation Army, 1976–80; Vice-Chm., 5th Nat. Cttee, Chinese People's Political Consultative Conf., 1978–80; Vice Premier, State Council, 1980, Premier, 1980–87. Mem., 10th Central Cttee, Chinese Communist Party, 1973; Alternate Mem., 1977, Mem., 1979, Mem. Standing Cttee, 1980, Political Bureau, and Vice Chm., 1981, 11th Central Cttee; Mem., 1982, and Mem. Standing Cttee, 1982, Political Bureau, 12th Central Cttee. *Address:* 6 Fuqiang Alley, Beijing, People's Republic of China.

ZHUKOV, Georgi Alexandrovich; Hero of Socialist Labour (1978); Orders of: Lenin (2); October Revolution; Red Banner of Labour (2); Red Star; Great Patriotic War, Grade 2; Friendship of Peoples; Joliot-Curie Medal; Columnist of Pravda, since 1962; Member Presidium, World Peace Council, since 1974; Vice-President, Soviet-American Institute, since 1961; President, Society USSR-France, since 1958; Secretary, Moscow writing organization, since 1970; *b* 1908. *Educ:* Lomonosov Inst., Moscow. Corresp.: local papers in Lugansk, Kharkov, 1927–32; Komsomolskaya Pravda, 1932–46 (Mem. Editorial Bd); Pravda in Paris, 1947–52; Foreign Editor of Pravda, 1952–57; Chairman, USSR Council of Ministers' State Committee for Cultural Relations with Foreign Countries, 1957–62. Mem., Central Auditing Cttee of CPSU, elected by XX, XXII, XXIII and XXIV Congresses of CPSU, 1956–89; Alternate Mem., Central Cttee of CPSU, elected by XXV, XXVI and XXVII Congresses of CPSU, 1976–89; Mem., Foreign Relations Cttee, USSR Supreme Soviet, 1966–89; MP, 1962–89; Chm., Soviet–French Parly Gp, 1966–89. Prizes: Lenin (for Journalism); Vorovsky; Union of Soviet Journalists; internat. organization of journalists. *Publications:* Border, 1938; Russians and Japan, 1945; Soldier's Life, 1946; American Notes (essays), 1947; The West After War, 1948; Three Months in Geneva, 1954; Taming Tigers, 1961; Japan, 1962; Meetings in Transcarpathia, 1962; One MIG from a Thousand, 1963, 2nd edn 1979; These Seventeen Years, 1963; Silent Art, 1964; The People of the Thirties, 1964; Vietnam, 1965; America, 1967; The People of the Forties, 1968, 2nd edn 1975; From Battle to Battle: letters from the ideological front, 1970; Chilean Diary, 1970; The USA on the Threshold of the Seventies, 1970; The People in the War (about Vietnam), 1972; 33 Visas, 1972; Times of Great Changes, 1973; Alex and others, 1974; Poisoners, 1975; The War: the beginning and the end, 1975; Letters from Rambouillet, 1975; European Horizons, 1975; Thirty Conversations with TV Viewers, 1977; Town's Beginning, 1977; Thoughts of Unthinkable, 1978; Society without Future, 1978; The Tale of Dirty Tricks, 1978; Roots, 1980; Pioneer Builders, 1982; Steep Steps, 1983 (English edn 1987); Journey through Indo-China, 1984; Journalists, 1984 (Chinese edn 1988); Where is peace—there life, 1985; Lack of Spirit, 1985; Dogs of War, 1986; Soldier's Thoughts, 1987; USSR–USA: the seventy years long way, 1988; Selected Works in Two Volumes, 1989.

ZIA, Hon. Khaleda; Prime Minister of Bangladesh, 1991–96 and since 2001; *b* 15 Aug. 1945; *m* 1960, Gen. Ziaur Rahman (*d* 1981), President of Bangladesh; two *s*. *Educ:* Surendranath Coll., Dinajpur. Vice-Chm., 1982–84, Chm., 1984–, Bangladesh Nat. Party. *Address:* Office of the Prime Minister, Tejgaon, Dhaka, Bangladesh.

ZIEGLER, Philip Sandeman, CVO 1991; author; *b* 24 Dec. 1929; *s* of Major Colin Louis Ziegler, DSO, DL, and Mrs Dora Ziegler (*née* Barnwell); *m* 1st, 1960, Sarah Collins; one *s* one *d*; 2nd, 1971, (Mary) Clare Charrington; one *s*. *Educ:* Eton; New Coll., Oxford (1st Cl. Hons Jurisprudence; Chancellor's Essay Prize). Entered Foreign Service, 1952; served in Vientiane, Paris, Pretoria and Bogotá; resigned 1967; joined William Collins and Sons Ltd, 1967, Editorial Dir 1972, Editor-in-Chief, 1979–80. Chairman: The London Library, 1979–85; Soc. of Authors, 1988–90; Public Lending Right Adv. Cttee, 1994–97. FRSL 1975; FRHS 1979. Hon. DLitt: Westminster Coll., Fulton, 1988; Buckingham, 2000. *Publications:* Duchess of Dino, 1962; Addington, 1965; The Black Death, 1968; William IV, 1971; Omdurman, 1973; Melbourne, 1976 (W. H. Heinemann Award); Crown and People, 1978; Diana Cooper, 1981; Mountbatten, 1985; Elizabeth's Britain 1926 to 1986, 1986; The Sixth Great Power: Barings 1762–1929, 1988; King Edward VIII, 1990; Harold Wilson: the authorised life, 1993; London at War 1939–45, 1995; Osbert Sitwell, 1998; Britain Then and Now, 1999; Soldiers, 2001; *edited:* the Diaries of Lord Louis Mountbatten 1920–1922, 1987; Personal Diary of Admiral the Lord Louis Mountbatten 1943–1946, 1988; From Shore to Shore: the diaries of Earl Mountbatten of Burma 1953–1979, 1989; (with Desmond Seward) Brooks's: a social history, 1991. *Address:* 22 Cottesmore Gardens, W8 5PR. *T:* (020) 7937 1903, *Fax:* (020) 7937 5458. *Club:* Brooks's.

ZIENKIEWICZ, Prof. Olgierd Cecil, CBE 1989; FRS 1979; FREng; Professor and Head of Civil Engineering Department, 1961–88, and Director, Institute for Numerical Methods in Engineering, 1976–88, University of Wales at Swansea, now Professor Emeritus; UNESCO Professor of Numerical Methods in Engineering, Universidad Politécnica de Cataluña, Barcelona; J. Walter Professor of Engineering, University of Texas, Austin, 1988–98; *b* Caterham, 18 May 1921; *s* of Casimir Zienkiewicz and Edith Violet (*née* Penny); *m* 1952, Helen Jean (*née* Fleming), Toronto; two *s* one *d*. *Educ:* Katowice, Poland; Imperial Coll., London (FIC 1993). BSc (Eng); ACGI; PhD; DIC; DSc (Eng); DipEng; FICE; FASCE; FREng (FEng 1979). Consulting engrg, 1945–49; Lectr, Univ. of Edinburgh, 1949–57; Prof. of Structural Mechanics, Northwestern Univ., 1957–61. Naval Sea Systems Comd Res. Prof., Monterey, Calif, 1979–80; Chalmers Jubilee Prof., Gothenburg, 1990, 1992. Hon. Founder Mem., GAMNI, France. Chairman: Cttee on Analysis and Design, Internat. Congress of Large Dams; Jt Computer Cttee, Instn of Civil Engineers. Mem. Council, ICE, 1972–75 (Chm., S Wales and Mon. Br.); Telford Premium, ICE, 1963–67. Pres., Internat. Assoc. Computational Mechanics,

1986–90. General Editor, Internat. Jl Numerical Methods in Engineering, 1968–98; Member Editorial Board: Internat. Jl Solids and Structures; Internat. Jl Earthquakes and Structural Mechanics; Internat. Jl Rock Mechanics, Numerical and Analytical Methods in Geomechanics. For. Associate, US Nat. Acad. of Engrg, 1981; Foreign Member: Polish Acad. of Sci., 1985; Chinese Acad. of Sci., 1998; Nat. Acad. of Sci., Italy, 1999. Hon. Prof., Dalian Inst. of Technology, China, 1987; Hon. Dr, Lisbon, 1972; Hon. DSc: NUI, 1975; Northwestern Univ., Illinois, 1984; Chalmers Univ. of Technology, Gothenburg, 1987; Univ. of Technol., Warsaw, 1989; Technical Univ., Krakow, 1989; Technical Univ., Budapest, 1992; Univ. of Hong Kong, 1992; Univ. of Padua, 1992; Aristotelian Univ. of Thessaloniki, 1993; Brunel Univ., 1993; Univ. of Wales, 1993; Ecole Normale Supérieure de Cachan, Paris, 1997; Technical Univ. of Madrid, 1998; Hon. DTech: Norwegian Inst. of Technol., Trondheim, 1985; Technische Univ., Vienna, 1993; Hon. DSci Free Univ., Brussels, 1982; Hon. LLD Dundee, 1987. FCGI 1979. James Clayton Fund Prizes, IMechE, 1967, 1973; James Alfred Ewing Medal, ICE, 1980; Newmark Medal, ASCE, 1980; Worcester Reed Warner Medal, ASME, 1980; Gauss Medal, Acad. of Science, Braunschweig, West Germany, 1987; Royal Medal, Royal Soc., 1990; Gold Medal, IStructE, 1992; Leonardo da Vinci Medal, FEANI, 1997; Timoshenko Medal, ASME, 1998. Chevalier, Ordre des Palmes Académiques (France), 1996. *Publications:* Stress Analysis, 1965; Rock Mechanics, 1968; Finite Element Method, 1967, 4th edn 1989; Optimum Design of Structures, 1973; Finite Elements in Fluids, 1975; Numerical Methods in Offshore Engineering, 1977; Finite Elements and Approximation, 1983; numerous papers in Jl ICE, Jl Mech. Sci., Proc. Royal Soc., Internat. Jl of Num. Methods in Engrg, etc. *Recreations:* sailing, skin-diving. *Address:* 29 Somerset Road, Langland, Swansea SA3 4PG. *T:* (01792) 368776. *Clubs:* Athenæum; Rotary (Mumbles); Mumbles Yacht.

ZIJLSTRA, Jelle; Central Banker; President, Netherlands Bank, 1967–81; Member, Supervisory Board, Royal Dutch Petroleum, since 1982; *b* 27 Aug. 1918; *s* of Ane Zijlstra and Pietje Postuma; *m* 1946, Hetty Bloksma; two *s* three *d*. *Educ:* Netherlands Sch. of Economics. Asst, Netherlands Sch. of Economics, 1945; Prof., Theoretical Economics, 1948–52; Prof., Public Finance, 1963–66, Free Univ. of Amsterdam; Minister of Economic Affairs, 1952–58; of Finance, 1959–63; Prime Minister, 1966–67. Mem., Chm. Board, and Pres., BIS, 1967–82; Governor, IMF, 1967–81. *Publications:* Planned Economy, 1947; The Velocity of Money and its Significance for the Value of Money and for Monetary Equilibrium, 1948; Economic Order and Economic Policy, 1952. *Recreations:* sailing, ski-ing. *Address:* Park Oud Wassenaar, flat 44, 2243 BX Wassenaar, Netherlands.

ZILKHA, Selim Khedoury; non-executive Director, El Paso Energy and Gas, since 2000; Principal, Zilkha Renewable Energy, since 2001; *b* 7 April 1927; *s* of Khedoury Aboodi Zilkha and Louise (*née* Bashi); *m* (marr. diss.); one *s* one *d*. *Educ:* English Sch., Heliopolis, Egypt; Horace Mann Sch. for Boys, USA; Williams Coll., USA (BA Major Philos.). Dir, Zilkha & Sons Inc., USA, 1947–87; Chm. and Man. Dir, Mothercare Ltd and associated cos, 1961–82; Dir, Habitat Mothercare Gp, 1982; Chairman: Amerfin Co. Ltd, GB, 1955–68; Spirella Co. of Great Britain Ltd, 1957–62; Chm./Jt Man. Dir, Lewis & Burrows Ltd, 1961–64; Chairman and Chief Executive Officer: Towner Petroleum Co., Houston, 1983–85; SKZ Inc., Houston, 1986; Zilkha Energy Co., Houston, 1987–98; non-exec. Dir, Sonat Inc., 1998–2000. *Recreations:* bridge, backgammon, tennis. *Address:* 750 Lausanne Road, Los Angeles, CA 90077–3316, USA. *Clubs:* Portland; Travellers (Paris).

ZILLMAN, Dr John William, AO 1996; Director of Meteorology, Australia, since 1978; President, World Meteorological Organization, since 1995; *b* 28 July 1939; *s* of late Charles H. S. Zillman and of Thelma Flora Fraser. *Educ:* Nudgee Coll.; Univ. of Queensland (BSc Hons 1960; BA 1970); Melbourne Univ. (MSc 1971); Univ. of Wisconsin (PhD 1972). Australian Bureau of Meteorology: forecaster and research scientist, 1957–74; Asst Dir (Res.), 1974–78. Commonwealth Dir of Meteorology and Perm. Rep. of Australia with WMO, 1978– (Mem., Exec. Council, 1979–). Pres., Royal Soc of Victoria, 1993–94; Vice-Pres., Aust. Acad. of Tech. Scis and Engineering, 1995–98. *Publications:* (ed jtly) Climate Change and Variability: a southern perspective, 1978; (ed jtly) Climate of the South Pacific, 1984; numerous contribs to learned jls. *Recreations:* reading, music. *Address:* Bureau of Meteorology, GPO Box 1289K, Melbourne, Vic 3001, Australia. *T:* (3) 96694558. *Club:* Melbourne (Melbourne).

ZIMAN, Prof. John Michael, FRS 1967; Emeritus Professor of Physics, University of Bristol, 1988; *b* 16 May 1925; *s* of late Solomon Netheim Ziman, ICS, retired, and Nellie Frances Ziman (*née* Gaster); *m* 1951, Rosemary Milnes Dixon; two adopted *s* two adopted *d*. *Educ:* Hamilton High Sch., NZ; Victoria University Coll., Wellington, NZ; Balliol Coll., Oxford. Junior Lectr in Mathematics, Oxford Univ., 1951–53; Pressed Steel Co. Ltd Research Fellow, Oxford Univ., 1953–54; Lectr in Physics, Cambridge Univ., 1954–64; Fellow of King's Coll., Cambridge, 1957–64; Editor of Cambridge Review, 1958–59; Tutor for Advanced Students, King's Coll., Cambridge, 1959–63; University of Bristol: Prof. of Theoretical Physics, 1964–69; Melville Wills Prof. of Physics, 1969–76; Dir, H. H. Wills Physics Lab., 1976–81; Henry Overton Wills Prof. of Physics, 1976–82. Vis.Prof., Dept of Social and Economic Studies, 1982–87, Dept of Humanities, 1982–, Imperial Coll., London. Rutherford Memorial Lectr in India and Pakistan, 1968. Dir, Sci. Policy Support Gp, 1986–91; Chairman: Council for Science and Society, 1976–90; European Assoc. for Study of Science and Technology, 1982–86; Member: Scientific Council, Internat. Centre for Theoretical Physics, Trieste, 1970–79; CNAA, 1982–87. Hon. DSc Victoria Univ. of Wellington, NZ, 1985. Jt Editor, Science Progress, 1965–92. *Publications:* Electrons and Phonons, 1960; Electrons in Metals, 1963; (with Jasper Rose) Camford Observed, 1964; Principles of the Theory of Solids, 1965; Public Knowledge, 1968; Elements of Advanced Quantum Theory, 1969; The Force of Knowledge, 1976; Reliable Knowledge, 1978; Models of Disorder, 1979; Teaching and Learning about Science and Society, 1980; Puzzles, Problems and Enigmas, 1981; An Introduction to Science Studies, 1984; (with Paul Sieghart and John Humphrey) The World of Science and the Rule of Law, 1986; Knowing Everything about Nothing, 1987; Prometheus Bound, 1994; Of One Mind, 1995; Real Science, 2000; numerous articles in scientific jls. *Address:* 27 Little London Green, Oakley, Aylesbury, Bucks HP18 9QL. *T:* and *Fax:* (0144) 237464.

ZINKERNAGEL, Prof. Rolf Martin, MD, PhD; Professor of Experimental Immunology, and Director, Institute of Experimental Immunology, University of Zürich, since 1992; *b* 6 Jan. 1944; *s* of Robert Zinkernagel and Susanne Zinkernagel-Staehlin; *m* 1968, Kathrin Lüdin; one *s* two *d*. *Educ:* Mathematisch-Naturwissenschaftliches Gymnasium; Univ. of Basel (MD 1970); Univ. of Zürich; ANU (PhD 1975). Extern, Glen Cove Community Hosp., Long Island, NY, 1966; Intern, Surgical Dept, Claraspital, Univ. of Basel, 1969; Fellow: Lab. for Electron Microscopy, Inst. of Anatomy, Univ. of Basel, 1969–70; Inst. of Biochemistry, Univ. of Lausanne, 1971–73; Vis. Fellow, Dept. of Microbiology, John Curtin Sch. of Med. Res., ANU, 1973–75; Asst Prof., subseq. Associate Prof., 1976–79, Prof., 1979, Dept of Immunopathology, Res. Inst. of Scripps Clinic, Calif; Adjunct Associate Prof., Dept of Pathology, UCSD, 1977–79; Associate Prof., 1979–88, Prof., 1988–92, Dept of Pathology, Univ. Hosp., Univ. of Zürich. Member: Swiss Soc. of Allergy and Immunology, 1971–; Amer. Assoc. of Immunologists, 1977–; Swiss Soc. of Pathology, 1981–; Sci. Adv. Council, Cancer Res. Inst., 1988–; Academia Europea, 1989–; Founding Cttee, Max-Planck-Inst. of Infectiology, 1990–92; US Acad. of Scis, 1996–; Foreign Mem., Royal Soc., 1998. Member: editl bd, numerous jls; numerous scientific adv. bds. Hon. DSc Liège, 1996. Awards include: Cloëtta Stiftung, Zürich, 1981; Paul Ehrlich Preis, Frankfurt, 1983; Lasker Award, 1995; (with Peter Doherty) Nobel Prize in Physiology or Medicine, 1996. *Address:* Institute of Experimental Immunology, University of Zürich, University Hospital, Schmelzbergstrasse 12, 8091 Zürich, Switzerland.

ZISSMAN, Sir Bernard (Philip), Kt 1996; Chief Executive Officer, Confident Communications, since 1997; *b* 11 Dec. 1934; *s* of Hannah and David Zissman; *m* 1958, Cynthia Glass; one *s* two *d*. *Educ:* King Edward's Grammar Sch., Five Ways. Sales Dir, 1960–70, Man. Dir, 1970–85, Zissman Bros (Birmingham); Dir, Hyatt Regency (Birmingham), 1992–95; Chm., Communication Hub Ltd, 1995–97; Dir of Communications, Bucknall Austin, 1996–99. Non-executive Director: Severn Trent Water Authy, 1983–89; Birmingham Broadcasting, 1994–2000; Capolito Roma, 1996–99. Birmingham City Council: Mem. (C), 1965–95; Lord Mayor, 1990–91; Leader, Conservative Gp, 1992–95; Hon. Alderman, 1995–. Chm., Edgbaston Cons. Assoc., 1996–99. Member: Council, Birmingham Chamber of Commerce and Industry, 1991–; W Midlands Police Authy, 1994–95. Chairman: Adv. Bd, Japan Centre, Birmingham Univ., 1992–; Midlands Cttee, Princess Royal Trust for Carers, 1999–. Trustee, CBSO, 1992–. Life Mem., Fedn of Clothing Designers and Execs, 1991–. Freeman, City of London. Mem., Repr. Council, Birmingham and Midland Jewry, 1992–2000; Pres., Birmingham Hebrew Congregation, 1999–. FRSA 1997. Hon. LLD Birmingham, 1997; DUniv Central England, 2000. *Recreations:* family, photography, travel. *Address:* 4 Petersham Place, Edgbaston, Birmingham B15 3RY. *T:* (0121) 454 1751.

ZOBEL de AYALA, Jaime; Chairman and President, Ayala Corporation, since 1983; Chairman, Bank of the Philippine Islands, since 1985; *b* 18 July 1934; *s* of Alfonso Zobel de Ayala and Carmen Pfitz y Herrero; *m* 1958, Beatriz Miranda; two *s* five *d*. *Educ:* La Salle, Madrid; Harvard Univ. (BA, Arch. Scis). Lt Col, Philippine Air Force (Res.). Philippine Ambassador to the Court of St James's and concurrently to Scandinavian countries, 1970–74. Mem., Camera Club of the Philippines, 1978–; Associate, RPS, 1984. Hon. Dr of Business Management De La Salle Univ., 1985; Hon. LLD Univ. of Philippines, 1991. Comendador de la Orden del Mérito Civil, Spain, 1968; Chevalier des Arts et des Lettres, 1980. *Recreation:* photography. *Address:* Ayala Corporation, 7/F Makati Stock Exchange Building, Ayala Avenue, 1254 Makati, Metro Manila 1200, Philippines. *Clubs:* White's; Fox (Harvard).

ZOCHONIS, Sir John (Basil), Kt 1997; DL; Chairman, Paterson Zochonis, 1970–93; Member, Commonwealth Development Corporation, 1992–95; *b* 2 Oct. 1929; *s* of Constantine and Octavia Nitza Zochonis; *m* 1990, Brigid Mary Evanson Demetriades. *Educ:* Rugby; Corpus Christi Coll., Oxford (BA Law). Joined Paterson Zochonis, 1953; Dir, 1957; retd, 1993. Founder, Zochonis Charitable Trust, 1977. Member Council: BESO, 1987–; Royal African Soc., 1984–. Mem., Court and Council, Manchester Univ., 1968–90 (Chm., Council, 1987–90); Chm. Govs, Withington Girls' Sch., 1995–98. President: Manchester E Co. Scout Council, 1994–; Adventure Farm Trust, 1994–99; Vice-Pres., Manchester YMCA, 1993–. Freeman, City of London, 1978; Liveryman, Tallow Chandlers' Co., 1978–. DL 1989, High Sheriff, 1994–95, Greater Manchester. Hon. RNCM 1991. Hon. LLD Manchester, 1991. *Recreations:* reading, watching cricket. *Address:* Cussons House, Bird Hall Lane, Stockport, Cheshire SK3 0XN. *T:* (0161) 491 8000. *Clubs:* Carlton, Travellers, MCC.

ZOLEVEKE, Sir Gideon (Asatori Pitabose), KBE 1983 (MBE 1968); retired as public servant, 1973 and as politician, 1980; farmer since 1980; *b* 3 Aug. 1922; *s* of Pita Pitabose and Mata Taburana; *m* 1954, Melody Sukuluta'a Watanamae; three *s* three *d* (and one *s* decd). *Educ:* primary schs, Solomon Is; secondary sch. and tertiary educn, Fiji. Dip. in Surgery and Medicine, Fiji Sch. of Medicine, Suva; DCMHE London. Served British Solomon Is Protectorate Defence Force, 1942–45 (Pacific Stars). Govt MO, 1951–62; Sen. Health Educn Officer, 1962–73; Mem., Governing Council, 1973–74 (Chm., Works and Public Utilities); MLA, 1974–78 (Backbencher, 1975–76); Minister of: Works and Public Utilities, 1974–75; Home Affairs, April-July 1975; Educn, July-Nov. 1975; Agriculture and Lands, 1976–78; Health and Med. Services, 1978–80. Mem. and leader, various govt delegns, 1953–. Mem., Solomon Is Public Service Commn, 1981–; Chairman: Solomon Is Electricity Authy Bd of Management, 1983–; Solomon Is Water Authy, 1994–. Dir, Boral Gas (SI), 1983–. Founder and first Pres., Solomon Is Med. Officers Assoc., 1952–69; President: W Pacific Br.,BMA, 1961–70; Choiseul People's Assoc., 1955–71; Civil Servants Assoc., British Solomon Is Protectorate, 1966–67; Solomon Is Br., BRCS, 1974–78 (BRCS award, 1978; Life Mem., 1982); Solomon Is Red Cross, 1978–82; St John's Primary Sch., Rove, Honiara, 1968–76; Honiara Club, 1963–68; Foundn Mem., 1967–, Pres. and Chm., 1980–, Sir Winston Churchill Trust Fund, Solomon Is. *Publications:* A Man from Choiseul (autobiog.), 1980; (contrib.) Lands in the Solomon Islands, 1982; (contrib.) Solomon Island Politics, 1983. *Recreations:* writing, reading. *Address:* Kaiti Hill, PO Box 243, Honiara, Solomon Islands. *T:* 22927.

ZOUCHE, 18th Baron *cr* 1308, of Haryngworth; **James Assheton Frankland;** Bt 1660; company director; President, Multiple Sclerosis Society of Victoria, 1981–84; *b* 23 Feb. 1943; *s* of Major Hon. Sir Thomas William Assheton Frankland, 11th Bt, and Mrs Robert Pardoe (*d* 1972), *d* of late Captain Hon. Edward Kay-Shuttleworth; *S* to father's Btcy, 1944; *S* grandmother, 17th Baroness Zouche, 1965; *m* 1978, Sally Olivia, *y d* of R. M. Barton, Bungay, Suffolk; one *s* one *d*. *Educ:* Lycée Jaccard, Lausanne. Served 15/19th the King's Royal Hussars, 1963–68. *Heir: s* Hon. William Thomas Assheton Frankland [*b* 23 July 1984]. *Address:* The Abbey, Charlton Adam, Somerton, Somerset TA11 7BE.

ZUCKER, Kenneth Harry, QC 1981; **His Honour Judge Zucker;** a Circuit Judge, since 1989; *b* 4 March 1935; *s* of Nathaniel and Norma Zucker; *m* 1961, Ruth Erica, *y d* of Dr H. Brudno; one *s* one *d*. *Educ:* Westcliff High Sch.; Exeter Coll., Oxford, 1955–58 (MA). Served in Royal Air Force, 1953–55. Bacon Scholar, Gray's Inn, 1958, called to Bar, Gray's Inn, 1959; Atkin Scholar, Gray's Inn, 1959. A Recorder, 1982–89. *Recreations:* reading, walking, photography, bookbinding.

ZUCKERMAN, Prof. Arie Jeremy, MD, DSc; FRCP, FRCPath, FMedSci; Professor of Medical Microbiology in the University of London, since 1975, and Dean, Royal Free Hospital School of Medicine, then Royal Free and University College Medical School, 1989–99. *Educ:* Birmingham Univ. (BSc 1953; MSc 1962; DSc 1973); London Univ. (MB BS 1957; MD 1963; DipBact 1965). MRCS, LRCP, 1957; DObst, RCOG, 1958; MRCPath 1965, FRCPath 1977; MRCP 1977, FRCP 1982. Ho. Surg., Royal Free Hosp., 1957–58; Ho. Phys., 1958, Casualty Surg. and Admissions Officer, 1958–59, Whittington Hosp.; Flt Lieut, then Sqn Leader, Medical Branch, RAF, 1959–62: Unit MO and Tutor in Aviation Medicine, Advanced Flying Sch., 1959–60; Epidemiol Res.

Lab., PHLS, 1960–62; seconded to Dept of Pathol., Guy's Hosp. Med. Sch., 1962–63; Sen. Registrar, PHLS, 1963–65; London School of Hygiene and Tropical Medicine: Sen. Lectr, Dept of Bacteriol. and Immunol., 1965–68; Reader in Virology, 1968–72; Prof. of Virology, 1972–75; Dir, Dept of Med. Microbiol., 1975–88; Member Council: Univ. of London, 1995– (Mem. Court, 1992–95); UCL, 1995–. Chm., Conf. of Metropolitan Deans, 1992–95. Hon. Consultant Microbiologist: UCH, 1982–89; Royal Free Hosp., 1989–; Hon. Consultant Virologist: Charing Cross Hosp., 1982–95; NE Thames Regl Blood Transfusion Centre, Brentwood, 1970–94; Nat. Blood Authy, 1994–99. World Health Organisation: Consultant on hepatitis, 1970–; Mem., Expert Adv. Panel on Virus Diseases, 1974–; Dir, Collaborating Centre for Ref. and Res. on Viral Diseases, 1990–; Dir, Collaborating Centre for Ref. and Res. on Viral Hepatitis, London, 1974–89. Non-exec. Dir, Royal Free Hampstead NHS Trust, 1990–99; Dir, Anthony Nolan Bone Marrow Trust, 1990–. Mem., expert advisory gps, DoH, 1970–. Mem. Council, Zool Soc. of London, 1989–92. Founder FMedSci 1998. Stewart Prize, BMA, 1981; James Blundell Medal and Award, British Blood Transfusion Soc., 1992. Editor: Jl of Med. Virology, 1976–; Jl of Virological Methods, 1979–. *Publications:* Virus Diseases of the Liver, 1970; Hepatitis-associated Antigen and Viruses, 1972, 2nd edn as Human Viral Hepatitis, 1975 (trans. Japanese, 1980); (with C. R. Howard) Hepatitis Viruses of Man, 1979 (trans. Japanese, 1981); A Decade of Viral Hepatitis: abstracts 1969–1979, 1980; (ed) Viral Hepatitis: clinics in tropical medicine and communicable diseases, 1986; (ed jtly) Principles and Practice of Clinical Virology, 1987 (trans. Italian, 1992), 4th edn 1999; (ed) Viral Hepatitis and Liver Disease, 1988; (ed) Recent Developments in Prophylactic Immunization, 1989; (ed) Viral Hepatitis, 1990 (trans. Spanish, 1991); (ed with H. Thomas) Viral Hepatitis: scientific basis and clinical management, 1993, 2nd edn 1998; (ed) Prevention of Hepatitis B in the Newborn, Children and Adolescents, 1996; (ed) Hepatitis B in the Asian-Pacific Region, vol. 1, 1997, vol. 2, 1998, vol. 3, 1999; contribs to many learned jls. *Address:* Royal Free and University College Medical School, Rowland Hill Street, Hampstead, NW3 2PF. *T:* (020) 7830 2579.

ZUKERMAN, Pinchas; conductor, concert violinist and violist; Music Director, National Arts Centre Orchestra, Canada, since 1999; *b* Tel Aviv, Israel, 16 July 1948; *s* of Jehuda and Miriam Zukerman; two *d* from former *m. Educ:* Juilliard School of Music. Début, USA, 1963, Europe, 1970. Violin soloist with every major orchestra in USA and Europe; tours of USA, Europe, Israel, Scandinavia, Australia; extensive recordings. Music Director: South Bank Festival, 1978–80; St Paul Chamber Orch., 1980–87; Principal Guest Conductor, Dallas Symph. Orch., 1993–95 (Principal Conductor, Internat. Summer Music Fest., 1990–95). First prize, Leventritt Internat. Violin Competition, 1967. *Recreation:* tennis. *Address:* c/o Kirshbaum Demler & Associates, 711 West End Avenue, New York, NY 10025, USA. *T:* (212) 222–4843.

ZUNZ, Sir Gerhard Jacob, (Sir Jack), Kt 1989; FREng; consulting engineer; *b* 25 Dec. 1923; *s* of Wilhelm Zunz and Helene (*née* Isenberg); *m* 1948, Babs Maisel; one *s* one *d* (and one *d* decd). *Educ:* Athlone High Sch., Johannesburg; Univ. of the Witwatersrand (BScCivEng); FICE, FIStructE; FREng (FEng 1983). War service, Egypt and Italy, with SA Artillery, 1943–46. Asst Engr, Alpheus, Williams & Dowse, 1948–50; Structural and Civil Engr with Ove Arup & Partners, London, 1950–54; Co-founder and Partner, Ove Arup & Partners (S Africa), 1954–61; Ove Arup & Partners: Associate Partner, 1961–65; Sen. Partner, and Partner in all overseas partnerships, 1965–77; Dir and Chm., 1977–84; Co-Chm., Ove Arup Partnership, and Dir, Ove Arup & Partners, 1984–89, Consultant, 1989–95. Non-exec. Dir, Innisfree PFI Fund, 1996–. Chairman: Ove Arup Foundn, 1992–96; AA Foundn, 1993–; Pres., CIRIA, 1996–98; former mem., various cttees associated with the construction industry. Industrial Fellow Commoner, Churchill Coll., Cambridge, 1967–68; Hon. Fellow, Trevelyan Coll., Durham Univ., 1996. Hon. FRIBA 1990; FCGI 1990. Hon. DSc W Ontario, 1993; Hon. DEng Glasgow, 1994. Oscar Faber Silver Medal (jtly, with Sir Ove Arup), 1969; IStructE Gold Medal, 1988. *Publications:* (some jtly) number of technical papers to learned socs, incl. papers on Sydney Opera House and Hongkong & Shanghai Bank. *Recreations:* theatre, music, golf, tribal art. *Address:* c/o 13 Fitzroy Street, W1P 6BQ.